# JOEL WHITBURN PRESENTS THE Billboard HOT 100 Charts

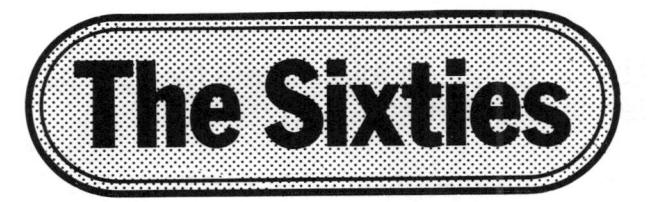

## The Sixties

Reproductions of *Billboard's* **Hot 100** charts, 1960 – 1969.

Record Research Inc.
P. O. Box 200
Menonomee Falls, Wisconsin 53051

Copyright © 1990 by Record Research Inc. and BPI Communications.

The charts used in this book are copyright © 1990 by BPI Communications and are used with permission of Billboard magazine. Both *Billboard* and *Hot 100* are registered trademarks of BPI Communications and are used with permission.

All Rights Reserved.

***** **NOTICE** *****

No part of this publication may be reproduced, stored in a retrieval system, or transmitted in any form by any means, electronic, mechanical, photocopying, recording or otherwise, without the prior written permission of Billboard magazine and Record Research Inc.

Compilation of Billboard's *Hot 100* chart information for publication or storage in a retrieval information system is prohibited.

Unauthorized copying, compiling, adapting or publication of Billboard's *Hot 100* charts is an infringement of copyright. Infringers are liable under law.

ISBN 0-89820-074-1

Published independently by Record Research Inc.
P.O. Box 200, Menomonee Falls, Wisconsin 53051

PRINTED IN CANADA

# AUTHOR'S NOTE

I am proud to introduce **Billboard Hot 100 Charts - The Sixties.** This book is the realization of a long-awaited dream: to view the *Hot 100* charts in a concise, bound volume. After searching the country for perfect condition back issues of *Billboard* to complement my Record Research library, I put together a pristine collection of *Hot 100s* for our readers.

We left the charts exactly as they were when they first rolled off *Billboard's* printing presses. To preserve the authenticity of the *Hot 100*, we did not correct any of the charts' original typesetting errors. You may notice a few chart entries that are titled differently than the way they actually appear on the record and thus, in the title section of this book and the other Record Research books. Please keep this in mind if you cross-reference the chart entries herein against the titles in our other publications. Some charts show the page numbers from the original issue.

Take note of the interesting graphic changes the *Hot 100* went through. At the same time, witness the whole history of the Beatles, the rise of Motown, the British invasion and the heyday of surf music. Examine a portion of any *Hot 100* chart of the Sixties and behold pop radio's mix of many musical tastes - from Bubble Gum to Acid Rock, from Country To Soul, from Folk to Psychedelic, from Easy Listening to Rock 'n Roll.

I found this to be a fascinating book to put together. Without lengthy narratives or critical commentaries, these 520 actual *Hot 100* charts tell the story of one of the most exciting eras in American popular music as its never been told.

JOEL WHITBURN

I am grateful to *Billboard* magazine for allowing me to publish this book. These charts are protected by *Billboard*. Any reproduction, transmission, sale or public use of these charts is strictly prohibited. This publication is intended solely for your personal enjoyment.

# THE HOT 100 CHARTS 1960-1969

Reproductions, in weekly chronological order, of every *Billboard Hot 100* chart published from January 4, 1960 through December 27, 1969.

### ISSUE / WEEK ENDING DATES

Differing issue dates and week ending dates appear at the top of each *Hot 100* chart through January 6, 1962. When both dates are shown, refer to the *issue date* as the date of reference. (All Record Research books use the issue date.) Please note that *Billboard* published an issue dated December 31, 1960 which did not follow the normal 7-day span between issues. Also, as of January 6, 1962, *Billboard* changed its issue date permanently from a Monday to a Saturday date. From January 13, 1962 on, a single date is shown, representing both the issue date and week ending date.

# The Billboard HOT 100

**FOR WEEK ENDING JANUARY 10**

*The Billboard's Music Popularity Charts ... POP RECORDS — JANUARY 4, 1960*

STAR PERFORMERS showed the greatest upward progress on the Hot 100 this week.
**S** Indicates that STEREO SINGLE version is available.

| This Week | 1 Wk Ago | 2 Wks Ago | 3 Wks Ago | TITLE, Artist, Company, Record No. | Weeks on Chart |
|---|---|---|---|---|---|
| 1 | 2 | 3 | 11 | EL PASO — Marty Robbins, Columbia 41511 | 9 |
| 2 | 1 | 2 | 5 | WHY — Frankie Avalon, Chancellor 1045 [S] | 7 |
| 3 | 3 | 4 | 10 | THE BIG HURT — Toni Fisher, Signet 275 | 8 |
| ★4 | 11 | 24 | 41 | RUNNING BEAR — Johnny Preston, Mercury 71474 | 12 |
| 5 | 5 | 5 | 13 | WAY DOWN YONDER IN NEW ORLEANS — Freddie Cannon, Swan 4043 | 7 |
| 6 | 6 | 1 | 1 | HEARTACHES BY THE NUMBER — Guy Mitchell, Columbia 41476 | 14 |
| 7 | 4 | 6 | 9 | IT'S TIME TO CRY — Paul Anka, ABC-Paramount 10064 [S] | 7 |
| 8 | 7 | 9 | 21 | AMONG MY SOUVENIRS — Connie Francis, M-G-M 12841 [S] | 7 |
| 9 | 10 | 19 | 20 | PRETTY BLUE EYES — Steve Lawrence, ABC-Paramount 10058 | 7 |
| ★10 | 19 | 35 | 74 | GO, JIMMY, GO — Jimmy Clanton, Ace 575 | 5 |
| 11 | 12 | 8 | 6 | WE GOT LOVE — Bobby Rydell, Cameo 169 | 13 |
| 12 | 8 | 7 | 3 | MACK THE KNIFE — Bobby Darin, Atco 6147 | 20 |
| ★13 | 28 | 56 | 70 | THE VILLAGE OF ST. BERNADETTE — Andy Williams, Cadence 1374 | 4 |
| 14 | 14 | 18 | 15 | UH! OH! (Part II) — The Nutty Squirrels, Hanover 4540 | 9 |
| 15 | 16 | 29 | 31 | SANDY — Larry Hall, Strand 25007 | 7 |
| 16 | 9 | 10 | 16 | HOUND DOG MAN — Fabian, Chancellor 1044 [S] | 8 |
| 17 | 13 | 14 | 18 | SCARLET RIBBONS — Browns, RCA Victor 7614 [S] | 10 |
| ★18 | 23 | 28 | 48 | SMOKIE (Part II) — Bill Black's Combo, Hi 2081 | 6 |
| ★19 | 32 | 52 | 81 | NOT ONE MINUTE MORE — Della Reese, RCA Victor 7644 [S] | 4 |
| 20 | 20 | 12 | 27 | FRIENDLY WORLD — Fabian, Chancellor 1044 [S] | 7 |
| 21 | 18 | 11 | 4 | IN THE MOOD — Ernie Fields, Rendezvous 110 | 16 |
| 22 | 15 | 47 | 99 | THE LITTLE DRUMMER BOY — Harry Simeone Chorale, 20th Fox 121 [S] | 4 |
| 23 | 27 | 25 | 43 | YOU GOT WHAT IT TAKES — Marv Johnson, United Artists 185 | 10 |
| 24 | 29 | 32 | 32 | FIRST NAME INITIAL — Annette, Vista 349 | 11 |
| 25 | 17 | 15 | 8 | SO MANY WAYS — Brook Benton, Mercury 71512 [S] | 12 |
| 26 | 25 | 16 | 14 | OH, CAROL — Neil Sedaka, RCA Victor 7595 | 13 |
| 27 | 24 | 21 | 12 | BE MY GUEST — Fats Domino, Imperial 5629 | 11 |
| 28 | 30 | 23 | 30 | TEARDROP — Santo and Johnny, Canadian-American 107 | 6 |
| ★29 | 50 | 100 | — | TEEN ANGEL — Mark Dinning, M-G-M 12845 | 3 |
| 30 | 31 | 26 | 25 | COME INTO MY HEART — Lloyd Price, ABC-Paramount 10062 [S] | 11 |
| 31 | 22 | 17 | 2 | MR. BLUE — Fleetwoods, Dolton 5 | 17 |
| 32 | 26 | 20 | 23 | I WANNA BE LOVED — Ricky Nelson, Imperial 5614 | 6 |
| 33 | 33 | 27 | 19 | DANNY BOY — Conway Twitty, M-G-M 12826 [S] | 15 |
| 34 | 21 | 13 | 7 | DON'T YOU KNOW — Della Reese, RCA Victor 7591 [S] | 15 |
| 35 | 43 | 44 | 56 | TALK THAT TALK — Jackie Wilson, Brunswick 55165 | 7 |
| 36 | 35 | 31 | 34 | MARINA — Rocco Granata, Laurie 3041 | 9 |
| 37 | 55 | 73 | 100 | JUST COME HOME — Hugo and Luigi, RCA Victor 7639 [S] | 4 |
| 38 | 49 | 61 | 88 | HOW ABOUT THAT — Dee Clark, Abner 1032 | 5 |
| 39 | 48 | 93 | — | SWINGIN' ON A RAINBOW — Frankie Avalon, Chancellor 1045 [S] | 3 |
| 40 | 36 | 22 | 17 | MISTY — Johnny Mathis, Columbia 41483 | 14 |
| 41 | 58 | — | — | HE'LL HAVE TO GO — Jim Reeves, RCA Victor 7643 | 2 |
| 42 | 47 | 40 | 36 | BELIEVE ME — Royal Teens, Capitol 4261 | 11 |
| 43 | 37 | 33 | 24 | DANCE WITH ME — The Drifters, Atlantic 2040 | 13 |
| 44 | 38 | 37 | 37 | JUST AS MUCH AS EVER — Bob Beckham, Decca 30861 | 22 |
| 45 | 34 | 76 | 80 | THE HAPPY REINDEER — Dancer, Prancer & Nervous, Capitol 4300 | 5 |
| 46 | 83 | — | — | BONNIE CAME BACK — Duane Eddy, Jamie 1144 | 2 |
| 47 | 53 | 78 | 77 | (NEW IN) THE WAYS OF LOVE — Tommy Edwards, M-G-M 12837 [S] | 8 |
| 48 | 62 | 98 | — | IF I HAD A GIRL — Rod Lauren, RCA Victor 7645 [S] | 3 |
| 49 | 45 | 38 | 55 | MIGHTY GOOD — Ricky Nelson, Imperial 5614 | 6 |
| 50 | 51 | 65 | 67 | WHAT ABOUT US — The Coasters, Atco 6153 | 5 |
| 51 | 72 | — | — | WHERE OR WHEN — Dion & the Belmonts, Laurie 3044 | 2 |
| 52 | 46 | 51 | 63 | CLOUDS — The Spacemen, Alton 254 | 12 |
| 53 | 61 | — | — | MARY, DON'T YOU WEEP — Stonewall Jackson, Columbia 41533 | 2 |
| 54 | 42 | 46 | 46 | MARINA — Willy Alberti, London 1888 | 6 |
| 55 | 56 | 39 | 33 | (IF YOU CRY) TRUE LOVE, TRUE LOVE — Drifters, Atlantic 2040 | 10 |
| 56 | 67 | — | — | NO LOVE HAVE I — Webb Pierce, Decca 31021 | 2 |
| 57 | 44 | 30 | 28 | REVEILLE ROCK — Johnny and the Hurricanes, Warwick 513 [S] | 10 |
| 58 | 65 | 45 | 54 | UH! OH! (Part I) — The Nutty Squirrels, Hanover 4540 | 5 |
| 59 | 40 | 34 | 22 | ALWAYS — Sammy Turner, Big Top 3029 | 10 |
| 60 | 76 | 90 | 90 | SHIMMY, SHIMMY, KO-KO BOP — Little Anthony & the Imperials, End 1060 | 5 |
| 61 | 41 | 68 | 89 | CHIPMUNK SONG — David Seville and the Chipmunks, Liberty 55250 [S] | 4 |
| 62 | 78 | — | — | DOWN BY THE STATION — Four Preps, Capitol 4312 | 2 |
| 63 | 52 | 57 | 65 | A YEAR AGO TONIGHT — The Crests, Coed 521 | 5 |
| 64 | 91 | — | — | HONEY HUSH — Joe Turner, Atlantic 1001 | 2 |
| 65 | 89 | — | — | LONELY BLUE BOY — Conway Twitty, M-G-M 12857 | 2 |
| 66 | 69 | 60 | 71 | WON'TCHA COME HOME — Lloyd Price, ABC-Paramount 10062 [S] | 9 |
| 67 | 87 | — | — | HANDY MAN — Jimmy Jones, Cub 9049 | |
| 68 | — | — | — | CRAZY ARMS — Bob Beckham, Decca 31029 | 1 |
| 69 | 54 | 49 | 47 | HIGH SCHOOL U.S.A. — Tommy Facenda, Atlantic 51 to 78 | 12 |
| 70 | 82 | 84 | 85 | LUCKY DEVIL — Carl Dobkins Jr., Decca 31020 | 5 |
| 71 | 74 | 94 | — | LET'S TRY AGAIN — Clyde McPhatter, M-G-M 12843 [S] | 3 |
| 72 | 73 | 85 | — | BACIARE, BACIARE — Dorothy Collins, Top Rank 2024 | 3 |
| 73 | 66 | 41 | 26 | 7 LITTLE GIRLS (SITTIN' IN THE BACK SEAT) — Paul Evans & the Curls, Guaranteed 200 | 17 |
| 74 | 60 | 50 | 39 | PRIMROSE LANE — Jerry Wallace, Challenge 59047 | 21 |
| 75 | 77 | 96 | — | THIS TIME OF THE YEAR — Brook Benton, Mercury 71558 [S] | 3 |
| 76 | 71 | 53 | 52 | LOVE POTION #9 — Clovers, United Artists 180 | 17 |
| 77 | 81 | 82 | — | CLIMB EV'RY MOUNTAIN — Tony Bennett, Columbia 41520 | 3 |
| 78 | — | — | — | SKOKIAAN — Bill Haley & the Comets, Decca 31030 | 1 |
| 79 | 90 | 99 | — | SWEET NUTHIN'S — Brenda Lee, Decca 30967 | 3 |
| 80 | 84 | 88 | — | RUN, RED, RUN — Coasters, Atco 6153 | 3 |
| 81 | 88 | — | — | PROMISE ME A ROSE — Anita Bryant, Carlton 523 [S] | 2 |
| 82 | — | — | — | ROCKIN' LITTLE ANGEL — Ray Smith, Judd 1016 | 1 |
| 83 | 64 | 55 | 40 | I'M MOVING ON — Ray Charles, Atlantic 2043 | 9 |
| 84 | — | — | — | TRACY'S THEME — Spencer Ross, Columbia 41532 | 1 |
| 85 | 63 | 91 | — | THE LITTLE DRUMMER BOY — Johnny Cash, Columbia 41481 | 3 |
| 86 | 93 | — | — | LITTLE THINGS MEAN A LOT — Joni James, M-G-M 12849 [S] | 2 |
| 87 | — | — | — | RIVERBOAT — Faron Young, Capitol 4291 | 1 |
| 88 | 98 | — | — | HARLEM NOCTURNE — Viscounts, Madison 123 | 2 |
| 89 | 39 | 36 | 60 | GOD BLESS AMERICA — Connie Francis, M-G-M 12841 [S] | 8 |
| 90 | 99 | — | — | THE SOUND OF MUSIC — Patti Page, Mercury 71555 | 2 |
| 91 | 80 | 89 | 96 | I DON'T KNOW WHAT IT IS — The Blue Notes, Brooke 111 | 4 |
| 92 | 100 | — | — | DARLING LORRAINE — Knockouts, Shad 5013 | 2 |
| 93 | — | — | — | (I REMEMBER) IN THE STILL OF THE NIGHT — The Five Satins, Ember 1005 | 1 |
| 94 | 70 | 75 | 92 | DO-RE-MI — Mitch Miller and the Kids, Columbia 41499 | 4 |
| 95 | — | — | — | LITTLE COCO PALM — Jerry Wallace, Challenge 59060 | 1 |
| 96 | 68 | 48 | 38 | DECK OF CARDS — Wink Martindale, Dot 15968 | 17 |
| 97 | — | — | — | ONE MINT JULEP — Chet Atkins, RCA Victor 7684 | 1 |
| 98 | 57 | 86 | 94 | HAPPY ANNIVERSARY — Jane Morgan, Kapp 305 | 9 |
| 99 | — | — | — | SMOKIE (PART II) — Bill Doggett, King 5310 | 1 |
| 100 | 75 | 81 | 84 | ONE MORE CHANCE — Rod Bernard, Mercury 71507 | 9 |

# The Billboard HOT 100

**FOR WEEK ENDING JANUARY 17**

*January 11, 1960*

STAR PERFORMERS showed the greatest upward progress on the Hot 100 this week.

S — Indicates that STEREO SINGLE version is available.

Columns: THIS WEEK | ONE WEEK AGO | TWO WEEKS AGO | THREE WEEKS AGO | TITLE, Artist, Company, Record No. | STEREO | WEEKS ON CHART

| # | 1wk | 2wk | 3wk | Title / Artist / Label / No. | S | Wks |
|---|---|---|---|---|---|---|
| 1 | 1 | 2 | 3 | EL PASO — Marty Robbins, Columbia 41511 | | 10 |
| 2 | 2 | 1 | 2 | WHY — Frankie Avalon, Chancellor 1045 | S | 8 |
| 3 | 5 | 5 | 5 | WAY DOWN YONDER IN NEW ORLEANS — Freddy Cannon, Swan 4043 | | 8 |
| 4 | 4 | 11 | 24 | RUNNING BEAR — Johnny Preston, Mercury 71474 | | 13 |
| 5 | 3 | 3 | 4 | THE BIG HURT — Toni Fisher, Signet 275 | | 9 |
| 6 | 7 | 4 | 6 | IT'S TIME TO CRY — Paul Anka, ABC-Paramount 10064 | S | 8 |
| 7 | 10 | 19 | 35 | GO, JIMMY, GO — Jimmy Clanton, Ace 575 | | 6 |
| 8 | 8 | 7 | 9 | AMONG MY SOUVENIRS — Connie Francis, M-G-M 12841 | S | 8 |
| 9 | 9 | 10 | 19 | PRETTY BLUE EYES — Steve Lawrence, ABC-Paramount 10058 | | 8 |
| 10 | 6 | 6 | 1 | HEARTACHES BY THE NUMBER — Guy Mitchell, Columbia 41476 | | 15 |
| 11 | 16 | 9 | 10 | HOUND DOG MAN — Fabian, Chancellor 1044 | S | 9 |
| 12 | 13 | 28 | 56 | THE VILLAGE OF ST. BERNADETTE — Andy Williams, Cadence 1374 | | 5 |
| 13 | 12 | 8 | 7 | MACK THE KNIFE — Bobby Darin, Atco 6147 | | 21 |
| 14 | 29 | 50 | 100 | TEEN ANGEL — Mark Dinning, M-G-M 12845 | | 4 |
| 15 | 23 | 27 | 25 | YOU GOT WHAT IT TAKES — Marv Johnson, United Artists 185 | | 11 |
| 16 | 19 | 32 | 52 | NOT ONE MINUTE MORE — Della Reese, RCA Victor 7644 | S | 5 |
| 17 | 18 | 23 | 28 | SMOKIE (Part II) — Bill Black's Combo, Hi 2081 | | 7 |
| 18 | 11 | 12 | 8 | WE GOT LOVE — Bobby Rydell, Cameo 169 | | 14 |
| 19 | 15 | 16 | 29 | SANDY — Larry Hall, Strand 25007 | | 8 |
| 20 | 24 | 29 | 32 | FIRST NAME INITIAL — Annette, Vista 349 | | 12 |
| 21 | 20 | 20 | 12 | FRIENDLY WORLD — Fabian, Chancellor 1044 | S | 8 |
| 22 | 22 | 15 | 47 | THE LITTLE DRUMMER BOY — Harry Simeone Chorale, 20th Fox 121 | S | 5 |
| 23 | 17 | 13 | 14 | SCARLET RIBBONS — Browns, RCA Victor 7614 | S | 11 |
| 24 | 14 | 14 | 18 | UH! OH! (Part II) — The Nutty Squirrels, Hanover 4540 | | 10 |
| 25 | 21 | 18 | 11 | IN THE MOOD — Ernie Fields, Rendezvous 110 | | 17 |
| 26 | 32 | 26 | 20 | I WANNA BE LOVED — Ricky Nelson, Imperial 5614 | | 7 |
| 27 | 26 | 25 | 16 | OH, CAROL — Neil Sedaka, RCA Victor 7595 | | 14 |
| 28 | 51 | 72 | — | WHERE OR WHEN — Dion & the Belmonts, Laurie 3044 | | 3 |
| 29 | 41 | 58 | — | HE'LL HAVE TO GO — Jim Reeves, RCA Victor 7643 | | 3 |
| 30 | 28 | 30 | 23 | TEARDROP — Santo and Johnny, Canadian-American 107 | | 7 |
| 31 | 30 | 31 | 26 | COME INTO MY HEART — Lloyd Price, ABC-Paramount 10062 | S | 12 |
| 32 | 25 | 17 | 15 | SO MANY WAYS — Brook Benton, Mercury 71512 | S | 13 |
| 33 | 62 | 78 | — | DOWN BY THE STATION — Four Preps, Capitol 4312 | | 3 |
| 34 | 35 | 43 | 44 | TALK THAT TALK — Jackie Wilson, Brunswick 55165 | | 8 |
| 35 | 37 | 55 | 73 | JUST COME HOME — Hugo and Luigi, RCA Victor 7639 | S | 5 |
| 36 | 48 | 62 | 98 | IF I HAD A GIRL — Rod Lauren, RCA Victor 7645 | S | 4 |
| 37 | 38 | 49 | 61 | HOW ABOUT THAT — Dee Clark, Abner 1032 | | 6 |
| 38 | 27 | 24 | 21 | BE MY GUEST — Fats Domino, Imperial 5629 | | 12 |
| 39 | 34 | 21 | 13 | DON'T YOU KNOW — Della Reese, RCA Victor 7591 | S | 16 |
| 40 | 46 | 83 | — | BONNIE CAME BACK — Duane Eddy, Jamie 1144 | | 3 |
| 41 | 53 | 61 | — | MARY, DON'T YOU WEEP — Stonewall Jackson, Columbia 41533 | | 3 |
| 42 | 67 | 87 | — | HANDY MAN — Jimmy Jones, Cub 9049 | | 3 |
| 43 | 70 | 82 | 84 | LUCKY DEVIL — Cary Dobkins Jr., Decca 31020 | | 6 |
| 44 | 60 | 76 | 90 | SHIMMY, SHIMMY, KO-KO BOP — Little Anthony & the Imperials, End 1060 | | 6 |
| 45 | 63 | 52 | 57 | A YEAR AGO TONIGHT — The Crests, Coed 521 | | 6 |
| 46 | 80 | 84 | 88 | RUN, RED, RUN — Coasters, Atco 6153 | | 4 |
| 47 | 50 | 51 | 65 | WHAT ABOUT US — The Coasters, Atco 6153 | | 6 |
| 48 | 71 | 74 | 94 | LET'S TRY AGAIN — Clyde McPhatter, M-G-M 12843 | S | 4 |
| 49 | 49 | 45 | 38 | MIGHTY GOOD — Ricky Nelson, Imperial 5614 | | 7 |
| 50 | 52 | 46 | 51 | CLOUDS — The Spacemen, Alton 254 | | 13 |
| 51 | 47 | 53 | 78 | (NEW IN) THE WAYS OF LOVE — Tommy Edwards, M-G-M 12837 | S | 9 |
| 52 | 33 | 33 | 27 | DANNY BOY — Conway Twitty, M-G-M 12826 | S | 16 |
| 53 | 43 | 37 | 33 | DANCE WITH ME — The Drifters, Atlantic 2040 | | 14 |
| 54 | 36 | 35 | 31 | MARINA — Rocco Granata, Laurie 3041 | | 10 |
| 55 | 72 | 73 | 85 | BACIARE, BACIARE — Dorothy Collins, Top Rank 2024 | | 4 |
| 56 | 56 | 67 | — | NO LOVE HAVE I — Webb Pierce, Decca 31021 | | 3 |
| 57 | 42 | 47 | 40 | BELIEVE ME — Royal Teens, Capitol 4261 | | 12 |
| 58 | 40 | 36 | 22 | MISTY — Johnny Mathis, Columbia 41483 | | 15 |
| 59 | 86 | 93 | — | LITTLE THINGS MEAN A LOT — Joni James, M-G-M 12849 | S | 3 |
| 60 | 84 | — | — | TRACY'S THEME — Spencer Ross, Columbia 41532 | | 2 |
| 61 | 65 | 89 | — | LONELY BLUE BOY — Conway Twitty, M-G-M 12857 | | 3 |
| 62 | 61 | 41 | 68 | CHIPMUNK SONG — David Seville and the Chipmunks, Liberty 55250 | S | 5 |
| 63 | 64 | 91 | — | HONEY HUSH — Joe Turner, Atlantic 1001 | | 3 |
| 64 | 68 | — | — | CRAZY ARMS — Bob Beckham, Decca 31029 | | 2 |
| 65 | 54 | 42 | 46 | MARINA — Willy Alberti, London 1888 | | 7 |
| 66 | 79 | 90 | 99 | SWEET NOTHIN'S — Brenda Lee, Decca 30967 | | 4 |
| 67 | 59 | 40 | 34 | ALWAYS — Sammy Turner, Big Top 3029 | | *11 |
| 68 | 55 | 56 | 39 | (IF YOU CRY) TRUE LOVE, TRUE LOVE — Drifters, Atlantic 2040 | | 11 |
| 69 | 39 | 48 | 93 | SWINGIN' ON A RAINBOW — Frankie Avalon, Chancellor 1045 | S | 4 |
| 70 | 75 | 77 | 96 | THIS TIME OF THE YEAR — Brook Benton, Mercury 71558 | S | 4 |
| 71 | 78 | — | — | SKOKIAAN — Bill Haley & the Comets, Decca 31030 | | 2 |
| 72 | 66 | 69 | 60 | WON'TCHA COME HOME — Lloyd Price, ABC-Paramount 10062 | S | 10 |
| 73 | 31 | 22 | 17 | MR. BLUE — Fleetwoods, Dolton 5 | | 18 |
| 74 | 77 | 81 | 82 | CLIMB EV'RY MOUNTAIN — Tony Bennett, Columbia 41520 | | 4 |
| 75 | — | — | — | WHAT IN THE WORLD'S COME OVER YOU — Jack Scott, Top Rank 2028 | | 1 |
| 76 | — | — | — | LET IT BE ME — The Everly Brothers, Cadence 1376 | | 1 |
| 77 | 88 | 98 | — | HARLEM NOCTURNE — Viscounts, Madison 123 | | 3 |
| 78 | 81 | 88 | — | PROMISE ME A ROSE — Anita Bryant, Carlton 523 | S | 3 |
| 79 | 57 | 44 | 30 | REVEILLE ROCK — Johnny and the Hurricanes, Warwick 513 | S | 11 |
| 80 | 82 | — | — | ROCKIN' LITTLE ANGEL — Ray Smith, Judd 1016 | | 2 |
| 81 | 91 | 80 | 89 | I DON'T KNOW WHAT IT IS — The Blue Notes, Brooke 111 | | 5 |
| 82 | 73 | 66 | 41 | 7 LITTLE GIRLS (SITTIN' IN THE BACK SEAT) — Paul Evans & the Curls, Guaranteed 200 | | 18 |
| 83 | — | — | — | TENDER LOVE AND CARE — Jimmie Rodgers, Roulette 4218 | | 1 |
| 84 | 58 | 65 | 45 | UH! OH! (Part I) — The Nutty Squirrels, Hanover 4540 | | 6 |
| 85 | 87 | — | — | RIVERBOAT — Faron Young, Capitol 4291 | | 2 |
| 86 | 92 | 100 | — | DARLING LORRAINE — Knockouts, Shad 5013 | | 3 |
| 87 | 83 | 64 | 55 | I'M MOVIN' ON — Ray Charles, Atlantic 2043 | | 10 |
| 88 | 89 | 39 | 36 | GOD BLESS AMERICA — Connie Francis, M-G-M 12841 | S | 9 |
| 89 | 95 | — | — | LITTLE COCO PALM — Jerry Wallace, Challenge 59060 | | 2 |
| 90 | 90 | 99 | — | THE SOUND OF MUSIC — Patti Page, Mercury 71555 | | 3 |
| 91 | 69 | 54 | 49 | HIGH SCHOOL U.S.A. — Tommy Facenda, Atlantic 51 to 78 | | 13 |
| 92 | 93 | — | — | (I REMEMBER) IN THE STILL OF THE NIGHT — The Five Satins, Ember 1005 | | 2 |
| 93 | 45 | 34 | 76 | THE HAPPY REINDEER — Dancer, Prancer & Nervous, Capitol 4300 | | 6 |
| 94 | 97 | — | — | ONE MINT JULEP — Chet Atkins, RCA Victor 7684 | | 2 |
| 95 | 99 | — | — | SMOKIE (PART II) — Bill Doggett, King 5310 | | 2 |
| 96 | — | — | — | THEME FROM A SUMMER PLACE — Percy Faith, Columbia 41490 | | 1 |
| 97 | — | — | — | LET THE GOOD TIMES ROLL — Ray Charles, Atlantic 2047 | | 1 |
| 98 | — | — | — | TELL HER FOR ME — Adam Wade, Coed 520 | | 1 |
| 99 | — | — | — | BULLDOG — The Fireballs, Top Rank 2026 | | 1 |
| 100 | — | — | — | TEENAGE HAYRIDE — Tender Slim, Grey Cliff 723 | | 1 |

# The Billboard HOT 100

**FOR WEEK ENDING JANUARY 24**

*JANUARY 18, 1960*

| This Week | One Week Ago | Two Weeks Ago | Three Weeks Ago | Title, Artist, Company, Record No. | Stereo | Weeks on Chart |
|---|---|---|---|---|---|---|
| 1 | 4 | 4 | 11 | RUNNING BEAR — Johnny Preston, Mercury 71474 | | 14 |
| 2 | 2 | 2 | 1 | WHY — Frankie Avalon, Chancellor 1045 | S | 9 |
| 3 | 1 | 1 | 2 | EL PASO — Marty Robbins, Columbia 41511 | | 11 |
| 4 | 5 | 3 | 3 | THE BIG HURT — Toni Fisher, Signet 275 | | 10 |
| 5 | 3 | 5 | 5 | WAY DOWN YONDER IN NEW ORLEANS — Freddy Cannon, Swan 4043 | | 9 |
| 6 | 7 | 10 | 19 | GO, JIMMY, GO — Jimmy Clanton, Ace 575 | | 7 |
| 7 | 14 | 29 | 50 | TEEN ANGEL — Mark Dinning, M-G-M 12845 | | 5 |
| 8 | 12 | 13 | 28 | THE VILLAGE OF ST. BERNADETTE — Andy Williams, Cadence 1374 | | 6 |
| 9 | 9 | 9 | 10 | PRETTY BLUE EYES — Steve Lawrence, ABC-Paramount 10058 | S | 9 |
| 10 | 8 | 8 | 7 | AMONG MY SOUVENIRS — Connie Francis, M-G-M 12841 | S | 9 |
| 11 | 6 | 7 | 4 | IT'S TIME TO CRY — Paul Anka, ABC-Paramount 10064 | S | 9 |
| 12 | 10 | 6 | 6 | HEARTACHES BY THE NUMBER — Guy Mitchell, Columbia 41476 | | 16 |
| 13 | 28 | 51 | 72 | WHERE OR WHEN — Dion & the Belmonts, Laurie 3044 | | 4 |
| 14 | 15 | 23 | 27 | YOU GOT WHAT IT TAKES — Marv Johnson, United Artists 185 | | 12 |
| 15 | 11 | 16 | 9 | HOUND DOG MAN — Fabian, Chancellor 1044 | S | 10 |
| 16 | 19 | 15 | 16 | SANDY — Larry Hall, Strand 25007 | | 9 |
| 17 | 17 | 18 | 23 | SMOKIE (Part II) — Bill Black's Combo, Hi 2081 | | 8 |
| 18 | 16 | 19 | 32 | NOT ONE MINUTE MORE — Della Reese, RCA Victor 7644 | S | 6 |
| 19 | 13 | 12 | 8 | MACK THE KNIFE — Bobby Darin, Atco 6147 | | 22 |
| 20 | 33 | 62 | 78 | DOWN BY THE STATION — Four Preps, Capitol 4312 | | 4 |
| 21 | 21 | 20 | 20 | FRIENDLY WORLD — Fabian, Chancellor 1044 | S | 9 |
| 22 | 20 | 24 | 29 | FIRST NAME INITIAL — Annette, Vista 349 | | 13 |
| 23 | 18 | 11 | 12 | WE GOT LOVE — Bobby Rydell, Cameo 169 | | 15 |
| 24 | 29 | 41 | 58 | HE'LL HAVE TO GO — Jim Reeves, RCA Victor 7643 | S | 4 |
| 25 | 42 | 67 | 87 | HANDY MAN — Jimmy Jones, Cub 9049 | | 4 |
| 26 | 40 | 46 | 83 | BONNIE CAME BACK — Duane Eddy, Jamie 4144 | | 4 |
| 27 | 43 | 70 | 82 | LUCKY DEVIL — Carl Dobkins Jr., Decca 31020 | | 7 |
| 28 | 23 | 17 | 13 | SCARLET RIBBONS — Browns, RCA Victor 7614 | S | 12 |
| 29 | 60 | 84 | — | TRACY'S THEME — Spencer Ross, Columbia 41532 | | 3 |
| 30 | 75 | — | — | WHAT IN THE WORLD'S COME OVER YOU — Jack Scott, Top Rank 2028 | S | 2 |
| 31 | 61 | 65 | 89 | LONELY BLUE BOY — Conway Twitty, M-G-M 12857 | | 4 |
| 32 | 30 | 28 | 30 | TEARDROP — Santo and Johnny, Canadian-American 107 | | 8 |
| 33 | 36 | 48 | 62 | IF I HAD A GIRL — Rod Lauren, RCA Victor 7645 | S | 5 |
| 34 | 44 | 60 | 76 | SHIMMY, SHIMMY, KO-KO BOP — Little Anthony & the Imperials, End 1060 | | 7 |
| 35 | 35 | 37 | 55 | JUST COME HOME — Hugo and Luigi, RCA Victor 7639 | S | 6 |
| 36 | 26 | 32 | 26 | I WANNA BE LOVED — Ricky Nelson, Imperial 5614 | | 8 |
| 37 | 32 | 25 | 17 | SO MANY WAYS — Brook Benton, Mercury 71512 | S | 14 |
| 38 | 37 | 38 | 49 | HOW ABOUT THAT — Dee Clark, Abner 1032 | | 7 |
| 39 | 31 | 30 | 31 | COME INTO MY HEART — Lloyd Price, ABC-Paramount 10062 | S | 13 |
| 40 | 27 | 26 | 25 | OH, CAROL — Neil Sedaka, RCA Victor 7595 | | 15 |
| 41 | 34 | 35 | 43 | TALK THAT TALK — Jackie Wilson, Brunswick 55165 | | 9 |
| 42 | 45 | 63 | 52 | A YEAR AGO TONIGHT — The Crests, Coed 521 | | 7 |
| 43 | 96 | — | — | THEME FROM A SUMMER PLACE — Percy Faith, Columbia 41490 | | 2 |
| 44 | 25 | 21 | 18 | IN THE MOOD — Ernie Fields, Rendezvous 110 | | 18 |
| 45 | 46 | 80 | 84 | RUN, RED, RUN — Coasters, Atco 6153 | | 5 |
| 46 | 24 | 14 | 14 | UH! OH! (Part II) — The Nutty Squirrels, Hanover 4540 | | 11 |
| 47 | 59 | 86 | 93 | LITTLE THINGS MEAN A LOT — Joni James, M-G-M 12849 | S | 4 |
| 48 | 48 | 71 | 74 | LET'S TRY AGAIN — Clyde McPhatter, M-G-M 12843 | S | 5 |
| 49 | 55 | 72 | 73 | BACIARE, BACIARE — Dorothy Collins, Top Rank 2024 | | 5 |
| 50 | 66 | 79 | 90 | SWEET NOTHIN'S — Brenda Lee, Decca 30967 | | 5 |
| 51 | 49 | 49 | 45 | MIGHTY GOOD — Ricky Nelson, Imperial 5614 | | 8 |
| 52 | 89 | 95 | — | LITTLE COCO PALM — Jerry Wallace, Challenge 59060 | | 3 |
| 53 | 41 | 53 | 61 | MARY, DON'T YOU WEEP — Stonewall Jackson, Columbia 41533 | | 4 |
| 54 | 22 | 22 | 15 | THE LITTLE DRUMMER BOY — Harry Simeone Chorale, 20th Fox 121 | S | 6 |
| 55 | 56 | 56 | 67 | NO LOVE HAVE I — Webb Pierce, Decca 31021 | | 4 |
| 56 | 47 | 50 | 51 | WHAT ABOUT US — The Coasters, Atco 6153 | | 7 |
| 57 | 63 | 64 | 91 | HONEY HUSH — Joe Turner, Atlantic 2044 | | 4 |
| 58 | 57 | 42 | 47 | BELIEVE ME — Royal Teens, Capitol 4261 | | 13 |
| 59 | 64 | 68 | — | CRAZY ARMS — Bob Beckham, Decca 31029 | | 3 |
| 60 | 83 | — | — | TENDER LOVE AND CARE — Jimmie Rodgers, Roulette 4218 | | 2 |
| 61 | 76 | — | — | LET IT BE ME — The Everly Brothers, Cadence 1376 | | 2 |
| 62 | 52 | 33 | 33 | DANNY BOY — Conway Twitty, M-G-M 12826 | S | 17 |
| 63 | 38 | 27 | 24 | BE MY GUEST — Fats Domino, Imperial 5629 | | 13 |
| 64 | 77 | 88 | 98 | HARLEM NOCTURNE — Viscounts, Madison 123 | | 4 |
| 65 | 69 | 39 | 48 | SWINGIN' ON A RAINBOW — Frankie Avalon, Chancellor 1045 | S | 5 |
| 66 | 70 | 75 | 77 | THIS TIME OF THE YEAR — Brook Benton, Mercury 71558 | S | 5 |
| 67 | 54 | 36 | 35 | MARINA — Rocco Granata, Laurie 3041 | | 11 |
| 68 | 81 | 91 | 80 | I DON'T KNOW WHAT IT IS — The Blue Notes, Brooke 111 | | 6 |
| 69 | 99 | — | — | BULLDOG — The Fireballs, Top Rank 2026 | S | 2 |
| 70 | 71 | 78 | — | SKOKIAAN — Bill Haley & the Comets, Decca 31030 | | 3 |
| 71 | 53 | 43 | 37 | DANCE WITH ME — The Drifters, Atlantic 2040 | | 15 |
| 72 | 88 | 89 | 39 | GOD BLESS AMERICA — Connie Francis, M-G-M 12841 | S | 10 |
| 73 | 80 | 82 | — | ROCKIN' LITTLE ANGEL — Ray Smith, Judd 1016 | | 3 |
| 74 | — | — | — | BEYOND THE SEA — Bobby Darin, Atco 6158 | | 1 |
| 75 | — | — | — | WALTZING MATILDA — Jimmie Rodgers, Roulette 4218 | S | 1 |
| 76 | 74 | 77 | 81 | CLIMB EV'RY MOUNTAIN — Tony Bennett, Columbia 41520 | | 5 |
| 77 | 86 | 92 | 100 | DARLING LORRAINE — Knockouts, Shad 5013 | | 4 |
| 78 | 67 | 59 | 40 | ALWAYS — Sammy Turner, Big Top 3029 | | 12 |
| 79 | 79 | 57 | 44 | REVEILLE ROCK — Johnny and the Hurricanes, Warwick 513 | S | 12 |
| 80 | 58 | 40 | 36 | MISTY — Johnny Mathis, Columbia 41483 | | 16 |
| 81 | 65 | 54 | 42 | MARINA — Willy Alberti, London 1888 | | 8 |
| 82 | 97 | — | — | LET THE GOOD TIMES ROLL — Ray Charles, Atlantic 2047 | | 2 |
| 83 | 85 | 87 | — | RIVERBOAT — Faron Young, Capitol 4291 | | 3 |
| 84 | — | — | — | WHY DO I LOVE YOU SO — Johnny Tillotson, Cadence 1372 | | 1 |
| 85 | 92 | 93 | — | (I REMEMBER) IN THE STILL OF THE NIGHT — The Five Satins, Ember 1005 | | 3 |
| 86 | — | — | — | AM I THAT EASY TO FORGET — Debbie Reynolds, Dot 15985 | | 1 |
| 87 | 98 | — | — | TELL HER FOR ME — Adam Wade, Coed 520 | | 2 |
| 88 | — | — | — | AMAPOLA — Jacky Noguez, Jamie 1148 | | 1 |
| 89 | — | — | — | TOO MUCH TEQUILA — Champs, Challenge 59063 | | 1 |
| 90 | 94 | 97 | — | ONE MINT JULEP — Chet Atkins, RCA Victor 7684 | | 3 |
| 91 | — | — | — | CRY ME A RIVER — Janice Harper, Capitol 4324 | | 1 |
| 92 | 39 | 34 | 21 | DON'T YOU KNOW — Della Reese, RCA Victor 7591 | S | 17 |
| 93 | 100 | — | — | TEENAGE HAYRIDE — Tender Slim, Grey Cliff 723 | | 2 |
| 94 | 73 | 31 | 22 | MR. BLUE — Fleetwoods, Dolton 5 | | 19 |
| 95 | — | — | — | I FORGOT MORE THAN YOU'LL EVER KNOW — Sonny James, Capitol 4307 | | 1 |
| 96 | — | — | — | UPTOWN — Roy Orbison, Monument 412 | | 1 |
| 97 | — | — | — | TIME AFTER TIME — Frankie Ford, Ace 580 | | 1 |
| 98 | 50 | 52 | 46 | CLOUDS — The Spacemen, Alton 254 | | 14 |
| 99 | — | — | — | THE HAPPY MULETEER — Ivo Robic, Laurie 3045 | | 1 |
| 100 | — | — | — | SINCE I MADE YOU CRY — The Rivieras, Coed 522 | | 1 |

# The Billboard HOT 100

**For week ending January 31** — January 25, 1960

STAR PERFORMERS showed the greatest upward progress on the Hot 100 this week.

S indicates that STEREO SINGLE version is available.

Columns: THIS WEEK | ONE WEEK AGO | TWO WEEKS AGO | THREE WEEKS AGO | TITLE, Artist, Company, Record No. | STEREO | WEEKS ON CHART

| This | 1wk | 2wk | 3wk | Title / Artist / Label | Stereo | Wks |
|---|---|---|---|---|---|---|
| 1 | 1 | 4 | 4 | RUNNING BEAR — Johnny Preston, Mercury 71474 | | 15 |
| 2 | 3 | 1 | 1 | EL PASO — Marty Robbins, Columbia 41511 | | 12 |
| 3 | 2 | 2 | 2 | WHY — Frankie Avalon, Chancellor 1045 | S | 10 |
| 4 | 7 | 14 | 29 | TEEN ANGEL — Mark Dinning, M-G-M 12845 | | 6 |
| 5 | 5 | 3 | 5 | WAY DOWN YONDER IN NEW ORLEANS — Freddy Cannon, Swan 4043 | | 10 |
| 6 | 4 | 5 | 3 | THE BIG HURT — Toni Fisher, Signet 275 | | 11 |
| 7 | 8 | 12 | 13 | THE VILLAGE OF ST. BERNADETTE — Andy Williams, Cadence 1374 | | 7 |
| 8 | 6 | 7 | 10 | GO, JIMMY, GO — Jimmy Clanton, Ace 575 | | 8 |
| 9 | 9 | 9 | 9 | PRETTY BLUE EYES — Steve Lawrence, ABC-Paramount 10058 | S | 10 |
| 10 | 13 | 28 | 51 | WHERE OR WHEN — Dion & the Belmonts, Laurie 3044 | | 5 |
| 11 | 14 | 15 | 23 | YOU GOT WHAT IT TAKES — Marv Johnson, United Artists 185 | | 13 |
| 12 | 11 | 6 | 7 | IT'S TIME TO CRY — Paul Anka, ABC-Paramount 10064 | S | 10 |
| 13 | 10 | 8 | 8 | AMONG MY SOUVENIRS — Connie Francis, M-G-M 12841 | S | 10 |
| ★14 | 25 | 42 | 67 | HANDY MAN — Jimmy Jones, Cub 9049 | | 5 |
| 15 | 16 | 19 | 15 | SANDY — Larry Hall, Strand 25007 | | 10 |
| ★16 | 30 | 75 | — | WHAT IN THE WORLD'S COME OVER YOU — Jack Scott, Top Rank 2028 | S | 3 |
| 17 | 20 | 33 | 62 | DOWN BY THE STATION — Four Preps, Capitol 4312 | | 5 |
| 18 | 15 | 11 | 16 | HOUND DOG MAN — Fabian, Chancellor 1044 | S | 11 |
| 19 | 18 | 16 | 19 | NOT ONE MINUTE MORE — Della Reese, RCA Victor 7644 | | 7 |
| 20 | 24 | 29 | 41 | HE'LL HAVE TO GO — Jim Reeves, RCA Victor 7643 | S | 5 |
| ★21 | 31 | 61 | 65 | LONELY BLUE BOY — Conway Twitty, M-G-M 12857 | | 5 |
| 22 | 12 | 10 | 6 | HEARTACHES BY THE NUMBER — Guy Mitchell, Columbia 41476 | | 17 |
| ★23 | 61 | 76 | — | LET IT BE ME — The Everly Brothers, Cadence 1376 | | 3 |
| 24 | 29 | 60 | 84 | TRACY'S THEME — Spencer Ross, Columbia 41532 | | 4 |
| 25 | 27 | 43 | 70 | LUCKY DEVIL — Carl Dobkins Jr., Decca 31020 | | 8 |
| 26 | 21 | 21 | 20 | FRIENDLY WORLD — Fabian, Chancellor 1044 | S | 10 |
| 27 | 17 | 17 | 18 | SMOKIE (Part II) — Bill Black's Combo, Hi 2018 | | 9 |
| ★28 | 43 | 96 | — | THEME FROM A SUMMER PLACE — Percy Faith, Columbia 41490 | | 3 |
| 29 | 26 | 40 | 46 | BONNIE CAME BACK — Duane Eddy, Jamie 1144 | | 5 |
| 30 | 22 | 20 | 24 | FIRST NAME INITIAL — Annette, Vista 349 | | 14 |
| 31 | 33 | 36 | 48 | IF I HAD A GIRL — Rod Lauren, RCA Victor 7645 | S | 6 |
| 32 | 19 | 13 | 12 | MACK THE KNIFE — Bobby Darin, Atco 6147 | | 23 |
| 33 | 38 | 37 | 38 | HOW ABOUT THAT — Dee Clark, Abner 1032 | | 8 |
| ★34 | 74 | — | — | BEYOND THE SEA — Bobby Darin, Atco 6158 | | 2 |
| 35 | 23 | 18 | 11 | WE GOT LOVE — Bobby Rydell, Cameo 169 | | 16 |
| 36 | 45 | 46 | 80 | RUN, RED, RUN — Coasters, Atco 6153 | | 6 |
| 37 | 32 | 30 | 28 | TEARDROP — Santo and Johnny, Canadian-American 107 | | 9 |
| 38 | 47 | 59 | 86 | LITTLE THINGS MEAN A LOT — Joni James, M-G-M 12849 | S | 5 |
| 39 | 41 | 34 | 35 | TALK THAT TALK — Jackie Wilson, Brunswick 55165 | | 10 |
| 40 | 36 | 26 | 32 | I WANNA BE LOVED — Ricky Nelson, Imperial 5614 | | 9 |
| 41 | 34 | 44 | 60 | SHIMMY, SHIMMY, KO-KO BOP — Little Anthony & the Imperials, End 1060 | | 8 |
| ★42 | 60 | 83 | — | TENDER LOVE AND CARE — Jimmie Rodgers, Roulette 4218 | | 3 |
| 43 | 28 | 23 | 17 | SCARLET RIBBONS — Browns, RCA Victor 7614 | S | 13 |
| 44 | 50 | 66 | 79 | SWEET NOTHIN'S — Brenda Lee, Decca 30967 | | 6 |
| 45 | 49 | 55 | 72 | BACIARE, BACIARE — Dorothy Collins, Top Rank 2024 | | 6 |
| 46 | 52 | 89 | 95 | LITTLE COCO PALM — Jerry Wallace, Challenge 59060 | | 4 |
| 47 | 42 | 45 | 63 | A YEAR AGO TONIGHT — The Crests, Coed 521 | | 8 |
| ★48 | 69 | 99 | — | BULLDOG — The Fireballs, Top Rank 2026 | S | 3 |
| 49 | 40 | 27 | 26 | OH, CAROL — Neil Sedaka, RCA Victor 7595 | | 16 |
| ★50 | 75 | — | — | WALTZING MATILDA — Jimmie Rodgers, Roulette 4218 | S | 2 |
| 51 | 35 | 35 | 37 | JUST COME HOME — Hugo and Luigi, RCA Victor 7639 | | 7 |
| 52 | 56 | 47 | 50 | WHAT ABOUT US — The Coasters, Atco 6153 | | 8 |
| 53 | 57 | 63 | 64 | HONEY HUSH — Joe Turner, Atlantic 2044 | | 5 |
| 54 | 37 | 32 | 25 | SO MANY WAYS — Brook Benton, Mercury 71512 | S | 15 |
| 55 | 51 | 49 | 49 | MIGHTY GOOD — Ricky Nelson, Imperial 5614 | | 9 |
| 56 | 44 | 25 | 21 | IN THE MOOD — Ernie Fields, Rendezvous 110 | | 19 |
| ★57 | 73 | 80 | 82 | ROCKIN' LITTLE ANGEL — Ray Smith, Judd 1016 | | 4 |
| 58 | 64 | 77 | 88 | HARLEM NOCTURNE — Viscounts, Madison 123 | | 5 |
| 59 | 59 | 64 | 68 | CRAZY ARMS — Bob Beckham, Decca 31029 | | 4 |
| 60 | 48 | 48 | 71 | LET'S TRY AGAIN — Clyde McPhatter, M-G-M 12843 | S | 6 |
| 61 | 68 | 81 | 91 | I DON'T KNOW WHAT IT IS — The Blue Notes, Brooke 111 | | 7 |
| 62 | 58 | 57 | 42 | BELIEVE ME — Royal Teens, Capitol 4261 | | 14 |
| 63 | 39 | 31 | 30 | COME INTO MY HEART — Lloyd Price, ABC-Paramount 10062 | S | 14 |
| 64 | 54 | 22 | 22 | THE LITTLE DRUMMER BOY — Harry Simeone Chorale, 20th Fox 121 | S | 7 |
| ★65 | 84 | — | — | WHY DO I LOVE YOU SO — Johnny Tillotson, Cadence 1372 | | 2 |
| 66 | 72 | 88 | 89 | GOD BLESS AMERICA — Connie Francis, M-G-M 12841 | | 11 |
| 67 | 46 | 24 | 14 | UH! OH! (Part II) — The Nutty Squirrels, Hanover 4540 | | 12 |
| 68 | 88 | — | — | AMAPOLA — Jacky Noguez, Jamie 1148 | | 2 |
| 69 | 77 | 86 | 92 | DARLING LORRAINE — Knockouts, Shad 5013 | | 5 |
| ★70 | — | — | — | MIDNIGHT SPECIAL — Paul Evans, Guaranteed 205 | | 1 |
| 71 | 62 | 52 | 33 | DANNY BOY — Conway Twitty, M-G-M 12826 | S | 18 |
| 72 | 63 | 38 | 27 | BE MY GUEST — Fats Domino, Imperial 5629 | | 14 |
| 73 | 53 | 41 | 53 | MARY, DON'T YOU WEEP — Stonewall Jackson, Columbia 41533 | | 5 |
| 74 | 55 | 56 | 56 | NO LOVE HAVE I — Webb Pierce, Decca 31021 | | 5 |
| 75 | 89 | — | — | TOO MUCH TEQUILA — Champs, Challenge 59063 | | 2 |
| 76 | 96 | — | — | UPTOWN — Roy Orbison, Monument 412 | | 2 |
| 77 | — | — | — | FOREVER — Little Dippers, University 210 | | 1 |
| 78 | 82 | 97 | — | LET THE GOOD TIMES ROLL — Ray Charles, Atlantic 2047 | | 3 |
| 79 | — | — | — | BABY (YOU GOT WHAT IT TAKES) — Brook Benton and Dinah Washington, Mercury 71565 | | 1 |
| 80 | 86 | — | — | AM I THAT EASY TO FORGET — Debbie Reynolds, Dot 15985 | | 2 |
| 81 | 85 | 92 | 93 | (I REMEMBER) IN THE STILL OF THE NIGHT — The Five Satins, Ember 1005 | | 4 |
| 82 | 87 | 98 | — | TELL HER FOR ME — Adam Wade, Coed 520 | | 3 |
| 83 | 95 | — | — | I FORGOT MORE THAN YOU'LL EVER KNOW — Sonny James, Capitol 4307 | | 2 |
| 84 | — | — | — | ON THE BEACH — Frank Chacksfield, London 1901 | | 1 |
| 85 | 90 | 94 | 97 | ONE MINT JULEP — Chet Atkins, RCA Victor 7684 | | 4 |
| 86 | — | — | — | HARBOR LIGHTS — The Platters, Mercury 71563 | | 1 |
| 87 | 99 | — | — | THE HAPPY MULETEER — Ivo Robic, Laurie 3045 | | 2 |
| 88 | 97 | — | — | TIME AFTER TIME — Frankie Ford, Ace 580 | | 2 |
| 89 | — | — | — | MY LITTLE MARINE — Jamie Horton, Joy 234 | | 1 |
| ★90 | — | — | — | I CAN'T SAY GOODBYE — The Fireflies, Ribbon 6904 | | 1 |
| 91 | 91 | — | — | CRY ME A RIVER — Janice Harper, Capitol 4324 | | 2 |
| 92 | 80 | 58 | 40 | MISTY — Johnny Mathis, Columbia 41483 | | 17 |
| 93 | 100 | — | — | SINCE I MADE YOU CRY — The Rivieras, Coed 522 | | 2 |
| 94 | — | — | — | I WAS SUCH A FOOL — The Flamingos, End 1062 | | 1 |
| 95 | — | — | — | MEDITERRANEAN MOON — The Rays, XYZ 605 | | 1 |
| 96 | — | — | — | I'LL TAKE CARE OF YOU — Bobby (Blue) Bland, Duke 314 | | 1 |
| 97 | — | — | — | LIVIN' DANGEROUSLY — McGuire Sisters, Coral 62162 | | 1 |
| 98 | 79 | 79 | 57 | REVEILLE ROCK — Johnny and the Hurricanes, Warwick 513 | S | 13 |
| 99 | 65 | 69 | 39 | SWINGIN' ON A RAINBOW — Frankie Avalon, Chancellor 1045 | S | 6 |
| 100 | — | — | — | SECRET OF LOVE — Elton Anderson, Mercury 71542 | | 1 |

# The Billboard HOT 100

FOR WEEK ENDING FEBRUARY 7

*The Billboard's Music Popularity Charts... POP RECORDS* — FEBRUARY 1, 1960

STAR PERFORMERS showed the greatest upward progress on the Hot 100 this week.

S — Indicates that STEREO SINGLE version is available.

Columns: THIS WEEK | ONE WEEK AGO | TWO WEEKS AGO | THREE WEEKS AGO | TITLE, Artist, Company, Record No. | STEREO | WEEKS ON CHART

| This | 1wk | 2wk | 3wk | Title, Artist, Company, Record No. | Stereo | Wks |
|---|---|---|---|---|---|---|
| 1 | 1 | 1 | 4 | RUNNING BEAR — Johnny Preston, Mercury 71474 | | 16 |
| 2 | 4 | 7 | 14 | TEEN ANGEL — Mark Dinning, M-G-M 12845 | | 7 |
| 3 | 2 | 3 | 1 | EL PASO — Marty Robbins, Columbia 41511 | | 13 |
| ★4 | 10 | 13 | 28 | WHERE OR WHEN — Dion & the Belmonts, Laurie 3044 | | 6 |
| 5 | 8 | 6 | 7 | GO, JIMMY, GO — Jimmy Clanton, Ace 575 | | 9 |
| 6 | 3 | 2 | 2 | WHY — Frankie Avalon, Chancellor 1045 | S | 11 |
| ★7 | 14 | 25 | 42 | HANDY MAN — Jimmy Jones, Cub 9049 | | 6 |
| 8 | 6 | 4 | 5 | THE BIG HURT — Toni Fisher, Signet 275 | | 12 |
| 9 | 5 | 5 | 3 | WAY DOWN YONDER IN NEW ORLEANS — Freddy Cannon, Swan 4043 | | 11 |
| 10 | 9 | 9 | 9 | PRETTY BLUE EYES — Steve Lawrence, ABC-Paramount 10058 | S | 11 |
| 11 | 7 | 8 | 12 | THE VILLAGE OF ST. BERNADETTE — Andy Williams, Cadence 1374 | | 8 |
| 12 | 16 | 30 | 75 | WHAT IN THE WORLD'S COME OVER YOU — Jack Scott, Top Rank 2028 | S | 4 |
| 13 | 11 | 14 | 15 | YOU GOT WHAT IT TAKES — Marv Johnson, United Artists 185 | | 14 |
| ★14 | 21 | 31 | 61 | LONELY BLUE BOY — Conway Twitty, M-G-M 12857 | | 6 |
| 15 | 17 | 20 | 33 | DOWN BY THE STATION — Four Preps, Capitol 4312 | | 6 |
| ★16 | 23 | 61 | 76 | LET IT BE ME — The Everly Brothers, Cadence 1376 | | 4 |
| 17 | 20 | 24 | 29 | HE'LL HAVE TO GO — Jim Reeves, RCA Victor 7643 | S | 6 |
| 18 | 12 | 11 | 6 | IT'S TIME TO CRY — Paul Anka, ABC-Paramount 10064 | S | 11 |
| ★19 | 28 | 43 | 96 | THEME FROM A SUMMER PLACE — Percy Faith, Columbia 41490 | | 4 |
| 20 | 24 | 29 | 60 | TRACY'S THEME — Spencer Ross, Columbia 41532 | | 5 |
| 21 | 15 | 16 | 19 | SANDY — Larry Hall, Strand 25007 | | 11 |
| 22 | 13 | 10 | 8 | AMONG MY SOUVENIRS — Connie Francis, M-G-M 12841 | S | 11 |
| ★23 | 34 | 74 | — | BEYOND THE SEA — Bobby Darin, Atco 6158 | | 3 |
| 24 | 18 | 15 | 11 | HOUND DOG MAN — Fabian, Chancellor 1044 | S | 12 |
| 25 | 30 | 22 | 20 | FIRST NAME INITIAL — Annette, Vista 349 | | 15 |
| ★26 | 42 | 60 | 83 | TENDER LOVE AND CARE — Jimmie Rodgers, Roulette 4218 | | 4 |
| 27 | 19 | 18 | 16 | NOT ONE MINUTE MORE — Della Reese, RCA Victor 7644 | S | 8 |
| 28 | 22 | 12 | 10 | HEARTACHES BY THE NUMBER — Guy Mitchell, Columbia 41476 | | 18 |
| 29 | 25 | 27 | 43 | LUCKY DEVIL — Carl Dobkins Jr., Decca 31020 | | 9 |
| 30 | 27 | 17 | 17 | SMOKIE (Part II) — Bill Black's Combo, Hi 2081 | | 10 |
| 31 | 31 | 33 | 36 | IF I HAD A GIRL — Rod Lauren, RCA Victor 7645 | S | 7 |
| 32 | 41 | 34 | 44 | SHIMMY, SHIMMY, KO-KO BOP — Little Anthony & the Imperials, End 1060 | | 9 |
| 33 | 29 | 26 | 40 | BONNIE CAME BACK — Duane Eddy, Jamie 1144 | | 6 |
| ★34 | 57 | 73 | 80 | ROCKIN' LITTLE ANGEL — Ray Smith, Judd 1016 | | 5 |
| 35 | 38 | 47 | 59 | LITTLE THINGS MEAN A LOT — Joni James, M-G-M 12849 | S | 6 |
| 36 | 46 | 52 | 89 | LITTLE COCO PALM — Jerry Wallace, Challenge 59060 | | 5 |
| 37 | 26 | 21 | 21 | FRIENDLY WORLD — Fabian, Chancellor 1044 | S | 11 |
| 38 | 48 | 69 | 99 | BULLDOG — The Fireballs, Top Rank 2026 | S | 4 |
| 39 | 33 | 38 | 37 | HOW ABOUT THAT — Dee Clark, Abner 1032 | | 9 |
| 40 | 32 | 19 | 13 | MACK THE KNIFE — Bobby Darin, Atco 6147 | | 24 |
| 41 | 50 | 75 | — | WALTZING MATILDA — Jimmie Rodgers, Roulette 4218 | S | 3 |
| 42 | 36 | 45 | 46 | RUN, RED, RUN — Coasters, Atco 6153 | | 7 |
| 43 | 45 | 49 | 55 | BACIARE, BACIARE — Dorothy Collins, Top Rank 2024 | | 7 |
| ★44 | 80 | 86 | — | AM I THAT EASY TO FORGET — Debbie Reynolds, Dot 15985 | | 3 |
| ★45 | 75 | 89 | — | TOO MUCH TEQUILA — Champs, Challenge 59063 | | 3 |
| 46 | 77 | — | — | FOREVER — Little Dippers, University 210 | | 2 |
| 47 | 37 | 32 | 30 | TEARDROP — Santo and Johnny, Canadian-American 107 | | 10 |
| 48 | 44 | 50 | 66 | SWEET NOTHIN'S — Brenda Lee, Decca 30967 | | 7 |
| 49 | 39 | 41 | 34 | TALK THAT TALK — Jackie Wilson, Brunswick 55165 | | 11 |
| 50 | 65 | 84 | — | WHY DO I LOVE YOU SO — Johnny Tillotson, Cadence 1372 | | 3 |
| ★51 | 69 | 77 | 86 | DARLING LORRAINE — Knockouts, Shad 5013 | | 6 |
| 52 | 58 | 64 | 77 | HARLEM NOCTURNE — Viscounts, Madison 123 | | 6 |
| 53 | 51 | 35 | 35 | JUST COME HOME — Hugo and Luigi, RCA Victor 7639 | S | 8 |
| 54 | 74 | 55 | 56 | NO LOVE HAVE I — Webb Pierce, Decca 31021 | | 6 |
| 55 | 59 | 59 | 64 | CRAZY ARMS — Bob Beckham, Decca 31029 | | 5 |
| 56 | 47 | 42 | 45 | A YEAR AGO TONIGHT — The Crests, Coed 521 | | 9 |
| 57 | 52 | 56 | 47 | WHAT ABOUT US — The Coasters, Atco 6153 | | 9 |
| 58 | 70 | — | — | MIDNIGHT SPECIAL — Paul Evans, Guaranteed 205 | | 2 |
| 59 | 60 | 48 | 48 | LET'S TRY AGAIN — Clyde McPhatter, M-G-M 12843 | S | 7 |
| 60 | 86 | — | — | HARBOR LIGHTS — The Platters, Mercury 71563 | | 2 |
| ★61 | — | — | — | COUNTRY BOY — Fats Domino, Imperial 5645 | | 1 |
| 62 | 61 | 68 | 81 | I DON'T KNOW WHAT IT IS — The Blue Notes, Brooke 111 | | 8 |
| 63 | 73 | 53 | 41 | MARY, DON'T YOU WEEP — Stonewall Jackson, Columbia 41533 | | 6 |
| 64 | 68 | 88 | — | AMAPOLA — Jacky Nogeuez, Jamie 1148 | | 3 |
| 65 | 53 | 57 | 63 | HONEY HUSH — Joe Turner, Atlantic 2044 | | 6 |
| 66 | 40 | 36 | 26 | I WANNA BE LOVED — Ricky Nelson, Imperial 5614 | | 10 |
| 67 | 79 | — | — | BABY (YOU GOT WHAT IT TAKES) — Brook Benton and Dinah Washington, Mercury 71565 | | 2 |
| 68 | 35 | 23 | 18 | WE GOT LOVE — Bobby Rydell, Cameo 169 | | 17 |
| 69 | 49 | 40 | 27 | OH, CAROL — Neil Sedaka, RCA Victor 7595 | | 17 |
| 70 | — | — | — | CHINA DOLL — Ames Brothers, RCA Victor 7655 | | 1 |
| 71 | — | — | — | LADY LUCK — Lloyd Price, ABC-Paramount 10075 | S | 1 |
| 72 | — | — | — | WILD ONE — Bobby Rydell, Cameo 171 | | 1 |
| 73 | 82 | 87 | 98 | TELL HER FOR ME — Adam Wade, Coed 520 | | 4 |
| 74 | 84 | — | — | ON THE BEACH — Frank Chacksfield, London 1901 | | 2 |
| 75 | 76 | 96 | — | UPTOWN — Roy Orbison, Monument 412 | | 3 |
| 76 | 43 | 28 | 23 | SCARLET RIBBONS — Browns, RCA Victor 7614 | S | 14 |
| 77 | 87 | 99 | — | THE HAPPY MULETEER — Ivo Robic, Laurie 3045 | | 3 |
| 78 | 54 | 37 | 32 | SO MANY WAYS — Brook Benton, Mercury 71512 | S | 16 |
| 79 | — | 70 | 71 | SKOKIAAN — Bill Haley and His Comets, Decca 31030 | | 4 |
| 80 | 83 | 95 | — | I FORGOT MORE THAN YOU'LL EVER KNOW — Sonny James, Capitol 4307 | | 3 |
| 81 | — | — | — | LET IT ROCK — Chuck Berry, Chess 1747 | | 1 |
| 82 | 85 | 90 | 94 | ONE MINT JULEP — Chet Atkins, RCA Victor 7684 | | 5 |
| 83 | — | — | — | TIME AND THE RIVER — Nat King Cole, Capitol 4325 | | 1 |
| 84 | 89 | — | — | MY LITTLE MARINE — Jamie Horton, Joy 234 | | 2 |
| 85 | — | — | — | THAT OLD FEELING — Kitty Kallen, Columbia 41546 | | 1 |
| 86 | — | — | — | LITTLE BITTY GIRL — Bobby Rydell, Cameo 171 | | 1 |
| 87 | 88 | 97 | — | TIME AFTER TIME — Frankie Ford, Ace 580 | | 3 |
| 88 | 100 | — | — | SECRET OF LOVE — Elton Anderson, Mercury 71542 | | 2 |
| ★89 | — | — | — | SIXTEEN REASONS — Connie Stevens, Warner Bros. 5137 | | 1 |
| 90 | 90 | — | — | I CAN'T SAY GOODBYE — The Fireflies, Ribbon 6904 | | 2 |
| 91 | 62 | 58 | 57 | BELIEVE ME — Royal Teens, Capitol 4261 | | 15 |
| 92 | — | — | — | TALL OAK TREE — Dorsey Burnette, Era 3012 | | 1 |
| 93 | 93 | 100 | — | SINCE I MADE YOU CRY — The Rivieras, Coed 522 | | 3 |
| 94 | 96 | — | — | I'LL TAKE CARE OF YOU — Bobby (Blue) Bland, Duke 314 | | 2 |
| 95 | — | — | — | MONEY — Barrett Strong, Anna 1111 | | 1 |
| 96 | — | — | — | PEACE OF MIND — Teresa Brewer, Coral 62167 | | 1 |
| 97 | — | — | — | FANNIE MAE — Buster Brown, Fire 1008 | | 1 |
| 98 | — | — | — | HULLY GULLY — Olympics, Arvee 562 | | 1 |
| 99 | 95 | — | — | MEDITERRANEAN MOON — The Rays, XYZ 605 | | 2 |
| 100 | — | — | — | WHIFFENPOOF SONG — Bob Crewe, Warwick 519 | | 1 |

… Pop Records — February 8, 1960

# The Billboard HOT 100
**For Week Ending February 14**

| This Week | One Week Ago | Two Weeks Ago | Three Weeks Ago | Title — Artist, Company, Record No. | Stereo | Weeks on Chart |
|---|---|---|---|---|---|---|
| 1 | 2 | 4 | 7 | TEEN ANGEL — Mark Dinning, M-G-M 12845 | | 8 |
| 2 | 1 | 1 | 1 | RUNNING BEAR — Johnny Preston, Mercury 71474 | | 17 |
| 3 | 4 | 10 | 13 | WHERE OR WHEN — Dion & the Belmonts, Laurie 3044 | | 7 |
| 4 | 3 | 2 | 3 | EL PASO — Marty Robbins, Columbia 41511 | A | 14 |
| 5 | 7 | 14 | 25 | HANDY MAN — Jimmy Jones, Cub 9049 | | 7 |
| 6 | 14 | 21 | 31 | LONELY BLUE BOY — Conway Twitty, M-G-M 12857 | | 7 |
| 7 | 12 | 16 | 30 | WHAT IN THE WORLD'S COME OVER YOU — Jack Scott, Top Rank 2028 | S | 5 |
| 8 | 17 | 20 | 24 | HE'LL HAVE TO GO — Jim Reeves, RCA Victor 7643 | S | 7 |
| 9 | 6 | 3 | 2 | WHY — Frankie Avalon, Chancellor 1045 | S | 12 |
| 10 | 13 | 11 | 14 | YOU GOT WHAT IT TAKES — Marv Johnson, United Artists 185 | | 15 |
| 11 | 5 | 8 | 6 | GO, JIMMY, GO — Jimmy Clanton, Ace 575 | | 10 |
| 12 | 19 | 28 | 43 | THEME FROM A SUMMER PLACE — Percy Faith, Columbia 41490 | A | 5 |
| 13 | 16 | 23 | 61 | LET IT BE ME — The Everly Brothers, Cadence 1376 | | 5 |
| 14 | 10 | 9 | 9 | PRETTY BLUE EYES — Steve Lawrence, ABC-Paramount 10058 | S | 12 |
| 15 | 11 | 7 | 8 | THE VILLAGE OF ST. BERNADETTE — Andy Williams, Cadence 1374 | | 9 |
| 16 | 15 | 17 | 20 | DOWN BY THE STATION — Four Preps, Capitol 4312 | | 7 |
| 17 | 8 | 6 | 4 | THE BIG HURT — Toni Fisher, Signet 275 | | 13 |
| 18 | 9 | 5 | 5 | WAY DOWN YONDER IN NEW ORLEANS — Freddy Cannon, Swan 4043 | | 12 |
| 19 | 23 | 34 | 74 | BEYOND THE SEA — Bobby Darin, Atco 6158 | | 4 |
| 20 | 20 | 24 | 29 | TRACY'S THEME — Spencer Ross, Columbia 41532 | A | 6 |
| 21 | 18 | 12 | 11 | IT'S TIME TO CRY — Paul Anka, ABC-Paramount 10064 | S | 12 |
| 22 | 22 | 13 | 10 | AMONG MY SOUVENIRS — Connie Francis, M-G-M 12841 | S | 12 |
| 23 | 21 | 15 | 16 | SANDY — Larry Hall, Strand 25007 | | 12 |
| 24 | 32 | 41 | 34 | SHIMMY, SHIMMY, KO-KO BOP — Little Anthony & the Imperials, End 1060 | | 10 |
| 25 | 26 | 42 | 60 | TENDER LOVE AND CARE — Jimmie Rodgers, Roulette 4218 | | 5 |
| 26 | 34 | 57 | 73 | ROCKIN' LITTLE ANGEL — Ray Smith, Judd 1016 | | 6 |
| 27 | 46 | 77 | — | FOREVER — Little Dippers, University 210 | | 3 |
| 28 | 29 | 25 | 27 | LUCKY DEVIL — Carl Dobkins Jr., Decca 31020 | | 10 |
| 29 | 72 | — | — | WILD ONE — Bobby Rydell, Cameo 171 | | 2 |
| 30 | 27 | 19 | 18 | NOT ONE MINUTE MORE — Della Reese, RCA Victor 7644 | S | 9 |
| 31 | 24 | 18 | 15 | HOUND DOG MAN — Fabian, Chancellor 1044 | S | 13 |
| 32 | 25 | 30 | 22 | FIRST NAME INITIAL — Annette, Vista 349 | | 16 |
| 33 | 33 | 29 | 26 | BONNIE CAME BACK — Duane Eddy, Jamie 1144 | | 7 |
| 34 | 38 | 48 | 69 | BULLDOG — The Fireballs, Top Rank 2026 | S | 5 |
| 35 | 30 | 27 | 17 | SMOKIE (Part II) — Bill Black's Combo, Hi 2081 | | 11 |
| 36 | 35 | 38 | 47 | LITTLE THINGS MEAN A LOT — Joni James, M-G-M 12849 | S | 7 |
| 37 | 67 | 79 | — | BABY — Brook Benton and Dinah Washington, Mercury 71565 | S | 3 |
| 38 | 36 | 46 | 52 | LITTLE COCO PALM — Jerry Wallace, Challenge 59060 | | 6 |
| 39 | 45 | 75 | 89 | TOO MUCH TEQUILLA — Champs, Challenge 59063 | | 4 |
| 40 | 31 | 31 | 33 | IF I HAD A GIRL — Rod Lauren, RCA Victor 7645 | S | 8 |
| 41 | 60 | 86 | — | HARBOR LIGHTS — The Platters, Mercury 71563 | S | 3 |
| 42 | 48 | 44 | 50 | SWEET NOTHIN'S — Brenda Lee, Decca 30967 | | 8 |
| 43 | 41 | 50 | 75 | WALTZING MATILDA — Jimmie Rodgers, Roulette 4218 | S | 4 |
| 44 | 44 | 80 | 86 | AM I THAT EASY TO FORGET — Debbie Reynolds, Dot 15985 | | 4 |
| 45 | 58 | 70 | — | MIDNIGHT SPECIAL — Paul Evans, Guaranteed 205 | | 3 |
| 46 | 50 | 65 | 84 | WHY DO I LOVE YOU SO — Johnny Tillotson, Cadence 1372 | | 4 |
| 47 | 28 | 22 | 12 | HEARTACHES BY THE NUMBER — Guy Mitchell, Columbia 41476 | A | 19 |
| 48 | 70 | — | — | CHINA DOLL — Ames Brothers, RCA Victor 7655 | | 2 |
| 49 | 51 | 69 | 77 | DARLING LORRAINE — Knockouts, Shad 5013 | | 7 |
| 50 | 83 | — | — | TIME AND THE RIVER — Nat King Cole, Capitol 4325 | | 2 |
| 51 | 71 | — | — | LADY LUCK — Lloyd Price, ABC-Paramount 10075 | S | 2 |
| 52 | 37 | 26 | 21 | FRIENDLY WORLD — Fabian, Chancellor 1044 | S | 12 |
| 53 | 52 | 58 | 64 | HARLEM NOCTURNE — Viscounts, Madison 123 | | 7 |
| 54 | 86 | — | — | LITTLE BITTY GIRL — Bobby Rydell, Cameo 171 | | 2 |
| 55 | 61 | — | — | COUNTRY BOY — Fats Domino, Imperial 5645 | | 2 |
| 56 | 43 | 45 | 49 | BACIARE, BACIARE — Dorothy Collins, Top Rank 2024 | | 8 |
| 57 | 39 | 33 | 38 | HOW ABOUT THAT — Dee Clark, Abner 1032 | | 10 |
| 58 | 55 | 59 | 59 | CRAZY ARMS — Bob Beckham, Decca 31029 | | 6 |
| 59 | 40 | 32 | 19 | MACK THE KNIFE — Bobby Darin, Atco 6147 | | 25 |
| 60 | 85 | — | — | THAT OLD FEELING — Kitty Kallen, Columbia 41546 | | 2 |
| 61 | — | — | — | ETERNALLY — Sarah Vaughan, Mercury 71562 | S | 1 |
| 62 | 53 | 51 | 35 | JUST COME HOME — Hugo and Luigi, RCA Victor 7639 | S | 9 |
| 63 | 74 | 84 | — | ON THE BEACH — Frank Chacksfield, London 1901 | | 3 |
| 64 | 77 | 87 | 99 | THE HAPPY MULETEER — Ivo Robic, Laurie 3045 | | 4 |
| 65 | 64 | 68 | 88 | AMAPOLA — Jacky Noguez, Jamie 1148 | | 5 |
| 66 | 54 | 74 | 55 | NO LOVE HAVE I — Webb Pierce, Decca 31021 | | 8 |
| 67 | 65 | 53 | 57 | HONEY HUSH — Joe Turner, Atlantic 2044 | | 7 |
| 68 | 73 | 82 | 87 | TELL HER FOR ME — Adam Wade, Coed 520 | | 5 |
| 69 | 42 | 36 | 45 | RUN, RED, RUN — Coasters, Atco 6153 | | 8 |
| 70 | 96 | — | — | PEACE OF MIND — Teresa Brewer, Coral 62167 | | 2 |
| 71 | — | — | — | DELAWARE — Perry Como, RCA Victor 7670 | | 1 |
| 72 | — | — | — | I WAS SUCH A FOOL — Flamingoes, End 1062 | | 1 |
| 73 | 89 | — | — | SIXTEEN REASONS — Connie Stevens, Warner Bros. 5137 | | 2 |
| 74 | 92 | — | — | TALL OAK TREE — Dorsey Burnette, Era 3012 | | 2 |
| 75 | 75 | 76 | 96 | UPTOWN — Roy Orbison, Monument 412 | | 4 |
| 76 | 79 | — | 70 | SKOKIAAN — Bill Haley and His Comets, Decca 31030 | | 5 |
| 77 | 63 | 73 | 53 | MARY, DON'T YOU WEEP — Stonewall Jackson, Columbia 41533 | A | 8 |
| 78 | 56 | 47 | 42 | A YEAR AGO TONIGHT — The Crests, Coed 521 | | 10 |
| 79 | 97 | — | — | FANNIE MAE — Buster Brown, Fire 1008 | | 2 |
| 80 | 95 | — | — | MONEY — Barrett Strong, Anna 1111 | | 2 |
| 81 | 81 | — | — | LET IT ROCK — Chuck Berry, Chess 1747 | | 2 |
| 82 | 82 | 85 | 90 | ONE MINT JULEP — Chet Atkins, RCA Victor 7684 | | 6 |
| 83 | 98 | — | — | HULLY GULLY — Olympics, Arvee 562 | | 2 |
| 84 | 62 | 61 | 68 | I DON'T KNOW WHAT IT IS — The Blue Notes, Brooke 111 | | 9 |
| 85 | 47 | 37 | 32 | TEARDROP — Santo and Johnny, Canadian-American 107 | | 11 |
| 86 | 66 | 40 | 36 | I WANNA BE LOVED — Ricky Nelson, Imperial 5614 | | 11 |
| 87 | 59 | 60 | 48 | LET'S TRY AGAIN — Clyde McPhatter, M-G-M 12843 | S | 8 |
| 88 | 69 | 49 | 40 | OH, CAROL — Neil Sedaka, RCA Victor 7595 | | 18 |
| 89 | 94 | 96 | — | I'LL TAKE CARE OF YOU — Bobby (Blue) Bland, Duke 314 | | 3 |
| 90 | — | — | — | BAD BOY — Marty Wilde, Epic 9356 | | 1 |
| 91 | 88 | 100 | — | SECRET OF LOVE — Elton Anderson, Mercury 71542 | | 3 |
| 92 | 49 | 39 | 41 | TALK THAT TALK — Jackie Wilson, Brunswick 55165 | | 12 |
| 93 | 57 | 52 | 56 | WHAT ABOUT US — The Coasters, Atco 6153 | | 10 |
| 94 | — | — | — | CLOSER WALK — Pete Fountain, Coral 62154 | | 1 |
| 95 | — | — | — | I KNOW WHAT GOD IS — Perry Como, RCA Victor 7670 | | 1 |
| 96 | 100 | — | — | WHIFFENPOOF SONG — Bob Crewe, Warwick 519 | | 2 |
| 97 | 84 | 89 | — | MY LITTLE MARINE — Jamie Horton, Joy 234 | | 3 |
| 98 | — | — | — | DON'T LET THE SUN CATCH YOU CRYING — Ray Charles, Atlantic 2047 | | 1 |
| 99 | — | — | — | HONEY LOVE — Narvel Felts, Pink 702 | | 1 |
| 100 | — | — | — | CLEMENTINE — Jan and Dean, Dore 539 | | 1 |

STAR PERFORMERS showed the greatest upward progress on Hot 100 this week.
S — Indicates that 45 r.p.m. stereo single version is available.
A — Indicates that 33⅓ r.p.m. stereo single version is available.

# The Billboard HOT 100

**FOR WEEK ENDING FEBRUARY 21**

*STAR PERFORMERS showed the greatest upward progress on Hot 100 this week.*
(S) Indicates that 45 r.p.m. stereo single version is available.
(A) Indicates that 33⅓ r.p.m. stereo single version is available.

| This Week | 1 Wk Ago | 2 Wks Ago | 3 Wks Ago | Title / Artist, Company, Record No. | Stereo | Wks on Chart |
|---|---|---|---|---|---|---|
| 1 | 1 | 2 | 4 | TEEN ANGEL — Mark Dinning, M-G-M 12845 | | 9 |
| 2 | 2 | 1 | 1 | RUNNING BEAR — Johnny Preston, Mercury 71474 | | 18 |
| 3 | 5 | 7 | 14 | HANDY MAN — Jimmy Jones, Cub 9049 | | 8 |
| 4 | 8 | 17 | 20 | HE'LL HAVE TO GO — Jim Reeves, RCA Victor 7643 | S | 8 |
| 5 | 3 | 4 | 10 | WHERE OR WHEN — Dion & the Belmonts, Laurie 3044 | | 8 |
| ★6 | 12 | 19 | 28 | THEME FROM A SUMMER PLACE — Percy Faith, Columbia 41490 | A | 6 |
| 7 | 7 | 12 | 16 | WHAT IN THE WORLD'S COME OVER YOU — Jack Scott, Top Rank 2028 | S | 6 |
| 8 | 6 | 14 | 21 | LONELY BLUE BOY — Conway Twitty, M-G-M 12857 | | 8 |
| 9 | 13 | 16 | 23 | LET IT BE ME — The Everly Brothers, Cadence 1376 | | 6 |
| 10 | 4 | 3 | 2 | EL PASO — Marty Robbins, Columbia 41511 | A | 15 |
| ★11 | 19 | 23 | 34 | BEYOND THE SEA — Bobby Darin, Atco 6158 | | 5 |
| 12 | 14 | 10 | 9 | PRETTY BLUE EYES — Steve Lawrence, ABC-Paramount 10058 | S | 13 |
| 13 | 16 | 15 | 17 | DOWN BY THE STATION — Four Preps, Capitol 4312 | | 8 |
| 14 | 10 | 13 | 11 | YOU GOT WHAT IT TAKES — Marv Johnson, United Artists 185 | | 16 |
| 15 | 11 | 5 | 8 | GO, JIMMY, GO — Jimmy Clanton, Ace 575 | | 11 |
| 16 | 9 | 6 | 3 | WHY — Frankie Avalon, Chancellor 1045 | S | 13 |
| 17 | 15 | 11 | 7 | THE VILLAGE OF ST. BERNADETTE — Andy Williams, Cadence 1374 | | 10 |
| 18 | 17 | 8 | 6 | THE BIG HURT — Toni Fisher, Signet 275 | | 14 |
| 19 | 20 | 20 | 24 | TRACY'S THEME — Spencer Ross, Columbia 41532 | A | 7 |
| ★20 | 37 | 67 | 79 | BABY — Brook Benton and Dinah Washington, Mercury 71565 | S | 4 |
| 21 | 27 | 46 | 77 | FOREVER — Little Dippers, University 210 | | 4 |
| 22 | 18 | 9 | 5 | WAY DOWN YONDER IN NEW ORLEANS — Freddy Cannon, Swan 4043 | | 13 |
| 23 | 29 | 72 | — | WILD ONE — Bobby Rydell, Cameo 171 | | 3 |
| 24 | 26 | 34 | 57 | ROCKIN' LITTLE ANGEL — Ray Smith, Judd 1016 | | 7 |
| 25 | 25 | 26 | 42 | TENDER LOVE AND CARE — Jimmie Rodgers, Roulette 4218 | | 6 |
| 26 | 24 | 32 | 41 | SHIMMY, SHIMMY, KO-KO BOP — Little Anthony & the Imperials, End 1060 | | 11 |
| ★27 | 41 | 60 | 86 | HARBOR LIGHTS — The Platters, Mercury 71563 | S | 4 |
| 28 | 23 | 21 | 15 | SANDY — Larry Hall, Strand 25007 | | 13 |
| 29 | 34 | 38 | 48 | BULLDOG — The Fireballs, Top Rank 2026 | S | 6 |
| ★30 | 42 | 48 | 44 | SWEET NOTHIN'S — Brenda Lee, Decca 30967 | | 9 |
| 31 | 28 | 29 | 25 | LUCKY DEVIL — Carl Dobkins Jr., Decca 31020 | | 11 |
| 32 | 22 | 22 | 13 | AMONG MY SOUVENIRS — Connie Francis, M-G-M 12841 | S | 13 |
| 33 | 45 | 58 | 70 | MIDNIGHT SPECIAL — Paul Evans, Guaranteed 205 | | 4 |
| ★34 | 50 | 83 | — | TIME AND THE RIVER — Nat King Cole, Capitol 4325 | | 3 |
| 35 | 51 | 71 | — | LADY LUCK — Lloyd Price, ABC-Paramount 10075 | S | 3 |
| 36 | 39 | 45 | 75 | TOO MUCH TEQUILA — Champs, Challenge 59063 | | 5 |
| ★37 | 55 | 61 | — | COUNTRY BOY — Fats Domino, Imperial 5645 | | 3 |
| 38 | 30 | 27 | 19 | NOT ONE MINUTE MORE — Della Reese, RCA Victor 7644 | S | 10 |
| 39 | 21 | 18 | 12 | IT'S TIME TO CRY — Paul Anka, ABC-Paramount 10064 | S | 13 |
| 40 | 32 | 25 | 30 | FIRST NAME INITIAL — Annette, Vista 349 | | 17 |
| ★41 | 54 | 86 | — | LITTLE BITTY GIRL — Bobby Rydell, Cameo 171 | | 3 |
| 42 | 48 | 70 | — | CHINA DOLL — Ames Brothers, RCA Victor 7655 | S | 3 |
| 43 | 46 | 50 | 65 | WHY DO I LOVE YOU SO — Johnny Tillotson, Cadence 1372 | | 5 |
| 44 | 71 | — | — | DELAWARE — Perry Como, RCA Victor 7670 | S | 2 |
| 45 | 40 | 31 | 31 | IF I HAD A GIRL — Rod Lauren, RCA Victor 7645 | S | 9 |
| 46 | 38 | 36 | 46 | LITTLE COCO PALM — Jerry Wallace, Challenge 59060 | | 7 |
| 47 | 44 | 44 | 80 | AM I THAT EASY TO FORGET — Debbie Reynolds, Dot 15985 | | 5 |
| ★48 | 58 | 55 | 59 | CRAZY ARMS — Bob Beckham, Decca 31029 | | 7 |
| 49 | 33 | 33 | 29 | BONNIE CAME BACK — Duane Eddy, Jamie 1144 | | 8 |
| ★50 | 74 | 92 | — | TALL OAK TREE — Dorsey Burnette, Era 3012 | | 3 |
| 51 | 31 | 24 | 18 | HOUND DOG MAN — Fabian, Chancellor 1044 | S | 14 |
| 52 | 61 | — | — | ETERNALLY — Sarah Vaughan, Mercury 71562 | S | 2 |
| 53 | 36 | 35 | 38 | LITTLE THINGS MEAN A LOT — Joni James, M-G-M 12849 | S | 8 |
| 54 | 47 | 28 | 22 | HEARTACHES BY THE NUMBER — Guy Mitchell, Columbia 41476 | A | 20 |
| 55 | 35 | 30 | 27 | SMOKIE (Part II) — Bill Black's Combo, Hi 2081 | | 12 |
| ★56 | 80 | 95 | — | MONEY — Barrett Strong, Anna 1111 | | 3 |
| 57 | 60 | 85 | — | THAT OLD FEELING — Kitty Kallen, Columbia 41546 | | 3 |
| 58 | 64 | 77 | 87 | THE HAPPY MULETEER — Ivo Robic, Laurie 3045 | | 5 |
| 59 | 63 | 74 | 84 | ON THE BEACH — Frank Chacksfield, London 1901 | | 4 |
| 60 | 49 | 51 | 69 | DARLING LORRAINE — Knockouts, Shad 5013 | | 8 |
| 61 | 57 | 39 | 33 | HOW ABOUT THAT — Dee Clark, Abner 1032 | | 11 |
| ★62 | 90 | — | — | BAD BOY — Marty Wilde, Epic 9356 | | 2 |
| 63 | 65 | 64 | 68 | AMAPOLA — Jacky Noguez, Jamie 1148 | | 6 |
| ★64 | 79 | 97 | — | FANNIE MAE — Buster Brown, Fire 1008 | | 3 |
| 65 | 53 | 52 | 58 | HARLEM NOCTURNE — Viscounts, Madison 123 | | 8 |
| 66 | 68 | 73 | 82 | TELL HER FOR ME — Adam Wade, Coed 520 | | 6 |
| 67 | 70 | 96 | — | PEACE OF MIND — Teresa Brewer, Coral 62167 | | 3 |
| 68 | 73 | 89 | — | SIXTEEN REASONS — Connie Stevens, Warner Bros. 5137 | | 3 |
| 69 | — | — | — | BEATNIK FLY — Johnny and the Hurricanes, Warwick 520 | | 1 |
| 70 | 56 | 43 | 45 | BACIARE, BACIARE — Dorothy Collins, Top Rank 2024 | | 9 |
| 71 | 72 | — | — | I WAS SUCH A FOOL — Flamingoes, End 1062 | | 2 |
| 72 | 75 | 75 | 76 | UPTOWN — Roy Orbison, Monument 412 | | 5 |
| 73 | 43 | 41 | 50 | WALTZING MATILDA — Jimmie Rodgers, Roulette 4218 | S | 5 |
| 74 | — | — | — | OUTSIDE MY WINDOW — Fleetwoods, Dolton 15 | | 1 |
| 75 | 81 | 81 | — | LET IT ROCK — Chuck Berry, Chess 1747 | | 3 |
| 76 | 59 | 40 | 32 | MACK THE KNIFE — Bobby Darin, Atco 6147 | | 26 |
| 77 | 83 | 98 | — | HULLY GULLY — Olympics, Arvee 562 | | 3 |
| 78 | — | — | — | TOO POOPED TO POP — Chuck Berry, Chess 1747 | | 1 |
| 79 | — | — | — | TEENSVILLE — Chet Atkins, RCA Victor 7684 | S | 1 |
| 80 | — | — | — | MUMBLIN' MOSIE — Johnny Otis, Capitol 4326 | | 1 |
| 81 | 95 | — | — | I KNOW WHAT GOD IS — Perry Como, RCA Victor 7670 | S | 2 |
| 82 | — | — | — | BABY, WHAT DO YOU WANT ME TO DO — Jimmy Reed, Vee Jay 333 | | 1 |
| 83 | — | — | — | FOREVER — Billy Walker, Columbia 41548 | | 1 |
| 84 | — | — | — | (DO THE) MASHED POTATOES — Nat Kendrick & the Swans, Dade 1804 | | 1 |
| 85 | — | — | — | JUST A LITTLE BIT — Roscoe Gordon, Vee Jay 332 | | 1 |
| 86 | 76 | 79 | — | SKOKIAAN — Bill Haley and His Comets, Decca 31030 | | 6 |
| 87 | — | — | — | YOU'RE MY BABY — Sarah Vaughan, Mercury 71562 | S | 1 |
| 88 | 67 | 65 | 53 | HONEY HUSH — Joe Turner, Atlantic 2044 | | 8 |
| 89 | 66 | 54 | 74 | NO LOVE HAVE I — Webb Pierce, Decca 31021 | | 9 |
| 90 | 99 | — | — | HONEY LOVE — Narvel Felts, Pink 702 | | 2 |
| 91 | — | 90 | 90 | I CAN'T SAY GOODBYE — The Fireflies, Ribbon 6904 | | 3 |
| 92 | — | — | 91 | CRY ME A RIVER — Janice Harper, Capitol 4324 | | 3 |
| 93 | 100 | — | — | CLEMENTINE — Jan and Dean, Dore 539 | | 2 |
| 94 | 52 | 37 | 26 | FRIENDLY WORLD — Fabian, Chancellor 1047 | S | 13 |
| 95 | 98 | — | — | DON'T LET THE SUN CATCH YOU CRYING — Ray Charles, Atlantic 2047 | | 2 |
| 96 | — | 87 | 88 | TIME AFTER TIME — Frankie Ford, Ace 580 | | 4 |
| 97 | — | — | — | WHAT'S HAPPENING — Wade Flemons, Vee Jay 335 | | 1 |
| 98 | — | — | — | IF YOU NEED ME — Fats Domino, Imperial 5645 | | 1 |
| 99 | — | — | — | LET THE LITTLE GIRL DANCE — Billy Bland, Old Town 1076 | | 1 |
| 100 | — | — | — | PARADISE — Sammy Turner, Big Top 3032 | | 1 |

# The Billboard HOT 100

**FOR WEEK ENDING FEBRUARY 28**

*STAR PERFORMERS showed the greatest upward progress on Hot 100 this week.*
(S) Indicates that 45 r.p.m. stereo single version is available.
(A) Indicates that 33⅓ r.p.m. stereo single version is available.

| This Week | 1 Wk Ago | 2 Wks Ago | 3 Wks Ago | Title — Artist, Company, Record No. | Stereo | Weeks on Chart |
|---|---|---|---|---|---|---|
| ★1 | 6 | 12 | 19 | THEME FROM A SUMMER PLACE — Percy Faith, Columbia 41490 | (A) | 7 |
| 2 | 1 | 1 | 2 | TEEN ANGEL — Mark Dinning, M-G-M 12845 | | 10 |
| 3 | 3 | 5 | 7 | HANDY MAN — Jimmy Jones, Cub 9049 | | 9 |
| 4 | 4 | 8 | 17 | HE'LL HAVE TO GO — Jim Reeves, RCA Victor 7643 | (S) | 9 |
| 5 | 7 | 7 | 12 | WHAT IN THE WORLD'S COME OVER YOU — Jack Scott, Top Rank 2028 | (S) | 7 |
| 6 | 2 | 2 | 1 | RUNNING BEAR — Johnny Preston, Mercury 71474 | | 19 |
| 7 | 9 | 13 | 16 | LET IT BE ME — The Everly Brothers, Cadence 1376 | | 7 |
| 8 | 11 | 19 | 23 | BEYOND THE SEA — Bobby Darin, Atco 6158 | | 6 |
| 9 | 8 | 6 | 14 | LONELY BLUE BOY — Conway Twitty, M-G-M 12857 | | 9 |
| 10 | 5 | 3 | 4 | WHERE OR WHEN — Dion and the Belmonts, Laurie 3044 | | 9 |
| ★11 | 23 | 29 | 72 | WILD ONE — Bobby Rydell, Cameo 171 | | 4 |
| 12 | 20 | 37 | 67 | BABY — Brook Benton and Dinah Washington, Mercury 71565 | (S) | 5 |
| ★13 | 19 | 20 | 20 | TRACY'S THEME — Spencer Ross, Columbia 41532 | (A) | 8 |
| 14 | 13 | 16 | 15 | DOWN BY THE STATION — Four Preps, Capitol 4312 | | 9 |
| 15 | 14 | 10 | 13 | YOU GOT WHAT IT TAKES — Marv Johnson, United Artists 185 | | 17 |
| 16 | 10 | 4 | 3 | EL PASO — Marty Robbins, Columbia 41511 | (A) | 16 |
| 17 | 21 | 27 | 46 | FOREVER — Little Dippers, University 210 | | 5 |
| 18 | 12 | 14 | 10 | PRETTY BLUE EYES — Steve Lawrence, ABC-Paramount 10058 | (S) | 14 |
| 19 | 33 | 45 | 58 | MIDNIGHT SPECIAL — Paul Evans, Guaranteed 205 | | 5 |
| ★20 | 35 | 51 | 71 | LADY LUCK — Lloyd Price, ABC-Paramount 10075 | (S) | 4 |
| 21 | 27 | 41 | 60 | HARBOR LIGHTS — The Platters, Mercury 71563 | (S) | 5 |
| 22 | 24 | 26 | 34 | ROCKIN' LITTLE ANGEL — Ray Smith, Judd 1016 | | 8 |
| 23 | 15 | 11 | 5 | GO, JIMMY, GO — Jimmy Clanton, Ace 575 | | 12 |
| 24 | 25 | 25 | 26 | TENDER LOVE AND CARE — Jimmie Rodgers, Roulette 4218 | | 7 |
| 25 | 29 | 34 | 38 | BULLDOG — The Fireballs, Top Rank 2026 | (S) | 7 |
| 26 | 30 | 42 | 48 | SWEET NOTHIN'S — Brenda Lee, Decca 30967 | | 10 |
| ★27 | 41 | 54 | 86 | LITTLE BITTY GIRL — Bobby Rydell, Cameo 171 | | 4 |
| 28 | 16 | 9 | 6 | WHY — Frankie Avalon, Chancellor 1045 | (S) | 14 |
| 29 | 37 | 55 | 61 | COUNTRY BOY — Fats Domino, Imperial 5645 | | 4 |
| 30 | 34 | 50 | 83 | TIME AND THE RIVER — Nat King Cole, Capitol 4325 | | 4 |
| 31 | 31 | 28 | 29 | LUCKY DEVIL — Carl Dobkins Jr., Decca 31020 | | 12 |
| 32 | 36 | 39 | 45 | TOO MUCH TEQUILA — Champs, Challenge 59063 | | 6 |
| 33 | 26 | 24 | 32 | SHIMMY, SHIMMY, KO-KO BOP — Little Anthony & the Imperials, End 1060 | | 12 |
| ★34 | 44 | 71 | — | DELAWARE — Perry Como, RCA Victor 7670 | (S) | 3 |
| 35 | 50 | 74 | 92 | TALL OAK TREE — Dorsey Burnette, Era 3012 | | 4 |
| ★36 | 69 | — | — | BEATNIK FLY — Johnny and the Hurricanes, Warwick 520 | | 2 |
| 37 | 18 | 17 | 8 | THE BIG HURT — Toni Fisher, Signet 275 | | 15 |
| 38 | 17 | 15 | 11 | THE VILLAGE OF ST. BERNADETTE — Andy Williams, Cadence 1374 | | 11 |
| 39 | 47 | 44 | 44 | AM I THAT EASY TO FORGET — Debbie Reynolds, Dot 15985 | | 6 |
| 40 | 42 | 48 | 70 | CHINA DOLL — Ames Brothers, RCA Victor 7655 | (S) | 4 |
| 41 | 52 | 61 | — | ETERNALLY — Sarah Vaughan, Mercury 71562 | (S) | 3 |
| 42 | 43 | 46 | 50 | WHY DO I LOVE YOU SO — Johnny Tillotson, Cadence 1372 | | 6 |
| 43 | 48 | 58 | 55 | CRAZY ARMS — Bob Beckham, Decca 31029 | | 8 |
| 44 | 22 | 18 | 9 | WAY DOWN YONDER IN NEW ORLEANS — Freddy Cannon, Swan 4043 | | 14 |
| ★45 | 62 | 90 | — | BAD BOY — Marty Wilde, Epic 9356 | | 3 |
| 46 | 60 | 49 | 51 | DARLING LORRAINE — Knockouts, Shad 5013 | | 9 |
| 47 | 59 | 63 | 74 | ON THE BEACH — Frank Chacksfield, London 1901 | | 5 |
| 48 | 74 | — | — | OUTSIDE MY WINDOW — Fleetwoods, Dolton 15 | | 2 |
| 49 | 56 | 80 | 95 | MONEY — Barrett Strong, Anna 1111 | | 4 |
| 50 | 82 | — | — | BABY, WHAT DO YOU WANT ME TO DO — Jimmy Reed, Vee Jay 333 | | 2 |
| 51 | 78 | — | — | TOO POOPED TO POP — Chuck Berry, Chess 1747 | | 2 |
| 52 | 64 | 79 | 97 | FANNIE MAE — Buster Brown, Fire 1008 | | 4 |
| 53 | 46 | 38 | 46 | LITTLE COCO PALM — Jerry Wallace, Challenge 59060 | | 8 |
| 54 | 28 | 23 | 21 | SANDY — Larry Hall, Strand 25007 | | 14 |
| 55 | 57 | 60 | 85 | THAT OLD FEELING — Kitty Kallen, Columbia 41546 | | 4 |
| 56 | 65 | 53 | 52 | HARLEM NOCTURNE — Viscounts, Madison 123 | | 9 |
| 57 | 39 | 21 | 18 | IT'S TIME TO CRY — Paul Anka, ABC-Paramount 10064 | (S) | 14 |
| 58 | 68 | 73 | 89 | SIXTEEN REASONS — Connie Stevens, Warner Bros. 5137 | | 4 |
| 59 | 32 | 22 | 22 | AMONG MY SOUVENIRS — Connie Francis, M-G-M 12841 | (S) | 14 |
| 60 | — | — | — | (WELCOME) NEW LOVERS — Pat Boone, Dot 16048 | (S) | 1 |
| 61 | — | — | — | STRING ALONG — Fabian, Chancellor 1047 | (S) | 1 |
| 62 | — | — | — | PUPPY LOVE — Paul Anka, ABC-Paramount 10082 | (S) | 1 |
| 63 | — | — | — | MAMA — Connie Francis, M-G-M 12878 | (S) | 1 |
| 64 | 75 | 81 | 81 | LET IT ROCK — Chuck Berry, Chess 1747 | | 4 |
| 65 | 73 | 43 | 41 | WALTZING MATILDA — Jimmie Rodgers, Roulette 4218 | (S) | 6 |
| 66 | 67 | 70 | 96 | PEACE OF MIND — Teresa Brewer, Coral 62167 | | 4 |
| 67 | — | — | — | THIS MAGIC MOMENT — Drifters, Atlantic 2050 | | 1 |
| 68 | — | — | — | O, DIO MIO — Annette, Vista 354 | | 1 |
| 69 | 49 | 33 | 33 | BONNIE CAME BACK — Duane Eddy, Jamie 1144 | | 9 |
| 70 | — | — | — | CHATTANOOGA SHOE SHINE BOY — Freddy Cannon, Swan 4050 | | 1 |
| 71 | 40 | 32 | 25 | FIRST NAME INITIAL — Annette, Vista 349 | | 18 |
| 72 | 77 | 83 | 98 | HULLY GULLY — Olympics, Arvee 562 | | 4 |
| 73 | 63 | 65 | 64 | AMAPOLA — Jacky Noguez, Jamie 1148 | | 7 |
| 74 | 79 | — | — | TEENSVILLE — Chet Atkins, RCA Victor 7684 | (S) | 2 |
| ★75 | 96 | — | 87 | TIME AFTER TIME — Frankie Ford, Ace 580 | | 5 |
| 76 | 71 | 72 | — | I WAS SUCH A FOOL — Flamingoes, End 1062 | | 3 |
| 77 | 66 | 68 | 73 | TELL HER FOR ME — Adam Wade, Coed 520 | | 7 |
| 78 | 45 | 40 | 31 | IF I HAD A GIRL — Rod Lauren, RCA Victor 7645 | (S) | 10 |
| 79 | 53 | 36 | 35 | LITTLE THINGS MEAN A LOT — Joni James, M-G-M 12849 | (S) | 9 |
| 80 | 80 | — | — | MUMBLIN' MOSIE — Johnny Otis, Capitol 4326 | | 2 |
| 81 | 85 | — | — | JUST A LITTLE BIT — Roscoe Gordon, Vee Jay 332 | | 2 |
| 82 | 58 | 64 | 77 | THE HAPPY MULETEER — Ivo Robic, Laurie 3045 | | 6 |
| 83 | 93 | 100 | — | CLEMENTINE — Jan and Dean, Dore 539 | | 3 |
| 84 | 100 | — | — | PARADISE — Sammy Turner, Big Top 3032 | | 2 |
| 85 | 88 | 67 | 65 | HONEY HUSH — Joe Turner, Atlantic 2044 | | 9 |
| 86 | — | — | — | DON'T FENCE ME IN — Tommy Edwards, M-G-M 12871 | (S) | 1 |
| 87 | 38 | 30 | 27 | NOT ONE MINUTE MORE — Della Reese, RCA Victor 7644 | (S) | 11 |
| 88 | — | — | — | LAWDY MISS CLAWDY — Gary Stites, Carlton 525 | | 1 |
| 89 | 51 | 31 | 24 | HOUND DOG MAN — Fabian, Chancellor 1044 | (S) | 15 |
| 90 | 89 | 66 | 54 | NO LOVE HAVE I — Webb Pierce, Decca 31021 | | 10 |
| 91 | — | — | — | ANYWAY THE WIND BLOWS — Doris Day, Columbia 41565 | | 1 |
| 92 | — | — | — | ANGELA JONES — Johnny Ferguson, M-G-M 12855 | | 1 |
| 93 | — | — | — | SLEEPY LAGOON — Platters, Mercury 71563 | (S) | 1 |
| 94 | 97 | — | — | WHAT'S HAPPENING — Wade Flemons, Vee Jay 335 | | 2 |
| 95 | — | — | — | GREENFIELDS — Brothers Four, Columbia 41571 | | 1 |
| 96 | 99 | — | — | LET THE LITTLE GIRL DANCE — Billy Bland, Old Town 1076 | | 2 |
| 97 | 70 | 56 | 43 | BACIARE, BACIARE — Dorothy Collins, Top Rank 2024 | | 10 |
| 98 | — | — | — | ALVIN'S ORCHESTRA — David Seville and the Chipmunks, Liberty 55233 | | 1 |
| 99 | — | — | — | EL MATADOR — Kingston Trio, Capitol 4338 | | 1 |
| 100 | — | — | — | LET THEM TALK — Little Willie John, King 5274 | | 1 |

## The Billboard HOT 100

**FEBRUARY 29, 1960** — For Week Ending March 6

STAR PERFORMERS showed the greatest upward progress on Hot 100 this week.
Ⓢ Indicates that 45 r.p.m. stereo single version is available.
Ⓢ Indicates that 33⅓ r.p.m. stereo single version is available.

| This Week | One Week Ago | Two Weeks Ago | Three Weeks Ago | Title — Artist, Company — Record No. | Stereo | Weeks on Chart |
|---|---|---|---|---|---|---|
| 1 | 1 | 6 | 12 | THEME FROM A SUMMER PLACE — Percy Faith, Columbia 41490 | △ | 8 |
| 2 | 3 | 3 | 5 | HANDY MAN — Jimmy Jones, Cub 9049 | | 10 |
| 3 | 4 | 4 | 8 | HE'LL HAVE TO GO — Jim Reeves, RCA Victor 7643 | Ⓢ | 10 |
| 4 | 2 | 1 | 1 | TEEN ANGEL — Mark Dinning, M-G-M 12845 | | 11 |
| 5 | 5 | 7 | 7 | WHAT IN THE WORLD'S COME OVER YOU — Jack Scott, Top Rank 2028 | Ⓢ | 8 |
| 6 | 8 | 11 | 19 | BEYOND THE SEA — Bobby Darin, Atco 6158 | | 7 |
| 7 | 6 | 2 | 2 | RUNNING BEAR — Johnny Preston, Mercury 71474 | | 20 |
| 8 | 7 | 9 | 13 | LET IT BE ME — The Everly Brothers, Cadence 1376 | | 8 |
| 9 | 12 | 20 | 37 | BABY — Brook Benton and Dinah Washington, Mercury 71565 | Ⓢ | 6 |
| 10 | 11 | 23 | 29 | WILD ONE — Bobby Rydell, Cameo 171 | | 5 |
| 11 | 10 | 5 | 3 | WHERE OR WHEN — Dion and the Belmonts, Laurie 3044 | | 10 |
| 12 | 9 | 8 | 6 | LONELY BLUE BOY — Conway Twitty, M-G-M 12857 | | 10 |
| 13 | 17 | 21 | 27 | FOREVER — Little Dippers, University 210 | | 6 |
| 14 | 14 | 13 | 16 | DOWN BY THE STATION — Four Preps, Capitol 4312 | | 10 |
| 15 | 21 | 27 | 41 | HARBOR LIGHTS — The Platters, Mercury 71563 | Ⓢ | 6 |
| 16 | 26 | 30 | 42 | SWEET NOTHIN'S — Brenda Lee, Decca 30967 | | 11 |
| 17 | 13 | 19 | 20 | TRACY'S THEME — Spencer Ross, Columbia 41532 | △ | 9 |
| 18 | 19 | 33 | 45 | MIDNIGHT SPECIAL — Paul Evans, Guaranteed 205 | | 6 |
| 19 | 20 | 35 | 51 | LADY LUCK — Lloyd Price, ABC-Paramount 10075 | Ⓢ | 5 |
| 20 | 15 | 14 | 10 | YOU GOT WHAT IT TAKES — Marv Johnson, United Artists 185 | | 18 |
| 21 | 18 | 12 | 14 | PRETTY BLUE EYES — Steve Lawrence, ABC-Paramount 10058 | Ⓢ | 15 |
| 22 | 22 | 24 | 26 | ROCKIN' LITTLE ANGEL — Ray Smith, Judd 1016 | | 9 |
| 23 | 34 | 44 | 71 | DELAWARE — Perry Como, RCA Victor 7670 | Ⓢ | 4 |
| 24 | 25 | 29 | 34 | BULLDOG — The Fireballs, Top Rank 2026 | Ⓢ | 8 |
| 25 | 29 | 37 | 55 | COUNTRY BOY — Fats Domino, Imperial 5645 | | 5 |
| 26 | 24 | 25 | 25 | TENDER LOVE AND CARE — Jimmie Rodgers, Roulette 4218 | | 8 |
| 27 | 36 | 69 | — | BEATNIK FLY — Johnny and the Hurricanes, Warwick 520 | | 3 |
| 28 | 27 | 41 | 54 | LITTLE BITTY GIRL — Bobby Rydell, Cameo 171 | | 5 |
| 29 | 16 | 10 | 4 | EL PASO — Marty Robbins, Columbia 41511 | △ | 17 |
| 30 | 32 | 36 | 39 | TOO MUCH TEQUILA — Champs, Challenge 59063 | | 7 |
| 31 | 31 | 31 | 28 | LUCKY DEVIL — Carl Dobkins Jr., Decca 31020 | | 13 |
| 32 | 23 | 15 | 11 | GO, JIMMY, GO — Jimmy Clanton, Ace 575 | | 13 |
| 33 | 33 | 26 | 24 | SHIMMY, SHIMMY, KO-KO BOP — Little Anthony & the Imperials, End 1060 | | 13 |
| 34 | 35 | 50 | 74 | TALL OAK TREE — Dorsey Burnette, Era 3012 | | 5 |
| 35 | 30 | 34 | 50 | TIME AND THE RIVER — Nat King Cole, Capitol 4325 | | 5 |
| 36 | 43 | 48 | 58 | CRAZY ARMS — Bob Beckham, Decca 31029 | | 9 |
| 37 | 50 | 82 | — | BABY, WHAT DO YOU WANT ME TO DO — Jimmy Reed, Vee Jay 333 | | 3 |
| 38 | 40 | 42 | 48 | CHINA DOLL — Ames Brothers, RCA Victor 7655 | Ⓢ | 5 |
| 39 | 39 | 47 | 44 | AM I THAT EASY TO FORGET — Debbie Reynolds, Dot 15985 | | 7 |
| 40 | 48 | 74 | — | OUTSIDE MY WINDOW — Fleetwoods, Dolton 15 | | 3 |
| 41 | 62 | — | — | PUPPY LOVE — Paul Anka, ABC-Paramount 10082 | Ⓢ | 2 |
| 42 | 51 | 78 | — | TOO POOPED TO POP — Chuck Berry, Chess 1747 | | 3 |
| 43 | 49 | 56 | 80 | MONEY — Barrett Strong, Anna 1111 | | 5 |
| 44 | 28 | 16 | 9 | WHY — Frankie Avalon, Chancellor 1045 | Ⓢ | 15 |
| 45 | 37 | 18 | 17 | THE BIG HURT — Toni Fisher, Signet 275 | | 16 |
| 46 | 41 | 52 | 61 | ETERNALLY — Sarah Vaughan, Mercury 71562 | Ⓢ | 4 |
| 47 | 67 | — | — | THIS MAGIC MOMENT — Drifters, Atlantic 2050 | | 2 |
| 48 | 47 | 59 | 63 | ON THE BEACH — Frank Chacksfield, London 1901 | | 6 |
| 49 | 45 | 62 | 90 | BAD BOY — Marty Wilde, Epic 9356 | | 4 |
| 50 | 60 | — | — | (WELCOME) NEW LOVERS — Pat Boone, Dot 16048 | Ⓢ | 2 |
| 51 | 52 | 64 | 79 | FANNIE MAE — Buster Brown, Fire 1008 | | 5 |
| 52 | 70 | — | — | CHATTANOOGA SHOE SHINE BOY — Freddy Cannon, Swan 4050 | | 2 |
| 53 | — | — | — | ABOUT THIS THING CALLED LOVE — Fabian, Chancellor 1047 | Ⓢ | 1 |
| 54 | 42 | 43 | 46 | WHY DO I LOVE YOU SO — Johnny Tillotson, Cadence 1372 | | 7 |
| 55 | 58 | 68 | 73 | SIXTEEN REASONS — Connie Stevens, Warner Bros. 5137 | | 5 |
| 56 | 56 | 65 | 53 | HARLEM NOCTURNE — Viscounts, Madison 123 | | 10 |
| 57 | 46 | 60 | 49 | DARLING LORRAINE — Knockouts, Shad 5013 | | 10 |
| 58 | 65 | 73 | 43 | WALTZING MATILDA — Jimmie Rodgers, Roulette 4218 | Ⓢ | 7 |
| 59 | 38 | 17 | 15 | THE VILLAGE OF ST. BERNADETTE — Andy Williams, Cadence 1374 | | 12 |
| 60 | 61 | — | — | STRING ALONG — Fabian, Chancellor 1047 | Ⓢ | 2 |
| 61 | 68 | — | — | O, DIO MIO — Annette, Vista 354 | | 2 |
| 62 | 63 | — | — | MAMA — Connie Francis, M-G-M 12878 | Ⓢ | 2 |
| 63 | 88 | — | — | LAWDY MISS CLAWDY — Gary Stites, Carlton 525 | | 2 |
| 64 | 81 | 85 | — | JUST A LITTLE BIT — Roscoe Gordon, Vee Jay 332 | | 3 |
| 65 | 93 | — | — | SLEEPY LAGOON — Platters, Mercury 71563 | Ⓢ | 2 |
| 66 | 84 | 100 | — | PARADISE — Sammy Turner, Big Top 3032 | | 3 |
| 67 | 83 | 93 | 100 | CLEMENTINE — Jan and Dean, Dore 539 | | 4 |
| 68 | 92 | — | — | ANGELA JONES — Johnny Ferguson, M-G-M 12855 | | 2 |
| 69 | 53 | 46 | 38 | LITTLE COCO PALM — Jerry Wallace, Challenge 59060 | | 9 |
| 70 | 99 | — | — | EL MATADOR — Kingston Trio, Capitol 4338 | | 2 |
| 71 | 98 | — | — | ALVIN'S ORCHESTRA — David Seville and the Chipmunks, Liberty 55233 | | 2 |
| 72 | 91 | — | — | ANYWAY THE WIND BLOWS — Doris Day, Columbia 41569 | | 2 |
| 73 | 74 | 79 | — | TEENSVILLE — Chet Atkins, RCA Victor 7684 | Ⓢ | 3 |
| 74 | 76 | 71 | 72 | I WAS SUCH A FOOL — Flamingoes, End 1062 | | 4 |
| 75 | 86 | — | — | DON'T FENCE ME IN — Tommy Edwards, M-G-M 12871 | | 2 |
| 76 | 64 | 75 | 81 | LET IT ROCK — Chuck Berry, Chess 1747 | | 5 |
| 77 | — | — | — | TEDDY — Connie Francis, M-G-M 12878 | Ⓢ | 1 |
| 78 | 44 | 22 | 18 | WAY DOWN YONDER IN NEW ORLEANS — Freddy Cannon, Swan 4043 | | 15 |
| 79 | 54 | 28 | 23 | SANDY — Larry Hall, Strand 25007 | | 15 |
| 80 | 95 | — | — | GREENFIELDS — Brothers Four, Columbia 41571 | | 2 |
| 81 | 75 | 96 | — | TIME AFTER TIME — Frankie Ford, Ace 580 | | 6 |
| 82 | — | — | — | SUMMER SET — Monty Kelly, Carlton 527 | Ⓢ | 1 |
| 83 | — | — | — | WEREWOLF — Frantics, Dolton 16 | | 1 |
| 84 | — | — | — | STARBRIGHT — Johnny Mathis, Columbia 41583 | | 1 |
| 85 | — | — | — | CHATTANOOGA CHOO CHOO — Ernie Fields, Rendezvous 117 | | 1 |
| 86 | 72 | 77 | 83 | HULLY GULLY — Olympics, Arvee 562 | | 5 |
| 87 | 55 | 57 | 60 | THAT OLD FEELING — Kitty Kallen, Columbia 41546 | | 5 |
| 88 | 57 | 39 | 21 | IT'S TIME TO CRY — Paul Anka, ABC-Paramount 10064 | Ⓢ | 15 |
| 89 | — | — | — | THE SAME OLD ME — Guy Mitchell, Columbia 41576 | | 1 |
| 90 | — | — | — | STEP BY STEP — The Crests, Coed 575 | | 1 |
| 91 | — | — | 91 | SECRET OF LOVE — Elton Anderson, Mercury 71542 | | 4 |
| 92 | — | 84 | — | (DO THE) MASHED POTATOES — Nat Kendrick & the Swans, Dade 1804 | | 2 |
| 93 | 69 | 99 | — | LET THE LITTLE GIRL DANCE — Billy Bland, Old Town 1076 | | 3 |
| 94 | — | 72 | 75 | UPTOWN — Roy Orbison, Monument 412 | | 6 |
| 95 | — | — | — | YOU DON'T KNOW ME — Lennie Welch, Cadence 1373 | | 1 |
| 96 | — | — | — | MOUNTAIN OF LOVE — Harold Dorman, Rita 1003 | | 1 |
| 97 | — | — | — | ROAD RUNNER — Bo Diddley, Checker 942 | | 1 |
| 98 | 59 | 32 | 22 | AMONG MY SOUVENIRS — Connie Francis, M-G-M 12841 | Ⓢ | 15 |
| 99 | — | — | — | OLD PAYOLA ROLL BLUES — Stan Freberg & Jesse White, Capitol 4329 | | 1 |
| 100 | — | — | — | JUST GIVE ME A RING — Clyde McPhatter, Atlantic 2049 | | 1 |

## The Billboard HOT 100

**FOR WEEK ENDING MARCH 13**

*STAR PERFORMERS showed the greatest upward progress on Hot 100 this week.*
*S — Indicates that 45 r.p.m. stereo single version is available.*
*A — Indicates that 33⅓ r.p.m. stereo single version is available.*

| This Week | 1 Wk Ago | 2 Wks Ago | 3 Wks Ago | Title — Artist, Company, Record No. | Stereo | Weeks on Chart |
|---|---|---|---|---|---|---|
| 1 | 1 | 1 | 6 | THEME FROM A SUMMER PLACE — Percy Faith, Columbia 41490 | A | 9 |
| 2 | 3 | 4 | 4 | HE'LL HAVE TO GO — Jim Reeves, RCA Victor 7643 | S | 11 |
| 3 | 2 | 3 | 3 | HANDY MAN — Jimmy Jones, Cub 9049 | | 11 |
| 4 | 10 | 11 | 23 | WILD ONE — Bobby Rydell, Cameo 171 | | 6 |
| 5 | 5 | 5 | 7 | WHAT IN THE WORLD'S COME OVER YOU — Jack Scott, Top Rank 2028 | S | 9 |
| 6 | 4 | 2 | 1 | TEEN ANGEL — Mark Dinning, M-G-M 12845 | | 12 |
| 7 | 6 | 8 | 11 | BEYOND THE SEA — Bobby Darin, Atco 6158 | | 8 |
| 8 | 9 | 12 | 20 | BABY — Brook Benton and Dinah Washington, Mercury 71565 | S | 7 |
| 9 | 8 | 7 | 9 | LET IT BE ME — The Everly Brothers, Cadence 1376 | | 9 |
| 10 | 7 | 6 | 2 | RUNNING BEAR — Johnny Preston, Mercury 71474 | | 21 |
| 11 | 13 | 17 | 21 | FOREVER — Little Dippers, University 210 | | 7 |
| 12 | 15 | 21 | 27 | HARBOR LIGHTS — The Platters, Mercury 71563 | S | 7 |
| 13 | 16 | 26 | 30 | SWEET NOTHIN'S — Brenda Lee, Decca 30967 | | 12 |
| 14 | 12 | 9 | 8 | LONELY BLUE BOY — Conway Twitty, M-G-M 12857 | | 11 |
| 15 | 11 | 10 | 5 | WHERE OR WHEN — Dion and the Belmonts, Laurie 3044 | | 11 |
| 16 | 19 | 20 | 35 | LADY LUCK — Lloyd Price, ABC-Paramount 10075 | S | 6 |
| 17 | 41 | 62 | — | PUPPY LOVE — Paul Anka, ABC-Paramount 10082 | S | 3 |
| 18 | 14 | 14 | 13 | DOWN BY THE STATION — Four Preps, Capitol 4312 | | 11 |
| 19 | 27 | 36 | 69 | BEATNIK FLY — Johnny and the Hurricanes, Warwick 520 | | 4 |
| 20 | 17 | 13 | 19 | TRACY'S THEME — Spencer Ross, Columbia 41532 | A | 10 |
| 21 | 18 | 19 | 33 | MIDNIGHT SPECIAL — Paul Evans, Guaranteed 205 | | 7 |
| 22 | 23 | 34 | 44 | DELAWARE — Perry Como, RCA Victor 7670 | S | 5 |
| 23 | 34 | 35 | 50 | TALL OAK TREE — Dorsey Burnette, Era 3012 | | 6 |
| 24 | 20 | 15 | 14 | YOU GOT WHAT IT TAKES — Marv Johnson, United Artists 185 | | 19 |
| 25 | 25 | 29 | 37 | COUNTRY BOY — Fats Domino, Imperial 5645 | | 6 |
| 26 | 22 | 22 | 24 | ROCKIN' LITTLE ANGEL — Ray Smith, Judd 1016 | | 10 |
| 27 | 28 | 27 | 41 | LITTLE BITTY GIRL — Bobby Rydell, Cameo 171 | | 6 |
| 28 | 21 | 18 | 12 | PRETTY BLUE EYES — Steve Lawrence, ABC-Paramount 10058 | S | 16 |
| 29 | 61 | 68 | — | O, DIO MIO — Annette, Vista 354 | | 3 |
| 30 | 40 | 48 | 74 | OUTSIDE MY WINDOW — Fleetwoods, Dolton 15 | | 4 |
| 31 | 29 | 16 | 10 | EL PASO — Marty Robbins, Columbia 41511 | A | 18 |
| 32 | 31 | 31 | 31 | LUCKY DEVIL — Carl Dobkins Jr., Decca 31020 | | 14 |
| 33 | 71 | 98 | — | ALVIN'S ORCHESTRA — David Seville and the Chipmunks, Liberty 55233 | | 3 |
| 34 | 50 | 60 | — | (WELCOME) NEW LOVERS — Pat Boone, Dot 16048 | S | 2 |
| 35 | 52 | 70 | — | CHATTANOOGA SHOE SHINE BOY — Freddy Cannon, Swan 4050 | | 3 |
| 36 | 24 | 25 | 29 | BULLDOG — The Fireballs, Top Rank 2026 | S | 9 |
| 37 | 30 | 32 | 36 | TOO MUCH TEQUILA — Champs, Challenge 59063 | | 8 |
| 38 | 37 | 50 | 82 | BABY, WHAT DO YOU WANT ME TO DO — Jimmy Reed, Vee Jay 333 | | 4 |
| 39 | 39 | 39 | 47 | AM I THAT EASY TO FORGET — Debbie Reynolds, Dot 15983 | | 8 |
| 40 | 33 | 33 | 26 | SHIMMY, SHIMMY, KO-KO BOP — Little Anthony & the Imperials, End 1060 | | 14 |
| 41 | 53 | — | — | ABOUT THIS THING CALLED LOVE — Fabian, Chancellor 1047 | S | 2 |
| 42 | 36 | 43 | 48 | CRAZY ARMS — Bob Beckham, Decca 31029 | | 10 |
| 43 | 32 | 23 | 15 | GO, JIMMY, GO — Jimmy Clanton, Ace 575 | | 14 |
| 44 | 42 | 51 | 78 | TOO POOPED TO POP — Chuck Berry, Chess 1747 | | 4 |
| 45 | 43 | 49 | 56 | MONEY — Barrett Strong, Anna 1111 | | 6 |
| 46 | 62 | 63 | — | MAMA — Connie Francis, M-G-M 12878 | S | 3 |
| 47 | 47 | 67 | — | THIS MAGIC MOMENT — Drifters, Atlantic 2050 | | 3 |
| 48 | 49 | 45 | 62 | BAD BOY — Marty Wilde, Epic 9356 | | 5 |
| 49 | 70 | 99 | — | EL MATADOR — Kingston Trio, Capitol 4338 | | 3 |
| 50 | 55 | 58 | 68 | SIXTEEN REASONS — Connie Stevens, Warner Bros. 5137 | | 6 |
| 51 | 26 | 24 | 25 | TENDER LOVE AND CARE — Jimmie Rodgers, Roulette 4218 | | 9 |
| 52 | 35 | 30 | 34 | TIME AND THE RIVER — Nat King Cole, Capitol 4325 | | 6 |
| 53 | 38 | 40 | 42 | CHINA DOLL — Ames Brothers, RCA Victor 7655 | S | 6 |
| 54 | 46 | 41 | 52 | ETERNALLY — Sarah Vaughan, Mercury 71562 | S | 5 |
| 55 | 72 | 91 | — | ANYWAY THE WIND BLOWS — Doris Day, Columbia 41569 | | 3 |
| 56 | 63 | 88 | — | LAWDY MISS CLAWDY — Gary Stites, Carlton 525 | | 3 |
| 57 | 51 | 52 | 64 | FANNIE MAE — Buster Brown, Fire 1008 | | 6 |
| 58 | 54 | 42 | 43 | WHY DO I LOVE YOU SO — Johnny Tillotson, Cadence 1372 | | 8 |
| 59 | 48 | 47 | 59 | ON THE BEACH — Frank Chacksfield, London 1901 | | 2 |
| 60 | 66 | 84 | 100 | PARADISE — Sammy Turner, Big Top 3032 | | 4 |
| 61 | 68 | 92 | — | ANGELA JONES — Johnny Ferguson, M-G-M 12855 | | 3 |
| 62 | 77 | — | — | TEDDY — Connie Francis, M-G-M 12878 | S | 2 |
| 63 | 89 | — | — | THE SAME OLD ME — Guy Mitchell, Columbia 41576 | | 2 |
| 64 | 80 | 95 | — | GREENFIELDS — Brothers Four, Columbia 41571 | | 3 |
| 65 | 67 | 83 | 93 | CLEMENTINE — Jan and Dean, Dore 539 | | 5 |
| 66 | 60 | — | — | STRING ALONG — Fabian, Chancellor 1047 | S | 3 |
| 67 | 64 | 81 | 85 | JUST A LITTLE BIT — Roscoe Gordon, Vee Jay 332 | | 4 |
| 68 | 56 | 56 | 65 | HARLEM NOCTURNE — Viscounts, Madison 123 | | 11 |
| 69 | — | — | — | SINK THE BISMARCK — Johnny Horton, Columbia 41568 | | 1 |
| 70 | — | — | — | WHITE SILVER SANDS — Bill Black's Combo, Hi 2021 | | 1 |
| 71 | 84 | — | — | STARBRIGHT — Johnny Mathis, Columbia 41583 | | 2 |
| 72 | 82 | — | — | SUMMER SET — Monty Kelly, Carlton 527 | S | 2 |
| 73 | 58 | 65 | 73 | WALTZING MATILDA — Jimmie Rodgers, Roulette 4218 | S | 8 |
| 74 | 75 | 86 | — | DON'T FENCE ME IN — Tommy Edwards, M-G-M 12871 | S | 3 |
| 75 | 85 | — | — | CHATTANOOGA CHOO CHOO — Ernie Fields, Rendezvous 117 | | 2 |
| 76 | 65 | 93 | — | SLEEPY LAGOON — Platters, Mercury 71563 | S | 3 |
| 77 | 44 | 28 | 16 | WHY — Frankie Avalon, Chancellor 1045 | S | 16 |
| 78 | 76 | 64 | 75 | LET IT ROCK — Chuck Berry, Chess 1747 | | 6 |
| 79 | — | — | — | I LOVE THE WAY YOU LOVE — Marv Johnson, United Artists 208 | | 1 |
| 80 | — | — | — | JUST ONE TIME — Don Gibson, RCA Victor 7690 | S | 1 |
| 81 | 97 | — | — | ROAD RUNNER — Bo Diddley, Checker 942 | | 2 |
| 82 | — | — | — | NEVER LET ME GO — Lloyd Price, ABC-Paramount 10075 | S | 1 |
| 83 | 45 | 37 | 18 | THE BIG HURT — Toni Fisher, Signet 275 | | 17 |
| 84 | — | — | — | FOOTSTEPS — Steve Lawrence, ABC-Paramount 10085 | | 1 |
| 85 | 90 | — | — | STEP BY STEP — The Crests, Coed 525 | | 2 |
| 86 | 57 | 46 | 60 | DARLING LORRAINE — Knockouts, Shad 5013 | | 11 |
| 87 | 59 | 38 | 17 | THE VILLAGE OF ST. BERNADETTE — Andy Williams, Cadence 1374 | | 13 |
| 88 | 95 | — | — | YOU DON'T KNOW ME — Lennie Welch, Cadence 1373 | | 2 |
| 89 | — | — | — | APPLE GREEN — June Valli, Mercury 71588 | | 1 |
| 90 | 93 | 69 | 99 | LET THE LITTLE GIRL DANCE — Billy Bland, Old Town 1076 | | 4 |
| 91 | 96 | — | — | MOUNTAIN OF LOVE — Harold Dorman, Rita 1003 | | 2 |
| 92 | 83 | — | — | WEREWOLF — The Frantics, Dolton 16 | | 2 |
| 93 | — | — | — | CLOSER WALK — Pete Fountain, Coral 62154 | | 2 |
| 94 | — | — | — | WHAT'CHA GONNA DO — Nat King Cole, Capitol 4325 | | 1 |
| 95 | — | — | — | SUDDENLY — Nick Dematteo, Guyden 2024 | | 1 |
| 96 | 100 | — | — | JUST GIVE ME A RING — Clyde McPhatter, Atlantic 2049 | | 5 |
| 97 | — | 87 | — | YOU'RE MY BABY — Sarah Vaughan, Mercury 71562 | | 2 |
| 98 | 86 | 72 | 77 | HULLY GULLY — Olympics, Arvee 562 | | 6 |
| 99 | — | — | — | JAMBALAYA (On the Bayou) — Bobby Comstock & the Counts, Atlantic 2051 | | 1 |
| 100 | 74 | 76 | 71 | I WAS SUCH A FOOL — Flamingoes, End 1062 | | 5 |
| 100 | — | — | — | DOWN BY THE RIVERSIDE — Les Compagnons de la Chanson, Capitol 4342 | | 1 |

# The Billboard HOT 100

**FOR WEEK ENDING MARCH 20** — MARCH 14, 1960

STAR PERFORMERS showed the greatest upward progress on Hot 100 this week.
Ⓢ Indicates that 45 r.p.m. stereo single version is available.
Ⓐ Indicates that 33⅓ r.p.m. stereo single version is available.

| This Week | 1 Wk Ago | 2 Wks Ago | 3 Wks Ago | Title — Artist, Company, Record No. | Stereo | Wks on Chart |
|---|---|---|---|---|---|---|
| 1 | 1 | 1 | 1 | THEME FROM A SUMMER PLACE — Percy Faith, Columbia 41490 | Ⓐ | 10 |
| 2 | 2 | 3 | 4 | HE'LL HAVE TO GO — Jim Reeves, RCA Victor 7643 | Ⓢ | 12 |
| 3 | 4 | 10 | 11 | WILD ONE — Bobby Rydell, Cameo 171 | | 7 |
| 4 | 3 | 2 | 3 | HANDY MAN — Jimmy Jones, Cub 9049 | | 12 |
| 5 | 5 | 5 | 5 | WHAT IN THE WORLD'S COME OVER YOU — Jack Scott, Top Rank 2028 | Ⓢ | 10 |
| 6 | 8 | 9 | 12 | BABY — Brook Benton and Dinah Washington, Mercury 71565 | Ⓢ | 8 |
| 7 | 6 | 4 | 2 | TEEN ANGEL — Mark Dinning, M-G-M 12845 | | 13 |
| 8 | 7 | 6 | 8 | BEYOND THE SEA — Bobby Darin, Atco 6158 | | 9 |
| 9 | 17 | 41 | 62 | PUPPY LOVE — Paul Anka, ABC-Paramount 10082 | Ⓢ | 4 |
| 10 | 12 | 15 | 21 | HARBOR LIGHTS — The Platters, Mercury 71563 | Ⓢ | 8 |
| 11 | 13 | 16 | 26 | SWEET NOTHIN'S — Brenda Lee, Decca 30967 | | 13 |
| 12 | 11 | 13 | 17 | FOREVER — Little Dippers, University 210 | | 8 |
| 13 | 9 | 8 | 7 | LET IT BE ME — The Everly Brothers, Cadence 1376 | | 10 |
| 14 | 10 | 7 | 6 | RUNNING BEAR — Johnny Preston, Mercury 71474 | | 22 |
| 15 | 16 | 19 | 20 | LADY LUCK — Lloyd Price, ABC-Paramount 10075 | Ⓢ | 7 |
| 16 | 19 | 27 | 36 | BEATNIK FLY — Johnny and the Hurricanes, Warwick 520 | | 5 |
| 17 | 15 | 11 | 10 | WHERE OR WHEN — Dion and the Belmonts, Laurie 3044 | | 12 |
| 18 | 21 | 18 | 19 | MIDNIGHT SPECIAL — Paul Evans, Guaranteed 205 | | 8 |
| 19 | 29 | 61 | 68 | O, DIO MIO — Annette, Vista 354 | | 4 |
| 20 | 20 | 17 | 13 | TRACY'S THEME — Spencer Ross, Columbia 41532 | Ⓐ | 11 |
| 21 | 47 | 47 | 67 | THIS MAGIC MOMENT — Drifters, Atlantic 2050 | | 4 |
| 22 | 27 | 28 | 27 | LITTLE BITTY GIRL — Bobby Rydell, Cameo 171 | | 7 |
| 23 | 26 | 22 | 22 | ROCKIN' LITTLE ANGEL — Ray Smith, Judd 1016 | | 11 |
| 24 | 34 | 50 | 60 | (WELCOME) NEW LOVERS — Pat Boone, Dot 16048 | Ⓢ | 3 |
| 25 | 22 | 23 | 34 | DELAWARE — Perry Como, RCA Victor 7670 | Ⓢ | 6 |
| 26 | 18 | 14 | 14 | DOWN BY THE STATION — Four Preps, Capitol 4312 | | 12 |
| 27 | 14 | 12 | 9 | LONELY BLUE BOY — Conway Twitty, M-G-M 12857 | | 12 |
| 28 | 30 | 40 | 48 | OUTSIDE MY WINDOW — Fleetwoods, Dolton 15 | | 5 |
| 29 | 46 | 62 | 63 | MAMA — Connie Francis, M-G-M 12878 | Ⓢ | 4 |
| 30 | 69 | — | — | SINK THE BISMARCK — Johnny Horton, Columbia 41568 | | 2 |
| 31 | 23 | 34 | 35 | TALL OAK TREE — Dorsey Burnette, Era 3012 | | 7 |
| 32 | 50 | 55 | 58 | SIXTEEN REASONS — Connie Stevens, Warner Bros. 5137 | | 7 |
| 33 | 33 | 71 | 98 | ALVIN'S ORCHESTRA — David Seville and the Chipmunks, Liberty 55233 | | 4 |
| 34 | 35 | 52 | 70 | CHATTANOOGA SHOE SHINE BOY — Freddy Cannon, Swan 4050 | | 4 |
| 35 | 41 | 53 | — | ABOUT THIS THING CALLED LOVE — Fabian, Chancellor 1047 | Ⓢ | 3 |
| 36 | 39 | 39 | 39 | AM I THAT EASY TO FORGET — Debbie Reynolds, Dot 15985 | | 9 |
| 37 | 25 | 25 | 29 | COUNTRY BOY — Fats Domino, Imperial 5645 | | 7 |
| 38 | 31 | 29 | 16 | EL PASO — Marty Robbins, Columbia 41511 | Ⓐ | 19 |
| 39 | 66 | 60 | — | STRING ALONG — Fabian, Chancellor 1047 | Ⓢ | 4 |
| 40 | 49 | 70 | 99 | EL MATADOR — Kingston Trio, Capitol 4338 | | 4 |
| 41 | 38 | 37 | 50 | BABY, WHAT DO YOU WANT ME TO DO — Jimmy Reed, Vee Jay 333 | | 5 |
| 42 | 70 | — | — | WHITE SILVER SANDS — Bill Black's Combo, Hi 2021 | | 2 |
| 43 | 28 | 21 | 18 | PRETTY BLUE EYES — Steve Lawrence, ABC-Paramount 10058 | Ⓢ | 17 |
| 44 | 64 | 80 | 95 | GREENFIELDS — Brothers Four, Columbia 41571 | Ⓐ | 4 |
| 45 | 57 | 51 | 52 | FANNIE MAE — Buster Brown, Fire 1008 | | 7 |
| 46 | 32 | 31 | 31 | LUCKY DEVIL — Carl Dobkins Jr., Decca 31020 | | 15 |
| 47 | 56 | 63 | 88 | LAWDY MISS CLAWDY — Gary Stites, Carlton 525 | | 4 |
| 48 | 37 | 30 | 32 | TOO MUCH TEQUILA — Champs, Challenge 59063 | | 9 |
| 49 | 36 | 24 | 25 | BULLDOG — The Fireballs, Top Rank 2026 | Ⓢ | 10 |
| 50 | 74 | 75 | 86 | DON'T FENCE ME IN — Tommy Edwards, M-G-M 12871 | Ⓢ | 4 |
| 51 | 55 | 72 | 91 | ANYWAY THE WIND BLOWS — Doris Day, Columbia 41569 | | 4 |
| 52 | 45 | 43 | 49 | MONEY — Barrett Strong, Anna 1111 | | 7 |
| 53 | 79 | — | — | I LOVE THE WAY YOU LOVE — Marv Johnson, United Artists 208 | | 2 |
| 54 | 62 | 77 | — | TEDDY — Connie Francis, M-G-M 12878 | Ⓢ | 3 |
| 55 | 24 | 20 | 15 | YOU GOT WHAT IT TAKES — Marv Johnson, United Artists 185 | | 20 |
| 56 | 58 | 54 | 42 | WHY DO I LOVE YOU SO — Johnny Tillotson, Cadence 1372 | | 9 |
| 57 | 61 | 68 | 92 | ANGELA JONES — Johnny Ferguson, M-G-M 12855 | | 4 |
| 58 | 48 | 49 | 45 | BAD BOY — Marty Wilde, Epic 9356 | | 6 |
| 59 | 44 | 42 | 51 | TOO POOPED TO POP — Chuck Berry, Chess 1747 | | 5 |
| 60 | 71 | 84 | — | STARBRIGHT — Johnny Mathis, Columbia 41583 | Ⓐ | 3 |
| 61 | 63 | 89 | — | THE SAME OLD ME — Guy Mitchell, Columbia 41576 | | 3 |
| 62 | 42 | 36 | 43 | CRAZY ARMS — Bob Beckham, Decca 31029 | | 11 |
| 63 | 54 | 46 | 41 | ETERNALLY — Sarah Vaughan, Mercury 71562 | Ⓢ | 6 |
| 64 | 80 | — | — | JUST ONE TIME — Don Gibson, RCA Victor 7690 | Ⓢ | 2 |
| 65 | — | — | — | DON'T THROW AWAY ALL THOSE TEARDROPS — Frankie Avalon, Chancellor 1048 | | 1 |
| 66 | 72 | 82 | — | SUMMER SET — Monty Kelly, Carlton 527 | Ⓢ | 3 |
| 67 | 75 | 85 | — | CHATTANOOGA CHOO CHOO — Ernie Fields, Rendezvous 117 | | 3 |
| 68 | 84 | — | — | FOOTSTEPS — Steve Lawrence, ABC-Paramount 10085 | | 2 |
| 69 | 53 | 38 | 40 | CHINA DOLL — Ames Brothers, RCA Victor 7655 | Ⓢ | 7 |
| 70 | 40 | 33 | 33 | SHIMMY, SHIMMY, KO-KO BOP — Little Anthony & the Imperials, End 1060 | | 15 |
| 71 | 91 | 96 | — | MOUNTAIN OF LOVE — Harold Dorman, Rita 1003 | | 3 |
| 72 | 76 | 65 | 93 | SLEEPY LAGOON — Platters, Mercury 71563 | Ⓢ | 4 |
| 73 | 67 | 64 | 81 | JUST A LITTLE BIT — Roscoe Gordon, Vee Jay 332 | | 5 |
| 74 | 68 | 56 | 56 | HARLEM NOCTURNE — Viscounts, Madison 123 | | 12 |
| 75 | 89 | — | — | APPLE GREEN — June Valli, Mercury 71588 | | 2 |
| 76 | — | — | — | AT MY FRONT DOOR — Dee Clark, Abner 1037 | | 1 |
| 77 | 60 | 66 | 84 | PARADISE — Sammy Turner, Big Top 3032 | | 5 |
| 78 | 43 | 32 | 23 | GO, JIMMY, GO — Jimmy Clanton, Ace 575 | | 15 |
| 79 | 85 | 90 | — | STEP BY STEP — The Crests, Coed 525 | | 3 |
| 80 | 90 | 93 | 69 | LET THE LITTLE GIRL DANCE — Billy Bland, Old Town 1076 | | 5 |
| 81 | 81 | 97 | — | ROAD RUNNER — Bo Diddley, Checker 942 | | 3 |
| 82 | 88 | 95 | — | YOU DON'T KNOW ME — Lennie Welch, Cadence 1373 | | 3 |
| 83 | 59 | 48 | 47 | ON THE BEACH — Frank Chacksfield, London 1901 | | 8 |
| 84 | — | — | — | STRAIGHT "A's" IN LOVE — Johnny Cash, Sun 334 | | 1 |
| 85 | 52 | 35 | 30 | TIME AND THE RIVER — Nat King Cole, Capitol 4325 | | 7 |
| 86 | 100 | — | — | DOWN BY THE RIVERSIDE — Les Compagnons de la Chanson, Capitol 4342 | | 2 |
| 87 | 65 | 67 | 83 | CLEMENTINE — Jan and Dean, Dore 539 | | 6 |
| 88 | — | — | — | BIG IRON — Marty Robbins, Columbia 41589 | Ⓐ | 1 |
| 89 | — | — | — | CARAVAN — Santo & Johnny, Canadian-American 1111 | | 1 |
| 90 | 95 | — | — | SUDDENLY — Nick Dematteo, Guyden 2024 | | 2 |
| 91 | 51 | 26 | 24 | TENDER LOVE AND CARE — Jimmie Rodgers, Roulette 4218 | | 10 |
| 92 | 94 | — | — | WHAT'CHA GONNA DO — Nat King Cole, Capitol 4325 | | 2 |
| 93 | 93 | — | — | CLOSER WALK — Pete Fountain, Coral 62154 | | 3 |
| 94 | 78 | 76 | 64 | LET IT ROCK — Chuck Berry, Chess 1747 | | 7 |
| 95 | 99 | — | — | JAMBALAYA (On the Bayou) — Bobby Comstock & the Counts, Atlantic 2051 | | 2 |
| 96 | — | — | — | THE OLD LAMPLIGHTER — The Browns, RCA Victor 7700 | | 1 |
| 97 | — | — | — | RUBY — Adam Wade, Coed 526 | | 1 |
| 98 | — | — | — | DON'T DECEIVE ME — Ruth Brown, Atlantic 2052 | | 1 |
| 99 | — | — | — | LONELY WEEKENDS — Charlie Rich, Phillips 3552 | | 1 |
| 100 | — | — | — | TEENAGE SONATA — Sam Cooke, RCA Victor 7701 | Ⓢ | 1 |

# The Billboard HOT 100

**FOR WEEK ENDING MARCH 27**

*The Billboard's Music Popularity Charts ... POP RECORDS — MARCH 21, 1960*

STAR PERFORMERS showed the greatest upward progress on Hot 100 this week.
[S] Indicates that 45 r.p.m. stereo single version is available.
[A] Indicates that 33⅓ r.p.m. stereo single version is available.

| This Week | 1 Wk Ago | 2 Wks Ago | 3 Wks Ago | Title — Artist, Company, Record No. | Stereo | Wks on Chart |
|---|---|---|---|---|---|---|
| 1 | 1 | 1 | 1 | THEME FROM A SUMMER PLACE — Percy Faith, Columbia 41490 | [A] | 11 |
| 2 | 2 | 2 | 3 | HE'LL HAVE TO GO — Jim Reeves, RCA Victor 7643 | [S] | 13 |
| 3 | 3 | 4 | 10 | WILD ONE — Bobby Rydell, Cameo 171 | | 8 |
| 4 | 4 | 3 | 2 | HANDY MAN — Jimmy Jones, Cub 9049 | | 13 |
| 5 | 8 | 8 | 9 | BABY — Brook Benton and Dinah Washington, Mercury 71565 | [S] | 9 |
| 6 | 5 | 5 | 5 | WHAT IN THE WORLD'S COME OVER YOU — Jack Scott, Top Rank 2028 | [S] | 11 |
| 7 | 9 | 17 | 41 | PUPPY LOVE — Paul Anka, ABC-Paramount 10082 | [S] | 5 |
| 8 | 11 | 13 | 16 | SWEET NOTHIN'S — Brenda Lee, Decca 30967 | | 14 |
| 9 | 7 | 6 | 4 | TEEN ANGEL — Mark Dinning, M-G-M 12845 | | 14 |
| 10 | 10 | 12 | 15 | HARBOR LIGHTS — The Platters, Mercury 71563 | [S] | 9 |
| 11 | 8 | 7 | 6 | BEYOND THE SEA — Bobby Darin, Atco 6158 | | 10 |
| 12 | 12 | 11 | 13 | FOREVER — Little Dippers, University 210 | | 9 |
| 13 | 13 | 9 | 8 | LET IT BE ME — The Everly Brothers, Cadence 1376 | | 11 |
| 14 | 15 | 16 | 19 | LADY LUCK — Lloyd Price, ABC-Paramount 10075 | [S] | 8 |
| 15 | 16 | 19 | 27 | BEATNIK FLY — Johnny and the Hurricanes, Warwick 520 | | 6 |
| 16 | 18 | 21 | 18 | MIDNIGHT SPECIAL — Paul Evans, Guaranteed 205 | | 9 |
| 17 | 19 | 29 | 61 | O, DIO MIO — Annette, Vista 354 | | 5 |
| ★18 | 24 | 34 | 50 | (WELCOME) NEW LOVERS — Pat Boone, Dot 16048 | [S] | 4 |
| 19 | 21 | 47 | 47 | THIS MAGIC MOMENT — Drifters, Atlantic 2050 | | 5 |
| 20 | 22 | 27 | 28 | LITTLE BITTY GIRL — Bobby Rydell, Cameo 171 | | 8 |
| 21 | 29 | 46 | 62 | MAMA — Connie Francis, M-G-M 12878 | [S] | 5 |
| ★22 | 44 | 64 | 80 | GREENFIELDS — Brothers Four, Columbia 41571 | [A] | 5 |
| 23 | 14 | 10 | 7 | RUNNING BEAR — Johnny Preston, Mercury 71474 | | 23 |
| 24 | 25 | 22 | 23 | DELAWARE — Perry Como, RCA Victor 7670 | [S] | 7 |
| ★25 | 36 | 39 | 39 | AM I THAT EASY TO FORGET — Debbie Reynolds, Dot 15985 | | 10 |
| 26 | 27 | 14 | 12 | LONELY BLUE BOY — Conway Twitty, M-G-M 12857 | | 13 |
| ★27 | 52 | 45 | 43 | MONEY — Barrett Strong, Anna 1111 | | 8 |
| 28 | 30 | 69 | — | SINK THE BISMARCK — Johnny Horton, Columbia 41568 | | 3 |
| 29 | 32 | 50 | 55 | SIXTEEN REASONS — Connie Stevens, Warner Bros. 5137 | | 8 |
| ★30 | 42 | 70 | — | WHITE SILVER SANDS — Bill Black's Combo, Hi 2021 | | 3 |
| 31 | 17 | 15 | 11 | WHERE OR WHEN — Dion and the Belmonts, Laurie 3044 | | 13 |
| 32 | 40 | 49 | 70 | EL MATADOR — Kingston Trio, Capitol 4338 | | 5 |
| 33 | 23 | 26 | 22 | ROCKIN' LITTLE ANGEL — Ray Smith, Judd 1016 | | 12 |
| 34 | 35 | 41 | 53 | ABOUT THIS THING CALLED LOVE — Fabian, Chancellor 1047 | [S] | 4 |
| 35 | 26 | 18 | 14 | DOWN BY THE STATION — Four Preps, Capitol 4312 | | 13 |
| 36 | 20 | 20 | 17 | TRACY'S THEME — Spencer Ross, Columbia 41532 | [A] | 12 |
| 37 | 34 | 35 | 52 | CHATTANOOGA SHOE SHINE BOY — Freddy Cannon, Swan 4050 | | 5 |
| ★38 | 53 | 79 | — | I LOVE THE WAY YOU LOVE — Marv Johnson, United Artist 208 | | 3 |
| 39 | 39 | 66 | 60 | STRING ALONG — Fabian, Chancellor 1047 | [S] | 5 |
| 40 | 31 | 23 | 34 | TALL OAK TREE — Dorsey Burnette, Era 3012 | | 8 |
| 41 | 28 | 30 | 40 | OUTSIDE MY WINDOW — Fleetwoods, Dolton 15 | | 6 |
| 42 | 38 | 31 | 29 | EL PASO — Marty Robbins, Columbia 41511 | [A] | 20 |
| ★43 | 68 | 84 | — | FOOTSTEPS — Steve Lawrence, ABC-Paramount 10085 | | 3 |
| ★44 | 60 | 71 | 84 | STARBRIGHT — Johnny Mathis, Columbia 41583 | [A] | 4 |
| 45 | 37 | 25 | 25 | COUNTRY BOY — Fats Domino, Imperial 5645 | | 8 |
| ★46 | 64 | 80 | — | JUST ONE TIME — Don Gibson, RCA Victor 7690 | [S] | 3 |
| 47 | 54 | 62 | 77 | TEDDY — Connie Francis, M-G-M 12878 | [S] | 4 |
| 48 | 49 | 36 | 24 | BULLDOG — The Fireballs, Top Rank 2026 | [S] | 11 |
| 49 | 50 | 74 | 75 | DON'T FENCE ME IN — Tommy Edwards, M-G-M 12871 | [S] | 5 |
| 50 | 51 | 55 | 72 | ANYWAY THE WIND BLOWS — Doris Day, Columbia 41569 | | 5 |
| 51 | 41 | 38 | 37 | BABY, WHAT DO YOU WANT ME TO DO — Jimmy Reed, Vee Jay 333 | | 6 |
| 52 | 61 | 63 | 89 | THE SAME OLD ME — Guy Mitchell, Columbia 41576 | | 4 |
| 53 | 65 | — | — | DON'T THROW AWAY ALL THOSE TEARDROPS — Frankie Avalon, Chancellor 1048 | | 2 |
| 54 | 45 | 57 | 51 | FANNIE MAE — Buster Brown, Fire 1008 | | 8 |
| 55 | 47 | 56 | 63 | LAWDY MISS CLAWDY — Gary Stites, Carlton 525 | | 5 |
| ★56 | 74 | 68 | 56 | HARLEM NOCTURNE — Viscounts, Madison 123 | | 13 |
| 57 | 46 | 32 | 31 | LUCKY DEVIL — Carl Dobkins Jr., Decca 31020 | | 16 |
| 58 | 66 | 72 | 82 | SUMMER SET — Monty Kelly, Carlton 527 | [S] | 4 |
| 59 | 48 | 37 | 30 | TOO MUCH TEQUILA — Champs, Challenge 59063 | | 10 |
| 60 | 33 | 33 | 71 | ALVIN'S ORCHESTRA — David Seville and the Chipmunks, Liberty 55233 | | 5 |
| 61 | 56 | 58 | 54 | WHY DO I LOVE YOU SO — Johnny Tillotson, Cadence 1372 | | 10 |
| ★62 | 80 | 90 | 93 | LET THE LITTLE GIRL DANCE — Billy Bland, Old Town 1076 | | 6 |
| 63 | 69 | 53 | 38 | CHINA DOLL — Ames Brothers, RCA Victor 7655 | [S] | 8 |
| 64 | 75 | 89 | — | APPLE GREEN — June Valli, Mercury 71588 | | 3 |
| 65 | 55 | 24 | 20 | YOU GOT WHAT IT TAKES — Marv Johnson, United Artists 185 | | 21 |
| 66 | 67 | 75 | 85 | CHATTANOOGA CHOO CHOO — Ernie Fields, Rendezvous 117 | | 4 |
| ★67 | 88 | — | — | BIG IRON — Marty Robbins, Columbia 41589 | [A] | 2 |
| 68 | 71 | 91 | 96 | MOUNTAIN OF LOVE — Harold Dorman, Rita 1003 | | 4 |
| 69 | 76 | — | — | AT MY FRONT DOOR — Dee Clark, Abner 1037 | | 2 |
| 70 | 70 | 40 | 33 | SHIMMY, SHIMMY, KO-KO BOP — Little Anthony & the Imperials, End 1060 | | 16 |
| 71 | 79 | 85 | 90 | STEP BY STEP — The Crests, Coed 525 | | 4 |
| 72 | 62 | 42 | 36 | CRAZY ARMS — Bob Beckham, Decca 31029 | | 12 |
| 73 | 57 | 61 | 68 | ANGELA JONES — Johnny Ferguson, M-G-M 12855 | | 5 |
| 74 | 58 | 48 | 49 | BAD BOY — Marty Wilde, Epic 9356 | | 7 |
| 75 | 81 | 81 | 97 | ROAD RUNNER — Bo Diddley, Checker 942 | | 4 |
| 76 | 89 | — | — | CARAVAN — Santo and Johnny, Canadian-American 111 | | 2 |
| 77 | 86 | 100 | — | DOWN BY THE RIVERSIDE — Les Compagnons de la Chanson, Capitol 4342 | | 3 |
| ★78 | 99 | — | — | LONELY WEEKENDS — Charlie Rich, Philips International 3552 | | 2 |
| 79 | 100 | — | — | TEENAGE SONATA — Sam Cooke, RCA Victor 7701 | [S] | 2 |
| 80 | 77 | 60 | 66 | PARADISE — Sammy Turner, Big Top 3032 | | 6 |
| 81 | 96 | — | — | THE OLD LAMPLIGHTER — The Browns, RCA Victor 7700 | | 2 |
| 82 | — | — | — | SHAZAM — Duane Eddy, Jamie 1151 | | 1 |
| 83 | 97 | — | — | RUBY — Adam Wade, Coed 526 | | 2 |
| 84 | 43 | 28 | 21 | PRETTY BLUE EYES — Steve Lawrence, ABC-Paramount 10058 | [S] | 18 |
| 85 | 73 | 67 | 64 | JUST A LITTLE BIT — Roscoe Gordon, Vee Jay 332 | | 6 |
| 86 | — | — | — | CLEMENTINE — Bobby Darin, Atco 6161 | | 1 |
| 87 | 84 | — | — | STRAIGHT A's IN LOVE — Johnny Cash, Sun 334 | | 2 |
| 88 | 82 | 88 | 95 | YOU DON'T KNOW ME — Lennie Welch, Cadence 1373 | | 4 |
| 89 | 98 | — | — | DON'T DECEIVE ME — Ruth Brown, Atlantic 2052 | | 2 |
| 90 | — | — | — | NIGHT — Jackie Wilson, Brunswick 55166 | | 1 |
| 91 | 95 | 99 | — | JAMBALAYA (ON THE BAYOU) — Bobby Comstock, Atlantic 2051 | | 3 |
| 92 | — | — | — | WAKE ME WHEN IT'S OVER — Andy Williams, Cadence 1378 | | 1 |
| 93 | 59 | 44 | 42 | TOO POOPED TO POP — Chuck Berry, Chess 1747 | | 6 |
| 94 | — | — | — | WORDS — Pat Boone, Dot 16048 | [S] | 1 |
| 95 | 63 | 54 | 46 | ETERNALLY — Sarah Vaughan, Mercury 71562 | [S] | 7 |
| 96 | 94 | 78 | 76 | LET IT ROCK — Chuck Berry, Chess 1747 | | 8 |
| 97 | 78 | 43 | 32 | GO, JIMMY, GO — Jimmy Clanton, Ace 575 | | 16 |
| 98 | 72 | 76 | 65 | SLEEPY LAGOON — Platters, Mercury 71563 | [S] | 5 |
| 99 | 85 | 52 | 35 | TIME AND THE RIVER — Nat King Cole, Capitol 4325 | | 8 |
| 100 | — | — | — | SOMEDAY — Della Reese, RCA Victor 7706 | [S] | 1 |

# The Billboard HOT 100

**FOR WEEK ENDING APRIL 3**

MARCH 28, 1960

| This Week | One Week Ago | Two Weeks Ago | Three Weeks Ago | Title — Artist, Company, Record No. | Stereo | Weeks on Chart |
|---|---|---|---|---|---|---|
| 1 | 1 | 1 | 1 | THEME FROM A SUMMER PLACE — Percy Faith, Columbia 41490 | A | 12 |
| 2 | 3 | 3 | 4 | WILD ONE — Bobby Rydell, Cameo 171 | | 9 |
| 3 | 2 | 2 | 2 | HE'LL HAVE TO GO — Jim Reeves, RCA Victor 7643 | S | 14 |
| 4 | 7 | 9 | 17 | PUPPY LOVE — Paul Anka, ABC-Paramount 10082 | S | 6 |
| 5 | 8 | 11 | 13 | SWEET NOTHIN'S — Brenda Lee, Decca 30967 | | 15 |
| 6 | 5 | 8 | 8 | BABY — Brook Benton and Dinah Washington, Mercury 71565 | S | 10 |
| 7 | 4 | 4 | 3 | HANDY MAN — Jimmy Jones, Cub 9049 | | 14 |
| 8 | 10 | 10 | 12 | HARBOR LIGHTS — The Platters, Mercury 71563 | S | 10 |
| 9 | 12 | 12 | 11 | FOREVER — Little Dippers, University 210 | | 10 |
| 10 | 17 | 19 | 29 | O, DIO MIO — Annette, Vista 354 | | 6 |
| 11 | 21 | 29 | 46 | MAMA — Connie Francis, M-G-M 12878 | S | 6 |
| 12 | 6 | 5 | 5 | WHAT IN THE WORLD'S COME OVER YOU — Jack Scott, Top Rank 2028 | S | 12 |
| 13 | 11 | 8 | 7 | BEYOND THE SEA — Bobby Darin, Atco 6158 | | 11 |
| 14 | 28 | 30 | 69 | SINK THE BISMARCK — Johnny Horton, Columbia 41568 | | 4 |
| 15 | 38 | 53 | 79 | I LOVE THE WAY YOU LOVE — Marv Johnson, United Artists 208 | | 4 |
| 16 | 19 | 21 | 47 | THIS MAGIC MOMENT — Drifters, Atlantic 2050 | | 6 |
| 17 | 15 | 16 | 19 | BEATNIK FLY — Johnny and the Hurricanes, Warwick 520 | | 7 |
| 18 | 14 | 15 | 16 | LADY LUCK — Lloyd Price, ABC-Paramount 10075 | S | 9 |
| 19 | 20 | 22 | 27 | LITTLE BITTY GIRL — Bobby Rydell, Cameo 171 | | 9 |
| 20 | 30 | 42 | 70 | WHITE SILVER SANDS — Bill Black's Combo, Hi 2021 | | 4 |
| 21 | 22 | 44 | 64 | GREENFIELDS — Brothers Four, Columbia 41571 | A | 6 |
| 22 | 18 | 24 | 34 | (WELCOME) NEW LOVERS — Pat Boone, Dot 16048 | S | 5 |
| 23 | 29 | 32 | 50 | SIXTEEN REASONS — Connie Stevens, Warner Bros. 5137 | | 9 |
| 24 | 9 | 7 | 6 | TEEN ANGEL — Mark Dinning, M-G-M 12845 | | 15 |
| 25 | 43 | 68 | 84 | FOOTSTEPS — Steve Lawrence, ABC-Paramount 10085 | | 4 |
| 26 | 27 | 52 | 45 | MONEY — Barrett Strong, Anna 1111 | | 9 |
| 27 | 13 | 13 | 9 | LET IT BE ME — The Everly Brothers, Cadence 1376 | | 12 |
| 28 | 44 | 60 | 71 | STARBRIGHT — Johnny Mathis, Columbia 41583 | A | 5 |
| 29 | 47 | 54 | 62 | TEDDY — Connie Francis, M-G-M 12878 | | |
| 30 | 24 | 25 | 22 | DELAWARE — Perry Como, RCA Victor 7670 | S | 8 |
| 31 | 34 | 35 | 41 | ABOUT THIS THING CALLED LOVE — Fabian, Chancellor 1047 | S | 5 |
| 32 | 16 | 18 | 21 | MIDNIGHT SPECIAL — Paul Evans, Guaranteed 205 | | 10 |
| 33 | 25 | 36 | 39 | AM I THAT EASY TO FORGET — Debbie Reynolds, Dot 15985 | | 11 |
| 34 | 62 | 80 | 90 | LET THE LITTLE GIRL DANCE — Billy Bland, Old Town 1076 | | 7 |
| 35 | 81 | 96 | — | THE OLD LAMPLIGHTER — The Browns, RCA Victor 7700 | | 3 |
| 36 | 32 | 40 | 49 | EL MATADOR — Kingston Trio, Capitol 4338 | | 6 |
| 37 | 46 | 64 | 80 | JUST ONE TIME — Don Gibson, RCA Victor 7690 | S | 4 |
| 38 | 53 | 65 | — | DON'T THROW AWAY ALL THOSE TEARDROPS — Frankie Avalon, Chancellor 1048 | | 3 |
| 39 | 54 | 45 | 57 | FANNIE MAE — Buster Brown, Fire 1008 | | 9 |
| 40 | 40 | 31 | 23 | TALL OAK TREE — Dorsey Burnette, Era 3012 | | 9 |
| 41 | 39 | 39 | 66 | STRING ALONG — Fabian, Chancellor 1047 | S | 6 |
| 42 | 58 | 66 | 72 | SUMMER SET — Monty Kelly, Carlton 527 | S | 5 |
| 43 | 71 | 79 | 85 | STEP BY STEP — The Crests, Coed 525 | | 5 |
| 44 | 86 | — | — | CLEMENTINE — Bobby Darin, Atco 6161 | | 2 |
| 45 | 49 | 50 | 74 | DON'T FENCE ME IN — Tommy Edwards, M-G-M 12871 | S | 6 |
| 46 | 80 | 77 | 60 | PARADISE — Sammy Turner, Big Top 3032 | | 7 |
| 47 | 41 | 28 | 30 | OUTSIDE MY WINDOW — Fleetwoods, Dolton 15 | | 7 |
| 48 | 33 | 23 | 26 | ROCKIN' LITTLE ANGEL — Ray Smith, Judd 1016 | | 13 |
| 49 | 55 | 47 | 56 | LAWDY MISS CLAWDY — Gary Stites, Carlton 525 | | 6 |
| 50 | 50 | 51 | 55 | ANYWAY THE WIND BLOWS — Doris Day, Columbia 41569 | | 6 |
| 51 | 52 | 61 | 63 | THE SAME OLD ME — Guy Mitchell, Columbia 41576 | | 5 |
| 52 | 37 | 34 | 35 | CHATTANOOGA SHOE SHINE BOY — Freddy Cannon, Swan 4050 | | 6 |
| 53 | 23 | 14 | 10 | RUNNING BEAR — Johnny Preston, Mercury 71474 | | 24 |
| 54 | 31 | 17 | 15 | WHERE OR WHEN — Dion and the Belmonts, Laurie 3044 | | 14 |
| 55 | 79 | 100 | — | TEENAGE SONATA — Sam Cooke, RCA Victor 7701 | S | 3 |
| 56 | 26 | 27 | 14 | LONELY BLUE BOY — Conway Twitty, M-G-M 12857 | | 14 |
| 57 | 64 | 75 | 89 | APPLE GREEN — June Valli, Mercury 71588 | | 4 |
| 58 | 36 | 20 | 20 | TRACY'S THEME — Spencer Ross, Columbia 41532 | A | 13 |
| 59 | 67 | 88 | — | BIG IRON — Marty Robbins, Columbia 41589 | A | 3 |
| 60 | 90 | — | — | NIGHT — Jackie Wilson, Brunswick 55166 | | 2 |
| 61 | 69 | 76 | — | AT MY FRONT DOOR — Dee Clark, Abner 1037 | | 3 |
| 62 | 63 | 69 | 53 | CHINA DOLL — Ames Brothers, RCA Victor 7655 | S | 9 |
| 63 | 66 | 67 | 75 | CHATTANOOGA CHOO CHOO — Ernie Fields, Rendezvous 117 | | 5 |
| 64 | 77 | 86 | 100 | DOWN BY THE RIVERSIDE — Les Compagnons de la Chanson, Capitol 4342 | | 4 |
| 65 | 61 | 56 | 58 | WHY DO I LOVE YOU SO — Johnny Tillotson, Cadence 1372 | | 11 |
| 66 | 68 | 71 | 91 | MOUNTAIN OF LOVE — Harold Dorman, Rita 1003 | | 5 |
| 67 | 35 | 26 | 18 | DOWN BY THE STATION — Four Preps, Capitol 4312 | | 14 |
| 68 | 48 | 49 | 36 | BULLDOG — The Fireballs, Top Rank 2026 | S | 12 |
| 69 | 76 | 89 | — | CARAVAN — Santo and Johnny, Canadian-American 111 | | 3 |
| 70 | 92 | — | — | WAKE ME WHEN IT'S OVER — Andy Williams, Cadence 1378 | | 2 |
| 71 | 56 | 74 | 68 | HARLEM NOCTURNE — Viscounts, Madison 123 | | 14 |
| 72 | 45 | 37 | 25 | COUNTRY BOY — Fats Domino, Imperial 5645 | | 9 |
| 73 | 59 | 48 | 37 | TOO MUCH TEQUILA — Champs, Challenge 59063 | | 11 |
| 74 | 82 | — | — | SHAZAM — Duane Eddy, Jamie 1151 | | 2 |
| 75 | 73 | 57 | 61 | ANGELA JONES — Johnny Ferguson, M-G-M 12855 | | 6 |
| 76 | — | — | — | CRADLE OF LOVE — Johnny Preston, Mercury 71598 | | 1 |
| 77 | 83 | 97 | — | RUBY — Adam Wade, Coed 526 | | 3 |
| 78 | 57 | 46 | 32 | LUCKY DEVIL — Carl Dobkins Jr., Decca 31020 | | 17 |
| 79 | 88 | 82 | 88 | YOU DON'T KNOW ME — Lennie Welch, Cadence 1373 | | 5 |
| 80 | 72 | 62 | 42 | CRAZY ARMS — Bob Beckham, Decca 31029 | | 13 |
| 81 | — | — | — | OHH POO PAH DOO (Part 2) — Jessie Hill, Minit 607 | | 1 |
| 82 | 51 | 41 | 38 | BABY, WHAT DO YOU WANT ME TO DO — Jimmy Reed, Vee Jay 333 | | 7 |
| 83 | — | — | — | IT COULD HAPPEN TO YOU — Dinah Washington, Mercury 71560 | | 1 |
| 84 | — | — | — | TEEN EX — Browns, RCA Victor 7700 | | 1 |
| 85 | 100 | — | — | SOMEDAY — Della Reese, RCA Victor 7706 | S | 2 |
| 86 | 42 | 38 | 31 | EL PASO — Marty Robbins, Columbia 41511 | A | 21 |
| 87 | 89 | 98 | — | DON'T DECEIVE ME — Ruth Brown, Atlantic 2052 | | 3 |
| 88 | — | — | — | HOUSE OF BAMBOO — Earl Grant, Decca 31044 | | 1 |
| 89 | 85 | 73 | 67 | JUST A LITTLE BIT — Roscoe Gordon, Vee Jay 332 | | 7 |
| 90 | 91 | 95 | 99 | JAMBALAYA (ON THE BAYOU) — Bobby Comstock, Atlantic 2051 | | 4 |
| 91 | 75 | 81 | 81 | ROAD RUNNER — Bo Diddley, Checker 942 | | 5 |
| 92 | — | — | 98 | HULLY GULLY — Olympics, Arvee 562 | | 7 |
| 93 | — | — | — | WHAT AM I LIVING FOR — Conway Twitty, M-G-M 12866 | | 1 |
| 94 | 65 | 55 | 24 | YOU GOT WHAT IT TAKES — Marv Johnson, United Artists 185 | | 22 |
| 95 | 78 | 99 | — | LONELY WEEKENDS — Charlie Rich, Philips International 3552 | | 3 |
| 96 | — | — | — | WHY I'M WALKING — Stonewall Jackson, Columbia 41591 | | |
| 97 | 74 | 58 | 48 | BAD BOY — Marty Wilde, Epic 9356 | | 8 |
| 98 | — | — | — | I NEED YOU NOW — Joni James, M-G-M 12885 | | 1 |
| 99 | — | — | — | STAIRWAY TO HEAVEN — Neil Sedaka, RCA Victor 7079 | S | 1 |
| 100 | 95 | 63 | 54 | ETERNALLY — Sarah Vaughan, Mercury 71562 | S | 8 |

# The Billboard HOT 100

FOR WEEK ENDING APRIL 10

★ STAR PERFORMERS showed the greatest upward progress on Hot 100 this week.

[S] Indicates that 45 r.p.m. stereo single version is available.

△ Indicates that 33⅓ r.p.m. stereo single version is available.

| This Week | One Week Ago | Two Weeks Ago | Three Weeks Ago | Title | Artist, Company, Record No. | Stereo | Weeks on Chart |
|---|---|---|---|---|---|---|---|
| 1 | 1 | 1 | 1 | THEME FROM A SUMMER PLACE | Percy Faith, Columbia 41490 | △ | 13 |
| 2 | 4 | 7 | 9 | PUPPY LOVE | Paul Anka, ABC-Paramount 10082 | S | 7 |
| 3 | 2 | 3 | 3 | WILD ONE | Bobby Rydell, Cameo 171 | | 10 |
| 4 | 3 | 2 | 2 | HE'LL HAVE TO GO | Jim Reeves, RCA Victor 7643 | S | 15 |
| 5 | 5 | 8 | 11 | SWEET NOTHIN'S | Brenda Lee, Decca 30967 | | 16 |
| ★6 | 14 | 28 | 30 | SINK THE BISMARCK | Johnny Horton, Columbia 41568 | | 5 |
| ★7 | 25 | 43 | 68 | FOOTSTEPS | Steve Lawrence, ABC-Paramount 10085 | | 5 |
| 8 | 8 | 10 | 10 | HARBOR LIGHTS | The Platters, Mercury 71563 | S | 11 |
| 9 | 11 | 21 | 29 | MAMA | Connie Francis, M-G-M 12878 | S | 7 |
| 10 | 6 | 5 | 8 | BABY | Brook Benton and Dinah Washington, Mercury 71565 | S | 11 |
| 11 | 10 | 17 | 19 | O, DIO MIO | Annette, Vista 354 | | 7 |
| ★12 | 21 | 22 | 44 | GREENFIELDS | Brothers Four, Columbia 41571 | △ | 7 |
| 13 | 7 | 4 | 4 | HANDY MAN | Jimmy Jones, Cub 9049 | | 15 |
| 14 | 15 | 38 | 53 | I LOVE THE WAY YOU LOVE | Marv Johnson, United Artists 208 | | 5 |
| ★15 | 20 | 30 | 42 | WHITE SILVER SANDS | Bill Black's Combo, Hi 2021 | | 5 |
| ★16 | 23 | 29 | 32 | SIXTEEN REASONS | Connie Stevens, Warner Bros. 5137 | | 10 |
| ★17 | 29 | 47 | 54 | TEDDY | Connie Francis, M-G-M 12878 | S | 6 |
| 18 | 22 | 18 | 24 | (WELCOME) NEW LOVERS | Pat Boone, Dot 16048 | S | 6 |
| 19 | 17 | 15 | 16 | BEATNIK FLY | Johnny and the Hurricanes, Warwick 520 | | 8 |
| 20 | 18 | 14 | 15 | LADY LUCK | Lloyd Price, ABC-Paramount 10075 | S | 10 |
| 21 | 16 | 19 | 21 | THIS MAGIC MOMENT | Drifters, Atlantic 2050 | | 7 |
| 22 | 12 | 6 | 5 | WHAT IN THE WORLD'S COME OVER YOU | Jack Scott, Top Rank 2028 | S | 13 |
| 23 | 9 | 12 | 12 | FOREVER | Little Dippers, University 210 | | 11 |
| ★24 | 35 | 81 | 96 | THE OLD LAMPLIGHTER | The Browns, RCA Victor 7700 | | 4 |
| 25 | 28 | 44 | 60 | STARBRIGHT | Johnny Mathis, Columbia 41583 | △ | 6 |
| 26 | 13 | 11 | 8 | BEYOND THE SEA | Bobby Darin, Atco 6158 | | 12 |
| ★27 | 38 | 53 | 65 | DON'T THROW AWAY ALL THOSE TEARDROPS | Frankie Avalon, Chancellor 1048 | | 4 |
| 28 | 34 | 62 | 80 | LET THE LITTLE GIRL DANCE | Billy Bland, Old Town 1076 | | 8 |
| 29 | 19 | 20 | 22 | LITTLE BITTY GIRL | Bobby Rydell, Cameo 171 | | 10 |
| ★30 | 42 | 58 | 66 | SUMMER SET | Monty Kelly, Carlton 527 | S | 6 |
| 31 | 26 | 27 | 52 | MONEY | Barrett Strong, Anna 1111 | | 10 |
| 32 | 33 | 25 | 36 | AM I THAT EASY TO FORGET | Debbie Reynolds, Dot 15985 | | 12 |
| ★33 | 43 | 71 | 79 | STEP BY STEP | The Crests, Coed 525 | | 6 |
| ★34 | 44 | 86 | — | CLEMENTINE | Bobby Darin, Atco 6161 | | 3 |
| 35 | 24 | 9 | 7 | TEEN ANGEL | Mark Dinning, M-G-M 12845 | | 16 |
| 36 | 37 | 46 | 64 | JUST ONE TIME | Don Gibson, RCA Victor 7690 | S | 5 |
| 37 | 40 | 40 | 31 | TALL OAK TREE | Dorsey Burnette, Era 3012 | | 10 |
| ★38 | 76 | — | — | CRADLE OF LOVE | Johnny Preston, Mercury 71598 | | 2 |
| 39 | 36 | 32 | 40 | EL MATADOR | Kingston Trio, Capitol 4338 | | 7 |
| 40 | 27 | 13 | 13 | LET IT BE ME | The Everly Brothers, Cadence 1376 | | 13 |
| 41 | 32 | 16 | 18 | MIDNIGHT SPECIAL | Paul Evans, Guaranteed 205 | | 11 |
| ★42 | 59 | 67 | 88 | BIG IRON | Marty Robbins, Columbia 41589 | △ | 4 |
| 43 | 41 | 39 | 39 | STRING ALONG | Fabian, Chancellor 1047 | S | 7 |
| 44 | 31 | 34 | 35 | ABOUT THIS THING CALLED LOVE | Fabian, Chancellor 1047 | S | 6 |
| 45 | 47 | 41 | 28 | OUTSIDE MY WINDOW | Fleetwoods, Dolton 15 | | 8 |
| 46 | 46 | 80 | 77 | PARADISE | Sammy Turner, Big Top 3032 | | 8 |
| 47 | 30 | 24 | 25 | DELAWARE | Perry Como, RCA Victor 7670 | S | 9 |
| 48 | 39 | 54 | 45 | FANNIE MAE | Buster Brown, Fire 1008 | | 10 |
| 49 | 57 | 64 | 75 | APPLE GREEN | June Valli, Mercury 71588 | | 5 |
| 50 | 55 | 79 | 100 | TEENAGE SONATA | Sam Cooke, RCA Victor 7701 | S | 4 |
| ★51 | 69 | 76 | 89 | CARAVAN | Santo and Johnny, Canadian-American 111 | | 4 |
| 52 | 48 | 33 | 23 | ROCKIN' LITTLE ANGEL | Ray Smith, Judd 1016 | | 14 |
| 53 | 60 | 90 | — | NIGHT | Jackie Wilson, Brunswick 55166 | | 3 |
| 54 | 63 | 66 | 67 | CHATTANOOGA CHOO CHOO | Ernie Fields, Rendezvous 117 | | 6 |
| 55 | 49 | 55 | 47 | LAWDY MISS CLAWDY | Garry Stites, Carlton 525 | | 7 |
| 56 | 61 | 69 | 76 | AT MY FRONT DOOR | Dee Clark, Abner 1037 | | 4 |
| 57 | 45 | 49 | 50 | DON'T FENCE ME IN | Tommy Edwards, M-G-M 12871 | S | 7 |
| ★58 | 75 | 73 | 57 | ANGELA JONES | Johnny Ferguson, M-G-M 12855 | | 7 |
| 59 | 62 | 63 | 69 | CHINA DOLL | Ames Brothers, RCA Victor 7655 | S | 10 |
| 60 | 64 | 77 | 86 | DOWN BY THE RIVERSIDE | Les Compagnons de la Chanson, Capitol 4342 | | 5 |
| 61 | 66 | 68 | 71 | MOUNTAIN OF LOVE | Harold Dorman, Rita 1003 | | 6 |
| 62 | 70 | 92 | — | WAKE ME WHEN IT'S OVER | Andy Williams, Cadence 1378 | | 3 |
| 63 | 74 | 82 | — | SHAZAM | Duane Eddy, Jamie 1151 | | 3 |
| ★64 | 84 | — | — | TEEN EX | Browns, RCA Victor 7700 | | 2 |
| ★65 | 87 | 89 | 98 | DON'T DECEIVE ME | Ruth Brown, Atlantic 2052 | | 4 |
| 66 | 77 | 83 | 97 | RUBY | Adam Wade, Coed 526 | | 4 |
| 67 | 53 | 23 | 14 | RUNNING BEAR | Johnny Preston, Mercury 71474 | | 25 |
| 68 | 65 | 61 | 56 | WHY DO I LOVE YOU SO | Johnny Tillotson, Cadence 1372 | | 12 |
| 69 | 71 | 56 | 74 | HARLEM NOCTURNE | Viscounts, Madison 123 | | 15 |
| 70 | 50 | 51 | 55 | ANYWAY THE WIND BLOWS | Doris Day, Columbia 41569 | | 7 |
| 71 | 79 | 88 | 82 | YOU DON'T KNOW ME | Lennie Welch, Cadence 1373 | | 6 |
| 72 | 51 | 52 | 61 | THE SAME OLD ME | Guy Mitchell, Columbia 41576 | | 6 |
| 73 | 52 | 37 | 34 | CHATTANOOGA SHOE SHINE BOY | Freddy Cannon, Swan 4050 | | 7 |
| 74 | 81 | — | — | OOH POO PAH DOO (Part 2) | Jessie Hill, Minit 607 | | 2 |
| ★75 | 99 | — | — | STAIRWAY TO HEAVEN | Neil Sedaka, RCA Victor 7709 | S | 2 |
| 76 | 54 | 31 | 17 | WHERE OR WHEN | Dion and the Belmonts, Laurie 3044 | | 15 |
| 77 | 58 | 36 | 20 | TRACY'S THEME | Spencer Ross, Columbia 41532 | △ | 14 |
| 78 | 83 | — | — | IT COULD HAPPEN TO YOU | Dinah Washington, Mercury 71560 | | 2 |
| 79 | 85 | 100 | — | SOMEDAY | Della Reese, RCA Victor 7706 | S | 3 |
| 80 | 82 | 51 | 41 | BABY, WHAT DO YOU WANT ME TO DO | Jimmy Reed, Vee Jay 333 | | 8 |
| ★81 | — | — | — | DOGGIN' AROUND | Jackie Wilson, Brunswick 55166 | | 1 |
| 82 | 95 | 78 | 99 | LONELY WEEKENDS | Charlie Rich, Philips International 3552 | | 4 |
| ★83 | — | — | — | ROCKIN' RED WING | Sammy Masters, Lode 108 | | 1 |
| ★84 | — | — | — | STUCK ON YOU | Elvis Presley, RCA Victor 7740 | S | 1 |
| ★85 | — | — | — | LOVE YOU SO | Rod Holden, Donna 1315 | | 1 |
| 86 | 93 | — | — | WHAT AM I LIVING FOR | Conway Twitty, M-G-M 12866 | | 2 |
| 87 | 96 | — | — | WHY I'M WALKIN' | Stonewall Jackson, Columbia 41591 | | 2 |
| 88 | 88 | — | — | HOUSE OF BAMBOO | Earl Grant, Decca 31044 | | 2 |
| ★89 | — | — | — | MADISON | Al Brown's Tunetoppers, Amy 804 | | 1 |
| ★90 | — | — | — | THINK ME A KISS | Clyde McPhatter, M-G-M 12877 | | 1 |
| 91 | 72 | 45 | 37 | COUNTRY BOY | Fats Domino, Imperial 5645 | | 10 |
| 92 | — | — | — | CHERRY PIE | Skip and Flip, Brent 7010 | | 1 |
| 93 | — | — | — | NEVER LET ME GO | Lloyd Price, ABC-Paramount 10075 | | 2 |
| 94 | — | — | — | ADAM AND EVE | Paul Anka, ABC-Paramount 10082 | | 1 |
| 95 | — | — | — | MR. LUCKY | Henry Mancini, RCA Victor 7705 | S | 1 |
| 96 | — | — | — | WHAT DO YOU WANT | Bobby Vee, Liberty 55234 | | 1 |
| 97 | 86 | 42 | 38 | EL PASO | Marty Robbins, Columbia 41511 | △ | 22 |
| 98 | 67 | 35 | 26 | DOWN BY THE STATION | The Four Preps, Capitol 4312 | | 15 |
| 99 | 91 | 75 | 81 | ROAD RUNNER | Bo Diddley, Checker 942 | | 6 |
| 100 | 56 | 26 | 27 | LONELY BLUE BOY | Conway Twitty, M-G-M 12857 | | 15 |

# The Billboard HOT 100

**FOR WEEK ENDING APRIL 17**

*APRIL 11, 1960*

| This Week | 1 Wk Ago | 2 Wks Ago | 3 Wks Ago | Title — Artist, Company, Record No. | Stereo | Weeks on Chart |
|---|---|---|---|---|---|---|
| 1 | 1 | 1 | 1 | THEME FROM A SUMMER PLACE — Percy Faith, Columbia 41490 | A | 14 |
| 2 | 2 | 4 | 7 | PUPPY LOVE — Paul Anka, ABC-Paramount 10082 | S | 8 |
| 3 | 4 | 3 | 2 | HE'LL HAVE TO GO — Jim Reeves, RCA Victor 7643 | S | 16 |
| 4 | 3 | 2 | 3 | WILD ONE — Bobby Rydell, Cameo 171 | | 11 |
| 5 | 12 | 21 | 22 | GREENFIELDS — Brothers Four, Columbia 41571 | A | 8 |
| 6 | 5 | 5 | 8 | SWEET NOTHIN'S — Brenda Lee, Decca 30967 | | 17 |
| 7 | 6 | 14 | 28 | SINK THE BISMARCK — Johnny Horton, Columbia 41568 | | 6 |
| 8 | 9 | 11 | 21 | MAMA — Connie Francis, M-G-M 12878 | S | 8 |
| 9 | 14 | 15 | 38 | I LOVE THE WAY YOU LOVE — Marv Johnson, United Artists 208 | | 6 |
| 10 | 7 | 25 | 43 | FOOTSTEPS — Steve Lawrence, ABC-Paramount 10085 | | 6 |
| 11 | 16 | 23 | 29 | SIXTEEN REASONS — Connie Stevens, Warner Bros. 5137 | | 11 |
| 12 | 15 | 20 | 30 | WHITE SILVER SANDS — Bill Black's Combo, Hi 2021 | | 6 |
| 13 | 10 | 6 | 5 | BABY — Brook Benton and Dinah Washington, Mercury 71565 | S | 12 |
| 14 | 11 | 10 | 17 | O, DIO MIO — Annette, Vista 354 | | 8 |
| 15 | 8 | 8 | 10 | HARBOR LIGHTS — The Platters, Mercury 71563 | S | 12 |
| 16 | 24 | 35 | 81 | THE OLD LAMPLIGHTER — The Browns, RCA Victor 7700 | | 5 |
| 17 | 84 | — | — | STUCK ON YOU — Elvis Presley, RCA Victor 7740 | S | 2 |
| 18 | 33 | 43 | 71 | STEP BY STEP — The Crests, Coed 525 | | 7 |
| 19 | 38 | 76 | — | CRADLE OF LOVE — Johnny Preston, Mercury 71598 | | 3 |
| 20 | 13 | 7 | 4 | HANDY MAN — Jimmy Jones, Cub 9049 | | 16 |
| 21 | 19 | 17 | 15 | BEATNIK FLY — Johnny and the Hurricanes, Warwick 520 | | 9 |
| 22 | 18 | 22 | 18 | (WELCOME) NEW LOVERS — Pat Boone, Dot 16048 | S | 7 |
| 23 | 27 | 38 | 53 | DON'T THROW AWAY ALL THOSE TEARDROPS — Frankie Avalon, Chancellor 1048 | | 5 |
| 24 | 31 | 26 | 27 | MONEY — Barrett Strong, Anna 1111 | | 11 |
| 25 | 25 | 28 | 44 | STARBRIGHT — Johnny Mathis, Columbia 41583 | A | 7 |
| 26 | 28 | 34 | 62 | LET THE LITTLE GIRL DANCE — Billy Bland, Old Town 1076 | | 9 |
| 27 | 17 | 29 | 47 | TEDDY — Connie Francis, M-G-M 12878 | S | 7 |
| 28 | 53 | 60 | 90 | NIGHT — Jackie Wilson, Brunswick 55166 | | 4 |
| 29 | 21 | 16 | 19 | THIS MAGIC MOMENT — Drifters, Atlantic 2050 | | 8 |
| 30 | 34 | 44 | 86 | CLEMENTINE — Bobby Darin, Atco 6161 | | 4 |
| 31 | 30 | 42 | 58 | SUMMER SET — Monty Kelly, Carlton 527 | S | 7 |
| 32 | 20 | 18 | 14 | LADY LUCK — Lloyd Price, ABC-Paramount 10075 | S | 11 |
| 33 | 29 | 19 | 20 | LITTLE BITTY GIRL — Bobby Rydell, Cameo 171 | | 11 |
| 34 | 22 | 12 | 6 | WHAT IN THE WORLD'S COME OVER YOU — Jack Scott, Top Rank 2028 | S | 14 |
| 35 | 36 | 37 | 46 | JUST ONE TIME — Don Gibson, RCA Victor 7690 | S | 6 |
| 36 | 23 | 9 | 12 | FOREVER — Little Dippers, University 210 | | 12 |
| 37 | 37 | 40 | 40 | TALL OAK TREE — Dorsey Burnette, Era 3012 | | 11 |
| 38 | 39 | 36 | 32 | EL MATADOR — Kingston Trio, Capitol 4338 | | 8 |
| 39 | 42 | 59 | 67 | BIG IRON — Marty Robbins, Columbia 41589 | A | 5 |
| 40 | 32 | 33 | 25 | AM I THAT EASY TO FORGET — Debbie Reynolds, Dot 15985 | | 13 |
| 41 | 26 | 13 | 11 | BEYOND THE SEA — Bobby Darin, Atco 6158 | | 13 |
| 42 | 75 | 99 | — | STAIRWAY TO HEAVEN — Neil Sedaka, RCA Victor 7709 | S | 3 |
| 43 | 48 | 39 | 54 | FANNIE MAE — Buster Brown, Fire 1008 | | 11 |
| 44 | 61 | 66 | 68 | MOUNTAIN OF LOVE — Harold Dorman, Rita 1003 | | 7 |
| 45 | 49 | 57 | 64 | APPLE GREEN — June Valli, Mercury 71588 | | 6 |
| 46 | 58 | 75 | 73 | ANGELA JONES — Johnny Ferguson, M-G-M 12855 | | 8 |
| 47 | 46 | 46 | 80 | PARADISE — Sammy Turner, Big Top 3032 | | 9 |
| 48 | 40 | 27 | 13 | LET IT BE ME — The Everly Brothers, Cadence 1376 | | 14 |
| 49 | 81 | — | — | DOGGIN' AROUND — Jackie Wilson, Brunswick 55166 | | 2 |
| 50 | 51 | 69 | 76 | CARAVAN — Santo and Johnny, Canadian-American 111 | | 5 |
| 51 | 41 | 32 | 16 | MIDNIGHT SPECIAL — Paul Evans, Guaranteed 205 | | 12 |
| 52 | 85 | — | — | LOVE YOU SO — Rod Holden, Donna 1315 | | 2 |
| 53 | 82 | 95 | 78 | LONELY WEEKENDS — Charlie Rich, Philips International 3552 | | 5 |
| 54 | 63 | 74 | 82 | SHAZAM — Duane Eddy, Jamie 1151 | | 4 |
| 55 | 92 | — | — | CHERRY PIE — Skip and Flip, Brent 7010 | | 2 |
| 56 | 59 | 62 | 63 | CHINA DOLL — Ames Brothers, RCA Victor 7655 | S | 11 |
| 57 | 62 | 70 | 92 | WAKE ME WHEN IT'S OVER — Andy Williams, Cadence 1378 | | 4 |
| 58 | 79 | 85 | 100 | SOMEDAY — Della Reese, RCA Victor 7706 | S | 4 |
| 59 | 56 | 61 | 69 | AT MY FRONT DOOR — Dee Clark, Abner 1037 | | 5 |
| 60 | 71 | 79 | 88 | YOU DON'T KNOW ME — Lennie Welch, Cadence 1373 | | 7 |
| 61 | 44 | 31 | 34 | ABOUT THIS THING CALLED LOVE — Fabian, Chancellor 1047 | S | 7 |
| 62 | 65 | 87 | 89 | DON'T DECEIVE ME — Ruth Brown, Atlantic 2052 | | 5 |
| 63 | 86 | 93 | — | WHAT AM I LIVING FOR — Conway Twitty, M-G-M 12886 | | 3 |
| 64 | 68 | 65 | 61 | WHY DO I LOVE YOU SO — Johnny Tillotson, Cadence 1372 | | 13 |
| 65 | 43 | 41 | 39 | STRING ALONG — Fabian, Chancellor 1047 | S | 8 |
| 66 | 66 | 77 | 83 | RUBY — Adam Wade, Coed 526 | | 5 |
| 67 | 55 | 49 | 55 | LAWDY MISS CLAWDY — Garry Stites, Carlton 525 | | 8 |
| 68 | 47 | 30 | 24 | DELAWARE — Perry Como, RCA Victor 7670 | S | 10 |
| 69 | 35 | 24 | 9 | TEEN ANGEL — Mark Dinning, M-G-M 12845 | | 17 |
| 70 | 57 | 45 | 49 | DON'T FENCE ME IN — Tommy Edwards, M-G-M 12871 | S | 8 |
| 71 | — | — | — | FAME AND FORTUNE — Elvis Presley, RCA Victor 7740 | S | 1 |
| 72 | 74 | 81 | — | OOH POO PAH DOO (Part 2) — Jessie Hill, Minit 607 | | 3 |
| 73 | 64 | 84 | — | TEEN EX — Browns, RCA Victor 7700 | | 3 |
| 74 | — | — | — | EARTH ANGEL — Johnny Tillotson, Cadence 1377 | | 1 |
| 75 | 60 | 64 | 77 | DOWN BY THE RIVERSIDE — Les Compagnons de la Chanson, Capitol 4342 | | 6 |
| 76 | 50 | 55 | 79 | TEENAGE SONATA — Sam Cooke, RCA Victor 7701 | S | 5 |
| 77 | 54 | 63 | 66 | CHATTANOOGA CHOO CHOO — Ernie Fields, Rendezvous 117 | | 7 |
| 78 | 78 | 83 | — | IT COULD HAPPEN TO YOU — Dinah Washington, Mercury 71560 | S | 3 |
| 79 | 95 | — | — | MR. LUCKY — Henry Mancini, RCA Victor 7705 | S | 2 |
| 80 | 83 | — | — | ROCKIN' RED WING — Sammy Masters, Lode 108 | | 2 |
| 81 | 67 | 53 | 23 | RUNNING BEAR — Johnny Preston, Mercury 71474 | | 26 |
| 82 | 52 | 48 | 33 | ROCKIN' LITTLE ANGEL — Ray Smith, Judd 1016 | | 15 |
| 83 | 87 | 96 | — | WHY I'M WALKIN' — Stonewall Jackson, Columbia 41591 | | 3 |
| 84 | 90 | — | — | THINK ME A KISS — Clyde McPhatter, M-G-M 12877 | | 2 |
| 85 | 89 | — | — | MADISON — Al Brown's Tunetoppers, Amy 804 | | 2 |
| 86 | — | — | — | PLEDGING MY LOVE — Johnny Tillotson, Cadence 1377 | | 1 |
| 87 | 80 | 82 | 51 | BABY, WHAT DO YOU WANT ME TO DO — Jimmy Reed, Vee Jay 333 | | 9 |
| 88 | — | — | — | TIES THAT BIND — Brook Benton, Mercury 71566 | S | 1 |
| 89 | 45 | 47 | 41 | OUTSIDE MY WINDOW — Fleetwoods, Dolton 15 | | 9 |
| 90 | 94 | — | — | ADAM AND EVE — Paul Anka, ABC-Paramount 10082 | | 2 |
| 91 | — | — | — | JENNY LOU — Sonny James, NRC 50 | | 1 |
| 92 | 76 | 54 | 31 | WHERE OR WHEN — Dion and the Belmonts, Laurie 3044 | | 16 |
| 93 | 96 | — | — | WHAT DO YOU WANT — Bobby Vee, Liberty 55234 | | 2 |
| 94 | — | — | — | PAPER ROSES — Anita Bryant, Carlton 528 | S | 1 |
| 95 | — | — | — | HOW DEEP IS THE OCEAN — Toni Fisher, Signet 276 | | 1 |
| 96 | 93 | — | — | NEVER LET ME GO — Lloyd Price, ABC-Paramount 10075 | | 3 |
| 97 | 88 | 88 | — | HOUSE OF BAMBOO — Earl Grant, Decca 31044 | | 3 |
| 98 | — | — | — | JUST A CLOSER WALK WITH THEE — Jimmie Rodgers, Roulette 4234 | | 1 |
| 99 | — | — | — | MADISON TIME — Ray Bryant, Columbia 41628 | | 1 |
| 100 | 69 | 71 | 56 | HARLEM NOCTURNE — Viscounts, Madison 123 | | 16 |

# The Billboard HOT 100

**FOR WEEK ENDING APRIL 24**

*STAR PERFORMERS showed the greatest upward progress on Hot 100 this week.*
*(S) Indicates that 45 r.p.m. stereo single version is available.*
*(A) Indicates that 33⅓ r.p.m. stereo single version is available.*

Columns: THIS WEEK | ONE WEEK AGO | TWO WEEKS AGO | THREE WEEKS AGO | TITLE — Artist, Company, Record No. | STEREO | WEEKS ON CHART

| # | 1wk | 2wk | 3wk | Title — Artist, Company, Record No. | Stereo | Wks |
|---|---|---|---|---|---|---|
| 1 | 1 | 1 | 1 | THEME FROM A SUMMER PLACE — Percy Faith, Columbia 41490 | A | 15 |
| 2 | 5 | 12 | 21 | GREENFIELDS — Brothers Four, Columbia 41571 | A | 9 |
| 3 | 2 | 2 | 4 | PUPPY LOVE — Paul Anka, ABC-Paramount 10082 | S | 9 |
| 4 | 6 | 5 | 5 | SWEET NOTHIN'S — Brenda Lee, Decca 30967 | | 18 |
| 5 | 7 | 6 | 14 | SINK THE BISMARCK — Johnny Horton, Columbia 41568 | | 7 |
| 6 | 17 | 84 | — | STUCK ON YOU — Elvis Presley, RCA Victor 7740 | S | 3 |
| 7 | 4 | 3 | 2 | WILD ONE — Bobby Rydell, Cameo 171 | | 12 |
| 8 | 3 | 4 | 3 | HE'LL HAVE TO GO — Jim Reeves, RCA Victor 7643 | S | 17 |
| 9 | 11 | 16 | 23 | SIXTEEN REASONS — Connie Stevens, Warner Bros. 5137 | | 12 |
| 10 | 8 | 9 | 11 | MAMA — Connie Francis, M-G-M 12878 | S | 9 |
| 11 | 10 | 7 | 25 | FOOTSTEPS — Steve Lawrence, ABC-Paramount 10085 | | 7 |
| 12 | 12 | 15 | 20 | WHITE SILVER SANDS — Bill Black's Combo, Hi 2021 | | 7 |
| 13 | 9 | 14 | 15 | I LOVE THE WAY YOU LOVE — Marv Johnson, United Artists 208 | | 7 |
| 14 | 19 | 38 | 76 | CRADLE OF LOVE — Johnny Preston, Mercury 71598 | | 4 |
| 15 | 18 | 33 | 43 | STEP BY STEP — The Crests, Coed 525 | | 8 |
| 16 | 16 | 24 | 35 | THE OLD LAMPLIGHTER — The Browns, RCA Victor 7700 | | 6 |
| 17 | 13 | 10 | 6 | BABY — Brook Benton and Dinah Washington, Mercury 71565 | S | 13 |
| 18 | 26 | 28 | 34 | LET THE LITTLE GIRL DANCE — Billy Bland, Old Town 1076 | | 10 |
| 19 | 28 | 53 | 60 | NIGHT — Jackie Wilson, Brunswick 55166 | | 5 |
| 20 | 15 | 8 | 8 | HARBOR LIGHTS — The Platters, Mercury 71563 | S | 13 |
| 21 | 30 | 34 | 44 | CLEMENTINE — Bobby Darin, Atco 6161 | | 5 |
| 22 | 23 | 27 | 38 | DON'T THROW AWAY ALL THOSE TEARDROPS — Frankie Avalon, Chancellor 1048 | | 6 |
| 23 | 24 | 31 | 26 | MONEY — Barrett Strong, Anna 1111 | | 12 |
| 24 | 14 | 11 | 10 | O, DIO MIO — Annette, Vista 354 | | 9 |
| 25 | 27 | 17 | 29 | TEDDY — Connie Francis, M-G-M 12878 | S | 8 |
| 26 | 39 | 42 | 59 | BIG IRON — Marty Robbins, Columbia 41589 | A | 6 |
| 27 | 42 | 75 | 99 | STAIRWAY TO HEAVEN — Neil Sedaka, RCA Victor 7709 | S | 4 |
| 28 | 21 | 19 | 17 | BEATNIK FLY — Johnny and the Hurricanes, Warwick 520 | | 10 |
| 29 | 35 | 36 | 37 | JUST ONE TIME — Don Gibson, RCA Victor 7690 | S | 7 |
| 30 | 25 | 25 | 28 | STARBRIGHT — Johnny Mathis, Columbia 41583 | A | 8 |
| 31 | 46 | 58 | 75 | ANGELA JONES — Johnny Ferguson, M-G-M 12855 | | 9 |
| 32 | 33 | 29 | 19 | LITTLE BITTY GIRL — Bobby Rydell, Cameo 171 | | 12 |
| 33 | 79 | 95 | — | MR. LUCKY — Henry Mancini, RCA Victor 7705 | S | 3 |
| 34 | 31 | 30 | 42 | SUMMER SET — Monty Kelly, Carlton 527 | S | 8 |
| 35 | 22 | 18 | 22 | (WELCOME) NEW LOVERS — Pat Boone, Dot 16048 | S | 8 |
| 36 | 45 | 49 | 57 | APPLE GREEN — June Valli, Mercury 71588 | | 7 |
| 37 | 20 | 13 | 7 | HANDY MAN — Jimmy Jones, Cub 9049 | | 17 |
| 38 | 29 | 21 | 16 | THIS MAGIC MOMENT — Drifters, Atlantic 2050 | | 9 |
| 39 | 44 | 61 | 66 | MOUNTAIN OF LOVE — Harold Dorman, Rita 1003 | | 8 |
| 40 | 37 | 37 | 40 | TALL OAK TREE — Dorsey Burnette, Era 3012 | | 12 |
| 41 | 52 | 85 | — | LOVE YOU SO — Rod Holden, Donna 1315 | | 3 |
| 42 | 36 | 23 | 9 | FOREVER — Little Dippers, University 210 | | 13 |
| 43 | 40 | 32 | 33 | AM I THAT EASY TO FORGET — Debbie Reynolds, Dot 15985 | | 14 |
| 44 | 71 | — | — | FAME AND FORTUNE — Elvis Presley, RCA Victor 7740 | S | 2 |
| 45 | 54 | 63 | 74 | SHAZAM — Duane Eddy, Jamie 1151 | | 5 |
| 46 | 49 | 81 | — | DOGGIN' AROUND — Jackie Wilson, Brunswick 55166 | | 3 |
| 47 | 63 | 86 | 93 | WHAT AM I LIVING FOR — Conway Twitty, M-G-M 12886 | | 4 |
| 48 | 50 | 51 | 69 | CARAVAN — Santo and Johnny, Canadian-American 111 | | 6 |
| 49 | 43 | 48 | 39 | FANNIE MAE — Buster Brown, Fire 1008 | | 12 |
| 50 | 38 | 39 | 36 | EL MATADOR — Kingston Trio, Capitol 4338 | | 9 |
| 51 | 55 | 92 | — | CHERRY PIE — Skip and Flip, Brent 7010 | | 3 |
| 52 | 73 | 64 | 84 | TEEN EX — Browns, RCA Victor 7700 | | 4 |
| 53 | 34 | 22 | 12 | WHAT IN THE WORLD'S COME OVER YOU — Jack Scott, Top Rank 2028 | S | 15 |
| 54 | 57 | 62 | 70 | WAKE ME WHEN IT'S OVER — Andy Williams, Cadence 1378 | | 5 |
| 55 | 72 | 74 | 81 | OOH POO PAH DOO (Part 2) — Jessie Hill, Minit 607 | | 4 |
| 56 | 58 | 79 | 85 | SOMEDAY — Della Reese, RCA Victor 7706 | S | 5 |
| 57 | 60 | 71 | 79 | YOU DON'T KNOW ME — Lennie Welch, Cadence 1373 | | 8 |
| 58 | 66 | 66 | 77 | RUBY — Adam Wade, Coed 526 | | 6 |
| 59 | 59 | 56 | 61 | AT MY FRONT DOOR — Dee Clark, Abner 1037 | | 6 |
| 60 | 78 | 78 | 83 | IT COULD HAPPEN TO YOU — Dinah Washington, Mercury 71560 | S | 4 |
| 61 | 53 | 82 | 95 | LONELY WEEKENDS — Charlie Rich, Philips International 3552 | | 6 |
| 62 | 47 | 46 | 46 | PARADISE — Sammy Turner, Big Top 3032 | | 10 |
| 63 | 67 | 55 | 49 | LAWDY MISS CLAWDY — Garry Stites, Carlton 525 | | 9 |
| 64 | 80 | 83 | — | ROCKIN' RED WING — Sammy Masters, Lode 108 | | 3 |
| 65 | 74 | — | — | EARTH ANGEL — Johnny Tillotson, Cadence 1377 | | 2 |
| 66 | 75 | 60 | 64 | DOWN BY THE RIVERSIDE — Les Compagnons de la Chanson, Capitol 4342 | | 7 |
| 67 | — | — | — | GOOD TIMIN' — Jimmy Jones, Cub 9067 | | 1 |
| 68 | 62 | 65 | 87 | DON'T DECEIVE ME — Ruth Brown, Atlantic 2052 | | 6 |
| 69 | 32 | 20 | 18 | LADY LUCK — Lloyd Price, ABC-Paramount 10075 | S | 12 |
| 70 | 51 | 41 | 32 | MIDNIGHT SPECIAL — Paul Evans, Guaranteed 205 | | 13 |
| 71 | 98 | — | — | JUST A CLOSER WALK WITH THEE — Jimmie Rodgers, Roulette 4234 | | 2 |
| 72 | 56 | 59 | 62 | CHINA DOLL — Ames Brothers, RCA Victor 7655 | S | 12 |
| 73 | 84 | 90 | — | THINK ME A KISS — Clyde McPhatter, M-G-M 12877 | | 3 |
| 74 | 87 | 80 | 82 | BABY, WHAT DO YOU WANT ME TO DO — Jimmy Reed, Vee Jay 333 | | 10 |
| 75 | 41 | 26 | 13 | BEYOND THE SEA — Bobby Darin, Atco 6158 | | 14 |
| 76 | — | — | — | WAY OF A CLOWN — Teddy Randazzo, ABC-Paramount 10088 | | 1 |
| 77 | 77 | 54 | 63 | CHATTANOOGA CHOO CHOO — Ernie Fields, Rendezvous 117 | | 8 |
| 78 | 48 | 40 | 27 | LET IT BE ME — The Everly Brothers, Cadence 1376 | | 15 |
| 79 | 85 | 89 | — | MADISON — Al Brown's Tunetoppers, Amy 804 | | 3 |
| 80 | 76 | 50 | 55 | TEENAGE SONATA — Sam Cooke, RCA Victor 7701 | S | 6 |
| 81 | 88 | — | — | TIES THAT BIND — Brook Benton, Mercury 71566 | S | 2 |
| 82 | — | — | — | NOBODY LOVES ME LIKE YOU — Flamingos, End 1068 | | 1 |
| 83 | 64 | 68 | 65 | WHY DO I LOVE YOU SO — Johnny Tillotson, Cadence 1372 | | 14 |
| 84 | 68 | 47 | 30 | DELAWARE — Perry Como, RCA Victor 7670 | S | 11 |
| 85 | 86 | — | — | PLEDGING MY LOVE — Johnny Tillotson, Cadence 1377 | | 2 |
| 86 | 69 | 35 | 24 | TEEN ANGEL — Mark Dinning, M-G-M 12845 | | 18 |
| 87 | 99 | — | — | MADISON TIME — Ray Bryant, Columbia 41628 | | 2 |
| 88 | 91 | — | — | JENNY LOU — Sonny James, NRC 50 | | 2 |
| 89 | 94 | — | — | PAPER ROSES — Anita Bryant, Carlton 528 | S | 2 |
| 90 | — | — | — | MY EMPTY ROOM — Little Anthony and the Imperials, End 1067 | | 1 |
| 91 | 81 | 67 | 53 | RUNNING BEAR — Johnny Preston, Mercury 71474 | | 27 |
| 92 | — | — | — | HITHER, THITHER AND YON — Brook Benton, Mercury 71566 | S | 1 |
| 93 | 95 | — | — | HOW DEEP IS THE OCEAN — Toni Fisher, Signet 276 | | 2 |
| 94 | — | — | — | CATHY'S CLOWN — Everly Brothers, Warner Bros. 5151 | S | 1 |
| 95 | — | — | — | BARBARA — Temptations, Goldisc 3001 | | 1 |
| 96 | 82 | 52 | 48 | ROCKIN' LITTLE ANGEL — Ray Smith, Judd 1016 | | 16 |
| 97 | — | — | — | BURNING BRIDGES — Jack Scott, Top Rank 2041 | | 1 |
| 98 | — | — | — | A STAR IS BORN (A LOVE HAS DIED) — Mark Dinning, M-G-M 12888 | | 1 |
| 99 | — | — | — | SOMEONE LOVES YOU, JOE — The Singing Belles, Madison 126 | | 1 |
| 100 | — | — | — | GOT A GIRL — Four Preps, Capitol 4362 | | 1 |

# The Billboard HOT 100

**For Week Ending May 1** — April 25, 1960

| This Week | 1 Wk Ago | 2 Wks Ago | 3 Wks Ago | Title / Artist, Company, Record No. | Wks on Chart |
|---|---|---|---|---|---|
| 1 ★ | 6 | 17 | 84 | STUCK ON YOU — Elvis Presley, RCA Victor 7740 | 4 |
| 2 | 2 | 5 | 12 | GREENFIELDS — Brothers Four, Columbia 41571 | 10 |
| 3 | 5 | 7 | 6 | SINK THE BISMARCK — Johnny Horton, Columbia 41568 | 8 |
| 4 | 1 | 1 | 1 | THEME FROM A SUMMER PLACE — Percy Faith, Columbia 41490 | 16 |
| 5 | 8 | 3 | 4 | HE'LL HAVE TO GO — Jim Reeves, RCA Victor 7643 | 18 |
| 6 | 9 | 11 | 16 | SIXTEEN REASONS — Connie Stevens, Warner Bros. 5137 | 13 |
| 7 | 3 | 2 | 2 | PUPPY LOVE — Paul Anka, ABC-Paramount 10082 | 10 |
| 8 ★ | 16 | 16 | 24 | THE OLD LAMPLIGHTER — The Browns, RCA Victor 7700 | 7 |
| 9 | 12 | 12 | 15 | WHITE SILVER SANDS — Bill Black's Combo, Hi 2021 | 8 |
| 10 | 4 | 6 | 5 | SWEET NOTHIN'S — Brenda Lee, Decca 30967 | 19 |
| 11 | 13 | 9 | 14 | I LOVE THE WAY YOU LOVE — Marv Johnson, United Artists 208 | 8 |
| 12 | 14 | 19 | 38 | CRADLE OF LOVE — Johnny Preston, Mercury 71598 | 5 |
| 13 | 19 | 28 | 53 | NIGHT — Jackie Wilson, Brunswick 55166 | 6 |
| 14 | 11 | 10 | 7 | FOOTSTEPS — Steve Lawrence, ABC-Paramount 10085 | 8 |
| 15 | 10 | 8 | 9 | MAMA — Connie Francis, M-G-M 12878 | 10 |
| 16 | 7 | 4 | 3 | WILD ONE — Bobby Rydell, Cameo 171 | 13 |
| 17 | 15 | 18 | 33 | STEP BY STEP — The Crests, Coed 525 | 9 |
| 18 | 18 | 26 | 28 | LET THE LITTLE GIRL DANCE — Billy Bland, Old Town 1076 | 11 |
| 19 | 27 | 42 | 75 | STAIRWAY TO HEAVEN — Neil Sedaka, RCA Victor 7709 | 5 |
| 20 ★ | 44 | 71 | — | FAME AND FORTUNE — Elvis Presley, RCA Victor 7740 | 3 |
| 21 | 21 | 30 | 34 | CLEMENTINE — Bobby Darin, Atco 6161 | 6 |
| 22 ★ | 33 | 79 | 95 | MR. LUCKY — Henry Mancini, RCA Victor 7705 | 4 |
| 23 | 22 | 23 | 27 | DON'T THROW AWAY ALL THOSE TEARDROPS — Frankie Avalon, Chancellor 1048 | 7 |
| 24 | 25 | 27 | 17 | TEDDY — Connie Francis, M-G-M 12878 | 9 |
| 25 | 23 | 24 | 31 | MONEY — Barrett Strong, Anna 1111 | 13 |
| 26 ★ | 46 | 49 | 81 | DOGGIN' AROUND — Jackie Wilson, Brunswick 55166 | 4 |
| 27 | 28 | 21 | 19 | BEATNIK FLY — Johnny and the Hurricanes, Warwick 520 | 11 |
| 28 | 31 | 46 | 58 | ANGELA JONES — Johnny Ferguson, M-G-M 12855 | 10 |
| 29 | 36 | 45 | 49 | APPLE GREEN — June Valli, Mercury 71588 | 8 |
| 30 | 26 | 39 | 42 | BIG IRON — Marty Robbins, Columbia 41589 | 7 |
| 31 | 29 | 35 | 36 | JUST ONE TIME — Don Gibson, RCA Victor 7690 | 8 |
| 32 | 30 | 25 | 25 | STARBRIGHT — Johnny Mathis, Columbia 41583 | 9 |
| 33 | 24 | 14 | 11 | O, DIO MIO — Annette, Vista 354 | 10 |
| 34 | 20 | 15 | 8 | HARBOR LIGHTS — The Platters, Mercury 71563 | 14 |
| 35 | 51 | 55 | 92 | CHERRY PIE — Skip and Flip, Brent 7010 | 4 |
| 36 | 47 | 63 | 86 | WHAT AM I LIVING FOR — Conway Twitty, M-G-M 12886 | 5 |
| 37 | 32 | 33 | 29 | LITTLE BITTY GIRL — Bobby Rydell, Cameo 171 | 13 |
| 38 | 17 | 13 | 10 | BABY — Brook Benton and Dinah Washington, Mercury 71565 | 14 |
| 39 | 41 | 52 | 85 | LOVE YOU SO — Rod Holden, Donna 1315 | 4 |
| 40 | 39 | 44 | 61 | MOUNTAIN OF LOVE — Harold Dorman, Rita 1003 | 9 |
| 41 | 61 | 53 | 82 | LONELY WEEKENDS — Charlie Rich, Philips International 3552 | 7 |
| 42 | 43 | 40 | 32 | AM I THAT EASY TO FORGET — Debbie Reynolds, Dot 15985 | 15 |
| 43 | 34 | 31 | 30 | SUMMER SET — Monty Kelly, Carlton 527 | 9 |
| 44 | 79 | 85 | 89 | MADISON — Al Brown's Tunetoppers, Amy 804 | 4 |
| 45 | 49 | 43 | 48 | FANNIE MAE — Buster Brown, Fire 1008 | 13 |
| 46 | 35 | 22 | 18 | (WELCOME) NEW LOVERS — Pat Boone, Dot 16048 | 9 |
| 47 | 52 | 73 | 64 | TEEN EX — Browns, RCA Victor 7700 | 5 |
| 48 ★ | 67 | — | — | GOOD TIMIN' — Jimmy Jones, Cub 9067 | 2 |
| 49 | 57 | 60 | 71 | YOU DON'T KNOW ME — Lennie Welch, Cadence 1373 | 9 |
| 50 | 48 | 50 | 51 | CARAVAN — Santo and Johnny, Canadian-American 111 | 7 |
| 51 | 40 | 37 | 37 | TALL OAK TREE — Dorsey Burnette, Era 3012 | 13 |
| 52 | 71 | 98 | — | JUST A CLOSER WALK WITH THEE — Jimmie Rodgers, Roulette 4234 | 3 |
| 53 | 60 | 78 | 78 | IT COULD HAPPEN TO YOU — Dinah Washington, Mercury 71560 | 5 |
| 54 | 54 | 57 | 62 | WAKE ME WHEN IT'S OVER — Andy Williams, Cadence 1378 | 6 |
| 55 | 87 | 99 | — | MADISON TIME — Ray Bryant, Columbia 41628 | 3 |
| 56 | 56 | 58 | 79 | SOMEDAY — Della Reese, RCA Victor 7706 | 6 |
| 57 | 89 | 94 | — | PAPER ROSES — Anita Bryant, Carlton 528 | 3 |
| 58 | 58 | 66 | 66 | RUBY — Adam Wade, Coed 526 | 7 |
| 59 | 37 | 20 | 13 | HANDY MAN — Jimmy Jones, Cub 9049 | 18 |
| 60 | 66 | 75 | 60 | DOWN BY THE RIVERSIDE — Les Compagnons de la Chanson, Capitol 4342 | 8 |
| 61 | 45 | 54 | 63 | SHAZAM — Duane Eddy, Jamie 1151 | 6 |
| 62 | 42 | 36 | 23 | FOREVER — Little Dippers, University 210 | 14 |
| 63 | 65 | 74 | — | EARTH ANGEL — Johnny Tillotson, Cadence 1377 | 3 |
| 64 | 55 | 72 | 74 | OOH POO PAH DOO (Part 2) — Jessie Hill, Minit 607 | 5 |
| 65 | 68 | 62 | 65 | DON'T DECEIVE ME — Ruth Brown, Atlantic 2052 | 7 |
| 66 ★ | 81 | 88 | — | TIES THAT BIND — Brook Benton, Mercury 71566 | 3 |
| 67 | 50 | 38 | 39 | EL MATADOR — Kingston Trio, Capitol 4338 | 10 |
| 68 | 38 | 29 | 21 | THIS MAGIC MOMENT — Drifters, Atlantic 2050 | 10 |
| 69 | 73 | 84 | 90 | THINK ME A KISS — Clyde McPhatter, M-G-M 12877 | 4 |
| 70 | 76 | — | — | WAY OF A CLOWN — Teddy Randazzo, ABC-Paramount 10088 | 2 |
| 71 | 82 | — | — | NOBODY LOVES ME LIKE YOU — Flamingos, End 1068 | 2 |
| 72 | 69 | 32 | 20 | LADY LUCK — Lloyd Price, ABC-Paramount 10075 | 13 |
| 73 | 72 | 56 | 59 | CHINA DOLL — Ames Brothers, RCA Victor 7655 | 13 |
| 74 ★ | 94 | — | — | CATHY'S CLOWN — Everly Brothers, Warner Bros. 5151 | 2 |
| 75 | 85 | 86 | — | PLEDGING MY LOVE — Johnny Tillotson, Cadence 1377 | 3 |
| 76 | 53 | 34 | 22 | WHAT IN THE WORLD'S COME OVER YOU — Jack Scott, Top Rank 2028 | 16 |
| 77 | 62 | 47 | 46 | PARADISE — Sammy Turner, Big Top 3032 | 11 |
| 78 | 92 | — | — | HITHER, THITHER AND YON — Brook Benton, Mercury 71566 | 2 |
| 79 | 59 | 59 | 56 | AT MY FRONT DOOR — Dee Clark, Abner 1037 | 7 |
| 80 | 80 | 76 | 50 | TEENAGE SONATA — Sam Cooke, RCA Victor 7701 | 7 |
| 81 | 88 | 91 | — | JENNY LOU — Sonny James, NRC 50 | 3 |
| 82 | 64 | 80 | 83 | ROCKIN' RED WING — Sammy Masters, Lode 108 | 4 |
| 83 | 95 | — | — | BARBARA — Temptations, Goldisc 3001 | 2 |
| 84 | 100 | — | — | GOT A GIRL — Four Preps, Capitol 4362 | 2 |
| 85 | — | — | — | WHEN YOU WISH UPON A STAR — Dion & the Belmonts, Laurie 3052 | 1 |
| 86 | 90 | — | — | MY EMPTY ROOM — Little Anthony & the Imperials, End 1067 | 2 |
| 87 | 98 | — | — | A STAR IS BORN (A LOVE HAS DIED) — Mark Dinning, M-G-M 12888 | 2 |
| 88 | 97 | — | — | BURNING BRIDGES — Jack Scott, Top Rank 2041 | 2 |
| 89 | — | — | — | TELL ME THAT YOU LOVE ME — Fats Domino, Imperial 5660 | 1 |
| 90 | 74 | 87 | 80 | BABY, WHAT DO YOU WANT ME TO DO — Jimmy Reed, Vee Jay 333 | 11 |
| 91 | 99 | — | — | SOMEONE LOVES YOU, JOE — The Singing Belles, Madison 126 | 2 |
| 92 | — | — | — | EASY LOVIN' — Wade Flemons, Vee Jay 344 | 1 |
| 93 | — | — | — | NO IF'S—NO AND'S — Lloyd Price, ABC-Paramount 10102 | 1 |
| 94 | — | — | — | LAST CHANCE — Collay and His Satellites, Sho-Biz 1002 | 1 |
| 95 | — | — | — | ANOTHER SLEEPLESS NIGHT — Jimmy Clanton, Ace 585 | 1 |
| 96 | — | — | — | (DOIN' THE) LOVER'S LEAP — Webb Pierce, Decca 31058 | 1 |
| 97 | — | — | — | TWO THOUSAND, TWO HUNDRED AND TWENTY-THREE MILES — Patti Page, Mercury 71597 | 1 |
| 98 | — | — | — | YOUNG EMOTIONS — Ricky Nelson, Imperial 5663 | 1 |
| 99 | — | — | — | BEAUTIFUL OBSESSION — Sir Chauncey, Warner Bros. 5150 | 1 |
| 100 | — | — | — | DUTCHMAN'S GOLD — Walter Brennan, Dot 16066 | 1 |

# The Billboard HOT 100

**FOR WEEK ENDING MAY 8**

*The Billboard's Music Popularity Charts... POP RECORDS — MAY 2, 1960*

STAR PERFORMERS showed the greatest upward progress on Hot 100 this week.
(S) Indicates that 45 r.p.m. stereo single version is available.
(A) Indicates that 33⅓ r.p.m. stereo single version is available.

| This Week | 1 Wk Ago | 2 Wks Ago | 3 Wks Ago | Title — Artist, Company, Record No. | Stereo | Weeks on Chart |
|---|---|---|---|---|---|---|
| 1 | 1 | 6 | 17 | STUCK ON YOU — Elvis Presley, RCA Victor 7740 | S | 5 |
| 2 | 2 | 2 | 5 | GREENFIELDS — Brothers Four, Columbia 41571 | A | 11 |
| 3 | 6 | 9 | 11 | SIXTEEN REASONS — Connie Stevens, Warner Bros. 5137 | | 14 |
| 4 | 3 | 5 | 7 | SINK THE BISMARCK — Johnny Horton, Columbia 41568 | | 9 |
| 5 | 8 | 16 | 16 | THE OLD LAMPLIGHTER — The Browns, RCA Victor 7700 | | 8 |
| 6 | 13 | 9 | 28 | NIGHT — Jackie Wilson, Brunswick 55166 | | 7 |
| 7 | 12 | 14 | 19 | CRADLE OF LOVE — Johnny Preston, Mercury 71598 | | 6 |
| 8 | 18 | 18 | 26 | LET THE LITTLE GIRL DANCE — Billy Bland, Old Town 1076 | | 12 |
| 9 | 4 | 1 | 1 | THEME FROM A SUMMER PLACE — Percy Faith, Columbia 41490 | A | 17 |
| 10 | 10 | 4 | 6 | SWEET NOTHIN'S — Brenda Lee, Decca 30967 | | 20 |
| 11 | 19 | 27 | 42 | STAIRWAY TO HEAVEN — Neil Sedaka, RCA Victor 7709 | S | 6 |
| 12 | 5 | 8 | 3 | HE'LL HAVE TO GO — Jim Reeves, RCA Victor 7643 | S | 19 |
| 13 | 11 | 13 | 9 | I LOVE THE WAY YOU LOVE — Marv Johnson, United Artists 208 | | 9 |
| 14 | 9 | 12 | 12 | WHITE SILVER SANDS — Bill Black's Combo, Hi 2021 | | 9 |
| 15 | 74 | 94 | — | CATHY'S CLOWN — Everly Brothers, Warner Bros. 5151 | S | 3 |
| 16 | 7 | 3 | 2 | PUPPY LOVE — Paul Anka, ABC-Paramount 10082 | S | 11 |
| 17 | 17 | 15 | 18 | STEP BY STEP — The Crests, Coed 525 | | 10 |
| 18 | 14 | 11 | 10 | FOOTSTEPS — Steve Lawrence, ABC-Paramount 10085 | | 9 |
| 19 | 35 | 51 | 55 | CHERRY PIE — Skip and Flip, Brent 7010 | | 5 |
| 20 | 20 | 44 | 71 | FAME AND FORTUNE — Elvis Presley, RCA Victor 7740 | S | 4 |
| 21 | 22 | 33 | 79 | MR. LUCKY — Henry Mancini, RCA Victor 7705 | S | 5 |
| 22 | 15 | 10 | 8 | MAMA — Connie Francis, M-G-M 12878 | S | 11 |
| 23 | 16 | 7 | 4 | WILD ONE — Bobby Rydell, Cameo 171 | | 14 |
| 24 | 21 | 21 | 30 | CLEMENTINE — Bobby Darin, Atco 6161 | | 7 |
| 25 | 41 | 61 | 53 | LONELY WEEKENDS — Charlie Rich, Phillips International 3552 | | 8 |
| 26 | 36 | 47 | 63 | WHAT AM I LIVING FOR — Conway Twitty, M-G-M 12886 | | 6 |
| 27 | 28 | 31 | 46 | ANGELA JONES — Johnny Ferguson, M-G-M 12855 | | 11 |
| 28 | 25 | 23 | 24 | MONEY — Barrett Strong, Anna 1111 | | 14 |
| 29 | 23 | 22 | 23 | DON'T THROW AWAY ALL THOSE TEARDROPS — Frankie Avalon, Chancellor 1048 | | 8 |
| 30 | 44 | 79 | 85 | MADISON — Al Brown's Tunetoppers, Amy 804 | | 5 |
| 31 | 29 | 36 | 45 | APPLE GREEN — June Valli, Mercury 71588 | | 9 |
| 32 | 30 | 26 | 39 | BIG IRON — Marty Robbins, Columbia 41589 | A | 8 |
| 33 | 39 | 41 | 52 | LOVE YOU SO — Rod Holden, Donna 1315 | | 5 |
| 34 | 57 | 89 | 94 | PAPER ROSES — Anita Bryant, Carlton 528 | S | 4 |
| 35 | 26 | 46 | 49 | DOGGIN' AROUND — Jackie Wilson, Brunswick 55166 | | 5 |
| 36 | 40 | 39 | 44 | MOUNTAIN OF LOVE — Harold Dorman, Rita 1003 | | 10 |
| 37 | — | — | — | HE'LL HAVE TO STAY — Jeanne Black, Capitol 4368 | | 1 |
| 38 | 45 | 49 | 43 | FANNIE MAE — Buster Brown, Fire 1008 | | 14 |
| 39 | 31 | 29 | 35 | JUST ONE TIME — Don Gibson, RCA Victor 7690 | S | 9 |
| 40 | 24 | 25 | 27 | TEDDY — Connie Francis, M-G-M 12878 | S | 10 |
| 41 | 64 | 55 | 72 | OOH POO PAH DOO (Part 2) — Jessie Hill, Minit 607 | | 6 |
| 42 | 48 | 67 | — | GOOD TIMIN' — Jimmy Jones, Cub 9067 | | 3 |
| 43 | 42 | 43 | 40 | AM I THAT EASY TO FORGET — Debbie Reynolds, Dot 15985 | | 16 |
| 44 | 52 | 71 | 98 | JUST A CLOSER WALK WITH THEE — Jimmie Rodgers, Roulette 4234 | | 4 |
| 45 | 66 | 81 | 88 | TIES THAT BIND — Brook Benton, Mercury 71566 | S | 4 |
| 46 | 33 | 24 | 14 | O, DIO MIO — Annette, Vista 354 | | 11 |
| 47 | 43 | 34 | 31 | SUMMER SET — Monty Kelly, Carlton 527 | S | 10 |
| 48 | 49 | 57 | 60 | YOU DON'T KNOW ME — Lennie Welch, Cadence 1373 | | 10 |
| 49 | 32 | 30 | 25 | STARBRIGHT — Johnny Mathis, Columbia 41583 | A | 10 |
| 50 | 54 | 54 | 57 | WAKE ME WHEN IT'S OVER — Andy Williams, Cadence 1378 | | 7 |
| 51 | 83 | 95 | — | BARBARA — Temptations, Goldisc 3001 | | 3 |
| 52 | 46 | 35 | 22 | (WELCOME) NEW LOVERS — Pat Boone, Dot 16048 | S | 10 |
| 53 | 55 | 87 | 99 | MADISON TIME — Ray Bryant, Columbia 41628 | | 4 |
| 54 | 37 | 32 | 33 | LITTLE BITTY GIRL — Bobby Rydell, Cameo 171 | | 14 |
| 55 | — | — | — | FOR LOVE — Lloyd Price, ABC-Paramount 10102 | | 1 |
| 56 | 27 | 28 | 21 | BEATNIK FLY — Johnny and the Hurricanes, Warwick 520 | | 12 |
| 57 | 98 | — | — | YOUNG EMOTIONS — Ricky Nelson, Imperial 5663 | | 2 |
| 58 | 34 | 20 | 15 | HARBOR LIGHTS — The Platters, Mercury 71563 | S | 15 |
| 59 | 88 | 97 | — | BURNING BRIDGES — Jack Scott, Top Rank 2041 | | 3 |
| 60 | 47 | 52 | 73 | TEEN EX — Browns, RCA Victor 7700 | | 6 |
| 61 | 63 | 65 | 74 | EARTH ANGEL — Johnny Tillotson, Cadence 1377 | | 4 |
| 62 | 71 | 82 | — | NOBODY LOVES ME LIKE YOU — Flamingos, End 1068 | | 3 |
| 63 | 78 | 92 | — | HITHER, THITHER AND YON — Brook Benton, Mercury 71566 | S | 3 |
| 64 | — | 95 | — | ANOTHER SLEEPLESS NIGHT — Jimmy Clanton, Ace 585 | | 2 |
| 65 | 38 | 17 | 13 | BABY — Brook Benton and Dinah Washington, Mercury 71565 | S | 15 |
| 66 | 69 | 73 | 84 | THINK ME A KISS — Clyde McPhatter, M-G-M 12877 | | 5 |
| 67 | 97 | — | — | TWO THOUSAND, TWO HUNDRED AND TWENTY-THREE MILES — Patti Page, Mercury 71597 | | 2 |
| 68 | 87 | 98 | — | A STAR IS BORN (A LOVE HAS DIED) — Mark Dinning, M-G-M 12888 | | 3 |
| 69 | 53 | 60 | 78 | IT COULD HAPPEN TO YOU — Dinah Washington, Mercury 71560 | S | 6 |
| 70 | 51 | 40 | 37 | TALL OAK TREE — Dorsey Burnette, Era 3012 | | 14 |
| 71 | 85 | — | — | WHEN YOU WISH UPON A STAR — Dion and the Belmonts, Laurie 3052 | | 2 |
| 72 | 100 | — | — | DUTCHMAN'S GOLD — Walter Brennan, Dot 16066 | | 2 |
| 73 | 81 | 88 | 91 | JENNY LOU — Sonny James, NRC 050 | | 4 |
| 74 | — | — | — | THEME FROM THE UNFORGIVEN — Don Costa, United Artists 221 | | 1 |
| 75 | — | — | — | IS IT WRONG (FOR LOVING YOU) — Webb Pierce, Decca 31058 | | 1 |
| 76 | 75 | 85 | 86 | PLEDGING MY LOVE — Johnny Tillotson, Cadence 1377 | | 4 |
| 77 | 84 | 100 | — | GOT A GIRL — Four Preps, Capitol 4362 | | 3 |
| 78 | 67 | 50 | 38 | EL MATADOR — Kingston Trio, Capitol 4338 | | 11 |
| 79 | 58 | 58 | 66 | RUBY — Adam Wade, Coed 526 | | 8 |
| 80 | — | — | — | ALL I COULD DO WAS CRY — Etta James, Argo 5359 | | 1 |
| 81 | 56 | 56 | 58 | SOMEDAY — Della Reese, RCA Victor 7706 | S | 7 |
| 82 | 90 | 74 | 87 | BABY, WHAT DO YOU WANT ME TO DO — Jimmy Reed, Vee Jay 333 | | 12 |
| 83 | — | — | — | RIGHT BY MY SIDE — Ricky Nelson, Imperial 5663 | | 1 |
| 84 | 68 | 38 | 29 | THIS MAGIC MOMENT — Drifters, Atlantic 2050 | | 11 |
| 85 | 50 | 48 | 50 | CARAVAN — Santo & Johnny, Canadian-American 111 | | 8 |
| 86 | — | — | — | OH, LITTLE ONE — Jack Scott, Top Rank 2041 | | 1 |
| 87 | 93 | — | — | NO IF'S—NO AND'S — Lloyd Price, ABC-Paramount 10102 | | 2 |
| 88 | 70 | 76 | — | WAY OF A CLOWN — Teddy Randazzo, ABC-Paramount 10088 | | 3 |
| 89 | — | — | — | BESAME MUCHO — Coasters, Atco 6163 | | 1 |
| 90 | 65 | 68 | 62 | DON'T DECEIVE ME — Ruth Brown, Atlantic 2052 | | 8 |
| 91 | 92 | — | — | EASY LOVIN' — Wade Flemons, Vee Jay 344 | | 2 |
| 92 | 82 | 64 | 80 | ROCKIN' RED WING — Sammy Masters, Lode 108 | | 5 |
| 93 | 96 | — | — | (DOIN' THE) LOVER'S LEAP — Webb Pierce, Decca 31058 | | 2 |
| 94 | — | — | — | MACK THE KNIFE — Ella Fitzgerald, Verve 10209 | S | 1 |
| 95 | — | — | — | CITY LIGHTS — Debbie Reynolds, Dot 16071 | | 1 |
| 96 | 89 | — | — | TELL ME THAT YOU LOVE ME — Fats Domino, Imperial 5660 | | 2 |
| 97 | — | — | — | THINK — James Brown & Famous Flames, Federal 12370 | | 1 |
| 98 | 61 | 45 | 54 | SHAZAM — Duane Eddy, Jamie 1151 | | 7 |
| 99 | — | — | — | HAPPY GO LUCKY ME — Paul Evans, Guaranteed 208 | S | 1 |
| 100 | — | — | — | WHEEL OF FORTUNE — LaVern Baker, Atlantic 2059 | | 1 |

# The Billboard HOT 100

**FOR WEEK ENDING MAY 15**

★ STAR PERFORMERS showed the greatest upward progress on Hot 100 this week.
Ⓢ Indicates that 45 r.p.m. stereo single version is available.
Ⓐ Indicates that 33⅓ r.p.m. stereo single version is available.

| This Week | One Week Ago | Two Weeks Ago | Three Weeks Ago | Title — Artist, Company, Record No. | Stereo | Weeks on Chart |
|---|---|---|---|---|---|---|
| 1 | 1 | 1 | 6 | STUCK ON YOU — Elvis Presley, RCA Victor 7740 | Ⓢ | 6 |
| 2 | 2 | 2 | 2 | GREENFIELDS — Brothers Four, Columbia 41571 | Ⓐ | 12 |
| ★3 | 15 | 74 | 94 | CATHY'S CLOWN — Everly Brothers, Warner Bros. 5151 | | 4 |
| 4 | 6 | 13 | 9 | NIGHT — Jackie Wilson, Brunswick 55166 | | 8 |
| 5 | 3 | 6 | 9 | SIXTEEN REASONS — Connie Stevens, Warner Bros. 5137 | | 15 |
| 6 | 4 | 3 | 5 | SINK THE BISMARCK — Johnny Horton, Columbia 41568 | Ⓐ | 10 |
| 7 | 5 | 8 | 16 | THE OLD LAMPLIGHTER — The Browns, RCA Victor 7700 | Ⓢ | 9 |
| 8 | 7 | 12 | 14 | CRADLE OF LOVE — Johnny Preston, Mercury 71598 | | 7 |
| 9 | 11 | 19 | 27 | STAIRWAY TO HEAVEN — Neil Sedaka, RCA Victor 7709 | Ⓢ | 7 |
| 10 | 8 | 18 | 18 | LET THE LITTLE GIRL DANCE — Billy Bland, Old Town 1076 | | 13 |
| 11 | 14 | 9 | 12 | WHITE SILVER SANDS — Bill Black's Combo, Hi 2021 | | 10 |
| 12 | 13 | 11 | 13 | I LOVE THE WAY YOU LOVE — Marv Johnson, United Artists 208 | | 10 |
| ★13 | 42 | 48 | 67 | GOOD TIMIN' — Jimmie Jones, Cub 9067 | | 4 |
| 14 | 17 | 17 | 15 | STEP BY STEP — The Crests, Coed 525 | | 11 |
| ★15 | 35 | 26 | 46 | DOGGIN' AROUND — Jackie Wilson, Brunswick 55166 | | 6 |
| 16 | 10 | 10 | 4 | SWEET NOTHIN'S — Brenda Lee, Decca 30967 | | 21 |
| 17 | 20 | 20 | 44 | FAME AND FORTUNE — Elvis Presley, RCA Victor 7740 | Ⓢ | 5 |
| 18 | 9 | 4 | 1 | THEME FROM A SUMMER PLACE — Percy Faith, Columbia 41490 | Ⓐ | 18 |
| 19 | 18 | 14 | 11 | FOOTSTEPS — Steve Lawrence, ABC-Paramount 10085 | | 10 |
| 20 | 12 | 5 | 8 | HE'LL HAVE TO GO — Jim Reeves, RCA Victor 7643 | Ⓢ | 20 |
| ★21 | 37 | — | — | HE'LL HAVE TO STAY — Jeanne Black, Capitol 4368 | | 2 |
| 22 | 19 | 35 | 51 | CHERRY PIE — Skip and Flip, Brent 7010 | | 6 |
| ★23 | 34 | 57 | 89 | PAPER ROSES — Anita Bryant, Carlton 528 | Ⓢ | 5 |
| 24 | 16 | 7 | 3 | PUPPY LOVE — Paul Anka, ABC-Paramount 10082 | Ⓢ | 12 |
| 25 | 25 | 41 | 61 | LONELY WEEKENDS — Charlie Rich, Philips International 3552 | | 9 |
| ★26 | 36 | 40 | 39 | MOUNTAIN OF LOVE — Harold Dorman, Rita 1003 | | 11 |
| 27 | 33 | 39 | 41 | LOVE YOU SO — Rod Holden, Donna 1315 | | 6 |
| 28 | 21 | 22 | 33 | MR. LUCKY — Henry Mancini, RCA Victor 7705 | Ⓢ | 6 |
| 29 | 26 | 36 | 47 | WHAT AM I LIVING FOR — Conway Twitty, M-G-M 12886 | | 7 |
| ★30 | 59 | 88 | 97 | BURNING BRIDGES — Jack Scott, Top Rank 2041 | | 4 |
| ★31 | 51 | 83 | 95 | BARBARA — Temptations, Goldise 3001 | | 4 |
| 32 | 30 | 44 | 79 | MADISON — Al Brown's Tunetoppers, Amy 804 | | 6 |
| ★33 | 57 | 98 | — | YOUNG EMOTIONS — Ricky Nelson, Imperial 5663 | | 3 |
| 34 | 41 | 64 | 55 | OOH POO PAH DOO (Part 2) — Jessie Hill, Minit 607 | | 7 |
| 35 | 22 | 15 | 10 | MAMA — Connie Francis, M-G-M 12878 | Ⓢ | 12 |
| 36 | 28 | 25 | 23 | MONEY — Barrett Strong, Anna 1111 | | 15 |
| 37 | 45 | 66 | 81 | TIES THAT BIND — Brook Benton, Mercury 71566 | Ⓢ | 5 |
| ★38 | 53 | 55 | 87 | MADISON TIME — Ray Bryant, Columbia 41628 | | 5 |
| 39 | 24 | 21 | 21 | CLEMENTINE — Bobby Darin, Atco 6161 | | 8 |
| 40 | 38 | 45 | 49 | FANNIE MAE — Buster Brown, Fire 1008 | | 15 |
| 41 | 27 | 28 | 31 | ANGELA JONES — Johnny Ferguson, M-G-M 12885 | | 12 |
| 42 | 29 | 23 | 22 | DON'T THROW AWAY ALL THOSE TEARDROPS — Frankie Avalon, Chancellor 1048 | | 9 |
| 43 | 32 | 30 | 26 | BIG IRON — Marty Robbins, Columbia 41589 | Ⓐ | 9 |
| 44 | 31 | 29 | 36 | APPLE GREEN — June Valli, Mercury 71588 | | 10 |
| 45 | 48 | 49 | 57 | YOU DON'T KNOW ME — Lennie Welch, Cadence 1373 | | 11 |
| 46 | 39 | 31 | 29 | JUST ONE TIME — Don Gibson, RCA Victor 7690 | Ⓢ | 10 |
| 47 | 23 | 16 | 7 | WILD ONE — Bobby Rydell, Cameo 171 | | 15 |
| ★48 | 77 | 84 | 100 | GOT A GIRL — Four Preps, Capitol 4362 | | 4 |
| 49 | 62 | 71 | 82 | NOBODY LOVES ME LIKE YOU — Flamingos, End 1068 | | 4 |
| 50 | 47 | 43 | 34 | SUMMER SET — Monty Kelly, Carlton 527 | Ⓢ | 11 |
| 51 | 55 | — | — | FOR LOVE — Lloyd Price, ABC-Paramount 10102 | | 2 |
| ★52 | — | — | — | EVERYBODY'S SOMEBODY'S FOOL — Connie Francis, M-G-M 12899 | | 1 |
| 53 | 52 | 46 | 35 | (WELCOME) NEW LOVERS — Pat Boone, Dot 16048 | Ⓢ | 11 |
| ★54 | — | — | — | DING-A-LING — Bobby Rydell, Cameo 175 | | 1 |
| 55 | 64 | 95 | — | ANOTHER SLEEPLESS NIGHT — Jimmy Clanton, Ace 585 | | 3 |
| 56 | 71 | 85 | — | WHEN YOU WISH UPON A STAR — Dion and the Belmonts, Laurie 3052 | | 3 |
| 57 | 40 | 24 | 25 | TEDDY — Connie Francis, M-G-M 12878 | Ⓢ | 11 |
| 58 | 61 | 63 | 65 | EARTH ANGEL — Johnny Tillotson, Cadence 1377 | | 5 |
| 59 | 96 | 89 | — | TELL ME THAT YOU LOVE ME — Fats Domino, Imperial 5660 | | 3 |
| 60 | 63 | 78 | 92 | HITHER, THITHER AND YON — Brook Benton, Mercury 71566 | Ⓢ | 4 |
| 61 | 97 | — | — | THINK — James Brown and Famous Flames, Federal 12370 | | 2 |
| 62 | 44 | 52 | 71 | JUST A CLOSER WALK WITH THEE — Jimmie Rodgers, Roulette 4234 | | 5 |
| 63 | 88 | 70 | 76 | WAY OF A CLOWN — Teddy Randazzo, ABC-Paramount 10088 | | 4 |
| 64 | 76 | 75 | 85 | PLEDGING MY LOVE — Johnny Tillotson, Cadence 1377 | | 5 |
| ★65 | 94 | — | — | MACK THE KNIFE — Ella Fitzgerald, Verve 10209 | Ⓢ | 2 |
| 66 | 46 | 33 | 24 | O, DIO MIO — Annette, Vista 354 | | 12 |
| 67 | 73 | 81 | 88 | JENNY LOU — Sonny James, NRC 050 | | 5 |
| 68 | 72 | 100 | — | DUTCHMAN'S GOLD — Walter Brennan, Dot 16066 | | 3 |
| 69 | 75 | — | — | IS IT WRONG (FOR LOVING YOU) — Webb Pierce, Decca 31058 | | 2 |
| 70 | 91 | 92 | — | EASY LOVIN' — Wade Flemons, Vee Jay 344 | | 3 |
| ★71 | — | — | — | SWINGING SCHOOL — Bobby Rydell, Cameo 175 | | 1 |
| 72 | 82 | 90 | 74 | BABY, WHAT DO YOU WANT ME TO DO — Jimmy Reed, Vee Jay 333 | | 13 |
| 73 | 60 | 47 | 52 | TEEN EX — Browns, RCA Victor 7700 | | 7 |
| 74 | 43 | 42 | 43 | AM I THAT EASY TO FORGET — Debbie Reynolds, Dot 15985 | | 17 |
| 75 | 68 | 87 | 98 | A STAR IS BORN (A LOVE HAS DIED) — Mark Dinning, M-G-M 12888 | | 4 |
| 76 | 89 | — | — | BESAME MUCHO — Coasters, Atco 6163 | | 2 |
| 77 | 56 | 27 | 28 | BEATNIK FLY — Johnny and the Hurricanes, Warwick 520 | | 13 |
| 78 | 86 | — | — | OH, LITTLE ONE — Jack Scott, Top Rank 2041 | | 2 |
| 79 | 87 | 93 | — | NO IF'S—NO AND'S — Lloyd Price, ABC-Paramount 10102 | | 3 |
| 80 | 80 | — | — | ALL I COULD DO WAS CRY — Etta James, Argo 5359 | | 2 |
| 81 | 74 | — | — | THEME FROM THE UNFORGIVEN — Don Costa, United Artists 221 | | 2 |
| ★82 | — | — | — | PINK CHIFFON — Mitchell Torok, Guyden 2034 | | 1 |
| 83 | 54 | 37 | 32 | LITTLE BITTY GIRL — Bobby Rydell, Cameo 171 | | 15 |
| 84 | 70 | 51 | 40 | TALL OAK TREE — Dorsey Burnette, Era 3012 | | 15 |
| ★85 | — | — | — | THEME FOR YOUNG LOVERS — Percy Faith, Columbia 41655 | | 1 |
| ★86 | — | — | — | JUMP OVER — Freddy Cannon, Swan 4053 | | 1 |
| 87 | 100 | — | — | WHEEL OF FORTUNE — LaVern Baker, Atlantic 2059 | | 2 |
| 88 | 49 | 32 | 30 | STARBRIGHT — Johnny Mathis, Columbia 41583 | Ⓐ | 11 |
| 89 | 58 | 34 | 20 | HARBOR LIGHTS — The Platters, Mercury 71563 | Ⓢ | 16 |
| 90 | 99 | — | — | HAPPY-GO-LUCKY ME — Paul Evans, Guaranteed 208 | Ⓢ | 2 |
| ★91 | — | — | — | PUT YOUR ARMS AROUND ME, HONEY — Ray Smith, Judd 1017 | | 1 |
| 92 | — | 99 | — | BEAUTIFUL OBSESSION — Sir Chauncey, Warner Bros. 5150 | | 2 |
| 93 | — | — | — | BEFORE I GROW TOO OLD — Fats Domino, Imperial 5660 | | 1 |
| 94 | — | — | — | HOT ROD LINCOLN — Charlie Ryan, Four Star 1733 | | 1 |
| 95 | — | — | — | COTTAGE FOR SALE — Little Willie John, King 5342 | | 1 |
| 96 | 50 | 54 | 54 | WAKE ME WHEN IT'S OVER — Andy Williams, Cadence 1378 | | 8 |
| 97 | — | — | — | WONDERFUL WORLD — Sam Cooke, Keen 82112 | | 1 |
| 98 | 66 | 69 | 73 | THINK ME A KISS — Clyde McPhatter, M-G-M 12877 | | 6 |
| 99 | — | — | — | I'LL BE SEEING YOU — Five Satins, Ember 1061 | | 1 |
| 100 | — | — | — | PENNIES FROM HEAVEN — Skyliners, Calico 117 | | 1 |

# The Billboard HOT 100

**FOR WEEK ENDING MAY 22**

Columns: THIS WEEK | ONE WEEK AGO | TWO WEEKS AGO | THREE WEEKS AGO | TITLE — Artist, Company, Record No. | STEREO | WEEKS ON CHART

STAR PERFORMERS showed the greatest upward progress on Hot 100 this week.
S — Indicates that 45 r.p.m. stereo single version is available.
A — Indicates that 33⅓ r.p.m. stereo single version is available.

| # | 1wk | 2wk | 3wk | Title — Artist, Company, Record No. | Stereo | Wks |
|---|---|---|---|---|---|---|
| 1 | 1 | 1 | 1 | STUCK ON YOU — Elvis Presley, RCA Victor 7740 | S | 7 |
| 2 | 3 | 15 | 74 | CATHY'S CLOWN — Everly Brothers, Warner Bros. 5151 | S | 5 |
| 3 | 2 | 2 | 2 | GREENFIELDS — Brothers Four, Columbia 41571 | A | 13 |
| 4 | 4 | 6 | 13 | NIGHT — Jackie Wilson, Brunswick 55166 | | 9 |
| ★5 | 13 | 42 | 48 | GOOD TIMIN' — Jimmie Jones, Cub 9076 | | 5 |
| 6 | 5 | 3 | 6 | SIXTEEN REASONS — Connie Stevens, Warner Bros. 5137 | | 16 |
| 7 | 10 | 8 | 18 | LET THE LITTLE GIRL DANCE — Billy Bland, Old Town 1076 | | 14 |
| 8 | 8 | 7 | 12 | CRADLE OF LOVE — Johnny Preston, Mercury 71598 | | 8 |
| 9 | 6 | 4 | 3 | SINK THE BISMARCK — Johnny Horton, Columbia 41568 | A | 11 |
| ★10 | 21 | 37 | — | HE'LL HAVE TO STAY — Jeanne Black, Capitol 4368 | | 3 |
| 11 | 7 | 5 | 8 | THE OLD LAMPLIGHTER — The Browns, RCA Victor 7700 | S | 10 |
| 12 | 23 | 34 | 57 | PAPER ROSES — Anita Bryant, Carlton 528 | S | 6 |
| 13 | 9 | 11 | 19 | STAIRWAY TO HEAVEN — Neil Sedaka, RCA Victor 7709 | S | 8 |
| 14 | 11 | 14 | 9 | WHITE SILVER SANDS — Bill Black's Combo, Hi 2021 | | 11 |
| 15 | 22 | 19 | 35 | CHERRY PIE — Skip and Flip, Brent 7010 | | 7 |
| 16 | 27 | 33 | 39 | LOVE YOU SO — Rod Holden, Donna 1315 | | 7 |
| 17 | 30 | 59 | 88 | BURNING BRIDGES — Jack Scott, Top Rank 2041 | | 5 |
| 18 | 14 | 17 | 17 | STEP BY STEP — The Crests, Coed 525 | | 12 |
| 19 | 12 | 13 | 11 | I LOVE THE WAY YOU LOVE — Marv Johnson, United Artists 208 | | 11 |
| 20 | 17 | 20 | 20 | FAME AND FORTUNE — Elvis Presley, RCA Victor 7740 | S | 6 |
| 21 | 16 | 10 | 10 | SWEET NOTHIN'S — Brenda Lee, Decca 30967 | | 22 |
| ★22 | 33 | 57 | 98 | YOUNG EMOTIONS — Ricky Nelson, Imperial 5663 | | 4 |
| 23 | 32 | 30 | 44 | MADISON — Al Brown's Tunetoppers, Amy 804 | | 7 |
| 24 | 28 | 21 | 22 | MR. LUCKY — Henry Mancini, RCA Victor 7705 | S | 7 |
| 25 | 25 | 25 | 41 | LONELY WEEKENDS — Charlie Rich, Philips International 3552 | | 10 |
| 26 | 26 | 36 | 40 | MOUNTAIN OF LOVE — Harold Dorman, Rita 1003 | | 12 |
| 27 | 19 | 18 | 14 | FOOTSTEPS — Steve Lawrence, ABC-Paramount 10085 | | 11 |
| 28 | 15 | 35 | 26 | DOGGIN' AROUND — Jackie Wilson, Brunswick 55166 | | 7 |
| 29 | 31 | 51 | 83 | BARBARA — Temptations, Goldisc 3001 | | 5 |
| 30 | 38 | 53 | 55 | MADISON TIME — Ray Bryant, Columbia 41628 | | 6 |
| ★31 | 56 | 71 | 85 | WHEN YOU WISH UPON A STAR — Dion and the Belmonts, Laurie 3052 | | 4 |
| ★32 | 48 | 77 | 84 | GOT A GIRL — Four Preps, Capitol 4362 | | 5 |
| 33 | 34 | 41 | 64 | OOH POO PAH DOO (Part 2) — Jessie Hill, Minit 607 | | 8 |
| 34 | 20 | 12 | 5 | HE'LL HAVE TO GO — Jim Reeves, RCA Victor 7643 | S | 21 |
| 35 | 18 | 9 | 4 | THEME FROM A SUMMER PLACE — Percy Faith, Columbia 41490 | A | 19 |
| 36 | 44 | 31 | 29 | APPLE GREEN — June Valli, Mercury 71588 | | 11 |
| ★37 | 54 | — | — | DING-A-LING — Bobby Rydell, Cameo 175 | | 2 |
| 38 | 29 | 26 | 36 | WHAT AM I LIVING FOR — Conway Twitty, M-G-M 12886 | | 8 |
| ★39 | 52 | — | — | EVERYBODY'S SOMEBODY'S FOOL — Connie Francis, M-G-M 12899 | | 2 |
| 40 | 24 | 16 | 7 | PUPPY LOVE — Paul Anka, ABC-Paramount 10082 | S | 13 |
| ★41 | 71 | — | — | SWINGING SCHOOL — Bobby Rydell, Cameo 175 | | 2 |
| 42 | 36 | 28 | 25 | MONEY — Barrett Strong, Anna 1111 | | 16 |
| 43 | 51 | 55 | — | FOR LOVE — Lloyd Price, ABC-Paramount 10102 | | 3 |
| 44 | 35 | 22 | 15 | MAMA — Connie Francis, M-G-M 12878 | S | 13 |
| 45 | 39 | 24 | 21 | CLEMENTINE — Bobby Darin, Atco 6161 | | 9 |
| 46 | 37 | 45 | 66 | TIES THAT BIND — Brook Benton, Mercury 71566 | S | 6 |
| 47 | 41 | 27 | 28 | ANGELA JONES — Johnny Ferguson, M-G-M 12885 | | 13 |
| 48 | 40 | 38 | 45 | FANNIE MAE — Buster Brown, Fire 1008 | | 16 |
| 49 | 49 | 62 | 71 | NOBODY LOVES ME LIKE YOU — Flamingos, End 1068 | | 5 |
| 50 | 63 | 88 | 70 | WAY OF A CLOWN — Teddy Randazzo, ABC-Paramount 10088 | | 5 |
| 51 | 59 | 96 | 89 | TELL ME THAT YOU LOVE ME — Fats Domino, Imperial 8660 | | 4 |
| ★52 | 65 | 94 | — | MACK THE KNIFE — Ella Fitzgerald, Verve 10209 | S | 3 |
| 53 | 61 | 97 | — | THINK — James Brown and Famous Flames, Federal 12370 | | 3 |
| 54 | 55 | 64 | 95 | ANOTHER SLEEPLESS NIGHT — Jimmy Clanton, Ace 585 | | 4 |
| 55 | 43 | 32 | 30 | BIG IRON — Marty Robbins, Columbia 41589 | A | 10 |
| ★56 | 97 | — | — | WONDERFUL WORLD — Sam Cooke, Keen 82112 | | 2 |
| 57 | 58 | 61 | 63 | EARTH ANGEL — Johnny Tillotson, Cadence 1377 | | 6 |
| 58 | 60 | 63 | 78 | HITHER, THITHER AND YON — Brook Benton, Mercury 71566 | S | 5 |
| 59 | 45 | 48 | 49 | YOU DON'T KNOW ME — Lennie Welch, Cadence 1373 | | 12 |
| ★60 | — | 95 | — | CITY LIGHTS — Debbie Reynolds, Dot 16071 | | 2 |
| 61 | 42 | 29 | 23 | DON'T THROW AWAY ALL THOSE TEARDROPS — Frankie Avalon, Chancellor 1048 | | 10 |
| 62 | 80 | 80 | — | ALL I COUULD DO WAS CRY — Etta James, Argo 5359 | | 3 |
| 63 | 64 | 76 | 75 | PLEDGING MY LOVE — Johnny Tillotson, Cadence 1377 | | 6 |
| 64 | 47 | 23 | 16 | WILD ONE — Bobby Rydell, Cameo 171 | | 16 |
| 65 | 68 | 72 | 100 | DUTCHMAN'S GOLD — Walter Brennan, Dot 16066 | | 4 |
| 66 | 46 | 39 | 31 | JUST ONE TIME — Don Gibson, RCA Victor 7690 | S | 11 |
| 67 | 86 | — | — | JUMP OVER — Freddy Cannon, Swan 4053 | | 2 |
| 68 | 78 | 86 | — | OH, LITTLE ONE — Jack Scott, Top Rank 2041 | | 3 |
| 69 | 75 | 68 | 87 | A STAR IS BORN (A LOVE HAS DIED) — Mark Dinning, M-G-M 12888 | | 5 |
| 70 | 76 | 89 | — | BESAME MUCHO — Coasters, Atco 6163 | | 3 |
| 71 | — | — | — | ALWAYS IT'S YOU — Everly Brothers, Warner Bros. 5151 | S | 1 |
| 72 | — | 83 | — | RIGHT BY MY SIDE — Ricky Nelson, Imperial 5663 | | 2 |
| 73 | 90 | 99 | — | HAPPY-GO-LUCKY ME — Paul Evans, Guaranteed 208 | S | 2 |
| 74 | 62 | 44 | 52 | JUST A CLOSER WALK WITH THEE — Jimmie Rodgers, Roulette 4234 | | 6 |
| 75 | 79 | 87 | 93 | NO IF'S—NO AND'S — Lloyd Price, ABC-Paramount 10102 | | 4 |
| 76 | 85 | — | — | THEME FOR YOUNG LOVERS — Percy Faith, Columbia 41655 | | 2 |
| 77 | — | — | — | EBB TIDE — Platters, Mercury 71624 | | 1 |
| 78 | — | — | — | THE URGE — Freddy Cannon, Swan 4053 | | 1 |
| 79 | 69 | 75 | — | IS IT WRONG (FOR LOVING YOU) — Webb Pierce, Decca 31058 | | 3 |
| 80 | — | — | — | NATIONAL CITY — Joiner, Arkansas Jr. High School Band, Liberty 55244 | | 1 |
| 81 | — | — | — | FINGER POPPIN' TIME — Hank Ballard and the Midnighters, King 5341 | | 1 |
| 82 | 82 | — | — | PINK CHIFFON — Mitchell Torok, Guyden 2034 | | 2 |
| 83 | 87 | 100 | — | WHEEL OF FORTUNE — LaVern Baker, Atlantic 2059 | | 3 |
| 84 | 93 | — | — | BEFORE I GROW TOO OLD — Fats Domino, Imperial 5660 | | 2 |
| 85 | — | — | 94 | LAST CHANCE — Collay and His Satellites, Sho-Biz 1002 | | 2 |
| 86 | 95 | — | — | COTTAGE FOR SALE — Little Willie John, King 5342 | | 2 |
| 87 | 94 | — | — | HOT ROD LINCOLN — Charlie Ryan, Four Star 1733 | | 2 |
| 88 | 70 | 91 | 92 | EASY LOVIN' — Wade Flemons, Vee Jay 344 | | 4 |
| 89 | 92 | — | 99 | BEAUTIFUL OBSESSION — Sir Chauncey, Warner Bros. 5150 | | 3 |
| 90 | 67 | 73 | 81 | JENNY LOU — Sonny James, NRC 050 | | 6 |
| 91 | 91 | — | — | PUT YOUR ARMS AROUND ME, HONEY — Ray Smith, Judd 1017 | | 2 |
| 92 | — | — | — | LA MONTANA — Frank De Vol, Columbia 41620 | | 1 |
| 93 | 72 | 82 | 90 | BABY, WHAT DO YOU WANT ME TO DO — Jimmy Reed, Vee Jay 333 | | 14 |
| 94 | 99 | — | — | I'LL BE SEEING YOU — Five Satins, Ember 1061 | | 2 |
| 95 | 81 | 74 | — | THEME FROM THE UNFORGIVEN — Don Costa, United Artists 221 | | 3 |
| 96 | 100 | — | — | PENNIES FROM HEAVEN — Skyliners, Calico 117 | | 2 |
| 97 | — | — | 91 | SOMEONE LOVES YOU, JOE — The Singing Belles, Madison 126 | | 3 |
| 98 | — | — | — | EXCLUSIVELY YOURS — Carl Dobkins Jr., Decca 31088 | | 1 |
| 99 | — | — | — | CLAP YOUR HANDS — Beau-Marks, Shad 5017 | | 1 |
| 100 | — | — | — | MOJO WORKOUT — Larry Bright, Tide 006 | | 1 |

## The Billboard HOT 100

**For Week Ending May 22** — May 23, 1960

Columns: THIS WEEK | ONE WEEK AGO | TWO WEEKS AGO | THREE WEEKS AGO | TITLE — Artist, Company, Record No. | STEREO | WEEKS ON CHART

| # | 1wk | 2wk | 3wk | Title — Artist, Company, Record No. | Stereo | Wks |
|---|-----|-----|-----|-------------------------------------|--------|-----|
| 1 | 2 | 3 | 15 | CATHY'S CLOWN — Everly Brothers, Warner Bros. 5151 | S | 6 |
| 2 | 1 | 1 | 1 | STUCK ON YOU — Elvis Presley, RCA Victor 7740 | S | 8 |
| 3 | 5 | 13 | 42 | GOOD TIMIN' — Jimmie Jones, Cub 9067 | | 6 |
| 4 | 3 | 2 | 2 | GREENFIELDS — Brothers Four, Columbia 41571 | △ | 14 |
| 5 | 4 | 4 | 6 | NIGHT — Jackie Wilson, Brunswick 55166 | | 10 |
| 6 | 6 | 5 | 3 | SIXTEEN REASONS — Connie Stevens, Warner Bros. 5137 | | 17 |
| 7 | 8 | 8 | 7 | CRADLE OF LOVE — Johnny Preston, Mercury 71598 | | 9 |
| 8 | 10 | 21 | 37 | HE'LL HAVE TO STAY — Jeanne Black, Capitol 4368 | | 4 |
| 9 | 7 | 10 | 8 | LET THE LITTLE GIRL DANCE — Billy Bland, Old Town 1076 | | 15 |
| 10 | 12 | 23 | 34 | PAPER ROSES — Anita Bryant, Carlton 528 | S | 7 |
| 11 | 17 | 30 | 59 | BURNING BRIDGES — Jack Scott, Top Rank 2041 | | 6 |
| 12 | 16 | 27 | 33 | LOVE YOU SO — Rod Holden, Donna 1315 | | 8 |
| 13 | 15 | 22 | 19 | CHERRY PIE — Skip and Flip, Brent 7010 | | 8 |
| 14 | 13 | 9 | 11 | STAIRWAY TO HEAVEN — Neil Sedaka, RCA Victor 7709 | S | 9 |
| 15 | 9 | 6 | 4 | SINK THE BISMARCK — Johnny Horton, Columbia 41568 | △ | 12 |
| 16 | 22 | 33 | 57 | YOUNG EMOTIONS — Ricky Nelson, Imperial 5663 | | 5 |
| 17 | 11 | 7 | 5 | THE OLD LAMPLIGHTER — The Browns, RCA Victor 7700 | S | 11 |
| 18 | 41 | 71 | — | SWINGING SCHOOL — Bobby Rydell, Cameo 175 | | 3 |
| 19 | 14 | 11 | 14 | WHITE SILVER SANDS — Bill Black's Combo, Hi 2021 | | 12 |
| 20 | 20 | 17 | 20 | FAME AND FORTUNE — Elvis Presley, RCA Victor 7740 | S | 7 |
| 21 | 26 | 26 | 36 | MOUNTAIN OF LOVE — Harold Dorman, Rita 1003 | | 13 |
| 22 | 25 | 25 | 25 | LONELY WEEKENDS — Charlie Rich, Philips International 3552 | | 11 |
| 23 | 24 | 28 | 21 | MR. LUCKY — Henry Mancini, RCA Victor 7705 | S | 8 |
| 24 | 32 | 48 | 77 | GOT A GIRL — Four Preps, Capitol 4362 | | 6 |
| 25 | 37 | 54 | — | DING-A-LING — Bobby Rydell, Cameo 175 | | 3 |
| 26 | 28 | 15 | 35 | DOGGIN' AROUND — Jackie Wilson, Brunswick 55166 | | 8 |
| 27 | 39 | 52 | — | EVERYBODY'S SOMEBODY'S FOOL — Connie Francis, M-G-M 12899 | | 3 |
| 28 | 33 | 34 | 41 | OOH POO PAH DOO (Part 2) — Jessie Hill, Minit 607 | | 9 |
| 29 | 56 | 97 | — | WONDERFUL WORLD — Sam Cooke, Keen 82112 | | 3 |
| 30 | 31 | 56 | 71 | WHEN YOU WISH UPON A STAR — Dion and the Belmonts, Laurie 3052 | | 5 |
| 31 | 23 | 32 | 30 | MADISON — Al Brown's Tunetoppers, Amy 804 | | 8 |
| 32 | 21 | 16 | 10 | SWEET NOTHIN'S — Brenda Lee, Decca 30967 | | 23 |
| 33 | 27 | 19 | 18 | FOOTSTEPS — Steve Lawrence, ABC-Paramount 10085 | | 12 |
| 34 | 30 | 38 | 53 | MADISON TIME — Ray Bryant, Columbia 41628 | | 7 |
| 35 | 38 | 29 | 26 | WHAT AM I LIVING FOR — Conway Twitty, M-G-M 12886 | | 9 |
| 36 | 29 | 31 | 51 | BARBARA — Temptations, Goldisc 3001 | | 6 |
| 37 | 34 | 20 | 12 | HE'LL HAVE TO GO — Jim Reeves, RCA Victor 7643 | S | 22 |
| 38 | 49 | 49 | 62 | NOBODY LOVES ME LIKE YOU — Flamingos, End 1068 | | 6 |
| 39 | 18 | 14 | 17 | STEP BY STEP — The Crests, Coed 525 | | 13 |
| 40 | 19 | 12 | 13 | I LOVE THE WAY YOU LOVE — Marv Johnson, United Artists 208 | | 12 |
| 41 | 73 | 90 | 99 | HAPPY-GO-LUCKY ME — Paul Evans, Guaranteed 208 | S | 3 |
| 42 | 54 | 55 | 64 | ANOTHER SLEEPLESS NIGHT — Jimmy Clanton, Ace 585 | | 5 |
| 43 | 36 | 44 | 31 | APPLE GREEN — June Valli, Mercury 71588 | | 12 |
| 44 | 65 | 68 | 72 | DUTCHMAN'S GOLD — Walter Brennan, Dot 16066 | | 5 |
| 45 | 53 | 61 | 97 | THINK — James Brown and the Famous Flames, Federal 12370 | | 4 |
| 46 | 43 | 51 | 55 | FOR LOVE — Lloyd Price, ABC-Paramount 10102 | | 4 |
| 47 | 52 | 65 | 94 | MACK THE KNIFE — Ella Fitzgerald, Verve 10209 | S | 4 |
| 48 | 47 | 41 | 27 | ANGELA JONES — Johnny Ferguson, M-G-M 12855 | | 14 |
| 49 | 68 | 78 | 86 | OH, LITTLE ONE — Jack Scott, Top Rank 2041 | | 4 |
| 50 | 50 | 63 | 88 | WAY OF A CLOWN — Teddy Randazzo, ABC-Paramount 10088 | | 6 |
| 51 | 46 | 37 | 45 | TIES THAT BIND — Brook Benton, Mercury 71566 | S | 7 |
| 52 | 35 | 18 | 9 | THEME FROM A SUMMER PLACE — Percy Faith, Columbia 41490 | △ | 20 |
| 53 | 67 | 86 | — | JUMP OVER — Freddy Cannon, Swan 4053 | | 3 |
| 54 | 75 | 79 | 87 | NO IF'S—NO AND'S — Lloyd Price, ABC-Paramount 10102 | | 5 |
| 55 | 60 | — | 95 | CITY LIGHTS — Debbie Reynolds, Dot 16071 | | 3 |
| 56 | 71 | — | — | ALWAYS IT'S YOU — Everly Brothers, Warner Bros. 5151 | S | 2 |
| 57 | 51 | 59 | 96 | TELL ME THAT YOU LOVE ME — Fats Domino, Imperial 5660 | | 5 |
| 58 | 62 | 80 | 80 | ALL I COULD DO WAS CRY — Etta James, Argo 5359 | | 4 |
| 59 | 72 | — | 83 | RIGHT BY MY SIDE — Ricky Nelson, Imperial 5663 | | 3 |
| 60 | 78 | — | — | THE URGE — Freddy Cannon, Swan 4053 | | 2 |
| 61 | — | — | — | A ROCKIN' GOOD WAY — Dinah Washington and Brook Benton, Mercury 11629 | | 1 |
| 62 | — | — | — | (WON'T YOU COME HOME) BILL BAILEY — Bobby Darin, Atco 6167 | | 1 |
| 63 | 40 | 24 | 16 | PUPPY LOVE — Paul Anka, ABC-Paramount 10082 | S | 14 |
| 64 | 77 | — | — | EBB TIDE — Platters, Mercury 71624 | | 2 |
| 65 | 57 | 58 | 61 | EARTH ANGEL — Johnny Tillotson, Cadence 1377 | | 7 |
| 66 | 42 | 36 | 28 | MONEY — Barrett Strong, Anna 1111 | | 17 |
| 67 | 48 | 40 | 38 | FANNIE MAE — Buster Brown, Fire 1008 | | 17 |
| 68 | 58 | 60 | 63 | HITHER, THITHER AND YON — Brook Benton, Mercury 71566 | S | 6 |
| 69 | 74 | 62 | 44 | JUST A CLOSER WALK WITH THEE — Jimmie Rodgers, Roulette 4234 | | 7 |
| 70 | 76 | 85 | — | THEME FOR YOUNG LOVERS — Percy Faith, Columbia 41655 | | 3 |
| 71 | 59 | 45 | 48 | YOU DON'T KNOW ME — Lennie Welch, Cadence 1373 | | 13 |
| 72 | 80 | — | — | NATIONAL CITY — Joiner, Arkansas Jr. High School Band, Liberty 55244 | | 2 |
| 73 | 81 | — | — | FINGER POPPIN' TIME — Hank Ballard and the Midnighters, King 5341 | | 2 |
| 74 | — | — | — | MY HOME TOWN — Paul Anka, ABC-Paramount 10106 | | 1 |
| 75 | — | — | — | JEALOUS OF YOU — Connie Francis, M-G-M 12899 | | 1 |
| 76 | 69 | 75 | 68 | A STAR IS BORN (A LOVE HAS DIED) — Mark Dinning, M-G-M 12888 | | 6 |
| 77 | — | — | — | PLEASE HELP ME I'M FALLING — Hank Locklin, RCA Victor 7692 | | 1 |
| 78 | 87 | 94 | — | HOT ROD LINCOLN — Charlie Ryan, Four Star 1733 | | 3 |
| 79 | 82 | 82 | — | PINK CHIFFON — Mitchell Torok, Guyden 2034 | | 3 |
| 80 | — | — | — | MULE SKINNER BLUES — Fenderman, Soma 1137 | | 1 |
| 81 | 95 | 81 | 74 | THEME FROM THE UNFORGIVEN — Don Costa, United Artists 221 | | 4 |
| 82 | 85 | — | — | LAST CHANCE — Collay and His Satellites, Sho-Biz 1002 | | 3 |
| 83 | 86 | 95 | — | COTTAGE FOR SALE — Little Willie John, King 5342 | | 3 |
| 84 | — | — | — | I'M WALKIN' THE FLOOR OVER YOU — Pat Boone, Dot 16073 | | 1 |
| 85 | — | — | — | BECAUSE THEY'RE YOUNG — Duane Eddy, Jamie 1156 | | 1 |
| 86 | 98 | — | — | EXCLUSIVELY YOURS — Carl Dobkins Jr., Decca 31088 | | 2 |
| 87 | 94 | 99 | — | I'LL BE SEEING YOU — Five Satins, Ember 1061 | | 3 |
| 88 | — | — | — | RUNAROUND — Fleetwoods, Dolton 22 | | 1 |
| 89 | 89 | 92 | — | BEAUTIFUL OBSESSION — Sir Chauncey, Warner Bros. 5150 | | 4 |
| 90 | 100 | — | — | MOJO WORKOUT — Larry Bright, Tide 006 | | 2 |
| 91 | 92 | — | — | LA MONTANA — Frank De Vol, Columbia 41620 | | 2 |
| 92 | 96 | 100 | — | PENNIES FROM HEAVEN — Skyliners, Calico 117 | | 3 |
| 93 | 99 | — | — | CLAP YOUR HANDS — Beau-Marks, Shad 5017 | | 2 |
| 94 | — | — | — | I REALLY DON'T WANT TO KNOW — Tommy Edwards, M-G-M 12890 | | 1 |
| 95 | — | — | — | DOWN THE AISLE — Ike Clanton, Ace 583 | | 1 |
| 96 | 83 | 87 | 100 | WHEEL OF FORTUNE — LaVern Baker, Atlantic 2059 | | 4 |
| 97 | — | — | — | BIG BOY PETE — The Olympics, Arvee 595 | | 1 |
| 98 | — | — | — | SHADOWS OF LOVE — LaVern Baker, Atlantic 2059 | | 1 |
| 99 | — | — | — | FOUND LOVE — Jimmy Reed, Veejay 347 | | 1 |
| 100 | — | — | — | LONELY WINDS — Drifters, Atlantic 2062 | | 1 |

## The Billboard HOT 100

**For week ending June 5** — MAY 30, 1960

| This Week | 1 Wk Ago | 2 Wks Ago | 3 Wks Ago | Title — Artist, Company, Record No. | Stereo | Weeks on Chart |
|---|---|---|---|---|---|---|
| 1 | 1 | 2 | 3 | CATHY'S CLOWN — Everly Brothers, Warner Bros. 5151 | S | 7 |
| 2 | 2 | 1 | 1 | STUCK ON YOU — Elvis Presley, RCA Victor 7740 | S | 9 |
| 3 | 3 | 5 | 13 | GOOD TIMIN' — Jimmie Jones, Cub 9067 | | 7 |
| 4 | 8 | 10 | 21 | HE'LL HAVE TO STAY — Jeanne Black, Capitol 4368 | | 5 |
| 5 | 4 | 3 | 2 | GREENFIELDS — Brothers Four, Columbia 41571 | A | 15 |
| 6 | 5 | 4 | 4 | NIGHT — Jackie Wilson, Brunswick 55166 | | 11 |
| 7 | 10 | 12 | 23 | PAPER ROSES — Anita Bryant, Carlton 528 | S | 8 |
| 8 | 6 | 6 | 5 | SIXTEEN REASONS — Connie Stevens, Warner Bros. 5137 | | 18 |
| 9 | 11 | 17 | 30 | BURNING BRIDGES — Jack Scott, Top Rank 2041 | | 7 |
| 10 | 7 | 8 | 8 | CRADLE OF LOVE — Johnny Preston, Mercury 71598 | | 10 |
| 11 | 13 | 15 | 22 | CHERRY PIE — Skip and Flip, Brent 7010 | | 9 |
| 12 | 16 | 22 | 33 | YOUNG EMOTIONS — Ricky Nelson, Imperial 5663 | | 6 |
| 13 | 9 | 7 | 10 | LET THE LITTLE GIRL DANCE — Billy Bland, Old Town 1076 | | 16 |
| 14 | 12 | 16 | 27 | LOVE YOU SO — Rod Holden, Donna 1315 | | 9 |
| 15 | 18 | 41 | 71 | SWINGING SCHOOL — Bobby Rydell, Cameo 175 | | 4 |
| 16 | 15 | 9 | 6 | SINK THE BISMARCK — Johnny Horton, Columbia 41568 | A | 13 |
| 17 | 14 | 13 | 9 | STAIRWAY TO HEAVEN — Neil Sedaka, RCA Victor 7709 | S | 10 |
| 18 | 25 | 37 | 54 | DING-A-LING — Bobby Rydell, Cameo 175 | | 4 |
| 19 | 17 | 11 | 7 | THE OLD LAMPLIGHTER — The Browns, RCA Victor 7700 | S | 12 |
| 20 | 27 | 39 | 52 | EVERYBODY'S SOMEBODY'S FOOL — Connie Francis, M-G-M 12899 | | 4 |
| 21 | 29 | 56 | 97 | WONDERFUL WORLD — Sam Cooke, Keen 82112 | | 4 |
| 22 | 21 | 26 | 26 | MOUNTAIN OF LOVE — Harold Dorman, Rita 1003 | | 14 |
| 23 | 20 | 20 | 17 | FAME AND FORTUNE — Elvis Presley, RCA Victor 7740 | S | 8 |
| 24 | 19 | 14 | 11 | WHITE SILVER SANDS — Bill Black's Combo, Hi 2021 | | 12 |
| 25 | 26 | 28 | 15 | DOGGIN' AROUND — Jackie Wilson, Brunswick 55166 | | 9 |
| 26 | 22 | 25 | 25 | LONELY WEEKENDS — Charlie Rich, Philips International 3552 | | 12 |
| 27 | 41 | 73 | 90 | HAPPY-GO-LUCKY ME — Paul Evans, Guaranteed 208 | S | 4 |
| 28 | 31 | 23 | 32 | MADISON — Al Brown's Tunetoppers, Amy 804 | | 9 |
| 29 | 24 | 32 | 48 | GOT A GIRL — Four Preps, Capitol 4362 | | 7 |
| 30 | 38 | 49 | 49 | NOBODY LOVES ME LIKE YOU — Flamingos, End 1068 | | 7 |
| 31 | 44 | 65 | 68 | DUTCHMAN'S GOLD — Walter Brennan and Billy Vaughn, Dot 16066 | | 6 |
| 32 | 53 | 67 | 86 | JUMP OVER — Freddy Cannon, Swan 4053 | | 4 |
| 33 | 34 | 30 | 38 | MADISON TIME — Ray Bryant, Columbia 41628 | | 8 |
| 34 | 28 | 33 | 34 | OOH POO PAH DOO (Part 2) — Jessie Hill, Minit 607 | | 10 |
| 35 | 45 | 53 | 61 | THINK — James Brown and the Famous Flames, Federal 12370 | | 5 |
| 36 | 47 | 52 | 65 | MACK THE KNIFE — Ella Fitzgerald, Verve 10209 | S | 5 |
| 37 | 49 | 68 | 78 | OH, LITTLE ONE — Jack Scott, Top Rank 2041 | | 5 |
| 38 | 42 | 54 | 55 | ANOTHER SLEEPLESS NIGHT — Jimmy Clanton, Ace 585 | | 6 |
| 39 | 23 | 24 | 28 | MR. LUCKY — Henry Mancini, RCA Victor 7705 | S | 9 |
| 40 | 54 | 75 | 79 | NO IF'S—NO AND'S — Lloyd Price, ABC-Paramount 10102 | | 6 |
| 41 | 39 | 18 | 14 | STEP BY STEP — The Crests, Coed 525 | | 14 |
| 42 | 85 | — | — | BECAUSE THEY'RE YOUNG — Duane Eddy, Jamie 1156 | | 2 |
| 43 | 75 | — | — | JEALOUS OF YOU — Connie Francis, M-G-M 12899 | | 2 |
| 44 | 35 | 38 | 29 | WHAT AM I LIVING FOR — Conway Twitty, M-G-M 12886 | | 10 |
| 45 | 40 | 19 | 12 | I LOVE THE WAY YOU LOVE — Marv Johnson, United Artists 208 | | 13 |
| 46 | 36 | 29 | 31 | BARBARA — Temptations, Goldise 3001 | | 7 |
| 47 | 50 | 50 | 63 | WAY OF A CLOWN — Teddy Randazzo, ABC-Paramount 10088 | | 7 |
| 48 | 58 | 62 | 80 | ALL I COULD DO WAS CRY — Etta James, Argo 5359 | | 5 |
| 49 | 61 | — | — | A ROCKIN' GOOD WAY — Dinah Washington and Brook Benton, Mercury 11629 | | 2 |
| 50 | 30 | 31 | 56 | WHEN YOU WISH UPON A STAR — Dion and the Belmonts, Laurie 3052 | | 6 |
| 51 | 57 | 51 | 59 | TELL ME THAT YOU LOVE ME — Fats Domino, Imperial 5660 | | 6 |
| 52 | 62 | — | — | (WON'T YOU COME HOME) BILL BAILEY — Bobby Darin, Atco 6167 | | 2 |
| 53 | — | — | — | PLEASE HELP ME, I'M FALLING — Hank Locklin, RCA Victor 7692 | | 2 |
| 54 | 37 | 34 | 20 | HE'LL HAVE TO GO — Jim Reeves, RCA Victor 7643 | S | 23 |
| 55 | 33 | 27 | 19 | FOOTSTEPS — Steve Lawrence, ABC-Paramount 10085 | | 13 |
| 56 | 64 | 77 | — | EBB TIDE — Platters, Mercury 71624 | | 3 |
| 57 | 74 | — | — | MY HOME TOWN — Paul Anka, ABC-Paramount 10106 | | 2 |
| 58 | 69 | 74 | 62 | JUST A CLOSER WALK WITH THEE — Jimmie Rodgers, Roulette 4234 | | 8 |
| 59 | 84 | — | — | I'M WALKIN' THE FLOOR OVER YOU — Pat Boone, Dot 16073 | | 2 |
| 60 | 51 | 46 | 37 | TIES THAT BIND — Brook Benton, Mercury 71566 | S | 8 |
| 61 | 46 | 43 | 51 | FOR LOVE — Lloyd Price, ABC-Paramount 10102 | | 5 |
| 62 | 43 | 36 | 44 | APPLE GREEN — June Valli, Mercury 71588 | | 13 |
| 63 | 32 | 21 | 16 | SWEET NOTHIN'S — Brenda Lee, Decca 30967 | | 24 |
| 64 | 94 | — | — | I REALLY DON'T WANT TO KNOW — Tommy Edwards, M-G-M 12890 | | 2 |
| 65 | 70 | 76 | 85 | THEME FOR YOUNG LOVERS — Percy Faith, Columbia 41655 | | 4 |
| 66 | 72 | 80 | — | NATIONAL CITY — Joiner, Arkansas Jr. High School Band, Liberty 55244 | | 3 |
| 67 | 73 | 81 | — | FINGER POPPIN' TIME — Hank Ballard and the Midnighters, King 5341 | | 3 |
| 68 | 55 | 60 | — | CITY LIGHTS — Debbie Reynolds, Dot 16071 | | 4 |
| 69 | 83 | 86 | 95 | COTTAGE FOR SALE — Little Willie John, King 5342 | | 4 |
| 70 | 79 | 82 | 82 | PINK CHIFFON — Mitchell Torok, Guyden 2034 | | 4 |
| 71 | 56 | 71 | — | ALWAYS IT'S YOU — Everly Brothers, Warner Bros. 5151 | S | 3 |
| 72 | 80 | — | — | MULE SKINNER BLUES — Fendermen, Soma 1137 | | 2 |
| 73 | 59 | 72 | — | RIGHT BY MY SIDE — Ricky Nelson, Imperial 5663 | | 4 |
| 74 | 52 | 35 | 18 | THEME FROM A SUMMER PLACE — Percy Faith, Columbia 41490 | A | 21 |
| 75 | 86 | 98 | — | EXCLUSIVELY YOURS — Carl Dobkins Jr., Decca 31088 | | 3 |
| 76 | — | — | — | I'M SORRY — Brenda Lee, Decca 31093 | | 1 |
| 77 | 81 | 95 | 81 | THEME FROM THE UNFORGIVEN — Don Costa, United Artists 221 | | 5 |
| 78 | 78 | 87 | 94 | HOT ROD LINCOLN — Charlie Ryan, Four Star 1733 | | 4 |
| 79 | 87 | 94 | 99 | I'LL BE SEEING YOU — Five Satins, Ember 1061 | | 4 |
| 80 | 92 | 96 | 100 | PENNIES FROM HEAVEN — Skyliners, Calico 117 | | 4 |
| 81 | — | — | — | DOWN YONDER — Johnny and the Hurricanes, Big Top 3036 | | 1 |
| 82 | — | — | — | RIVER STAY AWAY FROM MY DOOR — Frank Sinatra, Capitol 7376 | | 1 |
| 83 | 88 | — | — | RUNAROUND — Fleetwoods, Dolton 22 | | 2 |
| 84 | 48 | 47 | 41 | ANGELA JONES — Johnny Ferguson, M-G-M 12855 | | 15 |
| 85 | — | — | — | ALLEY-OOP — Hollywood Argyles, Lute 5905 | | 1 |
| 86 | — | — | — | SPRING RAIN — Pat Boone, Dot 221 | | 1 |
| 87 | 93 | 99 | — | CLAP YOUR HANDS — Beau-Marks, Shad 5017 | | 3 |
| 88 | 98 | — | — | SHADOWS OF LOVE — LaVern Baker, Atlantic 2059 | | 2 |
| 89 | 100 | — | — | LONELY WINDS — Drifters, Atlantic 2062 | | 2 |
| 90 | — | — | — | HEARTBREAK (IT'S HURTIN' ME) — Little Willie John, King 5356 | | 1 |
| 91 | 95 | — | — | DOWN THE AISLE — Ike Clanton, Ace 583 | | 2 |
| 92 | 91 | 92 | — | LA MONTANA — Frank De Vol, Columbia 41620 | | 3 |
| 93 | 99 | — | — | FOUND LOVE — Jimmy Reed, Vee-Jay 347 | | 2 |
| 94 | — | — | — | ALLEY OOP — Dante and the Evergreens, Madison 130 | | 1 |
| 95 | — | — | — | COMIN' DOWN WITH LOVE — Mel Gadson, Big Top 3034 | | 1 |
| 96 | — | — | — | WHEN WILL I BE LOVED — Everly Brothers, Cadence 1586 | | 1 |
| 97 | 60 | 78 | — | THE URGE — Freddy Cannon, Swan 4053 | | 3 |
| 98 | — | — | — | SOMETHING HAPPENED — Paul Anka, ABC-Paramount 10106 | | 1 |
| 99 | — | — | — | AIN'T GONNA BE THAT WAY — Marv Johnson, United Artists 262 | | 1 |
| 100 | — | — | — | MARIA — Johnny Mathis, Columbia 41684 | | 1 |

STAR PERFORMERS showed the greatest upward progress on Hot 100 this week.
S — Indicates that 45 r.p.m. stereo single version is available.
A — Indicates that 33⅓ r.p.m. stereo single version is available.

# The Billboard HOT 100

**FOR WEEK ENDING JUNE 12**

JUNE 6, 1960

| This Week | 1 Wk Ago | 2 Wks Ago | 3 Wks Ago | Title — Artist, Company, Record No. | Stereo | Weeks on Chart |
|---|---|---|---|---|---|---|
| 1 | 1 | 1 | 2 | CATHY'S CLOWN — Everly Brothers, Warner Bros. 5151 | S | 8 |
| 2 | 2 | 2 | 1 | STUCK ON YOU — Elvis Presley, RCA Victor 7740 | S | 10 |
| 3 | 3 | 3 | 5 | GOOD TIMIN' — Jimmy Jones, Cub 9067 | | 8 |
| 4 | 4 | 8 | 10 | HE'LL HAVE TO STAY — Jeanne Black, Capitol 4368 | | 6 |
| 5 | 9 | 11 | 17 | BURNING BRIDGES — Jack Scott, Top Rank 2041 | | 8 |
| 6 | 7 | 10 | 12 | PAPER ROSES — Anita Bryant, Carlton 528 | S | 9 |
| 7 | 6 | 5 | 4 | NIGHT — Jackie Wilson, Brunswick 55166 | | 12 |
| 8 | 20 | 27 | 39 | EVERYBODY'S SOMEBODY'S FOOL — Connie Francis, M-G-M 12899 | | 5 |
| 9 | 14 | 12 | 16 | LOVE YOU SO — Rod Holden, Donna 1315 | | 10 |
| 10 | 5 | 4 | 3 | GREENFIELDS — Brothers Four, Columbia 41571 | A | 16 |
| 11 | 8 | 6 | 6 | SIXTEEN REASONS — Connie Stevens, Warner Bros. 5137 | | 19 |
| 12 | 10 | 7 | 8 | CRADLE OF LOVE — Johnny Preston, Mercury 71598 | | 11 |
| 13 | 15 | 18 | 41 | SWINGING SCHOOL — Bobby Rydell, Cameo 175 | | 5 |
| 14 | 12 | 16 | 22 | YOUNG EMOTIONS — Ricky Nelson, Imperial 5663 | | 7 |
| 15 | 13 | 9 | 7 | LET THE LITTLE GIRL DANCE — Billy Bland, Old Town 1076 | | 17 |
| 16 | 11 | 13 | 15 | CHERRY PIE — Skip and Flip, Brent 7010 | | 10 |
| 17 | 27 | 41 | 73 | HAPPY-GO-LUCKY ME — Paul Evans, Guaranteed 208 | S | 5 |
| 18 | 18 | 25 | 37 | DING-A-LING — Bobby Rydell, Cameo 175 | | 5 |
| 19 | 21 | 29 | 56 | WONDERFUL WORLD — Sam Cooke, Keen 82112 | | 5 |
| 20 | 17 | 14 | 13 | STAIRWAY TO HEAVEN — Neil Sedaka, RCA Victor 7709 | S | 11 |
| 21 | 25 | 26 | 28 | DOGGIN' AROUND — Jackie Wilson, Brunswick 55166 | | 10 |
| 22 | 43 | 75 | — | JEALOUS OF YOU — Connie Francis, M-G-M 12899 | | 3 |
| 23 | 42 | 85 | — | BECAUSE THEY'RE YOUNG — Duane Eddy, Jamie 1156 | | 3 |
| 24 | 22 | 21 | 26 | MOUNTAIN OF LOVE — Harold Dorman, Rita 1003 | | 15 |
| 25 | 23 | 20 | 20 | FAME AND FORTUNE — Elvis Presley, RCA Victor 7740 | S | 9 |
| 26 | 19 | 17 | 11 | THE OLD LAMPLIGHTER — The Browns, RCA Victor 7700 | S | 13 |
| 27 | 49 | 61 | — | A ROCKIN' GOOD WAY — Dinah Washington and Brook Benton, Mercury 71629 | S | 3 |
| 28 | 16 | 15 | 9 | SINK THE BISMARCK — Johnny Horton, Columbia 41568 | A | 14 |
| 29 | 32 | 53 | 67 | JUMP OVER — Freddy Cannon, Swan 4053 | | 5 |
| 30 | 31 | 44 | 65 | DUTCHMAN'S GOLD — Walter Brennan and Billy Vaughn, Dot 16066 | | 7 |
| 31 | 36 | 47 | 52 | MACK THE KNIFE — Ella Fitzgerald, Verve 10209 | S | 6 |
| 32 | 38 | 42 | 54 | ANOTHER SLEEPLESS NIGHT — Jimmy Clanton, Ace 585 | | 7 |
| 33 | 35 | 45 | 53 | THINK — James Brown and the Famous Flames, Federal 12370 | | 6 |
| 34 | 37 | 49 | 68 | OH, LITTLE ONE — Jack Scott, Top Rank 2041 | | 6 |
| 35 | 26 | 22 | 25 | LONELY WEEKENDS — Charlie Rich, Philips International 3552 | | 13 |
| 36 | 30 | 38 | 49 | NOBODY LOVES ME LIKE YOU — Flamingos, End 1068 | | 8 |
| 37 | 57 | 74 | — | MY HOME TOWN — Paul Anka, ABC-Paramount 10106 | | 3 |
| 38 | 76 | — | — | I'M SORRY — Brenda Lee, Decca 31093 | | 2 |
| 39 | 48 | 58 | 62 | ALL I COULD DO WAS CRY — Etta James, Argo 5359 | | 6 |
| 40 | 64 | 94 | — | I REALLY DON'T WANT TO KNOW — Tommy Edwards, M-G-M 12890 | | 3 |
| 41 | 39 | 23 | 24 | MR. LUCKY — Henry Mancini, RCA Victor 7705 | S | 10 |
| 42 | 53 | — | — | PLEASE HELP ME, I'M FALLING — Hank Locklin, RCA Victor 7692 | | 3 |
| 43 | 52 | 62 | — | (WON'T YOU COME HOME) BILL BAILEY — Bobby Darin, Atco 6167 | | 3 |
| 44 | 47 | 50 | 50 | WAY OF A CLOWN — Teddy Randazzo, ABC-Paramount 10088 | | 8 |
| 45 | 65 | 70 | 76 | THEME FOR YOUNG LOVERS — Percy Faith, Columbia 41655 | | 5 |
| 46 | 46 | 36 | 29 | BARBARA — Temptations, Goldisc 3001 | | 8 |
| 47 | 50 | 30 | 31 | WHEN YOU WISH UPON A STAR — Dion and the Belmonts, Laurie 3052 | | 7 |
| 48 | 34 | 28 | 33 | OOH POO PAH DOO (Part 2) — Jesse Hill, Minit 607 | | 11 |
| 49 | 41 | 39 | 18 | STEP BY STEP — The Crests, Coed 525 | | 15 |
| 50 | 77 | 81 | 95 | THEME FROM THE UNFORGIVEN — Don Costa, United Artists 221 | | 6 |
| 51 | 24 | 19 | 14 | WHITE SILVER SANDS — Bill Black's Combo, Hi 2021 | | 13 |
| 52 | 28 | 31 | 23 | MADISON — Al Brown's Tunetoppers, Amy 804 | | 10 |
| 53 | 66 | 72 | 80 | NATIONAL CITY — Joiner, Arkansas Jr. High School Band, Liberty 55244 | | 4 |
| 54 | 86 | — | — | SPRING RAIN — Pat Boone, Dot 221 | | 2 |
| 55 | 85 | — | — | ALLEY-OOP — Hollywood Argyles, Lute 5905 | | 3 |
| 56 | 59 | 84 | — | I'M WALKIN' THE FLOOR OVER YOU — Pat Boone, Dot 16073 | | 3 |
| 57 | 72 | 80 | — | MULE SKINNER BLUES — Fendermen, Soma 1137 | | 3 |
| 58 | 33 | 34 | 30 | MADISON TIME — Ray Bryant, Columbia 41628 | | 9 |
| 59 | 56 | 64 | 77 | EBB TIDE — Platters, Mercury 71624 | | 4 |
| 60 | 60 | 51 | 46 | TIES THAT BIND — Brook Benton, Mercury 71566 | S | 9 |
| 61 | 29 | 24 | 32 | GOT A GIRL — Four Preps, Capitol 4362 | | 8 |
| 62 | 98 | — | — | SOMETHING HAPPENED — Paul Anka, ABC-Paramount 10106 | | 2 |
| 63 | 69 | 83 | 86 | COTTAGE FOR SALE — Little Willie John, King 5342 | | 5 |
| 64 | 67 | 73 | 81 | FINGER POPPIN' TIME — Hank Ballard and the Midnighters, King 5341 | | 4 |
| 65 | 58 | 69 | 74 | JUST A CLOSER WALK WITH THEE — Jimmie Rodgers, Roulette 4234 | | 9 |
| 66 | 73 | 59 | 72 | RIGHT BY MY SIDE — Ricky Nelson, Imperial 5663 | | 5 |
| 67 | 80 | 92 | 96 | PENNIES FROM HEAVEN — Skyliners, Calico 117 | | 5 |
| 68 | 70 | 79 | 82 | PINK CHIFFON — Mitchell Torok, Guyden 2034 | | 5 |
| 69 | 61 | 46 | 43 | FOR LOVE — Lloyd Price, ABC-Paramount 10102 | | 6 |
| 70 | 51 | 57 | 51 | TELL ME THAT YOU LOVE ME — Pats Domino, Imperial 5660 | | 7 |
| 71 | 83 | 88 | — | RUNAROUND — Fleetwoods, Dolton 22 | | 3 |
| 72 | 75 | 86 | 98 | EXCLUSIVELY YOURS — Carl Dobkins Jr., Decca 31088 | | 4 |
| 73 | 40 | 54 | 75 | NO IF'S — NO AND'S — Lloyd Price, ABC-Paramount 10102 | | 7 |
| 74 | 71 | 56 | 71 | ALWAYS IT'S YOU — Everly Brothers, Warner Bros. 5151 | S | 4 |
| 75 | 94 | — | — | ALLEY-OOP — Dante and the Evergreens, Madison 130 | | 2 |
| 76 | 81 | — | — | DOWN YONDER — Johnny and the Hurricanes, Big Top 3036 | | 2 |
| 77 | 44 | 35 | 38 | WHAT AM I LIVING FOR — Conway Twitty, M-G-M 12886 | | 11 |
| 78 | — | — | — | THAT'S ALL YOU GOTTA DO — Brenda Lee, Decca 31093 | | 1 |
| 79 | 90 | — | — | HEARTBREAK (IT'S HURTIN' ME) — Little Willie John, King 5356 | | 2 |
| 80 | 89 | 100 | — | LONELY WINDS — Drifters, Atlantic 2062 | | 3 |
| 81 | 78 | 78 | 87 | HOT ROD LINCOLN — Charlie Ryan, Four Star 1733 | | 5 |
| 82 | 96 | — | — | WHEN WILL I BE LOVED — Everly Brothers, Cadence 1586 | | 2 |
| 83 | 87 | 93 | 99 | CLAP YOUR HANDS — Beau-Marks, Shad 5017 | | 4 |
| 84 | 88 | 98 | — | SHADOWS OF LOVE — LaVern Baker, Atlantic 2059 | | 3 |
| 85 | 82 | — | — | RIVER STAY AWAY FROM MY DOOR — Frank Sinatra, Capitol 7376 | | 2 |
| 86 | 92 | 91 | 92 | LA MONTANA — Frank De Vol, Columbia 41620 | | 4 |
| 87 | 79 | 87 | 94 | I'LL BE SEEING YOU — Five Satins, Ember 1061 | | 5 |
| 88 | — | — | — | ONLY THE LONELY — Roy Orbison, Monument 421 | | 1 |
| 89 | — | — | — | HEY, LITTLE ONE — Dorsey Burnette, Era 3019 | | 1 |
| 90 | — | — | — | TRAIN OF LOVE — Annette, Vista 359 | | 1 |
| 91 | 99 | — | — | AIN'T GONNA BE THAT WAY — Marv Johnson, United Artists 262 | | 2 |
| 92 | — | — | — | ALLEY-OOP — Dyna-Sores, Rendezvous 120 | | 1 |
| 93 | — | — | — | HEARTBREAK (IT'S HURTIN' ME) — Jon Thomas, ABC-Paramount 10122 | | 1 |
| 94 | 95 | — | — | COMIN' DOWN WITH LOVE — Mel Gadson, Big Top 3034 | | 2 |
| 95 | — | — | — | IMAGE OF A GIRL — Safaris, Eldo 101 | | 1 |
| 96 | — | — | — | BANJO BOY — Jan & Kjeld, Kapp 336 | | 1 |
| 97 | — | — | — | BIOLOGY — Danny Valentino, M-G-M 12881 | | 1 |
| 98 | — | — | — | LA MONTANA — Roger Williams, Kapp 331 | | 1 |
| 99 | — | — | — | YEN YET SONG — Gary Cane, Shell 719 | | 1 |
| 100 | — | — | — | ONE OF US (WILL WEEP TONIGHT) — Patti Page, Mercury 71639 | S | 1 |

# The Billboard HOT 100

**POP SONGS — JUNE 13, 1960**
**For Week Ending June 19**

| This Week | 1 Wk Ago | 2 Wks Ago | 3 Wks Ago | Title / Artist, Company, Record No. | Stereo | Weeks on Chart |
|---|---|---|---|---|---|---|
| 1 | 1 | 1 | 1 | CATHY'S CLOWN — Everly Brothers, Warner Bros. 5151 | S | 9 |
| 2 | 8 | 20 | 27 | EVERYBODY'S SOMEBODY'S FOOL — Connie Francis, M-G-M 12899 | | 6 |
| 3 | 5 | 9 | 11 | BURNING BRIDGES — Jack Scott, Top Rank 2041 | | 9 |
| 4 | 3 | 3 | 3 | GOOD TIMIN' — Jimmy Jones, Cub 9067 | | 9 |
| 5 | 6 | 7 | 10 | PAPER ROSES — Anita Bryant, Carlton 528 | S | 10 |
| 6 | 4 | 4 | 8 | HE'LL HAVE TO STAY — Jeanne Black, Capitol 4368 | | 7 |
| 7 | 9 | 14 | 12 | LOVE YOU SO — Rod Holden, Donna 1315 | | 11 |
| 8 | 2 | 2 | 2 | STUCK ON YOU — Elvis Presley, RCA Victor 7740 | S | 11 |
| 9 | 13 | 15 | 18 | SWINGING SCHOOL — Bobby Rydell, Cameo 175 | | 6 |
| 10 | 17 | 27 | 41 | HAPPY-GO-LUCKY ME — Paul Evans, Guaranteed 208 | S | 6 |
| 11 | 7 | 6 | 5 | NIGHT — Jackie Wilson, Brunswick 55166 | | 13 |
| 12 | 55 | 85 | — | ALLEY-OOP — Hollywood Argyles, Lute 5905 | | 3 |
| 13 | 23 | 42 | 85 | BECAUSE THEY'RE YOUNG — Duane Eddy, Jamie 1156 | | 4 |
| 14 | 14 | 12 | 16 | YOUNG EMOTIONS — Ricky Nelson, Imperial 5663 | | 8 |
| 15 | 10 | 5 | 4 | GREENFIELDS — Brothers Four, Columbia 41571 | A | 17 |
| 16 | 37 | 57 | 74 | MY HOME TOWN — Paul Anka, ABC-Paramount 10106 | | 4 |
| 17 | 11 | 8 | 6 | SIXTEEN REASONS — Connie Stevens, Warner Bros. 5137 | | 20 |
| 18 | 16 | 11 | 13 | CHERRY PIE — Skip and Flip, Brent 7010 | | 11 |
| 19 | 19 | 21 | 29 | WONDERFUL WORLD — Sam Cooke, Keen 82112 | | 6 |
| 20 | 27 | 49 | 61 | A ROCKIN' GOOD WAY — Dinah Washington and Brook Benton, Mercury 71629 | S | 4 |
| 21 | 21 | 25 | 26 | DOGGIN' AROUND — Jackie Wilson, Brunswick 55166 | | 11 |
| 22 | 18 | 18 | 25 | DING-A-LING — Bobby Rydell, Cameo 175 | | 6 |
| 23 | 38 | 76 | — | I'M SORRY — Brenda Lee, Decca 31093 | | 3 |
| 24 | 22 | 43 | 75 | JEALOUS OF YOU — Connie Francis, M-G-M 12899 | | 4 |
| 25 | 57 | 72 | 80 | MULE SKINNER BLUES — Fendermen, Soma 1137 | | 4 |
| 26 | 15 | 13 | 9 | LET THE LITTLE GIRL DANCE — Billy Bland, Old Town 1076 | | 18 |
| 27 | 12 | 10 | 7 | CRADLE OF LOVE — Johnny Preston, Mercury 71598 | | 12 |
| 28 | 75 | 94 | — | ALLEY-OOP — Dante and the Evergreens, Madison 130 | | 3 |
| 29 | 29 | 32 | 53 | JUMP OVER — Freddy Cannon, Swan 4053 | | 6 |
| 30 | 32 | 38 | 42 | ANOTHER SLEEPLESS NIGHT — Jimmy Clanton, Ace 585 | | 8 |
| 31 | 31 | 36 | 47 | MACK THE KNIFE — Ella Fitzgerald, Verve 10209 | S | 7 |
| 32 | 35 | 26 | 22 | LONELY WEEKENDS — Charlie Rich, Philips International 3552 | | 14 |
| 33 | 39 | 48 | 58 | ALL I COULD DO WAS CRY — Etta James, Argo 5359 | | 7 |
| 34 | 40 | 64 | 94 | I REALLY DON'T WANT TO KNOW — Tommy Edwards, M-G-M 12890 | | 4 |
| 35 | 24 | 22 | 21 | MOUNTAIN OF LOVE — Harold Dorman, Rita 1003 | | 16 |
| 36 | 30 | 31 | 44 | DUTCHMAN'S GOLD — Walter Brennan and Billy Vaughn, Dot 16066 | | 8 |
| 37 | 41 | 39 | 23 | MR. LUCKY — Henry Mancini, RCA Victor 7705 | S | 11 |
| 38 | 42 | 53 | — | PLEASE HELP ME, I'M FALLING — Hank Locklin, RCA Victor 7692 | | 4 |
| 39 | 20 | 17 | 14 | STAIRWAY TO HEAVEN — Neil Sedaka, RCA Victor 7709 | S | 12 |
| 40 | 26 | 19 | 17 | THE OLD LAMPLIGHTER — The Browns, RCA Victor 7700 | S | 14 |
| 41 | 43 | 52 | 62 | (WON'T YOU COME HOME) BILL BAILEY — Bobby Darin, Atco 6167 | | 4 |
| 42 | 71 | 83 | 88 | RUNAROUND — Fleetwoods, Dolton 22 | | 4 |
| 43 | 45 | 65 | 70 | THEME FOR YOUNG LOVERS — Percy Faith, Columbia 41655 | | 6 |
| 44 | 88 | — | — | ONLY THE LONELY — Roy Orbison, Monument 421 | | 2 |
| 45 | 90 | — | — | TRAIN OF LOVE — Annette, Vista 359 | | 2 |
| 46 | 33 | 35 | 45 | THINK — James Brown and the Famous Flames, Federal 12370 | | 7 |
| 47 | 56 | 59 | 84 | I'M WALKIN' THE FLOOR OVER YOU — Pat Boone, Dot 16073 | | 4 |
| 48 | 28 | 16 | 15 | SINK THE BISMARCK — Johnny Horton, Columbia 41568 | A | 15 |
| 49 | 50 | 77 | 81 | THEME FROM THE UNFORGIVEN — Don Costa, United Artists 221 | | 7 |
| 50 | 67 | 80 | 92 | PENNIES FROM HEAVEN — Skyliners, Calico 117 | | 6 |
| 51 | 48 | 34 | 28 | OOH POO PAH DOO (Part 2) — Jessie Hill, Minit 607 | | 12 |
| 52 | 62 | 98 | — | SOMETHING HAPPENED — Paul Anka, ABC-Paramount 10106 | | 3 |
| 53 | 34 | 37 | 49 | OH, LITTLE ONE — Jack Scott, Top Rank 2041 | | 7 |
| 54 | 54 | 86 | — | SPRING RAIN — Pat Boone, Dot 16073 | | 3 |
| 55 | 78 | — | — | THAT'S ALL YOU GOTTA DO — Brenda Lee, Decca 31093 | | 2 |
| 56 | 53 | 66 | 72 | NATIONAL CITY — Joiner, Arkansas Jr. High School Band, Liberty 55244 | | 5 |
| 57 | 47 | 50 | 30 | WHEN YOU WISH UPON A STAR — Dion and the Belmonts, Laurie 3052 | | 8 |
| 58 | 83 | 87 | 93 | CLAP YOUR HANDS — Beau-Marks, Shad 5017 | | 5 |
| 59 | 92 | — | — | ALLEY-OOP — Dyna-Sores, Rendezvous 120 | | 2 |
| 60 | 46 | 46 | 36 | BARBARA — Temptations, Goldisc 3001 | | 9 |
| 61 | 52 | 28 | 31 | MADISON — Al Brown's Tunetoppers, Amy 804 | | 11 |
| 62 | 61 | 29 | 24 | GOT A GIRL — Four Preps, Capitol 4362 | | 9 |
| 63 | 76 | 81 | — | DOWN YONDER — Johnny and the Hurricanes, Big Top 3036 | | 3 |
| 64 | 68 | 70 | 79 | PINK CHIFFON — Mitchell Torok, Guyden 2034 | | 6 |
| 65 | 36 | 30 | 38 | NOBODY LOVES ME LIKE YOU — Flamingos, End 1068 | | 9 |
| 66 | 59 | 56 | 64 | EBB TIDE — Platters, Mercury 71624 | | 5 |
| 67 | 25 | 23 | 20 | FAME AND FORTUNE — Elvis Presley, RCA Victor 7740 | S | 10 |
| 68 | 44 | 47 | 50 | WAY OF A CLOWN — Teddy Randazzo, ABC-Paramount 10088 | | 9 |
| 69 | 72 | 75 | 86 | EXCLUSIVELY YOURS — Carl Dobkins Jr., Decca 31088 | | 5 |
| 70 | 80 | 89 | 100 | LONELY WINDS — Drifters, Atlantic 2062 | | 4 |
| 71 | 82 | 96 | — | WHEN WILL I BE LOVED — Everly Brothers, Cadence 1380 | | 3 |
| 72 | 89 | — | — | HEY, LITTLE ONE — Dorsey Burnett, Era 3019 | | 2 |
| 73 | 95 | — | — | IMAGE OF A GIRL — Safaris, Eldo 101 | | 2 |
| 74 | 64 | 67 | 73 | FINGER POPPIN' TIME — Hank Ballard and the Midnighters, King 5341 | | 5 |
| 75 | 74 | 71 | 56 | ALWAYS IT'S YOU — Everly Brothers, Warner Bros. 5151 | S | 5 |
| 76 | — | — | — | MR. LONELY — Videls, JDS 5004 | | 1 |
| 77 | 79 | 90 | — | HEARTBREAK (IT'S HURTIN' ME) — Little Willie John, King 5356 | | 3 |
| 78 | 100 | — | — | ONE OF US (WILL WEEP TONIGHT) — Patti Page, Mercury 71639 | S | 2 |
| 79 | 63 | 69 | 83 | COTTAGE FOR SALE — Little Willie John, King 5342 | | 6 |
| 80 | 86 | 92 | 91 | LA MONTANA — Frank De Vol, Columbia 41620 | | 5 |
| 81 | 96 | — | — | BANJO BOY — Jan and Kjeld, Kapp 336 | | 2 |
| 82 | — | — | — | TUXEDO JUNCTION — Frankie Avalon, Chancellor 1052 | | 1 |
| 83 | 84 | 88 | 98 | SHADOWS OF LOVE — LaVern Baker, Atlantic 2059 | | 4 |
| 84 | — | — | — | MISSION BELL — Donnie Brooks, Era 3018 | | 1 |
| 85 | 94 | 95 | — | COMIN' DOWN WITH LOVE — Mel Gadson, Big Top 3034 | | 3 |
| 86 | — | — | — | TELL LAURA I LOVE HER — Ray Peterson, RCA Victor 7745 | | 1 |
| 87 | — | — | — | ALL THE LOVE I GOT — Marv Johnson, United Artists 226 | | 1 |
| 88 | — | — | — | BANJO BOY — Dorothy Collins, Top Rank 2052 | | 1 |
| 89 | — | — | — | WHERE ARE YOU — Frankie Avalon, Chancellor 1052 | | 1 |
| 90 | — | — | — | TROUBLE IN PARADISE — Crests, Coed 531 | | 1 |
| 91 | 93 | — | — | HEARTBREAK (IT'S HURTIN' ME) — Jon Thomas, ABC-Paramount 10122 | | 2 |
| 92 | — | 97 | — | BIG BOY PETE — The Olympics, Arvee 595 | | 2 |
| 93 | — | — | — | IS A BLUEBIRD BLUE — Conway Twitty, M-G-M 12911 | | 1 |
| 94 | — | 90 | 100 | MOJO WORKOUT — Larry Bright, Tide 006 | | 3 |
| 95 | 97 | — | — | BIOLOGY — Danny Valentino, M-G-M 12881 | | 2 |
| 96 | 91 | 99 | — | AIN'T GONNA BE THAT WAY — Marv Johnson, United Artists 262 | | 3 |
| 97 | 87 | 79 | 87 | I'LL BE SEEING YOU — Five Satins, Ember 1061 | | 6 |
| 98 | 66 | 73 | 59 | RIGHT BY MY SIDE — Ricky Nelson, Imperial 5663 | | 6 |
| 99 | — | — | — | THERE IS SOMETHING ON YOUR MIND — Bobby Marchan, Fire 1022 | | 1 |
| 100 | — | — | — | BANJO BOY — Art Mooney, M-G-M 12908 | | 1 |

STAR PERFORMERS showed the greatest upward progress on Hot 100 this week.
S — Indicates that 45 r.p.m. stereo single version is available.
A — Indicates that 33⅓ r.p.m. stereo single version is available.

# The Billboard HOT 100

**JUNE 20, 1960** — For Week Ending June 26

STAR PERFORMERS showed the greatest upward progress on Hot 100 this week.
Ⓢ Indicates that 45 r.p.m. stereo single version is available.
Ⓐ Indicates that 33⅓ r.p.m. stereo single version is available.

Columns: THIS WEEK | ONE WEEK AGO | TWO WEEKS AGO | THREE WEEKS AGO | TITLE — Artist, Company, Record No. | STEREO | WEEKS ON CHART

| TW | 1W | 2W | 3W | Title — Artist, Company, Record No. | Stereo | Wks |
|---|---|---|---|---|---|---|
| 1 | 1 | 1 | 1 | CATHY'S CLOWN — Everly Brothers, Warner Bros. 5151 | S | 10 |
| 2 | 2 | 8 | 20 | EVERYBODY'S SOMEBODY'S FOOL — Connie Francis, M-G-M 12899 | | 7 |
| 3 | 3 | 5 | 9 | BURNING BRIDGES — Jack Scott, Top Rank 2041 | | 10 |
| 4 | 4 | 3 | 3 | GOOD TIMIN' — Jimmy Jones, Cub 9067 | | 10 |
| 5 | 9 | 13 | 15 | SWINGING SCHOOL — Bobby Rydell, Cameo 175 | | 7 |
| ★6 | 12 | 55 | 85 | ALLEY-OOP — Hollywood Argyles, Lute 5905 | | 4 |
| 7 | 5 | 6 | 7 | PAPER ROSES — Anita Bryant, Carlton 528 | S | 11 |
| 8 | 7 | 9 | 14 | LOVE YOU SO — Rod Holden, Donna 1315 | | 12 |
| 9 | 6 | 4 | 4 | HE'LL HAVE TO STAY — Jeanne Black, Capitol 4368 | | 8 |
| 10 | 8 | 2 | 2 | STUCK ON YOU — Elvis Presley, RCA Victor 740 | S | 12 |
| 11 | 13 | 23 | 42 | BECAUSE THEY'RE YOUNG — Duane Eddy, Jamie 1156 | | 5 |
| 12 | 16 | 37 | 57 | MY HOME TOWN — Paul Anka, ABC-Paramount 10106 | | 5 |
| 13 | 20 | 27 | 49 | A ROCKIN' GOOD WAY — Dinah Washington and Brook Benton, Mercury 71629 | S | 5 |
| ★14 | 23 | 38 | 76 | I'M SORRY — Brenda Lee, Decca 31093 | | 4 |
| 15 | 19 | 19 | 21 | WONDERFUL WORLD — Sam Cooke, Keen 82112 | | 7 |
| 16 | 10 | 17 | 27 | HAPPY-GO-LUCKY ME — Paul Evans, Guaranteed 208 | S | 7 |
| 17 | 11 | 7 | 6 | NIGHT — Jackie Wilson, Brunswick 55166 | | 14 |
| 18 | 14 | 14 | 12 | YOUNG EMOTIONS — Ricky Nelson, Imperial 5663 | | 9 |
| ★19 | 24 | 22 | 43 | JEALOUS OF YOU — Connie Francis, M-G-M 12899 | | 5 |
| ★20 | 28 | 75 | 94 | ALLEY-OOP — Dante and the Evergreens, Madison 130 | | 4 |
| 21 | 25 | 57 | 72 | MULE SKINNER BLUES — Fendermen, Soma 1137 | | 5 |
| 22 | 30 | 32 | 38 | ANOTHER SLEEPLESS NIGHT — Jimmy Clanton, Ace 585 | | 9 |
| 23 | 15 | 10 | 5 | GREENFIELDS — Brothers Four, Columbia 41571 | A | 18 |
| 24 | 17 | 11 | 8 | SIXTEEN REASONS — Connie Stevens, Warner Bros. 5137 | | 21 |
| 25 | 32 | 35 | 26 | LONELY WEEKENDS — Charlie Rich, Philips International 3552 | | 15 |
| 26 | 18 | 16 | 11 | CHERRY PIE — Skip and Flip, Brent 7010 | | 12 |
| 27 | 22 | 18 | 18 | DING-A-LING — Bobby Rydell, Cameo 175 | | 7 |
| 28 | 29 | 29 | 32 | JUMP OVER — Freddy Cannon, Swan 4053 | | 7 |
| 29 | 31 | 31 | 36 | MACK THE KNIFE — Ella Fitzgerald, Verve 10209 | S | 8 |
| 30 | 34 | 40 | 64 | I REALLY DON'T WANT TO KNOW — Tommy Edwards, M-G-M 12890 | | 5 |
| ★31 | 44 | 88 | — | ONLY THE LONELY — Roy Orbison, Monument 421 | | 2 |
| 32 | 27 | 12 | 10 | CRADLE OF LOVE — Johnny Preston, Mercury 71598 | | 13 |
| 33 | 41 | 43 | 52 | (WON'T YOU COME HOME) BILL BAILEY — Bobby Darin, Atco 6167 | | 5 |
| 34 | 38 | 42 | 53 | PLEASE HELP ME, I'M FALLING — Hank Locklin, RCA Victor 7692 | | 5 |
| 35 | 21 | 21 | 25 | DOGGIN' AROUND — Jackie Wilson, Brunswick 55166 | | 12 |
| ★36 | 55 | 78 | — | THAT'S ALL YOU GOTTA DO — Brenda Lee, Decca 31093 | | 3 |
| 37 | 45 | 90 | — | TRAIN OF LOVE — Annette, Vista 359 | | 3 |
| 38 | 26 | 15 | 13 | LET THE LITTLE GIRL DANCE — Billy Bland, Old Town 1076 | | 19 |
| ★39 | 50 | 67 | 80 | PENNIES FROM HEAVEN — Skyliners, Calico 117 | | 7 |
| 40 | 33 | 39 | 48 | ALL I COULD DO WAS CRY — Etta James, Argo 5359 | | 8 |
| 41 | 42 | 71 | 83 | RUNAROUND — Fleetwoods, Dolton 22 | | 5 |
| 42 | 43 | 45 | 65 | THEME FOR YOUNG LOVERS — Percy Faith, Columbia 41655 | | 7 |
| 43 | 48 | 28 | 16 | SINK THE BISMARCK — Johnny Horton, Columbia 41568 | A | 16 |
| 44 | 49 | 50 | 77 | THEME FROM THE UNFORGIVEN — Don Costa, United Artists 221 | | 8 |
| 45 | 47 | 56 | 59 | I'M WALKIN' THE FLOOR OVER YOU — Pat Boone, Dot 16073 | | 5 |
| 46 | 36 | 30 | 31 | DUTCHMAN'S GOLD — Walter Brennan and Billy Vaughn, Dot 16066 | | 9 |
| 47 | 52 | 62 | 98 | SOMETHING HAPPENED — Paul Anka, ABC-Paramount 10106 | | 4 |
| 48 | 37 | 41 | 39 | MR. LUCKY — Henry Mancini, RCA Victor 7705 | S | 12 |
| ★49 | 63 | 76 | 81 | DOWN YONDER — Johnny and the Hurricanes, Big Top 3036 | | 4 |
| 50 | 54 | 54 | 86 | SPRING RAIN — Pat Boone, Dot 16073 | | 4 |
| 51 | 39 | 20 | 17 | STAIRWAY TO HEAVEN — Neil Sedaka, RCA Victor 7709 | S | 13 |
| 52 | 78 | 100 | — | ONE OF US (WILL WEEP TONIGHT) — Patti Page, Mercury 71639 | S | 3 |
| 53 | 58 | 83 | 87 | CLAP YOUR HANDS — Beau-Marks, Shad 5017 | | 6 |
| 54 | 40 | 26 | 19 | THE OLD LAMPLIGHTER — The Browns, RCA Victor 7700 | S | 15 |
| 55 | 35 | 24 | 22 | MOUNTAIN OF LOVE — Harold Dorman, Rita 1003 | | 17 |
| 56 | 51 | 48 | 34 | OOH POO PAH DOO (Part 2) — Jessie Hill, Minit 607 | | 13 |
| 57 | — | — | — | WALKING TO NEW ORLEANS — Fats Domino, Imperial 5675 | | 1 |
| 58 | 56 | 53 | 66 | NATIONAL CITY — Joiner, Arkansas Jr. High School Band, Liberty 55244 | | 6 |
| 59 | 57 | 47 | 50 | WHEN YOU WISH UPON A STAR — Dion and the Belmonts, Laurie 3052 | | 9 |
| 60 | — | — | — | I'M GETTIN' BETTER — Jim Reeves, RCA Victor 7756 | | 1 |
| 61 | 64 | 68 | 70 | PINK CHIFFON — Mitchell Torok, Guyden 2034 | | 7 |
| 62 | 73 | 95 | — | IMAGE OF A GIRL — Safaris, Eldo 101 | | 3 |
| 63 | 71 | 82 | 96 | WHEN WILL I BE LOVED — Everly Brothers, Cadence 1380 | | 4 |
| 64 | 70 | 80 | 89 | LONELY WINDS — Drifters, Atlantic 2062 | | 5 |
| 65 | 69 | 72 | 75 | EXCLUSIVELY YOURS — Carl Dobkins Jr., Decca 31088 | | 6 |
| 66 | 60 | 46 | 46 | BARBARA — Temptations, Goldisc 3001 | | 10 |
| 67 | 72 | 89 | — | HEY, LITTLE ONE — Dorsey Burnett, Era 3019 | | 3 |
| 68 | 59 | 92 | — | ALLEY-OOP — Dyna-Sores, Rendezvous 120 | | 3 |
| 69 | 66 | 59 | 56 | EBB TIDE — Platters, Mercury 71624 | | 6 |
| 70 | 81 | 96 | — | BANJO BOY — Jan aad Kjeld, Kapp 335 | | 3 |
| 71 | 61 | 52 | 28 | MADISON — Al Brown's Tunetoppers, Amy 804 | | 12 |
| 72 | 86 | — | — | TELL LAURA I LOVE HER — Ray Peterson, RCA Victor 7745 | | 2 |
| 73 | 76 | — | — | MR. LONELY — Videls, JDS 5004 | | 2 |
| 74 | 74 | 64 | 67 | FINGER POPPIN' TIME — Hank Ballard and the Midnighters, King 5341 | | 6 |
| 75 | 85 | 94 | 95 | COMIN' DOWN WITH LOVE — Mel Gadson, Big Top 3034 | | 4 |
| ★76 | 93 | — | — | IS A BLUEBIRD BLUE — Conway Twitty, M-G-M 12911 | | 2 |
| 77 | 80 | 86 | 92 | LA MONTANA — Frank De Vol, Columbia 41620 | | 6 |
| 78 | 65 | 36 | 30 | NOBODY LOVES ME LIKE YOU — Flamingos, End 1068 | | 10 |
| 79 | 88 | — | — | BANJO BOY — Dorothy Collins, Top Rank 2052 | | 2 |
| 80 | 87 | — | — | ALL THE LOVE I GOT — Marv Johnson, United Artists 226 | | 2 |
| 81 | 75 | 74 | 71 | ALWAYS IT'S YOU — Everly Brothers, Warner Bros. 5151 | S | 6 |
| 82 | 62 | 61 | 29 | GOT A GIRL — Four Preps, Capitol 4362 | | 10 |
| 83 | 90 | — | — | TROUBLE IN PARADISE — Crests, Coed 531 | | 2 |
| 84 | 89 | — | — | WHERE ARE YOU — Frankie Avalon, Chancellor 1052 | | 2 |
| 85 | — | — | — | LOOK FOR A STAR — Dean Hawley, Dore 554 | | 1 |
| 86 | — | 81 | 78 | HOT ROD LINCOLN — Charlie Ryan, Four Star 1733 | | 6 |
| 87 | — | — | — | WAKE ME, SHAKE ME — Coasters, Atco 6168 | | 1 |
| 88 | — | — | — | LOOK FOR A STAR — Garry Miles, Liberty 55261 | | 1 |
| 89 | — | — | — | THIS BITTER EARTH — Dinah Washington, Mercury 71635 | | 1 |
| 90 | 99 | — | — | THERE IS SOMETHING ON YOUR MIND — Bobby Marchan, Fire 1022 | | 2 |
| 91 | 96 | 91 | 99 | AIN'T GONNA BE THAT WAY — Marv Johnson, United Artists 262 | | 4 |
| 92 | — | — | — | LOOK FOR A STAR — Billy Vaughn, Dot 16106 | | 1 |
| 93 | 82 | — | — | TUXEDO JUNCTION — Frankie Avalon, Chancellor 1052 | | 2 |
| 94 | — | — | — | I CAN'T HELP IT — Adam Wade, Coed 530 | | 1 |
| 95 | — | — | — | BAD MAN BLUNDER — Kingston Trio, Capitol 4379 | | 1 |
| 96 | 84 | — | — | MISSION BELL — Donnie Brooks, Era 3018 | | 2 |
| 97 | — | — | — | IS THERE ANY CHANCE — Marty Robbins, Columbia 41686 | | 1 |
| 98 | — | — | — | FEEL SO FINE — Johnny Preston, Mercury 71651 | | 1 |
| 99 | — | — | — | LOOK FOR A STAR — Gary Mills, Imperial 5674 | | 1 |
| 100 | 100 | — | — | BANJO BOY — Art Mooney, M-G-M 12908 | | 2 |

# The Billboard HOT 100

**FOR WEEK ENDING JULY 3** — June 27, 1960

STAR PERFORMERS showed the greatest upward progress on Hot 100 this week.
(S) Indicates that 45 r.p.m. stereo single version is available.
(A) Indicates that 33⅓ r.p.m. stereo single version is available.

| This Week | 1 Wk Ago | 2 Wks Ago | 3 Wks Ago | Title / Artist, Company, Record No. | Stereo | Weeks on Chart |
|---|---|---|---|---|---|---|
| 1 | 2 | 2 | 8 | EVERYBODY'S SOMEBODY'S FOOL — Connie Francis, M-G-M 12899 | | 8 |
| 2 | 1 | 1 | 1 | CATHY'S CLOWN — Everly Brothers, Warner Bros. 5151 | S | 11 |
| 3 | 6 | 12 | 55 | ALLEY-OOP — Hollywood Argyles, Lute 5905 | | 5 |
| 4 | 3 | 3 | 5 | BURNING BRIDGES — Jack Scott, Top Rank 2041 | | 11 |
| ★5 | 11 | 13 | 23 | BECAUSE THEY'RE YOUNG — Duane Eddy, Jamie 1156 | | 6 |
| 6 | 14 | 23 | 38 | I'M SORRY — Brenda Lee, Decca 31093 | | 5 |
| 7 | 13 | 20 | 27 | A ROCKIN' GOOD WAY — Dinah Washington and Brook Benton, Mercury 71629 | S | 6 |
| 8 | 7 | 5 | 6 | PAPER ROSES — Anita Bryant, Carlton 528 | S | 12 |
| 9 | 4 | 4 | 3 | GOOD TIMIN' — Jimmy Jones, Cub 9067 | | 11 |
| 10 | 5 | 9 | 13 | SWINGING SCHOOL — Bobby Rydell, Cameo 175 | | 8 |
| 11 | 12 | 16 | 37 | MY HOME TOWN — Paul Anka, ABC-Paramount 10106 | | 6 |
| 12 | 15 | 19 | 19 | WONDERFUL WORLD — Sam Cooke, Keen 82112 | | 8 |
| 13 | 8 | 7 | 9 | LOVE YOU SO — Rod Holden, Donna 1315 | | 13 |
| 14 | 16 | 10 | 17 | HAPPY-GO-LUCKY ME — Paul Evans, Guaranteed 208 | S | 8 |
| ★15 | 21 | 25 | 57 | MULE SKINNER BLUES — Fendermen, Soma 1137 | | 6 |
| 16 | 20 | 28 | 75 | ALLEY-OOP — Dante and the Evergreens, Madison 130 | | 5 |
| ★17 | 36 | 55 | 78 | THAT'S ALL YOU GOTTA DO — Brenda Lee, Decca 31093 | | 4 |
| 18 | 18 | 14 | 14 | YOUNG EMOTIONS — Ricky Nelson, Imperial 5663 | | 10 |
| 19 | 9 | 6 | 4 | HE'LL HAVE TO STAY — Jeanne Black, Capitol 4368 | | 9 |
| 20 | 19 | 24 | 22 | JEALOUS OF YOU — Connie Francis, M-G-M 12899 | | 6 |
| ★21 | 33 | 41 | 43 | (WON'T YOU COME HOME) BILL BAILEY — Bobby Darin, Atco 6167 | | 6 |
| 22 | 10 | 8 | 2 | STUCK ON YOU — Elvis Presley, RCA Victor 7740 | S | 13 |
| 23 | 31 | 44 | 88 | ONLY THE LONELY — Roy Orbison, Monument 421 | | 3 |
| ★24 | 34 | 38 | 42 | PLEASE HELP ME, I'M FALLING — Hank Locklin, RCA Victor 7692 | | 6 |
| 25 | 30 | 34 | 40 | I REALLY DON'T WANT TO KNOW — Tommy Edwards, M-G-M 12890 | | 6 |
| 26 | 27 | 22 | 18 | DING-A-LING — Bobby Rydell, Cameo 175 | | 8 |
| 27 | 29 | 31 | 31 | MACK THE KNIFE — Ella Fitzgerald, Verve 10209 | S | 9 |
| 28 | 22 | 30 | 32 | ANOTHER SLEEPLESS NIGHT — Jimmy Clanton, Ace 585 | | 10 |
| ★29 | 41 | 42 | 71 | RUNAROUND — Fleetwoods, Dolton 22 | | 6 |
| 30 | 17 | 11 | 7 | NIGHT — Jackie Wilson, Brunswick 55166 | | 15 |
| 31 | 24 | 17 | 11 | SIXTEEN REASONS — Connie Stevens, Warner Bros. 5137 | | 22 |
| 32 | 39 | 50 | 67 | PENNIES FROM HEAVEN — Skyliners, Calico 117 | | 8 |
| 33 | 26 | 18 | 16 | CHERRY PIE — Skip and Flip, Brent 7010 | | 13 |
| 34 | 25 | 32 | 35 | LONELY WEEKENDS — Charlie Rich, Philips International 3552 | | 16 |
| 35 | 42 | 43 | 45 | THEME FOR YOUNG LOVERS — Percy Faith, Columbia 41655 | | 8 |
| ★36 | 63 | 71 | 82 | WHEN WILL I BE LOVED — Everly Brothers, Cadence 1380 | | 5 |
| 37 | 44 | 49 | 50 | THEME FROM THE UNFORGIVEN — Don Costa, United Artists 221 | | 9 |
| 38 | 23 | 15 | 10 | GREENFIELDS — Brothers Four, Columbia 41571 | A | 19 |
| 39 | 40 | 33 | 39 | ALL I COULD DO WAS CRY — Etta James, Argo 5359 | | 9 |
| ★40 | 72 | 86 | — | TELL LAURA I LOVE HER — Ray Peterson, RCA Victor 7745 | | 3 |
| 41 | 47 | 52 | 62 | SOMETHING HAPPENED — Paul Anka, ABC-Paramount 10106 | | 5 |
| 42 | 52 | 78 | 100 | ONE OF US (WILL WEEP TONIGHT) — Patti Page, Mercury 71639 | S | 4 |
| 43 | 37 | 45 | 90 | TRAIN OF LOVE — Annette, Vista 359 | | 4 |
| 44 | 45 | 47 | 56 | I'M WALKIN' THE FLOOR OVER YOU — Pat Boone, Dot 16073 | | 6 |
| 45 | 32 | 27 | 12 | CRADLE OF LOVE — Johnny Preston, Mercury 71598 | | 14 |
| ★46 | 57 | — | — | WALKIN' TO NEW ORLEANS — Fats Domino, Imperial 5675 | | 2 |
| 47 | 55 | 35 | 24 | MOUNTAIN OF LOVE — Harold Dorman, Rita 1003 | | 18 |
| ★48 | 60 | — | — | I'M GETTIN' BETTER — Jim Reeves, RCA Victor 7756 | | 2 |
| 49 | 49 | 63 | 76 | DOWN YONDER — Johnny and the Hurricanes, Big Top 3036 | | 5 |
| 50 | 50 | 54 | 54 | SPRING RAIN — Pat Boone, Dot 16073 | | 5 |
| 51 | 53 | 58 | 83 | CLAP YOUR HANDS — Beau-Marks, Shad 5017 | | 7 |
| 52 | 28 | 29 | 29 | JUMP OVER — Freddy Cannon, Swan 4053 | | 8 |
| 53 | 62 | 73 | 95 | IMAGE OF A GIRL — Safaris, Eldo 101 | | 4 |
| 54 | 46 | 36 | 30 | DUTCHMAN'S GOLD — Walter Brennan and Billy Vaughn, Dot 16066 | | 10 |
| 55 | 35 | 21 | 21 | DOGGIN' AROUND — Jackie Wilson, Brunswick 55166 | | 13 |
| 56 | 38 | 26 | 15 | LET THE LITTLE GIRL DANCE — Billy Bland, Old Town 1076 | | 20 |
| 57 | 64 | 70 | 80 | LONELY WINDS — Drifters, Atlantic 2062 | | 6 |
| 58 | 56 | 51 | 48 | OOH POO PAH DOO (Part 2) — Jessie Hill, Minit 607 | | 14 |
| 59 | 58 | 56 | 53 | NATIONAL CITY — Joiner, Arkansas Jr. High School Band, Liberty 55244 | | 7 |
| 60 | 61 | 64 | 68 | PINK CHIFFON — Mitchell Torok, Guyden 2034 | | 8 |
| ★61 | 76 | 93 | — | IS A BLUEBIRD BLUE — Conway Twitty, M-G-M 12911 | | 3 |
| 62 | 65 | 69 | 72 | EXCLUSIVELY YOURS — Carl Dobkins Jr., Decca 31088 | | 7 |
| 63 | 70 | 81 | 96 | BANJO BOY — Jan and Kjeld, Kapp 335 | | 4 |
| 64 | 74 | 74 | 64 | FINGER POPPIN' TIME — Hank Ballard and the Midnighters, King 5341 | | 7 |
| 65 | 67 | 72 | 89 | HEY, LITTLE ONE — Dorsey Burnett, Era 3019 | | 4 |
| ★66 | 88 | — | — | LOOK FOR A STAR — Garry Miles, Liberty 55261 | | 2 |
| 67 | 51 | 39 | 20 | STAIRWAY TO HEAVEN — Neil Sedaka, RCA Victor 7709 | S | 14 |
| 68 | 85 | — | — | LOOK FOR A STAR — Dean Hawley, Dore 554 | | 2 |
| 69 | 75 | 85 | 94 | COMIN' DOWN WITH LOVE — Mel Gadson, Big Top 3034 | | 5 |
| 70 | 43 | 48 | 28 | SINK THE BISMARCK — Johnny Horton, Columbia 41568 | A | 17 |
| 71 | — | — | — | JOSEPHINE — Bill Black's Combo, Hi 2022 | | 1 |
| 72 | 84 | 89 | — | WHERE ARE YOU — Frankie Avalon, Chancellor 1052 | | 3 |
| 73 | 92 | — | — | LOOK FOR A STAR — Billy Vaughn, Dot 16106 | | 2 |
| 74 | 83 | 90 | — | TROUBLE IN PARADISE — Crests, Coed 531 | | 3 |
| 75 | 80 | 87 | — | ALL THE LOVE I GOT — Marv Johnson, United Artists 226 | | 3 |
| 76 | 95 | — | — | BAD MAN BLUNDER — Kingston Trio, Capitol 4375 | | 2 |
| 77 | 87 | — | — | WAKE ME, SHAKE ME — Coasters, Atco 6168 | | 2 |
| 78 | 99 | — | — | LOOK FOR A STAR — Gary Mills, Imperial 5674 | | 2 |
| 79 | 94 | — | — | I CAN'T HELP IT — Adam Wade, Coed 530 | | 2 |
| 80 | 90 | 99 | — | THERE IS SOMETHING ON YOUR MIND — Bobby Marchan, Fire 1022 | | 3 |
| 81 | 89 | — | — | THIS BITTER EARTH — Dinah Washington, Mercury 71635 | | 2 |
| 82 | 91 | 96 | 91 | AIN'T GONNA BE THAT WAY — Marv Johnson, United Artists 226 | | 5 |
| 83 | 97 | — | — | IS THERE ANY CHANCE — Marty Robbins, Columbia 41686 | | 2 |
| 84 | 79 | 88 | — | BANJO BOY — Dorothy Collins, Top Rank 2052 | | 3 |
| 85 | — | — | — | QUESTION — Lloyd Price, ABC-Paramount 10123 | | 1 |
| 86 | — | — | — | YOU'VE GOT THE POWER — James Brown and the Famous Flames, Federal 12370 | | 1 |
| 87 | — | 77 | 79 | HEARTBREAK (IT'S HURTIN' ME) — Little Willie John, King 5356 | | 4 |
| 88 | — | — | — | FOUND LOVE — Jimmy Reed, Vee Jay 347 | | 3 |
| 89 | — | — | — | THERE'S A STAR-SPANGLED BANNER WAVING SOMEWHERE, NO. 2 (THE BALLAD OF FRANCIS G. POWERS) — Red River Dave, Savoy 3020 | | 1 |
| 90 | — | 91 | 93 | HEARTBREAK (IT'S HURTIN' ME) — Jon Thomas, ABC-Paramount 10122 | | 3 |
| 91 | — | — | — | MARIA — Johnny Mathis, Columbia 41684 | | 2 |
| 92 | — | — | — | STICKS AND STONES — Ray Charles, ABC-Paramount 10118 | | 1 |
| 93 | 48 | 37 | 41 | MR. LUCKY — Henry Mancini, RCA Victor 7705 | S | 13 |
| 94 | — | 46 | 33 | THINK — James Brown and the Famous Flames, Federal 12370 | | 8 |
| 95 | 98 | — | — | FEEL SO FINE — Johnny Preston, Mercury 71651 | | 2 |
| 96 | — | — | — | DON'T COME KNOCKIN' — Fats Domino, Imperial 5675 | | 1 |
| 97 | — | — | — | BORN TO BE LOVED — Billy Bland, Old Town 1082 | | 1 |
| 98 | — | — | — | I'VE BEEN LOVED BEFORE — Shirley and Lee, Warwick 535 | | 1 |
| 99 | 73 | 76 | — | MR. LONELY — Videls, JDS 5004 | | 3 |
| 100 | 96 | 84 | — | MISSION BELL — Donnie Brooks, Era 3018 | | 3 |

# The Billboard HOT 100

**FOR WEEK ENDING JULY 10**

*July 4, 1960*

STAR PERFORMERS showed the greatest upward progress on Hot 100 this week.
Ⓢ Indicates that 45 r.p.m. stereo single version is available.
Ⓐ Indicates that 33⅓ r.p.m. stereo single version is available.

Columns: THIS WEEK | ONE WEEK AGO | TWO WEEKS AGO | THREE WEEKS AGO | TITLE — Artist, Company, Record No. | STEREO | WEEKS ON CHART

| # | 1wk | 2wk | 3wk | Title — Artist, Company, Record No. | Stereo | Wks |
|---|---|---|---|---|---|---|
| 1 | 1 | 2 | 2 | EVERYBODY'S SOMEBODY'S FOOL — Connie Francis, M-G-M 12899 | | 9 |
| 2 | 3 | 6 | 12 | ALLEY-OOP — Hollywood Argyles, Lute 5905 | | 6 |
| 3 | 6 | 14 | 23 | I'M SORRY — Brenda Lee, Decca 31092 | | 6 |
| 4 | 5 | 11 | 13 | BECAUSE THEY'RE YOUNG — Duane Eddy, Jamie 1156 | | 7 |
| 5 | 2 | 1 | 1 | CATHY'S CLOWN — Everly Brothers, Warner Bros. 5151 | Ⓢ | 12 |
| 6 | 17 | 36 | 55 | THAT'S ALL YOU GOTTA DO — Brenda Lee, Decca 31093 | | 5 |
| 7 | 4 | 3 | 3 | BURNING BRIDGES — Jack Scott, Top Rank 2041 | | 12 |
| 8 | 11 | 12 | 16 | MY HOME TOWN — Paul Anka, ABC-Paramount 10106 | | 7 |
| 9 | 15 | 21 | 25 | MULE SKINNER BLUES — Fendermen, Soma 1137 | | 7 |
| 10 | 7 | 13 | 20 | A ROCKIN' GOOD WAY — Dinah Washington and Brook Benton, Mercury 71629 | Ⓢ | 7 |
| 11 | 23 | 31 | 44 | ONLY THE LONELY — Roy Orbison, Monument 421 | | 4 |
| 12 | 12 | 15 | 19 | WONDERFUL WORLD — Sam Cooke, Keen 82112 | | 9 |
| 13 | 8 | 7 | 5 | PAPER ROSES — Anita Bryant, Carlton 528 | Ⓢ | 13 |
| 14 | 14 | 16 | 10 | HAPPY-GO-LUCKY ME — Paul Evans, Guaranteed 208 | Ⓢ | 9 |
| 15 | 16 | 20 | 28 | ALLEY-OOP — Dante and the Evergreens, Madison 130 | | 6 |
| 16 | 24 | 34 | 38 | PLEASE HELP ME, I'M FALLING — Hank Locklin, RCA Victor 7692 | | 7 |
| 17 | 9 | 4 | 4 | GOOD TIMIN' — Jimmy Jones, Cub 9067 | | 12 |
| 18 | 25 | 30 | 34 | I REALLY DON'T WANT TO KNOW — Tommy Edwards, M-G-M 12890 | | 7 |
| 19 | 21 | 33 | 41 | (WON'T YOU COME HOME) BILL BAILEY — Bobby Darin, Atco 6167 | | 7 |
| 20 | 36 | 63 | 71 | WHEN WILL I BE LOVED — Everly Brothers, Cadence 1380 | | 6 |
| 21 | 10 | 5 | 9 | SWINGING SCHOOL — Bobby Rydell, Cameo 175 | | 9 |
| 22 | 40 | 72 | 86 | TELL LAURA I LOVE HER — Ray Peterson, RCA Victor 7745 | | 4 |
| 23 | 20 | 19 | 24 | JEALOUS OF YOU — Connie Francis, M-G-M 12899 | | 7 |
| 24 | 13 | 8 | 7 | LOVE YOU SO — Rod Holden, Donna 1315 | | 14 |
| 25 | 29 | 41 | 42 | RUNAROUND — Fleetwoods, Dolton 22 | | 7 |
| 26 | 18 | 18 | 14 | YOUNG EMOTIONS — Ricky Nelson, Imperial 5663 | | 11 |
| 27 | 37 | 44 | 49 | THEME FROM THE UNFORGIVEN — Don Costa, United Artists 221 | | 10 |
| 28 | 27 | 29 | 31 | MACK THE KNIFE — Ella Fitzgerald, Verve 10209 | Ⓢ | 10 |
| 29 | 32 | 39 | 50 | PENNIES FROM HEAVEN — Skyliners, Calico 117 | | 9 |
| 30 | 19 | 9 | 6 | HE'LL HAVE TO STAY — Jeanne Black, Capitol 4368 | | 10 |
| 31 | 46 | 57 | — | WALKIN' TO NEW ORLEANS — Fats Domino, Imperial 5675 | | 3 |
| 32 | 26 | 27 | 22 | DING-A-LING — Bobby Rydell, Cameo 175 | | 9 |
| 33 | 71 | — | — | JOSEPHINE — Bill Black's Combo, Hi 2022 | | 2 |
| 34 | 42 | 52 | 78 | ONE OF US (WILL WEEP TONIGHT) — Patti Page, Mercury 71639 | Ⓢ | 5 |
| 35 | 66 | 88 | — | LOOK FOR A STAR — Garry Miles, Liberty 55261 | | 3 |
| 36 | 28 | 22 | 30 | ANOTHER SLEEPLESS NIGHT — Jimmy Clanton, Ace 585 | | 11 |
| 37 | 68 | 85 | — | LOOK FOR A STAR — Dean Hawley, Dore 554 | | 3 |
| 38 | 43 | 37 | 45 | TRAIN OF LOVE — Annette, Vista 359 | | 5 |
| 39 | 22 | 10 | 8 | STUCK ON YOU — Elvis Presley, RCA Victor 7740 | Ⓢ | 14 |
| 40 | 31 | 24 | 17 | SIXTEEN REASONS — Connie Stevens, Warner Bros. 5137 | | 23 |
| 41 | 41 | 47 | 52 | SOMETHING HAPPENED — Paul Anka, ABC-Paramount 10106 | | 6 |
| 42 | 48 | 60 | — | I'M GETTIN' BETTER — Jim Reeves, RCA Victor 7756 | | 3 |
| 43 | 53 | 62 | 73 | IMAGE OF A GIRL — Safaris, Eldo 101 | | 5 |
| 44 | 30 | 17 | 11 | NIGHT — Jackie Wilson, Brunswick 55166 | | 16 |
| 45 | 38 | 23 | 15 | GREENFIELDS — Brothers Four, Columbia 41571 | Ⓐ | 20 |
| 46 | 80 | 90 | 99 | THERE IS SOMETHING ON YOUR MIND — Bobby Marchan, Fire 1022 | | 4 |
| 47 | 34 | 25 | 32 | LONELY WEEKENDS — Charlie Rich, Philips International 3552 | | 17 |
| 48 | 49 | 49 | 63 | DOWN YONDER — Johnny and the Hurricanes, Big Top 3036 | | 6 |
| 49 | 51 | 53 | 58 | CLAP YOUR HANDS — Beau-Marks, Shad 5017 | | 8 |
| 50 | 61 | 76 | 93 | IS A BLUEBIRD BLUE — Conway Twitty, M-G-M 12911 | | 4 |
| 51 | 39 | 40 | 33 | ALL I COULD DO WAS CRY — Etta James, Argo 5359 | | 10 |
| 52 | 35 | 42 | 43 | THEME FOR YOUNG LOVERS — Percy Faith, Columbia 41655 | | 9 |
| 53 | 44 | 45 | 47 | I'M WALKIN' THE FLOOR OVER YOU — Pat Boone, Dot 16073 | | 7 |
| 54 | 57 | 64 | 70 | LONELY WINDS — Drifters, Atlantic 2062 | | 7 |
| 55 | 55 | 35 | 21 | DOGGIN' AROUND — Jackie Wilson, Brunswick 55166 | | 14 |
| 56 | 73 | 92 | — | LOOK FOR A STAR — Billy Vaughn, Dot 16106 | | 3 |
| 57 | 33 | 26 | 18 | CHERRY PIE — Skip and Flip, Brent 7010 | | 14 |
| 58 | 63 | 70 | 81 | BANJO BOY — Jan and Kjeld, Kapp 335 | | 5 |
| 59 | — | — | — | ITSY BITSY TEENIE WEENIE YELLOW POLKA DOT BIKINI — Brian Hyland, Leader 805 | | 1 |
| 60 | 64 | 74 | 74 | FINGER POPPIN' TIME — Hank Ballard and the Midnighters, King 5341 | | 8 |
| 61 | 65 | 67 | 72 | HEY, LITTLE ONE — Dorsey Burnette, Era 3019 | | 5 |
| 62 | 78 | 99 | — | LOOK FOR A STAR — Gary Mills, Imperial 5674 | | 3 |
| 63 | 50 | 50 | 54 | SPRING RAIN — Pat Boone, Dot 16073 | | 6 |
| 64 | 58 | 56 | 51 | OOH POO PAH DOO (Part 2) — Jessie Hill, Minit 607 | | 15 |
| 65 | 75 | 80 | 87 | ALL THE LOVE I GOT — Marv Johnson, United Artists 226 | | 4 |
| 66 | 76 | 95 | — | BAD MAN BLUNDER — Kingston Trio, Capitol 4375 | | 3 |
| 67 | 72 | 84 | 89 | WHERE ARE YOU — Frankie Avalon, Chancellor 1052 | | 4 |
| 68 | 74 | 83 | 90 | TROUBLE IN PARADISE — Crests, Coed 531 | | 4 |
| 69 | 79 | 94 | — | I CAN'T HELP IT — Adam Wade, Coed 530 | | 3 |
| 70 | 54 | 46 | 36 | DUTCHMAN'S GOLD — Walter Brennan and Billy Vaughn, Dot 16066 | | 11 |
| 71 | 77 | 87 | — | WAKE ME, SHAKE ME — Coasters, Atco 6168 | | 3 |
| 72 | 70 | 43 | 48 | SINK THE BISMARCK — Johnny Horton, Columbia 41568 | Ⓐ | 18 |
| 73 | 45 | 32 | 27 | CRADLE OF LOVE — Johnny Preston, Mercury 71598 | | 15 |
| 74 | 82 | 91 | 96 | I AIN'T GONNA BE THAT WAY — Marv Johnson, United Artists 226 | | 6 |
| 75 | 81 | 89 | — | THIS BITTER EARTH — Dinah Washington, Mercury 71635 | | 3 |
| 76 | 83 | 97 | — | IS THERE ANY CHANCE — Marty Robbins, Columbia 41686 | | 3 |
| 77 | 52 | 28 | 29 | JUMP OVER — Freddy Cannon, Swan 4053 | | 9 |
| 78 | — | — | — | MY TANI — Brothers Four, Columbia 41692 | | 1 |
| 79 | 100 | 96 | 84 | MISSION BELL — Donnie Brooks, Era 3018 | | 4 |
| 80 | 85 | — | — | QUESTION — Lloyd Price, ABC-Paramount 10123 | | 2 |
| 81 | 89 | — | — | THERE'S A STAR-SPANGLED BANNER WAVING SOMEWHERE, NO. 2 (THE BALLAD OF FRANCIS G. POWERS) — Red River Dave, Savoy 3020 | | 2 |
| 82 | — | — | — | JOHNNY FREEDOM — Johnny Horton, Columbia 41685 | | 1 |
| 83 | 87 | — | 77 | HEARTBREAK (IT'S HURTIN' ME) — Little Willie John, King 5356 | | 5 |
| 84 | 91 | — | — | MARIA — Johnny Mathis, Columbia 41684 | | 3 |
| 85 | 59 | 58 | 56 | NATIONAL CITY — Joiner, Arkansas, Jr. High School Band, Liberty 55244 | | 8 |
| 86 | 92 | — | — | STICKS AND STONES — Ray Charles, ABC-Paramount 10118 | | 2 |
| 87 | 62 | 65 | 69 | EXCLUSIVELY YOURS — Carl Dobkins Jr., Decca 31088 | | 8 |
| 88 | 47 | 55 | 35 | MOUNTAIN OF LOVE — Harold Dorman, Rita 1003 | | 19 |
| 89 | 90 | — | 91 | HEARTBREAK (IT'S HURTIN' ME) — Jon Thomas, ABC-Paramount 10122 | | 4 |
| 90 | 96 | — | — | DON'T COME KNOCKIN' — Fats Domino, Imperial 5675 | | 2 |
| 91 | — | — | — | ONE BOY — Joanie Sommers, Warner Bros. 5157 | | 1 |
| 92 | 95 | 98 | — | FEEL SO FINE — Johnny Preston, Mercury 71651 | | 3 |
| 93 | — | — | — | DO YOU MIND — Andy Williams, Cadence 1381 | | 1 |
| 94 | 97 | — | — | BORN TO BE LOVED — Billy Bland, Old Town 1082 | | 2 |
| 95 | — | — | — | I SHOT MR. LEE — Bobbettes, Triple-X 104 | | 1 |
| 96 | — | — | — | SECOND HONEYMOON — Johnny Cash, Columbia 41707 | | 1 |
| 97 | 67 | 51 | 39 | STAIRWAY TO HEAVEN — Neil Sedaka, RCA Victor 7709 | Ⓢ | 15 |
| 98 | — | — | — | TOO YOUNG TO GO STEADY — Connie Stevens, Warner Bros. 5159 | | 1 |
| 99 | 60 | 61 | 64 | PINK CHIFFON — Mitchell Torok, Guyden 2034 | | 9 |
| 100 | — | — | — | OVER THE RAINBOW — Dimensions, Mohawk 116 | | 1 |

# The Billboard HOT 100

**FOR WEEK ENDING JULY 17**

| This Week | 1 Wk Ago | 2 Wks Ago | 3 Wks Ago | Title / Artist, Company, Record No. | Weeks on Chart |
|---|---|---|---|---|---|
| 1 | 2 | 3 | 6 | ALLEY-OOP — Hollywood Argyles, Lute 5905 | 7 |
| 2 | 3 | 6 | 14 | I'M SORRY — Brenda Lee, Decca 31093 | 7 |
| 3 | 1 | 1 | 2 | EVERYBODY'S SOMEBODY'S FOOL — Connie Francis, M-G-M 12899 | 10 |
| 4 | 4 | 5 | 11 | BECAUSE THEY'RE YOUNG — Duane Eddy, Jamie 1156 | 8 |
| 5 | 9 | 15 | 21 | MULE SKINNER BLUES — Fendermen, Soma 1137 | 8 |
| 6 | 11 | 23 | 31 | ONLY THE LONELY — Roy Orbison, Monument 421 | 5 |
| 7 | 6 | 17 | 36 | THAT'S ALL YOU GOTTA DO — Brenda Lee, Decca 31093 | 6 |
| 8 | 8 | 11 | 12 | MY HOME TOWN — Paul Anka, ABC-Paramount 10106 | 8 |
| 9 | 10 | 7 | 13 | A ROCKIN' GOOD WAY — Dinah Washington and Brook Benton, Mercury 71629 | 8 |
| 10 | 20 | 36 | 63 | WHEN WILL I BE LOVED — Everly Brothers, Cadence 1380 | 7 |
| 11 | 7 | 4 | 3 | BURNING BRIDGES — Jack Scott, Top Rank 2041 | 13 |
| 12 | 22 | 40 | 72 | TELL LAURA I LOVE HER — Ray Peterson, RCA Victor 7745 | 5 |
| 13 | 5 | 2 | 1 | CATHY'S CLOWN — Everly Brothers, Warner Bros. 5151 | 13 |
| 14 | 16 | 24 | 34 | PLEASE HELP ME, I'M FALLING — Hank Locklin, RCA Victor 7692 | 8 |
| 15 | 15 | 16 | 20 | ALLEY-OOP — Dante and the Evergreens, Madison 130 | 7 |
| 16 | 13 | 8 | 7 | PAPER ROSES — Anita Bryant, Carlton 528 | 14 |
| 17 | 43 | 53 | 62 | IMAGE OF A GIRL — Safaris, Eldo 101 | 6 |
| 18 | 12 | 12 | 15 | WONDERFUL WORLD — Sam Cooke, Keen 82112 | 10 |
| 19 | 14 | 14 | 16 | HAPPY-GO-LUCKY ME — Paul Evans, Guaranteed 208 | 10 |
| 20 | 59 | — | — | ITSY BITSY TEENIE WEENIE YELLOW POLKA DOT BIKINI — Brian Hyland, Leader 805 | 2 |
| 21 | 31 | 46 | 57 | WALKIN' TO NEW ORLEANS — Fats Domino, Imperial 5675 | 4 |
| 22 | 24 | 13 | 8 | LOVE YOU SO — Rod Holden, Donna 1315 | 15 |
| 23 | 25 | 29 | 41 | RUNAROUND — Fleetwoods, Dolton 22 | 8 |
| 24 | 23 | 20 | 19 | JEALOUS OF YOU — Connie Francis, M-G-M 12899 | 8 |
| 25 | 35 | 66 | 88 | LOOK FOR A STAR — Garry Miles, Liberty 55261 | 4 |
| 26 | 29 | 32 | 39 | PENNIES FROM HEAVEN — Skyliners, Calico 117 | 10 |
| 27 | 27 | 37 | 44 | THEME FROM THE UNFORGIVEN — Don Costa, United Artists 221 | 11 |
| 28 | 33 | 71 | — | JOSEPHINE — Bill Black's Combo, Hi 2022 | 3 |
| 29 | 18 | 25 | 30 | I REALLY DON'T WANT TO KNOW — Tommy Edwards, M-G-M 12890 | 8 |
| 30 | 19 | 21 | 33 | (WON'T YOU COME HOME) BILL BAILEY — Bobby Darin, Atco 6167 | 8 |
| 31 | 34 | 42 | 52 | ONE OF US (WILL WEEP TONIGHT) — Patti Page, Mercury 71639 | 6 |
| 32 | 37 | 68 | 85 | LOOK FOR A STAR — Dean Hawley, Dore 554 | 4 |
| 33 | 46 | 80 | 90 | THERE IS SOMETHING ON YOUR MIND — Bobby Marchan, Fire 1022 | 5 |
| 34 | 79 | 100 | 96 | MISSION BELL — Donnie Brooks, Era 3018 | 5 |
| 35 | 17 | 9 | 4 | GOOD TIMIN' — Jimmy Jones, Cub 9067 | 13 |
| 36 | 38 | 43 | 37 | TRAIN OF LOVE — Annette, Vista 359 | 6 |
| 37 | 42 | 48 | 60 | I'M GETTIN' BETTER — Jim Reeves, RCA Victor 7756 | 4 |
| 38 | 21 | 10 | 5 | SWINGING SCHOOL — Bobby Rydell, Cameo 175 | 10 |
| 39 | 28 | 27 | 29 | MACK THE KNIFE — Ella Fitzgerald, Verve 10209 | 11 |
| 40 | 50 | 61 | 76 | IS A BLUEBIRD BLUE — Conway Twitty, M-G-M 12911 | 5 |
| 41 | 26 | 18 | 18 | YOUNG EMOTIONS — Ricky Nelson, Imperial 5663 | 12 |
| 42 | 75 | 81 | 89 | THIS BITTER EARTH — Dinah Washington, Mercury 71635 | 4 |
| 43 | 32 | 26 | 27 | DING-A-LING — Bobby Rydell, Cameo 175 | 10 |
| 44 | 36 | 28 | 22 | ANOTHER SLEEPLESS NIGHT — Jimmy Clanton, Ace 585 | 12 |
| 45 | 49 | 51 | 53 | CLAP YOUR HANDS — Beau-Marks, Shad 5017 | 9 |
| 46 | 56 | 73 | 92 | LOOK FOR A STAR — Billy Vaughn, Dot 16106 | 4 |
| 47 | 55 | 55 | 35 | DOGGIN' AROUND — Jackie Wilson, Brunswick 55166 | 15 |
| 48 | 51 | 39 | 40 | ALL I COULD DO WAS CRY — Etta James, Argo 5359 | 11 |
| 49 | 30 | 19 | 9 | HE'LL HAVE TO STAY — Jeanne Black, Capitol 4368 | 11 |
| 50 | 39 | 22 | 10 | STUCK ON YOU — Elvis Presley, RCA Victor 7740 | 15 |
| 51 | 41 | 41 | 47 | SOMETHING HAPPENED — Paul Anka, ABC-Paramount 10106 | 7 |
| 52 | 90 | 96 | — | DON'T COME KNOCKIN' — Fats Domino, Imperial 5675 | 3 |
| 53 | 60 | 64 | 74 | FINGER POPPIN' TIME — Hank Ballard and the Midnighters, King 5341 | 9 |
| 54 | 63 | 50 | 50 | SPRING RAIN — Pat Boone, Dot 16073 | 7 |
| 55 | 61 | 65 | 67 | HEY, LITTLE ONE — Dorsey Burnette, Era 3019 | 6 |
| 56 | 62 | 78 | 99 | LOOK FOR A STAR — Garry Mills, Imperial 5674 | 4 |
| 57 | 68 | 74 | 83 | TROUBLE IN PARADISE — Crests, Coed 531 | 5 |
| 58 | 80 | 85 | — | QUESTION — Lloyd Price, ABC-Paramount 10123 | 3 |
| 59 | 58 | 63 | 70 | BANJO BOY — Jan and Kjeld, Kapp 335 | 6 |
| 60 | 67 | 72 | 84 | WHERE ARE YOU — Frankie Avalon, Chancellor 1052 | 5 |
| 61 | 40 | 31 | 24 | SIXTEEN REASONS — Connie Stevens, Warner Bros. 5137 | 24 |
| 62 | 48 | 49 | 49 | DOWN YONDER — Johnny and the Hurricanes, Big Top 3036 | 7 |
| 63 | 65 | 75 | 80 | ALL THE LOVE I GOT — Marv Johnson, United Artists 226 | 5 |
| 64 | 66 | 76 | 95 | BAD MAN BLUNDER — Kingston Trio, Capitol 4375 | 4 |
| 65 | 47 | 34 | 25 | LONELY WEEKENDS — Charlie Rich, Philips International 3552 | 18 |
| 66 | 86 | 92 | — | STICKS AND STONES — Ray Charles, ABC-Paramount 10118 | 3 |
| 67 | 54 | 57 | 64 | LONELY WINDS — Drifters, Atlantic 2062 | 8 |
| 68 | 69 | 79 | 94 | I CAN'T HELP IT — Adam Wade, Coed 530 | 4 |
| 69 | 71 | 77 | 87 | WAKE ME, SHAKE ME — Coasters, Atco 6168 | 4 |
| 70 | 44 | 30 | 17 | NIGHT — Jackie Wilson, Brunswick 55166 | 17 |
| 71 | 76 | 83 | 97 | IS THERE ANY CHANCE — Marty Robbins, Columbia 41686 | 4 |
| 72 | 52 | 35 | 42 | THEME FOR YOUNG LOVERS — Percy Faith, Columbia 41655 | 10 |
| 73 | 92 | 95 | 98 | FEEL SO FINE — Johnny Preston, Mercury 71651 | 4 |
| 74 | 82 | — | — | JOHNNY FREEDOM — Johnny Horton, Columbia 41685 | 2 |
| 75 | 78 | — | — | MY TANI — Brothers Four, Columbia 41692 | 2 |
| 76 | 81 | 89 | — | THERE'S A STAR-SPANGLED BANNER WAVING SOMEWHERE, NO. 2 (THE BALLAD OF FRANCIS G. POWERS) — Red River Dave, Savoy 3020 | 3 |
| 77 | 83 | 87 | — | HEARTBREAK (IT'S HURTIN' ME) — Little Willie John, King 5356 | 6 |
| 78 | 84 | 91 | — | MARIA — Johnny Mathis, Columbia 41684 | 4 |
| 79 | — | — | — | I'LL BE THERE — Bobby Darin, Atco 6167 | 1 |
| 80 | — | — | — | (YOU WERE MADE FOR) ALL MY LOVE — Jackie Wilson, Brunswick 55167 | 4 |
| 81 | 93 | — | — | DO YOU MIND — Andy Williams, Cadence 1381 | 2 |
| 82 | — | — | — | BE BOP-A-LULA — Everly Brothers, Cadence 13880 | 1 |
| 83 | 64 | 58 | 56 | OOH POO PAH DOO (Part 2) — Jessie Hill, Minit 607 | 16 |
| 84 | 53 | 44 | 45 | I'M WALKIN' THE FLOOR OVER YOU — Pat Boone, Dot 16073 | 8 |
| 85 | 91 | — | — | ONE BOY — Joanie Sommers, Warner Bros. 5157 | 2 |
| 86 | 96 | — | — | SECOND HONEYMOON — Johnny Cash, Columbia 41707 | 2 |
| 87 | 98 | — | — | TOO YOUNG TO GO STEADY — Connie Stevens, Warner Bros. 5159 | 2 |
| 88 | 95 | — | — | I SHOT MR. LEE — Bobbettes, Triple-X 104 | 2 |
| 89 | — | — | — | DOWN THE STREET TO 301 — Johnny Cash, Sun 343 | 1 |
| 90 | — | — | — | A WOMAN, A LOVER, A FRIEND — Jackie Wilson, Brunswick 55167 | 1 |
| 91 | 77 | 52 | 28 | JUMP OVER — Freddy Cannon, Swan 4053 | 10 |
| 92 | — | — | 86 | HOT ROD LINCOLN — Charlie Ryan, Four Star 1733 | 7 |
| 93 | 70 | 54 | 46 | DUTCHMAN'S GOLD — Walter Brennan and Billy Vaughn, Dot 16066 | 12 |
| 94 | — | — | — | IN MY LITTLE CORNER OF THE WORLD — Anita Bryant, Carlton 530 | 1 |
| 95 | 74 | 82 | 91 | I AIN'T GONNA BE THAT WAY — Marv Johnson, United Artists 226 | 7 |
| 96 | — | 98 | — | I'VE BEEN LOVED BEFORE — Shirley and Lee, Warwick 535 | 2 |
| 97 | 100 | — | — | OVER THE RAINBOW — Dimensions, Mohawk 116 | 2 |
| 98 | — | — | — | THAT'S WHEN I CRIED — Jimmy Jones, Cub 9072 | 1 |
| 99 | 57 | 33 | 26 | CHERRY PIE — Skip and Flip, Brent 7010 | 15 |
| 100 | — | — | — | MY SHOES KEEP WALKING BACK TO YOU — Guy Mitchell, Columbia 41725 | 1 |

# The Billboard HOT 100

**FOR WEEK ENDING JULY 24**

STAR PERFORMERS showed the greatest upward progress on Hot 100 this week.
[S] Indicates that 45 r.p.m. stereo single version is available.
[A] Indicates that 33⅓ r.p.m. stereo single version is available.

Columns: THIS WEEK | ONE WEEK AGO | TWO WEEKS AGO | THREE WEEKS AGO | TITLE — Artist, Company, Record No. | STEREO | WEEKS ON CHART

| This | 1wk | 2wk | 3wk | Title — Artist, Company, Record No. | Wks |
|---|---|---|---|---|---|
| 1 | 2 | 3 | 6 | I'M SORRY — Brenda Lee, Decca 31093 | 8 |
| 2 | 1 | 2 | 3 | ALLEY-OOP — Hollywood Argyles, Lute 5905 | 8 |
| 3 | 3 | 1 | 1 | EVERYBODY'S SOMEBODY'S FOOL — Connie Francis, M-G-M 12899 | 11 |
| 4 | 6 | 11 | 23 | ONLY THE LONELY — Roy Orbison, Monument 421 | 6 |
| 5 | 4 | 4 | 5 | BECAUSE THEY'RE YOUNG — Duane Eddy, Jamie 1156 | 9 |
| 6 | 7 | 6 | 17 | THAT'S ALL YOU GOTTA DO — Brenda Lee, Decca 31093 | 7 |
| 7 | 5 | 9 | 15 | MULE SKINNER BLUES — Fendermen, Soma 1137 | 9 |
| 8 | 10 | 20 | 36 | WHEN WILL I BE LOVED — Everly Brothers, Cadence 1380 | 8 |
| 9 | 12 | 22 | 40 | TELL LAURA I LOVE HER — Ray Peterson, RCA Victor 7745 | 6 |
| 10 | 20 | 59 | — | ITSY BITSY TEENIE WEENIE YELLOW POLKA DOT BIKINI — Brian Hyland, Leader 805 | 3 |
| 11 | 9 | 10 | 7 | A ROCKIN' GOOD WAY — Dinah Washington and Brook Benton, Mercury 71629 [S] | 9 |
| 12 | 8 | 8 | 11 | MY HOME TOWN — Paul Anka, ABC-Paramount 10106 | 9 |
| 13 | 21 | 31 | 46 | WALKIN' TO NEW ORLEANS — Fats Domino, Imperial 5675 | 5 |
| 14 | 17 | 43 | 53 | IMAGE OF A GIRL — Safaris, Eldo 101 | 7 |
| 15 | 14 | 16 | 24 | PLEASE HELP ME, I'M FALLING — Hank Locklin, RCA Victor 7692 | 9 |
| 16 | 13 | 5 | 2 | CATHY'S CLOWN — Everly Brothers, Warner Bros. 5151 [S] | 14 |
| 17 | 18 | 12 | 12 | WONDERFUL WORLD — Sam Cooke, Keen 82112 | 11 |
| 18 | 28 | 33 | 71 | JOSEPHINE — Bill Black's Combo, Hi 2022 | 4 |
| 19 | 11 | 7 | 4 | BURNING BRIDGES — Jack Scott, Top Rank 2041 | 14 |
| 20 | 15 | 15 | 16 | ALLEY-OOP — Dante and the Evergreens, Madison 130 | 8 |
| 21 | 22 | 24 | 13 | LOVE YOU SO — Rod Holden, Donna 1315 | 16 |
| 22 | 25 | 35 | 66 | LOOK FOR A STAR — Garry Miles, Liberty 55261 | 5 |
| 23 | 16 | 13 | 8 | PAPER ROSES — Anita Bryant, Carlton 528 [S] | 15 |
| 24 | 26 | 29 | 32 | PENNIES FROM HEAVEN — Skyliners, Calico 117 | 11 |
| 25 | 34 | 79 | 100 | MISSION BELL — Donnie Brooks, Era 3018 | 6 |
| 26 | 57 | 68 | 74 | TROUBLE IN PARADISE — Crests, Coed 531 | 6 |
| 27 | 24 | 23 | 20 | JEALOUS OF YOU — Connie Francis, M-G-M 12899 | 9 |
| 28 | 53 | 60 | 64 | FINGER POPPIN' TIME — Hank Ballard and the Midnighters, King 5341 | 10 |
| 29 | 19 | 14 | 14 | HAPPY-GO-LUCKY ME — Paul Evans, Guaranteed 208 [S] | 11 |
| 30 | 32 | 37 | 68 | LOOK FOR A STAR — Dean Hawley, Dore 554 | 5 |
| 31 | 33 | 46 | 80 | THERE IS SOMETHING ON YOUR MIND — Bobby Marchan, Fire 1022 | 6 |
| 32 | 30 | 19 | 21 | (WON'T YOU COME HOME) BILL BAILEY — Bobby Darin, Atco 6167 | 9 |
| 33 | 23 | 25 | 29 | RUNAROUND — Fleetwoods, Dolton 22 | 9 |
| 34 | 27 | 27 | 37 | THEME FROM THE UNFORGIVEN — Don Costa, United Artists 221 | 12 |
| 35 | 40 | 50 | 61 | IS A BLUEBIRD BLUE — Conway Twitty, M-G-M 12911 | 6 |
| 36 | 58 | 80 | 85 | QUESTION — Lloyd Price, ABC-Paramount 10123 | 4 |
| 37 | 42 | 75 | 81 | THIS BITTER EARTH — Dinah Washington, Mercury 71635 | 5 |
| 38 | 52 | 90 | 96 | DON'T COME KNOCKIN' — Fats Domino, Imperial 5675 | 4 |
| 39 | 46 | 56 | 73 | LOOK FOR A STAR — Billy Vaughn, Dot 16106 | 5 |
| 40 | 56 | 62 | 78 | LOOK FOR A STAR — Garry Mills, Imperial 5674 | 5 |
| 41 | 73 | 92 | 95 | FEEL SO FINE — Johnny Preston, Mercury 71651 | 5 |
| 42 | 37 | 42 | 48 | I'M GETTIN' BETTER — Jim Reeves, RCA Victor 7756 | 5 |
| 43 | 66 | 86 | 92 | STICKS AND STONES — Ray Charles, ABC-Paramount 10118 | 4 |
| 44 | — | — | — | IT'S NOW OR NEVER — Elvis Presley, RCA Victor 7777 | 1 |
| 45 | 29 | 18 | 25 | I REALLY DON'T WANT TO KNOW — Tommy Edwards, M-G-M 12890 | 9 |
| 46 | 38 | 21 | 10 | SWINGING SCHOOL — Bobby Rydell, Cameo 175 | 11 |
| 47 | 51 | 41 | 41 | SOMETHING HAPPENED — Paul Anka, ABC-Paramount 10106 | 8 |
| 48 | 31 | 34 | 42 | ONE OF US (WILL WEEP TONIGHT) — Patti Page, Mercury 71639 [S] | 7 |
| 49 | 45 | 49 | 51 | CLAP YOUR HANDS — Beau-Marks, Shad 5017 | 10 |
| 50 | 55 | 61 | 65 | HEY, LITTLE ONE — Dorsey Burnette, Era 3019 | 7 |
| 51 | 60 | 67 | 72 | WHERE ARE YOU — Frankie Avalon, Chancellor 1052 | 6 |
| 52 | 39 | 28 | 27 | MACK THE KNIFE — Ella Fitzgerald, Verve 10209 [S] | 12 |
| 53 | 35 | 17 | 9 | GOOD TIMIN' — Jimmy Jones, Cub 9067 | 14 |
| 54 | 36 | 38 | 43 | TRAIN OF LOVE — Annette, Vista 359 | 7 |
| 55 | 48 | 51 | 39 | ALL I COULD DO WAS CRY — Etta James, Argo 5359 | 12 |
| 56 | 41 | 26 | 18 | YOUNG EMOTIONS — Ricky Nelson, Imperial 5663 | 13 |
| 57 | 65 | 47 | 34 | LONELY WEEKENDS — Charlie Rich, Philips International 3552 | 19 |
| 58 | 43 | 32 | 26 | DING-A-LING — Bobby Rydell, Cameo 175 | 11 |
| 59 | 69 | 71 | 77 | WAKE ME, SHAKE ME — Coasters, Atco 6168 | 5 |
| 60 | — | — | — | VOLARE (NEL BLU DI PINTO DI BLU) — Bobby Rydell, Cameo 179 | 1 |
| 61 | 94 | — | — | IN MY LITTLE CORNER OF THE WORLD — Anita Bryant, Carlton 530 | 2 |
| 62 | 80 | — | — | (YOU WERE MADE FOR) ALL MY LOVE — Jackie Wilson, Brunswick 55167 | 2 |
| 63 | 44 | 36 | 28 | ANOTHER SLEEPLESS NIGHT — Jimmy Clanton, Ace 585 | 13 |
| 64 | 68 | 69 | 79 | I CAN'T HELP IT — Adam Wade, Coed 530 | 5 |
| 65 | 64 | 66 | 76 | BAD MAN BLUNDER — Kingston Trio, Capitol 4375 | 5 |
| 66 | 71 | 76 | 83 | IS THERE ANY CHANCE — Marty Robbins, Columbia 41686 | 5 |
| 67 | 63 | 65 | 75 | ALL THE LOVE I GOT — Marv Johnson, United Artists 226 | 6 |
| 68 | 76 | 81 | 89 | THERE'S A STAR-SPANGLED BANNER WAVING SOMEWHERE, NO. 2 (THE BALLAD OF FRANCIS G. POWERS) — Red River Dave, Savoy 3020 | 4 |
| 69 | 74 | 82 | — | JOHNNY FREEDOM — Johnny Horton, Columbia 41685 | 3 |
| 70 | — | 90 | — | HEARTBREAK (IT'S HURTIN' ME) — Jon Thomas, ABC-Paramount 10122 | 4 |
| 71 | 81 | 93 | — | DO YOU MIND — Andy Williams, Cadence 1381 | 3 |
| 72 | 75 | 78 | — | MY TANI — Brothers Four, Columbia 41692 | 3 |
| 73 | 88 | 95 | — | I SHOT MR. LEE — Bobbettes, Triple-X 104 | 3 |
| 74 | 82 | — | — | BE BOP-A-LULA — Everly Brothers, Cadence 13880 | 2 |
| 75 | 77 | 83 | 87 | HEARTBREAK (IT'S HURTIN' ME) — Little Willie John, King 5356 | 7 |
| 76 | 62 | 48 | 49 | DOWN YONDER — Johnny and the Hurricanes, Big Top 3036 | 8 |
| 77 | 59 | 58 | 63 | BANJO BOY — Jan and Kjeld, Kapp 335 | 7 |
| 78 | 97 | 100 | — | OVER THE RAINBOW — Dimensions, Mohawk 116 | 3 |
| 79 | 85 | 91 | — | ONE BOY — Joanie Sommers, Warner Bros. 5157 | 3 |
| 80 | 47 | 55 | 55 | DOGGIN' AROUND — Jackie Wilson, Brunswick 55166 | 16 |
| 81 | 87 | 98 | — | TOO YOUNG TO GO STEADY — Connie Stevens, Warner Bros. 5159 | 3 |
| 82 | — | — | — | PLEASE HELP ME, I'M FALLING — Rusty Draper, Mercury 71634 | 1 |
| 83 | 92 | — | — | HOT ROD LINCOLN — Charlie Ryan, Four Star 1733 | 8 |
| 84 | 79 | — | — | I'LL BE THERE — Bobby Darin, Atco 6167 | 2 |
| 85 | 86 | 96 | — | SECOND HONEYMOON — Johnny Cash, Columbia 41707 | 3 |
| 86 | 89 | — | — | DOWN THE STREET TO 301 — Johnny Cash, Sun 343 | 2 |
| 87 | — | — | — | TWIST — Hank Ballard and the Midnighters, King 5171 | 1 |
| 88 | — | — | — | WALK—DON'T RUN — Ventures, Dolton 25 | 1 |
| 89 | 90 | — | — | A WOMAN, A LOVER, A FRIEND — Jackie Wilson, Brunswick 55167 | 2 |
| 90 | — | — | — | TA-TA — Clyde McPhatter, Mercury 71660 | 1 |
| 91 | 98 | — | — | THAT'S WHEN I CRIED — Jimmy Jones, Cub 9072 | 2 |
| 92 | — | — | — | DO YOU MIND — Anthony Newley, London 1918 | 1 |
| 93 | 50 | 39 | 22 | STUCK ON YOU — Elvis Presley, RCA Victor 7740 [S] | 16 |
| 94 | 96 | — | 98 | I'VE BEEN LOVED BEFORE — Shirley and Lee, Warwick 535 | 3 |
| 95 | — | — | — | IN THE STILL OF THE NIGHT — Dion and the Belmonts, Laurie 3059 | 1 |
| 96 | 67 | 54 | 57 | LONELY WINDS — Drifters, Atlantic 2062 | 9 |
| 97 | — | — | — | BIG BOY PETE — Olympics, Arvee 595 | 3 |
| 98 | — | — | — | MIO AMORE — Flamingos, End 1073 | — |
| 99 | 54 | 63 | 50 | SPRING RAIN — Pat Boone, Dot 16073 | 8 |
| 100 | — | — | — | NIGHT TRAIN — Viscounts, Madison 133 | 1 |

# The Billboard HOT 100

**FOR WEEK ENDING JULY 31**

| This Week | One Week Ago | Two Weeks Ago | Three Weeks Ago | Title / Artist, Company, Record No. | Weeks on Chart |
|---|---|---|---|---|---|
| 1 | 1 | 2 | 3 | I'M SORRY — Brenda Lee, Decca 31093 | 9 |
| 2 | 4 | 6 | 11 | ONLY THE LONELY — Roy Orbison, Monument 421 | 7 |
| 3 | 2 | 1 | 2 | ALLEY-OOP — Hollywood Argyles, Lute 5905 | 9 |
| 4 | 3 | 3 | 1 | EVERYBODY'S SOMEBODY'S FOOL — Connie Francis, M-G-M 12899 | 12 |
| ☆5 | 10 | 20 | 59 | ITSY BITSY TEENIE WEENIE YELLOW POLKA DOT BIKINI — Brian Hyland, Leader 805 | 4 |
| 6 | 7 | 5 | 9 | MULE SKINNER BLUES — Fendermen, Soma 1137 | 10 |
| 7 | 14 | 17 | 43 | IMAGE OF A GIRL — Safaris, Eldo 101 | 8 |
| 8 | 9 | 12 | 22 | TELL LAURA I LOVE HER — Ray Peterson, RCA Victor 7745 | 7 |
| ☆9 | 15 | 14 | 16 | PLEASE HELP ME, I'M FALLING — Hank Locklin, RCA Victor 7692 | 10 |
| 10 | 6 | 7 | 6 | THAT'S ALL YOU GOTTA DO — Brenda Lee, Decca 31093 | 8 |
| 11 | 8 | 10 | 20 | WHEN WILL I BE LOVED — Everly Brothers, Cadence 1380 | 9 |
| 12 | 5 | 4 | 4 | BECAUSE THEY'RE YOUNG — Duane Eddy, Jamie 1156 | 10 |
| 13 | 13 | 21 | 31 | WALKIN' TO NEW ORLEANS — Fats Domino, Imperial 5675 | 6 |
| ☆14 | 44 | — | — | IT'S NOW OR NEVER — Elvis Presley, RCA Victor 7777 | 2 |
| 15 | 11 | 9 | 10 | A ROCKIN' GOOD WAY — Dinah Washington and Brook Benton, Mercury 71629 | 10 |
| 16 | 12 | 8 | 8 | MY HOME TOWN — Paul Anka, ABC-Paramount 10106 | 10 |
| ☆17 | 28 | 53 | 60 | FINGER POPPIN' TIME — Hank Ballard and the Midnighters, King 5341 | 11 |
| 18 | 22 | 25 | 35 | LOOK FOR A STAR — Garry Miles, Liberty 55261 | 6 |
| 19 | 18 | 28 | 33 | JOSEPHINE — Bill Black's Combo, Hi 2022 | 5 |
| 20 | 25 | 34 | 79 | MISSION BELL — Donnie Brooks, Era 3018 | 7 |
| 21 | 26 | 57 | 68 | TROUBLE IN PARADISE — Crests, Coed 531 | 7 |
| ☆22 | 38 | 52 | 90 | DON'T COME KNOCKIN' — Fats Domino, Imperial 5675 | 5 |
| ☆23 | 36 | 58 | 80 | QUESTION — Lloyd Price, ABC-Paramount 10123 | 5 |
| ☆24 | 39 | 46 | 56 | LOOK FOR A STAR — Billy Vaughn, Dot 16106 | 6 |
| ☆25 | 41 | 73 | 92 | FEEL SO FINE — Johnny Preston, Mercury 71651 | 6 |
| 26 | 40 | 56 | 62 | LOOK FOR A STAR — Garry Mills, Imperial 5674 | 6 |
| 27 | 37 | 42 | 75 | THIS BITTER EARTH — Dinah Washington, Mercury 71635 | 6 |
| 28 | 20 | 15 | 15 | ALLEY-OOP — Dante and the Evergreens, Madison 130 | 9 |
| 29 | 30 | 32 | 37 | LOOK FOR A STAR — Dean Hawley, Dore 554 | 6 |
| 30 | 17 | 18 | 12 | WONDERFUL WORLD — Sam Cooke, Keen 82112 | 12 |
| 31 | 16 | 13 | 5 | CATHY'S CLOWN — Everly Brothers, Warner Bros. 5151 | 15 |
| 32 | 24 | 26 | 29 | PENNIES FROM HEAVEN — Skyliners, Calico 117 | 12 |
| 33 | 19 | 11 | 7 | BURNING BRIDGES — Jack Scott, Top Rank 2041 | 15 |
| 34 | 45 | 29 | 18 | I REALLY DON'T WANT TO KNOW — Tommy Edwards, M-G-M 12890 | 10 |
| ☆35 | 48 | 31 | 34 | ONE OF US (WILL WEEP TONIGHT) — Patti Page, Mercury 71639 | 8 |
| 36 | 27 | 24 | 23 | JEALOUS OF YOU — Connie Francis, M-G-M 12899 | 10 |
| 37 | 35 | 40 | 50 | IS A BLUEBIRD BLUE — Conway Twitty, M-G-M 12911 | 7 |
| ☆38 | 75 | 77 | 83 | HEARTBREAK (IT'S HURTIN' ME) — Little Willie John, King 5356 | 8 |
| ☆39 | 88 | — | — | WALK—DON'T RUN — Ventures, Dolton 25 | 2 |
| 40 | 31 | 33 | 46 | THERE IS SOMETHING ON YOUR MIND — Bobby Marchan, Fire 1022 | 7 |
| 41 | 66 | 71 | 76 | IS THERE ANY CHANCE — Marty Robbins, Columbia 41686 | 6 |
| 42 | 21 | 22 | 24 | LOVE YOU SO — Rod Holden, Donna 1315 | 17 |
| 43 | 42 | 37 | 42 | I'M GETTIN' BETTER — Jim Reeves, RCA Victor 7756 | 6 |
| 44 | 23 | 16 | 13 | PAPER ROSES — Anita Bryant, Carlton 528 | 16 |
| 45 | 51 | 60 | 67 | WHERE ARE YOU — Frankie Avalon, Chancellor 1052 | 7 |
| 46 | 33 | 23 | 25 | RUNAROUND — Fleetwoods, Dolton 22 | 10 |
| 47 | 29 | 19 | 14 | HAPPY-GO-LUCKY ME — Paul Evans, Guaranteed 208 | 12 |
| ☆48 | 60 | — | — | VOLARE (NEL BLU DI PINTO DI BLU) — Bobby Rydell, Cameo 179 | 2 |
| 49 | 62 | 80 | — | (YOU WERE MADE FOR) ALL MY LOVE — Jackie Wilson, Brunswick 55167 | 3 |
| 50 | 61 | 94 | — | IN MY LITTLE CORNER OF THE WORLD — Anita Bryant, Carlton 530 | 3 |
| 51 | 59 | 69 | 71 | WAKE ME, SHAKE ME — Coasters, Atco 6168 | 6 |
| 52 | 55 | 48 | 51 | ALL I COULD DO WAS CRY — Etta James, Argo 5359 | 13 |
| 53 | — | — | — | A MESS OF BLUES — Elvis Presley, RCA Victor 7777 | 1 |
| 54 | 32 | 30 | 19 | (WON'T YOU COME HOME) BILL BAILEY — Bobby Darin, Atco 6167 | 10 |
| 55 | 83 | 92 | — | HOT ROD LINCOLN — Charlie Ryan, Four Star 1733 | 9 |
| 56 | 50 | 55 | 61 | HEY, LITTLE ONE — Dorsey Burnette, Era 3019 | 8 |
| 57 | 73 | 88 | 95 | I SHOT MR. LEE — Bobbettes, Triple-X 104 | 4 |
| 58 | 43 | 66 | 86 | STICKS AND STONES — Ray Charles, ABC-Paramount 10118 | 5 |
| 59 | 49 | 45 | 49 | CLAP YOUR HANDS — Beau-Marks, Shad 5017 | 11 |
| 60 | 70 | — | 90 | HEARTBREAK (IT'S HURTIN' ME) — Jon Thomas, ABC-Paramount 10122 | 5 |
| 61 | 87 | — | — | TWIST — Hank Ballard and the Midnighters, King 5171 | 2 |
| 62 | 65 | 64 | 66 | BAD MAN BLUNDER — Kingston Trio, Capitol 4375 | 6 |
| 63 | 90 | — | — | TA-TA — Clyde McPhatter, Mercury 71660 | 2 |
| 64 | 68 | 76 | 81 | THERE'S A STAR-SPANGLED BANNER WAVING SOMEWHERE, NO. 2 (THE BALLAD OF FRANCIS G. POWERS) — Red River Dave, Savoy 3020 | 5 |
| 65 | 78 | 97 | 100 | OVER THE RAINBOW — Dimensions, Mohawk 116 | 4 |
| 66 | 82 | — | — | PLEASE HELP ME, I'M FALLING — Rusty Draper, Mercury 71634 | 2 |
| 67 | 52 | 39 | 28 | MACK THE KNIFE — Ella Fitzgerald, Verve 10209 | 13 |
| 68 | 47 | 51 | 41 | SOMETHING HAPPENED — Paul Anka, ABC-Paramount 10106 | 9 |
| 69 | 72 | 75 | 78 | MY TANI — Brothers Four, Columbia 41692 | 4 |
| 70 | 71 | 81 | 93 | DO YOU MIND — Andy Williams, Cadence 1381 | 4 |
| 71 | 81 | 87 | 98 | TOO YOUNG TO GO STEADY — Connie Stevens, Warner Bros. 5159 | 4 |
| 72 | 64 | 68 | 69 | I CAN'T HELP IT — Adam Wade, Coed 530 | 6 |
| 73 | 57 | 65 | 47 | LONELY WEEKENDS — Charlie Rich, Philips International 3552 | 20 |
| 74 | 53 | 35 | 17 | GOOD TIMIN' — Jimmy Jones, Cub 9067 | 15 |
| 75 | 79 | 85 | 91 | ONE BOY — Jeanne Sommers, Warner Bros. 5157 | 4 |
| 76 | 46 | 38 | 21 | SWINGING SCHOOL — Bobby Rydell, Cameo 175 | 12 |
| 77 | 69 | 74 | 82 | JOHNNY FREEDOM — Johnny Horton, Columbia 41685 | 4 |
| 78 | 95 | — | — | IN THE STILL OF THE NIGHT — Dion and the Belmonts, Laurie 3059 | 2 |
| 79 | 85 | 86 | 96 | SECOND HONEYMOON — Johnny Cash, Columbia 41707 | 4 |
| 80 | 89 | 90 | — | A WOMAN, A LOVER, A FRIEND — Jackie Wilson, Brunswick 55167 | 3 |
| 81 | 74 | 82 | — | BE BOP-A-LULA — Everly Brothers, Cadence 1380 | 3 |
| 82 | — | — | — | I KNOW ONE — Jim Reeves, RCA Victor 7756 | 1 |
| 83 | 54 | 36 | 38 | TRAIN OF LOVE — Annette, Vista 359 | 8 |
| 84 | 76 | 62 | 48 | DOWN YONDER — Johnny and the Hurricanes, Big Top 3036 | 9 |
| 85 | 86 | 89 | — | DOWN THE STREET TO 301 — Johnny Cash, Sun 343 | 3 |
| 86 | — | — | — | DREAMIN' — Johnny Burnette, Liberty 55258 | 1 |
| 87 | 91 | 98 | — | THAT'S WHEN I CRIED — Jimmy Jones, Cub 9072 | 3 |
| 88 | — | 100 | — | MY SHOES KEEP WALKING BACK TO YOU — Guy Mitchell, Columbia 41725 | 2 |
| 89 | — | — | — | LISA — Jeanne Black, Capitol 4396 | 1 |
| 90 | 34 | 27 | 27 | THEME FROM THE UNFORGIVEN — Don Costa, United Artists 221 | 13 |
| 91 | — | — | — | WHIP IT ON ME — Jessie Hill, Minit 611 | 1 |
| 92 | — | — | — | HONKY TONK GIRL — Johnny Cash, Columbia 41707 | 1 |
| 93 | 97 | — | — | BIG BOY PETE — Olympics, Arvee 595 | 4 |
| 94 | 98 | — | — | MIO AMORE — Flamingos, End 1073 | 2 |
| 95 | — | — | — | HAPPY SHADES OF BLUE — Freddy Cannon, Swan 4057 | 1 |
| 96 | — | — | — | THEME FROM THE APARTMENT — Ferrante and Teicher, United Artists 231 | 1 |
| 97 | 94 | 96 | — | I'VE BEEN LOVED BEFORE — Shirley and Lee, Warwick 535 | 4 |
| 98 | 100 | — | — | NIGHT TRAIN — Viscounts, Madison 133 | 2 |
| 99 | — | — | — | SHE'S A WHOLE LOT LIKE YOU — Hank Thompson, Capitol 4386 | 1 |
| 100 | — | — | — | COOL WATER — Jack Scott, Top Rank 2055 | 1 |

# The Billboard HOT 100

**FOR WEEK ENDING AUGUST 7**

AUGUST 1, 1960

| This Week | 1 Wk Ago | 2 Wks Ago | 3 Wks Ago | Title — Artist, Company, Record No. | Weeks on Chart |
|---|---|---|---|---|---|
| 1 | 1 | 1 | 2 | I'M SORRY — Brenda Lee, Decca 31093 | 10 |
| 2 | 5 | 10 | 20 | ITSY BITSY TEENIE WEENIE YELLOW POLKA DOT BIKINI — Brian Hyland, Leader 805 | 5 |
| ★3 | 14 | 44 | — | IT'S NOW OR NEVER — Elvis Presley, RCA Victor 7777 | 3 |
| 4 | 2 | 4 | 6 | ONLY THE LONELY — Roy Orbison, Monument 421 | 8 |
| 5 | 3 | 2 | 1 | ALLEY-OOP — Hollywood Argyles, Lute 5905 | 10 |
| 6 | 7 | 14 | 17 | IMAGE OF A GIRL — Safaris, Eldo 101 | 9 |
| 7 | 8 | 9 | 12 | TELL LAURA I LOVE HER — Ray Peterson, RCA Victor 7745 | 8 |
| 8 | 9 | 15 | 14 | PLEASE HELP ME, I'M FALLING — Hank Locklin, RCA Victor 7692 | 11 |
| 9 | 6 | 7 | 5 | MULE SKINNER BLUES — Fendermen, Soma 1137 | 11 |
| 10 | 10 | 6 | 7 | THAT'S ALL YOU GOTTA DO — Brenda Lee, Decca 31093 | 9 |
| 11 | 4 | 3 | 3 | EVERYBODY'S SOMEBODY'S FOOL — Connie Francis, M-G-M 12899 | 13 |
| 12 | 11 | 8 | 10 | WHEN WILL I BE LOVED — Everly Brothers, Cadence 1380 | 10 |
| 13 | 13 | 13 | 21 | WALKIN' TO NEW ORLEANS — Fats Domino, Imperial 5675 | 7 |
| 14 | 17 | 28 | 53 | FINGER POPPIN' TIME — Hank Ballard and the Midnighters, King 5341 | 12 |
| ★15 | 25 | 41 | 73 | FEEL SO FINE — Johnny Preston, Mercury 71651 | 7 |
| 16 | 18 | 22 | 25 | LOOK FOR A STAR — Garry Miles, Liberty 55261 | 7 |
| 17 | 12 | 5 | 4 | BECAUSE THEY'RE YOUNG — Duane Eddy, Jamie 1156 | 11 |
| ★18 | 39 | 88 | — | WALK, DON'T RUN — Ventures, Dolton 25 | 3 |
| ★19 | 24 | 39 | 46 | LOOK FOR A STAR — Billy Vaughn, Dot 16106 | 7 |
| 20 | 21 | 26 | 57 | TROUBLE IN PARADISE — Crests, Coed 531 | 8 |
| 21 | 22 | 38 | 52 | DON'T COME KNOCKIN' — Fats Domino, Imperial 5675 | 6 |
| 22 | 23 | 36 | 58 | QUESTION — Lloyd Price, ABC-Paramount 10123 | 6 |
| 23 | 19 | 18 | 28 | JOSEPHINE — Bill Black's Combo, Hi 2022 | 6 |
| 24 | 20 | 25 | 34 | MISSION BELL — Donnie Brooks, Era 3018 | 8 |
| 25 | 15 | 11 | 9 | A ROCKIN' GOOD WAY — Dinah Washington and Brook Benton, Mercury 71629 | 11 |
| ★26 | 49 | 62 | 80 | (YOU WERE MADE FOR) ALL MY LOVE — Jackie Wilson, Brunswick 55167 | 4 |
| 27 | 16 | 12 | 8 | MY HOME TOWN — Paul Anka, ABC-Paramount 10106 | 11 |
| 28 | 28 | 20 | 15 | ALLEY-OOP — Dante and the Evergreens, Madison 130 | 10 |
| 29 | 26 | 40 | 56 | LOOK FOR A STAR — Garry Mills, Imperial 5674 | 7 |
| 30 | 48 | 60 | — | VOLARE (NEL BLU DI PINTO DI BLU) — Bobby Rydell, Cameo 179 | 3 |
| 31 | 27 | 37 | 42 | THIS BITTER EARTH — Dinah Washington, Mercury 71635 | 7 |
| 32 | 45 | 51 | 60 | WHERE ARE YOU — Frankie Avalon, Chancellor 1052 | 8 |
| 33 | 41 | 66 | 71 | IS THERE ANY CHANCE — Marty Robbins, Columbia 41686 | 7 |
| 34 | 80 | 89 | 90 | A WOMAN, A LOVER, A FRIEND — Jackie Wilson, Brunswick 55167 | 4 |
| 35 | 40 | 31 | 33 | THERE IS SOMETHING ON YOUR MIND — Bobby Marchan, Fire 1022 | 8 |
| 36 | 29 | 30 | 32 | LOOK FOR A STAR — Dean Hawley, Dore 554 | 7 |
| 37 | 37 | 35 | 40 | IS A BLUEBIRD BLUE — Conway Twitty, M-G-M 12911 | 8 |
| 38 | 30 | 17 | 18 | WONDERFUL WORLD — Sam Cooke, Keen 82112 | 13 |
| 39 | 35 | 48 | 31 | ONE OF US (WILL WEEP TONIGHT) — Patti Page, Mercury 71639 | 9 |
| 40 | 53 | — | — | A MESS OF BLUES — Elvis Presley, RCA Victor 7777 | 2 |
| 41 | 50 | 61 | 94 | IN MY LITTLE CORNER OF THE WORLD — Anita Bryant, Carlton 530 | 4 |
| 42 | 38 | 75 | 77 | HEARTBREAK (IT'S HURTIN' ME) — Little Willie John, King 5356 | 9 |
| 43 | 62 | 65 | 64 | BAD MAN BLUNDER — Kingston Trio, Capitol 4375 | 7 |
| 44 | 34 | 45 | 29 | I REALLY DON'T WANT TO KNOW — Tommy Edwards, M-G-M 12890 | 11 |
| 45 | 31 | 16 | 13 | CATHY'S CLOWN — Everly Brothers, Warner Bros. 5151 | 16 |
| 46 | 33 | 19 | 11 | BURNING BRIDGES — Jack Scott, Top Rank 2041 | 16 |
| 47 | 46 | 33 | 23 | RUNAROUND — Fleetwoods, Dolton 22 | 11 |
| 48 | 56 | 50 | 55 | HEY, LITTLE ONE — Dorsey Burnette, Era 3019 | 9 |
| 49 | — | — | — | TWIST — Chubby Checker, Parkway 811 | 1 |
| 50 | 43 | 42 | 37 | I'M GETTIN' BETTER — Jim Reeves, RCA Victor 7756 | 7 |
| 51 | 36 | 27 | 24 | JEALOUS OF YOU — Connie Francis, M-G-M 12899 | 11 |
| 52 | 57 | 73 | 88 | I SHOT MR. LEE — Bobbettes, Triple-X 104 | 5 |
| 53 | 61 | 87 | — | TWIST — Hank Ballard and the Midnighters, King 5171 | 3 |
| 54 | 66 | 82 | — | PLEASE HELP ME, I'M FALLING — Rusty Draper, Mercury 71634 | 3 |
| 55 | 60 | 70 | — | HEARTBREAK (IT'S HURTIN' ME) — Jon Thomas, ABC-Paramount 10122 | 6 |
| 56 | 51 | 59 | 69 | WAKE ME, SHAKE ME — Coasters, Atco 6168 | 7 |
| 57 | 55 | 83 | 92 | HOT ROD LINCOLN — Charlie Ryan, Four Star 1733 | 10 |
| 58 | 65 | 78 | 97 | OVER THE RAINBOW — Dimensions, Mohawk 116 | 5 |
| 59 | 86 | — | — | DREAMIN' — Johnny Burnette, Liberty 55258 | 2 |
| 60 | 69 | 72 | 75 | MY TANI — Brothers Four, Columbia 41692 | 5 |
| 61 | 63 | 90 | — | TA-TA — Clyde McPhatter, Mercury 71660 | 3 |
| 62 | 44 | 23 | 16 | PAPER ROSES — Anita Bryant, Carlton 528 | 17 |
| 63 | 42 | 21 | 22 | LOVE YOU SO — Rod Holden, Donna 1315 | 18 |
| 64 | 32 | 24 | 26 | PENNIES FROM HEAVEN — Skyliners, Calico 117 | 13 |
| 65 | 52 | 55 | 48 | ALL I COULD DO WAS CRY — Etta James, Argo 5359 | 14 |
| 66 | 78 | 95 | — | IN THE STILL OF THE NIGHT — Dion and the Belmonts, Laurie 3059 | 3 |
| 67 | 58 | 43 | 66 | STICKS AND STONES — Ray Charles, ABC-Paramount 10118 | 6 |
| 68 | 75 | 79 | 85 | ONE BOY — Joanie Sommers, Warner Bros. 5157 | 5 |
| 69 | 59 | 49 | 45 | CLAP YOUR HANDS — Beau-Marks, Shad 5017 | 12 |
| 70 | 67 | 52 | 39 | MACK THE KNIFE — Ella Fitzgerald, Verve 10209 | 14 |
| 71 | 47 | 29 | 19 | HAPPY-GO-LUCKY ME — Paul Evans, Guaranteed 208 | 13 |
| 72 | 54 | 32 | 30 | (WON'T YOU COME HOME) BILL BAILEY — Bobby Darin, Atco 6167 | 11 |
| 73 | — | — | — | I LOVE YOU IN THE SAME OLD WAY — Paul Anka, ABC-Paramount 10132 | 1 |
| 74 | 72 | 64 | 68 | I CAN'T HELP IT — Adam Wade, Coed 530 | 7 |
| 75 | 71 | 81 | 87 | TOO YOUNG TO GO STEADY — Connie Stevens, Warner Bros. 5159 | 5 |
| 76 | — | — | — | RED SAILS IN THE SUNSET — Platters and Tony Williams, Mercury 71656 | 1 |
| 77 | — | — | — | MY LOVE — Nat King Cole, Capitol 4393 | 1 |
| 78 | 89 | — | — | LISA — Jeanne Black, Capitol 4396 | 2 |
| 79 | — | — | — | HELLO YOUNG LOVERS — Paul Anka, ABC-Paramount 10132 | 1 |
| 80 | 73 | 57 | 65 | LONELY WEEKENDS — Charlie Rich, Philips International 3552 | 21 |
| 81 | 64 | 68 | 76 | THERE'S A STAR-SPANGLED BANNER WAVING SOMEWHERE, NO. 2 (THE BALLAD OF FRANCIS G. POWERS) — Red River Dave, Savoy 3020 | 6 |
| 82 | 88 | —100 | | MY SHOES KEEP WALKING BACK TO YOU — Guy Mitchell, Columbia 41725 | 3 |
| 83 | 87 | 91 | 98 | THAT'S WHEN I CRIED — Jimmy Jones, Cub 9072 | 4 |
| 84 | 70 | 71 | 81 | DO YOU MIND — Andy Williams, Cadence 1381 | 5 |
| 85 | 96 | — | — | THEME FROM THE APARTMENT — Ferrante and Teicher, United Artists 231 | 2 |
| 86 | — | — | — | FAR FAR AWAY — Don Gibson, RCA Victor 7762 | 1 |
| 87 | 100 | — | — | COOL WATER — Jack Scott, Top Rank 2055 | 2 |
| 88 | 94 | 98 | — | MIO AMORE — Flamingos, End 1073 | 3 |
| 89 | — | — | — | SWINGING DOWN THE LANE — Jerry Wallace, Challenge 59082 | 1 |
| 90 | 81 | 74 | 82 | BE BOP-A-LULA — Everly Brothers, Cadence 1380 | 4 |
| 91 | 93 | 97 | — | BIG BOY PETE — Olympics, Arvee 595 | 5 |
| 92 | — | — | — | IF I CAN'T HAVE YOU — Etta James and Harvey, Chess 1760 | 1 |
| 93 | 95 | — | — | HAPPY SHADES OF BLUE — Freddy Cannon, Swan 4057 | 2 |
| 94 | 97 | 94 | 96 | I'VE BEEN LOVED BEFORE — Shirley and Lee, Warwick 535 | 5 |
| 95 | — | — | — | IT ONLY HAPPENED YESTERDAY — Jack Scott, Top Rank 2055 | 1 |
| 96 | — | — | — | WE GO TOGETHER — Jan and Dean, Dore 555 | 1 |
| 97 | — | — | — | THEME FROM ADVENTURES IN PARADISE — Jerry Byrd, Monument 419 | 1 |
| 98 | — | — | — | WRECK OF THE "JOHN B" — Jimmie Rodgers, Roulette 4260 | 1 |
| 99 | — | — | — | DEVIL OR ANGEL — Bobby Vee, Liberty 55270 | 1 |
| 100 | 98 | 100 | — | NIGHT TRAIN — Viscounts, Madison 133 | 3 |

# The Billboard HOT 100

**For Week Ending August 14**

*Billboard Music Popularity Charts ... POP RECORDS — August 8, 1960*

STAR PERFORMERS showed the greatest upward progress on Hot 100 this week.
(S) Indicates that 45 r.p.m. stereo single version is available.
(A) Indicates that 33⅓ r.p.m. stereo single version is available.

Columns: THIS WEEK | ONE WEEK AGO | TWO WEEKS AGO | THREE WEEKS AGO | TITLE — Artist, Company, Record No. | STEREO | WEEKS ON CHART

| This | 1wk | 2wk | 3wk | Title — Artist, Company, Record No. | Wks |
|---|---|---|---|---|---|
| 1 | 2 | 5 | 10 | ITSY BITSY TEENIE WEENIE YELLOW POLKA DOT BIKINI — Brian Hyland, Leader 805 | 6 |
| 2 | 1 | 1 | 1 | I'M SORRY — Brenda Lee, Decca 31093 | 11 |
| 3 | 3 | 14 | 44 | IT'S NOW OR NEVER — Elvis Presley, RCA Victor 7777 | 4 |
| 4 | 4 | 2 | 4 | ONLY THE LONELY — Roy Orbison, Monument 421 | 9 |
| 5 | 5 | 3 | 2 | ALLEY-OOP — Hollywood Argyles, Lute 5905 | 11 |
| 6 | 6 | 7 | 14 | IMAGE OF A GIRL — Safaris, Eldo 101 | 10 |
| ★7 | 18 | 39 | 88 | WALK, DON'T RUN — Ventures, Dolton 25 | 4 |
| 8 | 7 | 8 | 9 | TELL LAURA I LOVE HER — Ray Peterson, RCA Victor 7745 | 9 |
| 9 | 8 | 9 | 15 | PLEASE HELP ME, I'M FALLING — Hank Locklin, RCA Victor 7692 | 12 |
| 10 | 13 | 13 | 13 | WALKIN' TO NEW ORLEANS — Fats Domino, Imperial 5675 | 8 |
| ★11 | 49 | — | — | TWIST — Chubby Checker, Parkway 811 | 2 |
| 12 | 11 | 4 | 3 | EVERYBODY'S SOMEBODY'S FOOL — Connie Francis, M-G-M 12899 | 14 |
| 13 | 9 | 6 | 7 | MULE SKINNER BLUES — Fendermen, Soma 1137 | 12 |
| 14 | 15 | 25 | 41 | FEEL SO FINE — Johnny Preston, Mercury 71651 | 8 |
| 15 | 14 | 17 | 28 | FINGER POPPIN' TIME — Hank Ballard and the Midnighters, King 5341 | 13 |
| 16 | 16 | 18 | 22 | LOOK FOR A STAR — Garry Miles, Liberty 55261 | 8 |
| 17 | 17 | 12 | 5 | BECAUSE THEY'RE YOUNG — Duane Eddy, Jamie 1156 | 12 |
| ★18 | 24 | 20 | 25 | MISSION BELL — Donnie Brooks, Era 3018 | 9 |
| 19 | 22 | 23 | 36 | QUESTION — Lloyd Price, ABC-Paramount 10123 | 7 |
| 20 | 20 | 21 | 26 | TROUBLE IN PARADISE — Crests, Coed 531 | 9 |
| 21 | 12 | 11 | 8 | WHEN WILL I BE LOVED — Everly Brothers, Cadence 1380 | 11 |
| 22 | 23 | 19 | 18 | JOSEPHINE — Bill Black's Combo, Hi 2022 | 7 |
| ★23 | 41 | 50 | 61 | IN MY LITTLE CORNER OF THE WORLD — Anita Bryant, Carlton 530 | 5 |
| 24 | 26 | 49 | 62 | (YOU WERE MADE FOR) ALL MY LOVE — Jackie Wilson, Brunswick 55167 | 5 |
| ★25 | 58 | 65 | 78 | OVER THE RAINBOW — Demensions, Mohawk 116 | 6 |
| 26 | 31 | 27 | 37 | THIS BITTER EARTH — Dinah Washington, Mercury 71635 | 8 |
| 27 | 30 | 48 | 60 | VOLARE (NEL BLU DI PINTO DI BLU) — Bobby Rydell, Cameo 179 | 4 |
| 28 | 19 | 24 | 39 | LOOK FOR A STAR — Billy Vaughn, Dot 16106 | 8 |
| 29 | 34 | 80 | 89 | A WOMAN, A LOVER, A FRIEND — Jackie Wilson, Brunswick 55165 | 5 |
| 30 | 21 | 22 | 38 | DON'T COME KNOCKIN' — Fats Domino, Imperial 5675 | 7 |
| 31 | 33 | 41 | 66 | IS THERE ANY CHANCE — Marty Robbins, Columbia 41686 | 8 |
| 32 | 32 | 45 | 51 | WHERE ARE YOU — Frankie Avalon, Chancellor 1052 | 9 |
| 33 | 10 | 10 | 6 | THAT'S ALL YOU GOTTA DO — Brenda Lee, Decca 31093 | 10 |
| 34 | 25 | 15 | 11 | A ROCKIN' GOOD WAY — Dinah Washington and Brook Benton, Mercury 71629 | 12 |
| 35 | 29 | 26 | 40 | LOOK FOR A STAR — Garry Mills, Imperial 5674 | 8 |
| ★36 | 85 | 96 | — | THEME FROM THE APARTMENT — Ferrante and Teicher, United Artists 231 | 3 |
| 37 | 43 | 62 | 65 | BAD MAN BLUNDER — Kingston Trio, Capitol 4375 | 3 |
| 38 | 37 | 37 | 35 | IS A BLUEBIRD BLUE — Conway Twitty, M-G-M 12911 | 9 |
| 39 | 57 | 55 | 83 | HOT ROD LINCOLN — Charlie Ryan, Four Star 1733 | 11 |
| 40 | 67 | 58 | 43 | STICKS AND STONES — Ray Charles, ABC-Paramount 10118 | 7 |
| 41 | 59 | 86 | — | DREAMIN' — Johnny Burnette, Liberty 55258 | 3 |
| 42 | 28 | 28 | 20 | ALLEY-OOP — Dante and the Evergreens, Madison 130 | 11 |
| 43 | 36 | 29 | 30 | LOOK FOR A STAR — Dean Hawley, Dore 554 | 8 |
| 44 | 39 | 35 | 48 | ONE OF US (WILL WEEP TONIGHT) — Patti Page, Mercury 71639 | 10 |
| 45 | 35 | 40 | 31 | THERE IS SOMETHING ON YOUR MIND — Bobby Marchan, Fire 1022 | 9 |
| ★46 | 66 | 78 | 95 | IN THE STILL OF THE NIGHT — Dion and the Belmonts, Laurie 3059 | 4 |
| 47 | 44 | 34 | 45 | I REALLY DON'T WANT TO KNOW — Tommy Edwards, M-G-M 12890 | 12 |
| 48 | 55 | 60 | 70 | HEARTBREAK (IT'S HURTIN' ME) — Jon Thomas, ABC-Paramount 10122 | 7 |
| 49 | 42 | 38 | 75 | HEARTBREAK (IT'S HURTIN' ME) — Little Willie John, King 5356 | 10 |
| 50 | 60 | 69 | 72 | MY TANI — Brothers Four, Columbia 41692 | 6 |
| 51 | 40 | 53 | — | A MESS OF BLUES — Elvis Presley, RCA Victor 7777 | 3 |
| 52 | 45 | 31 | 16 | CATHY'S CLOWN — Everly Brothers, Warner Bros. 5151 | 17 |
| 53 | 52 | 57 | 73 | I SHOT MR. LEE — Bobbettes, Triple-X 104 | 6 |
| 54 | 27 | 16 | 12 | MY HOME TOWN — Paul Anka, ABC-Paramount 10106 | 12 |
| 55 | 61 | 63 | 90 | TA-TA — Clyde McPhatter, Mercury 71660 | 4 |
| 56 | 46 | 33 | 19 | BURNING BRIDGES — Jack Scott, Top Rank 2041 | 17 |
| 57 | 56 | 51 | 59 | WAKE ME, SHAKE ME — Coasters, Atco 6168 | 8 |
| ★58 | 76 | — | — | RED SAILS IN THE SUNSET — Platters and Tony Williams, Mercury 71656 | 2 |
| 59 | — | — | — | KIDDIO — Brook Benton, Mercury 71652 | 1 |
| 60 | 68 | 75 | 79 | ONE BOY — Joanie Sommers, Warner Bros. 5157 | 6 |
| 61 | 47 | 46 | 33 | RUNAROUND — Fleetwoods, Dolton 22 | 12 |
| 62 | 78 | 89 | — | LISA — Jeanne Black, Capitol 4396 | 3 |
| ★63 | 79 | — | — | HELLO, YOUNG LOVERS — Paul Anka, ABC-Paramount 10132 | 2 |
| 64 | 77 | — | — | MY LOVE — Nat King Cole, Capitol 4393 | 2 |
| 65 | 48 | 56 | 50 | HEY, LITTLE ONE — Dorsey Burnette, Era 3019 | 10 |
| 66 | 50 | 43 | 42 | I'M GETTIN' BETTER — Jim Reeves, RCA Victor 7756 | 8 |
| 67 | 54 | 66 | 82 | PLEASE HELP ME, I'M FALLING — Rusty Draper, Mercury 71634 | 4 |
| 68 | 38 | 30 | 17 | WONDERFUL WORLD — Sam Cooke, Keen 82112 | 14 |
| 69 | 65 | 52 | 55 | ALL I COULD DO WAS CRY — Etta James, Argo 5359 | 15 |
| 70 | 69 | 59 | 49 | CLAP YOUR HANDS — Beau-Marks, Shad 5017 | 13 |
| 71 | 84 | 70 | 71 | DO YOU MIND — Andy Williams, Cadence 1381 | 6 |
| 72 | 86 | — | — | FAR FAR AWAY — Don Gibson, RCA Victor 7762 | 2 |
| 73 | 63 | 42 | 21 | LOVE YOU SO — Rod Holden, Donna 1317 | 19 |
| 74 | 88 | 94 | 98 | MIO AMORE — Flamingos, End 1073 | 4 |
| 75 | — | — | — | NEVER ON SUNDAY — Don Costa, United Artists 234 | 1 |
| 76 | 95 | — | — | IT ONLY HAPPENED YESTERDAY — Jack Scott, Top Rank 2055 | 2 |
| 77 | 91 | 93 | 97 | BIG BOY PETE — Olympics, Arvee 595 | 6 |
| 78 | 98 | — | — | WRECK OF THE "JOHN B" — Jimmie Rodgers, Roulette 4260 | 2 |
| 79 | 89 | — | — | SWINGING DOWN THE LANE — Jerry Wallace, Challenge 59082 | 2 |
| 80 | — | — | — | YOGI — Ivy Three, Shell 720 | 1 |
| 81 | — | — | — | ANYMORE — Teresa Brewer, Coral 62219 | 1 |
| 82 | 100 | 98 | 100 | NIGHT TRAIN — Viscounts, Madison 133 | 4 |
| 83 | 93 | 95 | — | HAPPY SHADES OF BLUE — Freddy Cannon, Swan 40578 | 3 |
| 84 | — | — | — | LITTLE BITTY PRETTY ONE — Frankie Lyman, Roulette 4257 | 1 |
| 85 | 87 | 100 | — | COOL WATER — Jack Scott, Top Rank 2055 | 3 |
| 86 | 73 | — | — | I LOVE YOU IN THE SAME OLD WAY — Paul Anka, ABC-Paramount 10132 | 2 |
| 87 | — | — | — | YOU MEAN EVERYTHING TO ME — Neil Sedaka, RCA Victor 7781 | 1 |
| 88 | 94 | 97 | 94 | I'VE BEEN LOVED BEFORE — Shirley and Lee, Warwick 535 | 6 |
| 89 | 92 | — | — | IF I CAN'T HAVE YOU — Etta James and Harvey, Chess 1760 | 2 |
| 90 | — | — | — | BRIGADE OF BROKEN HEARTS — Paul Evans, Guaranteed 210 | 1 |
| 91 | 83 | 87 | 91 | THAT'S WHEN I CRIED — Jimmy Jones, Cub 9072 | 5 |
| 92 | 96 | — | — | WE GO TOGETHER — Jan and Dean, Dore 555 | 2 |
| 93 | — | — | — | HOT ROD LINCOLN — Johnny Bond, Republic 2005 | 1 |
| 94 | 90 | 81 | 74 | BE BOP-A-LULA — Everly Brothers, Cadence 1380 | 5 |
| 95 | 53 | 61 | 87 | TWIST — Hank Ballard and the Midnighters, King 5171 | 4 |
| 96 | — | — | — | BLUE VELVET — Statues, Liberty 55245 | 1 |
| 97 | 99 | — | — | DEVIL OR ANGEL — Bobby Vee, Liberty 55270 | 2 |
| 98 | — | — | — | SHE'S MINE — Conway Twitty, M-G-M 12911 | 1 |
| 99 | — | — | — | NO — Dodie Stevens, Dot 16103 | 1 |
| 100 | — | — | — | RUN, SAMSON, RUN — Neil Sedaka, RCA Victor 7781 | 1 |

# The Billboard HOT 100

**AUGUST 15, 1960**

FOR WEEK ENDING AUGUST 21

| This Week | 1 Wk Ago | 2 Wks Ago | 3 Wks Ago | Title / Artist, Company, Record No. | Weeks on Chart |
|---|---|---|---|---|---|
| 1 | 3 | 3 | 14 | IT'S NOW OR NEVER — Elvis Presley, RCA Victor 7777 | 5 |
| 2 | 1 | 2 | 5 | ITSY BITSY TEENIE WEENIE YELLOW POLKA DOT BIKINI — Brian Hyland, Leader 805 | 7 |
| 3 | 2 | 1 | 1 | I'M SORRY — Brenda Lee, Decca 31093 | 12 |
| 4 | 4 | 4 | 2 | ONLY THE LONELY — Roy Orbison, Monument 421 | 10 |
| 5 | 7 | 18 | 39 | WALK, DON'T RUN — Ventures, Dolton 25 | 5 |
| 6 | 10 | 13 | 13 | WALKIN' TO NEW ORLEANS — Fats Domino, Imperial 5675 | 9 |
| 7 | 15 | 14 | 17 | FINGER POPPIN' TIME — Hank Ballard and the Midnighters, King 5341 | 14 |
| 8 | 11 | 49 | — | TWIST — Chubby Checker, Parkway 811 | 3 |
| 9 | 8 | 7 | 8 | TELL LAURA I LOVE HER — Ray Peterson, RCA Victor 7745 | 10 |
| 10 | 6 | 6 | 7 | IMAGE OF A GIRL — Safaris, Eldo 101 | 11 |
| 11 | 27 | 30 | 48 | VOLARE (NEL BLU DI PINTO DI BLU) — Bobby Rydell, Cameo 179 | 5 |
| 12 | 18 | 24 | 20 | MISSION BELL — Donnie Brooks, Era 3018 | 10 |
| 13 | 9 | 8 | 9 | PLEASE HELP ME, I'M FALLING — Hank Locklin, RCA Victor 7692 | 13 |
| 14 | 24 | 26 | 49 | (YOU WERE MADE FOR) ALL MY LOVE — Jackie Wilson, Brunswick 55167 | 6 |
| 15 | 23 | 41 | 50 | IN MY LITTLE CORNER OF THE WORLD — Anita Bryant, Carlton 530 | 6 |
| 16 | 5 | 5 | 3 | ALLEY-OOP — Hollywood Argyles, Lute 5905 | 12 |
| 17 | 13 | 9 | 6 | MULE SKINNER BLUES — Fendermen, Soma 1137 | 13 |
| 18 | 14 | 15 | 25 | FEEL SO FINE — Johnny Preston, Mercury 71651 | 9 |
| 19 | 29 | 34 | 80 | A WOMAN, A LOVER, A FRIEND — Jackie Wilson, Brunswick 55167 | 6 |
| 20 | 12 | 11 | 4 | EVERYBODY'S SOMEBODY'S FOOL — Connie Francis, M-G-M 12899 | 15 |
| 21 | 20 | 20 | 21 | TROUBLE IN PARADISE — Crests, Coed 531 | 10 |
| 22 | 16 | 16 | 18 | LOOK FOR A STAR — Garry Miles, Liberty 55261 | 9 |
| 23 | 36 | 85 | 96 | THEME FROM THE APARTMENT — Ferrante and Teicher, United Artists 231 | 4 |
| 24 | 26 | 31 | 27 | THIS BITTER EARTH — Dinah Washington, Mercury 71635 | 9 |
| 25 | 17 | 17 | 12 | BECAUSE THEY'RE YOUNG — Duane Eddy, Jamie 1156 | 13 |
| 26 | 19 | 22 | 23 | QUESTION — Lloyd Price, ABC-Paramount 10123 | 8 |
| 27 | 25 | 58 | 65 | OVER THE RAINBOW — Demensions, Mohawk 116 | 7 |
| 28 | 41 | 59 | 86 | DREAMIN' — Johnny Burnette, Liberty 55258 | 4 |
| 29 | 22 | 23 | 19 | JOSEPHINE — Bill Black's Combo, Hi 2022 | 8 |
| 30 | 21 | 12 | 11 | WHEN WILL I BE LOVED — Everly Brothers, Cadence 1380 | 12 |
| 31 | 28 | 19 | 24 | LOOK FOR A STAR — Billy Vaughn, Dot 16106 | 9 |
| 32 | 51 | 40 | 53 | A MESS OF BLUES — Elvis Presley, RCA Victor 7777 | 4 |
| 33 | 30 | 21 | 22 | DON'T COME KNOCKIN' — Fats Domino, Imperial 5675 | 8 |
| 34 | 32 | 32 | 45 | WHERE ARE YOU — Frankie Avalon, Chancellor 1052 | 10 |
| 35 | 33 | 10 | 10 | THAT'S ALL YOU GOTTA DO — Brenda Lee, Decca 31093 | 11 |
| 36 | 31 | 33 | 41 | IS THERE ANY CHANCE — Marty Robbins, Columbia 41686 | 9 |
| 37 | 44 | 39 | 35 | ONE OF US (WILL WEEP TONIGHT) — Patti Page, Mercury 71639 | 11 |
| 38 | 46 | 66 | 78 | IN THE STILL OF THE NIGHT — Dion and the Belmonts, Laurie 3059 | 5 |
| 39 | 35 | 29 | 26 | LOOK FOR A STAR — Garry Mills, Imperial 5674 | 9 |
| 40 | 37 | 43 | 62 | BAD MAN BLUNDER — Kingston Trio, Capitol 4375 | 4 |
| 41 | 59 | — | — | KIDDIO — Brook Benton, Mercury 71652 | 2 |
| 42 | 93 | — | — | HOT ROD LINCOLN — Johnny Bond, Republic 2005 | 2 |
| 43 | 38 | 37 | 37 | IS A BLUEBIRD BLUE — Conway Twitty, M-G-M 12911 | 10 |
| 44 | 58 | 76 | — | RED SAILS IN THE SUNSET — Platters and Tony Williams, Mercury 71656 | 3 |
| 45 | 42 | 28 | 28 | ALLEY-OOP — Dante and the Evergreens, Madison 130 | 12 |
| 46 | 49 | 42 | 38 | HEARTBREAK (IT'S HURTIN' ME) — Little Willie John, King 5536 | 11 |
| 47 | 55 | 61 | 63 | TA-TA — Clyde McPhatter, Mercury 71660 | 5 |
| 48 | 43 | 36 | 29 | LOOK FOR A STAR — Dean Hawley, Dore 554 | 9 |
| 49 | 48 | 55 | 60 | HEARTBREAK (IT'S HURTIN' ME) — Jon Thomas, ABC-Paramount 10122 | 8 |
| 50 | 39 | 57 | 55 | HOT ROD LINCOLN — Charlie Ryan, Four Star 1733 | 12 |
| 51 | 63 | 79 | — | HELLO, YOUNG LOVERS — Paul Anka, ABC-Paramount 10132 | 3 |
| 52 | 53 | 52 | 57 | I SHOT MR. LEE — Bobbettes, Triple-X 104 | 7 |
| 53 | 45 | 35 | 40 | THERE IS SOMETHING ON YOUR MIND — Bobby Marchan, Fire 1022 | 10 |
| 54 | 60 | 68 | 75 | ONE BOY — Joanie Sommers, Warner Bros. 5157 | 7 |
| 55 | 62 | 78 | 89 | LISA — Jeanne Black, Capitol 4396 | 4 |
| 56 | — | — | — | MY HEART HAS A MIND OF ITS OWN — Connie Francis, M-G-M 12923 | 1 |
| 57 | 80 | — | — | YOGI — Ivy Three, Shell 720 | 2 |
| 58 | 84 | — | — | LITTLE BITTY PRETTY ONE — Frankie Lyman, Roulette 4257 | 2 |
| 59 | 86 | 73 | — | I LOVE YOU IN THE SAME OLD WAY — Paul Anka, ABC-Paramount 10132 | 3 |
| 60 | 47 | 44 | 34 | I REALLY DON'T WANT TO KNOW — Tommy Edwards, M-G-M 12890 | 13 |
| 61 | 95 | 53 | 61 | TWIST — Hank Ballard and the Midnighters, Kings 5171 | 5 |
| 62 | 64 | 77 | — | MY LOVE — Nat King Cole, Capitol 4393 | 3 |
| 63 | 57 | 56 | 51 | WAKE ME, SHAKE ME — Coasters, Atco 6168 | 9 |
| 64 | 76 | 95 | — | IT ONLY HAPPENED YESTERDAY — Jack Scott, Top Rank 2055 | 3 |
| 65 | 75 | — | — | NEVER ON SUNDAY — Don Costa, United Artists 234 | 2 |
| 66 | 65 | 48 | 56 | HEY, LITTLE ONE — Dorsey Burnette, Era 3019 | 11 |
| 67 | 34 | 25 | 15 | A ROCKIN' GOOD WAY — Dinah Washington and Brook Benton, Mercury 71629 | 13 |
| 68 | 54 | 27 | 16 | MY HOME TOWN — Paul Anka, ABC-Paramount 10106 | 13 |
| 69 | 87 | — | — | YOU MEAN EVERYTHING TO ME — Neil Sedaka, RCA Victor 7781 | 2 |
| 70 | 40 | 67 | 58 | STICKS AND STONES — Ray Charles, ABC-Paramount 10118 | 8 |
| 71 | 78 | 98 | — | WRECK OF THE "JOHN B" — Jimmie Rodgers, Roulette 4260 | 3 |
| 72 | 77 | 91 | 93 | BIG BOY PETE — Olympics, Arvee 595 | 7 |
| 73 | 61 | 47 | 46 | RUNAROUND — Fleetwoods, Dolton 22 | 13 |
| 74 | 67 | 54 | 66 | PLEASE HELP ME, I'M FALLING — Rusty Draper, Mercury 71634 | 5 |
| 75 | 81 | — | — | ANYMORE — Teresa Brewer, Coral 62119 | 2 |
| 76 | 72 | 86 | — | FAR FAR AWAY — Don Gibson, RCA Victor 7762 | 3 |
| 77 | 74 | 88 | 94 | MIO AMORE — Flamingos, End 1073 | 5 |
| 78 | 89 | 92 | — | IF I CAN'T HAVE YOU — Etta James and Harvey, Chess 1760 | 3 |
| 79 | — | — | — | CHAIN GANG — Sam Cooke, RCA Victor 7783 | 1 |
| 80 | 50 | 60 | 69 | MY TANI — Brothers Four, Columbia 41692 | 7 |
| 81 | — | — | — | YOU'RE LOOKIN' GOOD — Dee Clark, Vee-Jay 623 | 1 |
| 82 | 90 | — | — | BRIGADE OF BROKEN HEARTS — Paul Evans, Guaranteed 210 | 2 |
| 83 | — | — | — | (I DO THE) SHIMMY-SHIMMY — Bobby Freeman, King 5373 | 1 |
| 84 | 96 | — | — | BLUE VELVET — Statues, Liberty 55245 | 2 |
| 85 | — | — | — | BONGO, BONGO, BONGO — Preston Epps, Original Sound 09 | 1 |
| 86 | 83 | 93 | 95 | HAPPY SHADES OF BLUE — Freddy Cannon, Swan 4057 | 4 |
| 87 | 70 | 69 | 59 | CLAP YOUR HANDS — Beau-Marks, Shad 5017 | 14 |
| 88 | 82 | 100 | 98 | NIGHT TRAIN — Viscounts, Madison 133 | 5 |
| 89 | 68 | 38 | 30 | WONDERFUL WORLD — Sam Cooke, Keen 82112 | 15 |
| 90 | — | — | — | KOOKIE LITTLE PARADISE — Jo-Ann Campbell, ABC-Paramount 10135 | 1 |
| 91 | — | — | — | DO YOU MIND — Anthony Newley, London 1918 | 2 |
| 92 | 66 | 50 | 43 | I'M GETTIN' BETTER — Jim Reeves, RCA Victor 7756 | 9 |
| 93 | 97 | 99 | — | DEVIL OR ANGEL — Bobby Vee, Liberty 55270 | 3 |
| 94 | — | — | — | HONEST I DO — Innocents, Indigo 1055 | 1 |
| 95 | — | — | — | PINEAPPLE PRINCESS — Annette, Vista 362 | 1 |
| 96 | 71 | 84 | 70 | DO YOU MIND — Andy Williams, Cadence 1381 | 7 |
| 97 | 99 | — | — | NO — Dodie Stevens, Dot 16103 | 2 |
| 98 | — | — | — | KOOKIE LITTLE PARADISE — Tree Swingers, Guyden 2036 | 1 |
| 99 | — | — | — | THE LAST DANCE — McGuire Sisters, Coral 62216 | 1 |
| 100 | — | — | — | HOW HIGH THE MOON — Ella Fitzgerald, Verve 10220 | 1 |

# The Billboard HOT 100

**FOR WEEK ENDING AUGUST 28**

*STAR PERFORMERS showed the greatest upward progress on Hot 100 this week.*
*S — Indicates that 45 r.p.m. stereo single version is available.*
*SS — Indicates that 33⅓ r.p.m. stereo single version is available.*

Columns: THIS WEEK | ONE WEEK AGO | TWO WEEKS AGO | THREE WEEKS AGO | TITLE — Artist, Company, Record No. | WEEKS ON CHART

| TW | 1W | 2W | 3W | TITLE — Artist, Company, Record No. | Wks |
|---|---|---|---|---|---|
| 1 | 1 | 3 | 3 | IT'S NOW OR NEVER — Elvis Presley, RCA Victor 7777 | 6 |
| 2 | 2 | 1 | 2 | ITSY BITSY TEENIE WEENIE YELLOW POLKA DOT BIKINI — Brian Hyland, Kapp 342 | 8 |
| 3 | 5 | 7 | 18 | WALK, DON'T RUN — Ventures, Dolton 25 | 6 |
| 4 | 8 | 11 | 49 | TWIST — Chubby Checker, Parkway 811 | 4 |
| 5 | 3 | 2 | 1 | I'M SORRY — Brenda Lee, Decca 31093 | 13 |
| 6 | 4 | 4 | 4 | ONLY THE LONELY — Roy Orbison, Monument 421 | 11 |
| 7 | 11 | 27 | 30 | VOLARE (NEL BLU DI PINTO DI BLU) — Bobby Rydell, Cameo 179 | 6 |
| 8 | 7 | 15 | 14 | FINGER POPPIN' TIME — Hank Ballard and the Midnighters, King 5341 | 15 |
| 9 | 12 | 18 | 24 | MISSION BELL — Donnie Brooks, Era 3018 | 11 |
| 10 | 10 | 6 | 6 | IMAGE OF A GIRL — Safaris, Eldo 101 | 12 |
| 11 | 6 | 10 | 13 | WALKIN' TO NEW ORLEANS — Fats Domino, Imperial 5675 | 10 |
| 12 | 14 | 24 | 26 | (YOU WERE MADE FOR) ALL MY LOVE — Jackie Wilson, Brunswick 55167 | 7 |
| 13 | 13 | 9 | 8 | PLEASE HELP ME, I'M FALLING — Hank Locklin, RCA Victor 7692 | 14 |
| 14 | 15 | 23 | 41 | IN MY LITTLE CORNER OF THE WORLD — Anita Bryant, Carlton 530 | 7 |
| 15 | 19 | 29 | 34 | A WOMAN, A LOVER, A FRIEND — Jackie Wilson, Brunswick 55167 | 7 |
| 16 | 9 | 8 | 7 | TELL LAURA I LOVE HER — Ray Peterson, RCA Victor 7745 | 11 |
| ★17 | 28 | 41 | 59 | DREAMIN' — Johnny Burnette, Liberty 55258 | 5 |
| 18 | 17 | 13 | 9 | MULE SKINNER BLUES — Fendermen, Soma 1137 | 14 |
| 19 | 18 | 14 | 15 | FEEL SO FINE — Johnny Preston, Mercury 71651 | 10 |
| ★20 | 27 | 25 | 58 | OVER THE RAINBOW — Demensions, Mohawk 116 | 8 |
| 21 | 31 | 28 | 19 | LOOK FOR A STAR — Billy Vaughn, Dot 16106 | 10 |
| 22 | 22 | 16 | 16 | LOOK FOR A STAR — Garry Miles, Liberty 55261 | 10 |
| 23 | 16 | 5 | 5 | ALLEY-OOP — Hollywood Argyles, Lute 5905 | 13 |
| 24 | 20 | 12 | 11 | EVERYBODY'S SOMEBODY'S FOOL — Connie Francis, M-G-M 12899 | 16 |
| ★25 | 47 | 55 | 61 | TA-TA — Clyde McPhatter, Mercury 71660 | 6 |
| 26 | 21 | 20 | 20 | TROUBLE IN PARADISE — Crests, Coed 531 | 11 |
| 27 | 23 | 36 | 85 | THEME FROM THE APARTMENT — Ferrante and Teicher, United Artists 231 | 5 |
| 28 | 25 | 17 | 17 | BECAUSE THEY'RE YOUNG — Duane Eddy, Jamie 1156 | 14 |
| 29 | 26 | 19 | 22 | QUESTION — Lloyd Price, ABC-Paramount 10123 | 9 |
| 30 | 29 | 22 | 23 | JOSEPHINE — Bill Black's Combo, Hi 2022 | 9 |
| ★31 | 41 | 59 | — | KIDDIO — Brook Benton, Mercury 71652 | 3 |
| ★32 | 42 | 93 | — | HOT ROD LINCOLN — Johnny Bond, Republic 2005 | 3 |
| 33 | 33 | 30 | 21 | DON'T COME KNOCKIN' — Fats Domino, Imperial 5675 | 9 |
| ★34 | 56 | — | — | MY HEART HAS A MIND OF ITS OWN — Connie Francis, M-G-M 12923 | 2 |
| 35 | 51 | 63 | 79 | HELLO, YOUNG LOVERS — Paul Anka, ABC-Paramount 10132 | 4 |
| 36 | 44 | 58 | 76 | RED SAILS IN THE SUNSET — Platters and Tony Williams, Mercury 71656 | 4 |
| 37 | 24 | 26 | 31 | THIS BITTER EARTH — Dinah Washington, Mercury 71635 | 10 |
| 38 | 34 | 32 | 32 | WHERE ARE YOU — Frankie Avalon, Chancellor 1052 | 11 |
| 39 | 30 | 21 | 12 | WHEN WILL I BE LOVED — Everly Brothers, Cadence 1380 | 13 |
| 40 | 39 | 35 | 29 | LOOK FOR A STAR — Garry Mills, Imperial 5674 | 10 |
| 41 | 38 | 46 | 66 | IN THE STILL OF THE NIGHT — Dion and the Belmonts, Laurie 3059 | 6 |
| 42 | 35 | 33 | 10 | THAT'S ALL YOU GOTTA DO — Brenda Lee, Decca 31093 | 12 |
| 43 | 36 | 31 | 33 | IS THERE ANY CHANCE — Marty Robbins, Columbia 41686 | 10 |
| 44 | 40 | 37 | 43 | BAD MAN BLUNDER — Kingston Trio, Capitol 4375 | 5 |
| 45 | 32 | 51 | 40 | A MESS OF BLUES — Elvis Presley, RCA Victor 7777 | 5 |
| 46 | 43 | 38 | 37 | IS A BLUEBIRD BLUE — Conway Twitty, M-G-M 12911 | 11 |
| ★47 | 57 | 80 | — | YOGI — Ivy Three, Shell 720 | 3 |
| 48 | 45 | 42 | 28 | ALLEY-OOP — Dante and the Evergreens, Madison 130 | 13 |
| 49 | 62 | 64 | 77 | MY LOVE — Nat King Cole, Capitol 4393 | 4 |
| ★50 | 64 | 76 | 95 | IT ONLY HAPPENED YESTERDAY — Jack Scott, Top Rank 2055 | 4 |
| 51 | 59 | 86 | 73 | I LOVE YOU IN THE SAME OLD WAY — Paul Anka, ABC-Paramount 10132 | 4 |
| 52 | 48 | 43 | 36 | LOOK FOR A STAR — Dean Hawley, Dore 554 | 10 |
| 53 | 50 | 39 | 57 | HOT ROD LINCOLN — Charlie Ryan, Four Star 1733 | 13 |
| ★54 | 79 | — | — | CHAIN GANG — Sam Cooke, RCA Victor 7783 | 2 |
| 55 | 37 | 44 | 39 | ONE OF US (WILL WEEP TONIGHT) [S] — Patti Page, Mercury 71639 | 12 |
| 56 | 55 | 62 | 78 | LISA — Jeanne Black, Capitol 4396 | 5 |
| ★57 | 69 | 87 | — | YOU MEAN EVERYTHING TO ME — Neil Sedaka, RCA Victor 7781 | 3 |
| 58 | 61 | 95 | 53 | TWIST — Hank Ballard and the Midnighters, King 5171 | 6 |
| 59 | 72 | 77 | 91 | BIG BOY PETE — Olympics, Arvee 595 | 8 |
| 60 | 65 | 75 | — | NEVER ON SUNDAY — Don Costa, United Artists 234 | 3 |
| ★61 | — | — | — | SAME ONE — Brook Benton, Mercury 71652 | 1 |
| 62 | 54 | 60 | 68 | ONE BOY — Joanie Sommers, Warner Bros. 5157 | 8 |
| 63 | 75 | 81 | — | ANYMORE — Teresa Brewer, Coral 62218 | 3 |
| 64 | 78 | 89 | 92 | IF I CAN'T HAVE YOU — Etta James and Harvey, Chess 1760 | 4 |
| 65 | 52 | 53 | 52 | I SHOT MR. LEE — Bobbettes, Triple-X 104 | 8 |
| 66 | 53 | 45 | 35 | THERE IS SOMETHING ON YOUR MIND — Bobby Marchan, Fire 1022 | 11 |
| 67 | 58 | 84 | — | LITTLE BITTY PRETTY ONE — Frankie Lymon, Roulette 4257 | 3 |
| ★68 | — | — | — | DELIA GONE — Pat Boone, Dot 16122 | 1 |
| 69 | 46 | 49 | 42 | HEARTBREAK (IT'S HURTIN' ME) — Little Willie John, King 5356 | 12 |
| 70 | 71 | 78 | 98 | WRECK OF THE "JOHN B" — Jimmie Rodgers, Roulette 4260 | 4 |
| 71 | 83 | — | — | (I DO THE) SHIMMY SHIMMY — Bobby Freeman, King 5373 | 2 |
| 72 | 49 | 48 | 55 | HEARTBREAK (IT'S HURTIN' ME) — Jon Thomas, ABC-Paramount 10122 | 9 |
| ★73 | 98 | — | — | KOOKIE LITTLE PARADISE — Tree Swingers, Guyden 2036 | 2 |
| 74 | — | — | — | (I CAN'T HELP YOU) I'M FALLING TOO — Skeeter Davis, RCA Victor 7767 | 1 |
| 75 | 81 | — | — | YOU'RE LOOKIN' GOOD — Dee Clark, Vee-Jay 623 | 2 |
| 76 | 93 | 97 | 99 | DEVIL OR ANGEL — Bobby Vee, Liberty 55270 | 4 |
| 77 | 74 | 67 | 54 | PLEASE HELP ME, I'M FALLING — Rusty Draper, Mercury 71634 | 6 |
| 78 | 85 | — | — | BONGO, BONGO BONGO — Preston Epps, Original Sound 09 | 2 |
| 79 | 76 | 72 | 86 | FAR, FAR AWAY — Don Gibson, RCA Victor 7762 | 4 |
| 80 | — | — | — | CANDY SWEET — Pat Boone, Dot 16122 | 1 |
| 81 | 82 | 90 | — | BRIGADE OF BROKEN HEARTS — Paul Evans, Guaranteed 210 | 3 |
| 82 | — | 92 | 96 | WE GO TOGETHER — Jan and Dean, Dore 555 | 3 |
| 83 | 77 | 74 | 88 | MIO AMORE — Flamingos, End 1073 | 6 |
| 84 | — | — | 82 | MY SHOES KEEP WALKING BACK TO YOU — Guy Mitchell, Columbia 41725 | 4 |
| 85 | 92 | 66 | 50 | I'M GETTIN' BETTER — Jim Reeves, RCA Victor 7756 | 10 |
| 86 | — | — | — | MALAGUENA — Connie Francis, M-G-M 12923 | 1 |
| 87 | — | — | — | OLD OAKEN BUCKET — Tommy Sands, Capitol 4405 | 1 |
| 88 | 94 | — | — | HONEST I DO — Innocents, Indigo 1055 | 2 |
| 89 | — | — | — | KOMMOTION — Duane Eddy, Jamie 1163 | 1 |
| 90 | — | — | — | COME BACK — Jimmy Clanton, Ace 600 | 1 |
| 91 | 95 | — | — | PINEAPPLE PRINCESS — Annette, Vista 362 | 2 |
| 92 | 90 | — | — | KOOKIE LITTLE PARADISE — Jo-Ann Campbell, ABC-Paramount 10134 | 2 |
| 93 | 97 | 99 | — | NO — Dodie Stevens, Dot 16103 | 3 |
| 94 | — | — | — | I KNOW ONE — Jim Reeves, RCA Victor 7756 | 2 |
| 95 | — | — | — | A MILLION TO ONE — Jimmy Charles, Promo 1002 | 1 |
| 96 | 100 | — | — | HOW HIGH THE MOON — Ella Fitzgerald, Verve 10220 | 2 |
| 97 | 84 | 96 | — | BLUE VELVET — Statues, Liberty 55245 | 3 |
| 98 | 86 | 83 | 93 | HAPPY SHADES OF BLUE — Freddy Cannon, Swan 4057 | 5 |
| 99 | — | — | — | DIAMONDS AND PEARLS — Paradons, Milestone 2003 | 1 |
| 100 | — | — | — | LOVING TOUCH — Mark Dinning, M-G-M 12929 | 1 |

## The Billboard HOT 100

**FOR WEEK ENDING SEPTEMBER 4**

*STAR PERFORMERS showed the greatest upward progress on Hot 100 this week.*
[S] Indicates that 45 r.p.m. stereo single version is available.
[S] Indicates that 33⅓ r.p.m. stereo single version is available.

Columns: THIS WEEK | ONE WEEK AGO | TWO WEEKS AGO | THREE WEEKS AGO | TITLE — Artist, Company — Record No. | STEREO | WEEKS ON CHART

| This | 1wk | 2wk | 3wk | Title — Artist, Company, Record No. | Weeks |
|---|---|---|---|---|---|
| 1 | 1 | 1 | 3 | IT'S NOW OR NEVER — Elvis Presley, RCA Victor 7777 | 7 |
| 2 | 3 | 5 | 7 | WALK, DON'T RUN — Ventures, Dolton 25 | 7 |
| 3 | 4 | 8 | 11 | TWIST — Chubby Checker, Parkway 811 | 5 |
| 4 | 5 | 3 | 2 | I'M SORRY — Brenda Lee, Decca 31093 | 14 |
| 5 | 7 | 11 | 27 | VOLARE (NEL BLU DI PINTO DI BLU) — Bobby Rydell, Cameo 179 | 7 |
| 6 | 2 | 2 | 1 | ITSY BITSY TEENIE WEENIE YELLOW POLKA DOT BIKINI — Brian Hyland, Kapp 342 | 9 |
| 7 | 8 | 7 | 15 | FINGER POPPIN' TIME — Hank Ballard and the Midnighters, King 5341 | 16 |
| 8 | 9 | 12 | 18 | MISSION BELL — Donnie Brooks, Era 3018 | 12 |
| 9 | 6 | 4 | 4 | ONLY THE LONELY — Roy Orbison, Monument 421 | 12 |
| 10 | 14 | 15 | 23 | IN MY LITTLE CORNER OF THE WORLD — Anita Bryant, Carlton 530 | 8 |
| 11 | 17 | 28 | 41 | DREAMIN' — Johnny Burnette, Liberty 55258 | 6 |
| 12 | 27 | 23 | 36 | THEME FROM THE APARTMENT — Ferrante and Teicher, United Artists 231 | 6 |
| 13 | 11 | 6 | 10 | WALKIN' TO NEW ORLEANS — Fats Domino, Imperial 5675 | 11 |
| 14 | 13 | 13 | 9 | PLEASE HELP ME, I'M FALLING — Hank Locklin, RCA Victor 7692 | 15 |
| 15 | 47 | 57 | 80 | YOGI — Ivy Three, Shell 720 | 4 |
| 16 | 34 | 56 | — | MY HEART HAS A MIND OF ITS OWN — Connie Francis, M-G-M 12923 | 3 |
| 17 | 20 | 27 | 25 | OVER THE RAINBOW — Demensions, Mohawk 116 | 9 |
| 18 | 10 | 10 | 6 | IMAGE OF A GIRL — Safaris, Eldo 101 | 13 |
| 19 | 12 | 14 | 24 | (YOU WERE MADE FOR) ALL MY LOVE — Jackie Wilson, Brunswick 55167 | 8 |
| 20 | 19 | 18 | 14 | FEEL SO FINE — Johnny Preston, Mercury 71651 | 11 |
| 21 | 15 | 19 | 29 | A WOMAN, A LOVER, A FRIEND — Jackie Wilson, Brunswick 55167 | 8 |
| 22 | 21 | 31 | 28 | LOOK FOR A STAR — Billy Vaughn, Dot 16106 | 11 |
| 23 | 35 | 51 | 63 | HELLO, YOUNG LOVERS — Paul Anka, ABC-Paramount 10132 | 5 |
| 24 | 22 | 22 | 16 | LOOK FOR A STAR — Garry Miles, Liberty 55261 | 11 |
| 25 | 25 | 47 | 55 | TA-TA — Clyde McPhatter, Mercury 71660 | 7 |
| 26 | 16 | 9 | 8 | TELL LAURA I LOVE HER — Ray Peterson, RCA Victor 7745 | 12 |
| 27 | 31 | 41 | 59 | KIDDIO — Brook Benton, Mercury 71652 | 4 |
| 28 | 60 | 65 | 75 | NEVER ON SUNDAY — Don Costa, United Artists 234 | 4 |
| 29 | 32 | 42 | 93 | HOT ROD LINCOLN — Johnny Bond, Republic 2005 | 4 |
| 30 | 24 | 20 | 12 | EVERYBODY'S SOMEBODY'S FOOL — Connie Francis, M-G-M 12899 | 17 |
| 31 | 23 | 16 | 5 | ALLEY-OOP — Hollywood Argyles, Lute 5905 | 14 |
| 32 | 18 | 17 | 13 | MULE SKINNER BLUES — Fendermen, Soma 1137 | 15 |
| 33 | 54 | 79 | — | CHAIN GANG — Sam Cooke, RCA Victor 7783 | 3 |
| 34 | 29 | 26 | 19 | QUESTION — Lloyd Price, ABC-Paramount 10123 | 10 |
| 35 | 26 | 21 | 20 | TROUBLE IN PARADISE — Crests, Coed 531 | 12 |
| 36 | 57 | 69 | 87 | YOU MEAN EVERYTHING TO ME — Neil Sedaka, RCA Victor 7781 | 4 |
| 37 | 33 | 33 | 30 | DON'T COME KNOCKIN' — Fats Domino, Imperial 5675 | 10 |
| 38 | 53 | 50 | 39 | HOT ROD LINCOLN — Charlie Ryan, Four Star 1733 | 14 |
| 39 | 61 | — | — | THE SAME ONE — Brook Benton, Mercury 71652 | 2 |
| 40 | 58 | 61 | 95 | TWIST — Hank Ballard and the Midnighters, King 5171 | 7 |
| 41 | 51 | 59 | 86 | I LOVE YOU IN THE SAME OLD WAY — Paul Anka, ABC-Paramount 10132 | 5 |
| 42 | 74 | — | — | (I CAN'T HELP YOU) I'M FALLING TOO — Skeeter Davis, RCA Victor 7677 | 2 |
| 43 | 42 | 35 | 33 | THAT'S ALL YOU GOTTA DO — Brenda Lee, Decca 31093 | 13 |
| 44 | 50 | 64 | 76 | IT ONLY HAPPENED YESTERDAY — Jack Scott, Top Rank 2055 | 5 |
| 45 | 76 | 93 | 97 | DEVIL OR ANGEL — Bobby Vee, Liberty 55270 | 5 |
| 46 | 36 | 44 | 58 | RED SAILS IN THE SUNSET — Platters and Tony Williams, Mercury 71656 | 11 |
| 47 | 49 | 62 | 64 | MY LOVE — Nat King Cole, Capitol 4393 | 5 |
| 48 | 43 | 36 | 31 | IS THERE ANY CHANCE — Marty Robbins, Columbia 41686 | 11 |
| 49 | 37 | 24 | 26 | THIS BITTER EARTH — Dinah Washington, Mercury 71635 | 11 |
| 50 | 41 | 38 | 46 | IN THE STILL OF THE NIGHT — Dion and the Belmonts, Laurie 3059 | 7 |
| 51 | 59 | 72 | 77 | BIG BOY PETE — Olympics, Arvee 595 | 9 |
| 52 | 95 | — | — | A MILLION TO ONE — Jimmy Charles, Promo 1002 | 2 |
| 53 | 38 | 34 | 32 | WHERE ARE YOU — Frankie Avalon, Chancellor 1052 | 12 |
| 54 | 63 | 75 | 81 | ANYMORE — Teresa Brewer, Coral 62219 | 4 |
| 55 | 52 | 48 | 43 | LOOK FOR A STAR — Dean Hawley, Dore 554 | 11 |
| 56 | 40 | 39 | 35 | LOOK FOR A STAR — Garry Mills, Imperial 5674 | 11 |
| 57 | 91 | 95 | — | PINEAPPLE PRINCESS — Annette, Vista 362 | 3 |
| 58 | 56 | 55 | 62 | LISA — Jeanne Black, Capitol 4396 | 6 |
| 59 | 71 | 83 | — | (I DO THE) SHIMMY, SHIMMY — Bobby Freeman, King 5373 | 3 |
| 60 | 82 | — | 92 | WE GO TOGETHER — Jan and Dean, Dore 555 | 4 |
| 61 | 55 | 37 | 44 | ONE OF US (WILL WEEP TONIGHT) — Patti Page, Mercury 71639 [S] | 13 |
| 62 | 64 | 78 | 89 | IF I CAN'T HAVE YOU — Etta James and Harvey, Chess 1760 | 5 |
| 63 | 45 | 32 | 51 | A MESS OF BLUES — Elvis Presley, RCA Victor 7777 | 6 |
| 64 | 84 | — | — | MY SHOES KEEP WALKING BACK TO YOU — Guy Mitchell, Columbia 41725 | 5 |
| 65 | — | — | — | MR. CUSTER — Larry Verne, Era 3024 | 1 |
| 66 | 68 | — | — | DELIA GONE — Pat Boone, Dot 16122 | 2 |
| 67 | 86 | — | — | MALAGUENA — Connie Francis, M-G-M 12923 | 2 |
| 68 | 70 | 71 | 78 | WRECK OF THE "JOHN B" — Jimmie Rodgers, Roulette 4260 | 5 |
| 69 | — | — | — | LET'S HAVE A PARTY — Wanda Jackson, Capitol 4397 | 1 |
| 70 | 62 | 54 | 60 | ONE BOY — Joanie Sommers, Warner Bros. 5157 | 9 |
| 71 | — | — | — | I WALK THE LINE — Jaye P. Morgan, M-G-M 12924 | 1 |
| 72 | 80 | — | — | CANDY SWEET — Pat Boone, Dot 16122 | 2 |
| 73 | 87 | — | — | OLD OAKEN BUCKET — Tommy Sands, Capitol 4405 | 2 |
| 74 | 67 | 58 | 84 | LITTLE BITTY PRETTY ONE — Frankie Lyman, Roulette 4257 | 4 |
| 75 | 73 | 98 | — | KOOKIE LITTLE PARADISE — Tree Swingers, Guyden 2036 | 3 |
| 76 | 30 | 29 | 22 | JOSEPHINE — Bill Black's Combo, Hi 2022 | 10 |
| 77 | 88 | 94 | — | HONEST I DO — Innocents, Indigo 1055 | 3 |
| 78 | 89 | — | — | KOMMOTION — Duane Eddy, Jamie 1163 | 2 |
| 79 | 75 | 81 | — | YOU'RE LOOKIN' GOOD — Dee Clark, Vee Jay 623 | 3 |
| 80 | 93 | 97 | 99 | NO — Dodie Stevens, Dot 16103 | 4 |
| 81 | 99 | — | — | DIAMONDS AND PEARLS — Paradons, Milestone 2003 | 2 |
| 82 | — | — | — | SHORTNIN' BREAD — Paul Chaplin, Harper 100 | 1 |
| 83 | 81 | 82 | 90 | BRIGADE OF BROKEN HEARTS — Paul Evans, Guaranteed 210 | 4 |
| 84 | 92 | 90 | — | KOOKIE LITTLE PARADISE — Jo Ann Campbell, ABC-Paramount 10134 | 3 |
| 85 | 90 | — | — | COME BACK — Jimmy Clanton, Ace 600 | 2 |
| 86 | — | — | — | MANY A WONDERFUL MOMENT — Rosemary Clooney, RCA Victor 7754 | 1 |
| 87 | — | — | — | A FOOL IN LOVE — Ike and Tina Turner, Sue 730 | 1 |
| 88 | — | — | — | THIS OLD HEART — James Brown and the Famous Flames, Federal 12323 | 1 |
| 89 | 77 | 74 | 67 | PLEASE HELP ME, I'M FALLING — Rusty Draper, Mercury 71634 | 7 |
| 90 | 28 | 25 | 17 | BECAUSE THEY'RE YOUNG — Duane Eddy, Jamie 1156 | 15 |
| 91 | 96 | 100 | — | HOW HIGH THE MOON — Ella Fitzgerald, Verve 1020 | 3 |
| 92 | 100 | — | — | LOVING TOUCH — Mark Dinning, M-G-M 12929 | 2 |
| 93 | — | — | — | NICE AND EASY — Frank Sinatra, Capitol 4408 | 1 |
| 94 | 78 | 85 | — | BONGO, BONGO, BONGO — Preston Epps, Original Sound 09 | 3 |
| 95 | — | — | — | MY LOVE FOR YOU — Johnny Mathis, Columbia 41764 | 1 |
| 96 | — | — | — | SHORTNIN' BREAD — Bellnotes, Madison 136 | 1 |
| 97 | — | — | — | REVIVAL — Johnny and the Hurricanes, Big Top 3051 | 1 |
| 98 | 79 | 76 | 72 | FAR, FAR AWAY — Don Gibson, RCA Victor 7762 | 5 |
| 99 | — | — | — | VAQUERO — Fireballs, Top Rank 2054 | 1 |
| 100 | — | — | — | A TEENAGER FEELS IT TOO — Denny Reed, Trey 3007 | 1 |

# The Billboard HOT 100

**FOR WEEK ENDING SEPTEMBER 11**

SEPTEMBER 5, 1960

STAR PERFORMERS showed the greatest upward progress on Hot 100 this week.
S — Indicates that 45 r.p.m. stereo single version is available.
Ⓢ — Indicates that 33⅓ r.p.m. stereo single version is available.

Columns: THIS WEEK | ONE WEEK AGO | TWO WEEKS AGO | THREE WEEKS AGO | TITLE — Artist, Company, Record No. | STEREO | WEEKS ON CHART

| # | 1wk | 2wk | 3wk | Title — Artist, Company, Record No. | Wks |
|---|---|---|---|---|---|
| 1 | 1 | 1 | 1 | IT'S NOW OR NEVER — Elvis Presley, RCA Victor 7777 | 8 |
| 2 | 3 | 4 | 8 | TWIST — Chubby Checker, Parkway 811 | 6 |
| 3 | 2 | 3 | 5 | WALK, DON'T RUN — Ventures, Dolton 25 | 8 |
| 4 | 5 | 7 | 11 | VOLARE (NEL BLU DI PINTO DI BLU) — Bobby Rydell, Cameo 179 | 8 |
| 5 | 4 | 5 | 3 | I'M SORRY — Brenda Lee, Decca 31093 | 15 |
| 6 | 6 | 2 | 2 | ITSY BITSY TEENIE WEENIE YELLOW POLKA DOT BIKINI — Brian Hyland, Kapp 342 | 10 |
| 7 | 8 | 9 | 12 | MISSION BELL — Donnie Brooks, Era 3018 | 13 |
| 8 | 7 | 8 | 7 | FINGER POPPIN' TIME — Hank Ballard and the Midnighters, King 5341 | 17 |
| 9 ★ | 16 | 34 | 56 | MY HEART HAS A MIND OF ITS OWN — Connie Francis, M-G-M 12923 | 4 |
| 10 | 12 | 27 | 23 | THEME FROM THE APARTMENT — Ferrante and Teicher, United Artists 231 | 7 |
| 11 | 10 | 14 | 15 | IN MY LITTLE CORNER OF THE WORLD — Anita Bryant, Carlton 530 | 9 |
| 12 | 9 | 6 | 4 | ONLY THE LONELY — Roy Orbison, Monument 421 | 13 |
| 13 ★ | 65 | — | — | MR. CUSTER — Larry Verne, Era 3024 | 2 |
| 14 | 15 | 47 | 57 | YOGI — Ivy Three, Shell 720 | 5 |
| 15 | 14 | 13 | 13 | PLEASE HELP ME, I'M FALLING — Hank Locklin, RCA Victor 7692 | 16 |
| 16 | 17 | 20 | 27 | OVER THE RAINBOW — Demensions, Mohawk 116 | 10 |
| 17 ★ | 27 | 31 | 41 | KIDDIO — Brook Benton, Mercury 71652 | 5 |
| 18 | 11 | 17 | 28 | DREAMIN' — Johnny Burnette, Liberty 55258 | 7 |
| 19 | 19 | 12 | 14 | (YOU WERE MADE FOR) ALL MY LOVE — Jackie Wilson, Brunswick 55167 | 9 |
| 20 ★ | 52 | 95 | — | A MILLION TO ONE — Jimmy Charles, Promo 1002 | 3 |
| 21 ★ | 39 | 61 | — | THE SAME ONE — Brook Benton, Mercury 71652 | 3 |
| 22 ★ | 33 | 54 | 79 | CHAIN GANG — Sam Cooke, RCA Victor 7783 | 4 |
| 23 | 23 | 35 | 51 | HELLO, YOUNG LOVERS — Paul Anka, ABC-Paramount 10132 | 6 |
| 24 | 25 | 25 | 47 | TA-TA — Clyde McPhatter, Mercury 71660 | 8 |
| 25 | 13 | 11 | 6 | WALKIN' TO NEW ORLEANS — Fats Domino, Imperial 5675 | 12 |
| 26 | 28 | 60 | 65 | NEVER ON SUNDAY — Don Costa, United Artists 234 | 5 |
| 27 | 18 | 10 | 10 | IMAGE OF A GIRL — Safaris, Eldo 101 | 14 |
| 28 | 36 | 57 | 69 | YOU MEAN EVERYTHING TO ME — Neil Sedaka, RCA Victor 7781 | 5 |
| 29 | 20 | 19 | 18 | FEEL SO FINE — Johnny Preston, Mercury 71651 | 12 |
| 30 | 21 | 15 | 19 | A WOMAN, A LOVER, A FRIEND — Jackie Wilson, Brunswick 55167 | 9 |
| 31 | 40 | 58 | 61 | TWIST — Hank Ballard and the Midnighters, King 5171 | 8 |
| 32 ★ | 45 | 76 | 93 | DEVIL OR ANGEL — Bobby Vee, Liberty 55270 | 6 |
| 33 | 38 | 53 | 50 | HOT ROD LINCOLN — Charlie Ryan, Four Star 1733 | 15 |
| 34 | 32 | 18 | 17 | MULE SKINNER BLUES — Fendermen, Soma 1137 | 16 |
| 35 | 26 | 16 | 9 | TELL LAURA I LOVE HER — Ray Peterson, RCA Victor 7745 | 13 |
| 36 | 29 | 32 | 42 | HOT ROD LINCOLN — Johnny Bond, Republic 2005 | 5 |
| 37 ★ | 57 | 91 | 95 | PINEAPPLE PRINCESS — Annette, Vista 362 | 4 |
| 38 | 44 | 50 | 64 | IT ONLY HAPPENED YESTERDAY — Jack Scott, Top Rank 2055 | 6 |
| 39 | 42 | 74 | — | (I CAN'T HELP YOU) I'M FALLING TOO — Skeeter Davis, RCA Victor 7767 | 3 |
| 40 | 35 | 26 | 21 | TROUBLE IN PARADISE — Crests, Coed 531 | 13 |
| 41 | 31 | 23 | 16 | ALLEY-OOP — Hollywood Argyles, Lute 5905 | 15 |
| 42 | 30 | 24 | 20 | EVERYBODY'S SOMEBODY'S FOOL — Connie Francis, M-G-M 12899 | 18 |
| 43 | 58 | 56 | 55 | LISA — Jeanne Black, Capitol 4396 | 7 |
| 44 | 41 | 51 | 59 | I LOVE YOU IN THE SAME OLD WAY — Paul Anka, ABC-Paramount 10132 | 6 |
| 45 | 24 | 22 | 22 | LOOK FOR A STAR — Garry Miles, Liberty 55261 | 12 |
| 46 | 54 | 63 | 75 | ANYMORE — Teresa Brewer, Coral 62219 | 5 |
| 47 ★ | — | — | — | SO SAD — Everly Brothers, Warner Bros. 5163 | 1 |
| 48 | 34 | 29 | 26 | QUESTION — Lloyd Price, ABC-Paramount 10123 | 11 |
| 49 | 37 | 33 | 33 | DON'T COME KNOCKIN' — Fats Domino, Imperial 5675 | 11 |
| 50 | 22 | 21 | 31 | LOOK FOR A STAR — Billy Vaughn, Dot 16106 | 12 |
| 51 | 47 | 49 | 62 | MY LOVE — Nat King Cole, Capitol 4393 | 6 |
| 52 | 69 | — | — | LET'S HAVE A PARTY — Wanda Jackson, Capitol 4397 | 2 |
| 53 | 64 | 84 | — | MY SHOES KEEP WALKING BACK TO YOU — Guy Mitchell, Columbia 41725 | 6 |
| 54 | 51 | 59 | 72 | BIG BOY PETE — Olympics, Arvee 595 | 10 |
| 55 | 63 | 45 | 32 | A MESS OF BLUES — Elvis Presley, RCA Victor 7777 | 7 |
| 56 | 46 | 36 | 44 | RED SAILS IN THE SUNSET — Platters and Tony Williams, Mercury 71656 | 12 |
| 57 | 60 | 82 | — | WE GO TOGETHER — Jan and Dean, Dore 555 | 5 |
| 58 | 59 | 71 | 83 | (I DO THE) SHIMMY, SHIMMY — Bobby Freeman, King 5373 | 4 |
| 59 | 67 | 86 | — | MALAGUENA — Connie Francis, M-G-M 12923 | 3 |
| 60 ★ | — | — | — | LET THE GOOD TIMES ROLL — Shirley and Lee, Warwick 581 | 1 |
| 61 | 79 | 75 | 81 | YOU'RE LOOKIN' GOOD — Dee Clark, Vee Jay 355 | 4 |
| 62 | 62 | 64 | 78 | IF I CAN'T HAVE YOU — Etta James and Harvey, Chess 1760 | 6 |
| 63 | 43 | 42 | 35 | THAT'S ALL YOU GOTTA DO — Brenda Lee, Decca 31093 | 14 |
| 64 | 49 | 37 | 24 | THIS BITTER EARTH — Dinah Washington, Mercury 71635 | 12 |
| 65 | 61 | 55 | 37 | ONE OF US (WILL WEEP TONIGHT) — Patti Page, Mercury 71639 | 14 |
| 66 ★ | — | — | — | LUCILLE — Everly Brothers, Warner Bros. 5163 | 1 |
| 67 | 87 | — | — | A FOOL IN LOVE — Ike and Tina Turner, Sue 730 | 2 |
| 68 | 93 | — | — | NICE AND EASY — Frank Sinatra, Capitol 4408 | 2 |
| 69 | 77 | 88 | 94 | HONEST I DO — Innocents, Indigo 1055 | 4 |
| 70 | 84 | 93 | 90 | KOOKIE LITTLE PARADISE — Jo Ann Campbell, ABC-Paramount 10134 | 4 |
| 71 | 71 | — | — | I WALK THE LINE — Jaye P. Morgan, M-G-M 12924 | 2 |
| 72 | 95 | — | — | MY LOVE FOR YOU — Johnny Mathis, Columbia 41764 | 2 |
| 73 | 68 | 70 | 71 | WRECK OF THE "JOHN B" — Jimmie Rodgers, Roulette 4260 | 6 |
| 74 | 66 | 68 | — | DELIA GONE — Pat Boone, Dot 16122 | 3 |
| 75 ★ | — | — | — | I'M NOT AFRAID — Ricky Nelson, Imperial 5685 | 1 |
| 76 ★ | — | — | — | THREE NIGHTS A WEEK — Fats Domino, Imperial 5687 | 1 |
| 77 | 80 | 93 | 97 | NO — Dodie Stevens, Dot 16103 | 5 |
| 78 ★ | — | — | — | SAVE THE LAST DANCE FOR ME — Drifters, Atlantic 2071 | 1 |
| 79 | 48 | 43 | 36 | IS THERE ANY CHANCE — Marty Robbins, Columbia 41686 | 12 |
| 80 | 81 | 99 | — | DIAMONDS AND PEARLS — Paradons, Milestone 2003 | 3 |
| 81 | 75 | 73 | 98 | KOOKIE LITTLE PARADISE — Tree Swingers, Guyden 2036 | 4 |
| 82 | 88 | — | — | THIS OLD HEART — James Brown and the Famous Flames, Federal 12323 | 2 |
| 83 | 82 | — | — | SHORTNIN' BREAD — Paul Chaplain, Harper 100 | 2 |
| 84 ★ | — | — | — | SLEEP — Little Willie John, King 5394 | 1 |
| 85 ★ | — | — | — | AND NOW — Della Reese, RCA Victor 7784 | 1 |
| 86 | 91 | 96 | 100 | HOW HIGH THE MOON — Ella Fitzgerald, Verve 10220 | 4 |
| 87 ★ | — | — | — | LET'S THINK ABOUT LIVIN' — Bob Luman, Warner Bros. 5172 | 1 |
| 88 ★ | — | — | — | PUT YOUR ARMS AROUND ME, HONEY — Fats Domino, Imperial 5687 | 1 |
| 89 | 78 | 89 | — | KOMMOTION — Duane Eddy, Jamie 1163 | 3 |
| 90 ★ | — | — | — | MOVE TWO MOUNTAINS — Marv Johnson, United Artists 241 | 1 |
| 91 | 72 | 80 | — | CANDY SWEET — Pat Boone, Dot 16122 | 3 |
| 92 | 85 | 90 | — | COME BACK — Jimmy Clanton, Ace 600 | 3 |
| 93 | 86 | — | — | MANY A WONDERFUL MOMENT — Rosemary Clooney, RCA Victor 7754 | 2 |
| 94 | 73 | 87 | — | OLD OAKEN BUCKET — Tommy Sands, Capitol 4405 | 3 |
| 95 ★ | — | — | — | ROCKING GOOSE — Johnny and the Hurricanes, Big Top 3051 | 1 |
| 96 | 96 | — | — | SHORTNIN' BREAD — Bellnotes, Madison 136 | 2 |
| 97 ★ | — | — | — | A TEENAGER FEELS IT TOO — Denny Reed, Trey 3007 | 2 |
| 98 ★ | — | — | — | ALVIN FOR PRESIDENT — David Seville and the Chipmunks, Liberty 55277 | 1 |
| 99 ★ | — | — | — | NOBODY KNOWS YOU WHEN YOU'RE DOWN AND OUT — Nina Simone, Colpix 158 | 1 |
| 100 ★ | — | — | — | BEACHCOMBER — Bobby Darin, Atco 6173 | 1 |

# The Billboard HOT 100

**FOR WEEK ENDING SEPTEMBER 18**

*September 12, 1960*

| This Week | One Week Ago | Two Weeks Ago | Three Weeks Ago | Title / Artist, Company / Record No. | Weeks on Chart |
|---|---|---|---|---|---|
| 1 | 1 | 1 | 1 | IT'S NOW OR NEVER — Elvis Presley, RCA Victor 7777 | 9 |
| 2 | 2 | 3 | 4 | TWIST — Chubby Checker, Parkway 811 | 7 |
| 3 | 9 | 16 | 34 | MY HEART HAS A MIND OF ITS OWN — Connie Francis, M-G-M 12923 | 5 |
| 4 | 13 | 65 | — | MR. CUSTER — Larry Verne, Era 3024 | 3 |
| 5 | 3 | 2 | 3 | WALK, DON'T RUN — Ventures, Dolton 25 | 9 |
| 6 | 22 | 33 | 54 | CHAIN GANG — Sam Cooke, RCA Victor 7783 | 5 |
| 7 | 4 | 5 | 7 | VOLARE (NEL BLU DI PINTO DI BLU) — Bobby Rydell, Cameo 179 | 9 |
| 8 | 17 | 27 | 31 | KIDDIO — Brook Benton, Mercury 71652 | 6 |
| 9 | 14 | 15 | 47 | YOGI — Ivy Three, Shell 720 | 6 |
| 10 | 7 | 8 | 9 | MISSION BELL — Donnie Brooks, Era 3018 | 14 |
| 11 | 18 | 11 | 17 | DREAMIN' — Johnny Burnette, Liberty 55258 | 8 |
| 12 | 10 | 12 | 27 | THEME FROM THE APARTMENT — Ferrante and Teicher, United Artists 231 | 8 |
| 13 | 20 | 52 | 95 | A MILLION TO ONE — Jimmy Charles, Promo 1002 | 4 |
| 14 | 6 | 6 | 2 | ITSY BITSY TEENIE WEENIE YELLOW POLKA DOT BIKINI — Brian Hyland, Kapp 342 | 11 |
| 15 | 8 | 7 | 8 | FINGER POPPIN' TIME — Hank Ballard and the Midnighters, King 5341 | 18 |
| 16 | 11 | 10 | 14 | IN MY LITTLE CORNER OF THE WORLD — Anita Bryant, Carlton 530 | 10 |
| 17 | 47 | — | — | SO SAD — Everly Brothers, Warner Bros. 5163 | 2 |
| 18 | 16 | 17 | 20 | OVER THE RAINBOW — Demensions, Mohawk 116 | 11 |
| 19 | 21 | 39 | 61 | THE SAME ONE — Brook Benton, Mercury 71652 | 4 |
| 20 | 5 | 4 | 5 | I'M SORRY — Brenda Lee, Decca 31093 | 16 |
| 21 | 15 | 14 | 13 | PLEASE HELP ME, I'M FALLING — Hank Locklin, RCA Victor 7692 | 17 |
| 22 | 28 | 36 | 57 | YOU MEAN EVERYTHING TO ME — Neil Sedaka, RCA Victor 7781 | 6 |
| 23 | 24 | 25 | 25 | TA-TA — Clyde McPhatter, Mercury 71660 | 9 |
| 24 | 23 | 23 | 35 | HELLO, YOUNG LOVERS — Paul Anka, ABC-Paramount 10132 | 7 |
| 25 | 12 | 9 | 6 | ONLY THE LONELY — Roy Orbison, Monument 421 | 14 |
| 26 | 32 | 45 | 76 | DEVIL OR ANGEL — Bobby Vee, Liberty 55270 | 7 |
| 27 | 19 | 19 | 12 | (YOU WERE MADE FOR) ALL MY LOVE — Jackie Wilson, Brunswick 55167 | 10 |
| 28 | 37 | 57 | 91 | PINEAPPLE PRINCESS — Annette, Vista 362 | 5 |
| 29 | 31 | 40 | 58 | TWIST — Hank Ballard and the Midnighters, King 5171 | 9 |
| 30 | 27 | 18 | 10 | IMAGE OF A GIRL — Safaris, Eldo 101 | 15 |
| 31 | 30 | 21 | 15 | A WOMAN, A LOVER, A FRIEND — Jackie Wilson, Brunswick 55167 | 10 |
| 32 | 25 | 13 | 11 | WALKIN' TO NEW ORLEANS — Fats Domino, Imperial 5675 | 13 |
| 33 | 66 | — | — | LUCILLE — Everly Brothers, Warner Bros. 5163 | 2 |
| 34 | 46 | 54 | 63 | ANYMORE — Teresa Brewer, Coral 62219 | 6 |
| 35 | 76 | — | — | THREE NIGHTS A WEEEK — Fats Domino, Imperial 5687 | 2 |
| 36 | 33 | 38 | 53 | HOT ROD LINCOLN — Charlie Ryan, Four Star 1733 | 16 |
| 37 | 26 | 28 | 60 | NEVER ON SUNDAY — Don Costa, United Artists 234 | 6 |
| 38 | 36 | 29 | 32 | HOT ROD LINCOLN — Johnny Bond, Republic 2005 | 6 |
| 39 | 38 | 44 | 50 | IT ONLY HAPPENED YESTERDAY — Jack Scott, Top Rank 2055 | 7 |
| 40 | 44 | 41 | 51 | I LOVE YOU IN THE SAME OLD WAY — Paul Anka, ABC-Paramount 10132 | 7 |
| 41 | 39 | 42 | 74 | (I CAN'T HELP YOU) I'M FALLING TOO — Skeeter Davis, RCA Victor 7767 | 4 |
| 42 | 29 | 20 | 19 | FEEL SO FINE — Johnny Preston, Mercury 71651 | 13 |
| 43 | 34 | 32 | 18 | MULE SKINNER BLUES — Fendermen, Soma 1137 | 17 |
| 44 | 78 | — | — | SAVE THE LAST DANCE FOR ME — Drifters, Atlantic 2071 | 2 |
| 45 | 53 | 64 | 84 | MY SHOES KEEP WALKING BACK TO YOU — Guy Mitchell, Columbia 41725 | 7 |
| 46 | 58 | 59 | 71 | (I DO THE) SHIMMY, SHIMMY — Bobby Freeman, King 5373 | 5 |
| 47 | 67 | 87 | — | A FOOL IN LOVE — Ike and Tina Turner, Sue 730 | 3 |
| 48 | 60 | — | — | LET THE GOOD TIMES ROLL — Shirley and Lee, Warwick 581 | 2 |
| 49 | 43 | 58 | 56 | LISA — Jeanne Black, Capitol 4396 | 8 |
| 50 | 54 | 51 | 59 | BIG BOY PETE — Olympics, Arvee 595 | 11 |
| 51 | 52 | 69 | — | LET'S HAVE A PARTY — Wanda Jackson, Capitol 4397 | 3 |
| 52 | 55 | 63 | 45 | A MESS OF BLUES — Elvis Presley, RCA Victor 7777 | 8 |
| 53 | 57 | 60 | 82 | WE GO TOGETHER — Jan and Dean, Dore 555 | 6 |
| 54 | 62 | 62 | 64 | IF I CAN'T HAVE YOU — Etta James and Harvey, Chess 1760 | 7 |
| 55 | 61 | 79 | 75 | YOU'RE LOOKIN' GOOD — Dee Clark, Vee Jay 355 | 5 |
| 56 | 35 | 26 | 16 | TELL LAURA I LOVE HER — Ray Peterson, RCA Victor 7745 | 14 |
| 57 | 45 | 24 | 22 | LOOK FOR A STAR — Garry Miles, Liberty 55261 | 13 |
| 58 | 56 | 46 | 36 | RED SAILS IN THE SUNSET — Platters and Tony Williams, Mercury 71656 | 13 |
| 59 | 69 | 77 | 88 | HONEST I DO — Innocents, Indigo 1055 | 5 |
| 60 | 68 | 93 | — | NICE AND EASY — Frank Sinatra, Capitol 4408 | 3 |
| 61 | 80 | 81 | 99 | DIAMONDS AND PEARLS — Paradons, Milestone 2003 | 4 |
| 62 | 51 | 47 | 49 | MY LOVE — Nat King Cole, Capitol 4393 | 7 |
| 63 | 75 | — | — | I'M NOT AFRAID — Ricky Nelson, Imperial 5685 | 2 |
| 64 | 73 | 68 | 70 | WRECK OF THE "JOHN B" — Jimmie Rodgers, Roulette 4260 | 7 |
| 65 | 72 | 95 | — | MY LOVE FOR YOU — Johnny Mathis, Columbia 41764 | 3 |
| 66 | 71 | 71 | — | I WALK THE LINE — Jaye P. Morgan, M-G-M 12924 | 3 |
| 67 | — | — | — | I WANT TO BE WANTED — Brenda Lee, Decca 31149 | 1 |
| 68 | 64 | 49 | 37 | THIS BITTER EARTH — Dinah Washington, Mercury 71635 | 13 |
| 69 | 59 | 67 | 86 | MALAGUENA — Connie Francis, M-G-M 12923 | 4 |
| 70 | 70 | 84 | 93 | KOOKIE LITTLE PARADISE — Jo Ann Campbell, ABC-Paramount 10134 | 5 |
| 71 | 87 | — | — | LET'S THINK ABOUT LIVIN' — Bob Luman, Warner Bros. 5172 | 2 |
| 72 | 85 | — | — | AND NOW — Della Reese, RCA Victor 7784 | 2 |
| 73 | 77 | 80 | 93 | NO — Dodie Stevens, Dot 16103 | 6 |
| 74 | — | — | — | RUN, SAMPSON, RUN — Neil Sedaka, RCA Victor 7781 | 2 |
| 75 | 84 | — | — | SLEEP — Little Willie John, King 5394 | 2 |
| 76 | 86 | 91 | 96 | HOW HIGH THE MOON — Ella Fitzgerald, Verve 10220 | 5 |
| 77 | 90 | — | — | MOVE TWO MOUNTAINS — Marv Johnson, United Artists 241 | 2 |
| 78 | 88 | — | — | PUT YOUR ARMS AROUND ME, HONEY — Fats Domino, Imperial 5687 | 2 |
| 79 | 82 | 88 | — | THIS OLD HEART — James Brown and the Famous Flames, Federal 12323 | 3 |
| 80 | — | — | — | YES SIR, THAT'S MY BABY — Ricky Nelson, Imperial 5685 | 1 |
| 81 | — | — | — | SINCE I MET YOU BABY — Bobby Vee, Liberty 55270 | 1 |
| 82 | 95 | — | — | ROCKING GOOSE — Johnny and the Hurricanes, Big Top 3051 | 2 |
| 83 | — | — | — | BRONTOSAURUS STOMP — Piltdown Men, Capitol 4414 | 1 |
| 84 | 93 | 86 | — | MANY A WONDERFUL MOMENT — Rosemary Clooney, RCA Victor 7754 | 3 |
| 85 | — | — | — | JOURNEY OF LOVE — Crests, Coed 535 | 1 |
| 86 | 89 | 78 | 89 | KOMMOTION — Duane Eddy, Jamie 1163 | 4 |
| 87 | 92 | 85 | 90 | COME BACK — Jimmy Clanton, Ace 600 | 4 |
| 88 | 83 | 72 | — | SHORTNIN' BREAD — Paul Chaplain, Harper 100 | 3 |
| 89 | — | — | — | TONIGHT'S THE NIGHT — Chiffons, Big Deal 6003 | 1 |
| 90 | 81 | 75 | 73 | KOOKIE LITTLE PARADISE — Tree Swingers, Guyden 2036 | 5 |
| 91 | — | 92 | 100 | LOVIN' TOUCH — Mark Dinning, M-G-M 12929 | 3 |
| 92 | 94 | 73 | 87 | OLD OAKEN BUCKET — Tommy Sands, Capitol 4405 | 4 |
| 93 | 99 | — | — | NOBODY KNOWS YOU WHEN YOU'RE DOWN AND OUT — Nina Simone, Colpix 158 | 2 |
| 94 | 97 | 100 | — | A TEENAGER FEELS IT TOO — Denny Reed, Trey 3007 | 3 |
| 95 | — | — | — | FIVE BROTHERS — Marty Robbins, Columbia 41771 | 1 |
| 96 | — | — | — | DON'T BE CRUEL — Bill Black's Combo, Hi 2026 | 1 |
| 97 | — | — | — | TONIGHT'S THE NIGHT — Shirelles, Scepter 1208 | 1 |
| 98 | — | — | — | SHIMMY LIKE KATE — Olympics, Arvee 5006 | 1 |
| 99 | — | — | — | JUST CALL ME — Lloyd Price, ABC-Paramount 10139 | 1 |
| 100 | — | — | — | THE MACHINE — Dante and the Evergreens, Madison 135 | 1 |

# The Billboard HOT 100

**For week ending September 25** — September 19, 1960

STAR PERFORMERS showed the greatest upward progress on Hot 100 this week.
[S] Indicates that 45 r.p.m. stereo single version is available.
[A] Indicates that 33⅓ r.p.m. stereo single version is available.

Columns: THIS WEEK | ONE WEEK AGO | TWO WEEKS AGO | THREE WEEKS AGO | TITLE — Artist, Company, Record No. | STEREO | WEEKS ON CHART

| This | 1wk | 2wk | 3wk | Title — Artist, Company, Record No. | Stereo | Wks |
|---|---|---|---|---|---|---|
| 1 | 2 | 2 | 3 | TWIST — Chubby Checker, Parkway 811 | | 8 |
| 2 | 3 | 9 | 16 | MY HEART HAS A MIND OF ITS OWN — Connie Francis, M-G-M 12923 | | 6 |
| 3 | 1 | 1 | 1 | IT'S NOW OR NEVER — Elvis Presley, RCA Victor 7777 | S | 10 |
| 4 | 4 | 13 | 65 | MR. CUSTER — Larry Verne, Era 3024 | | 4 |
| 5 | 6 | 22 | 33 | CHAIN GANG — Sam Cooke, RCA Victor 7783 | S | 6 |
| 6 | 5 | 3 | 2 | WALK, DON'T RUN — Ventures, Dolton 25 | | 10 |
| 7 | 8 | 17 | 27 | KIDDIO — Brook Benton, Mercury 71652 | S | 7 |
| 8 | 9 | 14 | 15 | YOGI — Ivy Three, Shell 720 | | 7 |
| 9 | 7 | 4 | 5 | VOLARE (NEL BLU DI PINTO DI BLU) — Bobby Rydell, Cameo 179 | | 10 |
| 10 | 13 | 20 | 52 | A MILLION TO ONE — Jimmy Charles, Promo 1002 | | 5 |
| 11 | 17 | 47 | — | SO SAD — Everly Brothers, Warner Bros. 5163 | | 3 |
| 12 | 12 | 10 | 12 | THEME FROM THE APARTMENT — Ferrante and Teicher, United Artists 231 | | 9 |
| 13 | 11 | 18 | 11 | DREAMIN' — Johnny Burnette, Liberty 55258 | | 9 |
| 14 | 10 | 7 | 8 | MISSION BELL — Donnie Brooks, Era 3018 | | 15 |
| 15 | 26 | 32 | 45 | DEVIL OR ANGEL — Bobby Vee, Liberty 55270 | | 8 |
| 16 | 19 | 21 | 39 | THE SAME ONE — Brook Benton, Mercury 71652 | S | 5 |
| 17 | 28 | 37 | 57 | PINEAPPLE PRINCESS — Annette, Vista 362 | | 6 |
| 18 | 44 | 78 | — | SAVE THE LAST DANCE FOR ME — Drifters, Atlantic 2071 | | 3 |
| 19 | 15 | 8 | 7 | FINGER POPPIN' TIME — Hank Ballard and the Midnighters, King 5341 | | 19 |
| 20 | 16 | 11 | 10 | IN MY LITTLE CORNER OF THE WORLD — Anita Bryant, Carlton 530 | | 11 |
| 21 | 18 | 16 | 17 | OVER THE RAINBOW — Demensions, Mohawk 116 | | 12 |
| 22 | 35 | 76 | — | THREE NIGHTS A WEEK — Fats Domino, Imperial 5687 | | 3 |
| 23 | 22 | 28 | 36 | YOU MEAN EVERYTHING TO ME — Neil Sedaka, RCA Victor 7781 | S | 7 |
| 24 | 20 | 5 | 4 | I'M SORRY — Brenda Lee, Decca 31093 | | 17 |
| 25 | 14 | 6 | 6 | ITSY BITSY TEENIE WEENIE YELLOW POLKA DOT BIKINI — Brian Hyland, Kapp 342 | | 12 |
| 26 | 38 | 36 | 29 | HOT ROD LINCOLN — Johnny Bond, Republic 2005 | | 7 |
| 27 | 33 | 66 | — | LUCILLE — Everly Brothers, Warner Bros. 5163 | | 3 |
| 28 | 29 | 31 | 40 | TWIST — Hank Ballard and the Midnighters, King 5171 | | 10 |
| 29 | 27 | 19 | 19 | (YOU WERE MADE FOR) ALL MY LOVE — Jackie Wilson, Brunswick 55167 | | 11 |
| 30 | 25 | 12 | 9 | ONLY THE LONELY — Roy Orbison, Monument 421 | | 15 |
| 31 | 37 | 26 | 28 | NEVER ON SUNDAY — Don Costa, United Artists 234 | | 7 |
| 32 | 24 | 23 | 23 | HELLO, YOUNG LOVERS — Paul Anka, ABC-Paramount 10132 | S | 8 |
| 33 | 67 | — | — | I WANT TO BE WANTED — Brenda Lee, Decca 31149 | | 2 |
| 34 | 34 | 46 | 54 | ANYMORE — Teresa Brewer, Coral 62219 | | 7 |
| 35 | 30 | 27 | 18 | IMAGE OF A GIRL — Safaris, Eldo 101 | | 16 |
| 36 | 23 | 24 | 25 | TA-TA — Clyde McPhatter, Mercury 71660 | S | 10 |
| 37 | 31 | 30 | 21 | A WOMAN, A LOVER, A FRIEND — Jackie Wilson, Brunswick 55167 | | 11 |
| 38 | 63 | 75 | — | I'M NOT AFRAID — Ricky Nelson, Imperial 5685 | | 3 |
| 39 | 59 | 69 | 77 | HONEST I DO — Innocents, Indigo 1055 | | 6 |
| 40 | 21 | 15 | 14 | PLEASE HELP ME, I'M FALLING — Hank Locklin, RCA Victor 7692 | S | 18 |
| 41 | 39 | 38 | 44 | IT ONLY HAPPENED YESTERDAY — Jack Scott, Top Rank 2055 | | 8 |
| 42 | 41 | 39 | 42 | (I CAN'T HELP YOU) I'M FALLING TOO — Skeeter Davis, RCA Victor 7767 | S | 5 |
| 43 | 80 | — | — | YES SIR, THAT'S MY BABY — Ricky Nelson, Imperial 5685 | | 2 |
| 44 | 32 | 25 | 13 | WALKIN' TO NEW ORLEANS — Fats Domino, Imperial 5675 | | 14 |
| 45 | 36 | 33 | 38 | HOT ROD LINCOLN — Charlie Ryan, Four Star 1733 | | 17 |
| 46 | 40 | 44 | 41 | I LOVE YOU IN THE SAME OLD WAY — Paul Anka, ABC-Paramount 10132 | S | 8 |
| 47 | 46 | 58 | 59 | (I DO THE) SHIMMY, SHIMMY — Bobby Freeman, King 5373 | | 6 |
| 48 | 74 | — | — | RUN, SAMPSON, RUN — Neil Sedaka, RCA Victor 7781 | S | 3 |
| 49 | 47 | 67 | 87 | A FOOL IN LOVE — Ike and Tina Turner, Sue 730 | | 4 |
| 50 | 55 | 61 | 79 | YOU'RE LOOKIN' GOOD — Dee Clark, Vee Jay 355 | | 6 |
| 51 | 51 | 52 | 69 | LET'S HAVE A PARTY — Wanda Jackson, Capitol 4397 | | 4 |
| 52 | 54 | 62 | 62 | IF I CAN'T HAVE YOU — Etta James and Harvey, Chess 1760 | | 8 |
| 53 | 50 | 54 | 51 | BIG BOY PETE — Olympics, Arvee 595 | | 12 |
| 54 | 48 | 60 | — | LET THE GOOD TIMES ROLL — Shirley and Lee, Warwick 581 | | 3 |
| 55 | 69 | 59 | 67 | MALAGUENA — Connie Francis, M-G-M 12923 | | 5 |
| 56 | 71 | 87 | — | LET'S THINK ABOUT LIVIN' — Bob Luman, Warner Bros. 5172 | | 3 |
| 57 | 45 | 53 | 64 | MY SHOES KEEP WALKING BACK TO YOU — Guy Mitchell, Columbia 41725 | A | 8 |
| 58 | 78 | 88 | — | PUT YOUR ARMS AROUND ME, HONEY — Fats Domino, Imperial 5687 | | 3 |
| 59 | 52 | 55 | 63 | A MESS OF BLUES — Elvis Presley, RCA Victor 7777 | | 9 |
| 60 | 61 | 80 | 81 | DIAMONDS AND PEARLS — Paradons, Milestone 2003 | | 5 |
| 61 | 70 | 70 | 84 | KOOKIE LITTLE PARADISE — Jo Ann Campbell, ABC-Paramount 10134 | S | 6 |
| 62 | 43 | 34 | 32 | MULE SKINNER BLUES — Fendermen, Soma 1137 | | 18 |
| 63 | 65 | 72 | 95 | MY LOVE FOR YOU — Johnny Mathis, Columbia 41764 | A | 4 |
| 64 | 49 | 43 | 58 | LISA — Jeanne Black, Capitol 4396 | | 9 |
| 65 | 75 | 84 | — | SLEEP — Little Willie John, King 5394 | | 3 |
| 66 | 77 | 90 | — | MOVE TWO MOUNTAINS — Marv Johnson, United Artists 241 | | 3 |
| 67 | 60 | 68 | 93 | NICE AND EASY — Frank Sinatra, Capitol 4408 | | 4 |
| 68 | 66 | 71 | 71 | I WALK THE LINE — Jaye P. Morgan, M-G-M 12924 | | 4 |
| 69 | 42 | 29 | 20 | FEEL SO FINE — Johnny Preston, Mercury 71651 | S | 14 |
| 70 | 98 | — | — | SHIMMY LIKE KATE — Olympics, Arvee 5006 | | 2 |
| 71 | 64 | 73 | 68 | WRECK OF THE "JOHN B" — Jimmie Rodgers, Roulette 4260 | | 8 |
| 72 | 72 | 85 | — | AND NOW — Della Reese, RCA Victor 7784 | S | 3 |
| 73 | 82 | 95 | — | ROCKING GOOSE — Johnny and the Hurricanes, Big Top 3051 | | 3 |
| 74 | 87 | 92 | 85 | COME BACK — Jimmy Clanton, Ace 600 | | 5 |
| 75 | 83 | — | — | BRONTOSAURUS STOMP — Piltdown Men, Capitol 4414 | | 2 |
| 76 | 96 | — | — | DON'T BE CRUEL — Bill Black's Combo, Hi 2026 | | 2 |
| 77 | 95 | — | — | FIVE BROTHERS — Marty Robbins, Columbia 41771 | A | 2 |
| 78 | 89 | — | — | TONIGHT'S THE NIGHT — Chiffons, Big Deal 6003 | | 2 |
| 79 | 62 | 51 | 47 | MY LOVE — Nat King Cole, Capitol 4393 | | 8 |
| 80 | 73 | 77 | 80 | NO — Dodie Stevens, Dot 16103 | S | 7 |
| 81 | 85 | — | — | JOURNEY OF LOVE — Crests, Coed 535 | | 2 |
| 82 | 88 | 83 | 72 | SHORTNIN' BREAD — Paul Chaplain, Harper 100 | | 4 |
| 83 | 86 | 89 | 78 | KOMMOTION — Duane Eddy, Jamie 1163 | | 5 |
| 84 | 58 | 56 | 46 | RED SAILS IN THE SUNSET — Platters and Tony Williams, Mercury 71656 | S | 14 |
| 85 | 79 | 82 | 88 | THIS OLD HEART — James Brown and the Famous Flames, Federal 12378 | | 4 |
| 86 | 53 | 57 | 60 | WE GO TOGETHER — Jan and Dean, Dore 555 | | 7 |
| 87 | — | — | — | LET'S GO, LET'S GO, LET'S GO — Hank Ballard and the Midnighters, King 5400 | | 1 |
| 88 | 91 | — | 92 | LOVIN' TOUCH — Mark Dinning, M-G-M 12929 | | 4 |
| 89 | 90 | 81 | 75 | KOOKIE LITTLE PARADISE — Tree Swingers, Guyden 2036 | | 6 |
| 90 | 97 | — | — | TONIGHT'S THE NIGHT — Shirelles, Scepter 1208 | | 2 |
| 91 | — | — | — | YOU TALK TOO MUCH — Joe Jones, Ric 972 | | 1 |
| 92 | 99 | — | — | JUST CALL ME — Lloyd Price, ABC-Paramount 10139 | | 2 |
| 93 | — | — | — | NORTH TO ALASKA — Johnny Horton, Columbia 41782 | | 1 |
| 94 | — | — | — | IS YOU IS OR IS YOU AIN'T MY BABY — Buster Brown, Fire 1023 | | 1 |
| 95 | 100 | — | — | TIME MACHINE — Dante and the Evergreens, Madison 135 | | 2 |
| 96 | — | — | — | BLUE ANGEL — Roy Orbison, Monument 425 | | 1 |
| 97 | 68 | 64 | 49 | THIS BITTER EARTH — Dinah Washington, Mercury 71635 | S | 14 |
| 98 | — | — | — | TWISTIN' U.S.A. — Danny and the Juniors, Swan 4060 | | 1 |
| 99 | — | — | — | MY DEAREST DARLING — Etta James, Argo 5368 | | 1 |
| 100 | — | — | — | TOGETHERNESS — Frankie Avalon, Chancellor 1056 | | 1 |

# The Billboard HOT 100

**FOR WEEK ENDING OCTOBER 2** — SEPTEMBER 26, 1960

| This Week | 1 Wk Ago | 2 Wks Ago | 3 Wks Ago | Title — Artist, Company, Record No. | Weeks on Chart |
|---|---|---|---|---|---|
| 1 | 2 | 3 | 9 | MY HEART HAS A MIND OF ITS OWN — Connie Francis, M-G-M 12923 | 7 |
| 2 | 1 | 2 | 2 | TWIST — Chubby Checker, Parkway 811 | 9 |
| 3 | 5 | 6 | 22 | CHAIN GANG — Sam Cooke, RCA Victor 7783 | 7 |
| 4 | 4 | 4 | 13 | MR. CUSTER — Larry Verne, Era 3024 | 5 |
| ★5 | 10 | 13 | 20 | A MILLION TO ONE — Jimmy Charles, Promo 1002 | 6 |
| 6 | 3 | 1 | 1 | IT'S NOW OR NEVER — Elvis Presley, RCA Victor 7777 | 11 |
| 7 | 6 | 5 | 3 | WALK, DON'T RUN — Ventures, Dolton 25 | 11 |
| 8 | 7 | 8 | 17 | KIDDIO — Brook Benton, Mercury 71652 | 8 |
| 9 | 11 | 17 | 47 | SO BAD — Everly Brothers, Warner Bros. 5163 | 4 |
| ★10 | 18 | 44 | 78 | SAVE THE LAST DANCE FOR ME — Drifters, Atlantic 2071 | 4 |
| ★11 | 17 | 28 | 37 | PINEAPPLE PRINCESS — Annette, Vista 362 | 7 |
| 12 | 12 | 12 | 10 | THEME FROM THE APARTMENT — Ferrante and Teicher, United Artists 231 | 10 |
| 13 | 15 | 26 | 32 | DEVIL OR ANGEL — Bobby Vee, Liberty 55270 | 9 |
| 14 | 9 | 7 | 4 | VOLARE (NEL BLU DI PINTO DI BLU) — Bobby Rydell, Cameo 179 | 11 |
| 15 | 13 | 11 | 18 | DREAMIN' — Johnny Burnette, Liberty 55258 | 10 |
| 16 | 8 | 9 | 14 | YOGI — Ivy Three, Shell 720 | 8 |
| 17 | 16 | 19 | 21 | THE SAME ONE — Brook Benton, Mercury 71652 | 6 |
| 18 | 14 | 10 | 7 | MISSION BELL — Donnie Brooks, Era 3018 | 16 |
| 19 | 23 | 22 | 28 | YOU MEAN EVERYTHING TO ME — Neil Sedaka, RCA Victor 7781 | 8 |
| 20 | 19 | 15 | 8 | FINGER POPPIN' TIME — Hank Ballard and the Midnighters, King 5341 | 20 |
| 21 | 22 | 35 | 76 | THREE NIGHTS A WEEEK — Fats Domino, Imperial 5687 | 4 |
| 22 | 27 | 33 | 36 | LUCILLE — Everly Brothers, Warner Bros. 5163 | 4 |
| ★23 | 33 | 67 | — | I WANT TO BE WANTED — Brenda Lee, Decca 31149 | 3 |
| 24 | 21 | 18 | 16 | OVER THE RAINBOW — Demensions, Mohawk 116 | 13 |
| 25 | 20 | 16 | 11 | IN MY LITTLE CORNER OF THE WORLD — Anita Bryant, Carlton 530 | 12 |
| 26 | 31 | 37 | 26 | NEVER ON SUNDAY — Don Costa, United Artists 234 | 8 |
| ★27 | 38 | 63 | 75 | I'M NOT AFRAID — Ricky Nelson, Imperial 5685 | 4 |
| 28 | 39 | 59 | 69 | HONEST I DO — Innocents, Indigo 1055 | 7 |
| 29 | 25 | 14 | 6 | ITSY BITSY TEENIE WEENIE YELLOW POLKA DOT BIKINI — Brian Hyland, Kapp 342 | 13 |
| 30 | 24 | 20 | 5 | I'M SORRY — Brenda Lee, Decca 31093 | 18 |
| 31 | 34 | 34 | 46 | ANYMORE — Teresa Brewer, Coral 62219 | 8 |
| 32 | 26 | 38 | 36 | HOT ROD LINCOLN — Johnny Bond, Republic 2005 | 8 |
| 33 | 56 | 71 | 87 | LET'S THINK ABOUT LIVIN' — Bob Luman, Warner Bros. 5172 | 4 |
| 34 | 43 | 80 | — | YES SIR, THAT'S MY BABY — Ricky Nelson, Imperial 5685 | 3 |
| 35 | 28 | 29 | 31 | TWIST — Hank Ballard and the Midnighters, King 5171 | 11 |
| 36 | 29 | 27 | 19 | (YOU WERE MADE FOR) ALL MY LOVE — Jackie Wilson, Brunswick 85167 | 12 |
| ★37 | 60 | 61 | 80 | DIAMONDS AND PEARLS — Paradons, Milestone 2003 | 6 |
| 38 | 30 | 25 | 12 | ONLY THE LONELY — Roy Orbison, Monument 421 | 16 |
| 39 | 32 | 24 | 23 | HELLO, YOUNG LOVERS — Paul Anka, ABC-Paramount 10132 | 9 |
| 40 | 47 | 46 | 58 | (I DO THE) SHIMMY, SHIMMY — Bobby Freeman, King 5373 | 7 |
| 41 | 36 | 23 | 24 | TA-TA — Clyde McPhatter, Mercury 71660 | 11 |
| 42 | 37 | 31 | 30 | A WOMAN, A LOVER, A FRIEND — Jackie Wilson, Brunswick 85167 | 12 |
| 43 | 50 | 55 | 61 | YOU'RE LOOKIN' GOOD — Dee Clark, Vee Jay 355 | 7 |
| 44 | 49 | 47 | 67 | A FOOL IN LOVE — Ike and Tina Turner, Sue 730 | 5 |
| 45 | 51 | 51 | 52 | LET'S HAVE A PARTY — Wanda Jackson, Capitol 4397 | 5 |
| 46 | 40 | 21 | 15 | PLEASE HELP ME, I'M FALLING — Hank Locklin, RCA Victor 7692 | 19 |
| ★47 | 76 | 96 | — | DON'T BE CRUEL — Bill Black's Combo, Hi 2026 | 3 |
| 48 | 46 | 40 | 44 | I LOVE YOU IN THE SAME OLD WAY — Paul Anka, ABC-Paramount 10132 | 9 |
| 49 | 35 | 30 | 27 | IMAGE OF A GIRL — Safaris, Eldo 101 | 17 |
| 50 | 53 | 50 | 54 | BIG BOY PETE — Olympics, Arvee 595 | 13 |
| 51 | 42 | 41 | 39 | (I CAN'T HELP YOU) I'M FALLING TOO — Skeeter Davis, RCA Victor 7767 | 6 |
| 52 | 45 | 36 | 33 | HOT ROD LINCOLN — Charlie Ryan, Four Star 1733 | 18 |
| ★53 | 65 | 75 | 84 | SLEEP — Little Willie John, King 5394 | 4 |
| 54 | 48 | 74 | — | RUN, SAMPSON, RUN — Neil Sedaka, RCA Victor 7781 | 4 |
| 55 | 55 | 69 | 59 | MALAGUENA — Connie Francis, M-G-M 12923 | 6 |
| 56 | 91 | — | — | YOU TALK TOO MUCH — Joe Jones, Ric 972 | 2 |
| 57 | 70 | 98 | — | SHIMMY LIKE KATE — Olympics, Arvee 5006 | 3 |
| 58 | 52 | 54 | 62 | IF I CAN'T HAVE YOU — Etta James and Harvey, Chess 1760 | 9 |
| 59 | 58 | 78 | 88 | PUT YOUR ARMS AROUND ME, HONEY — Fats Domino, Imperial 5687 | 4 |
| 60 | 66 | 77 | 90 | MOVE TWO MOUNTAINS — Marv Johnson, United Artists 241 | 4 |
| 61 | 63 | 65 | 72 | MY LOVE FOR YOU — Johnny Mathis, Columbia 41764 | 5 |
| 62 | 73 | 82 | 95 | ROCKING GOOSE — Johnny and the Hurricanes, Big Top 3051 | 4 |
| 63 | 41 | 39 | 38 | IT ONLY HAPPENED YESTERDAY — Jack Scott, Top Rank 2055 | 9 |
| 64 | 59 | 52 | 55 | A MESS OF BLUES — Elvis Presley, RCA Victor 7777 | 10 |
| 65 | 54 | 48 | 60 | LET THE GOOD TIMES ROLL — Shirley and Lee, Warwick 581 | 4 |
| 66 | 74 | 87 | 92 | COME BACK — Jimmy Clanton, Ace 600 | 6 |
| 67 | 100 | — | — | TOGETHERNESS — Frankie Avalon, Chancellor 1056 | 2 |
| 68 | 57 | 45 | 53 | MY SHOES KEEP WALKING BACK TO YOU — Guy Mitchell, Columbia 41725 | 9 |
| 69 | 72 | 72 | 85 | AND NOW — Della Reese, RCA Victor 7784 | 4 |
| 70 | 61 | 70 | 70 | KOOKIE LITTLE PARADISE — Jo Ann Campbell, ABC-Paramount 10134 | 7 |
| ★71 | 98 | — | — | TWISTIN' U.S.A. — Danny and the Juniors, Swan 4060 | 2 |
| 72 | 68 | 66 | 71 | I WALK THE LINE — Jaye P. Morgan, M-G-M 12924 | 5 |
| ★73 | 95 | 100 | — | TIME MACHINE — Dante and the Evergreens, Madison 135 | 3 |
| 74 | 77 | 95 | — | FIVE BROTHERS — Marty Robbins, Columbia 41771 | 3 |
| ★75 | — | — | — | SOMEBODY TO LOVE — Bobby Darin, Atco 6179 | 1 |
| 76 | 78 | 89 | — | TONIGHT'S THE NIGHT — Chiffons, Big Deal 6003 | 3 |
| 77 | 87 | — | — | LET'S GO, LET'S GO, LET'S GO — Hank Ballard and the Midnighters, King 5400 | 2 |
| 78 | 90 | 97 | — | TONIGHT'S THE NIGHT — Shirelles, Scepter 1208 | 3 |
| 79 | 92 | 99 | — | JUST CALL ME — Lloyd Price, ABC-Paramount 10139 | 3 |
| 80 | 75 | 83 | — | BRONTOSAURUS STOMP — Piltdown Men, Capitol 4414 | 3 |
| 81 | 96 | — | — | BLUE ANGEL — Roy Orbison, Monument 425 | 2 |
| 82 | 67 | 60 | 68 | NICE AND EASY — Frank Sinatra, Capitol 4408 | 5 |
| 83 | 81 | 85 | — | JOURNEY OF LOVE — Crests, Coed 835 | 3 |
| 84 | 88 | 91 | — | LOVIN' TOUCH — Mark Dinning, M-G-M 12929 | 5 |
| 85 | 93 | — | — | NORTH TO ALASKA — Johnny Horton, Columbia 41782 | 2 |
| 86 | 85 | 79 | 82 | THIS OLD HEART — James Brown and the Famous Flames, Federal 12378 | 5 |
| 87 | 83 | 86 | 89 | KOMMOTION — Duane Eddy, Jamie 1163 | 6 |
| 88 | 94 | — | — | IS YOU IS OR IS YOU AIN'T MY BABY — Buster Brown, Fire 1023 | 2 |
| 89 | 99 | — | — | MY DEAREST DARLING — Etta James, Argo 5368 | 2 |
| 90 | — | — | — | ARTIFICIAL FLOWERS — Bobby Darin, Atco 6179 | 1 |
| 91 | — | — | — | TEMPTATION — Roger Williams, Kapp 347 | 1 |
| 92 | — | — | — | OVER THE MOUNTAIN — Johnnie and Joe, Chess 1654 | 1 |
| 93 | 80 | 73 | 77 | NO — Dodie Stevens, Dot 16103 | 8 |
| 94 | — | — | — | GEORGIA ON MY MIND — Ray Charles, ABC-Paramount 10135 | 1 |
| 95 | — | 98 | — | ALVIN FOR PRESIDENT — David Seville and the Chipmunks, Liberty 55277 | 2 |
| 96 | 71 | 64 | 73 | WRECK OF THE "JOHN B" — Jimmie Rodgers, Roulette 4260 | 9 |
| 97 | — | — | — | SUMMER'S GONE — Paul Anka, ABC-Paramount 10147 | 1 |
| 98 | — | — | — | ALABAM — Cowboy Copas, Starday 501 | 1 |
| 99 | — | — | — | YOU TALK TOO MUCH — Frankie Ford, Imperial 5686 | 1 |
| 100 | — | — | — | WAIT — Jimmy Clanton, Ace 600 | 1 |

# The Billboard HOT 100

**For Week Ending October 9** — October 3, 1960

| This Week | 1 Wk Ago | 2 Wks Ago | 3 Wks Ago | Title — Artist, Company, Record No. | Weeks on Chart |
|---|---|---|---|---|---|
| 1 | 1 | 2 | 3 | MY HEART HAS A MIND OF ITS OWN — Connie Francis, M-G-M 12923 | 8 |
| 2 | 3 | 5 | 6 | CHAIN GANG — Sam Cooke, RCA Victor 7783 | 8 |
| 3 | 4 | 4 | 4 | MR. CUSTER — Larry Verne, Era 3024 | 6 |
| 4 | 2 | 1 | 2 | TWIST — Chubby Checker, Parkway 811 | 10 |
| 5 | 5 | 10 | 13 | A MILLION TO ONE — Jimmy Charles, Promo 1002 | 7 |
| 6 | 10 | 18 | 44 | SAVE THE LAST DANCE FOR ME — Drifters, Atlantic 2071 | 5 |
| 7 | 6 | 3 | 1 | IT'S NOW OR NEVER — Elvis Presley, RCA Victor 7777 | 12 |
| 8 | 7 | 6 | 5 | WALK, DON'T RUN — Ventures, Dolton 25 | 12 |
| 9 | 9 | 11 | 17 | SO SAD — Everly Brothers, Warner Bros. 5163 | 5 |
| 10 | 12 | 12 | 12 | THEME FROM THE APARTMENT — Ferrante and Teicher, United Artists 231 | 11 |
| 11 | 8 | 7 | 8 | KIDDIO — Brook Benton, Mercury 71652 | 9 |
| 12 | 13 | 15 | 26 | DEVIL OR ANGEL — Bobby Vee, Liberty 55270 | 10 |
| 13 | 11 | 17 | 28 | PINEAPPLE PRINCESS — Annette, Vista 362 | 8 |
| 14 | 23 | 33 | 67 | I WANT TO BE WANTED — Brenda Lee, Decca 31149 | 4 |
| 15 | 14 | 9 | 7 | VOLARE (NEL BLU DI PINTO DI BLU) — Bobby Rydell, Cameo 179 | 12 |
| 16 | 17 | 16 | 19 | THE SAME ONE — Brook Benton, Mercury 71652 | 7 |
| 17 | 19 | 23 | 22 | YOU MEAN EVERYTHING TO ME — Neil Sedaka, RCA Victor 7781 | 9 |
| 18 | 15 | 13 | 11 | DREAMIN' — Johnny Burnette, Liberty 55258 | 11 |
| 19 | 33 | 56 | 71 | LET'S THINK ABOUT LIVIN' — Bob Luman, Warner Bros. 5172 | 5 |
| 20 | 16 | 8 | 9 | YOGI — Ivy Three, Shell 720 | 9 |
| 21 | 21 | 22 | 35 | THREE NIGHTS A WEEK — Fats Domino, Imperial 5687 | 5 |
| 22 | 37 | 60 | 61 | DIAMONDS AND PEARLS — Paradons, Milestone 2003 | 7 |
| 23 | 47 | 76 | 96 | DON'T BE CRUEL — Bill Black's Combo, Hi 2026 | 4 |
| 24 | 20 | 19 | 15 | FINGER POPPIN' TIME — Hank Ballard and the Midnighters, King 5341 | 21 |
| 25 | 26 | 31 | 37 | NEVER ON SUNDAY — Don Costa, United Artists 234 | 9 |
| 26 | 22 | 27 | 33 | LUCILLE — Everly Brothers, Warner Bros. 5163 | 5 |
| 27 | 24 | 21 | 18 | OVER THE RAINBOW — Demensions, Mohawk 116 | 14 |
| 28 | 18 | 14 | 10 | MISSION BELL — Donnie Brooks, Era 3018 | 17 |
| 29 | 27 | 38 | 63 | I'M NOT AFRAID — Ricky Nelson, Imperial 5685 | 5 |
| 30 | 35 | 28 | 29 | TWIST — Hank Ballard and the Midnighters, King 5171 | 12 |
| 31 | 28 | 39 | 59 | HONEST I DO — Innocents, Indigo 105 | 8 |
| 32 | 25 | 20 | 16 | IN MY LITTLE CORNER OF THE WORLD — Anita Bryant, Carlton 530 | 13 |
| 33 | 32 | 26 | 38 | HOT ROD LINCOLN — Johnny Bond, Republic 2005 | 9 |
| 34 | 34 | 43 | 80 | YES SIR, THAT'S MY BABY — Ricky Nelson, Imperial 5685 | 4 |
| 35 | 54 | 48 | 74 | RUN, SAMPSON, RUN — Neil Sedaka, RCA Victor 7781 | 5 |
| 36 | 31 | 34 | 34 | ANYMORE — Teresa Brewer, Coral 62219 | 9 |
| 37 | 40 | 47 | 46 | (I DO THE) SHIMMY, SHIMMY — Bobby Freeman, King 5373 | 8 |
| 38 | 30 | 24 | 20 | I'M SORRY — Brenda Lee, Decca 31093 | 19 |
| 39 | 29 | 25 | 14 | ITSY BITSY TEENIE WEENIE YELLOW POLKA DOT BIKINI — Brian Hyland, Kapp 342 | 14 |
| 40 | 44 | 49 | 47 | A FOOL IN LOVE — Ike and Tina Turner, Sue 730 | 6 |
| 41 | 53 | 65 | 75 | SLEEP — Little Willie John, King 5394 | 5 |
| 42 | 55 | 55 | 69 | MALAGUENA — Connie Francis, M-G-M 12923 | 7 |
| 43 | 41 | 36 | 23 | TA-TA — Clyde McPhatter, Mercury 71660 | 12 |
| 44 | 60 | 66 | 77 | MOVE TWO MOUNTAINS — Marv Johnson, United Artists 241 | 5 |
| 45 | 39 | 32 | 24 | HELLO, YOUNG LOVERS — Paul Anka, ABC-Paramount 10132 | 10 |
| 46 | 38 | 30 | 25 | ONLY THE LONELY — Roy Orbison, Monument 421 | 17 |
| 47 | 45 | 51 | 51 | LET'S HAVE A PARTY — Wanda Jackson, Capitol 4397 | 6 |
| 48 | 48 | 46 | 40 | I LOVE YOU IN THE SAME OLD WAY — Paul Anka, ABC-Paramount 10132 | 10 |
| 49 | 56 | 91 | — | YOU TALK TOO MUCH — Joe Jones, Ric 972 | 3 |
| 50 | 46 | 40 | 21 | PLEASE HELP ME, I'M FALLING — Hank Locklin, RCA Victor 7692 | 20 |
| 51 | 50 | 53 | 50 | BIG BOY PETE — Olympics, Arvee 595 | 14 |
| 52 | 36 | 29 | 27 | (YOU WERE MADE FOR) ALL MY LOVE — Jackie Wilson, Brunswick 55167 | 13 |
| 53 | 57 | 70 | 98 | SHIMMY LIKE KATE — Olympics, Arvee 5006 | 4 |
| 54 | 43 | 50 | 55 | YOU'RE LOOKIN' GOOD — Dee Clark, Vee Jay 355 | 8 |
| 55 | 90 | — | — | ARTIFICIAL FLOWERS — Bobby Darin, Atco 6179 | 2 |
| 56 | 61 | 63 | 65 | MY LOVE FOR YOU — Johnny Mathis, Columbia 41764 | 6 |
| 57 | 67 | 100 | — | TOGETHERNESS — Frankie Avalon, Chancellor 1056 | 3 |
| 58 | 58 | 52 | 54 | IF I CAN'T HAVE YOU — Etta James and Harvey, Chess 1760 | 10 |
| 59 | 94 | — | — | GEORGIA ON MY MIND — Ray Charles, ABC-Paramount 10135 | 2 |
| 60 | 62 | 73 | 82 | ROCKING GOOSE — Johnny and the Hurricanes, Big Top 3051 | 5 |
| 61 | 71 | 98 | — | TWISTIN' U.S.A. — Danny and the Juniors, Swan 4060 | 3 |
| 62 | 78 | 90 | 97 | TONIGHT'S THE NIGHT — Shirelles, Scepter 1208 | 4 |
| 63 | 66 | 74 | 87 | COME BACK — Jimmy Clanton, Ace 600 | 7 |
| 64 | 85 | 93 | — | NORTH TO ALASKA — Johnny Horton, Columbia 41782 | 3 |
| 65 | 77 | 87 | — | LET'S GO, LET'S GO, LET'S GO — Hank Ballard and the Midnighters, King 5400 | 3 |
| 66 | 75 | — | — | SOMEBODY TO LOVE — Bobby Darin, Atco 6179 | 2 |
| 67 | 52 | 45 | 36 | HOT ROD LINCOLN — Charlie Ryan, Four Star 1733 | 19 |
| 68 | 81 | 96 | — | BLUE ANGEL — Roy Orbison, Monument 425 | 3 |
| 69 | 97 | — | — | SUMMER'S GONE — Paul Anka, ABC-Paramount 10147 | 2 |
| 70 | 49 | 35 | 30 | IMAGE OF A GIRL — Safaris, Eldo 101 | 18 |
| 71 | 70 | 61 | 70 | KOOKIE LITTLE PARADISE — Jo Ann Campbell, ABC-Paramount 10134 | 8 |
| 72 | 59 | 58 | 78 | PUT YOUR ARMS AROUND ME, HONEY — Fats Domino, Imperial 5687 | 5 |
| 73 | 64 | 59 | 52 | A MESS OF BLUES — Elvis Presley, RCA Victor 7777 | 11 |
| 74 | 65 | 54 | 48 | LET THE GOOD TIMES ROLL — Shirley and Lee, Warwick 581 | 5 |
| 75 | 68 | 57 | 45 | MY SHOES KEEP WALKING BACK TO YOU — Guy Mitchell, Columbia 41725 | 10 |
| 76 | 73 | 95 | 100 | TIME MACHINE — Dante and the Evergreens, Madison 135 | 4 |
| 77 | 72 | 68 | 66 | I WALK THE LINE — Jaye P. Morgan, M-G-M 12924 | 6 |
| 78 | — | — | — | LOVE WALKED IN — Dinah Washington, Mercury 71696 | 1 |
| 79 | 91 | — | — | TEMPTATION — Roger Williams, Kapp 347 | 2 |
| 80 | 51 | 42 | 41 | (I CAN'T HELP YOU) I'M FALLING TOO — Skeeter Davis, RCA Victor 7767 | 7 |
| 81 | 88 | 94 | — | IS YOU IS OR IS YOU AIN'T MY BABY — Buster Brown, Fire 1023 | 3 |
| 82 | 74 | 77 | 95 | FIVE BROTHERS — Marty Robbins, Columbia 41771 | 4 |
| 83 | — | — | — | I WISH I'D NEVER BEEN BORN — Patti Page, Mercury 71695 | 1 |
| 84 | — | — | — | JUST A LITTLE — Brenda Lee, Decca 31149 | 1 |
| 85 | 89 | 99 | — | MY DEAREST DARLING — Etta James, Argo 5368 | 3 |
| 86 | — | — | — | STAY — Maurice Williams, Herald 552 | 1 |
| 87 | 82 | 67 | 60 | NICE 'N' EASY — Frank Sinatra, Capitol 4408 | 6 |
| 88 | 98 | — | — | ALABAM — Cowboy Copas, Starday 501 | 2 |
| 89 | 92 | — | — | OVER THE MOUNTAIN; ACROSS THE SEA — Johnnie and Joe, Chess 1654 | 2 |
| 90 | 79 | 92 | 99 | JUST CALL ME — Lloyd Price, ABC-Paramount 10139 | 4 |
| 91 | 69 | 72 | 72 | AND NOW — Della Reese, RCA Victor 7784 | 5 |
| 92 | 84 | 88 | 91 | LOVIN' TOUCH — Mark Dinning, M-G-M 12929 | 4 |
| 93 | 76 | 78 | 89 | TONIGHT'S THE NIGHT — Chiffons, Big Deal 6003 | 4 |
| 94 | 100 | — | — | WAIT — Jimmy Clanton, Ace 600 | 2 |
| 95 | 99 | — | — | YOU TALK TOO MUCH — Frankie Ford, Imperial 5686 | 2 |
| 96 | — | — | — | THEME FROM THE SUNDOWNERS — Felix Slatkin, Liberty 55282 | 1 |
| 97 | — | — | — | THEME FROM THE SUNDOWNERS — Billy Vaughn, Dot 16133 | 1 |
| 98 | 83 | 81 | 85 | JOURNEY OF LOVE — Crests, Coed 535 | 4 |
| 99 | — | — | — | SHOPPIN' FOR CLOTHES — Coasters, Atco 6178 | 1 |
| 100 | — | — | — | MY HERO — Bluenotes, Value 213 | 1 |

# The Billboard HOT 100

**FOR WEEK ENDING OCTOBER 16**

| TW | 1WA | 2WA | 3WA | TITLE — Artist, Company, Record No. | WoC |
|---|---|---|---|---|---|
| 1 | 3 | 4 | 4 | MR. CUSTER — Larry Verne, Era 3024 | 7 |
| 2 | 2 | 3 | 5 | CHAIN GANG — Sam Cooke, RCA Victor 7783 [S] | 9 |
| 3 | 1 | 1 | 2 | MY HEART HAS A MIND OF ITS OWN — Connie Francis, M-G-M 12923 | 9 |
| 4 | 6 | 10 | 18 | SAVE THE LAST DANCE FOR ME — Drifters, Atlantic 2071 | 6 |
| 5 | 4 | 2 | 1 | TWIST — Chubby Checker, Parkway 811 | 11 |
| 6 | 5 | 5 | 10 | A MILLION TO ONE — Jimmy Charles, Promo 1002 | 8 |
| 7 | 9 | 9 | 11 | SO SAD — Everly Brothers, Warner Bros. 5163 | 6 |
| 8 | 12 | 13 | 15 | DEVIL OR ANGEL — Bobby Vee, Liberty 55270 | 11 |
| 9 | 14 | 23 | 33 | I WANT TO BE WANTED — Brenda Lee, Decca 31149 | 5 |
| 10 | 11 | 8 | 7 | KIDDIO — Brook Benton, Mercury 71652 | 10 |
| 11 | 7 | 6 | 3 | IT'S NOW OR NEVER — Elvis Presley, RCA Victor 7777 [S] | 13 |
| 12 | 8 | 7 | 6 | WALK, DON'T RUN — Ventures, Dolton 25 | 13 |
| 13 | 19 | 33 | 56 | LET'S THINK ABOUT LIVIN' — Bob Luman, Warner Bros. 5172 | 6 |
| 14 | 10 | 12 | 12 | THEME FROM THE APARTMENT — Ferrante and Teicher, United Artists 231 | 12 |
| 15 | 21 | 21 | 22 | THREE NIGHTS A WEEK — Fats Domino, Imperial 5687 | 6 |
| 16 | 13 | 11 | 17 | PINEAPPLE PRINCESS — Annette, Vista 362 | 9 |
| 17 | 17 | 19 | 23 | YOU MEAN EVERYTHING TO ME — Neil Sedaka, RCA Victor 7781 [S] | 10 |
| 18 | 23 | 47 | 76 | DON'T BE CRUEL — Bill Black's Combo, Hi 2026 | 5 |
| 19 | 22 | 37 | 60 | DIAMONDS AND PEARLS — Paradons, Milestone 2003 | 8 |
| 20 | 16 | 17 | 16 | THE SAME ONE — Brook Benton, Mercury 71652 [S] | 8 |
| 21 | 26 | 22 | 27 | LUCILLE — Everly Brothers, Warner Bros. 5163 | 6 |
| 22 | 25 | 26 | 31 | NEVER ON SUNDAY — Don Costa, United Artists 234 | 10 |
| 23 | 18 | 15 | 13 | DREAMIN' — Johnny Burnette, Liberty 55258 | 12 |
| 24 | — | 59 | 94 | GEORGIA ON MY MIND — Ray Charles, ABC-Paramount 10135 | 3 |
| 25 | 20 | 16 | 8 | YOGI — Ivy Three, Shell 720 | 10 |
| 26 | 41 | 53 | 65 | SLEEP — Little Willie John, King 5394 | 6 |
| 27 | 61 | 71 | 98 | TWISTIN' U.S.A. — Danny and the Juniors, Swan 4060 | 4 |
| 28 | 28 | 18 | 14 | MISSION BELL — Donnie Brooks, Era 3018 | 18 |
| 29 | 44 | 60 | 66 | MOVE TWO MOUNTAINS — Marv Johnson, United Artists 241 | 6 |
| 30 | 40 | 44 | 49 | A FOOL IN LOVE — Ike and Tina Turner, Sue 730 | 7 |
| 31 | 15 | 14 | 9 | VOLARE (NEL BLU DI PINTO DI BLU) — Bobby Rydell, Cameo 179 | 13 |
| 32 | 35 | 54 | 48 | RUN, SAMPSON, RUN — Neil Sedaka, RCA Victor 7781 [S] | 6 |
| 33 | 49 | 56 | 91 | YOU TALK TOO MUCH — Joe Jones, Roulette 4304 | 4 |
| 34 | 24 | 20 | 19 | FINGER POPPIN' TIME — Hank Ballard and the Midnighters, King 5341 | 22 |
| 35 | 36 | 31 | 34 | ANYMORE — Teresa Brewer, Coral 62219 | 10 |
| 36 | 69 | 97 | — | SUMMER'S GONE — Paul Anka, ABC-Paramount 10147 | 3 |
| 37 | 47 | 45 | 51 | LET'S HAVE A PARTY — Wanda Jackson, Capitol 4397 | 7 |
| 38 | 29 | 27 | 38 | I'M NOT AFRAID — Ricky Nelson, Imperial 5685 | 6 |
| 39 | 37 | 40 | 47 | (I DO THE) SHIMMY, SHIMMY — Bobby Freeman, King 5373 | 9 |
| 40 | 86 | — | — | STAY — Maurice Williams and the Zodiacs, Herald 552 | 2 |
| 41 | 55 | 90 | — | ARTIFICIAL FLOWERS — Bobby Darin, Atco 6179 | 3 |
| 42 | 31 | 28 | 39 | HONEST I DO — Innocents, Indigo 1055 | 9 |
| 43 | 57 | 67 | 100 | TOGETHERNESS — Frankie Avalon, Chancellor 1056 | 4 |
| 44 | 42 | 55 | 55 | MALAGUENA — Connie Francis, M-G-M 12923 | 8 |
| 45 | 30 | 35 | 28 | TWIST — Hank Ballard and the Midnighters, King 5171 | 13 |
| 46 | 38 | 30 | 24 | I'M SORRY — Brenda Lee, Decca 31093 | 20 |
| 47 | 56 | 61 | 63 | MY LOVE FOR YOU — Johnny Mathis, Columbia 41764 | 7 |
| 48 | 68 | 81 | 96 | BLUE ANGEL — Roy Orbison, Monument 425 | 4 |
| 49 | 65 | 77 | 87 | LET'S GO, LET'S GO, LET'S GO — Hank Ballard and the Midnighters, King 5400 | 4 |
| 50 | 53 | 57 | 70 | SHIMMY LIKE KATE — Olympics, Arvee 5006 | 5 |
| 51 | 45 | 39 | 32 | HELLO, YOUNG LOVERS — Paul Anka, ABC-Paramount 10132 [S] | 11 |
| 52 | 34 | 34 | 43 | YES SIR, THAT'S MY BABY — Ricky Nelson, Imperial 5685 | 5 |
| 53 | 62 | 78 | 90 | TONIGHT'S THE NIGHT — Shirelles, Scepter 1208 | 5 |
| 54 | 39 | 29 | 25 | ITSY BITSY TEENIE WEENIE YELLOW POLKA DOT BIKINI — Brian Hyland, Kapp 342 | 15 |
| 55 | 32 | 25 | 20 | IN MY LITTLE CORNER OF THE WORLD — Anita Bryant, Carlton 530 | 14 |
| 56 | 27 | 24 | 21 | OVER THE RAINBOW — Demensions, Mohawk 116 | 15 |
| 57 | 33 | 32 | 26 | HOT ROD LINCOLN — Johnny Bond, Republic 2005 | 10 |
| 58 | 66 | 75 | — | SOMEBODY TO LOVE — Bobby Darin, Atco 6179 | 3 |
| 59 | 64 | 85 | 93 | NORTH TO ALASKA — Johnny Horton, Columbia 41782 | 4 |
| 60 | 46 | 38 | 30 | ONLY THE LONELY — Roy Orbison, Monument 421 | 18 |
| 61 | 48 | 48 | 46 | I LOVE YOU IN THE SAME OLD WAY — Paul Anka, ABC-Paramount 10132 [S] | 11 |
| 62 | 43 | 41 | 36 | TA-TA — Clyde McPhatter, Mercury 71660 [S] | 13 |
| 63 | 78 | — | — | LOVE WALKED IN — Dinah Washington, Mercury 71696 | 2 |
| 64 | 63 | 66 | 74 | COME BACK — Jimmy Clanton, Ace 600 | 8 |
| 65 | 54 | 43 | 50 | YOU'RE LOOKIN' GOOD — Dee Clark, Vee Jay 355 | 9 |
| 66 | 85 | 89 | 99 | MY DEAREST DARLING — Etta James, Argo 5368 | 4 |
| 67 | 79 | 91 | — | TEMPTATION — Roger Williams, Kapp 347 | 3 |
| 68 | 58 | 58 | 52 | IF I CAN'T HAVE YOU — Etta James and Harvey, Chess 1760 | 11 |
| 69 | 50 | 46 | 40 | PLEASE HELP ME, I'M FALLING — Hank Locklin, RCA Victor 7692 [S] | 21 |
| 70 | 84 | — | — | JUST A LITTLE — Brenda Lee, Decca 31149 | 2 |
| 71 | 83 | — | — | I WISH I'D NEVER BEEN BORN — Patti Page, Mercury 71695 | 2 |
| 72 | — | — | — | TO EACH HIS OWN — Platters, Mercury 71697 | 1 |
| 73 | — | — | — | HUCKLEBUCK — Chubby Checker, Parkway 813 | 1 |
| 74 | — | — | — | PETER GUNN — Duane Eddy, Jamie 1168 | 1 |
| 75 | — | — | — | ALONE AT LAST — Jackie Wilson, Brunswick 55170 | 1 |
| 76 | — | — | — | POETRY IN MOTION — Johnny Tillotson, Cadence 1384 | 1 |
| 77 | 76 | 73 | 95 | TIME MACHINE — Dante and the Evergreens, Madison 135 | 5 |
| 78 | — | — | — | IT'S NOT THE END OF EVERYTHING — Tommy Edwards, M-G-M 12916 | 1 |
| 79 | 60 | 62 | 73 | ROCKING GOOSE — Johnny and the Hurricanes, Big Top 3051 | 6 |
| 80 | 88 | 98 | — | ALABAM — Cowboy Copas, Starday 501 | 3 |
| 81 | 97 | — | — | THEME FROM THE SUNDOWNERS — Billy Vaughn, Dot 16133 | 2 |
| 82 | — | — | — | HUMDINGER — Freddie Cannon, Swan 4061 | 1 |
| 83 | 99 | — | — | SHOPPIN' FOR CLOTHES — Coasters, Atco 6178 | 2 |
| 84 | 100 | — | — | MY HERO — Bluenotes, Value 213 | 2 |
| 85 | 72 | 59 | 58 | PUT YOUR ARMS AROUND ME, HONEY — Fats Domino, Imperial 5687 | 6 |
| 86 | — | — | — | HUSH HUSH — Jimmy Reed, Vee Jay 357 | 1 |
| 87 | — | — | — | EVERGLADES — Kingston Trio, Capitol 4441 | 1 |
| 88 | 96 | — | — | THEME FROM THE SUNDOWNERS — Felix Slatkin, Liberty 55282 | 2 |
| 89 | — | — | — | SERENATA — Sarah Vaughan, Roulette 4285 | 1 |
| 90 | — | — | — | WHOLE LOTTA SHAKIN' GOIN' ON — Chubby Checker, Parkway 813 | 1 |
| 91 | 94 | 100 | — | WAIT — Jimmy Clanton, Ace 600 | 3 |
| 92 | 95 | 99 | — | YOU TALK TOO MUCH — Frankie Ford, Imperial 5686 | 3 |
| 93 | — | — | — | DON'T LET LOVE PASS ME BY — Frankie Avalon, Chancellor 1056 | 1 |
| 94 | — | — | — | HARMONY — Billy Bland, Old Town 1088 | 1 |
| 95 | 71 | 70 | 61 | KOOKIE LITTLE PARADISE — Jo Ann Campbell, ABC-Paramount 10134 [S] | 9 |
| 96 | — | — | — | HAVE MERCY BABY — Bobbettes, Triple X 106 | 1 |
| 97 | — | — | — | FOUR LITTLE HEELS (THE CLICKETY CLACK SONG) — Brian Hyland, Kapp 352 | 1 |
| 98 | — | — | — | ONE OF THE LUCKY ONES — Anita Bryant, Carlton 535 | 1 |
| 99 | — | — | — | LAST DATE — Floyd Cramer, RCA Victor 7775 | 1 |
| 100 | — | — | — | IF SHE SHOULD COME TO YOU (LA MONTANA) — Anthony Newley, London 1929 | 1 |

# The Billboard HOT 100

**FOR WEEK ENDING OCTOBER 23**

| This Week | One Week Ago | Two Weeks Ago | Three Weeks Ago | Title — Artist, Company, Record No. | Weeks on Chart |
|---|---|---|---|---|---|
| 1 | 4 | 6 | 10 | SAVE THE LAST DANCE FOR ME — Drifters, Atlantic 2071 | 7 |
| 2 | 3 | 1 | 1 | MY HEART HAS A MIND OF ITS OWN — Connie Francis, M-G-M 12923 | 10 |
| 3 | 2 | 2 | 3 | CHAIN GANG — Sam Cooke, RCA Victor 7783 | 10 |
| 4 | 9 | 14 | 23 | I WANT TO BE WANTED — Brenda Lee, Decca 31149 | 6 |
| 5 | 5 | 4 | 2 | TWIST — Chubby Checker, Parkway 811 | 12 |
| 6 | 8 | 12 | 13 | DEVIL OR ANGEL — Bobby Vee, Liberty 55270 | 12 |
| 7 | 1 | 3 | 4 | MR. CUSTER — Larry Verne, Era 3024 | 8 |
| 8 | 6 | 5 | 5 | A MILLION TO ONE — Jimmy Charles, Promo 1002 | 9 |
| 9 | 7 | 9 | 9 | SO SAD — Everly Brothers, Warner Bros. 5163 | 7 |
| 10 | 11 | 7 | 6 | IT'S NOW OR NEVER — Elvis Presley, RCA Victor 7777 | 14 |
| 11 | 13 | 19 | 33 | LET'S THINK ABOUT LIVIN' — Bob Luman, Warner Bros. 5172 | 7 |
| 12 | 10 | 11 | 8 | KIDDIO — Brook Benton, Mercury 71652 | 11 |
| 13 | 24 | 59 | 94 | GEORGIA ON MY MIND — Ray Charles, ABC-Paramount 10135 | 4 |
| 14 | 14 | 10 | 12 | THEME FROM THE APARTMENT — Ferrante and Teicher, United Artists 231 | 13 |
| 15 | 12 | 8 | 7 | WALK, DON'T RUN — Ventures, Dolton 25 | 14 |
| 16 | 15 | 21 | 21 | THREE NIGHTS A WEEK — Fats Domino, Imperial 5687 | 7 |
| 17 | 16 | 13 | 11 | PINEAPPLE PRINCESS — Annette, Vista 362 | 10 |
| 18 | 18 | 23 | 47 | DON'T BE CRUEL — Bill Black's Combo, Hi 2026 | 6 |
| 19 | 19 | 22 | 37 | DIAMONDS AND PEARLS — Paradons, Milestone 2003 | 9 |
| 20 | 29 | 44 | 60 | MOVE TWO MOUNTAINS — Marv Johnson, United Artists 241 | 7 |
| 21 | 26 | 41 | 53 | SLEEP — Little Willie John, King 5394 | 7 |
| 22 | 22 | 25 | 26 | NEVER ON SUNDAY — Don Costa, United Artists 234 | 11 |
| 23 | 17 | 17 | 19 | YOU MEAN EVERYTHING TO ME — Neil Sedaka, RCA Victor 7781 | 11 |
| 24 | 36 | 69 | 97 | SUMMER'S GONE — Paul Anka, ABC-Paramount 10147 | 4 |
| 25 | 33 | 49 | 56 | YOU TALK TOO MUCH — Joe Jones, Roulette 4304 | 5 |
| 26 | 41 | 55 | 90 | ARTIFICIAL FLOWERS — Bobby Darin, Atco 6179 | 4 |
| 27 | 30 | 40 | 44 | A FOOL IN LOVE — Ike and Tina Turner, Sue 730 | 8 |
| 28 | 32 | 35 | 54 | RUN, SAMPSON, RUN — Neil Sedaka, RCA Victor 7781 | 7 |
| 29 | 27 | 61 | 71 | TWISTIN' U.S.A. — Danny and the Juniors, Swan 4060 | 5 |
| 30 | 23 | 18 | 15 | DREAMIN' — Johnny Burnette, Liberty 55258 | 13 |
| 31 | 43 | 57 | 67 | TOGETHERNESS — Frankie Avalon, Chancellor 1056 | 5 |
| 32 | 21 | 26 | 22 | LUCILLE — Everly Brothers, Warner Bros. 5163 | 7 |
| 33 | 48 | 68 | 81 | BLUE ANGEL — Roy Orbison, Monument 425 | 5 |
| 34 | 49 | 65 | 77 | LET'S GO, LET'S GO, LET'S GO — Hank Ballard and the Midnighters, King 5400 | 5 |
| 35 | 20 | 16 | 17 | THE SAME ONE — Brook Benton, Mercury 71652 | 9 |
| 36 | 40 | 86 | — | STAY — Maurice Williams and the Zodiacs, Herald 552 | 3 |
| 37 | 59 | 64 | 85 | NORTH TO ALASKA — Johnny Horton, Columbia 41782 | 5 |
| 38 | 28 | 28 | 18 | MISSION BELL — Donnie Brooks, Era 3018 | 19 |
| 39 | 35 | 36 | 31 | ANYMORE — Teresa Brewer, Coral 62219 | 11 |
| 40 | 53 | 62 | 78 | TONIGHT'S THE NIGHT — Shirelles, Scepter 1208 | 6 |
| 41 | 76 | — | — | POETRY IN MOTION — Johnny Tillotson, Cadence 1384 | 2 |
| 42 | 34 | 24 | 20 | FINGER POPPIN' TIME — Hank Ballard and the Midnighters, King 5341 | 23 |
| 43 | 31 | 15 | 14 | VOLARE (NEL BLU DI PINTO DI BLU) — Bobby Rydell, Cameo 179 | 14 |
| 44 | 42 | 31 | 28 | HONEST I DO — Innocents, Indigo 1055 | 10 |
| 45 | 75 | — | — | ALONE AT LAST — Jackie Wilson, Brunswick 55170 | 2 |
| 46 | 39 | 37 | 40 | (I DO THE) SHIMMY, SHIMMY — Bobby Freeman, King 5373 | 10 |
| 47 | 50 | 53 | 57 | SHIMMY LIKE KATE — Olympics, Arvee 5006 | 6 |
| 48 | 37 | 47 | 45 | LET'S HAVE A PARTY — Wanda Jackson, Capitol 4397 | 8 |
| 49 | 72 | — | — | TO EACH HIS OWN — Platters, Mercury 71697 | 2 |
| 50 | 45 | 30 | 35 | TWIST — Hank Ballard and the Midnighters, King 5171 | 14 |
| 51 | 46 | 38 | 30 | I'M SORRY — Brenda Lee, Decca 91093 | 21 |
| 52 | 44 | 42 | 55 | MALAGUENA — Connie Francis, M-G-M 12923 | 9 |
| 53 | 58 | 66 | 75 | SOMEBODY TO LOVE — Bobby Darin, Atco 6179 | 4 |
| 54 | 66 | 85 | 89 | MY DEAREST DARLING — Etta James, Argo 5368 | 5 |
| 55 | 70 | 84 | — | JUST A LITTLE — Brenda Lee, Decca 31149 | 3 |
| 56 | 47 | 56 | 61 | MY LOVE FOR YOU — Johnny Mathis, Columbia 41764 | 8 |
| 57 | 38 | 29 | 27 | I'M NOT AFRAID — Ricky Nelson, Imperial 5685 | 7 |
| 58 | 52 | 34 | 34 | YES SIR, THAT'S MY BABY — Ricky Nelson, Imperial 5685 | 6 |
| 59 | 73 | — | — | HUCKLEBUCK — Chubby Checker, Parkway 813 | 2 |
| 60 | 71 | 83 | — | I WISH I'D NEVER BEEN BORN — Patti Page, Mercury 71695 | 3 |
| 61 | 63 | 78 | — | LOVE WALKED IN — Dinah Washington, Mercury 71696 | 3 |
| 62 | 67 | 79 | 91 | TEMPTATION — Roger Williams, Kapp 347 | 4 |
| 63 | 99 | — | — | LAST DATE — Floyd Cramer, RCA Victor 7775 | 2 |
| 64 | 51 | 45 | 39 | HELLO, YOUNG LOVERS — Paul Anka, ABC-Paramount 10132 | 12 |
| 65 | 87 | — | — | EVERGLADES — Kingston Trio, Capitol 4441 | 2 |
| 66 | 82 | — | — | HUMDINGER — Freddie Cannon, Swan 4061 | 2 |
| 67 | 74 | — | — | PETER GUNN — Duane Eddy, Jamie 1168 | 2 |
| 68 | 62 | 43 | 41 | TA-TA — Clyde McPhatter, Mercury 71660 | 14 |
| 69 | 68 | 58 | 58 | IF I CAN'T HAVE YOU — Etta James and Harvey, Chess 1760 | 12 |
| 70 | 65 | 54 | 43 | YOU'RE LOOKIN' GOOD — Dee Clark, Vee Jay 355 | 10 |
| 71 | — | — | — | NEW ORLEANS — U. S. Bonds, Lagrand 819 | 1 |
| 72 | 60 | 46 | 38 | ONLY THE LONELY — Roy Orbison, Monument 421 | 19 |
| 73 | 81 | 97 | — | THEME FROM THE SUNDOWNERS — Billy Vaughn, Dot 16133 | 3 |
| 74 | 80 | 88 | 98 | ALABAM — Cowboy Copas, Starday 501 | 4 |
| 75 | 86 | — | — | HUSH HUSH — Jimmy Reed, Vee Jay 357 | 2 |
| 76 | 88 | 96 | — | THEME FROM THE SUNDOWNERS — Felix Slatkin, Liberty 55282 | 3 |
| 77 | 90 | — | — | WHOLE LOTTA SHAKIN' GOIN' ON — Chubby Checker, Parkway 813 | 2 |
| 78 | 84 | 100 | — | MY HERO — Bluenotes, Value 213 | 3 |
| 79 | 77 | 76 | 73 | TIME MACHINE — Dante and the Evergreens, Madison 135 | 6 |
| 80 | 98 | — | — | ONE OF THE LUCKY ONES — Anita Bryant, Carlton 535 | 2 |
| 81 | 97 | — | — | FOUR LITTLE HEELS (THE CLICKETY CLACK SONG) — Brian Hyland, Kapp 352 | 2 |
| 82 | — | — | — | LONELY TEENAGER — Dion, Laurie 3070 | 1 |
| 83 | — | — | — | PATSY — Jack Scott, Top Rank 2075 | 1 |
| 84 | 78 | — | — | IT'S NOT THE END OF EVERYTHING — Tommy Edwards, M-G-M 12916 | 2 |
| 85 | 93 | — | — | DON'T LET LOVE PASS ME BY — Frankie Avalon, Chancellor 1056 | 2 |
| 86 | 89 | — | — | SERENATA — Sarah Vaughan, Roulette 4285 | 2 |
| 87 | 92 | 95 | 99 | YOU TALK TOO MUCH — Frankie Ford, Imperial 5686 | 4 |
| 88 | 96 | — | — | HAVE MERCY BABY — Bobbettes, Triple X 106 | 2 |
| 89 | 83 | 99 | — | SHOPPIN' FOR CLOTHES — Coasters, Atco 6178 | 3 |
| 90 | 69 | 50 | 46 | PLEASE HELP ME, I'M FALLING — Hank Locklin, RCA Victor 7692 | 22 |
| 91 | 94 | — | — | HARMONY — Billy Bland, Old Town 1088 | 2 |
| 92 | — | — | — | BALLAD OF THE ALAMO — Marty Robbins, Columbia 41809 | 1 |
| 93 | — | — | — | GIRL WITH THE STORY IN HER EYES — Safaris, Eldo 105 | 1 |
| 94 | — | — | — | SIDE CAR CYCLE — Charlie Ryan, Four Star 1745 | 1 |
| 95 | — | — | — | MIDNIGHT LACE — Ray Ellis, M-G-M 12942 | 1 |
| 96 | — | — | — | LAST ONE TO KNOW — Fleetwoods, Dolton 27 | 1 |
| 97 | — | — | — | NIGHT THEME — Mark II, Wye 1001 | 1 |
| 98 | 100 | — | — | IF SHE SHOULD COME TO YOU (LA MONTANA) — Anthony Newley, London 1929 | 2 |
| 99 | — | — | — | BALLAD OF THE ALAMO — Bud and Travis, Liberty 55284 | 1 |
| 100 | — | — | — | MIDNIGHT LACE — Ray Conniff, Columbia 41180 | 1 |

## The Billboard HOT 100

**FOR WEEK ENDING OCTOBER 30**

| This Week | 1wk | 2wk | 3wk | Title / Artist / Company / Record No. | Weeks on Chart |
|---|---|---|---|---|---|
| 1 | 4 | 9 | 14 | I WANT TO BE WANTED — Brenda Lee, Decca 31149 | 7 |
| 2 | 1 | 4 | 6 | SAVE THE LAST DANCE FOR ME — Drifters, Atlantic 2071 | 8 |
| 3 | 5 | 5 | 4 | TWIST — Chubby Checker, Parkway 811 | 13 |
| 4 | 2 | 3 | 1 | MY HEART HAS A MIND OF ITS OWN — Connie Francis, M-G-M 12923 | 11 |
| 5 | 3 | 2 | 2 | CHAIN GANG — Sam Cooke, RCA Victor 7783 | 11 |
| 6 | 6 | 8 | 12 | DEVIL OR ANGEL — Bobby Vee, Liberty 55270 | 13 |
| 7 | 11 | 13 | 19 | LET'S THINK ABOUT LIVIN' — Bob Luman, Warner Bros. 5172 | 8 |
| 8 | 9 | 7 | 9 | SO SAD — Everly Brothers, Warner Bros. 5163 | 8 |
| 9 | 7 | 1 | 3 | MR. CUSTER — Larry Verne, Era 3024 | 9 |
| 10 | 14 | 14 | 10 | THEME FROM THE APARTMENT — Ferrante and Teicher, United Artists 231 | 14 |
| 11 | 13 | 24 | 59 | GEORGIA ON MY MIND — Ray Charles, ABC-Paramount 10135 | 5 |
| 12 | 25 | 33 | 49 | YOU TALK TOO MUCH — Joe Jones, Roulette 4304 | 6 |
| 13 | 12 | 10 | 11 | KIDDIO — Brook Benton, Mercury 71652 | 12 |
| 14 | 8 | 6 | 5 | A MILLION TO ONE — Jimmy Charles, Promo 1002 | 10 |
| 15 | 18 | 18 | 23 | DON'T BE CRUEL — Bill Black's Combo, Hi 2026 | 7 |
| 16 | 10 | 11 | 7 | IT'S NOW OR NEVER — Elvis Presley, RCA Victor 7777 | 15 |
| 17 | 16 | 15 | 21 | THREE NIGHTS A WEEK — Fats Domino, Imperial 5687 | 8 |
| 18 | 19 | 19 | 22 | DIAMONDS AND PEARLS — Paradons, Milestone 2003 | 10 |
| 19 | 22 | 22 | 25 | NEVER ON SUNDAY — Don Costa, United Artists 234 | 12 |
| 20 | 24 | 36 | 69 | SUMMER'S GONE — Paul Anka, ABC-Paramount 10147 | 5 |
| 21 | 21 | 26 | 41 | SLEEP — Little Willie John, King 5394 | 8 |
| 22 | 33 | 48 | 68 | BLUE ANGEL — Roy Orbison, Monument 425 | 6 |
| 23 | 26 | 41 | 55 | ARTIFICIAL FLOWERS — Bobby Darin, Atco 6179 | 5 |
| 24 | 20 | 29 | 44 | MOVE TWO MOUNTAINS — Marv Johnson, United Artists 241 | 8 |
| 25 | 34 | 49 | 65 | LET'S GO, LET'S GO, LET'S GO — Hank Ballard and the Midnighters, King 5400 | 6 |
| 26 | 41 | 76 | — | POETRY IN MOTION — Johnny Tillotson, Cadence 1384 | 3 |
| 27 | 36 | 40 | 86 | STAY — Maurice Williams and the Zodiacs, Herald 552 | 4 |
| 28 | 30 | 23 | 18 | DREAMIN' — Johnny Burnette, Liberty 55258 | 14 |
| 29 | 17 | 16 | 13 | PINEAPPLE PRINCESS — Annette, Vista 362 | 11 |
| 30 | 31 | 43 | 57 | TOGETHERNESS — Frankie Avalon, Chancellor 1056 | 6 |
| 31 | 37 | 59 | 64 | NORTH TO ALASKA — Johnny Horton, Columbia 41782 | 6 |
| 32 | 49 | 72 | — | TO EACH HIS OWN — Platters, Mercury 71697 | 3 |
| 33 | 32 | 21 | 26 | LUCILLE — Everly Brothers, Warner Bros. 5163 | 8 |
| 34 | 15 | 12 | 8 | WALK, DON'T RUN — Ventures, Dolton 25 | 15 |
| 35 | 29 | 27 | 61 | TWISTIN' U.S.A. — Danny and the Juniors, Swan 4060 | 6 |
| 36 | 45 | 75 | — | ALONE AT LAST — Jackie Wilson, Brunswick 55170 | 3 |
| 37 | 35 | 20 | 16 | THE SAME ONE — Brook Benton, Mercury 71652 | 10 |
| 38 | 23 | 17 | 17 | YOU MEAN EVERYTHING TO ME — Neil Sedaka, RCA Victor 7781 | 12 |
| 39 | 40 | 53 | 62 | TONIGHT'S THE NIGHT — Shirelles, Scepter 1208 | 7 |
| 40 | 27 | 30 | 40 | A FOOL IN LOVE — Ike and Tina Turner, Sue 730 | 9 |
| 41 | 67 | 74 | — | PETER GUNN — Duane Eddy, Jamie 1168 | 3 |
| 42 | 47 | 50 | 53 | SHIMMY LIKE KATE — Olympics, Arvee 5006 | 7 |
| 43 | 55 | 70 | 84 | JUST A LITTLE — Brenda Lee, Decca 31149 | 4 |
| 44 | 39 | 35 | 36 | ANYMORE — Teresa Brewer, Coral 62219 | 12 |
| 45 | 53 | 58 | 66 | SOMEBODY TO LOVE — Bobby Darin, Atco 6179 | 5 |
| 46 | 46 | 39 | 37 | (I DO THE) SHIMMY, SHIMMY — Bobby Freeman, King 5373 | 11 |
| 47 | 28 | 32 | 35 | RUN, SAMPSON, RUN — Neil Sedaka, RCA Victor 7781 | 8 |
| 48 | 71 | — | — | NEW ORLEANS — U. S. Bonds, Legrand 819 | 2 |
| 49 | 48 | 37 | 47 | LET'S HAVE A PARTY — Wanda Jackson, Capitol 4397 | 9 |
| 50 | 54 | 66 | 85 | MY DEAREST DARLING — Etta James, Argo 5368 | 6 |
| 51 | 59 | 73 | — | HUCKLEBUCK — Chubby Checker, Parkway 813 | 3 |
| 52 | 60 | 71 | 83 | I WISH I'D NEVER BEEN BORN — Patti Page, Mercury 71695 | 4 |
| 53 | 42 | 34 | 24 | FINGER POPPIN' TIME — Hank Ballard and the Midnighters, King 5341 | 24 |
| 54 | 61 | 63 | 78 | LOVE WALKED IN — Dinah Washington, Mercury 71696 | 4 |
| 55 | 63 | 99 | — | LAST DATE — Floyd Cramer, RCA Victor 7775 | 3 |
| 56 | 62 | 67 | 79 | TEMPTATION — Roger Williams, Kapp 347 | 5 |
| 57 | 43 | 31 | 15 | VOLARE (NEL BLU DI PINTO DI BLU) — Bobby Rydell, Cameo 179 | 15 |
| 58 | 50 | 45 | 30 | TWIST — Hank Ballard and the Midnighters, King 5171 | 15 |
| 59 | 66 | 82 | — | HUMDINGER — Freddie Cannon, Swan 4061 | 3 |
| 60 | 65 | 87 | — | EVERGLADES — Kingston Trio, Capitol 4441 | 3 |
| 61 | 56 | 47 | 56 | MY LOVE FOR YOU — Johnny Mathis, Columbia 41764 | 9 |
| 62 | 57 | 38 | 29 | I'M NOT AFRAID — Ricky Nelson, Imperial 5685 | 8 |
| 63 | 51 | 46 | 38 | I'M SORRY — Brenda Lee, Decca 31093 | 22 |
| 64 | 38 | 28 | 28 | MISSION BELL — Donnie Brooks, Era 3018 | 20 |
| 65 | 77 | 90 | — | WHOLE LOTTA SHAKIN' GOIN' ON — Chubby Checker, Parkway 813 | 3 |
| 66 | 73 | 81 | 97 | THEME FROM THE SUNDOWNERS — Billy Vaughn, Dot 16133 | 4 |
| 67 | — | — | — | A THOUSAND STARS — Cathy Young, Indigo 108 | 1 |
| 68 | 80 | 98 | — | ONE OF THE LUCKY ONES — Anita Bryant, Carlton 535 | 3 |
| 69 | 74 | 80 | 88 | ALABAM — Cowboy Copas, Starday 501 | 5 |
| 70 | 76 | 88 | 96 | THEME FROM THE SUNDOWNERS — Felix Slatkin, Liberty 55282 | 4 |
| 71 | 83 | — | — | PATSY — Jack Scott, Top Rank 2075 | 2 |
| 72 | 82 | — | — | LONELY TEENAGER — Dion, Laurie 3070 | 2 |
| 73 | 81 | 97 | — | FOUR LITTLE HEELS (THE CLICKETY CLACK SONG) — Brian Hyland, Kapp 352 | 3 |
| 74 | — | — | — | THAT'S HOW MUCH — Brian Hyland, Kapp 352 | 1 |
| 75 | 98 | 100 | — | IF SHE SHOULD COME TO YOU (LA MONTANA) — Anthony Newley, London 1929 | 3 |
| 76 | — | — | — | SAILOR (YOUR HOME IS IN THE SEA.) — Lolita, Kapp 349 | 1 |
| 77 | — | — | — | MY GIRL, JOSEPHINE — Fats Domino, Imperial 5704 | 1 |
| 78 | — | — | — | AM I LOSING YOU — Jim Reeves, RCA Victor 7800 | 1 |
| 79 | — | — | — | DEAR JOHN — Pat Boone, Dot 16152 | 1 |
| 80 | 78 | 84 | 100 | MY HERO — Bluenotes, Value 213 | 4 |
| 81 | — | — | — | LAST DATE — Lawrence Welk, Dot 16145 | 1 |
| 82 | 86 | 89 | — | SERENATA — Sarah Vaughan, Roulette 4285 | 3 |
| 83 | 92 | — | — | BALLAD OF THE ALAMO — Marty Robbins, Columbia 41809 | 2 |
| 84 | 99 | — | — | BALLAD OF THE ALAMO — Bud and Travis, Liberty 55284 | 2 |
| 85 | 93 | — | — | GIRL WITH THE STORY IN HER EYES — Safaris, Eldo 105 | 2 |
| 86 | 88 | 96 | — | HAVE MERCY BABY — Bobbettes, Triple X 106 | 3 |
| 87 | 95 | — | — | MIDNIGHT LACE — Ray Ellis, M-G-M 12942 | 2 |
| 88 | 89 | 83 | 99 | SHOPPIN' FOR CLOTHES — Coasters, Atco 6178 | 4 |
| 89 | — | — | — | ALABAM — Pat Boone, Dot 16152 | 1 |
| 90 | — | — | — | I'LL SAVE THE LAST DANCE FOR YOU — Damita Jo, Mercury 71690 | 1 |
| 91 | 94 | — | — | SIDE CAR CYCLE — Charlie Ryan, Four Star 1745 | 2 |
| 92 | — | — | — | WAIT FOR ME — Playmates, Roulette 4276 | 1 |
| 93 | 97 | — | — | NIGHT THEME — Mark II, Wye 1001 | 2 |
| 94 | 100 | — | — | MIDNIGHT LACE — Ray Conniff, Columbia 41180 | 2 |
| 95 | — | — | — | DANCE WITH ME, GEORGIE — Bobbettes, Triple X 106 | 1 |
| 96 | 72 | 60 | 46 | ONLY THE LONELY — Roy Orbison, Monument 421 | 20 |
| 97 | — | — | — | THEME FROM THE DARK AT THE TOP OF THE STAIRS — Ernie Freeman, Imperial 5693 | 1 |
| 98 | — | — | — | MIDNIGHT LACE — David Carroll, Mercury 71703 | 1 |
| 99 | — | — | — | AM I THE MAN — Jackie Wilson, Brunswick 55170 | 1 |
| 100 | — | — | — | ISN'T IT AMAZING — Crests, Coed 537 | 1 |

# The Billboard HOT 100

**FOR WEEK ENDING NOVEMBER 6**

*STAR PERFORMERS showed the greatest upward progress on Hot 100 this week.*
*S — Indicates that 45 r.p.m. stereo single version is available.*
*A — Indicates that 33⅓ r.p.m. stereo single version is available.*

Columns: THIS WEEK | ONE WEEK AGO | TWO WEEKS AGO | THREE WEEKS AGO | TITLE — Artist, Company, Record No. | STEREO | WEEKS ON CHART

| This | 1wk | 2wk | 3wk | Title — Artist, Company, Record No. | Stereo | Wks |
|---|---|---|---|---|---|---|
| 1 | 2 | 1 | 4 | SAVE THE LAST DANCE FOR ME — Drifters, Atlantic 2071 | | 9 |
| 2 | 1 | 4 | 9 | I WANT TO BE WANTED — Brenda Lee, Decca 31149 | | 8 |
| 3 | 4 | 2 | 3 | MY HEART HAS A MIND OF ITS OWN — Connie Francis, M-G-M 12923 | | 12 |
| 4 | 3 | 5 | 5 | TWIST — Chubby Checker, Parkway 811 | | 14 |
| 5 | 5 | 3 | 2 | CHAIN GANG — Sam Cooke, RCA Victor 7783 | S | 12 |
| ★6 | 12 | 25 | 33 | YOU TALK TOO MUCH — Joe Jones, Roulette 4304 | | 7 |
| 7 | 6 | 6 | 8 | DEVIL OR ANGEL — Bobby Vee, Liberty 55270 | | 14 |
| 8 | 7 | 11 | 13 | LET'S THINK ABOUT LIVIN' — Bob Luman, Warner Bros. 5172 | | 9 |
| ★9 | 26 | 41 | 76 | POETRY IN MOTION — Johnny Tillotson, Cadence 1384 | | 4 |
| 10 | 11 | 13 | 24 | GEORGIA ON MY MIND — Ray Charles, ABC-Paramount 10135 | S | 6 |
| 11 | 20 | 24 | 36 | SUMMER'S GONE — Paul Anka, ABC-Paramount 10147 | S | 6 |
| 12 | 15 | 18 | 18 | DON'T BE CRUEL — Bill Black's Combo, Hi 2026 | | 8 |
| 13 | 8 | 9 | 7 | SO SAD — Everly Brothers, Warner Bros. 5163 | | 9 |
| ★14 | 25 | 34 | 49 | LET'S GO, LET'S GO, LET'S GO — Hank Ballard and the Midnighters, King 5400 | | 7 |
| 15 | 22 | 33 | 48 | BLUE ANGEL — Roy Orbison, Monument 425 | | 7 |
| 16 | 14 | 8 | 6 | A MILLION TO ONE — Jimmy Charles, Promo 1002 | | 11 |
| 17 | 10 | 14 | 14 | THEME FROM THE APARTMENT — Ferrante and Teicher, United Artists 231 | | 15 |
| 18 | 21 | 21 | 26 | SLEEP — Little Willie John, King 5394 | | 9 |
| ★19 | 27 | 36 | 40 | STAY — Maurice Williams and the Zodiacs, Herald 552 | | 5 |
| 20 | 23 | 26 | 41 | ARTIFICIAL FLOWERS — Bobby Darin, Atco 6179 | | 6 |
| 21 | 9 | 7 | 1 | MR. CUSTER — Larry Verne, Era 3024 | | 10 |
| 22 | 13 | 12 | 10 | KIDDIO — Brook Benton, Mercury 71652 | S | 13 |
| 23 | 31 | 37 | 59 | NORTH TO ALASKA — Johnny Horton, Columbia 41782 | | 7 |
| 24 | 32 | 49 | 72 | TO EACH HIS OWN — Platters, Mercury 71697 | S | 4 |
| ★25 | 36 | 45 | 75 | ALONE AT LAST — Jackie Wilson, Brunswick 55170 | | 4 |
| 26 | 30 | 31 | 43 | TOGETHERNESS — Frankie Avalon, Chancellor 1056 | S | 7 |
| 27 | 16 | 10 | 11 | IT'S NOW OR NEVER — Elvis Presley, RCA Victor 7777 | S | 16 |
| 28 | 55 | 63 | 99 | LAST DATE — Floyd Cramer, RCA Victor 7775 | S | 4 |
| 29 | 19 | 22 | 22 | NEVER ON SUNDAY — Don Costa, United Artists 234 | | 13 |
| ★30 | 48 | 71 | — | NEW ORLEANS — U. S. Bonds, Legrand 819 | | 3 |
| 31 | 17 | 16 | 15 | THREE NIGHTS A WEEK — Fats Domino, Imperial 5687 | | 9 |
| 32 | 41 | 67 | 74 | PETER GUNN — Duane Eddy, Jamie 1168 | | 4 |
| 33 | 18 | 19 | 19 | DIAMONDS AND PEARLS — Paradons, Milestone 2003 | | 11 |
| 34 | 40 | 27 | 30 | A FOOL IN LOVE — Ike and Tina Turner, Sue 730 | | 10 |
| 35 | 24 | 20 | 29 | MOVE TWO MOUNTAINS — Marv Johnson, United Artists 241 | | 9 |
| ★36 | 51 | 59 | 73 | HUCKLEBUCK — Chubby Checker, Parkway 813 | | 4 |
| ★37 | 67 | — | — | A THOUSAND STARS — Kathy Young and the Innocents, Indigo 108 | | 2 |
| 38 | 37 | 35 | 20 | THE SAME ONE — Brook Benton, Mercury 71652 | S | 11 |
| 39 | 29 | 17 | 16 | PINEAPPLE PRINCESS — Annette, Vista 362 | | 12 |
| 40 | 43 | 55 | 70 | JUST A LITTLE — Brenda Lee, Decca 31149 | | 5 |
| 41 | 50 | 54 | 66 | MY DEAREST DARLING — Etta James, Argo 5368 | | 7 |
| 42 | 33 | 32 | 21 | LUCILLE — Everly Brothers, Warner Bros. 5163 | | 9 |
| 43 | 34 | 15 | 12 | WALK, DON'T RUN — Ventures, Dolton 25 | | 16 |
| 44 | 44 | 39 | 35 | ANYMORE — Teresa Brewer, Coral 62219 | | 13 |
| 45 | 35 | 29 | 27 | TWISTIN' U.S.A. — Danny and the Juniors, Swan 4060 | | 7 |
| 46 | 45 | 53 | 58 | SOMEBODY TO LOVE — Bobby Darin, Atco 6179 | | 6 |
| 47 | 42 | 47 | 50 | SHIMMY LIKE KATE — Olympics, Arvee 5006 | | 8 |
| 48 | 39 | 40 | 53 | TONIGHT'S THE NIGHT — Shirelles, Scepter 1208 | | 8 |
| 49 | 47 | 28 | 32 | RUN, SAMPSON, RUN — Neil Sedaka, RCA Victor 7781 | S | 9 |
| ★50 | 65 | 77 | 90 | WHOLE LOT OF SHAKIN' GOIN ON — Chubby Checker, Parkway 813 | | 4 |
| 51 | 38 | 23 | 17 | YOU MEAN EVERYTHING TO ME — Neil Sedaka, RCA Victor 7781 | S | 13 |
| 52 | 77 | — | — | MY GIRL, JOSEPHINE — Fats Domino, Imperial 5704 | | 2 |
| 53 | 66 | 73 | 81 | THEME FROM THE SUNDOWNERS — Billy Vaughn, Dot 16133 | S | 5 |
| 54 | 52 | 60 | 71 | I WISH I'D NEVER BEEN BORN — Patti Page, Mercury 71695 | S | 5 |
| 55 | 54 | 61 | 63 | LOVE WALKED IN — Dinah Washington, Mercury 71696 | | 5 |
| 56 | 46 | 46 | 39 | (I DO THE) SHIMMY, SHIMMY — Bobby Freeman, King 5373 | | 12 |
| 57 | 53 | 42 | 34 | FINGER POPPIN' TIME — Hank Ballard and the Midnighters, King 5341 | | 25 |
| 58 | 49 | 48 | 37 | LET'S HAVE A PARTY — Wanda Jackson, Capitol 4397 | | 10 |
| ★59 | 90 | — | — | I'LL SAVE THE LAST DANCE FOR YOU — Damita Jo, Mercury 71690 | | 2 |
| 60 | 28 | 30 | 23 | DREAMIN' — Johnny Burnette, Liberty 55258 | | 15 |
| ★61 | 79 | — | — | DEAR JOHN — Pat Boone, Dot 16152 | | 2 |
| ★62 | 78 | — | — | AM I LOSING YOU — Jim Reeves, RCA Victor 7800 | | 2 |
| ★63 | — | — | — | HE WILL BREAK YOUR HEART — Jerry Butler, Vee Jay 354 | | 1 |
| 64 | 68 | 80 | 98 | ONE OF THE LUCKY ONES — Anita Bryant, Carlton 535 | | 4 |
| 65 | 71 | 83 | — | PATSY — Jack Scott, Top Rank 2075 | | 3 |
| 66 | 69 | 74 | 80 | ALABAM — Cowboy Copas, Starday 501 | | 6 |
| 67 | 75 | 98 | 100 | IF SHE SHOULD COME TO YOU (LA MONTANA) — Anthony Newley, London 1929 | | 4 |
| 68 | 60 | 65 | 87 | EVERGLADES — Kingston Trio, Capitol 4441 | | 4 |
| 69 | 89 | — | — | ALABAM — Pat Boone, Dot 16152 | | 2 |
| 70 | 72 | 82 | — | LONELY TEENAGER — Dion, Laurie 3070 | | 3 |
| 71 | 70 | 76 | 88 | THEME FROM THE SUNDOWNERS — Felix Slatkin, Liberty 55282 | | 5 |
| 72 | 92 | — | — | WAIT FOR ME — Playmates, Roulette 4276 | | 2 |
| 73 | 76 | — | — | SAILOR (YOUR HOME IS IN THE SEA) — Lolita, Kapp 349 | | 2 |
| 74 | 97 | — | — | THEME FROM THE DARK AT THE TOP OF THE STAIRS — Ernie Freeman, Imperial 5693 | | 2 |
| 75 | 59 | 66 | 82 | HUMDINGER — Freddie Cannon, Swan 4061 | | 4 |
| 76 | 74 | — | — | THAT'S HOW MUCH — Brian Hyland, Kapp 352 | | 2 |
| 77 | 99 | — | — | AM I THE MAN — Jackie Wilson, Brunswick 55170 | | 2 |
| 78 | — | — | — | PERFIDIA — Ventures, Dolton 28 | | 1 |
| 79 | 58 | 50 | 45 | TWIST — Hank Ballard and the Midnighters, King 5171 | | 16 |
| 80 | 61 | 56 | 47 | MY LOVE FOR YOU — Johnny Mathis, Columbia 41764 | A | 10 |
| 81 | 84 | 99 | — | BALLAD OF THE ALAMO — Marty Robbins, Columbia 41809 | A | 3 |
| 82 | 86 | 88 | 96 | HAVE MERCY, BABY — Bobbettes, Triple X 106 | | 4 |
| 83 | 84 | 99 | — | BALLAD OF THE ALAMO — Bud and Travis, Liberty 55284 | | 3 |
| 84 | 87 | 95 | — | MIDNIGHT LACE — Ray Ellis, M-G-M 12942 | | 3 |
| 85 | 63 | 51 | 46 | I'M SORRY — Brenda Lee, Decca 31093 | | 23 |
| 86 | — | — | — | NATURAL BORN LOVER — Fats Domino, Imperial 5704 | | 1 |
| 87 | 85 | 93 | — | GIRL WITH THE STORY IN HER EYES — Safaris, Eldo 105 | | 3 |
| 88 | — | — | — | LIKE STRANGERS — Everly Brothers, Cadence 1388 | | 1 |
| 89 | 91 | 94 | — | SIDE CAR CYCLE — Charlie Ryan, Four Star 1745 | | 3 |
| 90 | 93 | 97 | — | NIGHT THEME — Mark II, Wye 1001 | | 3 |
| 91 | 56 | 62 | 67 | TEMPTATION — Roger Williams, Kapp 347 | | 6 |
| 92 | 94 | 100 | — | MIDNIGHT LACE — Ray Conniff, Columbia 41180 | | 3 |
| 93 | — | — | — | A WHOLE LOT OF SHAKIN' GOIN' ON — Conway Twitty, M-G-M 12962 | | 1 |
| 94 | — | — | — | YOU'RE SIXTEEN — Johnny Burnette, Liberty 55285 | | 1 |
| 95 | — | — | — | RUBY DUBY DU — Tobin Matthews, Chief 7022 | | 1 |
| 96 | — | — | — | IRRESISTIBLE YOU — Bobby Peterson, V-Tone 214 | | 1 |
| 97 | — | — | — | RUBY DUBY DU — Charles Wolcott, M-G-M 12944 | | 1 |
| 98 | — | — | — | ONCE IN A WHILE — Chimes, Tag 444 | | 1 |
| 99 | — | — | — | A KISSIN' AND A TWISTIN' — Fabian, Chancellor 1061 | | 1 |
| 100 | — | — | — | GREEN LEAVES OF SUMMER — Brothers Four, Columbia 41808 | | 1 |

# The Billboard HOT 100

**FOR WEEK ENDING NOVEMBER 13**

*The Billboard's Music Popularity Charts ... POP RECORDS — NOVEMBER 7, 1960*

STAR PERFORMERS showed the greatest upward progress on Hot 100 this week.
(S) Indicates that 45 r.p.m. stereo single version is available.
(A) Indicates that 33⅓ r.p.m. stereo single version is available.

Columns: THIS WEEK | ONE WEEK AGO | TWO WEEKS AGO | THREE WEEKS AGO | TITLE — Artist, Company, Record No. | STEREO | WEEKS ON CHART

| # | 1wk | 2wk | 3wk | Title — Artist, Company, Record No. | Stereo | Wks |
|---|---|---|---|---|---|---|
| 1 | 1 | 2 | 1 | SAVE THE LAST DANCE FOR ME — Drifters, Atlantic 2071 | | 10 |
| 2 | 2 | 1 | 4 | I WANT TO BE WANTED — Brenda Lee, Decca 31149 | | 9 |
| ★3 | 9 | 26 | 41 | POETRY IN MOTION — Johnny Tillotson, Cadence 1384 | | 5 |
| 4 | 10 | 11 | 13 | GEORGIA ON MY MIND — Ray Charles, ABC-Paramount 10135 | S | 7 |
| 5 | 6 | 12 | 25 | YOU TALK TOO MUCH — Joe Jones, Roulette 4304 | | 8 |
| 6 | 3 | 4 | 2 | MY HEART HAS A MIND OF ITS OWN — Connie Francis, M-G-M 12923 | | 13 |
| ★7 | 19 | 27 | 36 | STAY — Maurice Williams and the Zodiacs, Herald 552 | | 6 |
| ★8 | 14 | 25 | 34 | LET'S GO, LET'S GO, LET'S GO — Hank Ballard and the Midnighters, King 5400 | | 8 |
| 9 | 15 | 22 | 23 | BLUE ANGEL — Roy Orbison, Monument 425 | | 8 |
| 10 | 7 | 6 | 6 | DEVIL OR ANGEL — Bobby Vee, Liberty 55270 | | 15 |
| 11 | 12 | 15 | 18 | DON'T BE CRUEL — Bill Black's Combo, Hi 2026 | | 9 |
| 12 | 5 | 5 | 3 | CHAIN GANG — Sam Cooke, RCA Victor 7783 | S | 13 |
| 13 | 8 | 7 | 11 | LET'S THINK ABOUT LIVIN' — Bob Luman, Warner Bros. 5172 | | 10 |
| 14 | 18 | 21 | 21 | SLEEP — Little Willie John, King 5394 | | 10 |
| 15 | 11 | 20 | 24 | SUMMER'S GONE — Paul Anka, ABC-Paramount 10147 | S | 7 |
| ★16 | 28 | 55 | 63 | LAST DATE — Floyd Cramer, RCA Victor 7775 | S | 5 |
| ★17 | 30 | 48 | 71 | NEW ORLEANS — U. S. Bonds, Legrand 819 | | 4 |
| 18 | 23 | 31 | 37 | NORTH TO ALASKA — Johnny Horton, Columbia 41782 | | 8 |
| 19 | 25 | 36 | 45 | ALONE AT LAST — Jackie Wilson, Brunswick 55170 | | 5 |
| 20 | 17 | 10 | 14 | THEME FROM THE APARTMENT — Ferrante and Teicher, United Artists 231 | | 16 |
| 21 | 24 | 32 | 49 | TO EACH HIS OWN — Platters, Mercury 71697 | S | 5 |
| ★22 | 37 | 67 | — | A THOUSAND STARS — Kathy Young and the Innocents, Indigo 108 | | 3 |
| 23 | 20 | 23 | 26 | ARTIFICIAL FLOWERS — Bobby Darin, Atco 6179 | | 7 |
| 24 | 4 | 3 | 5 | TWIST — Chubby Checker, Parkway 811 | | 15 |
| 25 | 22 | 13 | 12 | KIDDIO — Brook Benton, Mercury 71652 | S | 14 |
| 26 | 13 | 8 | 9 | SO SAD — Everly Brothers, Warner Bros. 5163 | | 10 |
| 27 | 26 | 30 | 31 | TOGETHERNESS — Frankie Avalon, Chancellor 1056 | S | 8 |
| 28 | 16 | 14 | 8 | A MILLION TO ONE — Jimmy Charles, Promo 1022 | | 12 |
| 29 | 36 | 51 | 59 | HUCKLEBUCK — Chubby Checker, Parkway 813 | | 5 |
| 30 | 32 | 41 | 67 | PETER GUNN — Duane Eddy, Jamie 1168 | | 5 |
| 31 | 29 | 19 | 22 | NEVER ON SUNDAY — Don Costa, United Artists 234 | | 14 |
| 32 | 27 | 16 | 10 | IT'S NOW OR NEVER — Elvis Presley, RCA Victor 7777 | S | 17 |
| 33 | 34 | 40 | 27 | A FOOL IN LOVE — Ike and Tina Turner, Sue 730 | | 11 |
| 34 | 21 | 9 | 7 | MR. CUSTER — Larry Verne, Era 3024 | | 11 |
| ★35 | 63 | — | — | HE WILL BREAK YOUR HEART — Jerry Butler, Vee Jay 354 | | 2 |
| 36 | 31 | 17 | 16 | THREE NIGHTS A WEEK — Fats Domino, Imperial 5687 | | 10 |
| 37 | 33 | 18 | 19 | DIAMONDS AND PEARLS — Paradons, Milestone 2003 | | 12 |
| 38 | 55 | 54 | 61 | LOVE WALKED IN — Dinah Washington, Mercury 71696 | | 6 |
| 39 | 59 | 90 | — | I'LL SAVE THE LAST DANCE FOR YOU — Damita Jo, Mercury 71690 | | 3 |
| 40 | 48 | 39 | 40 | TONIGHT'S THE NIGHT — Shirelles, Scepter 1208 | | 9 |
| 41 | 52 | 77 | — | MY GIRL JOSEPHINE — Fats Domino, Imperial 5704 | | 3 |
| 42 | 50 | 65 | 77 | WHOLE LOT OF SHAKIN' GOIN' ON — Chubby Checker, Parkway 813 | | 5 |
| 43 | 41 | 50 | 54 | MY DEAREST DARLING — Etta James, Argo 5368 | | 8 |
| ★44 | 78 | — | — | PERFIDIA — Ventures, Dolton 28 | | 2 |
| 45 | 46 | 45 | 53 | SOMEBODY TO LOVE — Bobby Darin, Atco 6179 | | 7 |
| 46 | 44 | 44 | 39 | ANYMORE — Teresa Brewer, Coral 62219 | | 14 |
| 47 | 35 | 24 | 20 | MOVE TWO MOUNTAINS — Marv Johnson, United Artists 241 | | 10 |
| ★48 | 72 | 92 | — | WAIT FOR ME — Playmates, Roulette 4276 | | 3 |
| 49 | 39 | 29 | 17 | PINEAPPLE PRINCESS — Annette, Vista 362 | | 13 |
| 50 | 70 | 72 | 82 | LONELY TEENAGER — Dion, Laurie 3070 | | 4 |
| 51 | 53 | 66 | 73 | THEME FROM THE SUNDOWNERS — Billy Vaughn, Dot 16133 | S | 6 |
| 52 | 86 | — | — | NATURAL BORN LOVER — Fats Domino, Imperial 5704 | | 2 |
| 53 | 47 | 42 | 47 | SHIMMY LIKE KATE — Olympics, Arvee 5006 | | 9 |
| 54 | — | — | — | SWAY — Bobby Rydell, Cameo 182 | | 1 |
| 55 | 42 | 33 | 32 | LUCILLE — Everly Brothers, Warner Bros. 5163 | | 10 |
| 56 | 61 | 79 | — | DEAR JOHN — Pat Boone, Dot 16152 | | 3 |
| 57 | 43 | 34 | 15 | WALK, DON'T RUN — Ventures, Dolton 25 | | 17 |
| 58 | 62 | 78 | — | AM I LOSING YOU — Jim Reeves, RCA Victor 7800 | | 3 |
| 59 | 45 | 35 | 29 | TWISTIN' U.S.A. — Danny and the Juniors, Swan 4060 | | 8 |
| 60 | 81 | 84 | 99 | BALLAD OF THE ALAMO — Marty Robbins, Columbia 41809 | A | 4 |
| 61 | 77 | 99 | — | AM I THE MAN — Jackie Wilson, Brunswick 55170 | | 3 |
| 62 | 94 | — | — | YOU'RE SIXTEEN — Johnny Burnette, Liberty 55285 | | 2 |
| 63 | 66 | 69 | 74 | ALABAM — Cowboy Copas, Starday 501 | | 7 |
| 64 | 95 | — | — | RUBY DUBY DU — Tobin Matthews, Chief 7022 | | 2 |
| 65 | 73 | 76 | — | THEME FROM THE DARK AT THE TOP OF THE STAIRS — Lolita, Kapp 349 | | 3 |
| 66 | 97 | — | — | RUBY DUBY DU — Charles Wolcott, M-G-M 12944 | | 2 |
| 67 | 64 | 68 | 80 | ONE OF THE LUCKY ONES — Anita Bryant, Carlton 535 | | 5 |
| 68 | 69 | 89 | — | ALABAM — Pat Boone, Dot 16152 | | 3 |
| 69 | 57 | 53 | 42 | FINGER POPPIN' TIME — Hank Ballard and the Midnighters, King 5341 | | 26 |
| ★70 | 88 | — | — | LIKE STRANGERS — Everly Brothers, Cadence 1388 | | 2 |
| 71 | 49 | 47 | 28 | RUN, SAMPSON, RUN — Neil Sedaka, RCA Victor 7781 | S | 10 |
| 72 | 71 | 70 | 76 | THEME FROM THE SUNDOWNERS — Felix Slatkin, Liberty 55282 | | 6 |
| 73 | 54 | 52 | 60 | I WISH I'D NEVER BEEN BORN — Patti Page, Mercury 71695 | S | 6 |
| 74 | 67 | 75 | 98 | IF SHE SHOULD COME TO YOU (LA MONTANA) — Anthony Newley, London 1929 | | 5 |
| 75 | 76 | 74 | — | THAT'S HOW MUCH — Brian Hyland, Kapp 352 | | 3 |
| 76 | 83 | 84 | 99 | BALLAD OF THE ALAMO — Bud and Travis, Liberty 55284 | | 4 |
| 77 | 65 | 71 | 83 | PATSY — Jack Scott, Top Rank 2075 | | 4 |
| 78 | 82 | 86 | 88 | HAVE MERCY, BABY — Bobbettes, Triple X 106 | | 5 |
| ★79 | — | — | — | MANY TEARS AGO — Connie Francis, M-G-M 12964 | | 1 |
| 80 | 90 | 93 | 97 | NIGHT THEME — Mark II, Wye 1001 | | 4 |
| 81 | 74 | 97 | — | THEME FROM THE DARK AT THE TOP OF THE STAIRS — Ernie Freeman, Imperial 5693 | | 3 |
| 82 | 93 | — | — | A WHOLE LOT OF SHAKIN' GOIN' ON — Conway Twitty, M-G-M 12962 | | 2 |
| 83 | 56 | 46 | 46 | (I DO THE) SHIMMY, SHIMMY — Bobby Freeman, King 5373 | | 13 |
| 84 | 89 | 91 | 94 | SIDE CAR CYCLE — Charlie Ryan, Four Star 1745 | | 4 |
| 85 | 84 | 87 | 95 | MIDNIGHT LACE — Ray Ellis, M-G-M 12942 | | 4 |
| 86 | — | — | — | GONZO — James Booker, Peacock 1697 | | 1 |
| 87 | — | — | — | SENZA MAMA (WITH NO ONE) — Connie Francis, M-G-M 12964 | | 1 |
| 88 | — | — | — | PSYCHO — Bobby Hendricks, Sue 732 | | 1 |
| 89 | 68 | 60 | 65 | EVERGLADES — Kingston Trio, Capitol 4441 | | 5 |
| 90 | 100 | — | — | GREEN LEAVES OF SUMMER — Brothers Four, Columbia 41808 | | 2 |
| 91 | 99 | — | — | A KISSIN' AND A TWISTIN' — Fabian, Chancellor 1061 | | 2 |
| 92 | — | — | — | OL' Mac DONALD — Frank Sinatra, Capitol 4466 | | 1 |
| 93 | — | — | — | THEME FROM THE SUNDOWNERS — Mantovani, London 1946 | | 1 |
| 94 | 98 | — | — | ONCE IN A WHILE — Chimes, Tag 444 | | 2 |
| 95 | 92 | 94 | 100 | MIDNIGHT LACE — Ray Conniff, Columbia 41860 | | 4 |
| 96 | — | — | — | A THOUSAND MILES AWAY — Heartbeats, Rama 216 | | 1 |
| 97 | 80 | 61 | 56 | MY LOVE FOR YOU — Johnny Mathis, Columbia 41764 | A | 11 |
| 98 | 38 | 37 | 35 | THE SAME ONE — Brook Benton, Mercury 71652 | S | 12 |
| 99 | — | — | — | DON'T GO TO STRANGERS — Etta Jones, Prestige 180 | | 1 |
| 100 | — | — | — | CRY, CRY, CRY — Bobby (Blue) Bland, Duke 327 | | 1 |

# The Billboard HOT 100

**FOR WEEK ENDING NOVEMBER 20**

*November 14, 1960*

Columns: THIS WEEK | ONE WEEK AGO | TWO WEEKS AGO | THREE WEEKS AGO | TITLE — Artist, Company, Record No. | STEREO | WEEKS ON CHART

★ STAR PERFORMERS showed the greatest upward progress on Hot 100 this week.
Ⓢ Indicates that 45 r.p.m. stereo single version is available.
△ Indicates that 33⅓ r.p.m. stereo single version is available.

| # | 1wk | 2wk | 3wk | Title — Artist, Company, Record No. | Stereo | Wks |
|---|---|---|---|---|---|---|
| 1 | 4 | 10 | 11 | GEORGIA ON MY MIND — Ray Charles, ABC-Paramount 10135 | Ⓢ | 8 |
| 2 | 3 | 9 | 26 | POETRY IN MOTION — Johnny Tillotson, Cadence 1384 | | 6 |
| 3 | 5 | 6 | 12 | YOU TALK TOO MUCH — Joe Jones, Roulette 4304 | | 9 |
| 4 | 2 | 2 | 1 | I WANT TO BE WANTED — Brenda Lee, Decca 31149 | | 10 |
| 5 | 1 | 1 | 2 | SAVE THE LAST DANCE FOR ME — Drifters, Atlantic 2071 | | 11 |
| 6 | 7 | 19 | 27 | STAY — Maurice Williams and the Zodiacs, Herald 552 | | 7 |
| 7 | 8 | 14 | 25 | LET'S GO, LET'S GO, LET'S GO — Hank Ballard and the Midnighters, King 5400 | | 9 |
| ★8 | 16 | 28 | 55 | LAST DATE — Floyd Cramer, RCA Victor 7775 | Ⓢ | 6 |
| ★9 | 22 | 37 | 67 | A THOUSAND STARS — Kathy Young and the Innocents, Indigo 108 | | 4 |
| 10 | 9 | 15 | 22 | BLUE ANGEL — Roy Orbison, Monument 425 | | 9 |
| 11 | 17 | 30 | 48 | NEW ORLEANS — U.S. Bonds, Legrand 819 | | 5 |
| 12 | 18 | 23 | 31 | NORTH TO ALASKA — Johnny Horton, Columbia 41782 | | 9 |
| 13 | 14 | 18 | 21 | SLEEP — Little Willie John, King 5394 | | 11 |
| 14 | 11 | 12 | 15 | DON'T BE CRUEL — Bill Black's Combo, Hi 2026 | | 10 |
| 15 | 19 | 25 | 36 | ALONE AT LAST — Jackie Wilson, Brunswick 55170 | | 6 |
| 16 | 13 | 8 | 7 | LET'S THINK ABOUT LIVIN' — Bob Luman, Warner Bros. 5172 | | 11 |
| 17 | 10 | 7 | 6 | DEVIL OR ANGEL — Bobby Vee, Liberty 55270 | | 16 |
| ★18 | 29 | 36 | 51 | HUCKLEBUCK — Chubby Checker, Parkway 813 | | 6 |
| 19 | 6 | 3 | 4 | MY HEART HAS A MIND OF ITS OWN — Connie Francis, M-G-M 12923 | | 14 |
| 20 | 12 | 5 | 5 | CHAIN GANG — Sam Cooke, RCA Victor 7783 | Ⓢ | 14 |
| 21 | 23 | 20 | 23 | ARTIFICIAL FLOWERS — Bobby Darin, Atco 6179 | | 8 |
| 22 | 21 | 24 | 32 | TO EACH HIS OWN — Platters, Mercury 71697 | Ⓢ | 6 |
| ★23 | 35 | 63 | — | HE WILL BREAK YOUR HEART — Jerry Butler, Vee Jay 354 | | 3 |
| 24 | 15 | 11 | 20 | SUMMER'S GONE — Paul Anka, ABC-Paramount 10147 | Ⓢ | 8 |
| 25 | 20 | 17 | 10 | THEME FROM THE APARTMENT — Ferrante and Teicher, United Artists 231 | | 17 |
| 26 | 25 | 22 | 13 | KIDDIO — Brook Benton, Mercury 71652 | Ⓢ | 15 |
| 27 | 30 | 32 | 41 | PETER GUNN — Duane Eddy, Jamie 1168 | | 6 |
| ★28 | 39 | 59 | 90 | I'LL SAVE THE LAST DANCE FOR YOU — Damita Jo, Mercury 71690 | | 4 |
| 29 | 24 | 4 | 3 | TWIST — Chubby Checker, Parkway 811 | | 16 |
| 30 | 38 | 55 | 54 | LOVE WALKED IN — Dinah Washington, Mercury 71696 | | 7 |
| 31 | 44 | 78 | — | PERFIDIA — Ventures, Dolton 28 | | 3 |
| 32 | 26 | 13 | 8 | SO SAD — Everly Brothers, Warner Bros. 5163 | | 11 |
| 33 | 27 | 26 | 30 | TOGETHERNESS — Frankie Avalon, Chancellor 1066 | | 9 |
| ★34 | 65 | 73 | 76 | SAILOR (YOUR HOME IS IN THE SEA) — Lolita, Kapp 349 | | 4 |
| ★35 | — | — | — | ARE YOU LONESOME TONIGHT — Elvis Presley, RCA Victor 7810 | | 1 |
| ★36 | 50 | 70 | 72 | LONELY TEENAGER — Dion, Laurie 5070 | | 5 |
| 37 | 41 | 52 | 77 | MY GIRL JOSEPHINE — Fats Domino, Imperial 5704 | | 4 |
| ★38 | 64 | 95 | — | RUBY DUBY DU — Tobin Matthews, Chief 7022 | | 3 |
| 39 | 28 | 16 | 14 | A MILLION TO ONE — Jimmy Charles, Promo 1022 | | 13 |
| 40 | 54 | — | — | SWAY — Bobby Rydell, Cameo 182 | | 2 |
| 41 | 62 | 94 | — | YOU'RE SIXTEEN — Johnny Burnette, Liberty 55285 | | 3 |
| 42 | 61 | 77 | 99 | AM I THE MAN — Jackie Wilson, Brunswick 55170 | | 4 |
| 43 | 43 | 41 | 50 | MY DEAREST DARLING — Etta James, Argo 5368 | | 9 |
| 44 | 48 | 72 | 92 | WAIT FOR ME — Playmates, Roulette 4276 | | 4 |
| 45 | 40 | 48 | 39 | TONIGHT'S THE NIGHT — Shirelles, Scepter 1208 | | 10 |
| 46 | 37 | 33 | 18 | DIAMONDS AND PEARLS — Paradons, Milestone 2003 | | 13 |
| 47 | 32 | 27 | 16 | IT'S NOW OR NEVER — Elvis Presley, RCA Victor 7777 | Ⓢ | 18 |
| 48 | 34 | 21 | 9 | MR. CUSTER — Larry Verne, Era 3024 | | 12 |
| ★49 | 79 | — | — | MANY TEARS AGO — Connie Francis, M-G-M 12964 | | 2 |
| 50 | — | — | — | WONDERLAND BY NIGHT — Bert Kaempfert, Decca 31141 | | 1 |
| 51 | 92 | — | — | OL' MAC DONALD — Frank Sinatra, Capitol 4466 | | 2 |
| 52 | 56 | 61 | 79 | DEAR JOHN — Pat Boone, Dot 16152 | | 4 |
| 53 | 58 | 62 | 78 | AM I LOSING YOU — Jim Reeves, RCA Victor 7800 | | 4 |
| ★54 | — | — | — | FOOLS RUSH IN — Brook Benton, Mercury 71722 | | 1 |
| 55 | 60 | 81 | 84 | BALLAD OF THE ALAMO — Marty Robbins, Columbia 41809 | △ | 5 |
| 56 | 33 | 34 | 40 | A FOOL IN LOVE — Ike and Tina Turner, Sue 730 | | 12 |
| 57 | 52 | 86 | — | NATURAL BORN LOVER — Fats Domino, Imperial 5704 | | 3 |
| 58 | 47 | 35 | 24 | MOVE TWO MOUNTAINS — Marv Johnson, United Artists 241 | | 11 |
| 59 | 51 | 53 | 66 | THEME FROM THE SUNDOWNERS — Billy Vaughn, Dot 16133 | Ⓢ | 7 |
| 60 | 36 | 31 | 17 | THREE NIGHTS A WEEK — Fats Domino, Imperial 5687 | | 11 |
| 61 | 45 | 46 | 45 | SOMEBODY TO LOVE — Bobby Darin, Atco 6179 | | 8 |
| 62 | 67 | 64 | 68 | ONE OF THE LUCKY ONES — Anita Bryant, Carlton 535 | | 6 |
| 63 | 42 | 50 | 65 | WHOLE LOT OF SHAKIN' GOIN' ON — Chubby Checker, Parkway 813 | | 6 |
| 64 | 76 | 83 | 84 | BALLAD OF THE ALAMO — Bud and Travis, Liberty 55284 | | 5 |
| 65 | — | — | — | I GOTTA KNOW — Elvis Presley, RCA Victor 7810 | | 1 |
| 66 | 70 | 88 | — | LIKE STRANGERS — Everly Brothers, Cadence 1388 | | 3 |
| 67 | 46 | 44 | 44 | ANYMORE — Teresa Brewer, Coral 62239 | | 15 |
| 68 | 53 | 47 | 42 | SHIMMY LIKE KATE — Olympics, Arvee 5006 | | 10 |
| 69 | 82 | 93 | — | WHOLE LOT OF SHAKIN' GOIN' ON — Conway Twitty, M-G-M 12962 | | 3 |
| 70 | 81 | 74 | 97 | THEME FROM THE DARK AT THE TOP OF THE STAIRS — Ernie Freeman, Imperial 5693 | | 4 |
| ★71 | — | — | — | EXODUS — Ferrante and Teicher, United Artists 274 | | 1 |
| 72 | 78 | 82 | 86 | HAVE MERCY, BABY — Bobbettes, Triple X 106 | | 6 |
| ★73 | 88 | — | — | PSYCHO — Bobby Hendricks, Sue 732 | | 2 |
| 74 | 59 | 45 | 35 | TWISTIN' U.S.A. — Danny and the Juniors, Swan 4060 | | 9 |
| 75 | 68 | 69 | 89 | ALABAM — Pat Boone, Dot 16152 | | 4 |
| 76 | 63 | 66 | 69 | ALABAM — Lloyd (Cowboy) Copas, Starday 501 | | 8 |
| 77 | 86 | — | — | GONZO — James Booker, Peacock 1697 | | 2 |
| 78 | 80 | 90 | 93 | NIGHT THEME — Mark II, Wye 1001 | | 5 |
| 79 | 31 | 29 | 19 | NEVER ON SUNDAY — Don Costa, United Artists 234 | | 15 |
| 80 | 57 | 43 | 34 | WALK, DON'T RUN — Ventures, Dolton 25 | | 18 |
| 81 | 73 | 54 | 52 | I WISH I'D NEVER BEEN BORN — Patti Page, Mercury 71695 | Ⓢ | 7 |
| 82 | 90 | 100 | — | GREEN LEAVES OF SUMMER — Brothers Four, Columbia 41808 | | 3 |
| 83 | 94 | 98 | — | ONCE IN A WHILE — Chimes, Tag 444 | | 3 |
| 84 | 84 | 89 | 91 | SIDE CAR CYCLE — Charlie Ryan, Four Star 1745 | | 5 |
| 85 | 99 | — | — | DON'T GO TO STRANGERS — Etta Jones, Prestige 180 | | 2 |
| 86 | 71 | 49 | 47 | RUN, SAMPSON, RUN — Neil Sedaka, RCA Victor 7781 | Ⓢ | 11 |
| 87 | 100 | — | — | CRY, CRY, CRY — Bobby (Blue) Bland, Duke 327 | | 2 |
| 88 | — | — | — | WONDERLAND BY NIGHT — Louis Prima, Dot 16151 | | 1 |
| 89 | — | — | — | I MISSED ME — Jim Reeves, RCA Victor 7800 | | 1 |
| 90 | — | — | — | PUSH, PUSH — Austin Taylor, Laurie 3068 | | 1 |
| 91 | — | — | — | THE BELLS — James Brown, King 5423 | | 1 |
| 92 | 66 | 97 | — | RUBY DUBY DU — Charles Wolcott, M-G-M 12944 | | 3 |
| 93 | 72 | 71 | 70 | THEME FROM THE SUNDOWNERS — Felix Slatkin, Liberty 55282 | | 7 |
| 94 | — | — | — | LAST OF THE BIG TIME SPENDERS — Cornbread and the Biscuits, Maske 102 | | 1 |
| 95 | — | — | — | GEE — Jan and Dean, Dore 576 | | 1 |
| 96 | — | — | — | BUMBLE BEE — La Vern Baker, Atlantic 2077 | | 1 |
| 97 | — | — | — | SWEET DREAMS — Don Gibson, RCA Victor 7805 | | 1 |
| 98 | 75 | 76 | 74 | THAT'S HOW MUCH — Brian Hyland, Kapp 352 | | 4 |
| 99 | — | — | — | SEND THE PILLOW (THAT YOU DREAM ON) — Browns, RCA Victor 7804 | | 1 |
| 100 | 49 | 39 | 29 | PINEAPPLE PRINCESS — Annette, Vista 362 | | 14 |

## The Billboard HOT 100

**FOR WEEK ENDING NOVEMBER 27**
**NOVEMBER 21, 1960**

STAR PERFORMERS showed the greatest upward progress on Hot 100 this week.
(S) Indicates that 45 r.p.m. stereo single version is available.
(S) Indicates that 33⅓ r.p.m. stereo single version is available.

Columns: THIS WEEK | ONE WEEK AGO | TWO WEEKS AGO | THREE WEEKS AGO | TITLE — Artist, Company, Record No. | STEREO | WEEKS ON CHART

| # | 1wk | 2wk | 3wk | Title / Artist | Wks |
|---|---|---|---|---|---|
| 1 | 6 | 7 | 19 | STAY — Maurice Williams and the Zodiacs, Herald 552 | 8 |
| 2 | 35 | — | — | ARE YOU LONESOME TONIGHT — Elvis Presley, RCA Victor 7810 | 2 |
| 3 | 2 | 3 | 9 | POETRY IN MOTION — Johnny Tillotson, Cadence 1384 | 7 |
| 4 | 8 | 16 | 28 | LAST DATE — Floyd Cramer, RCA Victor 7775 (S) | 7 |
| 5 | 1 | 4 | 10 | GEORGIA ON MY MIND — Ray Charles, ABC-Paramount 10135 (S) | 7 |
| 6 | 7 | 8 | 14 | LET'S GO, LET'S GO, LET'S GO — Hank Ballard and the Midnighters, King 5400 | 10 |
| 7 | 9 | 22 | 37 | A THOUSAND STARS — Kathy Young and the Innocents, Indigo 108 | 5 |
| 8 | 11 | 17 | 30 | NEW ORLEANS — U. S. Bonds, Legrand 819 | 6 |
| 9 | 3 | 5 | 6 | YOU TALK TOO MUCH — Joe Jones, Roulette 4304 | 10 |
| 10 | 5 | 1 | 1 | SAVE THE LAST DANCE FOR ME — Drifters, Atlantic 2071 | 12 |
| 11 | 4 | 2 | 2 | I WANT TO BE WANTED — Brenda Lee, Decca 31149 | 11 |
| 12 | 12 | 18 | 23 | NORTH TO ALASKA — Johnny Horton, Columbia 41782 | 10 |
| 13 | 15 | 19 | 25 | ALONE AT LAST — Jackie Wilson, Brunswick 55170 | 7 |
| 14 | 18 | 29 | 36 | HUCKLEBUCK — Chubby Checker, Parkway 813 | 7 |
| 15 | 23 | 35 | 63 | HE WILL BREAK YOUR HEART — Jerry Butler, Vee Jay 354 | 4 |
| 16 | 14 | 11 | 12 | DON'T BE CRUEL — Bill Black's Combo, Hi 2026 | 11 |
| 17 | 10 | 9 | 15 | BLUE ANGEL — Roy Orbison, Monument 425 | 10 |
| 18 | 13 | 14 | 18 | SLEEP — Little Willie John, King 5394 | 12 |
| 19 | 49 | 79 | — | MANY TEARS AGO — Connie Francis, M-G-M 12964 | 3 |
| 20 | 40 | 54 | — | SWAY — Bobby Rydell, Cameo 182 | 3 |
| 21 | 31 | 44 | 78 | PERFIDIA — Ventures, Dolton 28 | 4 |
| 22 | 22 | 21 | 24 | TO EACH HIS OWN — Platters, Mercury 71697 (S) | 7 |
| 23 | 17 | 10 | 7 | DEVIL OR ANGEL — Bobby Vee, Liberty 55270 | 17 |
| 24 | 34 | 65 | 73 | SAILOR (YOUR HOME IS IN THE SEA) — Lolita, Kapp 349 | 5 |
| 25 | 20 | 12 | 5 | CHAIN GANG — Sam Cooke, RCA Victor 7783 (S) | 15 |
| 26 | 50 | — | — | WONDERLAND BY NIGHT — Bert Kaempfert, Decca 31141 | 2 |
| 27 | 37 | 41 | 52 | MY GIRL JOSEPHINE — Fats Domino, Imperial 5704 | 5 |
| 28 | 19 | 6 | 3 | MY HEART HAS A MIND OF ITS OWN — Connie Francis, M-G-M 12923 | 15 |
| 29 | 16 | 13 | 8 | LET'S THINK ABOUT LIVIN' — Bob Luman, Warner Bros. 5172 | 12 |
| 30 | 28 | 39 | 59 | I'LL SAVE THE LAST DANCE FOR YOU — Damita Jo, Mercury 71690 | 5 |
| 31 | 21 | 23 | 20 | ARTIFICIAL FLOWERS — Bobby Darin, Atco 6179 | 9 |
| 32 | 41 | 62 | 94 | YOU'RE SIXTEEN — Johnny Burnette, Liberty 55285 | 4 |
| 33 | 38 | 64 | 95 | RUBY DUBY DU — Tobin Matthews, Chief 7022 | 4 |
| 34 | 36 | 50 | 70 | LONELY TEENAGER — Dion, Laurie 3070 | 6 |
| 35 | 27 | 30 | 32 | PETER GUNN — Duane Eddy, Jamie 1168 | 7 |
| 36 | 33 | 27 | 26 | TOGETHERNESS — Frankie Avalon, Chancellor 1056 (S) | 10 |
| 37 | 44 | 48 | 72 | WAIT FOR ME — Playmates, Roulette 4276 | 5 |
| 38 | 43 | 43 | 41 | MY DEAREST DARLING — Etta James, Argo 5368 | 10 |
| 39 | 24 | 15 | 11 | SUMMER'S GONE — Paul Anka, ABC-Paramount 10147 (S) | 9 |
| 40 | 54 | — | — | FOOLS RUSH IN — Brook Benton, Mercury 71722 | 2 |
| 41 | 53 | 58 | 62 | AM I LOSING YOU — Jim Reeves, RCA Victor 7800 | 5 |
| 42 | 32 | 26 | 13 | SO SAD — Everly Brothers, Warner Bros. 5163 | 12 |
| 43 | 51 | 92 | — | OL' Mac DONALD — Frank Sinatra, Capitol 4466 | 3 |
| 44 | 30 | 38 | 55 | LOVE WALKED IN — Dinah Washington, Mercury 71696 | 8 |
| 45 | 25 | 20 | 17 | THEME FROM THE APARTMENT — Ferrante and Teicher, United Artists 231 | 18 |
| 46 | 52 | 56 | 61 | DEAR JOHN — Pat Boone, Dot 16152 | 5 |
| 47 | 26 | 25 | 22 | KIDDIO — Brook Benton, Mercury 71652 (S) | 16 |
| 48 | 39 | 28 | 16 | A MILLION TO ONE — Jimmy Charles, Promo 1022 | 14 |
| 49 | 42 | 61 | 77 | AM I THE MAN — Jackie Wilson, Brunswick 55170 | 5 |
| 50 | 66 | 70 | 88 | LIKE STRANGERS — Everly Brothers, Cadence 1388 | 4 |
| 51 | 71 | — | — | EXODUS — Ferrante and Teicher, United Artists 274 | 2 |
| 52 | 29 | 24 | 4 | TWIST — Chubby Checker, Parkway 811 | 17 |
| 53 | 55 | 60 | 81 | BALLAD OF THE ALAMO — Marty Robbins, Columbia 41809 | 6 |
| 54 | 45 | 40 | 48 | TONIGHT'S THE NIGHT — Shirelles, Scepter 1208 | 11 |
| 55 | 46 | 37 | 33 | DIAMONDS AND PEARLS — Paradons, Milestone 2003 | 14 |
| 56 | 65 | — | — | I GOTTA KNOW — Elvis Presley, RCA Victor 7810 | 2 |
| 57 | 48 | 34 | 21 | MR. CUSTER — Larry Verne, Era 3024 | 13 |
| 58 | 57 | 52 | 86 | NATURAL BORN LOVER — Fats Domino, Imperial 5704 | 4 |
| 59 | 75 | 68 | 69 | ALABAM — Pat Boone, Dot 16152 | 5 |
| 60 | 77 | 86 | — | GONZO — James Booker, Peacock 1697 | 3 |
| 61 | 69 | 82 | 93 | WHOLE LOT OF SHAKIN' GOIN' ON — Conway Twitty, M-G-M 12962 | 4 |
| 62 | 56 | 33 | 34 | A FOOL IN LOVE — Ike and Tina Turner, Sue 730 | 13 |
| 63 | 61 | 45 | 46 | SOMEBODY TO LOVE — Bobby Darin, Atco 6179 | 9 |
| 64 | — | — | — | RUBY — Ray Charles, ABC-Paramount 10164 | 1 |
| 65 | 92 | 66 | 97 | RUBY DUBY DU — Charles Wolcott, M-G-M 12944 | 4 |
| 66 | 72 | 78 | 82 | HAVE MERCY, BABY — Bobbettes, Triple X 106 | 7 |
| 67 | — | — | — | GEE WHIZ — Innocents, Indigo 111 | 1 |
| 68 | 89 | — | — | I MISSED ME — Jim Reeves, RCA Victor 7800 | 2 |
| 69 | 63 | 42 | 50 | WHOLE LOT OF SHAKIN' GOIN' ON — Chubby Checker, Parkway 813 | 7 |
| 70 | 47 | 32 | 27 | IT'S NOW OR NEVER — Elvis Presley, RCA Victor 7777 (S) | 19 |
| 71 | — | — | — | EXODUS — Mantovani, London 1953 | 1 |
| 72 | 83 | 94 | 98 | ONCE IN A WHILE — Chimes, Tag 444 | 4 |
| 73 | — | — | — | HARD HEARTED HANNAH — Ray Charles, ABC-Paramount 10164 | 1 |
| 74 | 68 | 53 | 47 | SHIMMY LIKE KATE — Olympics, Arvee 5006 | 11 |
| 75 | 78 | 80 | 90 | NIGHT THEME — Mark II, Wye 1001 | 6 |
| 76 | 85 | 99 | — | DON'T GO TO STRANGERS — Etta Jones, Prestige 180 | 3 |
| 77 | 64 | 76 | 83 | BALLAD OF THE ALAMO — Bud and Travis, Liberty 55284 | 6 |
| 78 | 82 | 90 | 100 | GREEN LEAVES OF SUMMER — Brothers Four, Columbia 41808 | 4 |
| 79 | 87 | 100 | — | CRY, CRY, CRY — Bobby (Blue) Bland, Duke 327 | 3 |
| 80 | 70 | 81 | 74 | THEME FROM THE DARK AT THE TOP OF THE STAIRS — Ernie Freeman, Imperial 5693 | 5 |
| 81 | 59 | 51 | 53 | THEME FROM THE SUNDOWNERS — Billy Vaughn, Dot 16133 (S) | 8 |
| 82 | 76 | 63 | 66 | ALABAM — Lloyd (Cowboy) Copas, Starday 501 | 9 |
| 83 | 99 | — | — | SEND ME THE PILLOW (THAT YOU DREAM ON) — Browns, RCA Victor 7804 | 2 |
| 84 | 91 | — | — | THE BELLS — James Brown, King 5423 | 2 |
| 85 | 84 | 84 | 89 | SIDE CAR CYCLE — Charlie Ryan, Four Star 1745 | 6 |
| 86 | 94 | — | — | LAST OF THE BIG TIME SPENDERS — Cornbread and the Biscuits, Maske 102 | 2 |
| 87 | — | — | — | (WILL YOU LOVE ME) TOMORROW — Shirelles, Scepter 1211 | 1 |
| 88 | 88 | — | — | WONDERLAND BY NIGHT — Louis Prima, Dot 16151 | 2 |
| 89 | 67 | 46 | 44 | ANYMORE — Teresa Brewer, Coral 62219 | 16 |
| 90 | 90 | — | — | PUSH, PUSH — Austin Taylor, Laurie 3068 | 2 |
| 91 | — | — | — | STRANGER FROM DURANGO — Richie Allen, Imperial 5683 | 1 |
| 92 | — | — | — | SERENATA — Sarah Vaughan, Roulette 4285 | 4 |
| 93 | 95 | — | — | GEE — Jan and Dean, Dore 576 | 2 |
| 94 | — | — | — | LAST DATE — Lawrence Welk, Dot 16145 | 1 |
| 95 | 96 | — | — | BUMBLE BEE — La Vern Baker, Atlantic 2077 | 2 |
| 96 | — | — | — | CORINNA, CORINNA — Ray Peterson, Dunes 2002 | 1 |
| 97 | 97 | — | — | SWEET DREAMS — Don Gibson, RCA Victor 7805 | 2 |
| 98 | 62 | 67 | 64 | ONE OF THE LUCKY ONES — Anita Bryant, Carlton 535 | 1 |
| 99 | — | — | — | FALLEN ANGEL — Webb Pierce, Decca 31165 | 1 |
| 100 | — | — | — | GLORIA'S THEME — Adam Wade, Coed 541 | 1 |

# The Billboard HOT 100

**For Week Ending December 4** — November 28, 1960

STAR PERFORMERS showed the greatest upward progress on Hot 100 this week.
[S] Indicates that 45 r.p.m. stereo single version is available.
[A] Indicates that 33⅓ r.p.m. stereo single version is available.

Columns: THIS WEEK | ONE WEEK AGO | TWO WEEKS AGO | THREE WEEKS AGO | TITLE — Artist, Company, Record No. | STEREO | WEEKS ON CHART

| TW | 1WA | 2WA | 3WA | Title — Artist, Company, Record No. | Stereo | Wks |
|---|---|---|---|---|---|---|
| 1 | 2 | 35 | — | ARE YOU LONESOME TONIGHT — Elvis Presley, RCA Victor 7810 | S | 3 |
| 2 | 4 | 8 | 16 | LAST DATE — Floyd Cramer, RCA Victor 7775 | S | 8 |
| 3 | 1 | 6 | 7 | STAY — Maurice Williams and the Zodiacs, Herald 552 | | 9 |
| 4 | 3 | 2 | 3 | POETRY IN MOTION — Johnny Tillotson, Cadence 1384 | | 8 |
| 5 | 7 | 9 | 22 | A THOUSAND STARS — Kathy Young and the Innocents, Indigo 108 | | 6 |
| 6 | 8 | 11 | 17 | NEW ORLEANS — U. S. Bonds, Legrand 819 | | 7 |
| ★7 | 12 | 12 | 18 | NORTH TO ALASKA — Johnny Horton, Columbia 41782 | | 11 |
| 8 | 13 | 15 | 19 | ALONE AT LAST — Jackie Wilson, Brunswick 55170 | | 8 |
| 9 | 6 | 7 | 8 | LET'S GO, LET'S GO, LET'S GO — Hank Ballard and the Midnighters, King 5400 | | 11 |
| 10 | 5 | 1 | 4 | GEORGIA ON MY MIND — Ray Charles, ABC-Paramount 10135 | S | 8 |
| 11 | 15 | 23 | 35 | HE WILL BREAK YOUR HEART — Jerry Butler, Vee Jay 354 | | 5 |
| ★12 | 24 | 34 | 65 | SAILOR (YOUR HOME IS IN THE SEA) — Lolita, Kapp 349 | | 6 |
| 13 | 10 | 5 | 1 | SAVE THE LAST DANCE FOR ME — Drifters, Atlantic 2071 | | 13 |
| ★14 | 19 | 49 | 79 | MANY TEARS AGO — Connie Francis, M-G-M 12964 | | 4 |
| 15 | 14 | 18 | 29 | HUCKLEBUCK — Chubby Checker, Parkway 813 | | 8 |
| 16 | 20 | 40 | 54 | SWAY — Bobby Rydell, Cameo 182 | | 4 |
| 17 | 11 | 4 | 2 | I WANT TO BE WANTED — Brenda Lee, Decca 31149 | | 12 |
| 18 | 21 | 31 | 44 | PERFIDIA — Ventures, Dolton 28 | | 5 |
| 19 | 9 | 3 | 5 | YOU TALK TOO MUCH — Joe Jones, Roulette 4304 | | 11 |
| ★20 | 26 | 50 | — | WONDERLAND BY NIGHT — Bert Kaempfert, Decca 31141 | S | 3 |
| ★21 | 32 | 41 | 62 | YOU'RE SIXTEEN — Johnny Burnette, Liberty 55285 | | 5 |
| ★22 | 50 | 66 | 70 | LIKE STRANGERS — Everly Brothers, Cadence 1388 | | 5 |
| 23 | 18 | 13 | 14 | SLEEP — Little Willie John, King 5394 | | 13 |
| 24 | 27 | 37 | 41 | MY GIRL JOSEPHINE — Fats Domino, Imperial 5704 | | 6 |
| ★25 | 43 | 51 | 92 | OL' MAC DONALD — Frank Sinatra, Capitol 4466 | | 4 |
| 26 | 23 | 17 | 10 | DEVIL OR ANGEL — Bobby Vee, Liberty 55270 | | 18 |
| 27 | 17 | 10 | 9 | BLUE ANGEL — Roy Orbison, Monument 425 | | 11 |
| 28 | 22 | 22 | 21 | TO EACH HIS OWN — Platters, Mercury 71697 | S | 8 |
| 29 | 30 | 28 | 39 | I'LL SAVE THE LAST DANCE FOR YOU — Damita Jo, Mercury 71690 | | 6 |
| 30 | 33 | 38 | 64 | RUBY DUBY DU — Tobin Matthews, Chief 7022 | | 5 |
| 31 | 40 | 54 | — | FOOLS RUSH IN — Brook Benton, Mercury 71722 | | 3 |
| 32 | 34 | 36 | 50 | LONELY TEENAGER — Dion, Laurie 3070 | | 7 |
| 33 | 41 | 53 | 58 | AM I LOSING YOU — Jim Reeves, RCA Victor 7800 | | 6 |
| 34 | 56 | 65 | — | I GOTTA KNOW — Elvis Presley, RCA Victor 7810 | S | 3 |
| 35 | 16 | 14 | 11 | DON'T BE CRUEL — Bill Black's Combo, Hi 2026 | | 12 |
| 36 | 36 | 33 | 27 | TOGETHERNESS — Frankie Avalon, Chancellor 1056 | S | 11 |
| ★37 | 49 | 42 | 61 | AM I THE MAN — Jackie Wilson, Brunswick 55170 | | 6 |
| 38 | 31 | 21 | 23 | ARTIFICIAL FLOWERS — Bobby Darin, Atco 6179 | | 10 |
| 39 | 37 | 44 | 48 | WAIT FOR ME — Playmates, Roulette 4276 | | 6 |
| ★40 | 51 | 71 | — | EXODUS — Ferrante and Teicher, United Artists 274 | S | 3 |
| 41 | 65 | 92 | 66 | RUBY DUBY DU — Charles Wolcott, M-G-M 12944 | S | 5 |
| 42 | 38 | 43 | 43 | MY DEAREST DARLING — Etta James, Argo 5368 | | 11 |
| 43 | 29 | 16 | 13 | LET'S THINK ABOUT LIVIN' — Bob Luman, Warner Bros. 5172 | | 13 |
| 44 | 46 | 52 | 56 | DEAR JOHN — Pat Boone, Dot 16152 | S | 6 |
| 45 | 28 | 19 | 6 | MY HEART HAS A MIND OF ITS OWN — Connie Francis, M-G-M 12923 | | 16 |
| 46 | 25 | 20 | 12 | CHAIN GANG — Sam Cooke, RCA Victor 7783 | S | 16 |
| 47 | 44 | 30 | 38 | LOVE WALKED IN — Dinah Washington, Mercury 71696 | | 9 |
| 48 | 53 | 55 | 60 | BALLAD OF THE ALAMO — Marty Robbins, Columbia 41809 | A | 7 |
| ★49 | 60 | 77 | 86 | GONZO — James Booker, Peacock 1697 | | 4 |
| 50 | 58 | 57 | 52 | NATURAL BORN LOVER — Fats Domino, Imperial 5704 | | 5 |
| 51 | 39 | 24 | 15 | SUMMER'S GONE — Paul Anka, ABC-Paramount 10147 | S | 10 |
| 52 | 35 | 27 | 30 | PETER GUNN — Duane Eddy, Jamie 1168 | | 8 |
| 53 | 68 | 89 | — | I MISSED ME — Jim Reeves, RCA Victor 7800 | | 3 |
| 54 | 59 | 75 | 68 | ALABAM — Pat Boone, Dot 16152 | | 6 |
| 55 | 61 | 69 | 82 | WHOLE LOT OF SHAKIN' GOIN' ON — Conway Twitty, M-G-M 12962 | S | 5 |
| 56 | 52 | 29 | 24 | TWIST — Chubby Checker, Parkway 811 | | 18 |
| 57 | 55 | 46 | 37 | DIAMONDS AND PEARLS — Paradons, Milestone 2003 | | 15 |
| 58 | 45 | 25 | 20 | THEME FROM THE APARTMENT — Ferrante and Teicher, United Artists 231 | | 19 |
| 59 | 67 | — | — | GEE WHIZ — Innocents, Indigo 111 | | 2 |
| 60 | 47 | 26 | 25 | KIDDIO — Brook Benton, Mercury 71652 | S | 17 |
| 61 | 64 | — | — | RUBY — Ray Charles, ABC-Paramount 10164 | | 2 |
| 62 | 71 | — | — | EXODUS — Mantovani, London 1953 | S | 2 |
| 63 | 54 | 45 | 40 | TONIGHT'S THE NIGHT — Shirelles, Scepter 1208 | | 12 |
| 64 | 72 | 83 | 94 | ONCE IN A WHILE — Chimes, Tag 444 | | 5 |
| 65 | 78 | 82 | 90 | GREEN LEAVES OF SUMMER — Brothers Four, Columbia 41808 | A | 5 |
| 66 | 73 | — | — | HARD HEARTED HANNAH — Ray Charles, ABC-Paramount 10164 | | 2 |
| 67 | — | — | — | RUBBER BALL — Bobby Vee, Liberty 55287 | | 1 |
| 68 | 81 | 59 | 51 | THEME FROM THE SUNDOWNERS — Billy Vaughn, Dot 16133 | S | 9 |
| 69 | 82 | 76 | 63 | ALABAM — Lloyd (Cowboy) Copas, Starday 501 | | 10 |
| ★70 | 94 | — | — | LAST DATE — Lawrence Welk, Dot 16145 | S | 2 |
| 71 | 79 | 87 | 100 | CRY, CRY, CRY — Bobby (Blue) Bland, Duke 327 | | 4 |
| 72 | 76 | 85 | 99 | DON'T GO TO STRANGERS — Etta Jones, Prestige 180 | | 4 |
| 73 | 87 | — | — | (WILL YOU LOVE ME) TOMORROW — Shirelles, Sceptor 1211 | | 2 |
| 74 | 84 | 91 | — | THE BELLS — James Brown, King 5423 | | 3 |
| 75 | — | — | — | BLUE TANGO — Bill Black, Hi 2027 | | 1 |
| 76 | 83 | 99 | — | SEND ME THE PILLOW (THAT YOU DREAM ON) — Browns, RCA Victor 7804 | S | 3 |
| 77 | 86 | 94 | — | LAST OF THE BIG TIME SPENDERS — Cornbread and Biscuits, Maske 102 | | 3 |
| 78 | 88 | 88 | — | WONDERLAND BY NIGHT — Louis Prima, Dot 16151 | S | 3 |
| 79 | — | — | — | WINGS OF A DOVE — Ferlin Husky, Capitol 4406 | | 1 |
| 80 | 48 | 39 | 28 | A MILLION TO ONE — Jimmy Charles, Promo 1022 | | 15 |
| 81 | — | — | — | WALK SLOW — Little Willie John, King 5428 | | 1 |
| 82 | 75 | 78 | 80 | NIGHT THEME — Mark II, Wye 1001 | | 7 |
| 83 | 66 | 72 | 78 | HAVE MERCY, BABY — Bobbettes, Triple X 106 | | 8 |
| 84 | 96 | — | — | CORINNA, CORINNA — Ray Peterson, Dunes 2002 | | 2 |
| 85 | 77 | 64 | 76 | BALLAD OF THE ALAMO — Bud and Travis, Liberty 55284 | | 7 |
| 86 | — | — | — | DOLL HOUSE — Donnie Brooks, Era 3028 | | 1 |
| 87 | — | — | — | RAMONA — Blue Diamonds, London 1954 | | 1 |
| 88 | 69 | 63 | 42 | WHOLE LOT OF SHAKIN' GOIN' ON — Chubby Checker, Parkway 813 | | 8 |
| 89 | 93 | 95 | — | GEE — Jan and Dean, Dore 576 | | 3 |
| 90 | 91 | — | — | STRANGER FROM DURANGO — Richie Allen, Imperial 5683 | | 2 |
| 91 | 92 | — | — | SERENATA — Sarah Vaughan, Roulette 4285 | | 5 |
| 92 | — | 93 | 72 | THEME FROM THE SUNDOWNERS — Felix Slatkin, Liberty 55282 | | 8 |
| 93 | 95 | 96 | — | BUMBLE BEE — La Vern Baker, Atlantic 2077 | | 3 |
| 94 | 100 | — | — | GLORIA'S THEME — Adam Wade, Coed 541 | | 2 |
| 95 | — | — | — | COME RAIN OR COME SHINE — Ray Charles, Atlantic 2084 | | 1 |
| 96 | 97 | 97 | — | SWEET DREAMS — Don Gibson, RCA Victor 7805 | S | 3 |
| 97 | — | 73 | 88 | PSYCHO — Bobby Hendricks, Sue 732 | | 3 |
| 98 | 80 | 70 | 81 | THEME FROM THE DARK AT THE TOP OF THE STAIRS — Ernie Freeman, Imperial 5693 | | 6 |
| 99 | 70 | 47 | 32 | IT'S NOW OR NEVER — Elvis Presley, RCA Victor 7777 | S | 20 |
| 100 | — | — | — | HAVE YOU EVER BEEN LONELY — Teresa Brewer, Coral 62236 | | 1 |

# The Billboard HOT 100

FOR WEEK ENDING DECEMBER 11

DECEMBER 5, 1960

| This Week | One Week Ago | Two Weeks Ago | Three Weeks Ago | Title / Artist, Company, Record No. | Stereo | Weeks on Chart |
|---|---|---|---|---|---|---|
| 1 | 1 | 2 | 35 | ARE YOU LONESOME TONIGHT — Elvis Presley, RCA Victor 7810 | S | 4 |
| 2 | 2 | 4 | 8 | LAST DATE — Floyd Cramer, RCA Victor 7775 | S | 9 |
| 3 | 4 | 3 | 2 | POETRY IN MOTION — Johnny Tillotson, Cadence 1384 | | 9 |
| 4 | 3 | 1 | 6 | STAY — Maurice Williams and the Zodiacs, Herald 552 | | 10 |
| 5 | 5 | 7 | 9 | A THOUSAND STARS — Kathy Young and the Innocents, Indigo 108 | | 7 |
| 6 | 7 | 12 | 12 | NORTH TO ALASKA — Johnny Horton, Columbia 41782 | | 12 |
| 7 | 11 | 15 | 23 | HE WILL BREAK YOUR HEART — Jerry Butler, Vee Jay 354 | | 6 |
| 8 | 6 | 8 | 11 | NEW ORLEANS — U. S. Bonds, Legrand 819 | | 8 |
| 9 | 12 | 24 | 34 | SAILOR (YOUR HOME IS IN THE SEA) — Lolita, Kapp 349 | | 7 |
| 10 | 9 | 6 | 7 | LET'S GO, LET'S GO, LET'S GO — Hank Ballard and the Midnighters, King 5400 | | 12 |
| 11 | 14 | 19 | 49 | MANY TEARS AGO — Connie Francis, M-G-M 12964 | | 5 |
| 12 | 8 | 13 | 15 | ALONE AT LAST — Jackie Wilson, Brunswick 55170 | | 9 |
| 13 | 20 | 26 | 50 | WONDERLAND BY NIGHT — Bert Kaempfert, Decca 31141 | S | 4 |
| 14 | 24 | 27 | 37 | MY GIRL JOSEPHINE — Fats Domino, Imperial 5704 | | 7 |
| 15 | 10 | 5 | 1 | GEORGIA ON MY MIND — Ray Charles, ABC-Paramount 10135 | S | 9 |
| 16 | 16 | 20 | 40 | SWAY — Bobby Rydell, Cameo 182 | | 5 |
| 17 | 21 | 32 | 41 | YOU'RE SIXTEEN — Johnny Burnette, Liberty 55285 | | 6 |
| 18 | 13 | 10 | 5 | SAVE THE LAST DANCE FOR ME — Drifters, Atlantic 2071 | | 14 |
| 19 | 18 | 21 | 31 | PERFIDIA — Ventures, Dolton 28 | | 6 |
| 20 | 15 | 14 | 18 | HUCKLEBUCK — Chubby Checker, Parkway 813 | | 9 |
| 21 | 32 | 34 | 36 | LONELY TEENAGER — Dion, Laurie 3070 | | 8 |
| 22 | 29 | 30 | 28 | I'LL SAVE THE LAST DANCE FOR YOU — Damita Jo, Mercury 71690 | | 7 |
| 23 | 22 | 50 | 66 | LIKE STRANGERS — Everly Brothers, Cadence 1388 | | 6 |
| 24 | 31 | 40 | 54 | FOOLS RUSH IN — Brook Benton, Mercury 71722 | | 4 |
| 25 | 17 | 11 | 4 | I WANT TO BE WANTED — Brenda Lee, Decca 31149 | | 13 |
| 26 | 28 | 22 | 22 | TO EACH HIS OWN — Platters, Mercury 71697 | S | 9 |
| 27 | 34 | 56 | 65 | I GOTTA KNOW — Elvis Presley, RCA Victor 7810 | S | 4 |
| 28 | 19 | 9 | 3 | YOU TALK TOO MUCH — Joe Jones, Roulette 4304 | | 12 |
| 29 | 23 | 18 | 13 | SLEEP — Little Willie John, King 5394 | | 14 |
| 30 | 40 | 51 | 71 | EXODUS — Ferrante and Teicher, United Artists 274 | S | 4 |
| 31 | 25 | 43 | 51 | OL' MAC DONALD — Frank Sinatra, Capitol 4466 | | 5 |
| 32 | 37 | 49 | 42 | AM I THE MAN — Jackie Wilson, Brunswick 55170 | | 7 |
| 33 | 38 | 31 | 21 | ARTIFICIAL FLOWERS — Bobby Darin, Atco 6179 | | 11 |
| 34 | 42 | 38 | 43 | MY DEAREST DARLING — Etta James, Argo 5368 | | 12 |
| 35 | 30 | 33 | 38 | RUBY DUBY DU — Tobin Matthews, Chief 7022 | | 6 |
| 36 | 27 | 17 | 10 | BLUE ANGEL — Roy Orbison, Monument 425 | | 12 |
| 37 | 33 | 41 | 53 | AM I LOSING YOU — Jim Reeves, RCA Victor 7800 | | 7 |
| 38 | 50 | 58 | 57 | NATURAL BORN LOVER — Fats Domino, Imperial 5704 | | 6 |
| 39 | 70 | 94 | — | LAST DATE — Lawrence Welk, Dot 16145 | S | 3 |
| 40 | 48 | 53 | 55 | BALLAD OF THE ALAMO — Marty Robbins, Columbia 41809 | A | 8 |
| 41 | 75 | — | — | BLUE TANGO — Bill Black's Combo, Hi 2027 | | 2 |
| 42 | 36 | 36 | 33 | TOGETHERNESS — Frankie Avalon, Chancellor 1056 | S | 12 |
| 43 | 49 | 60 | 77 | GONZO — James Booker, Peacock 1697 | | 5 |
| 44 | 39 | 37 | 44 | WAIT FOR ME — Playmates, Roulette 4276 | | 7 |
| 45 | 61 | 64 | — | RUBY — Ray Charles, ABC-Paramount 10164 | | 3 |
| 46 | 44 | 46 | 52 | DEAR JOHN — Pat Boone, Dot 16152 | S | 7 |
| 47 | 54 | 59 | 75 | ALABAM — Pat Boone, Dot 16152 | | 7 |
| 48 | 26 | 23 | 17 | DEVIL OR ANGEL — Bobby Vee, Liberty 55270 | | 19 |
| 49 | 53 | 68 | 89 | I MISSED ME — Jim Reeves, RCA Victor 7800 | | 4 |
| 50 | 41 | 65 | 92 | RUBY DUBY DU — Charles Wolcott, M-G-M 12944 | S | 6 |
| 51 | 78 | 88 | 88 | WONDERLAND BY NIGHT — Louis Prima, Dot 16151 | S | 4 |
| 52 | 35 | 16 | 14 | DON'T BE CRUEL — Bill Black's Combo, Hi 2026 | | 13 |
| 53 | 67 | — | — | RUBBER BALL — Bobby Vee, Liberty 55287 | | 2 |
| 54 | 62 | 71 | — | EXODUS — Mantovani, London 1953 | S | 3 |
| 55 | 66 | 73 | — | HARD HEARTED HANNAH — Ray Charles, ABC-Paramount 10164 | | 3 |
| 56 | 59 | 67 | — | GEE WHIZ — Innocents, Indigo 111 | | 3 |
| 57 | 52 | 35 | 27 | PETER GUNN — Duane Eddy, Jamie 1168 | | 9 |
| 58 | 73 | 87 | — | (WILL YOU LOVE ME) TOMORROW — Shirelles, Scepter 1211 | | 3 |
| 59 | 64 | 72 | 83 | ONCE IN A WHILE — Chimes, Tag 444 | | 6 |
| 60 | 45 | 28 | 19 | MY HEART HAS A MIND OF ITS OWN — Connie Francis, M-G-M 12923 | | 17 |
| 61 | 51 | 39 | 24 | SUMMER'S GONE — Paul Anka, ABC-Paramount 10147 | S | 11 |
| 62 | 79 | — | — | WINGS OF A DOVE — Ferlin Husky, Capitol 4406 | | 2 |
| 63 | 43 | 29 | 16 | LET'S THINK ABOUT LIVIN' — Bob Luman, Warner Bros. 5172 | | 14 |
| 64 | 47 | 44 | 30 | LOVE WALKED IN — Dinah Washington, Mercury 71696 | | 10 |
| 65 | 65 | 78 | 82 | GREEN LEAVES OF SUMMER — Brothers Four, Columbia 41808 | A | 6 |
| 66 | 68 | 81 | 59 | THEME FROM THE SUNDOWNERS — Billy Vaughn, Dot 16133 | S | 10 |
| 67 | 81 | — | — | WALK SLOW — Little Willie John, King 5428 | | 2 |
| 68 | 76 | 83 | 99 | SEND ME THE PILLOW (THAT YOU DREAM ON) — Browns, RCA Victor 7804 | S | 4 |
| 69 | — | — | — | SAD MOOD — Sam Cooke, RCA Victor 7816 | | 1 |
| 70 | 74 | 84 | 91 | THE BELLS — James Brown, King 5423 | | 4 |
| 71 | 84 | 96 | — | CORINNA, CORINNA — Ray Peterson, Dunes 2002 | | 3 |
| 72 | 86 | — | — | DOLL HOUSE — Donnie Brooks, Era 3028 | | 2 |
| 73 | 69 | 82 | 76 | ALABAM — Cowboy Copas, Starday 501 | | 11 |
| 74 | 72 | 76 | 85 | DON'T GO TO STRANGERS — Etta Jones, Prestige 180 | | 5 |
| 75 | 77 | 86 | 94 | LAST OF THE BIG TIME SPENDERS — Cornbread and Biscuits, Maske 1102 | | 4 |
| 76 | 71 | 79 | 87 | CRY, CRY, CRY — Bobby (Blue) Bland, Duke 327 | | 5 |
| 77 | 85 | 77 | 64 | BALLAD OF THE ALAMO — Bud and Travis, Liberty 55284 | | 8 |
| 78 | 58 | 45 | 25 | THEME FROM THE APARTMENT — Ferrante and Teicher, United Artists 231 | | 20 |
| 79 | — | — | — | GROOVY TONIGHT — Bobby Rydell, Cameo 182 | | 1 |
| 80 | 87 | — | — | RAMONA — Blue Diamonds, London 1954 | | 2 |
| 81 | 89 | 93 | 95 | GEE — Jan and Dean, Dore 576 | | 4 |
| 82 | 93 | 95 | 96 | BUMBLE BEE — La Vern Baker, Atlantic 2077 | | 4 |
| 83 | 95 | — | — | COME RAIN OR COME SHINE — Ray Charles, Atlantic 2084 | | 2 |
| 84 | — | — | — | HOOCHI COOCHI COO — Hank Ballard and the Midnighters, King 5430 | | 1 |
| 85 | 91 | 92 | — | SERENATA — Sarah Vaughan, Roulette 4285 | | 6 |
| 86 | 94 | 100 | — | GLORIA'S THEME — Adam Wade, Coed 541 | | 3 |
| 87 | — | — | — | MAGNIFICENT SEVEN — Al Cariola, United Artists 261 | | 1 |
| 88 | — | — | — | RAMBLIN' — Ramblers, Addit 1257 | | 1 |
| 89 | — | — | — | WONDERLAND BY NIGHT — Anita Bryant, Carlton 537 | | 1 |
| 90 | — | — | — | DANCE BY THE LIGHT OF THE MOON — Olympics, Arvee 5020 | | 1 |
| 91 | — | — | — | YOU ARE MY SUNSHINE — Johnny and the Hurricanes, Big Top 3056 | | 1 |
| 92 | 100 | — | — | HAVE YOU EVER BEEN LONELY — Teresa Brewer, Coral 62236 | | 2 |
| 93 | 96 | 97 | 97 | SWEET DREAMS — Don Gibson, RCA Victor 7805 | S | 4 |
| 94 | 97 | — | 73 | PSYCHO — Bobby Hendricks, Sue 732 | | 4 |
| 95 | 57 | 55 | 46 | DIAMONDS AND PEARLS — Paradons, Milestone 2003 | | 16 |
| 96 | — | — | — | LITTLE MISS BLUE — Dion, Laurie 3070 | | 1 |
| 97 | — | — | — | AGE FOR LOVE — Jimmy Charles, Promo 1003 | | 1 |
| 98 | — | — | — | YOU BETTER KNOW WHAT YOU'RE DOING — Lloyd Price, ABC-Paramount 10162 | | 1 |
| 99 | — | — | — | WABASH BLUES — Viscounts, Madison 140 | | 1 |
| 100 | — | — | — | ROCKIN' ROLLIN' OCEAN — Hank Snow, RCA Victor 7702 | | 1 |

# The Billboard HOT 100

**FOR WEEK ENDING DECEMBER 18**

*The Billboard's Music Popularity Charts ... POP RECORDS — DECEMBER 12, 1960*

STAR PERFORMERS showed the greatest upward progress on Hot 100 this week.
[S] Indicates that 45 r.p.m. stereo single version is available.
[A] Indicates that 33⅓ r.p.m. stereo single version is available.

Columns: THIS WEEK | ONE WEEK AGO | TWO WEEKS AGO | THREE WEEKS AGO | TITLE — Artist, Company Record No. | STEREO | WEEKS ON CHART

| This | 1wk | 2wk | 3wk | Title — Artist, Company, Record No. | Stereo | Wks |
|---|---|---|---|---|---|---|
| 1 | 1 | 1 | 2 | ARE YOU LONESOME TONIGHT — Elvis Presley, RCA Victor 7810 | S | 5 |
| 2 | 2 | 2 | 4 | LAST DATE — Floyd Cramer, RCA Victor 7775 | S | 10 |
| 3 | 5 | 5 | 7 | A THOUSAND STARS — Kathy Young and the Innocents, Indigo 108 | | 8 |
| 4 | 13 | 20 | 26 | WONDERLAND BY NIGHT — Bert Kaempfert, Decca 31141 | S | 5 |
| 5 | 6 | 7 | 12 | NORTH TO ALASKA — Johnny Horton, Columbia 41782 | | 13 |
| 6 | 9 | 12 | 24 | SAILOR (YOUR HOME IS IN THE SEA) — Lolita, Kapp 349 | | 8 |
| 7 | 7 | 11 | 15 | HE WILL BREAK YOUR HEART — Jerry Butler, Vee Jay 354 | | 7 |
| 8 | 11 | 14 | 19 | MANY TEARS AGO — Connie Francis, M-G-M 12964 | | 6 |
| 9 | 3 | 4 | 3 | POETRY IN MOTION — Johnny Tillotson, Cadence 1384 | | 10 |
| 10 | 30 | 40 | 51 | EXODUS — Ferrante and Teicher, United Artists 274 | S | 5 |
| 11 | 4 | 3 | 1 | STAY — Maurice Williams and the Zodiacs, Herald 552 | | 11 |
| 12 | 17 | 21 | 32 | YOU'RE SIXTEEN — Johnny Burnette, Liberty 55285 | | 7 |
| 13 | 8 | 6 | 8 | NEW ORLEANS — U.S. Bonds, Legrand 819 | | 9 |
| 14 | 16 | 16 | 20 | SWAY — Bobby Rydell, Cameo 182 | | 6 |
| 15 | 10 | 9 | 6 | LET'S GO, LET'S GO, LET'S GO — Hank Ballard and the Midnighters, King 5400 | | 13 |
| 16 | 12 | 8 | 13 | ALONE AT LAST — Jackie Wilson, Brunswick 55170 | | 10 |
| 17 | 14 | 24 | 27 | MY GIRL JOSEPHINE — Fats Domino, Imperial 5704 | | 8 |
| 18 | 21 | 32 | 34 | LONELY TEENAGER — Dion, Laurie 3070 | | 9 |
| 19 | 19 | 18 | 21 | PERFIDIA — Ventures, Dolton 28 | | 7 |
| 20 | 27 | 34 | 56 | I GOTTA KNOW — Elvis Presley, RCA Victor 7810 | S | 5 |
| 21 | 39 | 70 | 94 | LAST DATE — Lawrence Welk, Dot 16145 | S | 4 |
| 22 | 41 | 75 | — | BLUE TANGO — Bill Black's Combo, Hi 2027 | | 3 |
| 23 | 53 | 67 | — | RUBBER BALL — Bobby Vee, Liberty 55287 | | 3 |
| 24 | 20 | 15 | 14 | HUCKLEBUCK — Chubby Checker, Parkway 813 | | 10 |
| 25 | 51 | 78 | 88 | WONDERLAND BY NIGHT — Louis Prima, Dot 16151 | S | 5 |
| 26 | 24 | 31 | 40 | FOOLS RUSH IN — Brook Benton, Mercury 71722 | | 5 |
| 27 | 22 | 29 | 30 | I'LL SAVE THE LAST DANCE FOR YOU — Damita Jo, Mercury 71690 | | 8 |
| 28 | 15 | 10 | 5 | GEORGIA ON MY MIND — Ray Charles, ABC-Paramount 10135 | S | 10 |
| 29 | 18 | 13 | 10 | SAVE THE LAST DANCE FOR ME — Drifters, Atlantic 2071 | | 15 |
| 30 | 23 | 22 | 50 | LIKE STRANGERS — Everly Brothers, Cadence 1388 | | 7 |
| 31 | 37 | 33 | 41 | AM I LOSING YOU — Jim Reeves, RCA Victor 7800 | | 8 |
| 32 | 25 | 17 | 11 | I WANT TO BE WANTED — Brenda Lee, Decca 31149 | | 14 |
| 33 | 58 | 73 | 87 | (WILL YOU LOVE ME) TOMORROW — Shirelles, Scepter 1211 | | 4 |
| 34 | 40 | 48 | 53 | BALLAD OF THE ALAMO — Marty Robbins, Columbia 41809 | A | 9 |
| 35 | 45 | 61 | 64 | RUBY — Ray Charles, ABC-Paramount 10164 | | 4 |
| 36 | 74 | 72 | 76 | DON'T GO TO STRANGERS — Etta Jones, Prestige 180 | | 6 |
| 37 | 26 | 28 | 22 | TO EACH HIS OWN — Platters, Mercury 71697 | S | 10 |
| 38 | 29 | 23 | 18 | SLEEP — Little Willie John, King 5394 | | 15 |
| 39 | 38 | 50 | 58 | NATURAL BORN LOVER — Fats Domino, Imperial 5704 | | 7 |
| 40 | — | — | — | ANGEL BABY — Rosie and the Originals, Highland 1011 | | 1 |
| 41 | 36 | 27 | 17 | BLUE ANGEL — Roy Orbison, Monument 425 | | 13 |
| 42 | 71 | 84 | 96 | CORINNA, CORINNA — Ray Peterson, Dunes 2002 | | 4 |
| 43 | 32 | 37 | 49 | AM I THE MAN — Jackie Wilson, Brunswick 55170 | | 8 |
| 44 | 49 | 53 | 68 | I MISSED ME — Jim Reeves, RCA Victor 7800 | | 5 |
| 45 | 54 | 62 | 71 | EXODUS — Mantovani, London 1953 | S | 4 |
| 46 | 35 | 30 | 33 | RUBY DUBY DU — Tobin Matthews, Chief 7022 | | 7 |
| 47 | 31 | 25 | 43 | OL' MAC DONALD — Frank Sinatra, Capitol 4466 | | 6 |
| 48 | 28 | 19 | 9 | YOU TALK TOO MUCH — Joe Jones, Roulette 4304 | | 13 |
| 49 | 59 | 64 | 72 | ONCE IN A WHILE — Chimes, Tag 444 | | 7 |
| 50 | 43 | 49 | 60 | GONZO — James Booker, Peacock 1697 | | 6 |
| 51 | 69 | — | — | SAD MOOD — Sam Cooke, RCA Victor 7816 | | 2 |
| 52 | 56 | 59 | 67 | GEE WHIZ — Innocents, Indigo 111 | | 4 |
| 53 | — | — | — | LITTLE DRUMMER BOY — Harry Simeone Chorale, 20th Fox 121 | | 1 |
| 54 | 67 | 81 | — | WALK SLOW — Little Willie John, King 5428 | | 3 |
| 55 | — | — | — | WHITE CHRISTMAS — Bing Crosby, Decca 23778 | | 1 |
| 56 | 33 | 38 | 31 | ARTIFICIAL FLOWERS — Bobby Darin, Atco 6179 | | 12 |
| 57 | 89 | — | — | WONDERLAND BY NIGHT — Anita Bryant, Carlton 537 | | 2 |
| 58 | 84 | — | — | HOOCHIE COOCHIE COO — Hank Ballard and Midnighters, King 5430 | | 2 |
| 59 | 62 | 79 | — | WINGS OF A DOVE — Ferlin Husky, Capitol 4406 | | 3 |
| 60 | 68 | 76 | 83 | SEND ME THE PILLOW (THAT YOU DREAM ON) — Browns, RCA Victor 7804 | S | 5 |
| 61 | 47 | 54 | 59 | ALABAM — Pat Boone, Dot 16152 | | 8 |
| 62 | 42 | 36 | 36 | TOGETHERNESS — Frankie Avalon, Chancellor 1056 | S | 13 |
| 63 | 34 | 42 | 38 | MY DEAREST DARLING — Etta James, Argo 5368 | | 13 |
| 64 | — | — | — | ROCKIN' AROUND THE CHRISTMAS TREE — Brenda Lee, Decca 30776 | | 1 |
| 65 | 72 | 86 | — | DOLL HOUSE — Donnie Brooks, Era 3028 | | 3 |
| 66 | — | — | — | CHIPMUNK SONG — David Seville and Chipmunks, Liberty 55168 | | 1 |
| 67 | 46 | 44 | 46 | DEAR JOHN — Pat Boone, Dot 16152 | S | 8 |
| 68 | 44 | 39 | 37 | WAIT FOR ME — Playmates, Roulette 4276 | | 8 |
| 69 | — | — | — | JINGLE BELL ROCK — Bobby Helms, Decca 30513 | | 1 |
| 70 | 79 | — | — | GROOVY TONIGHT — Bobby Rydell, Cameo 182 | | 2 |
| 71 | — | — | — | SHOP AROUND — Miracles, Tamla 54034 | | 1 |
| 72 | 90 | — | — | DANCE BY THE LIGHT OF THE MOON — Olympics, Arvee 5020 | | 2 |
| 73 | 70 | 74 | 84 | THE BELLS — James Brown, King 5423 | | 5 |
| 74 | 82 | 93 | 95 | BUMBLE BEE — La Vern Baker, Atlantic 2077 | | 5 |
| 75 | 87 | — | — | MAGNIFICENT SEVEN — Al Caiola, United Artists 261 | | 2 |
| 76 | 50 | 41 | 65 | RUBY DUBY DU — Charles Wolcott, M-G-M 12944 | S | 7 |
| 77 | 80 | 87 | — | RAMONA — Blue Diamonds, London 1954 | | 3 |
| 78 | 88 | — | — | RAMBLIN' — Ramblers, Addit 1257 | | 2 |
| 79 | — | — | — | ADESTE FIDELES — Bing Crosby, Decca 23777 | | 1 |
| 80 | 86 | 94 | 100 | GLORIA'S THEME — Adam Wade, Coed 541 | | 4 |
| 81 | 73 | 69 | 82 | ALABAM — Lloyd (Cowboy) Copas, Starday 501 | | 12 |
| 82 | 81 | 89 | 93 | GEE — Jan and Dean, Dore 576 | | 5 |
| 83 | 55 | 66 | 73 | HARD HEARTED HANNAH — Ray Charles, ABC-Paramount 10164 | | 4 |
| 84 | — | — | — | I'M HURTIN' — Roy Orbison, Monument 433 | | 1 |
| 85 | 65 | 65 | 78 | GREEN LEAVES OF SUMMER — Brothers Four, Columbia 41808 | A | 7 |
| 86 | — | — | — | PUPPET SONG — Frankie Avalon, Chancellor 1065 | | 1 |
| 87 | 92 | 100 | — | HAVE YOU EVER BEEN LONELY — Teresa Brewer, Coral 62236 | | 3 |
| 88 | — | — | — | A PERFECT LOVE — Frankie Avalon, Chancellor 1065 | | 1 |
| 89 | 97 | — | — | AGE FOR LOVE — Jimmy Charles, Promo 1003 | | 2 |
| 90 | 98 | — | — | YOU BETTER KNOW WHAT YOU'RE DOING — Lloyd Price, ABC-Paramount 10162 | | 2 |
| 91 | 75 | 77 | 86 | LAST OF THE BIG TIME SPENDERS — Cornbread and Biscuits, Maske 102 | | 5 |
| 92 | 100 | — | — | ROCKIN' ROLLIN' OCEAN — Hank Snow, RCA Victor 7702 | | 2 |
| 93 | — | — | — | HAPPY DAYS — Marv Johnson, United Artists 273 | | 1 |
| 94 | — | — | — | I IDOLIZE YOU — Ike and Tina Turner, Imperial 5686 | | 5 |
| 95 | — | — | — | CALCUTTA — Lawrence Welk, Dot 16161 | | 1 |
| 96 | — | — | — | YOU DON'T WANT MY LOVE — Andy Williams, Cadence 1398 | | 1 |
| 97 | 77 | 85 | 77 | BALLAD OF THE ALAMO — Bud and Travis, Liberty 55284 | | 9 |
| 98 | — | — | — | (MY) LAST DATE (WITH YOU) — Skeeter Davis, RCA Victor 7825 | | 1 |
| 99 | 99 | — | — | WABASH BLUES — Viscounts, Madison 140 | | 2 |
| 100 | — | — | — | CHRISTMAS SONG — Nat King Cole, Capitol 3561 | | 1 |

# The Billboard HOT 100

**FOR WEEK ENDING DECEMBER 25**

Columns show: THIS WEEK | ONE WEEK AGO | TWO WEEKS AGO | THREE WEEKS AGO | TITLE — Artist, Company, Record No. | STEREO | WEEKS ON CHART

| # | 1wk | 2wk | 3wk | Title / Artist | Stereo | Wks |
|---|---|---|---|---|---|---|
| 1 | 1 | 1 | 1 | ARE YOU LONESOME TONIGHT — Elvis Presley, RCA Victor 7810 | S | 6 |
| 2 | 2 | 2 | 2 | LAST DATE — Floyd Cramer, RCA Victor 7775 | S | 11 |
| 3 | 4 | 13 | 20 | WONDERLAND BY NIGHT — Bert Kaempfert, Decca 31141 | S | 6 |
| 4 | 5 | 6 | 7 | NORTH TO ALASKA — Johnny Horton, Columbia 41782 | | 14 |
| 5 | 6 | 9 | 12 | SAILOR (YOUR HOME IS IN THE SEA) — Lolita, Kapp 349 | | 9 |
| 6 | 10 | 30 | 40 | EXODUS — Ferrante and Teicher, United Artists 274 | S | 6 |
| 7 | 3 | 5 | 5 | A THOUSAND STARS — Kathy Young and the Innocents, Indigo 108 | | 9 |
| 8 | 8 | 11 | 14 | MANY YEARS AGO — Connie Francis, M-G-M 12964 | | 7 |
| 9 | 12 | 17 | 21 | YOU'RE SIXTEEN — Johnny Burnette, Liberty 55285 | | 8 |
| 10 | 7 | 7 | 11 | HE WILL BREAK YOUR HEART — Jerry Butler, Vee Jay 354 | | 8 |
| 11 | 9 | 3 | 4 | POETRY IN MOTION — Johnny Tillotson, Cadence 1384 | | 11 |
| 12 | 18 | 21 | 32 | LONELY TEENAGER — Dion, Laurie 3070 | | 10 |
| 13 | 11 | 4 | 3 | STAY — Maurice Williams and the Zodiacs, Herald 552 | | 12 |
| 14 | 14 | 16 | 16 | SWAY — Bobby Rydell, Cameo 182 | | 7 |
| 15 | 23 | 53 | 67 | RUBBER BALL — Bobby Vee, Liberty 55287 | | 4 |
| 16 | 22 | 41 | 75 | BLUE TANGO — Bill Black's Combo, Hi 2027 | | 4 |
| 17 | 19 | 19 | 18 | PERFIDIA — Ventures, Dolton 28 | | 8 |
| 18 | 13 | 8 | 6 | NEW ORLEANS — U. S. Bonds, Legrand 819 | | 10 |
| 19 | 17 | 14 | 24 | MY GIRL JOSEPHINE — Fats Domino, Imperial 5704 | | 9 |
| 20 | 25 | 51 | 78 | WONDERLAND BY NIGHT — Louis Prima, Dot 16151 | S | 6 |
| 21 | 16 | 12 | 8 | ALONE AT LAST — Jackie Wilson, Brunswick 55170 | | 11 |
| 22 | 33 | 58 | 73 | (WILL YOU LOVE ME) TOMORROW — Shirelles, Scepter 1211 | | 5 |
| 23 | 40 | — | — | ANGEL BABY — Rosie and the Originals, Highland 1011 | | 2 |
| 24 | 21 | 39 | 70 | LAST DATE — Lawrence Welk, Dot 16145 | S | 5 |
| 25 | 15 | 10 | 9 | LET'S GO, LET'S GO, LET'S GO — Hank Ballard and the Midnighters, King 5400 | | 14 |
| 26 | 64 | — | — | ROCKIN' AROUND THE CHRISTMAS TREE — Brenda Lee, Decca 30776 | | 2 |
| 27 | 42 | 71 | 84 | CORINNA, CORINNA — Ray Peterson, Dunes 2002 | | 5 |
| 28 | 53 | — | — | LITTLE DRUMMER BOY — Harry Simeone Chorale, 20th Fox 121 | | 2 |
| 29 | 51 | 69 | — | SAD MOOD — Sam Cooke, RCA Victor 7816 | | 3 |
| 30 | 20 | 27 | 34 | I GOTTA KNOW — Elvis Presley, RCA Victor 7810 | S | 6 |
| 31 | 27 | 22 | 29 | I'LL SAVE THE LAST DANCE FOR YOU — Damita Jo, Mercury 71690 | | 9 |
| 32 | 55 | — | — | WHITE CHRISTMAS — Bing Crosby, Decca 23778 | | 2 |
| 33 | 26 | 24 | 31 | FOOLS RUSH IN — Brook Benton, Mercury 71722 | | 6 |
| 34 | 34 | 40 | 48 | BALLAD OF THE ALAMO — Marty Robbins, Columbia 41809 | A | 10 |
| 35 | 29 | 18 | 13 | SAVE THE LAST DANCE FOR ME — Drifters, Atlantic 2071 | | 16 |
| 36 | 35 | 45 | 61 | RUBY — Ray Charles, ABC-Paramount 10164 | | 5 |
| 37 | 30 | 23 | 22 | LIKE STRANGERS — Everly Brothers, Cadence 1388 | | 8 |
| 38 | 24 | 20 | 15 | HUCKLEBUCK — Chubby Checker, Parkway 813 | | 11 |
| 39 | 31 | 37 | 33 | AM I LOSING YOU — Jim Reeves, RCA Victor 7800 | | 9 |
| 40 | 39 | 38 | 50 | NATURAL BORN LOVER — Fats Domino, Imperial 5704 | | 8 |
| 41 | 65 | 72 | 86 | DOLL HOUSE — Donnie Brooks, Era 3028 | | 4 |
| 42 | 59 | 62 | 79 | WINGS OF A DOVE — Ferlin Husky, Capitol 4406 | | 4 |
| 43 | 58 | 84 | — | HOOCHIE COOCHIE COO — Hank Ballard and the Midnighters, King 5430 | | 3 |
| 44 | 49 | 59 | 64 | ONCE IN A WHILE — Chimes, Tag 444 | | 8 |
| 45 | 66 | — | — | CHIPMUNK SONG — David Seville and Chipmunks, Liberty 55168 | | 2 |
| 46 | 69 | — | — | JINGLE BELL ROCK — Bobby Helms, Decca 30513 | | 2 |
| 47 | 57 | 89 | — | WONDERLAND BY NIGHT — Anita Bryant, Carlton 537 | | 3 |
| 48 | 54 | 67 | 81 | WALK SLOW — Little Willie John, King 5428 | | 4 |
| 49 | 28 | 15 | 10 | GEORGIA ON MY MIND — Ray Charles, ABC-Paramount 10135 | S | 11 |
| 50 | 45 | 54 | 62 | EXODUS — Mantovani, London 1953 | S | 5 |
| 51 | 50 | 43 | 49 | GONZO — James Booker, Peacock 1697 | | 7 |
| 52 | 32 | 25 | 17 | I WANT TO BE WANTED — Brenda Lee, Decca 31149 | | 15 |
| 53 | 43 | 32 | 37 | AM I THE MAN — Jackie Wilson, Brunswick 55170 | | 9 |
| 54 | 52 | 56 | 59 | GEE WHIZ — Innocents, Indigo 111 | | 5 |
| 55 | 36 | 74 | 72 | DON'T GO TO STRANGERS — Etta Jones, Prestige 180 | | 7 |
| 56 | 60 | 68 | 76 | SEND ME THE PILLOW (THAT YOU DREAM ON) — Browns, RCA Victor 7804 | S | 6 |
| 57 | 84 | — | — | I'M HURTIN' — Roy Orbison, Monument 433 | | 2 |
| 58 | 79 | — | — | ADESTE FIDELES (O COME ALL YE FAITHFUL) — Bing Crosby, Decca 23777 | | 2 |
| 59 | 71 | — | — | SHOP AROUND — Miracles, Tamla 54034 | | 2 |
| 60 | 75 | 87 | — | MAGNIFICENT SEVEN — Al Cariola, United Artists 261 | | 3 |
| 61 | 74 | 82 | 93 | BUMBLE BEE — La Vern Baker, Atlantic 2077 | | 6 |
| 62 | — | — | — | RUDOLPH, THE RED-NOSED REINDEER — David Seville and Chipmunks, Liberty 55289 | | 1 |
| 63 | 38 | 29 | 23 | SLEEP — Little Willie John, King 5394 | | 16 |
| 64 | — | — | — | SILENT NIGHT — Bing Crosby, Decca 23777 | | 1 |
| 65 | 95 | — | — | CALCUTTA — Lawrence Welk, Dot 16161 | | 2 |
| 66 | 47 | 31 | 25 | OL' Mac DONALD — Frank Sinatra, Capitol 4466 | | 7 |
| 67 | 41 | 36 | 27 | BLUE ANGEL — Roy Orbison, Monument 425 | | 14 |
| 68 | 73 | 70 | 74 | THE BELLS — James Brown, King 5423 | | 6 |
| 69 | 72 | 90 | — | DANCE BY THE LIGHT OF THE MOON — Olympics, Arvee 5020 | | 3 |
| 70 | 37 | 26 | 28 | TO EACH HIS OWN — Platters, Mercury 71697 | S | 11 |
| 71 | 44 | 49 | 53 | I MISSED ME — Jim Reeves, RCA Victor 7800 | | 6 |
| 72 | 77 | 80 | 87 | RAMONA — Blue Diamonds, London 1954 | | 4 |
| 73 | 78 | 88 | — | RAMBLIN' — Ramblers, Addit 1257 | | 3 |
| 74 | — | — | — | RUDOLPH, THE RED-NOSED REINDEER — Melodeers, Studio 9908 | | 1 |
| 75 | 88 | — | — | A PERFECT LOVE — Frankie Avalon, Chancellor 1065 | | 2 |
| 76 | 80 | 86 | 94 | GLORIA'S THEME — Adam Wade, Coed 541 | | 5 |
| 77 | — | — | — | I COUNT THE TEARS — Drifters, Atlantic 2087 | | 1 |
| 78 | — | — | — | TWISTIN' BELLS — Santo and Johnny, Canadian-American 120 | | 1 |
| 79 | 98 | — | — | (MY) LAST DATE (WITH YOU) — Skeeter Davis, RCA Victor 7825 | | 2 |
| 80 | 100 | — | — | CHRISTMAS SONG — Nat King Cole, Capitol 3561 | | 2 |
| 81 | 86 | — | — | PUPPET SONG — Frankie Avalon, Chancellor 1065 | | 2 |
| 82 | — | — | — | YOUR OTHER LOVE — Flamingos, End 1081 | | 1 |
| 83 | 46 | 35 | 30 | RUBY DUBY DU — Tobin Matthews, Chief 7022 | | 8 |
| 84 | 87 | 92 | 100 | HAVE YOU EVER BEEN LONELY — Teresa Brewer, Coral 62236 | | 4 |
| 85 | 96 | — | — | YOU DON'T WANT MY LOVE — Andy Williams, Cadence 1398 | | 2 |
| 86 | 89 | 97 | — | AGE FOR LOVE — Jimmy Charles, Promo 1003 | | 3 |
| 87 | 92 | 100 | — | ROCKIN', ROLLIN' OCEAN — Hank Snow, RCA Victor 7702 | | 3 |
| 88 | 93 | — | — | HAPPY DAYS — Marv Johnson, United Artists 273 | | 2 |
| 89 | — | — | — | CHRISTMAS AULD LANG SYNE — Bobby Darin, Atco 6183 | | 1 |
| 90 | — | — | — | (MY) LAST DATE (WITH YOU) — Joni James, M-G-M 12933 | | 1 |
| 91 | — | — | — | UTOPIA — Frankie Gari, Crusade 1020 | | 1 |
| 92 | 94 | — | — | I IDOLIZE YOU — Ike and Tina Turner, Sue 735 | | 6 |
| 93 | — | — | — | BABY, O' BABY — Shells, Johnson 104 | | 1 |
| 94 | 99 | 99 | — | WABASH BLUES — Viscounts, Madison 140 | | 3 |
| 95 | — | — | — | PEPE — Duane Eddy, Jamie 1175 | | 1 |
| 96 | — | — | — | WHITE CHRISTMAS — Clyde McPhatter and the Drifters, Atlantic 1048 | | 1 |
| 97 | — | — | — | BLUE CHRISTMAS — Browns, RCA Victor 7820 | | 1 |
| 98 | — | — | — | LOVEY DOVEY — Buddy Knox, Liberty 55290 | | 1 |
| 99 | — | — | — | MISTER LIVINGSTON — Larry Verne, Era 3034 | | 1 |
| 100 | — | — | — | CALENDAR GIRL — Neil Sedaka, RCA Victor 7829 | | 1 |

# The Billboard HOT 100

**FOR WEEK ENDING JANUARY 1**

*STAR PERFORMERS showed the greatest upward progress on Hot 100 this week.*
(S) Indicates that 45 r.p.m. stereo single version is available.
(A) Indicates that 33⅓ r.p.m. stereo single version is available.

Columns: THIS WEEK | ONE WEEK AGO | TWO WEEKS AGO | THREE WEEKS AGO | TITLE — Artist, Company, Record No. | STEREO | WEEKS ON CHART

| TW | 1W | 2W | 3W | Title — Artist, Company, Record No. | Stereo | Wks |
|---|---|---|---|---|---|---|
| 1 | 1 | 1 | 1 | ARE YOU LONESOME TONIGHT — Elvis Presley, RCA Victor 7810 | S | 7 |
| 2 | 3 | 4 | 13 | WONDERLAND BY NIGHT — Bert Kaempfert, Decca 31141 | S | 7 |
| 3 | 2 | 2 | 2 | LAST DATE — Floyd Cramer, RCA Victor 7775 | S | 12 |
| 4 | 7 | 3 | 5 | A THOUSAND STARS — Kathy Young and the Innocents, Indigo 108 | | 10 |
| 5 | 6 | 10 | 30 | EXODUS — Ferrante and Teicher, United Artists 274 | S | 7 |
| 6 | 4 | 5 | 6 | NORTH TO ALASKA — Johnny Horton, Columbia 41782 | | 15 |
| 7 | 8 | 8 | 11 | MANY TEARS AGO — Connie Francis, M-G-M 12964 | | 8 |
| 8 | 9 | 12 | 17 | YOU'RE SIXTEEN — Johnny Burnette, Liberty 55285 | | 9 |
| 9 | 5 | 6 | 9 | SAILOR (YOUR HOME IS IN THE SEA) — Lolita, Kapp 349 | | 10 |
| 10 | 27 | 42 | 71 | CORINNA, CORINNA — Ray Peterson, Dunes 2002 | | 6 |
| 11 | 10 | 7 | 7 | HE WILL BREAK YOUR HEART — Jerry Butler, Vee Jay 354 | | 9 |
| 12 | 12 | 18 | 21 | LONELY TEENAGER — Dion, Laurie 3070 | | 11 |
| 13 | 23 | 40 | — | ANGEL BABY — Rosie and the Originals, Highland 1011 | | 3 |
| 14 | 26 | 64 | — | ROCKIN' AROUND THE CHRISTMAS TREE — Brenda Lee, Decca 30776 | | 3 |
| 15 | 17 | 19 | 19 | PERFIDIA — Ventures, Dolton 28 | | 9 |
| 16 | 15 | 23 | 53 | RUBBER BALL — Bobby Vee, Liberty 55287 | | 5 |
| 17 | 20 | 25 | 51 | WONDERLAND BY NIGHT — Louis Prima, Dot 16151 | S | 7 |
| 18 | 11 | 9 | 3 | POETRY IN MOTION — Johnny Tillotson, Cadence 1384 | | 12 |
| 19 | 18 | 13 | 8 | NEW ORLEANS — U. S. Bonds, Legrand 819 | | 11 |
| 20 | 22 | 33 | 58 | (WILL YOU LOVE ME) TOMORROW — Shirelles, Scepter 1211 | | 6 |
| 21 | 62 | — | — | RUDOLPH, THE RED-NOSED REINDEER — David Seville and Chipmunks, Liberty 55289 | | 2 |
| 22 | 19 | 17 | 14 | MY GIRL JOSEPHINE — Fats Domino, Imperial 5704 | | 10 |
| 23 | 14 | 14 | 16 | SWAY — Bobby Rydell, Cameo 182 | | 8 |
| 24 | 28 | 53 | — | LITTLE DRUMMER BOY — Harry Simeone Chorale, 20th Fox 121 | | 3 |
| 25 | 16 | 22 | 41 | BLUE TANGO — Bill Black's Combo, Hi 2027 | | 5 |
| 26 | 32 | 55 | — | WHITE CHRISTMAS — Bing Crosby, Decca 23778 | | 3 |
| 27 | 47 | 57 | 89 | WONDERLAND BY NIGHT — Anita Bryant, Carlton 537 | | 4 |
| 28 | 21 | 16 | 12 | ALONE AT LAST — Jackie Wilson, Brunswick 55170 | | 12 |
| 29 | 33 | 26 | 24 | FOOLS RUSH IN — Brook Benton, Mercury 71722 | | 7 |
| 30 | 13 | 11 | 4 | STAY — Maurice Williams and the Zodiacs, Herald 552 | | 13 |
| 31 | 41 | 65 | 72 | DOLL HOUSE — Donnie Brooks, Era 3028 | | 5 |
| 32 | 36 | 35 | 45 | RUBY — Ray Charles, ABC-Paramount 10164 | | 6 |
| 33 | 25 | 15 | 10 | LET'S GO, LET'S GO, LET'S GO — Hank Ballard and the Midnighters, King 5400 | | 15 |
| 34 | 29 | 51 | 69 | SAD MOOD — Sam Cooke, RCA Victor 7816 | | 4 |
| 35 | 42 | 59 | 62 | WINGS OF A DOVE — Ferlin Husky, Capitol 4406 | | 5 |
| 36 | 46 | 69 | — | JINGLE BELL ROCK — Bobby Helms, Decca 30513 | | 3 |
| 37 | 31 | 27 | 22 | I'LL SAVE THE LAST DANCE FOR YOU — Damita Jo, Mercury 71690 | | 10 |
| 38 | 34 | 34 | 40 | BALLAD OF THE ALAMO — Marty Robbins, Columbia 41809 | A | 11 |
| 39 | 30 | 20 | 27 | I GOTTA KNOW — Elvis Presley, RCA Victor 7810 | S | 7 |
| 40 | 38 | 24 | 20 | HUCKLEBUCK — Chubby Checker, Parkway 813 | | 12 |
| 41 | 24 | 21 | 39 | LAST DATE — Lawrence Welk, Dot 16145 | S | 6 |
| 42 | 65 | 95 | — | CALCUTTA — Lawrence Welk, Dot 16161 | | 3 |
| 43 | 39 | 31 | 37 | AM I LOSING YOU — Jim Reeves, RCA Victor 7800 | | 10 |
| 44 | 35 | 29 | 18 | SAVE THE LAST DANCE FOR ME — Drifters, Atlantic 2071 | | 17 |
| 45 | 58 | 79 | — | ADESTE FIDELES (O COME ALL YE FAITHFUL) — Bing Crosby, Decca 23777 | | 3 |
| 46 | 66 | 47 | 31 | OL' MAC DONALD — Frank Sinatra, Capitol 4466 | | 8 |
| 47 | 37 | 30 | 23 | LIKE STRANGERS — Everly Brothers, Cadence 1388 | | 9 |
| 48 | 54 | 52 | 56 | GEE WHIZ — Innocents, Indigo 111 | | 6 |
| 49 | 44 | 49 | 59 | ONCE IN A WHILE — Chimes, Tag 444 | | 9 |
| 50 | 75 | 88 | — | A PERFECT LOVE — Frankie Avalon, Chancellor 1065 | | 3 |
| 51 | 57 | 84 | — | I'M HURTIN' — Roy Orbison, Monument 433 | | 3 |
| 52 | 51 | 50 | 43 | GONZO — James Booker, Peacock 1697 | | 8 |
| 53 | 59 | 71 | — | SHOP AROUND — Miracles, Tamla 54034 | | 3 |
| 54 | 64 | — | — | SILENT NIGHT — Bing Crosby, Decca 23777 | | 2 |
| 55 | 77 | — | — | I COUNT THE TEARS — Drifters, Atlantic 2087 | | 2 |
| 56 | 69 | 72 | 90 | DANCE BY THE LIGHT OF THE MOON — Olympics, Arvee 5020 | | 4 |
| 57 | 100 | — | — | CALENDAR GIRL — Neil Sedaka, RCA Victor 7829 | | 2 |
| 58 | 89 | — | — | CHRISTMAS AULD LANG SYNE — Bobby Darin, Atco 6183 | | 2 |
| 59 | 61 | 74 | 82 | BUMBLE BEE — La Vern Baker, Atlantic 2077 | | 7 |
| 60 | 45 | 66 | — | CHIPMUNK SONG — David Seville and Chipmunks, Liberty 55168 | | 3 |
| 61 | 78 | — | — | TWISTIN' BELLS — Santo and Johnny, Canadian-American 120 | | 2 |
| 62 | 93 | — | — | BABY, O' BABY — Shells, Johnson 104 | | 2 |
| 63 | — | — | — | YOU ARE THE ONLY ONE — Ricky Nelson, Imperial 5707 | | 1 |
| 64 | 53 | 43 | 32 | AM I THE MAN — Jackie Wilson, Brunswick 55170 | | 10 |
| 65 | 40 | 39 | 38 | NATURAL BORN LOVER — Fats Domino, Imperial 5704 | | 9 |
| 66 | 82 | — | — | YOUR OTHER LOVE — Flamingos, End 1081 | | 2 |
| 67 | 60 | 75 | 87 | MAGNIFICENT SEVEN — Al Caiola, United Artists 261 | | 4 |
| 68 | 79 | 98 | — | (MY) LAST DATE (WITH YOU) — Skeeter Davis, RCA Victor 7825 | | 3 |
| 69 | 81 | 86 | — | PUPPET SONG — Frankie Avalon, Chancellor 1065 | | 3 |
| 70 | 50 | 45 | 54 | EXODUS — Mantovani, London 1953 | S | 6 |
| 71 | 74 | — | — | RUDOLPH, THE RED-NOSED REINDEER — Melodeers, Studio 9908 | | 2 |
| 72 | 43 | 58 | 84 | HOOCHIE COOCHIE COO — Hank Ballard and the Midnighters, King 5430 | | 4 |
| 73 | 73 | 78 | 88 | RAMBLIN' — The Ramblers, Addit 1257 | | 4 |
| 74 | 76 | 80 | 86 | GLORIA'S THEME — Adam Wade, Coed 541 | | 6 |
| 75 | — | — | — | HOW TO HANDLE A WOMAN — Johnny Mathis, Columbia 41866 | | 1 |
| 76 | 56 | 60 | 68 | SEND ME THE PILLOW (THAT YOU DREAM ON) — Browns, RCA Victor 7804 | S | 7 |
| 77 | 99 | — | — | MISTER LIVINGSTON — Larry Verne, Era 3034 | | 2 |
| 78 | 72 | 77 | 80 | RAMONA — Blue Diamonds, London 1954 | | 5 |
| 79 | 85 | 96 | — | YOU DON'T WANT MY LOVE — Andy Williams, Cadence 1398 | | 3 |
| 80 | — | — | — | (LET'S DO THE) HULLY GULLY — Bill Doggett, Warner Bros. 5181 | | 1 |
| 81 | 48 | 54 | 67 | WALK SLOW — Little Willie John, King 5428 | | 5 |
| 82 | — | — | — | CHERRY PINK AND APPLE BLOSSOM WHITE — Jerry Murad's Harmonicats, Columbia 41816 | | 1 |
| 83 | 90 | — | — | (MY) LAST DATE (WITH YOU) — Joni James, M-G-M 12933 | | 2 |
| 84 | 84 | 87 | 92 | HAVE YOU EVER BEEN LONELY — Teresa Brewer, Coral 62236 | | 5 |
| 85 | 86 | 89 | 97 | AGE FOR LOVE — Jimmy Charles, Promo 1003 | | 4 |
| 86 | 88 | 93 | — | HAPPY DAYS — Marv Johnson, United Artists 273 | | 3 |
| 87 | 91 | — | — | UTOPIA — Frank Gari, Crusade 1020 | | 2 |
| 88 | 95 | — | — | PEPE — Duane Eddy, Jamie 1175 | | 2 |
| 89 | 98 | — | — | LOVEY DOVEY — Buddy Knox, Liberty 55290 | | 2 |
| 90 | 92 | 94 | — | I IDOLIZE YOU — Ike and Tina Turner, Sue 735 | | 7 |
| 91 | 94 | 99 | 99 | WABASH BLUES — Viscounts, Madison 140 | | 4 |
| 92 | — | — | — | TALK TO ME BABY — Annette, Vista 369 | | 1 |
| 93 | — | — | — | SOMEDAY (YOU'LL WANT ME TO WANT YOU) — Brook Benton, Mercury 71722 | | 1 |
| 94 | — | — | — | ANGEL ON MY SHOULDER — Shelby Flint, Valiant 111 | | 1 |
| 95 | — | — | — | CHILD OF GOD — Bobby Darin, Atco 6183 | | 1 |
| 96 | — | — | — | WE HAVE LOVE — Dinah Washington, Mercury 71744 | | 1 |
| 97 | — | — | — | MAKE SOMEONE HAPPY — Perry Como, RCA Victor 7812 | | 1 |
| 98 | — | — | — | THERE SHE GOES — Jerry Wallace, Challenge 59098 | | 1 |
| 99 | — | — | — | OH, HOW I MISS YOU TONIGHT — Jeanne Black, Capitol 4492 | | 1 |
| 100 | — | — | — | SPOONFUL — Etta and Harvey, Chess 1771 | | 1 |

## The Billboard HOT 100

**FOR WEEK ENDING JANUARY 8**

*December 31, 1960*

STAR PERFORMERS showed the greatest upward progress on Hot 100 this week.
[S] Indicates that 45 r.p.m. stereo single version is available.
[A] Indicates that 33⅓ r.p.m. stereo single version is available.

| This Week | One Week Ago | Two Weeks Ago | Three Weeks Ago | Title — Artist, Company, Record No. | Stereo | Weeks on Chart |
|---|---|---|---|---|---|---|
| 1 | 1 | 1 | 1 | ARE YOU LONESOME TONIGHT — Elvis Presley, RCA Victor 7810 | S | 8 |
| 2 | 2 | 3 | 4 | WONDERLAND BY NIGHT — Bert Kaempfert, Decca 31141 | S | 8 |
| 3 | 3 | 2 | 2 | LAST DATE — Floyd Cramer, RCA Victor 7775 | S | 13 |
| 4 | 5 | 6 | 10 | EXODUS — Ferrante and Teicher, United Artists 274 | S | 8 |
| 5 | 4 | 7 | 3 | A THOUSAND STARS — Kathy Young and the Innocents, Indigo 108 | | 11 |
| 6 | 6 | 4 | 5 | NORTH TO ALASKA — Johnny Horton, Columbia 41782 | | 16 |
| 7 | 7 | 8 | 8 | MANY TEARS AGO — Connie Francis, M-G-M 12964 | | 9 |
| 8 | 8 | 9 | 12 | YOU'RE SIXTEEN — Johnny Burnette, Liberty 55285 | | 10 |
| 9 | 13 | 23 | 40 | ANGEL BABY — Rosie and the Originals, Highland 1011 | | 4 |
| 10 | 10 | 27 | 42 | CORINNA, CORINNA — Ray Peterson, Dunes 2002 | | 7 |
| ★11 | 16 | 15 | 23 | RUBBER BALL — Bobby Vee, Liberty 55287 | | 6 |
| 12 | 9 | 5 | 6 | SAILOR (YOUR HOME IS IN THE SEA) — Lolita, Kapp 349 | | 11 |
| 13 | 11 | 10 | 7 | HE WILL BREAK YOUR HEART — Jerry Butler, Vee Jay 354 | | 10 |
| ★14 | 20 | 22 | 33 | (WILL YOU LOVE ME) TOMORROW — Shirelles, Scepter 1211 | | 7 |
| 15 | 12 | 12 | 18 | LONELY TEENAGER — Dion, Laurie 3070 | | 12 |
| 16 | 17 | 20 | 25 | WONDERLAND BY NIGHT — Louis Prima, Dot 16151 | S | 8 |
| 17 | 15 | 17 | 19 | PERFIDIA — Ventures, Dolton 28 | | 10 |
| 18 | 14 | 26 | 64 | ROCKIN' AROUND THE CHRISTMAS TREE — Brenda Lee, Decca 30776 | | 4 |
| ★19 | 27 | 47 | 57 | WONDERLAND BY NIGHT — Anita Bryant, Carlton 537 | | 5 |
| 20 | 23 | 14 | 14 | SWAY — Bobby Rydell, Cameo 182 | | 9 |
| 21 | 18 | 11 | 9 | POETRY IN MOTION — Johnny Tillotson, Cadence 1384 | | 13 |
| ★22 | 42 | 65 | 95 | CALCUTTA — Lawrence Welk, Dot 16161 | | 4 |
| 23 | 35 | 42 | 59 | WINGS OF A DOVE — Ferlin Husky, Capitol 4406 | | 6 |
| 24 | 19 | 18 | 13 | NEW ORLEANS — U. S. Bonds, Legrand 819 | | 12 |
| ★25 | 22 | 19 | 17 | MY GIRL JOSEPHINE — Fats Domino, Imperial 5704 | | 11 |
| 26 | 25 | 16 | 22 | BLUE TANGO — Bill Black's Combo, Hi 2027 | | 6 |
| ★27 | 62 | 93 | — | BABY, O' BABY — Shells, Johnson 104 | | 3 |
| 28 | 32 | 36 | 35 | RUBY — Ray Charles, ABC-Paramount 10164 | | 7 |
| 29 | 24 | 28 | 53 | LITTLE DRUMMER BOY — Harry Simeone Chorale, 20th Fox 121 | | 4 |
| 30 | 29 | 33 | 26 | FOOLS RUSH IN — Brook Benton, Mercury 71722 | | 8 |
| 31 | 28 | 21 | 16 | ALONE AT LAST — Jackie Wilson, Brunswick 55170 | | 13 |
| ★32 | 53 | 59 | 71 | SHOP AROUND — Miracles, Tamla 54034 | | 4 |
| 33 | 39 | 30 | 20 | I GOTTA KNOW — Elvis Presley, RCA Victor 7810 | S | 8 |
| 34 | 31 | 41 | 65 | DOLL HOUSE — Donnie Brooks, Era 3028 | | 6 |
| 35 | 30 | 13 | 11 | STAY — Maurice Williams and the Zodiacs, Herald 552 | | 14 |
| 36 | 34 | 29 | 51 | SAD MOOD — Sam Cooke, RCA Victor 7816 | | 5 |
| ★37 | 55 | 77 | — | I COUNT THE TEARS — Drifters, Atlantic 2087 | | 3 |
| ★38 | 57 | 100 | — | CALENDAR GIRL — Neil Sedaka, RCA Victor 7829 | | 3 |
| 39 | 38 | 34 | 34 | BALLAD OF THE ALAMO — Marty Robbins, Columbia 41809 | A | 12 |
| 40 | 51 | 57 | 84 | I'M HURTIN' — Roy Orbison, Monument 433 | | 4 |
| 41 | 37 | 31 | 27 | I'LL SAVE THE LAST DANCE FOR YOU — Damita Jo, Mercury 71690 | | 11 |
| ★42 | 63 | — | — | YOU ARE THE ONLY ONE — Ricky Nelson, Imperial 5707 | | 2 |
| 43 | 52 | 51 | 50 | GONZO — James Booker, Peacock 1697 | | 9 |
| 44 | 48 | 54 | 52 | GEE WHIZ — Innocents, Indigo 111 | | 7 |
| 45 | 40 | 38 | 24 | HUCKLEBUCK — Chubby Checker, Parkway 813 | | 13 |
| ★46 | 59 | 61 | 74 | BUMBLE BEE — La Vern Baker, Atlantic 2077 | | 8 |
| 47 | 56 | 69 | 72 | DANCE BY THE LIGHT OF THE MOON — Olympics, Arvee 5020 | | 5 |
| 48 | 43 | 39 | 31 | AM I LOSING YOU — Jim Reeves, RCA Victor 7800 | | 11 |
| ★49 | 61 | 78 | — | TWISTIN' BELLS — Santo and Johnny, Canadian-American 120 | | 3 |
| 50 | 49 | 44 | 49 | ONCE IN A WHILE — Chimes, Tag 444 | | 10 |
| 51 | 58 | 89 | — | CHRISTMAS AULD LANG SYNE — Bobby Darin, Atco 6183 | | 3 |
| 52 | 33 | 25 | 15 | LET'S GO, LET'S GO, LET'S GO — Hank Ballard and the Midnighters, King 5400 | | 16 |
| 53 | 47 | 37 | 30 | LIKE STRANGERS — Everly Brothers, Cadence 1388 | | 10 |
| 54 | 50 | 75 | 88 | A PERFECT LOVE — Frankie Avalon, Chancellor 1065 | | 4 |
| 55 | 41 | 24 | 21 | LAST DATE — Lawrence Welk, Dot 16145 | S | 7 |
| ★56 | 69 | 81 | 86 | PUPPET SONG — Frankie Avalon, Chancellor 1065 | | 4 |
| 57 | 68 | 79 | 98 | MY LAST DATE (WITH YOU) — Skeeter Davis, RCA Victor 7825 | | 4 |
| 58 | 67 | 60 | 75 | MAGNIFICENT SEVEN — Al Caiola, United Artists 261 | | 5 |
| 59 | 70 | 50 | 45 | EXODUS — Mantovani, London 1953 | S | 7 |
| ★60 | 89 | 98 | — | LOVEY DOVEY — Buddy Knox, Liberty 55290 | | 3 |
| ★61 | 98 | — | — | THERE SHE GOES — Jerry Wallace, Challenge 59098 | | 2 |
| 62 | 72 | 43 | 58 | HOOCHIE COOCHIE COO — Hank Ballard and the Midnighters, King 5430 | | 5 |
| 63 | 66 | 82 | — | YOUR OTHER LOVE — Flamingos, End 1081 | | 3 |
| 64 | 75 | — | — | HOW TO HANDLE A WOMAN — Johnny Mathis, Columbia 41866 | | 2 |
| 65 | 46 | 66 | 47 | OL' MacDONALD — Frank Sinatra, Capitol 4466 | | 9 |
| 66 | 80 | — | — | (LET'S DO) THE HULLY GULLY — Bill Doggett, Warner Bros. 5181 | | 2 |
| 67 | 44 | 35 | 29 | SAVE THE LAST DANCE FOR ME — Drifters, Atlantic 2071 | | 18 |
| 68 | 79 | 85 | 96 | YOU DON'T WANT MY LOVE — Andy Williams, Cadence 1398 | | 4 |
| 69 | 83 | 90 | — | MY LAST DATE (WITH YOU) — Joni James, M-G-M 12933 | | 3 |
| 70 | 82 | — | — | CHERRY PINK AND APPLE BLOSSOM WHITE — Jerry Murad's Harmonicats, Columbia 41816 | | 2 |
| 71 | 86 | 88 | 93 | HAPPY DAYS — Marv Johnson, United Artists 273 | | 4 |
| 72 | — | — | — | C'EST SI BON — Conway Twitty, M-G-M 12969 | | 1 |
| 73 | 81 | 48 | 54 | WALK SLOW — Little Willie John, King 5428 | | 6 |
| 74 | 88 | 95 | — | PEPE — Duane Eddy, Jamie 1175 | | 3 |
| 75 | 77 | 99 | — | MISTER LIVINGSTON — Larry Verne, Era 3034 | | 3 |
| 76 | 96 | — | — | WE HAVE LOVE — Dinah Washington, Mercury 71744 | | 2 |
| 77 | 94 | — | — | ANGEL ON MY SHOULDER — Shelby Flint, Valiant WB 6001 | | 2 |
| 78 | 100 | — | — | SPOONFUL — Etta and Harvey, Chess 1771 | | 2 |
| 79 | 87 | 91 | — | UTOPIA — Frank Gari, Crusade 1020 | | 3 |
| 80 | 97 | — | — | MAKE SOMEONE HAPPY — Perry Como, RCA Victor 7812 | | 2 |
| 81 | — | — | — | MILK COW BLUES — Ricky Nelson, Imperial 5707 | | 1 |
| 82 | 90 | 92 | 94 | I IDOLIZE YOU — Ike and Tina Turner, Sue 735 | | 4 |
| 83 | — | — | — | EMOTIONS — Brenda Lee, Decca 31195 | | 1 |
| 84 | — | — | — | WHAT WOULD I DO — Mickey and Sylvia, RCA Victor 7811 | | 1 |
| 85 | — | — | — | YES, I'M LONESOME TONIGHT — Thelma Carpenter, Coral 62241 | | 1 |
| 86 | — | — | — | SPANISH HARLEM — Ben E. King, Atco 6185 | | 1 |
| 87 | 99 | — | — | OH, HOW I MISS YOU TONIGHT — Jeanne Black, Capitol 4492 | | 2 |
| 88 | — | — | — | THERE'S A MOON OUT TONIGHT — Capris, Old Town 1094 | | 1 |
| 89 | 91 | 94 | 99 | WABASH BLUES — Viscounts, Madison 140 | | 5 |
| 90 | — | — | — | FIRST TASTE OF LOVE — Ben E. King, Atco 7185 | | 1 |
| 91 | — | — | — | IF I KNEW — Nat King Cole, Capitol 4482 | | 1 |
| 92 | — | — | — | ALL IN MY MIND — Maxine Brown, Nomar 102 | | 1 |
| 93 | 92 | — | — | TALK TO ME BABY — Annette, Vista 369 | | 2 |
| 94 | — | — | — | DON'T BELIEVE HIM, DONNA — Lenny Miles, Sceptor 1212 | | 1 |
| 95 | — | — | — | DON'T READ THE LETTER — Patti Page, Mercury 71745 | | 1 |
| 96 | — | — | — | I DON'T WANT NOBODY — Ella Johnson and Buddy Johnson Ork, Mercury 71723 | | 1 |
| 97 | — | — | — | OH LONESOME ME — Johnny Cash, Sun 355 | | 1 |
| 98 | — | — | — | YES, I'M LONESOME TONIGHT — Dodie Stevens, Dot 16167 | | 1 |
| 99 | — | — | — | SUGAR BEE — Cleveland Crochet, Goldband 1106 | | 1 |
| 100 | — | — | — | THIS IS MY STORY — Mickey and Sylvia, RCA Victor 7811 | | 1 |

# BILLBOARD HOT 100

**FOR WEEK ENDING JANUARY 15** — January 9, 1961

| This Week | 1 Wk Ago | 2 Wks Ago | 3 Wks Ago | Title / Artist, Company, Record No. | Stereo | Weeks on Chart |
|---|---|---|---|---|---|---|
| 1 | 2 | 2 | 3 | WONDERLAND BY NIGHT — Bert Kaempfert, Decca 31141 | S | 9 |
| 2 | 1 | 1 | 1 | ARE YOU LONESOME TONIGHT — Elvis Presley, RCA Victor 7810 | S | 9 |
| 3 | 4 | 5 | 6 | EXODUS — Ferrante and Teicher, United Artists 274 | S | 9 |
| 4 | 3 | 3 | 2 | LAST DATE — Floyd Cramer, RCA Victor 7775 | S | 14 |
| 5 | 14 | 20 | 22 | (WILL YOU LOVE ME) TOMORROW — Shirelles, Scepter 1211 | | 8 |
| 6 | 11 | 16 | 15 | RUBBER BALL — Bobby Vee, Liberty 55287 | | 7 |
| 7 | 9 | 13 | 23 | ANGEL BABY — Rosie and the Originals, Highland 1011 | | 5 |
| 8 | 6 | 6 | 4 | NORTH TO ALASKA — Johnny Horton, Columbia 41782 | | 17 |
| 9 | 10 | 10 | 27 | CORINNA, CORINNA — Ray Peterson, Dunes 2002 | | 8 |
| 10 | 8 | 8 | 9 | YOU'RE SIXTEEN — Johnny Burnette, Liberty 55285 | | 11 |
| 11 | 5 | 4 | 7 | A THOUSAND STARS — Kathy Young and the Innocents, Indigo 108 | | 12 |
| 12 | 7 | 7 | 8 | MANY TEARS AGO — Connie Francis, M-G-M 12964 | | 10 |
| 13 | 22 | 42 | 65 | CALCUTTA — Lawrence Welk, Dot 16161 | | 5 |
| 14 | 13 | 11 | 10 | HE WILL BREAK YOUR HEART — Jerry Butler, Vee Jay 354 | | 11 |
| 15 | 16 | 17 | 20 | WONDERLAND BY NIGHT — Louis Prima, Dot 16151 | S | 9 |
| 16 | 12 | 9 | 5 | SAILOR (YOUR HOME IS IN THE SEA) — Lolita, Kapp 349 | | 12 |
| 17 | 15 | 12 | 12 | LONELY TEENAGER — Dion, Laurie 3070 | | 13 |
| 18 | 19 | 27 | 47 | WONDERLAND BY NIGHT — Anita Bryant, Carlton 537 | | 6 |
| 19 | 32 | 53 | 59 | SHOP AROUND — Miracles, Tamla 54034 | | 5 |
| 20 | 23 | 35 | 42 | WINGS OF A DOVE — Ferlin Husky, Capitol 4406 | | 7 |
| 21 | 26 | 25 | 16 | BLUE TANGO — Bill Black's Combo, Hi 2027 | | 7 |
| 22 | 27 | 62 | 93 | BABY, O' BABY — Shells, Johnson 104 | | 4 |
| 23 | 38 | 57 | 100 | CALENDAR GIRL — Neil Sedaka, RCA Victor 7829 | | 4 |
| 24 | 17 | 15 | 17 | PERFIDIA — Ventures, Dolton 28 | | 11 |
| 25 | 42 | 63 | — | YOU ARE THE ONLY ONE — Ricky Nelson, Imperial 5707 | | 3 |
| 26 | 20 | 23 | 14 | SWAY — Bobby Rydell, Cameo 182 | | 10 |
| 27 | 40 | 51 | 57 | I'M HURTIN' — Roy Orbison, Monument 433 | | 5 |
| 28 | 28 | 32 | 36 | RUBY — Ray Charles, ABC-Paramount 10164 | | 8 |
| 29 | 25 | 22 | 19 | MY GIRL JOSEPHINE — Fats Domino, Imperial 5704 | | 12 |
| 30 | 37 | 55 | 77 | I COUNT THE TEARS — Drifters, Atlantic 2087 | | 4 |
| 31 | 21 | 18 | 11 | POETRY IN MOTION — Johnny Tillotson, Cadence 1384 | | 14 |
| 32 | 33 | 39 | 30 | I GOTTA KNOW — Elvis Presley, RCA Victor 7810 | | 9 |
| 33 | 24 | 19 | 18 | NEW ORLEANS — U.S. Bonds, Legrand 819 | | 13 |
| 34 | 44 | 48 | 54 | GEE WHIZ — Innocents, Indigo 111 | | 8 |
| 35 | 35 | 30 | 13 | STAY — Maurice Williams and the Zodiacs, Herald 552 | | 15 |
| 36 | 60 | 89 | 98 | LOVEY DOVEY — Buddy Knox, Liberty 55290 | | 4 |
| 37 | 34 | 31 | 41 | DOLL HOUSE — Donnie Brooks, Era 3028 | | 7 |
| 38 | 36 | 34 | 29 | SAD MOOD — Sam Cooke, RCA Victor 7816 | | 6 |
| 39 | 31 | 28 | 21 | ALONE AT LAST — Jackie Wilson, Brunswick 55170 | | 14 |
| 40 | 61 | 98 | — | THERE SHE GOES — Jerry Wallace, Challenge 59098 | | 3 |
| 41 | 50 | 49 | 44 | ONCE IN A WHILE — Chimes, Tag 444 | | 11 |
| 42 | 74 | 88 | 95 | PEPE — Duane Eddy, Jamie 1175 | | 4 |
| 43 | 62 | 72 | 43 | HOOCHIE COOCHIE COO — Hank Ballard and the Midnighters, King 5430 | | 6 |
| 44 | 58 | 67 | 60 | MAGNIFICENT SEVEN — Al Caiola, United Artists 261 | | 6 |
| 45 | 57 | 68 | 79 | MY LAST DATE (WITH YOU) — Skeeter Davis, RCA Victor 7825 | | 5 |
| 46 | 39 | 38 | 34 | BALLAD OF THE ALAMO — Marty Robbins, Columbia 41809 | AS | 13 |
| 47 | 54 | 50 | 75 | A PERFECT LOVE — Frankie Avalon, Chancellor 1065 | | 5 |
| 48 | 83 | — | — | EMOTIONS — Brenda Lee, Decca 31195 | | 2 |
| 49 | 46 | 59 | 61 | BUMBLE BEE — La Vern Baker, Atlantic 2077 | | 9 |
| 50 | 47 | 56 | 69 | DANCE BY THE LIGHT OF THE MOON — Olympics, Arvee 5020 | | 6 |
| 51 | 30 | 29 | 33 | FOOLS RUSH IN — Brook Benton, Mercury 71722 | | 9 |
| 52 | 43 | 52 | 51 | GONZO — James Booker, Peacock 1697 | | 10 |
| 53 | 59 | 70 | 50 | EXODUS — Mantovani, London 1953 | S | 8 |
| 54 | 63 | 66 | 82 | YOUR OTHER LOVE — Flamingos, End 1081 | | 4 |
| 55 | 69 | 83 | 90 | MY LAST DATE (WITH YOU) — Joni James, M-G-M 12933 | | 4 |
| 56 | 70 | 82 | — | CHERRY PINK AND APPLE BLOSSOM WHITE — Jerry Murad's Harmonicats, Columbia 41816 | | 3 |
| 57 | 72 | — | — | C'EST SI BON — Conway Twitty, M-G-M 12969 | | 2 |
| 58 | 55 | 41 | 24 | LAST DATE — Lawrence Welk, Dot 16145 | S | 8 |
| 59 | 73 | 81 | 48 | WALK SLOW — Little Willie John, King 5428 | | 7 |
| 60 | — | — | — | MY EMPTY ARMS — Jackie Wilson, Brunswick 55201 | | 1 |
| 61 | 56 | 69 | 81 | PUPPET SONG — Frankie Avalon, Chancellor 1065 | | 5 |
| 62 | 71 | 86 | 88 | HAPPY DAYS — Marv Johnson, United Artists 273 | | 5 |
| 63 | 79 | 87 | 91 | UTOPIA — Frank Gari, Crusade 1020 | | 4 |
| 64 | 68 | 79 | 85 | YOU DON'T WANT MY LOVE — Andy Williams, Cadence 1398 | | 5 |
| 65 | 87 | 99 | — | OH, HOW I MISS YOU TONIGHT — Jeanne Black, Capitol 4492 | | 3 |
| 66 | 92 | — | — | ALL IN MY MIND — Maxine Brown, Nomar 102 | | 2 |
| 67 | 94 | — | — | DON'T BELIEVE HIM, DONNA — Lenny Miles, Scepter 1212 | | 2 |
| 68 | 64 | 75 | — | HOW TO HANDLE A WOMAN — Johnny Mathis, Columbia 41866 | | 3 |
| 69 | 66 | 80 | — | (LET'S DO) THE HULLY GULLY — Bill Doggett, Warner Bros. 5181 | | 3 |
| 70 | 77 | 94 | — | ANGEL ON MY SHOULDER — Shelby Flint, Valiant WB 6001 | | 3 |
| 71 | 84 | — | — | WHAT WOULD I DO — Mickey and Sylvia, RCA Victor 7811 | | 2 |
| 72 | 86 | — | — | SPANISH HARLEM — Ben E. King, Atco 6185 | | 2 |
| 73 | 88 | — | — | THERE'S A MOON OUT TONIGHT — Capris, Old Town 1094 | | 2 |
| 74 | 85 | — | — | YES, I'M LONESOME TONIGHT — Thelma Carpenter, Coral 62241 | | 2 |
| 75 | 90 | — | — | FIRST TASTE OF LOVE — Ben E. King, Atco 6185 | | 2 |
| 76 | 95 | — | — | DON'T READ THE LETTER — Patti Page, Mercury 71745 | | 2 |
| 77 | 89 | 91 | 94 | WABASH BLUES — Viscounts, Madison 140 | | 6 |
| 78 | 98 | — | — | YES, I'M LONESOME TONIGHT — Dodie Stevens, Dot 16167 | | 2 |
| 79 | 81 | — | — | MILK COW BLUES — Ricky Nelson, Imperial 5707 | | 2 |
| 80 | — | — | — | LOST LOVE — H. B. Barnum, Eldo 111 | | 1 |
| 81 | — | — | — | WHEELS — String-A-Longs, Warwick 603 | | 1 |
| 82 | — | 86 | 89 | AGE FOR LOVE — Jimmy Charles, Promo 1003 | | 4 |
| 83 | 96 | — | — | I DON'T WANT NOBODY — Ella Johnson and Buddy Johnson Ork, Mercury 71723 | | 2 |
| 84 | — | — | — | AND THE HEAVENS CRIED — Ronnie Savoy, M-G-M 12955 | | 1 |
| 85 | 76 | 96 | — | WE HAVE LOVE — Dinah Washington, Mercury 71744 | | 3 |
| 86 | 91 | — | — | IF I KNEW — Nat King Cole, Capitol 4481 | | 2 |
| 87 | — | — | — | IF I DIDN'T CARE — Platters, Mercury 71749 | | 1 |
| 88 | — | — | — | WHAT AM I GONNA DO — Jimmy Clanton, Atco 607 | | 1 |
| 89 | — | — | — | IS THERE SOMETHING ON YOUR MIND — Jack Scott, Top Rank 2093 | | 1 |
| 90 | 41 | 37 | 31 | I'LL SAVE THE LAST DANCE FOR YOU — Damita Jo, Mercury 71690 | | 12 |
| 91 | 99 | — | — | SUGAR BEE — Cleveland Crochet, Goldband 1106 | | 2 |
| 92 | — | — | — | GHOST RIDERS IN THE SKY — Ramrods, Amy 813 | | 1 |
| 93 | 97 | — | — | OH LONESOME ME — Johnny Cash, Sun 355 | | 2 |
| 94 | — | — | — | CHILLS AND FEVER — Ronnie Love, Dot 16144 | | 1 |
| 95 | — | — | — | JIMMY'S GIRL — Johnny Tillotson, Cadence 1391 | | 1 |
| 96 | — | — | — | BABY SITTIN' BOOGIE — Buzz Clifford, Columbia 41876 | | 1 |
| 97 | — | — | — | YOU GOTTA LOVE HER WITH A FEELING — Freddy King, Federal 12384 | | 1 |
| 98 | — | — | — | THE MUSKRAT RAMBLE — Freddy Cannon, Swan 4066 | | 1 |
| 99 | — | — | 87 | ROCKIN' ROLLIN' OCEAN — Hank Snow, RCA Victor 7702 | | 4 |
| 100 | 78 | 100 | — | SPOONFUL — Etta and Harvey, Chess 1771 | | 3 |

# BILLBOARD HOT 100

**FOR WEEK ENDING JANUARY 22**

JANUARY 16, 1961

STAR PERFORMERS showed the greatest upward progress on Hot 100 this week.
S — Indicates that 45 r.p.m. stereo single version is available.
△ — Indicates that 33⅓ r.p.m. stereo single version is available.

Columns: THIS WEEK | ONE WEEK AGO | TWO WEEKS AGO | THREE WEEKS AGO | TITLE — Artist, Company, Record No. | STEREO | WEEKS ON CHART

| This | 1wk | 2wk | 3wk | Title — Artist, Company, Record No. | Wks |
|---|---|---|---|---|---|
| 1 | 1 | 2 | 2 | WONDERLAND BY NIGHT — Bert Kaempfert, Decca 31141 [S] | 10 |
| 2 | 2 | 1 | 1 | ARE YOU LONESOME TONIGHT — Elvis Presley, RCA Victor 7810 [S] | 10 |
| 3 | 3 | 4 | 5 | EXODUS — Ferrante and Teicher, United Artists 274 [S] | 10 |
| 4 | 5 | 14 | 20 | (WILL YOU LOVE ME) TOMORROW — Shirelles, Scepter 1211 | 9 |
| ★5 | 13 | 22 | 42 | CALCUTTA — Lawrence Welk, Dot 16161 | 6 |
| 6 | 7 | 9 | 13 | ANGEL BABY — Rosie and the Originals, Highland 1011 | 6 |
| 7 | 6 | 11 | 16 | RUBBER BALL — Bobby Vee, Liberty 55287 | 8 |
| 8 | 4 | 3 | 3 | LAST DATE — Floyd Cramer, RCA Victor 7775 [S] | 15 |
| 9 | 9 | 10 | 10 | CORINNA, CORINNA — Ray Peterson, Dunes 2002 | 9 |
| 10 | 8 | 6 | 6 | NORTH TO ALASKA — Johnny Horton, Columbia 41782 | 18 |
| 11 | 11 | 5 | 4 | A THOUSAND STARS — Kathy Young and the Innocents, Indigo 108 | 13 |
| ★12 | 19 | 32 | 53 | SHOP AROUND — Miracles, Tamla 54034 | 6 |
| 13 | 10 | 8 | 8 | YOU'RE SIXTEEN — Johnny Burnette, Liberty 55285 | 12 |
| ★14 | 23 | 38 | 57 | CALENDAR GIRL — Neil Sedaka, RCA Victor 7829 | 5 |
| 15 | 15 | 16 | 17 | WONDERLAND BY NIGHT — Louis Prima, Dot 16151 [S] | 10 |
| 16 | 16 | 12 | 9 | SAILOR (YOUR HOME IS IN THE SEA) — Lolita, Kapp 349 | 13 |
| 17 | 12 | 7 | 7 | MANY TEARS AGO — Connie Francis, M-G-M 12964 | 11 |
| 18 | 14 | 13 | 11 | HE WILL BREAK YOUR HEART — Jerry Butler, Vee Jay 354 | 12 |
| 19 | 17 | 15 | 12 | LONELY TEENAGER — Dion, Laurie 3070 | 14 |
| 20 | 18 | 19 | 27 | WONDERLAND BY NIGHT — Anita Bryant, Carlton 537 | 7 |
| 21 | 22 | 27 | 62 | BABY, O' BABY — Shells, Johnson 104 | 5 |
| 22 | 21 | 26 | 25 | BLUE TANGO — Bill Black's Combo, Hi 2027 | 8 |
| 23 | 20 | 23 | 35 | WINGS OF A DOVE — Ferlin Husky, Capitol 4406 | 8 |
| 24 | 30 | 37 | 55 | I COUNT THE TEARS — Drifters, Atlantic 2087 | 5 |
| ★25 | 41 | 50 | 49 | ONCE IN A WHILE — Chimes, Tag 444 | 12 |
| ★26 | 48 | 83 | — | EMOTIONS — Brenda Lee, Decca 31195 | 3 |
| 27 | 25 | 42 | 63 | YOU ARE THE ONLY ONE — Ricky Nelson, Imperial 5707 | 4 |
| 28 | 34 | 44 | 48 | GEE WHIZ — Innocents, Indigo 111 | 9 |
| ★29 | 60 | — | — | MY EMPTY ARMS — Jackie Wilson, Brunswick 55201 | 2 |
| 30 | 27 | 40 | 51 | I'M HURTIN' — Roy Orbison, Monument 433 | 6 |
| 31 | 36 | 60 | 89 | LOVEY DOVEY — Buddy Knox, Liberty 55290 | 5 |
| 32 | 29 | 25 | 22 | MY GIRL JOSEPHINE — Fats Domino, Imperial 5704 | 13 |
| 33 | 24 | 17 | 15 | PERFIDIA — Ventures, Dolton 28 | 12 |
| ★34 | 45 | 57 | 68 | MY LAST DATE (WITH YOU) — Skeeter Davis, RCA Victor 7825 | 6 |
| 35 | 43 | 62 | 72 | HOOCHIE COOCHIE COO — Hank Ballard and the Midnighters, King 5430 | 7 |
| 36 | 26 | 20 | 23 | SWAY — Bobby Rydell, Cameo 182 | 11 |
| 37 | 32 | 33 | 39 | I GOTTA KNOW — Elvis Presley, RCA Victor 7810 | 10 |
| 38 | 42 | 74 | 88 | PEPE — Duane Eddy, Jamie 1175 | 5 |
| ★39 | 57 | 72 | — | C'EST SI BON — Conway Twitty, M-G-M 12969 | 3 |
| 40 | 44 | 58 | 67 | MAGNIFICENT SEVEN — Al Caiola, United Artists 261 | 7 |
| 41 | 53 | 59 | 70 | EXODUS — Mantovani, London 1953 [S] | 9 |
| 42 | 40 | 61 | 98 | THERE SHE GOES — Jerry Wallace, Challenge 59098 | 4 |
| 43 | 37 | 34 | 31 | DOLL HOUSE — Donnie Brooks, Era 3028 | 8 |
| 44 | 35 | 35 | 30 | STAY — Maurice Williams and the Zodiacs, Herald 552 | 16 |
| ★45 | 55 | 69 | 83 | MY LAST DATE (WITH YOU) — Joni James, M-G-M 12933 | 5 |
| 46 | 73 | 88 | — | THERE'S A MOON OUT TONIGHT — Capris, Old Town 1094 | 3 |
| 47 | 31 | 21 | 18 | POETRY IN MOTION — Johnny Tillotson, Cadence 1384 | 15 |
| ★48 | 81 | — | — | WHEELS — String-A-Longs, Warwick 603 | 2 |
| 49 | 38 | 36 | 34 | SAD MOOD — Sam Cooke, RCA Victor 7816 | 7 |
| 50 | 28 | 28 | 32 | RUBY — Ray Charles, ABC-Paramount 10164 | 9 |
| 51 | 49 | 46 | 59 | BUMBLE BEE — La Verne Baker, Atlantic 2077 | 10 |
| ★52 | 63 | 79 | 87 | UTOPIA — Frank Gari, Crusade 1020 | 5 |
| 53 | 47 | 54 | 50 | A PERFECT LOVE — Frankie Avalon, Chancellor 1065 | 6 |
| 54 | 66 | 92 | — | ALL IN MY MIND — Maxine Brown, Nomar 102 | 3 |
| 55 | 52 | 43 | 52 | GONZO — James Booker, Peacock 1697 | 11 |
| 56 | 39 | 31 | 28 | ALONE AT LAST — Jackie Wilson, Brunswick 55170 | 15 |
| 57 | 61 | 56 | 69 | PUPPET SONG — Frankie Avalon, Chancellor 1065 | 6 |
| 58 | 62 | 71 | 86 | HAPPY DAYS — Marv Johnson, United Artists 273 | 6 |
| 59 | 72 | 86 | — | SPANISH HARLEM — Ben E. King, Atco 6185 | 3 |
| 60 | 67 | 94 | — | DON'T BELIEVE HIM, DONNA — Lenny Miles, Scepter 1212 | 3 |
| 61 | 70 | 77 | 94 | ANGEL ON MY SHOULDER — Shelby Flint, Valiant WB 6001 | 4 |
| 62 | 58 | 55 | 41 | LAST DATE — Lawrence Welk, Dot 16145 [S] | 9 |
| 63 | 65 | 87 | 99 | OH, HOW I MISS YOU TONIGHT — Jeanne Black, Capitol 4492 | 4 |
| 64 | 64 | 68 | 79 | YOU DON'T WANT MY LOVE — Andy Williams, Cadence 1398 | 6 |
| 65 | 76 | 95 | — | DON'T READ THE LETTER — Patti Page, Mercury 71745 | 3 |
| 66 | 56 | 70 | 82 | CHERRY PINK AND APPLE BLOSSOM WHITE — Jerry Murad's Harmonicats, Columbia 41816 | 4 |
| 67 | 74 | 85 | — | YES, I'M LONESOME TONIGHT — Thelma Carpenter, Coral 62241 | 3 |
| 68 | 59 | 73 | 81 | WALK SLOW — Little Willie John, King 5428 | 8 |
| 69 | 75 | 90 | — | FIRST TASTE OF LOVE — Ben E. King, Atco 6185 | 3 |
| 70 | 80 | — | — | LOST LOVE — H. B. Barnum, Eldo 111 | 2 |
| 71 | 54 | 63 | 66 | YOUR OTHER LOVE — Flamingos, End 1081 | 5 |
| 72 | — | — | — | NO ONE — Connie Francis, M-G-M 12971 | 1 |
| ★73 | 88 | — | — | WHAT AM I GONNA DO — Jimmy Clanton, Ace 607 | 2 |
| 74 | 78 | 98 | — | YES, I'M LONESOME TONIGHT — Dodie Stevens, Dot 16167 | 3 |
| 75 | — | — | — | AT LAST — Etta James, Argo 5380 | 1 |
| 76 | 71 | 84 | — | WHAT WOULD I DO — Mickey and Sylvia, RCA Victor 7811 | 3 |
| 77 | 96 | — | — | BABY SITTIN' BOOGIE — Buzz Clifford, Columbia 41876 | 2 |
| 78 | 83 | 96 | — | I DON'T WANT NOBODY — Ella Johnson and Buddy Johnson Ork, Mercury 71723 | 3 |
| 79 | 87 | — | — | IF I DIDN'T CARE — Platters, Mercury 71749 | 2 |
| 80 | 79 | 81 | — | MILK COW BLUES — Ricky Nelson, Imperial 5707 | 3 |
| 81 | 82 | — | 86 | AGE FOR LOVE — Jimmy Charles, Promo 1003 | 5 |
| 82 | 50 | 47 | 56 | DANCE BY THE LIGHT OF THE MOON — Olympics, Arvee 5020 | 7 |
| 83 | — | — | — | SOUND-OFF — Titus Turner, Jamis 1174 | 1 |
| 84 | 92 | — | — | GHOST RIDERS IN THE SKY — Ramrods, Amy 813 | 2 |
| 85 | 91 | 99 | — | SUGAR BEE — Cleveland Crochet, Goldband 1106 | 3 |
| 86 | 94 | — | — | CHILLS AND FEVER — Ronnie Love, Dot 16144 | 2 |
| 87 | — | — | — | FLAMINGO EXPRESS — Royaltones, Goldisc 3011 | 1 |
| 88 | 77 | 89 | 91 | WABASH BLUES — Viscounts, Madison 140 | 7 |
| 89 | — | — | — | THE STORY OF MY LOVE — Paul Anka, ABC-Paramount 10168 | 1 |
| 90 | — | — | — | WHERE THE BOYS ARE — Connie Francis, M-G-M 12971 | 1 |
| 91 | 98 | — | — | THE MUSKRAT RAMBLE — Freddy Cannon, Swan 4066 | 2 |
| 92 | 95 | — | — | JIMMY'S GIRL — Johnny Tillotson, Cadence 1391 | 2 |
| 93 | 97 | — | — | YOU GOTTA LOVE HER WITH A FEELING — Freddy King, Federal 12384 | 2 |
| 94 | 51 | 30 | 29 | FOOLS RUSH IN — Brook Benton, Mercury 71722 | 10 |
| 95 | — | — | — | THEM THAT GOT — Ray Charles, ABC-Paramount 10141 | 1 |
| 96 | 84 | — | — | AND THE HEAVENS CRIED — Ronnie Savoy, M-G-M 12955 | 2 |
| 97 | 33 | 24 | 19 | NEW ORLEANS — U. S. Bonds, Legrand 1003 | 14 |
| 98 | — | — | — | GIFT OF LOVE — Van Dykes, Donna 1333 | 1 |
| 99 | — | — | — | WHEN I FALL IN LOVE — Etta Jones, King 5424 | 1 |
| 100 | — | — | — | I REMEMBER — Maurice Williams and the Zodiacs, Herald 556 | 1 |

# BILLBOARD HOT 100

**For Week Ending January 29** — January 23, 1961

| This Week | 1 Wk | 2 Wks | 3 Wks | Title / Artist / Company / Record No. | Weeks on Chart |
|---|---|---|---|---|---|
| 1 | 1 | 1 | 2 | WONDERLAND BY NIGHT — Bert Kaempfert, Decca 31141 | 11 |
| 2 | 3 | 3 | 4 | EXODUS — Ferrante and Teicher, United Artists 274 | 11 |
| 3 | 5 | 13 | 22 | CALCUTTA — Lawrence Welk, Dot 16161 | 7 |
| 4 | 4 | 5 | 14 | (WILL YOU LOVE ME) TOMORROW — Shirelles, Scepter 1211 | 10 |
| 5 | 6 | 7 | 9 | ANGEL BABY — Rosie and the Originals, Highland 1011 | 7 |
| 6 | 2 | 2 | 1 | ARE YOU LONESOME TONIGHT — Elvis Presley, RCA Victor 7810 | 11 |
| 7 | 12 | 19 | 32 | SHOP AROUND — Miracles, Tamla 54034 | 7 |
| 8 | 14 | 23 | 38 | CALENDAR GIRL — Neil Sedaka, RCA Victor 7829 | 6 |
| 9 | 7 | 6 | 11 | RUBBER BALL — Bobby Vee, Liberty 55287 | 9 |
| 10 | 9 | 9 | 10 | CORINNA, CORINNA — Ray Peterson, Dunes 2002 | 10 |
| 11 | 8 | 4 | 3 | LAST DATE — Floyd Cramer, RCA Victor 7775 | 16 |
| 12 | 10 | 8 | 6 | NORTH TO ALASKA — Johnny Horton, Columbia 41782 | 19 |
| 13 | 26 | 48 | 83 | EMOTIONS — Brenda Lee, Decca 31195 | 4 |
| 14 | 25 | 41 | 50 | ONCE IN A WHILE — Chimes, Tag 444 | 13 |
| 15 | 11 | 11 | 5 | A THOUSAND STARS — Kathy Young and the Innocents, Indigo 108 | 14 |
| 16 | 23 | 20 | 23 | WINGS OF A DOVE — Ferlin Husky, Capitol 4406 | 9 |
| 17 | 29 | 60 | — | MY EMPTY ARMS — Jackie Wilson, Brunswick 55201 | 3 |
| 18 | 16 | 16 | 12 | SAILOR (YOUR HOME IS IN THE SEA) — Lolita, Kapp 349 | 14 |
| 19 | 15 | 15 | 16 | WONDERLAND BY NIGHT — Louis Prima, Dot 16151 | 11 |
| 20 | 13 | 10 | 8 | YOU'RE SIXTEEN — Johnny Burnette, Liberty 55285 | 13 |
| 21 | 18 | 14 | 13 | HE WILL BREAK YOUR HEART — Jerry Butler, Vee Jay 354 | 13 |
| 22 | 24 | 30 | 37 | I COUNT THE TEARS — Drifters, Atlantic 2087 | 6 |
| 23 | 19 | 17 | 15 | LONELY TEENAGER — Dion, Laurie 3070 | 15 |
| 24 | 21 | 22 | 27 | BABY, O' BABY — Shells, Johnson 104 | 6 |
| 25 | 31 | 36 | 60 | LOVEY DOVEY — Buddy Knox, Liberty 55290 | 6 |
| 26 | 34 | 45 | 57 | MY LAST DATE (WITH YOU) — Skeeter Davis, RCA Victor 7825 | 7 |
| 27 | 20 | 18 | 19 | WONDERLAND BY NIGHT — Anita Bryant, Carlton 537 | 8 |
| 28 | 32 | 29 | 25 | MY GIRL JOSEPHINE — Fats Domino, Imperial 5704 | 14 |
| 29 | 38 | 42 | 74 | PEPE — Duane Eddy, Jamie 1175 | 6 |
| 30 | 35 | 43 | 62 | HOOCHIE COOCHIE COO — Hank Ballard and the Midnighters, King 5430 | 8 |
| 31 | 41 | 53 | 59 | EXODUS — Mantovani, London 1953 | 10 |
| 32 | 39 | 57 | 72 | C'EST SI BON — Conway Twitty, MGM 12969 | 4 |
| 33 | 27 | 25 | 42 | YOU ARE THE ONLY ONE — Ricky Nelson, Imperial 5707 | 5 |
| 34 | 48 | 81 | — | WHEELS — String-A-Longs, Warwick 603 | 3 |
| 35 | 40 | 44 | 58 | MAGNIFICENT SEVEN — Al Caiola, United Artists 261 | 8 |
| 36 | 46 | 73 | 88 | THERE'S A MOON OUT TONIGHT — Capris, Old Town 1094 | 4 |
| 37 | 17 | 12 | 7 | MANY TEARS AGO — Connie Francis, MGM 12964 | 12 |
| 38 | 45 | 55 | 69 | MY LAST DATE (WITH YOU) — Joni James, MGM 12933 | 6 |
| 39 | 28 | 34 | 44 | GEE WHIZ — Innocents, Indigo 111 | 10 |
| 40 | 22 | 21 | 26 | BLUE TANGO — Bill Black's Combo, Hi 2027 | 9 |
| 41 | 42 | 40 | 61 | THERE SHE GOES — Jerry Wallace, Challenge 59098 | 5 |
| 42 | 90 | — | — | WHERE THE BOYS ARE — Connie Francis, MGM 12971 | 2 |
| 43 | 37 | 32 | 33 | I GOTTA KNOW — Elvis Presley, RCA Victor 7810 | 11 |
| 44 | 52 | 63 | 79 | UTOPIA — Frank Gari, Crusade 1020 | 6 |
| 45 | 59 | 72 | 86 | SPANISH HARLEM — Ben E. King, Atco 6185 | 4 |
| 46 | 30 | 27 | 40 | I'M HURTIN' — Roy Orbison, Monument 433 | 7 |
| 47 | 54 | 66 | 92 | ALL IN MY MIND — Maxine Brown, Nomar 102 | 4 |
| 48 | 43 | 37 | 34 | DOLL HOUSE — Donnie Brooks, Era 3028 | 9 |
| 49 | — | — | — | PONY TIME — Chubby Checker, Parkway 818 | 1 |
| 50 | 79 | 87 | — | IF I DIDN'T CARE — Platters, Mercury 71749 | 3 |
| 51 | 60 | 67 | 94 | DON'T BELIEVE HIM, DONNA — Lenny Miles, Scepter 1212 | 4 |
| 52 | 51 | 49 | 46 | BUMBLE BEE — La Verne Baker, Atlantic 2077 | 11 |
| 53 | — | — | — | GOOD TIME BABY — Bobby Rydell, Cameo 186 | 1 |
| 54 | 33 | 24 | 17 | PERFIDIA — Ventures, Dolton 28 | 13 |
| 55 | 77 | 96 | — | BABY SITTIN' BOOGIE — Buzz Clifford, Columbia 41876 | 3 |
| 56 | 73 | 88 | — | WHAT AM I GONNA DO — Jimmy Clanton, Ace 607 | 3 |
| 57 | 61 | 70 | 77 | ANGEL ON MY SHOULDER — Shelby Flint, Valiant WB 6001 | 5 |
| 58 | 67 | 74 | 85 | YES, I'M LONESOME TONIGHT — Thelma Carpenter, Coral 62241 | 4 |
| 59 | 44 | 35 | 35 | STAY — Maurice Williams and the Zodiacs, Herald 552 | 17 |
| 60 | — | — | — | TEAR OF THE YEAR — Jackie Wilson, Brunswick 55201 | 1 |
| 61 | 69 | 75 | 90 | FIRST TASTE OF LOVE — Ben E. King, Atco 6185 | 4 |
| 62 | 70 | 80 | — | LOST LOVE — H. B. Barnum, Eldo 111 | 3 |
| 63 | 74 | 78 | 98 | YES, I'M LONESOME TONIGHT — Dodie Stevens, Dot 16167 | 4 |
| 64 | 75 | — | — | AT LAST — Etta James, Argo 5380 | 2 |
| 65 | 91 | 98 | — | THE MUSKRAT RAMBLE — Freddy Cannon, Swan 4066 | 3 |
| 66 | 72 | — | — | NO ONE — Connie Francis, MGM 12971 | 2 |
| 67 | 89 | — | — | THE STORY OF MY LOVE — Paul Anka, ABC-Paramount 10168 | 2 |
| 68 | — | — | — | DEDICATED TO THE ONE I LOVE — Shirelles, Scepter 1203 | 1 |
| 69 | 81 | 82 | — | AGE FOR LOVE — Jimmy Charles, Promo 1003 | 6 |
| 70 | 65 | 76 | 95 | DON'T READ THE LETTER — Patti Page, Mercury 71745 | 4 |
| 71 | 58 | 62 | 71 | HAPPY DAYS — Marv Johnson, United Artists 273 | 7 |
| 72 | 86 | 94 | — | CHILLS AND FEVER — Ronnie Love, Dot 16144 | 3 |
| 73 | 76 | 71 | 84 | WHAT WOULD I DO — Mickey and Sylvia, RCA Victor 7811 | 4 |
| 74 | 92 | 95 | — | JIMMY'S GIRL — Johnny Tillotson, Cadence 1391 | 3 |
| 75 | 62 | 58 | 55 | LAST DATE — Lawrence Welk, Dot 16145 | 10 |
| 76 | 49 | 38 | 36 | SAD MOOD — Sam Cooke, RCA Victor 7816 | 8 |
| 77 | 83 | — | — | SOUND-OFF — Titus Turner, Jamie 1174 | 2 |
| 78 | — | — | — | WHAT A PRICE — Fats Domino, Imperial 5723 | 1 |
| 79 | — | — | — | LEAVE MY KITTEN ALONE — Little Willie John, King 5452 | 1 |
| 80 | 85 | 91 | 99 | SUGAR BEE — Cleveland Crochet, Goldband 1106 | 4 |
| 81 | 84 | 92 | — | GHOST RIDERS IN THE SKY — Ramrods, Amy 813 | 3 |
| 82 | 87 | — | — | FLAMINGO EXPRESS — Royaltones, Goldisc 3011 | 2 |
| 83 | — | — | — | AIN'T THAT JUST LIKE A WOMAN — Fats Domino, Imperial 5723 | 1 |
| 84 | 99 | — | — | WHEN I FALL IN LOVE — Etta Jones, King 5424 | 2 |
| 85 | 95 | — | — | THEM THAT GOT — Ray Charles, ABC-Paramount 10141 | 2 |
| 86 | 100 | — | — | I REMEMBER — Maurice Williams and the Zodiacs, Herald 556 | 2 |
| 87 | — | — | — | PONY TIME — Don Covay and the Goodtimers, Arnold 1002 | 1 |
| 88 | — | — | — | DEDICATED TO THE ONE I LOVE — Five Royales, King 5453 | 1 |
| 89 | 64 | 64 | 68 | YOU DON'T WANT MY LOVE — Andy Williams, Cadence 1398 | 7 |
| 90 | — | — | — | EXODUS SONG (THIS LAND IS MINE) — Pat Boone, Dot 16187 | 1 |
| 91 | 98 | — | — | GIFT OF LOVE — Van Dykes, Donna 1333 | 2 |
| 92 | — | — | — | TROUBLE IN MIND — Nina Simone, Colpix 175 | 1 |
| 93 | — | — | — | RAM-BUNK-SHUSH — Ventures, Dolton 32 | 1 |
| 94 | — | — | — | APACHE — Jorgen Ingmann, Atco 6184 | 1 |
| 95 | — | — | — | TONIGHT—TONIGHT — Melo Kings, Herald 502 | 1 |
| 96 | 57 | 61 | 56 | PUPPET SONG — Frankie Avalon, Chancellor 1065 | 7 |
| 97 | 63 | 65 | 87 | OH, HOW I MISS YOU TONIGHT — Jeanne Black, Capitol 4492 | 5 |
| 98 | — | — | — | GINNIE BELL — Paul Dino, Promo 2180 | 1 |
| 99 | — | — | — | I REMEMBER (IN THE STILL OF THE NIGHT) — Five Satins, Ember 1005 | 1 |
| 100 | — | — | — | CHARLENA — The Sevilles, J C D 116 | 1 |

# BILLBOARD HOT 100

**For Week Ending February 5** — January 30, 1961

| This Week | 1 Wk Ago | 2 Wks Ago | 3 Wks Ago | Title / Artist, Company, Record No. | Weeks on Chart |
|---|---|---|---|---|---|
| 1 | 4 | 4 | 5 | (WILL YOU LOVE ME) TOMORROW — Shirelles, Scepter 1211 | 11 |
| 2 | 3 | 5 | 13 | CALCUTTA — Lawrence Welk, Dot 16161 | 8 |
| 3 | 2 | 3 | 3 | EXODUS — Ferrante and Teicher, United Artists 274 | 12 |
| 4 | 1 | 1 | 1 | WONDERLAND BY NIGHT — Bert Kaempfert, Decca 31141 | 12 |
| 5 | 7 | 12 | 19 | SHOP AROUND — Miracles, Tamla 54034 | 8 |
| 6 | 5 | 6 | 7 | ANGEL BABY — Rosie and the Originals, Highland 1011 | 8 |
| 7 | 8 | 14 | 23 | CALENDAR GIRL — Neil Sedaka, RCA Victor 7829 | 7 |
| 8 | 13 | 26 | 48 | EMOTIONS — Brenda Lee, Decca 31195 | 5 |
| 9 | 9 | 7 | 6 | RUBBER BALL — Bobby Vee, Liberty 55287 | 10 |
| 10 | 6 | 2 | 2 | ARE YOU LONESOME TONIGHT — Elvis Presley, RCA Victor 7810 | 12 |
| 11 | 10 | 9 | 9 | CORINNA, CORINNA — Ray Peterson, Dunes 2002 | 11 |
| 12 | 14 | 25 | 41 | ONCE IN A WHILE — Chimes, Tag 444 | 14 |
| 13 | 12 | 10 | 8 | NORTH TO ALASKA — Johnny Horton, Columbia 41782 | 20 |
| 14 | 11 | 8 | 4 | LAST DATE — Floyd Cramer, RCA Victor 7775 | 17 |
| 15 | 17 | 29 | 60 | MY EMPTY ARMS — Jackie Wilson, Brunswick 55201 | 4 |
| 16 | 16 | 23 | 20 | WINGS OF A DOVE — Ferlin Husky, Capitol 4406 | 10 |
| 17 | 22 | 24 | 30 | I COUNT THE TEARS — Drifters, Atlantic 2087 | 7 |
| 18 | 15 | 11 | 11 | A THOUSAND STARS — Kathy Young and the Innocents, Indigo 108 | 15 |
| 19 | 18 | 16 | 16 | SAILOR (YOUR HOME IS IN THE SEA) — Lolita, Kapp 349 | 15 |
| 20 | 29 | 38 | 42 | PEPE — Duane Eddy, Jamie 1175 | 7 |
| 21 | 36 | 46 | 73 | THERE'S A MOON OUT TONIGHT — Capris, Old Town 1094 | 5 |
| 22 | 34 | 48 | 81 | WHEELS — String-A-Longs, Warwick 603 | 4 |
| 23 | 30 | 35 | 43 | HOOCHIE COOCHIE COO — Hank Ballard and the Midnighters, King 5430 | 9 |
| 24 | 20 | 13 | 10 | YOU'RE SIXTEEN — Johnny Burnette, Liberty 55285 | 14 |
| 25 | 32 | 39 | 57 | C'EST SI BON — Conway Twitty, MGM 12969 | 5 |
| 26 | 41 | 42 | 40 | THERE SHE GOES — Jerry Wallace, Challenge 59098 | 6 |
| 27 | 21 | 18 | 14 | HE WILL BREAK YOUR HEART — Jerry Butler, Vee Jay 354 | 14 |
| 28 | 19 | 15 | 15 | WONDERLAND BY NIGHT — Louis Prima, Dot 16151 | 12 |
| 29 | 24 | 21 | 22 | BABY, O' BABY — Shells, Johnson 104 | 7 |
| 30 | 42 | 90 | — | WHERE THE BOYS ARE — Connie Francis, MGM 12071 | 3 |
| 31 | 49 | — | — | PONY TIME — Chubby Checker, Parkway 818 | 2 |
| 32 | 27 | 20 | 18 | WONDERLAND BY NIGHT — Anita Bryant, Carlton 537 | 9 |
| 33 | 47 | 54 | 66 | ALL IN MY MIND — Maxine Brown, Nomar 103 | 5 |
| 34 | 45 | 59 | 72 | SPANISH HARLEM — Ben E. King, Atco 6185 | 5 |
| 35 | 55 | 77 | 96 | BABY SITTIN' BOOGIE — Buzz Clifford, Columbia 41876 | 4 |
| 36 | 25 | 31 | 36 | LOVEY DOVEY — Buddy Knox, Liberty 55290 | 7 |
| 37 | 31 | 41 | 53 | EXODUS — Mantovani, London 1953 | 11 |
| 38 | 33 | 27 | 25 | YOU ARE THE ONLY ONE — Ricky Nelson, Imperial 5707 | 6 |
| 39 | 35 | 40 | 44 | MAGNIFICENT SEVEN — Al Caiola, United Artists 261 | 9 |
| 40 | 50 | 79 | 87 | IF I DIDN'T CARE — Platters, Mercury 71749 | 4 |
| 41 | 51 | 60 | 67 | DON'T BELIEVE HIM, DONNA — Lenny Miles, Scepter 1212 | 5 |
| 42 | 53 | — | — | GOOD TIME BABY — Bobby Rydell, Cameo 186 | 2 |
| 43 | — | — | — | I'M LEARNING ABOUT LOVE — Brenda Lee, Decca 31195 | 1 |
| 44 | 60 | — | — | TEAR OF THE YEAR — Jackie Wilson, Brunswick 55201 | 2 |
| 45 | 44 | 52 | 63 | UTOPIA — Frank Gari, Crusade 1020 | 7 |
| 46 | 67 | 89 | — | THE STORY OF MY LOVE — Paul Anka, ABC-Paramount 10168 | 3 |
| 47 | 68 | — | — | DEDICATED TO THE ONE I LOVE — Shirelles, Scepter 1203 | 2 |
| 48 | 37 | 17 | 12 | MANY TEARS AGO — Connie Francis, MGM 12964 | 13 |
| 49 | 64 | 75 | — | AT LAST — Etta James, Argo 5380 | 3 |
| 50 | 56 | 73 | 88 | WHAT AM I GONNA DO — Jimmy Clanton, Ace 607 | 4 |
| 51 | 66 | 72 | — | NO ONE — Connie Francis, MGM 12971 | 3 |
| 52 | 78 | — | — | WHAT A PRICE — Fats Domino, Imperial 5723 | 2 |
| 53 | 57 | 61 | 70 | ANGEL ON MY SHOULDER — Shelby Flint, Valiant WB 6001 | 6 |
| 54 | 61 | 69 | 75 | FIRST TASTE OF LOVE — Ben E. King, Atco 6185 | 5 |
| 55 | 58 | 67 | 74 | YES, I'M LONESOME TONIGHT — Thelma Carpenter, Coral 62241 | 5 |
| 56 | 65 | 91 | 98 | THE MUSKRAT RAMBLE — Freddy Cannon, Swan 4066 | 4 |
| 57 | 62 | 70 | 80 | LOST LOVE — H. B. Barnum, Eldo 111 | 4 |
| 58 | 48 | 43 | 37 | DOLL HOUSE — Donnie Brooks, Era 3028 | 10 |
| 59 | 83 | — | — | AIN'T THAT JUST LIKE A WOMAN — Fats Domino, Imperial 5723 | 2 |
| 60 | 63 | 74 | 78 | YES, I'M LONESOME TONIGHT — Dodie Stevens, Dot 16167 | 5 |
| 61 | 59 | 44 | 35 | STAY — Maurice Williams and the Zodiacs, Herald 552 | 18 |
| 62 | — | — | — | YOU CAN HAVE HER — Roy Hamilton, Epic 9434 | 1 |
| 63 | 85 | 95 | — | THEM THAT GOT — Ray Charles, ABC-Paramount 10141 | 3 |
| 64 | 73 | 76 | 71 | WHAT WOULD I DO — Mickey and Sylvia, RCA Victor 7811 | 5 |
| 65 | 23 | 19 | 17 | LONELY TEENAGER — Dion, Laurie 3070 | 16 |
| 66 | 69 | 81 | 82 | AGE FOR LOVE — Jimmy Charles, Promo 1003 | 7 |
| 67 | — | — | — | EBONY EYES — Everly Brothers, Warner Bros. 5199 | 1 |
| 68 | 81 | 84 | 92 | GHOST RIDERS IN THE SKY — Ramrods, Amy 813 | 4 |
| 69 | 79 | — | — | LEAVE MY KITTEN ALONE — Little Willie John, King 5452 | 2 |
| 70 | 26 | 34 | 45 | MY LAST DATE (WITH YOU) — Skeeter Davis, RCA Victor 7825 | 8 |
| 71 | 74 | 92 | 95 | JIMMY'S GIRL — Johnny Tillotson, Cadence 1391 | 4 |
| 72 | — | — | — | DON'T WORRY (LIKE ALL THE OTHER TIMES) — Marty Robbins, Columbia 41922 | 1 |
| 73 | 93 | — | — | RAM-BUNK-SHUSH — Ventures, Dolton 32 | 2 |
| 74 | 40 | 22 | 21 | BLUE TANGO — Bill Black's Combo, Hi 2027 | 10 |
| 75 | 39 | 28 | 34 | GEE WHIZ — Innocents, Indigo 111 | 11 |
| 76 | 46 | 30 | 27 | I'M HURTIN' — Roy Orbison, Monument 433 | 8 |
| 77 | — | — | — | (I WANNA) LOVE MY LIFE AWAY — Gene Pitney, Musicor 1002 | 1 |
| 78 | — | — | — | CLOSE TOGETHER — Jimmy Reed, Vee Jay 373 | 1 |
| 79 | 77 | 83 | — | SOUND-OFF — Titus Turner, Jamie 1174 | 3 |
| 80 | 84 | 99 | — | WHEN I FALL IN LOVE — Etta Jones, King 5424 | 3 |
| 81 | — | 66 | 56 | CHERRY PINK AND APPLE BLOSSOM WHITE — Jerry Murad's Harmonicats, Columbia 41816 | 5 |
| 82 | 90 | — | — | EXODUS SONG (THIS LAND IS MINE) — Pat Boone, Dot 16176 | 2 |
| 83 | 94 | — | — | APACHE — Jorgen Ingmann, Atco 6184 | 2 |
| 84 | — | 82 | 50 | DANCE BY THE LIGHT OF THE MOON — Olympics, Arvee 5020 | 8 |
| 85 | 88 | — | — | DEDICATED TO THE ONE I LOVE — Five Royales, King 5453 | 2 |
| 86 | — | — | — | LEAVE MY KITTEN ALONE — Johnny Preston, Mercury 71761 | 1 |
| 87 | 87 | — | — | PONY TIME — Don Corvay and the Goodtimers, Arnold 1002 | 2 |
| 88 | 38 | 45 | 55 | MY LAST DATE (WITH YOU) — Joni James, MGM 12933 | 7 |
| 89 | 86 | 100 | — | I REMEMBER — Maurice Williams and the Zodiacs, Herald 556 | 3 |
| 90 | 98 | — | — | GINNIE BELL — Paul Dino, Promo 2180 | 2 |
| 91 | 80 | 85 | 91 | SUGAR BEE — Cleveland Crochet, Goldband 1106 | 5 |
| 92 | 72 | 86 | 94 | CHILLS AND FEVER — Ronnie Love, Dot 16144 | 4 |
| 93 | 92 | — | — | TROUBLE IN MIND — Nina Simone, Colpix 175 | 2 |
| 94 | 28 | 32 | 29 | MY GIRL JOSEPHINE — Fats Domino, Imperial 5704 | 15 |
| 95 | 100 | — | — | CHARLENA — The Sevilles, JCD 116 | 2 |
| 96 | — | — | — | GEE WHIZ (LOOK AT HIS EYES) — Carla Thomas, Atlantic 2086 | 1 |
| 97 | 82 | 87 | — | FLAMINGO EXPRESS — Royaltones, Goldisc 3011 | 3 |
| 98 | — | — | — | HONKY TONK, PART II — Bill Doggett, King 5444 | 1 |
| 99 | — | — | — | BYE, BYE, BABY — Mary Wells, Motown 1003 | 1 |
| 100 | — | — | — | WAIT A MINUTE — Coasters, Atco 6186 | 1 |

# BILLBOARD HOT 100

**For Week Ending February 12**

*STAR PERFORMERS showed the greatest upward progress on Hot 100 this week.*
S — Indicates that 45 r.p.m. stereo single version is available.
△ — Indicates that 33⅓ r.p.m. stereo single version is available.

Columns: THIS WEEK | ONE WEEK AGO | TWO WEEKS AGO | THREE WEEKS AGO | TITLE — Artist, Company, Record No. | STEREO | WEEKS ON CHART

| This | 1wk | 2wk | 3wk | Title — Artist, Company, Record No. | Stereo | Wks |
|---|---|---|---|---|---|---|
| 1 | 1 | 4 | 4 | (WILL YOU LOVE ME) TOMORROW — Shirelles, Scepter 1211 | | 12 |
| 2 | 2 | 3 | 5 | CALCUTTA — Lawrence Welk, Dot 16161 | | 9 |
| 3 | 3 | 2 | 3 | EXODUS — Ferrante and Teicher, United Artists 274 | S | 13 |
| 4 | 5 | 7 | 12 | SHOP AROUND — Miracles, Tamla 54034 | | 9 |
| 5 | 7 | 8 | 14 | CALENDAR GIRL — Neil Sedaka, RCA Victor 7829 | S | 8 |
| 6 | 4 | 1 | 1 | WONDERLAND BY NIGHT — Bert Kaempfert, Decca 31141 | S | 13 |
| 7 | 6 | 5 | 6 | ANGEL BABY — Rosie and the Originals, Highland 1011 | | 9 |
| 8 | 8 | 13 | 26 | EMOTIONS — Brenda Lee, Decca 31195 | | 6 |
| ★9 | 15 | 17 | 29 | MY EMPTY ARMS — Jackie Wilson, Brunswick 55201 | | 5 |
| 10 | 9 | 9 | 7 | RUBBER BALL — Bobby Vee, Liberty 55287 | | 11 |
| 11 | 10 | 6 | 2 | ARE YOU LONESOME TONIGHT — Elvis Presley, RCA Victor 7810 | S | 13 |
| 12 | 12 | 14 | 25 | ONCE IN A WHILE — Chimes, Tag 444 | | 15 |
| 13 | 16 | 16 | 23 | WINGS OF A DOVE — Ferlin Husky, Capitol 4406 | | 11 |
| 14 | 11 | 10 | 9 | CORINNA, CORINNA — Ray Peterson, Dunes 2002 | | 12 |
| ★15 | 31 | 49 | — | PONY TIME — Chubby Checker, Parkway 818 | | 3 |
| ★16 | 21 | 36 | 46 | THERE'S A MOON OUT TONIGHT — Capris, Old Town 1094 | | 6 |
| 17 | 17 | 22 | 24 | I COUNT THE TEARS — Drifters, Atlantic 2087 | | 8 |
| 18 | 20 | 29 | 38 | PEPE — Duane Eddy, Jamie 1175 | | 8 |
| 19 | 13 | 12 | 10 | NORTH TO ALASKA — Johnny Horton, Columbia 41782 | S | 21 |
| ★20 | 30 | 42 | 90 | WHERE THE BOYS ARE — Connie Francis, MGM 12071 | | 4 |
| ★21 | 46 | 67 | 89 | THE STORY OF MY LOVE — Paul Anka, ABC-Paramount 10168 | S | 4 |
| 22 | 25 | 32 | 39 | C'EST SI BON — Conway Twitty, MGM 12969 | | 6 |
| 23 | 14 | 11 | 8 | LAST DATE — Floyd Cramer, RCA Victor 7775 | S | 18 |
| ★24 | 35 | 55 | 77 | BABY SITTIN' BOOGIE — Buzz Clifford, Columbia 41876 | S | 5 |
| 25 | 19 | 18 | 16 | SAILOR (YOUR HOME IS IN THE SEA) — Lolita, Kapp 349 | | 16 |
| 26 | 26 | 41 | 42 | THERE SHE GOES — Jerry Wallace, Challenge 59098 | | 7 |
| ★27 | 47 | 68 | — | DEDICATED TO THE ONE I LOVE — Shirelles, Scepter 1203 | | 3 |
| 28 | 33 | 47 | 54 | ALL IN MY MIND — Maxine Brown, Nomar 102 | | 6 |
| 29 | 34 | 45 | 59 | SPANISH HARLEM — Ben E. King, Atco 6185 | | 6 |
| ★30 | 40 | 50 | 79 | IF I DIDN'T CARE — Platters, Mercury 71749 | S | 5 |
| ★31 | 42 | 53 | — | GOOD TIME BABY — Bobby Rydell, Cameo 186 | | 3 |
| 32 | 22 | 34 | 48 | WHEELS — String-A-Longs, Warwick 603 | | 5 |
| ★33 | 43 | — | — | I'M LEARNING ABOUT LOVE — Brenda Lee, Decca 31195 | | 2 |
| 34 | 23 | 30 | 35 | HOOCHIE COOCHIE COO — Hank Ballard and the Midnighters, King 5430 | | 10 |
| ★35 | 57 | 62 | 70 | LOST LOVE — H. B. Barnum, Eldo 111 | | 5 |
| 36 | 39 | 35 | 40 | MAGNIFICENT SEVEN — Al Caiola, United Artists 261 | | 10 |
| 37 | 53 | 57 | 61 | ANGEL ON MY SHOULDER — Shelby Flint, Valiant WB 6001 | | 7 |
| ★38 | 52 | 78 | — | WHAT A PRICE — Fats Domino, Imperial 5723 | | 3 |
| 39 | 18 | 15 | 11 | A THOUSAND STARS — Kathy Young and the Innocents, Indigo 108 | | 16 |
| 40 | 71 | 74 | 92 | JIMMY'S GIRL — Johnny Tillotson, Cadence 1391 | | 5 |
| 41 | 45 | 44 | 52 | UTOPIA — Frank Gari, Crusade 1020 | | 8 |
| ★42 | 59 | 83 | — | AIN'T THAT JUST LIKE A WOMAN — Fats Domino, Imperial 5723 | | 3 |
| 43 | 37 | 31 | 41 | EXODUS — Mantovani, London 1953 | S | 12 |
| 44 | 62 | — | — | YOU CAN HAVE HER — Roy Hamilton, Epic 9434 | | 2 |
| 45 | 41 | 51 | 60 | DON'T BELIEVE HIM, DONNA — Lenny Miles, Scepter 1212 | | 6 |
| 46 | 51 | 66 | 72 | NO ONE — Connie Francis, MGM 12971 | | 4 |
| 47 | 49 | 64 | 75 | AT LAST — Etta James, Argo 5380 | | 4 |
| 48 | 72 | — | — | DON'T WORRY (LIKE ALL THE OTHER TIMES) — Marty Robbins, Columbia 41922 | S | 2 |
| 49 | 73 | 93 | — | RAM-BUNK-SHUSH — Ventures, Dolton 32 | | 3 |
| 50 | 64 | 73 | 76 | WHAT WOULD I DO — Mickey and Sylvia, RCA Victor 7811 | S | 6 |
| 51 | 44 | 60 | — | TEAR OF THE YEAR — Jackie Wilson, Brunswick 55201 | | 3 |
| 52 | 67 | — | — | EBONY EYES — Everly Brothers, Warner Bros. 5199 | | 2 |
| 53 | 54 | 61 | 69 | FIRST TASTE OF LOVE — Ben E. King, Atco 6185 | | 6 |
| 54 | 56 | 65 | 91 | THE MUSKRAT RAMBLE — Freddy Cannon, Swan 4066 | | 5 |
| 55 | 68 | 81 | 84 | GHOST RIDERS IN THE SKY — Ramrods, Amy 813 | | 5 |
| 56 | 84 | — | 82 | DANCE BY THE LIGHT OF THE MOON — Olympics, Arvee 5020 | | 9 |
| 57 | 29 | 24 | 21 | BABY, O' BABY — Shells, Johnson 104 | | 8 |
| 58 | 63 | 85 | 95 | THEM THAT GOT — Ray Charles, ABC-Paramount 10141 | S | 4 |
| 59 | 28 | 19 | 15 | WONDERLAND BY NIGHT — Louis Prima, Dot 16151 | S | 13 |
| 60 | 36 | 25 | 31 | LOVEY DOVEY — Buddy Knox, Liberty 55290 | | 8 |
| 61 | 66 | 69 | 81 | AGE FOR LOVE — Jimmy Charles, Promo 1003 | | 8 |
| ★62 | 77 | — | — | (I WANNA) LOVE MY LIFE AWAY — Gene Pitney, Musicor 1002 | | 2 |
| 63 | 38 | 33 | 27 | YOU ARE THE ONLY ONE — Ricky Nelson, Imperial 5707 | | 7 |
| 64 | 50 | 56 | 73 | WHAT AM I GONNA DO — Jimmy Clanton, Ace 607 | | 5 |
| 65 | 69 | 79 | — | LEAVE MY KITTEN ALONE — Little Willie John, King 5452 | | 3 |
| 66 | — | — | — | LITTLE BOY SAD — Johnny Burnette, Liberty 55298 | | 1 |
| 67 | 83 | 94 | — | APACHE — Jorgen Ingmann, Atco 6184 | | 3 |
| 68 | 27 | 21 | 18 | HE WILL BREAK YOUR HEART — Jerry Butler, Vee Jay 354 | | 15 |
| 69 | 81 | — | 66 | CHERRY PINK AND APPLE BLOSSOM WHITE — Jerry Murad's Harmonicats, Columbia 41816 | S | 6 |
| 70 | 82 | 90 | — | EXODUS SONG (THIS LAND IS MINE) — Pat Boone, Dot 16176 | | 3 |
| ★71 | — | — | — | WALK RIGHT BACK — Everly Brothers, Warner Bros. 5199 | | 1 |
| 72 | 32 | 27 | 20 | WONDERLAND BY NIGHT — Anita Bryant, Carlton 537 | | 10 |
| 73 | — | — | — | WHEELS — Billy Vaughn, Dot 16174 | | 1 |
| 74 | 55 | 58 | 67 | YES, I'M LONESOME TONIGHT — Thelma Carpenter, Coral 62241 | | 6 |
| 75 | 80 | 84 | 99 | WHEN I FALL IN LOVE — Etta Jones, King 5424 | | 4 |
| 76 | 78 | — | — | CLOSE TOGETHER — Jimmy Reed, Vee Jay 373 | | 2 |
| 77 | 86 | — | — | LEAVE MY KITTEN ALONE — Johnny Preston, Mercury 71761 | | 2 |
| 78 | 96 | — | — | GEE WHIZ (LOOK AT HIS EYES) — Carla Thomas, Atlantic 2086 | | 2 |
| 79 | — | — | — | YOUR FRIENDS — Dee Clark, Vee Jay 372 | | 1 |
| 80 | 100 | — | — | WAIT A MINUTE — Coasters, Atco 6186 | | 2 |
| ★81 | — | — | — | MOST BEAUTIFUL WORDS — Della Reese, RCA Victor 7833 | | 1 |
| 82 | 85 | 88 | — | DEDICATED TO THE ONE I LOVE — Five Royales, King 5453 | | 3 |
| 83 | 60 | 63 | 74 | YES, I'M LONESOME TONIGHT — Dodie Stevens, Dot 16167 | | 6 |
| 84 | 87 | 87 | — | PONY TIME — Don Corvay and the Goodtimers, Arnold 1002 | | 3 |
| 85 | 90 | 98 | — | GINNIE BELL — Paul Dino, Promo 2180 | | 3 |
| 86 | — | — | — | HAVIN' FUN — Dion, Laurie 3081 | | 1 |
| 87 | 98 | — | — | HONKY TONK, PART II — Bill Doggett, King 5444 | | 2 |
| 88 | 95 | 100 | — | CHARLENA — The Sevilles, JCD 116 | | 3 |
| 89 | 99 | — | — | BYE, BYE, BABY — Mary Wells, Motown 1003 | | 2 |
| ★90 | — | — | — | MODEL GIRL — Johnny Maestro, Coed 545 | | 1 |
| 91 | 79 | 77 | 83 | SOUND-OFF — Titus Turner, Jamie 1174 | | 4 |
| 92 | — | — | — | KEEP YOUR HANDS OFF OF HIM — Damita Jo, Mercury 71760 | | 1 |
| 93 | 24 | 20 | 13 | YOU'RE SIXTEEN — Johnny Burnette, Liberty 55285 | | 15 |
| 94 | — | — | — | LAZY RIVER — Bobby Darin, Atco 6188 | | 1 |
| 95 | — | — | — | ONCE UPON A TIME — Rochell and the Candles, Swingin' 623 | | 1 |
| 96 | — | — | — | CALCUTTA — Four Preps, Capitol 4508 | | 1 |
| 97 | — | — | — | FOR MY BABY — Brook Benton, Mercury 71774 | | 1 |
| 98 | — | — | — | CERVEZA — Bert Kaempfert, Decca 30866 | | 1 |
| 99 | — | — | — | COWBOY JIMMY JOE — Lolita, Kapp 370 | | 1 |
| 100 | — | — | — | DON'T LET HIM SHOP AROUND — Debbie Dean, Motown 1007 | | 1 |

# BILLBOARD HOT 100
## For Week Ending February 19

| This Week | One Week Ago | Two Weeks Ago | Three Weeks Ago | Title / Artist, Company, Record No. | Stereo | Weeks on Chart |
|---|---|---|---|---|---|---|
| 1 | 2 | 2 | 3 | CALCUTTA — Lawrence Welk, Dot 16161 | | 10 |
| 2 | 1 | 1 | 4 | (WILL YOU LOVE ME) TOMORROW — Shirelles, Scepter 1211 | | 13 |
| 3 | 4 | 5 | 7 | SHOP AROUND — Miracles, Tamla 54034 | | 10 |
| 4 | 5 | 7 | 8 | CALENDAR GIRL — Neil Sedaka, RCA Victor 7829 | S | 9 |
| 5 | 3 | 3 | 2 | EXODUS — Ferrante and Teicher, United Artists 274 | S | 14 |
| 6 | 7 | 6 | 5 | ANGEL BABY — Rosie and the Originals, Highland 1011 | | 10 |
| 7 | 8 | 8 | 13 | EMOTIONS — Brenda Lee, Decca 31195 | | 7 |
| 8 | 6 | 4 | 1 | WONDERLAND BY NIGHT — Bert Kaempfert, Decca 31141 | S | 14 |
| 9 | 15 | 31 | 49 | PONY TIME — Chubby Checker, Parkway 818 | | 4 |
| 10 | 16 | 21 | 36 | THERE'S A MOON OUT TONIGHT — Capris, Old Town 1094 | | 7 |
| 11 | 12 | 12 | 14 | ONCE IN A WHILE — Chimes, Tag 444 | | 16 |
| 12 | 13 | 16 | 16 | WINGS OF A DOVE — Ferlin Husky, Capitol 4406 | | 12 |
| 13 | 27 | 47 | 68 | DEDICATED TO THE ONE I LOVE — Shirelles, Scepter 1203 | | 4 |
| 14 | 24 | 35 | 55 | BABY SITTIN' BOOGIE — Buzz Clifford, Columbia 41876 | S | 6 |
| 15 | 32 | 22 | 34 | WHEELS — String-A-Longs, Warwick 603 | | 6 |
| 16 | 20 | 30 | 42 | WHERE THE BOYS ARE — Connie Francis, MGM 12071 | | 5 |
| 17 | 21 | 46 | 67 | THE STORY OF MY LOVE — Paul Anka, ABC-Paramount 10168 | S | 5 |
| 18 | 9 | 15 | 17 | MY EMPTY ARMS — Jackie Wilson, Brunswick 55201 | | 6 |
| 19 | 28 | 33 | 47 | ALL IN MY MIND — Maxine Brown, Nomar 102 | | 7 |
| 20 | 10 | 9 | 9 | RUBBER BALL — Bobby Vee, Liberty 55287 | | 12 |
| 21 | 11 | 10 | 6 | ARE YOU LONESOME TONIGHT — Elvis Presley, RCA Victor 7810 | S | 14 |
| 22 | 18 | 20 | 29 | PEPE — Duane Eddy, Jamie 1175 | | 9 |
| 23 | 17 | 17 | 22 | I COUNT THE TEARS — Drifters, Atlantic 2087 | | 9 |
| 24 | 14 | 11 | 10 | CORINNA, CORINNA — Ray Peterson, Dunes 2002 | | 13 |
| 25 | 31 | 42 | 53 | GOOD TIME BABY — Bobby Rydell, Cameo 186 | | 4 |
| 26 | 29 | 34 | 45 | SPANISH HARLEM — Ben E. King, Atco 6185 | | 7 |
| 27 | 38 | 52 | 78 | WHAT A PRICE — Fats Domino, Imperial 5723 | | 4 |
| 28 | 48 | 72 | — | DON'T WORRY (LIKE ALL THE OTHER TIMES) — Marty Robbins, Columbia 41922 | S | 3 |
| 29 | 26 | 26 | 41 | THERE SHE GOES — Jerry Wallace, Challenge 59098 | | 8 |
| 30 | 22 | 25 | 32 | C'EST SI BON — Conway Twitty, MGM 12969 | | 7 |
| 31 | 40 | 71 | 74 | JIMMY'S GIRL — Johnny Tillotson, Cadence 1391 | | 3 |
| 32 | 44 | 62 | — | YOU CAN HAVE HER — Roy Hamilton, Epic 9434 | | 3 |
| 33 | 33 | 43 | — | I'M LEARNING ABOUT LOVE — Brenda Lee, Decca 31195 | | 3 |
| 34 | 37 | 53 | 57 | ANGEL ON MY SHOULDER — Shelby Flint, Valiant WB 6001 | | 8 |
| 35 | 19 | 13 | 12 | NORTH TO ALASKA — Johnny Horton, Columbia 41782 | S | 22 |
| 36 | 42 | 59 | 83 | AIN'T THAT JUST LIKE A WOMAN — Fats Domino, Imperial 5723 | | 4 |
| 37 | 25 | 19 | 18 | SAILOR (YOUR HOME IS IN THE SEA) — Lolita, Kapp 349 | | 17 |
| 38 | 41 | 45 | 44 | UTOPIA — Frank Gari, Crusade 1020 | | 9 |
| 39 | 49 | 73 | 93 | RAM-BUNK-SHUSH — Ventures, Dolton 32 | | 4 |
| 40 | 52 | 67 | — | EBONY EYES — Everly Brothers, Warner Bros. 5199 | | 3 |
| 41 | 46 | 51 | 66 | NO ONE — Connie Francis, MGM 12971 | | 5 |
| 42 | 35 | 57 | 62 | LOST LOVE — H. B. Barnum, Eldo 111 | | 6 |
| 43 | 55 | 56 | 81 | GHOST RIDERS IN THE SKY — Ramrods, Amy 813 | | 6 |
| 44 | 71 | — | — | WALK RIGHT BACK — Everly Brothers, Warner Bros. 5199 | | 2 |
| 45 | 78 | 96 | — | GEE WHIZ (LOOK AT HIS EYES) — Carla Thomas, Atlantic 2086 | | 3 |
| 46 | 66 | — | — | LITTLE BOY SAD — Johnny Burnette, Liberty 55298 | | 2 |
| 47 | 50 | 64 | 73 | WHAT WOULD I DO — Mickey and Sylvia, RCA Victor 7811 | S | 7 |
| 48 | 67 | 83 | 94 | APACHE — Jorgen Ingmann, Atco 6184 | | 4 |
| 49 | 80 | 100 | — | WAIT A MINUTE — Coasters, Atco 6186 | | 3 |
| 50 | 94 | — | — | LAZY RIVER — Bobby Darin, Atco 6188 | | 2 |
| 51 | 61 | 66 | 69 | AGE FOR LOVE — Jimmy Charles, Promo 1003 | | 9 |
| 52 | 56 | 84 | — | DANCE BY THE LIGHT OF THE MOON — Olympics, Arvee 5020 | | 10 |
| 53 | 51 | 44 | 60 | TEAR OF THE YEAR — Jackie Wilson, Brunswick 55201 | | 4 |
| 54 | 36 | 39 | 35 | MAGNIFICENT SEVEN — Al Caiola, United Artists 261 | | 11 |
| 55 | 62 | 77 | — | (I WANNA) LOVE MY LIFE AWAY — Gene Pitney, Musicor 1002 | | 3 |
| 56 | 23 | 14 | 11 | LAST DATE — Floyd Cramer, RCA Victor 7775 | S | 19 |
| 57 | 39 | 18 | 15 | A THOUSAND STARS — Kathy Young and the Innocents, Indigo 108 | | 17 |
| 58 | 58 | 63 | 85 | THEM THAT GOT — Ray Charles, ABC-Paramount 10141 | S | 5 |
| 59 | 30 | 40 | 50 | IF I DIDN'T CARE — Platters, Mercury 71749 | S | 6 |
| 60 | 45 | 41 | 51 | DON'T BELIEVE HIM, DONNA — Lenny Miles, Scepter 1212 | | 7 |
| 61 | 65 | 69 | 75 | LEAVE MY KITTEN ALONE — Little Willie John, King 5452 | | 4 |
| 62 | 34 | 23 | 30 | HOOCHIE COOCHIE COO — Hank Ballard and the Midnighters, King 5430 | | 11 |
| 63 | 53 | 54 | 61 | FIRST TASTE OF LOVE — Ben E. King, Atco 6185 | | 7 |
| 64 | 70 | 82 | 90 | EXODUS SONG (THIS LAND IS MINE) — Pat Boone, Dot 16176 | | 4 |
| 65 | 47 | 49 | 64 | AT LAST — Etta James, Argo 5380 | | 5 |
| 66 | 73 | — | — | WHEELS — Billy Vaughn, Dot 16174 | | 2 |
| 67 | 86 | — | — | HAVIN' FUN — Dion, Laurie 3081 | | 2 |
| 68 | 76 | 78 | — | CLOSE TOGETHER — Jimmy Reed, Vee Jay 373 | | 3 |
| 69 | — | — | — | STAYIN' IN — Bobby Vee, Liberty 55296 | | 1 |
| 70 | 75 | 80 | 84 | WHEN I FALL IN LOVE — Etta Jones, King 5424 | | 5 |
| 71 | 79 | — | — | YOUR FRIENDS — Dee Clark, Vee Jay 372 | | 2 |
| 72 | 90 | — | — | MODEL GIRL — Johnny Maestro, Coed 545 | | 2 |
| 73 | — | — | — | THINK TWICE — Brook Benton, Mercury 71774 | | 1 |
| 74 | 85 | 90 | 98 | GINNIE BELL — Paul Dino, Promo 2180 | | 4 |
| 75 | 77 | 86 | — | LEAVE MY KITTEN ALONE — Johnny Preston, Mercury 71761 | | 3 |
| 76 | 81 | — | — | MOST BEAUTIFUL WORDS — Della Reese, RCA Victor 7833 | | 2 |
| 77 | 95 | — | — | ONCE UPON A TIME — Rochell and the Candles, Swingin' 623 | | 2 |
| 78 | 69 | 81 | — | CHERRY PINK AND APPLE BLOSSOM WHITE — Jerry Murad's Harmonicats, Columbia 41816 | S | 7 |
| 79 | 84 | 87 | 87 | PONY TIME — Don Covay and the Goodtimers, Arnold 1002 | | 4 |
| 80 | 87 | 98 | — | HONKY TONK, PART II — Bill Doggett, King 5444 | | 3 |
| 81 | 82 | 85 | 88 | DEDICATED TO THE ONE I LOVE — Five Royales, King 5453 | | 4 |
| 82 | 54 | 56 | 65 | THE MUSKRAT RAMBLE — Freddy Cannon, Swan 4066 | | 6 |
| 83 | 89 | 99 | — | BYE, BYE, BABY — Mary Wells, Motown 1003 | | 3 |
| 84 | 88 | 95 | 100 | CHARLENA — The Sevilles, J C 116 | | 4 |
| 85 | 92 | — | — | KEEP YOUR HANDS OFF OF HIM — Damita Jo, Mercury 71760 | | 2 |
| 86 | 43 | 37 | 31 | EXODUS — Mantovani, London 1953 | S | 13 |
| 87 | — | — | — | YOU'RE THE BOSS — La Vern Baker and Jimmy Ricks, Atlantic 2090 | | 1 |
| 88 | 64 | 50 | 56 | WHAT AM I GONNA DO — Jimmy Clanton, Ace 607 | | 6 |
| 89 | 59 | 28 | 19 | WONDERLAND BY NIGHT — Louis Prima, Dot 16151 | S | 14 |
| 90 | — | — | — | TUNES OF GLORY — Cambridge Strings, London 1960 | | 1 |
| 91 | 63 | 38 | 33 | YOU ARE THE ONLY ONE — Ricky Nelson, Imperial 5707 | | 8 |
| 92 | 100 | — | — | DON'T LET HIM SHOP AROUND — Debbie Dean, Motown 1007 | | 2 |
| 93 | 97 | — | — | FOR MY BABY — Brook Benton, Mercury 71774 | | 2 |
| 94 | 99 | — | — | COWBOY JIMMY JOE — Lolita, Kapp 370 | | 2 |
| 95 | 60 | 36 | 25 | LOVEY DOVEY — Buddy Knox, Liberty 55290 | | 9 |
| 96 | 98 | — | — | CERVEZA — Bert Kaempfert, Decca 30866 | | 2 |
| 97 | — | — | — | CHEERIE — Bobby Rydell, Cameo 186 | | 1 |
| 98 | — | — | — | A TEXAN AND A GIRL FROM MEXICO — Anita Bryant, Carlton 538 | | 1 |
| 99 | 96 | — | — | CALCUTTA — Four Preps, Capitol 4508 | | 2 |
| 100 | — | — | — | WHAT ABOUT ME — Don Gibson, RCA Victor 7841 | | 1 |

# BILLBOARD HOT 100

**For Week Ending February 26** — February 20, 1961

| This Week | 1 Wk Ago | 2 Wks Ago | 3 Wks Ago | Title / Artist, Company, Record No. | Stereo | Weeks on Chart |
|---|---|---|---|---|---|---|
| 1 | 1 | 2 | 2 | CALCUTTA — Lawrence Welk, Dot 16161 | | 11 |
| 2 | 3 | 4 | 5 | SHOP AROUND — Miracles, Tamla 54034 | | 11 |
| 3 | 2 | 1 | 1 | (WILL YOU LOVE ME) TOMORROW — Shirelles, Scepter 1211 | | 14 |
| 4 | 9 | 15 | 31 | PONY TIME — Chubby Checker, Parkway 818 | | 5 |
| 5 | 10 | 16 | 21 | THERE'S A MOON OUT TONIGHT — Capris, Old Town 1094 | | 8 |
| 6 | 4 | 5 | 7 | CALENDAR GIRL — Neil Sedaka, RCA Victor 7829 | S | 10 |
| 7 | 7 | 8 | 8 | EMOTIONS — Brenda Lee, Decca 31195 | | 8 |
| 8 | 5 | 3 | 3 | EXODUS — Ferrante and Teicher, United Artists 274 | S | 15 |
| 9 | 13 | 27 | 47 | DEDICATED TO THE ONE I LOVE — Shirelles, Scepter 1203 | | 5 |
| 10 | 15 | 32 | 22 | WHEELS — String-A-Longs, Warwick 603 | | 7 |
| 11 | 16 | 20 | 30 | WHERE THE BOYS ARE — Connie Francis, MGM 12071 | | 6 |
| 12 | 14 | 24 | 35 | BABY SITTIN' BOOGIE — Buzz Clifford, Columbia 41876 | S | 7 |
| 13 | 12 | 13 | 16 | WINGS OF A DOVE — Ferlin Husky, Capitol 4406 | | 13 |
| 14 | 25 | 31 | 42 | GOOD TIME BABY — Bobby Rydell, Cameo 186 | | 5 |
| 15 | 28 | 48 | 72 | DON'T WORRY (LIKE ALL THE OTHER TIMES) — Marty Robbins, Columbia 41922 | S | 4 |
| 16 | 17 | 21 | 46 | THE STORY OF MY LOVE — Paul Anka, ABC-Paramount 10168 | S | 6 |
| 17 | 6 | 7 | 6 | ANGEL BABY — Rosie and the Originals, Highland 1011 | | 11 |
| 18 | 40 | 52 | 67 | EBONY EYES — Everly Brothers, Warner Bros. 5199 | | 4 |
| 19 | 19 | 28 | 33 | ALL IN MY MIND — Maxine Brown, Nomar 102 | | 8 |
| 20 | 8 | 6 | 4 | WONDERLAND BY NIGHT — Bert Kaempfert, Decca 31141 | S | 15 |
| 21 | 26 | 29 | 34 | SPANISH HARLEM — Ben E. King, Atco 6185 | | 8 |
| 22 | 27 | 38 | 52 | WHAT A PRICE — Fats Domino, Imperial 5723 | | 5 |
| 23 | 18 | 9 | 15 | MY EMPTY ARMS — Jackie Wilson, Brunswick 55201 | | 7 |
| 24 | — | — | — | SURRENDER — Elvis Presley, RCA Victor 7850 | | 1 |
| 25 | 46 | 66 | — | LITTLE BOY SAD — Johnny Burnette, Liberty 55298 | | 3 |
| 26 | 48 | 67 | 83 | APACHE — Jorgen Ingmann, Atco 6184 | | 5 |
| 27 | 31 | 40 | 71 | JIMMY'S GIRL — Johnny Tillotson, Cadence 1391 | | 7 |
| 28 | 34 | 37 | 53 | ANGEL ON MY SHOULDER — Shelby Flint, Valiant WB 6001 | | 9 |
| 29 | 11 | 12 | 12 | ONCE IN A WHILE — Chimes, Tag 444 | | 17 |
| 30 | 43 | 55 | 56 | GHOST RIDERS IN THE SKY — Ramrods, Amy 813 | | 7 |
| 31 | 32 | 44 | 62 | YOU CAN HAVE HER — Roy Hamilton, Epic 9434 | | 4 |
| 32 | 39 | 49 | 73 | RAM-BUNK-SHUSH — Ventures, Dolton 32 | | 5 |
| 33 | 22 | 18 | 20 | PEPE — Duane Eddy, Jamie 1175 | | 10 |
| 34 | 38 | 41 | 45 | UTOPIA — Frank Gari, Crusade 1020 | | 10 |
| 35 | 36 | 42 | 59 | AIN'T THAT JUST LIKE A WOMAN — Fats Domino, Imperial 5723 | | 5 |
| 36 | 20 | 10 | 9 | RUBBER BALL — Bobby Vee, Liberty 55287 | | 12 |
| 37 | 50 | 94 | — | LAZY RIVER — Bobby Darin, Atco 6188 | | 3 |
| 38 | 41 | 46 | 51 | NO ONE — Connie Francis, MGM 12971 | | 6 |
| 39 | 44 | 71 | — | WALK RIGHT BACK — Everly Brothers, Warner Bros. 5199 | | 3 |
| 40 | 45 | 78 | 96 | GEE WHIZ (LOOK AT HIS EYES) — Carla Thomas, Atlantic 2086 | | 4 |
| 41 | 49 | 80 | 100 | WAIT A MINUTE — Coasters, Atco 6186 | | 4 |
| 42 | 24 | 14 | 11 | CORINNA, CORINNA — Ray Peterson, Dunes 2002 | | 14 |
| 43 | 55 | 62 | 77 | (I WANNA) LOVE MY LIFE AWAY — Gene Pitney, Musicor 1002 | | 4 |
| 44 | 23 | 17 | 17 | I COUNT THE TEARS — Drifters, Atlantic 2087 | | 10 |
| 45 | 69 | — | — | STAYIN' IN — Bobby Vee, Liberty 55296 | | 2 |
| 46 | 47 | 50 | 64 | WHAT WOULD I DO — Mickey and Sylvia, RCA Victor 7811 | S | 8 |
| 47 | 51 | 61 | 66 | AGE FOR LOVE — Jimmy Charles, Promo 1003 | | 10 |
| 48 | 29 | 26 | 26 | THERE SHE GOES — Jerry Wallace, Challenge 59098 | | 9 |
| 49 | 42 | 35 | 57 | LOST LOVE — H. B. Barnum, Eldo 111 | | 7 |
| 50 | 35 | 19 | 13 | NORTH TO ALASKA — Johnny Horton, Columbia 41782 | S | 23 |
| 51 | 33 | 33 | 43 | I'M LEARNING ABOUT LOVE — Brenda Lee, Decca 31195 | | 4 |
| 52 | 30 | 22 | 25 | C'EST SI BON — Conway Twitty, MGM 12969 | | 8 |
| 53 | 71 | 79 | — | YOUR FRIENDS — Dee Clark, Vee Jay 372 | | 3 |
| 54 | 67 | 86 | — | HAVIN' FUN — Dion, Laurie 3081 | | 3 |
| 55 | 66 | 73 | — | WHEELS — Billy Vaughn, Dot 16174 | | 3 |
| 56 | 73 | — | — | THINK TWICE — Brook Benton, Mercury 71774 | | 2 |
| 57 | 97 | — | — | CHERIE — Bobby Rydell, Cameo 186 | | 2 |
| 58 | 21 | 11 | 10 | ARE YOU LONESOME TONIGHT — Elvis Presley, RCA Victor 7810 | S | 15 |
| 59 | 72 | 90 | — | MODEL GIRL — Johnny Maestro, Coed 545 | | 3 |
| 60 | 61 | 65 | 69 | LEAVE MY KITTEN ALONE — Little Willie John, King 5452 | | 5 |
| 61 | 53 | 51 | 44 | TEAR OF THE YEAR — Jackie Wilson, Brunswick 55201 | | 5 |
| 62 | 65 | 47 | 49 | AT LAST — Etta James, Argo 5380 | | 6 |
| 63 | 74 | 85 | 90 | GINNIE BELL — Paul Dino, Promo 2180 | | 5 |
| 64 | 56 | 23 | 14 | LAST DATE — Floyd Cramer, RCA Victor 7775 | S | 20 |
| 65 | 59 | 30 | 40 | IF I DIDN'T CARE — Platters, Mercury 71749 | S | 7 |
| 66 | 64 | 70 | 82 | EXODUS SONG (THIS LAND IS MINE) — Pat Boone, Dot 16176 | | 5 |
| 67 | 70 | 75 | 80 | WHEN I FALL IN LOVE — Etta Jones, King 5424 | | 6 |
| 68 | 93 | 97 | — | FOR MY BABY — Brook Benton, Mercury 717774 | | 3 |
| 69 | 77 | 95 | — | ONCE UPON A TIME — Rochell and the Candles, Swingin' 623 | | 3 |
| 70 | — | — | — | HEARTS OF STONE — Bill Black's Combo, Hi 2028 | | 1 |
| 71 | 76 | 81 | — | MOST BEAUTIFUL WORDS — Della Reese, RCA Victor 7833 | S | 3 |
| 72 | 83 | 89 | 99 | BYE, BYE, BABY — Mary Wells, Motown 1003 | | 4 |
| 73 | 75 | 77 | 86 | LEAVE MY KITTEN ALONE — Johnny Preston, Mercury 71761 | | 4 |
| 74 | 79 | 84 | 87 | PONY TIME — Don Corvay and the Goodtimers, Arnold 1002 | | 5 |
| 75 | — | — | — | ASIA MINOR — Kokomo, Felsted 8612 | | 1 |
| 76 | — | — | — | I DON'T WANT TO CRY — Chuck Jackson, Wand 106 | | 1 |
| 77 | 85 | 92 | — | KEEP YOUR HANDS OFF OF HIM — Damita Jo, Mercury 71760 | | 3 |
| 78 | 80 | 87 | 98 | HONKY TONK, PART II — Bill Doggett, King 5444 | | 4 |
| 79 | — | — | — | HAPPY BIRTHDAY BLUES — Kathy Young, Indigo 115 | | 1 |
| 80 | — | — | — | WATUSI — Vibrations, Checker 969 | | 1 |
| 81 | 68 | 76 | 78 | CLOSE TOGETHER — Jimmy Reed, Vee Jay 373 | | 4 |
| 82 | 37 | 25 | 19 | SAILOR (YOUR HOME IS IN THE SEA) — Lolita, Kapp 349 | | 18 |
| 83 | — | — | — | TOUCHABLES — Dickie Goodman, Mark X 8009 | | 1 |
| 84 | — | — | — | TO BE LOVED (FOREVER) — Pentagons, Donna 1337 | | 1 |
| 85 | 58 | 58 | 63 | THEM THAT GOT — Ray Charles, ABC-Paramount 10141 | S | 6 |
| 86 | 87 | — | — | YOU'RE THE BOSS — La Vern Baker and Jimmy Ricks, Atlantic 2090 | | 2 |
| 87 | 54 | 36 | 39 | MAGNIFICENT SEVEN — Al Caiola, United Artists 261 | | 12 |
| 88 | 78 | 69 | 81 | CHERRY PINK AND APPLE BLOSSOM WHITE — Jerry Murad's Harmonicats, Columbia 41816 | S | 8 |
| 89 | — | — | — | LET'S GO AGAIN (WHERE WE WENT LAST NIGHT) — Hank Ballard and the Midnighters, King 5459 | | 1 |
| 90 | — | — | — | I DON'T KNOW WHY — Clarence (Frogman) Henry, Argo 5378 | | 1 |
| 91 | 98 | — | — | A TEXAN AND A GIRL FROM MEXICO — Anita Bryant, Carlton 538 | | 2 |
| 92 | 96 | 98 | — | CERVEZA — Bert Kaempfert, Decca 30866 | | 3 |
| 93 | 84 | 88 | 95 | CHARLENA — The Sevilles, J C 116 | | 5 |
| 94 | 52 | 56 | 84 | DANCE BY THE LIGHT OF THE MOON — Olympics, Arvee 5020 | | 11 |
| 95 | 90 | — | — | TUNES OF GLORY — Cambridge Strings, London 1960 | | 2 |
| 96 | — | — | — | ORANGE BLOSSOM SPECIAL — Billy Vaughn, Dot 16174 | | 1 |
| 97 | — | — | — | PONY EXPRESS — Danny and the Juniors, Swan 468 | | 1 |
| 98 | — | — | — | I PITY THE FOOL — Bobby Bland, Duke 332 | | 1 |
| 99 | — | — | — | TOP FORTY, NEWS, WEATHER & SPORTS — Mark Dinning, MGM 12980 | | 1 |
| 100 | — | — | — | DREAM BOY — Annette, Vista 374 | | 1 |

# BILLBOARD HOT 100

**FOR WEEK ENDING MARCH 5** — FEBRUARY 27, 1961

STAR PERFORMERS showed the greatest upward progress on Hot 100 this week.
S — Indicates that 45 r.p.m. stereo single version is available.
A — Indicates that 33⅓ r.p.m. stereo single version is available.

| This Week | 1 Wk Ago | 2 Wks Ago | 3 Wks Ago | Title — Artist, Company, Record No. | Stereo | Weeks on Chart |
|---|---|---|---|---|---|---|
| 1 | 4 | 9 | 15 | PONY TIME — Chubby Checker, Parkway 818 | | 6 |
| 2 | 1 | 1 | 2 | CALCUTTA — Lawrence Welk, Dot 16161 | | 12 |
| 3 | 5 | 10 | 16 | THERE'S A MOON OUT TONIGHT — Capris, Old Town 1094 | | 9 |
| 4 | 24 | — | — | SURRENDER — Elvis Presley, RCA Victor 7850 | | 2 |
| 5 | 15 | 28 | 48 | DON'T WORRY (LIKE ALL THE OTHER TIMES) — Marty Robbins, Columbia 41922 | S | 5 |
| 6 | 9 | 13 | 27 | DEDICATED TO THE ONE I LOVE — Shirelles, Scepter 1203 | | 6 |
| 7 | 11 | 16 | 20 | WHERE THE BOYS ARE — Connie Francis, MGM 12971 | | 7 |
| 8 | 2 | 3 | 4 | SHOP AROUND — Miracles, Tamla 54034 | | 12 |
| 9 | 18 | 40 | 52 | EBONY EYES — Everly Brothers, Warner Bros. 5199 | | 5 |
| 10 | 10 | 15 | 32 | WHEELS — String-A-Longs, Warwick 603 | | 8 |
| 11 | 3 | 2 | 1 | (WILL YOU LOVE ME) TOMORROW — Shirelles, Scepter 1211 | | 15 |
| 12 | 12 | 14 | 24 | BABY SITTIN' BOOGIE — Buzz Clifford, Columbia 41876 | S | 8 |
| 13 | 14 | 25 | 31 | GOOD TIME BABY — Bobby Rydell, Cameo 186 | | 6 |
| 14 | 8 | 5 | 3 | EXODUS — Ferrante and Teicher, United Artists 274 | S | 16 |
| 15 | 6 | 4 | 5 | CALENDAR GIRL — Neil Sedaka, RCA Victor 7829 | S | 11 |
| 16 | 7 | 7 | 8 | EMOTIONS — Brenda Lee, Decca 31195 | | 9 |
| 17 | 13 | 12 | 13 | WINGS OF A DOVE — Ferlin Husky, Capitol 4406 | | 14 |
| 18 | 21 | 26 | 29 | SPANISH HARLEM — Ben E. King, Atco 6185 | | 9 |
| 19 | 19 | 19 | 28 | ALL IN MY MIND — Maxine Brown, Nomar 102 | | 9 |
| 20 | 26 | 48 | 67 | APACHE — Jorgen Ingmann, Atco 6184 | | 6 |
| 21 | 25 | 46 | 66 | LITTLE BOY SAD — Johnny Burnette, Liberty 55298 | | 4 |
| 22 | 28 | 34 | 37 | ANGEL ON MY SHOULDER — Shelby Flint, Valiant WB 6001 | | 10 |
| 23 | 16 | 17 | 21 | THE STORY OF MY LOVE — Paul Anka, ABC-Paramount 10168 | S | 7 |
| 24 | 31 | 32 | 44 | YOU CAN HAVE HER — Roy Hamilton, Epic 9434 | | 5 |
| 25 | 27 | 31 | 40 | JIMMY'S GIRL — Johnny Tillotson, Cadence 1391 | | 8 |
| 26 | 40 | 45 | 78 | GEE WHIZ (LOOK AT HIS EYES) — Carla Thomas, Atlantic 2086 | | 5 |
| 27 | 22 | 27 | 38 | WHAT A PRICE — Fats Domino, Imperial 5723 | | 6 |
| 28 | 39 | 44 | 71 | WALK RIGHT BACK — Everly Brothers, Warner Bros. 5199 | | 4 |
| 29 | 56 | 73 | — | THINK TWICE — Brook Benton, Mercury 71774 | | 3 |
| 30 | 17 | 6 | 7 | ANGEL BABY — Rosie and the Originals, Highland 1011 | | 12 |
| 31 | 32 | 39 | 49 | RAM-BUNK-SHUSH — Ventures, Dolton 32 | | 5 |
| 32 | 34 | 38 | 41 | UTOPIA — Frank Gari, Crusade 1020 | | 11 |
| 33 | 35 | 36 | 42 | AIN'T THAT JUST LIKE A WOMAN — Fats Domino, Imperial 5723 | | 6 |
| 34 | 38 | 41 | 46 | NO ONE — Connie Francis, MGM 12971 | | 7 |
| 35 | 37 | 50 | 94 | LAZY RIVER — Bobby Darin, Atco 6188 | | 4 |
| 36 | 20 | 8 | 6 | WONDERLAND BY NIGHT — Bert Kaempfert, Decca 31141 | S | 16 |
| 37 | 41 | 49 | 80 | WAIT A MINUTE — Coasters, Atco 6186 | | 5 |
| 38 | 45 | 69 | — | STAYIN' IN — Bobby Vee, Liberty 55296 | | 3 |
| 39 | 43 | 55 | 62 | (I WANNA) LOVE MY LIFE AWAY — Gene Pitney, Musicor 1002 | | 5 |
| 40 | 33 | 22 | 18 | PEPE — Duane Eddy, Jamie 1175 | | 11 |
| 41 | 23 | 18 | 9 | MY EMPTY ARMS — Jackie Wilson, Brunswick 55201 | | 8 |
| 42 | 53 | 71 | 79 | YOUR FRIENDS — Dee Clark, Vee Jay 372 | | 4 |
| 43 | 55 | 66 | 73 | WHEELS — Billy Vaughn, Dot 16174 | | 4 |
| 44 | 70 | — | — | HEARTS OF STONE — Bill Black's Combo, Hi 2028 | | 2 |
| 45 | 36 | 20 | 10 | RUBBER BALL — Bobby Vee, Liberty 55287 | | 13 |
| 46 | 75 | — | — | ASIA MINOR — Kokomo, Felsted 8612 | | 2 |
| 47 | 29 | 11 | 12 | ONCE IN A WHILE — Chimes, Tag 444 | | 18 |
| 48 | 30 | 43 | 55 | GHOST RIDERS IN THE SKY — Ramrods, Amy 813 | | 8 |
| 49 | 54 | 67 | 86 | HAVIN' FUN — Dion, Laurie 3081 | | 4 |
| 50 | 68 | 93 | 97 | FOR MY BABY — Brook Benton, Mercury 71774 | | 4 |
| 51 | 62 | 65 | 47 | AT LAST — Etta James, Argo 5380 | | 7 |
| 52 | 61 | 53 | 51 | TEAR OF THE YEAR — Jackie Wilson, Brunswick 55201 | | 6 |
| 53 | 44 | 23 | 17 | I COUNT THE TEARS — Drifters, Atlantic 2087 | | 11 |
| 54 | 57 | 97 | — | CHERIE — Bobby Rydell, Cameo 186 | | 3 |
| 55 | 52 | 30 | 22 | C'EST SI BON — Conway Twitty, MGM 12969 | | 9 |
| 56 | 48 | 29 | 26 | THERE SHE GOES — Jerry Wallace, Challenge 59098 | | 10 |
| 57 | 69 | 77 | 95 | ONCE UPON A TIME — Rochell and the Candles, Swingin' 623 | | 4 |
| 58 | 79 | — | — | HAPPY BIRTHDAY BLUES — Kathy Young and the Innocents, Indigo 115 | | 2 |
| 59 | 47 | 51 | 61 | AGE FOR LOVE — Jimmy Charles, Promo 1003 | | 11 |
| 60 | 80 | — | — | WATUSI — Vibrations, Checker 969 | | 2 |
| 61 | 76 | — | — | I DON'T WANT TO CRY — Chuck Jackson, Wand 106 | | 2 |
| 62 | 58 | 21 | 11 | ARE YOU LONESOME TONIGHT — Elvis Presley, RCA Victor 7810 | S | 16 |
| 63 | 97 | — | — | PONY EXPRESS — Danny and the Juniors, Swan 468 | | |
| 64 | 46 | 47 | 50 | WHAT WOULD I DO — Mickey and Sylvia, RCA Victor 7811 | S | 9 |
| 65 | 67 | 70 | 75 | WHEN I FALL IN LOVE — Etta Jones, King 5424 | | 7 |
| 66 | 42 | 24 | 14 | CORINNA, CORINNA — Ray Peterson, Dunes 2002 | | 15 |
| 67 | 71 | 76 | 81 | MOST BEAUTIFUL WORDS — Della Reese, RCA Victor 7833 | | 4 |
| 68 | 59 | 72 | 90 | MODEL GIRL — Johnny Mastro, Coed 545 | | 4 |
| 69 | 63 | 74 | 85 | GINNIE BELL — Paul Dino, Promo 2180 | | 6 |
| 70 | 72 | 83 | 89 | BYE, BYE, BABY — Mary Wells, Motown 1003 | | 5 |
| 71 | — | — | — | PLEASE LOVE ME FOREVER — Cathy Jean and Roomates, Valmor 007 | | 1 |
| 72 | 83 | — | — | TOUCHABLES — Dickie Goodman, Mark X 8009 | | 2 |
| 73 | 74 | 79 | 84 | PONY TIME — Don Covay and the Goodtimers, Arnold 1002 | | 6 |
| 74 | 95 | 90 | — | TUNES OF GLORY — Cambridge Strings, London 1960 | | 3 |
| 75 | 77 | 85 | 92 | KEEP YOUR HANDS OFF OF HIM — Damita Jo, Mercury 71760 | | 4 |
| 76 | 84 | — | — | TO BE LOVED (FOREVER) — Pentagons, Donna 1337 | | 2 |
| 77 | 90 | — | — | I DON'T KNOW WHY — Clarence (Frogman) Henry, Argo 5378 | | 2 |
| 78 | 60 | 61 | 65 | LEAVE MY KITTEN ALONE — Little Willie John, King 5452 | | 6 |
| 79 | 98 | — | — | I PITY THE FOOL — Bobby Bland, Duke 332 | | 2 |
| 80 | 78 | 80 | 87 | HONKY TONK, PART II — Bill Doggett, King 5444 | | 5 |
| 81 | 86 | 87 | — | YOU'RE THE BOSS — La Vern Baker and Jimmy Ricks, Atlantic 2090 | | 3 |
| 82 | 89 | — | — | LET'S GO AGAIN (WHERE WE WENT LAST NIGHT) — Hank Ballard and the Midnighters, King 5459 | | 2 |
| 83 | 96 | — | — | ORANGE BLOSSOM SPECIAL — Billy Vaughn, Dot 16174 | | 2 |
| 84 | — | — | — | LONELY MAN — Elvis Presley, RCA Victor 7850 | | 1 |
| 85 | 91 | 98 | — | A TEXAN AND A GIRL FROM MEXICO — Anita Bryant, Carlton 538 | | 3 |
| 86 | — | — | — | JA-DA — Johnny and the Hurricanes, Big Top 3063 | | 1 |
| 87 | 100 | — | — | DREAM BOY — Annette, Vista 374 | | 2 |
| 88 | 65 | 59 | 30 | IF I DIDN'T CARE — Platters, Mercury 71749 | S | 8 |
| 89 | 92 | 96 | 98 | CERVEZA — Bert Kaempfert, Decca 30866 | | 4 |
| 90 | 99 | — | — | TOP FORTY, NEWS, WEATHER & SPORTS — Mark Dinning, MGM 12980 | | 2 |
| 91 | — | — | — | ALL OF EVERYTHING — Frankie Avalon, Chancellor 1071 | | 1 |
| 92 | 73 | 75 | 77 | LEAVE MY KITTEN ALONE — Johnny Preston, Mercury 71761 | | 5 |
| 93 | 66 | 64 | 70 | EXODUS SONG (THIS LAND IS MINE) — Pat Boone, Dot 16176 | | 6 |
| 94 | — | — | — | BEWILDERED — James Brown, King 5442 | | 1 |
| 95 | — | — | — | WON'T BE LONG — Aretha Franklin, Columbia 41923 | | 1 |
| 96 | — | — | — | MORE THAN I CAN SAY — Bobby Vee, Liberty 55296 | | 1 |
| 97 | — | — | — | TUNES OF GLORY — Mitch Miller, Columbia 41941 | | 1 |
| 98 | — | — | — | A LOVER'S QUESTION — Ernestine Anderson, Mercury 71772 | | 1 |
| 99 | — | — | — | CHERRY BERRY WINE — Charley McCoy, Cadence 1390 | | 1 |
| 100 | — | — | — | BATTLE OF GETTYSBURG — Fred Darian, J.A.F. 2020 | | 1 |

# BILLBOARD HOT 100

**FOR WEEK ENDING MARCH 12**

STAR PERFORMERS showed the greatest upward progress on Hot 100 this week.
[S] Indicates that 45 r.p.m. stereo single version is available.
[△] Indicates that 33⅓ r.p.m. stereo single version is available.

| This Week | 1 Wk Ago | 2 Wks Ago | 3 Wks Ago | Title — Artist, Company, Record No. | Stereo | Weeks on Chart |
|---|---|---|---|---|---|---|
| 1 | 1 | 4 | 9 | PONY TIME — Chubby Checker, Parkway 818 | | 7 |
| 2 | 4 | 24 | — | SURRENDER — Elvis Presley, RCA Victor 7850 | | 3 |
| 3 | 10 | 10 | 15 | WHEELS — String-A-Longs, Warwick 603 | | 9 |
| 4 | 5 | 15 | 28 | DON'T WORRY (LIKE ALL THE OTHER TIMES) — Marty Robbins, Columbia 41922 | [S] | 6 |
| 5 | 7 | 11 | 16 | WHERE THE BOYS ARE — Connie Francis, MGM 12071 | | 8 |
| 6 | 2 | 1 | 1 | CALCUTTA — Lawrence Welk, Dot 16161 | | 13 |
| 7 | 12 | 12 | 14 | BABY SITTIN' BOOGIE — Buzz Clifford, Columbia 41876 | [S] | 9 |
| 8 | 6 | 9 | 13 | DEDICATED TO THE ONE I LOVE — Shirelles, Scepter 1203 | | 7 |
| 9 | 3 | 5 | 10 | THERE'S A MOON OUT TONIGHT — Capris, Old Town 1094 | | 10 |
| 10 | 9 | 18 | 40 | EBONY EYES — Everly Brothers, Warner Bros. 5199 | | 6 |
| 11 | 13 | 14 | 25 | GOOD TIME BABY — Bobby Rydell, Cameo 186 | | 7 |
| 12 | 24 | 31 | 32 | YOU CAN HAVE HER — Roy Hamilton, Epic 9434 | | 6 |
| 13 | 18 | 21 | 26 | SPANISH HARLEM — Ben E. King, Atco 6185 | | 10 |
| 14 | 8 | 2 | 3 | SHOP AROUND — Miracles, Tamla 54034 | | 13 |
| 15 | 20 | 26 | 48 | APACHE — Jorgen Ingmann, Atco 6184 | | 7 |
| 16 | 11 | 3 | 2 | (WILL YOU LOVE ME) TOMORROW — Shirelles, Scepter 1211 | | 16 |
| 17 | 28 | 39 | 44 | WALK RIGHT BACK — Everly Brothers, Warner Bros. 5199 | | 5 |
| 18 | 14 | 8 | 5 | EXODUS — Ferrante and Teicher, United Artists 274 | [S] | 17 |
| 19 | 15 | 6 | 4 | CALENDAR GIRL — Neil Sedaka, RCA Victor 7829 | [S] | 12 |
| 20 | 17 | 13 | 12 | WINGS OF A DOVE — Ferlin Husky, Capitol 4406 | | 15 |
| 21 | 21 | 25 | 46 | LITTLE BOY SAD — Johnny Burnette, Liberty 55298 | | 5 |
| 22 | 26 | 40 | 45 | GEE WHIZ (LOOK AT HIS EYES) — Carla Thomas, Atlantic 2086 | | 6 |
| 23 | 29 | 56 | 73 | THINK TWICE — Brook Benton, Mercury 71774 | | 4 |
| 24 | 16 | 7 | 7 | EMOTIONS — Brenda Lee, Decca 31195 | | 10 |
| 25 | 19 | 19 | 19 | ALL IN MY MIND — Maxine Brown, Nomar 102 | | 10 |
| 26 | 44 | 70 | — | HEARTS OF STONE — Bill Black's Combo, Hi 2028 | | 3 |
| 27 | 27 | 22 | 27 | WHAT A PRICE — Fats Domino, Imperial 5723 | | 7 |
| 28 | 22 | 28 | 34 | ANGEL ON MY SHOULDER — Shelby Flint, Valiant WB 6001 | | 11 |
| 29 | 31 | 32 | 39 | RAM-BUNK-SHUSH — Ventures, Dolton 32 | | 7 |
| 30 | 32 | 34 | 38 | UTOPIA — Frank Gari, Crusade 1020 | | 12 |
| 31 | 35 | 37 | 50 | LAZY RIVER — Bobby Darin, Atco 6188 | | 5 |
| 32 | 58 | 79 | — | HAPPY BIRTHDAY BLUES — Kathy Young and the Innocents, Indigo 115 | | 3 |
| 33 | 25 | 27 | 31 | JIMMY'S GIRL — Johnny Tillotson, Cadence 1391 | | 9 |
| 34 | 38 | 45 | 69 | STAYIN' IN — Bobby Vee, Liberty 55296 | | 4 |
| 35 | 71 | — | — | PLEASE LOVE ME FOREVER — Cathy Jean and Roomates, Valmor 007 | | 2 |
| 36 | 42 | 53 | 71 | YOUR FRIENDS — Dee Clark, Vee Jay 372 | | 5 |
| 37 | 43 | 55 | 66 | WHEELS — Billy Vaughn, Dot 16174 | | 5 |
| 38 | 37 | 41 | 49 | WAIT A MINUTE — Coasters, Atco 6186 | | 6 |
| 39 | 46 | 75 | — | ASIA MINOR — Kokomo, Felsted 8612 | | 3 |
| 40 | 23 | 16 | 17 | THE STORY OF MY LOVE — Paul Anka, ABC-Paramount 10168 | [S] | 8 |
| 41 | 34 | 38 | 41 | NO ONE — Connie Francis, MGM 12971 | | 8 |
| 42 | 49 | 54 | 67 | HAVIN' FUN — Dion, Laurie 3081 | | 5 |
| 43 | 33 | 35 | 36 | AIN'T THAT JUST LIKE A WOMAN — Fats Domino, Imperial 5723 | | 7 |
| 44 | 84 | — | — | LONELY MAN — Elvis Presley, RCA Victor 7850 | | 2 |
| 45 | 36 | 20 | 8 | WONDERLAND BY NIGHT — Bert Kaempfert, Decca 31141 | [S] | 17 |
| 46 | 50 | 68 | 93 | FOR MY BABY — Brook Benton, Mercury 71774 | | 5 |
| 47 | 61 | 76 | — | I DON'T WANT TO CRY — Chuck Jackson, Wand 106 | | 3 |
| 48 | 57 | 69 | 77 | ONCE UPON A TIME — Rochell and the Candles, Swingin' 623 | | 5 |
| 49 | 60 | 80 | — | WATUSI — Vibrations, Checker 969 | | 3 |
| 50 | 40 | 33 | 22 | PEPE — Duane Eddy, Jamie 1175 | | 12 |
| 51 | — | — | — | ON THE REBOUND — Floyd Cramer, RCA Victor 7840 | | 1 |
| 52 | 39 | 43 | 55 | (I WANNA) LOVE MY LIFE AWAY — Gene Pitney, Musicor 1002 | | 6 |
| 53 | 79 | 98 | — | I PITY THE FOOL — Bobby Bland, Duke 332 | | 3 |
| 54 | 30 | 17 | 6 | ANGEL BABY — Rosie and the Originals, Highland 1011 | | 13 |
| 55 | 68 | 59 | 72 | MODEL GIRL — Johnny Mastro, Coed 545 | | 5 |
| 56 | 41 | 23 | 18 | MY EMPTY ARMS — Jackie Wilson, Brunswick 55201 | | 9 |
| 57 | 52 | 61 | 53 | TEAR OF THE YEAR — Jackie Wilson, Brunswick 55201 | | 7 |
| 58 | 76 | 84 | — | TO BE LOVED (FOREVER) — Pentagons, Donna 1337 | | 3 |
| 59 | 54 | 57 | 97 | CHERIE — Bobby Rydell, Cameo 186 | | 4 |
| 60 | 74 | 95 | 90 | TUNES OF GLORY — Cambridge Strings, London 1960 | | 4 |
| 61 | 63 | 97 | — | PONY EXPRESS — Danny and the Juniors, Swan 468 | | 3 |
| 62 | 48 | 30 | 43 | GHOST RIDERS IN THE SKY — Ramrods, Amy 813 | | 9 |
| 63 | 51 | 62 | 65 | AT LAST — Etta James, Argo 5386 | | 8 |
| 64 | 82 | 89 | — | LET'S GO AGAIN (WHERE WE WENT LAST NIGHT) — Hank Ballard and the Midnighters, King 5459 | | 3 |
| 65 | — | — | — | BABY BLUE — Echoes, Segway 103 | | 1 |
| 66 | — | — | — | THAT'S IT—I QUIT—I'M MOVIN' ON — Sam Cooke, RCA Victor 7853 | | 1 |
| 67 | 77 | 90 | — | I DON'T KNOW WHY — Clarence (Frogman) Henry, Argo 5378 | | 3 |
| 68 | 72 | 83 | — | TOUCHABLES — Dickie Goodman, Mark X 8009 | | 3 |
| 69 | 73 | 74 | 79 | PONY TIME — Don Corvay and the Goodtimers, Arnold 1002 | | 7 |
| 70 | — | — | — | ONE MINT JULEP — Ray Charles, Impulse 200 | | 1 |
| 71 | 80 | 78 | 80 | HONKY TONK, PART II — Bill Doggett, King 5444 | | 6 |
| 72 | 65 | 67 | 70 | WHEN I FALL IN LOVE — Etta Jones, King 5424 | | 8 |
| 73 | 89 | 92 | 96 | CERVEZA — Bert Kaempfert, Decca 30866 | | 5 |
| 74 | — | — | — | FIND ANOTHER GIRL — Jerry Butler, Vee Jay 375 | | 1 |
| 75 | 91 | — | — | ALL OF EVERYTHING — Frankie Avalon, Chancellor 1071 | | 2 |
| 76 | — | — | — | PORTRAIT OF MY LOVE — Steve Lawrence, United Artists 291 | | 1 |
| 77 | — | — | — | RUNAWAY — Del Shannon, Big Top 3067 | | 1 |
| 78 | — | — | — | IT'S UNBELIEVABLE — Larks, Sheryl 334 | | 1 |
| 79 | 94 | — | — | BEWILDERED — James Brown, King 5442 | | 2 |
| 80 | 55 | 52 | 30 | C'EST SI BON — Conway Twitty, MGM 12969 | | 10 |
| 81 | — | — | — | HIDEAWAY — Freddy King, Federal 12401 | | 1 |
| 82 | 75 | 77 | 85 | KEEP YOUR HANDS OFF OF HIM — Damita Jo, Mercury 71760 | | 5 |
| 83 | 99 | — | — | WON'T BE LONG — Aretha Franklin, Columbia 41923 | | 2 |
| 84 | 96 | — | — | MORE THAN I CAN SAY — Bobby Vee, Liberty 55296 | | 2 |
| 85 | 83 | 96 | — | ORANGE BLOSSOM SPECIAL — Billy Vaughn, Dot 16174 | | 3 |
| 86 | — | — | — | SECOND TIME AROUND — Frank Sinatra, Reprise 20001 | | 1 |
| 87 | — | — | — | BLUE MOON — Marcels, Colpix 186 | | 1 |
| 88 | 97 | — | — | TUNES OF GLORY — Mitch Miller, Columbia 41941 | | 2 |
| 89 | — | — | — | BLUE MOON — Classics, Promo 1010 | | 1 |
| 90 | 70 | 72 | 83 | BYE, BYE, BABY — Mary Wells, Motown 1003 | | 6 |
| 91 | 67 | 71 | 76 | MOST BEAUTIFUL WORDS — Della Reese, RCA Victor 7833 | | 5 |
| 92 | — | — | — | LITTLE MISS STUCKUP — Playmates, Roulette 4322 | | 1 |
| 93 | — | — | — | TONIGHT I FELL IN LOVE — Tokens, Warwick 615 | | 1 |
| 94 | 90 | 99 | — | TOP FORTY, NEWS, WEATHER & SPORTS — Mark Dinning, MGM 12980 | | 3 |
| 95 | — | — | — | MILORD — Edith Piaf, Capitol 4493 | | 1 |
| 96 | 85 | 91 | 98 | A TEXAN AND A GIRL FROM MEXICO — Anita Bryant, Carlton 538 | | 4 |
| 97 | — | — | — | LING TING TONG — Buddy Knox, Liberty 55305 | | 1 |
| 98 | 86 | — | — | JA-DA — Johnny and the Hurricanes, Big Top 3063 | | 2 |
| 99 | — | — | — | I LIED TO MY HEART — Enchanters, Musitron 1072 | | 1 |
| 100 | — | — | — | APACHE — Sonny James, RCA Victor 7858 | | 1 |

# BILLBOARD HOT 100

**FOR WEEK ENDING MARCH 19**

MARCH 13, 1961

STAR PERFORMERS showed the greatest upward progress on Hot 100 this week.
Ⓢ Indicates that 45 r.p.m. stereo single version is available.
Ⓐ Indicates that 33⅓ r.p.m. stereo single version is available.

| This Week | 1 Wk Ago | 2 Wks Ago | 3 Wks Ago | Title — Artist, Company, Record No. | Weeks on Chart |
|---|---|---|---|---|---|
| 1 | 1 | 1 | 4 | PONY TIME — Chubby Checker, Parkway 818 | 8 |
| 2 | 2 | 4 | 24 | SURRENDER — Elvis Presley, RCA Victor 7850 | 4 |
| 3 | 3 | 10 | 10 | WHEELS — String-A-Longs, Warwick 603 | 10 |
| 4 | 4 | 5 | 15 | DON'T WORRY (LIKE ALL THE OTHER TIMES) — Marty Robbins, Columbia 41922 | 7 |
| 5 | 5 | 7 | 11 | WHERE THE BOYS ARE — Connie Francis, MGM 12071 | 9 |
| 6 | 7 | 12 | 12 | BABY SITTIN' BOOGIE — Buzz Clifford, Columbia 41876 | 10 |
| 7 | 8 | 6 | 9 | DEDICATED TO THE ONE I LOVE — Shirelles, Scepter 1203 | 8 |
| 8 | 6 | 2 | 1 | CALCUTTA — Lawrence Welk, Dot 16161 | 14 |
| 9 | 10 | 9 | 18 | EBONY EYES — Everly Brothers, Warner Bros. 5199 | 7 |
| 10 | 13 | 18 | 21 | SPANISH HARLEM — Ben E. King, Atco 6185 | 11 |
| 11 | 15 | 20 | 26 | APACHE — Jorgen Ingmann, Atco 6184 | 8 |
| 12 | 11 | 13 | 14 | GOOD TIME BABY — Bobby Rydell, Cameo 186 | 8 |
| 13 | 17 | 28 | 39 | WALK RIGHT BACK — Everly Brothers, Warner Bros. 5199 | 6 |
| 14 | 9 | 3 | 5 | THERE'S A MOON OUT TONIGHT — Capris, Old Town 1094 | 11 |
| ★15 | 22 | 26 | 40 | GEE WHIZ (LOOK AT HIS EYES) — Carla Thomas, Atlantic 2086 | 7 |
| 16 | 12 | 24 | 31 | YOU CAN HAVE HER — Roy Hamilton, Epic 9434 | 7 |
| 17 | 21 | 21 | 25 | LITTLE BOY SAD — Johnny Burnette, Liberty 55298 | 6 |
| 18 | 16 | 11 | 3 | (WILL YOU LOVE ME) TOMORROW — Shirelles, Scepter 1211 | 17 |
| 19 | 18 | 14 | 8 | EXODUS — Ferrante and Teicher, United Artists 274 | 18 |
| 20 | 23 | 29 | 56 | THINK TWICE — Brook Benton, Mercury 71774 | 5 |
| 21 | 26 | 44 | 70 | HEARTS OF STONE — Bill Black's Combo, Hi 2028 | 4 |
| ★22 | 35 | 71 | — | PLEASE LOVE ME FOREVER — Cathy Jean and Roomates, Valmor 007 | 3 |
| 23 | 14 | 8 | 2 | SHOP AROUND — Miracles, Tamla 54034 | 14 |
| ★24 | 51 | — | — | ON THE REBOUND — Floyd Cramer, RCA Victor 7840 | 2 |
| 25 | 31 | 35 | 37 | LAZY RIVER — Bobby Darin, Atco 6188 | 6 |
| 26 | 19 | 15 | 6 | CALENDAR GIRL — Neil Sedaka, RCA Victor 7829 | 13 |
| 27 | 30 | 32 | 34 | UTOPIA — Frank Gari, Crusade 1020 | 13 |
| 28 | 37 | 43 | 55 | WHEELS — Billy Vaughn, Dot 16174 | 6 |
| 29 | 27 | 27 | 22 | WHAT A PRICE — Fats Domino, Imperial 5723 | 8 |
| 30 | 20 | 17 | 13 | WINGS OF A DOVE — Ferlin Husky, Capitol 4406 | 16 |
| 31 | 29 | 31 | 32 | RAM-BUNK-SHUSH — Ventures, Dolton 32 | 8 |
| 32 | 32 | 58 | 79 | HAPPY BIRTHDAY BLUES — Kathy Young and the Innocents, Indigo 115 | 4 |
| 33 | 34 | 38 | 45 | STAYIN' IN — Bobby Vee, Liberty 55296 | 5 |
| 34 | 24 | 16 | 7 | EMOTIONS — Brenda Lee, Decca 31195 | 11 |
| 35 | 44 | 84 | — | LONELY MAN — Elvis Presley, RCA Victor 7850 | 3 |
| 36 | 39 | 46 | 75 | ASIA MINOR — Kokomo, Felsted 8612 | 4 |
| 37 | 43 | 33 | 35 | AIN'T THAT JUST LIKE A WOMAN — Fats Domino, Imperial 5723 | 8 |
| 38 | 36 | 42 | 53 | YOUR FRIENDS — Dee Clark, Vee Jay 372 | 6 |
| 39 | 49 | 60 | 80 | WATUSI — Vibrations, Checker 969 | 4 |
| 40 | 47 | 61 | 76 | I DON'T WANT TO CRY — Chuck Jackson, Wand 106 | 4 |
| 41 | 55 | 68 | 59 | MODEL GIRL — Johnny Mastro, Coed 545 | 6 |
| 42 | 28 | 22 | 28 | ANGEL ON MY SHOULDER — Shelby Flint, Valiant WB 6001 | 12 |
| 43 | 38 | 37 | 41 | WAIT A MINUTE — Coasters, Atco 6186 | 7 |
| 44 | 25 | 19 | 19 | ALL IN MY MIND — Maxine Brown, Nomar 102 | 11 |
| 45 | 48 | 57 | 69 | ONCE UPON A TIME — Rochell and the Candles, Swingin' 623 | 6 |
| 46 | 53 | 79 | 98 | I PITY THE FOOL — Bobby Bland, Duke 332 | 4 |
| 47 | 66 | — | — | THAT'S IT—I QUIT—I'M MOVIN' ON — Sam Cooke, RCA Victor 7853 | 2 |
| 48 | 33 | 25 | 27 | JIMMY'S GIRL — Johnny Tillotson, Cadence 1391 | 10 |
| 49 | 46 | 50 | 68 | FOR MY BABY — Brook Benton, Mercury 71774 | 6 |
| 50 | 64 | 82 | 89 | LET'S GO AGAIN (WHERE WE WENT LAST NIGHT) — Hank Ballard and the Midnighters, King 5459 | 4 |
| 51 | 65 | — | — | BABY BLUE — Echoes, Segway 103 | 2 |
| 52 | 67 | 77 | 90 | BUT I DO — Clarence (Frogman) Henry, Argo 5378 | 4 |
| 53 | 52 | 39 | 43 | (I WANNA) LOVE MY LIFE AWAY — Gene Pitney, Musicor 1002 | 7 |
| 54 | 70 | — | — | ONE MINT JULEP — Ray Charles, Impulse 200 | 2 |
| 55 | 74 | — | — | FIND ANOTHER GIRL — Jerry Butler, Vee Jay 375 | 2 |
| 56 | — | — | — | TONIGHT MY LOVE, TONIGHT — Paul Anka, ABC-Paramount 10194 | 1 |
| 57 | 77 | — | — | RUNAWAY — Del Shannon, Big Top 3067 | 2 |
| 58 | 58 | 76 | 84 | TO BE LOVED (FOREVER) — Pentagons, Donna 1337 | 4 |
| 59 | 87 | — | — | BLUE MOON — Marcels, Colpix 186 | 2 |
| 60 | 61 | 63 | 97 | PONY EXPRESS — Danny and the Juniors, Swan 468 | 4 |
| 61 | 71 | 80 | 78 | HONKY TONK, PART II — Bill Doggett, King 5444 | 7 |
| 62 | 76 | — | — | PORTRAIT OF MY LOVE — Steve Lawrence, United Artists 291 | 2 |
| 63 | — | — | — | TAKE GOOD CARE OF HER — Adam Wade, Coed 546 | 1 |
| 64 | 68 | 72 | 83 | TOUCHABLES — Dickie Goodman, Mark X 8009 | 4 |
| 65 | 89 | — | — | BLUE MOON — Classics, Promo 1010 | 2 |
| 66 | 69 | 73 | 74 | PONY TIME — Don Corvay and the Goodtimers, Arnold 1002 | 8 |
| 67 | 42 | 49 | 54 | HAVIN' FUN — Dion, Laurie 3081 | 6 |
| 68 | 81 | — | — | HIDEAWAY — Freddy King, Federal 12401 | 2 |
| 69 | 78 | — | — | IT'S UNBELIEVABLE — Larks, Sheryl 334 | 2 |
| 70 | 75 | 91 | — | ALL OF EVERYTHING — Frankie Avalon, Chancellor 1071 | 3 |
| 71 | 60 | 74 | 95 | TUNES OF GLORY — Cambridge Strings, London 1960 | 5 |
| 72 | 79 | 94 | — | BEWILDERED — James Brown, King 5442 | 3 |
| 73 | 73 | 89 | 92 | CERVEZA — Bert Kaempfert, Decca 30866 | 6 |
| 74 | 85 | 83 | 96 | ORANGE BLOSSOM SPECIAL — Billy Vaughn, Dot 16174 | 4 |
| ★75 | — | 69 | 63 | GINNIE BELL — Paul Dino, Promo 2180 | 7 |
| 76 | 83 | 99 | — | WON'T BE LONG — Aretha Franklin, Columbia 41923 | 3 |
| 77 | — | — | — | PLEASE TELL ME WHY — Jackie Wilson, Brunswick 55208 | 1 |
| 78 | — | — | — | TRUST IN ME — Etta James, Argo 5385 | 1 |
| 79 | 93 | — | — | TONIGHT I FELL IN LOVE — Tokens, Warwick 615 | 2 |
| 80 | 84 | 96 | — | MORE THAN I CAN SAY — Bobby Vee, Liberty 55296 | 3 |
| 81 | 94 | 90 | 99 | TOP FORTY, NEWS, WEATHER & SPORTS — Mark Dinning, MGM 12980 | 4 |
| 82 | 97 | — | — | LING TING TONG — Buddy Knox, Liberty 55305 | 2 |
| 83 | 92 | — | — | LITTLE MISS STUCKUP — Playmates, Roulette 4322 | 2 |
| 84 | — | — | — | LONELY BLUE NIGHTS — Rosie, Brunswick 55205 | 1 |
| 85 | 86 | — | — | SECOND TIME AROUND — Frank Sinatra, Reprise 20001 | 2 |
| 86 | — | — | — | I'VE TOLD EVERY LITTLE STAR — Linda Scott, Canadian-American 123 | 1 |
| 87 | 100 | — | — | APACHE — Sonny James, RCA Victor 7858 | 2 |
| 88 | 95 | — | — | MILORD — Edith Piaf, Capitol 4493 | 2 |
| 89 | — | — | — | JUST FOR OLD TIME'S SAKE — McGuire Sisters, Coral 62249 | 1 |
| 90 | — | — | — | MERRY-GO-ROUND — Marv Johnson, United Artists 294 | 1 |
| 91 | — | — | — | CANADIAN SUNSET — Etta Jones, Prestige 191 | 1 |
| 92 | — | — | — | MEMPHIS — Donnie Brooks, Era 3042 | 1 |
| 93 | — | — | — | VERY THOUGHT OF YOU — Little Willie John, King 5458 | 1 |
| 94 | — | — | — | OH MEIN PAPA — Dickie Lee, Blue Bell 503 | 1 |
| 95 | — | — | — | EARLY EVERY MORNING — Dinah Washington, Mercury 71778 | 1 |
| 96 | 99 | — | — | I LIED TO MY HEART — Enchanters, Musitron 1072 | 2 |
| 97 | — | — | — | COWBOY JIMMY JOE — Lolita, Kapp 370 | 3 |
| 98 | — | — | — | KOKOMO — Flamingos, End 1085 | 1 |
| 99 | — | — | — | LITTLE TURTLE DOVE — Otis Williams and the Charms, King 5455 | 1 |
| 100 | — | — | — | YOUR ONE AND ONLY LOVE — Jackie Wilson, Brunswick 55208 | 1 |

# BILLBOARD HOT 100

**FOR WEEK ENDING MARCH 26**

*MARCH 20, 1961*

STAR PERFORMERS showed the greatest upward progress on Hot 100 this week.
(S) Indicates that 45 r.p.m. stereo single version is available.
(A) Indicates that 33⅓ r.p.m. stereo single version is available.

| This Week | 1 Wk Ago | 2 Wks Ago | 3 Wks Ago | Title / Artist, Company, Record No. | Stereo | Weeks on Chart |
|---|---|---|---|---|---|---|
| 1 | 2 | 2 | 4 | SURRENDER — Elvis Presley, RCA Victor 7850 | | 5 |
| 2 | 1 | 1 | 1 | PONY TIME — Chubby Checker, Parkway 818 | | 9 |
| 3 | 4 | 4 | 5 | DON'T WORRY (LIKE ALL THE OTHER TIMES) — Marty Robbins, Columbia 41922 | S | 8 |
| 4 | 5 | 5 | 7 | WHERE THE BOYS ARE — Connie Francis, MGM 12071 | | 10 |
| 5 | 7 | 8 | 6 | DEDICATED TO THE ONE I LOVE — Shirelles, Scepter 1203 | | 9 |
| ★6 | 11 | 15 | 20 | APACHE — Jorgen Ingmann, Atco 6184 | | 9 |
| 7 | 3 | 3 | 10 | WHEELS — String-A-Longs, Warwick 603 | | 11 |
| 8 | 9 | 10 | 9 | EBONY EYES — Everly Brothers, Warner Bros. 5199 | | 8 |
| 9 | 13 | 17 | 28 | WALK RIGHT BACK — Everly Brothers, Warner Bros. 5199 | | 7 |
| 10 | 6 | 7 | 12 | BABY SITTIN' BOOGIE — Buzz Clifford, Columbia 41876 | S | 11 |
| ★11 | 10 | 13 | 18 | SPANISH HARLEM — Ben E. King, Atco 6185 | | 12 |
| 12 | 15 | 22 | 26 | GEE WHIZ (LOOK AT HIS EYES) — Carla Thomas, Atlantic 2086 | | 8 |
| ★13 | 20 | 23 | 29 | THINK TWICE — Brook Benton, Mercury 71774 | | 6 |
| 14 | 8 | 6 | 2 | CALCUTTA — Lawrence Welk, Dot 16161 | | 15 |
| 15 | 24 | 51 | — | ON THE REBOUND — Floyd Cramer, RCA Victor 7840 | | 3 |
| 16 | 12 | 11 | 13 | GOOD TIME BABY — Bobby Rydell, Cameo 186 | | 9 |
| 17 | 17 | 21 | 21 | LITTLE BOY SAD — Johnny Burnette, Liberty 55298 | | 7 |
| ★18 | 25 | 31 | 35 | LAZY RIVER — Bobby Darin, Atco 6188 | | 7 |
| 19 | 14 | 9 | 3 | THERE'S A MOON OUT TONIGHT — Capris, Old Town 1094 | | 12 |
| 20 | 21 | 26 | 44 | HEARTS OF STONE — Bill Black's Combo, Hi 2028 | | 5 |
| ★21 | 59 | 87 | — | BLUE MOON — Marcels, Colpix 186 | | 3 |
| 22 | 22 | 35 | 71 | PLEASE LOVE ME FOREVER — Cathy Jean and Roomates, Valmor 007 | | 4 |
| 23 | 16 | 12 | 24 | YOU CAN HAVE HER — Roy Hamilton, Epic 9434 | | 8 |
| 24 | 18 | 16 | 11 | (WILL YOU LOVE ME) TOMORROW — Shirelles, Scepter 1211 | | 18 |
| ★25 | 39 | 49 | 60 | WATUSI — Vibrations, Checker 969 | | 5 |
| 26 | 23 | 14 | 8 | SHOP AROUND — Miracles, Tamla 54034 | | 15 |
| 27 | 19 | 18 | 14 | EXODUS — Ferrante and Teicher, United Artists 274 | S | 19 |
| ★28 | 49 | 46 | 50 | FOR MY BABY — Brook Benton, Mercury 71774 | | 7 |
| ★29 | 41 | 55 | 68 | MODEL GIRL — Johnny Mastro, Coed 545 | | 7 |
| 30 | 32 | 32 | 58 | HAPPY BIRTHDAY BLUES — Kathy Young and the Innocents, Indigo 115 | | 5 |
| 31 | 28 | 37 | 43 | WHEELS — Billy Vaughn, Dot 16174 | | 7 |
| 32 | 35 | 44 | 84 | LONELY MAN — Elvis Presley, RCA Victor 7850 | | 4 |
| 33 | 36 | 39 | 46 | ASIA MINOR — Kokomo, Felsted 8612 | | 5 |
| 34 | 38 | 36 | 42 | YOUR FRIENDS — Dee Clark, Vee Jay 371 | | 7 |
| 35 | 26 | 19 | 15 | CALENDAR GIRL — Neil Sedaka, RCA Victor 7829 | S | 14 |
| 36 | 40 | 47 | 61 | I DON'T WANT TO CRY — Chuck Jackson, Wand 106 | | 5 |
| ★37 | 47 | 66 | — | THAT'S IT—I QUIT—I'M MOVIN' ON — Sam Cooke, RCA Victor 7853 | | 3 |
| 38 | 30 | 20 | 17 | WINGS OF A DOVE — Ferlin Husky, Capitol 4406 | | 17 |
| 39 | 50 | 64 | 82 | LET'S GO AGAIN (WHERE WE WENT LAST NIGHT) — Hank Ballard and the Midnighters, King 5459 | | 5 |
| 40 | 52 | 67 | 77 | BUT I DO — Clarence (Frogman) Henry, Argo 5378 | | 5 |
| 41 | 51 | 65 | — | BABY BLUE — Echoes, Segway 103 | | 3 |
| 42 | 45 | 48 | 57 | ONCE UPON A TIME — Rochell and the Candles, Swingin' 623 | | 7 |
| ★43 | 63 | — | — | TAKE GOOD CARE OF HER — Adam Wade, Coed 546 | | 2 |
| 44 | 54 | 70 | — | ONE MINT JULEP — Ray Charles, Impulse 200 | | 3 |
| 45 | 56 | — | — | TONIGHT MY LOVE, TONIGHT — Paul Anka, ABC-Paramount 10194 | | 2 |
| 46 | 29 | 27 | 27 | WHAT A PRICE — Fats Domino, Imperial 5723 | | 9 |
| 47 | 57 | 77 | — | RUNAWAY — Del Shannon, Big Top 3067 | | 3 |
| 48 | 46 | 53 | 79 | I PITY THE FOOL — Bobby Bland, Duke 332 | | 5 |
| 49 | 33 | 34 | 38 | STAYIN' IN — Bobby Vee, Liberty 55296 | | 6 |
| 50 | 55 | 74 | — | FIND ANOTHER GIRL — Jerry Butler, Vee Jay 375 | | 3 |
| 51 | 31 | 29 | 31 | RAM-BUNK-SHUSH — Ventures, Dolton 32 | | 9 |
| 52 | 77 | — | — | PLEASE TELL ME WHY — Jackie Wilson, Brunswick 55208 | | 2 |
| 53 | 68 | 81 | — | HIDEAWAY — Freddy King, Federal 12401 | | 3 |
| 54 | 62 | 76 | — | PORTRAIT OF MY LOVE — Steve Lawrence, United Artists 291 | | 3 |
| 55 | 65 | 89 | — | BLUE MOON — Classics, Promo 1010 | | 3 |
| 56 | 58 | 58 | 76 | TO BE LOVED (FOREVER) — Pentagons, Donna 1337 | | 5 |
| 57 | 61 | 71 | 80 | HONKY TONK, PART II — Bill Doggett, King 5444 | | 7 |
| 58 | 34 | 24 | 16 | EMOTIONS — Brenda Lee, Decca 31195 | | 12 |
| 59 | 72 | 79 | 94 | BEWILDERED — James Brown, King 5442 | | 4 |
| 60 | 66 | 69 | 73 | PONY TIME — Don Corvay and the Goodtimers, Arnold 1002 | | 9 |
| 61 | 80 | 84 | 96 | MORE THAN I CAN SAY — Bobby Vee, Liberty 55296 | | 4 |
| 62 | 64 | 68 | 72 | TOUCHABLES — Dickie Goodman, Mark X 8009 | | 5 |
| 63 | 74 | 85 | 83 | ORANGE BLOSSOM SPECIAL — Billy Vaughn, Dot 16174 | | 5 |
| 64 | 100 | — | — | YOUR ONE AND ONLY LOVE — Jackie Wilson, Brunswick 55208 | | 2 |
| 65 | 86 | — | — | I'VE TOLD EVERY LITTLE STAR — Linda Scott, Canadian-American 123 | | 2 |
| 66 | 84 | — | — | LONELY BLUE NIGHTS — Rosie, Brunswick 55205 | | 2 |
| 67 | 78 | — | — | TRUST IN ME — Etta James, Argo 5385 | | 2 |
| 68 | 75 | — | 69 | GINNIE BELL — Paul Dino, Promo 2180 | | 8 |
| 69 | 69 | 78 | — | IT'S UNBELIEVABLE — Larks, Sheryl 334 | | 3 |
| 70 | 60 | 61 | 63 | PONY EXPRESS — Danny and the Juniors, Swan 468 | | 5 |
| 71 | 71 | 60 | 74 | TUNES OF GLORY — Cambridge Strings, London 1960 | | 6 |
| 72 | 48 | 33 | 25 | JIMMY'S GIRL — Johnny Tillotson, Cadence 1391 | | 11 |
| 73 | 44 | 25 | 19 | ALL IN MY MIND — Maxine Brown, Nomar 102 | | 12 |
| 74 | 70 | 75 | 91 | ALL OF EVERYTHING — Frankie Avalon, Chancellor 1071 | | 4 |
| 75 | — | — | — | ONE-EYED JACKS — Ferrante and Teicher, United Artists 300 | | 1 |
| 76 | 27 | 30 | 32 | UTOPIA — Frank Gari, Crusade 1020 | | 14 |
| 77 | 79 | 93 | — | TONIGHT I FELL IN LOVE — Tokens, Warwick 615 | | 3 |
| 78 | 83 | 92 | — | LITTLE MISS STUCKUP — Playmates, Roulette 4322 | | 3 |
| 79 | — | 90 | 70 | BYE, BYE, BABY — Mary Wells, Motown 1003 | | 7 |
| 80 | 85 | 86 | — | SECOND TIME AROUND — Frank Sinatra, Reprise 20001 | | 3 |
| 81 | 82 | 97 | — | LING TING TONG — Buddy Knox, Liberty 55305 | | 3 |
| 82 | 43 | 38 | 37 | WAIT A MINUTE — Coasters, Atco 6186 | | 8 |
| 83 | 93 | — | — | VERY THOUGHT OF YOU — Little Willie John, King 5458 | | 2 |
| 84 | — | — | — | FELL IN LOVE ON MONDAY — Fats Domino, Imperial 5734 | | 1 |
| 85 | 81 | 94 | 90 | TOP FORTY, NEWS, WEATHER & SPORTS — Mark Dinning, MGM 12980 | | 5 |
| 86 | 53 | 52 | 39 | (I WANNA) LOVE MY LIFE AWAY — Gene Pitney, Musicor 1002 | | 8 |
| 87 | 90 | — | — | MERRY-GO-ROUND — Marv Johnson, United Artists 294 | | 2 |
| 88 | 89 | — | — | JUST FOR OLD TIME'S SAKE — McGuire Sisters, Coral 62249 | | 2 |
| 89 | — | — | — | FOOLIN' AROUND — Kay Starr, Capitol 4542 | | 1 |
| 90 | 92 | — | — | MEMPHIS — Donnie Brooks, Era 3042 | | 2 |
| 91 | — | — | — | ONE HUNDRED POUNDS OF CLAY — Gene McDaniels, Liberty 55308 | | 1 |
| 92 | 88 | 95 | — | MILORD — Edith Piaf, Capitol 4493 | | 3 |
| 93 | — | — | — | DIXIE — Duane Eddy, Jamie 1183 | | 1 |
| 94 | — | — | — | MY THREE SONS — Lawrence Welk, Dot 16198 | | 1 |
| 95 | — | — | — | SOME KIND OF WONDERFUL — Drifters, Atlantic 2096 | | 1 |
| 96 | 98 | — | — | KOKOMO — Flamingos, End 1085 | | 2 |
| 97 | — | — | — | SHU RAH — Fats Domino, Imperial 5734 | | 1 |
| 98 | 99 | — | — | LITTLE TURTLE DOVE — Otis Williams and the Charms, King 5455 | | 2 |
| 99 | — | — | — | SEVENTEEN — Frankie Ford, Imperial 5735 | | 1 |
| 100 | — | — | — | THE BLIZZARD — Jim Reeves, RCA Victor 7855 | | 1 |

# BILLBOARD HOT 100

**FOR WEEK ENDING APRIL 2**

*STAR PERFORMERS showed the greatest upward progress on Hot 100 this week.*
*S — Indicates that 45 r.p.m. stereo single version is available.*
*A — Indicates that 33⅓ r.p.m. stereo single version is available.*

| This Week | 1 Wk Ago | 2 Wks Ago | 3 Wks Ago | Title — Artist, Company, Record No. | Weeks on Chart |
|---|---|---|---|---|---|
| 1 | 1 | 2 | 2 | SURRENDER — Elvis Presley, RCA Victor 7850 | 6 |
| 2 | 2 | 1 | 1 | PONY TIME — Chubby Checker, Parkway 818 | 10 |
| 3 | 5 | 7 | 8 | DEDICATED TO THE ONE I LOVE — Shirelles, Scepter 1203 | 10 |
| 4 | 6 | 11 | 15 | APACHE — Jorgen Ingmann, Atco 6184 | 10 |
| 5 | 3 | 4 | 4 | DON'T WORRY (LIKE ALL THE OTHER TIMES) — Marty Robbins, Columbia 41922 | 9 |
| ★6 | 21 | 59 | 87 | BLUE MOON — Marcels, Colpix 186 | 4 |
| 7 | 9 | 13 | 17 | WALK RIGHT BACK — Everly Brothers, Warner Bros. 5199 | 8 |
| 8 | 7 | 3 | 3 | WHEELS — String-A-Longs, Warwick 603 | 12 |
| 9 | 4 | 5 | 5 | WHERE THE BOYS ARE — Connie Francis, MGM 12971 | 11 |
| 10 | 12 | 15 | 22 | GEE WHIZ (LOOK AT HIS EYES) — Carla Thomas, Atlantic 2086 | 9 |
| 11 | 15 | 24 | 51 | ON THE REBOUND — Floyd Cramer, RCA Victor 7840 | 4 |
| 12 | 13 | 20 | 23 | THINK TWICE — Brook Benton, Mercury 71774 | 7 |
| 13 | 8 | 9 | 10 | EBONY EYES — Everly Brothers, Warner Bros. 5199 | 9 |
| 14 | 18 | 25 | 31 | LAZY RIVER — Bobby Darin, Atco 6188 | 8 |
| ★15 | 33 | 36 | 39 | ASIA MINOR — Kokomo, Felsted 8612 | 6 |
| 16 | 11 | 10 | 13 | SPANISH HARLEM — Ben E. King, Atco 6185 | 13 |
| ★17 | 40 | 52 | 67 | BUT I DO — Clarence (Frogman) Henry, Argo 5378 | 6 |
| 18 | 17 | 17 | 21 | LITTLE BOY SAD — Johnny Burnette, Liberty 55298 | 8 |
| 19 | 10 | 6 | 7 | BABY SITTIN' BOOGIE — Buzz Clifford, Columbia 41876 | 12 |
| ★20 | 29 | 41 | 55 | MODEL GIRL — Johnny Mastro, Coed 545 | 8 |
| ★21 | 47 | 57 | 77 | RUNAWAY — Del Shannon, Big Top 3067 | 4 |
| 22 | 22 | 22 | 35 | PLEASE LOVE ME FOREVER — Cathy Jean and Roomates, Valmor 007 | 5 |
| 23 | 14 | 8 | 6 | CALCUTTA — Lawrence Welk, Dot 16161 | 16 |
| ★24 | 43 | 63 | — | TAKE GOOD CARE OF HER — Adam Wade, Coed 546 | 3 |
| 25 | 16 | 12 | 11 | GOOD TIME BABY — Bobby Rydell, Cameo 186 | 10 |
| 26 | 20 | 21 | 26 | HEARTS OF STONE — Bill Black's Combo, Hi 2028 | 6 |
| 27 | 41 | 51 | 65 | BABY BLUE — Echoes, Segway 103 | 4 |
| 28 | 25 | 39 | 49 | WATUSI — Vibrations, Checker 969 | 6 |
| 29 | 19 | 14 | 9 | THERE'S A MOON OUT TONIGHT — Capris, Old Town 1094 | 13 |
| 30 | 23 | 16 | 12 | YOU CAN HAVE HER — Roy Hamilton, Epic 9434 | 9 |
| 31 | 37 | 47 | 66 | THAT'S IT — I QUIT — I'M MOVIN' ON — Sam Cooke, RCA Victor 7853 | 4 |
| 32 | 44 | 54 | 70 | ONE MINT JULEP — Ray Charles, Impulse 200 | 4 |
| 33 | 52 | 77 | — | PLEASE TELL ME WHY — Jackie Wilson, Brunswick 55208 | 3 |
| ★34 | 45 | 56 | — | TONIGHT MY LOVE, TONIGHT — Paul Anka, ABC-Paramount 10194 | 3 |
| 35 | 42 | 45 | 48 | ONCE UPON A TIME — Rochell and the Candles, Swingin' 623 | 8 |
| 36 | 27 | 19 | 18 | EXODUS — Ferrante and Teicher, United Artists 274 | 20 |
| 37 | 30 | 32 | 32 | HAPPY BIRTHDAY BLUES — Kathy Young and the Innocents, Indigo 16174 | 6 |
| 38 | 26 | 23 | 14 | SHOP AROUND — Miracles, Tamla 54034 | 16 |
| 39 | 34 | 38 | 36 | YOUR FRIENDS — Dee Clark, Vee Jay 372 | 8 |
| ★40 | 64 | 100 | — | YOUR ONE AND ONLY LOVE — Jackie Wilson, Brunswick 55208 | 3 |
| ★41 | 84 | — | — | FELL IN LOVE ON MONDAY — Fats Domino, Imperial 5734 | 2 |
| 42 | 24 | 18 | 16 | (WILL YOU LOVE ME) TOMORROW — Shirelles, Scepter 1211 | 19 |
| ★43 | 67 | 78 | — | TRUST IN ME — Etta James, Argo 5385 | 3 |
| 44 | 39 | 50 | 64 | LET'S GO AGAIN (WHERE WE WENT LAST NIGHT) — Hand Ballard and the Midnighters, King 5459 | 6 |
| 45 | 53 | 68 | 81 | HIDEAWAY — Freddy King, Federal 12401 | 4 |
| ★46 | 65 | 86 | — | I'VE TOLD EVERY LITTLE STAR — Linda Scott, Canadian-American 123 | 3 |
| 47 | 48 | 46 | 53 | I PITY THE FOOL — Bobby Bland, Duke 332 | 6 |
| 48 | 54 | 62 | 76 | PORTRAIT OF MY LOVE — Steve Lawrence, United Artists 291 | 4 |
| 49 | 59 | 7 | 79 | BEWILDERED — James Brown, King 5442 | 5 |
| 50 | 55 | 65 | 89 | BLUE MOON — Classics, Promo 1010 | 4 |
| 51 | 68 | 75 | — | GINNIE BELL — Paul Dino, Promo 2180 | 9 |
| 52 | 31 | 28 | 37 | WHEELS — Billy Vaughn, Dot 16174 | 8 |
| 53 | 36 | 40 | 47 | I DON'T WANT TO CRY — Chuck Jackson, Wand 106 | 6 |
| 54 | 97 | — | — | SHU RAH — Fats Domino, Imperial 5734 | 2 |
| 55 | — | — | — | MOTHER-IN-LAW — Ernie K. Doe, Minit 623 | 1 |
| 56 | 50 | 55 | 74 | FIND ANOTHER GIRL — Jerry Butler, Vee Jay 375 | 4 |
| 57 | 38 | 30 | 20 | WINGS OF A DOVE — Ferlin Husky, Capitol 4406 | 18 |
| 58 | 28 | 49 | 46 | FOR MY BABY — Brook Benton, Mercury 71774 | 8 |
| 59 | 57 | 61 | 71 | HONKY TONK, PART II — Bill Doggett, King 5444 | 8 |
| 60 | 62 | 64 | 68 | TOUCHABLES — Dickie Goodman, Mark X 8009 | 6 |
| 61 | 75 | — | — | ONE-EYED JACKS — Ferrante and Teicher, United Artists 300 | 2 |
| 62 | — | — | — | YOU CAN DEPEND ON ME — Brenda Lee, Decca 31231 | 1 |
| 63 | 32 | 35 | 44 | LONELY MAN — Elvis Presley, RCA Victor 7850 | 5 |
| 64 | 95 | — | — | SOME KIND OF WONDERFUL — Drifters, Atlantic 2096 | 2 |
| 65 | 80 | 85 | 86 | SECOND TIME AROUND — Frank Sinatra, Reprise 20001 | 4 |
| 66 | 94 | — | — | MY THREE SONS — Lawrence Welk, Dot 16198 | 2 |
| 67 | 35 | 26 | 19 | CALENDAR GIRL — Neil Sedaka, RCA Victor 7829 | 15 |
| 68 | 70 | 60 | 61 | PONY EXPRESS — Danny and the Juniors, Swan 468 | 6 |
| 69 | 61 | 80 | 84 | MORE THAN I CAN SAY — Bobby Vee, Liberty 55296 | 5 |
| 70 | 81 | 82 | 97 | LING TING TONG — Buddy Knox, Liberty 55305 | 4 |
| ★71 | 91 | — | — | ONE HUNDRED POUNDS OF CLAY — Gene McDaniels, Liberty 55308 | 2 |
| 72 | 78 | 83 | 92 | LITTLE MISS STUCKUP — Playmates, Roulette 4322 | 4 |
| 73 | 83 | 93 | — | VERY THOUGHT OF YOU — Little Willie John, King 5458 | 3 |
| 74 | 66 | 84 | — | LONELY BLUE NIGHTS — Rosie, Brunswick 55205 | 3 |
| 75 | 79 | — | 90 | BYE, BYE, BABY — Mary Wells, Motown 1003 | 8 |
| 76 | 77 | 79 | 93 | TONIGHT I FELL IN LOVE — Tokens, Warwick 615 | 4 |
| 77 | 93 | — | — | DIXIE — Duane Eddy, Jamie 1183 | 2 |
| 78 | 88 | 89 | — | JUST FOR OLD TIME'S SAKE — McGuire Sisters, Coral 62249 | 3 |
| 79 | 49 | 33 | 34 | STAYIN' IN — Bobby Vee, Liberty 55296 | 7 |
| 80 | — | — | — | BRASS BUTTONS — String-A-Longs, Warwick 625 | 1 |
| 81 | 89 | — | — | FOOLIN' AROUND — Kay Starr, Capitol 4542 | 2 |
| 82 | 100 | — | — | THE BLIZZARD — Jim Reeves, RCA Victor 7855 | 2 |
| 83 | — | — | — | FUNNY — Maxine Brown, Nomar 106 | 1 |
| 84 | 87 | 90 | — | MERRY-GO-ROUND — Marv Johnson, United Artists 294 | 3 |
| 85 | — | — | — | AIN'T IT BABY — Miracles, Tamla 54036 | 1 |
| 86 | 56 | 58 | 58 | TO BE LOVED (FOREVER) — Pentagons, Donna 1337 | 6 |
| 87 | — | — | — | TENDERLY — Bert Kaempfert, Decca 31236 | 1 |
| 88 | — | — | — | DADDY'S HOME — Shep and the Limelites, Hull 740 | 1 |
| 89 | — | — | — | SLEEPY-EYED JOHN — Johnny Horton, Columbia 41963 | 1 |
| 90 | — | — | — | BUMBLE BOOGIE — B. Bumble, Rendezvous 140 | 1 |
| 91 | 99 | — | — | SEVENTEEN — Frankie Ford, Imperial 5735 | 2 |
| 92 | — | — | — | I'M IN THE MOOD FOR LOVE — Chimes, Tag 445 | 1 |
| 93 | — | — | — | I TOLD YOU SO — Jimmy Jones, Cub 9085 | 1 |
| 94 | — | — | — | LIKE LONG HAIR — Paul Revere and the Raiders, Gardena 116 | 1 |
| 95 | 63 | 74 | 85 | ORANGE BLOSSOM SPECIAL — Billy Vaughn, Dot 16174 | 6 |
| 96 | — | — | — | TRIANGLE — Janie Grant, Caprice 104 | 1 |
| 97 | — | — | — | WHERE I FELL IN LOVE — Capris, Old Town 1099 | 1 |
| 98 | — | — | — | LITTLE PEDRO — Olympics, Arvee 5023 | 1 |
| 99 | 85 | 81 | 94 | TOP FORTY, NEWS, WEATHER & SPORTS — Mark Dinning, MGM 12980 | 6 |
| 100 | — | — | — | GREEN GRASS OF TEXAS — Texans, Infinity 001 | 1 |

# BILLBOARD HOT 100

**APRIL 3, 1961**
**FOR WEEK ENDING APRIL 9, 1961**

| This Week | 1 Wk Ago | 2 Wks Ago | 3 Wks Ago | Title | Artist, Company, Record No. | Weeks on Chart |
|---|---|---|---|---|---|---|
| 1 | 6 | 21 | 59 | BLUE MOON | Marcels, Colpix 186 | 5 |
| 2 | 4 | 6 | 11 | APACHE | Jorgen Ingmann, Atco 6184 | 11 |
| 3 | 1 | 1 | 2 | SURRENDER | Elvis Presley, RCA Victor 7850 | 7 |
| 4 | 2 | 2 | 1 | PONY TIME | Chubby Checker, Parkway 818 | 11 |
| 5 | 3 | 5 | 7 | DEDICATED TO THE ONE I LOVE | Shirelles, Scepter 1203 | 11 |
| 6 | 5 | 3 | 4 | DON'T WORRY (LIKE ALL THE OTHER TIMES) | Marty Robbins, Columbia 41922 | 10 |
| 7 | 11 | 15 | 24 | ON THE REBOUND | Floyd Cramer, RCA Victor 7840 | 5 |
| 8 | 7 | 9 | 13 | WALK RIGHT BACK | Everly Brothers, Warner Bros. 5199 | 9 |
| 9 | 21 | 47 | 57 | RUNAWAY | Del Shannon, Big Top 3067 | 5 |
| 10 | 17 | 40 | 52 | BUT I DO | Clarence (Frogman) Henry, Argo 5378 | 7 |
| 11 | 12 | 13 | 20 | THINK TWICE | Brook Benton, Mercury 71774 | 8 |
| 12 | 8 | 7 | 3 | WHEELS | String-A-Longs, Warwick 603 | 13 |
| 13 | 15 | 33 | 36 | ASIA MINOR | Kokomo, Felsted 8612 | 7 |
| 14 | 10 | 12 | 15 | GEE WHIZ (LOOK AT HIS EYES) | Carla Thomas, Atlantic 2086 | 10 |
| 15 | 9 | 4 | 5 | WHERE THE BOYS ARE | Connie Francis, MGM 12971 | 12 |
| 16 | 22 | 22 | 22 | PLEASE LOVE ME FOREVER | Cathy Jean and Roomates, Valmor 007 | 6 |
| 17 | 13 | 8 | 9 | EBONY EYES | Everly Brothers, Warner Bros. 5199 | 10 |
| 18 | 24 | 43 | 63 | TAKE GOOD CARE OF HER | Adam Wade, Coed 546 | 4 |
| 19 | 27 | 41 | 51 | BABY BLUE | Echoes, Segway 103 | 5 |
| 20 | 20 | 29 | 41 | MODEL GIRL | Johnny Mastro, Coed 545 | 9 |
| 21 | 32 | 44 | 54 | ONE MINT JULEP | Ray Charles, Impulse 200 | 5 |
| 22 | 34 | 45 | 56 | TONIGHT MY LOVE, TONIGHT | Paul Anka, ABC-Paramount 10194 | 4 |
| 23 | 55 | — | — | MOTHER-IN-LAW | Ernie K. Doe, Minit 623 | 2 |
| 24 | 16 | 11 | 10 | SPANISH HARLEM | Ben E. King, Atco 6185 | 14 |
| 25 | 46 | 65 | 86 | I'VE TOLD EVERY LITTLE STAR | Linda Scott, Canadian-American 123 | 4 |
| 26 | 71 | 91 | — | ONE HUNDRED POUNDS OF CLAY | Gene McDaniels, Liberty 55308 | 3 |
| 27 | 33 | 52 | 77 | PLEASE TELL ME WHY | Jackie Wilson, Brunswick 55208 | 4 |
| 28 | 14 | 18 | 25 | LAZY RIVER | Bobby Darin, Atco 6188 | 9 |
| 29 | 62 | — | — | YOU CAN DEPEND ON ME | Brenda Lee, Decca 31231 | 2 |
| 30 | 35 | 42 | 45 | ONCE UPON A TIME | Rochell and the Candles, Swingin' 623 | 9 |
| 31 | 31 | 37 | 47 | THAT'S IT—I QUIT—I'M MOVIN' ON | Sam Cooke, RCA Victor 7853 | 5 |
| 32 | 41 | 84 | — | FELL IN LOVE ON MONDAY | Fats Domino, Imperial 5734 | 3 |
| 33 | 37 | 30 | 32 | HAPPY BIRTHDAY BLUES | Kathy Young and the Innocents, Indigo 115 | 7 |
| 34 | 56 | 50 | 55 | FIND ANOTHER GIRL | Jerry Butler, Vee Jay 375 | 5 |
| 35 | 45 | 53 | 68 | HIDEAWAY | Freddy King, Federal 12401 | 5 |
| 36 | 19 | 10 | 6 | BABY SITTIN' BOOGIE | Buzz Clifford, Columbia 41876 | 13 |
| 37 | 48 | 54 | 62 | PORTRAIT OF MY LOVE | Steve Lawrence, United Artists 291 | 5 |
| 38 | 43 | 67 | 78 | TRUST IN ME | Etta James, Argo 5385 | 4 |
| 39 | 28 | 25 | 39 | WATUSI | Vibrations, Checker 969 | 7 |
| 40 | 49 | 59 | 72 | BEWILDERED | James Brown, King 5442 | 6 |
| 41 | 26 | 20 | 21 | HEARTS OF STONE | Bill Black's Combo, Hi 2028 | 7 |
| 42 | 23 | 14 | 8 | CALCUTTA | Lawrence Welk, Dot 16161 | 17 |
| 43 | 18 | 17 | 17 | LITTLE BOY SAD | Johnny Burnette, Liberty 55298 | 9 |
| 44 | 40 | 64 | 100 | YOUR ONE AND ONLY LOVE | Jackie Wilson, Brunswick 55208 | 4 |
| 45 | 30 | 23 | 16 | YOU CAN HAVE HER | Roy Hamilton, Epic 9434 | 10 |
| 46 | 64 | 95 | — | SOME KIND OF WONDERFUL | Drifters, Atlantic 2096 | 3 |
| 47 | 54 | 97 | — | SHU RAH | Fats Domino, Imperial 5734 | 3 |
| 48 | 25 | 16 | 12 | GOOD TIME BABY | Bobby Rydell, Cameo 186 | 11 |
| 49 | 36 | 27 | 19 | EXODUS | Ferrante and Teicher, United Artists 274 | 21 |
| 50 | 65 | 80 | 85 | SECOND TIME AROUND | Frank Sinatra, Reprise 20001 | 5 |
| 51 | 29 | 19 | 14 | THERE'S A MOON OUT TONIGHT | Capris, Old Town 1094 | 14 |
| 52 | 86 | 56 | 58 | TO BE LOVED (FOREVER) | Pentagons, Donna 1337 | 7 |
| 53 | 77 | 93 | — | DIXIE | Duane Eddy, Jamie 1183 | 3 |
| 54 | 78 | 88 | 89 | JUST FOR OLD TIME'S SAKE | McGuire Sisters, Coral 62249 | 4 |
| 55 | 51 | 68 | 75 | GINNIE BELL | Paul Dino, Promo 2180 | 10 |
| 56 | 76 | 77 | 79 | TONIGHT I FELL IN LOVE | Tokens, Warwick 615 | 5 |
| 57 | 61 | 75 | — | ONE-EYED JACKS | Ferrante and Teicher, United Artists 300 | 3 |
| 58 | 66 | 94 | — | MY THREE SONS | Lawrence Welk, Dot 16198 | 3 |
| 59 | 87 | — | — | TENDERLY | Bert Kaempfert, Decca 31236 | 2 |
| 60 | 88 | — | — | DADDY'S HOME | Shep and the Limelites, Hull 740 | 2 |
| 61 | 73 | 83 | 93 | VERY THOUGHT OF YOU | Little Willie John, King 5458 | 4 |
| 62 | 82 | 100 | — | THE BLIZZARD | Jim Reeves, RCA Victor 7855 | 3 |
| 63 | 50 | 55 | 65 | BLUE MOON | Herb Lance and the Classics, Promo 1010 | 5 |
| 64 | 80 | — | — | BRASS BUTTONS | String-A-Longs, Warwick 625 | 2 |
| 65 | 75 | 79 | — | BYE, BYE, BABY | Mary Wells, Motown 1003 | 9 |
| 66 | 83 | — | — | FUNNY | Maxine Brown, Nomar 106 | 2 |
| 67 | 84 | 87 | 90 | MERRY-GO-ROUND | Marv Johnson, United Artists 294 | 4 |
| 68 | 85 | — | — | AIN'T IT BABY | Miracles, Tamla 54034 | 2 |
| 69 | 70 | 81 | 82 | LING TING TONG | Buddy Knox, Liberty 55305 | 5 |
| 70 | 72 | 78 | 83 | LITTLE MISS STUCKUP | Playmates, Roulette 4322 | 5 |
| 71 | 89 | — | — | SLEEPY-EYED JOHN | Johnny Horton, Columbia 41963 | 2 |
| 72 | 89 | — | — | WELCOME HOME | Sammy Kaye Ork, Decca 31204 | 2 |
| 73 | — | — | — | CONTINENTAL WALK | Hank Ballard and the Midnighters, King 5491 | 1 |
| 74 | 81 | 89 | — | FOOLIN' AROUND | Kay Starr, Capitol 4542 | 3 |
| 75 | 92 | — | — | I'M IN THE MOOD FOR LOVE | Chimes, Tag 445 | 2 |
| 76 | 98 | — | — | LITTLE PEDRO | Olympics, Arvee 5023 | 2 |
| 77 | 39 | 34 | 38 | YOUR FRIENDS | Dee Clark, Vee Jay 372 | 9 |
| 78 | 68 | 70 | 60 | PONY EXPRESS | Danny and the Juniors, Swan 468 | 7 |
| 79 | 60 | 62 | 64 | TOUCHABLES | Dickie Goodman, Mark X 8009 | 7 |
| 80 | 91 | 99 | — | SEVENTEEN | Frankie Ford, Imperial 5735 | 3 |
| 81 | 97 | — | — | WHERE I FELL IN LOVE | Capris, Old Town 1099 | 2 |
| 82 | — | — | — | TREES | Platters, Mercury 71791 | 1 |
| 83 | 94 | — | — | LIKE LONG HAIR | Paul Revere and the Raiders, Gardena 116 | 2 |
| 84 | 90 | — | — | BUMBLE BOOGIE | B. Bumble and the Stingers, Rendezvous 140 | 2 |
| 85 | 93 | — | — | I TOLD YOU SO | Jimmy Jones, Cub 9085 | 2 |
| 86 | 74 | 66 | 84 | LONELY BLUE NIGHTS | Rosie, Brunswick 55205 | 4 |
| 87 | 96 | — | — | TRIANGLE | Janie Grant, Caprice 104 | 2 |
| 88 | 59 | 57 | 61 | HONKY TONK, PART II | Bill Doggett, King 5444 | 9 |
| 89 | — | — | — | WHAT'D I SAY | Jerry Lee Lewis, Sun 356 | 1 |
| 90 | — | — | — | THEME FROM THE GREAT IMPOSTER | Henry Mancini, RCA Victor 7830 | 1 |
| 91 | 47 | 48 | 46 | I PITY THE FOOL | Bobby Bland, Duke 332 | 7 |
| 92 | — | 96 | 98 | KOKOMO | Flamingos, End 1085 | 3 |
| 93 | — | — | — | UNDERWATER | Frogman, Candix 3314 | 1 |
| 94 | — | — | — | SCOTTISH SOLDIER | Andy Stewart, Warwick 627 | 1 |
| 95 | — | 98 | 99 | LITTLE TURTLE DOVE | Otis Williams and the Charms, King 5455 | 3 |
| 96 | 53 | 36 | 40 | I DON'T WANT TO CRY | Chuck Jackson, Wand 106 | 7 |
| 97 | — | — | — | BONANZA | Al Caiola, United Artists 302 | 1 |
| 98 | — | — | — | CALIFORNIA SUN | Joe Jones, Roulette 4344 | 1 |
| 99 | — | — | — | THE NEXT KISS | Conway Twitty, MGM 12998 | 1 |
| 100 | — | — | — | SWEET LITTLE KATHY | Ray Peterson, Dunes 2004 | 1 |

## HOT 100 — A to Z

Ain't It Baby ... 68
Apache ... 2
Asia Minor ... 13
Baby Blue ... 19
Baby Sittin' Boogie ... 36
Bewildered ... 40
Blizzard (The) ... 62
Blue Moon (Herb Lance and the Classics) ... 63
Blue Moon (Marcels) ... 1
Bonanza ... 97
Brass Buttons ... 64
Bumble Boogie ... 84
But I Do ... 10
Bye, Bye, Baby ... 65
Calcutta ... 42
California Sun ... 98
Continental Walk ... 73
Daddy's Home ... 60
Dedicated to the One I Love ... 5
Dixie ... 53
Don't Worry (Like All the Other Times) ... 6
Ebony Eyes ... 17
Exodus ... 49
Fell in Love on Monday ... 32
Find Another Girl ... 34
Foolin' Around ... 74
Funny ... 66
Gee Whiz (Look at His Eyes) ... 14
Ginnie Bell ... 55
Good Time Baby ... 48
Happy Birthday Blues ... 33
Hearts of Stone ... 41
Hideaway ... 35
Honky Tonk, Part II ... 88
I Don't Want to Cry ... 96
I Pity the Fool ... 91
I Told You So ... 85
I'm in the Mood for Love ... 75
I've Told Every Little Star ... 25
Just For Old Time's Sake ... 54
Kokomo ... 92
Lazy River ... 28
Like Long Hair ... 83
Ling Ting Tong ... 69
Little Boy Sad ... 43
Little Miss Stuckup ... 70
Little Pedro ... 76
Little Turtle Dove ... 95
Lonely Blue Nights ... 86
Merry-Go-Round ... 67
Model Girl ... 20
Mother-In-Law ... 23
My Three Sons ... 58
Next Kiss (The) ... 99
On the Rebound ... 7
Once Upon a Time ... 30
One-Eyed Jacks ... 57
One Hundred Pounds of Clay ... 26
One Mint Julep ... 21
Please Love Me Forever ... 16
Please Tell Me Why ... 27
Pony Express ... 78
Pony Time ... 4
Portrait of My Love ... 37
Runaway ... 9
Scottish Soldier ... 94
Second Time Around ... 50
Seventeen ... 80
Shu Rah ... 47
Sleepy-Eyed John ... 71
Some Kind of Wonderful ... 46
Spanish Harlem ... 24
Surrender ... 3
Sweet Little Kathy ... 100
Take Good Care of Her ... 18
Tenderly ... 59
That's It—I Quit—I'm Movin' On ... 31
Theme From the Great Imposter ... 90
There's a Moon Out Tonight ... 51
Think Twice ... 11
To Be Loved (Forever) ... 52
Tonight I Fell in Love ... 56
Tonight My Love, Tonight ... 22
Touchables ... 79
Trees ... 82
Triangle ... 87
Trust in Me ... 38
Underwater ... 93
Very Thought of You ... 61
Walk Right Back ... 8
Watusi ... 39
Welcome Home ... 72
What'd I Say ... 89
Wheels (String-A-Longs) ... 12
Where I Fell in Love ... 81
Where the Boys Are ... 15
You Can Depend on Me ... 29
You Can Have Her ... 45
Your Friends ... 77
Your One and Only Love ... 44

# BILLBOARD HOT 100

**APRIL 10, 1961**

**FOR WEEK ENDING APRIL 16, 1961**

STAR PERFORMERS showed the greatest upward progress on Hot 100 this week.
Ⓢ Indicates that 45 r.p.m. stereo single version is available.
△ Indicates that 33⅓ r.p.m. stereo single version is available.

Columns: THIS WEEK | ONE WEEK AGO | TWO WEEKS AGO | THREE WEEKS AGO | TITLE — Artist, Company, Record No. | STEREO | WEEKS ON CHART

| # | 1wk | 2wk | 3wk | Title — Artist, Company, Record No. | Wks |
|---|---|---|---|---|---|
| 1 | 1 | 6 | 21 | BLUE MOON — Marcels, Colpix 186 | 6 |
| 2 | 2 | 4 | 6 | APACHE — Jorgen Ingmann, Atco 6184 | 12 |
| 3 | 5 | 3 | 5 | DEDICATED TO THE ONE I LOVE — Shirelles, Scepter 1203 | 12 |
| 4 | 9 | 21 | 47 | RUNAWAY — Del Shannon, Big Top 3067 | 6 |
| 5 | 7 | 11 | 15 | ON THE REBOUND — Floyd Cramer, RCA Victor 7840 | 6 |
| 6 | 10 | 17 | 40 | BUT I DO — Clarence (Frogman) Henry, Argo 5378 | 8 |
| 7 | 3 | 1 | 1 | SURRENDER — Elvis Presley, RCA Victor 7850 | 7 |
| 8 | 6 | 5 | 3 | DON'T WORRY (LIKE ALL THE OTHER TIMES) — Marty Robbins, Columbia 41922 | 11 |
| 9 | 23 | 55 | — | MOTHER-IN-LAW — Ernie K. Doe, Minit 623 | 3 |
| 10 | 8 | 7 | 9 | WALK RIGHT BACK — Everly Brothers, Warner Bros. 5199 | 10 |
| 11 | 4 | 2 | 2 | PONY TIME — Chubby Checker, Parkway 818 | 12 |
| 12 | 13 | 15 | 33 | ASIA MINOR — Kokomo, Felsted 8612 | 8 |
| 13 | 18 | 24 | 43 | TAKE GOOD CARE OF HER — Adam Wade, Coed 546 | 5 |
| 14 | 16 | 22 | 22 | PLEASE LOVE ME FOREVER — Cathy Jean and Roomates, Valmor 007 | 7 |
| 15 | 11 | 12 | 13 | THINK TWICE — Brook Benton, Mercury 71774 | 9 |
| 16 | 21 | 32 | 44 | ONE MINT JULEP — Ray Charles, Impulse 200 | 6 |
| 17 | 14 | 10 | 12 | GEE WHIZ (LOOK AT HIS EYES) — Carla Thomas, Atlantic 2086 | 11 |
| 18 | 19 | 27 | 41 | BABY BLUE — Echoes, Segway 103 | 6 |
| 19 | 29 | 62 | — | YOU CAN DEPEND ON ME — Brenda Lee, Decca 31231 | 3 |
| 20 | 26 | 71 | 91 | ONE HUNDRED POUNDS OF CLAY — Gene McDaniels, Liberty 55308 | 4 |
| 21 | 12 | 8 | 7 | WHEELS — String-A-Longs, Warwick 603 | 14 |
| 22 | 27 | 33 | 52 | PLEASE TELL ME WHY — Jackie Wilson, Brunswick 55208 | 5 |
| 23 | 25 | 46 | 65 | I'VE TOLD EVERY LITTLE STAR — Linda Scott, Canadian-American 123 | 5 |
| 24 | 37 | 48 | 54 | PORTRAIT OF MY LOVE — Steve Lawrence, United Artists 291 | 6 |
| 25 | 15 | 9 | 4 | WHERE THE BOYS ARE — Connie Francis, MGM 12971 | 13 |
| 26 | 30 | 35 | 42 | ONCE UPON A TIME — Rochell and the Candles, Swingin' 623 | 10 |
| 27 | 20 | 20 | 29 | MODEL GIRL — Johnny Mastro, Coed 545 | 10 |
| 28 | 22 | 34 | 45 | TONIGHT MY LOVE, TONIGHT — Paul Anka, ABC-Paramount 10194 | 5 |
| 29 | 35 | 45 | 53 | HIDEAWAY — Freddy King, Federal 12401 | 6 |
| 30 | 34 | 56 | 50 | FIND ANOTHER GIRL — Jerry Butler, Vee Jay 375 | 5 |
| 31 | 17 | 13 | 8 | EBONY EYES — Everly Brothers, Warner Bros. 5199 | 11 |
| 32 | 38 | 43 | 67 | TRUST IN ME — Etta James, Argo 5385 | 4 |
| 33 | 32 | 41 | 84 | FELL IN LOVE ON MONDAY — Fats Domino, Imperial 5734 | 4 |
| 34 | 33 | 37 | 30 | HAPPY BIRTHDAY BLUES — Kathy Young and the Innocents, Indigo 115 | 8 |
| 35 | 59 | 87 | — | TENDERLY — Bert Kaempfert, Decca 31236 | 3 |
| 36 | 46 | 64 | 95 | SOME KIND OF WONDERFUL — Drifters, Atlantic 2096 | 4 |
| 37 | 60 | 88 | — | DADDY'S HOME — Shep and the Limelites, Hull 740 | 3 |
| 38 | 55 | 51 | 68 | GINNIE BELL — Paul Dino, Promo 2180 | 11 |
| 39 | 31 | 31 | 37 | THAT'S IT — I QUIT — I'M MOVIN' ON — Sam Cooke, RCA Victor 7853 | 6 |
| 40 | 40 | 49 | 59 | BEWILDERED — James Brown, King 5442 | 7 |
| 41 | 54 | 78 | 88 | JUST FOR OLD TIME'S SAKE — McGuire Sisters, Coral 62249 | 5 |
| 42 | 47 | 54 | 97 | SHU RAH — Fats Domino, Imperial 5734 | 4 |
| 43 | 57 | 61 | 75 | ONE-EYED JACKS — Ferrante and Teicher, United Artists 300 | 4 |
| 44 | 24 | 16 | 11 | SPANISH HARLEM — Ben E. King, Atco 6185 | 15 |
| 45 | 65 | 75 | 79 | BYE, BYE, BABY — Mary Wells, Motown 1003 | 10 |
| 46 | 53 | 77 | 93 | DIXIE — Duane Eddy, Jamie 1183 | 4 |
| 47 | 56 | 76 | 77 | TONIGHT I FELL IN LOVE — Tokens, Warwick 615 | 6 |
| 48 | 83 | 94 | — | LIKE LONG HAIR — Paul Revere and the Raiders, Gardena 116 | 3 |
| 49 | 64 | 80 | — | BRASS BUTTONS — String-A-Longs, Warwick 625 | 3 |
| 50 | 52 | 86 | 56 | TO BE LOVED (FOREVER) — Pentagons, Donna 1337 | 8 |
| 51 | 50 | 65 | 80 | SECOND TIME AROUND — Frank Sinatra, Reprise 20001 | 6 |
| 52 | 66 | 83 | — | FUNNY — Maxine Brown, Nomar 106 | 3 |
| 53 | 75 | 92 | — | I'M IN THE MOOD FOR LOVE — Chimes, Tag 445 | 3 |
| 54 | 68 | 85 | — | AIN'T IT BABY — Miracles, Tamla 54034 | 3 |
| 55 | 28 | 14 | 18 | LAZY RIVER — Bobby Darin, Atco 6188 | 10 |
| 56 | 58 | 66 | 94 | MY THREE SONS — Lawrence Welk, Dot 16198 | 4 |
| 57 | 84 | 90 | — | BUMBLE BOOGIE — B. Bumble and the Stingers, Rendezvous 140 | 3 |
| 58 | 36 | 19 | 10 | BABY SITTIN' BOOGIE — Buzz Clifford, Columbia 41876 | 14 |
| 59 | 73 | — | — | CONTINENTAL WALK — Hank Ballard and the Midnighters, King 5491 | 2 |
| 60 | 44 | 40 | 64 | YOUR ONE AND ONLY LOVE — Jackie Wilson, Brunswick 55208 | 5 |
| 61 | 67 | 84 | 87 | MERRY-GO-ROUND — Marv Johnson, United Artists 294 | 5 |
| 62 | — | — | — | FROGG — Brothers Four, Columbia 41958 | 1 |
| 63 | 71 | 89 | — | SLEEPY-EYED JOHN — Johnny Horton, Columbia 41963 | 3 |
| 64 | 61 | 73 | 83 | VERY THOUGHT OF YOU — Little Willie John, King 5458 | 5 |
| 65 | 69 | 70 | 81 | LING TING TONG — Buddy Knox, Liberty 55305 | 6 |
| 66 | 74 | 81 | 89 | FOOLIN' AROUND — Kay Starr, Capitol 4542 | 4 |
| 67 | 39 | 28 | 25 | WATUSI — Vibrations, Checker 969 | 8 |
| 68 | 72 | — | — | WELCOME HOME — Sammy Kaye Ork, Decca 31204 | 2 |
| 69 | — | — | — | AFRICAN WALTZ — Cannonball Adderley, Riverside 45457 | 1 |
| 70 | 82 | — | — | TREES — Platters, Mercury 71791 | 2 |
| 71 | — | — | — | RUNNING SCARED — Roy Orbison, Monument 328 | 1 |
| 72 | 80 | 91 | 99 | SEVENTEEN — Frankie Ford, Imperial 5735 | 4 |
| 73 | — | — | — | EXODUS (In Jazz) — Eddie Harris, Vee Jay 378 | 1 |
| 74 | 81 | 97 | — | WHERE I FELL IN LOVE — Capris, Old Town 1099 | 3 |
| 75 | — | — | — | (IT NEVER HAPPENS) IN REAL LIFE — Chuck Jackson, Wand 108 | 1 |
| 76 | 76 | 98 | — | LITTLE PEDRO — Olympics, Arvee 5023 | 3 |
| 77 | 62 | 82 | 100 | THE BLIZZARD — Jim Reeves, RCA Victor 7855 | 4 |
| 78 | — | — | — | THE CHARANGA — Merv Griffin, Carlton 545 | 1 |
| 79 | 89 | — | — | WHAT'D I SAY — Jerry Lee Lewis, Sun 356 | 2 |
| 80 | — | — | — | GLORY OF LOVE — Roomates, Valmor 008 | 1 |
| 81 | 87 | 96 | — | TRIANGLE — Janie Grant, Caprice 104 | 3 |
| 82 | 99 | — | — | THE NEXT KISS (IS THE LAST GOODBYE) — Conway Twitty, MGM 12998 | 2 |
| 83 | 97 | — | — | BONANZA — Al Caiola, United Artists 302 | 2 |
| 84 | 93 | — | — | UNDERWATER — Frogmen, Candix 3314 | 2 |
| 85 | — | — | — | CONTINENTAL WALK — Rollers, Liberty 55320 | 1 |
| 86 | — | — | — | I'LL JUST HAVE ANOTHER CUP OF COFFEE — Claude Gray, Mercury 71732 | 1 |
| 87 | — | — | — | COME ALONG — Maurice Williams and the Zodiacs, Herald 559 | 1 |
| 88 | — | — | — | LA PACHANGA — Audrey Arno and the Hazy Osterwald Sextet, Decca 31238 | 1 |
| 89 | — | — | — | LULLABYE OF LOVE — Frank Gari, Crusade 1021 | 1 |
| 90 | — | — | — | A CITY GIRL STOLE MY COUNTRY BOY — Patti Page, Mercury 71792 | 1 |
| 91 | — | — | — | MR. PRIDE — Chuck Jackson, Beltone 1005 | 1 |
| 92 | 94 | — | — | SCOTTISH SOLDIER — Andy Stewart, Warwick 627 | 2 |
| 93 | 85 | 93 | — | I TOLD YOU SO — Jimmy Jones, Cub 9085 | 3 |
| 94 | — | — | — | COME ON OVER — Strollers, Carlton 546 | 1 |
| 95 | — | — | — | SAVED — LaVern Baker, Atlantic 2099 | 1 |
| 96 | 98 | — | — | CALIFORNIA SUN — Joe Jones, Roulette 4344 | 2 |
| 97 | — | — | — | HELLO WALLS — Faron Young, Capitol 4533 | 1 |
| 98 | — | — | — | THREE HEARTS IN A TANGLE — Roy Drusky, Decca 31193 | 1 |
| 99 | 41 | 26 | 20 | HEARTS OF STONE — Bill Black's Combo, Hi 2028 | 8 |
| 100 | — | — | — | GROUND HOG — Browns, RCA Victor 7866 | 1 |

## HOT 100 — A to Z

| Title | # | Title | # |
|---|---|---|---|
| A City Girl Stole My Country Boy | 90 | Ling Ting Tong | 65 |
| African Waltz | 69 | Little Pedro | 76 |
| Ain't It Baby | 54 | Lullaby of Love | 89 |
| Apache | 2 | Merry-Go-Round | 61 |
| Asia Minor | 12 | Mr. Pride | 91 |
| Baby Blue | 18 | Model Girl | 27 |
| Baby Sittin' Boogie | 58 | My Three Sons | 56 |
| Bewildered | 40 | Mother-in-Law | 9 |
| Blizzard, The | 77 | Next Kiss, The (Is the Last Goodbye) | 82 |
| Blue Moon | 1 | On the Rebound | 5 |
| Bonanza | 83 | Once Upon a Time | 26 |
| Brass Buttons | 49 | One-Eyed Jacks | 43 |
| Bumble Boogie | 57 | One Hundred Pounds of Clay | 20 |
| But I Do | 6 | One Mint Julep | 16 |
| Bye, Bye, Baby | 45 | Please Love Me Forever | 14 |
| California Sun | 96 | Please Tell Me Why | 22 |
| Charanga, The | 78 | Pony Time | 11 |
| Come Along | 87 | Portrait of My Love | 24 |
| Come On Over | 94 | Running Scared | 71 |
| Continental Walk (Ballard) | 59 | Saved | 95 |
| Continental Walk (Rollers) | 85 | Scottish Soldier | 92 |
| Daddy's Home | 37 | Second Time Around | 51 |
| Dedicated to the One I Love | 3 | Seventeen | 72 |
| Dixie | 46 | Shu Rah | 42 |
| Don't Worry (Like All the Other Times) | 8 | Sleepy-Eyed John | 63 |
| Ebony Eyes | 31 | Some Kind of Wonderful | 36 |
| Exodus (In Jazz) | 73 | Spanish Harlem | 44 |
| Fell in Love on Monday | 33 | Surrender | 7 |
| Find Another Girl | 30 | Take Good Care of Her | 13 |
| Foolin' Around | 66 | Tenderly | 35 |
| Frogg | 62 | That's It — I Quit — I'm Movin' On | 39 |
| Funny | 52 | Think Twice | 15 |
| Gee Whiz (Look at His Eyes) | 17 | Three Hearts in a Tangle | 98 |
| Ginnie Bell | 38 | To Be Loved (Forever) | 50 |
| Glory of Love | 80 | Tonight I Fell in Love | 47 |
| Ground Hog | 100 | Tonight, My Love, Tonight | 28 |
| Happy Birthday Blues | 34 | Trees | 70 |
| Hearts of Stone | 99 | Triangle | 81 |
| Hello Walls | 97 | Trust in Me | 32 |
| Hideaway | 29 | Underwater | 84 |
| I Told You So | 93 | Very Thought of You | 64 |
| I'll Just Have Another Cup of Coffee | 86 | Walk Right Back | 10 |
| I'm in the Mood for Love | 53 | Watusi | 67 |
| (It Never Happens) In Real Life | 75 | Welcome Home | 68 |
| I've Told Every Little Star | 23 | What'd I Say | 79 |
| Just for Old Time's Sake | 41 | Wheels | 21 |
| La Pachanga | 88 | Where I Fell in Love | 74 |
| Lazy River | 55 | Where the Boys Are | 25 |
| Like Long Hair | 48 | You Can Depend on Me | 19 |
|  |  | Your One and Only Love | 60 |

# BILLBOARD HOT 100

**APRIL 17, 1961**

**FOR WEEK ENDING APRIL 23, 1961**

| This Week | 1 Wk Ago | 2 Wks Ago | 3 Wks Ago | Title — Artist, Company, Record No. | Wks on Chart |
|---|---|---|---|---|---|
| 1 | 1 | 1 | 6 | BLUE MOON — Marcels, Colpix 186 | 7 |
| 2 | 4 | 9 | 21 | RUNAWAY — Del Shannon, Big Top 3067 | 7 |
| 3 | 9 | 23 | 55 | MOTHER-IN-LAW — Ernie K. Doe, Minit 623 | 4 |
| 4 | 5 | 7 | 11 | ON THE REBOUND — Floyd Cramer, RCA Victor 7840 | 7 |
| 5 | 6 | 10 | 17 | BUT I DO — Clarence (Frogman) Henry, Argo 5378 | 9 |
| 6 | 2 | 2 | 4 | APACHE — Jorgen Ingmann, Atco 6184 | 13 |
| 7 | 3 | 5 | 3 | DEDICATED TO THE ONE I LOVE — Shirelles, Scepter 1203 | 13 |
| 8 | 12 | 13 | 15 | ASIA MINOR — Kokomo, Felsted 8612 | 9 |
| 9 | 20 | 26 | 71 | ONE HUNDRED POUNDS OF CLAY — Gene McDaniels, Liberty 55308 | 5 |
| 10 | 7 | 3 | 1 | SURRENDER — Elvis Presley, RCA Victor 7850 | 9 |
| 11 | 13 | 18 | 24 | TAKE GOOD CARE OF HER — Adam Wade, Coed 546 | 6 |
| 12 | 8 | 6 | 5 | DON'T WORRY (LIKE ALL THE OTHER TIMES) — Marty Robbins, Columbia 41922 | 12 |
| 13 | 14 | 16 | 22 | PLEASE LOVE ME FOREVER — Cathy Jean and Roomates, Valmor 007 | 8 |
| 14 | 16 | 21 | 32 | ONE MINT JULEP — Ray Charles, Impulse 200 | 7 |
| 15 | 11 | 4 | 2 | PONY TIME — Chubby Checker, Parkway 818 | 13 |
| 16 | 19 | 29 | 62 | YOU CAN DEPEND ON ME — Brenda Lee, Decca 31231 | 4 |
| 17 | 18 | 19 | 27 | BABY BLUE — Echoes, Segway 103 | 7 |
| 18 | 23 | 25 | 46 | I'VE TOLD EVERY LITTLE STAR — Linda Scott, Canadian-American 123 | 6 |
| 19 | 28 | 22 | 34 | TONIGHT MY LOVE, TONIGHT — Paul Anka, ABC-Paramount 10194 | 6 |
| 20 | 22 | 27 | 33 | PLEASE TELL ME WHY — Jackie Wilson, Brunswick 55208 | 6 |
| 21 | 10 | 8 | 7 | WALK RIGHT BACK — Everly Brothers, Warner Bros. 5199 | 11 |
| 22 | 15 | 11 | 12 | THINK TWICE — Brook Benton, Mercury 71774 | 10 |
| 23 | 24 | 37 | 48 | PORTRAIT OF MY LOVE — Steve Lawrence, United Artists 291 | 6 |
| 24 | 17 | 14 | 10 | GEE WHIZ (LOOK AT HIS EYES) — Carla Thomas, Atlantic 2086 | 12 |
| 25 | 41 | 54 | 78 | JUST FOR OLD TIME'S SAKE — McGuire Sisters, Coral 62249 | 6 |
| 26 | 21 | 12 | 8 | WHEELS — String-A-Longs, Warwick 603 | 15 |
| 27 | 37 | 60 | 88 | DADDY'S HOME — Shep and the Limelites, Hull 740 | 4 |
| 28 | 26 | 30 | 35 | ONCE UPON A TIME — Rochell and the Candles, Swingin' 623 | 11 |
| 29 | 25 | 15 | 9 | WHERE THE BOYS ARE — Connie Francis, MGM 12971 | 14 |
| 30 | 32 | 38 | 43 | TRUST IN ME — Etta James, Argo 5385 | 6 |
| 31 | 30 | 34 | 56 | FIND ANOTHER GIRL — Jerry Butler, Vee Jay 375 | 7 |
| 32 | 35 | 59 | 87 | TENDERLY — Bert Kaempfert, Decca 31236 | 4 |
| 33 | 29 | 35 | 45 | HIDEAWAY — Freddy King, Federal 12401 | 7 |
| 34 | 42 | 47 | 54 | SHU RAH — Fats Domino, Imperial 5734 | 4 |
| 35 | 49 | 64 | 80 | BRASS BUTTONS — String-A-Longs, Warwick 625 | 4 |
| 36 | 36 | 46 | 64 | SOME KIND OF WONDERFUL — Drifters, Atlantic 2096 | 5 |
| 37 | 43 | 57 | 61 | ONE-EYED JACKS — Ferrante and Teicher, United Artists 300 | 5 |
| 38 | 48 | 83 | 94 | LIKE LONG HAIR — Paul Revere and the Raiders, Gardena 116 | 4 |
| 39 | 46 | 53 | 77 | THEME FROM DIXIE — Duane Eddy, Jamie 1183 | 5 |
| 40 | 27 | 20 | 20 | MODEL GIRL — Johnny Maestro, Coed 545 | 11 |
| 41 | 31 | 17 | 13 | EBONY EYES — Everly Brothers, Warner Bros. 5199 | 12 |
| 42 | 57 | 84 | 90 | BUMBLE BOOGIE — B. Bumble and the Stingers, Rendezvous 140 | 4 |
| 43 | 33 | 32 | 41 | FELL IN LOVE ON MONDAY — Fats Domino, Imperial 5734 | 5 |
| 44 | 47 | 56 | 76 | TONIGHT I FELL IN LOVE — Tokens, Warwick 615 | 7 |
| 45 | 53 | 75 | 92 | I'M IN THE MOOD FOR LOVE — Chimes, Tag 445 | 4 |
| 46 | 52 | 66 | 83 | FUNNY — Maxine Brown, Nomar 106 | 4 |
| 47 | 62 | — | — | FROGG — Brothers Four, Columbia 41958 | 2 |
| 48 | 50 | 52 | 86 | TO BE LOVED (FOREVER) — Pentagons, Donna 1337 | 9 |
| 49 | 39 | 31 | 31 | THAT'S IT—I QUIT—I'M MOVIN' ON — Sam Cooke, RCA Victor 7853 | 7 |
| 50 | 38 | 55 | 51 | GINNIE BELL — Paul Dino, Promo 2180 | 12 |
| 51 | 59 | 73 | — | CONTINENTAL WALK — Hank Ballard and the Midnighters, King 5491 | 3 |
| 52 | 54 | 68 | 85 | AIN'T IT BABY — Miracles, Tamla 54034 | 4 |
| 53 | 79 | 89 | — | WHAT'D I SAY — Jerry Lee Lewis, Sun 356 | 3 |
| 54 | 71 | — | — | RUNNING SCARED — Roy Orbison, Monument 328 | 2 |
| 55 | 56 | 58 | 66 | MY THREE SONS — Lawrence Welk, Dot 16198 | 5 |
| 56 | — | — | — | BREAKIN' IN A BRAND NEW HEART — Connie Francis, MGM 12995 | 1 |
| 57 | 34 | 33 | 37 | HAPPY BIRTHDAY BLUES — Kathy Young and the Innocents, Indigo 115 | 9 |
| 58 | 63 | 71 | 89 | SLEEPY-EYED JOHN — Johnny Horton, Columbia 41963 | 4 |
| 59 | 45 | 65 | 75 | BYE BYE BABY — Mary Wells, Motown 1003 | 11 |
| 60 | 66 | 74 | 81 | FOOLIN' AROUND — Kay Starr, Capitol 4542 | 5 |
| 61 | 44 | 24 | 16 | SPANISH HARLEM — Ben E. King, Atco 6185 | 16 |
| 62 | 70 | 82 | — | TREES — Platters, Mercury 71791 | 2 |
| 63 | 83 | 97 | — | BONANZA — Al Caiola, United Artists 302 | 3 |
| 64 | 69 | — | — | AFRICAN WALTZ — Cannonball Adderley, Riverside 45457 | 2 |
| 65 | 40 | 40 | 49 | BEWILDERED — James Brown, King 5442 | 8 |
| 66 | 61 | 67 | 84 | MERRY-GO-ROUND — Marv Johnson, United Artists 294 | 6 |
| 67 | 75 | — | — | (IT NEVER HAPPENS) IN REAL LIFE — Chuck Jackson, Wand 108 | 2 |
| 68 | 73 | — | — | EXODUS (In Jazz) — Eddie Harris, Vee Jay 378 | 2 |
| 69 | — | — | — | GOOD, GOOD LOVIN' — Chubby Checker, Parkway 822 | 1 |
| 70 | 51 | 50 | 65 | SECOND TIME AROUND — Frank Sinatra, Reprise 20001 | 7 |
| 71 | 78 | — | — | THE CHARANGA — Merv Griffin, Carlton 545 | 2 |
| 72 | 82 | 99 | — | THE NEXT KISS (IS THE LAST GOODBYE) — Conway Twitty, MGM 12998 | 3 |
| 73 | 81 | 87 | 96 | TRIANGLE — Janie Grant, Caprice 104 | 4 |
| 74 | 84 | 93 | — | UNDERWATER — Frogman, Candix 314 | 3 |
| 75 | 89 | — | — | LULLABYE OF LOVE — Frank Gari, Crusade 1021 | 2 |
| 76 | 80 | — | — | GLORY OF LOVE — Roomates, Valmor 008 | 2 |
| 77 | 97 | — | — | HELLO WALLS — Faron Young, Capitol 4533 | 2 |
| 78 | — | — | — | MAMA SAID — Shirelles, Scepter 1217 | 1 |
| 79 | 95 | — | — | SAVED — LaVern Baker, Atlantic 2099 | 2 |
| 80 | 85 | — | — | CONTINENTAL WALK — Rollers, Liberty 55320 | 2 |
| 81 | 72 | 80 | 91 | SEVENTEEN — Frankie Ford, Imperial 9735 | 5 |
| 82 | — | — | — | GIRL OF MY BEST FRIEND — Ral Donner, Gone 5102 | 1 |
| 83 | 87 | — | — | COME ALONG — Maurice Williams and the Zodiacs, Herald 559 | 2 |
| 84 | 86 | — | — | I'LL JUST HAVE ANOTHER CUP OF COFFEE — Claude Gray, Mercury 71732 | 2 |
| 85 | — | — | — | FLAMING STAR — Elvis Presley, RCA Victor LPC 128 (33 compact) | 1 |
| 86 | 64 | 61 | 73 | VERY THOUGHT OF YOU — Little Willie John, King 5458 | 6 |
| 87 | 88 | — | — | LA PACHANGA — Audrey Arno and the Hazy Osterwald Sextet, Decca 31238 | 2 |
| 88 | 92 | 94 | — | SCOTTISH SOLDIER — Andy Stewart, Warwick 627 | 3 |
| 89 | 96 | 98 | — | CALIFORNIA SUN — Joe Jones, Roulette 4344 | 3 |
| 90 | 65 | 69 | 70 | LING TING TONG — Buddy Knox, Liberty 55305 | 7 |
| 91 | 94 | — | — | COME ON OVER — Strollers, Carlton 546 | 2 |
| 92 | 68 | 72 | — | WELCOME HOME — Sammy Kaye Ork, Decca 31204 | 3 |
| 93 | 98 | — | — | THREE HEARTS IN A TANGLE — Roy Drusky, Decca 31193 | 2 |
| 94 | 60 | 44 | 40 | YOUR ONE AND ONLY LOVE — Jackie Wilson, Brunswick 55208 | 6 |
| 95 | — | — | — | MESS AROUND — Bobby Freeman, Josie 887 | 1 |
| 96 | — | — | — | HOP SCOTCH — Santo and Johnny, Canadian-American 124 | 1 |
| 97 | 100 | — | — | GROUND HOG — Browns, RCA Victor 7866 | 2 |
| 98 | 74 | 81 | 97 | WHERE I FELL IN LOVE — Capris, Old Town 1099 | 4 |
| 99 | — | — | — | TRAGEDY — Fleetwoods, Dolton 40 | 1 |
| 100 | 76 | 76 | 98 | LITTLE PEDRO — Olympics, Arvee 5023 | 4 |

## HOT 100 — A to Z

| Title | # | Title | # |
|---|---|---|---|
| African Waltz | 64 | Mama Said | 78 |
| Ain't It Baby | 52 | Merry-Go-Round | 66 |
| Apache | 6 | Mess Around | 95 |
| Asia Minor | 8 | Model Girl | 40 |
| Baby Blue | 17 | Mother-in-Law | 3 |
| Bewildered | 65 | My "Three Sons" | 55 |
| Blue Moon | 1 | Next Kiss, The | 72 |
| Bonanza | 63 | On the Rebound | 4 |
| Brass Buttons | 35 | Once Upon a Time | 28 |
| Breakin' in a Brand New Heart | 56 | One-Eyed Jacks | 37 |
| Bumble Boogie | 42 | One Hundred Pounds of Clay | 9 |
| But I Do | 5 | One Mint Julep | 14 |
| Bye Bye Baby | 59 | Please Love Me Forever | 13 |
| California Sun | 89 | Please Tell Me Why | 20 |
| Charanga, The | 71 | Pony Time | 15 |
| Come Along | 83 | Portrait of My Love | 23 |
| Come On Over | 91 | Runaway | 2 |
| Continental Walk (Ballard) | 51 | Running Scared | 54 |
| Continental Walk (Rollers) | 80 | Saved | 79 |
| Daddy's Home | 27 | Scottish Soldier | 88 |
| Dedicated to the One I Love | 7 | Second Time Around | 70 |
| Don't Worry (Like All the Other Times) | 12 | Seventeen | 81 |
| Ebony Eyes | 41 | Shu Rah | 34 |
| Exodus (In Jazz) | 68 | Sleepy-Eyed John | 58 |
| Fell in Love on Monday | 43 | Some Kind of Wonderful | 36 |
| Find Another Girl | 31 | Spanish Harlem | 61 |
| Flaming Star | 85 | Surrender | 10 |
| Foolin' Around | 60 | Take Good Care of Her | 11 |
| Frogg | 47 | Tenderly | 32 |
| Funny | 46 | That's It—I Quit—I'm Movin' On | 49 |
| Gee Whiz (Look at His Eyes) | 24 | Theme From Dixie | 39 |
| Ginnie Bell | 50 | Think Twice | 22 |
| Girl of My Best Friend | 82 | Three Hearts in a Tangle | 93 |
| Glory of Love | 76 | To Be Loved (Forever) | 48 |
| Good, Good Lovin' | 69 | Tonight I Fell in Love | 44 |
| Ground Hog | 97 | Tonight, My Love, Tonight | 19 |
| Happy Birthday Blues | 57 | Tragedy | 99 |
| Hello Walls | 77 | Trees | 62 |
| Hideaway | 33 | Triangle | 73 |
| Hop Scotch | 96 | Trust in Me | 30 |
| I'll Just Have Another Cup of Coffee | 84 | Underwater | 74 |
| I'm in the Mood for Love | 45 | Very Thought of You | 86 |
| It Never Happens in Real Life | 67 | Walk Right Back | 21 |
| I've Told Every Little Star | 18 | Welcome Home | 92 |
| Just For Old Time's Sake | 25 | What'd I Say | 53 |
| La Pachanga | 87 | Where I Fell in Love | 98 |
| Like Long Hair | 38 | Where the Boys Are | 29 |
| Ling Ting Tong | 90 | Wheels | 26 |
| Little Pedro | 100 | You Can Depend on Me | 16 |
| Lullabye of Love | 75 | Your One and Only Love | 94 |

# BILLBOARD HOT 100

**APRIL 24, 1961**

**FOR WEEK ENDING APRIL 30, 1961**

*STAR PERFORMERS showed the greatest upward progress on Hot 100 this week.*
*S — Indicates that 45 r.p.m. stereo single version is available.*
*▲ — Indicates that 33⅓ r.p.m. stereo single version is available.*

| This Week | One Week Ago | Two Weeks Ago | Three Weeks Ago | Title — Artist, Company, Record No. | Weeks on Chart |
|---|---|---|---|---|---|
| 1 | 2 | 4 | 9 | RUNAWAY — Del Shannon, Big Top 3067 | 8 |
| 2 | 1 | 1 | 1 | BLUE MOON — Marcels, Colpix 186 | 8 |
| 3 | 3 | 9 | 23 | MOTHER-IN-LAW — Ernie K-Doe, Minit 623 | 5 |
| 4 | 5 | 6 | 10 | BUT I DO — Clarence (Frogman) Henry, Argo 5378 | 10 |
| 5 | 4 | 5 | 7 | ON THE REBOUND — Floyd Cramer, RCA Victor 7840 | 8 |
| 6 | 9 | 20 | 26 | ONE HUNDRED POUNDS OF CLAY — Gene McDaniels, Liberty 55308 | 6 |
| ★7 | 18 | 23 | 25 | I'VE TOLD EVERY LITTLE STAR — Linda Scott, Canadian-American 123 | 7 |
| ★8 | 16 | 19 | 29 | YOU CAN DEPEND ON ME — Brenda Lee, Decca 31231 | 5 |
| 9 | 11 | 13 | 18 | TAKE GOOD CARE OF HER — Adam Wade, Coed 546 | 7 |
| 10 | 14 | 16 | 21 | ONE MINT JULEP — Ray Charles, Impulse 200 | 8 |
| 11 | 6 | 2 | 2 | APACHE — Jorgen Ingmann, Atco 6184 | 14 |
| 12 | 13 | 14 | 16 | PLEASE LOVE ME FOREVER — Cathy Jean and Roomates, Valmor 007 | 9 |
| 13 | 7 | 3 | 5 | DEDICATED TO THE ONE I LOVE — Shirelles, Scepter 1203 | 14 |
| 14 | 17 | 18 | 19 | BABY BLUE — Echoes, Segway 103 | 8 |
| 15 | 8 | 12 | 13 | ASIA MINOR — Kokomo, Felsted 8612 | 10 |
| 16 | 19 | 28 | 22 | TONIGHT MY LOVE, TONIGHT — Paul Anka, ABC-Paramount 10194 | 7 |
| ★17 | 23 | 24 | 37 | PORTRAIT OF MY LOVE — Steve Lawrence, United Artists 291 | 7 |
| 18 | 12 | 8 | 6 | DON'T WORRY (LIKE ALL THE OTHER TIMES) — Marty Robbins, Columbia 41922 | 13 |
| 19 | 10 | 7 | 3 | SURRENDER — Elvis Presley, RCA Victor 7850 | 10 |
| ★20 | 27 | 37 | 60 | DADDY'S HOME — Shep and the Limelites, Hull 740 | 5 |
| ★21 | 56 | — | — | BREAKIN' IN A BRAND NEW BROKEN HEART — Connie Francis, MGM 12995 | 2 |
| 22 | 20 | 22 | 27 | PLEASE TELL ME WHY — Jackie Wilson, Brunswick 55208 | 7 |
| 23 | 15 | 11 | 4 | PONY TIME — Chubby Checker, Parkway 818 | 14 |
| 24 | 21 | 10 | 8 | WALK RIGHT BACK — Everly Brothers, Warner Bros. 5199 | 12 |
| 25 | 24 | 17 | 14 | GEE WHIZ (LOOK AT HIS EYES) — Carla Thomas, Atlantic 2086 | 13 |
| 26 | 25 | 41 | 54 | JUST FOR OLD TIME'S SAKE — McGuire Sisters, Coral 62249 | 7 |
| 27 | 31 | 30 | 34 | FIND ANOTHER GIRL — Jerry Butler, Vee Jay 375 | 8 |
| ★28 | 44 | 47 | 56 | TONIGHT I FELL IN LOVE — Tokens, Warwick 615 | 8 |
| 29 | 22 | 15 | 11 | THINK TWICE — Brook Benton, Mercury 71774 | 11 |
| ★30 | 46 | 52 | 66 | FUNNY — Maxine Brown, Nomar 106 | 5 |
| 31 | 32 | 35 | 59 | TENDERLY — Bert Kaempfert, Decca 31236 | 5 |
| 32 | 34 | 42 | 47 | SHU RAH — Fats Domino, Imperial 5734 | 6 |
| 33 | 42 | 57 | 84 | BUMBLE BOOGIE — B. Bumble and the Stingers, Rendezvous 140 | 5 |
| ★34 | 85 | — | — | FLAMING STAR — Elvis Presley, RCA Victor LPC 128 (33 compact) | 2 |
| 35 | 47 | 62 | — | FROGG — Brothers Four, Columbia 41958 | 3 |
| ★36 | 35 | 49 | 64 | BRASS BUTTONS — String-A-Longs, Warwick 625 | 5 |
| 37 | 33 | 29 | 35 | HIDEAWAY — Freddy King, Federal 12401 | 8 |
| 38 | 54 | 71 | — | RUNNING SCARED — Roy Orbison, Monument 328 | 3 |
| 39 | 53 | 79 | 89 | WHAT'D I SAY — Jerry Lee Lewis, Sun 356 | 4 |
| 40 | 30 | 32 | 38 | TRUST IN ME — Etta James, Argo 5385 | 7 |
| 41 | 28 | 26 | 30 | ONCE UPON A TIME — Rochell and the Candles, Swingin' 623 | 12 |
| ★42 | 78 | — | — | MAMA SAID — Shirelles, Scepter 1217 | 2 |
| 43 | 29 | 25 | 15 | WHERE THE BOYS ARE — Connie Francis, MGM 12971 | 15 |
| 44 | 36 | 36 | 46 | SOME KIND OF WONDERFUL — Drifters, Atlantic 2096 | 6 |
| 45 | 26 | 21 | 12 | WHEELS — String-A-Longs, Warwick 603 | 16 |
| 46 | 43 | 33 | 32 | FELL IN LOVE ON MONDAY — Fats Domino, Imperial 5734 | 6 |
| 47 | 51 | 59 | 73 | CONTINENTAL WALK — Hank Ballard and the Midnighters, King 5491 | 4 |
| 48 | 38 | 48 | 83 | LIKE LONG HAIR — Paul Revere and the Raiders, Gardena 116 | 5 |
| 49 | 52 | 54 | 68 | AIN'T IT BABY — Miracles, Tamla 54036 | 5 |
| 50 | 37 | 43 | 57 | LOVE THEME FROM ONE-EYED JACKS — Ferrante and Teicher, United Artists 300 | 6 |
| 51 | 45 | 53 | 75 | I'M IN THE MOOD FOR LOVE — Chimes, Tag 445 | 5 |
| 52 | 39 | 46 | 53 | THEME FROM DIXIE — Duane Eddy, Jamie 1183 | 6 |
| ★53 | 69 | — | — | GOOD, GOOD LOVIN' — Chubby Checker, Parkway 822 | 2 |
| 54 | 79 | 95 | — | SAVED — La Vern Baker, Atlantic 2099 | 3 |
| ★55 | 82 | — | — | GIRL OF MY BEST FRIEND — Ral Donner, Gone 5102 | 2 |
| 56 | 58 | 63 | 71 | SLEEPY-EYED JOHN — Johnny Horton, Columbia 41963 | 5 |
| 57 | 55 | 56 | 58 | MY THREE SONS — Lawrence Welk, Dot 16198 | 6 |
| 58 | 63 | 83 | 97 | BONANZA — Al Caiola, United Artists 302 | 4 |
| 59 | 60 | 66 | 74 | FOOLIN' AROUND — Kay Starr, Capitol 4542 | 6 |
| 60 | 57 | 34 | 33 | HAPPY BIRTHDAY BLUES — Kathy Young and the Innocents, Indigo 115 | 10 |
| 61 | 68 | 73 | — | EXODUS — Eddie Harris, Vee Jay 378 | 3 |
| ★62 | 77 | 97 | — | HELLO WALLS — Faron Young, Capitol 4533 | 3 |
| 63 | 67 | 75 | — | (IT NEVER HAPPENS) IN REAL LIFE — Chuck Jackson, Wand 108 | 3 |
| 64 | 64 | 69 | — | AFRICAN WALTZ — Cannonball Adderley, Riverside 45457 | 3 |
| 65 | 73 | 81 | 87 | TRIANGLE — Janie Grant, Caprice 104 | 5 |
| 66 | 75 | 89 | — | LULLABYE OF LOVE — Frank Gari, Crusade 1021 | 3 |
| 67 | 76 | 80 | — | GLORY OF LOVE — Roomates, Valmor 008 | 3 |
| 68 | 74 | 84 | 93 | UNDERWATER — Frogman, Candix 314 | 4 |
| 69 | 71 | 78 | — | THE CHARANGA — Merv Griffin, Carlton 545 | 3 |
| 70 | 62 | 70 | 82 | TREES — Platters, Mercury 71791 | 4 |
| 71 | — | — | — | TRAVELIN' MAN — Ricky Nelson, Imperial 5741 | 1 |
| 72 | 48 | 50 | 52 | TO BE LOVED (FOREVER) — Pentagons, Donna 1337 | 10 |
| 73 | — | — | — | A DOLLAR DOWN — Limeliters, RCA Victor 7859 | 1 |
| 74 | 99 | — | — | TRAGEDY — Fleetwoods, Dolton 40 | 2 |
| 75 | 49 | 39 | 31 | THAT'S IT—I QUIT—I'M MOVIN' ON — Sam Cooke, RCA Victor 7853 | 8 |
| 76 | 40 | 27 | 20 | MODEL GIRL — Johnny Maestro, Coed 545 | 12 |
| 77 | 72 | 82 | 99 | THE NEXT KISS (IS THE LAST GOODBYE) — Conway Twitty, MGM 12998 | 4 |
| ★78 | — | — | — | TOUCHABLES IN BROOKLYN — Dickie Goodman, Mark-X 8010 | 1 |
| ★79 | — | — | — | (DANCE THE) MESS AROUND — Chubby Checker, Parkway 822 | 1 |
| ★80 | — | — | — | BE MY BOY — Paris Sisters, Gregmark 2 | 1 |
| 81 | — | — | — | PEANUT BUTTER — Marathons, Arvee 5027 | 1 |
| ★82 | — | — | — | WAYWARD WIND — Gogi Grant, Era 3046 | 1 |
| ★83 | — | — | — | THAT'S THE WAY WITH LOVE — Pierio Soffici, Kip 224 | 1 |
| ★84 | — | — | — | WHAT A SURPRISE — Johnny Maestro, Coed 549 | 1 |
| ★85 | — | — | — | LULLABY OF THE LEAVES — Ventures, Dolton 41 | 1 |
| 86 | — | — | — | BILBAO SONG — Andy Williams, Cadence 1398 | 1 |
| 87 | 80 | 85 | — | CONTINENTAL WALK — Rollers, Liberty 55320 | 3 |
| 88 | 93 | 98 | — | THREE HEARTS IN A TANGLE — Roy Drusky, Decca 31193 | 3 |
| 89 | 95 | — | — | MESS AROUND — Bobby Freeman, Josie 887 | 2 |
| 90 | 96 | — | — | HOP SCOTCH — Santo and Johnny, Canadian-American 124 | 2 |
| 91 | — | — | — | TOSSIN' AND TURNIN' — Bobby Lewis, Beltone 1002 | 1 |
| 92 | — | — | — | BETTER TELL HIM NO — Starlets, Pam 1003 | 1 |
| 93 | — | — | — | SHY AWAY — Jerry Fuller, Challenge 59104 | 1 |
| 94 | — | — | — | I'M A FOOL TO CARE — Oscar Black, Savoy 1600 | 1 |
| 95 | — | — | — | JURA (I SWEAR I LOVE YOU) — Les Paul and Mary Ford, Columbia 41994 | 1 |
| 96 | — | — | — | LITTLE EGYPT — Coasters, Atco 6192 | 1 |
| 97 | — | — | — | EIN SCHIFF WIRD KOMMEN (A Ship Will Come) — Lale Anderson, King 5478 | 1 |
| 98 | — | — | — | BILL BAILEY — Della Reese, RCA Victor 7867 | 1 |
| 99 | — | — | — | I'M A FOOL TO CARE — Joe Barry, Smash 1702 | 1 |
| 100 | — | — | — | NOBODY CARES — Jeanette (Baby) Washington, Neptune 122 | 1 |

## HOT 100 — A to Z

| Title | Pos. |
|---|---|
| A Dollar Down | 73 |
| African Waltz | 64 |
| Ain't It Baby | 49 |
| Apache | 11 |
| Asia Minor | 15 |
| Baby Blue (Echoes) | 14 |
| Be My Boy | 80 |
| Better Tell Him No | 92 |
| Bilbao Song | 86 |
| Bill Bailey | 98 |
| Blue Moon | 2 |
| Bonanza | 58 |
| Brass Buttons | 36 |
| Breakin' in a Brand New Broken Heart | 21 |
| Bumble Boogie | 33 |
| But I Do | 4 |
| Charanga, The | 69 |
| Continental Walk (Ballard) | 47 |
| Continental Walk (Rollers) | 87 |
| Daddy's Home | 20 |
| (Dance The) Mess Around | 79 |
| Dedicated to the One I Love | 13 |
| Don't Worry (Like All the Other Times) | 18 |
| Ein Schiff Wird Kommen | 97 |
| Exodus | 61 |
| Fell in Love on Monday | 46 |
| Find Another Girl | 27 |
| Flaming Star | 34 |
| Foolin' Around | 59 |
| Frogg | 35 |
| Funny | 30 |
| Gee Whiz (Look at His Eyes) | 25 |
| Girl of My Best Friend | 55 |
| Glory of Love | 67 |
| Good, Good Lovin' | 53 |
| Happy Birthday Blues | 60 |
| Hello Walls | 62 |
| Hideaway | 37 |
| Hop Scotch | 90 |
| I'm a Fool to Care (Barry) | 99 |
| I'm a Fool to Care (Black) | 94 |
| I'm in the Mood for Love | 51 |
| (It Never Happens) in Real Life | 63 |
| I've Told Every Little Star | 7 |
| Jura (I Swear I Love You) | 95 |
| Just for Old Time's Sake | 26 |
| Like Long Hair | 48 |
| Little Egypt | 96 |
| Love Theme From One-Eyed Jacks | 50 |
| Lullaby of Love | 66 |
| Lullaby of the Leaves | 85 |
| Mama Said | 42 |
| Mess Around | 89 |
| Model Girl | 76 |
| Mother-in-Law | 3 |
| My Three Sons | 57 |
| Next Kiss (Is the Last Goodbye), The | 77 |
| Nobody Cares | 100 |
| On the Rebound | 5 |
| Once Upon a Time | 41 |
| One Hundred Pounds of Clay | 6 |
| One Mint Julep | 10 |
| Peanut Butter | 81 |
| Please Love Me Forever | 12 |
| Please Tell Me Why | 22 |
| Pony Time | 23 |
| Portrait of My Love | 17 |
| Runaway | 1 |
| Running Scared | 38 |
| Saved | 54 |
| Shu Rah | 32 |
| Shy Away | 93 |
| Sleepy-Eyed John | 56 |
| Some Kind of Wonderful | 44 |
| Surrender | 19 |
| Take Good Care of Her | 9 |
| Tenderly | 31 |
| That's It—I Quit—I'm Movin' On | 75 |
| That's the Way With Love | 83 |
| Theme From Dixie | 52 |
| Think Twice | 29 |
| Three Hearts in a Tangle | 88 |
| To Be Loved (Forever) | 72 |
| Tonight I Fell in Love | 28 |
| Tonight My Love, Tonight | 16 |
| Tossin' and Turnin' | 91 |
| Touchables in Brooklyn | 78 |
| Tragedy | 74 |
| Travelin' Man | 71 |
| Trees | 70 |
| Triangle | 65 |
| Trust in Me | 40 |
| Underwater | 68 |
| Walk Right Back | 24 |
| Wayward Wind | 82 |
| What a Surprise | 84 |
| What'd I Say | 39 |
| Wheels | 45 |
| Where the Boys Are | 43 |
| You Can Depend on Me | 8 |

MAY 1, 1961

# BILLBOARD HOT 100

FOR WEEK ENDING MAY 7, 1961

**STAR PERFORMERS** showed the greatest upward progress on Hot 100 this week.
S — Indicates that 45 r.p.m. stereo single version is available.
△ — Indicates that 33⅓ r.p.m. stereo single version is available.

Columns: THIS WEEK | ONE WEEK AGO | TWO WEEKS AGO | THREE WEEKS AGO | TITLE — Artist, Company, Record No. | STEREO | WEEKS ON CHART

| This Wk | 1 Wk | 2 Wk | 3 Wk | Title — Artist, Company, Record No. | Wks |
|---|---|---|---|---|---|
| 1 | 1 | 2 | 4 | RUNAWAY — Del Shannon, Big Top 3067 | 9 |
| 2 | 3 | 3 | 9 | MOTHER-IN-LAW — Ernie K-Doe, Minit 623 | 6 |
| 3 | 7 | 18 | 23 | I'VE TOLD EVERY LITTLE STAR — Linda Scott, Canadian-American 123 | 8 |
| 4 | 6 | 9 | 20 | ONE HUNDRED POUNDS OF CLAY — Gene McDaniels, Liberty 55308 | 7 |
| 5 | 2 | 1 | 1 | BLUE MOON — Marcels, Colpix 186 | 9 |
| 6 | 4 | 5 | 6 | BUT I DO — Clarence (Frogman) Henry, Argo 5378 | 11 |
| 7 | 9 | 11 | 13 | TAKE GOOD CARE OF HER — Adam Wade, Coed 546 | 8 |
| 8 | 10 | 14 | 16 | ONE MINT JULEP — Ray Charles, Impulse 200 | 9 |
| 9 | 8 | 16 | 19 | YOU CAN DEPEND ON ME — Brenda Lee, Decca 31231 | 6 |
| 10 | 5 | 4 | 5 | ON THE REBOUND — Floyd Cramer, RCA Victor 7840 | 9 |
| 11 | 17 | 23 | 24 | PORTRAIT OF MY LOVE — Steve Lawrence, United Artists 291 | 8 |
| 12 | 14 | 17 | 18 | BABY BLUE — Echoes, Seg-way 103 | 9 |
| 13 | 16 | 19 | 28 | TONIGHT MY LOVE, TONIGHT — Paul Anka, ABC-Paramount 10194 | 8 |
| 14 | 11 | 6 | 2 | APACHE — Jorgen Ingmann, Atco 6184 | 15 |
| 15 | 20 | 27 | 37 | DADDY'S HOME — Shep and the Limelites, Hull 740 | 6 |
| 16 | 21 | 56 | — | BREAKIN' IN A BRAND NEW BROKEN HEART — Connie Francis, MGM 12995 | 3 |
| 17 | 28 | 44 | 47 | TONIGHT I FELL IN LOVE — Tokens, Warwick 615 | 9 |
| 18 | 42 | 78 | — | MAMA SAID — Shirelles, Scepter 1217 | 3 |
| 19 | 34 | 85 | — | FLAMING STAR — Elvis Presley, RCA Victor LPC 128 (33 compact) | 3 |
| 20 | 12 | 13 | 14 | PLEASE LOVE ME FOREVER — Cathy Jean and Roomates, Valmor 007 | 10 |
| 21 | 15 | 8 | 12 | ASIA MINOR — Kokomo, Felsted 8612 | 11 |
| 22 | 18 | 12 | 8 | DON'T WORRY (LIKE ALL THE OTHER TIMES) — Marty Robbins, Columbia 41922 | 14 |
| 23 | 26 | 25 | 41 | JUST FOR OLD TIME'S SAKE — McGuire Sisters, Coral 62249 | 8 |
| 24 | 38 | 54 | 71 | RUNNING SCARED — Roy Orbison, Monument 328 | 4 |
| 25 | 19 | 10 | 7 | SURRENDER — Elvis Presley, RCA Victor 7850 | 11 |
| 26 | 33 | 42 | 57 | BUMBLE BOOGIE — B. Bumble and the Stingers, Rendezvous 140 | 6 |
| 27 | 13 | 7 | 3 | DEDICATED TO THE ONE I LOVE — Shirelles, Scepter 1203 | 15 |
| 28 | 79 | — | — | (DANCE THE) MESS AROUND — Chubby Checker, Parkway 822 | 2 |
| 29 | 30 | 46 | 52 | FUNNY — Maxine Brown, Nomar 106 | 6 |
| 30 | 23 | 15 | 11 | PONY TIME — Chubby Checker, Parkway 818 | 15 |
| 31 | 39 | 53 | 79 | WHAT'D I SAY — Jerry Lee Lewis, Sun 356 | 5 |
| 32 | 35 | 47 | 62 | FROGG — Brothers Four, Columbia 41958 | 4 |
| 33 | 58 | 63 | 83 | BONANZA — Al Caiola, United Artists 302 | 5 |
| 34 | 71 | — | — | TRAVELIN' MAN — Ricky Nelson, Imperial 5741 | 2 |
| 35 | 31 | 32 | 35 | TENDERLY — Bert Kaempfert, Decca 31236 | 6 |
| 36 | 55 | 82 | — | GIRL OF MY BEST FRIEND — Ral Donner, Gone 5102 | 3 |
| 37 | 47 | 51 | 59 | CONTINENTAL WALK — Hank Ballard and the Midnighters, King 5491 | 5 |
| 38 | 54 | 79 | 95 | SAVED — La Vern Baker, Atlantic 2099 | 4 |
| 39 | 62 | 77 | 97 | HELLO WALLS — Faron Young, Capitol 4533 | 4 |
| 40 | 44 | 36 | 36 | SOME KIND OF WONDERFUL — Drifters, Atlantic 2096 | 7 |
| 41 | 51 | 45 | 53 | I'M IN THE MOOD FOR LOVE — Chimes, Tag 445 | 6 |
| 42 | 40 | 30 | 32 | TRUST IN ME — Etta James, Argo 5385 | 8 |
| 43 | 53 | 69 | — | GOOD, GOOD LOVIN' — Chubby Checker, Parkway 822 | 3 |
| 44 | 27 | 31 | 30 | FIND ANOTHER GIRL — Jerry Butler, Vee Jay 375 | 9 |
| 45 | 64 | 64 | 69 | AFRICAN WALTZ — Cannonball Adderley, Riverside 45457 | 4 |
| 46 | 74 | 99 | — | TRAGEDY — Fleetwoods, Dolton 40 | 3 |
| 47 | 37 | 33 | 29 | HIDEAWAY — Freddy King, Federal 12401 | 9 |
| 48 | 65 | 73 | 81 | TRIANGLE — Janie Grant, Caprice 104 | 6 |
| 49 | 59 | 60 | 66 | FOOLIN' AROUND — Kay Starr, Capitol 4542 | 7 |
| 50 | 24 | 21 | 10 | WALK RIGHT BACK — Everly Brothers, Warner Bros. 5199 | 13 |
| 51 | 36 | 35 | 49 | BRASS BUTTONS — String-A-Longs, Warwick 625 | 6 |
| 52 | 22 | 20 | 22 | PLEASE TELL ME WHY — Jackie Wilson, Brunswick 55208 | 8 |
| 53 | — | — | — | OLD BLACK MAGIC — Bobby Rydell, Cameo 190 | 1 |
| 54 | 56 | 58 | 63 | SLEEPY-EYED JOHN — Johnny Horton, Columbia 41963 | 6 |
| 55 | 66 | 75 | 89 | LULLABYE OF LOVE — Frank Gari, Crusade 1021 | 4 |
| 56 | — | — | — | LITTLE DEVIL — Neil Sedaka, RCA Victor 7874 | 1 |
| 57 | 61 | 68 | 73 | EXODUS — Eddie Harris, Vee Jay 378 | 4 |
| 58 | 63 | 67 | 75 | (IT NEVER HAPPENS) IN REAL LIFE — Chuck Jackson, Wand 108 | 4 |
| 59 | 29 | 22 | 15 | THINK TWICE — Brook Benton, Mercury 71774 | 12 |
| 60 | 73 | — | — | A DOLLAR DOWN — Limeliters, RCA Victor 7859 | 2 |
| 61 | 50 | 37 | 43 | LOVE THEME FROM ONE-EYED JACKS — Ferrante and Teicher, United Artists 300 | 7 |
| 62 | 48 | 38 | 48 | LIKE LONG HAIR — Paul Revere and the Raiders, Gardena 116 | 6 |
| 63 | 81 | — | — | PEANUT BUTTER — Marathons, Arvee 5027 | 2 |
| 64 | 68 | 74 | 84 | UNDERWATER — Frogman, Candix 314 | 5 |
| 65 | 32 | 34 | 42 | SHU RAH — Fats Domino, Imperial 5734 | 7 |
| 66 | 67 | 76 | 80 | GLORY OF LOVE — Roomates, Valmor 007 | 5 |
| 67 | 57 | 55 | 56 | MY THREE SONS — Lawrence Welk, Dot 16198 | 6 |
| 68 | 25 | 24 | 17 | GEE WHIZ (LOOK AT HIS EYES) — Carla Thomas, Atlantic 2086 | 14 |
| 69 | 84 | — | — | WHAT A SURPRISE — Johnny Maestro, Coed 549 | 2 |
| 70 | 80 | — | — | BE MY BOY — Paris Sisters, Gregmark 2 | 2 |
| 71 | 86 | — | — | BILBAO SONG — Andy Williams, Cadence 1398 | 2 |
| 72 | 78 | — | — | TOUCHABLES IN BROOKLYN — Dickie Goodman, Mark-X 8010 | 2 |
| 73 | — | — | — | HELLO MARY LOU — Ricky Nelson, Imperial 5741 | 1 |
| 74 | 52 | 39 | 46 | THEME FROM DIXIE — Duane Eddy, Jamie 1183 | 7 |
| 75 | 41 | 28 | 26 | ONCE UPON A TIME — Rochell and the Candles, Swingin' 623 | 13 |
| 76 | 85 | — | — | LULLABY OF THE LEAVES — Ventures, Dolton 41 | 2 |
| 77 | 49 | 52 | 54 | AIN'T IT BABY — Miracles, Tamla 54036 | 6 |
| 78 | 82 | — | — | WAYWARD WIND — Gogi Grant, Era 3046 | 2 |
| 79 | 83 | — | — | THAT'S THE WAY WITH LOVE — Pierio Soffici, Kip 224 | 2 |
| 80 | — | — | — | THOSE OLDIES BUT GOODIES — Caesar and the Romans, Del Fi 4158 | 1 |
| 81 | 91 | — | — | TOSSIN' AND TURNIN' — Bobby Lewis, Beltone 1002 | 2 |
| 82 | 93 | — | — | SHY AWAY — Jerry Fuller, Challenge 59104 | 2 |
| 83 | 69 | 71 | 78 | THE CHARANGA — Merv Griffin, Carlton 545 | 4 |
| 84 | 88 | 93 | 98 | THREE HEARTS IN A TANGLE — Roy Drusky, Decca 31193 | 4 |
| 85 | 95 | — | — | JURA (I SWEAR I LOVE YOU) — Les Paul and Mary Ford, Columbia 41994 | 2 |
| 86 | 92 | — | — | BETTER TELL HIM NO — Starlets, Pam 1003 | 2 |
| 87 | 99 | — | — | I'M A FOOL TO CARE — Joe Barry, Smash 1702 | 2 |
| 88 | — | — | — | BUZZ ZUZZ A-DIDDLE-IT — Freddy Cannon, Swan 4071 | 1 |
| 89 | 96 | — | — | LITTLE EGYPT — Coasters, Atco 6192 | 2 |
| 90 | — | — | — | RAINDROPS — Dee Clark, Vee Jay 383 | 1 |
| 91 | 97 | — | — | EIN SCHIFF WIRD KOMMEN (A Ship Will Come—Never on Sunday) — Lale Anderson, King 5478 | 2 |
| 92 | — | — | — | BIG BIG WORLD — Johnny Burnette, Liberty 55318 | 1 |
| 93 | — | — | — | YOU'RE GONNA NEED MAGIC — Roy Hamilton, Epic 9443 | 1 |
| 94 | — | — | — | COUNT EVERY STAR — Donnie and the Dreamers, Whale 500 | 1 |
| 95 | — | — | — | MOODY RIVER — Pat Boone, Dot 16209 | 1 |
| 96 | — | — | — | HALFWAY TO PARADISE — Tony Orlando, Epic 9441 | 1 |
| 97 | — | — | — | A CROSS STANDS ALONE — Jimmy Witter, United Artists 301 | 1 |
| 98 | 100 | — | — | NOBODY CARES — Jeanette (Baby) Washington, Neptune 122 | 2 |
| 99 | — | — | — | KISSIN' GAME — Dion, Laurie 3090 | 1 |
| 100 | — | — | — | RAMA LAMA DING DONG — Edsels, Twin 700 | 1 |

# BILLBOARD HOT 100

**MAY 8, 1961**

**FOR WEEK ENDING MAY 14, 1961**

STAR PERFORMERS—Selections registering greatest upward progress this week.

S Indicates that 45 r.p.m. stereo single version is available.
△ Indicates that 33⅓ r.p.m. mono single version is available.
Ⓢ Indicates that 33⅓ r.p.m. stereo single version is available.

| This Week | Wk. Ago / 2 Wks. Ago / 3 Wks. Ago | TITLE — Artist, Label & Number | Weeks On Chart |
|---|---|---|---|
| 1 | 1 1 2 | RUNAWAY — Del Shannon, Big Top 3067 | 10 |
| 2 | 2 3 3 | MOTHER-IN-LAW — Ernie K-Doe, Minit 623 | 7 |
| 3 | 4 6 9 | ONE HUNDRED POUNDS OF CLAY — Gene McDaniels, Liberty 55308 | 8 |
| 4 | 3 7 18 | I'VE TOLD EVERY LITTLE STAR — Linda Scott, Canadian-American 123 | 9 |
| 5 | 5 2 1 | BLUE MOON — Marcels, Colpix 186 | 10 |
| 6 | 9 8 16 | YOU CAN DEPEND ON ME — Brenda Lee, Decca 31231 | 7 |
| 7 | 7 9 11 | TAKE GOOD CARE OF HER — Adam Wade, Coed 546 | 9 |
| 8 | 8 10 14 | ONE MINT JULEP — Ray Charles, Impulse 200 | 10 |
| 9 | 11 17 23 | PORTRAIT OF MY LOVE — Steve Lawrence, United Artists 291 | 9 |
| 10 | 10 5 4 | ON THE REBOUND — Floyd Cramer, RCA Victor 7840 | 10 |
| 11 | 6 4 5 | BUT I DO — Clarence (Frogman) Henry, Argo 5378 | 12 |
| 12 | 15 20 27 | DADDY'S HOME — Shep and the Limelites, Hull 740 | 7 |
| 13 | 16 21 56 | BREAKIN' IN A BRAND NEW BROKEN HEART — Connie Francis, MGM 12995 | 4 |
| 14 | 18 42 78 | MAMA SAID — Shirelles, Scepter 1217 | 4 |
| 15 | 17 28 44 | TONIGHT I FELL IN LOVE — Tokens, Warwick 615 | 10 |
| 16 | 19 34 85 | FLAMING STAR — Elvis Presley, RCA Victor LPC 128 (33 compact) | 4 |
| 17 | 13 16 19 | TONIGHT MY LOVE, TONIGHT — Paul Anka, ABC-Paramount 10194 | 9 |
| 18 | 34 71 — | TRAVELIN' MAN — Ricky Nelson, Imperial 5741 | 3 |
| 19 | 24 38 54 | RUNNING SCARED — Roy Orbison, Monument 328 | 5 |
| 20 | 12 14 17 | BABY BLUE — Echoes, Seg-way 103 | 10 |
| 21 | 26 33 42 | BUMBLE BOOGIE — B. Bumble and the Stingers, Rendezvous 140 | 7 |
| 22 | 23 26 25 | JUST FOR OLD TIME'S SAKE — McGuire Sisters, Coral 62249 | 9 |
| 23 | 33 58 63 | BONANZA — Al Caiola, United Artists 302 | 6 |
| 24 | 28 79 — | (DANCE THE) MESS AROUND — Chubby Checker, Parkway 822 | 3 |
| 25 | 29 30 46 | FUNNY — Maxine Brown, Nomar 106 | 7 |
| 26 | 36 55 82 | GIRL OF MY BEST FRIEND — Ral Donner, Gone 5102 | 4 |
| 27 | 73 — — | HELLO MARY LOU — Ricky Nelson, Imperial 5741 | 2 |
| 28 | 21 15 8 | ASIA MINOR — Kokomo, Felsted 8612 | 12 |
| 29 | 39 62 77 | HELLO WALLS — Faron Young, Capitol 4533 | 5 |
| 30 | 31 39 53 | WHAT'D I SAY — Jerry Lee Lewis, Sun 356 | 6 |
| 31 | 46 74 99 | TRAGEDY — Fleetwoods, Dolton 40 | 4 |
| 32 | 14 11 6 | APACHE — Jorgen Ingmann, Atco 6184 | 16 |
| 33 | 20 12 13 | PLEASE LOVE ME FOREVER — Cathy Jean and Roomates, Valmor 007 | 11 |
| 34 | 56 — — | LITTLE DEVIL — Neil Sedaka, RCA Victor 7874 | 2 |
| 35 | 37 47 51 | CONTINENTAL WALK — Hank Ballard and the Midnighters, King 5491 | 6 |
| 36 | 40 44 36 | SOME KIND OF WONDERFUL — Drifters, Atlantic 2096 | 8 |
| 37 | 38 54 79 | SAVED — La Vern Baker, Atlantic 2099 | 5 |
| 38 | 53 — — | THAT OLD BLACK MAGIC — Bobby Rydell, Cameo 190 | 2 |
| 39 | 32 35 47 | FROGG — Brothers Four, Columbia 41958 | 5 |
| 40 | 27 13 7 | DEDICATED TO THE ONE I LOVE — Shirelles, Scepter 1203 | 16 |
| 41 | 45 64 64 | AFRICAN WALTZ — Cannonball Adderley, Riverside 45457 | 5 |
| 42 | 25 19 10 | SURRENDER — Elvis Presley, RCA Victor 7850 | 12 |
| 43 | 55 66 75 | LULLABYE OF LOVE — Frank Gari, Crusade 1021 | 5 |
| 44 | 64 68 74 | UNDERWATER — Frogmen, Candix 314 | 6 |
| 45 | 43 53 69 | GOOD, GOOD LOVIN' — Chubby Checker, Parkway 822 | 4 |
| 46 | 57 61 68 | EXODUS — Eddie Harris, Vee Jay 378 | 5 |
| 47 | 41 51 45 | I'M IN THE MOOD FOR LOVE — Chimes, Tag 445 | 7 |
| 48 | 48 65 73 | TRIANGLE — Janie Grant, Caprice 104 | 7 |
| 49 | 49 59 60 | FOOLIN' AROUND — Kay Starr, Capitol 4542 | 8 |
| 50 | 72 78 — | TOUCHABLES IN BROOKLYN — Dickie Goodman, Mark-X 8010 | 3 |
| 51 | 63 81 — | PEANUT BUTTER — Marathons, Arvee 5027 | 3 |
| 52 | 58 63 67 | (IT NEVER HAPPENS) IN REAL LIFE — Chuck Jackson, Wand 108 | 5 |
| 53 | 42 40 30 | TRUST IN ME — Etta James, Argo 5385 | 9 |
| 54 | 30 23 15 | PONY TIME — Chubby Checker, Parkway 818 | 16 |
| 55 | 66 67 76 | GLORY OF LOVE — Roomates, Valmor 008 | 5 |
| 56 | 69 84 — | WHAT A SURPRISE — Johnny Maestro, Coed 549 | 3 |
| 57 | 87 99 — | I'M A FOOL TO CARE — Joe Barry, Smash 1702 | 3 |
| 58 | 70 80 — | BE MY BOY — Paris Sisters, Gregmark 2 | 3 |
| 59 | 22 18 12 | DON'T WORRY — Marty Robbins, Columbia 41922 | 15 |
| 60 | 80 — — | THOSE OLDIES BUT GOODIES — Caesar and the Romans, Del Fi 4158 | 2 |
| 61 | 71 86 — | BILBAO SONG — Andy Williams, Cadence 1398 | 3 |
| 62 | 90 — — | RAINDROPS — Dee Clark, Vee Jay 383 | 2 |
| 63 | 44 27 31 | FIND ANOTHER GIRL — Jerry Butler, Vee Jay 375 | 10 |
| 64 | 35 41 32 | TENDERLY — Bert Kaempfert, Decca 3236 | 7 |
| 65 | 54 56 58 | SLEEPY-EYED JOHN — Johnny Horton, Columbia 41963 | 7 |
| 66 | 81 91 — | TOSSIN' AND TURNIN' — Bobby Lewis, Beltone 1002 | 3 |
| 67 | 88 — — | BUZZ BUZZ A-DIDDLE-IT — Freddy Cannon, Swan 4071 | 2 |
| 68 | 79 83 — | THAT'S THE WAY WITH LOVE — Pierino Soffici, Kip 224 | 3 |
| 69 | 60 73 — | A DOLLAR DOWN — Limeliters, RCA Victor 7859 | 3 |
| 70 | 47 37 33 | HIDEAWAY — Freddy King, Federal 12401 | 10 |
| 71 | 82 93 — | SHY AWAY — Jerry Fuller, Challenge 9104 | 3 |
| 72 | 76 85 — | LULLABY OF THE LEAVES — Ventures, Dolton 41 | 3 |
| 73 | 84 88 93 | THREE HEARTS IN A TANGLE — Roy Drusky, Decca 31193 | 2 |
| 74 | 95 — — | MOODY RIVER — Pat Boone, Dot 16209 | 2 |
| 75 | — — — | STAND BY ME — Ben E. King, Atco 6194 | 1 |
| 76 | 89 96 — | LITTLE EGYPT — Coasters, Atco 6192 | 3 |
| 77 | 78 82 — | WAYWARD WIND — Gogi Grant, Era 3046 | 3 |
| 78 | 96 — — | HALFWAY TO PARADISE — Tony Orlando, Epic 9441 | 2 |
| 79 | — — — | NEVER ON SUNDAY — Don Costa, United Artists 234 | 16 |
| 80 | 93 — — | YOU'RE GONNA NEED MAGIC — Roy Hamilton, Epic 9443 | 2 |
| 81 | — — — | A LOVE OF MY OWN — Carla Thomas, Atlantic 2101 | 1 |
| 82 | 86 92 — | BETTER TELL HIM NO — Starlets, Pam 1003 | 3 |
| 83 | — — — | IN MY HEART — Time-Tones, Times Square 421 | 1 |
| 84 | 92 — — | BIG BIG WORLD — Johnny Burnette, Liberty 55318 | 2 |
| 85 | 94 — — | COUNT EVERY STAR — Donnie and the Dreamers, Whale 500 | 2 |
| 86 | — — — | YOU'D BETTER COME HOME — Russell Byrd, Wand 107 | 1 |
| 87 | 51 36 35 | BRASS BUTTONS — String-A-Longs, Warwick 625 | 7 |
| 88 | 91 97 — | EIN SCHIFF WIRD KOMMEN (A Ship Will Come—Never on Sunday) — Lale Anderson, King 5478 | 3 |
| 89 | — — — | IN BETWEEN TEARS — Lenny Myles, Scepter 1218 | 1 |
| 90 | — — — | THIS WORLD WE LOVE IN — Mina, Time 1030 | 1 |
| 91 | — — — | LIFE'S A HOLIDAY — Jerry Wallace, Challenge 9107 | 1 |
| 92 | 99 — — | KISSIN' GAME — Dion, Laurie 3090 | 2 |
| 93 | 98 100 — | NOBODY CARES — Jeanette (Baby) Washington, Neptune 122 | 3 |
| 94 | 85 95 — | JURA (I SWEAR I LOVE YOU) — Les Paul and Mary Ford, Columbia 41994 | 3 |
| 95 | 100 — — | RAMA LAMA DING DONG — Edsels, Twin 700 | 2 |
| 96 | 97 — — | A CROSS STANDS ALONE — Jimmy Witter, United Artists 301 | 2 |
| 97 | — — — | SON-IN-LAW — Blossoms, Challenge 9109 | 1 |
| 98 | — — — | WHAT WILL I TELL MY HEART — Harptones, Companion 103 | 1 |
| 99 | — — — | OUR LOVE IS HERE TO STAY — Dinah Washington, Mercury 71812 | 1 |
| 100 | — — — | SON-IN-LAW — Louise Brown, Witch 1 | 1 |

## BUBBLING UNDER THE HOT 100

1. SPRING FEVER .................. Little Willie John, King 5503
2. FOR YOUR LOVE ................. Wanderers, Cub 9089
3. BARBARA ANN .................. Regents, Gee 1065
4. SUCU SUCU .................... Ping Ping, Kapp 377
5. MY KIND OF GIRL ............... Matt Monro, Warwick 636
6. HERE'S MY CONFESSION .......... Wyatt (Earp) McPherson, Savoy 1599
7. SPARKLE AND SHINE ............. Four Coquettes, Capitol 4534
8. WHITE CLIFFS OF DOVER ......... Robins, Lavender 001
9. I DON'T MIND .................. James Brown, King 5466
10. MISS FINE .................... New Yorkers, Wall 547
11. UNCHAINED MELODY ............. Jerry Granahan, Caprice 106
12. JUNKERNOO ................... Vibrations, Checker 974
13. RONNIE ...................... Marcy Jo, Robbee 110
14. LULLABYE OF THE BELLS ......... Deltairs, Ivy 101
15. LONESOME WHISTLE BLUES ....... Freddy King, Federal 12415
16. HE NEEDS ME .................. Gloria Lynne, Everest 19409
17. THE GIRL'S A DEVIL ............ Dukays, Nat 1003
18. MILORD ...................... Teresa Brewer, Coral 62265
19. BABY FACE .................... Bobby Vee, Liberty 55325
20. ABDUL'S PARTY ................ Larry Verne, Era 3044

## HOT 100 — A TO Z

| Title | # | Title | # |
|---|---|---|---|
| A Cross Stands Alone | 96 | Little Egypt | 76 |
| A Dollar Down | 69 | Lullabye of Love | 43 |
| A Love of My Own | 81 | Lullaby of the Leaves | 72 |
| African Waltz | 41 | Mama Said | 14 |
| Apache | 32 | Moody River | 74 |
| Asia Minor | 28 | Mother-In-Law | 2 |
| Baby Blue | 20 | Never on Sunday | 79 |
| Be My Boy | 58 | Nobody Cares | 93 |
| Better Tell Him No | 82 | On the Rebound | 10 |
| Big Big World | 84 | One Hundred Pounds of Clay | 3 |
| Bilbao | 61 | One Mint Julep | 8 |
| Blue Moon | 5 | Our Love Is Here to Stay | 99 |
| Bonanza | 23 | Peanut Butter | 51 |
| Brass Buttons | 87 | Please Love Me Forever | 33 |
| Breakin' in a Brand-New Broken Heart | 13 | Portrait of My Love | 9 |
| Bumble Boogie | 21 | Pony Time | 54 |
| But I Do | 11 | Rama Lama Ding Dong | 95 |
| Buzz Buzz A-Diddle-It | 67 | Raindrops | 62 |
| Continental Walk | 35 | Runaway | 1 |
| Count Every Star | 85 | Running Scared | 19 |
| Daddy's Home | 12 | Saved | 37 |
| (Dance the) Mess Around | 24 | Shy Away | 71 |
| Dedicated to the One I Love | 40 | Sleepy-Eyed John | 65 |
| Don't Worry | 59 | Some Kind of Wonderful | 36 |
| Ein Schiff Wird Kommen (A Ship Will Come—Never on Sunday) | 88 | Son-In-Law (Blossoms) | 97 |
| Exodus | 46 | Son-In-Law (Brown) | 100 |
| Find Another Girl | 63 | Stand By Me | 75 |
| Flaming Star | 16 | Surrender | 42 |
| Foolin' Around | 49 | Take Good Care of Her | 7 |
| Frogg | 39 | Tenderly | 64 |
| Funny | 25 | That Old Black Magic | 38 |
| Girl of My Best Friend | 26 | That's the Way With Love | 68 |
| Glory of Love | 55 | This World We Love In | 90 |
| Good, Good Lovin' | 45 | Those Oldies But Goodies | 60 |
| Halfway to Paradise | 78 | Three Hearts in a Tangle | 73 |
| Hello Mary Lou | 27 | Tonight I Fell in Love | 15 |
| Hello Walls | 29 | Tonight My Love, Tonight | 17 |
| Hideaway | 70 | Tossin' and Turnin' | 66 |
| I'm a Fool to Care | 57 | Touchables in Brooklyn | 50 |
| I'm in the Mood for Love | 47 | Tragedy | 31 |
| In Between Tears | 89 | Travelin' Man | 18 |
| In My Heart | 83 | Triangle | 48 |
| (It Never Happens) in Real Life | 52 | Trust in Me | 53 |
| I've Told Every Little Star | 4 | Underwater | 44 |
| Jura (I Swear I Love You) | 94 | Wayward Wind | 77 |
| Just for Old Time's Sake | 22 | What a Surprise | 56 |
| Kissin' Game | 92 | What Will I Tell My Heart | 98 |
| Life's a Holiday | 91 | What'd I Say | 30 |
| Little Devil | 34 | You Can Depend on Me | 6 |
|  |  | You'd Better Come Home | 86 |
|  |  | You're Gonna Need Magic | 80 |

# BILLBOARD HOT 100

**MAY 15, 1961**

**FOR WEEK ENDING MAY 21, 1961**

| # | Wks Ago | TITLE — Artist, Label & Number | Wks on Chart |
|---|---|---|---|
| 1 | 1 1 1 | RUNAWAY — Del Shannon, Big Top 3067 | 11 |
| 2 | 2 2 3 | MOTHER-IN-LAW — Ernie K-Doe, Minit 623 | 8 |
| 3 | 3 4 6 | ONE HUNDRED POUNDS OF CLAY — Gene McDaniels, Liberty 55308 | 9 |
| 4 | 4 3 7 | I'VE TOLD EVERY LITTLE STAR — Linda Scott, Canadian-American 123 | 10 |
| 5 | 12 15 20 | DADDY'S HOME — Shep and the Limelites, Hull 740 | 8 |
| 6 | 6 9 8 | YOU CAN DEPEND ON ME — Brenda Lee, Decca 31231 | 8 |
| 7 | 5 5 2 | BLUE MOON — Marcels, Colpix 186 | 11 |
| 8 | 18 34 71 | TRAVELIN' MAN — Ricky Nelson, Imperial 5741 | 4 |
| 9 | 14 18 42 | MAMA SAID — Shirelles, Scepter 1217 | 5 |
| 10 | 7 7 9 | TAKE GOOD CARE OF HER — Adam Wade, Coed 546 | 10 |
| 11 | 13 16 21 | BREAKIN' IN A BRAND NEW BROKEN HEART — Connie Francis, MGM 12995 | 5 |
| 12 | 9 11 17 | PORTRAIT OF MY LOVE — Steve Lawrence, United Artists 291 | 10 |
| 13 | 8 8 10 | ONE MINT JULEP — Ray Charles, Impulse 200 | 11 |
| 14 | 16 19 34 | FLAMING STAR — Elvis Presley, RCA Victor LPC 128 (33 compact) | 5 |
| 15 | 27 73 — | HELLO MARY LOU — Ricky Nelson, Imperial 5741 | 3 |
| 16 | 19 24 38 | RUNNING SCARED — Roy Orbison, Monument 328 | 6 |
| 17 | 10 10 5 | ON THE REBOUND — Floyd Cramer, RCA Victor 7840 | 11 |
| 18 | 15 17 28 | TONIGHT I FELL IN LOVE — Tokens, Warwick 615 | 11 |
| 19 | 23 33 58 | BONANZA — Al Caiola, United Artists 302 | 7 |
| 20 | 22 23 26 | JUST FOR OLD TIME'S SAKE — McGuire Sisters, Coral 62249 | 10 |
| 21 | 11 6 4 | BUT I DO — Clarence (Frogman) Henry, Argo 5378 | 13 |
| 22 | 31 46 74 | TRAGEDY — Fleetwoods, Dolton 40 | 5 |
| 23 | 34 56 — | LITTLE DEVIL — Neil Sedaka, RCA Victor 7874 | 3 |
| 24 | 26 36 55 | GIRL OF MY BEST FRIEND — Ral Donner, Gone 5102 | 5 |
| 25 | 25 29 30 | FUNNY — Maxine Brown, Nomar 106 | 8 |
| 26 | 29 39 62 | HELLO WALLS — Faron Young, Capitol 4533 | 6 |
| 27 | 24 28 79 | (DANCE THE) MESS AROUND — Chubby Checker, Parkway 822 | 4 |
| 28 | 21 26 33 | BUMBLE BOOGIE — B. Bumble and the Stingers, Rendezvous 140 | 8 |
| 29 | 20 12 14 | BABY BLUE — Echoes, Seg-way 103 | 11 |
| 30 | 17 13 16 | TONIGHT MY LOVE, TONIGHT — Paul Anka, ABC-Paramount 10194 | 10 |
| 31 | 36 53 — | THAT OLD BLACK MAGIC — Bobby Rydell, Cameo 190 | 3 |
| 32 | 36 40 44 | SOME KIND OF WONDERFUL — Drifters, Atlantic 2096 | 9 |
| 33 | 35 37 47 | CONTINENTAL WALK — Hank Ballard and the Midnighters, King 5491 | 7 |
| 34 | 30 31 39 | WHAT'D I SAY — Jerry Lee Lewis, Sun 356 | 7 |
| 35 | 43 55 66 | LULLABYE OF LOVE — Frank Gari, Crusade 1021 | 6 |
| 36 | 48 48 65 | TRIANGLE — Janie Grant, Caprice 104 | 8 |
| 37 | 28 21 15 | ASIA MINOR — Kokomo, Felsted 8612 | 13 |
| 38 | 47 41 51 | I'M IN THE MOOD FOR LOVE — Chimes, Tag 445 | 8 |
| 39 | 32 14 11 | APACHE — Jorgen Ingmann, Atco 6184 | 17 |
| 40 | 37 38 54 | SAVED — La Vern Baker, Atlantic 2099 | 6 |
| 41 | 75 — — | STAND BY ME — Ben E. King, Atco 6194 | 2 |
| 42 | 56 69 84 | WHAT A SURPRISE — Johnny Maestro, Coed 549 | 4 |
| 43 | — — — | I FEEL SO BAD — Elvis Presley, RCA Victor 7880 | 1 |
| 44 | 46 57 61 | EXODUS — Eddie Harris, Vee Jay 378 | 6 |
| 45 | 50 72 78 | TOUCHABLES IN BROOKLYN — Dickie Goodman, Mark-X 8010 | 4 |
| 46 | 52 58 62 | (IT NEVER HAPPENS) IN REAL LIFE — Chuck Jackson, Wand 108 | 6 |
| 47 | 45 43 53 | GOOD, GOOD LOVIN' — Chubby Checker, Parkway 822 | 5 |
| 48 | 51 63 81 | PEANUT BUTTER — Marathons, Argo 5389 | 4 |
| 49 | 44 64 68 | UNDERWATER — Frogmen, Candix 314 | 7 |
| 50 | 33 20 12 | PLEASE LOVE ME FOREVER — Cathy Jean and Roommates, Valmor 007 | 12 |
| 51 | 62 90 — | RAINDROPS — Dee Clark, Vee Jay 383 | 3 |
| 52 | 57 87 99 | I'M A FOOL TO CARE — Joe Barry, Smash 1702 | 4 |
| 53 | 55 66 67 | GLORY OF LOVE — Roommates, Valmor 008 | 6 |
| 54 | 74 95 — | MOODY RIVER — Pat Boone, Dot 16209 | 3 |
| 55 | 66 81 91 | TOSSIN' AND TURNIN' — Bobby Lewis, Beltone 1002 | 4 |
| 56 | 58 70 80 | BE MY BOY — Paris Sisters, Gregmark 2 | 4 |
| 57 | 60 80 — | THOSE OLDIES BUT GOODIES — Caesar and the Romans, Del Fi 4158 | 3 |
| 58 | 95 100 — | RAMA LAMA DING DONG — Edsels, Twin 700 | 3 |
| 59 | — — — | BARBARA ANN — Regents, Gee 1065 | 1 |
| 60 | 49 49 59 | FOOLIN' AROUND — Kay Starr, Capitol 4542 | 9 |
| 61 | 79 — — | NEVER ON SUNDAY — Don Costa, United Artists 234 | 17 |
| 62 | 67 88 — | BUZZ BUZZ A-DIDDLE-IT — Freddy Cannon, Swan 4071 | 4 |
| 63 | 61 71 86 | BILBAO SONG — Andy Williams, Cadence 1398 | 4 |
| 64 | 68 79 83 | THAT'S THE WAY WITH LOVE — Pierio Soffici, Kip 224 | 4 |
| 65 | 86 — — | YOU'D BETTER COME HOME — Russell Byrd, Wand 107 | 2 |
| 66 | 41 45 64 | AFRICAN WALTZ — Cannonball Adderley, Riverside 45457 | 6 |
| 67 | 77 78 82 | WAYWARD WIND — Gogi Grant, Era 3046 | 4 |
| 68 | 76 89 96 | LITTLE EGYPT — Coasters, Atco 6192 | 4 |
| 69 | 72 76 85 | LULLABY OF THE LEAVES — Ventures, Dolton 41 | 4 |
| 70 | 73 84 88 | THREE HEARTS IN A TANGLE — Roy Drusky, Decca 31193 | 6 |
| 71 | 81 — — | A LOVE OF MY OWN — Carla Thomas, Atlantic 2101 | 2 |
| 72 | 78 96 — | HALFWAY TO PARADISE — Tony Orlando, Epic 9441 | 3 |
| 73 | 84 92 — | BIG BIG WORLD — Johnny Burnette, Liberty 55318 | 3 |
| 74 | 83 — — | IN MY HEART — Time-Tones, Times Square 421 | 2 |
| 75 | 85 94 — | COUNT EVERY STAR — Donnie and the Dreamers, Whale 500 | 3 |
| 76 | — — — | YOU ALWAYS HURT THE ONE YOU LOVE — Clarence Henry, Argo 5388 | 1 |
| 77 | — — — | THE WRITING ON THE WALL — Adam Wade, Coed 550 | 1 |
| 78 | — — — | SPRING FEVER — Little Willie John, King 5503 | 1 |
| 79 | 82 86 92 | BETTER TELL HIM NO — Starlets, Pam 1003 | 4 |
| 80 | 71 82 93 | SHY AWAY — Jerry Fuller, Challenge 9104 | 4 |
| 81 | — — — | EVERY BEAT OF MY HEART — Pips, Vee Jay 386 | 1 |
| 82 | 92 99 — | KISSIN' GAME — Dion, Laurie 3090 | 3 |
| 83 | — — — | EVERY BEAT OF MY HEART — Gladys Knight, Fury 1050 | 1 |
| 84 | 89 — — | IN BETWEEN TEARS — Lenny Myles, Scepter 1218 | 2 |
| 85 | — — — | I DON'T MIND — James Brown, King 5466 | 1 |
| 86 | 97 — — | SON-IN-LAW — Blossoms, Challenge 9109 | 2 |
| 87 | — — — | MISS FINE — New Yorkers, Wall 547 | 1 |
| 88 | 100 — — | SON-IN-LAW — Louise Brown, Witch 1 | 2 |
| 89 | 96 97 — | A CROSS STANDS ALONE — Jimmy Witter, United Artists 301 | 3 |
| 90 | — — — | BOLL WEEVIL SONG — Brook Benton, Mercury 71820 | 1 |
| 91 | — — — | I CAN'T DO IT BY MYSELF — Anita Bryant, Carlton 547 | 1 |
| 92 | 80 93 — | YOU'RE GONNA NEED MAGIC — Roy Hamilton, Epic 9443 | 3 |
| 93 | 99 — — | OUR LOVE IS HERE TO STAY — Dinah Washington, Mercury 71812 | 2 |
| 94 | — — — | IT KEEPS RAININ' — Fats Domino, Imperial 5753 | 1 |
| 95 | — — — | FOR YOUR LOVE — Wanderers, Cub 9089 | 1 |
| 96 | 98 — — | WHAT WILL I TELL MY HEART — Harptones, Companion 103 | 2 |
| 97 | 88 91 97 | EIN SCHIFF WIRD KOMMEN (A Ship Will Come—Never on Sunday) — Lale Anderson, King 5478 | 4 |
| 98 | — — — | BROTHER-IN-LAW (He's a Moocher) — Paul Peek, Fairlane 702 | 1 |
| 99 | — — — | THE GIRL'S A DEVIL — Dukays, Nat 1003 | 1 |
| 100 | — — — | HERE'S MY CONFESSION — Wyatt (Earp) McPherson, Savoy 1599 | 1 |

## BUBBLING UNDER THE HOT 100

1. THIS WORLD WE LOVE IN .... Mina, Time 1030
2. LONESOME WHISTLE BLUES .... Freddy King, Federal 12415
3. SUCU SUCU .... Ping Ping, Kapp 377
4. MY KIND OF GIRL .... Matt Monro, Warwick 636
5. RONNIE .... Marcy Jo, Robbee 110
6. I FALL TO PIECES .... Patsy Cline, Decca 31205
7. I LIKE IT LIKE THAT .... Chris Kenner, Instant 3229
8. PICK ME UP ON YOUR WAY DOWN .... Pat Zill, Indigo 119
9. UNCHAINED MELODY .... Gerry Granahan, Caprice 106
10. ANNA .... Jorgen Ingmann, Atco 6195
11. HE NEEDS ME .... Gloria Lynne, Everest 19409
12. SUMMERTIME .... Marcels, Colpix 196
13. ABDUL'S PARTY .... Larry Verne, Era 3044
14. HEART AND SOUL .... Cleftones, Gee 1064
15. WATCH YOUR STEP .... Bobby Parker, V-Tone 223
16. HOW MANY TEARS .... Bobby Vee, Liberty 55325
17. LOCKED UP .... Sonny Fulton, Big Daddy 102
18. BIG BOSS MAN .... Jimmy Reed, Vee Jay 380
19. EVERY BEAT OF MY HEART .... Henry Booth and the Midnighters, ...
19. EVERY BEAT OF MY HEART .... Henry Booth and the Midnighters, Deluxe 6190
20. EXODUS .... Edith Piaf, Capitol 4564

## HOT 100—A TO Z

| Title | # | Title | # |
|---|---|---|---|
| A Cross Stands Alone | 89 | Just for Old Time's Sake | 20 |
| A Love of My Own | 71 | Kissin' Game | 82 |
| African Waltz | 66 | Little Devil | 23 |
| Apache | 39 | Little Egypt | 68 |
| Asia Minor | 37 | Lullabye of Love | 35 |
| Baby Blue | 29 | Lullaby of the Leaves | 69 |
| Barbara Ann | 59 | Mama Said | 9 |
| Be My Boy | 56 | Miss Fine | 87 |
| Better Tell Him No | 79 | Moody River | 54 |
| Big Big World | 73 | Mother-in-Law | 2 |
| Bilbao Song | 63 | Never on Sunday | 61 |
| Blue Moon | 7 | On the Rebound | 17 |
| Boll Weevil Song | 90 | One Hundred Pounds of Clay | 3 |
| Bonanza | 19 | One Mint Julep | 13 |
| Breakin' in a Brand-New Broken Heart | 11 | Our Love Is Here to Stay | 93 |
| Brother-in-Law (He's a Moocher) | 98 | Peanut Butter | 48 |
| Bumble Boogie | 28 | Please Love Me Forever | 50 |
| But I Do | 21 | Portrait of My Love | 12 |
| Buzz Buzz A-Diddle-It | 62 | Raindrops | 51 |
| Continental Walk | 33 | Rama Lama Ding Dong | 58 |
| Count Every Star | 75 | Runaway | 1 |
| Daddy's Home | 5 | Running Scared | 16 |
| (Dance The) Mess Around | 27 | Saved | 40 |
| Ein Schiff Wird Kommen (A Ship Will Come—Never on Sunday) | 97 | Shy Away | 80 |
| Every Beat of My Heart (Knight) | 83 | Some Kind of Wonderful | 32 |
| Every Beat of My Heart (Pips) | 81 | Son-in-Law (Blossoms) | 86 |
| Exodus | 44 | Son-in-Law (Brown) | 88 |
| Flaming Star | 14 | Spring Fever | 78 |
| Foolin' Around | 60 | Stand by Me | 41 |
| For Your Love | 95 | Take Good Care of Her | 10 |
| Funny | 25 | That Old Black Magic | 31 |
| Girl of My Best Friend | 24 | That's the Way With Love | 64 |
| Girl's a Devil, The | 99 | Those Oldies But Goodies | 57 |
| Glory of Love | 53 | Three Hearts in a Tangle | 70 |
| Good, Good Lovin' | 47 | Tonight I Fell in Love | 18 |
| Halfway to Paradise | 72 | Tonight My Love, Tonight | 30 |
| Hello Mary Lou | 15 | Tossin' and Turnin' | 55 |
| Hello Walls | 26 | Touchables in Brooklyn | 45 |
| Here's My Confession | 100 | Tragedy | 22 |
| I Can't Do It By Myself | 91 | Travelin' Man | 8 |
| I Don't Mind | 85 | Triangle | 36 |
| I Feel So Bad | 43 | Underwater | 49 |
| I'm a Fool to Care | 52 | Wayward Wind | 67 |
| I'm in the Mood for Love | 38 | What a Surprise | 42 |
| In Between Tears | 84 | What Will I Tell My Heart | 96 |
| In My Heart | 74 | What'd I Say | 34 |
| It Keeps Raining | 94 | Writing on the Wall, The | 77 |
| (It Never Happens) In Real Life | 46 | You Always Hurt the One You Love | 76 |
| I've Told Every Little Star | 4 | You'd Better Come Home | 65 |
|  |  | You Can Depend on Me | 6 |
|  |  | You're Gonna Need Magic | 92 |

# BILLBOARD HOT 100

**MAY 22, 1961**

**FOR WEEK ENDING MAY 28, 1961**

★ STAR PERFORMERS—Selections registering greatest upward progress this week.
Ⓢ indicates that 45 r.p.m. stereo single version is available.
△ indicates that 33⅓ r.p.m. mono single version is available.
▲ indicates that 33⅓ r.p.m. stereo single version is available.

| This Week | Wk. Ago | 2 Wks. Ago | 3 Wks. Ago | TITLE — Artist, Label & Number | Weeks On Chart |
|---|---|---|---|---|---|
| 1 | 2 | 2 | 2 | MOTHER-IN-LAW — Ernie K-Doe, Minit 623 | 9 |
| 2 | 1 | 1 | 1 | RUNAWAY — Del Shannon, Big Top 3067 | 12 |
| 3 | 5 | 12 | 15 | DADDY'S HOME — Shep and the Limelites, Hull 740 | 9 |
| 4 | 3 | 3 | 4 | ONE HUNDRED POUNDS OF CLAY — Gene McDaniels, Liberty 55308 | 10 |
| 5 | 8 | 18 | 34 | TRAVELIN' MAN — Ricky Nelson, Imperial 5741 | 5 |
| 6 | 9 | 14 | 18 | MAMA SAID — Shirelles, Scepter 1217 | 6 |
| ★7 | 16 | 19 | 24 | RUNNING SCARED — Roy Orbison, Monument 328 | 7 |
| 8 | 11 | 13 | 16 | BREAKIN' IN A BRAND NEW BROKEN HEART — Connie Francis, MGM 12995 | 6 |
| ★9 | 15 | 27 | 73 | HELLO MARY LOU — Ricky Nelson, Imperial 5741 | 5 |
| 10 | 4 | 4 | 3 | I'VE TOLD EVERY LITTLE STAR — Linda Scott, Canadian-American 123 | 11 |
| 11 | 6 | 6 | 9 | YOU CAN DEPEND ON ME — Brenda Lee, Decca 31231 | 9 |
| 12 | 7 | 5 | 5 | BLUE MOON — Marcels, Colpix 186 | 12 |
| 13 | 12 | 9 | 11 | PORTRAIT OF MY LOVE — Steve Lawrence, United Artists 291 | 11 |
| 14 | 10 | 7 | 7 | TAKE GOOD CARE OF HER — Adam Wade, Coed 546 | 11 |
| ★15 | 23 | 34 | 56 | LITTLE DEVIL — Neil Sedaka, RCA Victor 7874 | 4 |
| ★16 | 22 | 31 | 46 | TRAGEDY — Fleetwoods, Dolton 40 | 6 |
| 17 | 43 | — | — | I FEEL SO BAD — Elvis Presley, RCA Victor 7880 | 2 |
| ★18 | 26 | 29 | 39 | HELLO WALLS — Faron Young, Capitol 4533 | 7 |
| 19 | 18 | 15 | 17 | TONIGHT I FELL IN LOVE — Tokens, Warwick 615 | 12 |
| 20 | 19 | 23 | 23 | BONANZA — Al Caiola, United Artists 302 | 8 |
| 21 | 20 | 22 | 23 | JUST FOR OLD TIME'S SAKE — McGuire Sisters, Coral 62249 | 11 |
| 22 | 24 | 26 | 36 | GIRL OF MY BEST FRIEND — Ral Donner, Gone 5102 | 6 |
| 23 | 17 | 10 | 10 | ON THE REBOUND — Floyd Cramer, RCA Victor 7840 | 12 |
| 24 | 21 | 11 | 6 | BUT I DO — Clarence (Frogman) Henry, Argo 5378 | 14 |
| 25 | 31 | 36 | 53 | THAT OLD BLACK MAGIC — Bobby Rydell, Cameo 190 | 4 |
| 26 | 13 | 8 | 8 | ONE MINT JULEP — Ray Charles, Impulse 200 | 12 |
| 27 | 14 | 16 | 19 | FLAMING STAR — Elvis Presley, RCA Victor LPC 128 (33 compact) | 6 |
| ★28 | 41 | 75 | — | STAND BY ME — Ben E. King, Atco 6194 | 3 |
| 29 | 25 | 25 | 29 | FUNNY — Maxine Brown, Nomar 106 | 9 |
| 30 | 28 | 21 | 26 | BUMBLE BOOGIE — B. Bumble and the Stingers, Rendezvous 140 | 9 |
| ★31 | 54 | 74 | 95 | MOODY RIVER — Pat Boone, Dot 16209 | 4 |
| 32 | 27 | 24 | 28 | (DANCE THE) MESS AROUND — Chubby Checker, Parkway 822 | 5 |
| 33 | 35 | 43 | 55 | LULLABYE OF LOVE — Frank Gari, Crusade 1021 | 7 |
| 34 | 36 | 48 | 48 | TRIANGLE — Janie Grant, Caprice 104 | 9 |
| ★35 | 59 | — | — | BARBARA ANN — Regents, Gee 1065 | 2 |
| ★36 | 48 | 51 | 63 | PEANUT BUTTER — Marathons, Arvee 5027 | 5 |
| 37 | 32 | 36 | 40 | SOME KIND OF WONDERFUL — Drifters, Atlantic 2096 | 10 |
| 38 | 51 | 62 | 90 | RAINDROPS — Dee Clark, Vee Jay 383 | 4 |
| 39 | 42 | 56 | 69 | WHAT A SURPRISE — Johnny Maestro, Coed 549 | 5 |
| 40 | 29 | 20 | 12 | BABY BLUE — Echoes, Seg-way 103 | 12 |
| 41 | 44 | 46 | 57 | EXODUS — Eddie Harris, Vee Jay 378 | 7 |
| 42 | 45 | 50 | 72 | TOUCHABLES IN BROOKLYN — Dickie Goodman, Mark-X 8010 | 5 |
| 43 | 58 | 95 | 100 | RAMA LAMA DING DONG — Edsels, Twin 700 | 4 |
| 44 | 55 | 66 | 81 | TOSSIN' AND TURNIN' — Bobby Lewis, Beltone 1002 | 5 |
| 45 | 52 | 57 | 87 | I'M A FOOL TO CARE — Joe Barry, Smash 1702 | 5 |
| 46 | 57 | 60 | 80 | THOSE OLDIES BUT GOODIES — Caesar and the Romans, Del Fi 4158 | 4 |
| 47 | 46 | 52 | 58 | (IT NEVER HAPPENS) IN REAL LIFE — Chuck Jackson, Wand 108 | 7 |
| 48 | 76 | — | — | YOU ALWAYS HURT THE ONE YOU LOVE — Clarence Henry, Argo 5388 | 2 |
| 49 | 33 | 35 | 37 | CONTINENTAL WALK — Hank Ballard and the Midnighters, King 5491 | 8 |
| 50 | 30 | 17 | 13 | TONIGHT MY LOVE, TONIGHT — Paul Anka, ABC-Paramount 10194 | 11 |
| 51 | 37 | 28 | 21 | ASIA MINOR — Kokomo, Felsted 8612 | 14 |
| 52 | 61 | 79 | — | NEVER ON SUNDAY — Don Costa, United Artists 234 | 18 |
| 53 | 53 | 55 | 66 | GLORY OF LOVE — Roomates, Valmor 008 | 7 |
| 54 | 62 | 67 | 88 | BUZZ BUZZ A-DIDDLE-IT — Freddy Cannon, Swan 4071 | 4 |
| 55 | 65 | 86 | — | YOU'D BETTER COME HOME — Russell Byrd, Wand 107 | 3 |
| 56 | 77 | — | — | THE WRITING ON THE WALL — Adam Wade, Coed 550 | 2 |
| 57 | 68 | 76 | 89 | LITTLE EGYPT — Coasters, Atco 6192 | 5 |
| 58 | 75 | 85 | 94 | COUNT EVERY STAR — Donnie and the Dreamers, Whale 500 | 4 |
| 59 | 63 | 61 | 71 | BILBAO SONG — Andy Williams, Cadence 1398 | 5 |
| 60 | 74 | 83 | — | IN MY HEART — Time-Tones, Times Square 421 | 3 |
| 61 | 64 | 68 | 79 | THAT'S THE WAY WITH LOVE — Pierio Soffici, Kip 224 | 5 |
| 62 | 67 | 77 | 78 | WAYWARD WIND — Gogi Grant, Era 3046 | 5 |
| 63 | 81 | — | — | EVERY BEAT OF MY HEART — Pips, Vee Jay 386 | 2 |
| 64 | 79 | 82 | 86 | BETTER TELL HIM NO — Starlets, Pam 1003 | 5 |
| 65 | 72 | 78 | 96 | HALFWAY TO PARADISE — Tony Orlando, Epic 9441 | 4 |
| 66 | 73 | 84 | 92 | BIG BIG WORLD — Johnny Burnette, Liberty 55318 | 4 |
| 67 | 83 | — | — | EVERY BEAT OF MY HEART — Gladys Knight, Fury 1050 | 2 |
| 68 | 71 | 81 | — | A LOVE OF MY OWN — Carla Thomas, Atlantic 2101 | 3 |
| 69 | 56 | 58 | 70 | BE MY BOY — Paris Sisters, Gregmark 2 | 5 |
| 70 | 70 | 73 | 84 | THREE HEARTS IN A TANGLE — Roy Drusky, Decca 31193 | 5 |
| 71 | 90 | — | — | BOLL WEEVIL SONG — Brook Benton, Mercury 71820 | 2 |
| 72 | 47 | 45 | 43 | GOOD, GOOD LOVIN' — Chubby Checker, Parkway 822 | 6 |
| 73 | 94 | — | — | IT KEEPS RAININ' — Fats Domino, Imperial 5753 | 2 |
| 74 | 78 | — | — | SPRING FEVER — Little Willie John, King 5503 | 2 |
| 75 | 34 | 30 | 31 | WHAT'D I SAY — Jerry Lee Lewis, Sun 356 | 8 |
| 76 | 87 | — | — | MISS FINE — New Yorkers, Wall 547 | 2 |
| 77 | 85 | — | — | I DON'T MIND — James Brown, King 5466 | 2 |
| 78 | 49 | 44 | 64 | UNDERWATER — Frogman, Candix 314 | 8 |
| 79 | 69 | 72 | 76 | LULLABY OF THE LEAVES — Ventures, Dolton 41 | 5 |
| 80 | 88 | 100 | — | SON-IN-LAW — Louise Brown, Witch 1 | 3 |
| 81 | — | — | — | TELL ME WHY — Belmonts, Sabrina 500 | 1 |
| 82 | — | — | — | ANNA — Jorgen Ingmann, Atco 6195 | 1 |
| 83 | — | — | — | MILORD — Teresa Brewer, Coral 62265 | 1 |
| 84 | 86 | 97 | — | SON-IN-LAW — Blossoms, Challenge 9109 | 3 |
| 85 | 40 | 37 | 38 | SAVED — La Vern Baker, Atlantic 2099 | 7 |
| 86 | 98 | — | — | BROTHER-IN-LAW (He's a Moocher) — Paul Peek, Fairlane 702 | 2 |
| 87 | 91 | — | — | I CAN'T DO IT BY MYSELF — Anita Bryant, Carlton 547 | 2 |
| 88 | 38 | 47 | 41 | I'M IN THE MOOD FOR LOVE — Chimes, Tag 445 | 9 |
| 89 | 93 | 99 | — | OUR LOVE IS HERE TO STAY — Dinah Washington, Mercury 71812 | 3 |
| 90 | 89 | 96 | 97 | A CROSS STANDS ALONE — Jimmy Witter, United Artists 301 | 4 |
| 91 | — | — | — | PICK ME UP ON YOUR WAY DOWN — Pat Zell, Indigo 119 | 1 |
| 92 | — | — | — | RONNIE — Marcy Jo, Robbee 110 | 1 |
| 93 | 95 | — | — | FOR YOUR LOVE — Wanderers, Cub 9089 | 2 |
| 94 | — | — | — | LONESOME WHISTLE BLUES — Freddy King, Federal 12415 | 1 |
| 95 | 99 | — | — | THE GIRL'S A DEVIL — Dukays, Nat 1003 | 2 |
| 96 | — | — | — | I FALL TO PIECES — Patsy Cline, Decca 31205 | 1 |
| 97 | — | 93 | 98 | NOBODY CARES — Jeanette (Baby) Washington, Neptune 122 | 4 |
| 98 | — | — | — | HEART AND SOUL — Cleftones, Gee 1064 | 1 |
| 99 | — | — | — | QUARTER TO THREE — U. S. Bonds, Le Grand 1008 | 1 |
| 100 | — | — | — | DRIVING WHEEL — Little Junior Parker, Duke 335 | 1 |

## BUBBLING UNDER THE HOT 100

1. MY KIND OF GIRL ............................ Matt Monro, Warwick 636
2. HERE'S MY CONFESSION .... Wyatt (Earp) McPherson, Savoy 1599
3. SUMMERTIME ................................. Marcels, Colpix 196
4. JURA (I SWEAR I LOVE YOU) .. Les Paul & Mary Ford, Columbia 41994
5. I LIKE IT LIKE THAT ................. Chris Kenner, Instant 3229
6. HOW MANY TEARS ..................... Bobby Vee, Liberty 55325
7. DREAM ........................................ Etta James, Argo 5390
8. RING OF FIRE ............................. Duane Eddy, Jamie 1187
9. RESPECTABLE ............................. Chants, MGM 13008
10. HONEYDRIPPER ...................... Clovers, United Artists 307
11. LONELY CROWD .................... Teddy Vann, Columbia 41996
12. WATCH YOUR STEP ............... Bobby Parker, V-Tone 223
13. EVERY BEAT OF MY HEART ...... Henry Booth and the Midnighters, Deluxe 6190
14. LOCKED UP ............................. Sonny Fulton, Big Daddy 102
15. HOLD BACK THE TEARS ......... Delacardos, United Artists 310
16. BIG BOSS MAN ........................ Jimmy Reed, Vee Jay 380
17. EXODUS ..................................... Edith Piaf, Capitol 4564
18. BACARDI .................................. Ralph Marterie, United Artists 315
19. CAN'T HELP LOVIN' THAT GIRL OF MINE ...... Excels, R.S.V.P. 111
20. BRING BACK YOUR HEART ...... Del Vikings, ABC-Paramount 10208

## HOT 100 — A TO Z

| Title | # | Title | # |
|---|---|---|---|
| A Cross Stands Alone | 90 | Lonesome Whistle Blues | 94 |
| A Love of My Own | 68 | Lullabye of Love | 33 |
| Anna | 82 | Lullaby of the Leaves | 79 |
| Asia Minor | 51 | Mama Said | 6 |
| Baby Blue | 40 | Milord | 83 |
| Barbara Ann | 35 | Miss Fine | 76 |
| Be My Boy | 69 | Moody River | 31 |
| Better Tell Him No | 64 | Mother-in-Law | 1 |
| Big Big World | 66 | Never on Sunday | 52 |
| Bilbao | 59 | Nobody Cares | 97 |
| Blue Moon | 12 | On the Rebound | 23 |
| Boll Weevil | 71 | One Hundred Pounds of Clay | 4 |
| Bonanza | 20 | One Mint Julep | 26 |
| Breakin' in a Brand-New Broken Heart | 8 | Our Love Is Here to Stay | 89 |
| Brother-in-Law (He's a Moocher) | 86 | Peanut Butter | 36 |
| Bumble Boogie | 30 | Pick Me Up on Your Way Down | 91 |
| But I Do | 24 | Portrait of My Love | 13 |
| Buzz Buzz A-Diddle It | 54 | Quarter to Three | 99 |
| Continental Walk | 49 | Raindrops | 38 |
| Count Every Star | 58 | Rama Lama Ding Dong | 43 |
| Daddy's Home | 3 | Ronnie | 92 |
| (Dance the) Mess Around | 32 | Runaway | 2 |
| Driving Wheel | 100 | Running Scared | 7 |
| Every Beat of My Heart (Knight) | 67 | Saved | 85 |
| Every Beat of My Heart (Pips) | 63 | Some Kind of Wonderful | 37 |
| Exodus | 41 | Son-in-Law (Blossoms) | 84 |
| Flaming Star | 27 | Son-in-Law (Brown) | 80 |
| For Your Love | 93 | Spring Fever | 74 |
| Funny | 29 | Stand by Me | 28 |
| Girl of My Best Friend | 22 | Take Good Care of Her | 14 |
| Girl's a Devil, The | 95 | Tell Me Why | 81 |
| Glory of Love | 53 | That Old Black Magic | 25 |
| Good, Good Lovin' | 72 | That's the Way With Love | 61 |
| Halfway to Paradise | 65 | Those Oldies But Goodies | 46 |
| Heart and Soul | 98 | Three Hearts in a Tangle | 70 |
| Hello Mary Lou | 9 | Tonight I Fell in Love | 19 |
| Hello Walls | 18 | Tonight My Love, Tonight | 50 |
| I Can't Do It by Myself | 87 | Tossin' and Turnin' | 44 |
| I Don't Mind | 77 | Touchables in Brooklyn | 42 |
| I Fall to Pieces | 96 | Tragedy | 16 |
| I Feel So Bad | 17 | Travelin' Man | 5 |
| I'm a Fool to Care | 45 | Triangle | 34 |
| I'm in the Mood for Love | 88 | Underwater | 78 |
| In My Heart | 60 | What a Surprise | 39 |
| It Keeps Rainin' | 73 | Wayward Wind | 62 |
| (It Never Happens) in Real Life | 47 | What'd I Say | 75 |
| I've Told Every Little Star | 10 | Writing on the Wall, The | 56 |
| Just for Old Time's Sake | 21 | You Always Hurt the One You Love | 48 |
| Little Devil | 15 | You Can Depend on Me | 11 |
| Little Egypt | 57 | You'd Better Come Home | 55 |

# BILLBOARD HOT 100

**MAY 29, 1961**
**FOR WEEK ENDING JUNE 4, 1961**

| This Week | Wk Ago | 2 Wks Ago | Title | Artist, Label & Number | Weeks On Chart |
|---|---|---|---|---|---|
| 1 | 5 | 8 | TRAVELIN' MAN — Ricky Nelson, Imperial 5741 | | 6 |
| 2 | 3 | 5 | DADDY'S HOME — Shep and the Limelites, Hull 740 | | 10 |
| 3 | 7 | 16 | RUNNING SCARED — Roy Orbison, Monument 328 | | 8 |
| 4 | 6 | 9 | MAMA SAID — Shirelles, Scepter 1217 | | 7 |
| 5 | 1 | 2 | MOTHER-IN-LAW — Ernie K-Doe, Minit 623 | | 10 |
| 6 | 2 | 1 | RUNAWAY — Del Shannon, Big Top 3067 | | 13 |
| 7 | 8 | 11 | BREAKIN' IN A BRAND NEW BROKEN HEART — Connie Francis, MGM 12995 | | 7 |
| 8 | 4 | 3 | ONE HUNDRED POUNDS OF CLAY — Gene McDaniels, Liberty 55308 | | 11 |
| 9 | 17 | 43 | I FEEL SO BAD — Elvis Presley, RCA Victor 7880 | | 3 |
| 10 | 16 | 22 | TRAGEDY — Fleetwoods, Dolton 40 | | 7 |
| 11 | 15 | 23 | LITTLE DEVIL — Neil Sedaka, RCA Victor 7874 | | 5 |
| 12 | 18 | 26 | HELLO WALLS — Faron Young, Capitol 4533 | | 8 |
| 13 | 28 | 41 | STAND BY ME — Ben E. King, Atco 6194 | | 4 |
| 14 | 31 | 54 | MOODY RIVER — Pat Boone, Dot 16209 | | 5 |
| 15 | 38 | 51 | RAINDROPS — Dee Clark, Vee Jay 383 | | 5 |
| 16 | 9 | 15 | HELLO MARY LOU — Ricky Nelson, Imperial 5741 | | 5 |
| 17 | 10 | 4 | I'VE TOLD EVERY LITTLE STAR — Linda Scott, Canadian-American 123 | | 12 |
| 18 | 13 | 12 | PORTRAIT OF MY LOVE — Steve Lawrence, United Artists 291 | | 12 |
| 19 | 22 | 24 | GIRL OF MY BEST FRIEND — Ral Donner, Gone 5102 | | 7 |
| 20 | 35 | 59 | BARBARA ANN — Regents, Gee 1065 | | 3 |
| 21 | 25 | 31 | THAT OLD BLACK MAGIC — Bobby Rydell, Cameo 190 | | 5 |
| 22 | 11 | 6 | YOU CAN DEPEND ON ME — Brenda Lee, Decca 31231 | | 10 |
| 23 | 19 | 18 | TONIGHT I FELL IN LOVE — Tokens, Warwick 615 | | 13 |
| 24 | 33 | 35 | LULLABYE OF LOVE — Frank Gari, Crusade 1021 | | 8 |
| 25 | 48 | 76 | YOU ALWAYS HURT THE ONE YOU LOVE — Clarence Henry, Argo 5388 | | 3 |
| 26 | 12 | 7 | BLUE MOON — Marcels, Colpix 186 | | 13 |
| 27 | 21 | 20 | JUST FOR OLD TIME'S SAKE — McGuire Sisters, Coral 62249 | | 12 |
| 28 | 14 | 10 | TAKE GOOD CARE OF HER — Adam Wade, Coed 546 | | 12 |
| 29 | 34 | 36 | TRIANGLE — Janie Grant, Caprice 104 | | 10 |
| 30 | 36 | 48 | PEANUT BUTTER — Marathons, Arvee 5027 | | 6 |
| 31 | 20 | 19 | BONANZA — Al Caiola, United Artists 302 | | 9 |
| 32 | 56 | 77 | THE WRITING ON THE WALL — Adam Wade, Coed 550 | | 3 |
| 33 | 46 | 57 | THOSE OLDIES BUT GOODIES — Caesar and the Romans, Del Fi 4158 | | 5 |
| 34 | 44 | 55 | TOSSIN' AND TURNIN' — Bobby Lewis, Beltone 1002 | | 6 |
| 35 | 45 | 52 | I'M A FOOL TO CARE — Joe Barry, Smash 1702 | | 6 |
| 36 | 39 | 42 | WHAT A SURPRISE — Johnny Maestro, Coed 549 | | 6 |
| 37 | 41 | 44 | EXODUS — Eddie Harris, Vee Jay 378 | | 8 |
| 38 | 57 | 68 | LITTLE EGYPT — Coasters, Atco 6192 | | 6 |
| 39 | 24 | 21 | BUT I DO — Clarence (Frogman) Henry, Argo 5378 | | 15 |
| 40 | 65 | 72 | HALFWAY TO PARADISE — Tony Orlando, Epic 9441 | | 5 |
| 41 | 43 | 58 | RAMA LAMA DING DONG — Edsels, Twin 700 | | 5 |
| 42 | 71 | 90 | BOLL WEEVIL SONG — Brook Benton, Mercury 71820 | | 3 |
| 43 | 63 | 81 | EVERY BEAT OF MY HEART — Pips, Vee Jay 386 | | 3 |
| 44 | 59 | 63 | BILBAO SONG — Andy Williams, Cadence 1398 | | 6 |
| 45 | 52 | 61 | NEVER ON SUNDAY — Don Costa, United Artists 234 | | 19 |
| 46 | 32 | 27 | (DANCE THE) MESS AROUND — Chubby Checker, Parkway 822 | | 6 |
| 47 | 27 | 14 | FLAMING STAR — Elvis Presley, RCA Victor LPC 128 | | 7 |
| 48 | 37 | 32 | SOME KIND OF WONDERFUL — Drifters, Atlantic 2096 | | 11 |
| 49 | 53 | 53 | GLORY OF LOVE — Roomates, Valmor 008 | | 8 |
| 50 | 55 | 65 | YOU'D BETTER COME HOME — Russell Byrd, Wand 107 | | 4 |
| 51 | 60 | 74 | IN MY HEART — Time-Tones, Times Square 421 | | 4 |
| 52 | 54 | 62 | BUZZ BUZZ A-DIDDLE-IT — Freddy Cannon, Swan 4071 | | 5 |
| 53 | 58 | 75 | COUNT EVERY STAR — Donnie and the Dreamers, Whale 500 | | 5 |
| 54 | 64 | 79 | BETTER TELL HIM NO — Starlets, Pam 1003 | | 6 |
| 55 | 62 | 67 | WAYWARD WIND — Gogi Grant, Era 3046 | | 6 |
| 56 | 26 | 13 | ONE MINT JULEP — Ray Charles, Impulse 200 | | 13 |
| 57 | 67 | 83 | EVERY BEAT OF MY HEART — Gladys Knight, Fury 1050 | | 3 |
| 58 | 66 | 73 | BIG BIG WORLD — Johnny Burnette, Liberty 55318 | | 5 |
| 59 | 61 | 64 | THAT'S THE WAY WITH LOVE — Pierro Soffici, Kip 224 | | 6 |
| 60 | 30 | 28 | BUMBLE BOOGIE — B. Bumble and the Stingers, Rendezvous 140 | | 10 |
| 61 | 29 | 25 | FUNNY — Maxine Brown, Nomar 106 | | 10 |
| 62 | 68 | 71 | A LOVE OF MY OWN — Carla Thomas, Atlantic 2101 | | 4 |
| 63 | 23 | 17 | ON THE REBOUND — Floyd Cramer, RCA Victor 7840 | | 13 |
| 64 | 73 | 94 | IT KEEPS RAININ' — Fats Domino, Imperial 5753 | | 3 |
| 65 | 99 | — | QUARTER TO THREE — U. S. Bonds, Le Grand 1008 | | 2 |
| 66 | 70 | 70 | THREE HEARTS IN A TANGLE — Roy Drusky, Decca 31193 | | 8 |
| 67 | — | — | DANCE ON LITTLE GIRL — Paul Anka, ABC-Paramount 10220 | | 1 |
| 68 | 81 | — | TELL ME WHY — Belmonts, Sabrina 500 | | 2 |
| 69 | 77 | 85 | I DON'T MIND — James Brown, King 5466 | | 3 |
| 70 | 82 | — | ANNA — Jorgen Ingmann, Atco 6195 | | 2 |
| 71 | — | — | YELLOW BIRD — Arthur Lyman, Hi Fi 5024 | | 1 |
| 72 | 42 | 45 | TOUCHABLES IN BROOKLYN — Dickie Goodman, Mark-X 8010 | | 6 |
| 73 | 74 | 78 | SPRING FEVER — Little Willie John, King 5503 | | 3 |
| 74 | 76 | 87 | MISS FINE — New Yorkers, Wall 547 | | 3 |
| 75 | 83 | — | MILORD — Teresa Brewer, Coral 62265 | | 2 |
| 76 | 80 | 88 | SON-IN-LAW — Louise Brown, Witch 1 | | 4 |
| 77 | — | — | HOW MANY TEARS — Bobby Vee, Liberty 55325 | | 1 |
| 78 | 98 | — | HEART AND SOUL — Cleftones, Gee 1064 | | 2 |
| 79 | 84 | 86 | SON-IN-LAW — Blossoms, Challenge 9109 | | 4 |
| 80 | — | — | MY KIND OF GIRL — Matt Monro, Warwick 636 | | 1 |
| 81 | 92 | — | RONNIE — Marcy Jo, Robbee 110 | | 2 |
| 82 | 97 | 93 | NOBODY CARES — Jeanette (Baby) Washington, Neptune 122 | | 5 |
| 83 | — | — | JIMMY MARTINEZ — Marty Robbins, Columbia 42008 | | 1 |
| 84 | 86 | 98 | BROTHER-IN-LAW (He's a Moocher) — Paul Peek, Fairlane 702 | | 3 |
| 85 | 100 | — | DRIVING WHEEL — Little Junior Parker, Duke 335 | | 2 |
| 86 | — | — | I LIKE IT LIKE THAT — Chris Kenner, Instant 3229 | | 1 |
| 87 | — | — | RAININ' IN MY HEART — Slim Harpo, Excello 2194 | | 1 |
| 88 | 96 | — | I FALL TO PIECES — Patsy Cline, Decca 31205 | | 2 |
| 89 | — | — | WHO ELSE BUT YOU — Frankie Avalon, Chancellor 1077 | | 1 |
| 90 | — | — | SUMMERTIME — Marcels, Colpix 196 | | 1 |
| 91 | 94 | — | LONESOME WHISTLE BLUES — Freddy King, Federal 12415 | | 2 |
| 92 | 95 | 99 | THE GIRL'S A DEVIL — Dukays, Nat 1003 | | 3 |
| 93 | — | — | BIG BOSS MAN — Jimmy Reed, Vee Jay 380 | | 1 |
| 94 | — | — | TEMPTATION — Everly Brothers, Warner Bros. 5220 | | 1 |
| 95 | — | — | SACRED — Castelles, Era 3048 | | 1 |
| 96 | — | — | TONIGHT (COULD BE THE NIGHT) — Velvets, Monument 4410 | | 1 |
| 97 | — | 100 | HERE'S MY CONFESSION — Wyatt (Earp) McPherson, Savoy 1599 | | 2 |
| 98 | — | — | RING OF FIRE — Duane Eddy, Jamie 1187 | | 1 |
| 99 | — | 94 | JURA (I SWEAR I LOVE YOU) — Les Paul and Mary Ford, Columbia 41994 | | 4 |
| 100 | — | — | A LITTLE FEELING — Jack Scott, Capitol 4554 | | 1 |

## BUBBLING UNDER THE HOT 100

1. RESPECTABLE — Chants, MGM 13008
2. I CAN'T DO IT BY MYSELF — Anita Bryant, Carlton 547
3. WATCH YOUR STEP — Bobby Parker, V-Tone 223
4. BRING BACK YOUR HEART — Del-Vikings, ABC-Paramount 10208
5. FOOL THAT I AM — Etta James, Argo 5390
6. BOOK OF LOVE — Bobby Bare, Fraternity 878
7. DREAM — Etta James, Argo 5390
8. LOCKED UP — Sonny Fulton, Big Daddy 102
9. CHARLIE WASN'T THERE — Barbara Evans, Pioneer 1002
10. LONELY CROWD — Teddy Vann, Columbia 41996
11. REBEL—JOHNNY YUMA — Johnny Cash, Columbia 41995
12. BLUE TOMORROW — Billy Vaughn, Dot 16220
13. YOU CAN'T SIT DOWN — Phillip Upchurch Combo, Boyd 1026
14. HOLD BACK THE TEARS — Delacardos, United Artists 310
15. BICARDI — Ralph Marterie, United Artists 315
16. EXODUS — Edith Piaf, Capitol 4564
17. MONDAY TO SUNDAY — Alan Dale, Sinclair 1003
18. CAN'T HELP LOVIN' THAT GIRL OF MINE — Excels, R.S.V.P. 111
19. SHOULD I — String-A-Longs, Warwick 654
20. CUPID — Sam Cooke, RCA Victor 7883

JUNE 5, 1961

# BILLBOARD HOT 100

FOR WEEK ENDING JUNE 11, 1961

**STAR PERFORMERS**—Selections registering greatest upward progress this week.

S — Indicates that 45 r.p.m. stereo single version is available.
△ — Indicates that 33⅓ r.p.m. mono single version is available.
Ⓢ — Indicates that 33⅓ r.p.m. stereo single version is available.

| This Week | Wk. Ago | 2 Wks. Ago | 3 Wks. Ago | TITLE — Artist, Label & Number | Weeks On Chart |
|---|---|---|---|---|---|
| 1 | 3 | 7 | 16 | RUNNING SCARED — Roy Orbison, Monument 438 | 9 |
| 2 | 1 | 5 | 8 | TRAVELIN' MAN — Ricky Nelson, Imperial 5741 | 7 |
| 3 | 2 | 3 | 5 | DADDY'S HOME — Shep and the Limelites, Hull 740 | 11 |
| 4 | 4 | 6 | 9 | MAMA SAID — Shirelles, Scepter 1217 | 8 |
| 5 | 9 | 17 | 43 | I FEEL SO BAD — Elvis Presley, RCA Victor 7880 | 4 |
| ★6 | 13 | 28 | 41 | STAND BY ME — Ben E. King, Atco 6194 | 5 |
| ★7 | 14 | 31 | 54 | MOODY RIVER — Pat Boone, Dot 16209 | 6 |
| 8 | 8 | 4 | 3 | ONE HUNDRED POUNDS OF CLAY — Gene McDaniels, Liberty 55308 | 12 |
| ★9 | 15 | 38 | 51 | RAINDROPS — Dee Clark, Vee Jay 383 | 6 |
| 10 | 7 | 8 | 11 | BREAKIN' IN A BRAND NEW BROKEN HEART — Connie Francis, MGM 12995 | 8 |
| 11 | 10 | 16 | 22 | TRAGEDY — Fleetwoods, Dolton 40 | 8 |
| 12 | 12 | 18 | 26 | HELLO WALLS — Faron Young, Capitol 4533 | 9 |
| 13 | 11 | 15 | 23 | LITTLE DEVIL — Neil Sedaka, RCA Victor 7874 | 6 |
| 14 | 16 | 9 | 15 | HELLO MARY LOU — Ricky Nelson, Imperial 5741 | 6 |
| 15 | 6 | 2 | 1 | RUNAWAY — Del Shannon, Big Top 3067 | 14 |
| 16 | 20 | 35 | 59 | BARBARA ANN — Regents, Gee 1065 | 4 |
| 17 | 25 | 48 | 76 | YOU ALWAYS HURT THE ONE YOU LOVE — Clarence Henry, Argo 5388 | 4 |
| 18 | 32 | 56 | 77 | THE WRITING ON THE WALL — Adam Wade, Coed 550 | 4 |
| 19 | 5 | 1 | 2 | MOTHER-IN-LAW — Ernie K-Doe, Minit 623 | 11 |
| 20 | 19 | 22 | 24 | GIRL OF MY BEST FRIEND — Ral Donner, Gone 5102 | 8 |
| 21 | 43 | 63 | 81 | EVERY BEAT OF MY HEART — Pips, Vee Jay 386 | 4 |
| 22 | 33 | 46 | 57 | THOSE OLDIES BUT GOODIES — Caesar and the Romans, Del Fi 4158 | 6 |
| 23 | 24 | 33 | 35 | LULLABYE OF LOVE — Frank Gari, Crusade 1021 | 9 |
| ★24 | 34 | 44 | 55 | TOSSIN' AND TURNIN' — Bobby Lewis, Beltone 1002 | 7 |
| 25 | 35 | 45 | 52 | I'M A FOOL TO CARE — Joe Barry, Smash 1702 | 7 |
| 26 | 42 | 71 | 90 | BOLL WEEVIL SONG — Brook Benton, Mercury 71820 | 4 |
| ★27 | 38 | 57 | 68 | LITTLE EGYPT — Coasters, Atco 6192 | 7 |
| 28 | 30 | 36 | 48 | PEANUT BUTTER — Marathons, Arvee 5027 | 7 |
| 29 | 29 | 34 | 36 | TRIANGLE — Janie Grant, Caprice 104 | 11 |
| 30 | 18 | 13 | 12 | PORTRAIT OF MY LOVE — Steve Lawrence, United Artists 291 | 13 |
| 31 | 41 | 43 | 58 | RAMA LAMA DING DONG — Edsels, Twin 700 | 6 |
| 32 | 21 | 25 | 31 | THAT OLD BLACK MAGIC — Bobby Rydell, Cameo 190 | 6 |
| 33 | 65 | 99 | — | QUARTER TO THREE — U. S. Bonds, Le Grand 1008 | 3 |
| 34 | 17 | 10 | 4 | I'VE TOLD EVERY LITTLE STAR — Linda Scott, Canadian-American 123 | 13 |
| 35 | 36 | 39 | 42 | WHAT A SURPRISE — Johnny Maestro, Coed 549 | 7 |
| 36 | 37 | 41 | 44 | EXODUS — Eddie Harris, Vee Jay 378 | 9 |
| 37 | 44 | 59 | 63 | BILBAO SONG — Andy Williams, Cadence 1398 | 7 |
| 38 | 45 | 52 | 61 | NEVER ON SUNDAY — Don Costa, United Artists 234 | 20 |
| 39 | 40 | 65 | 72 | HALFWAY TO PARADISE — Tony Orlando, Epic 9441 | 6 |
| 40 | 22 | 11 | 6 | YOU CAN DEPEND ON ME — Brenda Lee, Decca 31231 | 11 |
| 41 | 28 | 14 | 10 | TAKE GOOD CARE OF HER — Adam Wade, Coed 546 | 13 |
| ★42 | 71 | — | — | YELLOW BIRD — Arthur Lyman, Hi Fi 5024 | 3 |
| 43 | 23 | 19 | 18 | TONIGHT I FELL IN LOVE — Tokens, Warwick 615 | 14 |
| 44 | 27 | 21 | 20 | JUST FOR OLD TIME'S SAKE — McGuire Sisters, Coral 62249 | 13 |
| 45 | 53 | 58 | 75 | COUNT EVERY STAR — Donnie and the Dreamers, Whale 500 | 6 |
| ★46 | 57 | 67 | 83 | EVERY BEAT OF MY HEART — Gladys Knight, Fury 1050 | 4 |
| 47 | 26 | 12 | 7 | BLUE MOON — Marcels, Colpix 186 | 14 |
| 48 | 67 | — | — | DANCE ON LITTLE GIRL — Paul Anka, ABC-Paramount 10220 | 2 |
| 49 | 54 | 64 | 79 | BETTER TELL HIM NO — Starlets, Pam 1003 | 7 |
| 50 | 55 | 62 | 67 | WAYWARD WIND — Gogi Grant, Era 3046 | 7 |
| 51 | 52 | 54 | 62 | BUZZ BUZZ A-DIDDLE-IT — Freddy Cannon, Swan 4071 | 6 |
| 52 | 31 | 20 | 19 | BONANZA — Al Caiola, United Artists 302 | 10 |
| 53 | 39 | 24 | 21 | BUT I DO — Clarence (Frogman) Henry, Argo 5378 | 16 |
| 54 | 64 | 73 | 94 | IT KEEPS RAININ' — Fats Domino, Imperial 5753 | 4 |
| 55 | 78 | 98 | — | HEART AND SOUL — Cleftones, Gee 1064 | 3 |
| 56 | 62 | 68 | 71 | A LOVE OF MY OWN — Carla Thomas, Atlantic 2101 | 4 |
| 57 | 49 | 53 | 53 | GLORY OF LOVE — Roomates, Valmor 008 | 9 |
| 58 | 68 | 81 | — | TELL ME WHY — Belmonts, Sabrina 500 | 3 |
| 59 | 94 | — | — | TEMPTATION — Everly Brothers, Warner Bros. 5220 | 2 |
| 60 | 70 | 82 | — | ANNA — Jorgen Ingmann, Atco 6195 | 3 |
| 61 | 69 | 77 | 85 | I DON'T MIND — James Brown, King 5466 | 4 |
| 62 | 58 | 66 | 73 | BIG BIG WORLD — Johnny Burnette, Liberty 55318 | 6 |
| 63 | 83 | — | — | JIMMY MARTINEZ — Marty Robbins, Columbia 42008 | 2 |
| 64 | 59 | 61 | 64 | THAT'S THE WAY WITH LOVE — Pierio Soffici, Kip 224 | 7 |
| 65 | 82 | 97 | — | NOBODY CARES — Jeanette (Baby) Washington, Neptune 122 | 6 |
| 66 | 46 | 32 | 27 | (DANCE THE) MESS AROUND — Chubby Checker, Parkway 822 | 7 |
| 67 | 51 | 60 | 74 | IN MY HEART — Time-Tones, Times Square 421 | 5 |
| 68 | 80 | — | — | MY KIND OF GIRL — Matt Monro, Warwick 636 | 2 |
| 69 | 74 | 76 | 87 | MISS FINE — New Yorkers, Wall 547 | 4 |
| 70 | 77 | — | — | HOW MANY TEARS — Bobby Vee, Liberty 55325 | 2 |
| 71 | 73 | 74 | 78 | SPRING FEVER — Little Willie John, King 5503 | 4 |
| ★72 | 87 | — | — | RAININ' IN MY HEART — Slim Harpo, Excello 2194 | 2 |
| 73 | — | — | — | WILD IN THE COUNTRY — Elvis Presley, RCA Victor 7880 | 1 |
| 74 | 75 | 83 | — | MILORD — Teresa Brewer, Coral 62265 | 3 |
| 75 | 86 | — | — | I LIKE IT LIKE THAT — Chris Kenner, Instant 3229 | 2 |
| 76 | 66 | 70 | 70 | THREE HEARTS IN A TANGLE — Roy Drusky, Decca 31193 | 9 |
| 77 | 88 | 96 | — | I FALL TO PIECES — Patsy Cline, Decca 31205 | 3 |
| 78 | 90 | — | — | SUMMERTIME — Marcels, Colpix 196 | 2 |
| 79 | 92 | 95 | 99 | THE GIRL'S A DEVIL — Dukays, Nat 1003 | 4 |
| ★80 | 95 | — | — | SACRED — Castelles, Era 3048 | 2 |
| 81 | 93 | — | — | BIG BOSS MAN — Jimmy Reed, Vee Jay 380 | 2 |
| 82 | 89 | — | — | WHO ELSE BUT YOU — Frankie Avalon, Chancellor 1077 | 2 |
| 83 | 99 | — | — | JURA (I SWEAR I LOVE YOU) — Les Paul and Mary Ford, Columbia 41994 | 5 |
| 84 | 98 | — | — | RING OF FIRE — Duane Eddy, Jamie 1187 | 2 |
| 85 | — | — | — | CUPID — Sam Cooke, RCA Victor 7883 | 1 |
| 86 | 50 | 55 | 65 | YOU'D BETTER COME HOME — Russell Byrd, Wand 107 | 5 |
| 87 | — | — | — | RIGHT OR WRONG — Wanda Jackson, Capitol 4553 | 1 |
| 88 | 91 | 94 | — | LONESOME WHISTLE BLUES — Freddy King, Federal 12415 | 3 |
| 89 | 96 | — | — | TONIGHT (COULD BE THE NIGHT) — Velvets, Monument 441 | 2 |
| 90 | — | — | — | SAN ANTONIO ROSE — Floyd Cramer, RCA Victor 7893 | 1 |
| 91 | 100 | — | — | A LITTLE FEELING — Jack Scott, Capitol 4554 | 2 |
| 92 | — | — | — | HATS OFF TO LARRY — Del Shannon, Big Top 3075 | 1 |
| 93 | — | — | — | PLEASE STAY — Drifters, Atlantic 2105 | 1 |
| 94 | — | — | — | OLE BUTTERMILK SKY — Bill Black's Combo, Hi 2036 | 1 |
| 95 | — | — | — | LONELY CROWD — Teddy Vann, Columbia 41996 | 1 |
| 96 | 81 | 92 | — | RONNIE — Marcy Jo, Robbee 110 | 3 |
| 97 | — | — | — | STICK WITH ME BABY — Everly Brothers, Warner Bros. 5220 | 1 |
| 98 | — | — | — | HOLD BACK THE TEARS — Delacardos, United Artists 310 | 1 |
| 99 | 76 | 80 | 88 | SON-IN-LAW — Louise Brown, Witch 1 | 5 |
| 100 | — | — | — | CAN'T HELP LOVIN' THAT GIRL OF MINE — Excels, R.S.V.P. 111 | 1 |

## BUBBLING UNDER THE HOT 100

1. BRING BACK YOUR HEART .......... Del-Vikings, ABC-Paramount 10208
2. DREAM .......... Etta James, Argo 5390
3. WATCH YOUR STEP .......... Bobby Parker, V-Tone 223
4. FOOL THAT I AM .......... Etta James, Argo 5390
5. BLUE TOMORROW .......... Billy Vaughn, Dot 16220
6. LOCKED UP .......... Sonny Fulton, Big Daddy 102
7. SHOULD I .......... String-A-Longs, Warwick 654
8. REBEL-JOHNNY YUMA .......... Johnny Cash, Columbia 41995
9. CHARLIE WASN'T THERE .......... Barbara Evans, Pioneer 1002
10. YOU CAN'T SIT DOWN .......... Phillip Upchurch Combo, Boyd 1026
11. MONDAY TO SUNDAY .......... Alan Dale, Sinclair 1003
12. YELLOW BIRD .......... Lawrence Welk, Dot 16222
13. LIFE IS BUT A DREAM .......... Earls, Rome 101
14. LOUISIANA MAN .......... Rusty and Doug, Hickory 1137
15. I'M GONNA KNOCK ON YOUR DOOR .......... Eddie Hodges, Cadence 1397
16. YOU'VE GOT TO SHOW ME .......... Tony Lawrence, Silver Bid 1025
17. THEME FROM GOODBYE AGAIN .......... Ferrante & Teicher, United Artists 319
18. NATURE BOY .......... Bobby Darin, Atco 6196
19. LIFE IS BUT A DREAM, SWEETHEART .......... Classics, Mercury 71829
20. BOBBY .......... Neil Scott, Portrait 102

## HOT 100 — A TO Z

| Title | # | Title | # |
|---|---|---|---|
| Anna | 60 | Lullabye of Love | 23 |
| Barbara Ann | 16 | Mama Said | 4 |
| Better Tell Him No | 49 | Milord | 74 |
| Big Big World | 62 | Miss Fine | 69 |
| Big Boss Man | 81 | Moody River | 7 |
| Bilbao Song | 37 | Mother-In-Law | 19 |
| Blue Moon | 47 | My Kind of Girl | 68 |
| Boll Weevil Song | 26 | Never on Sunday | 38 |
| Bonanza | 52 | Nobody Cares | 65 |
| Breakin' in a Brand New Broken Heart | 10 | Ole Buttermilk Sky | 94 |
| But I Do | 53 | One Hundred Pounds of Clay | 8 |
| Buzz Buzz A-Diddle-It | 51 | Peanut Butter | 28 |
| Can't Help Lovin' That Girl of Mine | 100 | Please Stay | 93 |
| | | Portrait of My Love | 30 |
| Count Every Star | 45 | Quarter to Three | 33 |
| Cupid | 85 | Raindrops | 9 |
| Daddy's Home | 3 | Rainin' in My Heart | 72 |
| Dance on Little Girl | 48 | Rama Lama Ding Dong | 31 |
| (Dance the) Mess Around | 66 | Right or Wrong | 87 |
| Every Beat of My Heart (Knight) | 46 | Ring of Fire | 84 |
| Every Beat of My Heart (Pips) | 21 | Ronnie | 96 |
| Exodus | 36 | Runaway | 15 |
| Girl of My Best Friend | 20 | Running Scared | 1 |
| Girl's a Devil, The | 79 | Sacred | 80 |
| Glory of Love | 57 | San Antonio Rose | 90 |
| Halfway to Paradise | 39 | Son-In-Law (Brown) | 99 |
| Hats Off to Larry | 92 | Spring Fever | 71 |
| Heart and Soul | 55 | Stand by Me | 6 |
| Hello Mary Lou | 14 | Stick With Me Baby | 97 |
| Hello Walls | 12 | Summertime | 78 |
| Hold Back the Tears | 98 | Take Good Care of Her | 41 |
| How Many Tears | 70 | Tell Me Why | 58 |
| I Don't Mind | 61 | Temptation | 59 |
| I Fall to Pieces | 77 | That Old Black Magic | 32 |
| I Feel So Bad | 5 | That's the Way With Love | 64 |
| I Like It Like That | 75 | Those Oldies But Goodies | 22 |
| I'm a Fool to Care | 25 | Three Hearts in a Tangle | 76 |
| In My Heart | 67 | Tonight | 89 |
| It Keeps Rainin' | 54 | Tonight I Fell in Love | 43 |
| I've Told Every Little Star | 34 | Tragedy | 11 |
| Jimmy Martinez | 63 | Travelin' Man | 2 |
| Jura | 83 | Wayward Wind | 50 |
| Just for Old Time's Sake | 44 | What a Surprise | 35 |
| Little Devil | 13 | Who Else But You | 82 |
| Little Egypt | 27 | Wild in the Country | 73 |
| Little Feeling, A | 91 | Writing on the Wall, The | 18 |
| Lonely Crowd | 95 | Yellow Bird | 42 |
| Lonesome Whistle Blues | 88 | You Always Hurt the One You Love | 17 |
| Love of My Own, A | 56 | You Can Depend on Me | 40 |
| | | You'd Better Come Home | 86 |

# BILLBOARD HOT 100

**JUNE 12, 1961** — FOR WEEK ENDING JUNE 18, 1961

STAR PERFORMERS—Selections registering greatest upward progress this week.

| This Week | Wk Ago | 2 Wks Ago | 3 Wks Ago | Title — Artist, Label & Number | Weeks on Chart |
|---|---|---|---|---|---|
| 1 | 2 | 1 | 5 | TRAVELIN' MAN — Ricky Nelson, Imperial 5741 | 8 |
| 2 | 7 | 14 | 31 | MOODY RIVER — Pat Boone, Dot 16209 | 7 |
| 3 | 1 | 3 | 7 | RUNNING SCARED — Roy Orbison, Monument 438 | 10 |
| 4 | 6 | 13 | 28 | STAND BY ME — Ben E. King, Atco 6194 | 6 |
| 5 | 9 | 15 | 38 | RAINDROPS — Dee Clark, Vee Jay 383 | 7 |
| 6 | 18 | 32 | 56 | THE WRITING ON THE WALL — Adam Wade, Coed 550 | 5 |
| 7 | 5 | 9 | 17 | I FEEL SO BAD — Elvis Presley, RCA Victor 7880 | 5 |
| 8 | 21 | 43 | 63 | EVERY BEAT OF MY HEART — Pips, Vee Jay 386 | 5 |
| 9 | 33 | 65 | 99 | QUARTER TO THREE — U. S. Bonds, Le Grand 1008 | 4 |
| 10 | 26 | 42 | 71 | BOLL WEEVIL SONG — Brook Benton, Mercury 71820 | 5 |
| 11 | 22 | 33 | 46 | THOSE OLDIES BUT GOODIES — Little Caesar and the Romans, Del Fi 4158 | 7 |
| 12 | 4 | 4 | 6 | MAMA SAID — Shirelles, Scepter 1217 | 9 |
| 13 | 16 | 20 | 35 | BARBARA ANN — Regents, Gee 1065 | 5 |
| 14 | 17 | 25 | 48 | YOU ALWAYS HURT THE ONE YOU LOVE — Clarence Henry, Argo 5388 | 5 |
| 15 | 14 | 16 | 9 | HELLO MARY LOU — Ricky Nelson, Imperial 5741 | 7 |
| 16 | 3 | 2 | 3 | DADDY'S HOME — Shep and the Limelites, Hull 740 | 12 |
| 17 | 24 | 34 | 44 | TOSSIN' AND TURNIN' — Bobby Lewis, Beltone 1002 | 8 |
| 18 | 12 | 12 | 18 | HELLO WALLS — Faron Young, Capitol 4533 | 10 |
| 19 | 8 | 8 | 4 | ONE HUNDRED POUNDS OF CLAY — Gene McDaniels, Liberty 55308 | 13 |
| 20 | 11 | 10 | 16 | TRAGEDY — Fleetwoods, Dolton 40 | 9 |
| 21 | 48 | 67 | — | DANCE ON LITTLE GIRL — Paul Anka, ABC-Paramount 10220 | 3 |
| 22 | 19 | 5 | 1 | MOTHER-IN-LAW — Ernie K-Doe, Minit 623 | 12 |
| 23 | 42 | 71 | — | YELLOW BIRD — Arthur Lyman, Hi Fi 5024 | 3 |
| 24 | 28 | 30 | 36 | PEANUT BUTTER — Marathons, Arvee 5027 | 8 |
| 25 | 27 | 38 | 57 | LITTLE EGYPT — Coasters, Atco 6192 | 8 |
| 26 | 31 | 41 | 43 | RAMA LAMA DING DONG — Edsels, Twin 700 | 7 |
| 27 | 25 | 35 | 45 | I'M A FOOL TO CARE — Joe Barry, Smash 1702 | 8 |
| 28 | 10 | 7 | 8 | BREAKIN' IN A BRAND NEW BROKEN HEART — Connie Francis, MGM 12995 | 9 |
| 29 | 15 | 6 | 2 | RUNAWAY — Del Shannon, Big Top 3067 | 15 |
| 30 | 13 | 11 | 15 | LITTLE DEVIL — Neil Sedaka, RCA Victor 7874 | 7 |
| 31 | 23 | 24 | 33 | LULLABYE OF LOVE — Frank Gari, Crusade 1021 | 10 |
| 32 | 59 | 94 | — | TEMPTATION — Everly Brothers, Warner Bros. 5220 | 3 |
| 33 | 35 | 36 | 39 | WHAT A SURPRISE — Johnny Maestro, Coed 549 | 8 |
| 34 | 20 | 19 | 22 | GIRL OF MY BEST FRIEND — Ral Donner, Gone 5102 | 9 |
| 35 | 29 | 29 | 34 | TRIANGLE — Janie Grant, Caprice 104 | 12 |
| 36 | 36 | 37 | 41 | EXODUS — Eddie Harris, Vee Jay 378 | 10 |
| 37 | 38 | 45 | 52 | NEVER ON SUNDAY — Don Costa, United Artists 234 | 21 |
| 38 | 45 | 53 | 58 | COUNT EVERY STAR — Donnie and the Dreamers, Whale 500 | 7 |
| 39 | 37 | 44 | 59 | BILBAO SONG — Andy Williams, Cadence 1398 | 8 |
| 40 | 49 | 54 | 64 | BETTER TELL HIM NO — Starlets, Pam 1003 | 8 |
| 41 | 58 | 68 | 81 | TELL ME WHY — Belmonts, Sabrina 500 | 4 |
| 42 | 39 | 40 | 65 | HALFWAY TO PARADISE — Tony Orlando, Epic 9441 | 7 |
| 43 | 55 | 78 | 98 | HEART AND SOUL — Cleftones, Gee 1064 | 4 |
| 44 | 54 | 64 | 73 | IT KEEPS RAININ' — Fats Domino, Imperial 5753 | 5 |
| 45 | 46 | 57 | 67 | EVERY BEAT OF MY HEART — Gladys Knight, Fury 1050 | 5 |
| 46 | 30 | 18 | 13 | PORTRAIT OF MY LOVE — Steve Lawrence, United Artists 291 | 14 |
| 47 | 32 | 21 | 25 | THAT OLD BLACK MAGIC — Bobby Rydell, Cameo 190 | 7 |
| 48 | 73 | — | — | WILD IN THE COUNTRY — Elvis Presley, RCA Victor 7880 | 2 |
| 49 | 34 | 17 | 10 | I'VE TOLD EVERY LITTLE STAR — Linda Scott, Canadian-American 123 | 14 |
| 50 | 97 | — | — | STICK WITH ME BABY — Everly Brothers, Warner Bros. 5220 | 2 |
| 51 | 68 | 80 | — | MY KIND OF GIRL — Matt Monro, Warwick 636 | 3 |
| 52 | 50 | 55 | 62 | WAYWARD WIND — Gogi Grant, Era 3046 | 8 |
| 53 | 63 | 83 | — | JIMMY MARTINEZ — Marty Robbins, Columbia 42008 | 3 |
| 54 | 60 | 70 | 82 | ANNA — Jorgen Ingmann, Atco 6195 | 4 |
| 55 | 61 | 69 | 77 | I DON'T MIND — James Brown, King 5466 | 5 |
| 56 | 40 | 22 | 11 | YOU CAN DEPEND ON ME — Brenda Lee, Decca 31231 | 12 |
| 57 | 56 | 62 | 68 | A LOVE OF MY OWN — Carla Thomas, Atlantic 2101 | 6 |
| 58 | 51 | 52 | 54 | BUZZ BUZZ A-DIDDLE-IT — Freddy Cannon, Swan 4071 | 7 |
| 59 | 41 | 28 | 14 | TAKE GOOD CARE OF HER — Adam Wade, Coed 546 | 14 |
| 60 | 44 | 27 | 21 | JUST FOR OLD TIME'S SAKE — McGuire Sisters, Coral 62249 | 14 |
| 61 | 76 | 66 | 70 | THREE HEARTS IN A TANGLE — Roy Drusky, Decca 31193 | 10 |
| 62 | 65 | 82 | 97 | NOBODY CARES — Jeanette (Baby) Washington, Neptune 122 | 7 |
| 63 | 70 | 77 | — | HOW MANY TEARS — Bobby Vee, Liberty 55325 | 3 |
| 64 | 85 | — | — | CUPID — Sam Cooke, RCA Victor 7883 | 2 |
| 65 | 93 | — | — | PLEASE STAY — Drifters, Atlantic 2105 | 2 |
| 66 | 83 | 99 | — | JURA (I SWEAR I LOVE YOU) — Les Paul and Mary Ford, Columbia 41994 | 6 |
| 67 | 89 | 96 | — | TONIGHT (COULD BE THE NIGHT) — Velvets, Monument 441 | 3 |
| 68 | 77 | 88 | 96 | I FALL TO PIECES — Patsy Cline, Decca 31205 | 4 |
| 69 | 72 | 87 | — | RAININ' IN MY HEART — Slim Harpo, Excello 2194 | 3 |
| 70 | 92 | — | — | HATS OFF TO LARRY — Del Shannon, Big Top 3075 | 2 |
| 71 | 80 | 95 | — | SACRED — Castelles, Era 3048 | 3 |
| 72 | — | — | — | I'M COMIN' ON BACK TO YOU — Jackie Wilson, Brunswick 55216 | 1 |
| 73 | 62 | 58 | 66 | BIG BIG WORLD — Johnny Burnette, Liberty 55318 | 7 |
| 74 | 90 | — | — | SAN ANTONIO ROSE — Floyd Cramer, RCA Victor 7893 | 2 |
| 75 | 75 | 86 | — | I LIKE IT LIKE THAT — Chris Kenner, Instant 3229 | 3 |
| 76 | 79 | 92 | 95 | THE GIRL'S A DEVIL — Dukays, Nat 1003 | 4 |
| 77 | 94 | — | — | OLE BUTTERMILK SKY — Bill Black's Combo, Hi 2036 | 2 |
| 78 | 81 | 93 | — | BIG BOSS MAN — Jimmy Reed, Vee Jay 380 | 3 |
| 79 | — | — | — | YELLOW BIRD — Lawrence Welk, Dot 16222 | 1 |
| 80 | — | — | — | LONELY LIFE — Jackie Wilson, Brunswick 55216 | 1 |
| 81 | 74 | 75 | 83 | MILORD — Teresa Brewer, Coral 62265 | 4 |
| 82 | 87 | — | — | RIGHT OR WRONG — Wanda Jackson, Capitol 4553 | 2 |
| 83 | — | — | — | FOOL THAT I AM — Etta James, Argo 5390 | 1 |
| 84 | — | — | — | NATURE BOY — Bobby Darin, Atco 6196 | 1 |
| 85 | 78 | 90 | — | SUMMERTIME — Marcels, Colpix 196 | 3 |
| 86 | 98 | — | — | HOLD BACK THE TEARS — Delacardos, United Artists 310 | 2 |
| 87 | 95 | — | — | LONELY CROWD — Teddy Vann, Columbia 41996 | 2 |
| 88 | — | — | — | DAYDREAMS — Johnny Crawford, Del Fi 4162 | 1 |
| 89 | 69 | 74 | 76 | MISS FINE — New Yorkers, Wall 547 | 5 |
| 90 | 88 | 91 | 94 | LONESOME WHISTLE BLUES — Freddy King, Federal 12415 | 4 |
| 91 | — | — | — | THEME FROM GOODBYE AGAIN — Ferrante and Teicher, United Artists 319 | 1 |
| 92 | — | — | — | WATCH YOUR STEP — Bobby Parker, V-Tone 223 | 1 |
| 93 | 71 | 73 | 74 | SPRING FEVER — Little Willie John, King 5503 | 5 |
| 94 | — | — | — | MOM AND DAD'S WALTZ — Patti Page, Mercury 71823 | 1 |
| 95 | — | — | — | SAD EYES — Echoes, Seg-Way 106 | 1 |
| 96 | 84 | 98 | — | RING OF FIRE — Duane Eddy, Jamie 1187 | 3 |
| 97 | — | — | — | JOANIE — Frankie Calen, Spark 902 | 1 |
| 98 | — | — | — | SHOULD I — String-A-Longs, Warwick 654 | 1 |
| 99 | — | — | — | BLUE TOMORROW — Billy Vaughn, Dot 16220 | 1 |
| 100 | — | — | — | BOBBY — Neil Scott, Portrait 102 | 1 |

## BUBBLING UNDER THE HOT 100

1. DOOLEY — Olympics, Arvee 5031
2. DREAM — Etta James, Argo 5390
3. QUITE A PARTY — Fireballs, Warwick 644
4. MATADOR — George Scott, Fairlane 701
5. I'M GONNA KNOCK ON YOUR DOOR — Eddie Hodges, Cadence 1397
6. CHARLESTON — Ernie Fields, Rendezvous 150
7. YOU'LL ANSWER TO ME — Patti Page, Mercury 71823
8. YOU CAN'T SIT DOWN — Phillip Upchurch Combo, Boyd 1026
9. TE-TA-TE-TA-TA — Ernie K-Doe, Minit 627
10. MARY AND MAN-O — Lloyd Price, ABC-Paramount 10221
11. MONDAY TO SUNDAY — Alan Dale, Sinclair 1003
12. LIFE IS BUT A DREAM — Earls, Rome 101
13. NEVER ON SUNDAY — Chordettes, Cadence 1402
14. YOU'VE GOTTA SHOW ME — Tony Lawrence, Silver Bid 1025
15. HILLBILLY HEAVEN — Tex Ritter, Capitol 4567
16. ONE SUMMER NIGHT — Diamonds, Mercury 71831
17. LIFE IS BUT A DREAM, SWEETHEART — Classics, Mercury 71829
18. SEA OF HEARTBREAK — Don Gibson, RCA Victor 7890
19. OFF TO WORK AGAIN — Wilbert Harrison, Neptune 123
20. SOLITAIRE — Embers, Empress 101

JUNE 19, 1961

# BILLBOARD HOT 100

FOR WEEK ENDING JUNE 25

1961

★ STAR PERFORMERS—Selections registering greatest upward progress this week.

S Indicates that 45 r.p.m. stereo single version is available.

△ Indicates that 33⅓ r.p.m. mono single version is available.

△S Indicates that 33⅓ r.p.m. stereo single version is available.

| This Week | 1 Wk. Ago | 2 Wks. Ago | 3 Wks. Ago | TITLE Artist, Label & Number | Weeks On Chart |
|---|---|---|---|---|---|
| 1 | 2 | 7 | 14 | MOODY RIVER — Pat Boone, Dot 16209 | 8 |
| 2 | 1 | 2 | 1 | TRAVELIN' MAN — Ricky Nelson, Imperial 5741 | 9 |
| ★3 | 9 | 33 | 65 | QUARTER TO THREE — U. S. Bonds, Le Grand 1008 | 5 |
| 4 | 4 | 6 | 13 | STAND BY ME — Ben E. King, Atco 6194 | 7 |
| 5 | 5 | 9 | 15 | RAINDROPS — Dee Clark, Vee Jay 383 | 8 |
| 6 | 6 | 18 | 32 | THE WRITING ON THE WALL — Adam Wade, Coed 550 | 6 |
| ★7 | 17 | 24 | 34 | TOSSIN' AND TURNIN' — Bobby Lewis, Beltone 1002 | 9 |
| 8 | 8 | 21 | 43 | EVERY BEAT OF MY HEART — Pips, Vee Jay 386 | 6 |
| 9 | 10 | 26 | 42 | BOLL WEEVIL SONG — Brook Benton, Mercury 71820 | 6 |
| 10 | 11 | 22 | 33 | THOSE OLDIES BUT GOODIES — Little Caesar and the Romans, Del Fi 4158 | 8 |
| 11 | 3 | 1 | 3 | RUNNING SCARED — Roy Orbison, Monument 438 | 11 |
| 12 | 14 | 17 | 25 | YOU ALWAYS HURT THE ONE YOU LOVE — Clarence Henry, Argo 5388 | 6 |
| 13 | 13 | 16 | 20 | BARBARA ANN — Regents, Gee 1065 | 6 |
| 14 | 7 | 5 | 9 | I FEEL SO BAD — Elvis Presley, RCA Victor 7880 | 6 |
| ★15 | 23 | 42 | 71 | YELLOW BIRD — Arthur Lyman, Hi Fi 5024 | 4 |
| ★16 | 21 | 48 | 67 | DANCE ON LITTLE GIRL — Paul Anka, ABC-Paramount 10220 | 4 |
| 17 | 15 | 14 | 16 | HELLO MARY LOU — Ricky Nelson, Imperial 5741 | 8 |
| ★18 | 43 | 55 | 78 | HEART AND SOUL — Cleftones, Gee 1064 | 5 |
| 19 | 18 | 12 | 12 | HELLO WALLS — Faron Young, Capitol 4533 | 11 |
| 20 | 24 | 28 | 30 | PEANUT BUTTER — Marathons, Arvee 5027 | 9 |
| 21 | 26 | 31 | 41 | RAMA LAMA DING DONG — Edsels, Twin 700 | 8 |
| 22 | 12 | 4 | 4 | MAMA SAID — Shirelles, Scepter 1217 | 10 |
| 23 | 25 | 27 | 38 | LITTLE EGYPT — Coasters, Atco 6192 | 9 |
| 24 | 16 | 3 | 2 | DADDY'S HOME — Shep and the Limelites, Hull 740 | 13 |
| 25 | 27 | 25 | 35 | I'M A FOOL TO CARE — Joe Barry, Smash 1702 | 9 |
| 26 | 19 | 8 | 8 | ONE HUNDRED POUNDS OF CLAY — Gene McDaniels, Liberty 55308 | 14 |
| ★27 | 48 | 73 | — | WILD IN THE COUNTRY — Elvis Presley, RCA Victor 7880 | 3 |
| 28 | 22 | 19 | 5 | MOTHER-IN-LAW — Ernie K-Doe, Minit 623 | 13 |
| 29 | 32 | 59 | 94 | TEMPTATION — Everly Brothers, Warner Bros. 5220 | 4 |
| ★30 | 41 | 58 | 68 | TELL ME WHY — Belmonts, Sabrina 500 | 5 |
| 31 | 20 | 11 | 10 | TRAGEDY — Fleetwoods, Dolton 40 | 10 |
| 32 | 30 | 13 | 11 | LITTLE DEVIL — Neil Sedaka, RCA Victor 7874 | 8 |
| ★33 | 70 | 92 | — | HATS OFF TO LARRY — Del Shannon, Big Top 3075 | 3 |
| 34 | 28 | 10 | 7 | BREAKIN' IN A BRAND NEW BROKEN HEART — Connie Francis, MGM 12995 | 10 |
| 35 | 38 | 45 | 53 | COUNT EVERY STAR — Donnie and the Dreamers, Whale 500 | 8 |
| 36 | 34 | 20 | 19 | GIRL OF MY BEST FRIEND — Ral Donner, Gone 5102 | 10 |
| 37 | 31 | 23 | 24 | LULLABYE OF LOVE — Frank Gari, Crusade 1021 | 11 |
| 38 | 40 | 49 | 54 | BETTER TELL HIM NO — Starlets, Pam 1003 | 9 |
| 39 | 37 | 38 | 45 | NEVER ON SUNDAY — Don Costa, United Artists 234 | 22 |
| 40 | 44 | 54 | 64 | IT KEEPS RAININ' — Fats Domino, Imperial 5753 | 6 |
| 41 | 50 | 97 | — | STICK WITH ME BABY — Everly Brothers, Warner Bros. 5220 | 3 |
| 42 | 29 | 15 | 6 | RUNAWAY — Del Shannon, Big Top 3067 | 16 |
| ★43 | 74 | 90 | — | SAN ANTONIO ROSE — Floyd Cramer, RCA Victor 7893 | 3 |
| 44 | 39 | 37 | 44 | BILBAO SONG — Andy Williams, Cadence 1398 | 9 |
| 45 | 35 | 29 | 29 | TRIANGLE — Janie Grant, Caprice 104 | 13 |
| 46 | 51 | 68 | 80 | MY KIND OF GIRL — Matt Monro, Warwick 636 | 4 |
| ★47 | 64 | 85 | — | CUPID — Sam Cooke, RCA Victor 7883 | 3 |
| ★48 | 61 | 76 | 66 | THREE HEARTS IN A TANGLE — Roy Drusky, Decca 31193 | 11 |
| ★49 | 72 | — | — | I'M COMIN' ON BACK TO YOU — Jackie Wilson, Brunswick 55216 | 2 |
| 50 | 33 | 35 | 36 | WHAT A SURPRISE — Johnny Maestro, Coed 549 | 9 |
| 51 | 53 | 63 | 83 | JIMMY MARTINEZ — Marty Robbins, Columbia 42008 | 4 |
| 52 | 55 | 61 | 69 | I DON'T MIND — James Brown, King 5466 | 6 |
| ★53 | 65 | 93 | — | PLEASE STAY — Drifters, Atlantic 2105 | 3 |
| 54 | 42 | 39 | 40 | HALFWAY TO PARADISE — Tony Orlando, Epic 9441 | 8 |
| ★55 | 77 | 94 | — | OLE BUTTERMILK SKY — Bill Black's Combo, Hi 2036 | 3 |
| 56 | 36 | 36 | 37 | EXODUS — Eddie Harris, Vee Jay 378 | 11 |
| ★57 | 67 | 89 | 96 | TONIGHT (COULD BE THE NIGHT) — Velvets, Monument 441 | 4 |
| 58 | 45 | 46 | 57 | EVERY BEAT OF MY HEART — Gladys Knight, Fury 1050 | 6 |
| 59 | 54 | 60 | 70 | ANNA — Jorgen Ingmann, Atco 6195 | 5 |
| 60 | 62 | 65 | 82 | NOBODY CARES — Jeanette (Baby) Washington, Neptune 122 | 8 |
| 61 | 71 | 80 | 95 | SACRED — Castells, Era 3048 | 4 |
| 62 | 66 | 83 | 99 | JURA (I SWEAR I LOVE YOU) — Les Paul and Mary Ford, Columbia 41994 | 7 |
| 63 | 46 | 30 | 18 | PORTRAIT OF MY LOVE — Steve Lawrence, United Artists 291 | 15 |
| 64 | 68 | 77 | 88 | I FALL TO PIECES — Patsy Cline, Decca 31205 | 5 |
| 65 | 52 | 50 | 55 | WAYWARD WIND — Gogi Grant, Era 3046 | 9 |
| ★66 | 84 | — | — | NATURE BOY — Bobby Darin, Atco 6196 | 2 |
| 67 | 47 | 32 | 21 | THAT OLD BLACK MAGIC — Bobby Rydell, Cameo 190 | 8 |
| ★68 | — | — | — | YOU CAN'T SIT DOWN (Part II) — Phillip Upchurch Combo, Boyd 1026 | 1 |
| ★69 | — | — | — | DUM DUM — Brenda Lee, Decca 31272 | 1 |
| 70 | 83 | — | — | FOOL THAT I AM — Etta James, Argo 5390 | 2 |
| 71 | 75 | 75 | 86 | I LIKE IT LIKE THAT — Chris Kenner, Instant 3229 | 4 |
| 72 | 79 | — | — | YELLOW BIRD — Lawrence Welk, Dot 16222 | 2 |
| 73 | 76 | 79 | 92 | THE GIRL'S A DEVIL — Dukays, Nat 1003 | 6 |
| 74 | 63 | 70 | 77 | HOW MANY TEARS — Bobby Vee, Liberty 55325 | 4 |
| ★75 | 98 | — | — | SHOULD I — String-A-Longs, Warwick 654 | 2 |
| 76 | 82 | 87 | — | RIGHT OR WRONG — Wanda Jackson, Capitol 4553 | 3 |
| ★77 | 92 | — | — | WATCH YOUR STEP — Bobby Parker, V-Tone 223 | 2 |
| 78 | 58 | 51 | 52 | BUZZ BUZZ A-DIDDLE-IT — Freddy Cannon, Swan 4071 | 8 |
| 79 | 87 | 95 | — | LONELY CROWD — Teddy Vann, Columbia 41996 | 3 |
| 80 | 88 | — | — | DAYDREAMS — Johnny Crawford, Del Fi 4162 | 2 |
| 81 | 94 | — | — | MOM AND DAD'S WALTZ — Patti Page, Mercury 71823 | 2 |
| 82 | 86 | 98 | — | HOLD BACK THE TEARS — Delacardos, United Artists 310 | 3 |
| ★83 | — | — | — | A SCOTTISH SOLDIER — Andy Stewart, Warwick 627 | 4 |
| ★84 | — | — | — | I'VE GOT NEWS FOR YOU — Ray Charles, Impulse 202 | 1 |
| ★85 | — | — | — | LET'S TWIST AGAIN — Chubby Checker, Parkway 824 | 1 |
| 86 | 100 | — | — | BOBBY — Neil Scott, Portrait 102 | 2 |
| ★87 | — | — | — | I'M GONNA MOVE TO THE OUTSKIRTS OF TOWN — Ray Charles, Impulse 202 | 1 |
| 88 | 91 | — | — | THEME FROM GOODBYE AGAIN — Ferrante and Teicher, United Artists 319 | 2 |
| 89 | 95 | — | — | SAD EYES — Echoes, Seg-Way 106 | 2 |
| 90 | 99 | — | — | BLUE TOMORROW — Billy Vaughn, Dot 16220 | 2 |
| 91 | — | — | — | I'M GONNA KNOCK ON YOUR DOOR — Eddie Hodges, Cadence 1397 | 1 |
| 92 | — | — | — | THE FLOAT — Hank Ballard and the Midnighters, King 5510 | 1 |
| 93 | — | — | — | POINT OF NO RETURN — Adam Wade, Coed 550 | 1 |
| 94 | — | — | — | DOOLEY — Olympics, Arvee 5031 | 1 |
| 95 | — | — | — | SEA OF HEARTBREAK — Don Gibson, RCA Victor 7890 | 1 |
| 96 | 97 | — | — | JOANIE — Frankie Calen, Spark 902 | 2 |
| 97 | — | — | — | THE CHARLESTON — Ernie Fields, Rendezvous 150 | 1 |
| 98 | — | — | — | NEVER ON SUNDAY — Chordettes, Cadence 1402 | 1 |
| 99 | — | — | — | NO, NO, NO — Chanters, Deluxe 6191 | 1 |
| 100 | — | — | — | I'LL NEVER BE FREE — Kay Starr, Capitol 4583 | 1 |

## BUBBLING UNDER THE HOT 100

1. DREAM ........ Etta James, Argo 5390
2. YOU'LL ANSWER TO ME ........ Patti Page, Mercury 71823
3. QUITE A PARTY ........ Fireballs, Warwick 644
4. MATADOR ........ George Scott, Fairlane 701
5. TE-TA-TE-TA-TA ........ Ernie K-Doe, Minit 627
6. THAT'S WHAT GIRLS ARE MADE FOR ........ Spinners, Tri-Phi 1001
7. TAKE A FOOL'S ADVICE ........ Nat King Cole, Capitol 4582
8. LIFE IS BUT A DREAM ........ Earls, Rome 101
9. LONELY LIFE ........ Jackie Wilson, Brunswick 55216
10. EVENTUALLY ........ Brenda Lee, Decca 31272
11. TIME WAS ........ Flamingos, End 1092
12. ONE SUMMER NIGHT ........ Diamonds, Mercury 71831
13. HILLBILLY HEAVEN ........ Tex Ritter, Capitol 4567
14. OFF TO WORK AGAIN ........ Wilbert Harrison, Neptune 123
15. LIFE IS BUT A DREAM, SWEETHEART ........ Classics, Mercury 71829
16. SWITCH-A-ROO ........ Hank Ballard and the Midnighters, King 5510
17. POMP AND CIRCUMSTANCE ........ Adrian Kimberly, Calliope 6501
18. OLD SMOKIE ........ Johnny and the Hurricanes, Big Top 3076
19. WOODEN HEART ........ Joe Dowell, Smash 1708
20. BOOGIE WOOGIE ........ B. Bumble and the Stingers, Rendezvous 151

## HOT 100—A TO Z


Anna ........ 59
Barbara Ann ........ 13
Better Tell Him No ........ 38
Bilbao Song ........ 44
Blue Tomorrow ........ 90
Bobby ........ 86
Boll Weevil Song ........ 9
Breakin' in a Brand New Broken Heart ........ 34
Buzz Buzz A-Diddle-It ........ 78
Charleston, The ........ 97
Count Every Star ........ 35
Cupid ........ 47
Daddy's Home ........ 24
Dance on Little Girl ........ 16
Daydreams ........ 80
Dooley ........ 94
Dum Dum ........ 69
Every Beat of My Heart (Knight) ........ 58
Every Beat of My Heart (Pips) ........ 8
Exodus ........ 56
Float, The ........ 92
Fool That I Am ........ 70
Girl of My Best Friend ........ 36
Girl's a Devil, The ........ 73
Halfway to Paradise ........ 54
Hats Off to Larry ........ 33
Heart and Soul ........ 18
Hello Mary Lou ........ 17
Hello Walls ........ 19
Hold Back the Tears ........ 82
How Many Tears ........ 74
I Don't Mind ........ 52
I Fall to Pieces ........ 64
I Feel So Bad ........ 14
I Like It Like That ........ 71
I'll Never Be Free ........ 100
I'm a Fool to Care ........ 25
I'm Coming on Back to You ........ 49
I'm Gonna Knock on Your Door ........ 91
I'm Gonna Move to the Outskirts of Town ........ 87
It Keeps Rainin' ........ 40
I've Got News for You ........ 84
Jimmy Martinez ........ 51
Joanie ........ 96
Jura (I Swear I Love You) ........ 62
Let's Twist Again ........ 85
Little Devil ........ 32
Little Egypt ........ 23
Lonely Crowd ........ 79
Lullabye of Love ........ 37
Mama Said ........ 22
Moody River ........ 1
Mom and Dad's Waltz ........ 81
Mother-in-Law ........ 28
My Kind of Girl ........ 46
Nature Boy ........ 66
Never on Sunday (Chordettes) ........ 98
Never on Sunday (Costa) ........ 39
No, No, No ........ 99
Nobody Cares ........ 60
Ole Buttermilk Sky ........ 55
One Hundred Pounds of Clay ........ 26
Peanut Butter ........ 20
Please Stay ........ 53
Point of No Return ........ 93
Portrait of My Love ........ 63
Quarter to Three ........ 3
Raindrops ........ 5
Rama Lama Ding Dong ........ 21
Right or Wrong ........ 76
Runaway ........ 42
Running Scared ........ 11
Sacred ........ 61
Sad Eyes ........ 89
San Antonio Rose ........ 43
Scottish Soldier, A ........ 83
Sea of Heartbreak ........ 95
Should I ........ 75
Stand By Me ........ 4
Stick With Me Baby ........ 41
Tell Me Why ........ 30
Temptation ........ 29
That Old Black Magic ........ 67
Theme From Goodbye Again ........ 88
Those Oldies But Goodies ........ 10
Three Hearts in a Tangle ........ 48
Tonight ........ 57
Tossin' and Turnin' ........ 7
Tragedy ........ 31
Travelin' Man ........ 2
Triangle ........ 45
Watch Your Step ........ 77
Wayward Wind ........ 65
What a Surprise ........ 50
Wild in the Country ........ 27
Writing on the Wall, The ........ 6
Yellow Bird (Lyman) ........ 15
Yellow Bird (Welk) ........ 72
You Always Hurt the One You Love ........ 12
You Can't Sit Down (Part II) ........ 68

# BILLBOARD HOT 100

**JUNE 26, 1961** — FOR WEEK ENDING JULY 2, 1961

| This Week | Wk Ago / 2 Wks / 3 Wks | Title — Artist, Label & Number | Weeks on Chart |
|---|---|---|---|
| 1 | 3 9 33 | QUARTER TO THREE — U. S. Bonds, Le Grand 1008 | 6 |
| 2 | 5 5 9 | RAINDROPS — Dee Clark, Vee Jay 383 | 9 |
| 3 | 1 2 7 | MOODY RIVER — Pat Boone, Dot 16209 | 9 |
| 4 | 7 17 24 | TOSSIN' AND TURNIN' — Bobby Lewis, Beltone 1002 | 10 |
| 5 | 2 1 2 | TRAVELIN' MAN — Ricky Nelson, Imperial 5741 | 10 |
| 6 | 6 6 18 | THE WRITING ON THE WALL — Adam Wade, Coed 550 | 7 |
| 7 | 9 10 26 | BOLL WEEVIL SONG — Brook Benton, Mercury 71820 | 7 |
| 8 | 8 8 21 | EVERY BEAT OF MY HEART — Pips, Vee Jay 386 | 7 |
| 9 | 10 11 22 | THOSE OLDIES BUT GOODIES — Little Caesar and the Romans, Del Fi 4158 | 9 |
| 10 | 4 4 6 | STAND BY ME — Ben E. King, Atco 6194 | 8 |
| 11 | 15 23 42 | YELLOW BIRD — Arthur Lyman, Hi Fi 5024 | 5 |
| 12 | 12 14 17 | YOU ALWAYS HURT THE ONE YOU LOVE — Clarence Henry, Argo 5388 | 7 |
| 13 | 16 21 48 | DANCE ON LITTLE GIRL — Paul Anka, ABC-Paramount 10220 | 5 |
| 14 | 11 3 1 | RUNNING SCARED — Roy Orbison, Monument 438 | 12 |
| 15 | 14 7 5 | I FEEL SO BAD — Elvis Presley, RCA Victor 7880 | 7 |
| 16 | 17 15 14 | HELLO MARY LOU — Ricky Nelson, Imperial 5741 | 9 |
| 17 | 13 13 16 | BARBARA ANN — Regents, Gee 1065 | 7 |
| 18 | 33 70 92 | HATS OFF TO LARRY — Del Shannon, Big Top 3075 | 4 |
| 19 | 43 74 90 | SAN ANTONIO ROSE — Floyd Cramer, RCA Victor 7893 | 4 |
| 20 | 30 41 58 | TELL ME WHY — Belmonts, Sabrina 500 | 6 |
| 21 | 19 18 12 | HELLO WALLS — Faron Young, Capitol 4533 | 12 |
| 22 | 18 43 55 | HEART AND SOUL — Cleftones, Gee 1064 | 6 |
| 23 | 20 24 28 | PEANUT BUTTER — Marathons, Arvee 5027 | 10 |
| 24 | 25 27 25 | I'M A FOOL TO CARE — Joe Barry, Smash 1702 | 10 |
| 25 | 21 26 31 | RAMA LAMA DING DONG — Edsels, Twin 700 | 9 |
| 26 | 27 48 73 | WILD IN THE COUNTRY — Elvis Presley, RCA Victor 7880 | 4 |
| 27 | 29 32 59 | TEMPTATION — Everly Brothers, Warner Bros. 5220 | 5 |
| 28 | 40 44 54 | IT KEEPS RAININ' — Fats Domino, Imperial 5753 | 7 |
| 29 | 23 25 27 | LITTLE EGYPT — Coasters, Atco 6192 | 10 |
| 30 | 57 67 89 | TONIGHT (COULD BE THE NIGHT) — Velvets, Monument 441 | 5 |
| 31 | 69 — — | DUM DUM — Brenda Lee, Decca 31272 | 2 |
| 32 | 49 72 — | I'M COMIN' ON BACK TO YOU — Jackie Wilson, Brunswick 55216 | 3 |
| 33 | 46 51 68 | MY KIND OF GIRL — Matt Monro, Warwick 636 | 5 |
| 34 | 55 77 94 | OLE BUTTERMILK SKY — Bill Black's Combo, Hi 2036 | 4 |
| 35 | 48 61 76 | THREE HEARTS IN A TANGLE — Roy Drusky, Decca 31193 | 12 |
| 36 | 47 64 85 | CUPID — Sam Cooke, RCA Victor 7883 | 4 |
| 37 | 31 20 11 | TRAGEDY — Fleetwoods, Dolton 40 | 11 |
| 38 | 53 65 93 | PLEASE STAY — Drifters, Atlantic 2105 | 4 |
| 39 | 68 — — | YOU CAN'T SIT DOWN (Part II) — Phillip Upchurch Combo, Boyd 1026 | 2 |
| 40 | 35 38 45 | COUNT EVERY STAR — Donnie and the Dreamers, Whale 500 | 9 |
| 41 | 71 75 75 | I LIKE IT LIKE THAT — Chris Kenner, Instant 3229 | 5 |
| 42 | 24 16 3 | DADDY'S HOME — Shep and the Limelites, Hull 740 | 14 |
| 43 | 62 66 83 | JURA (I SWEAR I LOVE YOU) — Les Paul and Mary Ford, Columbia 41994 | 8 |
| 44 | 38 40 49 | BETTER TELL HIM NO — Starlets, Pam 1003 | 10 |
| 45 | 26 19 8 | ONE HUNDRED POUNDS OF CLAY — Gene McDaniels, Liberty 55308 | 15 |
| 46 | 28 22 19 | MOTHER-IN-LAW — Ernie K-Doe, Minit 623 | 14 |
| 47 | 52 55 61 | I DON'T MIND — James Brown, King 5466 | 7 |
| 48 | — — — | TOGETHER — Connie Francis, MGM 13019 | 1 |
| 49 | 32 30 13 | LITTLE DEVIL — Neil Sedaka, RCA Victor 7874 | 9 |
| 50 | 61 71 80 | SACRED — Castells, Era 3048 | 5 |
| 51 | 66 84 — | NATURE BOY — Bobby Darin, Atco 6196 | 3 |
| 52 | 75 98 — | SHOULD I — String-A-Longs, Warwick 654 | 3 |
| 53 | 22 12 4 | MAMA SAID — Shirelles, Scepter 1217 | 11 |
| 54 | 64 68 77 | I FALL TO PIECES — Patsy Cline, Decca 31205 | 6 |
| 55 | 42 29 15 | RUNAWAY — Del Shannon, Big Top 3067 | 17 |
| 56 | 41 50 97 | STICK WITH ME BABY — Everly Brothers, Warner Bros. 5220 | 4 |
| 57 | 36 34 20 | GIRL OF MY BEST FRIEND — Ral Donner, Gone 5102 | 11 |
| 58 | 37 31 23 | LULLABYE OF LOVE — Frank Gari, Crusade 1021 | 12 |
| 59 | 39 37 38 | NEVER ON SUNDAY — Don Costa, United Artists 234 | 23 |
| 60 | 58 45 46 | EVERY BEAT OF MY HEART — Gladys Knight, Fury 1050 | 7 |
| 61 | 70 83 — | FOOL THAT I AM — Etta James, Argo 5390 | 3 |
| 62 | 85 — — | LET'S TWIST AGAIN — Chubby Checker, Parkway 824 | 2 |
| 63 | — — — | POMP AND CIRCUMSTANCE — Adrian Kimberly, Calliope 6501 | 1 |
| 64 | 44 39 37 | BILBAO SONG — Andy Williams, Cadence 1398 | 10 |
| 65 | 77 92 — | WATCH YOUR STEP — Bobby Parker, V-Tone 223 | 3 |
| 66 | 84 — — | I'VE GOT NEWS FOR YOU — Ray Charles, Impulse 202 | 2 |
| 67 | — — — | YOU'LL ANSWER TO ME — Patti Page, Mercury 71823 | 1 |
| 68 | 98 — — | NEVER ON SUNDAY — Chordettes, Cadence 1402 | 2 |
| 69 | 83 — — | A SCOTTISH SOLDIER — Andy Stewart, Warwick 627 | 2 |
| 70 | 80 88 — | DAYDREAMS — Johnny Crawford, Del Fi 4162 | 3 |
| 71 | 73 76 79 | THE GIRL'S A DEVIL — Dukays, Nat 1003 | 4 |
| 72 | — — — | DREAM — Etta James, Argo 5390 | 1 |
| 73 | 95 — — | SEA OF HEARTBREAK — Don Gibson, RCA Victor 7890 | 2 |
| 74 | 86 100 — | BOBBY — Neil Scott, Portrait 102 | 3 |
| 75 | 81 94 — | MOM AND DAD'S WALTZ — Patti Page, Mercury 71823 | 3 |
| 76 | 79 87 95 | LONELY CROWD — Teddy Vann, Columbia 41996 | 4 |
| 77 | — — — | THE SWITCH-A-ROO — Hank Ballard and the Midnighters, King 5510 | 1 |
| 78 | 99 — — | NO, NO, NO — Chanters, Deluxe 6191 | 2 |
| 79 | 91 — — | I'M GONNA KNOCK ON YOUR DOOR — Eddie Hodges, Cadence 1397 | 2 |
| 80 | 97 — — | THE CHARLESTON — Ernie Fields, Rendezvous 150 | 2 |
| 81 | 82 86 98 | HOLD BACK THE TEARS — Delacardos, United Artists 310 | 4 |
| 82 | — — — | THAT'S WHAT GIRLS ARE MADE FOR — Spinners, Tri-Phi 1001 | 1 |
| 83 | — — — | QUITE A PARTY — Fireballs, Warwick 644 | 1 |
| 84 | 87 — — | I'M GONNA MOVE TO THE OUTSKIRTS OF TOWN — Ray Charles, Impulse 202 | 2 |
| 85 | 88 91 — | THEME FROM GOODBYE AGAIN — Ferrante and Teicher, United Artists 319 | 3 |
| 86 | 96 97 — | JOANIE — Frankie Calen, Spark 902 | 3 |
| 87 | — — — | HEART AND SOUL — Jan and Dean, Challenge 9111 | 1 |
| 88 | 89 95 — | SAD EYES — Echoes, Seg-Way 106 | 3 |
| 89 | 90 99 — | BLUE TOMORROW — Billy Vaughn, Dot 16220 | 3 |
| 90 | — — — | TE-TA-TE-TA-TA — Ernie K-Doe, Minit 627 | 1 |
| 91 | 93 — — | POINT OF NO RETURN — Adam Wade, Coed 550 | 2 |
| 92 | 51 53 63 | JIMMY MARTINEZ — Marty Robbins, Columbia 42008 | 5 |
| 93 | 60 62 65 | NOBODY CARES — Jeanette (Baby) Washington, Neptune 122 | 9 |
| 94 | 72 79 — | YELLOW BIRD — Lawrence Welk, Dot 16222 | 3 |
| 95 | 59 54 60 | ANNA — Jorgen Ingmann, Atco 6195 | 6 |
| 96 | 100 — — | I'LL NEVER BE FREE — Kay Starr, Capitol 4583 | 2 |
| 97 | 76 82 87 | RIGHT OR WRONG — Wanda Jackson, Capitol 4553 | 4 |
| 98 | — — — | WOODEN HEART (Muss I Denn) — Joe Dowell, Smash 1702 | 1 |
| 99 | — 69 72 | RAININ' IN MY HEART — Slim Harpo, Excello 2194 | 4 |
| 100 | — — — | TAKE A FOOL'S ADVICE — Nat King Cole, Capitol 4582 | 1 |

## BUBBLING UNDER THE HOT 100

1. HILLBILLY HEAVEN — Tex Ritter, Capitol 4567
2. MONDAY TO SUNDAY — Alan Dale, Sinclair 1003
3. BOOGIE WOOGIE — B. Bumble and the Stingers, Rendezvous 151
4. LOUISIANA MAN — Rusty and Doug, Hickory 1137
5. PRESIDENTIAL PRESS CONFERENCE — Sicknicks, Amy 824
6. TIME WAS — Flamingos, End 1092
7. DOOLEY — Olympics, Arvee 5031
8. LAST NIGHT — Mar-Keys, Satellite 107
9. LIFE IS BUT A DREAM — Earls, Rome 101
10. TENDER YEARS — George Jones, Mercury 71804
11. THE FLOAT — Hank Ballard and the Midnighters, King 5510
12. LIFE IS BUT A DREAM, SWEETHEART — Classics, Mercury 71829
13. MATADOR — George Scott, Fairlane 701
14. EVENTUALLY — Brenda Lee, Decca 31272
15. ONE SUMMER NIGHT — Diamonds, Mercury 71831
16. OLD SMOKIE — Johnny and the Hurricanes, Big Top 3076
17. OFF TO WORK AGAIN — Wilbert Harrison, Neptune 123
18. LONELY LIFE — Jackie Wilson, Brunswick 55216
19. PEACE OF MIND — B. B. King, Kent 360
20. GRANADA — Frank Sinatra, Reprise 20010

JULY 3, 1961

# BILLBOARD HOT 100

FOR WEEK ENDING JULY 9

1961

★ STAR PERFORMERS—Selections registering greatest upward progress this week.

S Indicates that 45 r.p.m. stereo single version is available.

△ Indicates that 33⅓ r.p.m. mono single version is available.

△S Indicates that 33⅓ r.p.m. stereo single version is available.

| This Week | 1 Wk. Ago | 2 Wks. Ago | 3 Wks. Ago | Title | Artist, Label & Number | Weeks On Chart |
|---|---|---|---|---|---|---|
| 1 | 1 | 3 | 9 | QUARTER TO THREE | U. S. Bonds, Le Grand 1008 | 7 |
| 2 | 4 | 7 | 17 | TOSSIN' AND TURNIN' | Bobby Lewis, Beltone 1002 | 11 |
| 3 | 7 | 9 | 10 | BOLL WEEVIL SONG | Brook Benton, Mercury 71820 | 8 |
| 4 | 2 | 5 | 5 | RAINDROPS | Dee Clark, Vee Jay 383 | 10 |
| 5 | 6 | 6 | 6 | THE WRITING ON THE WALL | Adam Wade, Coed 550 | 8 |
| 6 | 3 | 1 | 2 | MOODY RIVER | Pat Boone, Dot 16209 | 10 |
| 7 | 5 | 2 | 1 | TRAVELIN' MAN | Ricky Nelson, Imperial 5741 | 11 |
| 8 | 8 | 8 | 8 | EVERY BEAT OF MY HEART | Pips, Vee Jay 386 | 8 |
| 9 | 9 | 10 | 11 | THOSE OLDIES BUT GOODIES | Little Caesar and the Romans, Del Fi 4158 | 10 |
| 10 | 11 | 15 | 23 | YELLOW BIRD | Arthur Lyman, Hi Fi 5024 | 6 |
| 11 | 10 | 4 | 4 | STAND BY ME | Ben E. King, Atco 6194 | 9 |
| 12 | 13 | 16 | 21 | DANCE ON LITTLE GIRL | Paul Anka, ABC-Paramount 10220 | 6 |
| 13 ★ | 18 | 33 | 70 | HATS OFF TO LARRY | Del Shannon, Big Top 3075 | 5 |
| 14 | 14 | 11 | 3 | RUNNING SCARED | Roy Orbison, Monument 438 | 13 |
| 15 | 16 | 17 | 15 | HELLO MARY LOU | Ricky Nelson, Imperial 5741 | 10 |
| 16 | 19 | 43 | 74 | SAN ANTONIO ROSE | Floyd Cramer, RCA Victor 7893 | 5 |
| 17 | 12 | 12 | 14 | YOU ALWAYS HURT THE ONE YOU LOVE | Clarence Henry, Argo 5388 | 8 |
| 18 | 17 | 13 | 13 | BARBARA ANN | Regents, Gee 1065 | 8 |
| 19 | 20 | 30 | 41 | TELL ME WHY | Belmonts, Sabrina 500 | 7 |
| 20 ★ | 31 | 69 | — | DUM DUM | Brenda Lee, Decca 31272 | 3 |
| 21 ★ | 38 | 53 | 65 | PLEASE STAY | Drifters, Atlantic 2105 | 5 |
| 22 | 22 | 18 | 43 | HEART AND SOUL | Cleftones, Gee 1064 | 7 |
| 23 | 32 | 49 | 72 | I'M COMIN' ON BACK TO YOU | Jackie Wilson, Brunswick 55216 | 4 |
| 24 | 28 | 40 | 44 | IT KEEPS RAININ' | Fats Domino, Imperial 5753 | 8 |
| 25 ★ | 41 | 71 | 75 | I LIKE IT LIKE THAT | Chris Kenner, Instant 3229 | 6 |
| 26 | 34 | 55 | 77 | OLE BUTTERMILK SKY | Bill Black's Combo, Hi 2036 | 5 |
| 27 | 21 | 19 | 18 | HELLO WALLS | Faron Young, Capitol 4533 | 13 |
| 28 | 30 | 57 | 67 | TONIGHT (COULD BE THE NIGHT) | Velvets, Monument 441 | 6 |
| 29 ★ | 39 | 68 | — | YOU CAN'T SIT DOWN (Part II) | Phillip Upchurch Combo, Boyd 1026 | 3 |
| 30 | 25 | 21 | 26 | RAMA LAMA DING DONG | Edsels, Twin 700 | 10 |
| 31 | 23 | 20 | 24 | PEANUT BUTTER | Marathons, Arvee 5027 | 11 |
| 32 | 33 | 46 | 51 | MY KIND OF GIRL | Matt Monro, Warwick 636 | 6 |
| 33 ★ | 48 | — | — | TOGETHER | Connie Francis, MGM 13019 | 2 |
| 34 | 36 | 47 | 64 | CUPID | Sam Cooke, RCA Victor 7883 | 5 |
| 35 | 15 | 14 | 7 | I FEEL SO BAD | Elvis Presley, RCA Victor 7880 | 8 |
| 36 ★ | 68 | 98 | — | NEVER ON SUNDAY | Chordettes, Cadence 1402 | 3 |
| 37 | 43 | 62 | 66 | JURA (I SWEAR I LOVE YOU) | Les Paul and Mary Ford, Columbia 41994 | 9 |
| 38 ★ | 50 | 61 | 71 | SACRED | Castells, Era 3048 | 6 |
| 39 ★ | 62 | 85 | — | LET'S TWIST AGAIN | Chubby Checker, Parkway 824 | 3 |
| 40 | 29 | 23 | 25 | LITTLE EGYPT | Coasters, Atco 6192 | 11 |
| 41 | 35 | 48 | 61 | THREE HEARTS IN A TANGLE | Roy Drusky, Decca 31193 | 13 |
| 42 | 24 | 25 | 27 | I'M A FOOL TO CARE | Joe Barry, Smash 1702 | 11 |
| 43 ★ | 63 | — | — | POMP AND CIRCUMSTANCE | Adrian Kimberly, Calliope 6501 | 2 |
| 44 | 27 | 29 | 32 | TEMPTATION | Everly Brothers, Warner Bros. 5220 | 6 |
| 45 ★ | 59 | 39 | 37 | NEVER ON SUNDAY | Don Costa, United Artists 234 | 24 |
| 46 | 44 | 38 | 40 | BETTER TELL HIM NO | Starlets, Pam 1003 | 11 |
| 47 | 51 | 66 | 84 | NATURE BOY | Bobby Darin, Atco 6196 | 4 |
| 48 ★ | 87 | — | — | HEART AND SOUL | Jan and Dean, Challenge 9111 | 2 |
| 49 | 54 | 64 | 68 | I FALL TO PIECES | Patsy Cline, Decca 31205 | 7 |
| 50 ★ | 61 | 70 | 83 | FOOL THAT I AM | Etta James, Argo 5390 | 4 |
| 51 | 52 | 75 | 98 | SHOULD I | String-A-Longs, Warwick 654 | 4 |
| 52 ★ | 77 | — | — | THE SWITCH-A-ROO | Hank Ballard and the Midnighters, King 5510 | 2 |
| 53 ★ | 67 | — | — | YOU'LL ANSWER TO ME | Patti Page, Mercury 71823 | 2 |
| 54 | 26 | 27 | 48 | WILD IN THE COUNTRY | Elvis Presley, RCA Victor 7880 | 5 |
| 55 ★ | 72 | — | — | DREAM | Etta James, Argo 5390 | 2 |
| 56 | 65 | 77 | 92 | WATCH YOUR STEP | Bobby Parker, V-Tone 223 | 4 |
| 57 | 47 | 52 | 55 | I DON'T MIND | James Brown, King 5466 | 8 |
| 58 ★ | 73 | 95 | — | SEA OF HEARTBREAK | Don Gibson, RCA Victor 7890 | 3 |
| 59 ★ | 99 | — | 69 | RAININ' IN MY HEART | Slim Harpo, Excello 2194 | 5 |
| 60 ★ | — | — | — | THE FISH | Bobby Rydell, Cameo 192 | 1 |
| 61 ★ | 82 | — | — | THAT'S WHAT GIRLS ARE MADE FOR | Spinners, Tri-Phi 1001 | 2 |
| 62 | 40 | 35 | 38 | COUNT EVERY STAR | Donnie and the Dreamers, Whale 500 | 10 |
| 63 ★ | 83 | — | — | QUITE A PARTY | Fireballs, Warwick 644 | 2 |
| 64 | 37 | 31 | 20 | TRAGEDY | Fleetwoods, Dolton 40 | 12 |
| 65 ★ | 80 | 97 | — | THE CHARLESTON | Ernie Fields, Rendezvous 150 | 3 |
| 66 | 74 | 86 | 100 | BOBBY | Neil Scott, Portrait 102 | 4 |
| 67 | 71 | 73 | 76 | THE GIRL'S A DEVIL | Dukays, Nat 1003 | 8 |
| 68 ★ | — | — | — | LAST NIGHT | Mar-Keys, Satellite 107 | 1 |
| 69 ★ | 98 | — | — | WOODEN HEART (Muss I Denn) | Joe Dowell, Smash 1708 | 2 |
| 70 | 78 | 99 | — | NO, NO, NO | Chanters, Deluxe 6191 | 3 |
| 71 | 66 | 84 | — | I'VE GOT NEWS FOR YOU | Ray Charles, Impulse 202 | 3 |
| 72 ★ | — | — | — | EVENTUALLY | Brenda Lee, Decca 31272 | 1 |
| 73 | 75 | 81 | 94 | MOM AND DAD'S WALTZ | Patti Page, Mercury 71823 | 4 |
| 74 ★ | — | — | — | PRETTY LITTLE ANGEL EYES | Curtis Lee, Dunes 2007 | 1 |
| 75 ★ | 94 | 72 | 79 | YELLOW BIRD | Lawrence Welk, Dot 16222 | 4 |
| 76 | 69 | 83 | — | A SCOTTISH SOLDIER | Andy Stewart, Warwick 627 | 6 |
| 77 | 90 | — | — | TE-TA-TE-TA-TA | Ernie K-Doe, Minit 627 | 2 |
| 78 | 81 | 82 | 86 | HOLD BACK THE TEARS | Delacardos, United Artists 310 | 5 |
| 79 | 79 | 91 | — | I'M GONNA KNOCK ON YOUR DOOR | Eddie Hodges, Cadence 1397 | 3 |
| 80 | 70 | 80 | 88 | DAYDREAMS | Johnny Crawford, Del Fi 4162 | 4 |
| 81 ★ | — | — | — | I'LL BE THERE | Damita Jo, Mercury 71840 | 1 |
| 82 | 86 | 96 | 97 | JOANIE | Frankie Calen, Spark 902 | 4 |
| 83 ★ | — | — | — | TIME WAS | Flamingos, End 1092 | 1 |
| 84 ★ | — | — | — | A TEAR | Gene McDaniels, Liberty 55344 | 1 |
| 85 ★ | — | — | — | DON'T BET MONEY HONEY | Linda Scott, Canadian-American 127 | 1 |
| 86 ★ | — | — | — | HILLBILLY HEAVEN | Tex Ritter, Capitol 4567 | 1 |
| 87 | 89 | 90 | 99 | BLUE TOMORROW | Billy Vaughn, Dot 16220 | 4 |
| 88 | 100 | — | — | TAKE A FOOL'S ADVICE | Nat King Cole, Capitol 4582 | 2 |
| 89 | 91 | 93 | — | POINT OF NO RETURN | Adam Wade, Coed 550 | 3 |
| 90 ★ | — | — | — | TENDER YEARS | George Jones, Mercury 71804 | 1 |
| 91 | — | — | — | GRANADA | Frank Sinatra, Reprise 20010 | 1 |
| 92 | — | — | — | MY TRUE STORY | Jive Five, Beltone 1006 | 1 |
| 93 | 85 | 88 | 91 | THEME FROM GOODBYE AGAIN | Ferrante and Teicher, United Artists 319 | 4 |
| 94 | 96 | 100 | — | I'LL NEVER BE FREE | Kay Starr, Capitol 4583 | 3 |
| 95 | — | — | — | PRINCESS | Frank Gari, Crusade 1022 | 1 |
| 96 | — | — | — | LA DOLCE VITA | Ray Ellis, RCA Victor 7888 | 1 |
| 97 | — | — | — | BROKEN HEARTED | Miracles, Tamla 54044 | 1 |
| 98 | — | — | — | ONE SUMMER NIGHT | Diamonds, Mercury 71831 | 1 |
| 99 | — | — | — | PEANUTS | Rick and the Keens, Smash 1705 | 1 |
| 100 | — | — | — | THE GUNS OF NAVARONE | Joe Reisman, Landa 674 | 1 |

## BUBBLING UNDER THE HOT 100

1. MONDAY TO SUNDAY ... Alan Dale, Sinclair 1003
2. BOOGIE WOOGIE ... B. Bumble and the Stingers, Rendezvous 151
3. WOODEN HEART (Muss I Denn) ... Gus Backus, Fono-Graf 1234
4. THE ASTRONAUT ... Jose Jimenez, Kapp 409
5. MICHAEL ... Highwaymen, United Artists 258
6. PITTER PATTER ... Four Sportsmen, Sunnybrook 4
7. LIFE IS BUT A DREAM ... Earls, Rome 101
8. LONESOME FOR YOU MAMA ... Anita Bryant, Carlton 553
9. LIFE IS BUT A DREAM, SWEETHEART ... Classics, Mercury 71829
10. THE FLOAT ... Hank Ballard and the Midnighters, King 5510
11. VOYAGE TO THE BOTTOM OF THE SEA ... Frankie Avalon, Chancellor 1081
12. A THING OF THE PAST ... Shirelles, Scepter 1220
13. DON'T FORGET I LOVE YOU ... Butanes, Enrica 1007
14. STARLIGHT ... Preludes Five, Pik 231
15. SOMEBODY NOBODY WANTS ... Dion, Laurie 3101
16. NOW YOU KNOW ... Little Willie John, King 5516
17. STRANDED IN THE JUNGLE ... Vibrations, Checker 982
18. I DON'T WANT TO TAKE A CHANCE ... Mary Wells, Motown 1011
19. MY CLAIRE DE LUNE ... Steve Lawrence, United Artists 335
20. IF ... Paragons, Tap 101

## HOT 100—A TO Z


| Title | No. |
|---|---|
| Barbara Ann | 18 |
| Better Tell Him No | 46 |
| Blue Tomorrow | 87 |
| Bobby | 66 |
| Boll Weevil Song | 3 |
| Broken Hearted | 97 |
| Charleston, The | 65 |
| Count Every Star | 62 |
| Cupid | 34 |
| Dance on Little Girl | 12 |
| Daydreams | 80 |
| Don't Bet Money Honey | 85 |
| Dream | 55 |
| Dum Dum | 20 |
| Eventually | 72 |
| Every Beat of My Heart | 8 |
| Fish, The | 60 |
| Fool That I Am | 50 |
| Girl's a Devil, The | 67 |
| Granada | 91 |
| Guns of Navarone, The | 100 |
| Hats Off to Larry | 13 |
| Heart and Soul (Cleftones) | 22 |
| Heart and Soul (Jan & Dean) | 48 |
| Hello Mary Lou | 15 |
| Hello Walls | 27 |
| Hillbilly Heaven | 86 |
| Hold Back the Tears | 78 |
| I Don't Mind | 57 |
| I Fall to Pieces | 49 |
| I Feel So Bad | 35 |
| I Like It Like That | 25 |
| I'll Be There | 81 |
| I'll Never Be Free | 94 |
| I'm a Fool to Care | 42 |
| I'm Comin' on Back to You | 23 |
| I'm Gonna Knock on Your Door | 79 |
| It Keeps Rainin' | 24 |
| I've Got News for You | 71 |
| Joanie | 82 |
| Jura (I Swear I Love You) | 37 |
| La Dolce Vita | 96 |
| Last Night | 68 |
| Let's Twist Again | 39 |
| Little Egypt | 40 |
| Moody River | 6 |
| Mom and Dad's Waltz | 73 |
| My Kind of Girl | 32 |
| My True Story | 92 |
| Nature Boy | 47 |
| Never on Sunday (Chordettcs) | 36 |
| Never on Sunday (Costa) | 45 |
| No, No, No, | 45 |
| Ole Buttermilk Sky | 26 |
| One Summer Night | 98 |
| Peanut Butter | 31 |
| Peanuts | 99 |
| Please Stay | 21 |
| Point of No Return | 89 |
| Pomp and Circumstance | 43 |
| Pretty Little Angel Eyes | 74 |
| Princess | 95 |
| Quarter to Three | 1 |
| Quite a Party | 63 |
| Raindrops | 4 |
| Rain' in My Heart | 59 |
| Rama Lama Ding Dong | 30 |
| Running Scared | 14 |
| Sacred | 38 |
| San Antonio Rose | 16 |
| Sea of Heartbreak | 58 |
| Scottish Soldier, A | 76 |
| Should I | 51 |
| Stand By Me | 11 |
| Switch-A-Roo, The | 52 |
| Take a Fool's Advice | 88 |
| Te-Ta-Te-Ta-Ta | 77 |
| Tear, A | 84 |
| Tell Me Why | 19 |
| Temptation | 44 |
| Tender Years | 90 |
| That's What Girls Are Made For | 61 |
| Theme From Goodbye Again | 93 |
| Those Oldies But Goodies | 9 |
| Three Hearts in a Tangle | 41 |
| Time Was | 83 |
| Together | 33 |
| Tonight | 28 |
| Tossin' and Turnin' | 2 |
| Tragedy | 64 |
| Travelin' Man | 7 |
| Watch Your Step | 56 |
| Wild in the Country | 54 |
| Wooden Heart | 69 |
| Writing on the Wall, The | 5 |
| Yellow Bird (Lyman) | 10 |
| Yellow Bird (Welk) | 75 |
| You Always Hurt the One You Love | 17 |
| You Can't Sit Down (Part II) | 29 |
| You'll Answer to Me | 53 |

# BILLBOARD HOT 100

JULY 10, 1961
FOR WEEK ENDING JULY 16, 1961

| This Week | Wk Ago | 2 Wks Ago | 3 Wks Ago | TITLE — Artist, Label & Number | Weeks On Chart |
|---|---|---|---|---|---|
| 1 | 2 | 4 | 7 | TOSSIN' AND TURNIN' — Bobby Lewis, Beltone 1002 | 12 |
| 2 | 3 | 7 | 9 | BOLL WEEVIL SONG — Brook Benton, Mercury 71820 | 9 |
| 3 | 1 | 1 | 3 | QUARTER TO THREE — U.S. Bonds, Le Grand 1008 | 8 |
| 4 | 4 | 2 | 5 | RAINDROPS — Dee Clark, Vee Jay 383 | 11 |
| 5 | 5 | 6 | 6 | THE WRITING ON THE WALL — Adam Wade, Coed 550 | 9 |
| 6 | 8 | 8 | 8 | EVERY BEAT OF MY HEART — Pips, Vee Jay 386 | 9 |
| 7 | 6 | 3 | 1 | MOODY RIVER — Pat Boone, Dot 16209 | 11 |
| 8 | 10 | 11 | 15 | YELLOW BIRD — Arthur Lyman, Hi Fi 5024 | 7 |
| 9 | 13 | 18 | 33 | HATS OFF TO LARRY — Del Shannon, Big Top 3075 | 6 |
| 10 | 12 | 13 | 16 | DANCE ON LITTLE GIRL — Paul Anka, ABC-Paramount 10220 | 7 |
| 11 | 16 | 19 | 43 | SAN ANTONIO ROSE — Floyd Cramer, RCA Victor 7893 | 6 |
| 12 | 7 | 5 | 2 | TRAVELIN' MAN — Ricky Nelson, Imperial 5741 | 12 |
| 13 | 20 | 31 | 69 | DUM DUM — Brenda Lee, Decca 31272 | 4 |
| 14 | 25 | 41 | 71 | I LIKE IT LIKE THAT — Chris Kenner, Instant 3229 | 7 |
| 15 | 9 | 9 | 10 | THOSE OLDIES BUT GOODIES — Little Caesar and the Romans, Del Fi 4158 | 11 |
| 16 | 11 | 10 | 4 | STAND BY ME — Ben E. King, Atco 6194 | 10 |
| 17 | 21 | 38 | 53 | PLEASE STAY — Drifters, Atlantic 2105 | 6 |
| 18 | 19 | 20 | 30 | TELL ME WHY — Belmonts, Sabrina 500 | 8 |
| 19 | 23 | 32 | 49 | I'M COMIN' ON BACK TO YOU — Jackie Wilson, Brunswick 55216 | 5 |
| 20 | 33 | 48 | — | TOGETHER — Connie Francis, MGM 13019 | 3 |
| 21 | 15 | 16 | 17 | HELLO MARY LOU — Ricky Nelson, Imperial 5741 | 11 |
| 22 | 14 | 14 | 11 | RUNNING SCARED — Roy Orbison, Monument 438 | 14 |
| 23 | 24 | 28 | 40 | IT KEEPS RAININ' — Fats Domino, Imperial 5753 | 6 |
| 24 | 36 | 68 | 98 | NEVER ON SUNDAY — Chordettes, Cadence 1402 | 4 |
| 25 | 26 | 34 | 55 | OLE BUTTERMILK SKY — Bill Black's Combo, Hi 2036 | 6 |
| 26 | 28 | 30 | 52 | TONIGHT (COULD BE THE NIGHT) — Velvets, Monument 441 | 7 |
| 27 | 39 | 62 | 85 | LET'S TWIST AGAIN — Chubby Checker, Parkway 824 | 4 |
| 28 | 34 | 36 | 47 | CUPID — Sam Cooke, RCA Victor 7883 | 6 |
| 29 | 29 | 39 | 68 | YOU CAN'T SIT DOWN (Part II) — Phillip Upchurch Combo, Boyd 1026 | 4 |
| 30 | 22 | 22 | 18 | HEART AND SOUL — Cleftones, Gee 1064 | 8 |
| 31 | 38 | 50 | 61 | SACRED — Castells, Era 3048 | 5 |
| 32 | 32 | 33 | 46 | MY KIND OF GIRL — Matt Monro, Warwick 636 | 7 |
| 33 | 48 | 87 | — | HEART AND SOUL — Jan and Dean, Challenge 9111 | 3 |
| 34 | 43 | 63 | — | POMP AND CIRCUMSTANCE — Adrian Kimberly, Calliope 6501 | 3 |
| 35 | 17 | 12 | 12 | YOU ALWAYS HURT THE ONE YOU LOVE — Clarence Henry, Argo 5388 | 9 |
| 36 | 59 | 99 | — | RAININ' IN MY HEART — Slim Harpo, Excello 2194 | 6 |
| 37 | 60 | — | — | THE FISH — Bobby Rydell, Cameo 192 | 2 |
| 38 | 58 | 73 | 95 | SEA OF HEARTBREAK — Don Gibson, RCA Victor 7890 | 4 |
| 39 | 27 | 21 | 19 | HELLO WALLS — Faron Young, Capitol 4533 | 14 |
| 40 | 47 | 51 | 66 | NATURE BOY — Bobby Darin, Atco 6196 | 5 |
| 41 | 52 | 77 | — | THE SWITCH-A-ROO — Hank Ballard and the Midnighters, King 5510 | 3 |
| 42 | 18 | 17 | 13 | BARBARA ANN — Regents, Gee 1065 | 9 |
| 43 | 68 | — | — | LAST NIGHT — Mar-Keys, Satellite 107 | 2 |
| 44 | 49 | 54 | 64 | I FALL TO PIECES — Patsy Cline, Decca 31205 | 8 |
| 45 | 61 | 82 | — | THAT'S WHAT GIRLS ARE MADE FOR — Spinners, Tri-Phi 1001 | 3 |
| 46 | 74 | — | — | PRETTY LITTLE ANGEL EYES — Curtis Lee, Dunes 2007 | 2 |
| 47 | 53 | 67 | — | YOU'LL ANSWER TO ME — Patti Page, Mercury 71823 | 3 |
| 48 | 31 | 23 | 20 | PEANUT BUTTER — Marathons, Arvee 5027 | 12 |
| 49 | 51 | 52 | 75 | SHOULD I — String-A-Longs, Warwick 654 | 5 |
| 50 | 46 | 44 | 38 | BETTER TELL HIM NO — Starlets, Pam 1003 | 12 |
| 51 | 56 | 65 | 77 | WATCH YOUR STEP — Bobby Parker, V-Tone 223 | 5 |
| 52 | 37 | 43 | 62 | JURA (I SWEAR I LOVE YOU) — Les Paul and Mary Ford, Columbia 41994 | 10 |
| 53 | 41 | 35 | 48 | THREE HEARTS IN A TANGLE — Roy Drusky, Decca 31193 | 14 |
| 54 | 50 | 61 | 70 | FOOL THAT I AM — Etta James, Argo 5390 | 5 |
| 55 | 69 | 98 | — | WOODEN HEART (Muss I Denn) — Joe Dowell, Smash 1708 | 3 |
| 56 | 72 | — | — | EVENTUALLY — Brenda Lee, Decca 31272 | 2 |
| 57 | 81 | — | — | I'LL BE THERE — Damita Jo, Mercury 71840 | 2 |
| 58 | 73 | 75 | 81 | MOM AND DAD'S WALTZ — Patti Page, Mercury 71823 | 5 |
| 59 | 45 | 59 | 39 | NEVER ON SUNDAY — Don Costa, United Artists 234 | 25 |
| 60 | 77 | 90 | — | TE-TA-TE-TA-TA — Ernie K-Doe, Minit 627 | 3 |
| 61 | 70 | 78 | 99 | NO, NO, NO — Chanters, Deluxe 6191 | 4 |
| 62 | 63 | 83 | — | QUITE A PARTY — Fireballs, Warwick 644 | 3 |
| 63 | 79 | 79 | 91 | I'M GONNA KNOCK ON YOUR DOOR — Eddie Hodges, Cadence 1397 | 4 |
| 64 | 67 | 71 | 73 | THE GIRL'S A DEVIL — Dukays, Nat 1003 | 9 |
| 65 | 66 | 74 | 86 | BOBBY — Neil Scott, Portrait 102 | 5 |
| 66 | 85 | — | — | DON'T BET MONEY HONEY — Linda Scott, Canadian-American 127 | 2 |
| 67 | 86 | — | — | HILLBILLY HEAVEN — Tex Ritter, Capitol 4567 | 2 |
| 68 | 84 | — | — | A TEAR — Gene McDaniels, Liberty 55344 | 2 |
| 69 | 83 | — | — | TIME WAS — Flamingos, End 1092 | 2 |
| 70 | 30 | 25 | 21 | RAMA LAMA DING DONG — Edsels, Twin 700 | 11 |
| 71 | 75 | 94 | 72 | YELLOW BIRD — Lawrence Welk, Dot 16222 | 5 |
| 72 | 71 | 66 | 84 | I'VE GOT NEWS FOR YOU — Ray Charles, Impulse 202 | 4 |
| 73 | 99 | — | — | PEANUTS — Rick and the Keens, Smash 1705 | 2 |
| 74 | 91 | — | — | GRANADA — Frank Sinatra, Reprise 20010 | 2 |
| 75 | 65 | 80 | 97 | THE CHARLESTON — Ernie Fields, Rendezvous 150 | 4 |
| 76 | 55 | 72 | — | DREAM — Etta James, Argo 5390 | 3 |
| 77 | 92 | — | — | MY TRUE STORY — Jive Five, Beltone 1006 | 2 |
| 78 | 95 | — | — | PRINCESS — Frank Gari, Crusade 1022 | 2 |
| 79 | — | — | — | READY FOR YOUR LOVE — Shep and the Limelites, Hull 742 | 1 |
| 80 | 82 | 86 | 96 | JOANIE — Frankie Calen, Spark 902 | 5 |
| 81 | 90 | — | — | TENDER YEARS — George Jones, Mercury 71804 | 2 |
| 82 | 40 | 29 | 23 | LITTLE EGYPT — Coasters, Atco 6192 | 12 |
| 83 | — | — | — | YOU DON'T KNOW WHAT YOU'VE GOT (Until You Lose It) — Ral Donner, Gone 5108 | 1 |
| 84 | 87 | 89 | 90 | BLUE TOMORROW — Billy Vaughn, Dot 16220 | 5 |
| 85 | 89 | 91 | 93 | POINT OF NO RETURN — Adam Wade, Coed 550 | 4 |
| 86 | 35 | 15 | 14 | I FEEL SO BAD — Elvis Presley, RCA Victor 7880 | 9 |
| 87 | 88 | 100 | — | TAKE A FOOL'S ADVICE — Nat King Cole, Capitol 4582 | 3 |
| 88 | — | — | — | RUNAROUND — Regents, Gee 1071 | 1 |
| 89 | — | — | — | BOOGIE WOOGIE — B. Bumble and the Stingers, Rendezvous 151 | 1 |
| 90 | 96 | — | — | LA DOLCE VITA — Ray Ellis, RCA Victor 7888 | 2 |
| 91 | — | — | — | MIGHTY GOOD LOVIN' — Miracles, Tamla 54044 | 1 |
| 92 | — | — | — | A THING OF THE PAST — Shirelles, Scepter 1220 | 1 |
| 93 | — | — | — | THE ASTRONAUT — Jose Jimenez, Kapp 409 | 1 |
| 94 | 98 | — | — | ONE SUMMER NIGHT — Diamonds, Mercury 71831 | 2 |
| 95 | — | — | — | WISHIN' ON A RAINBOW — Phill Wilson, Huron 22000 | 1 |
| 96 | 100 | — | — | THE GUNS OF NAVARONE — Joe Reisman, Landa 674 | 2 |
| 97 | — | — | — | BLACKLAND FARMER — Frankie Miller, Starday 424 | 1 |
| 98 | 42 | 24 | 25 | I'M A FOOL TO CARE — Joe Barry, Smash 1702 | 12 |
| 99 | — | — | — | WHAT WOULD YOU DO — Jim Reeves, RCA Victor 7905 | 1 |
| 100 | — | — | — | MICHAEL — Highwaymen, United Artists 258 | 1 |

## BUBBLING UNDER THE HOT 100

1. VOYAGE TO THE BOTTOM OF THE SEA — Frankie Avalon, Chancellor 1081
2. WOODEN HEART (Muss I Denn) — Gus Backus, Fono-Graf 1234
3. PITTER PATTER — Four Sportsmen, Sunnybrook 4
4. I'LL NEVER BE FREE — Kay Starr, Capitol 4583
5. NOW YOU KNOW — Little Willie John, King 5516
6. DEDICATED (TO THE SONGS I LOVE) — Three Friends, Imperial 5763
7. I DON'T WANT TO TAKE A CHANCE — Mary Wells, Motown 1011
8. THEME FROM COME SEPTEMBER — Dick Jacobs, Coral 62275
9. AROUND THE WORLD — Buddy Greco, Epic 9451
10. MY CLAIRE DE LUNE — Steve Lawrence, United Artists 335
11. DON'T FORGET I LOVE YOU — Butanes, Enrica 1007
12. STARLIGHT — Preludes Five, Pik 231
13. DRIVIN' HOME — Duane Eddy, Jamie 1195
14. BIG RIVER, BIG MAN — Claude King, Columbia 42043
15. LONESOME FOR YOU MAMA — Anita Bryant, Carlton 553
16. IF — Paragons, Tap 101
17. LIFE IS BUT A DREAM — Earls, Rome 101
18. TAKE FIVE — Dave Brubeck, Columbia 41479
19. LIFE IS BUT A DREAM, SWEETHEART — Classics, Mercury 71829
20. MR. JOHNNY Q — Bobbettes, End 1093

## HOT 100 — A TO Z

Astronaut, The ... 93
Barbara Ann ... 42
Better Tell Him No ... 50
Blackland Farmer ... 97
Blue Tomorrow ... 84
Bobby ... 65
Boll Weevil Song ... 2
Boogie Woogie ... 89
Charleston, The ... 75
Cupid ... 28
Dance on Little Girl ... 10
Don't Bet Money Honey ... 66
Dream ... 76
Dum Dum ... 13
Eventually ... 56
Every Beat of My Heart ... 6
Fish, The ... 37
Fool That I Am ... 54
Girl's a Devil, The ... 64
Granada ... 74
Guns of Navarone, The ... 96
Hats Off to Larry ... 9
Heart and Soul (Cleftones) ... 30
Heart and Soul (Jan and Dean) ... 33
Hello Mary Lou ... 21
Hello Walls ... 39
Hillbilly Heaven ... 67
I Fall to Pieces ... 44
I Feel So Bad ... 86
I Like It Like That ... 14
I'll Be There ... 57
I'm a Fool to Care ... 98
I'm Comin' on Back to You ... 19
I'm Gonna Knock on Your Door ... 63
It Keeps Rainin' ... 23
I've Got News for You ... 72
Joanie ... 80
Jura ... 52
La Dolce Vita ... 90
Last Night ... 43
Let's Twist Again ... 27
Little Egypt ... 82
Michael ... 100
Mighty Good Lovin' ... 91
Mom and Dad's Waltz ... 58
Moody River ... 7
My Kind of Girl ... 32
My True Story ... 77
Nature Boy ... 40
Never on Sunday (Chordettes) ... 24
Never on Sunday (Costa) ... 59
No, No, No ... 61
Ole Buttermilk Sky ... 25
One Summer Night ... 94
Peanut Butter ... 48
Peanuts ... 73
Please Stay ... 17
Point of No Return ... 85
Pomp and Circumstance ... 34
Pretty Little Angel Eyes ... 46
Princess ... 78
Quarter to Three ... 3
Quite a Party ... 62
Raindrops ... 4
Rainin' in My Heart ... 36
Rama Lama Ding Dong ... 70
Ready for Your Love ... 79
Runaround ... 88
Running Scared ... 22
Sacred ... 31
San Antonio Rose ... 11
Sea of Heartbreak ... 38
Should I ... 49
Stand by Me ... 16
Switch-A-Roo, The ... 41
Take a Fool's Advice ... 87
Te-Ta-Te-Ta-Ta ... 60
Tear, A ... 68
Tell Me Why ... 18
Tender Years ... 81
That's What Girls Are Made For ... 45
Thing of the Past, A ... 92
Those Oldies but Goodies ... 15
Three Hearts in a Tangle ... 53
Time Was ... 69
Together ... 20
Tonight ... 26
Tossin' and Turnin' ... 1
Travelin' Man ... 12
Watch Your Step ... 51
What Would You Do ... 99
Wishin' on a Rainbow ... 95
Wooden Heart ... 55
Writing on the Wall, The ... 5
Yellow Bird (Lyman) ... 8
Yellow Bird (Welk) ... 71
You Always Hurt the One You Love ... 35
You Can't Sit Down (Part II) ... 29
You Don't Know What You've Got (Until You Lose It) ... 83
You'll Answer to Me ... 47

# BILLBOARD HOT 100

**JULY 17, 1961**
**FOR WEEK ENDING JULY 23, 1961**

| This Week | Wk. Ago | 2 Wks. Ago | 3 Wks. Ago | TITLE — Artist, Label & Number | Weeks On Chart |
|---|---|---|---|---|---|
| 1 | 1 | 2 | 4 | TOSSIN' AND TURNIN' — Bobby Lewis, Beltone 1002 | 13 |
| 2 | 3 | 7 | — | BOLL WEEVIL SONG — Brook Benton, Mercury 71820 | 10 |
| 3 | 1 | 1 | 1 | QUARTER TO THREE — U.S. Bonds, Le Grand 1008 | 9 |
| 4 | 4 | 4 | 2 | RAINDROPS — Dee Clark, Vee Jay 383 | 12 |
| 5 | 8 | 10 | 11 | YELLOW BIRD — Arthur Lyman, Hi Fi 5024 | 8 |
| 6 | 9 | 13 | 18 | HATS OFF TO LARRY — Del Shannon, Big Top 3075 | 7 |
| 7 | 6 | 8 | 8 | EVERY BEAT OF MY HEART — Pips, Vee Jay 386 | 10 |
| 8 | 11 | 16 | 19 | SAN ANTONIO ROSE — Floyd Cramer, RCA Victor 7893 | 7 |
| 9 | 14 | 25 | 41 | I LIKE IT LIKE THAT — Chris Kenner, Instant 3229 | 8 |
| 10 | 13 | 20 | 31 | DUM DUM — Brenda Lee, Decca 31272 | 5 |
| 11 | 10 | 12 | 13 | DANCE ON LITTLE GIRL — Paul Anka, ABC-Paramount 10220 | 8 |
| 12 | 7 | 6 | 3 | MOODY RIVER — Pat Boone, Dot 16209 | 12 |
| 13 | 5 | 5 | 6 | THE WRITING ON THE WALL — Adam Wade, Coed 550 | 10 |
| 14 | 20 | 33 | 48 | TOGETHER — Connie Francis, MGM 13019 | 4 |
| 15 | 27 | 39 | 62 | LET'S TWIST AGAIN — Chubby Checker, Parkway 824 | 5 |
| 16 | 17 | 21 | 38 | PLEASE STAY — Drifters, Atlantic 2105 | 7 |
| 17 | 12 | 7 | 5 | TRAVELIN' MAN — Ricky Nelson, Imperial 5741 | 13 |
| 18 | 18 | 19 | 20 | TELL ME WHY — Belmonts, Sabrina 500 | 9 |
| 19 | 24 | 36 | 68 | NEVER ON SUNDAY — Chordettes, Cadence 1402 | 5 |
| 20 | 15 | 9 | 9 | THOSE OLDIES BUT GOODIES — Little Caesar and the Romans, Del Fi 4158 | 12 |
| 21 | 19 | 23 | 32 | I'M COMIN' ON BACK TO YOU — Jackie Wilson, Brunswick 55216 | 6 |
| 22 | 32 | 32 | 33 | MY KIND OF GIRL — Matt Monro, Warwick 636 | 8 |
| 23 | 16 | 11 | 10 | STAND BY ME — Ben E. King, Atco 6194 | 11 |
| 24 | 22 | 14 | 14 | RUNNING SCARED — Roy Orbison, Monument 438 | 15 |
| 25 | 21 | 15 | 16 | HELLO MARY LOU — Ricky Nelson, Imperial 5741 | 12 |
| 26 | 26 | 28 | 30 | TONIGHT (COULD BE THE NIGHT) — Velvets, Monument 441 | 8 |
| 27 | 28 | 34 | 36 | CUPID — Sam Cooke, RCA Victor 7883 | 7 |
| 28 | 23 | 24 | 28 | IT KEEPS RAININ' — Fats Domino, Imperial 5753 | 10 |
| 29 | 31 | 38 | 50 | SACRED — Castells, Era 3048 | 8 |
| 30 | 43 | 68 | — | LAST NIGHT — Mar-Keys, Satellite 107 | 3 |
| 31 | 33 | 48 | 87 | HEART AND SOUL — Jan and Dean, Challenge 9111 | 4 |
| 32 | 37 | 60 | — | THE FISH — Bobby Rydell, Cameo 192 | 3 |
| 33 | 41 | 52 | 77 | THE SWITCH-A-ROO — Hank Ballard and the Midnighters, King 5510 | 4 |
| 34 | 36 | 59 | 99 | RAININ' IN MY HEART — Slim Harpo, Excello 2194 | 7 |
| 35 | 55 | 69 | 98 | WOODEN HEART (Muss I Denn) — Joe Dowell, Smash 1708 | 4 |
| 36 | 46 | 74 | — | PRETTY LITTLE ANGEL EYES — Curtis Lee, Dunes 2007 | 3 |
| 37 | 45 | 61 | 82 | THAT'S WHAT GIRLS ARE MADE FOR — Spinners, Tri-Phi 1001 | 4 |
| 38 | 38 | 58 | 73 | SEA OF HEARTBREAK — Don Gibson, RCA Victor 7890 | 5 |
| 39 | 57 | 81 | — | I'LL BE THERE — Damita Jo, Mercury 71840 | 3 |
| 40 | 25 | 26 | 34 | OLE BUTTERMILK SKY — Bill Black's Combo, Hi 2036 | 7 |
| 41 | 30 | 22 | 22 | HEART AND SOUL — Cleftones, Gee 1064 | 9 |
| 42 | 49 | 51 | 52 | SHOULD I — String-A-Longs, Warwick 654 | 6 |
| 43 | 29 | 29 | 39 | YOU CAN'T SIT DOWN (Part II) — Phillip Upchurch Combo, Boyd 1026 | 5 |
| 44 | 34 | 43 | 63 | POMP AND CIRCUMSTANCE — Adrian Kimberly, Calliope 6501 | 4 |
| 45 | 53 | 41 | 35 | THREE HEARTS IN A TANGLE — Roy Drusky, Decca 31193 | 15 |
| 46 | 47 | 53 | 67 | YOU'LL ANSWER TO ME — Patti Page, Mercury 71823 | 4 |
| 47 | 35 | 17 | 12 | YOU ALWAYS HURT THE ONE YOU LOVE — Clarence Henry, Argo 5388 | 10 |
| 48 | 40 | 47 | 51 | NATURE BOY — Bobby Darin, Atco 6196 | 6 |
| 49 | 66 | 85 | — | DON'T BET MONEY HONEY — Linda Scott, Canadian-American 127 | 3 |
| 50 | 61 | 70 | 78 | NO, NO, NO — Chanters, Deluxe 6191 | 4 |
| 51 | 44 | 49 | 54 | I FALL TO PIECES — Patsy Cline, Decca 31205 | 9 |
| 52 | 62 | 63 | 83 | QUITE A PARTY — Fireballs, Warwick 644 | 4 |
| 53 | 60 | 77 | 90 | TE-TA-TE-TA-TA — Ernie K-Doe, Minit 627 | 4 |
| 54 | 63 | 79 | 79 | I'M GONNA KNOCK ON YOUR DOOR — Eddie Hodges, Cadence 1397 | 5 |
| 55 | 39 | 27 | 21 | HELLO WALLS — Faron Young, Capitol 4533 | 15 |
| 56 | 68 | 84 | — | A TEAR — Gene McDaniels, Liberty 55344 | 3 |
| 57 | 83 | — | — | YOU DON'T KNOW WHAT YOU'VE GOT (Until You Lose It) — Ral Donner, Gone 5108 | 2 |
| 58 | 77 | 92 | — | MY TRUE STORY — Jive Five, Beltone 1006 | 3 |
| 59 | 58 | 73 | 75 | MOM AND DAD'S WALTZ — Patti Page, Mercury 71823 | 6 |
| 60 | 65 | 66 | 74 | BOBBY — Neil Scott, Portrait 102 | 6 |
| 61 | 69 | 83 | — | TIME WAS — Flamingos, End 1092 | 3 |
| 62 | 50 | 46 | 44 | BETTER TELL HIM NO — Starlets, Pam 1003 | 13 |
| 63 | 67 | 86 | — | HILLBILLY HEAVEN — Tex Ritter, Capitol 4567 | 3 |
| 64 | 74 | 91 | — | GRANADA — Frank Sinatra, Reprise 20010 | 3 |
| 65 | 94 | 98 | — | ONE SUMMER NIGHT — Diamonds, Mercury 71831 | 2 |
| 66 | 78 | 95 | — | PRINCESS — Frank Gari, Crusade 1022 | 3 |
| 67 | 75 | 65 | 80 | THE CHARLESTON — Ernie Fields, Rendezvous 150 | 5 |
| 68 | 64 | 67 | 71 | THE GIRL'S A DEVIL — Dukays, Nat 1003 | 10 |
| 69 | 100 | — | — | MICHAEL — Highwaymen, United Artists 258 | 2 |
| 70 | 51 | 56 | 65 | WATCH YOUR STEP — Bobby Parker, V-Tone 223 | 6 |
| 71 | 73 | 99 | — | PEANUTS — Rick and the Keens, Smash 1705 | 3 |
| 72 | 91 | — | — | MIGHTY GOOD LOVIN' — Miracles, Tamla 54044 | 2 |
| 73 | 79 | — | — | READY FOR YOUR LOVE — Shep and the Limelites, Hull 742 | 2 |
| 74 | 59 | 45 | 59 | NEVER ON SUNDAY — Don Costa, United Artists 234 | 26 |
| 75 | 42 | 18 | 17 | BARBARA ANN — Regents, Gee 1065 | 10 |
| 76 | 56 | 72 | — | EVENTUALLY — Brenda Lee, Decca 31272 | 3 |
| 77 | 81 | 90 | — | TENDER YEARS — George Jones, Mercury 71804 | 3 |
| 78 | 80 | 82 | 86 | JOANIE — Frankie Calen, Spark 902 | 6 |
| 79 | 88 | — | — | RUNAROUND — Regents, Gee 1071 | 2 |
| 80 | 72 | 71 | 66 | I'VE GOT NEWS FOR YOU — Ray Charles, Impulse 202 | 5 |
| 81 | 87 | 88 | 100 | TAKE A FOOL'S ADVICE — Nat King Cole, Capitol 4582 | 4 |
| 82 | — | — | — | MY MEMORIES OF YOU — Donnie and the Dreamers, Whale 505 | 1 |
| 83 | — | — | — | NAG — Halos, Seven Arts 709 | 1 |
| 84 | — | — | — | TOO MANY RULES — Connie Francis, MGM 13019 | 1 |
| 85 | 90 | 96 | — | LA DOLCE VITA — Ray Ellis, RCA Victor 7888 | 3 |
| 86 | 97 | — | — | BLACKLAND FARMER — Frankie Miller, Starday 424 | 2 |
| 87 | — | — | — | WHAT A SWEET THING THAT WAS — Shirelles, Scepter 1220 | 1 |
| 88 | 54 | 50 | 61 | FOOL THAT I AM — Etta James, Argo 5390 | 6 |
| 89 | 99 | — | — | WHAT WOULD YOU DO — Jim Reeves, RCA Victor 7905 | 2 |
| 90 | 93 | — | — | THE ASTRONAUT — Jose Jimenez, Kapp 409 | 2 |
| 91 | 95 | — | — | WISHIN' ON A RAINBOW — Phill Wilson, Huron 22000 | 2 |
| 92 | 92 | — | — | A THING OF THE PAST — Shirelles, Scepter 1220 | 2 |
| 93 | — | — | — | WATER BOY — Don Shirley Trio, Cadence 1392 | 1 |
| 94 | — | — | — | BIG RIVER, BIG MAN — Claude King, Columbia 42043 | 1 |
| 95 | — | — | — | IF — Paragons, Tap 101 | 1 |
| 96 | — | — | — | STARLIGHT, STARBRIGHT — Linda Scott, Canadian-American 127 | 1 |
| 97 | — | — | — | MY CLAIRE DE LUNE — Steve Lawrence, United Artists 335 | 1 |
| 98 | — | — | — | I DON'T WANT TO TAKE A CHANCE — Mary Wells, Motown 1011 | 1 |
| 99 | — | — | — | DRIVIN' HOME — Duane Eddy, Jamie 1195 | 1 |
| 100 | — | — | — | NOW YOU KNOW — Little Willie John, King 5516 | 1 |

## BUBBLING UNDER THE HOT 100

1. VOYAGE TO THE BOTTOM OF THE SEA — Frankie Avalon, Chancellor 1081
2. PITTER PATTER — Four Sportsmen, Sunnybrook 4
3. SOMEBODY NOBODY WANTS — Dion, Laurie 3101
4. THEME FROM COME SEPTEMBER — Dick Jacobs, Coral 62275
5. I NEVER KNEW — Clyde McPhatter, Mercury 71841
6. DEDICATED (TO THE SONGS I LOVE) — Three Friends, Imperial 5763
7. LOVER'S ISLAND — Blue Jays, Milestone 2008
8. IN TIME — Steve Lawrence, United Artists 335
9. DON'T FORGET I LOVE YOU — Butanes, Enrica 1007
10. STARLIGHT — Preludes Five, Pik 231
11. SOLIDAIRE (SINCE YOU'RE GONE) — Embers, Empress 101
12. ALL I HAVE TO DO IS DREAM — Everly Brothers, Cadence 1348
13. THEME FROM COME SEPTEMBER — Bobby Darin & His Ork, Atco 6200
14. I JUST DON'T UNDERSTAND — Ann Margaret, RCA Victor 7894
15. I'M SO HAPPY — Ducanes, Goldisc 3024
16. BACK BEAT NO. 1 — Rondels, Amy 825
17. THE BELLS ARE RINGING — Van Dykes, DeLuxe 6193
18. S.O.S. (I LOVE YOU) — Ronnie Hayden, Camay 1001
19. HERE IN MY HEART — Al Martino, Capitol 4593
20. ST. LOUIS BLUES — Cousins, Parkway 823

## HOT 100 — A TO Z

| Title | # | Title | # |
|---|---|---|---|
| Astronaut, The | 90 | No, No, No | 50 |
| Barbara Ann | 75 | Now You Know | 100 |
| Better Tell Him No | 62 | Ole Buttermilk Sky | 40 |
| Big River, Big Man | 94 | One Summer Night | 65 |
| Blackland Farmer | 86 | Peanuts | 71 |
| Bobby | 60 | Please Stay | 16 |
| Boll Weevil Song | 2 | Pomp and Circumstance | 44 |
| Charleston, The | 67 | Pretty Little Angel Eyes | 36 |
| Cupid | 27 | Princess | 66 |
| Dance on Little Girl | 11 | Quarter to Three | 3 |
| Don't Bet Money Honey | 49 | Quite a Party | 52 |
| Drivin' Home | 99 | Raindrops | 4 |
| Dum Dum | 10 | Rainin' in My Heart | 34 |
| Eventually | 76 | Ready for Your Love | 73 |
| Every Beat of My Heart | 7 | Runaround | 79 |
| Fish, The | 32 | Running Scared | 24 |
| Fool That I Am | 88 | Sacred | 29 |
| Girl's a Devil, The | 68 | San Antonio Rose | 8 |
| Granada | 64 | Sea of Heartbreak | 38 |
| Hats Off to Larry | 6 | Should I | 42 |
| Heart and Soul (Cleftones) | 41 | Stand By Me | 23 |
| Heart and Soul (Jan and Dean) | 31 | Starlight, Starbright | 96 |
| Hello Mary Lou | 25 | Switch-A-Roo, The | 33 |
| Hello Walls | 55 | Take a Fool's Advice | 81 |
| Hillbilly Heaven | 63 | Te-Ta-Te-Ta-Ta | 53 |
| I Don't Want to Take a Chance | 98 | Tell Me Why | 18 |
| I Fall to Pieces | 51 | Tender Years | 77 |
| I Like It Like That | 9 | That's What Girls Are Made For | 37 |
| If | 95 | Thing of the Past, A | 92 |
| I'll Be There | 39 | Those Oldies But Goodies | 20 |
| I'm Comin' On Back to You | 21 | Three Hearts in a Tangle | 45 |
| I'm Gonna Knock on Your Door | 54 | Time Was | 61 |
| It Keeps Rainin' | 28 | Together | 14 |
| I've Got News for You | 80 | Too Many Rules | 84 |
| Joanie | 78 | Tonight (Could Be the Night) | 26 |
| La Dolce Vita | 85 | Tossin' and Turnin' | 1 |
| Last Night | 30 | Travelin' Man | 17 |
| Let's Twist Again | 15 | Watch Your Step | 70 |
| Michael | 69 | Water Boy | 93 |
| Mighty Good Lovin' | 72 | What a Sweet Thing That Was | 87 |
| Moody River | 12 | What Would You Do | 89 |
| Mom and Dad's Waltz | 59 | Wishin' On a Rainbow | 91 |
| My Claire De Lune | 97 | Wooden Heart | 35 |
| My Kind of Girl | 22 | Writing on the Wall, The | 13 |
| My Memories of You | 82 | Yellow Bird | 5 |
| My True Story | 58 | You Always Hurt the One You Love | 47 |
| Nag | 83 | You Can't Sit Down (Part II) | 43 |
| Nature Boy | 48 | You Don't Know What You've Got | 57 |
| Never on Sunday (Chordettes) | 19 | You'll Answer to Me | 46 |
| Never on Sunday (Costa) | 74 | | |

# BILLBOARD HOT 100

**JULY 24, 1961**
**FOR WEEK ENDING JULY 30, 1961**

| # | Wks Ago | Title | Artist, Label & Number | Weeks On Chart |
|---|---|---|---|---|
| 1 | 1 1 2 | TOSSIN' AND TURNIN' | Bobby Lewis, Beltone 1002 | 14 |
| 2 | 2 2 3 | BOLL WEEVIL SONG | Brook Benton, Mercury 71820 | 11 |
| 3 | 3 3 1 | QUARTER TO THREE | Gary (U.S.) Bonds, LeGrand 1008 | 10 |
| 4 | 5 8 10 | YELLOW BIRD | Arthur Lyman, Hi Fi 5024 | 9 |
| 5 | 9 14 25 | I LIKE IT LIKE THAT | Chris Kenner, Instant 3229 | 9 |
| 6 | 6 9 13 | HATS OFF TO LARRY | Del Shannon, Big Top 3075 | 8 |
| 7 | 4 4 4 | RAINDROPS | Dee Clark, Vee Jay 383 | 13 |
| 8 | 10 13 20 | DUM DUM | Brenda Lee, Decca 31272 | 6 |
| 9 | 14 20 33 | TOGETHER | Connie Francis, MGM 13019 | 5 |
| 10 | 15 27 39 | LET'S TWIST AGAIN | Chubby Checker, Parkway 824 | 6 |
| 11 | 8 11 16 | SAN ANTONIO ROSE | Floyd Cramer, RCA Victor 7893 | 8 |
| 12 | 30 43 68 | LAST NIGHT | Mar-Keys, Satellite 107 | 4 |
| 13 | 7 6 8 | EVERY BEAT OF MY HEART | Pips, Vee Jay 386 | 11 |
| 14 | 16 17 21 | PLEASE STAY | Drifters, Atlantic 2105 | 8 |
| 15 | 19 24 36 | NEVER ON SUNDAY | Chordettes, Cadence 1402 | 6 |
| 16 | 12 7 6 | MOODY RIVER | Pat Boone, Dot 16209 | 13 |
| 17 | 27 28 34 | CUPID | Sam Cooke, RCA Victor 7883 | 8 |
| 18 | 35 55 69 | WOODEN HEART (Muss I Denn) | Joe Dowell, Smash 1708 | 5 |
| 19 | 17 12 7 | TRAVELIN' MAN | Ricky Nelson, Imperial 5741 | 14 |
| 20 | 29 31 38 | SACRED | Castells, Era 3048 | 9 |
| 21 | 22 32 32 | MY KIND OF GIRL | Matt Monro, Warwick 636 | 9 |
| 22 | 18 18 19 | TELL ME WHY | Belmonts, Sabrina 500 | 10 |
| 23 | 25 21 15 | HELLO MARY LOU | Ricky Nelson, Imperial 5741 | 13 |
| 24 | 36 46 74 | PRETTY LITTLE ANGEL EYES | Curtis Lee, Dunes 2007 | 4 |
| 25 | 31 33 48 | HEART AND SOUL | Jan and Dean, Challenge 9111 | 5 |
| 26 | 33 41 52 | THE SWITCH-A-ROO | Hank Ballard and the Midnighters, King 5510 | 5 |
| 27 | 32 37 60 | THE FISH | Bobby Rydell, Cameo 192 | 4 |
| 28 | 39 57 81 | I'LL BE THERE | Damita Jo, Mercury 71840 | 4 |
| 29 | 23 16 11 | STAND BY ME | Ben E. King, Atco 6194 | 12 |
| 30 | 24 22 14 | RUNNING SCARED | Roy Orbison, Monument 438 | 16 |
| 31 | 37 45 61 | THAT'S WHAT GIRLS ARE MADE FOR | Spinners, Tri-Phi 1001 | 5 |
| 32 | 21 19 23 | I'M COMIN' ON BACK TO YOU | Jackie Wilson, Brunswick 55216 | 7 |
| 33 | 38 38 58 | SEA OF HEARTBREAK | Don Gibson, RCA Victor 7890 | 6 |
| 34 | 11 10 12 | DANCE ON LITTLE GIRL | Paul Anka, ABC Paramount 10220 | 9 |
| 35 | 57 83 — | YOU DON'T KNOW WHAT YOU'VE GOT (Until You Lose It) | Ral Donner, Gone 5108 | 3 |
| 36 | 49 66 85 | DON'T BET MONEY HONEY | Linda Scott, Canadian-American 127 | 4 |
| 37 | 51 44 49 | I FALL TO PIECES | Patsy Cline, Decca 31205 | 10 |
| 38 | 54 63 79 | I'M GONNA KNOCK ON YOUR DOOR | Eddie Hodges, Cadence 1397 | 6 |
| 39 | 20 15 9 | THOSE OLDIES BUT GOODIES | Little Caesar and the Romans, Del Fi 4158 | 13 |
| 40 | 13 5 5 | THE WRITING ON THE WALL | Adam Wade, Coed 550 | 11 |
| 41 | 69 100 — | MICHAEL | Highwaymen, United Artists 258 | 3 |
| 42 | 41 30 22 | HEART AND SOUL | Cleftones, Gee 1064 | 10 |
| 43 | 26 26 28 | TONIGHT (COULD BE THE NIGHT) | Velvets, Monument 441 | 9 |
| 44 | 43 29 29 | YOU CAN'T SIT DOWN (Part II) | Phillip Upchurch Combo, Boyd 1026 | 6 |
| 45 | 50 61 70 | NO, NO, NO | Chanters, Deluxe 6191 | 6 |
| 46 | 46 47 53 | YOU'LL ANSWER TO ME | Patti Page, Mercury 71823 | 5 |
| 47 | 79 88 — | RUNAROUND | Regents, Gee 1071 | 3 |
| 48 | 42 49 51 | SHOULD I | String-A-Longs, Warwick 654 | 7 |
| 49 | 52 62 63 | QUITE A PARTY | Fireballs, Warwick 644 | 5 |
| 50 | 73 79 — | READY FOR YOUR LOVE | Shep and the Limelites, Hull 742 | 3 |
| 51 | 56 68 84 | A TEAR | Gene McDaniels, Liberty 55344 | 4 |
| 52 | — — — | SCHOOL IS OUT | Gary (U.S.) Bonds, LeGrand 1009 | 1 |
| 53 | 62 50 46 | BETTER TELL HIM NO | Starlets, Pam 1003 | 14 |
| 54 | 58 77 92 | MY TRUE STORY | Jive Five, Beltone 1006 | 4 |
| 55 | 67 75 65 | THE CHARLESTON | Ernie Fields, Rendezvous 150 | 6 |
| 56 | — — — | LET THE FOUR WINDS BLOW | Fats Domino, Imperial 5764 | 1 |
| 57 | 63 67 86 | HILLBILLY HEAVEN | Tex Ritter, Capitol 4567 | 4 |
| 58 | 60 65 66 | BOBBY | Neil Scott, Portrait 102 | 7 |
| 59 | 61 69 83 | TIME WAS | Flamingos, End 1092 | 4 |
| 60 | 87 — — | WHAT A SWEET THING THAT WAS | Shirelles, Scepter 1220 | 2 |
| 61 | 65 94 98 | ONE SUMMER NIGHT | Diamonds, Mercury 71831 | 4 |
| 62 | 66 78 95 | PRINCESS | Frank Gari, Crusade 1022 | 4 |
| 63 | 45 53 41 | THREE HEARTS IN A TANGLE | Roy Drusky, Decca 31193 | 16 |
| 64 | 92 92 — | A THING OF THE PAST | Shirelles, Scepter 1220 | 3 |
| 65 | 68 64 67 | THE GIRL'S A DEVIL | Dukays, Nat 4001 | 11 |
| 66 | — — — | HURT | Timi Yuro, Liberty 55343 | 1 |
| 67 | 34 36 59 | RAININ' IN MY HEART | Slim Harpo, Excello 2194 | 8 |
| 68 | 72 91 — | MIGHTY GOOD LOVIN' | Miracles, Tamla 54044 | 3 |
| 69 | 71 73 99 | PEANUTS | Rick and the Keens, Smash 1705 | 4 |
| 70 | 83 — — | NAG | Halos, Seven Arts 709 | 2 |
| 71 | 44 34 43 | POMP AND CIRCUMSTANCE | Adrian Kimberly, Calliope 6501 | 5 |
| 72 | 84 — — | TOO MANY RULES | Connie Francis, MGM 13019 | 2 |
| 73 | — — — | I'M A TELLING YOU | Jerry Butler, Vee Jay 390 | 1 |
| 74 | — — — | RIGHT OR WRONG | Wanda Jackson, Capitol 4553 | 5 |
| 75 | 98 — — | I DON'T WANT TO TAKE A CHANCE | Mary Wells, Motown 1011 | 2 |
| 76 | 77 81 90 | TENDER YEARS | George Jones, Mercury 71804 | 4 |
| 77 | 81 87 88 | TAKE A FOOL'S ADVICE | Nat King Cole, Capitol 4582 | 5 |
| 78 | — — — | AS IF I DIDN'T KNOW | Adam Wade, Coed 553 | 2 |
| 79 | 82 — — | MY MEMORIES OF YOU | Donnie and the Dreamers, Whale 505 | 2 |
| 80 | 93 — — | WATER BOY | Don Shirley Trio, Cadence 1392 | 2 |
| 81 | 64 74 91 | GRANADA | Frank Sinatra, Reprise 20010 | 4 |
| 82 | 28 23 24 | IT KEEPS RAININ' | Fats Domino, Imperial 5753 | 11 |
| 83 | 86 97 — | BLACKLAND FARMER | Frankie Miller, Starday 424 | 3 |
| 84 | 40 25 26 | OLE BUTTERMILK SKY | Bill Black's Combo, Hi 2036 | 8 |
| 85 | 85 90 96 | LA DOLCE VITA | Ray Ellis, RCA Victor 7888 | 4 |
| 86 | 89 99 — | WHAT WOULD YOU DO | Jim Reeves, RCA Victor 7905 | 3 |
| 87 | 99 — — | DRIVIN' HOME | Duane Eddy, Jamie 1195 | 2 |
| 88 | 96 — — | STARLIGHT, STARBRIGHT | Linda Scott, Canadian-American 127 | 2 |
| 89 | 95 — — | IF | Paragons, Tap 101 | 2 |
| 90 | — — — | I NEVER KNEW | Clyde McPhatter, Mercury 71841 | 1 |
| 91 | — 96 100 | THE GUNS OF NAVARONE | Joe Reisman, Landa 674 | 3 |
| 92 | — — — | TEARS ON MY PILLOW | McGuire Sisters, Coral 62276 | 1 |
| 93 | 94 — — | BIG RIVER, BIG MAN | Claude King, Columbia 42043 | 2 |
| 94 | 53 60 77 | TE-TA-TE-TA-TA | Ernie K-Doe, Minit 627 | 5 |
| 95 | 97 — — | MY CLAIRE DE LUNE | Steve Lawrence, United Artists 335 | 2 |
| 96 | 100 — — | NOW YOU KNOW | Little Willie John, King 5516 | 2 |
| 97 | — — — | I JUST DON'T UNDERSTAND | Ann-Margret, RCA Victor 7894 | 1 |
| 98 | — — — | MR. HAPPINESS | Johnny Maestro, Coed 552 | 1 |
| 99 | — — — | HERE IN MY HEART | Al Martino, Capitol 4593 | 1 |
| 100 | — — — | ALL I HAVE TO DO IS DREAM | Everly Brothers, Cadence 1348 | 18 |

## BUBBLING UNDER THE HOT 100

1. IT'S GONNA WORK OUT FINE ............ Ike & Tina Turner, Sue 749
2. IN TIME ............ Steve Lawrence, United Artists 335
3. STARLIGHT ............ Preludes Five, Pik 231
4. THEME FROM COME SEPTEMBER ...... Dick Jacobs, Coral 62275
5. DEDICATED (TO THE SONGS I LOVE) .. Three Friends, Imperial 5763
6. THE BELLS ARE RINGING ............ Van Dykes, Deluxe 6193
7. WHEN WE GET MARRIED ............ Dreamlovers, Heritage 102
8. BACK BEAT NO. 1 ............ Rondells, Amy 825
9. DON'T FORGET I LOVE YOU ............ Butanes, Enrica 1007
10. RUN, RUN, RUN ............ Ronny Douglas, Everest 19413
11. I'LL NEVER SMILE AGAIN ............ Platters, Mercury 71847
12. A LITTLE BIT OF SOAP ............ Jarmels, Laurie 3098
13. I'M SO HAPPY (TRA LA LA) ............ Ducanes, Goldisc 3024
14. ST. LOUIS BLUES ............ Cousins, Goldisc 3024
15. TEARDROPS IN MY HEART ............ Joe Barry, Smash 1710
16. S. O. S. (I LOVE YOU) ............ Ronnie Hayden, Camay 1001
17. DOES YOUR CHEWING GUM LOSE ITS FLAVOR (ON THE BEDPOST OVER NIGHT) ....Lonnie Donegan, Dot 15911
18. TENNESSEE WALTZ ............ Don Robertson, RCA Victor 7909
19. SUMMER SOUVENIRS ............ Karl Hammel Jr., Arliss 1007
20. WHO PUT THE BOMP (IN THE BOMP, BOMP, BOMP) ............ Barry Mann, ABC Paramount ABC 10237

# Billboard HOT 100

**JULY 31, 1961**
**FOR WEEK ENDING AUGUST 6, 1961**

| This Week | Wk. Ago | 2 Wks. Ago | 3 Wks. Ago | Title | Artist, Label & Number | Weeks On Chart |
|---|---|---|---|---|---|---|
| 1 | 1 | 1 | 1 | TOSSIN' AND TURNIN' | Bobby Lewis, Beltone 1002 | 15 |
| 2 | 5 | 9 | 14 | I LIKE IT LIKE THAT | Chris Kenner, Instant 3229 | 10 |
| 3 | 2 | 2 | 2 | BOLL WEEVIL SONG | Brook Benton, Mercury 71820 | 12 |
| 4 | 8 | 10 | 13 | DUM DUM | Brenda Lee, Decca 31272 | 7 |
| 5 | 6 | 6 | 9 | HATS OFF TO LARRY | Del Shannon, Big Top 3075 | 9 |
| 6 | 3 | 3 | 3 | QUARTER TO THREE | Gary (U.S.) Bonds, LeGrand 1008 | 11 |
| 7 | 12 | 30 | 43 | LAST NIGHT | Mar-Keys, Satellite 107 | 5 |
| 8 | 9 | 14 | 20 | TOGETHER | Connie Francis, MGM 13019 | 6 |
| 9 | 10 | 15 | 27 | LET'S TWIST AGAIN | Chubby Checker, Parkway 824 | 7 |
| 10 | 4 | 5 | 8 | YELLOW BIRD | Arthur Lyman, Hi Fi 5024 | 10 |
| 11 | 11 | 8 | 11 | SAN ANTONIO ROSE | Floyd Cramer, RCA Victor 7893 | 9 |
| 12 | 7 | 4 | 4 | RAINDROPS | Dee Clark, Vee Jay 383 | 14 |
| 13 | 18 | 35 | 55 | WOODEN HEART (Muss I Denn) | Joe Dowell, Smash 1708 | 6 |
| 14 | 15 | 19 | 24 | NEVER ON SUNDAY | Chordettes, Cadence 1402 | 7 |
| 15 | 14 | 16 | 17 | PLEASE STAY | Drifters, Atlantic 2105 | 9 |
| 16 | 24 | 36 | 46 | PRETTY LITTLE ANGEL EYES | Curtis Lee, Dunes 2007 | 5 |
| 17 | 17 | 27 | 28 | CUPID | Sam Cooke, RCA Victor 7883 | 9 |
| 18 | 21 | 22 | 32 | MY KIND OF GIRL | Matt Monro, Warwick 636 | 10 |
| 19 | 28 | 39 | 57 | I'LL BE THERE | Damita Jo, Mercury 71840 | 5 |
| 20 | 20 | 29 | 31 | SACRED | Castells, Era 3048 | 10 |
| 21 | 13 | 7 | 6 | EVERY BEAT OF MY HEART | Pips, Vee Jay 386 | 12 |
| 22 | 16 | 12 | 7 | MOODY RIVER | Pat Boone, Dot 16209 | 14 |
| 23 | 41 | 69 | 100 | MICHAEL | Highwaymen, United Artists 258 | 4 |
| 24 | 35 | 57 | 83 | YOU DON'T KNOW WHAT YOU'VE GOT (Until You Lose It) | Ral Donner, Gone 5108 | 4 |
| 25 | 27 | 32 | 37 | THE FISH | Bobby Rydell, Cameo 192 | 5 |
| 26 | 26 | 33 | 41 | THE SWITCH-A-ROO | Hank Ballard and the Midnighters, King 5510 | 6 |
| 27 | 19 | 17 | 12 | TRAVELIN' MAN | Ricky Nelson, Imperial 5741 | 15 |
| 28 | 52 | — | — | SCHOOL IS OUT | Gary (U.S.) Bonds, LeGrand 1009 | 2 |
| 29 | 31 | 37 | 45 | THAT'S WHAT GIRLS ARE MADE FOR | Spinners, Tri-Phi 1001 | 6 |
| 30 | 36 | 49 | 66 | DON'T BET MONEY HONEY | Linda Scott, Canadian-American 127 | 5 |
| 31 | 38 | 54 | 63 | I'M GONNA KNOCK ON YOUR DOOR | Eddie Hodges, Cadence 1397 | 7 |
| 32 | 23 | 25 | 21 | HELLO MARY LOU | Ricky Nelson, Imperial 5741 | 14 |
| 33 | 37 | 51 | 44 | I FALL TO PIECES | Patsy Cline, Decca 31205 | 11 |
| 34 | 33 | 38 | 38 | SEA OF HEARTBREAK | Don Gibson, RCA Victor 7890 | 7 |
| 35 | 66 | — | — | HURT | Timi Yuro, Liberty 55343 | 2 |
| 36 | 56 | — | — | LET THE FOUR WINDS BLOW | Fats Domino, Imperial 5764 | 2 |
| 37 | 47 | 79 | 88 | RUNAROUND | Regents, Gee 1071 | 4 |
| 38 | 29 | 23 | 16 | STAND BY ME | Ben E. King, Atco 6194 | 13 |
| 39 | 25 | 31 | 33 | HEART AND SOUL | Jan and Dean, Challenge 9111 | 6 |
| 40 | 30 | 24 | 22 | RUNNING SCARED | Roy Orbison, Monument 438 | 17 |
| 41 | 45 | 50 | 61 | NO, NO, NO | Chanters, Deluxe 6191 | 7 |
| 42 | 50 | 73 | 79 | READY FOR YOUR LOVE | Shep and the Limelites, Hull 742 | 4 |
| 43 | 51 | 56 | 68 | A TEAR | Gene McDaniels, Liberty 55344 | 5 |
| 44 | 22 | 18 | 18 | TELL ME WHY | Belmonts, Sabrina 500 | 11 |
| 45 | 49 | 52 | 62 | QUITE A PARTY | Fireballs, Warwick 644 | 6 |
| 46 | 54 | 58 | 77 | MY TRUE STORY | Jive Five, Beltone 1006 | 5 |
| 47 | 48 | 42 | 49 | SHOULD I | String-A-Longs, Warwick 654 | 8 |
| 48 | 44 | 43 | 29 | YOU CAN'T SIT DOWN (Part II) | Phillip Upchurch Combo, Boyd 1026 | 7 |
| 49 | 32 | 21 | 19 | I'M COMIN' ON BACK TO YOU | Jackie Wilson, Brunswick 55216 | 8 |
| 50 | 53 | 62 | 50 | BETTER TELL HIM NO | Starlets, Pam 1003 | 15 |
| 51 | 55 | 67 | 75 | THE CHARLESTON | Ernie Fields, Rendezvous 150 | 7 |
| 52 | 62 | 66 | 78 | PRINCESS | Frank Gari, Crusade 1022 | 5 |
| 53 | 61 | 65 | 94 | ONE SUMMER NIGHT | Diamonds, Mercury 71831 | 5 |
| 54 | 60 | 87 | — | WHAT A SWEET THING THAT WAS | Shirelles, Scepter 1220 | 3 |
| 55 | 74 | — | — | RIGHT OR WRONG | Wanda Jackson, Capitol 4553 | 6 |
| 56 | 57 | 63 | 67 | HILLBILLY HEAVEN | Tex Ritter, Capitol 4567 | 5 |
| 57 | 59 | 61 | 69 | TIME WAS | Flamingos, End 1092 | 5 |
| 58 | 64 | 92 | 92 | A THING OF THE PAST | Shirelles, Scepter 1220 | 4 |
| 59 | 78 | — | — | AS IF I DIDN'T KNOW | Adam Wade, Coed 553 | 2 |
| 60 | 75 | 98 | — | I DON'T WANT TO TAKE A CHANCE | Mary Wells, Motown 1011 | 3 |
| 61 | 73 | — | — | I'M A-TELLING YOU | Jerry Butler, Vee Jay 390 | 2 |
| 62 | 68 | 72 | 91 | MIGHTY GOOD LOVIN' | Miracles, Tamla 54044 | 4 |
| 63 | 70 | 83 | — | NAG | Halos, Seven Arts 709 | 3 |
| 64 | 65 | 68 | 64 | THE GIRL'S A DEVIL | Dukays, Nat 4001 | 12 |
| 65 | 58 | 60 | 65 | BOBBY | Neil Scott, Portrait 102 | 8 |
| 66 | 46 | 46 | 47 | YOU'LL ANSWER TO ME | Patti Page, Mercury 71823 | 6 |
| 67 | 69 | 71 | 73 | PEANUTS | Rick and the Keens, Smash 1705 | 5 |
| 68 | 90 | — | — | I NEVER KNEW | Clyde McPhatter, Mercury 71841 | 2 |
| 69 | 95 | 97 | — | MY CLAIRE DE LUNE | Steve Lawrence, United Artists 335 | 3 |
| 70 | 34 | 11 | 10 | DANCE ON LITTLE GIRL | Paul Anka, ABC Paramount 10220 | 10 |
| 71 | 77 | 81 | 87 | TAKE A FOOL'S ADVICE | Nat King Cole, Capitol 4582 | 6 |
| 72 | — | — | — | AMOR | Ben E. King, Atco 6203 | 1 |
| 73 | 80 | 93 | — | WATER BOY | Don Shirley Trio, Cadence 1392 | 3 |
| 74 | 98 | — | — | MR. HAPPINESS | Johnny Maestro, Coed 552 | 2 |
| 75 | 86 | 89 | 99 | WHAT WOULD YOU DO | Jim Reeves, RCA Victor 7905 | 4 |
| 76 | — | — | — | IT'S GONNA WORK OUT FINE | Ike and Tina Turner, Sue 749 | 1 |
| 77 | 92 | — | — | TEARS ON MY PILLOW | McGuire Sisters, Coral 62276 | 2 |
| 78 | 97 | — | — | I JUST DON'T UNDERSTAND | Ann-Margret, RCA Victor 7894 | 2 |
| 79 | 79 | 82 | — | MY MEMORIES OF YOU | Donnie and the Dreamers, Whale 505 | 3 |
| 80 | 91 | 96 | 100 | THE GUNS OF NAVARONE | Joe Reisman, Landa 674 | 4 |
| 81 | 85 | 85 | 90 | LA DOLCE VITA | Ray Ellis, RCA Victor 7888 | 5 |
| 82 | 83 | 86 | 97 | BLACKLAND FARMER | Frankie Miller, Starday 424 | 4 |
| 83 | 93 | 94 | — | BIG RIVER, BIG MAN | Claude King, Columbia 42043 | 3 |
| 84 | 89 | 95 | — | IF | Paragons, Tap 101 | 3 |
| 85 | — | — | — | MISSING YOU | Ray Peterson, Dunes 2006 | 1 |
| 86 | — | — | — | TEARDROPS IN MY HEART | Joe Barry, Smash 1710 | 1 |
| 87 | — | — | — | I'LL NEVER SMILE AGAIN | Platters, Mercury 71847 | 1 |
| 88 | 99 | — | — | HERE IN MY HEART | Al Martino, Capitol 4593 | 2 |
| 89 | — | — | — | A LITTLE BIT OF SOAP | Jarmels, Laurie 3098 | 1 |
| 90 | — | — | — | THE MOUNTAIN'S HIGH | Dick and Deedee, Liberty 55350 | 1 |
| 91 | — | — | — | DEDICATED (TO THE SONGS I LOVE) | Three Friends, Imperial 5763 | 1 |
| 92 | — | — | — | RUN, RUN, RUN | Ronny Douglas, Everest 19413 | 1 |
| 93 | 96 | 100 | — | NOW YOU KNOW | Little Willie John, King 5516 | 3 |
| 94 | — | — | — | NOW AND FOREVER | Bert Kaempfert, Decca 31279 | 1 |
| 95 | — | — | — | TRANSISTOR SISTER | Freddy Cannon, Swan 4078 | 1 |
| 96 | 100 | — | — | ALL I HAVE TO DO IS DREAM | Everly Brothers, Cadence 1348 | 19 |
| 97 | — | — | — | WHEN WE GET MARRIED | Dreamlovers, Heritage 102 | 1 |
| 98 | — | — | — | DON'T FORGET I LOVE YOU | Butanes, Enrica 1007 | 1 |
| 99 | — | — | — | SUMMER SOUVENIRS | Karl Hammil Jr., Arliss 1007 | 1 |
| 100 | — | — | — | THE BELLS ARE RINGING | Van Dykes, Deluxe 6193 | 1 |

## BUBBLING UNDER THE HOT 100

1. STARLIGHT — Preludes Five, Pik 231
2. BACK BEAT NO. 1 — Rondells, Amy 825
3. SOLITAIRE (SINCE YOU'RE GONE) — Embers, Empress 101
4. THEME FROM COME SEPTEMBER — Dick Jacobs, Coral 62275
5. DON'T CRY NO MORE — Bobby (Blue) Bland, Duke 340
6. WHO PUT THE BOMP (IN THE BOMP, BOMP, BOMP) — Barry Mann, ABC Paramount 10237
7. LET ME BELONG TO YOU — Brian Hyland, ABC Paramount 10236
8. PRETTY, PRETTY GIRL — Time Tones, Atco 6201
9. I'M SO HAPPY (TRA LA LA) — Ducanes, Goldisc 3024
10. ST. LOUIS BLUES — Cousins, Parkway 823
11. I'VE GOT A LOT OF THINGS TO DO — Johnny Burnette, Liberty 55345
12. DOES YOUR CHEWING GUM LOSE ITS FLAVOR (ON THE BEDPOST OVER NIGHT) — Lonnie Donegan, Dot 15911
13. THEME FROM SILVER CITY — Ventures, Dolton 44
14. EVERY BREATH I TAKE — Gene Pitney, Musicor 1011
15. BLACKLAND FARMER — Wink Martindale, Dot 16243
16. WITHOUT YOU — Johnny Tillotson, Cadence 1404
17. LOVE AND WAR — Jerry Reed, Columbia 42047
18. LOOK IN MY EYES — Chantels, Carlton 555
19. BAND OF GOLD — Roomates, Valmor 10
20. JOHNNY WILLOW — Fred Darian, JAF 2023

## HOT 100 — A TO Z

All I Have to Do Is Dream 96
Amor 72
As If I Didn't Know 59
Bells Are Ringing, The 100
Better Tell Him No 50
Big River, Big Man 83
Blackland Farmer 82
Bobby 65
Boll Weevil Song 3
Charleston, The 51
Cupid 17
Dance on Little Girl 70
Dedicated (to the Songs I Love) 91
Don't Bet Money Honey 30
Don't Forget I Love You 98
Dum Dum 4
Every Beat of My Heart 21
Fish, The 25
Girl's a Devil, The 64
Guns of Navarone, The 80
Hats Off to Larry 5
Heart and Soul 39
Hello Mary Lou 32
Here in My Heart 88
Hillbilly Heaven 56
Hurt 35
I Don't Want to Take a Chance 60
I Fall to Pieces 33
I Never Knew 68
I Just Don't Understand 78
I Like It Like That 2
I'll Be There 19
I'll Never Smile Again 87
I'm A-Telling You 61
I'm Comin' on Back to You 49
I'm Gonna Knock on Your Door 31
It's Gonna Work Out Fine 76
La Dolce Vita 81
Last Night 7
Let the Four Winds Blow 36
Let's Twist Again 9
Little Bit of Soap 89
Michael 23
Mighty Good Lovin' 62
Missing You 85
Moody River 22
Mountain's High, The 90
Mr. Happiness 74
My Claire De Lune 69
My Kind of Girl 18
My Memories of You 79
My True Story 46
Nag 63
Never on Sunday 14
No, No, No 41
Now and Forever 94
Now You Know 93
One Summer Night 53
Peanuts 67
Please Stay 15
Pretty Little Angel Eyes 16
Princess 52
Quarter to Three 6
Quite a Party 45
Raindrops 12
Ready for Your Love 42
Right or Wrong 55
Run, Run, Run 92
Runaround 37
Running Scared 40
Sacred 20
San Antonio Rose 11
School Is Out 28
Sea of Heartbreak 34
Should I 47
Stand By Me 38
Summer Souvenirs 99
Switch-A-Roo, The 26
Take a Fool's Advice 71
Tear, A 43
Teardrops in My Heart 86
Tears on My Pillow 77
Tell Me Why 44
That's What Girls Are Made For 29
Thing of the Past, A 58
Time Was 57
Together 8
Tossin' and Turnin' 1
Transistor Sister 95
Travelin' Man 27
Water Boy 73
What a Sweet Thing That Was 54
What Would You Do 75
When We Get Married 97
Wooden Heart 13
Yellow Bird 10
You Can't Sit Down (Part II) 48
You Don't Know What You've Got 24
You'll Answer to Me 66

# BILLBOARD HOT 100

**AUGUST 7, 1961**
**FOR WEEK ENDING AUGUST 13, 1961**

★ STAR PERFORMERS—Selections registering greatest upward progress this week.
S Indicates that 45 r.p.m. stereo single version is available.
△ Indicates that 33⅓ r.p.m. mono single version is available.
Ⓢ Indicates that 33⅓ r.p.m. stereo single version is available.

| This Week | Wk. Ago | 2 Wks. Ago | 3 Wks. Ago | TITLE Artist, Label & Number | Weeks On Chart |
|---|---|---|---|---|---|
| 1 | 1 | 1 | 1 | TOSSIN' AND TURNIN' — Bobby Lewis, Beltone 1002 | 16 |
| 2 | 2 | 5 | 9 | I LIKE IT LIKE THAT — Chris Kenner, Instant 3229 | 11 |
| 3 | 7 | 12 | 30 | LAST NIGHT — Mar-Keys, Satellite 107 | 6 |
| 4 | 4 | 8 | 10 | DUM DUM — Brenda Lee, Decca 31272 | 8 |
| 5 | 5 | 6 | 6 | HATS OFF TO LARRY — Del Shannon, Big Top 3075 | 10 |
| 6 | 8 | 9 | 14 | TOGETHER — Connie Francis, MGM 13019 | 7 |
| ★7 | 16 | 24 | 36 | PRETTY LITTLE ANGEL EYES — Curtis Lee, Dunes 2007 | 6 |
| 8 | 9 | 10 | 15 | LET'S TWIST AGAIN — Chubby Checker, Parkway 824 | 8 |
| 9 | 13 | 18 | 35 | WOODEN HEART (Muss I Denn) — Joe Dowell, Smash 1708 | 7 |
| 10 | 23 | 41 | 69 | MICHAEL — Highwaymen, United Artists 258 | 5 |
| 11 | 3 | 2 | 2 | BOLL WEEVIL SONG — Brook Benton, Mercury 71820 | 13 |
| 12 | 6 | 3 | 3 | QUARTER TO THREE — Gary (U.S.) Bonds, LeGrand 1008 | 12 |
| 13 | 14 | 15 | 19 | NEVER ON SUNDAY — Chordettes, Cadence 1402 | 8 |
| ★14 | 19 | 28 | 39 | I'LL BE THERE — Damita Jo, Mercury 71840 | 6 |
| ★15 | 24 | 35 | 57 | YOU DON'T KNOW WHAT YOU'VE GOT (Until You Lose It) — Ral Donner, Gone 5108 | 5 |
| 16 | 28 | 52 | — | SCHOOL IS OUT — Gary (U.S.) Bonds, LeGrand 1009 | 3 |
| 17 | 17 | 17 | 27 | CUPID — Sam Cooke, RCA Victor 7883 △ | 10 |
| 18 | 18 | 21 | 22 | MY KIND OF GIRL — Matt Monro, Warwick 636 | 11 |
| 19 | 11 | 11 | 8 | SAN ANTONIO ROSE — Floyd Cramer, RCA Victor 7893 △ | 10 |
| 20 | 35 | 66 | — | HURT — Timi Yuro, Liberty 55343 | 3 |
| 21 | 10 | 4 | 5 | YELLOW BIRD — Arthur Lyman, Hi Fi 5024 | 11 |
| 22 | 36 | 56 | — | LET THE FOUR WINDS BLOW — Fats Domino, Imperial 5764 | 3 |
| 23 | 15 | 14 | 16 | PLEASE STAY — Drifters, Atlantic 2105 | 10 |
| 24 | 20 | 20 | 29 | SACRED — Castells, Era 3048 | 11 |
| 25 | 30 | 36 | 49 | DON'T BET MONEY HONEY — Linda Scott, Canadian-American 127 | 6 |
| 26 | 31 | 38 | 54 | I'M GONNA KNOCK ON YOUR DOOR — Eddie Hodges, Cadence 1397 | 8 |
| 27 | 29 | 31 | 37 | THAT'S WHAT GIRLS ARE MADE FOR — Spinners, Tri-Phi 1001 | 7 |
| 28 | 33 | 37 | 51 | I FALL TO PIECES — Patsy Cline, Decca 31205 | 12 |
| 29 | 37 | 47 | 79 | RUNAROUND — Regents, Gee 1071 | 5 |
| 30 | 25 | 27 | 32 | THE FISH — Bobby Rydell, Cameo 192 | 6 |
| 31 | 12 | 7 | 4 | RAINDROPS — Dee Clark, Vee Jay 383 | 15 |
| ★32 | 59 | 78 | — | AS IF I DIDN'T KNOW — Adam Wade, Coed 553 | 3 |
| ★33 | 45 | 49 | 52 | QUITE A PARTY — Fireballs, Warwick 644 | 7 |
| ★34 | 61 | 73 | — | I'M A-TELLING YOU — Jerry Butler, Vee Jay 390 | 3 |
| 35 | 26 | 26 | 33 | THE SWITCH-A-ROO — Hank Ballard and the Midnighters, King 5510 | 7 |
| 36 | 22 | 16 | 12 | MOODY RIVER — Pat Boone, Dot 16209 | 15 |
| 37 | 21 | 13 | 7 | EVERY BEAT OF MY HEART — Pips, Vee Jay 386 | 13 |
| 38 | 27 | 19 | 17 | TRAVELIN' MAN — Ricky Nelson, Imperial 5741 | 16 |
| 39 | 43 | 51 | 56 | A TEAR — Gene McDaniels, Liberty 55344 | 6 |
| 40 | 53 | 61 | 65 | ONE SUMMER NIGHT — Diamonds, Mercury 71831 | 6 |
| 41 | 46 | 54 | 58 | MY TRUE STORY — Jive Five, Beltone 1006 | 6 |
| 42 | 52 | 62 | 66 | PRINCESS — Frank Gari, Crusade 1022 | 6 |
| 43 | 34 | 33 | 38 | SEA OF HEARTBREAK — Don Gibson, RCA Victor 7890 △ | 8 |
| 44 | 56 | 57 | 63 | HILLBILLY HEAVEN — Tex Ritter, Capitol 4567 | 6 |
| 45 | 57 | 59 | 61 | TIME WAS — Flamingos, End 1092 | 6 |
| 46 | 55 | 74 | — | RIGHT OR WRONG — Wanda Jackson, Capitol 4553 | 7 |
| 47 | 50 | 53 | 62 | BETTER TELL HIM NO — Starlets, Pam 1003 | 16 |
| 48 | 51 | 55 | 67 | THE CHARLESTON — Ernie Fields, Rendezvous 150 | 8 |
| 49 | 32 | 23 | 25 | HELLO MARY LOU — Ricky Nelson, Imperial 5741 | 15 |
| 50 | 41 | 45 | 50 | NO, NO, NO — Chanters, Deluxe 6191 | 8 |
| 51 | 60 | 75 | 98 | I DON'T WANT TO TAKE A CHANCE — Mary Wells, Motown 1011 | 4 |
| 52 | 58 | 64 | 92 | A THING OF THE PAST — Shirelles, Scepter 1220 | 5 |
| 53 | 62 | 68 | 72 | MIGHTY GOOD LOVIN' — Miracles, Tamla 54044 | 5 |
| 54 | 54 | 60 | 87 | WHAT A SWEET THING THAT WAS — Shirelles, Scepter 1220 | 4 |
| 55 | 38 | 29 | 23 | STAND BY ME — Ben E. King, Atco 6194 | 14 |
| 56 | 47 | 48 | 42 | SHOULD I — String-A-Longs, Warwick 654 | 9 |
| 57 | 68 | 90 | — | I NEVER KNEW — Clyde McPhatter, Mercury 71841 | 3 |
| 58 | 72 | — | — | AMOR — Ben E. King, Atco 6203 | 2 |
| 59 | 48 | 44 | 43 | YOU CAN'T SIT DOWN (Part II) — Phillip Upchurch Combo, Boyd 1026 | 8 |
| 60 | 74 | 98 | — | MR. HAPPINESS — Johnny Maestro, Coed 552 | 3 |
| 61 | 63 | 70 | 83 | NAG — Halos, Seven Arts 709 | 4 |
| 62 | 78 | 97 | — | I JUST DON'T UNDERSTAND — Ann-Margret, RCA Victor 7894 | 3 |
| 63 | 42 | 50 | 73 | READY FOR YOUR LOVE — Shep and the Limelites, Hull 742 | 5 |
| 64 | 67 | 69 | 71 | PEANUTS — Rick and the Keens, Smash 1705 | 6 |
| 65 | 39 | 25 | 31 | HEART AND SOUL — Jan and Dean, Challenge 9111 | 7 |
| 66 | — | — | — | WHO PUT THE BOMP (In the Bomp, Bomp, Bomp) — Barry Mann, ABC-Paramount 10237 | 1 |
| 67 | — | — | — | DON'T CRY BABY — Etta James, Argo 5393 | 1 |
| 68 | 69 | 95 | 97 | MY CLAIRE DE LUNE — Steve Lawrence, United Artists 335 | 4 |
| 69 | 64 | 65 | 68 | THE GIRL'S A DEVIL — Dukays, Nat 4001 | 13 |
| 70 | 77 | 92 | — | TEARS ON MY PILLOW — McGuire Sisters, Coral 62276 | 3 |
| 71 | — | — | — | CANDY MAN — Roy Orbison, Monument 447 | 1 |
| 72 | 73 | 80 | 93 | WATER BOY — Don Shirley Trio, Cadence 1392 | 4 |
| 73 | 75 | 86 | 89 | WHAT WOULD YOU DO — Jim Reeves, RCA Victor 7905 △ | 5 |
| 74 | 76 | — | — | IT'S GONNA WORK OUT FINE — Ike and Tina Turner, Sue 749 | 2 |
| 75 | — | — | — | DOES YOUR CHEWING GUM LOSE ITS FLAVOR (On the Bedpost Over Night) — Lonnie Donegan, Dot 15911 | 1 |
| 76 | — | — | — | LET ME BELONG TO YOU — Brian Hyland, ABC-Paramount 10236 | 1 |
| 77 | 71 | 77 | 81 | TAKE A FOOL'S ADVICE — Nat King Cole, Capitol 4582 | 7 |
| 78 | — | — | — | WITHOUT YOU — Johnny Tillotson, Cadence 1404 | 1 |
| 79 | 80 | 91 | — | THE GUNS OF NAVARONE — Joe Reisman, Landa 674 | 5 |
| 80 | 86 | — | — | TEARDROPS IN MY HEART — Joe Barry, Smash 1710 | 2 |
| 81 | 92 | — | — | RUN, RUN, RUN — Ronny Douglas, Everest 19413 | 2 |
| 82 | 94 | — | — | NOW AND FOREVER — Bert Kaempfert, Decca 31279 | 2 |
| 83 | 84 | 89 | 95 | IF — Paragons, Tap 101 | 4 |
| 84 | 87 | — | — | I'LL NEVER SMILE AGAIN — Platters, Mercury 71847 | 2 |
| 85 | 90 | — | — | THE MOUNTAIN'S HIGH — Dick and Deedee, Liberty 55350 | 2 |
| 86 | 88 | 99 | — | HERE IN MY HEART — Al Martino, Capitol 4593 | 3 |
| ★87 | — | — | — | TAKE GOOD CARE OF MY BABY — Bobby Vee, Liberty 55354 | 1 |
| 88 | — | — | — | LONELY STREET — Clarence Henry, Argo 5395 | 1 |
| 89 | — | — | — | DON'T CRY NO MORE — Bobby (Blue) Bland, Duke 340 | 1 |
| 90 | — | — | — | HULLY GULLY AGAIN — Little Caesar & the Romans, Del-Fi 4164 | 1 |
| 91 | 97 | — | — | WHEN WE GET MARRIED — Dreamlovers, Heritage 102 | 2 |
| 92 | 99 | — | — | SUMMER SOUVENIRS — Karl Hammil Jr., Arliss 1007 | 2 |
| 93 | 85 | — | — | MISSING YOU — Ray Peterson, Dunes 2006 | 2 |
| 94 | 95 | — | — | TRANSISTOR SISTER — Freddy Cannon, Swan 4078 | 2 |
| 95 | — | — | — | EVERY BREATH I TAKE — Gene Pitney, Musicor 1011 | 1 |
| 96 | — | — | — | WELL-A, WELL-A — Shirley & Lee, Warwick 664 | 1 |
| 97 | — | — | — | LOVEDROPS — Mickey & Sylvia, Willow 23000 | 1 |
| 98 | — | — | — | SAN-HO-ZAY — Freddy King, Federal 12428 | 1 |
| 99 | 100 | — | — | THE BELLS ARE RINGING — Van Dykes, Deluxe 6193 | 2 |
| 100 | — | — | — | MY HEART'S ON FIRE — Billy Bland, Old Town 1105 | 1 |

## BUBBLING UNDER THE HOT 100

1. A LITTLE BIT OF SOAP ........ Jarmels, Laurie 3098
2. LOVER'S ISLAND ........ Blue Jays, Milestone 2008
3. BLESS YOU ........ Tony Orlando, Epic 9452
4. STARLIGHT ........ Preludes Five, Pik 231
5. DON'T FORGET I LOVE YOU ........ Butanes, Enrica 1007
6. PRETTY PRETTY GIRL ........ Tims Teens, Atco 6201
7. THEME FROM SILVER CITY ........ Ventures, Dolton 44
8. I'LL NEVER SMILE AGAIN ........ Wanderers, Cub 9094
9. I'VE GOT A LOT OF THINGS TO DO ........ Johnny Burnette, Liberty 55345
10. MEXICO ........ Bob Moore, Monument 446
11. JOHNNY WILLOW ........ Fred Darian, JAF 2023
12. TASTE OF A TEAR ........ Johnny & the Tokens, Warwick 658
13. BLACKLAND FARMER ........ Wink Martindale, Dot 16243
14. DEDICATED (TO THE SONGS I LOVE) ........ Three Friends, Imperial 5763
15. STICK SHIFT ........ Duals, Sue 745
16. GIRLS, GIRLS, GIRLS ........ Coasters, Atco 6204
17. MUSIC, MUSIC, MUSIC ........ Sensations, Argo 5391
18. MAGIC MOON ........ Rays, XYZ 607
19. LOOK IN MY EYES ........ Chantels, Carlton 555
20. BLACKLAND FARMER ........ Frankie Miller, Starday 424

## HOT 100 — A TO Z

| Title | # | Title | # |
|---|---|---|---|
| Amor | 58 | My Kind of Girl | 18 |
| As If I Didn't Know | 32 | My True Story | 41 |
| Bells Are Ringing, The | 99 | Nag | 61 |
| Better Tell Him No | 47 | Never on Sunday | 13 |
| Boll Weevil Song | 11 | No, No, No | 50 |
| Candy Man | 71 | Now and Forever | 82 |
| Charleston, The | 48 | One Summer Night | 40 |
| Cupid | 17 | Peanuts | 64 |
| Does Your Chewing Gum Lose Its Flavor | 75 | Please Stay | 23 |
| Don't Bet Money Honey | 25 | Pretty Little Angel Eyes | 7 |
| Don't Cry Baby | 67 | Princess | 42 |
| Don't Cry No More | 89 | Quarter to Three | 12 |
| Dum Dum | 4 | Quite a Party | 33 |
| Every Beat of My Heart | 37 | Raindrops | 31 |
| Every Breath I Take | 95 | Ready for Your Love | 63 |
| Fish, The | 30 | Right or Wrong | 46 |
| Girl's a Devil | 69 | Run, Run, Run | 81 |
| Guns of Navarone, The | 79 | Runaround | 29 |
| Hats Off to Larry | 5 | San Antonio Rose | 19 |
| Heart and Soul | 65 | San-Ho-Zay | 98 |
| Hello Mary Lou | 49 | School Is Out | 16 |
| Here in My Heart | 86 | Sea of Heartbreak | 43 |
| Hillbilly Heaven | 44 | Should I | 56 |
| Hully Gully Again | 90 | Stand By Me | 55 |
| Hurt | 20 | Summer Souvenirs | 92 |
| I Don't Want to Take a Chance | 51 | Switch-A-Roo, The | 35 |
| I Fall to Pieces | 28 | Take a Fool's Advice | 77 |
| I Never Knew | 57 | Take Good Care of My Baby | 87 |
| I Like It Like That | 2 | Tear, A | 39 |
| I Just Don't Understand | 62 | Teardrops in My Heart | 80 |
| If | 83 | Tears on My Pillow | 70 |
| I'll Be There | 14 | That's What Girls Are Made For | 27 |
| I'll Never Smile Again | 84 | Thing of the Past, A | 52 |
| I'm A-Telling You | 34 | Time Was | 45 |
| I'm Gonna Knock On Your Door | 26 | Together | 6 |
| It's Gonna Work Out Fine | 74 | Tossin' and Turnin' | 1 |
| Last Night | 3 | Transistor Sister | 94 |
| Let Me Belong to You | 76 | Travelin' Man | 38 |
| Let's Twist Again | 8 | Well-A, Well-A | 96 |
| Let the Four Winds Blow | 22 | What a Sweet Thing That Was | 54 |
| Lonely Street | 88 | What Would You Do | 73 |
| Lovedrops | 97 | When We Get Married | 91 |
| Michael | 10 | Who Put the Bomp | 66 |
| Mighty Good Lovin' | 53 | Without You | 78 |
| Missing You | 93 | Wooden Heart | 9 |
| Moody River | 36 | Yellow Bird | 21 |
| Mountain's High, The | 85 | You Can't Sit Down (Part II) | 59 |
| Mr. Happiness | 60 | You Don't Know What You've Got | 15 |
| My Claire De Lune | 68 | | |
| My Heart's on Fire | 100 | | |

# BILLBOARD HOT 100

**AUGUST 14, 1961**

FOR WEEK ENDING AUGUST 20, 1961

STAR PERFORMERS—Selections registering greatest upward progress this week.

S — Indicates that 45 r.p.m. stereo single version is available.
△ — Indicates that 33⅓ r.p.m. mono single version is available.
S — Indicates that 33⅓ r.p.m. stereo single version is available.

| This Week | Wk. Ago | 2 Wks. Ago | 3 Wks. Ago | Title | Artist, Label & Number | Weeks On Chart |
|---|---|---|---|---|---|---|
| 1 | 1 | 1 | 1 | TOSSIN' AND TURNIN' | Bobby Lewis, Beltone 1002 | 17 |
| 2 | 2 | 2 | 5 | I LIKE IT LIKE THAT | Chris Kenner, Instant 3229 | 12 |
| 3 | 3 | 7 | 12 | LAST NIGHT | Mar-Keys, Satellite 107 | 7 |
| 4 | 4 | 4 | 8 | DUM DUM | Brenda Lee, Decca 31272 | 9 |
| 5 | 9 | 13 | 18 | WOODEN HEART (Muss I Denn) | Joe Dowell, Smash 1708 | 8 |
| 6 | 10 | 23 | 41 | MICHAEL | Highwaymen, United Artists 258 | 6 |
| 7 | 7 | 16 | 24 | PRETTY LITTLE ANGEL EYES | Curtis Lee, Dunes 2007 | 7 |
| 8 | 8 | 9 | 10 | LET'S TWIST AGAIN | Chubby Checker, Parkway 824 | 9 |
| 9 | 6 | 8 | 9 | TOGETHER | Connie Francis, MGM 13019 | 8 |
| 10 | 16 | 28 | 52 | SCHOOL IS OUT | Gary (U.S.) Bonds, LeGrand 1009 | 4 |
| 11 | 15 | 24 | 35 | YOU DON'T KNOW WHAT YOU'VE GOT (Until You Lose It) | Ral Donner, Gone 5108 | 6 |
| 12 | 14 | 19 | 28 | I'LL BE THERE | Damita Jo, Mercury 71840 | 7 |
| 13 | 13 | 14 | 15 | NEVER ON SUNDAY | Chordettes, Cadence 1402 | 9 |
| 14 | 5 | 5 | 6 | HATS OFF TO LARRY | Del Shannon, Big Top 3075 | 11 |
| 15 | 20 | 35 | 66 | HURT | Timi Yuro, Liberty 55343 | 4 |
| 16 | 25 | 30 | 36 | DON'T BET MONEY HONEY | Linda Scott, Canadian-American 127 | 7 |
| 17 | 22 | 36 | 56 | LET THE FOUR WINDS BLOW | Fats Domino, Imperial 5764 | 4 |
| 18 | 18 | 18 | 21 | MY KIND OF GIRL | Matt Monro, Warwick 636 | 12 |
| 19 | 12 | 6 | 3 | QUARTER TO THREE | Gary (U.S.) Bonds, LeGrand 1008 | 13 |
| 20 | 11 | 3 | 2 | BOLL WEEVIL SONG | Brook Benton, Mercury 71820 | 14 |
| 21 | 32 | 59 | 72 | AS IF I DIDN'T KNOW | Adam Wade, Coed 553 | 4 |
| 22 | 26 | 31 | 38 | I'M GONNA KNOCK ON YOUR DOOR | Eddie Hodges, Cadence 1397 | 9 |
| 23 | 17 | 17 | 17 | CUPID | Sam Cooke, RCA Victor 7883 | 11 |
| 24 | 28 | 33 | 37 | I FALL TO PIECES | Patsy Cline, Decca 31205 | 13 |
| 25 | 40 | 53 | 61 | ONE SUMMER NIGHT | Diamonds, Mercury 71831 | 7 |
| 26 | 34 | 61 | 73 | I'M A-TELLING YOU | Jerry Butler, Vee Jay 390 | 4 |
| 27 | 33 | 45 | 49 | QUITE A PARTY | Fireballs, Warwick 644 | 8 |
| 28 | 29 | 37 | 47 | RUNAROUND | Regents, Gee 1071 | 6 |
| 29 | 19 | 11 | 11 | SAN ANTONIO ROSE | Floyd Cramer, RCA Victor 7893 | 11 |
| 30 | 23 | 15 | 14 | PLEASE STAY | Drifters, Atlantic 2105 | 11 |
| 31 | 39 | 43 | 51 | A TEAR | Gene McDaniels, Liberty 55344 | 7 |
| 32 | 41 | 46 | 54 | MY TRUE STORY | Jive Five, Beltone 1006 | 7 |
| 33 | 44 | 56 | 57 | HILLBILLY HEAVEN | Tex Ritter, Capitol 4567 | 7 |
| 34 | 21 | 10 | 4 | YELLOW BIRD | Arthur Lyman, Hi Fi 5024 | 12 |
| 35 | 24 | 20 | 20 | SACRED | Castells, Era 3048 | 12 |
| 36 | 42 | 52 | 62 | PRINCESS | Frank Gari, Crusade 1022 | 7 |
| 37 | 27 | 29 | 31 | THAT'S WHAT GIRLS ARE MADE FOR | Spinners, Tri-Phi 1001 | 8 |
| 38 | 46 | 55 | 74 | RIGHT OR WRONG | Wanda Jackson, Capitol 4553 | 8 |
| 39 | 43 | 34 | 33 | SEA OF HEARTBREAK | Don Gibson, RCA Victor 7890 | 9 |
| 40 | 75 | — | — | DOES YOUR CHEWING GUM LOSE ITS FLAVOR (On the Bedpost Over Night) | Lonnie Donegan, Dot 15911 | 2 |
| 41 | 87 | — | — | TAKE GOOD CARE OF MY BABY | Bobby Vee, Liberty 55354 | 2 |
| 42 | 51 | 60 | 75 | I DON'T WANT TO TAKE A CHANCE | Mary Wells, Motown 1011 | 5 |
| 43 | 62 | 78 | 97 | I JUST DON'T UNDERSTAND | Ann-Margret, RCA Victor 7894 | 4 |
| 44 | 66 | — | — | WHO PUT THE BOMP (In the Bomp, Bomp, Bomp) | Barry Mann, ABC-Paramount 10237 | 3 |
| 45 | 45 | 57 | 59 | TIME WAS | Flamingos, End 1092 | 7 |
| 46 | 52 | 58 | 64 | A THING OF THE PAST | Shirelles, Scepter 1220 | 6 |
| 47 | 48 | 51 | 55 | THE CHARLESTON | Ernie Fields, Rendezvous 150 | 6 |
| 48 | 58 | 72 | — | AMOR | Ben E. King, Atco 6203 | 3 |
| 49 | 84 | 87 | — | I'LL NEVER SMILE AGAIN | Platters, Mercury 71847 | 3 |
| 50 | 31 | 12 | 7 | RAINDROPS | Dee Clark, Vee Jay 383 | 16 |
| 51 | 53 | 62 | 68 | MIGHTY GOOD LOVIN' | Miracles, Tamla 54044 | 6 |
| 52 | 67 | — | — | DON'T CRY BABY | Etta James, Argo 5393 | 2 |
| 53 | — | — | 83 | STARLIGHT, STARBRIGHT | Linda Scott, Canadian-American 127 | 3 |
| 54 | 61 | 63 | 70 | NAG | Halos, Seven Arts 709 | 5 |
| 55 | 50 | 41 | 45 | NO, NO, NO | Chanters, Deluxe 6191 | 9 |
| 56 | 57 | 68 | 90 | I NEVER KNEW | Clyde McPhatter, Mercury 71841 | 4 |
| 57 | 60 | 74 | 98 | MR. HAPPINESS | Johnny Maestro, Coed 552 | 4 |
| 58 | 30 | 25 | 27 | THE FISH | Bobby Rydell, Cameo 192 | 7 |
| 59 | 70 | 77 | 92 | TEARS ON MY PILLOW | McGuire Sisters, Coral 62276 | 4 |
| 60 | 64 | 67 | 69 | PEANUTS | Rick and the Keens, Smash 1705 | 7 |
| 61 | 78 | — | — | WITHOUT YOU | Johnny Tillotson, Cadence 1404 | 2 |
| 62 | 94 | 95 | — | TRANSISTOR SISTER | Freddy Cannon, Swan 4078 | 3 |
| 63 | 93 | 85 | — | MISSING YOU | Ray Peterson, Dunes 2006 | 3 |
| 64 | 74 | 76 | — | IT'S GONNA WORK OUT FINE | Ike and Tina Turner, Sue 749 | 3 |
| 65 | 76 | — | — | LET ME BELONG TO YOU | Brian Hyland, ABC-Paramount 10236 | 2 |
| 66 | 72 | 73 | 80 | WATER BOY | Don Shirley Trio, Cadence 1392 | 5 |
| 67 | — | — | 90 | A LITTLE BIT OF SOAP | Jarmels, Laurie 3098 | 2 |
| 68 | 85 | 90 | — | THE MOUNTAIN'S HIGH | Dick and Deedee, Liberty 55350 | 3 |
| 69 | 71 | — | — | CANDY MAN | Roy Orbison, Monument 447 | 2 |
| 70 | 54 | 54 | 60 | WHAT A SWEET THING THAT WAS | Shirelles, Scepter 1220 | 5 |
| 71 | — | — | — | CRYIN' | Roy Orbison, Monument 447 | 1 |
| 72 | 88 | — | — | LONELY STREET | Clarence Henry, Argo 5395 | 2 |
| 73 | — | — | — | LOVER'S ISLAND | Bluejays, Milestone 2008 | 1 |
| 74 | 79 | 80 | 91 | THE GUNS OF NAVARONE | Joe Reisman, Landa 674 | 6 |
| 75 | 81 | 92 | — | RUN, RUN, RUN | Ronny Douglas, Everest 19413 | 3 |
| 76 | 91 | 97 | — | WHEN WE GET MARRIED | Dreamlovers, Heritage 102 | 3 |
| 77 | 80 | 86 | — | TEARDROPS IN MY HEART | Joe Barry, Smash 1710 | 3 |
| 78 | 68 | 69 | 95 | MY CLAIRE DE LUNE | Steve Lawrence, United Artists 335 | 4 |
| 79 | 90 | — | — | HULLY GULLY AGAIN | Little Caesar and the Romans, Del-Fi 4164 | 2 |
| 80 | 89 | — | — | DON'T CRY NO MORE | Bobby (Blue) Bland, Duke 340 | 2 |
| 81 | 82 | 94 | — | NOW AND FOREVER | Bert Kaempfert, Decca 31279 | 3 |
| 82 | 83 | 84 | 89 | IF | Paragons, Tap 101 | 5 |
| 83 | — | — | — | BACK BEAT NO. 1 | Rondells, Amy 825 | 1 |
| 84 | 98 | — | — | SAN-HO-ZAY | Freddy King, Federal 12428 | 2 |
| 85 | 92 | 99 | — | SUMMER SOUVENIRS | Karl Hammil Jr., Arliss 1007 | 3 |
| 86 | 86 | 88 | 99 | HERE IN MY HEART | Al Martino, Capitol 4593 | 4 |
| 87 | — | — | — | BLESS YOU | Tony Orlando, Epic 9452 | 1 |
| 88 | — | — | — | MAGIC MOON | Rays, XYZ 607 | 1 |
| 89 | — | — | 91 | DEDICATED (To the Songs I Love) | Three Friends, Imperial 5763 | 2 |
| 90 | — | — | 95 | EVERY BREATH I TAKE | Gene Pitney, Musicor 1011 | 2 |
| 91 | — | — | — | MEXICO | Bob Moore, Monument 446 | 1 |
| 92 | — | — | — | ROLL OVER BEETHOVEN | Velaires, Jamie 1198 | 1 |
| 93 | 96 | — | — | WELL-A, WELL-A | Shirley & Lee, Warwick 664 | 2 |
| 94 | — | — | — | IN TIME | Steve Lawrence, United Artists 335 | 1 |
| 95 | — | — | — | MUSIC, MUSIC, MUSIC | Sensations, Argo 5391 | 1 |
| 96 | — | — | — | STARLIGHT | Preludes Five, Pik 231 | 1 |
| 97 | 100 | — | — | MY HEART'S ON FIRE | Billy Bland, Old Town 1105 | 2 |
| 98 | — | — | — | MORE MONEY FOR YOU AND ME | Four Preps, Capitol 4599 | 1 |
| 99 | — | — | — | GIRLS, GIRLS, GIRLS | Coasters, Atco 6404 | 1 |
| 100 | — | — | — | PITTER PATTER | Four Sportsmen, Sunnybrook 4 | 1 |

## BUBBLING UNDER THE HOT 100

1. STICK SHIFT — Duals, Sue 745
2. THEME FROM SILVER CITY — Ventures, Dolton 44
3. JOHNNY WILLOW — Fred Darian, JAF 2023
4. BLACKLAND FARMER — Wink Martindale, Dot 16243
5. MR. PAGANINI — Ella Fitzgerald, Verve 10237
6. BABY, YOU'RE RIGHT — James Brown, King 5524
7. I'LL NEVER SMILE AGAIN — Wanderers, Cub 9094
8. LOOK IN MY EYES — Chantels, Carlton 555
9. PRETTY PRETTY GIRL — Time Tones, Atco 6201
10. NOTHIN' BUT GOOD — Hank Ballard and the Midnighters, King 5535
11. DON'T FORGET I LOVE YOU — Butanes, Enrica 1007
12. YOU DON'T KNOW WHAT IT MEANS — Jackie Wilson, Brunswick 55219
13. BIG COLD WIND — Pat Boone, Dot 16244
14. JEREMIAH PEABODY'S POLY UNSATURATED QUICK DISSOLVING FAST ACTING PLEASANT TASTING GREEN AND PURPLE PILLS — Ray Stevens, Mercury 71843
15. A FAR, FAR BETTER THING — Della Reese, RCA Victor 7884
16. THE WAY YOU LOOK TONIGHT — Lettermen, Capitol 4586
17. TENNESSEE WALTZ — Don Robertson, RCA Victor 7909
18. THE BELLS ARE RINGING — Van Dykes, Deluxe 6193
19. SOMEBODY CARES — Zorro, Maske 702
20. BLACKLAND FARMER — Frankie Miller, Starday 424

## HOT 100 — A TO Z

| Title | # | Title | # |
|---|---|---|---|
| Amor | 48 | Mountain's High, The | 68 |
| As If I Didn't Know | 21 | Mr. Happiness | 57 |
| Back Beat No. 1 | 83 | Music, Music, Music | 95 |
| Bless You | 87 | My Claire De Lune | 78 |
| Boll Weevil Song | 20 | My Heart's on Fire | 97 |
| Candy Man | 69 | My Kind of Girl | 18 |
| Charleston, The | 47 | My True Story | 32 |
| Cryin' | 71 | Nag | 54 |
| Cupid | 23 | Never on Sunday | 13 |
| Dedicated (To the Songs I Love) | 89 | No, No, No | 55 |
| Does Your Chewing Gum Lose Its Flavor | 40 | Now and Forever | 81 |
| Don't Bet Money Honey | 16 | One Summer Night | 25 |
| Don't Cry Baby | 52 | Peanuts | 60 |
| Don't Cry No More | 80 | Pitter Patter | 100 |
| Dum Dum | 4 | Please Stay | 30 |
| Every Breath I Take | 90 | Pretty Little Angel Eyes | 7 |
| Fish, The | 58 | Princess | 36 |
| Girls, Girls, Girls | 99 | Quarter to Three | 19 |
| Guns of Navarone, The | 74 | Quite a Party | 27 |
| Hats Off to Larry | 14 | Raindrops | 50 |
| Here in My Heart | 86 | Right or Wrong | 38 |
| Hillbilly Heaven | 33 | Roll Over Beethoven | 92 |
| Hully Gully Again | 79 | Runaround | 28 |
| Hurt | 15 | Sacred | 35 |
| I Don't Want to Take a Chance | 42 | San Antonio Rose | 29 |
| I Fall to Pieces | 24 | San-Ho-Zay | 84 |
| I Never Knew | 56 | School Is Out | 10 |
| I Like It Like That | 2 | Sea of Heartbreak | 39 |
| I Just Don't Understand | 43 | Starlight | 96 |
| If | 82 | Starlight, Starbright | 53 |
| I'll Be There | 12 | Summer Souvenirs | 85 |
| I'll Never Smile Again | 49 | Take Good Care of My Baby | 41 |
| I'm A-Telling You | 26 | Tear, A | 31 |
| I'm Gonna Knock on Your Door | 22 | Teardrops in My Heart | 77 |
| In Time | 94 | Tears on My Pillow | 59 |
| It's Gonna Work Out Fine | 64 | That's What Girls Are Made For | 37 |
| Last Night | 3 | Thing of the Past, A | 46 |
| Let Me Belong to You | 65 | Time Was | 45 |
| Let the Four Winds Blow | 17 | Together | 9 |
| Let's Twist Again | 8 | Tossin' and Turnin' | 1 |
| Little Bit of Soap, A | 67 | Transistor Sister | 62 |
| Lonely Street | 72 | Water Boy | 66 |
| Lover's Island | 73 | Well-A, Well-A | 93 |
| Magic Moon | 88 | What a Sweet Thing That Was | 70 |
| Mexico | 91 | When We Get Married | 76 |
| Michael | 6 | Who Put the Bomp | 44 |
| Mighty Good 'Lovin' | 51 | Without You | 61 |
| Missing You | 63 | Yellow Bird | 34 |
| More Money for You and Me | 98 | You Don't Know What You've Got | 11 |

# BILLBOARD HOT 100

**AUGUST 21, 1961**
**FOR WEEK ENDING AUGUST 27, 1961**

STAR PERFORMERS—Selections registering greatest upward progress this week.
S Indicates that 45 r.p.m. stereo single version is available.
△ Indicates that 33⅓ r.p.m. mono single version is available.
Ⓢ Indicates that 33⅓ r.p.m. stereo single version is available.

| This Week | Wk. Ago | 2 Wks. Ago | 3 Wks. Ago | Title — Artist, Label & Number | Weeks On Chart |
|---|---|---|---|---|---|
| 1 | 1 | 1 | 1 | TOSSIN' AND TURNIN' — Bobby Lewis, Beltone 1002 | 18 |
| 2 | 5 | 9 | 13 | WOODEN HEART (Muss I Denn) — Joe Dowell, Smash 1708 | 9 |
| 3 | 6 | 10 | 23 | MICHAEL — Highwaymen, United Artists 258 | 7 |
| 4 | 3 | 3 | 7 | LAST NIGHT — Mar-Keys, Satellite 107 | 7 |
| 5 | 2 | 2 | 2 | I LIKE IT LIKE THAT — Chris Kenner, Instant 3229 | 13 |
| 6 | 11 | 15 | 24 | YOU DON'T KNOW WHAT YOU'VE GOT (Until You Lose It) — Ral Donner, Gone 5108 | 7 |
| 7 | 7 | 7 | 16 | PRETTY LITTLE ANGEL EYES — Curtis Lee, Dunes 2007 | 8 |
| 8 | 4 | 4 | 4 | DUM DUM — Brenda Lee, Decca 31272 | 10 |
| 9 | 8 | 8 | 9 | LET'S TWIST AGAIN — Chubby Checker, Parkway 824 | 10 |
| 10 | 10 | 16 | 28 | SCHOOL IS OUT — Gary (U.S.) Bonds, LeGrand 1009 | 5 |
| 11 | 16 | 25 | 30 | DON'T BET MONEY HONEY — Linda Scott, Canadian-American 127 | 8 |
| 12 | 15 | 20 | 35 | HURT — Timi Yuro, Liberty 55343 | 5 |
| 13 | 9 | 6 | 8 | TOGETHER — Connie Francis, MGM 13019 | 9 |
| 14 | 21 | 32 | 59 | AS IF I DIDN'T KNOW — Adam Wade, Coed 553 | 5 |
| 15 | 17 | 22 | 36 | LET THE FOUR WINDS BLOW — Fats Domino, Imperial 5764 | 5 |
| 16 | 24 | 28 | 33 | I FALL TO PIECES — Patsy Cline, Decca 31205 | 14 |
| 17 | 22 | 26 | 31 | I'M GONNA KNOCK ON YOUR DOOR — Eddie Hodges, Cadence 1397 | 10 |
| 18 | 12 | 14 | 19 | I'LL BE THERE — Damita Jo, Mercury 71840 | 8 |
| 19 | 13 | 13 | 14 | NEVER ON SUNDAY — Chordettes, Cadence 1402 | 10 |
| 20 | 14 | 5 | 5 | HATS OFF TO LARRY — Del Shannon, Big Top 3075 | 12 |
| 21 | 32 | 41 | 46 | MY TRUE STORY — Jive Five, Beltone 1006 | 8 |
| 22 | 25 | 40 | 53 | ONE SUMMER NIGHT — Diamonds, Mercury 71831 | 8 |
| 23 | 18 | 18 | 18 | MY KIND OF GIRL — Matt Monro, Warwick 636 | 13 |
| 24 | 33 | 44 | 56 | HILLBILLY HEAVEN — Tex Ritter, Capitol 4567 | 8 |
| 25 | 26 | 34 | 61 | I'M A-TELLING YOU — Jerry Butler, Vee Jay 390 | 5 |
| 26 | 40 | 75 | — | DOES YOUR CHEWING GUM LOSE ITS FLAVOR (On the Bedpost Over Night) — Lonnie Donegan, Dot 15911 | 3 |
| 27 | 19 | 12 | 6 | QUARTER TO THREE — Gary (U.S.) Bonds, LeGrand 1008 | 14 |
| 28 | 20 | 11 | 3 | BOLL WEEVIL SONG — Brook Benton, Mercury 71820 | 15 |
| 29 | 38 | 46 | 55 | RIGHT OR WRONG — Wanda Jackson, Capitol 4553 | 9 |
| 30 | 27 | 33 | 45 | QUITE A PARTY — Fireballs, Warwick 644 | 9 |
| 31 | 41 | 87 | — | TAKE GOOD CARE OF MY BABY — Bobby Vee, Liberty 55354 | 3 |
| 32 | 36 | 42 | 52 | PRINCESS — Frank Gari, Crusade 1022 | 8 |
| 33 | 44 | 66 | — | WHO PUT THE BOMP (In the Bomp, Bomp, Bomp) — Barry Mann, ABC-Paramount 10237 | 6 |
| 34 | 49 | 84 | 87 | I'LL NEVER SMILE AGAIN — Platters, Mercury 71847 | 4 |
| 35 | 42 | 51 | 60 | I DON'T WANT TO TAKE A CHANCE — Mary Wells, Motown 1011 | 6 |
| 36 | 39 | 43 | 34 | SEA OF HEARTBREAK — Don Gibson, RCA Victor 7890 △ | 10 |
| 37 | 43 | 62 | 78 | I JUST DON'T UNDERSTAND — Ann-Margret, RCA Victor 7894 △ | 5 |
| 38 | 28 | 29 | 37 | RUNAROUND — Regents, Gee 1071 | 7 |
| 39 | 23 | 17 | 17 | CUPID — Sam Cooke, RCA Victor 7883 △ | 12 |
| 40 | 48 | 58 | 72 | AMOR — Ben E. King, Atco 6203 | 4 |
| 41 | 46 | 52 | 58 | A THING OF THE PAST — Shirelles, Scepter 1220 | 7 |
| 42 | 68 | 85 | 90 | THE MOUNTAIN'S HIGH — Dick and Deedee, Liberty 55350 | 4 |
| 43 | 54 | 61 | 63 | NAG — Halos, Seven Arts 709 | 6 |
| 44 | 61 | 78 | — | WITHOUT YOU — Johnny Tillotson, Cadence 1404 | 3 |
| 45 | 52 | 67 | — | DON'T CRY BABY — Etta James, Argo 5393 | 3 |
| 46 | 76 | 91 | 97 | WHEN WE GET MARRIED — Dreamlovers, Heritage 102 | 4 |
| 47 | 53 | — | — | STARLIGHT, STARBRIGHT — Linda Scott, Canadian-American 127 | 4 |
| 48 | 67 | — | 90 | A LITTLE BIT OF SOAP — Jarmels, Laurie 3098 | 3 |
| 49 | 71 | — | — | CRYIN' — Roy Orbison, Monument 447 | 2 |
| 50 | 30 | 23 | 15 | PLEASE STAY — Drifters, Atlantic 2105 | 12 |
| 51 | 29 | 19 | 11 | SAN ANTONIO ROSE — Floyd Cramer, RCA Victor 7893 △ | 12 |
| 52 | 31 | 39 | 43 | A TEAR — Gene McDaniels, Liberty 55344 | 8 |
| 53 | 62 | 94 | 95 | TRANSISTOR SISTER — Freddy Cannon, Swan 4078 | 4 |
| 54 | 79 | 90 | — | HULLY GULLY AGAIN — Little Caesar and the Romans, Del-Fi 4164 | 3 |
| 55 | 65 | 76 | — | LET ME BELONG TO YOU — Brian Hyland, ABC-Paramount 10236 | 3 |
| 56 | 64 | 74 | 76 | IT'S GONNA WORK OUT FINE — Ike and Tina Turner, Sue 749 | 4 |
| 57 | 73 | — | — | LOVER'S ISLAND — Bluejays, Milestone 2008 | 2 |
| 58 | 66 | 72 | 73 | WATER BOY — Don Shirley Trio, Cadence 1392 | 6 |
| 59 | 63 | 93 | 85 | MISSING YOU — Ray Peterson, Dunes 2006 | 4 |
| 60 | 69 | 71 | — | CANDY MAN — Roy Orbison, Monument 447 | 3 |
| 61 | — | — | — | LITTLE SISTER — Elvis Presley, RCA Victor 7908 | 1 |
| 62 | 56 | 57 | 68 | I NEVER KNEW — Clyde McPhatter, Mercury 71841 | 5 |
| 63 | 47 | 48 | 51 | THE CHARLESTON — Ernie Fields, Rendezvous 150 | 8 |
| 64 | 59 | 70 | 77 | TEARS ON MY PILLOW — McGuire Sisters, Coral 62276 | 4 |
| 65 | 45 | 45 | 57 | TIME WAS — Flamingos, End 1092 | 8 |
| 66 | 77 | 80 | 86 | TEARDROPS IN MY HEART — Joe Barry, Smash 1710 | 4 |
| 67 | 81 | 82 | 94 | NOW AND FOREVER — Bert Kaempfert, Decca 31279 | 4 |
| 68 | 84 | 98 | — | SAN-HO-ZAY — Freddy King, Federal 12428 | 3 |
| 69 | 91 | — | — | MEXICO — Bob Moore, Monument 446 | 2 |
| 70 | 72 | 88 | — | LONELY STREET — Clarence Henry, Argo 5395 | 3 |
| 71 | 88 | — | — | MAGIC MOON — Rays, XYZ 607 | 2 |
| 72 | 83 | — | — | BACK BEAT NO. 1 — Rondells, Amy 825 | 2 |
| 73 | 87 | — | — | BLESS YOU — Tony Orlando, Epic 9452 | 2 |
| 74 | — | — | — | NOTHIN' BUT GOOD — Hank Ballard and the Midnighters, King 5535 | 1 |
| 75 | — | — | — | FRANKIE AND JOHNNY — Brook Benton, Mercury 71859 | 1 |
| 76 | — | — | — | BIG COLD WIND — Pat Boone, Dot 16244 | 1 |
| 77 | 70 | 54 | 54 | WHAT A SWEET THING THAT WAS — Shirelles, Scepter 1220 | 6 |
| 78 | 98 | — | — | MORE MONEY FOR YOU AND ME — Four Preps, Capitol 4599 | 2 |
| 79 | 80 | 89 | — | DON'T CRY NO MORE — Bobby (Blue) Bland, Duke 340 | 3 |
| 80 | 85 | 92 | 99 | SUMMER SOUVENIRS — Karl Hammil Jr., Arliss 1007 | 4 |
| 81 | 92 | — | — | ROLL OVER BEETHOVEN — Velaires, Jamie 1198 | 2 |
| 82 | 90 | 95 | — | EVERY BREATH I TAKE — Gene Pitney, Musicor 1011 | 3 |
| 83 | 95 | — | — | MUSIC, MUSIC, MUSIC — Sensations, Argo 5391 | 2 |
| 84 | 93 | 96 | — | WELL-A, WELL-A — Shirley & Lee, Warwick 664 | 3 |
| 85 | 60 | 64 | 67 | PEANUTS — Rick and the Keens, Smash 1705 | 8 |
| 86 | 100 | — | — | PITTER PATTER — Four Sportsmen, Sunnybrook 4 | 2 |
| 87 | 57 | 60 | 74 | MR. HAPPINESS — Johnny Maestro, Coed 552 | 5 |
| 88 | — | — | — | BABY, YOU'RE SO FINE — Mickey and Sylvia, Willow 23000 | 1 |
| 89 | 96 | — | — | STARLIGHT — Preludes Five, Pik 231 | 2 |
| 90 | — | — | — | JEREMIAH PEABODY'S POLY UNSATURATED QUICK DISSOLVING FAST ACTING PLEASANT TASTING GREEN AND PURPLE PILLS — Ray Stevens, Mercury 71843 | 1 |
| 91 | — | — | — | YEARS FROM NOW — Jackie Wilson, Brunswick 55219 | 1 |
| 92 | — | — | — | BLACKLAND FARMER — Wink Martindale, Dot 16243 | 1 |
| 93 | 97 | 100 | — | MY HEART'S ON FIRE — Billy Bland, Old Town 1105 | 3 |
| 94 | — | — | — | BABY, YOU'RE RIGHT — James Brown, King 5524 | 1 |
| 95 | — | — | — | I WAKE UP CRYING — Chuck Jackson, Wand 110 | 1 |
| 96 | 99 | — | — | GIRLS, GIRLS, GIRLS — Coasters, Atco 6404 | 2 |
| 97 | — | — | — | KEEP ON DANCING — Hank Ballard and the Midnighters, King 5535 | 1 |
| 98 | — | 97 | — | DON'T FORGET I LOVE YOU — Butanes, Enrico 1007 | 2 |
| 99 | — | — | — | WIZARD OF LOVE — Ly-Dells, Master 251 | 1 |
| 100 | — | — | — | DONALD, WHERE'S YOUR TROOSERS — Andy Stewart, Warwick 665 | 1 |

## BUBBLING UNDER THE HOT 100

1. YOU'RE THE REASON ........ Joe South, Fairlans 21006
2. THEME FROM SILVER CITY ........ Ventures, Dolton 44
3. KISSIN' ON THE PHONE ........ Paul Anka, ABC-Paramount 10239
4. LOOK IN MY EYES ........ Chantels, Carlton 555
5. JOHNNY WILLOW ........ Fred Darian, JAF 2023
6. MR. PAGANINI ........ Ella Fitzgerald, Verve 10237
7. BLUE MU MU ........ Annette, Vista 384
8. GOLDEN TEARDROPS ........ Flamingos, Vee Jay 384
9. STICK SHIFT ........ Duals, Sue 745
10. YOU'RE THE REASON ........ Bobby Edwards, Crest 1075
11. SWEET LITTLE YOU ........ Neil Sedaka, RCA Victor 7922
12. GEE OH GEE ........ Echoes, Seg-Way 1002
13. S.O.S. I LOVE YOU ........ Ronnie Hayden, Camay 101
14. FOOT STOMPIN' (PART 1) ........ Flares, Felsted 8624
15. L-O-V-E ........ Craftys, Warwick 708
16. MY DREAM COME TRUE ........ Jack Scott, Seeco 6078
17. ANNIVERSARY OF LOVE ........ Caslons, Seeco 6078
18. THE WAY YOU LOOK TONIGHT ........ Lettermen, Capitol 4586
19. HUMAN ........ Tommy Hunt, Scepter 1219
20. IMPOSSIBLE ........ Gloria Lynne, Everest 19418

# Billboard HOT 100

**AUGUST 28, 1961**
**FOR WEEK ENDING SEPTEMBER 3, 1961**

| This Week | Last Week | 2 Wks Ago | 3 Wks Ago | Title / Artist, Label & Number | Weeks on Chart |
|---|---|---|---|---|---|
| 1 | 2 | 5 | 9 | WOODEN HEART (Muss I Denn) — Joe Dowell, Smash 1708 | 10 |
| 2 | 1 | 1 | 1 | TOSSIN' AND TURNIN' — Bobby Lewis, Beltone 1002 | 19 |
| 3 | 3 | 6 | 10 | MICHAEL — Highwaymen, United Artists 258 | 8 |
| 4 | 4 | 3 | 3 | LAST NIGHT — Mar-Keys, Satellite 107 | 8 |
| 5 | 6 | 11 | 15 | YOU DON'T KNOW WHAT YOU'VE GOT (Until You Lose It) — Ral Donner, Gone 5108 | 8 |
| 6 | 5 | 2 | 2 | I LIKE IT LIKE THAT — Chris Kenner, Instant 3229 | 14 |
| 7 | 10 | 10 | 16 | SCHOOL IS OUT — Gary (U.S.) Bonds, LeGrand 1009 | 6 |
| 8 | 7 | 7 | 7 | PRETTY LITTLE ANGEL EYES — Curtis Lee, Dunes 2007 | 9 |
| 9 | 11 | 16 | 25 | DON'T BET MONEY HONEY — Linda Scott, Canadian-American 127 | 9 |
| 10 | 12 | 15 | 20 | HURT — Timi Yuro, Liberty 55343 | 9 |
| 11 | 14 | 21 | 32 | AS IF I DIDN'T KNOW — Adam Wade, Coed 553 | 6 |
| 12 | 17 | 22 | 26 | I'M GONNA KNOCK ON YOUR DOOR — Eddie Hodges, Cadence 1397 | 11 |
| 13 | 21 | 32 | 41 | MY TRUE STORY — Jive Five, Beltone 1006 | 9 |
| 14 | 16 | 24 | 28 | I FALL TO PIECES — Patsy Cline, Decca 31205 | 15 |
| 15 | 15 | 17 | 22 | LET THE FOUR WINDS BLOW — Fats Domino, Imperial 5764 | 6 |
| 16 | 9 | 8 | 8 | LET'S TWIST AGAIN — Chubby Checker, Parkway 824 | 11 |
| 17 | 8 | 4 | 4 | DUM DUM — Brenda Lee, Decca 31272 | 11 |
| 18 | 13 | 9 | 6 | TOGETHER — Connie Francis, MGM 13019 | 10 |
| 19 | 26 | 40 | 75 | DOES YOUR CHEWING GUM LOSE ITS FLAVOR (On the Bedpost Over Night) — Lonnie Donegan, Dot 15911 | 4 |
| 20 | 24 | 33 | 44 | HILLBILLY HEAVEN — Tex Ritter, Capitol 4567 | 9 |
| 21 | 36 | 39 | 43 | SEA OF HEARTBREAK — Don Gibson, RCA Victor 7890 | 11 |
| 22 | 40 | 48 | 58 | AMOR — Ben E. King, Atco 6203 | 5 |
| 23 | 31 | 41 | 87 | TAKE GOOD CARE OF MY BABY — Bobby Vee, Liberty 55354 | 4 |
| 24 | 33 | 44 | 46 | WHO PUT THE BOMP (In the Bomp, Bomp, Bomp) — Barry Mann, ABC-Paramount 10237 | 4 |
| 25 | 25 | 26 | 34 | I'M A-TELLING YOU — Jerry Butler, Vee Jay 390 | 6 |
| 26 | 61 | — | — | LITTLE SISTER — Elvis Presley, RCA Victor 7908 | 2 |
| 27 | 37 | 43 | 62 | I JUST DON'T UNDERSTAND — Ann-Margret, RCA Victor 7894 | 6 |
| 28 | 44 | 61 | 78 | WITHOUT YOU — Johnny Tillotson, Cadence 1404 | 4 |
| 29 | 49 | 71 | — | CRYIN' — Roy Orbison, Monument 447 | 3 |
| 30 | 32 | 36 | 42 | PRINCESS — Frank Gari, Crusade 1022 | 9 |
| 31 | 34 | 49 | 84 | I'LL NEVER SMILE AGAIN — Platters, Mercury 71847 | 5 |
| 32 | 42 | 68 | 85 | THE MOUNTAIN'S HIGH — Dick and Deedee, Liberty 55350 | 5 |
| 33 | 35 | 42 | 51 | I DON'T WANT TO TAKE A CHANCE — Mary Wells, Motown 1011 | 7 |
| 34 | 46 | 76 | 91 | WHEN WE GET MARRIED — Dreamlovers, Heritage 102 | 5 |
| 35 | 48 | 67 | — | A LITTLE BIT OF SOAP — Jarmels, Laurie 3098 | 4 |
| 36 | 43 | 54 | 61 | NAG — Halos, Seven Arts 709 | 7 |
| 37 | 22 | 25 | 40 | ONE SUMMER NIGHT — Diamonds, Mercury 71831 | 9 |
| 38 | 29 | 38 | 46 | RIGHT OR WRONG — Wanda Jackson, Capitol 4553 | 10 |
| 39 | 18 | 12 | 14 | I'LL BE THERE — Damita Jo, Mercury 71840 | 9 |
| 40 | 20 | 14 | 5 | HATS OFF TO LARRY — Del Shannon, Big Top 3075 | 13 |
| 41 | 19 | 13 | 13 | NEVER ON SUNDAY — Chordettes, Cadence 1402 | 11 |
| 42 | 56 | 64 | 74 | IT'S GONNA WORK OUT FINE — Ike and Tina Turner, Sue 749 | 5 |
| 43 | 45 | 52 | 67 | DON'T CRY BABY — Etta James, Argo 5393 | 4 |
| 44 | 47 | 53 | — | STARLIGHT, STARBRIGHT — Linda Scott, Canadian-American 127 | 5 |
| 45 | 75 | — | — | FRANKIE AND JOHNNY — Brook Benton, Mercury 71859 | 2 |
| 46 | 53 | 62 | 94 | TRANSISTOR SISTER — Freddy Cannon, Swan 4078 | 5 |
| 47 | 68 | 84 | 98 | SAN-HO-ZAY — Freddy King, Federal 12428 | 4 |
| 48 | 55 | 65 | 76 | LET ME BELONG TO YOU — Brian Hyland, ABC-Paramount 10236 | 4 |
| 49 | 74 | — | — | NOTHIN' BUT GOOD — Hank Ballard and the Midnighters, King 5535 | 2 |
| 50 | 57 | 73 | — | LOVER'S ISLAND — Bluejays, Milestone 2008 | 3 |
| 51 | 58 | 66 | 72 | WATER BOY — Don Shirley Trio, Cadence 1392 | 7 |
| 52 | 78 | 98 | — | MORE MONEY FOR YOU AND ME — Four Preps, Capitol 4599 | 3 |
| 53 | 76 | — | — | BIG COLD WIND — Pat Boone, Dot 16244 | 2 |
| 54 | 54 | 79 | 90 | HULLY GULLY AGAIN — Little Caesar & the Romans, Del-Fi 4164 | 4 |
| 55 | 41 | 46 | 52 | A THING OF THE PAST — Shirelles, Scepter 1220 | 8 |
| 56 | 59 | 63 | 93 | MISSING YOU — Ray Peterson, Dunes 2006 | 5 |
| 57 | 73 | 87 | — | BLESS YOU — Tony Orlando, Epic 9452 | 3 |
| 58 | 67 | 81 | 82 | NOW AND FOREVER — Bert Kaempfert, Decca 31279 | 4 |
| 59 | 69 | 91 | — | MEXICO — Bob Moore, Monument 446 | 3 |
| 60 | — | — | — | KISSIN' ON THE PHONE — Paul Anka, ABC-Paramount 10239 | 1 |
| 61 | 71 | 88 | — | MAGIC MOON — Rays, XYZ 607 | 4 |
| 62 | 60 | 69 | 71 | CANDY MAN — Roy Orbison, Monument 447 | 4 |
| 63 | 66 | 77 | 80 | TEARDROPS IN MY HEART — Joe Barry, Smash 1710 | 4 |
| 64 | 70 | 72 | 88 | LONELY STREET — Clarence Henry, Argo 5395 | 4 |
| 65 | 94 | — | — | BABY, YOU'RE RIGHT — James Brown, King 5524 | 2 |
| 66 | — | — | — | (Marie's the Name) HIS LATEST FLAME — Elvis Presley, RCA Victor 7908 | 1 |
| 67 | 82 | 90 | 95 | EVERY BREATH I TAKE — Gene Pitney, Musicor 1011 | 4 |
| 68 | 81 | 92 | — | ROLL OVER BEETHOVEN — Velaires, Jamie 1198 | 3 |
| 69 | — | — | — | ONE TRACK MIND — Bobby Lewis, Beltone 1012 | 1 |
| 70 | 72 | 83 | — | BACK BEAT NO. 1 — Rondells, Amy 825 | 3 |
| 71 | 79 | 80 | 89 | DON'T CRY NO MORE — Bobby (Blue) Bland, Duke 340 | 4 |
| 72 | 80 | 85 | 92 | SUMMER SOUVENIRS — Karl Hammel Jr., Arliss 1007 | 5 |
| 73 | 88 | — | — | BABY, YOU'RE SO FINE — Mickey and Sylvia, Willow 23000 | 2 |
| 74 | 83 | 95 | — | MUSIC, MUSIC, MUSIC — Sensations, Argo 5391 | 3 |
| 75 | 90 | — | — | JEREMIAH PEABODY'S POLY UNSATURATED QUICK DISSOLVING FAST ACTING PLEASANT TASTING GREEN AND PURPLE PILLS — Ray Stevens, Mercury 71843 | 2 |
| 76 | 99 | — | — | WIZARD OF LOVE — Ly-Dells, Master 251 | 2 |
| 77 | — | — | — | SWEET LITTLE YOU — Neil Sedaka, RCA Victor 7922 | 1 |
| 78 | 95 | — | — | I WAKE UP CRYING — Chuck Jackson, Wand 110 | 2 |
| 79 | 86 | 100 | — | PITTER PATTER — Four Sportsmen, Sunnybrook 4 | 3 |
| 80 | — | — | — | LOOK IN MY EYES — Chantels, Carlton 555 | 1 |
| 81 | 84 | 93 | 96 | WELL-A, WELL-A — Shirley and Lee, Warwick 664 | 4 |
| 82 | 23 | 18 | 18 | MY KIND OF GIRL — Matt Monro, Warwick 636 | 14 |
| 83 | 27 | 19 | 12 | QUARTER TO THREE — Gary (U.S.) Bonds, LeGrand 1008 | 15 |
| 84 | 91 | — | — | YEARS FROM NOW — Jackie Wilson, Brunswick 55219 | 2 |
| 85 | 92 | — | — | BLACKLAND FARMER — Wink Martindale, Dot 16243 | 2 |
| 86 | 89 | 96 | — | STARLIGHT — Preludes Five, Pik 231 | 3 |
| 87 | 97 | — | — | KEEP ON DANCING — Hank Ballard and the Midnighters, King 5535 | 2 |
| 88 | — | — | — | MY BLUE HEAVEN — Duane Eddy, Jamie 1200 | 1 |
| 89 | — | — | — | BIG RIVER, BIG MAN — Claude King, Columbia 42043 | 4 |
| 90 | 93 | 97 | 100 | MY HEART'S ON FIRE — Billy Bland, Old Town 1105 | 4 |
| 91 | — | — | — | ROMEO — Janie Grant, Caprise 109 | 1 |
| 92 | 28 | 20 | 11 | BOLL WEEVIL SONG — Brook Benton, Mercury 71820 | 16 |
| 93 | — | — | — | MY DREAM COME TRUE — Jack Scott, Capitol 4597 | 1 |
| 94 | — | — | — | YOU'RE THE REASON — Joe South, Fairlane 21006 | 1 |
| 95 | 100 | — | — | DONALD, WHERE'S YOUR TROOSERS — Andy Stewart, Warwick 665 | 2 |
| 96 | 98 | — | — | DON'T FORGET I LOVE YOU — Butanes, Enrico 1007 | 3 |
| 97 | — | — | — | YOU'RE THE REASON — Bobby Edwards, Crest 1075 | 1 |
| 98 | — | — | — | THEME FROM SILVER CITY — Ventures, Dolton 44 | 1 |
| 99 | — | — | — | I CAN'T TAKE IT — Mary Ann Fisher, Seg-way 101 | 1 |
| 100 | 30 | 27 | 33 | QUITE A PARTY — Fireballs, Warwick 644 | 10 |

## BUBBLING UNDER THE HOT 100

| 101 | THE ASTRONAUT — Jose Jimenez, Kapp 409 |
| 102 | YOU MUST HAVE BEEN A BEAUTIFUL BABY — Bobby Darin, Atco 6206 |
| 103 | MR. PAGANINI — Ella Fitzgerald, Verve 10237 |
| 104 | CINDERELLA — Paul Anka, ABC-Paramount 10239 |
| 105 | IMPOSSIBLE — Gloria Lynne, Everest 19418 |
| 106 | JUKE BOX SATURDAY NIGHT — Nino and the Ebb Tides, Madison 166 |
| 107 | JOHNNY WILLOW — Fred Darian, JAF 2023 |
| 108 | S.O.S. I LOVE YOU — Ronnie Hayden, Camay 101 |
| 109 | BLUE MU MU — Annette, Vista 384 |
| 110 | STICK SHIFT — Duals, Sue 745 |
| 111 | YEARS FROM NOW — Tina Robin, Mercury 71852 |
| 112 | LET'S GET TOGETHER — Hayley Mills, Vista 385 |
| 113 | FOOT STOMPIN' (PART I) — Flares, Felsted 8624 |
| 114 | IT'S YOUR WORLD — Marty Robbins, Columbia 42065 |
| 115 | ANNIVERSARY OF LOVE — Caslons, Seeco 6078 |
| 116 | (HE'S THE) GREAT IMPOSTER — Fleetwoods, Dolton 45 |
| 117 | THAT'S WHY — Curtis Knight, Gulf 031 |
| 118 | SOMEBODY CARES — Zorro, Moske 107 |
| 119 | CRAZY FOR YOU — Aquatones, Fargo 1016 |
| 120 | YA YA — Lee Dorsey, Fury 1053 |

# BILLBOARD HOT 100

**SEPTEMBER 4, 1961**
**FOR WEEK ENDING SEPTEMBER 10, 1961**

★ STAR PERFORMERS—Selections registering greatest upward progress this week.
Ⓢ Indicates that 45 r.p.m. stereo single version is available.
△ Indicates that 33⅓ r.p.m. mono single version is available.
▲ Indicates that 33⅓ r.p.m. stereo single version is available.

| This Week | Wk. Ago | 2 Wks. Ago | 3 Wks. Ago | Title — Artist, Label & Number | Weeks On Chart |
|---|---|---|---|---|---|
| 1 | 3 | 3 | 6 | MICHAEL — Highwaymen, United Artists 258 | 9 |
| 2 | 1 | 2 | 5 | WOODEN HEART (Muss I Denn) — Joe Dowell, Smash 1708 | 11 |
| 3 | 2 | 1 | 1 | TOSSIN' AND TURNIN' — Bobby Lewis, Beltone 1002 | 20 |
| 4 | 5 | 6 | 11 | YOU DON'T KNOW WHAT YOU'VE GOT (Until You Lose It) — Ral Donner, Gone 5108 | 9 |
| 5 | 7 | 10 | 10 | SCHOOL IS OUT — Gary (U.S.) Bonds, LeGrand 1009 | 7 |
| ★6 | 23 | 31 | 41 | TAKE GOOD CARE OF MY BABY — Bobby Vee, Liberty 55354 | 5 |
| 7 | 13 | 21 | 32 | MY TRUE STORY — Jive Five, Beltone 1006 | 10 |
| 8 | 10 | 12 | 15 | HURT — Timi Yuro, Liberty 55343 | 7 |
| 9 | 9 | 11 | 16 | DON'T BET MONEY HONEY — Linda Scott, Canadian-American 127 | 10 |
| 10 | 11 | 14 | 21 | AS IF I DIDN'T KNOW — Adam Wade, Coed 553 | 7 |
| 11 | 19 | 26 | 40 | DOES YOUR CHEWING GUM LOSE ITS FLAVOR (On the Bedpost Over Night) — Lonnie Donegan, Dot 15911 | 5 |
| 12 | 14 | 16 | 24 | I FALL TO PIECES — Patsy Cline, Decca 31205 | 16 |
| 13 | 4 | 4 | 3 | LAST NIGHT — Mar-Keys, Satellite 107 | 9 |
| 14 | 24 | 33 | 44 | WHO PUT THE BOMP (In the Bomp, Bomp, Bomp) — Barry Mann, ABC-Paramount 10237 | 5 |
| 15 | 26 | 61 | — | LITTLE SISTER — Elvis Presley, RCA Victor 7908 | 3 |
| 16 | 29 | 49 | 71 | CRYIN' — Roy Orbison, Monument 447 | 4 |
| 17 | 12 | 17 | 22 | I'M GONNA KNOCK ON YOUR DOOR — Eddie Hodges, Cadence 1397 | 12 |
| 18 | 22 | 40 | 48 | AMOR — Ben E. King, Atco 6203 | 6 |
| 19 | 27 | 37 | 43 | I JUST DON'T UNDERSTAND — Ann-Margret, RCA Victor 7894 | 7 |
| 20 | 28 | 44 | 61 | WITHOUT YOU — Johnny Tillotson, Cadence 1404 | 5 |
| 21 | 32 | 42 | 68 | THE MOUNTAIN'S HIGH — Dick and Deedee, Liberty 55350 | 6 |
| 22 | 6 | 5 | 2 | I LIKE IT LIKE THAT — Chris Kenner, Instant 3229 | 15 |
| 23 | 34 | 46 | 76 | WHEN WE GET MARRIED — Dreamlovers, Heritage 102 | 6 |
| 24 | 35 | 48 | 67 | A LITTLE BIT OF SOAP — Jarmels, Laurie 3098 | 5 |
| 25 | 8 | 7 | 7 | PRETTY LITTLE ANGEL EYES — Curtis Lee, Dunes 2007 | 10 |
| 26 | 20 | 24 | 33 | HILLBILLY HEAVEN — Tex Ritter, Capitol 4567 | 10 |
| 27 | 15 | 15 | 17 | LET THE FOUR WINDS BLOW — Fats Domino, Imperial 5764 | 7 |
| 28 | 21 | 36 | 39 | SEA OF HEARTBREAK — Don Gibson, RCA Victor 7890 | 12 |
| 29 | 31 | 34 | 49 | I'LL NEVER SMILE AGAIN — Platters, Mercury 71847 | 6 |
| 30 | 36 | 43 | 54 | NAG — Halos, Seven Arts 709 | 8 |
| 31 | 45 | 75 | — | FRANKIE AND JOHNNY — Brook Benton, Mercury 71859 | 3 |
| 32 | 66 | — | — | (Marie's the Name) HIS LATEST FLAME — Elvis Presley, RCA Victor 7908 | 2 |
| 33 | 48 | 55 | 65 | LET ME BELONG TO YOU — Brian Hyland, ABC-Paramount 10236 | 5 |
| 34 | 53 | 76 | — | BIG COLD WIND — Pat Boone, Dot 16244 | 3 |
| 35 | 46 | 53 | 62 | TRANSISTOR SISTER — Freddy Cannon, Swan 4078 | 6 |
| 36 | 50 | 57 | 73 | LOVER'S ISLAND — Bluejays, Milestone 2008 | 4 |
| 37 | 33 | 35 | 42 | I DON'T WANT TO TAKE A CHANCE — Mary Wells, Motown 1011 | 8 |
| 38 | 42 | 56 | 64 | IT'S GONNA WORK OUT FINE — Ike and Tina Turner, Sue 749 | 6 |
| 39 | 43 | 45 | 52 | DON'T CRY BABY — Etta James, Argo 5393 | 5 |
| 40 | 57 | 73 | 87 | BLESS YOU — Tony Orlando, Epic 9452 | 4 |
| 41 | 52 | 78 | 98 | MORE MONEY FOR YOU AND ME MEDLEY — Four Preps, Capitol 4599 | 4 |
| 42 | 25 | 25 | 26 | I'M A-TELLING YOU — Jerry Butler, Vee Jay 390 | 7 |
| 43 | 60 | — | — | KISSIN' ON THE PHONE — Paul Anka, ABC-Paramount 10239 | 2 |
| 44 | 59 | 69 | 91 | MEXICO — Bob Moore, Monument 446 | 4 |
| 45 | 69 | — | — | ONE TRACK MIND — Bobby Lewis, Beltone 1012 | 2 |
| 46 | 51 | 58 | 66 | WATER BOY — Don Shirley Trio, Cadence 1392 | 8 |
| 47 | 80 | — | — | LOOK IN MY EYES — Chantels, Carlton 555 | 2 |
| 48 | 58 | 67 | 81 | NOW AND FOREVER — Bert Kaempfert, Decca 31279 | 6 |
| 49 | 65 | 94 | — | BABY, YOU'RE RIGHT — James Brown, King 5524 | 3 |
| 50 | 17 | 8 | 4 | DUM DUM — Brenda Lee, Decca 31272 | 12 |
| 51 | 56 | 59 | 63 | MISSING YOU — Ray Peterson, Dunes 2006 | 4 |
| 52 | 16 | 9 | 8 | LET'S TWIST AGAIN — Chubby Checker, Parkway 824 | 12 |
| 53 | 61 | 71 | 88 | MAGIC MOON — Rays, XYZ 607 | 4 |
| 54 | 44 | 47 | 53 | STARLIGHT, STARBRIGHT — Linda Scott, Canadian-American 127 | 6 |
| 55 | 67 | 82 | 90 | EVERY BREATH I TAKE — Gene Pitney, Musicor 1011 | 5 |
| 56 | 18 | 13 | 9 | TOGETHER — Connie Francis, MGM 13019 | 11 |
| 57 | 64 | 70 | 72 | LONELY STREET — Clarence Henry, Argo 5395 | 5 |
| 58 | 74 | 83 | 95 | MUSIC, MUSIC, MUSIC — Sensations, Argo 5391 | 4 |
| 59 | 73 | 88 | — | BABY, YOU'RE SO FINE — Mickey and Sylvia, Willow 23000 | 3 |
| 60 | 84 | 91 | — | YEARS FROM NOW — Jackie Wilson, Brunswick 55219 | 3 |
| 61 | 68 | 81 | 92 | ROLL OVER BEETHOVEN — Velaires, Jamie 1198 | 4 |
| 62 | 77 | — | — | SWEET LITTLE YOU — Neil Sedaka, RCA Victor 7922 | 2 |
| 63 | 78 | 95 | — | I WAKE UP CRYING — Chuck Jackson, Wand 110 | 3 |
| 64 | 75 | 90 | — | JEREMIAH PEABODY'S POLY UNSATURATED QUICK DISSOLVING FAST ACTING PLEASANT TASTING GREEN AND PURPLE PILLS — Ray Stevens, Mercury 71843 | 3 |
| 65 | 76 | 99 | — | WIZARD OF LOVE — Ly-Dells, Master 251 | 3 |
| 66 | 70 | 72 | 83 | BACK SEAT NO. 1 — Rondells, Amy 825 | 4 |
| 67 | — | — | — | YOU MUST HAVE BEEN A BEAUTIFUL BABY — Bobby Darin, Atco 6206 | 1 |
| 68 | 72 | 80 | 85 | SUMMER SOUVENIRS — Karl Hammil Jr., Arliss 1007 | 6 |
| 69 | 87 | 97 | — | KEEP ON DANCING — Hank Ballard and the Midnighters, King 5535 | 3 |
| 70 | 30 | 32 | 36 | PRINCESS — Frank Gari, Crusade 1022 | 10 |
| 71 | — | — | — | THE ASTRONAUT — Jose Jimenez, Kapp 409 | 3 |
| 72 | 47 | 68 | 84 | SAN-HO-ZAY — Freddy King, Federal 12428 | 5 |
| 73 | 88 | — | — | MY BLUE HEAVEN — Duane Eddy, Jamie 1200 | 2 |
| 74 | 49 | 74 | — | NOTHIN' BUT GOOD — Hank Ballard and the Midnighters, King 5535 | 3 |
| 75 | 62 | 60 | 69 | CANDY MAN — Roy Orbison, Monument 447 | 5 |
| 76 | 79 | 86 | 100 | PITTER PATTER — Four Sportsmen, Sunnybrook 4 | 4 |
| 77 | 81 | 84 | 93 | WELL-A, WELL-A — Shirley and Lee, Warwick 664 | 5 |
| 78 | — | — | — | DON'T GET AROUND MUCH ANYMORE — Belmonts, Sabrina 501 | 1 |
| 79 | 91 | — | — | ROMEO — Janie Grant, Caprise 109 | 2 |
| 80 | 86 | 89 | 96 | STARLIGHT — Preludes Five, Pik 231 | 4 |
| 81 | — | — | — | JUKE BOX SATURDAY NIGHT — Nino and the Ebb Tides, Madison 166 | 1 |
| 82 | 89 | — | — | BIG RIVER, BIG MAN — Claude King, Columbia 42043 | 5 |
| 83 | — | — | — | A LITTLE DOG CRIED — Jimmy Rodgers, Roulette 4384 | 1 |
| 84 | — | — | — | SAD MOVIES (Make Me Cry) — Sue Thompson, Hickory 1153 | 1 |
| 85 | 97 | — | — | YOU'RE THE REASON — Bobby Edwards, Crest 1075 | 2 |
| 86 | 93 | — | — | MY DREAM COME TRUE — Jack Scott, Capitol 4597 | 2 |
| 87 | 94 | — | — | YOU'RE THE REASON — Joe South, Fairlane 21006 | 2 |
| ★88 | — | — | — | (I Love You) FOR SENTIMENTAL REASONS — Cleftones, Gee 1067 | 1 |
| 89 | 95 | 100 | — | DONALD, WHERE'S YOUR TROOSERS — Andy Stewart, Warwick 665 | 3 |
| 90 | — | — | — | I DON'T LIKE IT LIKE THAT — Bobbettes, Gone 5112 | 1 |
| 91 | 98 | — | — | THEME FROM SILVER CITY — Ventures, Dolton 44 | 2 |
| 92 | — | — | — | LET'S GET TOGETHER — Hayley Mills, Vista 385 | 1 |
| 93 | — | — | — | THE WAY YOU LOOK TONIGHT — Lettermen, Capitol 4586 | 1 |
| 94 | 99 | — | — | I CAN'T TAKE IT — Mary Ann Fisher, Seg-way 101 | 2 |
| 95 | — | — | — | PLEASE MR. POSTMAN — Marvelettes, Tamla 54046 | 1 |
| 96 | — | — | — | I LOVE HOW YOU LOVE ME — Paris Sisters, Gregmark 6 | 1 |
| 97 | — | — | — | HUMAN — Tommy Hunt, Scepter 1219 | 1 |
| 98 | 38 | 29 | 38 | RIGHT OR WRONG — Wanda Jackson, Capitol 4553 | 11 |
| 99 | 41 | 19 | 13 | NEVER ON SUNDAY — Chordettes, Cadence 1402 | 12 |
| 100 | — | — | — | FOOT STOMPIN' (Part 1) — Flares, Felsted 8624 | 1 |

## BUBBLING UNDER THE HOT 100

| 101 | TAKE FIVE — Dave Brubeck, Columbia 41479 |
| 102 | YA YA — Lee Dorsey, Fury 1053 |
| 103 | BRISTOL STOMP — Dovells, Parkway 827 |
| 104 | PLAY IT AGAIN — Tina Robin, Mercury 71852 |
| 105 | CINDERELLA — Paul Anka, ABC-Paramount 10239 |
| 106 | IMPOSSIBLE — Gloria Lynne, Everest 19418 |
| 107 | STICK SHIFT — Duals, Sue 745 |
| 108 | IT'S YOUR WORLD — Marty Robbins, Columbia 42065 |
| 109 | MR. PAGANINI — Ella Fitzgerald, Verve 10237 |
| 110 | YOU'RE THE REASON — Hank Locklin, RCA Victor 7921 |
| 111 | (HE'S) THE GREAT IMPOSTOR — Fleetwoods, Dolton 45 |
| 112 | DRUMS — Kenny Chandler, United Artists 342 |
| 113 | ANNIVERSARY OF LOVE — Caslons, Seeco 6078 |
| 114 | MAGIC IS THE NIGHT — Kathy Young, Indigo 125 |
| 115 | THAT'S WHY — Curtis Knight, Gulf 031 |
| 116 | YOU AIN'T GONNA FIND — Cornell Blakely, Rich 71853 |
| 117 | A VERY TRUE STORY — Chris Kenner, Instant 3234 |
| 118 | YOU BROKE MY HEART — Gleems, Kip 236 |
| 119 | JUST OUT OF REACH (Of My Two Open Arms) — Solomon Burke, Atlantic 2114 |
| 120 | OLD SLEW-FOOT — Johnny Horton, Columbia 42063 |

# BILLBOARD HOT 100

FOR WEEK ENDING SEPTEMBER 17

1961

★ STAR PERFORMERS—Selections registering greatest upward progress this week.

[S] Indicates that 45 r.p.m. stereo single version is available.

△ Indicates that 33⅓ r.p.m. mono single version is available.

[S△] Indicates that 33⅓ r.p.m. stereo single version is available.

| This Week | 1 Wk. Ago | 2 Wks. Ago | 3 Wks. Ago | TITLE Artist, Label & Number | Weeks On Chart |
|---|---|---|---|---|---|
| 1 | 1 | 3 | 3 | MICHAEL — Highwaymen, United Artists 258 | 10 |
| 2 | 6 | 23 | 31 | TAKE GOOD CARE OF MY BABY — Bobby Vee, Liberty 55354 | 6 |
| 3 | 7 | 13 | 21 | MY TRUE STORY — Jive Five, Beltone 1006 | 11 |
| 4 | 8 | 10 | 12 | HURT — Timi Yuro, Liberty 55343 | 8 |
| 5 | 4 | 5 | 6 | YOU DON'T KNOW WHAT YOU'VE GOT (Until You Lose It) — Ral Donner, Gone 5108 | 10 |
| 6 | 2 | 1 | 2 | WOODEN HEART (Muss I Denn) — Joe Dowell, Smash 1708 | 12 |
| 7 | 11 | 19 | 26 | DOES YOUR CHEWING GUM LOSE ITS FLAVOR (On the Bedpost Over Night) — Lonnie Donegan, Dot 15911 | 6 |
| ★8 | 14 | 24 | 33 | WHO PUT THE BOMP (In the Bomp, Bomp, Bomp) — Barry Mann, ABC-Paramount 10237 | 6 |
| ★9 | 15 | 26 | 61 | LITTLE SISTER △ — Elvis Presley, RCA Victor 7908 | 4 |
| 10 | 10 | 11 | 14 | AS IF I DIDN'T KNOW — Adam Wade, Coed 553 | 8 |
| ★11 | 16 | 29 | 49 | CRYIN' — Roy Orbison, Monument 447 | 5 |
| ★12 | 21 | 32 | 42 | THE MOUNTAIN'S HIGH — Dick and Deedee, Liberty 55350 | 7 |
| ★13 | 23 | 34 | 46 | WHEN WE GET MARRIED — Dreamlovers, Heritage 102 | 7 |
| ★14 | 20 | 28 | 44 | WITHOUT YOU — Johnny Tillotson, Cadence 1404 | 6 |
| 15 | 3 | 2 | 1 | TOSSIN' AND TURNIN' — Bobby Lewis, Beltone 1002 | 21 |
| 16 | 5 | 7 | 10 | SCHOOL IS OUT — Gary (U. S.) Bonds, LeGrand 1009 | 8 |
| 17 | 19 | 27 | 37 | I JUST DON'T UNDERSTAND △ — Ann-Margret, RCA Victor 7894 | 8 |
| 18 | 9 | 9 | 11 | DON'T BET MONEY HONEY — Linda Scott, Canadian-American 127 | 11 |
| ★19 | 24 | 35 | 48 | A LITTLE BIT OF SOAP — Jarmels, Laurie 3098 | 6 |
| ★20 | 31 | 45 | 75 | FRANKIE AND JOHNNY — Brook Benton, Mercury 71859 | 4 |
| 21 | 12 | 14 | 16 | I FALL TO PIECES — Patsy Cline, Decca 31205 | 17 |
| ★22 | 32 | 66 | — | (Marie's the Name) HIS LATEST FLAME △ — Elvis Presley, RCA Victor 7908 | 3 |
| ★23 | 34 | 53 | 76 | BIG COLD WIND — Pat Boone, Dot 16244 | 4 |
| ★24 | 41 | 52 | 78 | MORE MONEY FOR YOU AND ME MEDLEY — Four Preps, Capitol 4599 | 5 |
| 25 | 29 | 31 | 34 | I'LL NEVER SMILE AGAIN — Platters, Mercury 71847 | 7 |
| 26 | 13 | 4 | 4 | LAST NIGHT — Mar-Keys, Satellite 107 | 10 |
| 27 | 18 | 22 | 40 | AMOR — Ben E. King, Atco 6203 | 7 |
| 28 | 30 | 36 | 43 | NAG — Halos, Seven Arts 709 | 9 |
| ★29 | 45 | 69 | — | ONE TRACK MIND — Bobby Lewis, Beltone 1012 | 3 |
| ★30 | 40 | 57 | 73 | BLESS YOU — Tony Orlando, Epic 9452 | 5 |
| 31 | 38 | 42 | 56 | IT'S GONNA WORK OUT FINE — Ike and Tina Turner, Sue 749 | 7 |
| 32 | 33 | 48 | 55 | LET ME BELONG TO YOU — Brian Hyland, ABC-Paramount 10236 | 6 |
| ★33 | 44 | 59 | 69 | MEXICO — Bob Moore, Monument 446 | 5 |
| ★34 | 67 | — | — | YOU MUST HAVE BEEN A BEAUTIFUL BABY — Bobby Darin, Atco 6206 | 2 |
| 35 | 43 | 60 | — | KISSIN' ON THE PHONE — Paul Anka, ABC-Paramount 10239 | 3 |
| 36 | 36 | 50 | 57 | LOVER'S ISLAND — Bluejays, Milestone 2008 | 5 |
| ★37 | 47 | 80 | — | LOOK IN MY EYES — Chantels, Carlton 555 | 3 |
| 38 | 17 | 12 | 17 | I'M GONNA KNOCK ON YOUR DOOR — Eddie Hodges, Cadence 1397 | 13 |
| 39 | 39 | 43 | 45 | DON'T CRY BABY — Etta James, Argo 5393 | 6 |
| ★40 | 60 | 84 | 91 | YEARS FROM NOW — Jackie Wilson, Brunswick 55219 | 4 |
| 41 | 22 | 6 | 5 | I LIKE IT LIKE THAT — Chris Kenner, Instant 3229 | 16 |
| ★42 | 55 | 67 | 82 | EVERY BREATH I TAKE — Gene Pitney, Musicor 1011 | 6 |
| 43 | 27 | 15 | 15 | LET THE FOUR WINDS BLOW — Fats Domino, Imperial 5764 | 8 |
| 44 | 35 | 46 | 53 | TRANSISTOR SISTER — Freddy Cannon, Swan 4078 | 7 |
| 45 | 28 | 21 | 36 | SEA OF HEARTBREAK △ — Don Gibson, RCA Victor 7890 | 13 |
| ★46 | 64 | 75 | 90 | JEREMIAH PEABODY'S POLY UNSATURATED QUICK DISSOLVING FAST ACTING PLEASANT TASTING GREEN AND PURPLE PILLS — Ray Stevens, Mercury 71843 | 4 |
| 47 | 26 | 20 | 24 | HILLBILLY HEAVEN — Tex Ritter, Capitol 4567 | 11 |
| ★48 | 71 | — | — | THE ASTRONAUT — Jose Jimenez, Kapp 409 | 4 |
| 49 | 53 | 61 | 71 | MAGIC MOON — Rays, XYZ 607 | 5 |
| 50 | 51 | 56 | 59 | MISSING YOU — Ray Peterson, Dunes 2006 | 7 |
| 51 | 25 | 8 | 7 | PRETTY LITTLE ANGEL EYES — Curtis Lee, Dunes 2007 | 11 |
| 52 | 46 | 51 | 58 | WATER BOY — Don Shirley Trio, Cadence 1392 | 9 |
| 53 | 61 | 68 | 81 | ROLL OVER BEETHOVEN — Velaires, Jamie 1198 | 5 |
| ★54 | 73 | 88 | — | MY BLUE HEAVEN — Duane Eddy, Jamie 1200 | 3 |
| ★55 | — | — | — | HIT THE ROAD JACK — Ray Charles, ABC-Paramount 10244 | 1 |
| 56 | 49 | 65 | 94 | BABY, YOU'RE RIGHT — James Brown, King 5524 | 4 |
| 57 | 59 | 73 | 88 | BABY, YOU'RE SO FINE — Mickey and Sylvia, Willow 23000 | 4 |
| 58 | 65 | 76 | 99 | WIZARD OF LOVE — Ly-Dells, Master 251 | 4 |
| 59 | 63 | 78 | 95 | I WAKE UP CRYING — Chuck Jackson, Wand 110 | 4 |
| 60 | 62 | 77 | — | SWEET LITTLE YOU △ — Neil Sedaka, RCA Victor 7922 | 3 |
| 61 | 58 | 74 | 83 | MUSIC, MUSIC, MUSIC — Sensations, Argo 5391 | 5 |
| 62 | 48 | 58 | 67 | NOW AND FOREVER — Bert Kaempfert, Decca 31279 | 7 |
| 63 | 54 | 44 | 47 | STARLIGHT, STARBRIGHT — Linda Scott, Canadian-American 127 | 7 |
| ★64 | — | — | — | TAKE FIVE △ — Dave Brubeck, Columbia 41479 | 1 |
| 65 | 37 | 33 | 35 | I DON'T WANT TO TAKE A CHANCE — Mary Wells, Motown 1011 | 9 |
| 66 | 69 | 87 | 97 | KEEP ON DANCING — Hank Ballard and the Midnighters, King 5535 | 4 |
| 67 | 57 | 64 | 70 | LONELY STREET — Clarence Henry, Argo 5395 | 6 |
| 68 | 42 | 25 | 25 | I'M A-TELLING YOU — Jerry Butler, Vee Jay 390 | 8 |
| ★69 | 92 | — | — | LET'S GET TOGETHER — Hayley Mills, Vista 385 | 2 |
| 70 | 81 | — | — | JUKE BOX SATURDAY NIGHT — Nino and the Ebb Tides, Madison 166 | 2 |
| 71 | 78 | — | — | DON'T GET AROUND MUCH ANYMORE — Belmonts, Sabrina 501 | 2 |
| 72 | 84 | — | — | SAD MOVIES (Make Me Cry) — Sue Thompson, Hickory 1153 | 2 |
| ★73 | 93 | — | — | THE WAY YOU LOOK TONIGHT — Lettermen, Capitol 4586 | 2 |
| ★74 | — | — | — | BRISTOL STOMP — Dovells, Parkway 827 | 1 |
| 75 | 79 | 91 | — | ROMEO — Janie Grant, Caprice 109 | 3 |
| ★76 | — | — | — | STICK SHIFT — Duals, Sue 745 | 1 |
| 77 | 89 | 95 | 100 | DONALD, WHERE'S YOUR TROOSERS — Andy Stewart, Warwick 665 | 4 |
| 78 | — | — | — | CINDERELLA — Paul Anka, ABC-Paramount 10239 | 1 |
| 79 | 83 | — | — | A LITTLE DOG CRIED — Jimmy Rodgers, Roulette 4384 | 2 |
| 80 | 80 | 86 | 89 | STARLIGHT — Preludes Five, Pik 231 | 5 |
| 81 | 85 | 97 | — | YOU'RE THE REASON — Bobby Edwards, Crest 1075 | 3 |
| 82 | 88 | — | — | (I Love You) FOR SENTIMENTAL REASONS — Cleftones, Gee 1067 | 2 |
| 83 | 91 | 98 | — | THEME FROM SILVER CITY — Ventures, Dolton 44 | 3 |
| 84 | 97 | — | — | HUMAN — Tommy Hunt, Scepter 1219 | 2 |
| 85 | 86 | 93 | — | MY DREAM COME TRUE — Jack Scott, Capitol 4597 | 3 |
| 86 | 90 | — | — | I DON'T LIKE IT LIKE THAT — Bobbettes, Gone 5112 | 2 |
| ★87 | — | — | — | SWEETS FOR MY SWEET — Drifters, Atlantic 2117 | 1 |
| 88 | 95 | — | — | PLEASE MR. POSTMAN — Marvelettes, Tamla 54046 | 2 |
| 89 | 96 | — | — | I LOVE HOW YOU LOVE ME — Paris Sisters, Gregmark 6 | 2 |
| 90 | 77 | 81 | 84 | WELL-A, WELL-A — Shirley and Lee, Warwick 664 | 6 |
| 91 | — | — | — | ANNIVERSARY OF LOVE — Caslons, Seeco 6078 | 1 |
| 92 | 94 | 99 | — | I CAN'T TAKE IT — Mary Ann Fisher, Seg-way 101 | 3 |
| 93 | — | — | — | (HE'S) THE GREAT IMPOSTOR — Fleetwoods, Dolton 45 | 1 |
| 94 | 100 | — | — | FOOT STOMPIN' (Part 1) — Flares, Felsted 8624 | 2 |
| 95 | — | — | — | YA YA — Lee Dorsey, Fury 1053 | 1 |
| 96 | 76 | 79 | 86 | PITTER PATTER — Four Sportsmen, Sunnybrook 4 | 5 |
| 97 | — | — | — | IT'S YOUR WORLD △ — Marty Robbins, Columbia 42065 | 1 |
| 98 | — | — | — | IMPOSSIBLE — Gloria Lynne, Everest 19418 | 1 |
| 99 | — | — | — | SIGNED, SEALED AND DELIVERED — Rusty Draper, Mercury 71854 | 1 |
| 100 | — | — | — | I LOVE YOU, YES I DO — Bullmoose Jackson, Seven Arts 705 | 1 |

## HOT 100—A TO Z—(Publisher-Licensee)


Amor (Peer, BMI) 27
Anniversary of Love (Woodstock, BMI) 91
As If I Didn't Know (Winneton-Glenville, BMI) 10
Astronaut, The (Bill Dana, ASCAP) 48
Baby, You're Right (Lois, BMI) 56
Baby, You're So Fine (Ben Ghazi, BMI) 57
Big Cold Wind (Gil, BMI) 23
Bless You (Aldon, BMI) 30
Bristol Stomp (Kalmann, ASCAP) 74
Cinderella (Spanka, BMI) 78
Cryin' (Acuff-Rose, BMI) 11
Does Your Chewing Gum Lose Its Flavor (Mills, ASCAP) 7
Donald, Where's Your Troosers (Kerr, BMI) 77
Don't Bet Money Honey (Figure, BMI) 18
Don't Cry Baby (Advance, ASCAP) 39
Don't Get Around Much Anymore (Robbins, ASCAP) 71
Every Breath I Take (Aldon, BMI) 42
Foot Stompin' (Part 1) (Argo, BMI) 94
Frankie and Johnny (Ben-Day, BMI) 20
(He's) the Great Imposter (Gold Cup-Cornerstone, BMI) 93
Hillbilly Heaven (Sage & Sand, SESAC-BMI) 47
Hit the Road Jack (Tangerine, BMI) 55
Human (Ludix, BMI) 84
Hurt (Miller, ASCAP) 4
I Can't Take It (Glodis-Good Songs, BMI) 92
I Don't Like It Like That (Kel, BMI) 86
I Don't Want to Take a Chance (Jobete, BMI) 65
I Fall to Pieces (Pamper, BMI) 21
I Just Don't Understand (Hill & Range, BMI) 17
I Like It Like That (Tune-Kel, BMI) 41
I Love How You Love Me (Aldon, BMI) 89
(I Love You) For Sentimental Reasons (Duchess, BMI) 82
I Love You, Yes I Do (BMI-Northern, ASCAP) 100
I Wake Up Crying (Belinda, CAPAC) 59
I'll Never Smile Aagain (Pickwick, ASCAP) 25
I'm A-Telling You (Conrad, BMI) 68
I'm Gonna Knock on Your Door (Sigma, ASCAP) 38
Impossible (Tippy, BMI) 98
It's Gonna Work Out Fine (Copa-Sona, ASCAP) 31
It's Your World (Marizona, BMI) 97
Jeremiah's Pills (Lowery, BMI) 46
Juke Box Saturday Night (Mutual, ASCAP) 70
Keep on Dancing (Lois, BMI) 66
Kissin' on the Phone (Brighton-Flanka, ASCAP) 35
Last Night (East, BMI) 26
Let Me Belong to You (East West, BMI) 32
Let the Four Winds Blow (Commodore, BMI) 43
Let's Get Together (Wonderland, BMI) 69
Little Bit of Soap, A (Mellin, BMI) 19
Little Dog Cried, A (E. V. Deane, ASCAP) 79
Little Sister (Elvis Presley, BMI) 9
Lonely Street (Arc, BMI) 67
Look in My Eyes (Atlantic, BMI) 37
Lover's Island (Code-Figure, BMI) 36
Magic Moon (Conley, ASCAP) 49
(Marie's the Name) His Latest Flame (Elvis Presley, BMI) 22
Mexico (Acuff-Rose, BMI) 33
Michael (United Artists, ASCAP) 1
Missing You (Copar, BMI) 50
More Money for You and Me Medley (Various) 24
Mountain's High, The (Odin, ASCAP) 12
Music, Music, Music (Cromwell, ASCAP) 61
My Blue Heaven (Feist, ASCAP) 54
My Dream Come True (Wolfpack, SESAC) 85
My True Story (Steven, BMI) 3
Nag (Selma, BMI) 28
Now and Forever (Roosevelt, BMI) 62
One Track Mind (Lescay, BMI) 29
Pitter Patter (Fury, BMI) 96
Please Mr. Postman (Jobete, BMI) 88
Pretty Little Angel Eyes (S-P-R, BMI) 51
Roll Over Beethoven (Arc, BMI) 53
Romeo (Good Songs, BMI) 75
Sad Movies (Acuff-Rose, BMI) 72
School Is Out (Pepe, BMI) 16
Sea of Heartbreak (Shapiro-Bernstein, ASCAP) 45
Signed, Sealed and Delivered (Lois, BMI) 99
Starlight (Lonnie-RoAnn, BMI) 80
Starlight, Starbright (Tybee, BMI) 63
Stick Shift (Hilde, BMI) 76
Sweet Little You (Aldon, BMI) 60
Sweets for My Sweet (Brenner-Progressive-Trio, BMI) 87
Take Five (Derry, BMI) 64
Take Good Care of My Baby (Aldon, BMI) 2
Theme From Silver City (Electron-Hollyvine, BMI) 83
Tossin' and Turnin' (Lescay, BMI) 15
Transistor Sister (Claridge, ASCAP) 44
Water Boy (Walbridge, BMI) 52
Way You Look Tonight, The (Harms, ASCAP) 73
Well-A, Well-A (Selma, BMI) 90
When We Get Married (Fisher, BMI) 13
Who Put the Bomp (Aldon, BMI) 8
Without You (Ridge, BMI) 14
Wizard of Love (Edith, BMI) 58
Wooden Heart (Gladys, ASCAP) 6
Ya Ya (Fast-Barich, BMI) 95
Years From Now (Merrimac, BMI) 40
You Don't Know What You've Got (Sequence, ASCAP) 5
You Must Have Been a Beautiful Baby (Remick, ASCAP) 34
You're the Reason (American, BMI) 81


## BUBBLING UNDER THE HOT 100

101. THIS TIME ........ Troy Shondell, Liberty 55353
102. MAGIC IS THE NIGHT ........ Kathy Young, Indigo 125
103. PLAY IT AGAIN ........ Tina Robin, Mercury 71852
104. L-O-V-E ........ Craftys, Seven Arts 708
105. A VERY TRUE STORY ........ Chris Kenner, Instant 3234
106. HEY LITTLE ONE ........ Bruce Bruno, Roulette 4386
107. I UNDERSTAND (JUST HOW YOU FEEL) ........ G-Clefs, Terrace 7500
108. NIGHT TRAIN ........ Richard Hayman, Mercury 71869
109. THAT'S WHY ........ Curtis Knight, Gulf 031
110. BACK TO THE HOP ........ Danny and the Juniors, Swan 4082
111. RIDERS IN THE SKY ........ Lawrence Welk, Dot 16237
112. SAD MOVIES (Make Me Cry) ........ Lennon Sisters, Dot 16255
113. FLYIN' BLUE ANGELS ........ George, Johnny and the Pilots, Coed 555
114. GIRL OF MY DREAMS ........ Capris, Old Town 1107
115. JUST OUT OF REACH (of My Two Open Arms) ........ Solomon Burke, Atlantic 2114
116. OLD SLEW-FOOT ........ Johnny Horton, Columbia 42063
117. YOU BROKE MY HEART ........ Gleems, Kip 236
118. GINHOUSE BLUES ........ Nina Simone, Colpix 608
119. BERLIN MELODY ........ Billy Vaughn, Dot 16119
120. DRUMS ........ Kenny Chandler, United Artists 342

# BILLBOARD HOT 100

**SEPTEMBER 18, 1961**
**FOR WEEK ENDING SEPTEMBER 24, 1961**

| This Week | Wk Ago | 2 Wks Ago | 3 Wks Ago | Title — Artist, Label & Number | Weeks On Chart |
|---|---|---|---|---|---|
| 1 | 2 | 6 | 23 | TAKE GOOD CARE OF MY BABY — Bobby Vee, Liberty 55354 | 7 |
| 2 | 1 | 1 | 3 | MICHAEL — Highwaymen, United Artists 258 | 11 |
| 3 | 3 | 7 | 13 | MY TRUE STORY — Jive Five, Beltone 1006 | 12 |
| 4 | 22 | 32 | 66 | (Marie's the Name) HIS LATEST FLAME — Elvis Presley, RCA Victor 7908 | 4 |
| 5 | 11 | 16 | 29 | CRYIN' — Roy Orbison, Monument 447 | 6 |
| 6 | 7 | 11 | 19 | DOES YOUR CHEWING GUM LOSE ITS FLAVOR (On the Bedpost Over Night) — Lonnie Donegan, Dot 15911 | 7 |
| 7 | 14 | 20 | 28 | WITHOUT YOU — Johnny Tillotson, Cadence 1404 | 7 |
| 8 | 6 | 2 | 1 | WOODEN HEART (Muss I Denn) — Joe Dowell, Smash 1708 | 13 |
| 9 | 29 | 45 | 69 | ONE TRACK MIND — Bobby Lewis, Beltone 1012 | 4 |
| 10 | 13 | 23 | 34 | WHEN WE GET MARRIED — Dreamlovers, Heritage 102 | 8 |
| 11 | 5 | 4 | 5 | YOU DON'T KNOW WHAT YOU'VE GOT (Until You Lose It) — Ral Donner, Gone 5108 | 11 |
| 12 | 19 | 24 | 35 | A LITTLE BIT OF SOAP — Jarmels, Laurie 3098 | 7 |
| 13 | 9 | 15 | 26 | LITTLE SISTER — Elvis Presley, RCA Victor 7908 | 5 |
| 14 | 31 | 38 | 42 | IT'S GONNA WORK OUT FINE — Ike and Tina Turner, Sue 749 | 8 |
| 15 | 12 | 21 | 32 | THE MOUNTAIN'S HIGH — Dick and Deedee, Liberty 55350 | 8 |
| 16 | 15 | 3 | 2 | TOSSIN' AND TURNIN' — Bobby Lewis, Beltone 1002 | 22 |
| 17 | 8 | 14 | 24 | WHO PUT THE BOMP (In the Bomp, Bomp, Bomp) — Barry Mann, ABC-Paramount 10237 | 7 |
| 18 | 4 | 8 | 10 | HURT — Timi Yuro, Liberty 55343 | 9 |
| 19 | 23 | 34 | 53 | BIG COLD WIND — Pat Boone, Dot 16244 | 5 |
| 20 | 20 | 31 | 45 | FRANKIE AND JOHNNY — Brook Benton, Mercury 71859 | 5 |
| 21 | 24 | 41 | 52 | MORE MONEY FOR YOU AND ME MEDLEY — Four Preps, Capitol 4599 | 6 |
| 22 | 33 | 44 | 59 | MEXICO — Bob Moore, Monument 446 | 6 |
| 23 | 34 | 67 | — | YOU MUST HAVE BEEN A BEAUTIFUL BABY — Bobby Darin, Atco 6206 | 3 |
| 24 | 21 | 12 | 14 | I FALL TO PIECES — Patsy Cline, Decca 31205 | 18 |
| 25 | 28 | 30 | 36 | NAG — Halos, Seven Arts 709 | 10 |
| 26 | 18 | 9 | 9 | DON'T BET MONEY HONEY — Linda Scott, Canadian-American 127 | 12 |
| 27 | 55 | — | — | HIT THE ROAD JACK — Ray Charles, ABC-Paramount 10244 | 2 |
| 28 | 26 | 13 | 4 | LAST NIGHT — Mar-Keys, Satellite 107 | 11 |
| 29 | 16 | 5 | 7 | SCHOOL IS OUT — Gary (U.S.) Bonds, LeGrand 1009 | 9 |
| 30 | 17 | 19 | 27 | I JUST DON'T UNDERSTAND — Ann-Margret, RCA Victor 7894 | 9 |
| 31 | 36 | 36 | 50 | LOVER'S ISLAND — Bluejays, Milestone 2008 | 6 |
| 32 | 10 | 10 | 11 | AS IF I DIDN'T KNOW — Adam Wade, Coed 553 | 8 |
| 33 | 48 | 71 | — | THE ASTRONAUT — Jose Jimenez, Kapp 409 | 3 |
| 34 | 27 | 18 | 22 | AMOR — Ben E. King, Atco 6203 | 8 |
| 35 | 46 | 64 | 75 | JEREMIAH PEABODY'S POLY UNSATURATED QUICK DISSOLVING FAST ACTING PLEASANT TASTING GREEN AND PURPLE PILLS — Ray Stevens, Mercury 71843 | 5 |
| 36 | 37 | 47 | 80 | LOOK IN MY EYES — Chantels, Carlton 555 | 4 |
| 37 | 40 | 60 | 84 | YEARS FROM NOW — Jackie Wilson, Brunswick 55219 | 5 |
| 38 | 32 | 33 | 48 | LET ME BELONG TO YOU — Brian Hyland, ABC-Paramount 10236 | 7 |
| 39 | 74 | — | — | BRISTOL STOMP — Dovells, Parkway 827 | 2 |
| 40 | 69 | 92 | — | LET'S GET TOGETHER — Hayley Mills, Vista 385 | 3 |
| 41 | 30 | 40 | 57 | BLESS YOU — Tony Orlando, Epic 9452 | 6 |
| 42 | 35 | 43 | 60 | KISSIN' ON THE PHONE — Paul Anka, ABC-Paramount 10239 | 4 |
| 43 | 25 | 29 | 31 | I'LL NEVER SMILE AGAIN — Platters, Mercury 71847 | 8 |
| 44 | 73 | 93 | — | THE WAY YOU LOOK TONIGHT — Lettermen, Capitol 4586 | 3 |
| 45 | 64 | — | — | TAKE FIVE — Dave Brubeck, Columbia 41479 | 2 |
| 46 | 42 | 55 | 67 | EVERY BREATH I TAKE — Gene Pitney, Musicor 1011 | 7 |
| 47 | 39 | 39 | 43 | DON'T CRY BABY — Etta James, Argo 5393 | 7 |
| 48 | 41 | 22 | 6 | I LIKE IT LIKE THAT — Chris Kenner, Instant 3229 | 17 |
| 49 | 43 | 27 | 15 | LET THE FOUR WINDS BLOW — Fats Domino, Imperial 5764 | 9 |
| 50 | 54 | 73 | 88 | MY BLUE HEAVEN — Duane Eddy, Jamie 1200 | 4 |
| 51 | 53 | 61 | 68 | ROLL OVER BEETHOVEN — Velaires, Jamie 1198 | 6 |
| 52 | 57 | 59 | 73 | BABY, YOU'RE SO FINE — Mickey and Sylvia, Willow 23000 | 5 |
| 53 | 76 | — | — | STICK SHIFT — Duals, Sue 745 | 2 |
| 54 | 61 | 58 | 74 | MUSIC, MUSIC, MUSIC — Sensations, Argo 5391 | 6 |
| 55 | 58 | 65 | 76 | WIZARD OF LOVE — Ly-Dells, Master 251 | 5 |
| 56 | 49 | 53 | 61 | MAGIC MOON — Rays, XYZ 607 | 6 |
| 57 | 71 | 78 | — | DON'T GET AROUND MUCH ANYMORE — Belmonts, Sabrina 501 | 3 |
| 58 | 50 | 51 | 56 | MISSING YOU — Ray Peterson, Dunes 2006 | 8 |
| 59 | 72 | 84 | — | SAD MOVIES (Make Me Cry) — Sue Thompson, Hickory 1153 | 3 |
| 60 | 45 | 28 | 21 | SEA OF HEARTBREAK — Don Gibson, RCA Victor 7890 | 14 |
| 61 | 47 | 26 | 20 | HILLBILLY HEAVEN — Tex Ritter, Capitol 4567 | 12 |
| 62 | 70 | 81 | — | JUKE BOX SATURDAY NIGHT — Nino and the Ebb Tides, Madison 166 | 3 |
| 63 | 89 | 96 | — | I LOVE HOW YOU LOVE ME — Paris Sisters, Gregmark 6 | 3 |
| 64 | 87 | — | — | SWEETS FOR MY SWEET — Drifters, Atlantic 2117 | 2 |
| 65 | 84 | 97 | — | HUMAN — Tommy Hunt, Scepter 1219 | 3 |
| 66 | 60 | 62 | 77 | SWEET LITTLE YOU — Neil Sedaka, RCA Victor 7922 | 4 |
| 67 | 44 | 35 | 46 | TRANSISTOR SISTER — Freddy Cannon, Swan 4078 | 8 |
| 68 | 59 | 63 | 78 | I WAKE UP CRYING — Chuck Jackson, Wand 110 | 5 |
| 69 | 52 | 46 | 51 | WATER BOY — Don Shirley Trio, Cadence 1392 | 10 |
| 70 | 82 | 88 | — | (I Love You) FOR SENTIMENTAL REASONS — Cleftones, Gee 1067 | 3 |
| 71 | 79 | 83 | — | A LITTLE DOG CRIED — Jimmie Rodgers, Roulette 4384 | 3 |
| 72 | 86 | 90 | — | I DON'T LIKE IT LIKE THAT — Bobbettes, Gone 5112 | 3 |
| 73 | 95 | — | — | YA YA — Lee Dorsey, Fury 1053 | 2 |
| 74 | 94 | 100 | — | FOOT STOMPIN' (Part 1) — Flares, Felsted 8624 | 3 |
| 75 | — | — | — | THIS TIME — Troy Shondell, Liberty 55353 | 1 |
| 76 | — | — | — | TONIGHT I WON'T BE THERE — Adam Wade, Coed 556 | 1 |
| 77 | — | — | — | LET TRUE LOVE BEGIN — Nat King Cole, Capitol 4623 | 1 |
| 78 | — | — | — | I UNDERSTAND (Just How You Feel) — G-Clefs, Terrace 7500 | 1 |
| 79 | 93 | — | — | (He's) THE GREAT IMPOSTOR — Fleetwoods, Dolton 45 | 2 |
| 80 | — | — | — | NIGHT TRAIN — Richard Hayman, Mercury 71869 | 1 |
| 81 | — | — | — | MAGIC IS THE NIGHT — Kathy Young, Indigo 125 | 1 |
| 82 | 88 | 95 | — | PLEASE MR. POSTMAN — Marvelettes, Tamla 54046 | 3 |
| 83 | 85 | 86 | 93 | MY DREAM COME TRUE — Jack Scott, Capitol 4597 | 4 |
| 84 | 66 | 69 | 87 | KEEP ON DANCING — Hank Ballard and the Midnighters, King 5535 | 5 |
| 85 | — | — | — | SO LONG BABY — Del Shannon, Big Top 3083 | 1 |
| 86 | 97 | — | — | IT'S YOUR WORLD — Marty Robbins, Columbia 42065 | 2 |
| 87 | — | — | — | TAKE MY LOVE — Little Willie John, King 5516 | 1 |
| 88 | 81 | 85 | 97 | YOU'RE THE REASON — Bobby Edwards, Crest 1075 | 4 |
| 89 | 91 | — | — | ANNIVERSARY OF LOVE — Caslons, Seeco 6078 | 2 |
| 90 | — | 68 | 72 | SUMMER SOUVENIRS — Karl Hammil Jr., Arliss 1007 | 7 |
| 91 | 99 | — | — | SIGNED, SEALED AND DELIVERED — Rusty Draper, Mercury 71854 | 2 |
| 92 | — | — | — | GIRL IN MY DREAMS — Capris, Old Town 1107 | 1 |
| 93 | — | — | — | BACK TO THE HOP — Danny and the Juniors, Swan 4082 | 1 |
| 94 | — | — | — | BERLIN MELODY — Billy Vaughn, Dot 16119 | 1 |
| 95 | — | — | — | PLAY IT AGAIN — Tina Robin, Mercury 71852 | 1 |
| 96 | — | — | — | JUST OUT OF REACH (of My Two Open Arms) — Solomon Burke, Atlantic 2114 | 1 |
| 97 | 98 | — | — | IMPOSSIBLE — Gloria Lynne, Everest 19418 | 2 |
| 98 | — | 100 | — | I LOVE YOU, YES I DO — Bullmoose Jackson, Seven Arts 705 | 1 |
| 99 | — | — | — | PANIC — Ods Williams, King 5527 | 1 |
| 100 | — | — | — | BRIGHT LIGHTS, BIG CITY — Jimmy Reed, Vee Jay 398 | 1 |

## BUBBLING UNDER THE HOT 100

101. EV'RYBODY PONY — Teddy and the Continentals, Pik 234
102. SAD MOVIES (Make Me Cry) — Lennon Sisters, Dot 16255
103. HEY LITTLE ONE — Bruce Bruno, Roulette 4386
104. MOVIN' — Bill Black's Combo, Hi 2038
105. A VERY TRUE STORY — Chris Kenner, Instant 3234
106. HOLLYWOOD — Connie Francis, MGM 13039
107. RIDERS IN THE SKY — Lawrence Welk, Dot 16237
108. BROKEN HEART AND A PILLOW FULL OF TEARS — Patti Page, Mercury 71870
109. LATE DATE — Parkays, ABC-Paramount 10242
110. FEEL IT — Sam Cooke, RCA Victor 7927
111. OLD SLEW-FOOT — Johnny Horton, Columbia 42063
112. DONALD, WHERE'S YOUR TROOSERS — Andy Stewart, Warwick 665
113. MEMORIES OF THOSE OLDIES BUT GOODIES — Little Caesar and the Romans, Del-Fi 4166
114. GINHOUSE BLUES — Nina Simone, Colpix 608
115. RUNAROUND SUE — Dion, Laurie 3110
116. (HE'S MY) DREAMBOAT — Connie Francis, MGM 13039
117. WHAT KIND OF GIRL — Charmaines, Fraternity 880
118. AUF WIEDERSEH'N — Gus Backus, Fono-Graf 1235
119. I CAN'T FORGET — Marvin Rainwater, Warwick 666
120. SINCERELY — Tokens, RCA Victor 7925

# BILLBOARD HOT 100

**SEPTEMBER 25, 1961**
**FOR WEEK ENDING OCTOBER 1, 1961**

| This Week | Wks. Ago (2,3) | Title | Artist, Label & Number | Weeks On Chart |
|---|---|---|---|---|
| 1 | 1 2 6 | TAKE GOOD CARE OF MY BABY | Bobby Vee, Liberty 55354 | 8 |
| 2 | 15 12 21 | THE MOUNTAIN'S HIGH | Dick and Deedee, Liberty 55350 | 9 |
| 3 | 2 1 1 | MICHAEL | Highwaymen, United Artists 258 | 12 |
| 4 | 5 11 16 | CRYIN' | Roy Orbison, Monument 447 | 7 |
| 5 | 6 7 11 | DOES YOUR CHEWING GUM LOSE ITS FLAVOR (On the Bedpost Over Night) | Lonnie Donegan, Dot 15911 | 8 |
| 6 | 13 9 15 | LITTLE SISTER | Elvis Presley, RCA Victor 7908 | 6 |
| 7 | 17 8 14 | WHO PUT THE BOMP (In the Bomp, Bomp, Bomp) | Barry Mann, ABC-Paramount 10237 | 8 |
| 8 | 3 3 7 | MY TRUE STORY | Jive Five, Beltone 1006 | 13 |
| 9 | 7 14 20 | WITHOUT YOU | Johnny Tillotson, Cadence 1404 | 8 |
| 10 | 4 22 32 | (Marie's the Name) HIS LATEST FLAME | Elvis Presley, RCA Victor 7908 | 5 |
| 11 | 9 29 45 | ONE TRACK MIND | Bobby Lewis, Beltone 1012 | 5 |
| 12 | 22 33 44 | MEXICO | Bob Moore, Monument 446 | 7 |
| 13 | 27 55 — | HIT THE ROAD JACK | Ray Charles, ABC-Paramount 10244 | 3 |
| 14 | 39 74 — | BRISTOL STOMP | Dovells, Parkway 827 | 3 |
| 15 | 10 13 23 | WHEN WE GET MARRIED | Dreamlovers, Heritage 102 | 9 |
| 16 | 23 34 67 | YOU MUST HAVE BEEN A BEAUTIFUL BABY | Bobby Darin, Atco 6206 | 4 |
| 17 | 21 24 41 | MORE MONEY FOR YOU AND ME MEDLEY | Four Preps, Capitol 4599 | 7 |
| 18 | 14 31 38 | IT'S GONNA WORK OUT FINE | Ike and Tina Turner, Sue 749 | 9 |
| 19 | 19 23 34 | BIG COLD WIND | Pat Boone, Dot 16244 | 6 |
| 20 | 38 32 33 | LET ME BELONG TO YOU | Brian Hyland, ABC-Paramount 10236 | 8 |
| 21 | 18 4 8 | HURT | Timi Yuro, Liberty 55343 | 10 |
| 22 | 41 30 40 | BLESS YOU | Tony Orlando, Epic 9452 | 7 |
| 23 | 8 6 2 | WOODEN HEART (Muss I Denn) | Joe Dowell, Smash 1708 | 14 |
| 24 | 75 — — | THIS TIME | Troy Shondell, Liberty 55353 | 2 |
| 25 | 33 48 71 | THE ASTRONAUT | Jose Jimenez, Kapp 409 | 6 |
| 26 | 28 26 13 | LAST NIGHT | Mar-Keys, Satellite 107 | 12 |
| 27 | 12 19 24 | A LITTLE BIT OF SOAP | Jarmels, Laurie 3098 | 8 |
| 28 | 20 20 31 | FRANKIE AND JOHNNY | Brook Benton, Mercury 71859 | 6 |
| 29 | 58 50 51 | MISSING YOU | Ray Peterson, Dunes 2006 | 9 |
| 30 | 40 69 92 | LET'S GET TOGETHER | Hayley Mills, Vista 385 | 4 |
| 31 | 24 21 12 | I FALL TO PIECES | Patsy Cline, Decca 31205 | 19 |
| 32 | 30 17 19 | I JUST DON'T UNDERSTAND | Ann-Margret, RCA Victor 7894 | 10 |
| 33 | 73 95 — | YA YA | Lee Dorsey, Fury 1053 | 3 |
| 34 | 29 16 5 | SCHOOL IS OUT | Gary (U.S.) Bonds, LeGrand 1009 | 10 |
| 35 | 31 36 36 | LOVER'S ISLAND | Bluejays, Milestone 2008 | 7 |
| 36 | 26 18 9 | DON'T BET MONEY HONEY | Linda Scott, Canadian-American 127 | 13 |
| 37 | 64 87 — | SWEETS FOR MY SWEET | Drifters, Atlantic 2117 | 3 |
| 38 | 44 73 93 | THE WAY YOU LOOK TONIGHT | Lettermen, Capitol 4586 | 4 |
| 39 | 59 72 84 | SAD MOVIES (Make Me Cry) | Sue Thompson, Hickory 1153 | 4 |
| 40 | 45 64 — | TAKE FIVE | Dave Brubeck, Columbia 41479 | 3 |
| 41 | 63 89 96 | I LOVE HOW YOU LOVE ME | Paris Sisters, Gregmark 6 | 4 |
| 42 | — — — | RUNAROUND SUE | Dion, Laurie 3110 | 1 |
| 43 | 34 27 18 | AMOR | Ben E. King, Atco 6203 | 9 |
| 44 | 11 5 4 | YOU DON'T KNOW WHAT YOU'VE GOT (Until You Lose It) | Ral Donner, Gone 5108 | 12 |
| 45 | 49 43 27 | LET THE FOUR WINDS BLOW | Fats Domino, Imperial 5764 | 10 |
| 46 | 53 76 — | STICK SHIFT | Duals, Sue 745 | 3 |
| 47 | 79 93 — | (He's) THE GREAT IMPOSTOR | Fleetwoods, Dolton 45 | 3 |
| 48 | 37 40 60 | YEARS FROM NOW | Jackie Wilson, Brunswick 55219 | 6 |
| 49 | 35 46 64 | JEREMIAH PEABODY'S POLY UNSATURATED QUICK DISSOLVING FAST ACTING PLEASANT TASTING GREEN AND PURPLE PILLS | Ray Stevens, Mercury 71843 | 6 |
| 50 | 36 37 47 | LOOK IN MY EYES | Chantels, Carlton 555 | 5 |
| 51 | 32 10 10 | AS IF I DIDN'T KNOW | Adam Wade, Coed 553 | 10 |
| 52 | 16 15 3 | TOSSIN' AND TURNIN' | Bobby Lewis, Beltone 1002 | 23 |
| 53 | 65 84 97 | HUMAN | Tommy Hunt, Scepter 1219 | 4 |
| 54 | 55 58 65 | WIZARD OF LOVE | Ly-Dells, Master 251 | 6 |
| 55 | 46 42 55 | EVERY BREATH I TAKE | Gene Pitney, Musicor 1011 | 8 |
| 56 | 69 52 46 | WATER BOY | Don Shirley Trio, Cadence 1392 | 11 |
| 57 | 62 70 81 | JUKE BOX SATURDAY NIGHT | Nino and the Ebb Tides, Madison 166 | 4 |
| 58 | 74 94 100 | FOOT STOMPIN' (Part 1) | Flares, Felsted 8624 | 3 |
| 59 | 66 60 62 | SWEET LITTLE YOU | Neil Sedaka, RCA Victor 7922 | 5 |
| 60 | — — — | THE FLY | Chubby Checker, Parkway 830 | 1 |
| 61 | 57 71 78 | DON'T GET AROUND MUCH ANYMORE | Belmonts, Sabrina 501 | 4 |
| 62 | 68 59 63 | I WAKE UP CRYING | Chuck Jackson, Wand 110 | 4 |
| 63 | 70 82 88 | (I Love You) FOR SENTIMENTAL REASONS | Cleftones, Gee 1067 | 4 |
| 64 | 25 28 30 | NAG | Halos, Seven Arts 709 | 11 |
| 65 | 52 57 59 | BABY, YOU'RE SO FINE | Mickey and Sylvia, Willow 23000 | 6 |
| 66 | 56 49 53 | MAGIC MOON | Rays, XYZ 607 | 7 |
| 67 | — — — | HOLLYWOOD | Connie Francis, MGM 13039 | 1 |
| 68 | 85 — — | SO LONG BABY | Del Shannon, Big Top 3083 | 2 |
| 69 | 50 54 73 | MY BLUE HEAVEN | Duane Eddy, Jamie 1200 | 5 |
| 70 | 86 97 — | IT'S YOUR WORLD | Marty Robbins, Columbia 42065 | 3 |
| 71 | — — — | MOVIN' | Bill Black's Combo, Hi 2038 | 1 |
| 72 | — — — | (He's My) DREAMBOAT | Connie Francis, MGM 13039 | 1 |
| 73 | 71 79 83 | A LITTLE DOG CRIED | Jimmie Rodgers, Roulette 4384 | 4 |
| 74 | 78 — — | I UNDERSTAND (Just How You Feel) | G-Clefs, Terrace 7500 | 2 |
| 75 | — — — | FEEL IT | Sam Cooke, RCA Victor 7927 | 1 |
| 76 | 42 35 43 | KISSIN' ON THE PHONE | Paul Anka, ABC-Paramount 10239 | 5 |
| 77 | 72 86 90 | I DON'T LIKE IT LIKE THAT | Bobbettes, Gone 5112 | 4 |
| 78 | 51 53 61 | ROLL OVER BEETHOVEN | Velaires, Jamie 1198 | 7 |
| 79 | 82 88 95 | PLEASE MR. POSTMAN | Marvelettes, Tamla 54046 | 4 |
| 80 | 81 — — | MAGIC IS THE NIGHT | Kathy Young, Indigo 125 | 2 |
| 81 | — — — | PLEASE DON'T GO | Ral Donner, Gone 5114 | 1 |
| 82 | 54 61 58 | MUSIC, MUSIC, MUSIC | Sensations, Argo 5391 | 7 |
| 83 | 100 — — | BRIGHT LIGHTS, BIG CITY | Jimmy Reed, Vee Jay 398 | 2 |
| 84 | 76 — — | TONIGHT I WON'T BE THERE | Adam Wade, Coed 556 | 2 |
| 85 | — — — | I REALLY LOVE YOU | Stereos, Cub 9095 | 1 |
| 86 | 93 — — | BACK TO THE HOP | Danny and the Juniors, Swan 4082 | 2 |
| 87 | — — — | DON'T BLAME ME | Everly Brothers, Warner Bros. 5501 | 1 |
| 88 | — — — | SAD MOVIES (Make Me Cry) | Lennon Sisters, Dot 16255 | 1 |
| 89 | 90 — 68 | SUMMER SOUVENIRS | Karl Hammil Jr., Arliss 1007 | 8 |
| 90 | — — — | FARAWAY STAR | Chordettes, Cadence 1402 | 1 |
| 91 | — — — | RIDERS IN THE SKY | Lawrence Welk, Dot 16237 | 1 |
| 92 | — — — | TRUE, TRUE LOVE | Frankie Avalon, Chancellor 1087 | 1 |
| 93 | — — — | IT'S ALL RIGHT | Sam Cooke, RCA Victor 7927 | 1 |
| 94 | 96 — — | JUST OUT OF REACH (of My Two Open Arms) | Solomon Burke, Atlantic 2114 | 2 |
| 95 | 88 81 85 | YOU'RE THE REASON | Bobby Edwards, Crest 1075 | 4 |
| 96 | — — — | JOHNNY WILLOW | Fred Darian, JAF 2023 | 1 |
| 97 | — — — | HONKY TRAIN | Bill Black's Combo, Hi 2038 | 1 |
| 98 | 97 98 — | IMPOSSIBLE | Gloria Lynne, Everest 19418 | 3 |
| 99 | — — — | YOUR LAST GOODBYE | Floyd Cramer, RCA Victor 7907 | 1 |
| 100 | — 78 — | CINDERELLA | Paul Anka, ABC-Paramount 10239 | 2 |

## BUBBLING UNDER THE HOT 100

101. MEMORIES OF THOSE OLDIES BUT GOODIES — Little Caesar and the Romans, Del-Fi 4166
102. LET TRUE LOVE BEGIN — Nat King Cole, Capitol 4623
103. A VERY TRUE STORY — Chris Kenner, Instant 3234
104. BERLIN MELODY — Billy Vaughn, Dot 16119
105. HANG ON — Little Willie John, King 5516
106. HANG ON — Floyd Cramer, RCA Victor 7907
107. YOU'RE THE REASON — Hank Locklin, RCA Victor 7921
108. LATE DATE — Parkays, ABC-Paramount 10242
109. LINDA — Adam Wade, Coed 556
110. OLD SLEW-FOOT — Johnny Horton, Columbia 42063
111. DONALD, WHERE'S YOUR TROOSERS — Andy Stewart, Warwick 665
112. NIGHT TRAIN — Richard Hayman, Mercury 71869
113. GINHOUSE BLUES — Nina Simone, Colpix 608
114. SONG OF THE NAIROBI TRIO — Fortune Tellers, Music Makers 105
115. YOU DON'T KNOW WHAT IT MEANS — Jackie Wilson, Brunswick 55219
116. GUILTY OF LOVING YOU — Jerry Fuller, Challenge 9114
117. SATIN DOLL — Billy Maxted, K&H 501
118. PLAY IT AGAIN — Tina Robin, Mercury 71852
119. MR. DJ — Van McCoy, Rockin' 101
120. A BROKEN HEART AND A PILLOW FILLED WITH TEARS — Patti Page, Mercury 71870

# BILLBOARD HOT 100

FOR WEEK ENDING OCTOBER 8

1961

★ STAR PERFORMERS—Selections registering greatest upward progress this week.

S Indicates that 45 r.p.m. stereo single version is available.

△ Indicates that 33⅓ r.p.m. mono single version is available.

△S Indicates that 33⅓ r.p.m. stereo single version is available.

| This Week | 1 Wk. Ago | 2 Wks. Ago | 3 Wks. Ago | Title | Artist, Label & Number | Weeks On Chart |
|---|---|---|---|---|---|---|
| 1 | 1 | 1 | 2 | TAKE GOOD CARE OF MY BABY | Bobby Vee, Liberty 55354 | 9 |
| 2 | 2 | 15 | 12 | THE MOUNTAIN'S HIGH | Dick and Deedee, Liberty 55350 | 10 |
| 3 | 4 | 5 | 11 | CRYIN' | Roy Orbison, Monument 447 | 8 |
| 4 | 13 | 27 | 55 | HIT THE ROAD JACK | Ray Charles, ABC-Paramount 10244 | 4 |
| 5 | 6 | 13 | 9 | LITTLE SISTER △ | Elvis Presley, RCA Victor 7908 | 7 |
| 6 | 3 | 2 | 1 | MICHAEL | Highwaymen, United Artists 258 | 13 |
| 7 | 12 | 22 | 33 | MEXICO | Bob Moore, Monument 446 | 8 |
| 8 | 16 | 23 | 34 | YOU MUST HAVE BEEN A BEAUTIFUL BABY | Bobby Darin, Atco 6206 | 5 |
| 9 | 5 | 6 | 7 | DOES YOUR CHEWING GUM LOSE ITS FLAVOR (On the Bedpost Over Night) | Lonnie Donegan, Dot 15911 | 9 |
| 10 | 14 | 39 | 74 | BRISTOL STOMP | Dovells, Parkway 827 | 4 |
| 11 | 7 | 17 | 8 | WHO PUT THE BOMP (In the Bomp, Bomp, Bomp) | Barry Mann, ABC-Paramount 10237 | 9 |
| 12 | 9 | 7 | 14 | WITHOUT YOU | Johnny Tillotson, Cadence 1404 | 9 |
| 13 | 11 | 9 | 29 | ONE TRACK MIND | Bobby Lewis, Beltone 1012 | 6 |
| 14 | 33 | 73 | 95 | YA YA | Lee Dorsey, Fury 1053 | 4 |
| 15 | 30 | 40 | 69 | LET'S GET TOGETHER | Hayley Mills, Vista 385 | 5 |
| 16 | 38 | 44 | 73 | THE WAY YOU LOOK TONIGHT | Lettermen, Capitol 4586 | 5 |
| 17 | 24 | 75 | — | THIS TIME | Troy Shondell, Liberty 55353 | 3 |
| 18 | 22 | 41 | 30 | BLESS YOU | Tony Orlando, Epic 9452 | 8 |
| 19 | 25 | 33 | 48 | THE ASTRONAUT | Jose Jimenez, Kapp 409 | 7 |
| 20 | 8 | 3 | 3 | MY TRUE STORY | Jive Five, Beltone 1006 | 14 |
| 21 | 42 | — | — | RUNAROUND SUE | Dion, Laurie 3110 | 2 |
| 22 | 17 | 21 | 24 | MORE MONEY FOR YOU AND ME MEDLEY | Four Preps, Capitol 4599 | 8 |
| 23 | 50 | 36 | 37 | LOOK IN MY EYES | Chantels, Carlton 555 | 6 |
| 24 | 39 | 59 | 72 | SAD MOVIES (Make Me Cry) | Sue Thompson, Hickory 1153 | 5 |
| 25 | 20 | 38 | 32 | LET ME BELONG TO YOU | Brian Hyland, ABC-Paramount 10236 | 9 |
| 26 | 10 | 4 | 22 | (Marie's the Name) HIS LATEST FLAME △ | Elvis Presley, RCA Victor 7908 | 6 |
| 27 | 19 | 19 | 23 | BIG COLD WIND | Pat Boone, Dot 16244 | 7 |
| 28 | 37 | 64 | 87 | SWEETS FOR MY SWEET | Drifters, Atlantic 2117 | 4 |
| 29 | 15 | 10 | 13 | WHEN WE GET MARRIED | Dreamlovers, Heritage 102 | 10 |
| 30 | 29 | 58 | 50 | MISSING YOU | Ray Peterson, Dunes 2006 | 10 |
| 31 | 21 | 18 | 4 | HURT | Timi Yuro, Liberty 55343 | 11 |
| 32 | 41 | 63 | 89 | I LOVE HOW YOU LOVE ME | Paris Sisters, Gregmark 6 | 5 |
| 33 | 46 | 53 | 76 | STICK SHIFT | Duals, Sue 745 | 4 |
| 34 | 26 | 28 | 26 | LAST NIGHT | Mar-Keys, Satellite 107 | 13 |
| 35 | 18 | 14 | 31 | IT'S GONNA WORK OUT FINE | Ike and Tina Turner, Sue 749 | 10 |
| 36 | 60 | — | — | THE FLY | Chubby Checker, Parkway 830 | 2 |
| 37 | 23 | 8 | 6 | WOODEN HEART (Muss I Denn) | Joe Dowell, Smash 1708 | 15 |
| 38 | 40 | 45 | 64 | TAKE FIVE △ | Dave Brubeck, Columbia 41479 | 4 |
| 39 | 47 | 79 | 93 | (He's) THE GREAT IMPOSTOR | Fleetwoods, Dolton 45 | 4 |
| 40 | 27 | 12 | 19 | A LITTLE BIT OF SOAP | Jarmels, Laurie 3098 | 9 |
| 41 | 32 | 30 | 11 | I JUST DON'T UNDERSTAND △ | Ann-Margret, RCA Victor 7894 | 11 |
| 42 | 35 | 31 | 36 | LOVER'S ISLAND | Bluejays, Milestone 2008 | 8 |
| 43 | 68 | 85 | — | SO LONG BABY | Del Shannon, Big Top 3083 | 3 |
| 44 | 28 | 20 | 20 | FRANKIE AND JOHNNY | Brook Benton, Mercury 71859 | 7 |
| 45 | 34 | 29 | 16 | SCHOOL IS OUT | Gary (U. S.) Bonds, LeGrand 1009 | 11 |
| 46 | 87 | — | — | DON'T BLAME ME | Everly Brothers, Warner Bros. 5501 | 2 |
| 47 | 36 | 26 | 18 | DON'T BET MONEY HONEY | Linda Scott, Canadian-American 127 | 14 |
| 48 | 31 | 24 | 21 | I FALL TO PIECES | Patsy Cline, Decca 31205 | 20 |
| 49 | 56 | 69 | 52 | WATER BOY | Don Shirley Trio, Cadence 1392 | 12 |
| 50 | 58 | 74 | 94 | FOOT STOMPIN' (Part 1) | Flares, Felsted 8624 | 5 |
| 51 | 53 | 65 | 84 | HUMAN | Tommy Hunt, Scepter 1219 | 5 |
| 52 | 43 | 34 | 27 | AMOR | Ben E. King, Atco 6203 | 10 |
| 53 | — | — | — | BIG BAD JOHN △ | Jimmy Dean, Columbia 42175 | 1 |
| 54 | 45 | 49 | 43 | LET THE FOUR WINDS BLOW | Fats Domino, Imperial 5764 | 11 |
| 55 | — | — | — | CANDY MAN | Roy Orbison, Monument 447 | 6 |
| 56 | 85 | — | — | I REALLY LOVE YOU | Stereos, Cub 9095 | 2 |
| 57 | 71 | — | — | MOVIN' | Bill Black's Combo, Hi 2038 | 2 |
| 58 | 61 | 57 | 71 | DON'T GET AROUND MUCH ANYMORE | Belmonts, Sabrina 501 | 5 |
| 59 | 72 | — | — | (He's My) DREAMBOAT | Connie Francis, MGM 13039 | 2 |
| 60 | 63 | 70 | 82 | (I Love You) FOR SENTIMENTAL REASONS | Cleftones, Gee 1067 | 5 |
| 61 | 88 | — | — | SAD MOVIES (Make Me Cry) | Lennon Sisters, Dot 16255 | 2 |
| 62 | 57 | 62 | 70 | JUKE BOX SATURDAY NIGHT | Nino and the Ebb Tides, Madison 166 | 5 |
| 63 | — | — | — | WHAT A PARTY | Fats Domino, Imperial 5779 | 1 |
| 64 | 70 | 86 | 97 | IT'S YOUR WORLD △ | Marty Robbins, Columbia 42065 | 4 |
| 65 | 62 | 68 | 59 | I WAKE UP CRYING | Chuck Jackson, Wand 110 | 7 |
| 66 | — | — | — | "OOL #1 | Brenda Lee, Decca 31309 | 1 |
| 67 | 74 | 78 | — | I UNDERSTAND (Just How You Feel) | G-Clefs, Terrace 7500 | 3 |
| 68 | — | — | — | EVERLOVIN' | Rick Nelson, Imperial 5770 | 1 |
| 69 | 95 | 88 | 81 | YOU'RE THE REASON | Bobby Edwards, Crest 1075 | 6 |
| 70 | 66 | 56 | 49 | MAGIC MOON | Rays, XYZ 607 | 8 |
| 71 | 59 | 66 | 60 | SWEET LITTLE YOU △ | Neil Sedaka, RCA Victor 7922 | 6 |
| 72 | 75 | — | — | FEEL IT △ | Sam Cooke, RCA Victor 7927 | 2 |
| 73 | — | — | — | A WONDER LIKE YOU | Rick Nelson, Imperial 5770 | 1 |
| 74 | 83 | 100 | — | BRIGHT LIGHTS, BIG CITY | Jimmy Reed, Vee Jay 398 | 3 |
| 75 | — | — | — | BIG JOHN | Shirelles, Scepter 1223 | 1 |
| 76 | — | — | — | IT'S JUST A HOUSE WITHOUT YOU | Brook Benton, Mercury 71859 | 1 |
| 77 | — | — | — | ANYBODY BUT ME | Brenda Lee, Decca 31309 | 1 |
| 78 | 67 | — | — | HOLLYWOOD | Connie Francis, MGM 13039 | 2 |
| 79 | 99 | — | — | YOUR LAST GOODBYE △ | Floyd Cramer, RCA Victor 7907 | 2 |
| 80 | 82 | 54 | 61 | MUSIC, MUSIC, MUSIC | Sensations, Argo 5391 | 8 |
| 81 | 79 | 82 | 88 | PLEASE MR. POSTMAN | Marvelettes, Tamla 54046 | 5 |
| 82 | 81 | — | — | PLEASE DON'T GO | Ral Donner, Gone 5114 | 2 |
| 83 | 94 | 96 | — | JUST OUT OF REACH (of My Two Open Arms) | Solomon Burke, Atlantic 2114 | 3 |
| 84 | — | — | — | TOWER OF STRENGTH | Gene McDaniels, Liberty 55371 | 1 |
| 85 | — | — | — | MUSKRAT | Everly Brothers, Warner Bros. 5501 | 1 |
| 86 | 100 | — | 78 | CINDERELLA | Paul Anka, ABC-Paramount 10239 | 3 |
| 87 | 91 | — | — | RIDERS IN THE SKY | Lawrence Welk, Dot 16237 | 2 |
| 88 | — | — | — | YOU DON'T KNOW WHAT IT MEANS | Jackie Wilson, Brunswick 55219 | 1 |
| 89 | 80 | 81 | — | MAGIC IS THE NIGHT | Kathy Young, Indigo 125 | 3 |
| 90 | 92 | — | — | TRUE, TRUE LOVE | Frankie Avalon, Chancellor 1087 | 2 |
| 91 | 84 | 76 | — | TONIGHT I WON'T BE THERE | Adam Wade, Coed 556 | 3 |
| 92 | 86 | 93 | — | BACK TO THE HOP | Danny and the Juniors, Swan 4082 | 3 |
| 93 | — | — | — | POCKETFUL OF RAINBOWS | Deane Hawley, Liberty 55359 | 1 |
| 94 | — | — | — | LINDA | Adam Wade, Coed 556 | 1 |
| 95 | 98 | 97 | 98 | IMPOSSIBLE | Gloria Lynne, Everest 19418 | 4 |
| 96 | 76 | 42 | 35 | KISSIN' ON THE PHONE | Paul Anka, ABC-Paramount 10239 | 6 |
| 97 | — | — | — | HANG ON △ | Floyd Cramer, RCA Victor 7907 | 1 |
| 98 | — | 94 | — | BERLIN MELODY | Billy Vaughn, Dot 16119 | 2 |
| 99 | — | — | — | A BROKEN HEART AND A PILLOW FILLED WITH TEARS | Patti Page, Mercury 71870 | 1 |
| 100 | — | — | — | THREE STEPS TO THE ALTAR | Shep and the Limelites, Hull 747 | 1 |

## HOT 100—A TO Z—(Publisher-Licensee)


Amor (Peer, BMI) .... 52
Anybody But Me (Champion, BMI) .... 77
Astronaut, The (Bill Dana, ASCAP) .... 19
Back to the Hop (Claridge, ASCAP) .... 92
Berlin Melody (Symphony House, ASCAP) .... 98
Big Bad John (Cigma, BMI) .... 53
Big Cold Wind (Gil, BMI) .... 27
Big John (Ludix, BMI) .... 75
Bless You (Aldon, BMI) .... 18
Bright Lights, Big City (Conrad, BMI) .... 74
Bristol Stomp (Kalmann, ASCAP) .... 10
Broken Heart and a Pillow Filled With Tears, A (Spanka, BMI) .... 99
Candy Man (January, BMI) .... 55
Cinderella (Spanka, BMI) .... 86
Cryin' (Acuff-Rose, BMI) .... 3
Does Your Chewing Gum Lose Its Flavor (Mills, ASCAP) .... 9
Don't Bet Money Honey (Figure, BMI) .... 47
Don't Blame Me (Robbins, ASCAP) .... 46
Don't Get Around Much Anymore (Robbins, ASCAP) .... 58
Dreamboat (Acuff-Rose, BMI) .... 59
Everlovin' (Jat, BMI) .... 68
Feel It (Kags, BMI) .... 72
Fly, The (Woodcrest-Mured, BMI) .... 36
Fool #1 (Sure Fire, BMI) .... 66
Foot Stompin' (Part 1) (Argo, BMI) .... 50
For Sentimental Reasons (Duchess, BMI) .... 60
Frankie and Johnny (Ben-Day, BMI) .... 44
Great Impostor, The (Gold Cup-Cornerstone, BMI) .... 39
Hang On (Cigma, BMI) .... 97
His Latest Flame (Elvis Presley, BMI) .... 26
Hit the Road Jack (Tangerine, BMI) .... 4
Hollywood (Acuff-Rose, BMI) .... 78
Human (Ludix, BMI) .... 51
Hurt (Miller, ASCAP) .... 31
I Fall to Pieces (Pamper, BMI) .... 48
I Just Don't Understand (Cedarwood, BMI) .... 41
I Love How You Love Me (Aldon, BMI) .... 32
I Really Love You (Shalimar, BMI) .... 56
I Understand (Jubilee, ASCAP) .... 67
I Wake Up Crying (Belinda, CAPAC) .... 65
Impossible (Tippy, BMI) .... 95
It's Gonna Work Out Fine (Copa-Sona, ASCAP) .... 35
It's Just a House Without You (Play, BMI) .... 76
It's Your World (Marizona, BMI) .... 64
Juke Box Saturday Night (Mutual, ASCAP) .... 62
Just Out of Reach (Four Star, BMI) .... 83
Kissin' on the Phone (Brighton-Flanka, ASCAP) .... 96
Last Night (East, BMI) .... 34
Let Me Belong to You (East-West, BMI) .... 25
Let the Four Winds Blow (Commodore, BMI) .... 54
Let's Get Together (Wonderland, BMI) .... 15
Linda (Warock, ASCAP) .... 94
Little Bit of Soap, A (Mellin, BMI) .... 40
Little Sister (Elvis Presley, BMI) .... 5
Look in My Eyes (Atlantic, BMI) .... 23
Lover's Island (Code-Figure, BMI) .... 42
Magic Is the Night (Blue Indigo, BMI) .... 89
Magic Moon (Conley, ASCAP) .... 70
Mexico (Acuff-Rose, BMI) .... 7
Michael (United Artists, ASCAP) .... 6
Missing You (Copar, BMI) .... 30
More Money for You and Me Medley (Various) .... 22
Mountain's High, The (Odin, ASCAP) .... 2
Movin' (Jec, BMI) .... 57
Music, Music, Music (Cromwell, ASCAP) .... 80
Muskrat (American, BMI) .... 85
My True Story (Steven, BMI) .... 20
One Track Mind (Lescay, BMI) .... 13
Please Don't Go (Alan K., BMI) .... 82
Please Mr. Postman (Jobete, BMI) .... 81
Pocketful of Rainbows (Gladys, ASCAP) .... 93
Riders in the Sky (Morris, ASCAP) .... 87
Runaround Sue (Just-Mubon, BMI) .... 21
Sad Movies—Lennons (Acuff-Rose, BMI) .... 61
Sad Movies—Thompson (Acuff-Rose, BMI) .... 24
School Is Out (Pepe, BMI) .... 45
So Long Baby (Vicki-McLaughlin, BMI) .... 43
Stick Shift (Hilde, BMI) .... 33
Sweet Little You (Aldon, BMI) .... 71
Sweets for My Sweet (Brenner-Progressive-Trio, BMI) .... 28
Take Five (Derry, BMI) .... 38
Take Good Care of My Baby (Aldon, BMI) .... 1
This Time (Tree, BMI) .... 17
Three Steps to the Altar (Keel, BMI) .... 100
Tonight I Won't Be There (Paxton, ASCAP) .... 91
Tower of Strength (Famous, ASCAP) .... 84
True, True Love (Mar-Nick, BMI) .... 90
Water Boy (Walbridge, BMI) .... 49
Way You Look Tonight, The (Harms, ASCAP) .... 16
What a Party (Travis, BMI) .... 63
When We Get Married (Fisher, BMI) .... 29
Who Put the Bomp (Aldon, BMI) .... 11
Without You (Ridge, BMI) .... 12
Wonder Like You, A (Four Star, BMI) .... 73
Wooden Heart (Gladys, ASCAP) .... 37
Ya Ya (Fast-Barich, BMI) .... 14
You Don't Know What It Means (Pearl, BMI) .... 88
You Must Have Been a Beautiful Baby (Remick, ASCAP) .... 8
You're the Reason (American, BMI) .... 69
Your Last Goodbye (Cigma, BMI) .... 79


## BUBBLING UNDER THE HOT 100

101. JOHNNY WILLOW .... Fred Darian, JAF 2023
102. MORNING AFTER .... Mar-Keys, Stax 112
103. LATE DATE .... Parkays, ABC-Paramount 10242
104. HONKY TRAIN .... Bill Black's Combo, Hi 2038
105. GYPSY WOMAN .... Impressions, ABC-Paramount 10241
106. GUILTY OF LOVING YOU .... Jerry Fuller, Challenge 9114
107. AWARE OF LOVE .... Jerry Butler, Vee Jay 405
108. ROCKIN' BICYCLE .... Fats Domino, Imperial 5779
109. MOON RIVER .... Jerry Butler, Vee Jay 405
110. MR. DJ .... Van McCoy, Rockin' 101
111. WASN'T SUMMER SHORT? .... Johnny Mathis, Columbia 42156
112. MAKE BELIEVE WEDDING .... Castells, Era 3057
113. SUMMER SOUVENIRS .... Karl Jammil Jr., Arliss 1007
114. DANCE WITH A DOLLY .... Damita Jo, Mercury 71871
115. SOFT RAIN .... Ray Price, Columbia 42132
116. ANNIVERSARY OF LOVE .... Caslons, Seeco 6078
117. SOOTHE ME .... Sims Twins, Sar 117
118. LAUGH .... Velvets, Monument 448
119. WELL I ASK YOU .... Eden Kane, London 1993
120. WHY NOT NOW .... Matt Monro, Warwick 669

# BILLBOARD HOT 100

**OCTOBER 9, 1961**
**FOR WEEK ENDING OCTOBER 15, 1961**

| This Week | Wk Ago | 2 Wks Ago | 3 Wks Ago | Title — Artist, Label & Number | Weeks On Chart |
|---|---|---|---|---|---|
| 1 | 4 | 13 | 27 | HIT THE ROAD JACK — Ray Charles, ABC-Paramount 10244 | 5 |
| 2 | 3 | 4 | 5 | CRYIN' — Roy Orbison, Monument 447 | 9 |
| 3 | 1 | 1 | 1 | TAKE GOOD CARE OF MY BABY — Bobby Vee, Liberty 55354 | 10 |
| 4 | 21 | 42 | — | RUNAROUND SUE — Dion, Laurie 3110 | 3 |
| 5 | 10 | 14 | 39 | BRISTOL STOMP — Dovells, Parkway 827 | 5 |
| 6 | 8 | 16 | 23 | YOU MUST HAVE BEEN A BEAUTIFUL BABY — Bobby Darin, Atco 6206 | 6 |
| 7 | 2 | 2 | 15 | THE MOUNTAIN'S HIGH — Dick and Deedee, Liberty 55350 | 11 |
| 8 | 5 | 6 | 13 | LITTLE SISTER — Elvis Presley, RCA Victor 7908 | 8 |
| 9 | 15 | 30 | 40 | LET'S GET TOGETHER — Hayley Mills, Vista 385 | 6 |
| 10 | 7 | 12 | 22 | MEXICO — Bob Moore, Monument 446 | 9 |
| 11 | 6 | 3 | 2 | MICHAEL — Highwaymen, United Artists 258 | 14 |
| 12 | 32 | 41 | 63 | I LOVE HOW YOU LOVE ME — Paris Sisters, Gregmark 6 | 6 |
| 13 | 17 | 24 | 75 | THIS TIME — Troy Shondell, Liberty 55353 | 4 |
| 14 | 14 | 33 | 73 | YA YA — Lee Dorsey, Fury 1053 | 5 |
| 15 | 18 | 22 | 41 | BLESS YOU — Tony Orlando, Epic 9452 | 9 |
| 16 | 16 | 38 | 44 | THE WAY YOU LOOK TONIGHT — Lettermen, Capitol 4586 | 6 |
| 17 | 53 | — | — | BIG BAD JOHN — Jimmy Dean, Columbia 42175 | 2 |
| 18 | 24 | 39 | 59 | SAD MOVIES (Make Me Cry) — Sue Thompson, Hickory 1153 | 6 |
| 19 | 23 | 50 | 36 | LOOK IN MY EYES — Chantels, Carlton 555 | 7 |
| 20 | 12 | 9 | 7 | WITHOUT YOU — Johnny Tillotson, Cadence 1404 | 10 |
| 21 | 26 | 10 | 4 | (Marie's the Name) HIS LATEST FLAME — Elvis Presley, RCA Victor 7908 | 7 |
| 22 | 36 | 60 | — | THE FLY — Chubby Checker, Parkway 830 | 3 |
| 23 | 9 | 5 | 6 | DOES YOUR CHEWING GUM LOSE ITS FLAVOR (On the Bedpost Over Night) — Lonnie Donegan, Dot 15911 | 10 |
| 24 | 28 | 37 | 64 | SWEETS FOR MY SWEET — Drifters, Atlantic 2117 | 5 |
| 25 | 38 | 40 | 45 | TAKE FIVE — Dave Brubeck, Columbia 41479 | 5 |
| 26 | 33 | 46 | 53 | STICK SHIFT — Duals, Sue 745 | 5 |
| 27 | 11 | 7 | 17 | WHO PUT THE BOMP (In the Bomp, Bomp, Bomp) — Barry Mann, ABC-Paramount 10237 | 10 |
| 28 | 46 | 87 | — | DON'T BLAME ME — Everly Brothers, Warner Bros. 5501 | 3 |
| 29 | 55 | — | — | CANDY MAN — Roy Orbison, Monument 447 | 7 |
| 30 | 13 | 11 | 9 | ONE TRACK MIND — Bobby Lewis, Beltone 1012 | 7 |
| 31 | 43 | 68 | 85 | SO LONG BABY — Del Shannon, Big Top 3083 | 4 |
| 32 | 59 | 72 | — | (He's My) DREAMBOAT — Connie Francis, MGM 13039 | 3 |
| 33 | 20 | 8 | 3 | MY TRUE STORY — Jive Five, Beltone 1006 | 15 |
| 34 | 30 | 29 | 58 | MISSING YOU — Ray Peterson, Dunes 2006 | 11 |
| 35 | 19 | 25 | 33 | THE ASTRONAUT — Jose Jimenez, Kapp 409 | 8 |
| 36 | 66 | — | — | FOOL #1 — Brenda Lee, Decca 31309 | 2 |
| 37 | 50 | 58 | 74 | FOOT STOMPIN' (Part 1) — Flares, Felsted 8624 | 6 |
| 38 | 39 | 47 | 79 | (He's) THE GREAT IMPOSTOR — Fleetwoods, Dolton 45 | 5 |
| 39 | 68 | — | — | EVERLOVIN' — Rick Nelson, Imperial 5770 | 2 |
| 40 | 49 | 56 | 69 | WATER BOY — Don Shirley Trio, Cadence 1392 | 13 |
| 41 | 57 | 71 | — | MOVIN' — Bill Black's Combo, Hi 2038 | 3 |
| 42 | 67 | 74 | 78 | I UNDERSTAND (Just How You Feel) — G-Clefs, Terrace 7500 | 4 |
| 43 | 56 | 85 | — | I REALLY LOVE YOU — Stereos, Cub 9095 | 3 |
| 44 | 63 | — | — | WHAT A PARTY — Fats Domino, Imperial 5779 | 2 |
| 45 | 84 | — | — | TOWER OF STRENGTH — Gene McDaniels, Liberty 55371 | 2 |
| 46 | 69 | 95 | 88 | YOU'RE THE REASON — Bobby Edwards, Crest 1075 | 7 |
| 47 | 22 | 17 | 21 | MORE MONEY FOR YOU AND ME MEDLEY — Four Preps, Capitol 4599 | 9 |
| 48 | 51 | 53 | 65 | HUMAN — Tommy Hunt, Scepter 1219 | 6 |
| 49 | 25 | 20 | 38 | LET ME BELONG TO YOU — Brian Hyland, ABC-Paramount 10236 | 10 |
| 50 | 29 | 15 | 10 | WHEN WE GET MARRIED — Dreamlovers, Heritage 102 | 11 |
| 51 | 64 | 70 | 86 | IT'S YOUR WORLD — Marty Robbins, Columbia 42065 | 5 |
| 52 | 81 | 79 | 82 | PLEASE MR. POSTMAN — Marvelettes, Tamla 54046 | 6 |
| 53 | 27 | 19 | 19 | BIG COLD WIND — Pat Boone, Dot 16244 | 8 |
| 54 | 73 | — | — | A WONDER LIKE YOU — Rick Nelson, Imperial 5770 | 2 |
| 55 | 35 | 18 | 14 | IT'S GONNA WORK OUT FINE — Ike and Tina Turner, Sue 749 | 11 |
| 56 | 61 | 88 | — | SAD MOVIES (Make Me Cry) — Lennon Sisters, Dot 16255 | 3 |
| 57 | 58 | 61 | 57 | DON'T GET AROUND MUCH ANYMORE — Belmonts, Sabrina 501 | 6 |
| 58 | 77 | — | — | ANYBODY BUT ME — Brenda Lee, Decca 31309 | 2 |
| 59 | 75 | — | — | BIG JOHN — Shirelles, Scepter 1223 | 2 |
| 60 | 76 | — | — | IT'S JUST A HOUSE WITHOUT YOU — Brook Benton, Mercury 71859 | 2 |
| 61 | 40 | 27 | 12 | A LITTLE BIT OF SOAP — Jarmels, Laurie 3098 | 10 |
| 62 | 31 | 21 | 18 | HURT — Timi Yuro, Liberty 55343 | 12 |
| 63 | 37 | 23 | 8 | WOODEN HEART (Muss I Denn) — Joe Dowell, Smash 1708 | 16 |
| 64 | 74 | 83 | 100 | BRIGHT LIGHTS, BIG CITY — Jimmy Reed, Vee Jay 398 | 4 |
| 65 | 72 | 75 | — | FEEL IT — Sam Cooke, RCA Victor 7927 | 3 |
| 66 | 65 | 62 | 68 | I WAKE UP CRYING — Chuck Jackson, Wand 110 | 8 |
| 67 | — | — | — | MOON RIVER — Jerry Butler, Vee Jay 405 | 1 |
| 68 | 41 | 32 | 30 | I JUST DON'T UNDERSTAND — Ann-Margret, RCA Victor 7894 | 12 |
| 69 | 71 | 59 | 66 | SWEET LITTLE YOU — Neil Sedaka, RCA Victor 7922 | 7 |
| 70 | 86 | 100 | — | CINDERELLA — Paul Anka, ABC-Paramount 10239 | 4 |
| 71 | 78 | 67 | — | HOLLYWOOD — Connie Francis, MGM 13039 | 3 |
| 72 | 79 | 99 | — | YOUR LAST GOODBYE — Floyd Cramer, RCA Victor 7907 | 3 |
| 73 | 60 | 63 | 70 | (I Love You) FOR SENTIMENTAL REASONS — Cleftones, Gee 1067 | 6 |
| 74 | — | — | — | MORNING AFTER — Mar-Keys, Stax 112 | 1 |
| 75 | 44 | 28 | 20 | FRANKIE AND JOHNNY — Brook Benton, Mercury 71859 | 8 |
| 76 | 82 | 81 | — | PLEASE DON'T GO — Ral Donner, Gone 5114 | 3 |
| 77 | 42 | 35 | 31 | LOVER'S ISLAND — Bluejays, Milestone 2008 | 9 |
| 78 | 83 | 94 | 96 | JUST OUT OF REACH (of My Two Open Arms) — Solomon Burke, Atlantic 2114 | 4 |
| 79 | — | — | — | HEARTACHES — Marcels, Colpix 612 | 1 |
| 80 | 88 | — | — | YOU DON'T KNOW WHAT IT MEANS — Jackie Wilson, Brunswick 55219 | 2 |
| 81 | 96 | 76 | 42 | KISSIN' ON THE PHONE — Paul Anka, ABC-Paramount 10239 | 7 |
| 82 | 85 | — | — | MUSKRAT — Everly Brothers, Warner Bros. 5501 | 2 |
| 83 | 91 | 84 | 76 | TONIGHT I WON'T BE THERE — Adam Wade, Coed 556 | 4 |
| 84 | — | — | — | HERE COMES THE NIGHT — Ben E. King, Atco 6207 | 1 |
| 85 | — | — | — | DOOR TO PARADISE — Bobby Rydell, Cameo 201 | 1 |
| 86 | — | — | — | THEME FROM COME SEPTEMBER — Billy Vaughn, Dot 16119 | 1 |
| 87 | 87 | 91 | — | RIDERS IN THE SKY — Lawrence Welk, Dot 16237 | 3 |
| 88 | 92 | 86 | 93 | BACK TO THE HOP — Danny and the Juniors, Swan 4082 | 4 |
| 89 | — | — | — | ROCK-A-BYE YOUR BABY WITH A DIXIE MELODY — Aretha Franklin, Columbia 42157 | 1 |
| 90 | — | — | — | LAUGH — Velvets, Monument 448 | 1 |
| 91 | 98 | 94 | — | BERLIN MELODY — Billy Vaughn, Dot 16119 | 3 |
| 92 | — | 97 | — | HONKY TRAIN — Bill Black's Combo, Hi 2038 | 2 |
| 93 | — | — | — | MOON RIVER — Henry Mancini, RCA Victor 7916 | 1 |
| 94 | — | — | — | I APOLOGIZE — Timi Yuro, Liberty 55343 | 1 |
| 95 | 97 | — | — | HANG ON — Floyd Cramer, RCA Victor 7907 | 2 |
| 96 | — | 77 | — | LET TRUE LOVE BEGIN — Nat King Cole, Capitol 4623 | 2 |
| 97 | — | — | — | GUILTY OF LOVING YOU — Jerry Fuller, Challenge 9114 | 1 |
| 98 | — | — | — | IMAGE (Part 1) — Hank Levine, ABC-Paramount 10256 | 1 |
| 99 | — | — | — | LATE DATE — Parkays, ABC-Paramount 10242 | 1 |
| 100 | — | — | — | MAKE BELIEVE WEDDING — Castells, Era 3057 | 1 |

## BUBBLING UNDER THE HOT 100

101. JOHNNY WILLOW — Fred Darian, JAF 2023
102. POCKETFUL OF RAINBOWS — Deane Hawley, Liberty 55359
103. LINDA — Adam Wade, Coed 556
104. MR. DJ — Van McCoy, Rockin' 101
105. DANCE WITH A DOLLY — Damita Jo, Mercury 71871
106. ROCKIN' BICYCLE — Fats Domino, Imperial 5779
107. GYPSY WOMAN — Impressions, ABC-Paramount 10241
108. WASN'T SUMMER SHORT — Johnny Mathis, Columbia 42156
109. A BROKEN HEART AND A PILLOW FILLED WITH TEARS — Patti Page, Mercury 71870
110. 'TIL — Angels, Caprice 107
111. SOOTHE ME — Sims Twins, Sar 117
112. THREE STEPS FROM THE ALTAR — Shep and the Limelites, Hull 747
113. AWARE OF LOVE — Jerry Butler, Vee Jay 405
114. EVERYBODY'S GOTTA PAY SOME DUES — Miracles, Tamla 54048
115. CAPPUCCINA — Nat King Cole, Capitol 4623
116. BACKTRACK — Faron Young, Capitol 4616
117. LOVERS NEVER SAY GOODBYE — Flamingos, End 1035
118. IN THE MIDDLE OF A HEARTACHE — Wanda Jackson, Capitol 4635
119. UNDER THE MOON OF LOVE — Curtis Lee, Dunes 2008
120. WANTED, ONE GIRL — Jan and Dean, Challenge 9120

# BILLBOARD HOT 100

**OCTOBER 16, 1961**
**FOR WEEK ENDING OCTOBER 22, 1961**

| This Week | Wk Ago | 2 Wks Ago | 3 Wks Ago | Title / Artist, Label & Number | Weeks On Chart |
|---|---|---|---|---|---|
| 1 | 1 | 4 | 13 | HIT THE ROAD JACK — Ray Charles, ABC-Paramount 10244 | 6 |
| 2 | 4 | 21 | 42 | RUNAROUND SUE — Dion, Laurie 3110 | 4 |
| 3 | 5 | 10 | 14 | BRISTOL STOMP — Dovells, Parkway 827 | 6 |
| 4 | 2 | 3 | 4 | CRYIN' — Roy Orbison, Monument 447 | 10 |
| 5 | 6 | 8 | 16 | YOU MUST HAVE BEEN A BEAUTIFUL BABY — Bobby Darin, Atco 6206 | 7 |
| 6 | 3 | 1 | 1 | TAKE GOOD CARE OF MY BABY — Bobby Vee, Liberty 55354 | 11 |
| 7 | 18 | 24 | 39 | SAD MOVIES (Make Me Cry) — Sue Thompson, Hickory 1153 | 7 |
| 8 | 17 | 53 | — | BIG BAD JOHN — Jimmy Dean, Columbia 42175 | 3 |
| 9 | 10 | 7 | 12 | MEXICO — Bob Moore, Monument 446 | 10 |
| 10 | 14 | 14 | 33 | YA YA — Lee Dorsey, Fury 1053 | 6 |
| 11 | 13 | 17 | 24 | THIS TIME — Troy Shondell, Liberty 55353 | 7 |
| 12 | 12 | 32 | 41 | I LOVE HOW YOU LOVE ME — Paris Sisters, Gregmark 6 | 7 |
| 13 | 9 | 15 | 30 | LET'S GET TOGETHER — Hayley Mills, Vista 385 | 8 |
| 14 | 22 | 36 | 60 | THE FLY — Chubby Checker, Parkway 830 | 4 |
| 15 | 16 | 16 | 38 | THE WAY YOU LOOK TONIGHT — Lettermen, Capitol 4586 | 7 |
| 16 | 7 | 2 | 2 | THE MOUNTAIN'S HIGH — Dick and Deedee, Liberty 55350 | 12 |
| 17 | 8 | 5 | 6 | LITTLE SISTER — Elvis Presley, RCA Victor 7908 | 9 |
| 18 | 19 | 23 | 50 | LOOK IN MY EYES — Chantels, Carlton 555 | 8 |
| 19 | 24 | 28 | 37 | SWEETS FOR MY SWEET — Drifters, Atlantic 2117 | 7 |
| 20 | 28 | 46 | 87 | DON'T BLAME ME — Everly Brothers, Warner Bros. 5501 | 4 |
| 21 | 15 | 18 | 22 | BLESS YOU — Tony Orlando, Epic 9452 | 10 |
| 22 | 21 | 26 | 10 | (Marie's the Name) HIS LATEST FLAME — Elvis Presley, RCA Victor 7908 | 8 |
| 23 | 45 | 84 | — | TOWER OF STRENGTH — Gene McDaniels, Liberty 55371 | 3 |
| 24 | 46 | 69 | 95 | YOU'RE THE REASON — Bobby Edwards, Crest 1075 | 8 |
| 25 | 32 | 59 | 72 | (He's My) DREAMBOAT — Connie Francis, MGM 13039 | 4 |
| 26 | 26 | 33 | 46 | STICK SHIFT — Duals, Sue 745 | 6 |
| 27 | 33 | 20 | 8 | MY TRUE STORY — Jive Five, Beltone 1006 | 16 |
| 28 | 31 | 43 | 68 | SO LONG BABY — Del Shannon, Big Top 3083 | 5 |
| 29 | 30 | 13 | 11 | ONE TRACK MIND — Bobby Lewis, Beltone 1012 | 8 |
| 30 | 38 | 39 | 47 | (He's) THE GREAT IMPOSTOR — Fleetwoods, Dolton 45 | 6 |
| 31 | 36 | 66 | — | FOOL #1 — Brenda Lee, Decca 31309 | 3 |
| 32 | 37 | 50 | 58 | FOOT STOMPIN' (Part 1) — Flares, Felsted 8624 | 7 |
| 33 | 42 | 67 | 74 | I UNDERSTAND (Just How You Feel) — G-Clefs, Terrace 7500 | 7 |
| 34 | 39 | 68 | — | EVERLOVIN' — Rick Nelson, Imperial 5770 | 3 |
| 35 | 52 | 81 | 79 | PLEASE MR. POSTMAN — Marvelettes, Tamla 54046 | 7 |
| 36 | 27 | 11 | 7 | WHO PUT THE BOMP (In the Bomp, Bomp, Bomp) — Barry Mann, ABC-Paramount 10237 | 11 |
| 37 | 20 | 12 | 9 | WITHOUT YOU — Johnny Tillotson, Cadence 1404 | 11 |
| 38 | 58 | 77 | — | ANYBODY BUT ME — Brenda Lee, Decca 31309 | 3 |
| 39 | 54 | 73 | — | A WONDER LIKE YOU — Rick Nelson, Imperial 5770 | 3 |
| 40 | 43 | 56 | 85 | I REALLY LOVE YOU — Stereos, Cub 9095 | 4 |
| 41 | 59 | 75 | — | BIG JOHN — Shirelles, Scepter 1223 | 3 |
| 42 | 44 | 63 | — | WHAT A PARTY — Fats Domino, Imperial 5779 | 3 |
| 43 | 29 | 55 | — | CANDY MAN — Roy Orbison, Monument 447 | 8 |
| 44 | 11 | 6 | 3 | MICHAEL — Highwaymen, United Artists 258 | 15 |
| 45 | 34 | 30 | 29 | MISSING YOU — Ray Peterson, Dunes 2006 | 12 |
| 46 | 25 | 38 | 40 | TAKE FIVE — Dave Brubeck, Columbia 41479 | 6 |
| 47 | 35 | 19 | 25 | THE ASTRONAUT — Jose Jimenez, Kapp 409 | 9 |
| 48 | 71 | 78 | 67 | HOLLYWOOD — Connie Francis, MGM 13039 | 4 |
| 49 | 55 | 35 | 18 | IT'S GONNA WORK OUT FINE — Ike and Tina Turner, Sue 749 | 12 |
| 50 | 67 | — | — | MOON RIVER — Jerry Butler, Vee Jay 405 | 2 |
| 51 | 41 | 57 | 71 | MOVIN' — Bill Black's Combo, HI 2038 | 4 |
| 52 | 60 | 76 | — | IT'S JUST A HOUSE WITHOUT YOU — Brook Benton, Mercury 71859 | 3 |
| 53 | 23 | 9 | 5 | DOES YOUR CHEWING GUM LOSE ITS FLAVOR (On the Bedpost Over Night) — Lonnie Donegan, Dot 15911 | 11 |
| 54 | 49 | 25 | 20 | LET ME BELONG TO YOU — Brian Hyland, ABC-Paramount 10236 | 11 |
| 55 | 40 | 49 | 56 | WATER BOY — Don Shirley Trio, Cadence 1392 | 14 |
| 56 | 47 | 22 | 17 | MORE MONEY FOR YOU AND ME MEDLEY — Four Preps, Capitol 4599 | 10 |
| 57 | 53 | 27 | 19 | BIG COLD WIND — Pat Boone, Dot 16244 | 9 |
| 58 | 79 | — | — | HEARTACHES — Marcels, Colpix 612 | 2 |
| 59 | 56 | 61 | 88 | SAD MOVIES (Make Me Cry) — Lennon Sisters, Dot 16255 | 4 |
| 60 | 78 | 83 | 94 | JUST OUT OF REACH (of My Two Open Arms) — Solomon Burke, Atlantic 2114 | 5 |
| 61 | 57 | 58 | 61 | DON'T GET AROUND MUCH ANYMORE — Belmonts, Sabrina 501 | 7 |
| 62 | 64 | 74 | 83 | BRIGHT LIGHTS, BIG CITY — Jimmy Reed, Vee Jay 398 | 5 |
| 63 | 74 | — | — | MORNING AFTER — Mar-Keys, Stax 112 | 2 |
| 64 | 65 | 72 | 75 | FEEL IT — Sam Cooke, RCA Victor 7927 | 4 |
| 65 | 48 | 51 | 53 | HUMAN — Tommy Hunt, Scepter 1219 | 7 |
| 66 | 72 | 79 | 99 | YOUR LAST GOODBYE — Floyd Cramer, RCA Victor 7907 | 4 |
| 67 | 76 | 82 | 81 | PLEASE DON'T GO — Ral Donner, Gone 5114 | 4 |
| 68 | 89 | — | — | ROCK-A-BYE YOUR BABY WITH A DIXIE MELODY — Aretha Franklin, Columbia 42157 | 2 |
| 69 | 51 | 64 | 70 | IT'S YOUR WORLD — Marty Robbins, Columbia 42065 | 6 |
| 70 | 50 | 29 | 15 | WHEN WE GET MARRIED — Dreamlovers, Heritage 102 | 12 |
| 71 | 83 | 91 | 84 | TONIGHT I WON'T BE THERE — Adam Wade, Coed 556 | 5 |
| 72 | 94 | — | — | I APOLOGIZE — Timi Yuro, Liberty 55343 | 2 |
| 73 | 96 | — | — | LET TRUE LOVE BEGIN — Nat King Cole, Capitol 4623 | 3 |
| 74 | 91 | 98 | — | BERLIN MELODY — Billy Vaughn, Dot 16119 | 4 |
| 75 | — | — | — | YOUNG BOY BLUES — Ben E. King, Atco 6207 | 1 |
| 76 | — | — | — | I WANT TO THANK YOU — Bobby Rydell, Cameo 201 | 1 |
| 77 | — | — | — | SEPTEMBER IN THE RAIN — Dinah Washington, Mercury 71876 | 1 |
| 78 | — | — | — | I'LL BE SEEING YOU — Frank Sinatra, Reprise 20023 | 1 |
| 79 | 80 | 88 | — | YOU DON'T KNOW WHAT IT MEANS — Jackie Wilson, Brunswick 55219 | 3 |
| 80 | 88 | 92 | 86 | BACK TO THE HOP — Danny and the Juniors, Swan 4082 | 5 |
| 81 | — | — | — | GOD, COUNTRY AND MY BABY — Johnny Burnette, Liberty 55279 | 1 |
| 82 | — | — | — | DON'T CRY NO MORE — Bobby (Blue) Bland, Duke 340 | 5 |
| 83 | — | — | — | ROCKIN' BICYCLE — Fats Domino, Imperial 5779 | 1 |
| 84 | — | — | — | TONIGHT — Ferrante & Teicher, United Artists 373 | 1 |
| 85 | — | — | — | UNDER THE MOON OF LOVE — Curtis Lee, Dunes 2008 | 1 |
| 86 | — | — | — | BRIDGE OF LOVE — Joe Dowell, Smash 1717 | 1 |
| 87 | 86 | — | — | THEME FROM COME SEPTEMBER — Billy Vaughn, Dot 16119 | 2 |
| 88 | — | — | — | GOODBYE CRUEL WORLD — James Darren, Colpix 609 | 1 |
| 89 | 99 | — | — | LATE DATE — Parkays, ABC-Paramount 10242 | 2 |
| 90 | 93 | — | — | MOON RIVER — Henry Mancini, RCA Victor 7916 | 2 |
| 91 | — | — | — | 'TIL — Angels, Caprice 107 | 1 |
| 92 | 82 | 85 | — | MUSKRAT — Everly Brothers, Warner Bros. 5501 | 3 |
| 93 | — | 99 | — | A BROKEN HEART AND A PILLOW FILLED WITH TEARS — Patti Page, Mercury 71870 | 2 |
| 94 | 97 | — | — | GUILTY OF LOVING YOU — Jerry Fuller, Challenge 9114 | 2 |
| 95 | — | — | — | WHY NOT NOW — Matt Monro, Warwick 669 | 1 |
| 96 | — | — | — | IN THE MIDDLE OF A HEARTACHE — Wanda Jackson, Capitol 4635 | 1 |
| 97 | — | — | — | FOR ME AND MY GAL — Freddy Cannon, Swan 4083 | 1 |
| 98 | 100 | — | — | MAKE BELIEVE WEDDING — Castells, Era 3057 | 2 |
| 99 | — | — | — | GYPSY WOMAN — Impressions, ABC-Paramount 10241 | 1 |
| 100 | — | — | — | BACKTRACK — Faron Young, Capitol 4616 | 1 |

## BUBBLING UNDER THE HOT 100

101. I WONDER — Pentagons, Jamie 1201
102. JOHNNY WILLOW — Fred Darian, JAF 2023
103. POCKETFUL OF RAINBOWS — Deane Hawley, Liberty 55359
104. MR. DJ — Van McCoy, Rockin' 101
105. AWARE OF LOVE — Jerry Butler, Vee Jay 405
106. CRAZY — Patsy Cline, Decca 31317
107. SWEET SORROW — Conway Twitty, MGM 13034
108. YOUR MA SAID YOU CRIED IN YOUR SLEEP LAST NIGHT — Kenny Dino, Musicor 1013
109. WASN'T THE SUMMER SHORT? — Johnny Mathis, Columbia 42156
110. THREE STEPS FROM THE ALTAR — Shep and the Limelites, Hull 747
111. IMPOSSIBLE — Gloria Lynne, Everest 19418
112. DANCE WITH A DOLLY — Damita Jo, Mercury 71871
113. MEXICO — Miracles, Tamla 54048
114. EVERYBODY GOTTA PAY SOME DUES — Sims Twins, Sar 117
115. SOOTHE ME — Frankie Avalon, Chancellor 1087
116. MARRIED — Jan and Dean, Challenge 9120
117. WANTED, ONE GIRL — Jan and Dean, Challenge 9120
118. SOMEWHERE ALONG THE WAY — Steve Lawrence, United Artists 364
119. LONESOME — Jerry Wallace, Challenge 9117
120. JUST BECAUSE — McGuire Sisters, Coral 62288
121. REACH FOR THE STARS — Shirley Bassey, United Artists 363

# BILLBOARD HOT 100

**OCTOBER 23, 1961**
**FOR WEEK ENDING OCTOBER 29, 1961**

★ STAR PERFORMERS—Selections registering greatest upward progress this week.
Ⓢ Indicates that 45 r.p.m. stereo single version is available.
△ Indicates that 33⅓ r.p.m. mono single version is available.
▲ Indicates that 33⅓ r.p.m. stereo single version is available.

| This Week | Wk. Ago | 2 Wks. Ago | 3 Wks. Ago | TITLE — Artist, Label & Number | Weeks On Chart |
|---|---|---|---|---|---|
| 1 | 2 | 4 | 21 | RUNAROUND SUE — Dion, Laurie 3110 | 5 |
| 2 | 3 | 5 | 10 | BRISTOL STOMP — Dovells, Parkway 827 | 7 |
| ★3 | 8 | 17 | 53 | BIG BAD JOHN — Jimmy Dean, Columbia 42175 △ | 4 |
| 4 | 1 | 1 | 4 | HIT THE ROAD JACK — Ray Charles, ABC-Paramount 10244 | 7 |
| 5 | 7 | 18 | 24 | SAD MOVIES (Make Me Cry) — Sue Thompson, Hickory 1153 | 8 |
| 6 | 11 | 13 | 17 | THIS TIME — Troy Shondell, Liberty 55353 | 6 |
| 7 | 12 | 12 | 32 | I LOVE HOW YOU LOVE ME — Paris Sisters, Gregmark 6 | 8 |
| 8 | 13 | 9 | 15 | LET'S GET TOGETHER — Hayley Mills, Vista 385 | 8 |
| 9 | 10 | 14 | 14 | YA YA — Lee Dorsey, Fury 1053 | 7 |
| 10 | 14 | 22 | 36 | THE FLY — Chubby Checker, Parkway 830 | 5 |
| 11 | 4 | 2 | 3 | CRYIN' — Roy Orbison, Monument 447 | 11 |
| 12 | 9 | 10 | 7 | MEXICO — Bob Moore, Monument 446 | 11 |
| 13 | 15 | 16 | 16 | THE WAY YOU LOOK TONIGHT — Lettermen, Capitol 4586 | 8 |
| 14 | 18 | 19 | 23 | LOOK IN MY EYES — Chantels, Carlton 555 | 9 |
| 15 | 6 | 3 | 1 | TAKE GOOD CARE OF MY BABY — Bobby Vee, Liberty 55354 | 12 |
| 16 | 5 | 6 | 8 | YOU MUST HAVE BEEN A BEAUTIFUL BABY — Bobby Darin, Atco 6206 | 8 |
| 17 | 23 | 45 | 84 | TOWER OF STRENGTH — Gene McDaniels, Liberty 55371 | 4 |
| 18 | 19 | 24 | 28 | SWEETS FOR MY SWEET — Drifters, Atlantic 2117 | 7 |
| 19 | 25 | 32 | 59 | (He's My) DREAMBOAT — Connie Francis, MGM 13039 | 5 |
| 20 | 33 | 42 | 67 | I UNDERSTAND (Just How You Feel) — G-Clefs, Terrace 7500 | 6 |
| 21 | 31 | 36 | 66 | FOOL #1 — Brenda Lee, Decca 31309 | 4 |
| 22 | 34 | 39 | 68 | EVERLOVIN' — Rick Nelson, Imperial 5770 | 4 |
| 23 | 20 | 28 | 46 | DON'T BLAME ME — Everly Brothers, Warner Bros. 5501 | 5 |
| 24 | 24 | 46 | 69 | YOU'RE THE REASON — Bobby Edwards, Crest 1075 | 9 |
| 25 | 26 | 26 | 33 | STICK SHIFT — Duals, Sue 745 | 7 |
| 26 | 16 | 7 | 2 | THE MOUNTAIN'S HIGH — Dick and Deedee, Liberty 55350 | 13 |
| ★27 | 39 | 54 | 73 | A WONDER LIKE YOU — Rick Nelson, Imperial 5770 | 4 |
| 28 | 32 | 37 | 50 | FOOT STOMPIN' (Part 1) — Flares, Felsted 8624 | 8 |
| 29 | 40 | 43 | 56 | I REALLY LOVE YOU — Stereos, Cub 9095 | 5 |
| 30 | 35 | 52 | 81 | PLEASE MR. POSTMAN — Marvelettes, Tamla 54046 | 8 |
| 31 | 38 | 58 | 77 | ANYBODY BUT ME — Brenda Lee, Decca 31309 | 4 |
| 32 | 27 | 33 | 20 | MY TRUE STORY — Jive Five, Beltone 1006 | 17 |
| 33 | 41 | 59 | 75 | BIG JOHN — Shirelles, Scepter 1223 | 4 |
| 34 | 17 | 8 | 5 | LITTLE SISTER — Elvis Presley, RCA Victor 7908 △ | 10 |
| 35 | 30 | 38 | 39 | (He's) THE GREAT IMPOSTOR — Fleetwoods, Dolton 45 | 7 |
| 36 | 29 | 30 | 13 | ONE TRACK MIND — Bobby Lewis, Beltone 1012 | 9 |
| 37 | 43 | 29 | 55 | CANDY MAN — Roy Orbison, Monument 447 | 9 |
| 38 | 46 | 25 | 38 | TAKE FIVE — Dave Brubeck, Columbia 41479 △ | 7 |
| 39 | 42 | 44 | 63 | WHAT A PARTY — Fats Domino, Imperial 5779 | 4 |
| 40 | 21 | 15 | 18 | BLESS YOU — Tony Orlando, Epic 9452 | 11 |
| 41 | 22 | 21 | 26 | (Marie's the Name) HIS LATEST FLAME — Elvis Presley, RCA Victor 7908 △ | 9 |
| 42 | 28 | 31 | 43 | SO LONG BABY — Del Shannon, Big Top 3083 | 6 |
| 43 | 50 | 67 | — | MOON RIVER — Jerry Butler, Vee Jay 405 | 3 |
| ★44 | 58 | 79 | — | HEARTACHES — Marcels, Colpix 612 | 3 |
| 45 | 52 | 60 | 76 | IT'S JUST A HOUSE WITHOUT YOU — Brook Benton, Mercury 71859 | 4 |
| 46 | 48 | 71 | 78 | HOLLYWOOD — Connie Francis, MGM 13039 | 5 |
| 47 | 49 | 55 | 35 | IT'S GONNA WORK OUT FINE — Ike and Tina Turner, Sue 749 | 13 |
| 48 | 37 | 20 | 12 | WITHOUT YOU — Johnny Tillotson, Cadence 1404 | 12 |
| 49 | 77 | — | — | SEPTEMBER IN THE RAIN — Dinah Washington, Mercury 71876 | 2 |
| 50 | 45 | 34 | 30 | MISSING YOU — Ray Peterson, Dunes 2006 | 13 |
| 51 | 67 | 76 | 82 | PLEASE DON'T GO — Ral Donner, Gone 5114 | 4 |
| 52 | 44 | 11 | 6 | MICHAEL — Highwaymen, United Artists 258 | 16 |
| 53 | 51 | 41 | 57 | MOVIN' — Bill Black's Combo, Hi 2038 | 5 |
| 54 | 60 | 78 | 83 | JUST OUT OF REACH (of My Two Open Arms) — Solomon Burke, Atlantic 2114 | 6 |
| 55 | 36 | 27 | 11 | WHO PUT THE BOMP (in the Bomp, Bomp, Bomp) — Barry Mann, ABC-Paramount 10237 | 12 |
| 56 | 64 | 65 | 72 | FEEL IT — Sam Cooke, RCA Victor 7927 △ | 4 |
| 57 | 59 | 56 | 61 | SAD MOVIES (Make Me Cry) — Lennon Sisters, Dot 16255 | 5 |
| 58 | 62 | 64 | 74 | BRIGHT LIGHTS, BIG CITY — Jimmy Reed, Vee Jay 398 | 4 |
| 59 | — | — | — | SCHOOL IS IN — Gary (U.S.) Bonds, LeGrand 1012 | 1 |
| 60 | 76 | — | — | I WANT TO THANK YOU — Bobby Rydell, Cameo 201 | 2 |
| 61 | 71 | 83 | 91 | TONIGHT I WON'T BE THERE — Adam Wade, Coed 556 | 6 |
| 62 | 68 | 89 | — | ROCK-A-BYE YOUR BABY WITH A DIXIE MELODY — Aretha Franklin, Columbia 42157 △ | 3 |
| 63 | 66 | 72 | 79 | YOUR LAST GOODBYE — Floyd Cramer, RCA Victor 7907 △ | 5 |
| 64 | 81 | — | — | GOD, COUNTRY AND MY BABY — Johnny Burnette, Liberty 55279 | 2 |
| 65 | — | — | — | CRAZY — Patsy Cline, Decca 31317 | 1 |
| 66 | 84 | — | — | TONIGHT — Ferrante & Teicher, United Artists 373 | 2 |
| 67 | 75 | — | — | YOUNG BOY BLUES — Ben E. King, Atco 6207 | 2 |
| 68 | 90 | 93 | — | MOON RIVER — Henry Mancini, RCA Victor 7916 △ | 3 |
| 69 | 88 | — | — | GOODBYE CRUEL WORLD — James Darren, Colpix 609 | 2 |
| 70 | 63 | 74 | — | MORNING AFTER — Mar-Keys, Stax 112 | 3 |
| 71 | 78 | — | — | I'LL BE SEEING YOU — Frank Sinatra, Reprise 20023 | 2 |
| 72 | — | — | — | MY HEART BELONGS TO ONLY YOU — Jackie Wilson, Brunswick 55220 | 1 |
| 73 | 47 | 35 | 19 | THE ASTRONAUT — Jose Jimenez, Kapp 409 | 10 |
| 74 | 61 | 57 | 58 | DON'T GET AROUND MUCH ANYMORE — Belmonts, Sabrina 501 | 8 |
| 75 | 86 | — | — | BRIDGE OF LOVE — Joe Dowell, Smash 1717 | 2 |
| 76 | — | — | — | THE WAY I AM — Jackie Wilson, Brunswick 55220 | 1 |
| 77 | 74 | 91 | 98 | BERLIN MELODY — Billy Vaughn, Dot 16119 | 5 |
| 78 | 82 | — | — | DON'T CRY NO MORE — Bobby (Blue) Bland, Duke 340 | 2 |
| 79 | 87 | 86 | — | THEME FROM COME SEPTEMBER — Billy Vaughn, Dot 16119 | 3 |
| 80 | — | — | — | SOMEWHERE ALONG THE WAY — Steve Lawrence, United Artists 364 | 1 |
| 81 | — | 84 | — | HERE COMES THE NIGHT — Ben E. King, Atco 6207 | 2 |
| 82 | 85 | — | — | UNDER THE MOON OF LOVE — Curtis Lee, Dunes 2008 | 2 |
| 83 | 73 | 96 | — | LET TRUE LOVE BEGIN — Nat King Cole, Capitol 4623 | 4 |
| 84 | 96 | — | — | IN THE MIDDLE OF A HEARTACHE — Wanda Jackson, Capitol 4635 | 2 |
| 85 | 69 | 51 | 64 | IT'S YOUR WORLD — Marty Robbins, Columbia 42065 △ | 7 |
| 86 | — | — | — | EVERYBODY GOTTA PAY SOME DUES — Miracles, Tamla 54048 | 1 |
| 87 | 56 | 47 | 22 | MORE MONEY FOR YOU AND ME MEDLEY — Four Preps, Capitol 4599 | 11 |
| 88 | 99 | — | — | GYPSY WOMAN — Impressions, ABC-Paramount 10241 | 2 |
| 89 | — | — | — | WASN'T THE SUMMER SHORT! — Johnny Mathis, Columbia 42156 | 1 |
| 90 | 92 | 82 | 85 | MUSKRAT — Everly Brothers, Warner Bros. 5501 | 4 |
| 91 | 93 | — | 99 | A BROKEN HEART AND A PILLOW FILLED WITH TEARS — Patti Page, Mercury 71870 | 3 |
| 92 | 97 | — | — | FOR ME AND MY GAL — Freddy Cannon, Swan 4083 | 2 |
| 93 | 95 | — | — | WHY NOT NOW — Matt Monro, Warwick 669 | 2 |
| 94 | 65 | 48 | 51 | HUMAN — Tommy Hunt, Scepter 1219 | 8 |
| 95 | — | — | — | SOOTHE ME — Sims Twins, Sar 117 | 1 |
| 96 | 100 | — | — | BACKTRACK — Faron Young, Capitol 4616 | 2 |
| 97 | 72 | 94 | — | I APOLOGIZE — Timi Yuro, Liberty 55343 | 3 |
| 98 | — | 100 | — | THREE STEPS FROM THE ALTAR — Shep and the Limelites, Hull 747 | 2 |
| 99 | — | — | — | WHO CAN I COUNT ON — Patsy Cline, Decca 31317 | 1 |
| 100 | — | — | — | BLUE MOON — Ventures, Dolton 47 | 1 |

## BUBBLING UNDER THE HOT 100

| 101 | I WONDER — Pentagons, Jamie 1201 |
| 102 | FLY BY NIGHT — Andy Williams, Columbia 42199 |
| 103 | POCKETFUL OF RAINBOWS — Deane Hawley, Liberty 55359 |
| 104 | WANTED, ONE GIRL — Jan and Dean, Challenge 9120 |
| 105 | LET THERE BE DRUMS — Sandy Nelson, Imperial 5775 |
| 106 | YOUR MA SAID YOU CRIED IN YOUR SLEEP LAST NIGHT — Kenny Dino, Musicor 1013 |
| 107 | JUST BECAUSE — McGuire Sisters, Coral 62288 |
| 108 | DANCE WITH A DOLLY — Damita Jo, Mercury 71871 |
| 109 | A CERTAIN GIRL — Ernie K-Doe, Minit 634 |
| 110 | LONESOME — Jerry Wallace, Challenge 9107 |
| 111 | WITHOUT YOUR LOVE — Wendy Hill, Era 3055 |
| 112 | MARRIED — Frankie Avalon, Chancellor 1087 |
| 113 | BE CAREFUL HOW YOU DRIVE YOUNG JOEY — Jerry Keller, Capitol 4630 |
| 114 | GUILTY OF LOVING YOU — Jerry Fuller, Challenge 9111 |
| 115 | AWARE OF LOVE — Jerry Butler, Vee Jay 405 |
| 116 | BERLIN TOP TEN — Dickie Goodman, Rori 602 |
| 117 | WALK ON BY — Leroy Van Dyke, Mercury 71834 |
| 118 | SOMETIME — Gene Thomas, United Artists 338 |
| 119 | DOOR TO PARADISE — Bobby Rydell, Cameo 201 |
| 120 | ONE GRAIN OF SAND — Eddy Arnold, RCA Victor 7926 |

OCTOBER 30, 1961

# BILLBOARD HOT 100

FOR WEEK ENDING NOVEMBER 5

1961

★ STAR PERFORMERS—Selections registering greatest upward progress this week.

S Indicates that 45 r.p.m. stereo single version is available.

△ Indicates that 33⅓ r.p.m. mono single version is available.

S△ Indicates that 33⅓ r.p.m. stereo single version is available.

| This Week | 1 Wk. Ago | 2 Wks. Ago | 3 Wks. Ago | Title | Artist, Label & Number | | Weeks On Chart |
|---|---|---|---|---|---|---|---|
| 1 | 1 | 2 | 4 | RUNAROUND SUE | Dion, Laurie 3110 | | 6 |
| 2 | 2 | 3 | 5 | BRISTOL STOMP | Dovells, Parkway 827 | | 8 |
| 3 | 3 | 8 | 17 | BIG BAD JOHN | Jimmy Dean, Columbia 42175 | △ | 5 |
| 4 | 4 | 1 | 1 | HIT THE ROAD JACK | Ray Charles, ABC-Paramount 10244 | | 8 |
| 5 | 7 | 12 | 12 | I LOVE HOW YOU LOVE ME | Paris Sisters, Gregmark 6 | | 9 |
| 6 | 5 | 7 | 18 | SAD MOVIES (Make Me Cry) | Sue Thompson, Hickory 1153 | | 9 |
| 7 | 9 | 10 | 14 | YA YA | Lee Dorsey, Fury 1053 | | 8 |
| 8 | 8 | 13 | 9 | LET'S GET TOGETHER | Hayley Mills, Vista 385 | | 9 |
| 9 | 10 | 14 | 22 | THE FLY | Chubby Checker, Parkway 830 | | 6 |
| 10 | 6 | 11 | 13 | THIS TIME | Troy Shondell, Liberty 55353 | | 7 |
| ★ 11 | 17 | 23 | 45 | TOWER OF STRENGTH | Gene McDaniels, Liberty 55371 | | 5 |
| 12 | 12 | 9 | 10 | MEXICO | Bob Moore, Monument 446 | | 12 |
| 13 | 16 | 5 | 6 | YOU MUST HAVE BEEN A BEAUTIFUL BABY | Bobby Darin, Atco 6206 | | 9 |
| ★ 14 | 19 | 25 | 32 | (He's My) DREAMBOAT | Connie Francis, MGM 13039 | | 6 |
| 15 | 11 | 4 | 2 | CRYIN' | Roy Orbison, Monument 447 | | 12 |
| 16 | 18 | 19 | 24 | SWEETS FOR MY SWEET | Drifters, Atlantic 2117 | | 8 |
| 17 | 21 | 31 | 36 | FOOL #1 | Brenda Lee, Decca 31309 | | 5 |
| ★ 18 | 24 | 24 | 46 | YOU'RE THE REASON | Bobby Edwards, Crest 1075 | | 10 |
| 19 | 13 | 15 | 16 | THE WAY YOU LOOK TONIGHT | Lettermen, Capitol 4586 | | 9 |
| 20 | 14 | 18 | 19 | LOOK IN MY EYES | Chantels, Carlton 555 | | 10 |
| 21 | 27 | 39 | 54 | A WONDER LIKE YOU | Rick Nelson, Imperial 5770 | | 5 |
| 22 | 23 | 20 | 28 | DON'T BLAME ME | Everly Brothers, Warner Bros. 5501 | | 6 |
| 23 | 20 | 33 | 42 | I UNDERSTAND (Just How You Feel) | G-Clefs, Terrace 7500 | | 7 |
| 24 | 33 | 41 | 59 | BIG JOHN | Shirelles, Scepter 1223 | | 5 |
| 25 | 28 | 32 | 37 | FOOT STOMPIN' (Part 1) | Flares, Felsted 8624 | | 9 |
| 26 | 22 | 34 | 39 | EVERLOVIN' | Rick Nelson, Imperial 5770 | | 5 |
| 27 | 25 | 26 | 26 | STICK SHIFT | Duals, Sue 745 | | 8 |
| 28 | 15 | 6 | 3 | TAKE GOOD CARE OF MY BABY | Bobby Vee, Liberty 55354 | | 13 |
| ★ 29 | 44 | 58 | 79 | HEARTACHES | Marcels, Colpix 612 | | 4 |
| 30 | 37 | 43 | 29 | CANDY MAN | Roy Orbison, Monument 447 | | 10 |
| 31 | 31 | 38 | 58 | ANYBODY BUT ME | Brenda Lee, Decca 31309 | | 5 |
| 32 | 32 | 27 | 33 | MY TRUE STORY | Jive Five, Beltone 1006 | | 18 |
| 33 | 30 | 35 | 52 | PLEASE MR. POSTMAN | Marvelettes, Tamla 54046 | | 9 |
| 34 | 34 | 17 | 8 | LITTLE SISTER | Elvis Presley, RCA Victor 7908 | △ | 11 |
| 35 | 42 | 28 | 31 | SO LONG BABY | Del Shannon, Big Top 3083 | | 7 |
| 36 | 29 | 40 | 43 | I REALLY LOVE YOU | Stereos, Cub 9095 | | 6 |
| 37 | 39 | 42 | 44 | WHAT A PARTY | Fats Domino, Imperial 5779 | | 5 |
| 38 | 38 | 46 | 25 | TAKE FIVE | Dave Brubeck, Columbia 41479 | △ | 8 |
| 39 | 43 | 50 | 67 | MOON RIVER | Jerry Butler, Vee Jay 405 | | 4 |
| 40 | 26 | 16 | 7 | THE MOUNTAIN'S HIGH | Dick and Deedee, Liberty 55350 | | 14 |
| 41 | 49 | 77 | — | SEPTEMBER IN THE RAIN | Dinah Washington, Mercury 71876 | | 3 |
| ★ 42 | 59 | — | — | SCHOOL IS IN | Gary (U. S.) Bonds, LeGrand 1012 | | 2 |
| 43 | 51 | 67 | 76 | PLEASE DON'T GO | Ral Donner, Gone 5114 | | 6 |
| 44 | 46 | 48 | 71 | HOLLYWOOD | Connie Francis, MGM 13039 | | 6 |
| ★ 45 | 65 | — | — | CRAZY | Patsy Cline, Decca 31317 | | 2 |
| ★ 46 | 62 | 68 | 89 | ROCK-A-BYE YOUR BABY WITH A DIXIE MELODY | Aretha Franklin, Columbia 42157 | △ | 4 |
| 47 | 53 | 51 | 41 | MOVIN' | Bill Black's Combo, Hi 2038 | | 6 |
| ★ 48 | 69 | 88 | — | GOODBYE CRUEL WORLD | James Darren, Colpix 609 | | 3 |
| ★ 49 | 66 | 84 | — | TONIGHT | Ferrante & Teicher, United Artists 373 | | 3 |
| 50 | 54 | 60 | 78 | JUST OUT OF REACH (of My Two Open Arms) | Solomon Burke, Atlantic 2114 | | 7 |
| 51 | 45 | 52 | 60 | IT'S JUST A HOUSE WITHOUT YOU | Brook Benton, Mercury 71859 | | 5 |
| 52 | 60 | 76 | — | I WANT TO THANK YOU | Bobby Rydell, Cameo 201 | | 3 |
| ★ 53 | 54 | 81 | — | GOD, COUNTRY AND MY BABY | Johnny Burnette, Liberty 55279 | | 3 |
| ★ 54 | 68 | 90 | 93 | MOON RIVER | Henry Mancini, RCA Victor 7916 | △ | 4 |
| 55 | 41 | 22 | 21 | (Marie's the Name) HIS LATEST FLAME | Elvis Presley, RCA Victor 7908 | △ | 10 |
| 56 | 47 | 49 | 55 | IT'S GONNA WORK OUT FINE | Ike and Tina Turner, Sue 749 | | 14 |
| 57 | 35 | 30 | 38 | (He's) THE GREAT IMPOSTOR | Fleetwoods, Dolton 45 | | 8 |
| 58 | 36 | 29 | 30 | ONE TRACK MIND | Bobby Lewis, Beltone 1012 | | 10 |
| 59 | 50 | 45 | 34 | MISSING YOU | Ray Peterson, Dunes 2006 | | 14 |
| ★ 60 | 75 | 86 | — | BRIDGE OF LOVE | Joe Dowell, Smash 1717 | | 3 |
| 61 | 40 | 21 | 15 | BLESS YOU | Tony Orlando, Epic 9452 | | 12 |
| 62 | 52 | 44 | 11 | MICHAEL | Highwaymen, United Artists 258 | | 17 |
| 63 | 56 | 64 | 65 | FEEL IT | Sam Cooke, RCA Victor 7927 | △ | 6 |
| 64 | 48 | 37 | 20 | WITHOUT YOU | Johnny Tillotson, Cadence 1404 | | 13 |
| 65 | 71 | 78 | — | I'LL BE SEEING YOU | Frank Sinatra, Reprise 20023 | | 3 |
| 66 | 67 | 75 | — | YOUNG BOY BLUES | Ben E. King, Atco 6207 | | 3 |
| 67 | 63 | 66 | 72 | YOUR LAST GOODBYE | Floyd Cramer, RCA Victor 7907 | △ | 6 |
| 68 | 70 | 63 | 74 | MORNING AFTER | Mar-Keys, Stax 112 | | 4 |
| 69 | 73 | 47 | 35 | THE ASTRONAUT | Jose Jimenez, Kapp 409 | | 11 |
| 70 | 72 | — | — | MY HEART BELONGS TO ONLY YOU | Jackie Wilson, Brunswick 55220 | | 2 |
| ★ 71 | 88 | 99 | — | GYPSY WOMAN | Impressions, ABC-Paramount 10241 | | 3 |
| 72 | 77 | 74 | 91 | BERLIN MELODY | Billy Vaughn, Dot 16119 | | 6 |
| 73 | 82 | 85 | — | UNDER THE MOON OF LOVE | Curtis Lee, Dunes 2008 | | 3 |
| 74 | 76 | — | — | THE WAY I AM | Jackie Wilson, Brunswick 55220 | | 2 |
| 75 | 58 | 62 | 64 | BRIGHT LIGHTS, BIG CITY | Jimmy Reed, Vee Jay 398 | | 7 |
| 76 | 79 | 87 | 86 | THEME FROM COME SEPTEMBER | Billy Vaughn, Dot 16119 | | 4 |
| ★ 77 | 100 | — | — | BLUE MOON | Ventures, Dolton 47 | | 2 |
| 78 | 74 | 61 | 57 | DON'T GET AROUND MUCH ANYMORE | Belmonts, Sabrina 501 | | 9 |
| 79 | 80 | — | — | SOMEWHERE ALONG THE WAY | Steve Lawrence, United Artists 364 | | 2 |
| 80 | 85 | 69 | 51 | IT'S YOUR WORLD | Marty Robbins, Columbia 42065 | △ | 8 |
| 81 | 86 | — | — | EVERYBODY GOTTA PAY SOME DUES | Miracles, Tamla 54048 | | 2 |
| 82 | 84 | 96 | — | IN THE MIDDLE OF A HEARTACHE | Wanda Jackson, Capitol 4635 | | 3 |
| 83 | 78 | 82 | — | DON'T CRY NO MORE | Bobby (Blue) Bland, Duke 340 | | 7 |
| 84 | 94 | 65 | 48 | HUMAN | Tommy Hunt, Scepter 1219 | | 9 |
| 85 | 61 | 71 | 83 | TONIGHT I WON'T BE THERE | Adam Wade, Coed 556 | | 7 |
| ★ 86 | — | — | — | DANNY BOY | Andy Williams, Columbia 42199 | △ | 1 |
| 87 | 57 | 59 | 56 | SAD MOVIES (Make Me Cry) | Lennon Sisters, Dot 16255 | | 6 |
| 88 | 98 | — | — | THREE STEPS FROM THE ALTAR | Shep and the Limelites, Hull 747 | | 3 |
| 89 | 96 | 100 | — | BACKTRACK | Faron Young, Capitol 4616 | | 3 |
| ★ 90 | — | — | — | SOMETIME | Gene Thomas, United Artists 338 | | 1 |
| 91 | 92 | 97 | — | FOR ME AND MY GAL | Freddy Cannon, Swan 4083 | | 3 |
| 92 | 93 | 95 | — | WHY NOT NOW | Matt Monro, Warwick 669 | | 3 |
| 93 | — | — | — | I DON'T KNOW WHY | Linda Scott, Canadian-American 129 | | 1 |
| 94 | — | — | — | LET THERE BE DRUMS | Sandy Nelson, Imperial 5775 | | 1 |
| 95 | — | 91 | — | 'TIL | Angels, Caprice 107 | | 2 |
| 96 | — | — | — | TOWN WITHOUT PITY | Gene Pitney, Musicor 1009 | | 1 |
| 97 | — | — | — | TURN AROUND, LOOK AT ME | Glen Campbell, Crest 1087 | | 1 |
| 98 | — | — | — | WALK ON BY | Leroy Van Dyke, Mercury 71834 | | 1 |
| 99 | — | — | — | ON BENDED KNEES | Clarence Henry, Argo 5401 | | 1 |
| 100 | — | — | — | I WONDER | Pentagons, Jamie 1201 | | 1 |

## HOT 100—A TO Z—(Publisher-Licensee)


Anybody But Me (Champion, BMI) ... 31
Astronaut, The (Bill Dana, ASCAP) ... 69
Backtrack (Vanadore, BMI) ... 89
Berlin Melody (Symphony House, ASCAP) ... 72
Big Bad John (Cigma, BMI) ... 3
Big John (Ludix, BMI) ... 24
Bless You (Aldon, BMI) ... 61
Blue Moon (Robbins, ASCAP) ... 77
Bridge of Love (Belinda, CAPAC) ... 60
Bright Lights, Big City (Conrad, BMI) ... 75
Bristol Stomp (Kalmann, ASCAP) ... 2
Candy Man (January, BMI) ... 30
Crazy (Pamper, BMI) ... 45
Cryin' (Acuff-Rose, BMI) ... 15
Danny Boy (Boosey and Hawkes, ASCAP) ... 86
Don't Blame Me (Robbins, ASCAP) ... 22
Don't Cry No More (Lion, BMI) ... 83
Don't Get Around Much Anymore (Robbins, ASCAP) ... 78
Dreamboat (Acuff-Rose, BMI) ... 14
Everlovin' (Jat, BMI) ... 26
Everybody Gotta Pay Some Dues (Jobete, BMI) ... 81
Feel It (Kags, BMI) ... 63
Fly, The (Woodcrest-Mured, BMI) ... 9
Fool #1 (Sure Fire, BMI) ... 17
Foot Stompin' (Part 1) (Argo, BMI) ... 25
For Me and My Gal (Mills, ASCAP) ... 91
God, Country and My Baby (New Phoenix-Sarah, ASCAP) ... 53
Goodbye Cruel World (Aldon, BMI) ... 48
Great Impostor, The (Gold Cup-Cornerstone, BMI) ... 57
Gypsy Woman (Curtom, BMI) ... 71
Heartaches (Leeds, ASCAP) ... 29
His Latest Flame (Elvis Presley, BMI) ... 55
Hit the Road Jack (Tangerine, BMI) ... 4
Hollywood (Acuff-Rose, BMI) ... 44
Human (Ludix, BMI) ... 84
I Don't Know Why (Ahlert & Cromwell, ASCAP) ... 93
I Love How You Love Me (Aldon, BMI) ... 5
I Really Love You (Shalimar, BMI) ... 36
I Understand (Jubilee, ASCAP) ... 23
I Want to Thank You (Lowe, ASCAP) ... 52
I Wonder (Silmo, BMI) ... 100
I'll Be Seeing You (Williamson, ASCAP) ... 65
In the Middle of a Heartache (Central, BMI) ... 82
It's Gonna Work Out Fine (Copa-Sona, ASCAP) ... 56
It's Just a House Without You (Play, BMI) ... 51
It's Your World (Marizona, BMI) ... 80
Just Out of Reach (Four Star, BMI) ... 50
Let There Be Drums (Travis, BMI) ... 94
Let's Get Together (Wonderland, BMI) ... 8
Little Sister (Elvis Presley, BMI) ... 34
Look in My Eyes (Atlantic, BMI) ... 20
Mexico (Acuff-Rose, BMI) ... 12
Michael (United Artists, ASCAP) ... 62
Missing You (Copar, BMI) ... 59
Moon River—Butler (Famous, ASCAP) ... 39
Moon River—Mancini (Famous, ASCAP) ... 54
Morning After (East-Bais, BMI) ... 68
Mountain's High, The (Odin, ASCAP) ... 40
Movin' (Jec, BMI) ... 47
My Heart Belongs to Only You (Merrimac, BMI) ... 70
My True Story (Steven, BMI) ... 32
On Bended Knees (Arc, BMI) ... 99
One Track Mind (Lescay, BMI) ... 58
Please Don't Go (Alan K., BMI) ... 43
Please Mr. Postman (Jobete, BMI) ... 33
Rock-A-Bye Your Baby With a Dixie Melody (Warock-Mills, ASCAP) ... 46
Runaround Sue (Schwartz-Disal, ASCAP) ... 1
Sad Movies—Lennons (Acuff-Rose, BMI) ... 87
Sad Movies—Thompson (Acuff-Rose, BMI) ... 6
School Is In (Pepe, BMI) ... 42
September in the Rain (Remick, ASCAP) ... 41
So Long Baby (Vicki-McLaughlin, BMI) ... 35
Sometime (Grand Prize, BMI) ... 90
Somewhere Along the Way (United Artists, ASCAP) ... 79
Stick Shift (Hilde, BMI) ... 27
Sweets for My Sweet (Brenner-Progressive-Trio, BMI) ... 16
Take Five (Derry, BMI) ... 38
Take Good Care of My Baby (Aldon, BMI) ... 28
Theme From Come September (Adaris, BMI) ... 76
This Time (Tree, BMI) ... 10
Three Steps From the Altar (Keel, BMI) ... 88
'Til (Chappell, ASCAP) ... 95
Tonight (Shirmer, ASCAP) ... 49
Tonight I Won't Be There (Paxton, ASCAP) ... 85
Tower of Strength (Famous, ASCAP) ... 11
Town Without Pity (United Artists, ASCAP) ... 96
Turn Around, Look at Me (American, BMI) ... 97
Under the Moon of Love (S-P-R, BMI) ... 73
Walk on By (Lowery, BMI) ... 98
Way I Am, The (East-West, ASCAP) ... 74
Way You Look Tonight, The (Harms, ASCAP) ... 19
What a Party (Travis, BMI) ... 37
Why Not Now (Selma, BMI) ... 92
Without You (Ridge, BMI) ... 64
Wonder Like You, A (Four Star, BMI) ... 21
Ya Ya (Fast-Barich, BMI) ... 7
You Must Have Been a Beautiful Baby (Remick, ASCAP) ... 13
Young Boy Blues (Rumbalero-Progressive-Trio, BMI) ... 66
You're the Reason (American, BMI) ... 18
Your Last Goodbye (Cigma, BMI) ... 67


## BUBBLING UNDER THE HOT 100

101. A CERTAIN GIRL ... Ernie K-Doe, Minit 634
102. LET THEM LOVE ... Dreamlovers, Heritage 104
103. LANGUAGE OF LOVE ... John D. Loudermilk, RCA Victor 7938
104. DOOR TO PARADISE ... Bobby Rydell, Cameo 201
105. DANCE WITH A DOLLY ... Damita Jo, Mercury 71871
106. YOUR MA SAID YOU CRIED IN YOUR SLEEP LAST NIGHT ... Kenny Dino, Musicor 1013
107. ONE GRAIN OF SAND ... Eddy Arnold, RCA Victor 7926
108. DON'T WALK AWAY FROM ME ... Dee Clark, Vee Jay 409
109. WHAT I FEEL IN MY HEART ... Jim Reeves, RCA Victor 7950
110. I CRIED MY LAST TEAR ... Ernie K-Doe, Minit 634
111. STEPS 1 & 2 ... Jack Scott, Capitol 4637
112. BE CAREFUL HOW YOU DRIVE YOUNG JOEY ... Jerry Keller, Capitol 4630
113. LATE DATE ... Parkays, ABC-Paramount 10246
114. AFTER ALL WE'VE BEEN THROUGH ... Maxine Brown, ABC-Paramount 10255
115. JUST BECAUSE ... McGuire Sisters, Coral 62288
116. IT WILL STAND ... Showmen, Minit 632
117. THE ROACH ... Gene and Wendell, Ray Starr 777
118. GREETINGS (This Is Uncle Sam) ... Valadiers, Miracle 6
119. LOVE (I'm So Glad) I FOUND YOU ... Spinners, Tri-Phi 1004
120. IT'S TOO SOON TO KNOW ... Etta James, Argo 5402

# BILLBOARD HOT 100

FOR WEEK ENDING NOVEMBER 12

1961

★ STAR PERFORMERS—Selections registering greatest upward progress this week.
[S] Indicates that 45 r.p.m. stereo single version is available.
△ Indicates that 33⅓ r.p.m. mono single version is available.
[S with triangle] Indicates that 33⅓ r.p.m. stereo single version is available.

| This Week | 1 Wk. Ago | 2 Wks. Ago | 3 Wks. Ago | Title | Artist, Label & Number | Weeks On Chart |
|---|---|---|---|---|---|---|
| 1 | 3 | 3 | 8 | BIG BAD JOHN △ | Jimmy Dean, Columbia 42175 | 6 |
| 2 | 1 | 1 | 2 | RUNAROUND SUE | Dion, Laurie 3110 | 7 |
| 3 | 2 | 2 | 3 | BRISTOL STOMP | Dovells, Parkway 827 | 9 |
| 4 | 4 | 4 | 1 | HIT THE ROAD JACK | Ray Charles, ABC-Paramount 10244 | 9 |
| ★5 | 17 | 21 | 31 | FOOL #1 | Brenda Lee, Decca 31309 | 6 |
| 6 | 6 | 5 | 7 | SAD MOVIES (Make Me Cry) | Sue Thompson, Hickory 1153 | 10 |
| 7 | 10 | 6 | 11 | THIS TIME | Troy Shondell, Liberty 55353 | 8 |
| 8 | 9 | 10 | 14 | THE FLY | Chubby Checker, Parkway 830 | 7 |
| 9 | 5 | 7 | 12 | I LOVE HOW YOU LOVE ME | Paris Sisters, Gregmark 6 | 10 |
| 10 | 11 | 17 | 23 | TOWER OF STRENGTH | Gene McDaniels, Liberty 55371 | 6 |
| 11 | 8 | 8 | 13 | LET'S GET TOGETHER | Hayley Mills, Vista 385 | 10 |
| 12 | 7 | 9 | 10 | YA YA | Lee Dorsey, Fury 1053 | 9 |
| ★13 | 21 | 27 | 39 | A WONDER LIKE YOU | Rick Nelson, Imperial 5770 | 6 |
| ★14 | 19 | 13 | 15 | THE WAY YOU LOOK TONIGHT | Lettermen, Capitol 4586 | 10 |
| 15 | 18 | 24 | 24 | YOU'RE THE REASON | Bobby Edwards, Crest 1075 | 11 |
| 16 | 14 | 19 | 25 | (He's My) DREAMBOAT | Connie Francis, MGM 13039 | 7 |
| ★17 | 33 | 30 | 35 | PLEASE MR. POSTMAN | Marvelettes, Tamla 54046 | 10 |
| 18 | 15 | 11 | 4 | CRYIN' | Roy Orbison, Monument 447 | 13 |
| 19 | 12 | 12 | 9 | MEXICO | Bob Moore, Monument 446 | 13 |
| 20 | 23 | 20 | 33 | I UNDERSTAND (Just How You Feel) | G-Clefs, Terrace 7500 | 8 |
| 21 | 16 | 18 | 19 | SWEETS FOR MY SWEET | Drifters, Atlantic 2117 | 9 |
| ★22 | 37 | 39 | 42 | WHAT A PARTY | Fats Domino, Imperial 5779 | 6 |
| 23 | 26 | 22 | 34 | EVERLOVIN' | Rick Nelson, Imperial 5770 | 6 |
| 24 | 24 | 33 | 41 | BIG JOHN | Shirelles, Scepter 1223 | 6 |
| 25 | 30 | 37 | 43 | CANDY MAN | Roy Orbison, Monument 447 | 11 |
| ★26 | 45 | 65 | — | CRAZY | Patsy Cline, Decca 31317 | 3 |
| ★27 | 48 | 69 | 88 | GOODBYE CRUEL WORLD | James Darren, Colpix 609 | 4 |
| 28 | 29 | 44 | 58 | HEARTACHES | Marcels, Colpix 612 | 5 |
| 29 | 22 | 23 | 20 | DON'T BLAME ME | Everly Brothers, Warner Bros. 5501 | 7 |
| 30 | 25 | 28 | 32 | FOOT STOMPIN' (Part 1) | Flares, Felsted 8624 | 10 |
| 31 | 27 | 25 | 26 | STICK SHIFT | Duals, Sue 745 | 9 |
| ★32 | 42 | 59 | — | SCHOOL IS IN | Gary (U. S.) Bonds, LeGrand 1012 | 3 |
| 33 | 20 | 14 | 18 | LOOK IN MY EYES | Chantels, Carlton 555 | 11 |
| 34 | 13 | 16 | 5 | YOU MUST HAVE BEEN A BEAUTIFUL BABY | Bobby Darin, Atco 6206 | 10 |
| 35 | 35 | 42 | 28 | SO LONG BABY | Del Shannon, Big Top 3083 | 8 |
| 36 | 38 | 38 | 46 | TAKE FIVE △ | Dave Brubeck, Columbia 41479 | 9 |
| 37 | 39 | 43 | 50 | MOON RIVER | Jerry Butler, Vee Jay 405 | 5 |
| 38 | 41 | 49 | 77 | SEPTEMBER IN THE RAIN | Dinah Washington, Mercury 71876 | 4 |
| ★39 | 52 | 60 | 76 | I WANT TO THANK YOU | Bobby Rydell, Cameo 201 | 4 |
| ★40 | 53 | 64 | 81 | GOD, COUNTRY AND MY BABY | Johnny Burnette, Liberty 55379 | 4 |
| 41 | 43 | 51 | 67 | PLEASE DON'T GO | Ral Donner, Gone 5114 | 7 |
| 42 | 44 | 46 | 48 | HOLLYWOOD | Connie Francis, MGM 13039 | 7 |
| 43 | 31 | 31 | 38 | ANYBODY BUT ME | Brenda Lee, Decca 31309 | 6 |
| 44 | 46 | 62 | 68 | ROCK-A-BYE YOUR BABY WITH A DIXIE MELODY △ | Aretha Franklin, Columbia 42157 | 5 |
| 45 | 50 | 54 | 60 | JUST OUT OF REACH (of My Two Open Arms) | Solomon Burke, Atlantic 2114 | 8 |
| 46 | 49 | 66 | 84 | TONIGHT | Ferrante & Teicher, United Artists 373 | 4 |
| 47 | 28 | 15 | 6 | TAKE GOOD CARE OF MY BABY | Bobby Vee, Liberty 55354 | 14 |
| 48 | 34 | 34 | 17 | LITTLE SISTER △ | Elvis Presley, RCA Victor 7908 | 12 |
| 49 | 54 | 68 | 90 | MOON RIVER △ | Henry Mancini, RCA Victor 7916 | 5 |
| 50 | 36 | 29 | 40 | I REALLY LOVE YOU | Stereos, Cub 9095 | 7 |
| 51 | 40 | 26 | 16 | THE MOUNTAIN'S HIGH | Dick and Deedee, Liberty 55350 | 15 |
| 52 | 32 | 32 | 27 | MY TRUE STORY | Jive Five, Beltone 1006 | 19 |
| 53 | 60 | 75 | 86 | BRIDGE OF LOVE | Joe Dowell, Smash 1717 | 4 |
| ★54 | 82 | 84 | 96 | IN THE MIDDLE OF A HEARTACHE | Wanda Jackson, Capitol 4635 | 4 |
| 55 | 47 | 53 | 51 | MOVIN' | Bill Black's Combo, Hi 2038 | 7 |
| ★56 | 73 | 82 | 85 | UNDER THE MOON OF LOVE | Curtis Lee, Dunes 2008 | 4 |
| 57 | 55 | 41 | 22 | (Marie's the Name) HIS LATEST NAME △ | Elvis Presley, RCA Victor 7908 | 11 |
| 58 | 59 | 50 | 45 | MISSING YOU | Ray Peterson, Dunes 2006 | 15 |
| 59 | 65 | 71 | 78 | I'LL BE SEEING YOU | Frank Sinatra, Reprise 20023 | 4 |
| 60 | 68 | 70 | 63 | MORNING AFTER | Mar-Keys, Stax 112 | 5 |
| 61 | 72 | 77 | 74 | BERLIN MELODY | Billy Vaughn, Dot 16119 | 7 |
| ★62 | 77 | 100 | — | BLUE MOON | Ventures, Dolton 47 | 3 |
| 63 | 67 | 63 | 66 | YOUR LAST GOODBYE △ | Floyd Cramer, RCA Victor 7907 | 7 |
| 64 | 71 | 88 | 99 | GYPSY WOMAN | Impressions, ABC-Paramount 10241 | 4 |
| 65 | 74 | 76 | — | THE WAY I AM | Jackie Wilson, Brunswick 55220 | 3 |
| 66 | 63 | 56 | 64 | FEEL IT △ | Sam Cooke, RCA Victor 7927 | 7 |
| 67 | 75 | 58 | 62 | BRIGHT LIGHTS, BIG CITY | Jimmy Reed, Vee Jay 398 | 8 |
| 68 | 70 | 72 | — | MY HEART BELONGS TO ONLY YOU | Jackie Wilson, Brunswick 55220 | 3 |
| ★69 | 94 | — | — | LET THERE BE DRUMS | Sandy Nelson, Imperial 5775 | 2 |
| 70 | 81 | 86 | — | EVERYBODY GOTTA PAY SOME DUES | Miracles, Tamla 54048 | 3 |
| 71 | 79 | 80 | — | SOMEWHERE ALONG THE WAY | Steve Lawrence, United Artists 364 | 3 |
| 72 | 66 | 67 | 75 | YOUNG BOY BLUES | Ben E. King, Atco 6207 | 4 |
| 73 | 76 | 79 | 87 | THEME FROM COME SEPTEMBER | Billy Vaughn, Dot 16119 | 5 |
| 74 | 56 | 47 | 49 | IT'S GONNA WORK OUT FINE | Ike and Tina Turner, Sue 749 | 15 |
| ★75 | 90 | — | — | SOMETIME | Gene Thomas, United Artists 338 | 2 |
| 76 | 86 | — | — | DANNY BOY △ | Andy Williams, Columbia 42199 | 2 |
| ★77 | — | — | — | YOUR MA SAID YOU CRIED IN YOUR SLEEP LAST NIGHT | Kenny Dino, Musicor 1013 | 1 |
| 78 | 88 | 98 | — | THREE STEPS FROM THE ALTAR | Shep and the Limelites, Hull 747 | 4 |
| 79 | 80 | 85 | 69 | IT'S YOUR WORLD △ | Marty Robbins, Columbia 42065 | 9 |
| ★80 | — | — | — | SMILE | Timi Yuro, Liberty 55375 | 1 |
| ★81 | 96 | — | — | TOWN WITHOUT PITY | Gene Pitney, Musicor 1009 | 2 |
| ★82 | — | — | — | TONIGHT | Eddie Fisher, Seven Arts 719 | 1 |
| 83 | 95 | — | 91 | 'TIL | Angels, Caprice 107 | 3 |
| 84 | 93 | — | — | I DON'T KNOW WHY | Linda Scott, Canadian-American 129 | 2 |
| 85 | 91 | 92 | 97 | FOR ME AND MY GAL | Freddy Cannon, Swan 4083 | 4 |
| 86 | 99 | — | — | ON BENDED KNEES | Clarence Henry, Argo 5401 | 2 |
| 87 | 84 | 94 | 65 | HUMAN | Tommy Hunt, Scepter 1219 | 10 |
| ★88 | — | — | — | FLY BY NIGHT △ | Andy Williams, Columbia 42199 | 1 |
| 89 | 98 | — | — | WALK ON BY | Leroy Van Dyke, Mercury 71834 | 2 |
| 90 | 87 | 57 | 59 | SAD MOVIES (Make Me Cry) | Lennon Sisters, Dot 16255 | 7 |
| 91 | — | 91 | 93 | A BROKEN HEART AND A PILLOW FILLED WITH TEARS | Patti Page, Mercury 71870 | 4 |
| 92 | — | — | — | LANGUAGE OF LOVE △ | John D. Loudermilk, RCA Victor 7938 | 1 |
| 93 | — | — | — | I CRIED MY LAST TEAR | Ernie K-Doe, Minit 634 | 1 |
| 94 | — | — | — | IT'S TOO SOON TO KNOW | Etta James, Argo 5402 | 1 |
| 95 | — | — | — | GYPSY ROVER | Highwaymen, United Artists 370 | 1 |
| 96 | 100 | — | — | I WONDER | Pentagons, Jamie 1201 | 2 |
| 97 | 97 | — | — | TURN AROUND, LOOK AT ME | Glen Campbell, Crest 1087 | 2 |
| 98 | — | — | — | STEPS 1 AND 2 | Jack Scott, Capitol 4637 | 1 |
| 99 | — | — | — | JUST BECAUSE | McGuire Sisters, Coral 62288 | 1 |
| 100 | — | — | — | LOSING YOUR LOVE | Jim Reeves, RCA Victor 7950 | 1 |

## HOT 100—A TO Z—(Publisher-Licensee)


Anybody But Me (Champion, BMI ... 43
Berlin Melody (Symphony House, ASCAP) ... 61
Big Bad John (Cigma, BMI) ... 1
Big John (Ludix, BMI) ... 24
Blue Moon (Robbins, ASCAP) ... 62
Bridge of Love (Belinda, CAPAC) ... 53
Brights Lights, Big City (Conrad, BMI) ... 67
Bristol Stomp (Kalmann, ASCAP) ... 3
Broken Heart and a Pillow Filled With Tears, A (Spanka, BMI) ... 91
Candy Man (January, BMI) ... 25
Crazy (Pamper, BMI) ... 26
Cryin' (Acuff-Rose, BMI) ... 18
Danny Boy (Boosey and Hawkes, ASCAP) ... 76
Don't Blame Me (Robbins, ASCAP) ... 29
Dreamboat (Acuff-Rose, BMI) ... 16
Everlovin' (Jat, BMI) ... 23
Everybody Gotta Pay Some Dues (Jobete, BMI) ... 70
Feel It (Kags, BMI) ... 66
Fly, The (Woodcrest-Mured, BMI) ... 8
Fly By Night (Sea-Lark, BMI) ... 88
Fool #1 (Sure Fire, BMI) ... 5
Foot Stompin' (Part 1) (Argo, BMI) ... 30
For Me and My Gal (Mills, ASCAP) ... 85
God, Country and My Baby (New Phoenix-Sarah, ASCAP) ... 40
Goodbye Cruel World (Aldon, BMI) ... 27
Gypsy Rover (Box and Cox, ASCAP) ... 95
Gypsy Woman (Curtom, BMI) ... 64
Heartaches (Leeds, ASCAP) ... 28
His Latest Flame (Elvis Presley, BMI) ... 57
Hit the Road Jack (Tangerine, BMI) ... 4
Hollywood (Acuff-Rose, BMI) ... 42
Human (Ludix, BMI) ... 87
I Cried My Last Tear (Minit, BMI) ... 93
I Don't Know Why (Ahlert & Cromwell, ASCAP) ... 84
I Love How You Love Me (Aldon, BMI) ... 9
I Really Love You (Shalimar, BMI) ... 50
I Understand (Jubilee, ASCAP) ... 20
I Want to Thank You (Lowe, ASCAP) ... 39
I Wonder (Silmo, BMI) ... 96
I'll Be Seeing You (Williamson, ASCAP) ... 59
In the Middle of a Heartache (Central, BMI) ... 54
It's Gonna Work Out Fine (Copo-Sona, ASCAP) ... 74
It's Too Soon to Know (Morris, ASCAP) ... 94
It's Your World (Marizona, BMI) ... 79
Just Because (Northern, ASCAP) ... 99
Just Out of Reach (Four Star, BMI) ... 45
Language of Love (Acuff-Rose, BMI) ... 92
Let There Be Drums (Travis, BMI) ... 69
Let's Get Together (Wonderland, BMI) ... 11
Little Sister (Elvis Presley, BMI) ... 48
Look in My Eyes (Atlantic, BMI) ... 33
Losing Your Love (Tree, BMI) ... 100
Mexico (Acuff-Rose, BMI) ... 19
Missing You (Copar, BMI) ... 58
Moon River—Butler (Famous, ASCAP) ... 37
Moon River—Mancini (Famous, ASCAP) ... 49
Morning After (East-Bais, BMI) ... 60
Mountain's High, The (Odin, ASCAP) ... 51
Movin' (Jec, BMI) ... 55
My Heart Belongs to Only You (Merrimac, BMI) ... 68
My True Story (Steven, BMI) ... 52
On Bended Knees (Arc, BMI) ... 86
Please Don't Go (Alan K., BMI) ... 41
Please Mr. Postman (Jobete, BMI) ... 17
Rock-A-Bye Your Baby With a Dixie Melody (Warock-Mills, ASCAP) ... 44
Runaround Sue (Schwartz-Disal, ASCAP) ... 2
Sad Movies—Lennons (Acuff-Rose, BMI) ... 90
Sad Movies—Thompson (Acuff-Rose, BMI) ... 6
School Is In (Pepe, BMI) ... 32
September in the Rain (Remick, ASCAP) ... 38
Smile (Bourne, ASCAP) ... 80
So Long Baby (Vicki-McLaughlin, BMI) ... 35
Sometime (Grand Prize, BMI) ... 75
Somewhere Along the Way (United Artists, ASCAP) ... 71
Steps 1 & 2 (Wolfpack, SESAC) ... 98
Stick Shift (Hidle, BMI) ... 31
Sweets for My Sweet (Brenner-Progressive-Trio, BMI) ... 21
Take Five (Derry, BMI) ... 36
Take Good Care of My Baby (Aldon, BMI) ... 47
Theme From Come September (Adaris, BMI) ... 73
This Time (Tree, BMI) ... 7
Three Steps From the Altar (Keel, BMI) ... 78
'Til (Chappell, ASCAP) ... 83
Tonight—Ferrante & Teicher (Schirmer, ASCAP) ... 46
Tonight—Fisher (Schirmer, ASCAP) ... 82
Tower of Strength (Famous, ASCAP) ... 10
Town Without Pity (United Artists, ASCAP) ... 81
Turn Around, Look at Me (American, BMI) ... 97
Under the Moon of Love (S-P-R, BMI) ... 56
Walk on By (Lowery, BMI) ... 89
Way I Am, The (East-West, ASCAP) ... 65
Way You Look Tonight, The (Harms, ASCAP) ... 14
What a Party (Travis, BMI) ... 22
Wonder Like You, A (Four Star, BMI) ... 13
Ya Ya (Fast-Barich, BMI) ... 12
You Must Have Been a Beautiful Baby (Remick, ASCAP) ... 34
Young Boy Blues (Rumbalero-Progressive-Trio, BMI) ... 72
You're the Reason (American, BMI) ... 15
Your Last Goodbye (Cigma, BMI) ... 63
Your Ma Said You Cried in Your Sleep Last Night (Sea-Lark, BMI) ... 77


## BUBBLING UNDER THE HOT 100

101. IT'S ALL BECAUSE ... Linda Scott, Canadian-American 129
102. A CERTAIN GIRL ... Ernie K-Doe, Minit 634
103. DOOR TO PARADISE ... Bobby Rydell, Cameo 201
104. LET TRUE LOVE BEGIN ... Nat King Cole, Capitol 4623
105. DON'T WALK AWAY FROM ME ... Dee Clark, Vee Jay 409
106. SOOTHE ME ... Sims Twins, Sar 117
107. BACKTRACK ... Faron Young, Capitol 4616
108. LET THEM LOVE ... Dreamlovers, Heritage 104
109. TENNESSEE FLAT-TOP BOX ... Johnny Cash, Columbia 42147
110. IT WILL STAND ... Showmen, Minit 632
111. EV'RYBODY'S CRYIN' ... Jimmie Beaumont, May 112
112. I'LL NEVER STOP WANTING YOU ... Brian Hyland, ABC-Paramount 10262
113. AFTER ALL WE'VE BEEN THROUGH ... Maxine Brown, ABC-Paramount 10255
114. JUST LET ME DREAM ... Pat Boone, Dot 16284
115. IMPOSSIBLE ... Gloria Lynne, Everest 19418
116. LONELY SIXTEEN ... Janie Black, Capitol 4633
117. FEMININE TOUCH ... Dorsey Burnette, Dot 16265
118. I KNOW ... Barbara George, AFO 302
119. THE LION SLEEPS TONIGHT ... Tokens, RCA Victor 7954
120. GIVE MYSELF A PARTY ... Rosemary Clooney, RCA Victor 7948

# BILLBOARD HOT 100

**NOVEMBER 13, 1961**

**FOR WEEK ENDING NOVEMBER 19, 1961**

★ STAR PERFORMERS—Selections registering greatest upward progress this week.
S Indicates that 45 r.p.m. stereo single version is available.
△ Indicates that 33⅓ r.p.m. mono single version is available.
S Indicates that 33⅓ r.p.m. stereo single version is available.

| This Week | Wk. Ago | 2 Wks. Ago | 3 Wks. Ago | TITLE — Artist, Label & Number | Weeks On Chart |
|---|---|---|---|---|---|
| 1 | 1 | 3 | 3 | BIG BAD JOHN — Jimmy Dean, Columbia 42175 △ | 7 |
| 2 | 2 | 1 | 1 | RUNAROUND SUE — Dion, Laurie 3110 | 8 |
| 3 | 5 | 17 | 21 | FOOL #1 — Brenda Lee, Decca 31309 | 7 |
| 4 | 3 | 2 | 2 | BRISTOL STOMP — Dovells, Parkway 827 | 10 |
| ★5 | 10 | 11 | 17 | TOWER OF STRENGTH — Gene McDaniels, Liberty 55371 | 7 |
| 6 | 4 | 4 | 4 | HIT THE ROAD JACK — Ray Charles, ABC-Paramount 10244 | 10 |
| 7 | 8 | 9 | 10 | THE FLY — Chubby Checker, Parkway 830 | 8 |
| 8 | 7 | 10 | 6 | THIS TIME — Troy Shondell, Liberty 55353 | 9 |
| 9 | 17 | 33 | 30 | PLEASE MR. POSTMAN — Marvelettes, Tamla 54046 | 11 |
| 10 | 6 | 6 | 5 | SAD MOVIES (Make Me Cry) — Sue Thompson, Hickory 1153 | 11 |
| 11 | 13 | 21 | 27 | A WONDER LIKE YOU — Rick Nelson, Imperial 5770 | 7 |
| ★12 | 27 | 48 | 69 | GOODBYE CRUEL WORLD — James Darren, Colpix 609 | 5 |
| 13 | 15 | 18 | 24 | YOU'RE THE REASON — Bobby Edwards, Crest 1075 | 12 |
| 14 | 11 | 8 | 8 | LET'S GET TOGETHER — Hayley Mills, Vista 385 | 11 |
| 15 | 9 | 5 | 7 | I LOVE HOW YOU LOVE ME — Paris Sisters, Gregmark 6 | 11 |
| 16 | 23 | 26 | 22 | EVERLOVIN' — Rick Nelson, Imperial 5770 | 7 |
| 17 | 28 | 29 | 44 | HEARTACHES — Marcels, Colpix 612 | 6 |
| 18 | 12 | 7 | 9 | YA YA — Lee Dorsey, Fury 1053 | 10 |
| ★19 | 26 | 45 | 65 | CRAZY — Patsy Cline, Decca 31317 | 4 |
| 20 | 20 | 23 | 20 | I UNDERSTAND (Just How You Feel) — G-Clefs, Terrace 7500 | 9 |
| 21 | 24 | 24 | 33 | BIG JOHN — Shirelles, Scepter 1223 | 7 |
| 22 | 18 | 15 | 11 | CRYIN' — Roy Orbison, Monument 447 | 14 |
| 23 | 21 | 16 | 18 | SWEETS FOR MY SWEET — Drifters, Atlantic 2117 | 10 |
| ★24 | 40 | 53 | 64 | GOD, COUNTRY AND MY BABY — Johnny Burnette, Liberty 55379 | 5 |
| 25 | 14 | 19 | 13 | THE WAY YOU LOOK TONIGHT — Lettermen, Capitol 4586 | 11 |
| 26 | 37 | 39 | 43 | MOON RIVER — Jerry Butler, Vee Jay 405 | 6 |
| 27 | 25 | 30 | 37 | CANDY MAN — Roy Orbison, Monument 447 | 12 |
| 28 | 32 | 42 | 59 | SCHOOL IS IN — Gary (U.S.) Bonds, LeGrand 1012 | 4 |
| ★29 | 46 | 49 | 66 | TONIGHT — Ferrante & Teicher, United Artists 373 | 5 |
| 30 | 39 | 52 | 60 | I WANT TO THANK YOU — Bobby Rydell, Cameo 201 | 5 |
| 31 | 19 | 12 | 12 | MEXICO — Bob Moore, Monument 446 | 14 |
| 32 | 38 | 41 | 49 | SEPTEMBER IN THE RAIN — Dinah Washington, Mercury 71876 | 5 |
| 33 | 16 | 14 | 19 | (He's My) DREAMBOAT — Connie Francis, MGM 13039 | 8 |
| ★34 | 45 | 50 | 54 | JUST OUT OF REACH (of My Two Open Arms) — Solomon Burke, Atlantic 2114 | 7 |
| 35 | 22 | 37 | 39 | WHAT A PARTY — Fats Domino, Imperial 5779 | 7 |
| ★36 | 49 | 54 | 68 | MOON RIVER — Henry Mancini, RCA Victor 7916 | 6 |
| 37 | 36 | 38 | 38 | TAKE FIVE — Dave Brubeck, Columbia 41479 △ | 10 |
| 38 | 30 | 25 | 28 | FOOT STOMPIN' (Part 1) — Flares, Felsted 8624 | 11 |
| 39 | 41 | 43 | 51 | PLEASE DON'T GO — Ral Donner, Gone 5114 | 8 |
| 40 | 29 | 22 | 23 | DON'T BLAME ME — Everly Brothers, Warner Bros. 5501 | 8 |
| 41 | 35 | 35 | 42 | SO LONG BABY — Del Shannon, Big Top 3083 | 9 |
| 42 | 33 | 20 | 14 | LOOK IN MY EYES — Chantels, Carlton 555 | 12 |
| 43 | 44 | 46 | 62 | ROCK-A-BYE YOUR BABY WITH A DIXIE MELODY — Aretha Franklin, Columbia 42157 △ | 6 |
| ★44 | 69 | 94 | — | LET THERE BE DRUMS — Sandy Nelson, Imperial 5775 | 3 |
| 45 | 31 | 27 | 25 | STICK SHIFT — Duals, Sue 745 | 10 |
| ★46 | 89 | 98 | — | WALK ON BY — Leroy Van Dyke, Mercury 71834 | 3 |
| 47 | 34 | 13 | 16 | YOU MUST HAVE BEEN A BEAUTIFUL BABY — Bobby Darin, Atco 6206 | 11 |
| 48 | 43 | 31 | 31 | ANYBODY BUT ME — Brenda Lee, Decca 31309 | 7 |
| 49 | 64 | 71 | 88 | GYPSY WOMAN — Impressions, ABC-Paramount 10241 | 5 |
| 50 | 56 | 73 | 82 | UNDER THE MOON OF LOVE — Curtis Lee, Dunes 2008 | 5 |
| 51 | 50 | 36 | 29 | I REALLY LOVE YOU — Stereos, Cub 9095 | 8 |
| 52 | 54 | 82 | 84 | IN THE MIDDLE OF A HEARTACHE — Wanda Jackson, Capitol 4635 | 5 |
| 53 | 53 | 60 | 75 | BRIDGE OF LOVE — Joe Dowell, Smash 1717 | 5 |
| 54 | 47 | 28 | 15 | TAKE GOOD CARE OF MY BABY — Bobby Vee, Liberty 55354 | 15 |
| 55 | — | — | — | THE TWIST — Chubby Checker, Parkway 811 | 19 |
| 56 | 48 | 34 | 34 | LITTLE SISTER — Elvis Presley, RCA Victor 7908 △ | 13 |
| 57 | — | — | — | RUN TO HIM — Bobby Vee, Liberty 55388 | 1 |
| 58 | 65 | 74 | 76 | THE WAY I AM — Jackie Wilson, Brunswick 55220 | 4 |
| 59 | 59 | 65 | 71 | I'LL BE SEEING YOU — Frank Sinatra, Reprise 20023 | 5 |
| ★60 | 70 | 81 | 86 | EVERYBODY GOTTA PAY SOME DUES — Miracles, Tamla 54048 | 4 |
| 61 | 60 | 68 | 70 | MORNING AFTER — Mar-Keys, Stax 112 | 6 |
| ★62 | — | — | — | HAPPY BIRTHDAY, SWEET SIXTEEN — Neil Sedaka, RCA Victor 7957 △ | 1 |
| 63 | 80 | — | — | SMILE — Timi Yuro, Liberty 55375 | 2 |
| 64 | 76 | 86 | — | DANNY BOY — Andy Williams, Columbia 42199 △ | 3 |
| 65 | 62 | 77 | 100 | BLUE MOON — Ventures, Dolton 47 | 3 |
| 66 | 84 | 93 | — | I DON'T KNOW WHY — Linda Scott, Canadian-American 129 | 3 |
| 67 | 71 | 79 | 80 | SOMEWHERE ALONG THE WAY — Steve Lawrence, United Artists 364 | 4 |
| 68 | 77 | — | — | YOUR MA SAID YOU CRIED IN YOUR SLEEP LAST NIGHT — Kenny Dino, Musicor 1013 | 2 |
| 69 | 75 | 90 | — | SOMETIME — Gene Thomas, United Artists 338 | 3 |
| ★70 | — | — | — | THE LION SLEEPS TONIGHT — Tokens, RCA Victor 7954 △ | 1 |
| 71 | 82 | — | — | TONIGHT — Eddie Fisher, Seven Arts 719 | 2 |
| 72 | 81 | 96 | — | TOWN WITHOUT PITY — Gene Pitney, Musicor 1009 | 3 |
| 73 | 67 | 75 | 58 | BRIGHT LIGHTS, BIG CITY — Jimmy Reed, Vee Jay 398 | 9 |
| 74 | 85 | 91 | 92 | FOR ME AND MY GAL — Freddy Cannon, Swan 4083 | 5 |
| ★75 | 92 | — | — | LANGUAGE OF LOVE — John D. Loudermilk, RCA Victor 7938 △ | 2 |
| 76 | 78 | 88 | 98 | THREE STEPS FROM THE ALTAR — Shep and the Limelites, Hull 747 | 5 |
| 77 | 72 | 66 | 67 | YOUNG BOY BLUES — Ben E. King, Atco 6207 | 5 |
| 78 | 86 | 99 | — | ON BENDED KNEES — Clarence Henry, Argo 5401 | 3 |
| 79 | 73 | 76 | 79 | THEME FROM COME SEPTEMBER — Billy Vaughn, Dot 16119 | 6 |
| 80 | — | — | — | JOHNNY WILL — Pat Boone, Dot 16284 | 1 |
| 81 | 83 | 95 | — | 'TIL — Angels, Caprice 107 | 4 |
| 82 | 88 | — | — | FLY BY NIGHT — Andy Williams, Columbia 42199 △ | 2 |
| 83 | 95 | — | — | GYPSY ROVER — Highwaymen, United Artists 370 | 2 |
| 84 | — | — | — | UP A LAZY RIVER — Si Zentner, Liberty 55374 | 1 |
| 85 | — | — | — | COMMANCHEROS — Claude King, Columbia 42196 | 1 |
| 86 | — | — | — | IT'S ALL BECAUSE — Linda Scott, Canadian-American 129 | 1 |
| 87 | 93 | — | — | I CRIED MY LAST TEAR — Ernie K-Doe, Minit 634 | 2 |
| 88 | 68 | 70 | 72 | MY HEART BELONGS TO ONLY YOU — Jackie Wilson, Brunswick 55220 | 4 |
| 89 | — | — | — | IT WILL STAND — Showmen, Minit 632 | 1 |
| 90 | 94 | — | — | IT'S TOO SOON TO KNOW — Etta James, Argo 5402 | 2 |
| 91 | — | — | — | TENNESSEE FLAT-TOP BOX — Johnny Cash, Columbia 42147 △ | 1 |
| 92 | — | — | — | WELL I TOLD YOU — Chantels, Carlton 564 | 1 |
| 93 | 96 | 100 | — | I WONDER — Pentagons, Jamie 1201 | 3 |
| 94 | — | — | — | DOOR TO PARADISE — Bobby Rydell, Cameo 201 | 2 |
| 95 | — | — | — | A CERTAIN GIRL — Ernie K-Doe, Minit 634 | 1 |
| 96 | — | 95 | — | SOOTHE ME — Sims Twins, Sar 117 | 2 |
| 97 | — | — | — | IT DO ME SO GOOD — Ann-Margret, RCA Victor 7952 △ | 1 |
| 98 | — | — | — | NEVER, NEVER — Jive Five, Beltone 1014 | 1 |
| 99 | — | — | — | I KNOW — Barbara George, AFO 302 | 1 |
| 100 | — | — | — | FUNNY HOW TIME SLIPS AWAY — Jimmy Elledge, RCA Victor 7946 △ | 1 |

## BUBBLING UNDER THE HOT 100

101. THERE'S NO OTHER — Crystals, Philles 100
102. AFTER ALL WE'VE BEEN THROUGH — Maxine Brown, ABC-Paramount 10255
103. WHY NOT NOW — Matt Monro, Warwick 669
104. DON'T WALK AWAY FROM ME — Dee Clark, Vee Jay 409
105. STEPS 1 & 2 — Jack Scott, Capitol 4637
106. DREAMIN' ABOUT YOU — Annette, Vista 388
107. TRADE WINDS — Pete Bennett and the Embers, Reprise 20021
108. FEVER — Pete Bennett and the Embers, Sunset 1002
109. LITTLE MISS U.S.A. — Barry Mann, ABC-Paramount 10263
110. SEVEN DAY FOOL — Etta James, Argo 5402
111. EV'RYBODY'S CRYIN' — Jimmie Beaumont, May 112
112. LITTLE LONELY — Chad Allen, Smash 1720
113. JUST A LITTLE BIT SWEET — Charlie Rich, Phillips 3572
114. MY BUDDY — Eddie Harris, Vee Jay 407
115. LOVE (I'm So Glad) I FOUND YOU — Spinners, Tri-Phi 1004
116. POP GOES THE WEASEL — Anthony Newley, London 9501
117. LITTLE ALTAR BOY — Vic Dana, Dolton 48
118. PUSHIN' YOUR LUCK — Sonny King, Joy 257
119. GOD BLESS THE CHILD — Eddie Harris, Vee Jay 407
120. GREETINGS (This Is Uncle Sam) — Valadiers, Miracle 6

# BILLBOARD HOT 100

FOR WEEK ENDING NOVEMBER 26 1961

★ STAR PERFORMERS—Selections registering greatest upward progress this week.

S Indicates that 45 r.p.m. stereo single version is available.

△ Indicates that 33⅓ r.p.m. mono single version is available.

(S) Indicates that 33⅓ r.p.m. stereo single version is available.

| This Week | 1 Wk. Ago | 2 Wks. Ago | 3 Wks. Ago | TITLE | Artist, Label & Number | | Weeks On Chart |
|---|---|---|---|---|---|---|---|
| 1 | 1 | 1 | 3 | BIG BAD JOHN | Jimmy Dean, Columbia 42175 | △ | 8 |
| 2 | 2 | 2 | 1 | RUNAROUND SUE | Dion, Laurie 3110 | | 9 |
| 3 | 3 | 5 | 17 | FOOL #1 | Brenda Lee, Decca 31309 | | 8 |
| ★4 | 12 | 27 | 48 | GOODBYE CRUEL WORLD | James Darren, Colpix 609 | | 6 |
| 5 | 4 | 3 | 2 | BRISTOL STOMP | Dovells, Parkway 827 | | 11 |
| 6 | 5 | 10 | 11 | TOWER OF STRENGTH | Gene McDaniels, Liberty 55371 | | 8 |
| 7 | 6 | 4 | 4 | HIT THE ROAD JACK | Ray Charles, ABC-Paramount 10244 | | 11 |
| 8 | 9 | 17 | 33 | PLEASE MR. POSTMAN | Marvelettes, Tamla 54046 | | 12 |
| 9 | 8 | 7 | 10 | THIS TIME | Troy Shondell, Liberty 55353 | | 10 |
| 10 | 7 | 8 | 9 | THE FLY | Chubby Checker, Parkway 830 | | 9 |
| 11 | 13 | 15 | 18 | YOU'RE THE REASON | Bobby Edwards, Crest 1075 | | 13 |
| 12 | 15 | 9 | 5 | I LOVE HOW YOU LOVE ME | Paris Sisters, Gregmark 6 | | 12 |
| ★13 | 29 | 46 | 49 | TONIGHT | Ferrante & Teicher, United Artists 373 | | 6 |
| ★14 | 20 | 20 | 23 | I UNDERSTAND (Just How You Feel) | G-Clefs, Terrace 7500 | | 10 |
| 15 | 19 | 26 | 45 | CRAZY | Patsy Cline, Decca 31317 | | 5 |
| 16 | 16 | 23 | 26 | EVERLOVIN' | Rick Nelson, Imperial 5770 | | 8 |
| 17 | 10 | 6 | 6 | SAD MOVIES (Make Me Cry) | Sue Thompson, Hickory 1153 | | 12 |
| ★18 | 24 | 40 | 53 | GOD, COUNTRY AND MY BABY | Johnny Burnette, Liberty 55379 | | 6 |
| 19 | 17 | 28 | 29 | HEARTACHES | Marcels, Colpix 612 | | 7 |
| 20 | 11 | 13 | 21 | A WONDER LIKE YOU | Rick Nelson, Imperial 5770 | | 8 |
| 21 | 30 | 39 | 52 | I WANT TO THANK YOU | Bobby Rydell, Cameo 201 | | 6 |
| 22 | 26 | 37 | 39 | MOON RIVER | Jerry Butler, Vee Jay 405 | | 7 |
| 23 | 14 | 11 | 8 | LET'S GET TOGETHER | Hayley Mills, Vista 385 | | 12 |
| ★24 | 34 | 45 | 50 | JUST OUT OF REACH (of My Two Open Arms) | Solomon Burke, Atlantic 2114 | | 10 |
| 25 | 18 | 12 | 7 | YA YA | Lee Dorsey, Fury 1053 | | 11 |
| ★26 | 36 | 49 | 54 | MOON RIVER | Henry Mancini, RCA Victor 7916 | △ | 7 |
| ★27 | 55 | — | — | THE TWIST | Chubby Checker, Parkway 811 | | 20 |
| 28 | 32 | 38 | 41 | SEPTEMBER IN THE RAIN | Dinah Washington, Mercury 71876 | | 6 |
| ★29 | 57 | — | — | RUN TO HIM | Bobby Vee, Liberty 55388 | | 2 |
| ★30 | 44 | 69 | 94 | LET THERE BE DRUMS | Sandy Nelson, Imperial 5775 | | 4 |
| ★31 | 46 | 89 | 98 | WALK ON BY | Leroy Van Dyke, Mercury 71834 | | 4 |
| 32 | 38 | 30 | 25 | FOOT STOMPIN' (Part 1) | Flares, Felsted 8624 | | 12 |
| 33 | 21 | 24 | 24 | BIG JOHN | Shirelles, Scepter 1223 | | 8 |
| 34 | 22 | 18 | 15 | CRYIN' | Roy Orbison, Monument 447 | | 15 |
| 35 | 23 | 21 | 16 | SWEETS FOR MY SWEET | Drifters, Atlantic 2117 | | 11 |
| 36 | 25 | 14 | 19 | THE WAY YOU LOOK TONIGHT | Lettermen, Capitol 4586 | | 12 |
| ★37 | 49 | 64 | 71 | GYPSY WOMAN | Impressions, ABC-Paramount 10241 | | 6 |
| 38 | 33 | 16 | 14 | (He's My) DREAMBOAT | Connie Francis, MGM 13039 | | 9 |
| 39 | 43 | 44 | 46 | ROCK-A-BYE YOUR BABY WITH A DIXIE MELODY | Aretha Franklin, Columbia 42157 | △ | 7 |
| 40 | 41 | 35 | 35 | SO LONG BABY | Del Shannon, Big Top 3083 | | 10 |
| 41 | 48 | 43 | 31 | ANYBODY BUT ME | Brenda Lee, Decca 31309 | | 8 |
| ★42 | 52 | 54 | 82 | IN THE MIDDLE OF A HEARTACHE | Wanda Jackson, Capitol 4635 | | 6 |
| 43 | 27 | 25 | 30 | CANDY MAN | Roy Orbison, Monument 447 | | 13 |
| 44 | 39 | 41 | 43 | PLEASE DON'T GO | Ral Donner, Gone 5114 | | 9 |
| ★45 | 62 | — | — | HAPPY BIRTHDAY, SWEET SIXTEEN | Neil Sedaka, RCA Victor 7957 | △ | 2 |
| 46 | 28 | 32 | 42 | SCHOOL IS IN | Gary (U. S.) Bonds, LeGrand 1012 | | 5 |
| ★47 | 66 | 84 | 93 | I DON'T KNOW WHY | Linda Scott, Canadian-American 129 | | 4 |
| 48 | 50 | 56 | 73 | UNDER THE MOON OF LOVE | Curtis Lee, Dunes 2008 | | 6 |
| 49 | 35 | 22 | 37 | WHAT A PARTY | Fats Domino, Imperial 5779 | | 8 |
| 50 | 53 | 53 | 60 | BRIDGE OF LOVE | Joe Dowell, Smash 1717 | | 6 |
| ★51 | 84 | — | — | UP A LAZY RIVER | Si Zentner, Liberty 55374 | | 2 |
| 52 | 60 | 70 | 81 | EVERYBODY GOTTA PAY SOME DUES | Miracles, Tamla 54048 | | 5 |
| ★53 | 68 | 77 | — | YOUR MA SAID YOU CRIED IN YOUR SLEEP LAST NIGHT | Kenny Dino, Musicor 1013 | | 3 |
| ★54 | 65 | 62 | 77 | BLUE MOON | Ventures, Dolton 47 | | 5 |
| ★55 | 70 | — | — | THE LION SLEEPS TONIGHT | Tokens, RCA Victor 7954 | △ | 2 |
| ★56 | 72 | 81 | 96 | TOWN WITHOUT PITY | Gene Pitney, Musicor 1009 | | 4 |
| ★57 | 81 | 83 | 95 | 'TIL | Angels, Caprice 107 | | 5 |
| 58 | 59 | 59 | 65 | I'LL BE SEEING YOU | Frank Sinatra, Reprise 20023 | | 6 |
| 59 | 63 | 80 | — | SMILE | Timi Yuro, Liberty 55375 | | 3 |
| ★60 | 71 | 82 | — | TONIGHT | Eddie Fisher, Seven Arts 719 | | 3 |
| 61 | 75 | 92 | — | LANGUAGE OF LOVE | John D. Loudermilk, RCA Victor 7938 | △ | 3 |
| 62 | 37 | 36 | 38 | TAKE FIVE | Dave Brubeck, Columbia 41479 | △ | 11 |
| 63 | 58 | 65 | 74 | THE WAY I AM | Jackie Wilson, Brunswick 55220 | | 5 |
| 64 | 69 | 75 | 90 | SOMETIME | Gene Thomas, United Artists 338 | | 4 |
| ★65 | — | — | — | LET'S TWIST AGAIN | Chubby Checker, Parkway 824 | | 13 |
| 66 | 51 | 50 | 36 | I REALLY LOVE YOU | Stereos, Cub 9095 | | 9 |
| 67 | 31 | 19 | 12 | MEXICO | Bob Moore, Monument 446 | | 15 |
| ★68 | — | — | — | PEPPERMINT TWIST | Joey Dee and the Starliters, Roulette 4401 | | 1 |
| 69 | 80 | — | — | JOHNNY WILL | Pat Boone, Dot 16284 | | 2 |
| 70 | 76 | 78 | 88 | THREE STEPS FROM THE ALTAR | Shep and the Limelites, Hull 747 | | 6 |
| 71 | 74 | 85 | 91 | FOR ME AND MY GAL | Freddy Cannon, Swan 4083 | | 6 |
| 72 | 64 | 76 | 86 | DANNY BOY | Andy Williams, Columbia 42199 | △ | 4 |
| ★73 | 90 | 94 | — | IT'S TOO SOON TO KNOW | Etta James, Argo 5402 | | 3 |
| ★74 | 92 | — | — | WELL I TOLD YOU | Chantels, Carlton 564 | | 2 |
| 75 | 88 | 68 | 70 | MY HEART BELONGS TO ONLY YOU | Jackie Wilson, Brunswick 55220 | | 5 |
| ★76 | 95 | — | — | A CERTAIN GIRL | Ernie K-Doe, Minit 634 | | 2 |
| 77 | 78 | 86 | 99 | ON BENDED KNEES | Clarence Henry, Argo 5401 | | 4 |
| 78 | 83 | 95 | — | GYPSY ROVER | Highwaymen, United Artists 370 | | 3 |
| 79 | 67 | 71 | 79 | SOMEWHERE ALONG THE WAY | Steve Lawrence, United Artists 364 | | 5 |
| ★80 | — | — | — | WHEN THE BOY IN YOUR ARMS | Connie Francis, MGM 13051 | | 1 |
| 81 | 86 | — | — | IT'S ALL BECAUSE | Linda Scott, Canadian-American 129 | | 2 |
| 82 | 87 | 93 | — | I CRIED MY LAST TEAR | Ernie K-Doe, Minit 634 | | 3 |
| ★83 | — | — | — | REVENGE | Brook Benton, Mercury 71903 | | 1 |
| 84 | 85 | — | — | COMMANCHEROS | Claude King, Columbia 42196 | △ | 2 |
| 85 | 45 | 31 | 27 | STICK SHIFT | Duals, Sue 745 | | 11 |
| 86 | 93 | 96 | 100 | I WONDER | Pentagons, Jamie 1201 | | 4 |
| 87 | 100 | — | — | FUNNY HOW TIME SLIPS AWAY | Jimmy Elledge, RCA Victor 7946 | △ | 2 |
| 88 | 89 | — | — | IT WILL STAND | Showmen, Minit 632 | | 2 |
| ★89 | — | — | — | WHEN I FALL IN LOVE | Lettermen, Capitol 4658 | | 1 |
| ★90 | — | — | — | IF YOU GOTTA MAKE A FOOL OF SOMEBODY | James Ray, Caprice 110 | | 1 |
| 91 | — | — | — | LOVE (I'm So Glad) I FOUND YOU | Spinners, Tri-Phi 1004 | | 1 |
| 92 | — | — | — | THERE'S NO OTHER | Crystals, Philles 100 | | 1 |
| 93 | — | — | — | GREETINGS (This Is Uncle Sam) | Valadiers, Miracle 6 | | 1 |
| 94 | — | — | — | WHAT A WALK | Bobby Lewis, Beltone 1015 | | 1 |
| 95 | 99 | — | — | I KNOW | Barbara George, AFO 302 | | 2 |
| 96 | 98 | — | — | NEVER, NEVER | Jive Five, Beltone 1014 | | 2 |
| 97 | — | — | — | YOU'RE FOLLOWING ME | Perry Como, RCA Victor 7962 | △ | 1 |
| 98 | — | 97 | — | TURN AROUND, LOOK AT ME | Glen Campbell, Crest 1087 | | 2 |
| 99 | — | 98 | — | STEPS 1 & 2 | Jack Scott, Capitol 4637 | | 2 |
| 100 | 91 | — | — | TENNESSEE FLAT-TOP BOX | Johnny Cash, Columbia 42147 | △ | 2 |

## HOT 100—A TO Z—(Publisher-Licensee)


Anybody But Me (Champion, BMI) ... 41
Big Bad John (Cigma, BMI) ... 1
Big John (Ludix, BMI) ... 33
Blue Moon (Robbins, ASCAP) ... 54
Bridge of Love (Belinda, CAPAC) ... 50
Bristol Stomp (Kalman, ASCAP) ... 5
Candy Man (January, BMI) ... 43
Certain Girl, A (Minit, BMI) ... 76
Commancheros (Robbins, ASCAP) ... 84
Crazy (Pamper, BMI) ... 15
Cryin' (Acuff-Rose, BMI) ... 34
Danny Boy (Boosey & Hawkes, ASCAP) ... 72
Dreamboat (Acuff-Rose, BMI) ... 38
Everlovin' (Jat, BMI) ... 16
Everybody Gotta Pay Some Dues (Jobete, BMI) ... 52
Fly, The (Woodcrest-Mured, BMI) ... 10
Fool #1 (Sure Fire, BMI) ... 3
Foot Stompin' (Part 1) (Argo, BMI) ... 32
For Me and My Gal (Mills, ASCAP) ... 71
Funny How Time Slips Away (Golden West Melodies, BMI) ... 87
God, Country and My Baby (New Phoenix-Sarah, ASCAP) ... 18
Goodbye Cruel World (Aldon, BMI) ... 4
Greetings (Jobete, BMI) ... 93
Gypsy Rover (Box and Cox, ASCAP) ... 78
Gypsy Woman (Curtom, BMI) ... 37
Happy Birthday, Sweet Sixteen (Aldon, BMI) ... 45
Heartaches (Leeds, ASCAP) ... 19
Hit the Road Jack (Tangerine, BMI) ... 7
I Cried My Last Tear (Minit, BMI) ... 82
I Don't Know Why (Ahlert & Cromwell, ASCAP) ... 47
I Know (Saturn-At Last, BMI) ... 95
I Love How You Love Me (Aldon, BMI) ... 12
I Really Love You (Shalimar, BMI) ... 66
I Understand (Jubilee, ASCAP) ... 14
I Want to Thank You (Lowe, ASCAP) ... 21
I Wonder (Silmo, BMI) ... 86
If You Gotta Make a Fool of Somebody (Good Song, BMI) ... 90
I'll Be Seeing You (Williamson, ASCAP) ... 58
In the Middle of a Heartache (Central, BMI) ... 42
It Will Stand (Minit, BMI) ... 88
It's All Because (Kilt, BMI) ... 81
It's Too Soon to Know (Morris, ASCAP) ... 73
Johnny Will (Lyle & Hollyjo, ASCAP) ... 69
Just Out of Reach (Four Star, BMI) ... 24
Language of Love (Acuff-Rose, BMI) ... 61
Let There Be Drums (Travis, BMI) ... 30
Let's Get Together (Wonderland, BMI) ... 23
Let's Twist Again (Kalmann, ASCAP) ... 65
Lion Sleeps Tonight, The (Sanga, BMI) ... 55
Love (Fuqua, BMI) ... 91
Mexico (Acuff-Rose, BMI) ... 67
Moon River—Butler (Famous, ASCAP) ... 22
Moon River—Mancini (Famous, ASCAP) ... 26
My Heart Belongs to Only You (Merrimac, BMI) ... 75
Never, Never (Lescay, BMI) ... 96
On Bended Knees (Arc, BMI) ... 77
Peppermint Twist (Impact-Ware, BMI) ... 68
Please Don't Go (Alan K., BMI) ... 44
Please Mr. Postman (Jobete, BMI) ... 8
Revenge (Raleigh, BMI) ... 83
Rock-A-Bye Your Baby With a Dixie Melody (Warock-Mills, ASCAP) ... 39
Runaround Sue (Schwartz-Disal, ASCAP) ... 2
Run to Him (Aldon, BMI) ... 29
Sad Movies (Acuff-Rose, BMI) ... 17
School Is In (Pepe, BMI) ... 46
September in the Rain (Remick, ASCAP) ... 28
Smile (Bourne, ASCAP) ... 59
So Long Baby (Vicki-McLaughlin, BMI) ... 40
Sometime (Grand Prize, BMI) ... 64
Somewhere Along the Way (United Artists, ASCAP) ... 79
Steps 1 & 2 (Wolfpack, SESAC) ... 99
Stick Shift (Hidle, BMI) ... 85
Sweets for My Sweet (Brenner-Progressive-Trio, BMI) ... 35
Take Five (Derry, BMI) ... 62
Tennessee Flat-Top Box (Cash, BMI) ... 100
There's No Other (Bertha, BMI) ... 92
This Time (Tree, BMI) ... 9
Three Steps From the Altar (Keel, BMI) ... 70
'Til (Chappell, ASCAP) ... 57
Tonight—Ferrante & Teicher (Schirmer, ASCAP) ... 13
Tonight—Fisher (Schirmer, ASCAP) ... 60
Tower of Strength (Famous, ASCAP) ... 6
Town Without Pity (United Artists, ASCAP) ... 56
Turn Around, Look at Me (American, BMI) ... 98
Twist, The (Jay & Cee, BMI) ... 27
Under the Moon of Love (S-P-R, BMI) ... 48
Up a Lazy River (Peer Int'l, BMI) ... 51
Walk On By (Lowery, BMI) ... 31
Way I Am, The (East-West, ASCAP) ... 63
Way You Look Tonight, The (Harms, ASCAP) ... 36
Well I Told You (Barrett's Chantel, BMI) ... 74
What a Party (Travis, BMI) ... 49
What a Walk (Darnel, BMI) ... 94
When I Fall in Love (Northern, ASCAP) ... 89
When the Boy in Your Arms (Pickwick, ASCAP) ... 80
Wonder Like You, A (Four Star, BMI) ... 20
Ya Ya (Fast-Barich, BMI) ... 25
You're Following Me (Morris, ASCAP) ... 97
You're the Reason (American, BMI) ... 11
Your Ma Said You Cried in Your Sleep Last Night (Sea-Lark, BMI) ... 53


## BUBBLING UNDER THE HOT 100

101. TRADE WINDS ... Aki Aleong, Reprise 20021
102. LET'S GO TRIPPEN ... Dick Dale, Deltone 5017
103. HAPPY TIMES (Are Here to Stay) ... Tony Orlando, Epic 9476
104. WHAT I FEEL IN MY HEART ... Jim Reeves, RCA Victor 7950
105. WALKING WITH MY ANGEL ... Bobby Vee, Liberty 55388
106. SEVEN DAY FOOL ... Etta James, Argo 5402
107. EV'RYBODY'S CRYIN' ... Jimmy Beaumont, May 112
108. PREVIEW TO PARADISE ... Adam Wade, Coed 560
109. DON'T WALK AWAY FROM ME ... Dee Clark, Vee Jay 409
110. LITTLE ALTAR BOY ... Vic Dana, Dolton 48
111. JUST A LITTLE BIT SWEET ... Charlie Rich, Phillips 3572
112. LITTLE LONELY ... Chad Allen, Smash 1720
113. GIVE MYSELF A PARTY ... Rosemary Clooney, RCA Victor 7948
114. POP GOES THE WEASEL ... Anthony Newley, London 9501
115. MY BUDDY ... Eddie Harris, Vee Jay 407
116. SEARCHIN' ... Jack Eubanks, Monument 451
117. STANDING IN THE NEED OF LOVE ... Clarence Henry, Argo 5401
118. PEPPERMINT TWIST ... Danny Peppermint and the Jumping Jacks, Carlton 565
119. SHE PUT THE HURT ON ME ... Prince La La, AFO 101
120. KING OF KINGS ... Felix Slatkin, Liberty 55372

# BILLBOARD HOT 100

**NOVEMBER 27, 1961** — FOR WEEK ENDING DECEMBER 3, 1961

| This Week | Wk Ago | 2 Wks Ago | 3 Wks Ago | Title — Artist, Label & Number | Weeks On Chart |
|---|---|---|---|---|---|
| 1 | 1 | 1 | 1 | BIG BAD JOHN — Jimmy Dean, Columbia 42175 | 9 |
| 2 | 2 | 2 | 2 | RUNAROUND SUE — Dion, Laurie 3110 | 10 |
| 3 | 8 | 9 | 17 | PLEASE MR. POSTMAN — Marvelettes, Tamla 54046 | 13 |
| 4 | 4 | 12 | 27 | GOODBYE CRUEL WORLD — James Darren, Colpix 609 | 7 |
| 5 | 3 | 3 | 5 | FOOL #1 — Brenda Lee, Decca 31309 | 9 |
| 6 | 5 | 4 | 3 | BRISTOL STOMP — Dovells, Parkway 827 | 12 |
| 7 | 19 | 17 | 28 | HEARTACHES — Marcels, Colpix 612 | 8 |
| 8 | 6 | 5 | 10 | TOWER OF STRENGTH — Gene McDaniels, Liberty 55371 | 9 |
| 9 | 15 | 19 | 26 | CRAZY — Patsy Cline, Decca 31317 | 6 |
| 10 | 9 | 8 | 7 | THIS TIME — Troy Shondell, Liberty 55353 | 11 |
| 11 | 10 | 7 | 8 | THE FLY — Chubby Checker, Parkway 830 | 10 |
| 12 | 31 | 46 | 89 | WALK ON BY — Leroy Van Dyke, Mercury 71834 | 5 |
| 13 | 13 | 29 | 46 | TONIGHT — Ferrante & Teicher, United Artists 373 | 7 |
| 14 | 14 | 20 | 20 | I UNDERSTAND (Just How You Feel) — G-Clefs, Terrace 7500 | 11 |
| 15 | 11 | 13 | 15 | YOU'RE THE REASON — Bobby Edwards, Crest 1075 | 14 |
| 16 | 27 | 55 | — | THE TWIST — Chubby Checker, Parkway 811 | 21 |
| 17 | 29 | 57 | — | RUN TO HIM — Bobby Vee, Liberty 55388 | 3 |
| 18 | 20 | 11 | 13 | A WONDER LIKE YOU — Rick Nelson, Imperial 5770 | 9 |
| 19 | 12 | 15 | 9 | I LOVE HOW YOU LOVE ME — Paris Sisters, Gregmark 6 | 13 |
| 20 | 22 | 26 | 37 | MOON RIVER — Jerry Butler, Vee Jay 405 | 8 |
| 21 | 21 | 30 | 39 | I WANT TO THANK YOU — Bobby Rydell, Cameo 201 | 7 |
| 22 | 7 | 6 | 4 | HIT THE ROAD JACK — Ray Charles, ABC-Paramount 10244 | 12 |
| 23 | 28 | 32 | 38 | SEPTEMBER IN THE RAIN — Dinah Washington, Mercury 71876 | 7 |
| 24 | 24 | 34 | 45 | JUST OUT OF REACH (of My Two Open Arms) — Solomon Burke, Atlantic 2114 | 11 |
| 25 | 18 | 24 | 40 | GOD, COUNTRY AND MY BABY — Johnny Burnette, Liberty 55379 | 7 |
| 26 | 26 | 36 | 49 | MOON RIVER — Henry Mancini, RCA Victor 7916 | 8 |
| 27 | 30 | 44 | 69 | LET THERE BE DRUMS — Sandy Nelson, Imperial 5775 | 5 |
| 28 | 45 | 62 | — | HAPPY BIRTHDAY, SWEET SIXTEEN — Neil Sedaka, RCA Victor 7957 | 3 |
| 29 | 42 | 52 | 54 | IN THE MIDDLE OF A HEARTACHE — Wanda Jackson, Capitol 4635 | 7 |
| 30 | 16 | 16 | 23 | EVERLOVIN' — Rick Nelson, Imperial 5770 | 9 |
| 31 | 17 | 10 | 6 | SAD MOVIES (Made Me Cry) — Sue Thompson, Hickory 1153 | 13 |
| 32 | 37 | 49 | 64 | GYPSY WOMAN — Impressions, ABC-Paramount 10241 | 5 |
| 33 | 23 | 14 | 11 | LET'S GET TOGETHER — Hayley Mills, Vista 385 | 13 |
| 34 | 25 | 18 | 12 | YA YA — Lee Dorsey, Fury 1053 | 12 |
| 35 | 32 | 38 | 30 | FOOT STOMPIN' (Part 1) — Flares, Felsted 8624 | 13 |
| 36 | 55 | 70 | — | THE LION SLEEPS TONIGHT — Tokens, RCA Victor 7954 | 3 |
| 37 | 39 | 43 | 44 | ROCK-A-BYE YOUR BABY WITH A DIXIE MELODY — Aretha Franklin, Columbia 42157 | 8 |
| 38 | 47 | 66 | 84 | I DON'T KNOW WHY — Linda Scott, Canadian-American 129 | 5 |
| 39 | 34 | 22 | 18 | CRYIN' — Roy Orbison, Monument 447 | 16 |
| 40 | 65 | — | — | LET'S TWIST AGAIN — Chubby Checker, Parkway 824 | 14 |
| 41 | 61 | 75 | 92 | LANGUAGE OF LOVE — John D. Loudermilk, RCA Victor 7938 | 4 |
| 42 | 59 | 63 | 80 | SMILE — Timi Yuro, Liberty 55375 | 4 |
| 43 | 68 | — | — | PEPPERMINT TWIST — Joey Dee and the Starliters, Roulette 4401 | 2 |
| 44 | 56 | 72 | 81 | TOWN WITHOUT PITY — Gene Pitney, Musicor 1009 | 5 |
| 45 | 51 | 84 | — | UP A LAZY RIVER — Si Zentner, Liberty 55374 | 3 |
| 46 | 48 | 50 | 56 | UNDER THE MOON OF LOVE — Curtis Lee, Dunes 2008 | 7 |
| 47 | 57 | 81 | 83 | 'TIL — Angels, Caprice 107 | 6 |
| 48 | 41 | 48 | 43 | ANYBODY BUT ME — Brenda Lee, Decca 31309 | 9 |
| 49 | 43 | 27 | 25 | CANDY MAN — Roy Orbison, Monument 447 | 14 |
| 50 | 53 | 68 | 77 | YOUR MA SAID YOU CRIED IN YOUR SLEEP LAST NIGHT — Kenny Dino, Musicor 1013 | 4 |
| 51 | 33 | 21 | 24 | BIG JOHN — Shirelles, Scepter 1223 | 9 |
| 52 | 52 | 60 | 70 | EVERYBODY GOTTA PAY SOME DUES — Miracles, Tamla 54048 | 6 |
| 53 | 64 | 69 | 75 | SOMETIME — Gene Thomas, United Artists 338 | 5 |
| 54 | 80 | — | — | WHEN THE BOY IN YOUR ARMS — Connie Francis, MGM 13051 | 2 |
| 55 | 89 | — | — | WHEN I FALL IN LOVE — Lettermen, Capitol 4658 | 2 |
| 56 | 73 | 90 | 94 | IT'S TOO SOON TO KNOW — Etta James, Argo 5402 | 4 |
| 57 | 60 | 71 | 82 | TONIGHT — Eddie Fisher, Seven Arts 719 | 4 |
| 58 | 63 | 58 | 65 | THE WAY I AM — Jackie Wilson, Brunswick 55220 | 6 |
| 59 | 70 | 76 | 78 | THREE STEPS FROM THE ALTAR — Shep and the Limelites, Hull 747 | 7 |
| 60 | 74 | 92 | — | WELL I TOLD YOU — Chantels, Carlton 564 | 3 |
| 61 | 62 | 37 | 36 | TAKE FIVE — Dave Brubeck, Columbia 41479 | 12 |
| 62 | — | — | — | UNCHAIN MY HEART — Ray Charles, ABC-Paramount 10266 | 1 |
| 63 | 78 | 83 | 95 | GYPSY ROVER — Highwaymen, United Artists 370 | |
| 64 | 77 | 78 | 86 | ON BENDED KNEES — Clarence Henry, Argo 5401 | 5 |
| 65 | 75 | 88 | 68 | MY HEART BELONGS TO ONLY YOU — Jackie Wilson, Brunswick 55220 | 6 |
| 66 | 69 | 80 | — | JOHNNY WILL — Pat Boone, Dot 16284 | 3 |
| 67 | 72 | 64 | 76 | DANNY BOY — Andy Williams, Columbia 42199 | 5 |
| 68 | 92 | — | — | THERE'S NO OTHER — Crystals, Philles 100 | 2 |
| 69 | 50 | 53 | 53 | BRIDGE OF LOVE — Joe Dowell, Smash 1717 | 7 |
| 70 | 36 | 25 | 14 | THE WAY YOU LOOK TONIGHT — Lettermen, Capitol 4586 | 13 |
| 71 | 83 | — | — | REVENGE — Brook Benton, Mercury 71903 | 2 |
| 72 | 82 | 87 | 93 | I CRIED MY LAST TEAR — Ernie K-Doe, Minit 634 | 4 |
| 73 | 54 | 65 | 62 | BLUE MOON — Ventures, Dolton 47 | 6 |
| 74 | 81 | 86 | — | IT'S ALL BECAUSE — Linda Scott, Canadian-American 129 | 3 |
| 75 | 76 | 95 | — | A CERTAIN GIRL — Ernie K-Doe, Minit 634 | 3 |
| 76 | 87 | 100 | — | FUNNY HOW TIME SLIPS AWAY — Jimmy Elledge, RCA Victor 7946 | 3 |
| 77 | 96 | 98 | — | NEVER, NEVER — Jive Five, Beltone 1014 | 3 |
| 78 | — | — | — | HEY, LITTLE GIRL — Del Shannon, Big Top 3091 | 1 |
| 79 | 58 | 59 | 59 | I'LL BE SEEING YOU — Frank Sinatra, Reprise 20023 | 7 |
| 80 | 95 | 99 | — | I KNOW — Barbara George, AFO 302 | 3 |
| 81 | 94 | — | — | WHAT A WALK — Bobby Lewis, Beltone 1015 | 3 |
| 82 | 88 | 89 | — | IT WILL STAND — Showmen, Minit 632 | 3 |
| 83 | — | — | — | I'LL NEVER STOP WANTING YOU — Brian Hyland, ABC-Paramount 10262 | 1 |
| 84 | 86 | 93 | 96 | I WONDER — Pentagons, Jamie 1201 | 5 |
| 85 | 84 | 85 | — | THE COMMANCHEROS — Claude King, Columbia 42196 | 3 |
| 86 | 99 | — | 98 | STEPS 1 & 2 — Jack Scott, Capitol 4637 | 3 |
| 87 | 90 | — | — | IF YOU GOTTA MAKE A FOOL OF SOMEBODY — James Ray, Caprice 110 | 2 |
| 88 | — | 96 | — | SOOTHE ME — Sims Twins, Sar 117 | 3 |
| 89 | 93 | — | — | GREETINGS (This Is Uncle Sam) — Valadiers, Miracle 6 | 2 |
| 90 | 100 | 91 | — | TENNESSEE FLAT-TOP BOX — Johnny Cash, Columbia 42147 | 3 |
| 91 | — | — | — | SEARCHIN' — Jack Eubanks, Monument 451 | 1 |
| 92 | 97 | — | — | YOU'RE FOLLOWING ME — Perry Como, RCA Victor 7962 | 2 |
| 93 | — | — | — | HAPPY TIMES (Are Here to Stay) — Tony Orlando, Epic 9476 | 1 |
| 94 | — | — | — | LET'S GO TRIPPIN' — Dick Dale, Deltone 5017 | 1 |
| 95 | — | — | — | POOR FOOL — Ike and Tina Turner, Sue 753 | 1 |
| 96 | — | — | — | WALKIN' WITH MY ANGEL — Bobby Vee, Liberty 55388 | 1 |
| 97 | — | 77 | 72 | YOUNG BOY BLUES — Ben E. King, Atco 6207 | 6 |
| 98 | — | 97 | — | IT DO ME SO GOOD — Ann-Margret, RCA Victor 7952 | 2 |
| 99 | — | — | — | LITTLE ALTAR BOY — Vic Dana, Dolton 48 | 1 |
| 100 | — | — | — | COTTON FIELDS — Highwaymen, United Artists 370 | 1 |

## BUBBLING UNDER THE HOT 100

101. LETTER FULL OF TEARS — Gladys Knight and the Pips, Fury 1054
102. TURN ON YOUR LOVE LIGHT — Bobby Bland, Duke 344
103. FLY BY NIGHT — Andy Williams, Columbia 42199
104. WHAT I FEEL IN MY HEART — Jim Reeves, RCA Victor 7950
105. SEVEN DAY FOOL — Etta James, Argo 5402
106. LOSING YOUR LOVE — Jim Reeves, RCA Victor 7959
107. DON'T WALK AWAY FROM ME — Dee Clark, Vee Jay 409
108. LONESOME NUMBER ONE — Don Gibson, RCA Victor 7959
109. STANDING IN THE NEED OF LOVE — Clarence Henry, Argo 5401
110. GIVE MYSELF A PARTY — Rosemary Clooney, RCA Victor 7948
111. EV'RYBODY'S CRYIN' — Jimmy Beaumont, May 112
112. PREVIEW OF PARADISE — Adam Wade, Coed 560
113. PEPPERMINT TWIST — Danny Peppermint and the Jumping Jacks, Carlton 565
114. AFTER ALL WE'VE BEEN THROUGH — Maxine Brown, ABC-Paramount 10255
115. TURN AROUND, LOOK AT ME — Glen Campbell, Crest 1087
116. BUT ON THE OTHER HAND BABY — Ray Charles, ABC-Paramount 10266
117. FLYING CIRCLE — Frank Slay and Orch., Swan 4085
118. DREAMY EYES — Johnny Tillotson, Cadence 1409
119. SONG FOR THE LONELY — Platters, Mercury 71904
120. TONIGHT — Jay and the Americans, United Artists 353

# BILLBOARD HOT 100

FOR WEEK ENDING DECEMBER 10

1961

★ STAR PERFORMERS—Selections registering greatest upward progress this week.

[S] Indicates that 45 r.p.m. stereo single version is available.

△ Indicates that 33⅓ r.p.m. mono single version is available.

△S Indicates that 33⅓ r.p.m. stereo single version is available.

| This Week | 1 Wk. Ago | 2 Wks. Ago | 3 Wks. Ago | Title | Artist, Label & Number | Weeks On Chart |
|---|---|---|---|---|---|---|
| 1 | 1 | 1 | 1 | BIG BAD JOHN △ | Jimmy Dean, Columbia 42175 | 10 |
| 2 | 3 | 8 | 9 | PLEASE MR. POSTMAN | Marvelettes, Tamla 54046 | 14 |
| 3 | 4 | 4 | 12 | GOODBYE CRUEL WORLD | James Darren, Colpix 609 | 8 |
| 4 | 2 | 2 | 2 | RUNAROUND SUE | Dion, Laurie 3110 | 11 |
| 5 | 5 | 3 | 3 | FOOL #1 | Brenda Lee, Decca 31309 | 10 |
| ★6 | 16 | 27 | 55 | THE TWIST | Chubby Checker, Parkway 811 | 22 |
| ★7 | 12 | 31 | 46 | WALK ON BY | Leroy Van Dyke, Mercury 71834 | 6 |
| 8 | 8 | 6 | 5 | TOWER OF STRENGTH | Gene McDaniels, Liberty 55371 | 10 |
| ★9 | 14 | 14 | 20 | I UNDERSTAND (Just How You Feel) | G-Clefs, Terrace 7500 | 12 |
| 10 | 9 | 15 | 19 | CRAZY | Patsy Cline, Decca 31317 | 7 |
| ★11 | 17 | 29 | 57 | RUN TO HIM | Bobby Vee, Liberty 55388 | 4 |
| 12 | 13 | 13 | 29 | TONIGHT | Ferrante & Teicher, United Artists 373 | 8 |
| 13 | 7 | 19 | 17 | HEARTACHES | Marcels, Colpix 612 | 9 |
| ★14 | 20 | 22 | 26 | MOON RIVER | Jerry Butler, Vee Jay 405 | 9 |
| 15 | 11 | 10 | 7 | THE FLY | Chubby Checker, Parkway 830 | 11 |
| ★16 | 27 | 30 | 44 | LET THERE BE DRUMS | Sandy Nelson, Imperial 5775 | 6 |
| ★17 | 36 | 55 | 70 | THE LION SLEEPS TONIGHT △ | Tokens, RCA Victor 7954 | 4 |
| 18 | 6 | 5 | 4 | BRISTOL STOMP | Dovells, Parkway 827 | 13 |
| 19 | 10 | 9 | 8 | THIS TIME | Troy Shondell, Liberty 55353 | 12 |
| ★20 | 32 | 37 | 49 | GYPSY WOMAN | Impressions, ABC-Paramount 10241 | 8 |
| 21 | 28 | 45 | 62 | HAPPY BIRTHDAY, SWEET SIXTEEN △ | Neil Sedaka, RCA Victor 7957 | 4 |
| 22 | 19 | 12 | 15 | I LOVE HOW YOU LOVE ME | Paris Sisters, Gregmark 6 | 14 |
| 23 | 23 | 28 | 32 | SEPTEMBER IN THE RAIN | Dinah Washington, Mercury 71876 | 8 |
| 24 | 26 | 26 | 36 | MOON RIVER △ | Henry Mancini, RCA Victor 7916 | 9 |
| 25 | 18 | 20 | 11 | A WONDER LIKE YOU | Rick Nelson, Imperial 5770 | 10 |
| ★26 | 38 | 47 | 66 | I DON'T KNOW WHY | Linda Scott, Canadian-American 129 | 6 |
| 27 | 29 | 42 | 52 | IN THE MIDDLE OF A HEARTACHE | Wanda Jackson, Capitol 4635 | 8 |
| 28 | 15 | 11 | 13 | YOU'RE THE REASON | Bobby Edwards, Crest 1075 | 15 |
| ★29 | 43 | 68 | — | PEPPERMINT TWIST | Joey Dee and the Starliters, Roulette 4401 | 3 |
| 30 | 24 | 24 | 34 | JUST OUT OF REACH (of My Two Open Arms) | Solomon Burke, Atlantic 2114 | 12 |
| 31 | 21 | 21 | 30 | I WANT TO THANK YOU | Bobby Rydell, Cameo 201 | 8 |
| 32 | 40 | 65 | — | LET'S TWIST AGAIN | Chubby Checker, Parkway 824 | 15 |
| ★33 | 47 | 57 | 81 | 'TIL | Angels, Caprice 107 | 7 |
| 34 | 35 | 32 | 38 | FOOT STOMPIN' (Part 1) | Flares, Felsted 8624 | 14 |
| ★35 | 55 | 89 | — | WHEN I FALL IN LOVE | Lettermen, Capitol 4658 | 3 |
| 36 | 41 | 61 | 75 | LANGUAGE OF LOVE △ | John D. Loudermilk, RCA Victor 7938 | 5 |
| ★37 | 54 | 80 | — | WHEN THE BOY IN YOUR ARMS | Connie Francis, MGM 13051 | 3 |
| ★38 | 62 | — | — | UNCHAIN MY HEART | Ray Charles, ABC-Paramount 10266 | 2 |
| ★39 | 50 | 53 | 68 | YOUR MA SAID YOU CRIED IN YOUR SLEEP LAST NIGHT | Kenny Dino, Musicor 1013 | 5 |
| 40 | 31 | 17 | 10 | SAD MOVIES (Make Me Cry) | Sue Thompson, Hickory 1153 | 14 |
| ★41 | 60 | 74 | 92 | WELL I TOLD YOU | Chantels, Carlton 564 | 4 |
| 42 | 25 | 18 | 24 | GOD, COUNTRY AND MY BABY | Johnny Burnette, Liberty 55379 | 8 |
| ★43 | 68 | 92 | — | THERE'S NO OTHER (Like My Baby) | Crystals, Philles 100 | 3 |
| 44 | 44 | 56 | 72 | TOWN WITHOUT PITY | Gene Pitney, Musicor 1009 | 6 |
| 45 | 42 | 59 | 63 | SMILE | Timi Yuro, Liberty 55375 | 5 |
| ★46 | 57 | 60 | 71 | TONIGHT | Eddie Fisher, Seven Arts 719 | 5 |
| 47 | 22 | 7 | 6 | HIT THE ROAD JACK | Ray Charles, ABC-Paramount 10244 | 13 |
| 48 | 30 | 16 | 16 | EVERLOVIN' | Rick Nelson, Imperial 5770 | 10 |
| 49 | 37 | 39 | 43 | ROCK-A-BYE YOUR BABY WITH A DIXIE MELODY △ | Aretha Franklin, Columbia 42157 | 9 |
| 50 | 45 | 51 | 84 | UP A LAZY RIVER | Si Zentner, Liberty 55374 | 4 |
| 51 | 33 | 23 | 14 | LET'S GET TOGETHER | Hayley Mills, Vista 385 | 14 |
| 52 | 34 | 25 | 18 | YA YA | Lee Dorsey, Fury 1053 | 13 |
| ★53 | 63 | 78 | 83 | GYPSY ROVER | Highwaymen, United Artists 370 | 5 |
| 54 | 56 | 73 | 90 | IT'S TOO SOON TO KNOW | Etta James, Argo 5402 | 5 |
| ★55 | 66 | 69 | 80 | JOHNNY WILL | Pat Boone, Dot 16284 | 4 |
| ★56 | 71 | 83 | — | REVENGE | Brook Benton, Mercury 71903 | 3 |
| ★57 | — | — | — | CAN'T HELP FALLING IN LOVE △ | Elvis Presley, RCA Victor 7968 | 1 |
| 58 | 59 | 70 | 76 | THREE STEPS FROM THE ALTAR | Shep and the Limelites, Hull 747 | 8 |
| ★59 | — | — | — | PEPPERMINT TWIST | Danny Peppermint and the Jumping Jacks, Carlton 565 | 1 |
| ★60 | 88 | — | 96 | SOOTHE ME | Sims Twins, Sar 117 | 4 |
| 61 | 74 | 81 | 86 | IT'S ALL BECAUSE | Linda Scott, Canadian-American 129 | 4 |
| ★62 | — | — | — | ROCK-A-HULA BABY △ | Elvis Presley, RCA Victor 7968 | 1 |
| 63 | 76 | 87 | 100 | FUNNY HOW TIME SLIPS AWAY △ | Jimmy Elledge, RCA Victor 7946 | 4 |
| ★64 | — | — | — | THE MAJESTIC | Dion, Laurie 3115 | 1 |
| ★65 | 80 | 95 | 99 | I KNOW | Barbara George, AFO 302 | 4 |
| ★66 | — | — | — | LONESOME NUMBER ONE △ | Don Gibson, RCA Victor 7959 | 1 |
| ★67 | — | — | — | I HEAR YOU KNOCKING | Fats Domino, Imperial 5796 | 1 |
| 68 | 78 | — | — | HEY, LITTLE GIRL | Del Shannon, Big Top 3091 | 2 |
| 69 | 72 | 82 | 87 | I CRIED MY LAST TEAR | Ernie K-Doe, Minit 634 | 5 |
| 70 | 52 | 52 | 60 | EVERYBODY GOTTA PAY SOME DUES | Miracles, Tamla 54048 | 7 |
| 71 | 75 | 76 | 95 | A CERTAIN GIRL | Ernie K-Doe, Minit 634 | 4 |
| 72 | 67 | 72 | 64 | DANNY BOY △ | Andy Williams, Columbia 42199 | 6 |
| ★73 | 95 | — | — | POOR FOOL | Ike and Tina Turner, Sue 753 | 2 |
| 74 | 87 | 90 | — | IF YOU GOTTA MAKE A FOOL OF SOMEBODY | James Ray, Caprice 110 | 3 |
| 75 | 85 | 84 | 85 | THE COMMANCHEROS △ | Claude King, Columbia 42196 | 4 |
| 76 | 82 | 88 | 89 | IT WILL STAND | Showmen, Minit 632 | 4 |
| 77 | 81 | 94 | — | WHAT A WALK | Bobby Lewis, Beltone 1015 | 3 |
| ★78 | 99 | — | — | LITTLE ALTAR BOY | Vic Dana, Dolton 48 | 2 |
| ★79 | — | — | — | THE WANDERER | Dion, Laurie 3115 | 1 |
| 80 | 77 | 96 | 98 | NEVER, NEVER | Jive Five, Beltone 1014 | 4 |
| ★81 | — | — | — | TURN ON YOUR LOVE LIGHT | Bobby Bland, Duke 344 | 1 |
| 82 | 93 | — | — | HAPPY TIMES (Are Here to Stay) | Tony Orlando, Epic 9476 | 2 |
| 83 | 91 | — | — | SEARCHIN' | Jack Eubanks, Monument 451 | 2 |
| ★84 | 100 | — | — | COTTON FIELDS | Highwaymen, United Artists 370 | 2 |
| 85 | 96 | — | — | WALKIN' WITH MY ANGEL | Bobby Vee, Liberty 55388 | 2 |
| 86 | — | — | — | SMALL SAD SAM | Phil McLean, Versatile 107 | 1 |
| ★87 | — | — | — | UNSQUARE DANCE △ | Dave Brubeck Quartet, Columbia 42228 | 1 |
| 88 | 90 | 100 | 91 | TENNESSEE FLAT-TOP BOX △ | Johnny Cash, Columbia 42147 | 1 |
| 89 | 53 | 64 | 69 | SOMETIME | Gene Thomas, United Artists 338 | 6 |
| ★90 | — | — | — | LOSING YOUR LOVE △ | Jim Reeves, RCA Victor 7950 | 1 |
| 91 | 94 | — | — | LET'S GO TRIPPIN' | Dick Dale, Deltone 5017 | 2 |
| 92 | 92 | 97 | — | YOU'RE FOLLOWING ME △ | Perry Como, RCA Victor 7962 | 3 |
| 93 | — | 98 | — | TURN AROUND, LOOK AT ME | Glen Campbell, Crest 1087 | 3 |
| 94 | — | — | — | NORMAN | Sue Thompson, Hickory 1159 | 1 |
| 95 | — | — | — | WHAT I FEEL IN MY HEART △ | Jim Reeves, RCA Victor 7950 | 1 |
| 96 | — | — | — | POP GOES THE WEASEL | Anthony Newley, London 9501 | 1 |
| 97 | 98 | — | 97 | IT DO ME SO GOOD △ | Ann-Margret, RCA Victor 7952 | 3 |
| 98 | — | — | — | SHE REALLY LOVES YOU | Timi Yuro, Liberty 55375 | 1 |
| 99 | — | — | — | DREAMY EYES | Johnny Tillotson, Cadence 1409 | 1 |
| 100 | — | — | — | WALKIN' BACK TO HAPPINESS | Helen Shapiro, Capitol 4662 | 1 |

## HOT 100—A TO Z—(*Publisher-Licensee*)


Big Bad John (Cigma, BMI)........ 1
Bristol Stomp (Kalmann, ASCAP)........ 18
Can't Help Falling in Love (Gladys, ASCAP)........ 57
Certain Girl, A (Minit, BMI)........ 71
Commancheros, The (Robbins, ASCAP)........ 75
Cotton Fields (Westside, BMI)........ 84
Crazy (Pamper, BMI)........ 10
Danny Boy (Boosey & Hawkes, ASCAP)........ 72
Dreamy Eyes (Southern Belle, BMI)........ 99
Everlovin' (Jat, BMI)........ 48
Everybody Gotta Pay Some Dues (Jabete, BMI)........ 70
Fly, The (Woodcrest-Mured, BMI)........ 15
Fool #1 (Sure Fire, BMI)........ 5
Foot Stompin' (Part 1) (Argo, BMI)........ 34
Funny How Time Slips Away (Golden West Melodies, BMI)........ 63
God, Country and My Baby (New Phoenix-Sarah, ASCAP)........ 42
Goodbye Cruel World (Aldon, BMI)........ 3
Gypsy Rover (Box and Cox, ASCAP)........ 53
Gypsy Woman (Curtom, BMI)........ 20
Happy Birthday, Sweet Sixteen (Aldon, BMI)........ 21
Happy Times (Aldon, BMI)........ 82
Heartaches (Leeds, ASCAP)........ 13
Hey! Little Girl (Vicki-McLaughlin, BMI)........ 68
Hit the Road Jack (Tangerine, BMI)........ 47
I Cried My Last Tear (Minit, BMI)........ 69
I Don't Know Why (Ahlert & Cromwell, ASCAP)........ 26
I Hear You Knocking (Commodore, BMI)........ 67
I Know (Saturn-At Last, BMI)........ 65
I Love How You Love Me (Aldon, BMI)........ 22
I Understand (Jubilee, ASCAP)........ 9
I Want to Thank You (Lowe, ASCAP)........ 31
If You Gotta Make a Fool of Somebody (Good Song, BMI)........ 74
In the Middle of a Heartache (Central, BMI)........ 27
It Do Me So Good (Arc, BMI)........ 97
It Will Stand (Minit, BMI)........ 76
It's All Because (Kilt, BMI)........ 61
It's Too Soon to Know (Morris, ASCAP)........ 54
Johnny Will (Lyle & Hollyjo, ASCAP)........ 55
Just Out of Reach (Four Stars, BMI)........ 30
Language of Love (Acuff-Rose, BMI)........ 36
Let There Be Drums (Travis, BMI)........ 16
Let's Get Together (Wonderland, BMI)........ 51
Let's Go Trippin' (Monsour, ASCAP)........ 91
Let's Twist Again (Kalmann, ASCAP)........ 32
Lion Sleeps Tonight, The (Folkways, BMI)........ 17
Little Altar Boy (House of Sound-Bilya Bay, BMI). 78
Lonesome Number One (Acuff-Rose, BMI)........ 66
Losing Your Love (Tree, BMI)........ 90
Majestic, The (Just-Mubon, BMI)........ 64
Moon River—Butler (Famous, ASCAP)........ 14
Moon River—Mancini (Famous, ASCAP)........ 24
Never, Never (Lescay, BMI)........ 80
Norman (Acuff-Rose, BMI)........ 94
Peppermint Twist—Dee (Impact-Ware, BMI)........ 29
Peppermint Twist—Peppermint (Pambill, ASCAP)........ 59
Please Mr. Postman (Jobete, BMI)........ 2
Poor Fool (Saturn, BMI)........ 73
Pop Goes the Weasel (Hollis, BMI)........ 96
Revenge (Raleigh, BMI)........ 56
Rock-A-Bye Your Baby With a Dixie Melody (Warock-Mills, ASCAP)........ 49
Rock-A-Hula Baby (Gladys, ASCAP)........ 62
Runaround Sue (Schwartz-Disal, ASCAP)........ 4
Run to Him (Aldon, BMI)........ 11
Sad Movies (Acuff-Rose, BMI)........ 40
Searchin' (Tiger, BMI)........ 83
September in the Rain (Remick, ASCAP)........ 23
She Really Loves You (Eden, BMI)........ 98
Small Sad Sam (R.F.D., ASCAP)........ 86
Smile (Bourne, ASCAP)........ 45
Sometime (Grand Prize, BMI)........ 89
Soothe Me (Kags, BMI)........ 60
Tennessee Flat-Top Box (Cash, BMI)........ 88
There's No Other (Bertha, BMI)........ 43
This Time (Tree, BMI)........ 19
Three Steps From the Altar (Keel, BMI)........ 58
'Til (Chappell, ASCAP)........ 33
Tonight—Ferrante & Teicher (Schirmer, ASCAP)........ 12
Tonight—Fisher (Schirmer, ASCAP)........ 46
Tower of Strength (Famous, ASCAP)........ 8
Town Without Pity (United Artists, ASCAP)........ 44
Turn Around, Look at Me (American, BMI)........ 93
Turn on Your Love Light (Don, BMI)........ 81
Twist, The (Jay & Cee, BMI)........ 6
Unchain My Heart (Tee Pee, ASCAP)........ 38
Unsquare Dance (Derry, BMI)........ 87
Up a Lazy River (Peer Int'l, BMI)........ 50
Walk on By (Lowery, BMI)........ 7
Walkin' Back to Happiness (Bourne-Rank, ASCAP). 100
Walkin' With My Angel (Aldon, BMI)........ 85
Wanderer, The (Schwartz-Disal, ASCAP)........ 79
Well, I Told You (Barrett's Chantel-Trio, BMI)........ 41
What a Walk (Darnel, BMI)........ 77
What I Feel in My Heart (Tuckahoe, BMI)........ 95
When I Fall in Love (Northern, ASCAP)........ 35
When the Boy in Your Arms (Pickwick, ASCAP) 37
Wonder Like You, A (Four Star, BMI)........ 25
Ya Ya (Fast-Barich, BMI)........ 52
You're Following Me (Morris, ASCAP)........ 92
You're the Reason (American, BMI)........ 28
Your Ma Said You Cried in Your Sleep Last Night (Sea-Lark, BMI)........ 39


## BUBBLING UNDER THE HOT 100

101. MARIA........Roger Williams, Kapp 437
102. EV'RYBODY'S CRYIN'........Jimmy Beaumont, May 112
103. STEPS 1 & 2........Jack Scott, Capitol 4637
104. THE BELLS AT MY WEDDING....Paul Anka, ABC-Paramount 10279
105. BUT ON THE OTHER HAND....Ray Charles, ABC-Paramount 10266
106. FLYING CIRCLE........Frank Slay and Ork, Swan 4085
107. TRADE WINDS........Aki Aleong, Reprise 20021
108. GIVE MYSELF A PARTY.......Rosemary Clooney, RCA Victor 7948
109. PREVIEW OF PARADISE........Adam Wade, Coed 560
110. LOVELAND........Paul Anka, ABC-Paramount 10279
111. LETTER FULL OF TEARS......Gladys Knight and the Pips, Fury 1054
112. PUSHIN' YOUR LUCK........Sleepy King, Joy 257
113. FEVER........Pete Bennett and the Embers, Sunset 1002
114. LITTLE MISS U. S. A.........Barry Mann, ABC-Paramount 10263
115. THE WALTZ YOU SAVED FOR ME......Ferlin Husky, Capitol 4650
116. SWEETHEARTS IN HEAVEN........Chase Webster, Dot 16270
117. A-ONE A-TWO A-CHA CHA CHA.....Lawrence Welk, Dot 16285
118. SONG FOR THE LONELY........Platters, Mercury 71904
119. I NEED SOMEONE........Belmonts, Sabrina 502
120. JUST GOT TO KNOW........Jimmy McCracklin, Art-Tone 825

# BILLBOARD HOT 100

**DECEMBER 11, 1961**
**FOR WEEK ENDING DECEMBER 17, 1961**

★ STAR PERFORMERS—Selections registering greatest upward progress this week.
S Indicates that 45 r.p.m. stereo single version is available.
△ Indicates that 33⅓ r.p.m. mono single version is available.
Ⓢ Indicates that 33⅓ r.p.m. stereo single version is available.

| This Week | 1 Wk. Ago | 2 Wk. Ago | 3 Wk. Ago | TITLE — Artist, Label & Number | Weeks On Chart |
|---|---|---|---|---|---|
| 1 | 2 | 3 | 8 | PLEASE MR. POSTMAN — Marvelettes, Tamla 54046 | 15 |
| 2 | 1 | 1 | 1 | BIG BAD JOHN — Jimmy Dean, Columbia 42175 | 11 |
| 3 | 3 | 4 | 4 | GOODBYE CRUEL WORLD — James Darren, Colpix 609 | 9 |
| 4 | 6 | 16 | 27 | THE TWIST — Chubby Checker, Parkway 811 | 23 |
| 5 | 7 | 12 | 31 | WALK ON BY — Leroy Van Dyke, Mercury 71834 | 7 |
| ★6 | 17 | 36 | 55 | THE LION SLEEPS TONIGHT — Tokens, RCA Victor 7954 | 5 |
| 7 | 11 | 17 | 29 | RUN TO HIM — Bobby Vee, Liberty 55388 | 5 |
| 8 | 12 | 13 | 13 | TONIGHT — Ferrante & Teicher, United Artists 373 | 9 |
| ★9 | 16 | 27 | 30 | LET THERE BE DRUMS — Sandy Nelson, Imperial 5775 | 7 |
| ★10 | 21 | 28 | 45 | HAPPY BIRTHDAY, SWEET SIXTEEN — Neil Sedaka, RCA Victor 7957 | 5 |
| 11 | 14 | 20 | 22 | MOON RIVER — Jerry Butler, Vee Jay 405 | 10 |
| 12 | 4 | 2 | 2 | RUNAROUND SUE — Dion, Laurie 3110 | 12 |
| 13 | 5 | 5 | 3 | FOOL #1 — Brenda Lee, Decca 31309 | 11 |
| 14 | 10 | 9 | 15 | CRAZY — Patsy Cline, Decca 31317 | 8 |
| 15 | 29 | 43 | 68 | PEPPERMINT TWIST — Joey Dee and the Starliters, Roulette 4401 | 4 |
| 16 | 9 | 14 | 14 | I UNDERSTAND (Just How You Feel) — G-Clefs, Terrace 7500 | 13 |
| ★17 | 24 | 26 | 26 | MOON RIVER — Henry Mancini, RCA Victor 7916 | 10 |
| 18 | 8 | 8 | 6 | TOWER OF STRENGTH — Gene McDaniels, Liberty 55371 | 11 |
| 19 | 26 | 38 | 47 | I DON'T KNOW WHY — Linda Scott, Canadian-American 129 | 7 |
| 20 | 20 | 32 | 37 | GYPSY WOMAN — Impressions, ABC-Paramount 10241 | 9 |
| ★21 | 35 | 55 | 89 | WHEN I FALL IN LOVE — Lettermen, Capitol 4658 | 4 |
| 22 | 15 | 11 | 10 | THE FLY — Chubby Checker, Parkway 830 | 12 |
| 23 | 13 | 7 | 19 | HEARTACHES — Marcels, Colpix 612 | 10 |
| 24 | 37 | 54 | 80 | WHEN THE BOY IN YOUR ARMS — Connie Francis, MGM 13051 | 4 |
| 25 | 32 | 40 | 65 | LET'S TWIST AGAIN — Chubby Checker, Parkway 824 | 16 |
| 26 | 38 | 62 | — | UNCHAIN MY HEART — Ray Charles, ABC-Paramount 10266 | 3 |
| 27 | 18 | 6 | 5 | BRISTOL STOMP — Dovells, Parkway 827 | 14 |
| 28 | 23 | 23 | 28 | SEPTEMBER IN THE RAIN — Dinah Washington, Mercury 71876 | 9 |
| 29 | 33 | 47 | 57 | 'TIL — Angels, Caprice 107 | 8 |
| 30 | 27 | 29 | 42 | IN THE MIDDLE OF A HEARTACHE — Wanda Jackson, Capitol 4635 | 9 |
| ★31 | 41 | 60 | 74 | WELL I TOLD YOU — Chantels, Carlton 564 | 5 |
| 32 | 36 | 41 | 61 | LANGUAGE OF LOVE — John D. Loudermilk, RCA Victor 7938 | 6 |
| 33 | 39 | 50 | 53 | YOUR MA SAID YOU CRIED IN YOUR SLEEP LAST NIGHT — Kenny Dino, Musicor 1013 | 6 |
| 34 | 43 | 68 | 92 | THERE'S NO OTHER (Like My Baby) — Crystals, Philles 100 | 4 |
| 35 | 22 | 19 | 12 | I LOVE HOW YOU LOVE ME — Paris Sisters, Gregmark 6 | 15 |
| 36 | 19 | 10 | 9 | THIS TIME — Troy Shondell, Liberty 55353 | 13 |
| 37 | 28 | 15 | 11 | YOU'RE THE REASON — Bobby Edwards, Crest 1075 | 16 |
| 38 | 30 | 24 | 24 | JUST OUT OF REACH (of My Two Open Arms) — Solomon Burke, Atlantic 2114 | 13 |
| 39 | 25 | 18 | 20 | A WONDER LIKE YOU — Rick Nelson, Imperial 5770 | 11 |
| 40 | 31 | 21 | 21 | I WANT TO THANK YOU — Bobby Rydell, Cameo 201 | 9 |
| ★41 | 57 | — | — | CAN'T HELP FALLING IN LOVE — Elvis Presley, RCA Victor 7968 | 2 |
| 42 | 44 | 44 | 56 | TOWN WITHOUT PITY — Gene Pitney, Musicor 1009 | 5 |
| 43 | 50 | 45 | 51 | UP A LAZY RIVER — Si Zentner, Liberty 55374 | 5 |
| 44 | 46 | 57 | 60 | TONIGHT — Eddie Fisher, Seven Arts 719 | 6 |
| 45 | 34 | 35 | 32 | FOOT STOMPIN' (Part 1) — Flares, Felsted 8624 | 15 |
| ★46 | 56 | 71 | 83 | REVENGE — Brook Benton, Mercury 71903 | 4 |
| ★47 | 62 | — | — | ROCK-A-HULA BABY — Elvis Presley, RCA Victor 7968 | 2 |
| 48 | 64 | — | — | THE MAJESTIC — Dion, Laurie 3115 | 2 |
| 49 | 60 | 88 | — | SOOTHE ME — Sims Twins, Sar 117 | 5 |
| 50 | 55 | 66 | 69 | JOHNNY WILL — Pat Boone, Dot 16284 | 5 |
| 51 | 53 | 63 | 78 | GYPSY ROVER — Highwaymen, United Artists 370 | 6 |
| 52 | 61 | 74 | 81 | IT'S ALL BECAUSE — Linda Scott, Canadian-American 129 | 5 |
| ★53 | 63 | 76 | 87 | FUNNY HOW TIME SLIPS AWAY — Jimmy Elledge, RCA Victor 7946 | 5 |
| 54 | 59 | — | — | PEPPERMINT TWIST — Danny Peppermint and the Jumping Jacks, Carlton 565 | 2 |
| 55 | 68 | 78 | — | HEY, LITTLE GIRL — Del Shannon, Big Top 3091 | 3 |
| 56 | 65 | 80 | 95 | I KNOW — Barbara George, AFO 302 | 4 |
| 57 | 78 | 99 | — | LITTLE ALTAR BOY — Vic Dana, Dolton 48 | 3 |
| 58 | 73 | 95 | — | POOR FOOL — Ike and Tina Turner, Sue 753 | 3 |
| 59 | 66 | — | — | LONESOME NUMBER ONE — Don Gibson, RCA Victor 7959 | 2 |
| 60 | 86 | — | — | SMALL SAD SAM — Phil McLean, Versatile 107 | 2 |
| 61 | 74 | 87 | 90 | IF YOU GOTTA MAKE A FOOL OF SOMEBODY — James Ray, Caprice 110 | 4 |
| 62 | 45 | 42 | 59 | SMILE — Timi Yuro, Liberty 55375 | 6 |
| ★63 | — | — | — | JAMBALAYA — Fats Domino, Imperial 5796 | 1 |
| 64 | 42 | 25 | 18 | GOD, COUNTRY AND MY BABY — Johnny Burnette, Liberty 55379 | 9 |
| ★65 | — | — | — | DEAR LADY TWIST — Gary (U.S.) Bonds, LeGrand 1015 | 1 |
| 66 | — | — | — | WHITE CHRISTMAS — Bing Crosby, Decca 23778 | 1 |
| 67 | 84 | 100 | — | COTTON FIELDS — Highwaymen, United Artists 370 | 3 |
| 68 | — | — | — | JINGLE BELL ROCK — Bobby Helms, Decca 30513 | 1 |
| 69 | 54 | 56 | 73 | IT'S TOO SOON TO KNOW — Etta James, Argo 5402 | 6 |
| 70 | 79 | — | — | THE WANDERER — Dion, Laurie 3115 | 2 |
| 71 | — | — | — | JINGLE BELL ROCK — Bobby Rydell & Chubby Checker, Cameo 205 | 1 |
| 72 | 76 | 82 | 88 | IT WILL STAND — Showmen, Minit 632 | 4 |
| 73 | — | — | — | BABY'S FIRST CHRISTMAS — Connie Francis, MGM 13051 | 1 |
| 74 | 80 | 77 | 96 | NEVER, NEVER — Jive Five, Beltone 1014 | 5 |
| 75 | 58 | 59 | 70 | THREE STEPS FROM THE ALTAR — Shep and the Limelites, Hull 747 | 9 |
| 76 | 93 | — | 98 | TURN AROUND, LOOK AT ME — Glen Campbell, Crest 1087 | 4 |
| 77 | 67 | — | — | I HEAR YOU KNOCKING — Fats Domino, Imperial 5796 | 2 |
| 78 | — | — | — | TWISTIN' U.S.A. — Chubby Checker, Parkway 811 | 1 |
| 79 | 75 | 85 | 84 | THE COMMANCHEROS — Claude King, Columbia 42196 | 5 |
| 80 | 85 | 96 | — | WALKIN' WITH MY ANGEL — Bobby Vee, Liberty 55388 | 3 |
| 81 | 89 | 53 | 64 | SOMETIME — Gene Thomas, United Artists 338 | 7 |
| 82 | 82 | 93 | — | HAPPY TIMES (Are Here to Stay) — Tony Orlando, Epic 9476 | 3 |
| 83 | 94 | — | — | NORMAN — Sue Thompson, Hickory 1159 | 2 |
| 84 | 88 | 90 | 100 | TENNESSEE FLAT-TOP BOX — Johnny Cash, Columbia 42147 | 5 |
| 85 | — | — | — | ROCKIN' AROUND THE CHRISTMAS TREE — Brenda Lee, Decca 20777 | 1 |
| ★86 | — | — | — | MARIA — Roger Williams, Kapp 437 | 1 |
| 87 | 91 | 94 | — | LET'S GO TRIPPIN' — Dick Dale, Deltone 5017 | 3 |
| 88 | — | — | — | JUST GOT TO KNOW — Jimmy McCracklin, Art-Tone 825 | 1 |
| 89 | 90 | — | — | LOSING YOUR LOVE — Jim Reeves, RCA Victor 7950 | 2 |
| 90 | 99 | — | — | DREAMY EYES — Johnny Tillotson, Cadence 1409 | 2 |
| 91 | — | — | — | MARIA — Johnny Mathis, Columbia 41684 | 1 |
| 92 | 95 | — | — | WHAT I FEEL IN MY HEART — Jim Reeves, RCA Victor 7950 | 2 |
| 93 | 98 | — | — | SHE REALLY LOVES YOU — Timi Yuro, Liberty 55375 | 2 |
| 94 | — | — | — | BUT ON THE OTHER HAND — Ray Charles, ABC-Paramount 10266 | 1 |
| 95 | — | — | — | IRRESISTIBLE YOU — Bobby Darin, Atco 6214 | 1 |
| 96 | 81 | — | — | TURN ON YOUR LOVE LIGHT — Bobby Bland, Duke 344 | 2 |
| 97 | 87 | — | — | UNSQUARE DANCE — Dave Brubeck Quartet, Columbia 42228 | 2 |
| 98 | — | — | — | LITTLE DRUMMER BOY — Harry Simeone Chorale, 20th Fox 121 | 1 |
| 99 | — | — | — | LETTER FULL OF TEARS — Gladys Knight and the Pips, Fury 1054 | 1 |
| 100 | — | — | — | FLYING CIRCLE — Frank Slay Ork, Swan 4085 | 1 |

## BUBBLING UNDER THE HOT 100

101. LOST SOMEONE — James Brown & the Famous Flames, King 5573
102. EV'RYBODY'S CRYIN' — Jimmie Beaumont, May 112
103. I NEED SOMEONE — Belmonts, Sabina 502
104. BABY IT'S YOU — Shirelles, Scepter 1227
105. FEVER — Pete Bennett & the Embers, Sunset 1002
106. GO ON HOME — Patti Page, Mercury 71906
107. THE THINGS I WANT TO HEAR — Shirelles, Scepter 1227
108. POP GOES THE WEASEL — Anthony Newley, London 9501
109. PUSHIN' YOUR LUCK — Sleepy King, Joy 257
110. DON'T WALK AWAY FROM ME — Dee Clark, Vee Jay 409
111. YOU DON'T HAVE TO BE A TOWER OF STRENGTH — Gloria Lynne, Everest 19428
112. WALKIN' BACK TO HAPPINESS — Helen Shapiro, Capitol 4662
113. YOU'LL NEVER KNOW — Platters, Mercury 71904
114. IT DO ME SO GOOD — Ann-Margret, RCA Victor 7952
115. GIVE MYSELF A PARTY — Rosemary Clooney, RCA Victor 7948
116. TRADE WINDS — Aki Aleong, Reprise 20021
117. SANTA AND THE TOUCHABLES — Dickie Goodman, Rori 701
118. ROOM FULL OF TEARS — Drifters, Atlantic 2127
119. EVERYBODY'S TWISTIN' DOWN IN MEXICO — Billy Vaughn, Dot 16295
120. TUFF — Ace Cannon, Hi 2040
120. THAT'S MY PA — Sheb Wooley, MGM 13046

# BILLBOARD HOT 100

**DECEMBER 18, 1961**
**FOR WEEK ENDING DECEMBER 24, 1961**

★ STAR PERFORMERS—Selections registering greatest upward progress this week.
S Indicates that 45 r.p.m. stereo single version is available.
△ Indicates that 33⅓ r.p.m. mono single version is available.
Ⓢ Indicates that 33⅓ r.p.m. stereo single version is available.

| This Week | Wk Ago | 2 Wks Ago | 3 Wks Ago | Title / Artist, Label & Number | Weeks On Chart |
|---|---|---|---|---|---|
| 1 | 6 | 17 | 36 | THE LION SLEEPS TONIGHT — Tokens, RCA Victor 7954 △ | 6 |
| 2 | 1 | 2 | 3 | PLEASE MR. POSTMAN — Marvelettes, Tamla 54046 | 16 |
| 3 | 7 | 11 | 17 | RUN TO HIM — Bobby Vee, Liberty 55388 | 6 |
| 4 | 4 | 6 | 16 | THE TWIST — Chubby Checker, Parkway 811 | 24 |
| 5 | 5 | 7 | 12 | WALK ON BY — Leroy Van Dyke, Mercury 71834 | 8 |
| 6 | 3 | 3 | 4 | GOODBYE CRUEL WORLD — James Darren, Colpix 609 | 10 |
| 7 | 9 | 16 | 27 | LET THERE BE DRUMS — Sandy Nelson, Imperial 5775 | 8 |
| 8 | 10 | 21 | 28 | HAPPY BIRTHDAY, SWEET SIXTEEN — Neil Sedaka, RCA Victor 7957 △ | 6 |
| 9 | 2 | 1 | 1 | BIG BAD JOHN — Jimmy Dean, Columbia 42175 △ | 12 |
| 10 | 15 | 29 | 43 | PEPPERMINT TWIST — Joey Dee and the Starliters, Roulette 4401 | 5 |
| 11 | 8 | 12 | 13 | TONIGHT — Ferrante & Teicher, United Artists 373 | 10 |
| 12 | 17 | 24 | 26 | MOON RIVER — Henry Mancini, RCA Victor 7916 △ | 11 |
| 13 | 19 | 26 | 38 | I DON'T KNOW WHY — Linda Scott, Canadian-American 129 | 8 |
| 14 | 21 | 35 | 55 | WHEN I FALL IN LOVE — Lettermen, Capitol 4658 | 5 |
| 15 | 11 | 14 | 20 | MOON RIVER — Jerry Butler, Vee Jay 405 | 11 |
| 16 | 24 | 37 | 54 | WHEN THE BOY IN YOUR ARMS — Connie Francis, MGM 13051 | 5 |
| 17 | 26 | 38 | 62 | UNCHAIN MY HEART — Ray Charles, ABC-Paramount 10266 | 4 |
| 18 | 41 | 57 | — | CAN'T HELP FALLING IN LOVE — Elvis Presley, RCA Victor 7968 △ | 3 |
| 19 | 13 | 5 | 5 | FOOL #1 — Brenda Lee, Decca 31309 | 12 |
| 20 | 12 | 4 | 2 | RUNAROUND SUE — Dion, Laurie 3110 | 13 |
| 21 | 20 | 20 | 32 | GYPSY WOMAN — Impressions, ABC-Paramount 10241 | 10 |
| 22 | 25 | 32 | 40 | LET'S TWIST AGAIN — Chubby Checker, Parkway 824 | 17 |
| 23 | 29 | 33 | 47 | 'TIL — Angels, Caprice 107 | 9 |
| 24 | 16 | 9 | 14 | I UNDERSTAND (Just How You Feel) — G-Clefs, Terrace 7500 | 14 |
| 25 | 14 | 10 | 9 | CRAZY — Patsy Cline, Decca 31317 | 9 |
| 26 | 34 | 43 | 68 | THERE'S NO OTHER (Like My Baby) — Crystals, Philles 100 | 5 |
| 27 | 33 | 39 | 50 | YOUR MA SAID YOU CRIED IN YOUR SLEEP LAST NIGHT — Kenny Dino, Musicor 1013 | 7 |
| 28 | 46 | 56 | 71 | REVENGE — Brook Benton, Mercury 71903 | 5 |
| 29 | 31 | 41 | 60 | WELL I TOLD YOU — Chantels, Carlton 564 | 6 |
| 30 | 27 | 18 | 6 | BRISTOL STOMP — Dovells, Parkway 827 | 15 |
| 31 | 38 | 30 | 24 | JUST OUT OF REACH (of My Two Open Arms) — Solomon Burke, Atlantic 2114 | 14 |
| 32 | 47 | 62 | — | ROCK-A-HULA BABY — Elvis Presley, RCA Victor 7968 △ | 3 |
| 33 | 66 | — | — | WHITE CHRISTMAS — Bing Crosby, Decca 23778 | 2 |
| 34 | 18 | 8 | 8 | TOWER OF STRENGTH — Gene McDaniels, Liberty 55371 | 12 |
| 35 | 23 | 13 | 7 | HEARTACHES — Marcels, Colpix 612 | 11 |
| 36 | 48 | 64 | — | THE MAJESTIC — Dion, Laurie 3115 | 3 |
| 37 | 42 | 44 | 44 | TOWN WITHOUT PITY — Gene Pitney, Musicor 1009 | 8 |
| 38 | 56 | 65 | 80 | I KNOW — Barbara George, AFO 302 | 6 |
| 39 | 60 | 86 | — | SMALL SAD SAM — Phil McLean, Versatile 107 | 3 |
| 40 | 32 | 36 | 41 | LANGUAGE OF LOVE — John D. Loudermilk, RCA Victor 7938 △ | 7 |
| 41 | 63 | — | — | JAMBALAYA — Fats Domino, Imperial 5796 | 2 |
| 42 | 49 | 60 | 88 | SOOTHE ME — Sims Twins, Sar 117 | 6 |
| 43 | 51 | 53 | 63 | GYPSY ROVER — Highwaymen, United Artists 370 | 7 |
| 44 | 53 | 63 | 76 | FUNNY HOW TIME SLIPS AWAY — Jimmy Elledge, RCA Victor 7946 △ | 6 |
| 45 | 71 | — | — | JINGLE BELL ROCK — Bobby Rydell & Chubby Checker, Cameo 205 | 2 |
| 46 | 50 | 55 | 66 | JOHNNY WILL — Pat Boone, Dot 16284 | 6 |
| 47 | 58 | 73 | 95 | POOR FOOL — Ike and Tina Turner, Sue 753 | 4 |
| 48 | 67 | 84 | 100 | COTTON FIELDS — Highwaymen, United Artists 370 | 3 |
| 49 | 61 | 74 | 87 | IF YOU GOTTA MAKE A FOOL OF SOMEBODY — James Ray, Caprice 110 | 5 |
| 50 | 52 | 61 | 74 | IT'S ALL BECAUSE — Linda Scott, Canadian-American 129 | 6 |
| 51 | 57 | 78 | 99 | LITTLE ALTAR BOY — Vic Dana, Dolton 48 | 4 |
| 52 | — | — | — | RUDOLPH, THE RED-NOSED REINDEER — David Seville and the Chipmunks, Liberty 55289 | 1 |
| 53 | 65 | — | — | DEAR LADY TWIST — Gary (U.S.) Bonds, LeGrand 1015 | 2 |
| 54 | 73 | — | — | BABY'S FIRST CHRISTMAS — Connie Francis, MGM 13051 | 2 |
| 55 | 55 | 68 | 78 | HEY, LITTLE GIRL — Del Shannon, Big Top 3091 | 4 |
| 56 | 70 | 79 | — | THE WANDERER — Dion, Laurie 3115 | 3 |
| 57 | 22 | 15 | 11 | THE FLY — Chubby Checker, Parkway 830 | 13 |
| 58 | 68 | — | — | JINGLE BELL ROCK — Bobby Helms, Decca 30513 | 2 |
| 59 | 37 | 28 | 15 | YOU'RE THE REASON — Bobby Edwards, Crest 1091 | 17 |
| 60 | 30 | 27 | 29 | IN THE MIDDLE OF A HEARTACHE — Wanda Jackson, Capitol 4635 | 10 |
| 61 | 28 | 23 | 23 | SEPTEMBER IN THE RAIN — Dinah Washington, Mercury 71876 | 10 |
| 62 | 54 | 59 | — | PEPPERMINT TWIST — Danny Peppermint and the Jumping Jacks, Carlton 565 | 3 |
| 63 | — | — | — | THE CHIPMUNK SONG — David Seville and the Chipmunks, Liberty 55250 | 1 |
| 64 | 69 | 54 | 56 | IT'S TOO SOON TO KNOW — Etta James, Argo 5402 | 7 |
| 65 | — | — | — | BABY IT'S YOU — Shirelles, Scepter 1227 | 1 |
| 66 | 83 | 94 | — | NORMAN — Sue Thompson, Hickory 1159 | 3 |
| 67 | 72 | 76 | 82 | IT WILL STAND — Showmen, Minit 632 | 6 |
| 68 | 78 | — | — | TWISTIN' U.S.A. — Chubby Checker, Parkway 811 | 2 |
| 69 | 98 | — | — | LITTLE DRUMMER BOY — Harry Simeone Chorale, 20th Fox 121 | 2 |
| 70 | 76 | 93 | — | TURN AROUND, LOOK AT ME — Glen Campbell, Crest 1087 | 5 |
| 71 | 79 | 75 | 85 | THE COMMANCHEROS — Claude King, Columbia 42196 △ | 6 |
| 72 | 75 | 58 | 59 | THREE STEPS FROM THE ALTAR — Shep and the Limelites, Hull 747 | 10 |
| 73 | — | — | — | A LITTLE BITTY TEAR — Burl Ives, Decca 31330 | 1 |
| 74 | 96 | 81 | — | TURN ON YOUR LOVE LIGHT — Bobby Bland, Duke 344 | 3 |
| 75 | 59 | 66 | — | LONESOME NUMBER ONE — Don Gibson, RCA Victor 7959 △ | 3 |
| 76 | — | — | — | TWIST-HER — Bill Black's Combo, Hi 2042 | 1 |
| 77 | 86 | — | — | MARIA — Roger Williams, Kapp 437 | 2 |
| 78 | 100 | — | — | FLYING CIRCLE — Frank Slay Ork., Swan 4085 | 2 |
| 79 | 80 | 85 | 96 | WALKIN' WITH MY ANGEL — Bobby Vee, Liberty 55388 | 4 |
| 80 | 99 | — | — | LETTER FULL OF TEARS — Gladys Knight and the Pips, Fury 1054 | 2 |
| 81 | 88 | — | — | JUST GOT TO KNOW — Jimmy McCracklin, Art-Tone 825 | 2 |
| 82 | — | — | — | DO-RE-MI — Lee Dorsey, Fury 1056 | 1 |
| 83 | — | — | — | ROOM FULL OF TEARS — Drifters, Atlantic 2127 | 1 |
| 84 | 85 | — | — | ROCKIN' AROUND THE CHRISTMAS TREE — Brenda Lee, Decca 20777 | 2 |
| 85 | 90 | 99 | — | DREAMY EYES — Johnny Tillotson, Cadence 1409 | 3 |
| 86 | — | — | — | MULTIPLICATION — Bobby Darin, Atco 6214 | 1 |
| 87 | — | — | — | POCKETFUL OF MIRACLES — Frank Sinatra, Reprise 20040 | 1 |
| 88 | 97 | 87 | — | UNSQUARE DANCE — Dave Brubeck Quartet, Columbia 42228 △ | 3 |
| 89 | 95 | — | — | IRRESISTIBLE YOU — Bobby Darin, Atco 6214 | 2 |
| 90 | 94 | — | — | BUT ON THE OTHER HAND — Ray Charles, ABC-Paramount 10266 | 2 |
| 91 | 87 | 91 | 94 | LET'S GO TRIPPIN' — Dick Dale, Deltone 5017 | 4 |
| 92 | 74 | 80 | 77 | NEVER, NEVER — Jive Five, Beltone 1014 | 6 |
| 93 | 84 | 88 | 90 | TENNESSEE FLAT-TOP BOX — Johnny Cash, Columbia 42147 △ | 6 |
| 94 | 91 | — | — | MARIA — Johnny Mathis, Columbia 41684 △ | 2 |
| 95 | — | — | — | SEVEN DAY FOOL — Etta James, Argo 5402 | 1 |
| 96 | — | — | — | LOST SOMEONE — James Brown and the Famous Flames, King 5573 | 1 |
| 97 | — | 70 | 52 | EVERYBODY GOTTA PAY SOME DUES — Miracles, Tamla 54048 | 8 |
| 98 | — | — | — | PUSHIN' YOUR LUCK — Sleepy King, Joy 257 | 1 |
| 99 | — | — | — | I COULD HAVE LOVED YOU SO WELL — Ray Peterson, Dunes 2009 | 1 |
| 100 | — | — | — | YOU DON'T HAVE TO BE A TOWER OF STRENGTH — Gloria Lynne, Everest 19428 | 1 |

## BUBBLING UNDER THE HOT 100

101. EV'RYBODY'S CRYIN' — Jimmie Beaumont, May 112
102. I NEED SOMEONE — Belmonts, Sabrina 502
103. POP GOES THE WEASEL — Anthony Newley, London 9501
104. SEARCHIN' — Jack Eubanks, Monument 451
105. DON'T WALK AWAY FROM ME — Dee Clark, Vee Jay 409
106. TUFF — Ace Cannon, Hi 2040
107. THE THINGS I WANT TO HEAR — Shirelles, Scepter 1227
108. GO ON HOME — Patti Page, Mercury 71906
109. YOU'LL NEVER KNOW — Platters, Mercury 71904
110. SANTA AND THE TOUCHABLES — Dickie Goodman, Rori 701
111. TWIST — Ernie Freeman, Imperial 5793
112. YOU'RE FOLLOWING ME — Perry Como, RCA Victor 7962
113. HE'S NOT JUST A SOLDIER — Little Richard, Mercury 71884
114. AND THEN CAME LOVE — Ed Townsend, Challenge 9129
115. SONG FOR THE LONELY — Tony Orlando, Epic 9476
116. HAPPY TIMES (ARE HERE TO STAY) — Platters, Mercury 71904
117. SMOKY PLACES — Corsairs, Tuff 3030
118. DREAMIN' ABOUT YOU — Annette, Vista 388
119. CLOSE YOUR EYES — Skyliners, Colpix 613
120. HE'S OLD ENOUGH TO KNOW BETTER — Crickets, Liberty 55392

# BILLBOARD HOT 100

**DECEMBER 25, 1961**
**FOR WEEK ENDING DECEMBER 31, 1961**

STAR PERFORMERS—Selections registering greatest upward progress this week.
[S] Indicates that 45 r.p.m. stereo single version is available.
[△] Indicates that 33⅓ r.p.m. mono single version is available.
[Ⓢ] Indicates that 33⅓ r.p.m. stereo single version is available.

| This Week | 1 Wk. Ago | 2 Wks. Ago | 3 Wks. Ago | Title — Artist, Label & Number | Weeks On Chart |
|---|---|---|---|---|---|
| 1 | 1 | 6 | 17 | THE LION SLEEPS TONIGHT △ — Tokens, RCA Victor 7954 | 7 |
| 2 | 3 | 7 | 11 | RUN TO HIM — Bobby Vee, Liberty 55388 | 7 |
| 3 | 4 | 4 | 6 | THE TWIST — Chubby Checker, Parkway 811 | 25 |
| 4 | 6 | 3 | 3 | GOODBYE CRUEL WORLD — James Darren, Colpix 609 | 11 |
| 5 | 5 | 5 | 7 | WALK ON BY — Leroy Van Dyke, Mercury 71834 | 9 |
| 6 | 10 | 15 | 29 | PEPPERMINT TWIST — Joey Dee and the Starliters, Roulette 4401 | 6 |
| 7 | 2 | 1 | 2 | PLEASE MR. POSTMAN — Marvelettes, Tamla 54046 | 17 |
| 8 | 8 | 10 | 21 | HAPPY BIRTHDAY, SWEET SIXTEEN △ — Neil Sedaka, RCA Victor 7957 | 7 |
| 9 | 7 | 9 | 16 | LET THERE BE DRUMS — Sandy Nelson, Imperial 5775 | 9 |
| ★10 | 18 | 41 | 57 | CAN'T HELP FALLING IN LOVE △ — Elvis Presley, RCA Victor 7968 | 4 |
| 11 | 12 | 17 | 24 | MOON RIVER △ — Henry Mancini, RCA Victor 7916 | 12 |
| 12 | 13 | 19 | 26 | I DON'T KNOW WHY — Linda Scott, Canadian-American 129 | 9 |
| 13 | 14 | 21 | 35 | WHEN I FALL IN LOVE — Lettermen, Capitol 4658 | 6 |
| 14 | 17 | 26 | 38 | UNCHAIN MY HEART — Ray Charles, ABC-Paramount 10266 | 5 |
| 15 | 16 | 24 | 37 | WHEN THE BOY IN YOUR ARMS — Connie Francis, MGM 13051 | 6 |
| 16 | 15 | 11 | 14 | MOON RIVER — Jerry Butler, Vee Jay 405 | 12 |
| ★17 | 23 | 29 | 33 | 'TIL — Angels, Caprice 107 | 10 |
| 18 | 11 | 8 | 12 | TONIGHT — Ferrante & Teicher, United Artists 373 | 11 |
| 19 | 9 | 2 | 1 | BIG BAD JOHN △ — Jimmy Dean, Columbia 42175 | 13 |
| ★20 | 33 | 66 | — | WHITE CHRISTMAS — Bing Crosby, Decca 23778 | 3 |
| 21 | 21 | 20 | 20 | GYPSY WOMAN — Impressions, ABC-Paramount 10241 | 11 |
| 22 | 28 | 46 | 56 | REVENGE — Brook Benton, Mercury 71903 | 6 |
| 23 | 26 | 34 | 43 | THERE'S NO OTHER (Like My Baby) — Crystals, Phillies 100 | 6 |
| 24 | 27 | 33 | 39 | YOUR MA SAID YOU CRIED IN YOUR SLEEP LAST NIGHT — Kenny Dino, Musicor 1013 | 8 |
| 25 | 32 | 47 | 62 | ROCK-A-HULA BABY △ — Elvis Presley, RCA Victor 7968 | 4 |
| 26 | 38 | 56 | 65 | I KNOW — Barbara George, AFO 302 | 7 |
| 27 | 45 | 71 | — | JINGLE BELL ROCK — Bobby Rydell & Chubby Checker, Cameo 205 | 3 |
| 28 | 19 | 13 | 5 | FOOL #1 — Brenda Lee, Decca 31309 | 13 |
| 29 | 22 | 25 | 32 | LET'S TWIST AGAIN — Chubby Checker, Parkway 824 | 18 |
| 30 | 31 | 38 | 30 | JUST OUT OF REACH (of My Two Open Arms) — Solomon Burke, Atlantic 2114 | 15 |
| ★31 | 44 | 53 | 63 | FUNNY HOW TIME SLIPS AWAY △ — Jimmy Elledge, RCA Victor 7946 | 7 |
| 32 | 29 | 31 | 41 | WELL I TOLD YOU — Chantels, Carlton 564 | 7 |
| 33 | 39 | 60 | 86 | SMALL SAD SAM — Phil McLean, Versatile 107 | 4 |
| ★34 | 69 | 98 | — | LITTLE DRUMMER BOY — Harry Simeone Chorale, 20th Fox 121 | 3 |
| 35 | 41 | 63 | — | JAMBALAYA — Fats Domino, Imperial 5796 | 3 |
| 36 | 37 | 42 | 44 | TOWN WITHOUT PITY — Gene Pitney, Musicor 1009 | 9 |
| ★37 | 48 | 67 | 84 | COTTON FIELDS — Highwaymen, United Artists 370 | 5 |
| 38 | 24 | 16 | 9 | I UNDERSTAND (Just How You Feel) — G-Clefs, Terrace 7500 | 15 |
| ★39 | 49 | 61 | 74 | IF YOU GOTTA MAKE A FOOL OF SOMEBODY — James Ray, Caprice 110 | 6 |
| 40 | 46 | 50 | 55 | JOHNNY WILL — Pat Boone, Dot 16284 | 7 |
| 41 | 56 | 70 | 79 | THE WANDERER — Dion, Laurie 3115 | 4 |
| 42 | 43 | 51 | 53 | GYPSY ROVER — Highwaymen, United Artists 370 | 8 |
| ★43 | 54 | 73 | — | BABY'S FIRST CHRISTMAS — Connie Francis, MGM 13051 | 3 |
| 44 | 55 | 55 | 68 | HEY, LITTLE GIRL — Del Shannon, Big Top 3091 | 5 |
| 45 | 65 | — | — | BABY IT'S YOU — Shirelles, Scepter 1227 | 2 |
| 46 | 47 | 58 | 73 | POOR FOOL — Ike and Tina Turner, Sue 753 | 5 |
| ★47 | 63 | — | — | THE CHIPMUNK SONG — David Seville and the Chipmunks, Liberty 55250 | 3 |
| 48 | 51 | 57 | 78 | LITTLE ALTAR BOY — Vic Dana, Dolton 48 | 3 |
| 49 | 58 | 68 | — | JINGLE BELL ROCK — Bobby Helms, Decca 30513 | 3 |
| 50 | 53 | 65 | — | DEAR LADY TWIST — Gary (U.S.) Bonds, LeGrand 1015 | 3 |
| 51 | 52 | — | — | RUDOLPH, THE RED-NOSED REINDEER — David Seville and the Chipmunks, Liberty 55289 | 2 |
| 52 | 73 | — | — | A LITTLE BITTY TEAR — Burl Ives, Decca 31330 | 2 |
| 53 | 42 | 49 | 60 | SOOTHE ME — Sims Twins, Sar 117 | 7 |
| 54 | 36 | 48 | 64 | THE MAJESTIC — Dion, Laurie 3115 | 4 |
| 55 | 20 | 12 | 4 | RUNAROUND SUE — Dion, Laurie 3110 | 14 |
| 56 | 61 | 28 | 23 | SEPTEMBER IN THE RAIN — Dinah Washington, Mercury 71876 | 11 |
| 57 | 25 | 14 | 10 | CRAZY — Patsy Cline, Decca 31317 | 10 |
| ★58 | 84 | 85 | — | ROCKIN' AROUND THE CHRISTMAS TREE — Brenda Lee, Decca 20777 | 3 |
| 59 | 40 | 32 | 36 | LANGUAGE OF LOVE △ — John D. Loudermilk, RCA Victor 7938 | 8 |
| 60 | 66 | 83 | 94 | NORMAN — Sue Thompson, Hickory 1159 | 5 |
| 61 | 74 | 96 | 81 | TURN ON YOUR LOVE LIGHT — Bobby Bland, Duke 344 | 4 |
| 62 | 70 | 76 | 93 | TURN AROUND, LOOK AT ME — Glen Campbell, Crest 1087 | 6 |
| 63 | 89 | 95 | — | IRRESISTIBLE YOU — Bobby Darin, Atco 6214 | 2 |
| ★64 | 87 | — | — | POCKETFUL OF MIRACLES — Frank Sinatra, Reprise 20040 | 2 |
| 65 | 76 | — | — | TWIST-HER — Bill Black's Combo, Hi 2042 | 2 |
| 66 | 82 | — | — | DO-RE-MI — Lee Dorsey, Fury 1056 | 2 |
| 67 | — | 43 | 50 | UP A LAZY RIVER — Si Zentner, Liberty 55374 | 6 |
| 68 | 77 | 86 | — | MARIA — Roger Williams, Kapp 437 | 3 |
| 69 | 78 | 100 | — | FLYING CIRCLE — Frank Slay Ork, Swan 4085 | 3 |
| 70 | 80 | 99 | — | LETTER FULL OF TEARS — Gladys Knight and the Pips, Fury 1054 | 3 |
| 71 | 50 | 52 | 61 | IT'S ALL BECAUSE — Linda Scott, Canadian-American 129 | 7 |
| 72 | 83 | — | — | ROOM FULL OF TEARS — Drifters, Atlantic 2127 | 2 |
| 73 | 85 | 90 | 99 | DREAMY EYES — Johnny Tillotson, Cadence 1409 | 4 |
| 74 | 79 | 80 | 85 | WALKIN' WITH MY ANGEL — Bobby Vee, Liberty 55388 | 5 |
| 75 | 81 | 88 | — | JUST GOT TO KNOW — Jimmy McCracklin, Art-Tone 825 | 3 |
| ★76 | — | — | — | SHE'S EVERYTHING — Ral Donner, Gone 5121 | 1 |
| 77 | 30 | 27 | 18 | BRISTOL STOMP — Dovells, Parkway 827 | 16 |
| 78 | 67 | 72 | 76 | IT WILL STAND — Showmen, Minit 632 | 7 |
| 79 | 35 | 23 | 13 | HEARTACHES — Marcels, Colpix 612 | 12 |
| 80 | 34 | 18 | 8 | TOWER OF STRENGTH — Gene McDaniels, Liberty 55371 | 13 |
| 81 | 68 | 78 | — | TWISTIN' U.S.A. — Chubby Checker, Parkway 811 | 3 |
| 82 | 88 | 97 | 87 | UNSQUARE DANCE △ — Dave Brubeck Quartet, Columbia 42228 | 4 |
| 83 | 86 | — | — | MULTIPLICATION — Bobby Darin, Atco 6214 | 2 |
| ★84 | — | — | — | ALVIN'S HARMONICA — David Seville and the Chipmunks, Liberty 55250 | 1 |
| 85 | — | — | — | PLEASE COME HOME FOR CHRISTMAS — Charles Brown, King 5405 | 1 |
| 86 | 91 | 87 | 91 | LET'S GO TRIPPIN' — Dick Dale, Deltone 5017 | 5 |
| 87 | — | 96 | — | POP GOES THE WEASEL — Anthony Newley, London 9501 | 2 |
| 88 | 62 | 54 | 59 | PEPPERMINT TWIST — Danny Peppermint and the Jumping Jacks, Carlton 565 | 3 |
| 89 | 99 | — | — | I COULD HAVE LOVED YOU SO WELL — Ray Peterson, Dunes 2009 | 2 |
| 90 | 96 | — | — | LOST SOMEONE — James Brown and the Famous Flames, King 5573 | 2 |
| 91 | — | — | — | GO ON HOME — Patti Page, Mercury 71906 | 1 |
| 92 | — | — | — | TUFF — Ace Cannon, Hi 2040 | 1 |
| 93 | 98 | — | — | PUSHIN' YOUR LUCK — Sleepy King, Joy 257 | 2 |
| ★94 | — | — | — | I TOLD THE BROOK △ — Marty Robbins, Columbia 42246 | 1 |
| 95 | — | — | — | SMOKY PLACES — Corsairs, Tuff 3030 | 1 |
| 96 | — | — | — | TEARS FROM AN ANGEL — Troy Shondell, Liberty 55398 | 1 |
| 97 | — | — | — | FREE ME — Johnny Preston, Mercury 71908 | 1 |
| 98 | — | — | — | I NEED SOMEONE — Belmonts, Sabrina 502 | 1 |
| 99 | — | — | — | SANTA AND THE TOUCHABLES — Dickie Goodman, Rori 701 | 1 |
| 100 | — | — | — | EV'RYBODY'S CRYIN' — Jimmie Beaumont, May 112 | 1 |

## BUBBLING UNDER THE HOT 100

| 101 | IT DO ME SO GOOD — Ann-Margret, RCA Victor 7952 |
| 102 | WALKIN' BACK TO HAPPINESS — Helen Shapiro, Capitol 4662 |
| 103 | YOU DON'T HAVE TO BE A TOWER OF STRENGTH — Gloria Lynne, Everest 19428 |
| 104 | DEAR IVAN — Jimmy Dean, Columbia 42259 |
| 105 | SEARCHIN' — Jack Eubanks, Monument 451 |
| 106 | ISLAND IN THE SKY — Troy Shondell, Liberty 55398 |
| 107 | JINGLE BELL ROCK — Chet Atkins, RCA Victor 7971 |
| 108 | CLOSE YOUR EYES — Skyliners, Colpix 613 |
| 109 | TWIST — Ernie Freeman, Imperial 5793 |
| 110 | A KISS FOR CHRISTMAS — Joe Dowell, Smash 1728 |
| 111 | HE'S OLD ENOUGH TO KNOW BETTER — Crickets, Liberty 55392 |
| 112 | THE WALTZ YOU SAVED FOR ME — Ferlin Husky, Capitol 4650 |
| 113 | BYE BYE BABY — Bob Conrad, Warner Bros. 5242 |
| 114 | HAPPY TIMES (Are Here to Stay) — Tony Orlando, Epic 9476 |
| 115 | JINGLE BELL ROCK — Chubby Checker/Bobby Rydell, Cameo 205 |
| 116 | LONESOME ROAD — Don Shirley, Cadence 1408 |
| 117 | HAPPY JOSE — Jack Ross, Dot 16302 |
| 118 | BASIE TWIST — Count Basie, Roulette 4403 |
| 119 | FEVER — Pete Bennett and the Embers, Sunset 1002 |
| 120 | TWISTIN' ALL NIGHT LONG — Danny and the Juniors, Swan 4092 |

# BILLBOARD HOT 100

FOR WEEK ENDING JANUARY 7 1962

★ STAR PERFORMERS—Selections registering greatest upward progress this week.

Ⓢ Indicates that 45 r.p.m. stereo single version is available.

△ Indicates that 33⅓ r.p.m. mono single version is available.

Ⓢ△ Indicates that 33⅓ r.p.m. stereo single version is available.

| This Week | 1 Wk. Ago | 2 Wks. Ago | 3 Wks. Ago | Title | Artist, Label & Number | Weeks On Chart |
|---|---|---|---|---|---|---|
| 1 | 1 | 1 | 6 | THE LION SLEEPS TONIGHT △ | Tokens, RCA Victor 7954 | 8 |
| 2 | 3 | 4 | 4 | THE TWIST | Chubby Checker, Parkway 811 | 26 |
| 3 | 2 | 3 | 7 | RUN TO HIM | Bobby Vee, Liberty 55388 | 8 |
| 4 | 6 | 10 | 15 | PEPPERMINT TWIST | Joey Dee and the Starliters, Roulette 4401 | 7 |
| ★5 | 10 | 18 | 41 | CAN'T HELP FALLING IN LOVE △ | Elvis Presley, RCA Victor 7968 | 5 |
| 6 | 8 | 8 | 10 | HAPPY BIRTHDAY, SWEET SIXTEEN △ | Neil Sedaka, RCA Victor 7957 | 8 |
| 7 | 4 | 6 | 3 | GOODBYE CRUEL WORLD | James Darren, Colpix 609 | 12 |
| 8 | 5 | 5 | 5 | WALK ON BY | Leroy Van Dyke, Mercury 71834 | 10 |
| 9 | 13 | 14 | 21 | WHEN I FALL IN LOVE | Lettermen, Capitol 4658 | 7 |
| 10 | 14 | 17 | 26 | UNCHAIN MY HEART | Ray Charles, ABC-Paramount 10266 | 6 |
| 11 | 15 | 16 | 24 | WHEN THE BOY IN YOUR ARMS | Connie Francis, MGM 13051 | 7 |
| ★12 | 20 | 33 | 66 | WHITE CHRISTMAS | Bing Crosby, Decca 23778 | 4 |
| 13 | 7 | 2 | 1 | PLEASE MR. POSTMAN | Marvelettes, Tamla 54046 | 18 |
| 14 | 17 | 23 | 29 | 'TIL | Angels, Caprice 107 | 11 |
| ★15 | 26 | 38 | 56 | I KNOW | Barbara George, AFO 302 | 8 |
| 16 | 12 | 13 | 19 | I DON'T KNOW WHY | Linda Scott, Canadian-American 129 | 10 |
| 17 | 9 | 7 | 9 | LET THERE BE DRUMS | Sandy Nelson, Imperial 5775 | 10 |
| 18 | 22 | 28 | 46 | REVENGE | Brook Benton, Mercury 71903 | 7 |
| 19 | 11 | 12 | 17 | MOON RIVER △ | Henry Mancini, RCA Victor 7916 | 13 |
| 20 | 23 | 26 | 34 | THERE'S NO OTHER (Like My Baby) | Crystals, Philles 100 | 7 |
| 21 | 27 | 45 | 71 | JINGLE BELL ROCK | Bobby Rydell & Chubby Checker, Cameo 205 | 4 |
| ★22 | 34 | 69 | 98 | LITTLE DRUMMER BOY | Harry Simeone Chorale, 20th Fox 121 | 4 |
| 23 | 25 | 32 | 47 | ROCK-A-HULA BABY △ | Elvis Presley, RCA Victor 7968 | 5 |
| ★24 | 36 | 37 | 42 | TOWN WITHOUT PITY | Gene Pitney, Musicor 1009 | 10 |
| 25 | 21 | 21 | 20 | GYPSY WOMAN | Impressions, ABC-Paramount 10241 | 12 |
| ★26 | 43 | 54 | 73 | BABY'S FIRST CHRISTMAS | Connie Francis, MGM 13051 | 4 |
| 27 | 16 | 15 | 11 | MOON RIVER | Jerry Butler, Vee Jay 405 | 13 |
| ★28 | 52 | 73 | — | A LITTLE BITTY TEAR | Burl Ives, Decca 31330 | 3 |
| ★29 | 39 | 49 | 61 | IF YOU GOTTA MAKE A FOOL OF SOMEBODY | James Ray, Caprice 110 | 7 |
| ★30 | 41 | 56 | 70 | THE WANDERER | Dion, Laurie 3115 | 5 |
| 31 | 31 | 44 | 53 | FUNNY HOW TIME SLIPS AWAY △ | Jimmy Elledge, RCA Victor 7946 | 8 |
| 32 | 37 | 48 | 67 | COTTON FIELDS | Highwaymen, United Artists 370 | 6 |
| 33 | 35 | 41 | 63 | JAMBALAYA | Fats Domino, Imperial 5796 | 4 |
| ★34 | 45 | 65 | — | BABY IT'S YOU | Shirelles, Scepter 1227 | 3 |
| 35 | 24 | 27 | 33 | YOUR MA SAID YOU CRIED IN YOUR SLEEP LAST NIGHT | Kenny Dino, Musicor 1013 | 9 |
| 36 | 18 | 11 | 8 | TONIGHT | Ferrante & Teicher, United Artists 373 | 12 |
| 37 | 40 | 46 | 50 | JOHNNY WILL | Pat Boone, Dot 16284 | 8 |
| 38 | 44 | 55 | 55 | HEY, LITTLE GIRL | Del Shannon, Big Top 3091 | 6 |
| 39 | 47 | 63 | — | THE CHIPMUNK SONG | David Seville and the Chipmunks, Liberty 55250 | 3 |
| 40 | 19 | 9 | 2 | BIG BAD JOHN △ | Jimmy Dean, Columbia 42175 | 14 |
| 41 | 49 | 58 | 68 | JUNGLE BELL ROCK | Bobby Helms, Decca 30513 | 4 |
| 42 | 46 | 47 | 58 | POOR FOOL | Ike and Tina Turner, Sue 753 | 6 |
| 43 | 32 | 29 | 31 | WELL I TOLD YOU | Chantels, Carlton 564 | 8 |
| 44 | 33 | 39 | 60 | SMALL SAD SAM | Phil McLean, Versatile 107 | 5 |
| 45 | 48 | 51 | 57 | LITTLE ALTAR BOY | Vic Dana, Dolton 48 | 6 |
| ★46 | 60 | 66 | 83 | NORMAN | Sue Thompson, Hickory 1159 | 5 |
| 47 | 51 | 52 | — | RUDOLPH, THE RED-NOSED REINDEER | David Seville and the Chipmunks, Liberty 55289 | 3 |
| 48 | 50 | 53 | 65 | DEAR LADY TWIST | Gary (U. S.) Bonds, LeGrand 1015 | 4 |
| 49 | 30 | 31 | 38 | JUST OUT OF REACH (of My Two Open Arms) | Solomon Burke, Atlantic 2114 | 16 |
| 50 | 58 | 84 | 85 | ROCKIN' AROUND THE CHRISTMAS TREE | Brenda Lee, Decca 20777 | 4 |
| ★51 | 61 | 74 | 96 | TURN ON YOUR LOVE LIGHT | Bobby Bland, Duke 344 | 5 |
| ★52 | 65 | 76 | — | TWIST-HER | Bill Black's Combo, Hi 2042 | 3 |
| ★53 | 63 | 89 | 95 | IRRESISTIBLE YOU | Bobby Darin, Atco 6214 | 4 |
| ★54 | 73 | 85 | 90 | DREAMY EYES | Johnny Tillotson, Cadence 1409 | 5 |
| ★55 | — | — | — | DEAR IVAN △ | Jimmy Dean, Columbia 42259 | 1 |
| 56 | 42 | 43 | 51 | GYPSY ROVER | Highwaymen, United Artists 370 | 9 |
| ★57 | 67 | — | 43 | UP A LAZY RIVER | Si Zentner, Liberty 55374 | 7 |
| 58 | 64 | 87 | — | POCKETFUL OF MIRACLES | Frank Sinatra, Reprise 20040 | 3 |
| ★59 | 69 | 78 | 100 | FLYING CIRCLE | Frank Slay Ork, Swan 4085 | 4 |
| 60 | 66 | 82 | — | DO-RE-MI | Lee Dorsey, Fury 1056 | 3 |
| 61 | 68 | 77 | 86 | MARIA | Roger Williams, Kapp 437 | 4 |
| 62 | 70 | 80 | 99 | LETTER FULL OF TEARS | Gladys Knight and the Pips, Fury 1054 | 4 |
| ★63 | 83 | 86 | — | MULTIPLICATION | Bobby Darin, Atco 6214 | 3 |
| 64 | 76 | — | — | SHE'S EVERYTHING | Ral Donner, Gone 5121 | 2 |
| 65 | 29 | 22 | 25 | LET'S TWIST AGAIN | Chubby Checker, Parkway 824 | 19 |
| 66 | 62 | 70 | 76 | TURN AROUND, LOOK AT ME | Glen Campbell, Crest 1087 | 7 |
| 67 | 75 | 81 | 88 | JUST GOT TO KNOW | Jimmy McCracklin, Art-Tone 825 | 4 |
| 68 | 28 | 19 | 13 | FOOL #1 | Brenda Lee, Decca 31309 | 14 |
| 69 | 74 | 79 | 80 | WALKIN' WITH MY ANGEL | Bobby Vee, Liberty 55388 | 6 |
| 70 | 53 | 42 | 49 | SOOTHE ME | Sims Twins, Sar 117 | 8 |
| 71 | 78 | 67 | 72 | IT WILL STAND | Showmen, Minit 632 | 8 |
| 72 | 38 | 24 | 16 | I UNDERSTAND (Just How You Feel) | G-Clefs, Terrace 7500 | 16 |
| 73 | 84 | — | — | ALVIN'S HARMONICA | David Seville and the Chipmunks, Liberty 55250 | 2 |
| 74 | 82 | 88 | 97 | UNSQUARE DANCE △ | Dave Brubeck Quartet, Columbia 42228 | 5 |
| 75 | 59 | 40 | 32 | LANGUAGE OF LOVE △ | John D. Loudermilk, RCA Victor 7938 | 9 |
| 76 | 85 | — | — | PLEASE COME HOME FOR CHRISTMAS | Charles Brown, King 5405 | 2 |
| 77 | 86 | 91 | 87 | LET'S GO TRIPPIN' | Dick Dale, Deltone 5017 | 6 |
| 78 | 92 | — | — | TUFF | Ace Cannon, Hi 2040 | 2 |
| 79 | 54 | 36 | 48 | THE MAJESTIC | Dion, Laurie 3115 | 5 |
| 80 | 89 | 99 | — | I COULD HAVE LOVED YOU SO WELL | Ray Peterson, Dunes 2009 | 3 |
| ★81 | — | — | — | TWISTIN' ALL NIGHT LONG | Danny and the Juniors, Swan 4092 | 1 |
| 82 | 91 | — | — | GO ON HOME | Patti Page, Mercury 71906 | 2 |
| 83 | 95 | — | — | SMOKY PLACES | Corsairs, Tuff 1030 | 2 |
| 84 | 96 | — | — | TEARS FROM AN ANGEL | Troy Shondell, Liberty 55398 | 2 |
| 85 | 87 | — | — | POP GOES THE WEASEL | Anthony Newley, London 9501 | 3 |
| 86 | 90 | 96 | — | LOST SOMEONE | James Brown and the Famous Flames, King 5573 | 3 |
| 87 | 72 | 83 | — | ROOM FULL OF TEARS | Drifters, Atlantic 2127 | 3 |
| ★88 | — | 94 | 91 | MARIA △ | Johnny Mathis, Columbia 41684 | 3 |
| 89 | 98 | — | — | I NEED SOMEONE | Belmonts, Sabrina 502 | 2 |
| 90 | 71 | 50 | 52 | IT'S ALL BECAUSE | Linda Scott, Canadian-American 129 | 8 |
| 91 | 57 | 25 | 14 | CRAZY | Patsy Cline, Decca 31317 | 11 |
| 92 | 93 | 98 | — | PUSHIN' YOUR LUCK | Sleepy King, Joy 257 | 3 |
| 93 | — | — | — | THE TWIST | Ernie Freeman, Imperial 5793 | 1 |
| 94 | — | — | — | THE WALTZ YOU SAVED FOR ME | Ferlin Husky, Capitol 4650 | 1 |
| 95 | — | — | — | LET ME IN | Sensations, Argo 5405 | 1 |
| 96 | — | — | — | LITTLE DRUMMER BOY | Jack Halloran Singers, Dot 16275 | 1 |
| 97 | — | — | — | THAT'S MY PA | Sheb Wooley, MGM 13046 | 1 |
| 98 | — | — | — | SEARCHIN' | Jack Eubanks, Monument 451 | 3 |
| 99 | — | — | — | MOTORCYCLE | Tico and the Triumphs, Amy 835 | 1 |
| 100 | — | — | — | DROWN IN MY OWN TEARS | Don Shirley, Cadence 1408 | 1 |

## HOT 100—A TO Z—(Publisher-Licensee)


Alvin's Harmonica (Monarch, ASCAP) .......... 73
Baby It's You (Dolfi, ASCAP) .......... 34
Baby's First Christmas (Francon, ASCAP) .......... 26
Big Bad John (Cigma, BMI) .......... 40
Can't Help Falling in Love (Gladys, ASCAP) .......... 5
Chipmunk Song, The (Monarch, ASCAP) .......... 39
Cotton Fields (Westside, BMI) .......... 32
Crazy (Pamper, BMI) .......... 91
Dear Ivan (Plainview, BMI) .......... 55
Dear Lady Twist (Pepe, BMI) .......... 48
Do-Re-Mi (Fast, BMI) .......... 60
Dreamy Eyes (Southern Belle, BMI) .......... 54
Drown in My Own Tears (Jay & Cee, BMI) .......... 100
Flying Circle (Claridge, ASCAP) .......... 59
Fool #1 (Sure Fire, BMI) .......... 68
Funny How Time Slips Away (Pamper, BMI) .......... 31
Go on Home (Pamper, BMI) .......... 82
Goodbye Cruel World (Aldon, BMI) .......... 7
Gypsy Rover (Box & Cox, ASCAP) .......... 56
Gypsy Woman (Curtom, BMI) .......... 25
Happy Birthday, Sweet Sixteen (Aldon, BMI) .......... 6
Hey, Little Girl (Vicki-McLaughlin, BMI) .......... 25
I Could Have Loved You So Well (Aldon, BMI) .......... 80
I Don't Know Why (Ahlert & Cromwell, ASCAP) .......... 16
I Know (Saturn-At Last, BMI) .......... 15
I Need Someone (Frankkapp, BMI) .......... 89
I Understand (Jubilee, ASCAP) .......... 72
If You Gotta Make a Fool of Somebody (Good Song, BMI) .......... 29
Irresistible You (Lloyd-Logan, BMI) .......... 53
It Will Stand (Minit, BMI) .......... 71
It's All Because (Kilt, BMI) .......... 90
Jambalaya (Acuff-Rose, BMI) .......... 33
Jingle Bell Rock—Helms (Cornell, ASCAP) .......... 41
Jingle Bell Rock—Rydell & Checker (Cornell, ASCAP) .......... 21
Johnny Will (Lyle & Hollyjo, ASCAP) .......... 37
Just Got to Know (B-Flat, BMI) .......... 67
Just Out of Reach (Four Star, BMI) .......... 49
Language of Love (Acuff-Rose, BMI) .......... 75
Let Me In (Arc-Kae Williams, BMI) .......... 95
Let There Be Drums (Travis, BMI) .......... 17
Let's Go Trippin' (Monsour, ASCAP) .......... 77
Let's Twist Again (Kalmann, ASCAP) .......... 65
Letter Full of Tears (Betalbin, BMI) .......... 62
Lion Sleeps Tonight, The (Folkway, BMI) .......... 1
Little Altar Boy (House of Sound-Bilya Bah, BMI) .......... 45
Little Bitty Tear, A (Pamper, BMI) .......... 28
Little Drummer Boy—Halloran (Delaware-Mills, ASCAP) .......... 96
Little Drummer Boy—Simeone (Delaware-Mills, ASCAP) .......... 22
Lost Someone (Lois, BMI) .......... 86
Majestic, The (Just-Mubon, BMI) .......... 79
Maria—Mathis (Schirmer-Chappell, ASCAP) .......... 88
Maria—Williams (Schirmer-Chappell, ASCAP) .......... 61
Moon River—Butler (Famous, ASCAP) .......... 27
Moon River—Mancini (Famous, ASCAP) .......... 19
Motorcycle (Wajome, BMI) .......... 99
Multiplication (Adaris, BMI) .......... 63
Norman (Acuff-Rose, BMI) .......... 46
Peppermint Twist (Jon-Ware, BMI) .......... 4
Please Come Home for Christmas (Lois, BMI) .......... 76
Please Mr. Postman (Jobette, BMI) .......... 13
Pocketful of Miracles (Maraville, ASCAP) .......... 58
Poor Fool (Saturn, BMI) .......... 42
Pop Goes the Weasel (Hollis, BMI) .......... 85
Pushin' Your Luck (Drury Lane, BMI) .......... 92
Revenge (Raleigh, BMI) .......... 18
Rock-A-Hula Baby (Gladys, ASCAP) .......... 23
Rockin' Around the Christmas Tree (St. Nicholas ASCAP) .......... 50
Room Full of Tears (St. Louis-Progressive-Trio, BMI) .......... 87
Rudolph, the Red-Nosed Reindeer (St. Nicholas, ASCAP) .......... 47
Run to Him (Aldon, BMI) .......... 3
Searchin' (Tiger, BMI) .......... 98
She's Everything (Alan K., BMI) .......... 64
Small Sad Sam (R.F.D., ASCAP) .......... 44
Smoky Places (Annie-Earl & Sun Flower, ASCAP) .......... 83
Soothe Me (Kags, BMI) .......... 70
Tears From an Angel (Metric, BMI) .......... 84
That's My Pa (Channel, ASCAP) .......... 97
There's No Other (Bertha, BMI) .......... 20
'Til (Chappell, ASCAP) .......... 14
Tonight (Schirmer, ASCAP) .......... 36
Town Without Pity (United Artists, ASCAP) .......... 24
Tuff (Jec, BMI) .......... 78
Turn Around, Look at Me (American, BMI) .......... 66
Turn on Your Love Light (Don, BMI) .......... 51
Twist, The—Checker (Lois, BMI) .......... 2
Twist, The—Freeman (Lois, BMI) .......... 93
Twist-Her (Jec, BMI) .......... 52
Twistin' All Night Long (Conley, ASCAP) .......... 81
Unchain My Heart (Tee Pee, ASCAP) .......... 10
Unsquare Dance (Derry, BMI) .......... 74
Up a Lazy River (Peer Int'l, BMI) .......... 57
Walk on By (Lowery, BMI) .......... 8
Walkin' With My Angel (Aldon, BMI) .......... 69
Waltz You Saved for Me, The (Feist, ASCAP) .......... 94
Wanderer, The (Schwartz-Disal, ASCAP) .......... 30
Well I Told You (Barrett's Chantel-Trio, BMI) .......... 43
When I Fall in Love (Northern, ASCAP) .......... 9
When the Boy in Your Arms (Pickwick, ASCAP) .......... 11
White Christmas (Berlin, ASCAP) .......... 12
Your Ma Said You Cried in Your Sleep Last Night (Sea-Lark, BMI) .......... 35


## BUBBLING UNDER THE HOT 100

101. HAPPY JOSE..........Jack Ross, Dot 16302
102. FREE ME..........Johnny Preston, Mercury 71908
103. YOU DON'T HAVE TO BE A TOWER OF STRENGTH..........Gloria Lynne, Everest 19428
104. PORTRAIT OF A FOOL..........Conway Twitty, MGM 13050
105. HE'S OLD ENOUGH TO KNOW BETTER.....Crickets, Liberty 55392
106. JINGLE BELL ROCK..........Chet Atkins, RCA Victor 7971
107. HAPPY TIMES (Are Here to Stay)..........Tony Orlando, Epic 9476
108. BASIE TWIST..........Count Basie, Roulette 4403
109. WALKIN' BACK TO HAPPINESS......Helen Shapiro, Capitol 4662
110. IT DO ME SO GOOD..........Ann-Margret, RCA Victor 7952
111. THE COMMANCHEROS..........Claude King, Columbia 42196
112. FEVER..........Pete Bennett and the Embers, Sunset 1002
113. HE'S NOT JUST A SOLDIER..........Little Richard, Mercury 71884
114. LONESOME NUMBER ONE..........Don Gibson, RCA Victor 7959
115. A SUNDAY KIND OF LOVE..........Jan and Dean, Liberty 55397
116. BUT ON THE OTHER HAND BABY..........Ray Charles, ABC-Paramount 10266
117. THE BELLS AT MY WEDDING....Paul Anka, ABC-Paramount 10279
118. LOSING YOUR LOVE..........Jim Reeves, RCA Victor 7950
119. MY BOOMERANG WON'T COME BACK..........Charlie Drake, United Artists 398
120. THE AVENGER..........Duane Eddy, Jamie 1206

# BILLBOARD HOT 100
### FOR WEEK ENDING JANUARY 13, 1962

**STAR PERFORMERS**—Selections registering greatest upward progress this week.
**S** Indicates that 45 r.p.m. stereo single version is available.
△ Indicates that 33⅓ r.p.m. mono single version is available.
△S Indicates that 33⅓ r.p.m. stereo single version is available.

| This Week | Wk. Ago | 2 Wks. Ago | 3 Wks. Ago | Title — Artist, Label & Number | Weeks On Chart |
|---|---|---|---|---|---|
| 1 | 2 | 3 | 4 | THE TWIST — Chubby Checker, Parkway 811 | 27 |
| 2 | 1 | 1 | 1 | THE LION SLEEPS TONIGHT — Tokens, RCA Victor 7954 | 9 |
| 3 | 4 | 6 | 10 | PEPPERMINT TWIST — Joey Dee and the Starliters, Roulette 4401 | 8 |
| 4 | 5 | 10 | 18 | CAN'T HELP FALLING IN LOVE — Elvis Presley, RCA Victor 7968 | 6 |
| 5 | 15 | 26 | 38 | I KNOW — Barbara George, AFO 302 | 9 |
| 6 | 6 | 8 | 8 | HAPPY BIRTHDAY, SWEET SIXTEEN — Neil Sedaka, RCA Victor 7957 | 9 |
| 7 | 8 | 5 | 5 | WALK ON BY — Leroy Van Dyke, Mercury 71834 | 11 |
| 8 | 3 | 2 | 3 | RUN TO HIM — Bobby Vee, Liberty 55388 | 9 |
| 9 | 10 | 14 | 17 | UNCHAIN MY HEART — Ray Charles, ABC-Paramount 10266 | 7 |
| 10 | 11 | 15 | 16 | WHEN THE BOY IN YOUR ARMS — Connie Francis, MGM 13051 | 8 |
| 11 | 7 | 4 | 6 | GOODBYE CRUEL WORLD — James Darren, Colpix 609 | 13 |
| 12 | 9 | 13 | 14 | WHEN I FALL IN LOVE — Lettermen, Capitol 4658 | 8 |
| 13 | 13 | 7 | 2 | PLEASE MR. POSTMAN — Marvelettes, Tamla 54046 | 19 |
| 14 | 17 | 9 | 7 | LET THERE BE DRUMS — Sandy Nelson, Imperial 5775 | 11 |
| 15 | 18 | 22 | 28 | REVENGE — Brook Benton, Mercury 71903 | 8 |
| 16 | 34 | 45 | 65 | BABY IT'S YOU — Shirelles, Scepter 1227 | 4 |
| 17 | 46 | 60 | 66 | NORMAN — Sue Thompson, Hickory 1159 | 6 |
| 18 | 28 | 52 | 73 | A LITTLE BITTY TEAR — Burl Ives, Decca 31330 | 4 |
| 19 | 32 | 37 | 48 | COTTON FIELDS — Highwaymen, United Artists 370 | 7 |
| 20 | 30 | 41 | 56 | THE WANDERER — Dion, Laurie 3115 | 6 |
| 21 | 24 | 36 | 37 | TOWN WITHOUT PITY — Gene Pitney, Musicor 1009 | 11 |
| 22 | 14 | 17 | 23 | 'TIL — Angels, Caprice 107 | 12 |
| 23 | 21 | 27 | 45 | JINGLE BELL ROCK — Bobby Rydell & Chubby Checker, Cameo 205 | 5 |
| 24 | 25 | 21 | 21 | GYPSY WOMAN — Impressions, ABC-Paramount 10241 | 13 |
| 25 | 20 | 23 | 26 | THERE'S NO OTHER (Like My Baby) — Crystals, Phillies 100 | 8 |
| 26 | 16 | 12 | 13 | I DON'T KNOW WHY — Linda Scott, Canadian-American 129 | 11 |
| 27 | 29 | 39 | 49 | IF YOU GOTTA MAKE A FOOL OF SOMEBODY — James Ray, Caprice 110 | 8 |
| 28 | 44 | 33 | 39 | SMALL SAD SAM — Phil McLean, Versatile 107 | 6 |
| 29 | 31 | 31 | 44 | FUNNY HOW TIME SLIPS AWAY — Jimmy Elledge, RCA Victor 7946 | 9 |
| 30 | 33 | 35 | 41 | JAMBALAYA — Fats Domino, Imperial 5796 | 5 |
| 31 | 23 | 25 | 32 | ROCK-A-HULA BABY — Elvis Presley, RCA Victor 7968 | 6 |
| 32 | 19 | 11 | 12 | MOON RIVER — Henry Mancini, RCA Victor 7916 | 14 |
| 33 | 48 | 50 | 53 | DEAR LADY TWIST — Gary (U.S.) Bonds, LeGrand 1015 | 5 |
| 34 | 27 | 16 | 15 | MOON RIVER — Jerry Butler, Vee Jay 405 | 14 |
| 35 | 37 | 40 | 46 | JOHNNY WILL — Pat Boone, Dot 16284 | 9 |
| 36 | 53 | 63 | 89 | IRRESISTIBLE YOU — Bobby Darin, Atco 6214 | 5 |
| 37 | 65 | 29 | 22 | LET'S TWIST AGAIN — Chubby Checker, Parkway 824 | 20 |
| 38 | 35 | 24 | 27 | YOUR MA SAID YOU CRIED IN YOUR SLEEP LAST NIGHT — Kenny Dino, Musicor 1013 | 10 |
| 39 | 42 | 46 | 47 | POOR FOOL — Ike and Tina Turner, Sue 753 | 7 |
| 40 | 38 | 44 | 55 | HEY, LITTLE GIRL — Del Shannon, Big Top 3091 | 7 |
| 41 | 52 | 65 | 76 | TWIST-HER — Bill Black's Combo, Hi 2042 | 4 |
| 42 | 55 | — | — | DEAR IVAN — Jimmy Dean, Columbia 42259 | 2 |
| 43 | 60 | 66 | 82 | DO-RE-MI — Lee Dorsey, Fury 1056 | 4 |
| 44 | 54 | 73 | 85 | DREAMY EYES — Johnny Tillotson, Cadence 1409 | 6 |
| 45 | 36 | 18 | 11 | TONIGHT — Ferrante & Teicher, United Artists 373 | 13 |
| 46 | 51 | 61 | 74 | TURN ON YOUR LOVE LIGHT — Bobby Bland, Duke 344 | 6 |
| 47 | 58 | 64 | 87 | POCKETFUL OF MIRACLES — Frank Sinatra, Reprise 20040 | 4 |
| 48 | 45 | 48 | 51 | LITTLE ALTAR BOY — Vic Dana, Dolton 48 | 7 |
| 49 | 43 | 32 | 29 | WELL I TOLD YOU — Chantels, Carlton 564 | 9 |
| 50 | 63 | 83 | 86 | MULTIPLICATION — Bobby Darin, Atco 6214 | 4 |
| 51 | 62 | 70 | 80 | LETTER FULL OF TEARS — Gladys Knight and the Pips, Fury 1054 | 5 |
| 52 | 64 | 76 | — | SHE'S EVERYTHING — Ral Donner, Gone 5121 | 3 |
| 53 | 61 | 68 | 77 | MARIA — Roger Williams, Kapp 437 | 4 |
| 54 | 59 | 69 | 78 | FLYING CIRCLE — Frank Slay Ork, Swan 4085 | 5 |
| 55 | 40 | 19 | 9 | BIG BAD JOHN — Jimmy Dean, Columbia 42175 | 15 |
| 56 | — | — | — | BREAK IT TO ME GENTLY — Brenda Lee, Decca 31348 | 1 |
| 57 | 69 | 74 | 79 | WALKIN' WITH MY ANGEL — Bobby Vee, Liberty 55388 | 7 |
| 58 | 49 | 30 | 31 | JUST OUT OF REACH (of My Two Open Arms) — Solomon Burke, Atlantic 2114 | 17 |
| 59 | 56 | 42 | 43 | GYPSY ROVER — Highwaymen, United Artists 370 | 10 |
| 60 | 57 | 67 | — | UP A LAZY RIVER — Si Zentner, Liberty 55374 | 8 |
| 61 | 78 | 92 | — | TUFF — Ace Cannon, Hi 2040 | 3 |
| 62 | — | — | — | SHADRACK — Brook Benton, Mercury 71912 | 1 |
| 63 | 71 | 78 | 67 | IT WILL STAND — Showmen, Minit 632 | 9 |
| 64 | 67 | 75 | 81 | JUST GOT TO KNOW — Jimmy McCracklin, Art-Tone 825 | 7 |
| 65 | 77 | 86 | 91 | LET'S GO TRIPPIN' — Dick Dale, Deltone 5017 | 5 |
| 66 | — | — | — | SO DEEP — Brenda Lee, Decca 31348 | 1 |
| 67 | 66 | 62 | 70 | TURN AROUND, LOOK AT ME — Glen Campbell, Crest 1087 | 8 |
| 68 | 82 | 91 | — | GO ON HOME — Patti Page, Mercury 71906 | 3 |
| 69 | 83 | 95 | — | SMOKY PLACES — Corsairs, Tuff 3030 | 3 |
| 70 | 79 | 54 | 36 | THE MAJESTIC — Dion, Laurie 3115 | 6 |
| 71 | 26 | 43 | 54 | BABY'S FIRST CHRISTMAS — Connie Francis, MGM 13051 | 5 |
| 72 | — | — | — | THE GREATEST HURT — Jackie Wilson, Brunswick 55221 | 1 |
| 73 | 86 | 90 | 96 | LOST SOMEONE — James Brown and the Famous Flames, King 5573 | 4 |
| 74 | 80 | 89 | 99 | I COULD HAVE LOVED YOU SO WELL — Ray Peterson, Dunes 2009 | 4 |
| 75 | 95 | — | — | LET ME IN — Sensations, Argo 5405 | 2 |
| 76 | — | — | — | WHAT'S THE REASON — Bobby Edwards, Capitol 4674 | 1 |
| 77 | 89 | 98 | — | I NEED SOMEONE — Belmonts, Sabrina 502 | 2 |
| 78 | 81 | — | — | TWISTIN' ALL NIGHT LONG — Danny and the Juniors, Swan 4092 | 2 |
| 79 | — | — | — | MY BOOMERANG WON'T COME BACK — Charlie Drake, United Artists 398 | 1 |
| 80 | — | — | — | THE LOST PENNY — Brook Benton, Mercury 71912 | 1 |
| 81 | — | — | — | I'M BLUE (The Gong-Gong Song) — Ikettes, Atco 6212 | 1 |
| 82 | 87 | 72 | 83 | ROOM FULL OF TEARS — Drifters, Atlantic 2127 | 4 |
| 83 | 84 | 96 | — | TEARS FROM AN ANGEL — Troy Shondell, Liberty 55398 | 2 |
| 84 | — | 94 | — | I TOLD THE BROOK — Marty Robbins, Columbia 42246 | 2 |
| 85 | — | — | — | WHAT'S SO GOOD ABOUT GOODBYE — Miracles, Tamla 54053 | 1 |
| 86 | — | — | 90 | BUT ON THE OTHER HAND BABY — Ray Charles, ABC-Paramount 10266 | 3 |
| 87 | — | — | — | A LITTLE TOO MUCH — Clarence Henry, Argo 5408 | 1 |
| 88 | 85 | 87 | — | POP GOES THE WEASEL — Anthony Newley, London 9501 | 3 |
| 89 | — | — | — | CRYING IN THE RAIN — Everly Brothers, Warner Bros. 5250 | 1 |
| 90 | — | — | — | HAPPY JOSE — Jack Ross, Dot 16302 | 1 |
| 91 | 74 | 82 | 88 | UNSQUARE DANCE — Dave Brubeck Quartet, Columbia 42228 | 6 |
| 92 | — | — | — | ISLAND IN THE SKY — Troy Shondell, Liberty 55398 | 1 |
| 93 | — | — | — | DUKE OF EARL — Gene Chandler, Vee Jay 416 | 1 |
| 94 | 97 | — | — | THAT'S MY PA — Sheb Wooley, MGM 13046 | 2 |
| 95 | — | — | — | SURFER'S STOMP — Mar-Kets, Liberty 55401 | 1 |
| 96 | 98 | — | — | SEARCHIN' — Jack Eubanks, Monument 451 | 4 |
| 97 | — | — | — | BASIE TWIST — Count Basie, Roulette 4403 | 1 |
| 98 | — | — | 71 | THE COMMANCHEROS — Claude King, Columbia 42196 | 7 |
| 99 | — | — | 75 | LONESOME NUMBER ONE — Don Gibson, RCA Victor 7959 | 4 |
| 100 | — | — | — | PERCOLATOR (TWIST) — Billy Joe and the Checkmates, Dore 620 | 1 |

### BUBBLING UNDER THE HOT 100

101. THE AVENGER — Duane Eddy, Jamie 1206
102. DROWN IN MY OWN TEARS — Don Shirley, Cadence 1408
103. MARIA — Johnny Mathis, Columbia 41684
104. PORTRAIT OF A FOOL — Conway Twitty, MGM 13050
105. CLOSE YOUR EYES — Skyliners, Colpix 613
106. PUSHIN' YOUR LUCK — Sleepy King, Joy 257
107. A LITTLE BITTY TEAR — Wanda Jackson, Capitol 4681
108. NIGHT OWL — Dukays, Nat 4002
109. FLYING BLUE ANGELS — George, Johnny and the Pilots, Coed 555
110. JAMIE — Eddie Holland, Motown 1021
111. HAPPY JOSE — Dave Appell & Ork, Cameo 207
112. MOTORCYCLE — Tico and the Triumphs, Amy 835
113. THE BELLS AT MY WEDDING — Paul Anka, ABC-Paramount 10279
114. SOMETIMES I'M TEMPTED — Marty Robbins, Columbia 42246
115. AFRIKAAN BEAT — Bert Kaempfert, Decca 31350
116. BANDIT OF MY DREAMS — Eddie Hodges, Cadence 1410
117. WALKIN' BACK TO HAPPINESS — Helen Shapiro, Capitol 4662
118. SURFIN' — Beach Boys, Candix 331
119. GOODBYE TO TOYLAND — Vonnair Sisters, Vista 390
120. SHIMMY, SHIMMY WALK — Megatons, Checker 1005

# BILLBOARD HOT 100

**FOR WEEK ENDING JANUARY 20, 1962**

★ STAR PERFORMERS—Selections registering greatest upward progress this week.
S Indicates that 45 r.p.m. stereo single version is available.
△ Indicates that 33⅓ r.p.m. mono single version is available.
Ⓢ Indicates that 33⅓ r.p.m. stereo single version is available.

| This Week | Wk. Ago | 2 Wks. Ago | 3 Wks. Ago | TITLE — Artist, Label & Number | Weeks On Chart |
|---|---|---|---|---|---|
| 1 | 1 | 2 | 3 | THE TWIST — Chubby Checker, Parkway 811 | 28 |
| 2 | 3 | 4 | 6 | PEPPERMINT TWIST — Joey Dee and the Starliters, Roulette 4401 | 9 |
| 3 | 2 | 1 | 1 | THE LION SLEEPS TONIGHT △ — Tokens, RCA Victor 7954 | 10 |
| 4 | 4 | 5 | 10 | CAN'T HELP FALLING IN LOVE △ — Elvis Presley, RCA Victor 7968 | 7 |
| 5 | 5 | 15 | 26 | I KNOW — Barbara George, AFO 302 | 10 |
| 6 | 6 | 6 | 8 | HAPPY BIRTHDAY, SWEET SIXTEEN △ — Neil Sedaka, RCA Victor 7957 | 10 |
| 7 | 8 | 5 | — | WALK ON BY — Leroy Van Dyke, Mercury 71834 | 12 |
| 8 | 8 | 3 | 2 | RUN TO HIM — Bobby Vee, Liberty 55388 | 10 |
| 9 | 12 | 9 | 13 | WHEN I FALL IN LOVE — Lettermen, Capitol 4658 | 9 |
| ★10 | 17 | 46 | 60 | NORMAN — Sue Thompson, Hickory 1159 | 7 |
| 11 | 9 | 10 | 14 | UNCHAIN MY HEART — Ray Charles, ABC-Paramount 10266 | 8 |
| 12 | 10 | 11 | 15 | WHEN THE BOY IN YOUR ARMS — Connie Francis, MGM 13051 | 9 |
| 13 | 14 | 17 | 9 | LET THERE BE DRUMS — Sandy Nelson, Imperial 5775 | 12 |
| ★14 | 21 | 24 | 36 | TOWN WITHOUT PITY — Gene Pitney, Musicor 1009 | 12 |
| 15 | 16 | 34 | 45 | BABY IT'S YOU — Shirelles, Scepter 1227 | 5 |
| 16 | 19 | 32 | 37 | COTTON FIELDS — Highwaymen, United Artists 370 | 8 |
| 17 | 18 | 28 | 52 | A LITTLE BITTY TEAR — Burl Ives, Decca 31330 | 5 |
| 18 | 20 | 30 | 41 | THE WANDERER — Dion, Laurie 3115 | 7 |
| 19 | 13 | 13 | 7 | PLEASE MR. POSTMAN — Marvelettes, Tamla 54046 | 20 |
| 20 | 11 | 7 | 4 | GOODBYE CRUEL WORLD — James Darren, Colpix 609 | 14 |
| 21 | 28 | 44 | 33 | SMALL SAD SAM — Phil McLean, Versatile 107 | 7 |
| 22 | 29 | 31 | 31 | FUNNY HOW TIME SLIPS AWAY △ — Jimmy Elledge, RCA Victor 7946 | 10 |
| 23 | 27 | 29 | 39 | IF YOU GOTTA MAKE A FOOL OF SOMEBODY — James Ray, Caprice 110 | 9 |
| ★24 | 42 | 55 | — | DEAR IVAN △ — Jimmy Dean, Columbia 42259 | 3 |
| 25 | 15 | 18 | 22 | REVENGE — Brook Benton, Mercury 71903 | 9 |
| 26 | 33 | 48 | 50 | DEAR LADY TWIST — Gary (U.S.) Bonds, LeGrand 1015 | 6 |
| 27 | 36 | 53 | 63 | IRRESISTIBLE YOU — Bobby Darin, Atco 6214 | 6 |
| 28 | 32 | 19 | 11 | MOON RIVER △ — Henry Mancini, RCA Victor 7916 | 15 |
| ★29 | 56 | — | — | BREAK IT TO ME GENTLY — Brenda Lee, Decca 31348 | 2 |
| 30 | 31 | 23 | 25 | ROCK-A-HULA BABY △ — Elvis Presley, RCA Victor 7968 | 7 |
| ★31 | 41 | 52 | 65 | TWIST-HER — Bill Black's Combo, Hi 2042 | 5 |
| ★32 | 43 | 60 | 66 | DO-RE-MI — Lee Dorsey, Fury 1056 | 5 |
| 33 | 51 | 62 | 70 | LETTER FULL OF TEARS — Gladys Knight and the Pips, Fury 1054 | 6 |
| ★34 | 46 | 51 | 61 | TURN ON YOUR LOVE LIGHT — Bobby Bland, Duke 344 | 7 |
| 35 | 44 | 54 | 73 | DREAMY EYES — Johnny Tillotson, Cadence 1409 | 7 |
| ★36 | 47 | 58 | 64 | POCKETFUL OF MIRACLES — Frank Sinatra, Reprise 20040 | 5 |
| 37 | 25 | 20 | 23 | THERE'S NO OTHER (Like My Baby) — Crystals, Philles 100 | 9 |
| 38 | 22 | 14 | 17 | 'TIL — Angels, Caprice 107 | 13 |
| ★39 | 50 | 63 | 83 | MULTIPLICATION — Bobby Darin, Atco 6214 | 5 |
| 40 | 26 | 16 | 12 | I DON'T KNOW WHY — Linda Scott, Canadian-American 129 | 12 |
| 41 | 24 | 25 | 21 | GYPSY WOMAN — Impressions, ABC-Paramount 10241 | 14 |
| 42 | 30 | 33 | 35 | JAMBALAYA — Fats Domino, Imperial 5796 | 6 |
| 43 | 39 | 42 | 46 | POOR FOOL — Ike and Tina Turner, Sue 753 | 8 |
| 44 | 61 | 78 | 92 | TUFF — Ace Cannon, Hi 2040 | 4 |
| 45 | 62 | — | — | SHADRACK — Brook Benton, Mercury 71912 | 2 |
| ★46 | 69 | 83 | 95 | SMOKY PLACES — Corsairs, Tuff 1808 | 4 |
| 47 | 54 | 59 | 69 | FLYING CIRCLE — Frank Slay Ork, Swan 4085 | 6 |
| 48 | 52 | 64 | 76 | SHE'S EVERYTHING — Ral Donner, Gone 5121 | 4 |
| ★49 | 93 | — | — | DUKE OF EARL — Gene Chandler, Vee Jay 416 | 2 |
| 50 | 53 | 61 | 68 | MARIA — Roger Williams, Kapp 437 | 6 |
| 51 | 48 | 45 | 48 | LITTLE ALTAR BOY — Vic Dana, Dolton 48 | 8 |
| 52 | 66 | — | — | SO DEEP — Brenda Lee, Decca 31348 | 2 |
| 53 | 57 | 69 | 74 | WALKIN' WITH MY ANGEL — Bobby Vee, Liberty 55388 | 8 |
| 54 | 68 | 82 | 91 | GO ON HOME — Patti Page, Mercury 71906 | 4 |
| 55 | 40 | 38 | 44 | HEY, LITTLE GIRL — Del Shannon, Big Top 3091 | 8 |
| 56 | 34 | 27 | 16 | MOON RIVER — Jerry Butler, Vee Jay 405 | 15 |
| 57 | 72 | — | — | THE GREATEST HURT — Jackie Wilson, Brunswick 55221 | 2 |
| 58 | 37 | 65 | 29 | LET'S TWIST AGAIN — Chubby Checker, Parkway 824 | 21 |
| 59 | 35 | 37 | 40 | JOHNNY WILL — Pat Boone, Dot 16284 | 10 |
| 60 | 65 | 77 | 86 | LET'S GO TRIPPIN' — Dick Dale, Deltone 5017 | 8 |
| 61 | 63 | 71 | 78 | IT WILL STAND — Showmen, Minit 632 | 10 |
| 62 | 67 | 66 | 62 | TURN AROUND, LOOK AT ME — Glen Campbell, Crest 1087 | 9 |
| ★63 | 81 | — | — | I'M BLUE (The Gong-Gong Song) — Ikettes, Atco 6212 | 2 |
| 64 | 75 | 95 | — | LET ME IN — Sensations, Argo 5405 | 3 |
| 65 | 60 | 57 | 67 | UP A LAZY RIVER — Si Zentner, Liberty 55374 | 9 |
| 66 | 38 | 35 | 24 | YOUR MA SAID YOU CRIED IN YOUR SLEEP LAST NIGHT — Kenny Dino, Musicor 1013 | 11 |
| ★67 | 89 | — | — | CRYING IN THE RAIN — Everly Brothers, Warner Bros. 5250 | 2 |
| 68 | 78 | 81 | — | TWISTIN' ALL NIGHT LONG — Danny and the Juniors, Swan 4092 | 3 |
| 69 | 74 | 80 | 89 | I COULD HAVE LOVED YOU SO WELL — Ray Peterson, Dunes 2009 | 5 |
| 70 | 79 | — | — | MY BOOMERANG WON'T COME BACK — Charlie Drake, United Artists 398 | 2 |
| 71 | 73 | 86 | 90 | LOST SOMEONE — James Brown and the Famous Flames, King 5573 | 5 |
| 72 | 86 | — | — | BUT ON THE OTHER HAND BABY — Ray Charles, ABC-Paramount 10266 | 4 |
| 73 | 76 | — | — | WHAT'S THE REASON — Bobby Edwards, Capitol 4674 | 4 |
| 74 | 55 | 40 | 19 | BIG BAD JOHN △ — Jimmy Dean, Columbia 42175 | 16 |
| 75 | 77 | 89 | 98 | I NEED SOMEONE — Belmonts, Sabrina 502 | 4 |
| ★76 | 95 | — | — | SURFER'S STOMP — Mar-Kets, Liberty 55401 | 2 |
| 77 | 80 | — | — | THE LOST PENNY — Brook Benton, Mercury 71912 | 2 |
| 78 | — | — | — | WHAT'S SO GOOD ABOUT GOODBYE — Miracles, Tamla 54053 | 2 |
| 79 | 90 | — | — | HAPPY JOSE — Jack Ross, Dot 16302 | 2 |
| 80 | — | — | — | TO A SLEEPING BEAUTY △ — Jimmy Dean, Columbia 42282 | 1 |
| 81 | 83 | 84 | 96 | TEARS FROM AN ANGEL — Troy Shondell, Liberty 55398 | 4 |
| 82 | 100 | — | — | PERCOLATOR (TWIST) — Billy Joe and the Checkmates, Dore 620 | 2 |
| 83 | 84 | — | 94 | I TOLD THE BROOK △ — Marty Robbins, Columbia 42246 | 3 |
| 84 | 87 | — | — | A LITTLE TOO MUCH — Clarence Henry, Argo 5408 | 2 |
| 85 | — | — | — | CHATTANOOGA CHOO CHOO △ — Floyd Cramer, RCA Victor 7978 | 1 |
| 86 | — | — | — | AFRIKAAN BEAT — Bert Kaempfert, Decca 31350 | 1 |
| ★87 | — | — | — | THERE'LL BE NO NEXT TIME — Jackie Wilson, Brunswick 55221 | 1 |
| 88 | 94 | 97 | — | THAT'S MY PA — Sheb Wooley, MGM 13046 | 3 |
| 89 | 64 | 67 | 75 | JUST GOT TO KNOW — Jimmy McCracklin, Art-Tone 825 | 6 |
| 90 | 82 | 87 | 72 | ROOM FULL OF TEARS — Drifters, Atlantic 2127 | 5 |
| 91 | — | — | — | A LITTLE BITTY TEAR — Wanda Jackson, Capitol 4681 | 1 |
| 92 | — | — | — | JAMIE — Eddie Holland, Motown 1021 | 1 |
| 93 | — | — | — | BLUE WATER LINE △ — Brothers Four, Columbia 42256 | 1 |
| 94 | 97 | — | — | BASIE TWIST — Count Basie, Roulette 4403 | 2 |
| 95 | — | — | — | A SUNDAY KIND OF LOVE — Jan and Dean, Liberty 55397 | 1 |
| 96 | — | — | — | CHIP CHIP — Gene McDaniels, Liberty 55405 | 1 |
| 97 | — | — | — | NIGHT OWL — Dukays, Nat 4002 | 1 |
| 98 | — | — | — | PORTRAIT OF A FOOL — Conway Twitty, MGM 13050 | 1 |
| 99 | — | — | — | OLIVER TWIST — Rod McKuen, Spiral 14 | 1 |
| 100 | — | — | — | WHERE HAVE ALL THE FLOWERS GONE — Kingston Trio, Capitol 4671 | 1 |

## BUBBLING UNDER THE HOT 100

101. BANDIT OF MY DREAMS .................. Eddie Hodges, Cadence 1410
102. THE DOOR IS OPEN ...................... Tommy Hunt, Scepter 1226
103. DROWN IN MY OWN TEARS ................. Don Shirley, Cadence 1408
104. I'LL SEE YOU IN MY DREAMS .............. Pat Boone, Dot 16312
105. THE AVENGER .......................... Duane Eddy, Jamie 1206
106. CLOSE YOUR EYES ...................... Skyliners, Colpix 613
107. HAPPY JOSE ........................... Dave Appell Ork, Cameo 207
108. FLYING BLUE ANGELS ........ George, Johnny and the Pilots, Coed 555
109. MOTORCYCLE ........................... Tico and the Triumphs, Amy 835
110. THE COMMANCHEROS ..................... Claude King, Columbia 42196
111. MARIA ................................ Johnny Mathis, Columbia 41684
112. SURFIN' ............................. Beach Boys, Candix 331
113. HEY BABY ............................. Bruce Channel, Smash 1731
114. CRY TO ME ............................ Solomon Burke, Atlantic 2131
115. GOODBYE TO TOYLAND ................... Vonnair Sisters, Vista 390
116. SHIMMY, SHIMMY WALK .................. Megatons, Dodge 808
117. LOVE IS THE SWEETEST THING ........... Saverio Saridis, Warner Bros. 5243
118. TEEN QUEEN OF THE WEEK ............... Freddy Cannon, Swan 4096
119. ARCHIE'S MELODY ...................... Byliners, Felsted 8631
120. STEP RIGHT UP ........................ Nat King Cole, Capitol 4672

# BILLBOARD HOT 100

FOR WEEK ENDING JANUARY 27

1962

★ STAR PERFORMERS—Selections registering greatest upward progress this week.

S Indicates that 45 r.p.m. stereo single version is available.

△ Indicates that 33⅓ r.p.m. mono single version is available.

S△ Indicates that 33⅓ r.p.m. stereo single version is available.

| This Week | 1 Wk. Ago | 2 Wks. Ago | 3 Wks. Ago | Title | Artist, Label & Number | Weeks On Chart |
|---|---|---|---|---|---|---|
| 1 | 2 | 3 | 4 | PEPPERMINT TWIST | Joey Dee and the Starliters, Roulette 4401 | 10 |
| 2 | 1 | 1 | 2 | THE TWIST | Chubby Checker, Parkway 811 | 29 |
| 3 | 5 | 5 | 15 | I KNOW | Barbara George, AFO 302 | 11 |
| 4 | 4 | 4 | 5 | CAN'T HELP FALLING IN LOVE △ | Elvis Presley, RCA Victor 7968 | 8 |
| ★ 5 | 10 | 17 | 46 | NORMAN | Sue Thompson, Hickory 1159 | 8 |
| 6 | 3 | 2 | 1 | THE LION SLEEPS TONIGHT △ | Tokens, RCA Victor 7954 | 11 |
| 7 | 9 | 12 | 9 | WHEN I FALL IN LOVE | Lettermen, Capitol 4658 | 10 |
| ★ 8 | 18 | 20 | 30 | THE WANDERER | Dion, Laurie 3115 | 8 |
| ★ 9 | 15 | 16 | 34 | BABY IT'S YOU | Shirelles, Scepter 1227 | 6 |
| 10 | 7 | 7 | 8 | WALK ON BY | Leroy Van Dyke, Mercury 71834 | 13 |
| 11 | 6 | 6 | 6 | HAPPY BIRTHDAY, SWEET SIXTEEN △ | Neil Sedaka, RCA Victor 7957 | 11 |
| 12 | 8 | 8 | 3 | RUN TO HIM | Bobby Vee, Liberty 55388 | 11 |
| 13 | 14 | 21 | 24 | TOWN WITHOUT PITY | Gene Pitney, Musicor 1009 | 13 |
| 14 | 17 | 18 | 28 | A LITTLE BITTY TEAR | Burl Ives, Decca 31330 | 6 |
| ★ 15 | 26 | 33 | 48 | DEAR LADY TWIST | Gary (U. S.) Bonds, LeGrand 1015 | 7 |
| 16 | 11 | 9 | 10 | UNCHAIN MY HEART | Ray Charles, ABC-Paramount 10266 | 9 |
| ★ 17 | 29 | 56 | — | BREAK IT TO ME GENTLY | Brenda Lee, Decca 31348 | 3 |
| 18 | 16 | 19 | 32 | COTTON FIELDS | Highwaymen, United Artists 370 | 9 |
| 19 | 12 | 10 | 11 | WHEN THE BOY IN YOUR ARMS | Connie Francis, MGM 13051 | 10 |
| ★ 20 | 49 | 93 | — | DUKE OF EARL | Gene Chandler, Vee Jay 416 | 3 |
| 21 | 13 | 14 | 17 | LET THERE BE DRUMS | Sandy Nelson, Imperial 5775 | 13 |
| 22 | 23 | 27 | 29 | IF YOU GOTTA MAKE A FOOL OF SOMEBODY | James Ray, Caprice 110 | 10 |
| 23 | 27 | 36 | 53 | IRRESISTIBLE YOU | Bobby Darin, Atco 6214 | 7 |
| 24 | 24 | 42 | 55 | DEAR IVAN △ | Jimmy Dean, Columbia 42259 | 4 |
| 25 | 22 | 29 | 31 | FUNNY HOW TIME SLIPS AWAY △ | Jimmy Elledge, RCA Victor 7946 | 11 |
| 26 | 31 | 41 | 52 | TWIST-HER | Bill Black's Combo, Hi 2042 | 6 |
| 27 | 33 | 51 | 62 | LETTER FULL OF TEARS | Gladys Knight and the Pips, Fury 1054 | 7 |
| 28 | 34 | 46 | 51 | TURN ON YOUR LOVE LIGHT | Bobby Bland, Duke 344 | 8 |
| 29 | 21 | 28 | 44 | SMALL SAD SAM | Phil McLean, Versatile 107 | 8 |
| 30 | 32 | 43 | 60 | DO-RE-MI | Lee Dorsey, Fury 1056 | 6 |
| 31 | 28 | 32 | 19 | MOON RIVER △ | Henry Mancini, RCA Victor 7916 | 16 |
| 32 | 19 | 13 | 13 | PLEASE MR. POSTMAN | Marvelettes, Tamla 54046 | 21 |
| ★ 33 | 45 | 62 | — | SHADRACK | Brook Benton, Mercury 71912 | 3 |
| 34 | 36 | 47 | 58 | POCKETFUL OF MIRACLES | Frank Sinatra, Reprise 20040 | 6 |
| 35 | 44 | 61 | 78 | TUFF | Ace Cannon, Hi 2040 | 5 |
| 36 | 39 | 50 | 63 | MULTIPLICATION | Bobby Darin, Atco 6214 | 6 |
| 37 | 20 | 11 | 7 | GOODBYE CRUEL WORLD | James Darren, Colpix 609 | 15 |
| 38 | 43 | 39 | 42 | POOR FOOL | Ike and Tina Turner, Sue 753 | 9 |
| 39 | 46 | 69 | 83 | SMOKY PLACES | Corsairs, Tuff 3030 | 5 |
| 40 | 37 | 25 | 20 | THERE'S NO OTHER (Like My Baby) | Crystals, Philles 100 | 10 |
| 41 | 48 | 52 | 64 | SHE'S EVERYTHING | Ral Donner, Gone 5121 | 5 |
| ★ 42 | 67 | 89 | — | CRYING IN THE RAIN | Everly Brothers, Warner Bros. 5250 | 3 |
| 43 | 30 | 31 | 23 | ROCK-A-HULA BABY △ | Elvis Presley, RCA Victor 7968 | 8 |
| ★ 44 | 57 | 72 | — | THE GREATEST HURT | Jackie Wilson, Brunswick 55221 | 3 |
| 45 | 47 | 54 | 59 | FLYING CIRCLE | Frank Slay Ork, Swan 4085 | 7 |
| 46 | 25 | 15 | 18 | REVENGE | Brook Benton, Mercury 71903 | 10 |
| 47 | 54 | 68 | 82 | GO ON HOME | Patti Page, Mercury 71906 | 5 |
| 48 | 50 | 53 | 61 | MARIA | Roger Williams, Kapp 437 | 7 |
| 49 | 40 | 26 | 16 | I DON'T KNOW WHY | Linda Scott, Canadian-American 129 | 13 |
| ★ 50 | 63 | 81 | — | I'M BLUE (The Gong-Gong Song) | Ikettes, Atco 6212 | 3 |
| 51 | 35 | 44 | 54 | DREAMY EYES | Johnny Tillotson, Cadence 1409 | 8 |
| 52 | 58 | 37 | 65 | LET'S TWIST AGAIN | Chubby Checker, Parkway 824 | 22 |
| 53 | 42 | 30 | 33 | JAMBALAYA | Fats Domino, Imperial 5796 | 7 |
| 54 | 41 | 24 | 25 | GYPSY WOMAN | Impressions, ABC-Paramount 10241 | 15 |
| ★ 55 | 76 | 95 | — | SURFER'S STOMP | Mar-Kets, Liberty 55401 | 3 |
| 56 | 64 | 75 | 95 | LET ME IN | Sensations, Argo 5405 | 4 |
| ★ 57 | 69 | 74 | 80 | I COULD HAVE LOVED YOU SO WELL | Ray Peterson, Dunes 2009 | 6 |
| 58 | 56 | 34 | 27 | MOON RIVER | Jerry Butler, Vee Jay 405 | 16 |
| 59 | 52 | 66 | — | SO DEEP | Brenda Lee, Decca 31348 | 3 |
| 60 | 38 | 22 | 14 | 'TIL | Angels, Caprice 107 | 14 |
| ★ 61 | 80 | — | — | TO A SLEEPING BEAUTY △ | Jimmy Dean, Columbia 42282 | 2 |
| 62 | 53 | 57 | 69 | WALKIN' WITH MY ANGEL | Bobby Vee, Liberty 55388 | 9 |
| ★ 63 | 96 | — | — | CHIP CHIP | Gene McDaniels, Liberty 55405 | 2 |
| 64 | 61 | 63 | 71 | IT WILL STAND | Showmen, Minit 632 | 11 |
| ★ 65 | 82 | 100 | — | PERCOLATOR (TWIST) | Billy Joe and the Checkmates, Dore 620 | 3 |
| 66 | 79 | 90 | — | HAPPY JOSE | Jack Ross, Dot 16302 | 3 |
| 67 | 60 | 65 | 77 | LET'S GO TRIPPIN' | Dick Dale, Deltone 5017 | 9 |
| 68 | 71 | 73 | 86 | LOST SOMEONE | James Brown and the Famous Flames, King 5573 | 6 |
| ★ 69 | — | — | — | CAJUN QUEEN △ | Jimmy Dean, Columbia 42282 | 1 |
| 70 | 70 | 79 | — | MY BOOMERANG WON'T COME BACK | Charlie Drake, United Artists 398 | 3 |
| 71 | 73 | 76 | — | WHAT'S THE REASON | Bobby Edwards, Capitol 4674 | 3 |
| 72 | 78 | 85 | — | WHAT'S SO GOOD ABOUT GOODBYE | Miracles, Tamla 54053 | 3 |
| 73 | 86 | — | — | AFRIKAAN BEAT | Bert Kaempfert, Decca 31350 | 2 |
| ★ 74 | — | — | — | HEY BABY | Bruce Channell, Smash 1731 | 1 |
| 75 | 85 | — | — | CHATTANOOGA CHOO CHOO △ | Floyd Cramer, RCA Victor 7978 | 2 |
| 76 | 89 | 64 | 67 | JUST GOT TO KNOW | Jimmy McCracklin, Art-Tone 825 | 7 |
| 77 | 84 | 87 | — | A LITTLE TOO MUCH | Clarence Henry, Argo 5408 | 3 |
| 78 | 81 | 83 | 84 | TEARS FROM AN ANGEL | Troy Shondell, Liberty 55398 | 5 |
| 79 | 68 | 78 | 81 | TWISTIN' ALL NIGHT LONG | Danny and the Juniors, Swan 4092 | 4 |
| 80 | 87 | — | — | THERE'LL BE NO NEXT TIME | Jackie Wilson, Brunswick 55221 | 2 |
| 81 | 83 | 84 | — | I TOLD THE BROOK △ | Marty Robbins, Columbia 42246 | 4 |
| ★ 82 | 100 | — | — | WHERE HAVE ALL THE FLOWERS GONE | Kingston Trio, Capitol 4671 | 2 |
| ★ 83 | — | — | — | I'LL SEE YOU IN MY DREAMS | Pat Boone, Dot 16312 | 1 |
| 84 | 91 | — | — | A LITTLE BITTY TEAR | Wanda Jackson, Capitol 4681 | 2 |
| ★ 85 | — | — | — | CRY TO ME | Solomon Burke, Atlantic 2131 | 1 |
| 86 | 88 | 94 | 97 | THAT'S MY PA | Sheb Wooley, MGM 13046 | 4 |
| ★ 87 | — | — | — | LIZZIE BORDEN | Chad Mitchell Trio, Kapp 439 | 1 |
| ★ 88 | — | — | — | LOVE IS THE SWEETEST THING | Saverio Saridis, Warner Bros. 5243 | 1 |
| 89 | 92 | — | — | JAMIE | Eddie Holland, Motown 1021 | 2 |
| ★ 90 | — | — | — | DO THE NEW CONTINENTAL | Dovells, Parkway 833 | 1 |
| 91 | 93 | — | — | BLUE WATER LINE △ | Brothers Four, Columbia 42256 | 2 |
| 92 | — | — | — | THE DOOR IS OPEN | Tommy Hunt, Scepter 1226 | 1 |
| 93 | — | — | — | SHIMMY, SHIMMY WALK | Megatons, Checker 1005 | 1 |
| 94 | 97 | — | — | NIGHT OWL | Dukays, Nat 4002 | 2 |
| 95 | — | — | — | AW, SHUCKS, HUSH YOUR MOUTH | Jimmy Reed, Vee Jay 425 | 1 |
| 96 | — | — | — | SHE'S GOT YOU | Patsy Cline, Decca 31354 | 1 |
| 97 | — | — | — | TWISTIN' POSTMAN | Marvelettes, Tamla 54054 | 1 |
| 98 | 98 | — | — | PORTRAIT OF A FOOL | Conway Twitty, MGM 13050 | 2 |
| 99 | — | — | — | HE KNOWS I LOVE HIM TOO MUCH | Paris Sisters, Gregmark 10 | 1 |
| 100 | — | — | — | BANDIT OF MY DREAMS | Eddie Hodges, Cadence 1410 | 1 |

## HOT 100—A TO Z—(Publisher-Licensee)

Afrikaan Beat (Roosevelt, BMI) .... 73
Aw, Shucks, Hush Your Mouth (Conrad, BMI) .... 95
Baby It's You (Dolfi, ASCAP) .... 9
Bandit of My Dreams (Arch, ASCAP) .... 100
Blue Water Line (January, BMI) .... 91
Break It to Me Gently (Northern, ASCAP) .... 17
Cajun Queen (Cedarwood, BMI) .... 69
Can't Help Falling in Love (Gladys, ASCAP) .... 4
Chattanooga Choo Choo (Feist, ASCAP) .... 75
Chip Chip (Trinity & Glo-Mac, BMI) .... 63
Cotton Fields (Westside, BMI) .... 18
Cry to Me (Melvin-Progressive, BMI) .... 85
Crying in the Rain (Aldon, BMI) .... 42
Dear Ivan (Plainview, BMI) .... 24
Dear Lady Twist (Pepe, BMI) .... 15
Do-Re-Mi (Fast, BMI) .... 30
Do the New Continental (Kalmann, ASCAP) .... 90
Door Is Open, The (Aldon, BMI) .... 92
Dreamy Eyes (Southern Belle, BMI) .... 51
Duke of Earl (Conrad-Karlan, BMI) .... 20
Flying Circle (Claridge, ASCAP) .... 45
Funny How Time Slips Away (Pamper, BMI) .... 25
Go on Home (Pamper, BMI) .... 47
Goodbye Cruel World (Aldon, BMI) .... 37
Greatest Hurt, The (Pearl, BMI) .... 44
Gypsy Woman (Curtom, BMI) .... 54
Happy Birthday, Sweet Sixteen (Aldon, BMI) .... 11
Happy Jose (Lansdowne, ASCAP) .... 66
He Knows I Love Him Too Much (Aldon, BMI) .... 99
Hey Baby (LeBill, BMI) .... 74
I Could Have Loved You So Well (Aldon, BMI) .... 57
I Don't Know Why (Ahlert & Cromwell, ASCAP) .... 49
I Know (Saturn-At Last, BMI) .... 3
I Told the Brook (Marizona, BMI) .... 81
If You Gotta Make a Fool of Somebody (Good Song, BMI) .... 22
I'll See You in My Dreams (Feist, ASCAP) .... 83
I'm Blue (Progressive-Placid, BMI) .... 50
Irresistible You (Lloyd-Logan, BMI) .... 23
It Will Stand (Minit, BMI) .... 64
Jambalaya (Acuff-Rose, BMI) .... 53
Jamie (Jobette, BMI) .... 89
Just Got to Know (B-Flat, BMI) .... 76
Let Me In (Arc-Kae Williams, BMI) .... 56
Let There Be Drums (Travis, BMI) .... 21
Let's Go Trippin' (Monsour, ASCAP) .... 67
Let's Twist Again (Kalmann, ASCAP) .... 52
Letter Full of Tears (Betalbin, BMI) .... 27
Lion Sleeps Tonight, The (Folkways, BMI) .... 6
Little Bitty Tear, A—Ives (Pamper, BMI) .... 14
Little Bitty Tear, A—Jackson (Pamper, BMI) .... 84
Little Too Much, A (Bar-Mar, BMI) .... 77
Lizzie Borden (Hill & Range, BMI) .... 87
Lost Someone (Lois, BMI) .... 68
Love Is the Sweetest Thing (Harms, ASCAP) .... 88
Maria (Schirmer-Chappell, ASCAP) .... 48
Moon River—Butler (Famous, ASCAP) .... 58
Moon River—Mancini (Famous, ASCAP) .... 31
Multiplication (Adaris, BMI) .... 36
My Boomerang Won't Come Back (Picadilly, BMI) .... 70
Night Owl (Conrad, BMI) .... 94
Norman (Acuff-Rose, BMI) .... 5
Peppermint Twist (Jon-Ware, BMI) .... 1
Percolator (Meadowlark, ASCAP) .... 65
Please Mr. Postman (Jobette, BMI) .... 32
Pocketful of Miracles (Maraville, ASCAP) .... 34
Portrait of a Fool (Cigma, BMI) .... 98
Poor Fool (Saturn, BMI) .... 38
Revenge (Raleigh, BMI) .... 46
Rock-A-Hula Baby (Gladys, ASCAP) .... 43
Run to Him (Aldon, BMI) .... 12
Shadrack (Fisher, ASCAP) .... 33
She's Everything (Alan K., BMI) .... 41
She's Got You (Pamper, BMI) .... 96
Shimmy, Shimmy Walk (Star-Flite & Hut, BMI) .... 93
Small Sad Sam (R.F.D., ASCAP) .... 29
Smoky Places (Annie-Earl & Sun Flower, ASCAP) .... 39
So Deep (Metric, BMI) .... 59
Surfer's Stomp (Strat-E.D.M., ASCAP) .... 55
Tears From an Angel (Metric, BMI) .... 78
That's My Pa (Channel, ASCAP) .... 86
There'll Be No Next Time (Merrimac, BMI) .... 80
There's No Other (Bertha, BMI) .... 40
'Til (Chappell, ASCAP) .... 60
To a Sleeping Beauty (Songsmiths-Remick, ASCAP) .... 61
Town Without Pity (United Artists, ASCAP) .... 13
Tuff (Jec, BMI) .... 35
Turn on Your Love Light (Don, BMI) .... 28
Twist, The (Lois, BMI) .... 2
Twist-Her (Jec, BMI) .... 26
Twistin' All Night Long (Conley, ASCAP) .... 79
Twistin' Postman (Jobette, BMI) .... 97
Unchain My Heart (Tee Pee, ASCAP) .... 16
Walk on By (Lowery, BMI) .... 10
Walkin' With My Angel (Aldon, BMI) .... 62
Wanderer, The (Schartz-Disal, ASCAP) .... 8
What's So Good About Goodbye (Jobette, BMI) .... 72
What's the Reason (Bourne, ASCAP) .... 71
When I Fall in Love (Northern, ASCAP) .... 7
When the Boy in Your Arms (Pickwick, ASCAP) .... 19
Where Have All the Flowers Gone (Fall River, BMI) .... 82

## BUBBLING UNDER THE HOT 100

101. PICTURES IN THE FIRE .... Pat Boone, Dot 16312
102. MY MELANCHOLY BABY .... Marcels, Colpix 624
103. DROWN IN MY OWN TEARS .... Don Shirley, Cadence 1408
104. HAPPY JOSE .... Dave Appell Ork, Cameo 207
105. TEEN QUEEN OF THE WEEK .... Freddy Cannon, Swan 4096
106. STEP RIGHT UP .... Nat King Cole, Capitol 4672
107. LET'S GO .... Floyd Cramer, RCA Victor 7978
108. MOTORCYCLE .... Tico and the Triumphs, Amy 836
109. SOMETIMES I'M TEMPTED .... Marty Robbins, Columbia 42246
110. MOMENTS TO REMEMBER .... Jennell Hawkins, Amazon 1003
111. MARIA .... Johnny Mathis, Columbia 41684
112. OLIVER TWIST .... Rod McKuen, Spiral 1407
113. I GOT A FUNNY KIND OF FEELING .... Maxine Brown, ABC-Paramount 10290
114. FOOLS HALL OF FAME .... Paul Anka, ABC-Paramount 10282
115. MAMIE IN THE AFTERNOON .... Bobby Lewis, Beltone 1016
116. MIDNIGHT .... Johnny Gibson, Big Top 3088
117. AFTER YOU'VE GONE .... Frankie Avalon, Chancellor 1101
118. ALONG CAME LINDA .... Tommy Boyce, RCA Victor 7975
119. IMAGINATION .... Quotations, Verve 10245
120. FOR ALL WE KNOW .... Casions, Amy 836

# BILLBOARD HOT 100

FOR WEEK ENDING FEBRUARY 3

1962

★ STAR PERFORMERS—Selections registering greatest upward progress this week.

[S] Indicates that 45 r.p.m. stereo single version is available.

△ Indicates that 33⅓ r.p.m. mono single version is available.

[S△] Indicates that 33⅓ r.p.m. stereo single version is available.

| This Week | 1 Wk. Ago | 2 Wks. Ago | 3 Wks. Ago | Title | Artist, Label & Number | Weeks On Chart |
|---|---|---|---|---|---|---|
| 1 | 1 | 2 | 3 | PEPPERMINT TWIST | Joey Dee and the Starliters, Roulette 4401 | 11 |
| 2 | 4 | 4 | 4 | CAN'T HELP FALLING IN LOVE △ | Elvis Presley, RCA Victor 7968 | 9 |
| 3 | 2 | 1 | 1 | THE TWIST | Chubby Checker, Parkway 811 | 30 |
| 4 | 5 | 10 | 17 | NORMAN | Sue Thompson, Hickory 1159 | 9 |
| 5 | 3 | 5 | 5 | I KNOW | Barbara George, AFO 302 | 12 |
| 6 | 8 | 18 | 20 | THE WANDERER | Dion, Laurie 3115 | 9 |
| ★7 | 20 | 49 | 93 | DUKE OF EARL | Gene (Duke of Earl) Chandler, Vee Jay 416 | 4 |
| 8 | 9 | 15 | 16 | BABY IT'S YOU | Shirelles, Scepter 1227 | 7 |
| ★9 | 17 | 29 | 56 | BREAK IT TO ME GENTLY | Brenda Lee, Decca 31348 | 4 |
| 10 | 6 | 3 | 2 | THE LION SLEEPS TONIGHT △ | Tokens, RCA Victor 7954 | 12 |
| 11 | 15 | 26 | 33 | DEAR LADY TWIST | Gary (U. S.) Bonds, LeGrand 1015 | 8 |
| 12 | 14 | 17 | 18 | A LITTLE BITTY TEAR | Burl Ives, Decca 31330 | 7 |
| 13 | 13 | 14 | 21 | TOWN WITHOUT PITY | Gene Pitney, Musicor 1009 | 14 |
| 14 | 7 | 9 | 12 | WHEN I FALL IN LOVE | Lettermen, Capitol 4658 | 11 |
| 15 | 12 | 8 | 8 | RUN TO HIM | Bobby Vee, Liberty 55388 | 12 |
| 16 | 10 | 7 | 7 | WALK ON BY | Leroy Van Dyke, Mercury 71834 | 14 |
| ★17 | 23 | 27 | 36 | IRRESISTIBLE YOU | Bobby Darin, Atco 6214 | 8 |
| 18 | 18 | 16 | 19 | COTTON FIELDS | Highwaymen, United Artists 370 | 10 |
| 19 | 11 | 6 | 6 | HAPPY BIRTHDAY, SWEET SIXTEEN △ | Neil Sedaka, RCA Victor 7957 | 12 |
| ★20 | 42 | 67 | 89 | CRYING IN THE RAIN | Everly Brothers, Warner Bros. 5250 | 4 |
| 21 | 16 | 11 | 9 | UNCHAIN MY HEART | Ray Charles, ABC-Paramount 10266 | 10 |
| ★22 | 33 | 45 | 62 | SHADRACK | Brook Benton, Mercury 71912 | 4 |
| 23 | 21 | 13 | 14 | LET THERE BE DRUMS | Sandy Nelson, Imperial 5775 | 14 |
| 24 | 22 | 23 | 27 | IF YOU GOTTA MAKE A FOOL OF SOMEBODY | James Ray, Caprice 110 | 11 |
| 25 | 27 | 33 | 51 | LETTER FULL OF TEARS | Gladys Knight and the Pips, Fury 1054 | 8 |
| 26 | 26 | 31 | 41 | TWIST-HER | Bill Black's Combo, Hi 2042 | 7 |
| 27 | 30 | 32 | 43 | DO-RE-MI | Lee Dorsey, Fury 1056 | 7 |
| ★28 | 41 | 48 | 52 | SHE'S EVERYTHING | Ral Donner, Gone 5121 | 6 |
| 29 | 31 | 28 | 32 | MOON RIVER △ | Henry Mancini, RCA Victor 7916 | 17 |
| 30 | 19 | 12 | 10 | WHEN THE BOY IN YOUR ARMS | Connie Francis, MGM 13051 | 11 |
| 31 | 24 | 24 | 42 | DEAR IVAN △ | Jimmy Dean, Columbia 42259 | 5 |
| 32 | 28 | 34 | 46 | TURN ON YOUR LOVE LIGHT | Bobby Bland, Duke 344 | 9 |
| 33 | 39 | 46 | 69 | SMOKY PLACES | Corsairs, Tuff 3030 | 6 |
| ★34 | 50 | 63 | 81 | I'M BLUE (The Gong-Gong Song) | Ikettes, Atco 6212 | 4 |
| 35 | 36 | 39 | 50 | MULTIPLICATION | Bobby Darin, Atco 6214 | 7 |
| 36 | 25 | 22 | 29 | FUNNY HOW TIME SLIPS AWAY △ | Jimmy Elledge, RCA Victor 7946 | 12 |
| 37 | 35 | 44 | 61 | TUFF | Ace Cannon, Hi 2040 | 6 |
| 38 | 29 | 21 | 28 | SMALL SAD SAM | Phil McLean, Versatile 107 | 9 |
| 39 | 34 | 36 | 47 | POCKETFUL OF MIRACLES | Frank Sinatra, Reprise 20040 | 7 |
| 40 | 44 | 57 | 72 | THE GREATEST HURT | Jackie Wilson, Brunswick 55221 | 4 |
| ★41 | 69 | — | — | CAJUN QUEEN △ | Jimmy Dean, Columbia 42282 | 2 |
| 42 | 47 | 54 | 68 | GO ON HOME | Patti Page, Mercury 71906 | 6 |
| ★43 | 56 | 64 | 75 | LET ME IN | Sensations, Argo 5405 | 5 |
| 44 | 38 | 43 | 39 | POOR FOOL | Ike and Tina Turner, Sue 753 | 10 |
| 45 | 37 | 20 | 11 | GOODBYE CRUEL WORLD | James Darren, Colpix 609 | 16 |
| ★46 | 63 | 96 | — | CHIP CHIP | Gene McDaniels, Liberty 55405 | 3 |
| ★47 | 61 | 80 | — | TO A SLEEPING BEAUTY △ | Jimmy Dean, Columbia 42282 | 3 |
| 48 | 55 | 76 | 95 | SURFER'S STOMP | Mar-Kets, Liberty 55401 | 4 |
| 49 | 43 | 30 | 31 | ROCK-A-HULA BABY △ | Elvis Presley, RCA Victor 7968 | 9 |
| 50 | 32 | 19 | 13 | PLEASE MR. POSTMAN | Marvelettes, Tamla 54046 | 22 |
| 51 | 48 | 50 | 53 | MARIA | Roger Williams, Kapp 437 | 8 |
| ★52 | 74 | — | — | HEY! BABY | Bruce Channel, Smash 1731 | 2 |
| ★53 | 65 | 82 | 100 | PERCOLATOR (TWIST) | Billy Joe and the Checkmates, Dore 620 | 4 |
| 54 | 52 | 58 | 37 | LET'S TWIST AGAIN | Chubby Checker, Parkway 824 | 23 |
| 55 | 40 | 37 | 25 | THERE'S NO OTHER (Like My Baby) | Crystals, Philles 100 | 11 |
| ★56 | 75 | 85 | — | CHATTANOOGA CHOO CHOO △ | Floyd Cramer, RCA Victor 7978 | 3 |
| 57 | 45 | 47 | 54 | FLYING CIRCLE | Frank Slay Ork, Swan 4085 | 8 |
| ★58 | 70 | 70 | 79 | MY BOOMERANG WON'T COME BACK | Charlie Drake, United Artists 398 | 4 |
| ★59 | 83 | — | — | I'LL SEE YOU IN MY DREAMS | Pat Boone, Dot 16312 | 2 |
| 60 | 66 | 79 | 90 | HAPPY JOSE | Jack Ross, Dot 16302 | 4 |
| 61 | 73 | 86 | — | AFRIKAAN BEAT | Bert Kaempfert, Decca 31350 | 3 |
| 62 | 72 | 78 | 85 | WHAT'S SO GOOD ABOUT GOODBYE | Miracles, Tamla 54053 | 4 |
| 63 | 68 | 71 | 73 | LOST SOMEONE | James Brown and the Famous Flames, King 5573 | 7 |
| 64 | 57 | 69 | 74 | I COULD HAVE LOVED YOU SO WELL | Ray Peterson, Dunes 2009 | 7 |
| 65 | 49 | 40 | 26 | I DON'T KNOW WHY | Linda Scott, Canadian-American 129 | 14 |
| ★66 | — | — | — | HER ROYAL MAJESTY | James Darren, Colpix 622 | 1 |
| 67 | 58 | 56 | 34 | MOON RIVER | Jerry Butler, Vee Jay 405 | 17 |
| 68 | 51 | 35 | 44 | DREAMY EYES | Johnny Tillotson, Cadence 1409 | 9 |
| 69 | 64 | 61 | 63 | IT WILL STAND | Showmen, Minit 632 | 12 |
| ★70 | — | — | — | TWISTIN' THE NIGHT AWAY △ | Sam Cooke, RCA Victor 7983 | 1 |
| ★71 | 96 | — | — | SHE'S GOT YOU | Patsy Cline, Decca 31354 | 2 |
| 72 | 82 | 100 | — | WHERE HAVE ALL THE FLOWERS GONE | Kingston Trio, Capitol 4671 | 3 |
| ★73 | 97 | — | — | TWISTIN' POSTMAN | Marvelettes, Tamla 54054 | 2 |
| 74 | 71 | 73 | 76 | WHAT'S THE REASON | Bobby Edwards, Capitol 4674 | 4 |
| 75 | 80 | 87 | — | THERE'LL BE NO NEXT TIME | Jackie Wilson, Brunswick 55221 | 3 |
| 76 | 87 | — | — | LIZZIE BORDEN | Chad Mitchell Trio, Kapp 439 | 2 |
| 77 | 78 | 81 | 83 | TEARS FROM AN ANGEL | Troy Shondell, Liberty 55398 | 6 |
| 78 | 85 | — | — | CRY TO ME | Solomon Burke, Atlantic 2131 | 2 |
| ★79 | — | — | — | MIDNIGHT IN MOSCOW | Kenny Ball, Kapp 442 | 1 |
| 80 | 86 | 88 | 94 | THAT'S MY PA | Sheb Wooley, MGM 13046 | 5 |
| 81 | 77 | 84 | 87 | A LITTLE TOO MUCH | Clarence Henry, Argo 5408 | 4 |
| ★82 | 100 | — | — | BANDIT OF MY DREAMS | Eddie Hodges, Cadence 1410 | 2 |
| 83 | 79 | 68 | 78 | TWISTIN' ALL NIGHT LONG | Danny and the Juniors, Swan 4092 | 5 |
| ★84 | 99 | — | — | HE KNOWS I LOVE HIM TOO MUCH | Paris Sisters, Gregmark 10 | 2 |
| ★85 | — | 99 | — | OLIVER TWIST | Rod McKuen, Spiral 1407 | 2 |
| 86 | 88 | — | — | LOVE IS THE SWEETEST THING | Saverio Saridis, Warner Bros. 5243 | 2 |
| 87 | 84 | 91 | — | A LITTLE BITTY TEAR | Wanda Jackson, Capitol 4681 | 3 |
| 88 | 94 | 97 | — | NITE OWL | Nat Chandler and the Dukays, Nat 4002 | 3 |
| 89 | 91 | 93 | — | BLUE WATER LINE △ | Brothers Four, Columbia 42256 | 3 |
| ★90 | — | — | — | MIDNIGHT | Johnny Gibson, Big Top 3088 | 1 |
| 91 | — | — | — | MY MELANCHOLY BABY | Marcels, Colpix 624 | 1 |
| 92 | — | — | — | TEEN QUEEN OF THE WEEK | Freddy Cannon, Swan 4096 | 1 |
| 93 | 90 | — | — | DO THE NEW CONTINENTAL | Dovells, Parkway 833 | 2 |
| 94 | 89 | 92 | — | JAMIE | Eddie Holland, Motown 1021 | 3 |
| 95 | — | — | — | ECSTASY | Ben E. King, Atco 6215 | 1 |
| 96 | — | — | — | LET ME CALL YOU SWEETHEART | Timi Yuro, Liberty 55410 | 1 |
| 97 | — | — | — | I SURRENDER DEAR △ | Aretha Franklin, Columbia 42266 | 1 |
| 98 | — | — | — | LET'S GO △ | Floyd Cramer, RCA Victor 7978 | 1 |
| 99 | — | — | — | TEQUILA TWIST | Champs, Challenge 9131 | 1 |
| 100 | — | — | — | SUGAR BABE | Buster Brown, Fire 507 | 1 |

## HOT 100—A TO Z—(Publisher-Licensee)

Afrikaan Beat (Roosevelt, BMI) ... 61
Baby, It's You (Dolfi, ASCAP) ... 8
Bandit of My Dreams (Arch, ASCAP) ... 82
Blue Water Line (January, BMI) ... 89
Break It to Me Gently (Northern, ASCAP) ... 9
Cajun Queen (Cedarwood, BMI) ... 41
Can't Help Falling in Love (Gladys, ASCAP) ... 2
Chip Chip (Trinity & Glo-Mac, BMI) ... 46
Chattanooga Choo Choo (Feist, ASCAP) ... 56
Cotton Fields (Westside, BMI) ... 18
Cry to Me (Melvin-Progressive, BMI) ... 78
Crying in the Rain (Aldon, BMI) ... 20
Dear Ivan (Plainview, BMI) ... 31
Dear Lady Twist (Pepe, BMI) ... 11
Do-Re-Mi (Fast, BMI) ... 27
Do the New Continental (Kalmann, ASCAP) ... 93
Dreamy Eyes (Southern Belle, BMI) ... 68
Duke of Earl (Conrad-Karlan, BMI) ... 7
Ecstasy (Presley-Progressive-Trio, BMI) ... 95
Flying Circle (Claridge, ASCAP) ... 57
Funny How Time Slips Away (Pamper, BMI) ... 36
Go on Home (Pamper, BMI) ... 42
Goodbye Cruel World (Aldon, BMI) ... 45
Greatest Hurt, The (Pearl, BMI) ... 40
Happy Birthday, Sweet Sixteen (Aldon, BMI) ... 19
Happy Jose (Lansdowne, ASCAP) ... 60
He Knows I Love Him Too Much (Aldon, BMI) ... 84
Her Royal Majesty (Aldon, BMI) ... 66
Hey! Baby (LeBill, BMI) ... 52
I Could Have Loved You So Well (Aldon, BMI) ... 64
I Don't Know Why (Ahlert & Cromwell, ASCAP) ... 65
I Know (Saturn-At Last, BMI) ... 5
I Surrender Dear (Mills, ASCAP) ... 97
If You Gotta Make a Fool of Somebody (Good Song, BMI) ... 24
I'll See You in My Dreams (Feist, ASCAP) ... 59
I'm Blue (Progressive-Placid, BMI) ... 34
Irresistible You (Lloyd-Logan, BMI) ... 17
It Will Stand (Minit, BMI) ... 69
Jamie (Jobette, BMI) ... 94
Let Me Call You Sweetheart (Shapiro, Bernstein, ASCAP) ... 96
Let Me In (Arc-Kae Williams, BMI) ... 43
Let There Be Drums (Travis, BMI) ... 23
Let's Go (Cigma, BMI) ... 98
Let's Twist Again (Kalmann, ASCAP) ... 54
Letter Full of Tears Betalbin, BMI) ... 25
Lion Sleeps Tonight, The (Folkways, BMI) ... 10
Little Bitty Tear, A—Ives (Pamper, BMI) ... 12
Little Bitty Tear, A—Jackson (Pamper, BMI) ... 87
Little Too Much, A (Bar-Mar, BMI) ... 81
Lizzie Borden (Hill & Range, BMI) ... 76
Lost Someone (Lois, BMI) ... 63
Love Is the Sweetest Thing (Harms, ASCAP) ... 86
Maria (Schirmer-Chappell, ASCAP) ... 51
Midnight (Vicki, BMI) ... 90
Midnight in Moscow (Melody Trails, BMI) ... 79
Moon River—Butler (Famous, ASCAP) ... 67
Moon River—Mancini (Famous, ASCAP) ... 29
Multiplication (Adaris, BMI) ... 35
My Boomerang Won't Come Back (Picadilly, BMI) . 58
My Melancholy Baby (Shapiro-Bernstein & Vogel, ASCAP) ... 91
Nite Owl (Conrad, BMI) ... 88
Norman (Acuff-Rose, BMI) ... 4
Oliver Twist (Shelly, ASCAP) ... 85
Peppermint Twist (Jon-Ware, BMI) ... 1
Percolator (Meadowlark, ASCAP) ... 53
Please Mr. Postman (Jobette, BMI) ... 50
Pocketful of Miracles (Maraville, ASCAP) ... 39
Poor Fool (Saturn, BMI) ... 44
Rock-A-Hula Baby (Gladys, ASCAP) ... 49
Run to Him (Aldon, BMI) ... 15
Shadrack (Fisher, ASCAP) ... 22
She's Everything (Alan K., BMI) ... 28
She's Got You (Pamper, BMI) ... 71
Small Sad Sam (R.F.D., ASCAP) ... 38
Smoky Places (Annie-Earl & Sun Flower, ASCAP) . 33
Sugar Babe (Fast, BMI) ... 100
Surfer's Stomp (Strat-E.D.M., ASCAP) ... 48
Tears From an Angel (Metric, BMI) ... 77
Teen Queen of the Week (Conley, ASCAP) ... 92
Tequila Twist (Jat, BMI) ... 99
That's My Pa (Channel, ASCAP) ... 80
There'll Be No Next Time (Merrimac, BMI) ... 75
There's No Other (Bertha, BMI) ... 55
To a Sleeping Beauty (Songsmiths-Remick, ASCAP). 47
Town Without Pity (United Artists, ASCAP) ... 13
Tuff (Jec, BMI) ... 37
Turn on Your Love Light (Don, BMI) ... 32
Twist, The (Lois, BMI) ... 3
Twist-Her (Jec, BMI) ... 26
Twistin' All Night Long (Conley, ASCAP) ... 83
Twistin' Postman (Jobette, BMI) ... 73
Twistin' the Night Away (Kags, BMI) ... 70
Unchain My Heart (Tee Pee, ASCAP) ... 21
Walk on By (Lowery, BMI) ... 16
Wanderer, The (Schwartz-Disal, ASCAP) ... 6
What's So Good About Goodbye (Jobette, BMI) ... 62
What's the Reason (Bourne, ASCAP) ... 74
When I Fall in Love (Northern, ASCAP) ... 14
When the Boy in Your Arms (Pickwick, ASCAP) .. 30
Where Have All the Flowers Gone (Fall River, BMI) ... 72

## BUBBLING UNDER THE HOT 100

101. PICTURES IN THE FIRE ... Pat Boone, Dot 16312
102. AW SHUCKS, HUSH YOUR MOUTH ... Jimmy Reed, Vee Jay 425
103. TEARS AND LAUGHTER ... Dinah Washington, Mercury 71922
104. HAPPY JOSE ... Dave Appell, Cameo 207
105. SURFIN' ... Beach Boys, Candix 331
106. MOMENTS ... Jennell Hawkins, Amazon 1003
107. I GOT A FUNNY KIND OF FEELING ... Maxine Brown, ABC-Paramount 10290
108. FOOLS HALL OF FAME ... Paul Anka, ABC-Paramount 10282
109. SHIMMY, SHIMMY WALK ... Megatons, Checker 1005
110. ECHO IN THE NIGHT ... Bert Kaempfert, Decca 31350
111. DO YOU KNOW HOW TO TWIST ... Hank Ballard, King 5593
112. IT'S GOOD TO HAVE YOU BACK WITH ME .. Adam Wade, Coed 565
113. MAMIE IN THE AFTERNOON ... Bobby Lewis, Beltone 1016
114. IMAGINATION ... Quotations, Verve 10245
115. STEP RIGHT UP ... Nat King Cole, Capitol 4672
116. OUR CONCERTO ... Steve Lawrence, United Artists 403
117. JOEY BABY ... Anita and the So & So's, RCA Victor 7974
118. HOW ARE THINGS IN LOVER'S LANE ... Adam Wade, Coed 565
119. ROUGH LOVER ... Aretha Franklin, Columbia 42266
120. WALKING CANE ... Billy Duke, 20th Fox 296

# BILLBOARD HOT 100

FOR WEEK ENDING FEBRUARY 10

1962

★ STAR PERFORMERS—Selections registering greatest upward progress this week.

[S] Indicates that 45 r.p.m. stereo single version is available.

△ Indicates that 33⅓ r.p.m. mono single version is available.

[S]△ Indicates that 33⅓ r.p.m. stereo single version is available.

| This Week | 1 Wk. Ago | 2 Wks. Ago | 3 Wks. Ago | Title | Artist, Label & Number | | Weeks On Chart |
|---|---|---|---|---|---|---|---|
| 1 | 1 | 1 | 2 | PEPPERMINT TWIST | Joey Dee and the Starliters, Roulette 4401 | | 12 |
| ★ 2 | 7 | 20 | 49 | DUKE OF EARL | Gene (Duke of Earl) Chandler, Vee Jay 416 | | 5 |
| 3 | 3 | 2 | 1 | THE TWIST | Chubby Checker, Parkway 811 | | 31 |
| 4 | 2 | 4 | 4 | CAN'T HELP FALLING IN LOVE | Elvis Presley, RCA Victor 7968 | △ | 10 |
| 5 | 5 | 3 | 5 | I KNOW | Barbara George, AFO 302 | | 13 |
| 6 | 4 | 5 | 10 | NORMAN | Sue Thompson, Hickory 1159 | | 10 |
| 7 | 6 | 8 | 18 | THE WANDERER | Dion, Laurie 3115 | | 10 |
| 8 | 9 | 17 | 29 | BREAK IT TO ME GENTLY | Brenda Lee, Decca 31348 | | 5 |
| 9 | 12 | 14 | 17 | A LITTLE BITTY TEAR | Burl Ives, Decca 31330 | | 8 |
| 10 | 11 | 15 | 26 | DEAR LADY TWIST | Gary (U. S.) Bonds, LeGrand 1015 | | 9 |
| 11 | 8 | 9 | 15 | BABY IT'S YOU | Shirelles, Scepter 1227 | | 8 |
| 12 | 10 | 6 | 3 | THE LION SLEEPS TONIGHT | Tokens, RCA Victor 7954 | △ | 13 |
| ★ 13 | 18 | 18 | 16 | COTTON FIELDS | Highwaymen, United Artists 370 | | 11 |
| ★ 14 | 20 | 42 | 67 | CRYING IN THE RAIN | Everly Brothers, Warner Bros. 5250 | | 5 |
| 15 | 17 | 23 | 27 | IRRESISTIBLE YOU | Bobby Darin, Atco 6214 | | 9 |
| 16 | 14 | 7 | 9 | WHEN I FALL IN LOVE | Lettermen, Capitol 4658 | | 12 |
| 17 | 13 | 13 | 14 | TOWN WITHOUT PITY | Gene Pitney, Musicor 1009 | | 15 |
| 18 | 15 | 12 | 8 | RUN TO HIM | Bobby Vee, Liberty 55388 | | 13 |
| ★ 19 | 25 | 27 | 33 | LETTER FULL OF TEARS | Gladys Knight and the Pips, Fury 1054 | | 9 |
| ★ 20 | 28 | 41 | 48 | SHE'S EVERYTHING | Ral Donner, Gone 5121 | | 7 |
| ★ 21 | 52 | 74 | — | HEY! BABY | Bruce Channel, Smash 1731 | | 3 |
| 22 | 22 | 33 | 45 | SHADRACK | Brook Benton, Mercury 71912 | | 5 |
| 23 | 16 | 10 | 7 | WALK ON BY | Leroy Van Dyke, Mercury 71834 | | 15 |
| ★ 24 | 46 | 63 | 96 | CHIP CHIP | Gene McDaniels, Liberty 55405 | | 4 |
| 25 | 33 | 39 | 46 | SMOKY PLACES | Corsairs, Tuff 3030 | | 7 |
| ★ 26 | 37 | 35 | 44 | TUFF | Ace Cannon, Hi 2040 | | 7 |
| 27 | 24 | 22 | 23 | IF YOU GOTTA MAKE A FOOL OF SOMEBODY | James Ray, Caprice 110 | | 12 |
| 28 | 34 | 50 | 63 | I'M BLUE (The Gong-Gong Song) | Ikettes, Atco 6212 | | 5 |
| 29 | 26 | 26 | 31 | TWIST-HER | Bill Black's Combo, Hi 2042 | | 8 |
| 30 | 29 | 31 | 28 | MOON RIVER | Henry Mancini, RCA Victor 7916 | △ | 18 |
| 31 | 27 | 30 | 32 | DO-RE-MI | Lee Dorsey, Fury 1056 | | 8 |
| 32 | 35 | 36 | 39 | MULTIPLICATION | Bobby Darin, Atco 6214 | | 8 |
| 33 | 23 | 21 | 13 | LET THERE BE DRUMS | Sandy Nelson, Imperial 5775 | | 15 |
| 34 | 41 | 69 | — | CAJUN QUEEN | Jimmy Dean, Columbia 42282 | △ | 3 |
| 35 | 43 | 56 | 64 | LET ME IN | Sensations, Argo 5405 | | 6 |
| 36 | 21 | 16 | 11 | UNCHAIN MY HEART | Ray Charles, ABC-Paramount 10266 | | 11 |
| 37 | 40 | 44 | 57 | THE GREATEST HURT | Jackie Wilson, Brunswick 55221 | | 5 |
| 38 | 19 | 11 | 6 | HAPPY BIRTHDAY, SWEET SIXTEEN | Neil Sedaka, RCA Victor 7957 | △ | 13 |
| 39 | 36 | 25 | 22 | FUNNY HOW TIME SLIPS AWAY | Jimmy Elledge, RCA Victor 7946 | △ | 13 |
| 40 | 47 | 61 | 80 | TO A SLEEPING BEAUTY | Jimmy Dean, Columbia 42282 | △ | 4 |
| 41 | 48 | 55 | 76 | SURFER'S STOMP | Mar-Kets, Liberty 55401 | | 5 |
| ★ 42 | 58 | 70 | 70 | MY BOOMERANG WON'T COME BACK | Charlie Drake, United Artists 398 | | 5 |
| 43 | 31 | 24 | 24 | DEAR IVAN | Jimmy Dean, Columbia 42259 | △ | 6 |
| ★ 44 | 62 | 72 | 78 | WHAT'S SO GOOD ABOUT GOODBYE | Miracles, Tamla 54053 | | 5 |
| 45 | 53 | 65 | 82 | PERCOLATOR (TWIST) | Billy Joe and the Checkmates, Dore 620 | | 5 |
| 46 | 42 | 47 | 54 | GO ON HOME | Patti Page, Mercury 71906 | | 7 |
| ★ 47 | 79 | — | — | MIDNIGHT IN MOSCOW | Kenny Ball, Kapp 442 | | 2 |
| 48 | 56 | 75 | 85 | CHATTANOOGA CHOO CHOO | Floyd Cramer, RCA Victor 7978 | △ | 4 |
| ★ 49 | 70 | — | — | TWISTIN' THE NIGHT AWAY | Sam Cooke, RCA Victor 7983 | △ | 2 |
| ★ 50 | 66 | — | — | HER ROYAL MAJESTY | James Darren, Colpix 622 | | 2 |
| 51 | 59 | 83 | — | I'LL SEE YOU IN MY DREAMS | Pat Boone, Dot 16312 | | 3 |
| 52 | 45 | 37 | 20 | GOODBYE CRUEL WORLD | James Darren, Colpix 609 | | 17 |
| 53 | 39 | 34 | 36 | POCKETFUL OF MIRACLES | Frank Sinatra, Reprise 20040 | | 8 |
| 54 | 61 | 73 | 86 | AFRIKAAN BEAT | Bert Kaempfert, Decca 31350 | | 4 |
| 55 | 32 | 28 | 34 | TURN ON YOUR LOVE LIGHT | Bobby Bland, Duke 344 | | 10 |
| ★ 56 | 73 | 97 | — | TWISTIN' POSTMAN | Marvelettes, Tamla 54054 | | 3 |
| 57 | 60 | 66 | 79 | HAPPY JOSE | Jack Ross, Dot 16302 | | 5 |
| 58 | 44 | 38 | 43 | POOR FOOL | Ike and Tina Turner, Sue 753 | | 11 |
| 59 | 63 | 68 | 71 | LOST SOMEONE | James Brown and the Famous Flames, King 5573 | | 8 |
| ★ 60 | 71 | 96 | — | SHE'S GOT YOU | Patsy Cline, Decca 31354 | | 3 |
| 61 | 30 | 19 | 12 | WHEN THE BOY IN YOUR ARMS | Connie Francis, MGM 13051 | | 12 |
| 62 | 38 | 29 | 21 | SMALL SAD SAM | Phil McLean, Versatile 107 | | 10 |
| ★ 63 | 78 | 85 | — | CRY TO ME | Solomon Burke, Atlantic 2131 | | 3 |
| 64 | 72 | 82 | 100 | WHERE HAVE ALL THE FLOWERS GONE | Kingston Trio, Capitol 4671 | | 4 |
| 65 | 57 | 45 | 47 | FLYING CIRCLE | Frank Slay Ork, Swan 4085 | | 9 |
| ★ 66 | — | — | — | DON'T BREAK THE HEART THAT LOVES YOU | Connie Francis, MGM 13059 | | 1 |
| 67 | 50 | 32 | 19 | PLEASE MR. POSTMAN | Marvelettes, Tamla 54046 | | 23 |
| ★ 68 | 84 | 99 | — | HE KNOWS I LOVE HIM TOO MUCH | Paris Sisters, Gregmark 10 | | 3 |
| 69 | 64 | 57 | 69 | I COULD HAVE LOVED YOU SO WELL | Ray Peterson, Dunes 2009 | | 8 |
| ★ 70 | 91 | — | — | MY MELANCHOLY BABY | Marcels, Colpix 624 | | 2 |
| 71 | 68 | 51 | 35 | DREAMY EYES | Johnny Tillotson, Cadence 1409 | | 10 |
| ★ 72 | — | — | — | WHAT'S YOUR NAME | Don and Juan, Big Top 3079 | | 1 |
| ★ 73 | 88 | 94 | 97 | NITE OWL | Gene Chandler and the Dukays, Nat 4002 | | 4 |
| ★ 74 | 93 | 90 | — | DO THE NEW CONTINENTAL | Dovells, Parkway 833 | | 3 |
| 75 | 80 | 86 | 88 | THAT'S MY PA | Sheb Wooley, MGM 13046 | | 6 |
| ★ 76 | 95 | — | — | ECSTASY | Ben E. King, Atco 6215 | | 2 |
| ★ 77 | — | — | — | DRUMS ARE MY BEAT | Sandy Nelson, Imperial 5809 | | 1 |
| 78 | 85 | — | 99 | OLIVER TWIST | Rod McKuen, Spiral 1407 | | 3 |
| ★ 79 | — | — | — | THE MAJESTIC | Dion, Laurie 3115 | | 7 |
| ★ 80 | — | — | — | B'WA NINA | Tokens, RCA Victor 7991 | △ | 1 |
| 81 | 94 | 89 | 92 | JAMIE | Eddie Holland, Motown 1021 | | 4 |
| 82 | 76 | 87 | — | LIZZIE BORDEN | Chad Mitchell Trio, Kapp 439 | | 3 |
| 83 | 74 | 71 | 73 | WHAT'S THE REASON | Bobby Edwards, Capitol 4674 | | 5 |
| 84 | 96 | — | — | LET ME CALL YOU SWEETHEART | Timi Yuro, Liberty 55410 | | 2 |
| 85 | 89 | 91 | 93 | BLUE WATER LINE | Brothers Four, Columbia 42256 | △ | 4 |
| ★ 86 | — | — | — | TEARS AND LAUGHTER | Dinah Washington, Mercury 71922 | | 1 |
| 87 | 81 | 77 | 84 | A LITTLE TOO MUCH | Clarence Henry, Argo 5408 | | 5 |
| 88 | 82 | 100 | — | BANDIT OF MY DREAMS | Eddie Hodges, Cadence 1410 | | 3 |
| 89 | 90 | — | — | MIDNIGHT | Johnny Gibson, Big Top 3088 | | 2 |
| 90 | 98 | — | — | LET'S GO | Floyd Cramer, RCA Victor 7978 | △ | 2 |
| 91 | — | — | — | DO YOU KNOW HOW TO TWIST | Hank Ballard, King 5593 | | 1 |
| 92 | — | — | — | BERMUDA | Linda Scott, Canadian-American 134 | | 1 |
| 93 | — | 95 | — | AW, SHUCKS, HUSH YOUR MOUTH | Jimmy Reed, Vee Jay 425 | | 2 |
| 94 | — | — | — | ROUGH LOVER | Aretha Franklin, Columbia 42266 | △ | 1 |
| 95 | — | 93 | — | SHIMMY, SHIMMY WALK | Megatons, Checker 1005 | | 2 |
| 96 | — | — | — | YESSIREE | Linda Scott, Congress 101 | | 1 |
| 97 | 97 | — | — | I SURRENDER DEAR | Aretha Franklin, Columbia 42266 | △ | 2 |
| 98 | — | — | — | PICTURES IN THE FIRE | Pat Boone, Dot 16312 | | 1 |
| 99 | 100 | — | — | SUGAR BABE | Buster Brown, Fire 507 | | 2 |
| 100 | — | — | — | STRANGE | Patsy Cline, Decca 31354 | | 1 |

## HOT 100—A TO Z—(Publisher-Licensee)

Afrikaan Beat (Roosevelt, BMI) .... 54
Aw, Shucks, Hush Your Mouth (Conrad, BMI) .... 93
Baby, It's You (Dolfi, ASCAP) .... 11
Bandit of My Dreams (Arch, ASCAP) .... 88
Bermuda (Suffolk, BMI) .... 92
Blue Water Line (January, BMI) .... 85
Break It to Me Gently (Northern, ASCAP) .... 8
B'wa Nina (Lionel, ASCAP) .... 80
Cajun Queen (Cedarwood, BMI) .... 34
Can't Help Falling in Love (Gladys, ASCAP) .... 4
Chip Chip (Trinity & Glo-Mac, BMI) .... 24
Chattanooga Choo Choo (Feist, ASCAP) .... 48
Cotton Fields (Westside, BMI) .... 13
Cry to Me (Melvin-Progressive, BMI) .... 63
Crying in the Rain (Aldon, BMI) .... 14
Dear Ivan (Plainview, BMI) .... 43
Dear Lady Twist (Pepe, BMI) .... 10
Do-Re-Mi (Fast, BMI) .... 31
Do the New Continental (Kalmann, ASCAP) .... 74
Do You Know How to Twist (Lois, BMI) .... 91
Don't Break the Heart That Loves You (Francon, ASCAP) .... 66
Dreamy Eyes (Southern Belle, BMI) .... 71
Drums Are My Beat (Travis, BMI) .... 77
Duke of Earl (Conrad-Karlan, BMI) .... 2
Ecstasy (Presley-Progressive-Trio, BMI) .... 76
Flying Circle (Claridge, ASCAP) .... 65
Funny How Time Slips Away (Pamper, BMI) .... 39
Go on Home (Pamper, BMI) .... 46
Goodbye Cruel World (Aldon, BMI) .... 52
Greatest Hurt, The (Pearl, BMI) .... 37
Happy Birthday, Sweet Sixteen (Aldon, BMI) .... 68
Happy Jose (Lansdowne, ASCAP) .... 57
He Knows I Love Him Too Much (Aldon, BMI) .... 68
Her Royal Majesty (Aldon, BMI) .... 50
Hey! Baby (LeBill, BMI) .... 21
I Could Have Loved You So Well (Aldon, BMI) .... 69
I Know (Saturn-At Last, BMI) .... 5
I Surrender Dear (Mills, ASCAP) .... 97
If You Gotta Make a Fool of Somebody (Good Song, BMI) .... 27
I'll See You in My Dreams (Feist, ASCAP) .... 51
I'm Blue (Progressive-Placid, BMI) .... 28
Irresistible You (Lloyd-Logan, BMI) .... 15
Jamie (Jobette, BMI) .... 81
Let Me Call You Sweetheart (Shapiro-Bernstein, ASCAP) .... 84
Let Me In (Arc-Kae Williams, BMI) .... 35
Let There Be Drums (Travis, BMI) .... 33
Let's Go (Cigma, BMI) .... 90
Letter Full of Tears (Betalbin, BMI) .... 19
Lion Sleeps Tonight, The (Folkways, BMI) .... 12
Little Bitty Tear, A (Pamper, BMI) .... 9
Little Too Much, A (Bar-Mar, BMI) .... 87
Lizzie Borden (Hill & Range, BMI) .... 82
Lost Someone (Lois, BMI) .... 59
Majestic, The (Just-Mubon, BMI) .... 79
Midnight (Vicki, BMI) .... 89
Midnight in Moscow (Melody Trails, BMI) .... 47
Moon River (Famous, ASCAP) .... 30
Multiplication (Adaris, BMI) .... 32
My Boomerang Won't Come Back (Picadilly, BMI) .... 42
My Melancholy Baby (Shapiro-Bernstein & Vogel, ASCAP) .... 70
Nite Owl (Conrad, BMI) .... 73
Norman (Acuff-Rose, BMI) .... 6
Oliver Twist (Shelly, ASCAP) .... 78
Peppermint Twist (Jon-Ware, BMI) .... 1
Percolator (Twist) (Meadowlark, ASCAP) .... 45
Pictures in the Fire (Spoone, ASCAP) .... 98
Please Mr. Postman (Jobette, BMI) .... 67
Pocketful of Miracles (Maraville, ASCAP) .... 53
Poor Fool (Saturn, BMI) .... 58
Rough Lover (Danby, BMI) .... 94
Run to Him (Aldon, BMI) .... 18
Shadrack (Fisher, ASCAP) .... 22
She's Everything (Alan K., BMI) .... 20
She's Got You (Pamper, BMI) .... 60
Shimmy, Shimmy Walk (Star-Flite & Hut, BMI) .... 95
Small Sad Sam (R.F.D., ASCAP) .... 62
Smoky Places (Annie-Earl & Sun Flower, ASCAP) .... 25
Strange (Cedarwood, BMI) .... 100
Sugar Babe (Fast, BMI) .... 99
Surfer's Stomp (Strat-E.D.M., ASCAP) .... 41
Tears and Laughter (Gil, BMI) .... 86
That's My Pa (Channel, ASCAP) .... 75
To a Sleeping Beauty (Songsmiths-Remick, ASCAP) .... 40
Town Without Pity (United Artists, ASCAP) .... 17
Tuff (Jec, BMI) .... 26
Turn on Your Love Light (Don, BMI) .... 55
Twist, The (Lois, BMI) .... 3
Twist-Her (Jec, BMI) .... 29
Twistin' Postman (Jobette, BMI) .... 56
Twistin' the Night Away (Kags, BMI) .... 49
Unchain My Heart (Tee Pee, ASCAP) .... 36
Walk on By (Lowery, BMI) .... 23
Wanderer, The (Schwartz-Disal, ASCAP) .... 7
What's So Good About Goodbye (Jobette, BMI) .... 44
What's the Reason (Bourne, ASCAP) .... 83
What's Your Name (Hill & Range, BMI) .... 72
When I Fall in Love (Northern, ASCAP) .... 16
When the Boy in Your Arms (Pickwick, ASCAP) .... 61
Where Have All the Flowers Gone (Fall River, BMI) .... 64
Yessiree (Kilt, BMI) .... 96

## BUBBLING UNDER THE HOT 100

101. SURFIN' .... Beach Boys, Candix 331
102. LOVE LETTERS .... Ketty Lester, Era 3068
103. FOOLS HALL OF FAME .... Paul Anka, ABC-Paramount 10282
104. I GOT A FUNNY KIND OF FEELING .... Maxine Brown, ABC-Paramount 10290
105. HAPPY JOSE .... Dave Appell, Cameo 207
106. JOEY BABY .... Anita and the So and So's, RCA Victor 7974
107. OUR CONCERTO .... Steve Lawrence, United Artists 403
108. ECHO IN THE NIGHT .... Bert Kaempfert, Decca 31350
109. IT'S GOOD TO HAVE YOU BACK WITH ME .. Adam Wade, Coed 565
110. MAMIE IN THE AFTERNOON .... Bobby Lewis, Beltone 1016
111. POP-EYE .... Huey Smith and the Clowns, Ace 649
112. STEP RIGHT UP .... Nat King Cole, Capitol 4672
113. MOMENTS .... Jennell Hawkins, Amazon 1003
114. HOW ARE THINGS IN LOVER'S LANE .... Adam Wade, Coed 565
115. THE BATTLE .... Duane Eddy, Jamie 1209
116. IMAGINATION .... Quotations, Verve 10245
117. ARCHIE'S MELODY .... Byliners, Felsted 8631
118. LOVE IS THE SWEETEST THING .. Saverio Saridis, Warner Bros. 5243
119. AFTER YOU'VE GONE .... Frankie Avalon, Chancellor 1101
120. LOSE HER .... Bobby Rydell, Cameo 209

# BILLBOARD HOT 100

FOR WEEK ENDING FEBRUARY 17

1962

★ STAR PERFORMERS—Selections registering greatest upward progress this week.

(S) Indicates that 45 r.p.m. stereo single version is available.

△ Indicates that 33⅓ r.p.m. mono single version is available.

(S)△ Indicates that 33⅓ r.p.m. stereo single version is available.

| This Week | 1 Wk. Ago | 2 Wks. Ago | 3 Wks. Ago | Title, Artist, Label & Number | Weeks On Chart |
|---|---|---|---|---|---|
| 1 | 2 | 7 | 20 | DUKE OF EARL — Gene (Duke of Earl) Chandler, Vee Jay 416 | 6 |
| 2 | 1 | 1 | 1 | PEPPERMINT TWIST — Joey Dee and the Starliters, Roulette 4401 | 13 |
| 3 | 3 | 3 | 2 | THE TWIST — Chubby Checker, Parkway 811 | 32 |
| 4 | 6 | 4 | 5 | NORMAN — Sue Thompson, Hickory 1159 | 11 |
| 5 | 7 | 6 | 8 | THE WANDERER — Dion, Laurie 3115 | 11 |
| 6 | 8 | 9 | 17 | BREAK IT TO ME GENTLY — Brenda Lee, Decca 31348 | 6 |
| 7 | 5 | 5 | 3 | I KNOW — Barbara George, AFO 302 | 14 |
| 8 | 4 | 2 | 4 | CAN'T HELP FALLING IN LOVE △ — Elvis Presley, RCA Victor 7968 | 11 |
| ★ 9 | 14 | 20 | 42 | CRYING IN THE RAIN — Everly Brothers, Warner Bros. 5250 | 6 |
| 10 | 10 | 11 | 15 | DEAR LADY TWIST — Gary (U. S.) Bonds, LeGrand 1015 | 10 |
| 11 | 9 | 12 | 14 | A LITTLE BITTY TEAR — Burl Ives, Decca 31330 | 9 |
| 12 | 11 | 8 | 9 | BABY IT'S YOU — Shirelles, Scepter 1227 | 9 |
| ★ 13 | 21 | 52 | 74 | HEY! BABY — Bruce Channel, Smash 1731 | 4 |
| 14 | 13 | 18 | 18 | COTTON FIELDS — Highwaymen, United Artists 370 | 12 |
| ★ 15 | 24 | 46 | 63 | CHIP CHIP — Gene McDaniels, Liberty 55405 | 5 |
| 16 | 12 | 10 | 6 | THE LION SLEEPS TONIGHT △ — Tokens, RCA Victor 7954 | 14 |
| 17 | 15 | 17 | 23 | IRRESISTIBLE YOU — Bobby Darin, Atco 6214 | 10 |
| 18 | 20 | 28 | 41 | SHE'S EVERYTHING — Ral Donner, Gone 5121 | 8 |
| 19 | 22 | 22 | 33 | SHADRACK — Brook Benton, Mercury 71912 | 6 |
| ★ 20 | 28 | 34 | 50 | I'M BLUE (The Gong-Gong Song) — Ikettes, Atco 6212 | 6 |
| 21 | 19 | 25 | 27 | LETTER FULL OF TEARS — Gladys Knight and the Pips, Fury 1054 | 10 |
| 22 | 18 | 15 | 12 | RUN TO HIM — Bobby Vee, Liberty 55388 | 14 |
| 23 | 17 | 13 | 13 | TOWN WITHOUT PITY — Gene Pitney, Musicor 1009 | 16 |
| 24 | 16 | 14 | 7 | WHEN I FALL IN LOVE — Lettermen, Capitol 4658 | 13 |
| 25 | 34 | 41 | 69 | CAJUN QUEEN △ — Jimmy Dean, Columbia 42282 | 4 |
| 26 | 26 | 37 | 35 | TUFF — Ace Cannon, Hi 2040 | 8 |
| 27 | 35 | 43 | 56 | LET ME IN — Sensations, Argo 5405 | 7 |
| 28 | 25 | 33 | 39 | SMOKY PLACES — Corsairs, Tuff 3030 | 8 |
| ★ 29 | 47 | 79 | — | MIDNIGHT IN MOSCOW — Kenny Ball, Kapp 442 | 3 |
| 30 | 32 | 35 | 36 | MULTIPLICATION — Bobby Darin, Atco 6214 | 9 |
| ★ 31 | 50 | 66 | — | HER ROYAL MAJESTY — James Darren, Colpix 622 | 3 |
| 32 | 41 | 48 | 55 | SURFER'S STOMP — Mar-Kets, Liberty 55401 | 6 |
| ★ 33 | 45 | 53 | 65 | PERCOLATOR (TWIST) — Billy Joe and the Checkmates, Dore 620 | 6 |
| 34 | 37 | 40 | 44 | THE GREATEST HURT — Jackie Wilson, Brunswick 55221 | 6 |
| 35 | 40 | 47 | 61 | TO A SLEEPING BEAUTY △ — Jimmy Dean, Columbia 42282 | 5 |
| 36 | 30 | 29 | 31 | MOON RIVER △ — Henry Mancini, RCA Victor 7916 | 19 |
| 37 | 42 | 58 | 70 | MY BOOMERANG WON'T COME BACK — Charlie Drake, United Artists 398 | 6 |
| ★ 38 | 49 | 70 | — | TWISTIN' THE NIGHT AWAY △ — Sam Cooke, RCA Victor 7983 | 3 |
| 39 | 31 | 27 | 30 | DO-RE-MI — Lee Dorsey, Fury 1056 | 9 |
| 40 | 44 | 62 | 72 | WHAT'S SO GOOD ABOUT GOODBYE — Miracles, Tamla 54053 | 6 |
| 41 | 29 | 26 | 26 | TWIST-HER — Bill Black's Combo, Hi 2042 | 9 |
| ★ 42 | 60 | 71 | 96 | SHE'S GOT YOU — Patsy Cline, Decca 31354 | 4 |
| 43 | 48 | 56 | 75 | CHATTANOOGA CHOO CHOO △ — Floyd Cramer, RCA Victor 7978 | 5 |
| 44 | 27 | 24 | 22 | IF YOU GOTTA MAKE A FOOL OF SOMEBODY — James Ray, Caprice 110 | 13 |
| 45 | 51 | 59 | 83 | I'LL SEE YOU IN MY DREAMS — Pat Boone, Dot 16312 | 4 |
| ★ 46 | 66 | — | — | DON'T BREAK THE HEART THAT LOVES YOU — Connie Francis, MGM 13059 | 2 |
| ★ 47 | 72 | — | — | WHAT'S YOUR NAME — Don and Juan, Big Top 3079 | 2 |
| 48 | 56 | 73 | 97 | TWISTIN' POSTMAN — Marvelettes, Tamla 54054 | 4 |
| ★ 49 | 59 | 63 | 68 | LOST SOMEONE — James Brown and the Famous Flames, King 5573 | 9 |
| 50 | 54 | 61 | 73 | AFRIKAAN BEAT — Bert Kaempfert, Decca 31350 | 5 |
| ★ 51 | 64 | 72 | 82 | WHERE HAVE ALL THE FLOWERS GONE — Kingston Trio, Capitol 4671 | 5 |
| 52 | 33 | 23 | 21 | LET THERE BE DRUMS — Sandy Nelson, Imperial 5775 | 16 |
| ★ 53 | 68 | 84 | 99 | HE KNOWS I LOVE HIM TOO MUCH — Paris Sisters, Gregmark 10 | 4 |
| 54 | 23 | 16 | 10 | WALK ON BY — Leroy Van Dyke, Mercury 71834 | 16 |
| ★ 55 | 77 | — | — | DRUMS ARE MY BEAT — Sandy Nelson, Imperial 5809 | 2 |
| 56 | 38 | 19 | 11 | HAPPY BIRTHDAY, SWEET SIXTEEN △ — Neil Sedaka, RCA Victor 7957 | 14 |
| 57 | 36 | 21 | 16 | UNCHAIN MY HEART — Ray Charles, ABC-Paramount 10266 | 12 |
| ★ 58 | 74 | 93 | 90 | DO THE NEW CONTINENTAL — Dovells, Parkway 833 | 4 |
| 59 | 57 | 60 | 66 | HAPPY JOSE — Jack Ross, Dot 16302 | 6 |
| 60 | 63 | 78 | 85 | CRY TO ME — Solomon Burke, Atlantic 2131 | 4 |
| ★ 61 | 81 | 94 | 89 | JAMIE — Eddie Holland, Motown 1021 | 5 |
| 62 | 43 | 31 | 24 | DEAR IVAN △ — Jimmy Dean, Columbia 42259 | 7 |
| 63 | 71 | 68 | 51 | DREAMY EYES — Johnny Tillotson, Cadence 1409 | 11 |
| ★ 64 | — | — | — | HEY, LET'S TWIST — Joey Dee & the Starliters, Roulette 4408 | 1 |
| 65 | 75 | 80 | 86 | THAT'S MY PA — Sheb Wooley, MGM 13046 | 7 |
| 66 | 46 | 42 | 47 | GO ON HOME — Patti Page, Mercury 71906 | 8 |
| 67 | 70 | 91 | — | MY MELANCHOLY BABY — Marcels, Colpix 624 | 3 |
| 68 | 80 | — | — | B'WA NINA △ — Tokens, RCA Victor 7991 | 2 |
| 69 | 39 | 36 | 25 | FUNNY HOW TIME SLIPS AWAY △ — Jimmy Elledge, RCA Victor 7946 | 14 |
| 70 | 76 | 95 | — | ECSTASY — Ben E. King, Atco 6215 | 3 |
| 71 | 82 | 76 | 87 | LIZZIE BORDEN — Chad Mitchell Trio, Kapp 439 | 4 |
| 72 | 79 | — | — | THE MAJESTIC — Dion, Laurie 3115 | 8 |
| ★ 73 | — | — | — | COME BACK SILLY GIRL — Lettermen, Capitol 4699 | 1 |
| ★ 74 | — | — | — | OUR ANNIVERSARY — Shep & the Limelites, Hull 748 | 1 |
| 75 | 73 | 88 | 94 | NITE OWL — Gene Chandler and the Dukays, Nat 4002 | 5 |
| 76 | 78 | 85 | — | OLIVER TWIST — Rod McKuen, Spiral 1407 | 4 |
| ★ 77 | — | — | — | DREAM BABY — Roy Orbison, Monument 456 | 1 |
| 78 | 84 | 96 | — | LET ME CALL YOU SWEETHEART — Timi Yuro, Liberty 55410 | 3 |
| 79 | 83 | 74 | 71 | WHAT'S THE REASON — Bobby Edwards, Capitol 4674 | 6 |
| 80 | 89 | 90 | — | MIDNIGHT — Johnny Gibson, Big Top 3088 | 3 |
| ★ 81 | — | — | — | WALK ON THE WILD SIDE — Brook Benton, Mercury 71925 | 1 |
| 82 | 88 | 82 | 100 | BANDIT OF MY DREAMS — Eddie Hodges, Cadence 1410 | 4 |
| ★ 83 | — | — | — | I'VE GOT BONNIE — Bobby Rydell, Cameo 209 | 1 |
| 84 | 85 | 89 | 91 | BLUE WATER LINE △ — Brothers Four, Columbia 42256 | 5 |
| 85 | 92 | — | — | BERMUDA — Linda Scott, Canadian-American 134 | 2 |
| 86 | 86 | — | — | TEARS AND LAUGHTER — Dinah Washington, Mercury 71922 | 2 |
| 87 | 96 | — | — | YESSIREE — Linda Scott, Congress 101 | 2 |
| ★ 88 | — | — | — | CRY BABY CRY — Angels, Caprice 1018 | 1 |
| ★ 89 | — | — | — | POP-EYE — Huey Smith & the Clowns, Ace 649 | 1 |
| ★ 90 | — | — | — | LOSE HER — Bobby Rydell, Cameo 209 | 1 |
| 91 | 91 | — | — | DO YOU KNOW HOW TO TWIST — Hank Ballard, King 5593 | 2 |
| 92 | — | 86 | 88 | LOVE IS THE SWEETEST THING — Saverio Saridis, Warner Bros. 5243 | 3 |
| 93 | — | — | — | SURFIN' — Beach Boys, Candix 331 | 1 |
| 94 | — | — | — | IT'S MAGIC — Platters, Mercury 71921 | 1 |
| 95 | 95 | — | 93 | SHIMMY, SHIMMY WALK — Megatons, Checker 1005 | 3 |
| 96 | 97 | 97 | — | I SURRENDER DEAR △ — Aretha Franklin, Columbia 42266 | 3 |
| 97 | 100 | — | — | STRANGE — Patsy Cline, Decca 31354 | 2 |
| 98 | — | — | — | JOEY BABY △ — Anita & the So & So's, RCA Victor 7974 | 1 |
| 99 | — | — | — | GROW CLOSER TOGETHER — Impressions, ABC-Paramount 10289 | 1 |
| 100 | — | — | — | SOUL TWIST — King Curtis, Enjoy 1000 | 1 |

## HOT 100—A TO Z—(Publisher-Licensee)

Afrikaan Beat (Roosevelt, BMI) .... 50
Baby It's You (Dolfi, ASCAP) .... 12
Bandit of My Dreams (Arch, ASCAP) .... 82
Bermuda (Suffolk, BMI) .... 85
Blue Water Line (January, BMI) .... 84
Break It to Me Gently (Northern, ASCAP) .... 6
B'way Nina (Lionel, ASCAP) .... 68
Cajun Queen (Cedarwood, BMI) .... 25
Can't Help Falling in Love (Gladys, ASCAP) .... 8
Chip Chip (Trinity Glo-Mac, BMI) .... 15
Chattanooga Choo Choo (Feist, ASCAP) .... 43
Come Back Silly Girl (Aldon, BMI) .... 73
Cotton Fields (Westside, BMI) .... 14
Cry Baby Cry (Jersey-Central Songs, BMI) .... 88
Cry to Me (Melvin-Progressive, BMI) .... 60
Crying in the Rain (Aldon, BMI) .... 9
Dear Ivan (Plainview, BMI) .... 62
Dear Lady Twist (Pepe, BMI) .... 10
Do-Re-Mi (Fast, BMI) .... 39
Do the New Continental (Kalmann, ASCAP) .... 58
Do You Know How to Twist (Lois, BMI) .... 91
Don't Break the Heart That Loves You (Francon, ASCAP) .... 46
Dream Baby (Combine, BMI) .... 77
Dreamy Eyes (Southern Belle, BMI) .... 63
Drums Are My Beat (Travis, BMI) .... 55
Duke of Earl (Conrad-Karlan, BMI) .... 1
Ecstasy (Presley-Progressive-Trio, BMI) .... 70
Funny How Time Slips Away (Pamper, BMI) .... 69
Go on Home (Pamper, BMI) .... 66
Greatest Hurt, The (Pearl, BMI) .... 34
Grow Closer Together (Curtom, BMI) .... 99
Happy Birthday, Sweet Sixteen (Aldon, BMI) .... 56
Happy Jose (Lansdowne, ASCAP) .... 59
He Knows I Love Him Too Much (Aldon, BMI) .... 53
Her Royal Majesty (Aldon, BMI) .... 31
Hey! Baby (LeBill, BMI) .... 13
Hey, Let's Twist (Ware-Frost, BMI) .... 64
I Know (Saturn-At Last, BMI) .... 7
I Surrender Dear (Mills, ASCAP) .... 96
I'll See You in My Dreams (Feist, ASCAP) .... 45
I'm Blue (Progressive-Placid, BMI) .... 20
I've Got Bonnie (Aldon, BMI) .... 83
If You Gotta Make a Fool of Somebody (Good Song, BMI) .... 44
Irresistible You (Lloyd-Logan, BMI) .... 17
It's Magic (Witmark, ASCAP) .... 94
Jamie (Jobette, BMI) .... 61
Joey Baby (Tree, BMI) .... 98
Let Me Call You Sweetheart (Shapiro-Bernstein & Shawnee, ASCAP) .... 78
Let Me In (Arc-Kae Williams, BMI) .... 27
Let There Be Drums (Travis, BMI) .... 52
Letter Full of Tears (Betalbin, BMI) .... 21
Lion Sleeps Tonight, The (Folkways, BMI) .... 16
Little Bitty Tear, A (Pamper, BMI) .... 11
Lizzie Borden (Hill & Range, BMI) .... 71
Lose Her (Kalmann-Fajob, ASCAP) .... 90
Lost Someone (Lois, BMI) .... 49
Love Is the Sweetest Thing (Harms, ASCAP) .... 92
Majestic, The (Just-Mubon, BMI) .... 72
Midnight (Vicki, BMI) .... 80
Midnight in Moscow (Melody Trails, BMI) .... 29
Moon River (Famous, ASCAP) .... 36
Multiplication (Adaris, BMI) .... 30
My Boomerang Won't Come Back (Picadilly, BMI) .... 37
My Melancholy Baby (Shapiro-Bernstein & Vogel, ASCAP) .... 67
Nite Owl (Conrad, BMI) .... 75
Norman (Acuff-Rose, BMI) .... 4
Oliver Twist (Shelly, ASCAP) .... 76
Our Anniversary (Keel, BMI) .... 74
Peppermint Twist (Jon-Ware, BMI) .... 2
Percolator (Twist) (Meadowlark, ASCAP) .... 33
Pop-Eye (Ace, BMI) .... 89
Run to Him (Aldon, BMI) .... 22
Shadrack (Fisher, ASCAP) .... 19
She's Everything (Alan K., BMI) .... 18
She's Got You (Pamper, BMI) .... 42
Shimmy, Shimmy Walk (Star-Flite & Hut, BMI) .... 95
Smoky Places (Annie-Earl & Sun Flower, ASCAP) .... 28
Soul Twist (Dan-Kelyn, BMI) .... 100
Strange (Cedarwood, BMI) .... 97
Surfer's Stomp (Strat-E.D.M., ASCAP) .... 32
Surfin' (Drank-Guild, BMI) .... 93
Tears and Laughter (Gil, BMI) .... 86
That's My Pa (Channel, ASCAP) .... 65
To a Sleeping Beauty (Songsmiths-Remick, ASCAP) .... 35
Town Without Pity (United Artists, ASCAP) .... 23
Tuff (Jec, BMI) .... 26
Twist, The (Lois, BMI) .... 3
Twist-Her (Jec, BMI) .... 41
Twistin' Postman (Jobette, BMI) .... 48
Twistin' the Night Away (Kags, BMI) .... 38
Unchain My Heart (Tee Pee, ASCAP) .... 57
Wa'k on By (Lowery, BMI) .... 54
Walk on the Wild Side (Columbia, ASCAP) .... 81
Wanderer, The (Schwartz-Disal, ASCAP) .... 5
What's So Good About Goodbye (Jobette, BMI) .... 40
What's the Reason (Bourne, ASCAP) .... 79
What's Your Name (Hill & Range, BMI) .... 47
When I Fall in Love (Northern, ASCAP) .... 24
Where Have All the Flowers Gone (Fall River, BMI) .... 51
Yessiree (Kilt, BMI) .... 87

## BUBBLING UNDER THE HOT 100

101. SO DEEP .... Brenda Lee, Decca 31348
102. ROUGH LOVER .... Aretha Franklin, Columbia 42266
103. LOVE LETTERS .... Ketty Lester, Era 3068
104. LET'S GO .... Floyd Cramer, RCA Victor 7978
105. BIRTH OF THE BEAT .... Sandy Nelson, Imperial 5809
106. BABY DON'T LEAVE ME .... Joe Henderson, Todd 1066
107. OUR CONCERTO .... Steve Lawrence, United Artists 403
108. MOMENTS .... Jennell Hawkins, Amazon 1003
109. IMAGINATION .... Quotations, Verve 10245
110. IT'S GOOD TO HAVE YOU BACK WITH ME .. Adam Wade, Coed 565
111. MIDNIGHT IN MOSCOW .... Jan Bergens, London 10503
112. PATTI ANN .... Johnny Crawford, Del Fi 4172
113. THE BALLAD OF THUNDER ROAD .. Robert Mitchum, Capitol 3986
114. THE BATTLE .... Duane Eddy, Jamie 1209
115. QUARTER TO FOUR STOMP .... Stompers, Landa 684
116. TOWN CRIER .... Linda Scott, Congress 101
117. YOU DON'T MISS YOUR WATER .... William Bell, Stax 116
118. SUGAR BABE .... Buster Brown, Fire 507
119. THE MOON WAS YELLOW .... Frank Sinatra, Capitol 4677
120. HAPPY JOSE .... Dave Appell & Ork, Cameo 207

# BILLBOARD HOT 100

FOR WEEK ENDING FEBRUARY 24

1962

★ STAR PERFORMERS—Selections registering greatest upward progress this week.

S Indicates that 45 r.p.m. stereo single version is available.

△ Indicates that 33⅓ r.p.m. mono single version is available.

S△ Indicates that 33⅓ r.p.m. stereo single version is available.

| This Week | 1 Wk. Ago | 2 Wks. Ago | 3 Wks. Ago | Title, Artist, Label & Number | | Weeks On Chart |
|---|---|---|---|---|---|---|
| 1 | 1 | 2 | 7 | DUKE OF EARL — Gene (Duke of Earl) Chandler, Vee Jay 416 | | 7 |
| 2 | 5 | 7 | 6 | THE WANDERER — Dion, Laurie 3115 | | 12 |
| 3 | 4 | 6 | 4 | NORMAN — Sue Thompson, Hickory 1159 | | 12 |
| 4 | 3 | 3 | 3 | THE TWIST — Chubby Checker, Parkway 811 | | 33 |
| ★5 | 13 | 21 | 52 | HEY! BABY — Bruce Channel, Smash 1731 | | 5 |
| 6 | 6 | 8 | 9 | BREAK IT TO ME GENTLY — Brenda Lee, Decca 31348 | | 7 |
| 7 | 2 | 1 | 1 | PEPPERMINT TWIST — Joey Dee and the Starliters, Roulette 4401 | | 14 |
| 8 | 9 | 14 | 20 | CRYING IN THE RAIN — Everly Brothers, Warner Bros. 5250 | | 7 |
| 9 | 10 | 10 | 11 | DEAR LADY TWIST — Gary (U. S.) Bonds, LeGrand 1015 | | 11 |
| 10 | 11 | 9 | 12 | A LITTLE BITTY TEAR — Burl Ives, Decca 31330 | | 10 |
| 11 | 15 | 24 | 46 | CHIP CHIP — Gene McDaniels, Liberty 55405 | | 6 |
| 12 | 8 | 4 | 2 | CAN'T HELP FALLING IN LOVE — Elvis Presley, RCA Victor 7968 | △ | 12 |
| 13 | 14 | 13 | 18 | COTTON FIELDS — Highwaymen, United Artists 370 | | 13 |
| 14 | 12 | 11 | 8 | BABY IT'S YOU — Shirelles, Scepter 1227 | | 10 |
| 15 | 7 | 5 | 5 | I KNOW — Barbara George, AFO 302 | | 15 |
| ★16 | 29 | 47 | 79 | MIDNIGHT IN MOSCOW — Kenny Ball, Kapp 442 | | 4 |
| ★17 | 27 | 35 | 43 | LET ME IN — Sensations, Argo 5405 | | 8 |
| ★18 | 26 | 26 | 37 | TUFF — Ace Cannon, Hi 2040 | | 9 |
| ★19 | 33 | 45 | 53 | PERCOLATOR (TWIST) — Billy Joe and the Checkmates, Dore 620 | | 7 |
| 20 | 20 | 28 | 34 | I'M BLUE (The Gong-Gong Song) — Ikettes, Atco 6212 | | 7 |
| ★21 | 31 | 50 | 66 | HER ROYAL MAJESTY — James Darren, Colpix 622 | | 4 |
| 22 | 25 | 34 | 41 | CAJUN QUEEN — Jimmy Dean, Columbia 42282 | △ | 5 |
| ★23 | 46 | 66 | — | DON'T BREAK THE HEART THAT LOVES YOU — Connie Francis, MGM 13059 | | 3 |
| 24 | 28 | 25 | 33 | SMOKY PLACES — Corsairs, Tuff 3030 | | 9 |
| ★25 | 37 | 42 | 58 | MY BOOMERANG WON'T COME BACK — Charlie Drake, United Artists 398 | | 7 |
| ★26 | 47 | 72 | — | WHAT'S YOUR NAME — Don and Juan, Big Top 3079 | | 3 |
| 27 | 19 | 22 | 22 | SHADRACK — Brook Benton, Mercury 71912 | | 7 |
| 28 | 18 | 20 | 28 | SHE'S EVERYTHING — Ral Donner, Gone 5121 | | 9 |
| 29 | 35 | 40 | 47 | TO A SLEEPING BEAUTY — Jimmy Dean, Columbia 42282 | △ | 6 |
| 30 | 17 | 15 | 17 | IRRESISTIBLE YOU — Bobby Darin, Atco 6214 | | 11 |
| 31 | 32 | 41 | 48 | SURFER'S STOMP — Mar-Kets, Liberty 55401 | | 7 |
| 32 | 23 | 17 | 13 | TOWN WITHOUT PITY — Gene Pitney, Musicor 1009 | | 17 |
| 33 | 38 | 49 | 70 | TWISTIN' THE NIGHT AWAY — Sam Cooke, RCA Victor 7983 | △ | 4 |
| 34 | 34 | 37 | 40 | THE GREATEST HURT — Jackie Wilson, Brunswick 55221 | | 7 |
| 35 | 40 | 44 | 62 | WHAT'S SO GOOD ABOUT GOODBYE — Miracles, Tamla 54053 | | 7 |
| 36 | 42 | 60 | 71 | SHE'S GOT YOU — Patsy Cline, Decca 31354 | | 5 |
| 37 | 21 | 19 | 25 | LETTER FULL OF TEARS — Gladys Knight and the Pips, Fury 1054 | | 11 |
| 38 | 43 | 48 | 56 | CHATTANOOGA CHOO CHOO — Floyd Cramer, RCA Victor 7978 | △ | 6 |
| 39 | 16 | 12 | 10 | THE LION SLEEPS TONIGHT — Tokens, RCA Victor 7954 | △ | 15 |
| 40 | 45 | 51 | 59 | I'LL SEE YOU IN MY DREAMS — Pat Boone, Dot 16312 | | 5 |
| ★41 | 55 | 77 | — | DRUMS ARE MY BEAT — Sandy Nelson, Imperial 5809 | | 3 |
| 42 | 36 | 30 | 29 | MOON RIVER — Henry Mancini, RCA Victor 7916 | △ | 20 |
| 43 | 50 | 54 | 61 | AFRIKAAN BEAT — Bert Kaempfert, Decca 31350 | | 6 |
| 44 | 48 | 56 | 73 | TWISTIN' POSTMAN — Marvelettes, Tamla 54054 | | 5 |
| 45 | 51 | 64 | 72 | WHERE HAVE ALL THE FLOWERS GONE — Kingston Trio, Capitol 4671 | | 6 |
| ★46 | 64 | — | — | HEY, LET'S TWIST — Joey Dee & the Starliters, Roulette 4408 | | 2 |
| 47 | 30 | 32 | 35 | MULTIPLICATION — Bobby Darin, Atco 6214 | | 10 |
| 48 | 49 | 59 | 63 | LOST SOMEONE — James Brown and the Famous Flames, King 5573 | | 10 |
| 49 | 22 | 18 | 15 | RUN TO HIM — Bobby Vee, Liberty 55388 | | 15 |
| 50 | 53 | 68 | 84 | HE KNOWS I LOVE HIM TOO MUCH — Paris Sisters, Gregmark 10 | | 5 |
| ★51 | 65 | 75 | 80 | THAT'S MY PA — Sheb Wooley, MGM 13046 | | 8 |
| 52 | 58 | 74 | 93 | DO THE NEW CONTINENTAL — Dovells, Parkway 833 | | 5 |
| ★53 | 77 | — | — | DREAM BABY — Roy Orbison, Monument 456 | | 2 |
| 54 | 24 | 16 | 14 | WHEN I FALL IN LOVE — Lettermen, Capitol 4658 | | 14 |
| 55 | 60 | 63 | 78 | CRY TO ME — Solomon Burke, Atlantic 2131 | | 5 |
| 56 | 61 | 81 | 94 | JAMIE — Eddie Holland, Motown 1021 | | 6 |
| ★57 | 71 | 82 | 76 | LIZZIE BORDEN — Chad Mitchell Trio, Kapp 439 | | 5 |
| ★58 | 73 | — | — | COME BACK SILLY GIRL — Lettermen, Capitol 4699 | | 2 |
| 59 | 68 | 80 | — | B'WA NINA — Tokens, RCA Victor 7991 | △ | 3 |
| 60 | 44 | 27 | 24 | IF YOU GOTTA MAKE A FOOL OF SOMEBODY — James Ray, Caprice 110 | | 14 |
| 61 | 70 | 76 | 95 | ECSTASY — Ben E. King, Atco 6215 | | 4 |
| 62 | 67 | 70 | 91 | MY MELANCHOLY BABY — Marcels, Colpix 624 | | 4 |
| 63 | 74 | — | — | OUR ANNIVERSARY — Shep & the Limelites, Hull 748 | | 2 |
| ★64 | — | — | — | YOU WIN AGAIN — Fats Domino, Imperial 5816 | | 1 |
| 65 | 63 | 71 | 68 | DREAMY EYES — Johnny Tillotson, Cadence 1409 | | 12 |
| ★66 | 83 | — | — | I'VE GOT BONNIE — Bobby Rydell, Cameo 209 | | 2 |
| 67 | 78 | 84 | 96 | LET ME CALL YOU SWEETHEART — Timi Yuro, Liberty 55410 | | 4 |
| ★68 | — | — | — | SO DEEP — Brenda Lee, Decca 31348 | | 4 |
| ★69 | 89 | — | — | POP-EYE — Huey Smith & the Clowns, Ace 649 | | 2 |
| 70 | 84 | 85 | 89 | BLUE WATER LINE — Brothers Four, Columbia 42256 | △ | 6 |
| 71 | 81 | — | — | WALK ON THE WILD SIDE — Brook Benton, Mercury 71925 | | 2 |
| 72 | 82 | 88 | 82 | BANDIT OF MY DREAMS — Eddie Hodges, Cadence 1410 | | 5 |
| 73 | 86 | 86 | — | TEARS AND LAUGHTER — Dinah Washington, Mercury 71922 | | 3 |
| 74 | 87 | 96 | — | YESSIREE — Linda Scott, Congress 101 | | 3 |
| ★75 | — | — | — | BIRTH OF THE BEAT — Sandy Nelson, Imperial 5809 | | 1 |
| 76 | 80 | 89 | 90 | MIDNIGHT — Johnny Gibson, Big Top 3088 | | 4 |
| 77 | 76 | 78 | 85 | OLIVER TWIST — Rod McKuen, Spiral 1407 | | 5 |
| 78 | 85 | 92 | — | BERMUDA — Linda Scott, Canadian-American 134 | | 3 |
| 79 | 90 | — | — | LOSE HER — Bobby Rydell, Cameo 209 | | 2 |
| ★80 | — | — | — | YES INDEED — Pete Fountain, Coral 65549 | | 1 |
| ★81 | — | — | — | PLEASE DON'T ASK ABOUT BARBARA — Bobby Vee, Liberty 55419 | | 1 |
| ★82 | — | 98 | — | PICTURES IN THE FIRE — Pat Boone, Dot 16312 | | 2 |
| 83 | 88 | — | — | CRY BABY CRY — Angels, Caprice 1018 | | 2 |
| ★84 | — | — | — | LOVE LETTERS — Ketty Lester, Era 3068 | | 1 |
| ★85 | — | — | — | LOVE ME WARM AND TENDER — Paul Anka, RCA Victor 7977 | △ | 1 |
| ★86 | — | — | — | SOMETHING'S GOT A HOLD ON ME — Etta James, Argo 5409 | | 1 |
| ★87 | — | — | — | YOU BETTER MOVE ON — Arthur Alexander, Dot 16309 | | 1 |
| 88 | 95 | 95 | — | SHIMMY, SHIMMY WALK — Megatons, Checker 1005 | | 4 |
| 89 | 92 | — | 86 | LOVE IS THE SWEETEST THING — Saverio Saridis, Warner Bros. 5243 | | 4 |
| 90 | 93 | — | — | SURFIN' — Beach Boys, Candix 331 | | 2 |
| 91 | 94 | — | — | IT'S MAGIC — Platters, Mercury 71921 | | 2 |
| 92 | — | — | — | I CAN'T SAY GOODBYE — Bobby Vee, Liberty 55419 | | 1 |
| 93 | 96 | 97 | 97 | I SURRENDER DEAR — Aretha Franklin, Columbia 42266 | △ | 4 |
| 94 | — | — | — | WHEN MY LITTLE GIRL IS SMILING — Drifters, Atlantic 2134 | | 1 |
| 95 | 98 | — | — | JOEY BABY — Anita & the So & So's, RCA Victor 7974 | △ | 2 |
| 96 | — | — | — | WHITE ROSE OF ATHENS — David Carroll, Mercury 71917 | | 1 |
| 97 | — | 93 | — | AW, SHUCKS, HUSH YOUR MOUTH — Jimmy Reed, Vee Jay 425 | | 3 |
| 98 | — | — | — | THE BALLAD OF THUNDER ROAD — Robert Mitchum, Capitol 3986 | | 1 |
| 99 | — | — | — | POPEYE JOE — Ernie K-Doe, Minit 641 | | 1 |
| 100 | — | — | — | DEAR ONE — Larry Finnegan, Old Town 1113 | | 1 |

## HOT 100—A TO Z—(Publisher-Licensee)


Afrikaan Beat (Roosevelt, BMI) .... 43
Aw, Shucks, Hush Your Mouth (Conrad, BMI) .... 97
Baby It's You (Dolfi, ASCAP) .... 14
Ballad of Thunder Road, The (Leeds, ASCAP) .... 98
Bandit of My Dreams (Arch, ASCAP) .... 72
Bermuda (Suffolk, BMI) .... 78
Birth of the Beat (Travis, BMI) .... 75
Blue Water Line (January, BMI) .... 70
Break It to Me Gently (Northern, ASCAP) .... 6
B'wa Nina (Lionel, ASCAP) .... 59
Cajun Queen (Cedarwood, BMI) .... 22
Can't Help Falling in Love (Gladys, ASCAP) .... 12
Chip Chip (Trinity & Glo-Mac, BMI) .... 11
Chattanooga Choo Choo (Feist, ASCAP) .... 38
Come Back Silly Girl (Aldon, BMI) .... 58
Cotton Fields (Westside, BMI) .... 13
Cry Baby, Cry (Jersey-Central Songs, BMI) .... 83
Cry to Me (Melvin-Progressive, BMI) .... 55
Crying in the Rain (Aldon, BMI) .... 8
Dear Lady Twist (Pepe, BMI) .... 9
Dear One (Maureen, BMI) .... 100
Do the New Continental (Kalmann, ASCAP) .... 52
Don't Break the Heart That Loves You (Francon, ASCAP) .... 23
Dream Baby (Combine, BMI) .... 53
Dreamy Eyes (Southern Belle, BMI) .... 65
Drums Are My Beat (Travis, BMI) .... 41
Duke of Earl (Conrad-Karlan, BMI) .... 1
Ecstasy (Presley-Progressive-Trio, BMI) .... 61
Greatest Hurt, The (Pearl, BMI) .... 34
He Knows I Love Him Too Much (Aldon, BMI) .... 50
Her Royal Majesty (Aldon, BMI) .... 21
Hey! Baby (LeBill, BMI) .... 5
Hey, Let's Twist (Ware-Frost, BMI) .... 46
I Can't Say Goodbye (Aldon, BMI) .... 92
I Know (Saturn-At Last, BMI) .... 15
I Surrender Dear (Mills, ASCAP) .... 93
I'll See You in My Dreams (Feist, ASCAP) .... 40
I'm Blue (Progressive-Placid, BMI) .... 20
I've Got Bonnie (Aldon, BMI) .... 66
If You Gotta Make a Fool of Somebody (Good Song, BMI) .... 60
Irresistible You (Lloyd-Logan, BMI) .... 30
It's Magic (Witmark, ASCAP) .... 91
Jamie (Jobette, BMI) .... 56
Joey Baby (Tree, BMI) .... 95
Let Me Call You Sweetheart (Shapiro-Bernstein & Shawnee, ASCAP) .... 67
Let Me In (Arc-Kae Williams, BMI) .... 17
Letter Full of Tears (Betalbin, BMI) .... 37
Lion Sleeps Tonight, The (Folkways, BMI) .... 39
Little Bitty Tear, A (Pamper, BMI) .... 10
Lizzie Borden (Hill & Range, BMI) .... 57
Lose Her (Kalmann-Fajob, ASCAP) .... 79
Lost Someone (Lois, BMI) .... 48
Love Is the Sweetest Thing (Harms, ASCAP) .... 89
Love Letters (Famous, ASCAP) .... 84
Love Me Warm and Tender (Spanka, BMI) .... 85
Midnight (Vicki, BMI) .... 76
Midnight in Moscow (Melody Trails, BMI) .... 16
Moon River (Famous, ASCAP) .... 42
Multiplication (Adaris, BMI) .... 47
My Boomerang Won't Come Back (Picadilly, BMI). 25
My Melancholy Baby (Shapiro-Bernstein & Vogel, ASCAP) .... 62
Norman (Acuff-Rose, BMI) .... 3
Oliver Twist (Spiral, ASCAP) .... 77
Our Anniversary (Keel, BMI) .... 63
Peppermint Twist (Jon-Ware, BMI) .... 7
Percolator Twist (Meadowlark, ASCAP) .... 19
Pictures in the Fire (Spoone, ASCAP) .... 82
Please Don't Ask About Barbara (Aldon, BMI) .... 81
Pop-Eye (Ace, BMI) .... 69
Popeye Joe (Minit, BMI) .... 99
Run to Him (Aldon, BMI) .... 49
Shadrack (Fischer, ASCAP) .... 27
She's Everything (Alan K., BMI) .... 28
She's Got You (Pamper, BMI) .... 36
Shimmy, Shimmy Walk (Star-Flite & Hut, BMI) .... 88
Smoky Places (Annie-Earl & Sun Flower, ASCAP) .... 24
So Deep (Metric, BMI) .... 68
Something's Got a Hold on Me (Figure, BMI) .... 86
Surfer's Stomp (Strat-E.D.M., ASCAP) .... 31
Surfin' (Drank-Guild, BMI) .... 90
Tears and Laughter (Gil, BMI) .... 73
That's My Pa (Channel, ASCAP) .... 51
To a Sleeping Beauty (Songsmiths-Remick, ASCAP). 29
Town Without Pity (United Artists, ASCAP) .... 32
Tuff (Jec, BMI) .... 18
Twist, The (Lois, BMI) .... 4
Twistin' Postman (Jobette, BMI) .... 44
Twistin' the Night Away (Kags, BMI) .... 33
Walk on the Wild Side Columbia, ASCAP) .... 71
Wanderer, The (Schwartz-Disal, ASCAP) .... 2
What's So Good About Goodbye (Jobette, BMI) .... 35
What's Your Name (Hill & Range, BMI) .... 26
When I Fall in Love (Northern, ASCAP) .... 54
When My Little Girl Is Smiling (Aldon, BMI) .... 94
Where Have All the Flowers Gone (Fall River, BMI) .... 45
White Rose of Athens (Peter Schaeffers, BMI) .... 96
Yes Indeed (Embassy, BMI) .... 80
Yessiree (Kilt, BMI) .... 74
You Better Move On (Spartus-Keva, BMI) .... 87
You Win Again (Fred Rose, BMI) .... 64


## BUBBLING UNDER THE HOT 100

101. THE RAINS CAME .... Big Sambo, Eric 7003
102. PATTI ANN .... Johnny Crawford, Del Fi 4172
103. YOU DON'T MISS YOUR WATER .... William Bell, Stax 116
104. LOVER, PLEASE .... Clyde McPhatter, Mercury 71941
105. IMAGINATION .... Quotation, Verve 10245
106. NUT ROCKER .... B. Bumble and the Stingers, Rendezvous 166
107. OUR CONCERTO .... Steve Lawrence, United Artists 403
108. FOOLS HALL OF FAME .... Paul Anka, ABC-Paramount 10282
109. GROW CLOSER TOGETHER .... Impressions, ABC-Paramount 10289
110. SOUL TWIST .... King Curtis, Enjoy 1000
111. LOVE THEME FROM EL CID .... Billy Storm, Infinity 013
112. JOHNNY ANGEL .... Shelley Fabares, Colpix 621
113. CONCERTO FOR THE X-15 .... Elliot Evans, Reprise 20039
114. ANNIE GET YOUR YO YO .... Little Junior Parker, Duke 345
115. SHE CRIED .... Jay and the Americans, United Artists 415
116. ECHO IN THE NIGHT .... Bert Kaempfert, Decca 31350
117. MIDNIGHT SPECIAL .... Jimmy Smith, Blue Note 1819
118. BABY IT'S COLD OUTSIDE .. Ray Charles and Betty Carter .... ABC-Paramount 10290
119. MASHED POTATO TIME .... Dee Dee Sharp, Cameo 212
120. STRANGER ON THE SHORE .... Acker Bilk, Atco 6217

# BILLBOARD HOT 100

**FOR WEEK ENDING MARCH 3, 1962**

★ STAR PERFORMERS—Selections registering greatest upward progress this week.
S Indicates that 45 r.p.m. stereo single version is available.
△ Indicates that 33⅓ r.p.m. mono single version is available.
Ⓢ Indicates that 33⅓ r.p.m. stereo single version is available.

| This Week | Wk. Ago | 2 Wks. Ago | 3 Wks. Ago | TITLE — Artist, Label & Number | Weeks On Chart |
|---|---|---|---|---|---|
| 1 | 1 | 1 | 2 | DUKE OF EARL — Gene (Duke of Earl) Chandler, Vee Jay 416 | 8 |
| 2 | 5 | 13 | 21 | HEY! BABY — Bruce Channel, Smash 1731 | 6 |
| 3 | 2 | 5 | 7 | THE WANDERER — Dion, Laurie 3115 | 13 |
| 4 | 6 | 6 | 8 | BREAK IT TO ME GENTLY — Brenda Lee, Decca 31348 | 8 |
| 5 | 4 | 3 | 3 | THE TWIST — Chubby Checker, Parkway 811 | 34 |
| 6 | 8 | 9 | 14 | CRYING IN THE RAIN — Everly Brothers, Warner Bros. 5250 | 8 |
| 7 | 3 | 4 | 6 | NORMAN — Sue Thompson, Hickory 1159 | 13 |
| ★8 | 16 | 29 | 47 | MIDNIGHT IN MOSCOW — Kenny Ball, Kapp 442 | 5 |
| 9 | 7 | 2 | 1 | PEPPERMINT TWIST — Joey Dee and the Starliters, Roulette 4401 | 15 |
| 10 | 11 | 15 | 24 | CHIP CHIP — Gene McDaniels, Liberty 55405 | 7 |
| 11 | 9 | 10 | 10 | DEAR LADY TWIST — Gary (U.S.) Bonds, LeGrand 1015 | 12 |
| 12 | 17 | 27 | 35 | LET ME IN — Sensations, Argo 5405 | 9 |
| ★13 | 23 | 46 | 66 | DON'T BREAK THE HEART THAT LOVES YOU — Connie Francis, MGM 13059 | 4 |
| 14 | 10 | 11 | 9 | A LITTLE BITTY TEAR — Burl Ives, Decca 31330 | 11 |
| 15 | 14 | 12 | 11 | BABY IT'S YOU — Shirelles, Scepter 1227 | 11 |
| ★16 | 21 | 31 | 50 | HER ROYAL MAJESTY — James Darren, Colpix 622 | 5 |
| 17 | 19 | 33 | 45 | PERCOLATOR (TWIST) — Billy Joe and the Checkmates, Dore 620 | 8 |
| 18 | 18 | 26 | 26 | TUFF — Ace Cannon, Hi 2040 | 10 |
| 19 | 20 | 20 | 28 | I'M BLUE (The Gong-Gong Song) — Ikettes, Atco 6212 | 8 |
| ★20 | 26 | 47 | 72 | WHAT'S YOUR NAME — Don and Juan, Big Top 3079 | 4 |
| 21 | 24 | 28 | 25 | SMOKY PLACES — Corsairs, Tuff 3030 | 10 |
| 22 | 25 | 37 | 42 | MY BOOMERANG WON'T COME BACK — Charlie Drake, United Artists 398 | 8 |
| 23 | 15 | 7 | 5 | I KNOW — Barbara George, AFO 302 | 16 |
| 24 | 22 | 25 | 34 | CAJUN QUEEN — Jimmy Dean, Columbia 42282 | 6 |
| 25 | 13 | 14 | 13 | COTTON FIELDS — Highwaymen, United Artists 370 | 14 |
| 26 | 29 | 35 | 40 | TO A SLEEPING BEAUTY — Jimmy Dean, Columbia 42282 | 7 |
| 27 | 33 | 38 | 49 | TWISTIN' THE NIGHT AWAY — Sam Cooke, RCA Victor 7983 | 5 |
| 28 | 36 | 42 | 60 | SHE'S GOT YOU — Patsy Cline, Decca 31354 | 6 |
| 29 | 12 | 8 | 4 | CAN'T HELP FALLING IN LOVE — Elvis Presley, RCA Victor 7968 | 13 |
| ★30 | 53 | 77 | — | DREAM BABY — Roy Orbison, Monument 456 | 3 |
| 31 | 46 | 64 | — | HEY, LET'S TWIST — Joey Dee & the Starliters, Roulette 4408 | 4 |
| 32 | 40 | 45 | 51 | I'LL SEE YOU IN MY DREAMS — Pat Boone, Dot 16263 | 6 |
| 33 | 31 | 32 | 41 | SURFER'S STOMP — Mar-Kets, Liberty 55401 | 8 |
| ★34 | 44 | 48 | 56 | TWISTIN' POSTMAN — Marvelettes, Tamla 54054 | 6 |
| 35 | 41 | 55 | 77 | DRUMS ARE MY BEAT — Sandy Nelson, Imperial 5809 | 4 |
| 36 | 38 | 43 | 48 | CHATTANOOGA CHOO CHOO — Floyd Cramer, RCA Victor 7978 | 7 |
| 37 | 30 | 17 | 15 | IRRESISTIBLE YOU — Bobby Darin, Atco 6214 | 12 |
| 38 | 45 | 51 | 64 | WHERE HAVE ALL THE FLOWERS GONE — Kingston Trio, Capitol 4671 | 7 |
| 39 | 50 | 53 | 68 | HE KNOWS I LOVE HIM TOO MUCH — Paris Sisters, Gregmark 10 | 6 |
| 40 | 52 | 58 | 74 | DO THE NEW CONTINENTAL — Dovells, Parkway 833 | 6 |
| 41 | 58 | 73 | — | COME BACK SILLY GIRL — Lettermen, Capitol 4699 | 3 |
| 42 | 56 | 61 | 81 | JAMIE — Eddie Holland, Motown 1021 | 7 |
| 43 | 35 | 40 | 44 | WHAT'S SO GOOD ABOUT GOODBYE — Miracles, Tamla 54053 | 8 |
| ★44 | 57 | 71 | 82 | LIZZIE BORDEN — Chad Mitchell Trio, Kapp 439 | 6 |
| 45 | 66 | 83 | — | I'VE GOT BONNIE — Bobby Rydell, Cameo 209 | 3 |
| 46 | 27 | 19 | 22 | SHADRACK — Brook Benton, Mercury 71912 | 8 |
| 47 | 43 | 50 | 54 | AFRIKAAN BEAT — Bert Kaempfert, Decca 31350 | 7 |
| 48 | 32 | 23 | 17 | TOWN WITHOUT PITY — Gene Pitney, Musicor 1009 | 18 |
| 49 | 28 | 18 | 20 | SHE'S EVERYTHING — Ral Donner, Gone 5121 | 10 |
| 50 | 34 | 34 | 37 | THE GREATEST HURT — Jackie Wilson, Brunswick 55221 | 8 |
| 51 | 51 | 65 | 75 | THAT'S MY PA — Sheb Wooley, MGM 13046 | 9 |
| 52 | 55 | 60 | 63 | CRY TO ME — Solomon Burke, Atlantic 2131 | 6 |
| ★53 | 65 | 63 | 71 | DREAMY EYES — Johnny Tillotson, Cadence 1409 | 13 |
| ★54 | 64 | — | — | YOU WIN AGAIN — Fats Domino, Imperial 5816 | 2 |
| 55 | 59 | 68 | 80 | B'WA NINA — Tokens, RCA Victor 7991 | 4 |
| 56 | 61 | 70 | 76 | ECSTASY — Ben E. King, Atco 6215 | 5 |
| 57 | 81 | — | — | PLEASE DON'T ASK ABOUT BARBARA — Bobby Vee, Liberty 55419 | 2 |
| 58 | 62 | 67 | 70 | MY MELANCHOLY BABY — Marcels, Colpix 624 | 5 |
| 59 | 63 | 74 | — | OUR ANNIVERSARY — Shep & the Limelites, Hull 748 | 3 |
| ★60 | — | — | — | SLOW TWISTIN' — Chubby Checker, Parkway 835 | 1 |
| 61 | 71 | 81 | — | WALK ON THE WILD SIDE — Brook Benton, Mercury 71925 | 3 |
| 62 | 37 | 21 | 19 | LETTER FULL OF TEARS — Gladys Knight and the Pips, Fury 1054 | 12 |
| 63 | 69 | 89 | — | POP-EYE — Huey Smith & the Clowns, Ace 649 | 3 |
| ★64 | 85 | — | — | LOVE ME WARM AND TENDER — Paul Anka, RCA Victor 7977 | 2 |
| 65 | 72 | 82 | 88 | BANDIT OF MY DREAMS — Eddie Hodges, Cadence 1410 | 6 |
| 66 | 67 | 78 | 84 | LET ME CALL YOU SWEETHEART — Timi Yuro, Liberty 55410 | 5 |
| ★67 | 84 | — | — | LOVE LETTERS — Ketty Lester, Era 3068 | 2 |
| 68 | 70 | 84 | 85 | BLUE WATER LINE — Brothers Four, Columbia 42256 | 7 |
| 69 | 79 | 90 | — | LOSE HER — Bobby Rydell, Cameo 209 | 3 |
| 70 | 78 | 85 | 92 | BERMUDA — Linda Scott, Canadian-American 134 | 4 |
| 71 | 73 | 86 | 86 | TEARS AND LAUGHTER — Dinah Washington, Mercury 71922 | 4 |
| 72 | 74 | 87 | 96 | YESSIREE — Linda Scott, Congress 101 | 4 |
| 73 | 86 | — | — | SOMETHING'S GOT A HOLD ON ME — Etta James, Argo 5409 | 2 |
| 74 | 83 | 88 | — | CRY, BABY, CRY — Angels, Caprice 1018 | 3 |
| 75 | 87 | — | — | YOU BETTER MOVE ON — Arthur Alexander, Dot 16309 | 2 |
| ★76 | — | — | — | NUT ROCKER — B. Bumble & the Stingers, Rendezvous 166 | 1 |
| ★77 | — | — | — | MASHED POTATO TIME — Dee Dee Sharp, Cameo 212 | 1 |
| 78 | 80 | — | — | YES INDEED — Pete Fountain, Coral 65549 | 2 |
| 79 | — | — | — | ALVIN TWIST — Chipmunks, Liberty 55424 | 1 |
| 80 | 82 | — | 98 | PICTURES IN THE FIRE — Pat Boone, Dot 16312 | 3 |
| ★81 | — | — | — | JOHNNY ANGEL — Shelley Fabares, Colpix 621 | 1 |
| 82 | 77 | 76 | 78 | OLIVER TWIST — Rod McKuen, Spiral 1407 | 6 |
| 83 | 90 | 93 | — | SURFIN' — Beach Boys, Candix 331 | 3 |
| ★84 | — | — | — | YOUNG WORLD — Rick Nelson, Imperial 5805 | 1 |
| 85 | 94 | — | — | WHEN MY LITTLE GIRL IS SMILING — Drifters, Atlantic 2134 | 2 |
| 86 | 89 | 92 | — | LOVE IS THE SWEETEST THING — Saverio Saridis, Warner Bros. 5243 | 5 |
| 87 | 93 | 96 | 97 | I SURRENDER DEAR — Aretha Franklin, Columbia 42266 | 5 |
| ★88 | — | 91 | 91 | DO YOU KNOW HOW TO TWIST — Hank Ballard, King 5593 | 3 |
| 89 | — | — | — | LOVER, PLEASE — Clyde McPhatter, Mercury 71941 | 1 |
| 90 | — | — | — | SHE CAN'T FIND HER KEYS — Paul Peterson, Colpix 620 | 1 |
| ★91 | 95 | 98 | — | JOEY BABY — Anita & the So & So's, RCA Victor 7974 | 3 |
| 92 | 100 | — | — | DEAR ONE — Larry Finnegan, Old Town 1113 | 2 |
| 93 | — | — | — | IDA JANE — Fats Domino, Imperial 5816 | 1 |
| 94 | — | — | — | BABY, IT'S COLD OUTSIDE — Ray Charles & Betty Carter, ABC-Paramount 10298 | 1 |
| 95 | — | — | — | PATTI ANN — Johnny Crawford, Del Fi 4172 | 1 |
| 96 | 97 | — | 93 | AW, SHUCKS, HUSH YOUR MOUTH — Jimmy Reed, Vee Jay 425 | 4 |
| 97 | 98 | — | — | THE BALLAD OF THUNDER ROAD — Robert Mitchum, Capitol 3986 | 2 |
| 98 | — | — | — | MIDNIGHT SPECIAL — Jimmy Smith, Blue Note 1819 | 1 |
| 99 | — | — | — | LOLLIPOPS AND ROSES — Jack Jones, Kapp 435 | 1 |
| 100 | — | — | — | QUARTER TO FOUR STOMP — Stompers, Landa 684 | 1 |

## BUBBLING UNDER THE HOT 100

101. IT WASN'T GOD WHO MADE HONKY TONK ANGELS ... Kitty Kallen, Columbia 42247
102. YOU DON'T MISS YOUR WATER ... William Bell, Stax 116
103. THE RAINS CAME ... Big Sambo, Eric 7003
104. GROW CLOSER TOGETHER ... Impressions, ABC-Paramount 10289
105. TELL ME ... Dick and Deedee, Liberty 55412
106. ANNIE GET YOUR YO-YO ... Little Junior Parker, Duke 345
107. TEARS BROKE OUT ON ME ... Eddy Arnold, RCA Victor 7984
108. SWEET THURSDAY ... Johnny Mathis, Columbia 42261
109. A GIRL HAS TO KNOW ... G-Clefs, Terrace 7503
110. CONCERTO ON THE X-15 ... Elliot Evans, Reprise 20039
111. I CAN'T SAY GOODBYE ... Bobby Vee, Liberty 55419
112. OUR CONCERTO ... Steve Lawrence, United Artists 403
113. CLOWN SHOES ... Johnny Burnette, Liberty 55416
114. WHITE ROSE OF ATHENS ... David Carroll, Mercury 71917
115. SUMMERTIME ... Rick Nelson, Imperial 5805
116. WHAT AM I SUPPOSED TO DO ... Ann-Margret, RCA Victor 7986
117. IT'S MAGIC ... Platters, Mercury 71921
118. TEEN QUEEN OF THE WEEK ... Freddy Cannon, Swan 4906
119. MEMORIES OF MARIA ... Jerry Byrd, Monument 449
120. STEP BY STEP, LITTLE BY LITTLE ... Anita Bryant, Columbia 42257

# BILLBOARD HOT 100

FOR WEEK ENDING MARCH 10

1962

★ STAR PERFORMERS—Selections registering greatest upward progress this week.

[S] Indicates that 45 r.p.m. stereo single version is available.

△ Indicates that 33⅓ r.p.m. mono single version is available.

[S]△ Indicates that 33⅓ r.p.m. stereo single version is available.

| This Week | 1 Wk. Ago | 2 Wks. Ago | 3 Wks. Ago | Title | Artist, Label & Number | Weeks On Chart |
|---|---|---|---|---|---|---|
| 1 | 2 | 5 | 13 | HEY! BABY | Bruce Channel, Smash 1731 | 7 |
| 2 | 1 | 1 | 1 | DUKE OF EARL | Gene (Duke of Earl) Chandler, Vee Jay 416 | 9 |
| ★3 | 8 | 16 | 29 | MIDNIGHT IN MOSCOW | Kenny Ball, Kapp 442 | 6 |
| ★4 | 13 | 23 | 46 | DON'T BREAK THE HEART THAT LOVES YOU | Connie Francis, MGM 13059 | 5 |
| ★5 | 12 | 17 | 27 | LET ME IN | Sensations, Argo 5405 | 10 |
| 6 | 6 | 8 | 9 | CRYING IN THE RAIN | Everly Brothers, Warner Bros. 5250 | 9 |
| 7 | 4 | 6 | 6 | BREAK IT TO ME GENTLY | Brenda Lee, Decca 31348 | 9 |
| ★8 | 16 | 21 | 31 | HER ROYAL MAJESTY | James Darren, Colpix 622 | 6 |
| 9 | 3 | 2 | 5 | THE WANDERER | Dion, Laurie 3115 | 14 |
| ★10 | 20 | 26 | 47 | WHAT'S YOUR NAME | Don and Juan, Big Top 3079 | 5 |
| 11 | 11 | 9 | 10 | DEAR LADY TWIST | Gary (U. S.) Bonds, LeGrand 1015 | 13 |
| ★12 | 17 | 19 | 33 | PERCOLATOR (TWIST) | Billy Joe and the Checkmates, Dore 620 | 9 |
| 13 | 5 | 4 | 3 | THE TWIST | Chubby Checker, Parkway 811 | 35 |
| 14 | 10 | 11 | 15 | CHIP CHIP | Gene McDaniels, Liberty 55405 | 8 |
| 15 | 7 | 3 | 4 | NORMAN | Sue Thompson, Hickory 1159 | 14 |
| ★16 | 21 | 24 | 28 | SMOKY PLACES | Corsairs, Tuff 3030 | 11 |
| 17 | 18 | 18 | 26 | TUFF | Ace Cannon, Hi 2040 | 11 |
| 18 | 9 | 7 | 2 | PEPPERMINT TWIST | Joey Dee and the Starliters, Roulette 4401 | 16 |
| 19 | 15 | 14 | 12 | BABY IT'S YOU | Shirelles, Scepter 1227 | 12 |
| ★20 | 28 | 36 | 42 | SHE'S GOT YOU | Patsy Cline, Decca 31354 | 7 |
| 21 | 27 | 33 | 38 | TWISTIN' THE NIGHT AWAY △ | Sam Cooke, RCA Victor 7983 | 6 |
| 22 | 31 | 46 | 64 | HEY, LET'S TWIST | Joey Dee & the Starliters, Roulette 4408 | 4 |
| 23 | 30 | 53 | 77 | DREAM BABY | Roy Orbison, Monument 456 | 4 |
| 24 | 22 | 25 | 37 | MY BOOMERANG WON'T COME BACK | Charlie Drake, United Artists 398 | 9 |
| 25 | 19 | 20 | 20 | I'M BLUE (The Gong-Gong Song) | Ikettes, Atco 6212 | 9 |
| 26 | 14 | 10 | 11 | A LITTLE BITTY TEAR | Burl Ives, Decca 31330 | 12 |
| 27 | 25 | 13 | 14 | COTTON FIELDS | Highwaymen, United Artists 370 | 15 |
| 28 | 26 | 29 | 35 | TO A SLEEPING BEAUTY △ | Jimmy Dean, Columbia 42282 | 8 |
| 29 | 38 | 45 | 51 | WHERE HAVE ALL THE FLOWERS GONE | Kingston Trio, Capitol 4671 | 8 |
| 30 | 24 | 22 | 25 | CAJUN QUEEN △ | Jimmy Dean, Columbia 42282 | 7 |
| ★31 | 41 | 58 | 73 | COME BACK SILLY GIRL | Lettermen, Capitol 4699 | 4 |
| ★32 | 42 | 56 | 61 | JAMIE | Eddie Holland, Motown 1021 | 8 |
| 33 | 35 | 41 | 55 | DRUMS ARE MY BEAT | Sandy Nelson, Imperial 5809 | 5 |
| 34 | 39 | 50 | 53 | HE KNOWS I LOVE HIM TOO MUCH | Paris Sisters, Gregmark 10 | 7 |
| ★35 | 45 | 66 | 83 | I'VE GOT BONNIE | Bobby Rydell, Cameo 209 | 4 |
| 36 | 60 | — | — | SLOW TWISTIN' | Chubby Checker, Parkway 835 | 2 |
| 37 | 40 | 52 | 58 | DO THE NEW CONTINENTAL | Dovells, Parkway 833 | 7 |
| 38 | 32 | 40 | 45 | I'LL SEE YOU IN MY DREAMS | Pat Boone, Dot 16312 | 7 |
| ★39 | 67 | 84 | — | LOVE LETTERS | Ketty Lester, Era 3068 | 3 |
| 40 | 29 | 12 | 8 | CAN'T HELP FALLING IN LOVE △ | Elvis Presley, RCA Victor 7968 | 14 |
| 41 | 23 | 15 | 7 | I KNOW | Barbara George, AFO 302 | 17 |
| 42 | 47 | 43 | 50 | AFRIKAAN BEAT | Bert Kaempfert, Decca 31350 | 8 |
| 43 | 34 | 44 | 48 | TWISTIN' POSTMAN | Marvelettes, Tamla 54054 | 7 |
| ★44 | 54 | 64 | — | YOU WIN AGAIN | Fats Domino, Imperial 5816 | 3 |
| ★45 | 57 | 81 | — | PLEASE DON'T ASK ABOUT BARBARA | Bobby Vee, Liberty 55419 | 3 |
| 46 | 52 | 55 | 60 | CRY TO ME | Solomon Burke, Atlantic 2131 | 7 |
| ★47 | 64 | 85 | — | LOVE ME WARM AND TENDER △ | Paul Anka, RCA Victor 7977 | 3 |
| 48 | 36 | 38 | 43 | CHATTANOOGA CHOO CHOO △ | Floyd Cramer, RCA Victor 7978 | 8 |
| ★49 | 77 | — | — | MASHED POTATO TIME | Dee Dee Sharp, Cameo 212 | 2 |
| ★50 | 81 | — | — | JOHNNY ANGEL | Shelley Fabares, Colpix 621 | 2 |
| 51 | 44 | 57 | 71 | LIZZIE BORDEN | Chad Mitchell Trio, Kapp 439 | 7 |
| 52 | 48 | 32 | 23 | TOWN WITHOUT PITY | Gene Pitney, Musicor 1009 | 19 |
| 53 | 43 | 35 | 40 | WHAT'S SO GOOD ABOUT GOODBYE | Miracles, Tamla 54053 | 9 |
| 54 | 61 | 71 | 81 | WALK ON THE WILD SIDE | Brook Benton, Mercury 71925 | 4 |
| 55 | 51 | 51 | 65 | THAT'S MY PA | Sheb Wooley, MGM 13046 | 10 |
| 56 | 63 | 69 | 89 | POP-EYE | Huey Smith & the Clowns, Ace 649 | 4 |
| 57 | 50 | 34 | 34 | THE GREATEST HURT | Jackie Wilson, Brunswick 55221 | 9 |
| ★58 | 84 | — | — | YOUNG WORLD | Rick Nelson, Imperial 5805 | 2 |
| 59 | 37 | 30 | 17 | IRRESISTIBLE YOU | Bobby Darin, Atco 6214 | 13 |
| ★60 | 75 | 87 | — | YOU BETTER MOVE ON | Arthur Alexander, Dot 16309 | 3 |
| 61 | 74 | 83 | 88 | CRY, BABY, CRY | Angels, Caprice 1018 | 4 |
| 62 | 73 | 86 | — | SOMETHING'S GOT A HOLD ON ME | Etta James, Argo 5409 | 3 |
| 63 | 56 | 61 | 70 | ECSTASY | Ben E. King, Atco 6215 | 6 |
| 64 | 53 | 65 | 63 | DREAMY EYES | Johnny Tillotson, Cadence 1409 | 14 |
| 65 | 72 | 74 | 87 | YESSIREE | Linda Scott, Congress 101 | 5 |
| 66 | 55 | 59 | 68 | B'WA NINA △ | Tokens, RCA Victor 7991 | 5 |
| 67 | 46 | 27 | 19 | SHADRACK | Brook Benton, Mercury 71912 | 9 |
| 68 | 59 | 63 | 74 | OUR ANNIVERSARY | Shep & the Limelites, Hull 748 | 4 |
| ★69 | 85 | 94 | — | WHEN MY LITTLE GIRL IS SMILING | Drifters, Atlantic 2134 | 3 |
| 70 | 76 | — | — | NUT ROCKER | B. Bumble & the Stingers, Rendezvous 166 | 2 |
| 71 | 79 | — | — | ALVIN TWIST | Chipmunks, Liberty 55424 | 2 |
| 72 | 78 | 80 | — | YES INDEED | Pete Fountain, Coral 65549 | 3 |
| 73 | 33 | 31 | 32 | SURFER'S STOMP | Mar-Kets, Liberty 55401 | 9 |
| ★74 | 89 | — | — | LOVER, PLEASE | Clyde McPhatter, Mercury 71941 | 2 |
| ★75 | — | — | — | IF A WOMAN ANSWERS | Leroy Van Dyke, Mercury 71926 | 1 |
| 76 | 49 | 28 | 18 | SHE'S EVERYTHING | Ral Donner, Gone 5121 | 11 |
| 77 | 80 | 82 | — | PICTURES IN THE FIRE | Pat Boone, Dot 16312 | 4 |
| 78 | 68 | 70 | 84 | BLUE WATER LINE △ | Brothers Four, Columbia 42256 | 8 |
| 79 | 69 | 79 | 90 | LOSE HER | Bobby Rydell, Cameo 209 | 4 |
| ★80 | 95 | — | — | PATTI ANN | Johnny Crawford, Del Fi 4172 | 2 |
| 81 | 92 | 100 | — | DEAR ONE | Larry Finnegan, Old Town 1113 | 3 |
| 82 | 71 | 73 | 86 | TEARS AND LAUGHTER | Dinah Washington, Mercury 71922 | 5 |
| 83 | 83 | 90 | 93 | SURFIN' | Beach Boys, Candix 331 | 4 |
| 84 | 70 | 78 | 85 | BERMUDA | Linda Scott, Canadian-American 134 | 5 |
| 85 | 90 | — | — | SHE CAN'T FIND HER KEYS | Paul Peterson, Colpix 620 | 2 |
| ★86 | — | — | — | ANNIE GET YOUR YO-YO | Little Junior Parker, Duke 345 | 1 |
| 87 | 88 | — | 91 | DO YOU KNOW HOW TO TWIST | Hank Ballard, King 5593 | 4 |
| 88 | 99 | — | — | LOLLIPOPS AND ROSES | Jack Jones, Kapp 435 | 2 |
| ★89 | — | — | — | ROLY POLY | Joey Dee & the Starliters, Roulette 4408 | 1 |
| 90 | 93 | — | — | IDA JANE | Fats Domino, Imperial 5816 | 2 |
| 91 | 94 | — | — | BABY, IT'S COLD OUTSIDE | Ray Charles & Betty Carter, ABC-Paramount 10298 | 2 |
| 92 | 98 | — | — | MIDNIGHT SPECIAL | Jimmy Smith, Blue Note 1819 | 2 |
| 93 | 96 | 97 | — | AW SHUCKS, HUSH YOUR MOUTH | Jimmy Reed, Vee Jay 425 | 5 |
| 94 | 97 | 98 | — | THE BALLAD OF THUNDER ROAD | Robert Mitchum, Capitol 3986 | 3 |
| 95 | — | — | — | SUMMERTIME | Rick Nelson, Imperial 5805 | 1 |
| 96 | — | — | — | GINNY COME LATELY | Brian Hyland, ABC-Paramount 10294 | 1 |
| 97 | — | — | — | DUCHESS OF EARL | Pearlettes, Vee Jay 435 | 1 |
| 98 | — | — | — | A GIRL HAS TO KNOW | G-Clefs, Terrace 7503 | 1 |
| 99 | — | — | — | AMOR | Roger Williams, Kapp 447 | 1 |
| 100 | — | — | — | THE RAINS CAME | Big Sambo, Eric 7003 | 1 |

## HOT 100—A TO Z—*(Publisher-Licensee)*

Afrikaan Beat (Roosevelt, BMI) ... 42
Alvin Twist (Monarch, ASCAP) ... 71
Amor (Peer Int'l, BMI) ... 99
Annie Get Your Yo-Yo (Don, BMI) ... 86
Aw Shucks, Hush Your Mouth (Conrad, BMI) ... 93
Baby, It's Cold Outside (Frank, ASCAP) ... 91
Baby It's You (Dolfi, ASCAP) ... 19
Ballad of Thunder Road, The (Leeds, ASCAP) ... 94
Bermuda (Suffolk, BMI) ... 84
Blue Water Line (January, BMI) ... 78
Break It to Me Gently (Northern, ASCAP) ... 7
B'wa Nina (Lionel, ASCAP) ... 66
Cajun Queen (Cedarwood, BMI) ... 30
Can't Help Falling in Love (Gladys, ASCAP) ... 40
Chip Chip (Trinity & Glo-Mac, BMI) ... 14
Chattanooga Choo-Choo (Feist, ASCAP) ... 48
Come Back Silly Girl (Aldon, BMI) ... 31
Cotton Fields (Westside, BMI) ... 27
Cry, Baby, Cry (Jersey, BMI) ... 61
Cry to Me (Melvin-Progressive, BMI) ... 46
Crying in the Rain (Aldon, BMI) ... 6
Dear Lady Twist (Pepe, BMI) ... 11
Dear One (Maureen, BMI) ... 81
Do the New Continental (Kalmann, ASCAP) ... 37
Do You Know How to Twist (Lois, BMI) ... 87
Don't Break the Heart That Loves You (Francon, ASCAP) ... 4
Dream Baby (Combine, BMI) ... 23
Dreamy Eyes (Southern Belle, BMI) ... 64
Drums Are My Beat (Travis, BMI) ... 33
Duchess of Earl (Conrad, BMI) ... 97
Duke of Earl (Conrad-Karlan, BMI) ... 2
Ecstasy (Presley-Progressive-Trio, BMI) ... 63
Ginny Come Lately (Pogo, ASCAP) ... 96
Girl Has to Know, A (Aldon, BMI) ... 98
Greatest Hurt, The (Pearl, BMI) ... 57
He Knows I Love Him Too Much (Aldon, BMI) ... 34
Her Royal Majesty (Aldon, BMI) ... 8
Hey! Baby (LeBill, BMI) ... 1
Hey, Let's Twist (Ware-Frost, BMI) ... 22
I Know (Saturn-At Last, BMI) ... 41
I'll See You in My Dreams (Feist, ASCAP) ... 38
I'm Blue (Progressive-Placid, BMI) ... 25
I've Got Bonnie (Aldon, BMI) ... 35
Ida Jane (Travis, BMI) ... 90
If a Woman Answers (Aldon, BMI) ... 75
Irresistible You (Lloyd-Logan, BMI) ... 59
Jamie (Jobette, BMI) ... 32
Johnny Angel (Post, ASCAP) ... 50
Let Me In (Arc-Kae Williams, BMI) ... 5
Little Bitty Tear, A (Pamper, BMI) ... 26
Lizzie Borden (Hill & Range, BMI) ... 51
Lollipops and Roses (Garland, ASCAP) ... 88
Lose Her (Kalmann-Fajob, ASCAP) ... 79
Love Letters (Famous, ASCAP) ... 39
Love Me Warm and Tender (Spanka, BMI) ... 47
Lover, Please (Lyn-Lou, BMI) ... 74
Mashed Potato Time (Rice-Mill, BMI) ... 49
Midnight in Moscow (Melody Trails, BMI) ... 3
Midnight Special (Folkways, BMI) ... 92
My Boomerang Won't Come Back (Picadilly, BMI). 24
Norman (Acuff-Rose, BMI) ... 15
Nut Rocker (Fowley, BMI) ... 70
Our Anniversary (Keel, BMI) ... 68
Patti Ann (Maraville, BMI) ... 80
Peppermint Twist (Jon-Ware, BMI) ... 18
Percolator (Twist) (Meadowlark, ASCAP) ... 12
Pictures in the Fire (Spoone, ASCAP) ... 77
Please Don't Ask About Barbara (Aldon, BMI).. 45
Pop-Eye (Ace, BMI) ... 56
Rains Came, The (Crazy Cajun-Corette, BMI) ...100
Roly Poly (Ware-Frost, BMI) ... 89
Shadrack (Fischer, ASCAP) ... 67
She Can't Find Her Keys (Arch, ASCAP) ... 85
She's Everything (Alan K., BMI) ... 76
She's Got You (Pamper, BMI) ... 20
Slow Twistin' (Woodcrest, BMI) ... 36
Smoky Places (Annie-Earl & Sun Flower, ASCAP).16
Something's Got a Hold on Me (Figure, BMI) ... 62
Summertime (Gershwin, ASCAP) ... 95
Surfer's Stomp (Strat-E.D.M., ASCAP) ... 73
Surfin' (Drank-Guild, BMI) ... 83
Tears and Laughter (Gil, BMI) ... 82
That's My Pa (Channel, ASCAP) ... 55
To a Sleeping Beauty (Songsmiths-Remick, ASCAP). 28
Town Without Pity (United Artists, ASCAP) ... 52
Tuff (Jec, BMI) ... 17
Twist, The (Lois, BMI) ... 13
Twistin' Postman (Jobette, BMI) ... 43
Twistin' the Night Away (Kags, BMI) ... 21
Walk on the Wild Side (Columbia, ASCAP) ... 54
Wanderer, The (Schwartz-Disal, ASCAP) ... 9
What's So Good About Goodbye (Jobette, BMI) .. 53
What's Your Name (Hill & Range, BMI) ... 10
When My Little Girl Is Smiling (Aldon, BMI) .. 69
Where Have All the Flowers Gone (Fall River, BMI) ... 29
Yes Indeed (Embassy, BMI) ... 72
Yessiree (Kilt, BMI) ... 65
You Better Move On (Spartus-Keva, BMI) ... 60
You Win Again (Fred Rose, BMI) ... 44
Young World (Four Star, BMI) ... 58

## BUBBLING UNDER THE HOT 100

101. I CAN'T SAY GOODBYE ... Bobby Vee, Liberty 55419
102. SOUL TWIST ... King Curtis, Enjoy 1000
103. TELL ME ... Dick and Deedee, Liberty 55412
104. YOU DON'T MISS YOUR WATER ... William Bell, Stax 116
105. TEEN QUEEN OF THE WEEK ... Freddy Cannon, Swan 4096
106. GROW CLOSER TOGETHER ... Impressions, ABC-Paramount 10289
107. IT WASN'T GOD WHO MADE HONKY TONK ANGELS ... Kitty Kallen, Columbia 42247
108. JOEY BABY ... Anita and the So and So's, RCA Victor 7974
109. MEMORIES OF MARIA ... Jerry Byrd, Monument 449
110. TEARS BROKE OUT ON ME ... Eddy Arnold, RCA Victor 7984
111. WHITE ROSE OF ATHENS ... David Carroll, Mercury 71917
112. SWEET THURSDAY ... Johnny Mathis, Columbia 42261
113. WHAT AM I SUPPOSED TO DO ... Ann-Margret, RCA Victor 7986
114. STEP BY STEP, LITTLE BY LITTLE ... Anita Bryant, Columbia 42257
115. IT'S MAGIC ... Platters, Mercury 71921
116. LOVE THEME FROM EL CID ... Billy Storm, Infinity 013
117. MASHED POTATOES ... Steve Alaimo, Checker 1006
118. CHAPEL BY THE SEA ... Billy Vaughn, Dot 16329
119. QUARTER TO FOUR STOMP ... Stompers, Landa 684
120. I WISH THAT WE WERE MARRIED ... Ronnie and the Hi-Lites, Joy 260

# BILLBOARD HOT 100
**For Week Ending March 17, 1962**

| This Week | Wk Ago | 2 Wks Ago | 3 Wks Ago | Title / Artist, Label & Number | Weeks On Chart |
|---|---|---|---|---|---|
| 1 | 1 | 2 | 5 | HEY! BABY — Bruce Channel, Smash 1731 | 8 |
| 2 | 3 | 8 | 16 | MIDNIGHT IN MOSCOW — Kenny Ball, Kapp 442 | 7 |
| 3 | 4 | 13 | 23 | DON'T BREAK THE HEART THAT LOVES YOU — Connie Francis, MGM 13059 | 6 |
| 4 | 5 | 12 | 17 | LET ME IN — Sensations, Argo 5405 | 11 |
| 5 | 2 | 1 | 1 | DUKE OF EARL — Gene (Duke of Earl) Chandler, Vee Jay 416 | 10 |
| 6 | 8 | 16 | 21 | HER ROYAL MAJESTY — James Darren, Colpix 622 | 7 |
| 7 | 10 | 20 | 26 | WHAT'S YOUR NAME — Don and Juan, Big Top 3079 | 6 |
| 8 | 6 | 6 | 8 | CRYING IN THE RAIN — Everly Brothers, Warner Bros. 5250 | 10 |
| 9 | 7 | 4 | 6 | BREAK IT TO ME GENTLY — Brenda Lee, Decca 31348 | 10 |
| 10 | 12 | 17 | 19 | PERCOLATOR (TWIST) — Billy Joe and the Checkmates, Dore 620 | 10 |
| 11 | 9 | 3 | 2 | THE WANDERER — Dion, Laurie 3115 | 15 |
| 12 | 16 | 21 | 24 | SMOKY PLACES — Corsairs, Tuff 3030 | 12 |
| 13 | 21 | 27 | 33 | TWISTIN' THE NIGHT AWAY — Sam Cooke, RCA Victor 7983 | 7 |
| 14 | 36 | 60 | — | SLOW TWISTIN' — Chubby Checker, Parkway 835 | 3 |
| 15 | 11 | 11 | 9 | DEAR LADY TWIST — Gary (U.S.) Bonds, LeGrand 1015 | 14 |
| 16 | 20 | 28 | 36 | SHE'S GOT YOU — Patsy Cline, Decca 31354 | 8 |
| 17 | 17 | 18 | 18 | TUFF — Ace Cannon, Hi 2040 | 12 |
| 18 | 23 | 30 | 53 | DREAM BABY — Roy Orbison, Monument 456 | 5 |
| 19 | 14 | 10 | 11 | CHIP CHIP — Gene McDaniels, Liberty 55405 | 9 |
| 20 | 22 | 31 | 46 | HEY, LET'S TWIST — Joey Dee & the Starliters, Roulette 4408 | 5 |
| 21 | 24 | 22 | 25 | MY BOOMERANG WON'T COME BACK — Charlie Drake, United Artists 398 | 10 |
| 22 | 35 | 45 | 66 | I'VE GOT BONNIE — Bobby Rydell, Cameo 209 | 5 |
| 23 | 39 | 67 | 84 | LOVE LETTERS — Ketty Lester, Era 3068 | 4 |
| 24 | 13 | 5 | 4 | THE TWIST — Chubby Checker, Parkway 811 | 36 |
| 25 | 29 | 38 | 45 | WHERE HAVE ALL THE FLOWERS GONE — Kingston Trio, Capitol 4671 | 9 |
| 26 | 15 | 7 | 3 | NORMAN — Sue Thompson, Hickory 1159 | 15 |
| 27 | 31 | 41 | 58 | COME BACK SILLY GIRL — Lettermen, Capitol 4699 | 6 |
| 28 | 50 | 81 | — | JOHNNY ANGEL — Shelley Fabares, Colpix 621 | 3 |
| 29 | 33 | 35 | 41 | DRUMS ARE MY BEAT — Sandy Nelson, Imperial 5809 | 6 |
| 30 | 27 | 25 | 13 | COTTON FIELDS — Highwaymen, United Artists 370 | 16 |
| 31 | 32 | 42 | 56 | JAMIE — Eddie Holland, Motown 1021 | 9 |
| 32 | 49 | 77 | — | MASHED POTATO TIME — Dee Dee Sharp, Cameo 212 | 3 |
| 33 | 25 | 19 | 20 | I'M BLUE (The Gong-Gong Song) — Ikettes, Atco 6212 | 10 |
| 34 | 34 | 39 | 50 | HE KNOWS I LOVE HIM TOO MUCH — Paris Sisters, Gregmark 6 | 8 |
| 35 | 45 | 57 | 81 | PLEASE DON'T ASK ABOUT BARBARA — Bobby Vee, Liberty 55419 | 4 |
| 36 | 47 | 64 | 85 | LOVE ME WARM AND TENDER — Paul Anka, RCA Victor 7977 | 4 |
| 37 | 58 | 84 | — | YOUNG WORLD — Rick Nelson, Imperial 5805 | 3 |
| 38 | 26 | 14 | 10 | A LITTLE BITTY TEAR — Burl Ives, Decca 31330 | 13 |
| 39 | 44 | 54 | 64 | YOU WIN AGAIN — Fats Domino, Imperial 5816 | 4 |
| 40 | 19 | 15 | 14 | BABY IT'S YOU — Shirelles, Scepter 1227 | 13 |
| 41 | 18 | 9 | 7 | PEPPERMINT TWIST — Joey Dee and the Starliters, Roulette 4401 | 17 |
| 42 | 37 | 40 | 52 | DO THE NEW CONTINENTAL — Dovells, Parkway 833 | 8 |
| 43 | 30 | 24 | 22 | CAJUN QUEEN — Jimmy Dean, Columbia 42282 | 8 |
| 44 | 46 | 52 | 55 | CRY TO ME — Solomon Burke, Atlantic 2131 | 8 |
| 45 | 38 | 32 | 40 | I'LL SEE YOU IN MY DREAMS — Pat Boone, Dot 16312 | 8 |
| 46 | 43 | 34 | 44 | TWISTIN' POSTMAN — Marvelettes, Tamla 54054 | 8 |
| 47 | 54 | 61 | 71 | WALK ON THE WILD SIDE — Brook Benton, Mercury 71925 | 5 |
| 48 | 41 | 23 | 15 | I KNOW — Barbara George, AFO 302 | 18 |
| 49 | 60 | 75 | 87 | YOU BETTER MOVE ON — Arthur Alexander, Dot 16309 | 4 |
| 50 | 42 | 47 | 43 | AFRIKAAN BEAT — Bert Kaempfert, Decca 31350 | 9 |
| 51 | — | — | — | GOOD LUCK CHARM — Elvis Presley, RCA Victor 7992 | 1 |
| 52 | 69 | 85 | 94 | WHEN MY LITTLE GIRL IS SMILING — Drifters, Atlantic 2134 | 4 |
| 53 | 56 | 63 | 69 | POP-EYE — Huey Smith and the Clowns, Ace 649 | 5 |
| 54 | 28 | 26 | 29 | TO A SLEEPING BEAUTY — Jimmy Dean, Columbia 42282 | 9 |
| 55 | 62 | 73 | 86 | SOMETHING'S GOT A HOLD ON ME — Etta James, Argo 5409 | 4 |
| 56 | 74 | 89 | — | LOVER, PLEASE — Clyde McPhatter, Mercury 71941 | 3 |
| 57 | 61 | 74 | 83 | CRY, BABY, CRY — Angels, Caprice 1018 | 5 |
| 58 | 51 | 44 | 57 | LIZZIE BORDEN — Chad Mitchell Trio, Kapp 439 | 8 |
| 59 | 75 | — | — | IF A WOMAN ANSWERS — Leroy Van Dyke, Mercury 71926 | 2 |
| 60 | 65 | 72 | 74 | YESSIREE — Linda Scott, Congress 101 | 6 |
| 61 | 85 | 90 | — | SHE CAN'T FIND HER KEYS — Paul Peterson, Colpix 620 | 3 |
| 62 | 70 | 76 | — | NUT ROCKER — B. Bumble & the Stingers, Rendezvous 166 | 3 |
| 63 | 71 | 79 | — | ALVIN TWIST — Chipmunks, Liberty 55424 | 3 |
| 64 | 55 | 51 | 51 | THAT'S MY PA — Sheb Wooley, MGM 13046 | 11 |
| 65 | 80 | 95 | — | PATTI ANN — Johnny Crawford, Del Fi 4172 | 3 |
| 66 | 68 | 59 | 63 | OUR ANNIVERSARY — Shep & the Limelites, Hull 748 | 5 |
| 67 | 53 | 43 | 35 | WHAT'S SO GOOD ABOUT GOODBYE — Miracles, Tamla 54053 | 10 |
| 68 | 81 | 92 | 100 | DEAR ONE — Larry Finnegan, Old Town 1113 | 4 |
| 69 | 72 | 78 | 80 | YES INDEED — Pete Fountain, Coral 65549 | 4 |
| 70 | — | — | — | ANYTHING THAT'S PART OF YOU — Elvis Presley, RCA Victor 7992 | 1 |
| 71 | 88 | 99 | — | LOLLIPOPS AND ROSES — Jack Jones, Kapp 435 | 3 |
| 72 | — | — | — | TELL ME — Dick & Deedee, Liberty 55412 | 1 |
| 73 | 96 | — | — | GINNY COME LATELY — Brian Hyland, ABC-Paramount 10294 | 2 |
| 74 | 89 | — | — | ROLY POLY — Joey Dee & the Starliters, Roulette 4408 | 2 |
| 75 | — | — | — | SHE CRIED — Jay & the Americans, United Artists 415 | 1 |
| 76 | 86 | — | — | ANNIE GET YOUR YO-YO — Little Junior Parker, Duke 345 | 2 |
| 77 | 83 | 83 | 90 | SURFIN' — Beach Boys, Candix 331 | 5 |
| 78 | — | — | — | SOUL TWIST — King Curtis, Enjoy 1000 | 2 |
| 79 | — | — | — | LA PALOMA TWIST — Chubby Checker, Parkway 835 | 1 |
| 80 | — | — | — | STRANGER ON THE SHORE — Acker Bilk, Atco 6217 | 1 |
| 81 | — | — | — | MASHED POTATOES — Steve Alaimo, Checker 1006 | 1 |
| 82 | 92 | 98 | — | MIDNIGHT SPECIAL — Jimmy Smith, Blue Note 1819 | 3 |
| 83 | — | — | — | CINDERELLA — Jack Ross, Dot 16333 | 1 |
| 84 | 84 | 70 | 78 | BERMUDA — Linda Scott, Canadian-American 134 | 6 |
| 85 | — | — | — | THE JAM — Bobby Gregg, Cotton 1003 | 1 |
| 86 | 94 | 97 | 98 | THE BALLAD OF THUNDER ROAD — Robert Mitchum, Capitol 3986 | 4 |
| 87 | 98 | — | — | A GIRL HAS TO KNOW — G-Clefs, Terrace 7503 | 2 |
| 88 | — | — | 96 | WHITE ROSE OF ATHENS — David Carroll, Mercury 71917 | 2 |
| 89 | 95 | — | — | SUMMERTIME — Rick Nelson, Imperial 5805 | 2 |
| 90 | — | — | — | MEMORIES OF MARIA — Jerry Byrd, Monument 449 | 1 |
| 91 | — | — | — | TWO OF A KIND — Sue Thompson, Hickory 1166 | 1 |
| 92 | — | — | — | TEEN QUEEN OF THE WEEK — Freddy Cannon, Swan 4096 | 2 |
| 93 | 99 | — | — | AMOR — Roger Williams, Kapp 447 | 2 |
| 94 | — | — | — | CHAPEL BY THE SEA — Billy Vaughn, Dot 16329 | 1 |
| 95 | — | — | — | JOHNNY JINGO — Hayley Mills, Vista 395 | 1 |
| 96 | 97 | — | — | DUCHESS OF EARL — Pearlettes, Vee Jay 435 | 2 |
| 97 | 100 | — | — | THE RAINS CAME — Big Sambo, Eric 7003 | 2 |
| 98 | — | — | — | SMILE — Ferrante & Teicher, United Artists 431 | 1 |
| 99 | — | — | — | THE MOON WAS YELLOW — Frank Sinatra, Capitol 4677 | 1 |
| 100 | — | — | — | SWEET THURSDAY — Johnny Mathis, Columbia 42261 | 1 |

## BUBBLING UNDER THE HOT 100

101. I CAN'T SAY GOODBYE — Bobby Vee, Liberty 55419
102. TEARS BROKE OUT ON ME — Eddy Arnold, RCA Victor 7984
103. IT WASN'T GOD WHO MADE HONKY TONK ANGELS — Kitty Kallen, Columbia 42247
104. YOU DON'T MISS YOUR WATER — William Bell, Stax 116
105. IT'S MAGIC — Platters, Mercury 71921
106. STEP BY STEP, LITTLE BY LITTLE — Anita Bryant, Columbia 42257
107. LOVE THEME FROM EL CID — Billy Storm, Infinity 013
108. UPTOWN — Crystals, Philles 102
109. QUARTER TO FOUR STOMP — Stompers, Landa 684
110. THOU SHALT NOT STEAL — John D. Loudermilk, RCA Victor 7993
111. WHAT AM I SUPPOSED TO DO — Ann-Margret, RCA Victor 7986
112. JOEY BABY — Anita and the So and So's, RCA Victor 7974
113. I WON'T BE THERE — Del Shannon, Big Top 3098
114. MOMENTS — Jennell Hawkins, Amazon 1003
115. NUT ROCKER — Jack B. Nimble and the Quicks, Del-Rio 2302
116. SHOUT! SHOUT! — Ernie Maresca, Seville 117
117. GINNY IN THE MIRROR — Del Shannon, Big Top 3098
118. HERE IT COMES AGAIN — Chantels, Carlton 569
119. I WISH WE WERE MARRIED — Ronnie and the Hi-Lites, Joy 260
120. THE ONE WHO REALLY LOVES YOU — Mary Wells, Motown 1024

# BILLBOARD HOT 100
**FOR WEEK ENDING MARCH 24, 1962**

| This Week | 1 Wk. Ago | 2 Wks. Ago | 3 Wks. Ago | Title, Artist, Label & Number | Weeks On Chart |
|---|---|---|---|---|---|
| 1 | 1 | 1 | 2 | HEY! BABY — Bruce Channel, Smash 1731 | 9 |
| 2 | 3 | 4 | 13 | DON'T BREAK THE HEART THAT LOVES YOU — Connie Francis, MGM 13059 | 7 |
| 3 | 2 | 3 | 8 | MIDNIGHT IN MOSCOW — Kenny Ball, Kapp 442 | 8 |
| 4 | 4 | 5 | 12 | LET ME IN — Sensations, Argo 5405 | 12 |
| 5 | 5 | 2 | 1 | DUKE OF EARL — Gene (Duke of Earl) Chandler, Vee Jay 416 | 11 |
| 6 | 18 | 23 | 30 | DREAM BABY — Roy Orbison, Monument 456 | 6 |
| 7 | 14 | 36 | 60 | SLOW TWISTIN' — Chubby Checker, Parkway 835 | 4 |
| 8 | 7 | 10 | 20 | WHAT'S YOUR NAME — Don and Juan, Big Top 3079 | 7 |
| 9 | 13 | 21 | 27 | TWISTIN' THE NIGHT AWAY — Sam Cooke, RCA Victor 7983 | 8 |
| 10 | 6 | 8 | 16 | HER ROYAL MAJESTY — James Darren, Colpix 622 | 8 |
| 11 | 28 | 50 | 81 | JOHNNY ANGEL — Shelley Fabares, Colpix 621 | 4 |
| 12 | 23 | 39 | 67 | LOVE LETTERS — Ketty Lester, Era 3068 | 5 |
| 13 | 8 | 6 | 6 | CRYING IN THE RAIN — Everly Brothers, Warner Bros. 5250 | 11 |
| 14 | 51 | — | — | GOOD LUCK CHARM — Elvis Presley, RCA Victor 7992 | 2 |
| 15 | 16 | 20 | 28 | SHE'S GOT YOU — Patsy Cline, Decca 31354 | 9 |
| 16 | 37 | 58 | 84 | YOUNG WORLD — Rick Nelson, Imperial 5805 | 4 |
| 17 | 10 | 12 | 17 | PERCOLATOR (TWIST) — Billy Joe and the Checkmates, Dore 620 | 11 |
| 18 | 9 | 7 | 4 | BREAK IT TO ME GENTLY — Brenda Lee, Decca 31348 | 11 |
| 19 | 11 | 9 | 3 | THE WANDERER — Dion, Laurie 3115 | 16 |
| 20 | 12 | 16 | 21 | SMOKY PLACES — Corsairs, Tuff 3030 | 13 |
| 21 | 17 | 17 | 18 | TUFF — Ace Cannon, Hi 2040 | 13 |
| 22 | 35 | 45 | 57 | PLEASE DON'T ASK ABOUT BARBARA — Bobby Vee, Liberty 55419 | 5 |
| 23 | 36 | 47 | 64 | LOVE ME WARM AND TENDER — Paul Anka, RCA Victor 7977 | 5 |
| 24 | 27 | 31 | 41 | COME BACK SILLY GIRL — Lettermen, Capitol 4699 | 6 |
| 25 | 25 | 29 | 38 | WHERE HAVE ALL THE FLOWERS GONE — Kingston Trio, Capitol 4671 | 10 |
| 26 | 32 | 49 | 77 | MASHED POTATO TIME — Dee Dee Sharp, Cameo 212 | 4 |
| 27 | 15 | 11 | 11 | DEAR LADY TWIST — Gary (U.S.) Bonds, LeGrand 1015 | 15 |
| 28 | 22 | 35 | 45 | I'VE GOT BONNIE — Bobby Rydell, Cameo 209 | 6 |
| 29 | 19 | 14 | 10 | CHIP CHIP — Gene McDaniels, Liberty 55405 | 10 |
| 30 | 31 | 32 | 42 | JAMIE — Eddie Holland, Motown 1021 | 10 |
| 31 | 21 | 24 | 22 | MY BOOMERANG WON'T COME BACK — Charlie Drake, United Artists 398 | 11 |
| 32 | 24 | 13 | 5 | THE TWIST — Chubby Checker, Parkway 811 | 37 |
| 33 | 39 | 44 | 54 | YOU WIN AGAIN — Fats Domino, Imperial 5816 | 5 |
| 34 | 29 | 33 | 35 | DRUMS ARE MY BEAT — Sandy Nelson, Imperial 5809 | 7 |
| 35 | 56 | 74 | 89 | LOVER, PLEASE — Clyde McPhatter, Mercury 71941 | 4 |
| 36 | 30 | 27 | 25 | COTTON FIELDS — Highwaymen, United Artists 370 | 17 |
| 37 | 33 | 25 | 19 | I'M BLUE (The Gong-Gong Song) — Ikettes, Atco 6212 | 11 |
| 38 | 26 | 15 | 7 | NORMAN — Sue Thompson, Hickory 1159 | 16 |
| 39 | 52 | 69 | 85 | WHEN MY LITTLE GIRL IS SMILING — Drifters, Atlantic 2134 | 5 |
| 40 | 20 | 22 | 31 | HEY, LET'S TWIST — Joey Dee and the Starliters, Roulette 4408 | 9 |
| 41 | 34 | 34 | 39 | HE KNOWS I LOVE HIM TOO MUCH — Paris Sisters, Gregmark 10 | 9 |
| 42 | 49 | 60 | 75 | YOU BETTER MOVE ON — Arthur Alexander, Dot 16309 | 6 |
| 43 | 47 | 54 | 61 | WALK ON THE WILD SIDE — Brook Benton, Mercury 71925 | 6 |
| 44 | 55 | 62 | 73 | SOMETHING'S GOT A HOLD ON ME — Etta James, Argo 5409 | 5 |
| 45 | 59 | 75 | — | IF A WOMAN ANSWERS — Leroy Van Dyke, Mercury 71926 | 3 |
| 46 | 40 | 19 | 15 | BABY IT'S YOU — Shirelles, Scepter 1227 | 14 |
| 47 | 44 | 46 | 52 | CRY TO ME — Solomon Burke, Atlantic 2131 | 9 |
| 48 | 62 | 70 | 76 | NUT ROCKER — B. Bumble & the Stingers, Rendezvous 166 | 4 |
| 49 | 61 | 85 | 90 | SHE CAN'T FIND HER KEYS — Paul Peterson, Colpix 620 | 4 |
| 50 | 68 | 81 | 92 | DEAR ONE — Larry Finnegan, Old Town 1113 | 5 |
| 51 | 63 | 71 | 79 | ALVIN TWIST — Chipmunks, Liberty 55424 | 4 |
| 52 | 57 | 61 | 74 | CRY, BABY, CRY — Angels, Caprice 1018 | 6 |
| 53 | 53 | 56 | 63 | POP-EYE — Huey Smith and the Clowns, Ace 649 | 6 |
| 54 | 38 | 26 | 14 | A LITTLE BITTY TEAR — Burl Ives, Decca 31330 | 14 |
| 55 | 41 | 18 | 9 | PEPPERMINT TWIST — Joey Dee and the Starliters, Roulette 4401 | 18 |
| 56 | 42 | 37 | 40 | DO THE NEW CONTINENTAL — Dovells, Parkway 833 | 9 |
| 57 | 46 | 43 | 34 | TWISTIN' POSTMAN — Marvelettes, Tamla 54054 | 9 |
| 58 | 70 | — | — | ANYTHING THAT'S PART OF YOU — Elvis Presley, RCA Victor 7992 | 2 |
| 59 | 78 | — | — | SOUL TWIST — King Curtis, Enjoy 1000 | 3 |
| 60 | 73 | 96 | — | GINNY COME LATELY — Brian Hyland, ABC-Paramount 10294 | 3 |
| 61 | 65 | 80 | 95 | PATTI ANN — Johnny Crawford, Del Fi 4172 | 4 |
| 62 | 83 | — | — | CINDERELLA — Jack Ross, Dot 16333 | 2 |
| 63 | — | — | — | SOLDIER BOY — Shirelles, Scepter 1228 | 1 |
| 64 | 75 | — | — | SHE CRIED — Jay & the Americans, United Artists 415 | 2 |
| 65 | 48 | 41 | 23 | I KNOW — Barbara George, AFO 302 | 19 |
| 66 | 72 | — | — | TELL ME — Dick & Deedee, Liberty 55412 | 2 |
| 67 | 50 | 42 | 47 | AFRIKAAN BEAT — Bert Kaempfert, Decca 31350 | 10 |
| 68 | — | — | — | SHOUT — Joey Dee & the Starliters, Roulette 4416 | 1 |
| 69 | 80 | — | — | STRANGER ON THE SHORE — Acker Bilk, Atco 6217 | 2 |
| 70 | 71 | 88 | 99 | LOLLIPOPS AND ROSES — Jack Jones, Kapp 435 | 4 |
| 71 | 66 | 68 | 59 | OUR ANNIVERSARY — Shep & the Limelites, Hull 748 | 6 |
| 72 | 79 | — | — | LA PALOMA TWIST — Chubby Checker, Parkway 835 | 2 |
| 73 | 85 | — | — | THE JAM — Bobby Gregg, Cotton 1003 | 2 |
| 74 | 76 | 86 | — | ANNIE GET YOUR YO-YO — Little Junior Parker, Duke 345 | 3 |
| 75 | 77 | 83 | 83 | SURFIN' — Beach Boys, Candix 331 | 6 |
| 76 | 69 | 72 | 78 | YES INDEED — Pete Fountain, Coral 65549 | 5 |
| 77 | 60 | 65 | 72 | YESSIREE — Linda Scott, Congress 101 | 7 |
| 78 | 74 | 89 | — | ROLY POLY — Joey Dee & the Starliters, Roulette 4408 | 3 |
| 79 | 45 | 38 | 32 | I'LL SEE YOU IN MY DREAMS — Pat Boone, Dot 16312 | 9 |
| 80 | 82 | 92 | 98 | MIDNIGHT SPECIAL — Jimmy Smith, Blue Note 1819 | 4 |
| 81 | 95 | — | — | JOHNNY JINGO — Hayley Mills, Vista 395 | 2 |
| 82 | 91 | — | — | TWO OF A KIND — Sue Thompson, Hickory 1166 | 2 |
| 83 | 86 | 94 | 97 | THE BALLAD OF THUNDER ROAD — Robert Mitchum, Capitol 3986 | 5 |
| 84 | 87 | 98 | — | A GIRL HAS TO KNOW — G-Clefs, Terrace 7503 | 3 |
| 85 | — | — | — | MOMENTS — Jennell Hawkins, Amason 1003 | 1 |
| 86 | 88 | — | — | WHITE ROSE OF ATHENS — David Carroll, Mercury 71917 | 3 |
| 87 | 90 | — | — | MEMORIES OF MARIA — Jerry Byrd, Monument 449 | 2 |
| 88 | 93 | 99 | — | AMOR — Roger Williams, Kapp 447 | 3 |
| 89 | 94 | — | — | CHAPEL BY THE SEA — Billy Vaughn, Dot 16329 | 2 |
| 90 | — | — | — | TRA LA LA LA LA — Ike & Tina Turner, Sue 757 | 1 |
| 91 | — | — | — | WHAT AM I SUPPOSED TO DO — Ann-Margret, RCA Victor 7986 | 1 |
| 92 | 97 | 100 | — | THE RAINS CAME — Big Sam, Eric 7003 | 3 |
| 93 | — | — | — | THE ONE WHO REALLY LOVES YOU — Mary Wells, Motown 1024 | 1 |
| 94 | — | — | — | SHOUT — Isley Brothers, RCA Victor 7588 | 1 |
| 95 | 98 | — | — | SMILE — Ferrante & Teicher, United Artists 431 | 2 |
| 96 | — | — | — | GUITAR BOOGIE SHUFFLE TWIST — Virtues, Sure 1733 | 1 |
| 97 | — | — | — | (WHAT A SAD WAY) TO LOVE SOMEONE — Ral Donner, Gone 5125 | 1 |
| 98 | — | — | — | STARDUST — Frank Sinatra, Reprise 20059 | 1 |
| 99 | — | — | — | THE WONDERFUL WORLD OF THE YOUNG — Andy Williams, Columbia 42265 | 1 |
| 100 | — | — | — | YOU ARE MINE — Frankie Avalon, Chancellor 1107 | 1 |

## BUBBLING UNDER THE HOT 100

101. YOU DON'T MISS YOUR WATER ... William Bell, Stax 116
102. SWEET THURSDAY ... Johnny Mathis, Columbia 42261
103. TEARS AND LAUGHTER ... Dinah Washington, Mercury 71922
104. I FOUND A LOVE ... Falcons, LuPine 1003
105. QUARTER TO FOUR STOMP ... Stompers, Landa 684
106. LOVE THEME FROM EL CID ... Billy Storm, Infinity 013
107. UPTOWN ... Crystals, Philles 102
108. HONKY-TONK MAN ... Johnny Horton, Columbia 42302
109. DUCHESS OF EARL ... Pearlettes, Vee Jay 435
110. IT WASN'T GOD WHO MADE HONKY TONK ANGELS ... Kitty Kallen, Columbia 42247
111. TEARS BROKE OUT ON ME ... Eddy Arnold, RCA Victor 7984
112. SUGAR BLUES ... Don Costa, Columbia 42307
113. THOU SHALT NOT STEAL ... John D. Loudermilk, RCA Victor 7993
114. COLINDA ... Rod Bernard, Hall-Way 1902
115. SHOUT! SHOUT! (Knock Yourself Out) ... Ernie Maresca, Seville 117
116. WHAT'D I SAY ... Bobby Storm, AFO 304
117. YOU TALK ABOUT LOVE ... Barbara George, AFO 304
118. TWISTIN' MATILDA ... Jimmy Soul, SPQR 3300
119. ALONG CAME LINDA ... Tommy Boyce, RCA Victor 7975
120. I WON'T BE THERE ... Del Shannon, Big Top 3098

# BILLBOARD HOT 100

FOR WEEK ENDING MARCH 31

1962

★ STAR PERFORMERS—Selections registering greatest upward progress this week.

[S] Indicates that 45 r.p.m. stereo single version is available.

△ Indicates that 33⅓ r.p.m. mono single version is available.

[S in triangle] Indicates that 33⅓ r.p.m. stereo single version is available.

| This Week | 1 Wk. Ago | 2 Wks. Ago | 3 Wks. Ago | TITLE Artist, Label & Number | | Weeks On Chart |
|---|---|---|---|---|---|---|
| 1 | 2 | 3 | 4 | DON'T BREAK THE HEART THAT LOVES YOU — Connie Francis, MGM 13059 | | 8 |
| 2 | 1 | 1 | 1 | HEY! BABY — Bruce Channel, Smash 1731 | | 10 |
| ★3 | 11 | 28 | 50 | JOHNNY ANGEL — Shelley Fabares, Colpix 621 | | 5 |
| 4 | 6 | 18 | 23 | DREAM BABY — Roy Orbison, Monument 456 | | 7 |
| 5 | 3 | 2 | 3 | MIDNIGHT IN MOSCOW — Kenny Ball, Kapp 442 | | 9 |
| 6 | 7 | 14 | 36 | SLOW TWISTIN' — Chubby Checker, Parkway 835 | | 5 |
| 7 | 8 | 7 | 10 | WHAT'S YOUR NAME — Don and Juan, Big Top 3079 | | 8 |
| 8 | 4 | 4 | 5 | LET ME IN — Sensations, Argo 5405 | | 13 |
| ★9 | 14 | 51 | — | GOOD LUCK CHARM — Elvis Presley, RCA Victor 7992 | △ | 3 |
| 10 | 9 | 13 | 21 | TWISTIN' THE NIGHT AWAY — Sam Cooke, RCA Victor 7983 | △ | 9 |
| 11 | 12 | 23 | 39 | LOVE LETTERS — Ketty Lester, Era 3068 | | 6 |
| 12 | 16 | 37 | 58 | YOUNG WORLD — Rick Nelson, Imperial 5805 | | 5 |
| 13 | 5 | 5 | 2 | DUKE OF EARL — Gene (Duke of Earl) Chandler, Vee Jay 416 | | 12 |
| 14 | 15 | 16 | 20 | SHE'S GOT YOU — Patsy Cline, Decca 31354 | | 10 |
| ★15 | 26 | 32 | 49 | MASHED POTATO TIME — Dee Dee Sharp, Cameo 212 | | 5 |
| ★16 | 23 | 36 | 47 | LOVE ME WARM AND TENDER — Paul Anka, RCA Victor 7977 | △ | 6 |
| ★17 | 24 | 27 | 31 | COME BACK SILLY GIRL — Lettermen, Capitol 4699 | | 7 |
| 18 | 10 | 6 | 8 | HER ROYAL MAJESTY — James Darren, Colpix 622 | | 9 |
| 19 | 22 | 35 | 45 | PLEASE DON'T ASK ABOUT BARBARA — Bobby Vee, Liberty 55419 | | 6 |
| ★20 | 35 | 56 | 74 | LOVER, PLEASE — Clyde McPhatter, Mercury 71941 | | 5 |
| 21 | 28 | 22 | 35 | I'VE GOT BONNIE — Bobby Rydell, Cameo 209 | | 7 |
| 22 | 25 | 25 | 29 | WHERE HAVE ALL THE FLOWERS GONE — Kingston Trio, Capitol 4671 | | 11 |
| ★23 | 33 | 39 | 44 | YOU WIN AGAIN — Fats Domino, Imperial 5816 | | 6 |
| 24 | 13 | 8 | 6 | CRYING IN THE RAIN — Everly Brothers, Warner Bros. 5250 | | 12 |
| 25 | 19 | 11 | 9 | THE WANDERER — Dion, Laurie 3115 | | 17 |
| 26 | 18 | 9 | 7 | BREAK IT TO ME GENTLY — Brenda Lee, Decca 31348 | | 12 |
| 27 | 21 | 17 | 17 | TUFF — Ace Cannon, Hi 2040 | | 14 |
| 28 | 20 | 12 | 16 | SMOKY PLACES — Corsairs, Tuff 3030 | | 14 |
| 29 | 17 | 10 | 12 | PERCOLATOR (TWIST) — Billy Joe and the Checkmates, Dore 620 | | 12 |
| ★30 | 48 | 62 | 70 | NUT ROCKER — B. Bumble & the Stingers, Rendezvous 166 | | 5 |
| ★31 | 42 | 49 | 60 | YOU BETTER MOVE ON — Arthur Alexander, Dot 16309 | | 6 |
| ★32 | 50 | 68 | 81 | DEAR ONE — Larry Finnegan, Old Town 1113 | | 6 |
| 33 | 30 | 31 | 32 | JAMIE — Eddie Holland, Motown 1021 | | 11 |
| ★34 | 63 | — | — | SOLDIER BOY — Shirelles, Scepter 1228 | | 2 |
| 35 | 39 | 52 | 69 | WHEN MY LITTLE GIRL IS SMILING — Drifters, Atlantic 2134 | | 6 |
| ★36 | 68 | — | — | SHOUT — Joey Dee & the Starliters, Roulette 4416 | | 2 |
| 37 | 45 | 59 | 75 | IF A WOMAN ANSWERS — Leroy Van Dyke, Mercury 71926 | | 4 |
| ★38 | 49 | 61 | 85 | SHE CAN'T FIND HER KEYS — Paul Peterson, Colpix 620 | | 5 |
| 39 | 44 | 55 | 62 | SOMETHING'S GOT A HOLD ON ME — Etta James, Argo 5409 | | 6 |
| 40 | 51 | 63 | 71 | ALVIN TWIST — Chipmunks, Liberty 55424 | | 5 |
| ★41 | 59 | 78 | — | SOUL TWIST — King Curtis, Enjoy 1000 | | 4 |
| ★42 | 52 | 57 | 61 | CRY, BABY, CRY — Angels, Caprice 112 | | 7 |
| ★43 | 69 | 80 | — | STRANGER ON THE SHORE — Acker Bilk, Atco 6217 | | 3 |
| 44 | 32 | 24 | 13 | THE TWIST — Chubby Checker, Parkway 811 | | 38 |
| 45 | 37 | 33 | 25 | I'M BLUE (The Gong-Gong Song) — Ikettes, Atco 6212 | | 12 |
| ★46 | 62 | 83 | — | CINDERELLA — Jack Ross, Dot 16333 | | 3 |
| ★47 | 61 | 65 | 80 | PATTI ANN — Johnny Crawford, Del Fi 4172 | | 5 |
| ★48 | 58 | 70 | — | ANYTHING THAT'S PART OF YOU — Elvis Presley, RCA Victor 7992 | △ | 3 |
| 49 | 27 | 15 | 11 | DEAR LADY TWIST — Gary (U. S.) Bonds, LeGrand 1015 | | 16 |
| 50 | 60 | 73 | 96 | GINNY COME LATELY — Brian Hyland, ABC-Paramount 10294 | | 4 |
| 51 | 53 | 53 | 56 | POP-EYE — Huey Smith and the Clowns, Ace 649 | | 7 |
| ★52 | 81 | 95 | — | JOHNNY JINGO — Hayley Mills, Vista 395 | | 3 |
| ★53 | 64 | 75 | — | SHE CRIED — Jay & the Americans, United Artists 415 | | 3 |
| 54 | 47 | 44 | 46 | CRY TO ME — Solomon Burke, Atlantic 2131 | | 10 |
| 55 | 36 | 30 | 27 | COTTON FIELDS — Highwaymen, United Artists 370 | | 18 |
| ★56 | 73 | 85 | — | THE JAM — Bobby Gregg and His Friends, Cotton 100 | | 3 |
| 57 | 31 | 21 | 24 | MY BOOMERANG WON'T COME BACK — Charlie Drake, United Artists 398 | | 12 |
| 58 | 66 | 72 | — | TELL ME — Dick & Deedee, Liberty 55412 | | 3 |
| 59 | 29 | 19 | 14 | CHIP CHIP — Gene McDaniels, Liberty 55405 | | 11 |
| ★60 | 74 | 76 | 86 | ANNIE GET YOUR YO-YO — Little Junior Parker, Duke 34 | | 4 |
| 61 | 43 | 47 | 54 | WALK ON THE WILD SIDE — Brook Benton, Mercury 7192 | | 7 |
| 62 | 41 | 34 | 34 | HE KNOWS I LOVE HIM TOO MUCH — Paris Sisters, Gregmark 1 | | 10 |
| 63 | 56 | 42 | 37 | DO THE NEW CONTINENTAL — Dovells, Parkway 83 | | 10 |
| ★64 | — | — | — | AT THE CLUB — Ray Charles and His Ork, ABC-Paramount 103 | | 1 |
| ★65 | — | — | — | YOU TALK ABOUT LOVE — Barbara George, AFO 304 | | 1 |
| ★66 | 85 | — | — | MOMENTS — Jennell Hawkins, Amazon 1003 | | 2 |
| ★67 | 82 | 91 | — | TWO OF A KIND — Sue Thompson, Hickory 1166 | | 3 |
| ★68 | — | — | — | TWIST, TWIST SENORA — Gary (U. S.) Bonds, LeGrand 1018 | | 1 |
| 69 | 80 | 82 | 92 | MIDNIGHT SPECIAL — Jimmy Smith, Blue Note 1819 | | 5 |
| ★70 | — | — | — | WHAT'D I SAY — Bobby Darin, Atco 6221 | | 1 |
| ★71 | 93 | — | — | THE ONE WHO REALLY LOVES YOU — Mary Wells, Motown 1024 | | 2 |
| ★72 | 90 | — | — | TRA LA LA LA LA — Ike & Tina Turner, Sue 757 | | 2 |
| 73 | 71 | 66 | 68 | OUR ANNIVERSARY — Shep & the Limelites, Hull 748 | | 7 |
| 74 | 76 | 69 | 72 | YES INDEED — Pete Fountain, Coral 65549 | | 6 |
| 75 | 70 | 71 | 88 | LOLLIPOPS AND ROSES — Jack Jones, Kapp 435 | | 5 |
| 76 | 87 | 90 | — | MEMORIES OF MARIA — Jerry Byrd, Monument 449 | | 3 |
| ★77 | — | — | — | WHO WILL THE NEXT FOOL BE — Bobby Bland, Duke 347 | | 1 |
| 78 | 89 | 94 | — | CHAPEL BY THE SEA — Billy Vaughn, Dot 16329 | | 3 |
| 79 | 83 | 86 | 94 | THE BALLAD OF THUNDER ROAD — Robert Mitchum, Capitol 3986 | | 6 |
| ★80 | — | — | — | UPTOWN — Crystals, Philles 102 | | 1 |
| 81 | 84 | 87 | 98 | A GIRL HAS TO KNOW — G-Clefs, Terrace 7503 | | 4 |
| ★82 | — | — | — | I WISH THAT WE WERE MARRIED — Ronnie and the Hi-Lites, Joy 260 | | 1 |
| ★83 | — | — | — | SHOUT! SHOUT! (Knock Yourself Out) — Ernie Maresca, Seville 117 | | 1 |
| 84 | 86 | 88 | — | WHITE ROSE OF ATHENS — David Carroll, Mercury 71917 | | 4 |
| 85 | 91 | — | — | WHAT AM I SUPPOSED TO DO — Ann-Margret, RCA Victor 7986 | △ | 2 |
| ★86 | — | — | — | AIN'T THAT LOVING YOU — Bobby Bland, Duke 338 | | 1 |
| ★87 | — | — | — | I WILL — Vic Dana, Dolton 51 | | 1 |
| ★88 | — | — | — | NITE OWL — Dukays, Vee Jay 430 | | 1 |
| 89 | 92 | 97 | 100 | THE RAINS CAME — Big Sam, Eric 7003 | | 4 |
| ★90 | — | — | — | P. T. 109 — Jimmy Dean, Columbia 42338 | △ | 1 |
| 91 | — | — | — | CATERINA — Perry Como, RCA Victor 8004 | | 1 |
| 92 | 97 | — | — | (WHAT A SAD WAY) TO LOVE SOMEONE — Ral Donner, Gone 5125 | | 2 |
| 93 | 100 | — | — | YOU ARE MINE — Frankie Avalon, Chancellor 1107 | | 2 |
| 94 | — | — | — | POP-EYE STROLL — Mar-Keys, Stax 121 | | 1 |
| 95 | — | — | — | PLAY THE THING — Marlowe Morris Quintet, Columbia 42218 | △ | 1 |
| 96 | — | — | — | HONKY-TONK MAN — Johnny Horton, Columbia 42302 | △ | 1 |
| 97 | — | — | — | TWISTIN' MATILDA — Jimmy Soul, SPQR 3300 | | 1 |
| 98 | — | — | — | I FOUND A LOVE — Falcons, LuPine 1003 | | 1 |
| 99 | — | — | — | THE BIG DRAFT — Four Preps, Capitol 4716 | | 1 |
| 100 | — | — | — | KING OF CLOWNS — Neil Sedaka, RCA Victor 8007 | △ | 1 |

## HOT 100—A TO Z—(Publisher-Licensee)


Ain't That Loving You (Lion, BMI) .... 86
Alvin Twist (Monarch, ASCAP) .... 40
Annie Get Your Yo-Yo (Do, BMI) .... 60
Anything That's Part of You (Gladys, ASCAP) .... 48
At the Club (Tangerine, BMI) .... 64
Ballad of Thunder Road, The (Leeds, ASCAP) .... 79
Big Draft, The (Lar-Bell, BMI) .... 99
Break It to Me Gently (Northern, ASCAP) .... 26
Caterina (Roncom, ASCAP) .... 91
Chip Chip (Trinity & Gio-Mac, BMI) .... 59
Chapel by the Sea (Sun-Vine, BMI) .... 78
Cinderella (Vin-Sun, ASCAP) .... 46
Come Back Silly Girl (Aldon, BMI) .... 17
Cotton Fields (Westside, BMI) .... 55
Cry, Baby, Cry (Jersey, BMI) .... 42
Cry to Me (Melvin-Progressive, BMI) .... 54
Crying in the Rain (Aldon, BMI) .... 24
Dear Lady Twist (Pepe, BMI) .... 49
Dear One (Maureen, BMI) .... 32
Do the New Continental (Kalmann, ASCAP) .... 63
Don't Break the Heart That Loves You (Francon, ASCAP) .... 1
Dream Baby (Combine, BMI) .... 4
Duke of Earl (Conrad-Karlan, BMI) .... 13
Ginny Come Lately (Pogo, ASCAP) .... 50
Girl Has to Know, A (Aldon, BMI) .... 81
Good Luck Charm (Gladys, ASCAP) .... 9
He Knows I Love Him Too Much (Aldon, BMI) .... 62
Her Royal Majesty (Aldon, BMI) .... 18
Hey! Baby (LeBill, BMI) .... 2
Honky-Tonk Man (Cedarwood, BMI) .... 96
I Found a Love (LuPine-Progressive-Alibri, BMI) .... 98
I Will (Camarillo, BMI) .... 87
I Wish That We Were Married (Joy, ASCAP) .... 82
I'm Blue (Progressive-Placid, BMI) .... 45
I've Got Bonnie (Aldon, BMI) .... 21
If a Woman Aswers (Aldon, BMI) .... 37
Jam, The (Cheltenham, BMI) .... 56
Jamie (Jobette, BMI) .... 33
Johnny Angel (Post, ASCAP) .... 3
Johnny Jingo (Dickson, ASCAP) .... 52
King of Clowns (Aldon, BMI) .... 100
Let Me In (Arc-Kae Williams, BMI) .... 8
Lollipops and Roses (Garland, ASCAP) .... 75
Love Letters (Famous, ASCAP) .... 11
Love Me Warm and Tender (Spanka, BMI) .... 16
Lover, Please (Lyn-Lou, BMI) .... 20
Mashed Potato Time (Rice-Mill, BMI) .... 15
Memories of Maria (Acuff-Rose, BMI) .... 76
Midnight in Moscow (Melody Trails, BMI) .... 5
Midnight Special (Edmy, BMI) .... 69
Moments (Titanic, BMI) .... 66
My Boomerang Won't Come Back (Picadilly, BMI) .... 57
Nite Owl (Conrad, BMI) .... 88
Nut Rocker (Fowley, BMI) .... 30
One Who Really Loves You, The (Jobette, BMI) .... 71
Our Anniversary (Keel, BMI) .... 73
P.T. 109 (Cedarwood, BMI) .... 90
Patti Ann (Maraville, BMI) .... 47
Percolator (Twist) (Meadowlark, ASCAP) .... 29
Play the Thing (Hollis, BMI) .... 95
Please Don't Ask About Barbara (Aldon, BMI) .... 19
Pop-Eye (Ace, BMI) .... 51
Pop-Eye Stroll (East-Bais, BMI) .... 94
Rains Came, The (Crazy Cajun-Corette, BMI) .... 89
She Can't Find Her Keys (Arch, ASCAP) .... 38
She Cried (Trio, BMI) .... 53
She's Got You (Pamper, BMI) .... 14
Shout (Wemar-Nom, BMI) .... 36
Shout! Shout! (Knock Yourself Out) (Broadway, ASCAP) .... 83
Slow Twistin' (Woodcrest, BMI) .... 83
Smoky Places (Annie-Earl & Sun Flower, ASCAP) .... 28
Soldier Boy (Ludix, BMI) .... 34
Something's Got a Hold on Me (Figure, BMI) .... 39
Soul Twist (Dan-Kelyn, BMI) .... 41
Stranger on the Shore (Mellin, BMI) .... 43
Tell Me (Odin, ASCAP) .... 58
Tra La La La La (Saturn, BMI) .... 72
Tuff (Jec, BMI) .... 27
Twist, The (Lois, BMI) .... 44
Twist, Twist Senora (Rockmasters, BMI) .... 68
Twistin' Matilda (Pepe, BMI) .... 97
Twistin' the Night Away (Kags, BMI) .... 10
Two of a Kind (Acuff-Rose, BMI) .... 67
Uptown (Aldon, BMI) .... 80
Walk on the Wild Side (Columbia, ASCAP) .... 61
Wanderer, The (Schwartz-Disal, ASCAP) .... 25
(What a Sad Way) To Love Someone (Trinity-Recherche, ASCAP) .... 92
What Am I Supposed to Do (Pamper, BMI) .... 85
What'd I Say (Progressive, BMI) .... 70
What's Your Name (Hill & Range, BMI) .... 7
When My Little Girl Is Smiling (Aldon, BMI) .... 35
Where Have All the Flowers Gone (Fall River, BMI) .... 22
White Rose of Athens (Peter Schaeffer, BMI) .... 84
Who Will the Next Fool Be (Knox, BMI) .... 77
Yes Indeed (Embassy, BMI) .... 74
You Are Mine (Debmar, BMI) .... 93
You Better Move On (Keva, BMI) .... 31
You Talk About Love (Saturn, BMI) .... 65
You Win Again (Fred Rose, BMI) .... 23
Young World (Four Star, BMI) .... 12


## BUBBLING UNDER THE HOT 100

101. ITTY BITTY PIECES .... James Ray, Caprice 114
102. SWEET THURSDAY .... Johnny Mathis, Columbia 42261
103. TWISTIN' FEVER .... Marcels, Colpix 629
104. SHOUT .... Isley Brothers, RCA Victor 7588
105. LA PALOMA TWIST .... Chubby Checker, Parkway 835
106. YOU DON'T MISS YOUR WATER .... William Bell, Stax 116
107. COLINDA .... Rod Bernard, Hall-Way 1902
108. DUCHESS OF EARL .... Pearlettes, Vee Jay 435
109. FUNNY WAY OF LAUGHIN' .... Burl Ives, Decca 31371
110. LOVER COME BACK .... Doris Day, Columbia 42295
111. THOU SHALT NOT STEAL .... John D. Loudermilk, RCA Victor 7993
112. QUARTER TO FOUR STOMP .... Stompers, Landa 684
113. THE RIGHT THING TO DO .... Nat King Cole, Capitol 4714
114. MEET ME AT THE TWISTIN' PLACE .... Johnnie Morisette, Sar 126
115. THE TOWN I LIVE IN .... McKinley Mitchell, One-Derful 2030
116. HULLY GULLY CALLING TIME .... Jive Five, Beltone 2019
117. IF YOU WANT TO .... Carousels, Gone 5118
118. DOCTOR FEEL GOOD .... Dr. Feelgood and the Interns, Okeh 7144
119. GEE BABY .... Ben and Bea, Philips 40000
120. HERE IT COMES AGAIN .... Chantels, Carlton 569
120. SO THIS IS LOVE .... Castells, Era 3073

# BILLBOARD HOT 100

FOR WEEK ENDING APRIL 7

1962

★ STAR PERFORMERS—Selections registering greatest upward progress this week.

S Indicates that 45 r.p.m. stereo single version is available.

△ Indicates that 33⅓ r.p.m. mono single version is available.

S△ Indicates that 33⅓ r.p.m. stereo single version is available.

| This Week | 1 Wk. Ago | 2 Wks. Ago | 3 Wks. Ago | Title | Artist, Label & Number | | Weeks On Chart |
|---|---|---|---|---|---|---|---|
| 1 | 3 | 11 | 28 | JOHNNY ANGEL | Shelley Fabares, Colpix 621 | | 6 |
| 2 | 1 | 2 | 3 | DON'T BREAK THE HEART THAT LOVES YOU | Connie Francis, MGM 13059 | | 9 |
| ★3 | 9 | 14 | 51 | GOOD LUCK CHARM | Elvis Presley, RCA Victor 7992 | △ | 4 |
| 4 | 6 | 7 | 14 | SLOW TWISTIN' | Chubby Checker, Parkway 835 | | 6 |
| 5 | 4 | 6 | 18 | DREAM BABY | Roy Orbison, Monument 456 | | 8 |
| 6 | 2 | 1 | 1 | HEY! BABY | Bruce Channel, Smash 1731 | | 11 |
| 7 | 5 | 3 | 2 | MIDNIGHT IN MOSCOW | Kenny Ball, Kapp 442 | | 10 |
| 8 | 12 | 16 | 37 | YOUNG WORLD | Rick Nelson, Imperial 5805 | | 6 |
| 9 | 11 | 12 | 23 | LOVE LETTERS | Ketty Lester, Era 3068 | | 7 |
| ★10 | 15 | 26 | 32 | MASHED POTATO TIME | Dee Dee Sharp, Cameo 212 | | 6 |
| 11 | 7 | 8 | 7 | WHAT'S YOUR NAME | Don and Juan, Big Top 3079 | | 9 |
| 12 | 16 | 23 | 36 | LOVE ME WARM AND TENDER | Paul Anka, RCA Victor 7977 | △ | 7 |
| 13 | 8 | 4 | 4 | LET ME IN | Sensations, Argo 5405 | | 14 |
| 14 | 10 | 9 | 13 | TWISTIN' THE NIGHT AWAY | Sam Cooke, RCA Victor 7983 | △ | 10 |
| 15 | 19 | 22 | 35 | PLEASE DON'T ASK ABOUT BARBARA | Bobby Vee, Liberty 55419 | | 7 |
| 16 | 20 | 35 | 56 | LOVER, PLEASE | Clyde McPhatter, Mercury 71941 | | 6 |
| 17 | 17 | 24 | 27 | COME BACK SILLY GIRL | Lettermen, Capitol 4699 | | 8 |
| 18 | 21 | 28 | 22 | I'VE GOT BONNIE | Bobby Rydell, Cameo 209 | | 8 |
| 19 | 14 | 15 | 16 | SHE'S GOT YOU | Patsy Cline, Decca 31354 | | 11 |
| 20 | 13 | 5 | 5 | DUKE OF EARL | Gene (Duke of Earl) Chandler, Vee Jay 416 | | 13 |
| 21 | 22 | 25 | 25 | WHERE HAVE ALL THE FLOWERS GONE | Kingston Trio, Capitol 4671 | | 12 |
| 22 | 23 | 33 | 39 | YOU WIN AGAIN | Fats Domino, Imperial 5816 | | 7 |
| 23 | 30 | 48 | 62 | NUT ROCKER | B. Bumble & the Stingers, Rendezvous 166 | | 6 |
| ★24 | 34 | 63 | — | SOLDIER BOY | Shirelles, Scepter 1228 | | 3 |
| 25 | 32 | 50 | 68 | DEAR ONE | Larry Finnegan, Old Town 1113 | | 7 |
| ★26 | 36 | 68 | — | SHOUT | Joey Dee & the Starliters, Roulette 4416 | | 3 |
| 27 | 31 | 42 | 49 | YOU BETTER MOVE ON | Arthur Alexander, Dot 16309 | | 7 |
| 28 | 35 | 39 | 52 | WHEN MY LITTLE GIRL IS SMILING | Drifters, Atlantic 2134 | | 7 |
| 29 | 18 | 10 | 6 | HER ROYAL MAJESTY | James Darren, Colpix 622 | | 10 |
| 30 | 38 | 49 | 61 | SHE CAN'T FIND HER KEYS | Paul Peterson, Colpix 620 | | 6 |
| ★31 | 43 | 69 | 80 | STRANGER ON THE SHORE | Mr. Acker Bilk, Atco 6217 | | 4 |
| ★32 | 68 | — | — | TWIST, TWIST, SENORA | Gary (U. S.) Bonds, LeGrand 1018 | | 2 |
| 33 | 41 | 59 | 78 | SOUL TWIST | King Curtis, Enjoy 1000 | | 5 |
| ★34 | 53 | 64 | 75 | SHE CRIED | Jay & the Americans, United Artists 415 | | 4 |
| 35 | 37 | 45 | 59 | IF A WOMAN ANSWERS | Leroy Van Dyke, Mercury 71926 | | 5 |
| ★36 | 48 | 58 | 70 | ANYTHING THAT'S PART OF YOU | Elvis Presley, RCA Victor 7992 | △ | 4 |
| ★37 | 50 | 60 | 73 | GINNY COME LATELY | Brian Hyland, ABC-Paramount 10294 | | 5 |
| 38 | 42 | 52 | 57 | CRY, BABY, CRY | Angels, Caprice 112 | | 8 |
| 39 | 39 | 44 | 55 | SOMETHING'S GOT A HOLD ON ME | Etta James, Argo 5409 | | 7 |
| 40 | 46 | 62 | 83 | CINDERELLA | Jack Ross, Dot 16333 | | 4 |
| 41 | 33 | 30 | 31 | JAMIE | Eddie Holland, Motown 1021 | | 12 |
| ★42 | 52 | 81 | 95 | JOHNNY JINGO | Hayley Mills, Vista 395 | | 4 |
| 43 | 47 | 61 | 65 | PATTI ANN | Johnny Crawford, Del Fi 4172 | | 6 |
| ★44 | 56 | 73 | 85 | THE JAM | Bobby Gregg and His Friends, Cotton 1003 | | 4 |
| 45 | 40 | 51 | 63 | ALVIN TWIST | Chipmunks, Liberty 55424 | | 6 |
| 46 | 28 | 20 | 12 | SMOKY PLACES | Corsairs, Tuff 3030 | | 15 |
| ★47 | 58 | 66 | 72 | TELL ME | Dick & Deedee, Liberty 55412 | | 4 |
| 48 | 27 | 21 | 17 | TUFF | Ace Cannon, Hi 2040 | | 15 |
| 49 | 29 | 17 | 10 | PERCOLATOR (TWIST) | Billy Joe and the Checkmates, Dore 620 | | 13 |
| 50 | 25 | 19 | 11 | THE WANDERER | Dion, Laurie 3115 | | 18 |
| 51 | 26 | 18 | 9 | BREAK IT TO ME GENTLY | Brenda Lee, Decca 31348 | | 13 |
| ★52 | 70 | — | — | WHAT'D I SAY | Bobby Darin, Atco 6221 | | 2 |
| 53 | 24 | 13 | 8 | CRYING IN THE RAIN | Everly Brothers, Warner Bros. 5250 | | 13 |
| 54 | 51 | 53 | 53 | POP-EYE | Huey Smith and the Clowns, Ace 649 | | 8 |
| ★55 | 67 | 82 | 91 | TWO OF A KIND | Sue Thompson, Hickory 1166 | | 4 |
| 56 | 60 | 74 | 76 | ANNIE GET YOUR YO-YO | Little Junior Parker, Duke 345 | | 5 |
| 57 | 66 | 85 | — | MOMENTS | Jennell Hawkins, Amazon 1003 | | 3 |
| 58 | 65 | — | — | YOU TALK ABOUT LOVE | Barbara George, AFO 304 | | 2 |
| 59 | 64 | — | — | AT THE CLUB | Ray Charles and His Ork, ABC-Paramount 10314 | | 2 |
| 60 | 44 | 32 | 24 | THE TWIST | Chubby Checker, Parkway 811 | | 39 |
| ★61 | 84 | 86 | 88 | WHITE ROSE OF ATHENS | David Carroll, Mercury 71917 | | 5 |
| 62 | 71 | 93 | — | THE ONE WHO REALLY LOVES YOU | Mary Wells, Motown 1024 | | 3 |
| 63 | 72 | 90 | — | TRA LA LA LA LA | Ike & Tina Turner, Sue 757 | | 3 |
| ★64 | 83 | — | — | SHOUT! SHOUT! (Knock Yourself Out) | Ernie Marèsca, Seville 117 | | 2 |
| ★65 | — | — | — | FUNNY WAY OF LAUGHIN' | Burl Ives, Decca 31371 | | 1 |
| 66 | 75 | 70 | 71 | LOLLIPOPS AND ROSES | Jack Jones, Kapp 435 | | 6 |
| ★67 | — | — | — | HIDE NOR HAIR | Ray Charles and His Ork, ABC-Paramount 10314 | | 1 |
| 68 | 80 | — | — | UPTOWN | Crystals, Philles 102 | | 2 |
| 69 | 82 | — | — | I WISH THAT WE WERE MARRIED | Ronnie and the Hi-Lites, Joy 260 | | 2 |
| ★70 | 90 | — | — | P. T. 109 | Jimmy Dean, Columbia 42338 | △ | 2 |
| ★71 | 91 | — | — | CATERINA | Perry Como, RCA Victor 8004 | △ | 2 |
| 72 | 78 | 89 | 94 | CHAPEL BY THE SEA | Billy Vaughn, Dot 16329 | | 4 |
| 73 | 69 | 80 | 82 | MIDNIGHT SPECIAL | Jimmy Smith, Blue Note 1819 | | 6 |
| 74 | 76 | 87 | 90 | MEMORIES OF MARIA | Jerry Byrd, Monument 449 | | 4 |
| 75 | 79 | 83 | 86 | THE BALLAD OF THUNDER ROAD | Robert Mitchum, Capitol 3986 | | 7 |
| ★76 | 93 | 100 | — | YOU ARE MINE | Frankie Avalon, Chancellor 1107 | | 3 |
| 77 | 73 | 71 | 66 | OUR ANNIVERSARY | Shep & the Limelites, Hull 748 | | 8 |
| ★78 | 99 | — | — | THE BIG DRAFT | Four Preps, Capitol 4716 | | 2 |
| 79 | 77 | — | — | WHO WILL THE NEXT FOOL BE | Bobby Bland, Duke 347 | | 2 |
| ★80 | — | — | — | RUNAWAY | Lawrence Welk, Dot 16336 | | 1 |
| 81 | 87 | — | — | I WILL | Vic Dana, Dolton 51 | | 2 |
| ★82 | — | — | — | THOU SHALT NOT STEAL | John D. Loudermilk, RCA Victor 7993 | △ | 1 |
| 83 | 85 | 91 | — | WHAT AM I SUPPOSED TO DO | Ann-Margret, RCA Victor 7986 | △ | 3 |
| ★84 | — | — | — | PATRICIA TWIST | Perez Prado, RCA Victor 8006 | △ | 1 |
| ★85 | — | — | — | EV'RYBODY'S TWISTIN' | Frank Sinatra, Reprise 20063 | | 1 |
| 86 | 89 | 92 | 97 | THE RAINS CAME | Big Sam, Eric 7003 | | 5 |
| 87 | 81 | 84 | 87 | A GIRL HAS TO KNOW | G-Clefs, Terrace 7503 | | 5 |
| 88 | 92 | 97 | — | (WHAT A SAD WAY) TO LOVE SOMEONE | Ral Donner, Gone 5125 | | 3 |
| 89 | 97 | — | — | TWISTIN' MATILDA | Jimmy Soul, SPQR 3300 | | 2 |
| 90 | 100 | — | — | KING OF CLOWNS | Neil Sedaka, RCA Victor 8007 | △ | 2 |
| 91 | — | — | — | ITTY BITTY PIECES | James Ray, Caprice 114 | | 1 |
| 92 | — | — | — | COOKIN' | Al Casey Combo, Stacy 925 | | 1 |
| 93 | — | 88 | 93 | AMOR | Roger Williams, Kapp 447 | | 4 |
| 94 | — | 95 | 98 | SMILE | Ferrante and Teicher, United Artists 431 | | 3 |
| 95 | — | 94 | — | SHOUT | Isley Brothers, RCA Victor 7588 | | 2 |
| 96 | 96 | — | — | HONKY-TONK MAN | Johnny Horton, Columbia 42302 | △ | 2 |
| 97 | — | — | — | OLD RIVERS | Walter Brennan, Liberty 55436 | | 1 |
| 98 | — | — | — | LOVER COME BACK | Doris Day, Columbia 42295 | △ | 1 |
| 99 | — | — | 100 | SWEET THURSDAY | Johnny Mathis, Columbia 42261 | △ | 2 |
| 100 | — | — | — | COUNT EVERY STAR | Linda Scott, Canadian-American 133 | | 1 |

## HOT 100—A TO Z—(Publisher-Licensee)


Alvin Twist (Monarch, ASCAP) .... 45
Amor (Peer Int'l, BMI) .... 93
Annie Get Your Yo-Yo (Don, BMI) .... 56
Anything That's Part of You (Gladys, ASCAP) .... 36
At the Club (Tangerine, BMI) .... 59
Ballad of Thunder Road (Leeds, ASCAP) .... 75
Big Draft, The (Lar-Bell, BMI) .... 78
Break It to Me Gently (Northern, ASCAP) .... 51
Caterina (Roncom, ASCAP) .... 71
Chapel By the Sea (Sun-Vine, BMI) .... 72
Cinderella (Vin-Sun, ASCAP) .... 40
Come Back Silly Girl (Aldon, BMI) .... 17
Cookin' (Renda, BMI) .... 92
Count Every Star (Paxton, ASCAP) .... 100
Cry, Baby, Cry (Jersey, BMI) .... 38
Crying in the Rain (Aldon, BMI) .... 53
Dear One (Maureen, BMI) .... 25
Don't Break the Heart That Loves You (Francon, ASCAP) .... 2
Dream Baby (Combine, BMI) .... 5
Duke of Earl (Conrad-Karlan, BMI) .... 20
Ev'rybody's Twistin' (Barton, ASCAP) .... 85
Funny Way of Laughin' (Pamper, BMI) .... 65
Ginny Come Lately (Pogo, ASCAP) .... 37
Girl Has to Know, A (Aldon, BMI) .... 87
Good Luck Charm (Gladys, ASCAP) .... 3
Her Royal Majesty (Aldon, BMI) .... 29
Hey! Baby (LeBill, BMI) .... 6
Hide Nor Hair (Tangerine, BMI) .... 67
Honky-Tonk Man (Cedarwood, BMI) .... 96
I Will (Camarillo, BMI) .... 81
I Wish That We Were Married (Joy, ASCAP) .... 69
I've Got Bonnie (Aldon, BMI) .... 18
If a Woman Answers (Aldon, BMI) .... 35
Itty Bitty Pieces (Good Songs, BMI) .... 91
Jam, The (Cheltenham, BMI) .... 44
Jamie (Jobette, BMI) .... 41
Johnny Angel (Post, ASCAP) .... 1
Johnny Jingo (Dickson, ASCAP) .... 42
King of Clowns (Aldon, BMI) .... 90
Let Me In (Arc-Kae Williams, BMI) .... 13
Lollipops and Roses (Garland, ASCAP) .... 66
Love Letters (Famous, ASCAP) .... 9
Love Me Warm and Tender (Spanka, BMI) .... 12
Lover Come Back (Daywin, BMI) .... 98
Lover, Please (Lyn-Lou, BMI) .... 16
Mashed Potato Time (Rice-Mill, BMI) .... 10
Memories of Maria (Acuff-Rose, BMI) .... 74
Midnight in Moscow (Melody Trails, BMI) .... 7
Midnight Special (Edmy, BMI) .... 73
Moments (Titanic, BMI) .... 57
Nut Rocker (Fowley, BMI) .... 23
Old Rivers (Glo-Mac & Metric, BMI) .... 97
One Who Really Loves You, The (Jobete, BMI) .... 62
Our Anniversary (Keel, BMI) .... 77
P.T. 109 (Cedarwood, BMI) .... 70
Patricia Twist (Peer Int'l, BMI) .... 84
Patti Ann (Maraville, BMI) .... 43
Percolator (Twist) (Meadowlark, ASCAP) .... 49
Please Don't Ask About Barbara (Aldon, BMI) .... 15
Pop-Eye (Ace, BMI) .... 54
Rains Came, The (Crazy Cajun-Corette, BMI) .... 86
Runaway (Vicki, BMI) .... 80
She Can't Find Her Keys (Arch, ASCAP) .... 30
She Cried (Trio, BMI) .... 34
She's Got You (Pamper, BMI) .... 19
Shout—Dee (Wemar-Nom, BMI) .... 26
Shout—Isley Brothers (Wemar-Nom, BMI) .... 95
Shout! Shout! (Knock Yourself Out) (Broadway, ASCAP) .... 64
Slow Twistin' (Woodcrest, BMI) .... 4
Smile (Bourne, ASCAP) .... 94
Smoky Places (Annie-Earl & Sun Flower, ASCAP) .... 46
Soldier Boy (Ludix, BMI) .... 24
Something's Got a Hold on Me (Figure, BMI) .... 39
Soul Twist (Dan-Kelyn, BMI) .... 33
Stranger on the Shore (Mellin, BMI) .... 31
Sweet Thursday (Elm Drive, ASCAP) .... 99
Tell Me (Odin, ASCAP) .... 47
Thou Shalt Not Steal (Acuff-Rose, BMI) .... 82
Tra La La La La (Saturn, BMI) .... 63
Tuff (Jec, BMI) .... 48
Twist, The (Lois, BMI) .... 60
Twist, Twist Senora (Rockmasters, BMI) .... 32
Twistin' Matilda (Pepe, BMI) .... 89
Twistin' the Night Away (Kags, BMI) .... 14
Two of a Kind (Acuff-Rose, BMI) .... 55
Uptown (Aldon, BMI) .... 68
Wanderer, The (Schwartz-Disal, ASCAP) .... 50
(What a Sad Way) to Love Someone (Tricky-Recherche, ASCAP) .... 88
What Am I Supposed to Do (Pamper, BMI) .... 83
What'd I Say (Progressive, BMI) .... 52
What's Your Name (Hill & Range, BMI) .... 11
When My Little Girl Is Smiling (Aldon, BMI) .... 28
Where Have All the Flowers Gone (Fall River, BMI) .... 21
White Rose of Athens (Peter Schaeffer's, BMI) .... 61
Who Will the Next Fool Be (Knox, BMI) .... 79
You Are Mine (Debmar, BMI) .... 76
You Better Move On (Keva, BMI) .... 27
You Talk About Love (Saturn, BMI) .... 58
You Win Again (Fred Rose, BMI) .... 22
Young World (Four Star, BMI) .... 8


## BUBBLING UNDER THE HOT 100

101. QUARTER TO FOUR STOMP....Stompers, Landa 684
102. POP-EYE STROLL....Mar-Keys, Stax 121
103. I FOUND A LOVE....Falcons, LuPine 1003
104. BUTTONS AND BOWS....The Browns, RCA Victor 7997
105. BLUES (STAY AWAY FROM ME)....Ace Cannon, Hi 2051
106. I'D NEVER FIND ANOTHER YOU..Paul Anka, ABC-Paramount 10311
107. SUGARTIME TWIST....McGuire Sisters, Coral 62305
108. ALL YOU HAD TO DO (WAS TELL ME)..Chris Montez, Monogram 500
109. MEET ME AT THE TWISTIN' PLACE....Johnnie Morisette, Sar 126
110. THE RIGHT THING TO SAY....Nat King Cole, Capitol 4714
111. LOVE IS A SWINGIN' THING....Shirelles, Scepter 1228
112. I WANT TO LOVE YOU ....Renee Roberts, New Phoenix 6198
113. LOVE THEME FROM EL CID....Billy Storm, Infinity 013
114. DR. FEEL GOOD....Dr. Feelgood and the Internes, Okeh 7144
115. YOU DON'T MISS YOUR WATER....William Bell, Stax 116
116. JUST ANOTHER FOOL....Curtis Lee, Dunes 2012
117. DUCHESS OF EARL....Pearlettes, Vee Jay 435
118. PLAY THE THING....Marlowe Morris Quintet, Columbia 42218
119. GEE BABY....Ben and Bea, Philips 40000
120. LOVESICK BLUES....Floyd Cramer, RCA Victor 8013

# BILLBOARD HOT 100

FOR WEEK ENDING APRIL 14 1962

★ STAR PERFORMERS—Selections registering greatest upward progress this week.

S Indicates that 45 r.p.m. stereo single version is available.

△ Indicates that 33⅓ r.p.m. mono single version is available.

S△ Indicates that 33⅓ r.p.m. stereo single version is available.

| This Week | 1 Wk. Ago | 2 Wks. Ago | 3 Wks. Ago | Title | Artist, Label & Number | Weeks On Chart |
|---|---|---|---|---|---|---|
| 1 | 1 | 3 | 11 | JOHNNY ANGEL | Shelley Fabares, Colpix 621 | 7 |
| 2 | 3 | 9 | 14 | GOOD LUCK CHARM △ | Elvis Presley, RCA Victor 7992 | 5 |
| 3 | 4 | 6 | 7 | SLOW TWISTIN' | Chubby Checker, Parkway 835 | 7 |
| ★4 | 10 | 15 | 26 | MASHED POTATO TIME | Dee Dee Sharp, Cameo 212 | 7 |
| 5 | 9 | 11 | 12 | LOVE LETTERS | Ketty Lester, Era 3068 | 8 |
| 6 | 8 | 12 | 16 | YOUNG WORLD | Rick Nelson, Imperial 5805 | 7 |
| 7 | 2 | 1 | 2 | DON'T BREAK THE HEART THAT LOVES YOU | Connie Francis, MGM 13059 | 10 |
| ★8 | 16 | 20 | 35 | LOVER, PLEASE | Clyde McPhatter, Mercury 71941 | 7 |
| 9 | 7 | 5 | 3 | MIDNIGHT IN MOSCOW | Kenny Ball, Kapp 442 | 11 |
| 10 | 6 | 2 | 1 | HEY! BABY | Bruce Channel, Smash 1731 | 12 |
| ★11 | 24 | 34 | 63 | SOLDIER BOY | Shirelles, Scepter 1228 | 4 |
| 12 | 12 | 16 | 23 | LOVE ME WARM AND TENDER △ | Paul Anka, RCA Victor 7977 | 8 |
| 13 | 5 | 4 | 6 | DREAM BABY | Roy Orbison, Monument 456 | 9 |
| ★14 | 26 | 36 | 68 | SHOUT | Joey Dee & the Starliters, Roulette 4416 | 4 |
| 15 | 13 | 8 | 4 | LET ME IN | Sensations, Argo 5405 | 15 |
| ★16 | 25 | 32 | 50 | DEAR ONE | Larry Finnegan, Old Town 1113 | 8 |
| 17 | 14 | 10 | 9 | TWISTIN' THE NIGHT AWAY △ | Sam Cooke, RCA Victor 7983 | 11 |
| 18 | 11 | 7 | 8 | WHAT'S YOUR NAME | Don and Juan, Big Top 3079 | 10 |
| ★19 | 31 | 43 | 69 | STRANGER ON THE SHORE | Mr. Acker Bilk, Atco 6217 | 5 |
| ★20 | 32 | 68 | — | TWIST, TWIST, SENORA | Gary (U. S.) Bonds, LeGrand 1018 | 3 |
| ★21 | 40 | 46 | 62 | CINDERELLA | Jack Ross, Dot 16333 | 5 |
| ★22 | 34 | 53 | 64 | SHE CRIED | Jay & the Americans, United Artists 415 | 5 |
| 23 | 15 | 19 | 22 | PLEASE DON'T ASK ABOUT BARBARA | Bobby Vee, Liberty 55419 | 8 |
| 24 | 30 | 38 | 49 | SHE CAN'T FIND HER KEYS | Paul Peterson, Colpix 620 | 7 |
| 25 | 27 | 31 | 42 | YOU BETTER MOVE ON | Arthur Alexander, Dot 16309 | 8 |
| 26 | 17 | 17 | 24 | COME BACK SILLY GIRL | Lettermen, Capitol 4699 | 9 |
| ★27 | 37 | 50 | 60 | GINNY COME LATELY | Brian Hyland, ABC-Paramount 10294 | 6 |
| 28 | 18 | 21 | 28 | I'VE GOT BONNIE | Bobby Rydell, Cameo 209 | 9 |
| 29 | 23 | 30 | 48 | NUT ROCKER | B. Bumble & the Stingers, Rendezvous 166 | 7 |
| 30 | 19 | 14 | 15 | SHE'S GOT YOU | Patsy Cline, Decca 31354 | 12 |
| 31 | 33 | 41 | 59 | SOUL TWIST | King Curtis, Enjoy 1000 | 6 |
| ★32 | 44 | 56 | 73 | THE JAM | Bobby Gregg and His Friends, Cotton 1003 | 5 |
| 33 | 36 | 48 | 58 | ANYTHING THAT'S PART OF YOU △ | Elvis Presley, RCA Victor 7992 | 5 |
| 34 | 42 | 52 | 81 | JOHNNY JINGO | Hayley Mills, Vista 395 | 5 |
| 35 | 21 | 22 | 25 | WHERE HAVE ALL THE FLOWERS GONE | Kingston Trio, Capitol 4671 | 13 |
| 36 | 22 | 23 | 33 | YOU WIN AGAIN | Fats Domino, Imperial 5816 | 8 |
| 37 | 39 | 39 | 44 | SOMETHING'S GOT A HOLD ON ME | Etta James, Argo 5409 | 8 |
| 38 | 28 | 35 | 39 | WHEN MY LITTLE GIRL IS SMILING | Drifters, Atlantic 2134 | 8 |
| ★39 | 70 | 90 | — | P. T. 109 △ | Jimmy Dean, Columbia 42338 | 3 |
| ★40 | 52 | 70 | — | WHAT'D I SAY | Bobby Darin, Atco 6221 | 3 |
| ★41 | 65 | — | — | FUNNY WAY OF LAUGHIN' | Burl Ives, Decca 31371 | 2 |
| 42 | 20 | 13 | 5 | DUKE OF EARL | Gene (Duke of Earl) Chandler, Vee Jay 416 | 14 |
| 43 | 64 | 83 | — | SHOUT! SHOUT! (Knock Yourself Out) | Ernie Maresca, Seville 117 | 3 |
| 44 | 45 | 40 | 51 | ALVIN TWIST | Chipmunks, Liberty 55424 | 7 |
| 45 | 47 | 58 | 66 | TELL ME | Dick & Deedee, Liberty 55412 | 5 |
| 46 | 38 | 42 | 52 | CRY, BABY, CRY | Angels, Caprice 112 | 9 |
| 47 | 29 | 18 | 10 | HER ROYAL MAJESTY | James Darren, Colpix 622 | 11 |
| 48 | 35 | 37 | 45 | IF A WOMAN ANSWERS | Leroy Van Dyke, Mercury 71926 | 6 |
| ★49 | 67 | — | — | HIDE NOR HAIR | Ray Charles and His Ork, ABC-Paramount 10314 | 2 |
| 50 | 55 | 67 | 82 | TWO OF A KIND | Sue Thompson, Hickory 1166 | 5 |
| 51 | 56 | 60 | 74 | ANNIE GET YOUR YO-YO | Little Junior Parker, Duke 345 | 6 |
| 52 | 59 | 64 | — | AT THE CLUB | Ray Charles and His Ork, ABC-Paramount 10314 | 3 |
| ★53 | 69 | 82 | — | I WISH THAT WE WERE MARRIED | Ronnie and the Hi-Lites, Joy 260 | 3 |
| 54 | 58 | 65 | — | YOU TALK ABOUT LOVE | Barbara George, AFO 304 | 3 |
| 55 | 62 | 71 | 93 | THE ONE WHO REALLY LOVES YOU | Mary Wells, Motown 1024 | 4 |
| ★56 | 68 | 80 | — | UPTOWN | Crystals, Philles 102 | 3 |
| 57 | 57 | 66 | 85 | MOMENTS | Jennell Hawkins, Amazon 1003 | 4 |
| 58 | 43 | 47 | 61 | PATTI ANN | Johnny Crawford, Del Fi 4172 | 7 |
| 59 | 63 | 72 | 90 | TRA LA LA LA LA | Ike & Tina Turner, Sue 757 | 4 |
| ★60 | 71 | 91 | — | CATERINA △ | Perry Como, RCA Victor 8004 | 3 |
| ★61 | 97 | — | — | OLD RIVERS | Walter Brennan, Liberty 55436 | 2 |
| 62 | 41 | 33 | 30 | JAMIE | Eddie Holland, Motown 1021 | 13 |
| 63 | 76 | 93 | 100 | YOU ARE MINE | Frankie Avalon, Chancellor 1107 | 4 |
| 64 | 48 | 27 | 21 | TUFF | Ace Cannon, Hi 2040 | 16 |
| 65 | 75 | 79 | 83 | THE BALLAD OF THUNDER ROAD | Robert Mitchum, Capitol 3986 | 8 |
| ★66 | — | — | — | EVERYBODY LOVES ME BUT YOU | Brenda Lee, Decca 31379 | 1 |
| 67 | 78 | 99 | — | THE BIG DRAFT | Four Preps, Capitol 4716 | 3 |
| 68 | 81 | 87 | — | I WILL | Vic Dana, Dolton 51 | 3 |
| 69 | 72 | 78 | 89 | CHAPEL BY THE SEA | Billy Vaughn, Dot 16329 | 5 |
| 70 | 73 | 69 | 80 | MIDNIGHT SPECIAL | Jimmy Smith, Blue Note 1819 | 7 |
| ★71 | 89 | 97 | — | TWISTIN' MATILDA | Jimmy Soul, SPQR 3300 | 3 |
| 72 | 80 | — | — | RUNAWAY | Lawrence Welk, Dot 16336 | 2 |
| ★73 | 90 | 100 | — | KING OF CLOWNS △ | Neil Sedaka, RCA Victor 8007 | 3 |
| 74 | 86 | 89 | 92 | THE RAINS CAME | Big Sam, Eric 7003 | 6 |
| 75 | 85 | — | — | EV'RYBODY'S TWISTIN' | Frank Sinatra, Reprise 20063 | 2 |
| 76 | 79 | 77 | — | WHO WILL THE NEXT FOOL BE | Bobby Bland, Duke 347 | 3 |
| 77 | 66 | 75 | 70 | LOLLIPOPS AND ROSES | Jack Jones, Kapp 435 | 7 |
| 78 | 82 | — | — | THOU SHALT NOT STEAL △ | John D. Loudermilk, RCA Victor 7993 | 2 |
| 79 | 84 | — | — | PATRICIA TWIST △ | Perez Prado, RCA Victor 8006 | 2 |
| 80 | 61 | 84 | 86 | WHITE ROSE OF ATHENS | David Carroll, Mercury 71917 | 6 |
| ★81 | — | — | — | CONSCIENCE | James Darren, Colpix 630 | 1 |
| 82 | 83 | 85 | 91 | WHAT AM I SUPPOSED TO DO △ | Ann-Margret, RCA Victor 7986 | 4 |
| 83 | 91 | — | — | ITTY BITTY PIECES | James Ray, Caprice 114 | 2 |
| 84 | 88 | 92 | 97 | (WHAT A SAD WAY) TO LOVE SOMEONE | Ral Donner, Gone 5125 | 4 |
| ★85 | 100 | — | — | COUNT EVERY STAR | Linda Scott, Canadian-American 133 | 2 |
| ★86 | — | — | — | BLUES (Stay Away From Me) | Ace Cannon, Hi 2051 | 1 |
| 87 | 74 | 76 | 87 | MEMORIES OF MARIA | Jerry Byrd, Monument 449 | 5 |
| ★88 | — | — | — | MARCH OF THE SIAMESE CHILDREN | Kenny Ball, Kapp 451 | 1 |
| ★89 | — | — | — | NIGHT TRAIN | James Brown, King 5614 | 1 |
| ★90 | — | — | — | I'M ON MY WAY | Highwaymen, United Artists 439 | 1 |
| 91 | — | — | — | LOVESICK BLUES △ | Floyd Cramer, RCA Victor 8013 | 1 |
| 92 | — | — | — | SUGAR BLUES | Ace Cannon, Santo 503 | 1 |
| 93 | — | — | — | DOIN' THE CONTINENTAL WALK | Danny & the Juniors, Swan 4100 | 1 |
| 94 | 95 | — | 94 | SHOUT △ | Isley Brothers, RCA Victor 7588 | 3 |
| 95 | 92 | — | — | COOKIN' | Al Casey Combo, Stacy 925 | 2 |
| 96 | — | 98 | — | I FOUND A LOVE | Falcons, LuPine 1003 | 2 |
| 97 | — | — | — | OPERATOR | Gladys Knight & the Pips, Fury 1064 | 1 |
| 98 | — | — | — | MEET ME AT THE TWISTIN' PLACE | Johnnie Morisette, Sar 126 | 1 |
| 99 | — | — | — | I'LL TAKE YOU HOME | Corsairs, Tuff 1818 | 1 |
| 100 | — | — | — | SO THIS IS LOVE | Castells, Era 3073 | 1 |

## HOT 100—A TO Z—(Publisher-Licensee)

Alvin Twist (Monarch, ASCAP) .... 44
Annie Get Your Yo-Yo (Don, BMI) .... 51
Anything That's Part of You (Gladys, ASCAP) .... 33
At the Club (Tangerine, BMI) .... 52
Ballad of Thunder Road, The (Leeds, ASCAP) .... 65
Big Draft, The (Lar-Bell, BMI) .... 67
Blues (Stay Away From Me) (Lois, BMI) .... 86
Caterina (Roncom, ASCAP) .... 60
Chapel by the Sea (Sun-Vine, BMI) .... 69
Cinderella (Vin-Sun, ASCAP) .... 21
Come Back Silly Girl (Aldon, BMI) .... 26
Conscience (Aldon, BMI) .... 81
Cookin' (Renda, BMI) .... 95
Count Every Star (Paxton, ASCAP) .... 85
Cry, Baby, Cry (Jersey, BMI) .... 46
Dear One (Maureen, BMI) .... 16
Doin' the Continental Walk (Chicory, BMI) .... 93
Don't Break the Heart That Loves You (Francon, ASCAP) .... 7
Dream Baby (Combine, BMI) .... 13
Duke of Earl (Conrad-Karlan, BMI) .... 42
Everybody Loves Me But You (Champion, BMI) .... 66
Ev'rybody's Twistin' (Barton, ASCAP) .... 75
Funny Way of Laughin' (Pamper, BMI) .... 41
Ginny Come Lately (Pogo, ASCAP) .... 27
Good Luck Charm (Gladys, ASCAP) .... 2
Her Royal Majesty (Aldon, BMI) .... 47
Hey! Baby (LeBill, BMI) .... 10
Hide Nor Hair (Tangerine, BMI) .... 49
I Found a Love (LuPine-Progressive-Alibri, BMI) .... 96
I Will (Camarillo, BMI) .... 68
I Wish That We Were Married (Joy, ASCAP) .... 53
I'll Take You Home (Sunflower & Annie-Earl, BMI) .... 99
I'm on My Way (Westside, BMI) .... 90
I've Got Bonnie (Aldon, BMI) .... 28
If a Woman Answers (Aldon, BMI) .... 48
Itty Bitty Pieces (Good Songs, BMI) .... 83
Jam, The (Cheltenham, BMI) .... 32
Jamie (Jobete, BMI) .... 62
Johnny Angel (Post, ASCAP) .... 1
Johnny Jingo (Dickson, ASCAP) .... 34
King of Clowns (Aldon, BMI) .... 73
Let Me In (Arc-Kae Williams, BMI) .... 15
Lollipops and Roses (Garland, ASCAP) .... 77
Love Letters (Famous, ASCAP) .... 5
Love Me Warm and Tender (Spanka, BMI) .... 12
Lover, Please (Lyn-Lou, BMI) .... 8
Lovesick Blues (Mills, ASCAP) .... 91
March of the Siamese Children (Williamson, ASCAP) .... 88
Mashed Potato Time (Rice-Mill, BMI) .... 4
Meet Me at the Twistin' Place (Kags, BMI) .... 98
Memories of Maria (Acuff-Rose, BMI) .... 87
Midnight in Moscow (Melody Trails, BMI) .... 9
Midnight Special (Edmy, BMI) .... 70
Moments (Titanic, BMI) .... 57
Night Train (Pamlee, BMI) .... 89
Nut Rocker (Fowley, BMI) .... 29
Old Rivers (Glo-Mac & Metric, BMI) .... 61
One Who Really Loves You, The (Jobete, BMI) .... 55
Operator (Sylvia, BMI) .... 97
P.T. 109 (Cedarwood, BMI) .... 39
Patricia Twist (Peer Int'l, BMI) .... 79
Patti Ann (Maraville, BMI) .... 58
Please Don't Ask About Barbara (Aldon, BMI) .... 23
Rains Came, The (Crazy Cajun-Corette, BMI) .... 74
Runaway (Vicki, BMI) .... 72
She Can't Find Her Keys (Arch, ASCAP) .... 24
She Cried (Trio, BMI) .... 22
She's Got You (Pamper, BMI) .... 30
Shout—Dee (Wemar-Nom, BMI) .... 14
Shout—Isley Brothers (Wemar-Nom,BMI) .... 94
Shout! Shout! (Knock Yourself Out) (Broadway, ASCAP) .... 43
Slow Twistin' (Woodcrest, BMI) .... 3
So This Is Love (Pattern, ASCAP) .... 100
Soldier Boy (Ludix, BMI) .... 11
Something's Got a Hold on Me (Figure, BMI) .... 37
Soul Twist (Dan-Kelyn, BMI) .... 31
Stranger on the Shore (Mellin, BMI) .... 19
Sugar Blues (Pickwick, ASCAP) .... 92
Tell Me (Odin, ASCAP) .... 45
Thou Shalt Not Steal (Acuff-Rose, BMI) .... 78
Tra La La La La (Saturn, BMI) .... 59
Tuff (Jec, BMI) .... 64
Twist, Twist, Senora (Rockmasters, BMI) .... 20
Twistin' Matilda (General-Pickwick, ASCAP) .... 71
Twistin' the Night Away (Kags, BMI) .... 17
Two of a Kind (Acuff-Rose, BMI) .... 50
Uptown (Aldon, BMI) .... 56
(What a Sad Way) to Love Someone (Tricky-Recherche, ASCAP) .... 84
What Am I Supposed to Do (Pamper, BMI) .... 82
What'd I Say (Progressive, BMI) .... 40
What's Your Name (Hill & Range, BMI) .... 18
When My Little Girl Is Smiling (Aldon, BMI) .... 38
Where Have All the Flowers Gone (Fall River, BMI) .... 35
White Rose of Athens (Peter Schaeffer's, BMI) .... 80
Who Will the Next Fool Be (Knox, BMI) .... 76
You Are Mine (Debmar, BMI) .... 63
You Better Move On (Keva, BMI) .... 25
You Talk About Love (Saturn, BMI) .... 54
You Win Again (Fred Rose, BMI) .... 36
Young World (Four Star, BMI) .... 6

## BUBBLING UNDER THE HOT 100

101. POP-EYE STROLL .... Mar-Keys, Stax 121
102. HONKY-TONK MAN .... Johnny Horton, Columbia 42302
103. YOU DON'T MISS YOUR WATER .... William Bell, Stax 116
104. PLAY THE THING .... Marlowe Morris Quintet, Columbia 42218
105. MOST PEOPLE GET MARRIED .... Patti Page, Mercury 71950
106. I'VE BEEN GOOD TO YOU .... Miracles, Tamla 54053
107. I SOLD MY HEART TO THE JUNKMAN .. Blue Bells, Newtown 5000
108. DOCTOR FEEL GOOD .... Dr. Feelgood and the Internes, Okeh 7144
109. LOVE IS A SWINGIN' THING .... Shirelles, Scepter 1228
110. JUST ANOTHER FOOL .... Curtis Lee, Dunes 2012
111. LOVE THEME FROM EL CID .... Billy Storm, Infinity 013
112. THE RIGHT THING TO SAY .... Nat King Cole, Capitol 4714
113. BUTTONS AND BOWS .... The Browns, RCA Victor 7997
114. DUCHESS OF EARL .... Pearlettes, Vee Jay 435
115. QUARTER TO FOUR STOMP .... Stompers, Landa 684
116. SWEET THURSDAY .... Johnny Mathis, Columbia 42261
117. NEED YOUR LOVE .... Metallics, Baronet 2
118. LOVER COME BACK .... Doris Day, Columbia 42295
119. HERE IT COMES AGAIN .... Chantels, Carlton 569
120. SMILE .... Ferrante and Teicher, United Artists 431

# BILLBOARD HOT 100

FOR WEEK ENDING APRIL 21 1962

★ STAR PERFORMERS—Selections registering greatest upward progress this week.

S Indicates that 45 r.p.m. stereo single version is available.

△ Indicates that 33⅓ r.p.m. mono single version is available.

△S Indicates that 33⅓ r.p.m. stereo single version is available.

| This Week | 1 Wk. Ago | 2 Wks. Ago | 3 Wks. Ago | Title | Artist, Label & Number | | Weeks on Chart |
|---|---|---|---|---|---|---|---|
| 1 | 2 | 3 | 9 | GOOD LUCK CHARM | Elvis Presley, RCA Victor 7992 | △ | 6 |
| 2 | 1 | 1 | 3 | JOHNNY ANGEL | Shelley Fabares, Colpix 621 | | 8 |
| 3 | 4 | 10 | 15 | MASHED POTATO TIME | Dee Dee Sharp, Cameo 212 | | 8 |
| 4 | 3 | 4 | 6 | SLOW TWISTIN' | Chubby Checker, Parkway 835 | | 8 |
| 5 | 6 | 8 | 12 | YOUNG WORLD | Rick Nelson, Imperial 5805 | | 8 |
| ★ 6 | 11 | 24 | 34 | SOLDIER BOY | Shirelles, Scepter 1228 | | 5 |
| 7 | 8 | 16 | 20 | LOVER, PLEASE | Clyde McPhatter, Mercury 71941 | | 8 |
| 8 | 5 | 9 | 11 | LOVE LETTERS | Ketty Lester, Era 3068 | | 9 |
| ★ 9 | 14 | 26 | 36 | SHOUT | Joey Dee & the Starliters, Roulette 4416 | | 5 |
| ★ 10 | 19 | 31 | 43 | STRANGER ON THE SHORE | Mr. Acker Bilk, Atco 6217 | | 6 |
| ★ 11 | 18 | 25 | 32 | DEAR ONE | Larry Finnegan, Old Town 1113 | | 9 |
| ★ 12 | 20 | 32 | 68 | TWIST, TWIST, SENORA | Gary (U. S.) Bonds, LeGrand 1018 | | 4 |
| 13 | 7 | 2 | 1 | DON'T BREAK THE HEART THAT LOVES YOU | Connie Francis, MGM 13059 | | 11 |
| 14 | 12 | 12 | 16 | LOVE ME WARM AND TENDER | Paul Anka, RCA Victor 7977 | △ | 9 |
| ★ 15 | 22 | 34 | 53 | SHE CRIED | Jay & the Americans, United Artists 415 | | 6 |
| 16 | 9 | 7 | 5 | MIDNIGHT IN MOSCOW | Kenny Ball, Kapp 442 | | 12 |
| 17 | 17 | 14 | 10 | TWISTIN' THE NIGHT AWAY | Sam Cooke, RCA Victor 7983 | △ | 12 |
| 18 | 10 | 6 | 2 | HEY! BABY | Bruce Channel, Smash 1731 | | 13 |
| 19 | 21 | 40 | 46 | CINDERELLA | Jack Ross, Dot 16333 | | 6 |
| 20 | 13 | 5 | 4 | DREAM BABY | Roy Orbison, Monument 456 | | 10 |
| 21 | 24 | 30 | 38 | SHE CAN'T FIND HER KEYS | Paul Peterson, Colpix 620 | | 8 |
| ★ 22 | 39 | 70 | 90 | P. T. 109 | Jimmy Dean, Columbia 42338 | △ | 4 |
| 23 | 27 | 37 | 50 | GINNY COME LATELY | Brian Hyland, ABC-Paramount 10294 | | 7 |
| 24 | 25 | 27 | 31 | YOU BETTER MOVE ON | Arthur Alexander, Dot 16309 | | 9 |
| 25 | 29 | 23 | 30 | NUT ROCKER | B. Bumble & the Stingers, Rendezvous 166 | | 8 |
| 26 | 31 | 33 | 41 | SOUL TWIST | King Curtis, Enjoy 1000 | | 7 |
| 27 | 34 | 42 | 52 | JOHNNY JINGO | Hayley Mills, Vista 395 | | 6 |
| 28 | 15 | 13 | 8 | LET ME IN | Sensations, Argo 5405 | | 16 |
| 29 | 32 | 44 | 56 | THE JAM | Bobby Gregg and His Friends, Cotton 1003 | | 6 |
| ★ 30 | 41 | 65 | — | FUNNY WAY OF LAUGHIN' | Burl Ives, Decca 31371 | | 3 |
| 31 | 33 | 36 | 48 | ANYTHING THAT'S PART OF YOU | Elvis Presley, RCA Victor 7992 | △ | 6 |
| ★ 32 | 49 | 67 | — | HIDE NOR HAIR | Ray Charles and His Ork, ABC-Paramount 10314 | | 3 |
| ★ 33 | 43 | 64 | 83 | SHOUT! SHOUT! (Knock Yourself Out) | Ernie Maresca, Seville 117 | | 4 |
| 34 | 18 | 11 | 7 | WHAT'S YOUR NAME | Don and Juan, Big Top 3079 | | 11 |
| 35 | 40 | 52 | 70 | WHAT'D I SAY | Bobby Darin, Atco 6221 | | 4 |
| 36 | 28 | 18 | 21 | I'VE GOT BONNIE | Bobby Rydell, Cameo 209 | | 10 |
| 37 | 23 | 15 | 19 | PLEASE DON'T ASK ABOUT BARBARA | Bobby Vee, Liberty 55419 | | 9 |
| ★ 38 | 53 | 69 | 82 | I WISH THAT WE WERE MARRIED | Ronnie and the Hi-Lites, Joy 260 | | 4 |
| ★ 39 | 61 | 97 | — | OLD RIVERS | Walter Brennan, Liberty 55436 | | 3 |
| 40 | 26 | 17 | 17 | COME BACK SILLY GIRL | Lettermen, Capitol 4699 | | 10 |
| 41 | 37 | 39 | 39 | SOMETHING'S GOT A HOLD ON ME | Etta James, Argo 5409 | | 9 |
| 42 | 50 | 55 | 67 | TWO OF A KIND | Sue Thompson, Hickory 1166 | | 6 |
| ★ 43 | 56 | 68 | 80 | UPTOWN | Crystals, Philles 102 | | 4 |
| 44 | 38 | 28 | 35 | WHEN MY LITTLE GIRL IS SMILING | Drifters, Atlantic 2134 | | 9 |
| 45 | 45 | 47 | 58 | TELL ME | Dick & Deedee, Liberty 55412 | | 6 |
| 46 | 55 | 62 | 71 | THE ONE WHO REALLY LOVES YOU | Mary Wells, Motown 1024 | | 5 |
| ★ 47 | 66 | — | — | EVERYBODY LOVES ME BUT YOU | Brenda Lee, Decca 31379 | | 2 |
| ★ 48 | 60 | 71 | 91 | CATERINA | Perry Como, RCA Victor 8004 | △ | 4 |
| 49 | 35 | 21 | 22 | WHERE HAVE ALL THE FLOWERS GONE | Kingston Trio, Capitol 4671 | | 14 |
| 50 | 52 | 59 | 64 | AT THE CLUB | Ray Charles and His Ork, ABC-Paramount 10314 | | 4 |
| 51 | 46 | 38 | 42 | CRY, BABY, CRY | Angels, Caprice 112 | | 10 |
| 52 | 54 | 58 | 65 | YOU TALK ABOUT LOVE | Barbara George, AFO 304 | | 4 |
| ★ 53 | 63 | 76 | 93 | YOU ARE MINE | Frankie Avalon, Chancellor 1107 | | 5 |
| 54 | 30 | 19 | 14 | SHE'S GOT YOU | Patsy Cline, Decca 31354 | | 13 |
| 55 | 57 | 57 | 66 | MOMENTS | Jennell Hawkins, Amazon 1003 | | 5 |
| 56 | 59 | 63 | 72 | TRA LA LA LA LA | Ike & Tina Turner, Sue 757 | | 5 |
| 57 | 36 | 22 | 23 | YOU WIN AGAIN | Fats Domino, Imperial 5816 | | 9 |
| 58 | 51 | 56 | 60 | ANNIE GET YOUR YO-YO | Little Junior Parker, Duke 345 | | 7 |
| 59 | 68 | 81 | 87 | I WILL | Vic Dana, Dolton 51 | | 4 |
| 60 | 44 | 45 | 40 | ALVIN TWIST | Chipmunks, Liberty 55424 | | 8 |
| 61 | 42 | 20 | 13 | DUKE OF EARL | Gene (Duke of Earl) Chandler, Vee Jay 416 | | 15 |
| ★ 62 | 81 | — | — | CONSCIENCE | James Darren, Colpix 630 | | 2 |
| 63 | 71 | 89 | 97 | TWISTIN' MATILDA | Jimmy Soul, SPQR 3300 | | 4 |
| 64 | 58 | 43 | 47 | PATTI ANN | Johnny Crawford, Del Fi 4172 | | 8 |
| 65 | 72 | 80 | — | RUNAWAY | Lawrence Welk, Dot 16336 | | 3 |
| 66 | 67 | 78 | 99 | THE BIG DRAFT | Four Preps, Capitol 4716 | | 4 |
| 67 | 73 | 90 | 100 | KING OF CLOWNS | Neil Sedaka, RCA Victor 8007 | △ | 4 |
| 68 | 79 | 84 | — | PATRICIA TWIST | Perez Prado, RCA Victor 8006 | △ | 3 |
| 69 | 48 | 35 | 37 | IF A WOMAN ANSWERS | Leroy Van Dyke, Mercury 71926 | | 7 |
| 70 | 83 | 91 | — | ITTY BITTY PIECES | James Ray, Caprice 114 | | 3 |
| ★ 71 | 89 | — | — | NIGHT TRAIN | James Brown, King 5614 | | 2 |
| 72 | 65 | 75 | 79 | THE BALLAD OF THUNDER ROAD | Robert Mitchum, Capitol 3986 | | 9 |
| 73 | 86 | — | — | BLUES (Stay Away From Me) | Ace Cannon, Hi 2051 | | 2 |
| 74 | 69 | 72 | 78 | CHAPEL BY THE SEA | Billy Vaughn, Dot 16329 | | 6 |
| 75 | 85 | 100 | — | COUNT EVERY STAR | Linda Scott, Canadian-American 133 | | 3 |
| 76 | 78 | 82 | — | THOU SHALT NOT STEAL | John D. Loudermilk, RCA Victor 7993 | △ | 3 |
| 77 | 70 | 73 | 69 | MIDNIGHT SPECIAL | Jimmy Smith, Blue Note 1819 | | 8 |
| 78 | 74 | 86 | 89 | THE RAINS CAME | Big Sam, Eric 7003 | | 7 |
| 79 | 84 | 88 | 92 | (WHAT A SAD WAY) TO LOVE SOMEONE | Ral Donner, Gone 5125 | | 5 |
| ★ 80 | — | — | — | I SOLD MY HEART TO THE JUNKMAN | Blue Belles, Newtown 5000 | | 1 |
| ★ 81 | — | — | — | MOST PEOPLE GET MARRIED | Patti Page, Mercury 71950 | | 1 |
| ★ 82 | — | — | — | (I WAS) BORN TO CRY | Dion, Laurie 3123 | | 1 |
| 83 | 80 | 61 | 84 | WHITE ROSE OF ATHENS | David Carroll, Mercury 71917 | | 7 |
| 84 | 87 | 74 | 76 | MEMORIES OF MARIA | Jerry Byrd, Monument 449 | | 6 |
| 85 | 82 | 83 | 85 | WHAT AM I SUPPOSED TO DO | Ann-Margret, RCA Victor 7986 | △ | 5 |
| ★ 86 | — | — | — | LOVERS WHO WANDER | Dion, Laurie 3123 | | 1 |
| 87 | 91 | — | — | LOVESICK BLUES | Floyd Cramer, RCA Victor 8013 | △ | 2 |
| ★ 88 | — | — | — | IF I CRIED EVERY TIME YOU HURT ME | Wanda Jackson, Capitol 4723 | | 1 |
| 89 | 77 | 66 | 75 | LOLLIPOPS AND ROSES | Jack Jones, Kapp 435 | | 8 |
| 90 | 98 | — | — | MEET ME AT THE TWISTIN' PLACE | Johnnie Morisette, Sar 126 | | 2 |
| 91 | 100 | — | — | SO THIS IS LOVE | Castells, Era 3073 | | 2 |
| 92 | — | — | — | DOCTOR FEEL GOOD | Dr. Feelgood and the Internes, Okeh 7144 | | 1 |
| 93 | — | — | — | I FOUND LOVE | Jackie Wilson and Linda Hopkins, Brunswick 55224 | | 1 |
| 94 | 76 | 79 | 77 | WHO WILL THE NEXT FOOL BE | Bobby Bland, Duke 347 | | 4 |
| 95 | — | — | — | DON'T PLAY THAT SONG | Ben E. King, Atco 6222 | | 1 |
| 96 | 96 | — | 98 | I FOUND A LOVE | Falcons, LuPine 1003 | | 3 |
| 97 | 99 | — | — | I'LL TAKE YOU HOME | Corsairs, Tuff 1818 | | 2 |
| 98 | — | — | — | TEACH ME TONIGHT | George Maharis, Epic 9504 | | 1 |
| 99 | — | — | — | FUNNY | Gene McDaniels, Liberty 55444 | | 1 |
| 100 | — | — | — | DEEP IN THE HEART OF TEXAS | Duane Eddy, RCA Victor 7999 | △ | 1 |

## HOT 100—A TO Z—(Publisher-Licensee)

Alvin Twist (Monarch, ASCAP) .......... 60
Annie Get Your Yo-Yo (Don, BMI) .......... 58
Anything That's Part of You (Gladys, ASCAP) .... 31
At the Club (Tangerine, BMI) .......... 50
Ballad of Thunder Road, The (Leeds, ASCAP) .... 72
Big Draft, The (Lar-Bell, BMI) .......... 66
Blues (Stay Away From Me) (Lois, BMI) .......... 73
Caterina (Roncom, ASCAP) .......... 48
Chapel by the Sea (Sun-Vine, BMI) .......... 74
Cinderella (Vin-Sun, ASCAP) .......... 19
Come Back Silly Girl (Aldon, BMI) .......... 40
Conscience (Aldon, BMI) .......... 62
Count Every Star (Paxton, ASCAP) .......... 75
Cry, Baby, Cry (Jersey, BMI) .......... 51
Dear One (Maureen, BMI) .......... 11
Deep in the Heart of Texas (Melody Lane, BMI) ..100
Doctor Feel Good (Cigma, BMI) .......... 92
Don't Break the Heart That Loves You (Francon, ASCAP) .......... 13
Don't Play That Song (Progressive, BMI) .......... 95
Dream Baby (Combine, BMI) .......... 20
Duke of Earl (Conrad-Karlan, BMI) .......... 61
Everybody Loves Me But You (Champion, BMI) .. 47
Funny (Chappell, ASCAP) .......... 99
Funny Way of Laughin' (Pamper, BMI) .......... 30
Ginny Come Lately (Pogo, ASCAP) .......... 23
Good Luck Charm (Gladys, ASCAP) .......... 1
Hey! Baby (LeBill, BMI) .......... 18
Hide Nor Hair (Tangerine, BMI) .......... 32
I Found a Love (LuPine-Progressive-Alibri, BMI) .. 96
I Found Love (Pearl, BMI) .......... 93
I Sold My Heart to the Junkman (Mills, ASCAP) .. 80
(I Was) Born to Cry (Disal, ASCAP) .......... 82
I Will (Camarillo, BMI) .......... 59
I Wish That We Were Married (Joy, ASCAP) ...... 38
I'll Take You Home (Sunflower & Annie-Earl, BMI). 97
I've Got Bonnie (Aldon, BMI) .......... 36
If a Woman Answers (Aldon, BMI) .......... 69
If I Cried Every Time You Hurt Me (Central, BMI) .......... 88
Itty Bitty Pieces (Good Songs, BMI) .......... 70
Jam, The (Cheltenham, BMI) .......... 29
Johnny Angel (Post, ASCAP) .......... 2
Johnny Jingo (Dickson, ASCAP) .......... 27
King of Clowns (Aldon, BMI) .......... 67
Let Me In (Arc-Kae Williams, BMI) .......... 28
Lollipops and Roses (Garland, ASCAP) .......... 89
Love Letters (Famous, ASCAP) .......... 8
Love Me Warm and Tender (Spanka, BMI) ...... 14
Lover, Please (Lyn-Lou, BMI) .......... 7
Lovers Who Wander (Disal, ASCAP) .......... 86
Lovesick Blues (Mills, ASCAP) .......... 87
Mashed Potato Time (Rice-Mill, BMI) .......... 3
Meet Me at the Twistin' Place (Kags, BMI) .... 90
Memories of Maria (Acuff-Rose, BMI) .......... 84
Midnight in Moscow (Melody Trails, BMI) ...... 16
Midnight Special (Edmy, BMI) .......... 77
Moments (Titanic, BMI) .......... 55
Most People Get Married (Famous, ASCAP) ...... 81
Night Train (Pamlee, BMI) .......... 71
Nut Rocker (Fowley, BMI) .......... 25
Old Rivers (Glo-Mac & Metric, BMI) .......... 39
One Who Really Loves You, The (Jobete, BMI) .. 46
P.T. 109 (Cedarwood, BMI) .......... 22
Patricia Twist (Peer Int'l, BMI) .......... 68
Patti Ann (Maraville, BMI) .......... 64
Please Don't Ask About Barabara (Aldon, BMI) .... 37
Rains Came, The (Crazy Cajun-Corette, BMI) .... 78
Runaway (Vicki, BMI) .......... 65
She Can't Find Her Keys (Arch, ASCAP) .......... 21
She Cried (Trio, BMI) .......... 15
She's Got You (Pamper, BMI) .......... 54
Shout (Wemar-Nom, BMI) .......... 9
Shout! Shout! (Knock Yourself Out) (Broadway, ASCAP) .......... 33
Slow Twistin' (Woodcrest, BMI) .......... 4
So This Is Love (Pattern, ASCAP) .......... 91
Soldier Boy (Ludix, BMI) .......... 6
Something's Got a Hold on Me (Figure, BMI) .... 41
Soul Twist (Dan-Kelyn, BMI) .......... 26
Stranger on the Shore (Mellin, BMI) .......... 10
Teach Me Tonight (Hub, ASCAP) .......... 98
Tell Me (Odin, ASCAP) .......... 45
Thou Shalt Not Steal (Acuff-Rose, BMI) .......... 76
Tra La La La La (Saturn, BMI) .......... 56
Twist, Twist, Senora (Rockmasters, BMI) .......... 12
Twistin' Matilda (General-Pickwick, ASCAP) .... 63
Twistin' the Night Away (Kags, BMI) .......... 17
Two of a Kind (Acuff-Rose, BMI) .......... 42
Uptown (Aldon, BMI) .......... 43
(What a Sad Way) to Love Someone (Tricky-Recherche, ASCAP) .......... 79
What Am I Supposed to Do (Pamper, BMI) ...... 85
What'd I Say (Progressive, BMI) .......... 35
What's Your Name (Hill & Range, BMI) .......... 34
When My Little Girl Is Smiling (Aldon, BMI) .... 44
Where Have All the Flowers Gone (Fall River, BMI) 49
White Rose of Athens (Peter Schaeffer's, BMI) .. 83
Who Will the Next Fool Be (Knox, BMI) .......... 94
You Are Mine (Debmar, BMI) .......... 53
You Better Move On (Keva, BMI) .......... 24
You Talk About Love (Saturn, BMI) .......... 52
You Win Again (Fred Rose, BMI) .......... 57
Young World (Four Star, BMI) .......... 5

## BUBBLING UNDER THE HOT 100

101. NUMBER ONE MAN ................Bruce Channel, Smash 1752
102. WALK ON THE WILD SIDE..........Elmer Bernstein, Choreo 101
103. I'VE BEEN GOOD TO YOU..............Miracles, Tamla 54053
104. YOU DON'T MISS YOUR WATER..........William Bell, Stax 116
105. OPERATOR ..............Gladys Knight and the Pips, Fury 1064
106. HONKY-TONK MAN ............Johnny Horton, Columbia 42302
107. COOKIN' ......................Al Casey Combo, Stacy 925
108. MARCH OF THE SIAMESE CHILDREN........Kenny Ball, Kapp 451
109. HULLY GULLY CALLING TIME............Jive Five, Beltone 2019
110. LOVE THEME FROM EL CID............Billy Storm, Infinity 013
111. HERE COMES THAT FEELING...........Brenda Lee, Decca 31379
112. VILLAGE OF LOVE...........Nathaniel Mayer, United Artists 449
113. I LOVE YOU ............................Volumes, Chex 1002
114. I'M ON MY WAY.............Highwaymen, United Artists 439
115. QUARTER TO FOUR STOMP...............Stompers, Landa 684
116. LEMON TREE ..........Peter, Paul and Mary, Warner Bros. 5274
117. I LEFT MY HEART IN SAN FRANCISCO....................
..........................Tony Bennett, Columbia 42332
118. SPANISH HARLEM.....Santo and Johnny, Canadian-American 137
119. NEED YOUR LOVE.........................Metallics, Baronet 2
120. A WOMAN IS A MAN'S BEST FRIEND....................
.......................Teddy and the Twilights, Swan 4102

# BILLBOARD HOT 100

**FOR WEEK ENDING APRIL 28, 1962**

★ STAR PERFORMERS—Selections registering greatest upward progress this week.

S Indicates that 45 r.p.m. stereo single version is available.
△ Indicates that 33⅓ r.p.m. mono single version is available.
Ⓢ Indicates that 33⅓ r.p.m. stereo single version is available.

| This Week | Wk. Ago | 2 Wks. Ago | 3 Wks. Ago | Title, Artist, Label & Number | Weeks On Chart |
|---|---|---|---|---|---|
| 1 | 1 | 2 | 3 | GOOD LUCK CHARM — Elvis Presley, RCA Victor 7992 △ | 7 |
| 2 | 2 | 1 | 1 | JOHNNY ANGEL — Shelley Fabares, Colpix 621 | 9 |
| 3 | 3 | 4 | 10 | MASHED POTATO TIME — Dee Dee Sharp, Cameo 212 | 9 |
| 4 | 6 | 11 | 24 | SOLDIER BOY — Shirelles, Scepter 1228 | 6 |
| 5 | 4 | 3 | 4 | SLOW TWISTIN' — Chubby Checker, Parkway 835 | 9 |
| 6 | 5 | 6 | 8 | YOUNG WORLD — Rick Nelson, Imperial 5805 | 9 |
| 7 | 10 | 19 | 31 | STRANGER ON THE SHORE — Mr. Acker Bilk, Atco 6217 | 7 |
| 8 | 7 | 8 | 16 | LOVER, PLEASE — Clyde McPhatter, Mercury 71941 | 8 |
| 9 | 9 | 14 | 26 | SHOUT — Joey Dee & the Starliters, Roulette 4416 | 6 |
| 10 | 12 | 20 | 32 | TWIST, TWIST, SENORA — Gary (U.S.) Bonds, LeGrand 1018 | 5 |
| 11 | 8 | 5 | 9 | LOVE LETTERS — Ketty Lester, Era 3068 | 10 |
| ★12 | 22 | 39 | 70 | P. T. 109 — Jimmy Dean, Columbia 42338 △ | 5 |
| 13 | 11 | 18 | 25 | DEAR ONE — Larry Finnegan, Old Town 1113 | 10 |
| 14 | 15 | 22 | 34 | SHE CRIED — Jay & the Americans, United Artists 415 | 7 |
| 15 | 14 | 12 | 12 | LOVE ME WARM AND TENDER — Paul Anka, RCA Victor 7977 △ | 10 |
| 16 | 19 | 21 | 40 | CINDERELLA — Jack Ross, Dot 16333 | 6 |
| 17 | 26 | 31 | 33 | SOUL TWIST — King Curtis, Enjoy 1000 | 8 |
| 18 | 17 | 17 | 14 | TWISTIN' THE NIGHT AWAY — Sam Cooke, RCA Victor 7983 △ | 13 |
| 19 | 21 | 24 | 30 | SHE CAN'T FIND HER KEYS — Paul Peterson, Colpix 620 | 9 |
| 20 | 30 | 41 | 65 | FUNNY WAY OF LAUGHIN' — Burl Ives, Decca 31371 | 4 |
| 21 | 23 | 27 | 37 | GINNY COME LATELY — Brian Hyland, ABC-Paramount 10294 | 8 |
| 22 | 27 | 34 | 42 | JOHNNY JINGO — Hayley Mills, Vista 395 | 7 |
| 23 | 32 | 49 | 67 | HIDE NOR HAIR — Ray Charles and His Ork., ABC-Paramount 10314 | 4 |
| ★24 | 35 | 40 | 52 | WHAT'D I SAY — Bobby Darin, Atco 6221 | 5 |
| 25 | 39 | 61 | 97 | OLD RIVERS — Walter Brennan, Liberty 55436 | 4 |
| ★26 | 47 | 66 | — | EVERYBODY LOVES ME BUT YOU — Brenda Lee, Decca 31379 | 3 |
| 27 | 33 | 43 | 64 | SHOUT! SHOUT! (Knock Yourself Out) — Ernie Maresca, Seville 117 | 5 |
| 28 | 16 | 9 | 7 | MIDNIGHT IN MOSCOW — Kenny Ball, Kapp 442 | 13 |
| 29 | 24 | 25 | 27 | YOU BETTER MOVE ON — Arthur Alexander, Dot 16309 | 10 |
| 30 | 25 | 29 | 23 | NUT ROCKER — B. Bumble & the Stingers, Renderovus 166 | 9 |
| 31 | 29 | 32 | 44 | THE JAM — Bobby Gregg and His Friends, Cotton 1003 | 7 |
| 32 | 13 | 7 | 2 | I DON'T BREAK THE HEART THAT LOVES YOU — Connie Francis, MGM 13059 | 12 |
| 33 | 38 | 53 | 69 | I WISH THAT WE WERE MARRIED — Ronnie and the Hi-Lites, Joy 260 | 5 |
| ★34 | 48 | 60 | 71 | CATERINA — Perry Como, RCA Victor 8004 △ | 5 |
| 35 | 31 | 33 | 36 | ANYTHING THAT'S PART OF YOU — Elvis Presley, RCA Victor 7992 △ | 7 |
| 36 | 28 | 15 | 13 | LET ME IN — Sensations, Argo 5405 | 17 |
| 37 | 43 | 56 | 68 | UPTOWN — Crystals, Philles 102 | 5 |
| 38 | 20 | 13 | 5 | DREAM BABY — Roy Orbison, Monument 456 | 11 |
| 39 | 41 | 37 | 39 | SOMETHING'S GOT A HOLD ON ME — Etta James, Argo 5409 | 10 |
| 40 | 18 | 10 | 6 | HEY! BABY — Bruce Channel, Smash 1731 | 14 |
| 41 | 46 | 55 | 62 | THE ONE WHO REALLY LOVES YOU — Mary Wells, Motown 1024 | 6 |
| ★42 | 63 | 71 | 89 | TWISTIN' MATILDA — Jimmy Soul, SPQR 3300 | 5 |
| ★43 | 62 | 81 | — | CONSCIENCE — James Darren, Colpix 630 | 3 |
| 44 | 37 | 23 | 15 | PLEASE DON'T ASK ABOUT BARBARA — Bobby Vee, Liberty 55419 | 10 |
| 45 | 50 | 52 | 59 | AT THE CLUB — Ray Charles and His Ork., ABC-Paramount 10314 | 5 |
| 46 | 52 | 54 | 58 | YOU TALK ABOUT LOVE — Barbara George, AFO 304 | 5 |
| 47 | 42 | 50 | 55 | TWO OF A KIND — Sue Thompson, Hickory 1166 | 7 |
| 48 | 45 | 45 | 47 | TELL ME — Dick & Deedee, Liberty 55412 | 7 |
| 49 | 53 | 63 | 76 | YOU ARE MINE — Frankie Avalon, Chancellor 1107 | 6 |
| 50 | 56 | 59 | 63 | TRA LA LA LA LA — Ike & Tina Turner, Sue 757 | 6 |
| 51 | 34 | 18 | 11 | WHAT'S YOUR NAME — Don and Juan, Big Top 3079 | 12 |
| 52 | 55 | 57 | 57 | MOMENTS — Jennell Hawkins, Amazon 1003 | 6 |
| 53 | 36 | 28 | 18 | I'VE GOT BONNIE — Bobby Rydell, Cameo 209 | 11 |
| 54 | 59 | 68 | 81 | I WILL — Vic Dana, Dolton 51 | 5 |
| 55 | 40 | 26 | 17 | COME BACK SILLY GIRL — Lettermen, Capitol 4699 | 11 |
| ★56 | 67 | 73 | 90 | KING OF CLOWNS — Neil Sedaka, RCA Victor 8007 △ | 5 |
| 57 | 73 | 86 | — | BLUES (Stay Away From Me) — Ace Cannon, Hi 2051 | 3 |
| 58 | 71 | 89 | — | NIGHT TRAIN — James Brown, King 5614 | 3 |
| 59 | 65 | 72 | 80 | RUNAWAY — Lawrence Welk, Dot 16336 | 4 |
| 60 | 58 | 51 | 56 | ANNIE GET YOUR YO-YO — Little Junior Parker, Duke 345 | 8 |
| 61 | 44 | 38 | 28 | WHEN MY LITTLE GIRL IS SMILING — Drifters, Atlantic 2134 | 10 |
| 62 | 70 | 83 | 91 | ITTY BITTY PIECES — James Ray, Caprice 114 | 4 |
| 63 | 66 | 67 | 78 | THE BIG DRAFT — Four Preps, Capitol 4716 | 4 |
| 64 | — | 86 | — | LOVERS WHO WANDER — Dion, Laurie 3123 | 2 |
| 65 | 68 | 79 | 84 | PATRICIA TWIST — Perez Prado, RCA Victor 8006 △ | 4 |
| 66 | 80 | — | — | I SOLD MY HEART TO THE JUNKMAN — Blue Belles, Newtown 5000 | 2 |
| 67 | 51 | 46 | 38 | CRY, BABY, CRY — Angels, Caprice 112 | 11 |
| 68 | 64 | 58 | 43 | PATTI ANN — Johnny Crawford, Del Fi 4172 | 9 |
| 69 | 81 | — | — | MOST PEOPLE GET MARRIED — Patti Page, Mercury 71950 | 2 |
| 70 | 75 | 85 | 100 | COUNT EVERY STAR — Linda Scott, Canadian-American 133 | 4 |
| 71 | 82 | — | — | (I WAS) BORN TO CRY — Dion, Laurie 3123 | 2 |
| 72 | 57 | 36 | 22 | YOU WIN AGAIN — Fats Domino, Imperial 5816 | 10 |
| ★73 | 95 | — | — | DON'T PLAY THAT SONG — Ben E. King, Atco 6222 | 2 |
| 74 | 79 | 84 | 88 | (WHAT A SAD WAY) TO LOVE SOMEONE — Ral Donner, Gone 5125 | 6 |
| 75 | 76 | 78 | 82 | THOU SHALT NOT STEAL — John D. Loudermilk, RCA Victor 7993 △ | 4 |
| 76 | 72 | 65 | 75 | THE BALLAD OF THUNDER ROAD — Robert Mitchum, Capitol 3986 | 10 |
| 77 | 88 | — | — | IF I CRIED EVERY TIME YOU HURT ME — Wanda Jackson, Capitol 4723 | 2 |
| 78 | — | — | — | HEARTS — Jackie Wilson, Brunswick 55225 | 1 |
| 79 | 84 | 87 | 74 | MEMORIES OF MARIA — Jerry Byrd, Monument 449 | 7 |
| 80 | 91 | 100 | — | SO THIS IS LOVE — Castells, Era 3073 | 3 |
| 81 | 96 | 96 | — | I FOUND A LOVE — Falcons, LuPine 1003 | 4 |
| 82 | 90 | 98 | — | MEET ME AT THE TWISTIN' PLACE — Johnnie Morisette, Sar 126 | 3 |
| ★83 | — | — | — | VILLAGE OF LOVE — Nathaniel Mayer, United Artists 449 | 1 |
| ★84 | — | — | — | ANY DAY NOW — Chuck Jackson, Wand 122 | 1 |
| 85 | 92 | — | — | DOCTOR FEEL GOOD — Dr. Feelgood and the Internes, Okeh 7144 | 2 |
| ★86 | — | — | — | LOVE CAN'T WAIT — Marty Robbins, Columbia 42375 △ | 1 |
| 87 | 87 | 91 | — | LOVESICK BLUES — Floyd Cramer, RCA Victor 8013 △ | 3 |
| 88 | 100 | — | — | DEEP IN THE HEART OF TEXAS — Duane Eddy, RCA Victor 7999 △ | 2 |
| 89 | 98 | — | — | TEACH ME TONIGHT — George Maharis, Epic 9504 | 2 |
| ★90 | — | — | — | NUMBER ONE MAN — Bruce Channel, Smash 1752 | 1 |
| 91 | — | — | — | SCOTCH AND SODA — Kingston Trio, Capitol 4740 | 1 |
| 92 | 97 | 99 | — | I'LL TAKE YOU HOME — Corsairs, Tuff 1818 | 3 |
| 93 | — | — | — | WALK ON WITH THE DUKE — Duke of Earl, Vee Jay 440 | 1 |
| 94 | — | — | — | THE MAN WHO SHOT LIBERTY VALANCE — Gene Pitney, Musicor 1020 | 1 |
| 95 | — | — | — | YOU DON'T MISS YOUR WATER — William Bell, Stax 116 | 1 |
| 96 | — | — | — | HERE COMES THAT FEELING — Brenda Lee, Decca 31379 | 1 |
| 97 | — | — | — | I LOVE YOU — Volumes, Chex 1002 | 1 |
| 98 | — | — | — | BALBOA BLUE — Marketts, Liberty 55443 | 1 |
| 99 | — | — | — | DRUMMIN' UP A STORM — Sandy Nelson, Imperial 5829 | 1 |
| 100 | — | — | — | THAT'S MY DESIRE — Sensations, Argo 5412 | 1 |

## BUBBLING UNDER THE HOT 100

101. NEED YOUR LOVE ............ Metallics, Baronet 2
102. HONKY-TONK MAN ............ Johnny Horton, Columbia 42302
103. OPERATOR ............ Glady Knight and the Pips, Fury 1064
104. WHAT AM I SUPPOSED TO DO ............ Ann-Margret, RCA Victor 7986
105. LOVE THEME FROM EL CID ............ Billy Storm, Infinity 013
106. LIPSTICK TRACES ............ Benny Spellman, Minit 644
107. COOKIN' ............ Al Casey Combo, Stacy 925
108. THE PRINCE ............ Jackie DeShannon, Liberty 55425
109. HULLY GULLY CALLING TIME ............ Jive Five, Beltone 2019
110. I'VE BEEN GOOD TO YOU ............ Miracles, Tamla 54053
111. OH MY ANGEL ............ Bertha Tillman, Brent 7029
112. I LEFT MY HEART IN SAN FRANCISCO ............ Tony Bennett, Columbia 42332
113. LEMON TREE ............ Peter, Paul and Mary, Warner Bros. 5274
114. FUNNY ............ Gene McDaniels, Liberty 55444
115. ADIOS AMIGOS ............ Jim Reeves, RCA Victor 8019
116. TWISTIN' WHITE SILVER SANDS ............ Bill Black's Combo, Hi 2052
117. FORTUNE TELLER ............ Bobby Curtola, Del Fi 4177
118. FOR THE FIRST TIME IN MY LIFE ............ Adam Wade, Coed 567
119. SWINGIN' SHEPHERD BLUES TWIST ............ Moe Koffman, Ascot 2100
120. POP-EYE STROLL ............ Mar-Keys, Stax 121

# BILLBOARD HOT 100

FOR WEEK ENDING MAY 5

1962

★ STAR PERFORMERS—Selections registering greatest upward progress this week.

S Indicates that 45 r.p.m. stereo single version is available.

△ Indicates that 33⅓ r.p.m. mono single version is available.

△S Indicates that 33⅓ r.p.m. stereo single version is available.

| This Week | 1 Wk. Ago | 2 Wks. Ago | 3 Wks. Ago | TITLE Artist, Label & Number | Weeks On Chart |
|---|---|---|---|---|---|
| 1 | 4 | 6 | 11 | SOLDIER BOY — Shirelles, Scepter 1228 | 7 |
| 2 | 3 | 3 | 4 | MASHED POTATO TIME — Dee Dee Sharp, Cameo 212 | 10 |
| 3 | 2 | 2 | 1 | JOHNNY ANGEL — Shelley Fabares, Colpix 621 | 10 |
| 4 | 7 | 10 | 19 | STRANGER ON THE SHORE — Mr. Acker Bilk, Atco 6217 | 8 |
| 5 | 1 | 1 | 2 | GOOD LUCK CHARM △ — Elvis Presley, RCA Victor 7992 | 8 |
| 6 | 9 | 9 | 14 | SHOUT — Joey Dee & the Starliters, Roulette 4416 | 7 |
| 7 | 8 | 7 | 8 | LOVER, PLEASE — Clyde McPhatter, Mercury 71941 | 10 |
| 8 | 5 | 4 | 3 | SLOW TWISTIN' — Chubby Checker, Parkway 835 | 10 |
| 9 | 12 | 22 | 39 | P. T. 109 △ — Jimmy Dean, Columbia 42338 | 6 |
| 10 | 10 | 12 | 20 | TWIST, TWIST, SENORA — Gary (U. S.) Bonds, LeGrand 1018 | 6 |
| 11 | 6 | 5 | 6 | YOUNG WORLD — Rick Nelson, Imperial 5805 | 10 |
| 12 | 13 | 11 | 18 | DEAR ONE — Larry Finnegan, Old Town 1113 | 11 |
| 13 | 14 | 15 | 22 | SHE CRIED — Jay & the Americans, United Artists 415 | 8 |
| ★14 | 20 | 30 | 41 | FUNNY WAY OF LAUGHIN' — Burl Ives, Decca 31371 | 5 |
| ★15 | 25 | 39 | 61 | OLD RIVERS — Walter Brennan, Liberty 55436 | 5 |
| ★16 | 27 | 33 | 43 | SHOUT! SHOUT! (Knock Yourself Out) — Ernie Maresca, Seville 117 | 6 |
| 17 | 17 | 26 | 31 | SOUL TWIST — King Curtis, Enjoy 1000 | 9 |
| ★18 | 26 | 47 | 66 | EVERYBODY LOVES ME BUT YOU — Brenda Lee, Decca 31379 | 4 |
| 19 | 11 | 8 | 5 | LOVE LETTERS — Ketty Lester, Era 3068 | 11 |
| 20 | 23 | 32 | 49 | HIDE NOR HAIR — Ray Charles and His Ork, ABC-Paramount 10314 | 5 |
| 21 | 22 | 27 | 34 | JOHNNY JINGO — Hayley Mills, Vista 395 | 8 |
| 22 | 19 | 21 | 24 | SHE CAN'T FIND HER KEYS — Paul Peterson, Colpix 620 | 10 |
| 23 | 15 | 14 | 12 | LOVE ME WARM AND TENDER △ — Paul Anka, RCA Victor 7977 | 11 |
| ★24 | 37 | 43 | 56 | UPTOWN — Crystals, Philles 102 | 6 |
| 25 | 16 | 19 | 21 | CINDERELLA — Jack Ross, Dot 16333 | 8 |
| ★26 | 43 | 62 | 81 | CONSCIENCE — James Darren, Colpix 630 | 4 |
| 27 | 33 | 38 | 53 | I WISH THAT WE WERE MARRIED — Ronnie and the Hi-Lites, Joy 260 | 5 |
| 28 | 24 | 35 | 40 | WHAT'D I SAY — Bobby Darin, Atco 6221 | 6 |
| 29 | 34 | 48 | 60 | CATERINA △ — Perry Como, RCA Victor 8004 | 5 |
| 30 | 31 | 29 | 32 | THE JAM — Bobby Gregg and His Friends, Cotton 1003 | 8 |
| 31 | 21 | 23 | 27 | GINNY COME LATELY — Brian Hyland, ABC-Paramount 10294 | 9 |
| 32 | 18 | 17 | 17 | TWISTIN' THE NIGHT AWAY △ — Sam Cooke, RCA Victor 7983 | 14 |
| ★33 | 64 | 86 | — | LOVERS WHO WANDER — Dion, Laurie 3123 | 3 |
| 34 | 41 | 46 | 55 | THE ONE WHO REALLY LOVES YOU — Mary Wells, Motown 1024 | 7 |
| 35 | 30 | 25 | 29 | NUT ROCKER — B. Bumble & the Stingers, Rendezvous 166 | 10 |
| 36 | 42 | 63 | 71 | TWISTIN' MATILDA — Jimmy Soul, SPQR 3300 | 6 |
| ★37 | 49 | 53 | 63 | YOU ARE MINE — Frankie Avalon, Chancellor 1107 | 7 |
| 38 | 29 | 24 | 25 | YOU BETTER MOVE ON — Arthur Alexander, Dot 16309 | 11 |
| 39 | 28 | 16 | 9 | MIDNIGHT IN MOSCOW — Kenny Ball, Kapp 442 | 14 |
| 40 | 35 | 31 | 33 | ANYTHING THAT'S PART OF YOU △ — Elvis Presley, RCA Victor 7992 | 8 |
| 41 | 48 | 45 | 45 | TELL ME — Dick & Deedee, Liberty 55412 | 8 |
| 42 | 36 | 28 | 15 | LET ME IN — Sensations, Argo 5405 | 18 |
| 43 | 47 | 42 | 50 | TWO OF A KIND — Sue Thompson, Hickory 1166 | 8 |
| ★44 | 66 | 80 | — | I SOLD MY HEART TO THE JUNKMAN — Blue Belles, Newtown 5000 | 3 |
| 45 | 38 | 20 | 13 | DREAM BABY — Roy Orbison, Monument 456 | 12 |
| ★46 | 69 | 81 | — | MOST PEOPLE GET MARRIED — Patti Page, Mercury 71950 | 3 |
| 47 | 54 | 59 | 68 | I WILL — Vic Dana, Dolton 51 | 6 |
| 48 | 45 | 50 | 52 | AT THE CLUB — Ray Charles and His Ork, ABC-Paramount 10314 | 6 |
| 49 | 39 | 41 | 37 | SOMETHING'S GOT A HOLD ON ME — Etta James, Argo 5409 | 11 |
| 50 | 52 | 55 | 57 | MOMENTS — Jennell Hawkins, Amazon 1003 | 7 |
| 51 | 58 | 71 | 89 | NIGHT TRAIN — James Brown, King 5614 | 4 |
| 52 | 56 | 67 | 73 | KING OF CLOWNS △ — Neil Sedaka, RCA Victor 8007 | 6 |
| 53 | 57 | 73 | 86 | BLUES (Stay Away From Me) — Ace Cannon, Hi 2051 | 4 |
| 54 | 62 | 70 | 83 | ITTY BITTY PIECES — James Ray, Caprice 114 | 5 |
| 55 | 46 | 52 | 54 | YOU TALK ABOUT LOVE — Barbara George, AFO 304 | 6 |
| 56 | 59 | 65 | 72 | RUNAWAY — Lawrence Welk, Dot 16336 | 5 |
| 57 | 40 | 18 | 10 | HEY! BABY — Bruce Channel, Smash 1731 | 15 |
| ★58 | 71 | 82 | — | (I WAS) BORN TO CRY — Dion, Laurie 3123 | 3 |
| ★59 | 73 | 95 | — | DON'T PLAY THAT SONG — Ben E. King, Atco 6222 | 3 |
| ★60 | 70 | 75 | 85 | COUNT EVERY STAR — Linda Scott, Canadian-American 133 | 5 |
| 61 | 63 | 66 | 67 | THE BIG DRAFT — Four Preps, Capitol 4716 | 6 |
| 62 | 50 | 56 | 59 | TRA LA LA LA LA — Ike & Tina Turner, Sue 757 | 7 |
| 63 | 32 | 13 | 7 | DON'T BREAK THE HEART THAT LOVES YOU — Connie Francis, MGM 13059 | 13 |
| ★64 | — | — | — | MOON RIVER △ — Henry Mancini, RCA Victor 7916 | 21 |
| ★65 | 80 | 91 | 100 | SO THIS IS LOVE — Castells, Era 3073 | 4 |
| ★66 | 89 | 98 | — | TEACH ME TONIGHT — George Maharis, Epic 9504 | 3 |
| 67 | 44 | 37 | 23 | PLEASE DON'T ASK ABOUT BARBARA — Bobby Vee, Liberty 55419 | 11 |
| 68 | 78 | — | — | HEARTS — Jackie Wilson, Brunswick 55225 | 2 |
| 69 | 51 | 34 | 18 | WHAT'S YOUR NAME — Don and Juan, Big Top 3079 | 13 |
| 70 | 65 | 68 | 79 | PATRICIA TWIST △ — Perez Prado, RCA Victor 8006 | 5 |
| 71 | 82 | 90 | 98 | MEET ME AT THE TWISTIN' PLACE — Johnnie Morisette, Sar 126 | 4 |
| 72 | 83 | — | — | VILLAGE OF LOVE — Nathaniel Mayer, United Artists 449 | 2 |
| 73 | 75 | 76 | 78 | THOU SHALT NOT STEAL △ — John D. Loudermilk, RCA Victor 7993 | 5 |
| 74 | 77 | 88 | — | IF I CRIED EVERY TIME YOU HURT ME — Wanda Jackson, Capitol 4723 | 3 |
| 75 | 79 | 84 | 87 | MEMORIES OF MARIA — Jerry Byrd, Monument 449 | 8 |
| 76 | 86 | — | — | LOVE CAN'T WAIT △ — Marty Robbins, Columbia 42375 | 2 |
| 77 | 90 | — | — | NUMBER ONE MAN — Bruce Channel, Smash 1752 | 2 |
| ★78 | 94 | — | — | THE MAN WHO SHOT LIBERTY VALANCE — Gene Pitney, Musicor 1020 | 2 |
| 79 | 74 | 79 | 84 | (WHAT A SAD WAY) TO LOVE SOMEONE — Ral Donner, Gone 5125 | 7 |
| ★80 | — | — | — | LEMON TREE — Peter, Paul & Mary, Warner Bros. 5274 | 1 |
| 81 | 84 | — | — | ANY DAY NOW — Chuck Jackson, Wand 122 | 2 |
| 82 | 88 | 100 | — | DEEP IN THE HEART OF TEXAS △ — Duane Eddy, RCA Victor 7999 | 3 |
| ★83 | 99 | — | — | DRUMMIN' UP A STORM — Sandy Nelson, Imperial 5829 | 2 |
| 84 | 81 | 96 | 96 | I FOUND A LOVE — Falcons, LuPine 1003 | 5 |
| 85 | 92 | 97 | 99 | I'LL TAKE YOU HOME — Corsairs, Tuff 1818 | 4 |
| ★86 | — | — | — | I CAN'T STOP LOVING YOU — Ray Charles, ABC-Paramount 10330 | 1 |
| 87 | 97 | — | — | I LOVE YOU — Volumes, Chex 1002 | 2 |
| ★88 | — | — | — | PLAYBOY — Marvelettes, Tamla 54060 | 1 |
| 89 | 91 | — | — | SCOTCH AND SODA — Kingston Trio, Capitol 4740 | 2 |
| ★90 | — | — | — | HIT RECORD — Brook Benton, Mercury 71962 | 1 |
| 91 | 93 | — | — | WALK ON WITH THE DUKE — Duke of Earl, Vee Jay 440 | 2 |
| 92 | — | — | — | TWISTIN' WHITE SILVER SANDS — Bill Black's Combo, Hi 2052 | 1 |
| 93 | 96 | — | — | HERE COMES THAT FEELING — Brenda Lee, Decca 31379 | 2 |
| 94 | 85 | 92 | — | DOCTOR FEEL GOOD — Dr. Feelgood and the Internes, Okeh 7144 | 3 |
| 95 | — | — | — | OH, MY ANGEL — Bertha Tillman, Brent 7029 | 1 |
| 96 | 98 | — | — | BALBOA BLUE — Marketts, Liberty 55443 | 2 |
| 97 | — | — | — | FORTUNETELLER — Bobby Curtola, Del Fi 4177 | 1 |
| 98 | — | — | — | ADIOS AMIGO △ — Jim Reeves, RCA Victor 8019 | 1 |
| 99 | — | — | — | LIPSTICK TRACES — Benny Spellman, Minit 644 | 1 |
| 100 | — | — | — | WHY'D YOU WANNA MAKE ME CRY — Connie Stevens, Warner Bros. 5265 | 1 |

## HOT 100—A TO Z—*(Publisher-Licensee)*


Adios Amigo (Randy-Smith, ASCAP) .... 98
Any Day Now (Plan Two, ASCAP) .... 81
Anything That's Part of You (Gladys, ASCAP) .. 40
At the Club (Tangerine, BMI) .... 48
Balboa Blue (Lock-E.D.M., ASCAP) .... 96
Big Draft, The (Lar-Bell, BMI) .... 61
Blues (Stay Away From Me) (Lois, BMI) .... 53
Caterina (Roncom, ASCAP) .... 29
Cinderella (Vin-Sun, ASCAP) .... 25
Conscience (Aldon, BMI) .... 26
Count Every Star (Paxton, ASCAP) .... 60
Dear One (Maureen, BMI) .... 12
Deep in the Heart of Texas (Melody Lane, BMI) .. 82
Doctor Feel Good (Cigma, BMI) .... 94
Don't Break the Heart That Loves You (Francon, ASCAP) .... 63
Don't Play That Song (Progressive, BMI) .... 59
Dream Baby (Combine, BMI) .... 45
Drummin' Up a Storm (Travis, BMI) .... 83
Everybody Loves Me But You (Champion, BMI) .. 18
Funny Way of Laughin' (Pamper, BMI) .... 14
Fortuneteller (Kemo, BMI) .... 97
Ginny Come Lately (Pogo, ASCAP) .... 31
Good Luck Charm (Gladys, ASCAP) .... 5
Hearts (East-West, ASCAP) .... 68
Here Comes That Feeling (Doral, BMI) .... 93
Hey! Baby (LeBill, BMI) .... 57
Hide Nor Hair (Tangerine, BMI) .... 20
Hit Record (Luristan-Dreyer, ASCAP) .... 90
I Can't Stop Loving You (Acuff-Rose, BMI) .... 86
I Found a Love (LuPine-Progressive-Alibri, BMI) .. 84
I Love You (Chriss, BMI) .... 87
I Sold My Heart to the Junkman (Mills, ASCAP) .. 44
(I Was) Born to Cry (Disal, ASCAP) .... 58
I Will (Camarillo, BMI) .... 47
I Wish That We Were Married (Joy, ASCAP) .... 27
I'll Take You Home (Sunflower & Annie-Earl, BMI). 85
If I Cried Every Time You Hurt Me (Central, BMI). 74
Itty Bitty Pieces (Good Songs, BMI) .... 54
Jam, The (Cheltenham, BMI) .... 30
Johnny Angel (Post, ASCAP) .... 3
Johnny Jingo (Dickson, ASCAP) .... 21
King of Clowns (Aldon, BMI) .... 52
Lemon Tree (Boulder, ASCAP) .... 80
Let Me In (Arc-Kae Williams, BMI) .... 42
Lipstick Traces (Minit, BMI) .... 99
Love Can't Wait (Marty's, BMI) .... 76
Love Letters (Famous, ASCAP) .... 19
Love Me Warm and Tender (Spanka, BMI) .... 23
Lover, Please (Lyn-Lou, BMI) .... 7
Lovers Who Wander (Disal, ASCAP) .... 33
Man Who Shot Liberty Valance, The (Famous, ASCAP) .... 78
Mashed Potato Time (Rice-Mill, BMI) .... 2
Meet Me at the Twistin' Place (Kags, BMI) .... 7
Memories of Maria (Acuff-Rose, BMI) .... 75
Midnight in Moscow (Melody Trails, BMI) .... 39
Moments (Titanic, BMI) .... 50
Moon River (Famous, ASCAP) .... 64
Most People Get Married (Famous, ASCAP) .... 46
Night Train (Pamless, BMI) .... 51
Number One Man (LeBill, BMI) .... 77
Nut Rocker (Fowley, BMI) .... 35
Oh, My Angel (Clifton, BMI) .... 95
Old Rivers (Glo-Mac & Metric, BMI) .... 15
One Who Really Loves You, The (Jobete, BMI) .. 34
P. T. 109 (Cedarwood, BMI) .... 9
Patricia Twist (Peer Int'l, BMI) .... 70
Playboy (Jobete, BMI) .... 88
Please Don't Ask About Barbara (Aldon, BMI) .. 67
Runaway (Vicki, BMI) .... 56
Scotch and Soda (Beechwood, BMI) .... 89
She Can't Find Her Keys (Arch, ASCAP) .... 22
She Cried (Trio, BMI) .... 13
Shout (Wemar-Nom, BMI) .... 6
Shout! Shout! (Knock Yourself Out) (Broadway, ASCAP) .... 16
Slow Twistin' (Woodcrest, BMI) .... 8
So This Is Love (Pattern, ASCAP) .... 65
Soldier Boy (Ludix, BMI) .... 1
Something's Got a Hold on Me (Figure, BMI) .... 49
Soul Twist (Dan-Kelyn, BMI) .... 17
Stranger on the Shore (Mellin, BMI) .... 4
Teach Me Tonight (Hub-Leeds, ASCAP) .... 66
Tell Me (Odin, ASCAP) .... 41
Thou Shalt Not Steal (Acuff-Rose, BMI) .... 73
Tra La La La La (Saturn, BMI) .... 62
Twist, Twist, Senora (Rockmasters, BMI) .... 10
Twistin' Matilda (General-Pickwick, ASCAP) .... 36
Twistin' the Night Away (Kags, BMI) .... 32
Twistin' White Silver Sands (Sharina, BMI) .... 92
Two of a Kind (Acuff-Rose, BMI) .... 43
Uptown (Aldon, BMI) .... 24
Village of Love (Trianon, BMI) .... 72
(What a Sad Way) To Love Someone (Tricky-Recherche, ASCAP) .... 79
Walk on With the Duke (Conrad-Karlan, BMI) .. 91
What'd I Say (Progressive, BMI) .... 28
What's Your Name (Hill & Range, BMI) .... 69
Why'd You Wanna Make Me Cry (Aldon, BMI) ..100
You Are Mine (Debmar, BMI) .... 37
You Better Move On (Keva, BMI) .... 38
You Talk About Love (Saturn, BMI) .... 55
Young World (Four Star, BMI) .... 11


## BUBBLING UNDER THE HOT 100

101. SPANISH HARLEM....Santo and Johnny, Canadian-American 137
102. SUGAR BLUES ....Ace Cannon, Santo 513
103. I'M ON MY WAY....Highwaymen, United Artists 439
104. FUNNY ....Gene McDaniels, Liberty 55444
105. AFTER THE LIGHTS GO DOWN LOW....George Maharis, Epic 9504
106. DREAM ....Dinah Washington, Mercury 71958
107. I'VE BEEN GOOD TO YOU....Miracles, Tamla 54053
108. THANKS TO THE FOOL ....Brook Benton, Mercury 71962
109. THE STRIPPER....David Rose and His Ork, MGM 13064
110. I LEFT MY HEART IN SAN FRANCISCO....Tony Bennett, Columbia 42332
111. MARCH OF THE SIAMESE CHILDREN....Kenny Ball, Kapp 451
112. TEACH ME TO TWIST.Bobby Rydell and Chubby Checker, Cameo 214
113. THAT'S MY DESIRE ....Sensations, Argo 5412
114. JANE JANE JANE....Kingston Trio, Capitol 4740
115. SWINGIN' SHEPHERD BLUES TWIST.....Moe Koffman, Ascot 2100
116. LET ME BE THE ONE....Paris Sisters, Gregmark 12
117. WOLVERTON MOUNTAIN....Claude King, Columbia 42352
118. NEED YOUR LOVE....Metallics, Baronet 2
119. VIOLETTA ....Ray Adams, Laurie 3118
120. QUEEN OF MY HEART....Rene and Ray, Donna 1360

# BILLBOARD HOT 100

FOR WEEK ENDING MAY 12

1962

★ STAR PERFORMERS—Selections registering greatest upward progress this week.

[S] Indicates that 45 r.p.m. stereo single version is available.

△ Indicates that 33⅓ r.p.m. mono single version is available.

[S△] Indicates that 33⅓ r.p.m. stereo single version is available.

| This Week | 1 Wk. Ago | 2 Wks. Ago | 3 Wks. Ago | TITLE — Artist, Label & Number | | Weeks On Chart |
|---|---|---|---|---|---|---|
| 1 | 1 | 4 | 6 | SOLDIER BOY — Shirelles, Scepter 1228 | | 8 |
| 2 | 2 | 3 | 3 | MASHED POTATO TIME — Dee Dee Sharp, Cameo 212 | | 11 |
| 3 | 4 | 7 | 10 | STRANGER ON THE SHORE — Mr. Acker Bilk, Atco 6217 | | 9 |
| 4 | 3 | 2 | 2 | JOHNNY ANGEL — Shelley Fabares, Colpix 621 | | 11 |
| 5 | 5 | 1 | 1 | GOOD LUCK CHARM — Elvis Presley, RCA Victor 7992 | △ | 9 |
| ★6 | 13 | 14 | 15 | SHE CRIED — Jay & the Americans, United Artists 415 | | 9 |
| ★7 | 15 | 25 | 39 | OLD RIVERS — Walter Brennan, Liberty 55436 | | 6 |
| ★8 | 16 | 27 | 33 | SHOUT! SHOUT! (Knock Yourself Out) — Ernie Maresca, Seville 117 | | 7 |
| 9 | 10 | 10 | 12 | TWIST, TWIST, SENORA — Gary (U. S.) Bonds, LeGrand 1018 | | 7 |
| 10 | 6 | 9 | 9 | SHOUT — Joey Dee & the Starliters, Roulette 4416 | | 8 |
| 11 | 9 | 12 | 22 | P. T. 109 — Jimmy Dean, Columbia 42338 | △ | 7 |
| ★12 | 18 | 26 | 47 | EVERYBODY LOVES ME BUT YOU — Brenda Lee, Decca 31379 | | 5 |
| 13 | 8 | 5 | 4 | SLOW TWISTIN' — Chubby Checker, Parkway 835 | | 11 |
| 14 | 14 | 20 | 30 | FUNNY WAY OF LAUGHIN' — Burl Ives, Decca 31371 | | 6 |
| 15 | 7 | 8 | 7 | LOVER, PLEASE — Clyde McPhatter, Mercury 71941 | | 11 |
| ★16 | 26 | 43 | 62 | CONSCIENCE — James Darren, Colpix 630 | | 5 |
| ★17 | 34 | 41 | 46 | THE ONE WHO REALLY LOVES YOU — Mary Wells, Motown 1024 | | 8 |
| ★18 | 27 | 33 | 38 | I WISH THAT WE WERE MARRIED — Ronnie and the Hi-Lites, Joy 260 | | 6 |
| ★19 | 33 | 64 | 86 | LOVERS WHO WANDER — Dion, Laurie 3123 | | 4 |
| 20 | 24 | 37 | 43 | UPTOWN — Crystals, Philles 102 | | 7 |
| 21 | 12 | 13 | 11 | DEAR ONE — Larry Finnegan, Old Town 1113 | | 12 |
| 22 | 11 | 6 | 5 | YOUNG WORLD — Rick Nelson, Imperial 5805 | | 11 |
| 23 | 17 | 17 | 26 | SOUL TWIST — King Curtis, Enjoy 1000 | | 10 |
| 24 | 19 | 11 | 8 | LOVE LETTERS — Ketty Lester, Era 3068 | | 12 |
| 25 | 29 | 34 | 48 | CATERINA — Perry Como, RCA Victor 8004 | △ | 6 |
| 26 | 21 | 22 | 27 | JOHNNY JINGO — Hayley Mills, Vista 395 | | 9 |
| ★27 | 37 | 49 | 53 | YOU ARE MINE — Frankie Avalon, Chancellor 1107 | | 8 |
| 28 | 36 | 42 | 63 | TWISTIN' MATILDA — Jimmy Soul, SPQR 3300 | | 7 |
| ★29 | 41 | 48 | 45 | TELL ME — Dick & Deedee, Liberty 55412 | | 9 |
| ★30 | 44 | 66 | 80 | I SOLD MY HEART TO THE JUNKMAN — Blue Belles, Newtown 5000 | | 4 |
| 31 | 31 | 21 | 23 | GINNY COME LATELY — Brian Hyland, ABC-Paramount 10294 | | 10 |
| 32 | 20 | 23 | 32 | HIDE NOR HAIR — Ray Charles and His Ork, ABC-Paramount 10314 | | 6 |
| 33 | 22 | 19 | 21 | SHE CAN'T FIND HER KEYS — Paul Peterson, Colpix 620 | | 11 |
| 34 | 23 | 15 | 14 | LOVE ME WARM AND TENDER — Paul Anka, RCA Victor 7977 | △ | 12 |
| ★35 | 46 | 69 | 81 | MOST PEOPLE GET MARRIED — Patti Page, Mercury 71950 | | 4 |
| 36 | 25 | 16 | 19 | CINDERELLA — Jack Ross, Dot 16333 | | 9 |
| 37 | 30 | 31 | 29 | THE JAM — Bobby Gregg and His Friends, Cotton 1003 | | 9 |
| 38 | 35 | 30 | 25 | NUT ROCKER — B. Bumble & the Stingers, Rendezvous 166 | | 11 |
| 39 | 32 | 18 | 17 | TWISTIN' THE NIGHT AWAY — Sam Cooke, RCA Victor 7983 | △ | 15 |
| 40 | 28 | 24 | 35 | WHAT'D I SAY — Bobby Darin, Atco 6221 | | 7 |
| ★41 | 54 | 62 | 70 | ITTY BITTY PIECES — James Ray, Caprice 114 | | 6 |
| ★42 | 53 | 57 | 73 | BLUES (Stay Away From Me) — Ace Cannon, Hi 2051 | | 5 |
| ★43 | 59 | 73 | 95 | DON'T PLAY THAT SONG — Ben E. King, Atco 6222 | | 4 |
| 44 | 48 | 45 | 50 | AT THE CLUB — Ray Charles and His Ork, ABC-Paramount 10314 | | 7 |
| 45 | 38 | 29 | 24 | YOU BETTER MOVE ON — Arthur Alexander, Dot 16309 | | 12 |
| 46 | 51 | 58 | 71 | NIGHT TRAIN — James Brown, King 5614 | | 5 |
| 47 | 52 | 56 | 67 | KING OF CLOWNS — Neil Sedaka, RCA Victor 8007 | △ | 7 |
| 48 | 43 | 47 | 42 | TWO OF A KIND — Sue Thompson, Hickory 1166 | | 9 |
| ★49 | 60 | 70 | 75 | COUNT EVERY STAR — Linda Scott, Canadian-American 133 | | 6 |
| ★50 | 64 | — | — | MOON RIVER — Henry Mancini, RCA Victor 7916 | △ | 22 |
| 51 | 49 | 39 | 41 | SOMETHING'S GOT A HOLD ON ME — Etta James, Argo 5409 | | 12 |
| 52 | 58 | 71 | 82 | (I WAS) BORN TO CRY — Dion, Laurie 3123 | | 4 |
| ★53 | 86 | — | — | I CAN'T STOP LOVING YOU — Ray Charles, ABC-Paramount 10330 | | 2 |
| ★54 | 65 | 80 | 91 | SO THIS IS LOVE — Castells, Era 3073 | | 5 |
| ★55 | 78 | 94 | — | THE MAN WHO SHOT LIBERTY VALANCE — Gene Pitney, Musicor 1020 | | 3 |
| ★56 | 88 | — | — | PLAYBOY — Marvelettes, Tamla 54060 | | 2 |
| 57 | 50 | 52 | 55 | MOMENTS — Jennell Hawkins, Amazon 1003 | | 8 |
| ★58 | — | — | — | FOLLOW THAT DREAM — Elvis Presley, RCA Victor EPA 4368 (Extended Play) | | 1 |
| 59 | 47 | 54 | 59 | I WILL — Vic Dana, Dolton 51 | | 7 |
| 60 | 68 | 78 | — | HEARTS — Jackie Wilson, Brunswick 55225 | | 3 |
| 61 | 66 | 89 | 98 | TEACH ME TONIGHT — George Maharis, Epic 9504 | | 4 |
| ★62 | 77 | 90 | — | NUMBER ONE MAN — Bruce Channel, Smash 1752 | | 3 |
| 63 | 72 | 83 | — | VILLAGE OF LOVE — Nathaniel Mayer, United Artists 449 | | 3 |
| ★64 | — | — | — | IT KEEPS RIGHT ON A-HURTIN' — Johnny Tillotson, Cadence 1418 | | 1 |
| 65 | 56 | 59 | 65 | RUNAWAY — Lawrence Welk, Dot 16336 | | 6 |
| 66 | 71 | 82 | 90 | MEET ME AT THE TWISTIN' PLACE — Johnnie Morisette, Sar 126 | | 5 |
| 67 | 74 | 77 | 88 | IF I CRIED EVERY TIME YOU HURT ME — Wanda Jackson, Capitol 4723 | | 4 |
| 68 | 80 | — | — | LEMON TREE — Peter, Paul & Mary, Warner Bros. 5274 | | 2 |
| ★69 | — | — | — | PALISADES PARK — Freddy Cannon, Swan 4106 | | 1 |
| ★70 | 87 | 97 | — | I LOVE YOU — Volumes, Chex 1002 | | 3 |
| ★71 | — | — | — | THAT'S OLD FASHIONED — Everly Brothers, Warner Bros. 5273 | | 1 |
| 72 | 81 | 84 | — | ANY DAY NOW — Chuck Jackson, Wand 122 | | 3 |
| ★73 | — | — | — | STRANGER ON THE SHORE — Drifters, Atlantic 2143 | | 1 |
| 74 | 76 | 86 | — | LOVE CAN'T WAIT — Marty Robbins, Columbia 42375 | △ | 3 |
| ★75 | — | — | — | SECOND HAND LOVE — Connie Francis, MGM 13074 | | 1 |
| 76 | 90 | — | — | HIT RECORD — Brook Benton, Mercury 71962 | | 2 |
| 77 | 75 | 79 | 84 | MEMORIES OF MARIA — Jerry Byrd, Monument 449 | | 9 |
| 78 | 83 | 99 | — | DRUMMIN' UP A STORM — Sandy Nelson, Imperial 5829 | | 3 |
| ★79 | 96 | 98 | — | BALBOA BLUE — Marketts, Liberty 55443 | | 3 |
| 80 | 85 | 92 | 97 | I'LL TAKE YOU HOME — Corsairs, Tuff 1818 | | 5 |
| 81 | 82 | 88 | 100 | DEEP IN THE HEART OF TEXAS — Duane Eddy, RCA Victor 7999 | △ | 4 |
| 82 | 84 | 81 | 96 | I FOUND A LOVE — Falcons, LuPine 1003 | | 6 |
| ★83 | — | 100 | — | THAT'S MY DESIRE — Sensations, Argo 5412 | | 2 |
| ★84 | — | — | — | WALK ON THE WILD SIDE — Jimmy Smith, Verve 10255 | | 1 |
| ★85 | 100 | — | — | WHY'D YOU WANNA MAKE ME CRY — Connie Stevens, Warner Bros. 5265 | | 2 |
| ★86 | — | — | — | HOW IS JULIE! — Lettermen, Capitol 4746 | | 1 |
| ★87 | — | — | — | YOU'RE NOBODY 'TIL SOMEBODY LOVES YOU — Dinah Washington, Roulette 4424 | | 1 |
| ★88 | — | — | — | BORN TO LOSE — Ray Charles, ABC-Paramount 10330 | | 1 |
| ★89 | — | — | — | CINDY'S BIRTHDAY — Johnny Crawford, Del Fi 4178 | | 1 |
| ★90 | — | — | — | THE STRIPPER — David Rose & His Ork, MGM 13064 | | 1 |
| 91 | 95 | — | — | OH, MY ANGEL — Bertha Tillman, Brent 7029 | | 2 |
| 92 | — | — | — | IMAGINE THAT — Patsy Cline, Decca 31377 | | 1 |
| 93 | 97 | — | — | FORTUNETELLER — Bobby Curtola, Del Fi 4177 | | 2 |
| 94 | — | — | — | MY REAL NAME — Fats Domino, Imperial 5833 | | 1 |
| 95 | 98 | — | — | ADIOS AMIGO — Jim Reeves, RCA Victor 8019 | △ | 2 |
| 96 | 99 | — | — | LIPSTICK TRACES — Benny Spellman, Minit 644 | | 2 |
| 97 | — | — | — | LET ME BE THE ONE — Paris Sisters, Gregmark 12 | | 1 |
| 98 | — | — | — | OPERATOR — Gladys Knight & the Pips, Fury 1064 | | 2 |
| 99 | — | — | — | I'LL TRY SOMETHING NEW — Miracles, Tamla 54059 | | 1 |
| 100 | — | — | — | DREAM — Dinah Washington, Mercury 71958 | | 1 |

## HOT 100—A TO Z—(Publisher-Licensee)


Adios Amigo (Randy-Smith, ASCAP) .... 95
Any Day Now (Plan Two, ASCAP) .... 72
At the Club (Tangerine, BMI) .... 44
Balboa Blue (Lock-E. D. M., ASCAP) .... 79
Blues (Stay Away From Me) (Lois, BMI) .... 42
Born to Lose (Peer Int'l, BMI) .... 88
Caterina (Roncom, ASCAP) .... 25
Cinderella (Vin-Sun, ASCAP) .... 36
Cindy's Birthday (Maraville, BMI) .... 89
Conscience (Aldon, BMI) .... 16
Count Every Star (Paxton, ASCAP) .... 49
Dear One (Maureen, BMI) .... 21
Deep in the Heart of Texas (Melody Lane, BMI) .... 81
Don't Play That Song (Progressive, BMI) .... 43
Dream (Goldsen, ASCAP) .... 100
Drummin' Up a Storm (Travis, BMI) .... 78
Everybody Loves Me But You (Champion, BMI) .... 12
Funny Way of Laughin' (Pamper, BMI) .... 14
Follow That Dream (Gladys, ASCAP) .... 58
Fortuneteller (Kemo, BMI) .... 93
Ginny Come Lately (Pogo, ASCAP) .... 31
Good Luck Charm (Gladys, ASCAP) .... 5
Hearts (East-West, ASCAP) .... 60
Hide Nor Hair (Tangerine, BMI) .... 32
Hit Record (Luristan-Dreyer, ASCAP) .... 76
How Is Julie? (Sherman-DeVorzon, BMI) .... 86
I Can't Stop Loving You (Acuff-Rose, BMI) .... 53
I Found a Love (LuPine-Progressive-Alibri, BMI) .... 82
I Love You (Chriss, BMI) .... 70
I Sold My Heart to the Junkman (Mills, ASCAP) .... 30
(I Was) Born to Cry (Disal, ASCAP) .... 52
I Will (Camarillo, BMI) .... 59
I Wish That We Were Married (Joy, ASCAP) .... 18
I'll Take You Home (Sunflower & Annie-Earl, BMI) .... 80
I'll Try Something New (Jobete, BMI) .... 99
If I Cried Every Time You Hurt Me (Central, BMI) .... 67
Imagine That (Tree, BMI) .... 92
It Keeps Right on A-Hurtin' (Tanridge, BMI) .... 64
Itty Bitty Pieces (Good Songs, BMI) .... 41
Jam, The (Cheltenham, BMI) .... 37
Johnny Angel (Post, ASCAP) .... 4
Johnny Jingo (Dickson, ASCAP) .... 26
King of Clowns (Aldon, BMI) .... 47
Lemon Tree (Boulder, ASCAP) .... 8
Let Me Be the One (Aldon, BMI) .... 97
Lipstick Traces (Minit, BMI) .... 96
Love Can't Wait (Marty's, BMI) .... 74
Love Letters (Famous, ASCAP) .... 24
Love Me Warm and Tender (Spanka, BMI) .... 34
Lover, Please (Lyn-Lou, BMI) .... 15
Lovers Who Wander (Disal, ASCAP) .... 19
Man Who Shot Liberty Valance, The (Famous, ASCAP) .... 55
Mashed Potato Time (Rice-Mill, BMI) .... 2
Meet Me at the Twistin' Place (Kags, BMI) .... 66
Memories of Maria (Acuff-Rose, BMI) .... 77
Moments (Titanic, BMI) .... 57
Moon River (Famous, ASCAP) .... 50
Most People Get Married (Famous, ASCAP) .... 35
My Real Name (Travis, BMI) .... 94
Night Train (Pamless, BMI) .... 46
Number One Man (LeBill, BMI) .... 62
Nut Rocker (Fowley, BMI) .... 38
Oh, My Angel (Clifton, BMI) .... 91
Old Rivers (Glo-Mac & Metric, BMI) .... 7
One Who Really Loves You, The (Jobete, BMI) .... 17
Operator (Sylvia, BMI) .... 98
P. T. 109 (Cedarwood, BMI) .... 11
Palisades Park (Claridge, ASCAP) .... 69
Playboy (Jobete, BMI) .... 56
Runaway (Vicki, BMI) .... 65
Second Hand Love (Merna, BMI) .... 75
She Can't Find Her Keys (Arch, ASCAP) .... 33
She Cried (Trio, BMI) .... 6
Shout (Wemar-Nom, BMI) .... 10
Shout! Shout! (Knock Yourself Out) (Broadway, ASCAP) .... 8
Slow Twistin' (Woodcrest, BMI) .... 13
So This Is Love (Pattern, ASCAP) .... 54
Soldier Boy (Ludix, BMI) .... 1
Something's Got a Hold on Me (Figure, BMI) .... 51
Soul Twist (Dan-Kelyn, BMI) .... 23
Stranger on the Shore—Bilk (Mellin, BMI) .... 3
Stranger on the Shore—Drifters (Mellin, BMI) .... 73
Stripper, The (David Rose, ASCAP) .... 90
Teach Me Tonight (Hub-Leeds, ASCAP) .... 61
Tell Me (Odin, ASCAP) .... 29
That's My Desire (Mills, ASCAP) .... 83
That's Old Fashioned (Aberbach, BMI) .... 71
Twist, Twist Senora (Rockmasters, BMI) .... 9
Twistin' Matilda (General-Pickwick, ASCAP) .... 28
Twistin' the Night Away (Kags, BMI) .... 39
Two of a Kind (Acuff-Rose, BMI) .... 48
Uptown (Aldon, BMI) .... 20
Village of Love (Trianon, BMI) .... 63
Walk on the Wild Side (Columbia Pictures, ASCAP) .... 84
What'd I Say (Progressive, BMI) .... 40
Why'd You Wanna Make Me Cry (Aldon, BMI) .... 85
You Are Mine (Debmar, BMI) .... 27
You Better Move On (Keva, BMI) .... 45
You're Nobody 'Til Somebody Loves You (Southern, ASCAP) .... 87
Young World (Four Star, BMI) .... 22


## BUBBLING UNDER THE HOT 100

101. SCOTCH AND SODA.... Kingston Trio, Capitol 4740
102. TWISTIN' WHITE SILVER SANDS.... Bill Black's Combo, Hi 2052
103. COLINDA.... Rod Bernard, Hall-Way 1902
104. AFTER THE LIGHTS GO DOWN LOW.... George Maharis, Epic 9504
105. HULLY GULLY CALLING TIME.... Jive Five, Beltone 2019
106. FUNNY.... Gene McDaniels, Liberty 55444
107. LIMBO ROCK.... The Champs, Challenge 9131
108. I LEFT MY HEART IN SAN FRANCISCO.... Tony Bennett, Columbia 42332
109. TEACH ME TO TWIST.. Chubby Checker & Bobby Rydell, Cameo 214
110. SWINGIN' SHEPHERD BLUES TWIST.... Moe Koffman, Ascot 2100
111. SPANISH HARLEM.... Santo and Johnny, Canadian-American 137
112. WALK ON WITH THE DUKE.... Duke of Earl, Vee Jay 440
113. WILLING AND EAGER.... Pat Boone, Dot 16349
114. SNAP YOUR FINGERS.... Joe Henderson, Todd 1072
115. THE JOHN BIRCH SOCIETY.... Chad Mitchell Trio, Kapp 457
116. QUEEN OF MY HEART.... Rene and Ray, Donna 1360
117. NEED YOUR LOVE.... Metallics, Baronet 2
118. JANE JANE JANE.... Kingston Trio, Capitol 4740
119. VIOLETTA.... Ray Adams, Laurie 3118
120. THEME FROM BEN CASEY.... Valjean, Carlton 573

# BILLBOARD HOT 100

**FOR WEEK ENDING MAY 19, 1962**

STAR PERFORMERS—Selections registering greatest upward progress this week.

S indicates that 45 r.p.m. stereo single version is available.

△ indicates that 33⅓ r.p.m. mono single version is available.

Ⓢ indicates that 33⅓ r.p.m. stereo single version is available.

| This Week | Wk. Ago | 2 Wks. Ago | 3 Wks. Ago | Title — Artist, Label & Number | Weeks On Chart |
|---|---|---|---|---|---|
| 1 | 1 | 1 | 4 | SOLDIER BOY — Shirelles, Scepter 1228 | 9 |
| 2 | 3 | 4 | 7 | STRANGER ON THE SHORE — Mr. Acker Bilk, Atco 6217 | 10 |
| 3 | 2 | 2 | 3 | MASHED POTATO TIME — Dee Dee Sharp, Cameo 212 | 12 |
| 4 | 4 | 3 | 2 | JOHNNY ANGEL — Shelley Fabares, Colpix 621 | 12 |
| 5 | 6 | 13 | 14 | SHE CRIED — Jay & the Americans, United Artists 415 | 10 |
| 6 | 8 | 16 | 27 | SHOUT! SHOUT! (Knock Yourself Out) — Ernie Maresca, Seville 117 | 8 |
| 7 | 7 | 15 | 25 | OLD RIVERS — Walter Brennan, Liberty 55436 | 7 |
| 8 | 12 | 18 | 26 | EVERYBODY LOVES ME BUT YOU — Brenda Lee, Decca 31379 | 6 |
| 9 | 11 | 9 | 12 | P. T. 109 — Jimmy Dean, Columbia 42338 △ | 8 |
| 10 | 14 | 14 | 20 | FUNNY WAY OF LAUGHIN' — Burl Ives, Decca 31371 | 7 |
| 11 | 5 | 5 | 1 | GOOD LUCK CHARM — Elvis Presley, RCA Victor 7992 △ | 10 |
| 12 | 10 | 6 | 9 | SHOUT — Joey Dee & the Starliters, Roulette 4416 | 9 |
| ★13 | 19 | 33 | 64 | LOVERS WHO WANDER — Dion, Laurie 3123 | 5 |
| 14 | 17 | 34 | 41 | THE ONE WHO REALLY LOVES YOU — Mary Wells, Motown 1024 | 9 |
| 15 | 16 | 26 | 43 | CONSCIENCE — James Darren, Colpix 630 | 6 |
| 16 | 9 | 10 | 10 | TWIST, TWIST, SENORA — Gary (U.S.) Bonds, LeGrand 1018 | 8 |
| 17 | 18 | 27 | 33 | I WISH THAT WE WERE MARRIED — Ronnie and the Hi-Lites, Joy 260 | 7 |
| 18 | 20 | 24 | 37 | UPTOWN — Crystals, Philles 102 | 8 |
| 19 | 13 | 8 | 5 | SLOW TWISTIN' — Chubby Checker, Parkway 835 | 12 |
| 20 | 15 | 7 | 8 | LOVER, PLEASE — Clyde McPhatter, Mercury 71941 | 12 |
| ★21 | 53 | 86 | — | I CAN'T STOP LOVING YOU — Ray Charles, ABC-Paramount 10330 | 3 |
| 22 | 29 | 41 | 48 | TELL ME — Dick & Deedee, Liberty 55412 | 10 |
| 23 | 25 | 29 | 34 | CATERINA — Perry Como, RCA Victor 8004 △ | 7 |
| 24 | 30 | 44 | 66 | I SOLD MY HEART TO THE JUNKMAN — Blue Belles, Newtown 5000 | 5 |
| 25 | 28 | 36 | 42 | TWISTIN' MATILDA — Jimmy Soul, SPQR 3300 | 8 |
| 26 | 27 | 37 | 49 | YOU ARE MINE — Frankie Avalon, Chancellor 1107 | 9 |
| 27 | 35 | 46 | 69 | MOST PEOPLE GET MARRIED — Patti Page, Mercury 71950 | 5 |
| 28 | 23 | 17 | 17 | SOUL TWIST — King Curtis, Enjoy 1000 | 11 |
| 29 | 26 | 21 | 22 | JOHNNY JINGO — Hayley Mills, Vista 395 | 10 |
| 30 | 21 | 12 | 13 | DEAR ONE — Larry Finnegan, Old Town 1113 | 13 |
| 31 | 22 | 11 | 6 | YOUNG WORLD — Rick Nelson, Imperial 5805 | 12 |
| ★32 | 55 | 78 | 94 | THE MAN WHO SHOT LIBERTY VALANCE — Gene Pitney, Musicor 1020 | 4 |
| ★33 | 43 | 59 | 73 | DON'T PLAY THAT SONG — Ben E. King, Atco 6222 | 5 |
| ★34 | 64 | — | — | IT KEEPS RIGHT ON A-HURTIN' — Johnny Tillotson, Cadence 1418 | 2 |
| 35 | 24 | 19 | 11 | LOVE LETTERS — Ketty Lester, Era 3068 | 13 |
| 36 | 42 | 53 | 57 | BLUES (Stay Away From Me) — Ace Cannon, Hi 2051 | 6 |
| ★37 | 50 | 64 | — | MOON RIVER — Henry Mancini, RCA Victor 7916 △ | 23 |
| 38 | 58 | — | — | FOLLOW THAT DREAM — Elvis Presley, RCA Victor EPA 4368 (Extended Play) | 2 |
| 39 | 46 | 51 | 58 | NIGHT TRAIN — James Brown, King 5614 | 6 |
| ★40 | 75 | — | — | SECOND HAND LOVE — Connie Francis, MGM 13074 | 2 |
| 41 | 49 | 60 | 70 | COUNT EVERY STAR — Linda Scott, Canadian-American 133 | 7 |
| ★42 | 69 | — | — | PALISADES PARK — Freddy Cannon, Swan 4106 | 2 |
| 43 | 63 | 72 | 83 | VILLAGE OF LOVE — Nathaniel Mayer, Fortune/United Artists 449 | 4 |
| 44 | 54 | 65 | 80 | SO THIS IS LOVE — Castells, Era 3073 | 6 |
| 45 | 47 | 52 | 56 | KING OF CLOWNS — Neil Sedaka, RCA Victor 8007 △ | 8 |
| ★46 | 56 | 88 | — | PLAYBOY — Marvelettes, Tamla 54060 | 3 |
| 47 | 61 | 66 | 89 | TEACH ME TONIGHT — George Maharis, Epic 9504 | 5 |
| 48 | 32 | 20 | 23 | HIDE NOR HAIR — Ray Charles and His Ork, ABC-Paramount 10314 | 7 |
| 49 | 52 | 58 | 71 | (I WAS) BORN TO CRY — Dion, Laurie 3123 | 5 |
| 50 | 59 | 47 | 54 | I WILL — Vic Dana, Dolton 51 | 8 |
| 51 | 41 | 54 | 62 | ITTY BITTY PIECES — James Ray, Caprice 114 | 7 |
| 52 | 31 | 31 | 21 | GINNY COME LATELY — Brian Hyland, ABC-Paramount 10294 | 11 |
| 53 | 40 | 28 | 24 | WHAT'D I SAY — Bobby Darin, Atco 6221 | 8 |
| 54 | 33 | 22 | 19 | SHE CAN'T FIND HER KEYS — Paul Peterson, Colpix 620 | 12 |
| 55 | 37 | 30 | 31 | THE JAM — Bobby Gregg and His Friends, Cotton 1003 | 10 |
| ★56 | 71 | — | — | THAT'S OLD FASHIONED — Everly Brothers, Warner Bros. 5273 | 2 |
| 57 | 62 | 77 | 90 | NUMBER ONE MAN — Bruce Channel, Smash 1752 | 4 |
| 58 | 60 | 68 | 78 | HEARTS — Jackie Wilson, Brunswick 55225 | 4 |
| 59 | 67 | 74 | 77 | IF I CRIED EVERY TIME YOU HURT ME — Wanda Jackson, Capitol 4723 | 5 |
| ★60 | 76 | 90 | — | HIT RECORD — Brook Benton, Mercury 71962 | 3 |
| 61 | 72 | 81 | 84 | ANY DAY NOW — Chuck Jackson, Wand 122 | 4 |
| 62 | 70 | 87 | 97 | I LOVE YOU — Volumes, Chex 1002 | 4 |
| 63 | 68 | 80 | — | LEMON TREE — Peter, Paul & Mary, Warner Bros. 5274 | 3 |
| 64 | 66 | 71 | 82 | MEET ME AT THE TWISTIN' PLACE — Johnnie Morisette, Sar 126 | 6 |
| 65 | 89 | — | — | CINDY'S BIRTHDAY — Johnny Crawford, Del Fi 4178 | 2 |
| 66 | 79 | 96 | 98 | BALBOA BLUE — Marketts, Liberty 55443 | 4 |
| 67 | 78 | 83 | 99 | DRUMMIN' UP A STORM — Sandy Nelson, Imperial 5829 | 4 |
| 68 | 80 | 85 | 92 | I'LL TAKE YOU HOME — Corsairs, Tuff 1818 | 6 |
| 69 | 84 | — | — | WALK ON THE WILD SIDE — Jimmy Smith, Verve 10255 | 2 |
| 70 | 88 | — | — | BORN TO LOSE — Ray Charles, ABC-Paramount 10330 | 2 |
| 71 | 74 | 76 | 86 | LOVE CAN'T WAIT — Marty Robbins, Columbia 42375 △ | 4 |
| ★72 | — | — | — | WHERE ARE YOU — Dinah Washington, Roulette 4424 | 1 |
| 73 | 86 | — | — | HOW IS JULIE! — Lettermen, Capitol 4746 | 2 |
| ★74 | — | — | — | SHARING YOU — Bobby Vee, Liberty 55451 | 1 |
| 75 | 83 | — | 100 | THAT'S MY DESIRE — Sensations, Argo 5412 | 3 |
| ★76 | — | — | — | SNAP YOUR FINGERS — Joe Henderson, Todd 1072 | 1 |
| 77 | 93 | 97 | — | FORTUNETELLER — Bobby Curtola, Del Fi 4177 | 3 |
| 78 | 81 | 82 | 88 | DEEP IN THE HEART OF TEXAS — Duane Eddy, RCA Victor 7999 △ | 5 |
| 79 | 94 | — | — | MY REAL NAME — Fats Domino, Imperial 5833 | 2 |
| 80 | 82 | 84 | 81 | I FOUND A LOVE — Falcons, LuPine 1003 | 7 |
| 81 | 91 | 95 | — | OH, MY ANGEL — Bertha Tillman, Brent 7029 | 3 |
| 82 | — | 94 | 85 | DOCTOR FEEL GOOD — Dr. Feelgood & the Internes, Okeh 7144 | 4 |
| 83 | 85 | 100 | — | WHY'D YOU WANNA MAKE ME CRY — Connie Stevens, Warner Bros. 5265 | 3 |
| ★84 | — | — | — | THEME FROM BEN CASEY — Valjean, Carlton 573 | 1 |
| 85 | — | — | — | WHEN I GET THROUGH WITH YOU — Patsy Cline, Decca 31377 | 1 |
| 86 | — | — | — | WOMAN IS A MAN'S BEST FRIEND — Teddy & the Twilights, Swan 4102 | 1 |
| 87 | 90 | — | — | THE STRIPPER — David Rose & His Ork, MGM 13064 | 2 |
| 88 | — | 89 | 91 | SCOTCH AND SODA — Kingston Trio, Capitol 4740 | 3 |
| 89 | — | 93 | 96 | HERE COMES THAT FEELIN' — Brenda Lee, Decca 31379 | 3 |
| 90 | 92 | — | — | IMAGINE THAT — Patsy Cline, Decca 31377 | 2 |
| 91 | 97 | — | — | LET ME BE THE ONE — Paris Sisters, Gregmark 12 | 2 |
| 92 | 100 | — | — | DREAM — Dinah Washington, Mercury 71958 | 2 |
| 93 | — | — | — | JANE JANE JANE — Kingston Trio, Capitol 4740 | 1 |
| 94 | 99 | — | — | I'LL TRY SOMETHING NEW — Miracles, Tamla 54059 | 2 |
| 95 | — | — | — | QUANDO, QUANDO, QUANDO — Pat Boone, Dot 16349 | 1 |
| 96 | — | 92 | — | TWISTIN' WHITE SILVER SANDS — Bill Black's Combo, Hi 2052 | 2 |
| 97 | — | — | — | BRISTOL TWISTIN' ANNIE — Dovells, Parkway 838 | 1 |
| 98 | — | — | — | THAT HAPPY FEELING — Bert Kaempfert, Decca 31388 | 1 |
| 99 | — | — | — | JOHN BIRCH SOCIETY — Chad Mitchell Trio, Kapp 457 | 1 |
| 100 | — | — | — | AL DI LA' — Emilio Pericoli, Warner Bros. 5259 | 1 |

## BUBBLING UNDER THE HOT 100

101. LIMBO ROCK — Champs, Challenge 9131
102. COLINDA — Rod Bernard, Hall-Way 1902
103. WOLVERTON MOUNTAIN — Claude King, Columbia 42352
104. STRANGER ON THE SHORE — Drifters, Atlantic 2143
105. DRUM STOMP — Sandy Nelson, Imperial 5829
106. AFTER THE LIGHTS GO DOWN LOW — George Maharis, Epic 9504
107. LIPSTICK TRACES — Benny Spellman, Minit 644
108. WEST OF THE WALL — Toni Fisher, Big Top 3097
109. ADIOS AMIGO — Jim Reeves, RCA Victor 8019
110. HULLY GULLY CALLING TIME — Jive Five, Beltone 2019
111. HOW CAN I MEET HER? — Everly Brothers, Warner Bros. 5273
112. ARRIVEDERCI ROMA — Eddie Fisher, ABC-Paramount 10326
113. DANCIN' THE STRAND — Maureen Gray, Landa 689
114. QUEEN OF MY HEART — Rene and Ray, Donna 1360
115. I'M ON MY WAY — Highwaymen, United Artists 439
116. A STEEL GUITAR AND A GLASS OF WINE — Paul Anka, RCA Victor 8030
117. GREENLEAVES OF SUMMER — Kenny Ball, Kapp 460
118. TEACH ME TO TWIST — Chubby Checker & Bobby Rydell, Cameo 214
119. WILLING AND EAGER — Pat Boone, Dot 16349
120. THE LADY WANTS TO TWIST — Steve Lawrence, Columbia 42396

# BILLBOARD HOT 100

**FOR WEEK ENDING MAY 26, 1962**

| This Week | Last Week | 2 Wks. Ago | 3 Wks. Ago | Title | Artist, Label & Number | Weeks On Chart |
|---|---|---|---|---|---|---|
| 1 | 2 | 3 | 4 | STRANGER ON THE SHORE | Mr. Acker Bilk, Atco 6217 | 11 |
| 2 | 1 | 1 | 1 | SOLDIER BOY | Shirelles, Scepter 1228 | 10 |
| 3 | 3 | 2 | 2 | MASHED POTATO TIME | Dee Dee Sharp, Cameo 212 | 13 |
| ★4 | 21 | 53 | 86 | I CAN'T STOP LOVING YOU | Ray Charles, ABC-Paramount 10330 | 4 |
| 5 | 7 | 7 | 15 | OLD RIVERS | Walter Brennan, Liberty 55436 | 8 |
| 6 | 8 | 12 | 18 | EVERYBODY LOVES ME BUT YOU | Brenda Lee, Decca 31379 | 7 |
| 7 | 5 | 6 | 13 | SHE CRIED | Jay & the Americans, United Artists 415 | 11 |
| 8 | 9 | 11 | 9 | P. T. 109 | Jimmy Dean, Columbia 42338 | 9 |
| 9 | 4 | 4 | 3 | JOHNNY ANGEL | Shelley Fabares, Colpix 621 | 13 |
| 10 | 13 | 19 | 33 | LOVERS WHO WANDER | Dion, Laurie 3123 | 6 |
| 11 | 6 | 8 | 16 | SHOUT! SHOUT! (Knock Yourself Out) | Ernie Maresca, Seville 117 | 9 |
| 12 | 14 | 17 | 34 | THE ONE WHO REALLY LOVES YOU | Mary Wells, Motown 1024 | 10 |
| ★13 | 18 | 20 | 24 | UPTOWN | Crystals, Philles 102 | 9 |
| 14 | 10 | 14 | 14 | FUNNY WAY OF LAUGHIN' | Burl Ives, Decca 31371 | 8 |
| 15 | 15 | 16 | 26 | CONSCIENCE | James Darren, Colpix 630 | 7 |
| 16 | 17 | 18 | 27 | I WISH THAT WE WERE MARRIED | Ronnie and the Hi-Lites, Joy 260 | 8 |
| 17 | 11 | 5 | 5 | GOOD LUCK CHARM | Elvis Presley, RCA Victor 7992 | 11 |
| ★18 | 34 | 64 | — | IT KEEPS RIGHT ON A-HURTIN' | Johnny Tillotson, Cadence 1418 | 3 |
| 19 | 12 | 10 | 6 | SHOUT | Joey Dee & the Starliters, Roulette 4416 | 10 |
| 20 | 24 | 30 | 44 | I SOLD MY HEART TO THE JUNKMAN | Blue Belles, Newtown 5000 | 6 |
| ★21 | 32 | 55 | 78 | THE MAN WHO SHOT LIBERTY VALANCE | Gene Pitney, Musicor 1020 | 5 |
| 22 | 25 | 28 | 36 | TWISTIN' MATILDA | Jimmy Soul, SPQR 3300 | 9 |
| 23 | 16 | 9 | 10 | TWIST, TWIST, SEÑORA | Gary (U. S.) Bonds, LeGrand 1018 | 9 |
| ★24 | 40 | 75 | — | SECOND HAND LOVE | Connie Francis, MGM 13074 | 3 |
| 25 | 33 | 43 | 59 | DON'T PLAY THAT SONG | Ben E. King, Atco 6222 | 6 |
| 26 | 22 | 29 | 41 | TELL ME | Dick & Deedee, Liberty 55412 | 11 |
| 27 | 23 | 25 | 29 | CATERINA | Perry Como, RCA Victor 8004 | 8 |
| ★28 | 42 | 69 | — | PALISADES PARK | Freddy Cannon, Swan 4106 | 3 |
| 29 | 27 | 35 | 46 | MOST PEOPLE GET MARRIED | Patti Page, Mercury 71950 | 6 |
| 30 | 38 | 58 | — | FOLLOW THAT DREAM | Elvis Presley, RCA Victor EPA 4368 (Extended Play) | 3 |
| 31 | 26 | 27 | 37 | YOU ARE MINE | Frankie Avalon, Chancellor 1107 | 10 |
| 32 | 37 | 50 | 64 | MOON RIVER | Henry Mancini, RCA Victor 7916 | 24 |
| ★33 | 46 | 56 | 88 | PLAYBOY | Marvelettes, Tamla 54060 | 4 |
| 34 | 20 | 15 | 7 | LOVER, PLEASE | Clyde McPhatter, Mercury 71941 | 13 |
| 35 | 39 | 46 | 51 | NIGHT TRAIN | James Brown, King 5614 | 7 |
| 36 | 43 | 63 | 72 | VILLAGE OF LOVE | Nathaniel Mayer, Fortune/United Artists 449 | 5 |
| 37 | 19 | 13 | 8 | SLOW TWISTIN' | Chubby Checker, Parkway 835 | 13 |
| 38 | 47 | 61 | 66 | TEACH ME TONIGHT | George Maharis, Epic 9504 | 6 |
| 39 | 28 | 23 | 17 | SOUL TWIST | King Curtis, Enjoy 1000 | 12 |
| 40 | 44 | 54 | 65 | SO THIS IS LOVE | Castells, Era 3073 | 7 |
| ★41 | 56 | 71 | — | THAT'S OLD FASHIONED | Everly Brothers, Warner Bros. 5273 | 3 |
| 42 | 49 | 52 | 58 | (I WAS) BORN TO CRY | Dion, Laurie 3123 | 6 |
| 43 | 31 | 22 | 11 | YOUNG WORLD | Rick Nelson, Imperial 5805 | 13 |
| ★44 | 69 | 84 | — | WALK ON THE WILD SIDE | Jimmy Smith, Verve 10255 | 3 |
| 45 | 41 | 49 | 60 | COUNT EVERY STAR | Linda Scott, Canadian-American 133 | 6 |
| ★46 | 61 | 72 | 81 | ANY DAY NOW | Chuck Jackson, Wand 122 | 5 |
| 47 | 36 | 42 | 53 | BLUES (Stay Away From Me) | Ace Cannon, Hi 2051 | 7 |
| ★48 | 60 | 76 | 90 | HIT RECORD | Brook Benton, Mercury 71962 | 4 |
| ★49 | 62 | 70 | 87 | I LOVE YOU | Volumes, Chex 1002 | 5 |
| 50 | 51 | 41 | 54 | ITTY BITTY PIECES | James Ray, Caprice 114 | 8 |
| 51 | 65 | 89 | — | CINDY'S BIRTHDAY | Johnny Crawford, Del Fi 4178 | 3 |
| 52 | 30 | 21 | 12 | DEAR ONE | Larry Finnegan, Old Town 1113 | 14 |
| 53 | 45 | 47 | 52 | KING OF CLOWNS | Neil Sedaka, RCA Victor 8007 | 9 |
| ★54 | 76 | — | — | SNAP YOUR FINGERS | Joe Henderson, Todd 1072 | 2 |
| 55 | 57 | 62 | 77 | NUMBER ONE MAN | Bruce Channel, Smash 1782 | 5 |
| 56 | 35 | 24 | 19 | LOVE LETTERS | Ketty Lester, Era 3068 | 14 |
| ★57 | 74 | — | — | SHARING YOU | Bobby Vee, Liberty 55451 | 2 |
| 58 | 59 | 67 | 74 | IF I CRIED EVERY TIME YOU HURT ME | Wanda Jackson, Capitol 4723 | 6 |
| 59 | 63 | 68 | 80 | LEMON TREE | Peter, Paul & Mary, Warner Bros. 5274 | 4 |
| 60 | 66 | 79 | 96 | BALBOA BLUE | Marketts, Liberty 55443 | 5 |
| 61 | 70 | 88 | — | BORN TO LOSE | Ray Charles, ABC-Paramount 10330 | 3 |
| ★62 | 87 | 90 | — | THE STRIPPER | David Rose & His Ork, MGM 13064 | 3 |
| 63 | 64 | 66 | 71 | MEET ME AT THE TWISTIN' PLACE | Johnnie Morisette, Sar 126 | 7 |
| 64 | 50 | 59 | 47 | I WILL | Vic Dana, Dolton 51 | 9 |
| 65 | 58 | 60 | 68 | HEARTS | Jackie Wilson, Brunswick 55225 | 5 |
| 66 | 72 | — | — | WHERE ARE YOU | Dinah Washington, Roulette 4424 | 2 |
| 67 | 29 | 26 | 21 | JOHNNY JINGO | Hayley Mills, Vista 395 | 11 |
| 68 | 79 | 94 | — | MY REAL NAME | Fats Domino, Imperial 5833 | 3 |
| 69 | 71 | 74 | 76 | LOVE CAN'T WAIT | Marty Robbins, Columbia 42375 | 5 |
| 70 | 73 | 86 | — | HOW IS JULIE! | Lettermen, Capitol 4746 | 3 |
| 71 | 75 | 83 | — | THAT'S MY DESIRE | Sensations, Argo 5412 | 4 |
| 72 | 68 | 80 | 85 | I'LL TAKE YOU HOME | Corsairs, Tuff 1818 | 7 |
| 73 | 85 | — | — | WHEN I GET THROUGH WITH YOU | Patsy Cline, Decca 31377 | 2 |
| 74 | 77 | 93 | 97 | FORTUNETELLER | Bobby Curtola, Del Fi 4177 | 4 |
| 75 | 80 | 82 | 84 | I FOUND A LOVE | Falcons, LuPine 1003 | 8 |
| 76 | 84 | — | — | THEME FROM BEN CASEY | Valjean, Carlton 573 | 3 |
| 77 | 82 | — | 94 | DOCTOR FEEL GOOD | Dr. Feelgood & the Interns, Okeh 7144 | 5 |
| 78 | 81 | 91 | 95 | OH, MY ANGEL | Bertha Tillman, Brent 7029 | 4 |
| 79 | 83 | 85 | 100 | WHY'D YOU WANNA MAKE ME CRY | Connie Stevens, Warner Bros. 5265 | 4 |
| ★80 | — | — | — | WOLVERTON MOUNTAIN | Claude King, Columbia 42352 | 1 |
| 81 | 100 | — | — | AL DI LA' | Emilio Pericoli, Warner Bros. 5259 | 2 |
| 82 | 94 | 99 | — | I'LL TRY SOMETHING NEW | Miracles, Tamla 54059 | 3 |
| 83 | 67 | 78 | 83 | DRUMMIN' UP A STORM | Sandy Nelson, Imperial 5829 | 5 |
| 84 | 86 | — | — | WOMAN IS A MAN'S BEST FRIEND | Teddy & the Twilights, Swan 4102 | 3 |
| 85 | 97 | — | — | BRISTOL TWISTIN' ANNIE | Dovells, Parkway 838 | 3 |
| ★86 | — | — | — | DRUM STOMP | Sandy Nelson, Imperial 5829 | 1 |
| 87 | 91 | 97 | — | LET ME BE THE ONE | Paris Sisters, Gregmark 12 | 3 |
| ★88 | — | — | — | A STEEL GUITAR AND A GLASS OF WINE | Paul Anka, RCA Victor 8030 | 1 |
| ★89 | — | — | — | SWINGIN' GENTLY | Earl Grant, Decca 25560 | 1 |
| ★90 | 95 | 98 | — | ADIOS AMIGO | Jim Reeves, RCA Victor 8019 | 3 |
| ★91 | — | — | — | HAVING A PARTY | Sam Cooke, RCA Victor 8036 | 1 |
| 92 | — | — | — | DOWN IN THE VALLEY | Solomon Burke, Atlantic 2147 | 1 |
| 93 | — | — | — | WHERE HAVE YOU BEEN ALL MY LIFE | Arthur Alexander, Dot 16357 | 1 |
| 94 | — | 96 | 99 | LIPSTICK TRACES | Benny Spellman, Minit 644 | 3 |
| 95 | — | — | — | JOHNNY GETS ANGRY | Joanie Sommers, Warner Bros. 5275 | 1 |
| 96 | — | — | — | HOW CAN I MEET HER! | Everly Brothers, Warner Bros. 5273 | 1 |
| 97 | — | — | — | TENNESSEE | Jan and Dean, Liberty 55454 | 1 |
| 98 | — | — | — | LIMBO ROCK | Champs, Challenge 9131 | 1 |
| 99 | — | — | — | WEST OF THE WALL | Toni Fisher, Big Top 3097 | 1 |
| 100 | — | — | — | BOOM BOOM | John Lee Hooker, Vee Jay 438 | 1 |

## BUBBLING UNDER THE HOT 100

101. THAT HAPPY FEELING ..... Bert Kaempfert, Decca 31388
102. TWISTIN' WHITE SILVER SANDS ..... Bill Black's Combo, Hi 2052
103. DREAM ..... Dinah Washington, Mercury 71958
104. ONE O'CLOCK JUMP ..... Jimmy Smith, Blue Note 1820
105. I CAN MEND YOUR BROKEN HEART ..... Don Gibson, RCA Victor 8017
106. THANKS TO A FOOL ..... Brook Benton, Mercury 71962
107. JOHN BIRCH SOCIETY ..... Chad Mitchell Trio, Kapp 457
108. I'M ON MY WAY ..... Highwaymen, United Artists 439
109. EVERYBODY LOVES A LOVER ..... Angels, Caprice 116
110. QUEEN OF MY HEART ..... Rene and Ray, Donna 1360
111. DANCIN' THE STRAND ..... Maureen Gray, Landa 689
112. DREAM MYSELF A SWEETHEART ..... Clarence Henry, Argo 5414
113. I'LL NEVER DANCE AGAIN ..... Bobby Rydell, Cameo 217
114. ROUTE 66 THEME ..... Nelson Riddle, Capitol 4741
115. GEE, IT'S WONDERFUL ..... Bobby Rydell, Cameo 217
116. GREEN LEAVES OF SUMMER ..... Kenny Ball, Kapp 460
117. THE STORY OF MY LIFE ..... Big Al Downing, Chess 1817
118. TWIST AND SHOUT ..... Isley Brothers, Wand 653
119. LOVE, WHERE ARE YOU NOW ..... Al Martino, Capitol 4710
120. I NEED YOUR LOVING ..... Don Gardner and Dee Dee Ford, Fire 508

# BILLBOARD HOT 100

FOR WEEK ENDING JUNE 2

1962

★ STAR PERFORMERS—Selections registering greatest upward progress this week.

S Indicates that 45 r.p.m. stereo single version is available.

△ Indicates that 33⅓ r.p.m. mono single version is available.

Ⓢ Indicates that 33⅓ r.p.m. stereo single version is available.

| THIS WEEK | 1 Wk. Ago | 2 Wks. Ago | 3 Wks. Ago | TITLE Artist, Label & Number | Weeks On Chart |
|---|---|---|---|---|---|
| 1 | 4 | 21 | 53 | I CAN'T STOP LOVING YOU — Ray Charles, ABC-Paramount 10330 | 5 |
| 2 | 1 | 2 | 3 | STRANGER ON THE SHORE — Mr. Acker Bilk, Atco 6217 | 12 |
| 3 | 2 | 1 | 1 | SOLDIER BOY — Shirelles, Scepter 1228 | 11 |
| ★ 4 | 10 | 13 | 19 | LOVERS WHO WANDER — Dion, Laurie 3123 | 7 |
| 5 | 3 | 3 | 2 | MASHED POTATO TIME — Dee Dee Sharp, Cameo 212 | 14 |
| 6 | 6 | 8 | 12 | EVERYBODY LOVES ME BUT YOU — Brenda Lee, Decca 31379 | 8 |
| 7 | 11 | 6 | 8 | SHOUT! SHOUT! (Knock Yourself Out) — Ernie Maresca, Seville 117 | 10 |
| 8 | 5 | 7 | 7 | OLD RIVERS — Walter Brennan, Liberty 55436 | 9 |
| 9 | 12 | 14 | 17 | THE ONE WHO REALLY LOVES YOU — Mary Wells, Motown 1024 | 11 |
| ★ 10 | 21 | 32 | 35 | THE MAN WHO SHOT LIBERTY VALANCE — Gene Pitney, Musicor 1020 | 6 |
| 11 | 15 | 15 | 16 | CONSCIENCE — James Darren, Colpix 630 | 8 |
| ★ 12 | 18 | 34 | 64 | IT KEEPS RIGHT ON A-HURTIN' — Johnny Tillotson, Cadence 1418 | 4 |
| 13 | 13 | 18 | 20 | UPTOWN — Crystals, Philles 102 | 10 |
| 14 | 7 | 5 | 6 | SHE CRIED — Jay & the Americans, United Artists 415 | 12 |
| ★ 15 | 20 | 24 | 30 | I SOLD MY HEART TO THE JUNKMAN — Blue Belles, Newtown 5000 | 7 |
| ★ 16 | 24 | 40 | 75 | SECOND HAND LOVE — Connie Francis, MGM 13074 | 4 |
| ★ 17 | 28 | 42 | 69 | PALISADES PARK — Freddy Cannon, Swan 4106 | 4 |
| ★ 18 | 25 | 33 | 43 | DON'T PLAY THAT SONG — Ben E. King, Atco 6222 | 7 |
| ★ 19 | 33 | 46 | 56 | PLAYBOY — Marvelettes, Tamla 54060 | 5 |
| 20 | 8 | 9 | 11 | P. T. 109 — Jimmy Dean, Columbia 42338 △ | 10 |
| 21 | 9 | 4 | 4 | JOHNNY ANGEL — Shelley Fabares, Colpix 621 | 14 |
| 22 | 22 | 25 | 28 | TWISTIN' MATILDA — Jimmy Soul, SPQR 3300 | 10 |
| 23 | 16 | 17 | 18 | I WISH THAT WE WERE MARRIED — Ronnie and the Hi-Lites, Joy 260 | 9 |
| 24 | 30 | 38 | 58 | FOLLOW THAT DREAM — Elvis Presley, RCA Victor EPA 4368 (Extended Play) | 4 |
| 25 | 14 | 10 | 14 | FUNNY WAY OF LAUGHIN' — Burl Ives, Decca 31371 | 9 |
| 26 | 17 | 11 | 5 | GOOD LUCK CHARM — Elvis Presley, RCA Victor 7992 △ | 12 |
| 27 | 26 | 22 | 29 | TELL ME — Dick & Deedee, Liberty 55412 | 12 |
| ★ 28 | 62 | 87 | 90 | THE STRIPPER — David Rose & His Ork, MGM 13064 | 4 |
| ★ 29 | 40 | 44 | 54 | SO THIS IS LOVE — Castells, Era 3073 | 8 |
| 30 | 27 | 23 | 25 | CATERINA — Perry Como, RCA Victor 8004 △ | 9 |
| 31 | 38 | 47 | 61 | TEACH ME TONIGHT — George Maharis, Epic 9504 | 7 |
| 32 | 36 | 43 | 63 | VILLAGE OF LOVE — Nathaniel Mayer, Fortune/United Artists 449 | 6 |
| 33 | 41 | 56 | 71 | THAT'S OLD FASHIONED — Everly Brothers, Warner Bros. 5273 | 4 |
| 34 | 23 | 16 | 9 | TWIST, TWIST, SENORA — Gary (U. S.) Bonds, LeGrand 1018 | 10 |
| 35 | 29 | 27 | 35 | MOST PEOPLE GET MARRIED — Patti Page, Mercury 71950 | 7 |
| 36 | 35 | 39 | 46 | NIGHT TRAIN — James Brown, King 5614 | 8 |
| ★ 37 | 51 | 65 | 89 | CINDY'S BIRTHDAY — Johnny Crawford, Del Fi 4178 | 4 |
| ★ 38 | 54 | 76 | — | SNAP YOUR FINGERS — Joe Henderson, Todd 1072 | 3 |
| ★ 39 | 49 | 62 | 70 | I LOVE YOU — Volumes, Chex 1002 | 6 |
| 40 | 46 | 61 | 72 | ANY DAY NOW — Chuck Jackson, Wand 122 | 6 |
| 41 | 19 | 12 | 10 | SHOUT — Joey Dee & the Starliters, Roulette 4416 | 11 |
| 42 | 44 | 69 | 84 | WALK ON THE WILD SIDE — Jimmy Smith, Verve 10255 | 4 |
| 43 | 31 | 26 | 27 | YOU ARE MINE — Frankie Avalon, Chancellor 1107 | 11 |
| 44 | 32 | 37 | 50 | MOON RIVER — Henry Mancini, RCA Victor 7916 △ | 25 |
| 45 | 48 | 60 | 76 | HIT RECORD — Brook Benton, Mercury 71962 | 5 |
| ★ 46 | 57 | 74 | — | SHARING YOU — Bobby Vee, Liberty 55451 | 3 |
| 47 | 34 | 20 | 15 | LOVER, PLEASE — Clyde McPhatter, Mercury 71941 | 14 |
| 48 | 45 | 41 | 49 | COUNT EVERY STAR — Linda Scott, Canadian-American 133 | 9 |
| 49 | 37 | 19 | 13 | SLOW TWISTIN' — Chubby Checker, Parkway 835 | 14 |
| ★ 50 | 61 | 70 | 88 | BORN TO LOSE — Ray Charles, ABC-Paramount 10330 | 4 |
| 51 | 42 | 49 | 52 | (I WAS) BORN TO CRY — Dion, Laurie 3123 | 7 |
| 52 | 55 | 57 | 62 | NUMBER ONE MAN — Bruce Channel, Smash 1752 | 6 |
| ★ 53 | 76 | 84 | — | THEME FROM BEN CASEY — Valjean, Carlton 573 | 3 |
| ★ 54 | 70 | 73 | 86 | HOW IS JULIE? — Lettermen, Capitol 4746 | 4 |
| 55 | 39 | 28 | 23 | SOUL TWIST — King Curtis, Enjoy 1000 | 13 |
| 56 | 59 | 63 | 68 | LEMON TREE — Peter, Paul & Mary, Warner Bros. 5274 | 5 |
| 57 | 50 | 51 | 41 | ITTY BITTY PIECES — James Ray, Caprice 114 | 9 |
| 58 | 60 | 66 | 79 | BALBOA BLUE — Marketts, Liberty 55443 | 6 |
| 59 | 68 | 79 | 94 | MY REAL NAME — Fats Domino, Imperial 5833 | 4 |
| ★ 60 | 73 | 85 | — | WHEN I GET THROUGH WITH YOU — Patsy Cline, Decca 31377 | 3 |
| 61 | 58 | 59 | 67 | IF I CRIED EVERY TIME YOU HURT ME — Wanda Jackson, Capitol 4723 | 7 |
| ★ 62 | 81 | 100 | — | AL DI LA' — Emilio Pericoli, Warner Bros. 5259 | 3 |
| 63 | 66 | 72 | — | WHERE ARE YOU — Dinah Washington, Roulette 4424 | 3 |
| 64 | 65 | 58 | 60 | HEARTS — Jackie Wilson, Brunswick 55225 | 6 |
| 65 | 74 | 77 | 93 | FORTUNETELLER — Bobby Curtola, Del Fi 4177 | 5 |
| 66 | 77 | 82 | — | DOCTOR FEEL GOOD — Dr. Feelgood & the Interns, Okeh 7144 | 6 |
| 67 | 63 | 64 | 66 | MEET ME AT THE TWISTIN' PLACE — Johnnie Morisette, Sar 126 | 8 |
| ★ 68 | 88 | — | — | A STEEL GUITAR AND A GLASS OF WINE — Paul Anka, RCA Victor 8030 △ | 2 |
| 69 | 71 | 75 | 83 | THAT'S MY DESIRE — Yvonne Baker & the Sensations, Argo 5412 | 5 |
| 70 | 78 | 81 | 91 | OH, MY ANGEL — Bertha Tillman, Brent 7029 | 5 |
| 71 | 85 | 97 | — | BRISTOL TWISTIN' ANNIE — Dovells, Parkway 838 | 3 |
| ★ 72 | — | — | — | THEME FROM DOCTOR KILDARE — Richard Chamberlain, MGM 13075 | 1 |
| 73 | 83 | 67 | 78 | DRUMMIN' UP A STORM — Sandy Nelson, Imperial 5829 | 6 |
| ★ 74 | 89 | — | — | SWINGIN' GENTLY — Earl Grant, Decca 25560 | 2 |
| ★ 75 | 91 | — | — | HAVING A PARTY — Sam Cooke, RCA Victor 8036 △ | 2 |
| 76 | 79 | 83 | 85 | WHY'D YOU WANNA MAKE ME CRY — Connie Stevens, Warner Bros. 5265 | 5 |
| 77 | 80 | — | — | WOLVERTON MOUNTAIN — Claude King, Columbia 42352 △ | 2 |
| 78 | 82 | 94 | 99 | I'LL TRY SOMETHING NEW — Miracles, Tamla 54059 | 4 |
| 79 | 72 | 68 | 80 | I'LL TAKE YOU HOME — Corsairs, Tuff 1818 | 8 |
| 80 | 94 | — | 96 | LIPSTICK TRACES — Benny Spellman, Minit 644 | 4 |
| 81 | 84 | 86 | — | WOMAN IS A MAN'S BEST FRIEND — Teddy & the Twilights, Swan 4102 | 3 |
| 82 | 75 | 80 | 82 | I FOUND A LOVE — Falcons, LuPine 1003 | 9 |
| 83 | 69 | 71 | 74 | LOVE CAN'T WAIT — Marty Robbins, Columbia 42375 △ | 6 |
| ★ 84 | — | — | — | TWIST AND SHOUT — Isley Brothers, Wand 124 | 1 |
| ★ 85 | — | — | — | THE CROWD — Roy Orbison, Monument 461 | 1 |
| ★ 86 | — | — | — | I'LL NEVER DANCE AGAIN — Bobby Rydell, Cameo 217 | 1 |
| 87 | 99 | — | — | WEST OF THE WALL — Toni Fisher, Big Top 3097 | 2 |
| 88 | 95 | — | — | JOHNNY GETS ANGRY — Joanie Sommers, Warner Bros. 5275 | 2 |
| 89 | 98 | — | — | LIMBO ROCK — Champs, Challenge 9131 | 2 |
| 90 | 90 | — | 95 | ADIOS AMIGO — Jim Reeves, RCA Victor 8019 △ | 4 |
| 91 | 92 | — | — | DOWN IN THE VALLEY — Solomon Burke, Atlantic 2147 | 2 |
| 92 | 93 | — | — | WHERE HAVE YOU BEEN ALL MY LIFE — Arthur Alexander, Dot 16357 | 2 |
| 93 | — | — | — | ROUTE 66 THEME — Nelson Riddle, Capitol 4741 | 1 |
| 94 | 87 | 91 | 97 | LET ME BE THE ONE — Paris Sisters, Gregmark 12 | 4 |
| 95 | — | — | — | GREEN LEAVES OF SUMMER — Kenny Ball, Kapp 460 | 1 |
| 96 | 97 | — | — | TENNESSEE — Jan and Dean, Liberty 55454 | 2 |
| 97 | — | 98 | — | THAT HAPPY FEELING — Bert Kaempfert, Decca 31388 | 2 |
| 98 | — | — | 88 | SCOTCH AND SODA — Kingston Trio, Capitol 4740 | 4 |
| 99 | 100 | — | — | BOOM BOOM — John Lee Hooker, Vee Jay 438 | 2 |
| 100 | — | — | — | I NEED YOUR LOVING — Don Gardner and Dee Dee Ford, Fire 508 | 1 |

## HOT 100—A TO Z—(Publisher-Licensee)

Adios Amigo (Randy-Smith, ASCAP) .......... 90
Al Di La' (Witmark, ASCAP) .......... 62
Any Day Now (Plan Two, ASCAP) .......... 40
Balboa Blue (Lock-E.D.M., ASCAP) .......... 58
Boom Boom (Conrad, BMI) .......... 99
Born to Lose (Peer Int'l, BMI) .......... 50
Bristol Twistin' Annie (Schulman, BMI) .......... 71
Caterina (Roncom, ASCAP) .......... 30
Cindy's Birthday (Maraville, BMI) .......... 37
Conscience (Aldon, BMI) .......... 11
Count Every Star (Paxton, ASCAP) .......... 48
Crowd, The (Acuff-Rose, BMI) .......... 85
Doctor Feel Good (Cigma, BMI) .......... 66
Don't Play That Song (Progressive, BMI) .......... 18
Down in the Valley (Progressive, BMI) .......... 91
Drummin' Up a Storm (Travis, BMI) .......... 73
Everybody Loves Me But You (Champion, BMI) .......... 6
Funny Way of Laughin' (Pamper, BMI) .......... 25
Follow That Dream (Gladys, ASCAP) .......... 24
Fortuneteller (Kemo, BMI) .......... 65
Good Luck Charm (Gladys, ASCAP) .......... 26
Green Leaves of Summer (Feist, ASCAP) .......... 95
Having a Party (Kags, BMI) .......... 75
Hearts (East-West, ASCAP) .......... 64
Hit Record (Luristan-Dreyer, ASCAP) .......... 45
How Is Julie? (Sherman-DeVorzon, BMI) .......... 54
I Can't Stop Loving You (Acuff-Rose, BMI) .......... 1
I Found a Love (LuPine-Progressive-Alibri, BMI) .......... 82
I Love You (Criss, BMI) .......... 39
I Need Your Loving (Fast-Pete, BMI) .......... 100
I Sold My Heart to the Junkman (Mills, ASCAP) .......... 15
(I Was) Born to Cry (Disal, ASCAP) .......... 51
I Wish That We Were Married (Joy, ASCAP) .......... 23
I'll Never Dance Again (Aldon, BMI) .......... 86
I'll Take You Home (Sunflower & Annie-Earl, ASCAP) .......... 79
I'll Try Something New (Jobete, BMI) .......... 78
If I Cried Every Time You Hurt Me (Central, BMI) .......... 61
It Keeps Right on A-Hurtin' (Tanridge, BMI) .......... 12
Itty Bitty Pieces (Good Songs, BMI) .......... 57
Johnny Angel (Post, ASCAP) .......... 21
Johnny Gets Angry (Tod, ASCAP) .......... 88
Lemon Tree (Boulder, ASCAP) .......... 56
Let Me Be the One (Aldon, BMI) .......... 94
Limbo Rock (Four Star, BMI) .......... 89
Lipstick Traces (Minit, BMI) .......... 80
Love Can't Wait (Marty's, BMI) .......... 83
Lover, Please (Lyn-Lou, BMI) .......... 47
Lovers Who Wander (Disal, ASCAP) .......... 4
Man Who Shot Liberty Valance, The (Famous, ASCAP) .......... 10
Mashed Potato Time (Rice-Mill, BMI) .......... 5
Meet Me at the Twistin' Place (Kags, BMI) .......... 67
Moon River (Famous, ASCAP) .......... 44
Most People Get Married (Famous, ASCAP) .......... 35
My Real Name (Travis, BMI) .......... 59
Night Train (Pamless, BMI) .......... 36
Number One Man (LeBill, BMI) .......... 52
Oh, My Angel (Clifton, BMI) .......... 70
Old Rivers (Glo-Mac & Metric, BMI) .......... 8
One Who Really Loves You, The (Jobete, BMI) .......... 9
P. T. 109 (Cedarwood, BMI) .......... 20
Palisades Park (Claridge, ASCAP) .......... 17
Playboy (Jobete, BMI) .......... 19
Route 66 Theme (Gower, BMI) .......... 93
Scotch and Soda (Beechwood, BMI) .......... 98
Second Hand Love (Merna, BMI) .......... 16
Sharing You (Aldon, BMI) .......... 46
She Cried (Trio, BMI) .......... 14
Shout (Wemar-Nom, BMI) .......... 41
Shout! Shout! (Knock Yourself Out) (Broadway, ASCAP) .......... 7
Slow Twistin' (Woodcrest, BMI) .......... 49
Snap Your Fingers (Cigma, BMI) .......... 38
So This Is Love (Pattern, ASCAP) .......... 29
Soldier Boy (Ludix, BMI) .......... 3
Soul Twist (Dan-Kelyn, BMI) .......... 55
Steel Guitar and a Glass of Wine, A (Spanka, BMI) .......... 68
Stranger on the Shore (Mellin, BMI) .......... 2
Stripper, The (David Rose, ASCAP) .......... 28
Swingin' Gently (Maraville, BMI) .......... 74
Teach Me Tonight (Hub-Leeds, ASCAP) .......... 31
Tell Me (Odin, ASCAP) .......... 27
Tennessee (Wonder-Achlen, BMI) .......... 96
That Happy Feeling (Northern, ASCAP) .......... 97
That's My Desire (Mills, ASCAP) .......... 69
That's Old Fashioned (Aberbach, BMI) .......... 33
Theme From Ben Casey (Marfran, ASCAP) .......... 53
Theme From Doctor Kildare (Hastings, BMI) .......... 72
Twist and Shout (Russber, BMI) .......... 84
Twist, Twist Senora (Rockmasters, BMI) .......... 34
Twistin' Matilda (General-Pickwick, ASCAP) .......... 22
Uptown (Aldon, BMI) .......... 13
Village of Love (Trianon, BMI) .......... 32
Walk on the Wild Side (Columbia Pictures, ASCAP) .......... 42
West of the Wall (Music Productions, ASCAP) .......... 87
When I Get Through With You (Pamper, BMI) .......... 60
Where Are You (Feist, ASCAP) .......... 63
Where Have You Been All My Life (Aldon, BMI) .......... 92
Why'd You Wanna Make Me Cry (Aldon, BMI) .......... 76
Wolverton Mountain (Painted Desert, BMI) .......... 77
Woman Is a Man's Best Friend, A (Claridge, ASCAP) .......... 81
You Are Mine (Debmar, BMI) .......... 43

## BUBBLING UNDER THE HOT 100

101. DREAM .......... Dinah Washington, Mercury 71958
102. ROSES ARE RED .......... Bobby Vinton, Epic 9509
103. ONE O'CLOCK JUMP .......... Jimmy Smith, Blue Note 1820
104. QUEEN OF MY HEART .......... Rene and Ray, Donna 1360
105. JOHN BIRCH SOCIETY .......... Chad Mitchell Trio, Kapp 457
106. WHAT DID DADDY DO .......... Shep and the Limelites, Hull 751
107. NA-NE-NO .......... Troy Shondell, Liberty 55445
108. HOW CAN I MEET HER? .......... Everly Brothers, Warner Bros. 5273
109. EVERYBODY LOVES A LOVER .......... Angels, Caprice 116
110. DANCIN' THE STRAND .......... Maureen Gray, Landa 689
111. STRANGER ON THE SHORE .......... Drifters, Atlantic 2143
112. WORK OUT, PART I .......... Ricky Dee and the Embers, Newtown 5001
113. AIR TRAVEL .......... Ray and Bob, Ledo 1150
114. GEE, IT'S WONDERFUL .......... Bobby Rydell, Cameo 217
115. LISA .......... Ferrante and Teicher, United Artists 470
116. TURN AROUND, LOOK AT ME .......... Lettermen, Capitol 4746
117. BABY ELEPHANT WALK .......... Miniature Men, Dolton 57
118. STRANGER ON THE SHORE .......... Andy Williams, Columbia 42451
119. BABY ELEPHANT WALK .......... Lawrence Welk, Dot 16364
120. WORRIED MIND .......... Ray Anthony, Capitol 4742

# BILLBOARD HOT 100

FOR WEEK ENDING JUNE 9

1962

★ STAR PERFORMERS—Selections registering greatest upward progress this week.

S Indicates that 45 r.p.m. stereo single version is available.

△ Indicates that 33⅓ r.p.m. mono single version is available.

Ⓢ Indicates that 33⅓ r.p.m. stereo single version is available.

| This Week | 1 Wk. Ago | 2 Wks. Ago | 3 Wks. Ago | Title, Artist, Label & Number | Weeks On Chart |
|---|---|---|---|---|---|
| 1 | 1 | 4 | 21 | I CAN'T STOP LOVING YOU — Ray Charles, ABC-Paramount 10330 | 6 |
| 2 | 2 | 1 | 2 | STRANGER ON THE SHORE — Mr. Acker Bilk, Atco 6217 | 13 |
| 3 | 4 | 10 | 13 | LOVERS WHO WANDER — Dion, Laurie 3123 | 8 |
| 4 | 3 | 2 | 1 | SOLDIER BOY — Shirelles, Scepter 1228 | 12 |
| ★5 | 10 | 21 | 32 | THE MAN WHO SHOT LIBERTY VALANCE — Gene Pitney, Musicor 1020 | 7 |
| ★6 | 12 | 18 | 34 | IT KEEPS RIGHT ON A-HURTIN' — Johnny Tillotson, Cadence 1418 | 5 |
| ★7 | 16 | 24 | 40 | SECOND HAND LOVE — Connie Francis, MGM 13074 | 5 |
| 8 | 9 | 12 | 14 | THE ONE WHO REALLY LOVES YOU — Mary Wells, Motown 1024 | 12 |
| ★9 | 17 | 28 | 42 | PALISADES PARK — Freddy Cannon, Swan 4106 | 5 |
| ★10 | 19 | 33 | 46 | PLAYBOY — Marvelettes, Tamla 54060 | 6 |
| 11 | 11 | 15 | 15 | CONSCIENCE — James Darren, Colpix 630 | 9 |
| ★12 | 18 | 25 | 33 | DON'T PLAY THAT SONG — Ben E. King, Atco 6222 | 8 |
| 13 | 6 | 6 | 8 | EVERYBODY LOVES ME BUT YOU — Brenda Lee, Decca 31379 | 9 |
| 14 | 5 | 3 | 3 | MASHED POTATO TIME — Dee Dee Sharp, Cameo 212 | 15 |
| ★15 | 28 | 62 | 87 | THE STRIPPER — David Rose & His Ork, MGM 13064 | 5 |
| 16 | 14 | 7 | 5 | SHE CRIED — Jay & the Americans, United Artists 415 | 13 |
| 17 | 15 | 20 | 24 | I SOLD MY HEART TO THE JUNKMAN — Blue Belles, Newtown 5000 | 8 |
| 18 | 8 | 5 | 7 | OLD RIVERS — Walter Brennan, Liberty 55436 | 10 |
| 19 | 7 | 11 | 6 | SHOUT! SHOUT! (Knock Yourself Out) — Ernie Maresca, Seville 117 | 11 |
| 20 | 13 | 13 | 18 | UPTOWN — Crystals, Philles 102 | 11 |
| 21 | 29 | 40 | 44 | SO THIS IS LOVE — Castells, Era 3073 | 9 |
| 22 | 24 | 30 | 38 | FOLLOW THAT DREAM — Elvis Presley, RCA Victor EPA 4368 (Extended Play) | 5 |
| ★23 | 33 | 41 | 56 | THAT'S OLD FASHIONED — Everly Brothers, Warner Bros. 5273 | 5 |
| 24 | 22 | 22 | 25 | TWISTIN' MATILDA — Jimmy Soul, SPQR 3300 | 11 |
| ★25 | 37 | 51 | 65 | CINDY'S BIRTHDAY — Johnny Crawford, Del Fi 4178 | 5 |
| 26 | 31 | 38 | 47 | TEACH ME TONIGHT — George Maharis, Epic 9504 | 8 |
| ★27 | 38 | 54 | 76 | SNAP YOUR FINGERS — Joe Henderson, Todd 1072 | 4 |
| 28 | 32 | 36 | 43 | VILLAGE OF LOVE — Nathaniel Mayer, Fortune/United Artists 449 | 7 |
| 29 | 25 | 14 | 10 | FUNNY WAY OF LAUGHIN' — Burl Ives, Decca 31371 | 10 |
| ★30 | 62 | 81 | 100 | AL DI LA' — Emilio Pericoli, Warner Bros. 5259 | 4 |
| ★31 | 46 | 57 | 74 | SHARING YOU — Bobby Vee, Liberty 55451 | 4 |
| ★32 | 42 | 44 | 69 | WALK ON THE WILD SIDE — Jimmy Smith, Verve 10255 | 5 |
| 33 | 21 | 9 | 4 | JOHNNY ANGEL — Shelley Fabares, Colpix 621 | 15 |
| 34 | 40 | 46 | 61 | ANY DAY NOW — Chuck Jackson, Wand 122 | 7 |
| ★35 | 56 | 59 | 63 | LEMON TREE — Peter, Paul & Mary, Warner Bros. 5274 | 6 |
| 36 | 39 | 49 | 62 | I LOVE YOU — Volumes, Chex 1002 | 7 |
| 37 | 20 | 8 | 9 | P. T. 109 — Jimmy Dean, Columbia 42338 △ | 11 |
| 38 | 36 | 35 | 39 | NIGHT TRAIN — James Brown, King 5614 | 9 |
| 39 | 23 | 16 | 17 | I WISH THAT WE WERE MARRIED — Ronnie and the Hi-Lites, Joy 260 | 10 |
| 40 | 27 | 26 | 22 | TELL ME — Dick & Deedee, Liberty 55412 | 13 |
| ★41 | 68 | 88 | — | A STEEL GUITAR AND A GLASS OF WINE — Paul Anka, RCA Victor 8030 △ | 3 |
| 42 | 35 | 29 | 27 | MOST PEOPLE GET MARRIED — Patti Page, Mercury 71950 | 8 |
| 43 | 26 | 17 | 11 | GOOD LUCK CHARM — Elvis Presley, RCA Victor 7992 △ | 13 |
| 44 | 30 | 27 | 23 | CATERINA — Perry Como, RCA Victor 8004 △ | 10 |
| 45 | 53 | 76 | 84 | THEME FROM BEN CASEY — Valjean, Carlton 573 | 4 |
| ★46 | 75 | 91 | — | HAVING A PARTY — Sam Cooke, RCA Victor 8036 △ | 3 |
| 47 | 54 | 70 | 73 | HOW IS JULIE? — Lettermen, Capitol 4746 | 5 |
| ★48 | 71 | 85 | 97 | BRISTOL TWISTIN' ANNIE — Dovells, Parkway 838 | 4 |
| 49 | 45 | 48 | 60 | HIT RECORD — Brook Benton, Mercury 71962 | 6 |
| ★50 | 65 | 74 | 77 | FORTUNETELLER — Bobby Curtola, Del Fi 4177 | 6 |
| ★51 | 77 | 80 | — | WOLVERTON MOUNTAIN — Claude King, Columbia 42352 △ | 3 |
| ★52 | 72 | — | — | THEME FROM DOCTOR KILDARE — Richard Chamberlain, MGM 13075 | 2 |
| ★53 | 63 | 66 | 72 | WHERE ARE YOU — Dinah Washington, Roulette 4424 | 4 |
| 54 | 44 | 32 | 37 | MOON RIVER — Henry Mancini, RCA Victor 7916 △ | 26 |
| 55 | 60 | 73 | 85 | WHEN I GET THROUGH WITH YOU — Patsy Cline, Decca 31377 | 4 |
| 56 | 58 | 60 | 66 | BALBOA BLUE — Marketts, Liberty 55443 | 7 |
| 57 | 50 | 61 | 70 | BORN TO LOSE — Ray Charles, ABC-Paramount 10330 | 5 |
| 58 | 48 | 45 | 41 | COUNT EVERY STAR — Linda Scott, Canadian-American 133 | 10 |
| ★59 | 74 | 89 | — | SWINGIN' GENTLY — Earl Grant, Decca 25560 | 3 |
| ★60 | 88 | 95 | — | JOHNNY GETS ANGRY — Joanie Sommers, Warner Bros. 5275 | 3 |
| 61 | 70 | 78 | 81 | OH, MY ANGEL — Bertha Tillman, Brent 7029 | 6 |
| ★62 | 86 | — | — | I'LL NEVER DANCE AGAIN — Bobby Rydell, Cameo 217 | 2 |
| ★63 | 78 | 82 | 94 | I'LL TRY SOMETHING NEW — Miracles, Tamla 54059 | 5 |
| 64 | 52 | 55 | 57 | NUMBER ONE MAN — Bruce Channel, Smash 1752 | 7 |
| 65 | 41 | 19 | 12 | SHOUT — Joey Dee & the Starliters, Roulette 4416 | 12 |
| 66 | 59 | 68 | 79 | MY REAL NAME — Fats Domino, Imperial 5833 | 5 |
| 67 | 61 | 58 | 59 | IF I CRIED EVERY TIME YOU HURT ME — Wanda Jackson, Capitol 4723 | 8 |
| ★68 | — | — | — | ROSES ARE RED — Bobby Vinton, Epic 9509 | 1 |
| 69 | 73 | 83 | 67 | DRUMMIN' UP A STORM — Sandy Nelson, Imperial 5829 | 7 |
| 70 | 66 | 77 | 82 | DOCTOR FEEL GOOD — Dr. Feelgood & the Interns, Okeh 7144 | 7 |
| 71 | 57 | 50 | 51 | ITTY BITTY PIECES — James Ray, Caprice 114 | 10 |
| ★72 | 87 | 99 | — | WEST OF THE WALL — Toni Fisher, Big Top 3097 | 3 |
| 73 | 76 | 79 | 83 | WHY'D YOU WANNA MAKE ME CRY — Connie Stevens, Warner Bros. 5265 | 6 |
| 74 | 85 | — | — | THE CROWD — Roy Orbison, Monument 461 | 2 |
| 75 | 69 | 71 | 75 | THAT'S MY DESIRE — Yvonne Baker & the Sensations, Argo 5412 | 6 |
| ★76 | — | — | — | STRANGER ON THE SHORE — Andy Williams, Columbia 42451 △ | 1 |
| 77 | 89 | 98 | — | LIMBO ROCK — Champs, Challenge 9131 | 3 |
| ★78 | 97 | — | 98 | THAT HAPPY FEELING — Bert Kaempfert, Decca 31388 | 3 |
| 79 | 81 | 84 | 86 | WOMAN IS A MAN'S BEST FRIEND — Teddy & the Twilights, Swan 4102 | 4 |
| 80 | 80 | 94 | — | LIPSTICK TRACES — Benny Spellman, Minit 644 | 5 |
| ★81 | 98 | — | — | SCOTCH AND SODA — Kingston Trio, Capitol 4740 | 5 |
| 82 | 84 | — | — | TWIST AND SHOUT — Isley Brothers, Wand 124 | 2 |
| 83 | 67 | 63 | 64 | MEET ME AT THE TWISTIN' PLACE — Johnnie Morisette, Sar 126 | 9 |
| ★84 | — | — | — | JOHNNY LOVES ME — Shelley Fabares, Colpix 636 | 1 |
| ★85 | — | 96 | — | HOW CAN I MEET HER? — Everly Brothers, Warner Bros. 5273 | 2 |
| 86 | 96 | 97 | — | TENNESSEE — Jan and Dean, Liberty 55454 | 3 |
| ★87 | — | — | — | QUEEN OF MY HEART — Rene & Ray, Donna 1360 | 1 |
| 88 | 99 | 100 | — | BOOM BOOM — John Lee Hooker, Vee Jay 438 | 3 |
| 89 | 100 | — | — | I NEED YOUR LOVING — Don Gardner and Dee Dee Ford, Fire 508 | 2 |
| 90 | 94 | 87 | 91 | LET ME BE THE ONE — Paris Sisters, Gregmark 12 | 5 |
| 91 | 93 | — | — | ROUTE 66 THEME — Nelson Riddle, Capitol 4741 | 2 |
| 92 | — | — | — | KEEP YOUR LOVE LOCKED (Deep in Your Heart) — Paul Petersen, Colpix 632 | 1 |
| 93 | 92 | 93 | — | WHERE HAVE YOU BEEN ALL MY LIFE — Arthur Alexander, Dot 16357 | 3 |
| 94 | 95 | — | — | GREEN LEAVES OF SUMMER — Kenny Ball, Kapp 460 | 2 |
| 95 | — | 86 | — | DRUM STOMP — Sandy Nelson, Imperial 5829 | 2 |
| 96 | — | — | — | BABY ELEPHANT WALK — Lawrence Welk, Dot 16364 | 1 |
| 97 | — | — | — | THE WAH-WATUSI — Orlons, Cameo 218 | 1 |
| 98 | — | — | — | BABY ELEPHANT WALK — Miniature Men, Dolton 57 | 1 |
| 99 | — | — | — | DANCIN' THE STRAND — Maureen Gray, Landa 689 | 1 |
| 100 | — | — | — | SEALED WITH A KISS — Brian Hyland, ABC-Paramount 10336 | 1 |

## HOT 100—A TO Z—*(Publisher-Licensee)*

Al Di La' (Witmark, ASCAP) .... 30
Any Day Now (Plan Two, ASCAP) .... 34
Baby Elephant Walk—Miniature Men (Famous, ASCAP) .... 98
Baby Elephant Walk—Welk (Famous, ASCAP) .... 96
Balboa Blue (Lock-E.D.M., ASCAP) .... 56
Boom Boom (Conrad, BMI) .... 88
Born to Lose (Peer Int'l, BMI) .... 57
Bristol Twistin' Annie (Schulman, BMI) .... 48
Caterina (Roncom, ASCAP) .... 44
Cindy's Birthday (Maraville, BMI) .... 25
Conscience (Aldon, BMI) .... 11
Count Every Star (Paxton, ASCAP) .... 58
Crowd, The (Acuff-Rose, BMI) .... 74
Dancin' the Strand (Ponderosa, BMI) .... 99
Doctor Feel Good (Cigma, BMI) .... 70
Don't Play That Song (Progressive, BMI) .... 12
Drum Stomp (Travis, BMI) .... 95
Drummin' Up a Storm (Travis, BMI) .... 69
Everybody Loves Me But You (Champion, BMI) .... 13
Follow That Dream (Gladys, ASCAP) .... 22
Fortuneteller (Kemo, BMI) .... 50
Funny Way of Laughin' (Pamper, BMI) .... 29
Good Luck Charm (Gladys, ASCAP) .... 43
Green Leaves of Summer (Feist, ASCAP) .... 94
Having a Party (Kags, BMI) .... 46
Hit Record (Luristan-Dreyer, ASCAP) .... 49
How Can I Meet Her? (Aberbach, BMI) .... 85
How Is Julie? (Sherman-DeVorzon, BMI) .... 47
I Can't Stop Loving You (Acuff-Rose, BMI) .... 1
I Love You (Criss, BMI) .... 36
I Need Your Loving (Fast-Pete, BMI) .... 89
I Sold My Heart to the Junkman (Mills, ASCAP) .. 17
I Wish That We Were Married (Joy, ASCAP) .... 39
I'll Never Dance Again (Aldon, BMI) .... 62
I'll Try Something New (Jobete, BMI) .... 63
If I Cried Everytime You Hurt Me (Central, BMI) .. 67
It Keeps Righ on A-Hurtin' (Tandridge, BMI) .... 6
Itty Bitty Pieces (Good Songs, BMI) .... 71
Johnny Angel (Post, ASCAP) .... 33
Johnny Gets Angry (Tod, ASCAP) .... 60
Johnny Loves Me (Aldon, BMI) .... 84
Keep Your Love Locked (Aldon, BMI) .... 92
Lemon Tree (Boulder, (ASCAP) .... 35
Let Me Be the One (Aldon, BMI) .... 90
Limbo Rock (Four Star, BMI) .... 77
Lipstick Traces (Minit, BMI) .... 80
Lovers Who Wander (Disal, ASCAP) .... 3
Man Who Shot Liberty Valance, The (Famous, ASCAP) .... 5
Mashed Potato Time (Rice-Mill, BMI) .... 14
Meet Me at the Twistin' Place (Kags, BMI) .... 83
Moon River (Famous, ASCAP) .... 54
Most People Get Married (Famous, ASCAP) .... 42
My Real Name (Travis, BMI) .... 66
Night Train (Pamless, BMI) .... 38
Number One Man (LeBill, BMI) .... 64
Oh My Angel (Clifton, BMI) .... 61
Old Rivers (Glo-Mac & Metric, BMI) .... 18
One Who Really Loves You, The (Jobete, BMI) .. 8
P. T. 109 (Cedarwood, BMI) .... 37
Palisades Park (Claridge, ASCAP) .... 9
Playboy (Jobete, BMI) .... 10
Queen of My Heart (Maravilla, BMI) .... 87
Roses Are Red (Lyle, ASCAP) .... 68
Route 66 Theme (Gower, BMI) .... 91
Scotch and Soda (Beechwood, BMI) .... 81
Sealed With a Kiss (Post, ASCAP) .... 100
Second-Hand Love (Merna, BMI) .... 7
Sharing You (Aldon, BMI) .... 31
She Cried (Trio, BMI) .... 16
Shout (Womar-Nom, BMI) .... 65
Shout! Shout! (Knock Yourself Out) (Broadway, ASCAP) .... 19
Snap Your Fingers (Cigma, BMI) .... 27
So This Is Love (Pattern, ASCAP) .... 21
Soldier Boy (Ludix, BMI) .... 4
Steel Guitar and a Glass of Wine, A (Spanka, BMI) .... 41
Stranger on the Shore—Bilk (Mellin, BMI) .... 2
Stranger on the Shore—Williams (Mellin, BMI) .. 76
Stripper, The (David Rose, ASCAP) .... 15
Swingin' Gently (Maraville, BMI) .... 59
Teach Me Tonight (Hub-Leeds, ASCAP) .... 26
Tell Me (Odin, ASCAP) .... 40
Tennessee (Wonder Achlen, BMI) .... 86
That Happy Feeling (Northern, ASCAP) .... 78
That's My Desire (Mills, ASCAP) .... 75
That's Old Fashioned (Aberbach, BMI) .... 23
Theme From Ben Casey (Marfran, ASCAP) .... 45
Theme From Docter Kildare (Hastings, BMI) .... 52
Twist and Shout (Russber, BMI) .... 82
Twistin' Matilda (General-Pickwick, ASCAP) .... 24
Uptown (Aldon, BMI) .... 20
Village of Love (Trianon, BMI) .... 28
Wah-Watusi, The (Kalmann-Lowe, ASCAP) .... 97
Walk on the Wild Side (Columbia Pictures, ASCAP) .... 32
West of the Wall (Music Productions, ASCAP) .. 72
When I Get Through With You (Pamper, BMI) .. 55
Where Are You (Feist, ASCAP) .... 53
Where Have You Been All My Life (Aldon, BMI).. 93
Why'd You Wanna Make Me Cry (Aldon, BMI).. 73
Wolverton Mountain (Painted Desert, BMI) .... 51
Woman Is a Man's Best Friend, A (Claridge, ASCAP) .... 79

## BUBBLING UNDER THE HOT 100

101. DOWN IN THE VALLEY .... Solomon Burke, Atlantic 2147
102. JOHN BIRCH SOCIETY .... Chad Mitchell Trio, Kapp 457
103. WHAT DID DADDY DO .... Shep & the Limelites, Hull 751
104. DREAM .... Dinah Washington, Mercury 71958
105. ADIOS AMIGO .... Jim Reeves, RCA Victor 8019
106. SHAKE A HAND .... Ruth Brown, Philips 40028
107. NA-NE-NO .... Troy Shondell, Liberty 55445
108. EVERYBODY LOVES A LOVER .... Angels, Caprice 116
109. GEE, IT'S WONDERFUL .... Bobby Rydell, Cameo 217
110. AIR TRAVEL .... Ray & Bob, Ledo 1150
111. TURN AROUND, LOOK AT ME .... Lettermen, Capitol 4746
112. LISA .... Ferrante & Teicher, United Artists 470
113. INSTANT MASHED .... Ventures, Dolton 55
114. WORRIED MIND .... Ray Anthony, Capitol 4742
115. THAT GREASY KID STUFF .... Janie Grant, Caprice 115
116. GRAVY .... Dee Dee Sharp, Cameo 219
117. IF THE BOY ONLY KNEW .... Sue Thompson, Hickory 1174
118. BONGO STOMP .... Little Joey & the Flips, Joy 262
119. PLEASE MR. COLUMBUS (Turn the Ship Around) .... Lou Monte, Reprise 20085
120. DR. BEN BASEY .... Mickey Shorr, Tuba 8001
120. I DON'T LOVE YOU NO MORE .... Jimmy Norman, Little Star 113

# BILLBOARD HOT 100

**FOR WEEK ENDING JUNE 16, 1962**

STAR PERFORMERS—Selections registering greatest upward progress this week.
S indicates that 45 r.p.m. stereo single version is available.
△ indicates that 33⅓ r.p.m. mono single version is available.
△ indicates that 33⅓ r.p.m. stereo single version is available.

| This Week | Last Week | 2 Wk. Ago | 3 Wk. Ago | Title — Artist, Label & Number | Weeks On Chart |
|---|---|---|---|---|---|
| 1 | 1 | 1 | 4 | I CAN'T STOP LOVING YOU — Ray Charles, ABC-Paramount 10330 | 7 |
| 2 | 2 | 2 | 1 | STRANGER ON THE SHORE — Mr. Acker Bilk, Atco 6217 | 14 |
| 3 | 6 | 12 | 18 | IT KEEPS RIGHT ON A-HURTIN' — Johnny Tillotson, Cadence 1418 | 6 |
| 4 | 5 | 10 | 21 | THE MAN WHO SHOT LIBERTY VALANCE — Gene Pitney, Musicor 1020 | 8 |
| 5 | 9 | 17 | 28 | PALISADES PARK — Freddy Cannon, Swan 4106 | 6 |
| 6 | 3 | 4 | 10 | LOVERS WHO WANDER — Dion, Laurie 3123 | 9 |
| 7 | 7 | 16 | 24 | SECOND HAND LOVE — Connie Francis, MGM 13074 | 5 |
| 8 | 15 | 28 | 62 | THE STRIPPER — David Rose & His Ork, MGM 13064 | 6 |
| 9 | 10 | 19 | 33 | PLAYBOY — Marvelettes, Tamla 54060 | 7 |
| 10 | 8 | 9 | 12 | THE ONE WHO REALLY LOVES YOU — Mary Wells, Motown 1024 | 13 |
| 11 | 12 | 18 | 25 | DON'T PLAY THAT SONG — Ben E. King, Atco 6222 | 9 |
| 12 | 25 | 37 | 51 | CINDY'S BIRTHDAY — Johnny Crawford, Del Fi 4178 | 6 |
| 13 | 23 | 33 | 41 | THAT'S OLD FASHIONED — Everly Brothers, Warner Bros. 5273 | 6 |
| 14 | 4 | 3 | 2 | SOLDIER BOY — Shirelles, Scepter 1228 | 13 |
| 15 | 22 | 24 | 30 | FOLLOW THAT DREAM — Elvis Presley, RCA Victor EPA 4368 (Extended Play) | 6 |
| 16 | 30 | 62 | 81 | AL DI LA' — Emilio Pericoli, Warner Bros. 5259 | 5 |
| 17 | 14 | 5 | 3 | MASHED POTATO TIME — Dee Dee Sharp, Cameo 212 | 16 |
| 18 | 27 | 38 | 54 | SNAP YOUR FINGERS — Joe Henderson, Todd 1072 | 5 |
| 19 | 31 | 46 | 57 | SHARING YOU — Bobby Vee, Liberty 55451 | 5 |
| 20 | 41 | 68 | 88 | A STEEL GUITAR AND A GLASS OF WINE — Paul Anka, RCA Victor 8030 | 4 |
| 21 | 13 | 6 | 6 | EVERYBODY LOVES ME BUT YOU — Brenda Lee, Decca 31379 | 10 |
| 22 | 17 | 15 | 20 | I SOLD MY HEART TO THE JUNKMAN — Blue Belles, Newtown 5000 | 9 |
| 23 | 21 | 29 | 40 | SO THIS IS LOVE — Castells, Era 3073 | 10 |
| 24 | 34 | 40 | 46 | ANY DAY NOW — Chuck Jackson, Wand 122 | 8 |
| 25 | 28 | 32 | 36 | VILLAGE OF LOVE — Nathaniel Mayer, Fortune/United Artists 449 | 8 |
| 26 | 26 | 31 | 38 | TEACH ME TONIGHT — George Maharis, Epic 9504 | 9 |
| 27 | 24 | 22 | 22 | TWISTIN' MATILDA — Jimmy Soul, SPQR 3300 | 12 |
| 28 | 20 | 13 | 13 | UPTOWN — Crystals, Phillies 102 | 12 |
| 29 | 18 | 8 | 5 | OLD RIVERS — Walter Brennan, Liberty 55436 | 11 |
| 30 | 32 | 42 | 44 | WALK ON THE WILD SIDE — Jimmy Smith, Verve 10255 | 6 |
| 31 | 68 | — | — | ROSES ARE RED — Bobby Vinton, Epic 9509 | 2 |
| 32 | 16 | 14 | 7 | SHE CRIED — Jay & the Americans, United Artists 415 | 14 |
| 33 | 11 | 11 | 15 | CONSCIENCE — James Darren, Colpix 630 | 10 |
| 34 | 36 | 39 | 49 | I LOVE YOU — Volumes, Chex 1002 | 8 |
| 35 | 77 | 80 | — | WOLVERTON MOUNTAIN — Claude King, Columbia 42352 | 4 |
| 36 | 46 | 75 | 91 | HAVING A PARTY — Sam Cooke, RCA Victor 8036 | 4 |
| 37 | 45 | 53 | 76 | THEME FROM BEN CASEY — Valjean, Carlton 573 | 5 |
| 38 | 19 | 7 | 11 | SHOUT! SHOUT! (Knock Yourself Out) — Ernie Maresca, Seville 117 | 12 |
| 39 | 35 | 56 | 59 | LEMON TREE — Peter, Paul & Mary, Warner Bros. 5274 | 7 |
| 40 | 60 | 88 | 95 | JOHNNY GETS ANGRY — Joanie Sommers, Warner Bros. 5275 | 4 |
| 41 | 52 | 72 | — | THEME FROM DOCTOR KILDARE — Richard Chamberlain, MGM 13075 | 3 |
| 42 | 47 | 54 | 70 | HOW IS JULIE! — Lettermen, Capitol 4746 | 6 |
| 43 | 62 | 86 | — | I'LL NEVER DANCE AGAIN — Bobby Rydell, Cameo 217 | 3 |
| 44 | 48 | 71 | 85 | BRISTOL TWISTIN' ANNIE — Dovells, Parkway 838 | 5 |
| 45 | 50 | 65 | 74 | FORTUNETELLER — Bobby Curtola, Del Fi 4177 | 7 |
| 46 | 53 | 63 | 66 | WHERE ARE YOU — Dinah Washington, Roulette 4424 | 5 |
| 47 | 49 | 45 | 48 | HIT RECORD — Brook Benton, Mercury 71962 | 7 |
| 48 | 56 | 58 | 60 | BALBOA BLUE — Marketts, Liberty 55443 | 8 |
| 49 | 59 | 74 | 89 | SWINGIN' GENTLY — Earl Grant, Decca 25560 | 4 |
| 50 | 29 | 25 | 14 | FUNNY WAY OF LAUGHIN' — Burl Ives, Decca 31371 | 11 |
| 51 | 57 | 50 | 61 | BORN TO LOSE — Ray Charles, ABC-Paramount 10330 | 6 |
| 52 | 74 | 85 | — | THE CROWD — Roy Orbison, Monument 461 | 3 |
| 53 | 55 | 60 | 73 | WHEN I GET THROUGH WITH YOU — Patsy Cline, Decca 31377 | 5 |
| 54 | 40 | 27 | 26 | TELL ME — Dick & Deedee, Liberty 55412 | 14 |
| 55 | 38 | 36 | 35 | NIGHT TRAIN — James Brown, King 5614 | 10 |
| 56 | 39 | 23 | 16 | I WISH THAT WE WERE MARRIED — Ronnie and the Hi-Lites, Joy 260 | 11 |
| 57 | 63 | 78 | 82 | I'LL TRY SOMETHING NEW — Miracles, Tamla 54059 | 6 |
| 58 | 44 | 30 | 27 | CATERINA — Perry Como, RCA Victor 8004 | 11 |
| 59 | 72 | 87 | 99 | WEST OF THE WALL — Toni Fisher, Big Top 3097 | 4 |
| 60 | 97 | — | — | THE WAH-WATUSI — Orlons, Cameo 218 | 2 |
| 61 | — | — | — | GRAVY — Dee Dee Sharp, Cameo 219 | 1 |
| 62 | 84 | — | — | JOHNNY LOVES ME — Shelley Fabares, Colpix 636 | 2 |
| 63 | 66 | 59 | 68 | MY REAL NAME — Fats Domino, Imperial 5833 | 6 |
| 64 | 73 | 76 | 79 | WHY'D YOU WANNA MAKE ME CRY — Connie Stevens, Warner Bros. 5265 | 7 |
| 65 | 100 | — | — | SEALED WITH A KISS — Brian Hyland, ABC-Paramount 10336 | 2 |
| 66 | 77 | 89 | 98 | LIMBO ROCK — Champs, Challenge 9131 | 4 |
| 67 | 61 | 70 | 78 | OH, MY ANGEL — Bertha Tillman, Brent 7029 | 7 |
| 68 | 76 | — | — | STRANGER ON THE SHORE — Andy Williams, Columbia 42451 | 2 |
| 69 | 79 | 81 | 84 | WOMAN IS A MAN'S BEST FRIEND — Teddy & the Twilights, Swan 4102 | 5 |
| 70 | — | — | — | SPEEDY GONZALES — Pat Boone, Dot 16368 | 1 |
| 71 | 78 | 97 | — | THAT HAPPY FEELING — Bert Kaempfert, Decca 31388 | 4 |
| 72 | 82 | 84 | — | TWIST AND SHOUT — Isley Brothers, Wand 124 | 3 |
| 73 | 70 | 66 | 77 | DOCTOR FEEL GOOD — Dr. Feelgood & the Interns, Okeh 7144 | 8 |
| 74 | 86 | 96 | 97 | TENNESSEE — Jan and Dean, Liberty 55454 | 4 |
| 75 | 85 | — | 96 | HOW CAN I MEET HER! — Everly Brothers, Warner Bros. 5273 | 3 |
| 76 | 69 | 73 | 83 | DRUMMIN' UP A STORM — Sandy Nelson, Imperial 5829 | 8 |
| 77 | 92 | — | — | KEEP YOUR LOVE LOCKED (Deep in Your Heart) — Paul Petersen, Colpix 632 | 2 |
| 78 | — | — | — | LITTLE BITTY PRETTY ONE — Clyde McPhatter, Mercury 71987 | 1 |
| 79 | — | — | — | DOCTOR BEN BASEY — Mickey Shore & the Catnips, Tuba 8001 | 1 |
| 80 | 93 | 92 | 93 | WHERE HAVE YOU BEEN ALL MY LIFE — Arthur Alexander, Dot 16357 | 4 |
| 81 | 89 | 100 | — | I NEED YOUR LOVING — Don Gardner and Dee Dee Ford, Fire 508 | 3 |
| 82 | 87 | — | — | QUEEN OF MY HEART — Rene & Ray, Donna 1360 | 2 |
| 83 | 80 | 80 | 94 | LIPSTICK TRACES — Benny Spellman, Minit 644 | 6 |
| 84 | 88 | 99 | 100 | BOOM BOOM — John Lee Hooker, Vee Jay 438 | 4 |
| 85 | 96 | — | — | BABY ELEPHANT WALK — Lawrence Welk, Dot 16364 | 2 |
| 86 | — | — | — | MARIANNA — Johnny Mathis, Columbia 42420 | 1 |
| 87 | 81 | 98 | — | SCOTCH AND SODA — Kingston Trio, Capitol 4740 | 6 |
| 88 | 91 | 93 | — | ROUTE 66 THEME — Nelson Riddle, Capitol 4741 | 3 |
| 89 | — | 91 | 92 | DOWN IN THE VALLEY — Solomon Burke, Atlantic 2147 | 3 |
| 90 | — | — | — | I DON'T LOVE YOU NO MORE — Jimmy Norman, Little Star 113 | 1 |
| 91 | 99 | — | — | DANCIN' THE STRAND — Maureen Gray, Landa 689 | 2 |
| 92 | 94 | 95 | — | GREEN LEAVES OF SUMMER — Kenny Ball, Kapp 460 | 3 |
| 93 | — | — | — | HAVE A GOOD TIME — Sue Thompson, Hickory 1174 | 1 |
| 94 | 95 | — | 86 | DRUM STOMP — Sandy Nelson, Imperial 5829 | 3 |
| 95 | 98 | — | — | BABY ELEPHANT WALK — Miniature Men, Dolton 57 | 2 |
| 96 | — | — | — | YOU'LL LOSE A GOOD THING — Barbara Lynn, Jamie 1220 | 1 |
| 97 | — | — | — | BONGO STOMP — Little Joey & the Flips, Joy 262 | 1 |
| 98 | — | 90 | 90 | ADIOS AMIGO — Jim Reeves, RCA Victor 8019 | 5 |
| 99 | — | — | — | NEVER IN A MILLION YEARS — Linda Scott, Congress 103 | 1 |
| 100 | — | — | — | LISA — Ferrante & Teicher, United Artists 470 | 1 |

## BUBBLING UNDER THE HOT 100

101. WHAT DID DADDY DO — Shep & the Limelites, Hull 751
102. DREAM — Dinah Washington, Mercury 71958
103. SHAKE A HAND — Ruth Brown, Philips 40028
104. INSTANT MASHED — Ventures, Dolton 55
105. TURN AROUND, LOOK AT ME — Lettermen, Capitol 4746
106. THAT GREASY KID STUFF — Janie Grant, Caprice 115
107. LITTLE RED RENTED ROWBOAT — Joe Dowell, Smash 1759
108. AIR TRAVEL — Ray & Bob, Ledo 1150
109. MY TIME FOR CRYING — Maxine Brown, ABC-Paramount 10327
110. SEVEN-DAY WEEKEND — Gary (U. S.) Bonds, LeGrand 1019
111. BUT NOT FOR ME — Ketty Lester, Era 3080
112. THANKS TO THE FOOL — Brook Benton, Mercury 71962
113. WORK OUT, PART I — Ricky Dee & the Embers, Newtown 5001
114. PLEASE MR. COLUMBUS (Turn the Ship Around) — Lou Monte, Reprise 20085
115. EVERYTIME (I THINK ABOUT YOU), PART I — Joey Dee & the Starliters, Roulette 4431
116. EVERYBODY LOVES A LOVER — Angels, Caprice 116
117. (GIRLS, GIRLS, GIRLS) MADE TO LOVE — Eddie Hodges, Cadence 1421
118. SOUND OF THE HAMMER — Vicki Tasso, Colpix 638
119. A HEARTACHE NAMED JOHNNY — Jaye P. Morgan, MGM 13076
120. GOODNIGHT IRENE — Jerry Reed & the Hully Girlies, Columbia 42417

# BILLBOARD HOT 100

**FOR WEEK ENDING JUNE 23, 1962**

★ STAR PERFORMERS—Selections registering greatest upward progress this week.
Ⓢ indicates that 45 r.p.m. stereo single version is available.
△ indicates that 33⅓ r.p.m. mono single version is available.
Ⓐ indicates that 33⅓ r.p.m. stereo single version is available.

| This Week | Wk Ago | 3 Wks Ago | Title — Artist, Label & Number | Weeks On Chart |
|---|---|---|---|---|
| 1 | 1 | 1 | I CAN'T STOP LOVING YOU — Ray Charles, ABC-Paramount 10330 | 8 |
| ★2 | 8 | 15 | 28 | THE STRIPPER — David Rose & His Ork, MGM 13064 | 7 |
| 3 | 5 | 9 | 17 | PALISADES PARK — Freddy Cannon, Swan 4106 | 7 |
| 4 | 3 | 6 | 12 | IT KEEPS RIGHT ON A-HURTIN' — Johnny Tillotson, Cadence 1418 | 7 |
| 5 | 2 | 2 | 2 | STRANGER ON THE SHORE — Mr. Acker Bilk, Atco 6217 | 15 |
| 6 | 4 | 5 | 10 | THE MAN WHO SHOT LIBERTY VALANCE — Gene Pitney, Musicor 1020 | 9 |
| 7 | 9 | 10 | 19 | PLAYBOY — Marvelettes, Tamla 54060 | 8 |
| 8 | 12 | 25 | 37 | CINDY'S BIRTHDAY — Johnny Crawford, Del Fi 4178 | 7 |
| 9 | 13 | 33 | 44 | THAT'S OLD FASHIONED — Everly Brothers, Warner Bros. 5273 | 7 |
| 10 | 7 | 7 | 16 | SECOND HAND LOVE — Connie Francis, MGM 13074 | 7 |
| 11 | 18 | 27 | 38 | SNAP YOUR FINGERS — Joe Henderson, Todd 1072 | 6 |
| 12 | 16 | 30 | 62 | AL DI LA' — Emilio Pericoli, Warner Bros. 5259 | 6 |
| 13 | 10 | 8 | 9 | THE ONE WHO REALLY LOVES YOU — Mary Wells, Motown 1024 | 14 |
| 14 | 6 | 3 | 4 | LOVERS WHO WANDER — Dion, Laurie 3123 | 10 |
| 15 | 15 | 22 | 24 | FOLLOW THAT DREAM — Elvis Presley, RCA Victor EPA 4368 (Extended Play) | 7 |
| ★16 | 31 | 68 | — | ROSES ARE RED — Bobby Vinton, Epic 9509 | 3 |
| 17 | 20 | 41 | 68 | A STEEL GUITAR AND A GLASS OF WINE — Paul Anka, RCA Victor 8030 | 5 |
| 18 | 19 | 31 | 46 | SHARING YOU — Bobby Vee, Liberty 55451 | 6 |
| 19 | 11 | 12 | 18 | DON'T PLAY THAT SONG — Ben E. King, Atco 6222 | 10 |
| ★20 | 35 | 51 | 77 | WOLVERTON MOUNTAIN — Claude King, Columbia 42352 | 5 |
| 21 | 30 | 32 | 42 | WALK ON THE WILD SIDE — Jimmy Smith, Verve 10255 | 7 |
| 22 | 25 | 28 | 32 | VILLAGE OF LOVE — Nathaniel Mayer, Fortune/United Artists 449 | 9 |
| 23 | 24 | 34 | 40 | ANY DAY NOW — Chuck Jackson, Wand 122 | 9 |
| 24 | 34 | 36 | 39 | I LOVE YOU — Volumes, Chex 1002 | 9 |
| 25 | 26 | 31 | 38 | TEACH ME TONIGHT — George Maharis, Epic 9504 | 9 |
| 26 | 40 | 60 | 88 | JOHNNY GETS ANGRY — Joanie Sommers, Warner Bros. 5275 | 5 |
| 27 | 23 | 21 | 29 | SO THIS IS LOVE — Castells, Era 3073 | 11 |
| 28 | 37 | 45 | 53 | THEME FROM BEN CASEY — Valjean, Carlton 573 | 6 |
| 29 | 36 | 46 | 75 | HAVING A PARTY — Sam Cooke, RCA Victor 8036 | 4 |
| 30 | 60 | 97 | — | THE WAH-WATUSI — Orlons, Cameo 218 | 3 |
| 31 | 43 | 62 | 86 | I'LL NEVER DANCE AGAIN — Bobby Rydell, Cameo 217 | 4 |
| 32 | 14 | 4 | 3 | SOLDIER BOY — Shirelles, Scepter 1228 | 14 |
| 33 | 41 | 52 | 72 | THEME FROM DOCTOR KILDARE — Richard Chamberlain, MGM 13075 | 6 |
| ★34 | 61 | — | — | GRAVY — Dee Dee Sharp, Cameo 219 | |
| 35 | 27 | 24 | 22 | TWISTIN' MATILDA — Jimmy Soul, SPQR 3300 | 13 |
| 36 | 46 | 53 | 63 | WHERE ARE YOU — Dinah Washington, Roulette 4424 | 6 |
| 37 | 52 | 74 | 85 | THE CROWD — Roy Orbison, Monument 461 | 4 |
| 38 | 22 | 17 | 15 | I SOLD MY HEART TO THE JUNKMAN — Blue Belles, Newtown 5000 | 10 |
| 39 | 44 | 48 | 71 | BRISTOL TWISTIN' ANNIE — Dovells, Parkway 838 | 6 |
| 40 | 17 | 14 | 5 | MASHED POTATO TIME — Dee Dee Sharp, Cameo 212 | 17 |
| 41 | 45 | 50 | 65 | FORTUNETELLER — Bobby Curtola, Del Fi 4177 | 8 |
| ★42 | 65 | 100 | — | SEALED WITH A KISS — Brian Hyland, ABC-Paramount 10336 | 3 |
| 43 | 57 | 63 | 78 | I'LL TRY SOMETHING NEW — Miracles, Tamla 54059 | 7 |
| 44 | 49 | 59 | 74 | SWINGIN' GENTLY — Earl Grant, Decca 25560 | 5 |
| 45 | 38 | 19 | 7 | SHOUT! SHOUT! (Knock Yourself Out) — Ernie Maresca, Seville 117 | 13 |
| 46 | 51 | 57 | 50 | BORN TO LOSE — Ray Charles, ABC-Paramount 10330 | |
| 47 | 59 | 72 | 87 | WEST OF THE WALL — Toni Fisher, Big Top 3097 | 5 |
| 48 | 62 | 84 | — | JOHNNY LOVES ME — Shelley Fabares, Colpix 636 | 3 |
| 49 | 42 | 47 | 54 | HOW IS JULIE! — Lettermen, Capitol 4746 | 7 |
| 50 | 28 | 20 | 13 | UPTOWN — Crystals, Philles 102 | 13 |
| 51 | 78 | — | — | LITTLE BITTY PRETTY ONE — Clyde McPhatter, Mercury 71987 | 2 |
| 52 | 39 | 35 | 56 | LEMON TREE — Peter, Paul & Mary, Warner Bros. 5274 | 8 |
| 53 | 21 | 13 | 6 | EVERYBODY LOVES ME BUT YOU — Brenda Lee, Decca 31379 | 11 |
| 54 | 55 | 38 | 36 | NIGHT TRAIN — James Brown, King 5614 | 11 |
| 55 | 64 | 73 | 76 | WHY'D YOU WANNA MAKE ME CRY — Connie Stevens, Warner Bros. 5265 | 8 |
| 56 | 48 | 56 | 58 | BALBOA BLUE — Marketts, Liberty 55443 | 9 |
| ★57 | 70 | — | — | SPEEDY GONZALES — Pat Boone, Dot 16368 | 2 |
| 58 | 66 | 77 | 89 | LIMBO ROCK — Champs, Challenge 9131 | 5 |
| 59 | 72 | 82 | 84 | TWIST AND SHOUT — Isley Brothers, Wand 124 | 4 |
| 60 | 53 | 55 | 60 | WHEN I GET THROUGH WITH YOU — Patsy Cline, Decca 31377 | 6 |
| 61 | 47 | 49 | 45 | HIT RECORD — Brook Benton, Mercury 71962 | 8 |
| 62 | 80 | 93 | 92 | WHERE HAVE YOU BEEN ALL MY LIFE — Arthur Alexander, Dot 16357 | 4 |
| 63 | 81 | 89 | 100 | I NEED YOUR LOVING — Don Gardner and Dee Dee Ford, Fire 508 | 4 |
| 64 | 69 | 79 | 81 | WOMAN IS A MAN'S BEST FRIEND — Teddy & the Twilights, Swan 4102 | 6 |
| 65 | 77 | 92 | — | KEEP YOUR LOVE LOCKED (Deep in Your Heart) — Paul Petersen, Colpix 632 | 3 |
| 66 | 68 | 76 | — | STRANGER ON THE SHORE — Andy Williams, Columbia 42451 | 3 |
| 67 | 71 | 78 | 97 | THAT HAPPY FEELING — Bert Kaempfert, Decca 31388 | 5 |
| ★68 | — | — | — | SEVEN-DAY WEEKEND — Gary (U.S.) Bonds, LeGrand 1019 | 1 |
| ★69 | — | — | — | (GIRLS, GIRLS, GIRLS) MADE TO LOVE — Eddie Hodges, Cadence 1421 | 1 |
| 70 | 67 | 61 | 70 | OH, MY ANGEL — Bertha Tillman, Brent 7029 | 8 |
| 71 | 63 | 66 | 59 | MY REAL NAME — Fats Domino, Imperial 5833 | 7 |
| 72 | 74 | 86 | 96 | TENNESSEE — Jan and Dean, Liberty 55454 | 5 |
| ★73 | 90 | — | — | I DON'T LOVE YOU NO MORE — Jimmy Norman, Little Star 113 | 2 |
| 74 | 84 | 88 | 99 | BOOM BOOM — John Lee Hooker, Vee Jay 438 | 5 |
| 75 | 97 | — | — | BONGO STOMP — Little Joey & the Flips, Joy 262 | 2 |
| 76 | 96 | — | — | YOU'LL LOSE A GOOD THING — Barbara Lynn, Jamie 1220 | 2 |
| 77 | 79 | — | — | DOCTOR BEN BASEY — Mickey Shore & the Cutups, Tuba 8001 | 2 |
| ★78 | — | — | — | DANCIN' PARTY — Chubby Checker, Parkway 842 | 1 |
| 79 | 82 | 87 | — | QUEEN OF MY HEART — Rene & Ray, Donna 1360 | 3 |
| 80 | — | — | — | BUT NOT FOR ME — Ketty Lester, Era 3080 | 1 |
| 81 | — | — | — | GOOD LOVER — Jimmy Reed, Vee Jay 449 | 1 |
| 82 | 93 | — | — | HAVE A GOOD TIME — Sue Thompson, Hickory 1174 | 2 |
| 83 | 85 | 96 | — | BABY ELEPHANT WALK — Lawrence Welk, Dot 16364 | 3 |
| 84 | 88 | 91 | 93 | ROUTE 66 THEME — Nelson Riddle, Capitol 4741 | 4 |
| 85 | 89 | — | 91 | DOWN IN THE VALLEY — Solomon Burke, Atlantic 2147 | 4 |
| 86 | 99 | — | — | NEVER IN A MILLION YEARS — Linda Scott, Congress 103 | 2 |
| 87 | 73 | 70 | 66 | DOCTOR FEEL GOOD — Dr. Feelgood & the Interns, Okeh 7144 | 9 |
| 88 | — | — | — | WELCOME HOME BABY — Shirelles, Scepter 1234 | 1 |
| 89 | — | — | — | THAT GREASY KID STUFF — Janie Grant, Caprice 115 | 1 |
| 90 | — | — | — | LITTLE RED RENTED ROWBOAT — Joe Dowell, Smash 1759 | 1 |
| 91 | 92 | 94 | 95 | GREEN LEAVES OF SUMMER — Kenny Ball, Kapp 460 | 4 |
| 92 | 98 | — | 90 | ADIOS AMIGO — Jim Reeves, RCA Victor 8019 | 6 |
| 93 | 95 | 98 | — | BABY ELEPHANT WALK — Miniature Men, Dolton 57 | 3 |
| 94 | — | — | — | BRING IT ON HOME TO ME — Sam Cooke, RCA Victor 8036 | 1 |
| 95 | — | — | — | SUMMERTIME, SUMMERTIME — Jamies, Epic 9281 | 1 |
| 96 | — | — | — | STEEL MEN — Jimmy Dean, Columbia 42483 | 1 |
| 97 | 87 | 81 | 98 | SCOTCH AND SODA — Kingston Trio, Capitol 4740 | 7 |
| 98 | 100 | — | — | LISA — Ferrante & Teicher, United Artists 470 | 2 |
| 99 | — | — | — | AIR TRAVEL — Ray & Bob, Ledo 1150 | 1 |
| 100 | — | — | — | SHAKE A HAND — Ruth Brown, Philips 40028 | 1 |

## BUBBLING UNDER THE HOT 100

101. WHAT DID DADDY DO .......... Shep & the Limelites, Hull 751
102. BREAKING UP IS HARD TO DO .......... Neil Sedaka, RCA Victor 8046
103. EVERYBODY LOVES A LOVER .......... Angels, Caprice 116
104. WORKOUT (Part I) .......... Ricky Dee & the Embers, Newtown 5001
105. AHAB THE ARAB .......... Ray Stevens, Mercury 71966
106. EVERYTIME (I THINK ABOUT YOU) (Part 1) .......... Joey Dee & the Starliters, Roulette 4431
107. ARDINELLA .......... Mr. Acker Bilk, Reprise 20090
108. LITTLE YOUNG LOVER .......... Impressions, ABC-Paramount 10328
109. PLEASE MR. COLUMBUS (Turn the Ship Around) .......... Lou Monte, Reprise 20085
110. TOUCH ME .......... Willie Nelson, Liberty 55439
111. SWEET AND LOVELY .......... April Stevens & Nino Tempo, Atco 6224
112. ROME .......... Johnny Taylor, Sar 131
113. POTATO PEELER .......... Bobby Gregg & His Friends, Cotton 1006
114. GOODBYE DAD .......... Castle Sisters, Terrace 7506
115. I MISS YOU .......... Dreamlovers, End 1114
116. IF THE BOY ONLY KNEW .......... Sue Thompson, Hickory 1174
117. WORRIED MIND .......... Ray Anthony, Capitol 4742
118. GOODNIGHT IRENE .......... Jerry Reed & the Hully Girlies, Columbia 42417
119. LOVELESS LIFE .......... Ral Donner, Gone 5129
120. A LITTLE HEARTACHE .......... Eddy Arnold, RCA Victor 8048

# BILLBOARD HOT 100

FOR WEEK ENDING JUNE 30

1962

★ STAR PERFORMERS—Selections registering greatest upward progress this week.

S Indicates that 45 r.p.m. stereo single version is available.

△ Indicates that 33⅓ r.p.m. mono single version is available.

S△ Indicates that 33⅓ r.p.m. stereo single version is available.

| This Week | 1 Wk. Ago | 2 Wks. Ago | 3 Wks. Ago | Title | Artist, Label & Number | Weeks On Chart |
|---|---|---|---|---|---|---|
| 1 | 1 | 1 | 1 | I CAN'T STOP LOVING YOU | Ray Charles, ABC-Paramount 10330 | 9 |
| 2 | 2 | 8 | 15 | THE STRIPPER | David Rose & His Ork, MGM 13064 | 8 |
| 3 | 3 | 5 | 9 | PALISADES PARK | Freddy Cannon, Swan 4106 | 8 |
| 4 | 4 | 3 | 6 | IT KEEPS RIGHT ON A-HURTIN' | Johnny Tillotson, Cadence 1418 | 8 |
| ★5 | 16 | 31 | 68 | ROSES ARE RED | Bobby Vinton, Epic 9509 | 4 |
| 6 | 6 | 4 | 5 | THE MAN WHO SHOT LIBERTY VALANCE | Gene Pitney, Musicor 1020 | 10 |
| 7 | 7 | 9 | 10 | PLAYBOY | Marvelettes, Tamla 54060 | 9 |
| 8 | 8 | 12 | 25 | CINDY'S BIRTHDAY | Johnny Crawford, Del Fi 4178 | 8 |
| 9 | 5 | 2 | 2 | STRANGER ON THE SHORE | Mr. Acker Bilk, Atco 6217 | 16 |
| 10 | 12 | 16 | 30 | AL DI LA' | Emilio Pericoli, Warner Bros. 5259 | 7 |
| 11 | 11 | 18 | 27 | SNAP YOUR FINGERS | Joe Henderson, Todd 1072 | 7 |
| 12 | 9 | 13 | 23 | THAT'S OLD FASHIONED | Everly Brothers, Warner Bros. 5273 | 8 |
| ★13 | 20 | 35 | 51 | WOLVERTON MOUNTAIN △ | Claude King, Columbia 42352 | 6 |
| ★14 | 26 | 40 | 60 | JOHNNY GETS ANGRY | Joanie Sommers, Warner Bros. 5275 | 6 |
| 15 | 17 | 20 | 41 | A STEEL GUITAR AND A GLASS OF WINE △ | Paul Anka, RCA Victor 8030 | 6 |
| 16 | 18 | 19 | 31 | SHARING YOU | Bobby Vee, Liberty 55451 | 7 |
| ★17 | 33 | 41 | 52 | THEME FROM DOCTOR KILDARE | Richard Chamberlain, MGM 13075 | 5 |
| ★18 | 30 | 60 | 97 | THE WAH-WATUSI | Orlons, Cameo 218 | 4 |
| 19 | 10 | 7 | 7 | SECOND HAND LOVE | Connie Francis, MGM 13074 | 8 |
| ★20 | 31 | 43 | 62 | I'LL NEVER DANCE AGAIN | Bobby Rydell, Cameo 217 | 5 |
| ★21 | 34 | 61 | — | GRAVY | Dee Dee Sharp, Cameo 219 | 3 |
| 22 | 24 | 34 | 36 | I LOVE YOU | Volumes, Chex 1002 | 10 |
| 23 | 23 | 24 | 34 | ANY DAY NOW | Chuck Jackson, Wand 122 | 10 |
| 24 | 29 | 36 | 46 | HAVING A PARTY △ | Sam Cooke, RCA Victor 8036 | 5 |
| 25 | 13 | 10 | 8 | THE ONE WHO REALLY LOVES YOU | Mary Wells, Motown 1024 | 15 |
| 26 | 15 | 15 | 22 | FOLLOW THAT DREAM | Elvis Presley, RCA Victor EPA 4368 (Extended Play) | 8 |
| ★27 | 42 | 65 | 100 | SEALED WITH A KISS | Brian Hyland, ABC-Paramount 10336 | 4 |
| 28 | 21 | 30 | 32 | WALK ON THE WILD SIDE | Jimmy Smith, Verve 10255 | 8 |
| 29 | 37 | 52 | 74 | THE CROWD | Roy Orbison, Monument 461 | 5 |
| 30 | 14 | 6 | 3 | LOVERS WHO WANDER | Dion, Laurie 3123 | 11 |
| 31 | 39 | 44 | 48 | BRISTOL TWISTIN' ANNIE | Dovells, Parkway 838 | 7 |
| 32 | 19 | 11 | 12 | DON'T PLAY THAT SONG | Ben E. King, Atco 6222 | 11 |
| 33 | 22 | 25 | 28 | VILLAGE OF LOVE | Nathaniel Mayer, Fortune/United Artists 449 | 10 |
| ★34 | 57 | 70 | — | SPEEDY GONZALES | Pat Boone, Dot 16368 | 3 |
| ★35 | 48 | 62 | 84 | JOHNNY LOVES ME | Shelley Fabares, Colpix 636 | 4 |
| 36 | 28 | 37 | 45 | THEME FROM BEN CASEY | Valjean, Carlton 573 | 7 |
| ★37 | 59 | 72 | 82 | TWIST AND SHOUT | Isley Brothers, Wand 124 | 5 |
| ★38 | 51 | 78 | — | LITTLE BITTY PRETTY ONE | Clyde McPhatter, Mercury 71987 | 3 |
| 39 | 43 | 57 | 63 | I'LL TRY SOMETHING NEW | Miracles, Tamla 54059 | 8 |
| 40 | 36 | 46 | 53 | WHERE ARE YOU | Dinah Washington, Roulette 4424 | 7 |
| 41 | 46 | 51 | 57 | BORN TO LOSE | Ray Charles, ABC-Paramount 10330 | 8 |
| 42 | 35 | 27 | 24 | TWISTIN' MATILDA | Jimmy Soul, SPQR 3300 | 14 |
| 43 | 41 | 45 | 50 | FORTUNE TELLER | Bobby Curtola, Del Fi 4177 | 9 |
| 44 | 47 | 59 | 72 | WEST OF THE WALL | Toni Fisher, Big Top 3097 | 6 |
| 45 | 27 | 23 | 21 | SO THIS IS LOVE | Castells, Era 3073 | 11 |
| ★46 | 68 | — | — | SEVEN-DAY WEEKEND | Gary (U. S.) Bonds, LeGrand 1019 | 2 |
| ★47 | 78 | — | — | DANCIN' PARTY | Chubby Checker, Parkway 842 | 2 |
| 48 | 25 | 26 | 31 | TEACH ME TONIGHT | George Maharis, Epic 9504 | 10 |
| 49 | 44 | 49 | 59 | SWINGIN' GENTLY | Earl Grant, Decca 25560 | 6 |
| ★50 | 88 | — | — | WELCOME HOME BABY | Shirelles, Scepter 1234 | 2 |
| ★51 | 69 | — | — | (GIRLS, GIRLS, GIRLS) MADE TO LOVE | Eddie Hodges, Cadence 1421 | 2 |
| 52 | 55 | 64 | 73 | WHY'D YOU WANNA MAKE ME CRY | Connie Stevens, Warner Bros. 5265 | 9 |
| ★53 | 63 | 81 | 89 | I NEED YOUR LOVING | Don Gardner and Dee Dee Ford, Fire 508 | 5 |
| 54 | 58 | 66 | 77 | LIMBO ROCK | Champs, Challenge 9131 | 6 |
| ★55 | 66 | 68 | 76 | STRANGER ON THE SHORE △ | Andy Williams, Columbia 42451 | 4 |
| 56 | 49 | 42 | 47 | HOW IS JULIE! | Lettermen, Capitol 4746 | 8 |
| ★57 | — | — | — | IT STARTED ALL OVER AGAIN | Brenda Lee, Decca 31407 | 1 |
| 58 | 62 | 80 | 93 | WHERE HAVE YOU BEEN ALL MY LIFE | Arthur Alexander, Dot 16357 | 6 |
| 59 | 38 | 22 | 17 | I SOLD MY HEART TO THE JUNKMAN | Blue Belles, Newtown 5000 | 11 |
| 60 | 64 | 69 | 79 | WOMAN IS A MAN'S BEST FRIEND | Teddy & the Twilights, Swan 4102 | 7 |
| ★61 | 77 | 79 | — | DOCTOR BEN BASEY | Mickey Shore & the Cutups, Tuba 8001 | 3 |
| 62 | 65 | 77 | 92 | KEEP YOUR LOVE LOCKED (Deep in Your Heart) | Paul Petersen, Colpix 632 | 4 |
| 63 | 73 | 90 | — | I DON'T LOVE YOU NO MORE | Jimmy Norman, Little Star 113 | 3 |
| 64 | 76 | 96 | — | YOU'LL LOSE A GOOD THING | Barbara Lynn, Jamie 1220 | 3 |
| 65 | 75 | 97 | — | BONGO STOMP | Little Joey & the Flips, Joy 262 | 3 |
| ★66 | — | — | — | BREAKING UP IS HARD TO DO △ | Neil Sedaka, RCA Victor 8046 | 1 |
| ★67 | 96 | — | — | STEEL MEN △ | Jimmy Dean, Columbia 42483 | 2 |
| 68 | 80 | — | — | BUT NOT FOR ME | Ketty Lester, Era 3080 | 2 |
| 69 | 72 | 74 | 86 | TENNESSEE | Jan and Dean, Liberty 55454 | 6 |
| ★70 | — | — | — | AHAB THE ARAB | Ray Stevens, Mercury 71966 | 1 |
| 71 | 74 | 84 | 88 | BOOM BOOM | John Lee Hooker, Vee Jay 438 | 6 |
| 72 | 56 | 48 | 56 | BALBOA BLUE | Marketts, Liberty 55443 | 10 |
| 73 | 40 | 17 | 14 | MASHED POTATO TIME | Dee Dee Sharp, Cameo 212 | 18 |
| 74 | 45 | 38 | 19 | SHOUT! SHOUT! (Knock Yourself Out) | Ernie Maresca, Seville 117 | 14 |
| ★75 | 90 | — | — | LITTLE RED RENTED ROWBOAT | Joe Dowell, Smash 1759 | 2 |
| 76 | 83 | 85 | 96 | BABY ELEPHANT WALK | Lawrence Welk, Dot 16364 | 4 |
| 77 | 82 | 93 | — | HAVE A GOOD TIME | Sue Thompson, Hickory 1174 | 3 |
| 78 | 84 | 88 | 91 | ROUTE 66 THEME | Nelson Riddle, Capitol 4741 | 5 |
| 79 | 86 | 99 | — | NEVER IN A MILLION YEARS | Linda Scott, Congress 103 | 3 |
| ★80 | 95 | — | — | SUMMERTIME, SUMMERTIME | Jamies, Epic 9281 | 2 |
| 81 | 81 | — | — | GOOD LOVER | Jimmy Reed, Vee Jay 449 | 2 |
| 82 | 67 | 71 | 78 | THAT HAPPY FEELING | Bert Kaempfert, Decca 31388 | 6 |
| 83 | 70 | 67 | 61 | OH, MY ANGEL | Bertha Tillman, Brent 7029 | 9 |
| ★84 | — | — | — | IF I SHOULD LOSE YOU | Dreamlovers, End 1114 | 1 |
| 85 | 85 | 89 | — | DOWN IN THE VALLEY | Solomon Burke, Atlantic 2147 | 5 |
| ★86 | — | — | — | LOCO-MOTION | Little Eva, Dimension 1000 | 1 |
| 87 | 93 | 95 | 98 | BABY ELEPHANT WALK | Miniature Men, Dolton 57 | 4 |
| ★88 | — | — | — | NOTHING NEW (Same Old Thing) | Fats Domino, Imperial 5863 | 1 |
| ★89 | — | — | — | YOU SHOULD'A TREATED ME RIGHT | Ike & Tina Turner, Sue 765 | 1 |
| ★90 | — | — | — | MARY'S LITTLE LAMB | James Darren, Colpix 644 | 1 |
| 91 | 91 | 92 | 94 | GREEN LEAVES OF SUMMER | Kenny Ball, Kapp 460 | 5 |
| 92 | — | — | — | WORRIED MIND | Ray Anthony, Capitol 4742 | 1 |
| 93 | — | — | — | GOODNIGHT, IRENE △ | Jerry Reed & the Hully Girlies, Columbia 42417 | 1 |
| 94 | — | — | — | WHAT DID DADDY DO | Shep & the Limelites, Hull 751 | 1 |
| 95 | — | — | — | PARTY LIGHTS | Claudine Clark, Chancellor 1113 | 1 |
| 96 | — | — | — | LA BOMBA △ | Tokens, RCA Victor 8052 | 1 |
| 97 | 100 | — | — | SHAKE A HAND | Ruth Brown, Philips 40028 | 2 |
| 98 | — | — | — | MY TIME FOR CRYING | Maxine Brown, ABC-Paramount 10327 | 1 |
| 99 | — | — | — | CRY MYSELF TO SLEEP | Del Shannon, Big Top 3112 | 1 |
| 100 | — | — | — | POTATO PEELER | Bobby Gregg & His Friends, Cotton 1006 | 1 |

## HOT 100—A TO Z—(Publisher-Licensee)

Ahab the Arab (Lowery, BMI) .... 70
Al Di La' (Witmark, ASCAP) .... 10
Any Day Now (Plan Two, ASCAP) .... 23
Baby Elephant Walk—Miniature Men (Famous, ASCAP) .... 87
Baby Elephant Walk—Welk (Famous, ASCAP) .... 76
Balboa Blue (Lock-E.D.M., ASCAP) .... 71
Bongo Stomp (Drury Lane, BMI) .... 65
Boom Boom (Conrad, BMI) .... 71
Born to Lose (Peer Int'l, BMI) .... 41
Breaking Up Is Hard to Do (Aldon, BMI) .... 66
Bristol Twistin' Annie (Schulman, BMI) .... 31
But Not for Me (New World, ASCAP) .... 68
Cindy's Birthday (Maraville, BMI) .... 8
Crowd, The (Acuff-Rose, BMI) .... 29
Cry Myself to Sleep (Vicky-McLaughlin, BMI) .... 99
Dancing Party (Kalmann, ASCAP) .... 47
Doctor Ben Basey (Rambler, BMI) .... 61
Don't Play That Song (Progressive, BMI) .... 32
Down in the Valley (Progressive, BMI) .... 85
Follow That Dream (Gladys, ASCAP) .... 26
Fortune Teller (Kemo, BMI) .... 43
(Girls, Girls, Girls) Made to Love (Acuff-Rose, BMI) .... 51
Good Lover (Conrad, BMI) .... 81
Goodnight Irene (Ludlow, BMI) .... 93
Gravy (Kalmann, ASCAP) .... 21
Green Leaves of Summer (Feist, ASCAP) .... 91
Have a Good Time (Acuff-Rose, BMI) .... 77
Having a Party (Kags, BMI) .... 24
How Is Julie? (Sherman-DeVorzon, BMI) .... 56
I Can't Stop Loving You (Acuff-Rose, BMI) .... 1
I Don't Love You No More (Hidle, BMI) .... 63
I Love You (Criss, BMI) .... 22
I Need Your Loving (Fast-Pete, BMI) .... 53
I Sold My Heart to the Junkman (Mills, ASCAP) .. 59
If I Should Lose You (Alan K., BMI) .... 84
I'll Never Dance Again (Aldon, BMI) .... 20
I'll Try Something New (Jobete, BMI) .... 39
It Keeps Right on A-Hurtin' (Tanridge, BMI) .... 4
It Started All Over Again (Aldon, BMI) .... 57
Johnny Gets Angry (Tod, ASCAP) .... 14
Johnny Loves Me (Aldon, BMI) .... 35
Keep Your Love Locked (Aldon, BMI) .... 62
La Bomba (Bright Tunes, BMI) .... 96
Limbo Rock (Four Star, BMI) .... 54
Little Bitty Pretty One (Recordo, BMI) .... 38
Little Red Rented Rowboat (Reis, BMI) .... 75
Loco-Motion (Aldon, BMI) .... 86
Lovers Who Wander (Disal, ASCAP) .... 30
Man Who Shot Liberty Valance, The (Famous, ASCAP) .... 6
Mary's Little Lamb (Aldon, BMI) .... 90
Mashed Potato Time (Rice-Mill, BMI) .... 73
My Time for Crying (Saturday, BMI) .... 98
Never in a Million Years (Robbins, ASCAP) .... 79
Nothing New (Travis, BMI) .... 88
Oh, My Angel (Cilfton, BMI) .... 83
One Who Really Loves You, The (Jobete, BMI) .. 25
Palisades Park (Clardige, ASCAP) .... 3
Party Lights (Rambed, BMI) .... 95
Playboy (Jobete, BMI) .... 7
Potato Peeler (Cheltenham, BMI) .... 100
Roses Are Red (Lyle, ASCAP) .... 5
Route 66 Theme (Gower, BMI) .... 78
Sealed With a Kiss (Post, ASCAP) .... 27
Second Hand Love (Merna, BMI) .... 19
Seven-Day Weekend (Hill & Range, BMI) .... 46
Shake a Hand (Angel, BMI) .... 97
Sharing You (Aldon, BMI) .... 16
Shout! Shout! (Knock Yourself Out) (Broadway, ASCAP) .... 74
Snap Your Fingers (Cigma, BMI) .... 11
So This Is Love (Pattern, ASCAP) .... 45
Speedy Gonzales (Budd, ASCAP) .... 34
Steel Guitar and a Glass of Wine, A (Spanka, BMI) .... 15
Steel Men (Southside, BMI) .... 67
Stranger on the Shore—Bilk (Mellin, BMI) .... 9
Stranger on the Shore—Williams (Mellin, BMI) .. 55
Stripper, The (David Rose, ASCAP) .... 2
Summertime, Summertime (Selroy, BMI) .... 80
Swingin' Gently (Marvelle, BMI) .... 49
Teach Me Tonight (Hub-Leeds, ASCAP) .... 48
Tennessee (Wonder-Achlen, BMI) .... 69
That Happy Feeling (Northern, ASCAP) .... 82
That's Old Fashioned (Aberbach, BMI) .... 12
Theme From Ben Casey (Marfran, ASCAP) .... 36
Theme From Doctor Kildare (Hastings, BMI) .... 17
Twist and Shout (Mellin, BMI) .... 37
Twistin' Matilda (General-Pickwick, ASCAP) .... 42
Village of Love (Trianon, BMI) .... 33
Wah-Watusi, The (Kalmann-Lowe, ASCAP) .... 18
Walk on the Wild Side (Columbia Pictures, ASCAP. 28
Welcome Home Bay (Ludix, BMI) .... 50
West of the Wall (Music Productions, ASCAP) .. 44
What Did Daddy Do (Keel, BMI) .... 94
Where Are You (Feist, ASCAP) .... 40
Where Hve You Been All My Life (Aldon, BMI) .. 58
Why'd You Wanna Make Me Cry (Aldon, BMI) .. 52
Wolverton Mountain (Painted Desert, BMI) .... 13
Woman Is a Man's Best Friend (Claridge, ASCAP).. 60
Worried Mind (Peer Int'l, BMI) .... 92
You Should'A Treated Me Right (Saturn, BMI) .. 89
You'll Lose a Good Thing (David-Crazy Cajun-Jamie, BMI) .... 64

## BUBBLING UNDER THE HOT 100

101. TROUBLE'S BACK IN TOWN........Wilburn Brothers, Decca 31363
102. SWEET AND LOVELY....April Stevens and Nino Tempo, Atco 6224
103. EVERYBODY LOVES A LOVER...............Angels, Caprice 116
104. HOT PEPPER ..................Floyd Cramer, RCA Victor 8051
105. EVERYTIME (I THINK OF YOU) (PART I)..................Joey Dee and the Starliters, Roulette 4431
106. DARINELLA .....................Mr. Acker Bilk, Reprise 20090
107. LITTLE YOUNG LOVER........Impressions, ABC-Paramount 10328
108. MAKE IT EASY FOR YOURSELF.........Jerry Butler, Vee Jay 451
109. TOUCH ME .......................Willie Nelson, Liberty 55439
110. CHARLIE'S SHOES ......................Guy Mitchell, Joy 264
111. BALLAD OF PALADIN.............Duane Eddy, RCA Victor 8047
112. ROME ...........................Johnny Taylor, Sar 131
113. COME ON LITTLE ANGEL..................Belmonts, Sabina 505
114. IF THE BOY ONLY KNEW..........Sue Thompson, Hickory 1174
115. ALL NIGHT LONG..............Sandy Nelson, Imperial 5860
116. I WISH I COULD CRY...........Little Willie John, King 5641
117. LOVELESS LIFE ......................Ral Donna, Gone 5129
118. A LITTLE HEARTACHE ...........Eddy Arnold, RCA Victor 8048
119. LIFE'S TOO SHORT ...............Lafayettes, RCA Victor 8044
120. THE THIRD MAN ..............Highwaymen, United Artists 475

# BILLBOARD HOT 100

FOR WEEK ENDING JULY 7

1962

★ STAR PERFORMERS—Selections registering greatest upward progress this week.

S Indicates that 45 r.p.m. stereo single version is available.

△ Indicates that 33⅓ r.p.m. mono single version is available.

S△ Indicates that 33⅓ r.p.m. stereo single version is available.

| This Week | 1 Wk. Ago | 2 Wks. Ago | 3 Wks. Ago | TITLE Artist, Label & Number | | Weeks On Chart |
|---|---|---|---|---|---|---|
| 1 | 2 | 2 | 8 | THE STRIPPER — David Rose & His Ork, MGM 13064 | | 9 |
| 2 | 5 | 16 | 31 | ROSES ARE RED — Bobby Vinton, Epic 9509 | | 5 |
| 3 | 1 | 1 | 1 | I CAN'T STOP LOVING YOU — Ray Charles, ABC-Paramount 10330 | | 10 |
| 4 | 3 | 3 | 5 | PALISADES PARK — Freddy Cannon, Swan 4106 | | 9 |
| 5 | 4 | 4 | 3 | IT KEEPS RIGHT ON A-HURTIN' — Johnny Tillotson, Cadence 1418 | | 9 |
| 6 | 10 | 12 | 16 | AL DI LA' — Emilio Pericoli, Warner Bros. 5259 | | 8 |
| ★ 7 | 13 | 20 | 35 | WOLVERTON MOUNTAIN — Claude King, Columbia 42352 | △ | 7 |
| 8 | 11 | 11 | 18 | SNAP YOUR FINGERS — Joe Henderson, Todd 1072 | | 8 |
| ★ 9 | 14 | 26 | 40 | JOHNNY GET ANGRY — Joanie Sommers, Warner Bros. 5275 | | 7 |
| 10 | 7 | 7 | 9 | PLAYBOY — Marvelettes, Tamla 54060 | | 10 |
| 11 | 8 | 8 | 12 | CINDY'S BIRTHDAY — Johnny Crawford, Del Fi 4178 | | 9 |
| ★ 12 | 27 | 42 | 65 | SEALED WITH A KISS — Brian Hyland, ABC-Paramount 10336 | | 5 |
| 13 | 15 | 17 | 20 | A STEEL GUITAR AND A GLASS OF WINE — Paul Anka, RCA Victor 8030 | △ | 7 |
| 14 | 18 | 30 | 60 | THE WAH-WATUSI — Orlons, Cameo 218 | | 5 |
| 15 | 16 | 18 | 19 | SHARING YOU — Bobby Vee, Liberty 55451 | | 8 |
| ★ 16 | 21 | 34 | 61 | GRAVY — Dee Dee Sharp, Cameo 219 | | 4 |
| 17 | 17 | 33 | 41 | THEME FROM DOCTOR KILDARE — Richard Chamberlain, MGM 13075 | | 6 |
| 18 | 20 | 31 | 43 | I'LL NEVER DANCE AGAIN — Bobby Rydell, Cameo 217 | | 6 |
| 19 | 9 | 5 | 2 | STRANGER ON THE SHORE — Mr. Acker Bilk, Atco 6217 | | 17 |
| 20 | 6 | 6 | 4 | THE MAN WHO SHOT LIBERTY VALANCE — Gene Pitney, Musicor 1020 | | 11 |
| 21 | 24 | 29 | 36 | HAVING A PARTY — Sam Cooke, RCA Victor 8036 | △ | 6 |
| ★ 22 | 34 | 57 | 70 | SPEEDY GONZALES — Pat Boone, Dot 16368 | | 4 |
| 23 | 12 | 9 | 13 | THAT'S OLD FASHIONED — Everly Brothers, Warner Bros. 5273 | | 9 |
| ★ 24 | 35 | 48 | 62 | JOHNNY LOVES ME — Shelley Fabares, Colpix 636 | | 5 |
| 25 | 28 | 21 | 30 | WALK ON THE WILD SIDE — Jimmy Smith, Verve 10255 | | 9 |
| ★ 26 | 66 | — | — | BREAKING UP IS HARD TO DO — Neil Sedaka, RCA Victor 8046 | △ | 2 |
| 27 | 29 | 37 | 52 | THE CROWD — Roy Orbison, Monument 461 | | 6 |
| ★ 28 | 38 | 51 | 78 | LITTLE BITTY PRETTY ONE — Clyde McPhatter, Mercury 71987 | | 4 |
| 29 | 31 | 39 | 44 | BRISTOL TWISTIN' ANNIE — Dovells, Parkway 838 | | 8 |
| ★ 30 | 47 | 78 | — | DANCING PARTY — Chubby Checker, Parkway 842 | | 3 |
| 31 | 37 | 59 | 72 | TWIST AND SHOUT — Isley Brothers, Wand 124 | | 6 |
| 32 | 22 | 24 | 34 | I LOVE YOU — Volumes, Chex 1002 | | 11 |
| ★ 33 | 53 | 63 | 81 | I NEED YOUR LOVING — Don Gardner and Dee Dee Ford, Fire 508 | | 6 |
| 34 | 25 | 13 | 10 | THE ONE WHO REALLY LOVES YOU — Mary Wells, Motown 1024 | | 16 |
| 35 | 36 | 28 | 37 | THEME FROM BEN CASEY — Valjean, Carlton 573 | | 8 |
| ★ 36 | 46 | 68 | — | SEVEN-DAY WEEKEND — Gary (U. S.) Bonds, LeGrand 1019 | | 3 |
| 37 | 23 | 23 | 24 | ANY DAY NOW — Chuck Jackson, Wand 122 | | 11 |
| ★ 38 | 51 | 69 | — | (GIRLS, GIRLS, GIRLS) MADE TO LOVE — Eddie Hodges, Cadence 1421 | | 3 |
| ★ 39 | 50 | 88 | — | WELCOME HOME BABY — Shirelles, Scepter 1234 | | 3 |
| 40 | 40 | 36 | 46 | WHERE ARE YOU — Dinah Washington, Roulette 4424 | | 8 |
| 41 | 43 | 41 | 45 | FORTUNE TELLER — Bobby Curtola, Del Fi 4177 | | 10 |
| 42 | 44 | 47 | 59 | WEST OF THE WALL — Toni Fisher, Big Top 3097 | | 7 |
| ★ 43 | 64 | 76 | 96 | YOU'LL LOSE A GOOD THING — Barbara Lynn, Jamie 1220 | | 4 |
| 44 | 39 | 43 | 57 | I'LL TRY SOMETHING NEW — Miracles, Tamla 54059 | | 9 |
| ★ 45 | 55 | 66 | 68 | STRANGER ON THE SHORE — Andy Williams, Columbia 42451 | △ | 5 |
| ★ 46 | 65 | 75 | 97 | BONGO STOMP — Little Joey & the Flips, Joy 262 | | 4 |
| ★ 47 | 70 | — | — | AHAB THE ARAB — Ray Stevens, Mercury 71966 | | 2 |
| 48 | 41 | 46 | 51 | BORN TO LOSE — Ray Charles, ABC-Paramount 10330 | | 9 |
| 49 | 19 | 10 | 7 | SECOND HAND LOVE — Connie Francis, MGM 13074 | | 9 |
| 50 | 54 | 58 | 66 | LIMBO ROCK — Champs, Challenge 9131 | | 7 |
| 51 | 33 | 22 | 25 | VILLAGE OF LOVE — Nathaniel Mayer, Fortune/United Artists 449 | | 11 |
| 52 | 49 | 44 | 49 | SWINGIN' GENTLY — Earl Grant, Decca 25560 | | 7 |
| 53 | 57 | — | — | IT STARTED ALL OVER AGAIN — Brenda Lee, Decca 31407 | | 2 |
| 54 | 26 | 15 | 15 | FOLLOW THAT DREAM — Elvis Presley, RCA Victor EPA 4368 (Extended Play) | | 9 |
| ★ 55 | 68 | 80 | — | BUT NOT FOR ME — Ketty Lester, Era 3080 | | 3 |
| ★ 56 | 77 | 82 | 93 | HAVE A GOOD TIME — Sue Thompson, Hickory 1174 | | 4 |
| ★ 57 | 67 | 96 | — | STEEL MEN — Jimmy Dean, Columbia 42483 | △ | 3 |
| 58 | 62 | 65 | 77 | KEEP YOUR LOVE LOCKED (Deep in Your Heart) — Paul Petersen, Colpix 632 | | 5 |
| 59 | 60 | 64 | 69 | WOMAN IS A MAN'S BEST FRIEND — Teddy & the Twilights, Swan 4102 | | 8 |
| 60 | 61 | 77 | 79 | DOCTOR BEN BASEY — Mickey Shorr & the Cutups, Tuba 8001 | | 4 |
| 61 | 63 | 73 | 90 | I DON'T LOVE YOU NO MORE — Jimmy Norman, Little Star 113 | | 4 |
| 62 | 58 | 62 | 80 | WHERE HAVE YOU BEEN ALL MY LIFE — Arthur Alexander, Dot 16357 | | 7 |
| 63 | 30 | 14 | 6 | LOVERS WHO WANDER — Dion, Laurie 3123 | | 12 |
| 64 | 45 | 27 | 23 | SO THIS IS LOVE — Castells, Era 3073 | | 12 |
| ★ 65 | — | — | — | HEART IN HAND — Brenda Lee, Decca 31407 | | 1 |
| 66 | 78 | 84 | 88 | ROUTE 66 THEME — Nelson Riddle, Capitol 4741 | | 6 |
| 67 | 32 | 19 | 11 | DON'T PLAY THAT SONG — Ben E. King, Atco 6222 | | 12 |
| 68 | 80 | 95 | — | SUMMERTIME, SUMMERTIME — Jamies, Epic 9281 | | 3 |
| 69 | 52 | 55 | 64 | WHY'D YOU WANNA MAKE ME CRY — Connie Stevens, Warner Bros. 5265 | | 10 |
| 70 | 71 | 74 | 84 | BOOM BOOM — John Lee Hooker, Vee Jay 438 | | 7 |
| ★ 71 | 86 | — | — | LOCO-MOTION — Little Eva, Dimension 1000 | | 2 |
| ★ 72 | — | — | — | LITTLE DIANE — Dion, Laurie 3134 | | 1 |
| 73 | 76 | 83 | 85 | BABY ELEPHANT WALK — Lawrence Welk, Dot 16364 | | 5 |
| 74 | 75 | 90 | — | LITTLE RED RENTED ROWBOAT — Joe Dowell, Smash 1759 | | 3 |
| 75 | 79 | 86 | 99 | NEVER IN A MILLION YEARS — Linda Scott, Congress 103 | | 4 |
| 76 | 69 | 72 | 74 | TENNESSEE — Jan and Dean, Liberty 55454 | | 7 |
| 77 | 90 | — | — | MARY'S LITTLE LAMB — James Darren, Colpix 644 | | 2 |
| ★ 78 | 95 | — | — | PARTY LIGHTS — Claudine Clark, Chancellor 1113 | | 2 |
| 79 | 81 | 81 | — | GOOD LOVER — Jimmy Reed, Vee Jay 449 | | 3 |
| 80 | 84 | — | — | IF I SHOULD LOSE YOU — Dreamlovers, End 1114 | | 2 |
| ★ 81 | — | — | — | HOT PEPPER — Floyd Cramer, RCA Victor 8051 | △ | 1 |
| ★ 82 | — | — | — | WHY DID YOU LEAVE ME? — Vince Edwards, Russ-Fi 7001 | | 1 |
| ★ 83 | — | — | — | THE BALLAD OF PALADIN — Duane Eddy, RCA Victor 8047 | △ | 1 |
| 84 | 85 | 85 | 89 | DOWN IN THE VALLEY — Solomon Burke, Atlantic 2147 | | 6 |
| 85 | 88 | — | — | NOTHING NEW (Same Old Thing) — Fats Domino, Imperial 5863 | | 2 |
| ★ 86 | — | — | — | SHOUT AND SHIMMY — James Brown & the Famous Flames, King 5657 | | 1 |
| 87 | 91 | 91 | 92 | GREEN LEAVES OF SUMMER — Kenny Ball, Kapp 460 | | 6 |
| ★ 88 | — | — | — | THINGS — Bobby Darin, Atco 6229 | | 1 |
| 89 | 89 | — | — | YOU SHOULD'A TREATED ME RIGHT — Ike & Tina Turner, Sue 765 | | 2 |
| ★ 90 | — | 89 | — | THAT GREASY KID STUFF — Janie Grant, Caprice 115 | | 2 |
| 91 | 92 | — | — | WORRIED MIND — Ray Anthony, Capitol 4742 | | 2 |
| 92 | — | — | — | I JUST CAN'T HELP IT — Jackie Wilson, Brunswick 55229 | | 1 |
| 93 | 93 | — | — | GOODNIGHT IRENE — Jerry Reed & the Hully Girlies, Columbia 42417 | △ | 2 |
| 94 | — | — | — | MY DADDY IS PRESIDENT — Little Jo Ann, Kapp 467 | | 1 |
| 95 | — | — | 91 | DANCIN' THE STRAND — Maureen Gray, Landa 689 | | 3 |
| 96 | 94 | — | — | WHAT DID DADDY DO — Shep & the Limelites, Hull 751 | | 2 |
| 97 | 100 | — | — | POTATO PEELER — Bobby Gregg & His Friends, Cotton 1006 | | 2 |
| 98 | — | — | — | SWEET AND LOVELY — April Stevens & Nino Tempo, Atco 6224 | | 1 |
| 99 | — | — | — | I'M HANGING UP MY HEART FOR YOU — Solomon Burke, Atlantic 2147 | | 1 |
| 100 | — | — | — | MAKE IT EASY FOR YOURSELF — Jerry Butler, Vee Jay 451 | | 1 |

## HOT 100—A TO Z—*(Publisher-Licensee)*

Ahab the Arab (Lowery, BMI) ........ 47
Al Di La' (Witmark, ASCAP) ........ 6
Any Day Now (Plan Two, ASCAP) ........ 37
Baby Elephant Walk (Famous, ASCAP) ........ 73
Ballad of Paladin, The (Time, BMI) ........ 83
Bongo Stomp (Drury Lane, BMI) ........ 46
Boom Boom (Conrad, BMI) ........ 70
Born to Lose (Peer Int'l, BMI) ........ 48
Breaking Up Is Hard to Do (Aldon, BMI) ........ 26
Bristol Twistin' Annie (Schulman, BMI) ........ 29
But Not for Me (New World, ASCAP) ........ 55
Cindy's Birthday (Maraville, BMI) ........ 11
Crowd, The (Acuff-Rose, BMI) ........ 27
Dancin' the Strand (Ponderosa, BMI) ........ 95
Dancing Party (Kalmann, ASCAP) ........ 30
Doctor Ben Basey (Rambler, BMI) ........ 60
Don't Play That Song (Progressive, BMI) ........ 67
Down in the Valley (Progressive, BMI) ........ 84
Follow That Dream (Gladys, ASCAP) ........ 54
Fortune Teller (Kemo, BMI) ........ 41
(Girls, Girls, Girls) Made to Love (Acuff-Rose BMI) ........ 38
Good Lover (Conrad, BMI) ........ 79
Goodnight Irene (Ludlow, BMI) ........ 93
Gravy (Kalmann, ASCAP) ........ 16
Green Leaves of Summer (Feist, ASCAP) ........ 87
Have a Good Time (Acuff-Rose, BMI) ........ 56
Having a Party (Kags, BMI) ........ 21
Heart in Hand (Metric, BMI) ........ 65
Hot Pepper (Acuff-Rose, BMI) ........ 81
I Can't Stop Loving You (Acuff-Rose, BMI) ........ 3
I Don't Love Yop No More (Hidle, BMI) ........ 61
I Just Can't Help It (Pearl, BMI) ........ 92
I Love You (Criss, BMI) ........ 32
I Need Your Loving (Fast-Pete, BMI) ........ 33
If I Should Lose You (Alan K., BMI) ........ 80
I'll Never Dance Again (Aldon, BMI) ........ 18
I'll Try Something New (Jobete, BMI) ........ 44
I'm Hanging Up My Heart for You (Progressive, BMI) ........ 99
It Keeps Right on A-Hurtin' (Tanridge, BMI) ........ 5
It Started All Over Again (Aldon, BMI) ........ 53
Johnny Get Angry (Tod, ASCAP) ........ 9
Johnny Loves Me (Aldon, BMI) ........ 24
Keep Your Love Locked (Aldon, BMI) ........ 58
Limbo Rock (Four Star, BMI) ........ 50
Little Bitty Pretty One (Recordo, BMI) ........ 28
Little Diane (Disal, ASCAP) ........ 72
Little Red Rented Rowboat (Reis, BMI) ........ 74
Loco-Motion (Aldon, BMI) ........ 71
Lovers Who Wander (Disal, ASCAP) ........ 63
Make It Easy on Yourself (Famous, ASCAP) ........ 100
Man Who Shot Liberty Valance, The (Famous, ASCAP) ........ 20
Mary's Little Lamb (Adon, BMI) ........ 77
My Daddy Is President (Gretavic, ASCAP) ........ 94
Never in a Million Years (Robbins, ASCAP) ........ 75
Nothing New (Travis, BMI) ........ 85
One Who Really Loves You, The (Jobete, BMI) ........ 34
Palisades Park (Claridge, ASCAP) ........ 4
Party Lights (Rambed, BMI) ........ 78
Playboy (Jobete, BMI) ........ 10
Potato Peeler (Cheltenham, BMI) ........ 97
Roses Are Red (Lyle, ASCAP) ........ 2
Route 66 Theme (Gower, BMI) ........ 66
Sealed With a Kiss (Post, ASCAP) ........ 12
Second Hand Love (Merna, BMI) ........ 49
Seven-Day Weekend (Hill & Range, BMI) ........ 36
Sharing You (Aldon, BMI) ........ 15
Shout and Shimmy (Lois, BMI) ........ 86
Snap Your Fingers (Cigma, BMI) ........ 8
So This Is Love (Pattern, ASCAP) ........ 64
Speedy Gonzales (Budd, ASCAP) ........ 22
Steel Guitar & a Glass of Wine (Spanka, BMI) ........ 13
Steel Men (Southside, BMI) ........ 57
Stranger on the Shore—Bilk (Mellin, BMI) ........ 19
Stranger on the Shore—Williams (Mellin, BMI) ........ 45
Stripper, The (David Rose, ASCAP) ........ 1
Summertime, Summertime (Selroy, BMI) ........ 68
Sweet and Lovely (Robbins-Daniels, ASCAP) ........ 98
Swingin' Gently (Marvelle, BMI) ........ 52
Tennessee (Wonder-Achlen, BMI) ........ 76
That Greasy Kid Stuff (Geril, ASCAP) ........ 90
That's Old Fashioned (Aberbach, BMI) ........ 23
Theme From Ben Casey (Marfran, ASCAP) ........ 35
Theme From Doctor Kildare (Hastings, BMI) ........ 17
Things (Adaris, BMI) ........ 88
Twist and Shout (Mellin, BMI) ........ 31
Village of Love (Trianon, BMI) ........ 51
Wah-Watusi, The (Kalmann-Lowe, ASCAP) ........ 14
Walk on the Wild Side (Columbia Pictures, ASCAP) ........ 25
Welcome Home, Baby (Ludix, BMI) ........ 39
West of the Wall (Music Productions, ASCAP) ........ 42
What Did Daddy Do (Keel, BMI) ........ 96
Where Are You (Feist, ASCAP) ........ 40
Where Have You Been All My Life (Aldon, BMI) ........ 62
Why Did You Leave Me? (Mamaleen, BMI) ........ 82
Why'd You Wanna Make Me Cry (Aldon, BMI) ........ 69
Wolverton Mountain (Painted Desert, BMI) ........ 7
Woman Is a Man's Best Friend (Clardige, ASCAP) 59
Worried Mind (Peer Int'l, BMI) ........ 91
You Should'a Treated Me Right (Saturn, BMI) ........ 89
You'll Lose a Good Thing (David-Crazy Cajun-Jamie, BMI) ........ 43

## BUBBLING UNDER THE HOT 100

101. LIFE'S TOO SHORT ........ Lafayettes, RCA Victor 8044
102. A TASTE OF HONEY ........ Martin Denny, Liberty 55470
103. WORK OUT (PART I) ........ Rickey Dee & the Embers, Newtown 5001
104. LITTLE YOUNG LOVER ........ Impressions, ABC-Paramount 10328
105. DANDANELLA ........ Mr. Acker Bilk, Reprise 20090
106. EVERYBODY LOVES A LOVER ........ Angels, Caprice 116
107. DON'T CRY BABY ........ Aretha Franklin, Columbia 42456
108. THEME FROM "HATARI!" ........ Henry Mancini, RCA Victor 8037
109. TILL DEATH DO US PART ........ Bob Braun, Decca 31355
110. SHAME ON YOU ........ Bobby Bare, RCA Victor 8032
111. MY TIME FOR CRYING ........ Maxine Brown, ABC-Paramount 10327
112. IF THE BOY ONLY KNEW ........ Sue Thompson, Hickory 1174
113. REAP WHAT YOU SOW ........ Billy Stewart, Chess 1820
114. SHAKE A HAND ........ Ruth Brown, Philips 40028
115. QUEEN OF MY HEART ........ Rene & Ray, Donna 1360
116. YOU BELONG TO ME ........ The Duprees, Coed 569
117. LA BOMBA ........ Tokens, RCA Victor 8052
118. DING DING DING ........ Hayley Mills, Vista 401
119. GOODBYE DAD ........ Castle Sisters, Terrace 7506
120. THE BIRD MAN ........ Highwaymen, United Artists 475

# BILLBOARD HOT 100

**FOR WEEK ENDING JULY 14, 1962**

STAR PERFORMERS—Selections registering greatest upward progress this week.

S indicates that 45 r.p.m. stereo single version is available.
△ indicates that 33⅓ r.p.m. mono single version is available.
▲ indicates that 33⅓ r.p.m. stereo single version is available.

| This Week | Wk. Ago | 3 Wks. Ago | Title, Artist, Label & Number | Weeks On Chart |
|---|---|---|---|---|
| 1 | 2 | 5 | 16 | ROSES ARE RED — Bobby Vinton, Epic 9509 | 6 |
| 2 | 1 | 2 | 2 | THE STRIPPER — David Rose & His Ork, MGM 13064 | 10 |
| 3 | 3 | 1 | 1 | I CAN'T STOP LOVING YOU — Ray Charles, ABC-Paramount 10330 | 11 |
| 4 | 14 | 18 | 30 | THE WAH-WATUSI — Orlons, Cameo 218 | 6 |
| ★5 | 12 | 27 | 42 | SEALED WITH A KISS — Brian Hyland, ABC-Paramount 10336 | 6 |
| 6 | 4 | 3 | 3 | PALISADES PARK — Freddy Cannon, Swan 4106 | 10 |
| 7 | 7 | 13 | 20 | WOLVERTON MOUNTAIN — Claude King, Columbia 42352 | 8 |
| 8 | 5 | 4 | 4 | IT KEEPS RIGHT ON A-HURTIN' — Johnny Tillotson, Cadence 1418 | 10 |
| ★9 | 16 | 21 | 34 | GRAVY — Dee Dee Sharp, Cameo 219 | 5 |
| 10 | 6 | 10 | 12 | AL DI LA' — Emilio Pericoli, Warner Bros. 5259 | 9 |
| 11 | 9 | 14 | 26 | JOHNNY GET ANGRY — Joanie Sommers, Warner Bros. 5275 | 8 |
| 12 | 8 | 11 | 11 | SNAP YOUR FINGERS — Joe Henderson, Todd 1072 | 9 |
| ★13 | 22 | 34 | 57 | SPEEDY GONZALES — Pat Boone, Dot 16368 | 5 |
| 14 | 18 | 20 | 31 | I'LL NEVER DANCE AGAIN — Bobby Rydell, Cameo 217 | 7 |
| 15 | 17 | 17 | 33 | THEME FROM DOCTOR KILDARE — Richard Chamberlain, MGM 13075 | 7 |
| 16 | 10 | 7 | 7 | PLAYBOY — Marvelettes, Tamla 54060 | 11 |
| 17 | 21 | 24 | 29 | HAVING A PARTY — Sam Cooke, RCA Victor 8036 | 7 |
| ★18 | 47 | 70 | — | AHAB THE ARAB — Ray Stevens, Mercury 71966 | 3 |
| ★19 | 26 | 66 | — | BREAKING UP IS HARD TO DO — Neil Sedaka, RCA Victor 8046 | 3 |
| 20 | 30 | 47 | 78 | DANCING PARTY — Chubby Checker, Parkway 842 | 4 |
| 21 | 11 | 8 | 8 | CINDY'S BIRTHDAY — Johnny Crawford, Del Fi 4178 | 10 |
| 22 | 24 | 35 | 48 | JOHNNY LOVES ME — Shelley Fabares, Colpix 636 | 6 |
| 23 | 31 | 37 | 59 | TWIST AND SHOUT — Isley Brothers, Wand 124 | 7 |
| 24 | 33 | 53 | 63 | I NEED YOUR LOVING — Don Gardner and Dee Dee Ford, Fire 508 | 7 |
| 25 | 28 | 38 | 51 | LITTLE BITTY PRETTY ONE — Clyde McPhatter, Mercury 71987 | 5 |
| 26 | 27 | 29 | 37 | THE CROWD — Roy Orbison, Monument 461 | 7 |
| 27 | 29 | 31 | 39 | BRISTOL TWISTIN' ANNIE — Dovells, Parkway 838 | 9 |
| 28 | 13 | 15 | 17 | A STEEL GUITAR AND A GLASS OF WINE — Paul Anka, RCA Victor 8030 | 8 |
| 29 | 38 | 51 | 69 | (GIRLS, GIRLS, GIRLS) MADE TO LOVE — Eddie Hodges, Cadence 1421 | 4 |
| 30 | 15 | 16 | 18 | SHARING YOU — Bobby Vee, Liberty 55451 | 9 |
| 31 | 25 | 28 | 21 | WALK ON THE WILD SIDE — Jimmy Smith, Verve 10255 | 10 |
| 32 | 36 | 46 | 68 | SEVEN-DAY WEEKEND — Gary (U.S.) Bonds, LeGrand 1019 | 4 |
| ★33 | 43 | 64 | 76 | YOU'LL LOSE A GOOD THING — Barbara Lynn, Jamie 1220 | 5 |
| 34 | 39 | 50 | 88 | WELCOME HOME BABY — Shirelles, Scepter 1234 | 4 |
| 35 | 46 | 65 | 75 | BONGO STOMP — Little Joey & the Flips, Joy 262 | 5 |
| 36 | 19 | 9 | 5 | STRANGER ON THE SHORE — Mr. Acker Bilk, Atco 6217 | 18 |
| 37 | 42 | 44 | 47 | WEST OF THE WALL — Toni Fisher, Big Top 3097 | 8 |
| 38 | 45 | 55 | 66 | STRANGER ON THE SHORE — Andy Williams, Columbia 42451 | 6 |
| 39 | 23 | 12 | 9 | THAT'S OLD FASHIONED — Everly Brothers, Warner Bros. 5273 | 10 |
| 40 | 50 | 54 | 58 | LIMBO ROCK — Champs, Challenge 9131 | 8 |
| 41 | 53 | 57 | — | IT STARTED ALL OVER AGAIN — Brenda Lee, Decca 31407 | 3 |
| 42 | 20 | 6 | 6 | THE MAN WHO SHOT LIBERTY VALANCE — Gene Pitney, Musicor 1020 | 12 |
| 43 | 55 | 68 | 80 | BUT NOT FOR ME — Ketty Lester, Era 3080 | 4 |
| 44 | 32 | 22 | 24 | I LOVE YOU — Volumes, Chex 1002 | 12 |
| 45 | 34 | 25 | 13 | THE ONE WHO REALLY LOVES YOU — Mary Wells, Motown 1024 | 17 |
| 46 | 37 | 23 | 23 | ANY DAY NOW — Chuck Jackson, Wand 122 | 12 |
| 47 | 44 | 39 | 43 | I'LL TRY SOMETHING NEW — Miracles, Tamla 54059 | 10 |
| 48 | 40 | 40 | 36 | WHERE ARE YOU — Dinah Washington, Roulette 4424 | 9 |
| 49 | 41 | 43 | 41 | FORTUNE TELLER — Bobby Curtola, Del Fi 4177 | 11 |
| 50 | 56 | 77 | 82 | HAVE A GOOD TIME — Sue Thompson, Hickory 1174 | 5 |
| 51 | 57 | 67 | 96 | STEEL MEN — Jimmy Dean, Columbia 42483 | 4 |
| 52 | 71 | 86 | — | LOCO-MOTION — Little Eva, Dimension 1000 | 3 |
| 53 | 72 | — | — | LITTLE DIANE — Dion, Laurie 3134 | 2 |
| 54 | 66 | 78 | 84 | ROUTE 66 THEME — Nelson Riddle, Capitol 4741 | 7 |
| 55 | 65 | — | — | HEART IN HAND — Brenda Lee, Decca 31407 | 2 |
| 56 | 61 | 63 | 73 | I DON'T LOVE YOU NO MORE — Jimmy Norman, Little Star 113 | 5 |
| 57 | 52 | 49 | 44 | SWINGIN' GENTLY — Earl Grant, Decca 25560 | 8 |
| 58 | 74 | 75 | 90 | LITTLE RED RENTED ROWBOAT — Joe Dowell, Smash 1759 | 4 |
| 59 | 68 | 80 | 95 | SUMMERTIME, SUMMERTIME — Jamies, Epic 9281 | 4 |
| 60 | 78 | 95 | — | PARTY LIGHTS — Claudine Clark, Chancellor 1113 | 3 |
| 61 | 88 | — | — | THINGS — Bobby Darin, Atco 6229 | 2 |
| 62 | 77 | 90 | — | MARY'S LITTLE LAMB — James Darren, Colpix 644 | 3 |
| 63 | 35 | 36 | 28 | THEME FROM BEN CASEY — Valjean, Carlton 573 | 9 |
| 64 | 70 | 71 | 74 | BOOM BOOM — John Lee Hooker, Vee Jay 438 | 8 |
| 65 | 60 | 61 | 77 | DOCTOR BEN BASEY — Mickey Shorr & the Cutups, Tuba 8001 | 5 |
| 66 | 54 | 26 | 15 | FOLLOW THAT DREAM — Elvis Presley, RCA Victor EPA 4368 (Extended Play) | 10 |
| 67 | 69 | 52 | 55 | WHY'D YOU WANNA MAKE ME CRY — Connie Stevens, Warner Bros. 5265 | 11 |
| 68 | 51 | 33 | 22 | VILLAGE OF LOVE — Nathaniel Mayer, Fortune/United Artists 449 | 12 |
| 69 | 58 | 62 | 65 | KEEP YOUR LOVE LOCKED (Deep in Your Heart) — Paul Petersen, Colpix 632 | 6 |
| 70 | 75 | 79 | 86 | NEVER IN A MILLION YEARS — Linda Scott, Congress 103 | 5 |
| 71 | 73 | 76 | 83 | BABY ELEPHANT WALK — Lawrence Welk, Dot 16364 | 6 |
| 72 | 82 | — | — | WHY DID YOU LEAVE ME? — Vince Edwards, Russ-Fi 7001 | 2 |
| 73 | 86 | — | — | SHOUT AND SHIMMY — James Brown & the Famous Flames, King 5657 | 2 |
| 74 | 84 | 85 | 85 | DOWN IN THE VALLEY — Solomon Burke, Atlantic 2147 | 7 |
| 75 | 80 | 84 | — | IF I SHOULD LOSE YOU — Dreamlovers, End 1114 | 3 |
| 76 | 81 | — | — | HOT PEPPER — Floyd Cramer, RCA Victor 8051 | 2 |
| 77 | 79 | 81 | 81 | GOOD LOVER — Jimmy Reed, Vee Jay 449 | 4 |
| 78 | 83 | — | — | THE BALLAD OF PALADIN — Duane Eddy, RCA Victor 8047 | 2 |
| 79 | 62 | 58 | 62 | WHERE HAVE YOU BEEN ALL MY LIFE — Arthur Alexander, Dot 16357 | 8 |
| 80 | — | — | — | BEN CRAZY — Dickie Goodman & Dr. I. M. Ill, Diamond 119 | 1 |
| 81 | 91 | 92 | — | WORRIED MIND — Ray Anthony, Capitol 4742 | 3 |
| 82 | 85 | 88 | — | NOTHING NEW (Same Old Thing) — Fats Domino, Imperial 5863 | 3 |
| 83 | 94 | — | — | MY DADDY IS PRESIDENT — Little Jo Ann, Kapp 467 | 2 |
| 84 | 92 | — | — | I JUST CAN'T HELP IT — Jackie Wilson, Brunswick 55229 | 2 |
| 85 | — | — | 94 | BRING IT ON HOME TO ME — Sam Cooke, RCA Victor 8036 | 2 |
| 86 | 90 | — | 89 | THAT GREASY KID STUFF — Janie Grant, Caprice 115 | 3 |
| 87 | — | — | — | ABOVE THE STARS — Mr. Acker Bilk, Atco 6230 | 1 |
| 88 | — | — | — | WHAT'S A MATTER BABY — Timi Yuro, Liberty 55469 | 1 |
| 89 | — | — | — | ALL NIGHT LONG — Sandy Nelson, Imperial 5860 | 1 |
| 90 | 93 | 93 | — | GOODNIGHT IRENE — Jerry Reed & the Hully Girlies, Columbia 42417 | 3 |
| 91 | 97 | 100 | — | POTATO PEELER — Bobby Gregg & His Friends, Cotton 1006 | 3 |
| 92 | — | — | — | THE BIRD MAN — Highwaymen, United Artists 475 | 1 |
| 93 | 98 | — | — | SWEET AND LOVELY — April Stevens & Nino Tempo, Atco 6224 | 2 |
| 94 | — | — | — | KEEP YOUR HANDS IN YOUR POCKETS — Playmates, Roulette 4432 | 1 |
| 95 | — | — | — | A TASTE OF HONEY — Martin Denny, Liberty 55470 | 1 |
| 96 | 100 | — | — | MAKE IT EASY FOR YOURSELF — Jerry Butler, Vee Jay 451 | 2 |
| 97 | — | — | — | RINKY DINK — Dave (Baby) Cortez, Chess 1829 | 1 |
| 98 | — | — | — | THEME FROM HATARI — Henry Mancini, RCA Victor 8037 | 1 |
| 99 | — | 96 | — | LA BOMBA — Tokens, RCA Victor 8052 | 2 |
| 100 | — | — | — | A MIRACLE — Frankie Avalon, Chancellor 1115 | 1 |

## BUBBLING UNDER THE HOT 100

101. LIFE'S TOO SHORT — Lafayettes, RCA Victor 8044
102. LITTLE YOUNG LOVER — Impressions, ABC-Paramount 10328
103. BABY ELEPHANT WALK — Miniature Men, Dolton 57
104. I'M HANGING UP MY HEART FOR YOU — Solomon Burke, Atlantic 2147
105. DANCE WITH MR. DOMINO — Fats Domino, Imperial 5863
106. DON'T CRY BABY — Aretha Franklin, Columbia 42456
107. REAP WHAT YOU SOW — Billy Stewart, Chess 1820
108. SHAME ON ME — Bobby Bare, RCA Victor 8032
109. SHAKE A HAND — Ruth Brown, Philips 40028
110. MY TIME FOR CRYING — Maxine Brown, ABC-Paramount 10327
111. THEY KNEW ABOUT YOU — George Maharis, Epic 9522
112. THEME FROM A SUMMER PLACE — Dick Roman, Harmon 1004
113. QUEEN OF MY HEART — Rene & Ray, Donna 1360
114. BEACH PARTY — King Curtis, Capitol 4788
115. COME ON LITTLE ANGEL — Belmonts, Sabina 505
116. MAMA, HERE COMES THE BRIDE — Shirelles, Scepter 1234
117. SOFTLY AS I LEAVE YOU — Matt Monro, Liberty 55449
118. I MISUNDERSTOOD — Wanda Jackson, Capitol 4785
119. THIS IS IT — Jay & the Americans, United Artists 479
120. SHEILA — Tommy Roe, ABC-Paramount 10329

# BILLBOARD HOT 100

**FOR WEEK ENDING JULY 21, 1962**

STAR PERFORMERS—Selections registering greatest upward progress this week.
S — Indicates that 45 r.p.m. stereo single version is available.
△ — Indicates that 33⅓ r.p.m. mono single version is available.
Ⓢ — Indicates that 33⅓ r.p.m. stereo single version is available.

| This Week | Wk. Ago | 2 Wks. Ago | Title — Artist, Label & Number | Weeks On Chart |
|---|---|---|---|---|
| 1 | 1 | 2 | ROSES ARE RED — Bobby Vinton, Epic 9509 | 7 |
| 2 | 4 | 14 | THE WAH-WATUSI — Orlons, Cameo 218 | 7 |
| 3 | 3 | 3 | I CAN'T STOP LOVING YOU — Ray Charles, ABC-Paramount 10330 | 12 |
| 4 | 2 | 1 | THE STRIPPER — David Rose & His Ork, MGM 13064 | 11 |
| 5 | 5 | 12 | SEALED WITH A KISS — Brian Hyland, ABC-Paramount 10336 | 7 |
| 6 | 7 | 7 | WOLVERTON MOUNTAIN — Claude King, Columbia 42353 | 9 |
| 7 | 11 | 9 | JOHNNY GET ANGRY — Joanie Sommers, Warner Bros. 5275 | 9 |
| ☆8 | 13 | 22 | SPEEDY GONZALES — Pat Boone, Dot 16368 | 6 |
| 9 | 9 | 16 | GRAVY — Dee Dee Sharp, Cameo 219 | 6 |
| 10 | 6 | 4 | PALISADES PARK — Freddy Cannon, Swan 4106 | 11 |
| 11 | 10 | 6 | AL DI LA' — Emilio Pericoli, Warner Bros. 5259 | 10 |
| 12 | 18 | 47 | AHAB THE ARAB — Ray Stevens, Mercury 71966 | 4 |
| ☆13 | 19 | 26 | BREAKING UP IS HARD TO DO — Neil Sedaka, RCA Victor 8046 | 4 |
| 14 | 8 | 5 | IT KEEPS RIGHT ON A-HURTIN' — Johnny Tillotson, Cadence 1418 | 11 |
| 15 | 20 | 30 | DANCING PARTY — Chubby Checker, Parkway 842 | 5 |
| 16 | 14 | 18 | I'LL NEVER DANCE AGAIN — Bobby Rydell, Cameo 217 | 8 |
| 17 | 17 | 21 | HAVING A PARTY — Sam Cooke, RCA Victor 8036 | 8 |
| 18 | 15 | 17 | THEME FROM DOCTOR KILDARE — Richard Chamberlain, MGM 13075 | 8 |
| 19 | 29 | 38 | (GIRLS, GIRLS, GIRLS) MADE TO LOVE — Eddie Hodges, Cadence 1421 | 5 |
| 20 | 12 | 8 | SNAP YOUR FINGERS — Joe Henderson, Todd 1072 | 10 |
| 21 | 22 | 24 | JOHNNY LOVES ME — Shelley Fabares, Colpix 636 | 7 |
| 22 | 23 | 31 | TWIST AND SHOUT — Isley Brothers, Wand 124 | 8 |
| 23 | 33 | 43 | YOU'LL LOSE A GOOD THING — Barbara Lynn, Jamie 1220 | 6 |
| 24 | 24 | 33 | I NEED YOUR LOVING — Don Gardner and Dee Dee Ford, Fire 508 | 8 |
| 25 | 16 | 10 | PLAYBOY — Marvelettes, Tamla 54060 | 12 |
| ☆26 | 52 | 71 | LOCO-MOTION — Little Eva, Dimension 1000 | 4 |
| 27 | 32 | 36 | SEVEN-DAY WEEKEND — Gary (U.S.) Bonds, LeGrand 1019 | 5 |
| 28 | 34 | 39 | WELCOME HOME BABY — Shirelles, Scepter 1234 | 5 |
| 29 | 25 | 28 | LITTLE BITTY PRETTY ONE — Clyde McPhatter, Mercury 71987 | 6 |
| 30 | 21 | 11 | CINDY'S BIRTHDAY — Johnny Crawford, Del Fi 4178 | 11 |
| 31 | 41 | 53 | IT STARTED ALL OVER AGAIN — Brenda Lee, Decca 31407 | 4 |
| ☆32 | 60 | 78 | PARTY LIGHTS — Claudine Clark, Chancellor 1113 | 5 |
| 33 | 26 | 27 | THE CROWD — Roy Orbison, Monument 461 | 8 |
| ☆34 | 61 | 88 | THINGS — Bobby Darin, Atco 6229 | 3 |
| 35 | 28 | 13 | A STEEL GUITAR AND A GLASS OF WINE — Paul Anka, RCA Victor 8030 | 9 |
| ☆36 | 55 | 65 | HEART IN HAND — Brenda Lee, Decca 31407 | 3 |
| 37 | 53 | 72 | LITTLE DIANE — Dion, Laurie 3134 | 3 |
| 38 | 27 | 29 | BRISTOL TWISTIN' ANNIE — Dovells, Parkway 838 | 10 |
| 39 | 31 | 25 | WALK ON THE WILD SIDE — Jimmy Smith, Verve 10255 | 11 |
| ☆40 | 50 | 56 | HAVE A GOOD TIME — Sue Thompson, Hickory 1174 | 6 |
| 41 | 43 | 55 | BUT NOT FOR ME — Ketty Lester, Era 3080 | 6 |
| 42 | 35 | 46 | BONGO STOMP — Little Joey & the Flips, Joy 262 | 6 |
| ☆43 | 58 | 74 | LITTLE RED RENTED ROWBOAT — Joe Dowell, Smash 1759 | 5 |
| 44 | 36 | 19 | STRANGER ON THE SHORE — Mr. Acker Bilk, Atco 6217 | 19 |
| 45 | 37 | 42 | WEST OF THE WALL — Toni Fisher, Big Top 3097 | 9 |
| 46 | 51 | 57 | STEEL MEN — Jimmy Dean, Columbia 42483 | 5 |
| 47 | 49 | 41 | FORTUNE TELLER — Bobby Curtola, Del Fi 4177 | 12 |
| 48 | 40 | 50 | LIMBO ROCK — Champs, Challenge 9131 | 9 |
| ☆49 | 85 | — | BRING IT ON HOME TO ME — Sam Cooke, RCA Victor 8036 | 3 |
| 50 | 54 | 66 | ROUTE 66 THEME — Nelson Riddle, Capitol 4741 | 8 |
| 51 | 38 | 45 | STRANGER ON THE SHORE — Andy Williams, Columbia 42451 | 7 |
| 52 | 59 | 68 | SUMMERTIME, SUMMERTIME — Jamies, Epic 9281 | 5 |
| 53 | 56 | 61 | I DON'T LOVE YOU NO MORE — Jimmy Norman, Little Star 113 | 6 |
| 54 | 30 | 15 | SHARING YOU — Bobby Vee, Liberty 55451 | 10 |
| 55 | 62 | 77 | MARY'S LITTLE LAMB — James Darren, Colpix 644 | 4 |
| 56 | 48 | 40 | WHERE ARE YOU — Dinah Washington, Roulette 4424 | 10 |
| 57 | 57 | 52 | SWINGIN' GENTLY — Earl Grant, Decca 25560 | 9 |
| 58 | 42 | 20 | THE MAN WHO SHOT LIBERTY VALANCE — Gene Pitney, Musicor 1020 | 13 |
| 59 | 71 | 73 | BABY ELEPHANT WALK — Lawrence Welk, Dot 16364 | 7 |
| 60 | 64 | 70 | BOOM BOOM — John Lee Hooker, Vee Jay 438 | 9 |
| 61 | 73 | 86 | SHOUT AND SHIMMY — James Brown & the Famous Flames, King 5657 | 3 |
| 62 | 70 | 75 | NEVER IN A MILLION YEARS — Linda Scott, Congress 103 | 6 |
| ☆63 | 78 | 83 | THE BALLAD OF PALADIN — Duane Eddy, RCA Victor 8047 | 3 |
| 64 | 39 | 23 | THAT'S OLD FASHIONED — Everly Brothers, Warner Bros. 5273 | 11 |
| 65 | 76 | 81 | HOT PEPPER — Floyd Cramer, RCA Victor 8051 | 3 |
| ☆66 | 88 | — | WHAT'S A MATTER BABY — Timi Yuro, Liberty 55469 | 2 |
| 67 | 75 | 80 | IF I SHOULD LOSE YOU — Dreamlovers, End 1114 | 4 |
| 68 | 72 | 82 | WHY DID YOU LEAVE ME — Vince Edwards, Russ-Fi 7001 | 3 |
| 69 | 80 | — | BEN CRAZY — Dickie Goodman & Dr. I. M. Ill, Diamond 119 | 2 |
| ☆70 | — | — | A SWINGIN' SAFARI — Billy Vaughn, Dot 16374 | |
| 71 | 74 | 84 | DOWN IN THE VALLEY — Solomon Burke, Atlantic 2147 | 8 |
| 72 | 84 | 92 | I JUST CAN'T HELP IT — Jackie Wilson, Brunswick 55229 | 3 |
| 73 | 83 | 94 | MY DADDY IS PRESIDENT — Little Jo Ann, Kapp 467 | 3 |
| 74 | 86 | 90 | THAT GREASY KID STUFF — Janie Grant, Caprice 115 | 4 |
| ☆75 | 96 | 100 | MAKE IT EASY ON YOURSELF — Jerry Butler, Vee Jay 451 | 2 |
| 76 | 97 | — | RINKY DINK — Dave (Baby) Cortez, Chess 1829 | |
| 77 | 82 | 85 | NOTHING NEW (SAME OLD THING) — Fats Domino, Imperial 5863 | 4 |
| 78 | 81 | 91 | WORRIED MIND — Ray Anthony, Capitol 4742 | 4 |
| 79 | 89 | — | ALL NIGHT LONG — Sandy Nelson, Imperial 5860 | 2 |
| 80 | 93 | 98 | SWEET AND LOVELY — April Stevens & Nino Tempo, Atco 6224 | 3 |
| 81 | 90 | 93 | GOODNIGHT IRENE — Jerry Reed & the Hully Girlies, Columbia 42417 | 4 |
| 82 | 95 | — | A TASTE OF HONEY — Martin Denny, Liberty 55470 | 2 |
| ☆83 | — | — | SHAME ON ME — Bobby Bare, RCA Victor 8032 | 1 |
| 84 | 92 | — | THE BIRD MAN — Highwaymen, United Artists 475 | 2 |
| ☆85 | — | 99 | I'M HANGING UP MY HEART FOR YOU — Solomon Burke, Atlantic 2147 | 2 |
| 86 | 87 | — | ABOVE THE STARS — Mr. Acker Bilk, Atco 6230 | 2 |
| ☆87 | — | — | LIFE'S TOO SHORT — Lafayettes, RCA Victor 8044 | |
| 88 | 94 | — | KEEP YOUR HANDS IN YOUR POCKETS — Playmates, Roulette 4432 | 2 |
| 89 | 91 | 97 | POTATO PEELER — Bobby Gregg & His Friends, Cotton 1006 | 4 |
| 90 | 100 | — | A MIRACLE — Frankie Avalon, Chancellor 1115 | 2 |
| 91 | — | — | BEACH PARTY — King Curtis, Capitol 4788 | 1 |
| 92 | — | — | DON'T CRY BABY — Aretha Franklin, Columbia 42456 | 1 |
| 93 | — | — | CALL ME MR. IN-BETWEEN — Burl Ives, Decca 31405 | |
| 94 | — | — | COME ON LITTLE ANGEL — Belmonts, Sabina 505 | 1 |
| 95 | 99 | — | LA BOMBA — Tokens, RCA Victor 8052 | 3 |
| 96 | — | — | TILL DEATH DO US PART — Bob Braun, Decca 31355 | 1 |
| 97 | 98 | — | THEME FROM HATARI — Henry Mancini, RCA Victor 8037 | 2 |
| 98 | — | — | DANCE WITH MR. DOMINO — Fats Domino, Imperial 5863 | 1 |
| 99 | — | — | REAP WHAT YOU SOW — Billy Stewart, Chess 1820 | |
| 100 | — | — | GOODBYE DAD — Castle Sisters, Terrace 7506 | 1 |

## BUBBLING UNDER THE HOT 100

101. I'M TOSSIN' AND TURNIN' AGAIN — Bobby Lewis, Beltone 2023
102. LITTLE YOUNG LOVER — Impressions, ABC-Paramount 10328
103. SHEILA — Tommy Roe, ABC-Paramount 10329
104. MAMA, HERE COMES THE BRIDE — Shirelles, Scepter 1234
105. MY TIME FOR CRYING — Maxine Brown, ABC-Paramount 10327
106. SO WRONG — Patsy Cline, Decca 31406
107. YOU'RE STRONGER THAN ME — Patsy Cline, Decca 31406
108. SHAKE A HAND — Ruth Brown, Philips 40028
109. THEME FROM A SUMMER PLACE — Dick Roman, Harmon 1004
110. POOR LITTLE PUPPET — Cathy Carroll, Warner Bros. 5284
111. DON'T LET ME STAND IN YOUR WAY — Frankie Avalon, Chancellor 1115
112. CALLIN' DR. CASEY — John D. Loudermilk, RCA Victor 8054
113. THEY KNEW ABOUT YOU — George Maharis, Epic 9522
114. IF YOU THINK — Barbara George, Sue 763
115. RIGHT STRING BUT THE WRONG YO-YO — Dr. Feelgood and the Interns, Okeh 7156
116. I'LL COME RUNNING BACK TO YOU — Roy Hamilton, Epic 9520
117. I MISUNDERSTOOD — Wanda Jackson, Capitol 4785
118. THIS IS IT — Jay and the Americans, United Artists 479
119. THE MASQUERADE IS OVER — Five Satins, Chancellor 1110
120. BE KIND — Ronnie and the Hi-Lites, Joy 265

# BILLBOARD HOT 100

FOR WEEK ENDING JULY 28

1962

★ STAR PERFORMERS—Selections registering greatest upward progress this week.

S Indicates that 45 r.p.m. stereo single version is available.

△ Indicates that 33⅓ r.p.m. mono single version is available.

△S Indicates that 33⅓ r.p.m. stereo single version is available.

| This Week | 1 Wk. Ago | 2 Wks. Ago | 3 Wks. Ago | Title — Artist, Label & Number | | Weeks On Chart |
|---|---|---|---|---|---|---|
| 1 | 1 | 1 | 2 | ROSES ARE RED — Bobby Vinton, Epic 9509 | | 8 |
| 2 | 2 | 4 | 14 | THE WAH-WATUSI — Orlons, Cameo 218 | | 8 |
| 3 | 5 | 5 | 12 | SEALED WITH A KISS — Brian Hyland, ABC-Paramount 10336 | | 8 |
| 4 | 3 | 3 | 3 | I CAN'T STOP LOVING YOU — Ray Charles, ABC-Paramount 10330 | | 13 |
| 5 | 4 | 2 | 1 | THE STRIPPER — David Rose & His Ork, MGM 13064 | | 12 |
| 6 | 8 | 13 | 22 | SPEEDY GONZALES — Pat Boone, Dot 16368 | | 7 |
| 7 | 6 | 7 | 7 | WOLVERTON MOUNTAIN — Claude King, Columbia 42352 | △ | 10 |
| ★8 | 13 | 19 | 26 | BREAKING UP IS HARD TO DO — Neil Sedaka, RCA Victor 8046 | △ | 5 |
| 9 | 9 | 9 | 16 | GRAVY — Dee Dee Sharp, Cameo 219 | | 7 |
| 10 | 12 | 18 | 47 | AHAB THE ARAB — Ray Stevens, Mercury 71966 | | 5 |
| 11 | 7 | 11 | 9 | JOHNNY GET ANGRY — Joanie Sommers, Warner Bros. 5275 | | 10 |
| 12 | 15 | 20 | 30 | DANCING PARTY — Chubby Checker, Parkway 842 | | 6 |
| ★13 | 18 | 15 | 17 | THEME FROM DOCTOR KILDARE — Richard Chamberlain, MGM 13075 | | 9 |
| ★14 | 26 | 52 | 71 | LOCO-MOTION — Little Eva, Dimension 1000 | | 5 |
| ★15 | 23 | 33 | 43 | YOU'LL LOSE A GOOD THING — Barbara Lynn, Jamie 1220 | | 7 |
| 16 | 10 | 6 | 4 | PALISADES PARK — Freddy Cannon, Swan 4106 | | 12 |
| 17 | 11 | 10 | 6 | AL DI LA' — Emilio Pericoli, Warner Bros. 5259 | | 11 |
| 18 | 19 | 29 | 38 | (GIRLS, GIRLS, GIRLS) MADE TO LOVE — Eddie Hodges, Cadence 1421 | | 6 |
| 19 | 22 | 23 | 31 | TWIST AND SHOUT — Isley Brothers, Wand 124 | | 9 |
| 20 | 24 | 24 | 33 | I NEED YOUR LOVING — Don Gardner and Dee Dee Ford, Fire 508 | | 9 |
| 21 | 17 | 17 | 21 | HAVING A PARTY — Sam Cooke, RCA Victor 8036 | △ | 9 |
| 22 | 28 | 34 | 39 | WELCOME HOME BABY — Shirelles, Scepter 1234 | | 6 |
| 23 | 32 | 60 | 78 | PARTY LIGHTS — Claudine Clark, Chancellor 1113 | | 5 |
| ★24 | 34 | 61 | 88 | THINGS — Bobby Darin, Atco 6229 | | 4 |
| 25 | 16 | 14 | 18 | I'LL NEVER DANCE AGAIN — Bobby Rydell, Cameo 217 | | 9 |
| ★26 | 36 | 55 | 65 | HEART IN HAND — Brenda Lee, Decca 31407 | | 4 |
| ★27 | 37 | 53 | 72 | LITTLE DIANE — Dion, Laurie 3134 | | 4 |
| 28 | 14 | 8 | 5 | IT KEEPS RIGHT ON A-HURTIN' — Johnny Tillotson, Cadence 1418 | | 12 |
| 29 | 31 | 41 | 53 | IT STARTED ALL OVER AGAIN — Brenda Lee, Decca 31407 | | 5 |
| 30 | 21 | 22 | 24 | JOHNNY LOVES ME — Shelley Fabares, Colpix 636 | | 8 |
| 31 | 20 | 12 | 8 | SNAP YOUR FINGERS — Joe Henderson, Todd 1072 | | 11 |
| 32 | 29 | 25 | 28 | LITTLE BITTY PRETTY ONE — Clyde McPhatter, Mercury 71987 | | 7 |
| 33 | 42 | 35 | 46 | BONGO STOMP — Little Joey & the Flips, Joy 262 | | 7 |
| 34 | 43 | 58 | 74 | LITTLE RED RENTED ROWBOAT — Joe Dowell, Smash 1759 | | 6 |
| 35 | 40 | 50 | 56 | HAVE A GOOD TIME — Sue Thompson, Hickory 1174 | | 7 |
| 36 | 25 | 16 | 10 | PLAYBOY — Marvelettes, Tamla 54060 | | 13 |
| 37 | 33 | 26 | 27 | THE CROWD — Roy Orbison, Monument 461 | | 9 |
| 38 | 30 | 21 | 11 | CINDY'S BIRTHDAY — Johnny Crawford, Del Fi 4178 | | 12 |
| 39 | 35 | 28 | 13 | A STEEL GUITAR AND A GLASS OF WINE — Paul Anka, RCA Victor 8030 | △ | 10 |
| 40 | 27 | 32 | 36 | SEVEN-DAY WEEKEND — Gary (U. S.) Bonds, LeGrand 1019 | | 6 |
| 41 | 41 | 43 | 55 | BUT NOT FOR ME — Ketty Lester, Era 3080 | | 6 |
| 42 | 50 | 54 | 66 | ROUTE 66 THEME — Nelson Riddle, Capitol 4741 | | 9 |
| 43 | 46 | 51 | 57 | STEEL MEN — Jimmy Dean, Columbia 42483 | △ | 6 |
| 44 | 49 | 85 | — | BRING IT ON HOME TO ME — Sam Cooke, RCA Victor 8036 | △ | 4 |
| 45 | 52 | 59 | 68 | SUMMERTIME, SUMMERTIME — Jamies, Epic 9281 | | 6 |
| 46 | 39 | 31 | 25 | WALK ON THE WILD SIDE — Jimmy Smith, Verve 10255 | | 12 |
| 47 | 55 | 62 | 77 | MARY'S LITTLE LAMB — James Darren, Colpix 644 | | 5 |
| 48 | 45 | 37 | 42 | WEST OF THE WALL — Toni Fisher, Big Top 3097 | | 10 |
| 49 | 53 | 56 | 61 | I DON'T LOVE YOU NO MORE — Jimmy Norman, Little Star 113 | | 7 |
| 50 | 48 | 40 | 50 | LIMBO ROCK — Champs, Challenge 9131 | | 10 |
| 51 | 47 | 49 | 41 | FORTUNE TELLER — Bobby Curtola, Del Fi 4177 | | 13 |
| ★52 | 66 | 88 | — | WHAT'S A MATTER BABY — Timi Yuro, Liberty 55469 | | 3 |
| 53 | 44 | 36 | 19 | STRANGER ON THE SHORE — Mr. Acker Bilk, Atco 6217 | | 20 |
| 54 | 38 | 27 | 29 | BRISTOL TWISTIN' ANNIE — Dovells, Parkway 838 | | 11 |
| 55 | 63 | 78 | 83 | THE BALLAD OF PALADIN — Duane Eddy, RCA Victor 8047 | △ | 4 |
| ★56 | — | — | — | YOU DON'T KNOW ME — Ray Charles, ABC-Paramount 10345 | | 1 |
| 57 | 59 | 71 | 73 | BABY ELEPHANT WALK — Lawrence Welk, Dot 16364 | | 8 |
| 58 | 62 | 70 | 75 | NEVER IN A MILLION YEARS — Linda Scott, Congress 103 | | 7 |
| ★59 | 69 | 80 | — | BEN CRAZY — Dickie Goodman & Dr. I. M. Ill, Diamond 119 | | 3 |
| ★60 | 76 | 97 | — | RINKY DINK — Dave (Baby) Cortez, Chess 1829 | | 3 |
| 61 | 56 | 48 | 40 | WHERE ARE YOU — Dinah Washington, Roulette 4424 | | 11 |
| 62 | 67 | 75 | 80 | IF I SHOULD LOSE YOU — Dreamlovers, End 1114 | | 5 |
| 63 | 65 | 76 | 81 | HOT PEPPER — Floyd Cramer, RCA Victor 8051 | △ | 4 |
| 64 | 70 | — | — | A SWINGIN' SAFARI — Billy Vaughn, Dot 16374 | | 2 |
| 65 | 61 | 73 | 86 | SHOUT AND SHIMMY — James Brown & the Famous Flames, King 5657 | | 4 |
| 66 | 60 | 64 | 70 | BOOM BOOM — John Lee Hooker, Vee Jay 438 | | 10 |
| ★67 | 82 | 95 | — | A TASTE OF HONEY — Martin Denny, Liberty 55470 | | 3 |
| 68 | 75 | 96 | 100 | MAKE IT EASY ON YOURSELF — Jerry Butler, Vee Jay 451 | | 3 |
| 69 | 73 | 83 | 94 | MY DADDY IS PRESIDENT — Little Jo Ann, Kapp 467 | | 4 |
| 70 | 72 | 84 | 92 | I JUST CAN'T HELP IT — Jackie Wilson, Brunswick 55229 | | 4 |
| 71 | 57 | 57 | 52 | SWINGIN' GENTLY — Earl Grant, Decca 25560 | | 10 |
| 72 | 83 | — | — | SHAME ON ME — Bobby Bare, RCA Victor 8032 | △ | 2 |
| ★73 | — | — | — | SHEILA — Tommy Roe, ABC-Paramount 10329 | | 1 |
| 74 | 68 | 72 | 82 | WHY DID YOU LEAVE ME! — Vince Edwards, Russ-Fi 7001 | | 4 |
| 75 | 79 | 89 | — | ALL NIGHT LONG — Sandy Nelson, Imperial 5860 | | 3 |
| ★76 | 93 | — | — | CALL ME MR. IN-BETWEEN — Burl Ives, Decca 31405 | | 2 |
| 77 | 80 | 93 | 98 | SWEET AND LOVELY — April Stevens & Nino Tempo, Atco 6224 | | 4 |
| ★78 | — | — | — | VACATION — Connie Francis, MGM 13087 | | 1 |
| 79 | 81 | 90 | 93 | GOODNIGHT IRENE — Jerry Reed & the Hully Girlies, Columbia 42417 | △ | 5 |
| 80 | 91 | — | — | BEACH PARTY — King Curtis, Capitol 4788 | | 2 |
| 81 | 84 | 92 | — | THE BIRD MAN — Highwaymen, United Artists 475 | | 3 |
| 82 | 86 | 87 | — | ABOVE THE STARS — Mr. Acker Bilk, Atco 6230 | | 3 |
| 83 | 78 | 81 | 91 | WORRIED MIND — Ray Anthony, Capitol 4742 | | 5 |
| ★84 | — | — | — | ALLEY CAT — Bent Fabric, Atco 6226 | | 1 |
| 85 | 95 | 99 | — | LA BOMBA — Tokens, RCA Victor 8052 | △ | 4 |
| ★86 | — | — | — | DEVIL WOMAN — Marty Robbins, Columbia 42486 | △ | 1 |
| 87 | 90 | 100 | — | A MIRACLE — Frankie Avalon, Chancellor 1115 | | 3 |
| ★88 | — | — | — | CARELESS LOVE — Ray Charles, ABC-Paramount 10345 | | 1 |
| 89 | 94 | — | — | COME ON LITTLE ANGEL — Belmonts, Sabina 505 | | 2 |
| ★90 | — | — | — | STOP THE WEDDING — Etta James, Argo 5418 | | 1 |
| 91 | — | — | — | CALLIN' DOCTOR CASEY — John D. Loudermilk, RCA Victor 8054 | △ | 1 |
| 92 | 77 | 82 | 85 | NOTHING NEW (Same Old Thing) — Fats Domino, Imperial 5863 | | 5 |
| 93 | 96 | — | — | TILL DEATH DO US PART — Bob Braun, Decca 31355 | | 2 |
| 94 | 87 | — | — | LIFE'S TOO SHORT — Lafayettes, RCA Victor 8044 | △ | 2 |
| 95 | 99 | — | — | REAP WHAT YOU SOW — Billy Stewart, Chess 1820 | | 2 |
| 96 | — | — | — | LITTLE YOUNG LOVER — Impressions, ABC-Paramount 10328 | | 1 |
| 97 | 97 | 98 | — | THEME FROM HATARI — Henry Mancini, RCA Victor 8037 | △ | 3 |
| 98 | — | — | — | I'M TOSSIN' AND TURNIN' AGAIN — Bobby Lewis, Beltone 2023 | | 1 |
| 99 | — | — | — | JIVIN' AROUND — Al Casey Combo, Stacy 936 | | 1 |
| 100 | — | — | — | COME ON BABY — Bruce Channel, Smash 1769 | | 1 |

## HOT 100—A TO Z—(Publisher-Licensee)


Above the Stars (LeVan, ASCAP) .... 82
Ahab the Arab (Lowery, BMI) .... 10
Al Di La' (Witmark, ASCAP) .... 17
All Night Long (Golden State, BMI) .... 75
Alley Cat (Metorion, BMI) .... 84

Baby Elephant Walk (Famous, ASCAP) .... 57
Ballad of Paladin, The (Time, BMI) .... 55
Beach Party (Kilynn, BMI) .... 80
Ben Crazy (RX, BMI) .... 59
Bird Man, The (United Artists, ASCAP) .... 81
Bongo Stomp (Drury Lane, BMI) .... 33
Boom Boom (Conrad, BMI) .... 66
Breaking Up Is Hard to Do (Aldon, BMI) .... 8
Bring It on Home to Me (Kags, BMI) .... 44
Bristol Twistin' Annie (Schulman, BMI) .... 54
But Not for Me (New World, ASCAP) .... 41

Call Me Mr. In-Between (Pamper, BMI) .... 76
Callin' Doctor Casey (Acuff-Rose, BMI) .... 91
Careless Love (Tangerine, BMI) .... 88
Cindy's Birthday (Maraville, BMI) .... 38
Come On Baby (LeBill, BMI) .... 100
Come On Little Angel (Glenden, ASCAP) .... 89
Crowd, The (Acuff-Rose, BMI) .... 37

Dancing Party (Kalmann, ASCAP) .... 12
Devil Woman (Marty's, BMI) .... 86

Fortune Teller (Kemo, BMI) .... 51

(Girls, Girls, Girls) Made to Love (Acuff-Rose, BMI) .... 18
Goodnight Irene (Ludlow, BMI) .... 79
Gravy (Kalmann, ASCAP) .... 9

Have a Good Time (Acuff-Rose, BMI) .... 35
Having a Party (Kags, BMI) .... 21
Heart in Hand (Metric, BMI) .... 26
Hot Pepper (Acuff-Rose, BMI) .... 63

I Can't Stop Loving You (Acuff-Rose, BMI) .... 4
I Don't Love You No More (Hidle, BMI) .... 49
I Just Can't Help It (Pearl, BMI) .... 70
I Need Your Loving (Fast-Pete, BMI) .... 20
I'm Tossin' and Turnin' Again (Lescay, BMI) .... 98
I'll Never Dance Again (Aldon, BMI) .... 25
If I Should Lose You (Alan K., BMI) .... 62
It Keeps Right on A-Hurtin' (Tanridge, BMI) .... 28
It Started All Over Again (Aldon, BMI) .... 29

Jivin' Around (Reese, BMI) .... 99
Johnny Get Angry (Tod, ASCAP) .... 11
Johnny Loves Me (Aldon, BMI) .... 30

La Bomba (Bright Tunes, BMI) .... 85
Life's Too Short (Duchess, BMI) .... 94
Limbo Rock (Four Star, BMI) .... 50
Little Bitty Pretty One (Recordo, BMI) .... 32
Little Diane (Disal, ASCAP) .... 27
Little Red Rented Rowboat (Reis, BMI) .... 34
Little Young Lover (Curtom, BMI) .... 96
Loco-Motion (Aldon, BMI) .... 14

Make It Easy on Yourself (Famous, ASCAP) .... 68
Mary's Little Lamb (Aldon, BMI) .... 47
Miracle, A (South Mountain, BMI) .... 87
My Daddy Is President (Gretavic, ASCAP) .... 69

Never in a Million Years (Robbins, ASCAP) .... 58
Nothing New (Travis, BMI) .... 92

Palisades Park (Claridge, ASCAP) .... 16
Party Lights (Rambed, BMI) .... 23
Playboy (Jobete, BMI) .... 36

Reap What You Sow (Arc, BMI) .... 95
Rinky-Dink (Arc-Cortez, BMI) .... 60
Roses Are Red (Lyle, ASCAP) .... 1
Route 66 Theme (Gower, BMI) .... 42

Sealed With a Kiss (Post, ASCAP) .... 3
Seven-Day Weekend (Hill & Range, BMI) .... 40
Shame on Me (Western Hills-Lois-Saran, BMI) .... 72
Sheila (Eager-Nitetime, BMI) .... 73
Shout and Shimmy (Lois, BMI) .... 65
Snap Your Fingers (Cigma, BMI) .... 31
Speedy Gonzales (Budd, ASCAP) .... 6
Steel Guitar and a Glass of Wine, A (Spanka, BMI) .... 39
Steel Men (Southside, BMI) .... 43
Stop the Wedding (Figure, BMI) .... 90
Stranger on the Shore (Mellin, BMI) .... 53
Stripper, The (David Rose, ASCAP) .... 5
Summertime, Summertime (Roxbury, ASCAP) .... 45
Sweet and Lovely (Robbins-Daniels, ASCAP) .... 77
Swingin' Gently (Marvelle, BMI) .... 71
Swingin' Safari, A (Roosevelt, BMI) .... 64

Taste of Honey, A (Songfest, ASCAP) .... 67
Theme From Doctor Kildare (Hastings, BMI) .... 13
Theme From Hatari (Famous, ASCAP) .... 97
Things (Adaris, BMI) .... 24
Till Death Do Us Part (Karolyn, ASCAP) .... 93
Twist and Shout (Mellin, BMI) .... 19

Vacation (Merna, BMI) .... 78

Wah-Watusi, The (Kalmann-Lowe, ASCAP) .... 2
Walk on the Wild Side (Columbia Pictures, ASCAP) .... 46
Welcome Home Baby (Ludix, BMI) .... 22
West of the Wall (Music Productions, ASCAP) .... 48
What's a Matter Baby (Eden, BMI) .... 52
Where Are You (Feist, ASCAP) .... 61
Why Did You Leave Me? (Mamaleen, BMI) .... 74
Wolverton Mountain (Painted Desert, BMI) .... 7
Worried Mind (Peer Int'l, BMI) .... 83

You Don't Know Me (Hill & Range, BMI) .... 56
You'll Lose a Good Thing (David-Crazy Cajun-Jamie, BMI) .... 15


## BUBBLING UNDER THE HOT 100

101. I WANT TO BE LOVED........Dinah Washington, Mercury 72015
102. THE MASQUERADE IS OVER........Five Satins, Chancellor 1110
103. GOODBYE DAD ....................Castle Sisters, Terrace 7506
104. YOUR HEART BELONGS TO ME...........Supremes, Motown 1027
105. DON'T CRY BABY..............Aretha Franklin, Columbia 42456
106. POOR LITTLE PUPPET..........Cathy Carroll, Warner Bros. 5284
107. RIGHT STRING BUT THE WRONG YO-YO.........................Dr. Feelgood & the Interns, Okeh 7156
108. THEME FROM A SUMMER PLACE......Dick Roman, Harmon 1004
109. LOLITA YA-YA...........................Ventures, Dolton 60
110. I'LL COME RUNNING BACK TO YOU......Roy Hamilton, Epic 9520
111. YOU'RE STRONGER THAN ME..........Patsy Cline, Decca 31406
112. YOU BELONG TO ME....................Duprees, Coed 569
113. DON'T WORRY 'BOUT ME..........Vince Edwards, Decca 31413
114. I'M COMIN' HOME...........Paul Anka, ABC-Paramount 10338
115. SO WRONG..........................Patsy Cline, Decca 31406
116. THIS IS IT..............Jay & The Americans, United Artists 479
117. SILVER THREADS & GOLDEN NEEDLES..Springfields, Philips 40038
118. DON'T BREAK THE HEART THAT LOVES YOU..............................Bernie Leighton, Colpix 645
119. SWEET GEORGIA BROWN...........Carroll Brothers, Cameo 221
120. THE BIGGEST SIN OF ALL............Connie Francis, MGM 13087

# BILLBOARD HOT 100
**FOR WEEK ENDING AUGUST 4, 1962**

| This Week | Wk. Ago | 2 Wk. Ago | 3 Wk. Ago | TITLE — Artist, Label & Number | Weeks On Chart |
|---|---|---|---|---|---|
| 1 | 1 | 1 | 1 | ROSES ARE RED — Bobby Vinton, Epic 9509 | 9 |
| 2 | 8 | 13 | 19 | BREAKING UP IS HARD TO DO — Neil Sedaka, RCA Victor 8046 | 6 |
| 3 | 3 | 5 | 5 | SEALED WITH A KISS — Brian Hyland, ABC-Paramount 10336 | 9 |
| 4 | 2 | 2 | 4 | THE WAH-WATUSI — Orlons, Cameo 218 | 9 |
| 5 | 10 | 12 | 18 | AHAB THE ARAB — Ray Stevens, Mercury 71966 | 6 |
| 6 | 6 | 8 | 13 | SPEEDY GONZALES — Pat Boone, Dot 16368 | 8 |
| 7 | 4 | 3 | 3 | I CAN'T STOP LOVING YOU — Ray Charles, ABC-Paramount 10330 | 14 |
| 8 | 14 | 26 | 52 | LOCO-MOTION — Little Eva, Dimension 1000 | 6 |
| 9 | 5 | 4 | 2 | THE STRIPPER — David Rose & His Ork, MGM 13064 | 13 |
| 10 | 13 | 18 | 15 | THEME FROM DOCTOR KILDARE — Richard Chamberlain, MGM 13075 | 10 |
| 11 | 7 | 6 | 7 | WOLVERTON MOUNTAIN — Claude King, Columbia 42352 | 11 |
| 12 | 12 | 15 | 20 | DANCING PARTY — Chubby Checker, Parkway 842 | 7 |
| 13 | 15 | 23 | 33 | YOU'LL LOSE A GOOD THING — Barbara Lynn, Jamie 1220 | 8 |
| 14 | 11 | 7 | 11 | JOHNNY GET ANGRY — Joanie Sommers, Warner Bros. 5275 | 11 |
| 15 | 9 | 9 | 9 | GRAVY — Dee Dee Sharp, Cameo 219 | 8 |
| 16 | 24 | 34 | 61 | THINGS — Bobby Darin, Atco 6229 | 5 |
| 17 | 18 | 19 | 29 | (GIRLS, GIRLS, GIRLS) MADE TO LOVE — Eddie Hodges, Cadence 1421 | 7 |
| 18 | 19 | 22 | 23 | TWIST AND SHOUT — Isley Brothers, Wand 124 | 10 |
| 19 | 27 | 37 | 53 | LITTLE DIANE — Dion, Laurie 3134 | 5 |
| 20 | 20 | 24 | 24 | I NEED YOUR LOVING — Don Gardner and Dee Dee Ford, Fire 508 | 10 |
| 21 | 23 | 32 | 60 | PARTY LIGHTS — Claudine Clark, Chancellor 1113 | 6 |
| 22 | 26 | 36 | 55 | HEART IN HAND — Brenda Lee, Decca 31407 | 5 |
| 23 | 16 | 10 | 6 | PALISADES PARK — Freddy Cannon, Swan 4106 | 13 |
| 24 | 17 | 11 | 10 | AL DI LA' — Emilio Pericoli, Warner Bros. 5259 | 12 |
| 25 | 34 | 43 | 58 | LITTLE RED RENTED ROWBOAT — Joe Dowell, Smash 1759 | 7 |
| 26 | 21 | 17 | 17 | HAVING A PARTY — Sam Cooke, RCA Victor 8036 | 10 |
| 27 | 56 | — | — | YOU DON'T KNOW ME — Ray Charles, ABC-Paramount 10345 | 2 |
| 28 | 22 | 28 | 34 | WELCOME HOME BABY — Shirelles, Scepter 1234 | 7 |
| 29 | 25 | 16 | 14 | I'LL NEVER DANCE AGAIN — Bobby Rydell, Cameo 217 | 10 |
| 30 | 28 | 14 | 8 | IT KEEPS RIGHT ON A-HURTIN' — Johnny Tillotson, Cadence 1418 | 13 |
| 31 | 42 | 50 | 54 | ROUTE 66 THEME — Nelson Riddle, Capitol 4741 | 10 |
| 32 | 44 | 49 | 85 | BRING IT ON HOME TO ME — Sam Cooke, RCA Victor 8036 | 5 |
| 33 | 29 | 31 | 41 | IT STARTED ALL OVER AGAIN — Brenda Lee, Decca 31407 | 6 |
| 34 | 30 | 21 | 22 | JOHNNY LOVES ME — Shelley Fabares, Colpix 636 | 9 |
| 35 | 33 | 42 | 35 | BONGO STOMP — Little Joey & the Flips, Joy 262 | 8 |
| 36 | 31 | 20 | 12 | SNAP YOUR FINGERS — Joe Henderson, Todd 1072 | 12 |
| 37 | 35 | 40 | 50 | HAVE A GOOD TIME — Sue Thompson, Hickory 1174 | 8 |
| 38 | 45 | 52 | 59 | SUMMERTIME, SUMMERTIME — Jamies, Epic 9281 | 7 |
| 39 | 47 | 55 | 62 | MARY'S LITTLE LAMB — James Darren, Colpix 644 | 6 |
| 40 | 36 | 25 | 16 | PLAYBOY — Marvelettes, Tamla 54060 | 14 |
| 41 | 43 | 46 | 51 | STEEL MEN — Jimmy Dean, Columbia 42483 | 7 |
| 42 | 76 | 93 | — | CALL ME MR. IN-BETWEEN — Burl Ives, Decca 31405 | 3 |
| 43 | 73 | — | — | SHEILA — Tommy Roe, ABC-Paramount 10329 | 2 |
| 44 | 60 | 76 | 97 | RINKY DINK — Dave (Baby) Cortez, Chess 1829 | 4 |
| 45 | 55 | 63 | 78 | THE BALLAD OF PALADIN — Duane Eddy, RCA Victor 8047 | 5 |
| 46 | 52 | 66 | 88 | WHAT'S A MATTER BABY — Timi Yuro, Liberty 55469 | 4 |
| 47 | 49 | 53 | 56 | I DON'T LOVE YOU NO MORE — Jimmy Norman, Little Star 113 | 8 |
| 48 | 64 | 70 | — | A SWINGIN' SAFARI — Billy Vaughn, Dot 16374 | 3 |
| 49 | 41 | 41 | 43 | BUT NOT FOR ME — Ketty Lester, Era 3080 | 7 |
| 50 | 57 | 59 | 71 | BABY ELEPHANT WALK — Lawrence Welk, Dot 16364 | 9 |
| 51 | 59 | 69 | 80 | BEN CRAZY — Dickie Goodman & Dr. I. M. Ill, Diamond 119 | 4 |
| 52 | 68 | 75 | 96 | MAKE IT EASY ON YOURSELF — Jerry Butler, Vee Jay 451 | 4 |
| 53 | 32 | 29 | 25 | LITTLE BITTY PRETTY ONE — Clyde McPhatter, Mercury 71987 | 8 |
| 54 | 78 | — | — | VACATION — Connie Francis, MGM 13087 | 2 |
| 55 | 46 | 39 | 31 | WALK ON THE WILD SIDE — Jimmy Smith, Verve 10255 | 13 |
| 56 | 58 | 62 | 70 | NEVER IN A MILLION YEARS — Linda Scott, Congress 103 | 8 |
| 57 | — | — | — | SHE'S NOT YOU — Elvis Presley, RCA Victor 8041 | 1 |
| 58 | 37 | 33 | 26 | THE CROWD — Roy Orbison, Monument 461 | 10 |
| 59 | 72 | 83 | — | SHAME ON ME — Bobby Bare, RCA Victor 8032 | 3 |
| 60 | 50 | 48 | 40 | LIMBO ROCK — Champs, Challenge 9131 | 11 |
| 61 | 67 | 82 | 95 | A TASTE OF HONEY — Martin Denny, Liberty 55470 | 4 |
| 62 | 51 | 47 | 49 | FORTUNE TELLER — Bobby Curtola, Del Fi 4177 | 14 |
| 63 | 48 | 45 | 37 | WEST OF THE WALL — Toni Fisher, Big Top 3097 | 11 |
| 64 | 38 | 30 | 21 | CINDY'S BIRTHDAY — Johnny Crawford, Del Fi 4178 | 13 |
| 65 | 40 | 27 | 32 | SEVEN-DAY WEEKEND — Gary (U.S.) Bonds, LeGrand 1019 | 7 |
| 66 | 84 | — | — | ALLEY CAT — Bent Fabric, Atco 6226 | 2 |
| 67 | 69 | 73 | 83 | MY DADDY IS PRESIDENT — Little Jo Ann, Kapp 467 | 5 |
| 68 | 53 | 44 | 36 | STRANGER ON THE SHORE — Mr. Acker Bilk, Atco 6217 | 21 |
| 69 | 82 | 86 | 87 | ABOVE THE STARS — Mr. Acker Bilk, Atco 6230 | 4 |
| 70 | 86 | — | — | DEVIL WOMAN — Marty Robbins, Columbia 42486 | 2 |
| 71 | 93 | 96 | — | TILL DEATH DO US PART — Bob Braun, Decca 31355 | 3 |
| 72 | 81 | 84 | 92 | THE BIRD MAN — Highwaymen, United Artists 475 | 4 |
| 73 | 61 | 56 | 48 | WHERE ARE YOU — Dinah Washington, Roulette 4424 | 12 |
| 74 | 74 | 68 | 72 | WHY DID YOU LEAVE ME! — Vince Edwards, Russ-Fi 7001 | 5 |
| 75 | 88 | — | — | CARELESS LOVE — Ray Charles, ABC-Paramount 10345 | 2 |
| 76 | 83 | 78 | 81 | WORRIED MIND — Ray Anthony, Capitol 4742 | 6 |
| 77 | 71 | 57 | 57 | SWINGIN' GENTLY — Earl Grant, Decca 25560 | 11 |
| 78 | 80 | 91 | — | BEACH PARTY — King Curtis, Capitol 4788 | 3 |
| 79 | — | — | — | MR. SONGWRITER — Connie Stevens, Warner Bros. 5289 | 1 |
| 80 | 90 | — | — | STOP THE WEDDING — Etta James, Argo 5418 | 2 |
| 81 | 87 | 90 | 100 | A MIRACLE — Frankie Avalon, Chancellor 1115 | 4 |
| 82 | — | — | — | POINT OF NO RETURN — Gene McDaniels, Liberty 55480 | 1 |
| 83 | — | — | — | LET'S DANCE — Chris Montez, Monogram 505 | 1 |
| 84 | — | — | — | RIGHT STRING BUT THE WRONG YO-YO — Dr. Feelgood & the Interns, Okeh 7156 | 1 |
| 85 | 85 | 95 | 99 | LA BOMBA — Tokens, RCA Victor 8052 | 5 |
| 86 | 89 | 94 | — | COME ON LITTLE ANGEL — Belmonts, Sabina 505 | 3 |
| 87 | — | — | — | LOLITA YA-YA — Ventures, Dolton 60 | 1 |
| 88 | 91 | — | — | CALLIN' DOCTOR CASEY — John D. Loudermilk, RCA Victor 8054 | 2 |
| 89 | — | — | — | BOY'S NIGHT OUT — Patti Page, Mercury 72013 | 1 |
| 90 | — | — | — | THEME FROM A SUMMER PLACE — Dick Roman, Harmon 1004 | 1 |
| 91 | — | — | — | RAMBLIN' ROSE — Nat King Cole, Capitol 4804 | 1 |
| 92 | 94 | 87 | — | LIFE'S TOO SHORT — Lafayettes, RCA Victor 8044 | 3 |
| 93 | — | — | — | YOU BELONG TO ME — Duprees, Coed 569 | 1 |
| 94 | — | — | — | SILVER THREADS & GOLDEN NEEDLES — Springfields, Phillips 40038 | 1 |
| 95 | 97 | 97 | 98 | THEME FROM HATARI — Henry Mancini, RCA Victor 8037 | 4 |
| 96 | — | — | — | POOR LITTLE PUPPET — Cathy Carroll, Warner Bros. 5284 | 1 |
| 97 | — | — | — | SUGAR PLUM — Ike Clanton, Mercury 71975 | 1 |
| 98 | 100 | — | — | COME ON BABY — Bruce Channel, Smash 1769 | 2 |
| 99 | — | — | — | LOVE ME AS I LOVE YOU — George Maharis, Epic 9522 | 1 |
| 100 | — | — | — | HOUDINI — Walter Brennan, Liberty 55477 | 1 |

## BUBBLING UNDER THE HOT 100

101. JUST TELL HER JIM SAID HELLO .... Elvis Presley, RCA Victor 8041
102. DON'T CRY BABY .... Aretha Franklin, Columbia 42456
103. I WANT TO BE LOVED .... Dinah Washington, Mercury 72051
104. YOUR NOSE IS GONNA GROW .... Johnny Crawford, Del-Fi 4181
105. THE MASQUERADE IS OVER .... Five Satins, Chancellor 1110
106. DON'T BREAK THE HEART THAT LOVES YOU .... Bernie Leighton, Colpix 645
107. LITTLE YOUNG LOVER .... Impressions, ABC-Paramount 10328
108. GOODBYE DAD .... Castle Sisters, Terrace 7506
109. TOO BAD .... Ben E. King, Atco 6231
110. BEECHWOOD 4-5789 .... Marvelettes, Tamla 54065
111. I'M TOSSIN' AND TURNIN' AGAIN .... Bobby Lewis, Beltone 2023
112. A TASTE OF HONEY .... Victor Feldman Quartet, Infinity 020
113. YOU'RE STRONGER THAN ME .... Patsy Cline, Decca 31406
114. DON'T WORRY 'BOUT ME .... Vince Edwards, Decca 31413
115. I LOVE YOU THE WAY YOU ARE .... Bobby Vinton, Diamond 121
116. LOOKIN' FOR A LOVE .... Valentinos, Sar 132
117. BIGGEST SIN OF ALL .... Connie Francis, MGM 13087
118. GREEN ONIONS .... Booker T & the MG's, Stax 127
119. JIVIN' AROUND .... Al Casey Combo, Stacy 936
*120. SILLY BOY .... Lettermen, Capitol 4810
*120. BROKEN HEART .... Fiestas, Old Town 1122
*Tie

# BILLBOARD HOT 100

**FOR WEEK ENDING AUGUST 11, 1962**

| This Week | Wk 2 | Wk 3 | Wk 4 | Title — Artist, Label & Number | Weeks On Chart |
|---|---|---|---|---|---|
| 1 | 2 | 8 | 13 | BREAKING UP IS HARD TO DO — Neil Sedaka, RCA Victor 8046 | 7 |
| 2 | 1 | 1 | 1 | ROSES ARE RED — Bobby Vinton, Epic 9509 | 10 |
| 3 | 4 | 2 | 2 | THE WAH-WATUSI — Orlons, Cameo 218 | 10 |
| 4 | 8 | 14 | 26 | LOCO-MOTION — Little Eva, Dimension 1000 | 7 |
| 5 | 5 | 10 | 12 | AHAB THE ARAB — Ray Stevens, Mercury 71966 | 7 |
| 6 | 6 | 6 | 8 | SPEEDY GONZALES — Pat Boone, Dot 16368 | 9 |
| 7 | 3 | 3 | 5 | SEALED WITH A KISS — Brian Hyland, ABC-Paramount 10336 | 10 |
| 8 | 13 | 15 | 23 | YOU'LL LOSE A GOOD THING — Barbara Lynn, Jamie 1220 | 9 |
| 9 | 16 | 24 | 34 | THINGS — Bobby Darin, Atco 6229 | 6 |
| 10 | 9 | 5 | 4 | THE STRIPPER — David Rose & His Ork, MGM 13064 | 14 |
| 11 | 27 | 56 | — | YOU DON'T KNOW ME — Ray Charles, ABC-Paramount 10345 | 3 |
| 12 | 11 | 7 | 6 | WOLVERTON MOUNTAIN — Claude King, Columbia 42352 | 12 |
| 13 | 19 | 27 | 37 | LITTLE DIANE — Dion, Laurie 3134 | 6 |
| 14 | 17 | 18 | 19 | (GIRLS, GIRLS, GIRLS) MADE TO LOVE — Eddie Hodges, Cadence 1421 | 8 |
| 15 | 14 | 11 | 7 | JOHNNY GET ANGRY — Joanie Sommers, Warner Bros. 5275 | 12 |
| 16 | 10 | 13 | 18 | THEME FROM DOCTOR KILDARE — Richard Chamberlain, MGM 13075 | 11 |
| 17 | 18 | 19 | 22 | TWIST AND SHOUT — Isley Brothers, Wand 124 | 11 |
| 18 | 21 | 23 | 32 | PARTY LIGHTS — Claudine Clark, Chancellor 1113 | 7 |
| 19 | 7 | 4 | 3 | I CAN'T STOP LOVING YOU — Ray Charles, ABC-Paramount 10330 | 15 |
| 20 | 22 | 26 | 36 | HEART IN HAND — Brenda Lee, Decca 31407 | 6 |
| 21 | 12 | 12 | 15 | DANCING PARTY — Chubby Checker, Parkway 842 | 8 |
| 22 | 20 | 20 | 24 | I NEED YOUR LOVING — Don Gardner and Dee Dee Ford, Fire 508 | 11 |
| 23 | 25 | 34 | 43 | LITTLE RED RENTED ROWBOAT — Joe Dowell, Smash 1759 | 8 |
| 24 | 43 | 73 | — | SHEILA — Tommy Roe, ABC-Paramount 10329 | 3 |
| 25 | 15 | 9 | 9 | GRAVY — Dee Dee Sharp, Cameo 219 | 9 |
| 26 | 57 | — | — | SHE'S NOT YOU — Elvis Presley, RCA Victor 8041 | 2 |
| 27 | 32 | 44 | 49 | BRING IT ON HOME TO ME — Sam Cooke, RCA Victor 8036 | 6 |
| 28 | 42 | 76 | 93 | CALL ME MR. IN-BETWEEN — Burl Ives, Decca 31405 | 4 |
| 29 | 48 | 64 | 70 | A SWINGIN' SAFARI — Billy Vaughn, Dot 16374 | 4 |
| 30 | 31 | 42 | 50 | ROUTE 66 THEME — Nelson Riddle, Capitol 4741 | 11 |
| 31 | 37 | 35 | 40 | HAVE A GOOD TIME — Sue Thompson, Hickory 1174 | 9 |
| 32 | 54 | 78 | — | VACATION — Connie Francis, MGM 13087 | 3 |
| 33 | 46 | 52 | 66 | WHAT'S A MATTER BABY — Timi Yuro, Liberty 55469 | 5 |
| 34 | 44 | 60 | 76 | RINKY DINK — Dave (Baby) Cortez, Chess 1829 | 5 |
| 35 | 24 | 17 | 11 | AL DI LA' — Emilio Pericoli, Warner Bros. 5259 | 13 |
| 36 | 45 | 55 | 63 | THE BALLAD OF PALADIN — Duane Eddy, RCA Victor 8047 | 6 |
| 37 | 26 | 21 | 17 | HAVING A PARTY — Sam Cooke, RCA Victor 8036 | 11 |
| 38 | 33 | 29 | 31 | IT STARTED ALL OVER AGAIN — Brenda Lee, Decca 31407 | 7 |
| 39 | 23 | 16 | 10 | PALISADES PARK — Freddy Cannon, Swan 4106 | 14 |
| 40 | 28 | 22 | 28 | WELCOME HOME BABY — Shirelles, Scepter 1234 | 8 |
| 41 | 29 | 25 | 16 | I'LL NEVER DANCE AGAIN — Bobby Rydell, Cameo 217 | 11 |
| 42 | 52 | 68 | 75 | MAKE IT EASY ON YOURSELF — Jerry Butler, Vee Jay 451 | 5 |
| 43 | 39 | 47 | 55 | MARY'S LITTLE LAMB — James Darren, Colpix 644 | 7 |
| 44 | 51 | 59 | 69 | BEN CRAZY — Dickie Goodman & Dr. I. M. Ill, Diamond 119 | 5 |
| 45 | 35 | 33 | 42 | BONGO STOMP — Little Joey & the Flips, Joy 262 | 9 |
| 46 | 38 | 45 | 52 | SUMMERTIME, SUMMERTIME — Jamies, Epic 9281 | 9 |
| 47 | 30 | 28 | 14 | IT KEEPS RIGHT ON A-HURTIN' — Johnny Tillotson, Cadence 1418 | 14 |
| 48 | 41 | 43 | 46 | STEEL MEN — Jimmy Dean, Columbia 42483 | 8 |
| 49 | 70 | 86 | — | DEVIL WOMAN — Marty Robbins, Columbia 42486 | 3 |
| 50 | 71 | 93 | 96 | TILL DEATH DO US PART — Bob Braun, Decca 31355 | 4 |
| 51 | 59 | 72 | 83 | SHAME ON ME — Bobby Bare, RCA Victor 8032 | 4 |
| 52 | 40 | 36 | 25 | PLAYBOY — Marvelettes, Tamla 54060 | 15 |
| 53 | 34 | 30 | 21 | JOHNNY LOVES ME — Shelley Fabares, Colpix 636 | 10 |
| 54 | 66 | 84 | — | ALLEY CAT — Bent Fabric, Atco 6226 | 3 |
| 55 | 60 | 50 | 48 | LIMBO ROCK — Champs, Challenge 9131 | 12 |
| 56 | 50 | 57 | 59 | BABY ELEPHANT WALK — Lawrence Welk, Dot 16364 | 10 |
| 57 | 82 | — | — | POINT OF NO RETURN — Gene McDaniels, Liberty 55480 | 2 |
| 58 | 61 | 67 | 82 | A TASTE OF HONEY — Martin Denny, Liberty 55470 | 5 |
| 59 | 56 | 58 | 62 | NEVER IN A MILLION YEARS — Linda Scott, Congress 103 | 9 |
| 60 | 75 | 88 | — | CARELESS LOVE — Ray Charles, ABC-Paramount 10345 | 3 |
| 61 | 69 | 82 | 86 | ABOVE THE STARS — Mr. Acker Bilk, Atco 6230 | 5 |
| 62 | 80 | 90 | — | STOP THE WEDDING — Etta James, Argo 5418 | 3 |
| 63 | 91 | — | — | RAMBLIN' ROSE — Nat King Cole, Capitol 4804 | 2 |
| 64 | 72 | 81 | 84 | THE BIRD MAN — Highwaymen, United Artists 475 | 5 |
| 65 | 99 | — | — | LOVE ME AS I LOVE YOU — George Maharis, Epic 9522 | 2 |
| 66 | 78 | 80 | 91 | BEACH PARTY — King Curtis, Capitol 4788 | 4 |
| 67 | 79 | — | — | MR. SONGWRITER — Connie Stevens, Warner Bros. 5289 | 2 |
| 68 | 93 | — | — | YOU BELONG TO ME — Duprees, Coed 569 | 2 |
| 69 | — | — | — | YOUR NOSE IS GONNA GROW — Johnny Crawford, Del-Fi 4181 | 1 |
| 70 | — | — | — | SEND ME THE PILLOW YOU DREAM ON — Johnny Tillotson, Cadence 1424 | 1 |
| 71 | 86 | 89 | 94 | COME ON LITTLE ANGEL — Belmonts, Sabina 505 | 4 |
| 72 | — | — | — | DON'T WORRY 'BOUT ME — Vince Edwards, Decca 31413 | 1 |
| 73 | — | — | — | YOU BEAT ME TO THE PUNCH — Mary Wells, Motown 1032 | 1 |
| 74 | 76 | 83 | 78 | WORRIED MIND — Ray Anthony, Capitol 4742 | 7 |
| 75 | 81 | 87 | 90 | A MIRACLE — Frankie Avalon, Chancellor 1115 | 5 |
| 76 | — | — | — | TEEN AGE IDOL — Rick Nelson, Imperial 5864 | 1 |
| 77 | 74 | 74 | 68 | WHY DID YOU LEAVE ME! — Vince Edwards, Russ-Fi 7001 | 6 |
| 78 | — | — | — | I LOVE YOU THE WAY YOU ARE — Bobby Vinton, Diamond 212 | 1 |
| 79 | — | — | — | BEECHWOOD 4-5789 — Marvelettes, Tamla 54065 | 1 |
| 80 | — | — | — | JUST TELL HER JIM SAID HELLO — Elvis Presley, RCA Victor 8041 | 1 |
| 81 | 87 | — | — | LOLITA YA-YA — Ventures, Dolton 60 | 2 |
| 82 | 94 | — | — | SILVER THREADS & GOLDEN NEEDLES — Springfields, Philips 40038 | 2 |
| 83 | 88 | 91 | — | CALLIN' DOCTOR CASEY — John D. Loudermilk, RCA Victor 8054 | 3 |
| 84 | 90 | — | — | THEME FROM A SUMMER PLACE — Dick Roman, Harmon 1004 | 2 |
| 85 | — | — | — | SURFIN' SAFARI — Beach Boys, Capitol 4777 | 1 |
| 86 | — | — | — | WONDERFUL DREAM — Majors, Imperial 5855 | 1 |
| 87 | — | — | — | I LEFT MY HEART IN SAN FRANCISCO — Tony Bennett, Columbia 42332 | 1 |
| 88 | 89 | — | — | BOYS' NIGHT OUT — Patti Page, Mercury 72013 | 2 |
| 89 | — | — | — | TOO BAD — Ben E. King, Atco 6231 | 1 |
| 90 | — | — | — | GREEN ONIONS — Booker T & the MG's, Stax 127 | 1 |
| 91 | 84 | — | — | RIGHT STRING BUT THE WRONG YO-YO — Dr. Feelgood & the Interns, Okeh 7156 | 2 |
| 92 | 96 | — | — | POOR LITTLE PUPPET — Cathy Carroll, Warner Bros. 5284 | 2 |
| 93 | — | 99 | — | JIVIN' AROUND — Al Casey Combo, Stacy 936 | 2 |
| 94 | — | — | — | YIELD NOT TO TEMPTATION — Bobby Bland, Duke 352 | 1 |
| 95 | 97 | — | — | SUGAR PLUM — Ike Clanton, Mercury 71975 | 2 |
| 96 | — | — | — | YOUR HEART BELONGS TO ME — Supremes, Motown 1027 | 1 |
| 97 | — | — | — | HULLY GULLY BABY — Dovells, Parkway 845 | 1 |
| 98 | — | — | — | SO WHAT — Bill Black's Combo, Hi 2055 | 1 |
| 99 | — | — | — | GLORY OF LOVE — Don Gardner & Dee Dee Ford, KC 106 | 1 |
| 100 | — | — | — | DO YOU LOVE ME — Contours, Gordy 7005 | 1 |

## BUBBLING UNDER THE HOT 100

101. SO WRONG — Patsy Cline, Decca 31406
102. HOUDINI — Walter Brennan, Liberty 54477
103. A LITTLE HEARTACHE — Eddy Arnold, RCA Victor 8048
104. TOO LATE TO WORRY—TOO BLUE TO CRY — Glen Campbell, Capitol 4783
105. I WANNA BE LOVED — Dinah Washington, Mercury 72051
106. OH! WHAT IT SEEMS TO BE — Castells, Era 3083
107. LIMBO — Caprices, Mr. Peacock 118
108. BEACH PARTY — Dave York, PKM 6700
109. I'M TOSSIN' & TURIN' AGAIN — Bobby Lewis, Beltone 2023
110. SILLY BOY — Lettermen, Capitol 4810
111. THIS IS IT — Jay and the Americans, Ace 8001
112. VENUS IN BLUE JEANS — Jimmy Clanton, Ace 8001
113. BROKEN HEART — Fiestas, Old Town 1122
114. A TASTE OF HONEY — Victor Feldman Quartet, Infinity 020
115. LOOKIN' FOR A LOVE — Valentinos, Sar 132
116. BIGGEST SIN OF ALL — Connie Francis, MGM 13087
117. SEND FOR ME — Barbara George, Sue 766
118. COME BACK INTO MY HEART — Volumes, Chex 1005
119. WOBBLE TWIST — King Curtis, Enjoy 2001
120. WHO'S GONNA PICK UP THE PIECES — Chuck Jackson, Wand 126

# BILLBOARD HOT 100

**FOR WEEK ENDING AUGUST 18, 1962**

| This Week | Wk Ago | 2 Wks Ago | 3 Wks Ago | TITLE — Artist, Label & Number | Weeks On Chart |
|---|---|---|---|---|---|
| 1 | 1 | 2 | 8 | BREAKING UP IS HARD TO DO — Neil Sedaka, RCA Victor 8046 | 8 |
| 2 | 4 | 8 | 14 | LOCO-MOTION — Little Eva, Dimension 1000 | 8 |
| 3 | 2 | 1 | 1 | ROSES ARE RED — Bobby Vinton, Epic 9509 | 11 |
| 4 | 3 | 4 | 2 | THE WAH-WATUSI — Orlons, Cameo 218 | 11 |
| 5 | 11 | 27 | 56 | YOU DON'T KNOW ME — Ray Charles, ABC-Paramount 10345 | 4 |
| 6 | 9 | 16 | 24 | THINGS — Bobby Darin, Atco 6229 | 7 |
| 7 | 5 | 5 | 10 | AHAB THE ARAB — Ray Stevens, Mercury 71966 | 8 |
| 8 | 13 | 19 | 27 | LITTLE DIANE — Dion, Laurie 3134 | 7 |
| 9 | 6 | 6 | 6 | SPEEDY GONZALES — Pat Boone, Dot 16368 | 10 |
| 10 | 7 | 3 | 3 | SEALED WITH A KISS — Brian Hyland, ABC-Paramount 10336 | 11 |
| 11 | 18 | 21 | 23 | PARTY LIGHTS — Claudine Clark, Chancellor 1113 | 8 |
| 12 | 24 | 43 | 73 | SHEILA — Tommy Roe, ABC-Paramount 10329 | 4 |
| 13 | 26 | 57 | — | SHE'S NOT YOU — Elvis Presley, RCA Victor 8041 | 3 |
| 14 | 8 | 13 | 15 | YOU'LL LOSE A GOOD THING — Barbara Lynn, Jamie 1220 | 10 |
| 15 | 10 | 9 | 5 | THE STRIPPER — David Rose & His Ork, MGM 13064 | 15 |
| 16 | 12 | 11 | 7 | WOLVERTON MOUNTAIN — Claude King, Columbia 42352 | 13 |
| 17 | 32 | 54 | 78 | VACATION — Connie Francis, MGM 13087 | 4 |
| 18 | 20 | 22 | 26 | HEART IN HAND — Brenda Lee, Decca 31407 | 7 |
| 19 | 17 | 18 | 19 | TWIST AND SHOUT — Isley Brothers, Wand 124 | 12 |
| 20 | 14 | 17 | 18 | (GIRLS, GIRLS, GIRLS) MADE TO LOVE — Eddie Hodges, Cadence 1421 | 9 |
| 21 | 27 | 32 | 44 | BRING IT ON HOME TO ME — Sam Cooke, RCA Victor 8036 | 7 |
| 22 | 28 | 42 | 76 | CALL ME MR. IN-BETWEEN — Burl Ives, Decca 31405 | 5 |
| 23 | 33 | 46 | 52 | WHAT'S A MATTER BABY — Timi Yuro, Liberty 55469 | 6 |
| 24 | 15 | 14 | 11 | JOHNNY GET ANGRY — Joanie Sommers, Warner Bros. 5275 | 13 |
| 25 | 29 | 48 | 64 | A SWINGIN' SAFARI — Billy Vaughn, Dot 16374 | 5 |
| 26 | 16 | 10 | 13 | THEME FROM DOCTOR KILDARE — Richard Chamberlain, MGM 13075 | 12 |
| 27 | 34 | 44 | 60 | RINKY DINK — Dave (Baby) Cortez, Chess 1829 | 6 |
| 28 | 22 | 20 | 20 | I NEED YOUR LOVING — Don Gardner and Dee Dee Ford, Fire 508 | 12 |
| 29 | 19 | 7 | 4 | I CAN'T STOP LOVING YOU — Ray Charles, ABC-Paramount 10330 | 16 |
| 30 | 21 | 12 | 12 | DANCING PARTY — Chubby Checker, Parkway 842 | 9 |
| 31 | 42 | 52 | 68 | MAKE IT EASY ON YOURSELF — Jerry Butler, Vee Jay 451 | 6 |
| 32 | 30 | 31 | 42 | ROUTE 66 THEME — Nelson Riddle, Capitol 4741 | 12 |
| 33 | 49 | 70 | 86 | DEVIL WOMAN — Marty Robbins, Columbia 42486 | 4 |
| 34 | 63 | 91 | — | RAMBLIN' ROSE — Nat King Cole, Capitol 4804 | 3 |
| 35 | 36 | 45 | 55 | THE BALLAD OF PALADIN — Duane Eddy, RCA Victor 8047 | 7 |
| 36 | 23 | 25 | 34 | LITTLE RED RENTED ROWBOAT — Joe Dowell, Smash 1759 | 9 |
| 37 | 51 | 59 | 72 | SHAME ON ME — Bobby Bare, RCA Victor 8032 | 5 |
| 38 | 31 | 37 | 35 | HAVE A GOOD TIME — Sue Thompson, Hickory 1174 | 10 |
| 39 | 50 | 71 | 93 | TILL DEATH DO US PART — Bob Braun, Decca 31355 | 5 |
| 40 | 25 | 15 | 9 | GRAVY — Dee Dee Sharp, Cameo 219 | 10 |
| 41 | 68 | 93 | — | YOU BELONG TO ME — Duprees, Coed 569 | 3 |
| 42 | 54 | 66 | 84 | ALLEY CAT — Bent Fabric, Atco 6226 | 4 |
| 43 | 38 | 33 | 29 | IT STARTED ALL OVER AGAIN — Brenda Lee, Decca 31407 | 8 |
| 44 | 69 | — | — | YOUR NOSE IS GONNA GROW — Johnny Crawford, Del-Fi 4181 | 2 |
| 45 | 37 | 26 | 21 | HAVING A PARTY — Sam Cooke, RCA Victor 8036 | 12 |
| 46 | 57 | 82 | — | POINT OF NO RETURN — Gene McDaniels, Liberty 55480 | 3 |
| 47 | 35 | 24 | 17 | AL DI LA' — Emilio Pericoli, Warner Bros. 5259 | 14 |
| 48 | 70 | — | — | SEND ME THE PILLOW YOU DREAM ON — Johnny Tillotson, Cadence 1424 | 2 |
| 49 | 39 | 23 | 16 | PALISADES PARK — Freddy Cannon, Swan 4106 | 15 |
| 50 | 45 | 35 | 33 | BONGO STOMP — Little Joey & the Flips, Joy 262 | 10 |
| 51 | 71 | 86 | 89 | COME ON LITTLE ANGEL — Belmonts, Sabina 505 | 5 |
| 52 | 56 | 50 | 57 | BABY ELEPHANT WALK — Lawrence Welk, Dot 16364 | 11 |
| 53 | 55 | 60 | 50 | LIMBO ROCK — Champs, Challenge 9131 | 13 |
| 54 | 76 | — | — | TEEN AGE IDOL — Rick Nelson, Imperial 5864 | 2 |
| 55 | 62 | 80 | 90 | STOP THE WEDDING — Etta James, Argo 5418 | 4 |
| 56 | 58 | 61 | 67 | A TASTE OF HONEY — Martin Denny, Liberty 55470 | 6 |
| 57 | 44 | 51 | 59 | BEN CRAZY — Dickie Goodman & Dr. I. M. Ill, Diamond 119 | 6 |
| 58 | 73 | — | — | YOU BEAT ME TO THE PUNCH — Mary Wells, Motown 1032 | 2 |
| 59 | 61 | 69 | 82 | ABOVE THE STARS — Mr. Acker Bilk, Atco 6230 | 6 |
| 60 | 65 | 99 | — | LOVE ME AS I LOVE YOU — George Maharis, Epic 9522 | 3 |
| 61 | 67 | 79 | — | MR. SONGWRITER — Connie Stevens, Warner Bros. 5289 | 3 |
| 62 | 41 | 29 | 25 | I'LL NEVER DANCE AGAIN — Bobby Rydell, Cameo 217 | 12 |
| 63 | 66 | 78 | 80 | BEACH PARTY — King Curtis, Capitol 4788 | 5 |
| 64 | 79 | — | — | BEECHWOOD 4-5789 — Marvelettes, Tamla 54065 | 2 |
| 65 | 90 | — | — | GREEN ONIONS — Booker T & the MG's, Stax 127 | 2 |
| 66 | 82 | 94 | — | SILVER THREADS & GOLDEN NEEDLES — Springfields, Philips 40038 | 3 |
| 67 | 43 | 39 | 47 | MARY'S LITTLE LAMB — James Darren, Colpix 644 | 8 |
| 68 | 78 | — | — | I LOVE YOU THE WAY YOU ARE — Bobby Vinton, Diamond 121 | 2 |
| 69 | 64 | 72 | 81 | THE BIRD MAN — Highwaymen, United Artists 475 | 6 |
| 70 | 80 | — | — | JUST TELL HER JIM SAID HELLO — Elvis Presley, RCA Victor 8041 | 2 |
| 71 | 81 | 87 | — | LOLITA YA-YA — Ventures, Dolton 60 | 3 |
| 72 | 87 | — | — | I LEFT MY HEART IN SAN FRANCISCO — Tony Bennett, Columbia 42332 | 2 |
| 73 | 84 | 90 | — | THEME FROM A SUMMER PLACE — Dick Roman, Harmon 1004 | 3 |
| 74 | — | — | — | VENUS IN BLUE JEANS — Jimmy Clanton, Ace 8001 | 1 |
| 75 | 86 | — | — | WONDERFUL DREAM — Majors, Imperial 5855 | 2 |
| 76 | — | — | — | I'M THE GIRL FROM WOLVERTON MOUNTAIN — Jo Ann Campbell, Cameo 223 | 1 |
| 77 | 88 | 89 | — | BOYS' NIGHT OUT — Patti Page, Mercury 72013 | 3 |
| 78 | — | 83 | — | LET'S DANCE — Chris Montez, Monogram 505 | 2 |
| 79 | 85 | — | — | SURFIN' SAFARI — Beach Boys, Capitol 4777 | 2 |
| 80 | 75 | 81 | 87 | A MIRACLE — Frankie Avalon, Chancellor 1115 | 6 |
| 81 | 60 | 75 | 88 | CARELESS LOVE — Ray Charles, ABC-Paramount 10345 | 4 |
| 82 | 94 | — | — | YIELD NOT TO TEMPTATION — Bobby Bland, Duke 352 | 2 |
| 83 | 93 | — | 99 | JIVIN' AROUND — Al Casey Combo, Stacy 936 | 3 |
| 84 | 91 | 84 | — | RIGHT STRING BUT THE WRONG YO-YO — Dr. Feelgood & the Interns, Okeh 7156 | 3 |
| 85 | — | — | — | PAPA-OOM-MOW-MOW — Rivingtons, Liberty 55427 | 1 |
| 86 | 74 | 76 | 83 | WORRIED MIND — Ray Anthony, Capitol 4742 | 8 |
| 87 | — | — | — | I WANNA BE LOVED — Dinah Washington, Mercury 72015 | 1 |
| 88 | 89 | — | — | TOO BAD — Ben E. King, Atco 6231 | 2 |
| 89 | — | — | — | YOU CAN'T JUDGE A BOOK BY THE COVER — Bo Diddley, Checker 1019 | 1 |
| 90 | — | — | — | IF I HAD A HAMMER — Peter, Paul & Mary, Warner Bros. 5296 | 1 |
| 91 | 92 | 96 | — | POOR LITTLE PUPPET — Cathy Carroll, Warner Bros. 5284 | 3 |
| 92 | 97 | — | — | HULLY GULLY BABY — Dovells, Parkway 845 | 2 |
| 93 | 72 | — | — | DON'T WORRY 'BOUT ME — Vince Edwards, Decca 31413 | 2 |
| 94 | 100 | — | — | DO YOU LOVE ME — Contours, Gordy 7005 | 2 |
| 95 | 96 | — | — | YOUR HEART BELONGS TO ME — Supremes, Motown 1027 | 2 |
| 96 | 98 | — | — | SO WHAT — Bill Black's Combo, Hi 2055 | 2 |
| 97 | — | — | — | SILLY BOY — Lettermen, Capitol 4810 | 1 |
| 98 | — | — | — | LOOKIN' FOR A LOVE — Valentinos, Sar 132 | 1 |
| 99 | — | — | — | LIMBO — Caprices, Mr. Peeke 118 | 1 |
| 100 | — | — | — | SWEET GEORGIA BROWN — Carroll Brothers, Cameo 221 | 1 |

## BUBBLING UNDER THE HOT 100

101. BEACH PARTY — Dave York, PKM 6700
102. TOO LATE TO WORRY—TOO BLUE TO CRY — Glen Campbell, Capitol 4783
103. OH! WHAT IT SEEMED TO BE — Castells, Era 3063
104. THEME FROM HATARI — Henry Mancini, RCA Victor 8037
105. SO WRONG — Patsy Cline, Decca 31406
106. GLORY OF LOVE — Don Gardner and Dee Dee Ford, KC 16
107. HOUDINI — Walter Brennan, Liberty 55477
108. EVERY NIGHT (Without You) — Paul Anka, RCA Victor 8068
109. THIS IS IT — Jay and the Americans, United Artists 479
110. PATCHES — Dickey Dee, Smash 1758
111. A TASTE OF HONEY — Victor Feldman Quartet, Infinity 020
112. FOR ALL WE KNOW — Dinah Washington, Roulette 4444
113. DON'T BREAK THE HEART THAT LOVES YOU — Bernie Leighton, Colpix 645
114. I'M COMIN' HOME — Paul Anka, ABC-Paramount 10338
115. WHAT KIND OF LOVE IS THIS — Joey Dee & the Starliters, Roulette 4438
116. SOFTLY AS I LEAVE YOU — Matt Monro, Liberty 55440
117. MAMA, HE TREATS YOUR DAUGHTER MEAN — Ruth Brown, Philips 24619
118. COMIN' HOME BABY — Herbie Mann, Atlantis 5020
119. IT MIGHT AS WELL RAIN UNTIL SEPTEMBER — Carol King, Dimension 2000
*120. WITH THE TOUCH OF YOUR HAND — Brook Benton, Mercury 72024
*120. NO ONE WILL EVER KNOW — Jimmy Rodgers, Dot 16378

*Tie at 120

# BILLBOARD HOT 100

FOR WEEK ENDING AUGUST 25

1962

★ STAR PERFORMERS—Selections registering greatest upward progress this week.

S Indicates that 45 r.p.m. stereo single version is available.

△ Indicates that 33⅓ r.p.m. mono single version is available.

△S Indicates that 33⅓ r.p.m. stereo single version is available.

| This Week | 1 Wk. Ago | 2 Wks. Ago | 3 Wks. Ago | Title | Artist, Label & Number | | Weeks On Chart |
|---|---|---|---|---|---|---|---|
| 1 | 2 | 4 | 8 | LOCO-MOTION | Little Eva, Dimension 1000 | | 9 |
| 2 | 1 | 1 | 2 | BREAKING UP IS HARD TO DO | Neil Sedaka, RCA Victor 8046 | △ | 9 |
| 3 | 6 | 9 | 16 | THINGS | Bobby Darin, Atco 6229 | | 8 |
| 4 | 5 | 11 | 27 | YOU DON'T KNOW ME | Ray Charles, ABC-Paramount 10345 | | 5 |
| ★5 | 12 | 24 | 43 | SHEILA | Tommy Roe, ABC-Paramount 10329 | | 5 |
| 6 | 3 | 2 | 1 | ROSES ARE RED | Bobby Vinton, Epic 9509 | | 12 |
| 7 | 11 | 18 | 21 | PARTY LIGHTS | Claudine Clark, Chancellor 1113 | | 9 |
| ★8 | 13 | 26 | 57 | SHE'S NOT YOU | Elvis Presley, RCA Victor 8041 | △ | 4 |
| 9 | 7 | 5 | 5 | AHAB THE ARAB | Ray Stevens, Mercury 71966 | | 9 |
| 10 | 8 | 13 | 19 | LITTLE DIANE | Dion, Laurie 3134 | | 8 |
| 11 | 4 | 3 | 4 | THE WAH-WATUSI | Orlons, Cameo 218 | | 12 |
| ★12 | 17 | 32 | 54 | VACATION | Connie Francis, MGM 13087 | | 5 |
| ★13 | 21 | 27 | 32 | BRING IT ON HOME TO ME | Sam Cooke, RCA Victor 8036 | △ | 8 |
| 14 | 14 | 8 | 13 | YOU'LL LOSE A GOOD THING | Barbara Lynn, Jamie 1220 | | 11 |
| 15 | 18 | 20 | 22 | HEART IN HAND | Brenda Lee, Decca 31407 | | 8 |
| 16 | 16 | 12 | 11 | WOLVERTON MOUNTAIN | Claude King, Columbia 42352 | △ | 14 |
| 17 | 10 | 7 | 3 | SEALED WITH A KISS | Brian Hyland, ABC-Paramount 10336 | | 12 |
| ★18 | 23 | 33 | 46 | WHAT'S A MATTER BABY | Timi Yuro, Liberty 55469 | | 7 |
| 19 | 22 | 28 | 42 | CALL ME MR. IN-BETWEEN | Burl Ives, Decca 31405 | | 6 |
| 20 | 9 | 6 | 6 | SPEEDY GONZALES | Pat Boone, Dot 16368 | | 11 |
| 21 | 25 | 29 | 48 | A SWINGIN' SAFARI | Billy Vaughn, Dot 16374 | | 6 |
| ★22 | 34 | 63 | 91 | RAMBLIN' ROSE | Nat King Cole, Capitol 4804 | | 4 |
| ★23 | 33 | 49 | 70 | DEVIL WOMAN | Marty Robbins, Columbia 42486 | △ | 5 |
| 24 | 27 | 34 | 44 | RINKY DINK | Dave (Baby) Cortez, Chess 1829 | | 7 |
| 25 | 31 | 42 | 52 | MAKE IT EASY ON YOURSELF | Jerry Butler, Vee Jay 451 | | 7 |
| 26 | 19 | 17 | 18 | TWIST AND SHOUT | Isley Brothers, Wand 124 | | 13 |
| 27 | 15 | 10 | 9 | THE STRIPPER | David Rose & His Ork, MGM 13064 | | 16 |
| 28 | 20 | 14 | 17 | (GIRLS, GIRLS, GIRLS) MADE TO LOVE | Eddie Hodges, Cadence 1421 | | 10 |
| 29 | 26 | 16 | 10 | THEME FROM DOCTOR KILDARE | Richard Chamberlain, MGM 13075 | | 13 |
| ★30 | 44 | 69 | — | YOUR NOSE IS GONNA GROW | Johnny Crawford, Del-Fi 4181 | | 3 |
| ★31 | 41 | 68 | 93 | YOU BELONG TO ME | Duprees, Coed 569 | | 4 |
| 32 | 39 | 50 | 71 | TILL DEATH DO US PART | Bob Braun, Decca 31355 | | 6 |
| 33 | 35 | 36 | 45 | THE BALLAD OF PALADIN | Duane Eddy, RCA Victor 8047 | △ | 8 |
| 34 | 37 | 51 | 59 | SHAME ON ME | Bobby Bare, RCA Victor 8032 | △ | 6 |
| ★35 | 54 | 76 | — | TEEN AGE IDOL | Rick Nelson, Imperial 5864 | | 3 |
| 36 | 42 | 54 | 66 | ALLEY CAT | Bent Fabric, Atco 6226 | | 5 |
| ★37 | 48 | 70 | — | SEND ME THE PILLOW YOU DREAM ON | Johnny Tillotson, Cadence 1424 | | 3 |
| 38 | 24 | 15 | 14 | JOHNNY GET ANGRY | Joanie Sommers, Warner Bros. 5275 | | 14 |
| ★39 | 58 | 73 | — | YOU BEAT ME TO THE PUNCH | Mary Wells, Motown 1032 | | 3 |
| ★40 | 51 | 71 | 86 | COME ON LITTLE ANGEL | Belmonts, Sabina 505 | | 6 |
| 41 | 29 | 19 | 7 | I CAN'T STOP LOVING YOU | Ray Charles, ABC-Paramount 10330 | | 17 |
| 42 | 46 | 57 | 82 | POINT OF NO RETURN | Gene McDaniels, Liberty 55480 | | 4 |
| 43 | 30 | 21 | 12 | DANCING PARTY | Chubby Checker, Parkway 842 | | 10 |
| ★44 | 55 | 62 | 80 | STOP THE WEDDING | Etta James, Argo 5418 | | 5 |
| 45 | 28 | 22 | 20 | I NEED YOUR LOVING | Don Gardner and Dee Dee Ford, Fire 508 | | 13 |
| 46 | 45 | 37 | 26 | HAVING A PARTY | Sam Cooke, RCA Victor 8036 | △ | 13 |
| ★47 | 74 | — | — | VENUS IN BLUE JEANS | Jimmy Clanton, Ace 8001 | | 2 |
| ★48 | 65 | 90 | — | GREEN ONIONS | Booker T & the MG's, Stax 127 | | 3 |
| ★49 | 64 | 79 | — | BEECHWOOD 4-5789 | Marvelettes, Tamla 54065 | | 3 |
| ★50 | 66 | 82 | 94 | SILVER THREADS & GOLDEN NEEDLES | Springfields, Philips 40038 | | 4 |
| 51 | 52 | 56 | 50 | BABY ELEPHANT WALK | Lawrence Welk, Dot 16364 | | 12 |
| ★52 | 75 | 86 | — | WONDERFUL DREAM | Majors, Imperial 5855 | | 3 |
| 53 | 56 | 58 | 61 | A TASTE OF HONEY | Martin Denny, Liberty 55470 | | 7 |
| 54 | 60 | 65 | 99 | LOVE ME AS I LOVE YOU | George Maharis, Epic 9522 | | 4 |
| ★55 | 78 | — | 83 | LET'S DANCE | Chris Montez, Monogram 505 | | 3 |
| 56 | 61 | 67 | 79 | MR. SONGWRITER | Connie Stevens, Warner Bros. 5289 | | 4 |
| 57 | 38 | 31 | 37 | HAVE A GOOD TIME | Sue Thompson, Hickory 1174 | | 11 |
| ★58 | 76 | — | — | I'M THE GIRL FROM WOLVERTON MOUNTAIN | Jo Ann Campbell, Cameo 223 | | 2 |
| ★59 | 90 | — | — | IF I HAD A HAMMER | Peter, Paul & Mary, Warner Bros. 5296 | | 2 |
| 60 | 63 | 66 | 78 | BEACH PARTY | King Curtis, Capitol 4788 | | 6 |
| ★61 | — | — | — | PATCHES | Dickey Lee, Smash 1758 | | 1 |
| ★62 | 79 | 85 | — | SURFIN' SAFARI | Beach Boys, Capitol 4777 | | 3 |
| 63 | 77 | 88 | 89 | BOYS' NIGHT OUT | Patti Page, Mercury 72013 | | 4 |
| ★64 | 68 | 78 | — | I LOVE YOU THE WAY YOU ARE | Bobby Vinton, Diamond 121 | | 3 |
| ★65 | — | — | — | SHERRY | Four Seasons, Vee Jay 456 | | 1 |
| ★66 | 70 | 80 | — | JUST TELL HER JIM SAID HELLO | Elvis Presley, RCA Victor 8041 | △ | 3 |
| 67 | 71 | 81 | 87 | LOLITA YA-YA | Ventures, Dolton 60 | | 4 |
| 68 | 73 | 84 | 90 | THEME FROM A SUMMER PLACE | Dick Roman, Harmon 1004 | | 4 |
| ★69 | — | — | — | LIE TO ME | Brook Benton, Mercury 72024 | | 1 |
| 70 | 92 | 97 | — | HULLY GULLY BABY | Dovells, Parkway 845 | | 3 |
| ★71 | — | — | — | WHAT KIND OF LOVE IS THIS | Joey Dee and the Starlighters, Roulette 4438 | | 1 |
| ★72 | 89 | — | — | YOU CAN'T JUDGE A BOOK BY THE COVER | Bo Diddley, Checker 1019 | | 2 |
| 73 | 72 | 87 | — | I LEFT MY HEART IN SAN FRANCISCO | Tony Bennett, Columbia 42332 | △ | 3 |
| 74 | 85 | — | — | PAPA-OOM-MOW-MOW | Rivingtons, Liberty 55427 | | 2 |
| 75 | 83 | 93 | — | JIVIN' AROUND | Al Casey Combo, Stacy 936 | | 4 |
| 76 | 87 | — | — | I WANNA BE LOVED | Dinah Washington, Mercury 72015 | | 2 |
| ★77 | — | — | — | TOO LATE TO WORRY—TOO BLUE TO CRY | Glen Campbell, Capitol 4783 | | 1 |
| 78 | 82 | 94 | — | YIELD NOT TO TEMPTATION | Bobby Bland, Duke 352 | | 3 |
| ★79 | — | — | — | REAP WHAT YOU SOW | Billy Stewart, Chess 1820 | | 3 |
| ★80 | — | — | — | EVERY NIGHT (WITHOUT YOU) | Paul Anka, RCA Victor 8068 | △ | 1 |
| ★81 | — | 99 | — | GLORY OF LOVE | Don Gardner and Dee Dee Ford, KC 106 | | 2 |
| 82 | 94 | 100 | — | DO YOU LOVE ME | Contours, Gordy 7005 | | 3 |
| ★83 | — | — | — | DON'T YOU WORRY | Don Gardner and Dee Dee Ford, Fire 513 | | 1 |
| 84 | 98 | — | — | LOOKIN' FOR A LOVE | Valentinos, Sar 132 | | 2 |
| ★85 | — | — | — | SO WRONG | Patsy Cline, Decca 31406 | | 1 |
| ★86 | — | — | — | LONG AS THE ROSE IS RED | Florraine Darlin, Epic 9529 | | 1 |
| ★87 | — | — | — | LOLLIPOPS AND ROSES | Paul Petersen, Colpix 649 | | 1 |
| ★88 | — | — | — | FOR ALL WE KNOW | Dinah Washington, Roulette 4444 | | 1 |
| ★89 | — | — | — | RAIN, RAIN, GO AWAY | Bobby Vinton, Epic 9532 | | 1 |
| ★90 | — | — | — | IT MIGHT AS WELL RAIN UNTIL SEPTEMBER | Carole King, Dimension 2000 | | 1 |
| 91 | 96 | 98 | — | SO WHAT | Bill Black's Combo, Hi 2055 | | 3 |
| 92 | 97 | — | — | SILLY BOY | Lettermen, Capitol 4810 | | 2 |
| 93 | — | — | — | OH! WHAT IT SEEMED TO BE | Castells, Era 3083 | | 1 |
| 94 | — | — | — | I'M COMIN' HOME | Paul Anka, ABC-Paramount 10338 | | 1 |
| 95 | — | — | — | BEACH PARTY | Dave York, PKM 6700 | | 1 |
| 96 | — | — | — | COPY CAT | Gary (U.S.) Bonds, LeGrand 1020 | | 1 |
| 97 | — | — | — | BROKEN HEART | Fiestas, Old Town 1122 | | 1 |
| 98 | — | — | — | HIDE AND GO SEEK | Bunker Hill, Mala 451 | | 1 |
| 99 | — | — | — | THERE IS NO GREATER LOVE | Wanderers, MGM 13082 | | 1 |
| 100 | — | — | — | TILL THERE WAS YOU | Valjean, Carlton 576 | | 1 |

## HOT 100—A TO Z—(Publisher-Licensee)

Ahab the Arab (Lowery, BMI) .... 9
Alley Cat (Metorion, BMI) .... 36
Baby Elephant Walk (Famous, ASCAP) .... 51
Ballad of Paladin, The (Time, BMI) .... 33
Beach Party-Curtis (Kilynn, BMI) .... 60
Beach Party-York (Garpax-Cinch, BMI) .... 95
Beechwood 4-5789 (Jobete, BMI) .... 49
Boys' Night Out (Miller, ASCAP) .... 63
Breaking Up Is Hard to Do (Aldon, BMI) .... 2
Bring It on Home to Me (Kags, KMI) .... 13
Broken Heart (Maureen, BMI) .... 97
Call Me Mr. In-Between (Pamper, BMI) .... 19
Come On Little Angel (Glenden, ASCAP) .... 40
Copy Cat (Rock Masters, BMI) .... 95
Dancing Party (Kalmann, ASCAP) .... 43
Devil Woman (Marty's, BMI) .... 23
Do You Love Me (Jobete, BMI) .... 82
Don't You Worry (Fast-Pete, BMI) .... 83
Every Night (Without You) (Spanka, BMI) .... 80
For All We Know (Feist, ASCAP) .... 88
(Girls, Girls, Girls) Made to Love (Acuff-Rose, BMI) 28
Glory of Love (Shapiro-Bernstein, ASCAP) .... 81
Green Onions (East, BMI) .... 48
Have a Good Time (Acuff-Rose, BMI) .... 57
Having a Party (Kags, BMI) .... 46
Heart in Hand (Metric, BMI) .... 15
Hide and Go Seek (Florentine, BMI) .... 98
Hully Gully Baby (Kalmann, ASCAP) .... 70
I Can't Stop Loving You (Acuff-Rose, BMI) .... 41
I Left My Heart in San Francisco (General, ASCAP) .... 73
I Love You the Way You Are (Tobi-Ann, BMI) .... 64
I Need Your Loving (East-Pete, BMI) .... 45
I Wanna Be Loved (Melrose, ASCAP) .... 76
I'm Comin' Home (Spanka, BMI) .... 94
I'm the Girl From Wolverton Mountain (Painted Desert, BMI) .... 58
If I Had a Hammer (Ludlow, BMI) .... 59
It Might as Well Rain Until September (Aldon, BMI) .... 90
Jivin' Around (Reese, BMI) .... 75
Johnny Get Angry (Tod, ASCAP) .... 38
Just Tell Her Jim Said Hello (Presley, BMI) .... 66
Let's Dance (Rondell-Sherman-DeVorzon, BMI) .... 55
Lie to Me (Ben Day, BMI) .... 69
Little Diane (Disal, ASCAP) .... 10
Loco-Motion (Aldon, BMI) .... 1
Lolita Ya-Ya (Chappell, ASCAP) .... 67
Lollipops and Roses (Garland, ASCAP) .... 87
Long as the Rose Is Red (Lyle, ASCAP) .... 86
Lookin' for a Love (Kags, BMI) .... 84
Love Me as I Love You (Marielle, BMI) .... 54
Make It Easy on Yourself (Famous, ASCAP) .... 25
Mr. Songwriter (Gil, BMI) .... 56
Oh! What It Seemed to Be (Joy, ASCAP) .... 93
Papa-Oom-Mow-Mow (Beechwood, BMI) .... 74
Party Lights (Rambed, BMI) .... 7
Patches (Aldon, BMI) .... 61
Point of No Return (Aldon, BMI) .... 42
Rain, Rain, Go Away (Regent, BMI) .... 89
Ramblin' Rose (Comet, ASCAP) .... 22
Reap What You Sow (Arc, BMI) .... 79
Rinky Dink (Arc-Cortez, BMI) .... 24
Roses Are Red (Lyle, ASCAP) .... 6
Sealed With a Kiss (Post, ASCAP) .... 17
Send Me the Pillow You Dream On (Four Star, BMI) .... 37
Shame on Me (Western Hills-Lois-Saran, BMI) .... 34
She's Not You (Presley, BMI) .... 8
Sheila (Eager-Nitetime, BMI) .... 8
Sherry (Bobob, ASCAP) .... 65
Silly Boy (Four Star, BMI) .... 92
Silver Threads & Golden Needles (Central Songs, BMI) .... 50
So What (Jec, BMI) .... 91
So Wrong (Cedarwood, BMI) .... 85
Speedy Gonzales (Budd, ASCAP) .... 20
Stop the Wedding (Figure, BMI) .... 44
Stripper, The (David Rose, ASCAP) .... 27
Surfin' Safari (Guild, BMI) .... 62
Swingin' Safari, A (Roosevelt, BMI) .... 21
Taste of Honey, A (Songfest, ASCAP) .... 53
Teen Age Idol (Nelson, ASCAP) .... 35
Theme From Doctor Kildare (Hastings, BMI) .... 29
Theme From A Summer Place (Witmark, ASCAP) .. 68
There Is No Greater Love (Jones, ASCAP) .... 99
Things (Adaris, BMI) .... 3
Till Death Do Us Part (Karolyn, ASCAP) .... 32
Till There Was You (Frank, ASCAP) .... 100
Too Late to Worry-Too Blue to Cry (American, BMI) .... 77
Twist and Shout (Mellin, BMI) .... 26
Vacation (Merna, BMI) .... 12
Venus in Blue Jeans (Aldon, BMI) .... 47
Wah-Watusi, The (Kalmann-Lowe, ASCAP) .... 11
What Kind of Love Is This (Planetary-Gee, ASCAP) .... 71
What's a Matter Baby (Eden, BMI) .... 18
Wolverton Mountain (Painted Desert, BMI) .... 16
Wonderful Dream (Travis-Rittenhouse, BMI) .... 52
Yield Not to Temptation (Don, BMI) .... 78
You Beat Me to the Punch (Jobete, BMI) .... 39
You Belong to Me (Ridgeway, BMI) .... 31
You Can't Judge a Book By the Cover (Arc, BMI).. 72
You Don't Know Me (Hill & Range, BMI) .... 4
You'll Lose a Good Thing (David-Crazy Cajun-Jamie, BMI) .... 14
Your Nose Is Gonna Grow (Maraville, BMI) .... 30

## BUBBLING UNDER THE HOT 100

101. DON'T WORRY 'BOUT ME ....Vince Edwards, Decca 31413
102. LET THE GOOD TIMES ROLL....Velvets, Monument 464
103. HOUDINI ....Walter Brennan, Liberty 55477
104. YOUR HEART BELONGS TO ME ....Supremes, Motown 1027
105. I'VE GOT MY EYES ON YOU....Rick Nelson, Imperial 5864
106. NO ONE WILL EVER KNOW ....Jimmie Rodgers, Dot 16378
107. I KEEP FORGETTIN' ....Chuck Jackson, Wand 126
108. A TASTE OF HONEY ....Victor Feldman Quartet, Infinity 020
109. THEME FROM HATARI ....Henry Mancini, RCA Victor 8037
110. BONANZA ....Johnny Cash, Columbia 42512
111. WHAT TIME IS IT....Jive Five, Beltone 2024
112. MAMA, HE TREATS YOUR DAUGHTER MEAN ....Ruth Brown, Philips 40056
113. COMIN' HOME BABY ....Herbie Mann, Atlantic 5020
114. I WOULDN'T KNOW ....Dinah Washington, Roulette 4444
115. IF I DIDN'T HAVE A DIME....Gene Pitney, Musicor 1022
116. SEND FOR ME ....Barbara George, Sue 766
*117. I WANNA THANK YOUR FOLKS..Johnny Burnette, Chancellor 1116
*117. FORGIVE ME....Babs Tino, Kapp 472
*119. TORTURE ....Kris Jensen, Hickory 1173
*119. HANDFUL OF MEMORIES....Baby Washington, Sue 767
*119. WHO'S GONNA PICK UP THE PIECES.. Chuck Jackson, Wand 126
*119. ABIGAIL....Embers, Empress 107

*Tie

# BILLBOARD HOT 100

**FOR WEEK ENDING SEPTEMBER 1, 1962**

★ STAR PERFORMERS—Selections registering greatest upward progress this week.
S Indicates that 45 r.p.m. stereo single version is available.
△ Indicates that 33⅓ r.p.m. mono single version is available.
△ Indicates that 33⅓ r.p.m. stereo single version is available.

| This Week | Wk. Ago | 2 Wks. Ago | 3 Wks. Ago | TITLE — Artist, Label & Number | Weeks On Chart |
|---|---|---|---|---|---|
| 1 | 5 | 12 | 24 | SHEILA — Tommy Roe, ABC-Paramount 10329 | 6 |
| 2 | 1 | 2 | 4 | LOCO-MOTION — Little Eva, Dimension 1000 | 10 |
| 3 | 2 | 1 | 1 | BREAKING UP IS HARD TO DO △ — Neil Sedaka, RCA Victor 8046 | 10 |
| 4 | 4 | 5 | 11 | YOU DON'T KNOW ME — Ray Charles, ABC-Paramount 10345 | 6 |
| 5 | 7 | 11 | 18 | PARTY LIGHTS — Claudine Clark, Chancellor 1113 | 10 |
| 6 | 8 | 13 | 26 | SHE'S NOT YOU △ — Elvis Presley, RCA Victor 8041 | 5 |
| 7 | 3 | 6 | 9 | THINGS — Bobby Darin, Atco 6229 | 9 |
| 8 | 6 | 3 | 2 | ROSES ARE RED — Bobby Vinton, Epic 9509 | 13 |
| 9 | 12 | 17 | 32 | VACATION — Connie Francis, MGM 13087 | 6 |
| 10 | 10 | 8 | 13 | LITTLE DIANE — Dion, Laurie 3134 | 9 |
| 11 | 22 | 34 | 63 | RAMBLIN' ROSE — Nat King Cole, Capitol 4804 | 5 |
| 12 | 18 | 23 | 33 | WHAT'S A MATTER BABY — Timi Yuro, Liberty 55469 | 8 |
| 13 | 9 | 7 | 5 | AHAB THE ARAB — Ray Stevens, Mercury 71966 | 10 |
| 14 | 30 | 44 | 69 | YOUR NOSE IS GONNA GROW — Johnny Crawford, Del-Fi 4181 | 4 |
| 15 | 21 | 25 | 29 | A SWINGIN' SAFARI — Billy Vaughn, Dot 16374 | 7 |
| 16 | 24 | 27 | 34 | RINKY DINK — Dave (Baby) Cortez, Chess 1829 | 8 |
| 17 | 35 | 54 | 76 | TEEN AGE IDOL — Rick Nelson, Imperial 5864 | 4 |
| 18 | 23 | 33 | 49 | DEVIL WOMAN △ — Marty Robbins, Columbia 42486 | 6 |
| 19 | 31 | 41 | 68 | YOU BELONG TO ME — Duprees, Coed 569 | 5 |
| 20 | 25 | 31 | 42 | MAKE IT EASY ON YOURSELF — Jerry Butler, Vee Jay 451 | 8 |
| 21 | 17 | 10 | 7 | SEALED WITH A KISS — Brian Hyland, ABC-Paramount 10336 | 13 |
| 22 | 65 | — | — | SHERRY — Four Seasons, Vee Jay 456 | 2 |
| 23 | 19 | 22 | 28 | CALL ME MR. IN-BETWEEN — Burl Ives, Decca 31405 | 7 |
| 24 | 11 | 4 | 3 | THE WAH-WATUSI — Orlons, Cameo 218 | 13 |
| 25 | 37 | 48 | 70 | SEND ME THE PILLOW YOU DREAM ON — Johnny Tillotson, Cadence 1424 | 4 |
| 26 | 32 | 39 | 50 | TILL DEATH DO US PART — Bob Braun, Decca 31355 | 7 |
| 27 | 26 | 19 | 17 | TWIST AND SHOUT — Isley Brothers, Wand 124 | 14 |
| 28 | 14 | 14 | 8 | YOU'LL LOSE A GOOD THING — Barbara Lynn, Jamie 1220 | 12 |
| 29 | 13 | 21 | 27 | BRING IT ON HOME TO ME △ — Sam Cooke, RCA Victor 8036 | 9 |
| 30 | 36 | 42 | 54 | ALLEY CAT — Bent Fabric, Atco 6226 | 6 |
| 31 | 40 | 51 | 71 | COME ON LITTLE ANGEL — Belmonts, Sabina 505 | 7 |
| 32 | 39 | 58 | 73 | YOU BEAT ME TO THE PUNCH — Mary Wells, Motown 1032 | 4 |
| 33 | 34 | 37 | 51 | SHAME ON ME △ — Bobby Bare, RCA Victor 8032 | 7 |
| 34 | 15 | 18 | 20 | HEART IN HAND — Brenda Lee, Decca 31407 | 7 |
| 35 | 20 | 9 | 6 | SPEEDY GONZALES — Pat Boone, Dot 16368 | 12 |
| 36 | 42 | 46 | 57 | POINT OF NO RETURN — Gene McDaniels, Liberty 55480 | 5 |
| 37 | 50 | 66 | 82 | SILVER THREADS & GOLDEN NEEDLES — Springfields, Philips 40038 | 5 |
| 38 | 47 | 74 | — | VENUS IN BLUE JEANS — Jimmy Clanton, Ace 8001 | 3 |
| 39 | 49 | 64 | 79 | BEECHWOOD 4-5789 — Marvelettes, Tamla 54065 | 4 |
| 40 | 48 | 65 | 90 | GREEN ONIONS — Booker T & the MG's, Stax 127 | 4 |
| 41 | 44 | 55 | 62 | STOP THE WEDDING — Etta James, Argo 5418 | 6 |
| 42 | 52 | 75 | 86 | WONDERFUL DREAM — Majors, Imperial 5855 | 4 |
| 43 | 55 | 78 | — | LET'S DANCE — Chris Montez, Monogram 505 | 3 |
| 44 | 16 | 16 | 12 | WOLVERTON MOUNTAIN △ — Claude King, Columbia 42352 | 15 |
| 45 | 61 | — | — | PATCHES — Dickey Lee, Smash 1758 | 2 |
| 46 | 59 | 90 | — | IF I HAD A HAMMER — Peter, Paul & Mary, Warner Bros. 5296 | 3 |
| 47 | 27 | 15 | 10 | THE STRIPPER — David Rose & His Ork, MGM 13064 | 17 |
| 48 | 58 | 76 | — | I'M THE GIRL FROM WOLVERTON MOUNTAIN — Jo Ann Campbell, Cameo 223 | 3 |
| 49 | 51 | 52 | 56 | BABY ELEPHANT WALK — Lawrence Welk, Dot 16364 | 13 |
| 50 | 53 | 56 | 58 | A TASTE OF HONEY — Martin Denny, Liberty 55470 | 8 |
| 51 | 62 | 79 | 85 | SURFIN' SAFARI — Beach Boys, Capitol 4777 | 4 |
| 52 | 64 | 68 | 78 | I LOVE YOU THE WAY YOU ARE — Bobby Vinton, Diamond 121 | 4 |
| 53 | 56 | 61 | 67 | MR. SONGWRITER — Connie Stevens, Warner Bros. 5289 | 5 |
| 54 | 28 | 20 | 14 | (GIRLS, GIRLS, GIRLS) MADE TO LOVE — Eddie Hodges, Cadence 1421 | 11 |
| 55 | 66 | 70 | 80 | JUST TELL HER JIM SAID HELLO △ — Elvis Presley, RCA Victor 8041 | 4 |
| 56 | 69 | — | — | LIE TO ME — Brook Benton, Mercury 72024 | 2 |
| 57 | 71 | — | — | WHAT KIND OF LOVE IS THIS — Joey Dee and the Starlighters, Roulette 4438 | 2 |
| 58 | 63 | 77 | 88 | BOYS' NIGHT OUT — Patti Page, Mercury 72013 | 5 |
| 59 | 74 | 85 | — | PAPA-OOM-MOW-MOW — Rivingtons, Liberty 55427 | 3 |
| 60 | 70 | 92 | 97 | HULLY GULLY BABY — Dovells, Parkway 845 | 4 |
| 61 | 29 | 26 | 16 | THEME FROM DOCTOR KILDARE — Richard Chamberlain, MGM 13075 | 14 |
| 62 | 73 | 77 | 87 | I LEFT MY HEART IN SAN FRANCISCO △ — Tony Bennett, Columbia 42332 | 4 |
| 63 | 54 | 60 | 65 | LOVE ME AS I LOVE YOU — George Maharis, Epic 9522 | 5 |
| 64 | 41 | 29 | 19 | I CAN'T STOP LOVING YOU — Ray Charles, ABC-Paramount 10330 | 18 |
| 65 | 68 | 73 | 84 | THEME FROM A SUMMER PLACE — Dick Roman, Harmon 1004 | 5 |
| 66 | 72 | 89 | — | YOU CAN'T JUDGE A BOOK BY THE COVER — Bo Diddley, Checker 1019 | 3 |
| 67 | 33 | 35 | 36 | THE BALLAD OF PALADIN △ — Duane Eddy, RCA Victor 8047 | 9 |
| 68 | 89 | — | — | RAIN, RAIN GO AWAY — Bobby Vinton, Epic 9532 | 2 |
| 69 | 82 | 94 | 100 | DO YOU LOVE ME — Contours, Gordy 7005 | 4 |
| 70 | 46 | 45 | 37 | HAVING A PARTY △ — Sam Cooke, RCA Victor 8036 | 14 |
| 71 | 75 | 83 | 93 | JIVIN' AROUND — Al Casey Combo, Stacy 936 | 5 |
| 72 | 78 | 82 | 94 | YIELD NOT TO TEMPTATION — Bobby Bland, Duke 352 | 4 |
| 73 | 90 | — | — | IT MIGHT AS WELL RAIN UNTIL SEPTEMBER — Carole King, Dimension 2000 | 2 |
| 74 | 67 | 71 | 81 | LOLITA YA-YA — Ventures, Dolton 60 | 5 |
| 75 | 80 | — | — | EVERY NIGHT (WITHOUT YOU) △ — Paul Anka, RCA Victor 8068 | 2 |
| 76 | 77 | — | — | TOO LATE TO WORRY—TOO BLUE TO CRY — Glen Campbell, Capitol 4783 | 2 |
| 77 | 86 | — | — | LONG AS THE ROSE IS RED — Florraine Darlin, Epic 9529 | 2 |
| 78 | — | — | — | PUNISH HER — Bobby Vee, Liberty 55479 | 1 |
| 79 | 87 | — | — | LOLLIPOPS AND ROSES — Paul Petersen, Colpix 649 | 2 |
| 80 | 81 | — | 99 | GLORY OF LOVE — Don Gardner and Dee Dee Ford, KC 106 | 3 |
| 81 | 92 | 97 | — | SILLY BOY — Lettermen, Capitol 4810 | 3 |
| 82 | 84 | 98 | — | LOOKIN' FOR A LOVE — Valentinos, Sar 132 | 3 |
| 83 | 83 | — | — | DON'T YOU WORRY — Don Gardner and Dee Dee Ford, Fire 513 | 2 |
| 84 | 60 | 63 | 66 | BEACH PARTY — King Curtis, Capitol 4788 | 7 |
| 85 | 79 | — | — | REAP WHAT YOU SOW — Billy Stewart, Chess 1820 | 4 |
| 86 | — | — | — | TORTURE — Kris Jensen, Hickory 1173 | 1 |
| 87 | 91 | 96 | 98 | SO WHAT — Bill Black's Combo, Hi 2055 | 4 |
| 88 | — | — | — | A TASTE OF HONEY — Victor Feldman Quartet, Infinity 020 | 1 |
| 89 | 76 | 87 | — | I WANNA BE LOVED — Dinah Washington, Mercury 72015 | 3 |
| 90 | — | — | — | WHAT KIND OF FOOL AM I — Sammy Davis Jr., Reprise 20048 | 1 |
| 91 | 93 | — | — | OH! WHAT IT SEEMED TO BE — Castells, Era 3083 | 2 |
| 92 | 97 | — | — | BROKEN HEART — Fiestas, Old Town 1122 | 2 |
| 93 | — | — | — | I WOULDN'T KNOW — Dinah Washington, Roulette 4444 | 1 |
| 94 | — | — | — | NO ONE WILL EVER KNOW — Jimmie Rodgers, Dot 16378 | 1 |
| 95 | — | — | — | I KEEP FORGETTIN' — Chuck Jackson, Wand 126 | 1 |
| 96 | 98 | — | — | HIDE AND GO SEEK — Bunker Hill, Mala 451 | 2 |
| 97 | 88 | — | — | FOR ALL WE KNOW — Dinah Washington, Roulette 4444 | 2 |
| 98 | 99 | — | — | THERE IS NO GREATER LOVE — Wanderers, MGM 13082 | 2 |
| 99 | — | — | — | IF I DIDN'T HAVE A DIME — Gene Pitney, Musicor 1022 | 1 |
| 100 | — | — | — | OL' MAN RIVER — Jimmy Smith, Verve 10262 | 1 |

## BUBBLING UNDER THE HOT 100

101. COMIN' HOME BABY — Herbie Mann, Atlantic 5020
102. DON'T BREAK THE HEART THAT LOVES YOU — Bernie Leighton, Colpix 645
103. YOU HEART BELONGS TO ME — Supremes, Motown 1027
104. WHAT'S GONNA HAPPEN WHEN SUMMER'S GONE — Freddy Cannon, Swan 4117
105. I'VE GOT MY EYES ON YOU — Rick Nelson, Imperial 5864
106. TILL THERE WAS YOU — Valjean, Carlton 576
107. I'M COMING HOME — Paul Anka, ABC-Paramount 10338
108. ONLY LOVE CAN BREAK A HEART — Gene Pitney, Musicor 1022
109. STOP THE MUSIC — Shirelles, Scepter 1237
110. WHAT TIME IS IT? — Jive Five, Beltone 2024
111. MAMA, HE TREATS YOUR DAUGHTER MEAN — Ruth Brown, Philips 40056
112. COPY CAT — Gary (U. S.) Bonds, LeGrand 1020
113. OLD JOE CLARK — Kingston Trio, Capitol 4808
114. I REMEMBER YOU — Frank Ifield, Vee Jay 457
115. THE SWISS MAID — Del Shannon, Big Top 3117
116. HANDFUL OF MEMORIES — Baby Washington, Sue 767
117. SEND FOR ME — Barbara George, Sue 776
118. THE OLD MASTER PAINTER — Browns, RCA Victor 8066
119. SOFTLY AS I LEAVE YOU — Matt Monro, Liberty 55449
120. ABIGAIL — Embers, Empress 107

# BILLBOARD HOT 100
**FOR WEEK ENDING SEPTEMBER 8, 1962**

★ STAR PERFORMERS—Selections registering greatest upward progress this week.
[S] Indicates that 45 r.p.m. stereo single version is available.
△ Indicates that 33⅓ r.p.m. mono single version is available.
[Ⓢ] Indicates that 33⅓ r.p.m. stereo single version is available.

| This Week | Wk Ago | 2 Wks Ago | 3 Wks Ago | Title — Artist, Label & Number | Weeks On Chart |
|---|---|---|---|---|---|
| 1 | 1 | 5 | 12 | SHEILA — Tommy Roe, ABC-Paramount 10329 | 7 |
| 2 | 4 | 4 | 5 | YOU DON'T KNOW ME — Ray Charles, ABC-Paramount 10345 | 7 |
| 3 | 2 | 1 | 2 | LOCO-MOTION — Little Eva, Dimension 1000 | 11 |
| ★4 | 11 | 22 | 24 | RAMBLIN' ROSE — Nat King Cole, Capitol 4804 | 6 |
| 5 | 6 | 8 | 13 | SHE'S NOT YOU — Elvis Presley, RCA Victor 8041 △ | 6 |
| 6 | 3 | 2 | 1 | BREAKING UP IS HARD TO DO — Neil Sedaka, RCA Victor 8046 △ | 11 |
| 7 | 5 | 7 | 11 | PARTY LIGHTS — Claudine Clark, Chancellor 1113 | 11 |
| 8 | 7 | 3 | 6 | THINGS — Bobby Darin, Atco 6229 | 10 |
| ★9 | 17 | 35 | 54 | TEEN AGE IDOL — Rick Nelson, Imperial 5864 | 5 |
| 10 | 9 | 12 | 17 | VACATION — Connie Francis, MGM 13087 | 7 |
| ★11 | 22 | 65 | — | SHERRY — Four Seasons, Vee Jay 456 | 3 |
| 12 | 16 | 24 | 27 | RINKY DINK — Dave (Baby) Cortez, Chess 1829 | 9 |
| 13 | 15 | 21 | 25 | A SWINGIN' SAFARI — Billy Vaughn, Dot 16374 | 8 |
| 14 | 12 | 18 | 23 | WHAT'S A MATTER BABY — Timi Yuro, Liberty 55469 | 9 |
| 15 | 14 | 30 | 44 | YOUR NOSE IS GONNA GROW — Johnny Crawford, Del-Fi 4181 | 5 |
| 16 | 18 | 23 | 33 | DEVIL WOMAN — Marty Robbins, Columbia 42486 △ | 7 |
| 17 | 8 | 6 | 3 | ROSES ARE RED — Bobby Vinton, Epic 9509 | 14 |
| 18 | 19 | 31 | 41 | YOU BELONG TO ME — Duprees, Coed 569 | 6 |
| 19 | 30 | 36 | 42 | ALLEY CAT — Bent Fabric, Atco 6226 | 7 |
| ★20 | 45 | 61 | — | PATCHES — Dickey Lee, Smash 1758 | 3 |
| 21 | 25 | 37 | 48 | SEND ME THE PILLOW YOU DREAM ON — Johnny Tillotson, Cadence 1424 | 5 |
| ★22 | 40 | 48 | 65 | GREEN ONIONS — Booker T & the MG's, Stax 127 | 5 |
| ★23 | 36 | 42 | 46 | POINT OF NO RETURN — Gene McDaniels, Liberty 55480 | 5 |
| 24 | 37 | 50 | 66 | SILVER THREADS & GOLDEN NEEDLES — Springfields, Philips 40038 | 6 |
| 25 | 33 | 34 | 37 | SHAME ON ME — Bobby Bare, RCA Victor 8032 △ | 8 |
| 26 | 38 | 47 | 74 | VENUS IN BLUE JEANS — Jimmy Clanton, Ace 8001 | 4 |
| 27 | 26 | 32 | 39 | TILL DEATH DO US PART — Bob Braun, Decca 31355 | 8 |
| 28 | 32 | 39 | 58 | YOU BEAT ME TO THE PUNCH — Mary Wells, Motown 1032 | 5 |
| 29 | 20 | 25 | 31 | MAKE IT EASY ON YOURSELF — Jerry Butler, Vee Jay 451 | 9 |
| 30 | 13 | 9 | 7 | AHAB THE ARAB — Ray Stevens, Mercury 71966 | 11 |
| 31 | 39 | 49 | 64 | BEECHWOOD 4-5789 — Marvelettes, Tamla 54065 | 5 |
| ★32 | 43 | 55 | 78 | LET'S DANCE — Chris Montez, Monogram 505 | 5 |
| 33 | 31 | 40 | 51 | COME ON LITTLE ANGEL — Belmonts, Sabina 505 | 8 |
| 34 | 10 | 10 | 8 | LITTLE DIANE — Dion, Laurie 3134 | 10 |
| 35 | 42 | 52 | 75 | WONDERFUL DREAM — Majors, Imperial 5855 | 5 |
| ★36 | 46 | 59 | 90 | IF I HAD A HAMMER — Peter, Paul & Mary, Warner Bros. 5296 | 4 |
| 37 | 41 | 44 | 55 | STOP THE WEDDING — Etta James, Argo 5418 | 7 |
| 38 | 21 | 17 | 10 | SEALED WITH A KISS — Brian Hyland, ABC-Paramount 10336 | 14 |
| 39 | 27 | 26 | 19 | TWIST AND SHOUT — Isley Brothers, Wand 124 | 15 |
| 40 | 48 | 58 | 76 | I'M THE GIRL FROM WOLVERTON MOUNTAIN — Jo Ann Campbell, Cameo 223 | 4 |
| ★41 | 56 | 69 | — | LIE TO ME — Brook Benton, Mercury 72024 | 3 |
| 42 | 29 | 13 | 21 | BRING IT ON HOME TO ME — Sam Cooke, RCA Victor 8036 △ | 10 |
| 43 | 28 | 14 | 14 | YOU'LL LOSE A GOOD THING — Barbara Lynn, Jamie 1220 | 13 |
| 44 | 23 | 19 | 22 | CALL ME MR. IN-BETWEEN — Burl Ives, Decca 31405 | 8 |
| 45 | 53 | 56 | 61 | MR. SONGWRITER — Connie Stevens, Warner Bros. 5289 | 6 |
| 46 | 51 | 62 | 79 | SURFIN' SAFARI — Beach Boys, Capitol 4777 | 5 |
| ★47 | 57 | 71 | — | WHAT KIND OF LOVE IS THIS — Joey Dee and the Starlighters, Roulette 4438 | 3 |
| 48 | 60 | 70 | 92 | HULLY GULLY BABY — Dovells, Parkway 845 | 5 |
| 49 | 49 | 51 | 52 | BABY ELEPHANT WALK — Lawrence Welk, Dot 16364 | 14 |
| 50 | 68 | 89 | — | RAIN, RAIN GO AWAY — Bobby Vinton, Epic 9532 | 3 |
| 51 | 52 | 64 | 68 | I LOVE YOU THE WAY YOU ARE — Bobby Vinton, Diamond 121 | 5 |
| 52 | 73 | 90 | — | IT MIGHT AS WELL RAIN UNTIL SEPTEMBER — Carole King, Dimension 2000 | 3 |
| 53 | 59 | 74 | 85 | PAPA-OOM-MOW-MOW — Rivingtons, Liberty 55427 | 4 |
| 54 | 58 | 63 | 77 | BOYS' NIGHT OUT — Patti Page, Mercury 72013 | 6 |
| ★55 | 69 | 82 | 94 | DO YOU LOVE ME — Contours, Gordy 7005 | 5 |
| 56 | 50 | 53 | 56 | A TASTE OF HONEY — Martin Denny, Liberty 55470 | 9 |
| 57 | 35 | 20 | 9 | SPEEDY GONZALES — Pat Boone, Dot 16368 | 13 |
| 58 | 55 | 66 | 70 | JUST TELL HER JIM SAID HELLO — Elvis Presley, RCA Victor 8041 △ | 5 |
| 59 | 78 | — | — | PUNISH HER — Bobby Vee, Liberty 55479 | 2 |
| 60 | 66 | 72 | 89 | YOU CAN'T JUDGE A BOOK BY THE COVER — Bo Diddley, Checker 1019 | 4 |
| 61 | 34 | 15 | 18 | HEART IN HAND — Brenda Lee, Decca 31407 | 10 |
| 62 | 62 | 73 | 77 | I LEFT MY HEART IN SAN FRANCISCO — Tony Bennett, Columbia 42332 △ | 5 |
| 63 | 75 | 80 | — | EVERY NIGHT (WITHOUT YOU) — Paul Anka, RCA Victor 8068 △ | 3 |
| 64 | 65 | 68 | 73 | THEME FROM A SUMMER PLACE — Dick Roman, Harmon 1004 | 6 |
| 65 | 24 | 11 | 4 | THE WAH-WATUSI — Orlons, Cameo 218 | 14 |
| 66 | 63 | 54 | 60 | LOVE ME AS I LOVE YOU — George Maharis, Epic 9522 | 6 |
| 67 | 79 | 87 | — | LOLLIPOPS AND ROSES — Paul Petersen, Colpix 649 | 3 |
| 68 | 44 | 16 | 16 | WOLVERTON MOUNTAIN — Claude King, Columbia 42352 △ | 16 |
| 69 | 74 | 67 | 71 | LOLITA YA-YA — Ventures, Dolton 60 | 6 |
| 70 | 72 | 78 | 82 | YIELD NOT TO TEMPTATION — Bobby Bland, Duke 352 | 5 |
| 71 | 95 | — | — | I KEEP FORGETTIN' — Chuck Jackson, Wand 126 | 2 |
| 72 | — | — | — | MONSTER MASH — Bobby (Boris) Pickett and the Crypt Kickers, Garpax 44167 | 1 |
| 73 | 77 | 86 | — | LONG AS THE ROSE IS RED — Florraine Darlin, Epic 9529 | 3 |
| 74 | 71 | 75 | 83 | JIVIN' AROUND — Al Casey Combo, Stacy 936 | 6 |
| 75 | 99 | — | — | IF I DIDN'T HAVE A DIME — Gene Pitney, Musicor 1022 | 2 |
| 76 | — | — | — | I REMEMBER YOU — Frank Ifield, Vee Jay 457 | 1 |
| 77 | 83 | 83 | — | DON'T YOU WORRY — Don Gardner and Dee Dee Ford, Fire 513 | 3 |
| 78 | — | — | — | STOP THE MUSIC — Shirelles, Scepter 1237 | 1 |
| 79 | — | — | — | WHAT'S GONNA HAPPEN WHEN SUMMER'S GONE — Freddy Cannon, Swan 4117 | 1 |
| 80 | 85 | 79 | — | REAP WHAT YOU SOW — Billy Stewart, Chess 1820 | 5 |
| 81 | 96 | 98 | — | HIDE AND GO SEEK — Bunker Hill, Mala 451 | 3 |
| 82 | 87 | 91 | 96 | SO WHAT — Bill Black's Combo, Hi 2055 | 5 |
| 83 | 86 | — | — | TORTURE — Kris Jensen, Hickory 1173 | 2 |
| 84 | 89 | 76 | 87 | I WANNA BE LOVED — Dinah Washington, Mercury 72015 | 4 |
| 85 | — | — | — | LIMBO ROCK — Chubby Checker, Parkway 849 | 1 |
| 86 | 84 | 60 | 63 | BEACH PARTY — King Curtis, Capitol 4788 | 8 |
| 87 | 82 | 84 | 98 | LOOKIN' FOR A LOVE — Valentinos, Sar 132 | 4 |
| 88 | 94 | — | — | NO ONE WILL EVER KNOW — Jimmie Rodgers, Dot 16378 | 2 |
| 89 | 92 | 97 | — | BROKEN HEART — Flestas, Old Town 1122 | 3 |
| 90 | — | — | — | SWEET SIXTEEN BARS — Earl Grant, Decca 25574 | 1 |
| 91 | 81 | 92 | 97 | SILLY BOY — Lettermen, Capitol 4810 | 4 |
| 92 | 98 | 99 | — | THERE IS NO GREATER LOVE — Wanderers, MGM 13082 | 3 |
| 93 | — | — | — | STORMY MONDAY BLUES — Bobby Bland, Duke 355 | 1 |
| 94 | — | 96 | — | COPY CAT — Gary (U.S.) Bonds, LeGrand 1020 | 2 |
| 95 | — | — | — | I REALLY DON'T WANT TO KNOW — Solomon Burke, Atlantic 2157 | 1 |
| 96 | — | — | — | SEND FOR ME — Barbara George, Sue 766 | 1 |
| 97 | 90 | — | — | WHAT KIND OF FOOL AM I — Sammy Davis Jr., Reprise 20048 | 2 |
| 98 | — | — | — | HE'S A REBEL — Crystals, Philles 106 | 1 |
| 99 | — | — | — | MAMA, HE TREATS YOUR DAUGHTER MEAN — Ruth Brown, Philips 40056 | 1 |
| 100 | — | — | — | BIG LOVE — Joe Henderson, Todd 1077 | 1 |

## BUBBLING UNDER THE HOT 100

101. YOUR HEART BELONGS TO ME .......... Supremes, Motown 102
102. DON'T BREAK THE HEART THAT LOVES YOU ........ Bernie Leighton, Colpix 645
103. GLORY OF LOVE ........ Don Gardner and Dee Dee Ford, KC 106
104. LITTLE BLACK BOOK ........ Jimmy Dean, Columbia 42529
105. OL' MAN RIVER ........ Jimmy Smith, Verve 10262
106. ONLY LOVE CAN BREAK A HEART ........ Gene Pitney, Musicor 1022
107. BEACH PARTY ........ Dave York, PKM 6700
108. DON'T GO NEAR THE INDIANS ........ Rex Allen, Mercury 71997
109. OH! WHAT IT SEEMED TO BE ........ Castells, Era 3083
110. SOMEDAY ........ Bobby Vee and the Crickets, Liberty 55479
111. TIJUANA BORDER (WOLVERTON MOUNTAIN) ........ El Clod, Challenge 9159
112. WHAT TIME IS IT? ........ Jive Five, Beltone 2024
113. COMIN' HOME BABY ........ Herbie Mann, Atlantic 5020
114. A TASTE OF HONEY ........ Victor Feldman Quartet, Infinity 020
115. I'M GONNA CHANGE EVERYTHING ........ Jim Reeves, RCA Victor 8080
116. WHAT KIND OF FOOL AM I ........ Anthony Newley, London 9546
117. ABIGAIL ........ Embers, Empress 107
118. SOFTLY AS I LEAVE YOU ........ Matt Monro, Liberty 55449
119. CHILLS ........ Tony Orlando, Epic 9519
120. CLOSE TO CATHY ........ Mike Clifford, United Artists 489

# BILLBOARD HOT 100

FOR WEEK ENDING SEPTEMBER 15

1962

★ STAR PERFORMERS—Selections registering greatest upward progress this week.

S Indicates that 45 r.p.m. stereo single version is available.

△ Indicates that 33⅓ r.p.m. mono single version is available.

△S Indicates that 33⅓ r.p.m. stereo single version is available.

| THIS WEEK | 1 Wk. Ago | 2 Wks. Ago | 3 Wks. Ago | TITLE Artist, Label & Number | Weeks On Chart |
|---|---|---|---|---|---|
| ★1 | 11 | 22 | 65 | SHERRY — Four Seasons, Vee Jay 456 | 4 |
| 2 | 1 | 1 | 5 | SHEILA — Tommy Roe, ABC-Paramount 10329 | 8 |
| 3 | 4 | 11 | 22 | RAMBLIN' ROSE — Nat King Cole, Capitol 4804 | 7 |
| 4 | 3 | 2 | 1 | LOCO-MOTION — Little Eva, Dimension 1000 | 12 |
| ★5 | 22 | 40 | 48 | GREEN ONIONS — Booker T & the MG's, Stax 127 | 6 |
| 6 | 5 | 6 | 8 | SHE'S NOT YOU △ — Elvis Presley, RCA Victor 8041 | 7 |
| 7 | 9 | 17 | 35 | TEEN AGE IDOL — Rick Nelson, Imperial 5864 | 6 |
| 8 | 2 | 4 | 4 | YOU DON'T KNOW ME — Ray Charles, ABC-Paramount 10345 | 8 |
| ★9 | 20 | 45 | 61 | PATCHES — Dickey Lee, Smash 1758 | 4 |
| 10 | 12 | 16 | 24 | RINKY DINK — Dave (Baby) Cortez, Chess 1829 | 10 |
| 11 | 6 | 3 | 2 | BREAKING UP IS HARD TO DO △ — Neil Sedaka, RCA Victor 8046 | 12 |
| ★12 | 28 | 32 | 39 | YOU BEAT ME TO THE PUNCH — Mary Wells, Motown 1032 | 6 |
| ★13 | 18 | 19 | 31 | YOU BELONG TO ME — Duprees, Coed 569 | 7 |
| 14 | 7 | 5 | 7 | PARTY LIGHTS — Claudine Clark, Chancellor 1113 | 12 |
| ★15 | 32 | 43 | 55 | LET'S DANCE — Chris Montez, Monogram 505 | 6 |
| 16 | 16 | 18 | 23 | DEVIL WOMAN △ — Marty Robbins, Columbia 42486 | 8 |
| 17 | 21 | 25 | 37 | SEND ME THE PILLOW YOU DREAM ON — Johnny Tillotson, Cadence 1424 | 6 |
| 18 | 19 | 30 | 36 | ALLEY CAT — Bent Fabric, Atco 6226 | 8 |
| ★19 | 26 | 38 | 47 | VENUS IN BLUE JEANS — Jimmy Clanton, Ace 8001 | 5 |
| ★20 | 31 | 39 | 49 | BEECHWOOD 4-5789 — Marvelettes, Tamla 54065 | 6 |
| 21 | 23 | 36 | 42 | POINT OF NO RETURN — Gene McDaniels, Liberty 55480 | 7 |
| 22 | 24 | 37 | 50 | SILVER THREADS & GOLDEN NEEDLES — Springfields, Philips 40038 | 7 |
| 23 | 25 | 33 | 34 | SHAME ON ME △ — Bobby Bare, RCA Victor 8032 | 9 |
| 24 | 8 | 7 | 3 | THINGS — Bobby Darin, Atco 6229 | 11 |
| ★25 | 35 | 42 | 52 | WONDERFUL DREAM — Majors, Imperial 5855 | 6 |
| 26 | 13 | 15 | 21 | A SWINGIN' SAFARI — Billy Vaughn, Dot 16374 | 9 |
| ★27 | 41 | 56 | 69 | LIE TO ME — Brook Benton, Mercury 72024 | 4 |
| 28 | 33 | 31 | 40 | COME ON LITTLE ANGEL — Belmonts, Sabina 505 | 9 |
| 29 | 15 | 14 | 30 | YOUR NOSE IS GONNA GROW — Johnny Crawford, Del-Fi 4181 | 6 |
| ★30 | 46 | 51 | 62 | SURFIN' SAFARI — Beach Boys, Capitol 4777 | 6 |
| 31 | 14 | 12 | 18 | WHAT'S A MATTER BABY — Timi Yuro, Liberty 55469 | 10 |
| ★32 | 48 | 60 | 70 | HULLY GULLY BABY — Dovells, Parkway 845 | 6 |
| ★33 | 50 | 68 | 89 | RAIN, RAIN GO AWAY — Bobby Vinton, Epic 9532 | 4 |
| 34 | 37 | 41 | 44 | STOP THE WEDDING — Etta James, Argo 5418 | 8 |
| 35 | 36 | 46 | 59 | IF I HAD A HAMMER — Peter, Paul & Mary, Warner Bros. 5296 | 5 |
| ★36 | 47 | 57 | 71 | WHAT KIND OF LOVE IS THIS — Joey Dee and the Starliters, Roulette 4438 | 4 |
| ★37 | 72 | — | — | MONSTER MASH — Bobby (Boris) Pickett and the Crypt Kickers, Garpax 44167 | 2 |
| 38 | 10 | 9 | 12 | VACATION — Connie Francis, MGM 13087 | 8 |
| 39 | 40 | 48 | 58 | I'M THE GIRL FROM WOLVERTON MOUNTAIN — Jo Ann Campbell, Cameo 223 | 5 |
| ★40 | 59 | 78 | — | PUNISH HER — Bobby Vee, Liberty 55479 | 3 |
| ★41 | 52 | 73 | 90 | IT MIGHT AS WELL RAIN UNTIL SEPTEMBER — Carole King, Dimension 2000 | 4 |
| ★42 | 55 | 69 | 82 | DO YOU LOVE ME — Contours, Gordy 7005 | 6 |
| 43 | 45 | 53 | 56 | MR. SONGWRITER — Connie Stevens, Warner Bros. 5289 | 7 |
| 44 | 17 | 8 | 6 | ROSES ARE RED — Bobby Vinton, Epic 9509 | 15 |
| 45 | 34 | 10 | 10 | LITTLE DIANE — Dion, Laurie 3134 | 11 |
| 46 | 51 | 52 | 64 | I LOVE YOU THE WAY YOU ARE — Bobby Vinton, Diamond 121 | 6 |
| 47 | 39 | 27 | 26 | TWIST AND SHOUT — Isley Brothers, Wand 124 | 16 |
| 48 | 49 | 49 | 51 | BABY ELEPHANT WALK — Lawrence Welk, Dot 16364 | 15 |
| 49 | 54 | 58 | 63 | BOYS' NIGHT OUT — Patti Page, Mercury 72013 | 7 |
| 50 | 27 | 26 | 32 | TILL DEATH DO US PART — Bob Braun, Decca 31355 | 9 |
| 51 | 53 | 59 | 74 | PAPA-OOM-MOW-MOW — Rivingtons, Liberty 55427 | 5 |
| 52 | 29 | 20 | 25 | MAKE IT EASY ON YOURSELF — Jerry Butler, Vee Jay 451 | 10 |
| ★53 | 76 | — | — | I REMEMBER YOU — Frank Ifield, Vee Jay 457 | 2 |
| 54 | 62 | 62 | 73 | I LEFT MY HEART IN SAN FRANCISCO △ — Tony Bennett, Columbia 42332 | 6 |
| 55 | 63 | 75 | 80 | EVERY NIGHT (WITHOUT YOU) △ — Paul Anka, RCA Victor 8068 | 4 |
| ★56 | 67 | 79 | 87 | LOLLIPOPS AND ROSES — Paul Petersen, Colpix 649 | 4 |
| 57 | 60 | 66 | 72 | YOU CAN'T JUDGE A BOOK BY THE COVER — Bo Diddley, Checker 1019 | 5 |
| 58 | 42 | 29 | 13 | BRING IT ON HOME TO ME △ — Sam Cooke, RCA Victor 8036 | 11 |
| ★59 | 70 | 72 | 78 | YIELD NOT TO TEMPTATION — Bobby Bland, Duke 352 | 6 |
| 60 | 44 | 23 | 19 | CALL ME MR. IN-BETWEEN — Burl Ives, Decca 31405 | 9 |
| 61 | 69 | 74 | 67 | LOLITA YA-YA — Ventures, Dolton 60 | 7 |
| 62 | 73 | 77 | 86 | LONG AS THE ROSE IS RED — Florraine Darlin, Epic 9529 | 4 |
| ★63 | 83 | 86 | — | TORTURE — Kris Jensen, Hickory 1173 | 3 |
| ★64 | 81 | 96 | 98 | HIDE AND GO SEEK — Bunker Hill, Mala 451 | 4 |
| 65 | 71 | 95 | — | I KEEP FORGETTIN' — Chuck Jackson, Wand 126 | 3 |
| 66 | 79 | — | — | WHAT'S GONNA HAPPEN WHEN SUMMER'S GONE — Freddy Cannon, Swan 4117 | 2 |
| 67 | 64 | 65 | 68 | THEME FROM A SUMMER PLACE — Dick Roman, Harmon 1004 | 7 |
| ★68 | — | — | — | ONLY LOVE CAN BREAK A HEART — Gene Pitney, Musicor 1022 | 1 |
| 69 | 78 | — | — | STOP THE MUSIC — Shirelles, Scepter 1237 | 2 |
| ★70 | — | — | — | POPEYE THE HITCHHIKER — Chubby Checker, Parkway 849 | 1 |
| 71 | 75 | 99 | — | IF I DIDN'T HAVE A DIME — Gene Pitney, Musicor 1022 | 3 |
| 72 | 56 | 50 | 53 | A TASTE OF HONEY — Martin Denny, Liberty 55470 | 10 |
| 73 | 77 | 83 | 83 | DON'T YOU WORRY — Don Gardner and Dee Dee Ford, Fire 513 | 4 |
| ★74 | — | — | — | DON'T GO NEAR THE INDIANS — Rex Allen, Mercury 71997 | 1 |
| 75 | 86 | 84 | 60 | BEACH PARTY — King Curtis, Capitol 4788 | 9 |
| ★76 | — | 80 | 81 | GLORY OF LOVE — Don Gardner & Dee Dee Ford, KC 106 | 4 |
| ★77 | — | — | — | LITTLE BLACK BOOK △ — Jimmy Dean, Columbia 42529 | 1 |
| 78 | 82 | 87 | 91 | SO WHAT — Bill Black's Combo, Hi 2055 | 6 |
| 79 | 85 | — | — | LIMBO ROCK — Chubby Checker, Parkway 849 | 2 |
| 80 | 88 | 94 | — | NO ONE WILL EVER KNOW — Jimmie Rodgers, Dot 16378 | 3 |
| 81 | 87 | 82 | 84 | LOOKIN' FOR A LOVE — Valentinos, Sar 132 | 5 |
| ★82 | — | — | — | THE THINGS WE DID LAST SUMMER — Shelley Fabares, Colpix 654 | 1 |
| 83 | 93 | — | — | STORMY MONDAY BLUES — Bobby Bland, Duke 355 | 2 |
| ★84 | 100 | — | — | BIG LOVE — Joe Henderson, Todd 1077 | 2 |
| 85 | 90 | — | — | SWEET SIXTEEN BARS — Earl Grant, Decca 25574 | 2 |
| 86 | 89 | 92 | 97 | BROKEN HEART — Fiestas, Old Town 1122 | 4 |
| 87 | 97 | 90 | — | WHAT KIND OF FOOL AM I — Sammy Davis Jr., Reprise 20048 | 3 |
| 88 | 92 | 98 | 99 | THERE IS NO GREATER LOVE — Wanderers, MGM 13082 | 4 |
| ★89 | — | — | — | THE SWISS MAID — Del Shannon, Big Top 3117 | 1 |
| ★90 | — | — | — | WHAT TIME IS IT! — Jive Five, Beltone 2024 | 1 |
| 91 | 98 | — | — | HE'S A REBEL — Crystals, Philles 106 | 2 |
| 92 | 94 | — | 96 | COPY CAT — Gary (U. S.) Bonds, LeGrand 1020 | 3 |
| 93 | 95 | — | — | I REALLY DON'T WANT TO KNOW — Solomon Burke, Atlantic 2157 | 2 |
| 94 | — | — | — | BONANZA! △ — Johnny Cash, Columbia 42512 | 1 |
| 95 | — | — | — | WAY OVER THERE — Miracles, Tamla 54069 | 1 |
| 96 | — | — | — | DON'T YOU BELIEVE IT △ — Andy Williams, Columbia 42523 | 1 |
| 97 | — | — | — | SWEET LITTLE SIXTEEN — Jerry Lee Lewis, Sun 478 | 1 |
| 98 | — | — | — | CLOSE TO CATHY — Mike Clifford, United Artists 489 | 1 |
| 99 | — | 100 | — | OL' MAN RIVER — Jimmy Smith, Verve 10262 | 2 |
| 100 | — | — | — | YOUR HEART BELONGS TO ME — Supremes, Motown 1027 | 3 |

## HOT 100—A TO Z—*(Publisher-Licensee)*


Alley Cat (Metorion, BMI) .......... 18
Baby Elephant Walk (Famous, ASCAP) .......... 48
Beach Party (Kilynn, BMI) .......... 75
Beechwood 4-5789 (Jobete, BMI) .......... 20
Big Love (Cramort, BMI) .......... 84
Bonanza! (Livingston & Evans, ASCAP) .......... 94
Boys' Night Out (Miller, ASCAP) .......... 49
Breaking Up Is Hard to Do (Aldon, BMI) .......... 11
Bring It on Home to Me (Kags, BMI) .......... 58
Broken Heart (Maureen, BMI) .......... 86
Call Me Mr. In-Between (Pamper, BMI) .......... 60
Close to Cathy (Arch, ASCAP) .......... 98
Come on Little Angel (Glenden, ASCAP) .......... 28
Copy Cat (Rock Masters, BMI) .......... 92
Devil Woman (Marty's, BMI) .......... 16
Do You Love Me (Jobete, BMI) .......... 42
Don't Go Near the Indians (Buttercup, BMI) .......... 74
Don't You Believe It (Dolfi, ASCAP) .......... 96
Don't You Worry (Fast-Pete, BMI) .......... 73
Every Night (Without You) (Spanka, BMI) .......... 55
Glory of Love (Shapiro-Bernstein, ASCAP) .......... 76
Green Onions (East, BMI) .......... 5
He's a Rebel (January, BMI) .......... 91
Hide and Go Seek (Florentine, BMI) .......... 64
Hully Gully Baby (Kalmann, ASCAP) .......... 32
I Keep Forgettin' (Trio, BMI) .......... 65
I Left My Heart in San Francisco (General, ASCAP) .......... 54
I Love You the Way You Are (Tobi-Ann, BMI) .......... 46
I Really Don't Want to Know (Hill & Range, BMI) .......... 93
I Remember You (Paramount, ASCAP) .......... 53
I'm the Girl From Wolverton Mountain (Painted Desert, BMI) .......... 39
If I Didn't Have a Dime (January, BMI) .......... 71
If I Had a Hammer (Ludlow, BMI) .......... 35
It Might as Well Rain Until September (Aldon, BMI) .......... 41
Let's Dance (Rondell & Sherman-DeVorzon, BMI) .......... 15
Lie to Me (Ben Day, BMI) .......... 27
Limbo Rock (Twist, BMI) .......... 79
Little Black Book (Plainview, BMI) .......... 77
Little Diane (Disal, ASCAP) .......... 45
Loco-Motion (Aldon, BMI) .......... 4
Lolita Ya-Ya (Chappell, ASCAP) .......... 61
Lollipops and Roses (Garland, ASCAP) .......... 56
Long as the Rose Is Red (Lyle, ASCAP) .......... 62
Lookin' for a Love (Kags, BMI) .......... 81
Make It Easy on Yourself (Famous, ASCAP) .......... 52
Mr. Songwriter (Gil, BMI) .......... 43
Monster Mash (Garpax, BMI) .......... 37
No One Will Ever Know (Milene, ASCAP) .......... 80
Ol' Man River (Harms, ASCAP) .......... 99
Only Love Can Break a Heart (Arch, ASCAP) .......... 68
Papa-Oom-Mow-Mow (Beechwood, BMI) .......... 51
Party Lights (Rambed, BMI) .......... 14
Patches (Aldon, BMI) .......... 9
Point of No Return (Aldon, BMI) .......... 21
Popeye the Hitchhiker (Kalmann, ASCAP) .......... 70
Punish Her (January, BMI) .......... 40
Rain, Rain Go Away (Regent, BMI) .......... 33
Ramblin' Rose (Sweco, BMI) .......... 3
Rinky Dink (Arc-Cortez, BMI) .......... 10
Roses Are Red (Lyle, ASCAP) .......... 44
Send Me the Pillow You Dream on (Four Star, BMI) .......... 17
Shame on Me (Western Hills-Lois-Saran, BMI) .......... 23
She's Not You (Presley, BMI) .......... 6
Sheila (Eager-Nitetime, BMI) .......... 2
Sherry (Bobob, ASCAP) .......... 1
Silver Threads & Golden Needles (Central Songs, BMI) .......... 22
So What (Jec, BMI) .......... 78
Stop the Music (Vee-Ve, BMI) .......... 69
Stop the Wedding (Figure, BMI) .......... 34
Stormy Monday Blues (Gregmark, ASCAP) .......... 83
Surfin' Safari (Guild, BMI) .......... 30
Sweet Little Sixteen (Arc, BMI) .......... 97
Sweet Sixteen Bars (Progressive, BMI) .......... 85
Swingin' Safari, A (Roosevelt, BMI) .......... 26
Swiss Maid, The (Tree, BMI) .......... 89
Taste of Honey, A (Songfest, ASCAP) .......... 72
Teen Age Idol (Nelson, ASCAP) .......... 7
Theme From a Summer Place (Witmark, ASCAP) .......... 67
There Is No Greater Love (Jones, ASCAP) .......... 88
Things (Adaris, BMI) .......... 24
Things We Did Last Summer, The (Kerwin, ASCAP) .......... 82
Till Death Do Us Part (Karolyn, ASCAP) .......... 50
Torture (Acuff-Rose, BMI) .......... 63
Twist and Shout (Mellin, BMI) .......... 47
Vacation (Merna, BMI) .......... 38
Venus in Blue Jeans (Aldon, BMI) .......... 19
Way Over There (Jobete, BMI) .......... 95
What Kind of Fool Am I (Ludlow, BMI) .......... 87
What Kind of Love Is This (Planetary-Gee, ASCAP) .......... 36
What Time Is It? (Lescay, BMI) .......... 90
What's a Matter Baby (Eden, BMI) .......... 31
What's Gonna Happen When Summer's Gone (Roosevelt, BMI) .......... 66
Wonderful Dream (Travis-Rittenhouse, BMI) .......... 25
Yield Not to Temptation (Don, BMI) .......... 59
You Beat Me to the Punch (Jobete, BMI) .......... 12
You Belong to Me (Ridgeway, BMI) .......... 13
You Can't Judge a Book By the Cover (Arc, BMI) .......... 57
You Don't Know Me (Hill & Range, BMI) .......... 8
Your Heart Belongs to Me (Jobete, BMI) .......... 100
Your Nose Is Gonna Grow (Maraville, BMI) .......... 29


## BUBBLING UNDER THE HOT 100

101. DON'T BREAK THE HEART THAT LOVES YOU .......... Bernie Leighton, Colpix 645
102. COMIN' HOME BABY .......... Herbie Mann, Atlantic 5020
103. SILLY BOY .......... Lettermen, Capitol 4810
104. TRY A LITTLE TENDERNESS .......... Aretha Franklin, Columbia 42520
105. TILL THERE WAS YOU .......... Valjean, Carlton 576
106. TOO LATE TO WORRY—TOO BLUE TO CRY .......... Glen Campbell, Capitol 4783
107. EVERYBODY LOVES MY BABY .......... Jimmy Smith, Blue Note 1851
108. I'M GONNA CHANGE EVERYTHING .......... Jim Reeves, RCA Victor 8080
109. SOMEDAY .......... Bobby Vee and the Crickets, Liberty 55479
110. SEND FOR ME .......... Barbara George, Sue 766
111. I WOULDN'T KNOW .......... Dinah Washington, Roulette 4444
112. LIVE IT UP .......... Sandy Nelson, Imperial 5870
113. WADDLE WADDLE .......... Bracelets, Congress 104
114. FOR ALL WE KNOW .......... Dinah Washington, Roulette 4444
115. TIJUANA BORDER (WOLVERTON MOUNTAIN .......... El Clod, Challenge 9159
116. MAMA, HE TREATS YOUR DAUGHTER MEAN .......... Ruth Brown, Philips 40056
117. RICHIE .......... Gloria Dennis, Rust 5049
118. AND THEN THERE WERE DRUMS .......... Sandy Nelson, Imperial 5870
119. WHAT KIND OF FOOL AM I .......... Anthony Newley, London 9546
*120. OL' MAN RIVER .......... Johnny Nash, Warner Bros. 5301
*120. HANDFUL OF MEMORIES .......... Baby Washington, Sue 767

*Tie

# BILLBOARD HOT 100

FOR WEEK ENDING SEPTEMBER 22

1962

★ STAR PERFORMERS—Selections registering greatest upward progress this week.

S Indicates that 45 r.p.m. stereo single version is available.

△ Indicates that 33⅓ r.p.m. mono single version is available.

S△ Indicates that 33⅓ r.p.m. stereo single version is available.

| This Week | Wk. Ago | 2 Wks. Ago | 3 Wks. Ago | Title | Artist, Label & Number | | Weeks On Chart |
|---|---|---|---|---|---|---|---|
| 1 | 1 | 11 | 22 | SHERRY | Four Seasons, Vee Jay 456 | | 5 |
| 2 | 3 | 4 | 11 | RAMBLIN' ROSE | Nat King Cole, Capitol 4804 | | 8 |
| 3 | 2 | 1 | 1 | SHEILA | Tommy Roe, ABC-Paramount 10329 | | 9 |
| 4 | 5 | 22 | 40 | GREEN ONIONS | Booker T & the MG's, Stax 127 | | 7 |
| 5 | 7 | 9 | 17 | TEEN AGE IDOL | Rick Nelson, Imperial 5864 | | 7 |
| 6 ★ | 15 | 32 | 43 | LET'S DANCE | Chris Montez, Monogram 505 | | 7 |
| 7 ★ | 13 | 18 | 19 | YOU BELONG TO ME | Duprees, Coed 569 | | 8 |
| 8 | 9 | 20 | 45 | PATCHES | Dickey Lee, Smash 1758 | | 5 |
| 9 | 12 | 28 | 32 | YOU BEAT ME TO THE PUNCH | Mary Wells, Motown 1032 | | 7 |
| 10 | 6 | 5 | 6 | SHE'S NOT YOU | Elvis Presley, RCA Victor 8041 | △ | 8 |
| 11 | 4 | 3 | 2 | LOCO-MOTION | Little Eva, Dimension 1000 | | 13 |
| 12 ★ | 18 | 19 | 30 | ALLEY CAT | Bent Fabric, Atco 6226 | | 9 |
| 13 ★ | 37 | 72 | — | MONSTER MASH | Bobby (Boris) Pickett and the Crypt Kickers, Garpax 44167 | | 3 |
| 14 | 10 | 12 | 16 | RINKY DINK | Dave (Baby) Cortez, Chess 1829 | | 11 |
| 15 ★ | 35 | 36 | 46 | IF I HAD A HAMMER | Peter, Paul & Mary, Warner Bros. 5296 | | 6 |
| 16 | 19 | 26 | 38 | VENUS IN BLUE JEANS | Jimmy Clanton, Ace 8001 | | 6 |
| 17 | 20 | 31 | 39 | BEECHWOOD 4-5789 | Marvelettes, Tamla 54065 | | 7 |
| 18 | 17 | 21 | 25 | SEND ME THE PILLOW YOU DREAM ON | Johnny Tillotson, Cadence 1424 | | 7 |
| 19 ★ | 33 | 50 | 68 | RAIN, RAIN GO AWAY | Bobby Vinton, Epic 9532 | | 5 |
| 20 | 22 | 24 | 37 | SILVER THREADS & GOLDEN NEEDLES | Springfields, Philips 40038 | | 8 |
| 21 | 8 | 2 | 4 | YOU DON'T KNOW ME | Ray Charles, ABC-Paramount 10345 | | 9 |
| 22 | 25 | 35 | 42 | A WONDERFUL DREAM | Majors, Imperial 5855 | | 6 |
| 23 | 27 | 41 | 56 | LIE TO ME | Brook Benton, Mercury 72024 | | 5 |
| 24 | 26 | 13 | 15 | A SWINGIN' SAFARI | Billy Vaughn, Dot 16374 | | 10 |
| 25 | 29 | 15 | 14 | YOUR NOSE IS GONNA GROW | Johnny Crawford, Del-Fi 4181 | | 7 |
| 26 ★ | 36 | 47 | 57 | WHAT KIND OF LOVE IS THIS | Joey Dee and the Starliters, Roulette 4438 | | 5 |
| 27 ★ | 53 | 76 | — | I REMEMBER YOU | Frank Ifield, Vee Jay 457 | | 3 |
| 28 ★ | 42 | 55 | 59 | DO YOU LOVE ME | Contours, Gordy 7005 | | 7 |
| 29 | 30 | 46 | 51 | SURFIN' SAFARI | Beach Boys, Capitol 4777 | | 7 |
| 30 | 32 | 48 | 60 | HULLY GULLY BABY | Dovells, Parkway 845 | | 7 |
| 31 | 40 | 59 | 78 | PUNISH HER | Bobby Vee, Liberty 55479 | | 4 |
| 32 | 41 | 52 | 73 | IT MIGHT AS WELL RAIN UNTIL SEPTEMBER | Carole King, Dimension 2000 | | 5 |
| 33 | 16 | 16 | 18 | DEVIL WOMAN | Marty Robbins, Columbia 42486 | △ | 9 |
| 34 | 11 | 6 | 3 | BREAKING UP IS HARD TO DO | Neil Sedaka, RCA Victor 8046 | △ | 13 |
| 35 | 28 | 33 | 31 | COME ON LITTLE ANGEL | Belmonts, Sabina 505 | | 10 |
| 36 | 21 | 23 | 36 | POINT OF NO RETURN | Gene McDaniels, Liberty 55480 | | 8 |
| 37 | 14 | 7 | 5 | PARTY LIGHTS | Claudine Clark, Chancellor 1113 | | 13 |
| 38 | 39 | 40 | 48 | I'M THE GIRL FROM WOLVERTON MOUNTAIN | Jo Ann Campbell, Cameo 223 | | 6 |
| 39 | 23 | 25 | 33 | SHAME ON ME | Bobby Bare, RCA Victor 8032 | △ | 10 |
| 40 | 46 | 51 | 52 | I LOVE YOU THE WAY YOU ARE | Bobby Vinton, Diamond 121 | | 7 |
| 41 | 34 | 37 | 41 | STOP THE WEDDING | Etta James, Argo 5418 | | 9 |
| 42 ★ | 54 | 62 | 62 | I LEFT MY HEART IN SAN FRANCISCO | Tony Bennett, Columbia 42332 | △ | 7 |
| 43 ★ | 68 | — | — | ONLY LOVE CAN BREAK A HEART | Gene Pitney, Musicor 1022 | | 2 |
| 44 ★ | 69 | 78 | — | STOP THE MUSIC | Shirelles, Scepter 1237 | | 3 |
| 45 ★ | 66 | 79 | — | WHAT'S GONNA HAPPEN WHEN SUMMER'S GONE | Freddy Cannon, Swan 4117 | | 3 |
| 46 | 55 | 63 | 75 | EVERY NIGHT (WITHOUT YOU) | Paul Anka, RCA Victor 8068 | △ | 5 |
| 47 | 31 | 14 | 12 | WHAT'S A MATTER BABY | Timi Yuro, Liberty 55469 | | 11 |
| 48 | 51 | 53 | 59 | PAPA-OOM-MOW-MOW | Rivingtons, Liberty 55427 | | 6 |
| 49 | 24 | 8 | 7 | THINGS | Bobby Darin, Atco 6229 | | 12 |
| 50 | 43 | 45 | 53 | MR. SONGWRITER | Connie Stevens, Warner Bros. 5289 | | 8 |
| 51 | 57 | 60 | 66 | YOU CAN'T JUDGE A BOOK BY THE COVER | Bo Diddley, Checker 1019 | | 6 |
| 52 ★ | 70 | — | — | POPEYE The Hitchhiker | Chubby Checker, Parkway 849 | | 2 |
| 53 ★ | 64 | 81 | 96 | HIDE AND GO SEEK | Bunker Hill, Mala 451 | | 5 |
| 54 | 56 | 67 | 79 | LOLLIPOPS AND ROSES | Paul Petersen, Colpix 649 | | 5 |
| 55 ★ | 65 | 71 | 95 | I KEEP FORGETTIN' | Chuck Jackson, Wand 126 | | 4 |
| 56 | 59 | 70 | 72 | YIELD NOT TO TEMPTATION | Bobby Bland, Duke 352 | | 7 |
| 57 | 63 | 83 | 86 | TORTURE | Kris Jensen, Hickory 1173 | | 4 |
| 58 ★ | — | — | — | SAVE ALL YOUR LOVIN' FOR ME | Brenda Lee, Decca 31424 | | 1 |
| 59 | 49 | 54 | 58 | BOYS' NIGHT OUT | Patti Page, Mercury 72013 | | 8 |
| 60 ★ | 74 | — | — | DON'T GO NEAR THE INDIANS | Rex Allen, Mercury 71997 | | 2 |
| 61 ★ | 77 | — | — | LITTLE BLACK BOOK | Jimmy Dean, Columbia 42529 | △ | 2 |
| 62 ★ | 82 | — | — | THE THINGS WE DID LAST SUMMER | Shelley Fabares, Colpix 654 | | 2 |
| 63 | 72 | 56 | 50 | A TASTE OF HONEY | Martin Denny, Liberty 55470 | | 11 |
| 64 | 48 | 49 | 49 | BABY ELEPHANT WALK | Lawrence Welk, Dot 16364 | | 16 |
| 65 | 71 | 75 | 99 | IF I DIDN'T HAVE A DIME | Gene Pitney, Musicor 1022 | | 4 |
| 66 ★ | 91 | 98 | — | HE'S A REBEL | Crystals, Philles 106 | | 3 |
| 67 | 38 | 10 | 9 | VACATION | Connie Francis, MGM 13087 | | 9 |
| 68 | 79 | 85 | — | LIMBO ROCK | Chubby Checker, Parkway 849 | | 3 |
| 69 ★ | — | — | — | KING OF THE WHOLE WIDE WORLD | Elvis Presley, RCA Victor EPA 4371 (Extended Play) | | 1 |
| 70 | 62 | 73 | 77 | LONG AS THE ROSE IS RED | Florraine Darlin, Epic 9529 | | 5 |
| 71 ★ | 87 | 97 | 90 | WHAT KIND OF FOOL AM I | Sammy Davis Jr., Reprise 20048 | | 4 |
| 72 | 73 | 77 | 83 | DON'T YOU WORRY | Don Gardner and Dee Dee Ford, Fire 513 | | 5 |
| 73 | 50 | 27 | 26 | TILL DEATH DO US PART | Bob Braun, Decca 31355 | | 10 |
| 74 ★ | 89 | — | — | THE SWISS MAID | Del Shannon, Big Top 3117 | | 2 |
| 75 | 76 | — | 80 | GLORY OF LOVE | Don Gardner & Dee Dee Ford, KC 106 | | 5 |
| 76 | 80 | 88 | 94 | NO ONE WILL EVER KNOW | Jimmie Rodgers, Dot 16378 | | 4 |
| 77 | 90 | — | — | WHAT TIME IS IT! | Jive Five, Beltone 2024 | | 2 |
| 78 | 81 | 87 | 82 | LOOKIN' FOR A LOVE | Valentinos, Sar 132 | | 6 |
| 79 | 83 | 93 | — | STORMY MONDAY BLUES | Bobby Bland, Duke 355 | | 3 |
| 80 ★ | — | — | — | GINA | Johnny Mathis, Columbia 42582 | △ | 1 |
| 81 | 86 | 89 | 92 | BROKEN HEART | Fiestas, Old Town 1122 | | 5 |
| 82 | 85 | 90 | — | SWEET SIXTEEN BARS | Earl Grant, Decca 25574 | | 3 |
| 83 | 84 | 100 | — | BIG LOVE | Joe Henderson, Todd 1077 | | 3 |
| 84 | 98 | — | — | CLOSE TO CATHY | Mike Clifford, United Artists 489 | | 2 |
| 85 ★ | — | — | — | TEN LONELY GUYS | Pat Boone, Dot 16391 | | 1 |
| 86 ★ | — | — | — | WARMED OVER KISSES | Brian Hyland, ABC-Paramount 10359 | | 1 |
| 87 ★ | — | — | — | TWISTIN' WITH LINDA | Isley Brothers, Wand 127 | | 1 |
| 88 ★ | — | — | — | AND THEN THERE WERE DRUMS | Sandy Nelson, Imperial 5870 | | 1 |
| 89 | 78 | 82 | 87 | SO WHAT | Bill Black's Combo, Hi 2055 | | 7 |
| 90 ★ | — | — | — | WORKIN' FOR THE MAN | Roy Orbison, Monument 467 | | 1 |
| 91 | 96 | — | — | DON'T YOU BELIEVE IT | Andy Williams, Columbia 42523 | △ | 2 |
| 92 | — | — | — | FOREVER AND A DAY | Jackie Wilson, Brunswick 55233 | | 1 |
| 93 | 93 | 95 | — | I REALLY DON'T WANT TO KNOW | Solomon Burke, Atlantic 2157 | | 3 |
| 94 | 95 | — | — | WAY OVER THERE | Miracles, Tamla 54069 | | 2 |
| 95 | 97 | — | — | SWEET LITTLE SIXTEEN | Jerry Lee Lewis, Sun 478 | | 2 |
| 96 | — | — | — | MR. LONELY | Buddy Greco, Epic 9536 | | 1 |
| 97 | — | — | — | SECOND FIDDLE GIRL | Barbara Lynn, Jamie 1233 | | 1 |
| 98 | — | — | — | I LEFT MY HEART IN THE BALCONY | Linda Scott, Congress 106 | | 1 |
| 99 | — | — | — | WHAT KIND OF FOOL AM I | Anthony Newley, London 9546 | | 1 |
| 100 | — | — | — | SOMEDAY | Bobby Vee & the Crickets, Liberty 55479 | | 1 |

## HOT 100—A TO Z—(Publisher-Licensee)

Alley Cat (Metorion, BMI) ........ 12
And Then There Were Drums (Travis, BMI) ........ 88
Baby Elephant Walk (Famous, ASCAP) ........ 64
Beechwood 4-5789 (Jobete, BMI) ........ 17
Big Love (Cramort, BMI) ........ 83
Boys' Night Out (Miller, ASCAP) ........ 59
Breaking Up Is Hard to Do (Aldon, BMI) ........ 34
Broken Heart (Maureen, BMI) ........ 81
Close to Cathy (Arch, ASCAP) ........ 84
Come on Little Angel (Glenden, ASCAP) ........ 35
Devil Woman (Marty's BMI) ........ 33
Do You Love Me (Jobete, BMI) ........ 28
Don't Go Near the Indians (Buttercup, BMI) ........ 60
Don't You Believe It (Dolfi, ASCAP) ........ 91
Don't You Worry (Fast-Pete, BMI) ........ 72
Every Night (Without You) (Spanka, BMI) ........ 46
Forever and a Day (Merrimac, BMI) ........ 92
Gina (Elm Drive, ASCAP) ........ 80
Glory of Love (Shapiro-Bernstein, ASCAP) ........ 75
Green Onions (East, BMI) ........ 4
He's a Rebel (January, BMI) ........ 66
Hide and Go Seek (Florentine, BMI) ........ 53
Hully Gully Baby (Kalmann, ASCAP) ........ 30
I Keep Forgettin' (Trio, BMI) ........ 55
I Left My Heart in San Francisco (General, ASCAP) ........ 42
I Left My Heart in the Balcony (Trinity-Kilt, BMI) ........ 98
I Love the Way You Are (Tobi-Ann, BMI) ........ 40
I Really Don't Want to Know (Hill & Range, BMI) ........ 93
I Remcember You (Paramount, ASCAP) ........ 27
I'm the Girl From Wolverton Mountain (Painted Desert, BMI) ........ 38
If I Didn't Have a Dime (January, BMI) ........ 65
If I Had a Hammer (Ludlow, BMI) ........ 15
It Might As Well Rain Until September (Aldon, BMI) ........ 32
King of the Whole Wide World (Presley, BMI) ........ 69
Let's Dance (Rondell & Sherman-DeVorzon, BMI) ........ 6
Lie to Me (Ben Day, BMI) ........ 23
Limbo Rock (Twist, BMI) ........ 68
Little Black Book (Plainview, BMI) ........ 61
Loco-Motion (Aldon, BMI) ........ 11
Lollipops and Roses (Garland, ASCAP) ........ 54
Long As the Rose Is Red (Lyle, ASCAP) ........ 7
Lookin' for a Love (Kags, BMI) ........ 78
Mr. Lonely (Ripley, BMI) ........ 96
Mr. Songwriter (Gil, BMI) ........ 50
Monster Mash (Garpax, BMI) ........ 13
No One Will Ever Know (Milene, ASCAP) ........ 76
Only Love Can Break a Heart (Arch, ASCAP) ........ 43
Papa-Oom-Mow-Mow (Beechwood, BMI) ........ 48
Party Lights (Rambed, BMI) ........ 37
Patches (Aldon, BMI) ........ 8
Point of No Return (Aldon, BMI) ........ 36
Popeye the Hitchhiker (Kalmann, ASCAP) ........ 52
Punish Her (January, BMI) ........ 31
Rain, Rain Go Away (Regent, BMI) ........ 19
Ramblin' Rose (Sweco, BMI) ........ 2
Rinky Dink (Arc-Cortez, BMI) ........ 14
Save All Your Lovin' for Me (Champion, BMI) ........ 58
Second Fiddle Girl (Dandelion-Crazy Cajun, BMI) ........ 97
Send Me the Pillow You Dream on (Four Star, BMI) ........ 18
Shame on Me (Western Hills-Lois-Saran, BMI) ........ 39
She's Not You (Presley, BMI) ........ 10
Sheila (Eager-Nitetime, BMI) ........ 3
Sherry (Bobob, ASCAP) ........ 1
Silver Threads & Golden Needles (Central Songs, BMI) ........ 20
So What (Jec, BMI) ........ 89
Someday (Woodbury-Saima, BMI) ........ 100
Stop the Music (Vee-Ve, BMI) ........ 44
Stop the Wedding (Figure, BMI) ........ 41
Stormy Monday Blues (Gregmark, ASCAP) ........ 79
Surfin' Safari (Guild, BMI) ........ 29
Sweet Little Sixteen (Arc, BMI) ........ 95
Sweet Sixteen Bars (Progressive, BMI) ........ 82
Swingin' Safari, A (Roosevelt, BMI) ........ 24
Swiss Maid, The (Tree, BMI) ........ 74
Taste of Honey, A (Songfest, ASCAP) ........ 63
Teen Age Idol (Nelson, ASCAP) ........ 5
Ten Lonely Guys (Roosevelt, BMI) ........ 85
Things (Adaris, BMI) ........ 49
Things We Did Last Summer, The (Kerwin, ASCAP) ........ 62
Till Death Do Us Part (Karolyn, ASCAP) ........ 73
Torture (Acuff-Rose, BMI) ........ 57
Twistin' With Linda (Wemar, BMI) ........ 87
Vacation (Merna, BMI) ........ 67
Venus in Blue Jeans (Aldon, BMI) ........ 16
Warmed Over Kisses (Pogo, ASCAP) ........ 86
Way Over There (Jobete, BMI) ........ 94
What Kind of Fool Am I—Davis (Ludlow, BMI) ........ 71
What Kind of Fool Am I—Newley (Ludlow, BMI) ........ 99
What Kind of Love Is This (Planetary-Gee, ASCAP) ........ 26
What Time Is It? (Lescay, BMI) ........ 77
What's a Matter Baby (Eden, BMI) ........ 47
What's Gonna Happen When Summer's Gone (Roosevelt, BMI) ........ 45
Wonderful Dream, A (Travis-Rittenhouse, BMI) ........ 22
Workin' for the Man (Acuff-Rose, BMI) ........ 90
Yield Not to Temptation (Don, BMI) ........ 56
You Beat Me to the Punch (Jobete, BMI) ........ 9
You Belong to Me (Ridgeway, BMI) ........ 7
You Can't Judge a Book By the Cover (Arc, BMI) ........ 51
You Don't Know Me (Hill & Range, BMI) ........ 21
Your Nose Is Gonna Grow (Maraville, BMI) ........ 25

## BUBBLING UNDER THE HOT 100

101. LIVE IT UP........Sandy Nelson, Imperial 5870
102. COMIN' HOME BABY........Herbie Mann, Atlantic 5020
103. BONANZA!........Johnny Cash, Columbia 42512
104. YOUR HEART BELONGS TO ME........Supremes, Motown 1027
105. LEAH........Roy Orbison, Monument 467
106. THERE IS NO GREATER LOVE........Wanderers, MGM 13082
107. TRY A LITTLE TENDERNESS........Aretha Franklin, Columbia 42520
108. FOR ALL WE KNOW........Dinah Washington, Roulette 4444
109. CHILLS........Tony Orlando, Epic 9519
110. I WOULDN'T KNOW........Dinah Washington, Roulette 4444
111. JUST FOR A THRILL........Aretha Franklin, Columbia 42520
112. I'VE BEEN EVERYWHERE........Hank Snow, RCA Victor 8072
113. STUBBORN KIND OF FELLOW........Marvin Gaye, Tamla 54068
114. HOW'S MY EX TREATING YOU........Jerry Lee Lewis, Sun 478
115. MAMA, HE TREATS YOUR DAUGHTER MEAN........Ruth Brown, Philips 40056
116. MASHED POTATOES U.S.A.........James Brown & the Famous Flames, King 5672
117. THE GREATEST ACTOR........Wanda Jackson, Capitol 4833
118. HAIL TO THE CONQUERING HERO........James Darren, Colpix 655
119. YOU CAN'T LIE TO A LIAR........Ketty Lester, Era 3088
120. ONE MORE TOWN........Kingston Trio, Capitol 4842
*120. HE'S A REBEL........Vikki Carr, Liberty 55493

*Tie

# BILLBOARD HOT 100

**FOR WEEK ENDING SEPTEMBER 29, 1962**

★ STAR PERFORMERS—Selections registering greatest upward progress this week.
Ⓢ Indicates that 45 r.p.m. stereo single version is available.
△ Indicates that 33⅓ r.p.m. mono single version is available.
Ⓐ Indicates that 33⅓ r.p.m. stereo single version is available.

| This Week | Last Week | 2 Wks. Ago | 3 Wks. Ago | Title — Artist, Label & Number | Weeks On Chart |
|---|---|---|---|---|---|
| 1 | 1 | 1 | 11 | SHERRY — Four Seasons, Vee Jay 456 | 6 |
| 2 | 2 | 3 | 4 | RAMBLIN' ROSE — Nat King Cole, Capitol 4804 | 9 |
| 3 | 4 | 5 | 22 | GREEN ONIONS — Booker T & the MG's, Stax 127 | 8 |
| 4 | 13 | 37 | 72 | MONSTER MASH — Bobby (Boris) Pickett and the Crypt Kickers, Garpax 44167 | 4 |
| 5 | 3 | 2 | 1 | SHEILA — Tommy Roe, ABC-Paramount 10329 | 10 |
| 6 | 6 | 15 | 32 | LET'S DANCE — Chris Montez, Monogram 505 | 8 |
| 7 | 12 | 18 | 19 | ALLEY CAT — Bent Fabric, Atco 6226 | 10 |
| 8 | 8 | 9 | 20 | PATCHES — Dickey Lee, Smash 1758 | 6 |
| 9 | 7 | 13 | 18 | YOU BELONG TO ME — Duprees, Coed 569 | 9 |
| 10 | 5 | 7 | 9 | TEEN AGE IDOL — Rick Nelson, Imperial 5864 | 8 |
| 11 | 9 | 12 | 28 | YOU BEAT ME TO THE PUNCH — Mary Wells, Motown 1032 | 8 |
| 12 | 15 | 35 | 36 | IF I HAD A HAMMER — Peter, Paul & Mary, Warner Bros. 5296 | 7 |
| 13 | 16 | 19 | 26 | VENUS IN BLUE JEANS — Jimmy Clanton, Ace 8001 | 7 |
| 14 | 11 | 4 | 3 | LOCO-MOTION — Little Eva, Dimension 1000 | 14 |
| 15 | 23 | 27 | 41 | LIE TO ME — Brook Benton, Mercury 72024 | 6 |
| 16 | 10 | 6 | 5 | SHE'S NOT YOU — Elvis Presley, RCA Victor 8041 △ | 9 |
| 17 | 27 | 53 | 76 | I REMEMBER YOU — Frank Ifield, Vee Jay 457 | 4 |
| 18 | 19 | 33 | 50 | RAIN, RAIN GO AWAY — Bobby Vinton, Epic 9532 | 6 |
| 19 | 28 | 42 | 55 | DO YOU LOVE ME — Contours, Gordy 7005 | 8 |
| 20 | 20 | 22 | 24 | SILVER THREADS & GOLDEN NEEDLES — Springfields, Philips 40038 | 9 |
| 21 | 26 | 36 | 47 | WHAT KIND OF LOVE IS THIS — Joey Dee and the Starliters, Roulette 4438 | 6 |
| 22 | 22 | 25 | 35 | A WONDERFUL DREAM — Majors, Imperial 5855 | 7 |
| 23 | 17 | 20 | 31 | BEECHWOOD 4-5789 — Marvelettes, Tamla 54065 | 8 |
| 24 | 29 | 30 | 46 | SURFIN' SAFARI — Beach Boys, Capitol 4777 | 8 |
| 25 | 32 | 41 | 52 | IT MIGHT AS WELL RAIN UNTIL SEPTEMBER — Carole King, Dimension 2000 | 6 |
| 26 | 31 | 40 | 59 | PUNISH HER — Bobby Vee, Liberty 55479 | 5 |
| 27 | 30 | 32 | 48 | HULLY GULLY BABY — Dovells, Parkway 845 | 8 |
| 28 | 14 | 10 | 12 | RINKY DINK — Dave (Baby) Cortez, Chess 1829 | 12 |
| 29 | 21 | 8 | 2 | YOU DON'T KNOW ME — Ray Charles, ABC-Paramount 10345 | 10 |
| 30 | 43 | 68 | — | ONLY LOVE CAN BREAK A HEART — Gene Pitney, Musicor 1022 | 3 |
| 31 | 25 | 29 | 15 | YOUR NOSE IS GONNA GROW — Johnny Crawford, Del-Fi 4181 | 7 |
| 32 | 42 | 54 | 62 | I LEFT MY HEART IN SAN FRANCISCO — Tony Bennett, Columbia 42332 △ | 8 |
| 33 | 18 | 17 | 21 | SEND ME THE PILLOW YOU DREAM ON — Johnny Tillotson, Cadence 1424 | 8 |
| 34 | 24 | 26 | 13 | A SWINGIN' SAFARI — Billy Vaughn, Dot 16374 | 11 |
| 35 | 39 | 23 | 25 | SHAME ON ME — Bobby Bare, RCA Victor 8032 △ | 11 |
| 36 | 52 | 70 | — | POPEYE THE HITCHHIKER — Chubby Checker, Parkway 849 | 3 |
| 37 | 35 | 28 | 33 | COME ON LITTLE ANGEL — Belmonts, Sabina 505 | 11 |
| 38 | 40 | 46 | 51 | I LOVE YOU THE WAY YOU ARE — Bobby Vinton, Diamond 121 | 8 |
| 39 | 33 | 16 | 16 | DEVIL WOMAN — Marty Robbins, Columbia 42486 △ | 10 |
| 40 | 36 | 21 | 23 | POINT OF NO RETURN — Gene McDaniels, Liberty 55480 | 9 |
| 41 | 44 | 69 | 78 | STOP THE MUSIC — Shirelles, Scepter 1237 | 4 |
| 42 | 57 | 63 | 83 | TORTURE — Kris Jensen, Hickory 1173 | 5 |
| 43 | 34 | 11 | 6 | BREAKING UP IS HARD TO DO — Neil Sedaka, RCA Victor 8046 △ | 14 |
| 44 | 66 | 91 | 98 | HE'S A REBEL — Crystals, Philles 106 | 4 |
| 45 | 38 | 39 | 40 | I'M THE GIRL FROM WOLVERTON MOUNTAIN — Jo Ann Campbell, Cameo 223 | 7 |
| 46 | 60 | 74 | — | DON'T GO NEAR THE INDIANS — Rex Allen, Mercury 71997 | 3 |
| 47 | 45 | 66 | 79 | WHAT'S GONNA HAPPEN WHEN SUMMER'S GONE — Freddy Cannon, Swan 4117 | 4 |
| 48 | 51 | 57 | 60 | YOU CAN'T JUDGE A BOOK BY THE COVER — Bo Diddley, Checker 1019 | 7 |
| 49 | 53 | 64 | 81 | HIDE AND GO SEEK — Bunker Hill, Mala 451 | 6 |
| 50 | — | — | — | ALL ALONE AM I — Brenda Lee, Decca 31424 | 1 |
| 51 | 61 | 77 | — | LITTLE BLACK BOOK — Jimmy Dean, Columbia 42529 △ | 3 |
| 52 | 37 | 14 | 7 | PARTY LIGHTS — Claudine Clark, Chancellor 1113 | 14 |
| 53 | 69 | — | — | KING OF THE WHOLE WIDE WORLD — Elvis Presley, RCA Victor EPA 4371 (Extended Play) | 2 |
| 54 | 71 | 87 | 97 | WHAT KIND OF FOOL AM I — Sammy Davis Jr., Reprise 20048 | 5 |
| 55 | 62 | 82 | — | THE THINGS WE DID LAST SUMMER — Shelley Fabares, Colpix 654 | 3 |
| 56 | 58 | — | — | SAVE ALL YOUR LOVIN' FOR ME — Brenda Lee, Decca 31424 | 2 |
| 57 | 59 | 49 | 54 | BOYS' NIGHT OUT — Patti Page, Mercury 72013 | 9 |
| 58 | 48 | 51 | 53 | PAPA-OOM-MOW-MOW — Rivingtons, Liberty 55427 | 7 |
| 59 | 68 | 79 | 85 | LIMBO ROCK — Chubby Checker, Parkway 849 | 4 |
| 60 | 55 | 65 | 71 | I KEEP FORGETTIN' — Chuck Jackson, Wand 126 | 5 |
| 61 | 63 | 72 | 56 | A TASTE OF HONEY — Martin Denny, Liberty 55470 | 12 |
| 62 | 54 | 56 | 67 | LOLLIPOPS AND ROSES — Paul Petersen, Colpix 649 | 6 |
| 63 | 80 | — | — | GINA — Johnny Mathis, Columbia 42582 △ | 2 |
| 64 | 65 | 71 | 75 | IF I DIDN'T HAVE A DIME — Gene Pitney, Musicor 1022 | 5 |
| 65 | 82 | 85 | 90 | SWEET SIXTEEN BARS — Earl Grant, Decca 25574 | 4 |
| 66 | 84 | 98 | — | CLOSE TO CATHY — Mike Clifford, United Artists 489 | 3 |
| 67 | 76 | 80 | 88 | NO ONE WILL EVER KNOW — Jimmie Rodgers, Dot 16378 | 5 |
| 68 | 72 | 73 | 77 | DON'T YOU WORRY — Don Gardner and Dee Dee Ford, Fire 513 | 6 |
| 69 | 77 | 90 | — | WHAT TIME IS IT — Jive Five, Beltone 2024 | 3 |
| 70 | 74 | 89 | — | THE SWISS MAID — Del Shannon, Big Top 3117 | 3 |
| 71 | 88 | — | — | AND THEN THERE WERE DRUMS — Sandy Nelson, Imperial 5870 | 2 |
| 72 | 78 | 81 | 87 | LOOKIN' FOR A LOVE — Valentinos, Sar 132 | 7 |
| 73 | 79 | 83 | 93 | STORMY MONDAY — Bobby Bland, Duke 355 | 4 |
| 74 | 83 | 84 | 100 | BIG LOVE — Joe Henderson, Todd 1077 | 4 |
| 75 | 87 | — | — | TWISTIN' WITH LINDA — Isley Brothers, Wand 127 | 2 |
| 76 | 86 | — | — | WARMED OVER KISSES — Brian Hyland, ABC-Paramount 10359 | 2 |
| 77 | 70 | 62 | 73 | LONG AS THE ROSE IS RED — Florraine Darlin, Epic 9529 | 6 |
| 78 | 56 | 59 | 70 | YIELD NOT TO TEMPTATION — Bobby Bland, Duke 352 | 8 |
| 79 | 90 | — | — | WORKIN' FOR THE MAN — Roy Orbison, Monument 467 | 2 |
| 80 | 85 | — | — | TEN LONELY GUYS — Pat Boone, Dot 16391 | 2 |
| 81 | 46 | 55 | 63 | EVERY NIGHT (WITHOUT YOU) — Paul Anka, RCA Victor 8068 △ | 6 |
| 82 | — | 99 | — | OL' MAN RIVER — Jimmy Smith, Verve 10262 | 3 |
| 83 | — | — | — | JAMES (Hold the Ladder Steady) — Sue Thompson, Hickory 1183 | 1 |
| 84 | — | — | — | BABY FACE — Bobby Darin, Atco 6236 | 1 |
| 85 | 91 | 96 | — | DON'T YOU BELIEVE IT — Andy Williams, Columbia 42523 △ | 3 |
| 86 | 97 | — | — | SECOND FIDDLE GIRL — Barbara Lynn, Jamie 1233 | 2 |
| 87 | — | — | — | NOTHING CAN CHANGE THIS LOVE — Sam Cooke, RCA Victor 8088 | 1 |
| 88 | — | — | — | I'VE BEEN EVERYWHERE — Hank Snow, RCA Victor 8072 △ | 1 |
| 89 | — | — | — | MASHED POTATOES U.S.A. — James Brown and the Famous Flames, King 5672 | 1 |
| 90 | — | — | — | IF A MAN ANSWERS — Bobby Darin, Capitol 4837 | 1 |
| 91 | 92 | — | — | FOREVER AND A DAY — Jackie Wilson, Brunswick 55233 | 2 |
| 92 | 81 | 86 | 89 | BROKEN HEART — Fiestas, Old Town 1122 | 6 |
| 93 | — | — | — | DESAFINADO — Stan Getz and Charlie Byrd, Verve 10260 | 1 |
| 94 | 94 | 95 | — | WAY OVER THERE — Miracles, Tamla 54069 | 3 |
| 95 | 95 | 97 | — | SWEET LITTLE SIXTEEN — Jerry Lee Lewis, Sun 379 | 3 |
| 96 | 96 | — | — | MR. LONELY — Buddy Greco, Epic 9536 | 2 |
| 97 | 99 | — | — | WHAT KIND OF FOOL AM I — Anthony Newley, London 9546 | 2 |
| 98 | 98 | — | — | I LEFT MY HEART IN THE BALCONY — Linda Scott, Congress 106 | 2 |
| 99 | 100 | — | — | SOMEDAY — Bobby Vee & the Crickets, Liberty 55479 | 2 |
| 100 | — | — | — | TRY A LITTLE TENDERNESS — Aretha Franklin, Columbia 42520 △ | 1 |

## BUBBLING UNDER THE HOT 100

101. HAIL THE CONQUERING HERO ........ James Darren, Colpix 655
102. IT'S LOVE THAT REALLY COUNTS ........ Shirelles, Scepter 1237
103. LEAH ........ Roy Orbison, Monument 467
104. YOU CAN'T LIE TO A LIAR ........ Ketty Lester, Era 3088
105. I'M GONNA CHANGE EVERYTHING ........ Jim Reeves, RCA Victor 8080
106. WHAT'LL I DO ........ Johnny Tillotson, Cadence 1424
107. THERE IS NO GREATER LOVE ........ Wanderers, MGM 13082
108. YOUR HEART BELONGS TO ME ........ Supremes, Motown 1027
109. SO WHAT ........ Bill Black's Combo, Hi 2055
110. TILL THERE WAS YOU ........ Valjean, Carlton 576
111. I'M GOING BACK TO SCHOOL ........ Dee Clark, Vee Jay 462
112. BEACH PARTY ........ Dave York, PKM 6700
113. LOVERS BY NIGHT, STRANGERS BY DAY ........ Fleetwoods, Dolton 62
114. (DANCE WITH THE) GUITAR MAN ........ Duane Eddy, RCA Victor 8087
115. LET'S GO ........ Routers, Warner Bros. 5283
116. 409 ........ Beach Boys, Capitol 4777
117. RICHIE ........ Gloria Dennis, Rust 5049
118. STUBBORN KIND OF FELLOW ........ Marvin Gaye, Tamla 54068
119. SWING LOW ........ Floyd Cramer, RCA Victor 8084
120. MAGIC WAND ........ Don and Juan, Big Top 3121

# BILLBOARD HOT 100

FOR WEEK ENDING OCTOBER 6 1962

★ STAR PERFORMERS—Selections registering greatest upward progress this week.

S Indicates that 45 r.p.m. stereo single version is available.

△ Indicates that 33⅓ r.p.m. mono single version is available.

△S Indicates that 33⅓ r.p.m. stereo single version is available.

| This Week | 1 Wk. Ago | 2 Wks. Ago | 3 Wks. Ago | TITLE Artist, Label & Number | Weeks On Chart |
|---|---|---|---|---|---|
| 1 | 1 | 1 | 1 | SHERRY — Four Seasons, Vee Jay 456 | 7 |
| 2 | 4 | 13 | 37 | MONSTER MASH — Bobby (Boris) Pickett and the Crypt Kickers, Garpax 44167 | 5 |
| 3 | 2 | 2 | 3 | RAMBLIN' ROSE — Nat King Cole, Capitol 4804 | 10 |
| 4 | 6 | 6 | 15 | LET'S DANCE — Chris Montez, Monogram 505 | 9 |
| 5 | 3 | 4 | 5 | GREEN ONIONS — Booker T & the MG's, Stax 127 | 9 |
| 6 | 8 | 8 | 9 | PATCHES — Dickey Lee, Smash 1758 | 7 |
| ★7 | 13 | 16 | 19 | VENUS IN BLUE JEANS — Jimmy Clanton, Ace 8001 | 8 |
| ★8 | 17 | 27 | 53 | I REMEMBER YOU — Frank Ifield, Vee Jay 457 | 5 |
| 9 | 7 | 12 | 18 | ALLEY CAT — Bent Fabric, Atco 6226 | 11 |
| 10 | 11 | 9 | 12 | YOU BEAT ME TO THE PUNCH — Mary Wells, Motown 1032 | 9 |
| 11 | 5 | 3 | 2 | SHEILA — Tommy Roe, ABC-Paramount 10329 | 11 |
| ★12 | 18 | 19 | 33 | RAIN, RAIN GO AWAY — Bobby Vinton, Epic 9532 | 7 |
| 13 | 15 | 23 | 27 | LIE TO ME — Brook Benton, Mercury 72024 | 7 |
| 14 | 12 | 15 | 35 | IF I HAD A HAMMER — Peter, Paul & Mary, Warner Bros. 5296 | 8 |
| 15 | 19 | 28 | 42 | DO YOU LOVE ME — Contours, Gordy 7005 | 9 |
| 16 | 10 | 5 | 7 | TEEN AGE IDOL — Rick Nelson, Imperial 5864 | 9 |
| 17 | 9 | 7 | 13 | YOU BELONG TO ME — Duprees, Coed 569 | 10 |
| ★18 | 23 | 17 | 20 | BEECHWOOD 4-5789 — Marvelettes, Tamla 54065 | 9 |
| ★19 | 24 | 29 | 30 | SURFIN' SAFARI — Beach Boys, Capitol 4777 | 9 |
| 20 | 21 | 26 | 36 | WHAT KIND OF LOVE IS THIS — Joey Dee and the Starliters, Roulette 4438 | 7 |
| 21 | 26 | 31 | 40 | PUNISH HER — Bobby Vee, Liberty 55479 | 6 |
| 22 | 25 | 32 | 41 | IT MIGHT AS WELL RAIN UNTIL SEPTEMBER — Carole King, Dimension 2000 | 7 |
| ★23 | 44 | 66 | 91 | HE'S A REBEL — Crystals, Philles 106 | 5 |
| 24 | 30 | 43 | 68 | ONLY LOVE CAN BREAK A HEART — Gene Pitney, Musicor 1022 | 4 |
| ★25 | 36 | 52 | 70 | POPEYE (THE HITCHHIKER) — Chubby Checker, Parkway 849 | 3 |
| 26 | 27 | 30 | 32 | HULLY GULLY BABY — Dovells, Parkway 845 | 9 |
| 27 | 14 | 11 | 4 | LOCO-MOTION — Little Eva, Dimension 1000 | 15 |
| 28 | 32 | 42 | 54 | I LEFT MY HEART IN SAN FRANCISCO △ — Tony Bennett, Columbia 42332 | 9 |
| 29 | 22 | 22 | 25 | A WONDERFUL DREAM — Majors, Imperial 5855 | 8 |
| ★30 | 46 | 60 | 74 | DONT GO NEAR THE INDIANS — Rex Allen, Mercury 71997 | 4 |
| 31 | 20 | 20 | 22 | SILVER THREADS & GOLDEN NEEDLES — Springfields, Philips 40038 | 10 |
| 32 | 16 | 10 | 6 | SHE'S NOT YOU △ — Elvis Presley, RCA Victor 8041 | 10 |
| 33 | 28 | 14 | 10 | RINKY DINK — Dave (Baby) Cortez, Chess 1829 | 13 |
| 34 | 37 | 35 | 28 | COME ON LITTLE ANGEL — Belmonts, Sabina 505 | 12 |
| ★35 | 50 | — | — | ALL ALONE AM I — Brenda Lee, Decca 31424 | 2 |
| ★36 | 51 | 61 | 77 | LITTLE BLACK BOOK △ — Jimmy Dean, Columbia 42529 | 4 |
| ★37 | 53 | 69 | — | KING OF THE WHOLE WIDE WORLD — Elvis Presley, RCA Victor EPA 4371 (Extended Play) | 3 |
| 38 | 42 | 57 | 63 | TORTURE — Kris Jensen, Hickory 1173 | 6 |
| 39 | 41 | 44 | 69 | STOP THE MUSIC — Shirelles, Scepter 1237 | 5 |
| ★40 | 54 | 71 | 87 | WHAT KIND OF FOOL AM I — Sammy Davis Jr., Reprise 20048 | 6 |
| 41 | 39 | 33 | 16 | DEVIL WOMAN △ — Marty Robbins, Columbia 42486 | 11 |
| 42 | 29 | 21 | 8 | YOU DON'T KNOW ME — Ray Charles, ABC-Paramount 10345 | 11 |
| 43 | 35 | 39 | 23 | SHAME ON ME △ — Bobby Bare, RCA Victor 8032 | 12 |
| 44 | 49 | 53 | 64 | HIDE AND GO SEEK — Bunker Hill, Mala 451 | 7 |
| 45 | 40 | 36 | 21 | POINT OF NO RETURN — Gene McDaniels, Liberty 55480 | 10 |
| ★46 | 63 | 80 | — | GINA △ — Johnny Mathis, Columbia 42582 | 3 |
| ★47 | 59 | 68 | 79 | LIMBO ROCK — Chubby Checker, Parkway 849 | 5 |
| 48 | 34 | 24 | 26 | A SWINGIN' SAFARI — Billy Vaughn, Dot 16374 | 12 |
| ★49 | 76 | 86 | — | WARMED OVER KISSES — Brian Hyland, ABC-Paramount 10359 | 3 |
| 50 | 55 | 62 | 82 | THE THINGS WE DID LAST SUMMER — Shelley Fabares, Colpix 654 | 4 |
| 51 | 33 | 18 | 17 | SEND ME THE PILLOW YOU DREAM ON — Johnny Tillotson, Cadence 1424 | 9 |
| 52 | 31 | 25 | 29 | YOUR NOSE IS GONNA GROW — Johnny Crawford, Del-Fi 4181 | 9 |
| 53 | 56 | 58 | — | SAVE ALL YOUR LOVIN' FOR ME — Brenda Lee, Decca 31424 | 3 |
| 54 | 61 | 63 | 72 | A TASTE OF HONEY — Martin Denny, Liberty 55470 | 13 |
| 55 | 48 | 51 | 57 | YOU CAN'T JUDGE A BOOK BY THE COVER — Bo Diddley, Checker 1019 | 8 |
| ★56 | 66 | 84 | 98 | CLOSE TO CATHY — Mike Clifford, United Artists 489 | 4 |
| 57 | 52 | 37 | 14 | PARTY LIGHTS — Claudine Clark, Chancellor 1113 | 15 |
| 58 | 60 | 55 | 65 | I KEEP FORGETTIN' — Chuck Jackson, Wand 126 | 6 |
| 59 | 62 | 54 | 56 | LOLLIPOPS AND ROSES — Paul Petersen, Colpix 649 | 7 |
| ★60 | 73 | 79 | 83 | STORMY MONDAY — Bobby Bland, Duke 355 | 5 |
| 61 | 65 | 82 | 85 | SWEET SIXTEEN BARS — Earl Grant, Decca 25574 | 5 |
| 62 | 64 | 65 | 71 | IF I DIDN'T HAVE A DIME — Gene Pitney, Musicor 1022 | 6 |
| ★63 | 79 | 90 | — | WORKIN' FOR THE MAN — Roy Orbison, Monument 467 | 3 |
| 64 | 67 | 76 | 80 | NO ONE WILL EVER KNOW — Jimmie Rodgers, Dot 16378 | 6 |
| 65 | 71 | 88 | — | AND THEN THERE WERE DRUMS — Sandy Nelson, Imperial 5870 | 3 |
| 66 | 68 | 72 | 73 | DON'T YOU WORRY — Don Gardner and Dee Dee Ford, Fire 513 | 7 |
| ★67 | 87 | — | — | NOTHING CAN CHANGE THIS LOVE △ — Sam Cooke, RCA Victor 8088 | 2 |
| 68 | 80 | 85 | — | TEN LONELY GUYS — Pat Boone, Dot 16391 | 3 |
| ★69 | 84 | — | — | BABY FACE — Bobby Darin, Atco 6236 | 2 |
| 70 | 70 | 74 | 89 | THE SWISS MAID — Del Shannon, Big Top 3117 | 4 |
| 71 | 83 | — | — | JAMES (Hold the Ladder Steady) — Sue Thompson, Hickory 1183 | 2 |
| 72 | 75 | 87 | — | TWISTIN' WITH LINDA — Isley Brothers, Wand 127 | 3 |
| ★73 | 90 | — | — | IF A MAN ANSWERS — Bobby Darin, Capitol 4837 | 2 |
| 74 | 77 | 70 | 62 | LONG AS THE ROSE IS RED — Florraine Darlin, Epic 9529 | 7 |
| 75 | 69 | 77 | 90 | WHAT TIME IS IT! — Jive Five, Beltone 2024 | 4 |
| 76 | 38 | 40 | 46 | I LOVE YOU THE WAY YOU ARE — Bobby Vinton, Diamond 121 | 9 |
| ★77 | — | — | — | NEXT DOOR TO AN ANGEL △ — Neil Sedaka, RCA Victor 8086 | 1 |
| 78 | 85 | 91 | 96 | DON'T YOU BELIEVE IT △ — Andy Williams, Columbia 42523 | 4 |
| 79 | 72 | 78 | 81 | LOOKIN' FOR A LOVE — Valentinos, Sar 132 | 8 |
| 80 | 58 | 48 | 51 | PAPA-OOM-MOW-MOW — Rivingtons, Liberty 55427 | 8 |
| ★81 | — | — | — | SUSIE DARLIN' — Tommy Roe, ABC-Paramount 10362 | 1 |
| 82 | 89 | — | — | MASHED POTATOES U. S. A. — James Brown and the Famous Flames, King 5672 | 2 |
| 83 | 86 | 97 | — | SECOND FIDDLE GIRL — Barbara Lynn, Jamie 1233 | 3 |
| ★84 | — | — | — | THE BURNING OF ATLANTA △ — Claude King, Columbia 42581 | 1 |
| 85 | 97 | 99 | — | WHAT KIND OF FOOL AM I — Anthony Newley, London 9546 | 3 |
| 86 | 93 | — | — | DESAFINADO — Stan Getz and Charlie Byrd, Verve 10260 | 2 |
| ★87 | — | — | — | I'M GOING BACK TO SCHOOL — Dee Clark, Vee Jay 462 | 1 |
| ★88 | — | — | — | (DANCE WITH THE) GUITAR MAN △ — Duane Eddy, RCA Victor 8087 | 1 |
| ★89 | — | — | — | WHAT KIND OF FOOL AM I △ — Robert Goulet, Columbia 42519 | 1 |
| ★90 | — | — | — | POP POP POP-PIE — Sherrys, Guyden 2068 | 1 |
| 91 | 91 | 92 | — | FOREVER AND A DAY — Jackie Wilson, Brunswick 55233 | 3 |
| 92 | — | — | — | LOVE ME TENDER — Richard Chamberlain, MGM 13097 | 1 |
| 93 | 96 | 96 | — | MR. LONELY — Buddy Greco, Epic 9536 | 3 |
| 94 | — | — | — | I WAS SUCH A FOOL — Connie Francis, MGM 13096 | 1 |
| 95 | — | — | — | LEAH — Roy Orbison, Monument 467 | 1 |
| 96 | 98 | 98 | — | I LEFT MY HEART IN THE BALCONY — Linda Scott, Congress 106 | 3 |
| 97 | — | — | — | DID YOU EVER SEE A DREAM WALKING — Fats Domino, Imperial 5875 | 1 |
| 98 | — | — | — | WIGGLE WOBBLE — Les Cooper, Everlast 5019 | 1 |
| 99 | — | — | — | HE THINKS I STILL CARE — Connie Francis, MGM 13096 | 1 |
| 100 | — | — | — | WHEN THE BOYS GET TOGETHER — Joanie Sommers, Warner Bros. 5308 | 1 |

## HOT 100—A TO Z—*(Publisher-Licensee)*


All Alone Am I (Duchess, BMI) ... 35
Alley Cat (Metorion, BMI) ... 9
And Then There Were Drums (Travis, BMI) ... 65
Baby Face (Remick, ASCAP) ... 69
Beechwood 4-5789 (Jobete, BMI) ... 18
Burning of Atlanta, The (Conrad, BMI) ... 84
Close to Cathy (Arch, ASCAP) ... 56
Come on Little Angel (Glenden, ASCAP) ... 34
(Dance With the) Guitar Man (Linduane, BMI) ... 88
Desafinado (Hollis, BMI) ... 86
Devil Woman (Marty's, BMI) ... 41
Did You Ever See a Dream Walking (DeSylva, Brown & Henderson, ASCAP) ... 97
Do You Love Me (Jobete, BMI) ... 15
Don't Go Near the Indians (Buttercup, BMI) ... 30
Don't You Believe It (Dolfi, ASCAP) ... 78
Don't You Worry (Fast-Pete, BMI) ... 66
Forever and a Day (Merrimac, BMI) ... 91
Gina (Elm Drive, ASCAP) ... 46
Green Onions (East, BMI) ... 5
He Thinks I Still Care (Glad-Jack, BMI) ... 99
He's a Rebel (January, BMI) ... 23
Hide & Go Seek (Marks-Florentine, BMI) ... 44
Hully Gully Baby (Kalmann, ASCAP) ... 26
I Keep Forgettin' (Trio, BMI) ... 58
I Left My Heart in San Francisco (General, ASCAP) ... 28
I Left My Heart in the Balcony (Trinity-Kilt, BMI). 96
I Love You the Way You Are (Tobi-Ann, BMI) .. 76
I Remember You (Paramount, ASCAP) ... 8
I Was Such a Fool (Francon, ASCAP) ... 94
I'm Going Back to School (Conrad, BMI) ... 87
If a Man Answers (Adaris, BMI) ... 73
If I Didn't Have a Dime (January, BMI) ... 62
If I Had a Hammer (Ludlow, BMI) ... 14
It Might as Well Rain Until September (Aldon, BMI) ... 22
James (Acuff-Rose, BMI) ... 71
King of the Whole Wide World (Presley, BMI) ... 37
Leah (Acuff-Rose, BMI) ... 95
Let's Dance (Rondell & Sherman-DeVorzon, BMI).. 4
Lie to Me (Ben Day, BMI) ... 13
Limbo Rock (Twist, BMI) ... 47
Little Black Book (Plainview, BMI) ... 36
Loco-Motion (Aldon, BMI) ... 27
Lollipops and Roses (Garland, ASCAP) ... 59
Long as the Rose Is Red (Lyle, ASCAP) ... 74
Lookin' for a Love (Kags, BMI) ... 79
Love Me Tender (Presley, BMI) ... 92
Mashed Potatoes U.S.A. (Lois, BMI) ... 82
Mr. Lonely (Ripley, BMI) ... 93
Monster Mash (Garpax, BMI) ... 2
Next Door to an Angel (Aldon, BMI) ... 77
No One Will Ever Know (Milene, ASCAP) ... 64
Nothing Can Change This Love (Kags, BMI) ... 67
Only Love Can Break a Heart (Arch, ASCAP) ... 24
Papa-Oom-Mow-Mow (Beechwood, BMI) ... 80
Party Lights (Rambed, BMI) ... 57
Patches (Aldon, BMI) ... 6
Point of No Return (Aldon, BMI) ... 45
Pop Pop Pop-Pie (Dandelion, BMI) ... 90
Popeye the Hitchhiker (Kalmann, ASCAP) ... 25
Punish Her (January, BMI) ... 21
Rain, Rain Go Away (Regent, BMI) ... 12
Ramblin' Rose (Sweco, BMI) ... 3
Rinky Dink (Arc-Cortez, BMI) ... 33
Save All Your Lovin' for Me (Champion, BMI) .. 53
Second Fiddle Girl (Dandelion-Crazy Cajun, BMI). 83
Send Me the Pillow You Dream On (Four Star, BMI) ... 51
Shame on Me (Western Hills-Lois-Saran, BMI) ... 43
She's Not You (Presley, BMI) ... 32
Sheila (Eager-Nitetime, BMI) ... 11
Sherry (Bobob, ASCAP) ... 1
Silver Threads & Golden Needles (Central Songs, BMI) ... 31
Stop the Music (Vee-Ve, BMI) ... 39
Stormy Monday (Gregmark, BMI) ... 60
Surfin' Safari (Guild, BMI) ... 19
Susie Darlin' (Chancellor, ASCAP) ... 81
Sweet Sixteen Bars (Progressive, BMI) ... 61
Swingin' Safari, A (Roosevelt, BMI) ... 48
Swiss Maid, The (Tree, BMI) ... 70
Taste of Honey, A (Songfest, ASCAP) ... 54
Teen Age Idol (Nelson, ASCAP) ... 16
Ten Lonely Guys (Roosevelt, BMI) ... 68
Things We Did Last Summer, The (Kerwin, ASCAP). 50
Torture (Acuff-Rose, BMI) ... 38
Twistin' With Linda (Wemar, BMI) ... 72
Venus in Blue Jeans (Aldon, BMI) ... 7
Warmed Over Kisses (Pogo, ASCAP) ... 49
What Kind of Fool Am I—Davis (Ludlow, BMI) ... 40
What Kind of Fool Am I—Goulet (Ludlow, BMI) .. 89
What Kind of Fool Am I—Newley (Ludlow, BMI) .. 85
What Kind of Love Is This (Planetary-Gee, ASCAP). 20
What Time Is It? (Lescay, BMI) ... 75
When the Boys Get Together (Tod, ASCAP) ...100
Wiggle Wobble (Bob-Dan, BMI) ... 98
Wonderful Dream, A (Travis-Rittenhouse, BMI) .. 29
Workin' for the Man (Acuff-Rose, BMI) ... 63
You Beat Me to the Punch (Jobete, BMI) ... 10
You Belong to Me (Ridgeway, BMI) ... 17
You Can't Judge a Book by the Cover (Arc, BMI). 55
You Don't Know Me (Hill & Range, BMI) ... 42
Your Nose Is Gonna Grow (Maraville, BMI) ... 52


## BUBBLING UNDER THE HOT 100

101. I'LL REMEMBER CAROL ... Tommy Boyce, RCA Victor 8074
102. IT'S LOVE THAT REALLY COUNTS ... Shirelles, Scepter 1237
103. I'M GONNA CHANGE EVERYTHING ... Jim Reeves, RCA Victor 8080
104. I'VE BEEN EVERYWHERE ... Hank Snow, RCA Victor 8072
105. YOU CAN'T LIE TO A LIAR ... Ketty Lester, Era 3088
106. THERE IS NO GREATER LOVE ... Wanderers, MGM 13082
107. WHAT'LL I DO ... Johnny Tillotson, Cadence 1424
108. 409 ... Beach Boys, Capitol 4777
109. BEACH PARTY ... Dave York, PKM 6700
110. SWING LOW* ... Floyd Cramer, RCA Victor 8084
110. LOVERS BY NIGHT, Strangers by Day* ... Fleetwoods, Dolton 62
111. STUBBORN KIND OF FELLOW ... Marvin Gaye, Tamla 54068
112. TRY A LITTLE TENDERNESS ... Aretha Franklin, Columbia 42520
113. HAIL TO THE CONQUERING HERO ... James Darren, Colpix 655
114. LET'S GO ... Routers, Warner Bros. 5283
115. RICHIE ... Gloria Dennis, Rust 5049
116. THAT STRANGER USED TO BE MY GIRL ... Trade Martin, Coed 570
117. WAY OVER THERE ... Miracles, Tamla 54069
118. SOMEDAY ... Bobby Vee & the Crickets, Liberty 55479
119. BABY, THAT'S ALL ... Jackie Wilson, Brunswick 55233
120. HE'S A REBEL ... Vikki Carr, Liberty 55493
121. LIMBO DANCE ... Champs, Challenge 9162
122. YOU CAN RUN ... Jerry Butler, Vee Jay 463
123. SOMEBODY HAVE MERCY ... Sam Cooke, RCA Victor 8088
124. THE GREATEST ACTOR ... Wanda Jackson, Capitol 4833
125. FOR ALL WE KNOW ... Dinah Washington, Roulette 4444
126. ONE MORE TOWN ... Kingston Trio, Capitol 4842
127. THE CHA CHA CHA ... Bobby Rydell, Cameo 228
128. AFTER LOVING YOU ... Eddy Arnold, RCA Victor 8048
129. I'LL BRING IT HOME TO YOU ... Carla Thomas, Atlantic 2163
130. DON'T EVER LEAVE ME ... Bob & Earl, Tempe 102
131. WHAT KIND OF FOOL AM I ... Vic Damone, Capitol 4827
132. HULLY GULLY GUITARS ... Jerry Reed, Columbia 42533

*Tie

# BILLBOARD HOT 100

FOR WEEK ENDING OCTOBER 13 1962

★ STAR PERFORMERS—Selections registering greatest upward progress this week.

[S] Indicates that 45 r.p.m. stereo single version is available.

△ Indicates that 33⅓ r.p.m. mono single version is available.

[△S] Indicates that 33⅓ r.p.m. stereo single version is available.

| This Week | 1 Wk. Ago | 2 Wks. Ago | 3 Wks. Ago | Title | Artist, Label & Number | | Weeks On Chart |
|---|---|---|---|---|---|---|---|
| 1 | 1 | 1 | 1 | SHERRY | Four Seasons, Vee Jay 456 | | 8 |
| 2 | 2 | 4 | 13 | MONSTER MASH | Bobby (Boris) Pickett and the Crypt Kickers, Garpax 44167 | | 6 |
| 3 | 3 | 2 | 2 | RAMBLIN' ROSE | Nat King Cole, Capitol 4804 | | 11 |
| 4 | 4 | 6 | 6 | LET'S DANCE | Chris Montez, Monogram 505 | | 10 |
| 5 | 8 | 17 | 27 | I REMEMBER YOU | Frank Ifield, Vee Jay 457 | | 6 |
| 6 | 5 | 3 | 4 | GREEN ONIONS | Booker T & the MG's, Stax 127 | | 10 |
| ★7 | 15 | 19 | 28 | DO YOU LOVE ME | Contours, Gordy 7005 | | 10 |
| 8 | 6 | 8 | 8 | PATCHES | Dickey Lee, Smash 1758 | | 8 |
| 9 | 9 | 7 | 12 | ALLEY CAT | Bent Fabric, Atco 6226 | | 12 |
| 10 | 14 | 12 | 15 | IF I HAD A HAMMER | Peter, Paul & Mary, Warner Bros. 5296 | | 9 |
| ★11 | 23 | 44 | 66 | HE'S A REBEL | Crystals, Philles 106 | | 6 |
| 12 | 7 | 13 | 16 | VENUS IN BLUE JEANS | Jimmy Clanton, Ace 8001 | | 9 |
| ★13 | 24 | 30 | 43 | ONLY LOVE CAN BREAK A HEART | Gene Pitney, Musicor 1022 | | 5 |
| ★14 | 19 | 24 | 29 | SURFIN' SAFARI | Beach Boys, Capitol 4777 | | 10 |
| 15 | 10 | 11 | 9 | YOU BEAT ME TO THE PUNCH | Mary Wells, Motown 1032 | | 10 |
| 16 | 11 | 5 | 3 | SHEILA | Tommy Roe, ABC-Paramount 10329 | | 12 |
| 17 | 12 | 18 | 19 | RAIN, RAIN GO AWAY | Bobby Vinton, Epic 9532 | | 8 |
| 18 | 20 | 21 | 26 | WHAT KIND OF LOVE IS THIS | Joey Dee and the Starliters, Roulette 4438 | | 8 |
| 19 | 13 | 15 | 23 | LIE TO ME | Brook Benton, Mercury 72024 | | 8 |
| 20 | 21 | 26 | 31 | PUNISH HER | Bobby Vee, Liberty 55479 | | 7 |
| ★21 | 35 | 50 | — | ALL ALONE AM I | Brenda Lee, Decca 31424 | | 3 |
| 22 | 22 | 25 | 32 | IT MIGHT AS WELL RAIN UNTIL SEPTEMBER | Carole King, Dimension 2000 | | 8 |
| 23 | 28 | 32 | 42 | I LEFT MY HEART IN SAN FRANCISCO | Tony Bennett, Columbia 42332 | △ | 10 |
| 24 | 25 | 36 | 52 | POPEYE (THE HITCHHIKER) | Chubby Checker, Parkway 849 | | 4 |
| 25 | 26 | 27 | 30 | HULLY GULLY BABY | Dovells, Parkway 845 | | 10 |
| 26 | 30 | 46 | 60 | DON'T GO NEAR THE INDIANS | Rex Allen, Mercury 71997 | | 5 |
| 27 | 17 | 9 | 7 | YOU BELONG TO ME | Duprees, Coed 569 | | 11 |
| ★28 | 38 | 42 | 57 | TORTURE | Kris Jensen, Hickory 1173 | | 7 |
| 29 | 16 | 10 | 5 | TEEN AGE IDOL | Rick Nelson, Imperial 5864 | | 10 |
| ★30 | 40 | 54 | 71 | WHAT KIND OF FOOL AM I | Sammy Davis Jr., Reprise 20048 | | 7 |
| ★31 | 46 | 63 | 80 | GINA | Johnny Mathis, Columbia 42582 | △ | 4 |
| 32 | 18 | 23 | 17 | BEECHWOOD 4-5789 | Marvelettes, Tamla 54065 | | 10 |
| ★33 | 47 | 59 | 68 | LIMBO ROCK | Chubby Checker, Parkway 849 | | 6 |
| 34 | 36 | 51 | 61 | LITTLE BLACK BOOK | Jimmy Dean, Columbia 42529 | △ | 5 |
| 35 | 37 | 53 | 69 | KING OF THE WHOLE WIDE WORLD | Elvis Presley, RCA Victor EPA 4371 (Extended Play) | | 4 |
| 36 | 44 | 49 | 53 | HIDE AND GO SEEK | Bunker Hill, Mala 451 | | 8 |
| ★37 | 56 | 66 | 84 | CLOSE TO CATHY | Mike Clifford, United Artists 489 | | 5 |
| 38 | 39 | 41 | 44 | STOP THE MUSIC | Shirelles, Scepter 1237 | | 6 |
| ★39 | 49 | 76 | 86 | WARMED OVER KISSES | Brian Hyland, ABC-Paramount 10359 | | 4 |
| 40 | 34 | 37 | 35 | COME ON LITTLE ANGEL | Belmonts, Sabina 505 | | 13 |
| ★41 | 67 | 87 | — | NOTHING CAN CHANGE THIS LOVE | Sam Cooke, RCA Victor 8088 | △ | 3 |
| 42 | 29 | 22 | 22 | A WONDERFUL DREAM | Majors, Imperial 5855 | | 9 |
| 43 | 27 | 14 | 11 | LOCO-MOTION | Little Eva, Dimension 1000 | | 16 |
| ★44 | 77 | — | — | NEXT DOOR TO AN ANGEL | Neil Sedaka, RCA Victor 8086 | △ | 2 |
| 45 | 33 | 28 | 14 | RINKY DINK | Dave (Baby) Cortez, Chess 1829 | | 14 |
| 46 | 50 | 55 | 62 | THE THINGS WE DID LAST SUMMER | Shelley Fabares, Colpix 654 | | 5 |
| ★47 | 68 | 80 | 85 | TEN LONELY GUYS | Pat Boone, Dot 16391 | | 4 |
| ★48 | 69 | 84 | — | BABY FACE | Bobby Darin, Atco 6236 | | 3 |
| 49 | 55 | 48 | 51 | YOU CAN'T JUDGE A BOOK BY THE COVER | Bo Diddley, Checker 1019 | | 9 |
| ★50 | 64 | 67 | 76 | NO ONE WILL EVER KNOW | Jimmie Rodgers, Dot 16378 | | 7 |
| ★51 | 73 | 90 | — | IF A MAN ANSWERS | Bobby Darin, Capitol 4837 | | 3 |
| ★52 | 71 | 83 | — | JAMES (Hold the Ladder Steady) | Sue Thompson, Hickory 1183 | | 3 |
| ★53 | 63 | 79 | 90 | WORKIN' FOR THE MAN | Roy Orbison, Monument 467 | | 4 |
| 54 | 60 | 73 | 79 | STORMY MONDAY | Bobby Bland, Duke 355 | | 6 |
| 55 | 53 | 56 | 58 | SAVE ALL YOUR LOVIN' FOR ME | Brenda Lee, Decca 31424 | | 4 |
| ★56 | 78 | 85 | 91 | DON'T YOU BELIEVE IT | Andy Williams, Columbia 42523 | △ | 5 |
| 57 | 61 | 65 | 82 | SWEET SIXTEEN BARS | Earl Grant, Decca 25574 | | 6 |
| 58 | 62 | 64 | 65 | IF I DIDN'T HAVE A DIME | Gene Pitney, Musicor 1022 | | 7 |
| 59 | 54 | 61 | 63 | A TASTE OF HONEY | Martin Denny, Liberty 55470 | | 14 |
| ★60 | 92 | — | — | LOVE ME TENDER | Richard Chamberlain, MGM 13097 | | 2 |
| ★61 | 81 | — | — | SUSIE DARLIN' | Tommy Roe, ABC-Paramount 10362 | | 2 |
| ★62 | 84 | — | — | THE BURNING OF ATLANTA | Claude King, Columbia 42581 | △ | 2 |
| 63 | 72 | 75 | 87 | TWISTIN' WITH LINDA | Isley Brothers, Wand 127 | | 4 |
| 64 | 70 | 70 | 74 | THE SWISS MAID | Del Shannon, Big Top 3117 | | 5 |
| 65 | 58 | 60 | 55 | I KEEP FORGETTIN' | Chuck Jackson, Wand 126 | | 7 |
| ★66 | 87 | — | — | I'M GOING BACK TO SCHOOL | Dee Clark, Vee Jay 462 | | 2 |
| 67 | 75 | 69 | 77 | WHAT TIME IS IT? | Jive Five, Beltone 2024 | | 5 |
| 68 | 65 | 71 | 88 | AND THEN THERE WERE DRUMS | Sandy Nelson, Imperial 5870 | | 4 |
| ★69 | — | — | — | THE CHA CHA CHA | Bobby Rydell, Cameo 228 | | 1 |
| ★70 | 99 | — | — | HE THINKS I STILL CARE | Connie Francis, MGM 13096 | | 2 |
| ★71 | 86 | 93 | — | DESAFINADO | Stan Getz and Charlie Byrd, Verve 10260 | | 3 |
| ★72 | 90 | — | — | POP POP POP-PIE | Sherrys, Guyden 2068 | | 2 |
| 73 | 83 | 86 | 97 | SECOND FIDDLE GIRL | Barbara Lynn, Jamie 1233 | | 4 |
| ★74 | 95 | — | — | LEAH | Roy Orbison, Monument 467 | | 2 |
| 75 | 88 | — | — | (DANCE WITH THE) GUITAR MAN | Duane Eddy, RCA Victor 8087 | △ | 2 |
| ★76 | — | — | — | 409 | Beach Boys, Capitol 4777 | | 1 |
| ★77 | — | — | — | I'VE GOT A WOMAN | Jimmy McGriff, Sue 770 | | 1 |
| ★78 | — | — | — | NEXT DOOR TO THE BLUES | Etta James, Argo 5424 | | 1 |
| ★79 | — | — | — | YOU CAN RUN | Jerry Butler, Vee Jay 463 | | 1 |
| ★80 | — | — | — | I'LL BRING IT HOME TO YOU | Carla Thomas, Atlantic 2163 | | 1 |
| ★81 | 97 | — | — | DID YOU EVER SEE A DREAM WALKING | Fats Domino, Imperial 5875 | | 2 |
| 82 | 91 | 91 | 92 | FOREVER AND A DAY | Jackie Wilson, Brunswick 55233 | | 4 |
| ★83 | — | — | — | LOVERS BY NIGHT, STRANGERS BY DAY | Fleetwoods, Dolton 62 | | 1 |
| ★84 | — | — | — | I'M HERE TO GET MY BABY OUT OF JAIL | Everly Brothers, Cadence 1429 | | 1 |
| ★85 | — | — | — | MAMA SANG A SONG | Stan Kenton, Capitol 4847 | | 1 |
| 86 | 96 | 98 | 98 | I LEFT MY HEART IN THE BALCONY | Linda Scott, Congress 106 | | 4 |
| 87 | 93 | 96 | 96 | MR. LONELY | Buddy Greco, Epic 9536 | | 4 |
| 88 | 94 | — | — | I WAS SUCH A FOOL | Connie Francis, MGM 13096 | | 2 |
| ★89 | — | 88 | — | I'VE BEEN EVERYWHERE | Hank Snow, RCA Victor 8072 | △ | 2 |
| ★90 | — | — | — | YOU CAN'T LIE TO A LIAR | Ketty Lester, Era 3088 | | 1 |
| 91 | — | — | — | DON'T HANG UP | Orlons, Cameo 231 | | 1 |
| 92 | — | — | — | I'LL REMEMBER CAROL | Tommy Boyce, RCA Victor 8074 | △ | 1 |
| 93 | — | — | — | HAPPY WEEKEND | Dave (Baby) Cortez, Chess 1834 | | 1 |
| 94 | — | — | — | FOOLS RUSH IN | Etta James, Argo 5424 | | 1 |
| 95 | — | — | — | FURTHER MORE | Ray Stevens, Mercury 72039 | | 1 |
| 96 | 100 | — | — | WHEN THE BOYS GET TOGETHER | Joanie Sommers, Warner Bros. 5308 | | 2 |
| 97 | — | — | — | HAIL TO THE CONQUERING HERO | James Darren, Colpix 655 | | 1 |
| 98 | — | — | — | HEARTACHES | Patsy Cline, Decca 31429 | | 1 |
| 99 | — | — | — | HULLY GULLY GUITARS | Jerry Reed, Columbia 42533 | △ | 1 |
| 100 | — | — | — | I'M GONNA CHANGE EVERYTHING | Jim Reeves, RCA Victor 8080 | △ | 1 |

## HOT 100—A TO Z—*(Publisher-Licensee)*


All Alone Am I (Duchess, BMI) .... 21
Alley Cat (Metorion, BMI) .... 9
And Then There Were Drums (Travis, BMI) .... 68
Baby Face (Remick, ASCAP) .... 48
Beechwood 4-5789 (Jobete, BMI) .... 32
Burning of Atlanta, The (Conrad, BMI) .... 62
Cha-Cha-Cha, The (Fajob-Kalmann, ASCAP) .... 69
Close to Cathy (Arch, ASCAP) .... 37
Come on Little Angel (Glenden, ASCAP) .... 40
(Dance With the) Guitar Man (Linduane, BMI) .. 75
Desafinado (Hollis, BMI) .... 71
Did You Ever See a Dream Walking (DeSylva, Brown & Henderson, ASCAP) .... 81
Do You Love Me (Jobete, BMI) .... 7
Don't Go Near the Indians (Buttercup, BMI) ... 26
Don't Hang Up (Kalmann, ASCAP) .... 91
Don't You Believe It (Dolfi, ASCAP) .... 56
Fools Rush In (Bregman, Vocco & Conn, ASCAP). 94
Forever and a Day (Merrimac, BMI) .... 82
409 (Sea of Tunes, BMI) .... 76
Further More (Lowery, BMI) .... 95
Gina (Elm Drive, ASCAP) .... 31
Green Onions (East, BMI) .... 6
Hail to the Conquering Hero (Aldon, BMI) .... 97
Happy Weekend (Arc, BMI) .... 93
He Thinks I Still Care (Glad-Jack, BMI) .... 70
Heartaches (Leeds, ASCAP) .... 98
He's a Rebel (January, BMI) .... 11
Hide & Go Seek (Marks-Florentine, BMI) .... 36
Hully Gully Baby (Kalmann, ASCAP) .... 25
Hully Gully Guitars (Lowery, BMI) .... 99
I Keep Forgettin' (Trio, BMI) .... 65
I Left My Heart in San Francisco (General, ASCAP) .... 23
I Left My Heart in the Balcony (Trinity-Kilt, BMI). 86
I Remember You (Paramount, ASCAP) .... 5
I Was Such a Fool (Francon, ASCAP) .... 88
I'm Going Back to School (Conrad, BMI) .... 66
I'm Gonna Change Everything (Tuckahoe, BMI) ....100
I'm Here to Get My Baby Out of Jail (Cole, BMI). 84
I've Been Everywhere (Hill & Range, BMI) .... 89
I've Got a Woman (Progressive, BMI) .... 77
I'll Bring It Home to You (Kags, BMI) .... 80
I'll Remember Carol (Calboy, BMI) .... 92
If a Man Answers (Adaris, BMI) .... 51
If I Didn't Have a Dime (January, BMI) .... 58
If I Had a Hammer (Ludlow, BMI) .... 10
It Might as Well Rain Until September (Aldon, BMI) .... 22
James (Acuff-Rose, BMI) .... 52
King of the Whole Wide World (Presley, BMI) .... 35
Leah (Acuff-Rose, BMI) .... 74
Let's Dance (Rondell & Sherman-DeVorzon, BMI) . 4
Lie to Me (Ben Day, BMI) .... 19
Limbo Rock (Twist, BMI) .... 33
Little Black Book (Plainview, BMI) .... 34
Loco-Motion (Aldon, BMI) .... 43
Love Me Tender (Presley, BMI) .... 60
Lovers By Night, Strangers By Day (January, BMI). 83
Mama Sang a Song (Tree-Champion, BMI) .... 85
Mr. Lonely (Ripley, BMI) .... 87
Monster Mash (Garpax, BMI) .... 2
Next Door to an Angel (Aldon, BMI) .... 44
Next Door to the Blues (Figure, BMI) .... 78
No One Will Ever Know (Milene, ASCAP) .... 50
Nothing Can Change This Love (Kags, BMI) .... 41
Only Love Can Break a Heart (Arch, ASCAP) .... 13
Patches (Aldon, BMI) .... 8
Pop Pop Pop-Pie (Dandelion, BMI) .... 72
Popeye (The Hitchhiker) (Kalmann, ASCAP) .... 24
Punish Her (January, BMI) .... 20
Rain, Rain Go Away (Regent, BMI) .... 17
Ramblin' Rose (Sweco, BMI) .... 3
Rinky Dink (Arc-Cortez, BMI) .... 45
Save All Your Lovin' for Me (Champion, BMI) .... 55
Second Fiddle Girl (Dandelion-Crazy Cajun, BMI).. 73
Sheila (Eager-Nitetime, BMI) .... 16
Sherry (Bobob, ASCAP) .... 1
Stop the Music (Vee-Ve, BMI) .... 38
Stormy Monday (Gregmark, BMI) .... 54
Surfin' Safari (Guild, BMI) .... 14
Susie Darlin' (Chancellor, ASCAP) .... 61
Sweet Sixteen Bars (Progressive, BMI) .... 57
Swiss Maid, The (Tree, BMI) .... 64
Taste of Honey, A (Songfest, ASCAP) .... 59
Teen Age Idol (Nelson, ASCAP) .... 29
Ten Lonely Guys (Roosevelt, BMI) .... 47
Things We Did Last Summer, The (Kerwin, ASCAP). 46
Torture (Acuff-Rose, BMI) .... 28
Twistin' With Linda (Wemar, BMI) .... 63
Venus in Blue Jeans (Aldon, BMI) .... 12
Warmed Over Kisses (Pogo, ASCAP) .... 39
What Kind of Fool Am I (Ludlow, BMI) .... 30
What Kind of Love Is This (Planetary-Gee, ASCAP). 18
What Time Is It? (Lescay, BMI) .... 67
When the Boys Get Together (Tod, ASCAP) .... 96
Wonderful Dream, A (Travis-Rittenhouse, BMI) ... 42
Workin' for the Man (Acuff-Rose, BMI) .... 53
You Beat Me to the Punch (Jobete, BMI) .... 15
You Belong to Me (Ridgeway, BMI) .... 27
You Can Run (Armada, BMI) .... 79
You Can't Judge a Book by the Cover (Arc, BMI). 49
You Can't Lie to a Liar (Morris, ASCAP) .... 90


## BUBBLING UNDER THE HOT 100

101. UNTIE ME .... Tams, Arlen 711
102. COLD, COLD HEART .... Dinah Washington, Mercury 72040
103. STOP THE CLOCK .... Fats Domino, Imperial 5875
104. DON'T EVER LEAVE ME .... Bob & Earl, Tempe 102
105. WHAT KIND OF FOOL AM I .... Anthony Newley, London 9546
106. SOMEDAY .... Bobby Vee & the Crickets, Liberty 55479
107. WHAT KIND OF FOOL AM I .... Robert Goulet, Columbia 42519
108. A TRUE, TRUE LOVE .... Bobby Darin, Capitol 4837
109. THAT STRANGER USED TO BE MY GIRL .... Trade Martin, Coed 570
110. MARIA .... George Chakiris, Capitol 4844
111. FOUR WALLS .... Kay Starr, Capitol 4835
112. LET'S GO .... Routers, Warner Bros. 5283
113. ANNA .... Arthur Alexander, Dot 16387
114. AFTER LOVING YOU .... Eddy Arnold, RCA Victor 8048
115. HE'S A REBEL .... Vikki Carr, Liberty 55493
116. LIMBO DANCE .... Champs, Challenge 9162
117. BUSTIN' SURFBOARDS .... Tornados, Aertaun 1013
118. WONDERFUL ONE .... Shondells, King 5656
119. SOMEBODY HAVE MERCY .... Sam Cooke, RCA Victor 8088
120. UP ON THE ROOF .... Drifters, Atlantic 2162
121. SOMEWHERE IN THIS TOWN .... Bruce Channel, Smash 1780
122. ONE MORE TOWN .... Kingston Trio, Capitol 4842
123. RIGHT NOW .... Herbie Mann, Atlantic 5023
124. MIDNIGHT SUN .... Five Whispers, Dolton 61
125. I FOUND A NEW LOVE .... Blue Belles, Newtown 5006
126. MINSTREL & QUEEN .... Impressions, ABC-Paramount 10357
127. WHEN MY LITTLE GIRL IS SMILING .... Jimmy Justice, Kapp 482

# BILLBOARD HOT 100

FOR WEEK ENDING OCTOBER 20

1962

★ STAR PERFORMERS—Selections registering greatest upward progress this week.

S Indicates that 45 r.p.m. stereo single version is available.

△ Indicates that 33⅓ r.p.m. mono single version is available.

S△ Indicates that 33⅓ r.p.m. stereo single version is available.

| This Week | 1 Wk. Ago | 2 Wks. Ago | 3 Wks. Ago | TITLE Artist, Label & Number | Weeks On Chart |
|---|---|---|---|---|---|
| 1 | 2 | 2 | 4 | MONSTER MASH — Bobby (Boris) Pickett and the Crypt Kickers, Garpax 44167 | 7 |
| 2 | 1 | 1 | 1 | SHERRY — Four Seasons, Vee Jay 456 | 9 |
| 3 | 7 | 15 | 19 | DO YOU LOVE ME — Contours, Gordy 7005 | 11 |
| ★4 | 11 | 23 | 44 | HE'S A REBEL — Crystals, Philles 106 | 7 |
| 5 | 5 | 8 | 17 | I REMEMBER YOU — Frank Ifield, Vee Jay 457 | 7 |
| 6 | 8 | 6 | 8 | PATCHES — Dickey Lee, Smash 1758 | 9 |
| 7 | 3 | 3 | 2 | RAMBLIN' ROSE — Nat King Cole, Capitol 4804 | 12 |
| ★8 | 13 | 24 | 30 | ONLY LOVE CAN BREAK A HEART — Gene Pitney, Musicor 1022 | 6 |
| 9 | 6 | 5 | 3 | GREEN ONIONS — Booker T & the MG's, Stax 127 | 11 |
| 10 | 4 | 4 | 6 | LET'S DANCE — Chris Montez, Monogram 505 | 11 |
| 11 | 10 | 14 | 12 | IF I HAD A HAMMER — Peter, Paul & Mary, Warner Bros. 5296 | 10 |
| 12 | 12 | 7 | 13 | VENUS IN BLUE JEANS — Jimmy Clanton, Ace 8001 | 10 |
| 13 | 9 | 9 | 7 | ALLEY CAT — Bent Fabric, Atco 6226 | 13 |
| 14 | 14 | 19 | 24 | SURFIN' SAFARI — Beach Boys, Capitol 4777 | 11 |
| ★15 | 21 | 35 | 50 | ALL ALONE AM I — Brenda Lee, Decca 31424 | 4 |
| ★16 | 24 | 25 | 36 | POPEYE (The Hitchhiker) — Chubby Checker, Parkway 849 | 5 |
| ★17 | 26 | 30 | 46 | DON'T GO NEAR THE INDIANS — Rex Allen, Mercury 71997 | 6 |
| ★18 | 30 | 40 | 54 | WHAT KIND OF FOOL AM I — Sammy Davis Jr., Reprise 20048 | 8 |
| 19 | 23 | 28 | 32 | I LEFT MY HEART IN SAN FRANCISCO △ — Tony Bennett, Columbia 42332 | 11 |
| ★20 | 31 | 46 | 63 | GINA △ — Johnny Mathis, Columbia 42582 | 5 |
| 21 | 19 | 13 | 15 | LIE TO ME — Brook Benton, Mercury 72024 | 9 |
| ★22 | 37 | 56 | 66 | CLOSE TO CATHY — Mike Clifford, United Artists 489 | 6 |
| ★23 | 33 | 47 | 59 | LIMBO ROCK — Chubby Checker, Parkway 849 | 7 |
| 24 | 18 | 20 | 21 | WHAT KIND OF LOVE IS THIS — Joey Dee and the Starliters, Roulette 4438 | 9 |
| 25 | 25 | 26 | 27 | HULLY GULLY BABY — Dovells, Parkway 845 | 11 |
| 26 | 28 | 38 | 42 | TORTURE — Kris Jensen, Hickory 1173 | 8 |
| 27 | 17 | 12 | 18 | RAIN, RAIN GO AWAY — Bobby Vinton, Epic 9532 | 9 |
| 28 | 15 | 10 | 11 | YOU BEAT ME TO THE PUNCH — Mary Wells, Motown 1032 | 11 |
| ★29 | 44 | 77 | — | NEXT DOOR TO AN ANGEL △ — Neil Sedaka, RCA Victor 8086 | 3 |
| 30 | 35 | 37 | 53 | KING OF THE WHOLE WIDE WORLD — Elvis Presley, RCA Victor EPA 4371 (Extended Play) | 5 |
| ★31 | 41 | 67 | 87 | NOTHING CAN CHANGE THIS LOVE △ — Sam Cooke, RCA Victor 8088 | 4 |
| 32 | 34 | 36 | 51 | LITTLE BLACK BOOK △ — Jimmy Dean, Columbia 42529 | 6 |
| 33 | 39 | 49 | 76 | WARMED OVER KISSES — Brian Hyland, ABC-Paramount 10359 | 5 |
| 34 | 27 | 17 | 9 | YOU BELONG TO ME — Duprees, Coed 569 | 12 |
| 35 | 36 | 44 | 49 | HIDE AND GO SEEK — Bunker Hill, Mala 451 | 9 |
| 36 | 38 | 39 | 41 | STOP THE MUSIC — Shirelles, Scepter 1237 | 7 |
| ★37 | 52 | 71 | 83 | JAMES (Hold the Ladder Steady) — Sue Thompson, Hickory 1183 | 4 |
| 38 | 16 | 11 | 5 | SHEILA — Tommy Roe, ABC-Paramount 10329 | 13 |
| 39 | 20 | 21 | 26 | PUNISH HER — Bobby Vee, Liberty 55479 | 8 |
| 40 | 29 | 16 | 10 | TEEN AGE IDOL — Rick Nelson, Imperial 5864 | 11 |
| 41 | 22 | 22 | 25 | IT MIGHT AS WELL RAIN UNTIL SEPTEMBER — Carole King, Dimension 2000 | 9 |
| 42 | 51 | 73 | 90 | IF A MAN ANSWERS — Bobby Darin, Capitol 4837 | 4 |
| 43 | 50 | 64 | 67 | NO ONE WILL EVER KNOW — Jimmie Rodgers, Dot 16378 | 8 |
| 44 | 48 | 69 | 84 | BABY FACE — Bobby Darin, Atco 6236 | 4 |
| 45 | 47 | 68 | 80 | TEN LONELY GUYS — Pat Boone, Dot 16391 | 5 |
| ★46 | 56 | 78 | 85 | DON'T YOU BELIEVE IT △ — Andy Williams, Columbia 42523 | 6 |
| ★47 | 69 | — | — | THE CHA-CHA-CHA — Bobby Rydell, Cameo 228 | 2 |
| ★48 | 60 | 92 | — | LOVE ME TENDER — Richard Chamberlain, MGM 13097 | 3 |
| 49 | 54 | 60 | 73 | STORMY MONDAY — Bobby Bland, Duke 355 | 7 |
| 50 | 32 | 18 | 23 | BEECHWOOD 4-5789 — Marvelettes, Tamla 54065 | 11 |
| ★51 | 61 | 81 | — | SUSIE DARLIN' — Tommy Roe, ABC-Paramount 10362 | 3 |
| ★52 | 71 | 86 | 93 | DESAFINADO — Stan Getz and Charlie Byrd, Verve 10260 | 4 |
| 53 | 53 | 63 | 79 | WORKIN' FOR THE MAN — Roy Orbison, Monument 467 | 5 |
| 54 | 55 | 53 | 56 | SAVE ALL YOUR LOVIN' FOR ME — Brenda Lee, Decca 31424 | 5 |
| 55 | 57 | 61 | 65 | SWEET SIXTEEN BARS — Earl Grant, Decca 25574 | 7 |
| ★56 | 75 | 88 | — | (DANCE WITH THE) GUITAR MAN △ — Duane Eddy, RCA Victor 8087 | 3 |
| ★57 | 88 | 94 | — | I WAS SUCH A FOOL — Connie Francis, MGM 13096 | 3 |
| 58 | 62 | 84 | — | THE BURNING OF ATLANTA △ — Claude King, Columbia 42581 | 3 |
| 59 | 40 | 34 | 37 | COME ON LITTLE ANGEL — Belmonts, Sabina 505 | 14 |
| ★60 | 77 | — | — | I'VE GOT A WOMAN — Jimmy McGriff, Sue 770 | 2 |
| 61 | 63 | 72 | 75 | TWISTIN' WITH LINDA — Isley Brothers, Wand 127 | 5 |
| 62 | 46 | 50 | 55 | THE THINGS WE DID LAST SUMMER — Shelley Fabares, Colpix 654 | 6 |
| 63 | 42 | 29 | 22 | A WONDERFUL DREAM — Majors, Imperial 5855 | 10 |
| 64 | 66 | 87 | — | I'M GOING BACK TO SCHOOL — Dee Clark, Vee Jay 462 | 3 |
| 65 | 74 | 95 | — | LEAH — Roy Orbison, Monument 467 | 3 |
| ★66 | — | — | — | BIG GIRLS DON'T CRY — Four Seasons, Vee Jay 465 | 1 |
| 67 | 72 | 90 | — | POP POP POP-PIE — Sherrys, Guyden 2068 | 3 |
| ★68 | — | — | — | RETURN TO SENDER △ — Elvis Presley, RCA Victor 8100 | 1 |
| 69 | 70 | 99 | — | HE THINKS I STILL CARE — Connie Francis, MGM 13096 | 3 |
| 70 | 73 | 83 | 86 | SECOND FIDDLE GIRL — Barbara Lynn, Jamie 1233 | 5 |
| ★71 | 91 | — | — | DON'T HANG UP — Orlons, Cameo 231 | 2 |
| 72 | 59 | 54 | 61 | A TASTE OF HONEY — Martin Denny, Liberty 55470 | 15 |
| 73 | 80 | — | — | I'LL BRING IT HOME TO YOU — Carla Thomas, Atlantic 2163 | 2 |
| 74 | 85 | — | — | MAMA SANG A SONG — Stan Kenton, Capitol 4847 | 2 |
| 75 | 79 | — | — | YOU CAN RUN — Jerry Butler, Vee Jay 463 | 2 |
| 76 | 78 | — | — | NEXT DOOR TO THE BLUES — Etta James, Argo 5424 | 2 |
| 77 | 83 | — | — | LOVERS BY NIGHT, STRANGERS BY DAY — Fleetwoods, Dolton 62 | 2 |
| 78 | 87 | 93 | 96 | MR. LONELY — Buddy Greco, Epic 9536 | 5 |
| ★79 | — | — | — | THE ALLEY CAT SONG — David Thorne, Riverside 4530 | 1 |
| 80 | 81 | 97 | — | DID YOU EVER SEE A DREAM WALKING — Fats Domino, Imperial 5875 | 3 |
| 81 | 84 | — | — | I'M HERE TO GET MY BABY OUT OF JAIL — Everly Brothers, Cadence 1429 | 2 |
| ★82 | — | — | — | MY OWN TRUE LOVE — Duprees, Coed 571 | 1 |
| 83 | 86 | 96 | 98 | I LEFT MY HEART IN THE BALCONY — Linda Scott, Congress 106 | 5 |
| ★84 | — | — | — | RIDE! — Dee Dee Sharp, Cameo 230 | 1 |
| ★85 | — | — | — | THAT STRANGER USED TO BE MY GIRL — Trade Martin, Coed 570 | 1 |
| 86 | 89 | — | 88 | I'VE BEEN EVERYWHERE △ — Hank Snow, RCA Victor 8072 | 3 |
| ★87 | — | — | — | BOBBY'S GIRL — Marcie Blane, Seville 120 | 1 |
| 88 | 93 | — | — | HAPPY WEEKEND — Dave (Baby) Cortez, Chess 1834 | 2 |
| 89 | 49 | 55 | 48 | YOU CAN'T JUDGE A BOOK BY THE COVER — Bo Diddley, Checker 1019 | 10 |
| ★90 | — | — | — | MAMA SANG A SONG — Walter Brennan, Liberty 55508 | 1 |
| 91 | — | — | — | DON'T ASK ME TO BE FRIENDS — Everly Brothers, Warner Bros. 5297 | 1 |
| 92 | 95 | — | — | FURTHER MORE — Ray Stevens, Mercury 72039 | 2 |
| 93 | 94 | — | — | FOOLS RUSH IN — Etta James, Argo 5424 | 2 |
| 94 | 96 | 100 | — | WHEN THE BOYS GET TOGETHER — Joanie Sommers, Warner Bros. 5308 | 3 |
| 95 | 100 | — | — | I'M GONNA CHANGE EVERYTHING △ — Jim Reeves, RCA Victor 8080 | 2 |
| 96 | 98 | — | — | HEARTACHES — Patsy Cline, Decca 31429 | 2 |
| 97 | — | — | — | LIMBO DANCE — Champs, Challenge 9162 | 1 |
| 98 | — | — | — | STUBBORN KIND OF FELLOW — Marvin Gaye, Tamla 54068 | 1 |
| 99 | — | — | — | UNTIE ME — Tams, Arlen 711 | 1 |
| 100 | — | — | — | DON'T EVER LEAVE ME — Bob and Earl, Tempe 102 | 1 |

## HOT 100—A TO Z—(Publisher-Licensee)


Alley Cat (Metorion, BMI) .......... 13
Alley Cat Song, The (Metorion, BMI) .......... 79
Baby Face (Remick, ASCAP) .......... 44
Beechwood 4-5789 (Jobete, BMI) .......... 50
Big Girls Don't Cry (Bobob, ASCAP) .......... 66
Bobby's Girl (A. M. E., BMI) .......... 87
Burning of Atlanta, The (Conrad, BMI) .......... 58
Cha-Cha-Cha, The (Fajob-Kalmann, ASCAP) .......... 47
Close to Cathy (Arch, ASCAP) .......... 22
Come on Little Angel (Glenden, ASCAP) .......... 59
(Dance With the) Guitar Man (Linduane, BMI) .. 56
Desafinado (Hollis, BMI) .......... 52
Did You Every See a Dream Walking (De Sylva, Brown & Henderson, ASCAP) .......... 80
Do You Love Me (Jobete, BMI) .......... 3
Don't Ask Me to Be Friends (Aldon, BMI) .......... 91
Don't Ever Leave Me (Fore-Site, BMI) .......... 100
Don't Go Near the Indians (Buttercup, BMI) .... 17
Don't Hang Up (Kalmann, ASCAP) .......... 71
Don't You Believe It (Dolfi, ASCAP) .......... 46
Fools Rush In (Bregman, Vocco & Conn, ASCAP).. 93
Further More (Lowery, BMI) .......... 92
Gina (Elm Drive, ASCAP) .......... 20
Green Onions (East, BMI) .......... 9
Happy Weekend (Arc, BMI) .......... 88
He Thinks I Still Care (Glad-Jack, BMI) .......... 69
Heartaches (Leeds, ASCAP) .......... 96
He's a Rebel (January, BMI) .......... 4
Hide & Go Seek (Marks-Florentine, BMI) .......... 35
Hully Gully Baby (Kalmann, ASCAP) .......... 25
I Left My Heart in San Francisco (General, ASCAP) .......... 19
I Left My Heart in the Balcony (Trinity-Kilt, BMI). 83
I Remember You (Paramount, ASCAP) .......... 5
I Was Such a Fool (Francon, ASCAP) .......... 57
I'm Going Back to School (Conrad, BMI) .......... 64
I'm Gonna Change Everything (Tuckahoe, BMI) .. 95
I'm Here to Get My Baby Out of Jail (Cole, BMI). 81
I've Been Everywhere (Hill & Range, BMI) .......... 86
I've Got a Woman (Progressive, BMI) .......... 60
I'll Bring It Home to You (Kags, BMI) .......... 73
If a Man Answers (Adaris, BMI) .......... 42
If I Had a Hammer (Ludlow, BMI) .......... 11
It Might as Well Rain Until September (Aldon, BMI) .......... 41
James (Acuff-Rose, BMI) .......... 37
King of the Whole Wide World (Presley, BMI) .. 30
Leah (Acuff-Rose, BMI) .......... 65
Let's Dance (Rondell & Sherman-DeVorzon, BMI). 10
Lie to Me (Ben Day, BMI) .......... 21
Limbo Dance (Four Star, BMI) .......... 97
Limbo Rock (Twist, BMI) .......... 23
Little Black Book (Plainview, BMI) .......... 32
Love Me Tender (Presley, BMI) .......... 48
Lovers By Night, Strangers By Day (January, BMI). 77
Mama Sang a Song—Brennan (Tree-Champion, BMI) .......... 90
Mama Sang a Song—Kenton (Tree-Champion, BMI). 74
Mr. Lonely (Ripley, BMI) .......... 78
Monster Mash (Garpax, BMI) .......... 1
My Own True Love (Remick, ASCAP) .......... 82
Next Door to an Angel (Aldon, BMI) .......... 29
Next Door to the Blues (Figure, BMI) .......... 76
No One Will Ever Know (Milene, ASCAP) .......... 43
Nothing Can Change This Love (Kags, BMI) .... 31
Only Love Can Break a Heart (Arch, ASCAP) .. 8
Patches (Aldon, BMI) .......... 6
All Alone Am I (Duchess, BMI) .......... 15
Pop Pop Pop-Pie (Dandelion, BMI) .......... 67
Popeye (The Hitchhiker) (Kalmann, ASCAP) .... 16
Punish Her (January, BMI) .......... 39
Rain, Rain Go Away (Regent, BMI) .......... 27
Ramblin' Rose (Sweco, BMI) .......... 7
Return to Sender (Presley, BMI) .......... 68
Ride! (Woodcrest-Check-Colt, BMI) .......... 84
Save All Your Lovin' for Me (Champion, BMI) .. 54
Second Fiddle Girl (Dandelion-Crazy Cajun, BMI).. 70
Sheila (Eager-Nitetime, BMI) .......... 38
Sherry (Bobob, ASCAP) .......... 2
Stop the Music (Vee-Ve, BMI) .......... 36
Stormy Monday (Gregmark, BMI) .......... 49
Stubborn Kind of Fellow (Jobete, BMI) .......... 98
Surfin' Safari (Guild, BMI) .......... 14
Susie Darlin' (Chancellor, ASCAP) .......... 51
Sweet Sixteen Bars (Progressive, BMI) .......... 55
Taste of Honey, A (Songfest, ASCAP) .......... 72
Teen Age Idol (Nelson, ASCAP) .......... 40
Ten Lonely Guys (Roosevelt, BMI) .......... 45
That Stranger Used to Be My Girl (Winneton, BMI) .......... 85
Things We Did Last Summer, The (Kerwin, ASCAP). 62
Torture (Acuff-Rose, BMI) .......... 26
Twistin' With Linda (Wemar, BMI) .......... 61
Untie Me (Lowery, BMI) .......... 99
Venus in Blue Jeans (Aldon, BMI) .......... 12
Warmed Over Kisses (Pogo, ASCAP) .......... 33
What Kind of Fool Am I (Ludlow, BMI) .... 18
What Kind of Love Is This (Planetary-Gee, ASCAP). 24
When the Boys Get Together (Tod, ASCAP) .... 94
Wonderful Dream, A (Travis-Rittenhouse, BMI) .. 63
Workin' for the Man (Acuff-Rose, BMI) .......... 53
You Beat Me to the Punch (Jobete, BMI) .... 28
You Belong to Me (Ridgeway, BMI) .......... 34
You Can Run (Armada, BMI) .......... 75
You Can't Judge a Book by the Cover (Arc, BMI). 89


## BUBBLING UNDER THE HOT 100

101. COLD, COLD HEART .......... Dinah Washington, Mercury 72040
102. ANNA .......... Arthur Alexander, Dot 16387
103. WHAT KIND OF FOOL AM I .......... Robert Goulet, Columbia 42519
104. I'LL REMEMBER CAROL .......... Tommy Boyce, RCA Victor 8074
105. WHAT KIND OF FOOL AM I .......... Anthony Newley, London 9546
106. LET'S GO .......... Routers, Warner Bros. 5283
107. ONE MORE TOWN .......... Kingston Trio, Capitol 4842
108. WHERE DO YOU COME FROM .......... Elvis Presley, RCA Victor 8100
109. FIESTA .......... Dave (Baby) Cortez, Emit 301
110. DON'T STOP THE WEDDING .......... Ann Cole, Roulette 4452
111. RIGHT NOW .......... Herbie Mann, Atlantic 5023
112. AFTER LOVING YOU .......... Eddy Arnold, RCA Victor 8048
113. YOU CAN'T LIE TO A LIAR .......... Ketty Lester, Era 3088
114. A TRUE, TRUE LOVE .......... Bobby Darin, Capitol 4837
115. MIDNIGHT SUN .......... Five Whispers, Dolton 61
116. BUSTIN' SURFBOARDS .......... Tornados, Aertaun 1013
117. SOMEWHERE IN THIS TOWN .......... Bruce Channel, Smash 1780
118. UP ON THE ROOF .......... Drifters, Atlantic 2162
119. OL' MAN RIVER .......... Jimmy Smith, Verve 10262
120. HELLO OUT THERE .......... Carl Belew, RCA Victor 8058
121. SOMEBODY HAVE MERCY .......... Sam Cooke, RCA Victor 8088
122. I FOUND A NEW LOVE .......... Blue Belles, Newtown 5006
123. TEAR FOR TEAR .......... Gene (Duke of Earl) Chandler, Vee Jay 461
124. MAGIE WAND .......... Don and Juan, Big Top 3121
125. SHE'S A TROUBLEMAKER .......... Majors, Imperial 5879
126. WONDERFUL ONE .......... Shondells, King 5656
127. LOSERS WEEPERS .......... Floyd Cramer, RCA Victor 8084
128. THE LONELY BULL .......... Tijuana Brass, A. & M. 703
129. MINSTREL & QUEEN .......... Impressions, ABC-Paramount 10357
130. NAKED CITY THEME .......... Nelson Riddle, Capitol 4843
131. ANY OTHER WAY .......... William Bell, Stax 128

# BILLBOARD HOT 100

FOR WEEK ENDING OCTOBER 27

1962

★ STAR PERFORMERS—Selections registering greatest upward progress this week.

[S] Indicates that 45 r.p.m. stereo single version is available.

△ Indicates that 33⅓ r.p.m. mono single version is available.

[S△] Indicates that 33⅓ r.p.m. stereo single version is available.

| This Week | 1 Wk. Ago | 2 Wks. Ago | 3 Wks. Ago | Title | Artist, Label & Number | | Weeks On Chart |
|---|---|---|---|---|---|---|---|
| 1 | 1 | 2 | 2 | MONSTER MASH | Bobby (Boris) Pickett and the Crypt Kickers, Garpax 44167 | | 8 |
| 2 | 4 | 11 | 23 | HE'S A REBEL | Crystals, Philles 106 | | 8 |
| 3 | 3 | 7 | 15 | DO YOU LOVE ME | Contours, Gordy 7005 | | 12 |
| 4 | 8 | 13 | 24 | ONLY LOVE CAN BREAK A HEART | Gene Pitney, Musicor 1022 | | 7 |
| 5 | 2 | 1 | 1 | SHERRY | Four Seasons, Vee Jay 456 | | 10 |
| ★6 | 15 | 21 | 35 | ALL ALONE AM I | Brenda Lee, Decca 31424 | | 5 |
| 7 | 6 | 8 | 6 | PATCHES | Dickey Lee, Smash 1758 | | 10 |
| 8 | 7 | 3 | 3 | RAMBLIN' ROSE | Nat King Cole, Capitol 4804 | | 13 |
| ★9 | 20 | 31 | 46 | GINA | Johnny Mathis, Columbia 42582 | △ | 6 |
| 10 | 5 | 5 | 8 | I REMEMBER YOU | Frank Ifield, Vee Jay 457 | | 8 |
| ★11 | 16 | 24 | 25 | POPEYE (The Hitchhiker) | Chubby Checker, Parkway 849 | | 6 |
| 12 | 9 | 6 | 5 | GREEN ONIONS | Booker T & the MG's, Stax 127 | | 12 |
| 13 | 10 | 4 | 4 | LET'S DANCE | Chris Montez, Monogram 505 | | 12 |
| ★14 | 22 | 37 | 56 | CLOSE TO CATHY | Mike Clifford, United Artists 489 | | 7 |
| ★15 | 29 | 44 | 77 | NEXT DOOR TO AN ANGEL | Neil Sedaka, RCA Victor 8086 | △ | 4 |
| 16 | 12 | 12 | 7 | VENUS IN BLUE JEANS | Jimmy Clanton, Ace 8001 | | 11 |
| ★17 | 66 | — | — | BIG GIRLS DON'T CRY | Four Seasons, Vee Jay 465 | | 2 |
| ★18 | 23 | 33 | 47 | LIMBO ROCK | Chubby Checker, Parkway 849 | | 8 |
| 19 | 13 | 9 | 9 | ALLEY CAT | Bent Fabric, Atco 6226 | | 14 |
| ★20 | 68 | — | — | RETURN TO SENDER | Elvis Presley, RCA Victor 8100 | △ | 2 |
| 21 | 14 | 14 | 19 | SURFIN' SAFARI | Beach Boys, Capitol 4777 | | 12 |
| 22 | 31 | 41 | 67 | NOTHING CAN CHANGE THIS LOVE | Sam Cooke, RCA Victor 8088 | △ | 5 |
| 23 | 26 | 28 | 38 | TORTURE | Kris Jensen, Hickory 1173 | | 9 |
| 24 | 18 | 30 | 40 | WHAT KIND OF FOOL AM I | Sammy Davis Jr., Reprise 20048 | | 9 |
| ★25 | 37 | 52 | 71 | JAMES (Hold the Ladder Steady) | Sue Thompson, Hickory 1183 | | 5 |
| 26 | 33 | 39 | 49 | WARMED OVER KISSES | Brian Hyland, ABC-Paramount 10359 | | 6 |
| 27 | 19 | 23 | 28 | I LEFT MY HEART IN SAN FRANCISCO | Tony Bennett, Columbia 42332 | △ | 12 |
| ★28 | 47 | 69 | — | THE CHA-CHA-CHA | Bobby Rydell, Cameo 228 | | 3 |
| 29 | 32 | 34 | 36 | LITTLE BLACK BOOK | Jimmy Dean, Columbia 42529 | △ | 7 |
| 30 | 17 | 26 | 30 | DON'T GO NEAR THE INDIANS | Rex Allen, Mercury 71997 | | 7 |
| ★31 | 52 | 71 | 86 | DESAFINADO | Stan Getz and Charlie Byrd, Verve 10260 | | 5 |
| 32 | 11 | 10 | 14 | IF I HAD A HAMMER | Peter, Paul & Mary, Warner Bros. 5296 | | 11 |
| 33 | 35 | 36 | 44 | HIDE AND GO SEEK | Bunker Hill, Mala 451 | | 10 |
| ★34 | 60 | 77 | — | I'VE GOT A WOMAN | Jimmy McGriff, Sue 770 | | 3 |
| 35 | 25 | 25 | 26 | HULLY GULLY BABY | Dovells, Parkway 845 | | 12 |
| ★36 | 53 | 53 | 63 | WORKIN' FOR THE MAN | Roy Orbison, Monument 467 | | 6 |
| ★37 | 48 | 60 | 92 | LOVE ME TENDER | Richard Chamberlain, MGM 13097 | | 4 |
| 38 | 42 | 51 | 73 | IF A MAN ANSWERS | Bobby Darin, Capitol 4837 | | 5 |
| 39 | 30 | 35 | 37 | KING OF THE WHOLE WIDE WORLD | Elvis Presley, RCA Victor EPA 4371 (Extended Play) | | 6 |
| 40 | 27 | 17 | 12 | RAIN, RAIN GO AWAY | Bobby Vinton, Epic 9532 | | 10 |
| 41 | 46 | 56 | 78 | DON'T YOU BELIEVE IT | Andy Williams, Columbia 42523 | △ | 7 |
| 42 | 44 | 48 | 69 | BABY FACE | Bobby Darin, Atco 6236 | | 5 |
| 43 | 49 | 54 | 60 | STORMY MONDAY | Bobby Bland, Duke 355 | | 8 |
| ★44 | 57 | 88 | 94 | I WAS SUCH A FOOL | Connie Francis, MGM 13096 | | 4 |
| ★45 | 71 | 91 | — | DON'T HANG UP | Orlons, Cameo 231 | | 3 |
| 46 | 21 | 19 | 13 | LIE TO ME | Brook Benton, Mercury 72024 | | 10 |
| 47 | 51 | 61 | 81 | SUSIE DARLIN' | Tommy Roe, ABC-Paramount 10362 | | 4 |
| 48 | 24 | 18 | 20 | WHAT KIND OF LOVE IS THIS | Joey Dee and the Starliters, Roulette 4438 | | 10 |
| 49 | 28 | 15 | 10 | YOU BEAT ME TO THE PUNCH | Mary Wells, Motown 1032 | | 12 |
| 50 | 56 | 75 | 88 | (DANCE WITH THE) GUITAR MAN | Duane Eddy, RCA Victor 8087 | △ | 4 |
| 51 | 43 | 50 | 64 | NO ONE WILL EVER KNOW | Jimmie Rodgers, Dot 16378 | | 9 |
| ★52 | 67 | 72 | 90 | POP POP POP-PIE | Sherrys, Guyden 2068 | | 4 |
| 53 | 58 | 62 | 84 | THE BURNING OF ATLANTA | Claude King, Columbia 42581 | △ | 4 |
| 54 | 61 | 63 | 72 | TWISTIN' WITH LINDA | Isley Brothers, Wand 127 | | 6 |
| 55 | 34 | 27 | 17 | YOU BELONG TO ME | Duprees, Coed 569 | | 13 |
| 56 | 65 | 74 | 95 | LEAH | Roy Orbison, Monument 467 | | 4 |
| ★57 | 69 | 70 | 99 | HE THINKS I STILL CARE | Connie Francis, MGM 13096 | | 4 |
| 58 | 36 | 38 | 39 | STOP THE MUSIC | Shirelles, Scepter 1237 | | 8 |
| 59 | 38 | 16 | 11 | SHEILA | Tommy Roe, ABC-Paramount 10329 | | 14 |
| 60 | 45 | 47 | 68 | TEN LONELY GUYS | Pat Boone, Dot 16391 | | 6 |
| 61 | 74 | 85 | — | MAMA SANG A SONG | Stan Kenton, Capitol 4847 | | 3 |
| 62 | 64 | 66 | 87 | I'M GOING BACK TO SCHOOL | Dee Clark, Vee Jay 462 | | 4 |
| 63 | 55 | 57 | 61 | SWEET SIXTEEN BARS | Earl Grant, Decca 25574 | | 8 |
| 64 | 73 | 80 | — | I'LL BRING IT HOME TO YOU | Carla Thomas, Atlantic 2163 | | 3 |
| ★65 | 84 | — | — | RIDE! | Dee Dee Sharp, Cameo 230 | | 2 |
| ★66 | 87 | — | — | BOBBY'S GIRL | Marcie Blane, Seville 120 | | 2 |
| ★67 | 82 | — | — | MY OWN TRUE LOVE | Duprees, Coed 571 | | 2 |
| 68 | 54 | 55 | 53 | SAVE ALL YOUR LOVIN' FOR ME | Brenda Lee, Decca 31424 | | 6 |
| 69 | 70 | 73 | 83 | SECOND FIDDLE GIRL | Barbara Lynn, Jamie 1233 | | 6 |
| 70 | 77 | 83 | — | LOVERS BY NIGHT, STRANGERS BY DAY | Fleetwoods, Dolton 62 | | 3 |
| 71 | 85 | — | — | THAT STRANGER USED TO BE MY GIRL | Trade Martin, Coed 570 | | 2 |
| 72 | 76 | 78 | — | NEXT DOOR TO THE BLUES | Etta James, Argo 5424 | | 3 |
| 73 | 75 | 79 | — | YOU CAN RUN | Jerry Butler, Vee Jay 463 | | 3 |
| 74 | 88 | 93 | — | HAPPY WEEKEND | Dave (Baby) Cortez, Chess 1834 | | 3 |
| 75 | 78 | 87 | 93 | MR. LONELY | Buddy Greco, Epic 9536 | | 6 |
| 76 | 90 | — | — | MAMA SANG A SONG | Walter Brennan, Liberty 55508 | | 2 |
| ★77 | — | — | — | SOMEBODY HAVE MERCY | Sam Cooke, RCA Victor 8088 | △ | 1 |
| 78 | 81 | 84 | — | I'M HERE TO GET MY BABY OUT OF JAIL | Everly Brothers, Cadence 1429 | | 3 |
| 79 | 80 | 81 | 97 | DID YOU EVER SEE A DREAM WALKING | Fats Domino, Imperial 5875 | | 4 |
| ★80 | — | — | — | I CAN'T HELP IT | Johnny Tillotson, Cadence 1432 | | 1 |
| ★81 | 96 | 98 | — | HEARTACHES | Patsy Cline, Decca 31429 | | 3 |
| 82 | 83 | 86 | 96 | I LEFT MY HEART IN THE BALCONY | Linda Scott, Congress 106 | | 6 |
| ★83 | — | — | 98 | WIGGLE WOBBLE | Les Cooper, Everlast 5019 | | 2 |
| ★84 | 99 | — | — | UNTIE ME | Tams, Arlen 711 | | 2 |
| 85 | 86 | 89 | — | I'VE BEEN EVERYWHERE | Hank Snow, RCA Victor 8072 | △ | 4 |
| ★86 | — | — | 85 | WHAT KIND OF FOOL AM I | Anthony Newley, London 9546 | | 4 |
| 87 | 93 | 94 | — | FOOLS RUSH IN | Etta James, Argo 5424 | | 3 |
| 88 | 100 | — | — | DON'T EVER LEAVE ME | Bob and Earl, Tempe 102 | | 2 |
| 89 | 91 | — | — | DON'T ASK ME TO BE FRIENDS | Everly Brothers, Warner Bros. 5297 | | 2 |
| ★90 | — | — | — | RELEASE ME | "Little Esther" Phillips, Lenox 5555 | | 1 |
| 91 | 92 | 95 | — | FURTHER MORE | Ray Stevens, Mercury 72039 | | 3 |
| 92 | — | — | — | MAGIC WAND | Don & Juan, Big Top 3121 | | 1 |
| 93 | — | — | — | ALADDIN | Bobby Curtola, Del-Fi 4185 | | 1 |
| 94 | — | — | — | ANNA | Arthur Alexander, Dot 16387 | | 1 |
| 95 | — | — | — | THE LONELY BULL | Tijuana Brass, A. & M. 703 | | 1 |
| 96 | 98 | — | — | STUBBORN KIND OF FELLOW | Marvin Gaye, Tamla 54068 | | 2 |
| 97 | — | — | — | MAMA SANG A SONG | Bill Anderson, Decca 31404 | | 1 |
| 98 | — | — | — | ONE MORE TOWN | Kingston Trio, Capitol 4842 | | 1 |
| 99 | — | — | — | WHERE DO YOU COME FROM | Elvis Presley, RCA Victor 810 | △ | 1 |
| 100 | — | — | — | FOUR WALLS | Kay Starr, Capitol 4835 | | 1 |

## HOT 100—A TO Z—*(Publisher-Licensee)*

Aladdin (Kemo, BMI) .... 93
All Alone Am I (Duchess, BMI) .... 6
Alley Cat (Metorion, BMI) .... 19
Anna (Painted Desert, BMI) .... 94
Baby Face (Remick, ASCAP) .... 42
Big Girls Don't Cry (Bobob, ASCAP) .... 17
Bobby's Girl (A. M. E., BMI) .... 66
Burning of Atlanta, The (Conrad, BMI) .... 53
Cha-Cha-Cha, The (Fajob-Kalmann, ASCAP) .... 28
Close to Cathy (Arch, ASCAP) .... 14
(Dance With the) Guitar Man (Linduane, BMI) .... 50
Desafinado (Hollis, BMI) .... 31
Did You Ever See a Dream Walking (De Sylva, Brown & Henderson, ASCAP) .... 79
Do You Love Me (Jobete, BMI) .... 3
Don't Ask Me to Be Friends (Aldon, BMI) .... 89
Don't Ever Leave Me (Fore-Site, BMI) .... 88
Don't Go Near the Indians (Buttercup, BMI) .... 30
Don't Hang Up (Kalmann, ASCAP) .... 45
Don't You Believe It (Dolfi, ASCAP) .... 41
Fools Rush In (Bregman, Vocco & Conn, ASCAP) .. 87
Four Walls (Sheldon, BMI ) .... 100
Further More (Lowery, BMI) .... 91
Gina (Elm Drive, ASCAP) .... 9
Green Onions (East, BMI) .... 12
Happy Weekend (Arc, BMI) .... 74
He Thinks I Still Care (Glad-Jack, BMI) .... 57
Heartaches (Leeds, ASCAP) .... 81
He's a Rebel (January, BMI) .... 2
Hide & Go Seek (Marks-Florentine, BMI) .... 33
Hully Gully Baby (Kalmann, ASCAP) .... 35
I Can't Help It (Acuff-Rose, BMI) .... 80
I Left My Heart in San Francisco (General, ASCAP) .... 27
I Left My Heart in the Balcony (Trinity-Kilt, BMI). 82
I Remember You (Paramount, ASCAP) .... 10
I Was Such a Fool (Francon, ASCAP) .... 44
I'm Going Back to School (Conrad, BMI) .... 62
I'm Here to Get My Baby Out of Jail (Cole, BMI).. 78
I've Been Everywhere (Hill & Range, BMI) .... 85
I've Got a Woman (Progressive, BMI) .... 34
I'll Bring It Home to You (Kags, BMI) .... 64
If a Man Answers (Adaris, BMI) .... 38
If I Had a Hammer (Ludlow, BMI) .... 32
James (Acuff-Rose, BMI) .... 25
King of the Whole Wide World (Presley, BMI) .. 39
Leah (Acuff-Rose, BMI) .... 56
Let's Dance (Rondell & Sherman-DeVorzon, BMI).. 13
Lie to Me (Ben Day, BMI) .... 46
Limbo Rock (Twist-Four Star, BMI) .... 18
Little Black Book (Plainview, BMI) .... 29
Lonely Bull, The (Almo, ASCAP) .... 95
Love Me Tender (Presley, BMI) .... 37
Lovers By Night, Strangers By Day (January, BMI). 70
Magic Wand (Hill & Range-Nancoz, BMI) .... 92
Mama Sang a Song—Anderson (Tree-Champion, BMI) .... 97
Mama Sang a Song—Brennan (Tree-Champion, BMI) .... 76
Mama Sang a Song—Kenton (Tree-Champion, BMI). 61
Mr. Lonely (Ripley, BMI) .... 75
Monster Mash (Garpax, BMI) .... 1
My Own True Love (Remick, ASCAP) .... 67
Next Door to an Angel (Aldon, BMI) .... 15
Next Door to the Blues (Figure, BMI) .... 72
No One Will Ever Know (Milene, ASCAP) .... 51
Nothing Can Change This Love (Kags, BMI) .... 22
One More Town (Sausalito, BMI) .... 98
Only Love Can Break a Heart (Arch, ASCAP) .... 4
Patches (Aldon, BMI) .... 7
Pop Pop Pop-Pie (Dandelion, BMI) .... 52
Popeye (The Hitchhiker) (Kalmann, ASCAP) .... 11
Rain, Rain Go Away (Regent, BMI) .... 40
Ramblin' Rose (Sweco, BMI) .... 8
Release Me (Four Star, BMI) .... 90
Return to Sender (Presley, BMI) .... 20
Ride! (Woodcrest-Check-Colt, BMI) .... 65
Save All Your Lovin' for Me (Champion, BMI) .. 68
Second Fiddle Girl (Dandelion-Crazy Cajun, BMI).. 69
Sheila (Eager-Nitetime, BMI) .... 59
Sherry (Bobob, ASCAP) .... 5
Somebody Have Mercy (Kags, BMI) .... 77
Stop the Music (Vee-Ve, BMI) .... 58
Stormy Monday (Gregmark, BMI) .... 43
Stubborn Kind of Fellow (Jobete, BMI) .... 96
Surfin' Safari (Guild, BMI) .... 21
Susie Darlin' (Chancellor, ASCAP) .... 47
Sweet Sixteen Bars (Progressive, BMI) .... 63
Ten Lonely Guys (Roosevelt, BMI) .... 60
That Stranger Used to Be My Girl (Winneton, BMI) .... 71
Torture (Acuff-Rose, BMI) .... 23
Twistin' With Linda (Wemar, BMI) .... 54
Untie Me (Lowery, BMI) .... 84
Venus in Blue Jeans (Aldon, BMI) .... 16
Warmed Over Kisses (Pogo, ASCAP) .... 26
What Kind of Fool Am I—Davis (Ludlow, BMI) .... 24
What Kind of Fool Am I—Newley (Ludlow, BMI) .. 86
What Kind of Love Is This (Planetary-Gee, ASCAP). 48
Where Do You Come From (Presley, BMI) .... 99
Wiggle Wobble (Bob-Dan, BMI) .... 83
Workin' for the Man (Acuff-Rose, BMI) .... 36
You Beat Me to the Punch (Jobete, BMI) .... 49
You Belong to Me (Ridgeway, BMI) .... 55
You Can Run (Armada, BMI) .... 73

## BUBBLING UNDER THE HOT 100

101. WHAT KIND OF FOOL AM I ....Robert Goulet, Columbia 42519
102. I'LL REMEMBER CAROL ....Tommy Boyce, RCA Victor 8074
103. WHY CAN'T HE BE YOU ....Patsy Cline, Decca 31429
104. THE ALLEY CAT SONG ....David Thorne, Riverside 4530
105. A TRUE, TRUE LOVE ....Bobby Darin, Capitol 4837
106. LET'S GO ....Routers, Warner Bros. 5283
107. I'M SO LONESOME I COULD CRY ....Johnny Tillotson, Cadence 1432
108. KEEP YOUR HANDS OFF MY BABY ....Little Eva, Dimension 1003
109. DON'T STOP THE WEDDING ....Ann Cole, Roulette 4452
110. BLUE FLAME ....Billy Vaughn, Dot 16397
111. YOU CAN'T LIE TO A LIAR ....Ketty Lester, Era 3088
112. COLD, COLD HEART ....Dinah Washington, Mercury 72040
113. HEART BREAKER ....Dean Christie, Select 715
114. I DIG THIS STATION ....Gary (U. S.) Bonds, LeGrand 1022
115. AFTER LOVING YOU ....Eddy Arnold, RCA Victor 8048
116. WONDERFUL ONE ....Shondells, King 5656
117. UP ON THE ROOF ....Drifters, Atlantic 2162
118. TEAR FOR TEAR ....Gene (Duke of Earl) Chandler, Vee Jay 461
119. LIMBO DANCE ....Champs, Challenge 9162
120. SLIGHTLY OUT OF TUNE ....Julie London, Liberty 55512
121. WHEN THE BOYS GET TOGETHER ....Joanie Sommers, Warner Bros. 5308
122. BLUEBIRDS OVER THE MOUNTAIN ....Echoes, Smash 1766
123. MINSTREL & QUEEN ....Impressions, ABC-Paramount 10357

# BILLBOARD HOT 100

FOR WEEK ENDING NOVEMBER 3 1962

★ STAR PERFORMERS—Selections registering greatest upward progress this week.
S Indicates that 45 r.p.m. stereo single version is available.
△ Indicates that 33⅓ r.p.m. mono single version is available.
S△ Indicates that 33⅓ r.p.m. stereo single version is available.

| This Week | 1 Wk. Ago | 2 Wks. Ago | 3 Wks. Ago | Title | Artist, Label & Number | Weeks On Chart |
|---|---|---|---|---|---|---|
| 1 | 2 | 4 | 11 | HE'S A REBEL | Crystals, Philles 106 | 9 |
| 2 | 4 | 8 | 13 | ONLY LOVE CAN BREAK A HEART | Gene Pitney, Musicor 1022 | 8 |
| 3 | 3 | 3 | 7 | DO YOU LOVE ME | Contours, Gordy 7005 | 13 |
| 4 | 1 | 1 | 2 | MONSTER MASH | Bobby (Boris) Pickett and the Crypt Kickers, Garpax 44167 | 9 |
| 5 | 6 | 15 | 21 | ALL ALONE AM I | Brenda Lee, Decca 31424 | 6 |
| ★ 6 | 17 | 66 | — | BIG GIRLS DON'T CRY | Four Seasons, Vee Jay 465 | 3 |
| 7 | 9 | 20 | 31 | GINA △ | Johnny Mathis, Columbia 42582 | 7 |
| ★ 8 | 18 | 23 | 33 | LIMBO ROCK | Chubby Checker, Parkway 849 | 9 |
| ★ 9 | 15 | 29 | 44 | NEXT DOOR TO AN ANGEL △ | Neil Sedaka, RCA Victor 8086 | 5 |
| ★ 10 | 20 | 68 | — | RETURN TO SENDER △ | Elvis Presley, RCA Victor 8100 | 3 |
| 11 | 5 | 2 | 1 | SHERRY | Four Seasons, Vee Jay 456 | 11 |
| 12 | 14 | 22 | 37 | CLOSE TO CATHY | Mike Clifford, United Artists 489 | 8 |
| 13 | 7 | 6 | 8 | PATCHES | Dickey Lee, Smash 1758 | 11 |
| 14 | 11 | 16 | 24 | POPEYE (The Hitchhiker) | Chubby Checker, Parkway 849 | 7 |
| ★ 15 | 28 | 47 | 69 | THE CHA-CHA-CHA | Bobby Rydell, Cameo 228 | 4 |
| 16 | 8 | 7 | 3 | RAMBLIN' ROSE | Nat King Cole, Capitol 4804 | 14 |
| ★ 17 | 24 | 18 | 30 | WHAT KIND OF FOOL AM I | Sammy Davis Jr., Reprise 20048 | 10 |
| ★ 18 | 25 | 37 | 52 | JAMES (Hold the Ladder Steady) | Sue Thompson, Hickory 1183 | 6 |
| 19 | 12 | 9 | 6 | GREEN ONIONS | Booker T & the MG's, Stax 127 | 13 |
| 20 | 23 | 26 | 28 | TORTURE | Kris Jensen, Hickory 1173 | 10 |
| 21 | 10 | 5 | 5 | I REMEMBER YOU | Frank Ifield, Vee Jay 457 | 9 |
| 22 | 22 | 31 | 41 | NOTHING CAN CHANGE THIS LOVE △ | Sam Cooke, RCA Victor 8088 | 6 |
| 23 | 21 | 14 | 14 | SURFIN' SAFARI | Beach Boys, Capitol 4777 | 13 |
| 24 | 27 | 19 | 23 | I LEFT MY HEART IN SAN FRANCISCO △ | Tony Bennett, Columbia 42332 | 13 |
| 25 | 26 | 33 | 39 | WARMED OVER KISSES | Brian Hyland, ABC-Paramount 10359 | 7 |
| 26 | 31 | 52 | 71 | DESAFINADO | Stan Getz and Charlie Byrd, Verve 10260 | 6 |
| ★ 27 | 37 | 48 | 60 | LOVE ME TENDER | Richard Chamberlain, MGM 13097 | 5 |
| 28 | 13 | 10 | 4 | LET'S DANCE | Chris Montez, Monogram 505 | 13 |
| 29 | 34 | 60 | 77 | I'VE GOT A WOMAN | Jimmy McGriff, Sue 770 | 4 |
| 30 | 19 | 13 | 9 | ALLEY CAT | Bent Fabric, Atco 6226 | 15 |
| ★ 31 | 44 | 57 | 88 | I WAS SUCH A FOOL | Connie Francis, MGM 13096 | 5 |
| ★ 32 | 45 | 71 | 91 | DON'T HANG UP | Orlons, Cameo 231 | 4 |
| 33 | 36 | 53 | 53 | WORKIN' FOR THE MAN | Roy Orbison, Monument 467 | 7 |
| 34 | 38 | 42 | 51 | IF A MAN ANSWERS | Bobby Darin, Capitol 4837 | 6 |
| 35 | 16 | 12 | 12 | VENUS IN BLUE JEANS | Jimmy Clanton, Ace 8001 | 12 |
| ★ 36 | 47 | 51 | 61 | SUSIE DARLIN' | Tommy Roe, ABC-Paramount 10362 | 5 |
| 37 | 29 | 32 | 34 | LITTLE BLACK BOOK △ | Jimmy Dean, Columbia 42529 | 8 |
| ★ 38 | 56 | 65 | 74 | LEAH | Roy Orbison, Monument 467 | 5 |
| 39 | 41 | 46 | 56 | DON'T YOU BELIEVE IT △ | Andy Williams, Columbia 42523 | 8 |
| ★ 40 | 50 | 56 | 75 | (DANCE WITH THE) GUITAR MAN △ | Duane Eddy, RCA Victor 8087 | 5 |
| ★ 41 | 66 | 87 | — | BOBBY'S GIRL | Marcie Blane, Seville 120 | 3 |
| ★ 42 | 52 | 67 | 72 | POP POP POP-PIE | Sherrys, Guyden 2068 | 5 |
| 43 | 42 | 44 | 48 | BABY FACE | Bobby Darin, Atco 6236 | 6 |
| ★ 44 | 65 | 84 | — | RIDE! | Dee Dee Sharp, Cameo 230 | 3 |
| ★ 45 | 67 | 82 | — | MY OWN TRUE LOVE | Duprees, Coed 571 | 3 |
| 46 | 51 | 43 | 50 | NO ONE WILL EVER KNOW | Jimmie Rodgers, Dot 16378 | 10 |
| ★ 47 | 61 | 74 | 85 | MAMA SANG A SONG | Stan Kenton, Capitol 4847 | 4 |
| 48 | 30 | 17 | 26 | DON'T GO NEAR THE INDIANS | Rex Allen, Mercury 71997 | 8 |
| 49 | 33 | 35 | 36 | HIDE AND GO SEEK | Bunker Hill, Mala 451 | 11 |
| ★ 50 | 71 | 85 | — | THAT STRANGER USED TO BE MY GIRL | Trade Martin, Coed 570 | 3 |
| 51 | 43 | 49 | 54 | STORMY MONDAY | Bobby Bland, Duke 355 | 9 |
| 52 | 40 | 27 | 17 | RAIN, RAIN GO AWAY | Bobby Vinton, Epic 9532 | 11 |
| 53 | 32 | 11 | 10 | IF I HAD A HAMMER | Peter, Paul & Mary, Warner Bros. 5296 | 12 |
| ★ 54 | 64 | 73 | 80 | I'LL BRING IT HOME TO YOU | Carla Thomas, Atlantic 2163 | 4 |
| ★ 55 | 80 | — | — | I CAN'T HELP IT | Johnny Tillotson, Cadence 1432 | 2 |
| 56 | 62 | 64 | 66 | I'M GOING BACK TO SCHOOL | Dee Clark, Vee Jay 462 | 5 |
| 57 | 60 | 45 | 47 | TEN LONELY GUYS | Pat Boone, Dot 16391 | 7 |
| 58 | 39 | 30 | 35 | KING OF THE WHOLE WIDE WORLD | Elvis Presley, RCA Victor EPA 4371 (Extended Play) | 7 |
| ★ 59 | 83 | — | — | WIGGLE WOBBLE | Les Cooper, Everlast 5019 | 3 |
| ★ 60 | 70 | 77 | 83 | LOVERS BY NIGHT, STRANGERS BY DAY | Fleetwoods, Dolton 62 | 4 |
| ★ 61 | 76 | 90 | — | MAMA SANG A SONG | Walter Brennan, Liberty 55508 | 3 |
| ★ 62 | 89 | 91 | — | DON'T ASK ME TO BE FRIENDS | Everly Brothers, Warner Bros. 5297 | 3 |
| 63 | 69 | 70 | 73 | SECOND FIDDLE GIRL | Barbara Lynn, Jamie 1233 | 7 |
| ★ 64 | 95 | — | — | THE LONELY BULL | Tijuana Brass, A. & M. 703 | 2 |
| 65 | 53 | '58 | 62 | THE BURNING OF ATLANTA △ | Claude King, Columbia 42581 | 5 |
| 66 | 75 | 78 | 87 | MR. LONELY | Buddy Greco, Epic 9536 | 7 |
| 67 | 74 | 88 | 93 | HAPPY WEEKEND | Dave (Baby) Cortez, Chess 1834 | 4 |
| ★ 68 | 90 | — | — | RELEASE ME | "Little Esther" Phillips, Lenox 5555 | 2 |
| 69 | 54 | 61 | 63 | TWISTIN' WITH LINDA | Isley Brothers, Wand 127 | 7 |
| 70 | 73 | 75 | 79 | YOU CAN RUN | Jerry Butler, Vee Jay 463 | 4 |
| 71 | 85 | 86 | 89 | I'VE BEEN EVERYWHERE △ | Hank Snow, RCA Victor 8072 | 5 |
| 72 | 84 | 99 | — | UNTIE ME | Tams, Arlen 711 | 3 |
| 73 | 57 | 69 | 70 | HE THINKS I STILL CARE | Connie Francis, MGM 13096 | 5 |
| 74 | 82 | 83 | 86 | I LEFT MY HEART IN THE BALCONY | Linda Scott, Congress 106 | 7 |
| 75 | 81 | 96 | 98 | HEARTACHES | Patsy Cline, Decca 31429 | 4 |
| 76 | 78 | 81 | 84 | I'M HERE TO GET MY BABY OUT OF JAIL | Everly Brothers, Cadence 1429 | 4 |
| ★ 77 | 96 | 98 | — | STUBBORN KIND OF FELLOW | Marvin Gaye, Tamla 54068 | 3 |
| 78 | 72 | 76 | 78 | NEXT DOOR TO THE BLUES | Etta James, Argo 5424 | 4 |
| 79 | 77 | — | — | SOMEBODY HAVE MERCY △ | Sam Cooke, RCA Victor 8088 | 2 |
| ★ 80 | — | — | — | LET'S GO | Routers, Warner Bros. 5283 | 1 |
| ★ 81 | — | — | — | ESO BESO △ | Paul Anka, RCA Victor 8097 | 1 |
| ★ 82 | — | — | 92 | I'LL REMEMBER CAROL △ | Tommy Boyce, RCA Victor 8074 | 2 |
| 83 | 94 | — | — | ANNA (Go to Him) | Arthur Alexander, Dot 16387 | 2 |
| ★ 84 | — | 79 | — | THE ALLEY CAT SONG | David Thorne, Riverside 4530 | 2 |
| ★ 85 | — | — | — | TELSTAR | Tornadoes, London 9561 | 1 |
| 86 | 88 | 100 | — | DON'T EVER LEAVE ME | Bob and Earl, Tempe 102 | 3 |
| ★ 87 | — | — | — | MARY ANN REGRETS | Burl Ives, Decca 31433 | 1 |
| ★ 88 | — | — | — | COMIN' HOME BABY | Mel Torme, Atlantic 2165 | 1 |
| 89 | 97 | — | — | MAMA SANG A SONG | Bill Anderson, Decca 31404 | 2 |
| ★ 90 | — | — | — | KEEP YOUR HANDS OFF MY BABY | Little Eva, Dimension 1003 | 1 |
| 91 | 92 | — | — | MAGIC WAND | Don & Juan, Big Top 3121 | 2 |
| 92 | 93 | — | — | ALADDIN | Bobby Curtola, Del-Fi 4185 | 2 |
| 93 | — | — | — | UP ON THE ROOF | Drifters, Atlantic 2162 | 1 |
| 94 | 79 | 80 | 81 | DID YOU EVER SEE A DREAM WALKING | Fats Domino, Imperial 5875 | 5 |
| 95 | — | — | — | RUMORS | Johnny Crawford, Del-Fi 4188 | 1 |
| 96 | — | — | — | HEART BREAKER | Dean Christie, Select 715 | 1 |
| 97 | 100 | — | — | FOUR WALLS | Kay Starr, Capitol 4835 | 2 |
| 98 | — | — | — | I LOST MY BABY | Joey Dee, Roulette 4456 | 1 |
| 99 | — | — | — | DEAR HEARTS AND GENTLE PEOPLE | Springfields, Philips 40072 | 1 |
| 100 | — | — | — | FATHER KNOWS BEST | Radiants, Chess 1832 | 1 |

## HOT 100—A TO Z—*(Publisher-Licensee)*


Aladdin (Kemo, BMI) .... 92
All Alone Am I (Duchess, BMI) .... 5
Alley Cat (Metorion, BMI) .... 30
Alley Cat Song, The (Metorion, BMI) .... 84
Anna (Painted Desert, BMI) .... 83
Baby Face (Remick, ASCAP) .... 43
Big Girls Don't Cry (Bobob, ASCAP) .... 6
Bobby's Girl (A. M. E., BMI) .... 41
Burning of Atlanta, The (Conrad, BMI) .... 65
Cha-Cha-Cha, The (Fajob-Kalmann, ASCAP) .... 15
Close to Cathy (Arch, ASCAP) .... 12
Comin' Home Baby (Melotone, BMI) .... 88
(Dance With the) Guitar Man (Linduane, BMI) .... 40
Dear Hearts and Gentle People (Morris, ASCAP) .... 99
Desafinado (Hollis, BMI) .... 26
Did You Ever See a Dream Walking (De Sylva, Brown & Henderson, ASCAP) .... 94
Do You Love Me (Jobete, BMI) .... 3
Don't Ask Me to Be Friends (Aldon, BMI) .... 62
Don't Ever Leave Me (Fore-Site, BMI) .... 86
Don't Go Near the Indians (Buttercup, BMI) .... 48
Don't Hang Up (Kalmann, ASCAP) .... 32
Don't You Believe It (Dolfi, ASCAP) .... 39
Eso Beso (Flanka, ASCAP) .... 81
Father Knows Best (Arc, BMI) .... 100
Four Walls (Sheldon, BMI) .... 97
Gina (Elm Drive, ASCAP) .... 7
Green Onions (East, BMI) .... 19
Happy Weekend (Arc, BMI) .... 67
He Thinks I Still Care (Glad-Jack, BMI) .... 73
Heartaches (Leeds, ASCAP) .... 75
Heart Breaker (Drury Lane, BMI) .... 100
He's a Rebel (January, BMI) .... 1
Hide & Go Seek (Marks-Florentine, BMI) .... 49
I Can't Help It (Acuff-Rose, BMI) .... 55
I Left My Heart in San Francisco (General, ASCAP). 24
I Left My Heart in the Balcony (Trinity-Kilt, BMI). 74
I Lost My Baby (Planetary, ASCAP) .... 98
I Remember You (Paramount, ASCAP) .... 21
I Was Such a Fool (Francon, ASCAP) .... 31
I'm Going Back to School (Conrad, BMI) .... 56
I'm Here to Get My Baby Out of Jail (Cole, BMI). 76
I've Been Everywhere (Hill & Range, BMI) .... 71
I've Got a Woman (Progressive, BMI) .... 29
I'll Bring It Home to You (Kags, BMI) .... 54
I'll Remember Carol (Calboy, BMI) .... 82
If a Man Answers (Adaris, BMI) .... 34
If I Had a Hammer (Ludlow, BMI) .... 53
James (Acuff-Rose, BMI) .... 18
Keep Your Hands Off My Baby (Aldon, BMI) .... 90
King of the Whole Wide World (Presley, BMI) .. 58
Leah (Acuff-Rose, BMI) .... 38
Let's Dance (Rondell & Sherman-DeVorzon, BMI) .. 28
Let's Go (Wrist-Giant, BMI) .... 80
Limbo Rock (Twist-Four Star, BMI) .... 8
Little Black Book (Plainview, BMI) .... 37
Lonely Bull, The (Almo, ASCAP) .... 64
Love Me Tender (Presley, BMI) .... 27
Lovers By Night, Strangers By Day (January, BMI) .... 60
Magic Wand (Hill & Range-Nancoz, BMI) .... 91
Mama Sang a Song—Anderson (Tree-Champion, BMI) .... 89
Mama Sang a Song—Brennan (Tree-Champion, BMI) .... 61
Mama Sang a Song—Kenton (Tree-Champion, BMI) .... 47
Mary Ann Regrets (Pamper, BMI) .... 87
Mr. Lonely (Ripley, BMI) .... 66
Monster Mash (Garpax, BMI) .... 4
My Own True Love (Remick, ASCAP) .... 45
Next Door to an Angel (Aldon, BMI) .... 9
Next Door to the Blues (Figure, BMI) .... 78
No One Will Ever Know (Milene, ASCAP) .... 46
Nothing Can Change This Love (Kags, BMI) .... 22
Only Love Can Break a Heart (Arch, ASCAP) .... 2
Patches (Aldon, BMI) .... 13
Pop Pop Pop-Pie (Dandelion, BMI) .... 42
Popeye (The Hitchhiker) (Kalmann, ASCAP) .... 14
Rain, Rain Go Away (Regent, BMI) .... 52
Ramblin' Rose (Sweco, BMI) .... 16
Release Me (Four Star, BMI) .... 68
Return to Sender (Presley, BMI) .... 10
Ride! (Woodcrest-Check-Colt, BMI) .... 44
Rumors (Aldon, BMI) .... 95
Second Fiddle Girl (Dandelion-Crazy Cajun, BMI) .. 63
Sherry (Bobob, ASCAP) .... 11
Somebody Have Mercy (Kags, BMI) .... 79
Stormy Monday (Gregmark, BMI) .... 51
Stubborn Kind of Fellow (Jobete, BMI) .... 77
Surfin' Safari (Guild, BMI) .... 23
Susie Darlin' (Congressional, ASCAP) .... 36
Telstar (Ivy, ASCAP) .... 85
Ten Lonely Guys (Roosevelt, BMI) .... 57
That Stranger Used to Be My Girl (Winneton, BMI). 50
Torture (Acuff-Rose, BMI) .... 20
Twistin' With Linda (Wemar, BMI) .... 69
Untie Me (Lowery, BMI) .... 72
Up on the Roof (Aldon, BMI) .... 93
Venus in Blue Jeans (Aldon, BMI) .... 35
Warmed Over Kisses (Pogo, ASCAP) .... 25
What Kind of Fool Am I—Davis (Ludlow, BMI) .. 17
Wiggle Wobble (Bob-Dan, BMI) .... 59
Workin' for the Man (Acuff-Rose, BMI) .... 33
You Can Run (Armada, BMI) .... 70


## BUBBLING UNDER THE HOT 100

101. THE LOOK OF LOVE .... Frank Sinatra, Reprise 20107
102. SPANISH LACE .... Gene McDaniels, Liberty 55510
103. FURTHER MORE .... Ray Stevens, Mercury 72039
104. WHY CAN'T HE BE YOU .... Patsy Cline, Decca 31429
105. A TRUE, TRUE LOVE .... Bobby Darin, Capitol 4837
106. I DIG THIS STATION .... Gary (U. S.) Bonds, LeGrand 1022
107. BLUE FLAME .... Billy Vaughn, Dot 16397
108. PIDDLE DE PAT .... Tommy Roe, ABC-Paramount 10362
109. DESAFINADO .... Pat Thomas, MGM 13102
110. WHERE DO YOU COME FROM .... Elvis Presley, RCA Victor 8100
111. ONE MORE TOWN .... Kingston Trio, Capitol 4842
112. THE PUSH AND KICK .... Mark Valentino, Swan 4121
113. MINSTREL AND QUEEN .... Impressions, ABC-Paramount 10357
114. TEAR FOR TEAR .... Gene (Duke of Earl) Chandler, Vee Jay 461
115. SLIGHTLY OUT OF TUNE .... Julie London, Liberty 55512
116. WHEN THE BOYS GET TOGETHER .... Joanie Sommers, Warner Bros. 5308
117. SOMEONE .... Billy Vaughn, Dot 16397
118. BLUEBIRDS OVER THE MOUNTAIN .... Echoes, Smash 1766
119. I'M STANDING BY .... Ben E. King, Atco 6237
120. BUSTIN' SURFBOARDS .... Tornados, Aertaun 1013
121. NO ONE CAN MAKE MY SUNSHINE SMILE .... Everly Brothers, Warner Bros., 5297
122. WHAT KIND OF FOOL AM I .... Robert Goulet, Columbia 42519
123. I'M SO LONESOME I COULD CRY .... Johnny Tillotson, Cadence 1432
124. LOVE CAME TO ME .... Dion, Laurie 3145
125. GO AWAY LITTLE GIRL .... Steve Lawrence, Columbia 42601
126. MIDNIGHT SUN .... Five Whispers, Dolton 61
127. BEST MAN CRIED .... Clyde McPhatter, Mercury 72051
128. SHE'S A TROUBLEMAKER .... Majors, Imperial 5879
129. OUR ANNIVERSARY OF LOVE .... Bob Braun, Decca 31430
130. MIND OVER MATTER .... Nolan Strong, Fortune 546

# BILLBOARD HOT 100

**FOR WEEK ENDING NOVEMBER 10, 1962**

| This Week | Wk. Ago | 2 Wks. Ago | Title | Artist, Label & Number | Weeks On Chart |
|---|---|---|---|---|---|
| 1 | 1 | 2 | HE'S A REBEL | Crystals, Philles 106 | 10 |
| 2 | 6 | 17 | BIG GIRLS DON'T CRY | Four Seasons, Vee Jay 465 | 4 |
| 3 | 5 | 6 | ALL ALONE AM I | Brenda Lee, Decca 31424 | 7 |
| 4 | 10 | 20 | RETURN TO SENDER | Elvis Presley, RCA Victor 8100 | 4 |
| 5 | 2 | 4 | ONLY LOVE CAN BREAK A HEART | Gene Pitney, Musicor 1022 | 9 |
| 6 | 9 | 15 | NEXT DOOR TO AN ANGEL | Neil Sedaka, RCA Victor 8086 | 6 |
| 7 | 7 | 9 | GINA | Johnny Mathis, Columbia 42582 | 8 |
| 8 | 4 | 1 | MONSTER MASH | Bobby (Boris) Pickett and the Crypt Kickers, Garpax 44167 | 9 |
| 9 | 3 | 3 | DO YOU LOVE ME | Contours, Gordy 7005 | 14 |
| 10 | 14 | 11 | POPEYE (The Hitchhiker) | Chubby Checker, Parkway 849 | 8 |
| 11 | 8 | 18 | LIMBO ROCK | Chubby Checker, Parkway 849 | 10 |
| 12 | 12 | 14 | CLOSE TO CATHY | Mike Clifford, United Artists 489 | 9 |
| 13 | 22 | 22 | NOTHING CAN CHANGE THIS LOVE | Sam Cooke, RCA Victor 8088 | 7 |
| 14 | 15 | 28 | THE CHA-CHA-CHA | Bobby Rydell, Cameo 228 | 5 |
| 15 | 11 | 5 | SHERRY | Four Seasons, Vee Jay 456 | 12 |
| 16 | 32 | 45 | DON'T HANG UP | Orlons, Cameo 231 | 5 |
| 17 | 18 | 25 | JAMES (Hold the Ladder Steady) | Sue Thompson, Hickory 1183 | 7 |
| 18 | 17 | 24 | WHAT KIND OF FOOL AM I | Sammy Davis Jr., Reprise 20048 | 11 |
| 19 | 41 | 66 | BOBBY'S GIRL | Marcie Blane, Seville 120 | 4 |
| 20 | 26 | 31 | DESAFINADO | Stan Getz and Charlie Byrd, Verve 10260 | 7 |
| 21 | 13 | 7 | PATCHES | Dickey Lee, Smash 1758 | 12 |
| 22 | 24 | 27 | I LEFT MY HEART IN SAN FRANCISCO | Tony Bennett, Columbia 42332 | 14 |
| 23 | 29 | 34 | I'VE GOT A WOMAN | Jimmy McGriff, Sue 770 | 5 |
| 24 | 27 | 37 | LOVE ME TENDER | Richard Chamberlain, MGM 13097 | 6 |
| 25 | 23 | 21 | SURFIN' SAFARI | Beach Boys, Capitol 4777 | 14 |
| 26 | 19 | 12 | GREEN ONIONS | Booker T & the MG's, Stax 127 | 14 |
| 27 | 44 | 65 | RIDE! | Dee Dee Sharp, Cameo 230 | 4 |
| 28 | 31 | 44 | I WAS SUCH A FOOL | Connie Francis, MGM 13096 | 6 |
| 29 | 16 | 8 | RAMBLIN' ROSE | Nat King Cole, Capitol 4804 | 15 |
| 30 | 40 | 50 | (DANCE WITH THE) GUITAR MAN | Duane Eddy, RCA Victor 8087 | 6 |
| 31 | 38 | 56 | LEAH | Roy Orbison, Monument 467 | 6 |
| 32 | 34 | 38 | IF A MAN ANSWERS | Bobby Darin, Capitol 4837 | 7 |
| 33 | 33 | 36 | WORKIN' FOR THE MAN | Roy Orbison, Monument 467 | 8 |
| 34 | 21 | 10 | I REMEMBER YOU | Frank Ifield, Vee Jay 457 | 10 |
| 35 | 36 | 47 | SUSIE DARLIN' | Tommy Roe, ABC-Paramount 10362 | 6 |
| 36 | 30 | 19 | ALLEY CAT | Bent Fabric, Atco 6226 | 16 |
| 37 | 45 | 67 | MY OWN TRUE LOVE | Duprees, Coed 571 | 4 |
| 38 | 20 | 23 | TORTURE | Kris Jensen, Hickory 1173 | 11 |
| 39 | 64 | 95 | THE LONELY BULL | Tijuana Brass, A. & M. 703 | 3 |
| 40 | 42 | 52 | POP POP POP-PIE | Sherrys, Guyden 2068 | 6 |
| 41 | 28 | 13 | LET'S DANCE | Chris Montez, Monogram 505 | 14 |
| 42 | 47 | 61 | MAMA SANG A SONG | Stan Kenton, Capitol 4847 | 5 |
| 43 | 50 | 71 | THAT STRANGER USED TO BE MY GIRL | Trade Martin, Coed 570 | 4 |
| 44 | 55 | 80 | I CAN'T HELP IT | Johnny Tillotson, Cadence 1432 | 3 |
| 45 | 25 | 26 | WARMED OVER KISSES | Brian Hyland, ABC-Paramount 10359 | 8 |
| 46 | 37 | 29 | LITTLE BLACK BOOK | Jimmy Dean, Columbia 42529 | 9 |
| 47 | 54 | 64 | I'LL BRING IT HOME TO YOU | Carla Thomas, Atlantic 2163 | 5 |
| 48 | 59 | 83 | WIGGLE WOBBLE | Les Cooper, Everlast 5019 | 4 |
| 49 | 39 | 41 | DON'T YOU BELIEVE IT | Andy Williams, Columbia 42523 | 9 |
| 50 | 68 | 90 | RELEASE ME | "Little Esther" Phillips, Lenox 5555 | 3 |
| 51 | 61 | 76 | MAMA SANG A SONG | Walter Brennan, Liberty 55508 | 4 |
| 52 | 56 | 62 | I'M GOING BACK TO SCHOOL | Dee Clark, Vee Jay 462 | 6 |
| 53 | 35 | 16 | VENUS IN BLUE JEANS | Jimmy Clanton, Ace 8001 | 13 |
| 54 | 49 | 33 | HIDE AND GO SEEK | Bunker Hill, Mala 451 | 12 |
| 55 | 60 | 70 | LOVERS BY NIGHT, STRANGERS BY DAY | Fleetwoods, Dolton 62 | 5 |
| 56 | 43 | 42 | BABY FACE | Bobby Darin, Atco 6236 | 7 |
| 57 | 51 | 43 | STORMY MONDAY | Bobby Bland, Duke 355 | 10 |
| 58 | 62 | 89 | DON'T ASK ME TO BE FRIENDS | Everly Brothers, Warner Bros. 5297 | 4 |
| 59 | 46 | 51 | NO ONE WILL EVER KNOW | Jimmie Rodgers, Dot 16378 | 11 |
| 60 | 81 | — | ESO BESO | Paul Anka, RCA Victor 8097 | 2 |
| 61 | 69 | 54 | TWISTIN' WITH LINDA | Isley Brothers, Wand 127 | 8 |
| 62 | 90 | — | KEEP YOUR HANDS OFF MY BABY | Little Eva, Dimension 1003 | 2 |
| 63 | 65 | 53 | THE BURNING OF ATLANTA | Claude King, Columbia 42581 | 6 |
| 64 | 66 | 75 | MR. LONELY | Buddy Greco, Epic 9536 | 8 |
| 65 | 72 | 84 | UNTIE ME | Tams, Arlen 711 | 4 |
| 66 | 95 | — | RUMORS | Johnny Crawford, Del-Fi 4188 | 2 |
| 67 | 70 | 73 | YOU CAN RUN | Jerry Butler, Vee Jay 463 | 5 |
| 68 | 73 | 57 | HE THINKS I STILL CARE | Connie Francis, MGM 13096 | 6 |
| 69 | 71 | 85 | I'VE BEEN EVERYWHERE | Hank Snow, RCA Victor 8072 | 6 |
| 70 | 83 | 94 | ANNA (Go to Him) | Arthur Alexander, Dot 16387 | 3 |
| 71 | 85 | — | TELSTAR | Tornadoes, London 9561 | 2 |
| 72 | 63 | 69 | SECOND FIDDLE GIRL | Barbara Lynn, Jamie 1233 | 8 |
| 73 | 80 | — | LET'S GO | Routers, Warner Bros. 5283 | 2 |
| 74 | — | — | LOVE CAME TO ME | Dion, Laurie 3145 | 1 |
| 75 | 77 | 96 | STUBBORN KIND OF FELLOW | Marvin Gaye, Tamla 54068 | 4 |
| 76 | 76 | 78 | I'M HERE TO GET MY BABY OUT OF JAIL | Everly Brothers, Cadence 1429 | 5 |
| 77 | 87 | — | MARY ANN REGRETS | Burl Ives, Decca 31433 | 2 |
| 78 | 79 | 77 | SOMEBODY HAVE MERCY | Sam Cooke, RCA Victor 8088 | 3 |
| 79 | 67 | 74 | HAPPY WEEKEND | Dave (Baby) Cortez, Chess 1834 | 5 |
| 80 | 82 | — | I'LL REMEMBER CAROL | Tommy Boyce, RCA Victor 8074 | 3 |
| 81 | 84 | 79 | THE ALLEY CAT SONG | David Thorne, Riverside 4530 | 3 |
| 82 | 75 | 81 | HEARTACHES | Patsy Cline, Decca 31429 | 5 |
| 83 | — | — | SPANISH LACE | Gene McDaniels, Liberty 55510 | 1 |
| 84 | — | — | IF YOU WERE A ROCK & ROLL RECORD | Freddy Cannon, Swan 4122 | 1 |
| 85 | 86 | 88 | DON'T EVER LEAVE ME | Bob and Earl, Tempe 102 | 4 |
| 86 | 88 | — | COMIN' HOME BABY | Mel Torme, Atlantic 2165 | 2 |
| 87 | — | — | CHAINS | Cookies, Dimension 1002 | 1 |
| 88 | — | — | THE PUSH AND KICK | Mark Valentino, Swan 4121 | 1 |
| 89 | — | — | DEAR LONELY HEARTS | Nat King Cole, Capitol 4870 | 1 |
| 90 | 98 | — | I LOST MY BABY | Joey Dee, Roulette 4456 | 2 |
| 91 | 93 | — | UP ON THE ROOF | Drifters, Atlantic 2162 | 2 |
| 92 | 91 | 92 | MAGIC WAND | Don & Juan, Big Top 3121 | 3 |
| 93 | — | — | WHAT KIND OF FOOL AM I | Robert Goulet, Columbia 42519 | 1 |
| 94 | 96 | — | HEART BREAKER | Dean Christie, Select 715 | 2 |
| 95 | 74 | 82 | I LEFT MY HEART IN THE BALCONY | Linda Scott, Congress 106 | 8 |
| 96 | 89 | 97 | MAMA SANG A SONG | Bill Anderson, Decca 31404 | 3 |
| 97 | — | — | THAT'S LIFE | Gabriel & the Angels, Swan 4118 | 1 |
| 98 | 99 | — | DEAR HEARTS AND GENTLE PEOPLE | Springfields, Philips 40072 | 2 |
| 99 | 97 | 100 | FOUR WALLS | Kay Starr, Capitol 4835 | 3 |
| 100 | — | — | GO AWAY LITTLE GIRL | Steve Lawrence, Columbia 42601 | 1 |

## BUBBLING UNDER THE HOT 100

101. I DIG THIS STATION — Gary (U.S.) Bonds, LeGrand 1022
102. THIS LAND IS YOUR LAND — Christy Minstrels, Columbia 425592
103. WHAT KIND OF FOOL AM I — Anthony Newley, London 9546
104. WHERE DO YOU COME FROM — Elvis Presley, RCA Victor 8100
105. CONEY ISLAND BABY — Excellents, Blast 205
106. HOME TOWN — Kingston Trio, Capitol 4842
107. DESAFINADO — Pat Thomas, MGM 13102
108. THIS LAND IS YOUR LAND — Ketty Lester, Era 3094
109. FURTHER MORE — Ray Stevens, Mercury 72039
110. SLIGHTLY OUT OF TUNE — Julie London, Liberty 55512
111. ALADDIN — Bobby Curtola, Del-Fi 4185
112. BLUEBIRDS OVER THE MOUNTAIN — Echoes, Smash 1766
113. FATHER KNOWS BEST — Radiants, Chess 1832
114. VOLARE — Ace Cannon, Hi 2057
115. SOMEONE — Billy Vaughn, Dot 16397
116. THE LOOK OF LOVE — Frank Sinatra, Reprise 20107
117. TEAR FOR TEAR — Gene (Duke of Earl) Chandler, Vee Jay 461
118. NO ONE CAN MAKE MY SUNSHINE SMILE — Everly Brothers, Warner Bros. 5297
119. OUR ANNIVERSARY OF LOVE — Bob Braun, Decca 31430
120. KISS TOMORROW GOODBYE — Danny White, Fresco 104
121. I'M STANDING BY — Ben E. King, Atco 4237
122. WHEN THE BOYS GET TOGETHER — Joanie Sommers, Warner Bros. 5308
123. SHE'S A TROUBLEMAKER — Majors, Imperial 5879
124. DIDDLE-DE-DUM — Belmonts, Sabina 507
125. THE SEARCHING IS OVER — Joe Henderson, Todd 1079
126. SHUTTERS AND BOARDS — Jerry Wallace, Challenge 9171
127. AGAIN — Belmonts, Sabina 4851
128. TOMORROW NIGHT — B. B. King, ABC-Paramount 10367
129. COLD, COLD HEART — Dinah Washington, Mercury 72040
130. NAKED CITY THEME — Nelson Riddle, Capitol 4843

# BILLBOARD HOT 100

FOR WEEK ENDING NOVEMBER 17 1962

★ STAR PERFORMERS—Selections registering greatest upward progress this week.

S Indicates that 45 r.p.m. stereo single version is available.

△ Indicates that 33⅓ r.p.m. mono single version is available.

S△ Indicates that 33⅓ r.p.m. stereo single version is available.

| This Week | 1 Wk. Ago | 2 Wks. Ago | 3 Wks. Ago | Title | Artist, Label & Number | Weeks On Chart |
|---|---|---|---|---|---|---|
| 1 | 2 | 6 | 17 | BIG GIRLS DON'T CRY | Four Seasons, Vee Jay 465 | 5 |
| 2 | 4 | 10 | 20 | RETURN TO SENDER △ | Elvis Presley, RCA Victor 8100 | 5 |
| 3 | 1 | 1 | 2 | HE'S A REBEL | Crystals, Philles 106 | 11 |
| 4 | 3 | 5 | 6 | ALL ALONE AM I | Brenda Lee, Decca 31424 | 8 |
| 5 | 6 | 9 | 15 | NEXT DOOR TO AN ANGEL △ | Neil Sedaka, RCA Victor 8086 | 7 |
| 6 | 7 | 7 | 9 | GINA △ | Johnny Mathis, Columbia 42582 | 9 |
| ★ 7 | 19 | 41 | 66 | BOBBY'S GIRL | Marcie Blane, Seville 120 | 5 |
| ★ 8 | 16 | 32 | 45 | DON'T HANG UP | Orlons, Cameo 231 | 6 |
| 9 | 11 | 8 | 18 | LIMBO ROCK | Chubby Checker, Parkway 849 | 11 |
| 10 | 14 | 15 | 28 | THE CHA-CHA-CHA | Bobby Rydell, Cameo 228 | 6 |
| 11 | 5 | 2 | 4 | ONLY LOVE CAN BREAK A HEART | Gene Pitney, Musicor 1022 | 10 |
| 12 | 13 | 22 | 22 | NOTHING CAN CHANGE THIS LOVE △ | Sam Cooke, RCA Victor 8088 | 8 |
| ★ 13 | 27 | 44 | 65 | RIDE! | Dee Dee Sharp, Cameo 230 | 5 |
| 14 | 8 | 4 | 1 | MONSTER MASH | Bobby (Boris) Pickett and the Crypt Kickers, Garpax 44167 | 11 |
| 15 | 12 | 12 | 14 | CLOSE TO CATHY | Mike Clifford, United Artists 489 | 10 |
| 16 | 9 | 3 | 3 | DO YOU LOVE ME | Contours, Gordy 7005 | 15 |
| 17 | 17 | 18 | 25 | JAMES (Hold the Ladder Steady) | Sue Thompson, Hickory 1183 | 8 |
| 18 | 20 | 26 | 31 | DESAFINADO | Stan Getz and Charlie Byrd, Verve 10260 | 8 |
| ★ 19 | 39 | 64 | 95 | THE LONELY BULL | Tijuana Brass, A. & M. 703 | 4 |
| 20 | 10 | 14 | 11 | POPEYE (The Hitchhiker) | Chubby Checker, Parkway 849 | 9 |
| 21 | 24 | 27 | 37 | LOVE ME TENDER | Richard Chamberlain, MGM 13097 | 7 |
| 22 | 23 | 29 | 34 | I'VE GOT A WOMAN | Jimmy McGriff, Sue 770 | 6 |
| 23 | 30 | 40 | 50 | (DANCE WITH THE) GUITAR MAN △ | Duane Eddy, RCA Victor 8087 | 7 |
| 24 | 28 | 31 | 44 | I WAS SUCH A FOOL | Connie Francis, MGM 13096 | 7 |
| 25 | 18 | 17 | 24 | WHAT KIND OF FOOL AM I | Sammy Davis Jr., Reprise 20048 | 12 |
| ★ 26 | 37 | 45 | 67 | MY OWN TRUE LOVE | Duprees, Coed 571 | 5 |
| 27 | 22 | 24 | 27 | I LEFT MY HEART IN SAN FRANCISCO △ | Tony Bennett, Columbia 42332 | 15 |
| ★ 28 | 43 | 50 | 71 | THAT STRANGER USED TO BE MY GIRL | Trade Martin, Coed 570 | 5 |
| 29 | 31 | 38 | 56 | LEAH | Roy Orbison, Monument 467 | 7 |
| 30 | 21 | 13 | 7 | PATCHES | Dickey Lee, Smash 1758 | 13 |
| 31 | 25 | 23 | 21 | SURFIN' SAFARI | Beach Boys, Capitol 4777 | 15 |
| ★ 32 | 50 | 68 | 90 | RELEASE ME | "Little Esther" Phillips, Lenox 5555 | 4 |
| ★ 33 | 44 | 55 | 80 | I CAN'T HELP IT | Johnny Tillotson, Cadence 1432 | 4 |
| 34 | 15 | 11 | 5 | SHERRY | Four Seasons, Vee Jay 456 | 13 |
| 35 | 40 | 42 | 52 | POP POP POP-PIE | Sherrys, Guyden 2068 | 7 |
| 36 | 33 | 33 | 36 | WORKIN' FOR THE MAN | Roy Orbison, Monument 467 | 9 |
| ★ 37 | 48 | 59 | 83 | WIGGLE WOBBLE | Les Cooper, Everlast 5019 | 5 |
| 38 | 42 | 47 | 61 | MAMA SANG A SONG | Stan Kenton, Capitol 4847 | 6 |
| ★ 39 | 71 | 85 | — | TELSTAR | Tornadoes, London 9561 | 3 |
| 40 | 26 | 19 | 12 | GREEN ONIONS | Booker T & the MG's, Stax 127 | 15 |
| 41 | 47 | 54 | 64 | I'LL BRING IT HOME TO YOU | Carla Thomas, Atlantic 2163 | 6 |
| ★ 42 | 62 | 90 | — | KEEP YOUR HANDS OFF MY BABY | Little Eva, Dimension 1003 | 3 |
| ★ 43 | 66 | 95 | — | RUMORS | Johnny Crawford, Del-Fi 4188 | 3 |
| ★ 44 | 60 | 81 | — | ESO BESO △ | Paul Anka, RCA Victor 8097 | 3 |
| 45 | 32 | 34 | 38 | IF A MAN ANSWERS | Bobby Darin, Capitol 4837 | 8 |
| 46 | 35 | 36 | 47 | SUSIE DARLIN' | Tommy Roe, ABC-Paramount 10362 | 7 |
| 47 | 51 | 61 | 76 | MAMA SANG A SONG | Walter Brennan, Liberty 55508 | 5 |
| 48 | 36 | 30 | 19 | ALLEY CAT | Bent Fabric, Atco 6226 | 17 |
| 49 | 58 | 62 | 89 | DON'T ASK ME TO BE FRIENDS | Everly Brothers, Warner Bros. 5297 | 5 |
| 50 | 38 | 20 | 23 | TORTURE | Kris Jensen, Hickory 1173 | 12 |
| 51 | 55 | 60 | 70 | LOVERS BY NIGHT, STRANGERS BY DAY | Fleetwoods, Dolton 62 | 6 |
| ★ 52 | 89 | — | — | DEAR LONELY HEARTS | Nat King Cole, Capitol 4870 | 2 |
| 53 | 49 | 39 | 41 | DON'T YOU BELIEVE IT △ | Andy Williams, Columbia 42523 | 10 |
| 54 | 57 | 51 | 43 | STORMY MONDAY | Bobby Bland, Duke 355 | 11 |
| ★ 55 | 75 | 77 | 96 | STUBBORN KIND OF FELLOW | Marvin Gaye, Tamla 54068 | 5 |
| ★ 56 | 74 | — | — | LOVE CAME TO ME | Dion, Laurie 3145 | 2 |
| 57 | 52 | 56 | 62 | I'M GOING BACK TO SCHOOL | Dee Clark, Vee Jay 462 | 7 |
| 58 | 34 | 21 | 10 | I REMEMBER YOU | Frank Ifield, Vee Jay 457 | 11 |
| ★ 59 | 73 | 80 | — | LET'S GO | Routers, Warner Bros. 5283 | 3 |
| 60 | 65 | 72 | 84 | UNTIE ME | Tams, Arlen 711 | 5 |
| 61 | 29 | 16 | 8 | RAMBLIN' ROSE | Nat King Cole, Capitol 4804 | 16 |
| 62 | 54 | 49 | 33 | HIDE AND GO SEEK | Bunker Hill, Mala 451 | 13 |
| 63 | 67 | 70 | 73 | YOU CAN RUN | Jerry Butler, Vee Jay 463 | 6 |
| 64 | 77 | 87 | — | MARY ANN REGRETS | Burl Ives, Decca 31433 | 3 |
| ★ 65 | 87 | — | — | CHAINS | Cookies, Dimension 1002 | 2 |
| 66 | 68 | 73 | 57 | HE THINKS I STILL CARE | Connie Francis, MGM 13096 | 7 |
| 67 | 64 | 66 | 75 | MR. LONELY | Buddy Greco, Epic 9536 | 9 |
| 68 | 69 | 71 | 85 | I'VE BEEN EVERYWHERE △ | Hank Snow, RCA Victor 8072 | 7 |
| 69 | 61 | 69 | 54 | TWISTIN' WITH LINDA | Isley Brothers, Wand 127 | 9 |
| 70 | 70 | 83 | 94 | ANNA (Go to Him) | Arthur Alexander, Dot 16387 | 4 |
| 71 | 79 | 67 | 74 | HAPPY WEEKEND | Dave (Baby) Cortez, Chess 1834 | 6 |
| 72 | 78 | 79 | 77 | SOMEBODY HAVE MERCY △ | Sam Cooke, RCA Victor 8088 | 4 |
| 73 | 82 | 75 | 81 | HEARTACHES | Patsy Cline, Decca 31429 | 6 |
| 74 | 86 | 88 | — | COMIN' HOME BABY | Mel Torme, Atlantic 2165 | 3 |
| ★ 75 | — | — | — | ZIP-A-DEE-DOO-DAH | Bob B. Soxx & the Blue Jeans, Philles 107 | 1 |
| 76 | 81 | 84 | — | THE ALLEY CAT SONG | David Thorne, Riverside 4530 | 4 |
| ★ 77 | — | — | — | YOU ARE MY SUNSHINE | Ray Charles, ABC-Paramount 10375 | 1 |
| 78 | 90 | 98 | — | I LOST MY BABY | Joey Dee, Roulette 4456 | 3 |
| 79 | 83 | — | — | SPANISH LACE | Gene McDaniels, Liberty 55510 | 2 |
| 80 | 76 | 76 | 78 | I'M HERE TO GET MY BABY OUT OF JAIL | Everly Brothers, Cadence 1429 | 6 |
| ★ 81 | — | — | — | A LITTLE BIT NOW | Majors, Imperial 5879 | 1 |
| 82 | 84 | — | — | IF YOU WERE A ROCK & ROLL RECORD | Freddy Cannon, Swan 4122 | 2 |
| 83 | 88 | — | — | THE PUSH AND KICK | Mark Valentino, Swan 4121 | 2 |
| ★ 84 | — | — | — | YOUR CHEATING HEART | Ray Charles, ABC-Paramount 10375 | 1 |
| ★ 85 | 100 | — | — | GO AWAY LITTLE GIRL △ | Steve Lawrence, Columbia 42601 | 2 |
| 86 | 91 | 93 | — | UP ON THE ROOF | Drifters, Atlantic 2162 | 3 |
| 87 | 97 | — | — | THAT'S LIFE | Gabriel & the Angels, Swan 4118 | 2 |
| ★ 88 | — | — | — | RUBY ANN △ | Marty Robbins, Columbia 42614 | 1 |
| ★ 89 | — | — | — | DIDDLE-DE-DUM | Belmonts, Sabina 507 | 1 |
| ★ 90 | — | — | — | SHUTTERS AND BOARDS | Jerry Wallace, Challenge 9171 | 1 |
| 91 | — | — | — | GETTING READY FOR THE HEARTBREAK | Chuck Jackson, Wand 128 | 1 |
| 92 | 99 | 97 | 100 | FOUR WALLS | Kay Starr, Capitol 4835 | 4 |
| 93 | — | — | — | MY DAD | Paul Petersen, Colpix 663 | 1 |
| 94 | 96 | 89 | 97 | MAMA SANG A SONG | Bill Anderson, Decca 31404 | 4 |
| 95 | — | 78 | 72 | NEXT DOOR TO THE BLUES | Etta James, Argo 5424 | 5 |
| 96 | — | — | — | COLD, COLD HEART | Dinah Washington, Mercury 72040 | 1 |
| 97 | — | — | 98 | ONE MORE TOWN | Kingston Trio, Capitol 4842 | 2 |
| 98 | — | — | — | FIESTA | Dave (Baby) Cortez, Emit 301 | 1 |
| 99 | — | — | — | BABY HAS GONE BYE BYE | George Maharis, Epic 9555 | 1 |
| 100 | — | 92 | 93 | ALADDIN | Bobby Curtola, Del-Fi 4185 | 3 |

## HOT 100—A TO Z—(Publisher-Licensee)

Aladdin (Kemo, BMI) ... 100
All Alone Am I (Duchess, BMI) ... 4
Alley Cat (Metorion, BMI) ... 48
Alley Cat Song (Metorion, BMI) ... 76
Anna (Painted Desert, BMI) ... 70
Baby Has Gone Bye Bye (Dymor, ASCAP) ... 99
Big Girls Don't Cry (Bobob, ASCAP) ... 1
Bobby's Girl (A. M. E., BMI) ... 7
Cha-Cha-Cha, The (Fajob-Kalmann, ASCAP) ... 10
Chains (Aldon, BMI) ... 65
Close to Cathy (Arch, ASCAP) ... 15
Cold, Cold Heart (Acuff-Rose, BMI) ... 96
Comin' Home Baby (Melotone, BMI) ... 74
(Dance With the) Guitar Man (Linduane, BMI) ... 23
Dear Lonely Hearts (Sweco-Cetra, BMI) ... 52
Desafinado (Hollis-Bendig, BMI) ... 18
Diddle-De-Dum (Glenden, ASCAP) ... 89
Do You Love Me (Jobete, BMI) ... 16
Don't Ask Me to Be Friends (Aldon, BMI) ... 49
Don't Hang Up (Kalmann, ASCAP) ... 8
Don't You Believe It (Dolfi, ASCAP) ... 53
Eso Beso (Flanka, ASCAP) ... 44
Fiesta (Tobi-Ann & Emit, BMI) ... 98
Four Walls (Sheldon, BMI) ... 92
Getting Ready for the Heartbreak (Ludix, BMI) ... 91
Gina (Elm Drive, ASCAP) ... 6
Go Away Little Girl (Aldon, BMI) ... 85
Green Onions (East, BMI) ... 40
Happy Weekend (Arc, BMI) ... 71
He Thinks I Still Care (Glad-Jack, BMI) ... 66
Heartaches (Leeds, ASCAP) ... 73
He's a Rebel (January, BMI) ... 3
Hide & Go Seek (Marks-Florentine, BMI) ... 62
I Can't Help It (Acuff-Rose, BMI) ... 33
I Left My Heart in San Francisco (General, ASCAP) ... 27
I Lost My Baby (Planetary, ASCAP) ... 78
I Remember You (Paramount, ASCAP) ... 58
I Was Such a Fool (Francon, ASCAP) ... 24
I'm Going Back to School (Conrad, BMI) ... 57
I'm Here to Get My Baby Out of Jail (Cole, BMI) ... 80
I've Been Everywhere (Hill & Range, BMI) ... 68
I've Got a Woman (Progressive, BMI) ... 22
I'll Bring It Home to You (Kags, BMI) ... 41
If a Man Answers (Adaris, BMI) ... 45
If You Were a Rock & Roll Record (Claridge, ASCAP) ... 82
James (Acuff-Rose, BMI) ... 17
Keep Your Hands Off My Baby (Aldon, BMI) ... 42
Leah (Acuff-Rose, BMI) ... 29
Let's Go (Wrist-Giant, BMI) ... 59
Limbo Rock (Four Star-Twist, BMI) ... 9
Little Bit Now, A (Travis-Rittenhouse, BMI) ... 81
Lonely Bull, The (Almo, ASCAP) ... 19
Love Came to Me (Schwartz-Disal, ASCAP) ... 56
Love Me Tender (Presley, BMI) ... 21
Lovers By Night, Strangers By Day (January, BMI) 51
Mama Sang a Song—Anderson (Tree-Champion, BMI) ... 94
Mama Sang a Song—Brennan (Tree-Champion, BMI) ... 47
Mama Sang a Song—Kenton (Tree-Champion, BMI) ... 38
Mary Ann Regrets (Pamper, BMI) ... 64
Mr. Lonely (Ripley, BMI) ... 64
Monster Mash (Garpax, BMI) ... 14
My Dad (Aldon, BMI) ... 93
My Own True Love (Remick, ASCAP) ... 26
Next Door to an Angel (Aldon, BMI) ... 5
Next Door to the Blues (Figure, BMI) ... 95
Nothing Can Change This Love (Kags, BMI) ... 12
One More Town (Sausalito, BMI) ... 97
Only Love Can Break a Heart (Arch, ASCAP) ... 11
Patches (Aldon, BMI) ... 30
Pop Pop Pop-Pie (Dandelion, BMI) ... 35
Popeye (The Hitchhiker) (Kalmann, ASCAP) ... 20
Push and Kick, The (Claridge, ASCAP) ... 83
Ramblin' Rose (Sweco, BMI) ... 61
Release Me (Four Star, BMI) ... 32
Return to Sender (Presley, BMI) ... 2
Ride! (Woodcrest-Check-Colt, BMI) ... 13
Ruby Ann (Marizona, BMI) ... 88
Pumors (Aldon, BMI) ... 43
Sherry (Bobob, ASCAP) ... 34
Shutters and Boards (Camp & Canyon, BMI) ... 90
Somebody Have Mercy (Kags, BMI) ... 72
Spanish Lace (St. Louis, BMI) ... 79
Stormy Monday (Gregmark, BMI) ... 54
Stubborn Kind of Fellow (Jobete, BMI) ... 55
Surfin' Safari (Guild, BMI) ... 31
Susie Darlin' (Congressional, ASCAP) ... 46
Telstar (Campbell Connelly, ASCAP) ... 39
That Stranger Used to Be My Girl (Winneton, BMI) ... 28
That's Life (Mary Hill-Missile, BMI) ... 87
Torture (Acuff-Rose, BMI) ... 50
Twistin' With Linda (Wemar, BMI) ... 69
Untie Me (Lowery, BMI) ... 60
Up on the Roof (Aldon, BMI) ... 86
What Kind of Fool Am I (Ludlow, BMI) ... 25
Wiggle Wobble (Bob-Dan, BMI) ... 37
Workin' for the Man (Acuff-Rose, BMI) ... 36
You Are My Sunshine (Peer Int'l, BMI) ... 77
You Can Run (Armada, BMI) ... 63
Your Cheating Heart (Fred Rose, BMI) ... 84
Zip-A-Dee-Doo-Dah (Joy, ASCAP) ... 75

## BUBBLING UNDER THE HOT 100

101. WHERE DO YOU COME FROM ... Elvis Presley, RCA Victor 8100
102. 409 ... Beach Boys, Capitol 4777
103. DESAFINADO ... Pat Thomas, MGM 13102
104. THIS LAND IS YOUR LAND ... Ketty Lester, Era 3094
105. CONEY ISLAND BABY ... Excellents, Blast 205
106. WHAT KIND OF FOOL AM I ... Robert Goulet, Columbia 42519
107. VOLARE ... Ace Cannon, Hi 2057
108. LIMELIGHT ... Mr. Acker Bilk, Atco 6238
109. WHAT KIND OF FOOL AM I ... Anthony Newley, London 9546
110. HEART BREAKER ... Dean Christie, Select 715
111. DEAR HEARTS AND GENTLE PEOPLE ... Springfields, Philips 40072
112. THIS LAND IS YOUR LAND ... Christy Minstrels, Columbia 42592
113. HERE I AM ... Chip Taylor, Warner Bros. 5314
114. GOTTA TRAVEL ON ... Springfields, Philips 40072
115. I DIG THIS STATION ... Gary (U. S.) Bonds, LeGrand 1022
116. I'M STANDING BY ... Ben E. King, Atco 6237
117. NO ONE CAN MAKE MY SUNSHINE SMILE ... Everly Brothers, Warner Bros. 5297
118. I DON'T BELIEVE I'LL FALL IN LOVE TODAY ... Bobby Bare, RCA Victor 8083
119. DESAFINADO ... Ella Fitzgerald, Verve 10274
120. AGAIN ... Lettermen, Capitol 4851
121. I'M SO LONESOME I COULD CRY ... Johnny Tillotson, Cadence 1432
122. BLUEBIRDS OVER THE MOUNTAIN ... Echoes, Smash 1766
123. UNDER YOUR SPELL AGAIN ... Lloyd Price, ABC-Paramount 10372
124. BUSTIN' SURFBOARDS ... Tornados, Aertaun 1013
125. SHE'S A TROUBLEMAKER ... Majors, Imperial 5879
126. SCHOOL BELLS ARE RINGING ... Carole King, Dimension 1004
127. YOU'RE A SWEETHEART ... Dinah Washington, Roulette 4455
128. THE SEARCHING IS OVER ... Joe Henderson, Todd 1079

# BILLBOARD HOT 100

**FOR WEEK ENDING NOVEMBER 24, 1962**

S — Indicates that 45 r.p.m. stereo single version is available.
△ — Indicates that 33⅓ r.p.m. mono single version is available.
Ⓢ — Indicates that 33⅓ r.p.m. stereo single version is available.

| This Week | Last Week | 2 Wks. Ago | 3 Wks. Ago | TITLE — Artist, Label & Number | Weeks On Chart |
|---|---|---|---|---|---|
| 1 | 1 | 2 | 6 | BIG GIRLS DON'T CRY — Four Seasons, Vee Jay 465 | 6 |
| 2 | 2 | 4 | 10 | RETURN TO SENDER — Elvis Presley, RCA Victor 8100 | 6 |
| 3 | 4 | 3 | 5 | ALL ALONE AM I — Brenda Lee, Decca 31424 | 9 |
| 4 | 7 | 19 | 41 | BOBBY'S GIRL — Marcie Blane, Seville 120 | 6 |
| 5 | 5 | 6 | 9 | NEXT DOOR TO AN ANGEL — Neil Sedaka, RCA Victor 8086 | 8 |
| 6 | 9 | 11 | 8 | LIMBO ROCK — Chubby Checker, Parkway 849 | 12 |
| 7 | 8 | 16 | 32 | DON'T HANG UP — Orlons, Cameo 231 | 7 |
| 8 | 3 | 1 | 1 | HE'S A REBEL — Crystals, Philles 106 | 12 |
| 9 | 6 | 7 | 7 | GINA — Johnny Mathis, Columbia 42582 | 10 |
| 10 | 13 | 27 | 44 | RIDE! — Dee Dee Sharp, Cameo 230 | 6 |
| 11 | 19 | 39 | 64 | THE LONELY BULL — Tijuana Brass, A. & M. 703 | 5 |
| 12 | 10 | 14 | 15 | THE CHA-CHA-CHA — Bobby Rydell, Cameo 228 | 7 |
| 13 | 11 | 5 | 2 | ONLY LOVE CAN BREAK A HEART — Gene Pitney, Musicor 1022 | 11 |
| 14 | 12 | 13 | 22 | NOTHING CAN CHANGE THIS LOVE — Sam Cooke, RCA Victor 8088 | 9 |
| 15 | 18 | 20 | 26 | DESAFINADO — Stan Getz and Charlie Byrd, Verve 10260 | 9 |
| 16 | 15 | 12 | 12 | CLOSE TO CATHY — Mike Clifford, United Artists 489 | 11 |
| 17 | 32 | 50 | 68 | RELEASE ME — "Little Esther" Phillips, Lenox 5555 | 5 |
| 18 | 39 | 71 | 85 | TELSTAR — Tornadoes, London 9561 | 4 |
| 19 | 26 | 37 | 45 | MY OWN TRUE LOVE — Duprees, Coed 571 | 6 |
| 20 | 22 | 23 | 29 | I'VE GOT A WOMAN — Jimmy McGriff, Sue 770 | 7 |
| 21 | 14 | 8 | 4 | MONSTER MASH — Bobby (Boris) Pickett and the Crypt Kickers, Garpax 44167 | 12 |
| 22 | 23 | 30 | 40 | (DANCE WITH THE) GUITAR MAN — Duane Eddy, RCA Victor 8087 | 8 |
| 23 | 25 | 18 | 17 | WHAT KIND OF FOOL AM I — Sammy Davis Jr., Reprise 20048 | 13 |
| 24 | 16 | 9 | 3 | DO YOU LOVE ME — Contours, Gordy 7005 | 16 |
| 25 | 29 | 31 | 38 | LEAH — Roy Orbison, Monument 467 | 8 |
| 26 | 17 | 17 | 18 | JAMES (Hold the Ladder Steady) — Sue Thompson, Hickory 1183 | 9 |
| 27 | 24 | 28 | 31 | I WAS SUCH A FOOL — Connie Francis, MGM 13096 | 8 |
| 28 | 33 | 44 | 55 | I CAN'T HELP IT — Johnny Tillotson, Cadence 1432 | 5 |
| 29 | 42 | 62 | 90 | KEEP YOUR HANDS OFF MY BABY — Little Eva, Dimension 1003 | 4 |
| 30 | 43 | 66 | 95 | RUMORS — Johnny Crawford, Del-Fi 4188 | 4 |
| 31 | 20 | 10 | 14 | POPEYE (The Hitchhiker) — Chubby Checker, Parkway 849 | 10 |
| 32 | 21 | 24 | 27 | LOVE ME TENDER — Richard Chamberlain, MGM 13097 | 8 |
| 33 | 28 | 43 | 50 | THAT STRANGER USED TO BE MY GIRL — Trade Martin, Coed 570 | 7 |
| 34 | 37 | 48 | 59 | WIGGLE WOBBLE — Les Cooper, Everlast 5019 | 6 |
| 35 | 38 | 42 | 47 | MAMA SANG A SONG — Stan Kenton, Capitol 4847 | 7 |
| 36 | 44 | 60 | 81 | ESO BESO — Paul Anka, RCA Victor 8097 | 4 |
| 37 | 51 | 55 | 60 | LOVERS BY NIGHT, STRANGERS BY DAY — Fleetwoods, Dolton 62 | 7 |
| 38 | 27 | 22 | 24 | I LEFT MY HEART IN SAN FRANCISCO — Tony Bennett, Columbia 42332 | 16 |
| 39 | 56 | 74 | — | LOVE CAME TO ME — Dion, Laurie 3145 | 3 |
| 40 | 59 | 73 | 80 | LET'S GO — Routers, Warner Bros. 5283 | 4 |
| 41 | 52 | 89 | — | DEAR LONELY HEARTS — Nat King Cole, Capitol 4870 | 3 |
| 42 | 31 | 25 | 23 | SURFIN' SAFARI — Beach Boys, Capitol 4777 | 16 |
| 43 | 47 | 51 | 61 | MAMA SANG A SONG — Walter Brennan, Liberty 55508 | 6 |
| 44 | 36 | 33 | 33 | WORKIN' FOR THE MAN — Roy Orbison, Monument 467 | 10 |
| 45 | 35 | 40 | 42 | POP POP POP-PIE — Sherrys, Guyden 2068 | 8 |
| 46 | 65 | 87 | — | CHAINS — Cookies, Dimension 1002 | 3 |
| 47 | 34 | 15 | 11 | SHERRY — Four Seasons, Vee Jay 456 | 14 |
| 48 | 49 | 58 | 62 | DON'T ASK ME TO BE FRIENDS — Everly Brothers, Warner Bros. 5297 | 6 |
| 49 | 30 | 21 | 13 | PATCHES — Dickey Lee, Smash 1758 | 14 |
| 50 | 77 | — | — | YOU ARE MY SUNSHINE — Ray Charles, ABC-Paramount 10375 | 2 |
| 51 | 55 | 75 | 77 | STUBBORN KIND OF FELLOW — Marvin Gaye, Tamla 54068 | 6 |
| 52 | 41 | 47 | 54 | I'LL BRING IT HOME TO YOU — Carla Thomas, Atlantic 2163 | 7 |
| 53 | 40 | 26 | 19 | GREEN ONIONS — Booker T & the MG's, Stax 127 | 16 |
| 54 | 85 | 100 | — | GO AWAY LITTLE GIRL — Steve Lawrence, Columbia 42601 | 3 |
| 55 | 64 | 77 | 87 | MARY ANN REGRETS — Burl Ives, Decca 31433 | 4 |
| 56 | 54 | 57 | 51 | STORMY MONDAY — Bobby Bland, Duke 355 | 12 |
| 57 | 74 | 86 | 88 | COMIN' HOME BABY — Mel Torme, Atlantic 2165 | 4 |
| 58 | 46 | 35 | 36 | SUSIE DARLIN' — Tommy Roe, ABC-Paramount 10362 | 8 |
| 59 | 50 | 38 | 20 | TORTURE — Kris Jensen, Hickory 1173 | 13 |
| 60 | 60 | 65 | 72 | UNTIE ME — Tams, Arlen 711 | 6 |
| 61 | 83 | 88 | — | THE PUSH AND KICK — Mark Valentino, Swan 4121 | 3 |
| 62 | 48 | 36 | 30 | ALLEY CAT — Bent Fabric, Atco 6226 | 18 |
| 63 | 84 | — | — | YOUR CHEATING HEART — Ray Charles, ABC-Paramount 10375 | 2 |
| 64 | 75 | — | — | ZIP-A-DEE-DOO-DAH — Bob B. Soxx & the Blue Jeans, Philles 107 | 2 |
| 65 | — | — | — | HOTEL HAPPINESS — Brook Benton, Mercury 72055 | 1 |
| 66 | 88 | — | — | RUBY ANN — Marty Robbins, Columbia 42614 | 2 |
| 67 | 79 | 83 | — | SPANISH LACE — Gene McDaniels, Liberty 55510 | 3 |
| 68 | 70 | 70 | 83 | ANNA (Go to Him) — Arthur Alexander, Dot 16387 | 5 |
| 69 | — | — | — | YOU THREW A LUCKY PUNCH — Gene (Duke of Earl) Chandler, Vee Jay 468 | 1 |
| 70 | 72 | 78 | 79 | SOMEBODY HAVE MERCY — Sam Cooke, RCA Victor 8088 | 5 |
| 71 | 66 | 68 | 73 | HE THINKS I STILL CARE — Connie Francis, MGM 13096 | 8 |
| 72 | 87 | 97 | — | THAT'S LIFE — Gabriel & the Angels, Swan 4118 | 3 |
| 73 | 89 | — | — | DIDDLE-DE-DUM — Belmonts, Sabina 507 | 2 |
| 74 | 78 | 90 | 98 | I LOST MY BABY — Joey Dee, Roulette 4456 | 4 |
| 75 | 93 | — | — | MY DAD — Paul Petersen, Colpix 663 | 3 |
| 76 | 82 | 84 | — | IF YOU WERE A ROCK & ROLL RECORD — Freddy Cannon, Swan 4122 | 3 |
| 77 | 81 | — | — | A LITTLE BIT NOW — Majors, Imperial 5879 | 3 |
| 78 | 68 | 69 | 71 | I'VE BEEN EVERYWHERE — Hank Snow, RCA Victor 8072 | 8 |
| 79 | 67 | 64 | 66 | MR. LONELY — Buddy Greco, Epic 9536 | 10 |
| 80 | 99 | — | — | BABY HAS GONE BYE BYE — George Maharis, Epic 9555 | 2 |
| 81 | 86 | 91 | 93 | UP ON THE ROOF — Drifters, Atlantic 2162 | 4 |
| 82 | 90 | — | — | SHUTTERS AND BOARDS — Jerry Wallace, Challenge 9171 | 2 |
| 83 | 95 | — | 78 | NEXT DOOR TO THE BLUES — Etta James, Argo 5424 | 6 |
| 84 | 63 | 67 | 70 | YOU CAN RUN — Jerry Butler, Vee Jay 463 | 7 |
| 85 | — | — | — | RAINBOW AT MIDNIGHT — Jimmie Rodgers, Dot 16407 | 1 |
| 86 | 73 | 82 | 75 | HEARTACHES — Patsy Cline, Decca 31429 | 7 |
| 87 | — | — | — | I MAY NOT LIVE TO SEE TOMORROW — Brian Hyland, ABC-Paramount 10374 | 1 |
| 88 | 71 | 79 | 67 | HAPPY WEEKEND — Dave (Baby) Cortez, Chess 1834 | 7 |
| 89 | 91 | — | — | GETTING READY FOR THE HEARTBREAK — Chuck Jackson, Wand 128 | 2 |
| 90 | — | — | — | DON'T GO NEAR THE ESKIMOS — Ben Colder, MGM 13104 | 1 |
| 91 | — | 94 | 96 | HEART BREAKER — Dean Christie, Select 715 | 3 |
| 92 | — | — | — | THE JITTERBUG — Dovells, Parkway 855 | 1 |
| 93 | — | — | — | SHE'S A TROUBLEMAKER — Majors, Imperial 5879 | 1 |
| 94 | — | — | — | THE SEARCHING IS OVER — Joe Henderson, Todd 1079 | 1 |
| 95 | — | 98 | 99 | DEAR HEARTS AND GENTLE PEOPLE — Springfields, Philips 40072 | 3 |
| 96 | 98 | — | — | FIESTA — Dave (Baby) Cortez, Emit 301 | 2 |
| 97 | — | — | — | FOOLS RUSH IN — Etta James, Argo 5424 | 4 |
| 98 | — | — | — | YOU'RE A SWEETHEART — Dinah Washington, Roulette 4455 | 1 |
| 99 | — | — | — | DON'T STOP THE WEDDING — Ann Cole, Roulette 4452 | 1 |
| 100 | — | — | — | CONEY ISLAND BABY — Excellents, Blast 205 | 1 |

## BUBBLING UNDER THE HOT 100

101. 409 — Beach Boys, Capitol 4777
102. BUSTIN' SURFBOARDS — Tornados, Aertaun 1013
103. MAMA SANG A SONG — Bill Anderson, Decca 31404
104. MY MAN—HE'S A LOVIN' MAN — Betty Lavett, Atlantic 2160
105. WHAT KIND OF FOOL AM I — Robert Goulet, Columbia 42519
106. TOMORROW NIGHT — B. B. King, ABC-Paramount 10367
107. WHAT KIND OF FOOL AM I — Anthony Newley, London 9546
108. THIS LAND IS YOUR LAND — Ketty Lester, Era 3088
109. FOUR WALLS — Kay Starr, Capitol 4835
110. COLD, COLD HEART — Dinah Washington, Mercury 72040
111. ONE MORE TOWN — Kingston Trio, Capitol 4842
112. MIND OVER MATTER — Nolan Strong, Fortune 546
113. I'M SO LONESOME I COULD CRY — Johnny Tillotson, Cadence 1432
114. LIMELIGHT — Mr. Acker Bilk, Atco 6238
115. THIS LAND IS YOUR LAND — Christy Minstrels, Columbia 42592
116. WHERE DO YOU COME FROM — Elvis Presley, RCA Victor 8100
117. LET'S KISS AND MAKE UP — Bobby Vinton, Epic 9561
118. DESAFINADO — Ella Fitzgerald, Verve 10274
119. TWO LOVERS — Mary Wells, Motown 1035
120. SLIGHTLY OUT OF TUNE — Julie London, Liberty 55512
121. DESAFINADO — Pat Thomas, MGM 13102
122. THE BEST MAN CRIED — Clyde McPhatter, Mercury 72051
123. I FEEL GOOD ALL OVER — Fiestas, Old Town 1127
124. I'M STANDING BY — Ben E. King, Atco 6237
125. SCHOOL BELLS ARE RINGING — Carole King, Dimension 1004
126. ROAD KING — John D. Loudermilk, RCA Victor 8101
127. PEPINO THE ITALIAN MOUSE — Lou Monte, Reprise 20106
128. STILL WATERS RUN DEEP — Brook Benton, Mercury 72055
129. HEY, GOOD LOOKIN' — Connie Stevens, Warner Bros. 5318

# BILLBOARD HOT 100

FOR WEEK ENDING DECEMBER 1

1962

★ STAR PERFORMERS—Selections registering greatest upward progress this week.

S Indicates that 45 r.p.m. stereo single version is available.

△ Indicates that 33⅓ r.p.m. mono single version is available.

△S Indicates that 33⅓ r.p.m. stereo single version is available.

| This Week | 1 Wk. Ago | 2 Wks. Ago | 3 Wks. Ago | Title — Artist, Label & Number | Weeks On Chart |
|---|---|---|---|---|---|
| 1 | 1 | 1 | 2 | BIG GIRLS DON'T CRY — Four Seasons, Vee Jay 465 | 7 |
| 2 | 2 | 2 | 4 | RETURN TO SENDER — Elvis Presley, RCA Victor 8100 △ | 7 |
| 3 | 4 | 7 | 19 | BOBBY'S GIRL — Marcie Blane, Seville 120 | 7 |
| 4 | 6 | 9 | 11 | LIMBO ROCK — Chubby Checker, Parkway 849 | 13 |
| 5 | 3 | 4 | 3 | ALL ALONE AM I — Brenda Lee, Decca 31424 | 10 |
| 6 | 7 | 8 | 16 | DON'T HANG UP — Orlons, Cameo 231 | 8 |
| 7 | 11 | 19 | 39 | THE LONELY BULL — Tijuana Brass, A. & M. 703 | 6 |
| 8 | 10 | 13 | 27 | RIDE! — Dee Dee Sharp, Cameo 230 | 7 |
| 9 | 8 | 3 | 1 | HE'S A REBEL — Crystals, Philles 106 | 13 |
| 10 | 5 | 5 | 6 | NEXT DOOR TO AN ANGEL — Neil Sedaka, RCA Victor 8086 △ | 9 |
| 11 | 9 | 6 | 7 | GINA — Johnny Mathis, Columbia 42582 △ | 11 |
| 12 | 12 | 10 | 14 | THE CHA-CHA-CHA — Bobby Rydell, Cameo 228 | 8 |
| ★13 | 18 | 39 | 71 | TELSTAR — Tornadoes, London 9561 | 5 |
| ★14 | 19 | 26 | 37 | MY OWN TRUE LOVE — Duprees, Coed 571 | 7 |
| 15 | 15 | 18 | 20 | DESAFINADO — Stan Getz and Charlie Byrd, Verve 10260 | 10 |
| 16 | 17 | 32 | 50 | RELEASE ME — "Little Esther" Phillips, Lenox 5555 | 6 |
| 17 | 13 | 11 | 5 | ONLY LOVE CAN BREAK A HEART — Gene Pitney, Musicor 1022 | 12 |
| 18 | 22 | 23 | 30 | (DANCE WITH THE) GUITAR MAN — Duane Eddy, RCA Victor 8087 △ | 9 |
| ★19 | 29 | 42 | 62 | KEEP YOUR HANDS OFF MY BABY — Little Eva, Dimension 1003 | 5 |
| ★20 | 30 | 43 | 66 | RUMORS — Johnny Crawford, Del-Fi 4188 | 5 |
| 21 | 16 | 15 | 12 | CLOSE TO CATHY — Mike Clifford, United Artists 489 | 12 |
| 22 | 14 | 12 | 13 | NOTHING CAN CHANGE THIS LOVE — Sam Cooke, RCA Victor 8088 △ | 10 |
| ★23 | 36 | 44 | 60 | ESO BESO — Paul Anka, RCA Victor 8097 △ | 5 |
| 24 | 28 | 33 | 44 | I CAN'T HELP IT — Johnny Tillotson, Cadence 1432 | 6 |
| 25 | 23 | 25 | 18 | WHAT KIND OF FOOL AM I — Sammy Davis Jr., Reprise 20048 | 14 |
| 26 | 24 | 16 | 9 | DO YOU LOVE ME — Contours, Gordy 7005 | 17 |
| ★27 | 39 | 56 | 74 | LOVE CAME TO ME — Dion, Laurie 3145 | 4 |
| 28 | 34 | 37 | 48 | WIGGLE WOBBLE — Les Cooper, Everlast 5019 | 7 |
| 29 | 20 | 22 | 23 | I'VE GOT A WOMAN — Jimmy McGriff, Sue 770 | 8 |
| ★30 | 41 | 52 | 89 | DEAR LONELY HEARTS — Nat King Cole, Capitol 4870 | 4 |
| 31 | 21 | 14 | 8 | MONSTER MASH — Bobby (Boris) Pickett and the Crypt Kickers, Garpax 44167 | 13 |
| 32 | 35 | 38 | 42 | MAMA SANG A SONG — Stan Kenton, Capitol 4847 | 8 |
| 33 | 33 | 28 | 43 | THAT STRANGER USED TO BE MY GIRL — Trade Martin, Coed 570 | 7 |
| ★34 | 46 | 65 | 87 | CHAINS — Cookies, Dimension 1002 | 4 |
| 35 | 38 | 27 | 22 | I LEFT MY HEART IN SAN FRANCISCO — Tony Bennett, Columbia 42332 △ | 17 |
| 36 | 37 | 51 | 55 | LOVERS BY NIGHT, STRANGERS BY DAY — Fleetwoods, Dolton 62 | 8 |
| 37 | 40 | 59 | 73 | LET'S GO — Routers, Warner Bros. 5283 | 5 |
| 38 | 43 | 47 | 51 | MAMA SANG A SONG — Walter Brennan, Liberty 55508 | 7 |
| 39 | 25 | 29 | 31 | LEAH — Roy Orbison, Monument 467 | 9 |
| ★40 | 50 | 77 | — | YOU ARE MY SUNSHINE — Ray Charles, ABC-Paramount 10375 | 3 |
| ★41 | 54 | 85 | 100 | GO AWAY LITTLE GIRL — Steve Lawrence, Columbia 42601 △ | 4 |
| ★42 | 65 | — | — | HOTEL HAPPINESS — Brook Benton, Mercury 72055 | 2 |
| 43 | 31 | 20 | 10 | POPEYE (The Hitchhiker) — Chubby Checker, Parkway 849 | 11 |
| ★44 | 64 | 75 | — | ZIP-A-DEE-DOO-DAH — Bob B. Soxx & the Blue Jeans, Philles 107 | 3 |
| ★45 | 66 | 88 | — | RUBY ANN — Marty Robbins, Columbia 42614 △ | 3 |
| 46 | 51 | 55 | 75 | STUBBORN KIND OF FELLOW — Marvin Gaye, Tamla 54068 | 7 |
| 47 | 27 | 24 | 28 | I WAS SUCH A FOOL — Connie Francis, MGM 13096 | 9 |
| ★48 | 63 | 84 | — | YOUR CHEATING HEART — Ray Charles, ABC-Paramount 10375 | 3 |
| 49 | 55 | 64 | 77 | MARY ANN REGRETS — Burl Ives, Decca 31433 | 5 |
| ★50 | 61 | 83 | 88 | THE PUSH AND KICK — Mark Valentino, Swan 4121 | 4 |
| 51 | 26 | 17 | 17 | JAMES (Hold the Ladder Steady) — Sue Thompson, Hickory 1183 | 10 |
| 52 | 42 | 31 | 25 | SURFIN' SAFARI — Beach Boys, Capitol 4777 | 17 |
| 53 | 57 | 74 | 86 | COMIN' HOME BABY — Mel Torme, Atlantic 2165 | 5 |
| 54 | 32 | 21 | 24 | LOVE ME TENDER — Richard Chamberlain, MGM 13097 | 9 |
| ★55 | 75 | 93 | — | MY DAD — Paul Petersen, Colpix 663 | 3 |
| ★56 | 67 | 79 | 83 | SPANISH LACE — Gene McDaniels, Liberty 55510 | 4 |
| 57 | 48 | 49 | 58 | DON'T ASK ME TO BE FRIENDS — Everly Brothers, Warner Bros. 5297 | 7 |
| 58 | 52 | 41 | 47 | I'LL BRING IT HOME TO YOU — Carla Thomas, Atlantic 2163 | 8 |
| 59 | 44 | 36 | 33 | WORKIN' FOR THE MAN — Roy Orbison, Monument 467 | 11 |
| 60 | 69 | — | — | YOU THREW A LUCKY PUNCH — Gene (Duke of Earl) Chandler, Vee Jay 468 | 2 |
| 61 | 74 | 78 | 90 | I LOST MY BABY — Joey Dee, Roulette 4456 | 5 |
| 62 | 59 | 50 | 38 | TORTURE — Kris Jensen, Hickory 1173 | 14 |
| 63 | 73 | 89 | — | DIDDLE-DE-DUM — Belmonts, Sabina 507 | 3 |
| ★64 | — | — | — | TWO LOVERS — Mary Wells, Motown 1035 | 1 |
| 65 | 60 | 60 | 65 | UNTIE ME — Tams, Arlen 711 | 7 |
| 66 | 56 | 54 | 57 | STORMY MONDAY — Bobby Bland, Duke 355 | 13 |
| 67 | 72 | 87 | 97 | THAT'S LIFE — Gabriel & the Angels, Swan 4118 | 4 |
| 68 | 76 | 82 | 84 | IF YOU WERE A ROCK & ROLL RECORD — Freddy Cannon, Swan 4122 | 4 |
| 69 | 68 | 70 | 70 | ANNA (Go to Him) — Arthur Alexander, Dot 16387 | 6 |
| 70 | 81 | 86 | 91 | UP ON THE ROOF — Drifters, Atlantic 2162 | 5 |
| 71 | 83 | 95 | — | NEXT DOOR TO THE BLUES — Etta James, Argo 5424 | 7 |
| 72 | 85 | — | — | RAINBOW AT MIDNIGHT — Jimmie Rodgers, Dot 16407 | 2 |
| ★73 | — | — | — | LET'S KISS AND MAKE UP — Bobby Vinton, Epic 9561 | 1 |
| 74 | 80 | 99 | — | BABY HAS GONE BYE BYE — George Maharis, Epic 9555 | 3 |
| 75 | 77 | 81 | — | A LITTLE BIT NOW — Majors, Imperial 5879 | 3 |
| 76 | 82 | 90 | — | SHUTTERS AND BOARDS — Jerry Wallace, Challenge 9171 | 3 |
| ★77 | — | — | — | TEN LITTLE INDIANS — Beach Boys, Capitol 4880 | 1 |
| ★78 | 100 | — | — | CONEY ISLAND BABY — Excellents, Blast 205 | 2 |
| 79 | 79 | 67 | 64 | MR. LONELY — Buddy Greco, Epic 9536 | 11 |
| 80 | 90 | — | — | DON'T GO NEAR THE ESKIMOS — Ben Colder, MGM 13104 | 2 |
| ★81 | — | — | — | TELL HIM — Exciters, United Artists 544 | 1 |
| 82 | 87 | — | — | I MAY NOT LIVE TO SEE TOMORROW — Brian Hyland, ABC-Paramount 10374 | 2 |
| ★83 | — | — | — | ROAD HOG — John D. Loudermilk, RCA Victor 8101 △ | 1 |
| ★84 | — | — | — | THE LOVE OF A BOY — Timi Yuro, Liberty 55519 | 1 |
| 85 | 92 | — | — | THE JITTERBUG — Dovells, Parkway 855 | 2 |
| ★86 | — | — | — | SEE SEE RIDER — LaVern Baker, Atlantic 2167 | 1 |
| 87 | 91 | — | 94 | HEART BREAKER — Dean Christie, Select 715 | 4 |
| 88 | 89 | 91 | — | GETTING READY FOR THE HEARTBREAK — Chuck Jackson, Wand 128 | 3 |
| ★89 | — | — | — | I'M SO LONESOME I COULD CRY — Johnny Tillotson, Cadence 1432 | 1 |
| 90 | 70 | 72 | 78 | SOMEBODY HAVE MERCY — Sam Cooke, RCA Victor 8088 △ | 6 |
| 91 | — | — | — | STRANGE I KNOW — Marvelettes, Tamla 54072 | 1 |
| 92 | — | — | — | GONNA RAISE A RUCKUS TONIGHT — Jimmy Dean, Columbia 42600 △ | 1 |
| 93 | — | — | — | THIS LAND IS YOUR LAND — Christy Minstrels, Columbia 42592 △ | 1 |
| 94 | — | — | — | EVERYBODY LOVES A LOVER — Shirelles, Scepter 1243 | 1 |
| 95 | — | — | — | ME AND MY SHADOW — Frank Sinatra & Sammy Davis Jr., Reprise 20128 | 1 |
| 96 | — | — | — | ECHO — Emotions, Kapp 490 | 1 |
| 97 | — | — | — | THIS LAND IS YOUR LAND — Ketty Lester, Era 3094 | 1 |
| 98 | 98 | — | — | YOU'RE A SWEETHEART — Dinah Washington, Roulette 4455 | 2 |
| 99 | — | — | — | FROM THE BOTTOM OF MY HEART (DAMMI, DAMMI, DAMMI) — Dean Martin, Reprise 20116 | 1 |
| 100 | — | — | — | LIMELIGHT — Mr. Acker Bilk, Atco 6238 | 1 |

## HOT 100—A TO Z—(Publisher-Licensee)


All Alone Am I (Duchess, BMI) ... 5
Anna (Painted Desert, BMI) ... 69
Baby Has Gone Bye Bye (Dymor, ASCAP) ... 74
Big Girls Don't Cry (Bobob, ASCAP) ... 1
Bobby's Girl (A. M. E., BMI) ... 3
Cha-Cha-Cha, The (Fajob-Kalmann, ASCAP) ... 12
Chains (Aldon, BMI) ... 34
Close to Cathy (Arch, ASCAP) ... 21
Comin' Home Baby (Melotone, BMI) ... 53
Coney Island Baby (Original, BMI) ... 78
(Dance With the) Guitar Man (Linduane, BMI) ... 18
Dear Lonely Hearts (Sweco-Cetra, BMI) ... 30
Desafinado (Hollis-Bendig, BMI) ... 15
Diddle-De-Dum (Glenden, ASCAP) ... 63
Do You Love Me (Jobete, BMI) ... 26
Don't Ask Me to Be Friends (Aldon, BMI) ... 57
Don't Go Near the Eskimos (Buttercup, BMI) ... 80
Don't Hang Up (Kalmann, ASCAP) ... 6
Echo (Spare Rib, BMI) ... 96
Eso Beso (Flanka, ASCAP) ... 23
Everybody Loves a Lover (Korwin, ASCAP) ... 94
From the Bottom of My Heart (Laurel, ASCAP) ... 99
Getting Ready for the Heartbreak (Ludix, BMI) ... 88
Gina (Elm Drive, ASCAP) ... 11
Go Away Little Girl (Aldon, BMI) ... 41
Gonna Raise a Ruckus Tonight (Plainview, BMI) ... 92
Heart Breaker (Drury Lane, BMI) ... 87
He's a Rebel (January, BMI) ... 9
Hotel Happiness (Ben Day-Mansion, ASCAP) ... 42
I Can't Help It (Acuff-Rose, BMI) ... 24
I Left My Heart in San Francisco (General, ASCAP) 35
I Lost My Baby (Planetary, ASCAP) ... 61
I May Not Live to See Tomorrow (Pogo, ASCAP) ... 82
I Was Such a Fool (Francon, ASCAP) ... 47
I'm So Lonesome I Could Cry (Acuff-Rose, BMI) ... 89
I've Got a Woman (Progressive, BMI) ... 29
I'll Bring It Home to You (Kags, BMI) ... 58
If You Were a Rock and Roll Record (Claridge, ASCAP) ... 68
James (Acuff-Rose, BMI) ... 51
Jitterbug, The (Cameo-Parkway, BMI) ... 85
Keep Your Hands Off My Baby (Aldon, BMI) ... 19
Leah (Acuff-Rose, BMI) ... 39
Let's Go (Wrist-Giant, BMI) ... 37
Let's Kiss and Make Up (Trio, BMI) ... 73
Limbo Rock (Four Star-Twist, BMI) ... 4
Limelight (Bourne, ASCAP) ... 100
Little Bit Now, A (Travis-Rittenhouse, BMI) ... 75
Lonely Bull, The (Almo, ASCAP) ... 7
Love Came to Me (Schwartz-Disal, ASCAP) ... 27
Love of a Boy, The (U. S. Songs, ASCAP) ... 84
Love Me Tender (Presley, BMI) ... 54
Lovers By Night, Strangers By Day (January, BMI) 36
Mama Sang a Song—Brennan (Tree-Champion, BMI) 38
Mama Sang a Song—Kenton (Tree-Champion, BMI) 32
Mary Ann Regrets (Pamper, BMI) ... 49
Me and My Shadow (Bourne, ASCAP) ... 95
Mr. Lonely (Ripley, BMI) ... 79
Monster Mash (Garpax, BMI) ... 31
My Dad (Aldon, BMI) ... 55
My Own True Love (Remick, ASCAP) ... 14
Next Door to an Angel (Aldon, BMI) ... 10
Next Door to the Blues (Figure, BMI) ... 71
Nothing Can Change This Love (Kags, BMI) ... 22
Only Love Can Break a Heart (Arch, ASCAP) ... 17
Popeye (the Hitchhiker) (Kalmann, ASCAP) ... 43
Push and Kick, The (Claridge, ASCAP) ... 50
Rainbow at Midnight (Shapiro-Bernstein, ASCAP) 72
Release Me (Four Star, BMI) ... 16
Return to Sender (Presley, BMI) ... 2
Ride! (Woodcrest-Check-Colt, BMI) ... 8
Road Hog (Acuff-Rose, BMI) ... 83
Ruby Ann (Marizona, BMI) ... 45
Rumors (Aldon, BMI) ... 20
See See Rider (Cotillion, BMI) ... 86
Shutters and Boards (Camp & Canyon, BMI) ... 76
Somebody Have Mercy (Kags, BMI) ... 90
Spanish Lace (St. Louis, BMI) ... 56
Stormy Monday (Gregmark, BMI) ... 66
Strange I Know (Jobete, BMI) ... 91
Stubborn Kind of Fellow (Jobete, BMI) ... 46
Surfin' Safari (Guild, BMI) ... 52
Tell Him (Mellin, BMI) ... 81
Telstar (Campbell Connelly, ASCAP) ... 13
Ten Little Indians (Sea of Tunes, BMI) ... 77
That Stranger Used to Be My Girl (Winneton, BMI) ... 33
That's Life (Mary Hill-Missile, BMI) ... 67
This Land Is Your Land—Christy Minstrels (Ludlow, BMI) ... 93
This Land Is Your Land—Lester (Ludlow, BMI) .. 97
Torture (Acuff-Rose, BMI) ... 62
Two Lovers (Jobete, BMI) ... 64
Untie Me (Lowery, BMI) ... 65
Up on the Roof (Aldon, BMI) ... 70
What Kind of Fool Am I (Ludlow, BMI) ... 25
Wiggle Wobble (Bob-Dan, BMI) ... 28
Workin' for the Man (Acuff-Rose, BMI) ... 59
You Are My Sunshine (Peer Int'l, BMI) ... 40
You Threw a Lucky Punch (Jobete, BMI) ... 60
You're a Sweetheart (Robbins, ASCAP) ... 98
Your Cheating Heart (Fred Rose, BMI) ... 48
Zip-A-Dee-Doo-Dah (Joy, ASCAP) ... 44


## BUBBLING UNDER THE HOT 100

101. GO TIGER, GO! ... Guy Mitchell, Joy 270
102. 409 ... Beach Boys, Capitol 4777
103. I'M HERE TO GET MY BABY OUT OF JAIL .. Everly Brothers, Cadence 1429
104. FOOLS RUSH IN ... Etta James, Argo 5424
105. FIESTA ... Dave (Baby) Cortez, Emit 301
106. MY MAN—HE'S A LOVIN' MAN ... Betty Lavett, Atlantic 2160
107. MAMA SANG A SONG ... Bill Anderson, Decca 31404
108. DESAFINADO ... Ella Fitzgerald, Verve 10274
109. SHE'S A TROUBLEMAKER ... Majors, Imperial 5879
110. THREE HEARTS IN A TANGLE ... James Brown and the Famous Flames, King 5701
111. I'M STANDING BY ... Ben E. King, Atco 6237
112. THE SEARCHING IS OVER ... Joe Henderson, Todd 1079
113. DESAFINADO ... Pat Thomas, MGM 13102
114. STILL WATERS RUN DEEP ... Brook Benton, Mercury 72055
115. BUSTIN' SURFBOARDS ... Tornadoes, Aertaun 1013
116. SLIGHTLY OUT OF TUNE ... Julie London, Liberty 55512
117. PEPINO THE ITALIAN MOUSE ... Lou Monte, Reprise 20106
118. THE BEST MAN CRIED ... Clyde McPhatter, Mercury 72051
119. LONGEST DAY (Instrumental) ... Mitch Miller, His Ork and Chorus, Columbia 42585
120. MY WIFE CAN'T COOK ... Lonnie Russ, 4J 501
121. THE 2,000 POUND BEE ... Ventures, Dolton 67
122. PARADISE ... Temptations, Gordy 7010
123. SCHOOL BELLS ARE RINGING ... Carole King, Dimension 1004
124. CAST YOUR FATE TO THE WIND ... Martin Denny, Liberty 55514
125. TWILIGHT TIME ... Andy Williams, Cadence 1433
126. WILD WEEKEND ... Rebels, Swan 4125
127. CAST YOUR FATE TO THE WIND ... Vince Guaraldi Trio, Fantasy 563
128. YOU'VE REALLY GOT A HOLD ON ME ... Miracles, Tamla 54073
129. THE NIGHT HAS A THOUSAND EYES ... Bobby Vee, Liberty 55521

# BILLBOARD HOT 100

**FOR WEEK ENDING DECEMBER 8, 1962**

★ STAR PERFORMERS—Selections registering greatest upward progress this week.
Ⓢ Indicates that 45 r.p.m. stereo single version is available.
△ Indicates that 33⅓ r.p.m. mono single version is available.
△ Indicates that 33⅓ r.p.m. stereo single version is available.

| This Week | Wk. Ago | 2 Wks. Ago | 3 Wks. Ago | TITLE — Artist, Label & Number | Weeks On Chart |
|---|---|---|---|---|---|
| 1 | 1 | 1 | 1 | BIG GIRLS DON'T CRY — Four Seasons, Vee Jay 465 | 8 |
| 2 | 2 | 2 | 2 | RETURN TO SENDER — Elvis Presley, RCA Victor 8100 | 8 |
| 3 | 3 | 4 | 7 | BOBBY'S GIRL — Marcie Blane, Seville 120 | 8 |
| 4 | 6 | 7 | 8 | DON'T HANG UP — Orlons, Cameo 231 | 9 |
| 5 | 8 | 10 | 13 | RIDE! — Dee Dee Sharp, Cameo 230 | 8 |
| 6 | 7 | 11 | 19 | THE LONELY BULL — Tijuana Brass, A. & M. 703 | 7 |
| 7 | 13 | 18 | 39 | TELSTAR — Tornadoes, London 9561 | 6 |
| 8 | 4 | 6 | 9 | LIMBO ROCK — Chubby Checker, Parkway 849 | 14 |
| 9 | 5 | 3 | 4 | ALL ALONE AM I — Brenda Lee, Decca 31424 | 11 |
| 10 | 16 | 17 | 32 | RELEASE ME — "Little Esther" Phillips, Lenox 5555 | 7 |
| 11 | 9 | 8 | 3 | HE'S A REBEL — Crystals, Philles 106 | 14 |
| 12 | 18 | 22 | 23 | (DANCE WITH THE) GUITAR MAN — Duane Eddy, RCA Victor 8087 | 10 |
| 13 | 14 | 19 | 26 | MY OWN TRUE LOVE — Duprees, Coed 571 | 8 |
| 14 | 27 | 39 | 56 | LOVE CAME TO ME — Dion, Laurie 3145 | 5 |
| 15 | 20 | 30 | 43 | RUMORS — Johnny Crawford, Del-Fi 4188 | 6 |
| 16 | 19 | 29 | 42 | KEEP YOUR HANDS OFF MY BABY — Little Eva, Dimension 1003 | 6 |
| 17 | 12 | 12 | 10 | THE CHA-CHA-CHA — Bobby Rydell, Cameo 228 | 9 |
| 18 | 15 | 15 | 18 | DESAFINADO — Stan Getz and Charlie Byrd, Verve 10260 | 11 |
| 19 | 23 | 36 | 44 | ESO BESO — Paul Anka, RCA Victor 8097 | 6 |
| 20 | 41 | 54 | 85 | GO AWAY LITTLE GIRL — Steve Lawrence, Columbia 42601 | 5 |
| 21 | 10 | 5 | 5 | NEXT DOOR TO AN ANGEL — Neil Sedaka, RCA Victor 8086 | 10 |
| 22 | 40 | 50 | 77 | YOU ARE MY SUNSHINE — Ray Charles, ABC-Paramount 10375 | 4 |
| 23 | 37 | 40 | 59 | LET'S GO — Routers, Warner Bros. 5283 | 6 |
| 24 | 42 | 65 | — | HOTEL HAPPINESS — Brook Benton, Mercury 72055 | 3 |
| 25 | 30 | 41 | 52 | DEAR LONELY HEARTS — Nat King Cole, Capitol 4870 | 5 |
| 26 | 28 | 34 | 37 | WIGGLE WOBBLE — Les Cooper, Everlast 5019 | 8 |
| 27 | 17 | 13 | 11 | ONLY LOVE CAN BREAK A HEART — Gene Pitney, Musicor 1022 | 13 |
| 28 | 24 | 28 | 33 | I CAN'T HELP IT — Johnny Tillotson, Cadence 1432 | 7 |
| 29 | 34 | 46 | 65 | CHAINS — Cookies, Dimension 1002 | 5 |
| 30 | 44 | 64 | 75 | ZIP-A-DEE-DOO-DAH — Bob B. Soxx & the Blue Jeans, Philles 107 | 4 |
| 31 | 45 | 66 | 88 | RUBY ANN — Marty Robbins, Columbia 42614 | 4 |
| 32 | 11 | 9 | 6 | GINA — Johnny Mathis, Columbia 42582 | 12 |
| 33 | 50 | 61 | 83 | THE PUSH AND KICK — Mark Valentino, Swan 4121 | 4 |
| 34 | 22 | 14 | 12 | NOTHING CAN CHANGE THIS LOVE — Sam Cooke, RCA Victor 8088 | 11 |
| 35 | 48 | 63 | 84 | YOUR CHEATING HEART — Ray Charles, ABC-Paramount 10375 | 4 |
| 36 | 33 | 33 | 28 | THAT STRANGER USED TO BE MY GIRL — Trade Martin, Coed 570 | 8 |
| 37 | 25 | 23 | 25 | WHAT KIND OF FOOL AM I — Sammy Davis Jr., Reprise 20048 | 15 |
| 38 | 29 | 20 | 22 | I'VE GOT A WOMAN — Jimmy McGriff, Sue 770 | 9 |
| 39 | 49 | 55 | 64 | MARY ANN REGRETS — Burl Ives, Decca 31433 | 6 |
| 40 | 32 | 35 | 38 | MAMA SANG A SONG — Stan Kenton, Capitol 4847 | 9 |
| 41 | 21 | 16 | 15 | CLOSE TO CATHY — Mike Clifford, United Artists 489 | 13 |
| 42 | 26 | 24 | 16 | DO YOU LOVE ME — Contours, Gordy 7005 | 18 |
| 43 | 64 | — | — | TWO LOVERS — Mary Wells, Motown 1035 | 2 |
| 44 | 56 | 67 | 79 | SPANISH LACE — Gene McDaniels, Liberty 55510 | 5 |
| 45 | 55 | 75 | 93 | MY DAD — Paul Petersen, Colpix 663 | 4 |
| 46 | 39 | 25 | 29 | LEAH — Roy Orbison, Monument 467 | 10 |
| 47 | 36 | 37 | 51 | LOVERS BY NIGHT, STRANGERS BY DAY — Fleetwoods, Dolton 62 | 9 |
| 48 | 38 | 43 | 47 | MAMA SANG A SONG — Walter Brennan, Liberty 55508 | 8 |
| 49 | 53 | 57 | 74 | COMIN' HOME BABY — Mel Torme, Atlantic 2165 | 6 |
| 50 | 35 | 38 | 37 | I LEFT MY HEART IN SAN FRANCISCO — Tony Bennett, Columbia 42332 | 18 |
| 51 | 46 | 51 | 55 | STUBBORN KIND OF FELLOW — Marvin Gaye, Tamla 54068 | 8 |
| 52 | 76 | 82 | 90 | SHUTTERS AND BOARDS — Jerry Wallace, Challenge 9171 | 4 |
| 53 | 94 | — | — | EVERYBODY LOVES A LOVER — Shirelles, Scepter 1243 | 2 |
| 54 | 43 | 31 | 20 | POPEYE (The Hitchhiker) — Chubby Checker, Parkway 849 | 12 |
| 55 | 81 | — | — | TELL HIM — Exciters, United Artists 544 | 2 |
| 56 | 63 | 73 | 89 | DIDDLE-DE-DUM — Belmonts, Sabina 507 | 4 |
| 57 | 60 | 69 | — | YOU THREW A LUCKY PUNCH — Gene (Duke of Earl) Chandler, Vee Jay 468 | 3 |
| 58 | 70 | 81 | 86 | UP ON THE ROOF — Drifters, Atlantic 2162 | 6 |
| 59 | 31 | 21 | 14 | MONSTER MASH — Bobby (Boris) Pickett and the Crypt Kickers, Garpax 44167 | 14 |
| 60 | 67 | 72 | 87 | THAT'S LIFE — Gabriel & the Angels, Swan 4118 | 5 |
| 61 | 61 | 74 | 78 | I LOST MY BABY — Joey Dee, Roulette 4456 | 6 |
| 62 | 74 | 80 | 99 | BABY HAS GONE BYE BYE — George Maharis, Epic 9555 | 4 |
| 63 | 77 | — | — | TEN LITTLE INDIANS — Beach Boys, Capitol 4880 | 2 |
| 64 | 75 | 77 | 81 | A LITTLE BIT NOW — Majors, Imperial 5879 | 4 |
| 65 | 73 | — | — | LET'S KISS AND MAKE UP — Bobby Vinton, Epic 9561 | 2 |
| 66 | — | — | — | LITTLE DRUMMER BOY — Harry Simeone Chorale, 20th Fox 121 | 1 |
| 67 | 68 | 76 | 82 | IF YOU WERE A ROCK & ROLL RECORD — Freddy Cannon, Swan 4122 | 5 |
| 68 | 80 | 90 | — | DON'T GO NEAR THE ESKIMOS — Ben Colder, MGM 13104 | 3 |
| 69 | 72 | 85 | — | RAINBOW AT MIDNIGHT — Jimmie Rodgers, Dot 16407 | 3 |
| 70 | — | — | — | THE NIGHT HAS A THOUSAND EYES — Bobby Vee, Liberty 55521 | 1 |
| 71 | 83 | — | — | ROAD HOG — John D. Loudermilk, RCA Victor 8101 | 2 |
| 72 | — | — | — | PEPINO THE ITALIAN MOUSE — Lou Monte, Reprise 20106 | 1 |
| 73 | 86 | — | — | SEE SEE RIDER — LaVern Baker, Atlantic 2167 | 2 |
| 74 | — | — | — | I SAW LINDA YESTERDAY — Dickey Lee, Smash 1791 | 1 |
| 75 | 78 | 100 | — | CONEY ISLAND BABY — Excellents, Blast 205 | 3 |
| 76 | — | — | — | TROUBLE IS MY MIDDLE NAME — Bobby Vinton, Epic 9561 | 1 |
| 77 | 84 | — | — | THE LOVE OF A BOY — Timi Yuro, Liberty 55519 | 2 |
| 78 | — | — | — | DON'T MAKE ME OVER — Dionne Warwick, Scepter 1239 | 1 |
| 79 | 82 | 87 | — | I MAY NOT LIVE TO SEE TOMORROW — Brian Hyland, ABC-Paramount 10374 | 3 |
| 80 | — | — | — | MONSTERS' HOLIDAY — Bobby (Boris) Pickett & the Crypt Kickers, Garpax 44171 | 1 |
| 81 | — | — | — | MY WIFE CAN'T COOK — Lonnie Russ, 4 J 501 | 1 |
| 82 | 85 | 92 | — | THE JITTERBUG — Dovells, Parkway 855 | 3 |
| 83 | — | — | — | DESAFINADO — Pat Thomas, MGM 13102 | 1 |
| 84 | — | — | — | THE BALLAD OF JED CLAMPETT — Lester Flatt & Earl Scruggs, Columbia 42606 | 1 |
| 85 | 95 | — | — | ME AND MY SHADOW — Frank Sinatra & Sammy Davis Jr., Reprise 20128 | 2 |
| 86 | 92 | — | — | GONNA RAISE A RUCKUS TONIGHT — Jimmy Dean, Columbia 42600 | 2 |
| 87 | — | — | — | YOU'VE REALLY GOT A HOLD ON ME — Miracles, Tamla 54073 | 1 |
| 88 | — | — | — | SOME KINDA FUN — Chris Montez, Monogram 507 | 1 |
| 89 | — | — | — | STILL WATER RUNS DEEP — Brook Benton, Mercury 72055 | 1 |
| 90 | 91 | — | — | STRANGE I KNOW — Marvelettes, Tamla 54072 | 2 |
| 91 | — | — | — | LET ME GO THE RIGHT WAY — Supremes, Motown 1034 | 1 |
| 92 | — | — | — | THE CHIPMUNK SONG — David Seville & the Chipmunks, Liberty 55250 | 1 |
| 93 | 100 | — | — | LIMELIGHT — Mr. Acker Bilk, Atco 6238 | 2 |
| 94 | — | — | — | CAST YOUR FATE TO THE WIND — Vince Guaraldi Trio, Fantasy 563 | 1 |
| 95 | 88 | 89 | 91 | GETTING READY FOR THE HEARTBREAK — Chuck Jackson, Wand 128 | 4 |
| 96 | — | — | — | TWILIGHT TIME — Andy Williams, Cadence 1433 | 1 |
| 97 | — | — | — | THREE HEARTS IN A TANGLE — James Brown & the Famous Flames, King 5701 | 1 |
| 98 | — | — | — | ZERO-ZERO — Lawrence Welk, Dot 16420 | 1 |
| 99 | — | — | — | JINGLE BELL ROCK — Bobby Helms, Decca 30513 | 1 |
| 100 | — | — | — | NIGHT TIME — Pete Antell, Cameo 234 | 1 |

## BUBBLING UNDER THE HOT 100

101. WHITE CHRISTMAS — Bing Crosby, Decca 23778
102. THEME FROM TARAS BULBA (The Wishing Star) — Jerry Butler, Vee Jay 475
103. GO TIGER, GO! — Guy Mitchell, Joy 270
104. THE END OF THE WORLD — Skeeter Davis, RCA Victor 8089
105. MY MAN—HE'S A LOVIN' MAN — Betty Lavett, Atlantic 2160
106. THERE'LL BE NO TEARDROPS TONIGHT — Adam Wade, Epic 9557
107. ECHO — Emotions, Kapp 490
108. RUDOLPH, THE RED-NOSED REINDEER — David Seville and the Chipmunks, Liberty 8209
109. THE LONGEST DAY (Instrumental) — Mitch Miller, His Ork and Chorus, Columbia 42585
110. THIS LAND IS YOUR LAND — Christy Minstrels, Columbia 42592
111. I'VE GOT THE WORLD BY THE TAIL — Claude King, Columbia 42630
112. YOU'RE GONNA NEED ME — Jamie Lyons, Jamie 1240
113. THE 2,000 POUND BEE — Ventures, Dolton 57
114. BIG BOAT — Peter, Paul and Mary, Warner Bros. 5325
115. MAMA SANG A SONG — Bill Anderson, Decca 31404
116. FROM THE BOTTOM OF MY HEART — Dean Martin, Reprise 20116
117. ROCKIN' AROUND THE CHRISTMAS TREE — Brenda Lee, Decca 20777
118. THEME FROM TARAS BULBA (The Wishing Star) — Ferrante & Teicher, United Artists 537
119. I'M SO LONESOME I COULD CRY — Johnny Tillotson, Cadence 1432
120. REMEMBER THEN — Earls, Old Town 1130
121. SHE'S A TROUBLEMAKER — Majors, Imperial 5879
122. THE SEARCHING IS OVER — Joe Henderson, Todd 1079
123. THE BEST MAN CRIED — Clyde McPhatter, Mercury 72051
124. THIS LAND IS YOUR LAND — Ketty Lester, Era 3094
125. FROM A JACK TO A KING — Ned Miller, Fabor 114
126. CAST YOUR FATE TO THE WIND — Martin Denny, Liberty 55514
127. ALVIN'S HARMONICA — David Seville and the Chipmunks, Liberty 55250
128. SANTA CLAUS IS WATCHING YOU — Ray Stevens, Mercury 72058
129. WELCOME HOME — Frankie Avalon, Chancellor 1125
130. MOLLY — Bobby Goldsboro, Laurie 3130

# BILLBOARD HOT 100

FOR WEEK ENDING DECEMBER 15 1962

★ STAR PERFORMERS—Selections registering greatest upward progress this week.

S Indicates that 45 r.p.m. stereo single version is available.

△ Indicates that 33⅓ r.p.m. mono single version is available.

S△ Indicates that 33⅓ r.p.m. stereo single version is available.

| This Week | 1 Wk. Ago | 2 Wks. Ago | 3 Wks. Ago | Title | Artist, Label & Number | | Weeks On Chart |
|---|---|---|---|---|---|---|---|
| 1 | 1 | 1 | 1 | BIG GIRLS DON'T CRY | Four Seasons, Vee Jay 465 | | 9 |
| 2 | 2 | 2 | 2 | RETURN TO SENDER | Elvis Presley, RCA Victor 8100 | △ | 9 |
| 3 | 3 | 3 | 4 | BOBBY'S GIRL | Marcie Blane, Seville 120 | | 9 |
| 4 | 8 | 4 | 6 | LIMBO ROCK | Chubby Checker, Parkway 849 | | 15 |
| 5 | 7 | 13 | 18 | TELSTAR | Tornadoes, London 9561 | | 7 |
| 6 | 4 | 6 | 7 | DON'T HANG UP | Orlons, Cameo 231 | | 10 |
| 7 | 6 | 7 | 11 | THE LONELY BULL | Tijuana Brass, A. & M. 703 | | 8 |
| 8 | 5 | 8 | 10 | RIDE! | Dee Dee Sharp, Cameo 230 | | 9 |
| 9 | 10 | 16 | 17 | RELEASE ME | "Little Esther" Phillips, Lenox 5555 | | 8 |
| ★10 | 20 | 41 | 54 | GO AWAY LITTLE GIRL | Steve Lawrence, Columbia 42601 | △ | 6 |
| ★11 | 22 | 40 | 50 | YOU ARE MY SUNSHINE | Ray Charles, ABC-Paramount 10375 | | 5 |
| 12 | 15 | 20 | 30 | RUMORS | Johnny Crawford, Del-Fi 4188 | | 7 |
| 13 | 16 | 19 | 29 | KEEP YOUR HANDS OFF MY BABY | Little Eva, Dimension 1003 | | 7 |
| 14 | 14 | 27 | 39 | LOVE CAME TO ME | Dion, Laurie 3145 | | 6 |
| ★15 | 24 | 42 | 65 | HOTEL HAPPINESS | Brook Benton, Mercury 72055 | | 4 |
| 16 | 12 | 18 | 22 | (DANCE WITH THE) GUITAR MAN | Duane Eddy, RCA Victor 8087 | △ | 11 |
| ★17 | 25 | 30 | 41 | DEAR LONELY HEARTS | Nat King Cole, Capitol 4870 | | 6 |
| 18 | 9 | 5 | 3 | ALL ALONE AM I | Brenda Lee, Decca 31424 | | 12 |
| 19 | 11 | 9 | 8 | HE'S A REBEL | Crystals, Philles 106 | | 15 |
| 20 | 23 | 37 | 40 | LET'S GO | Routers, Warner Bros. 5283 | | 7 |
| 21 | 13 | 14 | 19 | MY OWN TRUE LOVE | Duprees, Coed 571 | | 9 |
| 22 | 29 | 34 | 46 | CHAINS | Cookies, Dimension 1002 | | 6 |
| 23 | 31 | 45 | 66 | RUBY ANN | Marty Robbins, Columbia 42614 | △ | 5 |
| 24 | 18 | 15 | 15 | DESAFINADO | Stan Getz and Charlie Byrd, Verve 10260 | | 12 |
| 25 | 30 | 44 | 64 | ZIP-A-DEE-DOO-DAH | Bob B. Soxx & the Blue Jeans, Philles 107 | | 5 |
| 26 | 19 | 23 | 36 | ESO BESO | Paul Anka, RCA Victor 8097 | △ | 7 |
| 27 | 33 | 50 | 61 | THE PUSH AND KICK | Mark Valentino, Swan 4121 | | 6 |
| 28 | 26 | 28 | 34 | WIGGLE WOBBLE | Les Cooper, Everlast 5019 | | 9 |
| 29 | 17 | 12 | 12 | THE CHA-CHA-CHA | Bobby Rydell, Cameo 228 | | 10 |
| 30 | 35 | 48 | 63 | YOUR CHEATING HEART | Ray Charles, ABC-Paramount 10375 | | 5 |
| ★31 | 44 | 56 | 67 | SPANISH LACE | Gene McDaniels, Liberty 55510 | | 6 |
| ★32 | 45 | 55 | 75 | MY DAD | Paul Petersen, Colpix 663 | | 5 |
| ★33 | 43 | 64 | — | TWO LOVERS | Mary Wells, Motown 1035 | | 3 |
| 34 | 28 | 24 | 28 | I CAN'T HELP IT | Johnny Tillotson, Cadence 1432 | | 8 |
| ★35 | 55 | 81 | — | TELL HIM | Exciters, United Artists 544 | | 3 |
| ★36 | 53 | 94 | — | EVERYBODY LOVES A LOVER | Shirelles, Scepter 1243 | | 3 |
| ★37 | 72 | — | — | PEPINO THE ITALIAN MOUSE | Lou Monte, Reprise 20106 | | 2 |
| ★38 | 66 | — | — | LITTLE DRUMMER BOY | Harry Simeone Chorale, 20th Fox 121 | | 2 |
| 39 | 21 | 10 | 5 | NEXT DOOR TO AN ANGEL | Neil Sedaka, RCA Victor 8086 | △ | 11 |
| 40 | 49 | 53 | 57 | COMIN' HOME BABY | Mel Torme, Atlantic 2165 | | 7 |
| ★41 | 52 | 76 | 82 | SHUTTERS AND BOARDS | Jerry Wallace, Challenge 9171 | | 5 |
| ★42 | 70 | — | — | THE NIGHT HAS A THOUSAND EYES | Bobby Vee, Liberty 55521 | | 2 |
| 43 | 27 | 17 | 13 | ONLY LOVE CAN BREAK A HEART | Gene Pitney, Musicor 1022 | | 14 |
| 44 | 39 | 49 | 55 | MARY ANN REGRETS | Burl Ives, Decca 31433 | | 7 |
| ★45 | 58 | 70 | 81 | UP ON THE ROOF | Drifters, Atlantic 2162 | | 7 |
| 46 | 50 | 35 | 38 | I LEFT MY HEART IN SAN FRANCISCO | Tony Bennett, Columbia 42332 | △ | 19 |
| ★47 | 65 | 73 | — | LET'S KISS AND MAKE UP | Bobby Vinton, Epic 9561 | | 3 |
| 48 | 51 | 46 | 51 | STUBBORN KIND OF FELLOW | Marvin Gaye, Tamla 54068 | | 9 |
| ★49 | 74 | — | — | I SAW LINDA YESTERDAY | Dickey Lee, Smash 1791 | | 2 |
| 50 | 47 | 36 | 37 | LOVERS BY NIGHT, STRANGERS BY DAY | Fleetwoods, Dolton 62 | | 10 |
| ★51 | 63 | 77 | — | TEN LITTLE INDIANS | Beach Boys, Capitol 4880 | | 3 |
| 52 | 57 | 60 | 69 | YOU THREW A LUCKY PUNCH | Gene (Duke of Earl) Chandler, Vee Jay 468 | | 4 |
| 53 | 56 | 63 | 73 | DIDDLE-DE-DUM | Belmonts, Sabina 507 | | 5 |
| 54 | 60 | 67 | 72 | THAT'S LIFE | Gabriel & the Angels, Swan 4118 | | 6 |
| ★55 | 73 | 86 | — | SEE SEE RIDER | LaVern Baker, Atlantic 2167 | | 3 |
| ★56 | — | — | — | SANTA CLAUS IS COMING TO TOWN | Four Seasons, Vee Jay 478 | | 1 |
| ★57 | 80 | — | — | MONSTERS' HOLIDAY | Bobby (Boris) Pickett & the Crypt Kickers, Garpax 44171 | | 2 |
| ★58 | — | — | — | IT'S UP TO YOU | Rick Nelson, Imperial 5901 | | 1 |
| ★59 | 92 | — | — | THE CHIPMUNK SONG | David Seville & the Chipmunks, Liberty 55250 | | 2 |
| ★60 | 75 | 78 | 100 | CONEY ISLAND BABY | Excellents, Blast 205 | | 4 |
| ★61 | 78 | — | — | DON'T MAKE ME OVER | Dionne Warwick, Scepter 1239 | | 2 |
| 62 | 68 | 80 | 90 | DON'T GO NEAR THE ESKIMOS | Ben Colder, MGM 13104 | | 4 |
| 63 | 64 | 75 | 77 | A LITTLE BIT NOW | Majors, Imperial 5879 | | 5 |
| 64 | 61 | 61 | 74 | I LOST MY BABY | Joey Dee, Roulette 4456 | | 7 |
| 65 | 71 | 83 | — | ROAD HOG | John D. Loudermilk, RCA Victor 8101 | △ | 3 |
| 66 | 69 | 72 | 85 | RAINBOW AT MIDNIGHT | Jimmie Rodgers, Dot 16407 | | 4 |
| 67 | 77 | 84 | — | THE LOVE OF A BOY | Timi Yuro, Liberty 55519 | | 3 |
| 68 | 76 | — | — | TROUBLE IS MY MIDDLE NAME | Bobby Vinton, Epic 9561 | | 2 |
| 69 | 62 | 74 | 80 | BABY HAS GONE BYE BYE | George Maharis, Epic 9555 | | 5 |
| ★70 | — | — | — | WHITE CHRISTMAS | Bing Crosby, Decca 23778 | | 1 |
| ★71 | 88 | — | — | SOME KINDA FUN | Chris Montez, Monogram 507 | | 2 |
| 72 | 85 | 95 | — | ME AND MY SHADOW | Frank Sinatra & Sammy Davis Jr., Reprise 20128 | | 3 |
| 73 | 79 | 82 | 87 | I MAY NOT LIVE TO SEE TOMORROW | Brian Hyland, ABC-Paramount 10374 | | 4 |
| 74 | 86 | 92 | — | GONNA RAISE A RUCKUS TONIGHT | Jimmy Dean, Columbia 42600 | △ | 3 |
| ★75 | — | — | — | THE CHRISTMAS SONG | Nat King Cole, Capitol 3561 | | 1 |
| 76 | 90 | 91 | — | STRANGE I KNOW | Marvelettes, Tamla 54072 | | 3 |
| ★77 | — | — | — | SANTA CLAUS IS WATCHING YOU | Ray Stevens, Mercury 72058 | | 1 |
| 78 | 83 | — | — | DESAFINADO | Pat Thomas, MGM 13102 | | 2 |
| 79 | 87 | — | — | YOU'VE REALLY GOT A HOLD ON ME | Miracles, Tamla 54073 | | 2 |
| 80 | 81 | — | — | MY WIFE CAN'T COOK | Lonnie Russ, 4 J 501 | | 2 |
| 81 | 84 | — | — | THE BALLAD OF JED CLAMPETT | Lester Flatt & Earl Scruggs, Columbia 42606 | △ | 2 |
| ★82 | — | — | — | I'M GONNA BE WARM THIS WINTER | Connie Francis, MGM 13116 | | 1 |
| ★83 | — | — | — | YOU'RE GONNA NEED ME | Barbara Lynn, Jamie 1240 | | 1 |
| ★84 | — | — | — | HALF HEAVEN—HALF HEARTACHE | Gene Pitney, Musicor 1026 | | 1 |
| ★85 | — | — | 93 | SHE'S A TROUBLEMAKER | Majors, Imperial 5879 | | 2 |
| 86 | 96 | — | — | TWILIGHT TIME | Andy Williams, Cadence 1433 | | 2 |
| 87 | 99 | — | — | JINGLE BELL ROCK | Bobby Helms, Decca 30513 | | 2 |
| ★88 | — | 96 | — | ECHO | Emotions, Kapp 490 | | 2 |
| ★89 | — | — | — | ROCKIN' AROUND THE CHRISTMAS TREE | Brenda Lee, Decca 30776 | | 1 |
| ★90 | — | — | — | I FOUND A NEW BABY | Bobby Darin, Atco 6244 | | 1 |
| 91 | 94 | — | — | CAST YOUR FATE TO THE WIND | Vince Guaraldi Trio, Fantasy 563 | | 2 |
| 92 | 93 | 100 | — | LIMELIGHT | Mr. Acker Bilk, Atco 6238 | | 3 |
| 93 | — | — | — | TROUBLE IN MIND | Aretha Franklin, Columbia 42625 | △ | 1 |
| 94 | — | — | — | REMEMBER THEN | Earls, Old Town 1130 | | 1 |
| 95 | 97 | — | — | THREE HEARTS IN A TANGLE | James Brown & the Famous Flames, King 5701 | | 2 |
| 96 | — | — | — | LET ME ENTERTAIN YOU | Ray Anthony, Capitol 4876 | | 1 |
| 97 | — | — | — | JINGLE BELL ROCK | Bobby Rydell/Chubby Checker, Cameo 205 | | 1 |
| 98 | — | — | — | BIG BOAT | Peter, Paul & Mary, Warner Bros. 5325 | | 1 |
| 99 | — | — | — | RUDOLPH, THE RED-NOSED REINDEER | David Seville & the Chipmunks, Liberty 55289 | | 1 |
| 100 | — | — | — | THEME FROM TARAS BULBA (The Wishing Star) | Jerry Butler, Vee Jay 475 | | 1 |

## HOT 100—A TO Z—(Publisher-Licensee)


All Alone Am I (Duchess, BMI) .... 18
Baby Has Gone Bye Bye (Dymor, ASCAP) .... 69
Ballad of Jed Clampett (Carolintone, BMI) .... 81
Big Boat (Pepamar, ASCAP) .... 98
Big Girls Don't Cry (Bobob, ASCAP) .... 1
Bobby's Girl (A. M. E., BMI) .... 3
Cast Your Fate to the Wind (Friendship, BMI) .... 91
Cha-Cha-Cha, The (Fajob-Kalmann, ASCAP) .... 29
Chains (Aldon, BMI) .... 22
Chipmunk Song, The (Monarch, ASCAP) .... 59
Christmas Song, The (Morris, ASCAP) .... 75
Comin' Home Baby (Melotone, BMI) .... 40
Coney Island Baby (Original, BMI) .... 60
(Dance With the) Guitar Man (Linduane, BMI) .... 16
Dear Lonely Hearts (Sweco-Cetra, BMI) .... 17
Desafinado—Getz & Byrd (Hollis-Bendig, BMI) .... 24
Desafinado—Thomas (Hollis-Bendig, BMI) .... 78
Diddle-De-Dum (Glenden, ASCAP) .... 53
Don't Go Near the Eskimos (Buttercup, BMI) .... 62
Don't Hang Up (Kalmann, ASCAP) .... 6
Don't Make Me Over (Bacharach-Jac, ASCAP) .... 61
Echo (Spare Rib, BMI) .... 88
Eso Beso (Flanka, ASCAP) .... 26
Everybody Loves a Lover (Korwin, ASCAP) .... 36
Go Away Little Girl (Aldon, BMI) .... 10
Gonna Raise a Ruckus Tonight (Plainview, BMI) .. 74
Half Heaven—Half Heartache (Arch, ASCAP) .... 84
He's a Rebel (January, BMI) .... 19
Hotel Happiness (Dayben-Mansion, ASCAP) .... 15
I Can't Help It (Acuff-Rose, BMI) .... 34
I Found a New Baby (Pickwick, ASCAP) .... 90
I Left My Heart in San Francisco (General, ASCAP) .... 46
I Lost My Baby (Planetary, ASCAP) .... 64
I May Not Live to See Tomorrow (Pogo, ASCAP) .. 73
I Saw Linda Yesterday (Jack, BMI) .... 49
I'm Gonna Be Warm This Winter (Merna, BMI) .. 82
It's Up to You (Four Star, BMI) .... 58
Jingle Bell Rock—Helms (Cornell, ASCAP) .... 87
Jingle Bell Rock—Rydell-Checker (Cornell, ASCAP). 97
Keep Your Hands Off My Baby (Aldon, BMI) .. 13
Let Me Entertain You (Williamson-Stratford, ASCAP) .... 96
Let's Go (Wrist-Giant, BMI) .... 20
Let's Kiss And Make Up (Trio, BMI) .... 47
Limbo Rock (Four Star Twist, BMI) .... 4
Limelight (Bourne, ASCAP) .... 92
Little Bit Now, A (Travis-Rittenhouse, BMI) .... 63
Little Drummer Boy (Delaware-Mills, ASCAP) .... 38
Lonely Bull, The (Almo, ASCAP) .... 7
Love Came to Me (Schwartz-Disal, ASCAP) .... 14
Love of a Boy, The (U. S. Songs, ASCAP) .... 67
Lovers By Night, Strangers By Day (January, BMI). 50
Mary Ann Regrets (Pamper, BMI) .... 44
Me And My Shadow (Bourne, ASCAP) .... 72
Monsters' Holiday (Garpax-Underwood, BMI) .... 57
My Dad (Aldon, BMI) .... 32
My Own True Love (Remick, ASCAP) .... 21
My Wife Can't Cook (Lajesse, BMI) .... 80
Next Door to an Angel (Aldon, BMI) .... 39
Night Has a Thousand Eyes, The (Blen-Mabs, ASCAP) .... 42
Only Love Can Break a Heart (Arch, ASCAP) .. 43
Pepino the Italian Mouse (Romance-Ding Dong, BMI) .... 37
Push and Kick, The (Claridge, ASCAP) .... 27
Rainbow at Midnight (Shapiro-Bernstein, ASCAP). 66
kelease Me (Four Star, BMI) .... 9
Remember Then (Maureen, BMI) .... 94
Return to Sender (Presley, BMI) .... 2
Ride! (Woodcrest-Check-Colt, BMI) .... 8
Road Hog (Acuff-Rose, BMI) .... 65
Rockin' Around the Christmas Tree (St. Nicholas, ASCAP) .... 89
Ruby Ann (Marizona, BMI) .... 23
Rudolph, the Red-Nosed Reindeer (St. Nicholas, ASCAP) .... 99
Rumors (Aldon, BMI) .... 12
Santa Claus Is Coming to Town (Feist, ASCAP) 56
Santa Claus Is Watching You (Lowery, BMI) .... 77
See See Rider (Cotillion, BMI) .... 55
She's a Troublemaker (Travis-Rittenhouse, BMI).. 85
Shutters and Boards (Camp & Canyon, BMI) .... 41
Some Kinda Fun (Rondell, BMI) .... 71
Spanish Lace (St. Louis, BMI) .... 31
Strange I Know (Jobete, BMI) .... 76
Stubborn Kind of Fellow (Jobete, BMI) .... 35
Telstar (Campbell Connelly, ASCAP) .... 5
Ten Little Indians (Sea of Tunes, BMI) .... 51
That's Life (Mary Hill-Missile, BMI) .... 54
Theme From Taras Bulba (The Wishing Star) (United Artists, ASCAP) ....100
Three Hearts in a Tangle (Sonlo, BMI) .... 95
Trouble in Mind (Leeds, ASCAP) .... 93
Trouble Is My Middle Name (January, BMI) .... 68
Twilight Time (Porgie, BMI) .... 86
Two Lovers (Jobete, BMI) .... 33
Up on the Roof (Aldon, BMI) .... 45
White Christmas (Berlin, ASCAP) .... 70
Wiggle Wobble (Bob-Dan, BMI) .... 28
You Are My Sunshine (Peer Int'l, BMI) .... 11
You Threw a Lucky Punch (Jobete, BMI) .... 52
You're Gonna Need Me (Dandelion-Crazy Cajun, BMI) .... 83
You've Really Got a Hold on Me (Jobete, BMI) .. 79
Your Cheating Heart (Fred Rose, BMI) .... 30
Zip-A-Dee-Doo-Dah (Joy, ASCAP) .... 25


## BUBBLING UNDER THE HOT 100

101. ALVIN'S HARMONICA .... David Seville & the Chipmunks, Liberty 55250
102. DESAFINADO ....Ella Fitzgerald, Verve 10274
103. MY MAN—HE'S A LOVIN' MAN ....Betty Lavett, Atlantic 2160
104. HEY, GOOD LOOKIN' ....Connie Stevens, Warner Bros. 5318
105. LOVESICK BLUES ....Frank Ifield, Vee Jay 477
106. JELLY BREAD ....Booker T. & the MG's, Stax 131
107. STILL WATER RUNS DEEP ....Brook Benton, Mercury 72055
108. THERE'LL BE NO TEARDROPS TONIGHT .... Adam Wade, Epic 9557
109. THE 2,000 POUND BEE ....Ventures, Dolton 67
110. THE END OF THE WORLD .... Skeeter Davis, RCA Victor 8089
111. GO TIGER, GO! ....Guy Mitchell, Joy 270
112. ZERO-ZERO ....Lawrence Welk, Dot 16420
113. LET ME GO THE RIGHT WAY .... Supremes, Motown 1034
114. GETTING READY FOR THE HEARTBREAK ....Chuck Jackson, Wand 128
115. FROM A JACK TO A KING ....Ned Miller, Fabor 114
116. THEME FROM TARAS BULBA (The Wishing Star) ....Ferrante & Teicher, United Artists 537
117. HUSH HEART ....Baby Washington, Sue 769
118. FROM THE BOTTOM OF MY HEART (Dammi, Dammi, Dammi) R....Dean Martin, Reprise 20116
119. THIS LAND IS YOUR LAND ....Christy Minstrels, Columbia 42592
120. DOES HE MEAN THAT MUCH TO YOU? ....Eddy Arnold, RCA Victor 8102
121. THE LONGEST DAY (Instrumental) ....Mitch Miller, His Ork & Chorus, Columbia 42585
122. JOEY'S SONG ....Bill Black's Combo, Hi 2059
123. WOULD IT MAKE ANY DIFFERENCE TO YOU ....Etta James, Argo 5430
124. CAST YOUR FATE TO THE WIND ....Martin Denny, Liberty 55514
125. MOLLY ....Bobby Goldsboro, Laurie 3130
126. MINSTREL AND QUEEN ....Impressions, ABC-Paramount 10357
127. MIND OVER MATTER ....Nolan Strong, Fortune 546
128. FLY ME TO THE MOON—BOSSA NOVA ....Joe Harnell & His Ork, Kapp 497
129. STARDUST BOSSA NOVA ....Ella Fitzgerald, Verve 10274
130. THE BEST MAN CRIED ....Clyde McPhatter, Mercury 72051
131. I'M SO LONESOME I COULD CRY ....Johnny Tillotson, Cadence 1432
132. THE JITTERBUG ....Dovells, Parkway 855
133. MATILDA ....String-A-Longs, Dot 16393

# BILLBOARD HOT 100

FOR WEEK ENDING DECEMBER 22

1962

★ STAR PERFORMERS—Selections registering greatest upward progress this week.

(S) Indicates that 45 r.p.m. stereo single version is available.

△ Indicates that 33⅓ r.p.m. mono single version is available.

(△S) Indicates that 33⅓ r.p.m. stereo single version is available.

| This Week | 1 Wk. Ago | 2 Wks. Ago | 3 Wks. Ago | Title | Artist, Label & Number | Weeks On Chart |
|---|---|---|---|---|---|---|
| 1 | 5 | 7 | 13 | TELSTAR | Tornadoes, London 9561 | 8 |
| 2 | 4 | 8 | 4 | LIMBO ROCK | Chubby Checker, Parkway 849 | 16 |
| 3 | 2 | 2 | 2 | RETURN TO SENDER △ | Elvis Presley, RCA Victor 8100 | 10 |
| 4 | 3 | 3 | 3 | BOBBY'S GIRL | Marcie Blane, Seville 120 | 10 |
| 5 | 1 | 1 | 1 | BIG GIRLS DON'T CRY | Four Seasons, Vee Jay 465 | 10 |
| 6 | 6 | 4 | 6 | DON'T HANG UP | Orlons, Cameo 231 | 11 |
| 7 | 10 | 20 | 41 | GO AWAY LITTLE GIRL △ | Steve Lawrence, Columbia 42601 | 7 |
| 8 | 9 | 10 | 16 | RELEASE ME | "Little Esther" Phillips, Lenox 5555 | 9 |
| 9 | 11 | 22 | 40 | YOU ARE MY SUNSHINE | Ray Charles, ABC-Paramount 10375 | 6 |
| 10 | 14 | 14 | 27 | LOVE CAME TO ME | Dion, Laurie 3145 | 7 |
| 11 | 7 | 6 | 7 | THE LONELY BULL | Tijuana Brass, A. & M. 703 | 9 |
| 12 | 13 | 16 | 19 | KEEP YOUR HANDS OFF MY BABY | Little Eva, Dimension 1003 | 8 |
| 13 | 8 | 5 | 8 | RIDE! | Dee Dee Sharp, Cameo 230 | 10 |
| 14 | 15 | 24 | 42 | HOTEL HAPPINESS | Brook Benton, Mercury 72055 | 5 |
| 15 | 17 | 25 | 30 | DEAR LONELY HEARTS | Nat King Cole, Capitol 4870 | 7 |
| ★16 | 25 | 30 | 44 | ZIP-A-DEE-DOO-DAH | Bob B. Soxx & the Blue Jeans, Philles 107 | 6 |
| 17 | 12 | 15 | 20 | RUMORS | Johnny Crawford, Del-Fi 4188 | 8 |
| ★18 | 23 | 31 | 45 | RUBY ANN △ | Marty Robbins, Columbia 42614 | 6 |
| 19 | 20 | 23 | 37 | LET'S GO | Routers, Warner Bros. 5283 | 8 |
| 20 | 22 | 29 | 34 | CHAINS | Cookies, Dimension 1002 | 7 |
| 21 | 16 | 12 | 18 | (DANCE WITH THE) GUITAR MAN △ | Duane Eddy, RCA Victor 8087 | 12 |
| ★22 | 35 | 55 | 81 | TELL HIM | Exciters, United Artists 544 | 4 |
| ★23 | 37 | 72 | — | PEPINO THE ITALIAN MOUSE | Lou Monte, Reprise 20106 | 3 |
| 24 | 28 | 26 | 28 | WIGGLE WOBBLE | Les Cooper, Everlast 5019 | 10 |
| 25 | 33 | 43 | 64 | TWO LOVERS | Mary Wells, Motown 1035 | 4 |
| 26 | 18 | 9 | 5 | ALL ALONE AM I | Brenda Lee, Decca 31424 | 13 |
| 27 | 32 | 45 | 55 | MY DAD | Paul Petersen, Colpix 663 | 6 |
| 28 | 36 | 53 | 94 | EVERYBODY LOVES A LOVER | Shirelles, Scepter 1243 | 4 |
| 29 | 30 | 35 | 48 | YOUR CHEATING HEART | Ray Charles, ABC-Paramount 10375 | 6 |
| 30 | 19 | 11 | 9 | HE'S A REBEL | Crystals, Philles 106 | 16 |
| 31 | 31 | 44 | 56 | SPANISH LACE | Gene McDaniels, Liberty 55510 | 7 |
| 32 | 24 | 18 | 15 | DESAFINADO | Stan Getz and Charlie Byrd, Verve 10260 | 13 |
| 33 | 38 | 66 | — | LITTLE DRUMMER BOY | Harry Simeone Chorale, 20th Fox 121 | 3 |
| ★34 | 56 | — | — | SANTA CLAUS IS COMING TO TOWN | Four Seasons, Vee Jay 478 | 2 |
| 35 | 42 | 70 | — | THE NIGHT HAS A THOUSAND EYES | Bobby Vee, Liberty 55521 | 3 |
| 36 | 26 | 19 | 23 | ESO BESO △ | Paul Anka, RCA Victor 8097 | 8 |
| 37 | 27 | 33 | 50 | THE PUSH AND KICK | Mark Valentino, Swan 4121 | 7 |
| 38 | 41 | 52 | 76 | SHUTTERS AND BOARDS | Jerry Wallace, Challenge 9171 | 6 |
| 39 | 40 | 49 | 53 | COMIN' HOME BABY | Mel Torme, Atlantic 2165 | 8 |
| ★40 | 57 | 80 | — | MONSTERS' HOLIDAY | Bobby (Boris) Pickett & the Crypt Kickers, Garpax 44171 | 3 |
| 41 | 45 | 58 | 70 | UP ON THE ROOF | Drifters, Atlantic 2162 | 8 |
| 42 | 49 | 74 | — | I SAW LINDA YESTERDAY | Dickey Lee, Smash 1791 | 3 |
| 43 | 47 | 65 | 73 | LET'S KISS AND MAKE UP | Bobby Vinton, Epic 9561 | 4 |
| 44 | 21 | 13 | 14 | MY OWN TRUE LOVE | Duprees, Coed 571 | 10 |
| ★45 | 58 | — | — | IT'S UP TO YOU | Rick Nelson, Imperial 5901 | 2 |
| ★46 | 70 | — | — | WHITE CHRISTMAS | Bing Crosby, Decca 23778 | 2 |
| ★47 | 59 | 92 | — | THE CHIPMUNK SONG | David Seville & the Chipmunks, Liberty 55250 | 3 |
| 48 | 55 | 73 | 86 | SEE SEE RIDER | LaVern Baker, Atlantic 2167 | 4 |
| 49 | 52 | 57 | 60 | YOU THREW A LUCKY PUNCH | Gene (Duke of Earl) Chandler, Vee Jay 468 | 5 |
| ★50 | 61 | 78 | — | DON'T MAKE ME OVER | Dionne Warwick, Scepter 1239 | 3 |
| 51 | 54 | 60 | 67 | THAT'S LIFE | Gabriel & the Angels, Swan 4118 | 7 |
| 52 | 29 | 17 | 12 | THE CHA-CHA-CHA | Bobby Rydell, Cameo 228 | 11 |
| 53 | 51 | 63 | 77 | TEN LITTLE INDIANS | Beach Boys, Capitol 4880 | 4 |
| 54 | 34 | 28 | 24 | I CAN'T HELP IT | Johnny Tillotson, Cadence 1432 | 9 |
| ★55 | 77 | — | — | SANTA CLAUS IS WATCHING YOU | Ray Stevens, Mercury 72058 | 2 |
| ★56 | 84 | — | — | HALF HEAVEN—HALF HEARTACHE | Gene Pitney, Musicor 1026 | 2 |
| 57 | 46 | 50 | 35 | I LEFT MY HEART IN SAN FRANCISCO △ | Tony Bennett, Columbia 42332 | 20 |
| 58 | 60 | 75 | 78 | CONEY ISLAND BABY | Excellents, Blast 205 | 5 |
| ★59 | 87 | 99 | — | JINGLE BELL ROCK | Bobby Helms, Decca 30513 | 3 |
| 60 | 71 | 88 | — | SOME KINDA FUN | Chris Montez, Monogram 507 | 3 |
| 61 | 67 | 77 | 84 | THE LOVE OF A BOY | Timi Yuro, Liberty 55519 | 4 |
| 62 | 68 | 76 | — | TROUBLE IS MY MIDDLE NAME | Bobby Vinton, Epic 9561 | 3 |
| 63 | 63 | 64 | 75 | A LITTLE BIT NOW | Majors, Imperial 5879 | 6 |
| ★64 | 89 | — | — | ROCKIN' AROUND THE CHRISTMAS TREE | Brenda Lee, Decca 30777 | 2 |
| ★65 | 82 | — | — | I'M GONNA BE WARM THIS WINTER | Connie Francis, MGM 13116 | 2 |
| 66 | 66 | 69 | 72 | RAINBOW AT MIDNIGHT | Jimmie Rodgers, Dot 16407 | 5 |
| 67 | 75 | — | — | THE CHRISTMAS SONG | Nat King Cole, Capitol 3561 | 2 |
| 68 | 53 | 56 | 63 | DIDDLE-DE-DUM | Belmonts, Sabina 507 | 6 |
| 69 | 72 | 85 | 95 | ME AND MY SHADOW | Frank Sinatra & Sammy Davis Jr., Reprise 20128 | 4 |
| 70 | 62 | 68 | 80 | DON'T GO NEAR THE ESKIMOS | Ben Colder, MGM 13104 | 5 |
| 71 | 73 | 79 | 82 | I MAY NOT LIVE TO SEE TOMORROW | Brian Hyland, ABC-Paramount 10374 | 5 |
| 72 | 81 | 84 | — | THE BALLAD OF JED CLAMPETT △ | Lester Flatt & Earl Scruggs, Columbia 42606 | 3 |
| 73 | 74 | 86 | 92 | GONNA RAISE A RUCKUS TONIGHT △ | Jimmy Dean, Columbia 42600 | 4 |
| 74 | 76 | 90 | 91 | STRANGE I KNOW | Marvelettes, Tamla 54072 | 4 |
| ★75 | 94 | — | — | REMEMBER THEN | Earls, Old Town 1130 | 2 |
| 76 | 79 | 87 | — | YOU'VE REALLY GOT A HOLD ON ME | Miracles, Tamla 54073 | 3 |
| 77 | 83 | — | — | YOU'RE GONNA NEED ME | Barbara Lynn, Jamie 1240 | 2 |
| 78 | 80 | 81 | — | MY WIFE CAN'T COOK | Lonnie Russ, 4 J 501 | 3 |
| 79 | 65 | 71 | 83 | ROAD HOG △ | John D. Loudermilk, RCA Victor 8101 | 4 |
| ★80 | — | — | — | LOOP DE LOOP | Johnny Thunder, Diamond 129 | 1 |
| ★81 | 99 | — | — | RUDOLPH, THE RED-NOSED REINDEER | David Seville & the Chipmunks, Liberty 55289 | 2 |
| ★82 | — | — | — | LOVESICK BLUES | Frank Ifield, Vee Jay 477 | 1 |
| 83 | 85 | — | — | SHE'S A TROUBLEMAKER | Majors, Imperial 5879 | 3 |
| ★84 | — | — | — | SHAKE SHERRY | Contours, Gordy 7012 | 1 |
| 85 | 91 | 94 | — | CAST YOUR FATE TO THE WIND | Vince Guaraldi Trio, Fantasy 563 | 3 |
| 86 | 88 | — | 96 | ECHO | Emotions, Kapp 490 | 3 |
| ★87 | — | — | — | ALVIN'S HARMONICA | David Seville & the Chipmunks, Liberty 55250 | 1 |
| ★88 | — | — | — | WHITE CHRISTMAS | Drifters, Atlantic 1048 | 1 |
| ★89 | — | — | — | MY COLORING BOOK △ | Kitty Kallen, RCA Victor 8124 | 1 |
| ★90 | — | — | — | JELLY BREAD | Booker T & the MG's, Stax 131 | 1 |
| 91 | 93 | — | — | TROUBLE IN MIND △ | Aretha Franklin, Columbia 42625 | 2 |
| 92 | 97 | — | — | JINGLE BELL ROCK | Bobby Rydell/Chubby Checker, Cameo 205 | 2 |
| 93 | 95 | 97 | — | THREE HEARTS IN A TANGLE | James Brown & the Famous Flames, King 5701 | 3 |
| 94 | 86 | 96 | — | TWILIGHT TIME | Andy Williams, Cadence 1433 | 3 |
| 95 | — | — | — | SAM'S SONG | Dean Martin & Sammy Davis Jr., Reprise 20128 | 1 |
| 96 | — | — | — | MOLLY | Bobby Goldsboro, Laurie 3148 | 1 |
| 97 | — | — | — | LITTLE TOWN FLIRT | Del Shannon, Big Top 3131 | 1 |
| 98 | — | — | — | DOES HE MEAN THAT MUCH TO YOU? △ | Eddy Arnold, RCA Victor 8102 | 1 |
| 99 | — | — | — | THE (BOSSA NOVA) BIRD | Dells, Argo 5428 | 1 |
| 100 | — | — | — | I NEED YOU | Rick Nelson, Imperial 5901 | 1 |

## HOT 100—A TO Z—(Publisher-Licensee)


All Alone Am I (Duchess, BMI) .... 26
Alvin's Harmonica (Monarch, ASCAP) .... 87
Ballad of Jed Clampett (Carolintone, BMI) .... 72
Big Girls Don't Cry (Bobob, ASCAP) .... 5
Bobby's Girl (A. M. E., BMI) .... 4
(Bossa Nova) Bird, The (Chevis, BMI) .... 99
Cast Your Fate to the Wind (Friendship, BMI) .... 85
Cha-Cha-Cha, The (Fajob-Kalmann, ASCAP) .... 52
Chains (Aldon, BMI) .... 20
Chipmunk Song, The (Monarch, ASCAP) .... 47
Christmas Song, The (Morris, ASCAP) .... 67
Comin' Home Baby (Melotone, BMI) .... 39
Coney Island Baby (Original, BMI) .... 58
(Dance With the) Guitar Man (Linduane, BMI) .... 21
Dear Lonely Hearts (Sweco-Cetra, BMI) .... 15
Desafinado (Hollis-Bendig, BMI) .... 32
Diddle-De-Dum (Glenden, ASCAP) .... 68
Does He Mean That Much to You? (Ross Jungnickel, ASCAP) .... 98
Don't Go Near the Eskimos (Buttercup, BMI) .... 70
Don't Hang Up (Kalmann, ASCAP) .... 6
Don't Make Me Over (Bacharach-Jac, ASCAP) .... 50
Echo (Spare-Rib, BMI) .... 86
Eso Beso (Flanka, ASCAP) .... 36
Everybody Loves a Lover (Korwin, ASCAP) .... 28
Go Away Little Girl (Aldon, BMI) .... 7
Gonna Raise a Ruckus Tonight (Plainview, BMI) .... 73
Half Heaven—Half Heartache (Arch, ASCAP) .... 56
He's a Rebel (January, BMI) .... 30
Hotel Happiness (Dayben-Mansion, ASCAP) .... 14
I Can't Help It (Acuff-Rose, BMI) .... 54
I Left My Heart in San Francisco (General ASCAP) .... 57
I May Not Live to See Tomorrow (Pogo, ASCAP) .... 71
I Need You (Hilliard, BMI) .... 100
I Saw Linda Yesterday (Jack, BMI) .... 42
I'm Gonna Be Warm This Winter (Merna, BMI) .... 65
It's Up to You (Four Star, BMI) .... 45
Jelly Bread (East, BMI) .... 90
Jingle Bell Rock—Helms (Cornell, ASCAP) .... 59
Jingle Bell Rock—Rydell-Checker (Cornell, ASCAP) .... 92
Keep Your Hands Off My Baby (Aldon, BMI) .... 12
Let's Go (Wrist-Giant, BMI) .... 19
Let's Kiss and Make Up (Trio, BMI) .... 43
Limbo Rock (Four Star-Twist, BMI) .... 2
Little Bit Now, A (Travis-Rittenhouse, BMI) .... 63
Little Drummer Boy (Delaware-Mills, ASCAP) .... 33
Little Town Flirt (Vicki-McLaughlin, BMI) .... 97
Lonely Bull, The (Almo, ASCAP) .... 11
Loop De Loop (Tobi-Ann & Vann, BMI) .... 80
Love Came to Me (Schwartz-Disal, ASCAP) .... 10
Love of a Boy, The (U. S. Songs, ASCAP) .... 61
Lovesick Blues (Mills, ASCAP) .... 82
Me & My Shadow (Bourne, ASCAP) .... 69
Molly (Aldon, BMI) .... 96
Monsters' Holiday (Garpax-Underwood, BMI) .... 40
My Coloring Book (Sunbeam, BMI) .... 89
My Dad (Aldon, BMI) .... 27
My Own True Love (Remick, ASCAP) .... 44
My Wife Can't Cook (Lajesse, BMI) .... 78
Night Has a Thousand Eyes, The (Blen-Mabs, ASCAP) .... 35
Pepino the Italian Mouse (Romance-Ding Dong, BMI) .... 23
Push and Kick, The (Claridge, ASCAP) .... 37
Rainbow at Midnight (Shapiro-Bernstein, ASCAP) .... 66
Release Me (Four Star, BMI) .... 8
Remember Then (Maureen, BMI) .... 75
Return to Sender (Presley, BMI) .... 3
Ride! (Woodcrest-Check-Colt, BMI) .... 13
Road Hog (Acuff-Rose, BMI) .... 79
Rockin' Around the Christmas Tree (St. Nicholas, ASCAP) .... 64
Ruby Ann (Marizona, BMI) .... 18
Rudolph, the Red-Nosed Reindeer (St. Nicholas, ASCAP) .... 81
Rumors (Aldon, BMI) .... 17
Sam's Song (Weiss, ASCAP) .... 95
Santa Claus Is Coming to Town (Feist, ASCAP) .... 34
Santa Claus Is Watching You (Lowery, BMI) .... 55
See See Rider (Cotillion, BMI) .... 48
Shake Sherry (Jobete, BMI) .... 84
She's a Troublemaker (Travis-Rittenhouse, BMI) .... 83
Shutters and Boards (Camp & Canyon, BMI) .... 38
Some Kinda Fun (Rondell, BMI) .... 60
Spanish Lace (St. Louis, BMI) .... 31
Strange I Know (Jobete, BMI) .... 74
Tell Him (Mellin, BMI) .... 22
Telstar (Campbell Connelly, ASCAP) .... 1
Ten Little Indians (Sea of Tunes, BMI) .... 53
That's Life (Mary Hill-Missile, BMI) .... 51
Three Hearts in a Tangle (Sonlo, BMI) .... 93
Trouble in Mind (Leeds, ASCAP) .... 91
Trouble Is My Middle Name (January, BMI) .... 62
Twilight Time (Porgie, BMI) .... 94
Two Lovers (Jobete, BMI) .... 25
Up on the Roof (Aldon, BMI) .... 41
White Christmas—Crosby (Berlin, ASCAP) .... 46
White Christmas—Drifters (Berlin, ASCAP) .... 88
Wiggle Wobble (Bob-Dan, BMI) .... 24
You Are My Sunshine (Peer Int'l, BMI) .... 9
You Threw a Lucky Punch (Jobete, BMI) .... 49
You're Gonna Need Me (Dandelion-Crazy Cajun, BMI) .... 77
You've Really Got a Hold on Me (Jobete, BMI) .... 76
Your Cheating Heart (Fred Rose, BMI) .... 29
Zip-A-Dee-Doo-Dah (Joy, ASCAP) .... 16


## BUBBLING UNDER THE HOT 100

101. MY MAN—HE'S A LOVIN' MAN .... Betty Lavett, Atlantic 2160
102. HUSH HEART .... Baby Washington, Sue 769
103. I FOUND A NEW BABY .... Bobby Darin, Atco 6244
104. BIG GIRLS DON'T CRY LIMBO .... David Carroll, Mercury 72070
105. END OF THE WORLD .... Skeeter Davis, RCA Victor 8098
106. DESAFINADO .... Pat Thomas, MGM 13102
107. BIG BOAT .... Peter, Paul & Mary, Warner Bros. 5325
108. PLEASE COME HOME FOR CHRISTMAS .... Charles Brown, King 5405
109. DESAFINADO .... Ella Fitzgerald, Verve 10274
110. 2,000 POUND BEE .... Ventures, Dolton 67
111. MY COLORING BOOK .... Sandy Stewart, Colpix 669
112. WOULD IT MAKE ANY DIFFERENCE TO YOU .... Etta James, Argo 5430
113. BABY'S FIRST CHRISTMAS .... Connie Francis, MGM 13051
114. THERE'LL BE NO TEARDROPS TONIGHT .... Adam Wade, Epic 9557
115. THEME FROM TARAS BULBA (The Wishing Star) .... Jerry Butler, Vee Jay 475
116. STILL WATERS RUN DEEP .... Brook Benton, Mercury 72055
117. FROM THE BOTTOM OF MY HEART (Dammi, Dammi, Dammi) .... Dean Martin, Reprise 20116
118. FROM A JACK TO A KING .... Ned Miller, Fabor 114
119. WILD WEEKEND .... Rebels, Swan 4126
120. OO-LA-LA-LIMBO .... Danny & the Juniors, Guyden 2076
121. MINSTREL & QUEEN .... Impressions, ABC-Paramount 10357
122. FLY ME TO THE MOON—BOSSA NOVA .... Joe Harnell & His Ork, Kapp 497
123. LET ME GO THE RIGHT WAY .... Supremes, Motown 1034
124. SHAKE ME I RATTLE (Squeeze Me I Cry) .... Marion Worth, Columbia 42640
125. NIGHT TIME .... Pete Antell, Cameo 234
126. LITTLE TIN SOLDIER .... Toy Dolls, Era 3093
127. CINNAMON CINDER .... Pastel Six, Zen 102
128. DARKEST STREET IN TOWN .... Jimmy Clanton, Ace 8005
129. I'M SO LONESOME I COULD CRY .... Johnny Tillotson, Cadence 1432
130. LOVER COME BACK TO ME .... Cleftones, Gee 1079

# BILLBOARD HOT 100

FOR WEEK ENDING DECEMBER 29

1962

★ STAR PERFORMERS—Selections registering greatest upward progress this week.

S Indicates that 45 r.p.m. stereo single version is available.

△ Indicates that 33⅓ r.p.m. mono single version is available.

△S Indicates that 33⅓ r.p.m. stereo single version is available.

| THIS WEEK | 1 Wk. Ago | 2 Wks. Ago | 3 Wks. Ago | TITLE — Artist, Label & Number | Weeks On Chart |
|---|---|---|---|---|---|
| 1 | 1 | 5 | 7 | TELSTAR — Tornadoes, London 9561 | 9 |
| 2 | 2 | 4 | 8 | LIMBO ROCK — Chubby Checker, Parkway 849 | 17 |
| 3 | 4 | 3 | 3 | BOBBY'S GIRL — Marcie Blane, Seville 120 | 11 |
| 4 | 7 | 10 | 20 | GO AWAY LITTLE GIRL △ — Steve Lawrence, Columbia 42601 | 8 |
| 5 | 5 | 1 | 1 | BIG GIRLS DON'T CRY — Four Seasons, Vee Jay 465 | 11 |
| 6 | 3 | 2 | 2 | RETURN TO SENDER △ — Elvis Presley, RCA Victor 8100 | 11 |
| 7 | 9 | 11 | 22 | YOU ARE MY SUNSHINE — Ray Charles, ABC-Paramount 10375 | 7 |
| 8 | 8 | 9 | 10 | RELEASE ME — "Little Esther" Phillips, Lenox 5555 | 10 |
| ★ 9 | 16 | 25 | 30 | ZIP-A-DEE-DOO-DAH — Bob B. Soxx & the Blue Jeans, Philles 107 | 7 |
| 10 | 14 | 15 | 24 | HOTEL HAPPINESS — Brook Benton, Mercury 72055 | 6 |
| ★ 11 | 23 | 37 | 72 | PEPINO THE ITALIAN MOUSE — Lou Monte, Reprise 20106 | 4 |
| 12 | 12 | 13 | 16 | KEEP YOUR HANDS OFF MY BABY — Little Eva, Dimension 1003 | 9 |
| 13 | 15 | 17 | 25 | DEAR LONELY HEARTS — Nat King Cole, Capitol 4870 | 8 |
| ★ 14 | 22 | 35 | 55 | TELL HIM — Exciters, United Artists 544 | 5 |
| 15 | 11 | 7 | 6 | THE LONELY BULL — Tijuana Brass, A. & M. 703 | 10 |
| 16 | 6 | 6 | 4 | DON'T HANG UP — Orlons, Cameo 231 | 12 |
| 17 | 20 | 22 | 29 | CHAINS — Cookies, Dimension 1002 | 8 |
| 18 | 10 | 14 | 14 | LOVE CAME TO ME — Dion, Laurie 3145 | 8 |
| ★ 19 | 25 | 33 | 43 | TWO LOVERS — Mary Wells, Motown 1035 | 5 |
| ★ 20 | 27 | 32 | 45 | MY DAD — Paul Petersen, Colpix 663 | 7 |
| ★ 21 | 35 | 42 | 70 | THE NIGHT HAS A THOUSAND EYES — Bobby Vee, Liberty 55521 | 4 |
| 22 | 18 | 23 | 31 | RUBY ANN △ — Marty Robbins, Columbia 42614 | 7 |
| ★ 23 | 34 | 56 | — | SANTA CLAUS IS COMING TO TOWN — Four Seasons, Vee Jay 478 | 3 |
| 24 | 24 | 28 | 26 | WIGGLE WOBBLE — Les Cooper, Everlast 5019 | 11 |
| 25 | 13 | 8 | 5 | RIDE! — Dee Dee Sharp, Cameo 230 | 11 |
| 26 | 17 | 12 | 15 | RUMORS — Johnny Crawford, Del-Fi 4188 | 9 |
| 27 | 28 | 36 | 53 | EVERYBODY LOVES A LOVER — Shirelles, Scepter 1243 | 5 |
| 28 | 33 | 38 | 66 | LITTLE DRUMMER BOY — Harry Simeone Chorale, 20th Fox 121 | 4 |
| ★ 29 | 41 | 45 | 58 | UP ON THE ROOF — Drifters, Atlantic 2162 | 9 |
| ★ 30 | 45 | 58 | — | IT'S UP TO YOU — Rick Nelson, Imperial 5901 | 3 |
| 31 | 40 | 57 | 80 | MONSTERS' HOLIDAY — Bobby (Boris) Pickett & the Crypt Kickers, Garpax 44171 | 4 |
| 32 | 29 | 30 | 35 | YOUR CHEATING HEART — Ray Charles, ABC-Paramount 10375 | 7 |
| 33 | 21 | 16 | 12 | (DANCE WITH THE) GUITAR MAN △ — Duane Eddy, RCA Victor 8087 | 13 |
| 34 | 38 | 41 | 52 | SHUTTERS AND BOARDS — Jerry Wallace, Challenge 9171 | 7 |
| 35 | 19 | 20 | 23 | LET'S GO — Routers, Warner Bros. 5283 | 9 |
| 36 | 39 | 40 | 49 | COMIN' HOME BABY — Mel Torme, Atlantic 2165 | 9 |
| 37 | 32 | 24 | 18 | DESAFINADO — Stan Getz and Charlie Byrd, Verve 10260 | 14 |
| 38 | 46 | 70 | — | WHITE CHRISTMAS — Bing Crosby, Decca 23778 | 3 |
| 39 | 42 | 49 | 74 | I SAW LINDA YESTERDAY — Dickey Lee, Smash 1791 | 4 |
| 40 | 47 | 59 | 92 | THE CHIPMUNK SONG — David Seville & the Chipmunks, Liberty 55250 | 4 |
| 41 | 37 | 27 | 33 | THE PUSH AND KICK — Mark Valentino, Swan 4121 | 8 |
| 42 | 43 | 47 | 65 | LET'S KISS AND MAKE UP — Bobby Vinton, Epic 9561 | 5 |
| ★ 43 | 56 | 84 | — | HALF HEAVEN—HALF HEARTACHE — Gene Pitney, Musicor 1026 | 3 |
| 44 | 48 | 55 | 73 | SEE SEE RIDER — LaVern Baker, Atlantic 2167 | 5 |
| ★ 45 | 55 | 77 | — | SANTA CLAUS IS WATCHING YOU — Ray Stevens, Mercury 72058 | 3 |
| 46 | 50 | 61 | 78 | DON'T MAKE ME OVER — Dionne Warwick, Scepter 1239 | 4 |
| 47 | 30 | 19 | 11 | HE'S A REBEL — Crystals, Philles 106 | 17 |
| 48 | 31 | 31 | 44 | SPANISH LACE — Gene McDaniels, Liberty 55510 | 8 |
| ★ 49 | 62 | 68 | 76 | TROUBLE IS MY MIDDLE NAME — Bobby Vinton, Epic 9561 | 4 |
| 50 | 53 | 51 | 63 | TEN LITTLE INDIANS — Beach Boys, Capitol 4880 | 5 |
| ★ 51 | 65 | 82 | — | I'M GONNA BE WARM THIS WINTER — Connie Francis, MGM 13116 | 3 |
| 52 | 60 | 71 | 88 | SOME KINDA FUN — Chris Montez, Monogram 507 | 4 |
| 53 | 61 | 67 | 77 | THE LOVE OF A BOY — Timi Yuro, Liberty 55519 | 5 |
| 54 | 49 | 52 | 57 | YOU THREW A LUCKY PUNCH — Gene (Duke of Earl) Chandler, Vee Jay 468 | 6 |
| 55 | 58 | 60 | 75 | CONEY ISLAND BABY — Excellents, Blast 205 | 6 |
| 56 | 59 | 87 | 99 | JINGLE BELL ROCK — Bobby Helms, Decca 30513 | 4 |
| 57 | 26 | 18 | 9 | ALL ALONE AM I — Brenda Lee, Decca 31424 | 14 |
| ★ 58 | 75 | 94 | — | REMEMBER THEN — Earls, Old Town 1130 | 3 |
| 59 | 64 | 89 | — | ROCKIN' AROUND THE CHRISTMAS TREE — Brenda Lee, Decca 20777 | 3 |
| 60 | 51 | 54 | 60 | THAT'S LIFE — Gabriel & the Angels, Swan 4118 | 8 |
| ★ 61 | 80 | — | — | LOOP DE LOOP — Johnny Thunder, Diamond 129 | 2 |
| 62 | 66 | 66 | 69 | RAINBOW AT MIDNIGHT — Jimmie Rodgers, Dot 16407 | 6 |
| 63 | 57 | 46 | 50 | I LEFT MY HEART IN SAN FRANCISCO △ — Tony Bennett, Columbia 42332 | 21 |
| 64 | 69 | 72 | 85 | ME AND MY SHADOW — Frank Sinatra & Sammy Davis Jr., Reprise 20128 | 5 |
| 65 | 67 | 75 | — | THE CHRISTMAS SONG — Nat King Cole, Capitol 3561 | 3 |
| 66 | 70 | 62 | 68 | DON'T GO NEAR THE ESKIMOS — Ben Colder, MGM 13104 | 6 |
| ★ 67 | 89 | — | — | MY COLORING BOOK △ — Kitty Kallen, RCA Victor 8124 | 2 |
| 68 | 72 | 81 | 84 | THE BALLAD OF JED CLAMPETT △ — Lester Flatt & Earl Scruggs, Columbia 42606 | 4 |
| 69 | 76 | 79 | 87 | YOU'VE REALLY GOT A HOLD ON ME — Miracles, Tamla 54073 | 4 |
| 70 | 71 | 73 | 79 | I MAY NOT LIVE TO SEE TOMORROW — Brian Hyland, ABC-Paramount 10374 | 6 |
| 71 | 84 | — | — | SHAKE SHERRY — Contours, Gordy 7012 | 2 |
| 72 | 74 | 76 | 90 | STRANGE I KNOW — Marvelettes, Tamla 54072 | 5 |
| 73 | 82 | — | — | LOVESICK BLUES — Frank Ifield, Vee Jay 477 | 2 |
| 74 | 78 | 80 | 81 | MY WIFE CAN'T COOK — Lonnie Russ, 4 J 501 | 4 |
| 75 | 85 | 91 | 94 | CAST YOUR FATE TO THE WIND — Vince Guaraldi Trio, Fantasy 563 | 4 |
| 76 | 77 | 83 | — | YOU'RE GONNA NEED ME — Barbara Lynn, Jamie 1240 | 3 |
| 77 | 81 | 99 | — | RUDOLPH, THE RED-NOSED REINDEER — David Seville & the Chipmunks, Liberty 55289 | 3 |
| 78 | 73 | 74 | 86 | GONNA RAISE A RUCKUS TONIGHT △ — Jimmy Dean, Columbia 42600 | 5 |
| ★ 79 | — | — | — | CINNAMON CINDER — Pastel Six, Zen 102 | 1 |
| ★ 80 | — | — | — | MY COLORING BOOK — Sandy Stewart, Colpix 669 | 1 |
| ★ 81 | 97 | — | — | LITTLE TOWN FLIRT — Del Shannon, Big Top 3131 | 2 |
| 82 | 86 | 88 | — | ECHO — Emotions, Kapp 490 | 4 |
| ★ 83 | — | — | — | FROM A JACK TO A KING — Ned Miller, Fabor 114 | 1 |
| ★ 84 | — | — | — | WILD WEEKEND — Rebels, Swan 4125 | 1 |
| 85 | 96 | — | — | MOLLY — Bobby Goldsboro, Laurie 3148 | 2 |
| ★ 86 | — | — | — | JAVA △ — Floyd Cramer, RCA Victor 8116 | 1 |
| 87 | 100 | — | — | I NEED YOU — Rick Nelson, Imperial 5901 | 2 |
| 88 | 91 | 93 | — | TROUBLE IN MIND △ — Aretha Franklin, Columbia 42625 | 3 |
| ★ 89 | — | — | — | LITTLE TIN SOLDIER — Toy Dolls, Era 3093 | 1 |
| ★ 90 | — | — | — | SHAKE ME I RATTLE (Squeeze Me I Cry) △ — Marion Worth, Columbia 42640 | 1 |
| 91 | — | — | — | FLY ME TO THE MOON—BOSSA NOVA — Joe Harnell & Ork, Kapp 497 | 1 |
| 92 | — | — | — | THE 2,000 POUND BEE — Ventures, Dolton 67 | 1 |
| 93 | — | — | — | HE'S SURE THE BOY I LOVE — Crystals, Philles 109 | 1 |
| 94 | 95 | — | — | SAM'S SONG — Dean Martin & Sammy Davis Jr., Reprise 20128 | 2 |
| 95 | — | — | — | LOVER COME BACK TO ME — Cleftones, Gee 1079 | 1 |
| 96 | — | — | — | HEY PAULA — Paul & Paula, Philips 40084 | 1 |
| 97 | 99 | — | — | THE (BOSSA NOVA) BIRD — Dells, Argo 5428 | 2 |
| 98 | — | — | — | WHAT TO DO WITH LAURIE — Mike Clifford, United Artists 557 | 1 |
| 99 | — | — | — | SILENT NIGHT — Mahalia Jackson, Apollo 750 | 1 |
| 100 | — | — | — | POPEYE WADDLE — Don Covay, Cameo 239 | 1 |

## HOT 100—A TO Z—(Publisher-Licensee)

All Alone Am I (Duchess, BMI) .......... 57
Ballad of Jed Clampett (Carolintone, BMI) .......... 68
Big Girls Don't Cry (Bobob, ASCAP) .......... 5
Bobby's Girl (A.M.E., BMI) .......... 3
(Bossa Nova) Bird, The (Chevis, BMI) .......... 97
Cast Your Fate to the Wind (Friendship, BMI) .......... 75
Chains (Aldon, BMI) .......... 17
Chipmunk Song, The (Monarch, ASCAP) .......... 40
Christmas Song, The (Morris, ASCAP) .......... 65
Cinnamon Cinder (Algrace, BMI) .......... 79
Comin' Home Baby (Melotone, BMI) .......... 36
Coney Island Baby (Original, BMI) .......... 55
(Dance With the) Guitar Man (Linduane, BMI) .......... 33
Dear Lonely Hearts (Sweco-Cetra, BMI) .......... 13
Desafinado (Hollis-Bendig, BMI) .......... 37
Don't Go Near the Eskimos (Buttercup, BMI) .......... 66
Don't Hang Up (Kalmann, ASCAP) .......... 16
Don't Make Me Over (Bacharach-Jac, ASCAP) .......... 46
Echo (Spare-Rib, BMI) .......... 82
Everybody Loves a Lover (Korwin, ASCAP) .......... 27
Fly Me to the Moon—Bossa Nova (Almanac, ASCAP) .......... 91
From a Jack to a King (Dandelion, BMI) .......... 83
Go Away Little Girl (Aldon, BMI) .......... 4
Gonna Raise a Ruckus Tonight (Plainview, BMI) .......... 78
Half Heaven-Half Heartache (Arch, ASCAP) .......... 43
He's a Rebel (January, BMI) .......... 47
He's Sure the Boy I Love (Aldon, BMI) .......... 93
Hey Paula (LeBill-Marbill, BMI) .......... 96
Hotel Happiness (Dayben-Mansion, ASCAP) .......... 10
I Left My Heart in San Francisco (General, ASCAP) 63
I May Not Live to See Tomorrow (Pogo, ASCAP) .......... 70
I Need You (Hilliard, BMI) .......... 87
I Saw Linda Yesterday (Jack, BMI) .......... 39
I'm Gonna Be Warm This Winter (Merna, BMI) .......... 51
It's Up to You (Four Star, BMI) .......... 30
Java (Rush, BMI) .......... 86
Jingle Bell Rock—Helms (Cornell, ASCAP) .......... 56
Keep Your Hands Off My Baby (Aldon, BMI) .......... 12
Let's Go (Wrist-Giant, BMI) .......... 35
Let's Kiss and Make Up (Trio, BMI) .......... 42
Limbo Rock (Four Star-Twist, BMI) .......... 2
Little Drummer Boy (Delaware-Mills, ASCAP) .......... 28
Little Tin Soldier (Pattern, ASCAP) .......... 89
Little Town Flirt (Vicki-McLaughlin, BMI) .......... 81
Lonely Bull, The (Almo, ASCAP) .......... 15
Loop De Loop (Tobi-Ann & Vann, BMI) .......... 61
Love Came to Me (Schwartz-Disal, ASCAP) .......... 18
Love of a Boy, The (U. S. Songs, ASCAP) .......... 53
Lover Come Back to Me (Harms, ASCAP) .......... 95
Lovesick Blues (Mills, ASCAP) .......... 73
Me & My Shadow (Bourne, ASCAP) .......... 64
Molly (Aldon, BMI) .......... 85
Monsters' Holiday (Garpax-Underwood, BMI) .......... 31
My Coloring Book—Kallen (Sunbeam, BMI) .......... 67
My Coloring Book—Stewart (Sunbeam, BMI) .......... 80
My Dad (Aldon, BMI) .......... 20
My Wife Can't Cook (Lajesse, BMI) .......... 74
Night Has a Thousand Eyes, The (Blen-Mabs, ASCAP) .......... 21
Pepino the Italian Mouse (Romance-Ding Dong, BMI) .......... 11
Popeye Waddle (Cameo-Parkway-Woodcrest, BMI) ..........100
Push and Kick. The (Claridge, ASCAP) .......... 41
Rainbow at Midnight (Shapiro-Bernstein, ASCAP) .......... 62
Release Me (Four Star, BMI) .......... 8
Remember Then (Maureen, BMI) .......... 58
Return to Sender (Presley, BMI) .......... 6
Ride! (Woodcrest-Check-Colt, BMI) .......... 25
Rockin' Around the Christmas Tree (St. Nicholas, ASCAP) .......... 59
Ruby Ann (Marizona, BMI) .......... 22
Rudolph, the Red-Nosed Reindeer (St. Nicholas, ASCAP) .......... 77
Rumors (Aldon, BMI) .......... 26
Sam's Song (Weiss, ASCAP) .......... 94
Santa Claus Is Coming to Town (Feist, ASCAP) .......... 23
Santa Claus Is Watching You (Lowery, BMI) .......... 45
See See Rider (Cotillion, BMI) .......... 44
Shake Me I Rattle (Squeeze Me I Cry) (Coliseum, BMI) .......... 90
Shake Sherry (Jobete, BMI) .......... 71
Shutters and Boards (Camp & Canyon, BMI) .......... 34
Silent Night (Public Domain) .......... 99
Some Kinda Fun (Rondell, BMI) .......... 52
Spanish Lace (St. Louis, BMI) .......... 48
Strange I Know (Jobete, BMI) .......... 72
Tell Him (Mellin, BMI) .......... 14
Telstar (Campbell Connelly, ASCAP) .......... 1
Ten Little Indians (Sea of Tunes, BMI) .......... 50
That's Life (Mary Hill-Missile, BMI) .......... 60
Trouble in Mind (Leeds, ASCAP) .......... 88
Trouble Is My Middle Name (January, BMI) .......... 49
Two Lovers (Jobete, BMI) .......... 19
2,000 Pound Bee, The (Electron, BMI) .......... 92
Up on the Roof (Aldon, BMI) .......... 29
What to Do With Laurie (Trio, BMI) .......... 98
White Christmas—Crosby (Berlin, ASCAP) .......... 38
Wiggle Wobble (Bob-Dan, BMI) .......... 24
Wild Weekend (Shan-Todd, BMI) .......... 84
You Are My Sunshine (Peer Int'l, BMI) .......... 7
You Threw a Lucky Punch (Jobete, BMI) .......... 54
You're Gonna Need Me (Dandelion-Crazy Cajun, BMI) .......... 76
You've Really Got a Hold on Me (Jobete, BMI) .......... 69
Your Cheating Heart (Fred Rose, BMI) .......... 32
Zip-A-Dee-Doo-Dah (Joy, ASCAP) .......... 9

## BUBBLING UNDER THE HOT 100

101. FROM THE BOTTOM OF MY HEART (Dammi, Dammi, Dammi) .......... Dean Martin, Reprise 20116
102. BIG GIRLS DON'T CRY LIMBO .......... David Carroll, Mercury 72070
103. SAILOR BOY .......... Cathy Carr, Laurie 3147
104. THERE'LL BE NO TEARDROPS TONIGHT .......... Adam Wade, Epic 957
105. LET ME GO THE RIGHT WAY .......... Supremes, Motown 1034
106. STILL WATERS RUN DEEP .......... Brook Benton, Mercury 72055
107. NIGHT TIME .......... Pete Antell, Cameo 234
108. CHICKEN FEED .......... Bent Fabric, Atco 6245
109. LET THE FOUR WINDS BLOW .......... Sandy Nelson, Imperial 5904
110. JELLY BREAD .......... Booker T & the MG's, Stax 131
111. MY MAN—HE'S A LOVIN' MAN .......... Betty Lavett, Atlantic 2160
112. THEME FROM TARAS-BULBA (The Wishing Star) .. Jerry Butler, Vee Jay 475
113. BIG BOAT .......... Peter, Paul and Mary, Warner Bros. 5325
114. KENTUCKY MEANS PARADISE .......... Glen Campbell & Green River Boys, Capitol 4867
115. RED PEPPER .. Roosevelt Fountain & the Pens of Rhythm, Prince-Adams 447
116. WALK RIGHT IN .......... Rooftop Singers, Vanguard 35017
117. PROUD .......... Johnny Crawford, Del-Fi 4193
118. LITTLE WHITE LIES .......... Kenjolairs, A&M 704
119. COME TO ME .......... Richard (Popcorn) Wylie, Epic 9543

# Billboard HOT 100
**FOR WEEK ENDING JAN. 5 1963**

★ STAR PERFORMERS—Selections registering greatest upward progress this week.
S Indicates that 45 r.p.m. stereo single version is available.
△ Indicates that 33⅓ r.p.m. mono single version is available.
Ⓢ Indicates that 33⅓ r.p.m. stereo single version is available.

| This Week | 1 Wk. Ago | 2 Wks. Ago | 3 Wks. Ago | TITLE, Artist, Label & Number | Weeks On Chart |
|---|---|---|---|---|---|
| 1 | 1 | 1 | 5 | TELSTAR — Tornadoes, London 9561 | 10 |
| 2 | 4 | 7 | 10 | GO AWAY LITTLE GIRL △ — Steve Lawrence, Columbia 42601 | 9 |
| 3 | 2 | 2 | 4 | LIMBO ROCK — Chubby Checker, Parkway 849 | 18 |
| 4 | 3 | 4 | 3 | BOBBY'S GIRL — Marcie Blane, Seville 120 | 12 |
| 5 | 5 | 5 | 1 | BIG GIRLS DON'T CRY — Four Seasons, Vee Jay 465 | 12 |
| ★6 | 10 | 14 | 15 | HOTEL HAPPINESS — Brook Benton, Mercury 72055 | 7 |
| 7 | 11 | 23 | 37 | PEPINO THE ITALIAN MOUSE — Lou Monte, Reprise 20106 | 5 |
| 8 | 6 | 3 | 2 | RETURN TO SENDER △ — Elvis Presley, RCA Victor 8100 | 12 |
| 9 | 9 | 16 | 25 | ZIP-A-DEE-DOO-DAH — Bob B. Soxx & the Blue Jeans, Philles 107 | 8 |
| 10 | 14 | 22 | 35 | TELL HIM — Exciters, United Artists 544 | 6 |
| ★11 | 20 | 27 | 32 | MY DAD — Paul Petersen, Colpix 663 | 8 |
| 12 | 7 | 9 | 11 | YOU ARE MY SUNSHINE — Ray Charles, ABC-Paramount 10375 | 8 |
| 13 | 8 | 8 | 9 | RELEASE ME — "Little Esther" Phillips, Lenox 5555 | 11 |
| ★14 | 21 | 35 | 42 | THE NIGHT HAS A THOUSAND EYES — Bobby Vee, Liberty 55521 | 5 |
| 15 | 19 | 25 | 33 | TWO LOVERS — Mary Wells, Motown 1035 | 6 |
| 16 | 15 | 11 | 7 | THE LONELY BULL — Tijuana Brass, A. & M. 703 | 11 |
| 17 | 13 | 15 | 17 | DEAR LONELY HEARTS — Nat King Cole, Capitol 4870 | 9 |
| 18 | 17 | 20 | 22 | CHAINS — Cookies, Dimension 1002 | 9 |
| 19 | 12 | 12 | 13 | KEEP YOUR HANDS OFF MY BABY — Little Eva, Dimension 1003 | 10 |
| ★20 | 30 | 45 | 58 | IT'S UP TO YOU — Rick Nelson, Imperial 5901 | 4 |
| 21 | 16 | 6 | 6 | DON'T HANG UP — Orlons, Cameo 231 | 13 |
| 22 | 29 | 41 | 45 | UP ON THE ROOF — Drifters, Atlantic 2162 | 10 |
| 23 | 24 | 24 | 28 | WIGGLE WOBBLE — Les Cooper, Everlast 5019 | 12 |
| 24 | 18 | 10 | 14 | LOVE CAME TO ME — Dion, Laurie 3145 | 9 |
| 25 | 39 | 42 | 49 | I SAW LINDA YESTERDAY — Dickey Lee, Smash 1791 | 5 |
| 26 | 27 | 28 | 36 | EVERYBODY LOVES A LOVER — Shirelles, Scepter 1243 | 6 |
| 27 | 22 | 18 | 23 | RUBY ANN △ — Marty Robbins, Columbia 42614 | 8 |
| ★28 | 34 | 38 | 41 | SHUTTERS AND BOARDS — Jerry Wallace, Challenge 9171 | 8 |
| 29 | 43 | 56 | 84 | HALF HEAVEN—HALF HEARTACHE — Gene Pitney, Musicor 1026 | 4 |
| 30 | 31 | 40 | 57 | MONSTERS' HOLIDAY — Bobby (Boris) Pickett & the Crypt Kickers, Garpax 44171 | 5 |
| 31 | 25 | 13 | 8 | RIDE! — Dee Dee Sharp, Cameo 230 | 12 |
| 32 | 46 | 50 | 61 | DON'T MAKE ME OVER — Dionne Warwick, Scepter 1239 | 5 |
| 33 | 33 | 21 | 16 | (DANCE WITH THE) GUITAR MAN △ — Duane Eddy, RCA Victor 8087 | 14 |
| 34 | 49 | 62 | 68 | TROUBLE IS MY MIDDLE NAME — Bobby Vinton, Epic 9561 | 5 |
| 35 | 61 | 80 | — | LOOP DE LOOP — Johnny Thunder, Diamond 129 | 3 |
| 36 | 32 | 29 | 30 | YOUR CHEATING HEART — Ray Charles, ABC-Paramount 10375 | 8 |
| 37 | 44 | 48 | 55 | SEE SEE RIDER — LaVern Baker, Atlantic 2167 | 6 |
| 38 | 26 | 17 | 12 | RUMORS — Johnny Crawford, Del-Fi 4188 | 10 |
| ★39 | 51 | 65 | 82 | I'M GONNA BE WARM THIS WINTER — Connie Francis, MGM 13116 | 4 |
| 40 | 35 | 19 | 20 | LET'S GO — Routers, Warner Bros. 5283 | 8 |
| 41 | 37 | 32 | 24 | DESAFINADO — Stan Getz and Charlie Byrd, Verve 10260 | 15 |
| ★42 | 58 | 75 | 94 | REMEMBER THEN — Earls, Old Town 1130 | 4 |
| 43 | 42 | 43 | 47 | LET'S KISS AND MAKE UP — Bobby Vinton, Epic 9561 | 6 |
| 44 | 52 | 60 | 71 | SOME KINDA FUN — Chris Montez, Monogram 507 | 4 |
| 45 | 36 | 39 | 40 | COMIN' HOME BABY — Mel Torme, Atlantic 2165 | 10 |
| ★46 | 69 | 76 | 79 | YOU'VE REALLY GOT A HOLD ON ME — Miracles, Tamla 54073 | 4 |
| 47 | 53 | 61 | 67 | THE LOVE OF A BOY — Timi Yuro, Liberty 55519 | 6 |
| 48 | 67 | 89 | — | MY COLORING BOOK △ — Kitty Kallen, RCA Victor 8124 | 3 |
| 49 | 50 | 53 | 51 | TEN LITTLE INDIANS — Beach Boys, Capitol 4880 | 6 |
| 50 | 41 | 37 | 27 | THE PUSH AND KICK — Mark Valentino, Swan 4121 | 9 |
| 51 | 55 | 58 | 60 | CONEY ISLAND BABY — Excellents, Blast 205 | 7 |
| 52 | 47 | 30 | 19 | HE'S A REBEL — Crystals, Philles 106 | 18 |
| 53 | 96 | — | — | HEY PAULA — Paul & Paula, Philips 40084 | 2 |
| 54 | 73 | 82 | — | LOVESICK BLUES — Frank Ifield, Vee Jay 477 | 3 |
| 55 | 60 | 51 | 54 | THAT'S LIFE — Gabriel & the Angels, Swan 4118 | 7 |
| ★56 | 68 | 72 | 81 | THE BALLAD OF JED CLAMPETT △ — Lester Flatt & Earl Scruggs, Columbia 42606 | 5 |
| 57 | 74 | 78 | 80 | MY WIFE CAN'T COOK — Lonnie Russ, 4 J 501 | 5 |
| 58 | 80 | — | — | MY COLORING BOOK — Sandy Stewart, Colpix 669 | 2 |
| 59 | 54 | 49 | 52 | YOU THREW A LUCKY PUNCH — Gene (Duke of Earl) Chandler, Vee Jay 468 | 7 |
| 60 | 57 | 26 | 18 | ALL ALONE AM I — Brenda Lee, Decca 31424 | 15 |
| 61 | 72 | 74 | 76 | STRANGE I KNOW — Marvelettes, Tamla 54072 | 6 |
| 62 | 48 | 31 | 31 | SPANISH LACE — Gene McDaniels, Liberty 55510 | 9 |
| 63 | 79 | — | — | CINNAMON CINDER — Pastel Six, Zen 102 | 2 |
| 64 | 86 | — | — | JAVA △ — Floyd Cramer, RCA Victor 8116 | 2 |
| 65 | 76 | 77 | 83 | YOU'RE GONNA NEED ME — Barbara Lynn, Jamie 1240 | 4 |
| 66 | 71 | 84 | — | SHAKE SHERRY — Contours, Gordy 7012 | 3 |
| 67 | 83 | — | — | FROM A JACK TO A KING — Ned Miller, Fabor 114 | 2 |
| 68 | 90 | — | — | SHAKE ME I RATTLE (Squeeze Me I Cry) △ — Marion Worth, Columbia 42640 | 2 |
| 69 | 70 | 71 | 73 | I MAY NOT LIVE TO SEE TOMORROW — Brian Hyland, ABC-Paramount 10374 | 7 |
| 70 | 75 | 85 | 91 | CAST YOUR FATE TO THE WIND — Vince Guaraldi Trio, Fantasy 563 | 5 |
| 71 | — | — | — | WALK RIGHT IN — Rooftop Singers, Vanguard 35017 | 1 |
| 72 | 91 | — | — | FLY ME TO THE MOON—BOSSA NOVA — Joe Harnell & Ork, Kapp 497 | 2 |
| 73 | 64 | 69 | 72 | ME AND MY SHADOW — Frank Sinatra & Sammy Davis Jr., Reprise 20128 | 4 |
| 74 | 93 | — | — | HE'S SURE THE BOY I LOVE — Crystals, Philles 109 | 2 |
| 75 | — | — | — | I'M A WOMAN — Peggy Lee, Capitol 4888 | 1 |
| 76 | 84 | — | — | WILD WEEKEND — Rebels, Swan 4125 | 2 |
| 77 | 62 | 66 | 66 | RAINBOW AT MIDNIGHT — Jimmie Rodgers, Dot 16407 | 5 |
| 78 | 81 | 97 | — | LITTLE TOWN FLIRT — Del Shannon, Big Top 3131 | 3 |
| 79 | — | — | — | CALL ON ME — Bobby Bland, Duke 360 | 1 |
| 80 | 82 | 86 | 88 | ECHO — Emotions, Kapp 490 | 4 |
| 81 | — | — | — | ALL ABOUT MY GIRL — Jimmy McGriff, Sue 777 | 1 |
| 82 | 85 | 96 | — | MOLLY — Bobby Goldsboro, Laurie 3148 | 3 |
| 83 | — | — | — | BOSSA NOVA U.S.A. △ — Dave Brubeck Quartet, Columbia 42651 | 1 |
| 84 | 87 | 100 | — | I NEED YOU — Rick Nelson, Imperial 5901 | 3 |
| 85 | 89 | — | — | LITTLE TIN SOLDIER — Toy Dolls, Era 3093 | 2 |
| 86 | — | — | — | DARKEST STREET IN TOWN — Jimmy Clanton, Ace 8005 | 1 |
| 87 | — | — | — | PROUD — Johnny Crawford, Del-Fi 4193 | 1 |
| 88 | — | — | — | RED PEPPER — Roosevelt Fountain, Prince-Adams 447 | 1 |
| 89 | 78 | 73 | 74 | GONNA RAISE A RUCKUS TONIGHT △ — Jimmy Dean, Columbia 42600 | 6 |
| 90 | — | — | — | AL DI LA — Connie Francis, MGM 13116 | 1 |
| 91 | — | — | — | THE GYPSY CRIED — Lou Christie, Roulette 4457 | 1 |
| 92 | — | — | — | EVERY DAY I HAVE TO CRY — Steve Alaimo, Checker 1032 | 1 |
| 93 | 88 | 91 | 93 | TROUBLE IN MIND △ — Aretha Franklin, Columbia 42625 | 4 |
| 94 | — | — | — | I WILL LIVE MY LIFE FOR YOU △ — Tony Bennett, Columbia 42634 | 1 |
| 95 | — | 90 | — | JELLY BREAD — Booker T & the MG's, Stax 131 | 2 |
| 96 | 94 | 95 | — | SAM'S SONG — Dean Martin & Sammy Davis Jr., Reprise 20128 | 3 |
| 97 | 97 | 99 | — | THE (BOSSA NOVA) BIRD — Dells, Argo 5428 | 3 |
| 98 | — | — | — | MAMA DIDN'T LIE — Jan Bradley, Chess 1845 | 1 |
| 99 | — | — | — | HOW MUCH IS THAT DOGGIE IN THE WINDOW — Baby Jane & the Rockabyes, United Artists 560 | 1 |
| 100 | — | — | 96 | LET ME ENTERTAIN YOU — Ray Anthony, Capitol 4876 | 2 |

## BUBBLING UNDER THE HOT 100

101. LET ME GO THE RIGHT WAY .......... Supremes, Motown 1034
102. WHAT TO DO WITH LAURIE .......... Mike Clifford, United Artists 557
103. SOMEONE, SOMEWHERE .......... Junior Parker, Duke 357
104. NIGHT TIME .......... Pete Antell, Cameo 234
105. BIG BOAT .......... Peter, Paul & Mary, Warner Bros. 5325
106. WOULD IT MAKE ANY DIFFERENCE TO YOU .......... Etta James, Argo 5430
107. LET THE FOUR WINDS BLOW .......... Sandy Nelson, Imperial 5904
108. FROM THE BOTTOM OF MY HEART .......... Dean Martin, Reprise 20116
109. HOW DO YOU TALK TO AN ANGEL .......... Etta James, Argo 5430
110. HITCH HIKE .......... Marvin Gaye, Tamla 54075
111. SAILOR BOY .......... Cathy Carr, Laurie 3147
112. POPEYE WADDLE .......... Don Covay, Cameo 239
113. COME TO ME .......... Richard (Popcorn) Wylie, Epic 9543
114. KENTUCKY MEANS PARADISE .......... Glen Campbell & the Green River Boys, Capitol 4867
115. END OF THE WORLD .......... Skeeter Davis, RCA Victor 8098
116. LITTLE WHITE LIES .......... Kenjolairs, A&M 704
117. RHYTHM OF THE RAIN .......... Cascades, Valiant 6026
118. THAT CERTAIN PARTY .......... Bent Fabric, Atco 6245
119. STILL WATERS RUN DEEP .......... Brook Benton, Mercury 72055
120. CHICKEN FEED .......... Bent Fabric, Atco 6245
121. WHAT GOOD AM I WITHOUT YOU? .......... Jackie Wilson, Brunswick 55236

# Billboard HOT 100

**FOR WEEK ENDING JAN. 12, 1963**

★ STAR PERFORMERS—Selections registering greatest upward progress this week.
S — Indicates that 45 r.p.m. stereo single version is available.
△ — Indicates that 33⅓ r.p.m. mono single version is available.
Ⓢ — Indicates that 33⅓ r.p.m. stereo single version is available.

| This Week | 1 Wk. Ago | 2 Wks. Ago | 3 Wks. Ago | Title — Artist, Label & Number | Weeks On Chart |
|---|---|---|---|---|---|
| 1 | 2 | 4 | 7 | GO AWAY LITTLE GIRL △ — Steve Lawrence, Columbia 42601 | 10 |
| 2 | 1 | 1 | 1 | TELSTAR — Tornadoes, London 9561 | 11 |
| 3 | 3 | 2 | 2 | LIMBO ROCK — Chubby Checker, Parkway 849 | 19 |
| 4 | 6 | 10 | 14 | HOTEL HAPPINESS — Brook Benton, Mercury 72055 | 8 |
| 5 | 7 | 11 | 23 | PEPINO THE ITALIAN MOUSE — Lou Monte, Reprise 20106 | 6 |
| ★6 | 10 | 14 | 22 | TELL HIM — Exciters, United Artists 544 | 7 |
| 7 | 14 | 21 | 35 | THE NIGHT HAS A THOUSAND EYES — Bobby Vee, Liberty 55521 | 6 |
| 8 | 9 | 9 | 16 | ZIP-A-DEE-DOO-DAH — Bob B. Soxx & the Blue Jeans, Philles 107 | 9 |
| ★9 | 15 | 19 | 25 | TWO LOVERS — Mary Wells, Motown 1035 | 7 |
| 10 | 11 | 20 | 27 | MY DAD — Paul Petersen, Colpix 663 | 9 |
| 11 | 5 | 5 | 5 | BIG GIRLS DON'T CRY — Four Seasons, Vee Jay 465 | 13 |
| 12 | 4 | 3 | 4 | BOBBY'S GIRL — Marcie Blane, Seville 120 | 13 |
| 13 | 8 | 6 | 3 | RETURN TO SENDER △ — Elvis Presley, RCA Victor 8100 | 13 |
| 14 | 20 | 30 | 45 | IT'S UP TO YOU — Rick Nelson, Imperial 5901 | 5 |
| 15 | 12 | 7 | 9 | YOU ARE MY SUNSHINE — Ray Charles, ABC-Paramount 10375 | 9 |
| ★16 | 22 | 29 | 41 | UP ON THE ROOF — Drifters, Atlantic 2162 | 11 |
| 17 | 25 | 39 | 42 | I SAW LINDA YESTERDAY — Dickey Lee, Smash 1791 | 6 |
| 18 | 16 | 15 | 11 | THE LONELY BULL — Tijuana Brass, A. & M. 703 | 12 |
| ★19 | 35 | 61 | 80 | LOOP DE LOOP — Johnny Thunder, Diamond 129 | 4 |
| ★20 | 29 | 43 | 56 | HALF HEAVEN—HALF HEARTACHE — Gene Pitney, Musicor 1026 | 5 |
| 21 | 26 | 27 | 28 | EVERYBODY LOVES A LOVER — Shirelles, Scepter 1243 | 7 |
| 22 | 23 | 24 | 24 | WIGGLE WOBBLE — Les Cooper, Everlast 5019 | 13 |
| 23 | 13 | 8 | 8 | RELEASE ME — "Little Esther" Phillips, Lenox 5555 | 12 |
| 24 | 28 | 34 | 38 | SHUTTERS AND BOARDS — Jerry Wallace, Challenge 9171 | 9 |
| 25 | 17 | 13 | 15 | DEAR LONELY HEARTS — Nat King Cole, Capitol 4870 | 10 |
| 26 | 18 | 17 | 20 | CHAINS — Cookies, Dimension 1002 | 10 |
| 27 | 24 | 18 | 10 | LOVE CAME TO ME — Dion, Laurie 3145 | 10 |
| 28 | 32 | 46 | 50 | DON'T MAKE ME OVER — Dionne Warwick, Scepter 1239 | 6 |
| 29 | 19 | 12 | 12 | KEEP YOUR HANDS OFF MY BABY — Little Eva, Dimension 1003 | 11 |
| ★30 | 53 | 96 | — | HEY PAULA — Paul & Paula, Philips 40084 | 3 |
| 31 | 21 | 16 | 6 | DON'T HANG UP — Orlons, Cameo 231 | 14 |
| ★32 | 42 | 58 | 75 | REMEMBER THEN — Earls, Old Town 1130 | 5 |
| 33 | 46 | 69 | 76 | YOU'VE REALLY GOT A HOLD ON ME — Miracles, Tamla 54073 | 6 |
| 34 | 34 | 49 | 62 | TROUBLE IS MY MIDDLE NAME — Bobby Vinton, Epic 9561 | 6 |
| ★35 | 71 | — | — | WALK RIGHT IN — Rooftop Singers, Vanguard 35017 | 2 |
| 36 | 37 | 44 | 48 | SEE SEE RIDER — LaVern Baker, Atlantic 2167 | 7 |
| 37 | 39 | 51 | 65 | I'M GONNA BE WARM THIS WINTER — Connie Francis, MGM 13116 | 5 |
| ★38 | 48 | 67 | 89 | MY COLORING BOOK △ — Kitty Kallen, RCA Victor 8124 | 4 |
| 39 | 30 | 31 | 40 | MONSTERS' HOLIDAY — Bobby (Boris) Pickett & the Crypt Kickers, Garpax 44171 | 6 |
| 40 | 43 | 42 | 43 | LET'S KISS AND MAKE UP — Bobby Vinton, Epic 9561 | 7 |
| 41 | 31 | 25 | 13 | RIDE! — Dee Dee Sharp, Cameo 230 | 13 |
| ★42 | 58 | 80 | — | MY COLORING BOOK — Sandy Stewart, Colpix 669 | 3 |
| 43 | 44 | 52 | 60 | SOME KINDA FUN — Chris Montez, Monogram 507 | 6 |
| 44 | 27 | 22 | 18 | RUBY ANN △ — Marty Robbins, Columbia 42614 | 9 |
| 45 | 33 | 33 | 21 | (DANCE WITH THE) GUITAR MAN △ — Duane Eddy, RCA Victor 8087 | 15 |
| 46 | 47 | 53 | 61 | THE LOVE OF A BOY — Timi Yuro, Liberty 55519 | 7 |
| 47 | 36 | 32 | 29 | YOUR CHEATING HEART — Ray Charles, ABC-Paramount 10375 | 9 |
| 48 | 40 | 35 | 19 | LET'S GO — Routers, Warner Bros. 5283 | 11 |
| ★49 | 63 | 79 | — | CINNAMON CINDER — Pastel Six, Zen 102 | 3 |
| 50 | 41 | 37 | 32 | DESAFINADO — Stan Getz and Charlie Byrd, Verve 10260 | 16 |
| ★51 | 67 | 83 | — | FROM A JACK TO A KING — Ned Miller, Fabor 114 | 3 |
| 52 | 54 | 73 | 82 | LOVESICK BLUES — Frank Ifield, Vee Jay 477 | 4 |
| ★53 | 78 | 81 | 97 | LITTLE TOWN FLIRT — Del Shannon, Big Top 3131 | 4 |
| 54 | 56 | 68 | 72 | THE BALLAD OF JED CLAMPETT △ — Lester Flatt & Earl Scruggs, Columbia 42606 | 6 |
| 55 | 51 | 55 | 58 | CONEY ISLAND BABY — Excellents, Blast 205 | 8 |
| 56 | 49 | 50 | 53 | TEN LITTLE INDIANS — Beach Boys, Capitol 4880 | 7 |
| ★57 | 74 | 93 | — | HE'S SURE THE BOY I LOVE — Crystals, Philles 109 | 3 |
| 58 | 55 | 60 | 51 | THAT'S LIFE — Gabriel & the Angels, Swan 4118 | 10 |
| 59 | 61 | 72 | 74 | STRANGE I KNOW — Marvelettes, Tamla 54072 | 7 |
| 60 | 45 | 36 | 39 | COMIN' HOME BABY — Mel Tormé, Atlantic 2165 | 11 |
| 61 | 66 | 71 | 84 | SHAKE SHERRY — Contours, Gordy 7012 | 4 |
| 62 | 64 | 86 | — | JAVA △ — Floyd Cramer, RCA Victor 8116 | 3 |
| 63 | 68 | 90 | — | SHAKE ME I RATTLE (Squeeze Me I Cry) △ — Marion Worth, Columbia 42640 | 3 |
| 64 | 57 | 74 | 78 | MY WIFE CAN'T COOK — Lonnie Russ, 4 J 501 | 6 |
| 65 | 65 | 76 | 77 | YOU'RE GONNA NEED ME — Barbara Lynn, Jamie 1220 | 5 |
| 66 | 72 | 91 | — | FLY ME TO THE MOON—BOSSA NOVA — Joe Harnell & Ork, Kapp 497 | 3 |
| 67 | 76 | 84 | — | WILD WEEKEND — Rebels, Swan 4125 | 3 |
| 68 | 75 | — | — | I'M A WOMAN — Peggy Lee, Capitol 4888 | 2 |
| 69 | 59 | 54 | 49 | YOU THREW A LUCKY PUNCH — Gene (Duke of Earl) Chandler, Vee Jay 468 | 8 |
| 70 | 70 | 75 | 85 | CAST YOUR FATE TO THE WIND — Vince Guaraldi Trio, Fantasy 563 | 6 |
| ★71 | 87 | — | — | PROUD — Johnny Crawford, Del-Fi 4193 | 2 |
| 72 | 81 | — | — | ALL ABOUT MY GIRL — Jimmy McGriff, Sue 777 | 2 |
| 73 | 82 | 85 | 96 | MOLLY — Bobby Goldsboro, Laurie 3148 | 4 |
| 74 | 79 | — | — | CALL ON ME — Bobby Bland, Duke 360 | 2 |
| ★75 | 98 | — | — | MAMA DIDN'T LIE — Jan Bradley, Chess 1845 | 1 |
| 76 | 80 | 82 | 86 | ECHO — Emotions, Kapp 490 | 4 |
| 77 | — | — | — | CHICKEN FEED — Bent Fabric, Atco 6245 | 1 |
| 78 | 88 | — | — | RED PEPPER — Roosevelt Fountain, Prince-Adams 447 | 2 |
| ★79 | — | — | — | WOULD IT MAKE ANY DIFFERENCE TO YOU — Etta James, Argo 5430 | 1 |
| ★80 | — | — | — | RHYTHM OF THE RAIN — Cascades, Valiant 6026 | 1 |
| 81 | 86 | — | — | DARKEST STREET IN TOWN — Jimmy Clanton, Ace 8005 | 2 |
| 82 | 95 | — | 90 | JELLY BREAD — Booker T & the MG's, Stax 131 | 3 |
| 83 | 91 | — | — | THE GYPSY CRIED — Lou Christie, Roulette 4457 | 2 |
| 84 | 92 | — | — | EVERY DAY I HAVE TO CRY — Steve Alaimo, Checker 1032 | 2 |
| 85 | 85 | 89 | — | LITTLE TIN SOLDIER — Toy Dolls, Era 3093 | 3 |
| 86 | 93 | 88 | 91 | TROUBLE IN MIND △ — Aretha Franklin, Columbia 42625 | 5 |
| ★87 | — | 98 | — | WHAT TO DO WITH LAURIE — Mike Clifford, United Artists 557 | 1 |
| 88 | — | — | — | PUDDIN' N' TAIN — Alley Cats, Philles 108 | 1 |
| 89 | — | — | — | WILLIE CAN — Sue Thompson, Hickory 1196 | 1 |
| ★90 | — | — | — | I WANNA BE AROUND △ — Tony Bennett, Columbia 42634 | 1 |
| 91 | — | — | — | LOOK AT ME — Dobie Gray, CorDak 1602 | 1 |
| 92 | 99 | — | — | HOW MUCH IS THAT DOGGIE IN THE WINDOW — Baby Jane & the Rockabyes, United Artists 560 | 2 |
| 93 | — | — | — | BIG BOAT — Peter, Paul & Mary, Warner Bros. 5325 | 2 |
| 94 | 94 | — | — | I WILL LIVE MY LIFE FOR YOU △ — Tony Bennett, Columbia 42634 | 1 |
| 95 | — | — | — | SOMEONE SOMEWHERE — Junior Parker, Duke 357 | 1 |
| 96 | — | — | — | HITCH HIKE — Marvin Gaye, Tamla 54075 | 1 |
| 97 | — | — | — | SLOP TIME — Sherrys, Guyden 2077 | 1 |
| 98 | — | 100 | — | POPEYE WADDLE — Don Covay, Cameo 239 | 2 |
| 99 | — | — | — | LET ME GO THE RIGHT WAY — Supremes, Motown 1034 | 1 |
| 100 | — | — | — | WALK RIGHT IN — Moments, Era 3099 | 1 |

## BUBBLING UNDER THE HOT 100

101. NIGHT TIME — Pete Antell, Cameo 234
102. GO HOME GIRL — Arthur Alexander, Dot 16425
103. THE (Bossa Nova) BIRD — Dells, Argo 5428
104. BIG WIDE WORLD — Teddy Randazzo, Colpix 662
105. END OF THE WORLD — Skeeter Davis, RCA Victor 8098
106. MAMA-OOM-MOW-MOW — Rivingtons, Liberty 55528
107. BLAME IT ON THE BOSSA NOVA — Eydie Gorme, Columbia 42661
108. MAMA DIDN'T LIE — Fascinations, ABC-Paramount 10387
109. COME TO ME — Richard (Popcorn) Wylie, Epic 9543
110. BOSSA NOVA U.S.A. — Dave Brubeck Quartet, Columbia 42651
111. ANONYMOUS PHONE CALL — Bobby Vee, Liberty 55521
112. DON'T TAKE HER FROM ME — Kris Jensen, Hickory 1195
113. OO-LA-LIMBO — Danny & the Juniors, Guyden 2076
114. JOEY'S SONG — Bill Black's Combo, Hi 2059
115. STILL WATERS RUN DEEP — Brook Benton, Mercury 72055
116. LET ME ENTERTAIN YOU — Ray Anthony, Capitol 4876
117. THAT CERTAIN PARTY — Bent Fabric, Atco 6245

# Billboard HOT 100
**FOR WEEK ENDING JAN. 19 1963**

| This Week | Wk Ago | 2 Wks Ago | TITLE — Artist, Label & Number | Weeks On Chart |
|---|---|---|---|---|
| 1 | 1 | 2 | GO AWAY LITTLE GIRL — Steve Lawrence, Columbia 42601 △ | 11 |
| 2 | 2 | 1 | TELSTAR — Tornadoes, London 9561 | 12 |
| 3 | 4 | 6 | HOTEL HAPPINESS — Brook Benton, Mercury 72055 | 9 |
| 4 | 6 | 10 | TELL HIM — Exciters, United Artists 544 | 8 |
| 5 | 7 | 14 | THE NIGHT HAS A THOUSAND EYES — Bobby Vee, Liberty 55521 | 7 |
| 6 | 3 | 3 | LIMBO ROCK — Chubby Checker, Parkway 849 | 20 |
| 7 | 9 | 15 | TWO LOVERS — Mary Wells, Motown 1035 | 8 |
| 8 | 10 | 11 | MY DAD — Paul Petersen, Colpix 663 | 10 |
| 9 | 5 | 7 | PEPINO THE ITALIAN MOUSE — Lou Monte, Reprise 20106 | 7 |
| ★10 | 30 | 53 | HEY PAULA — Paul & Paula, Phillips 40084 | 4 |
| ★11 | 35 | 71 | WALK RIGHT IN — Rooftop Singers, Vanguard 35017 | 3 |
| 12 | 14 | 20 | IT'S UP TO YOU — Rick Nelson, Imperial 5901 | 6 |
| 13 | 16 | 22 | UP ON THE ROOF — Drifters, Atlantic 2162 | 12 |
| 14 | 17 | 25 | I SAW LINDA YESTERDAY — Dickey Lee, Smash 1791 | 7 |
| 15 | 8 | 9 | ZIP-A-DEE-DOO-DAH — Bob B. Soxx & the Blue Jeans, Philles 107 | 10 |
| 16 | 19 | 35 | LOOP DE LOOP — Johnny Thunder, Diamond 129 | 5 |
| 17 | 20 | 29 | HALF HEAVEN—HALF HEARTACHE — Gene Pitney, Musicor 1026 | 6 |
| 18 | 11 | 5 | BIG GIRLS DON'T CRY — Four Seasons, Vee Jay 465 | 14 |
| 19 | 12 | 4 | BOBBY'S GIRL — Marcie Blane, Seville 120 | 14 |
| 20 | 21 | 26 | EVERYBODY LOVES A LOVER — Shirelles, Scepter 1243 | 8 |
| 21 | 13 | 8 | RETURN TO SENDER — Elvis Presley, RCA Victor 8100 △ | 14 |
| 22 | 15 | 12 | YOU ARE MY SUNSHINE — Ray Charles, ABC-Paramount 10375 | 10 |
| ★23 | 37 | 39 | I'M GONNA BE WARM THIS WINTER — Connie Francis, MGM 13116 | 6 |
| 24 | 24 | 28 | SHUTTERS AND BOARDS — Jerry Wallace, Challenge 9171 | 10 |
| ★25 | 32 | 42 | REMEMBER THEN — Earls, Old Town 1130 | 6 |
| 26 | 28 | 32 | DON'T MAKE ME OVER — Dionne Warwick, Scepter 1239 | 7 |
| ★27 | 38 | 48 | MY COLORING BOOK — Kitty Kallen, RCA Victor 8124 △ | 5 |
| ★28 | 33 | 46 | YOU'VE REALLY GOT A HOLD ON ME — Miracles, Tamla 54073 | 7 |
| 29 | 22 | 23 | WIGGLE WOBBLE — Les Cooper, Everlast 5019 | 14 |
| 30 | 18 | 16 | THE LONELY BULL — Tijuana Brass, A. & M. 703 | 13 |
| 31 | 23 | 13 | RELEASE ME — "Little Esther" Phillips, Lenox 5555 | 13 |
| ★32 | 42 | 58 | MY COLORING BOOK — Sandy Stewart, Colpix 669 | 4 |
| 33 | 34 | 34 | TROUBLE IS MY MIDDLE NAME — Bobby Vinton, Epic 9561 | 7 |
| 34 | 36 | 37 | SEE SEE RIDER — LaVern Baker, Atlantic 2167 | 8 |
| 35 | 26 | 18 | CHAINS — Cookies, Dimension 1002 | 11 |
| ★36 | 49 | 63 | CINNAMON CINDER — Pastel Six, Zen 102 | 4 |
| 37 | 27 | 24 | LOVE CAME TO ME — Dion, Laurie 3145 | 11 |
| 38 | 40 | 43 | LET'S KISS AND MAKE UP — Bobby Vinton, Epic 9561 | 8 |
| 39 | 25 | 17 | DEAR LONELY HEARTS — Nat King Cole, Capitol 4870 | 11 |
| ★40 | 57 | 74 | HE'S SURE THE BOY I LOVE — Crystals, Philles 109 | 4 |
| 41 | 51 | 67 | FROM A JACK TO A KING — Ned Miller, Fabor 114 | 5 |
| 42 | 53 | 78 | LITTLE TOWN FLIRT — Del Shannon, Big Top 3131 | 5 |
| 43 | 43 | 44 | SOME KINDA FUN — Chris Montez, Monogram 507 | 7 |
| 44 | 46 | 47 | THE LOVE OF A BOY — Timi Yuro, Liberty 55519 | 8 |
| 45 | 29 | 19 | KEEP YOUR HANDS OFF MY BABY — Little Eva, Dimension 1003 | 12 |
| 46 | 52 | 54 | LOVESICK BLUES — Frank Ifield, Vee Jay 477 | 5 |
| 47 | 31 | 21 | DON'T HANG UP — Orlons, Cameo 231 | 15 |
| 48 | 48 | 40 | LET'S GO — Routers, Warner Bros. 5283 | 12 |
| ★49 | 66 | 72 | FLY ME TO THE MOON—BOSSA NOVA — Joe Harnell & Ork, Kapp 497 | 4 |
| ★50 | 63 | 68 | SHAKE ME I RATTLE (Squeeze Me I Cry) — Marion Worth, Columbia 42640 △ | 4 |
| ★51 | 71 | 87 | PROUD — Johnny Crawford, Del-Fi 4193 | 3 |
| 52 | 67 | 76 | WILD WEEKEND — Rebels, Swan 4125 | 4 |
| 53 | 54 | 56 | THE BALLAD OF JED CLAMPETT — Lester Flatt & Earl Scruggs, Columbia 42606 △ | 7 |
| 54 | 61 | 66 | SHAKE SHERRY — Contours, Gordy 7012 | 5 |
| 55 | 62 | 64 | JAVA — Floyd Cramer, RCA Victor 8116 △ | 4 |
| 56 | 59 | 61 | STRANGE I KNOW — Marvelettes, Tamla 54072 | 8 |
| 57 | 44 | 27 | RUBY ANN — Marty Robbins, Columbia 42614 △ | 10 |
| 58 | 45 | 33 | (DANCE WITH THE) GUITAR MAN — Duane Eddy, RCA Victor 8087 △ | 16 |
| 59 | 56 | 49 | TEN LITTLE INDIANS — Beach Boys, Capitol 4880 | 8 |
| 60 | 70 | 70 | CAST YOUR FATE TO THE WIND — Vince Guaraldi Trio, Fantasy 563 | 7 |
| 61 | 68 | 75 | I'M A WOMAN — Peggy Lee, Capitol 4888 | 3 |
| 62 | 75 | 98 | MAMA DIDN'T LIE — Jan Bradley, Chess 1845 | 2 |
| 63 | 64 | 57 | MY WIFE CAN'T COOK — Lonnie Ross, 4 J 501 | 2 |
| 64 | 58 | 55 | THAT'S LIFE — Gabriel & the Angels, Swan 4118 | 11 |
| ★65 | 80 | — | RHYTHM OF THE RAIN — Cascades, Valiant 6026 | 2 |
| ★66 | — | — | LOVE (Makes the World Go 'Round) — Paul Anka, RCA Victor 8115 △ | 1 |
| 67 | 55 | 51 | CONEY ISLAND BABY — Excellents, Blast 205 | 9 |
| 68 | 79 | — | WOULD IT MAKE ANY DIFFERENCE TO YOU — Etta James, Argo 5430 | 2 |
| ★69 | — | — | RUBY BABY — Dion, Columbia 42662 △ | 1 |
| 70 | 77 | — | CHICKEN FEED — Bent Fabric, Atco 6245 | 2 |
| 71 | 73 | 82 | MOLLY — Bobby Goldsboro, Laurie 3148 | 5 |
| 72 | 74 | 79 | CALL ON ME — Bobby Bland, Duke 360 | 3 |
| 73 | 83 | 91 | THE GYPSY CRIED — Lou Christie, Roulette 4457 | 3 |
| 74 | 84 | 92 | EVERY DAY I HAVE TO CRY — Steve Alaimo, Checker 1032 | 3 |
| 75 | 88 | — | PUDDIN' N' TAIN — Alley Cats, Philles 108 | 2 |
| 76 | 72 | 81 | ALL ABOUT MY GIRL — Jimmy McGriff, Sue 777 | 3 |
| 77 | 65 | 65 | YOU'RE GONNA NEED ME — Barbara Lynn, Jamie 1240 | 6 |
| ★78 | — | — | SETTLE DOWN — Peter, Paul and Mary, Warner Bros. 5334 | 1 |
| 79 | 87 | — | WHAT TO DO WITH LAURIE — Mike Clifford, United Artists 557 | 3 |
| 80 | 81 | 86 | DARKEST STREET IN TOWN — Jimmy Clanton, Ace 8005 | 3 |
| ★81 | — | — | THAT'S THE WAY LOVE IS — Bobby Bland, Duke 360 | 1 |
| ★82 | — | — | BLAME IT ON THE BOSSA NOVA — Eydie Gorme, Columbia 42661 △ | 1 |
| 83 | 89 | — | WILLIE CAN — Sue Thompson, Hickory 1196 | 2 |
| 84 | 85 | 85 | LITTLE TIN SOLDIER — Toy Dolls, Era 3093 | 4 |
| 85 | 98 | 100 | POPEYE WADDLE — Don Covay, Cameo 239 | 3 |
| 86 | 90 | — | I WANNA BE AROUND — Tony Bennett, Columbia 42634 △ | 2 |
| ★87 | — | — | YOU'RE THE REASON I'M LIVING — Bobby Darin, Capitol 4897 | 1 |
| 88 | 82 | 95 | JELLY BREAD — Booker T & the MG's, Stax 131 | 4 |
| 89 | 92 | 99 | HOW MUCH IS THAT DOGGIE IN THE WINDOW — Baby Jane & the Rockabyes, United Artists 560 | 3 |
| 90 | 96 | — | HITCH HIKE — Marvin Gaye, Tamla 54075 | 2 |
| 91 | 91 | — | LOOK AT ME — Dobie Gray, CorDak 1602 | 2 |
| 92 | 94 | 94 | I WILL LIVE MY LIFE FOR YOU — Tony Bennett, Columbia 42634 △ | 3 |
| 93 | 99 | — | LET ME GO THE RIGHT WAY — Supremes, Motown 1034 | 3 |
| 94 | — | 90 | AL DI LA — Connie Francis, MGM 13116 | 2 |
| 95 | 78 | 88 | RED PEPPER — Roosevelt Fountain, Prince-Adams 447 | 3 |
| 96 | — | — | WHO STOLE THE KEESHKA — Matys Brothers, Select 719 | 1 |
| 97 | — | — | FROM THE BOTTOM OF MY HEART (Dammi, Dammi, Dammi) — Dean Martin, Reprise 20116 | 1 |
| 98 | 100 | — | WALK RIGHT IN — Moments, Era 3099 | 2 |
| 99 | — | — | OO-LA-LA-LIMBO — Danny and the Juniors, Guyden 2076 | 1 |
| 100 | — | — | LONE TEEN RANGER — Jerry Landis, Amy 875 | 1 |

## BUBBLING UNDER THE HOT 100

101. END OF THE WORLD — Skeeter Davis, RCA Victor 8098
102. THE (BOSSA NOVA) BIRD — Dells, Argo 5428
103. BIG WIDE WORLD — Teddy Randazzo, Colpix 662
104. TROUBLE IN MIND — Aretha Franklin, Columbia 42625
105. DAYS OF WINE AND ROSES — Henry Mancini, RCA Victor 8120
106. BOSSA NOVA U.S.A. — Dave Brubeck Quartet, Columbia 42651
107. I NEED YOU — Rick Nelson, Imperial 5901
108. SOMEONE SOMEWHERE — Junior Parker, Duke 357
109. GO HOME GIRL — Arthur Alexander, Dot 16425
110. ANONYMOUS PHONE CALL — Bobby Vee, Liberty 55521
111. TELEPHONE (WON'T YOU RING) — Shelley Fabares, Colpix 667
112. LET ME ENTERTAIN YOU — Ray Anthony, Capitol 4876
113. TWILIGHT TIME — Andy Williams, Cadence 1433
114. STILL WATERS RUN DEEP — Brook Benton, Mercury 72055
115. SLOP TIME — Sherrys, Guyden 2077
116. ECHO — Emotions, Kapp 490
117. THE SAME OLD HURT — Burl Ives, Decca 31453
118. HOW DO YOU TALK TO AN ANGEL — Etta James, Argo 5430
119. LEAVIN' ON YOUR MIND — Patsy Cline, Decca 31455
120. BABY, YOU'RE DRIVING ME CRAZY — Joey Dee, Roulette 4467
121. SEND ME SOME LOVIN' — Sam Cooke, RCA Victor 8129
122. TELL DADDY — Ben E. King, Atco 6246
123. FLY ME TO THE MOON — Mark Murphy, Riverside 4526
124. ANY OTHER WAY — Jackie Shane, Sue 776
125. BABY, BABY, BABY — Sam Cooke, RCA Victor 8129
126. MAYBE YOU'LL BE THERE — Billy & the Essentials, Jamie 1239

# Billboard HOT 100

**FOR WEEK ENDING JAN. 26, 1963**

STAR PERFORMERS—Selections registering greatest upward progress this week.

S — Indicates that 45 r.p.m. stereo single version is available.
△ — Indicates that 33⅓ r.p.m. mono single version is available.
Ⓢ — Indicates that 33⅓ r.p.m. stereo single version is available.

| This Week | Wk. Ago | 2 Wks. Ago | 3 Wks. Ago | Title, Artist, Label & Number | Weeks On Chart |
|---|---|---|---|---|---|
| 1 | 11 | 35 | 71 | **WALK RIGHT IN** — Rooftop Singers, Vanguard 35017 | 4 |
| 2 | 10 | 30 | 53 | **HEY PAULA** — Paul & Paula, Philips 40084 | 5 |
| 3 | 1 | 1 | 2 | **GO AWAY LITTLE GIRL** △ — Steve Lawrence, Columbia 42601 | 12 |
| 4 | 4 | 6 | 10 | **TELL HIM** — Exciters, United Artists 544 | 9 |
| 5 | 5 | 7 | 14 | **THE NIGHT HAS A THOUSAND EYES** — Bobby Vee, Liberty 55521 | 8 |
| 6 | 8 | 10 | 11 | **MY DAD** — Paul Petersen, Colpix 663 | 11 |
| 7 | 7 | 9 | 15 | **TWO LOVERS** — Mary Wells, Motown 1035 | 9 |
| 8 | 2 | 2 | 1 | **TELSTAR** — Tornadoes, London 9561 | 13 |
| 9 | 12 | 14 | 20 | **IT'S UP TO YOU** — Rick Nelson, Imperial 5901 | 7 |
| 10 | 6 | 3 | 3 | **LIMBO ROCK** — Chubby Checker, Parkway 849 | 21 |
| 11 | 13 | 16 | 22 | **UP ON THE ROOF** — Drifters, Atlantic 2162 | 13 |
| 12 | 3 | 4 | 6 | **HOTEL HAPPINESS** — Brook Benton, Mercury 72055 | 10 |
| 13 | 16 | 19 | 35 | **LOOP DE LOOP** — Johnny Thunder, Diamond 129 | 6 |
| 14 | 14 | 17 | 25 | **I SAW LINDA YESTERDAY** — Dickey Lee, Smash 1791 | 8 |
| 15 | 17 | 20 | 29 | **HALF HEAVEN—HALF HEARTACHE** — Gene Pitney, Musicor 1026 | 7 |
| 16 | 9 | 5 | 7 | **PEPINO THE ITALIAN MOUSE** — Lou Monte, Reprise 20106 | 8 |
| 17 | 28 | 33 | 46 | **YOU'VE REALLY GOT A HOLD ON ME** — Miracles, Tamla 54073 | 8 |
| 18 | 23 | 37 | 39 | **I'M GONNA BE WARM THIS WINTER** — Connie Francis, MGM 13116 | 7 |
| 19 | 20 | 21 | 26 | **EVERYBODY LOVES A LOVER** — Shirelles, Scepter 1243 | 9 |
| 20 | 15 | 8 | 9 | **ZIP-A-DEE-DOO-DAH** — Bob B. Soxx & the Blue Jeans, Philles 107 | 11 |
| 21 | 26 | 28 | 32 | **DON'T MAKE ME OVER** — Dionne Warwick, Scepter 1239 | 8 |
| 22 | 19 | 12 | 4 | **BOBBY'S GIRL** — Marcie Blane, Seville 120 | 15 |
| 23 | 27 | 38 | 48 | **MY COLORING BOOK** △ — Kitty Kallen, RCA Victor 8124 | 6 |
| 24 | 25 | 32 | 42 | **REMEMBER THEN** — Earls, Old Town 1130 | 7 |
| 25 | 32 | 42 | 58 | **MY COLORING BOOK** — Sandy Stewart, Colpix 669 | 5 |
| 26 | 24 | 24 | 28 | **SHUTTERS AND BOARDS** — Jerry Wallace, Challenge 9171 | 11 |
| 27 | 18 | 11 | 3 | **BIG GIRLS DON'T CRY** — Four Seasons, Vee Jay 465 | 15 |
| 28 | 41 | 51 | 67 | **FROM A JACK TO A KING** — Ned Miller, Fabor 114 | 5 |
| 29 | 36 | 49 | 63 | **CINNAMON CINDER** — Pastel Six, Zen 102 | 5 |
| 30 | 42 | 53 | 78 | **LITTLE TOWN FLIRT** — Del Shannon, Big Top 3131 | 6 |
| 31 | 69 | — | — | **RUBY BABY** △ — Dion, Columbia 42662 | 2 |
| 32 | 40 | 57 | 74 | **HE'S SURE THE BOY I LOVE** — Crystals, Philles 109 | 5 |
| 33 | 49 | 66 | 72 | **FLY ME TO THE MOON—BOSSA NOVA** — Joe Harnell & Ork, Kapp 497 | 4 |
| 34 | 21 | 13 | 8 | **RETURN TO SENDER** △ — Elvis Presley, RCA Victor 8100 | 15 |
| 35 | 65 | 80 | — | **RHYTHM OF THE RAIN** — Cascades, Valiant 6026 | 3 |
| 36 | 51 | 71 | 87 | **PROUD** — Johnny Crawford, Del-Fi 4193 | 4 |
| 37 | 29 | 22 | 23 | **WIGGLE WOBBLE** — Les Cooper, Everlast 5019 | 15 |
| 38 | 52 | 67 | 76 | **WILD WEEKEND** — Rebels, Swan 4125 | 5 |
| 39 | 22 | 15 | 12 | **YOU ARE MY SUNSHINE** — Ray Charles, ABC-Paramount 10375 | 11 |
| 40 | — | — | — | **WALK LIKE A MAN** — Four Seasons, Vee Jay 485 | 1 |
| 41 | 33 | 34 | 34 | **TROUBLE IS MY MIDDLE NAME** — Bobby Vinton, Epic 9561 | 8 |
| 42 | 34 | 36 | 37 | **SEE SEE RIDER** — LaVern Baker, Atlantic 2167 | 9 |
| 43 | 50 | 63 | 68 | **SHAKE ME I RATTLE (Squeeze Me I Cry)** △ — Marion Worth, Columbia 42640 | 5 |
| 44 | 46 | 52 | 54 | **LOVESICK BLUES** — Frank Ifield, Vee Jay 477 | 6 |
| 45 | 38 | 40 | 43 | **LET'S KISS AND MAKE UP** — Bobby Vinton, Epic 9561 | 9 |
| 46 | 43 | 43 | 44 | **SOME KINDA FUN** — Chris Montez, Monogram 507 | 8 |
| 47 | 62 | 75 | 98 | **MAMA DIDN'T LIE** — Jan Bradley, Chess 1845 | 4 |
| 48 | 35 | 26 | 18 | **CHAINS** — Cookies, Dimension 1002 | 12 |
| 49 | 56 | 59 | 61 | **STRANGE I KNOW** — Marvelettes, Tamla 54072 | 9 |
| 50 | 30 | 18 | 16 | **THE LONELY BULL** — Tijuana Brass, A. & M. 703 | 14 |
| 51 | 53 | 54 | 56 | **THE BALLAD OF JED CLAMPETT** △ — Lester Flatt & Earl Scruggs, Columbia 42606 | 8 |
| 52 | 55 | 62 | 64 | **JAVA** △ — Floyd Cramer, RCA Victor 8116 | 5 |
| 53 | 54 | 61 | 66 | **SHAKE SHERRY** — Contours, Gordy 7012 | 6 |
| 54 | 66 | — | — | **LOVE (Makes the World Go 'Round)** △ — Paul Anka, RCA Victor 8115 | 2 |
| 55 | 60 | 70 | 70 | **CAST YOUR FATE TO THE WIND** — Vince Guaraldi Trio, Fantasy 563 | 8 |
| 56 | 87 | — | — | **YOU'RE THE REASON I'M LIVING** — Bobby Darin, Capitol 4897 | 2 |
| 57 | 48 | 48 | 40 | **LET'S GO** — Routers, Warner Bros. 5283 | 13 |
| 58 | 75 | 88 | — | **PUDDIN' N' TAIN** — Alley Cats, Philles 108 | 3 |
| 59 | 31 | 23 | 13 | **RELEASE ME** — "Little Esther" Phillips, Lenox 5555 | 14 |
| 60 | 72 | 74 | 79 | **CALL ON ME** — Bobby Bland, Duke 360 | 4 |
| 61 | 61 | 68 | 75 | **I'M A WOMAN** — Peggy Lee, Capitol 4888 | 4 |
| 62 | 73 | 83 | 91 | **THE GYPSY CRIED** — Lou Christie, Roulette 4457 | 4 |
| 63 | — | — | — | **SEND ME SOME LOVIN'** △ — Sam Cooke, RCA Victor 8129 | 1 |
| 64 | 74 | 84 | 92 | **EVERY DAY I HAVE TO CRY** — Steve Alaimo, Checker 1032 | 4 |
| 65 | 68 | 79 | — | **WOULD IT MAKE ANY DIFFERENCE TO YOU** — Etta James, Argo 5430 | 3 |
| 66 | — | — | — | **SHE'LL NEVER KNOW** — Brenda Lee, Decca 31454 | 1 |
| 67 | 82 | — | — | **BLAME IT ON THE BOSSA NOVA** △ — Eydie Gorme, Columbia 42661 | 2 |
| 68 | 79 | 87 | — | **WHAT TO DO WITH LAURIE** — Mike Clifford, United Artists 557 | 4 |
| 69 | 70 | 77 | — | **CHICKEN FEED** — Bent Fabric, Atco 6245 | 3 |
| 70 | 71 | 73 | 82 | **MOLLY** — Bobby Goldsboro, Laurie 3148 | 6 |
| 71 | 89 | 92 | 99 | **HOW MUCH IS THAT DOGGIE IN THE WINDOW** — Baby Jane & the Rockabyes, United Artists 569 | 4 |
| 72 | 78 | — | — | **SETTLE DOWN** — Peter, Paul and Mary, Warner Bros. 5334 | 2 |
| 73 | — | — | — | **YOUR USED TO BE** — Brenda Lee, Decca 31454 | 1 |
| 74 | 63 | 64 | 57 | **MY WIFE CAN'T COOK** — Lonnie Russ, 4 J 501 | 8 |
| 75 | 86 | 90 | — | **I WANNA BE AROUND** — Tony Bennett, Columbia 42634 | 3 |
| 76 | 76 | 72 | 81 | **ALL ABOUT MY GIRL** — Jimmy McGriff, Sue 777 | 4 |
| 77 | 80 | 81 | 86 | **DARKEST STREET IN TOWN** — Jimmy Clanton, Ace 8005 | 4 |
| 78 | 85 | 98 | — | **POPEYE WADDLE** — Don Covay, Cameo 239 | 4 |
| 79 | 83 | 89 | — | **WILLIE CAN** — Sue Thompson, Hickory 1196 | 3 |
| 80 | 81 | — | — | **THAT'S THE WAY LOVE IS** — Bobby Bland, Duke 360 | 2 |
| 81 | — | — | — | **WHAT WILL MARY SAY** — Johnny Mathis, Columbia 42666 | 1 |
| 82 | — | — | — | **DAYS OF WINE AND ROSES** △ — Henry Mancini, RCA Victor 8120 | 1 |
| 83 | 90 | 96 | — | **HITCH HIKE** — Marvin Gaye, Tamla 54075 | 3 |
| 84 | 96 | — | — | **THE END OF THE WORLD** — Skeeter Davis, RCA Victor 8098 | 2 |
| 85 | 96 | — | — | **WHO STOLE THE KEESHKA** — Matys Brothers, Select 719 | 2 |
| 86 | — | — | — | **BIG WIDE WORLD** — Teddy Randazzo, Colpix 662 | 1 |
| 87 | 88 | 82 | 95 | **JELLY BREAD** — Booker T & the MG's, Stax 131 | 5 |
| 88 | 98 | 100 | — | **WALK RIGHT IN** — Moments, Era 3099 | 3 |
| 89 | — | — | — | **LEAVIN' ON YOUR MIND** — Patsy Cline, Decca 31455 | 1 |
| 90 | 92 | 94 | 94 | **I WILL LIVE MY LIFE FOR YOU** △ — Tony Bennett, Columbia 42634 | 4 |
| 91 | — | — | — | **THE SAME OLD HURT** — Burl Ives, Decca 31455 | 1 |
| 92 | 94 | — | 90 | **AL DI LA** — Connie Francis, MGM 13116 | 3 |
| 93 | 93 | 99 | — | **LET ME GO THE RIGHT WAY** — Supremes, Motown 1034 | 4 |
| 94 | 97 | — | — | **FROM THE BOTTOM OF MY HEART (Dammi, Dammi, Dammi)** — Dean Martin, Reprise 20116 | 3 |
| 95 | — | — | — | **AS LONG AS SHE NEEDS ME** — Sammy Davis Jr., Reprise 20138 | 1 |
| 96 | — | — | — | **GREENBACK DOLLAR** — Kingston Trio, Capitol 4898 | 1 |
| 97 | 100 | — | — | **LONE TEEN RANGER** — Jerry Landis, Amy 875 | 2 |
| 98 | — | — | — | **I'D RATHER BE HERE IN YOUR ARMS** — Duprees, Coed 574 | 1 |
| 99 | 99 | — | — | **OO-LA-LA-LIMBO** — Danny and the Juniors, Guyden 2076 | 1 |
| 100 | — | — | — | **MEDITACAO (Meditation)** — Charlie Byrd, Riverside 4544 | 1 |

## BUBBLING UNDER THE HOT 100

101. TROUBLE IN MIND — Aretha Franklin, Columbia 42625
102. THE (Bossa Nova) BIRD — Dells, Argo 5428
103. BABY, BABY, BABY — Sam Cooke, RCA Victor 8129
104. LOOK AT ME — Dobie Gray, Cordak 1602
105. OUR WINTER LOVE — Bill Pursell, Columbia 42619
106. RED PEPPER — Roosevelt Fountain, Prince-Adams 447
107. I NEED YOU — Rick Nelson, Imperial 5901
108. GO HOME GIRL — Arthur Alexander, Dot 16425
109. TELEPHONE (Won't You Ring) — Shelley Fabares, Colpix 667
110. LET ME ENTERTAIN YOU — Ray Anthony, Capitol 4876
111. JIVE SAMBA — Cannonball Adderley Sextet, Riverside 4541
112. SOMEONE SOMEWHERE — Junior Parker, Duke 357
113. SLOP TIME — Sherrys, Guyden 2077
114. ECHO — Emotions, Kapp 490
115. TELL HIM I'M NOT HOME — Chuck Jackson, Wand 132
116. TWILIGHT TIME — Andy Williams, Cadence 1433
117. MAYBE YOU'LL BE THERE — Billy & the Essentials, Jamie 1239
118. BABY, YOU'RE DRIVING ME CRAZY — Joey Dee, Roulette 4467
119. LOVE FOR SALE — Arthur Lyman Group, Hi-Fi 5066
120. NOBODY BUT ME — Isley Brothers, Wand 131
121. BIG NOISE FROM WINNETKA — Cozy Cole, Coral 62339
122. LET'S STOMP — Bobby Comstock, Lawn 202
123. I FOUND A NEW BABY — Bobby Darin, Atco 6244
124. MAGIC STAR (Telstar) — Margie Singleton, Mercury 72079
125. BOSS — The Rumblers, Highland 16421
126. LITTLE WHITE LIES — Knoplairs, A&M 704
127. COOL WATER — Blue Belles, Newtown 5009
128. ZING! WENT THE STRINGS OF MY HEART — Furys, Mack IV 712

# Billboard HOT 100
## FOR WEEK ENDING FEB. 2 1963

| # | Wks Ago | Title | Artist, Label & Number | Weeks On Chart |
|---|---|---|---|---|
| 1 | 1 11 35 | WALK RIGHT IN | Rooftop Singers, Vanguard 35017 | 5 |
| 2 | 2 10 30 | HEY PAULA | Paul & Paula, Philips 40084 | 6 |
| 3 | 5 5 7 | THE NIGHT HAS A THOUSAND EYES | Bobby Vee, Liberty 55521 | 9 |
| 4 | 3 1 1 | GO AWAY LITTLE GIRL | Steve Lawrence, Columbia 42601 | 13 |
| 5 | 13 16 19 | LOOP DE LOOP | Johnny Thunder, Diamond 129 | 7 |
| 6 | 9 12 14 | IT'S UP TO YOU | Rick Nelson, Imperial 5901 | 8 |
| 7 | 11 13 16 | UP ON THE ROOF | Drifters, Atlantic 2162 | 14 |
| 8 | 4 4 6 | TELL HIM | Exciters, United Artists 544 | 10 |
| 9 | 7 7 9 | TWO LOVERS | Mary Wells, Motown 1035 | 10 |
| 10 | 6 8 10 | MY DAD | Paul Petersen, Colpix 663 | 12 |
| 11 | 17 28 33 | YOU'VE REALLY GOT A HOLD ON ME | Miracles, Tamla 54073 | 9 |
| 12 | 31 69 — | RUBY BABY | Dion, Columbia 42662 | 3 |
| 13 | 15 17 20 | HALF HEAVEN—HALF HEARTACHE | Gene Pitney, Musicor 1026 | 8 |
| 14 | 14 14 17 | I SAW LINDA YESTERDAY | Dickey Lee, Smash 1791 | 9 |
| 15 | 40 — — | WALK LIKE A MAN | Four Seasons, Vee Jay 485 | 2 |
| 16 | 28 41 51 | FROM A JACK TO A KING | Ned Miller, Fabor 114 | 6 |
| 17 | 8 2 2 | TELSTAR | Tornadoes, London 9561 | 14 |
| 18 | 23 27 38 | MY COLORING BOOK | Kitty Kallen, RCA Victor 8124 | 7 |
| 19 | 35 65 80 | RHYTHM OF THE RAIN | Cascades, Valiant 6026 | 4 |
| 20 | 25 32 42 | MY COLORING BOOK | Sandy Stewart, Colpix 669 | 6 |
| 21 | 21 26 28 | DON'T MAKE ME OVER | Dionne Warwick, Scepter 1239 | 9 |
| 22 | 12 3 4 | HOTEL HAPPINESS | Brook Benton, Mercury 72055 | 11 |
| 23 | 18 23 37 | I'M GONNA BE WARM THIS WINTER | Connie Francis, MGM 13116 | 8 |
| 24 | 19 20 21 | EVERYBODY LOVES A LOVER | Shirelles, Scepter 1243 | 10 |
| 25 | 29 36 49 | CINNAMON CINDER | Pastel Six, Zen 102 | 6 |
| 26 | 30 42 53 | LITTLE TOWN FLIRT | Del Shannon, Big Top 3131 | 7 |
| 27 | 32 40 57 | HE'S SURE THE BOY I LOVE | Crystals, Philles 109 | 6 |
| 28 | 33 49 66 | FLY ME TO THE MOON—BOSSA NOVA | Joe Harnell & Ork, Kapp 497 | 6 |
| 29 | 10 6 3 | LIMBO ROCK | Chubby Checker, Parkway 849 | 22 |
| 30 | 56 87 — | YOU'RE THE REASON I'M LIVING | Bobby Darin, Capitol 4897 | 3 |
| 31 | 16 9 5 | PEPINO THE ITALIAN MOUSE | Lou Monte, Reprise 20106 | 9 |
| 32 | 36 51 71 | PROUD | Johnny Crawford, Del-Fi 4193 | 5 |
| 33 | 26 24 24 | SHUTTERS AND BOARDS | Jerry Wallace, Challenge 9171 | 12 |
| 34 | 24 25 32 | REMEMBER THEN | Earls, Old Town 1130 | 8 |
| 35 | 38 52 67 | WILD WEEKEND | Rebels, Swan 4125 | 6 |
| 36 | 47 62 75 | MAMA DIDN'T LIE | Jan Bradley, Chess 1845 | 5 |
| 37 | 20 15 8 | ZIP-A-DEE-DOO-DAH | Bob B. Soxx & the Blue Jeans, Philles 107 | 12 |
| 38 | 63 — — | SEND ME SOME LOVIN' | Sam Cooke, RCA Victor 8129 | 2 |
| 39 | 22 19 12 | BOBBY'S GIRL | Marcie Blane, Seville 120 | 16 |
| 40 | 60 72 74 | CALL ON ME | Bobby Bland, Duke 360 | 5 |
| 41 | 54 66 — | LOVE (Makes the World Go 'Round) | Paul Anka, RCA Victor 8115 | 3 |
| 42 | 43 50 63 | SHAKE ME I RATTLE (Squeeze Me I Cry) | Marion Worth, Columbia 42640 | 6 |
| 43 | 27 18 11 | BIG GIRLS DON'T CRY | Four Seasons, Vee Jay 465 | 16 |
| 44 | 55 60 70 | CAST YOUR FATE TO THE WIND | Vince Guaraldi Trio, Fantasy 563 | 9 |
| 45 | 37 29 22 | WIGGLE WOBBLE | Les Cooper, Everlast 5019 | 16 |
| 46 | 51 53 54 | THE BALLAD OF JED CLAMPETT | Lester Flatt & Earl Scruggs, Columbia 42606 | 9 |
| 47 | 67 82 — | BLAME IT ON THE BOSSA NOVA | Eydie Gorme, Columbia 42661 | 3 |
| 48 | 42 34 36 | SEE SEE RIDER | LaVern Baker, Atlantic 2167 | 10 |
| 49 | 52 55 62 | JAVA | Floyd Cramer, RCA Victor 8116 | 6 |
| 50 | 53 54 61 | SHAKE SHERRY | Contours, Gordy 7012 | 7 |
| 51 | 34 21 13 | RETURN TO SENDER | Elvis Presley, RCA Victor 8100 | 16 |
| 52 | 49 56 59 | STRANGE I KNOW | Marvelettes, Tamla 54072 | 10 |
| 53 | 44 46 52 | LOVESICK BLUES | Frank Ifield, Vee Jay 477 | 7 |
| 54 | 58 75 88 | PUDDIN' N' TAIN | Alley Cats, Philles 108 | 4 |
| 55 | 46 43 43 | SOME KINDA FUN | Chris Montez, Monogram 507 | 9 |
| 56 | 39 22 15 | YOU ARE MY SUNSHINE | Ray Charles, ABC-Paramount 10375 | 12 |
| 57 | 61 61 68 | I'M A WOMAN | Peggy Lee, Capitol 4888 | 5 |
| 58 | 73 — — | YOUR USED TO BE | Brenda Lee, Decca 31454 | 2 |
| 59 | 62 73 83 | THE GYPSY CRIED | Lou Christie, Roulette 4457 | 5 |
| 60 | 80 81 — | THAT'S THE WAY LOVE IS | Bobby Bland, Duke 360 | 3 |
| 61 | 72 78 — | SETTLE DOWN | Peter, Paul and Mary, Warner Bros. 5334 | 3 |
| 62 | 66 — — | SHE'LL NEVER KNOW | Brenda Lee, Decca 31454 | 2 |
| 63 | 75 86 90 | I WANNA BE AROUND | Tony Bennett, Columbia 42634 | 4 |
| 64 | 65 68 79 | WOULD IT MAKE ANY DIFFERENCE TO YOU | Etta James, Argo 5430 | 4 |
| 65 | 84 — — | THE END OF THE WORLD | Skeeter Davis, RCA Victor 8098 | 2 |
| 66 | 81 — — | WHAT WILL MARY SAY | Johnny Mathis, Columbia 42666 | 2 |
| 67 | 69 70 77 | CHICKEN FEED | Bent Fabric, Atco 6245 | 4 |
| 68 | 64 74 84 | EVERY DAY I HAVE TO CRY | Steve Alaimo, Checker 1032 | 5 |
| 69 | 41 33 34 | TROUBLE IS MY MIDDLE NAME | Bobby Vinton, Epic 9561 | 9 |
| 70 | 83 90 96 | HITCH HIKE | Marvin Gaye, Tamla 54075 | 4 |
| 71 | 71 89 92 | HOW MUCH IS THAT DOGGIE IN THE WINDOW | Baby Jane & the Rockabyes, United Artists 560 | 5 |
| 72 | 76 76 72 | ALL ABOUT MY GIRL | Jimmy McGriff, Sue 777 | 5 |
| 73 | 96 — — | GREENBACK DOLLAR | Kingston Trio, Capitol 4898 | 2 |
| 74 | 68 79 87 | WHAT TO DO WITH LAURIE | Mike Clifford, United Artists 557 | 5 |
| 75 | 82 — — | DAYS OF WINE AND ROSES | Henry Mancini, RCA Victor 8120 | 2 |
| 76 | 78 85 98 | POPEYE WADDLE | Don Covay, Cameo 239 | 5 |
| 77 | 85 96 — | WHO STOLE THE KEESHKA | Matys Brothers, Select 719 | 3 |
| 78 | 79 83 89 | WILLIE CAN | Sue Thompson, Hickory 1196 | 4 |
| 79 | 70 71 73 | MOLLY | Bobby Goldsboro, Laurie 3148 | 7 |
| 80 | — — — | ONLY YOU | Mr. Acker Bilk, Atco 6247 | 1 |
| 81 | 95 — — | AS LONG AS SHE NEEDS ME | Sammy Davis Jr., Reprise 20138 | 2 |
| 82 | — — — | LET'S TURKEY TROT | Little Eva, Dimension 1006 | 1 |
| 83 | — — — | TELL HIM I'M NOT HOME | Chuck Jackson, Wand 132 | 1 |
| 84 | 86 — — | BIG WIDE WORLD | Teddy Randazzo, Colpix 662 | 2 |
| 85 | — — — | ALICE IN WONDERLAND | Neil Sedaka, RCA Victor 8137 | 1 |
| 86 | 88 98 100 | WALK RIGHT IN | Moments, Era 3099 | 4 |
| 87 | 89 — — | LEAVIN' ON YOUR MIND | Patsy Cline, Decca 31455 | 2 |
| 88 | — — — | OUR WINTER LOVE | Bill Pursell, Columbia 42619 | 1 |
| 89 | 90 92 94 | I WILL LIVE MY LIFE FOR YOU | Tony Bennett, Columbia 42634 | 5 |
| 90 | 93 93 99 | LET ME GO THE RIGHT WAY | Supremes, Motown 1034 | 5 |
| 91 | 94 97 — | FROM THE BOTTOM OF MY HEART (Dammi, Dammi, Dammi) | Dean Martin, Reprise 20116 | 4 |
| 92 | 91 — — | THE SAME OLD HURT | Burl Ives, Decca 31455 | 2 |
| 93 | — — — | AIN'T GONNA KISS YA | Ribbons, Marsh 202 | 1 |
| 94 | 98 — — | I'D RATHER BE HERE IN YOUR ARMS | Duprees, Coed 574 | 2 |
| 95 | — — — | M. G. BLUES | Jimmy McGriff, Sue 777 | 1 |
| 96 | — — — | BOSSA NOVA U. S. A. | Dave Brubeck Quartet, Columbia 42651 | 2 |
| 97 | 97 100 — | LONE TEEN RANGER | Jerry Landis, Amy 875 | 3 |
| 98 | — — — | BABY, BABY, BABY | Sam Cooke, RCA Victor 8129 | 1 |
| 99 | — — — | LOVE FOR SALE | Arthur Lyman Group, Hi-Fi 5066 | 1 |
| 100 | — — — | THEME FROM LAWRENCE OF ARABIA | Ferrante & Teicher, United Artist 563 | 1 |

## BUBBLING UNDER THE HOT 100

101. RIDIN' THE WIND — Tornadoes, London 9581
102. AL DI LA — Connie Francis, MGM 13116
103. THE BOSSA NOVA WATUSI TWIST — Freddy King, Federal 12482
104. JELLY BREAD — Booker T & the MG's, Stax 131
105. SOMEONE SOMEWHERE — Junior Parker, Duke 357
106. BABY, YOU'RE DRIVING ME CRAZY — Joey Dee, Roulette 4467
107. THE 2,000 POUND BEE — Ventures, Dolton 67
108. BOSS — Rumblers, Dot 16421
109. RED PEPPER — Roosevelt Fountain, Prince-Adams 447
110. HI-LILI, HI-LO — Richard Chamberlain, MGM 13121
111. MR. COOL — Champs, Challenge 9180
112. LOOK AT ME — Dobie Gray, CorDak 1602
113. SLOP TIME — Sherrys, Guyden 2077
114. NOBODY BUT ME — Isley Brothers, Wand 131
115. LET'S STOMP — Bobby Comstock, Lawn 202
116. I FOUND A NEW BABY — Bobby Darin, Atco 6244
117. I NEED YOU — Rick Nelson, Imperial 5901
118. TROUBLE IN MIND — Aretha Franklin, Columbia 42625
119. DON'T LET ME CROSS OVER — Carl Butler, Columbia 42593
120. THE (BOSSA NOVA) BIRD — Dells, Argo 5428
121. TWILIGHT TIME — Andy Williams, Cadence 1433
122. ZING WENT THE STRINGS OF MY HEART — Furys, Mack IV 112
123. GUILTY — Crests, Selma 311
124. OUR DAY WILL COME — Ruby & the Romantics, Kapp 501
125. FEELIN' SAD — Ray Charles, Atlantic 2174
126. IS THIS ME? — Jim Reeves, RCA Victor 8127

# Billboard HOT 100

**FOR WEEK ENDING FEB. 9, 1963**

| This Week | Wk. Ago | 2 Wks. Ago | 3 Wks. Ago | Title / Artist, Label & Number | Weeks On Chart |
|---|---|---|---|---|---|
| 1 | 2 | 2 | 10 | HEY PAULA — Paul & Paula, Philips 40084 | 7 |
| 2 | 1 | 1 | 11 | WALK RIGHT IN — Rooftop Singers, Vanguard 35017 | 6 |
| 3 | 3 | 5 | 5 | THE NIGHT HAS A THOUSAND EYES — Bobby Vee, Liberty 55521 | 10 |
| 4 | 5 | 13 | 16 | LOOP DE LOOP — Johnny Thunder, Diamond 129 | 8 |
| 5 | 7 | 11 | 13 | UP ON THE ROOF — Drifters, Atlantic 2162 | 15 |
| 6 | 15 | 40 | — | WALK LIKE A MAN — Four Seasons, Vee Jay 485 | 3 |
| 7 | 12 | 31 | 69 | RUBY BABY — Dion, Columbia 42662 | 4 |
| 8 | 11 | 17 | 28 | YOU'VE REALLY GOT A HOLD ON ME — Miracles, Tamla 54073 | 10 |
| 9 | 19 | 35 | 65 | RHYTHM OF THE RAIN — Cascades, Valiant 6026 | 5 |
| 10 | 4 | 3 | 1 | GO AWAY LITTLE GIRL — Steve Lawrence, Columbia 42601 | 14 |
| 11 | 16 | 28 | 41 | FROM A JACK TO A KING — Ned Miller, Fabor 114 | 7 |
| 12 | 13 | 15 | 17 | HALF HEAVEN—HALF HEARTACHE — Gene Pitney, Musicor 1026 | 9 |
| 13 | 6 | 9 | 12 | IT'S UP TO YOU — Rick Nelson, Imperial 5901 | 9 |
| 14 | 8 | 4 | 4 | TELL HIM — Exciters, United Artists 544 | 11 |
| 15 | 9 | 7 | 7 | TWO LOVERS — Mary Wells, Motown 1035 | 11 |
| 16 | 27 | 32 | 40 | HE'S SURE THE BOY I LOVE — Crystals, Philles 109 | 7 |
| 17 | 10 | 6 | 8 | MY DAD — Paul Petersen, Colpix 663 | 13 |
| 18 | 28 | 33 | 49 | FLY ME TO THE MOON—BOSSA NOVA — Joe Harnell & Ork, Kapp 497 | 7 |
| 19 | 14 | 14 | 14 | I SAW LINDA YESTERDAY — Dickey Lee, Smash 1791 | 10 |
| 20 | 30 | 56 | 87 | YOU'RE THE REASON I'M LIVING — Bobby Darin, Capitol 4897 | 4 |
| 21 | 36 | 47 | 62 | MAMA DIDN'T LIE — Jan Bradley, Chess 1845 | 6 |
| 22 | 18 | 23 | 27 | MY COLORING BOOK — Kitty Kallen, RCA Victor 8134 | 8 |
| 23 | 35 | 38 | 52 | WILD WEEKEND — Rebels, Swan 4125 | 7 |
| 24 | 26 | 30 | 42 | LITTLE TOWN FLIRT — Del Shannon, Big Top 3131 | 8 |
| 25 | 25 | 29 | 36 | CINNAMON CINDER — Pastel Six, Zen 102 | 7 |
| 26 | 21 | 21 | 26 | DON'T MAKE ME OVER — Dionne Warwick, Scepter 1239 | 10 |
| 27 | 20 | 25 | 32 | MY COLORING BOOK — Sandy Stewart, Colpix 669 | 7 |
| 28 | 38 | 63 | — | SEND ME SOME LOVIN' — Sam Cooke, RCA Victor 8129 | 2 |
| 29 | 32 | 36 | 51 | PROUD — Johnny Crawford, Del-Fi 4193 | 6 |
| 30 | 41 | 54 | 66 | LOVE (Makes the World Go' Round) — Paul Anka, RCA Victor 8115 | 4 |
| 31 | 40 | 60 | 72 | CALL ON ME — Bobby Bland, Duke 360 | 6 |
| 32 | 23 | 18 | 23 | I'M GONNA BE WARM THIS WINTER — Connie Francis, MGM 13116 | 9 |
| 33 | 66 | 81 | — | WHAT WILL MARY SAY — Johnny Mathis, Columbia 42666 | 3 |
| 34 | 47 | 67 | 82 | BLAME IT ON THE BOSSA NOVA — Eydie Gorme, Columbia 42661 | 4 |
| 35 | 44 | 55 | 60 | CAST YOUR FATE TO THE WIND — Vince Guaraldi Trio, Fantasy 563 | 10 |
| 36 | 17 | 8 | 2 | TELSTAR — Tornadoes, London 9561 | 15 |
| 37 | 24 | 19 | 20 | EVERYBODY LOVES A LOVER — Shirelles, Scepter 1243 | 11 |
| 38 | 60 | 80 | 81 | THAT'S THE WAY LOVE IS — Bobby Bland, Duke 360 | 4 |
| 39 | 22 | 12 | 3 | HOTEL HAPPINESS — Brook Benton, Mercury 72055 | 12 |
| 40 | 31 | 16 | 9 | PEPINO THE ITALIAN MOUSE — Lou Monte, Reprise 20106 | 10 |
| 41 | 58 | 73 | — | YOUR USED TO BE — Brenda Lee, Decca 31454 | 3 |
| 42 | 59 | 62 | 73 | THE GYPSY CRIED — Lou Christie, Roulette 4457 | 6 |
| 43 | 50 | 53 | 54 | SHAKE SHERRY — Contours, Gordy 7012 | 8 |
| 44 | 46 | 51 | 53 | THE BALLAD OF JED CLAMPETT — Lester Flatt & Earl Scruggs, Columbia 42606 | 10 |
| 45 | 34 | 24 | 25 | REMEMBER THEN — Earls, Old Town 1130 | 9 |
| 46 | 54 | 58 | 75 | PUDDIN' N' TAIN — Alley Cats, Philles 108 | 7 |
| 47 | 29 | 10 | 6 | LIMBO ROCK — Chubby Checker, Parkway 849 | 23 |
| 48 | 65 | 84 | — | THE END OF THE WORLD — Skeeter Davis, RCA Victor 8098 | 3 |
| 49 | 63 | 75 | 86 | I WANNA BE AROUND — Tony Bennett, Columbia 42634 | 5 |
| 50 | 42 | 43 | 50 | SHAKE ME I RATTLE (Squeeze Me I Cry) — Marion Worth, Columbia 42640 | 7 |
| 51 | 62 | 66 | — | SHE'LL NEVER KNOW — Brenda Lee, Decca 31454 | 3 |
| 52 | 37 | 20 | 15 | ZIP-A-DEE-DOO-DAH — Bob B. Soxx & the Blue Jeans, Philles 107 | 13 |
| 53 | 49 | 52 | 55 | JAVA — Floyd Cramer, RCA Victor 8116 | 7 |
| 54 | 57 | 61 | 61 | I'M A WOMAN — Peggy Lee, Capitol 4880 | 6 |
| 55 | 70 | 83 | 90 | HITCH HIKE — Marvin Gaye, Tamla 54075 | 5 |
| 56 | 61 | 72 | 78 | SETTLE DOWN — Peter, Paul and Mary, Warner Bros. 5334 | 4 |
| 57 | 85 | — | — | ALICE IN WONDERLAND — Neil Sedaka, RCA Victor 8137 | 2 |
| 58 | 73 | 96 | — | GREENBACK DOLLAR — Kingston Trio, Capitol 4898 | 3 |
| 59 | 68 | 64 | 74 | EVERY DAY I HAVE TO CRY — Steve Alaimo, Checker 1032 | 6 |
| 60 | 75 | 82 | — | DAYS OF WINE AND ROSES — Henry Mancini, RCA Victor 8120 | 3 |
| 61 | 52 | 49 | 56 | STRANGE I KNOW — Marvelettes, Tamla 54072 | 11 |
| 62 | 82 | — | — | LET'S TURKEY TROT — Little Eva, Dimension 1006 | 2 |
| 63 | 67 | 69 | 70 | CHICKEN FEED — Bent Fabric, Atco 6245 | 5 |
| 64 | 83 | — | — | TELL HIM I'M NOT HOME — Chuck Jackson, Wand 132 | 2 |
| 65 | 77 | 85 | 96 | WHO STOLE THE KEESHKA — Matys Brothers, Select 719 | 4 |
| 66 | 64 | 65 | 68 | WOULD IT MAKE ANY DIFFERENCE TO YOU — Etta James, Argo 5430 | 5 |
| 67 | 72 | 76 | 76 | ALL ABOUT MY GIRL — Jimmy McGriff, Sue 777 | 6 |
| 68 | 48 | 42 | 34 | SEE SEE RIDER — LaVern Baker, Atlantic 2167 | 11 |
| 69 | 71 | 71 | 89 | HOW MUCH IS THAT DOGGIE IN THE WINDOW — Baby Jane & the Rockabyes, United Artists 560 | 6 |
| 70 | 88 | — | — | OUR WINTER LOVE — Bill Pursell, Columbia 42619 | 2 |
| 71 | 81 | 95 | — | AS LONG AS SHE NEEDS ME — Sammy Davis Jr., Reprise 20138 | 3 |
| 72 | — | — | — | I REALLY DON'T WANT TO KNOW — "Little Esther" Phillips, Lenox 5560 | 1 |
| 73 | 84 | 86 | — | BIG WIDE WORLD — Teddy Randazzo, Colpix 662 | 3 |
| 74 | — | — | — | BUTTERFLY BABY — Bobby Rydell, Cameo 242 | 1 |
| 75 | 76 | 78 | 85 | POPEYE WADDLE — Don Covay, Cameo 239 | 6 |
| 76 | 74 | 68 | 79 | WHAT TO DO WITH LAURIE — Mike Clifford, United Artists 557 | 6 |
| 77 | 80 | — | — | ONLY YOU — Mr. Acker Bilk, Atco 6247 | 2 |
| 78 | 78 | 79 | 83 | WILLIE CAN — Sue Thompson, Hickory 1196 | 5 |
| 79 | — | — | — | OUR DAY WILL COME — Ruby and the Romantics, Kapp 501 | 1 |
| 80 | — | — | — | I'M THE ONE WHO LOVES YOU — Impressions, ABC-Paramount 10386 | 1 |
| 81 | — | — | — | IN DREAMS — Roy Orbison, Monument 806 | 1 |
| 82 | 86 | 88 | 98 | WALK RIGHT IN — Moments, Era 3099 | 5 |
| 83 | — | — | — | I NEED YOU — Rick Nelson, Imperial 5901 | 4 |
| 84 | 87 | 89 | — | LEAVIN' ON YOUR MIND — Patsy Cline, Decca 31455 | 3 |
| 85 | 89 | 90 | 92 | I WILL LIVE MY LIFE FOR YOU — Tony Bennett, Columbia 42634 | 6 |
| 86 | — | — | — | BOSS GUITAR — Duane Eddy, RCA Victor 8131 | 1 |
| 87 | 98 | — | — | BABY, BABY, BABY — Sam Cooke, RCA Victor 8129 | 2 |
| 88 | — | — | — | DON'T LET ME CROSS OVER — Carl Butler, Columbia 42593 | 1 |
| 89 | — | — | — | ALL I HAVE TO DO IS DREAM — Richard Chamberlain, MGM 13121 | 1 |
| 90 | — | — | — | PIN A MEDAL ON JOEY — James Darren, Colpix 672 | 1 |
| 91 | — | — | — | REMEMBER BABY — Shep and the Limelites, Hull 756 | 1 |
| 92 | 94 | 98 | — | I'D RATHER BE HERE IN YOUR ARMS — Duprees, Coed 574 | 3 |
| 93 | 93 | — | — | AIN'T GONNA KISS YA — Ribbons, March 202 | 2 |
| 94 | 99 | — | — | LOVE FOR SALE — Arthur Lyman Group, Hi-Fi 5066 | 2 |
| 95 | 95 | — | — | M. G. BLUES — Jimmy McGriff, Sue 777 | 2 |
| 96 | 91 | 94 | 97 | FROM THE BOTTOM OF MY HEART (Dammi, Dammi, Dammi) — Dean Martin, Reprise 20116 | 5 |
| 97 | — | 92 | 94 | AL DI LA — Connie Francis, MGM 13116 | 4 |
| 98 | — | — | — | THE DOG — Rufus Thomas, Stax 130 | 1 |
| 99 | — | — | — | EVERY BEAT OF MY HEART — James Brown and the Famous Flames, King 5710 | 1 |
| 100 | — | — | — | ZINGI WENT THE STRINGS OF MY HEART — Furys, Mack IV 112 | 1 |

## BUBBLING UNDER THE HOT 100

101. RIDIN' THE WIND — Tornadoes, London 9581
102. LET ME GO THE RIGHT WAY — Miracles, Motown 1034
103. IS THIS ME? — Jim Reeves, RCA Victor 8127
104. RAINBOW — Gene Chandler, Vee Jay 468
105. WHY DO LOVERS BREAK EACH OTHERS HEARTS? — Bob B. Soxx & the Blue Jeans, Philles 110
106. THEME FROM LAWRENCE OF ARABIA — Ferrante & Teicher, United Artists 563
107. HI-LILI, HI-LO — Richard Chamberlain, MGM 13121
108. THE SAME OLD HURT — Burl Ives, Decca 31455
109. NOBODY BUT ME — Isley Brothers, Wand 131
110. SLOP TIME — Sherrys, Guyden 2077
111. MR. COOL — Champs, Challenge 9180
112. LET'S STOMP — Bobby Comstock, Lawn 202
113. JELLY BREAD — Booker T & the MG's, Stax 131
114. BOSSA NOVA U. S. A. — Dave Brubeck Quartet, Columbia 42675
115. YAKETY SAX — Boots Randolph, Monument 804
116. THE (Bossa Nova) BIRD — Dolls, Argo 5428
117. AM I THAT EASY TO FORGET — "Little Esther" Phillips, Lenox 5560
118. SOMEONE SOMEWHERE — Junior Parker, Duke 357
119. FEELIN' SAD — Ray Charles, Atlantic 2174
120. I FOUND A NEW BABY — Bobby Darin, Atco 6244
121. BABY, YOU'RE DRIVING ME CRAZY — Joey Dee, Roulette 4467
122. BOSS — Rumblers, Dot 16421
123. THE JIVE SAMBA — Cannonball Adderley Sextet, Riverside 4841
124. THE 2,000 POUND BEE — Ventures, Dolton 67
125. FOUR LETTER MAN — Freddy Cannon, Swan 4132
126. GUILTY — Crests, Selma 311

# Billboard HOT 100

**FOR WEEK ENDING FEB. 16 1963**

STAR PERFORMERS—Selections registering greatest upward progress this week.
S — Indicates that 45 r.p.m. stereo single version is available.
△ — Indicates that 33⅓ r.p.m. mono single version is available.
Ⓢ — Indicates that 33⅓ r.p.m. stereo single version is available.

| This Week | Wk. Ago | 2 Wks. Ago | TITLE — Artist, Label & Number | Weeks On Chart |
|---|---|---|---|---|
| 1 | 2 | 2 | HEY PAULA — Paul & Paula, Philips 40084 | 8 |
| 2 | 1 | 1 | WALK RIGHT IN — Rooftop Singers, Vanguard 35017 | 7 |
| 3 | 6 | 15 | WALK LIKE A MAN — Four Seasons, Vee Jay 485 | 4 |
| 4 | 7 | 12 | RUBY BABY — Dion, Columbia 42662 △ | 5 |
| 5 | 9 | 19 | RHYTHM OF THE RAIN — Cascades, Valiant 6026 | 6 |
| 6 | 11 | 16 | FROM A JACK TO A KING — Ned Miller, Fabor 114 | 8 |
| 7 | 3 | 3 | THE NIGHT HAS A THOUSAND EYES — Bobby Vee, Liberty 55521 | 11 |
| 8 | 8 | 11 | YOU'VE REALLY GOT A HOLD ON ME — Miracles, Tamla 54073 | 11 |
| 9 | 4 | 5 | LOOP DE LOOP — Johnny Thunder, Diamond 129 | 9 |
| 10 | 5 | 7 | UP ON THE ROOF — Drifters, Atlantic 2162 | 16 |
| 11 | 16 | 27 | HE'S SURE THE BOY I LOVE — Crystals, Philles 109 | 8 |
| 12 | 20 | 30 | YOU'RE THE REASON I'M LIVING — Bobby Darin, Capitol 4897 | 5 |
| 13 | 24 | 26 | LITTLE TOWN FLIRT — Del Shannon, Big Top 3131 | 9 |
| 14 | 10 | 4 | GO AWAY LITTLE GIRL — Steve Lawrence, Columbia 42601 △ | 15 |
| 15 | 23 | 35 | WILD WEEKEND — Rebels, Swan 4125 | 8 |
| 16 | 21 | 36 | MAMA DIDN'T LIE — Jan Bradley, Chess 1845 | 7 |
| 17 | 18 | 28 | FLY ME TO THE MOON—BOSSA NOVA — Joe Harnell & Ork, Kapp 497 | 8 |
| 18 | 34 | 47 | BLAME IT ON THE BOSSA NOVA — Eydie Gorme, Columbia 42661 △ | 5 |
| 19 | 12 | 13 | HALF HEAVEN—HALF HEARTACHE — Gene Pitney, Musicor 1026 | 10 |
| 20 | 28 | 38 | SEND ME SOME LOVIN' — Sam Cooke, RCA Victor 8129 △ | 3 |
| 21 | 13 | 6 | IT'S UP TO YOU — Rick Nelson, Imperial 5901 | 10 |
| 22 | 31 | 40 | CALL ON ME — Bobby Bland, Duke 360 | 7 |
| 23 | 33 | 66 | WHAT WILL MARY SAY — Johnny Mathis, Columbia 42666 △ | 4 |
| 24 | 17 | 10 | MY DAD — Paul Petersen, Colpix 663 | 14 |
| 25 | 19 | 14 | I SAW LINDA YESTERDAY — Dickey Lee, Smash 1791 | 11 |
| 26 | 30 | 41 | LOVE (Makes the World Go 'Round) — Paul Anka, RCA Victor 8115 △ | 5 |
| 27 | 25 | 25 | CINNAMON CINDER — Pastel Six, Zen 102 | 8 |
| 28 | 35 | 44 | CAST YOUR FATE TO THE WIND — Vince Guaraldi Trio, Fantasy 563 | 11 |
| 29 | 14 | 8 | TELL HIM — Exciters, United Artists 544 | 12 |
| 30 | 42 | 59 | THE GYPSY CRIED — Lou Christie, Roulette 4457 | 7 |
| 31 | 15 | 9 | TWO LOVERS — Mary Wells, Motown 1035 | 12 |
| 32 | 57 | 85 | ALICE IN WONDERLAND — Neil Sedaka, RCA Victor 8137 △ | 3 |
| 33 | 22 | 18 | MY COLORING BOOK — Kitty Kallen, RCA Victor 8124 △ | 9 |
| 34 | 41 | 58 | YOUR USED TO BE — Brenda Lee, Decca 31454 | 4 |
| 35 | 26 | 21 | DON'T MAKE ME OVER — Dionne Warwick, Scepter 1239 | 11 |
| 36 | 48 | 65 | THE END OF THE WORLD — Skeeter Davis, RCA Victor 8098 △ | 4 |
| 37 | 27 | 20 | MY COLORING BOOK — Sandy Stewart, Colpix 669 | 8 |
| 38 | 70 | 88 | OUR WINTER LOVE — Bill Pursell, Columbia 42619 △ | 3 |
| 39 | 29 | 32 | PROUD — Johnny Crawford, Del-Fi 4193 | 7 |
| 40 | 49 | 63 | I WANNA BE AROUND — Tony Bennett, Columbia 42634 △ | 6 |
| 41 | 58 | 73 | GREENBACK DOLLAR — Kingston Trio, Capitol 4898 | 4 |
| 42 | 32 | 23 | I'M GONNA BE WARM THIS WINTER — Connie Francis, MGM 13116 | 10 |
| 43 | 46 | 54 | PUDDIN' N' TAIN — Alley Cats, Philles 108 | 6 |
| 44 | 62 | 82 | LET'S TURKEY TROT — Little Eva, Dimension 1006 | 3 |
| 45 | 38 | 60 | THAT'S THE WAY LOVE IS — Bobby Bland, Duke 360 | 5 |
| 46 | 43 | 50 | SHAKE SHERRY — Contours, Gordy 7012 | 9 |
| 47 | 81 | — | IN DREAMS — Roy Orbison, Monument 806 | 2 |
| 48 | 51 | 62 | SHE'LL NEVER KNOW — Brenda Lee, Decca 31454 | 4 |
| 49 | 36 | 17 | TELSTAR — Tornadoes, London 9561 | 16 |
| 50 | 37 | 24 | EVERYBODY LOVES A LOVER — Shirelles, Scepter 1243 | 12 |
| 51 | 86 | — | BOSS GUITAR — Duane Eddy, RCA Victor 8131 △ | 2 |
| 52 | 74 | — | BUTTERFLY BABY — Bobby Rydell, Cameo 242 | 2 |
| 53 | 79 | — | OUR DAY WILL COME — Ruby and the Romantics, Kapp 501 | 2 |
| 54 | 55 | 70 | HITCH HIKE — Marvin Gaye, Tamla 54075 | 6 |
| 55 | 60 | 75 | DAYS OF WINE AND ROSES — Henry Mancini, RCA Victor 8120 △ | 4 |
| 56 | 59 | 68 | EVERY DAY I HAVE TO CRY — Steve Alaimo, Checker 1032 | 7 |
| 57 | 65 | 77 | WHO STOLE THE KEESHKA — Matys Brothers, Select 719 | 5 |
| 58 | 56 | 61 | SETTLE DOWN — Peter, Paul and Mary, Warner Bros. 5334 | 5 |
| 59 | — | — | ONE BROKEN HEART FOR SALE — Elvis Presley, RCA Victor 8134 | 1 |
| 60 | 64 | 83 | TELL HIM I'M NOT HOME — Chuck Jackson, Wand 132 | 3 |
| 61 | 53 | 49 | JAVA — Floyd Cramer, RCA Victor 8116 △ | 8 |
| 62 | 44 | 46 | THE BALLAD OF JED CLAMPETT — Lester Flatt & Earl Scruggs, Columbia 42606 △ | 11 |
| 63 | 73 | 84 | BIG WIDE WORLD — Teddy Randazzo, Colpix 662 | 4 |
| 64 | 67 | 72 | ALL ABOUT MY GIRL — Jimmy McGriff, Sue 777 | 7 |
| 65 | — | — | LET'S LIMBO SOME MORE — Chubby Checker, Parkway 862 | 1 |
| 66 | 54 | 57 | I'M A WOMAN — Peggy Lee, Capitol 4888 | 7 |
| 67 | 50 | 42 | SHAKE ME I RATTLE (Squeeze Me I Cry) — Marion Worth, Columbia 42640 △ | 8 |
| 68 | 72 | — | I REALLY DON'T WANT TO KNOW — "Little Esther" Phillips, Lenox 5560 | 2 |
| 69 | 69 | 71 | HOW MUCH IS THAT DOGGIE IN THE WINDOW — Baby Jane & the Rockabyes, United Artists 560 | 7 |
| 70 | 71 | 81 | AS LONG AS SHE NEEDS ME — Sammy Davis Jr., Reprise 20138 | 4 |
| 71 | 87 | 98 | BABY, BABY, BABY — Sam Cooke, RCA Victor 8129 △ | 3 |
| 72 | 61 | 52 | STRANGE I KNOW — Marvelettes, Tamla 54072 | 12 |
| 73 | 66 | 64 | WOULD IT MAKE ANY DIFFERENCE TO YOU — Etta James, Argo 5430 | 6 |
| 74 | 63 | 67 | CHICKEN FEED — Bent Fabric, Atco 6245 | 6 |
| 75 | 90 | — | PIN A MEDAL ON JOEY — James Darren, Colpix 672 | 2 |
| 76 | — | — | SOUTH STREET — Orlons, Cameo 243 | 1 |
| 77 | 94 | 99 | LOVE FOR SALE — Arthur Lyman Group, HI-FI 5066 | 3 |
| 78 | 75 | 76 | POPEYE WADDLE — Don Covay, Cameo 239 | 7 |
| 79 | 80 | — | I'M THE ONE WHO LOVES YOU — Impressions, ABC-Paramount 10386 | 2 |
| 80 | — | — | RIDIN' THE WIND — Tornadoes, London 9581 | 1 |
| 81 | — | — | WHY DO LOVERS BREAK EACH OTHERS HEARTS — Bob B. Soxx & the Blue Jeans, Philles 110 | 1 |
| 82 | 93 | 93 | AIN'T GONNA KISS YA — Ribbons, Marsh 202 | 3 |
| 83 | 89 | — | ALL I HAVE TO DO IS DREAM — Richard Chamberlain, MGM 13121 | 2 |
| 84 | 84 | 87 | LEAVIN' ON YOUR MIND — Patsy Cline, Decca 31455 | 4 |
| 85 | 76 | 74 | WHAT TO DO WITH LAURIE — Mike Clifford, United Artists 557 | 7 |
| 86 | 85 | 89 | I WILL LIVE MY LIFE FOR YOU — Tony Bennett, Columbia 42634 △ | 7 |
| 87 | — | — | BOSS — Rumblers, Dot 16421 | 1 |
| 88 | — | 100 | THEME FROM LAWRENCE OF ARABIA — Ferrante & Teicher, United Artists 563 | 2 |
| 89 | — | — | LET'S STOMP — Bobby Comstock, Lawn 202 | 1 |
| 90 | — | 90 | LET ME GO THE RIGHT WAY — Supremes, Motown 1034 | 5 |
| 91 | 92 | 94 | I'D RATHER BE HERE IN YOUR ARMS — Duprees, Coed 574 | 4 |
| 92 | 100 | — | ZING! WENT THE STRINGS OF MY HEART — Furys, Mack IV 112 | 2 |
| 93 | 98 | — | THE DOG — Rufus Thomas, Stax 130 | 2 |
| 94 | 97 | 92 | AL DI LA — Connie Francis, MGM 13116 | 5 |
| 95 | 95 | 95 | M. G. BLUES — Jimmy McGriff, Sue 777 | 2 |
| 96 | — | 96 | BOSSA NOVA U.S.A. — Dave Brubeck Quartet, Columbia 42675 △ | 2 |
| 97 | — | — | HI-LILI, HI-LO — Richard Chamberlain, MGM 13121 | 1 |
| 98 | — | — | JIVE SAMBA — Cannonball Adderley Sextet, Riverside 4541 | 1 |
| 99 | — | — | MR. BASS MAN — Johnny Cymbal, Kapp 503 | 1 |
| 100 | — | — | BABY, YOU'RE DRIVING ME CRAZY — Joey Dee, Roulette 4467 | 1 |

## BUBBLING UNDER THE HOT 100

101. DON'T LET ME CROSS OVER — Carl Butler, Columbia 42593
102. FROM THE BOTTOM OF MY HEART (Dammi, Dammi, Dammi) — Dean Martin, Reprise 20116
103. IS THIS ME? — Jim Reeves, RCA Victor 8127
104. RAINBOW — Gene Chandler, Vee Jay 468
105. MEDITACAO (Meditation) — Charlie Byrd, Riverside 4544
106. NOBODY BUT ME — Isley Brothers, Wand 131
107. REMEMBER BABY — Shep & the Limelites, Hull 756
108. MOLLY — Bobby Goldsboro, Laurie 3148
109. YAKETY SAX — Boots Randolph, Monument 804
110. MY FOOLISH HEART — Demensions, Coral 62344
111. WHAT DOES A GIRL DO? — Marcie Blane, Seville 123
112. JELLY BREAD — Booker T. & the MG's, Stax 131
113. ONLY YOU — Mr. Acker Bilk, Atco 6247
114. AM I THAT EASY TO FORGET — "Little Esther" Phillips, Lenox 5560
115. HALF TIME — Routers, Warner Bros. 5332
116. WILLIE CAN — Sue Thompson, Hickory 1196
117. I NEED YOU — Rick Nelson, Imperial 5901
118. WALK RIGHT IN — Moments, Era 3099
119. THEY REMIND ME TOO MUCH OF YOU — Elvis Presley, RCA Victor 8134
120. THE (Bossa Nova) BIRD — Dells, Argo 5428
121. EVERY BEAT OF MY HEART — James Brown & the Famous Flames, King 5710
122. FOUR LETTER MAN — Freddy Cannon, Swan 4132
123. I FOUND A NEW BABY — Jerry Landis, Amy 875
124. LONE TEEN RANGER — Jerry Landis, Amy 875
125. THE BIRD — Dutones, Columbia 42657
126. MR. COOL — Ventures, Dolton 67
127. SOMEONE SOMEWHERE — Junior Parker, Duke 357
128. COMES LOVE — Skyliners, Viscount 104
129. DON'T LET ME CROSS OVER — Adam Wade, Epic 9566
130. FADED LOVE — Jackie DeShannon, Liberty 55526

# Billboard HOT 100
**FOR WEEK ENDING FEB. 23, 1963**

| This Week | Wks Ago | Title — Artist, Label & Number | Weeks On Chart |
|---|---|---|---|
| 1 | 1 1 2 | HEY PAULA — Paul & Paula, Philips 40084 | 9 |
| 2 | 4 7 12 | RUBY BABY — Dion, Columbia 42662 | 6 |
| 3 | 3 6 15 | WALK LIKE A MAN — Four Seasons, Vee Jay 485 | 5 |
| 4 | 2 2 1 | WALK RIGHT IN — Rooftop Singers, Vanguard 35017 | 8 |
| 5 | 5 9 19 | RHYTHM OF THE RAIN — Cascades, Valiant 6026 | 7 |
| 6 | 6 11 16 | FROM A JACK TO A KING — Ned Miller, Fabor 114 | 9 |
| 7 | 12 20 30 | YOU'RE THE REASON I'M LIVING — Bobby Darin, Capitol 4897 | 6 |
| 8 | 18 34 47 | BLAME IT ON THE BOSSA NOVA — Eydie Gorme, Columbia 42661 | 6 |
| 9 | 8 8 11 | YOU'VE REALLY GOT A HOLD ON ME — Miracles, Tamla 54073 | 12 |
| 10 | 15 23 35 | WILD WEEKEND — Rebels, Swan 4125 | 9 |
| 11 | 11 16 27 | HE'S SURE THE BOY I LOVE — Crystals, Philles 109 | 9 |
| 12 | 13 24 26 | LITTLE TOWN FLIRT — Del Shannon, Big Top 3131 | 10 |
| 13 | 20 28 38 | SEND ME SOME LOVIN' — Sam Cooke, RCA Victor 8129 | 4 |
| 14 | 17 18 28 | FLY ME TO THE MOON—BOSSA NOVA — Joe Harnell & Ork, Kapp 497 | 6 |
| 15 | 7 3 3 | THE NIGHT HAS A THOUSAND EYES — Bobby Vee, Liberty 55521 | 12 |
| 16 | 16 21 36 | MAMA DIDN'T LIE — Jan Bradley, Chess 1845 | 8 |
| 17 | 23 33 36 | WHAT WILL MARY SAY — Johnny Mathis, Columbia 42666 | 5 |
| 18 | 10 5 7 | UP ON THE ROOF — Drifters, Atlantic 2162 | 17 |
| 19 | 9 4 5 | LOOP DE LOOP — Johnny Thunder, Diamond 129 | 10 |
| 20 | 14 10 4 | GO AWAY LITTLE GIRL — Steve Lawrence, Columbia 42601 | 16 |
| 21 | 36 48 65 | THE END OF THE WORLD — Skeeter Davis, RCA Victor 8098 | 5 |
| 22 | 28 35 44 | CAST YOUR FATE TO THE WIND — Vince Guaraldi Trio, Fantasy 563 | 12 |
| 23 | 47 81 — | IN DREAMS — Roy Orbison, Monument 806 | 3 |
| 24 | 32 57 85 | ALICE IN WONDERLAND — Neil Sedaka, RCA Victor 8137 | 4 |
| 25 | 59 — — | ONE BROKEN HEART FOR SALE — Elvis Presley, RCA Victor 8134 | 2 |
| 26 | 26 30 41 | LOVE (Makes the World Go 'Round) — Paul Anka, RCA Victor 8115 | 6 |
| 27 | 53 79 — | OUR DAY WILL COME — Ruby and the Romantics, Kapp 501 | 3 |
| 28 | 30 42 59 | THE GYPSY CRIED — Lou Christie, Roulette 4457 | 8 |
| 29 | 22 31 40 | CALL ON ME — Bobby Bland, Duke 360 | 8 |
| 30 | 38 70 88 | OUR WINTER LOVE — Bill Pursell, Columbia 42619 | 4 |
| 31 | 41 58 73 | GREENBACK DOLLAR — Kingston Trio, Capitol 4898 | 5 |
| 32 | 34 41 58 | YOUR USED TO BE — Brenda Lee, Decca 31454 | 5 |
| 33 | 40 49 63 | I WANNA BE AROUND — Tony Bennett, Columbia 42634 | 7 |
| 34 | 44 62 82 | LET'S TURKEY TROT — Little Eva, Dimension 1006 | 4 |
| 35 | 21 13 6 | IT'S UP TO YOU — Rick Nelson, Imperial 5901 | 11 |
| 36 | 51 86 — | BOSS GUITAR — Duane Eddy, RCA Victor 8131 | 3 |
| 37 | 52 74 — | BUTTERFLY BABY — Bobby Rydell, Cameo 242 | 3 |
| 38 | 19 12 13 | HALF HEAVEN—HALF HEARTACHE — Gene Pitney, Musicor 1026 | 11 |
| 39 | 45 38 60 | THAT'S THE WAY LOVE IS — Bobby Bland, Duke 360 | 6 |
| 40 | 65 — — | LET'S LIMBO SOME MORE — Chubby Checker, Parkway 862 | 2 |
| 41 | 27 25 25 | CINNAMON CINDER — Pastel Six, Zen 102 | 9 |
| 42 | 24 17 10 | MY DAD — Paul Petersen, Colpix 663 | 15 |
| 43 | 54 55 70 | HITCH HIKE — Marvin Gaye, Tamla 54075 | 7 |
| 44 | 37 27 20 | MY COLORING BOOK — Sandy Stewart, Colpix 669 | 9 |
| 45 | 25 19 14 | I SAW LINDA YESTERDAY — Dickey Lee, Smash 1791 | 12 |
| 46 | 55 60 75 | DAYS OF WINE AND ROSES — Henry Mancini, RCA Victor 8120 | 5 |
| 47 | 48 51 62 | SHE'LL NEVER KNOW — Brenda Lee, Decca 31454 | 5 |
| 48 | 43 46 54 | PUDDIN' N' TAIN — Alley Cats, Philles 108 | 7 |
| 49 | 56 59 68 | EVERY DAY I HAVE TO CRY — Steve Alaimo, Checker 1032 | 8 |
| 50 | 76 — — | SOUTH STREET — Orlons, Cameo 243 | 2 |
| 51 | 29 14 8 | TELL HIM — Exciters, United Artists 544 | 13 |
| 52 | 60 64 83 | TELL HIM I'M NOT HOME — Chuck Jackson, Wand 132 | 4 |
| 53 | 33 22 18 | MY COLORING BOOK — Kitty Kallen, RCA Victor 8124 | 10 |
| 54 | 64 67 72 | ALL ABOUT MY GIRL — Jimmy McGriff, Sue 777 | 8 |
| 55 | 57 65 77 | WHO STOLE THE KEESHKA — Matys Brothers, Select 719 | 6 |
| 56 | 58 56 61 | SETTLE DOWN — Peter, Paul and Mary, Warner Bros. 5334 | 6 |
| 57 | 61 53 49 | JAVA — Floyd Cramer, RCA Victor 8116 | 9 |
| 58 | 42 32 23 | I'M GONNA BE WARM THIS WINTER — Connie Francis, MGM 13116 | 11 |
| 59 | 83 89 — | ALL I HAVE TO DO IS DREAM — Richard Chamberlain, MGM 13121 | 3 |
| 60 | 39 29 32 | PROUD — Johnny Crawford, Del-Fi 4193 | 8 |
| 61 | 63 73 84 | BIG WIDE WORLD — Teddy Randazzo, Colpix 662 | 5 |
| 62 | 70 71 81 | AS LONG AS SHE NEEDS ME — Sammy Davis Jr., Reprise 20138 | 5 |
| 63 | 68 72 — | I REALLY DON'T WANT TO KNOW — "Little Esther" Phillips, Lenox 5560 | 3 |
| 64 | 66 54 57 | I'M A WOMAN — Peggy Lee, Capitol 4888 | 8 |
| 65 | 77 94 99 | LOVE FOR SALE — Arthur Lyman Group, Hi-Fi 5066 | 3 |
| 66 | 71 87 98 | BABY, BABY, BABY — Sam Cooke, RCA Victor 8129 | 4 |
| 67 | 35 26 21 | DON'T MAKE ME OVER — Dionne Warwick, Scepter 1239 | 12 |
| 68 | 72 61 52 | STRANGE I KNOW — Marvelettes, Tamla 54072 | 13 |
| 69 | 75 90 — | PIN A MEDAL ON JOEY — James Darren, Colpix 672 | 3 |
| 70 | 31 15 9 | TWO LOVERS — Mary Wells, Motown 1035 | 13 |
| 71 | 73 66 64 | WOULD IT MAKE ANY DIFFERENCE TO YOU — Etta James, Argo 5430 | 7 |
| 72 | 74 63 67 | CHICKEN FEED — Bent Fabric, Atco 6245 | 7 |
| 73 | 81 — — | WHY DO LOVERS BREAK EACH OTHERS HEARTS — Bob B. Soxx & the Blue Jeans, Philles 110 | 2 |
| 74 | — — — | THEY REMIND ME TOO MUCH OF YOU — Elvis Presley, RCA Victor 8134 | 1 |
| 75 | 80 — — | RIDIN' THE WIND — Tornadoes, London 9581 | 2 |
| 76 | 79 80 — | I'M THE ONE WHO LOVES YOU — Impressions, ABC-Paramount 10386 | 3 |
| 77 | — — — | TWENTY MILES — Chubby Checker, Parkway 862 | 1 |
| 78 | — — — | LAUGHING BOY — Mary Wells, Motown 1039 | 1 |
| 79 | 89 — — | LET'S STOMP — Bobby Comstock, Lawn 202 | 2 |
| 80 | 97 — — | HI-LILI, HI-LO — Richard Chamberlain, MGM 13121 | 2 |
| 81 | 82 93 93 | AIN'T GONNA KISS YA — Ribbons, Marsh 202 | 4 |
| 82 | — 99 — | MR. BASS MAN — Johnny Cymbal, Kapp 503 | 2 |
| 83 | 84 84 87 | LEAVIN' ON YOUR MIND — Patsy Cline, Decca 31455 | 5 |
| 84 | — — — | I'M IN LOVE AGAIN — Rick Nelson, Imperial 5910 | 1 |
| 85 | — — — | RAINBOW — Gene Chandler, Vee Jay 468 | 1 |
| 86 | — — — | DON'T SET ME FREE — Ray Charles, ABC-Paramount 10405 | 1 |
| 87 | — — — | HE'S SO FINE — Chiffons, Laurie 3152 | 1 |
| 88 | 88 — 100 | THEME FROM LAWRENCE OF ARABIA — Ferrante & Teicher, United Artists 563 | 3 |
| 89 | 96 — 96 | BOSSA NOVA U.S.A. — Dave Brubeck Quartet, Columbia 42675 | 4 |
| 90 | — — — | LINDA — Jan and Dean, Liberty 55531 | 1 |
| 91 | — — — | THE 2,000 POUND BEE — Ventures, Dolton 67 | 1 |
| 92 | — 96 91 | FROM THE BOTTOM OF MY HEART (Dammi, Dammi, Dammi) — Dean Martin, Reprise 20116 | 6 |
| 93 | — — — | DON'T FENCE ME IN — George Maharis, Epic 9569 | 1 |
| 94 | — — — | YAKETY SAX — Boots Randolph, Monument 804 | 1 |
| 95 | — — — | WHAT DOES A GIRL DO! — Marcie Blane, Seville 123 | 1 |
| 96 | — — — | DON'T BE CRUEL — Barbara Lynn, Jamie 1244 | 1 |
| 97 | 98 — — | JIVE SAMBA — Cannonball Adderley Sextet, Riverside 4541 | 2 |
| 98 | — — — | FADED LOVE — Jackie De Shannon, Liberty 55526 | 1 |
| 99 | — — — | MEDITACAO (MEDITATION) — Charlie Byrd, Riverside 4544 | 1 |
| 100 | 77 80 — | ONLY YOU — Mr. Acker Bilk, Atco 6247 | 3 |

## BUBBLING UNDER THE HOT 100

101. DON'T LET ME CROSS OVER — Carl Butler, Columbia 42593
102. M.G. BLUES — Jimmy McGriff, Sue 777
103. IS THIS ME — Jim Reeves, RCA Victor 8127
104. BABY, YOU'RE DRIVING ME CRAZY — Joey Dee, Roulette 4467
105. THE BIRD — Dutones, Columbia 42657
106. I WILL LIVE MY LIFE FOR YOU — Tony Bennett, Columbia 42634
107. JELLY BREAD — Booker T and MG's, Stax 131
108. THE (Bossa Nova) BIRD — Dells, Argo 5428
109. I'D RATHER BE HERE IN YOUR ARMS — Duprees, Coral 574
110. IF MARY'S THERE — Brian Hyland, ABC-Paramount 10400
111. DO THE BIRD — Dee Dee Sharp, Cameo 244
112. EVERY BEAT OF MY HEART — James Brown and the Famous Flames, King 5710
113. FEELIN' SAD — Ray Charles, Atlantic 2174
114. AM I THAT EASY TO FORGET — "Little Esther" Phillips, Lenox 5560
115. MY FOOLISH HEART — Demensions, Coral 62346
116. THAT'S ALL — Rick Nelson, Imperial 5910
117. ANYTHING YOU CAN DO — Majors, Imperial 5914
118. HALF TIME — Routers, Warner Bros. 5332
119. LIKE LOCOMOTION — Tornadoes, London 9579
120. MEDITATION — Pat Boone, Dot 16450
121. FOUR LETTER MAN — Freddy Cannon, Swan 4132
122. DON'T MENTION MY NAME — Shephard Sisters, Atlantic 2176
123. JUST A SIMPLE MELODY — Patti Page, Columbia 42671
124. DAYS OF WINE AND ROSES — Andy Williams, Columbia 42674
125. SAX FIFTH AVENUE — Johnny Beecher, Omega 5341
126. BOSS — Rumblers, Dot 16421
127. BRIGHTEST SMILE IN TOWN — Ray Charles, ABC-Paramount 10405
128. LITTLE STAR — Jimmie Rodgers, Roulette 4471
129. FACE IN THE CROWD — Bobby Calender, Roulette 4471
130. HE'S GOT THE POWER — Exciters, United Artists 572
131. BOSSA NOVA WATUSI TWIST — Freddy King, Federal 12482
132. ANY OTHER WAY — Jackie Shane, Dot 776
133. SHIRLEY — Tony Orlando, Epic 9570
134. I'LL RELEASE YOU — Ted Taylor, Okeh 7165

Billboard

# HOT 100

FOR WEEK ENDING MARCH 2 1963

★ STAR PERFORMERS—Selections registering greatest upward progress this week.

[S] Indicates that 45 r.p.m. stereo single version is available.

△ Indicates that 33⅓ r.p.m. mono single version is available.

[S in △] Indicates that 33⅓ r.p.m. stereo single version is available.

| This Week | 1 Wk. Ago | 2 Wks. Ago | 3 Wks. Ago | TITLE — Artist, Label & Number | | Weeks On Chart |
|---|---|---|---|---|---|---|
| 1 | 3 | 3 | 6 | WALK LIKE A MAN — Four Seasons, Vee Jay 485 | | 6 |
| 2 | 2 | 4 | 7 | RUBY BABY — Dion, Columbia 42662 | △ | 7 |
| 3 | 1 | 1 | 1 | HEY PAULA — Paul & Paula, Philips 40084 | | 10 |
| 4 | 5 | 5 | 9 | RHYTHM OF THE RAIN — Cascades, Valiant 6026 | | 8 |
| 5 | 4 | 2 | 2 | WALK RIGHT IN — Rooftop Singers, Vanguard 35017 | | 9 |
| 6 | 7 | 12 | 20 | YOU'RE THE REASON I'M LIVING — Bobby Darin, Capitol 4897 | | 7 |
| 7 | 8 | 18 | 34 | BLAME IT ON THE BOSSA NOVA — Eydie Gorme, Columbia 42661 | △ | 7 |
| 8 | 6 | 6 | 11 | FROM A JACK TO A KING — Ned Miller, Fabor 114 | | 10 |
| 9 | 10 | 15 | 23 | WILD WEEKEND — Rebels, Swan 4125 | | 10 |
| ★ | 17 | 33 | 36 | WHAT WILL MY MARY SAY — Johnny Mathis, Columbia 42666 | △ | 6 |
| ★ | 27 | 53 | 79 | OUR DAY WILL COME — Ruby and the Romantics, Kapp 501 | | 4 |
| ★ | 21 | 36 | 48 | THE END OF THE WORLD — Skeeter Davis, RCA Victor 8098 | △ | 6 |
| 13 | 13 | 20 | 28 | SEND ME SOME LOVIN' — Sam Cooke, RCA Victor 8129 | △ | 5 |
| 14 | 9 | 8 | 8 | YOU'VE REALLY GOT A HOLD ON ME — Miracles, Tamla 54073 | | 13 |
| 15 | 16 | 16 | 21 | MAMA DIDN'T LIE — Jan Bradley, Chess 1845 | | 9 |
| 16 | 14 | 17 | 18 | FLY ME TO THE MOON—BOSSA NOVA — Joe Harnell & Ork, Kapp 497 | | 10 |
| 17 | 11 | 11 | 16 | HE'S SURE THE BOY I LOVE — Crystals, Philles 109 | | 10 |
| 18 | 12 | 13 | 24 | LITTLE TOWN FLIRT — Del Shannon, Big Top 3131 | | 11 |
| ★ | 25 | 59 | — | ONE BROKEN HEART FOR SALE — Elvis Presley, RCA Victor 8134 | △ | 3 |
| 20 | 23 | 47 | 81 | IN DREAMS — Roy Orbison, Monument 806 | | 4 |
| 21 | 24 | 32 | 57 | ALICE IN WONDERLAND — Neil Sedaka, RCA Victor 8137 | △ | 5 |
| ★ | 30 | 37 | 70 | OUR WINTER LOVE — Bill Pursell, Columbia 42619 | △ | 5 |
| 23 | 18 | 10 | 5 | UP ON THE ROOF — Drifters, Atlantic 2162 | | 18 |
| 24 | 15 | 7 | 3 | THE NIGHT HAS A THOUSAND EYES — Bobby Vee, Liberty 55521 | | 13 |
| 25 | 22 | 28 | 35 | CAST YOUR FATE TO THE WIND — Vince Guaraldi Trio, Fantasy 563 | | 13 |
| ★ | 31 | 41 | 58 | GREENBACK DOLLAR — Kingston Trio, Capitol 4898 | | 6 |
| 27 | 28 | 30 | 42 | THE GYPSY CRIED — Lou Christie, Roulette 4457 | | 9 |
| 28 | 29 | 22 | 31 | CALL ON ME — Bobby Bland, Duke 360 | | 9 |
| ★ | 37 | 52 | 74 | BUTTERFLY BABY — Bobby Rydell, Cameo 242 | | 4 |
| ★ | 40 | 65 | — | LET'S LIMBO SOME MORE — Chubby Checker, Parkway 862 | | 3 |
| 31 | 34 | 44 | 62 | LET'S TURKEY TROT — Little Eva, Dimension 1006 | | 5 |
| 32 | 33 | 40 | 49 | I WANNA BE AROUND — Tony Bennett, Columbia 42634 | △ | 8 |
| ★ | 43 | 54 | 55 | HITCH HIKE — Marvin Gaye, Tamla 54075 | | 8 |
| 34 | 36 | 51 | 86 | BOSS GUITAR — Duane Eddy, RCA Victor 8131 | △ | 4 |
| ★ | 50 | 76 | — | SOUTH STREET — Orlons, Cameo 243 | | 3 |
| ★ | 46 | 55 | 60 | DAYS OF WINE AND ROSES — Henry Mancini, RCA Victor 8120 | △ | 6 |
| 37 | 39 | 45 | 38 | THAT'S THE WAY LOVE IS — Bobby Bland, Duke 360 | | 7 |
| 38 | 32 | 34 | 41 | YOUR USED TO BE — Brenda Lee, Decca 31454 | | 6 |
| 39 | 26 | 26 | 30 | LOVE (Makes the World Go 'Round) — Paul Anka, RCA Victor 8115 | △ | 7 |
| 40 | 19 | 9 | 4 | LOOP DE LOOP — Johnny Thunder, Diamond 129 | | 11 |
| ★ | 87 | — | — | HE'S SO FINE — Chiffons, Laurie 3152 | | 2 |
| 42 | 20 | 14 | 10 | GO AWAY LITTLE GIRL — Steve Lawrence, Columbia 42601 | △ | 17 |
| 43 | 35 | 21 | 13 | IT'S UP TO YOU — Rick Nelson, Imperial 5901 | | 12 |
| ★ | 59 | 83 | 89 | ALL I HAVE TO DO IS DREAM — Richard Chamberlain, MGM 13121 | | 4 |
| 45 | 38 | 19 | 12 | HALF HEAVEN—HALF HEARTACHE — Gene Pitney, Musicor 1026 | | 12 |
| 46 | 49 | 56 | 59 | EVERY DAY I HAVE TO CRY — Steve Alaimo, Checker 1032 | | 9 |
| 47 | 44 | 37 | 27 | MY COLORING BOOK — Sandy Stewart, Colpix 669 | | 10 |
| 48 | 41 | 27 | 25 | CINNAMON CINDER — Pastel Six, Zen 102 | | 10 |
| 49 | 52 | 60 | 64 | TELL HIM I'M NOT HOME — Chuck Jackson, Wand 132 | | 5 |
| 50 | 54 | 64 | 67 | ALL ABOUT MY GIRL — Jimmy McGriff, Sue 777 | | 9 |
| ★ | 78 | — | — | LAUGHING BOY — Mary Wells, Motown 1039 | | 2 |
| ★ | 65 | 77 | 94 | LOVE FOR SALE — Arthur Lyman Group, Hi-Fi 5066 | | 5 |
| 53 | 42 | 24 | 17 | MY DAD — Paul Petersen, Colpix 663 | | 16 |
| 54 | 47 | 48 | 51 | SHE'LL NEVER KNOW — Brenda Lee, Decca 31454 | | 6 |
| ★ | 69 | 75 | 90 | PIN A MEDAL ON JOEY — James Darren, Colpix 672 | | 4 |
| ★ | 73 | 81 | — | WHY DO LOVERS BREAK EACH OTHERS HEARTS — Bob B. Soxx & the Blue Jeans, Philles 110 | | 3 |
| 57 | 61 | 63 | 73 | BIG WIDE WORLD — Teddy Randazzo, Colpix 662 | | 6 |
| ★ | 77 | — | — | TWENTY MILES — Chubby Checker, Parkway 862 | | 2 |
| 59 | 62 | 70 | 71 | AS LONG AS SHE NEEDS ME — Sammy Davis Jr., Reprise 20138 | | 6 |
| 60 | 55 | 57 | 65 | WHO STOLE THE KEESHKA — Matys Brothers, Select 719 | | 7 |
| 61 | 63 | 68 | 72 | I REALLY DON'T WANT TO KNOW — "Little Esther" Phillips, Lenox 5560 | | 4 |
| ★ | 79 | 89 | — | LET'S STOMP — Bobby Comstock, Lawn 202 | | 3 |
| 63 | 57 | 61 | 53 | JAVA — Floyd Cramer, RCA Victor 8116 | △ | 10 |
| ★ | 86 | — | — | DON'T SET ME FREE — Ray Charles, ABC-Paramount 10405 | | 2 |
| ★ | — | — | — | DO THE BIRD — Dee Dee Sharp, Cameo 244 | | 1 |
| ★ | — | — | — | THAT'S ALL — Rick Nelson, Imperial 5910 | | 1 |
| 67 | 74 | — | — | THEY REMIND ME TOO MUCH OF YOU — Elvis Presley, RCA Victor 8134 | △ | 2 |
| ★ | 82 | 99 | — | MR. BASS MAN — Johnny Cymbal, Kapp 503 | | 3 |
| 69 | 64 | 66 | 54 | I'M A WOMAN — Peggy Lee, Capitol 4888 | | 9 |
| 70 | 66 | 71 | 87 | BABY, BABY, BABY — Sam Cooke, RCA Victor 8129 | △ | 5 |
| 71 | 68 | 72 | 61 | STRANGE I KNOW — Marvelettes, Tamla 54072 | | 14 |
| 72 | 84 | — | — | I'M IN LOVE AGAIN — Rick Nelson, Imperial 5910 | | 2 |
| 73 | 75 | 80 | — | RIDIN' THE WIND — Tornadoes, London 9581 | | 3 |
| 74 | 80 | 97 | — | HI-LILI, HI-LO — Richard Chamberlain, MGM 13121 | | 3 |
| 75 | 76 | 79 | 80 | I'M THE ONE WHO LOVES YOU — Impressions, ABC-Paramount 10386 | | 4 |
| 76 | 72 | 74 | 63 | CHICKEN FEED — Bent Fabric, Atco 6245 | | 8 |
| ★ 77 | — | — | — | OUT OF MY MIND — Johnny Tillotson, Cadence 1434 | | 1 |
| 78 | 89 | 96 | — | BOSSA NOVA U. S. A. — Dave Brubeck Quartet, Columbia 42675 | △ | 5 |
| 79 | 85 | — | — | RAINBOW — Gene Chandler, Vee Jay 468 | | 2 |
| ★ 80 | — | — | — | FOLLOW THE BOYS — Connie Francis, MGM 13127 | | 1 |
| ★ 81 | 99 | — | — | MEDITACAO (Meditation) — Charlie Byrd, Riverside 4544 | | 2 |
| ★ 82 | — | — | — | CAN'T GET USED TO LOSING YOU — Andy Williams, Columbia 42674 | △ | 1 |
| ★ 83 | — | — | — | SAX FIFTH AVENUE — Johnny Beecher, Warner Bros. 5341 | | 1 |
| 84 | 97 | 98 | — | JIVE SAMBA — Cannonball Adderley Sextet, Riverside 4541 | | 3 |
| 85 | 94 | — | — | YAKETY SAX — Boots Randolph, Monument 804 | | 2 |
| 86 | 90 | — | — | LINDA — Jan and Dean, Liberty 55531 | | 2 |
| 87 | 95 | — | — | WHAT DOES A GIRL DO? — Marcie Blane, Seville 123 | | 2 |
| ★ 88 | — | — | — | HE'S GOT THE POWER — Exciters, United Artists 572 | | 1 |
| ★ 89 | — | — | — | SANDY — Dion, Laurie 3153 | | 1 |
| ★ 90 | — | — | — | NOTHING GOES UP (Without Coming Down) — Nat King Cole, Capitol 4919 | | 1 |
| 91 | 91 | — | — | THE 2,000 POUND BEE — Ventures, Dolton 67 | | 2 |
| 92 | — | — | — | ALL OVER THE WORLD — Nat King Cole, Capitol 4919 | | 1 |
| 93 | — | — | — | PIPELINE — Chantays, Dot 16440 | | 1 |
| 94 | 96 | — | — | DON'T BE CRUEL — Barbara Lynn, Jamie 1244 | | 2 |
| 95 | 93 | — | — | DON'T FENCE ME IN — George Maharis, Epic 9569 | | 2 |
| 96 | — | — | — | DON'T SAY NOTHIN' BAD ABOUT MY BABY — Cookies, Demension 1008 | | 1 |
| 97 | 98 | — | — | FADED LOVE — Jackie De Shannon, Liberty 55526 | | 2 |
| 98 | — | — | — | MY FOOLISH HEART — Demensions, Coral 62344 | | 1 |
| 99 | — | — | — | IF MARY'S THERE — Brian Hyland, ABC-Paramount 10400 | | 1 |
| 100 | — | — | — | I'M JUST A COUNTRY BOY — George McCurn, A&M 705 | | 1 |

## HOT 100—A TO Z—(Publisher-Licensee)


Alice in Wonderland (Aldon, BMI) ... 21
All About My Girl (Saturn-Jell, BMI) ... 50
All I Have to Do Is Dream (Acuff-Rose, BMI) ... 44
All Over the World (Comet, ASCAP) ... 92
As Long as She Needs Me (Hollis, BMI) ... 59
Baby, Baby, Baby (Kags, BMI) ... 70
Big Wide World (South Mountain, BMI) ... 57
Blame It on the Bossa Nova (Aldon, BMI) ... 7
Boss Guitar (Linduane, BMI) ... 34
Bossa Nova U. S. A. (Derry, BMI) ... 78
Butterfly Baby (Kalmann, ASCAP) ... 29
Call on Me (Lion, BMI) ... 28
Can't Get Used to Losing You (Brenner, BMI) ... 82
Cast Your Fate to the Wind (Friendship, BMI) ... 25
Chicken Feed (Metorion, BMI) ... 76
Cinnamon Cinder (Algrace, BMI) ... 48
Days of Wine and Roses (Witmark, ASCAP) ... 36
Do the Bird (Kalmann, ASCAP) ... 65
Don't Be Cruel (Shalimar-Presley, BMI) ... 94
Don't Fence Me In (Harms, ASCAP) ... 95
Don't Say Nothin' Bad About My Baby (Aldon, BMI) ... 96
Don't Set Me Free (Tee-Pee, ASCAP) ... 64
End of the World, The (Summit, ASCAP) ... 12
Every Day I Have to Cry (Tiki, BMI) ... 46
Faded Love (Hill & Range, BMI) ... 97
Fly Me to the Moon—Bossa Nova (Almanac, ASCAP) ... 16
Follow the Boys (Francon, ASCAP) ... 80
From a Jack to a King (Dandelion, BMI) ... 8
Go Away Little Girl (Aldon, BMI) ... 42
Greenback Dollar (Davon, BMI) ... 26
Gypsy Cried, The (Painted Desert, BMI) ... 27
Half Heaven—Half Heartache (Arch, ASCAP) ... 45
He's Got the Power (Trio, BMI) ... 88
He's So Fine (Bright-Tunes, BMI) ... 41
He's Sure the Boy I Love (Aldon, BMI) ... 17
Hey Paula (LeBill-Marbill, BMI) ... 3
Hi-Lili, Hi-Lo (Robbins, ASCAP) ... 74
Hitch Hike (Jobete, BMI) ... 33
I Really Don't Want to Know (Hill & Range, BMI) 61
I Wanna Be Around (Commander, ASCAP) ... 32
I'm a Woman (Trio, BMI) ... 69
I'm in Love Again (Travis, BMI) ... 72
I'm Just a Country Boy (Folkways, BMI) ... 100
I'm the One Who Loves You (Curtom, BMI) ... 75
If Mary's There (Pogo, ASCAP) ... 99
In Dreams (Acuff-Rose, BMI) ... 20
It's Up to You (Four Star, BMI) ... 43
Java (Rush, BMI) ... 63
Jive Samba (Artillery, BMI) ... 84
Laughing Boy (Jobete, BMI) ... 51
Let's Limbo Some More (Kalmann, ASCAP) ... 30
Let's Stomp (Roosevelt, BMI) ... 62
Let's Turkey Trot (Aldon, BMI) ... 31
Linda (Warock, ASCAP) ... 86
Little Town Flirt (Vicki-McLaughlin, BMI) ... 18
Loop De Loop (Tobi-Ann & Vann, BMI) ... 40
Love (Spanka, BMI) ... 39
Love for Sale (Harms, ASCAP) ... 52
Mama Didn't Lie (Curtom, BMI) ... 15
Meditacao (Meditation) (Duchess, BMI) ... 81
Mr. Bass Man (Jalo, BMI) ... 68
My Coloring Book—Stewart (Sunbeam, BMI) ... 47
My Dad (Aldon, BMI) ... 53
My Foolish Heart (Joy, ASCAP) ... 98
Night Has a Thousand Eyes, The (Blen-Mabs, BMI) ... 24
Nothing Goes Up (Without Coming Down) (Eden, BMI) ... 90
One Broken Heart for Sale (Presley, BMI) ... 19
Our Day Will Come (Rosewood, ASCAP) ... 11
Our Winter Love (Cramart, BMI) ... 22
Out of My Mind (Ridge, BMI) ... 77
Pin a Medal on Joey (Gower, BMI) ... 55
Pipeline (Downey, BMI) ... 93
Rainbow (Conrad-Curtom, BMI) ... 79
Rhythm of the Rain (Sherman-DeVorzon, BMI) ... 4
Ridin' the Wind (Ivy, PRS, ASCAP) ... 73
Ruby Baby (Tiger, BMI) ... 2
Sandy (DiMucci-Brandt, ASCAP) ... 89
Sax Fifth Avenue (Radio Active, BMI) ... 83
Send Me Some Lovin' (Venice, BMI) ... 13
She'll Never Know (Fame, BMI) ... 54
South Street (Kalmann, ASCAP) ... 35
Strange I Know (Jobete, BMI) ... 71
Tell Him I'm Not Home (Figure, BMI) ... 49
That's All (Travis, BMI) ... 66
That's the Way Love Is (Lion, BMI) ... 37
They Remind Me Too Much of You (Gladys, ASCAP) ... 67
Twenty Miles (Wyncote-Kalmann, ASCAP) ... 58
The 2,000 Pound Bee (Electron, BMI) ... 91
Up on the Roof (Aldon, BMI) ... 23
Walk Like a Man (Saturday-Gavadema, ASCAP) ... 1
Walk Right In (Ryerson, BMI) ... 5
What Does a Girl Do (Ametrop, BMI) ... 87
What Will My Mary Say (Elm Drive, ASCAP) ... 10
Who Stole the Keeshka (Dana, BMI) ... 60
Why Do Lovers Break Each Others Hearts (January, BMI) ... 56
Wild Weekend (Shan-Todd & Tupper, BMI) ... 9
Yakety Sax (Tree, BMI) ... 85
You're the Reason I'm Living (Adaris, BMI) ... 6
You've Really Got a Hold on Me (Jobete, BMI) ... 14
Your Used to Be (Aldon, BMI) ... 38


## BUBBLING UNDER THE HOT 100

101. PEPINO'S FRIEND PASQUAL (The Italian Pussy-Cat) ... Lou Monte, Reprise 20146
102. THEME FROM LAWRENCE OF ARABIA ... Ferrante & Teicher, United Artists 563
103. DON'T MENTION MY NAME ... Shepard Sisters, Atlantic 2176
104. IS THIS ME? ... Jim Reeves, RCA Victor 8127
105. DON'T LET ME CROSS OVER ... Carl Butler, Columbia 42593
106. JELLY BREAD ... Booker T. & MG's, Stax 131
107. EVERY BEAT OF MY HEART ... James Brown & the Famous Flames, King 5710
108. LITTLE STAR ... Bobby Calendar, Roulette 4471
109. LET ME GO THE RIGHT WAY ... Supremes, Motown 1034
110. THE DOG ... Rufus Thomas, Stax 130
111. ONLY YOU ... Mr. Acker Bilk, Atco 6247
112. AM I THAT EASY TO FORGET ... "Little Esther" Phillips, Lenox 5560
113. DAYS OF WINE AND ROSES ... Andy Williams, Columbia 42674
114. BOSS ... Rumblers, Dot 16421
115. THE BIRD ... Dutones, Columbia 42657
116. PRETTY BOY LONELY ... Patti Page, Columbia 42671
117. BRIGHTEST SMILE IN TOWN ... Ray Charles, ABC-Paramount 10405
118. MEDITATION ... Pat Boone, Dot 16439
119. HOW CAN I FORGET ... Jimmy Holiday, Everest 2022
120. THE YELLOW BANDANA ... Faron Young, Mercury 72085
121. TWO WRONGS DON'T MAKE A RIGHT ... Mary Wells, Motown 1039
122. HEARTACHES OH HEARTACHES ... Lettermen, Capitol 4914
123. BABY DOLL ... Carlo, Laurie 3151
124. HUM DIDDY DOO ... Fats Domino, Imperial 5909
125. JUST A SIMPLE MELODY ... Patti Page, Columbia 42671
126. GONE WITH THE WIND ... Duprees, Coed 576
127. DENVER ... New Christy Minstrels, Columbia 42673
128. OUR LOVE WILL LAST ... Arthur Prysock, Old Town 1132

# Billboard HOT 100

FOR WEEK ENDING MARCH 9 1963

★ STAR PERFORMERS—Selections registering greatest upward progress this week.

[S] Indicates that 45 r.p.m. stereo single version is available.

△ Indicates that 33⅓ r.p.m. mono single version is available.

[S in triangle] Indicates that 33⅓ r.p.m. stereo single version is available.

| This Week | 1 Wk. Ago | 2 Wks. Ago | 3 Wks. Ago | Title | Artist, Label & Number | | Weeks On Chart |
|---|---|---|---|---|---|---|---|
| 1 | 1 | 3 | 3 | WALK LIKE A MAN | Four Seasons, Vee Jay 485 | | 7 |
| 2 | 2 | 2 | 4 | RUBY BABY | Dion, Columbia 42662 | △ | 8 |
| 3 | 4 | 5 | 5 | RHYTHM OF THE RAIN | Cascades, Valiant 6026 | | 9 |
| 4 | 3 | 1 | 1 | HEY PAULA | Paul & Paula, Philips 40084 | | 11 |
| 5 | 6 | 7 | 12 | YOU'RE THE REASON I'M LIVING | Bobby Darin, Capitol 4897 | | 8 |
| ★ 6 | 11 | 27 | 53 | OUR DAY WILL COME | Ruby and the Romantics, Kapp 501 | | 5 |
| ★ 7 | 12 | 21 | 36 | THE END OF THE WORLD | Skeeter Davis, RCA Victor 8098 | △ | 7 |
| 8 | 9 | 10 | 15 | WILD WEEKEND | Rebels, Swan 4125 | | 11 |
| 9 | 10 | 17 | 33 | WHAT WILL MY MARY SAY | Johnny Mathis, Columbia 42666 | △ | 7 |
| 10 | 5 | 4 | 2 | WALK RIGHT IN | Rooftop Singers, Vanguard 35017 | | 10 |
| 11 | 7 | 8 | 18 | BLAME IT ON THE BOSSA NOVA | Eydie Gorme, Columbia 42661 | △ | 8 |
| 12 | 8 | 6 | 6 | FROM A JACK TO A KING | Ned Miller, Fabor 114 | | 11 |
| ★ 13 | 20 | 23 | 47 | IN DREAMS | Roy Orbison, Monument 806 | | 5 |
| 14 | 15 | 16 | 16 | MAMA DIDN'T LIE | Jan Bradley, Chess 1845 | | 10 |
| ★ 15 | 22 | 30 | 37 | OUR WINTER LOVE | Bill Pursell, Columbia 42619 | △ | 6 |
| 16 | 19 | 25 | 59 | ONE BROKEN HEART FOR SALE | Elvis Presley, RCA Victor 8134 | △ | 4 |
| 17 | 21 | 24 | 32 | ALICE IN WONDERLAND | Neil Sedaka, RCA Victor 8137 | △ | 6 |
| 18 | 13 | 13 | 20 | SEND ME SOME LOVIN' | Sam Cooke, RCA Victor 8129 | △ | 6 |
| ★ 19 | 41 | 87 | — | HE'S SO FINE | Chiffons, Laurie 3152 | | 3 |
| 20 | 14 | 9 | 8 | YOU'VE REALLY GOT A HOLD ON ME | Miracles, Tamla 54073 | | 14 |
| ★ 21 | 35 | 50 | 76 | SOUTH STREET | Orions, Cameo 243 | | 4 |
| 22 | 26 | 31 | 41 | GREENBACK DOLLAR | Kingston Trio, Capitol 4898 | | 7 |
| ★ 23 | 29 | 37 | 52 | BUTTERFLY BABY | Bobby Rydell, Cameo 242 | | 5 |
| ★ 24 | 31 | 34 | 44 | LET'S TURKEY TROT | Little Eva, Dimension 1006 | | 6 |
| ★ 25 | 30 | 40 | 65 | LET'S LIMBO SOME MORE | Chubby Checker, Parkway 862 | | 4 |
| 26 | 27 | 28 | 30 | THE GYPSY CRIED | Lou Christie, Roulette 4457 | | 10 |
| 27 | 18 | 12 | 13 | LITTLE TOWN FLIRT | Del Shannon, Big Top 3131 | | 12 |
| 28 | 17 | 11 | 11 | HE'S SURE THE BOY I LOVE | Crystals, Philles 109 | | 11 |
| 29 | 16 | 14 | 17 | FLY ME TO THE MOON—BOSSA NOVA | Joe Harnell & Ork, Kapp 497 | | 11 |
| 30 | 32 | 33 | 40 | I WANNA BE AROUND | Tony Bennett, Columbia 42634 | △ | 9 |
| 31 | 34 | 36 | 51 | BOSS GUITAR | Duane Eddy, RCA Victor 8131 | △ | 5 |
| 32 | 33 | 43 | 54 | HITCH HIKE | Marvin Gaye, Tamla 54075 | | 9 |
| ★ 33 | 44 | 59 | 83 | ALL I HAVE TO DO IS DREAM | Richard Chamberlain, MGM 13121 | | 5 |
| 34 | 37 | 39 | 45 | THAT'S THE WAY LOVE IS | Bobby Bland, Duke 360 | | 8 |
| 35 | 36 | 46 | 55 | DAYS OF WINE AND ROSES | Henry Mancini, RCA Victor 8120 | △ | 7 |
| 36 | 23 | 18 | 10 | UP ON THE ROOF | Drifters, Atlantic 2162 | | 19 |
| 37 | 25 | 22 | 28 | CAST YOUR FATE TO THE WIND | Vince Guaraldi Trio, Fantasy 563 | | 14 |
| 38 | 28 | 29 | 22 | CALL ON ME | Bobby Bland, Duke 360 | | 10 |
| ★ 39 | 51 | 78 | — | LAUGHING BOY | Mary Wells, Motown 1039 | | 3 |
| ★ 40 | 65 | — | — | DO THE BIRD | Dee Dee Sharp, Cameo 244 | | 2 |
| ★ 41 | 64 | 86 | — | DON'T SET ME FREE | Ray Charles, ABC-Paramount 10405 | | 3 |
| ★ 42 | 56 | 73 | 81 | WHY DO LOVERS BREAK EACH OTHERS HEARTS | Bob B. Soxx & the Blue Jeans, Philles 110 | | 4 |
| 43 | 49 | 52 | 60 | TELL HIM I'M NOT HOME | Chuck Jackson, Wand 132 | | 6 |
| 44 | 38 | 32 | 34 | YOUR USED TO BE | Brenda Lee, Decca 31454 | | 7 |
| 45 | 24 | 15 | 7 | THE NIGHT HAS A THOUSAND EYES | Bobby Vee, Liberty 55521 | | 14 |
| 46 | 52 | 65 | 77 | LOVE FOR SALE | Arthur Lyman Group, Hi-Fi 5066 | | 6 |
| ★ 47 | 58 | 77 | — | TWENTY MILES | Chubby Checker, Parkway 862 | | 3 |
| ★ 48 | 68 | 82 | 99 | MR. BASS MAN | Johnny Cymbal, Kapp 503 | | 4 |
| 49 | 46 | 49 | 56 | EVERY DAY I HAVE TO CRY | Steve Alaimo, Checker 1032 | | 10 |
| ★ 50 | 66 | — | — | THAT'S ALL | Rick Nelson, Imperial 5910 | | 2 |
| 51 | 57 | 61 | 63 | BIG WIDE WORLD | Teddy Randazzo, Colpix 662 | | 7 |
| ★ 52 | 80 | — | — | FOLLOW THE BOYS | Connie Francis, MGM 13127 | | 2 |
| ★ 53 | 67 | 74 | — | THEY REMIND ME TOO MUCH OF YOU | Elvis Presley, RCA Victor 8134 | △ | 3 |
| 54 | 55 | 69 | 75 | PIN A MEDAL ON JOEY | James Darren, Colpix 672 | | 5 |
| 55 | 39 | 26 | 26 | LOVE (Makes the World Go 'Round) | Paul Anka, RCA Victor 8115 | △ | 8 |
| 56 | 50 | 54 | 64 | ALL ABOUT MY GIRL | Jimmy McGriff, Sue 777 | | 10 |
| ★ 57 | 85 | 94 | — | YAKETY SAX | Boots Randolph, Monument 804 | | 3 |
| ★ 58 | 82 | — | — | CAN'T GET USED TO LOSING YOU | Andy Williams, Columbia 42674 | △ | 2 |
| ★ 59 | 89 | — | — | SANDY | Dion, Laurie 3153 | | 2 |
| 60 | 62 | 79 | 89 | LET'S STOMP | Bobby Comstock, Lawn 202 | | 4 |
| 61 | 60 | 55 | 57 | WHO STOLE THE KEESHKA | Matys Brothers, Select 719 | | 8 |
| ★ 62 | 77 | — | — | OUT OF MY MIND | Johnny Tillotson, Cadence 1434 | | 2 |
| 63 | 73 | 75 | 80 | RIDIN' THE WIND | Tornadoes, London 9581 | | 4 |
| 64 | 74 | 80 | 97 | HI-LILI, HI-LO | Richard Chamberlain, MGM 13121 | | 4 |
| 65 | 59 | 62 | 70 | AS LONG AS SHE NEEDS ME | Sammy Davis Jr., Reprise 20138 | | 7 |
| 66 | 63 | 57 | 61 | JAVA | Floyd Cramer, RCA Victor 8116 | △ | 11 |
| 67 | 72 | 84 | — | I'M IN LOVE AGAIN | Rick Nelson, Imperial 5910 | | 3 |
| ★ 68 | 86 | 90 | — | LINDA | Jan and Dean, Liberty 55531 | | 3 |
| 69 | 78 | 89 | 96 | BOSSA NOVA U. S. A. | Dave Brubeck Quartet, Columbia 42675 | △ | 6 |
| ★ 70 | 88 | — | — | HE'S GOT THE POWER | Exciters, United Artists 572 | | 2 |
| 71 | 61 | 63 | 68 | I REALLY DON'T WANT TO KNOW | "Little Esther" Phillips, Lenox 5560 | | 5 |
| ★ 72 | 96 | — | — | DON'T SAY NOTHIN' BAD ABOUT MY BABY | Cookies, Demension 1008 | | 2 |
| 73 | 75 | 76 | 79 | I'M THE ONE WHO LOVES YOU | Impressions, ABC-Paramount 10386 | | 5 |
| 74 | 81 | 99 | — | MEDITACAO (Meditation) | Charlie Byrd, Riverside 4544 | | 3 |
| 75 | 79 | 85 | — | RAINBOW | Gene Chandler, Vee Jay 468 | | 3 |
| 76 | 70 | 66 | 71 | BABY, BABY, BABY | Sam Cooke, RCA Victor 8129 | △ | 6 |
| ★ 77 | — | — | — | YOU DON'T LOVE ME ANYMORE (And I Can Tell) | Rick Nelson, Decca 31475 | | 1 |
| ★ 78 | — | — | — | DON'T BE AFRAID, LITTLE DARLIN' | Steve Lawrence, Columbia 42699 | △ | 1 |
| 79 | 83 | — | — | SAX FIFTH AVENUE | Johnny Beecher, Warner Bros. 5341 | | 2 |
| 80 | 92 | — | — | ALL OVER THE WORLD | Nat King Cole, Capitol 4919 | | 2 |
| ★ 81 | — | — | — | BABY WORKOUT | Jackie Wilson, Brunswick 55239 | | 1 |
| 82 | 87 | 95 | — | WHAT DOES A GIRL DO! | Marcie Blane, Seville 123 | | 3 |
| 83 | 84 | 97 | 98 | JIVE SAMBA | Cannonball Adderley Sextet, Riverside 4541 | | 4 |
| ★ 84 | 100 | — | — | I'M JUST A COUNTRY BOY | George McCurn, A&M 705 | | 2 |
| 85 | — | — | — | PEPINO'S FRIEND PASQUAL (The Italian Pussy-Cat) | Lou Monte, Reprise 20146 | | 1 |
| ★ 86 | 93 | — | — | PIPELINE | Chantays, Dot 16440 | | 2 |
| ★ 87 | — | — | — | OVER THE MOUNTAIN (Across the Sea) | Bobby Vinton, Epic 9577 | | 1 |
| 88 | 99 | — | — | IF MARY'S THERE | Brian Hyland, ABC-Paramount 10400 | | 2 |
| ★ 89 | — | — | — | DEARER THAN LIFE | Brook Benton, Mercury 72099 | | 1 |
| ★ 90 | — | — | — | BACK AT THE CHICKEN SHACK | Jimmy Smith, Blue Note 1877 | | 1 |
| 91 | — | — | — | MEDITATIONS | Pat Boone, Dot 16439 | | 1 |
| 92 | — | 88 | 88 | THEME FROM LAWRENCE OF ARABIA | Ferrante & Teicher, United Artists 563 | | 4 |
| 93 | 94 | 96 | — | DON'T BE CRUEL | Barbara Lynn, Jamie 1244 | | 3 |
| 94 | — | — | — | DON'T MENTION MY NAME | Shepherd Sisters, Atlantic 2176 | | 1 |
| 95 | — | — | — | BRIGHTEST SMILE IN TOWN | Ray Charles, ABC-Paramount 10405 | | 1 |
| 96 | 91 | 91 | — | THE 2,000 POUND BEE | Ventures, Dolton 67 | | 3 |
| 97 | 98 | — | — | MY FOOLISH HEART | Demensions, Coral 62344 | | 2 |
| 98 | — | — | — | PRETTY BOY LONELY | Patti Page, Columbia 42671 | △ | 1 |
| 99 | — | — | 86 | I WILL LIVE MY LIFE FOR YOU | Tony Bennett, Columbia 42534 | △ | 8 |
| 100 | — | — | 87 | BOSS | Rumblers, Dot 16421 | | 2 |

## HOT 100—A TO Z—(Publisher-Licensee)

Alice in Wonderland (Aldon, BMI) .... 17
All About My Girl (Saturn-Jell, BMI) .... 56
All I Have to Do Is Dream (Acuff-Rose, BMI) .... 33
All Over the World (Comet, ASCAP) .... 80
As Long as She Needs Me (Hollis, BMI) .... 65
Baby, Baby, Baby (Kags, BMI) .... 76
Baby Workout (Merrimac, BMI) .... 81
Back at the Chicken Shack (Edmy, BMI) .... 90
Big Wide World (South Mountain, BMI) .... 51
Blame It on the Bossa Nova (Aldon, BMI) .... 11
Boss (Downey, BMI) .... 100
Boss Guitar (Linduane, BMI) .... 31
Bossa Nova U. S. A. (Derry, BMI) .... 69
Brightest Smile in Town (Sherman-DeVorzon, BMI) 95
Butterfly Baby (Kalmann, ASCAP) .... 23
Call on Me (Lion, BMI) .... 38
Can't Get Used to Losing You (Brenner, BMI) .. 58
Cast Your Fate to the Wind (Friendship, BMI) .. 37
Days of Wine and Roses (Witmark, ASCAP) .... 35
Dearer Than Life (Northridge, ASCAP) .... 89
Do the Bird (Kalmann, ASCAP) .... 40
Don't Be Afraid, Little Darlin' (Aldon, BMI) .... 78
Don't Be Cruel (Shalimar-Presley, BMI) .... 93
Don't Mention My Name (BoBob, ASCAP) .... 94
Don't Say Nothing' Bad About My Baby (Aldon, BMI) .... 72
Don't Set Me Free (Tee-Pee, ASCAP) .... 41
End of the World, The (Summit, ASCAP) .... 7
Every Day I Have to Cry (Tiki, BMI) .... 49
Fly Me to the Moon-Bossa Nova (Almanac, ASCAP) .... 29
Follow the Boys (Francon, ASCAP) .... 52
From a Jack to a King (Dandelion, BMI) .... 12
Greenback Dollar (Davon, BMI) .... 22
Gypsy Cried, The (Painted Desert, BMI) .... 26
He's Got the Power (Trio, BMI) .... 70
He's So Fine (Bright-Tunes, BMI) .... 19
He's Sure the Boy I Love (Aldon, BMI) .... 28
Hey Paula (LeBill-Marbill, BMI) .... 4
Hi-Lili, Hi-Lo (Robbins, ASCAP) .... 64
Hitch Hike (Jobete, BMI) .... 32
I Really Don't Want to Know (Hill & Range, BMI) 71
I Wanna Be Around (Commander, ASCAP) .... 30
I Will Live My Life for You (Tunetime-Gil, BMI).. 99
I'm in Love Again (Travis, BMI) .... 67
I'm Just a Country Boy (Folkways, BMI) .... 84
I'm the One Who Loves You (Curtom, BMI) .... 73
If Mary's There (Pogo, ASCAP) .... 88
In Dreams (Acuff-Rose, BMI) .... 13
Java (Rush, BMI) .... 66
Jive Samba (Artillery, BMI) .... 83
Laughing Boy (Jobete, BMI) .... 39
Let's Limbo Some More (Kalmann, ASCAP) .... 25
Let's Stomp (Roosevelt, BMI) .... 60
Let's Turkey Trot (Aldon, BMI) .... 24
Linda (Warock, ASCAP) .... 68
Little Town Flirt (Vicki-McLaughlin, BMI) .... 27
Love (Spanka, BMI) .... 55
Love for Sale (Harms, ASCAP) .... 46
Mama Didn't Lie (Curtom, BMI) .... 14
Meditacao (Meditation) (Duchess, BMI) .... 74
Meditations (Duchess, BMI) .... 91
Mr. Bass Man (Jalo, BMI) .... 48
My Foolish Heart (Joy, ASCAP) .... 97
Night Has a Thousand Eyes, The (Blen-Mabs, BMI) 45
One Broken Heart for Sale (Presley, BMI) .... 16
Our Day Will Come (Rosewood, ASCAP) .... 6
Our Winter Love (Cramart, BMI) .... 15
Out of My Mind (Ridge, BMI) .... 62
Over the Mountain (Arc, BMI) .... 87
Pepino's Friend Pasqual (Romance-Sal. Songs, BMI) .... 85
Pin a Medal on Joey (Gower, BMI) .... 54
Pipeline (Downey, BMI) .... 86
Pretty Boy Lonely (January, BMI) .... 98
Rainbow (Conrad-Curtom, BMI) .... 75
Rhythm of the Rain (Sherman-DeVorzon, BMI) .... 3
Ridin' the Wind (Ivy, PRS, ASCAP) .... 63
Ruby Baby (Tiger, BMI) .... 2
Sandy (DiMucci-Brandt, ASCAP) .... 59
Sax Fifth Avenue (Radio Active, BMI) .... 79
Send Me Some Lovin' (Venice, BMI) .... 18
South Street (Kalmann, ASCAP) .... 21
Tell Him I'm Not Home (Figure, BMI) .... 43
That's All (Travis, BMI) .... 50
That's the Way Love Is (Lion, BMI) .... 34
Theme From Lawrence of Arabia (Gower, BMI) .. 92
They Remind Me Too Much of You (Gladys, ASCAP) .... 53
Twenty Miles (Wyncote-Kalmann, ASCAP) .... 47
2,000 Pound Bee, The (Electron, BMI) .... 96
Up on the Roof (Aldon, BMI) .... 36
Walk Like a Man (Saturday-Gavadema, ASCAP) .. 1
Walk Right In (Ryerson, BMI) .... 10
What Does a Girl Do (Ametrop, BMI) .... 82
What Will My Mary Say (Elm Drive, ASCAP) .. 9
Who Stole the Keeshka (Dana, BMI) .... 61
Why Do Lovers Break Each Others Hearts (January, BMI) .... 42
Wild Weekend (Shan-Todd & Tupper, BMI) .... 8
Yakety Sax (Tree, BMI) .... 57
You Don't Love Me Anymore (Painted Desert) BMI) 77
You're the Reason I'm Living (Adaris, BMI) .... 5
You've Really Got a Hold on Me (Jobete, BMI) .... 20
Your Used to Be (Aldon, BMI) .... 44

## BUBBLING UNDER THE HOT 100

101. DAYS OF WINE AND ROSES ....Andy Williams, Columbia 42674
102. NOTHING GOES UP (Without Going Down)....Nat King Cole, Capitol 4919
103. DON'T LET ME CROSS OVER ....Carl Butler, Columbia 42593
104. LITTLE STAR ....Bobby Calendar, Roulette 4471
105. THE DOG ....Rufus Thomas, Stax 130
106. I GOT A WOMAN ....Rick Nelson, Decca 31475
107. ONLY YOU ....Mr. Acker Bilk, Atco 6247
108. THE BIRD ....Dutones, Columbia 42657
109. EVERY BEAT OF MY HEART ....James Brown and the Famous Flames, King 5710
110. DON'T FENCE ME IN ....George Maharis, Epic 9569
111. IS THIS ME? ....Jim Reeves, RCA Victor 8127
112. TWO WRONGS DON'T MAKE A RIGHT ....Mary Wells, Motown 1039
113. FADED LOVE ....Jackie De Shannon, Liberty 55526
114. JUST A SIMPLE MELODY ....Patti Page, Columbia 42671
115. THE YELLOW BANDANA ....Faron Young, Mercury 72085
116. DON'T WANT TO THINK ABOUT PAULA ....Dickey Lee, Smash 1808
117. DON'T LET ME CROSS OVER ....Adam Wade, Epic 9566
118. SUN ARISE ....Rolf Harris, Epic 9567
119. HOW CAN I FORGET ....Jimmy Holiday, Everest 2022
120. LET ME GO THE RIGHT WAY ....Supremes, Motown 1034
121. AMY ....Paul Petersen, Colpix 676
122. DAYS OF WINE AND ROSES ....Pat Boone, Dot 16439
123. THIS EMPTY PLACE ....Dionne Warwick, Scepter 1247
124. PUFF ....Paul & Mary, Warner Bros. 5348
125. YOUNG AND IN LOVE ....Dick & Deedee, Warner Bros. 5342
126. WHAT ARE BOYS MADE OF ....Purcells, ABC-Paramount 10401
127. WAITING FOR BILLY ....Connie Francis, MGM 13127
128. I GOT WHAT I WANTED ....Brook Benton, Mercury 72099
129. NEVER ....Earls, Old Town 1133
130. ETERNALLY ....Chantels, Ludix 101
131. BABY DOLL ....Carlo, Laurie 3151

# Billboard HOT 100

FOR WEEK ENDING MARCH 16 1963

★ STAR PERFORMERS—Selections registering greatest upward progress this week.

[S] Indicates that 45 r.p.m. stereo single version is available.

△ Indicates that 33⅓ r.p.m. mono single version is available.

[S△] Indicates that 33⅓ r.p.m. stereo single version is available.

| This Week | 1 Wk. Ago | 2 Wks. Ago | 3 Wks. Ago | Title | Artist, Label & Number | | Weeks On Chart |
|---|---|---|---|---|---|---|---|
| 1 | 1 | 1 | 3 | WALK LIKE A MAN | Four Seasons, Vee Jay 485 | | 8 |
| ★ 2 | 6 | 11 | 27 | OUR DAY WILL COME | Ruby and the Romantics, Kapp 501 | | 6 |
| 3 | 5 | 6 | 7 | YOU'RE THE REASON I'M LIVING | Bobby Darin, Capitol 4897 | | 9 |
| ★ 4 | 7 | 12 | 21 | THE END OF THE WORLD | Skeeter Davis, RCA Victor 8098 | △ | 8 |
| 5 | 3 | 4 | 5 | RHYTHM OF THE RAIN | Cascades, Valiant 6026 | | 10 |
| 6 | 2 | 2 | 2 | RUBY BABY | Dion, Columbia 42662 | △ | 9 |
| 7 | 4 | 3 | 1 | HEY PAULA | Paul & Paula, Philips 40084 | | 12 |
| ★ 8 | 11 | 7 | 8 | BLAME IT ON THE BOSSA NOVA | Eydie Gorme, Columbia 42661 | △ | 9 |
| 9 | 9 | 10 | 17 | WHAT WILL MY MARY SAY | Johnny Mathis, Columbia 42666 | △ | 8 |
| ★ 10 | 19 | 41 | 87 | HE'S SO FINE | Chiffons, Laurie 3152 | | 4 |
| ★ 11 | 16 | 19 | 25 | ONE BROKEN HEART FOR SALE | Elvis Presley, RCA Victor 8134 | △ | 5 |
| 12 | 8 | 9 | 10 | WILD WEEKEND | Rebels, Swan 4125 | | 12 |
| 13 | 13 | 20 | 23 | IN DREAMS | Roy Orbison, Monument 806 | | 6 |
| 14 | 14 | 15 | 16 | MAMA DIDN'T LIE | Jan Bradley, Chess 1845 | | 11 |
| 15 | 15 | 22 | 30 | OUR WINTER LOVE | Bill Pursell, Columbia 42619 | △ | 7 |
| ★ 16 | 21 | 35 | 50 | SOUTH STREET | Orlons, Cameo 243 | | 5 |
| 17 | 17 | 21 | 24 | ALICE IN WONDERLAND | Neil Sedaka, RCA Victor 8137 | △ | 7 |
| 18 | 18 | 13 | 13 | SEND ME SOME LOVIN' | Sam Cooke, RCA Victor 8129 | △ | 7 |
| 19 | 10 | 5 | 4 | WALK RIGHT IN | Rooftop Singers, Vanguard 35017 | | 11 |
| ★ 20 | 25 | 30 | 40 | LET'S LIMBO SOME MORE | Chubby Checker, Parkway 862 | | 5 |
| 21 | 22 | 26 | 31 | GREENBACK DOLLAR | Kingston Trio, Capitol 4898 | | 8 |
| 22 | 24 | 31 | 34 | LET'S TURKEY TROT | Little Eva, Dimension 1006 | | 7 |
| 23 | 23 | 29 | 37 | BUTTERFLY BABY | Bobby Rydell, Cameo 242 | | 6 |
| 24 | 26 | 27 | 28 | THE GYPSY CRIED | Lou Christie, Roulette 4457 | | 11 |
| ★ 25 | 30 | 32 | 33 | I WANNA BE AROUND | Tony Bennett, Columbia 42634 | △ | 10 |
| 26 | 12 | 8 | 6 | FROM A JACK TO A KING | Ned Miller, Fabor 114 | | 12 |
| ★ 27 | 33 | 44 | 59 | ALL I HAVE TO DO IS DREAM | Richard Chamberlain, MGM 13121 | | 6 |
| 28 | 31 | 34 | 36 | BOSS GUITAR | Duane Eddy, RCA Victor 8131 | △ | 6 |
| 29 | 20 | 14 | 9 | YOU'VE REALLY GOT A HOLD ON ME | Miracles, Tamla 54073 | | 15 |
| 30 | 32 | 33 | 43 | HITCH HIKE | Marvin Gaye, Tamla 54075 | | 10 |
| 31 | 39 | 51 | 78 | LAUGHING BOY | Mary Wells, Motown 1039 | | 4 |
| 32 | 40 | 65 | — | DO THE BIRD | Dee Dee Sharp, Cameo 244 | | 3 |
| 33 | 34 | 37 | 39 | THAT'S THE WAY LOVE IS | Bobby Bland, Duke 360 | | 9 |
| 34 | 35 | 36 | 46 | DAYS OF WINE AND ROSES | Henry Mancini, RCA Victor 8120 | △ | 8 |
| 35 | 37 | 25 | 22 | CAST YOUR FATE TO THE WIND | Vince Guaraldi Trio, Fantasy 563 | | 15 |
| 36 | 41 | 64 | 86 | DON'T SET ME FREE | Ray Charles, ABC-Paramount 10405 | | 4 |
| ★ 37 | 48 | 68 | 82 | MR. BASS MAN | Johnny Cymbal, Kapp 503 | | 5 |
| 38 | 38 | 28 | 29 | CALL ON ME | Bobby Bland, Duke 360 | | 11 |
| 39 | 29 | 16 | 14 | FLY ME TO THE MOON—BOSSA NOVA | Joe Harnell & Ork, Kapp 497 | | 12 |
| ★ 40 | 52 | 80 | — | FOLLOW THE BOYS | Connie Francis, MGM 13127 | | 3 |
| 41 | 42 | 56 | 73 | WHY DO LOVERS BREAK EACH OTHERS HEARTS | Bob B. Soxx & the Blue Jeans, Philles 110 | | 5 |
| 42 | 43 | 49 | 52 | TELL HIM I'M NOT HOME | Chuck Jackson, Wand 132 | | 7 |
| 43 | 47 | 58 | 77 | TWENTY MILES | Chubby Checker, Parkway 862 | | 4 |
| ★ 44 | 58 | 82 | — | CAN'T GET USED TO LOSING YOU | Andy Williams, Columbia 42674 | △ | 3 |
| ★ 45 | 57 | 85 | 94 | YAKETY SAX | Boots Randolph, Monument 804 | | 4 |
| 46 | 46 | 52 | 65 | LOVE FOR SALE | Arthur Lyman Group, Hi-Fi 5066 | | 7 |
| 47 | 27 | 18 | 12 | LITTLE TOWN FLIRT | Del Shannon, Big Top 3131 | | 13 |
| 48 | 50 | 66 | — | THAT'S ALL | Rick Nelson, Imperial 5910 | | 3 |
| 49 | 28 | 17 | 11 | HE'S SURE THE BOY I LOVE | Crystals, Philles 109 | | 12 |
| ★ 50 | 81 | — | — | BABY WORKOUT | Jackie Wilson, Brunswick 55239 | | 2 |
| ★ 51 | 78 | — | — | DON'T BE AFRAID, LITTLE DARLIN' | Steve Lawrence, Columbia 42699 | △ | 2 |
| ★ 52 | 62 | 77 | — | OUT OF MY MIND | Johnny Tillotson, Cadence 1434 | | 3 |
| 53 | 59 | 89 | — | SANDY | Dion, Laurie 3153 | | 3 |
| ★ 54 | 72 | 96 | — | DON'T SAY NOTHIN' BAD ABOUT MY BABY | Cookies, Demension 1008 | | 3 |
| ★ 55 | 80 | 92 | — | ALL OVER THE WORLD | Nat King Cole, Capitol 4919 | | 3 |
| ★ 56 | 87 | — | — | OVER THE MOUNTAIN (Across the Sea) | Bobby Vinton, Epic 9577 | | 2 |
| 57 | 60 | 62 | 79 | LET'S STOMP | Bobby Comstock, Lawn 202 | | 5 |
| ★ 58 | — | — | — | YOUNG LOVERS | Paul & Paula, Philips 40096 | | 1 |
| 59 | 36 | 23 | 18 | UP ON THE ROOF | Drifters, Atlantic 2162 | | 20 |
| 60 | 53 | 67 | 74 | THEY REMIND ME TOO MUCH OF YOU | Elvis Presley, RCA Victor 8134 | △ | 4 |
| ★ 61 | — | — | — | PUFF | Peter, Paul & Mary, Warner Bros. 5348 | | 1 |
| ★ 62 | 77 | — | — | YOU DON'T LOVE ME ANYMORE (And I Can Tell) | Rick Nelson, Decca 31475 | | 2 |
| 63 | 68 | 86 | 90 | LINDA | Jan and Dean, Liberty 55531 | | 4 |
| 64 | 51 | 57 | 61 | BIG WIDE WORLD | Teddy Randazzo, Colpix 662 | | 8 |
| 65 | 65 | 59 | 62 | AS LONG AS SHE NEEDS ME | Sammy Davis Jr., Reprise 20138 | | 8 |
| ★ 66 | 83 | 84 | 97 | JIVE SAMBA | Cannonball Adderley Sextet, Riverside 4541 | | 5 |
| 67 | 70 | 88 | — | HE'S GOT THE POWER | Exciters, United Artists 572 | | 3 |
| 68 | 63 | 73 | 75 | RIDIN' THE WIND | Tornadoes, London 9581 | | 5 |
| 69 | 69 | 78 | 89 | BOSSA NOVA U. S. A. | Dave Brubeck Quartet, Columbia 42675 | △ | 7 |
| 70 | 75 | 79 | 85 | RAINBOW | Gene Chandler, Vee Jay 468 | | 4 |
| ★ 71 | 86 | 93 | — | PIPELINE | Chantays, Dot 16440 | | 3 |
| 72 | 74 | 81 | 99 | MEDITATION (Meditacao) | Charlie Byrd, Riverside 4544 | | 3 |
| 73 | 73 | 75 | 76 | I'M THE ONE WHO LOVES YOU | Impressions, ABC-Paramount 10386 | | 6 |
| ★ 74 | — | — | — | I GOT WHAT I WANTED | Brook Benton, Mercury 72099 | | 1 |
| 75 | 56 | 50 | 54 | ALL ABOUT MY GIRL | Jimmy McGriff, Sue 777 | | 11 |
| 76 | 76 | 70 | 66 | BABY, BABY, BABY | Sam Cooke, RCA Victor 8129 | △ | 7 |
| 77 | 79 | 83 | — | SAX FIFTH AVENUE | Johnny Beecher, Warner Bros. 5341 | | 3 |
| 78 | 67 | 72 | 84 | I'M IN LOVE AGAIN | Rick Nelson, Imperial 5910 | | 4 |
| 79 | 54 | 55 | 69 | PIN A MEDAL ON JOEY | James Darren, Colpix 672 | | 6 |
| 80 | 84 | 100 | — | I'M JUST A COUNTRY BOY | George McCurn, A&M 705 | | 3 |
| 81 | 90 | — | — | BACK AT THE CHICKEN SHACK | Jimmy Smith, Blue Note 1877 | | 2 |
| 82 | 89 | — | — | DEARER THAN LIFE | Brook Benton, Mercury 72099 | | 2 |
| ★ 83 | — | — | — | WATERMELON MAN | Mongo Santamaria, Battle 45909 | | 1 |
| 84 | 85 | — | — | PEPINO'S FRIEND PASQUAL (The Italian Pussy-Cat) | Lou Monte, Reprise 20146 | | 2 |
| 85 | 64 | 74 | 80 | HI-LILI, HI-LO | Richard Chamberlain, MGM 13121 | | 5 |
| ★ 86 | — | — | — | I GOT A WOMAN | Rick Nelson, Decca 31475 | | 1 |
| 87 | 61 | 60 | 55 | WHO STOLE THE KEESHKA | Matys Brothers, Select 719 | | 9 |
| ★ 88 | — | — | — | SUN ARISE | Rolf Harris, Epic 9567 | | 1 |
| ★ 89 | — | — | — | YOUNG AND IN LOVE | Dick & Deedee, Warner Bros. 5342 | | 1 |
| ★ 90 | — | — | — | DAYS OF WINE AND ROSES | Andy Williams, Columbia 42674 | △ | 1 |
| 91 | 92 | — | 88 | THEME FROM LAWRENCE OF ARABIA | Ferrante & Teicher, United Artists 563 | | 5 |
| 92 | 95 | — | — | BRIGHTEST SMILE IN TOWN | Ray Charles, ABC-Paramount 10405 | | 2 |
| 93 | 93 | 94 | 96 | DON'T BE CRUEL | Barbara Lynn, Jamie 1244 | | 4 |
| 94 | — | — | — | HOW CAN I FORGET | Jimmy Holiday, Everest 2022 | | 1 |
| 95 | 97 | 98 | — | MY FOOLISH HEART | Demensions, Coral 62344 | | 3 |
| 96 | — | — | — | HOW CAN I FORGET | Ben E. King, Atco 6256 | | 1 |
| 97 | — | — | — | CIGARETTES AND COFFEE BLUES | Marty Robbins, Columbia 42701 | △ | 1 |
| 98 | — | — | — | LITTLE STAR | Bobby Calendar, Roulette 4471 | | 1 |
| 99 | — | — | — | DON'T WANNA THINK ABOUT PAULA | Dickey Lee, Smash 1808 | | 1 |
| 100 | — | 90 | — | NOTHING GOES UP (Without Coming Down) | Nat King Cole, Capitol 4919 | | 2 |

## HOT 100—A TO Z—(Publisher-Licensee)


Alice in Wonderland (Aldon, BMI) ... 17
All About My Girl (Saturn-Jell, BMI) ... 75
All I Have to Do Is Dream (Acuff-Rose, BMI) ... 27
All Over the World (Comet, ASCAP) ... 55
As Long as She Needs Me (Hollis, BMI) ... 65
Baby, Baby, Baby (Kags, BMI) ... 76
Baby Workout (Merrimac, BMI) ... 50
Back at the Chicken Shack (Edmy, BMI) ... 81
Big Wide World (South Mountain, BMI) ... 64
Blame It on the Bossa Nova (Aldon, BMI) ... 8
Boss Guitar (Linduane, BMI) ... 28
Boss Nova U. S. A. (Derry, BMI) ... 69
Brightest Smile in Town (Sherman-DeVorzon, BMI). 92
Butterfly Baby (Kalmann, ASCAP) ... 23
Call on Me (Lion, BMI) ... 38
Can't Get Used to Losing You (Brenner, BMI) ... 44
Cast Your Fate to the Wind (Friendship, BMI) ... 35
Cigarettes & Coffee Blues (Marty's, BMI) ... 97
Days of Wine and Roses—Mancini (Witmark, ASCAP) ... 34
Days of Wine and Roses—Williams (Witmark, ASCAP) ... 90
Dearer Than Life (Northridge, ASCAP) ... 82
Do the Bird (Kalmann, ASCAP) ... 32
Don't Be Afraid, Little Darlin' (Aldon, BMI) ... 51
Don't Be Cruel (Shalimar-Presley, BMI) ... 93
Don't Say Nothin' Bad About My Baby (Aldon, BMI) ... 54
Don't Set Me Free (Tee-Pee, ASCAP) ... 36
Don't Wanna Think About Paula (Jack, BMI) ... 99
End of the World, The (Summit, ASCAP) ... 4
Fly Me to the Moon—Bossa Nova (Almanac, ASCAP) ... 39
Follow the Boys (Francon, ASCAP) ... 40
From a Jack to a King (Dandelion, BMI) ... 26
Greenback Dollar (Davon, BMI) ... 21
Gypsy Cried, The (Painted Desert, BMI) ... 24
He's Got the Power (Trio, BMI) ... 67
He's So Fine (Bright-Tunes, BMI) ... 10
He's Sure the Boy I Love (Aldon, BMI) ... 49
Hey Paula (LeBill-Marbill, BMI) ... 7
Hi-Lili, Hi-Lo (Robbins, ASCAP) ... 85
Hitch Hike (Jobete, BMI) ... 30
How Can I Forget—Holiday (Arrowhead, BMI) ... 94
How Can I Forget—King (Arrowhead, BMI) ... 96
I Got a Woman (Progressive, BMI) ... 86
I Got What I Wanted (Ben Day, BMI) ... 74
I Wanna Be Around (Commander, ASCAP) ... 25
I'm in Love Again (Travis, BMI) ... 78
I'm Just a Country Boy (Folkways, BMI) ... 80
I'm the One Who Loves You (Curtom, BMI) ... 73
In Dreams (Acuff-Rose, BMI) ... 13
Jive Samba (Artillery, BMI) ... 66
Laughing Boy (Jobete, BMI) ... 31
Let's Limbo Some More (Kalmann, ASCAP) ... 20
Let's Stomp (Roosevelt, BMI) ... 57
Let's Turkey Trot (Aldon, BMI) ... 22
Linda (Warock, ASCAP) ... 63
Little Star (Patricia, BMI) ... 98
Little Town Flirt (Vicki-McLaughlin, BMI) ... 47
Love for Sale (Harms, ASCAP) ... 46
Mama Didn't Lie (Curtom, BMI) ... 14
Meditation (Meditacao) (Duchess, BMI) ... 72
Mr. Bass Man (Jalo, BMI) ... 37
My Foolish Heart (Joy, ASCAP) ... 95
Nothing Goes Up (Sweco-Eden, BMI) ... 100
One Broken Heart for Sale (Presley, BMI) ... 11
Our Day Will Come (Rosewood, ASCAP) ... 2
Our Winter Love (Cramart, BMI) ... 15
Out of My Mind (Ridge, BMI) ... 52
Over the Mountain (Arc, BMI) ... 56
Pepino's Friend Pasqual (Romance-Sal. Songs, BMI). 84
Pin a Medal on Joey (Gower, BMI) ... 79
Pipeline (Downey, BMI) ... 71
Puff (Pepamar, ASCAP) ... 61
Rainbow (Conrad-Curtom, BMI) ... 70
Rhythm of the Rain (Sherman-DeVorzon, BMI) ... 5
Ridin' the Wind (Ivy, PRS, ASCAP) ... 68
Ruby Baby (Tiger, BMI) ... 6
Sandy (DiMucci-Brandt, ASCAP) ... 53
Sax Fifth Avenue (Radio Active, BMI) ... 77
Send Me Some Lovin' (Venice, BMI) ... 18
South Street (Kalmann, ASCAP) ... 16
Sun Arise (Ardmore, ASCAP) ... 88
Tell Him I'm Not Home (Figure, BMI) ... 42
That's All (Travis, BMI) ... 48
That's the Way Love Is (Lion, BMI) ... 33
Theme From Lawrence of Arabia (Gower, BMI) ... 91
They Remind Me Too Much of You (Gladys, ASCAP). 60
Twenty Miles (Wyncote-Kalmann, ASCAP) ... 43
Up on the Roof (Aldon, BMI) ... 59
Walk Like a Man (Saturday-Gavadema, ASCAP) ... 1
Walk Right In (Ryerson, BMI) ... 19
Watermelon Man (Aries, BMI) ... 83
What Will My Mary Say (Elm Drive, ASCAP) ... 9
Who Stole the Keeshka (Dana, BMI) ... 87
Why Do Lovers Break Each Others Hearts (January, BMI) ... 41
Wild Weekend (Shan-Todd & Topper, BMI) ... 12
Yakety Sax (Tree, BMI) ... 45
You Don't Love Me Anymore (Painted Desert, BMI). 62
Young and in Love (Odin, ASCAP) ... 89
Young Lovers (LeBill-Marbill, BMI) ... 58
You're the Reason I'm Living (Adaris, BMI) ... 3
You've Really Got a Hold on Me (Jobete, BMI) ... 29


## BUBBLING UNDER THE HOT 100

101. DON'T LET ME CROSS OVER ... Carl Butler, Columbia 42593
102. THE DOG ... Rufus Thomas, Stax 130
103. I WILL LIVE MY LIFE FOR YOU ... Tony Bennett, Columbia 42534
104. DON'T MENTION MY NAME ... Shepherd Sisters, Atlantic 2176
105. ETERNALLY ... Chantels, Ludix 101
106. THE BIRD ... Dutones, Columbia 42657
107. AMY ... Paul Petersen, Colpix 676
108. LOCKING UP MY HEART ... Marvelettes, Tamla 54077
109. TWO WRONGS DON'T MAKE A RIGHT ... Mary Wells, Motown 1039
110. DON'T FENCE ME IN ... George Maharis, Epic 9569
111. IS THIS ME? ... Jim Reeves, RCA Victor 8127
112. MEDITATIONS ... Pat Boone, Dot 16439
113. PRETTY BOY LONELY ... Patti Page, Columbia 42671
114. THE YELLOW BANDANA ... Faron Young, Mercury 72085
115. WHAT DOES A GIRL DO ... Marcie Blane, Seville 123
116. WHAT ARE BOYS MADE OF? ... Purcells, ABC-Paramount 10401
117. DAYS OF WINE AND ROSES ... Pat Boone, Dot 16439
118. IF MARY'S THERE ... Brian Hyland, ABC-Paramount 10400
119. DON'T LET ME CROSS OVER ... Adam Wade, Epic 9566
120. THIS EMPTY PLACE ... Dionne Warwick, Scepter 1247
121. WORDS ... Solomon Burke, Atlantic 2180
122. FUNNY MAN ... Ray Stevens, Mercury 72098
123. HERE I STAND ... Rip Chords, Columbia 42687
124. ON BROADWAY ... Drifters, Atlantic 2182
125. SHOOK UP OVER YOU ... Dee Clark, Vee Jay 487
126. ANN-MARIE ... Belmonts, Sabina 509
127. IF YOU WANNA BE HAPPY ... Jimmy Soul, S.P.Q.R. 3305
128. SHE'LL NEVER, NEVER LOVE YOU ... Teresa Brewer, Philips 40095
129. NEVER ... Earls, Old Town 1133
130. LITTLE BAND OF GOLD ... James Gilreath, Joy 274
131. HELLO WALL NO. 2 ... Ben Colder, MGM 13122
132. KILLER JOE ... Rocky Fellers, Scepter 1246

# Billboard HOT 100

FOR WEEK ENDING MARCH 23 1963

★ STAR PERFORMERS—Selections registering greatest upward progress this week.

S Indicates that 45 r.p.m. stereo single version is available.

△ Indicates that 33⅓ r.p.m. mono single version is available.

Ⓢ Indicates that 33⅓ r.p.m. stereo single version is available.

| This Week | 1 Wk. Ago | 2 Wks. Ago | 3 Wks. Ago | TITLE Artist, Label & Number | | Weeks On Chart |
|---|---|---|---|---|---|---|
| 1 | 2 | 6 | 11 | OUR DAY WILL COME — Ruby and the Romantics, Kapp 501 | | 7 |
| 2 | 4 | 7 | 12 | THE END OF THE WORLD — Skeeter Davis, RCA Victor 8098 | △ | 9 |
| 3 | 3 | 5 | 6 | YOU'RE THE REASON I'M LIVING — Bobby Darin, Capitol 4897 | | 10 |
| ★ 4 | 10 | 19 | 41 | HE'S SO FINE — Chiffons, Laurie 3152 | | 5 |
| 5 | 1 | 1 | 1 | WALK LIKE A MAN — Four Seasons, Vee Jay 485 | | 9 |
| 6 | 5 | 3 | 4 | RHYTHM OF THE RAIN — Cascades, Valiant 6026 | | 11 |
| ★ 7 | 16 | 21 | 35 | SOUTH STREET — Orlons, Cameo 243 | | 6 |
| 8 | 8 | 11 | 7 | BLAME IT ON THE BOSSA NOVA — Eydie Gorme, Columbia 42661 | △ | 10 |
| 9 | 9 | 9 | 10 | WHAT WILL MY MARY SAY — Johnny Mathis, Columbia 42666 | △ | 9 |
| ★ 10 | 13 | 13 | 20 | IN DREAMS — Roy Orbison, Monument 806 | | 7 |
| 11 | 11 | 16 | 19 | ONE BROKEN HEART FOR SALE — Elvis Presley, RCA Victor 8134 | △ | 6 |
| 12 | 6 | 2 | 2 | RUBY BABY — Dion, Columbia 42662 | △ | 10 |
| 13 | 15 | 15 | 22 | OUR WINTER LOVE — Bill Pursell, Columbia 42619 | △ | 8 |
| 14 | 7 | 4 | 3 | HEY PAULA — Paul & Paula, Philips 40084 | | 13 |
| 15 | 12 | 8 | 9 | WILD WEEKEND — Rebels, Swan 4125 | | 13 |
| ★ 16 | 25 | 30 | 32 | I WANNA BE AROUND — Tony Bennett, Columbia 42634 | △ | 11 |
| ★ 17 | 27 | 33 | 44 | ALL I HAVE TO DO IS DREAM — Richard Chamberlain, MGM 13121 | | 7 |
| 18 | 14 | 14 | 15 | MAMA DIDN'T LIE — Jan Bradley, Chess 1845 | | 12 |
| 19 | 17 | 17 | 21 | ALICE IN WONDERLAND — Neil Sedaka, RCA Victor 8137 | △ | 8 |
| 20 | 22 | 24 | 31 | LET'S TURKEY TROT — Little Eva, Dimension 1006 | | 8 |
| 21 | 20 | 25 | 30 | LET'S LIMBO SOME MORE — Chubby Checker, Parkway 862 | | 6 |
| 22 | 19 | 10 | 5 | WALK RIGHT IN — Rooftop Singers, Vanguard 35017 | | 12 |
| ★ 23 | 31 | 39 | 51 | LAUGHING BOY — Mary Wells, Motown 1039 | | 5 |
| ★ 24 | 36 | 41 | 64 | DON'T SET ME FREE — Ray Charles, ABC-Paramount 10405 | | 5 |
| ★ 25 | 50 | 81 | — | BABY WORKOUT — Jackie Wilson, Brunswick 55239 | | 3 |
| ★ 26 | 32 | 40 | 65 | DO THE BIRD — Dee Dee Sharp, Cameo 244 | | 4 |
| 27 | 23 | 23 | 29 | BUTTERFLY BABY — Bobby Rydell, Cameo 242 | | 7 |
| ★ 28 | 43 | 47 | 58 | TWENTY MILES — Chubby Checker, Parkway 862 | | 5 |
| 29 | 21 | 22 | 26 | GREENBACK DOLLAR — Kingston Trio, Capitol 4898 | | 9 |
| 30 | 28 | 31 | 34 | BOSS GUITAR — Duane Eddy, RCA Victor 8131 | △ | 7 |
| ★ 31 | 44 | 58 | 82 | CAN'T GET USED TO LOSING YOU — Andy Williams, Columbia 42674 | △ | 4 |
| 32 | 40 | 52 | 80 | FOLLOW THE BOYS — Connie Francis, MGM 13127 | | 4 |
| 33 | 34 | 35 | 36 | DAYS OF WINE AND ROSES — Henry Mancini, RCA Victor 8120 | △ | 9 |
| ★ 34 | 54 | 72 | 96 | DON'T SAY NOTHIN' BAD ABOUT MY BABY — Cookies, Demension 1008 | | 4 |
| ★ 35 | 58 | — | — | YOUNG LOVERS — Paul & Paula, Philips 40096 | | 2 |
| 36 | 37 | 48 | 68 | MR. BASS MAN — Johnny Cymbal, Kapp 503 | | 6 |
| ★ 37 | 52 | 62 | 77 | OUT OF MY MIND — Johnny Tillotson, Cadence 1434 | | 4 |
| 38 | 24 | 26 | 27 | THE GYPSY CRIED — Lou Christie, Roulette 4457 | | 12 |
| 39 | 41 | 42 | 56 | WHY DO LOVERS BREAK EACH OTHERS HEARTS — Bob B. Soxx & the Blue Jeans, Philles 110 | | 6 |
| 40 | 18 | 18 | 13 | SEND ME SOME LOVIN' — Sam Cooke, RCA Victor 8129 | △ | 8 |
| 41 | 45 | 57 | 85 | YAKETY SAX — Boots Randolph, Monument 804 | | 5 |
| 42 | 42 | 43 | 49 | TELL HIM I'M NOT HOME — Chuck Jackson, Wand 132 | | 8 |
| ★ 43 | 53 | 59 | 89 | SANDY — Dion, Laurie 3153 | | 4 |
| 44 | 46 | 46 | 52 | LOVE FOR SALE — Arthur Lyman Group, Hi-Fi 5066 | | 8 |
| ★ 45 | 61 | — | — | PUFF — Peter, Paul & Mary, Warner Bros. 5348 | | 2 |
| ★ 46 | 56 | 87 | — | OVER THE MOUNTAIN (Across the Sea) — Bobby Vinton, Epic 9577 | | 3 |
| 47 | 51 | 78 | — | DON'T BE AFRAID, LITTLE DARLIN' — Steve Lawrence, Columbia 42699 | △ | 3 |
| 48 | 48 | 50 | 66 | THAT'S ALL — Rick Nelson, Imperial 5910 | | 4 |
| 49 | 26 | 12 | 8 | FROM A JACK TO A KING — Ned Miller, Fabor 114 | | 13 |
| 50 | 55 | 80 | 92 | ALL OVER THE WORLD — Nat King Cole, Capitol 4919 | | 4 |
| 51 | 29 | 20 | 14 | YOU'VE REALLY GOT A HOLD ON ME — Miracles, Tamla 54073 | | 16 |
| 52 | 39 | 29 | 16 | FLY ME TO THE MOON—BOSSA NOVA — Joe Harnell & Ork, Kapp 497 | | 13 |
| 53 | 35 | 37 | 25 | CAST YOUR FATE TO THE WIND — Vince Guaraldi Trio, Fantasy 563 | | 16 |
| 54 | 30 | 32 | 33 | HITCH HIKE — Marvin Gaye, Tamla 54075 | | 11 |
| 55 | 62 | 77 | — | YOU DON'T LOVE ME ANYMORE (And I Can Tell) — Rick Nelson, Decca 31475 | | 3 |
| 56 | 38 | 38 | 28 | CALL ON ME — Bobby Bland, Duke 360 | | 12 |
| 57 | 63 | 68 | 86 | LINDA — Jan and Dean, Liberty 55531 | | 5 |
| ★ 58 | 71 | 86 | 93 | PIPELINE — Chantays, Dot 16440 | | 4 |
| 59 | 47 | 27 | 18 | LITTLE TOWN FLIRT — Del Shannon, Big Top 3131 | | 14 |
| ★ 60 | 74 | — | — | I GOT WHAT I WANTED — Brook Benton, Mercury 72099 | | 2 |
| 61 | 67 | 70 | 88 | HE'S GOT THE POWER — Exciters, United Artists 572 | | 4 |
| 62 | 33 | 34 | 37 | THAT'S THE WAY LOVE IS — Bobby Bland, Duke 360 | | 10 |
| 63 | 65 | 65 | 59 | AS LONG AS SHE NEEDS ME — Sammy Davis Jr., Reprise 20138 | | 9 |
| ★ 64 | 89 | — | — | YOUNG AND IN LOVE — Dick & Deedee, Warner Bros. 5342 | | 2 |
| 65 | 57 | 60 | 62 | LET'S STOMP — Bobby Comstock, Lawn 202 | | 6 |
| 66 | 72 | 74 | 81 | MEDITATION (Meditacao) — Charlie Byrd, Riverside 4544 | | 4 |
| 67 | 77 | 79 | 83 | SAX FIFTH AVENUE — Johnny Beecher, Warner Bros. 5341 | | 4 |
| 68 | 70 | 75 | 79 | RAINBOW — Gene Chandler, Vee Jay 468 | | 5 |
| 69 | 80 | 84 | 100 | I'M JUST A COUNTRY BOY — George McCurn, A&M 705 | | 4 |
| ★ 70 | 86 | — | — | I GOT A WOMAN — Rick Nelson, Decca 31475 | | 2 |
| 71 | 66 | 83 | 84 | JIVE SAMBA — Cannonball Adderley Sextet, Riverside 4541 | | 6 |
| 72 | 81 | 90 | — | BACK AT THE CHICKEN SHACK — Jimmy Smith, Blue Note 1877 | | 3 |
| 73 | 82 | 89 | — | DEARER THAN LIFE — Brook Benton, Mercury 72099 | | 3 |
| ★ 74 | — | — | — | SURFIN' U. S. A. — Beach Boys, Capitol 4932 | | 1 |
| 75 | 83 | — | — | WATERMELON MAN — Mongo Santamaria, Battle 45909 | | 2 |
| 76 | 78 | 67 | 72 | I'M IN LOVE AGAIN — Rick Nelson, Imperial 5910 | | 5 |
| ★ 77 | — | — | — | ETERNALLY — Chantels, Ludix 101 | | 1 |
| 78 | 84 | 85 | — | PEPINO'S FRIEND PASQUAL (The Italian Pussy-Cat) — Lou Monte, Reprise 20146 | | 3 |
| 79 | 90 | — | — | DAYS OF WINE AND ROSES — Andy Williams, Columbia 42674 | △ | 2 |
| 80 | 88 | — | — | SUN ARISE — Rolf Harris, Epic 9567 | | 2 |
| ★ 81 | — | — | — | MECCA — Gene Pitney, Musicor 1028 | | 1 |
| ★ 82 | — | — | — | ON BROADWAY — Drifters, Atlantic 2182 | | 1 |
| ★ 83 | — | — | — | LOCKING UP MY HEART — Marvelettes, Tamla 54077 | | 1 |
| ★ 84 | — | — | — | KILLER JOE — Rocky Fellers, Scepter 1246 | | 1 |
| 85 | 94 | — | — | HOW CAN I FORGET — Jimmy Holiday, Everest 2022 | | 2 |
| ★ 86 | — | — | — | FOOLISH LITTLE GIRL — Shirelles, Scepter 1248 | | 1 |
| 87 | 100 | — | 90 | NOTHING GOES UP (Without Coming Down) — Nat King Cole, Capitol 4919 | | 3 |
| 88 | 91 | 92 | — | THEME FROM LAWRENCE OF ARABIA — Ferrante & Teicher, United Artists 563 | | 6 |
| 89 | 99 | — | — | DON'T WANNA THINK ABOUT PAULA — Dickey Lee, Smash 1808 | | 2 |
| ★ 90 | — | — | — | I WILL FOLLOW HIM — Little Peggy March, RCA Victor 8139 | △ | 1 |
| 91 | — | — | — | GONE WITH THE WIND — Duprees, Coed 576 | | 1 |
| 92 | — | — | — | THE DOG — Rufus Thomas, Stax 130 | | 3 |
| 93 | 97 | — | — | CIGARETTES AND COFFEE BLUES — Marty Robbins, Columbia 42701 | △ | 2 |
| 94 | — | — | — | THAT'S HOW HEARTACHES ARE MADE — Baby Washington, Sue 783 | | 1 |
| 95 | 98 | — | — | LITTLE STAR — Bobby Calendar, Roulette 4471 | | 2 |
| 96 | — | — | — | TOM CAT — Rooftop Singers, Vanguard 35019 | | 1 |
| 97 | — | — | — | THIS EMPTY PLACE — Dionne Warwick, Scepter 1247 | | 1 |
| 98 | — | — | — | DON'T LET ME CROSS OVER — Carl Butler, Columbia 42593 | △ | 2 |
| 99 | — | — | — | LITTLE BAND OF GOLD — James Gilreath, Joy 274 | | 1 |
| 100 | — | — | — | TWO WRONGS DON'T MAKE A RIGHT — Mary Wells, Motown 1039 | | 1 |

## HOT 100—A TO Z—(Publisher-Licensee)


Alice in Wonderland (Aldon, BMI) .......... 19
All I Have to Do Is Dream (Acuff-Rose, BMI) ... 17
All Over the World (Comet, ASCAP) ........ 50
As Long As She Needs Me (Hollis, BMI) ...... 63
Baby Workout (Merrimac, BMI) .......... 25
Back at the Chicken Shack (Edmy, BMI) .... 72
Blame It on the Bossa Nova (Aldon, BMI) .... 8
Boss Guitar (Linduane, BMI) ........ 30
Butterfly Baby (Kalmann, ASCAP) .......... 27
Call on Me (Lion, BMI) .......... 56
Can't Get Used to Losing You (Brenner, BMI) .. 31
Cast Your Fate to the Wind (Friendship, BMI) .. 53
Cigarettes & Coffee Blues (Marty's, BMI) .... 93
Days of Wine and Roses—Mancini (Witmark, ASCAP) .... 33
Days of Wine and Roses—Williams (Witmark, ASCAP) .... 79
Dearer Than Life (Northridge, ASCAP) ........ 73
Do the Bird (Kalmann, ASCAP) .......... 26
Dog, The (East, BMI) .......... 92
Don't Be Afraid, Little Darlin' (Aldon, BMI) .... 47
Don't Let Me Cross Over (Martin, BMI) ...... 98
Don't Say Nothin' Bad About My Baby (Aldon, BMI) .... 34
Don't Set Me Free (Tee-Pee, ASCAP) ........ 24
Don't Wanna Think About Paula (Jack, BMI) ... 89
End of the World, The (Summit, ASCAP) ........ 2
Eternally (Bix-Betalbin, BMI) .......... 77
Fly Me to the Moon—Bossa Nova (Almanac, ASCAP) .... 52
Follow the Boys (Francon, ASCAP) .......... 32
Foolish Little Girl (Aldon, BMI) .......... 86
From a Jack to a King (Dandelion, BMI) .... 49
Gone With the Wind (Bourne, ASCAP) ........ 91
Greenback Dollar (Davon, BMI) .......... 29
Gypsy Cried, The (Painted Desert, BMI) ........ 38
He's Got the Power (Trio, BMI) .......... 61
He's So Fine (Bright-Tunes, BMI) .......... 4
Hey Paula (LeBill-Marbill, BMI) .......... 14
Hitch Hike (Jobete, BMI) .......... 54
How Can I Forget (Arrowhead, BMI) .......... 85
I Got a Woman (Progressive, BMI) .......... 70
I Got What I Wanted (Ben Day, BMI) .......... 60
I Wanna Be Around (Commander, ASCAP) ...... 16
I Will Follow Him (Leeds, ASCAP) .......... 90
I'm in Love Again (Travis, BMI) .......... 76
I'm Just a Country Boy (Folkways, BMI) ........ 69
In Dreams (Acuff-Rose, BMI) .......... 10
Jive Samba (Artillery, BMI) .......... 71
Killer Joe (Mellin-White Castle, BMI) ........ 84
Laughing Boy (Jobete, BMI) .......... 23
Let's Limbo Some More (Kalmann, ASCAP) ...... 21
Let's Stomp (Roosevelt, BMI) .......... 65
Let's Turkey Trot (Aldon, BMI) .......... 20
Linda (Warock, ASCAP) .......... 57
Little Band of Gold (Beaik, BMI) .......... 99
Little Star (Patricia, BMI) .......... 95
Little Town Flirt (Vicki-McLaughlin, BMI) ...... 59
Locking Up My Heart (Jobete, BMI) .......... 83
Love for Sale (Harms, ASCAP) .......... 44
Mama Didn't Lie (Curtom, BMI) .......... 18
Mecca (January, BMI) .......... 81
Meditation (Meditacao) (Duchess, BMI) ........ 66
Mr. Bass Man (Jalo, BMI) .......... 36
Nothing Goes Up (Sweco-Eden, BMI) .......... 87
On Broadway (Aldon, BMI) .......... 82
One Broken Heart for Sale (Presley, BMI) ...... 11
Our Day Will Come (Rosewood, ASCAP) ........ 1
Our Winter Love (Cramart, BMI) .......... 13
Out of My Mind (Ridge, BMI) .......... 37
Over the Mountain (Arc, BMI) .......... 46
Pepino's Friend Pasqual (Romance-Sal. Songs, BMI) 78
Pipeline (Downey, BMI) .......... 58
Puff (Pepamar, ASCAP) .......... 45
Rainbow (Conrad-Curtom, BMI) .......... 68
Rhythm of the Rain (Sherman-DeVorzon, BMI) .... 6
Ruby Baby (Tiger, BMI) .......... 12
Sandy (DiMucci-Brandt, ASCAP) .......... 43
Sax Fifth Avenue (Radio Active, BMI) ........ 67
Send Me Some Lovin' (Venice, BMI) .......... 40
South Street (Kalmann, ASCAP) .......... 7
Sun Arise (Ardmore, ASCAP) .......... 80
Surfin' U. S. A. (Arc, BMI) .......... 74
Tell Him I'm Not Home (Figure, BMI) .......... 42
That's All (Travis, BMI) .......... 48
That's How Heartaches Are Made (Sea-Lark, BMI) . 94
That's the Way Love Is (Lion, BMI) .......... 62
Theme From Lawrence of Arabia (Gower, BMI) .. 88
This Empty Place (U. S. Songs, ASCAP) ...... 97
Tom Cat (Ryerson, BMI) .......... 96
Twenty Miles (Wyncote, Kalmann, ASCAP) .... 28
Two Wrongs Don't Make a Right (Jobete, BMI)..100
Walk Like a Man (Saturday-Gavadema, ASCAP) .. 5
Walk Right In (Ryerson, BMI) .......... 22
Watermelon Man (Aries, BMI) .......... 75
What Will My Mary Say (Elm Drive, ASCAP) .... 9
Why Do Lovers Break Each Others Hearts (January, BMI) .......... 39
Wild Weekend (Shan-Todd & Tupper, BMI) ...... 15
Yakety Sax (Tree, BMI) .......... 41
You Don't Love Me Anymore (Painted Desert, BMI) 55
Young and in Love (Odin, ASCAP) .......... 64
Young Lovers (LeBill-Marbill, BMI) .......... 35
You're the Reason I'm Living (Adaris, BMI) .... 3
You've Really Got a Hold on Me (Jobete, BMI) . 51


## BUBBLING UNDER THE HOT 100

101. THE BIRD .......... Dutones, Columbia 42657
102. STRUTTIN' WITH MARIA ......Herb Alpert & the Tijuana Brass, A&M 706
103. I WILL LIVE MY LIFE FOR YOU ...... Tony Bennett, Columbia 42534
104. DON'T MENTION MY NAME ..........Shepherd Sisters, Atlantic 2176
105. AMY .......... Paul Petersen, Colpix 676
106. FUNNY MAN ..........Ray Stevens, Mercury 72098
107. CALL ME IRRESPONSIBLE ..........Frank Sinatra, Reprise 20151
108. IF YOU WANNA BE HAPPY ..........Jimmy Soul, SPQR 3305
109. WHAT ARE BOYS MADE OF ..........Purcells, ABC-Paramount 10401
110. IS THIS ME? ..........Jim Reeves, RCA Victor 8127
111. WHAT DOES A GIRL DO ..........Marcie Blane, Seville 123
112. PRETTY BOY LONELY ..........Patti Page, Columbia 42671
113. IF MARY'S THERE .......... Brian Hyland, ABC-Paramount 10400
114. HOW CAN I FORGET ..........Ben E. King, Atco 6256
115. PEANUTS ..........4 Seasons, Vee Jay EP 901 (Extended Play)
116. HERE I STAND ..........Rip Chords, Columbia 42687
117. DON'T BE CRUEL ..........Barbara Lynn, Jamie 1244
118. DON'T LET ME CROSS OVER ..........Adam Wade, Epic 9566
119. NEVER ..........Earls, Old Town 1133
120. ANN-MARIE ..........Belmonts, Sabina 509
121. WATERMELON MAN ..........Herbie Hancock, Blue Note 1862
122. SHE'LL NEVER, NEVER LOVE YOU ..........Teresa Brewer, Philips 40095
123. PRIMA DONNA ..........Glen Campbell, Capitol 4925
124. MEMORY LANE ..........Hippies, Parkway 863
125. HEART ..........Kenny Chandler, Laurie 3158
126. TONIGHT I MET AN ANGEL ..........Tokens, RCA Victor 8148
127. DENVER ..........New Christy Minstrels, Columbia 42673
128. I'LL MAKE IT ALL RIGHT ..........Valentinos, Sar 137
129. I LOVE YOU BECAUSE ..........Al Martino, Capitol 4930
130. WORKOUT ..........Michael Clark, Imperial 5893
131. ANY WAY YOU WANNA ..........Harvey, Tri-Phi 1017
132. MARCHING THRU MADRID ....Herb Alpert & the Tijuana Brass, A&M 706
133. TORE UP ..........Hormonica Fats, Darcey 5000
134. MY LITTLE GIRL ..........Crickets, Liberty 55540
135. HEART ..........Wayne Newton, Capitol 4920

# Billboard HOT 100
**FOR WEEK ENDING MARCH 30, 1963**

| This Week | Last Week | 2 Wks Ago | 3 Wks Ago | Title, Artist, Label & Number | Weeks On Chart |
|---|---|---|---|---|---|
| 1 | 4 | 10 | 19 | HE'S SO FINE — Chiffons, Laurie 3152 | 6 |
| 2 | 1 | 2 | 6 | OUR DAY WILL COME — Ruby and the Romantics, Kapp 501 | 8 |
| 3 | 2 | 4 | 7 | THE END OF THE WORLD — Skeeter Davis, RCA Victor 8098 | 10 |
| 4 | 7 | 16 | 21 | SOUTH STREET — Orlons, Cameo 243 | 7 |
| 5 | 3 | 3 | 5 | YOU'RE THE REASON I'M LIVING — Bobby Darin, Capitol 4897 | 11 |
| 6 | 6 | 5 | 3 | RHYTHM OF THE RAIN — Cascades, Valiant 6026 | 12 |
| 7 | 10 | 13 | 13 | IN DREAMS — Roy Orbison, Monument 806 | 8 |
| 8 | 25 | 50 | 81 | BABY WORKOUT — Jackie Wilson, Brunswick 55239 | 4 |
| 9 | 13 | 15 | 15 | OUR WINTER LOVE — Bill Pursell, Columbia 42619 | 9 |
| 10 | 8 | 8 | 11 | BLAME IT ON THE BOSSA NOVA — Eydie Gorme, Columbia 42661 | 11 |
| 11 | 5 | 1 | 1 | WALK LIKE A MAN — 4 Seasons, Vee Jay 485 | 10 |
| 12 | 9 | 9 | 9 | WHAT WILL MY MARY SAY — Johnny Mathis, Columbia 42666 | 10 |
| 13 | 11 | 11 | 16 | ONE BROKEN HEART FOR SALE — Elvis Presley, RCA Victor 8134 | 7 |
| 14 | 16 | 25 | 30 | I WANNA BE AROUND — Tony Bennett, Columbia 42634 | 12 |
| 15 | 23 | 31 | 39 | LAUGHING BOY — Mary Wells, Motown 1039 | 6 |
| 16 | 17 | 27 | 33 | ALL I HAVE TO DO IS DREAM — Richard Chamberlain, MGM 13121 | 8 |
| 17 | 26 | 32 | 40 | DO THE BIRD — Dee Dee Sharp, Cameo 244 | 5 |
| 18 | 31 | 44 | 58 | CAN'T GET USED TO LOSING YOU — Andy Williams, Columbia 42674 | 5 |
| 19 | 45 | 61 | — | PUFF — Peter, Paul & Mary, Warner Bros. 5348 | 3 |
| 20 | 24 | 36 | 41 | DON'T SET ME FREE — Ray Charles, ABC-Paramount 10405 | 6 |
| 21 | 21 | 20 | 25 | LET'S LIMBO SOME MORE — Chubby Checker, Parkway 862 | 7 |
| 22 | 12 | 6 | 2 | RUBY BABY — Dion, Columbia 42662 | 11 |
| 23 | 28 | 43 | 47 | TWENTY MILES — Chubby Checker, Parkway 862 | 6 |
| 24 | 15 | 12 | 8 | WILD WEEKEND — Rebels, Swan 4125 | 14 |
| 25 | 32 | 40 | 52 | FOLLOW THE BOYS — Connie Francis, MGM 13127 | 5 |
| 26 | 35 | 58 | — | YOUNG LOVERS — Paul & Paula, Philips 40096 | 3 |
| 27 | 34 | 54 | 72 | DON'T SAY NOTHIN' BAD ABOUT MY BABY — Cookies, Dimension 1008 | 5 |
| 28 | 36 | 37 | 48 | MR. BASS MAN — Johnny Cymbal, Kapp 503 | 7 |
| 29 | 14 | 7 | 4 | HEY PAULA — Paul & Paula, Philips 40084 | 14 |
| 30 | 37 | 52 | 62 | OUT OF MY MIND — Johnny Tillotson, Cadence 1434 | 5 |
| 31 | 20 | 22 | 24 | LET'S TURKEY TROT — Little Eva, Dimension 1006 | 9 |
| 32 | 19 | 17 | 17 | ALICE IN WONDERLAND — Neil Sedaka, RCA Victor 8137 | 9 |
| 33 | 47 | 51 | 78 | DON'T BE AFRAID, LITTLE DARLIN' — Steve Lawrence, Columbia 42699 | 4 |
| 34 | 27 | 23 | 23 | BUTTERFLY BABY — Bobby Rydell, Cameo 242 | 8 |
| 35 | 46 | 56 | 87 | OVER THE MOUNTAIN (Across the Sea) — Bobby Vinton, Epic 9577 | 4 |
| 36 | 33 | 34 | 35 | DAYS OF WINE AND ROSES — Henry Mancini, RCA Victor 8120 | 10 |
| 37 | 41 | 45 | 57 | YAKETY SAX — Boots Randolph, Monument 804 | 6 |
| 38 | 39 | 41 | 42 | WHY DO LOVERS BREAK EACH OTHERS HEARTS — Bob B. Soxx & the Blue Jeans, Philles 110 | 7 |
| 39 | 43 | 53 | 59 | SANDY — Dion, Laurie 3153 | 5 |
| 40 | 18 | 14 | 14 | MAMA DIDN'T LIE — Jan Bradley, Chess 1845 | 13 |
| 41 | 29 | 21 | 22 | GREENBACK DOLLAR — Kingston Trio, Capitol 4898 | 10 |
| 42 | 30 | 28 | 31 | BOSS GUITAR — Duane Eddy, RCA Victor 8131 | 8 |
| 43 | 44 | 46 | 46 | LOVE FOR SALE — Arthur Lyman Group, Hi-Fi 5066 | 9 |
| 44 | 58 | 71 | 86 | PIPELINE — Chantays, Dot 16440 | 5 |
| 45 | 42 | 42 | 43 | TELL HIM I'M NOT HOME — Chuck Jackson, Wand 132 | 9 |
| 46 | 64 | 89 | — | YOUNG AND IN LOVE — Dick & Deedee, Warner Bros. 5342 | 3 |
| 47 | 57 | 63 | 68 | LINDA — Jan and Dean, Liberty 55531 | 6 |
| 48 | 22 | 19 | 10 | WALK RIGHT IN — Rooftop Singers, Vanguard 35017 | 13 |
| 49 | 60 | 74 | — | I GOT WHAT I WANTED — Brook Benton, Mercury 72099 | 3 |
| 50 | 50 | 55 | 80 | ALL OVER THE WORLD — Nat King Cole, Capitol 4919 | 5 |
| 51 | 38 | 24 | 26 | THE GYPSY CRIED — Lou Christie, Roulette 4457 | 13 |
| 52 | 70 | 86 | — | I GOT A WOMAN — Rick Nelson, Decca 31475 | 3 |
| 53 | 79 | 90 | — | DAYS OF WINE AND ROSES — Andy Williams, Columbia 42674 | 3 |
| 54 | 48 | 48 | 50 | THAT'S ALL — Rick Nelson, Imperial 5910 | 5 |
| 55 | 55 | 62 | 77 | YOU DON'T LOVE ME ANYMORE (And I Can Tell) — Rick Nelson, Decca 31475 | 4 |
| 56 | 82 | — | — | ON BROADWAY — Drifters, Atlantic 2182 | 2 |
| 57 | 61 | 67 | 70 | HE'S GOT THE POWER — Exciters, United Artists 572 | 5 |
| 58 | 54 | 30 | 32 | HITCH HIKE — Marvin Gaye, Tamla 54075 | 12 |
| 59 | 81 | — | — | MECCA — Gene Pitney, Musicor 1028 | 2 |
| 60 | 75 | 83 | — | WATERMELON MAN — Mongo Santamaria, Battle 45909 | 3 |
| 61 | 53 | 35 | 37 | CAST YOUR FATE TO THE WIND — Vince Guaraldi Trio, Fantasy 563 | 17 |
| 62 | 90 | — | — | I WILL FOLLOW HIM — Little Peggy March, RCA Victor 8139 | 2 |
| 63 | 74 | — | — | SURFIN' U.S.A. — Beach Boys, Capitol 4932 | 2 |
| 64 | 69 | 80 | 84 | I'M JUST A COUNTRY BOY — George McCurn, A&M 705 | 5 |
| 65 | 67 | 77 | 79 | SAX FIFTH AVENUE — Johnny Beecher, Warner Bros. 5341 | 5 |
| 66 | 68 | 70 | 75 | RAINBOW — Gene Chandler, Vee Jay 468 | 6 |
| 67 | 72 | 81 | 90 | BACK AT THE CHICKEN SHACK — Jimmy Smith, Blue Note 1877 | 4 |
| 68 | 71 | 66 | 83 | JIVE SAMBA — Cannonball Adderley Sextet, Riverside 4541 | 7 |
| 69 | 83 | — | — | LOCKING UP MY HEART — Marvelettes, Tamla 54077 | 2 |
| 70 | 73 | 82 | 89 | DEARER THAN LIFE — Brook Benton, Mercury 72099 | 4 |
| 71 | 80 | 88 | — | SUN ARISE — Rolf Harris, Epic 9567 | 3 |
| 72 | 66 | 72 | 74 | MEDITATION (Meditacao) — Charlie Byrd, Riverside 4544 | 5 |
| 73 | 89 | 99 | — | DON'T WANNA THINK ABOUT PAULA — Dickey Lee, Smash 1808 | 3 |
| 74 | 86 | — | — | FOOLISH LITTLE GIRL — Shirelles, Scepter 1248 | 2 |
| 75 | — | — | — | CHARMS — Bobby Vee, Liberty 55530 | 1 |
| 76 | — | — | — | HERE I STAND — Rip Chords, Columbia 42687 | 1 |
| 77 | — | — | — | A LOVE SHE CAN COUNT ON — Miracles, Tamla 54078 | 1 |
| 78 | — | — | — | AMY — Paul Petersen, Colpix 676 | 1 |
| 79 | 76 | 78 | 67 | I'M IN LOVE AGAIN — Rick Nelson, Imperial 5910 | 6 |
| 80 | 85 | 94 | — | HOW CAN I FORGET — Jimmy Holiday, Everest 2022 | 3 |
| 81 | — | — | — | INSULT TO INJURY — Timi Yuro, Liberty 55552 | 1 |
| 82 | 84 | — | — | KILLER JOE — Rocky Fellers, Scepter 1246 | 2 |
| 83 | 96 | — | — | TOM CAT — Rooftop Singers, Vanguard 35019 | 2 |
| 84 | — | — | — | IF YOU WANNA BE HAPPY — Jimmy Soul, S.P.Q.R. 3305 | 1 |
| 85 | 94 | — | — | THAT'S HOW HEARTACHES ARE MADE — Baby Washington, Sue 783 | 2 |
| 86 | — | — | — | WHAT ARE BOYS MADE OF — Percells, ABC-Paramount 10401 | 1 |
| 87 | 92 | — | — | THE DOG — Rufus Thomas, Stax 130 | 4 |
| 88 | — | — | — | WHATEVER YOU WANT — Jerry Butler, Vee Jay 486 | 1 |
| 89 | 91 | — | — | GONE WITH THE WIND — Duprees, Coed 576 | 2 |
| 90 | — | — | — | FUNNY MAN — Ray Stevens, Mercury 72098 | 1 |
| 91 | 99 | — | — | LITTLE BAND OF GOLD — James Gilreath, Joy 274 | 2 |
| 92 | — | 96 | — | HOW CAN I FORGET — Ben E. King, Atco 6256 | 2 |
| 93 | 97 | — | — | THIS EMPTY PLACE — Dionne Warwick, Scepter 1247 | 2 |
| 94 | — | — | — | THE BIRD'S THE WORD — Rivingtons, Liberty 5553 | 1 |
| 95 | 88 | 91 | 92 | THEME FROM LAWRENCE OF ARABIA — Ferrante & Teicher, United Artists 563 | 7 |
| 96 | — | — | — | MARCHING THRU MADRID — Herb Alpert's Tijuana Brass, A&M 706 | 1 |
| 97 | — | — | — | I'LL MAKE IT ALRIGHT — Valentinos, Sar 137 | 1 |
| 98 | — | — | — | BONY MORONIE — Appalachians, ABC-Paramount 10419 | 1 |
| 99 | — | — | — | TWO FACES HAVE I — Lou Christie, Roulette 4481 | 1 |
| 100 | — | — | — | PREACHERMAN — Charlie Russo, Diamond 131 | 1 |

## BUBBLING UNDER THE HOT 100

101. THE BIRD — Dutones, Columbia 42657
102. DON'T LET ME CROSS OVER — Carl Butler, Columbia 42593
103. TORE UP — Harmonica Fats, Darcey 3500
104. WAYWARD WIND — Frank Ifield, Vee Jay 499
105. CIGARETTES AND COFFEE BLUES — Marty Robbins, Columbia 42701
106. HEART — Kenny Chandler, Laurie 3158
107. NANCY'S MINUET — Everly Brothers, Warner Bros. 5346
108. SHE'LL NEVER, NEVER LOVE YOU — Teresa Brewer, Philips 40095
109. PRIMA DONNA — Glen Campbell, Capitol 4925
110. I LOVE YOU BECAUSE — Otis Redding, Volt 103
111. THESE ARMS OF MINE — Otis Redding, Volt 103
112. DON'T MENTION MY NAME — Shepherd Sisters, Atlantic 2176
113. CALL ME IRRESPONSIBLE — Frank Sinatra, Reprise 20151
114. WALKING AFTER MIDNIGHT — Patsy Cline, Everest 2020
115. HE'S A BAD BOY — Carole King, Dimension 1009
116. SKIP TO M'LIMBO — Ventures, Dolton 68
117. DON'T BE CRUEL — Barbara Lynn, Jamie 1244
118. (SO IT WAS . . . SO IT IS) SO IT ALWAYS WILL BE — Everly Brothers, Warner Bros.
119. I CAN TAKE A HINT — Belmonts, Sabina 509
120. ANN-MARIE — Olympics, Tri Disc 106
121. HEART — Wayne Newton, Capitol 4920
122. THIS EMPTY BED — Jim Reeves, RCA Victor 8177
123. PLEASE DON'T — Kitty Kallen, RCA Victor 8158
124. I LOVE YOU — Al Martino, Capitol 4930
125. RONNIE, CALL ME WHEN YOU GET A CHANCE — Shelley Fabares, Colpix 682
126. THE BOUNCE — Ti Disc 106
127. PARADISE — April Stevens & Nino Tempo, Atco 6253
128. SEAGREEN — Dean Martin, Reprise 20150
129. FACE IN THE CROWD — Viceroys, Reprise 20150
130. HALF A MAN — Willie Nelson, Liberty 55532
131. TEARDROP BY TEARDROP — Gerry Pitney, Musicor 1025
132. THE ROSY DANCE — Johnny Thunder, Diamond 122
133. SHE'S NEW TO YOU — Wilma Bea, Liberty 55543
134. IF YOU WANT IN (I'VE GOT IT) — "Little Esther" Phillips & "Big Al" Downing, Lenox 5565
135. I GOT BURNED — Ral Donner, Reprise 20141
136. WHAT'S WRONG BILL? — Sue Thompson, Hickory 1204

# Billboard HOT 100

**For Week Ending April 6, 1963**

| This Week | Wks Ago | Title, Artist, Label & Number | Weeks On Chart |
|---|---|---|---|
| 1 | 1 4 10 | **HE'S SO FINE** — Chiffons, Laurie 3152 | 7 |
| 2 | 2 1 2 | **OUR DAY WILL COME** — Ruby and the Romantics, Kapp 501 | 9 |
| 3 | 3 2 4 | **THE END OF THE WORLD** — Skeeter Davis, RCA Victor 8098 | 11 |
| 4 | 4 7 16 | **SOUTH STREET** — Orlons, Cameo 243 | 8 |
| 5 | 18 31 44 | **CAN'T GET USED TO LOSING YOU** — Andy Williams, Columbia 42674 | 6 |
| 6 | 8 25 50 | **BABY WORKOUT** — Jackie Wilson, Brunswick 55239 | 5 |
| 7 | 7 10 13 | **IN DREAMS** — Roy Orbison, Monument 806 | 9 |
| 8 | 5 3 3 | **YOU'RE THE REASON I'M LIVING** — Bobby Darin, Capitol 4897 | 12 |
| 9 | 6 6 5 | **RHYTHM OF THE RAIN** — Cascades, Valiant 6026 | 13 |
| 10 | 26 35 58 | **YOUNG LOVERS** — Paul & Paula, Philips 40096 | 4 |
| 11 | 19 45 61 | **PUFF** — Peter, Paul & Mary, Warner Bros. 5348 | 4 |
| 12 | 17 26 32 | **DO THE BIRD** — Dee Dee Sharp, Cameo 244 | 6 |
| 13 | 9 13 15 | **OUR WINTER LOVE** — Bill Pursell, Columbia 42619 | 10 |
| 14 | 16 17 27 | **ALL I HAVE TO DO IS DREAM** — Richard Chamberlain, MGM 13121 | 9 |
| 15 | 10 8 8 | **BLAME IT ON THE BOSSA NOVA** — Eydie Gorme, Columbia 42661 | 12 |
| 16 | 12 9 9 | **WHAT WILL MY MARY SAY** — Johnny Mathis, Columbia 42666 | 11 |
| 17 | 14 16 25 | **I WANNA BE AROUND** — Tony Bennett, Columbia 42634 | 13 |
| 18 | 28 36 37 | **MR. BASS MAN** — Johnny Cymbal, Kapp 524 | 8 |
| 19 | 15 23 31 | **LAUGHING BOY** — Mary Wells, Motown 1039 | 7 |
| 20 | 25 32 40 | **FOLLOW THE BOYS** — Connie Francis, MGM 13127 | 6 |
| 21 | 23 28 43 | **TWENTY MILES** — Chubby Checker, Parkway 862 | 7 |
| 22 | 27 34 54 | **DON'T SAY NOTHIN' BAD ABOUT MY BABY** — Cookies, Dimension 1008 | 6 |
| 23 | 11 5 1 | **WALK LIKE A MAN** — 4 Seasons, Vee Jay 485 | 11 |
| 24 | 21 21 20 | **LET'S LIMBO SOME MORE** — Chubby Checker, Parkway 862 | 8 |
| 25 | 30 37 52 | **OUT OF MY MIND** — Johnny Tillotson, Cadence 1434 | 6 |
| 26 | 44 58 71 | **PIPELINE** — Chantays, Dot 16440 | 6 |
| 27 | 33 47 51 | **DON'T BE AFRAID, LITTLE DARLIN'** — Steve Lawrence, Columbia 42699 | 5 |
| 28 | 24 15 12 | **WILD WEEKEND** — Rebels, Swan 4125 | 15 |
| 29 | 13 11 11 | **ONE BROKEN HEART FOR SALE** — Elvis Presley, RCA Victor 8134 | 8 |
| 30 | 62 90 — | **I WILL FOLLOW HIM** — Little Peggy March, RCA Victor 8139 | 3 |
| 31 | 39 43 53 | **SANDY** — Dion, Laurie 3153 | 6 |
| 32 | 35 46 56 | **OVER THE MOUNTAIN (Across the Sea)** — Bobby Vinton, Epic 9577 | 5 |
| 33 | 49 60 74 | **I GOT WHAT I WANTED** — Brook Benton, Mercury 72099 | 4 |
| 34 | 20 24 36 | **DON'T SET ME FREE** — Ray Charles, ABC-Paramount 10405 | 7 |
| 35 | 37 41 45 | **YAKETY SAX** — Boots Randolph, Monument 804 | 7 |
| 36 | 36 33 34 | **DAYS OF WINE AND ROSES** — Henry Mancini, RCA Victor 8120 | 11 |
| 37 | 56 82 — | **ON BROADWAY** — Drifters, Atlantic 2182 | 3 |
| 38 | 22 12 6 | **RUBY BABY** — Dion, Columbia 42662 | 12 |
| 39 | 46 64 89 | **YOUNG AND IN LOVE** — Dick & Deedee, Warner Bros. 5342 | 4 |
| 40 | 38 39 41 | **WHY DO LOVERS BREAK EACH OTHERS HEARTS** — Bob B. Soxx & the Blue Jeans, Philles 110 | 8 |
| 41 | 60 75 83 | **WATERMELON MAN** — Mongo Santamaria, Battle 45909 | 4 |
| 42 | 59 81 — | **MECCA** — Gene Pitney, Musicor 1028 | 3 |
| 43 | 50 50 55 | **ALL OVER THE WORLD** — Nat King Cole, Capitol 4919 | 6 |
| 44 | 47 57 63 | **LINDA** — Jan and Dean, Liberty 55531 | 7 |
| 45 | 63 74 — | **SURFIN' U.S.A.** — Beach Boys, Capitol 4932 | 3 |
| 46 | 75 — — | **CHARMS** — Bobby Vee, Liberty 55530 | 2 |
| 47 | 53 79 90 | **DAYS OF WINE AND ROSES** — Andy Williams, Columbia 42674 | 4 |
| 48 | 43 44 46 | **LOVE FOR SALE** — Arthur Lyman Group, Hi-Fi 5066 | 10 |
| 49 | 52 70 86 | **I GOT A WOMAN** — Rick Nelson, Decca 31475 | 4 |
| 50 | 29 14 7 | **HEY PAULA** — Paul & Paula, Philips 40084 | 15 |
| 51 | 55 55 62 | **YOU DON'T LOVE ME ANYMORE (And I Can Tell)** — Rick Nelson, Decca 31475 | 5 |
| 52 | 83 96 — | **TOM CAT** — Rooftop Singers, Vanguard 35019 | 3 |
| 53 | 31 20 22 | **LET'S TURKEY TROT** — Little Eva, Dimension 1006 | 10 |
| 54 | 74 86 — | **FOOLISH LITTLE GIRL** — Shirelles, Scepter 1248 | 3 |
| 55 | 41 29 21 | **GREENBACK DOLLAR** — Kingston Trio, Capitol 4898 | 11 |
| 56 | 64 69 80 | **I'M JUST A COUNTRY BOY** — George McCurn, A&M 705 | 6 |
| 57 | 40 18 14 | **MAMA DIDN'T LIE** — Jan Bradley, Chess 1845 | 14 |
| 58 | 42 30 28 | **BOSS GUITAR** — Duane Eddy, RCA Victor 8131 | 9 |
| 59 | 32 19 17 | **ALICE IN WONDERLAND** — Neil Sedaka, RCA Victor 8137 | 10 |
| 60 | 69 83 — | **LOCKING UP MY HEART** — Marvelettes, Tamla 54077 | 3 |
| 61 | 45 42 42 | **TELL HIM I'M NOT HOME** — Chuck Jackson, Wand 132 | 10 |
| 62 | 34 27 23 | **BUTTERFLY BABY** — Bobby Rydell, Cameo 242 | 9 |
| 63 | 67 72 81 | **BACK AT THE CHICKEN SHACK** — Jimmy Smith, Blue Note 1877 | 5 |
| 64 | 71 80 88 | **SUN ARISE** — Rolf Harris, Epic 9567 | 4 |
| 65 | 65 67 77 | **SAX FIFTH AVENUE** — Johnny Beecher, Warner Bros. 5341 | 6 |
| 66 | 78 — — | **AMY** — Paul Petersen, Colpix 676 | 2 |
| 67 | 57 61 67 | **HE'S GOT THE POWER** — Exciters, United Artists 572 | 6 |
| 68 | 73 89 99 | **DON'T WANNA THINK ABOUT PAULA** — Dickey Lee, Smash 1808 | 4 |
| 69 | 70 73 82 | **DEARER THAN LIFE** — Brook Benton, Mercury 72099 | 5 |
| 70 | 61 53 35 | **CAST YOUR FATE TO THE WIND** — Vince Guaraldi Trio, Fantasy 563 | 18 |
| 71 | — — — | **A LOVE SHE CAN COUNT ON** — Miracles, Tamla 54078 | 2 |
| 72 | 66 68 70 | **RAINBOW** — Gene Chandler, Vee Jay 468 | 7 |
| 73 | 76 — — | **HERE I STAND** — Rip Chords, Columbia 42687 | 2 |
| 74 | 72 66 72 | **MEDITATION (Meditacao)** — Charlie Byrd, Riverside 4544 | 6 |
| 75 | 91 99 — | **LITTLE BAND OF GOLD** — James Gilreath, Joy 274 | 3 |
| 76 | 80 85 94 | **HOW CAN I FORGET** — Jimmy Holiday, Everest 2022 | 4 |
| 77 | 86 — — | **WHAT ARE BOYS MADE OF** — Percells, ABC-Paramount 10401 | 2 |
| 78 | 84 — — | **IF YOU WANNA BE HAPPY** — Jimmy Soul, S.P.Q.R. 3305 | 2 |
| 79 | 85 94 — | **THAT'S HOW HEARTACHES ARE MADE** — Baby Washington, Sue 783 | 3 |
| 80 | 54 48 48 | **THAT'S ALL** — Rick Nelson, Imperial 5910 | 6 |
| 81 | 82 84 — | **KILLER JOE** — Rocky Fellers, Scepter 1246 | 3 |
| 82 | — — — | **LOSING YOU** — Brenda Lee, Decca 31478 | 1 |
| 83 | — — — | **BILL BAILEY, WON'T YOU PLEASE COME HOME** — Ella Fitzgerald, Verve 10288 | 1 |
| 84 | 95 88 91 | **THEME FROM LAWRENCE OF ARABIA** — Ferrante & Teicher, United Artists 563 | 8 |
| 85 | 88 — — | **WHATEVER YOU WANT** — Jerry Butler, Vee Jay 486 | 2 |
| 86 | 93 97 — | **THIS EMPTY PLACE** — Dionne Warwick, Scepter 1247 | 3 |
| 87 | — — — | **I LOVE YOU BECAUSE** — Al Martino, Capitol 4930 | 1 |
| 88 | — — — | **REVEREND MR. BLACK** — Kingston Trio, Capitol 4951 | 1 |
| 89 | 90 — — | **FUNNY MAN** — Ray Stevens, Mercury 72098 | 2 |
| 90 | — — — | **HEART** — Kenny Chandler, Laurie 3158 | 1 |
| 91 | — — — | **DON'T LET HER BE YOUR BABY** — Contours, Gordy 7016 | 1 |
| 92 | 92 — 96 | **HOW CAN I FORGET** — Ben E. King, Atco 6256 | 3 |
| 93 | 99 — — | **TWO FACES HAVE I** — Lou Christie, Roulette 4481 | 2 |
| 94 | 100 — — | **PREACHERMAN** — Charlie Russo, Diamond 131 | 2 |
| 95 | — — — | **CALL ME IRRESPONSIBLE** — Frank Sinatra, Reprise 20151 | 1 |
| 96 | 98 — — | **BONY MORONIE** — Appalachians, ABC-Paramount 10419 | 2 |
| 97 | — — — | **COME AND GET THESE MEMORIES** — Martha & the Vandellas, Gordy 7014 | 1 |
| 98 | — — — | **ASK ME** — Maxine Brown, Wand 135 | 1 |
| 99 | 97 — — | **I'LL MAKE IT ALRIGHT** — Valentinos, Sar 137 | 2 |
| 100 | — — — | **(Today I Met) THE BOY I'M GONNA MARRY** — Darlene Love, Philles 111 | 1 |

## BUBBLING UNDER THE HOT 100

101. MEMORY LANE — Hippies, Parkway 863
102. HEART — Wayne Newton, Capitol 4920
103. PRIMA DONNA — Glen Campbell, Capitol 4925
104. IT'S THE WORD — Rivingtons, Liberty 55553
105. SHUT DOWN — Beach Boys, Capitol 4932
106. WAYWARD WIND — Frank Ifield, Vee Jay 499
107. MARCHING THRU MADRID — Herb Alpert's Tijuana Brass, A&M 706
108. DON'T MENTION MY NAME — Shepherd Sisters, Atlantic 2176
109. ETERNALLY — Chantels, Ludix 101
110. THE DOG — Rufus Thomas, Stax 130
111. DON'T LET ME CROSS OVER — Earl Scott, Columbia 42593
112. WALKING AFTER MIDNIGHT — Patsy Cline, Everest 2020
113. INSULT TO INJURY — Timi Yuro, Liberty 55552
114. NANCY'S MINUET — Everly Brothers, Warner Bros. 5346
115. I CAN TAKE A HINT — Miracles, Tamla 54078
116. ANN-MARIE — Belmonts, Sabina 509
117. STILL — Bill Anderson, Decca 31458
118. CRYING IN THE CHAPEL — Little Richard, Atlantic 2181
119. NOT FOR ALL THE MONEY IN THE WORLD — Shirelles, Scepter 1248
120. PLEASE DON'T — Kitty Kallen, RCA Victor 8158
121. RONNIE, CALL ME WHEN YOU GET A CHANCE — Shelley Fabares, Colpix 682
122. HOT CAKES — Dave (Baby) Cortez, Chess 1850
123. I GOT BURNED — Ral Donner, Reprise 20141
124. THE ROSY DANCE — Johnny Thunder, Diamond 122
125. HOT PASTRAMI — Dartells, Dot 16453
126. LONESOME 7-7203 — Hawkshaw Hawkins, King 5712
127. SINCE I DON'T HAVE YOU — Vee Jay 902 (Extended Play)
128. IF YOU WANT IT (I've Got It) — "Little Esther" Phillips & "Big Al" Downing, Lenox 5565
129. SHE'S NEW TO YOU — Molly Bee, Liberty 55542
130. GRAVY WALTZ — Steve Allen, Dot 16457
131. SEAGREEN — Viceroys, Bethlehem 3045
132. MY HEART CAN'T TAKE IT NO MORE — Shirelles, Scepter 1248
133. THIS OLE HOUSE — Jimmy Dean, Columbia 42738
134. I GOT BURNED — Jo Ann Campbell, Cameo 249
135. MOTHER, PLEASE! — Jo Ann Campbell, Cameo 249
136. THE BOUNCE — Olympics, Tri Disc 106

# Billboard HOT 100
**FOR WEEK ENDING APRIL 13, 1963**

| This Week | Wk Ago | 2 Wks Ago | 3 Wks Ago | TITLE — Artist, Label & Number | Weeks On Chart |
|---|---|---|---|---|---|
| 1 | 1 | 1 | 4 | HE'S SO FINE — Chiffons, Laurie 3152 | 8 |
| 2 | 5 | 18 | 31 | CAN'T GET USED TO LOSING YOU — Andy Williams, Columbia 42674 | 7 |
| 3 | 4 | 4 | 7 | SOUTH STREET — Orlons, Cameo 243 | 9 |
| 4 | 3 | 3 | 2 | THE END OF THE WORLD — Skeeter Davis, RCA Victor 8098 | 12 |
| 5 | 6 | 8 | 25 | BABY WORKOUT — Jackie Wilson, Brunswick 55239 | 6 |
| 6 | 2 | 2 | 1 | OUR DAY WILL COME — Ruby and the Romantics, Kapp 501 | 10 |
| 7 | 30 | 62 | 90 | I WILL FOLLOW HIM — Little Peggy March, RCA Victor 8139 | 4 |
| 8 | 11 | 19 | 45 | PUFF (The Magic Dragon) — Peter, Paul & Mary, Warner Bros. 5348 | 5 |
| 9 | 10 | 26 | 35 | YOUNG LOVERS — Paul & Paula, Philips 40096 | 5 |
| 10 | 12 | 17 | 26 | DO THE BIRD — Dee Dee Sharp, Cameo 244 | 6 |
| 11 | 7 | 7 | 10 | IN DREAMS — Roy Orbison, Monument 806 | 10 |
| 12 | 26 | 44 | 58 | PIPELINE — Chantays, Dot 16440 | 7 |
| 13 | 22 | 27 | 34 | DON'T SAY NOTHIN' BAD ABOUT MY BABY — Cookies, Dimension 1008 | 7 |
| 14 | 9 | 6 | 6 | RHYTHM OF THE RAIN — Cascades, Valiant 6026 | 14 |
| 15 | 13 | 9 | 13 | OUR WINTER LOVE — Bill Pursell, Columbia 42619 | 11 |
| 16 | 18 | 28 | 36 | MR. BASS MAN — Johnny Cymbal, Kapp 503 | 9 |
| 17 | 21 | 23 | 28 | TWENTY MILES — Chubby Checker, Parkway 862 | 8 |
| 18 | 20 | 25 | 32 | FOLLOW THE BOYS — Connie Francis, MGM 13127 | 7 |
| 19 | 8 | 5 | 3 | YOU'RE THE REASON I'M LIVING — Bobby Darin, Capitol 4897 | 13 |
| 20 | 14 | 16 | 17 | ALL I HAVE TO DO IS DREAM — Richard Chamberlain, MGM 13121 | 10 |
| 21 | 15 | 10 | 8 | BLAME IT ON THE BOSSA NOVA — Eydie Gorme, Columbia 42661 | 13 |
| 22 | 37 | 56 | 82 | ON BROADWAY — Drifters, Atlantic 2182 | 4 |
| 23 | 17 | 14 | 16 | I WANNA BE AROUND — Tony Bennett, Columbia 42634 | 14 |
| 24 | 25 | 30 | 37 | OUT OF MY MIND — Johnny Tillotson, Cadence 1434 | 7 |
| 25 | 32 | 35 | 46 | OVER THE MOUNTAIN (Across the Sea) — Bobby Vinton, Epic 9577 | 5 |
| 26 | 27 | 33 | 47 | DON'T BE AFRAID, LITTLE DARLIN' — Steve Lawrence, Columbia 42699 | 6 |
| 27 | 31 | 39 | 43 | SANDY — Dion, Laurie 3153 | 5 |
| 28 | 39 | 46 | 64 | YOUNG AND IN LOVE — Dick & Deedee, Warner Bros. 5342 | 5 |
| 29 | 33 | 49 | 60 | I GOT WHAT I WANTED — Brook Benton, Mercury 72099 | 5 |
| 30 | 42 | 59 | 81 | MECCA — Gene Pitney, Musicor 1028 | 4 |
| 31 | 41 | 60 | 75 | WATERMELON MAN — Mongo Santamaria, Battle 45909 | 5 |
| 32 | 19 | 15 | 23 | LAUGHING BOY — Mary Wells, Motown 1039 | 8 |
| 33 | 45 | 63 | 74 | SURFIN' U.S.A. — Beach Boys, Capitol 4932 | 4 |
| 34 | 46 | 75 | — | CHARMS — Bobby Vee, Liberty 55530 | 3 |
| 35 | 35 | 37 | 41 | YAKETY SAX — Boots Randolph, Monument 804 | 8 |
| 36 | 24 | 21 | 21 | LET'S LIMBO SOME MORE — Chubby Checker, Parkway 862 | 9 |
| 37 | 28 | 24 | 15 | WILD WEEKEND — Rebels, Swan 4125 | 16 |
| 38 | 16 | 12 | 9 | WHAT WILL MY MARY SAY — Johnny Mathis, Columbia 42666 | 12 |
| 39 | 47 | 53 | 79 | DAYS OF WINE AND ROSES — Andy Williams, Columbia 42674 | 5 |
| 40 | 23 | 11 | 5 | WALK LIKE A MAN — 4 Seasons, Vee Jay 485 | 12 |
| 41 | 44 | 47 | 57 | LINDA — Jan and Dean, Liberty 55531 | 8 |
| 42 | 43 | 50 | 50 | ALL OVER THE WORLD — Nat King Cole, Capitol 4919 | 7 |
| 43 | 54 | 74 | 86 | FOOLISH LITTLE GIRL — Shirelles, Scepter 1248 | 4 |
| 44 | 52 | 83 | 96 | TOM CAT — Rooftop Singers, Vanguard 35019 | 4 |
| 45 | 36 | 36 | 33 | DAYS OF WINE AND ROSES — Henry Mancini, RCA Victor 8120 | 12 |
| 46 | 40 | 38 | 39 | WHY DO LOVERS BREAK EACH OTHERS HEARTS — Bob B. Soxx & the Blue Jeans, Philles 110 | 9 |
| 47 | 51 | 55 | 55 | YOU DON'T LOVE ME ANYMORE (And I Can Tell) — Rick Nelson, Decca 31475 | 6 |
| 48 | 29 | 13 | 11 | ONE BROKEN HEART FOR SALE — Elvis Presley, RCA Victor 8134 | 9 |
| 49 | 38 | 22 | 12 | RUBY BABY — Dion, Columbia 42662 | 13 |
| 50 | 78 | 84 | — | IF YOU WANNA BE HAPPY — Jimmy Soul, S.P.Q.R. 3305 | 3 |
| 51 | 48 | 43 | 44 | LOVE FOR SALE — Arthur Lyman Group, Hi-Fi 5066 | 11 |
| 52 | 34 | 20 | 24 | DON'T SET ME FREE — Ray Charles, ABC-Paramount 10405 | 8 |
| 53 | 49 | 52 | 70 | I GOT A WOMAN — Rick Nelson, Decca 31475 | 5 |
| 54 | 60 | 69 | 83 | LOCKING UP MY HEART — Marvelettes, Tamla 54077 | 4 |
| 55 | 56 | 64 | 69 | I'M JUST A COUNTRY BOY — George McCurn, A&M 705 | 7 |
| 56 | 82 | — | — | LOSING YOU — Brenda Lee, Decca 31478 | 2 |
| 57 | 72 | 66 | 68 | RAINBOW — Gene Chandler, Vee Jay 468 | 8 |
| 58 | 67 | 57 | 61 | HE'S GOT THE POWER — Exciters, United Artists 572 | 7 |
| 59 | 71 | 77 | — | A LOVE SHE CAN COUNT ON — Miracles, Tamla 54078 | 3 |
| 60 | 77 | 86 | — | WHAT ARE BOYS MADE OF — Percells, ABC-Paramount 10401 | 3 |
| 61 | 64 | 71 | 80 | SUN ARISE — Rolf Harris, Epic 9567 | 5 |
| 62 | 88 | — | — | REVEREND MR. BLACK — Kingston Trio, Capitol 4951 | 2 |
| 63 | 63 | 67 | 72 | BACK AT THE CHICKEN SHACK — Jimmy Smith, Blue Note 1877 | 6 |
| 64 | 69 | 70 | 73 | DEARER THAN LIFE — Brook Benton, Mercury 72099 | 6 |
| 65 | 66 | 78 | — | AMY — Paul Petersen, Colpix 676 | 3 |
| 66 | 75 | 91 | 99 | LITTLE BAND OF GOLD — James Gilreath, Joy 274 | 4 |
| 67 | 73 | 76 | — | HERE I STAND — Rip Chords, Columbia 42687 | 3 |
| 68 | 87 | — | — | I LOVE YOU BECAUSE — Al Martino, Capitol 4930 | 2 |
| 69 | 65 | 65 | 67 | SAX FIFTH AVENUE — Johnny Beecher, Warner Bros. 5341 | 7 |
| 70 | — | — | — | TAKE THESE CHAINS FROM MY HEART — Ray Charles, ABC-Paramount 10435 | 1 |
| 71 | 93 | 99 | — | TWO FACES HAVE I — Lou Christie, Roulette 4481 | 3 |
| 72 | 81 | 82 | 84 | KILLER JOE — Rocky Fellers, Scepter 1246 | 4 |
| 73 | 68 | 73 | 89 | DON'T WANNA THINK ABOUT PAULA — Dickey Lee, Smash 1808 | 5 |
| 74 | 76 | 80 | 85 | HOW CAN I FORGET — Jimmy Holiday, Everest 2022 | 5 |
| 75 | 83 | — | — | BILL BAILEY, WON'T YOU PLEASE COME HOME — Ella Fitzgerald, Verve 10281 | 2 |
| 76 | 85 | 88 | — | WHATEVER YOU WANT — Jerry Butler, Vee Jay 486 | 3 |
| 77 | 79 | 85 | 94 | THAT'S HOW HEARTACHES ARE MADE — Baby Washington, Sue 783 | 4 |
| 78 | — | — | — | TWO KINDS OF TEARDROPS — Del Shannon, Big Top 3143 | 1 |
| 79 | 74 | 72 | 66 | MEDITATION (Meditacao) — Charlie Byrd, Riverside 4544 | 6 |
| 80 | — | — | — | HOT PASTRAMI — Dartells, Dot 16453 | 1 |
| 81 | 89 | 90 | — | FUNNY MAN — Ray Stevens, Mercury 72098 | 3 |
| 82 | 98 | — | — | ASK ME — Maxine Brown, Wand 135 | 2 |
| 83 | 100 | — | — | (Today I Met) THE BOY I'M GONNA MARRY — Darlene Love, Philles 111 | 2 |
| 84 | 86 | 93 | 97 | THIS EMPTY PLACE — Dionne Warwick, Scepter 1247 | 4 |
| 85 | 96 | 98 | — | BONY MORONIE — Appalachians, ABC-Paramount 10419 | 3 |
| 86 | 91 | — | — | DON'T LET HER BE YOUR BABY — Contours, Gordy 7016 | 2 |
| 87 | 95 | — | — | CALL ME IRRESPONSIBLE — Frank Sinatra, Reprise 20151 | 2 |
| 88 | 90 | — | — | HEART — Kenny Chandler, Laurie 3158 | 2 |
| 89 | — | — | — | REMEMBER DIANA — Paul Anka, RCA Victor 8170 | 1 |
| 90 | — | — | — | MEMORY LANE — Hippies, Parkway 863 | 1 |
| 91 | — | — | — | HOT CAKES (1st Serving) — Dave (Baby) Cortez, Chess 1850 | 1 |
| 92 | 94 | 100 | — | PREACHERMAN — Charlie Russo, Diamond 131 | 3 |
| 93 | 84 | 95 | 88 | THEME FROM LAWRENCE OF ARABIA — Ferrante & Teicher, United Artists 563 | 9 |
| 94 | — | — | — | DON'T MENTION MY NAME — Shepherd Sisters, Atlantic 2176 | 1 |
| 95 | — | — | — | SHAME, SHAME, SHAME — Jimmy Reed, Vee Jay 509 | 1 |
| 96 | — | 87 | 92 | THE DOG — Rufus Thomas, Stax 130 | 5 |
| 97 | 97 | — | — | COME AND GET THESE MEMORIES — Martha & the Vandellas, Gordy 7014 | 2 |
| 98 | — | — | — | HE'S SO HEAVENLY — Brenda Lee, Decca 31478 | 1 |
| 99 | — | — | — | STILL — Bill Anderson, Decca 31458 | 1 |
| 100 | — | — | — | NOT FOR ALL THE MONEY IN THE WORLD — Shirelles, Scepter 1248 | 1 |

## BUBBLING UNDER THE HOT 100

101. THE LOVE OF MY MAN — Theola Kilgore, Serock 2004
102. BIRD'S THE WORD — Rivingtons, Liberty 55553
103. THE BOUNCE — Olympics, Tri Disc 106
104. SHUT DOWN — Beach Boys, Capitol 4932
105. WHAT A GUY — Raindrops, Jubilee 5444
106. HOW CAN I FORGET — Ben E. King, Atco 6256
107. I CAN TAKE A HINT — Miracles, Tamla 54078
108. WALKING AFTER MIDNIGHT — Patsy Cline, Everest 2020
109. DIANA — Joe Harnell & His Ork., Kapp 521
110. I'LL MAKE IT ALRIGHT — Valentinos, Sar 137
111. INSULT TO INJURY — Timi Yuro, Liberty 55552
112. HEART — Wayne Newton, Capitol 4920
113. DO IT-RAT NOW — Bill Black's Combo, Hi 2064
114. ANN-MARIE — Belmonts, Sabina 509
115. PRIMA DONNA — Glen Campbell, Capitol 4925
116. NO LETTER TODAY — Ray Charles, ABC-Paramount 10435
117. THESE ARMS OF MINE — Otis Redding, Volt 103
118. I'M MOVIN' ON — Matt Lucas, Smash 1813
119. THE FOLK SINGER — Tommy Roe, ABC-Paramount 10423
120. RONNIE, CALL ME WHEN YOU GET A CHANCE — Shelley Fabares, Colpix 682
121. CRYING IN THE CHAPEL — Little Richard, Atlantic 2181
122. THE ROSY DANCE — Johnny Thunder, Diamond 129
123. SINCE I DON'T HAVE YOU — 4 Seasons, Vee Jay 503 (Extended Play)
124. GONE WITH THE WIND — 4 Seasons, Vee Jay 503 (Extended Play)
125. MOTHER, PLEASE — Jo Ann Campbell, Cameo 249
126. HE'S A BAD BOY — Carole King, Dimension 1009
127. YOU SHOULD HAVE BEEN THERE — Fleetwoods, Dolton 74
128. SEAGREEN — Viceroys, Bethlehem 3045
129. MY HEART CAN'T TAKE IT NO MORE — Supremes, Motown 1040
130. GRAVY WALTZ — Steve Allen, Dot 16457
131. BABY COME HOME TO ME — Burl Ives, Decca 31479
132. TWO OF US — Robert Goulet, Columbia 42740
133. PRISONER OF LOVE — James Brown & the Famous Flames, King 5739

# Billboard HOT 100

**FOR WEEK ENDING APRIL 20, 1963**

| This Week | Wks Ago | Title — Artist, Label & Number | Wks on Chart |
|---|---|---|---|
| 1 | 1 1 1 | HE'S SO FINE — Chiffons, Laurie 3152 | 9 |
| 2 | 2 5 18 | CAN'T GET USED TO LOSING YOU — Andy Williams, Columbia 42674 | 8 |
| 3 | 7 30 62 | I WILL FOLLOW HIM — Little Peggy March, RCA Victor 8139 | 5 |
| 4 | 8 11 19 | PUFF (The Magic Dragon) — Peter, Paul & Mary, Warner Bros. 5348 | 6 |
| 5 | 5 6 8 | BABY WORKOUT — Jackie Wilson, Brunswick 55239 | 7 |
| 6 | 9 10 26 | YOUNG LOVERS — Paul & Paula, Philips 40096 | 6 |
| 7 | 3 4 4 | SOUTH STREET — Orlons, Cameo 243 | 10 |
| 8 | 13 22 27 | DON'T SAY NOTHIN' BAD ABOUT MY BABY — Cookies, Dimension 1008 | 8 |
| 9 | 12 26 44 | PIPELINE — Chantays, Dot 16440 | 8 |
| 10 | 10 12 17 | DO THE BIRD — Dee Dee Sharp, Cameo 244 | 8 |
| 11 | 4 3 3 | THE END OF THE WORLD — Skeeter Davis, RCA Victor 8098 | 13 |
| 12 | 22 37 56 | ON BROADWAY — Drifters, Atlantic 2182 | 5 |
| 13 | 6 2 2 | OUR DAY WILL COME — Ruby and the Romantics, Kapp 501 | 11 |
| 14 | 31 41 60 | WATERMELON MAN — Mongo Santamaria, Battle 45909 | 6 |
| 15 | 17 21 23 | TWENTY MILES — Chubby Checker, Parkway 862 | 9 |
| 16 | 30 42 59 | MECCA — Gene Pitney, Musicor 1028 | 5 |
| 17 | 18 20 25 | FOLLOW THE BOYS — Connie Francis, MGM 13127 | 8 |
| 18 | 11 7 7 | IN DREAMS — Roy Orbison, Monument 806 | 11 |
| 19 | 16 18 28 | MR. BASS MAN — Johnny Cymbal, Kapp 503 | 10 |
| 20 | 28 39 46 | YOUNG AND IN LOVE — Dick & Deedee, Warner Bros. 5342 | 6 |
| 21 | 27 31 39 | SANDY — Dion, Laurie 3153 | 8 |
| 22 | 25 32 35 | OVER THE MOUNTAIN (Across the Sea) — Bobby Vinton, Epic 9577 | 7 |
| 23 | 33 45 63 | SURFIN' U.S.A. — Beach Boys, Capitol 4932 | 5 |
| 24 | 24 25 30 | OUT OF MY MIND — Johnny Tillotson, Cadence 1434 | 8 |
| 25 | 34 46 75 | CHARMS — Bobby Vee, Liberty 55530 | 4 |
| 26 | 26 27 33 | DON'T BE AFRAID, LITTLE DARLIN' — Steve Lawrence, Columbia 42699 | 7 |
| 27 | 15 13 9 | OUR WINTER LOVE — Bill Pursell, Columbia 42619 | 12 |
| 28 | 29 33 49 | I GOT WHAT I WANTED — Brook Benton, Mercury 72099 | 6 |
| 29 | 43 54 74 | FOOLISH LITTLE GIRL — Shirelles, Scepter 1248 | 5 |
| 30 | 23 17 14 | I WANNA BE AROUND — Tony Bennett, Columbia 42634 | 15 |
| 31 | 62 88 — | REVEREND MR. BLACK — Kingston Trio, Capitol 4951 | 3 |
| 32 | 50 78 84 | IF YOU WANNA BE HAPPY — Jimmy Soul, S.P.Q.R. 3305 | 4 |
| 33 | 56 82 — | LOSING YOU — Brenda Lee, Decca 31478 | 3 |
| 34 | 44 52 83 | TOM CAT — Rooftop Singers, Vanguard 35019 | 5 |
| 35 | 41 44 47 | LINDA — Jan and Dean, Liberty 55531 | 9 |
| 36 | 14 9 6 | RHYTHM OF THE RAIN — Cascades, Valiant 6026 | 15 |
| 37 | 39 47 53 | DAYS OF WINE AND ROSES — Andy Williams, Columbia 42674 | 6 |
| 38 | 21 15 10 | BLAME IT ON THE BOSSA NOVA — Eydie Gorme, Columbia 42661 | 14 |
| 39 | 20 14 16 | ALL I HAVE TO DO IS DREAM — Richard Chamberlain, MGM 13121 | 11 |
| 40 | 19 8 5 | YOU'RE THE REASON I'M LIVING — Bobby Darin, Capitol 4897 | 14 |
| 41 | 45 36 36 | DAYS OF WINE AND ROSES — Henry Mancini, RCA Victor 8120 | 13 |
| 42 | 66 75 91 | LITTLE BAND OF GOLD — James Gilreath, Joy 274 | 5 |
| 43 | 35 35 37 | YAKETY SAX — Boots Randolph, Monument 804 | 9 |
| 44 | 42 43 50 | ALL OVER THE WORLD — Nat King Cole, Capitol 4919 | 8 |
| 45 | 70 — — | TAKE THESE CHAINS FROM MY HEART — Ray Charles, ABC-Paramount 10435 | 2 |
| 46 | 54 60 69 | LOCKING UP MY HEART — Marvelettes, Tamla 54077 | 5 |
| 47 | 37 28 24 | WILD WEEKEND — Rebels, Swan 4125 | 17 |
| 48 | 59 71 77 | A LOVE SHE CAN COUNT ON — Miracles, Tamla 54078 | 4 |
| 49 | 36 24 21 | LET'S LIMBO SOME MORE — Chubby Checker, Parkway 862 | 10 |
| 50 | 32 19 15 | LAUGHING BOY — Mary Wells, Motown 1039 | 9 |
| 51 | 71 93 99 | TWO FACES HAVE I — Lou Christie, Roulette 4481 | 4 |
| 52 | 57 72 66 | RAINBOW — Gene Chandler, Vee Jay 468 | 9 |
| 53 | 60 77 86 | WHAT ARE BOYS MADE OF — Percells, ABC-Paramount 10401 | 4 |
| 54 | 40 23 11 | WALK LIKE A MAN — 4 Seasons, Vee Jay 485 | 13 |
| 55 | 53 49 52 | I GOT A WOMAN — Rick Nelson, Decca 31475 | 6 |
| 56 | 68 87 — | I LOVE YOU BECAUSE — Al Martino, Capitol 4930 | 3 |
| 57 | 72 81 82 | KILLER JOE — Rocky Fellers, Scepter 1246 | 4 |
| 58 | 55 56 64 | I'M JUST A COUNTRY BOY — George McCurn, A&M 705 | 8 |
| 59 | 47 51 55 | YOU DON'T LOVE ME ANYMORE (And I Can Tell) — Rick Nelson, Decca 31475 | 7 |
| 60 | 80 — — | HOT PASTRAMI — Dartells, Dot 16453 | 2 |
| 61 | 77 79 85 | THAT'S HOW HEARTACHES ARE MADE — Baby Washington, Sue 783 | 5 |
| 62 | 64 69 70 | DEARER THAN LIFE — Brook Benton, Mercury 72099 | 7 |
| 63 | 61 64 71 | SUN ARISE — Rolf Harris, Epic 9567 | 6 |
| 64 | 67 73 76 | HERE I STAND — Rip Chords, Columbia 42687 | 4 |
| 65 | 58 67 57 | HE'S GOT THE POWER — Exciters, United Artists 572 | 8 |
| 66 | — — — | ANOTHER SATURDAY NIGHT — Sam Cooke, RCA Victor 8164 | 1 |
| 67 | 65 66 78 | AMY — Paul Petersen, Colpix 676 | 4 |
| 68 | 74 76 80 | HOW CAN I FORGET — Jimmy Holiday, Everest 2022 | 6 |
| 69 | — — — | THIS LITTLE GIRL — Dion, Columbia 42776 | 1 |
| 70 | 78 — — | TWO KINDS OF TEARDROPS — Del Shannon, Big Top 3143 | 2 |
| 71 | — — — | PUSHOVER — Etta James, Argo 5437 | 1 |
| 72 | — — 94 | BIRD'S THE WORD — Rivingtons, Liberty 55553 | 2 |
| 73 | 76 85 88 | WHATEVER YOU WANT — Jerry Butler, Vee Jay 486 | 4 |
| 74 | 85 96 98 | BONY MORONIE — Appalachians, ABC-Paramount 10419 | 4 |
| 75 | 83 100 — | (Today I Met) THE BOY I'M GONNA MARRY — Darlene Love, Philles 111 | 3 |
| 76 | 69 65 65 | SAX FIFTH AVENUE — Johnny Beecher, Warner Bros. 5341 | 8 |
| 77 | 86 91 — | DON'T LET HER BE YOUR BABY — Contours, Gordy 7016 | 3 |
| 78 | 89 — — | REMEMBER DIANA — Paul Anka, RCA Victor 8170 | 2 |
| 79 | 75 83 — | BILL BAILEY, WON'T YOU PLEASE COME HOME — Ella Fitzgerald, Verve 10288 | 3 |
| 80 | 82 98 — | ASK ME — Maxine Brown, Wand 135 | 3 |
| 81 | 88 90 — | HEART — Kenny Chandler, Laurie 3158 | 3 |
| 82 | 90 — — | MEMORY LANE — Hippies, Parkway 863 | 2 |
| 83 | 97 97 — | COME AND GET THESE MEMORIES — Martha & the Vandellas, Gordy 7014 | 3 |
| 84 | 84 86 93 | THIS EMPTY PLACE — Dionne Warwick, Scepter 1247 | 5 |
| 85 | — 92 92 | HOW CAN I FORGET — Ben E. King, Atco 6256 | 4 |
| 86 | — — — | AIN'T THAT A SHAME! — 4 Seasons, Vee Jay 512 | 1 |
| 87 | 87 95 — | CALL ME IRRESPONSIBLE — Frank Sinatra, Reprise 20151 | 3 |
| 88 | 99 — — | STILL — Bill Anderson, Decca 31458 | 2 |
| 89 | — — — | PRISONER OF LOVE — James Brown & the Famous Flames, King 5739 | 1 |
| 90 | — — — | ANN-MARIE — Belmonts, Sabina 509 | 1 |
| 91 | — — — | IF YOU NEED ME — Solomon Burke, Atlantic 2185 | 1 |
| 92 | 96 — 87 | THE DOG — Rufus Thomas, Stax 130 | 6 |
| 93 | 98 — — | HE'S SO HEAVENLY — Brenda Lee, Decca 31478 | 2 |
| 94 | — — — | ETERNALLY — Chantels, Ludix 101 | 2 |
| 95 | — — — | THE LOVE OF MY MAN — Theola Kilgore, Serock 2004 | 1 |
| 96 | 93 84 95 | THEME FROM LAWRENCE OF ARABIA — Ferrante & Teicher, United Artists 563 | 10 |
| 97 | — — — | DIANE — Joe Harnell & His Ork, Kapp 521 | 1 |
| 98 | 92 94 100 | PREACHERMAN — Charlie Russo, Diamond 131 | 4 |
| 99 | — — — | SWEET DREAMS (Of You) — Patsy Cline, Decca 31483 | 1 |
| 100 | — — — | IF YOU CAN'T ROCK ME — Rick Nelson, Imperial 5935 | 1 |

## BUBBLING UNDER THE HOT 100

101. SHUT DOWN — Beach Boys, Capitol 4932
102. THE BOUNCE — Olympics, Tri Disc 106
103. EL WATUSI — Ray Barretto, Tico 419
104. FUNNY MAN — Ray Stevens, Mercury 72098
105. WHAT A GUY — Raindrops, Jubilee 5444
106. SHAME, SHAME, SHAME — Jimmy Reed, Vee Jay 509
107. STING RAY — Routers, Warner Bros. 5349
108. HE'S A BAD BOY — Carole King, Dimension 1009
109. HEART — Wayne Newton, Capitol 4920
110. DON'T MENTION MY NAME — Shepherd Sisters, Atlantic 2176
111. LONESOME 7-7203 — Hawkshaw Hawkins, King 5712
112. DO IT-RAT NOW — Bill Black's Combo, Hi 2064
113. ARABIA — Del-Cos, Showcase 2501
114. I CAN TAKE A HINT — Matt Lucas, Smash 1812
115. PRIMA DONNA — Miracles, Tamla 54078
116. THE POLK SINGER — Glen Campbell, Capitol 4925
117. I'M MOVIN' ON — Tommy Roe, ABC-Paramount 10423
118. HOT CAKES (1st Serving) — Dave (Baby) Cortez, Chess 1850
119. CRYING IN THE CHAPEL — Little Richard, Atlantic 2181
120. HOT PASTRAMI AND MASHED POTATOES (Part I) — Joey Dee & the Starliters, Roulette 4488
121. MOTHER, PLEASE! — Jo Ann Campbell, Cameo 249
122. YOU SHOULD HAVE BEEN THERE — Fleetwoods, Dolton 74
123. YOU NEVER MISS YOUR WATER (Till the Well Runs Dry) — "Little Esther" Phillips & "Big Al" Downing, Lenox 5565
124. GRAVY WALTZ — Steve Allen, Dot 16457
125. EVERYBODY SOUTH STREET — Four Evers, Jamie 1247
126. CRY ON MY SHOULDER — Johnny Crawford, Del-Fi 4203
127. IF YOU NEED ME — Wilson Pickett, Double L 713
128. RAIN — Jive Five, Beltone 2034
129. COTTON FIELDS (Cotton Song) — Arthur Lyman Group, Hi-Fi 5071
130. SINCE I MET YOU BABY — Ace Cannon, Hi 2063
131. SHAMPOO — Les McCann, Pacific Jazz 350

# Billboard HOT 100
**FOR WEEK ENDING APRIL 27, 1963**

★ STAR PERFORMERS—Selections registering greatest upward progress this week.
[S] Indicates that 45 r.p.m. stereo single version is available.
△ Indicates that 33⅓ r.p.m. mono single version is available.
[Ⓢ] Indicates that 33⅓ r.p.m. stereo single version is available.

| This Week | 1 Wk. Ago | 2 Wks. Ago | 3 Wks. Ago | Title – Artist, Label & Number | Weeks on Chart |
|---|---|---|---|---|---|
| 1 ★ Billboard Award | 3 | 7 | 30 | I WILL FOLLOW HIM △ — Little Peggy March, RCA Victor 8139 | 6 |
| 2 | 2 | 2 | 5 | CAN'T GET USED TO LOSING YOU — Andy Williams, Columbia 42674 | 9 |
| 3 | 1 | 1 | 1 | HE'S SO FINE — Chiffons, Laurie 3152 | 10 |
| 4 | 4 | 8 | 11 | PUFF (The Magic Dragon) — Peter, Paul & Mary, Warner Bros. 5348 | 7 |
| 5 | 5 | 5 | 6 | BABY WORKOUT — Jackie Wilson, Brunswick 55239 | 7 |
| 6 ★ | 9 | 12 | 26 | PIPELINE — Chantays, Dot 16440 | 9 |
| 7 | 8 | 13 | 22 | DON'T SAY NOTHIN BAD ABOUT MY BABY — Cookies, Dimension 1008 | 9 |
| 8 | 6 | 9 | 10 | YOUNG LOVERS — Paul & Paula, Philips 40096 | 7 |
| 9 | 12 | 22 | 37 | ON BROADWAY — Drifters, Atlantic 2182 | 6 |
| 10 | 14 | 31 | 41 | WATERMELON MAN — Mongo Santamaria, Battle 45909 | 7 |
| 11 | 23 | 33 | 45 | SURFIN' U.S.A. — Beach Boys, Capitol 4932 | 6 |
| 12 | 7 | 3 | 4 | SOUTH STREET — Orions, Cameo 243 | 11 |
| 13 | 16 | 30 | 42 | MECCA — Gene Pitney, Musicor 1028 | 6 |
| 14 | 11 | 4 | 3 | THE END OF THE WORLD △ — Skeeter Davis, RCA Victor 8098 | 14 |
| 15 | 32 | 50 | 78 | IF YOU WANNA BE HAPPY — Jimmy Soul, S.P.Q.R. 3305 | 5 |
| 16 | 31 | 62 | 88 | REVEREND MR. BLACK — Kingston Trio, Capitol 4951 | 4 |
| 17 | 25 | 34 | 46 | CHARMS — Bobby Vee, Liberty 55530 | 5 |
| 18 | 29 | 43 | 54 | FOOLISH LITTLE GIRL — Shirelles, Scepter 1248 | 6 |
| 19 | 20 | 28 | 39 | YOUNG AND IN LOVE — Dick & Deedee, Warner Bros. 5342 | 7 |
| 20 | 10 | 10 | 12 | DO THE BIRD — Dee Dee Sharp, Cameo 244 | 9 |
| 21 | 22 | 25 | 32 | OVER THE MOUNTAIN (Across the Sea) — Bobby Vinton, Epic 9577 | 8 |
| 22 | 13 | 6 | 2 | OUR DAY WILL COME — Ruby and the Romantics, Kapp 501 | 12 |
| 23 | 15 | 17 | 21 | TWENTY MILES — Chubby Checker, Parkway 862 | 10 |
| 24 | 17 | 18 | 20 | FOLLOW THE BOYS — Connie Francis, MGM 13127 | 9 |
| 25 ★ | 34 | 44 | 52 | TOM CAT — Rooftop Singers, Vanguard 35019 | 6 |
| 26 ★ | 33 | 56 | 82 | LOSING YOU — Brenda Lee, Decca 31478 | 4 |
| 27 | 45 | 70 | — | TAKE THESE CHAINS FROM MY HEART — Ray Charles, ABC-Paramount 10435 | 3 |
| 28 | 21 | 27 | 31 | SANDY — Dion, Laurie 3153 | 9 |
| 29 | 18 | 11 | 7 | IN DREAMS — Roy Orbison, Monument 806 | 12 |
| 30 | 19 | 16 | 18 | MR. BASS MAN — Johnny Cymbal, Kapp 503 | 11 |
| 31 | 35 | 41 | 44 | LINDA — Jan and Dean, Liberty 55531 | 10 |
| 32 ★ | 42 | 66 | 75 | LITTLE BAND OF GOLD — James Gilreath, Joy 274 | 6 |
| 33 | 26 | 26 | 27 | DON'T BE AFRAID, LITTLE DARLIN' — Steve Lawrence, Columbia 42699 | 8 |
| 34 | 37 | 39 | 47 | DAYS OF WINE AND ROSES △ — Andy Williams, Columbia 42674 | 7 |
| 35 ★ | 51 | 71 | 93 | TWO FACES HAVE I — Lou Christie, Roulette 4481 | 5 |
| 36 | 24 | 24 | 25 | OUT OF MY MIND — Johnny Tillotson, Cadence 1434 | 9 |
| 37 | 28 | 29 | 33 | I GOT WHAT I WANTED — Brook Benton, Mercury 72099 | 7 |
| 38 | 41 | 45 | 36 | DAYS OF WINE AND ROSES △ — Henry Mancini, RCA Victor 8120 | 14 |
| 39 | 60 | 80 | — | HOT PASTRAMI — Dartells, Dot 16453 | 3 |
| 40 | 57 | 72 | 81 | KILLER JOE — Rocky Fellers, Scepter 1246 | 6 |
| 41 | 56 | 68 | 87 | I LOVE YOU BECAUSE — Al Martino, Capitol 4930 | 4 |
| 42 | 48 | 59 | 71 | A LOVE SHE CAN COUNT ON — Miracles, Tamla 54078 | 5 |
| 43 | 66 | — | — | ANOTHER SATURDAY NIGHT △ — Sam Cooke, RCA Victor 8164 | 2 |
| 44 | 46 | 54 | 60 | LOCKING UP MY HEART — Marvelettes, Tamla 54077 | 6 |
| 45 | 27 | 15 | 13 | OUR WINTER LOVE △ — Bill Pursell, Columbia 42619 | 13 |
| 46 | 36 | 14 | 9 | RHYTHM OF THE RAIN — Cascades, Valiant 6026 | 16 |
| 47 | 38 | 21 | 15 | BLAME IT ON THE BOSSA NOVA △ — Eydie Gorme, Columbia 42661 | 15 |
| 48 | 30 | 23 | 17 | I WANNA BE AROUND △ — Tony Bennett, Columbia 42634 | 16 |
| 49 | 44 | 42 | 43 | ALL OVER THE WORLD — Nat King Cole, Capitol 4919 | 9 |
| 50 | 39 | 20 | 14 | ALL I HAVE TO DO IS DREAM — Richard Chamberlain, MGM 13121 | 12 |
| 51 | 86 | — | — | AIN'T THAT A SHAME! — 4 Seasons, Vee Jay 512 | 2 |
| 52 | 52 | 57 | 72 | RAINBOW — Gene Chandler, Vee Jay 468 | 10 |
| 53 | 71 | — | — | PUSHOVER — Etta James, Argo 5437 | 2 |
| 54 | 75 | 83 | 100 | (Today I Met) THE BOY I'M GONNA MARRY — Darlene Love, Philles 111 | 4 |
| 55 ★ | 69 | — | — | THIS LITTLE GIRL △ — Dion, Columbia 42776 | 2 |
| 56 | 64 | 67 | 73 | HERE I STAND △ — Rip Chords, Columbia 42687 | 5 |
| 57 | 61 | 77 | 79 | THAT'S HOW HEARTACHES ARE MADE — Baby Washington, Sue 783 | 6 |
| 58 | 53 | 60 | 77 | WHAT ARE BOYS MADE OF — Percells, ABC-Paramount 10401 | 5 |
| 59 | 62 | 64 | 69 | DEARER THAN LIFE — Brook Benton, Mercury 72099 | 8 |
| 60 | 68 | 74 | 76 | HOW CAN I FORGET — Jimmy Holiday, Everest 2022 | 7 |
| 61 | 72 | — | — | BIRD'S THE WORD — Rivingtons, Liberty 55553 | 3 |
| 62 | 74 | 85 | 96 | BONY MORONIE — Appalachians, ABC-Paramount 10419 | 5 |
| 63 | 78 | 89 | — | REMEMBER DIANA — Paul Anka, RCA Victor 8170 | 3 |
| 64 | 77 | 86 | 91 | DON'T LET HER BE YOUR BABY — Contours, Gordy 7016 | 4 |
| 65 | 70 | 78 | — | TWO KINDS OF TEARDROPS — Del Shannon, Big Top 3143 | 3 |
| 66 | 63 | 61 | 64 | SUN ARISE — Rolf Harris, Epic 9567 | 7 |
| 67 ★ | — | — | — | YOU CAN'T SIT DOWN — Dovells, Parkway 867 | 1 |
| 68 | 73 | 76 | 85 | WHATEVER YOU WANT — Jerry Butler, Vee Jay 486 | 5 |
| 69 | 81 | 88 | 90 | HEART — Kenny Chandler, Laurie 3158 | 4 |
| 70 ★ | 95 | — | — | THE LOVE OF MY MAN — Theola Kilgore, Serock 2004 | 2 |
| 71 | 88 | 99 | — | STILL — Bill Anderson, Decca 31458 | 3 |
| 72 | 82 | 90 | — | MEMORY LANE — Hippies, Parkway 863 | 3 |
| 73 | 93 | 98 | — | HE'S SO HEAVENLY — Brenda Lee, Decca 31478 | 3 |
| 74 | — | — | — | SHUT DOWN — Beach Boys, Capitol 4932 | 1 |
| 75 | — | — | — | YOU NEVER MISS YOUR WATER (Till the Well Runs Dry) — "Little Esther" Phillips and "Big Al" Downing, Lenox 5565 | 1 |
| 76 | 83 | 97 | 97 | COME AND GET THESE MEMORIES — Martha & the Vandellas, Gordy 7014 | 4 |
| 77 | 80 | 82 | 98 | ASK ME — Maxine Brown, Wand 135 | 4 |
| 78 | 87 | 87 | 95 | CALL ME IRRESPONSIBLE — Frank Sinatra, Reprise 20151 | 4 |
| 79 | — | 89 | — | PRISONER OF LOVE — James Brown & the Famous Flames, King 5739 | 2 |
| 80 | — | — | — | DA DOO RON RON — Crystals, Philles 112 | 1 |
| 81 | — | — | — | STING RAY — Routers, Warner Bros. 5349 | 1 |
| 82 | 91 | — | — | IF YOU NEED ME — Solomon Burke, Atlantic 2185 | 2 |
| 83 | — | — | — | DO IT—RAT NOW — Bill Black's Combo, Hi 2064 | 1 |
| 84 | — | — | — | HEART — Wayne Newton, Capitol 4920 | 1 |
| 85 ★ | — | — | — | RONNIE, CALL ME WHEN YOU GET A CHANCE — Shelley Fabares, Colpix 682 | 1 |
| 86 ★ | — | — | — | WHAT A GUY — Raindrops, Jubilee 5444 | 1 |
| 87 | — | — | — | HOT PASTRAMI WITH MASHED POTATOES (Part I) — Joe Dee and the Starliters, Roulette 4488 | 1 |
| 88 | 90 | — | — | ANN-MARIE — Belmonts, Sabina 509 | 2 |
| 89 | — | — | — | LET'S GO STEADY AGAIN — Neil Sedaka, RCA Victor 8169 | 1 |
| 90 | — | — | — | EL WATUSI — Ray Barretto, Tico 419 | 1 |
| 91 | 96 | 93 | 84 | THEME FROM LAWRENCE OF ARABIA — Ferrante & Teicher, United Artists 563 | 11 |
| 92 | — | — | — | THE BOUNCE — Olympics, Tri Disc 106 | 1 |
| 93 | — | — | — | MOTHER, PLEASE! — Jo Ann Campbell, Cameo 249 | 1 |
| 94 | — | — | — | GRAVY WALTZ — Steve Allen, Dot 16457 | 1 |
| 95 | — | 91 | — | HOT CAKES (1st Serving) — Dave (Baby) Cortez, Chess 1850 | 2 |
| 96 | 98 | 92 | 94 | PREACHERMAN — Charlie Russo, Diamond 131 | 5 |
| 97 | 99 | — | — | SWEET DREAMS (Of You) — Patsy Cline, Decca 31483 | 2 |
| 98 | — | — | — | HE'S A BAD BOY — Carole King, Dimension 1009 | 1 |
| 99 | — | — | — | ROCKIN' CRICKETS — Rockin' Rebels, Swan 4140 | 1 |
| 100 | — | — | — | SHY GIRL — Cascades, Valiant 6028 | 1 |

## BUBBLING UNDER THE HOT 100

101. PATTY BABY ............ Freddy Cannon, Swan 4139
102. YOU ALWAYS HURT THE ONE YOU LOVE ............ Fats Domino, Imperial 5937
103. SHAME, SHAME, SHAME ............ Jimmy Reed, Vee Jay 509
104. DON'T MENTION MY NAME ............ Shepherd Sisters, Atlantic 2176
105. OLD ENOUGH TO LOVE ............ Rick Nelson, Imperial 5935
106. HOW CAN I FORGET ............ Ben E. King, Atco 6256
107. FUNNY MAN ............ Ray Stevens, Mercury 72098
108. I'M MOVIN' ON ............ Matt Lucas, Smash 1813
109. THE LAST LEAF ............ Cascades, Valiant 6028
110. THE FOLK SINGER ............ Tommy Roe, ABC-Paramount 10423
111. ARABIA ............ Del-Cos, Showcase 2501
112. LONESOME 7-7203 ............ Hawkshaw Hawkins, King 5712
113. IF YOU CAN'T ROCK ME ............ Rick Nelson, Imperial 5935
114. IF YOU NEED ME ............ Wilson Pickett, Double 1713
115. ONE BOY TOO LATE ............ Mike Clifford, United Artists 563
116. NOT FOR ALL THE MONEY IN THE WORLD ............ Shirelles, Scepter 1248
117. DIANE ............ Joe Harnell & His Ork, Kapp 521
118. YOU SHOULD HAVE BEEN THERE ............ Fleetwoods, Dolton 74
119. NO LETTER TODAY ............ Ray Charles, ABC-Paramount 10435
120. CRYING IN THE CHAPEL ............ Little Richard, Atlantic 2181
121. CALL ME IRRESPONSIBLE ............ Jack Jones, Kapp 516
122. LOVE WILL FIND A WAY ............ Sam Cooke, RCA Victor 8164
123. PEARL, PEARL, PEARL ............ Lester Flatt and Earl Scruggs, Columbia 42755
124. NEEDLES AND PINS ............ Jackie De Shannon, Liberty 55563
125. BO DIDDLEY ............ Buddy Holly, Coral 62352
126. GIVE LOVE A HINT ............ Miracles, Tamla 54078
127. HELLO STRANGER ............ Barbara Lewis, Atlantic 2184
128. THIS OLE HOUSE ............ Jimmy Dean, Columbia 42738
129. ISLAND OF DREAMS ............ Springfields, Philips 40099
130. THE SHAMPOO ............ Les McCann, Pacific Jazz 350

# Billboard HOT 100

**FOR WEEK ENDING MAY 4, 1963**

| This Week | Wk. Ago | 2 Wks. Ago | 3 Wks. Ago | TITLE — Artist, Label & Number | Weeks On Chart |
|---|---|---|---|---|---|
| 1 | 1 | 3 | 7 | I WILL FOLLOW HIM — Little Peggy March, RCA Victor 8139 △ | 7 |
| 2 | 2 | 2 | 2 | CAN'T GET USED TO LOSING YOU — Andy Williams, Columbia 42674 △ | 10 |
| 3 | 4 | 4 | 8 | PUFF (The Magic Dragon) — Peter, Paul & Mary, Warner Bros. 5348 | 8 |
| 4 | 6 | 9 | 12 | PIPELINE — Chantays, Dot 16440 | 10 |
| 5 | 3 | 1 | 1 | HE'S SO FINE — Chiffons, Laurie 3152 | 11 |
| 6 | 15 | 32 | 50 | IF YOU WANNA BE HAPPY — Jimmy Soul, S.P.Q.R. 3305 | 6 |
| 7 | 7 | 8 | 13 | DON'T SAY NOTHIN' BAD ABOUT MY BABY — Cookies, Dimension 1008 | 10 |
| 8 | 11 | 23 | 33 | SURFIN' U. S. A. — Beach Boys, Capitol 4932 | 7 |
| 9 | 9 | 12 | 22 | ON BROADWAY — Drifters, Atlantic 2182 | 7 |
| 10 | 10 | 14 | 31 | WATERMELON MAN — Mongo Santamaria, Battle 45909 | 8 |
| 11 | 5 | 5 | 5 | BABY WORKOUT — Jackie Wilson, Brunswick 55239 | 9 |
| 12 | 13 | 16 | 30 | MECCA — Gene Pitney, Musicor 1028 | 7 |
| 13 | 18 | 29 | 43 | FOOLISH LITTLE GIRL — Shirelles, Scepter 1248 | 7 |
| 14 | 16 | 31 | 62 | REVEREND MR. BLACK — Kingston Trio, Capitol 4951 | 5 |
| 15 | 17 | 25 | 34 | CHARMS — Bobby Vee, Liberty 55530 | 6 |
| 16 | 8 | 6 | 9 | YOUNG LOVERS — Paul & Paula, Philips 40096 | 8 |
| 17 | 19 | 20 | 28 | YOUNG AND IN LOVE — Dick & Deedee, Warner Bros. 5342 | 8 |
| 18 | 26 | 33 | 56 | LOSING YOU — Brenda Lee, Decca 31478 | 5 |
| 19 | 27 | 45 | 70 | TAKE THESE CHAINS FROM MY HEART — Ray Charles, ABC-Paramount 10435 | 4 |
| 20 | 25 | 34 | 44 | TOM CAT — Rooftop Singers, Vanguard 35019 | 5 |
| 21 | 39 | 60 | 80 | HOT PASTRAMI — Dartells, Dot 16453 | 4 |
| 22 | 12 | 7 | 3 | SOUTH STREET — Orlons, Cameo 243 | 12 |
| 23 | 35 | 51 | 71 | TWO FACES HAVE I — Lou Christie, Roulette 4481 | 6 |
| 24 | 14 | 11 | 4 | THE END OF THE WORLD — Skeeter Davis, RCA Victor 8098 △ | 15 |
| 25 | 32 | 42 | 66 | LITTLE BAND OF GOLD — James Gilreath, Joy 274 | 7 |
| 26 | 34 | 37 | 39 | DAYS OF WINE AND ROSES — Andy Williams, Columbia 42674 △ | 8 |
| 27 | 21 | 22 | 25 | OVER THE MOUNTAIN (Across the Sea) — Bobby Vinton, Epic 9577 | 9 |
| 28 | 31 | 35 | 41 | LINDA — Jan and Dean, Liberty 55531 | 11 |
| 29 | 41 | 56 | 68 | I LOVE YOU BECAUSE — Al Martino, Capitol 4930 | 5 |
| 30 | 43 | 66 | — | ANOTHER SATURDAY NIGHT — Sam Cooke, RCA Victor 8164 | 3 |
| 31 | 55 | 69 | — | THIS LITTLE GIRL — Dion, Columbia 42776 △ | |
| 32 | 20 | 10 | 10 | DO THE BIRD — Dee Dee Sharp, Cameo 244 | 10 |
| 33 | 38 | 41 | 45 | DAYS OF WINE AND ROSES — Henry Mancini, RCA Victor 8120 △ | 15 |
| 34 | 40 | 57 | 72 | KILLER JOE — Rocky Fellers, Scepter 1246 | 7 |
| 35 | 28 | 21 | 27 | SANDY — Dion, Laurie 3153 | 10 |
| 36 | 51 | 86 | — | AIN'T THAT A SHAME! — 4 Seasons, Vee Jay 512 | 3 |
| 37 | 42 | 48 | 59 | A LOVE SHE CAN COUNT ON — Miracles, Tamla 54078 | 6 |
| 38 | 30 | 19 | 16 | MR. BASS MAN — Johnny Cymbal, Kapp 503 | 12 |
| 39 | 23 | 15 | 17 | TWENTY MILES — Chubby Checker, Parkway 862 | 11 |
| 40 | 33 | 26 | 26 | DON'T BE AFRAID, LITTLE DARLIN' — Steve Lawrence, Columbia 42699 △ | 9 |
| 41 | 54 | 75 | 83 | (Today I Met) THE BOY I'M GONNA MARRY — Darlene Love, Philles 111 | 5 |
| 42 | 22 | 13 | 6 | OUR DAY WILL COME — Ruby and the Romantics, Kapp 501 | 13 |
| 43 | 37 | 28 | 29 | I GOT WHAT I WANTED — Brook Benton, Mercury 72099 | 8 |
| 44 | 44 | 46 | 54 | LOCKING UP MY HEART — Marvelettes, Tamla 54077 | 7 |
| 45 | 36 | 24 | 24 | OUT OF MY MIND — Johnny Tillotson, Cadence 1434 | 10 |
| 46 | 53 | 71 | — | PUSHOVER — Etta James, Argo 5437 | 4 |
| 47 | 52 | 52 | 57 | RAINBOW — Gene Chandler, Vee Jay 468 | 11 |
| 48 | 24 | 17 | 18 | FOLLOW THE BOYS — Connie Francis, MGM 13127 | 10 |
| 49 | 71 | 88 | 99 | STILL — Bill Anderson, Decca 31458 | 4 |
| 50 | 67 | — | — | YOU CAN'T SIT DOWN — Dovells, Parkway 867 | 2 |
| 51 | 70 | 95 | — | THE LOVE OF MY MAN — Theola Kilgore, Serock 2004 | 3 |
| 52 | 56 | 64 | 67 | HERE I STAND — Rip Chords, Columbia 42687 △ | 6 |
| 53 | 57 | 61 | 77 | THAT'S HOW HEARTACHES ARE MADE — Baby Washington, Sue 783 | 7 |
| 54 | 80 | — | — | DA DOO RON RON — Crystals, Philles 112 | 2 |
| 55 | 29 | 18 | 11 | IN DREAMS — Roy Orbison, Monument 806 | 13 |
| 56 | 63 | 78 | 89 | REMEMBER DIANA — Paul Anka, RCA Victor 8170 △ | 4 |
| 57 | 60 | 68 | 74 | HOW CAN I FORGET — Jimmy Holiday, Everest 2022 | 8 |
| 58 | 76 | 83 | 97 | COME AND GET THESE MEMORIES — Martha & the Vandellas, Gordy 7014 | 5 |
| 59 | 65 | 70 | 78 | TWO KINDS OF TEARDROPS — Del Shannon, Big Top 3143 | 4 |
| 60 | 61 | 72 | — | BIRD'S THE WORD — Rivingtons, Liberty 55553 | 4 |
| 61 | 58 | 53 | 60 | WHAT ARE BOYS MADE OF — Percells, ABC-Paramount 10401 | 6 |
| 62 | 62 | 74 | 85 | BONY MORONIE — Appalachians, ABC-Paramount 10419 | 6 |
| 63 | 74 | — | — | SHUT DOWN — Beach Boys, Capitol 4932 | |
| 64 | 79 | 89 | — | PRISONER OF LOVE — James Brown and the Famous Flames, King 5739 | 3 |
| 65 | 45 | 27 | 15 | OUR WINTER LOVE — Bill Pursell, Columbia 42619 △ | 14 |
| 66 | 69 | 81 | 88 | HEART — Kenny Chandler, Laurie 3158 | |
| 67 | 72 | 82 | 90 | MEMORY LANE — Hippies, Parkway 863 | 4 |
| 68 | 68 | 73 | 76 | WHATEVER YOU WANT — Jerry Butler, Vee Jay 486 | 6 |
| 69 | 64 | 77 | 86 | DON'T LET HER BE YOUR BABY — Contours, Gordy 7016 | 5 |
| 70 | 89 | — | — | LET'S GO STEADY AGAIN — Neil Sedaka, RCA Victor 8169 | 2 |
| 71 | 90 | — | — | EL WATUSI — Ray Barretto, Tico 419 | 2 |
| 72 | 81 | — | — | STING RAY — Routers, Warner Bros. 5349 | 2 |
| 73 | 75 | — | — | YOU NEVER MISS YOUR WATER (Till the Well Runs Dry) — "Little Esther" Phillips and "Big Al" Downing, Lenox 5565 | |
| 74 | 82 | 91 | — | IF YOU NEED ME — Solomon Burke, Atlantic 2185 | 3 |
| 75 | 77 | 80 | 82 | ASK ME — Maxine Brown, Wand 135 | 5 |
| 76 | — | — | 95 | SHAME, SHAME, SHAME — Jimmy Reed, Vee Jay 509 | |
| 77 | 87 | — | — | HOT PASTRAMI WITH MASHED POTATOES (Part I) — Joe Dee and the Starliters, Roulette 4488 | 2 |
| 78 | 86 | — | — | WHAT A GUY — Raindrops, Jubilee 5444 | 2 |
| 79 | 92 | — | — | THE BOUNCE — Olympics, Tri Disc 106 | 2 |
| 80 | — | — | — | HELLO STRANGER — Barbara Lewis, Atlantic 2184 | |
| 81 | 78 | 87 | 87 | CALL ME IRRESPONSIBLE — Frank Sinatra, Reprise 20151 | 5 |
| 82 | 83 | — | — | DO IT—RAT NOW — Bill Black's Combo, Hi 2064 | 2 |
| 83 | 85 | — | — | RONNIE, CALL ME WHEN YOU GET A CHANCE — Shelley Fabares, Colpix 682 | 2 |
| 84 | 84 | — | — | HEART — Wayne Newton, Capitol 4920 | 2 |
| 85 | — | — | — | PATTY BABY — Freddy Cannon, Swan 4139 | |
| 86 | 88 | 90 | — | ANN-MARIE — Belmonts, Sabina 509 | 3 |
| 87 | — | — | — | THE FOLK SINGER — Tommy Roe, ABC-Paramount 10423 | 1 |
| 88 | — | — | — | I'M MOVIN' ON — Matt Lucas, Smash 1813 | 1 |
| 89 | 91 | 96 | 93 | THEME FROM LAWRENCE OF ARABIA — Ferrante & Teicher, United Artists 563 | 12 |
| 90 | — | — | — | IF YOU NEED ME — Wilson Pickett, Double L 713 | |
| 91 | 93 | — | — | MOTHER, PLEASE! — Jo Ann Campbell, Cameo 249 | |
| 92 | — | — | — | CALL ME IRRESPONSIBLE — Jack Jones, Kapp 516 | |
| 93 | 94 | — | — | GRAVY WALTZ — Steve Allen, Dot 16457 | 2 |
| 94 | 98 | — | — | HE'S A BAD BOY — Carole King, Dimension 1009 | 2 |
| 95 | — | — | — | GOT YOU ON MY MIND — Cookie & His Cupcakes, Chess 1848 | 1 |
| 96 | — | — | — | OLD ENOUGH TO LOVE — Rick Nelson, Imperial 5935 | |
| 97 | 99 | — | — | ROCKIN' CRICKETS — Rockin' Rebels, Swan 4140 | |
| 98 | 97 | 99 | — | SWEET DREAMS (Of You) — Patsy Cline, Decca 31483 | 3 |
| 99 | 100 | — | — | SHY GIRL — Cascades, Valiant 6028 | 2 |
| 100 | — | — | — | FOREVER — Marvelettes, Tamla 54077 | |

## HOT 100 — A TO Z — (Publisher-Licensee)

## BUBBLING UNDER THE HOT 100

101. THE LAST LEAF — Cascades, Valiant 6026
102. HE'S SO HEAVENLY — Brenda Lee, Decca 31478
103. JACK THE RIPPER — Link Wray & His Ray Men, Swan 4137
104. DANGER — Vic Dana, Dolton 73
105. NO LETTER TODAY — Ray Charles, ABC-Paramount 10435
106. TEENAGE HEAVEN — Johnny Cymbal, Kapp 524
107. I KNOW BETTER — Flamingos, End 1121
108. LITTLE LATIN LUPE LU — Righteous Brothers, Moonglow 215
109. SAD, SAD GIRL AND BOY — Impressions, ABC-Paramount 10431
110. LONESOME 7-7203 — Hawkshaw Hawkins, King 5712
111. DIANE — Joe Harnell & His Ork, Kapp 521
112. SOON (I'll Be Home Again) — 4 Seasons, Vee Jay 512
113. FUNNY MAN — Ray Stevens, Mercury 72094
114. YOU SHOULD HAVE BEEN THERE — Fleetwoods, Dolton 74
115. HOW CAN I FORGET — Ben E. King, Atco 6256
116. BILL BAILEY WON'T YOU PLEASE COME HOME — Ella Fitzgerald, Verve 10288
117. HOT CAKES (1st Serving) — Dave (Baby) Cortez, Chess 1850
118. BO DIDDLEY — Buddy Holly, Coral 62352
119. ONE BOY TOO LATE — Mike Clifford, United Artists 588
120. NOT FOR ALL THE MONEY IN THE WORLD — Shirelles, Scepter 1248
121. YOU KNOW IT AIN'T RIGHT — Joe Hinton, Back Beat 537
122. DON'T MENTION MY NAME — Shepherd Sisters, Atlantic 2176
123. BE EVER WONDERFUL — Ted Taylor, Okeh 7171
124. THE SHAMPOO — Les McCann, Pacific Jazz 350
125. DIDDLEY-DO — Ronnie Hawkins, Roulette 4483
126. LOVE WILL FIND A WAY — Sam Cooke, RCA Victor 8164
127. HARDHEAD — Louis Jordan, Tangerine 930
128. LITTLE BIRD — Pete Jolly Trio, Ava 116
129. THE GOOD LIFE — Tony Bennett, Columbia 42779
130. YOU'LL NEED ANOTHER FAVOR — Les McCann, Pacific Jazz 350
131. THE YOUNG YEARS — Floyd Cramer, RCA Victor 8171
132. ON THE TRAIL — Roger Williams, Kapp 522

# Billboard HOT 100
**FOR WEEK ENDING MAY 11, 1963**

★ STAR PERFORMERS—Selections registering greatest upward progress this week.
S Indicates that 45 r.p.m. stereo single version is available.
△ Indicates that 33⅓ r.p.m. mono single version is available.
Ⓢ Indicates that 33⅓ r.p.m. stereo single version is available.

| This Week | Wk. Ago | 2 Wks. Ago | TITLE, Artist, Label & Number | Weeks On Chart |
|---|---|---|---|---|
| 1 | 1 | 3 | **I WILL FOLLOW HIM** — Little Peggy March, RCA Victor 8139 *(Billboard Award)* | 8 |
| 2 | 3 | 4 | PUFF (The Magic Dragon) — Peter, Paul & Mary, Warner Bros. 5348 | 9 |
| ★3 | 6 | 15 | IF YOU WANNA BE HAPPY — Jimmy Soul, S.P.Q.R. 3305 | 7 |
| 4 | 4 | 6 | PIPELINE — Chantays, Dot 16440 | 11 |
| 5 | 2 | 2 | CAN'T GET USED TO LOSING YOU △ — Andy Williams, Columbia 42674 | 11 |
| ★6 | 13 | 18 | FOOLISH LITTLE GIRL — Shirelles, Scepter 1248 | 8 |
| 7 | 8 | 11 | SURFIN' U.S.A. — Beach Boys, Capitol 4932 | 8 |
| 8 | 5 | 3 | HE'S SO FINE — Chiffons, Laurie 3152 | 12 |
| ★9 | 14 | 16 | REVEREND MR. BLACK — Kingston Trio, Capitol 4951 | 6 |
| ★10 | 18 | 26 | LOSING YOU — Brenda Lee, Decca 31478 | 6 |
| 11 | 9 | 9 | ON BROADWAY — Drifters, Atlantic 2182 | 8 |
| 12 | 12 | 16 | MECCA — Gene Pitney, Musicor 1028 | 8 |
| 13 | 15 | 17 | CHARMS — Bobby Vee, Liberty 55530 | 7 |
| 14 | 11 | 5 | BABY WORKOUT — Jackie Wilson, Brunswick 55239 | 10 |
| 15 | 7 | 7 | DON'T SAY NOTHIN' BAD ABOUT MY BABY — Cookies, Dimension 1008 | 11 |
| 16 | 19 | 27 | TAKE THESE CHAINS FROM MY HEART — Ray Charles, ABC-Paramount 10435 | 5 |
| ★17 | 23 | 35 | TWO FACES HAVE I — Lou Christie, Roulette 4481 | 7 |
| 18 | 10 | 10 | WATERMELON MAN — Mongo Santamaria, Battle 45909 | 9 |
| ★19 | 34 | 40 | KILLER JOE — Rocky Fellers, Scepter 1246 | 8 |
| 20 | 21 | 39 | HOT PASTRAMI — Dartells, Dot 16453 | 5 |
| 21 | 25 | 32 | LITTLE BAND OF GOLD — James Gilreath, Joy 274 | 8 |
| 22 | 20 | 25 | TOM CAT — Rooftop Singers, Vanguard 35019 | 8 |
| 23 | 29 | 41 | I LOVE YOU BECAUSE — Al Martino, Capitol 4930 | 6 |
| 24 | 30 | 43 | ANOTHER SATURDAY NIGHT — Sam Cooke, RCA Victor 8164 | 4 |
| 25 | 16 | 8 | YOUNG LOVERS — Paul & Paula, Philips 40096 | 9 |
| ★26 | 31 | 55 | THIS LITTLE GIRL △ — Dion, Columbia 42776 | 4 |
| ★27 | 36 | 51 | AIN'T THAT A SHAME! — 4 Seasons, Vee Jay 512 | 4 |
| 28 | 17 | 19 | YOUNG AND IN LOVE — Dick & Deedee, Warner Bros. 5342 | 9 |
| ★29 | 49 | 71 | STILL — Bill Anderson, Decca 31458 | 5 |
| 30 | 26 | 34 | DAYS OF WINE AND ROSES △ — Andy Williams, Columbia 42674 | 9 |
| 31 | 37 | 42 | A LOVE SHE CAN COUNT ON — Miracles, Tamla 54078 | 7 |
| 32 | 24 | 14 | THE END OF THE WORLD — Skeeter Davis, RCA Victor 8098 | 16 |
| 33 | 28 | 31 | LINDA — Jan and Dean, Liberty 55531 | 12 |
| ★34 | 51 | 70 | THE LOVE OF MY MAN — Theola Kilgore, Serock 2004 | 4 |
| 35 | 33 | 38 | DAYS OF WINE AND ROSES — Henry Mancini, RCA Victor 8120 | 16 |
| ★36 | 50 | 67 | YOU CAN'T SIT DOWN — Dovells, Parkway 867 | 3 |
| ★37 | 54 | 80 | DA DOO RON RON — Crystals, Philles 112 | 3 |
| 38 | 46 | 53 | PUSHOVER — Etta James, Argo 5437 | 4 |
| 39 | 41 | 54 | (Today I Met) THE BOY I'M GONNA MARRY — Darlene Love, Philles 111 | 6 |
| ★40 | 71 | 90 | EL WATUSI — Ray Barretto, Tico 419 | 3 |
| 41 | 22 | 12 | SOUTH STREET — Orlons, Cameo 243 | 13 |
| ★42 | 58 | 76 | COME AND GET THESE MEMORIES — Martha & the Vandellas, Gordy 7014 | 6 |
| 43 | 35 | 28 | SANDY — Dion, Laurie 3153 | 11 |
| 44 | 56 | 63 | REMEMBER DIANA — Paul Anka, RCA Victor 8170 | 5 |
| 45 | 27 | 21 | OVER THE MOUNTAIN (Across the Sea) — Bobby Vinton, Epic 9577 | 10 |
| 46 | 32 | 20 | DO THE BIRD — Dee Dee Sharp, Cameo 244 | 11 |
| 47 | 53 | 57 | THAT'S HOW HEARTACHES ARE MADE — Baby Washington, Sue 783 | 8 |
| 48 | 44 | 44 | LOCKING UP MY HEART — Marvelettes, Tamla 54071 | 8 |
| 49 | 63 | 74 | SHUT DOWN — Beach Boys, Capitol 4932 | 3 |
| 50 | 70 | 89 | LET'S GO STEADY AGAIN — Neil Sedaka, RCA Victor 8169 | 3 |
| 51 | 52 | 56 | HERE I STAND △ — Rip Chords, Columbia 42687 | 7 |
| 52 | 60 | 61 | BIRD'S THE WORD — Rivingtons, Liberty 55553 | 5 |
| 53 | 64 | 79 | PRISONER OF LOVE — James Brown & the Famous Flames, King 5739 | 4 |
| 54 | 59 | 65 | TWO KINDS OF TEARDROPS — Del Shannon, Big Top 3143 | 5 |
| 55 | 39 | 23 | TWENTY MILES — Chubby Checker, Parkway 862 | 12 |
| 56 | 47 | 52 | RAINBOW — Gene Chandler, Vee Jay 468 | 12 |
| 57 | 77 | 87 | HOT PASTRAMI WITH MASHED POTATOES (Part I) — Joe Dee and the Starliters, Roulette 4488 | — |
| 58 | 74 | 82 | IF YOU NEED ME — Solomon Burke, Atlantic 2185 | 4 |
| 59 | 38 | 30 | MR. BASS MAN — Johnny Cymbal, Kapp 503 | 13 |
| 60 | — | — | IT'S MY PARTY — Leslie Gore, Mercury 72119 | 1 |
| 61 | 78 | 86 | WHAT A GUY — Raindrops, Jubilee 5444 | 3 |
| 62 | 72 | 81 | STING RAY — Routers, Warner Bros. 5349 | 3 |
| 63 | 67 | 72 | MEMORY LANE — Hippies, Parkway 863 | 5 |
| 64 | 57 | 60 | HOW CAN I FORGET — Jimmy Holiday, Everest 2022 | 9 |
| 65 | 80 | — | HELLO STRANGER — Barbara Lewis, Atlantic 2184 | 2 |
| 66 | 66 | 69 | HEART — Kenny Chandler, Laurie 3158 | 6 |
| 67 | 82 | 83 | DO IT-RAT NOW — Bill Black's Combo, Hi 2064 | 3 |
| 68 | 69 | 64 | DON'T LET HER BE YOUR BABY — Contours, Gordy 7016 | 6 |
| 69 | 79 | 92 | THE BOUNCE — Olympics, Tri Disc 106 | 3 |
| ★70 | — | — | THOSE LAZY-HAZY-CRAZY DAYS OF SUMMER — Nat King Cole, Capitol 4965 | 1 |
| 71 | 76 | — | SHAME, SHAME, SHAME — Jimmy Reed, Vee Jay 509 | 3 |
| 72 | 83 | 85 | RONNIE, CALL ME WHEN YOU GET A CHANCE — Shelley Fabares, Colpix 682 | 3 |
| 73 | 62 | 62 | BONY MORONIE — Appalachians, ABC-Paramount 10419 | 7 |
| ★74 | — | — | WILDWOOD DAYS — Bobby Rydell, Cameo 252 | 1 |
| ★75 | — | — | THE GOOD LIFE △ — Tony Bennett, Columbia 42779 | 1 |
| 76 | 98 | 97 | SWEET DREAMS (Of You) — Patsy Cline, Decca 31483 | 4 |
| 77 | 85 | — | PATTY BABY — Freddy Cannon, Swan 4139 | 2 |
| ★78 | — | — | I'M SAVING MY LOVE — Skeeter Davis, RCA Victor 8176 | 1 |
| 79 | — | — | SUKIYAKI — Kyu Sakamoto, Capitol 4945 | 1 |
| 80 | 90 | — | IF YOU NEED ME — Wilson Pickett, Double L 713 | 1 |
| 81 | 81 | 78 | CALL ME IRRESPONSIBLE — Frank Sinatra, Reprise 20151 | 6 |
| 82 | 84 | 84 | HEART — Wayne Newton, Capitol 4920 | 3 |
| 83 | — | — | DON'T MAKE MY BABY BLUE △ — Frankie Laine, Columbia 42767 | 1 |
| 84 | 87 | — | THE FOLK SINGER — Tommy Roe, ABC-Paramount 10423 | 2 |
| 85 | 88 | — | I'M MOVIN' ON — Matt Lucas, Smash 1813 | 2 |
| 86 | 92 | — | CALL ME IRRESPONSIBLE — Jack Jones, Kapp 516 | 2 |
| ★87 | — | — | TEENAGE HEAVEN — Johnny Cymbal, Kapp 524 | 1 |
| 88 | 91 | 93 | MOTHER, PLEASE! — Jo Ann Campbell, Cameo 249 | 3 |
| 89 | 93 | 94 | GRAVY WALTZ — Steve Allen, Dot 16457 | 3 |
| ★90 | — | — | LITTLE LATIN LUPE LU — Righteous Brothers, Moonglow 215 | 1 |
| 91 | 99 | 100 | SHY GIRL — Cascades, Valiant 6028 | 3 |
| 92 | — | — | SOON (I'll Be Home Again) — 4 Seasons, Vee Jay 512 | 1 |
| 93 | — | — | 18 YELLOW ROSES — Bobby Darin, Capitol 4970 | 1 |
| 94 | 96 | — | OLD ENOUGH TO LOVE — Rick Nelson, Imperial 5935 | 1 |
| 95 | 97 | 99 | ROCKIN' CRICKETS — Rockin' Rebels, Swan 4140 | 3 |
| 96 | — | — | ONE BOY TOO LATE — Mike Clifford, United Artists 588 | 1 |
| 97 | 100 | — | FOREVER — Marvelettes, Tamla 54077 | 1 |
| 98 | — | — | THE LAST LEAF — Cascades, Valiant 6028 | 1 |
| 99 | — | — | A STRANGER IN YOUR TOWN — Shacklefords, Mercury 72112 | 1 |
| 100 | — | — | HOBO FLATS (Part I) — Jimmy Smith, Verve 10283 | 1 |

## HOT 100—A TO Z—(Publisher-Licensee)

## BUBBLING UNDER THE HOT 100

101. DANGER — Vic Dana, Dolton 75
102. NEEDLES AND PINS — Jackie DeShannon, Liberty 55563
103. THEME FROM LAWRENCE OF ARABIA — Ferrante & Teicher, United Artists 563
104. JACK THE RIPPER — Link Wray & His Ray Men, Swan 4137
105. LOVE WILL FIND A WAY — Sam Cooke, RCA Victor 8164
106. NO LETTER TODAY — Ray Charles, ABC-Paramount 10435
107. I KNOW BETTER — Flamingos, End 1121
108. LONESOME 7-7203 — Hawkshaw Hawkins, King 5712
109. HE'S A BAD BOY — Carole King, Dimension 1009
110. GOT YOU ON MY MIND — Cookie & His Cupcakes, Chess 1849
111. HE'S SO HEAVENLY — Brenda Lee, Decca 31478
112. SAD, SAD GIRL AND BOY — Impressions, ABC-Paramount 10431
113. PEARL PEARL PEARL — Lester Flatt & Earl Scruggs, Columbia 42755
114. YOU SHOULD HAVE BEEN THERE — Fleetwoods, Dolton 75
115. DIANE — Joe Harnell & His Ork, Kapp 521
116. BO DIDDLEY — Buddy Holly, Coral 62352
117. DON'T MENTION MY NAME — Shepherd Sisters, Atlantic 2176
118. NOT FOR ALL THE MONEY IN THE WORLD — Shirelles, Scepter 1248
119. HOT CAKES (1st Serving) — Dave (Baby) Cortez, Chess 1850
120. HOW CAN I FORGET — Ben E. King, Atco 6256
121. YOU KNOW IT AIN'T RIGHT — Joe Hinton, Back Beat 537
122. BO DIDDLEY — Ronnie Hawkins, Roulette 4483
123. LITTLE BIRD — Pete Jolly Trio, Ava 116
124. YOU ALWAYS HURT THE ONE YOU LOVE — Fats Domino, Imperial 5937
125. SPRING IN MANHATTAN — Tony Bennett, Columbia 42779
126. PRISONER IN LOVE — Ikettes, Teena 1701
127. BILL BAILEY, WON'T YOU PLEASE COME HOME — Ella Fitzgerald, Verve 10280
128. DIANE — Roger Williams, Kapp 522
129. LET IT BE ME — Roy Hamilton, MGM 13138
130. THIS OLE HOUSE — Joe Hinton, Back Beat 537
131. SATURDAY NIGHT — Sherrys, Guyden 2084
132. OUR SUMMER LOVE — Roby & the Romantics, Kapp 522
133. TAMOURE — Bill Justis, Smash 1812

# Billboard HOT 100

FOR WEEK ENDING MAY 18 1963

★ STAR PERFORMERS—Selections registering greatest upward progress this week.

S Indicates that 45 r.p.m. stereo single version is available.

△ Indicates that 33⅓ r.p.m. mono single version is available.

S△ Indicates that 33⅓ r.p.m. stereo single version is available.

| This Week | 1 Wk. Ago | 2 Wks. Ago | 3 Wks. Ago | Title — Artist, Label & Number | Weeks On Chart |
|---|---|---|---|---|---|
| 1 (Billboard Award) | 3 | 6 | 15 | IF YOU WANNA BE HAPPY — Jimmy Soul, S.P.Q.R. 3305 | 8 |
| 2 | 1 | 1 | 1 | I WILL FOLLOW HIM — Little Peggy March, RCA Victor 8139 | 9 |
| 3 | 2 | 3 | 4 | PUFF (The Magic Dragon) — Peter, Paul & Mary, Warner Bros. 5348 | 10 |
| ★4 | 7 | 8 | 11 | SURFIN' U. S. A. — Beach Boys, Capitol 4932 | 9 |
| 5 | 6 | 13 | 18 | FOOLISH LITTLE GIRL — Shirelles, Scepter 1248 | 9 |
| 6 | 4 | 4 | 6 | PIPELINE — Chantays, Dot 16440 | 12 |
| ★7 | 10 | 18 | 26 | LOSING YOU — Brenda Lee, Decca 31478 | 7 |
| 8 | 9 | 14 | 16 | REVEREND MR. BLACK — Kingston Trio, Capitol 4951 | 7 |
| 9 | 5 | 2 | 2 | CAN'T GET USED TO LOSING YOU △ — Andy Williams, Columbia 42674 | 12 |
| ★10 | 23 | 29 | 41 | I LOVE YOU BECAUSE — Al Martino, Capitol 4930 | 7 |
| ★11 | 17 | 23 | 35 | TWO FACES HAVE I — Lou Christie, Roulette 4481 | 8 |
| 12 | 16 | 19 | 27 | TAKE THESE CHAINS FROM MY HEART — Ray Charles, ABC-Paramount 10435 | 6 |
| ★13 | 20 | 21 | 39 | HOT PASTRAMI — Dartells, Dot 16453 | 6 |
| ★14 | 24 | 30 | 43 | ANOTHER SATURDAY NIGHT — Sam Cooke, RCA Victor 8164 | 5 |
| 15 | 12 | 12 | 13 | MECCA — Gene Pitney, Musicor 1028 | 9 |
| 16 | 19 | 34 | 40 | KILLER JOE — Rocky Fellers, Scepter 1246 | 9 |
| 17 | 8 | 5 | 3 | HE'S SO FINE — Chiffons, Laurie 3152 | 13 |
| ★18 | 36 | 50 | 67 | YOU CAN'T SIT DOWN — Dovells, Parkway 867 | 4 |
| ★19 | 37 | 54 | 80 | DA DOO RON RON — Crystals, Philles 112 | 4 |
| 20 | 13 | 15 | 17 | CHARMS — Bobby Vee, Liberty 55530 | 8 |
| ★21 | 26 | 31 | 55 | THIS LITTLE GIRL △ — Dion, Columbia 42776 | 5 |
| ★22 | 27 | 36 | 51 | AIN'T THAT A SHAME! — 4 Seasons, Vee Jay 512 | 5 |
| 23 | 21 | 25 | 32 | LITTLE BAND OF GOLD — James Gilreath, Joy 274 | 9 |
| ★24 | 29 | 49 | 71 | STILL — Bill Anderson, Decca 31458 | 6 |
| 25 | 11 | 9 | 9 | ON BROADWAY — Drifters, Atlantic 2182 | 9 |
| ★26 | 60 | — | — | IT'S MY PARTY — Lesley Gore, Mercury 72119 | 2 |
| ★27 | 40 | 71 | 90 | EL WATUSI — Ray Barretto, Tico 419 | 4 |
| 28 | 30 | 26 | 34 | DAYS OF WINE AND ROSES △ — Andy Williams, Columbia 42674 | 10 |
| 29 | 22 | 20 | 25 | TOM CAT — Rooftop Singers, Vanguard 35019 | 9 |
| 30 | 18 | 10 | 10 | WATERMELON MAN — Mongo Santamaria, Battle 45909 | 10 |
| 31 | 34 | 51 | 70 | THE LOVE OF MY MAN — Theola Kilgore, Serock 2004 | 5 |
| 32 | 14 | 11 | 5 | BABY WORKOUT — Jackie Wilson, Brunswick 55239 | 11 |
| 33 | 15 | 7 | 7 | DON'T SAY NOTHIN' BAD ABOUT MY BABY — Cookies, Dimension 1008 | 12 |
| 34 | 35 | 33 | 38 | DAYS OF WINE AND ROSES — Henry Mancini, RCA Victor 8120 | 17 |
| 35 | 38 | 46 | 53 | PUSHOVER — Etta James, Argo 5437 | 5 |
| 36 | 42 | 58 | 76 | COME AND GET THESE MEMORIES — Martha & the Vandellas, Gordy 7014 | 7 |
| ★37 | 53 | 64 | 79 | PRISONER OF LOVE — James Brown & the Famous Flames, King 5739 | 5 |
| 38 | 31 | 37 | 42 | A LOVE SHE CAN COUNT ON — Miracles, Tamla 54078 | 8 |
| ★39 | 50 | 70 | 89 | LET'S GO STEADY AGAIN — Neil Sedaka, RCA Victor 8169 | 4 |
| 40 | 33 | 28 | 31 | LINDA — Jan and Dean, Liberty 55531 | 13 |
| 41 | 44 | 56 | 63 | REMEMBER DIANA — Paul Anka, RCA Victor 8170 | 6 |
| 42 | 28 | 17 | 19 | YOUNG AND IN LOVE — Dick & Deedee, Warner Bros. 5342 | 10 |
| 43 | 49 | 63 | 74 | SHUT DOWN — Beach Boys, Capitol 4932 | 4 |
| 44 | 39 | 41 | 54 | (Today I Met) THE BOY I'M GONNA MARRY — Darlene Love, Philles 111 | 7 |
| ★45 | 79 | — | — | SUKIYAKI — Kyu Sakamoto, Capitol 4945 | 2 |
| 46 | 47 | 53 | 57 | THAT'S HOW HEARTACHES ARE MADE — Baby Washington, Sue 783 | 9 |
| ★47 | 70 | — | — | THOSE LAZY-HAZY-CRAZY DAYS OF SUMMER — Nat King Cole, Capitol 4965 | 2 |
| 48 | 25 | 16 | 8 | YOUNG LOVERS — Paul & Paula, Philips 40096 | 10 |
| 49 | 57 | 77 | 87 | HOT PASTRAMI WITH MASHED POTATOES (Part I) — Joe Dee and the Starliters, Roulette 4488 | 4 |
| 50 | 54 | 59 | 65 | TWO KINDS OF TEARDROPS — Del Shannon, Big Top 3143 | 6 |
| 51 | 58 | 74 | 82 | IF YOU NEED ME — Solomon Burke, Atlantic 2185 | 5 |
| 52 | 61 | 78 | 86 | WHAT A GUY — Raindrops, Jubilee 5444 | 4 |
| ★53 | 65 | 80 | — | HELLO STRANGER — Barbara Lewis, Atlantic 2184 | 3 |
| 54 | 62 | 72 | 81 | STING RAY — Routers, Warner Bros. 5349 | 4 |
| ★55 | 93 | — | — | 18 YELLOW ROSES — Bobby Darin, Capitol 4970 | 2 |
| ★56 | 67 | 82 | 83 | DO IT—RAT NOW — Bill Black's Combo, Hi 2064 | 4 |
| 57 | 52 | 60 | 61 | BIRD'S THE WORD — Rivingtons, Liberty 55553 | 6 |
| ★58 | 69 | 79 | 92 | THE BOUNCE — Olympics, Tri Disc 106 | 4 |
| ★59 | 75 | — | — | THE GOOD LIFE △ — Tony Bennett, Columbia 42779 | 2 |
| ★60 | 74 | — | — | WILDWOOD DAYS — Bobby Rydell, Cameo 252 | 2 |
| ★61 | 78 | — | — | I'M SAVING MY LOVE — Skeeter Davis, RCA Victor 8176 | 2 |
| 62 | 71 | 76 | — | SHAME, SHAME, SHAME — Jimmy Reed, Vee Jay 509 | 4 |
| 63 | 32 | 24 | 14 | THE END OF THE WORLD — Skeeter Davis, RCA Victor 8098 | 17 |
| 64 | 66 | 66 | 69 | HEART — Kenny Chandler, Laurie 3158 | 7 |
| 65 | 48 | 44 | 44 | LOCKING UP MY HEART — Marvelettes, Tamla 54077 | 9 |
| 66 | 51 | 52 | 56 | HERE I STAND △ — Rip Chords, Columbia 42687 | 8 |
| 67 | 76 | 98 | 97 | SWEET DREAMS (Of You) — Patsy Cline, Decca 31483 | 5 |
| ★68 | 83 | — | — | DON'T MAKE MY BABY BLUE △ — Frankie Laine, Columbia 42767 | 2 |
| 69 | 77 | 85 | — | PATTY BABY — Freddy Cannon, Swan 4139 | 3 |
| ★70 | 87 | — | — | TEENAGE HEAVEN — Johnny Cymbal, Kapp 524 | 2 |
| 71 | 73 | 62 | 62 | BONY MORONIE — Appalachians, ABC-Paramount 10419 | 8 |
| ★72 | — | — | — | MY SUMMER LOVE — Ruby & the Romantics, Kapp 525 | 1 |
| ★73 | 90 | — | — | LITTLE LATIN LUPE LU — Rightous Brothers, Moonglow 215 | 2 |
| 74 | 80 | 90 | — | IF YOU NEED ME — Wilson Pickett, Double L 713 | 3 |
| 75 | 85 | 88 | — | I'M MOVIN' ON — Matt Lucas, Smash 1813 | 3 |
| 76 | 89 | 93 | 94 | GRAVY WALTZ — Steve Allen, Dot 16457 | 4 |
| 77 | 72 | 83 | 85 | RONNIE, CALL ME WHEN YOU GET A CHANCE — Shelley Fabares, Colpix 682 | 4 |
| 78 | 81 | 81 | 78 | CALL ME IRRESPONSIBLE — Frank Sinatra, Reprise 20151 | 7 |
| ★79 | 98 | — | — | THE LAST LEAF — Cascades, Valiant 6028 | 2 |
| 80 | 92 | — | — | SOON (I'll Be Home Again) — 4 Seasons, Vee Jay 512 | 2 |
| ★81 | — | — | — | BIRDLAND — Chubby Checker, Parkway 873 | 1 |
| ★82 | 100 | — | — | HOBO FLATS (Part I) — Jimmy Smith, Verve 10283 | 2 |
| 83 | 86 | 92 | — | CALL ME IRRESPONSIBLE — Jack Jones, Kapp 516 | 3 |
| ★84 | 99 | — | — | A STRANGER IN YOUR TOWN — Shacklefords, Mercury 72112 | 2 |
| ★85 | — | — | — | BLUE ON BLUE — Bobby Vinton, Epic 9593 | 1 |
| 86 | 97 | 100 | — | FOREVER — Marvelettes, Tamla 54077 | 3 |
| 87 | 95 | 97 | 99 | ROCKIN' CRICKETS — Rockin' Rebels, Swan 4140 | 4 |
| ★88 | — | — | — | GYPSY WOMAN — Rick Nelson, Decca 31495 | 1 |
| ★89 | — | — | — | THERE GOES (MY HEART AGAIN) — Fats Domino, ABC-Paramount 10444 | 1 |
| ★90 | — | — | — | SHAKE A TAIL FEATHER — Five Du-Tones, One-der-ful 4815 | 1 |
| 91 | 91 | 99 | 100 | SHY GIRL — Cascades, Valiant 6028 | 4 |
| 92 | 82 | 84 | 84 | HEART — Wayne Newton, Capitol 4920 | 4 |
| 93 | 84 | 87 | — | THE FOLK SINGER — Tommy Roe, ABC-Paramount 10423 | 3 |
| 94 | — | 95 | — | GOT YOU ON MY MIND — Cookie & His Cupcakes, Chess 1848 | 2 |
| 95 | — | — | — | IF MY PILLOW COULD TALK — Connie Francis, MGM 13143 | 1 |
| 96 | — | — | — | LONELY BOY, LONELY GUITAR — Duane Eddy, RCA Victor 8180 | 1 |
| 97 | — | — | — | NEEDLES AND PINS — Jackie DeShannon, Liberty 55563 | 1 |
| 98 | — | 94 | 98 | HE'S A BAD BOY — Carole King, Dimension 1009 | 3 |
| 99 | — | — | — | PRIDE AND JOY — Marvin Gaye, Tamla 54079 | 1 |
| 100 | 94 | 96 | — | OLD ENOUGH TO LOVE — Rick Nelson, Imperial 5935 | 3 |

## HOT 100—A TO Z—(Publisher-Licensee)

Ain't That a Shame (Travis, BMI) .... 22
Another Saturday Night (Kags, BMI) .... 14
Baby Workout (Merrimac, BMI) .... 32
Birdland (Woodcrest—Ace, BMI) .... 81
Bird's the Word (Beechwood, BMI) .... 57
Blue on Blue (Famous, ASCAP) .... 85
Bony Moronie (Venice, BMI) .... 71
Bounce, The (Marc-Jean, BMI) .... 58
Call Me Irresponsible—Jones (Paramount, ASCAP). 83
Call Me Irresponsible—Sinatra (Paramount, ASCAP). 78
Can't Get Used to Losing You (Brenner, BMI) .... 9
Charms (Screen Gems-Columbia, BMI) .... 20
Come and Get These Memories (Jobete, BMI) .... 36
Da Doo Ron Ron (Mother Bertha-Trio, BMI) .... 19
Days of Wine and Roses—Mancini (Witmark, ASCAP) .... 34
Days of Wine and Roses—Williams (Witmark, ASCAP) .... 28
Do It—Rat Now (Wrist-Jec, BMI) .... 56
Don't Make My Baby Blue (Screen Gems-Columbia, BMI) .... 68
Don't Say Nothin' Bad About My Baby (Screen Gems-Columbia, BMI) .... 33
18 Yellow Roses (T. M., BMI) .... 55
El Watusi (Little Dipper, BMI) .... 27
End of the World, The (Summit, ASCAP) .... 63
Folk Singer, The (Painted Desert, BMI) .... 93
Foolish Little Girl (Screen Gems-Columbia, BMI) .. 5
Forever (Jobete, BMI) .... 86
Good Life, The (Paris, ASCAP) .... 59
Got You on My Mind (Raleigh, BMI) .... 94
Gravy Waltz (Brown, BMI) .... 76
Gypsy Woman (Hilliard-Doral, BMI) .... 88
He's a Bad Boy (Screen Gems-Columbia, BMI) .. 98
He's So Fine (Bright-Tunes, BMI) .... 17
Heart—Chandler (Screen Gems-Columbia, BMI) .. 64
Heart—Newton (Screen Gems-Columbia, BMI) .. 92
Hello Stranger (McLaughlin, BMI) .... 53
Here I Stand (Conrad, BMI) .... 66
Hobo Flats (Part 1) (Noslen, BMI) .... 82
Hot Pastrami (Sherlyn-Pent, BMI) .... 13
Hot Pastrami With Mashed Potatoes (Part 1) (Sherlyn-Pent, BMI) .... 49
I Love You Because (Rose, BMI) .... 10
I Will Follow Him (Leeds, ASCAP) .... 2
I'm Movin' On (Hill & Range, BMI) .... 75
I'm Saving My Love (Samos Island, BMI) .... 61
If My Pillow Could Talk (Merna, BMI) .... 95
If You Need Me—Burke (Cotillion, BMI) .... 51
If You Need Me—Pickett (Cotillion, BMI) .... 74
If You Wanna Be Happy (Rockmasters, BMI) .... 1
It's My Party (Arch, ASCAP) .... 26
Killer Joe (Mellin-White Castle, BMI) .... 16
Last Leaf, The (Sherman-DeVorzon, BMI) .... 79
Let's Go Steady Again (Screen Gems-Columbia, BMI) .... 39
Linda (Warock, ASCAP) .... 40
Little Band of Gold (Beaik, BMI) .... 23
Little Latin Lupe Lu (Maxwell-Conrad, BMI) .... 73
Locking Up My Heart (Jobete, BMI) .... 65
Lonely Boy, Lonely Guitar (Linduane, BMI) .... 96
Losing You (B. N. P., ASCAP) .... 7
Love of My Man, The (Sylvia, BMI) .... 31
Love She Can Count On, A (Jobete, BMI) .... 38
Mecca (January, BMI) .... 15
My Summer Love (Rosewood, ASCAP) .... 72
Needles and Pins (Metric, BMI) .... 97
Old Enough to Love (Eric, BMI) .... 100
On Broadway (Screen Gems-Columbia, BMI) .... 25
Patty Baby (Grand Canyon, BMI) .... 69
Pipeline (Downey, BMI) .... 6
Pride and Joy (Jobete, BMI) .... 99
Prisoner of Love (P.D.) .... 37
Puff (The Magic Dragon) (Pepamar, ASCAP) .... 3
Pushover (Chevis, BMI) .... 35
Remember Diana (Spanka, BMI) .... 41
Reverend Mr. Black (Quartet-Butterfield, BMI) .... 8
Rockin' Crickets (Shan-Todd, BMI) .... 87
Ronnie, Call Me When You Get a Chance (Screen Gems-Columbia, BMI) .... 77
Shake a Tail Feather (Vapac, BMI) .... 90
Shame, Shame, Shame (Conrad, BMI) .... 62
Shut Down (Sea of Tunes, BMI) .... 43
Shy Girl (Sherman-DeVorzon, BMI) .... 91
Soon (I'll Be Home Again) (BoBob, ASCAP) .... 80
Still (Moss Rose, BMI) .... 24
Sting Ray (Wrist-House of Joseph, BMI) .... 54
Stranger in Your Town, A (Hazlewood-Little Darlin', BMI) .... 84
Sukiyaki (Beechwood, BMI) .... 45
Surfin' U.S.A. (Arc, BMI) .... 4
Sweet Dreams (Acuff-Rose, BMI) .... 67
Take These Chains From My Heart (Milene, ASCAP) .... 12
Teenage Heaven (Jeanick, BMI) .... 70
That's How Heartaches Are Made (Sea-Lark, BMI). 46
There Goes (My Heart Again) (Anatole, BMI) .... 89
This Little Girl (Screen Gems-Columbia, BMI) .... 21
Those Lazy-Hazy-Crazy Days of Summer (Comet, ASCAP) .... 47
(Today I Met) the Boy I'm Gonna Marry (January, BMI) .... 44
Tom Cat (Ryerson, BMI) .... 29
Two Faces Have I (Painted Desert-RTD, BMI) .... 11
Two Kinds of Teardrops (Vicki-McLaughlin, BMI).. 50
Watermelon Man (Hancock, BMI) .... 30
What a Guy (Trinity, BMI) .... 52
Wildwood Days (Kalmann, ASCAP) .... 60
You Can't Sit Down (Dasher, BMI) .... 18
Young and in Love (Odin, ASCAP) .... 42
Young Lovers (LeBill-Marbill, BMI) .... 48

## BUBBLING UNDER THE HOT 100

101. DANGER .... Vic Dana, Dolton 73
102. JACK THE RIPPER .... Link Wray & His Ray Men, Swan 4137
103. SPRING IN MANHATTAN .... Tony Bennett, Columbia 42779
104. ONE BOY TOO LATE .... Mike Clifford, United Artists 588
105. SWINGING ON A STAR .... Big Dee Irwin, Dimension 1010
106. SAD, SAD GIRL AND BOY .... Impressions, ABC-Paramount 10431
107. TEN COMMANDMENTS OF LOVE .... James MacArthur, Scepter 1250
108. HOT CAKES (1st Serving) .... Dave (Baby) Cortez, Chess 1850
109. I KNOW BETTER .... Flamingos, End 1121
110. DIANE .... Joe Harnell & His Ork, Kapp 521
111. MOTHER, PLEASE! .... Jo Ann Campbell, Cameo 249
112. NO LETTER TODAY .... Ray Charles, ABC-Paramount 10435
113. ON THE TRAIL .... Roger Williams, Kapp 522
114. LONESOME 7-7203 .... Hawkshaw Hawkins, King 5712
115. LITTLE BIRD .... Pete Jolly Trio, Ava 116
116. SATURDAY NIGHT .... Sherrys, Guyden 2084
117. BO DIDDLEY .... Ronnie Hawkins, Roulette 4483
118. THEME FROM LAWRENCE OF ARABIA .. Ferrante & Teicher, United Artists 563
119. PEARL PEARL PEARL .... Lester Flatt & Earl Scruggs, Columbia 42755
120. BO DIDDLEY .... Buddy Holly, Coral 62352
121. YOU ALWAYS HURT THE ONE YOU LOVE .... Fats Domino, Imperial 5937
122. THE SHAMPOO .... Les McCann, Pacific Jazz 350
123. LOVE WILL FIND A WAY .... Sam Cooke, RCA Victor 8164
124. HE'S SO HEAVENLY .... Brenda Lee, Decca 31478
125. YOUR OLD STAND BY .... Mary Wells, Motown 1042
126. OLD SMOOTHY LOCOMOTION .... Little Eva, Dimension 1011
127. BILL BAILEY, WON'T YOU PLEASE COME HOME .. Ella Fitzgerald, Verve 10288
128. YOU KNOW IT AIN'T RIGHT .... Joe Hinton, Back Beat 537
129. BE EVER WONDERFUL .... Ted Taylor, Okeh 7171
130. THE LAST MINUTE (Part I) .... Jimmy McGriff, Sue 786
131. IF YOU DON'T LOVE ME .... Junior Parker, Duke 364

# Billboard HOT 100
**For Week Ending May 25, 1963**

**STAR PERFORMERS**—Selections registering greatest upward progress this week.
S — Indicates that 45 r.p.m. stereo single version is available.
△ — Indicates that 33⅓ r.p.m. mono single version is available.
Ⓢ — Indicates that 33⅓ r.p.m. stereo single version is available.

| This Week | 1 Wk. Ago | 2 Wks. Ago | 3 Wks. Ago | Title — Artist, Label & Number | Weeks On Chart |
|---|---|---|---|---|---|
| 1 | 1 | 3 | 6 | IF YOU WANNA BE HAPPY — Jimmy Soul, S.P.Q.R. 3305 | 9 |
| 2 | 2 | 1 | 1 | I WILL FOLLOW HIM — Little Peggy March, RCA Victor 8139 | 10 |
| 3 | 4 | 7 | 8 | SURFIN' U.S.A. — Beach Boys, Capitol 4932 | 10 |
| 4 | 5 | 6 | 13 | FOOLISH LITTLE GIRL — Shirelles, Scepter 1248 | 10 |
| ★5 | 10 | 23 | 29 | I LOVE YOU BECAUSE — Al Martino, Capitol 4930 | 8 |
| 6 | 7 | 10 | 18 | LOSING YOU — Brenda Lee, Decca 31478 | 8 |
| 7 | 11 | 17 | 23 | TWO FACES HAVE I — Lou Christie, Roulette 4481 | 9 |
| ★8 | 12 | 16 | 19 | TAKE THESE CHAINS FROM MY HEART — Ray Charles, ABC-Paramount 10435 | 7 |
| ★9 | 26 | 60 | — | IT'S MY PARTY — Lesley Gore, Mercury 72119 | 3 |
| 10 | 14 | 24 | 30 | ANOTHER SATURDAY NIGHT — Sam Cooke, RCA Victor 8164 | 6 |
| 11 | 13 | 20 | 21 | HOT PASTRAMI — Dartells, Dot 16453 | 7 |
| 12 | 3 | 2 | 3 | PUFF (The Magic Dragon) — Peter, Paul & Mary, Warner Bros. 5348 | 11 |
| 13 | 19 | 37 | 54 | DA DOO RON RON — Crystals, Philles 112 | 5 |
| 14 | 8 | 9 | 14 | REVEREND MR. BLACK — Kingston Trio, Capitol 4951 | 8 |
| 15 | 18 | 36 | 50 | YOU CAN'T SIT DOWN — Dovells, Parkway 867 | 5 |
| 16 | 6 | 4 | 4 | PIPELINE — Chantays, Dot 16440 | 13 |
| 17 | 24 | 29 | 49 | STILL — Bill Anderson, Decca 31458 | 7 |
| 18 | 9 | 5 | 2 | CAN'T GET USED TO LOSING YOU — Andy Williams, Columbia 42674 | 13 |
| 19 | 16 | 19 | 34 | KILLER JOE — Rocky Fellers, Scepter 1246 | 10 |
| ★20 | 45 | 79 | — | SUKIYAKI — Kyu Sakamoto, Capitol 4945 | 3 |
| 21 | 21 | 26 | 31 | THIS LITTLE GIRL — Dion, Columbia 42776 | 6 |
| 22 | 22 | 27 | 36 | AINT THAT A SHAME! — 4 Seasons, Vee Jay 512 | 6 |
| 23 | 31 | 34 | 51 | THE LOVE OF MY MAN — Theola Kilgore, Serock 2004 | 6 |
| 24 | 27 | 40 | 71 | EL WATUSI — Ray Barretto, Tico 419 | 5 |
| ★25 | 47 | 70 | — | THOSE LAZY-HAZY-CRAZY DAYS OF SUMMER — Nat King Cole, Capitol 4965 | 3 |
| ★26 | 35 | 38 | 46 | PUSHOVER — Etta James, Argo 5437 | 6 |
| ★27 | 37 | 53 | 64 | PRISONER OF LOVE — James Brown and the Famous Flames, King 5739 | 6 |
| 28 | 17 | 8 | 5 | HE'S SO FINE — Chiffons, Laurie 3152 | 14 |
| 29 | 23 | 21 | 25 | LITTLE BAND OF GOLD — James Gilreath, Joy 274 | 10 |
| 30 | 15 | 12 | 12 | MECCA — Gene Pitney, Musicor 1028 | 10 |
| 31 | 39 | 50 | 70 | LET'S GO STEADY AGAIN — Neil Sedaka, RCA Victor 8169 | 5 |
| 32 | 36 | 42 | 58 | COME AND GET THESE MEMORIES — Martha & the Vandellas, Gordy 7014 | 8 |
| ★33 | 53 | 65 | 80 | HELLO STRANGER — Barbara Lewis, Atlantic 2184 | 4 |
| ★34 | 55 | 93 | — | 18 YELLOW ROSES — Bobby Darin, Capitol 4970 | 3 |
| 35 | 20 | 13 | 15 | CHARMS — Bobby Vee, Liberty 55530 | 9 |
| 36 | 28 | 30 | 26 | DAYS OF WINE AND ROSES — Andy Williams, Columbia 42674 | 11 |
| 37 | 25 | 11 | 9 | ON BROADWAY — Drifters, Atlantic 2182 | 10 |
| 38 | 43 | 49 | 63 | SHUT DOWN — Beach Boys, Capitol 4932 | 5 |
| 39 | 41 | 44 | 56 | REMEMBER DIANA — Paul Anka, RCA Victor 8170 | 7 |
| 40 | 51 | 58 | 74 | IF YOU NEED ME — Solomon Burke, Atlantic 2185 | 6 |
| 41 | 49 | 57 | 77 | HOT PASTRAMI WITH MASHED POTATOES (Part I) — Joey Dee and the Starliters, Roulette 4488 | 5 |
| 42 | 46 | 47 | 53 | THAT'S HOW HEARTACHES ARE MADE — Baby Washington, Sue 783 | 10 |
| ★43 | 59 | 75 | — | THE GOOD LIFE — Tony Bennett, Columbia 42779 | 3 |
| 44 | 30 | 18 | 10 | WATERMELON MAN — Mongo Santamaria, Battle 45909 | 11 |
| 45 | 38 | 31 | 37 | A LOVE SHE CAN COUNT ON — Miracles, Tamla 54078 | 9 |
| 46 | 33 | 15 | 7 | DON'T SAY NOTHIN' BAD ABOUT MY BABY — Cookies, Dimension 1008 | 13 |
| 47 | 52 | 61 | 78 | WHAT A GUY — Raindrops, Jubilee 5444 | 5 |
| 48 | 29 | 22 | 20 | TOM CAT — Rooftop Singers, Vanguard 35019 | 10 |
| 49 | 60 | 74 | — | WILDWOOD DAYS — Bobby Rydell, Cameo 252 | 3 |
| 50 | 44 | 39 | 41 | (Today I Met) THE BOY I'M GONNA MARRY — Darlene Love, Philles 111 | 8 |
| 51 | 34 | 35 | 33 | DAYS OF WINE AND ROSES — Henry Mancini, RCA Victor 8120 | 18 |
| 52 | 62 | 71 | 76 | SHAME, SHAME, SHAME — Jimmy Reed, Vee Jay 509 | 5 |
| 53 | 56 | 67 | 82 | DO IT — RAT NOW — Bill Black's Combo, Hi 2064 | 5 |
| 54 | 58 | 69 | 79 | THE BOUNCE — Olympics, Tri Disc 106 | 5 |
| 55 | 61 | 78 | — | I'M SAVING MY LOVE — Skeeter Davis, RCA Victor 8176 | 3 |
| 56 | 67 | 76 | 98 | SWEET DREAMS (Of You) — Patsy Cline, Decca 31483 | 6 |
| 57 | 54 | 62 | 72 | STING RAY — Routers, Warner Bros. 5349 | 5 |
| 58 | 42 | 28 | 17 | YOUNG AND IN LOVE — Dick & Deedee, Warner Bros. 5342 | 11 |
| 59 | 32 | 14 | 11 | BABY WORKOUT — Jackie Wilson, Brunswick 55239 | 12 |
| 60 | 68 | 83 | — | DON'T MAKE MY BABY BLUE — Frankie Laine, Columbia 42767 | 3 |
| 61 | 50 | 54 | 59 | TWO KINDS OF TEARDROPS — Del Shannon, Big Top 3143 | 7 |
| ★62 | 85 | — | — | BLUE ON BLUE — Bobby Vinton, Epic 9593 | 2 |
| 63 | 81 | — | — | BIRDLAND — Chubby Checker, Parkway 873 | 2 |
| 64 | 76 | 89 | 93 | GRAVY WALTZ — Steve Allen, Dot 16457 | 5 |
| 65 | 73 | 90 | — | LITTLE LATIN LUPE LU — Righteous Brothers, Moonglow 215 | 3 |
| 66 | 69 | 77 | 85 | PATTY BABY — Freddy Cannon, Swan 4139 | 4 |
| 67 | 74 | 80 | 90 | IF YOU NEED ME — Wilson Pickett, Double L 713 | 4 |
| 68 | 70 | 87 | — | TEENAGE HEAVEN — Johnny Cymbal, Kapp 524 | 3 |
| 69 | 72 | — | — | MY SUMMER LOVE — Ruby & the Romantics, Kapp 525 | 2 |
| 70 | 57 | 52 | 60 | BIRD'S THE WORD — Rivingtons, Liberty 55553 | 7 |
| 71 | 79 | 98 | — | THE LAST LEAF — Cascades, Valiant 6028 | 3 |
| ★72 | — | — | — | STRING ALONG — Rick Nelson, Decca 31495 | 1 |
| 73 | 99 | — | — | PRIDE AND JOY — Marvin Gaye, Tamla 54079 | 2 |
| ★74 | — | — | — | EVERY STEP OF THE WAY — Johnny Mathis, Columbia 42799 | 1 |
| 75 | 83 | 86 | 92 | CALL ME IRRESPONSIBLE — Jack Jones, Kapp 516 | 4 |
| ★76 | — | — | — | POOR LITTLE RICH GIRL — Steve Lawrence, Columbia 42795 | 1 |
| 77 | — | — | — | YOUR OLD STAND BY — Mary Wells, Motown 1042 | 1 |
| 78 | 78 | 81 | 81 | CALL ME IRRESPONSIBLE — Frank Sinatra, Reprise 20151 | 8 |
| 79 | 95 | — | — | IF MY PILLOW COULD TALK — Connie Francis, MGM 13143 | 2 |
| 80 | 84 | 99 | — | A STRANGER IN YOUR TOWN — Shacklefords, Mercury 72112 | 3 |
| 81 | 75 | 85 | 88 | I'M MOVIN' ON — Matt Lucas, Smash 1813 | 4 |
| 82 | 90 | — | — | SHAKE A TAIL FEATHER — Five Du-Tones, One-der-ful 4815 | 2 |
| 83 | 77 | 72 | 83 | RONNIE, CALL ME WHEN YOU GET A CHANCE — Shelley Fabares, Colpix 682 | 5 |
| 84 | 86 | 97 | 100 | FOREVER — Marvelettes, Tamla 54077 | 4 |
| 85 | 88 | — | — | GYPSY WOMAN — Rick Nelson, Decca 31495 | 2 |
| 86 | 82 | 100 | — | HOBO FLATS (Part I) — Jimmy Smith, Verve 10283 | 3 |
| 87 | 89 | — | — | THERE GOES (MY HEART AGAIN) — Fats Domino, ABC-Paramount 10444 | 2 |
| ★88 | — | — | — | SAD, SAD GIRL AND BOY — Impressions, ABC-Paramount 10431 | 1 |
| ★89 | — | — | — | SHAKE A HAND — Jackie Wilson & Linda Hopkins, Brunswick 55243 | 1 |
| ★90 | — | — | — | SWINGIN' ON A STAR — Big Dee Irwin, Dimension 1010 | 1 |
| 91 | — | — | — | THESE ARMS OF MINE — Otis Redding, Volt 103 | 1 |
| 92 | 96 | — | — | LONELY BOY, LONELY GUITAR — Duane Eddy, RCA Victor 8180 | 2 |
| 93 | 80 | 92 | — | SOON (I'll Be Home Again) — 4 Seasons, Vee Jay 512 | 3 |
| 94 | 94 | — | 95 | GOT YOU ON MY MIND — Cookie & His Cupcakes, Chess 1848 | 3 |
| 95 | — | — | — | THE DOG — Rufus Thomas, Stax 130 | 7 |
| 96 | — | — | — | I KNOW I KNOW — "Pookie" Hudson, Double L 711 | 1 |
| 97 | 97 | — | — | NEEDLES AND PINS — Jackie DeShannon, Liberty 55563 | 2 |
| 98 | — | — | — | DANGER — Vic Dana, Dolton 73 | 1 |
| 99 | — | — | — | THE LAST MINUTE (Part 1) — Jimmy McGriff, Sue 786 | 1 |
| 100 | — | — | — | SOULVILLE — Dinah Washington, Roulette 4490 | 1 |

## BUBBLING UNDER THE HOT 100

101. IF YOU DON'T LOVE ME — Junior Parker, Duke 364
102. JACK THE RIPPER — Link Wray & His Ray Men, Swan 4137
103. ROCKIN' CRICKETS — Rockin' Rebels, Swan 4140
104. TEN COMMANDMENTS OF LOVE — James MacArthur, Scepter 1250
105. OLD SMOKEY LOCOMOTION — Little Eva, Dimension 1011
106. OLD ENOUGH TO LOVE — Rick Nelson, Imperial 5935
107. ONE BOY TOO LATE — Mike Clifford, United Artists 588
108. YOU ALWAYS HURT THE ONE YOU LOVE — Fats Domino, Imperial 5937
109. I KNOW BETTER — Tymes, Parkway 781
110. HE'S A BAD BOY — Carole King, Dimension 1009
111. TIPS OF MY FINGERS — Roy Clark, Capitol 4956
112. LITTLE BIRD — Pete Jolly Trio, Ava 116
113. SPRING IN MANHATTAN — Tony Bennett, Columbia 42779
114. HOT CAKES (1st Serving) — Dave (Baby) Cortez, Chess 1850
115. YOU KNOW IT AIN'T RIGHT — Joe Hinton, Back Beat 537
116. SATURDAY NIGHT — Sherrys, Guyden 2084
117. LONESOME 7-7203 — Hawkshaw Hawkins, King 5712
118. ON TOP OF SPAGHETTI — Tom Glazer & the Children's Chorus, Kapp 526
119. LOVERS — Blendtones, Success 101
120. LOVED — Bill Pursell, Columbia 42780
121. GIVE US YOUR BLESSING — Ray Peterson, Dunes 2025
122. BE EVER WONDERFUL — Ted Taylor, Okeh 7171
123. RING OF FIRE — Johnny Cash, Columbia 42788
124. DIANE — Joe Harnell & His Ork., Kapp 526
125. YOU'LL NEED ANOTHER FAVOR — Little Johnny Taylor, Galaxy 718
126. CHECK YOURSELF — Gene Chandler, Vee Jay 511
127. SPRING IN MANHATTAN — Ella Fitzgerald, Verve 10288
128. BILL BAILEY, WON'T YOU PLEASE COME HOME — Ella Fitzgerald, Verve 10288
129. DENISE — Randy & the Rainbows, Rust 5059

# Billboard HOT 100

**FOR WEEK ENDING JUNE 1, 1963**

| This Week | Wks Ago | Title — Artist, Label & Number | Weeks on Chart |
|---|---|---|---|
| 1 | 9, 26, 60 | IT'S MY PARTY — Lesley Gore, Mercury 72119 | 4 |
| 2 | 1, 1, 3 | IF YOU WANNA BE HAPPY — Jimmy Soul, S.P.Q.R. 3305 | 10 |
| 3 | 5, 10, 23 | I LOVE YOU BECAUSE — Al Martino, Capitol 4930 | 9 |
| 4 | 3, 4, 7 | SURFIN' U.S.A. — Beach Boys, Capitol 4932 | 11 |
| 5 | 13, 19, 37 | DA DOO RON RON — Crystals, Philles 112 | 6 |
| 6 | 7, 11, 17 | TWO FACES HAVE I — Lou Christie, Roulette 4481 | 10 |
| 7 | 15, 18, 36 | YOU CAN'T SIT DOWN — Dovells, Parkway 867 | 6 |
| 8 | 2, 2, 1 | I WILL FOLLOW HIM — Little Peggy March, RCA Victor 8139 | 11 |
| 9 | 6, 7, 10 | LOSING YOU — Brenda Lee, Decca 31478 | 9 |
| 10 | 20, 45, 79 | SUKIYAKI — Kyu Sakamoto, Capitol 4945 | 4 |
| 11 | 17, 24, 29 | STILL — Bill Anderson, Decca 31458 | 8 |
| 12 | 4, 5, 6 | FOOLISH LITTLE GIRL — Shirelles, Scepter 1248 | 11 |
| 13 | 8, 12, 16 | TAKE THESE CHAINS FROM MY HEART — Ray Charles, ABC-Paramount 10435 | 8 |
| 14 | 10, 14, 24 | ANOTHER SATURDAY NIGHT — Sam Cooke, RCA Victor 8164 | 7 |
| 15 | 11, 13, 20 | HOT PASTRAMI — Dartells, Dot 16453 | 8 |
| 16 | 25, 47, 70 | THOSE LAZY-HAZY-CRAZY DAYS OF SUMMER — Nat King Cole, Capitol 4965 | 4 |
| 17 | 24, 27, 40 | EL WATUSI — Ray Barretto, Tico 419 | 6 |
| 18 | 12, 3, 2 | PUFF (The Magic Dragon) — Peter, Paul and Mary, Warner Bros. 5348 | 12 |
| 19 | 14, 8, 9 | REVEREND MR. BLACK — Kingston Trio, Capitol 4951 | 9 |
| 20 | 16, 6, 4 | PIPELINE — Chantays, Dot 16440 | 14 |
| 21 | 23, 31, 34 | THE LOVE OF MY MAN — Theola Kilgore, Serock 2004 | 7 |
| 22 | 27, 37, 53 | PRISONER OF LOVE — James Brown & the Famous Flames, King 5739 | 7 |
| 23 | 34, 55, 93 | 18 YELLOW ROSES — Bobby Darin, Capitol 4970 | 5 |
| 24 | 18, 9, 5 | CAN'T GET USED TO LOSING YOU — Andy Williams, Columbia 42674 | 14 |
| 25 | 22, 22, 27 | AIN'T THAT A SHAME! — 4 Seasons, Vee Jay 512 | 7 |
| 26 | 31, 39, 50 | LET'S GO STEADY AGAIN — Neil Sedaka, RCA Victor 8169 | 6 |
| 27 | 19, 16, 19 | KILLER JOE — Rocky Fellers, Scepter 1246 | 11 |
| 28 | 33, 53, 65 | HELLO STRANGER — Barbara Lewis, Atlantic 2184 | 5 |
| 29 | 21, 21, 26 | THIS LITTLE GIRL — Dion, Columbia 42776 | 7 |
| 30 | 26, 35, 38 | PUSHOVER — Etta James, Argo 5437 | 7 |
| 31 | 62, 85, — | BLUE ON BLUE — Bobby Vinton, Epic 9593 | 3 |
| 32 | 43, 59, 75 | THE GOOD LIFE — Tony Bennett, Columbia 42779 | 4 |
| 33 | 38, 43, 49 | SHUT DOWN — Beach Boys, Capitol 4932 | 6 |
| 34 | 29, 23, 21 | LITTLE BAND OF GOLD — James Gilreath, Joy 274 | 11 |
| 35 | 63, 81, — | BIRDLAND — Chubby Checker, Parkway 873 | 3 |
| 36 | 41, 49, 57 | HOT PASTRAMI WITH MASHED POTATOES (Part I) — Joey Dee and the Starliters, Roulette 4488 | 6 |
| 37 | 40, 51, 58 | IF YOU NEED ME — Solomon Burke, Atlantic 2185 | 7 |
| 38 | 32, 36, 42 | COME AND GET THESE MEMORIES — Martha & the Vandellas, Gordy 7014 | 9 |
| 39 | 49, 60, 74 | WILDWOOD DAYS — Bobby Rydell, Cameo 252 | 4 |
| 40 | 42, 46, 47 | THAT'S HOW HEARTACHES ARE MADE — Baby Washington, Sue 783 | 11 |
| 41 | 36, 28, 30 | DAYS OF WINE AND ROSES — Andy Williams, Columbia 42674 | 12 |
| 42 | 47, 52, 61 | WHAT A GUY — Raindrops, Jubilee 5444 | 6 |
| 43 | 28, 17, 8 | HE'S SO FINE — Chiffons, Laurie 3152 | 15 |
| 44 | 54, 58, 69 | THE BOUNCE — Olympics, Tri Disc 106 | 5 |
| 45 | 79, 95, — | IF MY PILLOW COULD TALK — Connie Francis, MGM 13143 | 3 |
| 46 | 35, 20, 13 | CHARMS — Bobby Vee, Liberty 55530 | 10 |
| 47 | 74, —, — | EVERY STEP OF THE WAY — Johnny Mathis, Columbia 42799 | 2 |
| 48 | 55, 61, 78 | I'M SAVING MY LOVE — Skeeter Davis, RCA Victor 8176 | 4 |
| 49 | 30, 15, 12 | MECCA — Gene Pitney, Musicor 1028 | 11 |
| 50 | 57, 54, 62 | STING RAY — Routers, Warner Bros. 5349 | 6 |
| 51 | 53, 56, 67 | DO IT—RAT NOW — Bill Black's Combo, Hi 2064 | 6 |
| 52 | 65, 73, 90 | LITTLE LATIN LUPE LU — Righteous Brothers, Moonglow 215 | 4 |
| 53 | 72, —, — | STRING ALONG — Rick Nelson, Decca 31495 | 2 |
| 54 | 56, 67, 76 | SWEET DREAMS (Of You) — Patsy Cline, Decca 31483 | 7 |
| 55 | 69, 72, — | MY SUMMER LOVE — Ruby & the Romantics, Kapp 525 | 3 |
| 56 | 61, 50, 54 | TWO KINDS OF TEARDROPS — Del Shannon, Big Top 3143 | 8 |
| 57 | 60, 68, 83 | DON'T MAKE MY BABY BLUE — Frankie Laine, Columbia 42767 | 4 |
| 58 | 68, 70, 87 | TEENAGE HEAVEN — Johnny Cymbal, Kapp 524 | 4 |
| 59 | 39, 41, 44 | REMEMBER DIANA — Paul Anka, RCA Victor 8170 | 6 |
| 60 | 71, 79, 98 | THE LAST LEAF — Cascades, Valiant 6028 | 4 |
| 61 | 73, 99, — | PRIDE AND JOY — Marvin Gaye, Tamla 54079 | 3 |
| 62 | 76, —, — | POOR LITTLE RICH GIRL — Steve Lawrence, Columbia 42795 | 2 |
| 63 | 52, 62, 71 | SHAME, SHAME, SHAME — Jimmy Reed, Vee Jay 509 | 6 |
| 64 | 67, 74, 80 | IF YOU NEED ME — Wilson Pickett, Double L 713 | 5 |
| 65 | 66, 69, 77 | PATTY BABY — Freddy Cannon, Swan 4139 | 5 |
| 66 | —, —, — | ONE FINE DAY — Chiffons, Laurie 3179 | 1 |
| 67 | 77, —, — | YOUR OLD STAND BY — Mary Wells, Motown 1042 | 2 |
| 68 | —, —, — | ON TOP OF SPAGHETTI — Tom Glazer & the Children's Chorus, Kapp 526 | 1 |
| 69 | —, —, — | OLD SMOKEY LOCOMOTION — Little Eva, Dimension 1011 | 1 |
| 70 | 64, 76, 89 | GRAVY WALTZ — Steve Allen, Dot 16457 | 6 |
| 71 | 87, 89, — | THERE GOES (My Heart Again) — Fats Domino, ABC-Paramount 10444 | 3 |
| 72 | —, —, — | RING OF FIRE — Johnny Cash, Columbia 42788 | 1 |
| 73 | 89, —, — | SHAKE A HAND — Jackie Wilson & Linda Hopkins, Brunswick 55243 | 2 |
| 74 | 86, 82, 100 | HOBO FLATS — Jimmy Smith, Verve 10283 | 4 |
| 75 | 90, —, — | SWINGING ON A STAR — Big Dee Irwin, Dimension 1010 | 2 |
| 76 | 80, 84, 99 | A STRANGER IN YOUR TOWN — Shacklefords, Mercury 72112 | 4 |
| 77 | 81, 75, 85 | I'M MOVIN' ON — Matt Lucas, Smash 1813 | 5 |
| 78 | 84, 86, 97 | FOREVER — Marvelettes, Tamla 54077 | 5 |
| 79 | 82, 90, — | SHAKE A TAIL FEATHER — Five Du-Tones, One-der-ful 4815 | 3 |
| 80 | 85, 88, — | GYPSY WOMAN — Rick Nelson, Decca 31495 | 3 |
| 81 | —, —, — | GIVE US YOUR BLESSING — Ray Peterson, Dunes 2025 | 1 |
| 82 | —, —, — | I WISH I WERE A PRINCESS — Little Peggy March, RCA Victor 8189 | 1 |
| 83 | —, —, — | DON'T TRY TO FIGHT IT BABY — Eydie Gorme, Columbia 42790 | 1 |
| 84 | —, —, — | GOODNIGHT MY LOVE — Fleetwoods, Dolton 75 | 1 |
| 85 | 91, —, — | THESE ARMS OF MINE — Otis Redding, Volt 103 | 2 |
| 86 | —, —, — | SO MUCH IN LOVE — Tymes, Parkway 781 | 1 |
| 87 | 88, —, — | SAD, SAD GIRL AND BOY — Impressions, ABC-Paramount 10431 | 2 |
| 88 | 93, 80, 92 | SOON (I'll Be Home Again) — 4 Seasons, Vee Jay 512 | 4 |
| 89 | 92, 96, — | LONELY BOY, LONELY GUITAR — Duane Eddy, RCA Victor 8180 | 3 |
| 90 | —, —, — | FIRST QUARREL — Paul & Paula, Philips 40114 | 1 |
| 91 | —, —, — | YOU KNOW IT AIN'T RIGHT — Joe Hinton, Back Beat 537 | 1 |
| 92 | 97, 97, — | NEEDLES AND PINS — Jackie DeShannon, Liberty 55563 | 3 |
| 93 | —, —, — | (I Love You) DON'T YOU FORGET IT — Perry Como, RCA Victor 8186 | 1 |
| 94 | 95, —, — | THE DOG — Rufus Thomas, Stax 130 | 8 |
| 95 | 94, 94, — | GOT YOU ON MY MIND — Cookie & His Cupcakes, Chess 1848 | 4 |
| 96 | 98, —, — | DANGER — Vic Dana, Dolton 73 | 2 |
| 97 | 100, —, — | SOULVILLE — Dinah Washington, Roulette 4490 | 2 |
| 98 | —, —, — | SAY WONDERFUL THINGS — Patti Page, Columbia 42791 | 1 |
| 99 | —, —, — | RIVER'S INVITATION — Percy Mayfield, Tangerine 931 | 1 |
| 100 | —, —, — | I CAN'T STOP LOVING YOU — Count Basie, Reprise 20170 | 1 |

## BUBBLING UNDER THE HOT 100

- 101. ROCKIN' CRICKETS — Randy & the Rebels, Swan 4140
- 102. DENISE — Randy & the Rainbows, Rust 5059
- 103. JACK THE RIPPER — Link Wray & His Ray Men, Swan 4137
- 104. TEN COMMANDMENTS OF LOVE — James MacArthur, Scepter 1250
- 105. SPRING IN MANHATTAN — Tony Bennett, Columbia 42779
- 106. OLD OLD FASHIONED LOVE — Rick Nelson, Imperial 5935
- 107. HOT CAKES — Gene Dudley, Golden Wing 3020
- 108. EASIEST SAID THAN DONE — Essex, Roulette 4494
- 109. SAY WONDERFUL THINGS — Ronnie Carroll, Philips 40110
- 110. SIX DAYS ON THE ROAD — Dave Dudley, Golden Wing 3020
- 111. I KNOW I KNOW — "Pookie" Hudson, Double L 711
- 112. THE LAST MINUTE — Jimmy McGriff, Sue 783
- 113. IT'S BEEN NICE (Goodnight) — Everly Brothers, Warner Bros. 5362
- 114. WILL YOU BE MY BABY — Bobby Rydell, Cameo 252
- 115. NOT TOO YOUNG TO GET MARRIED — Bob B. Soxx & the Blue Jeans, Philles 113
- 116. TIPS OF MY FINGERS — Roy Clark, Capitol 4956
- 117. YOU ALWAYS HURT THE ONE YOU LOVE — Fats Domino, Imperial 5937
- 118. BILL BAILEY, WON'T YOU PLEASE COME HOME — Ella Fitzgerald, Verve 10288
- 119. LONESOME 7-7203 — Hawkshaw Hawkins, King 5712
- 120. MEMPHIS — Lonnie Mack, Fraternity 906
- 121. CHECK YOURSELF — Dee (Baby) Cortez, Chess 1850
- 122. JUST ONE LOOK — Doris Troy, Atlantic 2188
- 123. CAN'T GO ON WITHOUT YOU — Fats Domino, ABC-Paramount 10444
- 124. LITTLE BIRD — Pete Jolly Trio, Ava 116
- 125. SHY GIRL — Cascades, Valiant 6028
- 126. TAMOURE — Bill Justis, Smash 1812
- 127. FALLING — Roy Orbison, Monument 815
- 128. BOSSA NOVA ITALIANO — Lou Monte, Reprise 20171
- 129. THESE ARE THE YOUNG YEARS — Floyd Cramer, RCA Victor 8171
- 130. I WILL NEVER TURN MY BACK ON YOU — Chuck Jackson, Wand 138
- 131. I'M WALKIN' — Patti Page, Mercury 72123
- 132. YEH-YEH — Mongo Santamaria, Battle 45917

# Billboard HOT 100

FOR WEEK ENDING JUNE 8 1963

★ STAR PERFORMERS—Selections registering greatest upward progress this week.

[S] Indicates that 45 r.p.m. stereo single version is available.

△ Indicates that 33⅓ r.p.m. mono single version is available.

△S Indicates that 33⅓ r.p.m. stereo single version is available.

| This Week | 1 Wk. Ago | 2 Wks. Ago | 3 Wks. Ago | Title | Artist, Label & Number | | Weeks On Chart |
|---|---|---|---|---|---|---|---|
| 1 (Billboard Award) | 1 | 9 | 26 | IT'S MY PARTY | Lesley Gore, Mercury 72119 | | 5 |
| ★ 2 | 10 | 20 | 45 | SUKIYAKI | Kyu Sakamoto, Capitol 4945 | | 5 |
| 3 | 5 | 13 | 19 | DA DOO RON RON | Crystals, Philles 112 | | 7 |
| 4 | 3 | 5 | 10 | I LOVE YOU BECAUSE | Al Martino, Capitol 4930 | | 10 |
| 5 | 7 | 15 | 18 | YOU CAN'T SIT DOWN | Dovells, Parkway 867 | | 7 |
| 6 | 6 | 7 | 11 | TWO FACES HAVE I | Lou Christie, Roulette 4481 | | 11 |
| 7 | 2 | 1 | 1 | IF YOU WANNA BE HAPPY | Jimmy Soul, S.P.Q.R. 3305 | | 11 |
| ★ 8 | 11 | 17 | 24 | STILL | Bill Anderson, Decca 31458 | | 9 |
| ★ 9 | 16 | 25 | 47 | THOSE LAZY-HAZY-CRAZY DAYS OF SUMMER | Nat King Cole, Capitol 4965 | | 5 |
| 10 | 4 | 3 | 4 | SURFIN' U. S. A. | Beach Boys, Capitol 4932 | | 12 |
| ★ 11 | 23 | 34 | 55 | 18 YELLOW ROSES | Bobby Darin, Capitol 4970 | | 5 |
| 12 | 9 | 6 | 7 | LOSING YOU | Brenda Lee, Decca 31478 | | 10 |
| ★ 13 | 28 | 33 | 53 | HELLO STRANGER | Barbara Lewis, Atlantic 2184 | | 6 |
| ★ 14 | 31 | 62 | 85 | BLUE ON BLUE | Bobby Vinton, Epic 9593 | | 4 |
| 15 | 14 | 10 | 14 | ANOTHER SATURDAY NIGHT | Sam Cooke, RCA Victor 8164 | | 8 |
| 16 | 15 | 11 | 13 | HOT PASTRAMI | Dartells, Dot 16453 | | 9 |
| 17 | 8 | 2 | 2 | I WILL FOLLOW HIM | Little Peggy March, RCA Victor 8139 | | 12 |
| 18 | 12 | 4 | 5 | FOOLISH LITTLE GIRL | Shirelles, Scepter 1248 | | 12 |
| 19 | 13 | 8 | 12 | TAKE THESE CHAINS FROM MY HEART | Ray Charles, ABC-Paramount 10435 | | 9 |
| 20 | 17 | 24 | 27 | EL WATUSI | Ray Barretto, Tico 419 | | 7 |
| 21 | 22 | 27 | 37 | PRISONER OF LOVE | James Brown & the Famous Flames, King 5739 | | 8 |
| ★ 22 | 35 | 63 | 81 | BIRDLAND | Chubby Checker, Parkway 873 | | 4 |
| 23 | 21 | 23 | 31 | THE LOVE OF MY MAN | Theola Kilgore, Serock 2004 | | 8 |
| ★ 24 | 32 | 43 | 59 | THE GOOD LIFE | Tony Bennett, Columbia 42779 | △ | 5 |
| ★ 25 | 30 | 26 | 35 | PUSHOVER | Etta James, Argo 5437 | | 8 |
| 26 | 19 | 14 | 8 | REVEREND MR. BLACK | Kingston Trio, Capitol 4951 | | 10 |
| 27 | 20 | 16 | 6 | PIPELINE | Chantays, Dot 16440 | | 15 |
| 28 | 18 | 12 | 3 | PUFF (The Magic Dragon) | Peter, Paul & Mary, Warner Bros. 5348 | | 13 |
| ★ 29 | 38 | 32 | 36 | COME AND GET THESE MEMORIES | Martha & the Vandellas, Gordy 7014 | | 10 |
| ★ 30 | 39 | 49 | 60 | WILDWOOD DAYS | Bobby Rydell, Cameo 252 | | 5 |
| 31 | 26 | 31 | 39 | LET'S GO STEADY AGAIN | Neil Sedaka, RCA Victor 8169 | | 7 |
| 32 | 33 | 38 | 43 | SHUT DOWN | Beach Boys, Capitol 4932 | | 7 |
| 33 | 25 | 22 | 22 | AIN'T THAT A SHAME! | 4 Seasons, Vee Jay 512 | | 8 |
| 34 | 27 | 19 | 16 | KILLER JOE | Rocky Fellers, Scepter 1246 | | 12 |
| ★ 35 | 45 | 79 | 95 | IF MY PILLOW COULD TALK | Connie Francis, MGM 13143 | | 4 |
| ★ 36 | 66 | — | — | ONE FINE DAY | Chiffons, Laurie 3179 | | 2 |
| ★ 37 | 47 | 74 | — | EVERY STEP OF THE WAY | Johnny Mathis, Columbia 42799 | △ | 3 |
| 38 | 24 | 18 | 9 | CAN'T GET USED TO LOSING YOU | Andy Williams, Columbia 42674 | △ | 15 |
| 39 | 29 | 21 | 21 | THIS LITTLE GIRL | Dion, Columbia 42776 | △ | 8 |
| 40 | 44 | 54 | 58 | THE BOUNCE | Olympics, Tri Disc 106 | | 7 |
| 41 | 42 | 47 | 52 | WHAT A GUY | Raindrops, Jubilee 5444 | | 7 |
| ★ 42 | 53 | 12 | — | STRING ALONG | Rick Nelson, Decca 31495 | | 3 |
| 43 | 37 | 40 | 51 | IF YOU NEED ME | Solomon Burke, Atlantic 2185 | | 8 |
| 44 | 48 | 55 | 61 | I'M SAVING MY LOVE | Skeeter Davis, RCA Victor 8176 | | 5 |
| ★ 45 | 55 | 69 | 72 | MY SUMMER LOVE | Ruby & the Romantics, Kapp 525 | | 4 |
| 46 | 36 | 41 | 49 | HOT PASTRAMI WITH MASHED POTATOES (Part I) | Joey Dee and the Starliters, Roulette 4488 | | 7 |
| ★ 47 | 62 | 76 | — | POOR LITTLE RICH GIRL | Steve Lawrence, Columbia 42795 | △ | 3 |
| 48 | 54 | 56 | 67 | SWEET DREAMS (Of You) | Patsy Cline, Decca 31483 | | 8 |
| 49 | 52 | 65 | 73 | LITTLE LATIN LUPE LU | Righteous Brothers, Moonglow 215 | | 5 |
| ★ 50 | 73 | 89 | — | SHAKE A HAND | Jackie Wilson & Linda Hopkins, Brunswick 55243 | | 3 |
| 51 | 57 | 60 | 68 | DON'T MAKE MY BABY BLUE | Frankie Laine, Columbia 42767 | △ | 5 |
| 52 | 61 | 73 | 99 | PRIDE AND JOY | Marvin Gaye, Tamla 54079 | | 4 |
| 53 | 50 | 57 | 54 | STING RAY | Routers, Warner Bros. 5349 | | 7 |
| ★ 54 | 68 | — | — | ON TOP OF SPAGHETTI | Tom Glazer & the Children's Chorus, Kapp 526 | | 2 |
| ★ 55 | 90 | — | — | FIRST QUARREL | Paul & Paula, Philips 40114 | | 2 |
| ★ 56 | 67 | 77 | — | YOUR OLD STAND BY | Mary Wells, Motown 1042 | | 3 |
| ★ 57 | 69 | — | — | OLD SMOKEY LOCOMOTION | Little Eva, Dimension 1011 | | 2 |
| 58 | 51 | 53 | 56 | DO IT—RAT NOW | Bill Black's Combo, Hi 2064 | | 7 |
| ★ 59 | 72 | — | — | RING OF FIRE | Johnny Cash, Columbia 42788 | △ | 1 |
| 60 | 58 | 68 | 70 | TEENAGE HEAVEN | Johnny Cymbal, Kapp 524 | | 5 |
| 61 | 63 | 52 | 62 | SHAME, SHAME, SHAME | Jimmy Reed, Vee Jay 509 | | 7 |
| ★ 62 | 77 | 81 | 75 | I'M MOVIN' ON | Matt Lucas, Smash 1813 | | 6 |
| 63 | 56 | 61 | 50 | TWO KINDS OF TEARDROPS | Del Shannon, Big Top 3143 | | 9 |
| 64 | 75 | 90 | — | SWINGING ON A STAR | Big Dee Irwin, Dimension 1010 | | 3 |
| 65 | 65 | 66 | 69 | PATTY BABY | Freddy Cannon, Swan 4139 | | 6 |
| ★ 66 | 82 | — | — | I WISH I WERE A PRINCESS | Little Peggy March, RCA Victor 8189 | | 2 |
| 67 | 71 | 87 | 89 | THERE GOES (MY HEART AGAIN) | Fats Domino, ABC-Paramount 10444 | | 4 |
| 68 | 34 | 29 | 23 | LITTLE BAND OF GOLD | James Gilreath, Joy 274 | | 12 |
| 69 | 74 | 86 | 82 | HOBO FLATS | Jimmy Smith, Verve 10283 | | 5 |
| 70 | 76 | 80 | 84 | A STRANGER IN YOUR TOWN | Shacklefords, Mercury 72112 | | 5 |
| ★ 71 | 86 | — | — | SO MUCH IN LOVE | Tymes, Parkway 781 | | 2 |
| 72 | 40 | 42 | 46 | THAT'S HOW HEARTACHES ARE MADE | Baby Washington, Sue 783 | | 12 |
| 73 | 64 | 67 | 74 | IF YOU NEED ME | Wilson Pickett, Double L 713 | | 6 |
| 74 | 83 | — | — | DON'T TRY TO FIGHT IT BABY | Eydie Gorme, Columbia 42790 | △ | 2 |
| 75 | 84 | — | — | GOODNIGHT MY LOVE | Fleetwoods, Dolton 75 | | 2 |
| ★ 76 | — | — | — | FALLING | Roy Oribson, Monument 815 | | 1 |
| 77 | 79 | 82 | 90 | SHAKE A TAIL FEATHER | Five Du-Tones, One-der-ful 4815 | | 4 |
| 78 | 70 | 64 | 76 | GRAVY WALTZ | Steve Allen, Dot 16457 | | 7 |
| 79 | 80 | 85 | 88 | GYPSY WOMAN | Rick Nelson, Decca 31495 | | 4 |
| 80 | 81 | — | — | GIVE US YOUR BLESSING | Ray Peterson, Dunes 2025 | | 2 |
| ★ 81 | — | — | — | EASIER SAID THAN DONE | Essex, Roulette 4494 | | 1 |
| 82 | 89 | 92 | 96 | LONELY BOY, LONELY GUITAR | Duane Eddy, RCA Victor 8180 | | 4 |
| 83 | 88 | 93 | 80 | SOON (I'll Be Home Again) | 4 Seasons, Vee Jay 512 | | 5 |
| 84 | 92 | 97 | 97 | NEEDLES AND PINS | Jackie DeShannon, Liberty 55563 | | 4 |
| ★ 85 | — | — | — | SIX DAYS ON THE ROAD | Dave Dudley, Golden Wing 3020 | | 1 |
| 86 | 60 | 71 | 79 | THE LAST LEAF | Cascades, Valiant 6028 | | 5 |
| 87 | 87 | 88 | — | SAD, SAD GIRL AND BOY | Impressions, ABC-Paramount 10431 | | 3 |
| ★ 88 | — | — | — | TIE ME KANGAROO DOWN, SPORT | Rolf Harris, Epic 9596 | | 1 |
| 89 | 91 | — | — | YOU KNOW IT AIN'T RIGHT | Joe Hinton, Back Beat 537 | | 2 |
| ★ 90 | — | — | — | MEMPHIS | Lonnie Mack, Fraternity 906 | | 1 |
| 91 | 93 | — | — | (I Love You) DON'T YOU FORGET IT | Perry Como, RCA Victor 8186 | | 2 |
| 92 | 97 | 100 | — | SOULVILLE | Dinah Washington, Roulette 4490 | | 3 |
| 93 | — | — | — | SPRING IN MANHATTAN | Tony Bennett, Columbia 42779 | △ | 1 |
| 94 | 78 | 84 | 86 | FOREVER | Marvelettes, Tamla 54077 | | 6 |
| 95 | 98 | — | — | SAY WONDERFUL THINGS | Patti Page, Columbia 42791 | △ | 2 |
| 96 | — | — | — | NOT TOO YOUNG TO GET MARRIED | Bob B. Soxx & the Blue Jeans, Phillies 113 | | 1 |
| 97 | 100 | — | — | I CAN'T STOP LOVING YOU | Count Basie, Reprise 20170 | | 2 |
| 98 | 85 | 91 | — | THESE ARMS OF MINE | Otis Redding, Volt 103 | | 3 |
| 99 | — | — | — | SAY WONDERFUL THINGS | Ronnie Carroll, Philips 40110 | | 1 |
| 100 | — | — | — | JUST ONE LOOK | Doris Troy, Atlantic 2188 | | 1 |

## HOT 100—A TO Z—(Publisher-Licensee)


Ain't That a Shame (Travis, BMI) .... 33
Another Saturday Night (Kags, BMI) .... 15
Birdland (Woodcrest-Ace, BMI) .... 22
Blue on Blue (Famous, ASCAP) .... 14
Bounce, The (Marc-Jean, BMI) .... 40
Can't Get Used to Losing You (Brenner, BMI) .... 38
Come and Get These Memories (Jobete, BMI) .... 29
Da Doo Ron Ron (Mother Bertha-Trio, BMI) .... 3
Do It—Rat Now (Wrist-Jec, BMI) .... 58
Don't Make My Baby Blue (Screen Gems-Columbia, (BMI) .... 51
Don't Try to Fight It Baby (Screen Gems-Columbia, BMI) .... 74
Don't You Forget It (Northridge, ASCAP) .... 91
Easier Said Than Done (Nom, BMI) .... 81
18 Yellow Roses (T. M., BMI) .... 11
El Watusi (Little Dipper, BMI) .... 20
Every Step of the Way (Pauline, ASCAP) .... 37
Falling (Acuff-Rose, BMI) .... 76
First Quarrel (LeBill-Marbill, BMI) .... 55
Foolish Little Girl (Screen Gems-Columbia, BMI) .... 18
Forever (Jobete, BMI) .... 94
Give Us Your Blessing (Trio, BMI) .... 80
Good Life, The (Paris, ASCAP) .... 24
Goodnight My Love (House of Fortune-Quintet, BMI) .... 75
Gravy Waltz (Brown, BMI) .... 78
Gypsy Woman (Hilliard-Doral, BMI) .... 79
Hello Stranger (McLaughlin, BMI) .... 13
Hobo Flats (Noslen, BMI) .... 69
Hot Pastrami (Sherlyn-Pent, BMI) .... 16
Hot Pastrami With Mashed Potatoes (Sherlyn-Pent, BMI) .... 46
I Can't Stop Loving You (Acuff-Rose, BMI) .... 97
I Love You Because (Rose, BMI) .... 4
I Will Follow Him (Leeds, ASCAP) .... 17
I Wish I Were a Princess (Atrium, ASCAP) .... 66
I'm Movin' On (Hill & Range, BMI) .... 62
I'm Saving My Love (Samos Island, BMI) .... 44
If My Pillow Could Talk (Merna, BMI) .... 35
If You Need Me—Burke (Cotillion, BMI) .... 43
If You Need Me—Pickett (Cotillion, BMI) .... 73
If You Wanna Be Happy (Rockmasters, BMI) .... 7
It's My Party (Arch, ASCAP) .... 1
Just One Look (Premier, BMI) .... 100
Killer Joe (Mellin-White Castle, BMI) .... 34
Last Leaf, The (Sherman-DeVorzon, BMI) .... 86
Let's Go Steady Again (Screen Gems-Columbia, BMI) .... 31
Little Band of Gold (Beaik, BMI) .... 68
Little Latin Lupe Lu (Maxwell-Conrad, BMI) .... 49
Lonely Boy, Lonely Guitar (Linduane, BMI) .... 82
Losing You (B. N. P., ASCAP) .... 12
Love of My Man, The (Sylvia, BMI) .... 23
Memphis (Arc, BMI) .... 90
My Summer Love (Rosewood, ASCAP) .... 45
Needles and Pins (Metric, BMI) .... 84
Not Too Young to Get Married (Mother Bertha-Trio, BMI) .... 96
Old Smokey Locomotion (Screen Gems-Columbia, BMI) .... 57
On Top of Spaghetti (Songs, ASCAP) .... 54
One Fine Day (Screen Gems-Columbia, BMI) .... 36
Patty Baby (Grand Canyon, BMI) .... 65
Pipeline (Downey, BMI) .... 27
Poor Little Rich Girl (Screen Gems-Columbia, BMI) 47
Pride and Joy (Jobete, BMI) .... 52
Prisoner of Love (Mayfair-Sherwin, ASCAP) .... 21
Puff (The Magic Dragon) (Pepamar, ASCAP) .... 28
Pushover (Chevis, BMI) .... 25
Reverend Mr. Black (Quartet-Butterfield, ASCAP) 26
Ring of Fire (Painted Desert, BMI) .... 59
Sad, Sad Girl and Boy (Curtom, BMI) .... 87
Say Wonderful Things—Carroll (Hill & Range, BMI) 99
Say Wonderful Things—Page (Hill & Range, BMI) 95
Shake a Hand (Merrimac, BMI) .... 50
Shake a Tail Feather (Vapac, BMI) .... 77
Shame, Shame, Shame (Conrad, BMI) .... 61
Shut Down (Sea of Tunes, BMI) .... 32
Six Days on the Road (Newkeys-Tune, BMI) .... 85
So Much in Love (Cameo-Parkway, BMI) .... 71
Soon (I'll Be Home Again) (BoBob, ASCAP) .... 83
Soulville (DeLarue-Nom, BMI) .... 92
Spring in Manhattan (Bregman, Vocco & Conn, ASCAP) .... 93
Still (Moss Rose, BMI) .... 8
Sting Ray (Wrist-House of Joseph, BMI) .... 53
Stranger in Your Town, A (Hazelwood-Little Darlin', BMI) .... 70
String Along (Blue Grass, BMI) .... 42
Sukiyaki (Beechwood, BMI) .... 2
Surfin' U. S. A. (Arc, BMI) .... 10
Sweet Dreams (Acuff-Rose, BMI) .... 48
Swinging on a Star (Burke-Van Heusen, ASCAP) .. 64
Take These Chains From My Heart (Milene, ASCAP) .... 19
Teenage Heaven (Jeanick, BMI) .... 60
That's How Heartaches Are Made (Sea-Lark, BMI) . 72
There Goes (My Heart Again) (Anatole, BMI) .... 67
These Arms of Mine (East-Time, BMI) .... 98
This Little Girl (Screen Gems-Columbia, BMI) .... 39
Those Lazy-Hazy-Crazy Days of Summer (Comet, ASCAP) .... 9
Tie Me Kangaroo Down, Sport (Beechwood, BMI) 88
Two Faces Have I (Painted Desert-RTD, BMI) .... 6
Two Kinds of Teardrops (Vici-McLaughlin, BMI) .. 63
What a Guy (Trinity, BMI) .... 41
Wildwood Days (Kalmann, ASCAP) .... 30
You Can't Sit Down (Conrad-Dasher, BMI) .... 5
You Know It Ain't Right (Don, BMI) .... 89
Your Old Stand By (Jobete, BMI) .... 56


## BUBBLING UNDER THE HOT 100

101. KENTUCKY ....Bob Moore, Monument [illegible]
102. TEN COMMANDMENTS OF LOVE ....James MacArthur, Scepter 1250
103. IT'S BEEN NICE (Goodnight) ....Everly Brothers, Warner Bros. 5362
104. DENISE ....Randy & the Rainbows, Rust 5059
105. GOT YOU ON MY MIND ....Cookie & His Cupcakes, Chess 1848
106. JACK THE RIPPER ....Link Wray & His Ray Men, Swan 4237
107. SURF CITY ....Jan & Dean, Liberty 55580
108. ROCKIN' CRICKETS ....Rockin' Rebels, Swan 4140
109. RIVER'S INVITATION ....Percy Mayfield, Tangerine 931
110. THE LAST MINUTE ....Jimmy McGriff, Sue 786
111. I KNOW I KNOW ....Pookie Hudson, Double L 711
112. DETROIT CITY ....Bobby Bare, RCA Victor 8183
113. TILL THEN ....Classics, Music Note 1116
114. I WILL NEVER TURN MY BACK ON YOU ....Chuck Jackson, Wand 138
115. DANGER ....Vic Dana, Dolton 73
116. LONESOME 7-7203 ....Hawkshaw Hawkins, King 5712
117. HOT CAKES ....Dave (Baby) Cortez, Chess 1850
118. BLACK CLOUD ....Chubby Checker, Parkway 873
119. CHECK YOURSELF ....Gene Chandler, Vee Jay 511
120. NOT ME ....Orlons, Cameo 257
121. BILL BAILEY, WON'T YOU PLEASE COME HOME ....Ella Fitzgerald, Verve 10288
122. MOCKINBIRD ....Inez Foxx, Cymbol 919
123. TIPS OF MY FINGERS ....Roy Clark, Capitol 4956
124. SUMMER'S COMIN' ....Kirby St. Romaine, Inette 103
125. SPRING ....Birdlegs & Pauline, Vee Jay 510
126. LITTLE BIRD ....Pete Jolly Trio, Ava 116
127. I'M WALKIN' ....Patti Page, Mercury 72123
128. MY BLOCK ....Four Pennies, Rust 5071
129. (These Are) THE YOUNG YEARS ....Floyd Cramer, RCA Victor 8171
130. KING OF THE SURF GUITARS ....Dick Dale & the Del-Tones, Capitol 4963

# Billboard HOT 100
**FOR WEEK ENDING JUNE 15, 1963**

| This Week | Wk Ago | 2 Wks Ago | 3 Wks Ago | Title — Artist, Label & Number | Weeks On Chart |
|---|---|---|---|---|---|
| 1 | 2 | 10 | 20 | SUKIYAKI — Kyu Sakamoto, Capitol 4945 | 6 |
| 2 | 1 | 1 | 9 | IT'S MY PARTY — Lesley Gore, Mercury 72119 | 6 |
| 3 | 5 | 7 | 15 | YOU CAN'T SIT DOWN — Dovells, Parkway 867 | 8 |
| 4 | 3 | 5 | 13 | DA DOO RON RON — Crystals, Philles 112 | 8 |
| 5 | 4 | 3 | 5 | I LOVE YOU BECAUSE — Al Martino, Capitol 4930 | 11 |
| 6 | 14 | 31 | 62 | BLUE ON BLUE — Bobby Vinton, Epic 9593 | 5 |
| 7 | 9 | 16 | 25 | THOSE LAZY-HAZY-CRAZY DAYS OF SUMMER — Nat King Cole, Capitol 4965 | 6 |
| 8 | 8 | 11 | 17 | STILL — Bill Anderson, Decca 31458 | 10 |
| 9 | 13 | 28 | 33 | HELLO STRANGER — Barbara Lewis, Atlantic 2184 | 7 |
| 10 | 11 | 23 | 34 | 18 YELLOW ROSES — Bobby Darin, Capitol 4970 | 6 |
| 11 | 6 | 6 | 7 | TWO FACES HAVE I — Lou Christie, Roulette 4481 | 12 |
| 12 | 7 | 2 | 1 | IF YOU WANNA BE HAPPY — Jimmy Soul, S.P.Q.R. 3305 | 12 |
| 13 | 10 | 4 | 3 | SURFIN' U.S.A. — Beach Boys, Capitol 4932 | 13 |
| 14 | 22 | 35 | 63 | BIRDLAND — Chubby Checker, Parkway 873 | 5 |
| 15 | 12 | 9 | 6 | LOSING YOU — Brenda Lee, Decca 31478 | 11 |
| 16 | 15 | 14 | 10 | ANOTHER SATURDAY NIGHT — Sam Cooke, RCA Victor 8164 | 9 |
| 17 | 36 | 66 | — | ONE FINE DAY — Chiffons, Laurie 3179 | 3 |
| 18 | 21 | 22 | 27 | PRISONER OF LOVE — James Brown & the Famous Flames, King 5739 | 9 |
| 19 | 16 | 15 | 11 | HOT PASTRAMI — Dartells, Dot 16453 | 10 |
| 20 | 24 | 32 | 43 | THE GOOD LIFE — Tony Bennett, Columbia 42779 | 6 |
| 21 | 18 | 12 | 4 | FOOLISH LITTLE GIRL — Shirelles, Scepter 1248 | 13 |
| 22 | 20 | 17 | 24 | EL WATUSI — Ray Barretto, Tico 419 | 8 |
| 23 | 19 | 13 | 8 | TAKE THESE CHAINS FROM MY HEART — Ray Charles, ABC-Paramount 10435 | 10 |
| 24 | 23 | 21 | 23 | THE LOVE OF MY MAN — Theola Kilgore, Serock 2004 | 9 |
| 25 | 30 | 39 | 49 | WILDWOOD DAYS — Bobby Rydell, Cameo 252 | 6 |
| 26 | 35 | 45 | 79 | IF MY PILLOW COULD TALK — Connie Francis, MGM 13143 | 5 |
| 27 | 17 | 8 | 2 | I WILL FOLLOW HIM — Little Peggy March, RCA Victor 8139 | 13 |
| 28 | 42 | 53 | 12 | STRING ALONG — Rick Nelson, Decca 31495 | 4 |
| 29 | 25 | 30 | 26 | PUSHOVER — Etta James, Argo 5437 | 9 |
| 30 | 32 | 33 | 38 | SHUT DOWN — Beach Boys, Capitol 4932 | 8 |
| 31 | 37 | 47 | 74 | EVERY STEP OF THE WAY — Johnny Mathis, Columbia 42799 | 4 |
| 32 | 29 | 38 | 32 | COME AND GET THESE MEMORIES — Martha & the Vandellas, Gordy 7014 | 11 |
| 33 | 45 | 55 | 69 | MY SUMMER LOVE — Ruby & the Romantics, Kapp 525 | 4 |
| 34 | 27 | 20 | 16 | PIPELINE — Chantays, Dot 16440 | 16 |
| 35 | 31 | 26 | 31 | LET'S GO STEADY AGAIN — Neil Sedaka, RCA Victor 8169 | 8 |
| 36 | 47 | 62 | 76 | POOR LITTLE RICH GIRL — Steve Lawrence, Columbia 42795 | 4 |
| 37 | 52 | 61 | 73 | PRIDE AND JOY — Marvin Gaye, Tamla 54079 | 5 |
| 38 | 34 | 27 | 19 | KILLER JOE — Rocky Fellers, Scepter 1246 | 13 |
| 39 | 54 | 68 | — | ON TOP OF SPAGHETTI — Tom Glazer & the Children's Chorus, Kapp 526 | 3 |
| 40 | 40 | 44 | 54 | THE BOUNCE — Olympics, Tri Disc 106 | 8 |
| 41 | 44 | 48 | 55 | I'M SAVING MY LOVE — Skeeter Davis, RCA Victor 8176 | 6 |
| 42 | 55 | 90 | — | FIRST QUARREL — Paul & Paula, Philips 40114 | 3 |
| 43 | 41 | 42 | 47 | WHAT A GUY — Raindrops, Jubilee 5444 | 8 |
| 44 | 48 | 54 | 56 | SWEET DREAMS (Of You) — Patsy Cline, Decca 31483 | 9 |
| 45 | 26 | 19 | 14 | REVEREND MR. BLACK — Kingston Trio, Capitol 4951 | 11 |
| 46 | 50 | 73 | 89 | SHAKE A HAND — Jackie Wilson & Linda Hopkins, Brunswick 55243 | 4 |
| 47 | 28 | 18 | 12 | PUFF (The Magic Dragon) — Peter, Paul & Mary, Warner Bros. 5348 | 14 |
| 48 | 59 | 72 | — | RING OF FIRE — Johnny Cash, Columbia 42788 | 3 |
| 49 | 49 | 52 | 65 | LITTLE LATIN LUPE LU — Righteous Brothers, Moonglow 215 | 6 |
| 50 | 81 | — | — | EASIER SAID THAN DONE — Essex, Roulette 4494 | 2 |
| 51 | 56 | 67 | 77 | YOUR OLD STAND BY — Mary Wells, Motown 1042 | 4 |
| 52 | 57 | 69 | — | OLD SMOKEY LOCOMOTION — Little Eva, Dimension 1011 | 3 |
| 53 | 66 | 82 | — | I WISH I WERE A PRINCESS — Little Peggy March, RCA Victor 8189 | 3 |
| 54 | 64 | 75 | 90 | SWINGING ON A STAR — Big Dee Irwin, Dimension 1010 | 4 |
| 55 | 71 | 86 | — | SO MUCH IN LOVE — Tymes, Parkway 781 | 3 |
| 56 | 53 | 50 | 57 | STING RAY — Routers, Warner Bros. 5349 | 8 |
| 57 | 90 | — | — | MEMPHIS — Lonnie Mack, Fraternity 906 | 2 |
| 58 | 88 | — | — | TIE ME KANGAROO DOWN, SPORT — Rolf Harris, Epic 9596 | 2 |
| 59 | 76 | — | — | FALLING — Roy Orbison, Monument 815 | 2 |
| 60 | 62 | 77 | 81 | I'M MOVIN' ON — Matt Lucas, Smash 1813 | 7 |
| 61 | 61 | 63 | 52 | SHAME, SHAME, SHAME — Jimmy Reed, Vee Jay 509 | 8 |
| 62 | 60 | 58 | 68 | TEENAGE HEAVEN — Johnny Cymbal, Kapp 524 | 6 |
| 63 | 43 | 37 | 40 | IF YOU NEED ME — Solomon Burke, Atlantic 2185 | 9 |
| 64 | 67 | 71 | 87 | THERE GOES (MY HEART AGAIN) — Fats Domino, ABC-Paramount 10444 | 5 |
| 65 | 33 | 25 | 22 | AIN'T THAT A SHAME! — 4 Seasons, Vee Jay 512 | 9 |
| 66 | 75 | 84 | — | GOODNIGHT MY LOVE — Fleetwoods, Dolton 75 | 3 |
| 67 | 74 | 83 | — | DON'T TRY TO FIGHT IT BABY — Eydie Gorme, Columbia 42790 | 3 |
| 68 | — | — | — | SURF CITY — Jan & Dean, Liberty 55580 | 1 |
| 69 | 51 | 57 | 60 | DON'T MAKE MY BABY BLUE — Frankie Laine, Columbia 42767 | 6 |
| 70 | — | — | — | HARRY THE HAIRY APE — Ray Stevens, Mercury 72125 | 1 |
| 71 | 77 | 79 | 82 | SHAKE A TAIL FEATHER — Five Du-Tones, One-der-ful 4815 | 5 |
| 72 | 100 | — | — | JUST ONE LOOK — Doris Troy, Atlantic 2188 | 2 |
| 73 | 79 | 80 | 85 | GYPSY WOMAN — Rick Nelson, Decca 31495 | 5 |
| 74 | 65 | 65 | 66 | PATTY BABY — Freddy Cannon, Swan 4139 | 7 |
| 75 | 85 | — | — | SIX DAYS ON THE ROAD — Dave Dudley, Golden Wing 3020 | 2 |
| 76 | 91 | 93 | — | (I Love You) DON'T YOU FORGET IT — Perry Como, RCA Victor 8186 | 3 |
| 77 | 80 | 81 | — | GIVE US YOUR BLESSING — Ray Peterson, Dunes 2025 | 3 |
| 78 | 96 | — | — | NOT TOO YOUNG TO GET MARRIED — Bob B. Soxx & the Blue Jeans, Philles 113 | 2 |
| 79 | 83 | 88 | 93 | SOON (I'll Be Home Again) — 4 Seasons, Vee Jay 512 | 6 |
| 80 | 58 | 51 | 53 | DO IT—RAT NOW — Bill Black's Combo, Hi 2064 | 8 |
| 81 | 69 | 74 | 86 | HOBO FLATS — Jimmy Smith, Verve 10283 | 5 |
| 82 | 82 | 89 | 92 | LONELY BOY, LONELY GUITAR — Duane Eddy, RCA Victor 8180 | 5 |
| 83 | 70 | 76 | 80 | A STRANGER IN YOUR TOWN — Shackelfords, Mercury 72112 | 6 |
| 84 | 87 | 87 | 88 | SAD, SAD GIRL AND BOY — Impressions, ABC-Paramount 10431 | 4 |
| 85 | — | — | — | COME GO WITH ME — Dion, Laurie 3171 | 1 |
| 86 | — | — | — | NOT ME — Orlons, Cameo 257 | 1 |
| 87 | — | — | — | DETROIT CITY — Bobby Bare, RCA Victor 8183 | 1 |
| 88 | 89 | 91 | — | YOU KNOW IT AIN'T RIGHT — Joe Hinton, Back Beat 537 | 3 |
| 89 | — | — | — | DENISE — Randy & the Rainbows, Rust 5059 | 1 |
| 90 | — | — | — | JACK THE RIPPER — Link Wray & His Ray Men, Swan 4137 | 1 |
| 91 | 99 | — | — | SAY WONDERFUL THINGS — Ronnie Carroll, Philips 40110 | 2 |
| 92 | 93 | — | — | SPRING IN MANHATTAN — Tony Bennett, Columbia 42779 | 2 |
| 93 | — | — | — | SUMMER'S COMIN' — Kirby St. Romain, Inette 103 | 1 |
| 94 | 95 | 98 | — | SAY WONDERFUL THINGS — Patti Page, Columbia 42791 | 3 |
| 95 | — | — | — | RAT RACE — Drifters, Atlantic 2191 | 1 |
| 96 | — | — | — | DON'T SAY GOODNIGHT AND MEAN GOODBYE — Shirelles, Scepter 1255 | 1 |
| 97 | 97 | 100 | — | I CAN'T STOP LOVING YOU — Count Basie, Reprise 20170 | 3 |
| 98 | — | — | — | BLACK CLOUD — Chubby Checker, Parkway 873 | 1 |
| 99 | — | — | — | MY TRUE CONFESSION — Brook Benton, Mercury 72135 | 1 |
| 100 | — | — | — | HOOTENANNY — Glencoves, Select 724 | 1 |

## BUBBLING UNDER THE HOT 100

101. IT'S BEEN NICE (Goodnight) — Everly Brothers, Warner Bros. 5362
102. TEN COMMANDMENTS OF LOVE — James MacArthur, Scepter 1250
103. I KNOW I KNOW — Pookie Hudson, Double L 711
104. MY BLOCK — Four Pennies, Rust 5071
105. KENTUCKY — Bob Moore, Monument 814
106. RIVER'S INVITATION — Percy Mayfield, Tangerine 931
107. DANGER — Vic Dana, Dolton 73
108. ABILENE — George Hamilton IV, RCA Victor 8181
109. I WILL NEVER TURN MY BACK ON YOU — Chuck Jackson, Wand 138
110. SPRING — Birdlegs & Pauline, Vee Jay 510
111. TILL THEN — Classics, Music Note 1116
112. FOREVER — Marvelettes, Tamla 54077
113. THESE ARMS OF MINE — Otis Redding, Volt 103
114. HOPELESS — Andy Williams, Columbia 42784
115. NEEDLES AND PINS — Jackie DeShannon, Liberty 55563
116. ROCKIN' CRICKETS — Rockin' Rebels, Swan 4140
117. BE TRUE TO YOURSELF — Bobby Vee, Liberty 55581
118. I GOT MY MOJO WORKING — Cookie & His Cupcakes, Chess 1854
119. WITHOUT LOVE (There Is Nothing) — Ray Charles, ABC-Paramount 10453
120. TIPS OF MY FINGERS — Roy Clark, Capitol 4956
121. I WILL NEVER TURN MY BACK ON YOU — Frank Sinatra, Reprise 20184
122. COME BLOW YOUR HORN — Chuck Jackson, Wand 138
123. SUMMERTIME — Chris Columbo Quintet, Strand 25056
124. GRADUATION DAY — Bobby Pickett, Garpax 44175
125. HOT CAKES — Dave (Baby) Cortez, Chess 1850
126. MOCKINGBIRD — Inez Foxx, Symbol 919
127. THE LAST MINUTE — Jimmy McGriff, Sue 786
128. WIPE OUT — Safaris, Dot 16479
129. A LETTER FROM BETTY — Bobby Vee, Liberty 55581
130. THE LEAF — Cascades, Valiant 6028
131. THE DOG — Rufus Thomas, Stax 130
132. COTTONFIELDS — Ace Cannon, Hi 2065
133. THE NINTH WAVE — Mongo Santamaria, Battle 45917
134. YEH-YEH — Mongo Santamaria, Battle 45917
135. THE PEKING THEME — Andy Williams, Columbia 42784
136. TO LOVE OR NOT TO LOVE — Barbara Lynn, Jamie 1251

# Billboard HOT 100

FOR WEEK ENDING JUNE 22 1963

★ STAR PERFORMERS—Selections registering greatest upward progress this week.

[S] Indicates that 45 r.p.m. stereo single version is available.

△ Indicates that 33⅓ r.p.m. mono single version is available.

[S△] Indicates that 33⅓ r.p.m. stereo single version is available.

| This Week | 1 Wk. Ago | 2 Wks. Ago | 3 Wks. Ago | TITLE Artist, Label & Number | Weeks On Chart |
|---|---|---|---|---|---|
| 1 (Billboard Award) | 1 | 2 | 10 | SUKIYAKI — Kyu Sakamoto, Capitol 4945 | 7 |
| 2 | 2 | 1 | 1 | IT'S MY PARTY — Lesley Gore, Mercury 72119 | 7 |
| 3 ★ | 9 | 13 | 28 | HELLO STRANGER — Barbara Lewis, Atlantic 2184 | 8 |
| 4 | 3 | 5 | 7 | YOU CAN'T SIT DOWN — Dovells, Parkway 867 | 9 |
| 5 | 6 | 14 | 31 | BLUE ON BLUE — Bobby Vinton, Epic 9593 | 6 |
| 6 | 4 | 3 | 5 | DA DOO RON RON — Crystals, Philles 112 | 9 |
| 7 | 7 | 9 | 16 | THOSE LAZY-HAZY-CRAZY DAYS OF SUMMER — Nat King Cole, Capitol 4965 | 7 |
| 8 | 8 | 8 | 11 | STILL — Bill Anderson, Decca 31458 | 11 |
| 9 | 5 | 4 | 3 | I LOVE YOU BECAUSE — Al Martino, Capitol 4930 | 12 |
| 10 ★ | 17 | 36 | 66 | ONE FINE DAY — Chiffons, Laurie 3179 | 4 |
| 11 | 10 | 11 | 23 | 18 YELLOW ROSES — Bobby Darin, Capitol 4970 | 7 |
| 12 | 14 | 22 | 35 | BIRDLAND — Chubby Checker, Parkway 873 | 6 |
| 13 | 12 | 7 | 2 | IF YOU WANNA BE HAPPY — Jimmy Soul, S.P.Q.R. 3305 | 13 |
| 14 | 11 | 6 | 6 | TWO FACES HAVE I — Lou Christie, Roulette 4481 | 13 |
| 15 ★ | 50 | 81 | — | EASIER SAID THAN DONE — Essex, Roulette 4494 | 3 |
| 16 | 13 | 10 | 4 | SURFIN' U. S. A. — Beach Boys, Capitol 4932 | 14 |
| 17 ★ | 25 | 30 | 39 | WILDWOOD DAYS — Bobby Rydell, Cameo 252 | 7 |
| 18 | 20 | 24 | 32 | THE GOOD LIFE — Tony Bennett, Columbia 42779 △ | 7 |
| 19 | 18 | 21 | 22 | PRISONER OF LOVE — James Brown & the Famous Flames, King 5739 | 10 |
| 20 ★ | 68 | — | — | SURF CITY — Jan & Dean, Liberty 55580 | 2 |
| 21 | 16 | 15 | 14 | ANOTHER SATURDAY NIGHT — Sam Cooke, RCA Victor 8164 | 10 |
| 22 ★ | 33 | 45 | 55 | MY SUMMER LOVE — Ruby & the Romantics, Kapp 525 | 6 |
| 23 ★ | 30 | 32 | 33 | SHUT DOWN — Beach Boys, Capitol 4932 | 9 |
| 24 | 26 | 35 | 45 | IF MY PILLOW COULD TALK — Connie Francis, MGM 13143 | 6 |
| 25 ★ | 57 | 90 | — | MEMPHIS — Lonnie Mack, Fraternity 906 | 3 |
| 26 | 28 | 42 | 53 | STRING ALONG — Rick Nelson, Decca 31495 | 5 |
| 27 ★ | 58 | 88 | — | TIE ME KANGAROO DOWN, SPORT — Rolf Harris, Epic 9596 | 3 |
| 28 | 24 | 23 | 21 | THE LOVE OF MY MAN — Theola Kilgore, Serock 2004 | 10 |
| 29 ★ | 39 | 54 | 68 | ON TOP OF SPAGHETTI — Tom Glazer & the Children's Chorus, Kapp 526 | 4 |
| 30 ★ | 36 | 47 | 62 | POOR LITTLE RICH GIRL — Steve Lawrence, Columbia 42795 △ | 5 |
| 31 | 31 | 37 | 47 | EVERY STEP OF THE WAY — Johnny Mathis, Columbia 42799 △ | 5 |
| 32 ★ | 42 | 55 | 90 | FIRST QUARREL — Paul & Paula, Philips 40114 | 4 |
| 33 ★ | 55 | 71 | 86 | SO MUCH IN LOVE — Tymes, Parkway 781 | 4 |
| 34 | 32 | 29 | 38 | COME AND GET THESE MEMORIES — Martha & the Vandellas, Gordy 7014 | 12 |
| 35 | 37 | 52 | 61 | PRIDE AND JOY — Marvin Gaye, Tamla 54079 | 6 |
| 36 | 15 | 12 | 9 | LOSING YOU — Brenda Lee, Decca 31478 | 12 |
| 37 ★ | 48 | 59 | 72 | RING OF FIRE — Johnny Cash, Columbia 42788 △ | 4 |
| 38 | 22 | 20 | 17 | EL WATUSI — Ray Barretto, Tico 419 | 9 |
| 39 | 19 | 16 | 15 | HOT PASTRAMI — Dartells, Dot 16453 | 11 |
| 40 ★ | 59 | 76 | — | FALLING — Roy Orbison, Monument 815 | 3 |
| 41 | 29 | 25 | 30 | PUSHOVER — Etta James, Argo 5437 | 10 |
| 42 | 46 | 50 | 73 | SHAKE A HAND — Jackie Wilson & Linda Hopkins, Brunswick 55243 | 5 |
| 43 ★ | 53 | 66 | 82 | I WISH I WERE A PRINCESS — Little Peggy March, RCA Victor 8189 | 4 |
| 44 | 21 | 18 | 12 | FOOLISH LITTLE GIRL — Shirelles, Scepter 1248 | 14 |
| 45 | 40 | 40 | 44 | THE BOUNCE — Olympics, Tri Disc 106 | 9 |
| 46 | 41 | 44 | 48 | I'M SAVING MY LOVE — Skeeter Davis, RCA Victor 8176 | 7 |
| 47 | 51 | 56 | 67 | YOUR OLD STAND BY — Mary Wells, Motown 1042 | 5 |
| 48 | 54 | 64 | 75 | SWINGING ON A STAR — Big Dee Irwin, Dimension 1010 | 5 |
| 49 | 44 | 48 | 54 | SWEET DREAMS (Of You) — Patsy Cline, Decca 31483 | 10 |
| 50 | 23 | 19 | 13 | TAKE THESE CHAINS FROM MY HEART — Ray Charles, ABC-Paramount 10435 | 11 |
| 51 ★ | 70 | — | — | HARRY THE HAIRY APE — Ray Stevens, Mercury 72125 | 2 |
| 52 | 52 | 57 | 69 | OLD SMOKEY LOCOMOTION — Little Eva, Dimension 1011 | 4 |
| 53 | 35 | 31 | 26 | LET'S GO STEADY AGAIN — Neil Sedaka, RCA Victor 8169 | 9 |
| 54 ★ | 66 | 75 | 84 | GOODNIGHT MY LOVE — Fleetwoods, Dolton 75 | 4 |
| 55 ★ | 67 | 74 | 83 | DON'T TRY TO FIGHT IT BABY — Eydie Gorme, Columbia 42790 △ | 4 |
| 56 | 60 | 62 | 77 | I'M MOVIN' ON — Matt Lucas, Smash 1813 | 8 |
| 57 | 63 | 43 | 37 | IF YOU NEED ME — Solomon Burke, Atlantic 2185 | 10 |
| 58 | 27 | 17 | 8 | I WILL FOLLOW HIM — Little Peggy March, RCA Victor 8139 | 14 |
| 59 | 64 | 67 | 71 | —THERE GOES (My Heart Again) — Fats Domino, ABC-Paramount 10444 | 6 |
| 60 | 56 | 53 | 50 | STING RAY — Routers, Warner Bros. 5349 | 9 |
| 61 | 49 | 49 | 52 | LITTLE LATIN LUPE LU — Righteous Brothers, Moonglow 215 | 7 |
| 62 ★ | — | — | — | WITHOUT LOVE (There Is Nothing) — Ray Charles, ABC-Paramount 10453 | 1 |
| 63 | 76 | 91 | 93 | (I Love You) DON'T YOU FORGET IT — Perry Como, RCA Victor 8186 | 4 |
| 64 | 75 | 85 | — | SIX DAYS ON THE ROAD — Dave Dudley, Golden Wing 3020 | 3 |
| 65 | 69 | 51 | 57 | DON'T MAKE MY BABY BLUE — Frankie Laine, Columbia 42767 △ | 7 |
| 66 | 72 | 100 | — | JUST ONE LOOK — Doris Troy, Atlantic 2188 | 3 |
| 67 ★ | 85 | — | — | COME GO WITH ME — Dion, Laurie 3171 | 2 |
| 68 | 73 | 79 | 80 | GYPSY WOMAN — Rick Nelson, Decca 31495 | 6 |
| 69 ★ | 86 | — | — | NOT ME — Orlons, Cameo 257 | 2 |
| 70 ★ | 99 | — | — | MY TRUE CONFESSION — Brook Benton, Mercury 72135 | 2 |
| 71 ★ | — | — | — | HOPELESS — Andy Williams, Columbia 42784 △ | 1 |
| 72 ★ | 87 | — | — | DETROIT CITY — Bobby Bare, RCA Victor 8183 | 2 |
| 73 | 78 | 96 | — | NOT TOO YOUNG TO GET MARRIED — Bob B. Soxx & the Blue Jeans, Philles 113 | 3 |
| 74 ★ | 96 | — | — | DON'T SAY GOODNIGHT AND MEAN GOODBYE — Shirelles, Scepter 1255 | 2 |
| 75 | 71 | 77 | 79 | SHAKE A TAIL FEATHER — Five Du-Tones, One-der-ful 4815 | 6 |
| 76 | 77 | 80 | 81 | GIVE US YOUR BLESSING — Ray Peterson, Dunes 2025 | 4 |
| 77 | 79 | 83 | 88 | SOON (I'll Be Home Again) — 4 Seasons, Vee Jay 512 | 7 |
| 78 ★ | — | — | — | TILL THEN — Classics, Music Note 1116 | 1 |
| 79 | 89 | — | — | DENISE — Randy & the Rainbows, Rust 5059 | 2 |
| 80 | 93 | — | — | SUMMER'S COMIN' — Kirby St. Romain, Inette 103 | 2 |
| 81 ★ | — | — | — | NO ONE — Ray Charles, ABC-Paramount 10453 | 1 |
| 82 ★ | — | — | — | GET HIM — Exciters, United Artists 604 | 1 |
| 83 ★ | — | — | — | BE TRUE TO YOURSELF — Bobby Vee, Liberty 55581 | 1 |
| 84 | 95 | — | — | RAT RACE — Drifters, Atlantic 2191 | 2 |
| 85 ★ | — | — | — | FINGERTIPS (Part II) — Little Stevie Wonder, Tamla 54080 | 1 |
| 86 ★ | — | — | — | WIPE OUT — Safaris, Dot 16479 | 1 |
| 87 | 97 | 97 | 100 | I CAN'T STOP LOVING YOU — Count Basie, Reprise 20170 | 4 |
| 88 | 100 | — | — | HOOTENANNY — Glencoves, Select 724 | 2 |
| 89 | 94 | 95 | 98 | SAY WONDERFUL THINGS — Patti Page, Columbia 42791 △ | 4 |
| 90 ★ | — | — | — | MOCKINGBIRD — Inez Foxx, Symbol 919 | 1 |
| 91 | 91 | 99 | — | SAY WONDERFUL THINGS — Ronnie Carroll, Philips 40110 | 3 |
| 92 | — | — | — | YEH-YEH! — Mongo Santamaria, Battle 45917 | 1 |
| 93 | — | — | — | BANZAI PIPELINE — Henry Mancini, RCA Victor 8184 | 1 |
| 94 | — | — | — | TEN COMMANDMENTS OF LOVE — James MacArthur, Scepter 1250 | 1 |
| 95 | 90 | — | — | JACK THE RIPPER — Link Wray & His Ray Men, Swan 4137 | 2 |
| 96 | — | — | — | ABILENE — George Hamilton IV, RCA Victor 8181 | 1 |
| 97 | — | — | — | MY BLOCK — Four Pennies, Rust 5071 | 1 |
| 98 | — | — | — | COTTONFIELDS — Ace Cannon, Hi 2065 | 1 |
| 99 | — | — | — | GRADUATION DAY — Bobby Pickett, Garpax 44175 | 1 |
| 100 | — | — | — | BREAKWATER — Lawrence Welk, Dot 16488 | 1 |

## HOT 100—A TO Z—(Publisher-Licensee)

Abilene (Acuff-Rose, BMI) ... 96
Another Saturday Night (Kags, BMI) ... 21
Banzai Pipeline (Southdale, ASCAP) ... 93
Be True to Yourself (U. S. Songs, ASCAP) ... 83
Birdland (Woodcrest-Ace, BMI) ... 12
Blue on Blue (Famous, ASCAP) ... 5
Bounce, The (Marc-Jean, BMI) ... 45
Breakwater (Von Tilzer, ASCAP) ... 100
Come and Get These Memories (Jobete, BMI) ... 34
Come Go With Me (Gil-Febee, BMI) ... 67
Cottonfields (Jec, BMI) ... 98
Da Doo Ron Ron (Mother Bertha-Trio, BMI) ... 6
Denise (Bright-Tunes, BMI) ... 79
Detroit City (Cedarwood, BMI) ... 72
Don't Make My Baby Blue (Screen Gems-Columbia, BMI) ... 65
Don't Say Goodnight and Mean Goodbye (Maggie, BMI) ... 74
Don't Try to Fight It Baby (Screen Gems-Columbia, BMI) ... 55
Don't You Forget It (Northridge, ASCAP) ... 63
Easier Said Than Done (Nom, BMI) ... 15
18 Yellow Roses (T. M., BMI) ... 11
El Watusi (Little Dipper, BMI) ... 38
Every Step of the Way (Pauline, ASCAP) ... 31
Falling (Acuff-Rose, BMI) ... 40
Fingertips (Part II) (Jobete, BMI) ... 85
First Quarrel (LeBill-Marbill, BMI) ... 32
Foolish Little Girl (Screen Gems-Columbia, BMI) ... 44
Get Him (Mellin, BMI) ... 82
Give Us Your Blessing (Trio, BMI) ... 76
Good Life, The (Paris, ASCAP) ... 18
Goodnight My Love (House of Fortune-Quintet, BMI) ... 54
Graduation Day (Sheldon, BMI) ... 99
Gypsy Woman (Hilliard-Doral, BMI) ... 68
Harry the Hairy Ape (Lowery, BMI) ... 51
Hello Stranger (McLaughlin, BMI) ... 3
Hootenanny (Joy, ASCAP) ... 88
Hopeless (Brenner, BMI) ... 71
Hot Pastrami (Sherlyn-Pent, BMI) ... 39
I Can't Stop Loving You (Acuff-Rose, BMI) ... 87
I Love You Because (Rose, BMI) ... 9
I Will Follow Him (Leeds, ASCAP) ... 58
I Wish I Were a Princess (Atrium, ASCAP) ... 43
I'm Movin' On (Hill & Range, BMI) ... 56
I'm Saving My Love (Samos Island, BMI) ... 46
If My Pillow Could Talk (Merna, BMI) ... 24
If You Need Me (Cotillion, BMI) ... 57
If You Wanna Be Happy (Rock Masters, BMI) ... 13
It's My Party (Arch, ASCAP) ... 2
Jack the Ripper (Andval-Florentine, BMI) ... 95
Just One Look (Premier, BMI) ... 66
Let's Go Steady Again (Screen Gems-Columbia, BMI) ... 53
Little Latin Lupe Lu (Maxwell-Conrad, BMI) ... 61
Losing You (B. N. P., ASCAP) ... 36
Love of My Man, The (Sylvia, BMI) ... 28
Memphis (Arc, BMI) ... 25
Mockingbird (Saturn, BMI) ... 90
My Block (January, BMI) ... 97
My Summer Love (Rosewood, ASCAP) ... 22
My True Confession (Lowery, BMI) ... 70
No One (Hill & Range, BMI) ... 81
Not Me (Rock Masters, BMI) ... 69
Not Too Young to Get Married (Mother Bertha-Trio, BMI) ... 73
Old Smokey Locomotion (Screen Gems-Columbia, BMI) ... 52
On Top of Spaghetti (Songs, ASCAP) ... 29
One Fine Day (Screen Gems-Columbia, BMI) ... 10
Poor Little Rich Girl (Screen Gems-Columbia, BMI) 30
Pride and Joy (Jobete, BMI) ... 35
Prisoner of Love (Mayfair-Sherwin, ASCAP) ... 19
Pushover (Chevis, BMI) ... 41
Rat Race (Trio-Cotillion, BMI) ... 84
Ring of Fire (Painted Desert, BMI) ... 37
Say Wonderful Things—Carroll (Hill & Range, BMI). 91
Say Wonderful Things—Page (Hill & Range, BMI).. 89
Shake a Hand (Merrimac, BMI) ... 42
Shake a Tail Feather (Vapac, BMI) ... 75
Shut Down (Sea of Tunes, BMI) ... 23
Six Days on the Road (Newkeys-Tune, BMI) ... 64
So Much in Love (Cameo-Parkway, BMI) ... 33
Soon (I'll Be Home Again) (BoBob, ASCAP) ... 77
Still (Moss Rose, BMI) ... 8
Sting Ray (Wrist-House of Joseph, BMI) ... 60
String Along (Blue Grass, BMI) ... 26
Sukiyaki (Beechwood, BMI) ... 1
Summer's Comin' (Tobi-Ann & Inette, BMI) ... 80
Surf City (Screen Gems-Columbia, BMI) ... 20
Surfin' U.S.A. (Arc, BMI) ... 16
Sweet Dreams (Acuff-Rose, BMI) ... 49
Swinging on a Star (Burke-Van Heusen, ASCAP) ... 48
Take These Chains From My Heart (Milene, ASCAP). 50
Ten Commandments of Love (Arc, BMI) ... 94
There Goes (My Heart Again) (Anatole, BMI) ... 59
Those Lazy-Hazy-Crazy Days of Summer (Comet, ASCAP) ... 7
Tie Me Kangaroo Down, Sport (Beechwood, BMI) . 27
Till Then (Pickwick, ASCAP) ... 78
Two Faces Have I (Painted Desert-RTD, BMI) ... 14
Wildwood Days (Kalmann, ASCAP) ... 17
Wipe Out (Miraleste-Robin Hood, BMI) ... 86
Without Love (Suffolk-P.M.P.C., BMI) ... 62
Yeh-Yeh! (Mongo, BMI) ... 92
You Can't Sit Down (Conrad-Dasher, BMI) ... 4
Your Old Stand By (Jobete, BMI) ... 47

## BUBBLING UNDER THE HOT 100

101. TIPS OF MY FINGERS ... Roy Clark, Capitol 4956
102. IT'S BEEN NICE (Goodnight) ... Everly Brothers, Warner Bros. 5362
103. BRENDA ... Cupids, KC 115
104. SUMMERTIME ... Chris Columbo Quintet, Strand 25056
105. KENTUCKY ... Bob Moore, Monument 814
106. HOBO FLATS ... Jimmy Smith, Verve 10283
107. BLACK CLOUD ... Chubby Checker, Parkway 873
108. I KNOW I KNOW ... Pookie Hudson, Double L 711
109. LONELY BOY, LONELY GUITAR ... Duane Eddy, RCA Victor 8180
110. I WILL NEVER TURN MY BACK ON YOU ... Chuck Jackson, Wand 138
111. BE CAREFUL OF STONES THAT YOU THROW ... Dion, Columbia 42810
112. COME BLOW YOUR HORN ... Frank Sinatra, Reprise 20184
113. SPRING ... Birdlegs & Pauline, Vee Jay 510
114. LIKE THE BIG GUYS DO ... Rocky Fellers, Scepter 1254
115. GOT YOU ON MY MIND ... Cookie & His Cupcakes, Chess 1848
116. THESE ARMS OF MINE ... Otis Redding, Volt 103
117. RIVER'S INVITATION ... Percy Mayfield, Tangerine 931
118. SPRING IN MANHATTAN ... Tony Bennett, Columbia 42779
119. LOVE IS A ONCE IN A LIFETIME THING .. Dick & Deedee, Warner Bros. 5364
120. A LETTER FROM BETTY ... Bobby Vee, Liberty 55581
121. NEEDLES AND PINS ... Jackie DeShannon, Liberty 55563
122. THE NINTH WAVE ... Ventures, Dolton 78
123. TAMOURE ... Bill Justis, Smash 1812
124. POOR BOY ... Jimmy Holiday, Everest 2027
125. SCARLETT O'HARA ... Lawrence Welk, Dot 16488
126. ALLENTOWN JAIL ... Lettermen, Capitol 4976
127. THE PEKING THEME ... Andy Williams, Columbia 42784
128. ALL I WANT TO DO IS RUN ... Elektras, United Artists 594
129. I'M AFRAID TO GO HOME ... Brian Hyland, ABC-Paramount 10452
130. MORE ... Steve Lawrence, Columbia 42795
131. HAPPY COWBOY ... Billy Vaughn, Dot 16477
132. HERE'S WHERE I CAME IN (Here's Where I Walk Out) ... Aretha Franklin, Columbia 42796

# Billboard HOT 100

**FOR WEEK ENDING JUNE 29, 1963**

| This Week | Wk Ago | 2 Wks Ago | Title | Artist, Label & Number | Weeks On Chart |
|---|---|---|---|---|---|
| 1 | 1 | 2 | SUKIYAKI | Kyu Sakamoto, Capitol 4945 | 8 |
| 2 | 2 | 1 | IT'S MY PARTY | Lesley Gore, Mercury 72119 | 8 |
| 3 | 3 | 9 13 | HELLO STRANGER | Barbara Lewis, Atlantic 2184 | 9 |
| 4 | 5 | 6 14 | BLUE ON BLUE | Bobby Vinton, Epic 9593 | 7 |
| 5 | 15 | 50 81 | EASIER SAID THAN DONE | Essex, Roulette 4494 | 4 |
| 6 | 7 | 7 9 | THOSE LAZY-HAZY-CRAZY DAYS OF SUMMER | Nat King Cole, Capitol 4965 | 4 |
| 7 | 10 | 17 36 | ONE FINE DAY | Chiffons, Laurie 3179 | 5 |
| 8 | 4 | 3 5 | YOU CAN'T SIT DOWN | Dovells, Parkway 867 | 10 |
| 9 | 25 | 57 90 | MEMPHIS | Lonnie Mack, Fraternity 906 | 4 |
| 10 | 20 | 68 — | SURF CITY | Jan & Dean, Liberty 55580 | 3 |
| 11 | 6 | 4 3 | DA DOO RON RON | Crystals, Philles 112 | 10 |
| 12 | 12 | 14 22 | BIRDLAND | Chubby Checker, Parkway 873 | 7 |
| 13 | 33 | 55 71 | SO MUCH IN LOVE | Tymes, Parkway 781 | 5 |
| 14 | 27 | 58 88 | TIE ME KANGAROO DOWN, SPORT | Rolf Harris, Epic 9596 | 4 |
| 15 | 8 | 8 8 | STILL | Bill Anderson, Decca 31458 | 12 |
| 16 | 11 | 10 11 | 18 YELLOW ROSES | Bobby Darin, Capitol 4970 | 8 |
| 17 | 16 | 13 10 | SURFIN' U.S.A. | Beach Boys, Capitol 4932 | 15 |
| 18 | 22 | 33 45 | MY SUMMER LOVE | Ruby & the Romantics, Kapp 525 | 7 |
| 19 | 9 | 5 4 | I LOVE YOU BECAUSE | Al Martino, Capitol 4930 | 13 |
| 20 | 29 | 39 54 | ON TOP OF SPAGHETTI | Tom Glazer & the Children's Chorus, Kapp 526 | 5 |
| 21 | 17 | 25 30 | WILDWOOD DAYS | Bobby Rydell, Cameo 252 | 8 |
| 22 | 18 | 20 24 | THE GOOD LIFE | Tony Bennett, Columbia 42779 | 8 |
| 23 | 24 | 26 35 | IF MY PILLOW COULD TALK | Connie Francis, MGM 13143 | 7 |
| 24 | 35 | 37 52 | PRIDE AND JOY | Marvin Gaye, Tamla 54079 | 7 |
| 25 | 26 | 28 42 | STRING ALONG | Rick Nelson, Decca 31495 | 6 |
| 26 | 14 | 11 6 | TWO FACES HAVE I | Lou Christie, Roulette 4481 | 14 |
| 27 | 30 | 36 47 | POOR LITTLE RICH GIRL | Steve Lawrence, Columbia 42795 | 6 |
| 28 | 32 | 42 55 | FIRST QUARREL | Paul & Paula, Philips 40114 | 5 |
| 29 | 23 | 30 32 | SHUT DOWN | Beach Boys, Capitol 4932 | 10 |
| 30 | 31 | 31 37 | EVERY STEP OF THE WAY | Johnny Mathis, Columbia 42799 | 6 |
| 31 | 34 | 32 29 | COME AND GET THESE MEMORIES | Martha & the Vandellas, Gordy 7014 | 13 |
| 32 | 51 | 70 — | HARRY THE HAIRY APE | Ray Stevens, Mercury 72125 | 3 |
| 33 | 13 | 12 7 | IF YOU WANNA BE HAPPY | Jimmy Soul, S.P.Q.R. 3305 | 14 |
| 34 | 40 | 59 76 | FALLING | Roy Orbison, Monument 815 | 4 |
| 35 | 37 | 48 59 | RING OF FIRE | Johnny Cash, Columbia 42788 | 5 |
| 36 | 43 | 53 66 | I WISH I WERE A PRINCESS | Little Peggy March, RCA Victor 8189 | 5 |
| 37 | 19 | 18 21 | PRISONER OF LOVE | James Brown & the Famous Flames, King 5739 | 11 |
| 38 | 21 | 16 15 | ANOTHER SATURDAY NIGHT | Sam Cooke, RCA Victor 8164 | 11 |
| 39 | 72 | 87 — | DETROIT CITY | Bobby Bare, RCA Victor 8183 | 3 |
| 40 | 28 | 24 23 | THE LOVE OF MY MAN | Theola Kilgore, Serock 2004 | 11 |
| 41 | 36 | 15 12 | LOSING YOU | Brenda Lee, Decca 31478 | 13 |
| 42 | 42 | 46 50 | SHAKE A HAND | Jackie Wilson & Linda Hopkins, Brunswick 55243 | 6 |
| 43 | 69 | 86 — | NOT ME | Orlons, Cameo 257 | 3 |
| 44 | 47 | 51 56 | YOUR OLD STAND BY | Mary Wells, Motown 1042 | 6 |
| 45 | 48 | 54 64 | SWINGING ON A STAR | Big Dee Irwin, Dimension 1010 | 6 |
| 46 | 63 | 76 91 | (I Love You) DON'T YOU FORGET IT | Perry Como, RCA Victor 8186 | 5 |
| 47 | 62 | — — | WITHOUT LOVE (There Is Nothing) | Ray Charles, ABC-Paramount 10453 | 2 |
| 48 | 52 | 52 57 | OLD SMOKEY LOCOMOTION | Little Eva, Dimension 1011 | 5 |
| 49 | 66 | 72 100 | JUST ONE LOOK | Doris Troy, Atlantic 2188 | 3 |
| 50 | 54 | 66 75 | GOODNIGHT MY LOVE | Fleetwoods, Dolton 75 | 4 |
| 51 | 86 | — — | WIPE OUT | Safaris, Dot 16479 | 2 |
| 52 | 74 | 96 — | DON'T SAY GOODNIGHT AND MEAN GOODBYE | Shirelles, Scepter 1255 | 3 |
| 53 | 55 | 67 74 | DON'T TRY TO FIGHT IT BABY | Eydie Gorme, Columbia 42790 | 5 |
| 54 | 71 | — — | HOPELESS | Andy Williams, Columbia 42784 | 2 |
| 55 | 67 | 85 — | COME GO WITH ME | Dion, Laurie 3171 | 3 |
| 56 | 45 | 40 40 | THE BOUNCE | Olympics, Tri Disc 106 | 10 |
| 57 | 64 | 75 85 | SIX DAYS ON THE ROAD | Dave Dudley, Golden Wing 3020 | 4 |
| 58 | 85 | — — | FINGERTIPS (Part II) | Little Stevie Wonder, Tamla 54080 | 2 |
| 59 | 70 | 99 — | MY TRUE CONFESSION | Brook Benton, Mercury 72135 | 3 |
| 60 | 81 | — — | NO ONE | Ray Charles, ABC-Paramount 10453 | 2 |
| 61 | 83 | — — | BE TRUE TO YOURSELF | Bobby Vee, Liberty 55581 | 2 |
| 62 | 75 | 71 77 | SHAKE A TAIL FEATHER | Five Du-Tones, One-derful 4815 | 7 |
| 63 | 59 | 64 67 | THERE GOES (My Heart Again) | Fats Domino, ABC-Paramount 10444 | 7 |
| 64 | 56 | 60 62 | I'M MOVIN' ON | Matt Lucas, Smash 1813 | 9 |
| 65 | 68 | 73 79 | GYPSY WOMAN | Rick Nelson, Decca 31495 | 7 |
| 66 | 60 | 56 53 | STING RAY | Routers, Warner Bros. 5349 | 10 |
| 67 | 73 | 78 96 | NOT TOO YOUNG TO GET MARRIED | Bob B. Soxx & the Blue Jeans, Philles 113 | 4 |
| 68 | 79 | 89 — | DENISE | Randy & the Rainbows, Rust 5059 | 3 |
| 69 | 57 | 63 43 | IF YOU NEED ME | Solomon Burke, Atlantic 2185 | 11 |
| 70 | 76 | 77 80 | GIVE US YOUR BLESSING | Ray Peterson, Dunes 2025 | 5 |
| 71 | 78 | — — | TILL THEN | Classics, Music Note 1116 | 2 |
| 72 | 88 | 100 — | HOOTENANNY | Glencoves, Select 724 | 3 |
| 73 | 84 | 95 — | RAT RACE | Drifters, Atlantic 2191 | 3 |
| 74 | 80 | 93 — | SUMMER'S COMIN' | Kirby St. Romain, Inette 103 | 2 |
| 75 | 97 | — — | MY BLOCK | Four Pennies, Rust 5071 | 2 |
| 76 | 82 | — — | GET HIM | Exciters, United Artists 604 | 2 |
| 77 | — | — — | TIPS OF MY FINGERS | Roy Clark, Capitol 4956 | 1 |
| 78 | — | — — | LIKE THE BIG GUYS DO | Rocky Fellers, Scepter 1254 | 1 |
| 79 | 96 | — — | ABILENE | George Hamilton IV, RCA Victor 8181 | 2 |
| 80 | 95 | 90 — | JACK THE RIPPER | Link Wray & His Ray Men, Swan 4137 | 3 |
| 81 | 89 | 94 95 | SAY WONDERFUL THINGS | Patti Page, Columbia 42791 | 5 |
| 82 | 90 | — — | MOCKINGBIRD | Inez Foxx, Symbol 919 | 2 |
| 83 | — | — — | GREEN, GREEN | New Christy Minstrels, Columbia 42805 | 1 |
| 84 | — | — — | (You're the) DEVIL IN DISGUISE | Elvis Presley, RCA Victor 8188 | 1 |
| 85 | 87 | 97 97 | I CAN'T STOP LOVING YOU | Count Basie, Reprise 20170 | 5 |
| 86 | — | — — | BLOWIN' IN THE WIND | Peter, Paul and Mary, Warner Bros. 5368 | 1 |
| 87 | — | — — | ANTONY AND CLEOPATRA THEME | Ferrante & Teicher, United Artists 607 | 1 |
| 88 | 99 | — — | GRADUATION DAY | Bobby Pickett, Garpax 44175 | 2 |
| 89 | — | — — | SCARLETT O'HARA | Lawrence Welk, Dot 16488 | 1 |
| 90 | 98 | — — | COTTONFIELDS | Ace Cannon, Hi 2065 | 2 |
| 91 | — | — — | GUILTY | Jim Reeves, RCA Victor 8193 | 1 |
| 92 | — | — — | I'M AFRAID TO GO HOME | Brian Hyland, ABC-Paramount 10452 | 1 |
| 93 | — | — — | LAND OF 1,000 DANCES | Chris Kenner, Instant 3252 | 1 |
| 94 | — | — — | A LETTER FROM BETTY | Bobby Vee, Liberty 55581 | 1 |
| 95 | — | — — | SUMMERTIME | Chris Columbo Quintet, Strand 25056 | 1 |
| 96 | — | — — | FROM ME TO YOU | Del Shannon, Big Top 3152 | 1 |
| 97 | — | — — | HELLO JIM | Paul Anka, RCA Victor 8195 | 1 |
| 98 | 91 | 91 99 | SAY WONDERFUL THINGS | Ronnie Carroll, Philips 40110 | 4 |
| 99 | — | — — | I (Who Have Nothing) | Ben E. King, Atco 6267 | 1 |
| 100 | — | — — | ROCK ME IN THE CRADLE OF LOVE | Dee Dee Sharp, Cameo 260 | 1 |

## BUBBLING UNDER THE HOT 100

101. TAMOURE — Bill Justis, Smash 1812
102. BE CAREFUL OF STONES THAT YOU THROW — Dion, Columbia 42810
103. TEN COMMANDMENTS OF LOVE — James MacArthur, Scepter 1250
104. KENTUCKY — Bob Moore, Monument 814
105. BRENDA — Cupids, KC 115
106. WHEN A BOY FALLS IN LOVE — Mel Carter, Derby 1003
107. YEH-YEH! — Mongo Santamaria, Battle 45917
108. COME BLOW YOUR HORN — Frank Sinatra, Reprise 20184
109. BANZAI PIPELINE — Henry Mancini, RCA Victor 8184
110. DAUGHTER — Blenders, Witch 114
111. WHERE CAN YOU GO (For a Broken Heart) — George Maharis, Epic 9600
112. BLACK CLOUD — Chubby Checker, Parkway 873
113. SPRING — Birdlegs & Pauline, Vee Jay 510
114. LOVE IS A ONCE IN A LIFETIME — Dick & Deedee, Warner Bros. 5364
115. THE PEKING THEME — Andy Williams, Columbia 42784
116. CHARMAINE — Four Preps, Capitol 4974
117. SPRING IN MANHATTAN — Tony Bennett, Columbia 42779
118. I KNOW I KNOW — Pookie Hudson, Double L 711
119. THE MINUTE YOU'RE GONE — Sonny James, Capitol 4969
120. LOVE ME ALL THE WAY — Kim Weston, Tamla 54076
121. LOVERS — Blendtones, Success 101
122. RIVER'S INVITATION — Percy Mayfield, Tangerine 921
123. ALLENTOWN JAIL — Lettermen, Capitol 4976
124. KING OF THE SURF GUITARS — Dick Dale & the Del-Tones, Capitol 4963
125. TEARS OF JOY — Chuck Jackson, Wand 141
126. ALL I WANT TO DO IS RUN — Elektras, United Artists 574
127. THE NINTH WAVE — Ventures, Dolton 78
128. HERE'S A HEART — Nero's Men's Quartet, Walk 01
129. SANDS OF GOLD — Webb Pierce, Decca 31490
130. A LONG VACATION — Rick Nelson, Imperial 5935

# Billboard HOT 100
**FOR WEEK ENDING JULY 6 1963**

## This Week's Chart

| # | Last Wks | Title | Artist, Label & Number | Weeks on Chart |
|---|---|---|---|---|
| 1 | 5-15-50 | EASIER SAID THAN DONE | Essex, Roulette 4494 | 5 |
| 2 | 1-1-1 | SUKIYAKI | Kyu Sakamoto, Capitol 4945 | 9 |
| 3 | 4-5-6 | BLUE ON BLUE | Bobby Vinton, Epic 9593 | 8 |
| 4 | 3-3-9 | HELLO STRANGER | Barbara Lewis, Atlantic 2184 | 10 |
| 5 | 2-2-2 | IT'S MY PARTY | Lesley Gore, Mercury 72119 | 9 |
| 6 | 7-10-17 | ONE FINE DAY | Chiffons, Laurie 3179 | 7 |
| 7 | 10-20-68 | SURF CITY | Jan & Dean, Liberty 55580 | 4 |
| 8 | 9-25-57 | MEMPHIS | Lonnie Mack, Fraternity 906 | 5 |
| 9 | 13-33-35 | SO MUCH IN LOVE | Tymes, Parkway 781 | 6 |
| 10 | 14-27-58 | TIE ME KANGAROO DOWN, SPORT | Rolf Harris, Epic 9596 | 5 |
| 11 | 8-4-3 | YOU CAN'T SIT DOWN | Dovells, Parkway 867 | 11 |
| 12 | 6-7-7 | THOSE LAZY-HAZY-CRAZY DAYS OF SUMMER | Nat King Cole, Capitol 4965 | 9 |
| 13 | 11-6-4 | DA DOO RON RON | Crystals, Philles 112 | 11 |
| 14 | 20-29-39 | ON TOP OF SPAGHETTI | Tom Glazer & the Children's Chorus, Kapp 526 | 6 |
| 15 | 24-35-37 | PRIDE AND JOY | Marvin Gaye, Tamla 54079 | 8 |
| 16 | 18-22-23 | MY SUMMER LOVE | Ruby & the Romantics, Kapp 525 | 8 |
| 17 | 51-86-— | WIPE OUT | Safaris, Dot 16479 | 3 |
| 18 | 58-85-— | FINGERTIPS (Part II) | Little Stevie Wonder, Tamla 54080 | 3 |
| 19 | 15-8-8 | STILL | Bill Anderson, Decca 31458 | 13 |
| 20 | 43-69-86 | NOT ME | Orlons, Cameo 257 | 4 |
| 21 | 32-51-70 | HARRY THE HAIRY APE | Ray Stevens, Mercury 72125 | 4 |
| 22 | 12-12-14 | BIRDLAND | Chubby Checker, Parkway 873 | 8 |
| 23 | 34-40-59 | FALLING | Roy Orbison, Monument 815 | 5 |
| 24 | 35-37-48 | RING OF FIRE | Johnny Cash, Columbia 42788 | 6 |
| 25 | 25-26-28 | STRING ALONG | Rick Nelson, Decca 31495 | 7 |
| 26 | 16-11-10 | 18 YELLOW ROSES | Bobby Darin, Capitol 4970 | 9 |
| 27 | 28-32-42 | FIRST QUARREL | Paul & Paula, Philips 40114 | 6 |
| 28 | 49-66-72 | JUST ONE LOOK | Doris Troy, Atlantic 2188 | 5 |
| 29 | 31-34-32 | COME AND GET THESE MEMORIES | Martha & the Vandellas, Gordy 7014 | 14 |
| 30 | 19-9-5 | I LOVE YOU BECAUSE | Al Martino, Capitol 4930 | 14 |
| 31 | 29-23-30 | SHUT DOWN | Beach Boys, Capitol 4932 | 11 |
| 32 | 39-72-87 | DETROIT CITY | Bobby Bare, RCA Victor 8183 | 4 |
| 33 | 36-43-53 | I WISH I WERE A PRINCESS | Little Peggy March, RCA Victor 8189 | 6 |
| 34 | 23-24-26 | IF MY PILLOW COULD TALK | Connie Francis, MGM 13143 | 8 |
| 35 | 60-81-— | NO ONE | Ray Charles, ABC-Paramount 10453 | 3 |
| 36 | 17-16-13 | SURFIN' U.S.A. | Beach Boys, Capitol 4932 | 16 |
| 37 | 47-62-— | WITHOUT LOVE (There Is Nothing) | Ray Charles, ABC-Paramount 10453 | 3 |
| 38 | 54-71-— | HOPELESS | Andy Williams, Columbia 42784 | 3 |
| 39 | 22-18-20 | THE GOOD LIFE | Tony Bennett, Columbia 42779 | 9 |
| 40 | 44-47-51 | YOUR OLD STAND BY | Mary Wells, Motown 1042 | 7 |
| 41 | 21-17-25 | WILDWOOD DAYS | Bobby Rydell, Cameo 252 | 9 |
| 42 | 59-70-99 | MY TRUE CONFESSION | Brook Benton, Mercury 72135 | 4 |
| 43 | 27-30-36 | POOR LITTLE RICH GIRL | Steve Lawrence, Columbia 42795 | 7 |
| 44 | 45-48-54 | SWINGING ON A STAR | Big Dee Irwin, Dimension 1010 | 7 |
| 45 | 46-63-76 | (I Love You) DON'T YOU FORGET IT | Perry Como, RCA Victor 8186 | 6 |
| 46 | 52-74-96 | DON'T SAY GOODNIGHT AND MEAN GOODBYE | Shirelles, Scepter 1255 | 4 |
| 47 | 30-31-31 | EVERY STEP OF THE WAY | Johnny Mathis, Columbia 42799 | 7 |
| 48 | 50-54-66 | GOODNIGHT MY LOVE | Fleetwoods, Dolton 75 | 6 |
| 49 | 84-—-— | (You're the) DEVIL IN DISGUISE | Elvis Presley, RCA Victor 8188 | 2 |
| 50 | 26-14-11 | TWO FACES HAVE I | Lou Christie, Roulette 4481 | 15 |
| 51 | 62-75-71 | SHAKE A TAIL FEATHER | Five Du-Tones, One-der-ful 4815 | 8 |
| 52 | 55-67-85 | COME GO WITH ME | Dion, Laurie 3171 | 4 |
| 53 | 61-83-— | BE TRUE TO YOURSELF | Bobby Vee, Liberty 55581 | 3 |
| 54 | 57-64-75 | SIX DAYS ON THE ROAD | Dave Dudley, Golden Wing 3020 | 5 |
| 55 | 68-79-89 | DENISE | Randy & the Rainbows, Rust 5059 | 4 |
| 56 | 79-96-— | ABILENE | George Hamilton IV, RCA Victor 8181 | 3 |
| 57 | 42-42-46 | SHAKE A HAND | Jackie Wilson & Linda Hopkins, Brunswick 55243 | 7 |
| 58 | 48-52-52 | OLD SMOKEY LOCOMOTION | Little Eva, Dimension 1011 | 6 |
| 59 | 40-28-24 | THE LOVE OF MY MAN | Theola Kilgore, Serock 2004 | 12 |
| 60 | 74-80-93 | SUMMER'S COMIN' | Kirby St. Romain, Inette 103 | 4 |
| 61 | 72-88-100 | HOOTENANNY | Glencoves, Select 724 | 4 |
| 62 | 65-68-73 | GYPSY WOMAN | Rick Nelson, Decca 31495 | 8 |
| 63 | 78-—-— | LIKE THE BIG GUYS DO | Rocky Fellers, Scepter 1254 | 2 |
| 64 | 86-—-— | BLOWIN' IN THE WIND | Peter, Paul & Mary, Warner Bros. 6358 | 2 |
| 65 | 71-78-— | TILL THEN | Classics, Music Note 1116 | 3 |
| 66 | 77-—-— | TIPS OF MY FINGERS | Roy Clark, Capitol 4956 | 2 |
| 67 | 67-73-78 | NOT TOO YOUNG TO GET MARRIED | Bob B. Soxx & the Blue Jeans, Philles 113 | 5 |
| 68 | 53-55-67 | DON'T TRY TO FIGHT IT BABY | Eydie Gorme, Columbia 42790 | 6 |
| 69 | 80-95-90 | JACK THE RIPPER | Link Wray & His Ray Men, Swan 4137 | 4 |
| 70 | 99-—-— | I (Who Have Nothing) | Ben E. King, Atco 6267 | 2 |
| 71 | 73-84-95 | RAT RACE | Drifters, Atlantic 2191 | 4 |
| 72 | 83-—-— | GREEN, GREEN | New Christy Minstrels, Columbia 42805 | 2 |
| 73 | 75-97-— | MY BLOCK | Four Pennies, Rust 5071 | 3 |
| 74 | 100-—-— | ROCK ME IN THE CRADLE OF LOVE | Dee Dee Sharp, Cameo 260 | 2 |
| 75 | —-—-— | BE CAREFUL OF STONES THAT YOU THROW | Dion, Columbia 42810 | 1 |
| 76 | 82-90-— | MOCKINGBIRD | Inez Foxx, Symbol 919 | 3 |
| 77 | 85-87-97 | I CAN'T STOP LOVING YOU | Count Basie, Reprise 20170 | 6 |
| 78 | —-—-— | CANDY GIRL | 4 Seasons, Vee Jay 539 | 1 |
| 79 | 70-76-77 | GIVE US YOUR BLESSING | Ray Peterson, Dunes 2025 | 6 |
| 80 | —-—-— | JUDY'S TURN TO CRY | Lesley Gore, Mercury 72143 | 1 |
| 81 | —-—-— | WILL POWER | Cookies, Dimension 1012 | 1 |
| 82 | —-—-— | BRENDA | Cupids, KC 115 | 1 |
| 83 | 90-98-— | COTTONFIELDS | Ace Cannon, Hi 2065 | 3 |
| 84 | —-—-— | WHEN A BOY FALLS IN LOVE | Mel Carter, Derby 1003 | 1 |
| 85 | —-—-— | MY WHOLE WORLD IS FALLING APART | Brenda Lee, Decca 31510 | 1 |
| 86 | 76-82-— | GET HIM | Exciters, United Artists 604 | 3 |
| 87 | 96-—-— | FROM ME TO YOU | Del Shannon, Big Top 3152 | 2 |
| 88 | —-—-— | DAUGHTER | Blenders, Witch 114 | 1 |
| 89 | 93-—-— | LAND OF 1,000 DANCES | Chris Kenner, Instant 3252 | 2 |
| 90 | —-—-— | MORE | Kai Winding, Verve 10295 | 1 |
| 91 | 92-—-— | I'M AFRAID TO GO HOME | Brian Hyland, ABC-Paramount 10452 | 2 |
| 92 | —-—-— | DANCIN' HOLIDAY | Olympics, Tri Disc 107 | 1 |
| 93 | 87-—-— | ANTONY AND CLEOPATRA THEME | Ferrante & Teicher, United Artists 607 | 2 |
| 94 | —-—-— | SPRING | Birdlegs & Pauline, Vee Jay 510 | 1 |
| 95 | 81-89-94 | SAY WONDERFUL THINGS | Patti Page, Columbia 42791 | 6 |
| 96 | 89-—-— | SCARLETT O'HARA | Lawrence Welk, Dot 16488 | 2 |
| 97 | —-—-— | I WILL LOVE YOU | Richard Chamberlain, MGM 13148 | 1 |
| 98 | —-—-— | LOVE ME ALL THE WAY | Kim Weston, Tamla 54076 | 1 |
| 99 | —-—-— | TRUE LOVE NEVER RUNS SMOOTH | Gene Pitney, Musicor 1032 | 1 |
| 100 | —-—-— | TEARS OF JOY | Chuck Jackson, Wand 138 | 1 |

## BUBBLING UNDER THE HOT 100

- 101. I KNOW I KNOW — Pookie Hudson, Double L 711
- 102. WHERE CAN YOU GO (For a Broken Heart) — George Maharis, Epic 9600
- 103. LOVE IS A ONCE IN A LIFETIME THING — Dick & Deedee, Warner Bros. 5364
- 104. SAY WONDERFUL THINGS — Ronnie Carroll, Philips 40110
- 105. TEN COMMANDMENTS OF LOVE — James MacArthur, Scepter 1250
- 106. BANZAI PIPELINE — Henry Mancini, RCA Victor 8184
- 107. GUILTY — Jim Reeves, RCA Victor 8193
- 108. KENTUCKY — Bob Moore, Monument 814
- 109. DANKE SCHOEN — Wayne Newton, Capitol 4989
- 110. HELLO JIM — Paul Anka, RCA Victor 8195
- 111. A LETTER FROM BETTY — Bobby Vee, Liberty 55581
- 112. GRADUATION DAY — Bobby Pickett & Johnny Stiles, Cameo 253
- 113. CROSSROADS — Luther Randolph & Johnny Stiles, Cameo 253
- 114. THE MINUTE YOU'RE GONE — Sonny James, Capitol 4969
- 115. I WONDER — Brenda Lee, Decca 31510
- 116. MARLENA — 4 Seasons, Vee Jay 539
- 117. SUMMERTIME — Chris Columbo Quintet, Strand 25056
- 118. SANDS OF GOLD — Webb Pierce, Decca 31488
- 119. LOVERS — Blendtones, Success 101
- 120. RIVER'S INVITATION — Percy Mayfield, Tangerine 931
- 121. HOW MANY TEARS — Lou Christie, Roulette 4504
- 122. GROOVY BABY — Billy Abbott, Parkway 874
- 123. EYES — Earls, Old Town 1141
- 124. COME BLOW YOUR HORN — Frank Sinatra, Reprise 20184
- 125. THE BOSS — Burl Ives, Decca 31504
- 126. THE MONKEY TIME — Major Lance, Okeh 7175
- 127. DANCE DANCE DANCE — Joey Dee, Roulette 4503
- 128. SURFIN' HOOTENANNY — Al Casey, Stacy 962
- 129. LONG VACATION — Rick Nelson, Imperial 5765
- 130. SCARLETT O'HARA — Bobby Gregg, Epic 9601
- 131. SAY IT ISN'T SO — Aretha Franklin, Columbia 42776
- 132. BAJA — Astronauts, RCA Victor 8194

# Billboard HOT 100

FOR WEEK ENDING JULY 13, 1963

| This Week | Wk Ago | 2 Wks Ago | 3 Wks Ago | TITLE — Artist, Label & Number | Weeks On Chart |
|---|---|---|---|---|---|
| 1 | 1 | 5 | 15 | EASIER SAID THAN DONE — Essex, Roulette 4494 | 6 |
| 2 | 7 | 10 | 20 | SURF CITY — Jan & Dean, Liberty 55580 | 5 |
| 3 | 10 | 14 | 27 | TIE ME KANGAROO DOWN, SPORT — Rolf Harris, Epic 9596 | 6 |
| 4 | 9 | 13 | 33 | SO MUCH IN LOVE — Tymes, Parkway 781 | 7 |
| 5 | 6 | 7 | 10 | ONE FINE DAY — Chiffons, Laurie 3179 | 7 |
| 6 | 2 | 1 | 1 | SUKIYAKI — Kyu Sakamoto, Capitol 4945 | 10 |
| 7 | 8 | 9 | 25 | MEMPHIS — Lonnie Mack, Fraternity 906 | 6 |
| 8 | 3 | 4 | 5 | BLUE ON BLUE — Bobby Vinton, Epic 9593 | 9 |
| 9 | 4 | 3 | 3 | HELLO STRANGER — Barbara Lewis, Atlantic 2184 | 11 |
| 10 | 17 | 51 | 86 | WIPE OUT — Surfaris, Dot 16479 | 4 |
| 11 | 18 | 58 | 85 | FINGERTIPS (Part II) — Little Stevie Wonder, Tamla 54080 | 4 |
| 12 | 5 | 2 | 2 | IT'S MY PARTY — Lesley Gore, Mercury 72119 | 10 |
| 13 | 15 | 24 | 35 | PRIDE AND JOY — Marvin Gaye, Tamla 54079 | 9 |
| 14 | 14 | 20 | 29 | ON TOP OF SPAGHETTI — Tom Glazer & the Children's Chorus, Kapp 526 | 7 |
| 15 | 20 | 43 | 69 | NOT ME — Orlons, Cameo 257 | 5 |
| 16 | 49 | 84 | — | (You're the) DEVIL IN DISGUISE — Elvis Presley, RCA Victor 8188 | 3 |
| 17 | 21 | 32 | 51 | HARRY THE HAIRY APE — Ray Stevens, Mercury 72125 | 5 |
| 18 | 12 | 6 | 7 | THOSE LAZY-HAZY-CRAZY DAYS OF SUMMER — Nat King Cole, Capitol 4965 | 10 |
| 19 | 11 | 8 | 4 | YOU CAN'T SIT DOWN — Dovells, Parkway 867 | 12 |
| 20 | 28 | 49 | 66 | JUST ONE LOOK — Doris Troy, Atlantic 2188 | 6 |
| 21 | 16 | 18 | 22 | MY SUMMER LOVE — Ruby & the Romantics, Kapp 525 | 9 |
| 22 | 23 | 34 | 40 | FALLING — Roy Orbison, Monument 815 | 6 |
| 23 | 24 | 35 | 37 | RING OF FIRE — Johnny Cash, Columbia 42788 | 7 |
| 24 | 35 | 60 | 81 | NO ONE — Ray Charles, ABC-Paramount 10453 | 4 |
| 25 | 13 | 11 | 6 | DA DOO RON RON — Crystals, Philles 112 | 12 |
| 26 | 25 | 25 | 26 | STRING ALONG — Rick Nelson, Decca 31495 | 8 |
| 27 | 32 | 39 | 72 | DETROIT CITY — Bobby Bare, RCA Victor 8183 | 7 |
| 28 | 38 | 54 | 71 | HOPELESS — Andy Williams, Columbia 42784 | 4 |
| 29 | 19 | 15 | 8 | STILL — Bill Anderson, Decca 31458 | 14 |
| 30 | 27 | 28 | 32 | FIRST QUARREL — Paul & Paula, Philips 40114 | 7 |
| 31 | 42 | 59 | 70 | MY TRUE CONFESSION — Brook Benton, Mercury 72135 | 5 |
| 32 | 33 | 36 | 43 | I WISH I WERE A PRINCESS — Little Peggy March, RCA Victor 8189 | 7 |
| 33 | 31 | 29 | 23 | SHUT DOWN — Beach Boys, Capitol 4932 | 12 |
| 34 | 64 | 86 | — | BLOWIN' IN THE WIND — Peter, Paul & Mary, Warner Bros. 5368 | 3 |
| 35 | 37 | 47 | 62 | WITHOUT LOVE (There Is Nothing) — Ray Charles, ABC-Paramount 10453 | 4 |
| 36 | 46 | 52 | 74 | DON'T SAY GOODNIGHT AND MEAN GOODBYE — Shirelles, Scepter 1255 | 5 |
| 37 | 30 | 19 | 9 | I LOVE YOU BECAUSE — Al Martino, Capitol 4930 | 15 |
| 38 | 44 | 45 | 48 | SWINGING ON A STAR — Big Dee Irwin, Dimension 1010 | 8 |
| 39 | 22 | 12 | 12 | BIRDLAND — Chubby Checker, Parkway 873 | 9 |
| 40 | 48 | 50 | 54 | GOODNIGHT MY LOVE — Fleetwoods, Dolton 75 | 5 |
| 41 | 45 | 46 | 63 | (I Love You) DON'T YOU FORGET IT — Perry Como, RCA Victor 8186 | 7 |
| 42 | 29 | 31 | 34 | COME AND GET THESE MEMORIES — Martha & the Vandellas, Gordy 7014 | 15 |
| 43 | 53 | 61 | 83 | BE TRUE TO YOURSELF — Bobby Vee, Liberty 55581 | 4 |
| 44 | 54 | 57 | 64 | SIX DAYS ON THE ROAD — Dave Dudley, Golden Wing 3020 | 6 |
| 45 | 36 | 17 | 16 | SURFIN' U.S.A. — Beach Boys, Capitol 4932 | 17 |
| 46 | 55 | 68 | 79 | DENISE — Randy & the Rainbows, Rust 5059 | 5 |
| 47 | 61 | 72 | 88 | HOOTENANNY — Glencoves, Select 724 | 5 |
| 48 | 52 | 55 | 67 | COME GO WITH ME — Dion, Laurie 3171 | 5 |
| 49 | 65 | 71 | 78 | TILL THEN — Classics, Music Note 1116 | 4 |
| 50 | 60 | 74 | 80 | SUMMER'S COMIN' — Kirby St. Romain, Inette 103 | 5 |
| 51 | 56 | 79 | 96 | ABILENE — George Hamilton IV, RCA Victor 8181 | 4 |
| 52 | 80 | — | — | JUDY'S TURN TO CRY — Lesley Gore, Mercury 72143 | 2 |
| 53 | 39 | 22 | 18 | THE GOOD LIFE — Tony Bennett, Columbia 42779 | 10 |
| 54 | 78 | — | — | CANDY GIRL — 4 Seasons, Vee Jay 539 | 2 |
| 55 | 63 | 78 | — | LIKE THE BIG GUYS DO — Rocky Fellers, Scepter 1254 | 3 |
| 56 | 40 | 44 | 47 | YOUR OLD STAND BY — Mary Wells, Motown 1042 | 8 |
| 57 | 51 | 62 | 75 | SHAKE A TAIL FEATHER — Five Du-Tones, One-Derful 4815 | 9 |
| 58 | 75 | — | — | BE CAREFUL OF STONES THAT YOU THROW — Dion, Columbia 42810 | 2 |
| 59 | 74 | 100 | — | ROCK ME IN THE CRADLE OF LOVE — Dee Dee Sharp, Cameo 260 | 3 |
| 60 | 72 | 83 | — | GREEN, GREEN — New Christy Minstrels, Columbia 42805 | 3 |
| 61 | 26 | 16 | 11 | 18 YELLOW ROSES — Bobby Darin, Capitol 4970 | 10 |
| 62 | 43 | 27 | 30 | POOR LITTLE RICH GIRL — Steve Lawrence, Columbia 42795 | 8 |
| 63 | 67 | 67 | 73 | NOT TOO YOUNG TO GET MARRIED — Bob B. Soxx & the Blue Jeans, Philles 113 | 6 |
| 64 | 66 | 77 | — | TIPS OF MY FINGERS — Roy Clark, Capitol 4956 | 3 |
| 65 | 68 | 53 | 55 | DON'T TRY TO FIGHT IT BABY — Eydie Gorme, Columbia 42790 | 7 |
| 66 | 70 | 99 | — | I (Who Have Nothing) — Ben E. King, Atco 6267 | 3 |
| 67 | 73 | 75 | 97 | MY BLOCK — Four Pennies, Rust 5071 | 4 |
| 68 | 62 | 65 | 68 | GYPSY WOMAN — Rick Nelson, Decca 31495 | 9 |
| 69 | 34 | 23 | 24 | IF MY PILLOW COULD TALK — Connie Francis, MGM 13143 | 9 |
| 70 | — | — | — | I WONDER — Brenda Lee, Decca 31510 | 1 |
| 71 | 69 | 80 | 95 | JACK THE RIPPER — Link Wray & His Ray Men, Swan 4137 | 5 |
| 72 | 76 | 82 | 90 | MOCKINGBIRD — Inez Foxx, Symbol 919 | 4 |
| 73 | 90 | — | — | MORE — Kai Winding, Verve 10295 | 2 |
| 74 | 85 | — | — | MY WHOLE WORLD IS FALLING DOWN — Brenda Lee, Decca 31510 | 2 |
| 75 | — | — | — | DANKE SCHOEN — Wayne Newton, Capitol 4989 | 1 |
| 76 | 82 | — | — | BRENDA — Cupids, KC 115 | 2 |
| 77 | — | — | — | MARLENA — 4 Seasons, Vee Jay 539 | 1 |
| 78 | 83 | 90 | 98 | COTTONFIELDS — Ace Cannon, Hi 2065 | 4 |
| 79 | 84 | — | — | WHEN A BOY FALLS IN LOVE — Mel Carter, Derby 1003 | 2 |
| 80 | 81 | — | — | WILL POWER — Cookies, Dimension 1012 | 2 |
| 81 | — | — | — | SURF PARTY — Chubby Checker, Parkway 879 | 1 |
| 82 | 87 | 96 | — | FROM ME TO YOU — Del Shannon, Big Top 3152 | 3 |
| 83 | — | — | — | SHAKE, SHAKE, SHAKE — Jackie Wilson, Brunswick 55246 | 1 |
| 84 | 71 | 73 | 84 | RAT RACE — Drifters, Atlantic 2191 | 5 |
| 85 | 100 | — | — | TEARS OF JOY — Chuck Jackson, Wand 138 | 2 |
| 86 | 88 | — | — | DAUGHTER — Blenders, Witch 114 | 2 |
| 87 | 91 | 92 | — | I'M AFRAID TO GO HOME — Brian Hyland, ABC-Paramount 10452 | 3 |
| 88 | 89 | 93 | — | LAND OF 1,000 DANCES — Chris Kenner, Instant 3252 | 3 |
| 89 | 93 | 87 | — | ANTONY AND CLEOPATRA THEME — Ferrante & Teicher, United Artists 607 | 3 |
| 90 | — | — | — | THE MONKEY TIME — Major Lance, Okeh 7175 | 1 |
| 91 | 92 | — | — | DANCIN' HOLIDAY — Olympics, Tri Disc 107 | 2 |
| 92 | 99 | — | — | TRUE LOVE NEVER RUNS SMOOTH — Gene Pitney, Musicor 1032 | 2 |
| 93 | 97 | — | — | I WILL LOVE YOU — Richard Chamberlain, MGM 13148 | 2 |
| 94 | 94 | — | — | SPRING — Birdlegs & Pauline, Vee Jay 510 | 2 |
| 95 | 95 | 81 | 89 | SAY WONDERFUL THINGS — Patti Page, Columbia 42791 | 7 |
| 96 | 98 | — | — | LOVE ME ALL THE WAY — Kim Weston, Tamla 54076 | 2 |
| 97 | — | — | — | SURFIN' HOOTENANNY — Al Casey, Stacy 962 | 1 |
| 98 | 77 | 85 | 87 | I CAN'T STOP LOVING YOU — Count Basie, Reprise 20170 | 7 |
| 99 | — | — | — | GUILTY — Jim Reeves, RCA Victor 8193 | 1 |
| 100 | — | — | — | TEN COMMANDMENTS OF LOVE — James MacArthur, Scepter 1250 | 1 |

## BUBBLING UNDER THE HOT 100

101. BREAKWATER — Lawrence Welk, Dot 16488
102. A LETTER FROM BETTY — Bobby Vee, Liberty 55581
103. LOVE IS A ONCE IN A LIFETIME THING — Dick & Deedee, Warner Bros. 5364
104. KENTUCKY — Bob Moore, Monument 814
105. HELLO JIM — Paul Anka, RCA Victor 8195
106. IF YOU DON'T COME BACK — Drifters, Atlantic 2191
107. LEAVE ME ALONE — Baby Washington, Sue 790
108. HOW MANY TEARS — Lou Christie, Roulette 4504
109. THE MINUTE YOU'RE GONE — Sonny James, Capitol 4969
110. CAN'T NOBODY LOVE YOU — Solomon Burke, Atlantic 2196
111. SUMMERTIME — Chris Columbo Quintet, Strand 25056
112. DANCE DANCE DANCE — Joey Dee, Roulette 4503
113. CROSSROADS — Luther Randolph & Johnny Stiles, Cameo 253
114. BANZAI PIPELINE — Henry Mancini, RCA Victor 8184
115. TWIST IT UP — Chubby Checker, Parkway 879
116. MAKE THE WORLD GO AWAY — Timi Yuro, Liberty 55587
117. SCARLETT O'HARA — Lawrence Welk, Dot 16488
118. LOVERS — Blenders, Success 101
119. GROOVY BABY — Billy Abbott, Parkway 874
120. SCARLETT O'HARA — Bobby Gregg, Epic 9601
121. RIVER'S INVITATION — Percy Mayfield, Tangerine 931
122. I'M THE BOSS — Burl Ives, Decca 31504
123. A LONG VACATION — Rick Nelson, Imperial 5958
124. AIN'T IT FUNNY WHAT A FOOL WILL DO — George Jones, United Artists 578
125. BAJA — Astronauts, RCA Victor 8194
126. I WILL NEVER TURN MY BACK ON YOU — Chuck Jackson, Wand 138
127. GRADUATION DAY — Bobby Pickett, Garpax 44175

# Billboard HOT 100

**FOR WEEK ENDING JULY 20, 1963**

★ STAR PERFORMERS—Selections registering greatest upward progress this week.
Ⓢ Indicates that 45 r.p.m. stereo single version is available.
△ Indicates that 33⅓ r.p.m. mono single version is available.
Ⓢ Indicates that 33⅓ r.p.m. stereo single version is available.

| This Week | Wk. 1 Ago | Wk. 2 Ago | Wk. 3 Ago | TITLE, Artist, Label & Number | Weeks On Chart |
|---|---|---|---|---|---|
| 1 | 2 | 7 | 10 | SURF CITY — Jan & Dean, Liberty 55580 | 6 |
| 2 | 1 | 1 | 5 | EASIER SAID THAN DONE — Essex, Roulette 4494 | 7 |
| 3 | 4 | 9 | 13 | SO MUCH IN LOVE — Tymes, Parkway 781 | 8 |
| 4 | 3 | 10 | 14 | TIE ME KANGAROO DOWN, SPORT — Rolf Harris, Epic 9596 | 7 |
| 5 | 7 | 8 | 9 | MEMPHIS — Lonnie Mack, Fraternity 906 | 7 |
| ★6 | 11 | 18 | 58 | FINGERTIPS (Part II) — Little Stevie Wonder, Tamla 54080 | 5 |
| ★7 | 10 | 17 | 51 | WIPE OUT — Surfaris, Dot 16479 | 5 |
| 8 | 6 | 2 | 1 | SUKIYAKI — Kyu Sakamoto, Capitol 4945 | 11 |
| ★9 | 16 | 49 | 84 | (You're the) DEVIL IN DISGUISE — Elvis Presley, RCA Victor 8188 | 4 |
| 10 | 13 | 15 | 24 | PRIDE AND JOY — Marvin Gaye, Tamla 54079 | 10 |
| 11 | 8 | 3 | 4 | BLUE ON BLUE — Bobby Vinton, Epic 9593 | 10 |
| 12 | 5 | 6 | 7 | ONE FINE DAY — Chiffons, Laurie 3179 | 8 |
| 13 | 15 | 20 | 43 | NOT ME — Orlons, Cameo 257 | 6 |
| ★14 | 34 | 64 | 86 | BLOWIN' IN THE WIND — Peter, Paul & Mary, Warner Bros. 5368 | 4 |
| ★15 | 20 | 28 | 49 | JUST ONE LOOK — Doris Troy, Atlantic 2188 | 7 |
| 16 | 9 | 4 | 3 | HELLO STRANGER — Barbara Lewis, Atlantic 2184 | 12 |
| 17 | 17 | 21 | 32 | HARRY THE HAIRY APE — Ray Stevens, Mercury 72125 | 6 |
| ★18 | 28 | 38 | 54 | HOPELESS — Andy Williams, Columbia 42784 | 5 |
| 19 | 12 | 5 | 2 | IT'S MY PARTY — Lesley Gore, Mercury 72119 | 11 |
| ★20 | 23 | 24 | 35 | RING OF FIRE — Johnny Cash, Columbia 42788 | 8 |
| 21 | 24 | 35 | 60 | NO ONE — Ray Charles, ABC-Paramount 10453 | 5 |
| 22 | 14 | 14 | 20 | ON TOP OF SPAGHETTI — Tom Glazer & the Children's Chorus, Kapp 526 | 8 |
| ★23 | 52 | 80 | — | JUDY'S TURN TO CRY — Lesley Gore, Mercury 72143 | 3 |
| 24 | 27 | 32 | 39 | DETROIT CITY — Bobby Bare, RCA Victor 8183 | 6 |
| 25 | 31 | 42 | 59 | MY TRUE CONFESSION — Brook Benton, Mercury 72135 | 6 |
| 26 | 22 | 23 | 34 | FALLING — Roy Orbison, Monument 815 | 7 |
| 27 | 19 | 11 | 8 | YOU CAN'T SIT DOWN — Dovells, Parkway 867 | 13 |
| 28 | 21 | 16 | 18 | MY SUMMER LOVE — Ruby & the Romantics, Kapp 525 | 10 |
| 29 | 35 | 37 | 47 | WITHOUT LOVE (There Is Nothing) — Ray Charles, ABC-Paramount 10453 | 5 |
| ★30 | 54 | 78 | — | CANDY GIRL — 4 Seasons, Vee Jay 539 | 3 |
| 31 | 36 | 46 | 52 | DON'T SAY GOODNIGHT AND MEAN GOODBYE — Shirelles, Scepter 1255 | 6 |
| 32 | 40 | 48 | 50 | GOODNIGHT MY LOVE — Fleetwoods, Dolton 75 | 8 |
| 33 | 18 | 12 | 6 | THOSE LAZY-HAZY-CRAZY DAYS OF SUMMER — Nat King Cole, Capitol 4965 | 11 |
| 34 | 43 | 53 | 61 | BE TRUE TO YOURSELF — Bobby Vee, Liberty 55581 | 5 |
| ★35 | — | — | — | TILL THEN — Classics, Music Note 1116 | 5 |
| 36 | 29 | 19 | 15 | STILL — Bill Anderson, Decca 31458 | 15 |
| 37 | 44 | 54 | 57 | SIX DAYS ON THE ROAD — Dave Dudley, Golden Wing 3020 | 7 |
| 38 | 38 | 44 | 45 | SWINGING ON A STAR — Big Dee Irwin, Dimension 1010 | 9 |
| 39 | 41 | 45 | 46 | (I Love You) DON'T YOU FORGET IT — Perry Como, RCA Victor 8186 | 8 |
| ★40 | 51 | 56 | 79 | ABILENE — George Hamilton IV, RCA Victor 8181 | 5 |
| 41 | 33 | 31 | 29 | SHUT DOWN — Beach Boys, Capitol 4932 | 13 |
| 42 | 46 | 55 | 68 | DENISE — Randy & the Rainbows, Rust 5059 | 6 |
| 43 | 47 | 61 | 72 | HOOTENANNY — Glencoves, Select 724 | 6 |
| ★44 | 60 | 72 | 83 | GREEN, GREEN — New Christy Minstrels, Columbia 42805 △ | 4 |
| 45 | 26 | 25 | 25 | STRING ALONG — Rick Nelson, Decca 31495 | 9 |
| ★46 | 58 | 75 | — | BE CAREFUL OF STONES THAT YOU THROW — Dion, Columbia 42810 △ | 3 |
| ★47 | 59 | 74 | 100 | ROCK ME IN THE CRADLE OF LOVE — Dee Dee Sharp, Cameo 260 | 4 |
| 48 | 30 | 27 | 28 | FIRST QUARREL — Paul & Paula, Philips 40114 | 8 |
| 49 | 50 | 60 | 74 | SUMMER'S COMIN' — Kirby St. Romain, Inette 103 | 6 |
| ★50 | 73 | 90 | — | MORE — Kai Winding, Verve 10295 | 3 |
| 51 | 74 | 85 | — | MY WHOLE WORLD IS FALLING DOWN — Brenda Lee, Decca 31510 | 3 |
| 52 | 64 | 66 | 77 | TIPS OF MY FINGERS — Roy Clark, Capitol 4956 | 4 |
| 53 | 70 | — | — | I WONDER — Brenda Lee, Decca 31510 | 2 |
| 54 | 48 | 52 | 55 | COME GO WITH ME — Dion, Laurie 3171 | 6 |
| ★55 | 66 | 70 | 99 | I (Who Have Nothing) — Ben E. King, Atco 6267 | 4 |
| 56 | 25 | 13 | 11 | DA DOO RON RON — Crystals, Philles 112 | 13 |
| 57 | 75 | — | — | DANKE SCHOEN — Wayne Newton, Capitol 4989 | 2 |
| 58 | 42 | 29 | 31 | COME AND GET THESE MEMORIES — Martha & the Vandellas, Gordy 7014 | 16 |
| 59 | 72 | 76 | 82 | MOCKINGBIRD — Inez Foxx, Symbol 919 | 5 |
| 60 | 37 | 30 | 19 | I LOVE YOU BECAUSE — Al Martino, Capitol 4930 | 16 |
| 61 | 57 | 51 | 62 | SHAKE A TAIL FEATHER — Five Du-Tones, One-Derful 4815 | 10 |
| 62 | 81 | — | — | SURF PARTY — Chubby Checker, Parkway 879 | 2 |
| 63 | 92 | 99 | — | TRUE LOVE NEVER RUNS SMOOTH — Gene Pitney, Musicor 1032 | 3 |
| 64 | 55 | 63 | 78 | LIKE THE BIG GUYS DO — Rocky Fellers, Scepter 1254 | 4 |
| 65 | 83 | — | — | SHAKE, SHAKE, SHAKE — Jackie Wilson, Brunswick 55246 | 2 |
| 66 | 77 | — | — | MARLENA — 4 Seasons, Vee Jay 539 | 2 |
| ★67 | — | — | — | SOMETIMES YOU GOTTA CRY A LITTLE — Bobby Bland, Duke 366 | 1 |
| 68 | 79 | 84 | — | WHEN A BOY FALLS IN LOVE — Mel Carter, Derby 1003 | 3 |
| 69 | 67 | 73 | 75 | MY BLOCK — Four Pennies, Rust 5071 | 5 |
| 70 | 78 | 83 | 90 | COTTONFIELDS — Ace Cannon, Hi 2065 | 5 |
| ★71 | — | — | — | TWIST IT UP — Chubby Checker, Parkway 879 | 1 |
| ★72 | 90 | — | — | THE MONKEY TIME — Major Lance, Okeh 7175 | 2 |
| 73 | 76 | 82 | — | BRENDA — Cupids, KC 115 | 3 |
| 74 | 80 | 81 | — | WILL POWER — Cookies, Dimension 1012 | 3 |
| 75 | 93 | 97 | — | I WILL LOVE YOU — Richard Chamberlain, MGM 13148 | 3 |
| 76 | 71 | 69 | 80 | JACK THE RIPPER — Link Wray & His Ray Men, Swan 4137 | 6 |
| 77 | 82 | 87 | 96 | FROM ME TO YOU — Del Shannon, Big Top 3152 | 4 |
| ★78 | — | — | — | MAKE THE WORLD GO AWAY — Timi Yuro, Liberty 55587 | 1 |
| ★79 | — | — | — | LEAVE ME ALONE — Baby Washington, Sue 790 | 1 |
| ★80 | — | — | — | HOW MANY TEARDROPS — Lou Christie, Roulette 4504 | 1 |
| 81 | 87 | 91 | 92 | I'M AFRAID TO GO HOME — Brian Hyland, ABC-Paramount 10452 | 4 |
| 82 | 84 | 71 | 73 | RAT RACE — Drifters, Atlantic 2191 | 6 |
| 83 | 89 | 93 | 87 | ANTONY AND CLEOPATRA THEME — Ferrante & Teicher, United Artists 607 | 4 |
| 84 | 88 | 89 | 93 | LAND OF 1,000 DANCES — Chris Kenner, Instant 3252 | 4 |
| 85 | — | — | 94 | A LETTER FROM BETTY — Bobby Vee, Liberty 55581 | 2 |
| 86 | 97 | — | — | SURFIN' HOOTENANNY — Al Casey, Stacy 962 | 2 |
| 87 | — | — | — | CAN'T NOBODY LOVE YOU — Solomon Burke, Atlantic 2196 | 1 |
| 88 | 96 | 98 | — | LOVE ME ALL THE WAY — Kim Weston, Tamla 54076 | 3 |
| 89 | 91 | 92 | — | DANCIN' HOLIDAY — Olympics, Tri Disc 107 | 3 |
| ★90 | — | — | — | WAIT 'TIL MY BOBBY GETS HOME — Darlene Love, Philles 114 | 1 |
| 91 | — | — | — | GROOVY BABY — Billy Abbott, Parkway 874 | 1 |
| 92 | — | — | — | MAMA DON'T ALLOW — Rooftop Singers, Vanguard 35020 | 1 |
| 93 | — | 95 | — | SUMMERTIME — Chris Columbo Quintet, Strand 25056 | 2 |
| 94 | — | — | — | DANCE, DANCE, DANCE — Joey Dee, Roulette 4503 | 1 |
| 95 | 98 | 77 | 85 | I CAN'T STOP LOVING YOU — Count Basie, Reprise 20170 | 8 |
| 96 | — | — | — | IT HURTS TO BE SIXTEEN — Andrea Carroll, Big Top 3156 | 1 |
| 97 | — | — | — | THIS IS ALL I ASK — Tony Bennett, Columbia 42820 △ | 1 |
| 98 | — | — | — | STILL NO. 2 — Ben Colder, MGM 13147 | 1 |
| 99 | — | — | — | I WANT TO STAY HERE — Steve & Eydie, Columbia 42815 △ | 1 |
| 100 | — | — | — | WHAT A FOOL I'VE BEEN — Carla Thomas, Atlantic 2189 | 1 |

## BUBBLING UNDER THE HOT 100

101. IF YOU DON'T COME BACK ............ Drifters, Atlantic 2191
102. TEARS OF JOY ........................ Chuck Jackson, Wand 138
103. DAUGHTER ........................... Blenders, Witch 114
104. LOVE IS A ONCE IN A LIFETIME THING .. Dick & Deedee, Warner Bros. 5364
105. THE MINUTE YOU'RE GONE ............. Sonny Gibson, Capitol 4969
106. SATURDAY SUNSHINE .................. Burt Bacharach, Kapp 532
107. BREAKWATER ......................... Lawrence Welk, Dot 16488
108. SAY WONDERFUL THINGS ............... Patti Page, Columbia 42791
109. SCARLETT O'HARA .................... Lawrence Welk, Dot 16488
110. RIVER'S INVITATION ................. Percy Mayfield, Tangerine 931
111. CROSSROADS ......................... Luther Randolph & Johnny Stiles, Cameo 253
112. HEY GIRL ........................... Freddie Scott, Colpix 692
113. SAY IT ISN'T SO .................... Aretha Franklin, Columbia 42776
114. SCARLETT O'HARA .................... Kenny Gregg, Epic 9601
115. MARTIAN HOP ........................ Ran-Dells, Chairman 4403
116. LUCKY LIPS ......................... Cliff Richard, Epic 9597
117. HELLO JIM .......................... Paul Anka, RCA Victor 8195
118. PAINTED, TAINTED ROSE .............. Al Martino, Capitol 5000
119. BAJA ............................... Astronauts, RCA Victor 8194
120. A LONG VACATION .................... Rick Nelson, Imperial 5985
121. I WILL NEVER TURN MY BACK ON YOU ... Rip Chords, Columbia 42812
122. GONE ............................... Teena Montgomery, Try Me 26001
123. I CRIED ............................ Supremes, Motown 1044
124. A BREATH TAKING GUY ................ Aretha Franklin, Columbia 42796
125. HERE'S WHERE I CAME IN (Here's Where I Walk Out) .. Aretha Franklin, Columbia 42796
126. TRUE BLUE LOU ...................... Tony Bennett, Columbia 42820
127. FRAULEIN ........................... Bobby Helms, Columbia 42776
128. QUE SERA SERA ...................... High Keys, Atco 6268

# Billboard HOT 100
**FOR WEEK ENDING JULY 27, 1963**

| # | Wks Ago | Title | Artist, Label & Number | Weeks On Chart |
|---|---|---|---|---|
| 1 | 1 2 7 | SURF CITY | Jan & Dean, Liberty 55580 | 7 |
| 2 | 3 4 9 | SO MUCH IN LOVE | Tymes, Parkway 871 | 9 |
| 3 | 6 11 18 | FINGERTIPS (Part II) | Little Stevie Wonder, Tamla 54080 | 6 |
| 4 | 2 1 1 | EASIER SAID THAN DONE | Essex, Roulette 4494 | 8 |
| 5 | 7 10 17 | WIPE OUT | Surfaris, Dot 16479 | 6 |
| 6 | 4 3 10 | TIE ME KANGAROO DOWN, SPORT | Rolf Harris, Epic 9596 | 8 |
| 7 | 9 16 49 | (You're the) DEVIL IN DISGUISE | Elvis Presley, RCA Victor 8188 | 5 |
| 8 | 14 34 64 | BLOWIN' IN THE WIND | Peter, Paul & Mary, Warner Bros. 5368 | 5 |
| 9 | 5 7 8 | MEMPHIS | Lonnie Mack, Fraternity 906 | 8 |
| 10 | 15 20 28 | JUST ONE LOOK | Doris Troy, Atlantic 2188 | 8 |
| 11 | 23 52 80 | JUDY'S TURN TO CRY | Lesley Gore, Mercury 72143 | 4 |
| 12 | 13 15 20 | NOT ME | Orlons, Cameo 257 | 7 |
| 13 | 10 13 15 | PRIDE AND JOY | Marvin Gaye, Tamla 54079 | 11 |
| 14 | 8 6 2 | SUKIYAKI | Kyu Sakamoto, Capitol 4945 | 12 |
| 15 | 18 28 38 | HOPELESS | Andy Williams, Columbia 42784 | 6 |
| 16 | 30 54 78 | CANDY GIRL | 4 Seasons, Vee Jay 539 | 4 |
| 17 | 20 23 24 | RING OF FIRE | Johnny Cash, Columbia 42788 | 9 |
| 18 | 11 8 3 | BLUE ON BLUE | Bobby Vinton, Epic 9593 | 11 |
| 19 | 24 27 32 | DETROIT CITY | Bobby Bare, RCA Victor 8183 | 7 |
| 20 | 17 17 21 | HARRY THE HAIRY APE | Ray Stevens, Mercury 72125 | 7 |
| 21 | 21 24 35 | NO ONE | Ray Charles, ABC-Paramount 10453 | 6 |
| 22 | 25 31 42 | MY TRUE CONFESSION | Brook Benton, Mercury 72135 | 7 |
| 23 | 16 9 4 | HELLO STRANGER | Barbara Lewis, Atlantic 2184 | 13 |
| 24 | 35 49 65 | TILL THEN | Classics, Music Note 1116 | 6 |
| 25 | 12 5 6 | ONE FINE DAY | Chiffons, Laurie 3179 | 9 |
| 26 | 31 36 46 | DON'T SAY GOODNIGHT AND MEAN GOODBYE | Shirelles, Scepter 1255 | 7 |
| 27 | 19 12 5 | IT'S MY PARTY | Lesley Gore, Mercury 72119 | 12 |
| 28 | 50 73 90 | MORE | Kai Winding, Verve 10295 | 4 |
| 29 | 42 46 55 | DENISE | Randy & the Rainbows, Rust 5059 | 7 |
| 30 | 40 51 56 | ABILENE | George Hamilton IV, RCA Victor 8181 | 6 |
| 31 | 29 35 37 | WITHOUT LOVE (There Is Nothing) | Ray Charles, ABC-Paramount 10453 | 6 |
| 32 | 32 40 48 | GOODNIGHT MY LOVE | Fleetwoods, Dolton 75 | 9 |
| 33 | 37 44 54 | SIX DAYS ON THE ROAD | Dave Dudley, Golden Wing 3020 | 8 |
| 34 | 44 60 72 | GREEN, GREEN | New Christy Minstrels, Columbia 42805 | 5 |
| 35 | 51 74 85 | MY WHOLE WORLD IS FALLING DOWN | Brenda Lee, Decca 31510 | 4 |
| 36 | 22 14 14 | ON TOP OF SPAGHETTI | Tom Glazer & the Children's Chorus, Kapp 526 | 9 |
| 37 | 34 43 53 | BE TRUE TO YOURSELF | Bobby Vee, Liberty 55581 | 6 |
| 38 | 43 47 61 | HOOTENANNY | Glencoves, Select 724 | 7 |
| 39 | 46 58 75 | BE CAREFUL OF STONES THAT YOU THROW | Dion, Columbia 42810 | 4 |
| 40 | 53 70 — | I WONDER | Brenda Lee, Decca 31510 | 3 |
| 41 | 59 72 76 | MOCKINGBIRD | Inez Foxx, Symbol 919 | 6 |
| 42 | 28 21 16 | MY SUMMER LOVE | Ruby & the Romantics, Kapp 525 | 11 |
| 43 | 38 38 44 | SWINGING ON A STAR | Big Dee Irwin, Dimension 1010 | 10 |
| 44 | 47 59 74 | ROCK ME IN THE CRADLE OF LOVE | Dee Dee Sharp, Cameo 260 | 5 |
| 45 | 39 41 45 | (I Love You) DON'T YOU FORGET IT | Perry Como, RCA Victor 8186 | 7 |
| 46 | 55 66 70 | I (Who Have Nothing) | Ben E. King, Atco 6267 | 5 |
| 47 | 57 75 — | DANKE SCHOEN | Wayne Newton, Capitol 4989 | 3 |
| 48 | 52 64 66 | TIPS OF MY FINGERS | Roy Clark, Capitol 4956 | 5 |
| 49 | 63 92 99 | TRUE LOVE NEVER RUNS SMOOTH | Gene Pitney, Musicor 1032 | 4 |
| 50 | 66 77 — | MARLENA | 4 Seasons, Vee Jay 539 | 3 |
| 51 | 26 22 23 | FALLING | Roy Orbison, Monument 815 | 8 |
| 52 | 65 83 — | SHAKE, SHAKE, SHAKE | Jackie Wilson, Brunswick 55246 | 3 |
| 53 | 33 18 12 | THOSE LAZY-HAZY-CRAZY DAYS OF SUMMER | Nat King Cole, Capitol 4965 | 12 |
| 54 | 27 19 11 | YOU CAN'T SIT DOWN | Dovells, Parkway 867 | 14 |
| 55 | 62 81 — | SURF PARTY | Chubby Checker, Parkway 879 | 3 |
| 56 | 68 79 84 | WHEN A BOY FALLS IN LOVE | Mel Carter, Derby 1003 | 4 |
| 57 | 49 50 60 | SUMMER'S COMIN' | Kirby St. Romain, Inette 103 | 7 |
| 58 | 61 57 51 | SHAKE A TAIL FEATHER | Five Du-Tones, One-Derful 4815 | 11 |
| 59 | 71 — — | TWIST IT UP | Chubby Checker, Parkway 879 | 2 |
| 60 | 73 76 82 | BRENDA | Cupids, KC 115 | 4 |
| 61 | 67 — — | SOMETIMES YOU GOTTA CRY A LITTLE | Bobby Bland, Duke 366 | 2 |
| 62 | 72 90 — | THE MONKEY TIME | Major Lance, Okeh 7175 | 3 |
| 63 | 78 — — | MAKE THE WORLD GO AWAY | Timi Yuro, Liberty 55587 | 2 |
| 64 | 76 71 69 | JACK THE RIPPER | Link Wray & His Ray Men, Swan 4137 | 7 |
| 65 | 80 — — | HOW MANY TEARDROPS | Lou Christie, Roulette 4504 | 2 |
| 66 | 75 93 97 | I WILL LOVE YOU | Richard Chamberlain, MGM 13148 | 4 |
| 67 | 70 78 83 | COTTONFIELDS | Ace Cannon, Hi 2065 | 6 |
| 68 | — — — | HEY GIRL | Freddie Scott, Colpix 692 | 1 |
| 69 | 64 55 63 | LIKE THE BIG GUYS DO | Rocky Fellers, Scepter 1254 | 5 |
| 70 | 86 97 — | SURFIN' HOOTENANNY | Al Casey, Stacy 962 | 3 |
| 71 | — — — | PAINTED, TAINTED ROSE | Al Martino, Capitol 5000 | 1 |
| 72 | 79 — — | LEAVE ME ALONE | Baby Washington, Sue 790 | 2 |
| 73 | 81 87 91 | I'M AFRAID TO GO HOME | Brian Hyland, ABC-Paramount 10452 | 5 |
| 74 | 74 80 81 | WILL POWER | Cookies, Dimension 1012 | 4 |
| 75 | 90 — — | WAIT 'TIL MY BOBBY GETS HOME | Darlene Love, Philles 114 | 2 |
| 76 | — — — | IF I HAD A HAMMER | Trini Lopez, Reprise 20198 | 1 |
| 77 | 84 88 89 | LAND OF 1,000 DANCES | Chris Kenner, Instant 3252 | 5 |
| 78 | — 86 88 | DAUGHTER | Blenders, Witch 114 | 3 |
| 79 | 97 — — | THIS IS ALL I ASK | Tony Bennett, Columbia 42820 | 2 |
| 80 | 87 — — | CAN'T NOBODY LOVE YOU | Solomon Burke, Atlantic 2196 | 2 |
| 81 | 91 — — | GROOVY BABY | Billy Abbott, Parkway 874 | 2 |
| 82 | — — — | THE DREAMER | Neil Sedaka, RCA Victor 8209 | 1 |
| 83 | 99 — — | I WANT TO STAY HERE | Steve & Eydie, Columbia 42815 | 2 |
| 84 | — — — | QUE SERA, SERA (Whatever Will Be, Will Be) | High Keys, Atco 6268 | 1 |
| 85 | 96 — — | IT HURTS TO BE SIXTEEN | Andrea Carroll, Big Top 3156 | 2 |
| 86 | 89 91 92 | DANCIN' HOLIDAY | Olympics, Tri Disc 107 | 4 |
| 87 | 92 — — | MAMA DON'T ALLOW | Rooftop Singers, Vanguard 35020 | 2 |
| 88 | 83 89 93 | ANTONY AND CLEOPATRA THEME | Ferrante & Teicher, United Artists 607 | 5 |
| 89 | — — — | FRANKIE AND JOHNNY | Sam Cooke, RCA Victor 8215 | 1 |
| 90 | — — — | CHINESE CHECKERS | Booker T. & the MG's, Stax 137 | 1 |
| 91 | 94 — — | DANCE, DANCE, DANCE | Joey Dee, Roulette 4503 | 2 |
| 92 | 95 98 77 | I CAN'T STOP LOVING YOU | Count Basie, Reprise 20170 | 9 |
| 93 | 100 — — | WHAT A FOOL I'VE BEEN | Carla Thomas, Atlantic 2189 | 2 |
| 94 | — — — | BAJA | Astronauts, RCA Victor 8194 | 1 |
| 95 | — — — | A BREATH TAKING GUY | Supremes, Motown 1044 | 1 |
| 96 | — — — | IT'S TOO LATE | Wilson Pickett, Double L 717 | 1 |
| 97 | — — — | SATURDAY SUNSHINE | Burt Bacharach, Kapp 532 | 1 |
| 98 | — — — | TRUE LOVE | Richard Chamberlain, MGM 13148 | 1 |
| 99 | — — — | THESE FOOLISH THINGS | James Brown & The Famous Flames, King 5767 | 1 |
| 100 | — — — | TRUE BLUE LOU | Tony Bennett, Columbia 42820 | 1 |

## BUBBLING UNDER THE HOT 100

| # | Title | Artist, Label & Number |
|---|---|---|
| 101 | IT WON'T BE THIS WAY (ALWAYS) | King Pins, Federal 12484 |
| 102 | HELLO MUDDUH, HELLO FADDUH (Letter From Camp) | Allan Sherman, Warner Bros. 5378 |
| 103 | LUCKY LIPS | Cliff Richard, Epic 9597 |
| 104 | RIVER'S INVITATION | Percy Mayfield, Tangerine 931 |
| 105 | LITTLE DANCING DOLL | Shelby Flint, Valiant 6031 |
| 106 | SUMMERTIME | Chris Columbo Quintet, Strand 25056 |
| 107 | MINUTE YOU'RE GONE | Sonny James, Capitol 4969 |
| 108 | LOVE IS A ONCE IN A LIFETIME THING | Dick & Deedee, Warner Bros. 5364 |
| 109 | CROSSROADS | Luther Randolph & Johnny Stiles, Cameo 253 |
| 110 | THIS IS ALL I ASK | Burl Ives, Decca 31518 |
| 111 | MARTIAN HOP | Ran Dells, Chairman 4403 |
| 112 | SCARLETT O'HARA | Bobby Gregg, Epic 9601 |
| 113 | RAT RACE | Drifters, Atlantic 2191 |
| 114 | I'M THE BOSS | Burl Ives, Decca 31504 |
| 115 | TREAT 'EM TOUGH | Jimmy Soul, S.P.Q.R. 3310 |
| 116 | IF YOU DON'T COME BACK | Drifters, Atlantic 2191 |
| 117 | GONE | Rip Chords, Columbia 42812 |
| 118 | SURFER GIRL | Beach Boys, Capitol 5009 |
| 119 | LONELY SURFER | Jack Nitzsche, Reprise 20202 |
| 120 | WHAT I GOTTA DO (TO MAKE YOU JEALOUS) | Little Eva, Dimension 1013 |
| 121 | I CRIED | Tenna Montgomery, Try Me 28001 |
| 122 | DUM DUM DEE DUM | Johnny Cymbal, Kapp 539 |
| 123 | I'M NOT A FOOL ANYMORE | T. K. Hulin, Smash 1899 |
| 124 | DO THE MONKEY | King Curtis, Capitol 4998 |
| 125 | IT HURTS TO BE SIXTEEN | Barbara Chandler, Kapp 542 |
| 126 | EVERYBODY MONKEY | Freddy Cannon, Swan 4149 |
| 127 | MORE | Vic Dana, Dolton 81 |
| 128 | WHAT MAKES LITTLE GIRLS CRY | Victorians, Liberty 55574 |
| 129 | WHAT I GOTTA DO (TO MAKE YOU JEALOUS) | Little Eva, Dimension 1013 |
| 130 | PLEASE DON'T TALK TO THE LIFEGUARD | Diane Ray, Mercury 72117 |
| 131 | MAKE THE MUSIC PLAY | Dionne Warwick, Scepter 1253 |

# Billboard HOT 100

FOR WEEK ENDING AUGUST 3 1963

★ STAR PERFORMERS—Selections registering greatest upward progress this week.

S Indicates that 45 r.p.m. stereo single version is available.

△ Indicates that 33⅓ r.p.m. mono single version is available.

△S Indicates that 33⅓ r.p.m. stereo single version is available.

| This Week | 1 Wk. Ago | 2 Wks. Ago | 3 Wks. Ago | Title | Artist, Label & Number | | Weeks On Chart |
|---|---|---|---|---|---|---|---|
| 1 (Billboard Award) | 2 | 3 | 4 | SO MUCH IN LOVE | Tymes, Parkway 781 | | 10 |
| 2 | 3 | 6 | 11 | FINGERTIPS (Part II) | Little Stevie Wonder, Tamla 54080 | | 7 |
| 3 | 1 | 1 | 2 | SURF CITY | Jan & Dean, Liberty 55580 | | 8 |
| ★4 | 7 | 9 | 16 | (You're the) DEVIL IN DISGUISE | Elvis Presley, RCA Victor 8188 | | 6 |
| 5 | 5 | 7 | 10 | WIPE OUT | Surfaris, Dot 16479 | | 7 |
| 6 | 8 | 14 | 34 | BLOWIN' IN THE WIND | Peter, Paul & Mary, Warner Bros. 5368 | | 6 |
| 7 | 4 | 2 | 1 | EASIER SAID THAN DONE | Essex, Roulette 4494 | | 9 |
| ★8 | 11 | 23 | 52 | JUDY'S TURN TO CRY | Lesley Gore, Mercury 72143 | | 5 |
| 9 | 6 | 4 | 3 | TIE ME KANGAROO DOWN, SPORT | Rolf Harris, Epic 9596 | | 9 |
| 10 | 10 | 15 | 20 | JUST ONE LOOK | Doris Troy, Atlantic 2188 | | 9 |
| ★11 | 16 | 30 | 54 | CANDY GIRL | 4 Seasons, Vee Jay 539 | | 5 |
| 12 | 9 | 5 | 7 | MEMPHIS | Lonnie Mack, Fraternity 906 | | 9 |
| 13 | 15 | 18 | 28 | HOPELESS | Andy Williams, Columbia 42784 | △ | 7 |
| 14 | 13 | 10 | 13 | PRIDE AND JOY | Marvin Gaye, Tamla 54079 | | 12 |
| 15 | 12 | 13 | 15 | NOT ME | Orlons, Cameo 257 | | 8 |
| 16 | 19 | 24 | 27 | DETROIT CITY | Bobby Bare, RCA Victor 8183 | | 8 |
| 17 | 17 | 20 | 23 | RING OF FIRE | Johnny Cash, Columbia 42788 | △ | 10 |
| 18 | 14 | 8 | 6 | SUKIYAKI | Kyu Sakamoto, Capitol 4945 | | 13 |
| ★19 | 28 | 50 | 73 | MORE | Kai Winding, Verve 10295 | | 4 |
| 20 | 24 | 35 | 49 | TILL THEN | Classics, Music Note 1116 | | 7 |
| ★21 | 34 | 44 | 60 | GREEN, GREEN | New Christy Minstrels, Columbia 42805 | △ | 6 |
| 22 | 18 | 11 | 8 | BLUE ON BLUE | Bobby Vinton, Epic 9593 | | 12 |
| ★23 | 29 | 42 | 46 | DENISE | Randy & the Rainbows, Rust 5059 | | 8 |
| ★24 | 30 | 40 | 51 | ABILENE | George Hamilton IV, RCA Victor 8181 | | 7 |
| ★25 | 35 | 51 | 74 | MY WHOLE WORLD IS FALLING DOWN | Brenda Lee, Decca 31510 | | 5 |
| 26 | 22 | 25 | 31 | MY TRUE CONFESSION | Brook Benton, Mercury 72135 | | 8 |
| ★27 | 41 | 59 | 72 | MOCKINGBIRD | Inez Foxx, Symbol 919 | | 7 |
| 28 | 21 | 21 | 24 | NO ONE | Ray Charles, ABC-Paramount 10453 | | 7 |
| 29 | 26 | 31 | 36 | DON'T SAY GOODNIGHT AND MEAN GOODBYE | Shirelles, Scepter 1255 | | 8 |
| ★30 | 49 | 63 | 92 | TRUE LOVE NEVER RUNS SMOOTH | Gene Pitney, Musicor 1032 | | 5 |
| 31 | 39 | 46 | 58 | BE CAREFUL OF STONES THAT YOU THROW | Dion, Columbia 42810 | △ | 5 |
| 32 | 33 | 37 | 44 | SIX DAYS ON THE ROAD | Dave Dudley, Golden Wing 3020 | | 9 |
| 33 | 40 | 53 | 70 | I WONDER | Brenda Lee, Decca 31510 | | 4 |
| 34 | 20 | 17 | 17 | HARRY THE HAIRY APE | Ray Stevens, Mercury 72125 | | 8 |
| ★35 | 47 | 57 | 75 | DANKE SCHOEN | Wayne Newton, Capitol 4989 | | 4 |
| 36 | 25 | 12 | 5 | ONE FINE DAY | Chiffons, Laurie 3179 | | 10 |
| ★37 | 59 | 71 | — | TWIST IT UP | Chubby Checker, Parkway 879 | | 3 |
| 38 | 38 | 43 | 47 | HOOTENANNY | Glencoves, Select 724 | | 8 |
| 39 | 32 | 32 | 40 | GOODNIGHT MY LOVE | Fleetwoods, Dolton 75 | | 10 |
| 40 | 46 | 55 | 66 | I (Who Have Nothing) | Ben E. King, Atco 6267 | | 6 |
| 41 | 50 | 66 | 77 | MARLENA | 4 Seasons, Vee Jay 539 | | 4 |
| ★42 | 52 | 65 | 83 | SHAKE, SHAKE, SHAKE | Jackie Wilson, Brunswick 55246 | | 4 |
| 43 | 44 | 47 | 59 | ROCK ME IN THE CRADLE OF LOVE | Dee Dee Sharp, Cameo 260 | | 6 |
| 44 | 31 | 29 | 35 | WITHOUT LOVE (There Is Nothing) | Ray Charles, ABC-Paramount 10453 | | 7 |
| ★45 | — | — | — | HELLO MUDDUH, HELLO FADDUH | Allan Sherman, Warner Bros. 5378 | | 1 |
| 46 | 48 | 52 | 64 | TIPS OF MY FINGERS | Roy Clark, Capitol 4956 | | 6 |
| 47 | 23 | 16 | 9 | HELLO STRANGER | Barbara Lewis, Atlantic 2184 | | 14 |
| ★48 | 62 | 72 | 90 | THE MONKEY TIME | Major Lance, Okeh 7175 | | 4 |
| 49 | 37 | 34 | 43 | BE TRUE TO YOURSELF | Bobby Vee, Liberty 55581 | | 7 |
| 50 | 27 | 19 | 12 | IT'S MY PARTY | Lesley Gore, Mercury 72119 | | 13 |
| ★51 | 65 | 80 | — | HOW MANY TEARDROPS | Lou Christie, Roulette 4504 | | 3 |
| ★52 | 63 | 78 | — | MAKE THE WORLD GO AWAY | Timi Yuro, Liberty 55587 | | 3 |
| 53 | 56 | 68 | 79 | WHEN A BOY FALLS IN LOVE | Mel Carter, Derby 1003 | | 5 |
| ★54 | 68 | — | — | HEY GIRL | Freddie Scott, Colpix 692 | | 2 |
| 55 | 55 | 62 | 81 | SURF PARTY | Chubby Checker, Parkway 879 | | 4 |
| ★56 | 71 | — | — | PAINTED, TAINTED ROSE | Al Martino, Capitol 5000 | | 2 |
| 57 | 60 | 73 | 76 | BRENDA | Cupids, KC 115 | | 5 |
| ★58 | 76 | — | — | IF I HAD A HAMMER | Trini Lopez, Reprise 20198 | | 2 |
| ★59 | 70 | 86 | 97 | SURFIN' HOOTENANNY | Al Casey, Stacy 962 | | 4 |
| ★60 | 89 | — | — | FRANKIE AND JOHNNY | Sam Cooke, RCA Victor 8215 | | 2 |
| 61 | 61 | 67 | — | SOMETIMES YOU GOTTA CRY A LITTLE | Bobby Bland, Duke 366 | | 3 |
| 62 | 75 | 90 | — | WAIT 'TIL MY BOBBY GETS HOME | Darlene Love, Philles 114 | | 3 |
| ★63 | 87 | 92 | — | MAMA DON'T ALLOW | Rooftop Singers, Vanguard 35020 | | 3 |
| 64 | 58 | 61 | 57 | SHAKE A TAIL FEATHER | Five Du-Tones, One-Derful 4815 | | 12 |
| 65 | 66 | 75 | 93 | I WILL LOVE YOU | Richard Chamberlain, MGM 13148 | | 5 |
| ★66 | 83 | 99 | — | I WANT TO STAY HERE | Steve & Eydie, Columbia 42815 | △ | 3 |
| 67 | 67 | 70 | 78 | COTTONFIELDS | Ace Cannon, Hi 2065 | | 7 |
| 68 | 73 | 81 | 87 | I'M AFRAID TO GO HOME | Brian Hyland, ABC-Paramount 10452 | | 6 |
| 69 | 82 | — | — | THE DREAMER | Neil Sedaka, RCA Victor 8209 | | 2 |
| ★70 | — | — | — | DESERT PETE | Kingston Trio, Capitol 5005 | | 1 |
| 71 | 72 | 79 | — | LEAVE ME ALONE | Baby Washington, Sue 790 | | 3 |
| 72 | 74 | 74 | 80 | WILL POWER | Cookies, Dimension 1012 | | 5 |
| 73 | 78 | — | 86 | DAUGHTER | Blenders, Witch 114 | | 4 |
| 74 | 85 | 96 | — | IT HURTS TO BE SIXTEEN | Andrea Carroll, Big Top 3156 | | 3 |
| ★75 | — | — | — | MY BOY FRIEND'S BACK | Angels, Smash 1834 | | 1 |
| 76 | 81 | 91 | — | GROOVY BABY | Billy Abbott, Parkway 874 | | 3 |
| ★77 | — | — | — | EVERYBODY MONKEY | Freddy Cannon, Swan 4149 | | 1 |
| 78 | 80 | 87 | — | CAN'T NOBODY LOVE YOU | Solomon Burke, Atlantic 2196 | | 3 |
| 79 | 79 | 97 | — | THIS IS ALL I ASK | Tony Bennett, Columbia 42820 | △ | 3 |
| 80 | 84 | — | — | QUE SERA, SERA (Whatever Will Be, Will Be) | High Keys, Atco 6268 | | 2 |
| 81 | 64 | 76 | 71 | JACK THE RIPPER | Link Wray & His Ray Men, Swan 4137 | | 8 |
| ★82 | — | — | — | HEAT WAVE | Martha & the Vandellas, Gordy 7022 | | 1 |
| ★83 | 99 | — | — | THESE FOOLISH THINGS | James Brown & The Famous Flames, King 5767 | | 2 |
| 84 | 96 | — | — | IT'S TOO LATE | Wilson Pickett, Double L 717 | | 2 |
| ★85 | — | — | — | SURFER GIRL | Beach Boys, Capitol 5009 | | 1 |
| 86 | 77 | 84 | 88 | LAND OF 1,000 DANCES | Chris Kenner, Instant 3252 | | 6 |
| ★87 | — | — | — | MY DADDY KNOWS BEST | Marvelettes, Tamla 54082 | | 1 |
| 88 | 86 | 89 | 91 | DANCIN' HOLIDAY | Olympics, Tri Disc 107 | | 5 |
| 89 | 91 | 94 | — | DANCE, DANCE, DANCE | Joey Dee, Roulette 4503 | | 3 |
| ★90 | — | — | — | DUM DUM DEE DUM | Johnny Cymbal, Kapp 539 | | 1 |
| 91 | — | — | — | THIS IS ALL I ASK | Burl Ives, Decca 31518 | | 1 |
| 92 | 90 | — | — | CHINESE CHECKERS | Booker T. & the MG's, Stax 137 | | 2 |
| 93 | — | — | — | MARTIAN HOP | Ran-Dells, Chairman 4403 | | 1 |
| 94 | 95 | — | — | A BREATH TAKING GUY | Supremes, Motown 1044 | | 2 |
| 95 | — | — | — | LUCKY LIPS | Cliff Richard, Epic 9597 | | 1 |
| 96 | 97 | — | — | SATURDAY SUNSHINE | Burt Bacharach, Kapp 532 | | 2 |
| 97 | — | — | — | AT THE SHORE | Johnny Caswell, Smash 1833 | | 1 |
| 98 | — | — | — | PLEASE DON'T TALK TO THE LIFEGUARD | Diane Ray, Mercury 72117 | | 1 |
| 99 | 100 | — | — | TRUE BLUE LOU | Tony Bennett, Columbia 42820 | △ | 2 |
| 100 | — | — | — | MAKE THE MUSIC PLAY | Dionne Warwick, Scepter 1253 | | 1 |

## HOT 100—A TO Z—(Publisher-Licensee)

Abilene (Acuff-Rose, BMI) ... 24
At the Shore (Marjoda, BMI) ... 97
Be Careful of Stones That You Throw (Acuff-Rose, BMI) ... 31
Be True to Yourself (U. S. Songs, ASCAP) ... 49
Blowin' in the Wind (Witmark, ASCAP) ... 6
Blue on Blue (Famous, ASCAP) ... 22
A Breath Taking Guy (Jobete, BMI) ... 94
Brenda (Sweco, BMI) ... 57
Candy Girl (Saturday-Gavadima, ASCAP) ... 11
Can't Nobody Love You (Trio, BMI) ... 78
Chinese Checkers (East, BMI) ... 92
Cottonfields (Folkways, BMI) ... 67
Dance, Dance, Dance (Patricia, BMI) ... 89
Dancin' Holiday (Marc-Jean & Keymen, BMI) ... 88
Danke Schoen (Roosevelt, BMI) ... 35
Daughter (Venetia, BMI) ... 73
Denise (Bright-Tunes, BMI) ... 23
Desert Pete (Sleepy Hollow, ASCAP) ... 70
Detroit City (Cedarwood, BMI) ... 16
Devil in Disguise (Presley, BMI) ... 4
Don't Say Goodnight and Mean Goodbye (Maggie, BMI) ... 29
The Dreamer (Rondak, BMI) ... 69
Dum Dum Dee Dum (Haymarket, BMI) ... 90
Easier Said Than Done (Nom, BMI) ... 7
Everybody Monkey (Valley-Shelros, BMI) ... 77
Fingertips (Part II) (Jobete, BMI) ... 2
Frankie and Johnny (Kags, BMI) ... 60
Goodnight My Love (House of Fortune-Quintet, BMI) ... 39
Green, Green (New Christy, BMI) ... 21
Groovy Baby (Cameo-Parkway, BMI) ... 76
Harry the Hairy Ape (Lowery, BMI) ... 34
Heat Wave (Jobete, BMI) ... 82
Hello Mudduh, Hello Fadduh (Curtain Call, ASCAP). 45
Hello Stranger (McLaughlin, BMI) ... 47
Hey Girl (Screen Gems-Columbia, BMI) ... 54
Hootenanny (Joy, ASCAP) ... 38
Hopeless (Brenner, BMI) ... 13
How Many Teardrops (Nom, BMI) ... 51
I Want to Stay Here (Screen Gems-Columbia, BMI). 66
I Will Love You (DeVorzon, BMI) ... 65
I (Who Have Nothing) (Milky Way-Trio-Cotillion, BMI) ... 40
I Wonder (Leeds, ASCAP) ... 33
I'm Afraid to Go Home (Geld-Udell, ASCAP) ... 68
If I Had a Hammer (Ludlow, BMI) ... 58
It Hurts to Be Sixteen (Rondak, BMI) ... 74
It's My Party (Arch, ASCAP) ... 50
It's Too Late (Prigan-Correctone, BMI) ... 84
Jack the Ripper (Andaval-Florentine, BMI) ... 81
Judy's Turn to Cry (Glamorous, ASCAP) ... 8
Just One Look (Premier, BMI) ... 10
Land of 1,000 Dances (Anatole & Tune-Kel, BMI). 86
Leave Me Alone (Roosevelt, BMI) ... 71
Lucky Lips (Tiger, BMI) ... 95
Make the Music Play (11th Floor-U. S. Songs, ASCAP) ... 100
Make the World Go Away (Pamper, BMI) ... 52
Mama Don't Allow (Egypt Valley, BMI) ... 63
Marlena (Saturday-Gavadima, ASCAP) ... 41
Martian Hop (Screen Gems-Columbia, BMI) ... 93
Memphis (Arc, BMI) ... 12
Mockingbird (Saturn, BMI) ... 27
Monkey Time, The (Curtain-Palier, BMI) ... 48
More (Marks, BMI) ... 19
My Boy Friend's Back (Blackwood, BMI) ... 75
My Daddy Knows Best (Jobete, BMI) ... 87
My True Confession (Lowery, BMI) ... 26
My Whole World Is Falling Down (Champion-Moss Rose, BMI) ... 25
No One (Hill & Range, BMI) ... 28
Not Me (Rock Masters, BMI) ... 15
One Fine Day (Screen Gems-Columbia, BMI) ... 36
Painted, Tainted Rose (Damian, ASCAP) ... 56
Please Don't Talk to the Lifeguard (Joy, ASCAP). 98
Pride and Joy (Jobete, BMI) ... 14
Que Sera, Sera (Whatever Will Be, Will Be) (Artists, ASCAP) ... 80
Ring of Fire (Painted Desert, BMI) ... 17
Rock Me in the Cradle of Love (Kalmann, ASCAP). 43
Saturday Sunshine (U. S. Songs, ASCAP) ... 96
Shake a Tail Feather (Vapac, BMI) ... 64
Shake, Shake, Shake (Brunswick, BMI) ... 42
Six Days on the Road (Newkeys-Tune, BMI) ... 32
So Much in Love (Cameo-Parkway, BMI) ... 1
Sometimes You Gotta Cry a Little (Don, BMI) ... 61
Sukiyaki (Beechwood, BMI) ... 18
Surf City (Screen Gems-Columbia, BMI) ... 3
Surf Party (C. C.-Kalmann, ASCAP) ... 55
Surfer Girl (Sea of Tunes, BMI) ... 85
Surfin' Hootenanny (Renda, BMI) ... 59
These Foolish Things (Bourne, ASCAP) ... 83
This Is All I Ask—Bennett (Massey, ASCAP) ... 79
This Is All I Ask—Ives (Massey, ASCAP) ... 91
Tie Me Kangaroo Down, Sport (Beechwood, BMI).. 9
Till Then (Pickwick, ASCAP) ... 20
Tips of My Fingers (Tree, BMI) ... 46
True Blue Lou (Famous, ASCAP) ... 99
True Love Never Runs Smooth (Arch, ASCAP) ... 30
Twist It Up (Kalmann-C. C., ASCAP) ... 37
Wait 'Til My Bobby Gets Home (Mother Bertha-Trio, BMI) ... 62
When a Boy Falls in Love (Kags, BMI) ... 53
Will Power (Screen Gems-Columbia, BMI) ... 72
Wipe Out (Miraleste-Robin Hood, BMI) ... 5
Without Love (Suffolk-P.M.P.C., BMI) ... 44

## BUBBLING UNDER THE HOT 100

101. FROM ME TO YOU ... Del Shannon, Big Top 3152
102. BAJA ... Astronauts, RCA Victor 8194
103. LITTLE DANCING DOLL ... Shelby Flint, Valiant 6031
104. THE MINUTE YOU'RE GONE ... Sonny James, Capitol 4969
105. IT WON'T BE THIS WAY (ALWAYS) ... King Pins, Federal 12484
106. ANTONY AND CLEOPATRA THEME .. Ferrante & Teicher, United Artists 607
107. WHAT A FOOL I'VE BEEN ... Carla Thomas, Atlantic 2189
108. DROWNIN' MY SORROWS ... Connie Francis, MGM 13160
109. TREAT 'EM TOUGH ... Jimmy Soul, S.P.Q.R. 3310
110. LOVE ME ALL THE WAY ... Kim Weston, Tamla 54076
111. I'M THE BOSS ... Burl Ives, Decca 31504
112. CROSSROADS ... Luther Randolph & Johnny Stiles, Cameo 253
113. SCARLETT O'HARA ... Lawrence Welk, Dot 16488
114. STILL NO. 2 ... Ben Colder, MGM 13147
115. SUMMERTIME ... Chris Columbo Qintet, Strand 25056
116. WHAT I GOTTA DO (TO MAKE YOU JEALOUS) .. Little Eva, Dimension 1013
117. LONELY SURFER ... Jack Nitzsche, Reprise 20202
118. YOU CAN NEVER STOP ME LOVING YOU ... Johnny Tillotson, Cadence 1437
119. I'M NOT A FOOL ANYMORE ... T. K. Hulin, Smash 1830
120. IT HURTS TO BE SIXTEEN ... Barbara Chandler, Kapp 542
121. DO THE MONKEY ... King Curtis, Capitol 4998
122. MAN'S TEMPTATION ... Gene Chandler, Vee Jay 536
123. RIVER'S INVITATION ... Percy Mayfield, Tangerine 931
124. MORE ... Vic Dana, Dolton 81
125. FROM ME TO YOU ... Beattles, Vee Jay 522
126. GONE ... Rip Chords, Columbia 42812
127. SCARLETT O'HARA ... Bobby Gregg, Epic 9601
128. THE KIND OF BOY YOU CAN'T FORGET ... Raindrops, Jubilee 5455
129. PAYBACK ... Etta James, Argo 5445
130. BIRTHDAY PARTY ... Pixies Three, Mercury 72130
131. YOUR BABY'S GONE SURFIN' ... Duane Eddy, RCA Victor 8214
132. GREEN MONKEY ... Garnell Cooper & the Kinfolks, Jubilee 5445
133. THE HAPPY PUPPY ... Bent Fabric, Atco 6271

# Billboard HOT 100
### FOR WEEK ENDING AUGUST 10, 1963

| This Week | 1 Wk. Ago | 2 Wks. Ago | 3 Wks. Ago | TITLE — Artist, Label & Number | Weeks On Chart |
|---|---|---|---|---|---|
| 1 | 2 | 3 | 6 | FINGERTIPS (Part II) — Little Stevie Wonder, Tamla 54080 | 8 |
| 2 | 5 | 5 | 7 | WIPE OUT — Surfaris, Dot 16479 | 8 |
| 3 | 4 | 7 | 9 | (You're the) DEVIL IN DISGUISE — Elvis Presley, RCA Victor 8188 | 7 |
| 4 | 6 | 8 | 14 | BLOWIN' IN THE WIND — Peter, Paul & Mary, Warner Bros. 5368 | 7 |
| 5 | 1 | 2 | 3 | SO MUCH IN LOVE — Tymes, Parkway 781 | 11 |
| 6 | 8 | 11 | 23 | JUDY'S TURN TO CRY — Lesley Gore, Mercury 72143 | 6 |
| 7 | 3 | 1 | 1 | SURF CITY — Jan & Dean, Liberty 55580 | 9 |
| 8 | 11 | 16 | 30 | CANDY GIRL — 4 Seasons, Vee Jay 539 | 6 |
| 9 | 7 | 4 | 2 | EASIER SAID THAN DONE — Essex, Roulette 4494 | 10 |
| 10 | 19 | 28 | 50 | MORE — Kai Winding, Verve 10295 | 5 |
| 11 | 9 | 6 | 4 | TIE ME KANGAROO DOWN, SPORT — Rolf Harris, Epic 9596 | 10 |
| 12 | 10 | 10 | 15 | JUST ONE LOOK — Doris Troy, Atlantic 2188 | 10 |
| 13 | 13 | 15 | 18 | HOPELESS — Andy Williams, Columbia 42784 | 8 |
| 14 | 12 | 9 | 5 | MEMPHIS — Lonnie Mack, Fraternity 906 | 9 |
| 15 | 24 | 30 | 40 | ABILENE — George Hamilton IV, RCA Victor 8181 | 8 |
| 16 | 21 | 34 | 44 | GREEN, GREEN — New Christy Minstrels, Columbia 42805 | 7 |
| 17 | 45 | — | — | HELLO MUDDUH, HELLO FADDUH — Allan Sherman, Warner Bros. 5378 | 2 |
| 18 | 14 | 13 | 10 | PRIDE AND JOY — Marvin Gaye, Tamla 54079 | 13 |
| 19 | 17 | 17 | 20 | RING OF FIRE — Johnny Cash, Columbia 42788 | 11 |
| 20 | 16 | 19 | 24 | DETROIT CITY — Bobby Bare, RCA Victor 8183 | 9 |
| 21 | 23 | 29 | 42 | DENISE — Randy & the Rainbows, Rust 5059 | 9 |
| 22 | 27 | 41 | 59 | MOCKINGBIRD — Inez Foxx, Symbol 919 | 8 |
| 23 | 35 | 47 | 57 | DANKE SCHOEN — Wayne Newton, Capitol 4989 | 5 |
| 24 | 25 | 35 | 51 | MY WHOLE WORLD IS FALLING DOWN — Brenda Lee, Decca 31510 | 6 |
| 25 | 30 | 49 | 63 | TRUE LOVE NEVER RUNS SMOOTH — Gene Pitney, Musicor 1032 | 6 |
| 26 | 15 | 12 | 13 | NOT ME — Orlons, Cameo 257 | 9 |
| 27 | 20 | 24 | 35 | TILL THEN — Classics, Music Note 1116 | 8 |
| 28 | 33 | 40 | 53 | I WONDER — Brenda Lee, Decca 31510 | 6 |
| 29 | 58 | 76 | — | IF I HAD A HAMMER — Trini Lopez, Reprise 20198 | 3 |
| 30 | 37 | 59 | 71 | TWIST IT UP — Chubby Checker, Parkway 879 | 4 |
| 31 | 75 | — | — | MY BOYFRIEND'S BACK — Angels, Smash 1834 | 2 |
| 32 | 48 | 62 | 72 | THE MONKEY TIME — Major Lance, Okeh 7175 | 5 |
| 33 | 42 | 52 | 65 | SHAKE, SHAKE, SHAKE — Jackie Wilson, Brunswick 55246 | 5 |
| 34 | 31 | 39 | 46 | BE CAREFUL OF STONES THAT YOU THROW — Dion, Columbia 42810 | 6 |
| 35 | 40 | 46 | 55 | I (Who Have Nothing) — Ben E. King, Atco 6267 | 7 |
| 36 | 41 | 50 | 66 | MARLENA — 4 Seasons, Vee Jay 539 | 5 |
| 37 | 18 | 14 | 8 | SUKIYAKI — Kyu Sakamoto, Capitol 4945 | 14 |
| 38 | 32 | 33 | 37 | SIX DAYS ON THE ROAD — Dave Dudley, Golden Wing 3020 | 10 |
| 39 | 52 | 63 | 78 | MAKE THE WORLD GO AWAY — Timi Yuro, Liberty 55587 | 4 |
| 40 | 54 | 68 | — | HEY GIRL — Freddie Scott, Colpix 692 | 3 |
| 41 | 26 | 22 | 25 | MY TRUE CONFESSION — Brook Benton, Mercury 72135 | 9 |
| 42 | 56 | 71 | — | PAINTED, TAINTED ROSE — Al Martino, Capitol 5000 | 3 |
| 43 | 60 | 89 | — | FRANKIE AND JOHNNY — Sam Cooke, RCA Victor 8215 | 3 |
| 44 | 39 | 32 | 32 | GOODNIGHT MY LOVE — Fleetwoods, Dolton 75 | 11 |
| 45 | 46 | 48 | 52 | TIPS OF MY FINGERS — Roy Clark, Capitol 4956 | 7 |
| 46 | 51 | 65 | 80 | HOW MANY TEARDROPS — Lou Christie, Roulette 4504 | 4 |
| 47 | 53 | 56 | 68 | WHEN A BOY FALLS IN LOVE — Mel Carter, Derby 1003 | 6 |
| 48 | 22 | 18 | 11 | BLUE ON BLUE — Bobby Vinton, Epic 9593 | 13 |
| 49 | 85 | — | — | SURFER GIRL — Beach Boys, Capitol 5009 | 2 |
| 50 | 59 | 70 | 86 | SURFIN' HOOTENANNY — Al Casey, Stacy 962 | 5 |
| 51 | 82 | — | — | HEAT WAVE — Martha & the Vandellas, Gordy 7022 | 2 |
| 52 | 69 | 82 | — | THE DREAMER — Neil Sedaka, RCA Victor 8209 | 3 |
| 53 | 66 | 83 | 99 | I WANT TO STAY HERE — Steve & Eydie, Columbia 42815 | 4 |
| 54 | 62 | 75 | 90 | WAIT 'TIL MY BOBBY GETS HOME — Darlene Love, Philles 114 | 4 |
| 55 | 63 | 87 | 92 | MAMA DON'T ALLOW — Rooftop Singers, Vanguard 35020 | 4 |
| 56 | 61 | 61 | 67 | SOMETIMES YOU GOTTA CRY A LITTLE — Bobby Bland, Duke 366 | 4 |
| 57 | 43 | 44 | 47 | ROCK ME IN THE CRADLE OF LOVE — Dee Dee Sharp, Cameo 260 | 7 |
| 58 | 38 | 38 | 43 | HOOTENANNY — Glencoves, Select 724 | 9 |
| 59 | 28 | 21 | 21 | NO ONE — Ray Charles, ABC-Paramount 10453 | 8 |
| 60 | 55 | 55 | 62 | SURF PARTY — Chubby Checker, Parkway 879 | 5 |
| 61 | 70 | — | — | DESERT PETE — Kingston Trio, Capitol 5005 | 2 |
| 62 | 29 | 26 | 31 | DON'T SAY GOODNIGHT AND MEAN GOODBYE — Shirelles, Scepter 1255 | 9 |
| 63 | 68 | 73 | 81 | I'M AFRAID TO GO HOME — Brian Hyland, ABC-Paramount 10452 | 7 |
| 64 | 57 | 60 | 73 | BRENDA — Cupids, KC 115 | 6 |
| 65 | 74 | 85 | 96 | IT HURTS TO BE SIXTEEN — Andrea Carroll, Big Top 3156 | 4 |
| 66 | 71 | 72 | 79 | LEAVE ME ALONE — Baby Washington, Sue 790 | 4 |
| 67 | 34 | 20 | 17 | HARRY THE HAIRY APE — Ray Stevens, Mercury 72125 | 9 |
| 68 | 65 | 66 | 75 | I WILL LOVE YOU — Richard Chamberlain, MGM 13148 | 6 |
| 69 | 76 | 81 | 91 | GROOVY BABY — Billy Abbott, Parkway 874 | 4 |
| 70 | 77 | — | — | EVERYBODY MONKEY — Freddy Cannon, Swan 4149 | 2 |
| 71 | 84 | 96 | — | IT'S TOO LATE — Wilson Pickett, Double L 717 | 3 |
| 72 | 83 | 99 | — | THESE FOOLISH THINGS — James Brown & The Famous Flames, King 5767 | 3 |
| 73 | 80 | 84 | — | QUE SERA, SERA (Whatever Will Be, Will Be) — High Keys, Atco 6268 | 3 |
| 74 | 79 | 79 | 97 | THIS IS ALL I ASK — Tony Bennett, Columbia 42820 | 4 |
| 75 | — | — | — | YOU CAN NEVER STOP ME LOVING YOU — Johnny Tillotson, Cadence 1437 | 1 |
| 76 | 98 | — | — | PLEASE DON'T TALK TO THE LIFEGUARD — Diane Ray, Mercury 72117 | 2 |
| 77 | 78 | 80 | 87 | CAN'T NOBODY LOVE YOU — Solomon Burke, Atlantic 2196 | 4 |
| 78 | — | — | — | BLUE VELVET — Bobby Vinton, Epic 9614 | 1 |
| 79 | — | — | — | HEY THERE LONELY BOY — Ruby & the Romantics, Kapp 544 | 1 |
| 80 | — | — | — | THE KIND OF BOY YOU CAN'T FORGET — Raindrops, Jubilee 5455 | 1 |
| 81 | 93 | — | — | MARTIAN HOP — Ran-Dells, Chairman 4403 | 2 |
| 82 | 91 | — | — | THIS IS ALL I ASK — Burl Ives, Decca 31518 | 2 |
| 83 | — | — | — | PAY BACK — Etta James, Argo 5445 | 1 |
| 84 | 90 | — | — | DUM DUM DEE DUM — Johnny Cymbal, Kapp 539 | 2 |
| 85 | — | — | — | DROWNIN' MY SORROWS — Connie Francis, MGM 13160 | 1 |
| 86 | 73 | 78 | — | DAUGHTER — Blenders, Witch 114 | 5 |
| 87 | 87 | — | — | MY DADDY KNOWS BEST — Marvelettes, Tamla 54082 | 2 |
| 88 | 88 | 86 | 89 | DANCIN' HOLIDAY — Olympics, Tri Disc 107 | 6 |
| 89 | 95 | — | — | LUCKY LIPS — Cliff Richard, Epic 9597 | 2 |
| 90 | — | — | — | IT'S A LONELY TOWN — Gene McDaniels, Liberty 55597 | 1 |
| 91 | 100 | — | — | MAKE THE MUSIC PLAY — Dionne Warwick, Scepter 1253 | 2 |
| 92 | 94 | 95 | — | A BREATH TAKING GUY — Supremes, Motown 1044 | 3 |
| 93 | 96 | 97 | — | SATURDAY SUNSHINE — Bert Bacharach, Kapp 532 | 3 |
| 94 | — | — | — | MAN'S TEMPTATION — Gene Chandler, Vee Jay 536 | 1 |
| 95 | — | — | — | THE MINUTE YOU'RE GONE — Sonny James, Capitol 4969 | 1 |
| 96 | — | — | — | LONELY SURFER — Jack Nitzsche, Reprise 20202 | 1 |
| 97 | — | — | — | (I Cried at) LAURA'S WEDDING — Barbara Lynn, Jamie 1260 | 1 |
| 98 | — | — | — | THIS IS MY PRAYER — Theola Kilgore, Serock 2006 | 1 |
| 99 | — | 98 | — | STILL NO. 2 — Ben Colder, MGM 13147 | 2 |
| 100 | — | — | — | MORE — Vic Dana, Dolton 81 | 1 |

## BUBBLING UNDER THE HOT 100

- 101. WHAT I GOTTA DO (To Make You Jealous) — Little Eva, Dimension 1013
- 102. AT THE SHORE — Johnny Caswell, Smash 1833
- 103. FROM ME TO YOU — Del Shannon, Big Top 3152
- 104. DANCE, DANCE, DANCE — Joey Dee, Roulette 4503
- 105. TRUE BLUE LOU — Tony Bennett, Columbia 42820
- 106. GONE — Rip Chords, Columbia 42812
- 107. CHINESE CHECKERS — Booker T. & the MG's, Stax 137
- 108. TREAT 'EM TOUGH — Jimmy Soul, S.P.Q.R. 3310
- 109. CROSSROADS — Luther Randolph & Johnny Stiles, Cameo 253
- 110. IT WON'T BE THIS WAY (ALWAYS) — King Pins, Federal 12434
- 111. THEN HE KISSED ME — Crystals, Philles 115
- 112. STRAIGHTEN UP YOUR HEART — Barbara Lewis, Atlantic 2200
- 113. YOUR BABY'S GONE SURFIN' — Duane Eddy, RCA Victor 8214
- 114. SOMETIMES YOU GOTTA CRY A LITTLE — Connie Francis, MGM 13160
- 115. I'M THE BOSS — Burl Ives, Decca 31504
- 116. FROM ME TO YOU — Beatles, Vee Jay 522
- 117. BAJA — Astronauts, RCA Victor 8194
- 118. LOVE ME ALL THE WAY — Kim Weston, Tamla 54076
- 119. PRETTY GIRLS EVERYWHERE — Arthur Alexander, Dot 16509
- 120. SUMMERTIME — Chris Colombo Quintet, Strand 25056
- 121. LITTLE DANCING DOLL — Shelby Flint, Valiant 6031
- 122. WHY DON'T YOU BELIEVE ME — Duprees, Coed 584
- 123. BIRTHDAY PARTY — Pixies Three, Mercury 72130
- 124. A SLOW DANCE — Ronnie & the Hi-Lites, Win 250
- 125. DO THE MONKEY — King Curtis, Capitol 4998
- 126. LITTLE DEUCE COUPE — Beach Boys, Capitol 5009
- 127. RIVER'S INVITATION — Percy Mayfield, Tangerine 931
- 128. I'VE GOT A RIGHT TO CRY — Fats Domino, ABC-Paramount 10475
- 129. LOVE ME ALL THE WAY — Kim Weston, Tamla 54076
- 130. HAPPY PUPPY — Henri René, Decca
- 131. OLD CAPE COD — Jerry Vale, Columbia 42826
- 132. WHEN I'M WALKING (Let Me Walk) — Fats Domino, ABC-Paramount 10475
- 133. WHERE IS LOVE NOW — Sapphires, Swan 4143
- 134. SCARLETT O'HARA — Lawrence Welk, Dot 16488
- 135. MALA FEMMENA — Jimmy Roselli, Lenox 5571

# Billboard

For Week Ending August 17, 1963

# HOT 100

★ **STAR performer**—Sides registering greatest proportionate upward progress this week.

| This Week | 1 Wk. Ago | 2 Wks. Ago | 3 Wks. Ago | TITLE | Artist, Label & Number | Weeks On Chart |
|---|---|---|---|---|---|---|
| 1 | 1 | 2 | 3 | FINGERTIPS (Part II) | Little Stevie Wonder, Tamla 54080 | 9 |
| 2 | 4 | 6 | 8 | BLOWIN' IN THE WIND | Peter, Paul & Mary, Warner Bros. 5368 | 8 |
| 3 | 3 | 4 | 7 | (You're the) DEVIL IN DISGUISE | Elvis Presley, RCA Victor 8188 | 8 |
| 4 | 2 | 5 | 5 | WIPE OUT | Surfaris, Dot 16479 | 9 |
| 5 | 6 | 8 | 11 | JUDY'S TURN TO CRY | Lesley Gore, Mercury 72143 | 7 |
| 6 | 8 | 11 | 16 | CANDY GIRL | 4 Seasons, Vee Jay 539 | 7 |
| ★ 7 | 17 | 45 | — | HELLO MUDDUH, HELLO FADDUH | Allan Sherman, Warner Bros. 5378 | 3 |
| 8 | 5 | 1 | 2 | SO MUCH IN LOVE | Tymes, Parkway 781 | 12 |
| 9 | 10 | 19 | 28 | MORE | Kai Winding, Verve 10295 | 6 |
| ★ 10 | 31 | 75 | — | MY BOYFRIEND'S BACK | Angels, Smash 1834 | 3 |
| 11 | 7 | 3 | 1 | SURF CITY | Jan & Dean, Liberty 55580 | 10 |
| 12 | 9 | 7 | 4 | EASIER SAID THAN DONE | Essex, Roulette 4494 | 11 |
| ★ 13 | 22 | 27 | 41 | MOCKINGBIRD | Inez Foxx, Symbol 919 | 9 |
| 14 | 16 | 21 | 34 | GREEN, GREEN | New Christy Minstrels, Columbia 42805 | 8 |
| ★ 15 | 21 | 23 | 29 | DENISE | Randy & the Rainbows, Rust 5059 | 10 |
| 16 | 15 | 24 | 30 | ABILENE | George Hamilton IV, RCA Victor 8181 | 9 |
| ★ 17 | 29 | 58 | 76 | IF I HAD A HAMMER | Trini Lopez, Reprise 20198 | 4 |
| ★ 18 | 23 | 35 | 47 | DANKE SCHOEN | Wayne Newton, Capitol 4989 | 6 |
| 19 | 12 | 10 | 10 | JUST ONE LOOK | Doris Troy, Atlantic 2188 | 11 |
| 20 | 14 | 12 | 9 | MEMPHIS | Lonnie Mack, Fraternity 906 | 11 |
| ★ 21 | 40 | 54 | 68 | HEY GIRL | Freddie Scott, Colpix 692 | 4 |
| 22 | 13 | 13 | 15 | HOPELESS | Andy Williams, Columbia 32784 | 9 |
| 23 | 25 | 30 | 49 | TRUE LOVE NEVER RUNS SMOOTH | Gene Pitney, Musicor 1032 | 7 |
| 24 | 24 | 25 | 35 | MY WHOLE WORLD IS FALLING DOWN | Brenda Lee, Decca 31510 | 7 |
| 25 | 28 | 33 | 40 | I WONDER | Brenda Lee, Decca 31510 | 6 |
| ★ 26 | 32 | 48 | 62 | THE MONKEY TIME | Major Lance, Okeh 7175 | 6 |
| 27 | 30 | 37 | 59 | TWIST IT UP | Chubby Checker, Parkway 879 | 5 |
| ★ 28 | 49 | 85 | — | SURFER GIRL | Beach Boys, Capitol 5009 | 3 |
| 29 | 20 | 16 | 19 | DETROIT CITY | Bobby Bare, RCA Victor 8183 | 10 |
| 30 | 19 | 17 | 17 | RING OF FIRE | Johnny Cash, Columbia 42788 | 12 |
| 31 | 39 | 52 | 63 | MAKE THE WORLD GO AWAY | Timi Yuro, Liberty 55587 | 5 |
| 32 | 11 | 9 | 6 | TIE ME KANGAROO DOWN, SPORT | Rolf Harris, Epic 9596 | 11 |
| ★ 33 | 43 | 60 | 89 | FRANKIE AND JOHNNY | Sam Cooke, RCA Victor 8215 | 4 |
| ★ 34 | 51 | 82 | — | HEAT WAVE | Martha & the Vandellas, Gordy 7022 | 3 |
| 35 | 35 | 40 | 46 | I (Who Have Nothing) | Ben E. King, Atco 6267 | 8 |
| 36 | 36 | 41 | 50 | MARLENA | 4 Seasons, Vee Jay 539 | 6 |
| 37 | 42 | 56 | 71 | PAINTED, TAINTED ROSE | Al Martino, Capitol 5000 | 4 |
| 38 | 27 | 20 | 24 | TILL THEN | Classics, Music Note 1116 | 9 |
| 39 | 18 | 14 | 13 | PRIDE AND JOY | Marvin Gaye, Tamla 54079 | 14 |
| 40 | 26 | 15 | 12 | NOT ME | Orlons, Cameo 257 | 10 |
| 41 | 38 | 32 | 33 | SIX DAYS ON THE ROAD | Dave Dudley, Golden Wing 3020 | 11 |
| 42 | 33 | 42 | 52 | SHAKE, SHAKE, SHAKE | Jackie Wilson, Brunswick 55246 | 6 |
| ★ 43 | 53 | 66 | 83 | I WANT TO STAY HERE | Steve & Eydie, Columbia 42815 | 5 |
| ★ 44 | 54 | 62 | 75 | WAIT 'TIL MY BOBBY GETS HOME | Darlene Love, Philles 114 | 5 |
| 45 | 45 | 46 | 48 | TIPS OF MY FINGERS | Roy Clark, Capitol 4956 | 8 |
| 46 | 34 | 31 | 39 | BE CAREFUL OF STONES THAT YOU THROW | Dion, Columbia 42810 | 7 |
| 47 | 47 | 53 | 56 | WHEN A BOY FALLS IN LOVE | Mel Carter, Derby 1003 | 7 |
| 48 | 50 | 59 | 70 | SURFIN' HOOTENANNY | Al Casey, Stacy 962 | 6 |
| 49 | 46 | 51 | 65 | HOW MANY TEARDROPS | Lou Christie, Roulette 4504 | 5 |
| 50 | 52 | 69 | 82 | THE DREAMER | Neil Sedaka, RCA Victor 8209 | 4 |
| ★ 51 | 61 | 70 | — | DESERT PETE | Kingston Trio, Capitol 5005 | 3 |
| ★ 52 | 65 | 74 | 85 | IT HURTS TO BE SIXTEEN | Andrea Carroll, Big Top 3156 | 5 |
| ★ 53 | 78 | — | — | BLUE VELVET | Bobby Vinton, Epic 9614 | 2 |
| ★ 54 | 75 | — | — | YOU CAN NEVER STOP ME LOVING YOU | Johnny Tillotson, Cadence 1437 | 2 |
| ★ 55 | 79 | — | — | HEY THERE LONELY BOY | Ruby & the Romantics, Kapp 544 | 2 |
| 56 | 56 | 61 | 61 | SOMETIMES YOU GOTTA CRY A LITTLE | Bobby Bland, Duke 366 | 5 |
| ★ 57 | 72 | 83 | 99 | THESE FOOLISH THINGS | James Brown & The Famous Flames, King 5767 | 4 |
| 58 | 55 | 63 | 87 | MAMA DON'T ALLOW | Rooftop Singers, Vanguard 35020 | 5 |
| ★ 59 | 69 | 76 | 81 | GROOVY BABY | Billy Abbott, Parkway 874 | 5 |
| ★ 60 | 71 | 84 | 96 | IT'S TOO LATE | Wilson Pickett, Double L 717 | 4 |
| ★ 61 | 76 | 98 | — | PLEASE DON'T TALK TO THE LIFEGUARD | Diane Ray, Mercury 72117 | 3 |
| ★ 62 | 81 | 93 | — | MARTIAN HOP | Ran-Dells, Chairman 4403 | 3 |
| 63 | 63 | 68 | 73 | I'M AFRAID TO GO HOME | Brian Hyland, ABC-Paramount 10452 | 8 |
| ★ 64 | 80 | — | — | THE KIND OF BOY YOU CAN'T FORGET | Raindrops, Jubilee 5455 | 2 |
| 65 | 66 | 71 | 72 | LEAVE ME ALONE | Baby Washington, Sue 790 | 5 |
| 66 | 70 | 77 | — | EVERYBODY MONKEY | Freddy Cannon, Swan 4149 | 3 |
| 67 | 73 | 80 | 84 | QUE SERA, SERA (Whatever Will Be, Will be) | High Keys, Atco 6268 | 4 |
| 68 | 60 | 55 | 55 | SURF PARTY | Chubby Checker, Parkway 879 | 6 |
| ★ 69 | 85 | — | — | DROWNIN' MY SORROWS | Connie Francis, MGM 13160 | 2 |
| 70 | 68 | 65 | 66 | I WILL LOVE YOU | Richard Chamberlain, MGM 13148 | 7 |
| ★ 71 | — | — | — | THEN HE KISSED ME | Crystals, Philles 115 | 1 |
| 72 | 77 | 78 | 80 | CAN'T NOBODY LOVE YOU | Solomon Burke, Atlantic 2196 | 5 |
| 73 | 82 | 91 | — | THIS IS ALL I ASK | Burl Ives, Decca 31518 | 3 |
| 74 | 74 | 79 | 79 | THIS IS ALL I ASK | Tony Bennett, Columbia 42820 | 5 |
| 75 | 87 | 87 | — | MY DADDY KNOWS BEST | Marvelettes, Tamla 54082 | 3 |
| 76 | 89 | 95 | — | LUCKY LIPS | Cliff Richard, Epic 9597 | 3 |
| 77 | 86 | 73 | 78 | DAUGHTER | Blenders, Witch 114 | 6 |
| 78 | 83 | — | — | PAY BACK | Etta James, Argo 5445 | 2 |
| 79 | 90 | — | — | IT'S A LONELY TOWN | Gene McDaniels, Liberty 55597 | 2 |
| ★ 80 | — | — | — | LITTLE DEUCE COUPE | Beach Boys, Capitol 5009 | 1 |
| ★ 81 | 96 | — | — | LONELY SURFER | Jack Nitzsche, Reprise 20202 | 2 |
| 82 | 92 | 94 | 95 | A BREATH TAKING GUY | Supremes, Motown 1044 | 4 |
| 83 | 84 | 90 | — | DUM DUM DEE DUM | Johnny Cymbal, Kapp 539 | 3 |
| 84 | 94 | — | — | MAN'S TEMPTATION | Gene Chandler, Vee Jay 536 | 2 |
| ★ 85 | 100 | — | — | MORE | Vic Dana, Dolton 81 | 2 |
| ★ 86 | — | — | — | PART TIME LOVE | Little Johnny Taylor, Galaxy 722 | 1 |
| ★ 87 | — | — | — | ONLY IN AMERICA | Jay & the Americans, United Artists 626 | 1 |
| ★ 88 | — | — | — | MICKEY'S MONKEY | Miracles, Tamla 54083 | 1 |
| ★ 89 | — | — | — | WONDERFUL! WONDERFUL! | Tymes, Parkway 884 | 1 |
| ★ 90 | — | — | — | STRAIGHTEN UP YOUR HEART | Barbara Lewis, Atlantic 2200 | 1 |
| 91 | — | — | — | IT WON'T BE THIS WAY (Always) | King Pins, Federal 12484 | 1 |
| 92 | 97 | — | — | (I Cried at) LAURA'S WEDDING | Barbara Lynn, Jamie 1260 | 2 |
| 93 | 98 | — | — | THIS IS MY PRAYER | Theola Kilgore, Serock 2006 | 2 |
| 94 | — | — | — | I'M NOT A FOOL ANYMORE | T. K. Hulin, Smash 1830 | 1 |
| 95 | — | — | — | BIRTHDAY PARTY | Pixies Three, Mercury 72130 | 1 |
| 96 | — | 92 | 90 | CHINESE CHECKERS | Booker T. & MG's, Stax 137 | 3 |
| 97 | — | — | — | GONE | Rip Chords, Columbia 42812 | 1 |
| 98 | — | 86 | 77 | LAND OF 1,000 DANCES | Chris Kenner, Instant 3252 | 7 |
| 99 | — | — | — | I CRIED | Tina Montgomery, Try Me 28001 | 1 |
| 100 | — | — | — | CRY BABY | Garnet Mimms & the Enchanters, United Artists 629 | 1 |

## HOT 100—A TO Z—*(Publisher-Licensee)*

A Breath Taking Guy (Jobete, BMI) .......... 82
Abilene (Acuff-Rose) .......... 16
Be Careful of Stones That You Throw (Acuff-Rose, BMI) .......... 46
Birthday Party (Dandelion-Merjoda, BMI) .......... 95
Blowin' in the Wind (Witmark, ASCAP) .......... 2
Blue Velvet (Vogue, BMI) .......... 53
Candy Girl (Saturday-Gavadima, ASCAP) .......... 6
Can't Nobody Love You (Trio, BMI) .......... 72
Chinese Checkers (East, BMI) .......... 96
Cry Baby (Rittenhouse-Mellin, BMI) .......... 100
Danke Schoen (Roosevelt, BMI) .......... 18
Daughter (Venetia, BMI) .......... 77
Denise (Bright-Tunes, BMI) .......... 15
Desert Pete (Sleepy Hollow, ASCAP) .......... 51
Detroit City (Cedarwood, BMI) .......... 29
Devil in Disguise (Presley, BMI) .......... 3
The Dreamer (Rondak, BMI) .......... 50
Drowin' My Sorrows (Merna, BMI) .......... 69
Dum Dum Dee Dum (Haymarket, BMI) .......... 83
Easier Said Than Done (Nom, BMI) .......... 12
Everybody Monkey (Valley-Shelros, BMI) .......... 66
Fingertips (Part II) (Jobete, BMI) .......... 1
Frankie and Johnny (Kags, BMI) .......... 33
Gone (Daywin, BMI) .......... 97
Green, Green (New Christy, BMI) .......... 14
Groovy Baby (Cameo-Parkway, BMI) .......... 59
Heat Wave (Jobete, BMI) .......... 34
Hello Mudduh, Hello Fadduh (Curtain Call, ASCAP) .......... 7
Hey Girl (Screen Gems-Columbia, BMI) .......... 21
Hey There Lonely Boy (Famous, ASCAP) .......... 55
Hopeless (Brenner, BMI) .......... 22
How Many Teardrops (Nom, BMI) .......... 49
I Cried (Jim Jam, BMI) .......... 99
I Want to Stay Here (Screen Gems-Columbia, BMI) .......... 43
I Will Love You (DeVorzon, BMI) .......... 70
I (Who Have Nothing) (Milky Way-Trio-Cotillion, BMI) .......... 35
I Wonder (Leeds, ASCAP) .......... 25
I'm Afraid to Go Home (Geld-Udell, ASCAP) .......... 63
I'm Not a Fool Anymore (Crazy Cajun, BMI) .......... 94
If I Had a Hammer (Ludlow, BMI) .......... 17
It Hurts to Be Sixteen (Rondak, BMI) .......... 52
It Won't Be This Way (Alawys) (Sonlo, BMI) .......... 91
It's a Lonely Town (Valley, BMI) .......... 79
It's Too Late (Prigan-Correctone, BMI) .......... 60
Judy's Turn to Cry (Glamorous, ASCAP) .......... 5
Just One Look (Premier, BMI) .......... 19
The Kind of Boy You Can't Forget (Trio, BMI) .......... 64
Land of 1,000 Dances (Tune-Kel, BMI) .......... 98
Laura's Wedding (Dickson-Hansen, ASCAP) .......... 92
Leave Me Alone (Roosevelt, BMI) .......... 65
Little Deuce Coupe (Sea of Tunes, BMI) .......... 80
Lonely Surfer (Little Darlin', BMI) .......... 81
Lucky Lips (Tiger, BMI) .......... 76
Make the World Go Away (Pamper, BMI) .......... 31
Mama Don't Allow (Egypt Valley, BMI) .......... 58
Man's Temptation (Conrad-Karlan, BMI) .......... 84
Mar'ena (Saturday-Gavadima, ASCAP) .......... 36
Matian Hop (Screen Gems-Columbia, BMI) .......... 62
Memphis (Arc, BMI) .......... 20
Mickey's Monkey (Jobete, BMI) .......... 88
Mockingbird (Saturn, BMI) .......... 13
Monkey Time, The (Curtain-Palier, BMI) .......... 26
More—Dana (Marks, BMI) .......... 85
More—Winding (Marks, BMI) .......... 9
My Boyfriend's Back (Blackwood, BMI) .......... 10
My Daddy Knows Best (Jobete, BMI) .......... 75
My Whole World Is Falling Down (Champion-Moss Rose, BMI) .......... 24
Not Me (Rock Masters, BMI) .......... 40
Only in America (Screen Gems-Columbia) .......... 87
Pay Back (Chevis, BMI) .......... 78
Painted, Tainted Roce (Damian, ASCAP) .......... 37
Part Time Love (Cireco-Escort, BMI) .......... 86
Please Don't Talk to the Lifeguard (Joy, ASCAP) .......... 61
Pride and Joy (Jobete, BMI) .......... 39
Que Sera, Sera (Artists, ASCAP) .......... 67
Ring of Fire (Painted Desert, BMI) .......... 30
Shake, Shake, Shake (Brunswick, BMI) .......... 42
Six Days on the Road (Newkeys-Tune, BMI) .......... 41
So Much in Love (Cameo-Parkway, BMI) .......... 8
Sometimes You Gotta Cry a Little (Don, BMI) .......... 6
Straighten Up Your Heart (McLaughlin, BMI) .......... 90
Surf City (Screen Gems-Columbia, BMI) .......... 11
Surf Party (C. C. Kalmann, ASCAP) .......... 68
Surfer Girl (Sea of Tunes, BMI) .......... 28
Surfin' Hootenanny (Renda, BMI) .......... 48
Then He Kissed Me (Mother Bertha-Trio, BMI) .......... 71
These Foolish Things (Bourne, ASCAP) .......... 57
This Is All I Ask—Bennett (Massey, ASCAP) .......... 74
This Is All I Ask—Ives (Massey, ASCAP) .......... 73
This Is My Prayer (Sylvia, BMI) .......... 93
Tie Me Kangaroo Down, Sport (Beechwood, BMI) .......... 32
Til Then (Pickwick, ASCAP) .......... 38
Tips of My Fingers (Tree, BMI) .......... 45
True Love Never Runs Smooth (Arch, ASCAP) .......... 23
Twist It Up (Kalmann-C. C., ASCAP) .......... 27
Wait 'Til My Bobby Gets Home (Mother Bertha-Trio, BMI) .......... 44
When a Boy Falls in Love (Kags, BMI) .......... 47
Wipe Out (Micaleste-Robin Hood, BMI) .......... 4
Wonderful! Wonderful! (Marks, BMI) .......... 89
You Can Never Stop Me Loving You (Ridge, BMI) .......... 54

## BUBBLING UNDER THE HOT 100

101. LOVE ME ALL THE WAY .......... Kim Weston, Tamla 54076
102. FROM ME TO YOU .......... Del Shannon, Big Top 3152
103. YOUR BABY'S GONE SURFIN' .......... Duane Eddy, RCA Victor 8214
104. SUMERTIME .......... Chris Columbo Quintet, Strand 25056
105. WHAT I GOTTA DO (To Make You Jealous) .......... Little Eva, Dimension 1013
106. STILL NO. 2 .......... Ben Colder, MGM 13147
107. DO THE MONKEY .......... King Curtis, Capitol 4998
108. AT THE SHORE .......... Johnny Caswell, Smash 1833
109. SATURDAY SUNSHINE .......... Bert Bacharach, Kapp 532
110. CROSSROADS .......... Luther Randolph & Johnny Stiles, Cameo 253
111. TPEAT 'EM TOUGH .......... Jimmy Soul, S.P.Q.R. 3310
112. WHY DON'T YOU BELIEVE ME .......... Duprees, Coed 584
113. BAJA .......... Astronauts, RCA Victor 8194
114. THE MINUTE YOU'RE GONE .......... Sonny James, Capitol 4969
115. SOMETHING OLD, SOMETHING NEW .......... Paul & Paula, Philips 40130
116. A LITTLE LIKE LOVIN' .......... Cascades, RCA Victor 8206
117. DANCE, DANCE, DANCE .......... Joey Dee, Roulette 4503
118. OLD CAPE COD .......... Jerry Vale, Columbia 42826
119. MAKE THE MUSIC PLAY .......... Dionne Warwick, Scepter 1253
120. RIVER'S INVITATION .......... Percy Mayfield, Tangerine 931
121. SURFER JOE .......... Surfaris, Dot 16479
122. IT HURTS TO BE SIXTEEN .......... Barbara Chandler, Kapp 542
123. HEAR THE BELLS .......... Tokens, RCA Victor 8210
124. FROM ME TO YOU .......... Beatles, Vee Jay 522
125. DON'T LET THE SUN CATCH YOU CRYING .......... Steve Alaimo, Checker 1047
126. PPETTY GIRLS EVERYWHERE .......... Arthur Alexander, Dot 16509
127. MALA FEMMENA .......... Connie Francis, MGM 13160
128. HAPPY PUPPY .......... Bent Fabric, Atco 6271
129. CHINA NIGHTS .......... Kyu Sakamoto, Capitol 5016
130. ELEPHANT WALK .......... Donald Jenkins, Cortland 109
131. HOW HIGH THE MOON .......... Floyd Cramer, RCA Victor 8217
132. LOVER'S MEDLEY .......... Marcy Jo & Eddie Rambeau, Swan 4145
133. MORE .......... Steve Lawrence, Columbia 42795
134. STOP PRETENDING .......... Clovers, Porwin 1002

Compiled from national retail sales and radio station airplay by the Music Popularity Dept. of Record Market Research, Billboard.

# Billboard

For Week Ending August 24, 1963

# HOT 100

★ **STAR performer**—Sides registering greatest proportionate upward progress this week.

Billboard Award

| This Week | 1 Wk. Ago | 2 Wks. Ago | 3 Wks. Ago | TITLE Artist, Label & Number | Weeks On Chart |
|---|---|---|---|---|---|
| 1 | 1 | 1 | 2 | FINGERTIPS (Part II) — Little Stevie Wonder, Tamla 54080 | 10 |
| ★2 | 7 | 17 | 45 | HELLO MUDDUH, HELLO FADDUH — Allan Sherman, Warner Bros. 5378 | 4 |
| ★3 | 6 | 8 | 11 | CANDY GIRL — 4 Seasons, Vee Jay 539 | 8 |
| ★4 | 10 | 31 | 75 | MY BOYFRIEND'S BACK — Angels, Smash 1834 | 4 |
| 5 | 5 | 6 | 8 | JUDY'S TURN TO CRY — Lesley Gore, Mercury 72143 | 8 |
| 6 | 2 | 4 | 6 | BLOWIN' IN THE WIND — Peter, Paul & Mary, Warner Bros. 5368 | 9 |
| 7 | 4 | 2 | 5 | WIPE OUT — Surfaris, Dot 16479 | 10 |
| 8 | 9 | 10 | 19 | MORE — Kai Winding, Verve 10295 | 7 |
| 9 | 3 | 3 | 4 | (You're the) DEVIL IN DISGUISE — Elvis Presley, RCA Victor 8188 | 9 |
| ★10 | 15 | 21 | 23 | DENISE — Randy & the Rainbows, Rust 5059 | 11 |
| ★11 | 17 | 29 | 58 | IF I HAD A HAMMER — Trini Lopez, Reprise 20198 | 5 |
| 12 | 13 | 22 | 27 | MOCKINGBIRD — Inez Foxx, Symbol 919 | 10 |
| ★13 | 18 | 23 | 35 | DANKE SCHOEN — Wayne Newton, Capitol 4989 | 7 |
| 14 | 8 | 5 | 1 | SO MUCH IN LOVE — Tymes, Parkway 781 | 13 |
| 15 | 11 | 7 | 3 | SURF CITY — Jan & Dean, Liberty 55580 | 11 |
| ★16 | 21 | 40 | 54 | HEY GIRL — Freddie Scott, Colpix 692 | 5 |
| 17 | 14 | 16 | 21 | GREEN, GREEN — New Christy Minstrels, Columbia 42805 | 9 |
| ★18 | 28 | 49 | 85 | SURFER GIRL — Beach Boys, Capitol 5009 | 4 |
| ★19 | 34 | 51 | 82 | HEAT WAVE — Martha & the Vandellas, Gordy 7022 | 4 |
| ★20 | 26 | 32 | 48 | THE MONKEY TIME — Major Lance, Okeh 7175 | 7 |
| 21 | 23 | 25 | 30 | TRUE LOVE NEVER RUNS SMOOTH — Gene Pitney, Musicor 1032 | 8 |
| ★22 | 33 | 43 | 60 | FRANKIE AND JOHNNY — Sam Cooke, RCA Victor 8215 | 5 |
| ★23 | 37 | 42 | 56 | PAINTED, TAINTED ROSE — Al Martino, Capitol 5000 | 5 |
| 24 | 20 | 14 | 12 | MEMPHIS — Lonnie Mack, Fraternity 906 | 12 |
| 25 | 27 | 30 | 37 | TWIST IT UP — Chubby Checker, Parkway 879 | 6 |
| ★26 | 31 | 39 | 52 | MAKE THE WORLD GO AWAY — Timi Yuro, Liberty 55587 | 6 |
| 27 | 12 | 9 | 7 | EASIER SAID THAN DONE — Essex, Roulette 4494 | 12 |
| 28 | 24 | 24 | 25 | MY WHOLE WORLD IS FALLING DOWN — Brenda Lee, Decca 31510 | 8 |
| ★29 | 35 | 35 | 40 | I (Who Have Nothing) — Ben E. King, Atco 6267 | 9 |
| ★30 | 53 | 78 | — | BLUE VELVET — Bobby Vinton, Epic 9614 | 3 |
| ★31 | 43 | 53 | 66 | I WANT TO STAY HERE — Steve & Eydie, Columbia 42815 | 6 |
| 32 | 16 | 15 | 24 | ABILENE — George Hamilton IV, RCA Victor 8181 | 10 |
| ★33 | 44 | 54 | 62 | WAIT 'TIL MY BOBBY GETS HOME — Darlene Love, Philles 114 | 6 |
| 34 | 22 | 13 | 13 | HOPELESS — Andy Williams, Columbia 32784 | 10 |
| 35 | 29 | 20 | 16 | DETROIT CITY — Bobby Bare, RCA Victor 8183 | 11 |
| 36 | 19 | 12 | 10 | JUST ONE LOOK — Doris Troy, Atlantic 2188 | 12 |
| 37 | 25 | 28 | 33 | I WONDER — Brenda Lee, Decca 31510 | 7 |
| 38 | 36 | 36 | 41 | MARLENA — 4 Seasons, Vee Jay 539 | 7 |
| 39 | 30 | 19 | 17 | RING OF FIRE — Johnny Cash, Columbia 42788 | 13 |
| ★40 | 54 | 75 | — | YOU CAN NEVER STOP ME LOVING YOU — Johnny Tillotson, Cadence 1437 | 3 |
| ★41 | 71 | — | — | THEN HE KISSED ME — Crystals, Philles 115 | 2 |
| 42 | 42 | 33 | 42 | SHAKE, SHAKE, SHAKE — Jackie Wilson, Brunswick 55246 | 7 |
| ★43 | 62 | 81 | 93 | MARTIAN HOP — Ran-Dells, Chairman 4403 | 4 |
| ★44 | 64 | 80 | — | THE KIND OF BOY YOU CAN'T FORGET — Raindrops, Jubilee 5455 | 3 |
| 45 | 47 | 47 | 53 | WHEN A BOY FALLS IN LOVE — Mel Carter, Derby 1003 | 8 |
| 46 | 51 | 61 | 70 | DESERT PETE — Kingston Trio, Capitol 5005 | 4 |
| 47 | 50 | 52 | 69 | THE DREAMER — Neil Sedaka, RCA Victor 8209 | 5 |
| 48 | 52 | 65 | 74 | IT HURTS TO BE SIXTEEN — Andrea Carroll, Big Top 3156 | 6 |
| ★49 | 69 | 85 | — | DROWNIN' MY SORROWS — Connie Francis, MGM 13160 | 3 |
| 50 | 55 | 79 | — | HEY THERE LONELY BOY — Ruby & the Romantics, Kapp 544 | 3 |
| ★51 | 89 | — | — | WONDERFUL! WONDERFUL! — Tymes, Parkway 884 | 2 |
| 52 | 48 | 50 | 59 | SURFIN' HOOTENANNY — Al Casey, Stacy 962 | 7 |
| 53 | 61 | 76 | 98 | PLEASE DON'T TALK TO THE LIFEGUARD — Diane Ray, Mercury 72117 | 4 |
| ★54 | 66 | 70 | 77 | EVERYBODY MONKEY — Freddy Cannon, Swan 4149 | 4 |
| 55 | 57 | 72 | 83 | THESE FOOLISH THINGS — James Brown & The Famous Flames, King 5767 | 5 |
| 56 | 59 | 69 | 76 | GROOVY BABY — Billy Abbott, Parkway 874 | 6 |
| 57 | 60 | 71 | 84 | IT'S TOO LATE — Wilson Pickett, Double L 717 | 5 |
| 58 | 58 | 55 | 63 | MAMA DON'T ALLOW — Rooftop Singers, Vanguard 35020 | 6 |
| ★59 | 88 | — | — | MICKEY'S MONKEY — Miracles, Tamla 54083 | 2 |
| 60 | 67 | 73 | 80 | QUE SERA, SERA (Whatever Will Be, Will Be) — High Keyes, Atco 6268 | 5 |
| ★61 | 77 | 86 | 73 | DAUGHTER — Blenders, Witch 114 | 7 |
| 62 | 65 | 66 | 71 | LEAVE ME ALONE — Baby Washington, Sue 790 | 6 |
| ★63 | 80 | — | — | LITTLE DEUCE COUPE — Beach Boys, Capitol 5009 | 2 |
| ★64 | 81 | 96 | — | LONELY SURFER — Jack Nitzsche, Reprise 20202 | 3 |
| 65 | 56 | 56 | 61 | SOMETIMES YOU GOTTA CRY A LITTLE — Bobby Bland, Duke 366 | 6 |
| 66 | 72 | 77 | 78 | CAN'T NOBODY LOVE YOU — Solomon Burke, Atlantic 2196 | 6 |
| 67 | 75 | 87 | 87 | MY DADDY KNOWS BEST — Marvelettes, Tamla 54082 | 4 |
| ★68 | 90 | — | — | STRAIGHTEN UP YOUR HEART — Barbara Lewis, Atlantic 2200 | 2 |
| 69 | 76 | 89 | 95 | LUCKY LIPS — Cliff Richard, Epic 9597 | 4 |
| ★70 | — | — | — | WHY DON'T YOU BELIEVE ME — Duprees, Coed 584 | 1 |
| ★71 | 87 | — | — | ONLY IN AMERICA — Jay & the Americans, United Artists 625 | 2 |
| 72 | 73 | 82 | 91 | THIS IS ALL I ASK — Burl Ives, Decca 31518 | 4 |
| 73 | 74 | 74 | 79 | THIS IS ALL I ASK — Tony Bennett, Columbia 42820 | 6 |
| 74 | 85 | 100 | — | MORE — Vic Dana, Dolton 81 | 3 |
| 75 | 79 | 90 | — | IT'S A LONELY TOWN — Gene McDaniels, Liberty 55597 | 3 |
| 76 | 86 | — | — | PART TIME LOVE — Little Johnny Taylor, Galaxy 722 | 2 |
| 77 | 83 | 84 | 90 | DUM DUM DEE DUM — Johnny Cymbal, Kapp 539 | 4 |
| 78 | 78 | 83 | — | PAY BACK — Etta James, Argo 5445 | 3 |
| ★79 | 100 | — | — | CRY BABY — Garnet Mimms & the Enchanters, United Artists 629 | 2 |
| ★80 | 95 | — | — | BIRTHDAY PARTY — Pixies Three, Mercury 72130 | 2 |
| 81 | 82 | 92 | 94 | A BREATH TAKING GUY — Supremes, Motown 1044 | 5 |
| ★82 | — | 91 | — | MAKE THE MUSIC PLAY — Dionne Warwick, Scepter 1253 | 2 |
| ★83 | — | — | — | 8 X 10 — Bill Anderson, Decca 31521 | 1 |
| 84 | 84 | 94 | — | MAN'S TEMPTATION — Gene Chandler, Vee Jay 536 | 3 |
| ★85 | — | — | — | ORGAN SHOUT — Dave (Baby) Cortez, Chess 1861 | 1 |
| ★86 | — | — | — | CHINA NIGHTS (Shina No Yoru) — Kyu Sakamoto, Capitol 5016 | 1 |
| 87 | 92 | 97 | — | (I Cried at) LAURA'S WEDDING — Barbara Lynn, Jamie 1260 | 3 |
| 88 | 93 | 98 | — | THIS IS MY PRAYER — Theola Kilgore, Sereck 2006 | 3 |
| 89 | 91 | — | — | IT WON'T BE THIS WAY (Always) — King Pins, Federal 12484 | 2 |
| ★90 | — | — | — | A WALKIN' MIRACLE — Essex, Roulette 4515 | 1 |
| 91 | 97 | — | — | GONE — Rip Chords, Columbia 42812 | 2 |
| 92 | 94 | — | — | I'M NOT A FOOL ANYMORE — T. K. Hulin, Smash 1830 | 2 |
| 93 | — | — | — | SOMETHING OLD, SOMETHING NEW — Paul & Paula, Philips 40130 | 1 |
| 94 | — | — | — | TREAT MY BABY GOOD — Bobby Darin, Capitol 5019 | 1 |
| 95 | — | — | — | WHAM — Lonnie Mack, Fraternity 912 | 1 |
| 96 | — | — | — | YOUR BABY'S GONE SURFIN' — Duane Eddy, RCA Victor 8214 | 1 |
| 97 | — | — | — | HEAR THE BELLS — Tokens, RCA Victor 8210 | 1 |
| 98 | — | — | — | TELL ME THE TRUTH — Nancy Wilson, Capitol 4991 | 1 |
| 99 | — | — | — | DANCE, EVERYBODY, DANCE — Dartells, Dot 16502 | 1 |
| 100 | — | — | — | DO THE MONKEY — King Curtis, Capitol 4998 | 1 |

## HOT 100—A TO Z—(Publisher-Licensee)

Abilene (Acuff-Rose) ... 32
Birthday Party (Dandelion-Merjoda, BMI) ... 80
Blowin' in the Wind (Witmark, ASCAP) ... 6
Blue Velvet (Vogue, BMI) ... 30
Breath Taking Guy, A (Jobete, BMI) ... 81
Candy Girl (Saturday-Gavadima, ASCAP) ... 3
Can't Nobody Love You (Trio, BMI) ... 66
China Nights (Shina No Yoru) (Leeds, ASCAP) ... 86
Cry Baby (Rittenhouse-Mellin, BMI) ... 79
Dance, Everybody Dance (Trifid & Branna, BMI) ... 99
Danke Schoen (Roosevelt, BMI) ... 13
Daughter (Venetia, BMI) ... 61
Denise (Bright-Tunes, BMI) ... 10
Desert Pete (Sleepy Hollow, ASCAP) ... 46
Detroit City (Cedarwood, BMI) ... 35
Devil in Disguise (Presley, BMI) ... 9
Do the Monkey (T. M.-Old Lyne, BMI) ... 100
Dreamer, The (Rondak, BMI) ... 47
Drownin' My Sorrows (Merna, BMI) ... 49
Dum Dum Dee Dum (Haymarket, BMI) ... 77
Easier Said Than Done (Nom, BMI) ... 27
8 x 10 (Moss Rose, BMI) ... 83
Everybody Monkey (Valley-Shelros, BMI) ... 54
Fingertips (Part II) (Jobete, BMI) ... 1
Frankie and Johnny (Kags, BMI) ... 22
Gone (Daywin, BMI) ... 91
Green, Green (New Christy, BMI) ... 17
Groovy Baby (Cameo-Parkway, BMI) ... 56
Hear the Bells (Bright Tunes, BMI) ... 97
Heat Wave (Jobete, BMI) ... 19
Hello Mudduh, Hello Fadduh (Curtain Call, ASCAP) ... 2
Hey Girl (Screen Gems-Columbia, BMI) ... 16
Hey There Lonely Boy (Famous, ASCAP) ... 50
Hopeless (Brenner, BMI) ... 34
I Want to Stay Here (Screen Gems-Columbia, BMI) ... 31
I (Who Have Nothing) (Milky Way-Trio, BMI) ... 29
I Wonder (Leeds, ASCAP) ... 37
I'm Not a Fool Anymore (Crazy Cajun, BMI) ... 92
If I Had a Hammer (Ludlow, BMI) ... 11
It Hurts to Be Sixteen (Rondak, BMI) ... 48
It Won't Be This Way (Always) (Sonlo, BMI) ... 89
It's a Lonely Town (Valley, BMI) ... 75
It's Too Late (Prigan-Correctone, BMI) ... 57
Judy's Turn to Cry (Glamorous, ASCAP) ... 5
Just One Look (Premier, BMI) ... 36
Kind of Boy You Can't Forget, The (Trio, BMI) ... 44
Laura's Wedding (Dickson-Hansen, ASCAP) ... 87
Leave Me Alone (Roosevelt, BMI) ... 62
Little Deuce Coupe (Sea of Tunes, BMI) ... 63
Lonely Surfer (Little Darlin', BMI) ... 64
Lucky Lips (Tiger, BMI) ... 69
Make the Music Play (Eleventh Floor-U.S. Songs, ASCAP) ... 82
Make the World Go Away (Pamper, BMI) ... 26
Mama Don't Allow (Egypt Valley, BMI) ... 58
Man's Temptation (Conrad-Karlan, BMI) ... 84
Marlena (Saturday-Gavadima, ASCAP) ... 38
Matian Hop (Screen Gems-Columbia, BMI) ... 43
Memphis (Arc, BMI) ... 24
Mickey's Monkey (Jobete, BMI) ... 59
Mockingbird (Saturn, BMI) ... 12
Monkey Time, The (Curtain-Palier, BMI) ... 20
More—Dana (Marks, BMI) ... 74
More—Winding (Marks, BMI) ... 8
My Boyfriend's Back (Blackwood, BMI) ... 4
My Daddy Knows Best (Jobete, BMI) ... 67
My Whole World Is Falling Down (Champion-Moss Rose, BMI) ... 28
Only in America (Screen Gems-Columbia, BMI) ... 71
Organ Shout (Chevis-Cortez, BMI) ... 85
Pay Back (Chevis, BMI) ... 78
Painted, Tainted Rose (Damian, ASCAP) ... 23
Part Time Love (Cireco-Escort, BMI) ... 76
Please Don't Talk to the Lifeguard (Joy, ASCAP) ... 53
Que Sera, Sera (Artists, ASCAP) ... 60
Ring of Fire (Painted Desert, BMI) ... 39
Shake, Shake, Shake (Brunswick, BMI) ... 42
So Much in Love (Cameo-Parkway, BMI) ... 14
Something Old, Something New (LeBill-Marbill, BMI) ... 93
Sometimes You Gotta Cry a Little (Don, BMI) ... 65
Straighten Up Your Heart (McLaughlin, BMI) ... 68
Surf City (Screen Gems-Columbia, BMI) ... 15
Surfer Girl (Sea of Tunes, BMI) ... 18
Surfin' Hootenanny (Renda, BMI) ... 52
Tell Me the Truth (Kacy, BMI) ... 98
Then He Kissed Me (Mother Bertha-Trio, BMI) ... 41
These Foolish Things (Bourne, ASCAP) ... 55
This Is All I Ask—Bennett (Massey, ASCAP) ... 73
This Is All I Ask—Ives (Massey, ASCAP) ... 72
This Is My Prayer (Sylvia, BMI) ... 88
Treat My Baby Good (T. M., BMI) ... 94
True Love Never Runs Smooth (Arch, ASCAP) ... 21
Twist It Up (Kalmann-C. C., ASCAP) ... 25
Your Baby's Gone Surfin' (Linduane, BMI) ... 96
Wait 'Til My Bobby Gets Home (Mother Bertha-Trio, BMI) ... 33
Walkin' Miracle, A (Planteary, ASCAP) ... 90
Wham (Carlson-Edwood, BMI) ... 95
When a Boy Falls in Love (Kags, BMI) ... 45
Why Don't You Believe Me (Brandon, ASCAP) ... 70
Wipe Out (Miraleste-Robin Hood, BMI) ... 7
Wonderful! Wonderful! (Marks, BMI) ... 51
You Can Never Stop Me Loving You (Ridge, BMI) ... 40

## BUBBLING UNDER THE HOT 100

101. LONELY WORLD ... Dion, Laurie 3187
102. FROM ME TO YOU ... Del Shannon, Big Top 3152
103. SOONER OR LATER ... Johnnie Mathis, Columbia 42836
104. WHAT I GOTTA DO (To Make You Jealous) ... Little Eva, Dimension 1013
105. SATURDAY SUNSHINE ... Bert Bacharach, Kapp 532
106. SURFER JOE ... Surfaris, Dot 16479
107. TALK TO ME ... Sunny & Sunglows, Tear Drop 3014
108. THE MINUTE YOU'RE GONE ... Sonny James, Capitol 4969
109. CROSSROADS ... Luther Randolph & Johnny Stiles, Cameo 253
110. CHINESE CHECKERS ... Booker T & MG's, Stax 137
111. BUST OUT ... Busters, Arlen 735
112. DANCE, DANCE, DANCE ... Joey Dee, Roulette 4503
113. SUMMERTIME ... Chris Columbo Quintet, Strand 25056
114. IT HURTS TO BE SIXTEEN ... Barbara Chandler, Kapp 542
115. AT THE SHORE ... Johnny Caswell, Smash 1833
116. LOVE ME ALL THE WAY ... Kim Weston, Tamla 54076
117. ELEPHANT WALK ... Donald Jenkins, Cortland 109
118. PRETTY GIRLS EVERYWHERE ... Arthur Alexander, Dot 16509
119. WHEN I'M WALKIN' (Let Me Walk) ... Fats Domino, ABC-Paramount 10475
120. WHAT A FOOL I'VE BEEN ... Carla Thomas, Atlantic 2189
121. WHAT MAKES LITTLE GIRLS CRY ... Victorians, Liberty 55574
122. HOW HIGH THE MOON ... Floyd Cramer, RCA Victor 8217
123. HAPPY PUPPY ... Bent Fabric, Atco 6271
124. LAND OF 1,000 DANCES ... Chris Kenner, Instant 3252
125. DOWN THE AISLE ... Patty LaBelle & Blue Bells, King 5777
126. SALLY, GO 'ROUND THE ROSES ... Jaynetts, Tuff 369
127. MORE ... Steve Lawrence, Columbia 42795
128. A SLOW DANCE ... Ronnie & Hi-Lites, Win 250
129. MY BABY LOVES TO DANCE ... Chris Montez, Monogram 513
130. I'VE GOT A RIGHT TO CRY ... Fats Domino, ABC-Paramount 10475
131. IF YOU LOVE HER ... Barbara Lewis, Atlantic 2200
132. LITTLE GIRL BAD ... Joanie Sommers, Warner Bros. 5374
133. MAKE THE WORLD GO AWAY ... Ray Price, Columbia 42827
134. MY LAURA ... Harry Charles, Rowax 802
135. WHERE IS MY JOHNNY NOW ... Sapphires, Swan 4143
136. FLIPPED OVER YOU ... Paul & Paula, Philips 40130

Compiled from national retail sales and radio station airplay by the Music Popularity Dept. of Record Market Research, Billboard.

# Billboard HOT 100

*For Week Ending August 31, 1963*

★ **STAR** performer—Sides registering greatest proportionate upward progress this week.

| This Week | Wk. Ago | 2 Wks. Ago | 3 Wks. Ago | TITLE, Artist, Label & Number | Weeks On Chart |
|---|---|---|---|---|---|
| ★1 | 4 | 10 | 31 | MY BOYFRIEND'S BACK — Angels, Smash 1834 | 5 |
| 2 | 2 | 7 | 17 | HELLO MUDDUH, HELLO FADDUH — Allan Sherman, Warner Bros. 5378 | 5 |
| 3 | 1 | 1 | 1 | FINGERTIPS (Part II) — Little Stevie Wonder, Tamla 54080 | 11 |
| 4 | 3 | 6 | 8 | CANDY GIRL — 4 Seasons, Vee Jay 539 | 9 |
| 5 | 6 | 2 | 4 | BLOWIN' IN THE WIND — Peter, Paul & Mary, Warner Bros. 5368 | 10 |
| ★6 | 11 | 17 | 29 | IF I HAD A HAMMER — Trini Lopez, Reprise 20198 | 6 |
| 7 | 5 | 5 | 6 | JUDY'S TURN TO CRY — Lesley Gore, Mercury 72143 | 9 |
| 8 | 12 | 13 | 22 | MOCKINGBIRD — Inez Foxx, Symbol 919 | 11 |
| 9 | 8 | 9 | 10 | MORE — Kai Winding, Verve 10295 | 8 |
| 10 | 10 | 15 | 21 | DENISE — Randy & the Rainbows, Rust 5059 | 12 |
| ★11 | 30 | 53 | 78 | BLUE VELVET — Bobby Vinton, Epic 9614 | 4 |
| 12 | 20 | 26 | 32 | THE MONKEY TIME — Major Lance, Okeh 7175 | 8 |
| ★13 | 18 | 28 | 49 | SURFER GIRL — Beach Boys, Capitol 5009 | 5 |
| ★14 | 19 | 34 | 51 | HEAT WAVE — Martha & the Vandellas, Gordy 7022 | 5 |
| 15 | 16 | 21 | 40 | HEY GIRL — Freddie Scott, Colpix 692 | 6 |
| 16 | 13 | 18 | 23 | DANKE SCHOEN — Wayne Newton, Capitol 4989 | 8 |
| 17 | 9 | 3 | 3 | (You're the) DEVIL IN DISGUISE — Elvis Presley, RCA Victor 8188 | 10 |
| 18 | 7 | 4 | 2 | WIPE OUT — Surfaris, Dot 16479 | 11 |
| 19 | 22 | 33 | 43 | FRANKIE AND JOHNNY — Sam Cooke, RCA Victor 8215 | 6 |
| 20 | 41 | 71 | — | THEN HE KISSED ME — Crystals, Philles 115 | 3 |
| 21 | 23 | 37 | 42 | PAINTED, TAINTED ROSE — Al Martino, Capitol 5000 | 6 |
| 22 | 14 | 8 | 5 | SO MUCH IN LOVE — Tymes, Parkway 781 | 14 |
| 23 | 21 | 23 | 25 | TRUE LOVE NEVER RUNS SMOOTH — Gene Pitney, Musicor 1032 | 9 |
| 24 | 17 | 14 | 16 | GREEN, GREEN — New Christy Minstrels, Columbia 42805 | 10 |
| 25 | 15 | 11 | 7 | SURF CITY — Jan & Dean, Liberty 55580 | 12 |
| 26 | 26 | 31 | 39 | MAKE THE WORLD GO AWAY — Timi Yuro, Liberty 55587 | 7 |
| ★27 | 33 | 44 | 54 | WAIT 'TIL MY BOBBY GETS HOME — Darlene Love, Philles 114 | 7 |
| 28 | 25 | 27 | 30 | TWIST IT UP — Chubby Checker, Parkway 879 | 7 |
| 29 | 31 | 43 | 53 | I WANT TO STAY HERE — Steve & Eydie, Columbia 42815 | 7 |
| ★30 | 40 | 54 | 75 | YOU CAN NEVER STOP ME LOVING YOU — Johnny Tillotson, Cadence 1437 | 4 |
| 31 | 29 | 35 | 35 | I (Who Have Nothing) — Ben E. King, Atco 6267 | 10 |
| 32 | 32 | 16 | 15 | ABILENE — George Hamilton IV, RCA Victor 8181 | 11 |
| ★33 | 43 | 62 | 81 | MARTIAN HOP — Ran-Dells, Chairman 4403 | 5 |
| ★34 | 44 | 64 | 80 | THE KIND OF BOY YOU CAN'T FORGET — Raindrops, Jubilee 5455 | 4 |
| ★35 | 51 | 89 | — | WONDERFUL! WONDERFUL! — Tymes, Parkway 884 | 3 |
| ★36 | 46 | 51 | 61 | DESERT PETE — Kingston Trio, Capitol 5005 | 4 |
| 37 | 28 | 24 | 24 | MY WHOLE WORLD IS FALLING DOWN — Brenda Lee, Decca 31510 | 9 |
| ★38 | 49 | 69 | 85 | DROWNIN' MY SORROWS — Connie Francis, MGM 13160 | 3 |
| ★39 | 59 | 88 | — | MICKEY'S MONKEY — Miracles, Tamla 54083 | 3 |
| ★40 | 50 | 55 | 79 | HEY THERE LONELY BOY — Ruby & the Romantics, Kapp 544 | 4 |
| 41 | 27 | 12 | 9 | EASIER SAID THAN DONE — Essex, Roulette 4494 | 13 |
| 42 | 38 | 36 | 36 | MARLENA — 4 Seasons, Vee Jay 539 | 8 |
| ★43 | 53 | 61 | 76 | PLEASE DON'T TALK TO THE LIFEGUARD — Diane Ray, Mercury 72117 | 5 |
| 44 | 45 | 47 | 47 | WHEN A BOY FALLS IN LOVE — Mel Carter, Derby 1003 | 9 |
| 45 | 48 | 52 | 65 | IT HURTS TO BE SIXTEEN — Andrea Carroll, Big Top 3156 | 7 |
| 46 | 35 | 29 | 20 | DETROIT CITY — Bobby Bare, RCA Victor 8183 | 12 |
| 47 | 36 | 19 | 12 | JUST ONE LOOK — Doris Troy, Atlantic 2188 | 13 |
| 48 | 24 | 20 | 14 | MEMPHIS — Lonnie Mack, Fraternity 906 | 13 |
| 49 | 34 | 22 | 13 | HOPELESS — Andy Williams, Columbia 32784 | 11 |
| 50 | 63 | 80 | — | LITTLE DEUCE COUPE — Beach Boys, Capitol 5009 | 3 |
| 51 | 64 | 81 | 96 | LONELY SURFER — Jack Nitzsche, Reprise 20202 | 4 |
| 52 | 52 | 48 | 50 | SURFIN' HOOTENANNY — Al Casey, Stacy 962 | 8 |
| 53 | 57 | 60 | 71 | IT'S TOO LATE — Wilson Pickett, Double L 717 | 6 |
| 54 | 68 | 90 | — | STRAIGHTEN UP YOUR HEART — Barbara Lewis, Atlantic 2200 | 3 |
| 55 | 56 | 59 | 69 | GROOVY BABY — Billy Abbott, Parkway 874 | 7 |
| 56 | 60 | 67 | 73 | QUE SERA, SERA (Whatever Will Be, Will Be) — High Keyes, Atco 6268 | 6 |
| 57 | 47 | 50 | 52 | THE DREAMER — Neil Sedaka, RCA Victor 8209 | 6 |
| 58 | 54 | 66 | 70 | EVERYBODY MONKEY — Freddy Cannon, Swan 4149 | 5 |
| ★59 | 70 | — | — | WHY DON'T YOU BELIEVE ME — Duprees, Coed 584 | 2 |
| 60 | 58 | 58 | 55 | MAMA DON'T ALLOW — Rooftop Singers, Vanguard 35020 | 7 |
| 61 | 61 | 77 | 86 | DAUGHTER — Blenders, Witch 114 | 8 |
| 62 | 71 | 87 | — | ONLY IN AMERICA — Jay & the Americans, United Artists 625 | 3 |
| ★63 | — | — | — | SALLY, GO 'ROUND THE ROSES — Jaynetts, Tuff 369 | 1 |
| 64 | 37 | 25 | 28 | I WONDER — Brenda Lee, Decca 31510 | 8 |
| 65 | 62 | 65 | 66 | LEAVE ME ALONE — Baby Washington, Sue 790 | 7 |
| ★66 | 90 | — | — | A WALKIN' MIRACLE — Essex, Roulette 4515 | 2 |
| 67 | 72 | 73 | 82 | THIS IS ALL I ASK — Burl Ives, Decca 31518 | 5 |
| 68 | 69 | 76 | 89 | LUCKY LIPS — Cliff Richard, Epic 9597 | 5 |
| 69 | 79 | 100 | — | CRY BABY — Garnet Mimms and the Enchanters, United Artists 629 | 3 |
| 70 | 73 | 74 | 74 | THIS IS ALL I ASK — Tony Bennett, Columbia 42820 | 7 |
| 71 | 74 | 85 | 100 | MORE — Vic Dana, Dolton 81 | 6 |
| 72 | 83 | — | — | 8 X 10 — Bill Anderson, Decca 31521 | 2 |
| 73 | 80 | 95 | — | BIRTHDAY PARTY — Pixies Three, Mercury 72130 | 3 |
| 74 | 76 | 86 | — | PART TIME LOVE — Little Johnny Taylor, Galaxy 722 | 3 |
| 75 | 42 | 42 | 33 | SHAKE, SHAKE, SHAKE — Jackie Wilson, Brunswick 55246 | 8 |
| ★76 | 86 | — | — | CHINA NIGHTS (Shina No Yoru) — Kyu Sakamoto, Capitol 5016 | 2 |
| 77 | 55 | 57 | 72 | THESE FOOLISH THINGS — James Brown & The Famous Flames, King 5767 | 6 |
| 78 | 75 | 79 | 90 | IT'S A LONELY TOWN — Gene McDaniels, Liberty 55597 | 4 |
| 79 | 67 | 75 | 87 | MY DADDY KNOWS BEST — Marvelettes, Tamla 54082 | 5 |
| 80 | 81 | 82 | 92 | A BREATH TAKING GUY — Supremes, Motown 1044 | 6 |
| 81 | 82 | — | 91 | MAKE THE MUSIC PLAY — Dionne Warwick, Scepter 1253 | 3 |
| 82 | 87 | 92 | 97 | (I Cried at) LAURA'S WEDDING — Barbara Lynn, Jamie 1260 | 4 |
| 83 | 94 | — | — | TREAT MY BABY GOOD — Bobby Darin, Capitol 5019 | 2 |
| 84 | 95 | — | — | WHAM — Lonnie Mack, Fraternity 912 | 2 |
| 85 | 93 | — | — | SOMETHING OLD, SOMETHING NEW — Paul & Paula, Philips 40130 | 2 |
| 86 | 78 | 78 | 83 | PAY BACK — Etta James, Argo 5445 | 4 |
| 87 | 88 | 93 | 98 | THIS IS MY PRAYER — Theola Kilgore, Serock 2006 | 4 |
| 88 | 84 | 84 | 94 | MAN'S TEMPTATION — Gene Chandler, Vee Jay 536 | 4 |
| 89 | 85 | — | — | ORGAN SHOUT — Dave (Baby) Cortez, Chess 1861 | 2 |
| ★90 | — | — | — | BE MY BABY — Ronettes, Philles 116 | 1 |
| 91 | 91 | 97 | — | GONE — Rip Chords, Columbia 42812 | 3 |
| 92 | — | — | — | SURFER JOE — Surfaris, Dot 16479 | 1 |
| 93 | 98 | — | — | TELL ME THE TRUTH — Nancy Wilson, Capitol 4991 | 2 |
| 94 | 97 | — | — | HEAR THE BELLS — Tokens, RCA Victor 8210 | 2 |
| 95 | — | — | — | LOVE ME ALL THE WAY — Kim Weston, Tamla 54076 | 4 |
| 96 | — | 96 | — | CHINESE CHECKERS — Booker T. & the M.G.'s, Stax 137 | 4 |
| 97 | — | — | — | THAT SUNDAY, THAT SUMMER — Nat King Cole, Capitol 5027 | 1 |
| 98 | — | — | — | FADED LOVE — Patsy Cline, Decca 31522 | 1 |
| 99 | — | — | — | BETTY IN BERMUDAS — Dovell's, Parkway 882 | 1 |
| 100 | — | — | — | MAKE THE WORLD GO AWAY — Ray Price, Columbia 42827 | 1 |

## BUBBLING UNDER THE HOT 100

101. I CALL IT PRETTY MUSIC — Little Stevie Wonder, Tamla 54061
102. YOUR BABY'S GONE SURFIN' — Duane Eddy, RCA Victor 8214
103. DOWN THE AISLE — Patty LaBelle & Blue Bells, Newtown 5777
104. LONELY WORLD — Johnny Mathis, Columbia 42836
105. SOONER OR LATER — Sonny & Sunglows, Tear Drop 3014
106. TALK TO ME — Sunny & Sunglows, Tear Drop 3014
107. DO THE MONKEY — King Curtis, Capitol 4998
108. FROM ME TO YOU — Del Shannon, Big Top 3152
109. BUST OUT — Busters, Arlen 735
110. IT WON'T BE THIS WAY (Always) — King Pins, Federal 12484
111. THE MINUTE YOU'RE GONE — Sonny James, Capitol 4969
112. AT THE SHORE — Johnny Caswell, Smash 1833
113. MY LAURA — Marcy Charles, Rowax 802
114. WHEN I'M WALKIN' (Let Me Walk) — Fats Domino, ABC-Paramount 10475
115. I'M NOT A FOOL ANYMORE — T. K. Hulin, Smash 1830
116. IT HURTS TO BE SIXTEEN — Barbara Chandler, Kapp 542
117. GEE WHAT A GUY — Yvonne Carroll, Domain 1018
118. PRETTY GIRLS EVERYWHERE — Arthur Alexander, Dot 16509
119. DANCE, EVERYBODY, DANCE — Dartells, Dot 16502
120. HELLO HEARTACHE, GOODBYE LOVE — Little Peggy March, RCA Victor 8217
121. HOW HIGH THE MOON — Floyd Cramer, RCA Victor 8217
122. STILL NO. 2 — Bon Caler, MGM 13147
123. SUMMERTIME — Chris Columbo Quintet, Strand 25056
124. WHAT I GOTTA DO (To Make You Jealous) — Little Eva, Dimension 1013
125. I CAN'T STAY MAD AT YOU — Skeeter Davis, RCA Victor 8219
126. CROSSROADS — Luther Randolph & Johnny Stiles, Cameo 250
127. A SLOW DANCE — Ronnie & Hi-Lites, Win 250
128. DANCE — Steve Lawrence, Columbia 42795
129. TRUE BLUE LOU — Tony Bennett, Columbia 42820
130. I'M COMING BACK TO YOU — Julie London, Liberty 55605
131. SATURDAY SUNSHINE — Bert Bacharach, Kapp 532

*Compiled from national retail sales and radio station airplay by the Music Popularity Dept. of Record Market Research, Billboard.*

# Billboard HOT 100

For Week Ending September 7, 1963

★ STAR performer—Sides registering greatest proportionate upward progress this week.

| This Week | Last Week | 2 Wk. Ago | 3 Wk. Ago | TITLE Artist, Label & Number | Weeks On Chart |
|---|---|---|---|---|---|
| 1 | 1 | 4 | 10 | MY BOYFRIEND'S BACK — Angels, Smash 1834 | 6 |
| 2 | 2 | 2 | 7 | HELLO MUDDUH, HELLO FADDUH — Allan Sherman, Warner Bros. 5378 | 6 |
| 3 | 6 | 11 | 17 | IF I HAD A HAMMER — Trini Lopez, Reprise 20198 | 7 |
| ★4 | 11 | 30 | 53 | BLUE VELVET — Bobby Vinton, Epic 9614 | 5 |
| 5 | 4 | 3 | 6 | CANDY GIRL — 4 Seasons, Vee Jay 539 | 10 |
| ★6 | 14 | 19 | 34 | HEAT WAVE — Martha & the Vandellas, Gordy 7022 | 6 |
| 7 | 8 | 12 | 13 | MOCKINGBIRD — Inez Foxx, Symbol 919 | 12 |
| 8 | 12 | 20 | 26 | THE MONKEY TIME — Major Lance, Okeh 7175 | 9 |
| 9 | 5 | 6 | 2 | BLOWIN' IN THE WIND — Peter, Paul & Mary, Warner Bros. 5368 | 11 |
| 10 | 15 | 16 | 21 | HEY GIRL — Freddie Scott, Colpix 692 | 7 |
| 11 | 3 | 1 | 1 | FINGERTIPS (Part II) — Little Stevie Wonder, Tamla 54080 | 12 |
| 12 | 13 | 18 | 28 | SURFER GIRL — Beach Boys, Capitol 5009 | 6 |
| 13 | 10 | 10 | 15 | DENISE — Randy & the Rainbows, Rust 5059 | 13 |
| 14 | 19 | 22 | 33 | FRANKIE AND JOHNNY — Sam Cooke, RCA Victor 8215 | 7 |
| 15 | 20 | 41 | 71 | THEN HE KISSED ME — Crystals, Philles 115 | 4 |
| 16 | 16 | 13 | 18 | DANKE SCHOEN — Wayne Newton, Capitol 4989 | 9 |
| 17 | 9 | 8 | 9 | MORE — Kai Winding, Verve 10295 | 9 |
| 18 | 7 | 5 | 5 | JUDY'S TURN TO CRY — Lesley Gore, Mercury 72143 | 10 |
| ★19 | 30 | 40 | 54 | YOU CAN NEVER STOP ME LOVING YOU — Johnny Tillotson, Cadence 1437 | 5 |
| 20 | 21 | 23 | 37 | PAINTED, TAINTED ROSE — Al Martino, Capitol 5000 | 7 |
| 21 | 39 | 59 | 88 | MICKEY'S MONKEY — Miracles, Tamla 54083 | 4 |
| 22 | 35 | 51 | 89 | WONDERFUL! WONDERFUL! — Tymes, Parkway 884 | 4 |
| 23 | 18 | 7 | 4 | WIPE OUT — Surfaris, Dot 16479 | 12 |
| 24 | 26 | 26 | 31 | MAKE THE WORLD GO AWAY — Timi Yuro, Liberty 55587 | 8 |
| 25 | 24 | 17 | 14 | GREEN, GREEN — New Christy Minstrels, Columbia 42805 | 11 |
| 26 | 27 | 33 | 44 | WAIT 'TIL MY BOBBY GETS HOME — Darlene Love, Philles 114 | 8 |
| 27 | 34 | 44 | 64 | THE KIND OF BOY YOU CAN'T FORGET — Raindrops, Jubilee 5455 | 5 |
| 28 | 29 | 31 | 43 | I WANT TO STAY HERE — Steve & Eydie, Columbia 42815 | 8 |
| 29 | 63 | — | — | SALLY, GO 'ROUND THE ROSES — Jaynetts, Tuff 369 | 2 |
| 30 | 33 | 43 | 62 | MARTIAN HOP — Ran-Dells, Chairman 4403 | 6 |
| 31 | 69 | 79 | 100 | CRY BABY — Garnet Mimms & the Enchanters, United Artists 629 | 4 |
| 32 | 23 | 21 | 23 | TRUE LOVE NEVER RUNS SMOOTH — Gene Pitney, Musicor 1032 | 10 |
| 33 | 22 | 14 | 8 | SO MUCH IN LOVE — Tymes, Parkway 871 | 15 |
| 34 | 36 | 46 | 51 | DESERT PETE — Kingston Trio, Capitol 5005 | 6 |
| 35 | 40 | 50 | 55 | HEY THERE LONELY BOY — Ruby & the Romantics, Kapp 544 | 5 |
| 36 | 38 | 49 | 69 | DROWNIN' MY SORROWS — Connie Francis, MGM 13160 | 5 |
| 37 | 43 | 53 | 61 | PLEASE DON'T TALK TO THE LIFEGUARD — Diane Ray, Mercury 72117 | 6 |
| ★38 | 50 | 63 | 80 | LITTLE DEUCE COUPE — Beach Boys, Capitol 5009 | 4 |
| 39 | 31 | 29 | 35 | I (Who Have Nothing) — Ben E. King, Atco 4267 | 11 |
| ★40 | 51 | 64 | 81 | LONELY SURFER — Jack Nitzsche, Reprise 20202 | 5 |
| 41 | 28 | 25 | 27 | TWIST IT UP — Chubby Checker, Parkway 879 | 8 |
| 42 | 17 | 9 | 3 | (You're the) DEVIL IN DISGUISE — Elvis Presley, RCA Victor 8188 | 11 |
| 43 | 74 | 76 | 86 | PART TIME LOVE — Little Johnny Taylor, Galaxy 722 | 4 |
| 44 | 25 | 15 | 11 | SURF CITY — Jan & Dean, Liberty 55580 | 13 |
| 45 | 66 | 90 | — | A WALKIN' MIRACLE — Essex, Roulette 4515 | 3 |
| 46 | 62 | 71 | 87 | ONLY IN AMERICA — Jay & the Americans, United Artists 626 | 4 |
| 47 | 32 | 32 | 16 | ABILENE — George Hamilton IV, RCA Victor 8181 | 12 |
| 48 | 59 | 70 | — | WHY DON'T YOU BELIEVE ME — Duprees, Coed 584 | 3 |
| 49 | 53 | 57 | 60 | IT'S TOO LATE — Wilson Pickett, Double L 717 | 7 |
| 50 | 54 | 68 | 90 | STRAIGHTEN UP YOUR HEART — Barbara Lewis, Atlantic 2200 | 4 |
| 51 | 45 | 48 | 52 | IT HURTS TO BE SIXTEEN — Andrea Carroll, Big Top 3156 | 8 |
| 52 | 58 | 54 | 66 | EVERYBODY MONKEY — Freddy Cannon, Swan 4149 | 6 |
| 53 | 56 | 60 | 67 | QUE SERA, SERA (Whatever Will Be, Will Be) — High Keyes, Atco 6268 | 7 |
| 54 | 71 | 74 | 85 | MORE — Vic Dana, Dolton 81 | 5 |
| ★55 | 90 | — | — | BE MY BABY — Ronettes, Philles 116 | 2 |
| 56 | 84 | 95 | — | WHAM — Lonnie Mack, Fraternity 912 | 3 |
| 57 | 55 | 56 | 59 | GROOVY BABY — Billy Abbott, Parkway 874 | 8 |
| 58 | 47 | 36 | 19 | JUST ONE LOOK — Doris Troy, Atlantic 2188 | 14 |
| 59 | 44 | 45 | 47 | WHEN A BOY FALLS IN LOVE — Mel Carter, Derby 1003 | 10 |
| 60 | 57 | 47 | 50 | THE DREAMER — Neil Sedaka, RCA Victor 8209 | 7 |
| 61 | 73 | 80 | 95 | BIRTHDAY PARTY — Pixies Three, Mercury 72130 | 4 |
| 62 | 72 | 83 | — | 8 X 10 — Bill Anderson, Decca 31521 | 3 |
| 63 | 83 | 94 | — | TREAT MY BABY GOOD — Bobby Darin, Capitol 5019 | 3 |
| 64 | 68 | 69 | 76 | LUCKY LIPS — Cliff Richard, Epic 9597 | 6 |
| 65 | 76 | 86 | — | CHINA NIGHTS (Shina No Yoru) — Kyu Sakamoto, Capitol 5016 | 3 |
| ★66 | — | — | — | BUSTED — Ray Charles, ABC-Paramount 10481 | 1 |
| 67 | 87 | 88 | 93 | THIS IS MY PRAYER — Theola Kilgore, Serock 2006 | 5 |
| 68 | 78 | 75 | 79 | IT'S A LONELY TOWN — Gene McDaniels, Liberty 55597 | 5 |
| 69 | 65 | 62 | 65 | LEAVE ME ALONE — Baby Washington, Sue 790 | 8 |
| 70 | 82 | 87 | 92 | (I Cried at) LAURA'S WEDDING — Barbara Lynn, Jamie 1260 | 5 |
| 71 | 88 | 84 | 84 | MAN'S TEMPTATION — Gene Chandler, Vee Jay 536 | 5 |
| 72 | — | — | — | BUST OUT — Busters, Arlen 735 | 1 |
| 73 | 79 | 67 | 75 | MY DADDY KNOWS BEST — Marvelettes, Tamla 54082 | 6 |
| ★74 | — | — | — | HELLO HEARTACHE, GOODBYE LOVE — Little Peggy March, RCA Victor 8221 | 1 |
| 75 | 80 | 81 | 82 | A BREATH TAKING GUY — Supremes, Motown 1044 | 7 |
| 76 | 89 | 85 | — | ORGAN SHOUT — Dave (Baby) Cortez, Chess 1861 | 3 |
| 77 | — | — | — | I CAN'T STAY MAD AT YOU — Skeeter Davis, RCA Victor 8219 | 1 |
| 78 | 85 | 93 | — | SOMETHING OLD, SOMETHING NEW — Paul & Paula, Philips 40130 | 3 |
| 79 | 97 | — | — | THAT SUNDAY, THAT SUMMER — Nat King Cole, Capitol 5027 | 2 |
| 80 | — | — | — | TALK TO ME — Sunny and the Sunglows, Tear Drop 3014 | 1 |
| 81 | 92 | — | — | SURFER JOE — Surfaris, Dot 16479 | 2 |
| 82 | — | — | — | MY BABE — Righteous Brothers, Moonglow 223 | 1 |
| 83 | 93 | 98 | — | TELL ME THE TRUTH — Nancy Wilson, Capitol 4991 | 3 |
| 84 | — | — | — | I'LL TAKE YOU HOME — Drifters, Atlantic 2201 | 1 |
| 85 | 86 | 78 | 78 | PAY BACK — Etta James, Argo 5445 | 5 |
| 86 | 96 | — | 96 | CHINESE CHECKERS — Booker T. & the M. G.'s, Stax 137 | 3 |
| 87 | — | — | — | SOONER OR LATER — Johnny Mathis, Columbia 42836 | 1 |
| 88 | 91 | 91 | 97 | GONE — Rip Chords, Columbia 42812 | 4 |
| 89 | — | — | — | WHAT DOES A GIRL DO — Shirelles, Scepter 1259 | 1 |
| 90 | — | — | — | MEAN WOMAN BLUES — Roy Orbison, Monument 824 | 1 |
| 91 | 99 | — | — | BETTY IN BERMUDAS — Dovell's, Parkway 882 | 2 |
| 92 | — | 100 | — | DO THE MONKEY — King Curtis, Capitol 4998 | 2 |
| 93 | — | — | — | HONOLULU LULU — Jan & Dean, Liberty 55613 | 1 |
| 94 | — | 95 | — | LOVE ME ALL THE WAY — Kim Weston, Tamla 54076 | 5 |
| 95 | — | — | — | SEPTEMBER SONG — Jimmy Durante, Warner Bros. 5382 | 1 |
| 96 | 98 | — | — | FADED LOVE — Patsy Cline, Decca 31522 | 2 |
| 97 | — | — | — | I'M CONFESSIN' — Frank Ifield, Capitol 5032 | 1 |
| 98 | — | — | — | TWO TICKETS TO PARADISE — Brook Benton, Mercury 72177 | 1 |
| 99 | — | — | — | CINDY'S GONNA CRY — Johnny Crawford, Del-Fi 4221 | 1 |
| 100 | — | — | — | A LOVE SO FINE — Chiffons, Laurie 3195 | 1 |

## BUBBLING UNDER THE HOT 100

101. CAN'T NOBODY LOVE YOU — Solomon Burke, Atlantic 2196
102. IT WON'T BE THIS WAY (Always) — King Pins, Federal 12484
103. HEAR THE BELLS — Tokens, RCA Victor 8210
104. LONELY WORLD — Dion, Laurie 3187
105. DOWN THE AISLE — Patty LaBelle & Blue Bells, King 5777
106. MAKING BELIEVE — Ray Charles, ABC-Paramount 10481
107. MY LAURA — Harry Charles, Reveue 902
108. LET'S FALL IN LOVE — Linda Scott, Congress 209
109. THE MINUTE YOU'RE GONE — Sonny James, Capitol 4969
110. YOUR BABY'S GONE SURFIN' — Duane Eddy, RCA Victor 8214
111. AT THE SHORE — Johnny Caswell, Smash 1833
112. MAKE THE WORLD GO AWAY — Ray Price, Columbia 42827
113. I'M NOT A FOOL ANYMORE — T.K. Hulin, Smash 1817
114. FLIPPED OVER YOU — Paul & Paula, Philips 40128
115. IT HURTS TO BE SIXTEEN — Barbara Chandler, Kapp 543
116. BLUE BAYOU — Roy Orbison, Monument 824
117. MORE — Steve Lawrence, Columbia 42815
118. TRUE BLUE LOU — Tony Bennett, Columbia 42820
119. ELEPHANT WALK — Donald Jenkins & the Delighters, Cortland 109
120. LAND OF 1,000 DANCES — Chris Kenner, Instant 3229
121. SHE'S MINE — Alice Wonder Land, Bardell 774
122. A SLOW DANCE — Ronnie & Hi-Lites, Win 250
123. SIDE SUMMER — Seychelles, Chancer 1140
124. MICHAEL — Steve Alaimo, Checker 1054
125. CROSSROADS — Luther Randolph & Johnny Stiles, Cameo 262
126. TIGER'S NOT A MONKEY — Sally London, Liberty 55591
127. I'M COMING BACK TO YOU — George Maharis, Epic 42611
128. HALFWAY — James Brown, Smash 1853
129. THAT'S HOW IT GOES — George Maharis, Epic 9613
130. DEEP PURPLE — Nino Tempo & April Stevens, Atco 6273
131. ARE YOU SURE — Betty Logan, Academy 102

Compiled from national retail sales and radio station airplay by the Music Popularity Dept. of Record Market Research, Billboard.

# Billboard HOT 100

**For Week Ending September 14, 1963**

★ STAR performer—Sides registering greatest proportionate upward progress this week.

| This Week | Wks. Ago | 2 Wks. Ago | 3 Wks. Ago | TITLE Artist, Label & Number | Weeks On Chart |
|---|---|---|---|---|---|
| 1 | 1 | 1 | 4 | MY BOYFRIEND'S BACK — Angels, Smash 1834 | 7 |
| 2 | 4 | 11 | 30 | BLUE VELVET — Bobby Vinton, Epic 9614 | 6 |
| 3 | 3 | 6 | 11 | IF I HAD A HAMMER — Trini Lopez, Reprise 20198 | 8 |
| 4 | 2 | 2 | 2 | HELLO MUDDUH, HELLO FADDUH — Allan Sherman, Warner Bros. 5378 | 7 |
| 5 | 6 | 14 | 19 | HEAT WAVE — Martha & the Vandellas, Gordy 7022 | 7 |
| ★6 | 15 | 20 | 41 | THEN HE KISSED ME — Crystals, Philles 115 | 5 |
| 7 | 12 | 13 | 18 | SURFER GIRL — Beach Boys, Capitol 5009 | 7 |
| 8 | 8 | 12 | 20 | THE MONKEY TIME — Major Lance, Okeh 7175 | 10 |
| ★9 | 29 | 63 | — | SALLY, GO 'ROUND THE ROSES — Jaynetts, Tuff 369 | 3 |
| 10 | 7 | 8 | 12 | MOCKINGBIRD — Inez Foxx, Symbol 919 | 13 |
| 11 | 10 | 15 | 16 | HEY GIRL — Freddie Scott, Colpix 692 | 8 |
| 12 | 5 | 4 | 3 | CANDY GIRL — 4 Seasons, Vee Jay 539 | 11 |
| ★13 | 31 | 69 | 79 | CRY BABY — Garnet Mimms & the Enchanters, United Artists 629 | 5 |
| 14 | 14 | 19 | 22 | FRANKIE AND JOHNNY — Sam Cooke, RCA Victor 8215 | 8 |
| 15 | 21 | 39 | 59 | MICKEY'S MONKEY — Miracles, Tamla 54083 | 5 |
| 16 | 22 | 35 | 51 | WONDERFUL! WONDERFUL! — Tymes, Parkway 884 | 5 |
| 17 | 20 | 21 | 23 | PAINTED, TAINTED ROSE — Al Martino, Capitol 5000 | 8 |
| 18 | 13 | 10 | 10 | DENISE — Randy & the Rainbows, Rust 5059 | 14 |
| 19 | 19 | 30 | 40 | YOU CAN NEVER STOP ME LOVING YOU — Johnny Tillotson, Cadence 1437 | 6 |
| ★20 | 55 | 90 | — | BE MY BABY — Ronettes, Philles 116 | 3 |
| 21 | 9 | 5 | 6 | BLOWIN' IN THE WIND — Peter, Paul & Mary, Warner Bros. 5368 | 12 |
| ★22 | 27 | 34 | 44 | THE KIND OF BOY YOU CAN'T FORGET — Raindrops, Jubilee 5455 | 6 |
| 23 | 11 | 3 | 1 | FINGERTIPS (Part II) — Little Stevie Wonder, Tamla 54080 | 13 |
| 24 | 30 | 33 | 43 | MARTIAN HOP — Ran-Dells, Chairman 4403 | 7 |
| 25 | 38 | 50 | 63 | LITTLE DEUCE COUPE — Beach Boys, Capitol 5009 | 5 |
| 26 | 17 | 9 | 8 | MORE — Kai Winding, Verve 10295 | 10 |
| 27 | 24 | 26 | 26 | MAKE THE WORLD GO AWAY — Timi Yuro, Liberty 55587 | 9 |
| 28 | 16 | 16 | 13 | DANKE SCHOEN — Wayne Newton, Capitol 4989 | 10 |
| ★29 | 45 | 66 | 90 | A WALKIN' MIRACLE — Essex, Roulette 4515 | 4 |
| 30 | 26 | 27 | 33 | WAIT 'TIL MY BOBBY GETS HOME — Darlene Love, Philles 114 | 9 |
| 31 | 28 | 29 | 31 | I WANT TO STAY HERE — Steve & Eydie, Columbia 42815 | 9 |
| 32 | 35 | 40 | 50 | HEY THERE LONELY BOY — Ruby & the Romantics, Kapp 544 | 6 |
| 33 | 34 | 36 | 46 | DESERT PETE — Kingston Trio, Capitol 5005 | 7 |
| 34 | 37 | 43 | 53 | PLEASE DON'T TALK TO THE LIFEGUARD — Diane Ray, Mercury 72117 | 7 |
| 35 | 43 | 74 | 76 | PART TIME LOVE — Little Johnny Taylor, Galaxy 722 | 5 |
| 36 | 36 | 38 | 49 | DROWNIN' MY SORROWS — Connie Francis, MGM 13160 | 6 |
| 37 | 18 | 7 | 5 | JUDY'S TURN TO CRY — Lesley Gore, Mercury 72143 | 11 |
| 38 | 66 | — | — | BUSTED — Ray Charles, ABC-Paramount 10481 | 2 |
| 39 | 40 | 51 | 64 | LONELY SURFER — Jack Nitzsche, Reprise 20202 | 6 |
| 40 | 48 | 59 | 70 | WHY DON'T YOU BELIEVE ME — Duprees, Coed 584 | 4 |
| 41 | 23 | 18 | 7 | WIPE OUT — Surfaris, Dot 16479 | 13 |
| 42 | 46 | 62 | 71 | ONLY IN AMERICA — Jay & the Americans, United Artists 625 | 5 |
| 43 | 25 | 24 | 17 | GREEN, GREEN — New Christy Minstrels, Columbia 42805 | 12 |
| ★44 | 56 | 84 | 95 | WHAM — Lonnie Mack, Fraternity 912 | 4 |
| 45 | 32 | 23 | 21 | TRUE LOVE NEVER RUNS SMOOTH — Gene Pitney, Musicor 1032 | 11 |
| 46 | 50 | 54 | 68 | STRAIGHTEN UP YOUR HEART — Barbara Lewis, Atlantic 2200 | 5 |
| 47 | 39 | 31 | 29 | I (Who Have Nothing) — Ben E. King, Atco 6267 | 12 |
| 48 | 53 | 56 | 60 | QUE SERA, SERA (Whatever Will Be, Will Be) — High Keyes, Atco 6268 | 8 |
| 49 | 54 | 71 | 74 | MORE — Vic Dana, Dolton 81 | 6 |
| 50 | 47 | 32 | 32 | ABILENE — George Hamilton IV, RCA Victor 8181 | 13 |
| 51 | 49 | 53 | 57 | IT'S TOO LATE — Wilson Pickett, Double L 717 | 8 |
| 52 | 77 | — | — | I CAN'T STAY MAD AT YOU — Skeeter Davis, RCA Victor 8219 | 2 |
| 53 | 62 | 72 | 83 | 8 X 10 — Bill Anderson, Decca 31521 | 4 |
| 54 | 63 | 83 | 94 | TREAT MY BABY GOOD — Bobby Darin, Capitol 5019 | 4 |
| 55 | 61 | 73 | 80 | BIRTHDAY PARTY — Pixies Three, Mercury 72130 | 5 |
| 56 | 51 | 45 | 48 | IT HURTS TO BE SIXTEEN — Andrea Carroll, Big Top 3156 | 9 |
| 57 | 52 | 58 | 54 | EVERYBODY MONKEY — Freddy Cannon, Swan 4149 | 7 |
| 58 | 93 | — | — | HONOLULU LULU — Jan & Dean, Liberty 55613 | 2 |
| 59 | 74 | — | — | HELLO HEARTACHE, GOODBYE LOVE — Little Peggy March, RCA Victor 8221 | 2 |
| 60 | 67 | 87 | 88 | THIS IS MY PRAYER — Theola Kilgore, Serock 2006 | 6 |
| 61 | 65 | 76 | 86 | CHINA NIGHTS (Shina No Yoru) — Kyu Sakamoto, Capitol 5016 | 4 |
| 62 | 64 | 68 | 69 | LUCKY LIPS — Cliff Richard, Epic 9597 | 7 |
| 63 | 79 | 97 | — | THAT SUNDAY, THAT SUMMER — Nat King Cole, Capitol 5027 | 3 |
| 64 | 68 | 78 | 75 | IT'S A LONELY TOWN — Gene McDaniels, Liberty 55597 | 6 |
| 65 | 72 | — | — | BUST OUT — Busters, Arlen 735 | 2 |
| 66 | 69 | 65 | 62 | LEAVE ME ALONE — Baby Washington, Sue 790 | 9 |
| 67 | — | — | — | DON'T THINK TWICE IT'S ALL RIGHT — Peter, Paul & Mary, Warner Bros. 5385 | 1 |
| 68 | 70 | 82 | 87 | (I Cried at) LAURA'S WEDDING — Barbara Lynn, Jamie 1260 | 6 |
| 69 | 81 | 92 | — | SURFER JOE — Surfaris, Dot 16479 | 3 |
| 70 | 80 | — | — | TALK TO ME — Sunny and the Sunglows, Tear Drop 3014 | 2 |
| 71 | 90 | — | — | MEAN WOMAN BLUES — Roy Orbison, Monument 824 | 2 |
| 72 | 84 | — | — | I'LL TAKE YOU HOME — Drifters, Atlantic 2201 | 2 |
| 73 | 71 | 88 | 84 | MAN'S TEMPTATION — Gene Chandler, Vee Jay 536 | 6 |
| 74 | 91 | 99 | — | BETTY IN BERMUDAS — Dovell's, Parkway 883 | 3 |
| 75 | — | — | — | DONNA THE PRIMA DONNA — Dion Di Muci, Columbia 42852 | 1 |
| 76 | 89 | — | — | WHAT DOES A GIRL DO — Shirelles, Scepter 1259 | 2 |
| 77 | 78 | 85 | 93 | SOMETHING OLD, SOMETHING NEW — Paul & Paula, Philips 40130 | 4 |
| 78 | 86 | 96 | — | CHINESE CHECKERS — Booker T. & the M.G.'s, Stax 137 | 6 |
| 79 | 82 | — | — | MY BABE — Righteous Brothers, Moonglow 223 | 2 |
| 80 | — | — | — | HE'S MINE — Alice Wonder Land, Bardell 774 | 1 |
| 81 | 83 | 93 | 98 | TELL ME THE TRUTH — Nancy Wilson, Capitol 4991 | 4 |
| 82 | — | — | — | TEENAGE CLEOPATRA — Tracey Dey, Liberty 55604 | 1 |
| 83 | 98 | — | — | TWO TICKETS TO PARADISE — Brook Benton, Mercury 72177 | 2 |
| 84 | — | — | — | ENAMORADO — Keith Colley, Unical 3006 | 1 |
| 85 | 87 | — | — | SOONER OR LATER — Johnny Mathis, Columbia 42836 | 2 |
| 86 | — | — | — | BLUE BAYOU — Roy Orbison, Monument 824 | 1 |
| 87 | — | — | — | FOOLS RUSH IN — Rick Nelson, Decca 31533 | 1 |
| 88 | 95 | — | — | SEPTEMBER SONG — Jimmy Durante, Warner Bros. 5382 | 2 |
| 89 | 97 | — | — | I'M CONFESSIN' — Frank Ifield, Capitol 5032 | 2 |
| 90 | 100 | — | — | A LOVE SO FINE — Chiffons, Laurie 3195 | 2 |
| 91 | — | — | — | ELEPHANT WALK — Donald Jenkins & the Daylighters, Cortland 109 | 1 |
| 92 | 85 | 86 | 78 | PAY BACK — Etta James, Argo 5445 | 6 |
| 93 | — | 96 | — | YOUR BABY'S GONE SURFIN' — Duane Eddy, RCA Victor 8214 | 2 |
| 94 | — | — | — | DEEP PURPLE — Nino Tempo & April Stevens, Atco 6273 | 1 |
| 95 | — | — | — | DOWN THE AISLE — Patty LaBelle and the Blue Belles, Newtown 5777 | 1 |
| 96 | — | — | — | LONELY DRIFTER — O'Jays, Imperial 5976 | 1 |
| 97 | 99 | — | — | CINDY'S GONNA CRY — Johnny Crawford, Del-Fi 4221 | 2 |
| 98 | — | 94 | 97 | HEAR THE BELLS — Tokens, RCA Victor 8210 | 3 |
| 99 | — | — | — | MR. WISHING WELL — Nat King Cole, Capitol 5027 | 1 |
| 100 | — | — | — | YOUR BOYFRIEND'S BACK — Bobby Comstock & the Counts, Lawn 219 | 1 |

## BUBBLING UNDER THE HOT 100

101. MAKE THE WORLD GO AWAY — Ray Price, Columbia 42827
102. MAKING BELIEVE — Ray Charles, ABC-Paramount 10481
103. MY DADDY KNOWS BEST — Marvelettes, Tamla 54082
104. YOU GIVE ME NOTHING TO GO ON — Ted Taylor, Okeh 7176
105. IT WON'T BE THIS WAY (Always) — King Pins, Federal 12484
106. SUGAR SHACK — Jimmy Gilmer & the Fireballs, Dot 16487
107. FADED LOVE — Patsy Cline, Decca 31522
108. FLIPPED OVER YOU — Paul & Paula, Philips 40130
109. LONELY WORLD — Dion, Laurie 3187
110. LITTLE YELLOW ROSES — Jackie DeShannon, Liberty 55602
111. LET'S FALL IN LOVE — Linda Scott, Congress 200
112. I'M NOT A FOOL ANYMORE — T. K. Hulin, Smash 1830
113. I'LL BELIEVE IT WHEN I SEE IT — Sierras, Goldisc 4
114. LOVE ME ALL THE WAY — Kim Weston, Tamla 54076
115. GEE WHAT A GUY — Yvonne Carroll, Domain 1018
116. A SLOW DANCE — Ronnie & Hi-Lites, Win 250
117. MICHAEL — Steve Alaimo, Checker 1054
118. THAT'S HOW IT GOES — George Maharis, Epic 9613
119. NIGHT LIFE — Rusty Draper, Monument 823
120. WHAT MAKES LITTLE GIRLS CRY — Victorians, Liberty 55574
121. BLUE SUMMER — Royalettes, Chancellor 1140
122. RED SAILS IN THE SUNSET — Fats Domino, ABC-Paramount 10484
123. DOWN ON BENDING KNEES — Johnny Copland, Golden Eagle 101
124. TALK BACK TREMBLING LIPS — Ernest Ashworth, Hickory 1214
125. HOW HIGH THE MOON — Floyd Cramer, RCA Victor 8217

*Compiled from national retail sales and radio station airplay by the Music Popularity Dept. of Record Market Research, Billboard.*

# Billboard HOT 100

For Week Ending September 21, 1963

★ STAR performer—Sides registering greatest proportionate upward progress this week.

| This Wk | 1 Wk. Ago | 2 Wks. Ago | 3 Wks. Ago | TITLE, Artist, Label & Number | Weeks On Chart |
|---|---|---|---|---|---|
| 1 | 2 | 4 | 11 | BLUE VELVET — Bobby Vinton, Epic 9614 | 7 |
| 2 | 1 | 1 | 1 | MY BOYFRIENDS BACK — Angels, Smash 1834 | 8 |
| 3 | 3 | 3 | 6 | IF I HAD A HAMMER — Trini Lopez, Reprise 20198 | 9 |
| 4 | 5 | 6 | 14 | HEAT WAVE — Martha & the Vandellas, Gordy 7022 | 8 |
| ★5 | 9 | 29 | 63 | SALLY, GO 'ROUND THE ROSES — Jaynetts, Tuff 369 | 4 |
| 6 | 6 | 15 | 20 | THEN HE KISSED ME — Crystals, Philles 115 | 6 |
| 7 | 7 | 12 | 13 | SURFER GIRL — Beach Boys, Capitol 5009 | 8 |
| 8 | 15 | 21 | 39 | MICKEY'S MONKEY — Miracles, Tamla 54083 | 6 |
| 9 | 4 | 2 | 2 | HELLO MUDDUH, HELLO FADDUH — Allan Sherman, Warner Bros. 5378 | 6 |
| 10 | 13 | 31 | 69 | CRY BABY — Garnet Mimms & the Enchanters, United Artists 629 | 6 |
| 11 | 16 | 22 | 35 | WONDERFUL! WONDERFUL! — Tymes, Parkway 884 | 6 |
| 12 | 20 | 55 | 90 | BE MY BABY — Ronettes, Philles 116 | 4 |
| 13 | 8 | 8 | 12 | THE MONKEY TIME — Major Lance, Okeh 7175 | 11 |
| 14 | 29 | 45 | 66 | A WALKIN' MIRACLE — Essex, Roulette 4515 | 5 |
| 15 | 17 | 20 | 21 | PAINTED, TAINTED ROSE — Al Martino, Capitol 5000 | 9 |
| 16 | 11 | 10 | 15 | HEY GIRL — Freddie Scott, Colpix 692 | 9 |
| 17 | 10 | 7 | 8 | MOCKINGBIRD — Inez Foxx, Symbol 919 | 14 |
| 18 | 19 | 19 | 30 | YOU CAN NEVER STOP ME LOVING YOU — Johnny Tillotson, Cadence 1437 | 7 |
| ★19 | 24 | 30 | 33 | MARTIAN HOP — Ran-Dells, Chairman 4403 | 8 |
| 20 | 14 | 14 | 19 | FRANKIE AND JOHNNY — Sam Cooke, RCA Victor 8215 | 9 |
| 21 | 22 | 27 | 34 | THE KIND OF BOY YOU CAN'T FORGET — Raindrops, Jubilee 5455 | 7 |
| 22 | 25 | 38 | 50 | LITTLE DEUCE COUPE — Beach Boys, Capitol 5009 | 6 |
| 23 | 38 | 66 | — | BUSTED — Ray Charles, ABC-Paramount 10481 | 3 |
| 24 | 12 | 5 | 4 | CANDY GIRL — 4 Seasons, Vee Jay 539 | 12 |
| 25 | 18 | 13 | 10 | DENISE — Randy & the Rainbows, Rust 5059 | 15 |
| 26 | 35 | 43 | 74 | PART TIME LOVE — Little Johnny Taylor, Galaxy 722 | 6 |
| 27 | 58 | 93 | — | HONOLULU LULU — Jan & Dean, Liberty 55613 | 3 |
| 28 | 21 | 9 | 5 | BLOWIN' IN THE WIND — Peter, Paul & Mary, Warner Bros. 5368 | 13 |
| 29 | 32 | 35 | 40 | HEY THERE LONELY BOY — Ruby & the Romantics, Kapp 544 | 7 |
| 30 | 31 | 28 | 29 | I WANT TO STAY HERE — Steve & Eydie, Columbia 42815 | 10 |
| 31 | 34 | 37 | 43 | PLEASE DON'T TALK TO THE LIFEGUARD — Diane Ray, Mercury 72117 | 8 |
| ★32 | 44 | 56 | 84 | WHAM — Lonnie Mack, Fraternity 912 | 5 |
| 33 | 23 | 11 | 3 | FINGERTIPS (Part II) — Little Stevie Wonder, Tamla 54080 | 14 |
| 34 | 26 | 17 | 9 | MORE — Kai Winding, Verve 10295 | 11 |
| 35 | 42 | 46 | 62 | ONLY IN AMERICA — Jay & the Americans, United Artists 625 | 6 |
| 36 | 28 | 16 | 16 | DANKE SCHOEN — Wayne Newton, Capitol 4989 | 11 |
| 37 | 40 | 48 | 59 | WHY DON'T YOU BELIEVE ME — Duprees, Coed 584 | 5 |
| 38 | 27 | 24 | 26 | MAKE THE WORLD GO AWAY — Timi Yuro, Liberty 55587 | 10 |
| 39 | 33 | 34 | 36 | DESERT PETE — Kingston Trio, Capitol 5005 | 8 |
| ★40 | 52 | 77 | — | I CAN'T STAY MAD AT YOU — Skeeter Davis, RCA Victor 8219 | 3 |
| 41 | 65 | 72 | — | BUST OUT — Busters, Arlen 735 | 3 |
| 42 | 39 | 40 | 51 | LONELY SURFER — Jack Nitzsche, Reprise 20202 | 7 |
| 43 | 46 | 50 | 54 | STRAIGHTEN UP YOUR HEART — Barbara Lewis, Atlantic 2200 | 6 |
| ★44 | 55 | 61 | 73 | BIRTHDAY PARTY — Pixies Three, Mercury 72130 | 6 |
| 45 | 49 | 54 | 71 | MORE — Vic Dana, Dolton 81 | 7 |
| 46 | 54 | 63 | 83 | TREAT MY BABY GOOD — Bobby Darin, Capitol 5019 | 5 |
| 47 | 48 | 53 | 56 | QUE SERA, SERA (Whatever Will Be, Will Be) — High Keyes, Atco 6268 | 9 |
| ★48 | 59 | 74 | — | HELLO HEARTACHE, GOODBYE LOVE — Little Peggy March, RCA Victor 8221 | 3 |
| 49 | 30 | 26 | 27 | WAIT 'TIL MY BOBBY GETS HOME — Darlene Love, Philles 114 | 10 |
| 50 | 71 | 90 | — | MEAN WOMAN BLUES — Roy Orbison, Monument 824 | 3 |
| 51 | 67 | — | — | DON'T THINK TWICE IT'S ALL RIGHT — Peter, Paul & Mary, Warner Bros. 5385 | 2 |
| 52 | 75 | — | — | DONNA THE PRIMA DONNA — Dion Di Muci, Columbia 42852 | 2 |
| 53 | 63 | 79 | 97 | THAT SUNDAY, THAT SUMMER — Nat King Cole, Capitol 5027 | 4 |
| 54 | 51 | 49 | 53 | IT'S TOO LATE — Wilson Pickett, Double L 717 | 9 |
| 55 | 72 | 84 | — | I'LL TAKE YOU HOME — Drifters, Atlantic 2201 | 3 |
| 56 | 83 | 98 | — | TWO TICKETS TO PARADISE — Brook Benton, Mercury 72177 | 3 |
| 57 | 70 | 80 | — | TALK TO ME — Sunny and the Sunglows, Tear Drop 3014 | 3 |
| 58 | 61 | 65 | 76 | CHINA NIGHTS (Shina No Yoru) — Kyu Sakamoto, Capitol 5016 | 5 |
| 59 | 76 | 89 | — | WHAT DOES A GIRL DO — Shirelles, Scepter 1259 | 3 |
| 60 | 74 | 91 | 99 | BETTY IN BERMUDAS — Dovell's, Parkway 883 | 4 |
| 61 | 53 | 62 | 72 | 8 X 10 — Bill Anderson, Decca 31521 | 5 |
| 62 | 36 | 36 | 38 | DROWNIN' MY SORROWS — Connie Francis, MGM 13160 | 7 |
| 63 | 41 | 23 | 18 | WIPE OUT — Surfaris, Dot 16479 | 14 |
| 64 | 87 | — | — | FOOLS RUSH IN — Rick Nelson, Decca 31533 | 2 |
| 65 | — | — | — | SUGAR SHACK — Jimmy Gilmer and the Fireballs, Dot 16487 | 1 |
| 66 | 62 | 64 | 68 | LUCKY LIPS — Cliff Richard, Epic 9597 | 8 |
| 67 | 69 | 81 | 92 | SURFER JOE — Surfaris, Dot 16479 | 4 |
| 68 | 68 | 70 | 82 | (I Cried at) LAURA'S WEDDING — Barbara Lynn, Jamie 1260 | 7 |
| 69 | 50 | 47 | 32 | ABILENE — George Hamilton IV, RCA Victor 8181 | 14 |
| ★70 | 86 | — | — | BLUE BAYOU — Roy Orbison, Monument 824 | 2 |
| 71 | 66 | 69 | 65 | LEAVE ME ALONE — Baby Washington, Sue 790 | 10 |
| 72 | 60 | 67 | 87 | THIS IS MY PRAYER — Theola Kilgore, Sereck 2006 | 7 |
| 73 | 81 | 83 | 93 | TELL ME THE TRUTH — Nancy Wilson, Capitol 4991 | 5 |
| ★74 | 94 | — | — | DEEP PURPLE — Nino Tempo & April Stevens, Atco 6273 | 2 |
| 75 | 90 | 100 | — | A LOVE SO FINE — Chiffons, Laurie 3195 | 3 |
| 76 | 91 | — | — | ELEPHANT WALK — Donald Jenkins & the Daylighters, Cortland 109 | 2 |
| 77 | 80 | — | — | HE'S MINE — Alice Wonder Land, Bardell 774 | 2 |
| 78 | 89 | 97 | — | I'M CONFESSIN' — Frank Ifield, Capitol 5032 | 3 |
| 79 | 88 | 95 | — | SEPTEMBER SONG — Jimmy Durante, Warner Bros. 5382 | 3 |
| 80 | 82 | — | — | TEENAGE CLEOPATRA — Tracey Dey, Liberty 55604 | 2 |
| 81 | 84 | — | — | ENAMARADO — Keith Colley, Unical 3006 | 2 |
| ★82 | — | — | — | RED SAILS IN THE SUNSET — Fats Domino, ABC-Paramount 10484 | 1 |
| 83 | 64 | 68 | 78 | IT'S A LONELY TOWN — Gene McDaniels, Liberty 55597 | 7 |
| 84 | 85 | 87 | — | SOONER OR LATER — Johnny Mathis, Columbia 42836 | 3 |
| 85 | 78 | 86 | 96 | CHINESE CHECKERS — Booker T. & the M.G.'s, Stax 137 | 7 |
| 86 | 73 | 71 | 88 | MAN'S TEMPTATION — Gene Chandler, Vee Jay 536 | 7 |
| 87 | 79 | 82 | — | MY BABE — Righteous Brothers, Moonglow 223 | 3 |
| 88 | 97 | 99 | — | CINDY'S GONNA CRY — Johnny Crawford, Del-Fi 4221 | 3 |
| 89 | 77 | 78 | 85 | SOMETHING OLD, SOMETHING NEW — Paul & Paula, Philips 40130 | 5 |
| 90 | — | — | — | BABY GET IT (and Don't Quit It) — Jackie Wilson, Brunswick 55250 | 1 |
| 91 | 95 | — | — | DOWN THE AISLE — Patty LaBelle & the Blue Belles, Newtown 5777 | 2 |
| 92 | — | — | — | CRY TO ME — Betty Harris, Jubilee 4556 | 1 |
| 93 | 96 | — | — | LONELY DRIFTER — O'Jays, Imperial 5976 | 2 |
| 94 | — | — | — | THAT'S HOW IT GOES — George Maharis, Epic 9613 | 1 |
| 95 | 98 | — | 94 | HEAR THE BELLS — Tokens, RCA Victor 8210 | 4 |
| 96 | 99 | — | — | MR. WISHING WELL — Nat King Cole, Capitol 5027 | 2 |
| 97 | — | 96 | 98 | FADED LOVE — Patsy Cline, Decca 31522 | 3 |
| 98 | 100 | — | — | YOUR BOYFRIEND'S BACK — Bobby Comstock & the Counts, Lawn 219 | 2 |
| 99 | — | — | — | MARIA ELENA — Los Indios Tavajaras, RCA Victor 8216 | 1 |
| 100 | — | — | — | WASHINGTON SQUARE — Village Stompers, Epic 9617 | 1 |

## BUBBLING UNDER THE HOT 100

101. MY DADDY KNOWS BEST — Marvelettes, Tamla 54082
102. HAPPY PUPPY — Bent Fabric, Atco 6271
103. HOOTENANNY GRANNY — Jim Lowe, 20th Century-Fox 426
104. THE DAY THE SAWMILL CLOSED DOWN — Dickey Lee, Smash 1844
105. I'M NOT A FOOL ANYMORE — T. K. Hulin, Smash 1830
106. EVERYBODY GO HOME — Eydie Gorme, Columbia 42854
107. JENNY BROWN — Smothers Brothers, Mercury 72182
108. I'LL BELIEVE IT WHEN I SEE IT — Sierras, Goldisc 4
109. LONELY WORLD — Dion, Laurie 3187
110. NIGHT LIFE — Rusty Draper, Monument 823
111. MAKING BELIEVE — Ray Charles, ABC-Paramount 10481
112. MICHAEL — Steve Alaimo, Checker 1054
113. WHAT'D I SAY — Kenny Burrell & Jimmy Smith, Verve 10299
114. LITTLE YELLOW ROSES — Jackie DeShannon, Liberty 55602
115. THE SOUND OF SURF — Percy Faith & His Ork, Columbia 42844
116. SAD GIRL — Jay Wiggins, IPG 1006
117. NOT SO LONG AGO — Marty Robbins, Columbia 42831
118. I'M COMING BACK TO YOU — Julie London, Liberty 55605
119. COTTON FIELDS — Angels, Ascot 2139
120. STRANGE FEELING — Billy Stewart, Chess 1868
121. P. S. I LOVE YOU — Classics, Music Note 118
122. WHAT'S EASY FOR TWO IS SO HARD FOR ONE — Mary Wells, Motown 1048
123. REACH OUT FOR ME — Lou Johnson, Big Top 3153
124. YOU LOST THE SWEETEST BOY — Mary Wells, Motown 1048
125. HALFWAY — Eddie Hodges, Columbia 42811
126. CUT YOU A-LOOSE — Ricky Allen, Age 29118
127. FROM ONE TO ONE — Clyde McPhatter, Mercury 72166
128. LITTLE EEFIN ANNIE — Joe Perkins, Sound Stage 72511
129. MARY, MARY — Jimmy Reed, Vee Jay 552

# Billboard HOT 100

**For Week Ending September 28, 1963**

★ STAR performer—Sides registering greatest proportionate upward progress this week.

| This Week | Wks. Ago | 2 Wks. Ago | 3 Wks. Ago | TITLE — Artist, Label & Number | Weeks On Chart |
|---|---|---|---|---|---|
| 1 | 1 | 2 | 4 | BLUE VELVET — Bobby Vinton, Epic 9614 | 8 |
| 2 | 5 | 9 | 29 | SALLY, GO 'ROUND THE ROSES — Jaynetts, Tuff 369 | 5 |
| ★3 | 12 | 20 | 55 | BE MY BABY — Ronettes, Philles 116 | 5 |
| 4 | 4 | 5 | 6 | HEAT WAVE — Martha & the Vandellas, Gordy 7022 | 9 |
| 5 | 2 | 1 | 1 | MY BOYFRIEND'S BACK — Angels, Smash 1834 | 9 |
| 6 | 6 | 6 | 15 | THEN HE KISSED ME — Crystals, Philles 115 | 7 |
| 7 | 11 | 16 | 22 | WONDERFUL! WONDERFUL! — Tymes, Parkway 884 | 7 |
| 8 | 8 | 15 | 21 | MICKEY'S MONKEY — Miracles, Tamla 54083 | 7 |
| 9 | 10 | 13 | 31 | CRY BABY — Garnet Mimms & the Enchanters, United Artists 629 | 7 |
| 10 | 3 | 3 | 3 | IF I HAD A HAMMER — Trini Lopez, Reprise 20198 | 10 |
| 11 | 7 | 7 | 12 | SURFER GIRL — Beach Boys, Capitol 5009 | 9 |
| 12 | 14 | 29 | 45 | A WALKIN' MIRACLE — Essex, Roulette 4515 | 6 |
| ★13 | 23 | 38 | 66 | BUSTED — Ray Charles, ABC-Paramount 10481 | 4 |
| 14 | 13 | 8 | 8 | THE MONKEY TIME — Major Lance, Okeh 7175 | 12 |
| ★15 | 22 | 25 | 38 | LITTLE DEUCE COUPE — Beach Boys, Capitol 5009 | 7 |
| 16 | 19 | 24 | 30 | MARTIAN HOP — Ran-Dells, Chairman 4403 | 9 |
| 17 | 21 | 22 | 27 | THE KIND OF BOY YOU CAN'T FORGET — Raindrops, Jubilee 5455 | 8 |
| 18 | 9 | 4 | 2 | HELLO MUDDUH, HELLO FADDUH — Allan Sherman, Warner Bros. 5378 | 9 |
| ★19 | 65 | — | — | SUGAR SHACK — Jimmy Gilmer and the Fireballs, Dot 16487 | 2 |
| 20 | 27 | 58 | 93 | HONOLULU LULU — Jan & Dean, Liberty 55613 | 4 |
| 21 | 15 | 17 | 20 | PAINTED, TAINTED ROSE — Al Martino, Capitol 5000 | 10 |
| 22 | 16 | 11 | 10 | HEY GIRL — Freddie Scott, Colpix 692 | 10 |
| 23 | 18 | 19 | 19 | YOU CAN NEVER STOP ME LOVING YOU — Johnny Tillotson, Cadence 1437 | 8 |
| 24 | 26 | 35 | 43 | PART TIME LOVE — Little Johnny Taylor, Galaxy 722 | 7 |
| 25 | 35 | 42 | 46 | ONLY IN AMERICA — Jay & the Americans, United Artists 625 | 7 |
| ★26 | 32 | 44 | 56 | WHAM — Lonnie Mack, Fraternity 912 | 6 |
| 27 | 29 | 32 | 35 | HEY THERE LONELY BOY — Ruby & the Romantics, Kapp 544 | 8 |
| 28 | 17 | 10 | 7 | MOCKINGBIRD — Inez Foxx, Symbol 919 | 15 |
| 29 | 40 | 52 | 77 | I CAN'T STAY MAD AT YOU — Skeeter Davis, RCA Victor 8219 | 4 |
| 30 | 41 | 65 | 72 | BUST OUT — Busters, Arlen 735 | 5 |
| 31 | 57 | 70 | 80 | TALK TO ME — Sunny and the Sunglows, Tear Drop 3014 | 4 |
| ★32 | 50 | 71 | 90 | MEAN WOMAN BLUES — Roy Orbison, Monument 824 | 4 |
| ★33 | 52 | 75 | — | DONNA THE PRIMA DONNA — Dion Di Muci, Columbia 42852 | 3 |
| ★34 | 51 | 67 | — | DON'T THINK TWICE IT'S ALL RIGHT — Peter, Paul & Mary, Warner Bros. 5385 | 3 |
| ★35 | 53 | 63 | 79 | THAT SUNDAY, THAT SUMMER — Nat King Cole, Capitol 5027 | 5 |
| 36 | 28 | 21 | 9 | BLOWIN' IN THE WIND — Peter, Paul & Mary, Warner Bros. 5368 | 14 |
| 37 | 25 | 18 | 13 | DENISE — Randy & the Rainbows, Rust 5059 | 16 |
| ★38 | 48 | 59 | 74 | HELLO HEARTACHE, GOODBYE LOVE — Little Peggy March, RCA Victor 8221 | 4 |
| 39 | 37 | 40 | 48 | WHY DON'T YOU BELIEVE ME — Duprees, Coed 584 | 6 |
| 40 | 20 | 14 | 14 | FRANKIE AND JOHNNY — Sam Cooke, RCA Victor 8215 | 10 |
| ★41 | 55 | 72 | 84 | I'LL TAKE YOU HOME — Drifters, Atlantic 2201 | 4 |
| 42 | 45 | 49 | 54 | MORE — Vic Dana, Dolton 81 | 8 |
| 43 | 44 | 55 | 61 | BIRTHDAY PARTY — Pixies Three, Mercury 72130 | 7 |
| 44 | 46 | 54 | 63 | TREAT MY BABY GOOD — Bobby Darin, Capitol 5019 | 6 |
| ★45 | 70 | 86 | — | BLUE BAYOU — Roy Orbison, Monument 824 | 3 |
| 46 | 64 | 87 | — | FOOLS RUSH IN — Rick Nelson, Decca 31533 | 3 |
| 47 | 56 | 83 | 98 | TWO TICKETS TO PARADISE — Brook Benton, Mercury 72177 | 4 |
| 48 | 34 | 26 | 17 | MORE — Kai Winding, Verve 10295 | 12 |
| 49 | 31 | 34 | 37 | PLEASE DON'T TALK TO THE LIFEGUARD — Diane Ray, Mercury 72117 | 9 |
| 50 | 24 | 12 | 5 | CANDY GIRL — 4 Seasons, Vee Jay 539 | 13 |
| 51 | 30 | 31 | 28 | I WANT TO STAY HERE — Steve & Eydie, Columbia 42815 | 11 |
| 52 | 38 | 27 | 24 | MAKE THE WORLD GO AWAY — Timi Yuro, Liberty 55587 | 11 |
| 53 | 60 | 74 | 91 | BETTY IN BERMUDAS — Dovells, Parkway 883 | 5 |
| 54 | 42 | 39 | 40 | LONELY SURFER — Jack Nitzsche, Reprise 20202 | 8 |
| 55 | 59 | 76 | 89 | WHAT DOES A GIRL DO — Shirelles, Scepter 1259 | 4 |
| 56 | 36 | 28 | 16 | DANKE SCHOEN — Wayne Newton, Capitol 4989 | 12 |
| 57 | 43 | 46 | 50 | STRAIGHTEN UP YOUR HEART — Barbara Lewis, Atlantic 2200 | 7 |
| ★58 | 74 | 94 | — | DEEP PURPLE — Nino Tempo & April Stevens, Atco 6273 | 3 |
| ★59 | 75 | 90 | 100 | A LOVE SO FINE — Chiffons, Laurie 3195 | 4 |
| 60 | 61 | 53 | 62 | 8 X 10 — Bill Anderson, Decca 31521 | 6 |
| 61 | 33 | 23 | 11 | FINGERTIPS (Part II) — Little Stevie Wonder, Tamla 54080 | 15 |
| 62 | 67 | 69 | 81 | SURFER JOE — Surfaris, Dot 16479 | 5 |
| 63 | 72 | 60 | 67 | THIS IS MY PRAYER — Theola Kilgore, Serock 2006 | 8 |
| 64 | 58 | 61 | 65 | CHINA NIGHTS (Shina No Yoru) — Kyu Sakamoto, Capitol 5016 | 6 |
| 65 | 54 | 51 | 49 | IT'S TOO LATE — Wilson Pickett, Double L 717 | 10 |
| 66 | 99 | — | — | MARIA ELENA — Los Indios Tabajaras, RCA Victor 8216 | 2 |
| 67 | 78 | 89 | 97 | I'M CONFESSIN' — Frank Ifield, Capitol 5032 | 4 |
| 68 | 63 | 41 | 23 | WIPE OUT — Surfaris, Dot 16479 | 15 |
| 69 | 100 | — | — | WASHINGTON SQUARE — Village Stompers, Epic 9617 | 2 |
| ★70 | — | — | — | YOU LOST THE SWEETEST — Mary Wells, Motown 1048 | 1 |
| 71 | 79 | 88 | 95 | SEPTEMBER SONG — Jimmy Durante, Warner Bros. 5382 | 4 |
| 72 | 77 | 80 | — | HE'S MINE — Alice Wonder Land, Bardell 774 | 3 |
| 73 | 82 | — | — | RED SAILS IN THE SUNSET — Fats Domino, ABC-Paramount 10484 | 2 |
| ★74 | — | — | — | THE GRASS IS GREENER — Brenda Lee, Decca 31539 | 1 |
| 75 | 76 | 91 | — | ELEPHANT WALK — Donald Jenkins & the Daylighters, Cortland 109 | 3 |
| 76 | 81 | 84 | — | ENAMORADO — Keith Colley, Unical 3006 | 3 |
| 77 | 80 | 82 | — | TEENAGE CLEOPATRA — Tracey Dey, Liberty 55604 | 3 |
| 78 | 87 | 79 | 82 | MY BABE — Righteous Brothers, Moonglow 223 | 4 |
| 79 | 68 | 68 | 70 | (I Cried at) LAURA'S WEDDING — Barbara Lynn, Jamie 1260 | 8 |
| 80 | 92 | — | — | CRY TO ME — Betty Harris, Jubilee 4556 | 2 |
| 81 | — | — | — | SHE'S A FOOL — Lesley Gore, Mercury 72180 | 1 |
| 82 | — | — | — | CROSSFIRE! — Orlons, Cameo 273 | 1 |
| 83 | 91 | 95 | — | DOWN THE AISLE — Patty LaBelle & the Blue Belles, Newtown 5777 | 3 |
| 84 | 88 | 91 | 99 | CINDY'S GONNA CRY — Johnny Crawford, Del-Fi 4221 | 4 |
| 85 | 73 | 81 | 83 | TELL ME THE TRUTH — Nancy Wilson, Capitol 4991 | 6 |
| 86 | — | — | — | IT'S ALL RIGHT — Impressions, ABC-Paramount 10487 | 1 |
| 87 | 90 | — | — | BABY GET IT (And Don't Quit It) — Jackie Wilson, Brunswick 55250 | 2 |
| 88 | 94 | — | — | THAT'S HOW IT GOES — George Maharis, Epic 9613 | 2 |
| 89 | — | — | — | STRANGE FEELING — Billy Stewart, Chess 1868 | 1 |
| 90 | — | — | — | (Down at) PAPA JOE'S — Dixiebelles, Sound Stage 7 2507 | 1 |
| 91 | — | — | — | BLUE GUITAR — Richard Chamberlain, MGM 13170 | 1 |
| 92 | 96 | 99 | — | MR. WISHING WELL — Nat King Cole, Capitol 5027 | 3 |
| 93 | — | — | — | NIGHT LIFE — Rusty Draper, Monument 823 | 1 |
| 94 | — | — | — | JENNY BROWN — Smothers Brothers, Mercury 72182 | 1 |
| 95 | — | — | — | NICK TEEN AND AL K. HALL — Rolf Harris, Epic 9615 | 1 |
| 96 | — | — | — | SWEET IMPOSSIBLE YOU — Brenda Lee, Decca 31539 | 1 |
| 97 | — | — | — | LITTLE EEFIN ANNIE — Joe Perkins, Sound Stage 7 2511 | 1 |
| 98 | — | — | — | EVERYBODY GO HOME — Eydie Gorme, Columbia 42854 | 1 |
| 99 | — | — | — | POINT PANIC — Surfaris, Decca 31538 | 1 |
| 100 | — | — | — | LET'S MAKE LOVE TONIGHT — Bobby Rydell, Cameo 272 | 1 |

## BUBBLING UNDER THE HOT 100

101. FADED LOVE — Patsy Cline, Decca 31522
102. FIRST DAY BACK AT SCHOOL — Paul & Paula, Philips 40142
103. BLUE VELVET — Lawrence Welk, Dot 16526
104. LONELY WORLD — Dion, Laurie 3187
105. A PERFECT PAIR — Paul & Paula, Philips 40142
106. LONELY DRIFTER — O'Jays, Imperial 5976
107. THE DAY THE SAWMILL CLOSED DOWN — Dickey Lee, Smash 1844
108. WILD! — Dee Dee Sharp, Cameo 274
109. HYMN TO FREEDOM — Oscar Peterson Trio, Verve 10302
110. MY DADDY KNOWS BEST — Marvelettes, Tamla 54082
111. THE SOUND OF SURF — Percy Faith & His Ork, Columbia 42844
112. MICHAEL — Steve Alaimo, Checker 1054
113. SPEED BALL — Ray Stevens, Mercury 71830
114. I'M NOT A FOOL ANYMORE — T. K. Nulin, Smash 1830
115. HOT SO LONG AGO — Marty Robbins, Columbia 42831
116. MONKEY-SHINE — Bill Black & His Combo, Hi 2069
117. I'M LEAVING IT UP TO YOU — Dale & Grace, Montel 921
118. HALFWAY — Eddie Hodges, Columbia 42811
119. MARY, MARY — Jimmy Reed, Vee Jay 552
120. P. S. I LOVE YOU — Classics, Music Note 118
121. LET'S FALL IN LOVE — Linda Scott, Congress 200
122. COWBOY BOOTS — Dave Dudley, Golden Ring 3020
123. ON BENDING KNEES — Johnny Copeland, Golden Eagle 101
124. WHERE DID THE GOOD TIMES GO — Dick & Deedee, Warner Bros. 5383
125. YOUR LIFE BEGINS (At Sweet 16) — Majors, Imperial 5991
126. CUT YOU A-LOOSE — Ricky Allen, Age 29118
127. EEFANANNY — Ardells, Epic 9621
128. EVERYBODY — Tommy Roe, ABC-Paramount 10478
129. HOOTENANNY GRANNY — Jim Lowe, 20th Century-Fox 426

*Compiled from national retail sales and radio station airplay by the Music Popularity Dept. of Record Market Research, Billboard.*

# Billboard HOT 100

*For Week Ending October 5, 1963*

★ **STAR** performer—Sides registering greatest proportionate upward progress this week.

| This Wk | 2 Wk Ago | 3 Wk Ago | TITLE Artist, Label & Number | Weeks On Chart |
|---|---|---|---|---|
| 1 | 1 | 2 | BLUE VELVET — Bobby Vinton, Epic 9614 | 9 |
| 2 | 2 | 5 | SALLY, GO 'ROUND THE ROSES — Jaynetts, Tuff 369 | 6 |
| 3 | 3 | 12 | BE MY BABY — Ronettes, Philles 116 | 6 |
| ★4 | 19 | 65 | SUGAR SHACK — Jimmy Gilmer and the Fireballs, Dot 16487 | 3 |
| ★5 | 9 | 10 | CRY BABY — Garnet Mimms & the Enchanters, United Artists 629 | 8 |
| 6 | 5 | 2 | MY BOYFRIEND'S BACK — Angels, Smash 1834 | 10 |
| 7 | 7 | 11 | WONDERFUL! WONDERFUL! — Tymes, Parkway 884 | 8 |
| 8 | 4 | 4 | HEAT WAVE — Martha & the Vandellas, Gordy 7022 | 10 |
| ★9 | 13 | 23 | BUSTED — Ray Charles, ABC-Paramount 10481 | 5 |
| 10 | 6 | 6 | THEN HE KISSED ME — Crystals, Philles 115 | 8 |
| 11 | 8 | 8 | MICKEY'S MONKEY — Miracles, Tamla 54083 | 8 |
| 12 | 12 | 14 | A WALKIN' MIRACLE — Essex, Roulette 4515 | 7 |
| 13 | 20 | 27 | HONOLULU LULU — Jan & Dean, Liberty 55613 | 5 |
| 14 | 11 | 7 | SURFER GIRL — Beach Boys, Capitol 5009 | 10 |
| 15 | 10 | 3 | IF I HAD A HAMMER — Trini Lopez, Reprise 20198 | 11 |
| ★16 | 32 | 50 | MEAN WOMAN BLUES — Roy Orbison, Monument 824 | 5 |
| 17 | 33 | 52 | DONNA THE PRIMA DONNA — Dion Di Muci, Columbia 42852 | 4 |
| 18 | 16 | 19 | MARTIAN HOP — Ran-Dells, Chairman 4403 | 10 |
| 19 | 24 | 26 | PART TIME LOVE — Little Johnny Taylor, Galaxy 722 | 8 |
| 20 | 15 | 22 | LITTLE DEUCE COUPE — Beach Boys, Capitol 5009 | 8 |
| ★21 | 34 | 51 | DON'T THINK TWICE IT'S ALL RIGHT — Peter, Paul & Mary, Warner Bros. 5385 | 4 |
| 22 | 14 | 13 | THE MONKEY TIME — Major Lance, Okeh 7175 | 13 |
| 23 | 29 | 40 | I CAN'T STAY MAD AT YOU — Skeeter Davis, RCA Victor 8219 | 5 |
| 24 | 26 | 32 | WHAM — Lonnie Mack, Fraternity 912 | 7 |
| 25 | 25 | 35 | ONLY IN AMERICA — Jay & the Americans, United Artists 625 | 8 |
| ★26 | 31 | 57 | TALK TO ME — Sunny and the Sunglows, Tear Drop 3014 | 5 |
| 27 | 30 | 41 | BUST OUT — Busters, Arlen 735 | 5 |
| ★28 | 35 | 53 | THAT SUNDAY, THAT SUMMER — Nat King Cole, Capitol 5027 | 6 |
| 29 | 17 | 21 | THE KIND OF BOY YOU CAN'T FORGET — Raindrops, Jubilee 5455 | 9 |
| 30 | 21 | 15 | PAINTED, TAINTED ROSE — Al Martino, Capitol 5000 | 11 |
| 31 | 38 | 48 | HELLO HEARTACHE, GOODBYE LOVE — Little Peggy March, RCA Victor 8221 | 5 |
| 32 | 41 | 55 | I'LL TAKE YOU HOME — Drifters, Atlantic 2201 | 5 |
| 33 | 58 | 74 | DEEP PURPLE — Nino Tempo & April Stevens, Atco 6273 | 4 |
| 34 | 46 | 64 | FOOLS RUSH IN — Rick Nelson, Decca 31533 | 4 |
| 35 | 22 | 16 | HEY GIRL — Freddie Scott, Colpix 692 | 11 |
| ★36 | 47 | 56 | TWO TICKETS TO PARADISE — Brook Benton, Mercury 72177 | 5 |
| 37 | 23 | 18 | YOU CAN NEVER STOP ME LOVING YOU — Johnny Tillotson, Cadence 1437 | 9 |
| ★38 | 69 | 100 | WASHINGTON SQUARE — Village Stompers, Epic 9617 | 3 |
| 39 | 28 | 17 | MOCKINGBIRD — Inez Foxx, Symbol 919 | 16 |
| 40 | 43 | 44 | BIRTHDAY PARTY — Pixies Three, Mercury 72130 | 8 |
| 41 | 45 | 70 | BLUE BAYOU — Roy Orbison, Monument 824 | 4 |
| 42 | 42 | 45 | MORE — Vic Dana, Delton 81 | 9 |
| 43 | 44 | 46 | TREAT MY BABY GOOD — Bobby Darin, Capitol 5019 | 7 |
| 44 | 18 | 9 | HELLO MUDDUH; HELLO FADDUH — Allan Sherman, Warner Bros. 5378 | 10 |
| 45 | 27 | 29 | HEY THERE LONELY BOY — Ruby & the Romantics, Kapp 544 | 9 |
| ★46 | — | — | THE GRASS IS GREENER — Brenda Lee, Decca 31539 | 2 |
| 47 | 40 | 20 | FRANKIE AND JOHNNY — Sam Cooke, RCA Victor 8215 | 11 |
| 48 | 59 | 75 | A LOVE SO FINE — Chiffons, Laurie 3195 | 5 |
| 49 | 36 | 28 | BLOWIN' IN THE WIND — Peter, Paul & Mary, Warner Bros. 5368 | 15 |
| ★50 | 70 | — | YOU LOST THE SWEETEST BOY — Mary Wells, Motown 1048 | 2 |
| 51 | 53 | 60 | BETTY IN BERMUDAS — Dovells, Parkway 882 | 6 |
| 52 | 39 | 37 | WHY DON'T YOU BELIEVE ME — Duprees, Coed 584 | 7 |
| 53 | 55 | 59 | WHAT DOES A GIRL DO — Shirelles, Scepter 1259 | 6 |
| ★54 | 66 | 99 | MARIA ELENA — Los Indios Tabajaras, RCA Victor 8216 | 4 |
| 55 | 37 | 25 | DENISE — Randy & the Rainbows, Rust 5059 | 17 |
| 56 | 82 | — | CROSSFIRE! — Orlons, Cameo 273 | 2 |
| 57 | 48 | 34 | MORE — Kai Winding, Verve 10295 | 13 |
| 58 | 86 | — | IT'S ALL RIGHT — Impressions, ABC-Paramount 10487 | 2 |
| 59 | 81 | — | SHE'S A FOOL — Lesley Gore, Mercury 72180 | 2 |
| 60 | 67 | 78 | I'M CONFESSIN' — Frank Ifield, Capitol 5032 | 5 |
| 61 | 80 | 92 | CRY TO ME — Betty Harris, Jubilee 4456 | 3 |
| 62 | 71 | 79 | SEPTEMBER SONG — Jimmy Durante, Warner Bros. 5382 | 4 |
| ★63 | — | — | WORKOUT STEVIE, WORKOUT — Little Stevie Wonder, Tamla 54086 | 1 |
| 64 | 62 | 67 | SURFER JOE — Surfaris, Dot 16479 | 6 |
| 65 | 73 | 82 | RED SAILS IN THE SUNSET — Fats Domino, ABC-Paramount 10484 | 3 |
| ★66 | — | — | MONKEY-SHINE — Bill Black & His Combo, Hi 2069 | 1 |
| 67 | 72 | 77 | HE'S MINE — Alice Wonder Land, Bardell 774 | 4 |
| 68 | 75 | 76 | ELEPHANT WALK — Donald Jenkins & the Daylighters, Cortland 109 | 4 |
| ★69 | — | — | MISTY — Lloyd Price, Double L 722 | 1 |
| 70 | 76 | 81 | ENAMORADO — Keith Colley, Unical 3006 | 4 |
| 71 | 63 | 72 | THIS IS MY PRAYER — Theola Kilgore, Serock 2006 | 9 |
| 72 | 84 | 88 | CINDY'S GONNA CRY — Johnny Crawford, Del-Fi 4221 | 5 |
| 73 | 87 | 90 | BABY GET IT (And Don't Quit It) — Jackie Wilson, Brunswick 55250 | 3 |
| ★74 | — | — | TWO SIDES (To Every Story) — Etta James, Argo 5452 | 1 |
| 75 | 77 | 80 | TEENAGE CLEOPATRA — Tracey Dey, Liberty 55604 | 4 |
| 76 | 78 | 87 | MY BABE — Righteous Brothers, Moonglow 223 | 5 |
| 77 | 68 | 63 | WIPE OUT — Surfaris, Dot 16479 | 16 |
| 78 | 83 | 91 | DOWN THE AISLE — Patty LaBelle and the Blue Belles, Newtown 5777 | 4 |
| 79 | — | — | FIRST DAY BACK AT SCHOOL — Paul & Paula, Philips 40142 | 1 |
| 80 | — | — | WALKING THE DOG — Rufus Thomas, Stax 140 | 1 |
| 81 | 91 | — | BLUE GUITAR — Richard Chamberlain, MGM 13170 | 2 |
| 82 | 90 | — | (Down at) PAPA JOE'S — Dixiebelles, Sound Stage 7 2507 | 2 |
| 83 | 97 | — | LITTLE EEEFIN ANNIE — Joe Perkins, Sound Stage 7 2511 | 2 |
| 84 | 89 | — | STRANGE FEELING — Billy Stewart, Chess 1868 | 2 |
| 85 | 93 | — | NIGHT LIFE — Rusty Draper, Monument 823 | 2 |
| 86 | 94 | — | JENNY BROWN — Smothers Brothers, Mercury 72182 | 2 |
| 87 | 99 | — | POINT PANIC — Surfaris, Decca 31538 | 2 |
| 88 | 98 | — | EVERYBODY GO HOME — Eydie Gorme, Columbia 42854 | 2 |
| 89 | — | — | I'M LEAVING IT UP TO YOU — Dale & Grace, Montel-Michele 921 | 1 |
| 90 | — | — | WILD! — Dee Dee Sharp, Cameo 274 | 1 |
| 91 | 96 | — | SWEET IMPOSSIBLE YOU — Brenda Lee, Decca 31539 | 2 |
| 92 | — | — | TOYS IN THE ATTIC — Jack Jones, Kapp 551 | 1 |
| 93 | — | — | WHERE DID THE GOOD TIMES GO — Dick & Deedee, Warner Bros. 5383 | 1 |
| 94 | — | — | NEW MEXICAN ROSE — 4 Seasons, Vee Jay 562 | 1 |
| 95 | — | — | TOYS IN THE ATTIC — Joe Sherman, World Artists 1088 | 1 |
| 96 | — | — | 500 MILES AWAY FROM HOME — Bobby Bare, RCA Victor 8238 | 1 |
| 97 | 88 | 94 | THAT'S HOW IT GOES — George Maharis, Epic 9613 | 3 |
| 98 | 100 | — | LET'S MAKE LOVE TONIGHT — Bobby Rydell, Cameo 272 | 2 |
| 99 | — | — | THAT'S THE WAY IT GOES — 4 Seasons, Vee Jay 562 | 1 |
| 100 | — | — | MICHAEL — Steve Alaimo, Checker 1054 | 1 |

## BUBBLING UNDER THE HOT 100

101. SIGNED, SEALED AND DELIVERED — James Brown & the Famous Flames, King 5803
102. TALK BACK TREMBLING LIPS — Ernest Ashworth, Hickory 1214
103. MR. WISHING WELL — Nat King Cole, Capitol 5027
104. LONELY DRIFTER — O'Jays, Imperial 5976
105. DOWN ON BENDING KNEES — Johnny Copeland, Golden Eagle 101
106. NICK TEEN AND AL K. HALL — Rolf Harris, Epic 9615
107. DETROIT CITY NO. 2 — Ben Colder, MGM 13167
108. SPEED BALL — Ray Stevens, Mercury 72189
109. FADED LOVE — Patsy Cline, Decca 31522
110. COWBOY BOOTS — Dave Dudley, Golden King 3020
111. FIESTA — Lawrence Welk, Dot 16526
112. EEFANANNY — Ardells, Epic 9621
113. COME BACK — Johnny Mathis, Mercury 72184
114. BLUE VELVET — Lawrence Welk, Dot 16526
115. YOUR TEENAGE DREAMS — Johnny Mathis, Mercury 72184
116. A PERFECT PAIR — Paul & Paula, Philips 40142
117. BETTER TO GIVE THAN RECEIVE — Joe Hinton, Back Beat 539
118. LITTLE YELLOW ROSES — Jackie DeShannon, Liberty 55602
119. NOT SO LONG AGO — Marty Robbins, Columbia 42831
120. I WONDER WHAT SHE'S DOING TONIGHT — Barry & the Tamerlanes, Valiant 6034
121. BROWN-EYED HANDSOME MAN — Buddy Holly, Coral 62369
122. HYMN TO FREEDOM — Oscar Peterson Trio, Verve 10302
123. EVERYBODY — Tommy Roe, ABC-Paramount 10478
124. NINETY MILES AN HOUR (Down a Dead End Street) — Hank Snow, RCA Victor 8239

Compiled from national retail sales and radio station airplay by the Music Popularity Dept. of Record Market Research, Billboard.

For Week Ending October 12, 1963

# Billboard HOT 100

Billboard Award

★ STAR performer—Sides registering greatest proportionate upward progress this week.

| This Week | 1 Wk. Ago | 2 Wks. Ago | 3 Wks. Ago | TITLE | Artist, Label & Number | Weeks On Chart |
|---|---|---|---|---|---|---|
| ★ 1 | 4 | 19 | 65 | SUGAR SHACK | Jimmy Gilmer and the Fireballs, Dot 16487 | 4 |
| 2 | 3 | 3 | 12 | BE MY BABY | Ronettes, Philles 116 | 7 |
| 3 | 1 | 1 | 1 | BLUE VELVET | Bobby Vinton, Epic 9614 | 10 |
| 4 | 5 | 9 | 10 | CRY BABY | Garnet Mimms & the Enchanters, United Artists 629 | 9 |
| 5 | 2 | 2 | 5 | SALLY, GO 'ROUND THE ROSES | Jaynetts, Tuff 369 | 7 |
| ★ 6 | 9 | 13 | 23 | BUSTED | Ray Charles, ABC-Paramount 10481 | 6 |
| 7 | 6 | 5 | 2 | MY BOYFRIEND'S BACK | Angels, Smash 1834 | 11 |
| ★ 8 | 16 | 32 | 50 | MEAN WOMAN BLUES | Roy Orbison, Monument 824 | 6 |
| 9 | 8 | 4 | 4 | HEAT WAVE | Martha & the Vandellas, Gordy 7022 | 11 |
| ★ 10 | 17 | 33 | 52 | DONNA THE PRIMA DONNA | Dion Di Muci, Columbia 42852 | 5 |
| 11 | 13 | 20 | 27 | HONOLULU LULU | Jan & Dean, Liberty 55613 | 6 |
| 12 | 7 | 7 | 11 | WONDERFUL! WONDERFUL! | Tymes, Parkway 884 | 9 |
| ★ 13 | 28 | 35 | 53 | THAT SUNDAY, THAT SUMMER | Nat King Cole, Capitol 5027 | 7 |
| ★ 14 | 21 | 34 | 51 | DON'T THINK TWICE IT'S ALL RIGHT | Peter, Paul & Mary, Warner Bros. 5385 | 5 |
| 15 | 14 | 11 | 7 | SURFER GIRL | Beach Boys, Capitol 5009 | 11 |
| 16 | 10 | 6 | 6 | THEN HE KISSED ME | Crystals, Philles 115 | 9 |
| 17 | 11 | 8 | 8 | MICKEY'S MONKEY | Miracles, Tamla 54083 | 9 |
| ★ 18 | 23 | 29 | 40 | I CAN'T STAY MAD AT YOU | Skeeter Davis, RCA Victor 8219 | 6 |
| 19 | 19 | 24 | 26 | PART TIME LOVE | Little Johnny Taylor, Galaxy 722 | 9 |
| ★ 20 | 33 | 58 | 74 | DEEP PURPLE | Nino Tempo & April Stevens, Atco 6273 | 5 |
| ★ 21 | 26 | 31 | 57 | TALK TO ME | Sunny and the Sunglows, Tear Drop 3014 | 6 |
| 22 | 12 | 12 | 14 | A WALKIN' MIRACLE | Essex, Roulette 4515 | 8 |
| ★ 23 | 38 | 69 | 100 | WASHINGTON SQUARE | Village Stompers, Epic 9617 | 4 |
| 24 | 18 | 16 | 19 | MARTIAN HOP | Ran-Dells, Chairman 4403 | 11 |
| 25 | 27 | 30 | 41 | BUST OUT | Busters, Arlen 735 | 6 |
| ★ 26 | 34 | 46 | 64 | FOOLS RUSH IN | Rick Nelson, Decca 31533 | 5 |
| 27 | 15 | 10 | 3 | IF I HAD A HAMMER | Trini Lopez, Reprise 20198 | 12 |
| 28 | 31 | 38 | 48 | HELLO HEARTACHE, GOODBYE LOVE | Little Peggy March, RCA Victor 8221 | 6 |
| 29 | 32 | 41 | 55 | I'LL TAKE YOU HOME | Drifters, Atlantic 2201 | 6 |
| 30 | 20 | 15 | 22 | LITTLE DEUCE COUPE | Beach Boys, Capitol 5009 | 9 |
| ★ 31 | 41 | 45 | 70 | BLUE BAYOU | Roy Orbison, Monument 824 | 5 |
| ★ 32 | 54 | 66 | 99 | MARIA ELENA | Los Indios Tabajaras, RCA Victor 8216 | 4 |
| 33 | 22 | 14 | 13 | THE MONKEY TIME | Major Lance, Okeh 7175 | 14 |
| 34 | 36 | 47 | 56 | TWO TICKETS TO PARADISE | Brook Benton, Mercury 72177 | 6 |
| ★ 35 | 58 | 86 | — | IT'S ALL RIGHT | Impressions, ABC-Paramount 10487 | 3 |
| ★ 36 | 46 | 74 | — | THE GRASS IS GREENER | Brenda Lee, Decca 31539 | 3 |
| 37 | 25 | 25 | 35 | ONLY IN AMERICA | Jay & the Americans, United Artists 625 | 9 |
| 38 | 29 | 17 | 21 | THE KIND OF BOY YOU CAN'T FORGET | Raindrops, Jubilee 5455 | 10 |
| ★ 39 | 50 | 70 | — | YOU LOST THE SWEETEST BOY | Mary Wells, Motown 1048 | 3 |
| 40 | 24 | 26 | 32 | WHAM | Lonnie Mack, Fraternity 912 | 8 |
| 41 | 30 | 21 | 15 | PAINTED, TAINTED ROSE | Al Martino, Capitol 5000 | 12 |
| 42 | 48 | 59 | 75 | A LOVE SO FINE | Chiffons, Laurie 3195 | 6 |
| 43 | 37 | 23 | 18 | YOU CAN NEVER STOP ME LOVING YOU | Johnny Tillotson, Cadence 1437 | 10 |
| 44 | 42 | 42 | 45 | MORE | Vic Dana, Dolton 81 | 10 |
| ★ 45 | 56 | 82 | — | CROSSFIRE! | Orlons, Cameo 273 | 3 |
| ★ 46 | 59 | 81 | — | SHE'S A FOOL | Lesley Gore, Mercury 72180 | 3 |
| 47 | 35 | 22 | 16 | HEY GIRL | Freddie Scott, Colpix 692 | 12 |
| 48 | 40 | 43 | 44 | BIRTHDAY PARTY | Pixies Three, Mercury 72130 | 9 |
| ★ 49 | 63 | — | — | WORKOUT STEVIE, WORKOUT | Little Stevie Wonder, Tamla 54086 | 2 |
| 50 | 51 | 53 | 60 | BETTY IN BERMUDAS | Dovells, Parkway 883 | 7 |
| 51 | 39 | 28 | 17 | MOCKINGBIRD | Inez Foxx, Symbol 919 | 17 |
| 52 | 43 | 44 | 46 | TREAT MY BABY GOOD | Bobby Darin, Capitol 5019 | 8 |
| ★ 53 | 65 | 73 | 82 | RED SAILS IN THE SUNSET | Fats Domino, ABC-Paramount 10484 | 4 |
| 54 | 62 | 71 | 79 | SEPTEMBER SONG | Jimmy Durante, Warner Bros. 5382 | 6 |
| 55 | 53 | 55 | 59 | WHAT DOES A GIRL DO | Shirelles, Scepter 1259 | 6 |
| ★ 56 | 69 | — | — | MISTY | Lloyd Price, Double L 722 | 2 |
| 57 | 61 | 80 | 92 | CRY TO ME | Betty Harris, Jubilee 4556 | 4 |
| 58 | 60 | 67 | 78 | I'M CONFESSIN' | Frank Ifield, Capitol 5032 | 6 |
| 59 | 66 | — | — | MONKEY-SHINE | Bill Black & His Combo, Hi 2069 | 2 |
| 60 | 57 | 48 | 34 | MORE | Kai Winding, Verve 10295 | 14 |
| 61 | 73 | 87 | 90 | BABY GET IT (And Don't Quit It) | Jackie Wilson, Brunswick 55250 | 4 |
| 62 | 67 | 72 | 77 | HE'S MINE | Alice Wonder Land, Bardell 774 | 5 |
| 63 | 74 | — | — | TWO SIDES (To Every Story) | Etta James, Argo 5452 | 2 |
| 64 | 68 | 75 | 76 | ELEPHANT WALK | Donald Jenkins & the Daylighters, Cortland 109 | 5 |
| ★ 65 | 89 | — | — | I'M LEAVING IT UP TO YOU | Dale & Grace, Montel-Michele 921 | 2 |
| 66 | 78 | 83 | 91 | DOWN THE AISLE | Patty LaBelle & the Blue Belles, Newtown 5777 | 5 |
| 67 | 70 | 76 | 81 | ENAMORADO | Keith Colley, Unical 3006 | 5 |
| ★ 68 | — | — | — | EVERYBODY | Tommy Roe, ABC-Paramount 10478 | 1 |
| 69 | 80 | — | — | WALKING THE DOG | Rufus Thomas, Stax 140 | 2 |
| 70 | 79 | — | — | FIRST DAY BACK AT SCHOOL | Paul & Paula, Philips 40142 | 2 |
| ★ 71 | 96 | — | — | 500 MILES AWAY FROM HOME | Bobby Bare, RCA Victor 8238 | 2 |
| 72 | 85 | 93 | — | NIGHT LIFE | Rusty Draper, Monument 823 | 3 |
| 73 | 82 | 90 | — | (Down at) PAPA JOE'S | Dixiebelles, Sound Stage 7 2507 | 3 |
| 74 | 87 | 99 | — | POINT PANIC | Surfaris, Decca 31538 | 3 |
| 75 | 76 | 78 | 87 | MY BABE | Righteous Brothers, Moonglow 223 | 6 |
| 76 | 72 | 84 | 88 | CINDY'S GONNA CRY | Johnny Crawford, Del-Fi 4221 | 6 |
| 77 | 83 | 97 | — | LITTLE EEEFIN ANNIE | Joe Perkins, Sound Stage 7 2511 | 3 |
| 78 | 81 | 91 | — | BLUE GUITAR | Richard Chamberlain, MGM 13170 | 3 |
| ★ 79 | 94 | — | — | NEW MEXICAN ROSE | 4 Seasons, Vee Jay 562 | 2 |
| 80 | 91 | 96 | — | SWEET IMPOSSIBLE YOU | Brenda Lee, Decca 31539 | 3 |
| ★ 81 | — | — | — | SPEED BALL | Ray Stevens, Mercury 72189 | 1 |
| 82 | 84 | 89 | — | STRANGE FEELING | Billy Stewart, Chess 1868 | 3 |
| 83 | 90 | — | — | WILD! | Dee Dee Sharp, Cameo 274 | 2 |
| 84 | 86 | 94 | — | JENNY BROWN | Smothers Brothers, Mercury 72182 | 3 |
| 85 | 95 | — | — | TOYS IN THE ATTIC | Joe Sherman, World Artists 1088 | 2 |
| ★ 86 | — | — | — | YOUR TEEN-AGE DREAMS | Johnny Mathis, Mercury 72184 | 1 |
| 87 | 75 | 77 | 80 | TEENAGE CLEOPATRA | Tracey Dey, Liberty 55604 | 5 |
| 88 | 88 | 98 | — | EVERYBODY GO HOME | Eydie Gorme, Columbia 42854 | 3 |
| ★ 89 | — | — | — | BETTER TO GIVE THAN RECEIVE | Joe Hinton, Back Beat 539 | 1 |
| ★ 90 | — | — | — | DETROIT CITY NO. 2 | Ben Colder, MGM 13167 | 1 |
| 91 | 99 | — | — | THAT'S THE WAY IT GOES | 4 Seasons, Vee Jay 562 | 2 |
| 92 | — | — | — | COME BACK | Johnny Mathis, Mercury 72184 | 1 |
| 93 | — | — | — | CUANDO CALIENTA EL SOL | Steve Allen, Dot 16507 | 1 |
| 94 | — | — | — | GOTTA TRAVEL ON | Timi Yuro, Liberty 55634 | 1 |
| 95 | — | — | — | COWBOY BOOTS | Dave Dudley, Golden Ring 3030 | 1 |
| 96 | — | — | — | SIGNED, SEALED AND DELIVERED | James Brown & the Famous Flames, King 5083 | 1 |
| 97 | — | — | 93 | LONELY DRIFTER | O'Jays, Imperial 5976 | 2 |
| 98 | — | — | — | TWO-TEN, SIX-EIGHTEEN | Jimmie Rodgers, Dot 16527 | 1 |
| 99 | — | — | — | DON'T WAIT TOO LONG | Tony Bennett, Columbia 42886 | 1 |
| 100 | — | — | — | HEY LONELY ONE | Baby Washington, Sue 794 | 1 |

## HOT 100—A TO Z—(Publisher-Licensee)

Baby Get It (And Don't Quit It) (Merrimac, BMI) .. 61
Be My Baby (Mother Bertha-Trio, BMI) .... 2
Better to Give Than Receive (Don, BMI) .... 89
Betty in Bermudas (Cameo-Parkway, BMI) .... 50
Birthday Party (Dandelion-Marjoda, BMI) .... 48
Blue Bayou (Acuff-Rose, BMI) .... 31
Blue Guitar (U. S. Songs, ASCAP) .... 78
Blue Velvet (Vogue, BMI) .... 3
Bust Out (Lanny, BMI) .... 25
Busted (Pamper, BMI) .... 6
Cindy's Gonna Cry (Screen Gems-Columbia, BMI) .. 76
Come Back (Elm Drive, ASCAP) .... 92
Cowboy Boots (Four Star, BMI) .... 95
Crossfire! (Kalmann, ASCAP) .... 45
Cry Baby (Rittenhouse-Mellin, BMI) .... 4
Cry to Me (Mellin-Progressive, BMI) .... 57
Cuando Calienta El Sol (Peer Int'l, BMI) .... 93
Deep Purple (Robbins, ASCAP) .... 20
Detroit City No. 2 (Cedarwood, BMI) .... 90
Donna the Prima Donna (Disal, ASCAP) .... 10
Don't Think Twice It's All Right (Witmark, ASCAP) .... 14
Don't Wait Too Long (Panther, ASCAP) .... 99
(Down at) Papa Joe's (Tuneville, BMI) .... 73
Down the Aisle (Sixty-Six, BMI) .... 66
Elephant Walk (Colca, BMI) .... 64
Enamorado (Lenmar-Konwater, BMI) .... 67
Everybody (Low-Twi, BMI) .... 68
Everybody Go Home (Screen Gems-Columbia) .. 88
500 Miles Away From Home (Central Songs, BMI) 71
First Day Back at School (LeBill, BMI) .... 70
Fools Rush in (Bregman, Vocco & Conn, ASCAP) .. 26
Gotta Travel On (Sanga, BMI) .... 94
Grass is Greener, The (Screen Gems-Columbia, BMI) .... 36
Heat Wave (Jobete, BMI) .... 9
Hello Heartache, Goodbye Love (Atrium, ASCAP) .. 28
He's Mine (Scharber, BMI) .... 62
Hey Girl (Screen Gems-Columbia, BMI) .... 47
Hey Lonely One (Saturn, BMI) ....100
Honolulu Lulu (Screen Gems-Columbia, BMI) .... 11
I Can't Stay Mad at You (Screen Gems-Columbia) BMI) .... 18
I'm Confessin' (Bourne, ASCAP) .... 58
I'm Leaving It Up to You (Venice, BMI) .... 65
I'll Take You Home (Screen Gems-Columbia, BMI) 29
If I Had a Hammer (Ludlow, BMI) .... 27
It's All Right (Curtom, BMI) .... 35
Jenny Brown (Wolf-Mills, ASCAP) .... 84
Kind of Boy You Can't Forget, The (Trio, BMI) .. 38
Little Deuce Coupe (Sea of Tunes, BMI) .... 30
Little Eeefin Annie (Mimosa, BMI) .... 77
Lonely Drifter (Nidle, BMI) .... 97
Love So Fine, A (Jobete, BMI) .... 42
Maria Elena (Peer Int'l, BMI) .... 32
Martian Hop (Screen Gems-Columbia, BMI) .... 24
Mean Woman Blues (Gladys, BMI) .... 8
Mickey's Monkey (Jobete, BMI) .... 17
Misty (Vernon, BMI) .... 56
Mockingbird (Saturn, BMI) .... 51
Monkey-Shine (Jec, BMI) .... 59
Monkey Time (Curtain-Palier, BMI) .... 33
More—Dana (Marks, BMI) .... 44
More—Winding (Marks, BMI) .... 60
My Babe (Maxwell, BMI) .... 75
My Boyfriend's Back (Blackwood, BMI) .... 7
New Mexican Rose (Claridge, ASCAP) .... 79
Night Life (Pamper, BMI) .... 72
Only in America (Screen Gems-Columbia, BMI) ... 37
Painted, Tainted Rose (Damian, ASCAP) .... 41
Part Time Love (Circco-Escort, BMI) .... 19
Point Panic (Champion, BMI) ....74
Red Sails in the Sunset (Shapiro-Bernstein, ASCAP) .... 53
Sally, Go 'Round the Roses (Winlyn, BMI) .... 5
September Song (Henderson, ASCAP) .... 54
She's a Fool (Helios-MRC, BMI) .... 46
Signed, Sealed and Delivered (Lois, BMI) .... 96
Speed Ball (Lowery, BMI) .... 81
Strange Feeling (Arc, BMI) .... 82
Sugar Shack (Dundee, BMI) .... 1
Surfer Girl (Guild, BMI) .... 15
Sweet Impossible You (Champion, BMI) .... 80
Talk to Me (Jay & Cee, BMI) .... 21
Teenage Cleopatra (Saturday, ASCAP) .... 87
That Sunday, That Summer (Comet, ASCAP) .... 13
That's the Way It Goes (Claridge, ASCAP) .... 91
Then He Kissed Me (Mother Bertha-Trio, BMI) .. 16
Toys in the Attric (United Artists, ASCAP) .... 85
Treat My Baby Good (T. M., BMI) .... 52
Two Sides (To Every Story) (Chevis-Salaam, BMI) .. 63
Two-Ten, Six-Eighteen (Devon, BMI) .... 98
Two Tickets to Paradise (Benday, BMI) .... 34
Walkin' Miracle, A (Planetary, ASCAP) .... 22
Walking the Dog (East, BMI) .... 69
Washington Square (Rayven, BMI) .... 23
Wham (Carlson-Edwood, BMI) .... 40
What Does a Girl Do (Damic, BMI) .... 55
Wild! (Kalmann, ASCAP) .... 83
Wonderful! Wonderful! (Marks, BMI) .... 12
Workout Stevie, Workout (Jobete, BMI) .... 49
You Can Never Stop Me Loving You (Ridge, BMI) .. 43
You Lost the Sweetest Boy (Jobete, BMI) .... 39
Your Teenage Dream (Elm Drive, ASCAP) .... 86

## BUBBLING UNDER THE HOT 100

101. TALK BACK TREMBLING LIPS .... Ernest Ashworth, Hickory 1214
102. I WONDER WHAT SHE'S DOING TONIGHT .... Barry & the Tamerlanes, Valiant 6034
103. WALKING PROUD .... Steve Lawrence, Columbia 42865
104. TOYS IN THE ATTIC .... Jack Jones, Kapp 551
105. WHERE DID THE GOOD TIMES GO .... Dick & Deedee, Warner Bros. 5383
106. FIESTA .... Lawrence Welk, Dot 16526
107. YOUR OTHER LOVE .... Connie Francis, MGM 13176
108. PLEASE WRITE .... Tokens, Laurie 3180
109. EEFANANNY .... Ardells, Epic 9621
110. BLUE VELVET .... Lawrence Welk, Dot 16526
111. FADED LOVE .... Patsy Cline, Decca 31522
112. MICHAEL .... Steve Alaimo, Checker 1054
113. BROWN-EYED HANDSOME MAN .... Buddy Holly, Coral 62369
114. UNCHAINED MELODY .... Vito & the Salutations, Herald 583
115. WIVES AND LOVERS .... Jack Jones, Kapp 551
116. GUITARS, GUITARS, GUITARS .... Al Casey, Stacy 964
117. CAN I GET A WITNESS .... Marvin Gaye, Tamla 54087
118. A STORY UNTOLD .... Emotions, 20th Century-Fox 430
119. TOYS IN THE ATTIC .... Dennis Regor, Contempo 904
120. LET'S MAKE LOVE TONIGHT .... Bobby Rydell, Cameo 272
121. KICK OUT .... Safaris, Valiant 6036
122. A PERFECT PAIR .... Paul & Paula, Philips 40142
123. DOWN ON BENDING KNEES .... Johnny Copland, Golden Eagle 101
124. IT COMES AND GOES .... Burl Ives, Decca 31543
125. NOT SO LONG AGO .... Marty Robbins, Columbia 42831
126. DEAR ABBY .... Hearts, Tuff 5557
127. THE GORILLA .... Ideals, Cortland 110
128. UNDERTOW .... Fabulous Continentals, CB 5003
129. MARY MARY .... Jimmy Reed, Vee Jay 552
130. HE'S THE ONE YOU LOVE .... Inez Foxx, Symbol 922
131. THE MATADOR .... Johnny Cash, Columbia 42880

Compiled from national retail sales and radio station airplay by the Music Popularity Dept. of Record Market Research, Billboard.

# Billboard HOT 100

*For Week Ending October 19, 1963*

★ **STAR** performer—Sides registering greatest proportionate upward progress this week.

| This Week | 1 Wk. Ago | 2 Wks. Ago | 3 Wks. Ago | TITLE, Artist, Label & Number | Weeks On Chart |
|---|---|---|---|---|---|
| 1 | 1 | 4 | 19 | **SUGAR SHACK** — Jimmy Gilmer and the Fireballs, Dot 16487 | 5 |
| 2 | 2 | 3 | 3 | **BE MY BABY** — Ronettes, Philles 116 | 8 |
| 3 | 3 | 1 | 1 | **BLUE VELVET** — Bobby Vinton, Epic 9614 | 11 |
| 4 | 6 | 9 | 13 | **BUSTED** — Ray Charles, ABC-Paramount 10481 | 7 |
| 5 | 4 | 5 | 9 | **CRY BABY** — Garnet Mimms & the Enchanters, United Artists 629 | 10 |
| 6 | 5 | 2 | 2 | **SALLY, GO 'ROUND THE ROSES** — Jaynetts, Tuff 369 | 8 |
| 7 | 8 | 16 | 32 | **MEAN WOMAN BLUES** — Roy Orbison, Monument 824 | 7 |
| 8 | 10 | 17 | 33 | **DONNA THE PRIMA DONNA** — Dion Di Muci, Columbia 42852 | 6 |
| ★9 | 20 | 33 | 58 | **DEEP PURPLE** — Nino Tempo & April Stevens, Atco 6273 | 6 |
| ★10 | 14 | 21 | 34 | **DON'T THINK TWICE IT'S ALL RIGHT** — Peter, Paul & Mary, Warner Bros. 5385 | 6 |
| 11 | 11 | 13 | 20 | **HONOLULU LULU** — Jan & Dean, Liberty 55613 | 7 |
| 12 | 18 | 23 | 29 | **I CAN'T STAY MAD AT YOU** — Skeeter Davis, RCA Victor 8219 | 7 |
| 13 | 13 | 28 | 35 | **THAT SUNDAY, THAT SUMMER** — Nat King Cole, Capitol 5027 | 8 |
| ★14 | 26 | 34 | 46 | **FOOLS RUSH IN** — Rick Nelson, Decca 31533 | 6 |
| 15 | 7 | 6 | 5 | **MY BOYFRIEND'S BACK** — Angels, Smash 1834 | 12 |
| 16 | 21 | 26 | 31 | **TALK TO ME** — Sunny and the Sunglows, Tear Drop 3014 | 7 |
| 17 | 23 | 38 | 69 | **WASHINGTON SQUARE** — Village Stompers, Epic 9617 | 5 |
| 18 | 9 | 8 | 4 | **HEAT WAVE** — Martha & the Vandellas, Gordy 7022 | 12 |
| 19 | 16 | 10 | 6 | **THEN HE KISSED ME** — Crystals, Philles 115 | 10 |
| 20 | 15 | 14 | 11 | **SURFER GIRL** — Beach Boys, Capitol 5009 | 12 |
| ★21 | 32 | 54 | 66 | **MARIA ELENA** — Los Indios Tabajaras, RCA Victor 8216 | 5 |
| 22 | 19 | 19 | 24 | **PART TIME LOVE** — Little Johnny Taylor, Galaxy 722 | 10 |
| 23 | 17 | 11 | 8 | **MICKEY'S MONKEY** — Miracles, Tamla 54083 | 10 |
| ★24 | 35 | 58 | 86 | **IT'S ALL RIGHT** — Impressions, ABC-Paramount 10487 | 4 |
| 25 | 29 | 32 | 41 | **I'LL TAKE YOU HOME** — Drifters, Atlantic 2201 | 7 |
| 26 | 28 | 31 | 38 | **HELLO HEARTACHE, GOODBYE LOVE** — Little Peggy March, RCA Victor 8221 | 6 |
| 27 | 12 | 7 | 7 | **WONDERFUL! WONDERFUL!** — Tymes, Parkway 884 | 10 |
| ★28 | 45 | 56 | 82 | **CROSSFIRE!** — Orlons, Cameo 273 | 4 |
| 29 | 31 | 41 | 45 | **BLUE BAYOU** — Roy Orbison, Monument 824 | 6 |
| ★30 | 36 | 46 | 74 | **THE GRASS IS GREENER** — Brenda Lee, Decca 31539 | 4 |
| ★31 | 46 | 59 | 81 | **SHE'S A FOOL** — Lesley Gore, Mercury 72180 | 4 |
| 32 | 34 | 36 | 47 | **TWO TICKETS TO PARADISE** — Brook Benton, Mercury 72177 | 7 |
| 33 | 30 | 20 | 15 | **LITTLE DEUCE COUPE** — Beach Boys, Capitol 5009 | 10 |
| 34 | 22 | 12 | 12 | **A WALKIN' MIRACLE** — Essex, Roulette 4515 | 9 |
| 35 | 39 | 50 | 70 | **YOU LOST THE SWEETEST BOY** — Mary Wells, Motown 1048 | 4 |
| 36 | 25 | 27 | 30 | **BUST OUT** — Busters, Arlen 735 | 7 |
| ★37 | 49 | 63 | — | **WORKOUT STEVIE, WORKOUT** — Little Stevie Wonder, Tamla 54086 | 3 |
| 38 | 27 | 15 | 10 | **IF I HAD A HAMMER** — Trini Lopez, Reprise 20198 | 13 |
| 39 | 24 | 18 | 16 | **MARTIAN HOP** — Ran-Dells, Chairman 4403 | 12 |
| 40 | 42 | 48 | 59 | **A LOVE SO FINE** — Chiffons, Laurie 3195 | 7 |
| ★41 | 56 | 69 | — | **MISTY** — Lloyd Price, Double L 722 | 3 |
| 42 | 37 | 25 | 25 | **ONLY IN AMERICA** — Jay & the Americans, United Artists 625 | 10 |
| 43 | 53 | 65 | 73 | **RED SAILS IN THE SUNSET** — Fats Domino, ABC-Paramount 10484 | 5 |
| 44 | 33 | 22 | 14 | **THE MONKEY TIME** — Major Lance, Okeh 7175 | 15 |
| ★45 | 57 | 61 | 80 | **CRY TO ME** — Betty Harris, Jubilee 4556 | 5 |
| 46 | 73 | 82 | 90 | **(Down at) PAPA JOE'S** — Dixiebelles, Sound Stage 7 2507 | 4 |
| ★47 | 65 | 89 | — | **I'M LEAVING IT UP TO YOU** — Dale & Grace, Montel-Michele 921 | 3 |
| 48 | 71 | 96 | — | **500 MILES AWAY FROM HOME** — Bobby Bare, RCA Victor 8238 | 3 |
| 49 | 66 | 78 | 83 | **DOWN THE AISLE** — Patty LaBelle & the Blue Belles, Newtown 5777 | 6 |
| 50 | 79 | 94 | — | **NEW MEXICAN ROSE** — 4 Seasons, Vee Jay 562 | 3 |
| 51 | 54 | 62 | 71 | **SEPTEMBER SONG** — Jimmy Durante, Warner Bros. 5382 | 7 |
| 52 | 69 | 80 | — | **WALKING THE DOG** — Rufus Thomas, Stax 140 | 3 |
| 53 | 68 | — | — | **EVERYBODY** — Tommy Roe, ABC-Paramount 10478 | 2 |
| 54 | 38 | 29 | 17 | **THE KIND OF BOY YOU CAN'T FORGET** — Raindrops, Jubilee 5455 | 11 |
| 55 | 51 | 39 | 28 | **MOCKINGBIRD** — Inez Foxx, Symbol 919 | 18 |
| 56 | 59 | 66 | — | **MONKEY-SHINE** — Bill Black & His Combo, Hi 2069 | 3 |
| 57 | 52 | 43 | 44 | **TREAT MY BABY GOOD** — Bobby Darin, Capitol 5019 | 9 |
| 58 | 44 | 42 | 42 | **MORE** — Vic Dana, Dolton 81 | 11 |
| 59 | 40 | 24 | 26 | **WHAM** — Lonnie Mack, Fraternity 912 | 9 |
| ★60 | 83 | 90 | — | **WILD!** — Dee Dee Sharp, Cameo 274 | 3 |
| 61 | 78 | 81 | 91 | **BLUE GUITAR** — Richard Chamberlain, MGM 13170 | 4 |
| 62 | 70 | 79 | — | **FIRST DAY BACK TO SCHOOL** — Paul & Paula, Philips 40142 | 3 |
| 63 | 58 | 60 | 67 | **I'M CONFESSIN'** — Frank Ifield, Capitol 5032 | 7 |
| ★64 | 81 | — | — | **SPEED BALL** — Ray Stevens, Mercury 72189 | 2 |
| 65 | 63 | 74 | — | **TWO SIDES (To Every Story)** — Etta James, Argo 5452 | 3 |
| 66 | 62 | 67 | 72 | **HE'S MINE** — Alice Wonder Land, Bardell 774 | 6 |
| 67 | 67 | 70 | 76 | **ENAMORADO** — Keith Colley, Unical 3006 | 6 |
| 68 | 72 | 85 | 93 | **NIGHT LIFE** — Rusty Draper, Monument 823 | 4 |
| 69 | 64 | 68 | 75 | **ELEPHANT WALK** — Donald Jenkins & the Daylighters, Cortland 109 | 6 |
| 70 | 74 | 87 | 99 | **POINT PANIC** — Surfaris, Decca 31538 | 4 |
| 71 | 61 | 73 | 87 | **BABY GET IT (And Don't Quit It)** — Jackie Wilson, Brunswick 55250 | 5 |
| ★72 | — | — | — | **WITCHCRAFT** — Elvis Presley, RCA Victor 8243 | 1 |
| 73 | 80 | 91 | 96 | **SWEET IMPOSSIBLE YOU** — Brenda Lee, Decca 31539 | 4 |
| ★74 | — | — | — | **HEY LITTLE GIRL** — Major Lance, Okeh 7181 | 1 |
| 75 | 75 | 76 | 78 | **MY BABE** — Righteous Brothers, Moonglow 223 | 7 |
| 76 | 77 | 83 | 97 | **LITTLE EEEFIN ANNIE** — Joe Perkins, Sound Stage 7 2511 | 4 |
| 77 | — | — | — | **BOSSA NOVA BABY** — Elvis Presley, RCA Victor 8243 | 1 |
| 78 | 82 | 84 | 89 | **STRANGE FEELING** — Billy Stewart, Chess 1868 | 4 |
| ★79 | — | — | — | **YOUR OTHER LOVE** — Connie Francis, MGM 13176 | 1 |
| 80 | 76 | 72 | 84 | **CINDY'S GONNA CRY** — Johnny Crawford, Del-Fi 4221 | 7 |
| ★81 | — | — | — | **WALKING PROUD** — Steve Lawrence, Columbia 42865 | 1 |
| 82 | 86 | — | — | **YOUR TEEN-AGE DREAMS** — Johnny Mathis, Mercury 72184 | 2 |
| ★83 | — | — | — | **I WONDER WHAT SHE'S DOING TONIGHT** — Barry & the Tamerlanes, Valiant 6034 | 1 |
| ★84 | — | — | — | **I'M CRAZY 'BOUT MY BABY** — Marvin Gaye, Tamla 54087 | 1 |
| 85 | 92 | — | — | **COME BACK** — Johnny Mathis, Mercury 72184 | 2 |
| 86 | 88 | 88 | 98 | **EVERYBODY GO HOME** — Eydie Gorme, Columbia 42854 | 4 |
| ★87 | — | — | — | **WHAT'S EASY FOR TWO IS SO HARD FOR ONE** — Mary Wells, Motown 1048 | 1 |
| 88 | 91 | 99 | — | **THAT'S THE ONLY WAY** — 4 Seasons, Vee Jay 562 | 3 |
| 89 | 94 | — | — | **GOTTA TRAVEL ON** — Timi Yuro, Liberty 55634 | 2 |
| ★90 | — | — | — | **A FINE FINE BOY** — Darlene Love, Philles 117 | 1 |
| 91 | — | — | — | **FUNNY HOW TIME SLIPS AWAY** — Johnny Tillotson, Cadence 1441 | 1 |
| 92 | 93 | — | — | **CUANDO CALIENTA EL SOL** — Steve Allen, Dot 16507 | 2 |
| 93 | 98 | — | — | **TWO-TEN, SIX-EIGHTEEN** — Jimmie Rodgers, Dot 16527 | 2 |
| 94 | 96 | — | — | **SIGNED, SEALED AND DELIVERED** — James Brown & the Famous Flames, King 5083 | 2 |
| 95 | 99 | — | — | **DON'T WAIT TOO LONG** — Tony Bennett, Columbia 42886 | 2 |
| 96 | — | — | — | **IT'S A MAD, MAD, MAD, MAD WORLD** — Shirelles, Scepter 1260 | 1 |
| 97 | — | — | — | **CAN I GET A WITNESS** — Marvin Gay, Tamla 54087 | 1 |
| 98 | — | — | — | **DEAR ABBY** — Hearts, Tuff 5557 | 1 |
| 99 | — | — | — | **TWENTY-FOUR HOURS FROM TULSA** — Gene Pitney, Musicor 1034 | 1 |
| 100 | — | — | — | **REACH OUT FOR ME** — Lou Johnson, Big Top 3153 | 1 |

## BUBBLING UNDER THE HOT 100

101. TALK BACK TREMBLING LIPS ... Ernest Ashworth, Hickory 1214
102. WONDERFUL SUMMER ... Robin Ward, Dot 16530
103. I ADORE HIM ... Angels, Smash 1854
104. TOYS IN THE ATTIC ... Jack Jones, Kapp 551
105. COWBOY BOOTS ... Dave Dudley, Golden Ring 3020
106. ANY NUMBER CAN WIN ... Jimmy Smith, Verve 10299
107. DETROIT CITY NO. 2 ... Ben Colder, MGM 13154
108. JENNY BROWN ... Smothers Brothers, Mercury 72182
109. LONELY DRIFTER ... O'Jays, Imperial 5976
110. HEY LONELY ONE ... Baby Washington, Sue 794
111. TOYS IN THE ATTIC ... Joe Sherman, World Artists 1088
112. YOU'RE GOOD FOR ME ... Solomon Burke, Atlantic 2205
113. LITTLE RED ROOSTER ... Sam Cooke, RCA Victor 8247
114. WHERE DID THE GOOD TIMES GO ... Dick & Deedee, Warner Bros. 5383
115. TOYS IN THE ATTIC ... Donald Jager, Contempo 904
116. BETTER TO GIVE THAN RECEIVE ... Joe Hinton, Back Beat 539
117. ANY OTHER WAY ... Chuck Jackson, Wand 141
118. THE MATADOR ... Johnny Cash, Columbia 42880
119. LET'S MAKE LOVE TONIGHT ... Bobby Rydell, Cameo 272
120. KICK OUT ... Safaris, Valiant 6036
121. SATURDAY NIGHT ... New Christy Minstrels, Columbia 42887
122. DOWN ON BENDING KNEES ... Johnny Copland, Golden Eagle 101
123. PROMISE ME ANYTHING ... Annette, Vista 427
124. SHY BOY ... Lou Christie, Roulette 4527
125. HE'S THE ONE YOU LOVE ... Inez Foxx, Symbol 922
126. DOWN HOME ... Rick Nelson, Decca 31533
127. YOUNG WINGS CAN FLY ... Ruby & the Romantics, Kapp 557
128. JENNY BROWN ... Gene Thomas, United Artists 640
129. BABY'S GONE ... Gene Thomas, United Artists 640
130. HEY LOVER ... Debbie Dovale, Roulette 4521
131. TOMORROW IS ANOTHER DAY ... Doris Troy, Atlantic 2206
132. GUITARS, GUITARS, GUITARS ... Al Casey, Stacy 964
133. NINETY MILES AN HOUR (Down a Dead-End Street) ... Hank Snow, RCA Victor 8239
134. P.S.: I LOVE YOU ... Classics, Music Note 118

*Compiled from national retail sales and radio station airplay by the Music Popularity Dept. of Record Market Research, Billboard.*

# Billboard HOT 100

**For Week Ending October 26, 1963**

★ STAR performer—Sides registering greatest proportionate upward progress this week.

| This Week | Wk. Ago | 2 Wks. Ago | 3 Wks. Ago | TITLE — Artist, Label & Number | Weeks On Chart |
|---|---|---|---|---|---|
| 1 | 1 | 1 | 4 | SUGAR SHACK — Jimmy Gilmer and the Fireballs, Dot 16487 | 6 |
| 2 | 2 | 2 | 3 | BE MY BABY — Ronettes, Philles 116 | 9 |
| ★3 | 9 | 20 | 33 | DEEP PURPLE — Nino Tempo & April Stevens, Atco 6273 | 7 |
| 4 | 4 | 6 | 9 | BUSTED — Ray Charles, ABC-Paramount 10481 | 8 |
| 5 | 3 | 3 | 1 | BLUE VELVET — Bobby Vinton, Epic 9614 | 12 |
| 6 | 8 | 10 | 17 | DONNA THE PRIMA DONNA — Dion Di Muci, Columbia 42852 | 7 |
| 7 | 7 | 8 | 16 | MEAN WOMAN BLUES — Roy Orbison, Monument 824 | 8 |
| ★8 | 17 | 23 | 38 | WASHINGTON SQUARE — Village Stompers, Epic 9617 | 6 |
| 9 | 10 | 14 | 21 | DON'T THINK TWICE IT'S ALL RIGHT — Peter, Paul & Mary, Warner Bros. 5385 | 7 |
| 10 | 5 | 4 | 5 | CRY BABY — Garnet Mimms & the Enchanters, United Artists 629 | 11 |
| 11 | 16 | 21 | 26 | TALK TO ME — Sunny and the Sunglows, Tear Drop 3014 | 8 |
| 12 | 12 | 18 | 23 | I CAN'T STAY MAD AT YOU — Skeeter Davis, RCA Victor 8219 | 8 |
| 13 | 13 | 13 | 28 | THAT SUNDAY, THAT SUMMER — Nat King Cole, Capitol 5027 | 9 |
| 14 | 14 | 26 | 34 | FOOLS RUSH IN — Rick Nelson, Decca 31533 | 7 |
| ★15 | 24 | 35 | 58 | IT'S ALL RIGHT — Impressions, ABC-Paramount 10487 | 5 |
| 16 | 11 | 11 | 13 | HONOLULU LULU — Jan & Dean, Liberty 55613 | 8 |
| 17 | 6 | 5 | 2 | SALLY, GO 'ROUND THE ROSES — Jaynetts, Tuff 369 | 12 |
| 18 | 21 | 32 | 54 | MARIA ELENA — Los Indios Tabajaras, RCA Victor 8216 | 6 |
| ★19 | 47 | 65 | 89 | I'M LEAVING IT UP TO YOU — Dale & Grace, Montel-Michele 921 | 4 |
| 20 | 31 | 46 | 59 | SHE'S A FOOL — Lesley Gore, Mercury 72180 | 5 |
| 21 | 30 | 36 | 46 | THE GRASS IS GREENER — Brenda Lee, Decca 31539 | 5 |
| 22 | 28 | 45 | 56 | CROSSFIRE! — Orlons, Cameo 273 | 5 |
| 23 | 46 | 73 | 82 | (Down at) PAPA JOE'S — Dixiebelles, Sound Stage 7 2507 | 5 |
| 24 | 20 | 15 | 14 | SURFER GIRL — Beach Boys, Capitol 5009 | 10 |
| 25 | 15 | 7 | 6 | MY BOYFRIEND'S BACK — Angels, Smash 1834 | 13 |
| 26 | 22 | 19 | 19 | PART TIME LOVE — Little Johnny Taylor, Galaxy 722 | 11 |
| 27 | 18 | 9 | 8 | HEAT WAVE — Martha & the Vandellas, Gordy 7022 | 13 |
| 28 | 25 | 29 | 32 | I'LL TAKE YOU HOME — Drifters, Atlantic 2201 | 8 |
| ★29 | 35 | 39 | 50 | YOU LOST THE SWEETEST BOY — Mary Wells, Motown 1048 | 5 |
| ★30 | 53 | 68 | — | EVERYBODY — Tommy Roe, ABC-Paramount 10478 | 3 |
| 31 | 23 | 17 | 11 | MICKEY'S MONKEY — Miracles, Tamla 54083 | 11 |
| 32 | 19 | 16 | 10 | THEN HE KISSED ME — Crystals, Philles 115 | 11 |
| ★33 | 29 | 31 | 41 | BLUE BAYOU — Roy Orbison, Monument 824 | 7 |
| 34 | 36 | 25 | 27 | BUST OUT — Busters, Arlen 735 | 8 |
| 35 | 32 | 34 | 36 | TWO TICKETS TO PARADISE — Brook Benton, Mercury 72177 | 8 |
| 36 | 37 | 49 | 63 | WORKOUT STEVIE, WORKOUT — Little Stevie Wonder, Tamla 54086 | 4 |
| ★37 | 48 | 71 | 96 | 500 MILES AWAY FROM HOME — Bobby Bare, RCA Victor 8238 | 4 |
| 38 | 41 | 56 | 69 | MISTY — Lloyd Price, Double L 722 | 4 |
| 39 | 43 | 53 | 65 | RED SAILS IN THE SUNSET — Fats Domino, ABC-Paramount 10484 | 6 |
| 40 | 45 | 57 | 61 | CRY TO ME — Betty Harris, Jubilee 4556 | 6 |
| ★41 | 77 | — | — | BOSSA NOVA BABY — Elvis Presley, RCA Victor 8243 | 2 |
| 42 | 26 | 28 | 31 | HELLO HEARTACHE, GOODBYE LOVE — Little Peggy March, RCA Victor 8221 | 8 |
| 43 | 50 | 79 | 94 | NEW MEXICAN ROSE — 4 Seasons, Vee Jay 562 | 4 |
| 44 | 40 | 42 | 48 | A LOVE SO FINE — Chiffons, Laurie 3195 | 8 |
| 45 | 33 | 30 | 20 | LITTLE DEUCE COUPE — Beach Boys, Capitol 5009 | 11 |
| 46 | 27 | 12 | 7 | WONDERFUL! WONDERFUL! — Tymes, Parkway 884 | 11 |
| 47 | 49 | 66 | 78 | DOWN THE AISLE — Patty LaBelle & the Blue Belles, Newtown 5777 | 7 |
| 48 | 52 | 69 | 80 | WALKING THE DOG — Rufus Thomas, Stax 140 | 4 |
| 49 | 42 | 37 | 25 | ONLY IN AMERICA — Jay & the Americans, United Artists 625 | 11 |
| 50 | 60 | 83 | 90 | WILD! — Dee Dee Sharp, Cameo 274 | 4 |
| 51 | 38 | 27 | 15 | IF I HAD A HAMMER — Trini Lopez, Reprise 20198 | 14 |
| 52 | 34 | 22 | 12 | A WALKIN' MIRACLE — Essex, Roulette 4515 | 10 |
| 53 | 39 | 24 | 18 | MARTIAN HOP — Ran-Dells, Chairman 4403 | 13 |
| 54 | 56 | 59 | 66 | MONKEY-SHINE — Bill Black & His Combo, Hi 2069 | 4 |
| 55 | 61 | 78 | 81 | BLUE GUITAR — Richard Chamberlain, MGM 13170 | 5 |
| ★56 | 79 | — | — | YOUR OTHER LOVE — Connie Francis, MGM 13176 | 2 |
| ★57 | 72 | — | — | WITCHCRAFT — Elvis Presley, RCA Victor 8243 | 2 |
| 58 | 51 | 54 | 62 | SEPTEMBER SONG — Jimmy Durante, Warner Bros. 5382 | 8 |
| 59 | 64 | 81 | — | SPEED BALL — Ray Stevens, Mercury 72189 | 3 |
| 60 | 62 | 70 | 79 | FIRST DAY BACK AT SCHOOL — Paul & Paula, Philips 40142 | 4 |
| 61 | 70 | 74 | 87 | POINT PANIC — Surfaris, Decca 31538 | 5 |
| 62 | 74 | — | — | HEY LITTLE GIRL — Major Lance, Okeh 7181 | 2 |
| 63 | 65 | 63 | 74 | TWO SIDES (To Every Story) — Etta James, Argo 5452 | 4 |
| 64 | 69 | 64 | 68 | ELEPHANT WALK — Donald Jenkins & the Daylighters, Cortland 109 | 7 |
| 65 | 68 | 72 | 85 | NIGHT LIFE — Rusty Draper, Monument 823 | 5 |
| 66 | 67 | 67 | 70 | ENAMORADO — Keith Colley, Unical 3006 | 7 |
| ★67 | 83 | — | — | I WONDER WHAT SHE'S DOING TONIGHT — Barry & the Tamerlanes, Valiant 6034 | 2 |
| 68 | 66 | 62 | 67 | HE'S MINE — Alice Wonder Land, Bardell 774 | 7 |
| 69 | 81 | — | — | WALKING PROUD — Steve Lawrence, Columbia 42865 | 2 |
| 70 | 73 | 80 | 91 | SWEET IMPOSSIBLE YOU — Brenda Lee, Decca 31539 | 5 |
| ★71 | — | — | — | I ADORE HIM — Angels, Smash 1854 | 1 |
| 72 | 85 | 92 | — | COME BACK — Johnny Mathis, Mercury 72184 | 3 |
| 73 | — | — | — | LITTLE RED ROOSTER — Sam Cooke, RCA Victor 8247 | 1 |
| ★74 | 91 | — | — | FUNNY HOW TIME SLIPS AWAY — Johnny Tillotson, Cadence 1441 | 2 |
| 75 | 90 | — | — | A FINE FINE BOY — Darlene Love, Philles 117 | 2 |
| 76 | 82 | 86 | — | YOUR TEEN-AGE DREAMS — Johnny Mathis, Mercury 72184 | 3 |
| 77 | 99 | — | — | TWENTY-FOUR HOURS FROM TULSA — Gene Pitney, Musicor 1034 | 2 |
| 78 | 78 | 82 | 84 | STRANGE FEELING — Billy Stewart, Chess 1868 | 5 |
| 79 | 95 | 99 | — | DON'T WAIT TOO LONG — Tony Bennett, Columbia 42886 | 3 |
| 80 | 87 | — | — | WHAT'S EASY FOR TWO IS SO HARD FOR ONE — Mary Wells, Motown 1048 | 2 |
| 81 | — | — | — | SATURDAY NIGHT — New Christy Minstrels, Columbia 42868 | 1 |
| 82 | 84 | — | — | I'M CRAZY 'BOUT MY BABY — Marvin Gaye, Tamla 54087 | 2 |
| 83 | 86 | 88 | 88 | EVERYBODY GO HOME — Eydie Gorme, Columbia 42854 | 3 |
| 84 | — | — | — | YOUNG WINGS CAN FLY — Ruby & the Romantics, Kapp 557 | 1 |
| 85 | 89 | 94 | — | GOTTA TRAVEL ON — Timi Yuro, Liberty 55634 | 3 |
| 86 | — | — | — | THE MATADOR — Johnny Cash, Columbia 42880 | 1 |
| 87 | 76 | 77 | 83 | LITTLE EEEFIN ANNIE — Joe Perkins, Sound Stage 7 2511 | 5 |
| 88 | 93 | 98 | — | TWO-TEN, SIX-EIGHTEEN — Jimmie Rodgers, Dot 16527 | 3 |
| 89 | 92 | 93 | — | CUANDO CALIENTA EL SOL — Steve Allen, Dot 16507 | 3 |
| 90 | — | — | — | LIVING A LIE — Al Martino, Capitol 5060 | 1 |
| 91 | 97 | — | — | CAN I GET A WITNESS — Marvin Gaye, Tamla 54037 | 2 |
| 92 | 96 | — | — | IT'S A MAD, MAD, MAD, MAD WORLD — Shirelles, Scepter 1260 | 2 |
| 93 | 94 | 96 | — | SIGNED, SEALED & DELIVERED — James Brown & the Famous Flames, King 5083 | 3 |
| 94 | 100 | — | — | REACH OUT FOR ME — Lou Johnson, Big Top 3153 | 2 |
| 95 | — | — | — | SHIRL GIRL — Wayne Newton, Capitol 5058 | 1 |
| 96 | 98 | — | — | DEAR ABBY — Hearts, Tuff 5557 | 2 |
| 97 | — | — | — | UNCHAINED MELODY — Vito & the Salutations, Herald 583 | 1 |
| 98 | — | — | — | THE SCAVENGER — Dick Dale & the Del-Tones, Capitol 5048 | 1 |
| 99 | — | — | — | SINCE I FELL FOR YOU — Lenny Welch, Cadence 1439 | 1 |
| 100 | — | 84 | 86 | JENNY BROWN — Smothers Brothers, Mercury 72182 | 4 |

## BUBBLING UNDER THE HOT 100

101. 31 FLAVORS — Shirelles, Scepter 1260
102. WONDERFUL SUMMER — Robin Ward, Dot 16530
103. COWBOY BOOTS — Dave Dudley, Golden Ring 3030
104. HEY LOVER — Debbie Dovale, Roulette 4521
105. WIVES AND LOVERS — Jack Jones, Kapp 551
106. YOU'RE GOOD FOR ME — Solomon Burke, Atlantic 2205
107. HEY LONELY ONE — Baby Washington, Sue 794
108. TOYS IN THE ATTIC — Joe Sherman, World Artists 1088
109. MISERY — Dynamics, Big Top 3161
110. DETROIT CITY NO. 2 — Ben Colder, MGM 13167
111. LOVE ISN'T JUST FOR THE YOUNG — Frank Sinatra, Reprise 20209
112. I COULD HAVE DANCED ALL NIGHT — Ben E. King, Atco 6275
113. PLEASE DON'T KISS ME AGAIN — Charmettes, Kapp 547
114. LONELY DRIFTER — O'Jays, Imperial 5974
115. DOWN ON BENDING KNEES — Johnny Copland, Golden Eagle 101
116. HE'S THE ONE YOU LOVE — Inez Foxx, Symbol 922
117. ANY NUMBER CAN WIN — Jimmy Smith, Verve 10299
118. TOMORROW IS ANOTHER DAY — Doris Troy, Atlantic 2206
119. SHY BOY — Lou Christie, Roulette 4522
120. A STORY UNTOLD — Emotions, 20th Century-Fox 430
121. BABY'S GONE — Gene Thomas, Contempo 904
122. TOYS IN THE ATTIC — Dennis Regor, Contempo 904
123. LOVE HER — Everly Brothers, Warner Bros. 5389
124. FIESTA — Lawrence Welk, Dot 16526
125. SUE'S GOTTA BE MINE — Del Shannon, Berlee 501
126. YESTERDAY AND YOU — Bobby Vee, Liberty 55636
127. TOYS IN THE ATTIC — Jack Jones, Kapp 551
128. DAWN — David Rockingham Trio, Josie 913
129. WASHINGTON SQUARE — Ames Brothers, Epic 9630
130. ANY OTHER WAY — Chuck Jackson, Wand 141
131. HEY CHILD — Johnny Thunder, Diamond 148
132. BETTER TO GIVE THAN RECEIVE — Joe Hinton, Back Beat 529
133. FOUR STRONG WINDS — Brothers Four, Columbia 42888

Compiled from national retail sales and radio station airplay by the Music Popularity Dept. of Record Market Research, Billboard.

# Billboard HOT 100

For Week Ending November 2, 1963

★ STAR performer—Sides registering greatest proportionate upward progress this week.

| This Week | 1 Wk. Ago | 2 Wks. Ago | 3 Wks. Ago | TITLE — Artist, Label & Number | Weeks On Chart |
|---|---|---|---|---|---|
| 1 | 1 | 1 | 1 | SUGAR SHACK — Jimmy Gilmer and the Fireballs, Dot 16487 | 7 |
| 2 | 3 | 9 | 20 | DEEP PURPLE — Nino Tempo & April Stevens, Atco 6273 | 8 |
| ★3 | 8 | 17 | 23 | WASHINGTON SQUARE — Village Stompers, Epic 9617 | 7 |
| 4 | 4 | 4 | 6 | BUSTED — Ray Charles, ABC-Paramount 10481 | 9 |
| 5 | 7 | 7 | 8 | MEAN WOMAN BLUES — Roy Orbison, Monument 824 | 9 |
| 6 | 6 | 8 | 10 | DONNA THE PRIMA DONNA — Dion Di Muci, Columbia 42852 | 8 |
| ★7 | 12 | 12 | 18 | I CAN'T STAY MAD AT YOU — Skeeter Davis, RCA Victor 8219 | 9 |
| 8 | 2 | 2 | 2 | BE MY BABY — Ronettes, Philles 116 | 10 |
| 9 | 15 | 24 | 35 | IT'S ALL RIGHT — Impressions, ABC-Paramount 10487 | 6 |
| 10 | 18 | 21 | 32 | MARIA ELENA — Los Indios Tabajaras, RCA Victor 8216 | 7 |
| 11 | 19 | 47 | 65 | I'M LEAVING IT UP TO YOU — Dale & Grace, Montel-Michele 921 | 5 |
| 12 | 13 | 13 | 13 | THAT SUNDAY, THAT SUMMER — Nat King Cole, Capitol 5027 | 10 |
| 13 | 14 | 14 | 26 | FOOLS RUSH IN — Rick Nelson, Decca 31533 | 8 |
| 14 | 11 | 16 | 21 | TALK TO ME — Sunny and the Sunglows, Tear Drop 3014 | 9 |
| 15 | 5 | 3 | 3 | BLUE VELVET — Bobby Vinton, Epic 9614 | 13 |
| 16 | 20 | 31 | 46 | SHE'S A FOOL — Lesley Gore, Mercury 72180 | 6 |
| 17 | 10 | 5 | 4 | CRY BABY — Garnet Mimms & the Enchanters, United Artists 629 | 12 |
| 18 | 9 | 10 | 14 | DON'T THINK TWICE IT'S ALL RIGHT — Peter, Paul & Mary, Warner Bros. 5385 | 8 |
| 19 | 22 | 28 | 45 | CROSSFIRE! — Orlons, Cameo 273 | 6 |
| 20 | 21 | 30 | 36 | THE GRASS IS GREENER — Brenda Lee, Decca 31539 | 6 |
| 21 | 23 | 46 | 73 | (Down at) PAPA JOE'S — Dixiebelles, Sound Stage 7 2507 | 6 |
| ★22 | 30 | 53 | 68 | EVERYBODY — Tommy Roe, ABC-Paramount 10478 | 4 |
| ★23 | 37 | 48 | 71 | 500 MILES AWAY FROM HOME — Bobby Bare, RCA Victor 8238 | 5 |
| 24 | 29 | 35 | 39 | YOU LOST THE SWEETEST BOY — Mary Wells, Motown 1048 | 6 |
| ★25 | 41 | 77 | — | BOSSA NOVA BABY — Elvis Presley, RCA Victor 8243 | 3 |
| ★26 | 38 | 41 | 56 | MISTY — Lloyd Price, Double L 722 | 4 |
| 27 | 16 | 11 | 11 | HONOLULU LULU — Jan & Dean, Liberty 55613 | 9 |
| ★28 | 48 | 52 | 69 | WALKING THE DOG — Rufus Thomas, Stax 140 | 5 |
| 29 | 26 | 22 | 19 | PART TIME LOVE — Little Johnny Taylor, Galaxy 722 | 12 |
| 30 | 33 | 29 | 31 | BLUE BAYOU — Roy Orbison, Monument 824 | 8 |
| 31 | 40 | 45 | 57 | CRY TO ME — Betty Harris, Jubilee 4556 | 7 |
| 32 | 17 | 6 | 5 | SALLY, GO 'ROUND THE ROSES — Jaynetts, Tuff 369 | 10 |
| 33 | 36 | 37 | 49 | WORKOUT STEVIE, WORKOUT — Little Stevie Wonder, Tamla 54086 | 5 |
| 34 | 28 | 25 | 29 | I'LL TAKE YOU HOME — Drifters, Atlantic 2201 | 9 |
| 35 | 39 | 43 | 53 | RED SAILS IN THE SUNSET — Fats Domino, ABC-Paramount 10484 | 7 |
| 36 | 43 | 50 | 79 | NEW MEXICAN ROSE — 4 Seasons, Vee Jay 562 | 5 |
| 37 | 35 | 32 | 34 | TWO TICKETS TO PARADISE — Brook Benton, Mercury 72177 | 9 |
| ★38 | 50 | 60 | 83 | WILD! — Dee Dee Sharp, Cameo 274 | 5 |
| 39 | 62 | 74 | — | HEY LITTLE GIRL — Major Lance, Okeh 7181 | 3 |
| 40 | 47 | 49 | 66 | DOWN THE AISLE — Patty LaBelle & the Blue Belles, Newtown 5777 | 8 |
| 41 | 56 | 79 | — | YOUR OTHER LOVE — Connie Francis, MGM 13176 | 3 |
| 42 | 24 | 20 | 15 | SURFER GIRL — Beach Boys, Capitol 5009 | 14 |
| 43 | 31 | 23 | 17 | MICKEY'S MONKEY — Miracles, Tamla 54083 | 12 |
| ★44 | 73 | — | — | LITTLE RED ROOSTER — Sam Cooke, RCA Victor 8247 | 2 |
| 45 | 57 | 72 | — | WITCHCRAFT — Elvis Presley, RCA Victor 8243 | 3 |
| 46 | 27 | 18 | 9 | HEAT WAVE — Martha & the Vandellas, Gordy 7022 | 14 |
| 47 | 54 | 56 | 59 | MONKEY-SHINE — Bill Black & His Combo, Hi 2069 | 5 |
| 48 | 69 | 81 | — | WALKING PROUD — Steve Lawrence, Columbia 42865 | 3 |
| 49 | 32 | 19 | 16 | THEN HE KISSED ME — Crystals, Philles 115 | 12 |
| ★50 | 67 | 83 | — | I WONDER WHAT SHE'S DOING TONIGHT — Barry & the Tamerlanes, Valiant 6034 | 3 |
| 51 | 61 | 70 | 74 | POINT PANIC — Surfaris, Decca 31538 | 6 |
| 52 | 71 | — | — | I ADORE HIM — Angels, Smash 1854 | 2 |
| 53 | 34 | 36 | 25 | BUST OUT — Busters, Arlen 735 | 9 |
| 54 | 77 | 99 | — | TWENTY-FOUR HOURS FROM TULSA — Gene Pitney, Musicor 1034 | 3 |
| 55 | 55 | 61 | 78 | BLUE GUITAR — Richard Chamberlain, MGM 13170 | 6 |
| 56 | 74 | 91 | — | FUNNY HOW TIME SLIPS AWAY — Johnny Tillotson, Cadence 1441 | 3 |
| 57 | 44 | 40 | 42 | A LOVE SO FINE — Chiffons, Laurie 3195 | 9 |
| 58 | 81 | — | — | SATURDAY NIGHT — New Christy Minstrels, Columbia 42887 | 2 |
| 59 | 42 | 26 | 28 | HELLO HEARTACHE, GOODBYE LOVE — Little Peggy March, RCA Victor 8221 | 9 |
| 60 | 25 | 15 | 7 | MY BOYFRIEND'S BACK — Angels, Smash 1834 | 14 |
| 61 | 86 | — | — | THE MATADOR — Johnny Cash, Columbia 42880 | 2 |
| 62 | 65 | 68 | 72 | NIGHT LIFE — Rusty Draper, Monument 823 | 6 |
| 63 | 75 | 90 | — | A FINE FINE BOY — Darlene Love, Philles 117 | 3 |
| 64 | 64 | 69 | 64 | ELEPHANT WALK — Donald Jenkins & the Daylighters, Cortland 109 | 8 |
| 65 | 72 | 85 | 92 | COME BACK — Johnny Mathis, Mercury 72184 | 4 |
| 67 | 79 | 95 | 99 | DON'T WAIT TOO LONG — Tony Bennett, Columbia 42886 | 4 |
| 68 | 80 | 87 | — | WHAT'S EASY FOR TWO IS SO HARD FOR ONE — Mary Wells, Motown 1048 | 3 |
| 69 | 66 | 67 | 67 | ENAMORADO — Keith Colley, Unical 3006 | 8 |
| 70 | 78 | 78 | 82 | STRANGE FEELING — Billy Stewart, Chess 1868 | 6 |
| 71 | — | — | — | LODDY LO — Chubby Checker, Parkway 890 | 1 |
| 72 | 91 | 97 | — | CAN I GET A WITNESS — Marvin Gaye, Tamla 54037 | 3 |
| 73 | 99 | — | — | SINCE I FELL FOR YOU — Lenny Welch, Cadence 1439 | 2 |
| 74 | 90 | — | — | LIVING A LIE — Al Martino, Capitol 5060 | 2 |
| 75 | 84 | — | — | YOUNG WINGS CAN FLY — Ruby & the Romantics, Kapp 557 | 2 |
| 76 | 76 | 82 | 86 | YOUR TEEN-AGE DREAMS — Johnny Mathis, Mercury 72184 | 4 |
| 77 | 82 | 84 | — | I'M CRAZY 'BOUT MY BABY — Marvin Gaye, Tamla 54087 | 3 |
| 78 | 97 | — | — | UNCHAINED MELODY — Vito & the Salutations, Herald 583 | 2 |
| 79 | 85 | 89 | 94 | GOTTA TRAVEL ON — Timi Yuro, Liberty 55634 | 4 |
| 80 | 83 | 86 | 88 | EVERYBODY GO HOME — Eydie Gorme, Columbia 42854 | 6 |
| 81 | 93 | 94 | 96 | SIGNED, SEALED AND DELIVERED — James Brown & the Famous Flames, King 5083 | 4 |
| 82 | — | — | — | WIVES AND LOVERS — Jack Jones, Kapp 551 | 1 |
| 83 | — | — | — | BE TRUE TO YOUR SCHOOL — Beach Boys, Capitol 5069 | 1 |
| 84 | — | — | — | YOU DON'T HAVE TO BE A BABY TO CRY — Caravels, Smash 1852 | 1 |
| 85 | 89 | 92 | 93 | CUANDO CALIENTA EL SOL — Steve Allen, Dot 16507 | 4 |
| 86 | — | — | — | IN MY ROOM — Beach Boys, Capitol 5069 | 1 |
| 87 | 88 | 93 | 98 | TWO-TEN, SIX-EIGHTEEN — Jimmie Rodgers, Dot 16527 | 4 |
| 88 | — | — | — | ANY OTHER WAY — Chuck Jackson, Wand 141 | 1 |
| 89 | — | — | — | YOU'RE GOOD FOR ME — Solomon Burke, Atlantic 2205 | 1 |
| 90 | — | — | — | I COULD HAVE DANCED ALL NIGHT — Ben E. King, Atco 6275 | 1 |
| 91 | — | — | — | TRA LA LA LA SUZY — Dean & Jean, Rust 5067 | 1 |
| 92 | — | — | — | MISERY — Dynamics, Big Top 3161 | 1 |
| 93 | 94 | 100 | — | REACH OUT FOR ME — Lou Johnson, Big Top 3158 | 3 |
| 94 | 96 | 98 | — | DEAR ABBY — Hearts, Tuff 5557 | 3 |
| 95 | 95 | — | — | SHIRL GIRL — Wayne Newton, Capitol 5058 | 2 |
| 96 | — | — | — | ANY NUMBER CAN WIN — Jimmy Smith, Verve 10299 | 1 |
| 97 | — | — | — | 31 FLAVORS — Shirelles, Scepter 1260 | 1 |
| 98 | — | — | — | I GOT A WOMAN — Freddie Scott, Colpix 709 | 1 |
| 99 | — | — | — | CROSSFIRE TIME — Dee Clark, Constellation 108 | 1 |
| 100 | — | — | — | SUE'S GOTTA BE MINE — Del Shannon, Berlee 501 | 1 |

## BUBBLING UNDER THE HOT 100

101. HEY LOVER — Debbie Dovale, Roulette 4521
102. MIDNIGHT MARY — Joey Powers, Amy 892
103. YESTERDAY AND YOU — Bobby Vee, Liberty 55636
104. THE SCAVENGER — Dick Dale & the Del-Tones, Capitol 5048
105. WHAT'CHA GONNA DO ABOUT IT — Doris Troy, Atlantic 2206
106. TOYS IN THE ATTIC — Joe Sherman, World Artists 1088
107. BAD GIRL — Neil Sedaka, RCA Victor 8254
108. COWBOY BOOTS — Dave Dudley, Golden King 3030
109. BABY'S GONE — Gene Thomas, United Artists 640
110. DOMINIQUE — Singing Nun, Philips 40152
111. PLEASE DON'T KISS ME AGAIN — Charmettes, Kapp 547
112. HAVE YOU HEARD — Duprees, Coed 585
113. HE'S THE ONE YOU LOVE — Irene Foxx, Symbol 922
114. A STORY UNTOLD — Emotions, 20th Century-Fox 430
115. AS LONG AS I KNOW HE'S MINE — Marvelettes, Tamla 54088
116. SENATE HEARING — Dickie Goodman, 20th Century-Fox 443
117. LOVE HER — Everly Brothers, Warner Bros. 5389
118. HEY CHILD — Johnny Thunder, Diamond 148
119. LONG TALL TEXAN — Murry Kellum, M.O.C. 653
120. SALT WATER TAFFY — Morty Jay & the Surfin' Cats, Legend 124
121. DETROIT CITY NO. 2 — Ben Colder, MGM 13167
122. DAWN — David Rockingham Trio, Josie 913
123. THE BOY NEXT DOOR — Secrets, Philips 40146
124. WHEN THE BOY'S HAPPY THE GIRL'S HAPPY TOO — Four Pennies, Rust 5070
125. ROCK CANDY — Jack Mcduff, Prestige 273
126. STOP MONKEYIN' AROUN' — Dovells, Parkway 889
127. LOUIE, LOUIE — Paul Revere & the Raiders, Columbia 42814
128. SHY BOY — Linda Christy, Roulette 4527
129. SUMMER'S COME AND GONE — Brandywine Singers, Jay 281
130. I'M DOWN TO MY LAST HEART BREAK — Wilson Pickett, Double L 724
131. FORGET HIM — Bobby Rydell, Cameo 280
132. LOUIE, LOUIE — Kingsmen, Wand 143
133. NINETY MILES AN HOUR (DOWN A DEAD-END STREET) — Hank Snow, RCA Victor 8239
134. FOUND TRUE LOVE — Billy Butler & the Four Enchanters, Okeh 7178
135. I AM A WITNESS — Tommy Hunt, Scepter 1261

Compiled from national retail sales and radio station airplay by the Music Popularity Dept. of Record Market Research, Billboard.

# Billboard HOT 100

For Week Ending November 9, 1963

★ STAR performer—Sides registering greatest proportionate upward progress this week.

| This Week | 1 Wk. Ago | 2 Wks. Ago | 3 Wks. Ago | TITLE Artist, Label & Number | Weeks On Chart |
|---|---|---|---|---|---|
| 1 | 1 | 1 | 1 | **SUGAR SHACK** — Jimmy Gilmer and the Fireballs, Dot 16487 | 8 |
| 2 | 2 | 3 | 9 | **DEEP PURPLE** — Nino Tempo & April Stevens, Atco 6273 | 9 |
| 3 | 3 | 8 | 17 | **WASHINGTON SQUARE** — Village Stompers, Epic 9617 | 8 |
| ★4 | 9 | 15 | 24 | **IT'S ALL RIGHT** — Impressions, ABC-Paramount 10487 | 7 |
| 5 | 5 | 7 | 7 | **MEAN WOMAN BLUES** — Roy Orbison, Monument 824 | 10 |
| ★6 | 11 | 19 | 47 | **I'M LEAVING IT UP TO YOU** — Dale & Grace, Montel-Michele 921 | 6 |
| 7 | 10 | 18 | 21 | **MARIA ELENA** — Los Indios Tabajaras, RCA Victor 8216 | 8 |
| ★8 | 4 | 4 | 4 | **BUSTED** — Ray Charles, ABC-Paramount 10481 | 10 |
| 9 | 25 | 41 | 77 | **BOSSA NOVA BABY** — Elvis Presley, RCA Victor 8243 | 4 |
| 10 | 7 | 12 | 12 | **I CAN'T STAY MAD AT YOU** — Skeeter Davis, RCA Victor 8219 | 10 |
| 11 | 16 | 20 | 31 | **SHE'S A FOOL** — Lesley Gore, Mercury 72180 | 7 |
| 12 | 13 | 14 | 14 | **FOOLS RUSH IN** — Rick Nelson, Decca 31533 | 9 |
| 13 | 6 | 6 | 8 | **DONNA THE PRIMA DONNA** — Dion Di Muci, Columbia 42852 | 9 |
| ★14 | 22 | 30 | 53 | **EVERYBODY** — Tommy Roe, ABC-Paramount 10478 | 5 |
| ★15 | 23 | 37 | 48 | **500 MILES AWAY FROM HOME** — Bobby Bare, RCA Victor 8238 | 6 |
| 16 | 12 | 13 | 13 | **THAT SUNDAY, THAT SUMMER** — Nat King Cole, Capitol 5027 | 11 |
| 17 | 20 | 21 | 30 | **THE GRASS IS GREENER** — Brenda Lee, Decca 31539 | 7 |
| 18 | 14 | 11 | 16 | **TALK TO ME** — Sunny and the Sunglows, Tear Drop 3014 | 10 |
| 19 | 21 | 23 | 46 | **(Down at) PAPA JOE'S** — Dixiebelles, Sound Stage 7 2507 | 7 |
| 20 | 8 | 2 | 2 | **BE MY BABY** — Ronettes, Philles 116 | 11 |
| 21 | 19 | 22 | 28 | **CROSSFIRE!** — Orlons, Cameo 273 | 7 |
| 22 | 24 | 29 | 35 | **YOU LOST THE SWEETEST BOY** — Mary Wells, Motown 1048 | 6 |
| 23 | 26 | 38 | 41 | **MISTY** — Lloyd Price, Double L 722 | 6 |
| ★24 | 31 | 40 | 45 | **CRY TO ME** — Betty Harris, Jubilee 5456 | 8 |
| 25 | 28 | 48 | 52 | **WALKING THE DOG** — Rufus Thomas, Stax 140 | 6 |
| 26 | 15 | 5 | 3 | **BLUE VELVET** — Bobby Vinton, Epic 9614 | 14 |
| 27 | 18 | 9 | 10 | **DON'T THINK TWICE IT'S ALL RIGHT** — Peter, Paul & Mary, Warner Bros. 5385 | 9 |
| 28 | 17 | 10 | 5 | **CRY BABY** — Garnet Mimms & the Enchanters, United Artists 629 | 13 |
| 29 | 39 | 62 | 74 | **HEY LITTLE GIRL** — Major Lance, Okeh 7181 | 4 |
| ★30 | 48 | 69 | 81 | **WALKING PROUD** — Steve Lawrence, Columbia 42865 | 4 |
| ★31 | 44 | 73 | — | **LITTLE RED ROOSTER** — Sam Cooke, RCA Victor 8247 | 3 |
| 32 | 41 | 56 | 79 | **YOUR OTHER LOVE** — Connie Francis, MGM 13176 | 4 |
| 33 | 38 | 50 | 60 | **WILD!** — Dee Dee Sharp, Cameo 274 | 6 |
| ★34 | 30 | 33 | 29 | **BLUE BAYOU** — Roy Orbison, Monument 824 | 9 |
| ★35 | 27 | 16 | 11 | **HONOLULU LULU** — Jan & Dean, Liberty 55613 | 10 |
| ★36 | 45 | 57 | 72 | **WITCHCRAFT** — Elvis Presley, RCA Victor 8243 | 4 |
| ★37 | 40 | 47 | 49 | **DOWN THE AISLE** — Patty LaBelle & the Blue Belles, Newtown 5777 | 9 |
| 38 | 33 | 36 | 37 | **WORKOUT STEVIE, WORKOUT** — Little Stevie Wonder, Tamla 54086 | 6 |
| ★39 | 52 | 71 | — | **I ADORE HIM** — Angels, Smash 1854 | 3 |
| 40 | 36 | 43 | 50 | **NEW MEXICAN ROSE** — 4 Seasons, Vee Jay 562 | 6 |
| ★41 | 58 | 81 | — | **SATURDAY NIGHT** — New Christy Minstrels, Columbia 42887 | 3 |
| ★42 | 55 | 55 | 61 | **BLUE GUITAR** — Richard Chamberlain, MGM 13170 | 7 |
| ★43 | 54 | 77 | 99 | **TWENTY-FOUR HOURS FROM TULSA** — Gene Pitney, Musicor 1034 | 4 |
| ★44 | 50 | 67 | 83 | **I WONDER WHAT SHE'S DOING TONIGHT** — Barry & the Tamerlanes, Valiant 6034 | 4 |
| ★45 | 35 | 39 | 43 | **RED SAILS IN THE SUNSET** — Fats Domino, ABC-Paramount 10484 | 8 |
| 46 | 34 | 28 | 25 | **I'LL TAKE YOU HOME** — Drifters, Atlantic 2201 | 10 |
| ★47 | 61 | 86 | — | **THE MATADOR** — Johnny Cash, Columbia 42880 | 3 |
| ★48 | 74 | 90 | — | **LIVING A LIE** — Al Martino, Capitol 5060 | 3 |
| 49 | 51 | 61 | 70 | **POINT PANIC** — Surfaris, Decca 31538 | 7 |
| 50 | 47 | 54 | 56 | **MONKEY-SHINE** — Bill Black & His Combo, Hi 2069 | 6 |
| 51 | 56 | 74 | 91 | **FUNNY HOW TIME SLIPS AWAY** — Johnny Tillotson, Cadence 1441 | 4 |
| ★52 | 32 | 17 | 6 | **SALLY, GO 'ROUND THE ROSES** — Jaynetts, Tuff 369 | 11 |
| ★53 | 66 | — | — | **WONDERFUL SUMMER** — Robin Ward, Dot 16530 | 2 |
| 54 | 63 | 75 | 90 | **A FINE FINE BOY** — Darlene Love, Philles 117 | 4 |
| 55 | 37 | 35 | 32 | **TWO TICKETS TO PARADISE** — Brook Benton, Mercury 72177 | 10 |
| ★56 | 84 | — | — | **YOU DON'T HAVE TO BE A BABY TO CRY** — Caravels, Smash 1852 | 2 |
| 57 | 62 | 65 | 68 | **NIGHT LIFE** — Rusty Draper, Monument 823 | 7 |
| ★58 | 72 | 91 | 97 | **CAN I GET A WITNESS** — Marvin Gaye, Tamla 54087 | 4 |
| 59 | 67 | 79 | 95 | **DON'T WAIT TOO LONG** — Tony Bennett, Columbia 42886 | 5 |
| 60 | 29 | 26 | 22 | **PART TIME LOVE** — Little Johnny Taylor, Galaxy 722 | 13 |
| 61 | 65 | 72 | 85 | **COME BACK** — Johnny Mathis, Mercury 72184 | 5 |
| 62 | 53 | 34 | 36 | **BUST OUT** — Busters, Arlen 735 | 10 |
| ★63 | 71 | — | — | **LODDY LO** — Chubby Checker, Parkway 890 | 2 |
| ★64 | — | — | — | **DOMINIQUE** — Singing Nun, Philips 40152 | 1 |
| ★65 | 86 | — | — | **IN MY ROOM** — Beach Boys, Capitol 5069 | 2 |
| 66 | 73 | 99 | — | **SINCE I FELL FOR YOU** — Lenny Welch, Cadence 1439 | 3 |
| ★67 | 75 | 84 | — | **YOUNG WINGS CAN FLY** — Ruby & the Romantics, Kapp 557 | 3 |
| ★68 | 68 | 80 | 87 | **WHAT'S EASY FOR TWO IS SO HARD FOR ONE** — Mary Wells, Motown 1048 | 4 |
| ★69 | 83 | — | — | **BE TRUE TO YOUR SCHOOL** — Beach Boys, Capitol 5069 | 2 |
| 70 | 82 | — | — | **WIVES AND LOVERS** — Jack Jones, Kapp 551 | 2 |
| 71 | 78 | 97 | — | **UNCHAINED MELODY** — Vito & the Salutations, Herald 583 | 3 |
| ★72 | 92 | — | — | **MISERY** — Dynamics, Big Top 3161 | 2 |
| 73 | 79 | 85 | 89 | **GOTTA TRAVEL ON** — Timi Yuro, Liberty 55634 | 5 |
| 74 | 76 | 76 | 82 | **YOUR TEEN-AGE DREAMS** — Johnny Mathis, Mercury 72184 | 5 |
| 75 | 98 | — | — | **I GOT A WOMAN** — Freddie Scott, Colpix 709 | 2 |
| ★76 | — | — | — | **HAVE YOU HEARD** — Duprees, Coed 585 | 1 |
| 77 | 81 | 93 | 94 | **SIGNED, SEALED AND DELIVERED** — James Brown & the Famous Flames, King 5083 | 5 |
| 78 | 89 | — | — | **YOU'RE GOOD FOR ME** — Solomon Burke, Atlantic 2205 | 2 |
| ★79 | — | — | — | **MIDNIGHT MARY** — Joey Powers, Amy 892 | 1 |
| 80 | 91 | — | — | **TRA LA LA LA SUZY** — Dean & Jean, Rust 5067 | 2 |
| 81 | 90 | — | — | **I COULD HAVE DANCED ALL NIGHT** — Ben E. King, Atco 6275 | 2 |
| ★82 | — | — | — | **THE BOY NEXT DOOR** — Secrets, Philips 40146 | 1 |
| ★83 | — | — | — | **LOUIE LOUIE** — Kingsmen, Wand 143 | 1 |
| ★84 | — | — | — | **YESTERDAY AND YOU** — Bobby Vee, Liberty 55636 | 1 |
| 85 | 87 | 88 | 93 | **TWO-TEN, SIX-EIGHTEEN** — Jimmie Rodgers, Dot 16527 | 5 |
| ★86 | — | — | — | **DAWN** — David Rockingham Trio, Josie 913 | 1 |
| 87 | 88 | — | — | **ANY OTHER WAY** — Chuck Jackson, Wand 141 | 2 |
| 88 | 93 | 94 | 100 | **REACH OUT FOR ME** — Lou Johnson, Big Top 3153 | 4 |
| 89 | 100 | — | — | **SUE'S GOTTA BE MINE** — Del Shannon, Berlee 501 | 2 |
| ★90 | — | — | — | **WE SHALL OVERCOME** — Joan Baez, Vanguard 35023 | 1 |
| 91 | — | — | — | **TALK BACK TREMBLING LIPS** — Johnny Tillotson, MGM 13181 | 1 |
| 92 | 95 | 95 | — | **SHIRL GIRL** — Wayne Newton, Capitol 5058 | 3 |
| 93 | — | — | — | **SALTWATER TAFFY** — Morty Jay & the Surfin' Cats, Legend 124 | 1 |
| 94 | — | — | — | **FORGET HIM** — Bobby Rydell, Cameo 280 | 1 |
| 95 | — | — | — | **WHEN THE BOY'S HAPPY** — Four Pennies, Rust 5070 | 1 |
| 96 | — | — | — | **STOP MONKEYIN' AROUN'** — Dovells, Parkway 889 | 1 |
| 97 | — | — | — | **I AM A WITNESS** — Tommy Hunt, Scepter 1261 | 1 |
| 98 | — | — | — | **I'M DOWN TO MY LAST HEART BREAK** — Wilson Pickett, Double L 724 | 1 |
| 99 | — | — | — | **LONG TALL TEXAN** — Murry Kellum, M.O.C. 653 | 1 |
| 100 | — | — | — | **AS LONG AS I KNOW HE'S MINE** — Marvelettes, Tamla 54088 | 1 |

## BUBBLING UNDER THE HOT 100

101. HEY LOVER — Debbie Dovale, Roulette 4521
102. BAD GIRL — Neil Sedaka, RCA Victor 8254
103. TOYS IN THE ATTIC — Joe Sherman, World Artists 1088
104. CUANDO CALIENTA EL SOL — Steve Allen, Dot 16507
105. BABY'S GONE — Gene Thomas, United Artists 640
106. THE SCAVENGER — Dick Dale & the Del-Tones, Capitol 5048
107. BABY DON'T YOU WEEP — Garnet Mimms & the Enchanters, United Artists 658
108. SEE THE BIG MAN CRY — Paul Revere & the Raiders, Columbia 42814
109. LOUIE LOUIE — Paul Revere & the Raiders, Columbia 42814
110. WHAT'CHA GONNA DO ABOUT IT — Doris Troy, Atlantic 2206
111. A STORY UNTOLD — Emotions, 20th Century-Fox 430
112. ANY NUMBER CAN WIN — Jimmy Smith, Verve 10299
113. TALK BACK TREMBLING LIPS — Ernest Ashworth, Hickory 1214
114. FOR YOUR PRECIOUS LOVE — Garnet Mimms & the Enchanters, United Artists 658
115. THE NITTY GRITTY — Shirley Ellis, Congress 202
116. PLEASE DON'T KISS ME AGAIN — Shirelles, Scepter 1260
117. 31 FLAVORS — Shirelles, Scepter 1260
118. POPSICLES AND ICICLES — Murmaids, Chattahoochee 628
119. YOU'RE NO GOOD — Betty Everett, Vee Jay 566
120. IT'S A MAD, MAD, MAD, MAD WORLD — Shirelles, Scepter 1260
121. YOU'RE NOW GONE — Dee Dee Warwick, Jubilee 5459
122. BABY I DO LOVE YOU — Al Bruce, Wand 140
123. MY TRUE CARRIE LOVE — Tony Orlando, Epic 9622
124. LOVE MADE A FOOL OF YOU — Paul Peterson, Colpix 707
125. LET US MAKE OUR OWN MISTAKES — Brian Hyland, ABC-Paramount 10494
126. FOUR STRONG WINDS — Brothers Four, Columbia 42888
127. I HAVE A BOYFRIEND — Chiffons, Laurie 3212
128. TALK TO ME BABY — Barry Mann, JDS 5018
129. THERE'S MORE PRETTY GIRLS THAN ONE — George Hamilton IV, RCA Victor 8250
130. HE UNDERSTANDS ME — Teresa Brewer, Philips 40125
131. FOUR IN THE FLOOR — Shut Downs, Dimension 1016
132. HI DIDDLE DIDDLE — Inez Foxx, Symbol 924
133. THE MONKEY WALK — Flares, Press 2810
134. STOP FOOLIN' — Brook Benton & Damita Jo, Mercury 72207
135. SHE'S GOT EVERYTHING — Essex, Roulette 4530

Compiled from national retail sales and radio station airplay by the Music Popularity Dept. of Record Market Research, Billboard.

# Billboard HOT 100

**For Week Ending November 16, 1963**

★ STAR performer—Sides registering greatest proportionate upward progress this week.

| This Week | 1 Wk. Ago | 2 Wks. Ago | 3 Wks. Ago | TITLE, Artist, Label & Number | Weeks On Chart |
|---|---|---|---|---|---|
| 1 | 2 | 2 | 3 | DEEP PURPLE — Nino Tempo & April Stevens, Atco 6273 | 10 |
| 2 | 1 | 1 | 1 | SUGAR SHACK — Jimmy Gilmer and the Fireballs, Dot 16487 | 9 |
| 3 | 3 | 3 | 8 | WASHINGTON SQUARE — Village Stompers, Epic 9617 | 9 |
| 4 | 6 | 11 | 19 | I'M LEAVING IT UP TO YOU — Dale & Grace, Montel-Michele 921 | 7 |
| 5 | 4 | 9 | 15 | IT'S ALL RIGHT — Impressions, ABC-Paramount 10487 | 8 |
| 6 | 7 | 10 | 18 | MARIA ELENA — Los Indios Tabajaras, RCA Victor 8216 | 9 |
| 7 | 11 | 16 | 20 | SHE'S A FOOL — Lesley Gore, Mercury 72180 | 8 |
| 8 | 9 | 25 | 41 | BOSSA NOVA BABY — Elvis Presley, RCA Victor 8243 | 5 |
| 9 | 14 | 22 | 30 | EVERYBODY — Tommy Roe, ABC-Paramount 10478 | 6 |
| 10 | 15 | 23 | 37 | 500 MILES AWAY FROM HOME — Bobby Bare, RCA Victor 8238 | 7 |
| 11 | 5 | 5 | 7 | MEAN WOMAN BLUES — Roy Orbison, Monument 824 | 11 |
| 12 | 10 | 7 | 12 | I CAN'T STAY MAD AT YOU — Skeeter Davis, RCA Victor 8219 | 11 |
| 13 | 12 | 13 | 14 | FOOLS RUSH IN — Rick Nelson, Decca 31533 | 10 |
| 14 | 8 | 4 | 4 | BUSTED — Ray Charles, ABC-Paramount 10481 | 11 |
| 15 | 25 | 28 | 48 | WALKING THE DOG — Rufus Thomas, Stax 140 | 7 |
| 16 | 19 | 21 | 23 | (Down at) PAPA JOE'S — Dixiebelles, Sound Stage 7 2507 | 8 |
| 17 | 13 | 6 | 6 | DONNA THE PRIMA DONNA — Dion DiMuci, Columbia 42852 | 10 |
| 18 | 29 | 39 | 62 | HEY LITTLE GIRL — Major Lance, Okeh 7181 | 5 |
| 19 | 64 | — | — | DOMINIQUE — Singing Nun, Philips 40152 | 2 |
| 20 | 18 | 14 | 21 | TALK TO ME — Sunny and the Sunglows, Tear Drop 3014 | 11 |
| 21 | 23 | 26 | 38 | MISTY — Lloyd Price, Double L 722 | 7 |
| 22 | 20 | 8 | 2 | BE MY BABY — Ronettes, Philles 116 | 12 |
| 23 | 24 | 31 | 40 | CRY TO ME — Betty Harris, Jubilee 5456 | 9 |
| 24 | 22 | 24 | 29 | YOU LOST THE SWEETEST BOY — Mary Wells, Motown 1048 | 8 |
| 25 | 31 | 44 | 73 | LITTLE RED ROOSTER — Sam Cooke, RCA Victor 8247 | 4 |
| 26 | 43 | 54 | 77 | TWENTY-FOUR HOURS FROM TULSA — Gene Pitney, Musicor 1034 | 5 |
| 27 | 16 | 12 | 13 | THAT SUNDAY, THAT SUMMER — Nat King Cole, Capitol 5027 | 12 |
| 28 | 30 | 48 | 69 | WALKING PROUD — Steve Lawrence, Columbia 42865 | 5 |
| 29 | 32 | 41 | 56 | YOUR OTHER LOVE — Connie Francis, MGM 13176 | 5 |
| 30 | 21 | 19 | 22 | CROSSFIRE! — Orlons, Cameo 273 | 8 |
| 31 | 41 | 58 | 81 | SATURDAY NIGHT — New Christy Minstrels, Columbia 42887 | 4 |
| 32 | 36 | 45 | 57 | WITCHCRAFT — Elvis Presley, RCA Victor 8243 | 5 |
| 33 | 33 | 38 | 50 | WILD! — Dee Dee Sharp, Cameo 274 | 7 |
| 34 | 53 | 66 | — | WONDERFUL SUMMER — Robin Ward, Dot 16530 | 3 |
| 35 | 39 | 52 | 71 | I ADORE HIM — Angels, Smash 1854 | 4 |
| 36 | 48 | 74 | 90 | LIVING A LIE — Al Martino, Capitol 5060 | 4 |
| 37 | 27 | 18 | 9 | DON'T THINK TWICE IT'S ALL RIGHT — Peter, Paul & Mary, Warner Bros. 5385 | 10 |
| 38 | 44 | 50 | 67 | I WONDER WHAT SHE'S DOING TONIGHT — Barry & the Tamerlanes, Valiant 6034 | 5 |
| 39 | 28 | 17 | 10 | CRY BABY — Garnet Mimms & the Enchanters, United Artists 629 | 14 |
| 40 | 37 | 40 | 47 | DOWN THE AISLE — Patty LaBelle & the Blue Belles, Newtown 5777 | 10 |
| 41 | 56 | 84 | — | YOU DON'T HAVE TO BE A BABY TO CRY — Caravels, Smash 1852 | 3 |
| 42 | 17 | 20 | 21 | THE GRASS IS GREENER — Brenda Lee, Decca 31539 | 8 |
| 43 | 66 | 73 | 99 | SINCE I FELL FOR YOU — Lenny Welch, Cadence 1439 | 4 |
| 44 | 69 | 83 | — | BE TRUE TO YOUR SCHOOL — Beach Boys, Capitol 5069 | 3 |
| 45 | 63 | 71 | — | LODDY LO — Chubby Checker, Parkway 890 | 3 |
| 46 | 47 | 61 | 86 | THE MATADOR — Johnny Cash, Columbia 42880 | 4 |
| 47 | 58 | 73 | 91 | CAN I GET A WITNESS — Marvin Gaye, Tamla 54087 | 5 |
| 48 | 34 | 30 | 33 | BLUE BAYOU — Roy Orbison, Monument 824 | 10 |
| 49 | 26 | 15 | 5 | BLUE VELVET — Bobby Vinton, Epic 9614 | 15 |
| 50 | 51 | 56 | 74 | FUNNY HOW TIME SLIPS AWAY — Johnny Tillotson, Cadence 1441 | 5 |
| 51 | 40 | 36 | 43 | NEW MEXICAN ROSE — 4 Seasons, Vee Jay 562 | 7 |
| 52 | 42 | 55 | 55 | BLUE GUITAR — Richard Chamberlain, MGM 13170 | 8 |
| 53 | 49 | 51 | 61 | POINT PANIC — Surfaris, Decca 31538 | 8 |
| 54 | 54 | 63 | 75 | A FINE FINE BOY — Darlene Love, Philles 117 | 5 |
| 55 | 59 | 67 | 79 | DON'T WAIT TOO LONG — Tony Bennett, Columbia 42886 | 6 |
| 56 | 67 | 75 | 84 | YOUNG WINGS CAN FLY — Ruby & the Romantics, Kapp 557 | 4 |
| 57 | 65 | 86 | — | IN MY ROOM — Beach Boys, Capitol 5069 | 3 |
| 58 | 83 | — | — | LOUIE LOUIE — Kingsmen, Wand 143 | 2 |
| 59 | 91 | — | — | TALK BACK TREMBLING LIPS — Johnny Tillotson, MGM 13181 | 2 |
| 60 | 72 | 92 | — | MISERY — Dynamics, Big Top 3161 | 3 |
| 61 | 76 | — | — | HAVE YOU HEARD — Duprees, Coed 585 | 2 |
| 62 | 70 | 82 | — | WIVES AND LOVERS — Jack Jones, Kapp 551 | 3 |
| 63 | 57 | 62 | 65 | NIGHT LIFE — Rusty Draper, Monument 823 | 8 |
| 64 | 73 | 79 | 85 | GOTTA TRAVEL ON — Timi Yuro, Liberty 55634 | 6 |
| 65 | 61 | 65 | 72 | COME BACK — Johnny Mathis, Mercury 72184 | 6 |
| 66 | 52 | 32 | 17 | SALLY, GO 'ROUND THE ROSES — Jaynetts, Tuff 369 | 12 |
| 67 | 82 | — | — | THE BOY NEXT DOOR — Secrets, Philips 40146 | 2 |
| 68 | 74 | 76 | 76 | YOUR TEEN-AGE DREAMS — Johnny Mathis, Mercury 72184 | 6 |
| 69 | 79 | — | — | MIDNIGHT MARY — Joey Powers, Amy 892 | 2 |
| 70 | 71 | 78 | 97 | UNCHAINED MELODY — Vito & the Salutations, Herald 583 | 4 |
| 71 | 75 | 98 | — | I GOT A WOMAN — Freddie Scott, Colpix 709 | 3 |
| 72 | 78 | 89 | — | YOU'RE GOOD FOR ME — Solomon Burke, Atlantic 2205 | 3 |
| 73 | — | — | — | DRIP DROP — Dion DiMuci, Columbia 42917 | 1 |
| 74 | 84 | — | — | YESTERDAY AND YOU — Bobby Vee, Liberty 55636 | 2 |
| 75 | 68 | 68 | 80 | WHAT'S EASY FOR TWO IS SO HARD FOR ONE — Mary Wells, Motown 1048 | 5 |
| 76 | 81 | 90 | — | I COULD HAVE DANCED ALL NIGHT — Ben E. King, Atco 6275 | 3 |
| 77 | 92 | 95 | 95 | SHIRL GIRL — Wayne Newton, Capitol 5058 | 4 |
| 78 | 94 | — | — | FORGET HIM — Bobby Rydell, Cameo 280 | 2 |
| 79 | 80 | 91 | — | TRA LA LA LA SUZY — Dean & Jean, Rust 5067 | 3 |
| 80 | — | — | — | BAD GIRL — Neil Sedaka, RCA Victor 8254 | 1 |
| 81 | 87 | 88 | — | ANY OTHER WAY — Chuck Jackson, Wand 141 | 3 |
| 82 | 89 | 100 | — | SUE'S GOTTA BE MINE — Del Shannon, Berlee 501 | 3 |
| 83 | 85 | 87 | 88 | TWO-TEN, SIX-EIGHTEEN — Jimmie Rodgers, Dot 16527 | 6 |
| 84 | 86 | — | — | DAWN — David Rockingham Trio, Josie 913 | 2 |
| 85 | 100 | — | — | AS LONG AS I KNOW HE'S MINE — Marvelettes, Tamla 54088 | 2 |
| 86 | 88 | 93 | 94 | REACH OUT FOR ME — Lou Johnson, Big Top 3153 | 5 |
| 87 | — | — | — | SHE'S GOT EVERYTHING — Essex, Roulette 4530 | 1 |
| 88 | — | — | — | THE NITTY GRITTY — Shirley Ellis, Congress 202 | 1 |
| 89 | — | — | — | RAGS TO RICHES — Sunny and the Sunliners, Tear Drop 3022 | 1 |
| 90 | — | — | — | BABY DON'T YOU WEEP — Garnet Mimms and the Enchanters, United Artists 658 | 1 |
| 91 | — | — | — | KANSAS CITY — Trini Lopez, Reprise 20236 | 1 |
| 92 | — | — | — | I HAVE A BOYFRIEND — Chiffons, Laurie 3212 | 1 |
| 93 | 99 | — | — | LONG TALL TEXAN — Murry Kellum, M.O.C. 653 | 2 |
| 94 | 96 | — | — | STOP MONKEYIN' AROUN' — Dovells, Parkway 889 | 2 |
| 95 | 98 | — | — | I'M DOWN TO MY LAST HEART BREAK — Wilson Pickett, Double L 724 | 2 |
| 96 | 97 | — | — | I AM A WITNESS — Tommy Hunt, Scepter 1261 | 2 |
| 97 | — | — | — | GOTTA LOTTA LOVE — Steve Alaimo, Imperial 66003 | 1 |
| 98 | — | — | — | DUMB HEAD — Ginny Arnell, MGM 13177 | 1 |
| 99 | — | — | — | BABY'S GONE — Gene Thomas, United Artists 640 | 1 |
| 100 | — | — | — | HEY LOVER — Debbie Dovale, Roulette 4521 | 1 |

## BUBBLING UNDER THE HOT 100

101. CUANDO CALIENTA EL SOL ..... Steve Allen, Dot 16507
102. NOW ..... Lena Horne, 20th Century-Fox 449
103. TOYS IN THE ATTIC ..... Joe Sherman, World Artists 1088
104. SALTWATER TAFFY ..... Marty Jay & The Surfin' Cats, Legend 124
105. WE SHALL OVERCOME ..... Joan Baez, Vanguard 35023
106. WHEN THE BOY'S HAPPY ..... Four Pennies, Rust 5070
107. BABY I DO LOVE YOU ..... Galens, Challenge 9212
108. 31 FLAVORS ..... Shirelles, Scepter 1260
109. POPSICLES AND ICICLES ..... Murmaids, Chattahoochee 628
110. CROSSFIRE TIME ..... Dee Clark, Constellation 108
111. FOR YOUR PRECIOUS LOVE ..... Garnet Mimms & the Enchanters, United Artists 658
112. WE BELONG TOGETHER ..... Jimmy Velvet, ABC-Paramount 10488
113. SURFER STREET ..... Allisons, Tip 1011
114. SEE THE BIG MAN CRY ..... Ed Bruce, Wand 140
115. THE SCAVENGER ..... Dick Dale & the Del-Tones, Capitol 5048
116. YOU'RE NO GOOD ..... Betty Everett, Vee Jay 566
117. TALK BACK TREMBLING LIPS ..... Ernest Ashworth, Hickory 1214
118. NEAR TO YOU ..... Wilbert Harrison, Sea-Horn 502
119. THE CHEER LEADER ..... Paul Petersen, Colpix 707
120. TURN AROUND ..... Dick & Deedee, Warner Bros. 5396
121. SWANEE RIVER ..... Ace Cannon, Hi 2070
122. ALLY, ALLY OXEN FREE ..... Kingston Trio, Capitol 5078
123. BABY, YOU'VE GOT IT MADE ..... Brook Benton & Damita Jo, Mercury 72207
124. KEEP AN EYE ON HER ..... Jaynetts, Tuff 371
125. THERE'S MORE PRETTY GIRLS THAN ONE ..... George Hamilton IV, RCA Victor 8250
126. DON'T KISS ME AGAIN ..... Charmettes, Kapp 547
127. LET US MAKE OUR OWN MISTAKES ..... Brian Hyland, ABC-Paramount 10494
128. LET'S START THE PARTY AGAIN ..... Little Eva, Dimension 1019
129. THE IMPOSSIBLE HAPPENED ..... Little Peggy March, RCA Victor 8267
130. LIPSTICK PAINT A SMILE ON ME ..... Demetriss Tapp, Brunswick 55251

Compiled from national retail sales and radio station airplay by the Music Popularity Dept. of Record Market Research, Billboard.

# Billboard HOT 100

**For Week Ending November 23, 1963**

★ STAR performer—Sides registering greatest proportionate upward progress this week.

| This Week | 1 Wk. Ago | 2 Wks. Ago | 3 Wks. Ago | TITLE Artist, Label & Number | Weeks On Chart |
|---|---|---|---|---|---|
| 1 | 4 | 6 | 11 | I'M LEAVING IT UP TO YOU — Dale & Grace, Montel-Michele 921 | 8 |
| 2 | 3 | 3 | 3 | WASHINGTON SQUARE — Village Stompers, Epic 9617 | 10 |
| 3 | 1 | 2 | 2 | DEEP PURPLE — Nino Tempo & April Stevens, Atco 6273 | 11 |
| 4 | 2 | 1 | 1 | SUGAR SHACK — Jimmy Gilmer and the Fireballs, Dot 16487 | 10 |
| 5 | 5 | 4 | 9 | IT'S ALL RIGHT — Impressions, ABC-Paramount 10487 | 9 |
| 6 | 7 | 11 | 16 | SHE'S A FOOL — Lesley Gore, Mercury 72180 | 9 |
| 7 | 9 | 14 | 22 | EVERYBODY — Tommy Roe, ABC-Paramount 10478 | 7 |
| 8 | 8 | 9 | 25 | BOSSA NOVA BABY — Elvis Presley, RCA Victor 8243 | 6 |
| ★9 | 19 | 64 | — | DOMINIQUE — Singing Nun, Philips 40152 | 3 |
| 10 | 6 | 7 | 10 | MARIA ELENA — Los Indios Tabajaras, RCA Victor 8216 | 10 |
| 11 | 16 | 19 | 21 | (Down at) PAPA JOE'S — Dixiebelles, Sound Stage 7 2507 | 9 |
| 12 | 15 | 25 | 28 | WALKING THE DOG — Rufus Thomas, Stax 140 | 8 |
| 13 | 18 | 29 | 39 | HEY LITTLE GIRL — Major Lance, Okeh 7181 | 6 |
| 14 | 10 | 15 | 23 | 500 MILES AWAY FROM HOME — Bobby Bare, RCA Victor 8238 | 8 |
| 15 | 25 | 31 | 44 | LITTLE RED ROOSTER — Sam Cooke, RCA Victor 8247 | 5 |
| 16 | 13 | 12 | 13 | FOOLS RUSH IN — Rick Nelson, Decca 31533 | 11 |
| 17 | 11 | 5 | 5 | MEAN WOMAN BLUES — Roy Orbison, Monument 824 | 12 |
| ★18 | 34 | 53 | 66 | WONDERFUL SUMMER — Robin Ward, Dot 16530 | 4 |
| ★19 | 44 | 69 | 83 | BE TRUE TO YOUR SCHOOL — Beach Boys, Capitol 5069 | 4 |
| ★20 | 43 | 66 | 73 | SINCE I FELL FOR YOU — Lenny Welch, Cadence 1439 | 5 |
| 21 | 26 | 43 | 54 | TWENTY-FOUR HOURS FROM TULSA — Gene Pitney, Musicor 1034 | 6 |
| ★22 | 41 | 56 | 84 | YOU DON'T HAVE TO BE A BABY TO CRY — Caravelles, Smash 1852 | 4 |
| 23 | 38 | 44 | 50 | I WONDER WHAT SHE'S DOING TONIGHT — Barry & the Tamerlanes, Valiant 6034 | 6 |
| 24 | 12 | 10 | 7 | I CAN'T STAY MAD AT YOU — Skeeter Davis, RCA Victor 8219 | 12 |
| 25 | 45 | 63 | 71 | LODDY LO — Chubby Checker, Parkway 890 | 4 |
| 26 | 28 | 30 | 48 | WALKING PROUD — Steve Lawrence, Columbia 42865 | 5 |
| 27 | 36 | 48 | 74 | LIVING A LIE — Al Martino, Capitol 5060 | 5 |
| 28 | 29 | 32 | 41 | YOUR OTHER LOVE — Connie Francis, MGM 13176 | 6 |
| 29 | 21 | 23 | 26 | MISTY — Lloyd Price, Double L 722 | 8 |
| ★30 | 35 | 39 | 52 | I ADORE HIM — Angels, Smash 1854 | 5 |
| 31 | 31 | 41 | 58 | SATURDAY NIGHT — New Christy Minstrels, Columbia 42887 | 5 |
| 32 | 14 | 8 | 4 | BUSTED — Ray Charles, ABC-Paramount 10481 | 12 |
| ★33 | 47 | 58 | 73 | CAN I GET A WITNESS — Marvin Gaye, Tamla 54087 | 6 |
| 34 | 23 | 24 | 31 | CRY TO ME — Betty Harris, Jubilee 5456 | 10 |
| 35 | 27 | 16 | 12 | THAT SUNDAY, THAT SUMMER — Nat King Cole, Capitol 5027 | 13 |
| 36 | 24 | 22 | 24 | YOU LOST THE SWEETEST BOY — Mary Wells, Motown 1048 | 9 |
| 37 | 33 | 33 | 38 | WILD! — Dee Dee Sharp, Cameo 274 | 8 |
| ★38 | 73 | — | — | DRIP DROP — Dion DiMuci, Columbia 42917 | 2 |
| 39 | 32 | 36 | 45 | WITCHCRAFT — Elvis Presley, RCA Victor 8243 | 6 |
| 40 | 20 | 18 | 14 | TALK TO ME — Sunny and the Sunglows, Tear Drop 3014 | 12 |
| ★41 | 58 | 83 | — | LOUIE LOUIE — Kingsmen, Wand 143 | 3 |
| ★42 | 59 | 91 | — | TALK BACK TREMBLING LIPS — Johnny Tillotson, MGM 13181 | 3 |
| 43 | 61 | 76 | — | HAVE YOU HEARD — Duprees, Coed 585 | 3 |
| ★44 | 57 | 65 | 86 | IN MY ROOM — Beach Boys, Capitol 5069 | 4 |
| 45 | 40 | 37 | 40 | DOWN THE AISLE — Patty LaBelle & the Blue Belles, Newtown 5777 | 11 |
| 46 | 46 | 47 | 61 | THE MATADOR — Johnny Cash, Columbia 42880 | 5 |
| 47 | 62 | 70 | 82 | WIVES AND LOVERS — Jack Jones, Kapp 551 | 4 |
| 48 | 17 | 13 | 6 | DONNA THE PRIMA DONNA — Dion DiMuci, Columbia 42852 | 11 |
| 49 | 22 | 20 | 8 | BE MY BABY — Ronettes, Philles 116 | 13 |
| 50 | 30 | 21 | 19 | CROSSFIRE! — Orlons, Cameo 273 | 9 |
| ★51 | 80 | — | — | BAD GIRL — Neil Sedaka, RCA Victor 8254 | 2 |
| 52 | 56 | 67 | 75 | YOUNG WINGS CAN FLY — Ruby & the Romantics, Kapp 557 | 5 |
| 53 | 54 | 54 | 63 | A FINE FINE BOY — Darlene Love, Philles 117 | 6 |
| 54 | 55 | 59 | 67 | DON'T WAIT TOO LONG — Tony Bennett, Columbia 42886 | 7 |
| 55 | 50 | 51 | 56 | FUNNY HOW TIME SLIPS AWAY — Johnny Tillotson, Cadence 1441 | 6 |
| ★56 | 67 | 82 | — | THE BOY NEXT DOOR — Secrets, Philips 40146 | 3 |
| 57 | 60 | 72 | 92 | MISERY — Dynamics, Big Top 3161 | 4 |
| 58 | 69 | 79 | — | MIDNIGHT MARY — Joey Powers, Amy 892 | 3 |
| ★59 | 90 | — | — | BABY DON'T YOU WEEP — Garnet Mimms and the Enchanters, United Artists 658 | 2 |
| 60 | 78 | 94 | — | FORGET HIM — Bobby Rydell, Cameo 280 | 2 |
| 61 | 79 | 80 | 91 | TRA LA LA LA SUZY — Dean & Jean, Rust 5067 | 4 |
| 62 | 74 | 84 | — | YESTERDAY AND YOU — Bobby Vee, Liberty 55636 | 3 |
| 63 | 71 | 75 | 98 | I GOT A WOMAN — Freddie Scott, Colpix 709 | 4 |
| ★64 | 85 | 100 | — | AS LONG AS I KNOW HE'S MINE — Marvelettes, Tamla 54088 | 3 |
| ★65 | 87 | — | — | SHE'S GOT EVERYTHING — Essex, Roulette 4530 | 2 |
| ★66 | 89 | — | — | RAGS TO RICHES — Sunny and the Sunliners, Tear Drop 3022 | 2 |
| 67 | 77 | 92 | 95 | SHIRL GIRL — Wayne Newton, Capitol 5058 | 5 |
| 68 | 72 | 78 | 89 | YOU'RE GOOD FOR ME — Solomon Burke, Atlantic 2205 | 4 |
| 69 | 64 | 73 | 79 | GOTTA TRAVEL ON — Timi Yuro, Liberty 55634 | 7 |
| ★70 | 91 | — | — | KANSAS CITY — Trini Lopez, Reprise 20236 | 2 |
| ★71 | 88 | — | — | THE NITTY GRITTY — Shirley Ellis, Congress 202 | 2 |
| 72 | 76 | 81 | 90 | I COULD HAVE DANCED ALL NIGHT — Ben E. King, Atco 6275 | 4 |
| 73 | 70 | 71 | 78 | UNCHAINED MELODY — Vito & the Salutations, Herald 583 | 5 |
| 74 | 68 | 74 | 86 | YOUR TEEN-AGE DREAMS — Johnny Mathis, Mercury 72184 | 7 |
| ★75 | — | — | — | QUICKSAND — Martha & the Vandellas, Gordy 7025 | 1 |
| 76 | 82 | 89 | 100 | SUE'S GOTTA BE MINE — Del Shannon, Berlee 501 | 4 |
| 77 | 84 | 86 | — | DAWN — David Rockingham Trio, Josie 913 | 3 |
| 78 | 83 | 85 | 87 | TWO-TEN, SIX-EIGHTEEN — Jimmie Rodgers, Dot 16527 | 7 |
| 79 | — | — | — | NEED TO BELONG — Jerry Butler, Vee Jay 567 | 1 |
| 80 | — | — | — | POPSICLES AND ICICLES — Murmaids, Chattahoochee 628 | 1 |
| 81 | — | — | — | YOU'RE NO GOOD — Betty Everett, Vee Jay 566 | 1 |
| 82 | 86 | 88 | 93 | REACH OUT FOR ME — Lou Johnson, Big Top 3153 | 6 |
| 83 | 92 | — | — | I HAVE A BOYFRIEND — Chiffons, Laurie 3212 | 2 |
| 84 | — | — | — | THE IMPOSSIBLE HAPPENED — Little Peggy March, RCA Victor 8267 | 1 |
| 85 | — | — | — | TURN AROUND — Dick & Deedee, Warner Bros. 5396 | 1 |
| 86 | — | — | — | FOR YOUR PRECIOUS LOVE — Garnet Mimms & the Enchanters, United Artists 658 | 1 |
| 87 | 83 | 99 | — | LONG TALL TEXAN — Murry Kellum, M.O.C. 653 | 3 |
| 88 | — | — | — | BABY I DO LOVE YOU — Galens, Challenge 9212 | 1 |
| 89 | 97 | — | — | GOTTA LOTTA LOVE — Steve Alaimo, Imperial 66003 | 2 |
| 90 | — | — | — | BE MAD LITTLE GIRL — Bobby Darin, Capitol 5079 | 1 |
| 91 | — | — | — | RUMBLE — Jack Nitzsche, Reprise 20225 | 1 |
| 92 | — | — | — | I GOTTA DANCE TO KEEP FROM CRYING — Miracles, Tamla 54089 | 1 |
| 93 | 100 | — | — | HEY LOVER — Debbie Dovale, Roulette 4521 | 2 |
| 94 | 96 | 97 | — | I AM A WITNESS — Tommy Hunt, Scepter 1261 | 3 |
| 95 | — | — | — | NOW — Lena Horne, 20th Century-Fox 449 | 1 |
| 96 | — | — | — | ALLY, ALLY OXEN FREE — Kingston Trio, Capitol 5078 | 1 |
| 97 | — | 99 | — | CROSSFIRE TIME — Dee Clark, Constellation 108 | 2 |
| 98 | — | 85 | — | CUANDO CALIENTA EL SOL — Steve Allen, Dot 16507 | 5 |
| 99 | — | — | — | PAIN IN MY HEART — Otis Redding, Volt 112 | 1 |
| 100 | — | — | — | PLEASE DON'T KISS ME AGAIN — Charmettes, Kapp 547 | 1 |

## BUBBLING UNDER THE HOT 100

101. WE SHALL OVERCOME — Joan Baez, Vanguard 35023
102. BABY'S GONE — Gene Thomas, United Artists 640
103. TOYS IN THE ATTIC — Joe Sherman, World Artists 1088
104. SHY GUY — Four Pennies, Rust 5070
105. WHEN THE BOY'S HAPPY — Radiants, Chess 1872
106. DUMB HEAD — Ginny Arnell, MGM 13177
107. COME DANCE WITH ME — Jay & the Americans, United Artists 669
108. I'M DOWN TO MY LAST HEART BREAK — Wilson Pickett, Double L 724
109. SEE THE BIG MAN CRY — Ed Bruce, Wand 140
110. THE CHEER LEADER — Paul Petersen, Colpix 707
111. THE SCAVENGER — Dick Dale and the Del-Tones, Capitol 5048
112. WE BELONG TOGETHER — Jimmy Velvet, Duke 368
113. BLUE MONDAY — James Davis, Duke 368
114. WHAT'CHA GONNA DO ABOUT IT — Doris Troy, Atlantic 2206
115. SWANEE RIVER — Ace Cannon, Hi 2070
116. 31 FLAVORS — Shirelles, Scepter 1260
117. YOU'RE NO GOOD — Dee Dee Warwick, Jubilee 5459
118. I WORRY BOUT YOU — Etta James, Argo 5452
119. THERE'S MORE PRETTY GIRLS THAN ONE — George Hamilton IV, RCA Victor 8250
120. KEEP AN EYE ON HER — Jaynetts, Tuff 371
121. BABY YOU'VE GOT IT MADE — Brook Benton & Damita Jo, Mercury 72207
122. LETTER FROM SHERRY — Dale Ward, Dot 16520
123. SALTWATER TAFFY — Morty Jay & the Surfin' Cats, Legend 124
124. LIPSTICK PAINT A SMILE ON ME — Demetriss Tapp, Brunswick 55251
125. STEWBALL — Peter, Paul & Mary, Warner Bros. 5391
126. TOO HURT TO CRY, TOO MUCH IN LOVE TO SAY GOODBYE — Darnells, Gordy 7024
127. HIT THE ROAD JACK — Jerry Lee Lewis, Smash 1857
128. WHEN THE LOVELIGHT STARTS SHINING THROUGH HIS EYES — Supremes, Motown 1051
129. FOUR STRONG WINDS — Brothers Four, Columbia 42888
130. GIRLS GROW UP FASTER THAN BOYS — Cookies, Dimension 1020
131. THE MARVELOUS TOY — Chad Mitchell Trio, Mercury 72197
132. MOUNTAIN OF LOVE — David Houston, Epic 9625
133. SURFER STREET — Allisons, Tip 1011

Compiled from national retail sales and radio station airplay by the Music Popularity Dept. of Record Market Research, Billboard.

# Billboard HOT 100

For Week Ending November 30, 1963

★ STAR performer—Sides registering greatest proportionate upward progress this week.

| This Week | 2 Wks Ago | 3 Wks Ago | TITLE Artist, Label & Number | Weeks On Chart |
|---|---|---|---|---|
| 1 | 1 | 4 | I'M LEAVING IT UP TO YOU — Dale & Grace, Montel-Michele 921 | 9 |
| 2 | 9 | 19 | DOMINIQUE — Singing Nun, Philips 40152 | 4 |
| 3 | 2 | 3 | WASHINGTON SQUARE — Village Stompers, Epic 9617 | 11 |
| 4 | 4 | 2 | SUGAR SHACK — Jimmy Gilmer and the Fireballs, Dot 16487 | 11 |
| 5 | 5 | 5 | IT'S ALL RIGHT — Impressions, ABC-Paramount 10487 | 10 |
| 6 | 6 | 7 | SHE'S A FOOL — Lesley Gore, Mercury 72180 | 10 |
| 7 | 7 | 9 | EVERYBODY — Tommy Roe, ABC-Paramount 10478 | 8 |
| 8 | 3 | 1 | DEEP PURPLE — Nino Tempo & April Stevens, Atco 6273 | 12 |
| 9 | 11 | 16 | (Down at) PAPA JOE'S — Dixiebelles, Sound Stage 7 2507 | 10 |
| 10 | 8 | 8 | BOSSA NOVA BABY — Elvis Presley, RCA Victor 8243 | 7 |
| 11 | 12 | 15 | WALKING THE DOG — Rufus Thomas, Stax 140 | 9 |
| 12 | 15 | 25 | LITTLE RED ROOSTER — Sam Cooke, RCA Victor 8247 | 6 |
| 13 | 13 | 18 | HEY LITTLE GIRL — Major Lance, Okeh 7181 | 7 |
| 14 | 19 | 44 | BE TRUE TO YOUR SCHOOL — Beach Boys, Capitol 5069 | 5 |
| 15 | 10 | 6 | MARIA ELENA — Los Indios Tabajaras, RCA Victor 8216 | 11 |
| 16 | 20 | 43 | SINCE I FELL FOR YOU — Lenny Welch, Cadence 1439 | 6 |
| 17 | 18 | 34 | WONDERFUL SUMMER — Robin Ward, Dot 16530 | 5 |
| 18 | 21 | 26 | TWENTY-FOUR HOURS FROM TULSA — Gene Pitney, Musicor 1034 | 7 |
| 19 | 22 | 41 | YOU DON'T HAVE TO BE A BABY TO CRY — Caravelles, Smash 1852 | 5 |
| 20 | 14 | 10 | 500 MILES AWAY FROM HOME — Bobby Bare, RCA Victor 8238 | 9 |
| 21 | 25 | 45 | LODDY LO — Chubby Checker, Parkway 890 | 5 |
| 22 | 23 | 38 | I WONDER WHAT SHE'S DOING TONIGHT — Barry & the Tamerlanes, Valiant 6034 | 7 |
| 23 | 41 | 58 | LOUIE LOUIE — Kingsmen, Wand 143 | 4 |
| 24 | 27 | 36 | LIVING A LIE — Al Martino, Capitol 5060 | 6 |
| 25 | 30 | 35 | I ADORE HIM — Angels, Smash 1854 | 6 |
| 26 | 38 | 73 | DRIP DROP — Dion DiMuci, Columbia 42917 | 3 |
| 27 | 16 | 13 | FOOLS RUSH IN — Rick Nelson, Decca 31533 | 12 |
| 28 | 26 | 28 | WALKING PROUD — Steve Lawrence, Columbia 42865 | 6 |
| 29 | 31 | 31 | SATURDAY NIGHT — New Christy Minstrels, Columbia 42887 | 6 |
| 30 | 33 | 47 | CAN I GET A WITNESS — Marvin Gaye, Tamla 54087 | 7 |
| 31 | 42 | 59 | TALK BACK TREMBLING LIPS — Johnny Tillotson, MGM 13181 | 4 |
| 32 | 43 | 61 | HAVE YOU HEARD — Duprees, Coed 585 | 4 |
| 33 | 47 | 62 | WIVES AND LOVERS — Jack Jones, Kapp 551 | 5 |
| 34 | 24 | 12 | I CAN'T STAY MAD AT YOU — Skeeter Davis, RCA Victor 8219 | 13 |
| 35 | 17 | 11 | MEAN WOMAN BLUES — Roy Orbison, Monument 824 | 13 |
| 36 | 34 | 23 | CRY TO ME — Betty Harris, Jubilee 5456 | 11 |
| 37 | 28 | 29 | YOUR OTHER LOVE — Connie Francis, MGM 13176 | 7 |
| 38 | 44 | 57 | IN MY ROOM — Beach Boys, Capitol 5069 | 5 |
| 39 | 29 | 21 | MISTY — Lloyd Price, Double L 722 | 9 |
| 40 | 37 | 33 | WILD! — Dee Dee Sharp, Cameo 274 | 9 |
| 41 | 45 | 40 | DOWN THE AISLE — Patty LaBelle & the Blue Belles, Newtown 5777 | 12 |
| 42 | 51 | 80 | BAD GIRL — Neil Sedaka, RCA Victor 8254 | 3 |
| 43 | 39 | 32 | WITCHCRAFT — Elvis Presley, RCA Victor 8243 | 7 |
| 44 | 46 | 46 | THE MATADOR — Johnny Cash, Columbia 42880 | 6 |
| 45 | 75 | — | QUICKSAND — Martha & the Vandellas, Gordy 7025 | 2 |
| 46 | 58 | 69 | MIDNIGHT MARY — Joey Powers, Amy 892 | 4 |
| 47 | 52 | 56 | YOUNG WINGS CAN FLY — Ruby & the Romantics, Kapp 557 | 6 |
| 48 | 59 | 90 | BABY DON'T YOU WEEP — Garnet Mimms and the Enchanters, United Artists 658 | 3 |
| 49 | 60 | 78 | FORGET HIM — Bobby Rydell, Cameo 280 | 4 |
| 50 | — | — | THERE! I'VE SAID IT AGAIN — Bobby Vinton, Epic 9638 | 1 |
| 51 | 56 | 67 | THE BOY NEXT DOOR — Secrets, Philips 40146 | 4 |
| 52 | 70 | 91 | KANSAS CITY — Trini Lopez, Reprise 20236 | 3 |
| 53 | 71 | 88 | THE NITTY GRITTY — Shirley Ellis, Congress 202 | 3 |
| 54 | 66 | 89 | RAGS TO RICHES — Sunny and the Sunliners, Tear Drop 3022 | 3 |
| 55 | 57 | 60 | MISERY — Dynamics, Big Top 3161 | 5 |
| 56 | 63 | 71 | I GOT A WOMAN — Freddie Scott, Colpix 709 | 5 |
| 57 | 68 | 72 | YOU'RE GOOD FOR ME — Solomon Burke, Atlantic 2205 | 5 |
| 58 | 61 | 79 | TRA LA LA LA SUZY — Dean & Jean, Rust 5067 | 5 |
| 59 | 62 | 74 | YESTERDAY AND YOU — Bobby Vee, Liberty 55636 | 4 |
| 60 | 65 | 87 | SHE'S GOT EVERYTHING — Essex, Roulette 4530 | 3 |
| 61 | 64 | 85 | AS LONG AS I KNOW HE'S MINE — Marvelettes, Tamla 54088 | 4 |
| 62 | 67 | 77 | SHIRL GIRL — Wayne Newton, Capitol 5058 | 6 |
| 63 | 80 | — | POPSICLES AND ICICLES — Murmaids, Chattahoochee 628 | 2 |
| 64 | 83 | 92 | I HAVE A BOYFRIEND — Chiffons, Laurie 3212 | 3 |
| 65 | 85 | — | TURN AROUND — Dick & Deedee, Warner Bros. 5396 | 2 |
| 66 | 73 | 70 | UNCHAINED MELODY — Vito & the Salutations, Herald 583 | 6 |
| 67 | 79 | — | NEED TO BELONG — Jerry Butler, Vee Jay 567 | 2 |
| 68 | 84 | — | THE IMPOSSIBLE HAPPENED — Little Peggy March, RCA Victor 8267 | 2 |
| 69 | 77 | 84 | DAWN — David Rockingham Trio, Josie 913 | 4 |
| 70 | 92 | — | I GOTTA DANCE TO KEEP FROM CRYING — Miracles, Tamla 54089 | 2 |
| 71 | 76 | 82 | SUE'S GOTTA BE MINE — Del Shannon, Berlee 501 | 5 |
| 72 | — | — | STEWBALL — Peter, Paul & Mary, Warner Bros. 5399 | 1 |
| 73 | 87 | 99 | LONG TALL TEXAN — Murry Kellum, M.O.C. 653 | 4 |
| 74 | 96 | — | ALLY, ALLY OXEN FREE — Kingston Trio, Capitol 5078 | 2 |
| 75 | 81 | — | YOU'RE NO GOOD — Betty Everett, Vee Jay 546 | 2 |
| 76 | 94 | 96 | I AM A WITNESS — Tommy Hunt, Scepter 1261 | 4 |
| 77 | 90 | — | BE MAD LITTLE GIRL — Bobby Darin, Capitol 5079 | 2 |
| 78 | 86 | — | FOR YOUR PRECIOUS LOVE — Garnet Mimms & the Enchanters, United Artists 658 | 2 |
| 79 | 82 | 86 | REACH OUT FOR ME — Lou Johnson, Big Top 3153 | 7 |
| 80 | — | — | GIRLS GROW UP FASTER THAN BOYS — Cookies, Dimension 1020 | 1 |
| 81 | 93 | 100 | HEY LOVER — Debbie Dovale, Roulette 4521 | 3 |
| 82 | 89 | 97 | GOTTA LOTTA LOVE — Steve Alaimo, Imperial 66003 | 3 |
| 83 | — | — | BEGGING TO YOU — Marty Robbins, Columbia 42890 | 1 |
| 84 | 88 | — | BABY I DO LOVE YOU — Galens, Challenge 9212 | 2 |
| 85 | — | — | WHEN THE LOVELIGHT STARTS SHINING THROUGH HIS EYES — Supremes, Motown 1051 | 1 |
| 86 | 99 | — | PAIN IN MY HEART — Otis Redding, Volt 112 | 2 |
| 87 | — | — | THE MARVELOUS TOY — Chad Mitchell Trio, Mercury 72197 | 1 |
| 88 | — | 81 | ANY OTHER WAY — Chuck Jackson, Wand 141 | 4 |
| 89 | — | — | THAT BOY JOHN — Raindrops, Jubilee 5466 | 1 |
| 90 | — | — | COME DANCE WITH ME — Jay & the Americans, United Artists 669 | 1 |
| 91 | 91 | — | RUMBLE — Jack Nitzsche, Reprise 20225 | 2 |
| 92 | 95 | — | NOW — Lena Horne, 20th Century-Fox 449 | 2 |
| 93 | — | — | BABY, WHAT'S WRONG — Lonnie Mack, Fraternity 918 | 1 |
| 94 | — | — | TODAY'S TEARDROPS — Rick Nelson, Imperial 66004 | 1 |
| 95 | 97 | — | CROSSFIRE TIME — Dee Clark, Constellation 108 | 3 |
| 96 | — | 98 | DUMB HEAD — Ginny Arnell, MGM 13177 | 2 |
| 97 | — | 95 | I'M DOWN TO MY LAST HEART BREAK — Wilson Pickett, Double L 724 | 3 |
| 98 | — | — | BABY WE'VE GOT LOVE — Johnnie Taylor, Derby 1006 | 1 |
| 99 | — | — | THE CHEER LEADER — Paul Petersen, Colpix 707 | 1 |
| 100 | — | — | THE SHELTER OF YOUR ARMS — Sammy Davis Jr., Reprise 20216 | 1 |

## BUBBLING UNDER THE HOT 100

101. BABY'S GONE — Gene Thomas, United Artists 640
102. WHAT'CHA GONNA DO ABOUT IT — Doris Troy, Atlantic 2206
103. SWANEE RIVER — Ace Cannon, Hi 2075
104. 31 FLAVORS — Shirelles, Scepter 1260
105. SHY GUY — Radiants, Chess 1872
106. WHY DO KIDS GROW UP — Randy & the Rainbows, Rust 5073
107. DRAG CITY — Jan & Dean, Liberty 55641
108. I SHALL OVERCOME — Joan Baez, Vanguard 35023
109. WE BELONG TOGETHER — Jimmy Velvet, ABC-Paramount 10488
110. ROCK CANDY — Jack McDuff, Prestige 272
111. PRETTY PAPER — Roy Orbison, Monument 830
112. SEE THE BIG MAN CRY — Ed Bruce, Wand 140
113. BABY YOU'VE GOT IT MADE — Brook Benton & Damita Jo, Mercury 72207
114. HI DIDDLE DIDDLE — Inez Foxx, Symbol 924
115. FOUR STRONG WINDS — Brothers Four, Columbia 42888
116. THERE'S MORE PRETTY GIRLS THAN ONE — George Hamilton IV, RCA Victor 8250
117. TOO HURT TO CRY, TOO MUCH IN LOVE TO SAY GOODBYE — Darnells, Gordy 7024
118. BLUE MONDAY — James Davis, Duke 368
119. IT'S ALL IN THE GAME — Cliff Richard, Epic 9633
120. THE SCAVENGER — Dick Dale & the Del-Tones, Capitol 5048
121. HIT THE ROAD JACK — Jerry Lee Lewis, Smash 1857
122. LIPSTICK PAINT A SMILE ON ME — Demetriss Tapp, Brunswick 55251
123. WHERE THERE'S A WILL — Leonie Mack, Fraternity 918
124. HARLEM SHUFFLE — Bob & Earl, Marc 104
125. CHARADE — Henry Mancini & His Ork, RCA Victor 8256
126. LET'S START THE PARTY AGAIN — Little Eva, Dimension 1019
127. I CAN'T GIVE YOU ANYTHING BUT LOVE — Fats Domino, ABC-Paramount 10484
128. STOP FOOLIN' — Brook Benton & Damita Jo, Mercury 72207
129. SURFER STREET — Allisons, Scepter 1260
130. IT'S A MAD, MAD, MAD, MAD WORLD — Charlie Rich, Groove 0253
131. BIG BOSS MAN — Brooks O'Dell, Gold 214
132. WATCH YOUR STEP — Kenny Ball, Kapp 564
133. HEARTACHES — 
134. DON'T ENVY ME — George Hamilton, MGM 13178

Compiled from national retail sales and radio station airplay by the Music Popularity Dept. of Record Market Research, Billboard.

**Billboard** For Week Ending December 7, 1963

# HOT 100

★ **STAR performer—Sides registering greatest proportionate upward progress this week.**

Billboard Award

| THIS WEEK | 1 Wk. Ago | 2 Wks. Ago | 3 Wks. Ago | TITLE Artist, Label & Number | Weeks On Chart |
|---|---|---|---|---|---|
| 1 | 2 | 9 | 19 | DOMINIQUE — Singing Nun, Philips 40152 | 5 |
| 2 | 1 | 1 | 4 | I'M LEAVING IT UP TO YOU — Dale & Grace, Montel-Michele 921 | 10 |
| ★ 3 | 7 | 7 | 9 | EVERYBODY — Tommy Roe, ABC-Paramount 10478 | 9 |
| ★ 4 | 23 | 41 | 58 | LOUIE LOUIE — Kingsmen, Wand 143 | 5 |
| 5 | 6 | 6 | 7 | SHE'S A FOOL — Lesley Gore, Mercury 72180 | 11 |
| 6 | 4 | 4 | 2 | SUGAR SHACK — Jimmy Gilmer and the Fireballs, Dot 16487 | 12 |
| ★ 7 | 19 | 22 | 41 | YOU DON'T HAVE TO BE A BABY TO CRY — Caravelles, Smash 1852 | 6 |
| ★ 8 | 14 | 19 | 44 | BE TRUE TO YOUR SCHOOL — Beach Boys, Capitol 5069 | 6 |
| 9 | 3 | 2 | 3 | WASHINGTON SQUARE — Village Stompers, Epic 9617 | 12 |
| 10 | 11 | 12 | 15 | WALKING THE DOG — Rufus Thomas, Stax 140 | 10 |
| 11 | 8 | 3 | 1 | DEEP PURPLE — Nino Tempo & April Stevens, Atco 6273 | 13 |
| 12 | 12 | 15 | 25 | LITTLE RED ROOSTER — Sam Cooke, RCA Victor 8247 | 7 |
| 13 | 13 | 13 | 18 | HEY LITTLE GIRL — Major Lance, Okeh 7181 | 8 |
| 14 | 16 | 20 | 43 | SINCE I FELL FOR YOU — Lenny Welch, Cadence 1439 | 7 |
| ★ 15 | 26 | 38 | 73 | DRIP DROP — Dion DiMuci, Columbia 42917 | 4 |
| 16 | 5 | 5 | 5 | IT'S ALL RIGHT — Impressions, ABC-Paramount 10487 | 11 |
| 17 | 18 | 21 | 26 | TWENTY-FOUR HOURS FROM TULSA — Gene Pitney, Musicor 1034 | 8 |
| 18 | 9 | 11 | 16 | (Down at) PAPA JOE'S — Dixiebelles, Sound Stage 7 2507 | 11 |
| 19 | 17 | 18 | 34 | WONDERFUL SUMMER — Robin Ward, Dot 16530 | 6 |
| 20 | 21 | 25 | 45 | LODDY LO — Chubby Checker, Parkway 890 | 6 |
| 21 | 22 | 23 | 48 | I WONDER WHAT SHE'S DOING TONIGHT — Barry & the Tamerlanes, Valiant 6034 | 8 |
| ★ 22 | 50 | — | — | THERE! I'VE SAID IT AGAIN — Bobby Vinton, Epic 9638 | 2 |
| 23 | 15 | 10 | 6 | MARIA ELENA — Los Indios Tabajaras, RCA Victor 8216 | 12 |
| 24 | 24 | 27 | 36 | LIVING A LIE — Al Martino, Capitol 5060 | 7 |
| ★ 25 | 32 | 43 | 61 | HAVE YOU HEARD — Duprees, Coed 585 | 5 |
| ★ 26 | 31 | 42 | 59 | TALK BACK TREMBLING LIPS — Johnny Tillotson, MGM 13181 | 5 |
| 27 | 30 | 33 | 47 | CAN I GET A WITNESS — Marvin Gaye, Tamala 54087 | 8 |
| ★ 28 | 38 | 44 | 57 | IN MY ROOM — Beach Boys, Capitol 5069 | 6 |
| 29 | 10 | 8 | 8 | BOSSA NOVA BABY — Elvis Presley, RCA Victor 8243 | 8 |
| ★ 30 | 49 | 60 | 78 | FORGET HIM — Bobby Rydell, Cameo 280 | 5 |
| 31 | 33 | 47 | 62 | WIVES AND LOVERS — Jack Jones, Kapp 551 | 6 |
| ★ 32 | 63 | 80 | — | POPSICLES AND ICICLES — Murmaids, Chattahoochee 628 | 3 |
| 33 | 20 | 14 | 10 | 500 MILES AWAY FROM HOME — Bobby Bare, RCA Victor 8238 | 10 |
| ★ 34 | 45 | 75 | — | QUICKSAND — Martha & the Vandellas, Gordy 7025 | 3 |
| ★ 35 | 48 | 59 | 90 | BABY DON'T YOU WEEP — Garnet Mimms and the Enchanters, United Artists 658 | 4 |
| ★ 36 | 46 | 58 | 69 | MIDNIGHT MARY — Joey Powers, Amy 892 | 5 |
| 37 | 25 | 30 | 35 | I ADORE HIM — Angels, Smash 1854 | 7 |
| ★ 38 | 53 | 71 | 88 | THE NITTY GRITTY — Shirley Ellis, Congress 202 | 4 |
| ★ 39 | 51 | 56 | 67 | THE BOY NEXT DOOR — Secrets, Philips 40146 | 5 |
| 40 | 42 | 51 | 80 | BAD GIRL — Neil Sedaka, RCA Victor 8254 | 4 |
| 41 | 28 | 26 | 28 | WALKING PROUD — Steve Lawrence, Columbia 42865 | 8 |
| ★ 42 | 52 | 70 | 91 | KANSAS CITY — Trini Lopez, Reprise 20236 | 4 |
| 43 | 27 | 16 | 13 | FOOLS RUSH IN — Rick Nelson, Decca 31533 | 13 |
| 44 | 41 | 45 | 40 | DOWN THE AISLE — Patty LaBelle & the Blue Belles, Newtown 5777 | 13 |
| ★ 45 | 58 | 61 | 79 | TRA LA LA LA SUZY — Dean & Jean, Rust 5067 | 6 |
| 46 | 29 | 31 | 31 | SATURDAY NIGHT — New Christy Minstrels, Columbia 42887 | 7 |
| 47 | 47 | 52 | 56 | YOUNG WINGS CAN FLY — Ruby & the Romantics, Kapp 557 | 7 |
| 48 | 56 | 63 | 71 | I GOT A WOMAN — Freddie Scott, Colpix 709 | 6 |
| 49 | 44 | 46 | 46 | THE MATADOR — Johnny Cash, Columbia 42880 | 7 |
| 50 | 55 | 57 | 60 | MISERY — Dynamics, Big Top 3161 | 6 |
| 51 | 54 | 66 | 89 | RAGS TO RICHES — Sunny and the Sunliners, Tear Drop 3022 | 4 |
| ★ 52 | 64 | 83 | 92 | I HAVE A BOYFRIEND — Chiffons, Laurie 3212 | 4 |
| 53 | 57 | 68 | 72 | YOU'RE GOOD FOR ME — Solomon Burke, Atlantic 2205 | 6 |
| ★ 54 | 65 | 85 | — | TURN AROUND — Dick & Deedee, Warner Bros. 5396 | 3 |
| ★ 55 | 72 | — | — | STEWBALL — Peter, Paul & Mary, Warner Bros. 5399 | 2 |
| 56 | 61 | 64 | 85 | AS LONG AS I KNOW HE'S MINE — Marvelettes, Tamla 54088 | 5 |
| 57 | 60 | 65 | 87 | SHE'S GOT EVERYTHING — Essex, Roulette 4530 | 4 |
| 58 | 62 | 67 | 77 | SHIRL GIRL — Wayne Newton, Capitol 5058 | 7 |
| 59 | 59 | 62 | 74 | YESTERDAY AND YOU — Bobby Vee, Liberty 55636 | 5 |
| ★ 60 | 70 | 92 | — | I GOTTA DANCE TO KEEP FROM CRYING — Miracles, Tamla 54089 | 3 |
| 61 | 74 | 96 | — | ALLY, ALLY OXEN FREE — Kingston Trio, Capitol 5078 | 3 |
| 62 | 67 | 79 | — | NEED TO BELONG — Jerry Butler, Vee Jay 567 | 3 |
| 63 | 68 | 84 | — | THE IMPOSSIBLE HAPPENED — Little Peggy March, RCA Victor 8267 | 3 |
| 64 | 69 | 77 | 84 | DAWN — David Rockingham Trio, Josie 913 | 5 |
| 65 | 73 | 87 | 99 | LONG TALL TEXAN — Murry Kellum, M.O.C. 653 | 5 |
| 66 | 78 | 86 | — | FOR YOUR PRECIOUS LOVE — Garnet Mimms & the Enchanters, United Artists 658 | 3 |
| 67 | 77 | 90 | — | BE MAD LITTLE GIRL — Bobby Darin, Capitol 5079 | 3 |
| 68 | 75 | 81 | — | YOU'RE NO GOOD — Betty Everett, Vee Jay 566 | 3 |
| 69 | 80 | — | — | GIRLS GROW UP FASTER THAN BOYS — Cookies, Dimension 1020 | 2 |
| ★ 70 | — | — | — | DRAG CITY — Jan & Dean, Liberty 55641 | 1 |
| 71 | 76 | 94 | 96 | I AM A WITNESS — Tommy Hunt, Scepter 1261 | 5 |
| 72 | — | — | — | THAT LUCKY OLD SUN — Ray Charles, ABC-Paramount 10509 | 1 |
| 73 | 71 | 76 | 82 | SUE'S GOTTA BE MINE — Del Shannon, Berlee 501 | 6 |
| 74 | 79 | 82 | 86 | REACH OUT FOR ME — Lou Johnson, Big Top 3153 | 8 |
| 75 | 85 | — | — | WHEN THE LOVELIGHT STARTS SHINING THROUGH HIS EYES — Supremes, Motown 1051 | 2 |
| 76 | 84 | 88 | — | BABY I DO LOVE YOU — Galens, Challenge 9212 | 3 |
| 77 | 87 | — | — | THE MARVELOUS TOY — Chad Mitchell Trio, Mercury 72197 | 2 |
| 78 | 86 | 99 | — | PAIN IN MY HEART — Otis Redding, Volt 112 | 3 |
| 79 | 82 | 89 | 97 | GOTTA LOTTA LOVE — Steve Alaimo, Imperial 66003 | 4 |
| 80 | 83 | — | — | BEGGING TO YOU — Marty Robbins, Columbia 42890 | 2 |
| 81 | 90 | — | — | COME DANCE WITH ME — Jay & the Americans, United Artists 669 | 2 |
| ★ 82 | — | — | — | SOMEWHERE — Tymes, Parkway 891 | 1 |
| ★ 83 | — | — | — | HOOKA TOOKA — Chubby Checker, Parkway 890 | 1 |
| 84 | 94 | — | — | TODAY'S TEARDROPS — Rick Nelson, Imperial 66004 | 2 |
| ★ 85 | — | — | — | OUT OF LIMITS — Marketts, Warner Bros. 5391 | 1 |
| 86 | 89 | — | — | THAT BOY JOHN — Raindrops, Jubilee 5466 | 2 |
| ★ 87 | — | — | — | CHARADE — Henry Mancini & His Ork, RCA Victor 8256 | 1 |
| ★ 88 | — | 96 | — | BABY'S GONE — Gene Thomas, United Artists 640 | 2 |
| ★ 89 | — | — | — | IT'S ALL IN THE GAME — Cliff Richard, Epic 9633 | 1 |
| ★ 90 | — | — | — | THANK YOU AND GOODNIGHT — Angels, Smash 1854 | 1 |
| 91 | 99 | — | — | THE CHEER LEADER — Paul Petersen, Colpix 707 | 2 |
| 92 | 88 | — | 81 | ANY OTHER WAY — Chuck Jackson, Wand 141 | 5 |
| 93 | 96 | — | 98 | DUMB HEAD — Ginny Arnell, MGM 13177 | 3 |
| 94 | 95 | 97 | — | CROSSFIRE TIME — Dee Clark, Constellation 108 | 4 |
| 95 | 100 | — | — | THE SHELTER OF YOUR ARMS — Sammy Davis Jr., Reprise 20216 | 1 |
| 96 | 97 | — | 95 | I'M DOWN TO MY LAST HEART BREAK — Wilson Pickett, Double L 724 | 4 |
| 97 | — | — | — | SURFIN' BIRD — Trashmen, Garrett 4002 | 1 |
| 98 | — | — | — | HI DIDDLE DIDDLE — Inex Foxx, Symbol 924 | 1 |
| 99 | 81 | 93 | 100 | HEY LOVER — Debbie Dovale, Roulette 4521 | 4 |
| 100 | — | — | — | ANYONE WHO HAD A HEART — Dionne Warwick, Scepter 1262 | 1 |

## HOT 100—A TO Z—(Publisher-Licensee)

Ally, Ally Oxen Free (In, ASCAP) .... 61
Any Other Way (East-Bais, BMI) .... 92
Anyone Who Had a Heart (U. S. Songs, ASCAP) .. 100
As Long as I Know He's Mine (Jobete, BMI) .... 56
Baby Don't You Weep (Rittenhouse-Mellin, BMI) .. 35
Baby's Gone (Acuff-Rose, BMI) .... 88
Baby I Do Love You (4 Star-Sullivan, BMI) .... 76
Bad Girl (Screen Gems-Columbia, BMI) .... 40
Be Mad Little Girl (T. M., BMI) .... 67
Be True to Your School (Sea of Tunes, BMI) .... 8
Begging to You (Marty's, BMI) .... 80
Bossa Nova Baby (Presley, BMI) .... 29
Boy Next Door, The (Merjoda, BMI) .... 39
Can I Get a Witness (Jobete, BMI) .... 27
Charade (Southdale-Northern, ASCAP) .... 87
Cheer Leader, The (Northridge, ASCAP) .... 91
Come Dance With Me (Trio, BMI) .... 81
Crossfire Time (Vonglo-Joni, BMI) .... 94
Dawn (Nea-How, BMI) .... 64
Deep Purple (Robbins, ASCAP) .... 11
Dominique (General, ASCAP) .... 1
(Down at) Papa Joe's (Tuneville, BMI) .... 18
Down the Aisle (Sixty-Six, BMI) .... 44
Drag City (Screen Gems-Columbia, BMI) .... 70
Drip Drop (Progressive-Quintet, BMI) .... 15
Dumb Head (Peter Maurice, ASCAP) .... 93
Everybody (Low-Twi, BMI) .... 3
500 Miles Away From Home (Central Songs, BMI) . 33
Fools Rush In (Bregman, Vocco & Conn, ASCAP) .. 43
For Your Precious Love (Gladstone, ASCAP) .... 66
Forget Him (Leeds, ASCAP) .... 30
Girls Grow Up Faster Than Boys (Screen Gems-Columbia, BMI) .... 69
Gotta Lotta Love (Topper, ASCAP) .... 79
Have You Heard (Brandon, ASCAP) .... 25
Hey Little Girl (Curtom-Jalynne, BMI) .... 13
Hey Lover (Roosevelt, BMI) .... 99
Hi Diddle Diddle (Saturn, BMI) .... 98
Hooka Tooka (Evanston-Woodcrest, BMI) .... 83
I Adore Him (Screen Gems-Columbia, BMI) .... 37
I Am a Witness (Damic, BMI) .... 71
I Got a Woman (Progressive, BMI) .... 48
I Gotta Dance to Keep From Crying (Jobete, BMI). 60
I Have a Boyfriend (Trio, BMI) .... 52
I Wonder What She's Doing Tonight (Sherman-DeVorzon, BMI) .... 21
I'm Down to My Last Heart Break (Screen Gems-Columbia, BMI) .... 96
I'm Leaving It Up to You (Venice, BMI) .... 2
Impossible Happened, The (Atrium, ASCAP) .... 63
In My Room (Sea of Tunes, BMI) .... 28
It's All in the Game (Remick, ASCAP) .... 89
It's All Right (Curtom, BMI) .... 16
Kansas City (Lois, BMI) .... 42
Little Red Rooster (Ark, BMI) .... 12
Living a Lie (Damian, ASCAP) .... 24
Loddy Lo (Kalmann-C. C., ASCAP) .... 20
Long Tall Texan (Adams-Ethridge, BMI) .... 65
Louie Louie (Limax, BMI) .... 4
Maria Elena (Peer Int'l, BMI) .... 23
Marvelous Toy, The (Teena, ASCAP) .... 77
Matador, The (Cash, BMI) .... 49
Midnight Mary (Jimskip, BMI) .... 36
Misery (Noma & Dar-Bar, BMI) .... 50
Need to Belong (Curtom-Conrad, BMI) .... 62
Nitty Gritty, The (Gallico, BMI) .... 38
Out of Limits (Wrist, BMI) .... 85
Pain in My Heart (East-Time, BMI) .... 78
Popsicles and Icicles (Dragonwick, BMI) .... 32
Quicksand (Jobete, BMI) .... 34
Rags to Riches (Saunders, ASCAP) .... 51
Reach Out for Me (Ross Jungnickel, ASCAP) .... 74
Saturday Night (Cherrybell, ASCAP) .... 46
She's a Fool (Helios-MRC, BMI) .... 5
She's Got Everything (January, BMI) .... 57
Shelter of Your Arms, The (Pride, ASCAP) .... 95
Shirl Girl (T. H., BMI) .... 58
Since I Fell for You (Advanced, ASCAP) .... 14
Somewhere (Wyncote, ASCAP) .... 82
Stewball (Pepamar, ASCAP) .... 55
Sue's Gotta Be Mine (Shidel, BMI) .... 73
Sugar Shack (Dundee, BMI) .... 6
Surfin' Bird (Long, BMI) .... 97
Talk Back Trembling Lips (Acuff-Rose, BMI) .... 26
Thank You and Goodnight (Grand Canyon, BMI) .. 90
That Boy John (Trio, BMI) .... 86
That Lucky Old Sun (Robbins, ASCAP) .... 72
There! I've Said It Again (Valiant, ASCAP) .... 22
Today's Teardrops (Sea-Lark, BMI) .... 84
Tra La La La Suzy (Just, BMI) .... 45
Turn Around (Clara, ASCAP) .... 54
Twenty-Four Hours From Tulsa (Arch, ASCAP) .... 17
Walking Proud (Screen Gems-Columbia, BMI) .... 41
Walking the Dog (East, BMI) .... 60
Washington Square (Rayven, BMI) .... 9
When the Lovelight Starts Shining Through His Eyes (Jobete, BMI) .... 75
Wives and Lovers (Famous, ASCAP) .... 31
Wonderful Summer (Rock, BMI) .... 19
Yesterday and You (A.B.C., ASCAP) .... 59
You Don't Have to Be a Baby to Cry (R.F.D., ASCAP) .... 7
You're Good for Me (Cotillion-Vonglo, BMI) .... 53
You're No Good (Morris, ASCAP) .... 68
Young Wings Can Fly (Day-Hilliard, ASCAP) .... 47

## BUBBLING UNDER THE HOT 100

101. DID YOU HAVE A HAPPY BIRTHDAY ....Paul Anka, RCA Victor 8272
102. WE BELONG TOGETHER ....Jimmy Velvet, ABC-Paramount 10488
103. LOUIE LOUIE ....Paul Revere and the Raiders, Columbia 42814
104. PRETTY PAPER ....Roy Orbison, Monument 830
105. NOW.... Lena Horne, 20th Century-Fox 449
106. BABY WHAT'S WRONG ....Lonnie Mack, Fraternity 918
107. OH WHAT A NIGHT FOR LOVE ....Roy Tyson, Double L 723
108. STOP FOOLIN' ....Brook Benton and Damita Jo, Mercury 72207
109. SEE THE BIG MAN CRY ....Ed Bruce, Wand 140
110. I'LL SEARCH MY HEART ....Johnny Mathis, Columbia 42916
111. BABY YOU'VE GOT IT MADE ...Brook Benton and Damita Jo, Mercury 72207
112. BABY WE'VE GOT LOVE ....Johnnie Taylor, Derby 1006
113. WHO DO KIDS GROW UP ....Randy and the Rainbows, Rust 5073
114. FOUR STRONG WINDS ....Brothers Four, Columbia 42888
115. HARLEM SHUFFLE....Bob and Earl, Marc 104
116. SHY GUY ....Radiants, Chess 1872
117. SWANEE RIVER ....Ace Cannon, Hi 2070
118. LIPSTICK PAINT A SMILE ON ME ....Demetriss Tapp, Brunswick 55251
119. ROCK CANDY ....Jack McDuff, Prestige 273
120. HIT THE ROAD JACK ....Jerry Lee Lewis, Smash 1857
121. I CAN'T GIVE YOU ANYTHING BUT LOVE ....Fats Domino, Imperial 66005
122. WE SHALL OVERCOME ....Joan Baez, Vanguard 35023
123. LET'S START THE PARTY AGAIN ....Little Eva, Dimension 1019
124. WHAT'CHA GONNA DO ABOUT IT ....Doris Troy, Atlantic 2206
125. I CAN'T STOP TALKING ABOUT YOU ....Steve and Eydie, Columbia 42932
126. WATCH YOUR STEP ....Brooks O'Dell, Gold 214
127. DO-WAH-DIDDY ....Exciters, United Artists 662
128. HEARTACHES ....Kenny Ball, Kapp 554
129. FOR YOUR SWEET LOVE ....Cascades, RCA Victor 8268
130. BIG BOSS MAN....Charlie Rich, Groove 0025
131. SURFER STREET....Allisons, Tip 1011

Compiled from national retail sales and radio station airplay by the Music Popularity Dept. of Record Market Research, Billboard.

For Week Ending December 14, 1963

# Billboard HOT 100

★ STAR performer—Sides registering greatest proportionate upward progress this week.

Billboard Award

| THIS WEEK | 1 Wk. Ago | 2 Wks. Ago | 3 Wks. Ago | TITLE | Artist, Label & Number | Weeks On Chart |
|---|---|---|---|---|---|---|
| 1 | 1 | 2 | 9 | DOMINIQUE | Singing Nun, Philips 40152 | 6 |
| 2 | 4 | 23 | 41 | LOUIE LOUIE | Kingsmen, Wand 143 | 6 |
| 3 | 3 | 7 | 7 | EVERYBODY | Tommy Roe, ABC-Paramount 10478 | 10 |
| 4 | 2 | 1 | 1 | I'M LEAVING IT UP TO YOU | Dale & Grace, Montel/Michele 921 | 11 |
| 5 | 7 | 19 | 22 | YOU DON'T HAVE TO BE A BABY TO CRY | Caravelles, Smash 1852 | 7 |
| ★ 6 | 14 | 16 | 20 | SINCE I FELL FOR YOU | Lenny Welch, Cadence 1439 | 8 |
| 7 | 8 | 14 | 19 | BE TRUE TO YOUR SCHOOL | Beach Boys, Capitol 5069 | 7 |
| ★ 8 | 15 | 26 | 38 | DRIP DROP | Dion DiMuci, Columbia 42917 | 5 |
| ★ 9 | 22 | 50 | — | THERE! I'VE SAID IT AGAIN | Bobby Vinton, Epic 9638 | 3 |
| 10 | 10 | 11 | 12 | WALKING THE DOG | Rufus Thomas, Stax 140 | 11 |
| 11 | 12 | 12 | 15 | LITTLE RED ROOSTER | Sam Cooke, RCA Victor 8247 | 8 |
| 12 | 5 | 6 | 6 | SHE'S A FOOL | Lesley Gore, Mercury 72180 | 12 |
| 13 | 6 | 4 | 4 | SUGAR SHACK | Jimmy Gilmer and the Fireballs, Dot 16487 | 13 |
| ★ 14 | 19 | 17 | 18 | WONDERFUL SUMMER | Robin Ward, Dot 16530 | 7 |
| ★ 15 | 20 | 21 | 25 | LODDY LO | Chubby Checker, Parkway 890 | 7 |
| ★ 16 | 32 | 63 | 80 | POPSICLES AND ICICLES | Murmaids, Chattahoochee 628 | 4 |
| 17 | 9 | 3 | 2 | WASHINGTON SQUARE | Village Stompers, Epic 9617 | 13 |
| ★ 18 | 26 | 31 | 42 | TALK BACK TREMBLING LIPS | Johnny Tillotson, MGM 13181 | 6 |
| 19 | 16 | 5 | 5 | IT'S ALL RIGHT | Impressions, ABC-Paramount 10487 | 12 |
| ★ 20 | 25 | 32 | 43 | HAVE YOU HEARD | Duprees, Coed 585 | 6 |
| 21 | 11 | 8 | 3 | DEEP PURPLE | Nino Tempo & April Stevens, Atco 6273 | 14 |
| 22 | 24 | 24 | 27 | LIVING A LIE | Al Martino, Capitol 5060 | 8 |
| ★ 23 | 34 | 45 | 75 | QUICKSAND | Martha & the Vandellas, Gordy 7025 | 4 |
| 24 | 27 | 30 | 33 | CAN I GET A WITNESS | Marvin Gaye, Tamala 54087 | 9 |
| ★ 25 | 30 | 49 | 60 | FORGET HIM | Bobby Rydell, Cameo 280 | 6 |
| ★ 26 | 31 | 33 | 47 | WIVES AND LOVERS | Jack Jones, Kapp 551 | 7 |
| ★ 27 | 36 | 46 | 58 | MIDNIGHT MARY | Joey Powers, Amy 892 | 6 |
| ★ 28 | 38 | 53 | 71 | THE NITTY GRITTY | Shirley Ellis, Congress 202 | 5 |
| 29 | 13 | 13 | 13 | HEY LITTLE GIRL | Major Lance, Okeh 7181 | 9 |
| 30 | 21 | 22 | 23 | I WONDER WHAT SHE'S DOING TONIGHT | Barry & the Tamerlanes, Valiant 6034 | 9 |
| ★ 31 | 42 | 52 | 70 | KANSAS CITY | Trini Lopez, Reprise 20236 | 5 |
| 32 | 35 | 48 | 59 | BABY DON'T YOU WEEP | Garnet Mimms and the Enchanters, United Artists 658 | 5 |
| 33 | 28 | 38 | 44 | IN MY ROOM | Beach Boys, Capitol 5069 | 7 |
| 34 | 17 | 18 | 21 | TWENTY-FOUR HOURS FROM TULSA | Gene Pitney, Musicor 1034 | 9 |
| 35 | 39 | 51 | 56 | THE BOY NEXT DOOR | Secrets, Philips 40146 | 6 |
| 36 | 18 | 9 | 11 | (Down at) PAPA JOE'S | Dixiebelles, Sound Stage 7 2507 | 12 |
| 37 | 29 | 10 | 8 | BOSSA NOVA BABY | Elvis Presley, RCA Victor 8243 | 9 |
| 38 | 23 | 15 | 10 | MARIA ELENA | Los Indios Tabajaras, RCA Victor 8216 | 13 |
| 39 | 40 | 42 | 51 | BAD GIRL | Neil Sedaka, RCA Victor 8254 | 5 |
| 40 | 45 | 58 | 61 | TRA LA LA LA SUZY | Dean & Jean, Rust 5067 | 7 |
| 41 | 33 | 20 | 14 | 500 MILES AWAY FROM HOME | Bobby Bare, RCA Victor 8238 | 11 |
| ★ 42 | 66 | 78 | 86 | FOR YOUR PRECIOUS LOVE | Garnet Mimms & the Enchanters, United Artists 658 | 4 |
| 43 | 41 | 28 | 26 | WALKING PROUD | Steve Lawrence, Columbia 42865 | 9 |
| 44 | 50 | 55 | 57 | MISERY | Dynamics, Big Top 3161 | 7 |
| ★ 45 | 62 | 67 | 79 | NEED TO BELONG | Jerry Butler, Vee Jay 567 | 4 |
| 46 | 52 | 64 | 83 | I HAVE A BOYFRIEND | Chiffons, Laurie 3212 | 5 |
| 47 | 56 | 61 | 64 | AS LONG AS I KNOW HE'S MINE | Marvelettes, Tamla 54088 | 6 |
| 48 | 54 | 65 | 85 | TURN AROUND | Dick & Deedee, Warner Bros. 5396 | 4 |
| 49 | 53 | 57 | 68 | YOU'RE GOOD FOR ME | Solomon Burke, Atlantic 2205 | 7 |
| ★ 50 | 60 | 70 | 92 | I GOTTA DANCE TO KEEP FROM CRYING | Miracles, Tamla 54089 | 4 |
| 51 | 51 | 54 | 66 | RAGS TO RICHES | Sunny and the Sunliners, Tear Drop 3022 | 5 |
| 52 | 55 | 72 | — | STEWBALL | Peter, Paul & Mary, Warner Bros. 5399 | 3 |
| ★ 53 | 72 | — | — | THAT LUCKY OLD SUN | Ray Charles, ABC-Paramount 10509 | 2 |
| ★ 54 | 70 | — | — | DRAG CITY | Jan & Dean, Liberty 55641 | 2 |
| 55 | 59 | 59 | 62 | YESTERDAY AND YOU | Bobby Vee, Liberty 55636 | 6 |
| 56 | 57 | 60 | 65 | SHE'S GOT EVERYTHING | Essex, Roulette 4530 | 5 |
| 57 | 65 | 73 | 87 | LONG TALL TEXAN | Murry Kellum, M.O.C. 653 | 6 |
| ★ 58 | 68 | 75 | 81 | YOU'RE NO GOOD | Betty Everett, Vee Jay 566 | 4 |
| 59 | 63 | 68 | 84 | THE IMPOSSIBLE HAPPENED | Little Peggy March, RCA Victor 8267 | 4 |
| ★ 60 | — | — | — | PRETTY PAPER | Roy Orbison, Monument 830 | 1 |
| 61 | 61 | 74 | 96 | ALLY, ALLY OXEN FREE | Kingston Trio, Capitol 5078 | 4 |
| 62 | 64 | 69 | 77 | DAWN | David Rockingham Trio, Josie 913 | 6 |
| 63 | 75 | 85 | — | WHEN THE LOVELIGHT STARTS SHINING THROUGH HIS EYES | Supremes, Motown 1051 | 3 |
| 64 | 67 | 77 | 90 | BE MAD LITTLE GIRL | Bobby Darin, Capitol 5079 | 4 |
| 65 | 69 | 80 | — | GIRLS GROW UP FASTER THAN BOYS | Cookies, Dimension 1020 | 3 |
| 66 | 48 | 56 | 63 | I GOT A WOMAN | Freddie Scott, Colpix 709 | 7 |
| ★ 67 | 82 | — | — | SOMEWHERE | Tymes, Parkway 891 | 2 |
| 68 | 47 | 47 | 52 | YOUNG WINGS CAN FLY | Ruby & the Romantics, Kapp 557 | 8 |
| ★ 69 | 85 | — | — | OUT OF LIMITS | Marketts, Warner Bros. 5391 | 2 |
| ★ 70 | 97 | — | — | SURFIN' BIRD | Trashmen, Garrett 4002 | 2 |
| 71 | 83 | — | — | HOOKA TOOKA | Chubby Checker, Parkway 890 | 2 |
| 72 | 73 | 71 | 76 | SUE'S GOTTA BE MINE | Del Shannon, Berlee 501 | 7 |
| 73 | 77 | 87 | — | THE MARVELOUS TOY | Chad Mitchell Trio, Mercury 72197 | 3 |
| 74 | 76 | 84 | 88 | BABY I DO LOVE YOU | Galens, Challenge 9212 | 4 |
| ★ 75 | — | — | — | AS USUAL | Brenda Lee, Decca 31570 | 1 |
| 76 | 84 | 94 | — | TODAY'S TEARDROPS | Rick Nelson, Imperial 66004 | 3 |
| 77 | 79 | 82 | 89 | GOTTA LOTTA LOVE | Steve Alaimo, Imperial 66003 | 5 |
| 78 | 80 | 83 | — | BEGGING TO YOU | Marty Robbins, Columbia 42890 | 3 |
| 79 | 86 | 89 | — | THAT BOY JOHN | Raindrops, Jubilee 5466 | 3 |
| 80 | 87 | — | — | CHARADE | Henry Mancini & His Ork, RCA Victor 8256 | 2 |
| 81 | 81 | 90 | — | COME DANCE WITH ME | Jay & the Americans, United Artists 669 | 3 |
| ★ 82 | — | — | — | WATCH YOUR STEP | Brooks O'Dell, Gold 214 | 1 |
| ★ 83 | — | — | — | WHAT KIND OF FOOL (DO YOU THINK I AM) | Tams, ABC-Paramount 10502 | 1 |
| ★ 84 | — | — | — | HEY LITTLE COBRA | Rip Chords, Columbia 42921 | 1 |
| 85 | 89 | — | — | IT'S ALL IN THE GAME | Cliff Richard, Epic 9633 | 2 |
| 86 | 90 | — | — | THANK YOU AND GOODNIGHT | Angels, Smash 1854 | 2 |
| 87 | 91 | 99 | — | THE CHEER LEADER | Paul Petersen, Colpix 707 | 3 |
| ★ 88 | — | — | — | WE BELONG TOGETHER | Jimmy Velvet, ABC-Paramount 10488 | 1 |
| ★ 89 | — | — | — | DID YOU HAVE A HAPPY BIRTHDAY | Paul Anka, RCA Victor 8272 | 1 |
| ★ 90 | — | — | — | DAISY PETAL PICKIN' | Jimmy Gilmer & the Fireballs, Dot 16539 | 1 |
| 91 | 93 | 96 | — | DUMB HEAD | Ginny Arnell, MGM 13177 | 4 |
| 92 | 94 | 95 | 97 | CROSSFIRE TIME | Dee Clark, Constellation 108 | 5 |
| 93 | — | — | — | SURFER STREET | Allisons, Tip 1011 | 1 |
| 94 | — | — | — | PLEASE | Frank Ifield, Capitol 5089 | 1 |
| 95 | — | — | — | I'LL SEARCH MY HEART | Johnny Mathis, Columbia 42916 | 1 |
| 96 | 100 | — | — | ANYONE WHO HAD A HEART | Dionne Warwick, Scepter 1262 | 2 |
| 97 | — | — | — | HOOTENANNY SATURDAY NIGHT | Brothers Four, Columbia 42927 | 1 |
| 98 | — | — | — | BON-DOO-WAH | Orlons, Cameo 287 | 1 |
| 99 | — | — | — | WHY DO KIDS GROW UP | Randy & the Rainbows, Rust 5073 | 1 |
| 100 | — | — | — | COLD, COLD WINTER | Pixies Three, Mercury 72208 | 1 |

## HOT 100—A TO Z—(Publisher-Licensee)

Ally, Ally Oxen Free (In, ASCAP) ... 61
Anyone Who Had a Heart (U. S. Songs, ASCAP) ... 96
As Long As I Know He's Mine (Jobete, BMI) ... 47
As Usual (Samos Island, BMI) ... 75
Baby Don't You Weep (Rittenhouse-Mellin, BMI) ... 32
Baby I Do Love You (4 Star-Sullivan, BMI) ... 74
Bad Girl (Screen Gems-Columbia, BMI) ... 39
Be Mad Little Girl (T. M., BMI) ... 64
Be True to Your School (Sea of Tunes, BMI) ... 7
Begging to You (Marty's, BMI) ... 78
Bon-Doo-Wah (Kalmann, ASCAP) ... 98
Bossa Nova Baby (Presley, BMI) ... 37
Boy Next Door, The (Merjoda, BMI) ... 35
Can I Get a Witness (Jobete, BMI) ... 24
Charade (Southdale-Northern, ASCAP) ... 80
Cheer Leader, The (Northridge, ASCAP) ... 87
Cold Cold Winter (Merjoda, BMI) ... 100
Come Dance With Me (Trio, BMI) ... 81
Crossfire Time (Vonglo-Joni, BMI) ... 92
Daisy Petal Pickin' (Dundee, BMI) ... 90
Dawn (Nea-Now, BMI) ... 62
Deep Purple (Robbins, ASCAP) ... 21
Did You Have a Happy Birthday (Screen Gems-Columbia, BMI) ... 89
Dominique (General, ASCAP) ... 1
(Down at) Papa Joe's (Tuneville, BMI) ... 36
Drag City (Screen Gems-Columbia, BMI) ... 54
Drip Drop (Progressive-Qintet, BMI) ... 8
Dumb Head (Peter Maurice, ASCAP) ... 91
Everybody (Low-Twi, BMI) ... 3
500 Miles Away From Home (Central Songs, BMI) ... 41
For Your Precious Love (Gladstone, ASCAP) ... 42
Forget Him (Leeds, ASCAP) ... 25
Girls Grow Up Faster Than Boys (Screen Gems-Columbia, BMI) ... 65
Gotta Lotta Love (Topper, ASCAP) ... 77
Have You Heard (Brandon, ASCAP) ... 20
Hey Little Cobra (Vadim, BMI) ... 84
Hey Little Girl (Curtom-Jalynne, BMI) ... 29
Hooka Tooka (Evanston-Woodcrest, BMI) ... 71
Hootenanny Saturday Night (Saunders, ASCAP) ... 97
I Got a Woman (Progressive, BMI) ... 66
I Gotta Dance to Keep From Crying (Jobete, BMI) ... 50
I Have a Boyfriend (Trio, BMI) ... 46
I Wonder What She's Doing Tonight (Sherman-DeVorzon, BMI) ... 30
I'm Leaving It Up to You (Venice, BMI) ... 4
I'll Search My Heart (Elm Drive, ASCAP) ... 95
Impossible Happened, The (Atrium, ASCAP) ... 59
In My Room (Sea of Tunes, BMI) ... 33
It's All in the Game (Remick, ASCAP) ... 85
It's All Right (Curtom, BMI) ... 19
Kansas City (Lois, BMI) ... 31
Little Red Rooster (Ark, BMI) ... 11
Living a Lie (Damian, ASCAP) ... 22
Loddy Lo (Kalmann-C. C., ASCAP) ... 15
Long Tall Texan (Adams-Ethridge, BMI) ... 57
Louie Louie (Limax, BMI) ... 2
Maria Elena (Peer Int'l, BMI) ... 38
Marvelous Toy, The (Teena, ASCAP) ... 73
Midnight Mary (Jimskip, BMI) ... 27
Misery (Noma & Dar-Bar, BMI) ... 44
Need to Belong (Curtom-Conrad, BMI) ... 45
Nitty Gritty, The (Gallico, BMI) ... 28
Out of Limits (Wrist, BMI) ... 69
Please (Famous, ASCAP) ... 94
Pretty Paper (Pamper, BMI) ... 60
Popsicles and Icicles (Dragonwyck, BMI) ... 16
Quicksand (Jobete, BMI) ... 23
Rags to Riches (Saunders, ASCAP) ... 51
She's a Fool (Helios-MRC, BMI) ... 12
She's Got Everything (January, BMI) ... 56
Since I Fell for You (Advanced, ASCAP) ... 6
Somewhere (Wyncote, ASCAP) ... 67
Stewball (Pepamar, ASCAP) ... 52
Sue's Gotta Be Mine (Shidel, BMI) ... 72
Sugar Shack (Dundee, BMI) ... 13
Surfer Street (Dragonwyck-Venice, BMI) ... 93
Surfin' Bird (Long, BMI) ... 70
Talk Back Trembling Lips (Acuff-Rose, BMI) ... 18
Thank You and Goodnight (Grand Canyon, BMI) ... 86
That Boy John (Trio, BMI) ... 75
That Lucky Ole Sun (Robbins, ASCAP) ... 53
There! I've Said It Again (Valiant, ASCAP) ... 9
Today's Teardrops (Sea-Lark, BMI) ... 76
Tra La La Suzy (Just, BMI) ... 40
Turn Around (Clara, ASCAP) ... 48
Twenty-Four Hours From Tulsa (Arch, ASCAP) ... 34
Walking Proud (Screen Gems-Columbia, BMI) ... 43
Walking the Dog (East, BMI) ... 10
Washington Square (Rayven, BMI) ... 17
Watch You Step (Ludix, BMI) ... 82
We Belong Together (Figure, BMI) ... 88
What Kind of Fool Do You Think I Am (Low-Twi, BMI) ... 83
When the Lovelight Starts Shining Through His Eyes (Jobete, BMI) ... 63
Why Do Kids Grow Up (Just-Bright Tunes, BMI) ... 99
Wives and Lovers (Famous, ASCAP) ... 26
Wonderful Summer (Rock, BMI) ... 14
Yesterday and You (A.B.C., ASCAP) ... 55
You Don't Have to Be a Baby to Cry (R.F.D., ASCAP) ... 5
You're Good for Me (Cotillion-Vonglo, BMI) ... 49
You're No Good (Morris, ASCAP) ... 58
Young Wings Can Fly (Day-Hilliard, ASCAP) ... 68

## BUBBLING UNDER THE HOT 100

101. WE SHALL OVERCOME ... Joan Baez, Vanguard 35023
102. BABY'S GONE ... Gene Thomas, United Artists 640
103. HIT THE ROAD JACK ... Jerry Lee Lewis, Smash 1857
104. SWANEE RIVER ... Ace Cannon, Hi 2070
105. ANY OTHER WAY ... Chuck Jackson, Wand 141
106. OH WAT A NIGHT FOR LOVE ... Roy Tyson, Double L 723
107. HI DIDDLE DIDDLE ... Inez Foxx, Symbol 924
108. THE SON OF REBEL ROUSER ... Duane Eddy, RCA Victor 8276
109. ROCK CANDY ... Jack McDuff, Prestige 273
110. HARLEM SHUFFLE ... Bob & Earl, Marc 104
111. SHY GUY ... Radiants, Chess 1872
112. LIPSTICK PAINT A SMILE ON ME ... Demetriss Tapp, Brunswick 55251
113. I'M DOWN TO MY LAST HEART BREAK ... Wilson Pickett, Double L 724
114. BABY WHAT'S WRONG ... Lonnie Mack, Fraternity 918
115. TRUE LOVE GOES ON AND ON ... Burl Ives, Decca 31571
116. I CAN'T GIVE YOU ANYTHING BUT LOVE ... Fats Domino, Imperial 66005
117. THE SHELTER OF YOUR ARMS ... Sammy Davis Jr., Reprise 20216
118. NOW ... Lena Horne, 20th Century-Fox 449
119. HEARTACHES ... Kenny Ball, Kapp 554
120. WHAT'CHA GONNA DO ABOUT IT ... Doris Troy, Atlantic 2206
121. FOR YOUR SWEET LOVE ... Cascades, RCA Victor 8268
122. STOP FOOLIN' ... Brook Benton & Damita Jo, Mercury 72207
123. WHERE THERE'S A WILL ... Lonnie Mack, Fraternity 918
124. I CAN'T STOP TALKING ABOUT YOU ... Steve & Eydie, Columbia 42932
125. DO-WAH-DIDDY ... Exciters, United Artists 662
126. BIG BOSS MAN ... Charlie Rich, Groove 0025
127. MOMENT OF TRUTH ... Tony Bennett, Columbia 42931
128. LETTER FROM SHERRY ... Dale Ward, Dot 16520
129. WAITIN' FOR THE EVENING TRAIN ... Anita Kerr Quartet, RCA Victor 8246
130. THE LITTLE BOY ... Tony Bennett, Columbia 42931
131. WHEN YOU WALK IN THE ROOM ... Jackie DeShannon, Liberty 55645
132. CRYSTAL FINGERS ... Ferrante & Teicher, United Artists 660
133. LAST DAY IN THE MINES ... Dave Dudley, Mercury 72212

Compiled from national retail sales and radio station airplay by the Music Popularity Dept. of Record Market Research, Billboard.

# Billboard HOT 100

*For Week Ending December 21, 1963*

★ **STAR** performer—Sides registering greatest proportionate upward progress this week.

| This Week | 1 Wk. Ago | 2 Wk. Ago | 3 Wk. Ago | TITLE Artist, Label & Number | Weeks On Chart |
|---|---|---|---|---|---|
| 1 | 1 | 1 | 2 | DOMINIQUE — Singing Nun, Philips 40152 | 7 |
| 2 | 2 | 4 | 23 | LOUIE LOUIE — Kingsmen, Wand 143 | 7 |
| 3 | 5 | 7 | 19 | YOU DON'T HAVE TO BE A BABY TO CRY — Caravelles, Smash 1852 | 8 |
| 4 | 9 | 22 | 50 | THERE! I'VE SAID IT AGAIN — Bobby Vinton, Epic 9638 | 4 |
| 5 | 6 | 14 | 16 | SINCE I FELL FOR YOU — Lenny Welch, Cadence 1439 | 9 |
| 6 | 7 | 8 | 14 | BE TRUE TO YOUR SCHOOL — Beach Boys, Capitol 5069 | 8 |
| 7 | 8 | 15 | 26 | DRIP DROP — Dion DiMuci, Columbia 42917 | 6 |
| 8 | 4 | 2 | 1 | I'M LEAVING IT UP TO YOU — Dale & Grace, Montel/Michele 921 | 12 |
| 9 | 3 | 3 | 7 | EVERYBODY — Tommy Roe, ABC-Paramount 10478 | 11 |
| 10 | 16 | 32 | 63 | POPSICLES AND ICICLES — Murmaids, Chattahoochee 628 | 5 |
| 11 | 18 | 26 | 31 | TALK BACK TREMBLING LIPS — Johnny Tillotson, MGM 13181 | 7 |
| 12 | 15 | 20 | 21 | LODDY LO — Chubby Checker, Parkway 890 | 8 |
| 13 | 25 | 30 | 49 | FORGET HIM — Bobby Rydell, Cameo 280 | 7 |
| 14 | 14 | 19 | 17 | WONDERFUL SUMMER — Robin Ward, Dot 16530 | 8 |
| 15 | 12 | 5 | 6 | SHE'S A FOOL — Lesley Gore, Mercury 72180 | 13 |
| 16 | 10 | 10 | 11 | WALKING THE DOG — Rufus Thomas, Stax 140 | 12 |
| 17 | 23 | 34 | 45 | QUICKSAND — Martha & the Vandellas, Gordy 7025 | 5 |
| 18 | 20 | 25 | 32 | HAVE YOU HEARD — Duprees, Coed 585 | 7 |
| 19 | 11 | 12 | 12 | LITTLE RED ROOSTER — Sam Cooke, RCA Victor 8247 | 9 |
| 20 | 26 | 31 | 33 | WIVES AND LOVERS — Jack Jones, Kapp 551 | 8 |
| 21 | 35 | 39 | 51 | THE BOY NEXT DOOR — Secrets, Philips 40146 | 6 |
| 22 | 28 | 38 | 53 | THE NITTY GRITTY — Shirley Ellis, Congress 202 | 6 |
| 23 | 33 | 28 | 38 | IN MY ROOM — Beach Boys, Capitol 5069 | 8 |
| 24 | 27 | 36 | 46 | MIDNIGHT MARY — Joey Powers, Amy 892 | 7 |
| 25 | 31 | 42 | 52 | KANSAS CITY — Trini Lopez, Reprise 20236 | 6 |
| 26 | 24 | 27 | 30 | CAN I GET A WITNESS — Marvin Gaye, Tamla 54087 | 10 |
| 27 | 19 | 16 | 5 | IT'S ALL RIGHT — Impressions, ABC-Paramount 10487 | 13 |
| 28 | 13 | 6 | 4 | SUGAR SHACK — Jimmy Gilmer and the Fireballs, Dot 16487 | 14 |
| 29 | 22 | 24 | 24 | LIVING A LIE — Al Martino, Capitol 5060 | 9 |
| 30 | 32 | 35 | 48 | BABY DON'T YOU WEEP — Garnet Mimms and the Enchanters, United Artists 658 | 6 |
| 31 | 54 | 70 | — | DRAG CITY — Jan & Dean, Liberty 55641 | 3 |
| 32 | 17 | 9 | 3 | WASHINGTON SQUARE — Village Stompers, Epic 9617 | 14 |
| 33 | 60 | — | — | PRETTY PAPER — Roy Orbison, Monument 830 | 2 |
| 34 | 39 | 40 | 42 | BAD GIRL — Neil Sedaka, RCA Victor 8254 | 6 |
| 35 | 29 | 13 | 13 | HEY LITTLE GIRL — Major Lance, Okeh 7181 | 10 |
| 36 | 42 | 66 | 78 | FOR YOUR PRECIOUS LOVE — Garnet Mimms & the Enchanters, United Artists 658 | 5 |
| 37 | 34 | 17 | 18 | TWENTY-FOUR HOURS FROM TULSA — Gene Pitney, Musicor 1034 | 10 |
| 38 | 48 | 54 | 65 | TURN AROUND — Dick & Deedee, Warner Bros. 5396 | 5 |
| 39 | 21 | 11 | 8 | DEEP PURPLE — Nino Tempo & April Stevens, Atco 6273 | 15 |
| 40 | 53 | 72 | — | THAT LUCKY OLD SUN — Ray Charles, ABC-Paramount 10509 | 3 |
| 41 | 30 | 21 | 22 | I WONDER WHAT SHE'S DOING TONIGHT — Barry & the Tamerlanes, Valiant 6034 | 10 |
| 42 | 52 | 55 | 72 | STEWBALL — Peter, Paul & Mary, Warner Bros. 5399 | 4 |
| 43 | 45 | 62 | 67 | NEED TO BELONG — Jerry Butler, Vee Jay 567 | 5 |
| 44 | 46 | 52 | 64 | I HAVE A BOYFRIEND — Chiffons, Laurie 3212 | 6 |
| 45 | 51 | 51 | 54 | RAGS TO RICHES — Sunny and the Sunliners, Tear Drop 3022 | 6 |
| 46 | 40 | 45 | 58 | TRA LA LA LA SUZY — Dean & Jean, Rust 5067 | 8 |
| 47 | 50 | 60 | 70 | I GOTTA DANCE TO KEEP FROM CRYING — Miracles, Tamla 54089 | 5 |
| 48 | 75 | — | — | AS USUAL — Brenda Lee, Decca 31570 | 2 |
| 49 | 49 | 53 | 57 | YOU'RE GOOD FOR ME — Solomon Burke, Atlantic 2205 | 8 |
| 50 | 38 | 23 | 15 | MARIA ELENA — Los Indios Tabajaras, RCA Victor 8216 | 14 |
| 51 | 57 | 65 | 73 | LONG TALL TEXAN — Murry Kellum, M.O.C. 653 | 7 |
| 52 | 67 | 82 | — | SOMEWHERE — Tymes, Parkway 891 | 3 |
| 53 | 70 | 97 | — | SURFIN' BIRD — Trashmen, Garrett 4002 | 3 |
| 54 | 36 | 18 | 9 | (Down at) PAPA JOE'S — Dixiebelles, Sound Stage 7 2507 | 13 |
| 55 | 63 | 75 | 85 | WHEN THE LOVELIGHT STARTS SHINING THROUGH HIS EYES — Supremes, Motown 1051 | 4 |
| 56 | 37 | 29 | 10 | BOSSA NOVA BABY — Elvis Presley, RCA Victor 8243 | 10 |
| 57 | 65 | 69 | 80 | GIRLS GROW UP FASTER THAN BOYS — Cookies, Dimension 1020 | 4 |
| 58 | 44 | 50 | 55 | MISERY — Dynamics, Big Top 3161 | 8 |
| 59 | 69 | 85 | — | OUT OF LIMITS — Marketts, Warner Bros. 5391 | 3 |
| 60 | 55 | 59 | 59 | YESTERDAY AND YOU — Bobby Vee, Liberty 55636 | 7 |
| 61 | 59 | 63 | 68 | THE IMPOSSIBLE HAPPENED — Little Peggy March, RCA Victor 8267 | 5 |
| 62 | 71 | 83 | — | HOOKA TOOKA — Chubby Checker, Parkway 890 | 3 |
| 63 | 47 | 56 | 61 | AS LONG AS I KNOW HE'S MINE — Marvelettes, Tamla 54088 | 5 |
| 64 | 64 | 67 | 77 | BE MAD LITTLE GIRL — Bobby Darin, Capitol 5079 | 5 |
| 65 | 73 | 77 | 87 | THE MARVELOUS TOY — Chad Mitchell Trio, Mercury 72197 | 4 |
| 66 | 61 | 61 | 74 | ALLY, ALLY OXEN FREE — Kingston Trio, Capitol 5078 | 5 |
| 67 | 62 | 64 | 69 | DAWN — David Rockingham Trio, Josie 913 | 7 |
| 68 | 76 | 84 | 94 | TODAY'S TEARDROPS — Rick Nelson, Imperial 66004 | 4 |
| 69 | 84 | — | — | HEY LITTLE COBRA — Rip Chords, Columbia 42921 | 2 |
| 70 | 74 | 76 | 84 | BABY I DO LOVE YOU — Galens, Challenge 9212 | 5 |
| 71 | 79 | 86 | 89 | THAT BOY JOHN — Raindrops, Jubilee 5466 | 4 |
| 72 | 90 | — | — | DAISY PETAL PICKIN' — Jimmy Gilmer and the Fireballs, Dot 16539 | 2 |
| 73 | 80 | 87 | — | CHARADE — Henry Mancini & His Ork, RCA Victor 8256 | 3 |
| 74 | 77 | 79 | 82 | GOTTA LOTTA LOVE — Steve Alaimo, Imperial 66003 | 6 |
| 75 | 58 | 68 | 75 | YOU'RE NO GOOD — Betty Everett, Vee Jay 566 | 5 |
| 76 | 85 | 89 | — | IT'S ALL IN THE GAME — Cliff Richard, Epic 9633 | 3 |
| 77 | 96 | 100 | — | ANYONE WHO HAD A HEART — Dionne Warwick, Scepter 1262 | 3 |
| 78 | 78 | 80 | 83 | BEGGING TO YOU — Marty Robbins, Columbia 42890 | 4 |
| 79 | 81 | 81 | 90 | COME DANCE WITH ME — Jay & the Americans, United Artists 669 | 4 |
| 80 | — | — | — | WHISPERING — Nino Tempo & April Stevens, Atco 6281 | 1 |
| 81 | 82 | — | — | WATCH YOUR STEP — Brooks O'Dell, Gold 214 | 2 |
| 82 | 94 | — | — | PLEASE — Frank Ifield, Capitol 5089 | 2 |
| 83 | 83 | — | — | WHAT KIND OF FOOL (Do You Think I Am) — Tams, ABC-Paramount 10502 | 2 |
| 84 | 86 | 90 | — | THANK YOU AND GOODNIGHT — Angels, Smash 8854 | 3 |
| 85 | 88 | — | — | WE BELONG TOGETHER — Jimmy Velvet, ABC-Paramount 10488 | 2 |
| 86 | 91 | 93 | 96 | DUMB HEAD — Ginny Arnell, MGM 13177 | 5 |
| 87 | 87 | 91 | 99 | THE CHEER LEADER — Paul Petersen, Colpix 707 | 4 |
| 88 | — | — | — | I CAN'T STOP TALKING ABOUT YOU — Steve & Eydie, Columbia 42932 | 1 |
| 89 | 89 | — | — | DID YOU HAVE A HAPPY BIRTHDAY — Paul Anka, RCA Victor 8272 | 2 |
| 90 | — | — | — | THE LITTLE BOY — Tony Bennett, Columbia 42931 | 1 |
| 91 | 100 | — | — | COLD, COLD WINTER — Pixies Three, Mercury 72208 | 2 |
| 92 | 97 | — | — | HOOTENANNY SATURDAY NIGHT — Brothers Four, Columbia 42927 | 2 |
| 93 | 98 | — | — | BON-DOO-WAH — Orlons, Cameo 287 | 2 |
| 94 | 95 | — | — | I'LL SEARCH MY HEART — Johnny Mathis, Columbia 42916 | 2 |
| 95 | — | — | — | HARLEM SHUFFLE — Bob & Earl, Marc 104 | 1 |
| 96 | — | — | — | COMIN' IN THE BACK DOOR — Baja Marimba Band, Almo 201 | 1 |
| 97 | 99 | — | — | WHY DO KIDS GROW UP — Randy & the Rainbows, Rust 5073 | 2 |
| 98 | — | 78 | 86 | PAIN IN MY HEART — Otis Redding, Volt 112 | 4 |
| 99 | — | 95 | — | THE SHELTER OF YOUR ARMS — Sammy Davis Jr., Reprise 20216 | 2 |
| 100 | — | — | — | BABY I LOVE YOU — Ronettes, Philles 118 | 1 |

## BUBBLING UNDER THE HOT 100

101. BABY'S GONE — Gene Thomas, United Artists 640
102. HI DIDDLE DIDDLE — Inez Foxx, Symbol 924
103. TRUE LOVE GOES ON AND ON — Burl Ives, Decca 31571
104. IN THE SUMMER OF HIS YEARS — Connie Francis, MGM 13202
105. THE SON OF REBEL ROUSER — Duane Eddy, RCA Victor 8276
106. I CAN'T STOP SINGING — Bobby Bland, Duke 370
107. CROSSFIRE TIME — Dee Clark, Constellation 108
108. JUST A LONELY MAN — Fats Domino, ABC-Paramount 10512
109. SURFER STREET — Allisons, Tip 1011
110. COMING BACK TO YOU — Maxine Brown, Wand 142
111. THE FEELING IS GONE — Bobby Bland, Duke 370
112. I'M DOWN TO MY LAST HEART BREAK — Wilson Pickett, Double L 724
113. SHY GUY — Radiants, Chess 1872
114. I CAN'T GIVE YOU ANYTHING BUT LOVE — Fats Domino, Imperial 66005
115. ROCK CANDY — Jack McDuff, Prestige 271
116. IN THE SUMMER OF HIS YEARS — Mahalia Jackson, Columbia 42946
117. WHERE THERE'S A WILL — Lonnie Mack, Fraternity 918
118. LETTER FROM SHERRY — Dale Ward, Dot 16520
119. DO-WAH-DIDDY — Exciters, United Artists 662
120. BABY FOR SALE — Cascades, RCA Victor 8268
121. RED DON'T GO WITH BLUE — Jimmy Clanton, Philips 40161
122. SWANEE RIVER — Ace Cannon, Hi 2070
123. BABY WHAT'S WRONG — Lonnie Mack, Fraternity 918
124. BIG BOSS MAN — Charlie Rich, Groove 0025
125. THEME FROM "THE CARDINAL" — Jerome Courtland, United Artists
126. WHEN YOU WALK IN THE ROOM — Jackie DeShannon, Liberty 55645
127. (My One and Only) JIMMY BOY — Girlfriends, Colpix 712
128. LAST DAY IN THE MINES — Dave Dudley, Mercury 72212
129. HIT THE ROAD JACK — Jerry Lee Lewis, Smash 1857
130. HEARTLESS HEART — Floyd Cramer, RCA Victor 8265
131. MAMA WAS A COTTON PICKER — Jimmie Rodgers, Dot 16561

# Billboard HOT 100

*For Week Ending December 28, 1963*

★ **STAR** performer—Sides registering greatest proportionate upward progress this week.

| This Week | 1 Wk. Ago | 2 Wks. Ago | 3 Wks. Ago | TITLE, Artist, Label & Number | Weeks On Chart |
|---|---|---|---|---|---|
| 1 | 1 | 1 | 1 | **DOMINIQUE** — Singing Nun, Philips 40163 | 8 |
| 2 | 4 | 9 | 22 | **THERE! I'VE SAID IT AGAIN** — Bobby Vinton, Epic 9638 | 5 |
| 3 | 2 | 2 | 4 | **LOUIE LOUIE** — Kingsmen, Wand 143 | 8 |
| 4 | 5 | 6 | 14 | **SINCE I FELL FOR YOU** — Lenny Welch, Cadence 1439 | 10 |
| 5 | 3 | 5 | 7 | **YOU DON'T HAVE TO BE A BABY TO CRY** — Caravelles, Smash 1852 | 9 |
| 6 | 7 | 8 | 15 | **DRIP DROP** — Dion DiMuci, Columbia 42917 | 7 |
| ★7 | 13 | 25 | 30 | **FORGET HIM** — Bobby Rydell, Cameo 280 | 8 |
| 8 | 10 | 16 | 32 | **POPSICLES AND ICICLES** — Murmaids, Chattahoochee 628 | 6 |
| 9 | 11 | 18 | 26 | **TALK BACK TREMBLING LIPS** — Johnny Tillotson, MGM 13181 | 8 |
| 10 | 6 | 7 | 8 | **BE TRUE TO YOUR SCHOOL** — Beach Boys, Capitol 5069 | 9 |
| 11 | 24 | 27 | 36 | **MIDNIGHT MARY** — Joey Powers, Amy 892 | 8 |
| ★12 | 17 | 23 | 34 | **QUICKSAND** — Martha & the Vandellas, Gordy 7025 | 6 |
| 13 | 22 | 28 | 38 | **THE NITTY GRITTY** — Shirley Ellis, Congress 202 | 7 |
| 14 | 12 | 15 | 20 | **LODDY LO** — Chubby Checker, Parkway 890 | 9 |
| 15 | 20 | 26 | 31 | **WIVES AND LOVERS** — Jack Jones, Kapp 551 | 9 |
| 16 | 8 | 4 | 2 | **I'M LEAVING IT UP TO YOU** — Dale & Grace, Montel/Michele 921 | 13 |
| 17 | 9 | 3 | 3 | **EVERYBODY** — Tommy Roe, ABC-Paramount 10478 | 12 |
| 18 | 21 | 35 | 39 | **THE BOY NEXT DOOR** — Secrets, Philips 40146 | 8 |
| ★19 | 33 | 60 | — | **PRETTY PAPER** — Roy Orbison, Monument 830 | 3 |
| ★20 | 48 | 75 | — | **AS USUAL** — Brenda Lee, Decca 31570 | 3 |
| ★21 | 53 | 70 | 97 | **SURFIN' BIRD** — Trashmen, Garrett 4002 | 4 |
| 22 | 26 | 24 | 27 | **CAN I GET A WITNESS** — Marvin Gaye, Tamla 54087 | 11 |
| 23 | 18 | 20 | 25 | **HAVE YOU HEARD** — Duprees, Coed 585 | 8 |
| ★24 | 31 | 54 | 70 | **DRAG CITY** — Jan & Dean, Liberty 55641 | 4 |
| 25 | 25 | 31 | 42 | **KANSAS CITY** — Trini Lopez, Reprise 20236 | 7 |
| 26 | 14 | 14 | 19 | **WONDERFUL SUMMER** — Robin Ward, Dot 16530 | 9 |
| 27 | 23 | 33 | 28 | **IN MY ROOM** — Beach Boys, Capitol 5069 | 9 |
| 28 | 15 | 12 | 5 | **SHE'S A FOOL** — Lesley Gore, Mercury 72180 | 14 |
| 29 | 16 | 10 | 10 | **WALKING THE DOG** — Rufus Thomas, Stax 140 | 13 |
| 30 | 38 | 48 | 54 | **TURN AROUND** — Dick & Deedee, Warner Bros. 5396 | 6 |
| 31 | 36 | 42 | 66 | **FOR YOUR PRECIOUS LOVE** — Garnet Mimms & the Enchanters, United Artists 658 | 6 |
| 32 | 40 | 53 | 72 | **THAT LUCKY OLD SUN** — Ray Charles, ABC-Paramount 10509 | 4 |
| 33 | 34 | 39 | 40 | **BAD GIRL** — Neil Sedaka, RCA Victor 8254 | 7 |
| 34 | 19 | 11 | 12 | **LITTLE RED ROOSTER** — Sam Cooke, RCA Victor 8247 | 10 |
| 35 | 42 | 52 | 55 | **STEWBALL** — Peter, Paul & Mary, Warner Bros. 5399 | 5 |
| 36 | 30 | 32 | 35 | **BABY DON'T YOU WEEP** — Garnet Mimms and the Enchanters, United Artists 658 | 7 |
| ★37 | 80 | — | — | **WHISPERING** — Nino Tempo & April Stevens, Atco 6281 | 2 |
| 38 | 59 | 69 | 85 | **OUT OF LIMITS** — Marketts, Warner Bros. 5391 | 4 |
| 39 | 43 | 45 | 62 | **NEED TO BELONG** — Jerry Butler, Vee Jay 567 | 6 |
| ★40 | 55 | 63 | 75 | **WHEN THE LOVELIGHT STARTS SHINING THROUGH HIS EYES** — Supremes, Motown 1051 | 5 |
| 41 | 44 | 46 | 52 | **I HAVE A BOYFRIEND** — Chiffons, Laurie 3212 | 7 |
| ★42 | 52 | 67 | 82 | **SOMEWHERE** — Tymes, Parkway 891 | 4 |
| 43 | 29 | 22 | 24 | **LIVING A LIE** — Al Martino, Capitol 5060 | 10 |
| 44 | 37 | 34 | 17 | **TWENTY-FOUR HOURS FROM TULSA** — Gene Pitney, Musicor 1034 | 11 |
| 45 | 47 | 50 | 60 | **I GOTTA DANCE TO KEEP FROM CRYING** — Miracles, Tamla 54089 | 6 |
| ★46 | 69 | 84 | — | **HEY LITTLE COBRA** — Rip Chords, Columbia 42921 | 3 |
| 47 | 28 | 13 | 6 | **SUGAR SHACK** — Jimmy Gilmer and the Fireballs, Dot 16487 | 15 |
| 48 | 27 | 19 | 16 | **IT'S ALL RIGHT** — Impressions, ABC-Paramount 10487 | 14 |
| 49 | 46 | 40 | 45 | **TRA LA LA LA SUZY** — Dean & Jean, Rust 5067 | 9 |
| 50 | 45 | 51 | 51 | **RAGS TO RICHES** — Sunny and the Sunliners, Tear Drop 3022 | 7 |
| 51 | 57 | 65 | 69 | **GIRLS GROW UP FASTER THAN BOYS** — Cookies, Dimension 1020 | 5 |
| ★52 | 72 | 90 | — | **DAISY PETAL PICKIN'** — Jimmy Gilmer & the Fireballs, Dot 16539 | 3 |
| 53 | 51 | 57 | 65 | **LONG TALL TEXAN** — Murry Kellum, M.O.C. 653 | 8 |
| 54 | 58 | 44 | 50 | **MISERY** — Dynamics, Big Top 3161 | 9 |
| 55 | 62 | 71 | 83 | **HOOKA TOOKA** — Chubby Checker, Parkway 890 | 4 |
| 56 | 65 | 73 | 77 | **THE MARVELOUS TOY** — Chad Mitchell Trio, Mercury 72197 | 5 |
| 57 | 61 | 59 | 63 | **THE IMPOSSIBLE HAPPENED** — Little Peggy March, RCA Victor 8267 | 6 |
| 58 | 63 | 47 | 56 | **AS LONG AS I KNOW HE'S MINE** — Marvelettes, Tamla 54088 | 8 |
| 59 | 68 | 76 | 84 | **TODAY'S TEARDROPS** — Rick Nelson, Imperial 66004 | 5 |
| ★60 | 76 | 85 | 89 | **IT'S ALL IN THE GAME** — Cliff Richard, Epic 9633 | 4 |
| ★61 | — | — | — | **FOR YOU** — Rick Nelson, Decca 31574 | 1 |
| 62 | 66 | 61 | 61 | **ALLY, ALLY OXEN FREE** — Kingston Trio, Capitol 5078 | 6 |
| ★63 | 100 | — | — | **BABY I LOVE YOU** — Ronettes, Philles 118 | 2 |
| 64 | 77 | 96 | 100 | **ANYONE WHO HAD A HEART** — Dionne Warwick, Scepter 1262 | 3 |
| 65 | 73 | 80 | 87 | **CHARADE** — Henry Mancini & His Ork, RCA Victor 8256 | 4 |
| 66 | 64 | 64 | 67 | **BE MAD LITTLE GIRL** — Bobby Darin, Capitol 5079 | 6 |
| 67 | 88 | — | — | **I CAN'T STOP TALKING ABOUT YOU** — Steve & Eydie, Columbia 42932 | 2 |
| 68 | 71 | 79 | 86 | **THAT BOY JOHN** — Raindrops, Jubilee 5466 | 5 |
| 69 | 67 | 62 | 64 | **DAWN** — David Rockingham Trio, Josie 913 | 8 |
| 70 | 86 | 91 | 93 | **DUMB HEAD** — Ginny Arnell, MGM 13177 | 6 |
| 71 | 93 | 98 | — | **BON-DOO-WAH** — Orlons, Cameo 287 | 3 |
| ★72 | — | — | — | **YOU DON'T OWN ME** — Lesley Gore, Mercury 72206 | 1 |
| 73 | 96 | — | — | **COMIN' IN THE BACK DOOR** — Baja Marimba Band, Almo 201 | 2 |
| 74 | 78 | 78 | 80 | **BEGGING TO YOU** — Marty Robbins, Columbia 42890 | 5 |
| 75 | 83 | 83 | — | **WHAT KIND OF FOOL (Do You Think I Am)** — Tams, ABC-Paramount 10502 | 3 |
| 76 | 79 | 81 | 81 | **COME DANCE WITH ME** — Jay & the Americans, United Artists 669 | 5 |
| 77 | 81 | 82 | — | **WATCH YOUR STEP** — Brooks O'Dell, Gold 214 | 3 |
| ★78 | — | — | — | **TRUE LOVE GOES ON AND ON** — Burl Ives, Decca 31571 | 1 |
| 79 | — | — | — | **WHAT'S EASY FOR TWO IS SO HARD FOR ONE** — Mary Wells, Motown 1048 | 6 |
| 80 | 82 | 94 | — | **PLEASE** — Frank Ifield, Capitol 5089 | 3 |
| 81 | 90 | — | — | **THE LITTLE BOY** — Tony Bennett, Columbia 42931 | 2 |
| 82 | 85 | 88 | — | **WE BELONG TOGETHER** — Jimmy Velvet, ABC-Paramount 10488 | 3 |
| 83 | — | — | — | **LETTER FROM SHERRY** — Dale Ward, Dot 16520 | 1 |
| 84 | — | — | — | **MY ONE AND ONLY JIMMY BOY** — Girlfriends, Colpix 712 | 1 |
| 85 | — | — | — | **IN THE SUMMER OF HIS YEARS** — Connie Francis, MGM 13202 | 1 |
| 86 | 87 | 87 | 91 | **THE CHEER LEADER** — Paul Petersen, Colpix 707 | 5 |
| 87 | — | — | 88 | **BABY'S GONE** — Gene Thomas, United Artists 640 | |
| 88 | 91 | 100 | — | **COLD, COLD WINTER** — Pixies Three, Mercury 72208 | 3 |
| 89 | 92 | 97 | — | **HOOTENANNY SATURDAY NIGHT** — Brothers Four, Columbia 42927 | |
| 90 | 94 | 95 | — | **I'LL SEARCH MY HEART** — Johnny Mathis, Columbia 42916 | |
| 91 | 99 | — | 95 | **THE SHELTER OF YOUR ARMS** — Sammy Davis Jr., Reprise 20216 | 3 |
| 92 | 89 | 89 | — | **DID YOU HAVE A HAPPY BIRTHDAY** — Paul Anka, RCA Victor 8272 | 3 |
| 93 | — | — | — | **HERE COMES THE BOY** — Tracey Dey, Amy 894 | 1 |
| 94 | 95 | — | — | **HARLEM SHUFFLE** — Bob & Earl, Marc 104 | 2 |
| 95 | — | — | — | **PINK DOMINOES** — Crescents, Era 3116 | |
| 96 | — | — | — | **SNAP YOUR FINGERS** — Barbara Lewis, Atlantic 2214 | |
| 97 | — | — | — | **THE FEELING IS GONE** — Bobby Bland, Duke 379 | 1 |
| 98 | — | — | — | **FOR YOUR SWEET LOVE** — Cascades, RCA Victor 8268 | 1 |
| 99 | — | — | — | **NEVER LOVE A ROBIN** — Bobby Vee, Liberty 55636 | 1 |
| 100 | — | — | — | **WHERE OR WHEN** — Lettermen, Capitol 5091 | 1 |

## BUBBLING UNDER THE HOT 100

101. CROSSFIRE TIME ............ Dee Clark, Constellation 108
102. THE SON OF REBEL ROUSER ... Duane Eddy, RCA Victor 8276
103. WHY DO KIDS GROW UP ....... Randy & the Rainbows, Rust 5073
104. SNEAKY SUE ................ Patty Lace & the Petticoats, Kapp 563
105. DO-WAH-DIDDY .............. Exciters, United Artists 662
106. SINCE I FOUND A NEW LOVE .. Little Johnny Taylor, Galaxy 725
107. IN THE SUMMER OF HIS YEARS Millicent Martin, ABC-Paramount 10514
108. PAIN IN MY HEART .......... Otis Redding, Volt 112
109. THEME FROM "THE CARDINAL" .. Roger Williams, Kapp 560
110. JAVA ...................... Al Hirt, RCA Victor 8280
111. DEEP IN THE HEART OF HARLEM .. Clyde McPhatter, Mercury 72220
112. BIG BOSS MAN .............. Charlie Rich, Groove 0025
113. I CAN'T STOP SINGING ...... Bobby Bland, Duke 370
114. COMING BACK TO YOU ........ Maxine Brown, Wand 142
115. ROCK CANDY ................ Jack McDuff, Prestige 273
116. SLIPIN' AND SLIDIN' ....... Jim & Monica, Betty 1207
117. WHEN YOU WALK IN THE ROOM .. Jackie DeShannon, Liberty 55645
118. RED DON'T GO WITH BLUE .... Jimmy Clanton, Philips 40161
119. PUPPY LOVE ................ Barbara Lewis, Atlantic 2214
120. WERE THERE'S A WILL ....... Leonie Mack, Fraternity 918
121. I CAN'T GIVE ANY ANYTHING BUT LOVE ... Fats Domino, Imperial 66005
122. QUERIDITA MIA ............. Keith Colley, Unical 3011
123. SEE THE FUNNY LITTLE CLOWN Bobby Goldsboro, United Artists 672
124. HEARTLESS HEART ........... Floyd Cramer, RCA Victor 8265
125. LAST DAY IN THE MINES ..... Dave Dudley, Mercury 72213
126. HE WAS A FRIEND OF MINE ... Brierwood Singers, United Artists 641
127. CRYSTAL FINGERS ........... Ferrante & Teicher, United Artists 660
128. NEAR TO YOU ............... Wilbert Harrison, Sea-Horn 502
129. WAITIN' FOR THE EVENING TRAIN ... Anita Kerr Quartet, RCA Victor 8246
130. LITTLE BOXES .............. Pete Seeger, Columbia 42920
131. BLESS 'EM ALL ............. Jane Morgan, Colpix 713
132. JIMMY BOY ................. Carol Shaw, Atco 6278

*Compiled from national retail sales and radio station airplay by the Music Popularity Dept. of Record Market Research, Billboard.*

# Billboard HOT 100

**For Week Ending January 4, 1964**

★ STAR performer—Sides registering greatest proportionate upward progress this week.

| This Week | Wk. Ago | 2 Wks. Ago | 3 Wks. Ago | TITLE — Artist, Label & Number | Weeks On Chart |
|---|---|---|---|---|---|
| 1 | 2 | 4 | 9 | THERE! I'VE SAID IT AGAIN — Bobby Vinton, Epic 9638 | 6 |
| 2 | 3 | 2 | 2 | LOUIE LOUIE — Kingsmen, Wand 143 | 9 |
| 3 | 1 | 1 | 1 | DOMINIQUE — Singing Nun, Philips 40163 | 9 |
| 4 | 4 | 5 | 6 | SINCE I FELL FOR YOU — Lenny Welch, Cadence 1439 | 11 |
| 5 | 7 | 13 | 25 | FORGET HIM — Bobby Rydell, Cameo 280 | 7 |
| 6 | 8 | 10 | 16 | POPSICLES AND ICICLES — Murmaids, Chattahoochee 628 | 7 |
| 7 | 9 | 11 | 18 | TALK BACK TREMBLING LIPS — Johnny Tillotson, MGM 13181 | 9 |
| ★8 | 12 | 17 | 23 | QUICKSAND — Martha & the Vandellas, Gordy 7025 | 7 |
| 9 | 13 | 22 | 28 | THE NITTY GRITTY — Shirley Ellis, Congress 202 | 8 |
| 10 | 11 | 24 | 27 | MIDNIGHT MARY — Joey Powers, Amy 892 | 9 |
| 11 | 5 | 3 | 5 | YOU DON'T HAVE TO BE A BABY TO CRY — Caravelles, Smash 1852 | 10 |
| 12 | 6 | 7 | 8 | DRIP DROP — Dion DiMuci, Columbia 42917 | 8 |
| 13 | 21 | 53 | 70 | SURFIN' BIRD — Trashmen, Garrett 4002 | 5 |
| 14 | 20 | 48 | 75 | AS USUAL — Brenda Lee, Decca 31570 | 4 |
| 15 | 15 | 20 | 26 | WIVES AND LOVERS — Jack Jones, Kapp 551 | 10 |
| 16 | 19 | 33 | 60 | PRETTY PAPER — Roy Orbison, Monument 830 | 4 |
| 17 | 24 | 31 | 54 | DRAG CITY — Jan & Dean, Liberty 55641 | 5 |
| 18 | 10 | 6 | 7 | BE TRUE TO YOUR SCHOOL — Beach Boys, Capitol 5069 | 10 |
| 19 | 37 | 80 | — | WHISPERING — Nino Tempo & April Stevens, Atco 6281 | 3 |
| 20 | 18 | 21 | 35 | THE BOY NEXT DOOR — Secrets, Philips 40146 | 9 |
| 21 | 16 | 8 | 4 | I'M LEAVING IT UP TO YOU — Dale & Grace, Montel/Michele 921 | 14 |
| 22 | 14 | 12 | 15 | LODDY LO — Chubby Checker, Parkway 890 | 10 |
| 23 | 25 | 25 | 31 | KANSAS CITY — Trini Lopez, Reprise 20236 | 8 |
| 24 | 22 | 26 | 24 | CAN I GET A WITNESS — Marvin Gaye, Tamala 54087 | 12 |
| 25 | 17 | 9 | 3 | EVERYBODY — Tommy Roe, ABC-Paramount 10478 | 13 |
| ★26 | 32 | 40 | 53 | THAT LUCKY OLD SUN — Ray Charles, ABC-Paramount 10509 | 5 |
| 27 | 30 | 38 | 48 | TURN AROUND — Dick & Deedee, Warner Bros. 5396 | 7 |
| ★28 | 40 | 55 | 63 | WHEN THE LOVELIGHT STARTS SHINING THROUGH HIS EYES — Supremes, Motown 1051 | 5 |
| 29 | 31 | 36 | 42 | FOR YOUR PRECIOUS LOVE — Garnet Mimms & the Enchanters, United Artists 658 | 7 |
| 30 | 23 | 18 | 20 | HAVE YOU HEARD — Duprees, Coed 585 | 9 |
| 31 | 42 | 52 | 67 | SOMEWHERE — Tymes, Parkway 891 | 5 |
| ★32 | 64 | 77 | 96 | ANYONE WHO HAD A HEART — Dionne Warwick, Scepter 1262 | 5 |
| 33 | 38 | 59 | 69 | OUT OF LIMITS — Marketts, Warner Bros. 5391 | 5 |
| 34 | 39 | 43 | 45 | NEED TO BELONG — Jerry Butler, Vee Jay 567 | 7 |
| ★35 | 46 | 49 | 84 | HEY LITTLE COBRA — Rip Chords, Columbia 42921 | 4 |
| 36 | 41 | 44 | 46 | I HAVE A BOYFRIEND — Chiffons, Laurie 3212 | 8 |
| 37 | 27 | 23 | 33 | IN MY ROOM — Beach Boys, Capitol 5069 | 10 |
| 38 | 35 | 42 | 52 | STEWBALL — Peter, Paul & Mary, Warner Bros. 5399 | 6 |
| 39 | 45 | 47 | 50 | I GOTTA DANCE TO KEEP FROM CRYING — Miracles, Tamla 54089 | 7 |
| ★40 | 52 | 72 | 90 | DAISY PETAL PICKIN' — Jimmy Gilmer & the Fireballs, Dot 16539 | 4 |
| ★41 | 61 | — | — | FOR YOU — Rick Nelson, Decca 31574 | 2 |
| ★42 | 63 | 100 | — | BABY I LOVE YOU — Ronettes, Philles 118 | 3 |
| 43 | 26 | 14 | 14 | WONDERFUL SUMMER — Robin Ward, Dot 16530 | 10 |
| ★44 | 55 | 62 | 71 | HOOKA TOOKA — Chubby Checker, Parkway 890 | 5 |
| 45 | 49 | 46 | 40 | TRA LA LA LA SUZY — Dean & Jean, Rust 5067 | 10 |
| 46 | 36 | 30 | 32 | BABY DON'T YOU WEEP — Garnet Mimms and the Enchanters, United Artists 658 | 8 |
| 47 | 56 | 65 | 73 | THE MARVELOUS TOY — Chad Mitchell Trio, Mercury 72197 | 6 |
| 48 | 51 | 57 | 65 | GIRLS GROW UP FASTER THAN BOYS — Cookies, Dimension 1020 | 6 |
| ★49 | 72 | — | — | YOU DON'T OWN ME — Lesley Gore, Mercury 72206 | 2 |
| 50 | 29 | 16 | 10 | WALKING THE DOG — Rufus Thomas, Stax 140 | 14 |
| 51 | 58 | 63 | 47 | AS LONG AS I KNOW HE'S MINE — Marvelettes, Tamla 54088 | 9 |
| 52 | 33 | 34 | 39 | BAD GIRL — Neil Sedaka, RCA Victor 8254 | 8 |
| 53 | 53 | 51 | 57 | LONG TALL TEXAN — Murry Kellum, M.O.C. 653 | 9 |
| 54 | 28 | 15 | 12 | SHE'S A FOOL — Lesley Gore, Mercury 72180 | 15 |
| 55 | 67 | 88 | — | I CAN'T STOP TALKING ABOUT YOU — Steve & Eydie, Columbia 42932 | 3 |
| 56 | 60 | 75 | 85 | IT'S ALL IN THE GAME — Cliff Richard, Epic 9633 | 4 |
| 57 | 59 | 68 | 76 | TODAY'S TEARDROPS — Rick Nelson, Imperial 66004 | 6 |
| ★58 | — | — | — | UM, UM, UM, UM, UM, UM — Major Lance, Okeh 7187 | 1 |
| 59 | 54 | 58 | 44 | MISERY — Dynamics, Big Top 3161 | 10 |
| 60 | 79 | — | — | WHAT'S EASY FOR TWO IS SO HARD FOR ONE — Mary Wells, Motown 1048 | 7 |
| 61 | 65 | 73 | 80 | CHARADE — Henry Mancini & His Ork, RCA Victor 8256 | 5 |
| 62 | 75 | 83 | 83 | WHAT KIND OF FOOL (Do You Think I Am) — Tams, ABC-Paramount 10502 | 4 |
| 63 | 71 | 93 | 98 | BON-DOO-WAH — Orlons, Cameo 287 | 4 |
| 64 | 68 | 71 | 79 | THAT BOY JOHN — Raindrops, Jubilee 5466 | 6 |
| 65 | 62 | 66 | 61 | ALLY, ALLY OXEN FREE — Kingston Trio, Capitol 5078 | 7 |
| 66 | 77 | 81 | 82 | WATCH YOUR STEP — Brooks O'Dell, Gold 214 | 4 |
| 67 | 73 | 96 | — | COMIN' IN THE BACK DOOR — Baja Marimba Band, Almo 201 | 3 |
| ★68 | 84 | — | — | MY ONE AND ONLY JIMMY BOY — Girlfriends, Colpix 712 | 2 |
| ★69 | 85 | — | — | IN THE SUMMER OF HIS YEARS — Connie Francis, MGM 13202 | 2 |
| 70 | 70 | 86 | 91 | DUMB HEAD — Ginny Arnell, MGM 13177 | 7 |
| 71 | 78 | — | — | TRUE LOVE GOES ON AND ON — Burl Ives, Decca 31571 | 2 |
| 72 | 81 | 90 | — | THE LITTLE BOY — Tony Bennett, Columbia 42931 | 3 |
| 73 | 66 | 64 | 64 | BE MAD LITTLE GIRL — Bobby Darin, Capitol 5079 | 7 |
| 74 | 83 | — | — | LETTER FROM SHERRY — Dale Ward, Dot 16520 | 2 |
| 75 | 80 | 82 | 94 | PLEASE — Frank Ifield, Capitol 5089 | 4 |
| 76 | 76 | 79 | 81 | COME DANCE WITH ME — Jay & the Americans, United Artists 669 | 6 |
| 77 | — | — | — | IF SOMEBODY TOLD YOU — Anna King, Smash 1858 | 1 |
| 78 | 86 | 87 | 87 | THE CHEER LEADER — Paul Petersen, Colpix 707 | 6 |
| 79 | 88 | 91 | 100 | COLD, COLD WINTER — Pixies Three, Mercury 72208 | 4 |
| 80 | 82 | 85 | 88 | WE BELONG TOGETHER — Jimmy Velvet, ABC-Paramount 10488 | 4 |
| 81 | 96 | — | — | SNAP YOUR FINGERS — Barbara Lewis, Atlantic 2214 | 2 |
| ★82 | — | — | — | YOU'LL NEVER WALK ALONE — Patti LaBelle & the Blue Belles, Nicetown 5020 | 1 |
| 83 | 94 | 95 | — | HARLEM SHUFFLE — Bob & Earl, Marc 104 | 3 |
| 84 | 87 | — | — | BABY'S GONE — Gene Thomas, United Artists 640 | 4 |
| 85 | — | — | — | SINCE I FOUND A NEW LOVE — Little Johnny Taylor, Galaxy 725 | 1 |
| 86 | 98 | — | — | FOR YOUR SWEET LOVE — Cascades, RCA Victor 8268 | 2 |
| 87 | — | — | — | WHO CARES — Fats Domino, ABC-Paramount 10512 | 1 |
| 88 | 91 | 99 | — | THE SHELTER OF YOUR ARMS — Sammy Davis Jr., Reprise 20216 | 4 |
| 89 | — | 75 | 58 | YOU'RE NO GOOD — Betty Everett, Vee Jay 566 | 6 |
| 90 | — | — | — | DO-WAH-DIDDY — Exciters, United Artists 662 | 1 |
| 91 | 95 | — | — | PINK DOMINOES — Crescents, Era 3116 | 2 |
| 92 | 97 | — | — | THE FEELING IS GONE — Bobby Bland, Duke 379 | 2 |
| 93 | — | — | — | HIS KISS — Betty Harris, Jubilee 5465 | 1 |
| 94 | — | 98 | — | PAIN IN MY HEART — Otis Redding, Volt 112 | 5 |
| 95 | — | — | — | DEEP IN THE HEART OF HARLEM — Clyde McPhatter, Mercury 72220 | 1 |
| 96 | — | — | — | JAVA — Al Hirt, RCA Victor 8280 | 1 |
| 97 | 90 | 94 | 95 | I'LL SEARCH MY HEART — Johnny Mathis, Columbia 42916 | 4 |
| 98 | 100 | — | — | WHERE OR WHEN — Lettermen, Capitol 5091 | 2 |
| 99 | — | — | — | COMING BACK TO YOU — Maxine Brown, Wand 142 | 1 |
| 100 | — | — | — | THE SON OF REBEL-ROUSER — Duane Eddy, RCA Victor 8276 | 1 |

## BUBBLING UNDER THE HOT 100

101. HERE COMES THE BOY — Tracey Dey, Amy 894
102. A FOOL NEVER LEARNS — Andy Williams, Columbia 42950
103. I WISH YOU LOVE — Gloria Lynne, Everest 2036
104. BEGGING TO YOU — Marty Robbins, Columbia 42890
105. NEVER LOVE A ROBIN — Bobby Vee, Liberty 55636
106. IN THE SUMMER OF HIS YEARS — Millicent Martin, ABC-Paramount 10514
107. MY HOME TOWN — Steve Lawrence, Columbia 42952
108. BIG BOSS MAN — Charlie Rich, Groove 0025
109. TRIBUTE — Anthony Newley, Acapela 778
110. SLIPIN' AND SLIDIN' — Jim & Monica, Betty 1207
111. WHY DO KIDS GROW UP — Randy & the Rainbows, Rust 5073
112. I CAN'T STOP SINGING — Bobby Bland, Duke 370
113. ROCK CANDY — Jack McDuff, Prestige 273
114. HOOTENANNY SATURDAY NIGHT — Brothers Four, Columbia 42927
115. CHARADE — Andy Williams, Columbia 42950
116. WHERE THERE'S A WILL — Lonnie Mack, Fraternity 918
117. TONIGHT YOU'RE GONNA FALL IN LOVE WITH ME — Shirelles, Scepter 1264
118. SAGINAW, MICHIGAN — Lefty Frizzell, Columbia 42924
119. BILLIE BABY — Roger Williams, Kapp 560
120. THEME FROM "THE CARDINAL" — Al Caiola, United Artists
121. SEE THE FUNNY LITTLE CLOWN — Bobby Goldsboro, United Artists 672
122. NEAR TO YOU — Wilbert Harrison, Sea-Horn 502
123. LOVE LOVES ME — Johnny Crawford, Del-Fi 4231
124. PUPPY LOVE — Barbara Lewis, Atlantic 2214
125. WAITIN' FOR THE EVENING TRAIN — Anita Kerr Quartet, RCA Victor 8246
126. LITTLE BOXES — Pete Seeger, Columbia 42940
127. SOUL DANCE — Tommy Leonetti, RCA Victor 8251
128. RED DON'T GO WITH BLUE — Jimmy Clanton, Philips 40161
129. GONNA SEND YOU BACK TO GEORGIA (A CITY SLICK) — Timmy Shaw, Wand 146
130. CHICKEN POT PIE — Ken Jones, Almont 305
131. DON'T CROSS OVER (TO MY SIDE OF THE STREET) — Linda Brannon, Epic 9640
132. WHEN YOU WALK IN THE ROOM — Jackie DeShannon, Liberty 55645

Compiled from national retail sales and radio station airplay by the Music Popularity Dept. of Record Market Research, Billboard.

# Billboard HOT 100

**For Week Ending January 11, 1964**

★ STAR performer—Sides registering greatest proportionate upward progress this week.

| This Week | 1 Wk. Ago | 2 Wks. Ago | TITLE, Artist, Label & Number | Weeks On Chart |
|---|---|---|---|---|
| 1 | 1 | 2 | 4 | THERE! I'VE SAID IT AGAIN — Bobby Vinton, Epic 9638 | 7 |
| 2 | 2 | 3 | 2 | LOUIE LOUIE — Kingsmen, Wand 143 | 10 |
| ★3 | 6 | 8 | 10 | POPSICLES AND ICICLES — Murmaids, Chattahoochee 628 | 8 |
| 4 | 3 | 1 | 1 | DOMINIQUE — Singing Nun, Philips 40152 | 10 |
| 5 | 5 | 7 | 13 | FORGET HIM — Bobby Rydell, Cameo 280 | 10 |
| 6 | 4 | 4 | 5 | SINCE I FELL FOR YOU — Lenny Welch, Cadence 1439 | 12 |
| ★7 | 13 | 21 | 53 | SURFIN' BIRD — Trashmen, Garrett 4002 | 6 |
| 8 | 9 | 13 | 22 | THE NITTY GRITTY — Shirley Ellis, Congress 202 | 9 |
| 9 | 7 | 9 | 11 | TALK BACK TREMBLING LIPS — Johnny Tillotson, MGM 13181 | 10 |
| 10 | 10 | 11 | 24 | MIDNIGHT MARY — Joey Powers, Amy 892 | 10 |
| 11 | 8 | 12 | 17 | QUICKSAND — Martha & the Vandellas, Gordy 7025 | 8 |
| 12 | 14 | 20 | 48 | AS USUAL — Brenda Lee, Decca 31570 | 5 |
| 13 | 17 | 24 | 31 | DRAG CITY — Jan & Dean, Liberty 55641 | 6 |
| 14 | 15 | 15 | 20 | WIVES AND LOVERS — Jack Jones, Kapp 551 | 11 |
| 15 | 16 | 19 | 33 | PRETTY PAPER — Roy Orbison, Monument 830 | 5 |
| 16 | 19 | 37 | 80 | WHISPERING — Nino Tempo & April Stevens, Atco 6281 | 4 |
| 17 | 11 | 5 | 3 | YOU DON'T HAVE TO BE A BABY TO CRY — Caravelles, Smash 1852 | 11 |
| 18 | 12 | 6 | 7 | DRIP DROP — Dion DiMuci, Columbia 42917 | 8 |
| 19 | 35 | 35 | 46 | HEY LITTLE COBRA — Rip Chords, Columbia 42921 | 5 |
| 20 | 33 | 38 | 59 | OUT OF LIMITS — Marketts, Warner Bros. 5391 | 6 |
| ★21 | 26 | 32 | 40 | THAT LUCKY OLD SUN — Ray Charles, ABC-Paramount 10509 | 6 |
| 22 | 32 | 64 | 77 | ANYONE WHO HAD A HEART — Dionne Warwick, Scepter 1262 | 6 |
| 23 | 28 | 40 | 55 | WHEN THE LOVELIGHT STARTS SHINING THROUGH HIS EYES — Supremes, Motown 1051 | 7 |
| 24 | 24 | 22 | 26 | CAN I GET A WITNESS — Marvin Gaye, Tamala 54087 | 13 |
| 25 | 31 | 42 | 52 | SOMEWHERE — Tymes, Parkway 891 | 6 |
| 26 | 29 | 31 | 36 | FOR YOUR PRECIOUS LOVE — Garnet Mimms & the Enchanters, United Artists 658 | 8 |
| ★27 | 41 | 61 | — | FOR YOU — Rick Nelson, Decca 31574 | 3 |
| 28 | 22 | 14 | 12 | LODDY LO — Chubby Checker, Parkway 890 | 11 |
| 29 | 23 | 25 | 25 | KANSAS CITY — Trini Lopez, Reprise 20236 | 9 |
| ★30 | 40 | 52 | 72 | DAISY PETAL PICKIN' — Jimmy Gilmer & the Fireballs, Dot 16539 | 5 |
| 31 | 58 | — | — | UM, UM, UM, UM, UM, UM — Major Lance, Okeh 7187 | 2 |
| 32 | 42 | 63 | 100 | BABY I LOVE YOU — Ronettes, Philles 118 | 4 |
| 33 | 44 | 55 | 62 | HOOKA TOOKA — Chubby Checker, Parkway 890 | 6 |
| 34 | 34 | 39 | 43 | NEED TO BELONG — Jerry Butler, Vee Jay 567 | 8 |
| 35 | 39 | 45 | 47 | I GOTTA DANCE TO KEEP FROM CRYING — Miracles, Tamla 54089 | 7 |
| 36 | 27 | 30 | 38 | TURN AROUND — Dick & Deedee, Warner Bros. 5396 | 8 |
| ★37 | 49 | 72 | — | YOU DON'T OWN ME — Lesley Gore, Mercury 72206 | 3 |
| 38 | 18 | 10 | 6 | BE TRUE TO YOUR SCHOOL — Beach Boys, Capitol 5069 | 11 |
| 39 | 21 | 16 | 8 | I'M LEAVING IT UP TO YOU — Dale & Grace, Montel/Michele 921 | 15 |
| 40 | 20 | 18 | 21 | THE BOY NEXT DOOR — Secrets, Philips 40146 | 10 |
| 41 | 25 | 17 | 9 | EVERYBODY — Tommy Roe, ABC-Paramount 10478 | 14 |
| 42 | 45 | 49 | 46 | TRA LA LA LA SUZY — Dean & Jean, Rust 5067 | 11 |
| 43 | 48 | 51 | 57 | GIRLS GROW UP FASTER THAN BOYS — Cookies, Dimension 1020 | 7 |
| 44 | 37 | 27 | 23 | IN MY ROOM — Beach Boys, Capitol 5069 | 11 |
| 45 | 36 | 41 | 44 | I HAVE A BOYFRIEND — Chiffons, Laurie 3212 | 9 |
| 46 | 47 | 56 | 65 | THE MARVELOUS TOY — Chad Mitchell Trio, Mercury 72197 | 7 |
| 47 | 56 | 60 | 75 | IT'S ALL IN THE GAME — Cliff Richard, Epic 9633 | 6 |
| 48 | 38 | 35 | 42 | STEWBALL — Peter, Paul & Mary, Warner Bros. 5399 | 7 |
| 49 | 30 | 23 | 18 | HAVE YOU HEARD — Duprees, Coed 585 | 10 |
| 50 | 46 | 36 | 30 | BABY DON'T YOU WEEP — Garnet Mimms and the Enchanters, United Artists 658 | 9 |
| ★51 | 62 | 75 | 83 | WHAT KIND OF FOOL (Do You Think I Am) — Tams, ABC-Paramount 10502 | 5 |
| 52 | 55 | 67 | 88 | I CAN'T STOP TALKING ABOUT YOU — Steve & Eydie, Columbia 42932 | 4 |
| 53 | 61 | 65 | 73 | CHARADE — Henry Mancini & His Ork, RCA Victor 8256 | 6 |
| 54 | 60 | 79 | — | WHAT'S EASY FOR TWO IS SO HARD FOR ONE — Mary Wells, Motown 1048 | 8 |
| 55 | 63 | 71 | 93 | BON-DOO-WAH — Orlons, Cameo 287 | 5 |
| ★56 | 69 | 85 | — | IN THE SUMMER OF HIS YEARS — Connie Francis, MGM 13203 | 3 |
| 57 | 51 | 58 | 63 | AS LONG AS I KNOW HE'S MINE — Marvelettes, Tamla 54088 | 10 |
| 58 | 53 | 53 | 51 | LONG TALL TEXAN — Murry Kellum, M.O.C. 653 | 10 |
| 59 | 67 | 73 | 96 | COMIN' IN THE BACK DOOR — Baja Marimba Band, Almo 201 | 4 |
| 60 | 57 | 59 | 68 | TODAY'S TEARDROPS — Rick Nelson, Imperial 66004 | 7 |
| 61 | 68 | 84 | — | MY ONE AND ONLY JIMMY BOY — Girlfriends, Colpix 712 | 3 |
| 62 | 72 | 81 | 90 | THE LITTLE BOY — Tony Bennett, Columbia 42931 | 4 |
| 63 | 66 | 77 | 81 | WATCH YOUR STEP — Brooks O'Dell, Gold 214 | 5 |
| 64 | 64 | 68 | 71 | THAT BOY JOHN — Raindrops, Jubilee 5466 | 7 |
| 65 | — | — | — | A FOOL NEVER LEARNS — Andy Williams, Columbia 42950 | 1 |
| 66 | 71 | 78 | — | TRUE LOVE GOES ON AND ON — Burl Ives, Decca 31571 | 3 |
| 67 | 74 | 83 | — | LETTER FROM SHERRY — Dale Ward, Dot 16520 | 3 |
| 68 | 70 | 70 | 86 | DUMB HEAD — Ginny Arnell, MGM 13177 | 8 |
| 69 | 77 | — | — | IF SOMEBODY TOLD YOU — Anna King, Smash 1858 | 2 |
| 70 | 83 | 94 | 95 | HARLEM SHUFFLE — Bob & Earl, Marc 104 | 4 |
| 71 | 75 | 80 | 82 | PLEASE — Frank Ifield, Capitol 5089 | 5 |
| 72 | 82 | — | — | YOU'LL NEVER WALK ALONE — Patti LaBelle & Her Blue Belles, Parkway 896 | 2 |
| 73 | 81 | 96 | — | SNAP YOUR FINGERS — Barbara Lewis, Atlantic 2214 | 3 |
| 74 | 87 | — | — | WHO CARES — Fats Domino, ABC-Paramount 10512 | 2 |
| 75 | 88 | 91 | 99 | THE SHELTER OF YOUR ARMS — Sammy Davis Jr., Reprise 20216 | 5 |
| 76 | 80 | 82 | 85 | WE BELONG TOGETHER — Jimmy Velvet, ABC-Paramount 10488 | 5 |
| 77 | — | — | — | TONIGHT YOU'RE GONNA FALL IN LOVE WITH ME — Shirelles, Scepter 1264 | 1 |
| ★78 | 96 | — | — | JAVA — Al Hirt, RCA Victor 8280 | 2 |
| 79 | — | — | — | I WISH YOU LOVE — Gloria Lynn, Everest 2036 | 1 |
| 80 | 76 | 76 | 79 | COME DANCE WITH ME — Jay & the Americans, United Artists 669 | 7 |
| 81 | 89 | — | 75 | YOU'RE NO GOOD — Betty Everett, Vee Jay 566 | 7 |
| 82 | 85 | — | — | SINCE I FOUND A NEW LOVE — Little Johnny Taylor, Galaxy 725 | 2 |
| 83 | — | — | — | SEE THE FUNNY LITTLE CLOWN — Bobby Goldsboro, United Artists 672 | 1 |
| 84 | — | — | — | PUPPY LOVE — Barbara Lewis, Atlantic 2214 | 1 |
| 85 | 78 | 86 | 87 | THE CHEER LEADER — Paul Petersen, Colpix 707 | 7 |
| 86 | 86 | 98 | — | FOR YOUR SWEET LOVE — Cascades, RCA Victor 8268 | 3 |
| 87 | — | — | — | BILLIE BABY — Lloyd Price, Double L 729 | 1 |
| 88 | 91 | 95 | — | PINK DOMINOES — Crescents, Era 3116 | 3 |
| 89 | 90 | — | — | DO-WAH-DIDDY — Exciters, United Artists 662 | 2 |
| 90 | 94 | — | 98 | PAIN IN MY HEART — Otis Redding, Volt 112 | 6 |
| 91 | 92 | 97 | — | THE FEELING IS GONE — Bobby Bland, Duke 379 | 3 |
| 92 | 93 | — | — | HIS KISS — Betty Harris, Jubilee 5465 | 2 |
| 93 | 95 | — | — | DEEP IN THE HEART OF HARLEM — Clyde McPhatter, Mercury 72220 | 2 |
| 94 | 84 | 87 | — | BABY'S GONE — Gene Thomas, United Artists 640 | 5 |
| 95 | — | — | — | LITTLE BOXES — Pete Seeger, Columbia 42940 | 1 |
| 96 | — | — | — | JUDY LOVES ME — Johnny Crawford, Del-Fi 4231 | 1 |
| 97 | — | 100 | — | THE SON OF REBEL-ROUSER — Duane Eddy, RCA Victor 8276 | 2 |
| 98 | 79 | 88 | 91 | COLD, COLD WINTER — Pixies Three, Mercury 72208 | 4 |
| 99 | 99 | — | — | COMING BACK TO YOU — Maxine Brown, Wand 142 | 2 |
| 100 | — | — | — | WHO DO YOU LOVE — Sapphires, Swan 4162 | 1 |

## BUBBLING UNDER THE HOT 100

101. HERE COMES THE BOY ... Tracey Dey, Amy 894
102. BEGGING TO YOU ... Marty Robbins, Columbia 42890
103. SINNER NOT A SAINT ... Trini Lopez, United Modern 106
104. IN THE SUMMER OF HIS YEARS ... Millicent Martin, ABC-Paramount 10514
105. TRIBUTE ... Anthony Newley, Acapella 778
106. MY HOME TOWN ... Steve Lawrence, Columbia 42942
107. NEVER LOVE A ROBIN ... Bobby Vee, Liberty 55636
108. SLIPIN' AND SLIDIN' ... Jim & Monica, Betty 1207
109. CHARADE ... Andy Williams, Columbia 42950
110. PROMISES ... Ray Peterson, Dunes 2030
111. SOUL DANCE ... Tommy Leonetti, RCA Victor 8251
112. BIG BOSS MAN ... Charlie Rich, Groove 0025
113. WHERE THERE'S A WILL ... Lonnie Mack, Fraternity 918
114. I CAN'T STOP SINGING ... Bobby Bland, Duke 370
115. BIG TOWN BOY ... Shirley Matthews, Atlantic 2210
116. WHY DO KIDS GROW UP ... Randy & the Rainbows, Rust 5073
117. RED DON'T GO WITH BLUE ... Jimmy Clanton, Philips 40161
118. SAGINAW, MICHIGAN ... Lefty Frizzell, Columbia 42924
119. ROCK CANDY ... Jack McDuff, Prestige 273
120. HOOTENANNY SATURDAY NIGHT ... Brothers Four, Columbia 42927
121. WHEN YOU WALK IN THE ROOM ... Jackie DeShannon, Liberty 55645
122. I ONLY WANT TO BE WITH YOU ... Dusty Springfield, Philips 40162
123. GONNA SEND YOU BACK TO GEORGIA (A City Slick) ... Timmy Shaw, Wand 146
124. DON'T CROSS OVER ... Linda Brannon, Epic 9640
125. CHICKEN POT PIE ... Ken Jones, Almont 305
126. JUST A LONELY MAN ... Fats Domino, ABC-Paramount 10512

Compiled from national retail sales and radio station airplay by the Music Popularity Dept. of Record Market Research, Billboard.

# Billboard HOT 100

**For Week Ending January 18, 1964**

★ STAR performer—Sides registering greatest proportionate upward progress this week.

| This Week | 1 Wk. Ago | 2 Wks. Ago | 3 Wks. Ago | TITLE, Artist, Label & Number | Weeks On Chart |
|---|---|---|---|---|---|
| 1 | 1 | 1 | 2 | THERE! I'VE SAID IT AGAIN — Bobby Vinton, Epic 9638 | 8 |
| 2 | 2 | 2 | 3 | LOUIE LOUIE — Kingsmen, Wand 143 | 11 |
| 3 | 3 | 6 | 8 | POPSICLES AND ICICLES — Murmaids, Chattahoochee 628 | 9 |
| 4 | 5 | 5 | 7 | FORGET HIM — Bobby Rydell, Cameo 280 | 11 |
| 5 | 7 | 13 | 21 | SURFIN' BIRD — Trashmen, Garrett 4002 | 7 |
| 6 | 4 | 3 | 1 | DOMINIQUE — Singing Nun, Philips 40163 | 11 |
| ★7 | 19 | 19 | 35 | HEY LITTLE COBRA — Rip Chords, Columbia 42921 | 6 |
| 8 | 8 | 9 | 13 | THE NITTY GRITTY — Shirley Ellis, Congress 202 | 10 |
| ★9 | 20 | 33 | 38 | OUT OF LIMITS — Marketts, Warner Bros. 5391 | 7 |
| 10 | 13 | 17 | 24 | DRAG CITY — Jan & Dean, Liberty 55641 | 7 |
| 11 | 16 | 19 | 37 | WHISPERING — Nino Tempo & April Stevens, Atco 6281 | 5 |
| 12 | 12 | 14 | 20 | AS USUAL — Brenda Lee, Decca 31570 | 6 |
| 13 | 6 | 4 | 4 | SINCE I FELL FOR YOU — Lenny Welch, Cadence 1439 | 13 |
| ★14 | 31 | 58 | — | UM, UM, UM, UM, UM, UM — Major Lance, Okeh 7187 | 3 |
| 15 | 10 | 10 | 11 | MIDNIGHT MARY — Joey Powers, Amy 892 | 11 |
| 16 | 9 | 7 | 9 | TALK BACK TREMBLING LIPS — Johnny Tillotson, MGM 13181 | 11 |
| ★17 | 22 | 32 | 64 | ANYONE WHO HAD A HEART — Dionne Warwick, Scepter 1262 | 7 |
| 18 | 37 | 49 | 72 | YOU DON'T OWN ME — Lesley Gore, Mercury 72206 | 4 |
| 19 | 27 | 41 | 61 | FOR YOU — Rick Nelson, Decca 31574 | 4 |
| 20 | 21 | 26 | 32 | THAT LUCKY OLD SUN — Ray Charles, ABC-Paramount 10509 | 7 |
| 21 | 11 | 8 | 12 | QUICKSAND — Martha & the Vandellas, Gordy 7025 | 9 |
| 22 | 14 | 15 | 15 | WIVES AND LOVERS — Jack Jones, Kapp 551 | 12 |
| ★23 | 30 | 40 | 52 | DAISY PETAL PICKIN' — Jimmy Gilmer & the Fireballs, Dot 16539 | 6 |
| 24 | 25 | 31 | 42 | SOMEWHERE — Tymes, Parkway 891 | 7 |
| 25 | 23 | 28 | 40 | WHEN THE LOVELIGHT STARTS SHINING THROUGH HIS EYES — Supremes, Motown 1051 | 8 |
| 26 | 15 | 16 | 19 | PRETTY PAPER — Roy Orbison, Monument 830 | 6 |
| 27 | 17 | 11 | 5 | YOU DON'T HAVE TO BE A BABY TO CRY — Caravelles, Smash 1852 | 12 |
| 28 | 32 | 42 | 63 | BABY I LOVE YOU — Ronettes, Philles 118 | 5 |
| 29 | 18 | 12 | 2 | DRIP DROP — Dion DiMuci, Columbia 42917 | 10 |
| 30 | 33 | 44 | 55 | HOOKA TOOKA — Chubby Checker, Parkway 890 | 7 |
| 31 | 34 | 34 | 39 | NEED TO BELONG — Jerry Butler, Vee Jay 567 | 9 |
| 32 | 24 | 24 | 22 | CAN I GET A WITNESS — Marvin Gaye, Tamala 54087 | 14 |
| 33 | 29 | 23 | 25 | KANSAS CITY — Trini Lopez, Reprise 20236 | 10 |
| 34 | 43 | 48 | 51 | GIRLS GROW UP FASTER THAN BOYS — Cookies, Dimension 1020 | 8 |
| 35 | 42 | 45 | 49 | TRA LA LA LA SUZY — Dean & Jean, Rust 5067 | 12 |
| 36 | 28 | 22 | 14 | LODDY LO — Chubby Checker, Parkway 890 | 12 |
| 37 | 26 | 29 | 31 | FOR YOUR PRECIOUS LOVE — Garnet Mimms & the Enchanters, United Artists 658 | 9 |
| 38 | 35 | 39 | 45 | I GOTTA DANCE TO KEEP FROM CRYING — Miracles, Tamla 54089 | 9 |
| ★39 | 51 | 62 | 75 | WHAT KIND OF FOOL (Do You Think I Am) — Tams, ABC-Paramount 10502 | 6 |
| 40 | 47 | 56 | 60 | IT'S ALL IN THE GAME — Cliff Richard, Epic 9633 | 7 |
| 41 | 36 | 27 | 30 | TURN AROUND — Dick & Deedee, Warner Bros. 5396 | 9 |
| ★42 | 53 | 61 | 65 | CHARADE — Henry Mancini & His Ork, RCA Victor 8256 | 7 |
| 43 | 46 | 47 | 56 | THE MARVELOUS TOY — Chad Mitchell Trio, Mercury 72197 | 8 |
| 44 | 52 | 55 | 67 | I CAN'T STOP TALKING ABOUT YOU — Steve & Eydie, Columbia 42932 | 5 |
| ★45 | — | — | — | I WANT TO HOLD YOUR HAND — Beatles, Capitol 5112 | 1 |
| 46 | 38 | 18 | 10 | BE TRUE TO YOUR SCHOOL — Beach Boys, Capitol 5069 | 12 |
| 47 | 54 | 60 | 79 | WHAT'S EASY FOR TWO IS SO HARD FOR ONE — Mary Wells, Motown 1048 | 9 |
| ★48 | 65 | — | — | A FOOL NEVER LEARNS — Andy Williams, Columbia 42674 | 2 |
| 49 | 56 | 69 | 85 | IN THE SUMMER OF HIS YEARS — Connie Francis, MGM 13202 | 4 |
| 50 | — | — | — | TALKING ABOUT MY BABY — Impressions, ABC-Paramount 10511 | 1 |
| 51 | 67 | 74 | 83 | LETTER FROM SHERRY — Dale Ward, Dot 16520 | 4 |
| 52 | 45 | 36 | 41 | I HAVE A BOYFRIEND — Chiffons, Laurie 3212 | 10 |
| ★53 | 78 | 96 | — | JAVA — Al Hirt, RCA Victor 8280 | 3 |
| 54 | 60 | 57 | 59 | TODAY'S TEARDROPS — Rick Nelson, Imperial 66004 | 8 |
| 55 | 59 | 67 | 73 | COMIN' IN THE BACK DOOR — Baja Marimba Band, Almo 201 | 5 |
| 56 | 61 | 68 | 84 | MY ONE AND ONLY JIMMY BOY — Girlfriends, Colpix 712 | 4 |
| 57 | 55 | 63 | 71 | BON-DOO-WAH — Orlons, Cameo 287 | 6 |
| 58 | 62 | 72 | 81 | THE LITTLE BOY — Tony Bennett, Columbia 42931 | 5 |
| 59 | 68 | 70 | 70 | DUMB HEAD — Ginny Arnell, MGM 13177 | 9 |
| ★60 | 81 | 89 | — | YOU'RE NO GOOD — Betty Everett, Vee Jay 566 | 3 |
| 61 | 63 | 66 | 77 | WATCH YOUR STEP — Brooks O'Dell, Gold 214 | 6 |
| 62 | 58 | 53 | 53 | LONG TALL TEXAN — Murry Kellum, M.O.C. 653 | 11 |
| 63 | 70 | 83 | 94 | HARLEM SHUFFLE — Bob & Earl, Marc 104 | 5 |
| 64 | 57 | 51 | 58 | AS LONG AS I KNOW HE'S MINE — Marvelettes, Tamla 54088 | 11 |
| 65 | 75 | 88 | 91 | THE SHELTER OF YOUR ARMS — Sammy Davis Jr., Reprise 20216 | 4 |
| 66 | 72 | 82 | — | YOU'LL NEVER WALK ALONE — Patti LaBelle & Her Blue Belles, Parkway 896 | 3 |
| 67 | 69 | 77 | — | IF SOMEBODY TOLD YOU — Anna King, Smash 1858 | 3 |
| 68 | 64 | 64 | 68 | THAT BOY JOHN — Raindrops, Jubilee 5466 | 8 |
| 69 | 66 | 71 | 78 | TRUE LOVE GOES ON AND ON — Burl Ives, Decca 31571 | 4 |
| ★70 | 90 | 94 | — | PAIN IN MY HEART — Otis Redding, Volt 112 | 7 |
| 71 | 73 | 81 | 96 | SNAP YOUR FINGERS — Barbara Lewis, Atlantic 2214 | 4 |
| 72 | 74 | 87 | — | WHO CARES — Fats Domino, ABC-Paramount 10512 | 3 |
| 73 | 79 | — | — | I WISH YOU LOVE — Gloria Lynn, Everest 2036 | 2 |
| 74 | 77 | — | — | TONIGHT YOU'RE GONNA FALL IN LOVE WITH ME — Shirelles, Scepter 1264 | 2 |
| 75 | 76 | 80 | 82 | WE BELONG TOGETHER — Jimmy Velvet, ABC-Paramount 10488 | 6 |
| 76 | 71 | 75 | 80 | PLEASE — Frank Ifield, Capitol 5089 | 6 |
| 77 | 88 | 91 | 95 | PINK DOMINOES — Crescents, Era 3116 | 4 |
| 78 | 82 | 85 | — | SINCE I FOUND A NEW LOVE — Little Johnny Taylor, Galaxy 725 | 3 |
| 79 | 89 | 90 | — | DO-WAH-DIDDY — Exciters, United Artists 662 | 3 |
| 80 | 83 | — | — | SEE THE FUNNY LITTLE CLOWN — Bobby Goldsboro, United Artists 672 | 2 |
| 81 | 84 | — | — | PUPPY LOVE — Barbara Lewis, Atlantic 2214 | 2 |
| ★82 | — | — | — | COME ON — Tommy Roe, ABC-Paramount 10515 | 1 |
| 83 | 80 | 76 | 76 | COME DANCE WITH ME — Jay & the Americans, United Artists 669 | 8 |
| 84 | — | — | — | SOUTHTOWN, U.S.A. — Dixiebelles, Sound Stage 7 2517 | 1 |
| 85 | 87 | — | — | BILLIE BABY — Lloyd Price, Double L 729 | 2 |
| 86 | 95 | — | — | LITTLE BOXES — Pete Seeger, Columbia 42940 | 2 |
| 87 | — | — | — | THAT GIRL BELONGS TO YESTERDAY — Gene Pitney, Musicor 1036 | 1 |
| ★88 | — | — | — | STAY WITH ME — Frank Sinatra, Reprise 0249 | 1 |
| 89 | — | — | — | WOW WOW WEE — Angels, Smash 1870 | 1 |
| 90 | 93 | 95 | — | DEEP IN THE HEART OF HARLEM — Clyde McPhatter, Mercury 72220 | 3 |
| 91 | 92 | 93 | — | HIS KISS — Betty Harris, Jubilee 5465 | 3 |
| 92 | — | — | — | SAGINAW, MICHIGAN — Lefty Frizzell, Columbia 42924 | 1 |
| 93 | — | — | — | I'LL REMEMBER (In the Still of the Night) — Santo & Johnny, Canadian-American 164 | 1 |
| 94 | — | — | — | SO FAR AWAY — Hank Jacobs, Sue 795 | 1 |
| 95 | 96 | — | — | JUDY LOVES ME — Johnny Crawford, Del-Fi 4231 | 2 |
| 96 | — | — | — | 442 GLENWOOD AVENUE — Pixies Three, Mercury 72208 | 1 |
| 97 | — | — | — | SLIPIN' AND SLIDIN' — Jim & Monica, Betty 1207 | 1 |
| 98 | — | — | 93 | HERE COMES THE BOY — Tracey Dey, Amy 894 | 2 |
| 99 | 100 | — | — | WHO DO YOU LOVE — Sapphires, Swan 4162 | 2 |
| 100 | — | — | — | CHARADE — Andy Williams, Columbia 42950 | 1 |

## BUBBLING UNDER THE HOT 100

101. BABY WHAT YOU WANT ME TO DO — Etta James, Argo 5459
102. WHEN YOU WALK IN THE ROOM — Jackie DeShannon, Liberty 55645
103. THE COW — Bill Robinson, American 1023
104. COMING BACK TO YOU — Maxine Brown, Wand 142
105. SOUL DANCE — Tommy Leonetti, RCA Victor 8251
106. MY HOME TOWN — Steve Lawrence, Columbia 42952
107. THE FEELING IS GONE — Bobby Bland, Duke 379
108. PROMISES — Ray Peterson, Dunes 2030
109. FOR YOUR SWEET LOVE — Cascades, RCA Victor 8268
110. BIG TOWN BOY — Shirley Matthews, Atlantic 2210
111. THE SON OF REBEL-ROUSER — Duane Eddy, RCA Victor 8276
112. (It's No) SIN — Duprees, Coed 587
113. ASK ME — Inez Foxx, Symbol 926
114. NAVY BLUE — Diane Renay, 20th Century-Fox 456
115. RED DON'T GO WITH BLUE — Jimmy Clanton, Philips 40161
116. HE SAYS THE SAME THINGS TO ME — Skeeter Davis, RCA Victor 8288
117. PEANUTS — 4 Seasons, Vee Jay 901 (Extended Play)
118. DON'T CROSS OVER — Linda Brannon, Way 9640
119. I ONLY WANT TO BE WITH YOU — Dusty Springfield, Philips 40162
120. A ROOM WITHOUT WINDOWS — Steve Lawrence, Columbia 42952
121. HERE'S A HEART — Diplomats, Arock 1004
122. TELL HIM — Drew-Vels, Capitol 5055
123. CALIFORNIA SUN — Rivieras, Riviera 1401
124. PENETRATION — Pyramids, Best 13002
125. I DIDN'T KNOW WHAT TIME IT WAS — Crampton Sisters, DCP 1001
126. BEGGING TO YOU — Marty Robbins, Columbia 42890
127. THE GREASY SPOON — Hank Marr, Federal 12508
128. WHO NEEDS YOU — Bobby Paris, Chattahoochee 637

Compiled from national retail sales and radio station airplay by the Music Popularity Dept. of Record Market Research, Billboard.

# Billboard

For Week Ending January 25, 1964

# HOT 100

★ **STAR performer**—Sides registering greatest proportionate upward progress this week.

Billboard Award

| This Week | 1 Wk. Ago | 2 Wks. Ago | 3 Wks. Ago | TITLE Artist, Label & Number | Weeks On Chart |
|---|---|---|---|---|---|
| 1 | 1 | 1 | 1 | THERE! I'VE SAID IT AGAIN — Bobby Vinton, Epic 9638 | 9 |
| 2 | 2 | 2 | 2 | LOUIE LOUIE — Kingsmen, Wand 143 | 12 |
| ★3 | 45 | — | — | I WANT TO HOLD YOUR HAND — Beatles, Capitol 5112 | 2 |
| 4 | 5 | 7 | 13 | SURFIN' BIRD — Trashmen, Garrett 4002 | 8 |
| 5 | 3 | 3 | 6 | POPSICLES AND ICICLES — Murmaids, Chattahoochee 628 | 10 |
| ★6 | 9 | 20 | 33 | OUT OF LIMITS — Marketts, Warner Bros. 5391 | 8 |
| 7 | 7 | 19 | 35 | HEY LITTLE COBRA — Rip Chords, Columbia 42921 | 7 |
| 8 | 4 | 5 | 5 | FORGET HIM — Bobby Rydell, Cameo 280 | 12 |
| ★9 | 14 | 31 | 58 | UM, UM, UM, UM, UM, UM — Major Lance, Okeh 7187 | 4 |
| 10 | 10 | 13 | 17 | DRAG CITY — Jan & Dean, Liberty 55641 | 8 |
| 11 | 11 | 16 | 19 | WHISPERING — Nino Tempo & April Stevens, Atco 6281 | 6 |
| 12 | 12 | 12 | 14 | AS USUAL — Brenda Lee, Decca 31570 | 7 |
| ★13 | 18 | 37 | 49 | YOU DON'T OWN ME — Lesley Gore, Mercury 72206 | 5 |
| ★14 | 19 | 27 | 41 | FOR YOU — Rick Nelson, Decca 31574 | 5 |
| 15 | 6 | 4 | 3 | DOMINIQUE — Singing Nun, Philips 40163 | 12 |
| 16 | 17 | 22 | 32 | ANYONE WHO HAD A HEART — Dionne Warwick, Scepter 1262 | 8 |
| 17 | 8 | 8 | 9 | THE NITTY GRITTY — Shirley Ellis, Congress 202 | 11 |
| ★18 | 23 | 30 | 40 | DAISY PETAL PICKIN' — Jimmy Gilmer & the Fireballs, Dot 16539 | 7 |
| 19 | 13 | 6 | 4 | SINCE I FELL FOR YOU — Lenny Welch, Cadence 1439 | 14 |
| 20 | 20 | 21 | 26 | THAT LUCKY OLD SUN — Ray Charles, ABC-Paramount 10509 | 8 |
| 21 | 24 | 25 | 31 | SOMEWHERE — Tymes, Parkway 891 | 8 |
| 22 | 21 | 11 | 8 | QUICKSAND — Martha & the Vandellas, Gordy 7025 | 10 |
| 23 | 15 | 10 | 10 | MIDNIGHT MARY — Joey Powers, Amy 892 | 12 |
| 24 | 25 | 23 | 28 | WHEN THE LOVELIGHT STARTS SHINING THROUGH HIS EYES — Supremes, Motown 1051 | 9 |
| ★25 | 50 | — | — | TALKING ABOUT MY BABY — Impressions, ABC-Paramount 10511 | 2 |
| 26 | 28 | 32 | 42 | BABY I LOVE YOU — Ronettes, Philles 118 | 6 |
| 27 | 30 | 33 | 44 | HOOKA TOOKA — Chubby Checker, Parkway 890 | 8 |
| 28 | 22 | 14 | 15 | WIVES AND LOVERS — Jack Jones, Kapp 551 | 13 |
| 29 | 16 | 9 | 7 | TALK BACK TREMBLING LIPS — Johnny Tillotson, MGM 13181 | 12 |
| ★30 | 48 | 65 | — | A FOOL NEVER LEARNS — Andy Williams, Columbia 42950 | 3 |
| 31 | 27 | 17 | 11 | YOU DON'T HAVE TO BE A BABY TO CRY — Caravelles, Smash 1852 | 13 |
| 32 | 32 | 24 | 24 | CAN I GET A WITNESS — Marvin Gaye, Tamla 54087 | 15 |
| 33 | 39 | 51 | 62 | WHAT KIND OF FOOL (Do You Think I Am) — Tams, ABC-Paramount 10502 | 7 |
| 34 | 34 | 43 | 48 | GIRLS GROW UP FASTER THAN BOYS — Cookies, Dimension 1020 | 9 |
| 35 | 31 | 34 | 34 | NEED TO BELONG — Jerry Butler, Vee Jay 567 | 10 |
| ★36 | 53 | 78 | 96 | JAVA — Al Hirt, RCA Victor 8280 | 4 |
| 37 | 40 | 47 | 56 | IT'S ALL IN THE GAME — Cliff Richard, Epic 9633 | 8 |
| 38 | 47 | 54 | 60 | WHAT'S EASY FOR TWO IS SO HARD FOR ONE — Mary Wells, Motown 1048 | 10 |
| 39 | 44 | 52 | 55 | I CAN'T STOP TALKING ABOUT YOU — Steve & Eydie, Columbia 42932 | 6 |
| 40 | 42 | 53 | 61 | CHARADE — Henry Mancini & His Ork, RCA Victor 8256 | 8 |
| 41 | 29 | 18 | 12 | DRIP DROP — Dion DiMuci, Columbia 42917 | 11 |
| 42 | 38 | 35 | 39 | I GOTTA DANCE TO KEEP FROM CRYING — Miracles, Tamla 54089 | 10 |
| 43 | 26 | 15 | 16 | PRETTY PAPER — Roy Orbison, Monument 830 | 7 |
| 44 | 35 | 42 | 45 | TRA LA LA LA SUZY — Dean & Jean, Rust 5067 | 13 |
| ★45 | 55 | 59 | 67 | COMIN' IN THE BACK DOOR — Baja Marimba Band, Almo 201 | 6 |
| 46 | 49 | 56 | 69 | IN THE SUMMER OF HIS YEARS — Connie Francis, MGM 13202 | 5 |
| 47 | 36 | 28 | 22 | LODDY LO — Chubby Checker, Parkway 890 | 13 |
| ★48 | 66 | 72 | 82 | YOU'LL NEVER WALK ALONE — Patti LaBelle & Her Blue Belles, Parkway 896 | 4 |
| ★49 | 63 | 70 | 83 | HARLEM SHUFFLE — Bob & Earl, Marc 104 | 6 |
| ★50 | 65 | 75 | 88 | THE SHELTER OF YOUR ARMS — Sammy Davis Jr., Reprise 20216 | 7 |
| 51 | 60 | 81 | 89 | YOU'RE NO GOOD — Betty Everett, Vee Jay 566 | 9 |
| 52 | 56 | 61 | 68 | MY ONE AND ONLY JIMMY BOY — Girlfriends, Colpix 712 | 5 |
| 53 | 43 | 46 | 47 | THE MARVELOUS TOY — Chad Mitchell Trio, Mercury 72197 | 9 |
| 54 | 59 | 68 | 70 | DUMB HEAD — Ginny Arnell, MGM 13177 | 10 |
| 55 | 58 | 62 | 72 | THE LITTLE BOY — Tony Bennett, Columbia 42931 | 6 |
| 56 | 51 | 67 | 74 | LETTER FROM SHERRY — Dale Ward, Dot 16520 | 5 |
| 57 | 54 | 60 | 57 | TODAY'S TEARDROPS — Rick Nelson, Imperial 66004 | 9 |
| 58 | 64 | 57 | 51 | AS LONG AS I KNOW HE'S MINE — Marvelettes, Tamla 54088 | 12 |
| 59 | 61 | 63 | 66 | WATCH YOUR STEP — Brooks O'Dell, Gold 214 | 7 |
| ★60 | 74 | 77 | — | TONIGHT YOU'RE GONNA FALL IN LOVE WITH ME — Shirelles, Scepter 1264 | 3 |
| ★61 | 84 | — | — | SOUTHTOWN, U. S. A. — Dixiebelles, Sound Stage 7 2517 | 2 |
| 62 | 70 | 90 | 94 | PAIN IN MY HEART — Otis Redding, Volt 112 | 8 |
| 63 | 72 | 74 | 87 | WHO CARES — Fats Domino, ABC-Paramount 10512 | 4 |
| ★64 | 82 | — | — | COME ON — Tommy Roe, ABC-Paramount 10515 | 2 |
| ★65 | 80 | 83 | — | SEE THE FUNNY LITTLE CLOWN — Bobby Goldsboro, United Artists 672 | 3 |
| ★66 | — | — | — | STOP AND THINK IT OVER — Dale & Grace, Montel 922 | 1 |
| 67 | 69 | 66 | 71 | TRUE LOVE GOES ON AND ON — Burl Ives, Decca 31571 | 5 |
| 68 | 73 | 79 | — | I WISH YOU LOVE — Gloria Lynn, Everest 2036 | 3 |
| ★69 | — | — | — | SHE LOVES YOU — Beatles, Swan 4152 | 1 |
| ★70 | — | — | — | CALIFORNIA SUN — Rivieras, Riviera 1401 | 1 |
| ★71 | 87 | — | — | THAT GIRL BELONGS TO YESTERDAY — Gene Pitney, Musicor 1036 | 2 |
| 72 | 67 | 69 | 77 | IF SOMEBODY TOLD YOU — Anna King, Smash 1858 | 4 |
| ★73 | — | — | — | OH BABY DON'T YOU WEEP — James Brown & the Famous Flames, King 5842 | 1 |
| 74 | 71 | 73 | 81 | SNAP YOUR FINGERS — Barbara Lewis, Atlantic 2214 | 5 |
| 75 | 77 | 88 | 91 | PINK DOMINOES — Crescents, Era 3116 | 5 |
| ★76 | — | — | — | HE SAYS THE SAME THINGS TO ME — Skeeter Davis, RCA Victor 8288 | 1 |
| ★77 | — | — | — | I ONLY WANT TO BE WITH YOU — Dusty Springfield, Philips 40162 | 1 |
| 78 | 79 | 89 | 90 | DO-WAH-DIDDY — Exciters, United Artists 662 | 4 |
| 79 | 75 | 76 | 80 | WE BELONG TOGETHER — Jimmy Velvet, ABC-Paramount 10488 | 7 |
| 80 | 93 | — | — | I'LL REMEMBER (In the Still of the Night) — Santo & Johnny, Canadian-American 164 | 2 |
| 81 | 81 | 84 | — | PUPPY LOVE — Barbara Lewis, Atlantic 2214 | 3 |
| ★82 | — | — | — | GOING GOING GONE — Brook Benton, Mercury 72230 | 1 |
| ★83 | — | — | — | GONNA SEND YOU BACK TO GEORGIA — Timmy Shaw, Wand 146 | 1 |
| 84 | 85 | 87 | — | BILLIE BABY — Lloyd Price, Double L 729 | 3 |
| 85 | 92 | — | — | SAGINAW, MICHIGAN — Lefty Frizzell, Columbia 42924 | 2 |
| 86 | 86 | 95 | — | LITTLE BOXES — Pete Seeger, Columbia 42940 | 3 |
| 87 | 88 | — | — | STAY WITH ME — Frank Sinatra, Reprise 0249 | 2 |
| 88 | 89 | — | — | WOW WOW WEE — Angels, Smash 1870 | 2 |
| 89 | 91 | 92 | 93 | HIS KISS — Betty Harris, Jubilee 5465 | 4 |
| ★90 | — | — | — | NAVY BLUE — Diane Renay, 20th Century-Fox 456 | 1 |
| 91 | 96 | — | — | 442 GLENWOOD AVENUE — Pixies Three, Mercury 72208 | 2 |
| 92 | — | — | — | STRANGER IN YOUR ARMS — Bobby Vee, Liberty 55654 | 1 |
| 93 | — | — | — | GOOD NEWS — Sam Cooke, RCA Victor 8299 | 1 |
| 94 | — | — | — | (IT'S NO) SIN — Dupress, Coed 587 | 1 |
| 95 | 95 | 96 | — | JUDY LOVES ME — Johnny Crawford, Del-Fi 4231 | 3 |
| 96 | 97 | — | — | SLIPPIN' AND SLIDIN' — Jim & Monica, Betty 1207 | 2 |
| 97 | 99 | 100 | — | WHO DO YOU LOVE — Sapphires, Swan 4162 | 3 |
| 98 | — | — | — | ASK ME — Inez Foxx, Symbol 926 | 1 |
| 99 | — | — | — | WHEN YOU WALK IN THE ROOM — Jackie DeShannon, Liberty 55645 | 1 |
| 100 | — | — | — | WHO'S BEEN SLEEPING IN MY BED — Linda Scoot, Congress 204 | 1 |

## HOT 100—A TO Z—(Publisher-Licensee)

Anyone Who Had a Heart (U. S. Songs, ASCAP) .. 16
As Long as I Know He's Mine (Jobete, BMI) .... 58
As Usual (Samos Island, BMI) .... 12
Ask Me (Saturn, BMI) .... 98
Baby, I Love You (Mother Bertha-Trio, BMI) .... 26
Billie Baby (Prigan, BMI) .... 84
California Sun (Llyod & Logan, BMI) .... 70
Can I Get a Witness (Jobete, BMI) .... 32
Charade—Mancini (Southdale-Northern, ASCAP) .. 40
Come On (Fame, BMI) .... 64
Comin' in the Back Door (Irving, BMI) .... 45
Daisy Petal Pickin' (Dundee, BMI) .... 18
Do-Wha-Ditty (Trio, BMI) .... 78
Dominique (General, ASCAP) .... 15
Drag City (Screen Gems-Columbia, BMI) .... 10
Drip Drop (Progressive-Quintet, BMI) .... 41
Dumb Head (Peter Maurice, ASCAP) .... 54
Fool Never Learns, A (Cricket, BMI) .... 30
For You (Witmark, ASCAP) .... 14
Forget Him (Leeds, ASCAP) .... 8
442 Glenwood Avenue (Merjoda, BMI) .... 91
Girls Grow Up Faster Than Boys (Screen Gems-Columbia, BMI) .... 34
Going Going Gone (Gil, BMI) .... 82
Gonna Send You Back to Georgia (Zann, BMI) ... 83
Good News (Kags, BMI) .... 93
Harlem Shuffle (Marc Jean-Keyman, BMI) .... 49
He Says the Same Things to Me (Geld-Udell, ASCAP) .... 76
Hey Little Cobra (Vadim, BMI) .... 7
Hiss Kiss (Mellin-Trio, BMI) .... 89
Hooka Tooka (Evanston-Woodcrest, BMI) .... 27
I Can't Stop Talking About You (Screen Gems-Columbia, BMI) .... 39
I Gotta Dance to Keep From Crying (Jobete, BMI) .. 42
I Only Want to Be With You (Chappell. ASCAP) .. 77
I Want to Hold Your Hand (Duchess, BMI) .... 3
I Wish You Love (Leeds, ASCAP) .... 68
I'll Remember (in the Still of the Night) (Cherio, BMI) .... 80
If Somebody Told You (Jim Jam, BMI) .... 72
In the Summer of His Years (Leeds, ASCAP) .... 46
It's All in the Game (Remick, ASCAP) .... 37
(It's No) Sin (Algonquin, BMI) .... 94
Java (Tideland, BMI) .... 36
Judy Loves Me (Screen Gems-Columbia, BMI) .... 95
Letter From Sherry (NuStar, BMI) .... 56
Little Boxes (Schroder, ASCAP) .... 86
Little Boy, The (Morris, ASCAP) .... 55
Loddy Lo (Kalmann-C.C.C., ASCAP) .... 47
Louie Louie (Limax, BMI) .... 2
Marvelous Toy, The (Teena, ASCAP) .... 53
Midnight Mary (Jimskip, BMI) .... 23
My One and Only Jimmy Boy (Screen Gems-Columbia, BMI) .... 52
Navy Blue (Saturday, ASCAP) .... 90
Need to Belong (Curtom-Conrad, BMI) .... 35
Nitty Gritty, The (Gallico, BMI) .... 17
Oh Baby Don't You Weep (Jim Jam, BMI) .... 73
Out of Limits (Wrist, BMI) .... 6
Pain in My Heart (Jarb, BMI) .... 62
Pink Dominoes (Dimondaire-Room Seven, BMI) .. 75
Popsicles asd Icicles (Dragonwyck, BMI) .... 5
Pretty Paper (Pamper, BMI) .... 43
Puppy Love (McLaughlin, BMI) .... 81
Quicksand (Jobete, BMI) .... 22
Saginaw, Michigan (Tree, BMI) .... 85
See the Funny Little Clown (Unart, BMI) .... 65
She Loves You (Gil, BMI) .... 69
Shelter of Your Arms, The (Print, ASCAP) .... 50
Since I Fell for You (Advanced, ASCAP) .... 19
Slipin' and Slidin' (Venice, BMI) .... 96
Snap Your Fingers (Cigma, BMI) .... 74
Somewhere (Wyncote, ASCAP) .... 21
Southtown, U.S.A. (Gallico, BMI) .... 61
Stay With Me (Chappell, ASCAP) .... 87
Stop and Think It Over (Crazy Cajun-Red Sticy, BMI) .... 66
Stranger in Your Arms (Davilene-Saima, BMI) .... 92
Surfin' Bird (Willong, BMI) .... 4
Talk Back Trembling Lips (Acuff-Rose, BMI) ... 29
Talking About My Baby (Curtom, BMI) .... 25
That Girl Belongs to Yesterday (Pitfield, BMI) .... 71
That Lucky Old Sun (Robbins, ASCAP) .... 20
There! I've Said It Again (Valiant, ASCAP) ... 1
Today's Teardrops (Sea Lark, BMI) .... 57
Tonight You're Gonna Fall in Love With Me (Screen Gems-Columbia, BMI) .... 60
Tra La La La Suzy (Just, BMI) .... 44
True Loves Goes on and On (Frank, ASCAP) .... 67
Um, Um, Um, Um, Um, Um (Curtom-Jalynne, BMI). 9
Watch Your Step (Ludix, BMI) .... 59
We Belong Together (Figure, BMI) .... 79
What Kind of Fool (Do You Think I Am) (Low-Twi, BMI) .... 33
What's Easy for Two Is So Hard for One (Jobete, BMI) .... 38
When the Lovelight Starts Shining Through His Eyes (Jobete, BMI) .... 24
When You Walk in the Room (Metric, BMI) .... 99
Whispering (Fisher-Miller, ASCAP) .... 11
Who Cares (Acuff-Rose, BMI) .... 63
Who Do You Love (Hill & Range, BMI) .... 97
Who's Been Sleeping in My Bed (Famous, ASCAP).100
Wives and Lovers (Famous, ASCAP) .... 28
Wow Wow Wee (Grand Canyon, BMI) .... 88
You Don't Have to Be a Baby to Cry (R.F.D., ASCAP) .... 31
You Don't Own Me (Merjoda, BMI) .... 13
You'll Never Walk Alone (Williamson, ASCAP) .. 48
You're No Good (Morris, ASCAP) .... 51

## BUBBLING UNDER THE HOT 100

101. HERE COMES THE BOY .... Tracey Dey, Amy 894
102. BABY WHAT YOU WANT ME TO DO .... Etta James, Argo 5459
103. SO FAR AWAY .... Hank Jacobs, Sue 795
104. LONG GONE LONESOME BLUES .... Hank Williams Jr., MGM 13208
105. DEEP IN THE HEART OF HARLEM .... Clyde McPhatter, Mercury 72220
106. BIG TOWN BOY .... Shirley Matthews, Atlantic 2210
107. PENETRATION .... Pyramids, Best 13002
108. CAN YOUR MONKEY DO THE DOG .... Rufus Thomas, Stax 144
109. I DIDN'T KNOW WHAT TIME IT WAS .... Crampton Sisters, DCP 1001
110. (I'm Watching) EVERY LITTLE MOVE YOU MAKE .... Little Peggy March, RCA Victor 8302
111. FOR YOUR SWEET LOVE .... Cascades, RCA Victor 8268
112. CHARADE .... Andy Williams, Columbia 42950
113. THE GREASY SPOON .... Hank Marr, Federal 12508
114. THE COW .... Bill Robinson, American 1023
115. GO ON AND HAVE YOURSELF A BALL .... Mar-Vels, Butane 778
116. DON'T CROSS OVER .... Linda Brannon, Epic 9640
117. HERE'S A HEART .... Diplomats, Arock 1004
118. RED DON'T GO WITH BLUE .... Jimmy Clanton, Philips 40161
119. PEANUTS .... 4 Seasons, Vee Jay 901 (Extended Play)
120. LOOK HOMEWARD ANGEL .... Monarchs, Sound Stage 7 2516
121. VAYA CON DIOS .... Drifters, Atlantic 2216
122. LITTLE BOY .... Crystals, Philles 119X
123. COMIN' ON .... Bill Black's Combo, Hi 2072
124. I LOVE YOU MORE AND MORE EVERY DAY .... Al Martino, Capitol 5108
125. LEAVING HERE .... Eddie Holland, Motown 1052
126. WELCOME TO MY WORLD .... Jim Reeves, RCA Victor 8289
127. WHY, WHY, WON'T YOU BELIEVE ME .... Shep & the Limelites, Hull 761
128. THROUGH THE EYES OF A FOOL .... Roy Clark, Capitol 5099
129. OUTSIDE CITY LIMITS .... Cashelles, Decca 31575
130. LOVE WITH THE PROPER STRANGER .... Jack Jones, Kapp 571
131. WHAT NOW MY LOVE .... Ben E. King, Atco 6284
132. SINNER NOT A SAINT .... Trini Lopez, United Modern 106

Compiled from national retail sales and radio station airplay by the Music Popularity Dept. of Record Market Research, Billboard.

# Billboard HOT 100

*For Week Ending February 1, 1964*

★ **STAR** performer—Sides registering greatest proportionate upward progress this week.

| This Week | 1 Wk. Ago | 2 Wk. Ago | 3 Wk. Ago | TITLE Artist, Label & Number | Weeks On Chart |
|---|---|---|---|---|---|
| 1 | 3 | 45 | — | I WANT TO HOLD YOUR HAND — Beatles, Capitol 5112 | 3 |
| 2 | 13 | 18 | 37 | YOU DON'T OWN ME — Lesley Gore, Mercury 72206 | 6 |
| 3 | 6 | 9 | 20 | OUT OF LIMITS — Marketts, Warner Bros. 5391 | 9 |
| 4 | 4 | 5 | 7 | SURFIN' BIRD — Trashmen, Garrett 4002 | 9 |
| 5 | 7 | 7 | 19 | HEY LITTLE COBRA — Rip Chords, Columbia 42921 | 8 |
| 6 | 2 | 2 | 2 | LOUIE LOUIE — Kingsmen, Wand 143 | 13 |
| 7 | 1 | 1 | 1 | THERE! I'VE SAID IT AGAIN — Bobby Vinton, Epic 9638 | 10 |
| 8 | 9 | 14 | 31 | UM, UM, UM, UM, UM, UM — Major Lance, Okeh 7187 | 5 |
| 9 | 16 | 17 | 22 | ANYONE WHO HAD A HEART — Dionne Warwick, Scepter 1262 | 9 |
| 10 | 14 | 19 | 27 | FOR YOU — Rick Nelson, Decca 31574 | 6 |
| 11 | 5 | 3 | 3 | POPSICLES AND ICICLES — Murmaids, Chattahoochee 628 | 11 |
| 12 | 8 | 4 | 5 | FORGET HIM — Bobby Rydell, Cameo 280 | 13 |
| 13 | 10 | 10 | 13 | DRAG CITY — Jan & Dean, Liberty 55641 | 9 |
| 14 | 11 | 11 | 16 | WHISPERING — Nino Tempo & April Stevens, Atco 6281 | 7 |
| 15 | 25 | 50 | — | TALKING ABOUT MY BABY — Impressions, ABC-Paramount 10511 | 3 |
| 16 | 12 | 12 | 12 | AS USUAL — Brenda Lee, Decca 31570 | 8 |
| 17 | 33 | 39 | 51 | WHAT KIND OF FOOL (Do You Think I Am) — Tams, ABC-Paramount 10502 | 8 |
| 18 | 18 | 23 | 30 | DAISY PETAL PICKIN' — Jimmy Gilmer & the Fireballs, Dot 16539 | 8 |
| 19 | 21 | 24 | 25 | SOMEWHERE — Tymes, Parkway 891 | 9 |
| 20 | 27 | 30 | 33 | HOOKA TOOKA — Chubby Checker, Parkway 890 | 9 |
| 21 | 69 | — | — | SHE LOVES YOU — Beatles, Swan 4152 | 2 |
| 22 | 30 | 48 | 65 | A FOOL NEVER LEARNS — Andy Williams, Columbia 42950 | 4 |
| 23 | 36 | 53 | 78 | JAVA — Al Hirt, RCA Victor 8280 | 5 |
| 24 | 26 | 28 | 32 | BABY I LOVE YOU — Ronettes, Philles 118 | 7 |
| 25 | 17 | 8 | 8 | THE NITTY GRITTY — Shirley Ellis, Congress 202 | 12 |
| 26 | 19 | 13 | 6 | SINCE I FELL FOR YOU — Lenny Welch, Cadence 1439 | 15 |
| 27 | 24 | 25 | 23 | WHEN THE LOVELIGHT STARTS SHINING THROUGH HIS EYES — Supremes, Motown 1051 | 10 |
| 28 | 37 | 40 | 47 | IT'S ALL IN THE GAME — Cliff Richard, Epic 9633 | 9 |
| 29 | 23 | 15 | 10 | MIDNIGHT MARY — Joey Powers, Amy 892 | 13 |
| 30 | 15 | 6 | 4 | DOMINIQUE — Singing Nun, Philips 40163 | 13 |
| 31 | 22 | 21 | 11 | QUICKSAND — Martha & the Vandellas, Gordy 7025 | 11 |
| 32 | 28 | 22 | 14 | WIVES AND LOVERS — Jack Jones, Kapp 551 | 14 |
| 33 | 34 | 34 | 43 | GIRLS GROW UP FASTER THAN BOYS — Cookies, Dimension 1020 | 10 |
| 34 | 29 | 16 | 9 | TALK BACK TREMBLING LIPS — Johnny Tillotson, MGM 13181 | 13 |
| 35 | 56 | 51 | 67 | LETTER FROM SHERRY — Dale Ward, Dot 16520 | 6 |
| 36 | 40 | 42 | 53 | CHARADE — Henry Mancini & His Ork, RCA Victor 8256 | 9 |
| 37 | 39 | 44 | 52 | I CAN'T STOP TALKING ABOUT YOU — Steve & Eydie, Columbia 42932 | 7 |
| 38 | 70 | — | — | CALIFORNIA SUN — Rivieras, Riviera 1401 | 2 |
| 39 | 20 | 20 | 21 | THAT LUCKY OLD SUN — Ray Charles, ABC-Paramount 10509 | 9 |
| 40 | 50 | 65 | 75 | THE SHELTER OF YOUR ARMS — Sammy Davis Jr., Reprise 20216 | 8 |
| 41 | 48 | 66 | 72 | YOU'LL NEVER WALK ALONE — Patti LaBelle & Her Blue Belles, Parkway 896 | 5 |
| 42 | 45 | 55 | 59 | COMIN' IN THE BACK DOOR — Baja Marimba Band, Almo 201 | 7 |
| 43 | 66 | — | — | STOP AND THINK IT OVER — Dale & Grace, Montel 922 | 2 |
| 44 | 61 | 84 | — | SOUTHTOWN, U.S.A. — Dixiebelles, Sound Stage 7 2517 | 3 |
| 45 | 35 | 31 | 34 | NEED TO BELONG — Jerry Butler, Vee Jay 567 | 11 |
| 46 | 49 | 63 | 70 | HARLEM SHUFFLE — Bob & Earl, Marc 104 | 7 |
| 47 | 32 | 32 | 24 | CAN I GET A WITNESS — Marvin Gaye, Tamla 54087 | 16 |
| 48 | 38 | 47 | 54 | WHAT'S EASY FOR TWO IS SO HARD FOR ONE — Mary Wells, Motown 1048 | 11 |
| 49 | 52 | 56 | 61 | MY ONE AND ONLY JIMMY BOY — Girlfriends, Colpix 712 | 6 |
| 50 | 54 | 59 | 68 | DUMB HEAD — Ginny Arnell, MGM 13177 | 11 |
| 51 | 64 | 82 | — | COME ON — Tommy Roe, ABC-Paramount 10515 | 3 |
| 52 | 55 | 58 | 62 | THE LITTLE BOY — Tony Bennett, Columbia 42931 | 7 |
| 53 | 46 | 49 | 56 | IN THE SUMMER OF HIS YEARS — Connie Francis, MGM 13202 | 6 |
| 54 | 73 | — | — | OH BABY DON'T YOU WEEP — James Brown & the Famous Flames, King 5842 | 2 |
| 55 | 65 | 80 | 83 | SEE THE FUNNY LITTLE CLOWN — Bobby Goldsboro, United Artists 672 | 4 |
| 56 | 68 | 73 | 79 | I WISH YOU LOVE — Gloria Lynn, Everest 2036 | 4 |
| 57 | 60 | 74 | 77 | TONIGHT YOU'RE GONNA FALL IN LOVE WITH ME — Shirelles, Scepter 1264 | 4 |
| 58 | 59 | 61 | 63 | WATCH YOUR STEP — Brooks O'Dell, Gold 214 | 8 |
| 59 | 51 | 60 | 81 | YOU'RE NO GOOD — Betty Everett, Vee Jay 566 | 10 |
| 60 | 71 | 87 | — | THAT GIRL BELONGS TO YESTERDAY — Gene Pitney, Musicor 1036 | 3 |
| 61 | — | 82 | — | GOING GOING GONE — Brook Benton, Mercury 72230 | 2 |
| 62 | 62 | 70 | 90 | PAIN IN MY HEART — Otis Redding, Volt 112 | 9 |
| 63 | 76 | — | — | HE SAYS THE SAME THINGS TO ME — Skeeter Davis, RCA Victor 8288 | 2 |
| 64 | — | — | — | VAYA CON DIOS — Drifters, Atlantic 2216 | 1 |
| 65 | 63 | 72 | 74 | WHO CARES — Fats Domino, ABC-Paramount 10512 | 5 |
| 66 | — | — | — | ABIGAIL BEECHER — Freddy Cannon, Warner Bros. 5409 | 1 |
| 67 | 58 | 64 | 57 | AS LONG AS I KNOW HE'S MINE — Marvelettes, Tamla 54088 | 13 |
| 68 | — | — | — | PLEASE PLEASE ME — Beatles, Vee Jay 581 | 1 |
| 69 | 75 | 77 | 88 | PINK DOMINOES — Crescents, Era 3116 | 6 |
| 70 | 80 | 93 | — | I'LL REMEMBER (In the Still of the Night) — Santo & Johnny, Canadian-American 164 | 3 |
| 71 | 90 | — | — | NAVY BLUE — Diane Renay, 20th Century-Fox 456 | 2 |
| 72 | 83 | — | — | GONNA SEND YOU BACK TO GEORGIA — Timmy Shaw, Wand 146 | 2 |
| 73 | 77 | — | — | I ONLY WANT TO BE WITH YOU — Dusty Springfield, Philips 40162 | 2 |
| 74 | 81 | 81 | 84 | PUPPY LOVE — Barbara Lewis, Atlantic 2214 | 4 |
| 75 | — | — | — | DAWN — 4 Seasons, Philips 40166 | 1 |
| 76 | 88 | 89 | — | WOW WOW WEE — Angels, Smash 1870 | 3 |
| 77 | 93 | — | — | GOOD NEWS — Sam Cooke, RCA Victor 8299 | 2 |
| 78 | 97 | 99 | 100 | WHO DO YOU LOVE — Sapphires, Swan 4162 | 4 |
| 79 | — | — | — | I LOVE YOU MORE AND MORE EVERY DAY — Al Martino, Capitol 5108 | 1 |
| 80 | 72 | 67 | 69 | IF SOMEBODY TOLD YOU — Anna King, Smash 1858 | 5 |
| 81 | 87 | 88 | — | STAY WITH ME — Frank Sinatra, Reprise 0249 | 3 |
| 82 | 94 | — | — | (It's No) SIN — Dupress, Coed 587 | 2 |
| 83 | 86 | 86 | 95 | LITTLE BOXES — Pete Seeger, Columbia 42940 | 4 |
| 84 | 91 | 96 | — | 442 GLENWOOD AVENUE — Pixies Three, Mercury 72208 | 3 |
| 85 | — | — | — | CAN YOUR MONKEY DO THE DOG — Rufus Thomas, Stax 144 | 1 |
| 86 | 92 | — | — | STRANGER IN YOUR ARMS — Bobby Vee, Liberty 55654 | 2 |
| 87 | — | — | — | (I'm Watching) EVERY LITTLE MOVE YOU MAKE — Little Peggy March, RCA Victor 8302 | 1 |
| 88 | — | — | — | SHIMMY SHIMMY — Orlons, Cameo 295 | 1 |
| 89 | — | — | — | BABY WHAT YOU WANT ME TO DO — Etta James, Argo 5459 | 1 |
| 90 | — | — | — | PENETRATION — Pyramids, Best 13002 | 1 |
| 91 | — | 94 | — | SO FAR AWAY — Hank Jacobs, Sue 795 | 2 |
| 92 | — | — | — | COMIN' ON — Bill Black's Combo, Hi 2072 | 1 |
| 93 | — | 90 | 93 | DEEP IN THE HEART OF HARLEM — Clyde McPhatter, Mercury 72220 | 4 |
| 94 | 98 | — | — | ASK ME — Inez Foxx, Symbol 926 | 2 |
| 95 | — | — | — | LONG GONE LONESOME BLUES — Hank Williams Jr., MGM 13208 | 1 |
| 96 | — | 98 | — | HERE COMES THE BOY — Tracey Dey, Amy 894 | 3 |
| 97 | — | — | — | WHERE DID I GO WRONG — Dee Dee Sharp, Cameo 296 | 1 |
| 98 | — | — | — | LITTLE BOY — Crystals, Philles 119 | 1 |
| 99 | — | — | — | BYE BYE BARBARA — Johnny Mathis, Mercury 72229 | 1 |
| 100 | — | — | — | HERE'S A HEART — Diplomats, Arock 1004 | 1 |

## BUBBLING UNDER THE HOT 100

101. THE GREASY SPOON — Hank Marr, Federal 12508
102. I DIDN'T KNOW WHAT TIME IT WAS — Crampton Sisters, DCP 1001
103. HI-HEEL SNEAKERS — Tommy Tucker, Checker 1067
104. BIG TOWN BOY — Shirley Matthews, Atlantic 2210
105. WHAT NOW MY LOVE — Ben E. King, Atco 6284
106. HIS KYSS — Betty Harris, Jubilee 5465
107. SAGINAW, MICHIGAN — Lefty Frizzell, Columbia 42924
108. PEANUTS — 4 Seasons, Vee Jay 901 (Extended Play)
109. SLIPIN' AND SLIDIN' — Jim & Monica, Betty 1207
110. RIP VAN WINKLE — Devotions, Roulette 4541
111. JUDY LOVES ME — Johnny Crawford, Del-Fi 4231
112. BILLIE BABY — Lloyd Price, Double T 729
113. TELL HIM — Drew-Vels, Capitol 5055
114. WHEN YOU WALK IN THE ROOM — Jackie DeShannon, Liberty 55645
115. DON'T CROSS OVER — Linda Brannon, Sue 795
116. WHO'S BEEN SLEEPING IN MY BED — Linda Scott, Congress 204
117. LEAVING HERE — Eddie Holland, Motown 1052
118. GO ON AND HAVE YOURSELF A BALL — Mar-Vels, Butane 778
119. HAVE YOU EVER BEEN LONELY — Caravelles, Smash 1869
120. THE LA-DEE-DA SONG — Village Stompers, Epic 9655
121. GOING BACK TO LOUISIANA — Bruce Channel, LeCam 122
122. THROUGH THE EYES OF A FOOL — Jack Jones, Kapp 571
123. LOVE WITH THE PROPER STRANGER — Steve Lawrence, Columbia 42952
124. A ROOM WITHOUT WINDOWS — Shep & the Limelites, Hull 761
125. WHY, WHY, WON'T YOU BELIEVE ME — Bobby Bare, RCA Victor 8294
126. MAMA'S GAVE — Gene Thomas, United Artists 640
127. HE WALKS LIKE A MAN — Jody Miller, Capitol 5090
128. THROUGH THE EYES OF A FOOL — Roy Clark, Capitol 5099
129. GOTTA FIND A WAY — Theresa Lindsey, Correc-Tone 5040
130. SOUL DANCE — Tommy Leonetti, RCA Victor 8251
131. STAND TALL — O'Jays, Imperial 66007
132. ROBERTA — Barry & the Tamerlanes, Valiant 6040
133. BABY'S GONE — Gene Thomas, United Artists 640
134. WHO NEEDS IT — Gene Pitney, Musicor 1034
135. HIGH ON A HILL — Scott English, Spokane 4003

*Compiled from national retail sales and radio station airplay by the Music Popularity Dept. of Record Market Research, Billboard.*

**Billboard** For Week Ending February 8, 1964

# HOT 100

★ **STAR performer**—Sides registering greatest proportionate upward progress this week.

| This Week | 1 Wk. Ago | 2 Wks. Ago | 3 Wks. Ago | TITLE | Artist, Label & Number | Weeks On Chart |
|---|---|---|---|---|---|---|
| 1 (Billboard Award) | 1 | 3 | 45 | I WANT TO HOLD YOUR HAND | Beatles, Capitol 5112 | 4 |
| 2 | 2 | 13 | 18 | YOU DON'T OWN ME | Lesley Gore, Mercury 72206 | 7 |
| 3 | 3 | 6 | 9 | OUT OF LIMITS | Marketts, Warner Bros. 5391 | 10 |
| 4 | 5 | 7 | 7 | HEY LITTLE COBRA | Rip Chords, Columbia 42921 | 9 |
| ★5 | 8 | 9 | 14 | UM, UM, UM, UM, UM, UM | Major Lance, Okeh 7187 | 6 |
| 6 | 4 | 4 | 5 | SURFIN' BIRD | Trashmen, Garrett 4002 | 10 |
| ★7 | 21 | 69 | — | SHE LOVES YOU | Beatles, Swan 4152 | 3 |
| 8 | 10 | 14 | 19 | FOR YOU | Rick Nelson, Decca 31574 | 7 |
| 9 | 9 | 16 | 17 | ANYONE WHO HAD A HEART | Dionne Warwick, Scepter 1262 | 10 |
| 10 | 7 | 1 | 1 | THERE! I'VE SAID IT AGAIN | Bobby Vinton, Epic 9638 | 11 |
| ★11 | 17 | 33 | 39 | WHAT KIND OF FOOL | Tams, ABC-Paramount 10502 | 9 |
| 12 | 15 | 25 | 50 | TALKING ABOUT MY BABY | Impressions, ABC-Paramount 10511 | 4 |
| ★13 | 23 | 36 | 53 | JAVA | Al Hirt, RCA Victor 8280 | 6 |
| 14 | 6 | 2 | 2 | LOUIE LOUIE | Kingsmen, Wand 143 | 14 |
| 15 | 18 | 18 | 23 | DAISY PETAL PICKIN' | Jimmy Gilmer & the Fireballs, Dot 16539 | 9 |
| ★16 | 22 | 30 | 48 | A FOOL NEVER LEARNS | Andy Williams, Columbia 42950 | 5 |
| 17 | 20 | 27 | 30 | HOOKA TOOKA | Chubby Checker, Parkway 890 | 10 |
| 18 | 12 | 8 | 4 | FORGET HIM | Bobby Rydell, Cameo 280 | 14 |
| 19 | 11 | 5 | 3 | POPSICLES AND ICICLES | Murmaids, Chattahoochee 628 | 12 |
| 20 | 14 | 11 | 11 | WHISPERING | Nino Tempo & April Stevens, Atco 6281 | 8 |
| 21 | 13 | 10 | 10 | DRAG CITY | Jan & Dean, Liberty 55641 | 10 |
| 22 | 19 | 21 | 24 | SOMEWHERE | Tymes, Parkway 891 | 10 |
| ★23 | 38 | 70 | — | CALIFORNIA SUN | Rivieras, Riviera 1401 | 3 |
| ★24 | 75 | — | — | DAWN (Go Away) | 4 Seasons, Philips 40166 | 2 |
| 25 | 16 | 12 | 12 | AS USUAL | Brenda Lee, Decca 31570 | 9 |
| ★26 | 43 | 66 | — | STOP AND THINK IT OVER | Dale & Grace, Montel 922 | 3 |
| 27 | 28 | 37 | 40 | IT'S ALL IN THE GAME | Cliff Richard, Epic 9633 | 10 |
| 28 | 24 | 26 | 28 | BABY I LOVE YOU | Ronettes, Philles 118 | 8 |
| ★29 | 44 | 61 | 84 | SOUTHTOWN, U. S. A. | Dixiebelles, Sound Stage 7 2517 | 4 |
| ★30 | 35 | 56 | 51 | LETTER FROM SHERRY | Dale Ward, Dot 16520 | 7 |
| 31 | 25 | 17 | 8 | THE NITTY GRITTY | Shirley Ellis, Congress 202 | 13 |
| 32 | 26 | 19 | 13 | SINCE I FELL FOR YOU | Lenny Welch, Cadence 1439 | 16 |
| ★33 | 48 | 38 | 47 | WHAT'S EASY FOR TWO IS SO HARD FOR ONE | Mary Wells, Motown 1048 | 12 |
| 34 | 41 | 48 | 66 | YOU'LL NEVER WALK ALONE | Patti LaBelle & Her Blue Belles, Parkway 896 | 6 |
| 35 | 37 | 39 | 44 | I CAN'T STOP TALKING ABOUT YOU | Steve & Eydie, Columbia 42932 | 8 |
| 36 | 27 | 24 | 25 | WHEN THE LOVELIGHT STARTS SHINING THROUGH HIS EYES | Supremes, Motown 1051 | 11 |
| 37 | 33 | 34 | 34 | GIRLS GROW UP FASTER THAN BOYS | Cookies, Dimension 1020 | 11 |
| 38 | 40 | 50 | 65 | THE SHELTER OF YOUR ARMS | Sammy Davis Jr., Reprise 20216 | 9 |
| 39 | 36 | 40 | 42 | CHARADE | Henry Mancini & His Ork, RCA Victor 8256 | 10 |
| ★40 | 51 | 64 | 82 | COME ON | Tommy Roe, ABC-Paramount 10515 | 4 |
| 41 | 42 | 45 | 55 | COMIN' IN THE BACK DOOR | Baja Marimba Band, Almo 201 | 8 |
| ★42 | 71 | 90 | — | NAVY BLUE | Diane Renay, 20th Century-Fox 456 | 3 |
| 43 | 31 | 22 | 21 | QUICKSAND | Martha & the Vandellas, Gordy 7025 | 12 |
| 44 | 46 | 49 | 63 | HARLEM SHUFFLE | Bob & Earl, Marc 104 | 8 |
| ★45 | 55 | 65 | 80 | SEE THE FUNNY LITTLE CLOWN | Bobby Goldsboro, United Artists 672 | 5 |
| ★46 | 79 | — | — | I LOVE YOU MORE AND MORE EVERY DAY | Al Martino, Capitol 5108 | 2 |
| 47 | 54 | 73 | — | OH BABY DON'T YOU WEEP | James Brown & the Famous Flames, King 5842 | 3 |
| ★48 | 77 | 93 | — | GOOD NEWS | Sam Cooke, RCA Victor 8299 | 3 |
| ★49 | 76 | 88 | 89 | WOW WOW WEE | Angels, Smash 1870 | 4 |
| ★50 | 66 | — | — | ABIGAIL BEECHER | Freddy Cannon, Warner Bros. 5409 | 2 |
| ★51 | 61 | 82 | — | GOING GOING GONE | Brook Benton, Mercury 72230 | 3 |
| ★52 | 64 | — | — | VAYA CON DIOS | Drifters, Atlantic 2216 | 2 |
| 53 | 56 | 68 | 73 | I WISH YOU LOVE | Gloria Lynne, Everest 2036 | 5 |
| ★54 | 73 | 77 | — | I ONLY WANT TO BE WITH YOU | Dusty Springfield, Philips 40162 | 3 |
| 55 | 60 | 71 | 87 | THAT GIRL BELONGS TO YESTERDAY | Gene Pitney, Musicor 1036 | 4 |
| 56 | 63 | 76 | — | HE SAYS THE SAME THINGS TO ME | Skeeter Davis, RCA Victor 8288 | 3 |
| ★57 | 68 | — | — | PLEASE PLEASE ME | Beatles, Vee Jay 581 | 2 |
| ★58 | 78 | 97 | 99 | WHO DO YOU LOVE | Sapphires, Swan 4162 | 5 |
| ★59 | 70 | 80 | 93 | I'LL REMEMBER (In the Still of the Night) | Santo & Johnny, Canadian-American 164 | 4 |
| 60 | 49 | 52 | 56 | MY ONE AND ONLY JIMMY BOY | Girlfriends, Colpix 712 | 7 |
| 61 | 62 | 62 | 70 | PAIN IN MY HEART | Otis Redding, Volt 112 | 10 |
| 62 | 50 | 54 | 59 | DUMB HEAD | Ginny Arnell, MGM 13177 | 12 |
| 63 | 72 | 83 | — | GONNA SEND YOU BACK TO GEORGIA | Timmy Shaw, Wand 146 | 3 |
| 64 | 74 | 81 | 81 | PUPPY LOVE | Barbara Lewis, Atlantic 2214 | 5 |
| 65 | 57 | 60 | 74 | TONIGHT YOU'RE GONNA FALL IN LOVE WITH ME | Shirelles, Scepter 1264 | 5 |
| 66 | 52 | 55 | 58 | THE LITTLE BOY | Tony Bennett, Columbia 42931 | 8 |
| ★67 | 90 | — | — | PENETRATION | Pyramids, Best 13002 | 2 |
| ★68 | — | — | — | I SAW HER STANDING THERE | Beatles, Capitol 5112 | 1 |
| 69 | 69 | 75 | 77 | PINK DOMINOES | Crescents, Era 3116 | 7 |
| ★70 | 85 | — | — | CAN YOUR MONKEY DO THE DOG | Rufus Thomas, Stax 144 | 2 |
| ★71 | 99 | — | — | BYE BYE BARBARA | Johnny Mathis, Mercury 72229 | 2 |
| ★72 | 88 | — | — | SHIMMY SHIMMY | Orlons, Cameo 295 | 2 |
| 73 | 58 | 59 | 61 | WATCH YOUR STEP | Brooks O'Dell, Gold 214 | 9 |
| 74 | 82 | 94 | — | (It's No) SIN | Dupress, Coed 587 | 3 |
| 75 | 83 | 86 | 86 | LITTLE BOXES | Pete Seeger, Columbia 42940 | 5 |
| ★76 | 84 | 91 | 96 | 442 GLENWOOD AVENUE | Pixies Three, Mercury 72208 | 4 |
| ★77 | 92 | — | — | COMIN' ON | Bill Black's Combo, Hi 2072 | 2 |
| 78 | — | — | — | HI-HEEL SNEAKERS | Tommy Tucker, Checker 1067 | 1 |
| ★79 | — | — | — | MILLER'S CAVE | Bobby Bare, RCA Victor 8294 | 1 |
| 80 | 80 | 72 | 67 | IF SOMEBODY TOLD YOU | Anna King, Smash 1858 | 6 |
| ★81 | — | — | — | LIVE WIRE | Martha & the Vandellas, Gordy 7027 | 1 |
| 82 | 89 | — | — | BABY WHAT YOU WANT ME TO DO | Etta James, Argo 5459 | 2 |
| 83 | 86 | 92 | — | STRANGER IN YOUR ARMS | Bobby Vee, Liberty 55654 | 3 |
| 84 | 87 | — | — | (I'm Watching) EVERY LITTLE MOVE YOU MAKE | Little Peggy March, RCA Victor 8302 | 2 |
| 85 | 95 | — | — | LONG GONE LONESOME BLUES | Hank Williams Jr., MGM 13208 | 2 |
| ★86 | — | — | — | HE'LL HAVE TO GO | Solomon Burke, Atlantic 2218 | 1 |
| ★87 | — | — | — | LEAVING HERE | Eddie Holland, Motown 1052 | 1 |
| 88 | 97 | — | — | WHERE DID I GO WRONG | Dee Dee Sharp, Cameo 296 | 2 |
| 89 | 100 | — | — | HERE'S A HEART | Diplomats, Arock 1004 | 2 |
| ★90 | — | — | — | TELL HIM | Drew-Vels, Capitol 5055 | 1 |
| 91 | 94 | 98 | — | ASK ME | Inez Foxx, Symbol 926 | 3 |
| 92 | 98 | — | — | LITTLE BOY | Crystals, Philles 119 | 2 |
| 93 | 93 | — | 90 | DEEP IN THE HEART OF HARLEM | Clyde McPhatter, Mercury 72220 | 5 |
| 94 | — | — | — | I DIDN'T KNOW WHAT TIME IT WAS | Crampton Sisters, DCP 1001 | 1 |
| 95 | — | — | — | BIRD DANCE BEAT | Trashmen, Garrett 4003 | 1 |
| 96 | — | — | — | HE WALKS LIKE A MAN | Jody Miller, Capitol 5090 | 1 |
| 97 | — | — | 78 | SINCE I FOUND A NEW LOVE | Little Johnny Taylor, Galaxy 725 | 4 |
| 98 | — | — | — | HAVE YOU EVER BEEN LONELY | Caravelles, Smash 1869 | 1 |
| 99 | — | — | — | RIP VAN WINKLE | Devotions, Roulette 4541 | 1 |
| 100 | — | — | — | STRANGE THINGS HAPPENING | Little Junior Parker, Duke 371 | 1 |

## HOT 100—A TO Z—*(Publisher-Licensee)*

Abigail Beecher (Claridge-Halseon, ASCAP) ........ 50
Anyone Who Had a Heart (U. S. Songs, ASCAP) .. 9
As Usual (Samos Island, BMI) .......... 25
Ask Me (Saturn, BMI) .......... 91
Baby, I Love You (Mother Bertha-Trio, BMI) .... 28
Baby What You Want Me to Do (Conrad, BMI) .. 82
Bird Dance Beat (Willong, BMI) .......... 95
Bye Bye Barbara (Fisher-Elm Drive, ASCAP) ...... 71
California Sun (Lloyd & Logan, BMI) .......... 23
Can Your Monkey Do the Dog (East, BMI) ....... 70
Charade (Southdale-Northern, ASCAP) .......... 39
Come On (Fame, BMI) .......... 40
Comin' in the Back Door (Irving, BMI) .......... 41
Comin' On (Jec, BMI) .......... 77
Daisy Petal Pickin' (Dundee, BMI) .......... 15
Dawn (Go Away) (Saturday-Gavidima, ASCAP) ... 24
Deep in the Heart of Harlem (January, BMI) ..... 93
Drag City (Screen Gems-Columbia, BMI) .......... 21
Dumb Head (Peter Maurice, ASCAP) .......... 62
Fool Never Learns, A (Cricket, BMI) .......... 16
For You (Witmark, ASCAP) .......... 8
Forget Him (Leeds, ASCAP) .......... 18
442 Glenwood Avenue (Merjoda, BMI) .......... 76
Girls Grow Up Faster Than Boys (Screen Gems-Columbia, BMI) .......... 37
Going Going Gone (Gil, BMI) .......... 51
Gonna Send You Back to Georgia (Zann, BMI) .. 63
Good News (Kags, BMI) .......... 48
Harlem Shuffle (Marc Jean-Keyman, BMI) ....... 44
Have You Ever Been Lonely (Shapiro-Bernstein, ASCAP) .......... 98
He Says the Same Things to Me (Geld-Udell, ASCAP) .......... 56
He Walks Like a Man (Central Songs, BMI) ..... 96
He'll Have to Go (Central Songs, BMI) ....... 86
Here's a Heart (Sylvia, BMI) .......... 89
Hey Little Cobra (Vadim, BMI) .......... 4
Hi-Heel Sneakers (Medal, BMI) .......... 78
Hooka Tooka (Evanston-Woodcrest, BMI) ........ 17
I Can't Stop Talking About You (Screen Gems-Columbia, BMI) .......... 35
I Didn't Know What Time It Was (Chappell, ASCAP) .......... 94
I Love You More and More Every Day (Robertson, ASCAP) .......... 46
I Only Want to Be With You (Chappell, ASCAP) ... 54
I Saw Her Standing There (Hofer, BMI) ........ 68
I Want to Hold Your Hand (Duchess, BMI) ...... 1
I Wish You Love (Leeds, ASCAP) .......... 53
I'll Remember (in the Still of the Night) (Cherio, BMI) .......... 59
If Somebody Told You (Jim Jim, BMI) .......... 80
(I'm Watching) Every Little Move You Make (Spanka, BMI) .......... 84
It's All in the Game (Remick, ASCAP) ...... 27
(It's No) Sin (Algonquin, BMI) .......... 74
Java (Tideland, BMI) .......... 13
Leaving Here (Jobete, BMI) .......... 87
Letter From Sherry (NuStar, BMI) .......... 30
Little Boxes (Schroder, ASCAP) .......... 75
Little Boy, The—Bennett (Morris, ASCAP) ...... 66
Little Boy—Crystals (Mother Bertha-Trio, BMI) .. 92
Live Wire (Jobete, BMI) .......... 81
Long Gone Lonesome Blues (Acuff-Rose, BMI) .... 85
Louie Louie (Limax, BMI) .......... 14
Miller's Cave (Jack, BMI) .......... 79
My One and Only Jimmy Boy (Screen Gems-Columbia, BMI) .......... 60
Navy Blue (Saturday, ASCAP) .......... 42
Nitty Gritty, The (Gallico, BMI) .......... 31
Oh Baby Don't You Weep (Jim Jam, BMI) ...... 47
Out of Limits (Wrist, BMI) .......... 3
Pain in My Heart (Jarb, BMI) .......... 61
Penetration (Dorothy, ASCAP) .......... 67
Pink Dominoes (Dimondaire-Room Seven, BMI) ... 69
Please Please Me (Concertone, ASCAP) .......... 57
Popsicles and Icicles (Dragonwyck, BMI) ........ 19
Puppy Love (McLaughlin, BMI) .......... 64
Quicksand (Jobete, BMI) .......... 43
Rip Van Winkle (Skidmore, ASCAP) .......... 99
See the Funny Little Clown (Unart, BMI) ....... 45
She Loves You (Gil, BMI) .......... 7
Shelter of Your Arms, The (Prince, ASCAP) ..... 38
Shimmy Shimmy (Thin Man, BMI) .......... 72
Since I Fell For You (Advanced, ASCAP) ..... 32
Since I Found a New Love (Cireco-Voycon, BMI) .. 97
Somewhere (Wyncote, ASCAP) .......... 22
Southtown, U.S.A. (Gallico, BMI) .......... 29
Stop and Think It Over (Crazy Cajun-Red Sticy, BMI .......... 26
Strange Things Happening (Venice, BMI) .......100
Stranger in Your Arms (Davilene-Saima, BMI) .. 83
Surfin' Bird (Willong, BMI) .......... 6
Talking About My Baby (Curtom, BMI) .... 12
Tell Him (Beechwood, BMI) .......... 90
That Girl Belongs to Yesterday (Pitfield, BMI) ... 55
There! I've Said It Again (Valiant, ASCAP) ..... 10
Tonight You're Gonna Fall in Love With Me (Screen Gems-Columbia, BMI) .......... 65
Um, Um, Um, Um, Um, Um (Curtom-Jalynne, BMI) . 5
Vaya Con Dios (Ardmore, ASCAP) .......... 52
Watch Your Step (Ludix, BMI) .......... 73
What Kind of Fool (Do You Think I Am) (Low-Twi, BMI) .......... 11
What's Easy for Two Is So Hard for One (Jobete, BMI) .......... 33
When the Lovelight Starts Shining Through His Eyes (Jobete, BMI) .......... 36
Where Did I Go Wrong (Kalmann, ASCAP) ...... 88
Whispering (Fisher-Miller, ASCAP) .......... 20
Who Do You Love (Hill & Range, BMI) .......... 58
Wow Wow Wee (Grand Canyon, BMI) .......... 49
You Don't Own Me (Merjoda, BMI) .......... 2
You'll Never Walk Alone (Williamson, ASCAP) .. 34

## BUBBLING UNDER THE HOT 100

101. THE GREASY SPOON ..........Hank Marr, Federal 12508
102. WHAT NOW MY LOVE ..........Ben E. King, Atco 6284
103. SAGINAW, MICHIGAN.......... Lefty Frizzell, Columbia 42924
104. SLIPIN' AND SLIDIN'.......... Jim & Monica, Betty 1207
105. HERE COMES THE BOY ..........Tracey Dey, Amy 894
106. BIG TOWN BOY ..........Shirley Matthews, Atlantic 2210
107. MY BONNIE ..........Beatles, MGM 13213
108. BILLIE BABY ..........Lloyd Price, Double L 729
109. HIS KISS ..........Betty Harris, Jubilee 5465
110. STAY WITH ME ..........Frank Sinatra, Reprise 0249
111. SO FAR AWAY ..........Hank Jacobs, Sue 795
112. PLEASE DON'T GO AWAY ..........Johnny Tillotson, MGM 13193
113. THE LA-DEE-DA SONG ..........Village Stompers, Epic 9655
114. WHEN YOU WALK IN THE ROOM ......Jackie DeShannon, Liberty 55645
115. TOUS LES CHEMINS ........Soeur Sourire (Singing Nun), Philips 40165
116. FUN, FUN, FUN ..........Beach Boys, Capitol 5118
117. GOING BACK TO LOUISIANA ..........Bruce Channel, LeCam 122
118. TRUE LOVE GOES ON AND ON ..........Burl Ives, Decca 31571
119. DARK AS A DUNGEON ..........Johnny Cash, Columbia 42964
120. CHARADE ..........Andy Williams, Columbia 42950
121. GLAD ALL OVER ..........Dave Clark Five, Epic 9656
122. YOU CAN'T MISS NOTHING YOU NEVER HAD . . Ike & Tina Turner, Sonja 2005
123. UNDERSTAND YOUR MAN ..........Johnny Cash, Columbia 42964
124. JUDY LOVES ME ..........Johnny Crawford, Del-Fi 4231
125. THE HAREM ..........Mr. Acker Bilk, Atco 6282
126. WHY, WHY DON'T YOU BELIEVE ME ....Shep & the Limelites, Hull 761
127. ROBERTA ..........Barry & the Tamerlanes, Valiant 6040
128. STAY ..........4 Seasons, Vee Jay 582
129. GOTTA FIND A WAY ..........Theresa Lindsey, Correc-Tone 5840
130. SOUL DANCE ..........Tommy Leonetti, RCA Victor 8251
131. WHO NEEDS IT ..........Gene Pitney, Musicor 1036
132. LOOK HOMEWARD ANGEL ..........Monarchs, Sound Stage 7 2516
133. I'LL BE THERE ..........Majors, Imperial 66009
134. WELCOME TO MY WORLD .......... Jim Reeves, RCA Victor 8289

Compiled from national retail sales and radio station airplay by the Music Popularity Dept. of Record Market Research, Billboard.

Billboard

For Week Ending February 15, 1964

# HOT 100

★ STAR performer—Sides registering greatest proportionate upward progress this week.

| This Week | 1 Wk. Ago | 2 Wks. Ago | 3 Wks. Ago | TITLE Artist, Label & Number | Weeks On Chart |
|---|---|---|---|---|---|
| 1 (Billboard Award) | 1 | 1 | 3 | I WANT TO HOLD YOUR HAND — Beatles, Capitol 5112 | 5 |
| 2 | 2 | 2 | 13 | YOU DON'T OWN ME — Lesley Gore, Mercury 72206 | 8 |
| ★ 3 | 7 | 21 | 69 | SHE LOVES YOU — Beatles, Swan 4152 | 4 |
| 4 | 4 | 5 | 7 | HEY LITTLE COBRA — Rip Chords, Columbia 42921 | 10 |
| 5 | 5 | 8 | 9 | UM, UM, UM, UM, UM, UM — Major Lance, Okeh 7187 | 7 |
| 6 | 8 | 10 | 14 | FOR YOU — Rick Nelson, Decca 31574 | 8 |
| 7 | 3 | 3 | 6 | OUT OF LIMITS — Marketts, Warner Bros. 5391 | 11 |
| 8 | 9 | 9 | 16 | ANYONE WHO HAD A HEART — Dionne Warwick, Scepter 1262 | 11 |
| ★ 9 | 13 | 23 | 36 | JAVA — Al Hirt, RCA Victor 8280 | 7 |
| 10 | 11 | 17 | 33 | WHAT KIND OF FOOL (Do You Think I Am) — Tams, ABC-Paramount 10502 | 10 |
| ★ 11 | 24 | 75 | — | DAWN (Go Away) — 4 Seasons, Philips 40166 | 3 |
| 12 | 12 | 15 | 25 | TALKING ABOUT MY BABY — Impressions, ABC-Paramount 10511 | 5 |
| 13 | 16 | 22 | 30 | A FOOL NEVER LEARNS — Andy Williams, Columbia 42950 | 6 |
| ★ 14 | 23 | 38 | 70 | CALIFORNIA SUN — Rivieras, Riviera 1401 | 4 |
| 15 | 6 | 4 | 4 | SURFIN' BIRD — Trashmen, Garrett 4002 | 11 |
| ★ 16 | 26 | 43 | 66 | STOP AND THINK IT OVER — Dale & Grace, Montel 922 | 4 |
| 17 | 17 | 20 | 27 | HOOKA TOOKA — Chubby Checker, Parkway 890 | 11 |
| 18 | 10 | 7 | 1 | THERE! I'VE SAID IT AGAIN — Bobby Vinton, Epic 9638 | 12 |
| 19 | 15 | 18 | 18 | DAISY PETAL PICKIN' — Jimmy Gilmer & the Fireballs, Dot 16539 | 10 |
| ★ 20 | 29 | 44 | 61 | SOUTHTOWN, U. S. A. — Dixiebelles, Sound Stage 7 2517 | 5 |
| ★ 21 | 42 | 71 | 90 | NAVY BLUE — Diane Renay, 20th Century-Fox 456 | 4 |
| ★ 22 | 45 | 55 | 65 | SEE THE FUNNY LITTLE CLOWN — Bobby Goldsboro, United Artists 672 | 6 |
| 23 | 14 | 6 | 2 | LOUIE LOUIE — Kingsmen, Wand 143 | 15 |
| 24 | 18 | 12 | 8 | FORGET HIM — Bobby Rydell, Cameo 280 | 15 |
| 25 | 27 | 28 | 37 | IT'S ALL IN THE GAME — Cliff Richard, Epic 9633 | 11 |
| 26 | 30 | 35 | 56 | LETTER FROM SHERRY — Dale Ward, Dot 16520 | 8 |
| ★ 27 | 54 | 73 | 77 | I ONLY WANT TO BE WITH YOU — Dusty Springfield, Philips 40162 | 4 |
| 28 | 19 | 11 | 5 | POPSICLES AND ICICLES — Murmaids, Chattahoochee 628 | 13 |
| ★ 29 | 48 | 77 | 93 | GOOD NEWS — Sam Cooke, RCA Victor 8299 | 4 |
| ★ 30 | 38 | 40 | 50 | THE SHELTER OF YOUR ARMS — Sammy Davis Jr., Reprise 20216 | 10 |
| 31 | 33 | 48 | 38 | WHAT'S EASY FOR TWO IS SO HARD FOR ONE — Mary Wells, Motown 1048 | 13 |
| 32 | 28 | 24 | 26 | BABY I LOVE YOU — Ronettes, Philles 118 | 9 |
| ★ 33 | 46 | 79 | — | I LOVE YOU MORE AND MORE EVERY DAY — Al Martino, Capitol 5108 | 3 |
| 34 | 25 | 16 | 12 | AS USUAL — Brenda Lee, Decca 31570 | 10 |
| ★ 35 | 47 | 54 | 73 | OH BABY DON'T YOU WEEP — James Brown & the Famous Flames, King 5842 | 4 |
| ★ 36 | 50 | 66 | — | ABIGAIL BEECHER — Freddy Cannon, Warner Bros. 5409 | 3 |
| 37 | 39 | 36 | 40 | CHARADE — Henry Mancini & His Ork, RCA Victor 8256 | 11 |
| 38 | 40 | 51 | 64 | COME ON — Tommy Roe, ABC-Paramount 10515 | 5 |
| ★ 39 | 51 | 61 | 82 | GOING GOING GONE — Brook Benton, Mercury 72230 | 4 |
| 40 | 21 | 13 | 10 | DRAG CITY — Jan & Dean, Liberty 55641 | 11 |
| 41 | 49 | 76 | 88 | WOW WOW WEE — Angels, Smash 1870 | 5 |
| 42 | 22 | 19 | 21 | SOMEWHERE — Tymes, Parkway 891 | 11 |
| 43 | 34 | 41 | 48 | YOU'LL NEVER WALK ALONE — Patti LaBelle & Her Blue Belles, Parkway 896 | 7 |
| 44 | 20 | 14 | 11 | WHISPERING — Nino Tempo & April Stevens, Atco 6281 | 9 |
| ★ 45 | 57 | 68 | — | PLEASE PLEASE ME — Beatles, Vee Jay 581 | 3 |
| ★ 46 | 58 | 78 | 97 | WHO DO YOU LOVE — Sapphires, Swan 4162 | 6 |
| ★ 47 | 63 | 72 | 83 | GONNA SEND YOU BACK TO GEORGIA — Timmy Shaw, Wand 146 | 4 |
| 48 | 52 | 64 | — | VAYA CON DIOS — Drifters, Atlantic 2216 | 3 |
| 49 | 31 | 25 | 17 | THE NITTY GRITTY — Shirley Ellis, Congress 202 | 14 |
| 50 | 53 | 56 | 68 | I WISH YOU LOVE — Gloria Lynne, Everest 2036 | 6 |
| 51 | 55 | 60 | 71 | THAT GIRL BELONGS TO YESTERDAY — Gene Pitney, Musicor 1036 | 5 |
| 52 | 56 | 63 | 76 | HE SAYS THE SAME THINGS TO ME — Skeeter Davis, RCA Victor 8288 | 4 |
| 53 | 35 | 37 | 39 | I CAN'T STOP TALKING ABOUT YOU — Steve & Eydie, Columbia 42932 | 9 |
| ★ 54 | 68 | — | — | I SAW HER STANDING THERE — Beatles, Capitol 5112 | 2 |
| ★ 55 | 67 | 90 | — | PENETRATION — Pyramids, Best 13002 | 3 |
| 56 | 44 | 46 | 49 | HARLEM SHUFFLE — Bob & Earl, Marc 104 | 9 |
| ★ 57 | 78 | — | — | HI-HEEL SNEAKERS — Tommy Tucker, Checker 1067 | 2 |
| ★ 58 | 81 | — | — | LIVE WIRE — Martha & the Vandellas, Gordy 7027 | 2 |
| 59 | 59 | 70 | 80 | I'LL REMEMBER (In the Still of the Night) — Santo & Johnny, Canadian-American 164 | 5 |
| 60 | 64 | 74 | 81 | PUPPY LOVE — Barbara Lewis, Atlantic 2214 | 6 |
| ★ 61 | 95 | — | — | BIRD DANCE BEAT — Trashmen, Garrett 4003 | 2 |
| ★ 62 | 79 | — | — | MILLER'S CAVE — Bobby Bare, RCA Victor 8294 | 2 |
| 63 | 41 | 42 | 45 | COMIN' IN THE BACK DOOR — Baja Marimba Band, Almo 201 | 9 |
| 64 | 70 | 85 | — | CAN YOUR MONKEY DO THE DOG — Rufus Thomas, Stax 144 | 3 |
| 65 | 76 | 84 | 91 | 442 GLENWOOD AVENUE — Pixies Three, Mercury 72208 | 5 |
| 66 | 66 | 52 | 55 | THE LITTLE BOY — Tony Bennett, Columbia 42931 | 9 |
| ★ 67 | — | — | — | MY BONNIE — Beatles, MGM 13213 | 1 |
| 68 | 72 | 88 | — | SHIMMY SHIMMY — Orlons, Cameo 295 | 3 |
| ★ 69 | — | — | — | FUN, FUN, FUN — Beach Boys, Capitol 5118 | 1 |
| 70 | 71 | 99 | — | BYE BYE BARBARA — Johnny Mathis, Mercury 72229 | 3 |
| ★ 71 | — | — | — | BLUE WINTER — Connie Francis, MGM 13214 | 1 |
| 72 | 86 | — | — | HE'LL HAVE TO GO — Solomon Burke, Atlantic 2218 | 2 |
| 73 | 75 | 83 | 86 | LITTLE BOXES — Pete Seeger, Columbia 42940 | 6 |
| 74 | 61 | 62 | 62 | PAIN IN MY HEART — Otis Redding, Volt 112 | 11 |
| 75 | 77 | 92 | — | COMIN' ON — Bill Black's Combo, Hi 2072 | 3 |
| ★ 76 | — | — | — | HELLO, DOLLY! — Louis Armstrong, Kapp 573 | 1 |
| ★ 77 | — | — | — | GLAD ALL OVER — Dave Clark Five, Epic 9656 | 1 |
| 78 | 69 | 69 | 75 | PINK DOMINOES — Crescents, Era 3116 | 8 |
| 79 | 87 | — | — | LEAVING HERE — Eddie Holland, Motown 1052 | 2 |
| ★ 80 | — | — | — | YOUNG AND IN LOVE — Chris Crosby, MGM 13191 | 1 |
| ★ 81 | — | — | — | STAY — 4 Seasons, Vee Jay 582 | 1 |
| 82 | 88 | 97 | — | WHERE DID I GO WRONG — Dee Dee Sharp, Cameo 296 | 3 |
| 83 | 85 | 95 | — | LONG GONE LONESOME BLUES — Hank Williams Jr., MGM 13208 | 3 |
| ★ 84 | — | — | — | TELL ME BABY — Garnet Mimms and the Enchanters, United Artists 694 | 1 |
| 85 | 96 | — | — | HE WALKS LIKE A MAN — Jody Miller, Capitol 5090 | 2 |
| ★ 86 | — | — | — | UNDERSTAND YOUR MAN — Johnny Cash, Columbia 4296 | 1 |
| ★ 87 | — | — | — | LOVE WITH THE PROPER STRANGER — Jack Jones, Kapp 571 | 1 |
| 88 | 74 | 82 | 94 | (It's No) SIN — Dupress, Coed 587 | 4 |
| 89 | 99 | — | — | RIP VAN WINKLE — Devotions, Roulette 4541 | 2 |
| 90 | 90 | — | — | TELL HIM — Drew-Vels, Capitol 5055 | 2 |
| 91 | — | — | 85 | SAGINAW, MICHIGAN — Lefty Frizell, Columbia 42924 | 3 |
| 92 | 94 | — | — | I DIDN'T KNOW WHAT TIME IT WAS — Crampton Sisters, DCP 1001 | 2 |
| 93 | 84 | 87 | — | (I'm Watching) EVERY LITTLE MOVE YOU MAKE — Little Peggy March, RCA Victor 8302 | 3 |
| 94 | 82 | 89 | — | BABY WHAT YOU WANT ME TO DO — Etta James, Argo 5459 | 3 |
| 95 | 98 | — | — | HAVE YOU EVER BEEN LONELY — Caravelles, Smash 1869 | 2 |
| 96 | 92 | 98 | — | LITTLE BOY — Crystals, Philles 119 | 3 |
| 97 | — | — | — | PLEASE, PLEASE, PLEASE — James Brown and the Famous Flames, King 5853 | 1 |
| 98 | 89 | 100 | — | HERE'S A HEART — Diplomats, Arock 1004 | 3 |
| 99 | 100 | — | — | STRANGE THINGS HAPPENING — Little Junior Parker, Duke 371 | 2 |
| 100 | — | — | 67 | TRUE LOVE GOES ON AND ON — Burl Ives, Decca 31571 | 6 |

## HOT 100—A TO Z—(Publisher-Licensee)


Abigail Beecher (Claridge-Halseon, ASCAP) .......... 36
Anyone Who Had a Heart (U. S. Songs, ASCAP) 8
As Usual (Samos Island, BMI) .......... 34
Baby, I Love You (Mother Bertha-Trio, BMI) .......... 32
Baby What You Want Me to Do (Conrad, BMI) .......... 94
Bird Dance Beat (Willong, BMI) .......... 61
Blue Winter (January, BMI) .......... 71
Bye Bye Barbara (Fisher-Elm Drive, ASCAP) .......... 70
California Sun (Lloyd & Logan, BMI) .......... 14
Can Your Monkey Do the Dog (East, BMI) .......... 64
Charade (Southdale-Northern, ASCAP) .......... 37
Come On (Fame, BMI) .......... 38
Comin' in the Back Door (Irving, BMI) .......... 63
Comin' On (Jec, BMI) .......... 75
Daisy Petal Pickin' (Dundee, BMI) .......... 19
Dawn (Go Away) (Saturday-Gavidima, ASCAP) .......... 11
Drag City (Screen Gems-Columbia, BMI) .......... 40
Fool Never Learns, A (Cricket, BMI) .......... 13
For You (Witmark, ASCAP) .......... 6
Forget Him (Leeds, ASCAP) .......... 24
442 Glenwood Avenue (Merjoda, BMI) .......... 65
Fun, Fun, Fun (Sea of Tunes, BMI) .......... 69
Glad All Over (Ivy, ASCAP) .......... 77
Going Going Gone (Gil, BMI) .......... 39
Gonna Send You Back to Georgia (Zann, BMI) .......... 47
Good News (Kags, BMI) .......... 29
Harlem Shuffle (Marc Jean-Keyman, BMI) .......... 56
Have You Ever Been Lonely (Shapiro-Bernstein, ASCAP) .......... 95
He Says the Same Things to Me (Geld-Udell, ASCAP) .......... 52
He Walks Like a Man (Central Songs, BMI) .......... 85
He'll Have to Go (Central Songs, BMI) .......... 72
Hello, Dolly! (Morris, ASCAP) .......... 76
Here's a Heart (Sylvia, BMI) .......... 98
Hey Little Cobra (Vadim, BMI) .......... 4
Hi-Heel Sneakers (Medal, BMI) .......... 57
Hooka Tooka (Evanston-Woodcrest, BMI) .......... 17
I Can't Stop Talking About You (Screen Gems-Columbia, BMI) .......... 53
I Didn't Know What Time It Was (Chappell, ASCAP) .......... 92
I Love You More and More Every Day (Robertson, ASCAP) .......... 33
I Only Want to Be With You (Chappell, ASCAP) .......... 27
I Saw Her Standing There (Hofer, BMI) .......... 54
I Want to Hold Your Hand (Duchess, BMI) .......... 1
I Wish You Love (Leeds, ASCAP) .......... 50
I'll Remember (in the Still of the Night) (Cherio, BMI) .......... 59
(I'm Watching) Every Little Move You Make (Spanka, BMI) .......... 93
It's All in the Game (Remick, ASCAP) .......... 25
(It's No) Sin (Algonquin, BMI) .......... 88
Java (Tideland, BMI) .......... 9
Leaving Here (Jobete, BMI) .......... 79
Letter From Sherry (Nu Star, BMI) .......... 26
Little Boxes (Schroder, ASCAP) .......... 73
Little Boy, The—Bennett (Morris, ASCAP) .......... 66
Little Boy—Crystals (Mother Bertha-Trio, BMI) .......... 96
Live Wire (Jobete, BMI) .......... 58
Long Gone Lonesome Blues (Acuff-Rose, BMI) .......... 83
Louie Louie (Limax, BMI) .......... 23
Love With the Proper Stranger (Paramount, ASCAP) .......... 87
Miller's Cave (Jack, BMI) .......... 62
My Bonnie (P.D.) .......... 67
Navy Blue (Saturday, ASCAP) .......... 21
Nitty Gritty, The (Gallico, BMI) .......... 49
Oh Baby Don't You Weep (Jim Jam, BMI) .......... 35
Out of Limits (Wrist, BMI) .......... 7
Pain in My Heart (Jarb, BMI) .......... 74
Penetration (Dorothy, ASCAP) .......... 55
Pink Dominoes (Dimondaire-Room Seven, BMI) .......... 78
Please Please Me (Concertone, ASCAP) .......... 45
Please, Please, Please (Armo, BMI) .......... 97
Popsicles and Icicles (Dragonwyck, BMI) .......... 28
Puppy Love (McLaughlin, BMI) .......... 60
Rip Van Winkle (Skidmore, ASCAP) .......... 89
Saginaw, Michigan (Tree, BMI) .......... 91
See the Funny Little Clown (Unart, BMI) .......... 22
She Loves You (Gil, BMI) .......... 3
Shelter of Your Arms, The (Print, ASCAP) .......... 30
Shimmy Shimmy (Thin Man, BMI) .......... 68
Somewhere (Wyncote, ASCAP) .......... 42
Southtown U.S.A. (Gallico, BMI) .......... 20
Stay (Cherio, BMI) .......... 81
Stop and Think It Over (Crazy Cajun-Red Sticy, BMI) .......... 16
Strange Things Happening (Venice, BMI) .......... 99
Surfin' Bird (Willong, BMI) .......... 15
Talking About My Baby (Curtom, BMI) .......... 12
Tell Him (Beechwood, BMI) .......... 90
Tell Me Baby (Sealark, BMI) .......... 84
That Girl Belongs to Yesterday (Pitfield, BMI) .......... 51
There! I've Said It Again (Valiant, ASCAP) .......... 18
True Love Goes On and On (Frank, ASCAP) .......... 100
Um, Um, Um, Um, Um, Um (Curtom-Jalynne, BMI) .......... 5
Understand Your Man (Cash, BMI) .......... 86
Vaya Con Dios (Ardmore, ASCAP) .......... 48
What Kind of Fool (Do You Think I Am) (Low-Twi, BMI) .......... 10
What's Easy for Two Is So Hard for One (Jobete, BMI) .......... 31
Where Did I Go Wrong (Kalmann, ASCAP) .......... 82
Whispering (Fisher-Miller, ASCAP) .......... 44
Who Do You Love (Hill & Range, BMI) .......... 46
Wow Wow Wee (Grand Canyon, BMI) .......... 41
You Don't Own Me (Merjoda, BMI) .......... 2
You'll Never Walk Alone (Williamson, ASCAP) .......... 43
Young and in Love (Miller, ASCAP) .......... 80


## BUBBLING UNDER THE HOT 100

101. MY TRUE CARRIE LOVE .......... Nat King Cole, Capitol 5125
102. HOW MUCH CAN A LONELY HEART STAND .. Skeeter Davis, RCA Victor 8288
103. STAY WITH ME .......... Frank Sinatra, Reprise 0249
104. WORRIED GUY .......... Johnny Tillotson, MGM 13193
105. HIGH ON A HILL .......... Scott English, Spokane 4003
106. I CAN'T STAND IT .......... Soul Sisters, Sue 799
107. WHAT NOW MY LOVE .......... Ben E. King, Atco 6284
108. GOING BACK TO LOUISIANA .......... Bruce Channel, LeCam 122
109. SINCE I FOUND A NEW LOVE .......... Little Johnny Taylor, Galaxy 725
110. THE LA-DEE-DAH SONG .......... Village Stompers, Epic 9655
111. HERE COMES THE BOY .......... Tracey Dey, Amy 894
112. PLEASE DON'T GO AWAY .......... Johnny Tillotson, MGM 13193
113. I'LL BE THERE .......... Majors, Imperial 66009
114. BIG TOWN BOY .......... Shirley Matthews, Atlantic 2210
115. SO FAR AWAY .......... Hank Jacobs, Sue 795
116. LOOK HOMEWARD ANGEL .......... Monarchs, Sound Stage 7 2516
117. HE'S A GOOD GUY .......... Marvelettes, Tamla 54091
118. GREASY SPOON .......... Hank Marr, Federal 12508
119. WHO'S BEEN SLEEPING IN MY BED .......... Linda Scott, Congress 204
120. A ROOM WITHOUT WINDOWS .......... Steve Lawrence, Columbia 42952
121. WELCOME TO MY WORLD .......... Jim Reeves, RCA Victor 8289
122. MY BOYFRIEND GOT A BEATLE HAIRCUT .......... Donna Lynn, Capitol 5127
123. ON AND ON .......... Jerry Vale, Columbia 42951
124. CUSTOM MACHINE .......... Bruce & Terry, Columbia 42956
125. BABY COME ON HOME .......... Hoagy Lands, Atlantic 2217
126. OUT OF SIGHT—OUT OF MIND .... Sunny & the Sunliners, Tear Drop 3027
127. ALL MY TRIALS .......... Dick & Deedee, Warner Bros. 5411
128. COMPETITION COUPE .......... Astronauts, RCA Victor 8298
129. WHITE ON WHITE .......... Danny Williams, United Artists 685
130. YOU WERE WRONG .......... Z. Z. Hill, M&H 200
131. (The Story of) WOMAN, LOVE AND A MAN .......... Tony Clarke, Chess 1880

Compiled from national retail sales and radio station airplay by the Music Popularity Dept. of Record Market Research, Billboard.

# Billboard HOT 100

*For Week Ending February 22, 1964*

★ STAR performer—Sides registering greatest proportionate upward progress this week.

| This Week | Wk. Ago | 2 Wk. Ago | TITLE Artist, Label & Number | Weeks On Chart |
|---|---|---|---|---|
| 1 | 1 | 1 | **I WANT TO HOLD YOUR HAND** — Beatles, Capitol 5112 | 6 |
| 2 | 3 | 7 | **SHE LOVES YOU** — Beatles, Swan 4152 | 21 |
| ★3 | 11 | 24 | **DAWN (Go Away)** — 4 Seasons, Philips 40166 | 4 |
| 4 | 2 | 2 | **YOU DON'T OWN ME** — Lesley Gore, Mercury 72206 | 9 |
| 5 | 9 | 13 | **JAVA** — Al Hirt, RCA Victor 8280 | 8 |
| 6 | 5 | 5 | **UM, UM, UM, UM, UM, UM** — Major Lance, Okeh 7187 | 8 |
| 7 | 4 | 4 | **HEY LITTLE COBRA** — Rip Chords, Columbia 42921 | 11 |
| 8 | 14 | 23 | **CALIFORNIA SUN** — Rivieras, Riviera 1401 | 5 |
| 9 | 10 | 11 | **WHAT KIND OF FOOL (Do You Think I Am)** — Tams, ABC-Paramount 10502 | 11 |
| ★10 | 21 | 42 | **NAVY BLUE** — Diane Renay, 20th Century-Fox 456 | 5 |
| 11 | 6 | 8 | **FOR YOU** — Rick Nelson, Decca 31574 | 9 |
| 12 | 16 | 26 | **STOP AND THINK IT OVER** — Dale & Grace, Montel 922 | 5 |
| 13 | 7 | 3 | **OUT OF LIMITS** — Marketts, Warner Bros. 5391 | 12 |
| 14 | 12 | 12 | **TALKING ABOUT MY BABY** — Impressions, ABC-Paramount 10511 | 6 |
| 15 | 20 | 29 | **SOUTHTOWN, U.S.A.** — Dixiebelles, Sound Stage 7 2517 | 6 |
| 16 | 8 | 9 | **ANYONE WHO HAD A HEART** — Dionne Warwick, Scepter 1262 | 12 |
| 17 | 22 | 45 | **SEE THE FUNNY LITTLE CLOWN** — Bobby Goldsboro, United Artists 672 | 7 |
| 18 | 13 | 16 | **A FOOL NEVER LEARNS** — Andy Williams, Columbia 42950 | 7 |
| 19 | 17 | 17 | **HOOKA TOOKA** — Chubby Checker, Parkway 890 | 12 |
| 20 | 27 | 54 | **I ONLY WANT TO BE WITH YOU** — Dusty Springfield, Philips 40162 | 7 |
| 21 | 29 | 48 | **GOOD NEWS** — Sam Cooke, RCA Victor 8299 | 5 |
| 22 | 15 | 6 | **SURFIN' BIRD** — Trashmen, Garrett 4002 | 12 |
| 23 | 36 | 50 | **ABIGAIL BEECHER** — Freddy Cannon, Warner Bros. 5409 | 4 |
| 24 | 33 | 46 | **I LOVE YOU MORE AND MORE EVERY DAY** — Al Martino, Capitol 5108 | 4 |
| 25 | 26 | 30 | **LETTER FROM SHERRY** — Dale Ward, Dot 16520 | 9 |
| 26 | 30 | 38 | **THE SHELTER OF YOUR ARMS** — Sammy Davis Jr., Reprise 20216 | 11 |
| 27 | 69 | — | **FUN, FUN, FUN** — Beach Boys, Capitol 5118 | 2 |
| 28 | 23 | 14 | **LOUIE LOUIE** — Kingsmen, Wand 143 | 16 |
| 29 | 45 | 57 | **PLEASE PLEASE ME** — Beatles, Vee Jay 581 | 4 |
| 30 | 55 | 67 | **PENETRATION** — Pyramids, Best 13002 | 4 |
| 31 | 31 | 33 | **WHAT'S EASY FOR TWO IS SO HARD FOR ONE** — Mary Wells, Motown 1048 | 14 |
| 32 | 35 | 47 | **OH BABY DON'T YOU WEEP** — James Brown and the Famous Flames, King 5842 | 5 |
| 33 | 25 | 27 | **IT'S ALL IN THE GAME** — Cliff Richard, Epic 9633 | 12 |
| 34 | 24 | 18 | **FORGET HIM** — Bobby Rydell, Cameo 280 | 16 |
| ★35 | 54 | 68 | **I SAW HER STANDING THERE** — Beatles, Capitol 5112 | 3 |
| 36 | 39 | 51 | **GOING GOING GONE** — Brook Benton, Mercury 72230 | 5 |
| 37 | 46 | 58 | **WHO DO YOU LOVE** — Sapphires, Swan 4162 | 7 |
| 38 | 38 | 40 | **COME ON** — Tommy Roe, ABC-Paramount 10515 | 6 |
| 39 | 19 | 15 | **DAISY PETAL PICKIN'** — Jimmy Gilmer and the Fireballs, Dot 16539 | 11 |
| 40 | 18 | 10 | **THERE! I'VE SAID IT AGAIN** — Bobby Vinton, Epic 9638 | 13 |
| 41 | 41 | 49 | **WOW WOW WEE** — Angels, Smash 1870 | 6 |
| ★42 | 57 | 78 | **HI-HEEL SNEAKERS** — Tommy Tucker, Checker 1067 | 3 |
| ★43 | 61 | 95 | **BIRD DANCE BEAT** — Trashmen, Garrett 4008 | 3 |
| 44 | 50 | 53 | **I WISH YOU LOVE** — Gloria Lynne, Everest 2036 | 7 |
| 45 | 47 | 63 | **GONNA SEND YOU BACK TO GEORGIA** — Timmy Shaw, Wand 146 | 5 |
| 46 | 48 | 52 | **VAYA CON DIOS** — Drifters, Atlantic 2216 | 4 |
| 47 | 58 | 81 | **LIVE WIRE** — Martha & the Vandellas, Gordy 7027 | 3 |
| 48 | 34 | 25 | **AS USUAL** — Brenda Lee, Decca 31570 | 11 |
| 49 | 51 | 55 | **THAT GIRL BELONGS TO YESTERDAY** — Gene Pitney, Musicor 1036 | 6 |
| 50 | 28 | 19 | **POPSICLES AND ICICLES** — Murmaids, Chattahoochee 628 | 14 |
| ★51 | 62 | 79 | **MILLER'S CAVE** — Bobby Bare, RCA Victor 8294 | 3 |
| 52 | 52 | 56 | **HE SAYS THE SAME THINGS TO ME** — Skeeter Davis, RCA Victor 8288 | 5 |
| ★53 | 76 | — | **HELLO, DOLLY!** — Louis Armstrong, Kapp 573 | 2 |
| ★54 | 67 | — | **MY BONNIE** — Beatles, MGM 13213 | 2 |
| 55 | 60 | 64 | **PUPPY LOVE** — Barbara Lewis, Atlantic 2214 | 7 |
| 56 | 65 | 76 | **422 GLENWOOD AVENUE** — Pixies Three, Mercury 72208 | 6 |
| 57 | 64 | 70 | **CAN YOUR MONKEY DO THE DOG** — Rufus Thomas, Stax 144 | 5 |
| 58 | 59 | 59 | **I'LL REMEMBER (In the Still of the Night)** — Santo & Johnny, Canadian-American 164 | 6 |
| ★59 | 71 | — | **BLUE WINTER** — Connie Francis, MGM 13214 | 2 |
| 60 | 70 | 71 | **BYE BYE BARBARA** — Johnny Mathis, Mercury 72229 | 4 |
| 61 | 56 | 44 | **HARLEM SHUFFLE** — Bob & Earl, Marc 104 | 10 |
| 62 | 43 | 34 | **YOU'LL NEVER WALK ALONE** — Patti LaBelle & Her Blue Belles, Parkway 896 | 8 |
| ★63 | — | — | **KISSIN' COUSINS** — Elvis Presley, RCA Victor 8307 | 1 |
| 64 | 72 | 86 | **HE'LL HAVE TO GO** — Solomon Burke, Atlantic 2218 | 3 |
| ★65 | 77 | — | **GLAD ALL OVER** — Dave Clark Five, Epic 9656 | 2 |
| 66 | 68 | 72 | **SHIMMY SHIMMY** — Orlons, Cameo 295 | 4 |
| 67 | 80 | — | **YOUNG AND IN LOVE** — Chris Crosby, MGM 13191 | 2 |
| 68 | 75 | 77 | **COMIN' ON** — Bill Black's Combo, Hi 2072 | 4 |
| 69 | — | — | **WORRIED GUY** — Johnny Tillotson, MGM 13193 | 1 |
| 70 | 73 | 75 | **LITTLE BOXES** — Pete Seeger, Columbia 42940 | 7 |
| ★71 | 86 | — | **UNDERSTAND YOUR MAN** — Johnny Cash, Columbia 4296 | 2 |
| 72 | 81 | — | **STAY** — 4 Seasons, Vee Jay 582 | 2 |
| 73 | 85 | 96 | **HE WALKS LIKE A MAN** — Jody Miller, Capitol 5090 | 3 |
| 74 | 87 | — | **LOVE WITH THE PROPER STRANGER** — Jack Jones, Kapp 571 | 2 |
| 75 | 83 | 85 | **LONG GONE LONESOME BLUES** — Hank Williams Jr., MGM 13208 | 4 |
| 76 | 79 | 87 | **LEAVING HERE** — Eddie Holland, Motown 1052 | 3 |
| 77 | 89 | 99 | **RIP VAN WINKLE** — Devotions, Roulette 4541 | 3 |
| 78 | 78 | 69 | **PINK DOMINOES** — Crescents, Era 3116 | 9 |
| 79 | — | — | **STARDUST** — Nino Tempo & April Stevens, Atco 6286 | 1 |
| 80 | 84 | — | **TELL ME BABY** — Garnet Mimms and the Enchanters, United Artists 694 | 2 |
| 81 | — | — | **LOOK HOMEWARD ANGEL** — Monarchs, Sound Stage 7 2516 | 1 |
| 82 | — | — | **MY TRUE CARRIE LOVE** — Nat King Cole, Capitol 5125 | 1 |
| 83 | — | — | **BABY, DON'T YOU CRY** — Ray Charles, ABC-Paramount 10530 | 1 |
| 84 | 88 | 74 | **(It's No) SIN** — Duprees, Coed 587 | 5 |
| 85 | 82 | 88 | **WHERE DID I GO WRONG** — Dee Dee Sharp, Cameo 296 | 4 |
| 86 | — | — | **(That's) WHAT THE NUTTY GRITTY IS** — Shirley Ellis, Congress 208 | 1 |
| 87 | 91 | — | **SAGINAW, MICHIGAN** — Lefty Frizzell, Columbia 42924 | 4 |
| 88 | — | — | **HEY JEAN, HEY DEAN** — Dean & Jean, Rust 5075 | 1 |
| 89 | — | — | **ALL MY TRIALS** — Dick & Deedee, Warner Bros. 5411 | 1 |
| 90 | — | — | **OUT OF SIGHT—OUT OF MIND** — Sunny & the Sunliners, Tear Drop 3027 | 1 |
| 91 | — | — | **HIGH ON A HILL** — Scott English, Spokane 4003 | 1 |
| 92 | — | — | **HOW MUCH CAN A LONELY HEART STAND** — Skeeter Davis, RCA Victor 8288 | 1 |
| 93 | — | — | **I'LL MAKE YOU MINE** — Bobby Vee, Liberty 55670 | 1 |
| 94 | 95 | 98 | **HAVE YOU EVER BEEN LONELY** — Caravelles, Smash 1869 | 3 |
| 95 | 97 | — | **PLEASE, PLEASE, PLEASE** — James Brown and the Famous Flames, King 5853 | 2 |
| 96 | — | — | **CUSTOM MACHINE** — Bruce & Terry, Columbia 42956 | 1 |
| 97 | — | — | **MY BOY FRIEND GOT A BEATLE HAIRCUT** — Donna Lynn, Capitol 5127 | 1 |
| 98 | — | — | **HE'S A GOOD GUY** — Marvelettes, Tamla 54091 | 1 |
| 99 | — | — | **SUSPICION** — Terry Stafford, Crusader 101 | 1 |
| 100 | — | — | **MO' ONIONS** — Booker T & the MG's, Stax 142 | 1 |

## BUBBLING UNDER THE HOT 100

101. THERE'S A MEETIN' HERE TONITE — Joe & Eddie, Crescendo 195
102. THE WAY YOU DO THE THINGS YOU DO — Temptations, Gordy 7028
103. (I'm Watching) EVERY LITTLE MOVE YOU MAKE — Little Peggy March, RCA Victor 8302
104. GOING BACK TO LOUISIANA — Bruce Channel, LeCam 122
105. I CAN'T STAND IT — Soul Sisters, Sue 799
106. YOU WERE WRONG — Jim Reeves, RCA Victor 8289
107. MY HEART CRIES FOR YOU — Z. Z. Hill, M&H 200
108. I DIDN'T KNOW WHAT TIME IT WAS — Crampton Sisters, DCP 1001
109. SHOOP SHOOP SONG — Betty Everett, Vee Jay 585
110. TELL HIM — Drew-Vels, Capitol 5055
111. I WONDER WHO'S KISSING HER NOW — Bobby Darin, Capitol 5126
112. IT HURTS ME — Elvis Presley, RCA Victor 8307
113. I'LL BE THERE — Majors, Imperial 66009
114. HITCHHIKE BACK TO GEORGIA — Buddy Knox, Liberty 55650
115. GIRL FROM SPANISH TOWN — Marty Robbins, Columbia 42968
116. STRANGE THINGS HAPPENING — Little Junior Parker, Duke 371
117. THE LA-DEE-DAH SONG — Village Stompers, Epic 9655
118. WELCOME TO MY WORLD — Jim Reeves, RCA Victor 8289
119. WHO'S BEEN SLEEPING IN MY BED — Linda Scott, Congress 204
120. FROM ME TO YOU — Beatles, Vee Jay 522
121. SINCE I FOUND A NEW LOVE — Little Johnny Taylor, Galaxy 725
122. FIVE LITTLE FINGERS — Bill Anderson, Decca 31577
123. SO FAR AWAY — Hank Jacobs, Sue 795
124. COMPETITION COUPE — Astronauts, RCA Victor 8298
125. WHITE ON WHITE — Danny Williams, United Artists 685
126. I'M LOOKING OVER A FOUR-LEAF CLOVER — Wayne Newton, Capitol 5124
127. A ROOM WITHOUT WINDOWS — Steve Lawrence, Columbia 42952
128. BIG TOWN BOY — Shirley Mathews, Atlantic 2210
129. NEVER LEAVE ME — Stratfords, O'Dell 100
130. WILLYAM, WILLYAM — Dee Dee Sharp, Cameo 296
131. ROBERTA — Barry & the Tamerlanes, Valiant 6040
132. BIG DADDY — Sue Thompson, Hickory 1240

*Compiled from national retail sales and radio station airplay by the Music Popularity Dept. of Record Market Research, Billboard.*

For Week Ending February 29, 1964

# Billboard HOT 100

★ STAR performer—Sides registering greatest proportionate upward progress this week.

| This Week | 1 Wk. Ago | 2 Wks. Ago | 3 Wks. Ago | TITLE Artist, Label & Number | Weeks On Chart |
|---|---|---|---|---|---|
| 1 (Billboard Award) | 1 | 1 | 1 | I WANT TO HOLD YOUR HAND — Beatles, Capitol 5112 | 7 |
| 2 | 2 | 3 | 7 | SHE LOVES YOU — Beatles, Swan 4152 | 6 |
| 3 | 3 | 11 | 24 | DAWN (Go Away) — 4 Seasons, Philips 40166 | 5 |
| 4 | 5 | 9 | 13 | JAVA — Al Hirt, RCA Victor 8280 | 9 |
| ★5 | 8 | 14 | 23 | CALIFORNIA SUN — Rivieras, Riviera 1401 | 6 |
| ★6 | 29 | 45 | 57 | PLEASE PLEASE ME — Beatles, Vee Jay 581 | 5 |
| 7 | 4 | 2 | 2 | YOU DON'T OWN ME — Lesley Gore, Mercury 72206 | 10 |
| 8 | 10 | 21 | 42 | NAVY BLUE — Diane Renay, 20th Century-Fox 456 | 6 |
| ★9 | 12 | 16 | 26 | STOP AND THINK IT OVER — Dale & Grace, Montel 922 | 6 |
| 10 | 6 | 5 | 5 | UM, UM, UM, UM, UM, UM — Major Lance, Okeh 7187 | 9 |
| 11 | 7 | 4 | 4 | HEY LITTLE COBRA — Rip Chords, Columbia 42921 | 12 |
| ★12 | 17 | 22 | 45 | SEE THE FUNNY LITTLE CLOWN — Bobby Goldsboro, United Artists 672 | 8 |
| ★13 | 21 | 29 | 48 | GOOD NEWS — Sam Cooke, RCA Victor 8299 | 6 |
| ★14 | 20 | 27 | 54 | I ONLY WANT TO BE WITH YOU — Dusty Springfield, Philips 40162 | 6 |
| ★15 | 24 | 33 | 46 | I LOVE YOU MORE AND MORE EVERY DAY — Al Martino, Capitol 5108 | 5 |
| 16 | 18 | 13 | 16 | A FOOL NEVER LEARNS — Andy Williams, Columbia 42950 | 8 |
| ★17 | 27 | 69 | — | FUN, FUN, FUN — Beach Boys, Capitol 5118 | 3 |
| ★18 | 23 | 36 | 50 | ABIGAIL BEECHER — Freddy Cannon, Warner Bros. 5409 | 5 |
| 19 | 14 | 12 | 12 | TALKING ABOUT MY BABY — Impressions, ABC-Paramount 10511 | 7 |
| 20 | 9 | 10 | 11 | WHAT KIND OF FOOL (Do You Think I Am) — Tams, ABC-Paramount 10502 | 12 |
| 21 | 11 | 6 | 8 | FOR YOU — Rick Nelson, Decca 31574 | 10 |
| 22 | 15 | 20 | 29 | SOUTHTOWN, U. S. A. — Dixiebelles, Sound Stage 7 2517 | 7 |
| 23 | 26 | 30 | 38 | THE SHELTER OF YOUR ARMS — Sammy Davis Jr., Reprise 20216 | 12 |
| 24 | 13 | 7 | 3 | OUT OF LIMITS — Marketts, Warner Bros. 5391 | 13 |
| ★25 | 30 | 55 | 67 | PENETRATION — Pyramids, Best 13002 | 5 |
| ★26 | 32 | 35 | 47 | OH BABY DON'T YOU WEEP — James Brown & the Famous Flames, King 5842 | 6 |
| 27 | 19 | 17 | 17 | HOOKA TOOKA — Chubby Checker, Parkway 890 | 13 |
| ★28 | 35 | 54 | 68 | I SAW HER STANDING THERE — Beatles, Capitol 5112 | 4 |
| 29 | 31 | 31 | 33 | WHAT'S EASY FOR TWO IS SO HARD FOR ONE — Mary Wells, Motown 1048 | 15 |
| ★30 | 37 | 46 | 58 | WHO DO YOU LOVE — Sapphires, Swan 4162 | 8 |
| 31 | 16 | 8 | 9 | ANYONE WHO HAD A HEART — Dionne Warwick, Scepter 1262 | 13 |
| 32 | 25 | 26 | 30 | LETTER FROM SHERRY — Dale Ward, Dot 16520 | 10 |
| 33 | 42 | 57 | 78 | HI-HEEL SNEAKERS — Tommy Tucker, Checker 1067 | 4 |
| ★34 | 44 | 50 | 53 | I WISH YOU LOVE — Gloria Lynne, Everest 2036 | 8 |
| 35 | 36 | 39 | 51 | GOING GOING GONE — Brook Benton, Mercury 72230 | 6 |
| 36 | 38 | 38 | 40 | COME ON — Tommy Roe, ABC-Paramount 10515 | 7 |
| 37 | 43 | 61 | 95 | BIRD DANCE BEAT — Trashmen, Garrett 4003 | 4 |
| ★38 | 52 | 76 | — | HELLO, DOLLY! — Louis Armstrong, Kapp 573 | 3 |
| 39 | 33 | 25 | 27 | IT'S ALL IN THE GAME — Cliff Richard, Epic 9633 | 13 |
| 40 | 22 | 15 | 6 | SURFIN' BIRD — Trashmen, Garrett 4002 | 13 |
| 41 | 45 | 47 | 63 | GONNA SEND YOU BACK TO GEORGIA — Timmy Shaw, Wand 146 | 6 |
| ★42 | 54 | 67 | — | MY BONNIE — Beatles, MGM 13213 | 3 |
| 43 | 46 | 48 | 52 | VAYA CON DIOS — Drifters, Atlantic 2216 | 5 |
| 44 | 47 | 58 | 81 | LIVE WIRE — Martha & the Vandellas, Gordy 7027 | 4 |
| ★45 | 63 | — | — | KISSIN' COUSINS — Elvis Presley, RCA Victor 8307 | 2 |
| 46 | 51 | 62 | 79 | MILLER'S CAVE — Bobby Bare, RCA Victor 8294 | 4 |
| 47 | 52 | 52 | 56 | HE SAYS THE SAME THINGS TO ME — Skeeter Davis, RCA Victor 8288 | 6 |
| 48 | 41 | 41 | 49 | WOW WOW WEE — Angels, Smash 1870 | 7 |
| 49 | 57 | 64 | 70 | CAN YOUR MONKEY DO THE DOG — Rufus Thomas, Stax 144 | 5 |
| 50 | 59 | 71 | — | BLUE WINTER — Connie Francis, MGM 13214 | 3 |
| ★51 | 64 | 72 | 86 | HE'LL HAVE TO GO — Solomon Burke, Atlantic 2218 | 4 |
| ★52 | 72 | 81 | — | STAY — 4 Seasons, Vee Jay 582 | 3 |
| ★53 | 65 | 77 | — | GLAD ALL OVER — Dave Clark Five, Epic 9656 | 3 |
| 54 | 49 | 51 | 55 | THAT GIRL BELONGS TO YESTERDAY — Gene Pitney, Musicor 1036 | 7 |
| 55 | 60 | 70 | 71 | BYE BYE BARBARA — Johnny Mathis, Mercury 72229 | 5 |
| ★56 | 71 | 86 | — | UNDERSTAND YOUR MAN — Johnny Cash, Columbia 42964 | 3 |
| ★57 | 69 | — | — | WORRIED GUY — Johnny Tillotson, MGM 13193 | 2 |
| 58 | 55 | 60 | 64 | PUPPY LOVE — Barbara Lewis, Atlantic 2214 | 8 |
| ★59 | 79 | — | — | STARDUST — Nino Tempo & April Stevens, Atco 6286 | 2 |
| 60 | 58 | 59 | 59 | I'LL REMEMBER (In the Still of the Night) — Santo & Johnny, Canadian-American 164 | 7 |
| ★61 | 82 | — | — | MY TRUE CARRIE LOVE — Nat King Cole, Capitol 5125 | 2 |
| 62 | 56 | 65 | 76 | 422 GLENWOOD AVENUE — Pixies Three, Mercury 72208 | 7 |
| 63 | 67 | 80 | — | YOUNG AND IN LOVE — Chris Crosby, MGM 13191 | 3 |
| 64 | 61 | 56 | 44 | HARLEM SHUFFLE — Bob & Earl, Marc 104 | 11 |
| ★65 | — | — | — | MY HEART BELONGS TO ONLY YOU — Bobby Vinton, Epic 9662 | 1 |
| 66 | 66 | 68 | 72 | SHIMMY SHIMMY — Orlons, Cameo 295 | 5 |
| 67 | 68 | 75 | 77 | COMIN' ON — Bill Black's Combo, Hi 2072 | 5 |
| 68 | 74 | 87 | — | LOVE WITH THE PROPER STRANGER — Jack Jones, Kapp 571 | 3 |
| 69 | 81 | — | — | LOOK HOMEWARD ANGEL — Monarchs, Sound Stage 7 2516 | 2 |
| 70 | 73 | 85 | 96 | HE WALKS LIKE A MAN — Jody Miller, Capitol 5090 | 4 |
| 71 | 80 | 84 | — | TELL ME BABY — Garnet Mimms and the Enchanters, United Artists 694 | 3 |
| ★72 | 88 | — | — | HEY JEAN, HEY DEAN — Dean & Jean, Rust 5075 | 2 |
| 73 | 77 | 89 | 99 | RIP VAN WINKLE — Devotions, Roulette 4541 | 4 |
| 74 | 75 | 83 | 85 | LONG GONE LONESOME BLUES — Hank Williams Jr., MGM 13208 | 5 |
| 75 | 70 | 73 | 75 | LITTLE BOXES — Pete Seeger, Columbia 42940 | 8 |
| ★76 | — | — | — | THE WAY YOU DO THE THINGS YOU DO — Temptations, Gordy 7028 | 1 |
| 77 | 83 | — | — | BABY, DON'T YOU CRY — Ray Charles, ABC-Paramount 10530 | 2 |
| ★78 | — | — | — | IT HURTS ME — Elvis Presley, RCA Victor 8307 | 1 |
| 79 | 90 | — | — | OUT OF SIGHT—OUT OF MIND — Sunny & the Sunliners, Tear Drop 3027 | 2 |
| 80 | 78 | 78 | 69 | PINK DOMINOES — Crescents, Era 3116 | 10 |
| 81 | 76 | 79 | 87 | LEAVING HERE — Eddie Holland, Motown 1052 | 4 |
| ★82 | 99 | — | — | SUSPICION — Terry Stafford, Crusader 101 | 2 |
| ★83 | 98 | — | — | HE'S A GOOD GUY — Marvelettes, Tamla 54091 | 2 |
| ★84 | — | — | — | MY HEART CRIES FOR YOU — Ray Charles, ABC-Paramount 10530 | 1 |
| 85 | 86 | — | — | (That's) WHAT THE NITTY GRITTY IS — Shirley Ellis, Congress 208 | 2 |
| 86 | 87 | 91 | — | SAGINAW, MICHIGAN — Lefty Frizzell, Columbia 42924 | 5 |
| 87 | 93 | — | — | I'LL MAKE YOU MINE — Bobby Vee, Liberty 55670 | 2 |
| 88 | 91 | — | — | HIGH ON A HILL — Scott English, Spokane 4003 | 2 |
| ★89 | — | — | — | GOING BACK TO LOUISIANA — Bruce Channel, Le Cam 122 | 1 |
| ★90 | — | — | — | CROOKED LITTLE MAN — Serendipity Singers, Philips 40175 | 1 |
| 91 | 89 | — | — | ALL MY TRIALS — Dick & Deedee, Warner Bros. 5411 | 2 |
| 92 | — | — | — | I CAN'T STAND IT — Soul Sisters, Sue 799 | 1 |
| 93 | — | — | — | CASTLES IN THE SAND — Little Stevie Wonder, Tamla 54090 | 1 |
| 94 | 94 | 95 | 98 | HAVE YOU EVER BEEN LONELY — Caravelles, Smash 1869 | 4 |
| 95 | 97 | — | — | MY BOY FRIEND GOT A BEATLE HAIRCUT — Donna Lynn, Capitol 5127 | 2 |
| 96 | — | — | — | SHOOP SHOOP SONG — Betty Everett, Vee Jay 585 | 1 |
| 97 | — | — | — | WILLYAM, WILLYAM — Dee Dee Sharp, Cameo 296 | 1 |
| 98 | 100 | — | — | MO' ONIONS — Booker T & the MG's, Stax 142 | 2 |
| 99 | — | — | — | THE BOY WITH THE BEATLE HAIR — Swans, Cameo 302 | 1 |
| 100 | — | — | — | LAZY LADY — Fats Domino, ABC-Paramount 10531 | 1 |

## HOT 100—A TO Z—(Publisher-Licensee)


Abigail Beecher (Claridge-Halseon, ASCAP) ...... 18
All My Trials (Odin, ASCAP) ...... 91
Anyone Who Had a Heart (U. S. Songs, ASCAP) .. 31
Baby, Don't You Cry (Leeds, ASCAP) ...... 77
Bird Dance Beat (Willong, BMI) ...... 37
Blue Winter (January, BMI) ...... 50
Boy With the Beatle Hair, The (Hill & Range-Shelrose, BMI) ...... 99
Bye Bye Barbara (Fisher-Elm Drive, ASCAP) ...... 55
California Sun (Lloyd & Logan, BMI) ...... 5
Can Your Monkey Do the Dog (East, BMI) ...... 49
Castles in the Sand (Jobete, BMI) ...... 93
Come On (Fame, BMI) ...... 36
Comin' On (Jec, BMI) ...... 67
Crooked Little Man (Serendipity, BMI) ...... 90
Dawn (Go Away) (Saturday-Gavidima, ASCAP) ...... 3
Fool Never Learns, A (Cricket, BMI) ...... 16
For You (Witmark, ASCAP) ...... 21
442 Glenwood Avenue (Merjoda, BMI) ...... 62
Fun, Fun, Fun (Sea of Tunes, BMI) ...... 17
Glad All Over (Ivy, ASCAP) ...... 53
Going Back to Louisiana (LeBill-Marbill, BMI) .. 89
Going Going Gone (Gil, BMI) ...... 35
Gonna Send You Back to Georgia (Zann, BMI) ... 41
Good News (Kags, BMI) ...... 13
Harlem Shuffle (Marc Jean-Keyman, BMI) ...... 64
Have You Ever Been Lonely (Shapiro-Bernstein, ASCAP) ...... 94
He Says the Same Things to Me (Geld-Udell, ASCAP) ...... 47
He Walks Like a Man (Central Songs, BMI) ...... 70
He's a Good Guy (Jobete, BMI) ...... 83
He'll Have to Go (Central Songs, BMI) ...... 51
Hello, Dolly! (Morris, ASCAP) ...... 38
Hey Jean, Hey Dean (Schwartz, ASCAP) ...... 72
Hey Little Cobra (Vadim, BMI) ...... 11
Hi-Heel Sneakers (Medal, BMI) ...... 33
High on a Hill (Sultan, BMI) ...... 88
Hooka Tooka (Evanston-Woodcrest, BMI) ...... 27
I Can't Stand It (Saturn-Staccato, BMI) ...... 92
I Love You More and More Every Day (Robertson, ASCAP) ...... 15
I Only Want to Be With You (Chappell, ASCAP) .. 14
I Saw Her Standing There (Hofer, BMI) ...... 28
I Want to Hold Your Hand (Duchess, BMI) ...... 1
I Wish You Love (Leeds, ASCAP) ...... 34
I'll Make You Mine (Saima, BMI) ...... 87
I'll Remember (In the Still of the Night) (Cherió, BMI) ...... 60
It Hurts Me (Presley, BMI) ...... 78
It's All in the Game (Remick, ASCAP) ...... 39
Java (Tideland, BMI) ...... 4
Kissin' Cousins (Gladys, ASCAP) ...... 45
Lazy Lady (Anatole, BMI) ......100
Leaving Here (Jobete, BMI) ...... 81
Letter From Sherry (Nu Star, BMI) ...... 32
Little Boxes (Schroder, ASCAP) ...... 75
Live Wire (Jobete, BMI) ...... 44
Long Gone Lonesome Blues (Acuff-Rose, BMI) .... 74
Look Homeward Angel (Rogelle, BMI) ...... 69
Love With the Proper Stranger (Paramount, ASCAP) ...... 68
Miller's Cave (Jack, BMI) ...... 46
Mo' Onions (East-Bais, BMI) ...... 98
My Bonnie (Hill & Range, BMI) ...... 42
My Boyfriend Got a Beatle Haircut (Integrity-ASCAP) ...... 95
My Heart Belongs to Only You (Regent, BMI) ... 65
Massey, ASCAP) ...... 84
My Heart Cries for You (Ross-Jungnickel-Gladys-
My True Carrie Love (Comet, ASCAP) ...... 61
Navy Blue (Saturday, ASCAP) ...... 8
Oh Baby Don't You Weep (Jim Jam, BMI) ...... 26
Out of Limits (Wrist, BMI) ...... 24
Out of Sight—Out of Mind (Nome, BMI) ...... 79
Penetration (Dorothy, ASCAP) ...... 25
Pink Dominoes (Dimondaire-Room Seven, BMI) .. 80
Please Please Me (Concertone, ASCAP) ...... 6
Puppy Love (McLaughlin, BMI) ...... 58
Rip Van Winkle (Skidmore, ASCAP) ...... 73
Saginaw, Michigan (Tree, BMI) ...... 86
See the Funny Little Clown (Unart, BMI) ...... 12
She Loves You (Gil, BMI) ...... 2
Shelter of Your Arms, The (Print, ASCAP) ...... 23
Shimmy Shimmy (Thin Man, BMI) ...... 66
Shoop Shoop Song (Tim, BMI) ...... 96
Southtown U.S.A. (Gallico, BMI) ...... 22
Stardust (Mills, ASCAP) ...... 59
Stay (Cherio, BMI) ...... 52
Stop and Think It Over (Crazy Cajun-Red Sticy, BMI) ...... 9
Surfin' Bird (Willong, BMI) ...... 40
Suspicion (Presley, BMI) ...... 82
Talking About My Baby (Curtom, BMI) ...... 19
Tell Me Baby (Sealark, BMI) ...... 71
That Girl Belongs to Yesterday (Pitfield, BMI) .... 54
(That's) What the Nitty Gritty Is (Gallico, BMI) .. 85
Um, Um, Um, Um, Um, Um (Curtom-Jalynne, BMI). 10
Understand Your Man (Cash, BMI) ...... 56
Vaya Con Dios (Ardmore, ASCAP) ...... 43
Way You Do the Things You Do, The (Jobete, BMI). 76
What Kind of Fool (Do You Think I Am) (Low-Twi, BMI) ...... 20
What's Easy for Two Is So Hard for One (Jobete, BMI) ...... 29
Who Do You Love (Hill & Range, BMI) ...... 30
Willyam, Willyam (Wyncote, ASCAP) ...... 97
Worried Guy (Wood, ASCAP) ...... 57
Wow Wow Wee (Grand Canyon, BMI) ...... 48
You Don't Own Me (Merioda, BMI) ...... 7
Young and in Love (Miller, ASCAP) ...... 63


## BUBBLING UNDER THE HOT 100

101. FROM ME TO YOU ...... Beatles, Vee Jay 522
102. TELL HIM ...... Drew-Vels, Capitol 5055
103. PLEASE, PLEASE, PLEASE ... James Brown & the Famous Flames, King 5853
104. THE LA-DEE-DAH SONG ...... Village Stompers, Epic 9655
105. HERE'S A HEART ...... Diplomats, Arock 1004
106. YOU WERE WRONG ...... Z. Z. Hill, M&H 200
107. HOW MUCH CAN A LONELY HEART STAND .. Skeeter Davis, RCA Victor 8288
108. I WONDER WHO'S KISSING HER NOW ...... Bobby Darin, Capitol 5126
109. TIC-TAC-TOE ...... Booker T & the MG's, Stax 142
110. CUSTOM MACHINE ...... Bruce & Terry, Columbia 42956
111. STRANGE THINGS HAPPENING ...... Little Junior Parker, Duke 371
112. WELCOME TO MY WORLD ...... Jim Reeves, RCA Victor 8289
113. SEARCHIN' ...... Ace Cannon, Hi 2074
114. GIRL FROM SPANISH TOWN ...... Marty Robbins, Columbia 42968
115. RUN, RUN, RUN ...... Supremes, Motown 1054
116. NADINE ...... Chuck Berry, Chess 1883
117. NEEDLES AND PINS ...... Searchers, Kapp 577
118. FIVE LITTLE FINGERS ...... Bill Anderson, Decca 31577
119. SINCE I FOUND A NEW LOVE ...... Little Johnny Taylor, Galaxy 725
120. SO FAR AWAY ...... Hank Jacobs, Sue 795
121. OUR EVERLASTING LOVE ...... Ruby & the Romantics, Kapp 578
122. I DIDN'T KNOW WHAT TIME IT WAS ...... Crampton Sisters, DCP 1001
123. I'M LOOKING OVER A FOUR-LEAF CLOVER .... Wayne Newton, Capitol 5124
124. NEVER LEAVE ME ...... Stratfords, O'Dell 100
125. I'M TRAVELIN' ON ...... Jackie Wilson, Brunswick 55260
126. I CAN'T WAIT UNTIL I SEE MY BABY ...... Baby Washington, Sue 797
127. WHY DO FOOLS FALL IN LOVE ...... Beach Boys, Capitol 5118
128. LAST NIGHT I HAD THE STRANGEST DREAM .... Kingston Trio, Capitol 5132
129. WHO'S GOING TO TAKE CARE OF ME ...... Baby Washington, Sue 797
130. THINK NOTHING ABOUT IT ...... Gene Chandler, Constellation 112
131. I ADORE YOU ...... Patti Page, Columbia 42963
132. HIPPY HIPPY SHAKE ...... Swinging Blue Jeans, Imperial 66021
133. FRIENDLIEST THING ...... Eydie Gorme, Columbia 42953
134. JAILER, BRING ME WATER ...... Trini Lopez, Reprise 0260
135. BLUE MOON ...... Ray Conniff, His Ork & Chorus, Columbia 42967

Compiled from national retail sales and radio station airplay by the Music Popularity Dept. of Record Market Research, Billboard.

Billboard

For Week Ending March 7, 1964

# HOT 100

★ STAR performer—Sides registering greatest proportionate upward progress this week.

Billboard Award

| This Week | 1 Wk. Ago | 2 Wks. Ago | 3 Wks. Ago | TITLE Artist, Label & Number | Weeks On Chart |
|---|---|---|---|---|---|
| 1 | 1 | 1 | 1 | I WANT TO HOLD YOUR HAND — Beatles, Capitol 5112 | 8 |
| 2 | 2 | 2 | 3 | SHE LOVES YOU — Beatles, Swan 4152 | 7 |
| 3 | 3 | 3 | 11 | DAWN (Go Away) — 4 Seasons, Philips 40166 | 6 |
| 4 | 6 | 29 | 45 | PLEASE PLEASE ME — Beatles, Vee Jay 581 | 6 |
| 5 | 4 | 5 | 9 | JAVA — Al Hirt, RCA Victor 8280 | 10 |
| 6 | 5 | 8 | 14 | CALIFORNIA SUN — Rivieras, Riviera 1401 | 7 |
| 7 | 8 | 10 | 21 | NAVY BLUE — Diane Renay, 20th Century-Fox 456 | 7 |
| 8 | 9 | 12 | 16 | STOP AND THINK IT OVER — Dale & Grace, Montel 922 | 7 |
| ★9 | 17 | 27 | 69 | FUN, FUN, FUN — Beach Boys, Capitol 5118 | 4 |
| 10 | 12 | 17 | 22 | SEE THE FUNNY LITTLE CLOWN — Bobby Goldsboro, United Artists 672 | 9 |
| 11 | 15 | 24 | 33 | I LOVE YOU MORE AND MORE EVERY DAY — Al Martino, Capitol 5108 | 6 |
| 12 | 13 | 21 | 29 | GOOD NEWS — Sam Cooke, RCA Victor 8299 | 7 |
| 13 | 7 | 4 | 2 | YOU DON'T OWN ME — Lesley Gore, Mercury 72206 | 11 |
| 14 | 14 | 20 | 27 | I ONLY WANT TO BE WITH YOU — Dusty Springfield, Philips 40162 | 7 |
| 15 | 10 | 6 | 5 | UM, UM, UM, UM, UM, UM — Major Lance, Okeh 7187 | 10 |
| 16 | 18 | 23 | 36 | ABIGAIL BEECHER — Freddy Cannon, Warner Bros. 5409 | 6 |
| ★17 | 23 | 26 | 30 | THE SHELTER OF YOUR ARMS — Sammy Davis Jr., Reprise 20216 | 13 |
| ★18 | 28 | 35 | 54 | I SAW HER STANDING THERE — Beatles, Capitol 5112 | 5 |
| ★19 | 25 | 30 | 55 | PENETRATION — Pyramids, Best 13002 | 6 |
| 20 | 16 | 18 | 13 | A FOOL NEVER LEARNS — Andy Williams, Columbia 42950 | 9 |
| ★21 | 45 | 63 | — | KISSIN' COUSINS — Elvis Presley, RCA Victor 8307 | 3 |
| ★22 | 33 | 42 | 57 | HI-HEEL SNEAKERS — Tommy Tucker, Checker 1067 | 5 |
| ★23 | 53 | 65 | 77 | GLAD ALL OVER — Dave Clark Five, Epic 9656 | 4 |
| 24 | 26 | 32 | 35 | OH BABY DON'T YOU WEEP — James Brown & the Famous Flames, King 5842 | 7 |
| 25 | 19 | 14 | 12 | TALKING ABOUT MY BABY — Impressions, ABC-Paramount 10511 | 8 |
| 26 | 11 | 7 | 4 | HEY LITTLE COBRA — Rip Chords, Columbia 42921 | 13 |
| ★27 | 38 | 52 | 76 | HELLO, DOLLY! — Louis Armstrong, Kapp 573 | 4 |
| 28 | 30 | 37 | 46 | WHO DO YOU LOVE — Sapphires, Swan 4162 | 9 |
| ★29 | 34 | 44 | 50 | I WISH YOU LOVE — Gloria Lynne, Everest 2036 | 9 |
| ★30 | 37 | 43 | 61 | BIRD DANCE BEAT — Trashmen, Garrett 4003 | 5 |
| ★31 | 42 | 54 | 67 | MY BONNIE — Beatles, MGM 13213 | 4 |
| 32 | 20 | 9 | 10 | WHAT KIND OF FOOL (Do You Think I Am) — Tams, ABC-Paramount 10502 | 13 |
| 33 | 21 | 11 | 6 | FOR YOU — Rick Nelson, Decca 31574 | 11 |
| ★34 | 65 | — | — | MY HEART BELONGS TO ONLY YOU — Bobby Vinton, Epic 9662 | 2 |
| ★35 | 50 | 59 | 71 | BLUE WINTER — Connie Francis, MGM 13214 | 4 |
| ★36 | 46 | 51 | 62 | MILLER'S CAVE — Bobby Bare, RCA Victor 8294 | 5 |
| 37 | 29 | 31 | 31 | WHAT'S EASY FOR TWO IS SO HARD FOR ONE — Mary Wells, Motown 1048 | 16 |
| 38 | 22 | 15 | 20 | SOUTHTOWN, U. S. A. — Dixiebelles, Sound Stage 7 2517 | 8 |
| 39 | 24 | 13 | 7 | OUT OF LIMITS — Marketts, Warner Bros. 5391 | 14 |
| ★40 | 52 | 72 | 81 | STAY — 4 Seasons, Vee Jay 582 | 4 |
| 41 | 32 | 25 | 26 | LETTER FROM SHERRY — Dale Ward, Dot 16520 | 11 |
| ★42 | 56 | 71 | 86 | UNDERSTAND YOUR MAN — Johnny Cash, Columbia 42964 | 4 |
| 43 | 44 | 47 | 58 | LIVE WIRE — Martha & the Vandellas, Gordy 7027 | 5 |
| ★44 | 78 | — | — | IT HURTS ME — Elvis Presley, RCA Victor 8307 | 2 |
| ★45 | 58 | 55 | 60 | PUPPY LOVE — Barbara Lewis, Atlantic 2214 | 9 |
| ★46 | 59 | 79 | — | STARDUST — Nino Tempo & April Stevens, Atco 6286 | 3 |
| ★47 | 57 | 69 | — | WORRIED GUY — Johnny Tillotson, MGM 13193 | 3 |
| 48 | 49 | 57 | 64 | CAN YOUR MONKEY DO THE DOG — Rufus Thomas, Stax 144 | 6 |
| 49 | 31 | 16 | 8 | ANYONE WHO HAD A HEART — Dionne Warwick, Scepter 1262 | 14 |
| 50 | 27 | 19 | 17 | HOOKA TOOKA — Chubby Checker, Parkway 890 | 14 |
| 51 | 51 | 64 | 72 | HE'LL HAVE TO GO — Solomon Burke, Atlantic 2218 | 5 |
| ★52 | 76 | — | — | THE WAY YOU DO THE THINGS YOU DO — Temptations, Gordy 7028 | 2 |
| 53 | 55 | 60 | 70 | BYE BYE BARBARA — Johnny Mathis, Mercury 72229 | 6 |
| 54 | 41 | 45 | 47 | GONNA SEND YOU BACK TO GEORGIA — Timmy Shaw, Wand 146 | 7 |
| 55 | 61 | 82 | — | MY TRUE CARRIE LOVE — Nat King Cole, Capitol 5125 | 3 |
| 56 | 35 | 36 | 39 | GOING GOING GONE — Brook Benton, Mercury 72230 | 7 |
| 57 | 36 | 38 | 38 | COME ON — Tommy Roe, ABC-Paramount 10515 | 8 |
| ★58 | 84 | — | — | MY HEART CRIES FOR YOU — Ray Charles, ABC-Paramount 10530 | 2 |
| 59 | 47 | 52 | 52 | HE SAYS THE SAME THINGS TO ME — Skeeter Davis, RCA Victor 8288 | 7 |
| 60 | 43 | 46 | 48 | VAYA CON DIOS — Drifters, Atlantic 2216 | 6 |
| 61 | 73 | 77 | 89 | RIP VAN WINKLE — Devotions, Roulette 4541 | 5 |
| 62 | 63 | 67 | 80 | YOUNG AND IN LOVE — Chris Crosby, MGM 13191 | 4 |
| 63 | 68 | 74 | 87 | LOVE WITH THE PROPER STRANGER — Jack Jones, Kapp 571 | 4 |
| 64 | 69 | 81 | — | LOOK HOMEWARD ANGEL — Monarchs, Sound Stage 7 2516 | 3 |
| 65 | 72 | 88 | — | HEY JEAN, HEY DEAN — Dean & Jean, Rust 5075 | 3 |
| 66 | 70 | 73 | 85 | HE WALKS LIKES A MAN — Jody Miller, Capitol 5090 | 5 |
| 67 | 77 | 83 | — | BABY, DON'T YOU CRY — Ray Charles, ABC-Paramount 10530 | 3 |
| 68 | 74 | 75 | 83 | LONG GONE LONESOME BLUES — Hank Williams Jr., MGM 13208 | 6 |
| 69 | 71 | 80 | 84 | TELL ME BABY — Garnet Mimms and the Enchanters, United Artists 694 | 4 |
| ★70 | 96 | — | — | SHOOP SHOOP SONG — Betty Everett, Vee Jay 585 | 2 |
| 71 | 82 | 99 | — | SUSPICION — Terry Stafford, Crusader 101 | 3 |
| ★72 | — | — | — | (You Can't Let the Boy Over-power) THE MAN IN YOU — Miracles, Tamla 54092 | 1 |
| 73 | 79 | 90 | — | OUT OF SIGHT—OUT OF MIND — Sunny & the Sunliners, Tear Drop 3027 | 3 |
| 74 | 83 | 98 | — | HE'S A GOOD GUY — Marvelettes, Tamla 54091 | 3 |
| ★75 | — | — | — | NEEDLES AND PINS — Searchers, Kapp 577 | 1 |
| 76 | 87 | 93 | — | I'LL MAKE YOU MINE — Bobby Vee, Liberty 55670 | 3 |
| 77 | 88 | 91 | — | HIGH ON A HILL — Scott English, Spokane 4003 | 3 |
| ★78 | — | — | — | DEAD MAN'S CURVE — Jan & Dean, Liberty 55672 | 1 |
| 79 | 85 | 86 | — | (That's) WHAT THE NITTY GRITTY IS — Shirley Ellis, Congress 208 | 3 |
| 80 | — | — | — | HIPPY HIPPY SHAKE — Swinging Blue Jeans, Imperial 66021 | 1 |
| ★81 | — | — | — | WHITE ON WHITE — Danny Williams, United Artists 685 | 1 |
| ★82 | — | — | — | TELL IT ON THE MOUNTAIN — Peter, Paul & Mary, Warner Bros. 5418 | 1 |
| 83 | 90 | — | — | CROOKED LITTLE MAN — Serendipity Singers, Philips 40175 | 2 |
| 84 | 92 | — | — | I CAN'T STAND IT — Soul Sisters, Sue 799 | 2 |
| 85 | 93 | — | — | CASTLES IN THE SAND — Little Stevie Wonder, Tamla 54090 | 2 |
| ★86 | — | — | — | FROM ME TO YOU — Beatles, Vee Jay 581 | 1 |
| 87 | 81 | 76 | 79 | LEAVING HERE — Eddie Holland, Motown 1052 | 5 |
| ★88 | — | — | — | THINK — Brenda Lee, Decca 31599 | 1 |
| ★89 | — | — | — | AIN'T NOTHING YOU CAN DO — Bobby Bland, Duke 375 | 1 |
| ★90 | — | — | — | NADINE — Chuck Berry, Chess 1883 | 1 |
| 91 | 91 | 89 | — | ALL MY TRIALS — Dick & Deedee, Warner Bros. 5411 | 3 |
| 92 | — | 96 | — | CUSTOM MACHINE — Bruce & Terry, Columbia 42956 | 2 |
| 93 | — | — | — | SOUL SERENADE — King Curtis, Capitol 5109 | 1 |
| 94 | 89 | — | — | GOING BACK TO LOUISIANA — Bruce Channel, Le Cam 122 | 2 |
| 95 | — | — | — | SO FAR AWAY — Hank Jacobs, Sue 795 | 3 |
| 96 | 99 | — | — | THE BOY WITH THE BEATLE HAIR — Swans, Cameo 302 | 2 |
| 97 | 98 | 100 | — | MO' ONIONS — Booker T & the MG's, Stax 142 | 3 |
| 98 | — | — | — | I WONDER WHO'S KISSING HER NOW — Bobby Darin, Capitol 5126 | 1 |
| 99 | — | — | — | FOREVER — Pete Drake, Smash 1867 | 1 |
| 100 | — | — | — | YOU WERE WRONG — Z. Z. Hill, M & H 200 | 1 |

## 100—A TO Z—(Publisher-Licensee)

Abigail Beecher (Claridge-Halseon, ASCAP) .... 16
Ain't Nothing You Can Do (Don, BMI) .... 89
All My Trials (Odin, ASCAP) .... 91
Anyone Who Had a Heart (U. S. Songs, ASCAP) .. 49
Baby, Don't You Cry (Leeds, ASCAP) .... 67
Bird Dance Beat (Willong, BMI) .... 30
Blue Winter (January, BMI) .... 35
Boy With the Beatle Hair, The (Hill & Range-Shelrose, BMI) .... 96
Bye Bye Barbara (Fisher-Elm Drive, ASCAP) .... 53
California Sun (Lloyd & Logan, BMI) .... 6
Can Your Monkey Do the Dog (East, BMI) .... 48
Castles in the Sand (Jobete, BMI) .... 85
Come On (Fame, BMI) .... 57
Crooked Little Man (Serendipity, BMI) .... 83
Custom Machine (Sea of Tunes, BMI) .... 92
Dawn (Go Away) (Saturday-Gavidima, ASCAP) .. 3
Dead Man's Curve (Screen Gems-Columbia, BMI) . 78
Fool Never Learns, A (Cricket, BMI) .... 20
For You (Witmark, ASCAP) .... 33
Forever (Tree, BMI) .... 99
From Me to You (Gil, BMI) .... 86
Fun, Fun, Fun (Sea of Tunes, BMI) .... 10
Glad All Over (Ivy, ASCAP) .... 23
Going Back to Louisiana (LeBill-Marbill, BMI) 94
Going, Going, Gone (Gil, BMI) .... 56
Gonna Send You Back to Georgia (Zann, BMI).. 54
Good News (Kags, BMI) .... 12
He Says the Same Things to Me (Geld-Udell, ASCAP) .... 59
He Walks Like a Man (Central Songs, BMI) .... 66
He's a Good Guy (Jobete, BMI) .... 74
He'll Have to Go (Central Songs, BMI) .... 51
Hello, Dolly! (Morris, ASCAP) .... 27
Hey Jean, Hey Dean (Schwartz, ASCAP) .... 65
Hey Little Cobra (Vadim, BMI) .... 26
Hi-Hell Sneakers (Medal, BMI ).... 22
High on a Hill (Sultan, BMI) .... 77
Hippy Hippy Shake (Maraville, BMI) .... 80
Hooka Tooka (Evanston-Woodcrest, BMI) .... 50
I Can't Stand It (Saturn-Staccato, BMI) .... 84
I Love You More and More Every Day (Robertson, ASCAP) .... 11
I Only Want to Be With You (Chappell, ASCAP)... 14
I Saw Her Standing There (Hofer, BMI) .... 18
I Want to Hold Your Hand (Duchess, BMI) .... 1
I Wish You Love (Leeds, ASCAP) .... 29
I Wonder Who's Kissing Her Now (Vogel, ASCAP) . 93
I'll Make You Mine (Saima, BMI) .... 76
It Hurts Me (Presley, BMI) .... 44
Java (Tideland, BMI) .... 5
Kissin' Cousins (Gladys, ASCAP) .... 21
Leaving Here (Jobete, BMI) .... 87
Letter From Sherry (Nu Star, BMI) .... 41
Live Wire (Jobete, BMI) .... 43
Long Gone Lonesome Blues (Acuff-Rose, BMI) ... 68
Look Homeward Angel (Rogelle, BMI) .... 64
Love With the Proper Stranger (Paramount, ASCAP). 63
Miller's Cave (Jack, BMI) .... 36
Mo' Onions (East-Bias, BMI) .... 97
My Bonnie (Hill & Range, BMI) .... 31
My Heart Belongs to Only You (Regent, BMI) .... 34
My Heart Cries for You (Ross-Jungnickel-Gladys-Massey, ASCAP) .... 58
My True Carrie Love (Comet, ASCAP) .... 55
Nadine (Arc, BMI) .... 90
Navy Blue (Saturday, ASCAP) .... 7
Needles and Pins (Metric, BMI) .... 75
Oh Baby Don't You Weep (Jim Jam, BMI) .... 24
Out of Limits (Wrist, BMI) .... 39
Out of Sight—Out of Mind (Nome, BMI) .... 73
Penetration (Dorothy, ASCAP) .... 19
Please Please Me (Concertone, ASCAP) .... 4
Puppy Love (McLaughlin, BMI) .... 45
Rip Van Winkle (Llee, BMI) .... 61
See the Funny Little Clown (Unart, BMI) .... 10
She Loves You (Gil, BMI) .... 2
Shelter of Your Arms, The (Print, ASCAP) .... 17
Shoop, Shoop Song (T.M., BMI) .... 70
So Far Away (Saturn-Five Point, BMI) .... 95
Soul Serenade (Kilynn-VeeVee, BMI) .... 93
Southtown U. S. A. (Gallico, BMI) .... 38
Stardust (Mills, ASCAP) .... 46
Stay (Cherio, BMI) .... 40
Stop and Think It Over (Crazy Cajun-Red Sticy, BMI) .... 8
Suspicion (Presley, BMI) .... 71
Talking About My Baby (Curtom, BMI) .... 25
Tell It to the Mountain (Pepamar, ASCAP) .... 82
Tell Me Baby (Sealark, BMI) .... 69
(That's) What the Nitty Gritty Is (Gallico, BMI).. 79
Think (Forrest Hills-Rombre, BMI) .... 88
Um, Um, Um, Um, Um, Um, (Curtom-Jalynne, BMI). 15
Understand Your Man (Cash, BMI) .... 42
Vaya Con Dios (Ardmore, ASCAP) .... 60
Way You Do the Things You Do, The (Jobete, BMI) .... 52
What Kind of Fool (Do You Think I Am) (Low-Twi, BMI) .... 32
What's Easy for Two Is So Hard for One (Jobete, BMI) .... 37
White on White (Painted Desert, BMI) .... 81
Who Do You Love (Hill & Range, BMI) .... 28
Worried Guy (Wood, ASCAP) .... 47
(You Can't Let the Boy Overpower) The Man in You (Jobete, BMI) .... 72
You Don't Own Me (Merjoda, BMI) .... 13
You Were Wrong (Bria, BMI) .... 100
Young and in Love (Miller, ASCAP) .... 62

## BUBBLING UNDER THE HOT 100

101. HOW MUCH CAN A LONELY HEART STAND...Skeeter Davis, RCA Victor 8288
102. THE WAITING GAME ....Brenda Lee, Decca 31599
103. SAGINAW, MICHIGAN ....Lefty Frizzell, Columbia 42924
104. THE LA-DEE-DAH SONG ....Village Stompers, Epic 9655
105. STRANGE THINGS HAPPENING ....Little Junior Parker, Duke 371
106. WILLYAM, WILLYAM ....Dee Dee Sharp, Cameo 296
107. THINK NOTHING ABOUT IT ....Gene Chandler, Constellation 112
108. SANDY ....Johnny Crawford, Del-Fi 4229
109. MY BOYFRIEND GOT A BEATLE HAIRCUT ....Donna Lynn, Capitol 5127
110. HERE'S A HEART ....Diplomats, Arock 1004
111. SEARCHIN' ....Ace Cannon, Hi 2074
112. RUN, RUN, RUN ....Supremes, Motown 1054
113. TIC-TAC-TOE ....Booker T. & the MG's, Stax 142
114. LAZY LADY ....Fats Domino, ABC-Paramount 10531
115. COME TO ME ....Otis Redding, Volt 116
116. WELCOME TO MY WORLD ....Jim Reeves, RCA Victor 8289
117. IT AIN'T NO USE ....Lou Johnson, Hilltop 551
118. GIRL FROM SPANISH TOWN ....Marty Robbins, Columbia 42968
119. MIDNIGHT ....David Rockingham Trio, Josie 917
120. WHY DO FOOLS FALL IN LOVE ....Beach Boys, Capitol 5118
121. OUR EVERLASTING LOVE ....Ruby & the Romantics, Kapp 578
122. I CAN'T WAIT UNTIL I SEE MY BABY ....Baby Washington, Sue 797
123. I'M TRAVELIN' ON ....Jackie Wilson, Brunswick 55260
124. BABY COME ON HOME ....Hoagy Lands, Atlantic 2217
125. OUT OF THIS WORLD ....Gino Washington, Wand 147
126. WOMAN, LOVE AND A MAN ....Tony Clarke, Chess 1880
127. I'M YOUR HOOCHIE COOCHE MAN ....Dion Di Muci, Columbia 42977
128. STOCKHOLM ....Lawrence Welk, Dot 16582
129. LONNIE ON THE MOVE ....Lonnie Mack, Fraternity 920
130. SHANGRI-LA ....Robert Maxwell, His Harp & Ork, Decca 25622
131. JAILER, BRING ME WATER ....Trini Lopez, Reprise 0260
132. LAST NIGHT I HAD THE STRANGEST DREAM ....Kingston Trio, Capitol 5132
133. ALWAYS IN MY HEART ....Los Indios Tabajaras, RCA Victor 8313
134. WHERE DOES LOVE GO ....Freddie Scott, Colpix 724

Compiled from national retail sales and radio station airplay by the Music Popularity Dept. of Record Market Research, Billboard.

# Billboard HOT 100

For Week Ending March 14, 1964

★ STAR performer—Sides registering greatest proportionate upward progress this week.

| This Week | 1 Wk. Ago | 2 Wks. Ago | 3 Wks. Ago | TITLE — Artist, Label & Number | Weeks On Chart |
|---|---|---|---|---|---|
| 1 | 1 | 1 | 1 | I WANT TO HOLD YOUR HAND — Beatles, Capitol 5112 | 9 |
| 2 | 2 | 2 | 2 | SHE LOVES YOU — Beatles, Swan 4152 | 8 |
| 3 | 4 | 6 | 29 | PLEASE PLEASE ME — Beatles, Vee Jay 581 | 7 |
| 4 | 3 | 3 | 3 | DAWN (Go Away) — 4 Seasons, Philips 40166 | 7 |
| 5 | 5 | 4 | 5 | JAVA — Al Hirt, RCA Victor 8280 | 11 |
| 6 | 7 | 8 | 10 | NAVY BLUE — Diane Renay, 20th Century-Fox 456 | 8 |
| 7 | 9 | 17 | 27 | FUN, FUN, FUN — Beach Boys, Capitol 5118 | 5 |
| 8 | 6 | 5 | 8 | CALIFORNIA SUN — Rivieras, Riviera 1401 | 8 |
| 9 | 10 | 12 | 17 | SEE THE FUNNY LITTLE CLOWN — Bobby Goldsboro, United Artists 672 | 10 |
| 10 | 11 | 15 | 24 | I LOVE YOU MORE AND MORE EVERY DAY — Al Martino, Capitol 5108 | 7 |
| 11 | 12 | 13 | 21 | GOOD NEWS — Sam Cooke, RCA Victor 8299 | 8 |
| 12 | 14 | 14 | 20 | I ONLY WANT TO BE WITH YOU — Dusty Springfield, Philips 40162 | 8 |
| 13 | 27 | 38 | 52 | HELLO, DOLLY! — Louis Armstrong, Kapp 573 | 5 |
| 14 | 8 | 9 | 12 | STOP AND THINK IT OVER — Dale & Grace, Montel 922 | 8 |
| 15 | 18 | 28 | 35 | I SAW HER STANDING THERE — Beatles, Capitol 5112 | 5 |
| 16 | 21 | 45 | 63 | KISSIN' COUSINS — Elvis Presley, RCA Victor 8307 | 4 |
| 17 | 17 | 23 | 26 | THE SHELTER OF YOUR ARMS — Sammy Davis Jr., Reprise 20216 | 14 |
| 18 | 19 | 25 | 30 | PENETRATION — Pyramids, Best 13002 | 7 |
| 19 | 22 | 33 | 42 | HI-HEEL SNEAKERS — Tommy Tucker, Checker 1067 | 6 |
| 20 | 23 | 53 | 65 | GLAD ALL OVER — Dave Clark Five, Epic 9656 | 5 |
| 21 | 13 | 7 | 4 | YOU DON'T OWN ME — Lesley Gore, Mercury 72206 | 12 |
| 22 | 34 | 65 | — | MY HEART BELONGS TO ONLY YOU — Bobby Vinton, Epic 9662 | 3 |
| 23 | 24 | 26 | 32 | OH BABY DON'T YOU WEEP — James Brown & the Famous Flames, King 5842 | 8 |
| 24 | 16 | 18 | 23 | ABIGAIL BEECHER — Freddy Cannon, Warner Bros. 5409 | 7 |
| 25 | 28 | 30 | 37 | WHO DO YOU LOVE — Sapphires, Swan 4162 | 10 |
| 26 | 31 | 42 | 54 | MY BONNIE — Beatles, MGM 13213 | 5 |
| 27 | 35 | 50 | 59 | BLUE WINTER — Connie Francis, MGM 13214 | 5 |
| 28 | 29 | 34 | 44 | I WISH YOU LOVE — Gloria Lynne, Everest 2036 | 7 |
| 29 | 40 | 52 | 72 | STAY — 4 Seasons, Vee Jay 582 | 5 |
| 30 | 30 | 37 | 43 | BIRD DANCE BEAT — Trashmen, Garrett 4003 | 6 |
| 31 | 15 | 10 | 6 | UM, UM, UM, UM, UM, UM — Major Lance, Okeh 7187 | 11 |
| 32 | 20 | 16 | 18 | A FOOL NEVER LEARNS — Andy Williams, Columbia 42950 | 8 |
| 33 | 36 | 46 | 51 | MILLER'S CAVE — Bobby Bare, RCA Victor 8294 | 6 |
| 34 | 46 | 59 | 79 | STARDUST — Nino Tempo & April Stevens, Atco 6286 | 4 |
| 35 | 44 | 78 | — | IT HURTS ME — Elvis Presley, RCA Victor 8307 | 3 |
| 36 | 32 | 20 | 9 | WHAT KIND OF FOOL (Do You Think I Am) — Tams, ABC-Paramount 10502 | 14 |
| 37 | 26 | 11 | 7 | HEY LITTLE COBRA — Rip Chords, Columbia 42921 | 14 |
| 38 | 45 | 58 | 55 | PUPPY LOVE — Barbara Lewis, Atlantic 2214 | 10 |
| 39 | 47 | 57 | 69 | WORRIED GUY — Johnny Tillotson, MGM 13193 | 4 |
| 40 | 42 | 56 | 71 | UNDERSTAND YOUR MAN — Johnny Cash, Columbia 42964 | 5 |
| 41 | 52 | 76 | — | THE WAY YOU DO THE THINGS YOU DO — Temptations, Gordy 7028 | 3 |
| 42 | 43 | 44 | 47 | LIVE WIRE — Martha & the Vandellas, Gordy 7027 | 6 |
| 43 | 25 | 19 | 14 | TALKING ABOUT MY BABY — Impressions, ABC-Paramount 10511 | 9 |
| 44 | 37 | 29 | 31 | WHAT'S EASY FOR TWO IS SO HARD FOR ONE — Mary Wells, Motown 1048 | 17 |
| 45 | 67 | 77 | 83 | BABY, DON'T YOU CRY — Ray Charles, ABC-Paramount 10530 | 4 |
| 46 | 75 | — | — | NEEDLES AND PINS — Searchers, Kapp 577 | 2 |
| 47 | 65 | 72 | 88 | HEY JEAN, HEY DEAN — Dean & Jean, Rust 5075 | 4 |
| 48 | 58 | 84 | — | MY HEART CRIES FOR YOU — Ray Charles, ABC-Paramount 10530 | 3 |
| 49 | 71 | 82 | 99 | SUSPICION — Terry Stafford, Crusader 101 | 4 |
| 50 | 70 | 96 | — | SHOOP SHOOP SONG — Betty Everett, Vee Jay 585 | 3 |
| 51 | 48 | 49 | 57 | CAN YOUR MONKEY DO THE DOG — Rufus Thomas, Stax 144 | 7 |
| 52 | 55 | 61 | 82 | MY TRUE CARRIE LOVE — Nat King Cole, Capitol 5125 | 4 |
| 53 | 51 | 51 | 64 | HE'LL HAVE TO GO — Solomon Burke, Atlantic 2218 | 6 |
| 54 | 62 | 63 | 67 | YOUNG AND IN LOVE — Chris Crosby, MGM 13191 | 5 |
| 55 | — | — | — | TWIST AND SHOUT — Beatles, Tollie 9001 | 1 |
| 56 | 64 | 69 | 81 | LOOK HOMEWARD ANGEL — Monarchs, Sound Stage 7 2516 | 4 |
| 57 | 61 | 73 | 77 | RIP VAN WINKLE — Devotions, Roulette 4541 | 6 |
| 58 | 60 | 43 | 46 | VAYA CON DIOS — Drifters, Atlantic 2216 | 7 |
| 59 | 78 | — | — | DEAD MAN'S CURVE — Jan & Dean, Liberty 55672 | 2 |
| 60 | 88 | — | — | THINK — Brenda Lee, Decca 31599 | 2 |
| 61 | 80 | — | — | HIPPY HIPPY SHAKE — Swinging Blue Jeans, Imperial 66021 | 2 |
| 62 | 53 | 55 | 60 | BYE BYE BARBARA — Johnny Mathis, Mercury 72229 | 7 |
| 63 | 82 | — | — | TELL IT ON THE MOUNTAIN — Peter, Paul & Mary, Warner Bros. 5418 | 2 |
| 64 | 76 | 87 | 93 | I'LL MAKE YOU MINE — Bobby Vee, Liberty 55670 | 4 |
| 65 | 83 | 90 | — | CROOKED LITTLE MAN — Serendipity Singers, Philips 40175 | 3 |
| 66 | 81 | — | — | WHITE ON WHITE — Danny Williams, United Artists 685 | 2 |
| 67 | 63 | 68 | 74 | LOVE WITH THE PROPER STRANGER — Jack Jones, Kapp 571 | 5 |
| 68 | 68 | 74 | 75 | LONG GONE LONESOME BLUES — Hank Williams Jr., MGM 13208 | 7 |
| 69 | 66 | 70 | 73 | HE WALKS LIKES A MAN — Jody Miller, Capitol 5090 | 6 |
| 70 | 72 | — | — | (You Can't Let the Boy Overpower) THE MAN IN YOU — Miracles, Tamla 54092 | 2 |
| 71 | — | — | — | CONGRATULATIONS — Rick Nelson, Imperial 66017 | 1 |
| 72 | 74 | 83 | 98 | HE'S A GOOD GUY — Marvelettes, Tamla 54091 | 4 |
| 73 | 86 | — | — | FROM ME TO YOU — Beatles, Vee Jay 581 | 2 |
| 74 | 69 | 71 | 80 | TELL ME BABY — Garnet Mimms and the Enchanters, United Artists 694 | 5 |
| 75 | 73 | 79 | 90 | OUT OF SIGHT—OUT OF MIND — Sunny & the Sunliners, Tear Drop 3027 | 4 |
| 76 | 79 | 85 | 86 | (That's) WHAT THE NITTY GRITTY IS — Shirley Ellis, Congress 208 | 4 |
| 77 | 77 | 88 | 91 | HIGH ON A HILL — Scott English, Spokane 4003 | 4 |
| 78 | 85 | 93 | — | CASTLES IN THE SAND — Little Stevie Wonder, Tamla 54090 | 3 |
| 79 | 90 | — | — | NADINE — Chuck Berry, Chess 1883 | 2 |
| 80 | 99 | — | — | FOREVER — Pete Drake, Smash 1867 | 2 |
| 81 | — | — | — | YOU'RE A WONDERFUL ONE — Marvin Gaye, Tamla 54093 | 1 |
| 82 | — | — | — | MONEY — Kingsmen, Wand 150 | 1 |
| 83 | 84 | 92 | — | I CAN'T STAND IT — Soul Sisters, Sue 799 | 3 |
| 84 | — | — | — | HEY, BOBBA NEEDLE — Chubby Checker, Parkway 907 | 1 |
| 85 | 92 | — | 96 | CUSTOM MACHINE — Bruce & Terry, Columbia 42956 | 3 |
| 86 | 96 | 99 | — | THE BOY WITH THE BEATLE HAIR — Swans, Cameo 302 | 3 |
| 87 | — | 95 | 97 | MY BOYFRIEND GOT A BEATLE HAIRCUT — Donna Lynn, Capitol 5127 | 3 |
| 88 | — | — | — | WOMAN, LOVE AND A MAN — Tony Clarke, Chess 1880 | 1 |
| 89 | 89 | — | — | AIN'T NOTHING YOU CAN DO — Bobby Bland, Duke 375 | 2 |
| 90 | — | — | — | SEARCHIN' — Ace Cannon, Hi 2074 | 1 |
| 91 | — | — | — | STOCKHOLM — Lawrence Welk, Dot 16582 | 1 |
| 92 | 94 | 89 | — | GOING BACK TO LOUISIANA — Bruce Channel, Le Cam 122 | 3 |
| 93 | 98 | — | — | I WONDER WHO'S KISSING HER NOW — Bobby Darin, Capitol 5126 | 2 |
| 94 | — | — | — | ALWAYS IN MY HEART — Los Indios Tabajaras, RCA Victor 8313 | 1 |
| 95 | — | — | — | BOOK OF LOVE — Raindrops, Jubilee 5469 | 1 |
| 96 | — | — | — | AIN'T GONNA TELL NOBODY — Jimmy Gilmer, Dot 16583 | 1 |
| 97 | 93 | — | — | SOUL SERENADE — King Curtis, Capitol 5109 | 2 |
| 98 | — | — | — | TO EACH HIS OWN — Tymes, Parkway 908 | 1 |
| 99 | — | — | — | WHERE DOES LOVE GO — Freddie Scott, Colpix 724 | 1 |
| 100 | — | — | — | RUN, RUN, RUN — Supremes, Motown 1054 | 1 |

## BUBBLING UNDER THE HOT 100

101. WHEN JOANNA LOVED ME — Tony Bennett, Columbia 42996
102. ROLL OVER BEETHOVEN — Beatles, Capitol 72133
103. SAGINAW, MICHIGAN — Lefty Frizzell, Columbia 42924
104. WELCOME TO MY WORLD — Jim Reeves, RCA Victor 8289
105. WILLYAM, WILLYAM — Dee Dee Sharp, Cameo 296
106. THE WAITING GAME — Brenda Lee, Decca 31579
107. WE LOVE YOU BEATLES — Carefrees, London 10614
108. GIRL FROM SPANISH TOWN — Marty Robbins, Columbia 42968
109. YOU WERE WRONG — Z. Z. Hill, M & H 200
110. SO FAR AWAY — Hank Jacobs, Sue 795
111. JAILER, BRING ME WATER — Trini Lopez, Reprise 0260
112. STRANGE THINGS HAPPENING — Little Junior Parker, Duke 371
113. I'M YOUR HOOCHIE COOCHE MAN — Dion DiMuci, Columbia 42977
114. BLUE MOON — Ray Conniff, His Ork & Chorus, Columbia 42967
115. OUR EVERLASTING LOVE — Ruby and the Romantics, Kapp 578
116. SANDY — Johnny Crawford, Del-Fi 4229
117. LONNIE ON THE MOVE — Lonnie Mack, Fraternity 920
118. YOUR CHEATIN' HEART — Fats Domino, Imperial 66016
119. BLUE MOON — Ray Conniff, His Ork & Chorus, Columbia 42977
120. OUT OF THIS WORLD — Gino Washington, Wand 147
121. NOTHING NEW ABOUT IT — Gene Chandler, Constellation 1
122. LAZY LADY — Fats Domino, Imperial 10531
123. WINTER'S HERE — Robin Ward, Dot 16578
124. LAST NIGHT I HAD THE STRANGEST DREAM — Kingston Trio, Capitol 5132
125. NEVER LEAVE ME — Stratfords, O'Dell 100
126. NEW GIRL IN SCHOOL — Jan & Dean, Liberty 55672
127. SOMEDAY YOU'LL WANT ME TO WANT YOU — Patsy Cline, Decca 31588
128. HEARTBREAK AHEAD — Murmaids, Chattahoochee 636
129. HOLD IT UP — Chuck Jackson, Wand 149
130. MONDO CANE #2 — Kai Winding, Verve 10313
131. T'AIN'T NOTHIN' TO ME — Coasters, Atco 6287
132. I CAN'T WAIT UNTIL I SEE MY BABY — Baby Washington, Sue 797
133. THAT'S THE WAY LOVE IS — Del Shannon, Berlee 502
134. A LETTER TO THE BEATLES — 4 Preps, Capitol 5143

For Week Ending March 21, 1964

# Billboard

# HOT 100

★ STAR performer—Sides registering greatest proportionate upward progress this week.

Billboard Award

| This Week | 1 Wk. Ago | 2 Wks. Ago | 3 Wks. Ago | TITLE Artist, Label & Number | Weeks On Chart |
|---|---|---|---|---|---|
| 1 | 2 | 2 | 2 | **SHE LOVES YOU** — Beatles, Swan 4152 | 9 |
| 2 | 1 | 1 | 1 | **I WANT TO HOLD YOUR HAND** — Beatles, Capitol 5112 | 10 |
| 3 | 3 | 4 | 6 | **PLEASE PLEASE ME** — Beatles, Vee Jay 581 | 8 |
| 4 | 4 | 3 | 3 | **DAWN (Go Away)** — 4 Seasons, Philips 40166 | 8 |
| 5 | 7 | 9 | 17 | **FUN, FUN, FUN** — Beach Boys, Capitol 5118 | 6 |
| 6 | 6 | 7 | 8 | **NAVY BLUE** — Diane Renay, 20th Century-Fox 456 | 9 |
| ★7 | 55 | — | — | **TWIST AND SHOUT** — Beatles, Tollie 9001 | 2 |
| 8 | 5 | 5 | 4 | **JAVA** — Al Hirt, RCA Victor 8280 | 12 |
| 9 | 10 | 11 | 15 | **I LOVE YOU MORE AND MORE EVERY DAY** — Al Martino, Capitol 5108 | 8 |
| ★10 | 13 | 27 | 38 | **HELLO, DOLLY!** — Louis Armstrong, Kapp 573 | 6 |
| ★11 | 19 | 22 | 33 | **HI-HEEL SNEAKERS** — Tommy Tucker, Checker 1067 | 7 |
| 12 | 16 | 21 | 45 | **KISSIN' COUSINS** — Elvis Presley, RCA Victor 8307 | 5 |
| ★13 | 22 | 34 | 65 | **MY HEART BELONGS TO ONLY YOU** — Bobby Vinton, Epic 9662 | 4 |
| 14 | 15 | 18 | 28 | **I SAW HER STANDING THERE** — Beatles, Capitol 5112 | 7 |
| ★15 | 20 | 23 | 53 | **GLAD ALL OVER** — Dave Clark Five, Epic 9656 | 6 |
| 16 | 8 | 6 | 5 | **CALIFORNIA SUN** — Rivieras, Riviera 1401 | 9 |
| 17 | 9 | 10 | 12 | **SEE THE FUNNY LITTLE CLOWN** — Bobby Goldsboro, United Artists 672 | 11 |
| 18 | 11 | 12 | 13 | **GOOD NEWS** — Sam Cooke, RCA Victor 8299 | 9 |
| ★19 | 49 | 71 | 82 | **SUSPICION** — Terry Stafford, Crusader 101 | 5 |
| ★20 | 29 | 40 | 52 | **STAY** — 4 Seasons, Vee Jay 582 | 6 |
| 21 | 12 | 14 | 14 | **I ONLY WANT TO BE WITH YOU** — Dusty Springfield, Philips 40162 | 9 |
| ★22 | 50 | 70 | 96 | **SHOOP SHOOP SONG** — Betty Everett, Vee Jay 585 | 4 |
| ★23 | 41 | 52 | 76 | **THE WAY YOU DO THE THINGS YOU DO** — Temptations, Gordy 7028 | 4 |
| 24 | 27 | 35 | 50 | **BLUE WINTER** — Connie Francis, MGM 13214 | 6 |
| ★25 | 46 | 75 | — | **NEEDLES AND PINS** — Searchers, Kapp 577 | 3 |
| 26 | 17 | 17 | 23 | **THE SHELTER OF YOUR ARMS** — Sammy Davis Jr., Reprise 20216 | 15 |
| 27 | 25 | 28 | 30 | **WHO DO YOU LOVE** — Sapphires, Swan 4162 | 11 |
| 28 | 18 | 19 | 25 | **PENETRATIONS** — Pyramids, Best 13002 | 8 |
| 29 | 24 | 16 | 18 | **ABIGAIL BEECHER** — Freddy Cannon, Warner Bros. 5409 | 8 |
| 30 | 23 | 24 | 26 | **OH BABY DON'T YOU WEEP** — James Brown & the Famous Flames, King 5842 | 9 |
| 31 | 14 | 8 | 9 | **STOP AND THINK IT OVER** — Dale & Grace, Montel 922 | 9 |
| 32 | 34 | 46 | 59 | **STARDUST** — Nino Tempo & April Stevens, Atco 6286 | 5 |
| 33 | 35 | 44 | 78 | **IT HURTS ME** — Elvis Presley, RCA Victor 8307 | 4 |
| ★34 | 65 | 83 | 90 | **DON'T LET THE RAIN COME DOWN (Crooked Little Man)** — Serendipity Singers, Philips 40175 | 4 |
| 35 | 40 | 42 | 56 | **UNDERSTAND YOUR MAN** — Johnny Cash, Columbia 42964 | 6 |
| 36 | 30 | 30 | 37 | **BIRD DANCE BEAT** — Trashmen, Garrett 4003 | 7 |
| 37 | 39 | 47 | 57 | **WORRIED GUY** — Johnny Tillotson, MGM 13193 | 5 |
| 38 | 47 | 65 | 72 | **HEY JEAN, HEY DEAN** — Dean & Jean, Rust 5075 | 5 |
| 39 | 45 | 67 | 77 | **BABY, DON'T YOU CRY** — Ray Charles, ABC-Paramount 10530 | 5 |
| 40 | 28 | 29 | 34 | **I WISH YOU LOVE** — Gloria Lynne, Everest 2036 | 11 |
| ★41 | 61 | 80 | — | **HIPPY HIPPY SHAKE** — Swinging Blue Jeans, Imperial 66021 | 3 |
| 42 | 26 | 31 | 42 | **MY BONNIE** — Beatles, MGM 13213 | 6 |
| ★43 | 60 | 88 | — | **THINK** — Brenda Lee, Decca 31599 | 3 |
| ★44 | 59 | 78 | — | **DEAD MAN'S CURVE** — Jan & Dean, Liberty 55672 | 3 |
| 45 | 33 | 36 | 46 | **MILLER'S CAVE** — Bobby Bare, RCA Victor 8294 | 7 |
| 46 | 48 | 58 | 84 | **MY HEART CRIES FOR YOU** — Ray Charles, ABC-Paramount 10530 | 4 |
| ★47 | 57 | 61 | 73 | **RIP VAN WINKLE** — Devotions, Roulette 4541 | 7 |
| 48 | 21 | 13 | 7 | **YOU DON'T OWN ME** — Lesley Gore, Mercury 72206 | 13 |
| 49 | 52 | 55 | 61 | **MY TRUE CARRIE LOVE** — Nat King Cole, Capitol 5125 | 5 |
| ★50 | 63 | 82 | — | **TELL IT ON THE MOUNTAIN** — Peter, Paul & Mary, Warner Bros. 5418 | 3 |
| 51 | 51 | 48 | 49 | **CAN YOUR MONKEY DO THE DOG** — Rufus Thomas, Stax 144 | 8 |
| 52 | 53 | 51 | 51 | **HE'LL HAVE TO GO** — Solomon Burke, Atlantic 2218 | 7 |
| 53 | 54 | 62 | 63 | **YOUNG AND IN LOVE** — Chris Crosby, MGM 13191 | 6 |
| ★54 | 81 | — | — | **YOU'RE A WONDERFUL ONE** — Marvin Gaye, Tamla 54093 | 2 |
| 55 | 56 | 64 | 69 | **LOOK HOMEWARD ANGEL** — Monarchs, Sound Stage 7 2516 | 5 |
| 56 | 38 | 45 | 58 | **PUPPY LOVE** — Barbara Lewis, Atlantic 2214 | 11 |
| ★57 | 89 | 89 | — | **AIN'T NOTHING YOU CAN DO** — Bobby Bland, Duke 375 | 3 |
| ★58 | 73 | 86 | — | **FROM ME TO YOU** — Beatles, Vee Jay 581 | 3 |
| 59 | 66 | 81 | — | **WHITE ON WHITE** — Danny Williams, United Artists 685 | 3 |
| 60 | 64 | 76 | 87 | **I'LL MAKE YOU MINE** — Bobby Vee, Liberty 55670 | 5 |
| ★61 | 79 | 90 | — | **NADINE** — Chuck Berry, Chess 1883 | 3 |
| 62 | 42 | 43 | 44 | **LIVE WIRE** — Martha & the Vandellas, Gordy 7027 | 7 |
| ★63 | 82 | — | — | **MONEY** — Kingsmen, Wand 150 | 2 |
| 64 | 72 | 74 | 83 | **HE'S A GOOD GUY** — Marvelettes, Tamla 54091 | 5 |
| 65 | 67 | 63 | 68 | **LOVE WITH THE PROPER STRANGER** — Jack Jones, Kapp 571 | 6 |
| 66 | 70 | 72 | — | **(You Can't Let the Boy Over-power) THE MAN IN YOU** — Miracles, Tamla 54092 | 3 |
| 67 | 68 | 68 | 74 | **LONG GONE LONESOME BLUES** — Hank Williams Jr., MGM 13208 | 8 |
| ★68 | 84 | — | — | **HEY, BOBBA NEEDLE** — Chubby Checker, Parkway 907 | 2 |
| 69 | 71 | — | — | **CONGRATULATIONS** — Rick Nelson, Imperial 66017 | 2 |
| 70 | 80 | 99 | — | **FOREVER** — Pete Drake, Smash 1867 | 3 |
| 71 | 75 | 73 | 79 | **OUT OF SIGHT—OUT OF MIND** — Sunny & the Sunliners, Tear Drop 3027 | 5 |
| 72 | 76 | 79 | 85 | **(That's) WHAT THE NITTY GRITTY IS** — Shirley Ellis, Congress 208 | 5 |
| ★73 | — | — | — | **WE LOVE YOU BEATLES** — Carefrees, London Int'l 10614 | 1 |
| 74 | 78 | 85 | 93 | **CASTLES IN THE SAND** — Little Stevie Wonder, Tamla 54090 | 4 |
| ★75 | 96 | — | — | **AIN'T GONNA TELL NOBODY** — Jimmy Gilmer, Dot 16583 | 2 |
| 76 | 74 | 69 | 71 | **TELL ME BABY** — Garnet Mimms and the Enchanters, United Artists 694 | 6 |
| 77 | 83 | 84 | 92 | **I CAN'T STAND IT** — Soul Sisters, Sue 799 | 4 |
| ★78 | — | — | — | **NEW GIRL IN SCHOOL** — Jan & Dean, Liberty 55672 | 1 |
| ★79 | — | — | — | **ROLL OVER BEETHOVEN** — Beatles, Capitol of Canada 72133 | 1 |
| ★80 | — | — | — | **EBB TIDE** — Lenny Welch, Cadence 1422 | 1 |
| 81 | 95 | — | — | **BOOK OF LOVE** — Raindrops, Jubilee 5469 | 2 |
| 82 | 94 | — | — | **ALWAYS IN MY HEART** — Los Indios Tabajaras, RCA Victor 8313 | 2 |
| 83 | 87 | — | 95 | **MY BOYFRIEND GOT A BEATLE HAIRCUT** — Donna Lynn, Capitol 5127 | 4 |
| 84 | 90 | — | — | **SEARCHIN'** — Ace Cannon, Hi 2074 | 2 |
| 85 | 86 | 96 | 99 | **THE BOY WITH THE BEATLE HAIR** — Swans, Cameo 302 | 4 |
| ★86 | — | — | 100 | **LAZY LADY** — Fats Domino, ABC-Paramount 10531 | 2 |
| ★87 | — | — | — | **A LETTER TO THE BEATLES** — 4 Preps, Capitol 5143 | 1 |
| ★88 | — | — | — | **YOU LIED TO YOUR DADDY** — Tams, ABC-Paramount 10533 | 1 |
| 89 | 98 | — | — | **TO EACH HIS OWN** — Tymes, Parkway 908 | 2 |
| ★90 | — | — | — | **OUR EVERLASTING LOVE** — Rudy and the Romantics, Kapp 578 | 1 |
| 91 | 91 | — | — | **STOCKHOLM** — Lawrence Welk, Dot 16582 | 2 |
| 92 | — | — | — | **SHANGRI-LA** — Robert Maxwell, His Harp & Ork, Decca 25622 | 1 |
| 93 | 100 | — | — | **RUN, RUN, RUN** — Supremes, Motown 1054 | 2 |
| 94 | — | — | — | **COME TO ME** — Otis Redding, Volt 116 | 1 |
| 95 | — | — | — | **SHA-LA-LA** — Shirelles, Scepter 1267 | 1 |
| 96 | — | — | — | **JAILER, BRING ME WATER** — Trini Lopez, Reprise 0260 | 1 |
| 97 | 93 | 98 | — | **I WONDER WHO'S KISSING HER NOW** — Bobby Darin, Capitol 5126 | 3 |
| 98 | — | — | — | **I CAN'T WAIT UNTIL I SEE MY BABY** — Baby Washington, Sue 797 | 1 |
| 99 | 99 | — | — | **WHERE DOES LOVE GO** — Freddie Scott, Colpix 724 | 2 |
| 100 | — | — | — | **WHEN JOANNA LOVED ME** — Tony Bennett, Columbia 42996 | 1 |

## HOT 100—A TO Z—*(Publisher-Licensee)*


Abigail Beecher (Claridge-Halseon, ASCAP) ..... 29
Ain't Gonna Tell Nobody (Dundee, BMI) ..... 75
Ain't Nothing You Can Do (Don, BMI) ..... 57
Always in My Heart (Southern, ASCAP) ..... 82
Baby, Don't You Cry (Leeds, ASCAP) ..... 39
Bird Dance Beat (Willong, BMI) ..... 36
Blue Winter (January, BMI) ..... 24
Book of Love (Keel-Arc, BMI) ..... 81
Boy With the Beatle Hair, The (Hill & Range-Shelrose, BMI) ..... 85
California Sun (Lloyd & Logan, BMI) ..... 16
Can Your Monkey Do the Dog (East, BMI) ..... 51
Castles in the Sand (Jobete, BMI) ..... 74
Come to Me (East-Time, BMI) ..... 94
Congratulations (Four Star, BMI) ..... 69
Dawn (Go Away) (Saturday-Gavidima, ASCAP) ..... 4
Dead Man's Curve (Screen Gems-Columbia, BMI) ..... 44
Don't Let the Rain Come Down (Serendipity, BMI ..... 34
Ebb Tide (Robbins, ASCAP) ..... 80
Forever (Tree, BMI) ..... 70
From Me to You (Gil, BMI) ..... 58
Fun, Fun, Fun (Sea of Tunes, BMI) ..... 5
Glad All Over (Campbell-Connelly, ASCAP) ..... 15
Good News (Kags, BMI) ..... 18
He's a Good Guy (Jobete, BMI) ..... 64
He'll Have to Go (Central Songs, BMI) ..... 52
Hello, Dolly! (Morris, ASCAP) ..... 10
Hey, Bobba Needle (Kalman-C.C., ASCAP) ..... 68
Hey Jean, Hey Dean (Schwartz, ASCAP) ..... 38
Hi-Heel Sneakers (Medal, BMI) ..... 11
Hippy Hippy Shake (Maraville, BMI) ..... 41
I Can't Stand It (Saturn-Staccato, BMI) ..... 77
I Can't Wait Until I See My Baby (Picturetone, BMI) ..... 98
I Love You More and More Every Day (Robertson, ASCAP) ..... 9
I Only Want to Be With You (Chappell, ASCAP).. 21
I Saw Her Standing There (Hofer, BMI) ..... 14
I Want to Hold Your Hand (Duchess, BMI) ..... 2
I Wish You Love (Leeds, ASCAP) ..... 40
I Wonder Who's Kissing Her Now (Vogel, ASCAP).. 97
I'll Make You Mine (Saima, BMI) ..... 60
It Hurts Me (Presley, BMI) ..... 33
Jailer, Bring Me Water (T. M., BMI) ..... 96
Java (Tideland, BMI) ..... 8
Kissin' Cousins (Gladys, ASCAP) ..... 12
Lazy Lady (Anatole, BMI) ..... 86
Letter to the Beatles, A (Lar-Bell, BMI) ..... 87
Live Wire (Jobete, BMI) ..... 62
Long Gone Lonesome Blues (Acuff-Rose, BMI) ..... 67
Look Homeward Angel (Rogelle, BMI) ..... 55
Love With the Proper Stranger (Paramount, ASCAP) ..... 65
Miller's Cave (Jack, BMI) ..... 45
Money (Jobete, BMI) ..... 63
My Bonnie (Hill & Range, BMI) ..... 42
My Boyfriend Gat a Beatle Haircut (Integrity-Nancy, ASCAP) ..... 83
My Heart Belongs to Only You (Regent, BMI) .. 13
My Heart Cries for You (Ross-Jungnickel-Gladys-Massey, ASCAP) ..... 46
My True Carrie Love (Comet, ASCAP) ..... 49
Nadine (Arc, BMI) ..... 61
Navy Blue (Saturday, ASCAP) ..... 6
Needles and Pins (Metric, BMI) ..... 25
New Girl in School (Screen Gems-Columbia, BMI). 78
Oh Baby Don't You Weep (Jim Jam, BMI) ..... 30
Our Everlasting Love (Mansion, ASCAP) ..... 90
Out of Sight—Out of Mind (Nome, BMI) ..... 71
Penetration (Dorothy, ASCAP) ..... 28
Please Please Me (Concertone, ASCAP) ..... 3
Puppy Love (McLaughlin, BMI) ..... 56
Rip Van Winkle (Llee, BMI) ..... 47
Roll Over Beethoven (Arc, BMI) ..... 79
Run, Run, Run (Jobete, BMI) ..... 93
Searchin' (Tiger, BMI) ..... 84
See the Funny Little Clown (Unart, BMI) ..... 17
Sha-La-La (Ludix-Romarlu, BMI) ..... 95
Shangri-La (Robbins, ASCAP) ..... 92
She Loves You (Gil, BMI) ..... 1
Shelter of Your Arms, The (Print, ASCAP) ..... 26
Shoop, Shoop Song (T.M., BMI) ..... 22
Stardust (Mills, ASCAP) ..... 32
Stay (Cherio, BMI) ..... 20
Stockholm (Von Tilzer, ASCAP) ..... 91
Stop and Think It Over (Crazy Cajun-Red Sticy, BMI) ..... 31
Suspicion (Presley, BMI) ..... 19
Tell It to the Mountain (Pepamar, ASCAP) ..... 50
Tell Me Baby (Sealark, BMI) ..... 76
(That's) What the Nitty Gritty Is (Gallico, BMI) .. 72
Think (Forrest Hills-Rombre, BMI) ..... 43
To Each His Own (Paramount, ASCAP) ..... 89
Twist and Shout (Mellin-Progressive, BMI) ..... 7
Understand Your Man (Cash, BMI) ..... 35
Way Yo Do the Things You Do, The (Jobete, BMI). 23
We Love You Beatles (Morris, ASCAP) ..... 73
When Joanna Loved Me (Morris, ASCAP) .....100
Where Does Love Go (Screen Gems-Columbia, BMI). 99
White on White (Painted Desert, BMI) ..... 59
Who Do You love (Hill & Range, BMI) ..... 27
Worried Guy (Wood, ASCAP) ..... 37
(You Can't Let the Boy Overpower) The Man in You (Jobete, BMI) ..... 66
You Don't Own Me (Merjoda, BMI) ..... 48
You Lied to Your Daddy (Low-Twi BMI) ..... 88
You're a Wonderful One (Jobete, BMI) ..... 54
Young and in Love (Miller, ASCAP) ..... 53


## BUBBLING UNDER THE HOT 100

101. THE WAITING GAME ..... Brenda Lee, Decca 31599
102. WELCOME TO MY WORLD ..... Jim Reeves, RCA Victor 8289
103. SAGINAW, MICHIGAN ..... Lefty Frizzell, Columbia 42924
104. SOUL SERENADE ..... King Curtis, Capitol 5109
105. STAND BY ME ..... Cassius Clay, Columbia 43007
106. GIRL FROM SPANISH TOWN ..... Marty Robbins, Columbia 42968
107. HAND IT OVER ..... Chuck Jackson, Wand 149
108. THINK NOTHING ABOUT IT ..... Gene Chandler, Constellation 112
109. YOU WERE WRONG ..... Z. Z. Hill, M&H 200
110. STRANGE THINGS HAPPENING ..... Little Junior Parker, Duke 371
111. EASY TO LOVE ..... Chiffons, Laurie 3224
112. YOUR CHEATIN' HEART ..... Fats Domino, Imperial 66016
113. I AM THE GREATEST ..... Cassius Clay, Columbia 43007
114. WOMAN, LOVE AND A MAN ..... Tony Clarke, Chess 1880
114. TALL COOL ONE ..... Wailers, Golden Crest 518
116. HEARTBREAK AHEAD ..... Murmaids, Chattahoochee 636
117. T'AIN'T NOTHING TO ME ..... Coasters, Atco 6287
118. MEXICAN DRUMMER BOY ..... Herb Alpert's Tijuana Brass, A&M 732
119. I'M YOUR HOOCHIE COOCHE MAN ..... Dion Di Muci, Columbia 42977
120. MONDO CANE NO. 2 ..... Kai Winding, Verve 10313
121. LOOK WHO'S TALKING ..... Jim Reeves & Dottie West, RCA Victor 8324
122. I DON'T WANT TO SET THE WORLD ON FIRE ..... Fats Domino, ABC-Paramount 10531
123. SOMEDAY YOU'LL WANT ME TO WANT YOU ..... Patsy Cline, Decca 31588
124. WONDERLAND OF LOVE ..... Tymes, Parkway 908
125. AROUND THE CORNER ..... Ben E. King, Atco 6288
126. BLUE MOON ..... Ray Conniff, His Ork & Chorus, Columbia 42967
127. THAT'S WHEN IT HURTS ..... Ben E. King, Atco 6288
128. DON'T BLAME ME ..... Frank Ifield, Capitol 5134
129. NEVER LEAVE ME ..... Stratfords, O'Dell 100
130. HERE'S TO OUR LOVE ..... Brian Hyland, Philips 40179
131. THERE'S A MEETIN' HERE TONITE ..... Joe & Eddie, Crescendo 195
132. MOONGLOW/PICNIC THEME ..... Baja Marimba Band, Almo 203

Compiled from national retail sales and radio station airplay by the Music Popularity Dept. of Record Market Research, Billboard.

# Billboard HOT 100

For Week Ending March 28, 1964

★ STAR performer—Sides registering greatest proportionate upward progress this week.

| This Week | Wk. Ago | 2 Wks. Ago | TITLE, Artist, Label & Number | Weeks On Chart |
|---|---|---|---|---|
| 1 | 1 | 2 | SHE LOVES YOU — Beatles, Swan 4152 | 10 |
| 2 | 2 | 1 | I WANT TO HOLD YOUR HAND — Beatles, Capitol 5112 | 11 |
| ★3 | 7 | 55 | TWIST AND SHOUT — Beatles, Tollie 9001 | 3 |
| 4 | 3 | 3 | PLEASE PLEASE ME — Beatles, Vee Jay 581 | 9 |
| 5 | 4 | 3 | DAWN (Go Away) — 4 Seasons, Philips 40166 | 9 |
| 6 | 5 | 7 | FUN, FUN, FUN — Beach Boys, Capitol 5118 | 7 |
| 7 | 19 | 49 | SUSPICION — Terry Stafford, Crusader 101 | 6 |
| 8 | 10 | 13 | HELLO, DOLLY! — Louis Armstrong, Kapp 573 | 7 |
| 9 | 13 | 22 | MY HEART BELONGS TO ONLY YOU — Bobby Vinton, Epic 9662 | 5 |
| 10 | 15 | 20 | GLAD ALL OVER — Dave Clark Five, Epic 9656 | 7 |
| 11 | 11 | 19 | HI-HEEL SNEAKERS — Tommy Tucker, Checker 1067 | 8 |
| 12 | 12 | 16 | KISSIN' COUSINS — Elvis Presley, RCA Victor 8307 | 6 |
| 13 | 6 | 6 | NAVY BLUE — Diane Renay, 20th Century-Fox 456 | 10 |
| 14 | 8 | 5 | JAVA — Al Hirt, RCA Victor 8280 | 13 |
| 15 | 23 | 41 | THE WAY YOU DO THE THINGS YOU DO — Temptations, Gordy 7028 | 5 |
| 16 | 22 | 50 | SHOOP SHOOP SONG — Betty Everett, Vee Jay 585 | 5 |
| 17 | 9 | 10 | I LOVE YOU MORE AND MORE EVERY DAY — Al Martino, Capitol 5108 | 9 |
| 18 | 20 | 29 | STAY — 4 Seasons, Vee Jay 582 | 7 |
| 19 | 34 | 65 | DON'T LET THE RAIN COME DOWN (Crooked Little Man) — Serendipity Singers, Philips 40175 | 5 |
| 20 | 25 | 46 | NEEDLES AND PINS — Searchers, Kapp 577 | 4 |
| 21 | 16 | 8 | CALIFORNIA SUN — Rivieras, Riviera 1401 | 10 |
| 22 | 17 | 9 | SEE THE FUNNY LITTLE CLOWN — Bobby Goldsboro, United Artists 672 | 12 |
| 23 | 54 | 81 | YOU'RE A WONDERFUL ONE — Marvin Gaye, Tamla 54093 | 3 |
| 24 | 24 | 27 | BLUE WINTER — Connie Francis, MGM 13214 | 7 |
| 25 | 18 | 11 | GOOD NEWS — Sam Cooke, RCA Victor 8299 | 10 |
| 26 | 14 | 15 | I SAW HER STANDING THERE — Beatles, Capitol 5112 | 8 |
| 27 | — | — | CAN'T BUY ME LOVE — Beatles, Capitol 5150 | 1 |
| 28 | 28 | 18 | PENETRATION — Pyramids, Best 13002 | 9 |
| 29 | 33 | 35 | IT HURTS ME — Elvis Presley, RCA Victor 8307 | 4 |
| 30 | 21 | 12 | I ONLY WANT TO BE WITH YOU — Dusty Springfield, Philips 40162 | 10 |
| ★31 | 41 | 61 | HIPPY HIPPY SHAKE — Swinging Blue Jeans, Imperial 66021 | 4 |
| ★32 | 43 | 60 | THINK — Brenda Lee, Decca 31599 | 4 |
| 33 | 32 | 34 | STARDUST — Nino Tempo & April Stevens, Atco 6286 | 6 |
| ★34 | 44 | 59 | DEAD MAN'S CURVE — Jan & Dean, Liberty 55672 | 4 |
| 35 | 38 | 47 | HEY JEAN, HEY DEAN — Dean & Jean, Rust 5075 | 6 |
| 36 | 30 | 23 | OH BABY DON'T YOU WEEP — James Brown & the Famous Flames, King 5842 | 10 |
| ★37 | 57 | 89 | AIN'T NOTHING YOU CAN DO — Bobby Bland, Duke 375 | 4 |
| 38 | 26 | 17 | THE SHELTER OF YOUR ARMS — Sammy Davis Jr., Reprise 20216 | 16 |
| 39 | 35 | 40 | UNDERSTAND YOUR MAN — Johnny Cash, Columbia 42964 | 7 |
| 40 | 46 | 48 | MY HEART CRIES FOR YOU — Ray Charles, ABC-Paramount 10530 | 5 |
| ★41 | 61 | 79 | NADINE — Chuck Berry, Chess 1883 | 4 |
| ★42 | 63 | 82 | MONEY — Kingsmen, Wand 150 | 3 |
| 43 | 50 | 63 | TELL IT ON THE MOUNTAIN — Peter, Paul & Mary, Warner Bros. 5418 | 4 |
| 44 | 47 | 57 | RIP VAN WINKLE — Devotions, Roulette 4541 | 8 |
| 45 | 39 | 45 | BABY, DON'T YOU CRY — Ray Charles, ABC-Paramount 10530 | 4 |
| ★46 | 59 | 66 | WHITE ON WHITE — Danny Williams, United Artists 685 | 4 |
| 47 | 27 | 25 | WHO DO YOU LOVE — Sapphires, Swan 4162 | 12 |
| 48 | 37 | 39 | WORRIED GUY — Johnny Tillotson, MGM 13193 | 6 |
| 49 | 40 | 28 | I WISH YOU LOVE — Gloria Lynne, Everest 2036 | 12 |
| 50 | 58 | 73 | FROM ME TO YOU — Beatles, Vee Jay 581 | 4 |
| ★51 | 68 | 84 | HEY, BOBBA NEEDLE — Chubby Checker, Parkway 907 | 3 |
| ★52 | 78 | — | NEW GIRL IN SCHOOL — Jan & Dean, Liberty 55672 | 2 |
| 53 | 56 | 38 | PUPPY LOVE — Barbara Lewis, Atlantic 2214 | 12 |
| 54 | 51 | 51 | CAN YOUR MONKEY DO THE DOG — Rufus Thomas, Stax 144 | 9 |
| 55 | 60 | 64 | I'LL MAKE YOU MINE — Bobby Vee, Liberty 55670 | 6 |
| 56 | 64 | 72 | HE'S A GOOD GUY — Marvelettes, Tamla 54091 | 6 |
| 57 | 73 | — | WE LOVE THE BEATLES — Carefrees, London Int'l 10614 | 2 |
| 58 | 52 | 53 | HE'LL HAVE TO GO — Solomon Burke, Atlantic 2218 | 8 |
| 59 | 70 | 80 | FOREVER — Pete Drake, Smash 1867 | 4 |
| ★60 | 75 | 96 | AIN'T GONNA TELL NOBODY — Jimmy Gilmer, Dot 16583 | 3 |
| 61 | 53 | 54 | YOUNG AND IN LOVE — Chris Crosby, MGM 13191 | 7 |
| 62 | 74 | 78 | CASTLES IN THE SAND — Little Stevie Wonder, Tamla 54090 | 5 |
| 63 | 66 | 70 | (You Can't Let the Boy Overpower) THE MAN IN YOU — Miracles, Tamla 54092 | 4 |
| 64 | 69 | 71 | CONGRATULATIONS — Rick Nelson, Imperial 66017 | 3 |
| 65 | 65 | 67 | LOVE WITH THE PROPER STRANGER — Jack Jones, Kapp 571 | 7 |
| 66 | 49 | 52 | MY TRUE CARRIE LOVE — Nat King Cole, Capitol 5125 | 6 |
| 67 | 77 | 83 | I CAN'T STAND IT — Soul Sisters, Sue 799 | 5 |
| 68 | 80 | — | EBB TIDE — Lenny Welch, Cadence 1422 | 2 |
| 69 | 55 | 56 | LOOK HOMEWARD ANGEL — Monarchs, Sound Stage 7 2516 | 6 |
| 70 | 81 | 95 | BOOK OF LOVE — Raindrops, Jubilee 5469 | 3 |
| ★71 | — | — | ALL MY LOVING — Beatles, Capitol of Canada 72144 | 1 |
| ★72 | — | — | THAT'S THE WAY BOYS ARE — Lesley Gore, Mercury 72259 | 1 |
| 73 | 67 | 68 | LONG GONE LONESOME BLUES — Hank Williams Jr., MGM 13208 | 9 |
| 74 | 72 | 76 | (That's) WHAT THE NITTY GRITTY IS — Shirley Ellis, Congress 208 | 6 |
| 75 | 79 | — | ROLL OVER BEETHOVEN — Beatles, Capitol of Canada 72133 | 2 |
| ★76 | — | — | THE MATADOR — Major Lance, Okeh 7191 | 1 |
| ★77 | 95 | — | SHA-LA-LA — Shirelles, Scepter 1267 | 2 |
| ★78 | — | — | DO YOU WANT TO KNOW A SECRET — Beatles, Vee Jay 587 | 1 |
| 79 | 76 | 74 | TELL ME BABY — Garnet Mimms and the Enchanters, United Artists 694 | 7 |
| ★80 | — | — | STAY AWHILE — Dusty Springfield, Philips 40180 | 1 |
| 81 | 90 | — | OUR EVERLASTING LOVE — Rudy and the Romantics, Kapp 578 | 2 |
| ★82 | — | — | MAKE ME FORGET — Bobby Rydell, Cameo 309 | 1 |
| 83 | 89 | 98 | TO EACH HIS OWN — Tymes, Parkway 908 | 3 |
| ★84 | — | — | MY GIRL SLOOPY — Vibrations, Atlantic 2221 | 1 |
| 85 | 88 | — | YOU LIED TO YOUR DADDY — Tams, ABC-Paramount 10533 | 2 |
| 86 | 87 | — | A LETTER TO THE BEATLES — 4 Preps, Capitol 5143 | 2 |
| 87 | 92 | — | SHANGRI-LA — Robert Maxwell, His Harp & Ork, Decca 25622 | 2 |
| ★88 | — | 97 | SOUL SERENADE — King Curtis, Capitol 5109 | 93 |
| 89 | — | — | T'AIN'T NOTHIN' TO ME — Coasters, Atco 6287 | 1 |
| ★90 | — | — | WISH SOMEONE WOULD CARE — Irma Thomas, Imperial 66013 | 1 |
| 91 | 99 | 99 | WHERE DOES LOVE GO — Freddie Scott, Colpix 724 | 3 |
| 92 | — | — | MEXICAN DRUMMER MAN — Herb Alpert's Tijuana Brass, A&M 732 | 1 |
| 93 | 94 | — | COME TO ME — Otis Redding, Volt 116 | 2 |
| 94 | 96 | — | JAILER, BRING ME WATER — Trini Lopez, Reprise 0260 | 2 |
| 95 | 98 | — | I CAN'T WAIT UNTIL I SEE MY BABY — Baby Washington, Sue 797 | 2 |
| 96 | — | — | HAND IT OVER — Chuck Jackson, Wand 149 | 1 |
| 97 | — | — | HOW BLUE CAN YOU GET — B. B. King, ABC-Paramount 10527 | 1 |
| 98 | 100 | — | WHEN JOANNA LOVED ME — Tony Bennett, Columbia 42996 | 2 |
| 99 | — | — | VANISHING POINT — Marketts, Warner Bros. 5423 | 1 |
| 100 | — | — | SHANGRI-LA — Vic Dana, Dolton 92 | 1 |

## BUBBLING UNDER THE HOT 100

101. THE WAITING GAME — Brenda Lee, Decca 31599
102. STAND BY ME — Cassius Clay, Columbia 43007
103. BITS AND PIECES — Dave Clark Five, Epic 9671
104. THAT'S WHEN IT HURTS — Ben E. King, Atco 6288
105. CAN YOU DO IT — Contours, Gordy 7029
106. RUN, RUN, RUN — Supremes, Motown 1054
107. BABY BABY BABY — Anna King-Bobby Byrd, Smash 1884
108. PEOPLE — Barbra Streisand, Columbia 42965
109. GIVING UP ON LOVE — Jerry Butler, Vee Jay 588
110. EASY TO LOVE — Chiffons, Laurie 3224
111. SEARCHIN' — Ace Cannon, Hi 2074
112. HIGH ON A HILL — Scott English, Spokane 4003
113. ALWAYS IN MY HEART — Los Indios Tabajaras, RCA Victor 8313
114. I AM WOMAN — Barbra Streisand, Columbia 42965
115. YOU CAN'T DO THAT — Beatles, Capitol 5150
116. SAGINAW, MICHIGAN — Lefty Frizzell, Columbia 42924
117. LITTLE BOXES — Womenfolk, RCA Victor 8301
118. THERE'S A MEETIN' HERE TONITE — Joe & Eddie, Crescendo 195
119. STRANGE THINGS HAPPENING — Little Junior Parker, Duke 371
120. I AM THE GREATEST — Cassius Clay, Columbia 43007
121. WELCOME TO MY WORLD — Jim Reeves, RCA Victor 8289
122. KISS ME SAILOR — Diane Renay, 20th Century-Fox 477
123. SOMEDAY YOU'LL WANT ME TO WANT YOU — Patsy Cline, Decca 31588
124. TO THE AISLE — Jimmy Velvet, ABC-Paramount 10528
125. GREASE MONKEY — Brother Jack McDuff, Prestige 299
126. I'M LEAVING — Johnny Nash, Groove 0030
127. PUPPET ON A STRING — Bob & Earl, Marc 105
128. ALL MY LOVING — Jimmy Griffin, Reprise 0268
129. HERE'S TO OUR LOVE — Brian Hyland, Philips 40179
130. MOONGLOW/PICNIC THEME — Baja Marimba Band, Almo 203
131. PLEASE LITTLE ANGEL — Doris Troy, Atlantic 2222

Compiled from national retail sales and radio station airplay by the Music Popularity Dept. of Record Market Research, Billboard.

For Week Ending April 4, 1964

# Billboard HOT 100

★ STAR performer—Sides registering greatest proportionate upward progress this week.

Billboard Award: No. 1

| This Week | 1 Wk. Ago | 2 Wks. Ago | 3 Wks. Ago | TITLE | Artist, Label & Number | Weeks On Chart |
|---|---|---|---|---|---|---|
| ★1 | 27 | — | — | CAN'T BUY ME LOVE | Beatles, Capitol 5150 | 2 |
| 2 | 3 | 7 | 55 | TWIST AND SHOUT | Beatles, Tollie 9001 | 4 |
| 3 | 1 | 1 | 2 | SHE LOVES YOU | Beatles, Swan 4152 | 11 |
| 4 | 2 | 2 | 1 | I WANT TO HOLD YOUR HAND | Beatles, Capitol 5112 | 12 |
| 5 | 4 | 3 | 3 | PLEASE PLEASE ME | Beatles, Vee Jay 581 | 10 |
| 6 | 7 | 19 | 49 | SUSPICION | Terry Stafford, Crusader 101 | 7 |
| 7 | 8 | 10 | 13 | HELLO, DOLLY! | Louis Armstrong, Kapp 573 | 8 |
| ★8 | 16 | 22 | 50 | SHOOP SHOOP SONG | Betty Everett, Vee Jay 585 | 6 |
| 9 | 9 | 13 | 22 | MY HEART BELONGS TO ONLY YOU | Bobby Vinton, Epic 9662 | 6 |
| 10 | 10 | 15 | 20 | GLAD ALL OVER | Dave Clark Five, Epic 9656 | 8 |
| 11 | 5 | 4 | 4 | DAWN (Go Away) | 4 Seasons, Philips 40166 | 10 |
| 12 | 15 | 23 | 41 | THE WAY YOU DO THE THINGS YOU DO | Temptations, Gordy 7028 | 6 |
| 13 | 6 | 5 | 7 | FUN, FUN, FUN | Beach Boys, Capitol 5118 | 8 |
| ★14 | 19 | 34 | 65 | DON'T LET THE RAIN COME DOWN (Crooked Little Man) | Serendipity Singers, Philips 40175 | 6 |
| ★15 | 20 | 25 | 46 | NEEDLES AND PINS | Searchers, Kapp 577 | 5 |
| 16 | 18 | 20 | 29 | STAY | 4 Seasons, Vee Jay 582 | 8 |
| 17 | 12 | 12 | 16 | KISSIN' COUSINS | Elvis Presley, RCA Victor 8307 | 7 |
| ★18 | 23 | 54 | 81 | YOU'RE A WONDERFUL ONE | Marvin Gaye, Tamla 54093 | 4 |
| 19 | 14 | 8 | 5 | JAVA | Al Hirt, RCA Victor 8280 | 14 |
| 20 | 11 | 11 | 19 | HI-HEEL SNEAKERS | Tommy Tucker, Checker 1067 | 9 |
| ★21 | 37 | 57 | 89 | AIN'T NOTHING YOU CAN DO | Bobby Bland, Duke 375 | 5 |
| ★22 | 42 | 63 | 82 | MONEY | Kingsmen, Wand 150 | 4 |
| 23 | 17 | 9 | 10 | I LOVE YOU MORE AND MORE EVERY DAY | Al Martino, Capitol 5108 | 10 |
| ★24 | 31 | 41 | 61 | HIPPY HIPPY SHAKE | Swinging Blue Jeans, Imperial 66021 | 5 |
| ★25 | 34 | 44 | 59 | DEAD MAN'S CURVE | Jan & Dean, Liberty 55672 | 5 |
| ★26 | 32 | 43 | 60 | THINK | Brenda Lee, Decca 31599 | 5 |
| 27 | 13 | 6 | 6 | NAVY BLUE | Diane Renay, 20th Century-Fox 456 | 11 |
| 28 | 24 | 24 | 27 | BLUE WINTER | Connie Francis, MGM 13214 | 8 |
| 29 | 29 | 33 | 35 | IT HURTS ME | Elvis Presley, RCA Victor 8307 | 6 |
| ★30 | 41 | 61 | 79 | NADINE | Chuck Berry, Chess 1883 | 5 |
| 31 | 26 | 14 | 15 | I SAW HER STANDING THERE | Beatles, Capitol 5112 | 9 |
| 32 | 35 | 38 | 47 | HEY JEAN, HEY DEAN | Dean & Jean, Rust 5075 | 7 |
| ★33 | 43 | 50 | 63 | TELL IT ON THE MOUNTAIN | Peter, Paul & Mary, Warner Bros. 5418 | 5 |
| ★34 | 46 | 59 | 66 | WHITE ON WHITE | Danny Williams, United Artists 685 | 5 |
| ★35 | 51 | 68 | 84 | HEY, BOBBA NEEDLE | Chubby Checker, Parkway 907 | 4 |
| 36 | 44 | 47 | 57 | RIP VAN WINKLE | Devotions, Roulette 4541 | 9 |
| 37 | 22 | 17 | 9 | SEE THE FUNNY LITTLE CLOWN | Bobby Goldsboro, United Artists 672 | 13 |
| 38 | 40 | 46 | 48 | MY HEART CRIES FOR YOU | Ray Charles, ABC-Paramount 10530 | 6 |
| ★39 | 72 | — | — | THAT'S THE WAY BOYS ARE | Lesley Gore, Mercury 72259 | 2 |
| ★40 | 52 | 78 | — | NEW GIRL IN SCHOOL | Jan & Dean, Liberty 55672 | 3 |
| 41 | 50 | 58 | 73 | FROM ME TO YOU | Beatles, Vee Jay 581 | 5 |
| ★42 | 57 | 63 | — | WE LOVE YOU BEATLES | Carefrees, London Int'l 10614 | 3 |
| 43 | 39 | 35 | 40 | UNDERSTAND YOUR MAN | Johnny Cash, Columbia 42964 | 8 |
| ★44 | 59 | 70 | 80 | FOREVER | Pete Drake, Smash 1867 | 5 |
| 45 | 28 | 28 | 18 | PENETRATION | Pyramids, Best 13002 | 10 |
| ★46 | 78 | — | — | DO YOU WANT TO KNOW A SECRET | Beatles, Vee Jay 587 | 2 |
| ★47 | 68 | 80 | — | EBB TIDE | Lenny Welch, Cadcnce 1422 | 3 |
| ★48 | — | — | — | BITS AND PIECES | Dave Clark Five, Epic 9671 | 1 |
| 49 | 45 | 39 | 45 | BABY, DON'T YOU CRY | Ray Charles, ABC-Paramount 10530 | 7 |
| ★50 | — | — | — | MY GUY | Mary Wells, Motown 1056 | 1 |
| ★51 | 76 | — | — | THE MATADOR | Major Lance, Okeh 7191 | 2 |
| 52 | 55 | 60 | 64 | I'LL MAKE YOU MINE | Bobby Vee, Liberty 55670 | 7 |
| ★53 | 67 | 77 | 83 | I CAN'T STAND IT | Soul Sisters, Sue 799 | 6 |
| 54 | 48 | 37 | 39 | WORRIED GUY | Johnny Tillotson, MGM 13193 | 7 |
| 55 | 56 | 64 | 72 | HE'S A GOOD GUY | Marvelettes, Tamla 54091 | 7 |
| 56 | 62 | 74 | 78 | CASTLES IN THE SAND | Little Stevie Wonder, Tamla 54090 | 6 |
| 57 | 60 | 75 | 96 | AIN'T GONNA TELL NOBODY | Jimmy Gilmer, Dot 16583 | 4 |
| ★58 | 71 | — | — | ALL MY LOVING | Beatles, Capitol of Canada 72144 | 2 |
| 59 | 63 | 66 | 70 | (You Can't Let the Boy Over-power) THE MAN IN YOU | Miracles, Tamla 54092 | 5 |
| ★60 | 87 | 92 | — | SHANGRI-LA | Robert Maxwell, His Harp & Ork, Decca 25622 | 3 |
| ★61 | — | — | — | I'M SO PROUD | Impressions, ABC-Paramount 10544 | 1 |
| 62 | 65 | 65 | 67 | LOVE WITH THE PROPER STRANGER | Jack Jones, Kapp 571 | 8 |
| 63 | 64 | 69 | 71 | CONGRATULATIONS | Rick Nelson, Imperial 66017 | 4 |
| 64 | 70 | 81 | 95 | BOOK OF LOVE | Raindrops, Jubilee 5469 | 4 |
| ★65 | — | — | — | YOU CAN'T DO THAT | Beatles, Capitol 5150 | 1 |
| 66 | 69 | 55 | 56 | LOOK HOMEWARD ANGEL | Monarchs, Sound Stage 7 2516 | 7 |
| ★67 | 82 | — | — | MAKE ME FORGET | Bobby Rydell, Cameo 309 | 2 |
| 68 | 75 | 79 | — | ROLL OVER BEETHOVEN | Beatles, Capitol of Canada 72133 | 3 |
| 69 | 77 | 95 | — | SHA-LA-LA | Shirelles, Scepter 1267 | 3 |
| ★70 | 100 | — | — | SHANGRI-LA | Vic Dana, Dolton 92 | 2 |
| 71 | 84 | — | — | MY GIRL SLOOPY | Vibrations, Atlantic 2221 | 2 |
| ★72 | — | — | — | BABY BABY BABY | Anna King & Bobby Byrd, Smash 1884 | 1 |
| ★73 | 90 | — | — | WISH SOMEONE WOULD CARE | Irma Thomas, Imperial 66013 | 2 |
| ★74 | — | — | — | GIVING UP ON LOVE | Jerry Butler, Vee Jay 588 | 1 |
| 75 | 80 | — | — | STAY AWHILE | Dusty Springfield, Philips 40180 | 2 |
| 76 | 81 | 90 | — | OUR EVERLASTING LOVE | Rudy and the Romantics, Kapp 578 | 3 |
| 77 | 89 | — | — | T'AIN'T NOTHIN' TO ME | Coasters, Atco 6287 | 2 |
| 78 | 83 | 89 | 98 | TO EACH HIS OWN | Tymes, Parkway 908 | 4 |
| ★79 | — | — | — | THANK YOU GIRL | Beatles, Vee Jay 587 | 1 |
| ★80 | — | — | — | PINK PANTHER THEME | Henry Mancini & His Ork, RCA Victor 8286 | 1 |
| 81 | 85 | 88 | — | YOU LIED TO YOUR DADDY | Tams, ABC-Paramount 10533 | 3 |
| ★82 | — | — | — | I SHOULD CARE | Gloria Lynne, Everest 2042 | 1 |
| 83 | 91 | 99 | 99 | WHERE DOES LOVE GO | Freddie Scott, Colpix 724 | 4 |
| ★84 | — | — | — | CAN YOU DO IT | Contours, Gordy 7029 | 1 |
| 85 | 86 | 87 | — | A LETTER TO THE BEATLES | 4 Preps, Capitol 5143 | 3 |
| 86 | 88 | — | 97 | SOUL SERENADE | King Curtis, Capitol 5109 | 4 |
| ★87 | — | — | — | IT'S ALL RIGHT | Tams, ABC-Paramount 10533 | 1 |
| ★88 | — | — | — | THAT'S WHEN IT HURTS | Ben E. King, Atco 6288 | 1 |
| ★89 | — | — | — | CHARADE | Sammy Kaye & His Ork, Decca 31589 | 1 |
| ★90 | — | — | — | KISS ME SAILOR | Diane Renay, 20th Century-Fox 477 | 1 |
| 91 | 92 | — | — | MEXICAN DRUMMER MAN | Herb Alpert's Tijuana Brass, A&M 732 | 2 |
| 92 | 93 | 94 | — | COME TO ME | Otis Redding, Volt 116 | 3 |
| 93 | 95 | 98 | — | I CAN'T WAIT UNTIL I SEE MY BABY | Baby Washington, Sue 797 | 3 |
| 94 | — | — | — | BE ANYTHING (BUT BE MINE) | Gloria Lynne, Fontana 1890 | 1 |
| 95 | 96 | — | — | HAND IT OVER | Chuck Jackson, Wand 149 | 2 |
| 96 | 99 | — | — | VANISHING POINT | Marketts, Warner Bros. 5423 | 2 |
| 97 | 97 | — | — | HOW BLUE CAN YOU GET | B. B. King, ABC-Paramount 10527 | 2 |
| 98 | — | — | — | (THE BEST PART OF) BREAKIN' UP | Ronettes, Philles 120 | 1 |
| 99 | — | — | — | HEY, MR. SAX MAN | Boots Randolph, Monument 835 | 1 |
| 100 | — | — | — | PEOPLE | Barbra Streisand, Columbia 42965 | 1 |

## HOT 100—A TO Z—(Publisher-Licensee)

Ain't Gonna Tell Nobody (Dundee, BMI) ...... 57
Ain't Nothing You Can Do (Don, BMI) ...... 21
All My Loving (James (PRS), ASCAP) ...... 58
Baby Baby Baby (Try Me, BMI) ...... 72
Baby, Don't You Cry (Leeds, ASCAP) ...... 49
Be Anything (But Be Mine) (Shapiro-Bernstein, ASCAP) ...... 94
(The Best Part of) Breakin' Up (Mother Bertha-Hill & Range, BMI) ...... 98
Bits and Pieces (Beechwood, BMI) ...... 48
Blue Winter (January, BMI) ...... 28
Book of Love (Keel-Arc, BMI) ...... 64
Can You Do It (Jobete, BMI) ...... 84
Can't Buy Me Love (Northern, ASCAP) ...... 1
Castles in the Sand (Jobete, BMI) ...... 56
Charade (Northern-Southdale, ASCAP) ...... 89
Come to Me (East-Time, BMI) ...... 92
Congratulations (Four Star, BMI) ...... 63
Dawn (Go Away) (Saturday-Gavidima, ASCAP) ...... 11
Dead Man's Curve (Screen Gems-Columbia, BMI) ...... 25
Do You Want to Know a Secret (Metric, BMI) ...... 46
Don't Let the Rain Come Down (Serendipity, BMI) ...... 14
Ebb Tide (Robbins, ASCAP) ...... 47
Forever (Tree, BMI) ...... 44
From Me to You (Gil, BMI) ...... 41
Fun, Fun, Fun (Sea of Tunes, BMI) ...... 13
Giving Up on Love (Roosevelt, BMI) ...... 74
Glad All Over (Campbell-Connelly, ASCAP) ...... 10
Hand It Over (Ludix-Flo Mar Lu, BMI) ...... 95
He's a Good Guy (Jobete, BMI) ...... 55
Hello, Dolly! (Morris, ASCAP) ...... 7
Hey Bobba Needle (Kalmann-C.C., ASCAP) ...... 35
Hey Jean, Hey Dean (Schwartz, ASCAP) ...... 32
Hey, Mr. Sax Man (Forrest Hills, BMI) ...... 99
Hi-Heel Sneakers (Medal, BMI) ...... 20
Hippy Hippy Shake (Maraville, BMI) ...... 24
How Blue Can You Get (Big Bopper, BMI) ...... 97
I Can't Stand It (Saturn-Staccato, BMI) ...... 53
I Can't Wait Until I See My Baby (Picturetone, BMI) ...... 93
I Love You More and More Every Day (Robertson, ASCAP) ...... 23
I Saw Her Standing There (Gil, BMI) ...... 31
I Should Care (Dorsey, ASCAP) ...... 82
I Want to Hold Your Hand (Duchess, BMI) ...... 4
I'm So Proud (Curtom, BMI) ...... 61
I'll Make You Mine (Saima, BMI) ...... 52
It Hurts Me (Presley, BMI) ...... 29
It's All Right (Low Sal, BMI) ...... 87
Java (Tideland, BMI) ...... 19
Kiss Me Sailor (Saturday, ASCAP) ...... 90
Kissin' Cousins (Gladys, ASCAP) ...... 17
Letter to the Beatles, A (Lar-Bell, BMI) ...... 85
Look Homeward Angel (Rogelle, BMI) ...... 66
Love With the Proper Stranger (Paramount, ASCAP) ...... 62
Make Me Forget (Wood, ASCAP) ...... 67
Matador, The (Curtom-Jalynne, BMI) ...... 51
Mexican Drummer Man (Irving, BMI) ...... 91
Money (Jobete, BMI) ...... 22
My Girl Sloopy (Picturetone-Mellin, BMI) ...... 71
My Guy (Jobete, BMI) ...... 50
My Heart Belongs to Only You (Regent, BMI) ...... 9
My Heart Cries for You (Ross-Jungnickel-Gladys-Massey, ASCAP) ...... 38
Nadine (Arc, BMI) ...... 30
Navy Blue (Saturday, ASCAP) ...... 27
Needles and Pins (Metric, BMI) ...... 15
New Girl in School (Screen Gems-Columbia, BMI) ...... 40
Our Everlasting Love (Mansion, ASCAP) ...... 76
Penetration (Dorothy, ASCAP) ...... 45
People (Chappell, ASCAP) ...... 100
Pink Panther Theme (Northridge-United Artists, ASCAP) ...... 80
Please Please Me (Concertone, ASCAP) ...... 5
Rip Van Winkle (Lee, BMI) ...... 36
Roll Over Beethoven (Arc, BMI) ...... 68
See the Funny Little Clown (Unart, BMI) ...... 37
La-La-La (Ludix-Romarlu, BMI) ...... 69
Shangri-La—Dana (Robbins, ASCAP) ...... 70
Shangri-La—Maxwell (Robbins, ASCAP) ...... 60
She Loves You (Gil, BMI) ...... 3
Shoop, Shoop Song (T. M., BMI) ...... 8
Soul Serenade (Kilynn-VeeVee, BMI) ...... 86
Stay (Cherio, BMI) ...... 16
Stay Awhile (MRC, BMI) ...... 75
Suspicion (Presley, BMI) ...... 6
T'Aint Nothing to Me (Gregmark, BMI) ...... 77
Tell It on the Mountain (Pepamar, ASCAP) ...... 33
Thank You Girl (Conrad, BMI) ...... 79
That's the Way Poys Are (Earth, BMI) ...... 39
That's When It Hurts (Cotillion-Mellin, BMI) ...... 88
Think (Forrest Hills-Rombre, BMI) ...... 26
To Fach His Own (Paramount, ASCAP) ...... 78
Twist and Shout (Mellin-Progressive, BMI) ...... 2
Understand Your Man (Cash, BMI) ...... 43
Vanishing Point (Wrist, BMI) ...... 96
Way You Do the Things You Do, The (Jobete, BMI) ...... 12
We Love You Beatles (Morris, ASCAP) ...... 42
Where Does Love Go (Screen Gems-Columbia, BMI) ...... 83
White on White (Painted Desert, BMI) ...... 34
Wish Someone Would Care (Metric, BMI) ...... 73
Worried Guy (Wood, ASCAP) ...... 54
You Can't Do That (Northern, ASCAP) ...... 65
(You Can't Let the Boy Overpower) the Man in You (Jobete, BMI) ...... 59
You Lied to Your Daddy (Low-Twi, BMI) ...... 81
You're a Wonderful One (Jobete, BMI) ...... 18

## BUBBLING UNDER THE HOT 100

101. THE WAITING GAME ...... Brenda Lee, Decca 31599
102. STAND BY ME ...... Cassius Clay, Columbia 43007
103. WHEN JOANNA LOVED ME ...... Tony Bennett, Columbia 42996
104. JAILER, BRING ME WATER ...... Trini Lopez, Reprise 0260
105. EASY TO LOVE ...... Chiffons, Laurie 3224
106. RUN, RUN, RUN ...... Supremes, Motown 1054
107. THE WONDER OF YOU ...... Ray Peterson, RCA Victor 8333
108. TALL COOL ONE ...... Wailers, Golden Crest 518
109. TODAY ...... New Christy Minstrels, Columbia 43000
110. HIGH ON A HILL ...... Scott English, Spokane 4003
111. LITTLE BOXES ...... Womenfolk, RCA Victor 8301
112. OH BOY ...... Jackie DeShannon, Liberty 55678
113. DIANE ...... Bachelors, London 9639
114. I AM WOMAN ...... Barbra Streisand, Columbia 42965
115. LOVE IS NO EXCUSE ...... Jim Reeves & Dottie West, RCA Victor 7324
116. THERE'S A MEETIN' HERE TONITE ...... Joe & Eddie, Crescendo 195
117. WE'LL NEVER BREAK UP FOR GOOD ...... Paul & Paula, Philips 40168
118. TO THE AISLE ...... Jimmy Velvet, ABC-Paramount 10528
119. WALK, WALK ...... Freewheelers, Epic 9664
120. I'M LEAVING ...... Johnny Nash, Groove 0030
121. GREASE MONKEY ...... Brother Jack McDuff, Prestige 299
122. I'M GONNA LOVE THAT GUY ...... Linda Lloyd, Columbia 42990
123. ALL MY LOVING ...... Jimmy Griffin, Reprise 0268
124. WHERE ARE YOU ...... Duprees, Coed 591
125. WHO'S GOING TO TAKE CARE OF ME ...... Baby Washington, Sue 797
126. SEARCHIN' ...... Ace Cannon, Hi 2074
127. A THOUSAND MILES AWAY ...... Santo & Johnny, Canadian-American 167
128. PLEASE LITTLE ANGEL ...... Dorris Troy, Atlantic 2222
129. GEE ...... Pixies Three, Mercury 72250
130. PERMANENTLY LONELY ...... Timi Yuro, Liberty 55665
131. LOVING YOU MORE EVERY DAY ...... Etta James, Argo 5465
132. SOME THINGS ARE BETTER LEFT UNSAID ...... Ketty Lester, RCA Victor 8331
133. LONNIE ON THE MOVE ...... Lonnie Mack, Fraternity 920
134. BALTIMORE ...... Sonny James, Capitol 5129

Compiled from national retail sales and radio station airplay by the Music Popularity Dept. of Record Market Research, Billboard.

# Billboard

For Week Ending April 11, 1964

# HOT 100

★ **STAR performer**—Sides registering greatest proportionate upward progress this week.

| This Week | 1 Wk. Ago | 2 Wks. Ago | 3 Wks. Ago | TITLE Artist, Label & Number | Weeks On Chart |
|---|---|---|---|---|---|
| 1 (Billboard Award) | 1 | 27 | — | CAN'T BUY ME LOVE — Beatles, Capitol 5150 | 3 |
| 2 | 2 | 3 | 7 | TWIST AND SHOUT — Beatles, Tollie 9001 | 5 |
| ★3 | 6 | 7 | 19 | SUSPICION — Terry Stafford, Crusader 101 | 8 |
| 4 | 3 | 1 | 1 | SHE LOVES YOU — Beatles, Swan 4152 | 12 |
| 5 | 7 | 8 | 10 | HELLO, DOLLY! — Louis Armstrong, Kapp 573 | 9 |
| 6 | 8 | 16 | 22 | SHOOP SHOOP SONG — Betty Everett, Vee Jay 585 | 7 |
| 7 | 4 | 2 | 2 | I WANT TO HOLD YOUR HAND — Beatles, Capitol 5112 | 13 |
| 8 | 10 | 10 | 15 | GLAD ALL OVER — Dave Clark Five, Epic 9656 | 9 |
| 9 | 5 | 4 | 3 | PLEASE PLEASE ME — Beatles, Vee Jay 581 | 11 |
| ★10 | 14 | 19 | 34 | DON'T LET THE RAIN COME DOWN (Crooked Little Man) — Serendipity Singers, Philips 40175 | 7 |
| 11 | 12 | 15 | 23 | THE WAY YOU DO THE THINGS YOU DO — Temptations, Gordy 7028 | 7 |
| 12 | 9 | 9 | 13 | MY HEART BELONGS TO ONLY YOU — Bobby Vinton, Epic 9662 | 7 |
| 13 | 15 | 20 | 25 | NEEDLES AND PINS — Searchers, Kapp 577 | 6 |
| ★14 | 46 | 78 | — | DO YOU WANT TO KNOW A SECRET — Beatles, Vee Jay 587 | 3 |
| ★15 | 25 | 34 | 44 | DEAD MAN'S CURVE — Jan & Dean, Liberty 55672 | 6 |
| 16 | 16 | 18 | 20 | STAY — 4 Seasons, Vee Jay 582 | 9 |
| 17 | 18 | 23 | 54 | YOU'RE A WONDERFUL ONE — Marvin Gaye, Tamla 54093 | 5 |
| 18 | 13 | 6 | 5 | FUN, FUN, FUN — Beach Boys, Capitol 5118 | 9 |
| 19 | 22 | 42 | 63 | MONEY — Kingsmen, Wand 150 | 5 |
| 20 | 21 | 37 | 57 | AIN'T NOTHING YOU CAN DO — Bobby Bland, Duke 375 | 6 |
| 21 | 11 | 5 | 4 | DAWN (Go Away) — 4 Seasons, Philips 40166 | 11 |
| ★22 | 48 | — | — | BITS AND PIECES — Dave Clark Five, Epic 9671 | 2 |
| ★23 | 39 | 72 | — | THAT'S THE WAY BOYS ARE — Lesley Gore, Mercury 72259 | 3 |
| 24 | 24 | 31 | 41 | HIPPY HIPPY SHAKE — Swinging Blue Jeans, Imperial 66021 | 6 |
| 25 | 26 | 32 | 43 | THINK — Brenda Lee, Decca 31599 | 6 |
| ★26 | 50 | — | — | MY GUY — Mary Wells, Motown 1056 | 2 |
| ★27 | 34 | 46 | 59 | WHITE ON WHITE — Danny Williams, United Artists 685 | 6 |
| ★28 | 35 | 51 | 68 | HEY, BOBBA NEEDLE — Chubby Checker, Parkway 907 | 5 |
| 29 | 30 | 41 | 61 | NADINE — Chuck Berry, Chess 1883 | 6 |
| 30 | 20 | 11 | 11 | HI-HEEL SNEAKERS — Tommy Tucker, Checker 1067 | 10 |
| 31 | 19 | 14 | 8 | JAVA — Al Hirt, RCA Victor 8280 | 15 |
| ★32 | 51 | 76 | — | THE MATADOR — Major Lance, Okeh 7191 | 3 |
| 33 | 33 | 43 | 50 | TELL IT ON THE MOUNTAIN — Peter, Paul & Mary, Warner Bros. 5418 | 6 |
| 34 | 17 | 12 | 12 | KISSIN' COUSINS — Elvis Presley, RCA Victor 8307 | 8 |
| ★35 | 47 | 68 | 80 | EBB TIDE — Lenny Welch, Cadence 1422 | 4 |
| 36 | 44 | 59 | 70 | FOREVER — Pete Drake, Smash 1867 | 6 |
| 37 | 40 | 52 | 78 | NEW GIRL IN SCHOOL — Jan & Dean, Liberty 55672 | 4 |
| 38 | 31 | 26 | 14 | I SAW HER STANDING THERE — Beatles, Capitol 5112 | 10 |
| 39 | 42 | 57 | 63 | WE LOVE YOU BEATLES — Carefrees, London Int'l 10614 | 4 |
| 40 | 28 | 24 | 24 | BLUE WINTER — Connie Francis, MGM 13214 | 9 |
| 41 | 29 | 29 | 33 | IT HURTS ME — Elvis Presley, RCA Victor 8307 | 7 |
| ★42 | 60 | 87 | 92 | SHANGRI-LA — Robert Maxwell, His Harp & Ork, Decca 25622 | 4 |
| 43 | 27 | 13 | 6 | NAVY BLUE — Diane Renay, 20th Century-Fox 456 | 12 |
| 44 | 36 | 44 | 47 | RIP VAN WINKLE — Devotions, Roulette 4541 | 10 |
| 45 | 23 | 17 | 9 | I LOVE YOU MORE AND MORE EVERY DAY — Al Martino, Capitol 5108 | 11 |
| 46 | 32 | 35 | 38 | HEY JEAN, HEY DEAN — Dean & Jean, Rust 5075 | 8 |
| 47 | 38 | 40 | 46 | MY HEART CRIES FOR YOU — Ray Charles, ABC-Paramount 10530 | 7 |
| ★48 | 65 | — | — | YOU CAN'T DO THAT — Beatles, Capitol 5150 | 2 |
| 49 | 53 | 67 | 77 | I CAN'T STAND IT — Soul Sisters, Sue 799 | 7 |
| 50 | 58 | 71 | — | ALL MY LOVING — Beatles, Capitol of Canada 72144 | 3 |
| ★51 | 61 | — | — | I'M SO PROUD — Impressions, ABC-Paramount 10544 | 2 |
| 52 | 41 | 50 | 58 | FROM ME TO YOU — Beatles. Vee Jay 581 | 6 |
| ★53 | 73 | 90 | — | WISH SOMEONE WOULD CARE — Irma Thomas, Imperial 66013 | 3 |
| ★54 | 67 | 82 | — | MAKE ME FORGET — Bobby Rydell, Cameo 309 | 3 |
| 55 | 52 | 55 | 60 | I'LL MAKE YOU MINE — Bobby Vee, Liberty 55670 | 8 |
| 56 | 56 | 62 | 74 | CASTLES IN THE SAND — Little Stevie Wonder, Tamla 54090 | 7 |
| 57 | 57 | 60 | 75 | AIN'T GONNA TELL NOBODY — Jimmy Gilmer, Dot 16583 | 5 |
| ★58 | 70 | 100 | — | SHANGRI-LA — Vic Dana, Dolton 92 | 3 |
| ★59 | — | — | — | RONNIE — 4 Seasons, Philips 40185 | 1 |
| ★60 | 71 | 84 | — | MY GIRL SLOOPY — Vibrations, Atlantic 2221 | 3 |
| ★61 | 79 | — | — | THANK YOU GIRL — Beatles, Vee Jay 587 | 2 |
| 62 | 75 | 80 | — | STAY AWHILE — Dusty Springfield, Philips 40180 | 3 |
| 63 | 72 | — | — | BABY BABY BABY — Anna King & Bobby Byrd, Smash 1884 | 2 |
| 64 | 64 | 70 | 81 | BOOK OF LOVE — Raindrops, Jubilee 5469 | 5 |
| 65 | 66 | 69 | 55 | LOOK HOMEWARD ANGEL — Monarchs, Sound Stage 7 2516 | 8 |
| 66 | 74 | — | — | GIVING UP ON LOVE — Jerry Butler, Vee Jay 588 | 2 |
| 67 | 76 | 81 | 90 | OUR EVERLASTING LOVE — Ruby and the Romantics, Kapp 578 | 4 |
| 68 | 63 | 64 | 69 | CONGRATULATIONS — Rick Nelson, Imperial 66017 | 5 |
| ★69 | 84 | — | — | CAN YOU DO IT — Contours, Gordy 7029 | 2 |
| ★70 | 89 | — | — | CHARADE — Sammy Kaye & His Ork, Decca 31589 | 2 |
| 71 | 77 | 89 | — | T'AIN'T NOTHIN' TO ME — Coasters, Atco 6287 | 3 |
| 72 | 80 | — | — | PINK PANTHER THEME — Henry Mancini & His Ork, RCA Victor 8286 | 2 |
| 73 | 81 | 85 | 88 | YOU LIED TO YOUR DADDY — Tams, ABC-Paramount 10533 | 4 |
| ★74 | — | — | — | THERE'S A PLACE — Beatles, Tollie 9001 | 1 |
| 75 | 82 | — | — | I SHOULD CARE — Gloria Lynne, Everest 2042 | 2 |
| 76 | 69 | 77 | 95 | SHA-LA-LA — Shirelles, Sceptor 1267 | 4 |
| 77 | 90 | — | — | KISS ME SAILOR — Diane Renay, 20th Century-Fox 477 | 2 |
| 78 | 68 | 75 | 79 | ROLL OVER BEETHOVEN — Beatles, Capitol of Canada 72133 | 4 |
| 79 | 87 | — | — | IT'S ALL RIGHT — Tams, ABC-Paramount 10533 | 2 |
| ★80 | 98 | — | — | (The Best Part of) BREAKIN' UP — Ronettes, Philles 120 | 2 |
| ★81 | — | — | — | LOVE ME DO — Beatles, Capitol of Canada 72076 | 1 |
| 82 | 83 | 91 | 99 | WHERE DOES LOVE GO — Freddie Scott, Colpix 724 | 5 |
| ★83 | — | — | — | IN MY LONELY ROOM — Martha & the Vandellas, Gordy 7031 | 1 |
| 84 | 86 | 88 | — | SOUL SERENADE — King Curtis, Capitol 5109 | 5 |
| 85 | 88 | — | — | THAT'S WHEN IT HURTS — Ben E. King, Atco 6288 | 2 |
| ★86 | — | — | — | (Just Like) ROMEO & JULIET — Reflections, Golden World 9 | 1 |
| ★87 | — | — | — | COTTON CANDY — Al Hirt, RCA Victor 8346 | 1 |
| 88 | 92 | 93 | 94 | COME TO ME — Otis Redding, Volt 116 | 4 |
| 89 | 91 | 92 | — | MEXICAN DRUMMER MAN — Herb Alpert's Tijuana Brass, A&M 732 | 3 |
| ★90 | — | — | — | IT'S OVER — Roy Orbison, Monument 837 | 1 |
| 91 | — | — | — | SOMEBODY STOLE MY DOG — Rufus Thomas, Stax 149 | 1 |
| 92 | 95 | 96 | — | HAND IT OVER — Chuck Jackson, Wand 149 | 3 |
| 93 | 96 | 99 | — | VANISHING POINT — Marketts, Warner Bros. 5423 | 3 |
| 94 | 94 | — | — | BE ANYTHING (But Be Mine) — Gloria Lynne, Fontana 1890 | 2 |
| 95 | — | — | — | TALL COOL ONE — Wailers, Golden Crest 518 | 1 |
| 96 | — | 98 | 100 | WHEN JOANNA LOVED ME — Tony Bennett, Columbia 42996 | 3 |
| 97 | 100 | — | — | PEOPLE — Barbra Streisand, Columbia 42965 | 2 |
| 98 | — | — | — | I'M ON FIRE — Jerry Lee Lewis, Smash 1886 | 1 |
| 99 | — | — | — | LOVE ME WITH ALL YOUR HEART — Ray Charles Singers, Command 4046 | 1 |
| 100 | — | — | — | PEOPLE — Nat King Cole, Capitol 5155 | 1 |

## HOT 100—A TO Z—*(Publisher-Licensee)*

Ain't Gonna Tell Nobody (Dundee, BMI) ........ 57
Ain't Nothing You Can Do (Don, BMI) ........ 20
All My Loving (James (PRS), ASCAP) ........ 50
Baby, Baby, Baby (Try Me, BMI) ........ 63
Be Anything (But Be Mine) (Shapiro-Bernstein, ASCAP) ........ 94
(The Best Part of) Breakin' Up (Mother Bertha-Hill & Range, BMI) ........ 80
Bits and Pieces (Beechwood, BMI) ........ 22
Blue Winter (January, BMI) ........ 40
Book of Love (Keel-Arc, BMI) ........ 64
Can You Do It (Jobete, BMI) ........ 69
Can't Buy Me Love (Northern, ASCAP) ........ 1
Castles in the Sand (Jobete, BMI) ........ 56
Charade (Northern-Southdale, ASCAP) ........ 70
Come to Me (East-Time, BMI) ........ 88
Congratulations (Four Star, BMI) ........ 68
Cotton Candy (Gallico, BMI) ........ 87
Dawn (Go Away) (Saturday-Gavidima, ASCAP) ........ 21
Dead Man's Curve (Screen Gems-Columbia, BMI) ........ 15
Do You Want to Know a Secret (Metric, BMI) ........ 14
Don't Let the Rain Come Down (Serendipity, BMI) ........ 10
Ebb Tide (Robbins, ASCAP) ........ 35
Forever (Tree, BMI) ........ 36
From Me to You (Gil, BMI) ........ 52
Fun, Fun, Fun (Sea of Tunes, BMI) ........ 18
Giving Up on Love (Roosevelt, BMI) ........ 66
Glad All Over (Campbell-Connelly, ASCAP) ........ 8
Hand It Over (Ludix-Flo Mar Lu, BMI) ........ 92
Hello, Dolly! (Morris, ASCAP) ........ 5
Hey Bobba Needle (Kalmann-C.C., ASCAP) ........ 28
Hey Jean, Hey Dean (Schwartz, ASCAP) ........ 46
Hi-Heel Sneakers (Medal, BMI) ........ 30
Hippy Hippy Shake (Maraville, BMI) ........ 24
I Can't Stand It (Saturn-Staccato, BMI) ........ 49
I Love You More and More Every Day (Robertson, ASCAP) ........ 45
I Saw Her Standing There (Gil, BMI) ........ 38
I Should Care (Dorsey, ASCAP) ........ 75
I Want to Hold Your Hand (Duchess, BMI) ........ 7
I'm on Fire (Grand Canyon, BMI) ........ 98
I'm So Proud (Curtom, BMI) ........ 51
I'll Make You Mine (Saima, BMI) ........ 55
In My Lonely Room (Jobete, BMI) ........ 83
It Hurts Me (Presley, BMI) ........ 41
It's All Right (Low Sal, BMI) ........ 79
It's Over (Acuff-Rose, BMI) ........ 90
Java (Tideland, BMI) ........ 31
(Just Like) Romeo & Juliet (Myto, BMI) ........ 86
Kiss Me Sailor (Saturday, ASCAP) ........ 77
Kissin' Cousins (Gladys, ASCAP) ........ 34
Look Homeward Angel (Rogelle, BMI) ........ 65
Love Me Do (Ardmore-Beechwood, BMI) ........ 81
Love Me With All Your Heart (Peer Int'l, BMI) ........ 99
Make Me Forget (Wood, ASCAP) ........ 54
Matador, The (Curtom-Jalynne, BMI) ........ 32
Mexican Drummer Man (Irving, BMI) ........ 89
Money (Jobete, BMI) ........ 19
My Girl Sloopy (Picturetone-Mellin, BMI) ........ 60
My Guy (Jobete, BMI) ........ 26
My Heart Belongs to Only You (Regent, BMI) ........ 12
My Heart Cries for You (Ross-Jungnickel-Gladys-Massey, ASCAP) ........ 47
Nadine (Arc, BMI) ........ 29
Navy Blue (Saturday, ASCAP) ........ 43
Needles and Pins (Metric, BMI) ........ 13
New Girl in School (Screen Gems-Columbia, BMI) ........ 37
Our Everlasting Love (Mansion, ASCAP) ........ 67
People—Cole (Chappell, ASCAP) ........ 100
People—Streisand (Chappell, ASCAP) ........ 97
Pink Panther Theme (Northridge-United Artists, ASCAP) ........ 72
Please Please Me (Concertone, ASCAP) ........ 9
Rip Van Winkle (Lee, BMI) ........ 44
Roll Over Beethoven (Arc, BMI) ........ 78
Ronnie (Saturday-Gavadima, ASCAP) ........ 59
Sha-La-La (Ludix-Romarlu, BMI) ........ 76
Shangri-La—Dana (Robbins, ASCAP) ........ 58
Shangri-La—Maxwell (Robbins, ASCAP) ........ 42
She Loves You (Gil, BMI) ........ 4
Shoop, Shoop Song (T. M., BMI) ........ 6
Somebody Stole My Dog (East, BMI) ........ 91
Soul Serenade (Kilynn-VeeVee, BMI) ........ 84
Stay (Cherio, BMI) ........ 16
Stay Awhile (MRC, BMI) ........ 62
Suspicion (Presley, BMI) ........ 3
T'Ain't Nothin' to Me (Gregmark, BMI) ........ 71
Tall Cool One (C.F.G., BMI) ........ 95
Tell It to the Mountain (Pepamar, ASCAP) ........ 33
Thank You Girl (Conrad, BMI) ........ 61
That's the Way Boys Are (Earth, BMI) ........ 23
That's When It Hurts (Cotillion-Mellin, BMI) ........ 85
There's a Place (Gil, BMI) ........ 74
Think (Forrest Hills-Rombre, BMI) ........ 25
Twist and Shout (Mellin-Progressive, BMI) ........ 2
Vanishing Point (Wrist, BMI) ........ 93
Way You Do the Things You Do, The (Jobete, BMI) ........ 11
We Love You Beatles (Morris, ASCAP) ........ 39
When Joanna Loved Me (Morris, ASCAP) ........ 96
Where Does Love Go (Screen Gems-Columbia, BMI) ........ 82
White on White (Painted Desert, BMI) ........ 27
Wish Someone Would Care (Metric, BMI) ........ 53
You Can't Do That (Northern, ASCAP) ........ 48
You Lied to Your Daddy (Low-Twi, BMI) ........ 73
You're a Wonderful One (Jobete, BMI) ........ 17

## BUBBLING UNDER THE HOT 100

101. DIANE ........ Bachelors, London 9639
102. LITTLE BOXES ........ Womenfolk, RCA Victor 8301
103. IF YOU LOVE ME (Like You Say) ........ Little Johnny Taylor, Galaxy 729
104. HEY, MR. SAX MAN ........ Boots Randolph, Monument 835
105. WE'LL NEVER BREAK UP FOR GOOD ........ Paul & Paula, Philips 40168
106. THE WONDER OF YOU ........ Ray Peterson, RCA Victor 8333
107. FIRST CLASS LOVE ........ Little Johnny Taylor, Galaxy 729
108. STAND BY ME ........ Cassius Clay, Columbia 43007
109. SHOUT ........ Dion, Laurie 3240
110. WRONG FOR EACH OTHER ........ Andy Williams, Columbia 43015
111. EASY TO LOVE ........ Chiffons, Laurie 3224
112. WHENEVER HE HOLDS YOU ........ Bobby Goldsboro, United Artists 710
113. THE WAITING GAME ........ Brenda Lee, Decca 31599
114. OH BOY ........ Jackie DeShannon, Liberty 55678
115. PARTY GIRL ........ Bernadette Carroll, Laurie 3238
116. HOW BLUE CAN YOU GET ........ B. B. King, ABC-Paramount 10527
117. BEATLE MANIA BLUES ........ Roaches, Crossroads 447
118. GONNA GET ALONG WITHOUT YOU NOW ........ Tracey Dey, Amy 901
119. GREASE MONKEY ........ Brother Jack McDuff, Prestige 299
120. ALL MY LOVING ........ Jimmy Griffin, Reprise 0268
121. WHERE YOU ARE ........ Duprees, Coed 591
122. I'M GONNA LOVE THAT GUY ........ Linda Lloyd, Columbia 42990
123. TODAY ........ New Christy Minstrels, Columbia 43000
124. A THOUSAND MILES AWAY ........ Santo & Johnny, Canadian-American 167
125. ALL YOU HAD TO DO (Was Tell Me) ........ Chris & Kathy, Monogram 517
126. OUR FADED LOVE ........ Royaltones, Mala 473
127. GEE ........ Pixies Three, Mercury 72250
128. SOMETHINGS ARE BETTER LEFT UNSAID ........ Ketty Lester, RCA Victor 8331
129. LOVING YOU MORE EVERY DAY ........ Etta James, Argo 5465
130. JUST ONE LOOK ........ Hollies, Imperial 66026
131. WHY ........ Beatles with Tony Sheridan, MGM 13227
132. BLUE TRAIN (Of the Heartbreak Line) ........ John D. Loudermilk, RCA Victor 8308
133. PUPPET ON A STRING ........ Bob & Earl, Marc 105

Compiled from national retail sales and radio station airplay by the Music Popularity Dept. of Record Market Research, Billboard.

For Week Ending April 18, 1964

Billboard

# HOT 100

★ STAR performer—Sides registering greatest proportionate upward progress this week.

| This Week | 1 Wk. Ago | 2 Wks. Ago | 3 Wks. Ago | Title — Artist, Label & Number | Weeks On Chart |
|---|---|---|---|---|---|
| 1 | 1 | 1 | 27 | CAN'T BUY ME LOVE — Beatles, Capitol 5150 | 4 |
| 2 | 2 | 2 | 3 | TWIST AND SHOUT — Beatles, Tollie 9001 | 6 |
| 3 | 3 | 6 | 7 | SUSPICION — Terry Stafford, Crusader 101 | 9 |
| 4 | 5 | 7 | 8 | HELLO, DOLLY! — Louis Armstrong, Kapp 573 | 10 |
| ★ 5 | 14 | 46 | 78 | DO YOU WANT TO KNOW A SECRET — Beatles, Vee Jay 587 | 4 |
| 6 | 6 | 8 | 16 | SHOOP SHOOP SONG — Betty Everett, Vee Jay 585 | 8 |
| 7 | 8 | 10 | 10 | GLAD ALL OVER — Dave Clark Five, Epic 9656 | 10 |
| 8 | 4 | 3 | 1 | SHE LOVES YOU — Beatles, Swan 4152 | 13 |
| 9 | 10 | 14 | 19 | DON'T LET THE RAIN COME DOWN (Crooked Little Man) — Serendipity Singers, Philips 40175 | 8 |
| ★ 10 | 15 | 25 | 34 | DEAD MAN'S CURVE — Jan & Dean, Liberty 55672 | 7 |
| ★ 11 | 22 | 48 | — | BITS AND PIECES — Dave Clark Five, Epic 9671 | 3 |
| 12 | 11 | 12 | 15 | THE WAY YOU DO THE THINGS YOU DO — Temptations, Gordy 7028 | 8 |
| 13 | 13 | 15 | 20 | NEEDLES AND PINS — Searchers, Kapp 577 | 7 |
| ★ 14 | 26 | 50 | — | MY GUY — Mary Wells, Motown 1056 | 3 |
| 15 | 17 | 18 | 23 | YOU'RE A WONDERFUL ONE — Marvin Gaye, Tamla 54093 | 6 |
| 16 | 9 | 5 | 4 | PLEASE PLEASE ME — Beatles, Vee Jay 581 | 12 |
| ★ 17 | 23 | 39 | 72 | THAT'S THE WAY BOYS ARE — Lesley Gore, Mercury 72259 | 4 |
| 18 | 19 | 22 | 42 | MONEY — Kingsmen, Wand 150 | 6 |
| 19 | 7 | 4 | 2 | I WANT TO HOLD YOUR HAND — Beatles, Capitol 5112 | 14 |
| 20 | 20 | 21 | 37 | AIN'T NOTHING YOU CAN DO — Bobby Bland, Duke 375 | 7 |
| ★ 21 | 27 | 34 | 46 | WHITE ON WHITE — Danny Williams, United Artists 685 | 7 |
| 22 | 12 | 9 | 9 | MY HEART BELONGS TO ONLY YOU — Bobby Vinton, Epic 9662 | 8 |
| ★ 23 | 32 | 51 | 76 | THE MATADOR — Major Lance, Okeh 7191 | 4 |
| 24 | 16 | 16 | 18 | STAY — 4 Seasons, Vee Jay 582 | 10 |
| 25 | 25 | 26 | 32 | THINK — Brenda Lee, Decca 31599 | 7 |
| 26 | 28 | 35 | 51 | HEY, BOBBA NEEDLE — Chubby Checker, Parkway 907 | 6 |
| ★ 27 | 36 | 44 | 59 | FOREVER — Pete Drake, Smash 1867 | 7 |
| 28 | 29 | 30 | 41 | NADINE — Chuck Berry, Chess 1883 | 7 |
| ★ 29 | 59 | — | — | RONNIE — 4 Seasons, Philips 40185 | 2 |
| ★ 30 | 42 | 60 | 87 | SHANGRI-LA — Robert Maxwell, His Harp & Ork, Decca 25622 | 5 |
| 31 | 35 | 47 | 68 | EBB TIDE — Lenny Welch, Cadence 1422 | 5 |
| 32 | 24 | 24 | 31 | HIPPY HIPPY SHAKE — Swinging Blue Jeans, Imperial 66021 | 7 |
| 33 | 18 | 13 | 6 | FUN, FUN, FUN — Beach Boys, Capitol 5118 | 10 |
| 34 | 30 | 20 | 11 | HI-HEEL SNEAKERS — Tommy Tucker, Checker 1067 | 11 |
| 35 | 21 | 11 | 5 | DAWN (Go Away) — 4 Seasons, Philips 40166 | 12 |
| 36 | 33 | 33 | 43 | TELL IT ON THE MOUNTAIN — Peter, Paul & Mary, Warner Bros. 5418 | 7 |
| ★ 37 | 51 | 61 | — | I'M SO PROUD — Impressions, ABC-Paramount 10544 | 3 |
| 38 | 31 | 19 | 14 | JAVA — Al Hirt, RCA Victor 8280 | 16 |
| 39 | 34 | 17 | 12 | KISSIN' COUSINS — Elvis Presley, RCA Victor 8307 | 9 |
| 40 | 37 | 40 | 52 | NEW GIRL IN SCHOOL — Jan & Dean, Liberty 55672 | 5 |
| ★ 41 | 60 | 71 | | MY GIRL SLOOPY — Vibrations, Atlantic 2221 | 4 |
| ★ 42 | 53 | 73 | 90 | WISH SOMEONE WOULD CARE — Irma Thomas, Imperial 66013 | 4 |
| 43 | 39 | 42 | 57 | WE LOVE YOU BEATLES — Carefrees, London Int'l 10614 | 5 |
| ★ 44 | 77 | 90 | — | KISS ME SAILOR — Diane Renay, 20th Century-Fox 477 | 3 |
| 45 | 38 | 31 | 26 | I SAW HER STANDING THERE — Beatles, Capitol 5112 | 11 |
| 46 | 49 | 53 | 67 | I CAN'T STAND IT — Soul Sisters, Sue 799 | 8 |
| ★ 47 | 58 | 70 | 100 | SHANGRI-LA — Vic Dana, Dolton 92 | 4 |
| 48 | 50 | 58 | 71 | ALL MY LOVING — Beatles, Capitol of Canada 72144 | 4 |
| ★ 49 | 61 | 79 | — | THANK YOU GIRL — Beatles, Vee Jay 587 | 3 |
| 50 | 54 | 67 | 82 | MAKE ME FORGET — Bobby Rydell, Cameo 309 | 4 |
| ★ 51 | 62 | 75 | 80 | STAY AWHILE — Dusty Springfield, Philips 40180 | 4 |
| 52 | 56 | 56 | 62 | CASTLES IN THE SAND — Little Stevie Wonder, Tamla 54090 | 8 |
| 53 | 57 | 57 | 60 | AIN'T GONNA TELL NOBODY — Jimmy Gilmer, Dot 16583 | 6 |
| ★ 54 | 72 | 80 | — | PINK PANTHER THEME — Henry Mancini & His Ork, RCA Victor 8286 | 3 |
| 55 | 48 | 65 | — | YOU CAN'T DO THAT — Beatles, Capitol 5150 | 3 |
| ★ 56 | 70 | 89 | — | CHARADE — Sammy Kaye & His Ork, Decca 31589 | 3 |
| 57 | 63 | 72 | — | BABY BABY BABY — Anna King & Bobby Byrd, Smash 1884 | 3 |
| 58 | 65 | 66 | 69 | LOOK HOMEWARD ANGEL — Monarchs, Sound Stage 7 2516 | 9 |
| 59 | 66 | 74 | — | GIVING UP ON LOVE — Jerry Butler, Vee Jay 588 | 3 |
| ★ 60 | 90 | — | — | IT'S OVER — Roy Orbison, Monument 837 | 2 |
| 61 | 69 | 84 | — | CAN YOU DO IT — Contours, Gordy 7029 | 3 |
| 62 | 64 | 64 | 70 | BOOK OF LOVE — Raindrops, Jubilee 5469 | 6 |
| ★ 63 | 83 | — | — | IN MY LONELY ROOM — Martha & the Vandellas, Gordy 7031 | 2 |
| 64 | 67 | 76 | 81 | OUR EVERLASTING LOVE — Ruby and the Romantics, Kapp 578 | 5 |
| 65 | 71 | 77 | 89 | T'AIN'T NOTHIN' TO ME — Coasters, Atco 6287 | 4 |
| ★ 66 | — | — | — | SLIP-IN MULES — Sugar Pie De Santo, Checker 1073 | 1 |
| ★ 67 | 87 | — | — | COTTON CANDY — Al Hirt, RCA Victor 8346 | 2 |
| ★ 68 | 84 | 86 | 88 | SOUL SERENADE — King Curtis, Capitol 5109 | 6 |
| 69 | 75 | 82 | — | I SHOULD CARE — Gloria Lynne, Everest 2042 | 3 |
| 70 | 73 | 81 | 85 | YOU LIED TO YOUR DADDY — Tams, ABC-Paramount 10533 | 5 |
| 71 | 80 | 98 | — | (The Best Part of) BREAKIN' UP — Ronettes, Philles 120 | 3 |
| ★ 72 | — | — | — | WRONG FOR EACH OTHER — Andy Williams, Columbia 43015 | 1 |
| 73 | 81 | — | — | LOVE ME DO — Beatles, Capitol of Canada 72076 | 2 |
| ★ 74 | — | — | — | DIANE — Bachelors, London 9639 | 1 |
| 75 | 86 | — | — | (Just Like) ROMEO & JULIET — Reflections, Golden World 9 | 2 |
| 76 | 85 | 88 | — | THAT'S WHEN IT HURTS — Ben E. King, Atco 6288 | 3 |
| 77 | 89 | 91 | 92 | MEXICAN DRUMMER MAN — Herb Alpert's Tijuana Brass, A&M 732 | 4 |
| ★ 78 | — | — | — | GOODBYE BABY (Baby Goodbye) — Solomon Burke, Atlantic 2226 | 1 |
| 79 | 79 | 87 | — | IT'S ALL RIGHT — Tams, ABC-Paramount 10533 | 3 |
| ★ 80 | — | — | — | WHENEVER HE HOLDS YOU — Bobby Goldsboro, United Artists 710 | 1 |
| ★ 81 | — | — | — | LOVING YOU MORE EVERY DAY — Etta James, Argo 5465 | 1 |
| 82 | 82 | 83 | 91 | WHERE DOES LOVE GO — Freddie Scott, Colpix 724 | 6 |
| 83 | 88 | 92 | 93 | COME TO ME — Otis Redding, Volt 116 | 5 |
| ★ 84 | — | — | — | TODAY — New Christy Minstrels, Columbia 43000 | 1 |
| 85 | 95 | — | — | TALL COOL ONE — Wailers, Golden Crest 518 | 2 |
| 86 | 91 | — | — | SOMEBODY STOLE MY DOG — Rufus Thomas, Stax 149 | 2 |
| ★ 87 | — | — | — | LITTLE CHILDREN — Billy J. Kramer, Imperial 66027 | 1 |
| ★ 88 | — | — | — | WHY — Beatles with Tony Sheridan, MGM 13227 | 1 |
| 89 | 94 | 94 | — | BE ANYTHING (But Be Mine) — Gloria Lynne, Fontana 1890 | 3 |
| 90 | 93 | 96 | 99 | VANISHING POINT — Marketts, Warner Bros. 5423 | 4 |
| 91 | — | — | — | HIGH ON A HILL — Scott English, Spokane 4003 | 5 |
| 92 | — | — | — | I'M THE LONELY ONE — Cliff Richard, Epic 9670 | 1 |
| 93 | 99 | — | — | LOVE ME WITH ALL YOUR HEART — Ray Charles Singers, Command 4046 | 2 |
| 94 | — | — | — | GEE — Pixies Three, Mercury 72250 | 1 |
| 95 | — | — | — | AIN'T THAT JUST LIKE ME — Searchers, Kapp 584 | 1 |
| 96 | 96 | — | 98 | WHEN JOANNA LOVED ME — Tony Bennett, Columbia 42996 | 4 |
| 97 | — | — | — | DONNIE — Bermudas, Era 3125 | 1 |
| 98 | — | — | — | HEY, MR. SAX MAN — Boots Randolph, Monument 835 | 2 |
| 99 | 97 | 100 | — | PEOPLE — Barbra Streisand, Columbia 42965 | 3 |
| 100 | — | — | — | LITTLE BOXES — Womenfolk, RCA Victor 8301 | 1 |

## HOT 100—A TO Z—*(Publisher-Licensee)*


Ain't Gonna Tell Nobody (Dundee, BMI) ...... 53
Ain't Nothing You Can Do (Don, BMI) ...... 20
Ain't That Just Like Me (Trio-Progressive, BMI).. 95
All My Loving (James (PRS), ASCAP) ...... 48
Baby, Baby, Baby (Try Me, BMI) ...... 57
Be Anything (But Be Mine) (Shapiro-Bernstein, ASCAP) ...... 89
(The Best Part of) Breakin' Up (Mother Bertha-Hill & Range, BMI) ...... 71
Bits and Pieces (Beechwood, BMI) ...... 11
Book of Love (Keel-Arc, BMI) ...... 62
Can You Do It (Jobete, BMI) ...... 61
Can't Buy Me Love (Northern, ASCAP) ...... 1
Castles in the Sand (Jobete, BMI) ...... 52
Charade (Northern-Southdale, ASCAP) ...... 56
Come to Me (East-Time, BMI) ...... 83
Cotton Candy (Gallico, BMI) ...... 67
Dawn (Go Away) (Saturday-Gavidima, ASCAP) ...... 35
Dead Man's Curve (Screen Gems-Columbia, BMI).. 10
Diane (Miller, ASCAP) ...... 74
Do You Want to Know a Secret (Metric, BMI) .. 5
Don't Let the Rain Come Down (Serendipity, BMI) 9
Donnie (Rickland, BMI) ...... 97
Ebb Tide (Robbins, ASCAP) ...... 31
Forever (Tree, BMI) ...... 27
Fun, Fun, Fun (Sea of Tunes, BMI) ...... 33
Gee (Patricia, BMI) ...... 94
Giving Up on Love (Roosevelt, BMI) ...... 59
Glad All Over (Campbell-Connelly, ASCAP) ...... 7
Goodbye Baby (Picturetone-Mellin, BMI) ...... 78
Hello, Dolly! (Morris, ASCAP) ...... 4
Hey Bobba Needle (Kalmann-C.C., ASCAP) ...... 26
Hey, Mr. Sax Man (Forrest Hills, BMI) ...... 98
Hi-Heel Sneakers (Medal, BMI) ...... 34
High on a Hill (Sultan, BMI) ...... 91
Hippy Hippy Shake (Maraville, BMI) ...... 32
I Can't Stand It (Saturn-Staccato, BMI) ...... 46
I Saw Her Standing There (Gil, BMI) ...... 45
I Should Care (Dorsey, ASCAP) ...... 69
I Want to Hold Your Hand (Duchess, BMI) ...... 19
I'm the Lonely One (Duchess, BMI) ...... 92
I'm So Proud (Curtom, BMI) ...... 37
In My Lonely Room (Jobete, BMI) ...... 63
It's All Right (Low Sal, BMI) ...... 79
It's Over (Acuff-Rose, BMI) ...... 60
Java (Tideland, BMI) ...... 38
(Just Like) Romeo & Juliet (Myto, BMI) ...... 75
Kiss Me Sailor (Saturday, ASCAP) ...... 44
Kissin' Cousins (Gladys, ASCAP) ...... 39
Little Boxes (Schroeder, ASCAP) ......100
Little Children (Rumbalero, BMI) ...... 87
Look Homeward Angel (Rogelle, BMI) ...... 58
Love Me Do (Ardmore-Beechwood, BMI) ...... 73
Love Me With All Your Heart (Peer Int'l, BMI) .. 93
Loving You More Every Day (Trio, BMI) ...... 81
Make Me Forget (Wood, ASCAP) ...... 50
Matador, The (Curtom-Jalynne, BMI) ...... 23
Mexican Drummer Man (Irving, BMI) ...... 77
Money (Jobete, BMI) ...... 18
My Girl Sloopy (Picturetone-Mellin, BMI) ...... 41
My Guy (Jobete, BMI) ...... 14
My Heart Belongs to Only You (Regent, BMI) ... 22
Nadine (Arc, BMI) ...... 28
Needles and Pins (Metric, BMI) ...... 13
New Girl in School (Screen Gems-Columbia, BMI).. 40
Our Everlasting Love (Mansion, ASCAP) ...... 64
People (Chappell, ASCAP) ...... 99
Pink Panther Theme (Northridge-United Artists, ASCAP) ...... 54
Please Please Me (Concertone, ASCAP) ...... 16
Ronnie (Saturday-Gavidima, ASCAP) ...... 29
Shangri-La—Dana (Robbins, ASCAP) ...... 47
Shangri-La—Maxwlel (Robbins, ASCAP) ...... 30
She Loves You (Gil, BMI) ...... 8
Shoop Shoop Song (T. M., BMI) ...... 6
Slip-In Mules (Chevis-Medal, BMI) ...... 66
Somebody Stole My Dog (East, BMI) ...... 86
Soul Serenade (Kilynn-Vee Vee, BMI) ...... 68
Stay (Cherio, BMI) ...... 24
Stay Awhile (MRC, BMI) ...... 51
Suspicion (Presley, BMI) ...... 3
T'ain't Nothin' to Me (Gregmark, BMI) ...... 65
Tall Cool One (C.F.G., BMI ...... 85
Tell It on the Mountain, Pepamar, ASCAP) ...... 36
Thank You Girl (Conrad, BMI) ...... 49
That's the Way Boys Are (Earth, BMI) ...... 17
That's When It Hurts (Cotillion-Mellin, BMI) .... 76
Think (Forrest Hills-Rombre, BMI) ...... 25
Today (Miller-Heritage House, ASCAP) ...... 84
Twist and Shout (Mellin-Progressive, BMI) ...... 2
Vanishing Point (Wrist, BMI) ...... 90
Way You Do the Things You Do, The (Jobete, BMI) ...... 12
We Love You Beatles (Morris, ASCAP) ...... 43
When Joanna Loved Me (Morris, ASCAP) ...... 96
Whenever He Holds You (Unart, BMI) ...... 80
Where Does Love Go (Screen Gems-Columbia, BMI) 82
White on White (Painted Desert, BMI) ...... 21
Why (Gallico, BMI) ...... 88
Wish Someone Would Care (Metric, BMI) ...... 42
Wrong for Each Other (Valley, BMI) ...... 72
You Can't Do That (Northern, ASCAP) ...... 55
You Lied to Your Daddy (Low-Twi, BMI) ...... 70
You're a Wonderful One (Jobete, BMI) ...... 15


## BUBBLING UNDER THE HOT 100

101. SUGAR AND SPICE ......Searchers, Liberty 55689
102. I DON'T WANT TO HURT ANYMORE ......Nat King Cole, Capitol 5155
103. I'M ON FIRE ......Jerry Lee Lewis, Smash 1886
104. PEOPLE ......Nat King Cole, Capitol 5155
105. THE WONDER OF YOU ......Ray Peterson, RCA Victor 8333
106. WE'LL NEVER BREAK UP FOR GOOD ......Paul & Paula, Philips 40168
107. THE VERY THOUGHT OF YOU ......Rick Nelson, Decca 31612
108. SHOUT ......Dion, Laurie 3240
109. IF YOU LOVE ME (Like You Say) ......Little Johnny Taylor, Galaxy 729
110. CALL HER UP ......Jackie Wilson, Brunswick 55263
111. PUPPET ON A STRING ...... Bob & Earl, Marc 105
112. FIRST CLASS LOVE ......Little Johnny Taylor, Galaxy 729
113. OH BOY ......Jackie DeShannon, Liberty 55678
114. HOW BLUE CAN YOU GET ......B. B. King, ABC-Paramount 10527
115. GONNA GET ALONG WITHOUT YOU NOW ......Tracey Dey, Amy 901
116. GREASE MONKEY ......Brother Jack McDuff, Prestige 299
117. PARTY GIRL ......Bernadette Carroll, Laurie 3238
118. ALL MY LOVING ......Jimmy Griffin, Reprise 0268
119. WALK ON BY ......Dionne Warwick, Scepter 1274
120. THE FALL OF LOVE ......Johnny Mathis, Mercury 72263
121. WHERE ARE YOU ......Duprees, Coed 591
122. A THOUSAND MILES AWAY ......Santo & Johnny, Canadian-American 167
123. FROM RUSSIA WITH LOVE ......Al Caiol, United Artists 711
124. OUR FADED LOVE ......Royaltones, Mala 473
125. FROM RUSSIA WITH LOVE ......Village Stompers, Epic 9674
126. GONNA GET ALONG WITHOUT YOU NOW ......Skeeter Davis, RCA Victor 8347
127. SOMETHINGS ARE BETTER LEFT UNSAID ......Ketty Lester, RCA Victor 8331
128. I ONLY HAVE EYES FOR YOU ......Cliff Richard, Epic 9670
129. LITTLE DONNA ......Rivieras, Riviera 1402
130. I WISH I KNEW WHAT DRESS TO WEAR ......Ginny Arnell, MGM 13226
131. BLUESETTE ......Sarah Vaughan, Mercury 72249

Compiled from national retail sales and radio station airplay by the Music Popularity Dept. of Record Market Research, Billboard.

For Week Ending April 25, 1964

# Billboard HOT 100

★ **STAR** performer—Sides registering greatest proportionate upward progress this week.

Billboard Award

| This Week | 1 Wk. Ago | 2 Wks. Ago | 3 Wks. Ago | TITLE Artist, Label & Number | Weeks On Chart |
|---|---|---|---|---|---|
| 1 | 1 | 1 | 1 | **CAN'T BUY ME LOVE** Beatles, Capitol 5150 | 5 |
| 2 | 2 | 2 | 2 | **TWIST AND SHOUT** Beatles, Tollie 9001 | 7 |
| 3 | 5 | 14 | 46 | **DO YOU WANT TO KNOW A SECRET** Beatles, Vee Jay 587 | 5 |
| 4 | 4 | 5 | 7 | **HELLO, DOLLY!** Louis Armstrong, Kapp 573 | 11 |
| 5 | 3 | 3 | 6 | **SUSPICION** Terry Stafford, Crusader 101 | 10 |
| 6 | 7 | 8 | 10 | **GLAD ALL OVER** Dave Clark Five, Epic 9656 | 11 |
| ★7 | 11 | 22 | 48 | **BITS AND PIECES** Dave Clark Five, Epic 9671 | 4 |
| 8 | 9 | 10 | 14 | **DON'T LET THE RAIN COME DOWN (Crooked Little Man)** Serendipity Singers, Philips 40175 | 9 |
| ★9 | 14 | 26 | 50 | **MY GUY** Mary Wells, Motown 1056 | 4 |
| 10 | 10 | 15 | 25 | **DEAD MAN'S CURVE** Jan & Dean, Liberty 55672 | 8 |
| 11 | 6 | 6 | 8 | **SHOOP SHOOP SONG** Betty Everett, Vee Jay 585 | 9 |
| ★12 | 17 | 23 | 39 | **THAT'S THE WAY BOYS ARE** Lesley Gore, Mercury 72259 | 5 |
| 13 | 13 | 13 | 15 | **NEEDLES AND PINS** Searchers, Kapp 577 | 8 |
| 14 | 12 | 11 | 12 | **THE WAY YOU DO THE THINGS YOU DO** Temptations, Gordy 7028 | 9 |
| 15 | 15 | 17 | 18 | **YOU'RE A WONDERFUL ONE** Marvin Gaye, Tamla 54093 | 7 |
| ★16 | 21 | 27 | 34 | **WHITE ON WHITE** Danny Williams, United Artists 685 | 8 |
| ★17 | 29 | 59 | — | **RONNIE** 4 Seasons, Philips 40185 | 3 |
| 18 | 18 | 19 | 22 | **MONEY** Kingsmen, Wand 150 | 7 |
| 19 | 8 | 4 | 3 | **SHE LOVES YOU** Beatles, Swan 4152 | 14 |
| ★20 | 30 | 42 | 60 | **SHANGRI-LA** Robert Maxwell, His Harp & Ork, Decca 25622 | 6 |
| 21 | 23 | 32 | 51 | **THE MATADOR** Major Lance, Okeh 7191 | 5 |
| 22 | 20 | 20 | 21 | **AIN'T NOTHING YOU CAN DO** Bobby Bland, Duke 375 | 8 |
| 23 | 26 | 28 | 35 | **HEY, BOBBA NEEDLE** Chubby Checker, Parkway 907 | 7 |
| 24 | 19 | 7 | 4 | **I WANT TO HOLD YOUR HAND** Beatles, Capitol 5112 | 15 |
| 25 | 27 | 36 | 44 | **FOREVER** Pete Drake, Smash 1867 | 8 |
| 26 | 28 | 29 | 30 | **NADINE** Chuck Berry, Chess 1883 | 8 |
| 27 | 31 | 35 | 47 | **EBB TIDE** Lenny Welch, Cadence 1422 | 6 |
| ★28 | 60 | 90 | — | **IT'S OVER** Roy Orbison, Monument 837 | 3 |
| 29 | 16 | 9 | 5 | **PLEASE PLEASE ME** Beatles, Vee Jay 581 | 13 |
| 30 | 22 | 12 | 9 | **MY HEART BELONGS TO ONLY YOU** Bobby Vinton, Epic 9662 | 9 |
| 31 | 25 | 25 | 26 | **THINK** Brenda Lee, Decca 31599 | 8 |
| ★32 | 42 | 53 | 73 | **WISH SOMEONE WOULD CARE** Irma Thomas, Imperial 66013 | 5 |
| 33 | 37 | 51 | 61 | **I'M SO PROUD** Impressions, ABC-Paramount 10544 | 4 |
| ★34 | 44 | 77 | 90 | **KISS ME SAILOR** Diane Renay, 20th Century-Fox 477 | 4 |
| 35 | 41 | 60 | 71 | **MY GIRL SLOOPY** Vibrations, Atlantic 2221 | 5 |
| 36 | 24 | 16 | 16 | **STAY** 4 Seasons, Vee Jay 582 | 11 |
| ★37 | 49 | 61 | 79 | **THANK YOU GIRL** Beatles, Vee Jay 587 | 4 |
| 38 | 40 | 37 | 40 | **NEW GIRL IN SCHOOL** Jan & Dean, Liberty 55672 | 6 |
| 39 | 32 | 24 | 24 | **HIPPY HIPPY SHAKE** Swinging Blue Jeans, Imperial 66021 | 8 |
| 40 | 47 | 58 | 70 | **SHANGRI-LA** Vic Dana, Dolton 92 | 5 |
| ★41 | 67 | 87 | — | **COTTON CANDY** Al Hirt, RCA Victor 8346 | 3 |
| ★42 | 61 | 69 | 84 | **CAN YOU DO IT** Contours, Gordy 7029 | 4 |
| 43 | 50 | 54 | 67 | **MAKE ME FORGET** Bobby Rydell, Cameo 309 | 5 |
| 44 | 51 | 62 | 75 | **STAY AWHILE** Dusty Springfield, Philips 40180 | 5 |
| 45 | 48 | 50 | 58 | **ALL MY LOVING** Beatles, Capitol of Canada 72144 | 5 |
| ★46 | 56 | 70 | 89 | **CHARADE** Sammy Kaye & His Ork, Decca 31589 | 4 |
| 47 | 33 | 18 | 13 | **FUN, FUN, FUN** Beach Boys, Capitol 5118 | 11 |
| 48 | 54 | 72 | 80 | **PINK PANTHER THEME** Henry Mancini & His Ork, RCA Victor 8286 | 4 |
| 49 | 35 | 21 | 11 | **DAWN (Go Away)** 4 Seasons, Philips 40166 | 13 |
| ★50 | 75 | 86 | — | **(Just Like) ROMEO & JULIET** Reflections, Golden World 9 | 3 |
| 51 | 46 | 49 | 53 | **I CAN'T STAND IT** Soul Sisters, Sue 799 | 9 |
| ★52 | 63 | 83 | — | **IN MY LONELY ROOM** Martha & the Vandellas, Gordy 7031 | 3 |
| 53 | 58 | 65 | 66 | **LOOK HOMEWARD ANGEL** Monarchs, Sound Stage 7 2516 | 10 |
| 54 | 57 | 63 | 72 | **BABY BABY BABY** Anna King & Bobby Byrd, Smash 1884 | 4 |
| ★55 | 66 | — | — | **SLIP-IN MULES** Sugar Pie De Santo, Checker 1073 | 2 |
| 56 | 59 | 66 | 74 | **GIVING UP ON LOVE** Jerry Butler, Vee Jay 588 | 4 |
| ★57 | 71 | 80 | 98 | **(The Best Part of) BREAKIN' UP** Ronettes, Philles 120 | 4 |
| 58 | 53 | 57 | 57 | **AIN'T GONNA TELL NOBODY** Jimmy Gilmer, Dot 16583 | 7 |
| ★59 | 72 | — | — | **WRONG FOR EACH OTHER** Andy Williams, Columbia 43015 | 2 |
| 60 | 55 | 48 | 65 | **YOU CAN'T DO THAT** Beatles, Capitol 5150 | 4 |
| ★61 | 87 | — | — | **LITTLE CHILDREN** Billy J. Kramer, Imperial 66027 | 2 |
| ★62 | 93 | 99 | — | **LOVE ME WITH ALL YOUR HEART** Ray Charles Singers, Command 4046 | 3 |
| 63 | 74 | — | — | **DIANE** Bachelors, London 9639 | 2 |
| 64 | 69 | 75 | 82 | **I SHOULD CARE** Gloria Lynne, Everest 2042 | 4 |
| 65 | 65 | 71 | 77 | **T'AIN'T NOTHIN' TO ME** Coasters, Atco 6287 | 5 |
| 66 | 52 | 56 | 56 | **CASTLES IN THE SAND** Little Stevie Wonder, Tamla 54090 | 9 |
| 67 | 73 | 81 | — | **LOVE ME DO** Beatles, Capitol of Canada 72076 | 3 |
| 68 | 62 | 64 | 64 | **BOOK OF LOVE** Raindrops, Jubilee 5469 | 7 |
| ★69 | 84 | — | — | **TODAY** New Christy Minstrels, Columbia 43000 | 2 |
| 70 | 80 | — | — | **WHENEVER HE HOLDS YOU** Bobby Goldsboro, United Artists 710 | 2 |
| 71 | 64 | 67 | 76 | **OUR EVERLASTING LOVE** Ruby and the Romantics, Kapp 578 | 6 |
| 72 | 76 | 85 | 88 | **THAT'S WHEN IT HURTS** Ben E. King, Atco 6288 | 4 |
| 73 | 68 | 84 | 86 | **SOUL SERENADE** King Curtis, Capitol 5109 | 7 |
| 74 | 85 | 95 | — | **TALL COOL ONE** Wailers, Golden Crest 518 | 3 |
| 75 | 78 | — | — | **GOODBYE BABY (Baby Goodbye)** Solomon Burke, Atlantic 2226 | 2 |
| 76 | 81 | — | — | **LOVING YOU MORE EVERY DAY** Etta James, Argo 5465 | 2 |
| ★77 | — | — | — | **THE WONDER OF YOU** Ray Peterson, RCA Victor [illegible] | 1 |
| ★78 | — | — | — | **THE VERY THOUGHT OF YOU** Rick Nelson, Decca 31612 | 1 |
| 79 | 83 | 88 | 92 | **COME TO ME** Otis Redding, Volt 116 | 6 |
| ★80 | 95 | — | — | **AIN'T THAT JUST LIKE ME** Searchers, Kapp 584 | 2 |
| ★81 | — | — | — | **I DON'T WANT TO BE HURT ANY MORE** Nat King Cole, Capitol 5155 | 1 |
| 82 | 77 | 89 | 91 | **MEXICAN DRUMMER MAN** Herb Alpert's Tijuana Brass, A&M 732 | 5 |
| ★83 | 100 | — | — | **LITTLE BOXES** Womenfolk, RCA Victor 8301 | 2 |
| ★84 | 99 | 97 | 100 | **PEOPLE** Barbra Streisand, Columbia 42965 | 4 |
| ★85 | — | — | — | **WALK ON BY** Dionne Warwick, Scepter 1274 | 1 |
| 86 | 98 | — | — | **HEY, MR. SAX MAN** Boots Randolph, Monument 835 | 3 |
| 87 | 94 | — | — | **GEE** Pixies Three, Mercury 72250 | 2 |
| 88 | 89 | 94 | 94 | **BE ANYTHING (But Be Mine)** Gloria Lynne, Fontana 1890 | 4 |
| 89 | 97 | — | — | **DONNIE** Bermudas, Era 3125 | 2 |
| ★90 | — | — | — | **I KNEW IT ALL THE TIME** Dave Clark Five, Congress 212 | 1 |
| 91 | — | — | — | **GONNA GET ALONG WITHOUT YOU NOW** Tracey Dey, Amy 901 | 1 |
| 92 | — | — | — | **THREE WINDOW COUPE** Rip Chords, Columbia 43035 | 1 |
| 93 | — | — | — | **WHO'S AFRAID OF VIRGINIA WOOLF?** Jimmy Smith, Verve 10314 | 1 |
| 94 | 96 | 96 | — | **WHEN JOANNA LOVED ME** Tony Bennett, Columbia 42996 | 5 |
| 95 | — | — | — | **FROM RUSSIA WITH LOVE** Village Stompers, Epic 9674 | 1 |
| 96 | — | — | — | **CAROL** Tommy Roe, ABC-Paramount 10543 | 1 |
| 97 | 92 | — | — | **I'M THE LONELY ONE** Cliff Richard, Epic 9670 | 2 |
| 98 | — | — | — | **WINKIN', BLINKIN' AND NOD** Simon Sisters, Kapp 586 | 1 |
| 99 | — | — | — | **I'M CONFESSIN'** Nino Tempo & April Stevens, Atco 6294 | 1 |
| 100 | — | — | — | **HURT BY LOVE** Inez Foxx, Symbol 20-001 | 1 |

## HOT 100—A TO Z—*(Publisher-Licensee)*


Ain't Gonna Tell Nobody (Dundee, BMI) ........ 58
Ain't Nothing You Can Do (Don, BMI) ........ 22
Ain't That Just Like Me (Trio-Progressive, BMI) .. 80
All My Loving (James (PRS), ASCAP) ........ 45
Baby, Baby, Baby (Try Me, BMI) ........ 54
Be Anything (But Be Mine) (Shapiro-Bernstein, ASCAP) ........ 88
(The Best Part of) Breakin' Up (Mother Bertha-Hill & Range, BMI) ........ 57
Bits and Pieces (Beechwood, BMI) ........ 7
Book of Love (Keel-Arc, BMI) ........ 68
Can You Do It (Jobete, BMI) ........ 42
Can't Buy Me Love (Northern, ASCAP) ........ 1
Carol (Arc, BMI) ........ 96
Castles in the Sand (Jobete, BMI) ........ 66
Charade (Northern-Southdale, ASCAP) ........ 46
Come to Me (East-Time, BMI) ........ 79
Cotton Candy (Gallico, BMI) ........ 41
Dawn (Go Away) (Saturday-Gavidima, ASCAP) . 49
Dead Man's Curve (Screen Gems-Columbia, BMI)... 10
Diane (Miller, ASCAP) ........ 63
Do You Want to Know a Secret (Metric, BMI) ... 3
Don't Let the Rain Come Down (Serendipity, BMI). 8
Donnie (Rickland, BMI) ........ 89
Ebb Tide (Robbins, ASCAP) ........ 27
Forever (Tree, BMI) ........ 25
From Russia With Love (Unart, BMI) ........ 95
Fun, Fun, Fun (Sea of Tunes, BMI) ........ 47
Gee (Patricia, BMI) ........ 87
Giving Up On Love (Roosevelt, BMI) ........ 56
Glad All Over (Campbell-Connelly, ASCAP) ........ 6
Gonna Get Along Without You Now (Reliance, ASCAP) ........ 91
Goodbye Baby (Picturetone-Mellin, BMI) ........ 75
Hello, Dolly! (Morris, ASCAP) ........ 4
Hey Bobba Needle (Kalmann-C.C., ASCAP) ........ 23
Hey, Mr. Sax Man (Forrest Hills, BMI) ........ 86
Hippy Hippy Shake (Maraville, BMI) ........ 39
Hurt by Love (Saturn, BMI) ........ 51
I Can't Stand It (Saturn-Staccato, BMI) ........ 51
I Don't Want to Be Hurt Anymore (Bregman, Vocco & Conn, ASCAP) ........ 81
I Knew It All the Time (Gallico, BMI) ........ 90
I Should Care (Dorsey, ASCAP) ........ 64
I Want to Hold Your Hand (Duchess, BMI) ........ 24
I'm Confessin' (Bourne, ASCAP) ........ 99
I'm the Lonely One (Duchess, BMI) ........ 97
I'm So Proud (Curtom, BMI) ........ 33
In My Lonely Room (Jobete, BMI) ........ 52
It's Over (Acuff-Rose, BMI) ........ 28
(Just Like) Romeo & Juliet (Myto, BMI) ........ 50
Kiss Me Sailor (Saturday, ASCAP) ........ 34
Little Boxes (Schroeder, ASCAP) ........ 83
Little Children (Rumbalero, BMI) ........ 61
Look Homeward Angel (Rogelle, BMI) ........ 53
Love Me Do (Ardmore-Beechwood, BMI) ........ 67
Love Me With All Your Heart (Peer Int'l, BMI) .. 62
Loving You More Every Day (Trio, BMI) ........ 76
Make Me Forget (Wood, ASCAP) ........ 43
Matador, The (Curtom-Jalynne, BMI) ........ 21
Mexican Drummer Man (Irving, BMI) ........ 82
Money (Jobete, BMI) ........ 18
My Girl Sloopy (Picturestone-Mellin, BMI) ........ 35
My Guy (Jobete, BMI) ........ 9
My Heart Belongs to Only You (Regent, BMI) ... 30
Nadine (Arc, BMI) ........ 26
Needles and Pins (Metric, BMI) ........ 13
New Girl in School (Screen Gems-Columbia, BMI) .. 38
Our Everlasting Love (Mansion, ASCAP) ........ 71
People (Chappell, ASCAP) ........ 84
Pink Panther Theme (Northridge-United Artists, ASCAP) ........ 48
Please Please Me (Concertone, ASCAP) ........ 29
Ronnie (Saturday-Gavidima, ASCAP) ........ 17
Shangri-La—Dana (Robbins, ASCAP) ........ 40
Shangri-La—Maxwell (Robbins, ASCAP) ........ 20
She Loves You (Gil, BMI) ........ 19
Shoop Shoop Song (T. M., BMI) ........ 11
Slip-In Mules (Chevis-Medal, BMI) ........ 55
Soul Serenade (Kilynn-Vee Vee, BMI) ........ 73
Stay (Cherio, BMI) ........ 36
Stay Awhile (MRC, BMI) ........ 44
Suspicion (Presley, BMI) ........ 5
T'ain't Nothin' to Me (Gregmark, BMI) ........ 65
Tall Cool One (C.F.G., BMI) ........ 74
Thank You Girl (Conrad, BMI) ........ 37
That's the Way Boys Are (Earth, BMI) ........ 12
That's When It Hurts (Cotillion-Mellin, BMI) ........ 72
Think (Forrest Hills-Rombre, BMI) ........ 31
Three Window Coupe (Screen Gems-Columbia, BMI). 92
Today (Miller-Heritage House, ASCAP) ........ 69
Twist and Shout (Mellin-Progressive, BMI) ........ 2
Very Thought of You, The (Witmark, ASCAP) .... 78
Walk On By (Blue Seas-Jac, ASCAP) ........ 85
Way You Do the Things You Do, The (Jobete, BMI). 14
When Joanna Loved Me (Morris, ASCAP) ........ 94
Whenever He Holds You (Unart, BMI) ........ 70
White on White (Painted Desert, BMI) ........ 16
Winkin', Blinkin' and Nod (Ryerson, BMI) ........ 98
Wish Someone Would Care (Metric, BMI) ........ 32
Who's Afraid of Virginia Woolf? (Avant Garde, ASCAP) ........ 93
Wonder of You, The (Duchess, BMI) ........ 77
Wrong for Each Other (Valley, BMI) ........ 59
You Can't Do That (Northern, ASCAP) ........ 60
You're a Wonderful One (Jobete, BMI) ........ 15


## BUBBLING UNDER THE HOT 100

101. I RISE, I FALL ........ Johnny Tillotson, MGM 13232
102. EVERY LITTLE BIT HURTS ........ Brenda Holloway, Tamla 5494
103. PEOPLE ........ Nat King Cole, Capitol 5155
104. TEA FOR TWO ........ Nino Tempo & April Stevens, Atco 6294
105. HIGH ON A HILL ........ Scott English, Spokane 4003
106. CHAPEL OF LOVE ........ Dixie Cups, Red Bird 001
107. THE CLOSEST THING TO HEAVEN ........ Neil Sedaka, RCA Victor 8341
108. SUGAR AND SPICE ........ Searchers, Liberty 55689
109. IF YOU LOVE ME (LIKE YOU SAY) ........ Little Johnny Taylor, Galaxy 729
110. GONNA GET ALONG WITHOUT YOU NOW ........ Skeeter Davis, RCA Victor 8347
111. OUR FADED LOVE ........ Royaltones, Mala 473
112. OH BOY ........ Jackie De Shannon, Liberty 55678
113. PARTY GIRL ........ Bernadette Carroll, Laurie 3238
114. WHERE ARE YOU ........ Duprees, Coed 591
115. WHERE DOES LOVE GO ........ Freddie Scott, Colpix 724
116. SOMEBODY STOLE MY DOG ........ Rufus Thomas, Stax 149
117. IF YOU LOVE ME, REALLY LOVE ME ........ Jackie Trent, Kapp 583
118. I'LL FIND YOU ........ Valerie & Nick, Glover 3000
119. ONE WAY LOVE ........ Drifters, Atlantic 2225
120. THERE'S A PLACE ........ Beatles, Tollie 9001
121. MOONGLOW/PICNIC THEME ........ Baja Marimba Band, Almo 23
122. FROM RUSSIA WITH LOVE ........ Al Caiola, United Artists 711
123. JUST ONE LOOK ........ Hollies, Imperial 66026
124. LITTLE DONNA ........ Rivieras, Riviera 1402
125. IN THE WEE WEE HOURS (OF THE NITE) ........ James Brown and the Famous Flames, King 5853
126. LONG TALL SHORTY ........ Tommy Tucker, Checker 1075
127. GIVING UP ........ Gladys Knight and the Pips, Maxx 326
128. KIKO ........ Jimmy McGriff, Sue 10-001
129. ROSEMARIE ........ Pat Boone, Dot 16598
130. CALDONIA ........ James Brown and His Ork, Smash 1898
131. NOT FADE AWAY ........ Rolling Stones, London 9657
132. INVISIBLE TEARS ........ Ned Miller, Fabor 128
133. AGAIN ........ James Brown and the Famous Flames, King 5876
134. THE FRENCH SONG ........ Lucille Starr, Almo 204
135. THE WORLD I USED TO KNOW ........ Jimmie Rodgers, Dot 16595

Compiled from national retail sales and radio station airplay by the Music Popularity Dept. of Record Market Research, Billboard.

For Week Ending May 2, 1964

Billboard

# HOT 100

★ **STAR** performer—Sides registering greatest proportionate upward progress this week.

Billboard Award

| THIS WEEK | 1 Wk. Ago | 2 Wks. Ago | 3 Wks. Ago | TITLE Artist, Label & Number | Weeks On Chart |
|---|---|---|---|---|---|
| 1 | 1 | 1 | 1 | **CAN'T BUY ME LOVE** Beatles, Capitol 5150 | 6 |
| 2 | 4 | 4 | 5 | **HELLO, DOLLY!** Louis Armstrong, Kapp 573 | 12 |
| 3 | 3 | 5 | 14 | **DO YOU WANT TO KNOW A SECRET** Beatles, Vee Jay 587 | 6 |
| ★4 | 7 | 11 | 12 | **BITS AND PIECES** Dave Clark Five, Epic 9671 | 5 |
| ★5 | 9 | 14 | 26 | **MY GUY** Mary Wells, Motown 1056 | 5 |
| 6 | 8 | 9 | 10 | **DON'T LET THE RAIN COME DOWN (Crooked Little Man)** Serendipity Singers, Philips 40175 | 10 |
| 7 | 2 | 2 | 2 | **TWIST AND SHOUT** Beatles, Tollie 9001 | 8 |
| 8 | 5 | 3 | 3 | **SUSPICION** Terry Stafford, Crusader 101 | 11 |
| 9 | 10 | 10 | 15 | **DEAD MAN'S CURVE** Jan & Dean, Liberty 55672 | 9 |
| ★10 | 17 | 29 | 59 | **RONNIE** 4 Seasons, Philips 40185 | 4 |
| ★11 | 16 | 21 | 27 | **WHITE ON WHITE** Danny Williams, United Artists 685 | 9 |
| 12 | 12 | 17 | 23 | **THAT'S THE WAY BOYS ARE** Lesley Gore, Mercury 72259 | 6 |
| 13 | 6 | 7 | 8 | **GLAD ALL OVER** Dave Clark Five, Epic 9656 | 12 |
| 14 | 11 | 6 | 6 | **SHOOP SHOOP SONG** Betty Everett, Vee Jay 585 | 10 |
| ★15 | 20 | 30 | 42 | **SHANGRI-LA** Robert Maxwell, His Harp & Ork, Decca 25622 | 7 |
| 16 | 18 | 18 | 19 | **MONEY** Kingsmen, Wand 150 | 8 |
| 17 | 15 | 15 | 17 | **YOU'RE A WONDERFUL ONE** Marvin Gaye, Tamla 54093 | 8 |
| ★18 | 28 | 60 | 90 | **IT'S OVER** Roy Orbison, Monument 837 | 4 |
| 19 | 14 | 12 | 11 | **THE WAY YOU DO THE THINGS YOU DO** Temptations, Gordy 7028 | 10 |
| 20 | 21 | 23 | 32 | **THE MATADOR** Major Lance, Okeh 7191 | 6 |
| ★21 | 32 | 42 | 53 | **WISH SOMEONE WOULD CARE** Irma Thomas, Imperial 66013 | 6 |
| ★22 | 33 | 37 | 51 | **I'M SO PROUD** Impressions, ABC-Paramount 10544 | 5 |
| 23 | 26 | 28 | 29 | **NADINE** Chuck Berry, Chess 1883 | 9 |
| 24 | 13 | 13 | 13 | **NEEDLES AND PINS** Searchers, Kapp 577 | 9 |
| 25 | 25 | 27 | 36 | **FOREVER** Pete Drake, Smash 1867 | 9 |
| 26 | 22 | 20 | 20 | **AIN'T NOTHING YOU CAN DO** Bobby Bland, Duke 375 | 9 |
| 27 | 27 | 31 | 35 | **EBB TIDE** Lenny Welch, Cadence 1422 | 7 |
| ★28 | 62 | 93 | 99 | **LOVE ME WITH ALL YOUR HEART** Ray Charles Singers, Command 4046 | 4 |
| 29 | 35 | 41 | 60 | **MY GIRL SLOOPY** Vibrations, Atlantic 2221 | 6 |
| 30 | 34 | 44 | 77 | **KISS ME SAILOR** Diane Renay, 20th Century-Fox 477 | 5 |
| 31 | 40 | 47 | 58 | **SHANGRI-LA** Vic Dana, Dolton 92 | 6 |
| ★32 | 67 | 73 | 81 | **LOVE ME DO** Beatles, Tollie 9008/Capitol of Canada 72076 | 4 |
| ★33 | 50 | 75 | 86 | **(Just Like) ROMEO & JULIET** Reflections, Golden World 9 | 4 |
| 34 | 23 | 26 | 28 | **HEY, BOBBA NEEDLE** Chubby Checker, Parkway 907 | 8 |
| ★35 | 61 | 87 | — | **LITTLE CHILDREN** Billy J. Kramer, Imperial 66027 | 3 |
| 36 | 19 | 8 | 4 | **SHE LOVES YOU** Beatles, Swan 4152 | 15 |
| 37 | 41 | 67 | 87 | **COTTON CANDY** Al Hirt, RCA Victor 8346 | 4 |
| 38 | 46 | 56 | 70 | **CHARADE** Sammy Kaye & His Ork, Decca 31589 | 5 |
| 39 | 44 | 51 | 62 | **STAY AWHILE** Dusty Springfield, Philips 40180 | 6 |
| 40 | 37 | 49 | 61 | **THANK YOU GIRL** Beatles, Vee Jay 587 | 5 |
| 41 | 48 | 54 | 72 | **PINK PANTHER THEME** Henry Mancini & His Ork, RCA Victor 8286 | 5 |
| 42 | 42 | 61 | 69 | **CAN YOU DO IT** Contours, Gordy 7029 | 5 |
| 43 | 31 | 25 | 25 | **THINK** Brenda Lee, Decca 31599 | 9 |
| 44 | 52 | 63 | 83 | **IN MY LONELY ROOM** Martha & the Vandellas, Gordy 7031 | 4 |
| 45 | 38 | 40 | 37 | **NEW GIRL IN SCHOOL** Jan & Dean, Liberty 55672 | 7 |
| ★46 | 57 | 71 | 80 | **(The Best Part of) BREAKIN' UP** Ronettes, Philles 120 | 5 |
| 47 | 53 | 58 | 65 | **LOOK HOMEWARD ANGEL** Monarchs, Sound Stage 7 2516 | 11 |
| 48 | 43 | 50 | 54 | **MAKE ME FORGET** Bobby Rydell, Cameo 309 | 6 |
| ★49 | 59 | 72 | — | **WRONG FOR EACH OTHER** Andy Williams, Columbia 43015 | 3 |
| 50 | 55 | 66 | — | **SLIP-IN MULES** Sugar Pie De Santo, Checker 1073 | 3 |
| ★51 | 81 | — | — | **I DON'T WANT TO BE HURT ANY MORE** Nat King Cole, Capitol 5155 | 2 |
| 52 | 54 | 57 | 63 | **BABY BABY BABY** Anna King & Bobby Byrd, Smash 1884 | 5 |
| ★53 | — | — | — | **DO YOU LOVE ME** Dave Clark Five, Epic 9678 | 1 |
| ★54 | 78 | — | — | **THE VERY THOUGHT OF YOU** Rick Nelson, Decca 31612 | 2 |
| ★55 | 70 | 80 | — | **WHENEVER HE HOLDS YOU** Bobby Goldsboro, United Artists 710 | 3 |
| ★56 | 75 | 78 | — | **GOODBYE BABY (Baby Goodbye)** Solomon Burke, Atlantic 2226 | 3 |
| 57 | 63 | 74 | — | **DIANE** Bachelors, London 9639 | 3 |
| ★58 | 69 | 84 | — | **TODAY** New Christy Minstrels, Columbia 43000 | 3 |
| 59 | 45 | 48 | 50 | **ALL MY LOVING** Beatles, Capitol of Canada 72144 | 6 |
| ★60 | 74 | 85 | 95 | **TALL COOL ONE** Wailers, Golden Crest 518 | 4 |
| ★61 | 85 | — | — | **WALK ON BY** Dionne Warwick, Scepter 1274 | 2 |
| ★62 | 84 | 99 | 97 | **PEOPLE** Barbra Streisand, Columbia 42965 | 5 |
| 63 | 72 | 76 | 85 | **THAT'S WHEN IT HURTS** Ben E. King, Atco 6288 | 5 |
| 64 | 65 | 65 | 71 | **T'AIN'T NOTHIN' TO ME** Coasters, Atco 6287 | 6 |
| 65 | 56 | 59 | 66 | **GIVING UP ON LOVE** Jerry Butler, Vee Jay 588 | 5 |
| 66 | 73 | 68 | 84 | **SOUL SERENADE** King Curtis, Capitol 5109 | 8 |
| 67 | 64 | 69 | 75 | **I SHOULD CARE** Gloria Lynne, Everest 2042 | 5 |
| 68 | 80 | 95 | — | **AIN'T THAT JUST LIKE ME** Searchers, Kapp 584 | 3 |
| 69 | 79 | 83 | 88 | **COME TO ME** Otis Redding, Volt 116 | 7 |
| 70 | 77 | — | — | **THE WONDER OF YOU** Ray Peterson, RCA Victor 8333 | 2 |
| 71 | 76 | 81 | — | **LOVING YOU MORE EVERY DAY** Etta James, Argo 5465 | 3 |
| ★72 | — | — | — | **CHAPEL OF LOVE** Dixie Cups, Red Bird 001 | 1 |
| ★73 | — | — | — | **ONCE UPON A TIME** Marvin Gaye & Mary Wells, Motown 1057 | 1 |
| ★74 | 90 | — | — | **I KNEW IT ALL THE TIME** Dave Clark Five, Congress 212 | 2 |
| ★75 | 92 | — | — | **THREE WINDOW COUPE** Rip Chords, Columbia 43035 | 2 |
| ★76 | — | — | — | **EVERY LITTLE BIT HURTS** Brenda Holloway, Tamla 54094 | 1 |
| ★77 | 100 | — | — | **HURT BY LOVE** Inez Foxx, Symbol 20-001 | 2 |
| ★78 | — | — | — | **TEA FOR TWO** Nino Tempo & April Stevens, Atco 6294 | 1 |
| ★79 | — | — | — | **KISS ME QUICK** Elvis Presley, RCA Victor 0639 | 1 |
| 80 | 86 | 98 | — | **HEY, MR. SAX MAN** Boots Randolph, Monument 835 | 4 |
| 81 | 93 | — | — | **WHO'S AFRAID OF VIRGINIA WOOLF?** Jimmy Smith, Verve 10314 | 2 |
| ★82 | 98 | — | — | **WINKIN', BLINKIN' AND NOD** Simon Sisters, Kapp 586 | 2 |
| 83 | 83 | 100 | — | **LITTLE BOXES** Womenfolk, RCA Victor 8301 | 3 |
| ★84 | — | — | — | **ONE WAY LOVE** Drifters, Atlantic 2225 | 1 |
| 85 | 96 | — | — | **CAROL** Tommy Roe, ABC-Paramount 10543 | 2 |
| 86 | 89 | 97 | — | **DONNIE** Bermudas, Era 3125 | 3 |
| 87 | 87 | 94 | — | **GEE** Pixies Three, Mercury 72250 | 3 |
| 88 | 91 | — | — | **GONNA GET ALONG WITHOUT YOU NOW** Tracey Dey, Amy 901 | 2 |
| ★89 | — | — | — | **THE LONELIEST NIGHT** Dale & Grace, Montel 928 | 1 |
| ★90 | — | — | — | **GONNA GET ALONG WITHOUT YOU NOW** Skeeter Davis, RCA Victor 8347 | 1 |
| 91 | 95 | — | — | **FROM RUSSIA WITH LOVE** Village Stompers, Epic 9674 | 2 |
| 92 | — | — | — | **SOUL HOOTENANNY** Gene Chandler, Constellation 114 | 1 |
| 93 | — | — | — | **I RISE, I FALL** Johnny Tillotson, MGM 13232 | 1 |
| 94 | — | 82 | 82 | **WHERE DOES LOVE GO** Freddie Scott, Colpix 724 | 7 |
| 95 | — | — | — | **LITTLE DONNA** Rivieras, Riviera 1402 | 1 |
| 96 | — | — | — | **SUGAR AND SPICE** Searchers, Liberty 55689 | 1 |
| 97 | — | — | — | **BIG PARTY** Barbara & the Browns, Stax 150 | 1 |
| 98 | — | — | — | **NOT FADE AWAY** Rolling Stones, London 9657 | 1 |
| 99 | — | — | — | **THE LITTLE WHITE CLOUD THAT CRIED** Wayne Newton, Challenge 59238 | 1 |
| 100 | — | — | — | **CALDONIA** James Brown & His Ork, Smash 1898 | 1 |

## HOT 100—A TO Z—*(Publisher-Licensee)*


Ain't Nothing You Can Do (Don, BMI) ........ 26
Ain't That Just Like Me (Trio-Progressive, BMI). 68
All My Loving (James (PRS), ASCAP) ........ 59
Baby, Baby, Baby (Try Me, BMI) ........ 52
(The Best Part of) Breakin' Up (Mother Bertha-Hill & Range, BMI) ........ 46
Big Party (Beckie, BMI) ........ 97
Bits and Pieces (Beechwood, BMI) ........ 4
Caldonia (Cherio, BMI) ........ 100
Can You Do It (Jobete, BMI) ........ 42
Can't Buy Me Love (Northern, ASCAP) ........ 1
Carol (Arc, BMI) ........ 85
Chapel of Love (Trio, BMI) ........ 72
Charade (Northern-Southdale, ASCAP) ........ 38
Come to Me (East-Time, BMI) ........ 69
Cotton Candy (Gallico, BMI) ........ 37
Dead Man's Curve (Screen Gems-Columbia, BMI).. 9
Diane (Miller, ASCAP) ........ 57
Do You Love Me (Jobete, BMI) ........ 53
Do You Want to Know a Secret (Metric, BMI) ... 3
Don't Let the Rain Come Down (Serendipity, BMI). 6
Donnie (Rickland, BMI) ........ 86
Ebb Tide (Robbins, ASCAP) ........ 27
Every Little Bit Hurts (Jobete, BMI) ........ 76
Forever (Tree, BMI) ........ 25
From Russia With Love (Unart, BMI) ........ 91
Gee (Patricia, BMI) ........ 87
Giving Up on Love (Roosevelt, BMI) ........ 65
Glad All Over (Campbell-Connelly, ASCAP) ..... 13
Gonna Get Along Without You Now—Davis (Reliance, ASCAP) ........ 90
Gonna Get Along Without You Now—Dey (Reliance, ASCAP) ........ 88
Goodbye Baby (Picturetone-Mellin, BMI) ........ 56
Hello Dolly! (Morris, ASCAP) ........ 2
Hey Bobba Needle (Kalmann-C.C., ASCAP) ...... 34
Hey, Mr. Sax Man (Forrest Hills, BMI) ........ 80
Hurt By Love (Saturn, BMI) ........ 77
I Don't Want to Be Hurt Anymore (Bregman, Vocco & Conn, ASCAP) ........ 51
I Knew It All the Time (Gallico, BMI) ........ 74
I Rise, I Fall (Tod, ASCAP) ........ 93
I Should Care (Dorsey, ASCAP) ........ 67
I'm So Proud (Curtom, BMI) ........ 22
In My Lonely Room (Jobete, BMI) ........ 44
It's Over (Acuff-Rose, BMI) ........ 18
(Just Like) Romeo & Juliet (Myto, BMI)........ 33
Kiss Me Quick (Presley, BMI) ........ 79
Kiss Me Sailor (Saturday, ASCAP) ........ 30
Little Boxes (Schroeder, ASCAP) ........ 83
Little Children (Rumbalero, BMI) ........ 35
Little Donna (World Int'l, BMI) ........ 95
Little White Cloud That Cried, The (Carlyle, ASCAP) ........ 99
Loneliest Night, The (Acuff-Rose, BMI) ........ 89
Look Homeward Angel (Rogelle, BMI) ........ 47
Love Me Do (Ardmore-Beechwood, BMI) ........ 32
Love Me With All Your Heart (Peer Int'l, BMI).. 28
Loving You More Every Day (Trio, BMI) ........ 71
Make Me Forget (Wood, ASCAP) ........ 48
Matador, The (Curtom-Jalynne, BMI) ........ 20
Money (Jobete, BMI) ........ 16
My Girl Sloopy (Picturetone-Mellin, BMI) ...... 29
My Guy (Jobete, BMI) ........ 5
Nadine (Arc, BMI) ........ 23
Needles and Pins (Metric, BMI) ........ 24
New Girl in School (Screen Gems-Columbia, BMI). 45
Not Fade Away (Nor Va Jak, BMI) ........ 98
Once Upon a Time (Jobete, BMI) ........ 73
One Way Love (Keetch, Caesar & Dino, BMI) ..... 84
People (Chappell, ASCAP) ........ 62
Pink Panther Theme (Northridge-United Artists, ASCAP) ........ 41
Ronnie (Saturday-Gavidima, ASCAP) ........ 10
Shangri-La—Dana (Robbins, ASCAP) ........ 31
Shangri-La—Maxwell (Robbins, ASCAP) ........ 15
She Loves You (Gil, BMI) ........ 36
Shoop Shoop Song (T. M., BMI) ........ 14
Slip-in Mules (Chevis-Medal, BMI) ........ 50
Soul Hootenanny (Conrad, BMI) ........ 92
Soul Serenade (Kilynn-Vee Vee, BMI) ........ 66
Stay Awhile (MRC, BMI) ........ 39
Sugar and Spice (Duchess, BMI) ........ 96
Suspicion (Presley, BMI) ........ 8
T'ain't Nothin' to Me (Gregmark, BMI) ........ 64
Tall Cool One (C.F.G., BMI) ........ 60
Tea for Two (Harms, ASCAP) ........ 78
Thank You Girl (Conrad, BMI) ........ 40
That's the Way Boys Are (Earth, BMI) ........ 12
That's When It Hurts (Cotillion-Mellin, BMI) ... 63
Think (Forrest Hills-Rombre, BMI) ........ 43
Three Window Coupe (Screen Gems-Columbia, BMI). 75
Today (Miller-Heritage House, ASCAP) ........ 58
Twist and Shout (Mellin-Progressive, BMI) ...... 7
Very Thought of You, The (Witmark, ASCAP) ..... 54
Walk on By (Blue Seas-Jac, ASCAP) ........ 61
Way You Do the Things You Do, The (Jobete, BMI) ........ 19
Whenever He Holds You (Unart, BMI) ........ 55
Where Does Love Go (Screen Gems-Columbia, BMI) 94
White on White (Painted Desert, BMI) ........ 11
Winkin', Blinkin' and Nod (Ryerson, BMI) ...... 82
Wish Someone Would Care (Metric, BMI) ........ 21
Who's Afraid of Virginia Woolf? (Avant Garde, ASCAP) ........ 81
Wonder of You, The (Duchess, BMI) ........ 70
Wrong for Each Other (Valley, BMI) ........ 49
You're a Wonderful One (Jobete, BMI) ........ 17


## BUBBLING UNDER THE HOT 100

101. IF YOU LOVE ME (Like You Say) ........Little Johnny Taylor, Galaxy 729
102. GOOD GOLLY MISS MOLLY ........Swinging Blue Jeans, Imperial 66030
103. OUR FADED LOVE ........Royaltones, Mala 473
104. YESTERDAY'S GONE ......Chad Stuart & Jeremy Clyde, World Artists 1021
105. A WORLD WITHOUT LOVE ........Peter & Gordon, Capitol 5175
106. JUST ONE LOOK ........Hollies, Imperial 66026
107. THE CLOSEST THING TO HEAVEN ........Neil Sedaka, RCA Victor 8341
108. PARTY GIRL ........Bernadette Carroll, Laurie 3238
109. IF YOU LOVE ME, REALLY LOVE ME ........Jackie Trent, Kapp 583
110. PEOPLE ........Nat King Cole, Capitol 5155
111. THE FRENCH SONG ........Lucille Starr, Almo 204
112. BE ANYTHING (But Be Mine) ........Gloria Lynne, Fontana 1890
113. I'M THE LONELY ONE ........Cliff Richard, Epic 9670
114. WHAT'S THE MATTER WITH YOU BABY ........Marvin Faye & Mary Wells, Motown 1057
115. BE ANYTHING (But Be Mine) ........Connie Francis, MGM 13237
116. SWING ........Tokens, B.T. Puppy 500
117. I'LL FIND YOU ........Valerie & Nick, Glover 3000
118. MY BABY'S COMIN' HOME ........Paul Anka, RCA Victor 8349
119. LONG TALL SHORTY ........Tommy Tucker, Checker 1075
120. FROM RUSSIA WITH LOVE ........Al Caiola, United Artists 711
121. I ONLY HAVE EYES FOR YOU ........Cliff Richard, Epic 9670
122. TRY TO FIND ANOTHER MAN ........Righteous Brothers, Moonglow 231
123. SHOUT ........Dion, Laurie 3240
124. TOMORROW ........Chris Crosby, MGM 13234
125. GREASE MONKEY ........Jack McDuff, Prestige 299
126. KIKO ........Jimmy McGriff, Sue 10-001
127. A THOUSAND MILES AWAY ........Santo & Johnny, Canadian-American 167
128. I'VE HAD IT ........Lonnie Mack, Fraternity 925
129. JAVA JONES ........Donna Lynn, Capitol 5156
130. THE FUGITIVE ........Ventures, Dolton 94
131. TELL ME MAMA ........Christine Quaite, World Artists 1022
132. LOUIE—GO HOME ........Paul Revere & the Raiders, Columbia 43008
133. AIN'T THAT LOVIN' YOU, BABY ........Everly Brothers, Warner Bros. 5422
134. DRAGGIN' WAGON ........Surfer Girls, Columbia 43001
135. BLUESETTE ........Sarah Vaughan, Mercury 72249

Compiled from national retail sales and radio station airplay by the Music Popularity Dept. of Record Market Research, Billboard.

For Week Ending May 9, 1964

Billboard

# HOT 100

★ STAR performer—Sides registering greatest proportionate upward progress this week.

| THIS WEEK | 1 Wk. Ago | 2 Wks. Ago | 3 Wks. Ago | TITLE Artist, Label & Number | Weeks On Chart |
|---|---|---|---|---|---|
| 1 (Billboard Award) | 2 | 4 | 4 | HELLO, DOLLY! — Louis Armstrong, Kapp 573 | 13 |
| 2 | 3 | 3 | 5 | DO YOU WANT TO KNOW A SECRET — Beatles, Vee Jay 587 | 7 |
| 3 | 5 | 9 | 14 | MY GUY — Mary Wells, Motown 1056 | 6 |
| 4 | 4 | 7 | 11 | BITS AND PIECES — Dave Clark Five, Epic 9671 | 6 |
| 5 | 1 | 1 | 1 | CAN'T BUY ME LOVE — Beatles, Capitol 5150 | 7 |
| 6 | 6 | 8 | 9 | DON'T LET THE RAIN COME DOWN (Crooked Little Man) — Serendipity Singers, Philips 40175 | 10 |
| ★7 | 10 | 17 | 29 | RONNIE — 4 Seasons, Philips 40185 | 5 |
| 8 | 9 | 10 | 10 | DEAD MAN'S CURVE — Jan & Dean, Liberty 55672 | 10 |
| 9 | 8 | 5 | 3 | SUSPICION — Terry Stafford, Crusader 101 | 12 |
| 10 | 11 | 16 | 21 | WHITE ON WHITE — Danny Williams, United Artists 685 | 10 |
| 11 | 7 | 2 | 2 | TWIST AND SHOUT — Beatles, Tollie 9001 | 9 |
| ★12 | 32 | 67 | 73 | LOVE ME DO — Beatles, Tollie 9008 | 5 |
| ★13 | 18 | 28 | 60 | IT'S OVER — Roy Orbison, Monument 837 | 5 |
| 14 | 13 | 6 | 7 | GLAD ALL OVER — Dave Clark Five, Epic 9656 | 13 |
| 15 | 15 | 20 | 30 | SHANGRI-LA — Robert Maxwell, His Harp & Ork, Decca 25622 | 8 |
| 16 | 14 | 11 | 6 | SHOOP SHOOP SONG — Betty Everett, Vee Jay 585 | 11 |
| 17 | 12 | 12 | 17 | THAT'S THE WAY BOYS ARE — Lesley Gore, Mercury 72259 | 7 |
| 18 | 21 | 32 | 42 | WISH SOMEONE WOULD CARE — Irma Thomas, Imperial 66013 | 7 |
| 19 | 22 | 33 | 37 | I'M SO PROUD — Impressions, ABC-Paramount 10544 | 6 |
| 20 | 20 | 21 | 23 | THE MATADOR — Major Lance, Okeh 7191 | 7 |
| ★21 | 28 | 62 | 93 | LOVE ME WITH ALL YOUR HEART — Ray Charles Singers, Command 4046 | 5 |
| 22 | 16 | 18 | 18 | MONEY — Kingsmen, Wand 150 | 9 |
| ★23 | 35 | 61 | 87 | LITTLE CHILDREN — Billy J. Kramer, Imperial 66027 | 4 |
| 24 | 17 | 15 | 15 | YOU'RE A WONDERFUL ONE — Marvin Gaye, Tamla 54093 | 9 |
| 25 | 27 | 27 | 31 | EBB TIDE — Lenny Welch, Cadence 1422 | 8 |
| ★26 | 33 | 50 | 75 | (Just Like) ROMEO & JULIET — Reflections, Golden World 9 | 5 |
| 27 | 29 | 35 | 41 | MY GIRL SLOOPY — Vibrations, Atlantic 2221 | 7 |
| 28 | 31 | 40 | 47 | SHANGRI-LA — Vic Dana, Dolton 92 | 7 |
| 29 | 25 | 25 | 27 | FOREVER — Pete Drake, Smash 1867 | 10 |
| 30 | 30 | 34 | 44 | KISS ME SAILOR — Diane Renay, 20th Century-Fox 477 | 6 |
| ★31 | 41 | 48 | 54 | PINK PANTHER THEME — Henry Mancini & His Ork, RCA Victor 8286 | 6 |
| ★32 | 53 | — | — | DO YOU LOVE ME — Dave Clark Five, Epic 9678 | 2 |
| 33 | 37 | 41 | 67 | COTTON CANDY — Al Hirt, RCA Victor 8346 | 5 |
| 34 | 19 | 14 | 12 | THE WAY YOU DO THE THINGS YOU DO — Temptations, Gordy 7028 | 11 |
| 35 | 40 | 37 | 49 | THANK YOU GIRL — Beatles, Vee Jay 587 | 6 |
| 36 | 38 | 46 | 56 | CHARADE — Sammy Kaye & His Ork, Decca 31589 | 6 |
| 37 | 24 | 13 | 13 | NEEDLES AND PINS — Searchers, Kapp 577 | 10 |
| 38 | 39 | 44 | 51 | STAY AWHILE — Dusty Springfield, Philips 40180 | 7 |
| ★39 | 54 | 78 | — | THE VERY THOUGHT OF YOU — Rick Nelson, Decca 31612 | 3 |
| ★40 | 61 | 85 | — | WALK ON BY — Dionne Warwick, Scepter 1274 | 3 |
| 41 | 42 | 42 | 61 | CAN YOU DO IT — Contours, Gordy 7029 | 6 |
| ★42 | 72 | — | — | CHAPEL OF LOVE — Dixie Cups, Red Bird 001 | 2 |
| 43 | 51 | 81 | — | I DON'T WANT TO BE HURT ANY MORE — Nat King Cole, Capitol 5155 | 3 |
| 44 | 44 | 52 | 63 | IN MY LONELY ROOM — Martha & the Vandellas, Gordy 7031 | 5 |
| 45 | 46 | 57 | 71 | (The Best Part of) BREAKIN' UP — Ronettes, Philles 120 | 6 |
| ★46 | 57 | 63 | 74 | DIANE — Bachelors, London 9639 | 4 |
| ★47 | 58 | 69 | 84 | TODAY — New Christy Minstrels, Columbia 43000 | 4 |
| 48 | 50 | 55 | 66 | SLIP-IN MULES — Sugar Pie De Santo, Checker 1073 | 4 |
| 49 | 49 | 59 | 72 | WRONG FOR EACH OTHER — Andy Williams, Columbia 43015 | 4 |
| 50 | 34 | 23 | 26 | HEY, BOBBA NEEDLE — Chubby Checker, Parkway 907 | 9 |
| 51 | 47 | 53 | 58 | LOOK HOMEWARD ANGEL — Monarchs, Sound Stage 7 2516 | 12 |
| 52 | 55 | 70 | 80 | WHENEVER HE HOLDS YOU — Bobby Goldsboro, United Artists 710 | 4 |
| 53 | 23 | 26 | 28 | NADINE — Chuck Berry, Chess 1883 | 10 |
| 54 | 56 | 75 | 78 | GOODBYE BABY (Baby Goodbye) — Solomon Burke, Atlantic 2226 | 4 |
| ★55 | 73 | — | — | ONCE UPON A TIME — Marvin Gaye & Mary Wells, Motown 1057 | 2 |
| 56 | 45 | 38 | 40 | NEW GIRL IN SCHOOL — Jan & Dean, Liberty 55672 | 8 |
| 57 | 62 | 84 | 99 | PEOPLE — Barbra Streisand, Columbia 42965 | 6 |
| 58 | 60 | 74 | 85 | TALL COOL ONE — Wailers, Golden Crest 518 | 5 |
| ★59 | 75 | 92 | — | THREE WINDOW COUPE — Rip Chords, Columbia 43035 | 3 |
| 60 | 52 | 54 | 57 | BABY BABY BABY — Anna King & Bobby Byrd, Smash 1884 | 6 |
| ★61 | 76 | — | — | EVERY LITTLE BIT HURTS — Brenda Holloway, Tamla 54094 | 2 |
| 62 | 68 | 80 | 95 | AIN'T THAT JUST LIKE ME — Searchers, Kapp 584 | 4 |
| 63 | 66 | 73 | 68 | SOUL SERENADE — King Curtis, Capitol 5109 | 9 |
| ★64 | — | — | — | P.S.: I LOVE YOU — Beatles, Tollie 9008 | 1 |
| 65 | 78 | — | — | TEA FOR TWO — Nino Tempo & April Stevens, Atco 6294 | 2 |
| 66 | 79 | — | — | KISS ME QUICK — Elvis Presley, RCA Victor 0639 | 2 |
| 67 | 65 | 56 | 59 | GIVING UP ON LOVE — Jerry Butler, Vee Jay 588 | 6 |
| 68 | 71 | 76 | 81 | LOVING YOU MORE EVERY DAY — Etta James, Argo 5465 | 4 |
| 69 | 63 | 72 | 76 | THAT'S WHEN IT HURTS — Ben E. King, Atco 6288 | 6 |
| 70 | 74 | 90 | — | I KNEW IT ALL THE TIME — Dave Clark Five, Congress 212 | 3 |
| ★71 | 93 | — | — | I RISE, I FALL — Johnny Tillotson, MGM 13232 | 2 |
| 72 | 77 | 100 | — | HURT BY LOVE — Inez Foxx, Symbol 20-001 | 3 |
| ★73 | 88 | 91 | — | GONNA GET ALONG WITHOUT YOU NOW — Tracey Dey, Amy 901 | 3 |
| 74 | 86 | 89 | 97 | DONNIE — Bermudas, Era 3125 | 4 |
| 75 | 82 | 98 | — | WINKIN', BLINKIN' AND NOD — Simon Sisters, Kapp 586 | 3 |
| ★76 | — | — | — | A WORLD WITHOUT LOVE — Peter & Gordon, Capitol 5175 | 1 |
| 77 | 80 | 86 | 98 | HEY, MR. SAX MAN — Boots Randolph, Monument 835 | 5 |
| 78 | 84 | — | — | ONE WAY LOVE — Drifters, Atlantic 2225 | 2 |
| 79 | 85 | 96 | — | CAROL — Tommy Roe, ABC-Paramount 10543 | 3 |
| 80 | 70 | 77 | — | THE WONDER OF YOU — Ray Peterson, RCA Victor 8333 | 3 |
| 81 | 81 | 93 | — | WHO'S AFRAID OF VIRGINIA WOOLF? — Jimmy Smith, Verve 10314 | 3 |
| 82 | 89 | — | — | THE LONELIEST NIGHT — Dale & Grace, Montel 928 | 2 |
| ★83 | — | — | — | YESTERDAY'S HERO — Gene Pitney, Musicor 1038 | 1 |
| ★84 | — | — | — | BE ANYTHING (But Be Mine) — Connie Francis, MGM 13237 | 1 |
| 85 | 96 | — | — | SUGAR AND SPICE — Searchers, Liberty 55689 | 2 |
| 86 | 91 | 95 | — | FROM RUSSIA WITH LOVE — Village Stompers, Epic 9674 | 3 |
| ★87 | — | — | — | VIVA LAS VEGAS — Elvis Presley, RCA Victor 8360 | 1 |
| 88 | 90 | — | — | GONNA GET ALONG WITHOUT YOU NOW — Skeeter Davis, RCA Victor 8347 | 2 |
| ★89 | — | — | — | GOOD GOLLY MISS HOLLY — Swinging Blue Jeans, Imperial 66030 | 1 |
| 90 | — | — | — | ROCK ME BABY — B. B. King, Kent 393 | 1 |
| 91 | — | — | — | WHAT HAVE I GOT OF MY OWN — Trini Lopez, Reprise 0276 | 1 |
| 92 | 92 | — | — | SOUL HOOTENANNY — Gene Chandler, Constellation 114 | 2 |
| 93 | 95 | — | — | LITTLE DONNA — Rivieras, Riviera 1402 | 2 |
| 94 | — | — | — | GIVING UP — Gladys Knight & the Pips, Maxx 326 | 1 |
| 95 | 100 | — | — | CALDONIA — James Brown & His Ork, Smash 1898 | 2 |
| 96 | 98 | — | — | NOT FADE AWAY — Rolling Stones, London 9657 | 2 |
| 97 | 97 | — | — | BIG PARTY — Barbara & the Browns, Stax 150 | 2 |
| 98 | — | — | — | TOO LATE TO TURN BACK NOW — Brook Benton, Mercury 72266 | 1 |
| 99 | 99 | — | — | THE LITTLE WHITE CLOUD THAT CRIED — Wayne Newton, Challenge 59238 | 2 |
| 100 | — | — | — | A WORLD WITHOUT LOVE — Bobby Rydell, Cameo 320 | 1 |

## HOT 100—A TO Z—(Publisher-Licensee)

Ain't That Just Like Me (Trio-Progressive, BMI) .. 62
Baby, Baby, Baby (Try Me, BMI) .... 60
Be Anything (But Be Mine) (Shapiro-Bernstein, ASCAP) .... 84
(The Best Part of) Breakin' Up (Mother Bertha-Hill & Range, BMI) .... 45
Big Party (Beckie, BMI) .... 97
Bits and Pieces (Beechwood, BMI) .... 4
Caldonia (Cherio, BMI) .... 95
Can You Do It (Jobete, BMI) .... 41
Can't Buy Me Love (Northern, ASCAP) .... 5
Carol (Arc, BMI) .... 79
Chapel of Love (Trio, BMI) .... 42
Charade (Northern-Southdale, ASCAP) .... 36
Cotton Candy (Gallico, BMI) .... 33
Dead Man's Curve (Screen Gems-Columbia, BMI) .. 8
Diane (Miller, ASCAP) .... 46
Do You Love Me (Jobete, BMI) .... 32
Do You Want to Know a Secret (Metric, BMI) .. 2
Don't Let the Rain Come Down (Serendipity, BMI) 6
Donnie (Rickland, BMI) .... 74
Ebb Tide (Robbins, ASCAP) .... 25
Every Little Bit Hurts (Jobete, BMI) .... 61
Forever (Tree, BMI) .... 29
From Russia With Love (Unart, BMI) .... 86
Giving Up (Trio, BMI) .... 94
Giving Up on Love (Roosevelt, BMI) .... 67
Glad All Over (Campbell-Connelly, ASCAP) .... 4
Gonna Get Along Without You Now—Davis (Reliance, ASCAP) .... 88
Gonna Get Along Without You Now—Dey (Reliance, ASCAP) .... 73
Good Golly Miss Molly (Venice, BMI) .... 89
Goodbye Baby (Picturetone-Mellin, BMI) .... 54
Hello, Dolly! (Morris, ASCAP) .... 1
Hey Bobba Needle (Kalmann-C.C., ASCAP) .... 50
Hey, Mr. Sax Man (Forrest Hills, BMI) .... 77
Hurt by Love (Saturn, BMI) .... 72
I Don't Want to Be Hurt Anymore (Bregman, Vocco & Conn, ASCAP) .... 43
I Knew It All the Time (Gallico, BMI) .... 70
I Rise, I Fall (Tod, ASCAP) .... 71
I'm So Proud (Curtom, BMI) .... 19
In My Lonely Room (Jobete, BMI) .... 44
It's All Over (Acuff-Rose, BMI) .... 13
(Just Like) Romeo & Juliet (Myto, BMI) .... 26
Kiss Me Quick (Presley, BMI) .... 66
Kiss Me Sailor (Saturday, ASCAP) .... 30
Little Children (Rumbalero, BMI) .... 23
Little Donna (World Int'l, BMI) .... 93
Little White Cloud That Cried, The (Carlyle, ASCAP) 99
Loneliest Night, The (Acuff-Rose, BMI) .... 82
Look Homeward Angel (Rogelle, BMI) .... 51
Love Me Do (Ardmore-Beechwood, BMI) .... 12
Love Me With All Your Heart (Peer Int'l, BMI) ... 21
Loving You More Every Day (Trio, BMI) .... 68
Matador, The (Curtom-Jalynne, BMI) .... 20
Money (Jobete, BMI) .... 22
My Girl Sloopy (Picturetone-Mellin, BMI) .... 27
My Guy (Jobete, BMI) .... 3
Nadine (Arc, BMI) .... 53
Needles and Pins (Metric, BMI) .... 37
New Girl in School (Screen Gems, Columbia, BMI) 56
Not Fade Away (Nor Va Jak, BMI) .... 96
Once Upon a Time (Jobete, BMI) .... 55
One Way Love (Keetch, Caesar & Dino, BMI) ... 78
P.S.: I Love You (Beechwood, BMI) .... 64
People (Chappell, ASCAP) .... 57
Pink Panther Theme (Northridge-United Artists, ASCAP) .... 31
Rock Me Baby (Modern, BMI) .... 90
Ronnie (Saturday-Gavidima, ASCAP) .... 7
Shangri-La—Dana (Robbins, ASCAP) .... 28
Shangri-La—Maxwell (Robbins, ASCAP) .... 15
Shoop Shoop Song (T. M., BMI) .... 16
Slip-In Mules (Chevis-Medal, BMI) .... 48
Soul Hootenanny (Conrad, BMI) .... 92
Soul Serenade (Kilynn-Vee Vee, BMI) .... 63
Stay Awhile (MRC, BMI) .... 38
Sugar and Spice (Duchess, BMI) .... 85
Suspicion (Presley, BMI) .... 9
Tall Cool One (C.F.G., BMI) .... 58
Tea for Two (Harms, ASCAP) .... 65
Thank You Girl (Conrad, BMI) .... 35
That's the Way Boys Are (Earth, BMI) .... 17
That's When It Hurts (Cotillion-Mellin, BMI) .... 69
Three Window Coupe (Screen-Gems-Columbia, BMI) 59
Today (Miller-Heritage House, ASCAP) .... 47
Too Late to Turn Back Now (Play, BMI) .... 98
Twist and Shout (Mellin-Progressive, BMI) .... 11
Very Thought of You, The (Witmark, ASCAP) ... 39
Viva Las Vegas (Presley, BMI) .... 87
Walk on By (Blue-Seas-Jac, ASCAP) .... 40
Way You Do the Things You Do, The (Jobete, BMI) .... 34
What Have I Got of My Own (Sawtell-Herring, ASCAP) .... 91
Whenever He Holds You (Unart, BMI) .... 52
White on White (Painted Desert, BMI) .... 10
Winkin', Blinkin' and Nod (Ryerson, BMI) .... 75
Wish Someone Would Care (Metric, BMI) .... 18
Who's Afraid of Virginia Woolf? (Avant Garde, ASCAP) .... 81
Wonder of You, The (Duchess, BMI) .... 80
World Without Love, A—Peter & Gordon (Northern, ASCAP) .... 76
World Without Love, A—Rydell (Northern, ASCAP) .... 100
Wrong for Each Other (Valley, BMI) .... 49
Yesterday's Hero (Sea-Lark, BMI) .... 83
You're a Wonderful One (Jobete, BMI) .... 24

## BUBBLING UNDER THE HOT 100

101. PARTY GIRL ....Bernadette Carroll, Laurie 3238
102. KIKO ....Jimmy McGriff, Sue 10-001
103. OUR FADED LOVE ....Royaltones, Mala 473
104. YESTERDAY'S GONE ....Chad Stuart & Jeremy Clyde, World Artists 1021
105. THE FRENCH SONG ....Lucille Starr, Almo 204
106. IF YOU LOVE ME, REALLY LOVE ME ....Jackie Trent, Kapp 583
107. AGAIN ....James Brown & the Famous Flames, King 5876
108. IF YOU LOVE ME (Like You Say) ....Little Johnny Taylor, Galaxy 729
109. JUST ONE LOOK ....Hollies, Imperial 66026
110. SOMETHING YOU GOT ....Alvin Robinson, Tiger 104
111. BE ANYTHING (But Be Mine) ....Gloria Lynne, Fontana 1890
112. SUSPICION ....Elvis Presley, RCA Victor 0639
113. MY BABY'S COMIN' HOME ....Paul Anka, RCA Victor 8349
114. LONG TALL SHORTY ....Tommy Tucker, Checker 1075
115. SWING ....Tokens, B. T. Puppy 500
116. I ONLY HAVE EYES FOR YOU ....Cliff Richard, Epic 9670
117. I'LL FIND YOU ....Valerie & Nick, Glover 3000
118. WHAT'S THE MATTER WITH YOU BABY ....Marvin Gaye & Mary Wells, Motown 1057
119. TELL ME MAMMA ....Christine Quaite, World Artists 1022
120. ANOTHER CUP OF COFFEE ....Brook Benton, Mercury 72266
121. YO ME PREGUNTO ....Valrays, Parkway 904
122. TRY TO FIND ANOTHER MAN ....Righteous Brothers, Moonglow 231
123. I'M CONFESSIN' ....Nino Tempo & April Stevens, Atco 6294
124. SOMEDAY WE'RE GONNA LOVE AGAIN ....Barbara Lewis, Atlantic 2227
125. MY BABY WALKS ALL OVER ME ....Johnny Sea, Philips 40164
126. LITTLE TRACY ....Wynton Kelly, Verve 10316
127. FUGITIVE ....Ventures, Dolton 94
128. LOUIE—GO HOME ....Paul Revere & the Raiders, Columbia 43008
129. FUGITIVE ....Jan Davis, A&M 733
130. SHY ONE ....Shirley Ellis, Congress 210
131. THE WORLD I USED TO KNOW ....Jimmy Rodgers, Dot 16595
132. TEQUILA ....Bill Black's Combo, Hi 2077
133. SOULVILLE ....Aretha Franklin, Columbia 4309
134. NOMAD ....Louie Armstrong & Dave Brubeck, Columbia 43032
135. YOU CAN'T MISS NOTHING YOU NEVER HAD ....Ike & Tina Turner, Sonja 2005

Compiled from national retail sales and radio station airplay by the Music Popularity Dept. of Record Market Research, Billboard.

For Week Ending May 16, 1964

# Billboard HOT 100

★ STAR performer—Sides registering greatest proportionate upward progress this week.

| This Week | 1 Wk. Ago | 2 Wks. Ago | 3 Wks. Ago | TITLE Artist, Label & Number | Weeks On Chart |
|---|---|---|---|---|---|
| 1 (Billboard Award) | 3 | 5 | 9 | MY GUY — Mary Wells, Motown 1056 | 7 |
| 2 | 1 | 2 | 4 | HELLO, DOLLY! — Louis Armstrong, Kapp 573 | 14 |
| ★3 | 12 | 32 | 67 | LOVE ME DO — Beatles, Tollie 9008 | 6 |
| 4 | 4 | 4 | 7 | BITS AND PIECES — Dave Clark Five, Epic 9671 | 7 |
| 5 | 2 | 3 | 3 | DO YOU WANT TO KNOW A SECRET — Beatles, Vee Jay 587 | 8 |
| 6 | 7 | 10 | 17 | RONNIE — 4 Seasons, Philips 40185 | 6 |
| 7 | 6 | 6 | 8 | DON'T LET THE RAIN COME DOWN (Crooked Little Man) — Serendipity Singers, Philips 40175 | 11 |
| 8 | 8 | 9 | 10 | DEAD MAN'S CURVE — Jan & Dean, Liberty 55672 | 11 |
| 9 | 10 | 11 | 16 | WHITE ON WHITE — Danny Williams, United Artists 685 | 11 |
| ★10 | 13 | 18 | 28 | IT'S OVER — Roy Orbison, Monument 837 | 6 |
| 11 | 5 | 1 | 1 | CAN'T BUY ME LOVE — Beatles, Capitol 5150 | 8 |
| ★12 | 21 | 28 | 62 | LOVE ME WITH ALL YOUR HEART — Ray Charles Singers, Command 4046 | 6 |
| ★13 | 26 | 33 | 50 | (Just Like) ROMEO & JULIET — Reflections, Golden World 9 | 6 |
| ★14 | 42 | 72 | — | CHAPEL OF LOVE — Dixie Cups, Red Bird 001 | 3 |
| 15 | 15 | 15 | 20 | SHANGRI-LA — Robert Maxwell, His Harp & Ork, Decca 25622 | 9 |
| ★16 | 23 | 35 | 61 | LITTLE CHILDREN — Billy J. Kramer, Imperial 66027 | 5 |
| 17 | 18 | 21 | 32 | WISH SOMEONE WOULD CARE — Irma Thomas, Imperial 66013 | 8 |
| 18 | 19 | 22 | 33 | I'M SO PROUD — Impressions, ABC-Paramount 10544 | 7 |
| 19 | 9 | 8 | 5 | SUSPICION — Terry Stafford, Crusader 101 | 13 |
| 20 | 11 | 7 | 2 | TWIST AND SHOUT — Beatles, Tollie 9001 | 10 |
| ★21 | 40 | 61 | 85 | WALK ON BY — Dionne Warwick, Scepter 1274 | 4 |
| ★22 | 32 | 53 | — | DO YOU LOVE ME — Dave Clark Five, Epic 9678 | 3 |
| ★23 | 33 | 37 | 41 | COTTON CANDY — Al Hirt, RCA Victor 8346 | 6 |
| 24 | 22 | 16 | 18 | MONEY — Kingsmen, Wand 150 | 10 |
| 25 | 16 | 14 | 11 | SHOOP SHOOP SONG — Betty Everett, Vee Jay 585 | 12 |
| 26 | 27 | 29 | 35 | MY GIRL SLOOPY — Vibrations, Atlantic 2221 | 8 |
| 27 | 28 | 31 | 40 | SHANGRI-LA — Vic Dana, Dolton 92 | 8 |
| 28 | 17 | 12 | 12 | THAT'S THE WAY BOYS ARE — Lesley Gore, Mercury 72259 | 8 |
| 29 | 30 | 30 | 34 | KISS ME SAILOR — Diane Renay, 20th Century-Fox 477 | 7 |
| ★30 | 76 | — | — | A WORLD WITHOUT LOVE — Peter & Gordon, Capitol 5175 | 2 |
| 31 | 31 | 41 | 48 | PINK PANTHER THEME — Henry Mancini & His Ork, RCA Victor 8286 | 7 |
| 32 | 39 | 54 | 78 | THE VERY THOUGHT OF YOU — Rick Nelson, Decca 31612 | 4 |
| ★33 | 64 | — | — | P.S. I LOVE YOU — Beatles, Tollie 9008 | 2 |
| 34 | 14 | 13 | 6 | GLAD ALL OVER — Dave Clark Five, Epic 9656 | 14 |
| 35 | 43 | 51 | 81 | I DON'T WANT TO BE HURT ANY MORE — Nat King Cole, Capitol 5155 | 4 |
| ★36 | 46 | 57 | 63 | DIANE — Bachelors, London 9639 | 5 |
| ★37 | 47 | 58 | 69 | TODAY — New Christy Minstrels, Columbia 43000 | 5 |
| ★38 | 49 | 49 | 59 | WRONG FOR EACH OTHER — Andy Williams, Columbia 43015 | 5 |
| 39 | 45 | 46 | 57 | (The Best Part of) BREAKIN' UP — Ronettes, Philles 120 | 7 |
| 40 | 20 | 20 | 21 | THE MATADOR — Major Lance, Okeh 7191 | 8 |
| 41 | 36 | 38 | 46 | CHARADE — Sammy Kaye & His Ork, Decca 31589 | 7 |
| 42 | 25 | 27 | 27 | EBB TIDE — Lenny Welch, Cadence 1422 | 9 |
| ★43 | 66 | 79 | — | KISS ME QUICK — Elvis Presley, RCA Victor 0639 | 3 |
| ★44 | 55 | 73 | — | ONCE UPON A TIME — Marvin Gaye & Mary Wells, Motown 1057 | 3 |
| ★45 | 59 | 75 | 92 | THREE WINDOW COUPE — Rip Chords, Columbia 43035 | 4 |
| 46 | 52 | 55 | 70 | WHENEVER HE HOLDS YOU — Bobby Goldsboro, United Artists 710 | 5 |
| ★47 | 57 | 62 | 84 | PEOPLE — Barbra Streisand, Columbia 42965 | 7 |
| 48 | 54 | 56 | 75 | GOODBYE BABY (Baby Goodbye) — Solomon Burke, Atlantic 2226 | 5 |
| 49 | 35 | 40 | 37 | THANK YOU GIRL — Beatles, Vee Jay 587 | 7 |
| 50 | 24 | 17 | 15 | YOU'RE A WONDERFUL ONE — Marvin Gaye, Tamla 54093 | 10 |
| ★51 | 61 | 76 | — | EVERY LITTLE BIT HURTS — Brenda Holloway, Tamla 54094 | 3 |
| 52 | 29 | 25 | 25 | FOREVER — Pete Drake, Smash 1867 | 11 |
| 53 | 58 | 60 | 74 | TALL COOL ONE — Wailers, Golden Crest 518 | 6 |
| ★54 | 87 | — | — | VIVA LAS VEGAS — Elvis Presley, RCA Victor 8360 | 2 |
| 55 | 48 | 50 | 55 | SLIP-IN MULES — Sugar Pie De Santo, Checker 1073 | 5 |
| 56 | 44 | 44 | 52 | IN MY LONELY ROOM — Martha & the Vandellas, Gordy 7031 | 6 |
| 57 | 51 | 47 | 53 | LOOK HOMEWARD ANGEL — Monarchs, Sound Stage 7 2516 | 13 |
| 58 | 63 | 66 | 73 | SOUL SERENADE — King Curtis, Capitol 5109 | 10 |
| ★59 | 71 | 93 | — | I RISE, I FALL — Johnny Tillotson, MGM 13232 | 3 |
| ★60 | 70 | 74 | 90 | I KNEW IT ALL THE TIME — Dave Clark Five, Congress 212 | 4 |
| 61 | 62 | 68 | 80 | AIN'T THAT JUST LIKE ME — Searchers, Kapp 584 | 5 |
| 62 | 65 | 78 | — | TEA FOR TWO — Nino Tempo & April Stevens, Atco 6294 | 3 |
| 63 | 72 | 77 | 100 | HURT BY LOVE — Inez Foxx, Symbol 20-001 | 4 |
| ★64 | 84 | — | — | BE ANYTHING (But Be Mine) — Connie Francis, MGM 13237 | 2 |
| 65 | 68 | 71 | 76 | LOVING YOU MORE EVERY DAY — Etta James, Argo 5465 | 5 |
| 66 | 69 | 63 | 72 | THAT'S WHEN IT HURTS — Ben E. King, Atco 6288 | 7 |
| 67 | 78 | 84 | — | ONE WAY LOVE — Drifters, Atlantic 2225 | 3 |
| ★68 | 88 | 90 | — | GONNA GET ALONG WITHOUT YOU NOW — Skeeter Davis, RCA Victor 8347 | 3 |
| 69 | 79 | 85 | 96 | CAROL — Tommy Roe, ABC-Paramount 10543 | 4 |
| 70 | 73 | 88 | 91 | GONNA GET ALONG WITHOUT YOU NOW — Tracey Dey, Amy 901 | 4 |
| ★71 | 89 | — | — | GOOD GOLLY MISS MOLLY — Swinging Blue Jeans, Imperial 66030 | 2 |
| 72 | 85 | 96 | — | SUGAR AND SPICE — Searchers, Liberty 55689 | 3 |
| 73 | 75 | 82 | 98 | WINKIN', BLINKIN' AND NOD — Simon Sisters, Kapp 586 | 4 |
| 74 | 74 | 86 | 89 | DONNIE — Bermudas, Era 3125 | 5 |
| 75 | 81 | 81 | 93 | WHO'S AFRAID OF VIRGINIA WOOLF? — Jimmy Smith, Verve 10314 | 4 |
| ★76 | — | — | — | TEARS AND ROSES — Al Martino, Capitol 5183 | 1 |
| 77 | 83 | — | — | YESTERDAY'S HERO — Gene Pitney, Musicor 1038 | 2 |
| 78 | 82 | 89 | — | THE LONELIEST NIGHT — Dale & Grace, Montel 928 | 3 |
| ★79 | — | — | — | WHAT'S THE MATTER WITH YOU BABY — Marvin Gaye & Mary Wells, Motown 1057 | 1 |
| 80 | 90 | — | — | ROCK ME BABY — B. B. King, Kent 393 | 2 |
| 81 | 94 | — | — | GIVING UP — Gladys Knight & the Pips, Maxx 326 | 2 |
| ★82 | — | — | — | ONE GIRL — Garnet Mimms, United Artists 715 | 1 |
| 83 | 77 | 80 | 86 | HEY, MR. SAX MAN — Boots Randolph, Monument 835 | 6 |
| ★84 | — | — | — | PARTY GIRL — Bernadette Carroll, Laurie 3238 | 1 |
| 85 | 86 | 91 | 95 | FROM RUSSIA WITH LOVE — Village Stompers, Epic 9674 | 4 |
| 86 | 98 | — | — | TOO LATE TO TURN BACK NOW — Brook Benton, Mercury 72266 | 2 |
| ★87 | — | — | — | THE FRENCH SONG — Lucille Starr, Almo 204 | 1 |
| ★88 | — | — | — | ANOTHER CUP OF COFFEE — Brook Benton, Mercury 72266 | 1 |
| ★89 | — | — | — | KIKO — Jimmy McGriff, Sue 10-01 | 1 |
| ★90 | — | — | — | MILORD — Bobby Darin, Atco 6297 | 1 |
| 91 | 91 | — | — | WHAT HAVE I GOT OF MY OWN — Trini Lopez, Reprise 0276 | 2 |
| 92 | 100 | — | — | A WORLD WITHOUT LOVE — Bobby Rydell, Cameo 320 | 2 |
| 93 | 93 | 95 | — | LITTLE DONNA — Rivieras, Riviera 1402 | 3 |
| 94 | — | — | — | HAVE I STAYED AWAY TOO LONG — Bobby Bare, RCA Victor 8358 | 1 |
| 95 | — | — | — | THE WORLD OF LONELY PEOPLE — Anita Bryant, Columbia 43037 | 1 |
| 96 | 96 | 98 | — | NOT FADE AWAY — Rolling Stones, London 9657 | 3 |
| 97 | — | — | — | RULES OF LOVE — Orlons, Cameo 319 | 1 |
| 98 | — | — | — | JUST ONE LOOK — Hollies, Imperial 66026 | 1 |
| 99 | — | — | — | LONG TALL SHORTY — Tommy Tucker, Checker 1075 | 1 |
| 100 | — | — | — | TEQUILA — Bill Black's Combo, Hi 2077 | 1 |

## HOT 100—A TO Z—*(Publisher-Licensee)*

Ain't That Just Like Me (Trio-Progressive, BMI) .. 61
Another Cup of Coffee (Peter Maurice, ASCAP) ... 88
Be Anything (But Be Mine) (Shapiro-Bernstein, ASCAP) ... 64
(The Best Part of) Breakin' Up (Mother Bertha-Hill & Range, BMI) ... 39
Bits and Pieces (Beechwood, BMI) ... 4
Can't Buy Me Love (Northern, ASCAP) ... 11
Carol (Arc, BMI) ... 69
Chapel of Love (Trio, BMI) ... 14
Charade (Northern-Southdale, ASCAP) ... 41
Cotton Candy (Gallico, BMI) ... 23
Dead Man's Curve (Screen Gems-Columbia, BMI) .. 8
Diane (Miller, ASCAP) ... 36
Do You Love Me (Jobete, BMI) ... 22
Do You Want to Know a Secret (Metric, BMI) ... 5
Don't Let the Rain Come Down (Serendipity, BMI). 7
Donnie (Rickland, BMI) ... 74
Ebb Tide (Robbins, ASCAP) ... 42
Every Little Bit Hurts (Jobete, BMI) ... 51
Forever (Tree, BMI) ... 52
The French Song (Irving-Doral, BMI) ... 87
From Russia With Love (Unart, BMI) ... 85
Giving Up (Trio, BMI) ... 81
Glad All Over (Campbell-Connelly, ASCAP) ... 34
Gonna Get Along Without You Now—Davis (Reliance, ASCAP) ... 68
Gonna Get Along Without You Now—Dey (Reliance, ASCAP) ... 70
Good Golly Miss Molly (Venice, BMI) ... 71
Goodbye Baby (Picturetone-Mellin, BMI) ... 48
Have I Stayed Away Too Long (Frank, ASCAP) ... 94
Hello, Dolly! (Morris, ASCAP) ... 2
Hey, Mr. Sax Man (Forrest Hills, BMI) ... 83
Hurt By Love (Saturn, BMI) ... 63
I Don't Want to Be Hurt Anymore (Bregman, Vocco & Conn, ASCAP) ... 35
I Knew It All the Time (Gallico, BMI) ... 60
I Rise, I Fall (Tod, ASCAP) ... 59
I'm So Proud (Curtom, BMI) ... 18
In My Lonely Room (Jobete, BMI) ... 56
It's Over (Acuff-Rose, BMI) ... 10
(Just Like) Romeo & Juliet (Myto, BMI) ... 13
Just One Look (Premier, BMI) ... 98
Kiko (Saturn-Renner-Jell, BMI) ... 85
Kiss Me Quick (Presley, BMI) ... 43
Kiss Me Sailor (Saturday, ASCAP) ... 29
Little Children (Rumbalero, BMI) ... 16
Little Donna (World Int'l, BMI) ... 93
Loneliest Night, The (Acuff-Rose, BMI) ... 78
Long Tall Shorty (Medal, BMI) ... 99
Look Homeward Angel (Rogelle, BMI) ... 57
Love Me Do (Ardmore-Beechwood, BMI) ... 3
Love Me With All Your Heart (Peer Int'l, BMI) .. 12
Loving You More Every Day (Trio, BMI) ... 65
Matador, The (Curtom-Jalynne, BMI) ... 40
Milord (Alamo, ASCAP) ... 90
Money (Jobete, BMI) ... 24
My Girl Sloopy (Picturetone-Mellin, BMI) ... 26
My Guy (Jobete, BMI) ... 1
Not Fade Away (Nor Va Jak, BMI) ... 96
Once Upon a Time (Jobete, BMI) ... 44
One Girl (Mellin-Rittenhouse, BMI) ... 82
One Way Love (Keetch, Caesar & Dino, BMI) ... 67
P.S. I Love You (Beechwood, BMI) ... 33
Party Girl (Schwartz, ASCAP) ... 84
People (Chappell, ASCAP) ... 47
Pink Panther Theme (Northridge-United Artists, ASCAP) ... 31
Rock Me Baby (Modern, BMI) ... 80
Ronnie (Saturday-Gavidina, ASCAP) ... 6
Rules of Love (Kalmann, ASCAP) ... 97
Shangri-La—Dana (Robbins, ASCAP) ... 27
Shangri-La—Maxwell (Robbins, ASCAP) ... 15
Shoop Shoop Song (T.M., BMI) ... 25
Slip-In Mules (Chevis-Medal, BMI) ... 55
Soul Serenade (Kilynn-Vee Vee, BMI) ... 58
Sugar and Spice (Duchess, BMI) ... 72
Suspicion (Presley, BMI) ... 19
Tall Cool One (C.F.G., BMI) ... 53
Tea for Two (Harms, ASCAP) ... 62
Tears and Roses (Davilene, BMI) ... 76
Tequila (Jot, BMI) ... 100
Thank You Girl (Conrad, BMI) ... 49
That's the Way Boys Are (Earth, BMI) ... 28
That's When It Hurts (Cotillion-Mellin, BMI) ... 66
Three Window Coupe (Screen Gems-Columbia, BMI). 45
Today (Miller-Heritage House, ASCAP) ... 37
Too Late to Turn Back Now (Play, BMI) ... 86
Twist and Shout (Mellin-Progressive, BMI) ... 20
Very Thought of You, The (Witmark, ASCAP) ... 32
Viva Las Vegas (Presley, BMI) ... 54
Walk on By (Blue-Seas-Jac, ASCAP) ... 21
What Have I Got of My Own (Sawtell-Herring, ASCAP) ... 91
What's the Matter With You Baby (Jobete, BMI) .. 79
Whenever He Holds You (Unart, BMI) ... 46
White on White (Painted Desert, BMI) ... 9
Winkin', Blinkin' and Nod (Ryerson, BMI) ... 73
Wish Someone Would Care (Metric, BMI) ... 17
Who's Afraid of Virginia Woolf? (Avant Garde, ASCAP) ... 75
World of Lonely People, The (Ross Jungnickel, ASCAP) ... 95
World Without Love, A—Peter & Gordon (Northern, ASCAP) ... 30
World Without Love, A—Rydell (Northern, ASCAP) ... 92
Wrong for Each Other (Valley, BMI) ... 38
Yesterday's Hero (Sea-Lark, BMI) ... 77
You're a Wonderful One (Jobete, BMI) ... 50

## BUBBLING UNDER THE HOT 100

101. BE MY GIRL ... Four-Evers, Smash 1887
102. GOTTA GET AWAY ... Billy Butler & the Enchanters, Okeh 7192
103. SUSPICION ... Elvis Presley, RCA Victor 0639
104. BIG PARTY ... Barbara & the Browns, Stax 150
105. SWING ... Tokens, B. T. Puppy 500
106. SOMETHING YOU GOT ... Alvin Robinson, Tiger 104
107. IF YOU LOVE ME, REALLY LOVE ME ... Jackie Trent, Kapp 583
108. WHAT'D I SAY ... Elvis Presley, RCA Victor 8360
109. I ONLY HAVE EYES FOR YOU ... Cliff Richard, Epic 9670
110. DON'T LET THE SUN CATCH YOU CRYING ... Gerry & the Pacemakers, Laurie 3251
111. TELL ME MAMMA ... Christine Quaite, World Artists 1022
112. ACROSS THE STREET ... Lenny O'Henry, Atco 6291
113. YESTERDAY'S GONE ... Chad Stuart & Jeremy Clyde, World Artists 1021
114. SOUL HOOTENANNY ... Gene Chandler, Constellation 114
115. YESTERDAY'S GONE ... Overlanders, Hickory 1258
116. OUR FADED LOVE ... Royaltones, Mala 473
117. I'M CONFESSIN' ... Nino Tempo & April Stevens, Atco 6294
118. LOUIE—GO HOME ... Paul Revere & the Raiders, Columbia 43008
119. TRY TO FIND ANOTHER MAN ... Righteous Brothers, Moonglow 231
120. I'LL TOUCH A STAR ... Terry Stafford, Crusader 105
121. NEW YORK TOWN ... Dixiebelles, Sound Stage 7 2521
122. BY BABY WALKS ALL OVER ME ... Johnny Sea, Philips 40164
123. BE ANYTHING (But Be Mine) ... Gloria Lynne, Fontana 1890
124. AGAIN ... James Brown & the Famous Flames, King 5876
125. PRECIOUS WORDS ... Wallace Brothers, Sims 174
126. FUGITIVE ... Ventures, Dolton 94
127. THE WORLD I USED TO KNOW ... Jimmie Rodgers, Dot 16595
128. SOULVILLE ... Aretha Franklin, Columbia 4309
129. IF YOU LOVE ME (Like You Say) ... Little Johnny Taylor, Galaxy 729
130. EVERYBODY KNOWS ... Steve Lawrence, Columbia 43047
131. BIG BOSS LINE ... Jackie Wilson, Brunswick 55266
132. BAD NEWS ... Trashmen, Garrett 4005
133. SECURITY ... Otis Redding, Volt 117
134. RUBY RED, BABY BLUE ... Fleetwoods, Dolton 93

Compiled from national retail sales and radio station airplay by the Music Popularity Dept. of Record Market Research. Billboard.

# Billboard HOT 100

For Week Ending May 23, 1964

★ STAR performer—Sides registering greatest proportionate upward progress this week.

| This Week | Wk. Ago | 2 Wks. Ago | 3 Wks. Ago | TITLE, Artist, Label & Number | Weeks On Chart |
|---|---|---|---|---|---|
| 1 | 1 | 3 | 5 | MY GUY — Mary Wells, Motown 1056 | 8 |
| 2 | 3 | 12 | 32 | LOVE ME DO — Beatles, Tollie 9008 | 7 |
| 3 | 2 | 1 | 2 | HELLO, DOLLY! — Louis Armstrong, Kapp 573 | 15 |
| 4 | 14 | 42 | 72 | CHAPEL OF LOVE — Dixie Cups, Red Bird 001 | 4 |
| ★5 | 12 | 21 | 28 | LOVE ME WITH ALL YOUR HEART — Ray Charles Singers, Command 4046 | 7 |
| 6 | 4 | 4 | 4 | BITS AND PIECES — Dave Clark Five, Epic 9671 | 8 |
| 7 | 13 | 26 | 33 | (Just Like) ROMEO & JULIET — Reflections, Golden World 9 | 7 |
| 8 | 6 | 7 | 10 | RONNIE — 4 Seasons, Philips 40185 | 7 |
| 9 | 10 | 13 | 18 | IT'S OVER — Roy Orbison, Monument 837 | 7 |
| 10 | 30 | 76 | — | A WORLD WITHOUT LOVE — Peter & Gordon, Capitol 5175 | 3 |
| 11 | 16 | 23 | 35 | LITTLE CHILDREN — Billy J. Kramer, Imperial 66027 | 6 |
| 12 | 5 | 2 | 3 | DO YOU WANT TO KNOW A SECRET — Beatles, Vee Jay 587 | 9 |
| 13 | 8 | 8 | 9 | DEAD MAN'S CURVE — Jan & Dean, Liberty 55672 | 12 |
| 14 | 18 | 19 | 22 | I'M SO PROUD — Impressions, ABC-Paramount 10544 | 8 |
| ★15 | 33 | 64 | — | P.S. I LOVE YOU — Beatles, Tollie 9008 | 3 |
| 16 | 21 | 40 | 61 | WALK ON BY — Dionne Warwick, Scepter 1274 | 5 |
| 17 | 17 | 18 | 21 | WISH SOMEONE WOULD CARE — Irma Thomas, Imperial 66013 | 9 |
| 18 | 22 | 32 | 53 | DO YOU LOVE ME — Dave Clark Five, Epic 9678 | 4 |
| 19 | 9 | 10 | 11 | WHITE ON WHITE — Danny Williams, United Artists 685 | 12 |
| 20 | 7 | 6 | 6 | DON'T LET THE RAIN COME DOWN (Crooked Little Man) — Serendipity Singers, Philips 40175 | 12 |
| 21 | 15 | 15 | 15 | SHANGRI-LA — Robert Maxwell, His Harp & Ork, Decca 25622 | 10 |
| 22 | 23 | 33 | 37 | COTTON CANDY — Al Hirt, RCA Victor 8346 | 7 |
| 23 | 11 | 5 | 1 | CAN'T BUY ME LOVE — Beatles, Capitol 5150 | 9 |
| 24 | 19 | 9 | 8 | SUSPICION — Terry Stafford, Crusader 101 | 14 |
| ★25 | 35 | 43 | 51 | I DON'T WANT TO BE HURT ANY MORE — Nat King Cole, Capitol 5155 | 4 |
| 26 | 47 | 57 | 62 | PEOPLE — Barbra Streisand, Columbia 42965 | 8 |
| 27 | 36 | 46 | 57 | DIANE — Bachelors, London 9639 | 6 |
| 28 | 32 | 39 | 54 | THE VERY THOUGHT OF YOU — Rick Nelson, Decca 31612 | 5 |
| 29 | 24 | 22 | 16 | MONEY — Kingsmen, Wand 150 | 11 |
| 30 | 26 | 27 | 29 | MY GIRL SLOOPY — Vibrations, Atlantic 2221 | 9 |
| 31 | 27 | 28 | 31 | SHANGRI-LA — Vic Dana, Dolton 92 | 9 |
| 32 | 44 | 55 | 73 | ONCE UPON A TIME — Marvin Gaye & Mary Wells, Motown 1057 | 4 |
| ★33 | 51 | 61 | 76 | EVERY LITTLE BIT HURTS — Brenda Holloway, Tamla 54094 | 4 |
| 34 | 43 | 66 | 79 | KISS ME QUICK — Elvis Presley, RCA Victor 0639 | 4 |
| 35 | 37 | 47 | 58 | TODAY — New Christy Minstrels, Columbia 43000 | 6 |
| ★36 | 48 | 54 | 56 | GOODBYE BABY (Baby Goodbye) — Solomon Burke, Atlantic 2226 | 6 |
| 37 | 38 | 49 | 49 | WRONG FOR EACH OTHER — Andy Williams, Columbia 43015 | 6 |
| 38 | 25 | 16 | 14 | SHOOP SHOOP SONG — Betty Everett, Vee Jay 585 | 13 |
| 39 | 45 | 59 | 75 | THREE WINDOW COUPE — Rip Chords, Columbia 43035 | 5 |
| 40 | 46 | 52 | 55 | WHENEVER HE HOLDS YOU — Bobby Goldsboro, United Artists 710 | 6 |
| 41 | 20 | 11 | 7 | TWIST AND SHOUT — Beatles, Tollie 9001 | 11 |
| ★42 | 64 | 84 | — | BE ANYTHING (But Be Mine) — Connie Francis, MGM 13237 | 3 |
| 43 | 31 | 31 | 41 | PINK PANTHER THEME — Henry Mancini & His Ork, RCA Victor 8286 | 8 |
| 44 | 39 | 45 | 46 | (The Best Part of) BREAKIN' UP — Ronettes, Philles 120 | 8 |
| 45 | 53 | 58 | 60 | TALL COOL ONE — Wailers, Golden Crest 518 | 7 |
| 46 | 54 | 87 | — | VIVA LAS VEGAS — Elvis Presley, RCA Victor 8360 | 3 |
| 47 | 29 | 30 | 30 | KISS ME SAILOR — Diane Renay, 20th Century-Fox 477 | 8 |
| 48 | 59 | 71 | 93 | I RISE, I FALL — Johnny Tillotson, MGM 13232 | 4 |
| 49 | 28 | 17 | 12 | THAT'S THE WAY BOYS ARE — Lesley Gore, Mercury 72259 | 9 |
| 50 | — | — | — | WHAT'D I SAY — Elvis Presley, RCA Victor 8360 | 1 |
| 51 | 58 | 63 | 66 | SOUL SERENADE — King Curtis, Capitol 5109 | 11 |
| ★52 | 76 | — | — | TEARS AND ROSES — Al Martino, Capitol 5183 | 2 |
| ★53 | 71 | 89 | — | GOOD GOLLY MISS MOLLY — Swinging Blue Jeans, Imperial 66030 | 3 |
| 54 | 63 | 72 | 77 | HURT BY LOVE — Inez Foxx, Symbol 20-001 | 5 |
| 55 | 68 | 88 | 90 | GONNA GET ALONG WITHOUT YOU NOW — Skeeter Davis, RCA Victor 8347 | 4 |
| 56 | 62 | 65 | 78 | TEA FOR TWO — Nino Tempo & April Stevens, Atco 6294 | 4 |
| 57 | 80 | 90 | — | ROCK ME BABY — B. B. King, Kent 393 | 3 |
| 58 | 60 | 70 | 74 | I KNEW IT ALL THE TIME — Dave Clark Five, Congress 212 | 5 |
| 59 | 70 | 73 | 88 | GONNA GET ALONG WITHOUT YOU NOW — Tracey Dey, Amy 901 | 5 |
| 60 | 67 | 78 | 84 | ONE WAY LOVE — Drifters, Atlantic 2225 | 4 |
| 61 | 69 | 79 | 85 | CAROL — Tommy Roe, ABC-Paramount 10543 | 5 |
| 62 | 72 | 85 | 96 | SUGAR AND SPICE — Searchers, Liberty 55689 | 4 |
| ★63 | 79 | — | — | WHAT'S THE MATTER WITH YOU BABY — Marvin Gaye & Mary Wells, Motown 1057 | 2 |
| ★64 | 88 | — | — | ANOTHER CUP OF COFFEE — Brook Benton, Mercury 72266 | 2 |
| 65 | 78 | 82 | 89 | THE LONELIEST NIGHT — Dale & Grace, Montel 928 | 4 |
| 66 | 61 | 62 | 68 | AIN'T THAT JUST LIKE ME — Searchers, Kapp 584 | 6 |
| 67 | 74 | 74 | 86 | DONNIE — Bermudas, Era 3125 | 6 |
| 68 | — | — | — | TELL ME WHY — Bobby Vinton, Epic 9687 | 1 |
| 69 | 84 | — | — | PARTY GIRL — Bernadette Carroll, Laurie 3238 | 2 |
| 70 | 81 | 94 | — | GIVING UP — Gladys Knight & the Pips, Maxx 326 | 3 |
| 71 | 65 | 68 | 71 | LOVING YOU MORE EVERY DAY — Etta James, Argo 5465 | 6 |
| 72 | 75 | 81 | 81 | WHO'S AFRAID OF VIRGINIA WOOLF? — Jimmy Smith, Verve 10314 | 5 |
| 73 | 73 | 75 | 82 | WINKIN', BLINKIN' AND NOD — Simon Sisters, Kapp 586 | 5 |
| 74 | 77 | 83 | — | YESTERDAY'S HERO — Gene Pitney, Musicor 1038 | 3 |
| ★75 | — | — | — | I DON'T WANNA BE A LOSER — Lesley Gore, Mercury 72270 | 1 |
| ★76 | — | — | — | I GET AROUND — Beach Boys, Capitol 5174 | 1 |
| 77 | 86 | 98 | — | TOO LATE TO TURN BACK NOW — Brook Benton, Mercury 72266 | 3 |
| 78 | 82 | — | — | ONE GIRL — Garnet Mimms, United Artists 715 | 2 |
| ★79 | — | — | — | I'LL TOUCH A STAR — Terry Stafford, Crusader 105 | 1 |
| 80 | 95 | — | — | THE WORLD OF LONELY PEOPLE — Anita Bryant, Columbia 43037 | 2 |
| 81 | 85 | 86 | 91 | FROM RUSSIA WITH LOVE — Village Stompers, Epic 9674 | 5 |
| 82 | 91 | 91 | — | WHAT HAVE I GOT OF MY OWN — Trini Lopez, Reprise 0276 | 3 |
| 83 | 96 | 96 | 98 | NOT FADE AWAY — Rolling Stones, London 9657 | 4 |
| 84 | 97 | — | — | RULES OF LOVE — Orlons, Cameo 319 | 2 |
| 85 | 89 | — | — | KIKO — Jimmy McGriff, Sue 10-01 | 2 |
| 86 | 87 | — | — | THE FRENCH SONG — Lucille Starr, Almo 204 | 2 |
| ★87 | — | — | — | DON'T LET THE SUN CATCH YOU CRYING — Gerry & the Pacemakers, Laurie 3251 | 1 |
| 88 | 90 | — | — | MILORD — Bobby Darin, Atco 6297 | 2 |
| ★89 | — | — | — | BEANS IN MY EARS — Serendipity Singers, Philips 40198 | 1 |
| 90 | — | — | — | MY BOY LOLLIPOP — Millie Small, Smash 1893 | 1 |
| 91 | 100 | — | — | TEQUILA — Bill Black's Combo, Hi 2077 | 2 |
| 92 | — | — | — | YESTERDAY'S GONE — Chad Stuart & Jeremy Clyde, World Artists 1021 | 1 |
| 93 | — | — | — | BEG ME — Chuck Jackson, Wand 154 | 1 |
| 94 | — | — | — | BIG BOSS LINE — Jackie Wilson, Brunswick 55266 | 1 |
| 95 | — | — | — | TELL ME MAMMA — Christine Quaite, World Artists 1022 | 1 |
| 96 | 99 | — | — | LONG TALL SHORTY — Tommy Tucker, Checker 1075 | 2 |
| 97 | — | — | — | SECURITY — Otis Redding, Volt 117 | 1 |
| 98 | — | — | — | YESTERDAY'S GONE — Overlanders, Hickory 1258 | 1 |
| 99 | — | — | — | JUST AIN'T ENOUGH LOVE — Eddie Holland, Motown 1058 | 1 |
| 100 | — | — | — | NO PARTICULAR PLACE TO GO — Chuck Berry, Chess 1898 | 1 |

## BUBBLING UNDER THE HOT 100

101. GOTTA GET AWAY — Billy Butler & the Enchanters, Okeh 7192
102. KICK THAT LITTLE FOOT, SALLY ANN — Round Robin, Domain 1404
103. HAVE I STAYED AWAY TOO LONG — Bobby Bare, RCA Victor 8358
104. BE MY GIRL — Four-Evers, Smash 1887
105. SWING — Tokens, B. T. Puppy 500
106. SOMETHING YOU GOT — Alvin Robinson, Tiger 104
107. EVERYBODY KNOWS — Steve Lawrence, Columbia 43047
108. I'LL BE IN TROUBLE — Temptations, Gordy 7032
109. ACROSS THE STREET — Lenny O'Henry, Atco 6291
110. BLOWIN' IN THE WIND — Stan Getz, Verve 10323
111. BIG PARTY — Barbara & the Browns, Stax 150
112. A WORLD WITHOUT LOVE — Bobby Rydell, Cameo 320
113. JUST ONE LOOK — Hollies, Imperial 66026
114. THE GIRL'S ALRIGHT WITH ME — Temptations, Gordy 7032
115. THE WORLD I USED TO KNOW — Jimmie Rodgers, Dot 16595
116. LET'S HAVE A PARTY — Rivieras, Riviera 1402
117. I ONLY HAVE EYES FOR YOU — Cliff Richard, Epic 9670
118. I WANNA BE LOVED — Dean & Jean, Rust 5081
119. NEW YORK TOWN — Dixiebelles, Sound Stage 7 2521
120. BAD TO ME — Billy J. Kramer, Imperial 66027
121. MY BABY WALKS ALL OVER ME — Johnny Sea, Philips 40164
122. NOMAD — Louis Armstrong & Dave Brubeck, Columbia 43032
123. IF YOU DON'T LOOK AROUND — Kingston Trio, Capitol 5166
124. SOULVILLE — Aretha Franklin, Columbia 4309
125. PRECIOUS WORDS — Wallace Brothers, Sims 174
126. FUGITIVE — Ventures, Dolton 589
127. THE FIRST NIGHT OF THE FULL MOON — Jack Jones, Kapp 589
128. SOMEDAY WE'RE GONNA LOVE AGAIN — Barbara Lewis, Atlantic 4047
129. FRENCH RIVIERA — Webb Pierce, Decca 31617
130. SOUL HOOTENANNY — Gene Chandler, Constellation 114
131. INVISIBLE TEARS — Ned Miller, Fabor 128
132. SPEND A LITTLE TIME — Barbara Lewis, Atlantic 2227
133. LOOK AT ME — Jimmy Gilmer, Dot 16609
134. BABY BABY (I Still Love You) — Cinderellas, Dimension 1026
135. SHE'S A BAD MOTOCYCLE — Crestones, Markie 117

Compiled from national retail sales and radio station airplay by the Music Popularity Dept. of Record Market Research, Billboard.

For Week Ending May 30, 1964

# Billboard

# HOT 100

★ STAR performer—Sides registering greatest proportionate upward progress this week.

Billboard Award

| This Week | 1 Wk. Ago | 2 Wks. Ago | 3 Wks. Ago | TITLE Artist, Label & Number | Weeks On Chart |
|---|---|---|---|---|---|
| 1 | 2 | 3 | 12 | LOVE ME DO — Beatles, Tollie 9008 | 8 |
| 2 | 4 | 14 | 42 | CHAPEL OF LOVE — Dixie Cups, Red Bird 001 | 5 |
| 3 | 1 | 1 | 3 | MY GUY — Mary Wells, Motown 1056 | 9 |
| 4 | 5 | 12 | 21 | LOVE ME WITH ALL YOUR HEART — Ray Charles Singers, Command 4046 | 8 |
| 5 | 3 | 2 | 1 | HELLO, DOLLY! — Louis Armstrong, Kapp 573 | 16 |
| 6 | 7 | 13 | 26 | (Just Like) ROMEO & JULIET — Reflections, Golden World 9 | 8 |
| ★7 | 10 | 30 | 76 | A WORLD WITHOUT LOVE — Peter & Gordon, Capitol 5175 | 4 |
| ★8 | 11 | 16 | 23 | LITTLE CHILDREN — Billy J. Kramer, Imperial 66027 | 7 |
| 9 | 9 | 10 | 13 | IT'S OVER — Roy Orbison, Monument 837 | 8 |
| ★10 | 16 | 21 | 40 | WALK ON BY — Dionne Warwick, Scepter 1274 | 6 |
| 11 | 15 | 33 | 64 | P.S. I LOVE YOU — Beatles, Tollie 9008 | 4 |
| ★12 | 18 | 22 | 32 | DO YOU LOVE ME — Dave Clark Five, Epic 9678 | 5 |
| 13 | 8 | 6 | 7 | RONNIE — 4 Seasons, Philips 40185 | 8 |
| 14 | 6 | 4 | 4 | BITS AND PIECES — Dave Clark Five, Epic 9671 | 9 |
| ★15 | 22 | 23 | 33 | COTTON CANDY — Al Hirt, RCA Victor 8346 | 8 |
| ★16 | 26 | 47 | 57 | PEOPLE — Barbra Streisand, Columbia 42965 | 9 |
| ★17 | 33 | 51 | 61 | EVERY LITTLE BIT HURTS — Brenda Holloway, Tamla 54094 | 5 |
| 18 | 14 | 18 | 19 | I'M SO PROUD — Impressions, ABC-Paramount 10544 | 9 |
| 19 | 12 | 5 | 2 | DO YOU WANT TO KNOW A SECRET — Beatles, Vee Jay 587 | 10 |
| ★20 | 27 | 36 | 46 | DIANE — Bachelors, London 9639 | 7 |
| 21 | 17 | 17 | 18 | WISH SOMEONE WOULD CARE — Irma Thomas, Imperial 66013 | 10 |
| 22 | 25 | 35 | 43 | I DON'T WANT TO BE HURT ANY MORE — Nat King Cole, Capitol 5155 | 6 |
| 23 | 13 | 8 | 8 | DEAD MAN'S CURVE — Jan & Dean, Liberty 55672 | 13 |
| ★24 | 32 | 44 | 55 | ONCE UPON A TIME — Marvin Gaye & Mary Wells, Motown 1057 | 5 |
| 25 | 21 | 15 | 15 | SHANGRI-LA — Robert Maxwell, His Harp & Ork, Decca 25622 | 11 |
| 26 | 28 | 32 | 39 | THE VERY THOUGHT OF YOU — Rick Nelson, Decca 31612 | 6 |
| ★27 | 35 | 37 | 47 | TODAY — New Christy Minstrels, Columbia 43000 | 7 |
| 28 | 19 | 9 | 10 | WHITE ON WHITE — Danny Williams, United Artists 685 | 13 |
| ★29 | 50 | — | — | WHAT'D I SAY — Elvis Presley, RCA Victor 8360 | 2 |
| ★30 | 68 | — | — | TELL ME WHY — Bobby Vinton, Epic 9687 | 2 |
| 31 | 39 | 45 | 59 | THREE WINDOW COUPE — Rip Chords, Columbia 43035 | 6 |
| ★32 | 42 | 64 | 84 | BE ANYTHING (But Be Mine) — Connie Francis, MGM 13237 | 4 |
| ★33 | 46 | 54 | 87 | VIVA LAS VEGAS — Elvis Presley, RCA Victor 8360 | 4 |
| 34 | 34 | 43 | 66 | KISS ME QUICK — Elvis Presley, RCA Victor 0639 | 5 |
| 35 | 37 | 38 | 49 | WRONG FOR EACH OTHER — Andy Williams, Columbia 43015 | 7 |
| 36 | 36 | 48 | 54 | GOODBYE BABY (Baby Goodbye) — Solomon Burke, Atlantic 2226 | 7 |
| 37 | 20 | 7 | 6 | DON'T LET THE RAIN COME DOWN (Crooked Little Man) — Serendipity Singers, Philips 40175 | 13 |
| 38 | 45 | 53 | 58 | TALL COOL ONE — Wailers, Golden Crest 518 | 8 |
| 39 | 40 | 46 | 52 | WHENEVER HE HOLDS YOU — Bobby Goldsboro, United Artists 710 | 7 |
| ★40 | 52 | 76 | — | TEARS AND ROSES — Al Martino, Capitol 5183 | 3 |
| 41 | 24 | 19 | 9 | SUSPICION — Terry Stafford, Crusader 101 | 15 |
| 42 | 23 | 11 | 5 | CAN'T BUY ME LOVE — Beatles, Capitol 5150 | 10 |
| 43 | 48 | 59 | 71 | I RISE, I FALL — Johnny Tillotson, MGM 13232 | 5 |
| 44 | 31 | 27 | 28 | SHANGRI-LA — Vic Dana, Dolton 92 | 10 |
| ★45 | 76 | — | — | I GET AROUND — Beach Boys, Capitol 5174 | 2 |
| 46 | 53 | 71 | 89 | GOOD GOLLY MISS MOLLY — Swinging Blue Jeans, Imperial 66030 | 4 |
| ★47 | 87 | — | — | DON'T LET THE SUN CATCH YOU CRYING — Gerry & the Pacemakers, Laurie 3251 | 2 |
| ★48 | 90 | — | — | MY BOY LOLLIPOP — Millie Small, Smash 1893 | 2 |
| ★49 | 79 | — | — | I'LL TOUCH A STAR — Terry Stafford, Crusader 105 | 2 |
| ★50 | 62 | 72 | 85 | SUGAR AND SPICE — Searchers, Liberty 55689 | 5 |
| 51 | 55 | 68 | 88 | GONNA GET ALONG WITHOUT YOU NOW — Skeeter Davis, RCA Victor 8347 | 5 |
| ★52 | 75 | — | — | I DON'T WANNA BE A LOSER — Lesley Gore, Mercury 72270 | 2 |
| 53 | 59 | 70 | 73 | GONNA GET ALONG WITHOUT YOU NOW — Tracey Dey, Amy 901 | 6 |
| 54 | 58 | 60 | 70 | I KNEW IT ALL THE TIME — Dave Clark Five, Congress 212 | 6 |
| 55 | 63 | 79 | — | WHAT'S THE MATTER WITH YOU BABY — Marvin Gaye & Mary Wells, Motown 1057 | 3 |
| 56 | 57 | 80 | 90 | ROCK ME BABY — B. B. King, Kent 393 | 4 |
| ★57 | 77 | 86 | 98 | TOO LATE TO TURN BACK NOW — Brook Benton, Mercury 72266 | 4 |
| 58 | 60 | 67 | 78 | ONE WAY LOVE — Drifters, Atlantic 2225 | 5 |
| 59 | 54 | 63 | 72 | HURT BY LOVE — Inez Foxx, Symbol 20-001 | 6 |
| 60 | 56 | 62 | 65 | TEA FOR TWO — Nino Tempo & April Stevens, Atco 6294 | 5 |
| 61 | 64 | 88 | — | ANOTHER CUP OF COFFEE — Brook Benton, Mercury 72266 | 3 |
| 62 | 67 | 74 | 74 | DONNIE — Bermudas, Era 3125 | 7 |
| 63 | 69 | 84 | — | PARTY GIRL — Bernadette Carroll, Laurie 3238 | 3 |
| 64 | 74 | 77 | 83 | YESTERDAY'S HERO — Gene Pitney, Musicor 1038 | 4 |
| 65 | 51 | 58 | 63 | SOUL SERENADE — King Curtis, Capitol 5109 | 12 |
| 66 | 70 | 81 | 94 | GIVING UP — Gladys Knight & the Pips, Maxx 326 | 4 |
| 67 | 78 | 82 | — | ONE GIRL — Garnet Mimms, United Artists 715 | 3 |
| 68 | 65 | 78 | 82 | THE LONELIEST NIGHT — Dale & Grace, Montel 928 | 5 |
| ★69 | — | — | — | DON'T THROW YOUR LOVE AWAY — Searchers, Kapp 593 | 1 |
| 70 | 61 | 69 | 79 | CAROL — Tommy Roe, ABC-Paramount 10543 | 6 |
| ★71 | — | — | — | BAD TO ME — Billy J. Kramer, Imperial 66027 | 1 |
| ★72 | 92 | — | — | YESTERDAY'S GONE — Chad Stuart & Jeremy Clyde, World Artists 1021 | 2 |
| 73 | 86 | 87 | — | THE FRENCH SONG — Lucille Starr, Almo 204 | 3 |
| ★74 | 89 | — | — | BEANS IN MY EARS — Serendipity Singers, Philips 40198 | 2 |
| 75 | 80 | 95 | — | THE WORLD OF LONELY PEOPLE — Anita Bryant, Columbia 43037 | 3 |
| 76 | 82 | 91 | 91 | WHAT HAVE I GOT OF MY OWN — Trini Lopez, Reprise 0276 | 4 |
| 77 | 73 | 73 | 75 | WINKIN', BLINKIN' AND NOD — Simon Sisters, Kapp 586 | 6 |
| ★78 | 100 | — | — | NO PARTICULAR PLACE TO GO — Chuck Berry, Chess 1898 | 2 |
| 79 | 88 | 90 | — | MILORD — Bobby Darin, Atco 6297 | 3 |
| ★80 | — | — | — | I'LL BE IN TROUBLE — Temptations, Gordy 7032 | 1 |
| 81 | 81 | 85 | 86 | FROM RUSSIA WITH LOVE — Village Stompers, Epic 9674 | 6 |
| 82 | 83 | 96 | 96 | NOT FADE AWAY — Rolling Stones, London 9657 | 5 |
| 83 | 84 | 97 | — | RULES OF LOVE — Orlons, Cameo 319 | 3 |
| ★84 | — | — | — | HICKORY, DICK AND DOC — Bobby Vee, Liberty 55700 | 1 |
| 85 | 95 | — | — | TELL ME MAMMA — Christine Quaite, World Artists 1022 | 2 |
| ★86 | — | 92 | 100 | WORLD WITHOUT LOVE — Bobby Rydell, Cameo 320 | 3 |
| 87 | 98 | — | — | YESTERDAY'S GONE — Overlanders, Hickory 1258 | 2 |
| ★88 | — | — | — | MEMPHIS — Johnny Rivers, Imperial 66032 | 1 |
| ★89 | — | — | — | THE WORLD I USED TO KNOW — Jimmie Rodgers, Dot 16595 | 1 |
| ★90 | — | — | — | BE MY GIRL — Four-Evers, Smash 1887 | 1 |
| 91 | 91 | 100 | — | TEQUILA — Bill Black's Combo, Hi 2077 | 3 |
| 92 | 93 | — | — | BEG ME — Chuck Jackson, Wand 154 | 2 |
| 93 | — | — | — | DON'T WORRY BABY — Beach Boys, Capitol 5174 | 1 |
| 94 | — | — | — | MY BABY DON'T DIG ME — Ray Charles, ABC-Paramount 10557 | 1 |
| 95 | — | — | — | I WANNA BE LOVED — Dean & Jean, Rust 5081 | 1 |
| 96 | — | — | — | THE FIRST NIGHT OF THE FULL MOON — Jack Jones, Kapp 589 | 1 |
| 97 | — | — | — | KICK THAT LITTLE FOOL, SALLY ANN — Round Robin, Domain 1404 | 1 |
| 98 | — | — | — | ACROSS THE STREET — Lenny O'Henry, Atco 6291 | 1 |
| 99 | — | — | — | LET'S HAVE A PARTY — Rivieras, Riviera 1402 | 1 |
| 100 | — | — | — | EVERYBODY KNOWS — Steve Lawrence, Columbia 43047 | 1 |

## HOT 100—A TO Z—(Publisher-Licensee)

- Across the Street (Saturday, ASCAP) .... 98
- Another Cup of Coffee (Peter Maurice, ASCAP) .... 61
- Bad to Me (Metric, BMI) .... 71
- Be Anything (But Be Mine) (Shapiro-Bernstein, ASCAP) .... 32
- Be My Girl (Elephant-Jonic, BMI) .... 9
- Beans in My Ears (Fall River, BMI) .... 74
- Beg Me (T. M., BMI) .... 92
- Bits and Pieces (Beechwood, BMI) .... 14
- Can't Buy Me Love (Northern, ASCAP) .... 42
- Carol (Arc, BMI) .... 70
- Chapel of Love (Trio, BMI) .... 2
- Cotton Candy (Gallico, BMI) .... 15
- Dead Man's Curve (Screen Gems-Columbia, BMI). 23
- Diane (Miller, ASCAP) .... 20
- Do You Love Me (Jobete, BMI) .... 12
- Do You Want to Know a Secret (Metric, BMI) .... 19
- Don't Let the Rain Come Down (Serendipity, BMI). 37
- Don't Let the Sun Catch You Crying (Pacemaker, BMI) .... 47
- Don't Throw Your Love Away (Wyncote, ASCAP) .. 69
- Don't Worry Baby (Sea of Tunes, BMI) .... 93
- Donnie (Rickland, BMI) .... 62
- Every Little Bit Hurts (Jobete, BMI) .... 17
- Everybody Knows (Gil, BMI) ....100
- First Night of the Full Moon, The (Famous, ASCAP) .... 96
- French Song, The (Irving-Doral, BMI) .... 73
- From Russia With Love (Unart, BMI) .... 81
- Giving Up (Trio, BMI) .... 66
- Gonna Get Along Without You Now—Davis (Reliance, ASCAP) .... 51
- Gonna Get Along Without You Now—Dey (Reliance, ASCAP) .... 53
- Good Golly Miss Molly (Venice, BMI) .... 46
- Goodbye Baby (Picturetone-Mellin, BMI) .... 36
- Hello, Dolly! (Morris, ASCAP) .... 5
- Hickory, Dick and Doc (Rose, BMI) .... 84
- Hurt by Love (Saturn, BMI) .... 59
- I Don't Wanna Be a Loser (Earth, BMI) .... 52
- I Don't Want to Be Hurt Anymore (Brogman, Vecco & Conn, ASCAP) .... 22
- I Get Around (Sea of Tunes, BMI) .... 45
- I Knew It All the Time (Gallico, BMI) .... 54
- I Rise, I Fall (Tod, ASCAP) .... 43
- I Wanna Be Loved (Famous, ASCAP) .... 95
- I'm So Proud (Curtom, BMI) .... 18
- I'll Be in Trouble (Jobete, BMI) .... 80
- I'll Touch a Star (Blen-Holly Hill-Lesjohn, ASCAP) .... 49
- It's Over (Acuff-Rose, BMI) .... 9
- (Just Like) Romeo & Juliet (Myto, BMI) .... 6
- Kick That Little Foot, Sally Ann (Screen Gems-Columbia, BMI) .... 97
- Kiss Me Quick (Presley, BMI) .... 34
- Let's Have a Party (Gladys, ASCAP) .... 99
- Little Children (Rumbalero, BMI) .... 8
- Loneliest Night, The (Acuff-Rose, BMI) .... 68
- Love Me Do (Ardmore-Beechwood, BMI) .... 1
- Love Me With All of Your Heart (Peer Int'l, BMI). 4
- Memphis (Arc, BMI) .... 88
- Milord (Alamo, ASCAP) .... 79
- My Baby Don't Dig Me (Tangerine, BMI) .... 94
- My Boy Lollipop (Nom, BMI) .... 48
- My Guy (Jobete, BMI) .... 3
- No Particular Place to Go (Berry, BMI) .... 78
- Not Fade Away (Nor Va Jak, BMI) .... 82
- Once Upon a Time (Jobete, BMI) .... 24
- One Girl (Mellin-Rittenhouse, BMI) .... 67
- One Way Love (Keetch, Caesar & Dino, BMI) .... 58
- P.S. I Love You (Beechwood, BMI) .... 11
- Party Girl (Schwartz, ASCAP) .... 63
- People (Chappell, ASCAP) .... 16
- Rock Me Baby (Modern, BMI) .... 56
- Ronnie (Saturday-Gavidina, ASCAP) .... 13
- Rules of Love (Kalmann, ASCAP) .... 83
- Shangri-La—Dana (Robbins, ASCAP) .... 44
- Shangri-La—Maxwell (Robbins, ASCAP) .... 25
- Soul Serenade (Kilynn-Vee Vee, BMI) .... 65
- Sugar and Spice (Duchess, BMI) .... 50
- Suspicion (Presley, BMI) .... 41
- Tall Cool One (C.F.G., BMI) .... 38
- Tea for Two (Harms, ASCAP) .... 60
- Tears and Roses (Davilene, BMI) .... 40
- Tell Me Mama (Unart, BMI) .... 85
- Tell Me Why (Signet, BMI) .... 30
- Tequila (Jat, BMI) .... 91
- Three Window Coupe (Screen Gems-Columbia, BMI). 31
- Today (Miller-Heritage House, ASCAP) .... 27
- Too Late to Turn Back Now (Play, BMI) .... 57
- Very Thought of You, The (Witmark, ASCAP) .... 26
- Viva Las Vegas (Presley, BMI) .... 33
- Walk On By (Blue Seas-Jac, ASCAP) .... 10
- What Have I Got of My Own (Sawtell-Herring, ASCAP) .... 76
- What'd I Say (Progressive, BMI) .... 29
- What's the Matter With You Baby (Jobete, BMI).. 55
- Whenever He Holds You (Unart, BMI) .... 39
- White on White (Painted Desert, BMI) .... 28
- Winkin', Blinkin' and Nod (Ryerson, BMI) .... 77
- Wish Someone Would Care (Metric, BMI) .... 21
- World I Used to Know, The (In, ASCAP) .... 89
- World of Lonely People, The (Ross Jungnickel, ASCAP) .... 75
- World Without Love, A—Peter Gordon (Northern, ASCAP) .... 7
- World Without Love, A—Rydell (Northern, ASCAP).. 86
- Wrong for Each Other (Valley, BMI) .... 35
- Yesterday's Gone—Overlanders (Unart, BMI) .... 87
- Yesterday's Gone—Stuart/Clyde (Unart, BMI) .... 72
- Yesterday's Hero (See-Lark, BMI) .... 64

## BUBBLING UNDER THE HOT 100

101. GOTTA GET AWAY ....Billy Butler & the Enchanters, Okeh 7192
102. I WISH YOU LOVE ....Gloria Lynne, Everest 2036
103. HAVE I STAYED AWAY TOO LONG ....Bobby Bare, RCA Victor 8358
104. SOMETH'NG YOU GOT ....Alvin Robinson, Tiger 104
105. THAT'S REALLY SOME GOOD ....Rufus & Carla, Stax 151
106. DREAM LOVER ....Paris Sisters, MGM 13236
107. SECURITY ....Otis Redding, Volt 117
108. SIE LIEBT DICH ....Die Beatles, Swan 4182
109. MY DREAMS ....Brenda Lee, Decca 31628
110. SWING ....Tokens, B.T. Puppy 500
111. GIRL FROM IPANEMA ....Getz/Gilberto, Verve 10323
112. JUST AIN'T ENOUGH LOVE ....Eddie Holland, Motown 158
113. JUST ONE LOOK ....Hollies, Imperial 66026
114. BLOWIN' IN THE WIND ....Stan Getz, Verve 10323
115. I ONLY HAVE EYES FOR YOU ....Cliff Richard, Epic 9670
116. THE COURT OF KING CARACTACUS ....Rolf Harris, Epic 9682
117. LITTLE TRACY ....Wynton Kelly, Verve 10316
118. BIG BOSS LINE ....Jackie Wilson, Brunswick 55266
119. PRECIOUS WORDS ....Wallace Brothers, Sims 174
120. CHOOSE ....Sammy Davis Jr., Reprise 0278
121. MY BABY WALKS ALL OVER ME ....Johnny Sea, Philips 40164
122. SPEND A LITTLE TIME ....Barbara Lewis, Atlantic 2227
123. GOOD TIMES ....Sam Cooke, RCA Victor 8368
124. BAD NEWS ....Trashmen, Garrett 4005
125. THE GIRLS ALRIGHT WITH ME ....Temptations, Gordy 7032
126. GOOD TIME TONIGHT ....Soul Sisters, Sue 10-005
127. HELP THE POOR ....B. B. King, ABC-Paramount 10552
128. DEVIL WITH THE BLUE DRESS ....Shorty Long, Soul 35001
129. FRENCH RIVIERA ....Webb Pierce, Decca 31617
130. YOU TAKE ONE STEP (I'll Take Two) ....Joe Henderson, Todd 1096
131. LET'S GO TOGETHER ....Raindrops, Jubilee 5475
132. IF I'M A FOOL FOR LOVING YOU ....Bobby Wood, Joy 285
133. FUGITIVE ....Ventures, Dolton 94
134. DANG ME ....Roger Miller, Smash 1881
135. I'M INTO SOMETHIN' GOOD ....Pearl-Jean, Colpix 729

Compiled from national retail sales and radio station airplay by the Music Popularity Dept. of Record Market Research. Billboard.

For Week Ending June 6, 1964

Billboard

# HOT 100

★ **STAR performer**—Sides registering greatest proportionate upward progress this week.

| This Week | 1 Wk. Ago | 2 Wks. Ago | 3 Wks. Ago | TITLE Artist, Label & Number | Weeks On Chart |
|---|---|---|---|---|---|
| 1 | 2 | 4 | 14 | CHAPEL OF LOVE — Dixie Cups, Red Bird 001 | 6 |
| 2 | 1 | 2 | 3 | LOVE ME DO — Beatles, Tollie 9008 | 9 |
| 3 | 3 | 1 | 1 | MY GUY — Mary Wells, Motown 1056 | 10 |
| 4 | 4 | 5 | 12 | LOVE ME WITH ALL YOUR HEART — Ray Charles Singers, Command 4046 | 9 |
| 5 | 5 | 3 | 2 | HELLO, DOLLY! — Louis Armstrong, Kapp 573 | 17 |
| 6 | 7 | 10 | 30 | WORLD WITHOUT LOVE, A — Peter & Gordon, Capitol 5175 | 5 |
| ★7 | 10 | 16 | 21 | WALK ON BY — Dionne Warwick, Scepter 1274 | 7 |
| 8 | 8 | 11 | 16 | LITTLE CHILDREN — Billy J. Kramer, Imperial 66027 | 8 |
| 9 | 6 | 7 | 13 | (Just Like) ROMEO & JULIET — Reflections, Golden World 9 | 9 |
| 10 | 11 | 15 | 33 | P.S. I LOVE YOU — Beatles, Tollie 9008 | 5 |
| 11 | 12 | 18 | 22 | DO YOU LOVE ME — Dave Clark Five, Epic 9678 | 6 |
| 12 | 16 | 26 | 47 | PEOPLE — Barbra Streisand, Columbia 42965 | 10 |
| 13 | 17 | 33 | 51 | EVERY LITTLE BIT HURTS — Brenda Holloway, Tamla 54094 | 6 |
| ★14 | 20 | 27 | 36 | DIANE — Bachelors, London 9639 | 8 |
| 15 | 15 | 22 | 23 | COTTON CANDY — Al Hirt, RCA Victor 8346 | 9 |
| 16 | 9 | 9 | 10 | IT'S OVER — Roy Orbison, Monument 837 | 9 |
| ★17 | 45 | 76 | — | I GET AROUND — Beach Boys, Capitol 5174 | 3 |
| ★18 | 27 | 35 | 37 | TODAY — New Christy Minstrels, Columbia 43000 | 8 |
| ★19 | 24 | 32 | 44 | ONCE UPON A TIME — Marvin Gaye & Mary Wells, Motown 1057 | 6 |
| ★20 | 30 | 68 | — | TELL ME WHY — Bobby Vinton, Epic 9687 | 3 |
| 21 | 18 | 14 | 18 | I'M SO PROUD — Impressions, ABC-Paramount 10544 | 10 |
| 22 | 22 | 25 | 35 | I DON'T WANT TO BE HURT ANY MORE — Nat King Cole, Capitol 5155 | 7 |
| 23 | 13 | 8 | 6 | RONNIE — 4 Seasons, Philips 40185 | 9 |
| ★24 | 29 | 50 | — | WHAT'D I SAY — Elvis Presley, RCA Victor 8360 | 3 |
| 25 | 14 | 6 | 4 | BITS AND PIECES — Dave Clark Five, Epic 9671 | 10 |
| ★26 | 47 | 87 | — | DON'T LET THE SUN CATCH YOU CRYING — Gerry & the Pacemakers, Laurie 3251 | 3 |
| ★27 | 48 | 90 | — | MY BOY LOLLIPOP — Millie Small, Smash 1893 | 3 |
| 28 | 31 | 39 | 45 | THREE WINDOW COUPE — Rip Chords, Columbia 43035 | 7 |
| 29 | 32 | 42 | 64 | BE ANYTHING (But Be Mine) — Connie Francis, MGM 13237 | 5 |
| ★30 | 40 | 52 | 76 | TEARS AND ROSES — Al Martino, Capitol 5183 | 4 |
| 31 | 23 | 13 | 8 | DEAD MAN'S CURVE — Jan & Dean, Liberty 55672 | 14 |
| 32 | 21 | 17 | 17 | WISH SOMEONE WOULD CARE — Irma Thomas, Imperial 66013 | 11 |
| 33 | 33 | 46 | 54 | VIVA LAS VEGAS — Elvis Presley, RCA Victor 8360 | 5 |
| 34 | 35 | 37 | 38 | WRONG FOR EACH OTHER — Andy Williams, Columbia 43015 | 8 |
| 35 | 36 | 36 | 48 | GOODBYE BABY (Baby Goodbye) — Solomon Burke, Atlantic 2226 | 8 |
| 36 | 19 | 12 | 5 | DO YOU WANT TO KNOW A SECRET — Beatles, Vee Jay 587 | 11 |
| 37 | 28 | 19 | 9 | WHITE ON WHITE — Danny Williams, United Artists 685 | 14 |
| ★38 | 49 | 79 | — | I'LL TOUCH A STAR — Terry Stafford, Crusader 105 | 3 |
| 39 | 26 | 28 | 32 | THE VERY THOUGHT OF YOU — Rick Nelson, Decca 31612 | 7 |
| 40 | 43 | 48 | 59 | I RISE, I FALL — Johnny Tillotson, MGM 13232 | 6 |
| 41 | 38 | 45 | 53 | TALL COOL ONE — Wailers, Golden Crest 518 | 9 |
| ★42 | 55 | 63 | 79 | WHAT'S THE MATTER WITH YOU BABY — Marvin Gaye & Mary Wells, Motown 1057 | 4 |
| ★43 | 78 | 100 | — | NO PARTICULAR PLACE TO GO — Chuck Berry, Chess 1898 | 3 |
| 44 | 46 | 53 | 71 | GOOD GOLLY MISS MOLLY — Swinging Blue Jeans, Imperial 66030 | 5 |
| ★45 | 56 | 57 | 80 | ROCK ME BABY — B. B. King, Kent 393 | 5 |
| 46 | 52 | 75 | — | I DON'T WANNA BE A LOSER — Lesley Gore, Mercury 72270 | 3 |
| 47 | 50 | 62 | 72 | SUGAR AND SPICE — Searchers, Liberty 55689 | 6 |
| 48 | 51 | 55 | 68 | GONNA GET ALONG WITHOUT YOU NOW — Skeeter Davis, RCA Victor 8347 | 6 |
| 49 | 25 | 21 | 15 | SHANGRI-LA — Robert Maxwell, His Harp & Ork, Decca 25622 | 12 |
| 50 | 34 | 34 | 43 | KISS ME QUICK — Elvis Presley, RCA Victor 0639 | 6 |
| 51 | 53 | 59 | 70 | GONNA GET ALONG WITHOUT YOU NOW — Tracey Dey, Amy 901 | 7 |
| 52 | 57 | 77 | 86 | TOO LATE TO TURN BACK NOW — Brook Benton, Mercury 72266 | 5 |
| 53 | 54 | 58 | 60 | I KNEW IT ALL THE TIME — Dave Clark Five, Congress 212 | 7 |
| ★54 | 69 | — | — | DON'T THROW YOUR LOVE AWAY — Searchers, Kapp 593 | 2 |
| 55 | 59 | 54 | 63 | HURT BY LOVE — Inez Foxx, Symbol 20-001 | 7 |
| 56 | 58 | 60 | 67 | ONE WAY LOVE — Drifters, Atlantic 2225 | 6 |
| 57 | 61 | 64 | 88 | ANOTHER CUP OF COFFEE — Brook Benton, Mercury 72266 | 4 |
| 58 | 66 | 70 | 81 | GIVING UP — Gladys Knight & the Pips, Maxx 326 | 5 |
| 59 | 39 | 40 | 46 | WHENEVER HE HOLDS YOU — Bobby Goldsboro, United Artists 710 | 8 |
| ★60 | 74 | 89 | — | BEANS IN MY EARS — Serendipity Singers, Philips 40198 | 3 |
| 61 | 71 | — | — | BAD TO ME — Billy J. Kramer, Imperial 66027 | 2 |
| 62 | 63 | 69 | 84 | PARTY GIRL — Bernadette Carroll, Laurie 3238 | 4 |
| ★63 | 88 | — | — | MEMPHIS — Johnny Rivers, Imperial 66032 | 2 |
| 64 | 72 | 92 | — | YESTERDAY'S GONE — Chad Stuart & Jeremy Clyde, World Artists 1021 | 3 |
| ★65 | 80 | — | — | I'LL BE IN TROUBLE — Temptations, Gordy 7032 | 2 |
| 66 | 62 | 67 | 74 | DONNIE — Bermudas, Era 3125 | 8 |
| 67 | 67 | 78 | 82 | ONE GIRL — Garnet Mimms, United Artists 715 | 4 |
| 68 | 79 | 88 | 90 | MILORD — Bobby Darin, Atco 6297 | 3 |
| 69 | 75 | 80 | 95 | THE WORLD OF LONELY PEOPLE — Anita Bryant, Columbia 43037 | 4 |
| 70 | 73 | 86 | 87 | THE FRENCH SONG — Lucille Starr, Almo 204 | 4 |
| 71 | 76 | 82 | 91 | WHAT HAVE I GOT OF MY OWN — Trini Lopez, Reprise 0276 | 5 |
| 72 | 64 | 74 | 77 | YESTERDAY'S HERO — Gene Pitney, Musicor 1038 | 5 |
| 73 | 83 | 84 | 97 | RULES OF LOVE — Orlons, Cameo 319 | 4 |
| ★74 | 93 | — | — | DON'T WORRY BABY — Beach Boys, Capitol 5174 | 2 |
| ★75 | 94 | — | — | MY BABY DON'T DIG ME — Ray Charles, ABC-Paramount 10557 | 2 |
| ★76 | 92 | 83 | — | BEG ME — Chuck Jackson, Wand 154 | 3 |
| ★77 | — | — | — | GOOD TIMES — Sam Cooke, RCA Victor 8368 | 1 |
| ★78 | 100 | — | — | EVERYBODY KNOWS — Steve Lawrence, Columbia 43047 | 2 |
| ★79 | — | 85 | 89 | KIKO — Jimmy McGriff, Sue 10-001 | 3 |
| 80 | 86 | — | 92 | WORLD WITHOUT LOVE, A — Bobby Rydell, Cameo 320 | 4 |
| 81 | 84 | — | — | HICKORY, DICK AND DOC — Bobby Vee, Liberty 55700 | 2 |
| 82 | 82 | 83 | 96 | NOT FADE AWAY — Rolling Stones, London 9657 | 6 |
| ★83 | — | 99 | — | JUST AIN'T ENOUGH LOVE — Eddie Holland, Motown 1058 | 2 |
| 84 | 87 | 98 | — | YESTERDAY'S GONE — Overlanders, Hickory 1258 | 3 |
| ★85 | — | — | — | KEEP ON PUSHING — Impressions, ABC-Paramount 10554 | 1 |
| 86 | 89 | — | — | THE WORLD I USED TO KNOW — Jimmie Rodgers, Dot 16595 | 2 |
| ★87 | — | — | — | THE GIRL FROM IPANEMA — Getz/Gilberto, Verve 10323 | 1 |
| 88 | 90 | — | — | BE MY GIRL — Four-Evers, Smash 1887 | 2 |
| ★89 | — | — | — | IT AIN'T NO USE — Major Lance, Okeh 7197 | 1 |
| ★90 | — | — | — | SOMETHING YOU GOT — Alvin Robinson, Tiger 104 | 1 |
| 91 | 96 | — | — | THE FIRST NIGHT OF THE FULL MOON — Jack Jones, Kapp 589 | 2 |
| 92 | — | — | — | THAT'S REALLY SOME GOOD — Rufus & Carla, Stax 151 | 1 |
| 93 | 95 | — | — | I WANNA BE LOVED — Dean & Jean, Rust 5081 | 2 |
| 94 | — | — | — | REMEMBER ME — Rita Pavone, RCA Victor 8365 | 1 |
| 95 | 97 | — | — | KICK THAT LITTLE FOOT, SALLY ANN — Round Robin, Domain 1404 | 2 |
| 96 | — | — | — | MY DREAMS — Brenda Lee, Decca 31628 | 1 |
| 97 | — | — | — | LAZY ELSIE MOLLY — Chubby Checker, Parkway 920 | 1 |
| 98 | — | — | — | ALONE — Four Seasons, Vee Jay 597 | 1 |
| 99 | — | — | — | TROUBLE I'VE HAD — Clarence Ashe, Chess 1896 | 1 |
| 100 | — | — | — | TRY IT BABY — Marvin Gaye, Tamla 54095 | 1 |

## HOT 100—A TO Z—*(Publisher-Licensee)*


Alone (Selma, BMI) ... 98
Another Cup of Coffee (Peter Maurice, ASCAP) ... 57
Bad to Me (Metric, BMI) ... 61
Be Anything (But Be Mine) (Shapiro-Bernstein, ASCAP) ... 29
Be My Girl (Elephant-Jonic, BMI) ... 88
Beans in My Ears (Fall River, BMI) ... 60
Beg Me (T.M., BMI) ... 76
Bits and Pieces (Beechwood, BMI) ... 25
Chapel of Love (Trio, BMI) ... 1
Cotton Candy (Gallico, BMI) ... 15
Dead Man's Curve (Screen Gems-Columbia, BMI) ... 31
Diane (Miller, ASCAP) ... 14
Do You Love Me (Jobete, BMI) ... 11
Do You Want to Know a Secret (Metric, BMI) ... 36
Don't Let the Sun Catch You Crying (Pacemaker, BMI) ... 26
Don't Throw Your Love Away (Wyncote, ASCAP) ... 54
Don't Worry Baby (Sea of Tunes, BMI) ... 74
Donnie (Rickland, BMI) ... 66
Every Little Bit Hurts (Jobete, BMI) ... 13
Everybody Knows (Gil, BMI) ... 78
First Night of the Full Moon, The (Famous, ASCAP) ... 91
French Song, The (Irving-Doral, BMI) ... 70
Girl From Ipanema, The (Duchess, BMI) ... 87
Giving Up (Trio, BMI) ... 58
Gonna Get Along Without You Now—Davis (Reliance, ASCAP) ... 48
Gonna Get Along Without You Now—Dey Reliance, ASCAP) ... 51
Good Golly Miss Molly (Venice, BMI) ... 44
Good Times (Kags, BMI) ... 77
Goodbye Baby (Picturetone-Mellin, BMI) ... 35
Hello, Dolly! (Morris, ASCAP) ... 5
Hickory, Dick and Doc (Rose, BMI) ... 81
Hurt by Love (Saturn, BMI) ... 55
I Don't Wanna Be a Loser (Earth, BMI) ... 46
I Don't Want to Be Hurt Any More (Bregman, Vocco & Conn, ASCAP) ... 22
I Get Around (Sea of Tunes, BMI) ... 17
I Knew It All the Time (Gallico, BMI) ... 53
I Rise, I Fall (Tod, ASCAP) ... 40
I Wanna Be Loved (Famous, ASCAP) ... 93
I'm So Proud (Curtom, BMI) ... 21
I'll Be in Trouble (Jobete, BMI) ... 65
I'll Touch a Star (Blen-Holly Hill-Lesjohn, ASCAP) 38
It Ain't No Use (Curtom-Jalynne, BMI) ... 89
It's Over (Acuff-Rose, BMI) ... 16
Just Ain't Enough Love (Jobete, BMI) ... 83
(Just Like) Juliet & Romeo (Myto, BMI) ... 9
Kick That Little Foot, Sally Ann (Screen Gems-Columbia, BMI) ... 95
Kiko (Saturn-Renner-Jell, BMI) ... 83
Kiss Me Quick (Presley, BMI) ... 50
Lazy Elsie Molly (Evanston-Picturetone, BMI) ... 97
Little Children (Rumbalero, BMI) ... 8
Love Me Do (Ardmore-Beechwood, BMI) ... 2
Love Me With All of Your Heart (Peer Int'l, BMI) 4
Memphis (Arc, BMI) ... 63
Milord (Alamo, ASCAP) ... 68
My Baby Don't Dig Me (Tangerine, BMI) ... 75
My Boy Lollipop (Nom, BMI) ... 27
My Dreams (Fame, BMI) ... 96
My Guy (Jobete, BMI) ... 3
No Particular Place to Go (Arc, BMI) ... 43
Not Fade Away (Nor Va Jak, BMI) ... 82
Once Upon a Time (Jobete, BMI) ... 19
One Girl (Mellin-Rittenhouse, BMI) ... 67
One Way Love (Keetch, Caesar & Dino, BMI) ... 56
P.S. I Love You (Beechwood, BMI) ... 10
Party Girl (Schwartz, ASCAP) ... 62
People (Chappell, ASCAP) ... 12
Remember Me (Gil, BMI) ... 94
Rock Me Baby (Modern, BMI) ... 45
Ronnie (Saturday-Gavidina, ASCAP) ... 23
Rules of Love (Kalman, ASCAP) ... 73
Shangri-La (Robbins, ASCAP) ... 49
Something You Got (Tune Kel, BMI) ... 90
Sugar and Spice (Duchess, BMI) ... 47
Tall Cool One (C.F.G., BMI) ... 41
Tears and Roses (Davilene, BMI) ... 30
Tell Me Why (Signet, BMI) ... 20
That's Really Some Good (East, BMI) ... 92
Three Window Coupe (Screen Gems-Columbia, BMI) 28
Try It Baby (Jobete, BMI) ... 100
Today (Miller-Heritage House, ASCAP) ... 18
Too Late to Turn Back Now (Play, BMI) ... 52
Trouble I've Had (Zell's, BMI) ... 99
Very Thought of You, The (Witmark, ASCAP) ... 39
Viva Las Vegas (Presley, BMI) ... 33
Walk on By (Blue Seas-Jac, ASCAP) ... 7
What Have I Got of My Own (Sawtell-Herring, ASCAP) ... 71
What'd I Say (Progressive, BMI) ... 24
What's the Matter With You Baby (Jobete, BMI) .. 42
Whenever He Holds You (Unart, BMI) ... 59
White on White (Painted Desert, BMI) ... 37
Wish Someone Would Care (Metric, BMI) ... 32
World I Used to Know, The (In, ASCAP) ... 86
World of Lonely People, The (Ross Jungnickel, ASCAP) ... 69
World Without Love, A—Peter & Gordon (Northern, ASCAP) ... 6
World Without Love, A—Rydell (Northern, ASCAP) 80
Wrong for Each Other (Valley, BMI) ... 34
Yesterday's Gone—Overlanders (Unart, BMI) ... 84
Yesterday's Gone—Stuart-Clyde (Unart, BMI) ... 64
Yesterday's Hero (See-Lark, BMI) ... 72


## BUBBLING UNDER THE HOT 100

101. ALONE WITH YOU ... Brenda Lee, Decca 31628
102. I WISH YOU LOVE ... Gloria Lynne, Everest 2036
103. DREAM LOVER ... Paris Sisters, MGM 13236
104. SECURITY ... Otis Redding, Volt 117
105. FOUR BY THE BEATLES ... Capitol EAP 1-2121 (Extended Play)
106. TENNESSEE WALTZ ... Sam Cooke, RCA Victor 8368
107. BIG BOSS LINE ... Jackie Wilson, Brunswick 55266
108. SIE LIEBT DICH (She Love You) ... Die Beatles, Swan 4182
109. THE GIRL'S ALRIGHT WITH ME ... Temptations, Gordy 7032
110. A LITTLE TOY BALLOON ... Danny Williams, United Artists 729
111. TELL ME MAMMA ... Christine Quaite, World Artists 1022
112. GOTTA GET AWAY ... Billy Butler & the Enchanters, Okeh 7192
113. LITTLE TRACY ... Wynton Kelly, Verve 10316
114. CHOOSE ... Sammy Davis Jr., Reprise 0278
115. PRECIOUS WORDS ... Wallace Brothers, Sims 174
116. BLOWIN' IN THE WIND ... Stan Getz, Verve 10323
117. TEQUILA ... Bill Black's Combo, Hi 2077
118. RAUNCHY ... Bill Black's Combo, Hi 2077
119. WISHIN' AND HOPIN' ... Dusty Springfield, Philips 40207
120. SPEND A LITTLE TIME ... Barbara Lewis, Atlantic 2227
121. SOULVILLE ... Aretha Franklin, Columbia 43009
122. IT'S ALL OVER NOW ... Valentinos, Sar 152
123. QUIET PLACE ... Garnet Mimms, United Artists 715
124. GOOD TIME TONIGHT ... Soul Sisters, Sue 10-005
125. HELP THE POOR ... B. B. King, ABC-Paramount 10552
126. DANG ME ... Roger Miller, Smash 1881
127. DEVIL IN THE BLUE DRESS ... Shorty Long, Soul 35001
128. YOU TAKE ONE STEP (I'll Take Two) ... Joe Henderson, Todd 1096
129. I DON'T WANT TO HEAR ANYMORE ... Jerry Butler, Vee Jay 598
130. LET'S GO TOGETHER ... Raindrops, Jubilee 5475
131. IF I'M A FOOL FOR LOVING YOU ... Bobby Wood, Joy 285
132. THE MAGIC OF OUR SUMMER LOVE ... Tymes, Parkway 919
133. RUN LITTLE GIRL ... Donnie Elbert, Gateway 731
134. HOW LONG DARLING ... James Brown & the Famous Flames, King 5876
135. TELL ME WHEN ... Applejacks, London 9658

Compiled from national retail sales and radio station airplay by the Music Popularity Dept. of Record Market Research, Billboard.

For Week Ending June 13, 1964

# Billboard HOT 100

★ STAR performer—Sides registering greatest proportionate upward progress this week.

Billboard Award

| This Week | 1 Wk. Ago | 2 Wks. Ago | 3 Wks. Ago | TITLE Artist, Label & Number | Weeks On Chart |
|---|---|---|---|---|---|
| 1 | 1 | 2 | 4 | CHAPEL OF LOVE — Dixie Cups, Red Bird 001 | 7 |
| ★ 2 | 6 | 7 | 10 | A WORLD WITHOUT LOVE — Peter & Gordon, Capitol 5175 | 6 |
| 3 | 4 | 4 | 5 | LOVE ME WITH ALL YOUR HEART — Ray Charles Singers, Command 4046 | 10 |
| 4 | 2 | 1 | 2 | LOVE ME DO — Beatles, Tollie 9008 | 10 |
| 5 | 3 | 3 | 1 | MY GUY — Mary Wells, Motown 1056 | 11 |
| 6 | 7 | 10 | 16 | WALK ON BY — Dionne Warwick, Scepter 1274 | 8 |
| 7 | 8 | 8 | 11 | LITTLE CHILDREN — Billy J. Kramer, Imperial 66027 | 9 |
| 8 | 5 | 5 | 3 | HELLO, DOLLY! — Louis Armstrong, Kapp 573 | 18 |
| ★ 9 | 12 | 16 | 26 | PEOPLE — Barbra Streisand, Columbia 42965 | 11 |
| ★ 10 | 17 | 45 | 76 | I GET AROUND — Beach Boys, Capitol 5174 | 4 |
| 11 | 14 | 20 | 27 | DIANE — Bachelors, London 9639 | 9 |
| 12 | 9 | 6 | 7 | (Just Like) ROMEO & JULIET — Reflections, Golden World 9 | 10 |
| 13 | 13 | 17 | 33 | EVERY LITTLE BIT HURTS — Brenda Holloway, Tamla 54094 | 7 |
| 14 | 11 | 12 | 18 | DO YOU LOVE ME — Dave Clark Five, Epic 9678 | 7 |
| 15 | 10 | 11 | 15 | P.S. I LOVE YOU — Beatles, Tollie 9008 | 6 |
| ★ 16 | 27 | 48 | 90 | MY BOY LOLLIPOP — Millie Small, Smash 1893 | 4 |
| 17 | 20 | 30 | 68 | TELL ME WHY — Bobby Vinton, Epic 9687 | 4 |
| 18 | 18 | 27 | 35 | TODAY — New Christy Minstrels, Columbia 43000 | 9 |
| 19 | 19 | 24 | 32 | ONCE UPON A TIME — Marvin Gaye & Mary Wells, Motown 1057 | 7 |
| ★ 20 | 26 | 47 | 87 | DON'T LET THE SUN CATCH YOU CRYING — Gerry & the Pacemakers, Laurie 3251 | 4 |
| 21 | 24 | 29 | 50 | WHAT'D I SAY — Elvis Presley, RCA Victor 8360 | 4 |
| 22 | 15 | 15 | 22 | COTTON CANDY — Al Hirt, RCA Victor 8346 | 10 |
| 23 | 16 | 9 | 9 | IT'S OVER — Roy Orbison, Monument 837 | 10 |
| ★ 24 | 30 | 40 | 52 | TEARS AND ROSES — Al Martino, Capitol 5183 | 5 |
| 25 | 29 | 32 | 42 | BE ANYTHING (But Be Mine) — Connie Francis, MGM 13237 | 6 |
| ★ 26 | 61 | 71 | — | BAD TO ME — Billy J. Kramer, Imperial 66027 | 3 |
| 27 | 22 | 22 | 25 | I DON'T WANT TO BE HURT ANY MORE — Nat King Cole, Capitol 5155 | 8 |
| 28 | 28 | 31 | 39 | THREE WINDOW COUPE — Rip Chords, Columbia 43035 | 8 |
| 29 | 33 | 33 | 46 | VIVA LAS VEGAS — Elvis Presley, RCA Victor 8360 | 6 |
| ★ 30 | 43 | 78 | 100 | NO PARTICULAR PLACE TO GO — Chuck Berry, Chess 1898 | 4 |
| ★ 31 | 63 | 88 | — | MEMPHIS — Johnny Rivers, Imperial 66032 | 3 |
| 32 | 38 | 49 | 79 | I'LL TOUCH A STAR — Terry Stafford, Crusader 105 | 4 |
| 33 | 35 | 36 | 36 | GOODBYE BABY (Baby Goodbye) — Solomon Burke, Atlantic 2226 | 9 |
| 34 | 42 | 55 | 63 | WHAT'S THE MATTER WITH YOU BABY — Marvin Gaye & Mary Wells, Motown 1057 | 5 |
| ★ 35 | 64 | 72 | 92 | YESTERDAY'S GONE — Chad Stuart & Jeremy Clyde, World Artists 1021 | 4 |
| 36 | 40 | 43 | 48 | I RISE, I FALL — Johnny Tillotson, MGM 13232 | 7 |
| 37 | 45 | 56 | 57 | ROCK ME BABY — B. B. King, Kent 393 | 6 |
| 38 | 25 | 14 | 6 | BITS AND PIECES — Dave Clark Five, Epic 9671 | 11 |
| ★ 39 | 60 | 74 | 89 | BEANS IN MY EARS — Serendipity Singers, Philips 40198 | 4 |
| 40 | 21 | 18 | 14 | I'M SO PROUD — Impressions, ABC-Paramount 10544 | 11 |
| ★ 41 | 54 | 69 | — | DON'T THROW YOUR LOVE AWAY — Searchers, Kapp 593 | 3 |
| 42 | 46 | 52 | 75 | I DON'T WANNA BE A LOSER — Lesley Gore, Mercury 72270 | 4 |
| 43 | 44 | 46 | 53 | GOOD GOLLY MISS MOLLY — Swinging Blue Jeans, Imperial 66030 | 6 |
| 44 | 47 | 50 | 62 | SUGAR AND SPICE — Searchers, Liberty 55689 | 7 |
| 45 | 23 | 13 | 8 | RONNIE — 4 Seasons, Philips 40185 | 10 |
| 46 | 32 | 21 | 17 | WISH SOMEONE WOULD CARE — Irma Thomas, Imperial 66013 | 12 |
| 47 | 34 | 35 | 37 | WRONG FOR EACH OTHER — Andy Williams, Columbia 43015 | 9 |
| 48 | 41 | 38 | 45 | TALL COOL ONE — Wailers, Golden Crest 518 | 10 |
| 49 | 52 | 57 | 77 | TOO LATE TO TURN BACK NOW — Brook Benton, Mercury 72266 | 6 |
| 50 | 58 | 66 | 70 | GIVING UP — Gladys Knight & the Pips, Maxx 326 | 6 |
| 51 | 57 | 61 | 64 | ANOTHER CUP OF COFFEE — Brook Benton, Mercury 72266 | 5 |
| 52 | 48 | 51 | 55 | GONNA GET ALONG WITHOUT YOU NOW — Skeeter Davis, RCA Victor 8347 | 7 |
| ★ 53 | 74 | 93 | — | DON'T WORRY BABY — Beach Boys, Capitol 5174 | 3 |
| 54 | 51 | 53 | 59 | GONNA GET ALONG WITHOUT YOU NOW — Tracey Dey, Amy 901 | 8 |
| 55 | 55 | 59 | 54 | HURT BY LOVE — Inez Foxx, Symbol 20-001 | 8 |
| 56 | 62 | 63 | 69 | PARTY GIRL — Bernadette Carroll, Laurie 3238 | 5 |
| 57 | 65 | 80 | — | I'LL BE IN TROUBLE — Temptations, Gordy 7032 | 3 |
| ★ 58 | 70 | 73 | 86 | THE FRENCH SONG — Lucille Starr, Almo 204 | 5 |
| 59 | 53 | 54 | 58 | I KNEW IT ALL THE TIME — Dave Clark Five, Congress 212 | 8 |
| 60 | 69 | 75 | 80 | THE WORLD OF LONELY PEOPLE — Anita Bryant, Columbia 43037 | 5 |
| ★ 61 | 87 | — | — | THE GIRL FROM IPANEMA — Getz/Gilberto, Verve 10323 | 2 |
| ★ 62 | 77 | — | — | GOOD TIMES — Sam Cooke, RCA Victor 8368 | 2 |
| 63 | 68 | 79 | 88 | MILORD — Bobby Darin, Atco 6297 | 4 |
| 64 | 66 | 62 | 67 | DONNIE — Bermudas, Era 3125 | 9 |
| 65 | 75 | 94 | — | MY BABY DON'T DIG ME — Ray Charles, ABC-Paramount 10557 | 3 |
| 66 | 71 | 76 | 82 | WHAT HAVE I GOT OF MY OWN — Trini Lopez, Reprise 0276 | 6 |
| 67 | 73 | 83 | 84 | RULES OF LOVE — Orlons, Cameo 319 | 5 |
| ★ 68 | — | — | — | CAN'T YOU SEE THAT SHE'S MINE — Dave Clark Five, Epic 9692 | 1 |
| ★ 69 | 100 | — | — | TRY IT BABY — Marvin Gaye, Tamla 54095 | 2 |
| ★ 70 | 85 | — | — | KEEP ON PUSHING — Impressions, ABC-Paramount 10554 | 2 |
| 71 | 56 | 58 | 60 | ONE WAY LOVE — Drifters, Atlantic 2225 | 7 |
| 72 | 76 | 92 | 93 | BEG ME — Chuck Jackson, Wand 154 | 4 |
| 73 | 78 | 100 | — | EVERYBODY KNOWS — Steve Lawrence, Columbia 43047 | 3 |
| ★ 74 | — | — | — | TENNESSEE WALTZ — Sam Cooke, RCA Victor 8368 | 1 |
| 75 | 88 | 90 | — | BE MY GIRL — Four-Evers, Smash 1887 | 3 |
| 76 | 81 | 84 | — | HICKORY, DICK AND DOC — Bobby Vee, Liberty 55700 | 3 |
| ★ 77 | 94 | — | — | REMEMBER ME — Rita Pavone, RCA Victor 8365 | 2 |
| 78 | 82 | 82 | 83 | NOT FADE AWAY — Rolling Stones, London 9657 | 7 |
| 79 | 79 | — | 85 | KIKO — Jimmy McGriff, Sue 10-001 | 4 |
| 80 | 83 | — | 99 | JUST AIN'T ENOUGH LOVE — Eddie Holland, Motown 1058 | 3 |
| 81 | 84 | 87 | 98 | YESTERDAY'S GONE — Overlanders, Hickory 1258 | 4 |
| ★ 82 | 97 | — | — | LAZY ELSIE MOLLY — Chubby Checker, Parkway 920 | 2 |
| ★ 83 | 98 | — | — | ALONE — Four Seasons, Vee Jay 597 | 2 |
| 84 | 86 | 89 | — | THE WORLD I USED TO KNOW — Jimmie Rodgers, Dot 16595 | 3 |
| ★ 85 | — | — | — | ALONE WITH YOU — Brenda Lee, Decca 31628 | 1 |
| 86 | 89 | — | — | IT AIN'T NO USE — Major Lance, Okeh 7197 | 2 |
| 87 | 80 | 86 | — | A WORLD WITHOUT LOVE — Bobby Rydell, Cameo 320 | 5 |
| 88 | 90 | — | — | SOMETHING YOU GOT — Alvin Robinson, Tiger 104 | 2 |
| ★ 89 | — | — | — | SHARE YOUR LOVE WITH ME — Bobby Bland, Duke 377 | 1 |
| ★ 90 | — | — | — | HEY HARMONICA MAN — Stevie Wonder, Tamla 54096 | 1 |
| 91 | 91 | 96 | — | THE FIRST NIGHT OF THE FULL MOON — Jack Jones, Kapp 589 | 3 |
| 92 | 92 | — | — | THAT'S REALLY SOME GOOD — Rufus & Carla, Stax 151 | 2 |
| 93 | 93 | 95 | — | I WANNA BE LOVED — Dean & Jean, Rust 5081 | 3 |
| 94 | — | — | — | DANG ME — Roger Miller, Smash 1881 | 1 |
| 95 | 95 | 97 | — | KICK THAT LITTLE FOOT, SALLY ANN — Round Robin, Domain 1404 | 3 |
| 96 | 96 | — | — | MY DREAMS — Brenda Lee, Decca 31628 | 2 |
| 97 | — | — | — | FOUR BY THE BEATLES — Capitol EAP 1-2121 (Extended Play) | 1 |
| 98 | — | — | — | GOOD TIME TONIGHT — Soul Sisters, Sue 10-005 | 1 |
| 99 | — | — | — | THE MAGIC OF OUR SUMMER LOVE — Tymes, Parkway 919 | 1 |
| 100 | — | — | — | DREAM LOVER — Paris Sisters, MGM 13236 | 1 |

## HOT 100—A TO Z—(Publisher-Licensee)


Alone (Selma, BMI) .... 83
Alone With You (Metric, BMI) .... 85
Another Cup of Coffee (Peter Maurice, ASCAP) .... 51
Bad to Me (Metric, BMI) .... 26
Be Anything (But Be Mine) (Shapiro-Bernstein, ASCAP) .... 25
Be My Girl (Elephant-Jonic, BMI) .... 75
Beans in My Ears (Fall River, BMI) .... 39
Beg Me (T.M., BMI) .... 72
Bits and Pieces (Beechwood, BMI) .... 38
Can't You See That She's Mine (Beechwood, BMI) .... 68
Chapel of Love (Trio, BMI) .... 1
Cotton Candy (Gallico, BMI) .... 22
Dang Me (Tree, BMI) .... 94
Diane (Miller, ASCAP) .... 11
Do You Love Me (Jobete, BMI) .... 14
Don't Let the Sun Catch You Crying (Pacemaker, BMI) .... 20
Don't Throw Your Love Away (Wyncote, ASCAP) .... 41
Don't Worry Baby (Sea of Tunes, BMI) .... 53
Donnie (Rickland, BMI) .... 64
Dream Lover (Screen Gems-Columbia & T.M., BMI) .... 100
Every Little Bit Hurts (Jobete, BMI) .... 13
Everybody Knows (Gil, BMI) .... 73
First Night of the Full Moon (Famous, ASCAP) .... 91
Four By the Beatles (Various Publishers) .... 97
French Song, The (Irving-Doral, BMI) .... 58
Girl From Ipanema, The (Duchess, BMI) .... 61
Giving Up (Trio, BMI) .... 50
Gonna Get Along Without You Now—Davis (Reliance, ASCAP) .... 52
Gonna Get Along Without You Now—Dey (Reliance, ASCAP) .... 54
Good Golly Miss Molly (Venice, BMI) .... 43
Good Time Tonight (Saturn, BMI) .... 98
Good Times (Kags, BMI) .... 62
Goodbye Baby (Picturetone-Mellin, BMI) .... 33
Hello, Dolly! (Morris, ASCAP) .... 8
Hey Harmonica Man (Jobete-Little Darlin', BMI) .... 90
Hickory, Dick and Doc (Rose, BMI) .... 76
Hurt By Love (Saturn, BMI) .... 55
I Don't Wanna Be a Loser (Earth, BMI) .... 42
I Don't Want to Be Hurt Any More (Bregman, Vocco & Conn, ASCAP) .... 27
I Get Around (Sea of Tunes, BMI) .... 10
I Knew It All the Time (Gallico, BMI) .... 59
I Rise, I Fall (Ted, ASCAP) .... 36
I Wanna Be Loved (Famous, ASCAP) .... 93
I'm So Proud (Curtom, BMI) .... 40
I'll Be in Trouble (Jobete, BMI) .... 57
I'll Touch a Star (Blen-Holly Hill-Lesjohn, ASCAP) .... 32
It Ain't No Use (Curtom-Jalynne, BMI) .... 86
It's Over (Acuff-Rose, BMI) .... 23
Just Ain't Enough Love (Jobete, BMI) .... 80
(Just Like) Romeo & Juliet (Myto, BMI) .... 12
Keep on Pushing (Curtom, BMI) .... 70
Kick That Little Foot, Sally Ann (Screen Gems-Columbia, BMI) .... 95
Kiko (Saturn-Renner-Jell, BMI) .... 79
Lazy Elsie Molly (Evanston-Picturetone, BMI) .... 82
Little Children (Rumbalero, BMI) .... 7
Love Me Do (Ardmore-Beechwood, BMI) .... 4
Love Me With All Your Heart (Peer Int'l, BMI) .... 3
Magic of Our Summer Love, The (Wyncote, ASCAP) .... 99
Memphis (Arc, BMI) .... 31
Milord (Alamo, ASCAP) .... 63
My Baby Don't Dig Me (Tangerine, BMI) .... 65
My Boy Lollipop (Nom, BMI) .... 16
My Dreams (Fame, BMI) .... 96
My Guy (Jobete, BMI) .... 5
No Particular Place to Go (Arc, BMI) .... 30
Not Fade Away (Nor Va Jak, BMI) .... 78
Once Upon a Time (Jobete, BMI) .... 19
One Way Love (Keetch, Caesar & Dino, BMI) .... 71
P.S. I Love You (Beechwood, BMI) .... 15
Party Girl (Schwartz, ASCAP) .... 56
People (Chappell, ASCAP) .... 9
Remember Me (Gil, BMI) .... 77
Rock Me Baby (Modern, BMI) .... 37
Ronnie (Saturday-Gavidima, ASCAP) .... 45
Rules of Love (Kalmann, ASCAP) .... 67
Share Your Love With Me (Don, BMI) .... 89
Something You Got (Tune Kel, BMI) .... 88
Sugar and Spice (Duchess, BMI) .... 44
Tall Cool One (C.F.G., BMI) .... 48
Tears and Roses (Davilene, BMI) .... 24
Tell Me Why (Signet, BMI) .... 17
Tennessee Waltz (Acuff-Rose, BMI) .... 74
That's Really Some Good (East, BMI) .... 92
Three Window Coupe (Screen Gems-Columbia, BMI) .... 28
Try It Baby (Jobete, BMI) .... 69
Today (Miller-Heritage House, ASCAP) .... 18
Too Late to Turn Back Now (Play, BMI) .... 49
Viva Las Vegas (Presley, BMI) .... 29
Walk on By (Blue Seas-Jac, ASCAP) .... 6
What Have I Got of My Own (Sawtell-Herring, ASCAP) .... 66
What'd I Say (Progressive, BMI) .... 21
What's the Matter With You Baby (Jobete, BMI) .... 34
Wish Someone Would Care (Metric, BMI) .... 46
World I Used to Know, The (In, ASCAP) .... 84
World of Lonely People, The (Ross Jungnickel, ASCAP) .... 60
World Without Love, A—Peter & Gordon (Northern, ASCAP) .... 2
World Without Love, A—Rydell (Northern, ASCAP) .... 87
Wrong for Each Other (Valley, BMI) .... 47
Yesterday's Gone—Overlanders (Unart, BMI) .... 81
Yesterday's Gone—Stuart/Clyde (Unart, BMI) .... 35


## BUBBLING UNDER THE HOT 100

101. WISHIN' AND HOPIN' — Dusty Springfield, Philips 40207
102. SIE LIEBT DICH (She Loves You) — Die Beatles, Swan 4182
103. TROUBLE I'VE HAD — Clarence Ashe, Chess 1896
104. SECURITY — Otis Redding, Volt 117
105. A LITTLE TOY BALLOON — Danny Williams, United Artists 729
106. TELL ME MAMMA — Christine Quaite, World Artists 1022
107. I STILL GET JEALOUS — Louis Armstrong, Kapp 597
108. OH, ROCK MY SOUL — Peter, Paul & Mary, Warner Bros. 5442
109. LET'S GO TOGETHER — Raindrops, Jubilee 5475
110. THE THINGS THAT I USED TO DO — James Brown, Smash 1908
111. AFTER IT'S TOO LATE — Bobby Bland, Duke 377
112. CHOOSE — Sammy Davis Jr., Reprise 0278
113. PRECIOUS WORDS — Wallace Brothers, Sims 174
114. FARMER JOHN — Premiers, Warner Bros. 5443
115. I WISH YOU LOVE — Gloria Lynne, Everest 2036
116. BEACHCOMBER — Johnny Gibson Trio, Laurie 3256
117. HELP THE POOR — B. B. King, ABC-Paramount 10552
118. I DON'T WANT TO HEAR ANYMORE — Jerry Butler, Vee Jay 598
119. SPEND A LITTLE TIME — Barbara Lewis, Atlantic 2227
120. THE GIRL'S ALRIGHT WITH ME — Temptations, Gordy 7032
121. GOTTA GET AWAY — Billy Butler & the Enchanters, Okeh 7192
122. MIXED-UP, SHOOK-UP, GIRL — Patty & the Emblems, Herald 590
123. MY KIND OF TOWN — Frank Sinatra, Reprise 0279
124. NIGHT TIME IS THE RIGHT TIME — Rufus & Carla, Stax 151
125. IT WILL STAND — Showmen, Imperial 66033
126. FRENCH RIVIERA — Webb Pierce, Decca 31617
127. DEVIL WITH THE BLUE DRESS — Shorty Long, Soul 35001
128. IT'S ALL OVER NOW — Valentinos, Sar 152
129. SHE'S MY GIRL — Bobby Shafto, Rust 5082
130. RUN LITTLE GIRL — Donnie Elbert, Gateway 731
131. BIG PARTY — Barbara & the Browns, Stax 150
132. LONG LONELY NIGHTS — Four Seasons, Vee Jay 597
133. THREAD YOUR NEEDLE — Dean & Jean, Rust 5081
134. DANCE, DANCE, DANCE — Tommy Duncan, Falow 104

Compiled from national retail sales and radio station airplay by the Music Popularity Dept. of Record Market Research. Billboard.

For Week Ending June 20, 1964

# Billboard HOT 100

★ STAR performer—Sides registering greatest proportionate upward progress this week.

| This Week | 1 Wk. Ago | 2 Wks. Ago | 3 Wks. Ago | TITLE Artist, Label & Number | Weeks On Chart |
|---|---|---|---|---|---|
| 1 | 1 | 1 | 2 | CHAPEL OF LOVE — Dixie Cups, Red Bird 001 | 8 |
| 2 | 2 | 6 | 7 | A WORLD WITHOUT LOVE — Peter & Gordon, Capitol 5175 | 7 |
| ★3 | 10 | 17 | 45 | I GET AROUND — Beach Boys, Capitol 5174 | 5 |
| 4 | 3 | 4 | 4 | LOVE ME WITH ALL YOUR HEART — Ray Charles Singers, Command 4046 | 11 |
| ★5 | 16 | 27 | 48 | MY BOY LOLLIPOP — Millie Small, Smash 1893 | 5 |
| 6 | 6 | 7 | 10 | WALK ON BY — Dionne Warwick, Scepter 1274 | 9 |
| 7 | 4 | 2 | 1 | LOVE ME DO — Beatles, Tollie 9008 | 11 |
| 8 | 9 | 12 | 16 | PEOPLE — Barbra Streisand, Columbia 42965 | 12 |
| ★9 | 20 | 26 | 47 | DON'T LET THE SUN CATCH YOU CRYING — Gerry & the Pacemakers, Laurie 3251 | 5 |
| 10 | 11 | 14 | 20 | DIANE — Bachelors, London 9639 | 10 |
| 11 | 7 | 8 | 8 | LITTLE CHILDREN — Billy J. Kramer, Imperial 66027 | 10 |
| 12 | 5 | 3 | 3 | MY GUY — Mary Wells, Motown 1056 | 12 |
| 13 | 17 | 20 | 30 | TELL ME WHY — Bobby Vinton, Epic 9687 | 5 |
| 14 | 8 | 5 | 5 | HELLO, DOLLY! — Louis Armstrong, Kapp 573 | 19 |
| ★15 | 31 | 63 | 88 | MEMPHIS — Johnny Rivers, Imperial 66032 | 4 |
| ★16 | 26 | 61 | 71 | BAD TO ME — Billy J. Kramer, Imperial 66027 | 4 |
| 17 | 18 | 18 | 27 | TODAY — New Christy Minstrels, Columbia 43000 | 10 |
| 18 | 13 | 13 | 17 | EVERY LITTLE BIT HURTS — Brenda Holloway, Tamla 54094 | 8 |
| 19 | 19 | 19 | 24 | ONCE UPON A TIME — Marvin Gaye & Mary Wells, Motown 1057 | 8 |
| 20 | 24 | 30 | 40 | TEARS AND ROSES — Al Martino, Capitol 5183 | 6 |
| 21 | 21 | 24 | 29 | WHAT'D I SAY — Elvis Presley, RCA Victor 8360 | 5 |
| 22 | 15 | 10 | 11 | P.S. I LOVE YOU — Beatles, Tollie 9008 | 7 |
| 23 | 12 | 9 | 6 | (Just Like) ROMEO & JULIET — Reflections, Golden World 9 | 11 |
| 24 | 14 | 11 | 12 | DO YOU LOVE ME — Dave Clark Five, Epic 9678 | 8 |
| ★25 | 30 | 43 | 78 | NO PARTICULAR PLACE TO GO — Chuck Berry, Chess 1898 | 5 |
| ★26 | 32 | 38 | 49 | I'LL TOUCH A STAR — Terry Stafford, Crusader 105 | 5 |
| ★27 | 35 | 64 | 72 | YESTERDAY'S GONE — Chad Stuart & Jeremy Clyde, World Artists 1021 | 5 |
| ★28 | 41 | 54 | 69 | DON'T THROW YOUR LOVE AWAY — Searchers, Kapp 593 | 4 |
| 29 | 25 | 29 | 32 | BE ANYTHING (But Be Mine) — Connie Francis, MGM 13237 | 7 |
| ★30 | 39 | 60 | 74 | BEANS IN MY EARS — Serendipity Singers, Philips 40198 | 5 |
| ★31 | 68 | — | — | CAN'T YOU SEE THAT SHE'S MINE — Dave Clark Five, Epic 9692 | 2 |
| 32 | 34 | 42 | 55 | WHAT'S THE MATTER WITH YOU BABY — Marvin Gaye & Mary Wells, Motown 1057 | 6 |
| 33 | 28 | 28 | 31 | THREE WINDOW COUPE — Rip Chords, Columbia 43035 | 9 |
| 34 | 37 | 45 | 56 | ROCK ME BABY — B. B. King, Kent 393 | 7 |
| ★35 | 61 | 87 | — | THE GIRL FROM IPANEMA — Getz/Gilberto, Verve 10323 | 3 |
| 36 | 27 | 22 | 22 | I DON'T WANT TO BE HURT ANY MORE — Nat King Cole, Capitol 5155 | 9 |
| 37 | 42 | 46 | 52 | I DON'T WANNA BE A LOSER — Lesley Gore, Mercury 72270 | 5 |
| 38 | 22 | 15 | 15 | COTTON CANDY — Al Hirt, RCA Victor 8346 | 11 |
| 39 | 23 | 16 | 9 | IT'S OVER — Roy Orbison, Monument 837 | 11 |
| 40 | 29 | 33 | 33 | VIVA LAS VEGAS — Elvis Presley, RCA Victor 8360 | 7 |
| ★41 | 53 | 74 | 93 | DON'T WORRY BABY — Beach Boys, Capitol 5174 | 4 |
| 42 | 36 | 40 | 43 | I RISE, I FALL — Johnny Tillotson, MGM 13232 | 8 |
| 43 | 49 | 52 | 57 | TOO LATE TO TURN BACK NOW — Brook Benton, Mercury 72266 | 7 |
| ★44 | 62 | 77 | — | GOOD TIMES — Sam Cooke, RCA Victor 8368 | 3 |
| 45 | 43 | 44 | 46 | GOOD GOLLY MISS MOLLY — Swinging Blue Jeans, Imperial 66030 | 7 |
| ★46 | 69 | 100 | — | TRY IT BABY — Marvin Gaye, Tamla 54095 | 3 |
| 47 | 51 | 57 | 61 | ANOTHER CUP OF COFFEE — Brook Benton, Mercury 72266 | 6 |
| 48 | 57 | 65 | 80 | I'LL BE IN TROUBLE — Temptations, Gordy 7032 | 4 |
| 49 | 50 | 58 | 66 | GIVING UP — Gladys Knight & the Pips, Maxx 326 | 7 |
| 50 | 33 | 35 | 36 | GOODBYE BABY (Baby Goodbye) — Solomon Burke, Atlantic 2226 | 10 |
| ★51 | 83 | 98 | — | ALONE — Four Seasons, Vee Jay 597 | 3 |
| 52 | 56 | 62 | 63 | PARTY GIRL — Bernadette Carroll, Laurie 3238 | 6 |
| ★53 | — | — | — | RAG DOLL — 4 Seasons, Philips 40211 | 1 |
| 54 | 58 | 70 | 73 | THE FRENCH SONG — Lucille Starr, Almo 204 | 6 |
| ★55 | 66 | 71 | 76 | WHAT HAVE I GOT OF MY OWN — Trini Lopez, Reprise 0276 | 7 |
| 56 | 63 | 68 | 79 | MILORD — Bobby Darin, Atco 6297 | 5 |
| ★57 | 74 | — | — | TENNESSEE WALTZ — Sam Cooke, RCA Victor 8368 | 2 |
| 58 | 44 | 47 | 50 | SUGAR AND SPICE — Searchers, Liberty 55689 | 8 |
| 59 | 60 | 69 | 75 | THE WORLD OF LONELY PEOPLE — Anita Bryant, Columbia 43037 | 6 |
| 60 | 55 | 55 | 59 | HURT BY LOVE — Inez Foxx, Symbol 20-001 | 9 |
| 61 | 65 | 75 | 94 | MY BABY DON'T DIG ME — Ray Charles, ABC-Paramount 10557 | 4 |
| ★62 | 94 | — | — | DANG ME — Roger Miller, Smash 1881 | 2 |
| ★63 | 82 | 97 | — | LAZY ELSIE MOLLY — Chubby Checker, Parkway 920 | 3 |
| 64 | 64 | 66 | 62 | DONNIE — Bermudas, Era 3125 | 10 |
| 65 | 70 | 85 | — | KEEP ON PUSHING — Impressions, ABC-Paramount 10554 | 3 |
| 66 | 67 | 73 | 83 | RULES OF LOVE — Orlons, Cameo 319 | 6 |
| 67 | 77 | 94 | — | REMEMBER ME — Rita Pavone, RCA Victor 8365 | 3 |
| ★68 | — | — | — | FARMER JOHN — Premiers, Warner Bros. 5443 | 1 |
| 69 | 72 | 76 | 92 | BEG ME — Chuck Jackson, Wand 154 | 5 |
| ★70 | 90 | — | — | HEY HARMONICA MAN — Stevie Wonder, Tamla 54096 | 2 |
| 71 | 80 | 83 | — | JUST AIN'T ENOUGH LOVE — Eddie Holland, Motown 1058 | 4 |
| 72 | 73 | 78 | 100 | EVERYBODY KNOWS — Steve Lawrence, Columbia 43047 | 4 |
| 73 | 85 | — | — | ALONE WITH YOU — Brenda Lee, Decca 31628 | 2 |
| 74 | 78 | 82 | 82 | NOT FADE AWAY — Rolling Stones, London 9657 | 8 |
| 75 | 75 | 88 | 90 | BE MY GIRL — Four-Evers, Smash 1887 | 4 |
| 76 | 76 | 81 | 84 | HICKORY, DICK AND DOC — Bobby Vee, Liberty 55700 | 4 |
| ★77 | 95 | 95 | 97 | KICK THAT LITTLE FOOT, SALLY ANN — Round Robin, Domain 1404 | 4 |
| 78 | 84 | 86 | 89 | THE WORLD I USED TO KNOW — Jimmie Rodgers, Dot 16595 | 4 |
| ★79 | — | — | — | WISHIN' AND HOPIN' — Dusty Springfield, Philips 40207 | 1 |
| 80 | 89 | — | — | SHARE YOUR LOVE WITH ME — Bobby Bland, Duke 377 | 2 |
| 81 | 81 | 84 | 87 | YESTERDAY'S GONE — Overlanders, Hickory 1258 | 5 |
| ★82 | — | — | — | I STILL GET JEALOUS — Louis Armstrong, Kapp 597 | 1 |
| 83 | 87 | 80 | 86 | A WORLD WITHOUT LOVE — Bobby Rydell, Cameo 320 | 6 |
| 84 | 86 | 89 | — | IT AIN'T NO USE — Major Lance, Okeh 7197 | 3 |
| 85 | 96 | 96 | — | MY DREAMS — Brenda Lee, Decca 31628 | 3 |
| 86 | 88 | 90 | — | SOMETHING YOU GOT — Alvin Robinson, Tiger 104 | 3 |
| 87 | 91 | 91 | 96 | THE FIRST NIGHT OF THE FULL MOON — Jack Jones, Kapp 589 | 4 |
| ★88 | — | — | — | I WANNA LOVE HIM SO BAD — Jelly Beans, Red Bird 10-003 | 1 |
| ★89 | — | — | — | A LITTLE TOY BALLOON — Danny Williams, United Artists 729 | 1 |
| ★90 | — | — | — | DO I LOVE YOU? — Ronettes, Philles 121 | 1 |
| 91 | 93 | 93 | 95 | I WANNA BE LOVED — Dean & Jean, Rust 5081 | 4 |
| 92 | — | — | — | PEG O' MY HEART — Robert Maxwell, Decca 25637 | 1 |
| 93 | — | — | — | MIXED UP, SHOOK UP, GIRL — Patty & the Emblems, Herald 590 | 1 |
| 94 | — | — | — | NIGHT TIME IS THE RIGHT TIME — Rufus & Carla, Stax 151 | 1 |
| 95 | — | — | — | OH! BABY — Barbara Lynn, Jamie 1277 | 1 |
| 96 | — | — | — | TASTE OF TEARS — Johnny Mathis, Mercury 72287 | 1 |
| 97 | 97 | — | — | FOUR BY THE BEATLES — Capitol EAP 1-2121 (Extended Play) | 2 |
| 98 | — | — | — | THE FERRIS WHEEL — Everly Brothers, Warner Bros. 5441 | 1 |
| 99 | 100 | — | — | DREAM LOVER — Paris Sisters, MGM 13236 | 2 |
| 100 | — | — | — | STEAL AWAY — Jimmy Hughes, Fame 6401 | 1 |

## HOT 100—A TO Z—*(Publisher-Licensee)*

Alone (Selma, BMI) .... 51
Alone With You (Metric, BMI) .... 73
Another Cup of Coffee (Peter Maurice, ASCAP) .. 47
Bad to Me (Metric, BMI) .... 16
Be Anything (But Be Mine) (Shapiro-Bernstein, ASCAP) .... 29
Be My Girl (Elephant-Jonic, BMI) .... 75
Beans in My Ears (Fall River, BMI) .... 30
Beg Me (T. M., BMI) .... 69
Can't You See That She's Mine (Beechwood, BMI). 31
Chapel of Love (Trio, BMI) .... 1
Cotton Candy (Gallico, BMI) .... 38
Dang Me (Tree, BMI) .... 62
Diane (Miller, ASCAP) .... 10
Do I Love You? (Mother Bertha-Hill & Range, BMI) .... 90
Do You Love Me (Jobete, BMI) .... 24
Don't Let the Sun Catch You Crying (Pacemaker, BMI) .... 9
Don't Throw Your Love Away (Wyncote, ASCAP) .. 28
Don't Worry Baby (Sea of Tunes, BMI) .... 41
Donnie (Rickland, BMI) .... 64
Dream Lover (Screen Gems-Columbia & T.M., BMI). 99
Every Little Bit Hurts (Jobete, BMI) .... 18
Everybody Knows (Gil, BMI) .... 72
Farmer John (Venice, BMI) .... 68
Ferris Wheel, The (Rose, BMI) .... 98
First Night of the Full Moon (Famous, ASCAP) .. 87
Four By the Beatles (Various Publishers) .... 97
French Song, The (Irving-Doral, BMI) .... 54
Girl From Ipanema, The (Duchess, BMI) .... 35
Giving Up (Trio, BMI) .... 49
Good Golly Miss Molly (Venice, BMI) .... 45
Good Times (Kags, BMI) .... 44
Goodbye Baby (Picturetone-Mellin, BMI) .... 50
Hello, Dolly! (Morris, ASCAP) .... 14
Hey Harmonica Man (Jobete-Little Darlin', BMI) 70
Hickory, Dick and Doc (Rose, BMI) .... 76
Hurt By Love (Saturn, BMI) .... 60
I Don't Wanna Be a Loser (Earth, BMI) .... 37
I Don't Want to Be Hurt Any More (Bregman, Vocco & Conn, ASCAP) .... 36
I Get Around (Sea of Tunes, BMI) .... 3
I Rise, I Fall (Tod, ASCAP) .... 42
I Still Get Jealous (Morris, ASCAP) .... 82
I Wanna Be Loved (Famous, ASCAP) .... 91
I Wanna Love Him So Bad (Trio, BMI) .... 88
I'll Be in Trouble (Jobete, BMI) .... 48
I'll Touch a Star (Blen-Holly Hill-Lesjohn, ASCAP). 26
It Ain't No Use (Curtom-Jalynne, BMI) .... 84
It's Over (Acuff-Rose, BMI) .... 39
Just Ain't Enough Love (Jobete, BMI) .... 71
(Just Like) Romeo & Juliet (Myto, BMI) .... 23
Keep on Pushing (Curtom, BMI) .... 65
Kick That Little Foot, Sally Ann (Screen Gems-Columbia, BMI) .... 77
Lazy Elsie Molly (Evanston-Picturetone, BMI) ... 63
Little Children (Rumbalero, BMI) .... 11
Little Toy Balloon, A (Duchess, BMI) .... 89
Love Me Do (Ardmore-Beechwood, BMI) .... 7
Love Me With All Your Heart (Peer Int'l, BMI) .. 4
Memphis (Arc, BMI) .... 15
Milord (Alamo, ASCAP) .... 56
Mixed-Up, Shook-Up, Girl (Ben-Lee, BMI) .... 93
My Baby Don't Dig Me (Tangerine, BMI) .... 61
My Boy Lollipop (Nom, BMI) .... 5
My Dreams (Fame, BMI) .... 85
My Guy (Jobete, BMI) .... 12
Night Time Is the Right Time (Crossroads, BMI).. 94
No Particular Place to Go (Arc, BMI) .... 25
Not Fade Away (Nor Va Jak, BMI) .... 74
Oh! Baby (Nujac, BMI) .... 95
Once Upon a Time (Jobete, BMI) .... 19
P.S. I Love You (Beechwood, BMI) .... 22
Party Girl (Schwartz, ASCAP) .... 52
Peg o' My Heart (Feist, ASCAP) .... 92
People (Chappell, ASCAP) .... 8
Rag Doll (Saturday-Gavadima, ASCAP) .... 53
Remember Me (Gil, BMI) .... 67
Rock Me Baby (Modern, BMI) .... 34
Rules of Love (Kalmann, ASCAP) .... 66
Share Your Love With Me (Don, BMI) .... 80
Something You Got (Tune Kel, BMI) .... 86
Steal Away (Fame, BMI) .... 100
Sugar and Spice (Duchess, BMI) .... 58
Taste of Tears (Prize-Elm Drive, ASCAP) .... 96
Tears and Roses (Davilene, BMI) .... 20
Tell Me Why (Signet, BMI) .... 13
Tennessee Waltz (Acuff-Rose, BMI) .... 57
Three Window Coupe (Screen Gems-Columbia, BMI). 33
Today (Miller-Heritage House, ASCAP) .... 17
Too Late to Turn Back Now (Play, BMI) .... 43
Try It Baby (Jobete, BMI) .... 46
Viva Las Vegas (Presley, BMI) .... 40
Walk on By (Blue Seas-Jac, ASCAP) .... 6
What Have I Got of My Own (Sawtell-Herring, ASCAP) .... 55
What'd I Say (Progressive, BMI) .... 21
What's the Matter With You Baby (Jobete, BMI).. 32
Wishin' and Hopin' (Jonathan, BMI) .... 79
World I Used to Know, The (In, ASCAP) .... 78
World of Lonely People, The (Ross Jungnickel, ASCAP) .... 59
World Without Love, A—Peter & Gordon (MacLen, BMI) .... 2
World Without Love, A—Rydell (MacLen, BMI) ... 83
Yesterday's Gone—Overlanders (Unart, BMI) .... 81
Yesterday's Gone—Stuart-Clyde (Unart, BMI) .... 27

## BUBBLING UNDER THE HOT 100

101. SIE LIEBT DICH (She Loves You) .... Beatles, Swan 4182
102. THAT'S REALLY SOME GOOD .... Rufus & Carla, Stax 151
103. THE MAGIC OF OUR SUMMER LOVE .... Tymes, Parkway 919
104. GOOD TIME TONIGHT .... Soul Sisters, Sue 10-005
105. TELL ME MAMMA .... Christine Quaite, World Artists 1022
106. OH, ROCK MY SOUL .... Peter, Paul & Mary, Warner Bros. 5442
107. HELP THE POOR .... B. B. King, ABC-Paramount 10552
108. SECURITY .... Otis Redding, Volt 117
109. LET'S GO TOGETHER .... Raindrops, Jubilee 5475
110. TROUBLE I'VE HAD .... Clarence Ashe, Chess 1896
111. EVERYBODY LOVES SOMEBODY .... Dean Martin, Reprise 0281
112. ANYONE WHO KNOWS WHAT LOVE IS .... Irma Thomas, Imperial 66041
113. PRECIOUS WORDS .... Wallace Brothers, Sims 174
114. THE THINGS THAT I USED TO DO .... James Brown, Smash 1903
115. (You Don't Know) HOW GLAD I AM .... Nancy Wilson, Capitol 5198
116. BEACHCOMBER .... Johnny Gibson Trio, Laurie 3256
117. SHE'S MY GIRL .... Bobby Shafto, Rust 5082
118. IT WILL STAND .... Showmen, Imperial 66033
119. LONG LONELY NIGHTS .... 4 Seasons, Vee Jay 597
120. THE GIRL'S ALRIGHT WITH ME .... Temptations, Gordy 7032
121. ROSIE .... Chubby Checker, Parkway 920
122. MY KIND OF TOWN .... Frank Sinatra, Reprise 0279
123. THREAD YOUR NEEDLE .... Dean & Jean, Rust 5081
124. I DON'T WANT TO HEAR ANYMORE .... Jerry Butler, Vee Jay 598
125. DEVIL WITH THE BLUE DRESS .... Shorty Long, Soul 35001
126. ANGELITO .... Rene & Rene, Columbia 43045
127. IT'S ALL OVER NOW .... Valentinos, Sar 152
128. I CAN'T HEAR YOU .... Betty Everett, Vee Jay 599
129. JAMAICA SKA .... The Ska Kings, Atlantic 2232
130. RUN LITTLE GIRL .... Donnie Elbert, Gateway, 731
131. HELLO, DOLLY! (Italian Style) .... Lou Monte, Reprise 0284
132. GROWIN' UP TOO FAST .... Diane Renay, 20th Century-Fox 514
133. MY MAN .... Walter Gates, Swan 4180
134. BIG PARTY .... Barbara & the Browns, Stax 150
135. TEQUILA .... Bill Black's Combo, Hi 2077

Compiled from national retail sales and radio station airplay by the Music Popularity Dept. of Record Market Research, Billboard.

# Billboard HOT 100

**For Week Ending June 27, 1964**

★ STAR performer—Sides registering greatest proportionate upward progress this week.

| This Week | 1 Wk. Ago | 2 Wks. Ago | 3 Wks. Ago | TITLE — Artist, Label & Number | Weeks On Chart |
|---|---|---|---|---|---|
| 1 | 2 | 2 | 6 | A WORLD WITHOUT LOVE — Peter & Gordon, Capitol 5175 | 8 |
| 2 | 3 | 10 | 17 | I GET AROUND — Beach Boys, Capitol 5174 | 6 |
| 3 | 1 | 1 | 1 | CHAPEL OF LOVE — Dixie Cups, Red Bird 001 | 9 |
| 4 | 5 | 16 | 27 | MY BOY LOLLIPOP — Millie Small, Smash 1893 | 6 |
| ★5 | 8 | 9 | 12 | PEOPLE — Barbra Streisand, Columbia 42965 | 13 |
| ★6 | 15 | 31 | 63 | MEMPHIS — Johnny Rivers, Imperial 66032 | 5 |
| 7 | 9 | 20 | 26 | DON'T LET THE SUN CATCH YOU CRYING — Gerry & the Pacemakers, Laurie 3251 | 6 |
| 8 | 4 | 3 | 4 | LOVE ME WITH ALL YOUR HEART — Ray Charles Singers, Command 4046 | 12 |
| ★9 | 16 | 26 | 61 | BAD TO ME — Billy J. Kramer, Imperial 66027 | 5 |
| 10 | 6 | 6 | 7 | WALK ON BY — Dionne Warwick, Scepter 1274 | 10 |
| 11 | 7 | 4 | 2 | LOVE ME DO — Beatles, Tollie 9008 | 12 |
| 12 | 11 | 7 | 8 | LITTLE CHILDREN — Billy J. Kramer, Imperial 66027 | 11 |
| 13 | 13 | 17 | 20 | TELL ME WHY — Bobby Vinton, Epic 9687 | 6 |
| 14 | 25 | 30 | 43 | NO PARTICULAR PLACE TO GO — Chuck Berry, Chess 1898 | 6 |
| 15 | 12 | 5 | 3 | MY GUY — Mary Wells, Motown 1056 | 13 |
| ★16 | 31 | 68 | — | CAN'T YOU SEE THAT SHE'S MINE — Dave Clark Five, Epic 9692 | 3 |
| 17 | 10 | 11 | 14 | DIANE — Bachelors, London 9639 | 11 |
| 18 | 53 | — | — | RAG DOLL — 4 Seasons, Philips 40211 | 2 |
| 19 | 14 | 8 | 5 | HELLO, DOLLY! — Louis Armstrong, Kapp 573 | 20 |
| 20 | 35 | 61 | 87 | THE GIRL FROM IPANEMA — Getz/Gilberto, Verve 10323 | 4 |
| 21 | 17 | 18 | 18 | TODAY — New Christy Minstrels, Columbia 43000 | 11 |
| ★22 | 32 | 34 | 42 | WHAT'S THE MATTER WITH YOU BABY — Marvin Gaye & Mary Wells, Motown 1057 | 7 |
| 23 | 44 | 62 | 77 | GOOD TIMES — Sam Cooke, RCA Victor 8368 | 4 |
| 24 | 27 | 35 | 64 | YESTERDAY'S GONE — Chad Stuart & Jeremy Clyde, World Artists 1021 | 6 |
| 25 | 28 | 42 | 54 | DON'T THROW YOUR LOVE AWAY — Searchers, Kapp 593 | 5 |
| 26 | 26 | 32 | 38 | I'LL TOUCH A STAR — Terry Stafford, Crusader 105 | 6 |
| 27 | 46 | 69 | 100 | TRY IT BABY — Marvin Gaye, Tamla 54095 | 4 |
| 28 | 20 | 24 | 30 | TEARS AND ROSES — Al Martino, Capitol 5183 | 7 |
| 29 | 41 | 53 | 74 | DON'T WORRY BABY — Beach Boys, Capitol 5174 | 5 |
| 30 | 30 | 39 | 60 | BEANS IN MY EARS — Serendipity Singers, Philips 40198 | 6 |
| 31 | 18 | 13 | 13 | EVERY LITTLE BIT HURTS — Brenda Holloway, Tamla 54094 | 9 |
| ★32 | 65 | 70 | 85 | KEEP ON PUSHING — Impressions, ABC-Paramount 10554 | 4 |
| 33 | 19 | 19 | 19 | ONCE UPON A TIME — Marvin Gaye & Mary Wells, Motown 1057 | 9 |
| 34 | 24 | 14 | 11 | DO YOU LOVE ME — Dave Clark Five, Epic 9678 | 9 |
| 35 | 21 | 21 | 24 | WHAT'D I SAY — Elvis Presley, RCA Victor 8360 | 6 |
| 36 | 23 | 12 | 9 | (Just Like) ROMEO & JULIET — Reflections, Golden World 9 | 12 |
| 37 | 22 | 15 | 10 | P.S. I LOVE YOU — Beatles, Tollie 9008 | 8 |
| ★38 | 51 | 83 | 98 | ALONE — Four Seasons, Vee Jay 597 | 4 |
| 39 | 34 | 37 | 45 | ROCK ME BABY — B. B. King, Kent 393 | 8 |
| 40 | 29 | 25 | 29 | BE ANYTHING (But Be Mine) — Connie Francis, MGM 13237 | 8 |
| 41 | 48 | 57 | 65 | I'LL BE IN TROUBLE — Temptations, Gordy 7032 | 5 |
| 42 | 49 | 50 | 58 | GIVING UP — Gladys Knight & the Pips, Maxx 326 | 8 |
| 43 | 38 | 22 | 15 | COTTON CANDY — Al Hirt, RCA Victor 8346 | 12 |
| ★44 | 62 | 94 | — | DANG ME — Roger Miller, Smash 1881 | 3 |
| 45 | 67 | 77 | 94 | REMEMBER ME — Rita Pavone, RCA Victor 8365 | 4 |
| ★46 | 57 | 74 | — | TENNESSEE WALTZ — Sam Cooke, RCA Victor 8368 | 3 |
| 47 | 52 | 56 | 62 | PARTY GIRL — Bernadette Carroll, Laurie 3238 | 7 |
| 48 | 47 | 51 | 57 | ANOTHER CUP OF COFFEE — Brook Benton, Mercury 72266 | 7 |
| 49 | 56 | 63 | 68 | MILORD — Bobby Darin, Atco 6297 | 6 |
| 50 | 63 | 82 | 97 | LAZY ELSIE MOLLY — Chubby Checker, Parkway 920 | 4 |
| 51 | 61 | 65 | 75 | MY BABY DON'T DIG ME — Ray Charles, ABC-Paramount 10557 | 5 |
| 52 | 70 | 90 | — | HEY HARMONICA MAN — Stevie Wonder, Tamla 54096 | 3 |
| 53 | 55 | 66 | 71 | WHAT HAVE I GOT OF MY OWN — Trini Lopez, Reprise 0276 | 8 |
| 54 | 54 | 58 | 70 | THE FRENCH SONG — Lucille Starr, Almo 204 | 7 |
| 55 | 43 | 49 | 52 | TOO LATE TO TURN BACK NOW — Brook Benton, Mercury 72266 | 8 |
| 56 | 68 | — | — | FARMER JOHN — Premiers, Warner Bros. 5443 | 2 |
| 57 | 69 | 72 | 76 | BEG ME — Chuck Jackson, Wand 154 | 6 |
| 58 | 73 | 85 | — | ALONE WITH YOU — Brenda Lee, Decca 31628 | 3 |
| 59 | 59 | 60 | 69 | THE WORLD OF LONELY PEOPLE — Anita Bryant, Columbia 43037 | 7 |
| 60 | — | — | — | THE LITTLE OLD LADY (From Pasadena) — Jan & Dean, Liberty 55704 | 1 |
| 61 | 79 | — | — | WISHIN' AND HOPIN' — Dusty Springfield, Philips 40207 | 2 |
| 62 | 71 | 80 | 83 | JUST AIN'T ENOUGH LOVE — Eddie Holland, Motown 1058 | 5 |
| 63 | 74 | 78 | 82 | NOT FADE AWAY — Rolling Stones, London 9657 | 9 |
| 64 | 82 | — | — | I STILL GET JEALOUS — Louis Armstrong, Kapp 597 | 2 |
| 65 | 80 | 89 | — | SHARE YOUR LOVE WITH ME — Bobby Bland, Duke 377 | 3 |
| 66 | — | — | — | (YOU DON'T KNOW) HOW GLAD I AM — Nancy Wilson, Capitol 5198 | 1 |
| 67 | 86 | 88 | 90 | SOMETHING YOU GOT — Alvin Robinson, Tiger 104 | 4 |
| 68 | 77 | 95 | 95 | KICK THAT LITTLE FOOT, SALLY ANN — Round Robin, Domain 1404 | 5 |
| 69 | 76 | 76 | 81 | HICKORY, DICK AND DOC — Bobby Vee, Liberty 55700 | 5 |
| 70 | 78 | 84 | 86 | THE WORLD I USED TO KNOW — Jimmie Rodgers, Dot 16595 | 5 |
| 71 | 87 | 91 | 91 | THE FIRST NIGHT OF THE FULL MOON — Jack Jones, Kapp 589 | 5 |
| ★72 | — | — | — | EVERYBODY LOVES SOMEBODY — Dean Martin, Reprise 0281 | 1 |
| ★73 | — | — | — | NOBODY I KNOW — Peter & Gordon, Capitol 5211 | 1 |
| 74 | 72 | 73 | 78 | EVERYBODY KNOWS — Steve Lawrence, Columbia 43047 | 5 |
| 75 | 81 | 81 | 84 | YESTERDAY'S GONE — Overlanders, Hickory 1258 | 6 |
| 76 | 84 | 86 | 89 | IT AIN'T NO USE — Major Lance, Okeh 7197 | 4 |
| 77 | 100 | — | — | STEAL AWAY — Jimmy Hughes, Fame 6401 | 2 |
| 78 | 90 | — | — | DO I LOVE YOU? — Ronettes, Philles 121 | 2 |
| ★79 | — | — | — | I CAN'T HEAR YOU — Betty Everett, Vee Jay 599 | 1 |
| 80 | — | — | — | GIRLS — Major Lance, Okeh 7197 | 1 |
| 81 | — | — | — | UNDER THE BOARDWALK — Drifters, Atlantic 2237 | 1 |
| ★82 | — | — | — | I LIKE IT LIKE THAT — Miracles, Tamla 54098 | 1 |
| 83 | — | — | — | I BELIEVE — Bachelors, London 9672 | 1 |
| 84 | 88 | — | — | I WANNA LOVE HIM SO BAD — Jelly Beans, Red Bird 10-003 | 2 |
| 85 | 93 | — | — | MIXED-UP, SHOOK-UP GIRL — Patty & the Emblems, Herald 590 | 2 |
| 86 | 89 | — | — | A LITTLE TOY BALLOON — Danny Williams, United Artists 729 | 2 |
| 87 | 92 | — | — | PEG O' MY HEART — Robert Maxwell, Decca 25637 | 2 |
| 88 | 98 | — | — | THE FERRIS WHEEL — Everly Brothers, Warner Bros. 5441 | 2 |
| 89 | 95 | — | — | OH! BABY — Barbara Jean, Jamie 1277 | 2 |
| ★90 | — | — | — | I'M INTO SOMETHIN' GOOD — Earl-Jean, Colpix 729 | 1 |
| 91 | 91 | 93 | 93 | I WANNA BE LOVED — Dean & Jean, Rust 5081 | 5 |
| 92 | 97 | 97 | — | FOUR BY THE BEATLES — Capitol EAP 1-2121 (Extended Play) | 3 |
| 93 | 99 | 100 | — | DREAM LOVER — Paris Sisters, MGM 13236 | 3 |
| 94 | 96 | — | — | TASTE OF TEARS — Johnny Mathis, Mercury 72287 | 2 |
| 95 | — | — | — | THE MEXICAN SHUFFLE — Herb Alpert's Tijuana Brass, A&M 742 | 1 |
| 96 | — | — | — | OH, ROCK MY SOUL — Peter, Paul & Mary, Warner Bros. 5442 | 1 |
| 97 | — | — | — | SIE LIEBT DICH (She Loves You) — Die Beatles, Swan 4182 | 1 |
| 98 | — | — | — | I DON'T WANT TO HEAR ANYMORE — Jerry Butler, Vee Jay 598 | 1 |
| 99 | — | — | — | IT'S ALL OVER NOW — Valentinos, Sar 152 | 1 |
| 100 | — | — | — | HELP THE POOR — B. B. King, ABC-Paramount 10552 | 1 |

## BUBBLING UNDER THE HOT 100

101. IT WILL STAND — Showmen, Imperial 66033
102. LONG LONELY NIGHTS — 4 Seasons, Vee Jay 597
103. WALKIN' — Al Hirt, RCA Victor 8346
104. I WANT TO HOLD YOUR HAND — Boston Pops Ork, RCA Victor 8378
105. THE GIRL'S ALRIGHT WITH ME — Temptations, Gordy 7032
106. MY HEART SKIPS A BEAT — Buck Owens, Capitol 5136
107. THE COWBOY IN THE CONTINENTAL SUIT — Marty Robbins, Columbia 43049
108. C'MON AND SWIM — Bobby Freeman, Autumn 2
109. MY DREAMS — Brenda Lee, Decca 31628
110. NIGHT TIME IS THE RIGHT TIME — Rufus & Carla, Stax 151
111. ANYONE WHO KNOWS WHAT LOVE IS — Irma Thomas, Imperial 66041
112. SHE'S MY GIRL — Bobby Shafto, Rust 5082
113. ANGELITO — Rene & Rene, Columbia 43045
114. THE THINGS I USED TO DO — James Brown, Smash 1908
115. SECURITY — Otis Redding, Volt 117
116. ROSIE — Chubby Checker, Parkway 920
117. HANDY MAN — Del Shannon, Amy 905
118. THAT'S REALLY SOME GOOD — Rufus & Carla, Stax 151
119. LOVE IS ALL WE NEED — Vic Dana, Dolton 95
120. JAMAICA SKA — Ska Kings, Atlantic 2232
121. YOU'RE MY WORLD — Cilla Black, Capitol 5196
122. GOOD TIME TONIGHT — Sue Sisters, Sue 10-005
123. JUST ONE MORE — Rita Pavone, RCA Victor 8365
124. LET'S GO TOGETHER — Raindrops, Jubilee 5475
125. HELLO, DOLLY! — Ella Fitzgerald, Verve 10324
126. HAUNTED HOUSE — Gene Simmons, Hi 2076
127. MY KIND OF TOWN — Frank Sinatra, Reprise 0279
128. CLOSE YOUR EYES — Arthur Prysock, Old Town 1163
129. BIG PARTY — Four Pennies, Phillips 40202
130. GROWIN' UP TOO FAST — Diane Renay, 20th Century-Fox 514
131. SO LONG — James Brown, King 5899
132. JULIET — Four Pennies, Phillips 40202
133. HE'S COMING BACK TO ME — Theola Kilgore, KT 501
134. DANCE, DANCE, DANCE — Tommy Duncan, Falew 104
135. BEE-BOM — Sammy Davis Jr., Reprise 0278

Compiled from national retail sales and radio station airplay by the Music Popularity Dept. of Record Market Research, Billboard.

**Billboard**

For Week Ending July 4, 1964

# HOT 100

★ **STAR performer—Sides registering greatest proportionate upward progress this week.**

Billboard Award

| This Week | 1 Wk. Ago | 2 Wks. Ago | 3 Wks. Ago | TITLE Artist, Label & Number | Weeks On Chart |
|---|---|---|---|---|---|
| 1 | 2 | 3 | 10 | **I GET AROUND** Beach Boys, Capitol 5174 | 7 |
| 2 | 4 | 5 | 16 | **MY BOY LOLLIPOP** Millie Small, Smash 1893 | 7 |
| ★3 | 6 | 15 | 31 | **MEMPHIS** Johnny Rivers, Imperial 66032 | 6 |
| ★4 | 7 | 9 | 20 | **DON'T LET THE SUN CATCH YOU CRYING** Gerry & the Pacemakers, Laurie 3251 | 7 |
| 5 | 5 | 8 | 9 | **PEOPLE** Barbra Streisand, Columbia 42965 | 14 |
| 6 | 1 | 2 | 2 | **A WORLD WITHOUT LOVE** Peter & Gordon, Capitol 5175 | 9 |
| 7 | 3 | 1 | 1 | **CHAPEL OF LOVE** Dixie Cups, Red Bird 001 | 10 |
| ★8 | 18 | 53 | — | **RAG DOLL** 4 Seasons, Philips 40211 | 3 |
| 9 | 9 | 16 | 26 | **BAD TO ME** Billy J. Kramer, Imperial 66027 | 6 |
| ★10 | 16 | 31 | 68 | **CAN'T YOU SEE THAT SHE'S MINE** Dave Clark Five, Epic 9692 | 4 |
| 11 | 14 | 25 | 30 | **NO PARTICULAR PLACE TO GO** Chuck Berry, Chess 1898 | 7 |
| ★12 | 20 | 35 | 61 | **THE GIRL FROM IPANEMA** Getz/Gilberto, Verve 10323 | 5 |
| 13 | 8 | 4 | 3 | **LOVE ME WITH ALL YOUR HEART** Ray Charles Singers, Command 4046 | 13 |
| 14 | 12 | 11 | 7 | **LITTLE CHILDREN** Billy J. Kramer, Imperial 66027 | 12 |
| 15 | 10 | 6 | 6 | **WALK ON BY** Dionne Warwick, Scepter 1274 | 11 |
| ★16 | 23 | 44 | 62 | **GOOD TIMES** Sam Cooke, RCA Victor 8368 | 5 |
| ★17 | 22 | 32 | 34 | **WHAT'S THE MATTER WITH YOU BABY** Marvin Gaye & Mary Wells, Motown 1057 | 8 |
| ★18 | 25 | 28 | 41 | **DON'T THROW YOUR LOVE AWAY** Searchers, Kapp 593 | 6 |
| 19 | 11 | 7 | 4 | **LOVE ME DO** Beatles, Tollie 9008 | 13 |
| ★20 | 27 | 46 | 69 | **TRY IT BABY** Marvin Gaye, Tamla 54095 | 5 |
| 21 | 24 | 27 | 35 | **YESTERDAY'S GONE** Chad Stuart & Jeremy Clyde, World Artists 1021 | 7 |
| ★22 | 60 | — | — | **THE LITTLE OLD LADY (From Pasadena)** Jan & Dean, Liberty 55704 | 2 |
| ★23 | 32 | 65 | 70 | **KEEP ON PUSHING** Impressions, ABC-Paramount 10554 | 5 |
| ★24 | 29 | 41 | 53 | **DON'T WORRY BABY** Beach Boys, Capitol 5174 | 6 |
| 25 | 26 | 26 | 32 | **I'LL TOUCH A STAR** Terry Stafford, Crusader 105 | 7 |
| 26 | 13 | 13 | 17 | **TELL ME WHY** Bobby Vinton, Epic 9687 | 7 |
| 27 | 17 | 10 | 11 | **DIANE** Bachelors, London 9639 | 12 |
| 28 | 21 | 17 | 18 | **TODAY** New Christy Minstrels, Columbia 43000 | 12 |
| 29 | 15 | 12 | 5 | **MY GUY** Mary Wells, Motown 1056 | 14 |
| ★30 | 38 | 51 | 83 | **ALONE** Four Seasons, Vee Jay 597 | 5 |
| ★31 | 44 | 62 | 94 | **DANG ME** Roger Miller, Smash 1881 | 4 |
| 32 | 30 | 30 | 39 | **BEANS IN MY EARS** Serendipity Singers, Philips 40193 | 7 |
| 33 | 41 | 48 | 57 | **I'LL BE IN TROUBLE** Temptations, Gordy 7032 | 6 |
| 34 | 19 | 14 | 8 | **HELLO, DOLLY!** Louis Armstrong, Kapp 573 | 21 |
| ★35 | 46 | 57 | 74 | **TENNESSEE WALTZ** Sam Cooke, RCA Victor 8368 | 4 |
| 36 | 45 | 67 | 77 | **REMEMBER ME** Rita Pavone, RCA Victor 8365 | 5 |
| ★37 | 56 | 58 | — | **FARMER JOHN** Premiers, Warner Bros. 5443 | 3 |
| 38 | 42 | 49 | 50 | **GIVING UP** Gladys Knight & the Pips, Maxx 326 | 9 |
| 39 | 28 | 20 | 24 | **TEARS AND ROSES** Al Martino, Capitol 5183 | 8 |
| 40 | 34 | 24 | 14 | **DO YOU LOVE ME** Dave Clark Five, Epic 9678 | 10 |
| ★41 | 52 | 70 | 90 | **HEY HARMONICA MAN** Stevie Wonder, Tamla 54096 | 4 |
| 42 | 50 | 63 | 82 | **LAZY ELSIE MOLLY** Chubby Checker, Parkway 920 | 5 |
| 43 | 31 | 18 | 13 | **EVERY LITTLE BIT HURTS** Brenda Holloway, Tamla 54094 | 10 |
| ★44 | 61 | 79 | — | **WISHIN' AND HOPIN'** Dusty Springfield, Philips 40207 | 3 |
| 45 | 49 | 56 | 63 | **MILORD** Bobby Darin, Atco 6297 | 7 |
| ★46 | 72 | — | — | **EVERYBODY LOVES SOMEBODY** Dean Martin, Reprise 0281 | 2 |
| 47 | 47 | 52 | 56 | **PARTY GIRL** Bernadette Carroll, Laurie 3238 | 8 |
| ★48 | 73 | — | — | **NOBODY I KNOW** Peter & Gordon, Capitol 5211 | 2 |
| 49 | 57 | 69 | 72 | **BEG ME** Chuck Jackson, Wand 154 | 7 |
| 50 | 58 | 73 | 85 | **ALONE WITH YOU** Brenda Lee, Decca 31628 | 4 |
| 51 | 53 | 55 | 66 | **WHAT HAVE I GOT OF MY OWN** Trini Lopez, Reprise 0276 | 9 |
| ★52 | 77 | 100 | — | **STEAL AWAY** Jimmy Hughes, Fame 6401 | 3 |
| ★53 | 64 | 82 | — | **I STILL GET JEALOUS** Louis Armstrong, Kapp 597 | 3 |
| 54 | 62 | 71 | 80 | **JUST AIN'T ENOUGH LOVE** Eddie Holland, Motown 1058 | 6 |
| 55 | 63 | 74 | 78 | **NOT FADE AWAY** Rolling Stones, London 9657 | 10 |
| 56 | 51 | 61 | 65 | **MY BABY DON'T DIG ME** Ray Charles, ABC-Paramount 10557 | 6 |
| 57 | 54 | 54 | 58 | **THE FRENCH SONG** Lucille Starr, Almo 204 | 8 |
| 58 | 66 | — | — | **(You Don't Know) HOW GLAD I AM** Nancy Wilson, Capitol 5198 | 2 |
| ★59 | 70 | 78 | 84 | **THE WORLD I USED TO KNOW** Jimmie Rodgers, Dot 16595 | 6 |
| 60 | 65 | 80 | 89 | **SHARE YOUR LOVE WITH ME** Bobby Bland, Duke 377 | 4 |
| ★61 | 84 | 88 | — | **I WANNA LOVE HIM SO BAD** Jelly Beans, Red Bird 10-003 | 3 |
| ★62 | 81 | — | — | **UNDER THE BOARDWALK** Drifters, Atlantic 2237 | 2 |
| 63 | 68 | 77 | 95 | **KICK THAT LITTLE FOOT, SALLY ANN** Round Robin, Domain 1404 | 6 |
| 64 | 67 | 86 | 88 | **SOMETHING YOU GOT** Alvin Robinson, Tiger 104 | 5 |
| 65 | 69 | 76 | 76 | **HICKORY, DICK AND DOC** Bobby Vee, Liberty 55700 | 6 |
| 66 | 78 | 90 | — | **DO I LOVE YOU?** Ronettes, Philles 121 | 3 |
| ★67 | 82 | — | — | **I LIKE IT LIKE THAT** Miracles, Tamla 54098 | 2 |
| 68 | 76 | 84 | 86 | **IT AIN'T NO USE** Major Lance, Okeh 7197 | 5 |
| 69 | 71 | 87 | 91 | **THE FIRST NIGHT OF THE FULL MOON** Jack Jones, Kapp 589 | 6 |
| 70 | 80 | — | — | **GIRLS** Major Lance, Okeh 7197 | 2 |
| 71 | 83 | — | — | **I BELIEVE** Bachelors, London 9672 | 2 |
| 72 | 79 | — | — | **I CAN'T HEAR YOU** Betty Everett, Vee Jay 599 | 2 |
| 73 | 59 | 59 | 60 | **THE WORLD OF LONELY PEOPLE** Anita Bryant, Columbia 43037 | 8 |
| ★74 | — | — | — | **I WANT TO HOLD YOUR HAND** Boston Pops Ork, RCA Victor 8378 | 1 |
| 75 | 87 | 92 | — | **PEG O' MY HEART** Robert Maxwell, Decca 25637 | 3 |
| 76 | 89 | 95 | — | **OH! BABY** Barbara Lynn, Jamie 1277 | 3 |
| 77 | 75 | 81 | 81 | **YESTERDAY'S GONE** Overlanders, Hickory 1258 | 7 |
| 78 | 90 | — | — | **I'M INTO SOMETHIN' GOOD** Earl-Jean, Colpix 729 | 2 |
| 79 | 88 | 98 | — | **THE FERRIS WHEEL** Everly Brothers, Warner Bros. 5441 | 3 |
| ★80 | — | — | — | **YOU'RE MY WORLD** Cilla Black, Capitol 5195 | 1 |
| ★81 | — | — | — | **TELL ME** Rolling Stones, London 9682 | 1 |
| ★82 | — | — | — | **ANYONE WHO KNOWS WHAT LOVE IS** Irma Thomas, Imperial 66041 | 1 |
| 83 | 85 | 93 | — | **MIXED-UP, SHOOK-UP GIRL** Patty & the Emblems, Herald 590 | 3 |
| ★84 | — | — | — | **DON'T TAKE YOUR LOVE FROM ME** Gloria Lynne, Everest 2044 | 1 |
| ★85 | — | — | — | **HANDY MAN** Del Shannon, Amy 905 | 1 |
| 86 | 86 | 89 | — | **A LITTLE TOY BALLOON** Danny Williams, United Artists 729 | 3 |
| 87 | 94 | 96 | — | **TASTE OF TEARS** Johnny Mathis, Mercury 72287 | 3 |
| ★88 | — | — | — | **YOU'RE MY REMEDY** Marvelettes, Tamla 54097 | 1 |
| ★89 | — | — | — | **IT WILL STAND** Showmen, Imperial 66033 | 1 |
| 90 | 95 | — | — | **THE MEXICAN SHUFFLE** Herb Alpert's Tijuana Brass, A&M 742 | 2 |
| 91 | 93 | 99 | 100 | **DREAM LOVER** Paris Sisters, MGM 13236 | 4 |
| 92 | — | — | — | **VIVA LAS VEGAS EP** Elvis Presley, RCA Victor EPA 4382 | 1 |
| 93 | — | — | — | **ALL MY LOVING** Hollyridge Strings, Capitol 5207 | 1 |
| 94 | 99 | — | — | **IT'S ALL OVER NOW** Valentinos, Sar 152 | 2 |
| 95 | 98 | — | — | **I DON'T WANT TO HEAR ANYMORE** Jerry Butler, Vee Jay 598 | 2 |
| 96 | 96 | — | — | **OH, ROCK MY SOUL** Peter, Paul & Mary, Warner Bros. 5442 | 2 |
| 97 | — | — | — | **IF YOU SEE MY LOVE** Lenny Welch, Cadence 1446 | 1 |
| 98 | 100 | — | — | **HELP THE POOR** B. B. King, ABC-Paramount 10552 | 2 |
| 99 | — | — | — | **THE THINGS THAT I USED TO DO** James Brown, Smash 1908 | 1 |
| 100 | — | — | — | **MY HEART SKIPS A BEAT** Buck Owens, Capitol 5136 | 1 |

## HOT 100—A TO Z—*(Publisher-Licensee)*


All My Love (Northern, ASCAP) .......... 93
Alone (Selma, BMI) .......... 30
Alone With You (Metric, BMI) .......... 50
Anyone Who Knows What Love Is (Metric, BMI) .. 32
Bad to Me (Metric, BMI) .......... 9
Beans in My Ears (Fall River, BMI) .......... 32
Beg Me (T. M., BMI) .......... 49
Can't You See That She's Mine (Beechwood, BMI) .. 10
Chapel of Love (Trio, BMI) .......... 7
Dang Me (Tree, BMI) .......... 31
Diane (Miller, ASCAP) .......... 27
Do I Love You? (Mother Bertha-Hill & Range, BMI) .......... 66
Do You Love Me (Jobete, BMI) .......... 40
Don't Let the Sun Catch You Crying (Pacemaker, BMI) .......... 4
Don't Take Your Love From Me (Morris, ASCAP) .. 84
Don't Throw Your Love Away (Wyncote, ASCAP) .. 18
Don't Worry Baby (Sea of Tunes, BMI) .......... 24
Dream Lover (Screen Gems-Columbia & T. M., BMI) .......... 91
Every Little Bit Hurts (Jobete, BMI) .......... 43
Everybody Loves Somebody (Sands, ASCAP) .......... 46
Farmer John (Venice, BMI) .......... 37
Ferris Wheel, The (Rose, BMI) .......... 79
First Night of the Full Moon, The (Famous, ASCAP) .......... 69
French Song, The (Irving-Doral, BMI) .......... 57
Girl From Ipanema, The (Duchess, BMI) .......... 12
Girls (Curtom, BMI) .......... 70
Giving Up (Trio, BMI) .......... 38
Good Times (Kags, BMI) .......... 16
Handy Man (Travis-Bess, BMI) .......... 85
Hello, Dolly! (Morris, ASCAP) .......... 34
Help the Poor (Noma, BMI) .......... 98
Hey Harmonica Man (Jobete-Little Darlin', BMI) .. 41
Hickory, Dick and Doc (Rose, BMI) .......... 65
I Believe (Cromwell, ASCAP) .......... 71
I Can't Hear You (Screen Gems-Columbia, BMI) ... 72
I Don't Want to Hear Anymore (Metric, BMI) .... 95
I Get Around (Sea of Tunes, BMI) .......... 1
I Like It Like That (Jobete, BMI) .......... 67
I Still Get Jealous (Morris, ASCAP) .......... 53
I Wanna Love Him So Bad (Trio, BMI) .......... 61
I Want to Hold Your Hand (Duchess, BMI) .......... 74
I'm Into Somethin' Good (Screen Gems, Columbia, BMI) .......... 78
I'll Be in Trouble (Jobete, BMI) .......... 33
I'll Touch a Star (Blen-Les John-Trafalgar, ASCAP) 25
If You See My Love (Four Star, BMI) .......... 97
It Ain't No Use (Curtom-Jalynne, BMI) .......... 68
It's All Over Now (Kags, BMI) .......... 94
It Will Stand (Travis, BMI) .......... 89
Just Ain't Enough Love (Jobete, BMI) .......... 54
Keep on Pushing (Curtom, BMI) .......... 23
Kick That Little Foot, Sally Ann (Screen Gems-Columbia, BMI) .......... 63
Lazy Elsie Molly (Evanston-Picturetone, BMI) ... 42
Little Children (Rumbalero, BMI) .......... 14
Little Old Lady (From Pasadena), The (Trousdale, BMI) .......... 22
Little Toy Balloon, A (Duchess, BMI) .......... 86
Love Me Do (Ardmore-Beechwood, BMI) .......... 19
Love Me With All Your Heart (Peer Int'l, BMI) .. 13
Memphis (Arc, BMI) .......... 3
Mexican Shuffle, The (Alamo, ASCAP) .......... 90
Milord (Alamo, ASCAP) .......... 45
Mixed-Up, Shook-Up Girl (Ben-Lee, BMI) .......... 83
My Baby Don't Dig Me (Tangerine, BMI) .......... 56
My Boy Lollipop (Nom, BMI) .......... 2
My Guy (Jobete, BMI) .......... 29
My Heart Skips a Beat (Bluebook, BMI) .......... 100
No Particular Place to Go (Arc, BMI) .......... 11
Nobody I Know (Maclen, BMI) .......... 48
Not Fade Away (Nor Va Jak, BMI) .......... 55
Oh! Baby (Nujac, BMI) .......... 76
Oh, Rock My Soul (Pepamar, ASCAP) .......... 90
Party Girl (Schwartz, ASCAP) .......... 47
Peg 'o My Heart (Feist, ASCAP) .......... 15
People (Chappell, ASCAP) .......... 5
Rag Doll (Saturday-Gavadima, ASCAP) .......... 8
Remember Me (Gil, BMI) .......... 36
Share Your Love With Me (Don, BMI) .......... 60
Something You Got (Tune Kel, BMI) .......... 64
Steal Away (Fame, BMI) .......... 52
Taste of Tears (Prize-Elm Drive, ASCAP) .......... 87
Tears and Roses (Davilene, BMI) .......... 39
Tell Me (Southern, ASCAP) .......... 81
Tell Me Why (Signet, BMI) .......... 26
Tennessee Waltz (Acuff-Rose ,BMI) .......... 35
Things That I Used to Do, The (Music, BMI) .. 99
Today (Miller-Heritage House, ASCAP) .......... 28
Try It Baby (Jobete, BMI) .......... 20
Under the Boardwalk (T. M., BMI) .......... 62
Viva Las Vegas EP (Presley, BMI) .......... 92
Walk on By (Blue Seas-Jac, ASCAP) .......... 15
What Have I Got of My Own (Sawtell-Herring, ASCAP) .......... 51
What's the Matter With You Baby (Jobete, BMI) .. 17
Wishin' and Hopin' (Jonathan, BMI) .......... 44
World I Used to Know, The (In, ASCAP) .......... 59
World of Lonely People, The (Ross Jungnickel, ASCAP) .......... 73
World Without Love, A—Peter & Gordon (Maclen, BMI) ..........
Yesterday's Gone—Overlanders (Unart, BMI) ..... 77
Yesterday's Gone—Stuart-Clyde (Unart, BMI) ..... 21
(You Don't Know) How Glad I Am (Roosevelt, BMI). 58
You're My Remedy (Jobete, BMI) .......... 88
You're My World (Hill & Range, BMI) .......... 80


## BUBBLING UNDER THE HOT 100

101. ANGELITO .......... Rene & Rene, Columbia 43045
102. C'MON AND SWIN .......... Bobby Freeman, Autumn 2
103. THE COWBOY IN THE CONTINENTAL SUIT . Marty Robbins, Columbia 43049
104. SHE'S MY GIRL .......... Bobby Shafto, Rust 5082
105. A QUIET PLACE .......... Garnet Mimms, United Artists 715
106. LOVE IS ALL WE NEED .......... Vic Dana, Dolton 95
107. I WANNA BE LOVED .......... Dean & Jean, Rust 5081
108. I'M THE ONE .......... Gerry & the Pacemakers, Laurie 3233
109. WALK—DON'T RUN '64 .......... Ventures, Dolton 96
110. SOLE SOLE SOLE .......... Siw Malmkvist-Umberto Marcato, Jubilee 5479
111. JAMAICA SKA .......... Ska Kings, Atlantic 2232
112. SUMMER MEANS FUN .......... Bruce & Terry, Columbia 43055
113. LITTLE LATIN LUPE LU .......... Kingsmen, Wand 157
114. PRECIOUS WORDS .......... Wallace Bros., Sims 174
115. MY DREAMS .......... Brenda Lee, Decca 31628
116. JULIET .......... Four Pennies, Philips 40202
117. IT'S SUMMER TIME U.S.A. .......... Pixies Three, Mercury 72288
118. SUNNY .......... Neil Sedaka, RCA Victor 8382
119. GOOD TIME TONIGHT .......... Soul Sisters, Sue 10-005
120. MORE .......... Danny Williams, United Artists 601
121. WHAT CAN A MAN DO .......... Ben E. King, Atco 6303
122. HAUNTED HOUSE .......... Gene Simmons, Hi 2076
123. BACHELOR BOY .......... Cliff Richard & the Shadows, Epic 9691
124. GROWIN' UP TOO FAST .......... Diane Renay, 20th Century-Fox 514
125. BAMA LAMA BAMA LOO .......... Little Richard, Specialty 692
126. ONE GIRL .......... Garnet Mimms, United Artists 715
127. LUCKY STAR .......... Rick Nelson, Imperial 66039
128. CLOSE YOUR EYES .......... Arthur Prysock, Old Town 1163
129. JUST BE TRUE .......... Gene Chandler, Constellation 130
130. IN THE MISTY MOONLIGHT .......... Jerry Wallace, Challenge 59246
131. LIKE COLUMBUS DID .......... Reflections, Golden World 12
132. FATHER SEBASTIAN .......... Ramblers, Almont 311
133. HAPPY I LONG TO BE .......... Betty Everett, C. J. 619
134. SHE'S THE ONE .......... Chartbusters, Mutual 502
135. JOHNNY LOVES ME .......... Florraine Darlin, Ric 105-64

Compiled from national retail sales and radio station airplay by the Music Popularity Dept. of Record Market Research, Billboard.

For Week Ending July 11, 1964

# Billboard HOT 100

★ STAR performer—Sides registering greatest proportionate upward progress this week.

Billboard Award

| This Week | 1 Wk. Ago | 2 Wks. Ago | 3 Wks. Ago | TITLE Artist, Label & Number | Weeks On Chart |
|---|---|---|---|---|---|
| 1 | 1 | 2 | 3 | I GET AROUND — Beach Boys, Capitol 5174 | 8 |
| 2 | 3 | 6 | 15 | MEMPHIS — Johnny Rivers, Imperial 66032 | 7 |
| ★3 | 8 | 18 | 53 | RAG DOLL — 4 Seasons, Philips 40211 | 4 |
| 4 | 4 | 7 | 9 | DON'T LET THE SUN CATCH YOU CRYING — Gerry & the Pacemakers, Laurie 3251 | 8 |
| ★5 | 10 | 16 | 31 | CAN'T YOU SEE THAT SHE'S MINE — Dave Clark Five, Epic 9692 | 5 |
| 6 | 2 | 4 | 5 | MY BOY LOLLIPOP — Millie Small, Smash 1893 | 8 |
| 7 | 5 | 5 | 8 | PEOPLE — Barbra Streisand, Columbia 42965 | 15 |
| 8 | 6 | 1 | 2 | A WORLD WITHOUT LOVE — Peter & Gordon, Capitol 5175 | 10 |
| ★9 | 12 | 20 | 35 | THE GIRL FROM IPANEMA — Getz/Gilberto, Verve 10323 | 6 |
| 10 | 11 | 14 | 25 | NO PARTICULAR PLACE TO GO — Chuck Berry, Chess 1898 | 8 |
| 11 | 9 | 9 | 16 | BAD TO ME — Billy J. Kramer, Imperial 66027 | 7 |
| ★12 | 22 | 60 | — | THE LITTLE OLD LADY (From Pasadena) — Jan & Dean, Liberty 55704 | 3 |
| ★13 | 31 | 44 | 62 | DANG ME — Roger Miller, Smash 1881 | 5 |
| 14 | 7 | 3 | 1 | CHAPEL OF LOVE — Dixie Cups, Red Bird 001 | 11 |
| 15 | 16 | 23 | 44 | GOOD TIMES — Sam Cooke, RCA Victor 8368 | 6 |
| 16 | 18 | 25 | 28 | DON'T THROW YOUR LOVE AWAY — Searchers, Kapp 593 | 7 |
| 17 | 20 | 27 | 46 | TRY IT BABY — Marvin Gaye, Tamla 54095 | 6 |
| ★18 | 23 | 32 | 65 | KEEP ON PUSHING — Impressions, ABC-Paramount 10554 | 6 |
| 19 | 14 | 12 | 11 | LITTLE CHILDREN — Billy J. Kramer, Imperial 66027 | 13 |
| 20 | 15 | 10 | 6 | WALK ON BY — Dionne Warwick, Scepter 1274 | 12 |
| 21 | 17 | 22 | 32 | WHAT'S THE MATTER WITH YOU BABY — Marvin Gaye & Mary Wells, Motown 1057 | 9 |
| 22 | 13 | 8 | 4 | LOVE ME WITH ALL YOUR HEART — Ray Charles Singers, Command 4046 | 14 |
| ★23 | 48 | 73 | — | NOBODY I KNOW — Peter & Gordon, Capitol 5211 | 3 |
| 24 | 19 | 11 | 7 | LOVE ME DO — Beatles, Tollie 9008 | 14 |
| 25 | 21 | 24 | 27 | YESTERDAY'S GONE — Chad Stuart & Jeremy Clyde, World Artists 1021 | 8 |
| ★26 | 36 | 45 | 67 | REMEMBER ME — Rita Pavone, RCA Victor 8365 | 6 |
| ★27 | 44 | 61 | 79 | WISHIN' AND HOPIN' — Dusty Springfield, Philips 40207 | 4 |
| 28 | 24 | 29 | 41 | DON'T WORRY BABY — Beach Boys, Capitol 5174 | 7 |
| 29 | 30 | 38 | 51 | ALONE — Four Seasons, Vee Jay 597 | 6 |
| ★30 | 37 | 56 | 58 | FARMER JOHN — Premiers, Warner Bros. 5443 | 4 |
| ★31 | 62 | 81 | — | UNDER THE BOARDWALK — Drifters, Atlantic 2237 | 3 |
| 32 | 28 | 21 | 17 | TODAY — New Christy Minstrels, Columbia 43000 | 13 |
| 33 | 32 | 30 | 30 | BEANS IN MY EARS — Serendipity Singers, Philips 40198 | 8 |
| ★34 | 46 | 72 | — | EVERYBODY LOVES SOMEBODY — Dean Martin, Reprise 0281 | 3 |
| 35 | 41 | 52 | 70 | HEY HARMONICA MAN — Stevie Wonder, Tamla 54096 | 5 |
| 36 | 25 | 26 | 26 | I'LL TOUCH A STAR — Terry Stafford, Crusader 105 | 8 |
| 37 | 35 | 46 | 57 | TENNESSEE WALTZ — Sam Cooke, RCA Victor 8368 | 5 |
| ★38 | 52 | 77 | 100 | STEAL AWAY — Jimmy Hughes, Fame 6401 | 4 |
| 39 | 33 | 41 | 48 | I'LL BE IN TROUBLE — Temptations, Gordy 7032 | 7 |
| 40 | 42 | 50 | 63 | LAZY ELSIE MOLLY — Chubby Checker, Parkway 920 | 6 |
| ★41 | 58 | 66 | — | (You Don't Know) HOW GLAD I AM — Nancy Wilson, Capitol 5198 | 3 |
| ★42 | 61 | 84 | 88 | I WANNA LOVE HIM SO BAD — Jelly Beans, Red Bird 10-003 | 4 |
| 43 | 27 | 17 | 10 | DIANE — Bachelors, London 9639 | 13 |
| 44 | 34 | 19 | 14 | HELLO, DOLLY! — Louis Armstrong, Kapp 573 | 22 |
| 45 | 29 | 15 | 12 | MY GUY — Mary Wells, Motown 1056 | 15 |
| 46 | 26 | 13 | 13 | TELL ME WHY — Bobby Vinton, Epic 9687 | 8 |
| 47 | 49 | 57 | 69 | BEG ME — Chuck Jackson, Wand 154 | 8 |
| 48 | 50 | 58 | 73 | ALONE WITH YOU — Brenda Lee, Decca 31628 | 5 |
| 49 | 38 | 42 | 49 | GIVING UP — Gladys Knight & the Pips, Maxx 326 | 10 |
| 50 | 51 | 53 | 55 | WHAT HAVE I GOT OF MY OWN — Trini Lopez, Reprise 0276 | 10 |
| 51 | 53 | 64 | 82 | I STILL GET JEALOUS — Louis Armstrong, Kapp 597 | 4 |
| 52 | 55 | 63 | 74 | NOT FADE AWAY — Rolling Stones, London 9657 | 11 |
| 53 | 60 | 65 | 80 | SHARE YOUR LOVE WITH ME — Bobby Bland, Duke 377 | 5 |
| 54 | 59 | 70 | 78 | THE WORLD I USED TO KNOW — Jimmie Rodgers, Dot 16595 | 7 |
| 55 | 45 | 49 | 56 | MILORD — Bobby Darin, Atco 6297 | 8 |
| 56 | 47 | 47 | 52 | PARTY GIRL — Bernadette Carroll, Laurie 3238 | 9 |
| ★57 | 67 | 82 | — | I LIKE IT LIKE THAT — Miracles, Tamla 54098 | 3 |
| 58 | 64 | 67 | 86 | SOMETHING YOU GOT — Alvin Robinson, Tiger 104 | 6 |
| 59 | 54 | 62 | 71 | JUST AIN'T ENOUGH LOVE — Eddie Holland, Motown 1058 | 7 |
| 60 | 66 | 78 | 90 | DO I LOVE YOU? — Ronettes, Philles 121 | 4 |
| 61 | 63 | 68 | 77 | KICK THAT LITTLE FOOT, SALLY ANN — Round Robin, Domain 1404 | 7 |
| ★62 | 88 | — | — | YOU'RE MY REMEDY — Marvelettes, Tamla 54097 | 2 |
| 63 | 65 | 69 | 76 | HICKORY, DICK AND DOC — Bobby Vee, Liberty 55700 | 7 |
| 64 | 69 | 71 | 87 | THE FIRST NIGHT OF THE FULL MOON — Jack Jones, Kapp 589 | 7 |
| ★65 | 80 | — | — | YOU'RE MY WORLD — Cilla Black, Capitol 5196 | 2 |
| 66 | 71 | 83 | — | I BELIEVE — Bachelors, London 9672 | 3 |
| ★67 | 83 | 85 | 93 | MIXED-UP, SHOOK-UP GIRL — Patty & the Emblems, Herald 590 | 4 |
| 68 | 74 | — | — | I WANT TO HOLD YOUR HAND — Boston Pops Ork, RCA Victor 8378 | 2 |
| ★69 | 85 | — | — | HANDY MAN — Del Shannon, Amy 905 | 2 |
| 70 | 81 | — | — | TELL ME — Rolling Stones, London 9682 | 2 |
| 71 | 72 | 79 | — | I CAN'T HEAR YOU — Betty Everett, Vee Jay 599 | 3 |
| 72 | 78 | 90 | — | I'M INTO SOMETHIN' GOOD — Earl-Jean, Colpix 729 | 3 |
| 73 | 75 | 87 | 92 | PEG O' MY HEART — Robert Maxwell, Decca 25637 | 4 |
| 74 | 68 | 76 | 84 | IT AIN'T NO USE — Major Lance, Okeh 7197 | 6 |
| ★75 | — | — | — | SUGAR LIPS — Al Hirt, RCA Victor 8391 | 1 |
| 76 | 70 | 80 | — | GIRLS — Major Lance, Okeh 7197 | 3 |
| ★77 | — | — | — | WHERE DID OUR LOVE GO — Supremes, Motown 1060 | 1 |
| 78 | 76 | 89 | 95 | OH! BABY — Barbara Lynn, Jamie 1277 | 4 |
| 79 | 79 | 88 | 98 | THE FERRIS WHEEL — Everly Brothers, Warner Bros. 5441 | 4 |
| 80 | 82 | — | — | ANYONE WHO KNOWS WHAT LOVE IS — Irma Thomas, Imperial 66041 | 2 |
| ★81 | — | — | — | AL-DI-LA — Ray Charles Singers, Command 4049 | 1 |
| 82 | 84 | — | — | DON'T TAKE YOUR LOVE FROM ME — Gloria Lynne, Everest 2044 | 2 |
| ★83 | — | — | — | LITTLE LATIN LUPE LU — Kingsmen, Wand 157 | 1 |
| 84 | 86 | 86 | 89 | A LITTLE TOY BALLOON — Danny Williams, United Artists 729 | 4 |
| ★85 | — | — | — | HOW DO YOU DO IT — Gerry and the Pacemakers, Laurie 3261 | 1 |
| ★86 | — | — | — | WALK—DON'T RUN '64 — Ventures, Dolton 96 | 1 |
| 87 | 89 | — | — | IT WILL STAND — Showmen, Imperial 66033 | 2 |
| 88 | 90 | 95 | — | THE MEXICAN SHUFFLE — Herb Alpert's Tijuana Brass, A&M 742 | 3 |
| ★89 | — | — | — | JUST BE TRUE — Gene Chandler, Constellation 130 | 1 |
| ★90 | — | — | — | SHE'S THE ONE — Chartbusters, Mutual 502 | 1 |
| 91 | — | — | — | ANGELITO — Rene and Rene, Columbia 43045 | 1 |
| 92 | 97 | — | — | IF YOU SEE MY LOVE — Lenny Welch, Cadence 1446 | 2 |
| 93 | 96 | 96 | — | OH, ROCK MY SOUL — Peter, Paul & Mary, Warner Bros. 5442 | 3 |
| 94 | 100 | — | — | MY HEART SKIPS A BEAT — Buck Owens, Capitol 5136 | 2 |
| 95 | — | — | — | I'M THE ONE — Gerry and the Pacemakers, Laurie 3233 | 1 |
| 96 | — | — | — | LIKE COLUMBUS DID — Reflections, Golden World 12 | 1 |
| 97 | — | — | — | LOVE IS ALL WE NEED — Vic Dana, Dolton 95 | 1 |
| 98 | — | — | — | JAMAICA SKA — Ska Kings, Atlantic 2232 | 1 |
| 99 | — | — | — | IT'S A SIN TO TELL A LIE — Tony Bennett, Columbia 43073 | 1 |
| 100 | — | — | — | C'MON AND SWIM — Bobby Freeman, 8 Autumn 2 | 1 |

## HOT 100—A TO Z—(Publisher-Licensee)


Al-Di-La (Witmark, ASCAP) ... 81
Alone (Selma, BMI) ... 29
Alone With You (Metric, BMI) ... 48
Angelito (Gil-Epps, BMI) ... 91
Anyone Who Knows What Love Is (Metric, BMI) ... 80
Bad to Me (Metric, BMI) ... 11
Beans in My Ears (Fall River, BMI) ... 33
Beg Me (T. M., BMI) ... 47
Can't You See That She's Mine (Beechwood, BMI) ... 5
C'mon and Swim (Taracrest, BMI) ... 100
Chapel of Love (Trio, BMI) ... 14
Dang Me (Tree, BMI) ... 13
Diane (Miller, ASCAP) ... 43
Do I Love You? (Mother Bertha-Hill & Range, BMI) ... 60
Don't Let the Sun Catch You Crying (Pacemaker, BMI) ... 4
Don't Take Your Love From Me (Morris, ASCAP) ... 82
Don't Throw Your Love Away (Wyncote, ASCAP) ... 16
Don't Worry Baby (Sea of Tunes, BMI) ... 28
Everybody Loves Somebody (Sands, ASCAP) ... 34
Farmer John (Venice, BMI) ... 30
Ferris Wheel, The (Rose, BMI) ... 79
First Night of the Full Moon, The (Famous, ASCAP) ... 64
Girl From Ipanema, The (Duchess, BMI) ... 9
Girls (Curtom, BMI) ... 76
Giving Up (Trio, BMI) ... 49
Good Times (Kags, BMI) ... 15
Handy Man (Travis, BMI) ... 69
Hello, Dolly! (Morris, ASCAP) ... 44
Hey Harmonica Man (Jobete-Little Darlin', BMI) ... 35
Hickory, Dick and Doc (Rose, BMI) ... 63
How Do You Do It (Just, BMI) ... 85
I Believe (Cromwell, ASCAP) ... 66
I Can't Hear You (Screen Gems-Columbia, BMI) ... 71
I Get Around (Sea of Tunes, BMI) ... 1
I Like It Like That (Jobete, BMI) ... 57
I Still Get Jealous (Morris, ASCAP) ... 51
I Wanna Love Him So Bad (Trio, BMI) ... 42
I Want to Hold Your Hand (Duchess, BMI) ... 68
I'm Into Somethin' Good (Screen Gems-Columbia, BMI) ... 72
I'm the One (Pacer, BMI) ... 95
I'll Be in Trouble (Jobete, BMI) ... 39
I'll Touch a Star (Blen-Les John-Trafalgar, ASCAP) ... 36
If You See My Love (Four Star, BMI) ... 92
It Ain't No Use (Curtom-Jalynne, BMI) ... 74
It's a Sin to Tell a Lie (Bregman, Vocco & Conn, ASCAP) ... 99
It Will Stand (Travis, BMI) ... 87
Jamaica Ska (Benders, BMI) ... 98
Just Ain't Enough Love (Jobete, BMI) ... 59
Just Be True (Curtom-Camad, BMI) ... 89
Keep on Pushing (Curtom, BMI) ... 18
Kick That Little Foot, Sally Ann (Screen Gems-Columbia, BMI) ... 61
Lazy Elsie Molly (Evanston-Picturetone, BMI) ... 40
Like Columbus Did (Myto, BMI) ... 96
Little Children (Rumbalero, BMI) ... 19
Little Latin Lupe Lu (Conrad, BMI) ... 83
Little Old Lady (From Pasadena), The (Trousdale, BMI) ... 12
Little Toy Balloon, A (Duchess, BMI) ... 84
Love Is All We Need (Travis, BMI) ... 97
Love Me Do (Ardmore-Beechwood, BMI) ... 24
Love Me With All Your Heart (Peer Int'l, BMI) ... 22
Memphis (Arc, BMI) ... 2
Mexican Shuffle, The (Alamo, ASCAP) ... 88
Milord (Alamo, ASCAP) ... 55
Mixed-Up, Shook-Up Girl (Ben-Lee, BMI) ... 67
My Boy Lollipop (Nom, BMI) ... 6
My Guy (Jobete, BMI) ... 45
My Heart Skips a Beat (Bluebook, BMI) ... 94
No Particular Place to Go (Arc, BMI) ... 10
Nobody I Know (Maclen, BMI) ... 23
Not Fade Away (Nor Va Jak, BMI) ... 52
Oh! Baby (Nujac, BMI) ... 78
Oh, Rock My Soul (Pepamar, ASCAP) ... 93
Party Girl (Schwartz, ASCAP) ... 56
Peg o' My Heart (Feist, ASCAP) ... 73
People (Chappell, ASCAP) ... 7
Rag Doll (Saturday-Gavadima, ASCAP) ... 3
Remember Me (Gil, BMI) ... 26
Share Your Love With Me (Don, BMI) ... 53
She's the One (Eastwick-Chartbuster, BMI) ... 90
Something You Got (Tune Kel, BMI) ... 58
Steal Away (Fame, BMI) ... 38
Sugar Lips (Tree, BMI) ... 75
Tell Me (Southern, ASCAP) ... 70
Tell Me Why (Signet, BMI) ... 46
Tennessee Waltz (Acuff-Rose, BMI) ... 37
Today (Miller-Heritage House, ASCAP) ... 32
Try It Baby (Jobete, BMI) ... 17
Under the Boardwalk (T. M., BMI) ... 31
Walk—Don't Run '64 (Forshay, BMI) ... 86
Walk on By (Blue Seas-Jac, ASCAP) ... 20
What Have I Got of My Own (Sawtell-Herring, ASCAP) ... 50
What's the Matter With You Baby (Jobete, BMI) 21
Where Did Our Love Go (Jobete, BMI) ... 77
Wishin' and Hopin' (Jonathan, BMI) ... 27
World I Used to Know, The (In, ASCAP) ... 54
World Without Love, A (Maclen, BMI) ... 8
Yesterday's Gone (Unart, BMI) ... 25
(You Don't Know) How Glad I Am (Roosevelt, BMI). 41
You're My Remedy (Jobete, BMI) ... 62
You're My World (Hill & Range, BMI) ... 65


## BUBBLING UNDER THE HOT 100

101. SHE'S MY GIRL ... Bobby Shafto, Rust 5082
102. A QUIET PLACE ... Garnet Mimms, United Artists 715
103. DREAM LOVER ... Paris Sisters, MGM 13236
104. I DON'T WANT TO HEAR ANYMORE ... Jerry Butler, Vee Jay 598
105. HELP THE POOR ... B. B. King, ABC-Paramount 10552
106. IT'S ALL OVER NOW ... Valentinos, Sar 152
107. PRECIOUS WORDS ... Wallace Brothers, Sims 174
108. SOLE SOLE SOLE ... Siw Malmkvist & Umberto Marcato, Jubilee 5479
109. ALL MY LOVING ... Hollyridge Strings, Capitol 5207
110. MY KIND OF TOWN ... Frank Sinatra, Reprise 0279
111. BACHELOR BOY ... Cliff Richard and the Shadows, Epic 9691
112. THE COWBOY IN THE CONTINENTAL SUIT ... Marty Robbins, Columbia 43049
113. WHAT CAN A MAN DO ... Ben E. King, Atco 6303
114. SUNNY ... Neil Sedaka, RCA Victor 8382
115. LICORICE STICK ... Pete Fountain, Coral 62413
116. GOOD TIME TONIGHT ... Soul Sisters, Sue 10-005
117. IT'S SUMMER TIME U.S.A. ... Pixies Three, Mercury 72288
118. MORE ... Danny Williams, United Artists 601
119. BAMA LAMA BAMA LOO ... Little Richard, Specialty 692
120. OH WHAT A KISS ... Johnny Rivers, United Artists 741
121. GINO IS A COWARD ... Gino Washington, Ric-Tic 100
122. HANGIN' ON TO MY BABY ... Tracey Dey, Amy 908
123. I'M SORRY ... Pete Drake, Smash 1910
124. I'M GONNA CRY ... Wilson Pickett, Atlantic 2233
125. FATHER SEBASTIAN ... Ramblers, Almont 311
126. SHOUT ... Lulu and the Luvers, Parrot 9678
127. IN THE MISTY MOONLIGHT ... Jerry Wallace, Challenge 59246
128. JOHNNY LOVES ME ... Florraine Darlin', Ric 105-64
129. HAPPY I LONG TO BE ... Betty Everett, CJ 619
130. FRANKIE AND JOHNNY ... Greenwood County Singers, Kapp 591
131. GROWIN' UP TOO FAST ... Diane Renay, 20th Century-Fox 514
132. ALL GROWN UP ... Crystals, Philles 122
133. G.T.O. ... Ronnie & the Daytonas, Mala 481

Compiled from national retail sales and radio station airplay by the Music Popularity Dept. of Record Market Research, Billboard.

# Billboard HOT 100

For Week Ending July 18, 1964

★ STAR performer—Sides registering greatest proportionate upward progress this week.

| This Week | 1 Wk. Ago | 2 Wks. Ago | 3 Wks. Ago | TITLE, Artist, Label & Number | Weeks On Chart |
|---|---|---|---|---|---|
| 1 | 3 | 8 | 18 | RAG DOLL — 4 Seasons, Philips 40211 | 4 |
| 2 | 2 | 3 | 6 | MEMPHIS — Johnny Rivers, Imperial 66032 | 8 |
| 3 | 1 | 1 | 2 | I GET AROUND — Beach Boys, Capitol 5174 | 9 |
| 4 | 5 | 10 | 16 | CAN'T YOU SEE THAT SHE'S MINE — Dave Clark Five, Epic 9692 | 6 |
| ★5 | 9 | 12 | 20 | THE GIRL FROM IPANEMA — Getz/Gilberto, Verve 10323 | 7 |
| ★6 | 12 | 22 | 60 | THE LITTLE OLD LADY (From Pasadena) — Jan & Dean, Liberty 55704 | 4 |
| 7 | 4 | 4 | 7 | DON'T LET THE SUN CATCH YOU CRYING — Gerry & the Pacemakers, Laurie 3251 | 9 |
| 8 | 13 | 31 | 44 | DANG ME — Roger Miller, Smash 1881 | 6 |
| 9 | 6 | 2 | 4 | MY BOY LOLLIPOP — Millie Small, Smash 1893 | 9 |
| ★10 | 18 | 23 | 32 | KEEP ON PUSHING — Impressions, ABC-Paramount 10554 | 7 |
| 11 | 15 | 16 | 23 | GOOD TIMES — Sam Cooke, RCA Victor 8368 | 7 |
| 12 | 27 | 44 | 61 | WISHIN' AND HOPIN' — Dusty Springfield, Philips 40207 | 5 |
| 13 | 34 | 46 | 72 | EVERYBODY LOVES SOMEBODY — Dean Martin, Reprise 0281 | 4 |
| 14 | 7 | 5 | 5 | PEOPLE — Barbra Streisand, Columbia 42965 | 16 |
| ★15 | 23 | 48 | 73 | NOBODY I KNOW — Peter & Gordon, Capitol 5211 | 4 |
| 16 | 17 | 20 | 27 | TRY IT BABY — Marvin Gaye, Tamla 54095 | 7 |
| 17 | 10 | 11 | 14 | NO PARTICULAR PLACE TO GO — Chuck Berry, Chess 1898 | 9 |
| 18 | 11 | 9 | 9 | BAD TO ME — Billy J. Kramer, Imperial 66027 | 8 |
| 19 | 31 | 62 | 81 | UNDER THE BOARDWALK — Drifters, Atlantic 2237 | 4 |
| 20 | 16 | 18 | 25 | DON'T THROW YOUR LOVE AWAY — Searchers, Kapp 593 | 8 |
| 21 | — | — | — | A HARD DAY'S NIGHT — Beatles, Capitol 5222 | 1 |
| 22 | 8 | 6 | 1 | A WORLD WITHOUT LOVE — Peter & Gordon, Capitol 5175 | 11 |
| 23 | 30 | 37 | 56 | FARMER JOHN — Premiers, Warner Bros. 5443 | 5 |
| 24 | 42 | 61 | 84 | I WANNA LOVE HIM SO BAD — Jelly Beans, Red Bird 10-003 | 5 |
| 25 | 28 | 24 | 29 | DON'T WORRY BABY — Beach Boys, Capitol 5174 | 8 |
| 26 | 26 | 36 | 45 | REMEMBER ME — Rita Pavone, RCA Victor 8365 | 7 |
| 27 | 14 | 7 | 3 | CHAPEL OF LOVE — Dixie Cups, Red Bird 001 | 12 |
| 28 | 29 | 30 | 38 | ALONE — Four Seasons, Vee Jay 597 | 7 |
| 29 | 19 | 14 | 12 | LITTLE CHILDREN — Billy J. Kramer, Imperial 66027 | 14 |
| 30 | 38 | 52 | 77 | STEAL AWAY — Jimmy Hughes, Fame 6401 | 5 |
| 31 | 41 | 58 | 66 | (You Don't Know) HOW GLAD I AM — Nancy Wilson, Capitol 5198 | 4 |
| 32 | 22 | 13 | 8 | LOVE ME WITH ALL YOUR HEART — Ray Charles Singers, Command 4046 | 15 |
| 33 | 35 | 41 | 52 | HEY HARMONICA MAN — Stevie Wonder, Tamla 54096 | 6 |
| 34 | 25 | 21 | 24 | YESTERDAY'S GONE — Chad Stuart & Jeremy Clyde, World Artists 1021 | 9 |
| 35 | 37 | 35 | 46 | TENNESSEE WALTZ — Sam Cooke, RCA Victor 8368 | 6 |
| 36 | 20 | 15 | 10 | WALK ON BY — Dionne Warwick, Scepter 1274 | 13 |
| 37 | 21 | 17 | 22 | WHAT'S THE MATTER WITH YOU BABY — Marvin Gaye & Mary Wells, Motown 1057 | 10 |
| ★38 | 77 | — | — | WHERE DID OUR LOVE GO — Supremes, Motown 1060 | 2 |
| 39 | 60 | 66 | 78 | DO I LOVE YOU? — Ronettes, Philles 121 | 5 |
| 40 | 39 | 33 | 41 | I'LL BE IN TROUBLE — Temptations, Gordy 7032 | 8 |
| 41 | 57 | 67 | 82 | I LIKE IT LIKE THAT — Miracles, Tamla 54098 | 4 |
| 42 | 65 | 80 | — | YOU'RE MY WORLD — Cilla Black, Capitol 5196 | 3 |
| 43 | 50 | 51 | 53 | WHAT HAVE I GOT OF MY OWN — Trini Lopez, Reprise 0276 | 11 |
| 44 | 40 | 42 | 50 | LAZY ELSIE MOLLY — Chubby Checker, Parkway 920 | 7 |
| 45 | 47 | 49 | 57 | BEG ME — Chuck Jackson, Wand 154 | 9 |
| 46 | 51 | 53 | 64 | I STILL GET JEALOUS — Louis Armstrong, Kapp 597 | 5 |
| ★47 | 69 | 85 | — | HANDY MAN — Del Shannon, Amy 905 | 3 |
| 48 | 52 | 55 | 63 | NOT FADE AWAY — Rolling Stones, London 9657 | 12 |
| 49 | 53 | 60 | 65 | SHARE YOUR LOVE WITH ME — Bobby Bland, Duke 377 | 6 |
| 50 | 48 | 50 | 58 | ALONE WITH YOU — Brenda Lee, Decca 31628 | 6 |
| 51 | 54 | 59 | 70 | THE WORLD I USED TO KNOW — Jimmie Rodgers, Dot 16595 | 8 |
| 52 | 58 | 64 | 67 | SOMETHING YOU GOT — Alvin Robinson, Tiger 104 | 7 |
| 53 | 66 | 71 | 83 | I BELIEVE — Bachelors, London 9672 | 4 |
| 54 | 81 | — | — | AL-DI-LA — Ray Charles Singers, Command 4049 | 2 |
| 55 | 75 | — | — | SUGAR LIPS — Al Hirt, RCA Victor 8391 | 2 |
| 56 | 67 | 83 | 85 | MIXED-UP, SHOOK-UP GIRL — Patty & the Emblems, Herald 590 | 5 |
| 57 | 62 | 88 | — | YOU'RE MY REMEDY — Marvelettes, Tamla 54097 | 3 |
| 58 | 100 | — | — | C'MON AND SWIM — Bobby Freeman, 8 Autumn 2 | 2 |
| 59 | 64 | 69 | 71 | THE FIRST NIGHT OF THE FULL MOON — Jack Jones, Kapp 589 | 8 |
| ★60 | 72 | 78 | 90 | I'M INTO SOMETHIN' GOOD — Earl-Jean, Colpix 729 | 4 |
| 61 | 68 | 74 | — | I WANT TO HOLD YOUR HAND — Boston Pops Ork, RCA Victor 8378 | 3 |
| 62 | 70 | 81 | — | TELL ME — Rolling Stones, London 9682 | 3 |
| 63 | 85 | — | — | HOW DO YOU DO IT — Gerry and the Pacemakers, Laurie 3261 | 2 |
| 64 | 73 | 75 | 87 | PEG O' MY HEART — Robert Maxwell, Decca 25637 | 5 |
| ★65 | 86 | — | — | WALK—DON'T RUN '64 — Ventures, Dolton 96 | 2 |
| 66 | 71 | 72 | 79 | I CAN'T HEAR YOU — Betty Everett, Vee Jay 599 | 4 |
| 67 | 80 | 82 | — | ANYONE WHO KNOWS WHAT LOVE IS — Irma Thomas, Imperial 66041 | 3 |
| 68 | 61 | 63 | 68 | KICK THAT LITTLE FOOT, SALLY ANN — Round Robin, Domain 1404 | 8 |
| 69 | 74 | 68 | 76 | IT AIN'T NO USE — Major Lance, Okeh 7197 | 7 |
| 70 | 89 | — | — | JUST BE TRUE — Gene Chandler, Constellation 130 | 2 |
| 71 | 91 | — | — | ANGELITO — Rene and Rene, Columbia 43045 | 2 |
| 72 | — | — | — | PEOPLE SAY — Dixie Cups, Red Bird 10-006 | 1 |
| 73 | 79 | 79 | 88 | THE FERRIS WHEEL — Everly Brothers, Warner Bros. 5441 | 5 |
| 74 | 78 | 76 | 89 | OH! BABY — Barbara Lynn, Jamie 1277 | 5 |
| 75 | 76 | 70 | 80 | GIRLS — Major Lance, Okeh 7197 | 4 |
| 76 | 82 | 84 | — | DON'T TAKE YOUR LOVE FROM ME — Gloria Lynne, Everest 2044 | 3 |
| 77 | 63 | 65 | 69 | HICKORY, DICK AND DOC — Bobby Vee, Liberty 55700 | 8 |
| 78 | 83 | — | — | LITTLE LATIN LUPE LU — Kingsmen, Wand 157 | 2 |
| 79 | 97 | — | — | LOVE IS ALL WE NEED — Vic Dana, Dolton 95 | 2 |
| 80 | 87 | 89 | — | IT WILL STAND — Showmen, Imperial 66033 | 3 |
| 81 | — | — | — | EVERYBODY NEEDS SOMEBODY TO LOVE — Solomon Burke, Atlantic 2241 | 1 |
| 82 | 95 | — | — | I'M THE ONE — Gerry and the Pacemakers, Laurie 3233 | 2 |
| 83 | 90 | — | — | SHE'S THE ONE — Chartbusters, Mutual 502 | 2 |
| 84 | — | — | — | SOLE SOLE SOLE — Siw Malmkvist & Umberto Marcato, Jubilee 5479 | 1 |
| 85 | 88 | 90 | 95 | THE MEXICAN SHUFFLE — Herb Alpert's Tijuana Brass, A&M 742 | 4 |
| 86 | — | — | — | THANK YOU BABY — Shirelles, Scepter 1278 | 1 |
| 87 | — | — | — | LOOKING FOR LOVE — Connie Francis, MGM 13256 | 1 |
| 88 | — | — | — | INVISIBLE TEARS — Ray Conniff Singers, Columbia 43061 | 1 |
| 89 | — | — | — | HEY GIRL, DON'T BOTHER ME — Tams, ABC-Paramount 10573 | 1 |
| 90 | — | — | — | AIN'T SHE SWEET — Beatles, Atco 6308 | 1 |
| 91 | — | — | — | NO ONE TO CRY TO — Ray Charles, ABC-Paramount 10571 | 1 |
| 92 | — | — | — | BAMA LAMA BAMA LOO — Little Richard, Specialty 692 | 1 |
| 93 | — | — | — | IT HURTS TO BE IN LOVE — Gene Pitney, Musicor 1040 | 1 |
| 94 | — | — | — | A HOUSE IS NOT A HOME — Brook Benton, Mercury 72303 | 1 |
| 95 | — | — | — | A QUIET PLACE — Garnet Mimms, United Artists 715 | 1 |
| 96 | — | — | — | BABY COME HOME — Ruby & the Romantics, Kapp 601 | 1 |
| 97 | — | — | — | A SHOT IN THE DARK — Henry Mancini & His Ork, RCA Victor 8381 | 1 |
| 98 | — | — | — | WORRY — Johnny Tillotson, MGM 13255 | 1 |
| 99 | — | — | — | SHE'S MY GIRL — Bobby Shafto, Rust 5082 | 1 |
| 100 | — | — | — | SAY YOU — Ronnie Dove, Diamond 167 | 1 |

## HOT 100—A TO Z—(Publisher-Licensee)

Ain't She Sweet (Advance, ASCAP) .......... 90
Al-Di-La (Witmark, ASCAP) .......... 54
Alone (Selma, BMI) .......... 28
Alone With You (Metric, BMI) .......... 50
Angelito (Gil-Epps, BMI) .......... 71
Anyone Who Knows What Love Is (Metric, BMI) .......... 67
Baby Come Home (Rosewood-Day-Hilliard, ASCAP) .......... 96
Bad to Me (Metric, BMI) .......... 18
Bama Lama Bama Loo (Little Richard, BMI) .......... 92
Beg Me (T.M., BMI) .......... 45
Believe, I (Just, BMI) .......... 53
C'mon and Swim (Taracrest, BMI) .......... 58
Can't You See That She's Mine (Beechwood, BMI) .......... 4
Chapel of Love (Trio, BMI) .......... 27
Dang Me (Tree, BMI) .......... 8
Do I Love You? (Mother Bertha-Hill & Range, BMI) .......... 39
Don't Let the Sun Catch You Crying (Pacemaker, BMI) .......... 7
Don't Take Your Love From Me (Morris, ASCAP) .......... 76
Don't Throw Your Love Away (Wyncote, ASCAP) .......... 20
Don't Worry Baby (Sea of Tunes, BMI) .......... 25
Everybody Loves Somebody (Sands, ASCAP) .......... 13
Everybody Needs Somebody to Love (Keetch, Caesar & Dino, BMI) .......... 81
Farmer John (Venice, BMI) .......... 23
Ferris Wheel, The (Rose, BMI) .......... 73
First Night of the Full Moon, The (Famous, ASCAP) .......... 59
Girl From Ipanema, The (Duchess, BMI) .......... 5
Girls (Curtom, BMI) .......... 75
Good Times (Kags, BMI) .......... 11
Handy Man (Travis, BMI) .......... 47
Hard Day's Night, A (Unart-Maclen, BMI) .......... 21
Hey Girl Don't Bother Me (Low-Twi, BMI) .......... 89
Hey Harmonica Man (Jobete-Little Darlin', BMI) .......... 33
Hickory, Dick and Doc (Rose, BMI) .......... 77

House Is Not a Home, A (Diplomat, BMI) .......... 94
How Do You Do It (Just, BMI) .......... 63
How Glad I Am (Cromwell, ASCAP) .......... 31
I Believe (Cromwell, ASCAP) .......... 53
I Can't Hear You (Screen Gems-Columbia, BMI) .......... 66
I Get Around (Sea of Tunes, BMI) .......... 3
I Like It Like That (Jobete, BMI) .......... 41
I Still Get Jealous (Morris, ASCAP) .......... 46
I Wanna Love Him So Bad (Trio, BMI) .......... 24
I Want to Hold Your Hand (Maxwell-Conrad, BMI) .......... 61
I'm Into Somethin' Good (Screen Gems-Columbia, BMI) .......... 60
I'm the One (Pacer, BMI) .......... 82
I'll Be in Trouble (Jobete, BMI) .......... 40
Invisible Tears (Central Songs, BMI) .......... 88
It Ain't No Use (Curtom-Jalynne, BMI) .......... 69
It Hurts to Be in Love (Screen Gems-Columbia, BMI) .......... 93
It Will Stand (Travis, BMI) .......... 80
Just Be True (Curtom-Camad, BMI) .......... 70
Keep On Pushing (Curtom, BMI) .......... 10
Kick That Little Foot, Sally Ann (Screen Gems-Columbia, BMI) .......... 68
Lazy Elsie Molly (Evanston-Picturetone, BMI) .......... 44
Little Children (Rumbalero, BMI) .......... 29
Little Latin Lupe Lu (Maxwell-Conrad, BMI) .......... 78
Little Old Lady (From Pasadena), The (Trousdale, BMI) .......... 6
Looking for Love (Leeds, BMI) .......... 87
Love Is All We Need (Travis, BMI) .......... 79
Love Me With All Your Heart (Peer Int'l, BMI) .......... 32
Memphis (Arc, BMI) .......... 2
Mexican Shuffle, The (Almo, ASCAP) .......... 85
Mixed-Up, Shook-Up Girl (Ben-Lee, BMI) .......... 56
My Boy Lollipop (Nom, BMI) .......... 9
No One to Cry To (Hill & Range, BMI) .......... 91
No Particular Place to Go (Arc, BMI) .......... 17

Nobody I Know (Maclen, BMI) .......... 15
Not Fade Away (Nor Va Jak, BMI) .......... 48
Oh! Baby (Nujac, BMI) .......... 74
Peg o' My Heart (Feist, ASCAP) .......... 64
People (Chappell, ASCAP) .......... 14
People Say (Trio, ASCAP) .......... 72
Quiet Place, A (Rittenhouse, BMI) .......... 95
Rag Doll (Saturday-Gavadima, ASCAP) .......... 1
Remember Me (Gil, BMI) .......... 26
Say You (T.M., BMI) .......... 100
Share Your Love With Me (Don, BMI) .......... 49
She's My Girl (Spectorius, BMI) .......... 99
She's the One (Eastwick-Chartbuster, BMI) .......... 83
Shot in the Dark, A (Twin Chris, ASCAP) .......... 97
Sole Sole Sole (MRC, BMI) .......... 84
Something You Got (Tune Kel, BMI) .......... 52
Steal Away (Fame, BMI) .......... 30
Sugar Lips (Southern, ASCAP) .......... 55
Tell Me (Jobete, BMI) .......... 62
Tennessee Waltz (Acuff-Rose, BMI) .......... 35
Thank You Baby (Girl's, BMI) .......... 86
Try It Baby (Jobete, BMI) .......... 16
Under the Boardwalk (T.M., BMI) .......... 19
Walk—Don't Run '64 (Forshay, BMI) .......... 65
Walk on By (Blue Seas-Jac, ASCAP) .......... 36
What Have I Got of My Own (Sawtell-Herring, ASCAP) .......... 43
What's the Matter With You Baby (Jobete, BMI) .......... 37
Where Did Our Love Go (Jobete, BMI) .......... 38
Wishin' and Hopin' (Jonathan, BMI) .......... 12
World I Used to Know, The (Viva, BMI) .......... 51
World Without Love, A (Maclen, BMI) .......... 22
Worry (Ridge, BMI) .......... 98
Yesterday's Gone (Jobete, BMI) .......... 34
(You Don't Know) How Glad I Am (Roosevelt, BMI) .......... 31
You're My Remedy (Jobete, BMI) .......... 57
You're My World (Hill & Range, BMI) .......... 42

## BUBBLING UNDER THE HOT 100

101. LIKE COLUMBUS DID .......... Reflections, Golden World 14
102. MORE AND MORE OF YOUR AMOR .......... Nat King Cole, Capitol 5219
103. I DON'T WANT TO HEAR ANYMORE .......... Jerry Butler, Vee Jay 598
104. IF YOU SEE MY LOVE .......... Lenny Welch, Cadence 1446
105. A TASTE OF HONEY .......... Tony Bennett, Columbia 43073
106. MY HEART SKIPS A BEAT .......... Buck Owens, Capitol 5136
107. ALL MY LOVING .......... Hollyridge Strings, Capitol 5207
108. HANGIN' ON TO MY BABY .......... Tracey Dey, Amy 908
109. BACHELOR BOY .......... Cliff Richard and the Shadows, Epic 9691
110. DREAM LOVER .......... Marty Robbins, Columbia 43049
111. SUNNY .......... Neil Sedaka, RCA Victor 8382
112. NIGHTINGALE MELODY .......... Little Johnny Taylor, Galaxy 731
113. HELP THE POOR .......... B. B. King, ABC-Paramount 10552
114. A TEAR FELL .......... Ray Charles, ABC-Paramount 10571
115. PRECIOUS WORDS .......... Wallace Brothers, Sims 174
116. IT'S SUMMER TIME U.S.A. .......... Pixies Three, Mercury 72288
117. IT'S A SIN TO TELL A LIE .......... Tony Bennett, Columbia 43073
118. I SHOULD HAVE KNOWN BETTER .......... Beatles, Capitol 5222
119. I'M SORRY .......... Danny Williams, United Artists 601
120. SHOUT .......... Lulu and the Luvers, Parrot 9678
121. LICORICE STICK .......... Pete Fountain, Coral 62413
122. I'M SORRY .......... Pete Drake, Smash 1910
123. MY KIND OF TOWN .......... Frank Sinatra, Reprise 0279
124. JAMAICA SKA .......... Ska Kings, Atlantic 2232
125. IN THE MISTY MOONLIGHT .......... Jerry Wallace, Challenge 59246
126. HAPPY I LONG TO BE .......... Betty Everett, CJ 619
127. DREAM LOVER .......... Paris Sisters, MGM 13236
128. (You Don't Know) How Glad I Am .......... LaVern Baker, Atlantic 2243
129. YOU'D BETTER FIND YOURSELF ANOTHER FOOL .......... Arthur Prysock, Old Town 1163
130. GROWIN' UP TOO FAST .......... Diane Renay, 20th Century-Fox 514
131. SAILOR BOY .......... Chiffons, Laurie 3262
132. IF I'M A FOOL FOR LOVING YOU .......... Bobby Wood, Joy 285
133. SEVENTH DAWN .......... Ferrante & Teicher, United Artists 735
134. LOVE ME DO .......... Hollyridge Strings, Capitol 5207
135. I GUESS I'M CRAZY .......... Jim Reeves, RCA Victor 8383

Compiled from national retail sales and radio station airplay by the Music Popularity Dept. of Record Market Research, Billboard.

**Billboard**

For Week Ending July 25, 1964

# HOT 100

★ **STAR** performer—Sides registering greatest proportionate upward progress this week.

Billboard Award

| This Week | 1 Wk. Ago | 2 Wks. Ago | 3 Wks. Ago | TITLE Artist, Label & Number | Weeks On Chart |
|---|---|---|---|---|---|
| 1 | 1 | 3 | 8 | RAG DOLL — 4 Seasons, Philips 40211 | 5 |
| ★ 2 | 21 | — | — | A HARD DAY'S NIGHT — Beatles, Capitol 5222 | 2 |
| 3 | 3 | 1 | 1 | I GET AROUND — Beach Boys, Capitol 5174 | 10 |
| 4 | 2 | 2 | 3 | MEMPHIS — Johnny Rivers, Imperial 66032 | 9 |
| 5 | 5 | 9 | 12 | THE GIRL FROM IPANEMA — Getz/Gilberto, Verve 10323 | 8 |
| 6 | 6 | 12 | 22 | THE LITTLE OLD LADY (From Pasadena) — Jan & Dean, Liberty 55704 | 5 |
| 7 | 4 | 5 | 10 | CAN'T YOU SEE THAT SHE'S MINE — Dave Clark Five, Epic 9692 | 7 |
| 8 | 8 | 13 | 31 | DANG ME — Roger Miller, Smash 1881 | 7 |
| ★ 9 | 12 | 27 | 44 | WISHIN' AND HOPIN' — Dusty Springfield, Philips 40207 | 6 |
| 10 | 10 | 18 | 23 | KEEP ON PUSHING — Impressions, ABC-Paramount 10554 | 8 |
| 11 | 13 | 34 | 46 | EVERYBODY LOVES SOMEBODY — Dean Martin, Reprise 0281 | 5 |
| 12 | 11 | 15 | 16 | GOOD TIMES — Sam Cooke, RCA Victor 8368 | 8 |
| ★ 13 | 19 | 31 | 62 | UNDER THE BOARDWALK — Drifters, Atlantic 2237 | 5 |
| 14 | 15 | 23 | 48 | NOBODY I KNOW — Peter & Gordon, Capitol 5211 | 5 |
| 15 | 16 | 17 | 20 | TRY IT BABY — Marvin Gaye, Tamla 54095 | 8 |
| 16 | 9 | 6 | 2 | MY BOY LOLLIPOP — Millie Small, Smash 1893 | 10 |
| 17 | 7 | 4 | 4 | DON'T LET THE SUN CATCH YOU CRYING — Gerry & the Pacemakers, Laurie 3251 | 10 |
| ★ 18 | 38 | 77 | — | WHERE DID OUR LOVE GO — Supremes, Motown 1060 | 3 |
| 19 | 14 | 7 | 5 | PEOPLE — Barbra Streisand, Columbia 42965 | 17 |
| 20 | 24 | 42 | 61 | I WANNA LOVE HIM SO BAD — Jelly Beans, Red Bird 10-003 | 6 |
| 21 | 20 | 16 | 18 | DON'T THROW YOUR LOVE AWAY — Searchers, Kapp 593 | 9 |
| ★ 22 | 31 | 41 | 58 | (You Don't Know) HOW GLAD I AM — Nancy Wilson, Capitol 5198 | 5 |
| 23 | 23 | 30 | 37 | FARMER JOHN — Premiers, Warner Bros. 5443 | 6 |
| 24 | 18 | 11 | 9 | BAD TO ME — Billy J. Kramer, Imperial 66027 | 9 |
| ★ 25 | 30 | 38 | 52 | STEAL AWAY — Jimmy Hughes, Fame 6401 | 6 |
| 26 | 17 | 10 | 11 | NO PARTICULAR PLACE TO GO — Chuck Berry, Chess 1898 | 10 |
| 27 | 25 | 28 | 24 | DON'T WORRY BABY — Beach Boys, Capitol 5174 | 9 |
| 28 | 22 | 8 | 6 | A WORLD WITHOUT LOVE — Peter & Gordon, Capitol 5175 | 12 |
| 29 | 33 | 35 | 41 | HEY HARMONICA MAN — Stevie Wonder, Tamla 54096 | 7 |
| 30 | 26 | 26 | 36 | REMEMBER ME — Rita Pavone, RCA Victor 8365 | 8 |
| ★ 31 | 42 | 65 | 80 | YOU'RE MY WORLD — Cilla Black, Capitol 5196 | 4 |
| 32 | 27 | 14 | 7 | CHAPEL OF LOVE — Dixie Cups, Red Bird 001 | 13 |
| 33 | 28 | 29 | 30 | ALONE — Four Seasons, Vee Jay 597 | 8 |
| ★ 34 | 47 | 69 | 85 | HANDY MAN — Del Shannon, Amy 905 | 4 |
| 35 | 41 | 57 | 67 | I LIKE IT LIKE THAT — Miracles, Tamla 54098 | 5 |
| ★ 36 | 58 | 100 | — | C'MON AND SWIM — Bobby Freeman, Autumn 2 | 3 |
| 37 | 39 | 60 | 66 | DO I LOVE YOU? — Ronettes, Philles 121 | 6 |
| ★ 38 | 54 | 81 | — | AL-DI-LA — Ray Charles Singers, Command 4049 | 3 |
| 39 | 35 | 37 | 35 | TENNESSEE WALTZ — Sam Cooke, RCA Victor 8368 | 7 |
| 40 | 40 | 39 | 33 | I'LL BE IN TROUBLE — Temptations, Gordy 7032 | 9 |
| 41 | 29 | 19 | 14 | LITTLE CHILDREN — Billy J. Kramer, Imperial 66027 | 15 |
| 42 | 49 | 53 | 60 | SHARE YOUR LOVE WITH ME — Bobby Bland, Duke 377 | 7 |
| 43 | 43 | 50 | 51 | WHAT HAVE I GOT OF MY OWN — Trini Lopez, Reprise 0276 | 12 |
| ★ 44 | 55 | 75 | — | SUGAR LIPS — Al Hirt, RCA Victor 8391 | 3 |
| 45 | 46 | 51 | 53 | I STILL GET JEALOUS — Louis Armstrong, Kapp 597 | 6 |
| ★ 46 | 70 | 89 | — | JUST BE TRUE — Gene Chandler, Constellation 130 | 3 |
| ★ 47 | 72 | — | — | PEOPLE SAY — Dixie Cups, Red Bird 10-006 | 2 |
| ★ 48 | 65 | 86 | — | WALK—DON'T RUN '64 — Ventures, Dolton 96 | 3 |
| ★ 49 | 62 | 70 | 81 | TELL ME — Rolling Stones, London 9682 | 4 |
| 50 | 53 | 66 | 71 | I BELIEVE — Bachelors, London 9672 | 5 |
| 51 | 51 | 54 | 59 | THE WORLD I USED TO KNOW — Jimmie Rodgers, Dot 16595 | 9 |
| ★ 52 | 71 | 91 | — | ANGELITO — Rene and Rene, Columbia 43045 | 3 |
| ★ 53 | 63 | 85 | — | HOW DO YOU DO IT — Gerry and the Pacemakers, Laurie 3261 | 3 |
| 54 | 56 | 67 | 83 | MIXED-UP, SHOOK-UP GIRL — Patty & the Emblems, Herald 590 | 6 |
| ★ 55 | 67 | 80 | 82 | ANYONE WHO KNOWS WHAT LOVE IS — Irma Thomas, Imperial 66041 | 4 |
| 56 | 57 | 62 | 88 | YOU'RE MY REMEDY — Marvelettes, Tamla 54097 | 4 |
| 57 | 60 | 72 | 78 | I'M INTO SOMETHIN' GOOD — Earl-Jean, Colpix 729 | 5 |
| 58 | 48 | 52 | 55 | NOT FADE AWAY — Rolling Stones, London 9657 | 13 |
| 59 | 52 | 58 | 64 | SOMETHING YOU GOT — Alvin Robinson, Tiger 104 | 8 |
| 60 | 45 | 47 | 49 | BEG ME — Chuck Jackson, Wand 154 | 10 |
| 61 | 61 | 68 | 74 | I WANT TO HOLD YOUR HAND — Boston Pops Ork, RCA Victor 8378 | 4 |
| 62 | 59 | 64 | 69 | THE FIRST NIGHT OF THE FULL MOON — Jack Jones, Kapp 589 | 9 |
| ★ 63 | 83 | 90 | — | SHE'S THE ONE — Chartbusters, Mutual 502 | 3 |
| 64 | 64 | 73 | 75 | PEG O' MY HEART — Robert Maxwell, Decca 25637 | 6 |
| 65 | 78 | 83 | — | LITTLE LATIN LUPE LU — Kingsmen, Wand 157 | 3 |
| 66 | 66 | 71 | 72 | I CAN'T HEAR YOU — Betty Everett, Vee Jay 599 | 5 |
| ★ 67 | 90 | — | — | AIN'T SHE SWEET — Beatles, Atco 6308 | 2 |
| 68 | 75 | 76 | 70 | GIRLS — Major Lance, Okeh 7197 | 5 |
| ★ 69 | 87 | — | — | LOOKING FOR LOVE — Connie Francis, MGM 13256 | 2 |
| 70 | 79 | 97 | — | LOVE IS ALL WE NEED — Vic Dana, Dolton 95 | 3 |
| 71 | 74 | 78 | 76 | OH! BABY — Barbara Lynn, Jamie 1277 | 6 |
| 72 | 73 | 79 | 79 | THE FERRIS WHEEL — Everly Brothers, Warner Bros. 5441 | 6 |
| 73 | 69 | 74 | 68 | IT AIN'T NO USE — Major Lance, Okeh 7197 | 8 |
| ★ 74 | 89 | — | — | HEY GIRL, DON'T BOTHER — Tams, ABC-Paramount 10573 | 2 |
| ★ 75 | — | — | — | I SHOULD HAVE KNOWN BETTER — Beatles, Capitol 5222 | 1 |
| ★ 76 | 91 | — | — | NO ONE TO CRY TO — Ray Charles, ABC-Paramount 10571 | 2 |
| 77 | 84 | — | — | SOLE SOLE SOLE — Siw Malmkvist & Umberto Marcato, Jubilee 5479 | 2 |
| 78 | 86 | — | — | THANK YOU BABY — Shirelles, Scepter 1278 | 2 |
| 79 | 81 | — | — | EVERYBODY NEEDS SOMEBODY TO LOVE — Solomon Burke, Atlantic 2241 | 2 |
| ★ 80 | — | — | — | AND I LOVE HER — Beatles, Capitol 5235 | 1 |
| ★ 81 | 96 | — | — | BABY COME HOME — Ruby & the Romantics, Kapp 601 | 2 |
| ★ 82 | — | — | — | SUCH A NIGHT — Elvis Presley, RCA Victor 8400 | 1 |
| ★ 83 | — | — | — | IN THE MISTY MOONLIGHT — Jerry Wallace, Challenge 59246 | 1 |
| 84 | 98 | — | — | WORRY — Johnny Tillotson, MGM 13255 | 2 |
| ★ 85 | — | — | — | I'LL KEEP YOU SATISFIED — Billy J. Kramer, Imperial 66048 | 1 |
| 86 | 88 | — | — | INVISIBLE TEARS — Ray Conniff Singers, Columbia 43061 | 2 |
| 87 | 93 | — | — | IT HURTS TO BE IN LOVE — Gene Pitney, Musicor 1040 | 2 |
| ★ 88 | — | — | — | MAYBE I KNOW — Lesley Gore, Mercury 72309 | 1 |
| ★ 89 | — | — | — | I WANT YOU TO MEET MY BABY — Eydie Gorme, Columbia 43082 | 1 |
| ★ 90 | — | — | — | HELLO MUDDUH, HELLO FADDUH (1964 Version) — Allan Sherman, Warner Bros. 5449 | 1 |
| 91 | 95 | — | — | A QUIET PLACE — Garnet Mimms, United Artists 715 | 2 |
| 92 | 94 | — | — | A HOUSE IS NOT A HOME — Brook Benton, Mercury 72303 | 2 |
| 93 | 92 | — | — | BAMA LAMA BAMA LOO — Little Richard, Specialty 692 | 2 |
| 94 | — | — | — | RINGO'S THEME (THIS BOY) — George Martin & His Ork, United Artists 745 | 1 |
| 95 | — | — | — | SUMMER MEANS FUN — Bruce & Terry, Columbia 43055 | 1 |
| 96 | 85 | 88 | 90 | THE MEXICAN SHUFFLE — Herb Alpert's Tijuana Brass, A&M 742 | 5 |
| 97 | 97 | — | — | A SHOT IN THE DARK — Henry Mancini & His Ork, RCA Victor 8381 | 2 |
| 98 | 100 | — | — | SAY YOU — Ronnie Dove, Diamond 167 | 2 |
| 99 | — | — | — | SUNNY — Neil Sedaka, RCA Victor 8382 | 1 |
| 100 | — | — | — | IT'S ALL OVER NOW — Rolling Stones, London 9687 | 1 |

## HOT 100—A TO Z—(Publisher-Licensee)

Ain't She Sweet (Advance, ASCAP) ... 67
Al-Di-La (Witmark, ASCAP) ... 38
Alone (Selma, BMI) ... 33
And I Love Her (Unart-Maclen, BMI) ... 80
Angelito (Gil-Epps, BMI) ... 52
Anyone Who Knows What Love Is (Metric, BMI) ... 55
Baby Come Home (Rosewood-Day-Hilliard, ASCAP) ... 81
Bad to Me (Metric, BMI) ... 24
Bama Lama Bama Loo (Little Richard, BMI) ... 93
Beg Me (T. M., BMI) ... 60
Can't You See That She's Mine (Beechwood, BMI) ... 7
C'mon and Swim (Taracrest, BMI) ... 36
Chapel of Love (Trio, BMI) ... 32
Dang Me (Tree, BMI) ... 8
Do I Love You (Mother Bertha-Hill & Range, BMI) 37
Don't Let the Sun Catch You Crying (Pacemaker, BMI) ... 17
Don't Throw Your Love Away (Wyncote, ASCAP) ... 21
Don't Worry Baby (Sea of Tunes, BMI) ... 27
Everybody Loves Somebody (Sands, ASCAP) ... 11
Everybody Needs Somebody to Love (Keetch, Caesar & Dino, BMI) ... 79
Farmer John (Venice, BMI) ... 23
Ferris Wheel, The (Rose, BMI) ... 72
First Night of the Full Moon, The (Famous, ASCAP) ... 62
Girl From Ipanema, The (Duchess, BMI) ... 5
Girls (Curtom, BMI) ... 68
Good Times (Kags, BMI) ... 12
Handy Man (Travis, BMI) ... 34
Hard Day's Night, A (Unart-Maclen, BMI) ... 2
Hello Mudduh, Hello Fadduh (Curtain Call, ASCAP) 90
Hey Girl, Don't Bother Me (Low-Twi, BMI) ... 74
Hey Harmonica Man (Jobete-Little Darlin', BMI) ... 29
House Is Not a Home, A (Diplomat, ASCAP) ... 92
How Do You Do It (Just, BMI) ... 53
I Believe (Cromwell, ASCAP) ... 50
I Can't Hear You (Screen Gems-Columbia, BMI) ... 66
I Get Around (Sea of Tunes, BMI) ... 3
I Like It Like That (Jobete, BMI) ... 35
I Should Have Known Better (Unart-Maclen, BMI) ... 75
I Still Get Jealous (Morris, ASCAP) ... 45
I Wanna Love Him So Bad (Trio, BMI) ... 20
I Want to Hold Your Hand (Duchess, BMI) ... 61
I Want You to Meet My Baby (Screen Gems-Columbia, BMI) ... 89
I'm Into Something Good (Screen Gems-Columbia, BMI) ... 57
I'll Be in Trouble (Jobete, BMI) ... 40
I'll Keep You Satisfied (Metric, BMI) ... 85
In the Misty Moonlight (Four Star, BMI) ... 83
Invisible Tears (Central Songs, BMI) ... 86
It Ain't No Use (Curtom-Jalynne, BMI) ... 73
It Hurts to Be in Love (Screen Gems-Columbia, BMI) 87
It's All Over Now (Kags, BMI) ... 100
Just Be True (Curtom-Camad, BMI) ... 46
Keep on Pushing (Curtom, BMI) ... 10
Little Children (Rumbalero, BMI) ... 41
Little Latin Lupe Lu (Maxwell-Conrad, BMI) ... 65
Little Old Lady (From Pasadena), The (Trousdale, BMI) ... 6
Looking for Love (Merna, BMI) ... 69
Love Is All We Need (Travis, BMI) ... 70
Maybe I Know (Trio, BMI) ... 88
Memphis (Arc, BMI) ... 4
Mexican Shuffle, The (Alamo, ASCAP) ... 96
Mixed-Up, Shook-Up, Girl (Ben-Lee, BMI) ... 54
My Boy Lollipop (Nom, BMI) ... 16
No One to Cry To (Hill & Range, BMI) ... 76
No Particular Place to Go (Arc, BMI) ... 26
Nobody I Know (Maclen, BMI) ... 14
Not Fade Away (Nor Va Jak, BMI) ... 58
Oh! Baby (Nujac, BMI) ... 71
Peg o' My Heart (Feist, ASCAP) ... 64
People (Chappell, ASCAP) ... 19
People Say (Trio, BMI) ... 47
Quiet Place, A (Rittenhouse, BMI) ... 91
Rag Doll (Saturday-Gavadima, ASCAP) ... 1
Remember Me (Gil, BMI) ... 30
Ringo's Theme (This Boy) Maclen, BMI) ... 94
Say You (T.M., BMI) ... 98
Share Your Love With Me (Don, BMI) ... 42
She's the One (Eastwick-Chartbuster, BMI) ... 63
Shot in the Dark, A (Twin Chris, ASCAP) ... 97
Sole Sole Sole (MRC, BMI) ... 77
Something You Got (Tune Kel, BMI) ... 59
Steal Away (Fame, BMI) ... 25
Such a Night (Raleigh, BMI) ... 82
Sugar Lips (Tree, BMI) ... 44
Summer Means Fun (Trousdale, BMI) ... 95
Sunny (Screen Gems-Columbia, BMI) ... 99
Tell Me (Southern, ASCAP) ... 49
Tennessee Waltz (Acuff-Rose, BMI) ... 39
Thank You Baby (Girl's, BMI) ... 78
Try It Baby (Jobete, BMI) ... 15
Under the Boardwalk (T. M., BMI) ... 13
Walk—Don't Run '64 (Forshay, BMI) ... 48
What Have I Got of My Own (Sawtell-Herring, ASCAP) ... 43
Where Did Our Love Go (Jobete, BMI) ... 18
Wishin' and Hopin' (Jonathan, BMI) ... 9
World I Used to Know, The (In, ASCAP) ... 51
World Without Love, A (Maclen, BMI) ... 28
Worry (Ridge, BMI) ... 84
(You Don't Know) How Glad I Am (Roosevelt, BMI) 22
You're My Remedy (Jobete, BMI) ... 56
You're My World (Hill & Range, BMI) ... 31

## BUBBLING UNDER THE HOT 100

101. SHOUT ... Lulu & the Luvers, Parrot 9678
102. A TASTE OF HONEY ... Tony Bennett, Columbia 43073
103. ME JAPANESE BOY I LOVE YOU ... Bobby Goldsboro, United Artists 742
104. FATHER SEBASTIAN ... Ramblers, Almont 311
105. SHE'S MY GIRL ... Bobby Shafto, Rust 5082
106. LIKE COLUMBUS DID ... Reflections, Golden World 12
107. HANGIN' ON TO MY BABY ... Tracey Dey, Amy 908
108. A TEAR FELL ... Ray Charles, ABC-Paramount 10571
109. NIGHTINGALE MELODY ... Little Johnny Taylor, Galaxy 731
110. I STAND ACCUSED ... Jerry Butler, Vee Jay 598
111. NEVER ENDING ... Elvis Presley, RCA Victor 8400
112. PRECIOUS WORDS ... Wallace Brothers, Sims 174
113. I'M HAPPY JUST TO DANCE WITH YOU ... Beatles, Capitol 5234
114. BACHELOR BOY ... Cliff Richard & the Shadows, Epic 9691
115. I'LL CRY INSTEAD ... Beatles, Capitol 5234
116. THE NEW FRANKIE AND JOHNNY SONG ... Greenwood County Singers, Kapp 591
117. MORE ... Danny Williams, United Artists 601
118. G. T. O. ... Ronny and the Daytona, Mala 481
119. MY HEART SKIPS A BEAT ... Buck Owens, Capitol 516
120. ALL GROWN UP ... Crystals, Philles 122
121. IF I'M A FOOL FOR LOVING YOU ... Bobby Wood, Joy 285
122. JAMAICA SKA ... Ska Kings, Atlantic 2232
123. YOU NEVER CAN TELL ... Chuck Berry, Chess 1906
124. CLOSE YOUR EYES ... Arthur Prysock, Old Town 1163
125. DREAM LOVER ... Paris Sisters, MGM 13236
126. IT'S A COTTON CANDY WORLD ... Jerry Wallace, Mercury 72292
127. MARY, OH MARY ... Fats Domino, ABC-Paramount 10567
128. THE JAMES BOND THEME ... Billy Strange, Crescendo, 320
129. SEVENTH DAWN ... Ferrante & Teicher, United Artists 735
130. OH WHAT A KISS ... Johnny Rivers, United Artists 741
131. SELFISH ONE ... Jackie Ross, Chess 190
132. I'LL KEEP TRYING ... Theola Kilgore, KT 50
133. DANCE, DANCE, DANCE ... Tommy Duncan, Falew 104
134. SHRIMP BOATS ... Jerry Jackson, Columbia 43056
135. A CASUAL KISS ... Leon Peels, Whirlybird 2002

Compiled from national retail sales and radio station airplay by the Music Popularity Dept. of Record Market Research, Billboard.

# Billboard HOT 100

**For Week Ending August 1, 1964**

★ STAR performer—Sides registering greatest proportionate upward progress this week.

| This Week | 1 Wk. Ago | 2 Wks. Ago | 3 Wks. Ago | TITLE — Artist, Label & Number | Weeks On Chart |
|---|---|---|---|---|---|
| 1 | 2 | 21 | — | **A HARD DAY'S NIGHT** — Beatles, Capitol 5222 | 3 |
| 2 | 1 | 1 | 3 | **RAG DOLL** — 4 Seasons, Philips 40211 | 6 |
| ★3 | 6 | 6 | 12 | **THE LITTLE OLD LADY (From Pasadena)** — Jan & Dean, Liberty 55704 | 6 |
| ★4 | 11 | 13 | 34 | **EVERYBODY LOVES SOMEBODY** — Dean Martin, Reprise 0281 | 6 |
| ★5 | 18 | 38 | 77 | **WHERE DID OUR LOVE GO** — Supremes, Motown 1060 | 4 |
| 6 | 9 | 12 | 27 | **WISHIN' AND HOPIN'** — Dusty Springfield, Philips 40207 | 7 |
| 7 | 8 | 8 | 13 | **DANG ME** — Roger Miller, Smash 1881 | 8 |
| 8 | 3 | 3 | 1 | **I GET AROUND** — Beach Boys, Capitol 5174 | 11 |
| 9 | 4 | 2 | 2 | **MEMPHIS** — Johnny Rivers, Imperial 66032 | 10 |
| 10 | 5 | 5 | 9 | **THE GIRL FROM IPANEMA** — Getz/Gilberto, Verve 10323 | 9 |
| 11 | 13 | 19 | 31 | **UNDER THE BOARDWALK** — Drifters, Atlantic 2237 | 6 |
| 12 | 14 | 15 | 23 | **NOBODY I KNOW** — Peter & Gordon, Capitol 5211 | 6 |
| 13 | 7 | 4 | 5 | **CAN'T YOU SEE THAT SHE'S MINE** — Dave Clark Five, Epic 9692 | 8 |
| 14 | 10 | 10 | 18 | **KEEP ON PUSHING** — Impressions, ABC-Paramount 10554 | 9 |
| ★15 | 20 | 24 | 42 | **I WANNA LOVE HIM SO BAD** — Jelly Beans, Red Bird 10-003 | 7 |
| 16 | 12 | 11 | 15 | **GOOD TIMES** — Sam Cooke, RCA Victor 8368 | 9 |
| ★17 | 22 | 31 | 41 | **(You Don't Know) HOW GLAD I AM** — Nancy Wilson, Capitol 5198 | 6 |
| 18 | 15 | 16 | 17 | **TRY IT BABY** — Marvin Gaye, Tamla 54095 | 9 |
| 19 | 23 | 23 | 30 | **FARMER JOHN** — Premiers, Warner Bros. 5443 | 7 |
| 20 | 25 | 30 | 38 | **STEAL AWAY** — Jimmy Hughes, Fame 6401 | 7 |
| 21 | 16 | 9 | 6 | **MY BOY LOLLIPOP** — Millie Small, Smash 1893 | 11 |
| 22 | 17 | 7 | 4 | **DON'T LET THE SUN CATCH YOU CRYING** — Gerry & the Pacemakers, Laurie 3251 | 11 |
| 23 | 19 | 14 | 7 | **PEOPLE** — Barbra Streisand, Columbia 42965 | 18 |
| 24 | 36 | 58 | 100 | **C'MON AND SWIM** — Bobby Freeman, Autumn 2 | — |
| 25 | 21 | 20 | 16 | **DON'T THROW YOUR LOVE AWAY** — Searchers, Kapp 593 | 10 |
| ★26 | 31 | 42 | 65 | **YOU'RE MY WORLD** — Cilla Black, Capitol 5196 | 5 |
| 27 | 34 | 47 | 69 | **HANDY MAN** — Del Shannon, Amy 905 | 5 |
| 28 | 35 | 41 | 57 | **I LIKE IT LIKE THAT** — Miracles, Tamla 54098 | 6 |
| 29 | 48 | 65 | 86 | **WALK—DON'T RUN '64** — Ventures, Dolton 96 | 4 |
| 30 | 27 | 25 | 28 | **DON'T WORRY BABY** — Beach Boys, Capitol 5174 | 10 |
| 31 | 47 | 72 | — | **PEOPLE SAY** — Dixie Cups, Red Bird 10-006 | 3 |
| 32 | 38 | 54 | 81 | **AL-DI-LA** — Ray Charles Singers, Command 4049 | 4 |
| 33 | 46 | 70 | 89 | **JUST BE TRUE** — Gene Chandler, Constellation 130 | 4 |
| 34 | 37 | 39 | 60 | **DO I LOVE YOU?** — Ronettes, Philles 121 | 7 |
| 35 | 24 | 18 | 11 | **BAD TO ME** — Billy J. Kramer, Imperial 66027 | 10 |
| ★36 | 49 | 62 | 70 | **TELL ME** — Rolling Stones, London 9682 | 5 |
| 37 | 29 | 33 | 35 | **HEY HARMONICA MAN** — Stevie Wonder, Tamla 54096 | 8 |
| 38 | 44 | 55 | 75 | **SUGAR LIPS** — Al Hirt, RCA Victor 8391 | 5 |
| 39 | 50 | 53 | 66 | **I BELIEVE** — Bachelors, London 9672 | 6 |
| 40 | 67 | 90 | — | **AIN'T SHE SWEET** — Beatles, Atco 6308 | 3 |
| 41 | 33 | 28 | 29 | **ALONE** — Four Seasons, Vee Jay 597 | 9 |
| 42 | 54 | 56 | 67 | **MIXED-UP, SHOOK-UP GIRL** — Patty & the Emblems, Herald 590 | 7 |
| 43 | 53 | 63 | 85 | **HOW DO YOU DO IT** — Gerry and the Pacemakers, Laurie 3261 | 4 |
| 44 | 52 | 71 | 91 | **ANGELITO** — Rene and Rene, Columbia 43045 | 4 |
| 45 | 57 | 60 | 72 | **I'M INTO SOMETHIN' GOOD** — Earl-Jean, Colpix 729 | 5 |
| 46 | 43 | 43 | 50 | **WHAT HAVE I GOT OF MY OWN** — Trini Lopez, Reprise 0276 | 13 |
| 47 | 39 | 35 | 37 | **TENNESSEE WALTZ** — Sam Cooke, RCA Victor 8368 | 8 |
| 48 | 26 | 17 | 10 | **NO PARTICULAR PLACE TO GO** — Chuck Berry, Chess 1898 | 11 |
| 49 | 42 | 49 | 53 | **SHARE YOUR LOVE WITH ME** — Bobby Bland, Duke 377 | 8 |
| 50 | 63 | 83 | 90 | **SHE'S THE ONE** — Chartbusters, Mutual 502 | 4 |
| 51 | 56 | 57 | 62 | **YOU'RE MY REMEDY** — Marvelettes, Tamla 54097 | 5 |
| 52 | 55 | 67 | 80 | **ANYONE WHO KNOWS WHAT LOVE IS** — Irma Thomas, Imperial 66041 | 5 |
| 53 | 45 | 46 | 51 | **I STILL GET JEALOUS** — Louis Armstrong, Kapp 597 | 7 |
| 54 | 85 | — | — | **I'LL KEEP YOU SATISFIED** — Billy J. Kramer, Imperial 66048 | 2 |
| 55 | 61 | 61 | 68 | **I WANT TO HOLD YOUR HAND** — Boston Pops Ork, RCA Victor 8378 | 6 |
| 56 | 82 | — | — | **SUCH A NIGHT** — Elvis Presley, RCA Victor 8400 | 2 |
| 57 | 65 | 78 | 83 | **LITTLE LATIN LUPE LU** — Kingsmen, Wand 157 | 4 |
| 58 | 69 | 87 | — | **LOOKING FOR LOVE** — Connie Francis, MGM 13256 | 3 |
| 59 | 30 | 26 | 26 | **REMEMBER ME** — Rita Pavone, RCA Victor 8365 | 9 |
| 60 | — | — | — | **BECAUSE** — Dave Clark Five, Epic 9704 | 1 |
| 61 | 70 | 79 | 97 | **LOVE IS ALL WE NEED** — Vic Dana, Dolton 95 | 4 |
| 62 | — | — | — | **I'LL CRY INSTEAD** — Beatles, Capitol 5234 | 1 |
| 63 | 83 | — | — | **IN THE MISTY MOONLIGHT** — Jerry Wallace, Challenge 59246 | 2 |
| 64 | 88 | — | — | **MAYBE I KNOW** — Lesley Gore, Mercury 72309 | 2 |
| 65 | 80 | — | — | **AND I LOVE HER** — Beatles, Capitol 5235 | — |
| 66 | 75 | — | — | **I SHOULD HAVE KNOWN BETTER** — Beatles, Capitol 5222 | 2 |
| 67 | 74 | 89 | — | **HEY GIRL DON'T BOTHER ME** — Tams, ABC-Paramount 10573 | 3 |
| 68 | 76 | 91 | — | **NO ONE TO CRY TO** — Ray Charles, ABC-Paramount 10571 | 3 |
| 69 | 71 | 74 | 78 | **OH! BABY** — Barbara Lynn, Jamie 1277 | 7 |
| 70 | 77 | 84 | — | **SOLE SOLE SOLE** — Siw Malmkvist & Umberto Marcato, Jubilee 5479 | 3 |
| 71 | 78 | 86 | — | **THANK YOU BABY** — Shirelles, Scepter 1278 | 3 |
| 72 | 79 | 81 | — | **EVERYBODY NEEDS SOMEBODY TO LOVE** — Solomon Burke, Atlantic 2241 | 3 |
| ★73 | 89 | — | — | **I WANT YOU TO MEET MY BABY** — Eydie Gorme, Columbia 43082 | 2 |
| ★74 | — | — | — | **A TEAR FELL** — Ray Charles, ABC-Paramount 10571 | 1 |
| 75 | 81 | 96 | — | **BABY COME HOME** — Ruby & the Romantics, Kapp 601 | 3 |
| 76 | 86 | 88 | — | **INVISIBLE TEARS** — Ray Conniff Singers, Columbia 43061 | 3 |
| 77 | 90 | — | — | **HELLO MUDDUH, HELLO FADDUH (1964 Version)** — Allan Sherman, Warner Bros. 5449 | 2 |
| 78 | 84 | 98 | — | **WORRY** — Johnny Tillotson, MGM 13255 | — |
| 79 | 68 | 75 | 76 | **GIRLS** — Major Lance, Okeh 7197 | 6 |
| 80 | 87 | 93 | — | **IT HURTS TO BE IN LOVE** — Gene Pitney, Musicor 1040 | 3 |
| 81 | 100 | — | — | **IT'S ALL OVER NOW** — Rolling Stones, London 9687 | 2 |
| 82 | 95 | — | — | **SUMMER MEANS FUN** — Bruce & Terry, Columbia 43055 | 2 |
| 83 | — | — | — | **YOU NEVER CAN TELL** — Chuck Berry, Chess 1906 | 1 |
| 84 | — | — | — | **I STAND ACCUSED** — Jerry Butler, Vee Jay 598 | 1 |
| 85 | — | — | — | **I'VE GOT NO TIME TO LOSE** — Carla Thomas, Atlantic 2238 | 1 |
| 86 | — | — | — | **THE NEW FRANKIE & JOHNNY SONG** — Greenwood County Singers, Kapp 591 | 1 |
| 87 | 99 | — | — | **SUNNY** — Neil Sedaka, RCA Victor 8382 | 2 |
| 88 | — | — | — | **SELFISH ONE** — Jackie Ross, Chess 1903 | 1 |
| 89 | — | — | — | **G.T.O.** — Ronny & the Daytonas, Mala 481 | 1 |
| 90 | — | — | — | **SAILOR BOY** — Chiffons, Laurie 3262 | 1 |
| 91 | 92 | 94 | — | **A HOUSE IS NOT A HOME** — Brook Benton, Mercury 72303 | 3 |
| 92 | — | — | — | **IF I FELL** — Beatles, Capitol 5235 | 1 |
| 93 | 93 | 92 | — | **BAMA LAMA BAMA LOO** — Little Richard, Specialty 692 | 3 |
| 94 | 98 | 100 | — | **SAY YOU** — Ronnie Dove, Diamond 167 | 3 |
| 95 | — | — | — | **I'M HAPPY JUST TO DANCE WITH YOU** — Beatles, Capitol 5234 | 1 |
| 96 | — | — | — | **A HOUSE IS NOT A HOME** — Dionne Warwick, Scepter 1282 | 1 |
| 97 | — | — | — | **SHOUT** — Lulu & the Luvers, Parrot 9678 | 1 |
| 98 | — | — | — | **ALL GROWN UP** — Crystals, Philles 122 | 1 |
| 99 | — | — | — | **BACHELOR BOY** — Cliff Richard & the Shadows, Epic 9691 | 1 |
| 100 | — | — | — | **YOU'RE NO GOOD** — Swinging Blue Jeans, Imperial 66049 | 1 |

## BUBBLING UNDER THE HOT 100

101. FATHER SEBASTIAN — Ramblers, Almont 311
102. ME JAPANESE BOY I LOVE YOU — Bobby Goldsboro, United Artists 742
103. A QUIET PLACE — Garnet Mimms, United Artists 715
104. SWEET WILLIAM — Millie Small, Smash 1920
105. AND I LOVE HER — George Martin and His Ork, United Artists 745
106. THE GIRL'S ALRIGHT WITH ME — Temptations, Gordy 7032
107. HANGIN' ON TO MY BABY — Tracey Dey, Amy 908
108. I'LL KEEP TRYING — Theola Kilgore, KT 501
109. MY HEART SKIPS A BEAT — Buck Owens, Capitol 5136
110. MORE — Danny Williams, United Artists 601
111. I GUESS I'M CRAZY — Jim Reeves, RCA Victor 8383
112. SHE'S MY GIRL — Bobby Shafto, Rust 5082
113. NIGHTINGALE MELODY — Little Johnny Taylor, Galaxy 731
114. MORE AND MORE OF YOUR AMOR — Nat King Cole, Capitol 5219
115. BREAD AND BUTTER — Newbeats, Hickory 1269
116. WE'LL SING IN THE SUNSHINE — Gale Garnett, RCA Victor 8388
117. I'M A FOOL FOR LOVING YOU — Bobby Wood, Joy 285
118. A TASTE OF HONEY — Tony Bennett, Columbia 43073
119. IT'S A COTTON CANDY WORLD — Jerry Wallace, Mercury 72292
120. IF I FELL — Valentinos, Sar 152
121. PRECIOUS WORDS — Wallace Brothers, Sims 174
122. I'LL ALWAYS LOVE YOU — Brenda Holloway, Tamla 54099
123. HE'S IN TOWN — Tokens, B. T. Puppy 502
124. THE JAMES BOND THEME — Billy Strange, Crescendo 320
125. DREAM LOVER — Paris Sisters, MGM 13236
126. DOWN WHERE THE WINDS BLOW — Serendipity Singers, Philips 40215
127. DARLING IT'S WONDERFUL — Dale & Grace, Montel 930
128. SEVENTH DAWN — Ferrante & Teicher, United Artists 737
129. LET ME GET CLOSE TO YOU — Skeeter Davis, RCA Victor 8397
130. I'VE GOT A TIGER BY THE TAIL — Pete Drake, Smash 1910
131. HAUNTED HOUSE — Gene Simmons, HT 2076
132. 20—75 — Willie Mitchell, HI 2075
133. SILLY OL' SUMMERTIME — New Christy Minstrels, Columbia 43092
134. MARY, OH MARY — Fats Domino, ABC-Paramount 10567
135. YOU'D BETTER FIND YOURSELF ANOTHER FOOL — LaVern Baker, Atlantic 2234

*Compiled from national retail sales and radio station airplay by the Music Popularity Dept. of Record Market Research, Billboard.*

Billboard

For Week Ending August 8, 1964

# HOT 100

★ STAR performer—Sides registering greatest proportionate upward progress this week.

Billboard Award (No. 1)

| THIS WEEK | 1 Wk. Ago | 2 Wks. Ago | 3 Wks. Ago | TITLE | Artist, Label & Number | Weeks On Chart |
|---|---|---|---|---|---|---|
| 1 | 1 | 2 | 21 | A HARD DAY'S NIGHT | Beatles, Capitol 5222 | 4 |
| 2 | 4 | 11 | 13 | EVERYBODY LOVES SOMEBODY | Dean Martin, Reprise 0281 | 7 |
| 3 | 5 | 18 | 38 | WHERE DID OUR LOVE GO | Supremes, Motown 1060 | 5 |
| 4 | 3 | 6 | 6 | THE LITTLE OLD LADY (From Pasadena) | Jan & Dean, Liberty 55704 | 7 |
| 5 | 2 | 1 | 1 | RAG DOLL | 4 Seasons, Philips 40211 | 7 |
| 6 | 6 | 9 | 12 | WISHIN' AND HOPIN' | Dusty Springfield, Philips 40207 | 8 |
| ★7 | 11 | 13 | 19 | UNDER THE BOARDWALK | Drifters, Atlantic 2237 | 7 |
| 8 | 7 | 8 | 8 | DANG ME | Roger Miller, Smash 1881 | 9 |
| ★9 | 15 | 20 | 24 | I WANNA LOVE HIM SO BAD | Jelly Beans, Red Bird 10-003 | 8 |
| 10 | 8 | 3 | 3 | I GET AROUND | Beach Boys, Capitol 5174 | 12 |
| 11 | 10 | 5 | 5 | THE GIRL FROM IPANEMA | Getz/Gilberto, Verve 10323 | 10 |
| 12 | 9 | 4 | 2 | MEMPHIS | Johnny Rivers, Imperial 66032 | 11 |
| ★13 | 24 | 36 | 58 | C'MON AND SWIM | Bobby Freeman, Autumn 2 | 5 |
| 14 | 17 | 22 | 31 | (You Don't Know) HOW GLAD I AM | Nancy Wilson, Capitol 5198 | 7 |
| 15 | 12 | 14 | 15 | NOBODY I KNOW | Dave Clark Five, Epic 9692 | 7 |
| 16 | 13 | 7 | 4 | CAN'T YOU SEE THAT SHE'S MINE | Impressions, ABC-Paramount 10554 | 9 |
| 17 | 14 | 10 | 10 | KEEP ON PUSHING | Peter & Gordon, Capitol 5211 | 10 |
| ★18 | 31 | 47 | 72 | PEOPLE SAY | Dixie Cups, Red Bird 10-006 | 4 |
| 19 | 20 | 25 | 30 | STEAL AWAY | Jimmy Hughes, Fame 6401 | 8 |
| ★20 | 29 | 48 | 65 | WALK—DON'T RUN '64 | Ventures, Dolton 96 | 5 |
| ★21 | 43 | 53 | 63 | HOW DO YOU DO IT | Gerry and the Pacemakers, Laurie 3261 | 5 |
| ★22 | 60 | — | — | BECAUSE | Dave Clark Five, Epic 9704 | 2 |
| 23 | 27 | 34 | 47 | HANDY MAN | Del Shannon, Amy 905 | 6 |
| ★24 | 36 | 49 | 62 | TELL ME | Rolling Stones, London 9682 | 6 |
| ★25 | 40 | 67 | 90 | AIN'T SHE SWEET | Beatles, Atco 6308 | 4 |
| 26 | 26 | 31 | 42 | YOU'RE MY WORLD | Cilla Black, Capitol 5196 | 6 |
| 27 | 28 | 35 | 41 | I LIKE IT LIKE THAT | Miracles, Tamla 54098 | 7 |
| ★28 | 33 | 46 | 70 | JUST BE TRUE | Gene Chandler, Constellation 130 | 5 |
| 29 | 32 | 38 | 54 | AL-DI-LA | Ray Charles Singers, Command 4049 | 5 |
| 30 | 18 | 15 | 16 | TRY IT BABY | Marvin Gaye, Tamla 54095 | 10 |
| 31 | 38 | 44 | 55 | SUGAR LIPS | Al Hirt, RCA Victor 8391 | 5 |
| 32 | 19 | 23 | 23 | FARMER JOHN | Premiers, Warner Bros. 5443 | 8 |
| 33 | 39 | 50 | 53 | I BELIEVE | Bachelors, London 9672 | 7 |
| 34 | 34 | 37 | 39 | DO I LOVE YOU? | Ronettes, Philles 121 | 8 |
| ★35 | 56 | 82 | — | SUCH A NIGHT | Elvis Presley, RCA Victor 8400 | 3 |
| 36 | 23 | 19 | 14 | PEOPLE | Barbra Streisand, Columbia 42965 | 19 |
| 37 | 16 | 12 | 11 | GOOD TIMES | Sam Cooke, RCA Victor 8368 | 10 |
| 38 | 45 | 57 | 60 | I'M INTO SOMETHIN' GOOD | Earl-Jean, Colpix 729 | 7 |
| 39 | 25 | 21 | 20 | DON'T THROW YOUR LOVE AWAY | Searchers, Kapp 593 | 11 |
| ★40 | 65 | 80 | — | AND I LOVE HER | Beatles, Capitol 5235 | 3 |
| 41 | 21 | 16 | 9 | MY BOY LOLLIPOP | Millie Small, Smash 1893 | 12 |
| 42 | 42 | 54 | 56 | MIXED-UP, SHOOK-UP GIRL | Patty & the Emblems, Herald 590 | 8 |
| 43 | 44 | 52 | 71 | ANGELITO | Rene and Rene, Columbia 43045 | 5 |
| ★44 | 62 | — | — | I'LL CRY INSTEAD | Beatles, Capitol 5234 | 2 |
| 45 | 22 | 17 | 7 | DON'T LET THE SUN CATCH YOU CRYING | Gerry & the Pacemakers, Laurie 3251 | 12 |
| 46 | 54 | 85 | — | I'LL KEEP YOU SATISFIED | Billy J. Kramer, Imperial 66048 | 3 |
| 47 | 50 | 63 | 83 | SHE'S THE ONE | Chartbusters, Mutual 502 | 5 |
| 48 | 51 | 56 | 57 | YOU'RE MY REMEDY | Marvelettes, Tamla 54097 | 6 |
| ★49 | 63 | 83 | — | IN THE MISTY MOONLIGHT | Jerry Wallace, Challenge 59246 | 3 |
| ★50 | 64 | 88 | — | MAYBE I KNOW | Lesley Gore, Mercury 72309 | 3 |
| 51 | 57 | 65 | 78 | LITTLE LATIN LUPE LU | Kingsmen, Wand 157 | 5 |
| 52 | 52 | 55 | 67 | ANYONE WHO KNOWS WHAT LOVE IS | Irma Thomas, Imperial 66041 | 6 |
| 53 | 49 | 42 | 49 | SHARE YOUR LOVE WITH ME | Bobby Bland, Duke 377 | 9 |
| 54 | 58 | 69 | 87 | LOOKING FOR LOVE | Connie Francis, MGM 13256 | 4 |
| 55 | 55 | 61 | 61 | I WANT TO HOLD YOUR HAND | Boston Pops Ork, RCA Victor 8378 | 6 |
| ★56 | 67 | 74 | 89 | HEY GIRL DON'T BOTHER ME | Tams, ABC-Paramount 10573 | 4 |
| 57 | 61 | 70 | 79 | LOVE IS ALL WE NEED | Vic Dana, Dolton 95 | 5 |
| ★58 | 74 | — | — | A TEAR FELL | Ray Charles, ABC-Paramount 10571 | 2 |
| 59 | 66 | 75 | — | I SHOULD HAVE KNOWN BETTER | Beatles, Capitol 5222 | 3 |
| ★60 | — | — | — | THE HOUSE OF THE RISING SUN | Animals, MGM 13264 | 1 |
| 61 | 70 | 77 | 84 | SOLE SOLE SOLE | Siw Malmkvist & Umberto Marcato, Jubilee 5479 | 4 |
| 62 | 68 | 76 | 91 | NO ONE TO CRY TO | Ray Charles, ABC-Paramount 10571 | 4 |
| 63 | 71 | 78 | 86 | THANK YOU BABY | Shirelles, Scepter 1278 | 4 |
| ★64 | 80 | 87 | 93 | IT HURTS TO BE IN LOVE | Gene Pitney, Musicor 1040 | 4 |
| 65 | 73 | 89 | — | I WANT YOU TO MEET MY BABY | Eydie Gorme, Columbia 43082 | 3 |
| ★66 | 83 | — | — | YOU NEVER CAN TELL | Chuck Berry, Chess 1906 | 2 |
| 67 | 77 | 90 | — | HELLO MUDDUH, HELLO FADDUH (1964 Version) | Allan Sherman, Warner Bros. 5449 | 3 |
| 68 | 81 | 100 | — | IT'S ALL OVER NOW | Rolling Stones, London 9687 | 3 |
| 69 | 72 | 79 | 81 | EVERYBODY NEEDS SOMEBODY TO LOVE | Solomon Burke, Atlantic 2241 | 4 |
| ★70 | 88 | — | — | SELFISH ONE | Jackie Ross, Chess 1903 | 2 |
| 71 | 78 | 84 | 98 | WORRY | Johnny Tillotson, MGM 13255 | 4 |
| ★72 | 89 | — | — | G.T.O. | Ronny & the Daytonas, Mala 481 | 2 |
| ★73 | — | — | — | SWEET WILLIAM | Millie Small, Smash 1920 | 1 |
| 74 | 69 | 71 | 74 | OH! BABY | Barbara Lynn, Jamie 1277 | 8 |
| 75 | 75 | 81 | 96 | BABY COME HOME | Ruby & the Romantics, Kapp 601 | 4 |
| ★76 | — | — | — | I'LL ALWAYS LOVE YOU | Brenda Holloway, Tamla 54099 | 1 |
| 77 | 85 | — | — | I'VE GOT NO TIME TO LOSE | Carla Thomas, Atlantic 2238 | 2 |
| 78 | 76 | 86 | 88 | INVISIBLE TEARS | Ray Conniff Singers, Columbia 43061 | 4 |
| 79 | 82 | 95 | — | SUMMER MEANS FUN | Bruce & Terry, Columbia 43055 | 3 |
| 80 | 86 | — | — | THE NEW FRANKIE & JOHNNY SONG | Greenwood County Singers, Kapp 591 | 2 |
| ★81 | — | 94 | — | RINGO'S THEME (This Boy) | George Martin and His Ork, United Artists 745 | 2 |
| 82 | 93 | 93 | 92 | BAMA LAMA BAMA LOO | Little Richard, Specialty 692 | 4 |
| 83 | 90 | — | — | SAILOR BOY | Chiffons, Laurie 3262 | 2 |
| ★84 | — | — | — | HE'S IN TOWN | Tokens, B. T. Puppy 502 | 1 |
| 85 | 96 | — | — | A HOUSE IS NOT A HOME | Dionne Warwick, Scepter 1282 | 2 |
| 86 | 87 | 99 | — | SUNNY | Neil Sedaka, RCA Victor 8382 | 3 |
| 87 | 92 | — | — | IF I FELL | Beatles, Capitol 5235 | 2 |
| ★88 | — | — | — | CLINGING VINE | Bobby Vinton, Epic 9705 | 1 |
| 89 | 91 | 92 | 94 | A HOUSE IS NOT A HOME | Brook Benton, Mercury 72303 | 4 |
| ★90 | — | — | — | WHEN YOU LOVED ME | Brenda Lee, Decca 31654 | 1 |
| 91 | — | — | — | FATHER SEBASTIAN | Ramblers, Almont 311 | 1 |
| 92 | — | — | — | SILLY OL' SUMMERTIME | New Christy Minstrels, Columbia 43092 | 1 |
| 93 | 94 | 98 | 100 | SAY YOU | Ronnie Dove, Diamond 167 | 4 |
| 94 | 97 | — | — | SHOUT | Lulu & the Luvers, Parrot 9678 | 2 |
| 95 | — | — | — | WE'LL SING IN THE SUNSHINE | Gale Garnett, RCA Victor 8388 | 1 |
| 96 | — | — | — | ONE PIECE TOPLESS BATHING SUIT | Rip Chords, Columbia 43093 | 1 |
| 97 | 100 | — | — | YOU'RE NO GOOD | Swinging Blue Jeans, Imperial 66049 | 2 |
| 98 | — | — | — | ME JAPANESE BOY I LOVE YOU | Bobby Goldsboro, United Artists 742 | 1 |
| 99 | — | — | — | HAUNTED HOUSE | Gene Simmons, Hi 2076 | 1 |
| 100 | — | — | — | IF I'M A FOOL FOR LOVING YOU | Bobby Wood, Joy 285 | 1 |

## HOT 100—A TO Z—*(Publisher-Licensee)*

| | |
|---|---|
| Ain't She Sweet (Advance, ASCAP) | 25 |
| Al-Di-La (Witmark, ASCAP) | 29 |
| And I Loved Her (Unart-Maclen, BMI) | 40 |
| Angelito (Gil-Epps, BMI) | 43 |
| Anyone Who Knows What Love Is (Metric, BMI) | 52 |
| Baby Come Home (Rosewood-Day-Hilliard, ASCAP) | 75 |
| Bama Lama Bama Loo (Little Richard, BMI) | 82 |
| Because (Ivy, ASCAP) | 22 |
| Can't You See That She's Mine (Beechwood, BMI) | 16 |
| Clinging Vine (Peter Maurice, ASCAP) | 88 |
| C'mon and Swim (Taracrest, BMI) | 13 |
| Dang Me (Tree, BMI) | 8 |
| Do I Love You (Mother Bertha-Hill & Range, BMI) | 34 |
| Don't Let the Sun Catch You Crying (Pacemaker, BMI) | 45 |
| Don't Throw Your Love Away (Wyncote, ASCAP) | 39 |
| Everybody Loves Somebody (Sands, ASCAP) | 2 |
| Everybody Needs Somebody to Love (Keetch, Caesar & Dino, BMI) | 69 |
| Farmer John (Venice, BMI) | 32 |
| Father Sebastian (Four Star, BMI) | 91 |
| G.T.O. (Buckhorn, BMI) | 72 |
| Girl From Ipanema, The (Duchess, BMI) | 11 |
| Good Times (Kags, BMI) | 37 |
| Handy Man (Travis, BMI) | 23 |
| Hard Day's Night, A (Unart-Maclen, BMI) | 1 |
| Haunted House (Venice-B. Flat, BMI) | 99 |
| He's in Town (Screen-Gems-Columbia, BMI) | 84 |
| Hello Mudduh, Hello Fadduh (Curtain Call, ASCAP) | 67 |
| Hey Girl Don't Bother Me (Low-Twi, BMI) | 56 |
| House Is Not a Home, A—Benton (Diplomat, ASCAP) | 89 |
| House Is Not a Home, A—Warwick (Diplomat, ASCAP) | 85 |
| House of the Rising Sun, The (Gallico, BMI) | 60 |
| How Do You Do It (Just, BMI) | 21 |
| I Believe (Cromwell, ASCAP) | 33 |
| I Get Around (Sea of Tunes, BMI) | 10 |
| I Like It Like That (Jobete, BMI) | 27 |
| I Should Have Known Better (Unart-Maclen, BMI) | 59 |
| I Wanna Love Him So Bad (Trio, BMI) | 9 |
| I Want to Hold Your Hand (Duchess, BMI) | 55 |
| I Want You to Meet My Baby (Screen Gems-Columbia, BMI) | 65 |
| I'm Into Somethin' Good (Screen Gems-Columbia, BMI) | 38 |
| I've Got No Time to Lose (East, BMI) | 77 |
| I'll Always Love You (Jobete, BMI) | 76 |
| I'll Keep You Satisfied (Metric, BMI) | 46 |
| I'll Cry Instead (Unart-Maclen, BMI) | 44 |
| If I'm a Fool for Loving You (Drury Lane-Beckie, BMI) | 100 |
| If I Fell (Unart-Maclen, BMI) | 87 |
| In the Misty Moonlight (Four Star, BMI) | 49 |
| Invisible Tears (Central Songs, BMI) | 78 |
| It Hurts to Be in Love (Screen Gems-Columbia, BMI) | 64 |
| It's All Over Now (Kags, BMI) | 68 |
| Just Be True (Curtom-Camad, BMI) | 28 |
| Keep on Pushing (Curtom, BMI) | 17 |
| Little Latin Lupe Lu (Maxwell-Conrad, BMI) | 51 |
| Little Old Lady (From Pasadena), The (Screen Gems-Columbia, BMI) | 4 |
| Looking for Love (Merna, BMI) | 54 |
| Love Is All We Need (Travis, BMI) | 57 |
| Maybe I Know (Trio, BMI) | 50 |
| Me Japanese Boy I Love You (Jac-Blue Seas, ASCAP) | 98 |
| Memphis (Arc, BMI) | 12 |
| Mixed-Up, Shook-Up Girl (Ben-Lee, BMI) | 42 |
| My Boy Lollipop (Nom, BMI) | 41 |
| New Frankie & Johnny Song, The (Hollis, BMI) | 80 |
| No One to Cry To (Hill & Range, BMI) | 62 |
| Nobody I Know (Maclen, BMI) | 15 |
| Oh! Baby (Nujac, BMI) | 74 |
| One Piece Topless Bathing Suit (Trousdale, BMI) | 96 |
| People (Chappell, ASCAP) | 36 |
| Rag Doll (Saturday-Gavadima, ASCAP) | 5 |
| Ringo's Theme (This Boy) (Maclen, BMI) | 81 |
| Sailor Boy (Screen Gems-Columbia, BMI) | 83 |
| Say You (T.M., BMI) | 93 |
| Selfish One (Chevis, BMI) | 70 |
| Share Your Love With Me (Don, BMI) | 53 |
| She's the One (Eastwick-Chartbuster, BMI) | 47 |
| Shout (Wemar-Nom, BMI) | 94 |
| Silly Ol' Summertime (New Christy, BMI) | 92 |
| Sole Sole Sole (MRC, BMI) | 61 |
| Steal Away (Fame, BMI) | 19 |
| Such a Night (Raleigh, BMI) | 35 |
| Sugar Lips (Tree, BMI) | 31 |
| Summer Means Fun (Trousdale, BMI) | 79 |
| Sunny (Screen Gems-Columbia, BMI) | 86 |
| Sweet William (Budd, ASCAP) | 73 |
| Tear Fell, A (Progressive, BMI) | 58 |
| Tell Me (Southern, ASCAP) | 24 |
| Thank You Baby (Girl's, BMI) | 63 |
| Try It Baby (Jobete, BMI) | 30 |
| Under the Boardwalk (T.M., BMI) | 7 |
| Walk—Don't Run '64 (Forshay, BMI) | 20 |
| We'll Sing in the Sunshine (Lutercalia, BMI) | 95 |
| When You Loved Me (Hill & Range-Ron-Bre, BMI) | 90 |
| Where Did Our Love Go (Jobete, BMI) | 3 |
| Wishin' and Hopin' (Jonathan, ASCAP) | 6 |
| Worry (Ridge, BMI) | 71 |
| (You Don't Know) How Glad I Am (Roosevelt, BMI) | 14 |
| You Never Can Tell (Arc, BMI) | 66 |
| You're My Remedy (Jobete, BMI) | 48 |
| You're My World (Plan Two, ASCAP) | 26 |
| You're No Good (Morris, BMI) | 97 |

## BUBBLING UNDER THE HOT 100

101. YOU'LL NEVER GET TO HEAVEN (If You Break My Heart) ........ Dionne Warwick, Scepter 1282
102. THE GIRL'S ALRIGHT WITH ME ........ Temptations, Gordy 7032
103. BACHELOR BOY ........ Cliff Richard & the Shadows, Epic 9691
104. I'M HAPPY JUST TO DANCE WITH YOU ........ Beatles, Capitol 5234
105. BREAD AND BUTTER ........ Newbeats, Hickory 1269
106. MY HEART SKIPS A BEAT ........ Buck Owens, Capitol 5136
107. HERE I GO AGAIN ........ Hollies, Imperial 66044
108. OUT OF SIGHT ........ James Brown, Smash 1919
109. I STAND ACCUSED ........ Jerry Butler, Vee Jay 598
110. A TASTE OF HONEY ........ Tony Bennett, Columbia 43073
111. I GUESS I'M CRAZY ........ Jim Reeves, RCA Victor 8383
112. DOWN WHERE THE WINDS BLOW ........ Serendipity Singers, Philips 40215
113. IT'S A COTTON CANDY WORLD ........ Jerry Wallace, Mercury 72292
114. WHERE LOVE HAS GONE ........ Jack Jones, Kapp 608
115. SOMEONE, SOMEONE ........ Brian Poole, Monument 846
116. IT'S ALL OVER NOW ........ Valentinos, Sar 152
117. THE JAMES BOND THEME ........ Billy Strange, Crescendo 320
118. A SHOT IN THE DARK ........ Henry Mancini & His Ork, RCA Victor 8381
119. I'LL KEEP TRYING ........ Theola Kilgore, KT 501
120. A QUIET PLACE ........ Garnet Mimms, United Artists 715
121. LET ME GET CLOSE TO YOU ........ Skeeter Davis, RCA Victor 8397
122. SOMEDAY WE'RE GONNA LOVE AGAIN ........ Searchers, Kapp 609
123. AND I LOVE HER ........ George Martin & His Ork, United Artists 745
124. SEVENTH DAWN ........ Ferrante & Teicher, United Artists 735
125. CLOSE YOUR EYES ........ Arthur Prysock, Old Town 1163
126. MORE AND MORE OF YOUR AMOR ........ Nat King Cole, Capitol 5219
127. ONLY YOU ........ Wayne Newton, Capitol 5203
128. THEME FROM "A SUMMER PLACE" ........ J's With Jamie, Columbia 43068
129. UNDER PARIS SKIES ........ Andy Williams, Cadence 1447
130. YOU'RE GONNA MISS ME ........ B. B. King, Kent 396
131. NEVER PICK A PRETTY BOY ........ Dee Dee Sharp, Cameo 329
132. JOHNNY LOVES ME ........ Florraine Darlin, RIC 105-64
133. BETTER WATCH OUT BOY ........ Accents, Challenge 59254
134. HE WAS A FRIEND OF MINE ........ Bobby Bare, RCA Victor 8395
135. DARLIN' IT'S WONDERFUL ........ Dale & Grace, Montel 930

Compiled from national retail sales and radio station airplay by the Music Popularity Dept. of Record Market Research, Billboard.

Billboard

For Week Ending August 15, 1964

# HOT 100

★ STAR performer—Sides registering greatest proportionate upward progress this week.

Billboard Award

| This Week | 1 Wk. Ago | 2 Wks. Ago | 3 Wks. Ago | TITLE Artist, Label & Number | Weeks On Chart |
|---|---|---|---|---|---|
| 1 | 2 | 4 | 11 | EVERYBODY LOVES SOMEBODY — Dean Martin, Reprise 0281 | 8 |
| 2 | 3 | 5 | 18 | WHERE DID OUR LOVE GO — Supremes, Motown 1060 | 6 |
| 3 | 1 | 1 | 2 | A HARD DAY'S NIGHT — Beatles, Capitol 5222 | 5 |
| 4 | 5 | 2 | 1 | RAG DOLL — 4 Seasons, Philips 40211 | 8 |
| 5 | 7 | 11 | 13 | UNDER THE BOARDWALK — Drifters, Atlantic 2237 | 8 |
| 6 | 6 | 6 | 9 | WISHIN' AND HOPIN' — Dusty Springfield, Philips 40207 | 9 |
| 7 | 4 | 3 | 6 | THE LITTLE OLD LADY (From Pasadena) — Jan & Dean, Liberty 55704 | 8 |
| ★ 8 | 13 | 24 | 36 | C'MON AND SWIM — Bobby Freeman, Autumn 2 | 6 |
| 9 | 9 | 15 | 20 | I WANNA LOVE HIM SO BAD — Jelly Beans, Red Bird 10-003 | 9 |
| ★ 10 | 60 | — | — | THE HOUSE OF THE RISING SUN — Animals, MGM 13264 | 2 |
| 11 | 14 | 17 | 22 | (You Don't Know) HOW GLAD I AM — Nancy Wilson, Capitol 5198 | 8 |
| 12 | 10 | 8 | 3 | I GET AROUND — Beach Boys, Capitol 5174 | 13 |
| ★ 13 | 20 | 29 | 48 | WALK—DON'T RUN '64 — Ventures, Dolton 96 | 6 |
| ★ 14 | 22 | 60 | — | BECAUSE — Dave Clark Five, Epic 9704 | 3 |
| 15 | 18 | 31 | 47 | PEOPLE SAY — Dixie Cups, Red Bird 10-006 | 5 |
| ★ 16 | 21 | 43 | 53 | HOW DO YOU DO IT — Gerry and the Pacemakers, Laurie 3261 | 6 |
| 17 | 19 | 20 | 25 | STEAL AWAY — Jimmy Hughes, Fame 6401 | 9 |
| 18 | 8 | 7 | 8 | DANG ME — Roger Miller, Smash 1881 | 10 |
| 19 | 11 | 10 | 5 | THE GIRL FROM IPANEMA — Getz/Gilberto, Verve 10323 | 11 |
| ★ 20 | 28 | 33 | 46 | JUST BE TRUE — Gene Chandler, Constellation 130 | 6 |
| 21 | 17 | 14 | 10 | KEEP ON PUSHING — Impressions, ABC-Paramount 10554 | 11 |
| 22 | 25 | 40 | 67 | AIN'T SHE SWEET — Beatles, Atco 6308 | 5 |
| 23 | 23 | 27 | 34 | HANDY MAN — Del Shannon, Amy 905 | 7 |
| 24 | 24 | 36 | 49 | TELL ME — Rolling Stones, London 9682 | 7 |
| 25 | 15 | 12 | 14 | NOBODY I KNOW — Peter & Gordon, Capitol 5211 | 8 |
| 26 | 12 | 9 | 4 | MEMPHIS — Johnny Rivers, Imperial 66032 | 12 |
| ★ 27 | 40 | 65 | 80 | AND I LOVE HER — Beatles, Capitol 5235 | 4 |
| ★ 28 | 35 | 56 | 82 | SUCH A NIGHT — Elvis Presley, RCA Victor 8400 | 4 |
| 29 | 29 | 32 | 38 | AL-DI-LA — Ray Charles Singers, Command 4049 | 6 |
| 30 | 31 | 38 | 44 | SUGAR LIPS — Al Hirt, RCA Victor 8391 | 6 |
| 31 | 16 | 13 | 7 | CAN'T YOU SEE THAT SHE'S MINE — Dave Clark Five, Epic 9692 | 10 |
| 32 | 27 | 28 | 35 | I LIKE IT LIKE THAT — Miracles, Tamla 54098 | 8 |
| ★ 33 | 47 | 50 | 63 | SHE'S THE ONE — Chartbusters, Mutual 502 | 6 |
| ★ 34 | 44 | 62 | — | I'LL CRY INSTEAD — Beatles, Capitol 5234 | 3 |
| ★ 35 | 46 | 54 | 85 | I'LL KEEP YOU SATISFIED — Billy J. Kramer, Imperial 66048 | 4 |
| 36 | 26 | 26 | 31 | YOU'RE MY WORLD — Cilla Black, Capitol 5196 | 7 |
| 37 | 42 | 42 | 54 | MIXED-UP, SHOOK-UP, GIRL — Patty & the Emblems, Herald 590 | 9 |
| ★ 38 | 70 | 88 | — | SELFISH ONE — Jackie Ross, Chess 1903 | 3 |
| 39 | 30 | 18 | 15 | TRY IT BABY — Marvin Gaye, Tamla 54095 | 11 |
| ★ 40 | 50 | 64 | 88 | MAYBE I KNOW — Lesley Gore, Mercury 72309 | 4 |
| 41 | 33 | 39 | 50 | I BELIEVE — Bachelors, London 9672 | 8 |
| 42 | 32 | 19 | 23 | FARMER JOHN — Premiers, Warner Bros. 5443 | 9 |
| 43 | 43 | 44 | 52 | ANGELITO — Rene and Rene, Columbia 43045 | 6 |
| 44 | 34 | 34 | 37 | DO I LOVE YOU? — Ronettes, Philles 121 | 9 |
| 45 | 49 | 63 | 83 | IN THE MISTY MOONLIGHT — Jerry Wallace, Challenge 59246 | 4 |
| 46 | 38 | 45 | 57 | I'M INTO SOMETHIN' GOOD — Earl-Jean, Colpix 729 | 8 |
| ★ 47 | 66 | 83 | — | YOU NEVER CAN TELL — Chuck Berry, Chess 1906 | 3 |
| 48 | 54 | 58 | 69 | LOOKING FOR LOVE — Connie Francis, MGM 13256 | 5 |
| 49 | 56 | 67 | 74 | HEY GIRL DON'T BOTHER ME — Tams, ABC-Paramount 10573 | 5 |
| ★ 50 | 72 | 89 | — | G.T.O. — Ronny & the Daytonas, Mala 481 | 3 |
| 51 | 51 | 57 | 65 | LITTLE LATIN LUPE LU — Kingsmen, Wand 157 | 6 |
| ★ 52 | 64 | 80 | 87 | IT HURTS TO BE IN LOVE — Gene Pitney, Musicor 1040 | 5 |
| 53 | 59 | 66 | 75 | I SHOULD HAVE KNOWN BETTER — Beatles, Capitol 5222 | 4 |
| ★ 54 | 68 | 81 | 100 | IT'S ALL OVER NOW — Rolling Stones, London 9687 | 4 |
| 55 | 58 | 74 | — | A TEAR FELL — Ray Charles, ABC-Paramount 10571 | 3 |
| ★ 56 | — | — | — | BREAD AND BUTTER — Newbeats, Hickory 1269 | 1 |
| ★ 57 | 71 | 78 | 84 | WORRY — Johnny Tillotson, MGM 13255 | 5 |
| 58 | 61 | 70 | 77 | SOLE SOLE SOLE — Siw Malmkvist & Umberto Marcato, Jubilee 5479 | 5 |
| 59 | 57 | 61 | 70 | LOVE IS ALL WE NEED — Vic Dana, Dolton 95 | 6 |
| ★ 60 | 73 | — | — | SWEET WILLIAM — Millie Small, Smash 1920 | 2 |
| 61 | 62 | 68 | 76 | NO ONE TO CRY TO — Ray Charles, ABC-Paramount 10571 | 5 |
| 62 | 65 | 73 | 89 | I WANT YOU TO MEET MY BABY — Eydie Gorme, Columbia 43082 | 4 |
| ★ 63 | 88 | — | — | CLINGING VINE — Bobby Vinton, Epic 9705 | 2 |
| 64 | 69 | 72 | 79 | EVERYBODY NEEDS SOMEBODY TO LOVE — Solomon Burke, Atlantic 2241 | 5 |
| ★ 65 | 81 | — | 94 | RINGO'S THEME (This Boy) — George Martin and His Ork, United Artists 745 | 3 |
| 66 | 48 | 51 | 56 | YOU'RE MY REMEDY — Marvelettes, Tamla 54097 | 7 |
| 67 | 67 | 77 | 90 | HELLO MUDDUH, HELLO FADDUH (1964 Version) — Allan Sherman, Warner Bros. 5449 | 4 |
| ★ 68 | 99 | — | — | HAUNTED HOUSE — Gene Simmons, Hi 2076 | 2 |
| 69 | 76 | — | — | I'LL ALWAYS LOVE YOU — Brenda Holloway, Tamla 54099 | 2 |
| ★ 70 | — | — | — | MABELLINE — Johnny Rivers, Imperial 66056 | 1 |
| 71 | 78 | 76 | 86 | INVISIBLE TEARS — Ray Conniff Singers, Columbia 43061 | 5 |
| ★ 72 | 87 | 92 | — | IF I FELL — Beatles, Capitol 5235 | 3 |
| ★ 73 | — | — | — | OUT OF SIGHT — James Brown, Smash 1919 | 1 |
| 74 | 84 | — | — | HE'S IN TOWN — Tokens, B. T. Puppy 502 | 2 |
| ★ 75 | 90 | — | — | WHEN YOU LOVED ME — Brenda Lee, Decca 31654 | 2 |
| 76 | 77 | 85 | — | I'VE GOT NO TIME TO LOSE — Carla Thomas, Atlantic 2238 | 3 |
| 77 | 63 | 71 | 78 | THANK YOU BABY — Shirelles, Scepter 1278 | 5 |
| 78 | 80 | 86 | — | THE NEW FRANKIE & JOHNNIE SONG — Greenwood County Singers, Kapp 591 | 3 |
| 79 | 79 | 82 | 95 | SUMMER MEANS FUN — Bruce & Terry, Columbia 43055 | 4 |
| ★ 80 | 95 | — | — | WE'LL SING IN THE SUNSHINE — Gale Garnett, RCA Victor 8388 | 2 |
| 81 | 83 | 90 | — | SAILOR BOY — Chiffons, Laurie 3262 | 3 |
| 82 | 89 | 91 | 92 | A HOUSE IS NOT A HOME — Brook Benton, Mercury 72303 | 5 |
| 83 | 93 | 94 | 98 | SAY YOU — Ronnie Dove, Diamond 167 | 5 |
| ★ 84 | — | — | — | FUNNY — Joe Hinton, Back Beat 541 | 1 |
| 85 | 85 | 96 | — | A HOUSE IS NOT A HOME — Dionne Warwick, Scepter 1282 | 3 |
| ★ 86 | — | — | — | WHERE LOVE HAS GONE — Jack Jones, Kapp 608 | 1 |
| ★ 87 | — | — | — | YOU'LL NEVER GET TO HEAVEN (If You Break My Heart) — Dionne Warwick, Scepter 1282 | 1 |
| 88 | 100 | — | — | IF I'M A FOOL FOR LOVING YOU — Bobby Wood, Joy 285 | 2 |
| ★ 89 | — | — | — | SOME DAY WE'RE GONNA LOVE AGAIN — Searchers, Kapp 609 | 1 |
| ★ 90 | — | — | — | BABY I NEED YOUR LOVING — Four Tops, Motown 1062 | 1 |
| 91 | 91 | — | — | FATHER SEBASTIAN — Ramblers, Almont 311 | 2 |
| 92 | 92 | — | — | SILLY OL' SUMMERTIME — New Christy Minstrels, Columbia 43092 | 2 |
| 93 | — | — | 91 | QUIET PLACE — Garnet Mimms, United Artists 715 | 3 |
| 94 | 94 | 97 | — | SHOUT — Lulu & the Luvers, Parrot 9678 | 3 |
| 95 | 98 | — | — | ME JAPANESE BOY I LOVE YOU — Bobby Goldsboro, United Artists 742 | 2 |
| 96 | — | — | — | ALWAYS TOGETHER — Al Martino, Capitol 5239 | 1 |
| 97 | — | — | — | A SUMMER SONG — Chad Stuart & Jeremy Clyde, World Artists 1027 | 1 |
| 98 | — | — | — | SOUL DRESSING — Booker T. & MG's, Stax 153 | 1 |
| 99 | — | — | — | IT'S COTTON CANDY WORLD — Jerry Wallace, Mercury 72292 | 1 |
| 100 | — | — | — | I CAN'T GET YOU OUT OF MY HEART — Al Martino, 20th Century-Fox 530 | 1 |

## HOT 100—A TO Z—(Publisher-Licensee)


Ain't She Sweet (Advance, ASCAP) ........ 22
Al-Di-La (Witmark, ASCAP) ........ 29
Always Together (Damian, ASCAP) ........ 96
And I Love Her (Unart-Maclen, BMI) ........ 27
Angelito (Gil-Epps, BMI) ........ 43
Baby I Need Your Loving (Jobete, BMI) ........ 90
Because (Ivy, ASCAP) ........ 14
Bread and Butter (Acuff-Rose, BMI) ........ 56
Can't You See That She's Mine (Beechwood, BMI). 31
Clinging Vine (Peter Maurice, ASCAP) ........ 63
C'mon and Swim (Taracrest, BMI) ........ 8
Dang Me, (Tree, BMI) ........ 18
Do I Love You (Mother Bertha-Hill & Range, BMI) 44
Everybody Loves Somebody (Sands, ASCAP) ........ 1
Everybody Needs Somebody to Love (Keetch, Caesar & Dino, BMI) ........ 64
Farmer John (Venice, BMI) ........ 42
Father Sebastian (Four Star, BMI) ........ 91
Funny (Just & Geneva, BMI) ........ 84
G.T.O. (Buckhorn, BMI) ........ 50
Girl From Ipanema, The (Duchess, BMI) ........ 19
Handy Man (Travis, BMI) ........ 23
Hard Day's Night, A (Unart-Maclen, BMI) ........ 3
Haunted House (Venice-B. Flat, BMI) ........ 68
He's in Town (Screen Gems-Columbia, BMI) ........ 74
Hello Mudduh, Hello Fadduh (Curtain Call, ASCAP) 67
Hey Girl Don't Bother Me (Low-Twi, BMI) ........ 49
House Is Not a Home, A—Benton (Diplomat, ASCAP). 82
House Is Not a Home, A—Warwick (Diplomat, ASCAP) ........ 85
House of the Rising Sun, The (Gallico, BMI) ........ 10
How Do You Do It (Just, BMI) ........ 16
I Believe (Cromwell, ASCAP) ........ 41
I Can't Get You Out of My Heart (Southern, ASCAP) ........ 100
I Get Around (Sea of Tunes, BMI) ........ 12
I Like It Like That (Jobete, BMI) ........ 32
I Should Have Known Better (Unart-Maclen, BMI). 53
I Wanna Love Him So Bad (Trio, BMI) ........ 9
I Want You to Meet My Baby (Screen Gems-Columbia, BMI) ........ 62
I'm Into Somethin' Good (Screen Gems-Columbia, BMI) ........ 46
I've Got No Time to Lose (East, BMI) ........ 76
I'll Always Love You (Jobete, BMI) ........ 69
I'll Cry Instead (Unart-Maclen, BMI) ........ 34
I'll Keep You Satisfied (Metric, BMI) ........ 35
If I'm a Fool for Loving You (Drury Lane-Beckie, BMI) ........ 88
If I Fell (Unart-Maclen, BMI) ........ 72
In the Misty Moonlight (Four Star, BMI) ........ 45
Invisible Tears (Central Songs, BMI) ........ 71
It Hurts to Be in Love (Screen Gems-Columbia, BMI) 52
It's a Cotton Candy World (Feist, ASCAP) ........ 99
It's All Over Now (Kags, BMI) ........ 54
Just Be True (Curtom-Camad, BMI) ........ 20
Keep on Pushing (Curtom, BMI) ........ 21
Little Latin Lupe Lu (Maxwell-Conrad, BMI) ........ 51
Little Old Lady (From Pasadena), The (Screen Gems-Columbia, BMI) ........ 7
Looking for Love (Merna, BMI) ........ 48
Love Is All We Need (Travis, BMI) ........ 59
Maybe I Know (Trio, BMI) ........ 40
Mabelline (Arc, BMI) ........ 70
Me Japanese Boy I Love You (Jac-Blue Seas, ASCAP) ........ 95
Memphis (Arc, BMI) ........ 26
Mixed-Up, Shook-Up, Girl (Ben-Lee, BMI) ........ 37
New Frankie and Johnny Song, The (Hollis, BMI). 78
No One to Cry To (Hill & Range, BMI) ........ 61
Nobody I Know (Maclen, BMI) ........ 25
Out of Sight (Try Me, BMI) ........ 73
People Say (Trio, BMI) ........ 15
Quiet Place (Rittenhouse, BMI) ........ 93
Rag Doll (Saturday-Gavadima, ASCAP) ........ 4
Ringo's Theme (This Boy) (Maclen, BMI) ........ 65
Sailor Boy (Screen Gems-Columbia, BMI) ........ 81
Say You (T.M., BMI) ........ 83
Selfish One (Chevis, BMI) ........ 38
She's the One (Eastwick-Chartbuster, BMI) ........ 33
Shout (Wemar-Nom, BMI) ........ 94
Silly Ol' Summertime (New Christy, BMI) ........ 92
Sole Sole Sole (MRC, BMI) ........ 58
Some Day We're Gonna Love Again (McLaughlin, BMI) ........ 89
Soul Dressing (East, BMI) ........ 98
Steal Away (Fame, BMI) ........ 17
Such a Night (Raleigh, BMI) ........ 28
Sugar Lips (Tree, BMI) ........ 30
Summer Means Fun (Trousdale, BMI) ........ 79
Summer Song, A (Unart Woart, BMI) ........ 97
Sweet William (Budd, ASCAP) ........ 60
Tear Fell, A (Progressive, BMI) ........ 55
Tell Me (Southern, ASCAP) ........ 24
Thank You Baby (Girl's, BMI) ........ 77
Try It Baby, Jobete, BMI) ........ 39
Under the Boardwalk (T.M., BMI) ........ 5
Walk—Don't Run '64 (Forshay, BMI) ........ 13
We'll Sing in the Sunshine (Lutercalia, BMI) ........ 80
When You Loved Me (Hill & Range-Ron-Bre, BMI). 75
Where Did Our Love Go (Jobete, BMI) ........ 2
Where Love Has Gone (Paramount, ASCAP) ........ 86
Wishin' and Hopin' (Jonathan, ASCAP) ........ 6
Worry (Ridge, BMI) ........ 57
You Don't Know How Glad I Am (Roosevelt, BMI). . 11
You Never Can Tell (Arc, BMI) ........ 47
You're My Remedy (Jobete, BMI) ........ 66
You're My World (Plan Two, ASCAP) ........ 36
You'll Never Get to Heaven (Jac-Blue Seas, ASCAP) 87


## BUBBLING UNDER THE HOT 100

101. JAMES BOND THEME ........ Billy Strange, Crescendo 320
102. I'M HAPPY JUST TO DANCE WITH YOU ........ Beatles, Capitol 5234
103. I STAND ACCUSED ........ Jerry Butler, Vee Jay 598
104. A TASTE OF HONEY ........ Tony Bennett, Columbia 43073
105. MY HEART SKIPS A BEAT ........ Buck Owens, Capitol 5136
106. REMEMBER (Walkin' in the Sand) ........ Shangri-Las, Red Bird 10-008
107. SOMEONE, SOMEONE ........ Brian Poole, Monument 846
103. YOU'RE GONNA MISS ME ........ B. B. King, Kent 396
109. I GUESS I'M CRAZY ........ Jim Reeves, RCA Victor 8383
110. LET ME LOVE YOU ........ B. B. King, Kent 396
111. ONE PIECE TOPLESS BATHING SUIT ........ Rip Chords, Columbia 43093
112. BACHELOR BOY ........ Cliff Richard and the Shadows, Epic 9691
113. 20-75 ........ Willie Mitchell, Hi 2075
114. LET ME GET CLOSE TO YOU ........ Skeeter Davis, RCA Victor 8397
115. MICHAEL ........ Trini Lopez, Reprise 0300
116. I'LL KEEP TRYING ........ Theola Kilgore, KT 501
117. YOU PULLED A FAST ONE ........ V.I.P.'s, Big Top 518
118. THEME FROM "A SUMMER PLACE" ........ J's With Jamie, Columbia 43068
119. I JUST DON'T KNOW WHAT TO DO WITH MYSELF ........ Tommy Hunt, Scepter 1236
120. AND I LOVE HER ........ George Martin and His Ork, United Artists 745
121. UNDER PARIS SKIES ........ Andy Williams, Cadence 1447
122. THERE'S NOTHING I CAN SAY ........ Rick Nelson, Decca 31656
123. ONLY YOU ........ Wayne Newton, Capitol 5203
124. JOHNNY LOVES ME ........ Florraine Darlin, Ric 105-64
125. (There's) ALWAYS SOMETHING THERE TO REMIND ME ........ Lou Johnson, Big Hill 552
126. THE LONG SHIPS ........ Charles Albertine, Colpix 726
127. SQUEEZE HER—TEASE HER (But Love Her) ........ Jackie Wilson, Brunswick 55269
128. NEW GIRL ........ Accents, M-Pac 7216
129. NEVER ENDING ........ Elvis Presley, RCA Victor 8400
130. SOMETHING'S GOT A HOLD OF ME ........ Don and Alleyne Cole, Tollie 9015
131. DARLING IT'S WONDERFUL ........ Dale and Grace, Montel 930
132. PUT AWAY YOUR TEARDROPS ........ Lettermen, Capitol 5218
133. I'M ON THE OUTSIDE (LOOKING) ........ Little Anthony and the Imperials, DCP 1104
134. I'VE GOT A THING GOING ON ........ Bobby Marchan, Dial 3022
135. HE'S SURE TO REMEMBER ME ........ Brenda Lee, Decca 31654

Compiled from national retail sales and radio station airplay by the Music Popularity Dept. of Record Market Research, Billboard.

Billboard

For Week Ending August 22, 1964

# HOT 100

★ STAR performer—Sides registering greatest proportionate upward progress this week.

Billboard Award

| THIS WEEK | 1 Wk. Ago | 2 Wks. Ago | 3 Wks. Ago | TITLE — Artist, Label & Number | Weeks On Chart |
|---|---|---|---|---|---|
| 1 | 2 | 3 | 5 | WHERE DID OUR LOVE GO — Supremes, Motown 1060 | 7 |
| 2 | 1 | 2 | 4 | EVERYBODY LOVES SOMEBODY — Dean Martin, Reprise 0281 | 9 |
| 3 | 3 | 1 | 1 | A HARD DAY'S NIGHT — Beatles, Capitol 5222 | 6 |
| 4 | 5 | 7 | 11 | UNDER THE BOARDWALK — Drifters, Atlantic 2237 | 9 |
| ★ 5 | 10 | 60 | — | THE HOUSE OF THE RISING SUN — Animals, MGM 13264 | 3 |
| 6 | 8 | 13 | 24 | C'MON AND SWIM — Bobby Freeman, Autumn 2 | 7 |
| ★ 7 | 14 | 22 | 60 | BECAUSE — Dave Clark Five, Epic 9704 | 4 |
| ★ 8 | 13 | 20 | 29 | WALK—DON'T RUN '64 — Ventures, Dolton 96 | 7 |
| 9 | 6 | 6 | 6 | WISHIN' AND HOPIN' — Dusty Springfield, Philips 40207 | 10 |
| ★ 10 | 16 | 21 | 43 | HOW DO YOU DO IT — Gerry and the Pacemakers, Laurie 3261 | 7 |
| 11 | 4 | 5 | 2 | RAG DOLL — 4 Seasons, Philips 40211 | 9 |
| 12 | 15 | 18 | 31 | PEOPLE SAY — Dixie Cups, Red Bird 10-006 | 6 |
| 13 | 7 | 4 | 3 | THE LITTLE OLD LADY (From Pasadena) — Jan & Dean, Liberty 55704 | 9 |
| 14 | 9 | 9 | 15 | I WANNA LOVE HIM SO BAD — Jelly Beans, Red Bird 10-003 | 10 |
| 15 | 12 | 10 | 8 | I GET AROUND — Beach Boys, Capitol 5174 | 14 |
| ★ 16 | 28 | 35 | 56 | SUCH A NIGHT — Elvis Presley, RCA Victor 8400 | 5 |
| ★ 17 | 27 | 40 | 65 | AND I LOVE HER — Beatles, Capitol 5235 | 5 |
| 18 | 11 | 14 | 17 | (You Don't Know) HOW GLAD I AM — Nancy Wilson, Capitol 5198 | 9 |
| 19 | 22 | 25 | 40 | AIN'T SHE SWEET — Beatles, Atco 6308 | 6 |
| 20 | 20 | 28 | 33 | JUST BE TRUE — Gene Chandler, Constellation 130 | 7 |
| ★ 21 | 40 | 50 | 64 | MAYBE I KNOW — Lesley Gore, Mercury 72309 | 5 |
| 22 | 23 | 23 | 27 | HANDY MAN — Del Shannon, Amy 905 | 8 |
| ★ 23 | 56 | — | — | BREAD AND BUTTER — Newbeats, Hickory 1269 | 2 |
| 24 | 17 | 19 | 20 | STEAL AWAY — Jimmy Hughes, Fame 6401 | 10 |
| ★ 25 | 47 | 66 | 83 | YOU NEVER CAN TELL — Chuck Berry, Chess 1906 | 4 |
| 26 | 21 | 17 | 14 | KEEP ON PUSHING — Impressions, ABC-Paramount 10554 | 12 |
| 27 | 24 | 24 | 36 | TELL ME — Rolling Stones, London 9682 | 8 |
| ★ 28 | 50 | 72 | 89 | G.T.O. — Ronny & the Daytonas, Mala 481 | 4 |
| ★ 29 | 34 | 44 | 62 | I'LL CRY INSTEAD — Beatles, Capitol 5234 | 4 |
| ★ 30 | 35 | 46 | 54 | I'LL KEEP YOU SATISFIED — Billy J. Kramer, Imperial 66048 | 5 |
| ★ 31 | 45 | 49 | 63 | IN THE MISTY MOONLIGHT — Jerry Wallace, Challenge 59246 | 5 |
| 32 | 38 | 70 | 88 | SELFISH ONE — Jackie Ross, Chess 1903 | 4 |
| 33 | 33 | 47 | 50 | SHE'S THE ONE — Chartbusters, Mutual 502 | 7 |
| 34 | 18 | 8 | 7 | DANG ME — Roger Miller, Smash 1881 | 11 |
| 35 | 30 | 31 | 38 | SUGAR LIPS — Al Hirt, RCA Victor 8391 | 7 |
| 36 | 19 | 11 | 10 | THE GIRL FROM IPANEMA — Getz/Gilberto, Verve 10323 | 12 |
| 37 | 37 | 42 | 42 | MIXED-UP, SHOOK-UP, GIRL — Patty & the Emblems, Herald 590 | 10 |
| ★ 38 | 63 | 88 | — | CLINGING VINE — Bobby Vinton, Epic 9705 | 3 |
| ★ 39 | 70 | — | — | MABELLINE — Johnny Rivers, Imperial 66056 | 2 |
| ★ 40 | 54 | 68 | 81 | IT'S ALL OVER NOW — Rolling Stones, London 9687 | 5 |
| 41 | 25 | 15 | 12 | NOBODY I KNOW — Peter & Gordon, Capitol 5211 | 9 |
| ★ 42 | 52 | 64 | 80 | IT HURTS TO BE IN LOVE — Gene Pitney, Musicor 1040 | 6 |
| 43 | 49 | 56 | 67 | HEY GIRL DON'T BOTHER ME — Tams, ABC-Paramount 10573 | 6 |
| 44 | 32 | 27 | 28 | I LIKE IT LIKE THAT — Miracles, Tamla 54098 | 9 |
| 45 | 48 | 54 | 58 | LOOKING FOR LOVE — Connie Francis, MGM 13256 | 6 |
| 46 | 43 | 43 | 44 | ANGELITO — Rene and Rene, Columbia 43045 | 7 |
| ★ 47 | 68 | 99 | — | HAUNTED HOUSE — Gene Simmons, Hi 2076 | 3 |
| 48 | 51 | 51 | 57 | LITTLE LATIN LUPE LU — Kingsmen, Wand 157 | 7 |
| ★ 49 | 62 | 65 | 73 | I WANT YOU TO MEET MY BABY — Eydie Gorme, Columbia 43082 | 5 |
| 50 | 55 | 58 | 74 | A TEAR FELL — Ray Charles, ABC-Paramount 10571 | 4 |
| 51 | 60 | 73 | — | SWEET WILLIAM — Millie Small, Smash 1920 | 3 |
| 52 | 57 | 71 | 78 | WORRY — Johnny Tillotson, MGM 13255 | 6 |
| 53 | 59 | 57 | 61 | LOVE IS ALL WE NEED — Vic Dana, Dolton 95 | 7 |
| ★ 54 | 90 | — | — | BABY I NEED YOUR LOVING — Four Tops, Motown 1062 | 2 |
| 55 | 61 | 62 | 68 | NO ONE TO CRY TO — Ray Charles, ABC-Paramount 10571 | 6 |
| 56 | 65 | 81 | — | RINGO'S THEME (This Boy) — George Martin and His Ork, United Artists 745 | 4 |
| ★ 57 | 72 | 87 | 92 | IF I FELL — Beatles, Capitol 5235 | 4 |
| 58 | 64 | 69 | 72 | EVERYBODY NEEDS SOMEBODY TO LOVE — Solomon Burke, Atlantic 2241 | 6 |
| 59 | 67 | 67 | 77 | HELLO MUDDUH, HELLO FADDUH (1964 Version) — Allan Sherman, Warner Bros. 5449 | 5 |
| 60 | 69 | 76 | — | I'LL ALWAYS LOVE YOU — Brenda Holloway, Tamla 54099 | 3 |
| 61 | 73 | — | — | OUT OF SIGHT — James Brown, Smash 1919 | 2 |
| ★ 62 | 80 | 95 | — | WE'LL SING IN THE SUNSHINE — Gale Garnett, RCA Victor 8388 | 3 |
| 63 | 75 | 90 | — | WHEN YOU LOVED ME — Brenda Lee, Decca 31654 | 3 |
| 64 | 74 | 84 | — | HE'S IN TOWN — Tokens, B. T. Puppy 502 | 3 |
| ★ 65 | 96 | — | — | ALWAYS TOGETHER — Al Martino, Capitol 5239 | 2 |
| ★ 66 | — | — | — | I'M ON THE OUTSIDE (LOOKING IN) — Little Anthony & the Imperials, DCP 1104 | 1 |
| ★ 67 | 89 | — | — | SOME DAY WE'RE GONNA LOVE AGAIN — Searchers, Kapp 609 | 2 |
| ★ 68 | — | — | — | DANCING IN THE STREET — Martha & the Vandellas, Gordy 7033 | 1 |
| ★ 69 | 84 | — | — | FUNNY — Joe Hinton, Back Beat 541 | 2 |
| 70 | 71 | 78 | 76 | INVISIBLE TEARS — Ray Conniff Singers, Columbia 43061 | 6 |
| 71 | 76 | 77 | 85 | I'VE GOT NO TIME TO LOSE — Carla Thomas, Atlantic 2238 | 4 |
| 72 | 79 | 79 | 82 | SUMMER MEANS FUN — Bruce & Terry, Columbia 43055 | 5 |
| 73 | 85 | 85 | 96 | A HOUSE IS NOT A HOME — Dionne Warwick, Scepter 1282 | 4 |
| 74 | 83 | 93 | 94 | SAY YOU — Ronnie Dove, Diamond 167 | 6 |
| 75 | 78 | 80 | 86 | THE NEW FRANKIE & JOHNNIE SONG — Greenwood County Singers, Kapp 591 | 4 |
| 76 | 77 | 63 | 71 | THANK YOU BABY — Shirelles, Scepter 1278 | 6 |
| 77 | 88 | 100 | — | IF I'M A FOOL FOR LOVING YOU — Bobby Wood, Joy 285 | 3 |
| ★ 78 | — | — | — | REMEMBER (Walkin' in the Sand) — Shangri-La, Red Bird 10-008 | 1 |
| 79 | 82 | 89 | 91 | A HOUSE IS NOT A HOME — Brook Benton, Mercury 72303 | 6 |
| ★ 80 | — | — | 84 | I STAND ACCUSED — Jerry Butler, Vee Jay 598 | 2 |
| 81 | 86 | — | — | WHERE LOVE HAS GONE — Jack Jones, Kapp 608 | 2 |
| ★ 82 | — | — | — | (There's) ALWAYS SOMETHING THERE TO REMIND ME — Lou Johnson, Big Hill 552 | 1 |
| 83 | 87 | — | — | YOU'LL NEVER GET TO HEAVEN (If You Break My Heart) — Dionne Warwick, Scepter 1282 | 2 |
| ★ 84 | — | — | — | THERE'S NOTHING I CAN SAY — Rick Nelson, Decca 31656 | 1 |
| 85 | 97 | — | — | A SUMMER SONG — Chad Stuart & Jeremy Clyde, World Artists 1027 | 2 |
| ★ 86 | — | — | — | JOHNNY B. GOODE — Dion Di Muci, Columbia 43096 | 1 |
| 87 | 95 | 98 | — | ME JAPANESE BOY I LOVE YOU — Bobby Goldsboro, United Artists 742 | 3 |
| 88 | 91 | 91 | — | FATHER SEBASTIAN — Ramblers, Almont 311 | 3 |
| 89 | 93 | — | — | QUIET PLACE — Garnet Mimms, United Artists 715 | 4 |
| ★ 90 | — | — | — | MICHAEL — Trini Lopez, Reprise 0300 | 1 |
| 91 | — | — | — | I GUESS I'M CRAZY — Jim Reeves, RCA Victor 8383 | 1 |
| 92 | — | — | — | FROM A WINDOW — Billy J. Kramer, Imperial 66051 | 1 |
| 93 | — | — | — | I DON'T CARE — Buck Owens, Capitol 5240 | 1 |
| 94 | — | — | — | SQUEEZE HER—TEASE HER (But Love Her) — Jackie Wilson, Brunswick 55269 | 1 |
| 95 | 98 | — | — | SOUL DRESSING — Booker T. & MG's, Stax 153 | 2 |
| 96 | — | — | — | RHYTHM — Major Lance, Okeh 7203 | 1 |
| 97 | — | — | — | THE JAMES BOND THEME — Billy Strange, Crescendo 320 | 1 |
| 98 | — | — | — | LOVERS ALWAYS FORGIVE — Gladys Knight & the Pips, Maxx 329 | 1 |
| 99 | 100 | — | — | I CAN'T GET YOU OUT OF MY HEART — Al Martino, 20th Century-Fox 530 | 2 |
| 100 | — | — | — | A TASTE OF HONEY — Tony Bennett, Columbia 43073 | 1 |

## HOT 100—A TO Z—*(Publisher-Licensee)*


Ain't She Sweet (Advance, ASCAP) .......... 19
Always Together (Damian, ASCAP) .......... 65
And I Love Her (Unart-Maclen, BMI) .......... 17
Angelito (Gil-Epps, BMI) .......... 46
Baby I Need Your Loving (Jobete, BMI) .......... 54
Because (Ivy, ASCAP) .......... 7
Bread and Butter (Acuff-Rose, BMI) .......... 23
Clinging Vine (Peter Maurice, ASCAP) .......... 38
C'mon and Swim (Taracrest, BMI) .......... 6
Dancing in the Street (Jobete, BMI) .......... 68
Dang Me (Tree, BMI) .......... 34
Everybody Loves Somebody (Sands, ASCAP) .......... 2
Everybody Needs Somebody to Love (Keetch, Caesar & Dino, BMI) .......... 58
Father Sebastian (Four Star, BMI) .......... 88
From a Window (Northern, ASCAP) .......... 92
Funny (Just-Geneva, BMI) .......... 69
G.T.O. (Buckhorn, BMI) .......... 28
Girl From Ipanema, The (Duchess, BMI) .......... 36
Handy Man (Travis, BMI) .......... 22
Hard Day's Night, A (Unart-Maclen, BMI) .......... 3
Haunted House (Venice-B. Flat, BMI) .......... 47
He's in Town (Screen Gems-Columbia, BMI) .......... 64
Hello Mudduh, Hello Fadduh (Curtain Call, ASCAP). 59
Hey Girl Don't Bother Me (Low-Twi, BMI) .......... 43
House Is Not a Home, A—Benton (Diplomat, ASCAP) .......... 79
House Is Not a Home, A—Warwick (Diplomat, ASCAP) .......... 73
House of the Rising Sun, The (Gallico, BMI) .......... 5
How Do You Do It (Just, BMI) .......... 10
I Can't Get You Out of My Heart (Southern, ASCAP) .......... 99
I Don't Care (Bluebook, BMI) .......... 93
I Get Around (Sea of Tunes, BMI) .......... 15
I Guess I'm Crazy (Mallory, BMI) .......... 91
I Like It Like That (Jobete, BMI) .......... 44
I Stand Accused (Curtom, BMI) .......... 80
I Wanna Love Him So Bad (Trio, BMI) .......... 14
I Want You to Meet My Baby (Screen Gems-Columbia, BMI) .......... 49
I'm on the Outside (Looking In) (South Mountain, BMI) .......... 66
I've Got No Time to Lose (East, BMI) .......... 71
I'll Always Love You (Jobete, BMI) .......... 60
I'll Cry Instead (Unart-Maclen, BMI) .......... 29
I'll Keep You Satisfied (Metric, BMI) .......... 30
If I'm a Fool for Loving You (Drury Lane-Beckie, BMI) .......... 77
If I Fell (Unart-Maclen, BMI) .......... 57
In the Misty Moonlight (Four Star, BMI) .......... 31
Invisible Tears (Central Songs, BMI) .......... 70
It Hurts to Be in Love (Screen Gems-Columbia, BMI) .......... 42
It's All Over Now (Kags, BMI) .......... 40
James Bond Theme, The (Unart, BMI) .......... 97
Johnny B. Goode (Arc, BMI) .......... 86
Just Be True (Curtom-Camad, BMI) .......... 20
Keep on Pushing (Curtom, BMI) .......... 26
Little Latin Lupe Lu (Maxwell-Conrad, BMI) .......... 48
Little Old Lady (From Pasadena) (Screen Gems-Columbia, BMI) .......... 13
Looking for Love (Merna, BMI) .......... 45
Love Is All We Need (Travis, BMI) .......... 53
Lovers Always Forgive (Maxx, BMI) .......... 98
Mabelline (Arc, BMI) .......... 39
Maybe I Know (Trio, BMI) .......... 21
Me Japanese Boy I Love You (Jac-Blue Seas, ASCAP) .......... 87
Michael (United Artists, ASCAP) .......... 90
Mixed-Up, Shook-Up, Girl (Ben-Lee, BMI) .......... 37
New Frankie and Johnny Song, The (Hollis, BMI). 75
No One to Cry To (Hill & Range, BMI) .......... 55
Nobody I Know (Maclen, BMI) .......... 41
Out of Sight (Try Me, BMI) .......... 61
People Say (Trio, BMI) .......... 12
Quiet Place, A (Rittenhouse, BMI) .......... 89
Rag Doll (Saturday-Gavadima, ASCAP) .......... 11
Remember (Walkin' in the Sands) (Tender Tunes-Trio, BMI) .......... 78
Rhythm (Jalynne-Curtom, BMI) .......... 96
Ringo's Theme (This Boy) (Maclen, BMI) .......... 56
Say You (T. M., BMI) .......... 74
Selfish One (Chevis, BMI) .......... 32
She's the One (Eastwick-Chartbuster, BMI) .......... 33
Some Day We're Gonna Love Again (McLaughlin, BMI) .......... 67
Soul Dressing (East, BMI) .......... 95
Squeeze Her—Tease Her (But Love Her) (Merrimac, BMI) .......... 94
Steal Away (Fame, BMI) .......... 24
Such a Night (Raleigh, BMI) .......... 16
Sugar Lips (Tree, BMI) .......... 35
Summer Means Fun (Trousdale, BMI) .......... 72
Summer Song, A (Unart-Woart, BMI) .......... 85
Sweet William (Budd, ASCAP) .......... 51
Taste of Honey, A (Songfest, ASCAP) .......... 100
Tear Fell, A (Progressive, BMI) .......... 50
Tell Me (Southern, ASCAP) .......... 27
Thank You Baby (Girl's, BMI) .......... 76
(There's) Always Something There to Remind Me (Ross-Jungnickel & Blue Seas, ASCAP) .......... 82
There's Nothing I Can Say (Chappell, ASCAP) .......... 84
Under the Boardwalk (T. M., BMI) .......... 4
Walk—Don't Run '64 (Forshay, BMI) .......... 8
We'll Sing in the Sunshine (Lutercalia, BMI) .......... 62
When You Loved Me (Hill & Range-Ron-Bre, BMI). 63
Where Did Our Love Go (Jobete, BMI) .......... 1
Where Love Has Gone (Paramount, ASCAP) .......... 81
Wishin' and Hopin' (Jonathan, ASCAP) .......... 9
Worry (Ridge, BMI) .......... 52
(You Don't Know) How Glad I Am (Roosevelt, BMI) .......... 18
You Never Can Tell (Arc, BMI) .......... 25
You'll Never Get to Heaven (Jac-Blue Seas, ASCAP) .......... 83


## BUBBLING UNDER THE HOT 100

101. OH, PRETTY WOMAN .......... Roy Orbison, Monument 851
102. SAVE IT FOR ME .......... 4 Seasons, Philips 40225
103. CAN'T GET OVER (THE BOSSA NOVA) .......... Eydie Gorme, Columbia 43082
104. SILLY OL' SUMMERTIME .......... New Christy Minstrels, Columbia 43092
105. SINCERELY .......... 4 Seasons, Vee Jay 608
106. SOMEONE, SOMEONE .......... Brian Poole, Monument 846
107. YOU'RE GONNA MISS ME .......... B. B. King, Kent 396
103. LET ME GET CLOSE TO YOU .......... Skeeter Davis, RCA Victor 8397
109. BACHELOR BOY .......... Cliff Richard & the Shadows, Epic 9691
110. ONE PIECE TOPLESS BATHING SUIT .......... Rip Chords, Columbia 43039
111. IT'S A COTTON CANDY WORLD .......... Jerry Wallace, Mercury 72292
112. LET ME LOVE YOU .......... B. B. King, Kent 396
113. YOU'RE NO GOOD .......... Swinging Blue Jeans, Imperial 66049
114. DARLING IT'S WONDERFUL .......... Dale & Grace, Motel 930
115. THEME FROM "A SUMMERPLACE" .......... J's with Jamie, Columbia 43068
116. I GOT A THING GOING ON .......... Bobby Marchan, Dial 3022
117. YOU PULLED A FAST ONE .......... V.I.P.'s, Big Top 518
118. I'M HAPPY JUST TO DANCE WITH YOU .......... Beatles, Capitol 5234
119. I JUST DON'T KNOW WHAT TO DO WITH MYSELF .. Tommy Hunt, Scepter 1236
120. THE LONG SHIPS .......... Charles Albertine, Colpix 726
121. JOHNNY LOVES ME .......... Florraine Darlin, Ric 105-64
122. ONLY YOU .......... Wayne Newton, Capitol 5203
123. IF .......... Timi Yuro, Mercury 72316
124. LA LA LA LA LA .......... Blendells, Reprise 0291
125. I'LL FOLLOW THE RAINBOW .......... Terry Stafford, Crusader 109
126. LAST KISS .......... J. Frank Wilson & the Cavaliers, Josie 923
127. SOMETHING'S GOT A HOLD OF ME .......... Don & Alleyne Cole, Tollie 9015
128. GUITARS AND BONGOS .......... Lou Christie, Colpix 735
129. YET I KNOW (Et Pourtant) .......... Steve Lawrence, Columbia 43095
130. DON'T LET HER KNOW .......... Buck Owens, Capitol 5240
131. IT'S IN YOUR HANDS .......... Diane Renay, 20th Century-Fox 523
132. RINGO FOR PRESIDENT .......... Young World Singers, Decca 31660
133. HEARTBREAK .......... Dee Clark, Constellation 132
134. HOLD ME .......... P. J. Proby, London 9688
135. THE DARTELL STOMP .......... Mustangs, Providence 401

Compiled from national retail sales and radio station airplay by the Music Popularity Dept. of Record Market Research, Billboard.

# Billboard HOT 100

**For Week Ending August 29, 1964**

★ STAR performer—Sides registering greatest proportionate upward progress this week.

| This Week | Wk. Ago | 2 Wks. Ago | 3 Wks. Ago | TITLE Artist, Label & Number | Weeks On Chart |
|---|---|---|---|---|---|
| 1 | 1 | 2 | 3 | WHERE DID OUR LOVE GO — Supremes, Motown 1060 | 8 |
| 2 | 5 | 10 | 60 | THE HOUSE OF THE RISING SUN — Animals, MGM 13264 | 4 |
| 3 | 2 | 1 | 2 | EVERYBODY LOVES SOMEBODY — Dean Martin, Reprise 0281 | 10 |
| 4 | 3 | 3 | 1 | A HARD DAY'S NIGHT — Beatles, Capitol 5222 | 7 |
| 5 | 6 | 8 | 13 | C'MON AND SWIM — Bobby Freeman, Autumn 2 | |
| 6 | 4 | 5 | 7 | UNDER THE BOARDWALK — Drifters, Atlantic 2237 | 10 |
| 7 | 7 | 14 | 22 | BECAUSE — Dave Clark Five, Epic 9704 | 5 |
| 8 | 8 | 13 | 20 | WALK—DON'T RUN '64 — Ventures, Dolton 96 | 8 |
| 9 | 23 | 56 | — | BREAD AND BUTTER — Newbeats, Hickory 1269 | 3 |
| 10 | 10 | 16 | 21 | HOW DO YOU DO IT — Gerry and the Pacemakers, Laurie 3261 | 8 |
| 11 | 9 | 6 | 6 | WISHIN' AND HOPIN' — Dusty Springfield, Philips 40207 | 11 |
| 12 | 12 | 15 | 18 | PEOPLE SAY — Dixie Cups, Red Bird 10-006 | 7 |
| 13 | 17 | 27 | 40 | AND I LOVE HER — Beatles, Capitol 5235 | 6 |
| 14 | 32 | 38 | 70 | SELFISH ONE — Jackie Ross, Chess 1903 | 5 |
| 15 | 28 | 50 | 72 | G.T.O. — Ronny & the Daytonas, Mala 481 | 5 |
| 16 | 16 | 28 | 35 | SUCH A NIGHT — Elvis Presley, RCA Victor 8400 | 6 |
| 17 | 11 | 4 | 5 | RAG DOLL — 4 Seasons, Philips 40211 | 10 |
| 18 | 21 | 40 | 50 | MAYBE I KNOW — Lesley Gore, Mercury 72309 | 5 |
| 19 | 20 | 20 | 28 | JUST BE TRUE — Gene Chandler, Constellation 130 | 8 |
| 20 | 25 | 47 | 66 | YOU NEVER CAN TELL — Chuck Berry, Chess 1906 | 5 |
| 21 | 38 | 63 | 88 | CLINGING VINE — Bobby Vinton, Epic 9705 | 4 |
| 22 | 13 | 7 | 4 | THE LITTLE OLD LADY (From Pasadena) — Jan & Dean, Liberty 55704 | 10 |
| 23 | 18 | 11 | 14 | (You Don't Know) HOW GLAD I AM — Nancy Wilson, Capitol 5198 | 10 |
| 24 | 19 | 22 | 25 | AIN'T SHE SWEET — Beatles, Atco 6308 | 7 |
| 25 | 29 | 34 | 44 | I'LL CRY INSTEAD — Beatles, Capitol 5234 | 5 |
| 26 | 31 | 45 | 49 | IN THE MISTY MOONLIGHT — Jerry Wallace, Challenge 59246 | 6 |
| 27 | 15 | 12 | 10 | I GET AROUND — Beach Boys, Capitol 5174 | 15 |
| 28 | 14 | 9 | 9 | I WANNA LOVE HIM SO BAD — Jelly Beans, Red Bird 10-003 | 11 |
| 29 | 42 | 52 | 64 | IT HURTS TO BE IN LOVE — Gene Pitney, Musicor 1040 | 7 |
| 30 | 39 | 70 | — | MAYBELLINE — Johnny Rivers, Imperial 66056 | 3 |
| 31 | 22 | 23 | 23 | HANDY MAN — Del Shannon, Amy 905 | 9 |
| 32 | 54 | 90 | — | BABY I NEED YOUR LOVING — Four Tops, Motown 1062 | 3 |
| 33 | 24 | 17 | 19 | STEAL AWAY — Jimmy Hughes, Fame 6401 | 11 |
| 34 | 40 | 54 | 68 | IT'S ALL OVER NOW — Rolling Stones, London 9687 | 6 |
| 35 | 47 | 68 | 99 | HAUNTED HOUSE — Gene Simmons, Hi 2076 | 4 |
| 36 | 30 | 35 | 46 | I'LL KEEP YOU SATISFIED — Billy J. Kramer, Imperial 66048 | 6 |
| 37 | 33 | 33 | 47 | SHE'S THE ONE — Chartbusters, Mutual 502 | 8 |
| 38 | 27 | 24 | 24 | TELL ME — Rolling Stones, London 9682 | 9 |
| 39 | 26 | 21 | 17 | KEEP ON PUSHING — Impressions, ABC-Paramount 10554 | 13 |
| 40 | 37 | 37 | 42 | MIXED-UP, SHOOK-UP GIRL — Patty & the Emblems, Herald 590 | 11 |
| 41 | 43 | 49 | 56 | HEY GIRL DON'T BOTHER ME — Tams, ABC-Paramount 10573 | 7 |
| 42 | 68 | — | — | DANCING IN THE STREET — Martha & the Vandellas, Gordy 7033 | 2 |
| 43 | 51 | 60 | 73 | SWEET WILLIAM — Millie Small, Smash 1920 | 4 |
| 44 | 49 | 62 | 65 | I WANT YOU TO MEET MY BABY — Eydie Gorme, Columbia 43082 | 6 |
| 45 | 69 | 84 | — | FUNNY — Joe Hinton, Back Beat 541 | 3 |
| 46 | 48 | 51 | 51 | LITTLE LATIN LUPE LU — Kingsmen, Wand 157 | 8 |
| 47 | 78 | — | — | REMEMBER (Walkin' in the Sand) — Shangri-Las, Red Bird 10-008 | 2 |
| 48 | 62 | 80 | 95 | WE'LL SING IN THE SUNSHINE — Gale Garnett, RCA Victor 8388 | 4 |
| 49 | 52 | 57 | 71 | WORRY — Johnny Tillotson, MGM 13255 | 7 |
| 50 | 66 | — | — | I'M ON THE OUTSIDE (LOOKING IN) — Little Anthony & the Imperials, DCP 1104 | 2 |
| 51 | — | — | — | OH, PRETTY WOMAN — Roy Orbison, Monument 851 | 1 |
| 52 | 65 | 96 | — | ALWAYS TOGETHER — Al Martino, Capitol 5239 | 3 |
| 53 | 46 | 43 | 43 | ANGELITO — Rene and Rene, Columbia 43045 | 8 |
| 54 | 57 | 72 | 87 | IF I FELL — Beatles, Capitol 5235 | 5 |
| 55 | 56 | 65 | 81 | RINGO'S THEME (This Boy) — George Martin and His Ork, United Artists 745 | 5 |
| 56 | 67 | 89 | — | SOME DAY WE'RE GONNA LOVE AGAIN — Searchers, Kapp 609 | 3 |
| 57 | 63 | 75 | 90 | WHEN YOU LOVED ME — Brenda Lee, Decca 31654 | 3 |
| 58 | 64 | 74 | 84 | HE'S IN TOWN — Tokens, B. T. Puppy 502 | 4 |
| 59 | 50 | 55 | 58 | A TEAR FELL — Ray Charles, ABC-Paramount 10571 | 5 |
| 60 | 60 | 69 | 76 | I'LL ALWAYS LOVE YOU — Brenda Holloway, Tamla 54099 | 4 |
| 61 | 61 | 73 | — | OUT OF SIGHT — James Brown, Smash 1919 | 3 |
| 62 | 45 | 48 | 54 | LOOKING FOR LOVE — Connie Francis, MGM 13256 | 7 |
| 63 | 59 | 67 | 67 | HELLO MUDDUH, HELLO FADDUH (1964 Version) — Allan Sherman, Warner Bros. 5449 | 6 |
| 64 | — | — | — | SAVE IT FOR ME — 4 Seasons, Philips 40225 | 1 |
| 65 | 74 | 83 | 93 | SAY YOU — Ronnie Dove, Diamond 167 | |
| 66 | 58 | 64 | 69 | EVERYBODY NEEDS SOMEBODY TO LOVE — Solomon Burke, Atlantic 2241 | 7 |
| 67 | 71 | 76 | 77 | I'VE GOT NO TIME TO LOSE — Carla Thomas, Atlantic 2238 | 5 |
| 68 | 83 | 87 | — | YOU'LL NEVER GET TO HEAVEN (If You Break My Heart) — Dionne Warwick, Scepter 1282 | 3 |
| 69 | 70 | 71 | 78 | INVISIBLE TEARS — Ray Conniff Singers, Columbia 43061 | 7 |
| 70 | 85 | 97 | — | A SUMMER SONG — Chad Stuart & Jeremy Clyde, World Artists 1027 | |
| 71 | 73 | 85 | 85 | A HOUSE IS NOT A HOME — Dionne Warwick, Scepter 1282 | 5 |
| 72 | 80 | — | — | I STAND ACCUSED — Jerry Butler, Vee Jay 598 | 3 |
| 73 | 81 | 86 | — | WHERE LOVE HAS GONE — Jack Jones, Kapp 608 | 3 |
| 74 | 86 | — | — | JOHNNY B. GOODE — Dion Di Muci, Columbia 43096 | |
| 75 | 79 | 82 | 89 | A HOUSE IS NOT A HOME — Brook Benton, Mercury 72303 | |
| 76 | 84 | — | — | THERE'S NOTHING I CAN SAY — Rick Nelson, Decca 31656 | |
| 77 | 77 | 88 | 100 | IF I'M A FOOL FOR LOVING YOU — Bobby Wood, Joy 285 | 4 |
| 78 | 82 | — | — | (There's) ALWAYS SOMETHING THERE TO REMIND ME — Lou Johnson, Big Hill 552 | 2 |
| 79 | 92 | — | — | FROM A WINDOW — Billy J. Kramer, Imperial 66051 | 2 |
| 80 | 89 | 93 | — | QUIET PLACE — Garnet Mimms, United Artists 715 | 5 |
| 81 | 76 | 77 | 63 | THANK YOU BABY — Shirelles, Scepter 1278 | 7 |
| 82 | — | — | — | KNOCK! KNOCK! (Who's There) — Orlons, Cameo 332 | 1 |
| 83 | 96 | — | — | RHYTHM — Major Lance, Okeh 7203 | 2 |
| 84 | 90 | — | — | MICHAEL — Trini Lopez, Reprise 0300 | |
| 85 | 75 | 78 | 80 | THE NEW FRANKIE & JOHNNIE SONG — Greenwood County Singers, Kapp 591 | 5 |
| 86 | 88 | 91 | 91 | FATHER SEBASTIAN — Ramblers, Almont 311 | 4 |
| 87 | 87 | 95 | 98 | ME JAPANESE BOY I LOVE YOU — Bobby Goldsboro, United Artists 742 | |
| 88 | — | — | — | CANDY TO ME — Eddie Holland, Motown 1063 | 1 |
| 89 | 94 | — | — | SQUEEZE HER—TEASE HER (But Love Her) — Jackie Wilson, Brunswick 55269 | 2 |
| 90 | — | — | — | SHE WANTS T'SWIM — Chubby Checker, Parkway 922 | 1 |
| 91 | 91 | — | — | I GUESS I'M CRAZY — Jim Reeves, RCA Victor 8383 | 2 |
| 92 | 93 | — | — | I DON'T CARE — Buck Owens, Capitol 5240 | 2 |
| 93 | 97 | — | — | THE JAMES BOND THEME — Billy Strange, Crescendo 320 | 2 |
| 94 | 100 | — | — | A TASTE OF HONEY — Tony Bennett, Columbia 43073 | |
| 95 | — | — | — | SINCERELY — 4 Seasons, Vee Jay 608 | |
| 96 | 98 | — | — | LOVERS ALWAYS FORGIVE — Gladys Knight & the Pips, Maxx 329 | |
| 97 | — | — | — | 20-75 — Willie Mitchell, Hi 2075 | |
| 98 | — | — | — | YET… I KNOW (Et Pourtant) — Steve Lawrence, Columbia 43095 | 1 |
| 99 | — | — | — | LOVER'S PRAYER — Wallace Brothers, Sims 189 | |
| 100 | — | — | — | CAN'T GET OVER (The Bossa Nova) — Eydie Gorme, Columbia 43082 | |

## BUBBLING UNDER THE HOT 100

101. SOMEONE, SOMEONE — Brian Pole, Monument 846
102. SOUL DRESSING — Booker T. & MG's, Stax 153
103. I CAN'T GET YOU OUT OF MY HEART — Al Martino, 20th Century-Fox 530
104. MERCY, MERCY — Don Covay & the Goodtimers, Rosemart 801
105. LA LA LA LA — Blendells, Reprise 0291
106. LET ME GET CLOSE TO YOU — Skeeter Davis, RCA Victor 8397
107. LOOP DE LOOP — Soul Sisters, Sue 107
108. YOU'RE NO GOOD — Swinging Blue Jeans, Imperial 66049
109. YOU'RE GONNA MISS ME — B. B. King, Kent 396
110. LAST KISS — J. Frank Wilson & the Cavaliers, Josie 923
111. THE CLOCK — Baby Washington, Sue 104
112. THE LONG SHIPS — Charles Albertine, Colpix 726
113. LONELY CORNER — Rick Nelson, Decca 31656
114. BACHELOR BOY — Cliff Richard & the Shadows, Epic 9691
115. I'LL FOLLOW THE RAINBOW — Terry Stafford, Crusader 109
116. I'M HAPPY JUST TO DANCE WITH YOU — Beatles, Capitol 5234
117. HOLD ME — P. J. Proby, London 9688
118. THANK YOU FOR LOVING ME — Al Martino, Capitol 5239
119. MERCY'S GOT A HOLD OF ME — Don & Alleyne Cole, Tollie 9015
120. LET ME LOVE YOU — B. B. King, Kent 396
121. IF — Timi Yuro, Mercury 72316
122. I WANNA THANK YOU — Enchanters, Warner Bros. 5460
123. GUITARS AND BONGOS — Lou Christie, Colpix 735
124. IT HURTS TO BE IN LOVE — Betty Everett, Vee Jay 610
125. THAT'S HOW STRONG MY LOVE IS — O. V. Wright with the Keys, Goldwax 106
126. SOCIETY GIRL — Rag Dolls, Parkway 921
127. HEARTBREAK — Dee Clark, Constellation 132
128. IT'S FOR YOU — Cilla Black, Capitol 5258
129. AND I LOVE HER — George Martin & His Ork, United Artists 745
130. DOWN WHERE THE WINDS BLOW — Serendipity Singers, Philips 40215
131. LE DEA I LOVE YOU — Inez Foxx, Symbol 201
132. IN THE NAME OF LOVE — Peggy Lee, Capitol 5241
133. WHAT KINDA LOVE? — Jimmy Gilmer, Dot 16642
134. TOBACCO ROAD — Nashville Teens, London 9689
135. MR. SANDMAN — Fleetwoods, Dolton 98

Compiled from national retail sales and radio station airplay by the Music Popularity Dept. of Record Market Research, Billboard.

For Week Ending September 5, 1964

Billboard

# HOT 100

★ STAR performer—Sides registering greatest proportionate upward progress this week.

Billboard Award

| This Week | 1 Wk. Ago | 2 Wks. Ago | 3 Wks. Ago | TITLE Artist, Label & Number | Weeks On Chart |
|---|---|---|---|---|---|
| 1 | 2 | 5 | 10 | THE HOUSE OF THE RISING SUN — Animals, MGM 13264 | 5 |
| 2 | 1 | 1 | 2 | WHERE DID OUR LOVE GO — Supremes, Motown 1060 | 9 |
| 3 | 3 | 2 | 1 | EVERYBODY LOVES SOMEBODY — Dean Martin, Reprise 0281 | 11 |
| ★4 | 7 | 7 | 14 | BECAUSE — Dave Clark Five, Epic 9704 | 6 |
| 5 | 5 | 6 | 8 | C'MON AND SWIM — Bobby Freeman, Autumn 2 | 9 |
| ★6 | 9 | 23 | 56 | BREAD AND BUTTER — Newbeats, Hickory 1269 | 4 |
| 7 | 6 | 4 | 5 | UNDER THE BOARDWALK — Drifters, Atlantic 2237 | 11 |
| 8 | 4 | 3 | 3 | A HARD DAY'S NIGHT — Beatles, Capitol 5222 | 8 |
| 9 | 10 | 10 | 16 | HOW DO YOU DO IT — Gerry and the Pacemakers, Laurie 3261 | 9 |
| ★10 | 15 | 28 | 50 | G.T.O. — Ronny & the Daytonas, Mala 481 | 6 |
| 11 | 14 | 32 | 38 | SELFISH ONE — Jackie Ross, Chess 1903 | 6 |
| 12 | 13 | 17 | 27 | AND I LOVE HER — Beatles, Capitol 5235 | 7 |
| ★13 | 47 | 78 | — | REMEMBER (Walkin' in the Sand) — Shangri-Las, Red Bird 10-008 | 3 |
| ★14 | 20 | 25 | 47 | YOU NEVER CAN TELL — Chuck Berry, Chess 1906 | 6 |
| 15 | 8 | 8 | 13 | WALK—DON'T RUN '64 — Ventures, Dolton 96 | 9 |
| 16 | 18 | 21 | 40 | MAYBE I KNOW — Lesley Gore, Mercury 72309 | 7 |
| ★17 | 30 | 39 | 70 | MAYBELLINE — Johnny Rivers, Imperial 66056 | 4 |
| ★18 | 35 | 47 | 68 | HAUNTED HOUSE — Gene Simmons, Hi 2076 | 5 |
| 19 | 21 | 38 | 63 | CLINGING VINE — Bobby Vinton, Epic 9705 | 5 |
| 20 | 12 | 12 | 15 | PEOPLE SAY — Dixie Cups, Red Bird 10-006 | 8 |
| 21 | 16 | 16 | 28 | SUCH A NIGHT — Elvis Presley, RCA Victor 8400 | 7 |
| 22 | 26 | 31 | 45 | IN THE MISTY MOONLIGHT — Jerry Wallace, Challenge 59246 | 7 |
| 23 | 11 | 9 | 6 | WISHIN' AND HOPIN' — Dusty Springfield, Philips 40207 | 12 |
| ★24 | 48 | 62 | 80 | WE'LL SING IN THE SUNSHINE — Gale Garnett, RCA Victor 8388 | 5 |
| ★25 | 32 | 54 | 90 | BABY I NEED YOUR LOVING — Four Tops, Motown 1062 | 4 |
| 26 | 29 | 42 | 52 | IT HURTS TO BE IN LOVE — Gene Pitney, Musicor 1040 | 8 |
| ★27 | 51 | — | — | OH, PRETTY WOMAN — Roy Orbison, Monument 851 | 2 |
| 28 | 19 | 20 | 20 | JUST BE TRUE — Gene Chandler, Constellation 130 | 9 |
| ★29 | 34 | 40 | 54 | IT'S ALL OVER NOW — Rolling Stones, London 9687 | 7 |
| 30 | 24 | 19 | 22 | AIN'T SHE SWEET — Beatles, Atco 6308 | 8 |
| ★31 | 64 | — | — | SAVE IT FOR ME — 4 Seasons, Philips 40225 | 2 |
| ★32 | 42 | 68 | — | DANCING IN THE STREET — Martha & the Vandellas, Gordy 7033 | 3 |
| 33 | 17 | 11 | 4 | RAG DOLL — 4 Seasons, Philips 40211 | 12 |
| 34 | 25 | 29 | 34 | I'LL CRY INSTEAD — Beatles, Capitol 5234 | 6 |
| ★35 | 45 | 69 | 84 | FUNNY — Joe Hinton, Back Beat 541 | 4 |
| ★36 | 50 | 66 | — | I'M ON THE OUTSIDE (Looking In) — Little Anthony & the Imperials, DCP 1104 | 3 |
| 37 | 33 | 24 | 17 | STEAL AWAY — Jimmy Hughes, Fame 6401 | 12 |
| 38 | 22 | 13 | 7 | THE LITTLE OLD LADY (From Pasadena) — Jan & Dean, Liberty 55704 | 11 |
| 39 | 31 | 22 | 23 | HANDY MAN — Del Shannon, Amy 905 | 10 |
| 40 | 43 | 51 | 60 | SWEET WILLIAM — Millie Small, Smash 1920 | 5 |
| 41 | 41 | 43 | 49 | HEY GIRL DON'T BOTHER ME — Tams, ABC-Paramount 10573 | 8 |
| 42 | 28 | 14 | 9 | I WANNA LOVE HIM SO BAD — Jelly Beans, Red Bird 10-003 | 12 |
| 43 | 44 | 49 | 62 | I WANT YOU TO MEET MY BABY — Eydie Gorme, Columbia 43082 | 7 |
| 44 | 23 | 18 | 11 | (You Don't Know) HOW GLAD I AM — Nancy Wilson, Capitol 5198 | 11 |
| ★45 | 61 | 61 | 73 | OUT OF SIGHT — James Brown, Smash 1919 | 4 |
| ★46 | 56 | 67 | 89 | SOME DAY WE'RE GONNA LOVE AGAIN — Searchers, Kapp 609 | 4 |
| 47 | 52 | 65 | 96 | ALWAYS TOGETHER — Al Martino, Capitol 5239 | 4 |
| ★48 | 58 | 64 | 74 | HE'S IN TOWN — Tokens, B. T. Puppy 502 | 5 |
| 49 | 49 | 52 | 57 | WORRY — Johnny Tillotson, MGM 13255 | 8 |
| 50 | 38 | 27 | 24 | TELL ME — Rolling Stones, London 9682 | 10 |
| 51 | 36 | 30 | 35 | I'LL KEEP YOU SATISFIED — Billy J. Kramer, Imperial 66048 | 7 |
| ★52 | 68 | 83 | 87 | YOU'LL NEVER GET TO HEAVEN (If You Break My Heart) — Dionne Warwick, Scepter 1282 | 4 |
| 53 | 54 | 57 | 72 | IF I FELL — Beatles, Capitol 5235 | 6 |
| 54 | 57 | 63 | 75 | WHEN YOU LOVED ME — Brenda Lee, Decca 31654 | 5 |
| 55 | 55 | 56 | 65 | RINGO'S THEME (This Boy) — George Martin and His Ork, United Artists 745 | 6 |
| 56 | 46 | 48 | 51 | LITTLE LATIN LUPE LU — Kingsmen, Wand 157 | 9 |
| 57 | 65 | 74 | 83 | SAY YOU — Ronnie Dove, Diamond 167 | 8 |
| ★58 | — | — | — | DO WAH DIDDY DIDDY — Manfred Mann, Ascot 2157 | 1 |
| ★59 | 69 | 70 | 71 | INVISIBLE TEARS — Ray Conniff Singers, Columbia 43061 | 8 |
| ★60 | 70 | 85 | 97 | A SUMMER SONG — Chad Stuart & Jeremy Clyde, World Artists 1027 | 4 |
| ★61 | 76 | 84 | — | THERE'S NOTHING I CAN SAY — Rick Nelson, Decca 31656 | 3 |
| 62 | 72 | 80 | — | I STAND ACCUSED — Jerry Butler, Vee Jay 598 | 4 |
| ★63 | 78 | 82 | — | (There's) ALWAYS SOMETHING THERE TO REMIND ME — Lou Johnson, Big Hill 552 | 3 |
| ★64 | 79 | 92 | — | FROM A WINDOW — Billy J. Kramer, Imperial 66051 | 3 |
| 65 | 73 | 81 | 86 | WHERE LOVE HAS GONE — Jack Jones, Kapp 608 | 4 |
| 66 | 60 | 60 | 69 | I'LL ALWAYS LOVE YOU — Brenda Holloway, Tamla 54099 | 5 |
| ★67 | — | — | — | YOU MUST BELIEVE ME — Impressions, ABC-Paramount 10581 | 1 |
| ★68 | 83 | 96 | — | RHYTHM — Major Lance, Okeh 7203 | 3 |
| 69 | 66 | 58 | 64 | EVERYBODY NEEDS SOMEBODY TO LOVE — Solomon Burke, Atlantic 2241 | 8 |
| 70 | 67 | 71 | 76 | I'VE GOT NO TIME TO LOSE — Carla Thomas, Atlantic 2238 | 6 |
| 71 | 74 | 86 | — | JOHNNY B. GOODE — Dion Di Muci, Columbia 43096 | 3 |
| ★72 | — | — | — | LET IT BE ME — Betty Everett & Jerry Butler, Vee Jay 613 | 1 |
| ★73 | — | — | — | LAST KISS — J. Frank Wilson & the Cavaliers, Josie 923 | 1 |
| 74 | 77 | 77 | 88 | IF I'M A FOOL FOR LOVING YOU — Bobby Wood, Joy 285 | 5 |
| ★75 | 90 | — | — | SHE WANTS T'SWIM — Chubby Checker, Parkway 922 | 2 |
| 76 | 84 | 90 | — | MICHAEL — Trini Lopez, Reprise 0300 | 3 |
| 77 | 82 | — | — | KNOCK! KNOCK! (Who's There) — Orlons, Cameo 332 | 2 |
| 78 | 80 | 89 | 93 | QUIET PLACE — Garnet Mimms, United Artists 715 | 6 |
| 79 | 88 | — | — | CANDY TO ME — Eddie Holland, Motown 1063 | 2 |
| 80 | 71 | 73 | 85 | A HOUSE IS NOT A HOME — Dionne Warwick, Scepter 1282 | 6 |
| ★81 | — | — | — | MATCHBOX — Beatles, Capitol 5255 | 1 |
| ★82 | 97 | — | — | 20-75 — Willie Mitchell, Hi 2075 | 2 |
| ★83 | — | — | — | WHEN I GROW UP TO BE A MAN — Beach Boys, Capitol 5245 | 1 |
| 84 | 95 | — | — | SINCERELY — 4 Seasons, Vee Jay 608 | 2 |
| 85 | 87 | 87 | 95 | ME JAPANESE BOY I LOVE YOU — Bobby Goldsboro, United Artists 742 | 5 |
| 86 | 98 | — | — | YET . . . I KNOW (Et Pourtant) — Steve Lawrence, Columbia 43095 | 2 |
| ★87 | — | — | — | THE CAT — Jimmy Smith, Verve 10330 | 1 |
| ★88 | — | — | — | MERCY, MERCY — Don Covay & the Goodtimers, Rosemart 801 | 1 |
| ★89 | — | — | — | HOLD ME — P. J. Proby, London 9688 | 1 |
| ★90 | — | — | — | SOFTLY, AS I LEAVE YOU — Frank Sinatra, Reprise 0301 | 1 |
| 91 | 93 | 97 | — | THE JAMES BOND THEME — Billy Strange, Crescendo 320 | 3 |
| 92 | 92 | 93 | — | I DON'T CARE — Buck Owens, Capitol 5240 | 3 |
| 93 | 96 | 98 | — | LOVERS ALWAYS FORGIVE — Gladys Knight & the Pips, Maxx 329 | 3 |
| 94 | 94 | 100 | — | A TASTE OF HONEY — Tony Bennett, Columbia 43073 | 3 |
| 95 | 100 | — | — | CAN'T GET OVER (The Bossa Nova) — Eydie Gorme, Columbia 43082 | 2 |
| 96 | — | — | — | CHUG-A-LUG — Roger Miller, Smash 1926 | 1 |
| 97 | 99 | — | — | LOVER'S PRAYER — Wallace Brothers, Sims 189 | 2 |
| 98 | — | — | — | I WANNA THANK YOU — Enchanters, Warner Bros. 5460 | 1 |
| 99 | — | — | — | SLOW DOWN — Beatles, Capitol 5255 | 1 |
| 100 | — | — | — | ROCKIN' ROBIN — Rivieras, Rivera 1403 | 1 |

## HOT 100—A TO Z—*(Publisher-Licensee)*


Ain't She Sweet (Advance, ASCAP) .......... 30
Always Together (Damian, ASCAP) .......... 47
And I Love Her (Unart-Maclen, BMI) .......... 12
Baby I Need Your Loving (Jobete, BMI) .......... 25
Because (Ivy, ASCAP) .......... 4
Bread and Butter (Acuff-Rose, BMI) .......... 6
Can't Get Over (The Bossa Nova) (Maxana, ASCAP) .......... 95
Candy to Me (Jobete, BMI) .......... 79
Cat, The (Hastings, BMI) .......... 87
Chug-A-Lug (Tree, BMI) .......... 96
Clinging Vine (Peter Maurice, ASCAP) .......... 19
C'mon and Swim (Taracrest, BMI) .......... 5
Dancing in the Street (Jobete, BMI) .......... 32
Do Wah Diddy Diddy (Trio, BMI) .......... 58
Everybody Loves Somebody (Sands, ASCAP) .......... 3
Everybody Needs Somebody to Love (Keetch, Caesar & Dino, BMI) .......... 69
From a Window (Maclen, BMI) .......... 64
Funny (Pamper, BMI) .......... 35
G.T.O. (Buckhorn, BMI) .......... 10
Handy Man (Travis, BMI) .......... 39
Hard Day's Night, A (Unart-Maclen, BMI) .......... 8
Haunted House (Venice-B. Flat, BMI) .......... 18
He's in Town (Screen Gems-Columbia, BMI) .......... 48
Hey Girl, Don't Bother Me (Low-Twi, BMI) .......... 41
Hold Me (Ross Jungnickel-Robbins-World, ASCAP) .......... 89
House Is Not a Home, A (Diplomat, ASCAP) .......... 80
House of the Rising Sun, The (Gallico, BMI) .......... 1
How Do You Do It (Just, BMI) .......... 9
I Don't Care (Bluebook, BMI) .......... 92
I Stand Accused (Curtom, BMI) .......... 62
I Wanna Love Him So Bad (Trio, BMI) .......... 42
I Wanna Thank You (Rittenhouse, BMI) .......... 98
I Want You to Meet My Baby (Screen Gems-Columbia, BMI) .......... 43
I'm on the Outside (Looking In) (South Mountain, BMI) .......... 36
I've Got No Time to Lose (East, BMI) .......... 70
I'll Always Love You (Jobete, BMI) .......... 66
I'll Cry Instead (Unart-Maclen, BMI) .......... 34
I'll Keep You Satisfied (Metric, BMI) .......... 51
If I'm a Fool for Loving You (Drury Lane-Beckie, BMI) .......... 74
If I Fell (Unart-Maclen, BMI) .......... 53
In the Misty Moonlight (Four Star, BMI) .......... 22
Invisible Tears (Central Songs, BMI) .......... 59
It Hurts to Be in Love (Screen Gems-Columbia, BMI) .......... 26
It's All Over Now (Kags, BMI) .......... 29
James Bond Theme, The (Unart, BMI) .......... 91
Johnny B. Goode (Arc, BMI) .......... 71
Just Be True (Curtom-Camad, BMI) .......... 28
Knock! Knock! (Who's There) (Saturday, ASCAP) .......... 77
Last Kiss (Boblo, BMI) .......... 73
Let It Be Me (Leeds, ASCAP) .......... 72
Little Latin Lupe Lu (Maxwell-Conrad, BMI) .......... 56
Little Old Lady (From Pasadena) (Screen Gems-Columbia, BMI) .......... 38
Lover's Prayer (English, BMI) .......... 97
Lovers Always Forgive (Maxx, BMI) .......... 93
Matchbox (Knox, BMI) .......... 81
Maybe I Know (Trio, BMI) .......... 16
Maybelline (Arc, BMI) .......... 17
Me Japanese Boy I Love You (Jac-Blue Seas, ASCAP) .......... 85
Mercy, Mercy (Cotillion-Vonglo, BMI) .......... 88
Michael (Unart, BMI) .......... 76
Oh, Pretty Woman (Acuff-Rose, BMI) .......... 27
Out of Sight (Try Me, BMI) .......... 45
People Say (Trio, BMI) .......... 20
Quiet Place, A (Rittenhouse, BMI) .......... 78
Rag Doll (Saturday-Gavadima, ASCAP) .......... 33
Remember (Walkin' in the Sand) (Tender Tunes-Trio, BMI) .......... 13
Rhythm (Jalynne-Curtom, BMI) .......... 68
Ringo's Theme (This Boy) (Maclen, BMI) .......... 55
Rockin' Robin (Recordo, BMI) .......... 100
Save It for Me (Saturday-Gavadima, ASCAP) .......... 31
Say You (T. M., BMI) .......... 57
Selfish One (Chevis, BMI) .......... 11
She Wants T'Swim (Kalmann-C.C., ASCAP) .......... 75
Sincerely (Regent, BMI) .......... 84
Slow Down (Venice, BMI) .......... 99
Softly, As I Leave You (Miller, ASCAP) .......... 90
Some Day We're Gonna Love Again (McLaughlin, BMI) .......... 46
Steal Away (Fame, BMI) .......... 37
Such a Night (Raleigh, BMI) .......... 21
Summer Song, A (Unart-Woart, BMI) .......... 60
Sweet William (Budd, ASCAP) .......... 40
Taste of Honey, A (Songfest, ASCAP) .......... 94
Tell Me (Southern, ASCAP) .......... 50
(There's) Always Something There to Remind Me (Ross-Jungnickel & Blue Seas, ASCAP) .......... 63
There's Nothing I Can Say (Chappell, ASCAP) .......... 61
20-75 (Jec, BMI) .......... 82
Under the Boardwalk (T. M., BMI) .......... 7
Walk—Don't Run '64 (Forshay, BMI) .......... 15
We'll Sing in the Sunshine (Lupercalia, ASCAP) .......... 24
When I Grow Up to Be a Man (Sea of Tunes, BMI). 83
When You Loved Me (Hill & Range-Ron Bre, BMI). 54
Where Did Our Love Go (Jobete, BMI) .......... 2
Where Love Has Gone (Paramount, ASCAP) .......... 65
Wishin' and Hopin' (Jonathan, ASCAP) .......... 23
Worry (Ridge, BMI) .......... 49
Yet . . . I Know (Et Pourtant) (Leeds, ASCAP) .......... 86
(You Don't Know) How Glad I Am (Roosevelt, BMI). 44
You Must Believe Me (Curtom, BMI) .......... 67
You Never Can Tell (Arc, BMI) .......... 14
You'll Never Get to Heaven (Jac-Blue Seas, ASCAP). 52


## BUBBLING UNDER THE HOT 100

101. SOUL DRESSING .......... Booker T. & the MG's, Stax 153
102. WHY YOU WANNA MAKE ME BLUE .......... Temptations, Gordy 7035
103. SOMEONE, SOMEONE .......... Brian Poole, Monument 846
104. LA LA LA LA LA .......... Blendells, Reprise 0291
105. THE CLOCK .......... Baby Washington, Sue 104
106. I'LL FOLLOW THE RAINBOW .......... Terry Stafford, Crusader 109
107. LOOP DE LOOP .......... Soul Sisters, Sue 107
108. I CAN'T GET YOU OUT OF MY HEART .... Al Martino, 20th Century-Fox 530
109. SQUEEZE HER—TEASE HER (But Love Her) .. Jackie Wilson, Brunswick 55269
110. LET ME LOVE YOU .......... B. B. King, Kent 396
111. SOCIETY GIRL .......... Rag Dolls, Parkway 921
112. I'M HAPPY JUST TO DANCE WITH YOU .......... Beatles, Capitol 5234
113. MR. SANDMAN .......... Fleetwoods, Dolton 98
114. TOBACCO ROAD .......... Nashville Teens, London 9689
115. YOU'RE GONNA MISS ME .......... B. B. King, Kent 396
116. LITTLE HONDA .......... Hondells, Mercury 72324
117. SOMETHING'S GOT A HOLD ON ME .......... Don & Alleyne Cole, Tollie 9015
118. THANK YOU FOR LOVING ME .......... Al Martino, Capitol 5239
119. IT HURTS TO BE IN LOVE .......... Betty Everett, Vee Jay 610
120. IF .......... Timi Yuro, Mercury 72316
121. THAT'S HOW STRONG MY LOVE IS .. O. V. Wright with the Keys, Goldwax 106
122. GATOR TAILS AND MONKEY RIBS .......... Spats, ABC-Paramount 10585
123. SOON I'LL WED MY LOVE .......... John Gary, RCA Victor 8413
124. TROUBLE IN MIND .......... Jimmy Ricks, Atlantic 2246
125. HEARTBREAK .......... Dee Clark, Constellation 132
126. GOOD NIGHT BABY .......... Butterflys, Red Bird 10-009
127. I COULD CONQUER THE WORLD .......... Shevelles, World Artists 1025
128. GOODNIGHT IRENE .......... Little Richard, Vee Jay 612
129. PEARLY SHELLS .......... Burl Ives, Decca 31659
130. LA DE DA I LOVE YOU .......... Inez Foxx, Smybol 201
131. WHOLE LOTTA SHAKIN' GOIN' ON .......... Little Richard, Vee Jay 612
132. YOU PULLED A FAST ONE .......... V.I.P.'s, Big Top 518
133. I'VE GOT A THING GOING ON .......... Bobby Marchan, Dial 3022
134. LITTLE QUEENIE .......... Bill Black's Combo, Hi 2079
135. OPPORTUNITY .......... Jewels, Dimension 1034

Compiled from national retail sales and radio station airplay by the Music Popularity Dept. of Record Market Research, Billboard.

# Billboard HOT 100

For Week Ending September 12, 1964

★ STAR performer—Sides registering greatest proportionate upward progress this week.

| This Week | Wk. Ago | 2 Wks. Ago | 3 Wks. Ago | TITLE, Artist, Label & Number | Weeks On Chart |
|---|---|---|---|---|---|
| 1 | 1 | 2 | 5 | THE HOUSE OF THE RISING SUN — Animals, MGM 13264 | 6 |
| 2 | 2 | 1 | 1 | WHERE DID OUR LOVE GO — Supremes, Motown 1060 | 10 |
| 3 | 4 | 7 | 7 | BECAUSE — Dave Clark Five, Epic 9704 | 7 |
| 4 | 3 | 3 | 2 | EVERYBODY LOVES SOMEBODY — Dean Martin, Reprise 0281 | 11 |
| 5 | 6 | 9 | 23 | BREAD AND BUTTER — Newbeats, Hickory 1269 | 5 |
| 6 | 5 | 5 | 6 | C'MON AND SWIM — Bobby Freeman, Autumn 2 | 10 |
| ★7 | 10 | 15 | 28 | G.T.O. — Ronny & the Daytonas, Mala 481 | 7 |
| 8 | 8 | 4 | 3 | A HARD DAY'S NIGHT — Beatles, Capitol 5222 | 9 |
| 9 | 13 | 47 | 78 | REMEMBER (Walkin' in the Sand) — Shangri-Las, Red Bird 10-008 | 4 |
| ★10 | 27 | 51 | — | OH, PRETTY WOMAN — Roy Orbison, Monument 851 | 3 |
| 11 | 11 | 14 | 32 | SELFISH ONE — Jackie Ross, Chess 1903 | 7 |
| 12 | 12 | 13 | 17 | AND I LOVE HER — Beatles, Capitol 5235 | 8 |
| 13 | 7 | 6 | 4 | UNDER THE BOARDWALK — Drifters, Atlantic 2237 | 12 |
| 14 | 16 | 18 | 21 | MAYBE I KNOW — Lesley Gore, Mercury 72309 | 8 |
| 15 | 17 | 30 | 39 | MAYBELLINE — Johnny Rivers, Imperial 66056 | 5 |
| 16 | 18 | 35 | 47 | HAUNTED HOUSE — Gene Simmons, Hi 2076 | 6 |
| 17 | 19 | 21 | 38 | CLINGING VINE — Bobby Vinton, Epic 9705 | 6 |
| 18 | 9 | 10 | 10 | HOW DO YOU DO IT — Gerry and the Pacemakers, Laurie 3261 | 10 |
| 19 | 22 | 26 | 31 | IN THE MISTY MOONLIGHT — Jerry Wallace, Challenge 59246 | 8 |
| 20 | 14 | 20 | 25 | YOU NEVER CAN TELL — Chuck Berry, Chess 1906 | 7 |
| ★21 | 26 | 29 | 42 | IT HURTS TO BE IN LOVE — Gene Pitney, Musicor 1040 | 9 |
| ★22 | 31 | 64 | — | SAVE IT FOR ME — 4 Seasons, Philips 40225 | 3 |
| 23 | 24 | 48 | 62 | WE'LL SING IN THE SUNSHINE — Gale Garnett, RCA Victor 8388 | 6 |
| ★24 | 25 | 32 | 54 | BABY I NEED YOUR LOVING — Four Tops, Motown 1062 | 5 |
| ★25 | 32 | 42 | 68 | DANCING IN THE STREET — Martha and the Vandellas, Gordy 7033 | 4 |
| 26 | 15 | 8 | 8 | WALK—DON'T RUN '64 — Ventures, Dolton 96 | 10 |
| 27 | 29 | 34 | 40 | IT'S ALL OVER NOW — Rolling Stones, London 9687 | 8 |
| 28 | 35 | 45 | 69 | FUNNY — Joe Hinton, Back Beat 541 | 5 |
| 29 | 36 | 50 | 66 | I'M ON THE OUTSIDE — Little Anthony & the Imperials, DCP 1104 | 4 |
| 30 | 23 | 11 | 9 | WISHIN' AND HOPIN' — Dusty Springfield, Philips 40207 | 13 |
| ★31 | 58 | — | — | DO WAH DIDDY DIDDY — Manfred Mann, Ascot 2157 | 2 |
| 32 | 20 | 12 | 12 | PEOPLE SAY — Dixie Cups, Red Bird 10-006 | 9 |
| 33 | 21 | 16 | 16 | SUCH A NIGHT — Elvis Presley, RCA Victor 8400 | 8 |
| ★34 | 28 | 19 | 20 | JUST BE TRUE — Gene Chandler, Constellation 130 | 10 |
| ★35 | 45 | 61 | 61 | OUT OF SIGHT — James Brown, Smash 1919 | 5 |
| 36 | 34 | 25 | 29 | I'LL CRY INSTEAD — Beatles, Capitol 5234 | 7 |
| 37 | 30 | 24 | 19 | AIN'T SHE SWEET — Beatles, Atco 6308 | 9 |
| 38 | 46 | 56 | 67 | SOME DAY WE'RE GONNA LOVE AGAIN — Searchers, Kapp 609 | 5 |
| 39 | 47 | 52 | 65 | ALWAYS TOGETHER — Al Martino, Capitol 5239 | 5 |
| 40 | 40 | 43 | 51 | SWEET WILLIAM — Millie Small, Smash 1920 | 6 |
| ★41 | 52 | 68 | 83 | YOU'LL NEVER GET TO HEAVEN (If You Break My Heart) — Dionne Warwick, Scepter 1282 | 5 |
| ★42 | 81 | — | — | MATCHBOX — Beatles, Capitol 5255 | 2 |
| 43 | 43 | 44 | 49 | I WANT YOU TO MEET MY BABY — Eydie Gorme, Columbia 43082 | 8 |
| ★44 | 60 | 70 | 85 | A SUMMER SONG — Chad Stuart & Jeremy Clyde, World Artists 1027 | 5 |
| 45 | 49 | 49 | 52 | WORRY — Johnny Tillotson, MGM 13255 | 9 |
| 46 | 48 | 58 | 64 | HE'S IN TOWN — Tokens, B.T. Puppy 502 | 6 |
| 47 | 54 | 57 | 63 | WHEN YOU LOVED ME — Brenda Lee, Decca 31654 | 6 |
| ★48 | 67 | — | — | YOU MUST BELIEVE ME — Impressions, ABC-Paramount 10531 | 2 |
| ★49 | 76 | 84 | 90 | MICHAEL — Trini Lopez, Reprise 0300 | 4 |
| 50 | 61 | 76 | 84 | THERE'S NOTHING I CAN SAY — Rick Nelson, Decca 31656 | 4 |
| ★51 | 64 | 79 | 92 | FROM A WINDOW — Billy J. Kramer, Imperial 66051 | 4 |
| 52 | 57 | 65 | 74 | SAY YOU — Ronnie Dove, Diamond 167 | 9 |
| 53 | 55 | 55 | 56 | RINGO'S THEME (This Boy) — George Martin and His Ork, United Artists 745 | 7 |
| ★54 | 72 | — | — | LET IT BE ME — Betty Everett & Jerry Butler, Vee Jay 613 | 2 |
| 55 | 63 | 78 | 82 | (There's) ALWAYS SOMETHING THERE TO REMIND ME — Lou Johnson, Big Hill 552 | 4 |
| 56 | 68 | 83 | 96 | RHYTHM — Major Lance, Okeh 7203 | 4 |
| 57 | 59 | 69 | 70 | INVISIBLE TEARS — Ray Conniff Singers, Columbia 43061 | 9 |
| ★58 | 83 | — | — | WHEN I GROW UP TO BE A MAN — Beach Boys, Capitol 5245 | 2 |
| 59 | 53 | 54 | 57 | IF I FELL — Beatles, Capitol 5235 | 7 |
| ★60 | 73 | — | — | LAST KISS — J. Frank Wilson & the Cavalleers, Josie 923 | 2 |
| ★61 | 62 | 72 | 80 | I STAND ACCUSED — Jerry Butler, Vee Jay 598 | 4 |
| 62 | 65 | 73 | 81 | WHERE LOVE HAS GONE — Jack Jones, Kapp 608 | 5 |
| ★63 | 82 | 97 | — | 20-75 — Willie Mitchell, Hi 2075 | 3 |
| 64 | 75 | 90 | — | SHE WANTS T'SWIM — Chubby Checker, Parkway 922 | 3 |
| ★65 | — | — | — | WHY YOU WANNA MAKE ME BLUE — Temptations, Gordy 7035 | 1 |
| ★66 | — | — | — | ON THE STREET WHERE YOU LIVE — Andy Williams, Columbia 43128 | 1 |
| 67 | 99 | — | — | SLOW DOWN — Beatles, Capitol 5255 | 2 |
| 68 | 79 | 88 | — | CANDY TO ME — Eddie Holland, Motown 1063 | 3 |
| 69 | 77 | 82 | — | KNOCK! KNOCK! (Who's There) — Orlons, Cameo 332 | 3 |
| 70 | 89 | — | — | HOLD ME — P.J. Proby, London 9688 | 2 |
| 71 | 71 | 74 | 86 | JOHNNY B. GOODE — Dion Di Muci, Columbia 43096 | 4 |
| ★72 | — | — | — | GONNA SEND YOU BACK TO WALKER — Animals, MGM 13242 | 1 |
| 73 | 70 | 67 | 71 | I'VE GOT NO TIME TO LOSE — Carla Thomas, Atlantic 2238 | 7 |
| 74 | 85 | 87 | 87 | ME JAPANESE BOY I LOVE YOU — Bobby Goldsboro, United Artists 742 | 6 |
| 75 | 84 | 95 | — | SINCERELY — 4 Seasons, Vee Jay 608 | 3 |
| 76 | 91 | 93 | 97 | THE JAMES BOND THEME — Billy Strange, Crescendo 220 | 4 |
| 77 | 88 | — | — | MERCY, MERCY — Don Covay and the Goodtimers, Rosemart 801 | 2 |
| 78 | 96 | — | — | CHUG-A-LUG — Roger Miller, Smash 1926 | 2 |
| 79 | — | — | — | PEARLY SHELLS — Burl Ives, Decca 31659 | 1 |
| 80 | 86 | 98 | — | YET... I KNOW (Et Pourtant) — Steve Lawrence, Columbia 43095 | 3 |
| 81 | 78 | 80 | 89 | QUIET PLACE — Garnet Mimms, United Artists 715 | 7 |
| 82 | 87 | — | — | THE CAT — Jimmy Smith, Verve 10330 | 2 |
| 83 | 90 | — | — | SOFTLY, AS I LEAVE YOU — Frank Sinatra, Reprise 0301 | 2 |
| 84 | — | — | — | LITTLE HONDA — Hondells, Mercury 72224 | 1 |
| 85 | — | — | — | LA LA LA LA LA — Blendells, Reprise 0291 | 1 |
| 86 | — | — | — | COME A LITTLE BIT CLOSER — Jay & the Americans, United Artists 759 | 1 |
| 87 | 95 | 100 | — | CAN'T GET OVER (The Bossa Nova) — Eydie Gorme, Columbia 43082 | 3 |
| ★88 | — | — | — | I WOULDN'T TRADE YOU FOR THE WORLD — Bachelors, London 9693 | 1 |
| 89 | 93 | 96 | 98 | LOVERS ALWAYS FORGIVE — Gladys Knight and the Pips, Maxx 329 | 4 |
| ★90 | — | — | — | TOBACCO ROAD — Nashville Teens, London 9489 | 1 |
| 91 | — | — | — | IT'S ALL OVER — Ben E. King, Atco 6315 | 1 |
| 92 | — | — | — | GOOD NIGHT BABY — Butterflys, Red Bird 10-009 | 1 |
| 93 | 98 | — | — | I WANNA THANK YOU — Enchanters, Warner Bros. 5460 | 2 |
| 94 | — | — | — | SOON I'LL WED MY LOVE — John Gary, RCA Victor 8413 | 1 |
| 95 | — | — | — | SOCIETY GIRL — Rag Dolls, Parkway 921 | 1 |
| 96 | — | — | — | FUNNY GIRL — Barbra Streisand, Columbia 43127 | 1 |
| 97 | — | — | — | ONE MORE TEAR — Raindrops, Jubilee 5487 | 1 |
| 98 | — | — | — | DEATH OF AN ANGEL — Kingsmen, Wand 164 | 1 |
| 99 | — | — | — | SOMEONE, SOMEONE — Brian Poole, Monument 846 | 1 |
| 100 | 100 | — | — | ROCKIN' ROBIN — Rivieras, Rivera 1403 | 2 |

## BUBBLING UNDER THE HOT 100

101. I'LL FOLLOW THE RAINBOW — Terry Stafford, Crusader 109
102. BABY LET ME TAKE YOU HOME — Animals, MGM 13242
103. DERN YA — Ruby Wright, Ric 126-64
104. I DON'T KNOW — Steve Alaimo, ABC-Paramount 10580
105. I CAN'T GET YOU OUT OF MY HEART — Al Martino, 20th Century-Fox 530
106. A TASTE OF HONEY — Tony Bennett, Columbia 43078
107. SQUEEZE HER—TEASE HER (But Love Her) — Jackie Wilson, Brunswick 55269
108. AIN'T THAT LOVING YOU BABY — Betty Everett & Jerry Butler, Vee Jay 613
109. SHE KNOWS ME TOO WELL — Beach Boys, Capitol 5245
110. THE CLOCK — Baby Washington, Sue 104
111. HOW'S YOUR SISTER — Steve Allen, Brunswick
112. LOVER'S PRAYER — Wallace Brothers, Sims 189
113. OOH LA LA — Nino Tempo & April Stevens, Atco 6314
114. LITTLE QUEENIE — Bill Black's Combo, Hi 2079
115. THAT'S HOW STRONG MY LOVE IS — O.V. Wright with the Keys, Goldwax 106
116. SOUL DRESSING — Booker T. & the MG's, Stax 151
117. I'M TOO POOR TO DIE — Louisiana Red, Glover 3002
118. GATOR TAILS AND MONKEY RIBS — Spats, ABC-Paramount 10585
119. HEARTBREAK — Dee Clark, Constellation 132
120. WHERE IS SHE? — Bobby Vee, Liberty 55726
121. I COULD CONQUER THE WORLD — Shevelles, World Artists 1025
122. (Say I Love You) DOO BEE DUM — Four Evers, Smash 1921
123. MY ADORABLE ONE — Joe Simon, Vee Jay 609
124. (I'm Just) A HENPECKED GUY — Reflections, Golden World 16
125. GIRL FROM IPANEMA — Ernie Heckscher and His Ork, Columbia 43103
126. I HAD A TALK WITH MY MAN — Mitty Collier, Chess 1907
127. RUNNIN' OUT OF FOOLS — Aretha Franklin, Columbia 43113
128. THE LONG SHIPS — Sonny Knight, Aura 403
129. IF YOU WANT THIS LOVE — Sonny Knight, Aura 403
130. WELCOME, WELCOME HOME — Anita Bryant, Columbia 43106
131. NICE AND EASY — Charlie Rich, Groove 0041
132. SOFTLY AS I LEAVE YOU — Matt Monro, Liberty 55725
133. OH NO! — Ray Peterson, MGM 13269
134. IT'S IN YOUR HANDS — Diane Reney, 20th Century-Fox 533

Compiled from national retail sales and radio station airplay by the Music Popularity Dept. of Record Market Research, Billboard.

# Billboard HOT 100

**For Week Ending September 19, 1964**

★ STAR performer—Sides registering greatest proportionate upward progress this week.

| This Week | 1 Wk. Ago | 2 Wks. Ago | 3 Wks. Ago | TITLE Artist, Label & Number | Weeks On Chart |
|---|---|---|---|---|---|
| 1 | 1 | 1 | 2 | THE HOUSE OF THE RISING SUN — Animals, MGM 13264 | 7 |
| 2 | 5 | 6 | 9 | BREAD AND BUTTER — Newbeats, Hickory 1269 | 6 |
| 3 | 2 | 2 | 1 | WHERE DID OUR LOVE GO — Supremes, Motown 1060 | 11 |
| 4 | 10 | 27 | 51 | OH, PRETTY WOMAN — Roy Orbison, Monument 851 | 4 |
| 5 | 7 | 10 | 15 | G.T.O. — Ronny & the Daytonas, Mala 481 | 8 |
| 6 | 4 | 3 | 3 | EVERYBODY LOVES SOMEBODY — Dean Martin, Reprise 0281 | 12 |
| 7 | 9 | 13 | 47 | REMEMBER (Walkin' in the Sand) — Shangri-Las, Red Bird 10-008 | 5 |
| 8 | 3 | 4 | 7 | BECAUSE — Dave Clark Five, Epic 9704 | 8 |
| 9 | 31 | 58 | — | DO WAH DIDDY DIDDY — Manfred Mann, Ascot 2157 | 3 |
| 10 | 25 | 32 | 42 | DANCING IN THE STREET — Martha & the Vandellas, Gordy 7033 | 5 |
| 11 | 11 | 11 | 14 | SELFISH ONE — Jackie Ross, Chess 1903 | 8 |
| 12 | 8 | 8 | 4 | A HARD DAY'S NIGHT — Beatles, Capitol 5222 | 10 |
| 13 | 15 | 17 | 30 | MAYBELLINE — Johnny Rivers, Imperial 66056 | 6 |
| 14 | 16 | 18 | 35 | HAUNTED HOUSE — Gene Simmons, Hi 2076 | 7 |
| 15 | 24 | 25 | 32 | BABY I NEED YOUR LOVING — Four Tops, Motown 1062 | 6 |
| 16 | 21 | 26 | 29 | IT HURTS TO BE IN LOVE — Gene Pitney, Musicor 1040 | 10 |
| 17 | 17 | 19 | 21 | CLINGING VINE — Bobby Vinton, Epic 9705 | 7 |
| 18 | 22 | 31 | 64 | SAVE IT FOR ME — 4 Seasons, Philips 40225 | 4 |
| 19 | 19 | 22 | 26 | IN THE MISTY MOONLIGHT — Jerry Wallace, Challenge 59246 | 9 |
| 20 | 23 | 24 | 48 | WE'LL SING IN THE SUNSHINE — Gale Garnett, RCA Victor 8388 | 7 |
| 21 | 28 | 35 | 45 | FUNNY — Joe Hinton, Back Beat 541 | 6 |
| 22 | 14 | 16 | 18 | MAYBE I KNOW — Lesley Gore, Mercury 72309 | 9 |
| 23 | 6 | 5 | 5 | C'MON AND SWIM — Bobby Freeman, Autumn 2 | 11 |
| 24 | 13 | 7 | 6 | UNDER THE BOARDWALK — Drifters, Atlantic 2237 | 13 |
| 25 | 29 | 36 | 50 | I'M ON THE OUTSIDE (Looking In) — Little Anthony & the Imperials, DCP 1104 | 5 |
| 26 | 27 | 29 | 34 | IT'S ALL OVER NOW — Rolling Stones, London 9687 | 9 |
| 27 | 20 | 14 | 20 | YOU NEVER CAN TELL — Chuck Berry, Chess 1906 | 8 |
| 28 | 12 | 12 | 13 | AND I LOVE HER — Beatles, Capitol 5235 | 9 |
| 29 | 35 | 45 | 61 | OUT OF SIGHT — James Brown, Smash 1919 | 6 |
| 30 | 44 | 60 | 70 | A SUMMER SONG — Chad Stuart & Jeremy Clyde, World Artists 1027 | 6 |
| 31 | 18 | 9 | 10 | HOW DO YOU DO IT — Gerry and the Pacemakers, Laurie 3261 | 11 |
| 32 | 42 | 81 | — | MATCHBOX — Beatles, Capitol 5255 | 3 |
| 33 | 48 | 67 | — | YOU MUST BELIEVE ME — Impressions, ABC-Paramount 10531 | 3 |
| 34 | 58 | 83 | — | WHEN I GROW UP TO BE A MAN — Beach Boys, Capitol 5245 | 3 |
| 35 | 38 | 46 | 56 | SOME DAY WE'RE GONNA LOVE AGAIN — Searchers, Kapp 609 | 6 |
| 36 | 39 | 47 | 52 | ALWAYS TOGETHER — Al Martino, Capitol 5239 | 6 |
| 37 | 51 | 64 | 79 | FROM A WINDOW — Billy J. Kramer, Imperial 66051 | 5 |
| 38 | 41 | 52 | 68 | YOU'LL NEVER GET TO HEAVEN (If You Break My Heart) — Dionne Warwick, Scepter 1282 | 6 |
| 39 | 56 | 68 | 83 | RHYTHM — Major Lance, Okeh 7203 | 3 |
| 40 | 54 | 72 | — | LET IT BE ME — Betty Everett & Jerry Butler, Vee Jay 613 | 3 |
| 41 | 26 | 15 | 8 | WALK—DON'T RUN '64 — Ventures, Dolton 96 | 11 |
| 42 | 60 | 73 | — | LAST KISS — J. Frank Wilson & the Cavaliers, Josie 923 | 3 |
| 43 | 67 | 99 | — | SLOW DOWN — Beatles, Capitol 5255 | 3 |
| 44 | 49 | 76 | 84 | MICHAEL — Trini Lopez, Reprise 0300 | 5 |
| 45 | 52 | 57 | 65 | SAY YOU — Ronnie Dove, Diamond 167 | 10 |
| 46 | 46 | 48 | 58 | HE'S IN TOWN — Tokens, B. T. Puppy 502 | 7 |
| 47 | 50 | 61 | 76 | THERE'S NOTHING I CAN SAY — Rick Nelson, Decca 31656 | 5 |
| 48 | 40 | 40 | 43 | SWEET WILLIAM — Millie Small, Smash 1920 | 7 |
| 49 | 45 | 49 | 49 | WORRY — Johnny Tillotson, MGM 13255 | 10 |
| 50 | 65 | — | — | WHY YOU WANNA MAKE ME BLUE — Temptations, Gordy 7035 | 2 |
| 51 | 47 | 54 | 57 | WHEN YOU LOVED ME — Brenda Lee, Decca 31654 | 7 |
| 52 | 63 | 82 | 97 | 20-75 — Willie Mitchell, Hi 2075 | 4 |
| 53 | 55 | 63 | 78 | (There's) ALWAYS SOMETHING THERE TO REMIND ME — Lou Johnson, Big Hill 552 | 5 |
| 54 | 64 | 75 | 90 | SHE WANTS T'SWIM — Chubby Checker, Parkway 922 | 4 |
| 55 | 59 | 53 | 54 | IF I FELL — Beatles, Capitol 5235 | 8 |
| 56 | 66 | — | — | ON THE STREET WHERE YOU LIVE — Andy Williams, Columbia 43128 | 2 |
| 57 | 53 | 55 | 55 | RINGO'S THEME (This Boy) — George Martin and His Ork, United Artists 745 | 8 |
| 58 | 68 | 79 | 88 | CANDY TO ME — Eddie Holland, Motown 1063 | 4 |
| 59 | 57 | 59 | 69 | INVISIBLE TEARS — Ray Conniff Singers, Columbia 43061 | 10 |
| 60 | 84 | — | — | LITTLE HONDA — Hondells, Mercury 72324 | 2 |
| 61 | 77 | 88 | — | MERCY, MERCY — Don Covay & the Goodtimers, Rosemart 801 | 3 |
| 62 | 62 | 65 | 73 | WHERE LOVE HAS GONE — Jack Jones, Kapp 608 | 6 |
| 63 | 78 | 96 | — | CHUG-A-LUG — Roger Miller, Smash 1926 | 3 |
| 64 | 69 | 77 | 82 | KNOCK! KNOCK! (Who's There) — Orlons, Cameo 332 | 4 |
| 65 | 72 | — | — | GONNA SEND YOU BACK TO WALKER — Animals, MGM 13242 | 2 |
| 66 | 61 | 62 | 72 | I STAND ACCUSED — Jerry Butler, Vee Jay 598 | 6 |
| 67 | 76 | 91 | 93 | THE JAMES BOND THEME — Billy Strange, Crescendo 320 | 5 |
| 68 | 83 | 90 | — | SOFTLY, AS I LEAVE YOU — Frank Sinatra, Reprise 0301 | 3 |
| 69 | 73 | 70 | 67 | I'VE GOT NO TIME TO LOSE — Carla Thomas, Atlantic 2238 | 8 |
| 70 | 79 | — | — | PEARLY SHELLS — Burl Ives, Decca 31659 | 2 |
| 71 | 96 | — | — | FUNNY GIRL — Barbra Streisand, Columbia 43127 | 2 |
| 72 | 90 | — | — | TOBACCO ROAD — Nashville Teens, London 9689 | 2 |
| 73 | 82 | 87 | — | THE CAT — Jimmy Smith, Verve 10330 | 3 |
| 74 | 86 | — | — | COME A LITTLE BIT CLOSER — Jay & the Americans, United Artists 759 | 2 |
| 75 | 75 | 84 | 95 | SINCERELY — 4 Seasons, Vee Jay 608 | 4 |
| 76 | 91 | — | — | IT'S ALL OVER — Ben E. King, Atco 6315 | 2 |
| 77 | 80 | 86 | 98 | YET...I KNOW (Et Pourtant) — Steve Lawrence, Columbia 43095 | 4 |
| 78 | — | — | — | THAT'S WHAT LOVE IS MADE OF — Miracles, Tamla 54102 | 1 |
| 79 | 70 | 89 | — | HOLD ME — P. J. Proby, London 9688 | 3 |
| 80 | 88 | — | — | I WOULDN'T TRADE YOU FOR THE WORLD — Bachelors, London 9693 | 2 |
| 81 | — | — | — | BABY DON'T YOU DO IT — Marvin Gaye, Tamla 54101 | 1 |
| 82 | — | — | — | RIDE THE WILD SURF — Jan & Dean, Liberty 55724 | 1 |
| 83 | 85 | — | — | LA LA LA LA LA — Blendells, Reprise 0291 | 2 |
| 84 | — | — | — | IT'S FOR YOU — Cilla Black, Capitol 5258 | 1 |
| 85 | — | — | — | I DON'T WANT TO SEE TOMORROW — Nat King Cole, Capitol 5261 | 1 |
| 86 | 92 | — | — | GOOD NIGHT BABY — Butterflys, Red Bird 10-009 | 2 |
| 87 | — | — | — | DO YOU WANT TO DANCE — Del Shannon, Amy 911 | 1 |
| 88 | — | — | — | TEEN BEAT '65 — Sandy Nelson, Imperial 66060 | 1 |
| 89 | 89 | 93 | 96 | LOVERS ALWAYS FORGIVE — Gladys Knight & the Pips, Maxx 329 | 5 |
| 90 | — | — | — | HAVE I THE RIGHT? — Honeycombs, Interphon 7707 | 1 |
| 91 | 93 | 98 | — | I WANNA THANK YOU — Enchanters, Warner Bros. 5460 | 3 |
| 92 | 98 | — | — | DEATH OF AN ANGEL — Kingsmen, Wand 164 | 2 |
| 93 | 95 | — | — | SOCIETY GIRL — Rag Dolls, Parkway 921 | 2 |
| 94 | 94 | — | — | SOON I'LL WED MY LOVE — John Gary, RCA Victor 8413 | 2 |
| 95 | — | — | — | RUNNIN' OUT OF FOOLS — Aretha Franklin, Columbia 43113 | 1 |
| 96 | 100 | 100 | — | ROCKIN' ROBIN — Rivieras, Rivera 1403 | 3 |
| 97 | 99 | — | — | SOMEONE, SOMEONE — Brian Poole, Monument 846 | 2 |
| 98 | — | — | — | TILL THE END OF TIME — Ray Charles Singers, Command 4049 | 1 |
| 99 | — | — | — | SALLY WAS A GOOD OLD GIRL — Fats Domino, ABC-Paramount 10584 | 1 |
| 100 | — | — | — | THE CLOCK — Baby Washington, Sue 104 | 1 |

## HOT 100—A TO Z—(Publisher-Licensee)

Always Together (Damian, ASCAP) .... 36
And I Love Her (Unart-Maclen, BMI) .... 28
Baby Don't You Do It (Jobete, BMI) .... 81
Baby I Need Your Loving (Jobete, BMI) .... 15
Because (Ivy, BMI) .... 8
Bread and Butter (Acuff-Rose, BMI) .... 2
Candy to Me (Jobete, BMI) .... 58
Cat, The (Hastings, BMI) .... 73
Chug-A-Lug (Tree, BMI) .... 63
Clinging Vine (Peter Maurice, ASCAP) .... 17
Clock, The (Saturn & Mon-Ami, BMI) .... 100
C'mon and Swim (Taracrest, BMI) .... 23
Come a Little Bit Closer (Jobete, BMI) .... 74
Dancing in the Street (Jobete, BMI) .... 10
Death of an Angel (Pattern, ASCAP) .... 92
Do Wah Diddy Diddy (Trio, BMI) .... 9
Do You Want to Dance (Clockus, BMI) .... 87
Everybody Loves Somebody (Sands, ASCAP) .... 6
From a Window (Maclen, BMI) .... 37
Funny (Pamper, BMI) .... 21
Funny Girl (Chappell, ASCAP) .... 71
G.T.O. (Buckhorn, BMI) .... 5
Gonna Send You Back to Walker (Zann, BMI) .... 65
Good Night Baby (Trio, BMI) .... 86
Hard Day's Night, A (Unart-Maclen, BMI) .... 12
Haunted House (Venice-B. Flat, BMI) .... 14
Have I the Right? (Ivy, ASCAP) .... 90
He's in Town (Screen Gems-Columbia, BMI) .... 46
Hold Me (Ross Jungnickel-Robbins-World, ASCAP) .... 79
House of the Rising Sun, The (Gallico, BMI) .... 1
How Do You Do It (Just, BMI) .... 31
I Don't Want to See Tomorrow (Sweco, BMI) .... 85
I Stand Accused (Curtom, BMI) .... 66
I Wanna Thank You (Rittenhouse, BMI) .... 91
I Wouldn't Trade You for the World (LeBill, BMI) .... 80
I'm On the Outside (Looking In) (South Mountain, BMI) .... 25
I've Got No Time to Lose (East, BMI) .... 69
If I Fell (Unart-Maclen, BMI) .... 55
In the Misty Moonlight (Four Star, BMI) .... 19
Invisible Tears (Central Songs, BMI) .... 59
It Hurts to Be in Love (Screen Gems-Columbia, BMI) .... 16
It's All Over (Keetch, Caesar & Dino, BMI) .... 76
It's All Over Now (Kags, BMI) .... 26
It's For You (Maclen, BMI) .... 84
James Bond Theme, The (Unart, BMI) .... 67
Knock! Knock! (Who's There) (Saturday, ASCAP) .... 64
La La La La La (Jobete, BMI) .... 83
Last Kiss (Boblo, BMI) .... 42
Let It Be Me (Leeds, ASCAP) .... 40
Little Honda (Sea of Tunes, BMI) .... 60
Lovers Always Forgive (Maxx, BMI) .... 89
Matchbox (Knox, BMI) .... 32
Maybe I Know (Trio, BMI) .... 22
Maybelline (Arc, BMI) .... 13
Mercy, Mercy (Cotillion-Vonglo, BMI) .... 61
Michael (Unart, BMI) .... 44
Oh, Pretty Woman (Acuff-Rose, BMI) .... 4
On the Street Where You Live (Chappell, ASCAP) .... 56
Out of Sight (Try Me, BMI) .... 29
Pearly Shells (Criterion, BMI) .... 70
Remember (Walkin' in the Sand) (Tender Tunes-Trio, BMI) .... 7
Rhythm (Jalynne-Curtom, BMI) .... 39
Ride the Wild Surf (Screen Gems-Columbia, BMI) .... 82
Ringo's Theme (This Boy) (Maclen, BMI) .... 57
Rockin' Robin (Recordo, BMI) .... 96
Runnin' Out of Fools (Roosevelt, BMI) .... 95
Sally Was a Good Old Girl (Pamper, BMI) .... 99
Save It for Me (Saturday-Gavadima, ASCAP) .... 18
Say You (Chevis, BMI) .... 45
Selfish One (Chevis, BMI) .... 11
She Wants T'Swim (Kalmann-C.C., ASCAP) .... 54
Sincerely (Regent, BMI) .... 75
Slow Down (Venice, BMI) .... 43
Society Girl (Saturday, ASCAP) .... 93
Softly, As I Leave You (Miller, ASCAP) .... 68
Some Day We're Gonna Love Again (McLaughlin, BMI) .... 35
Someone, Someone (Nep, ASCAP) .... 97
Soon I'll Wed My Love (Laurel, ASCAP) .... 94
Summer Song, A (Unart-Woart, BMI) .... 30
Sweet William (Budd, ASCAP) .... 48
Teen Beat '65 (Drive-In, BMI) .... 88
That's What Love Is Made Of (Jobete, BMI) .... 78
(There's) Always Something There to Remind Me (Ross-Jungnickel & Blue Seas, ASCAP) .... 53
There's Nothing I Can Say (Chappell, ASCAP) .... 47
Till the End of Time (Joy, ASCAP) .... 98
Tobacco Road (Cedarwood, BMI) .... 72
20-75 (Jec, BMI) .... 52
Under the Boardwalk (T.M., BMI) .... 24
Walk—Don't Run '64 (Forshay, BMI) .... 41
We'll Sing in the Sunshine (Lupercalia, ASCAP) .... 20
When I Grow Up to Be a Man (Sea of Tunes, BMI) .... 34
When You Loved Me (Hill & Range-Ron Bre, BMI) .... 51
Where Did Our Love Go (Jobete, BMI) .... 3
Where Love Has Gone (Paramount, ASCAP) .... 62
Why You Wanna Make Me Blue (Jobete, BMI) .... 50
Worry (Ridge, BMI) .... 49
Yet...I Know (Et Pourtant) (Leeds, ASCAP) .... 77
You'll Never Get to Heaven (Jac-Blue Seas, ASCAP) .... 38
You Must Believe Me (Curtom, BMI) .... 33
You Never Can Tell (Arc, BMI) .... 27

## BUBBLING UNDER THE HOT 100

101. SHE KNOWS ME TOO WELL ........ Beach Boys, Capitol 5245
102. ONE MORE TEAR .................. Raindrops, Jubilee 5487
103. I DON'T KNOW ............ Steve Alaimo, ABC-Paramount 10580
104. LOVER'S PRAYER .......... Wallace Brothers, Sims 189
105. LITTLE QUEENIE ............ Bill Black's Combo, Hi 2079
106. SOUL DRESSING .......... Booker T. & the MG's, Stax 153
107. SQUEEZE HER-TEASE HER (BUT LOVE HER) ...... Jackie Wilson, Brunswick 55269
108. I COULD CONQUER THE WORLD ...... Shevelles, World Artists 1025
109. ALL CRIED OUT .......... Dusty Springfield, Philips 40229
110. THAT'S HOW STRONG MY LOVE IS ... O. V. Wright with the Keys, Goldwax 106
111. BEACH GIRL .............. Pat Boone, Dot 16658
112. LUMBERJACK ............ Brook Benton, Mercury 72333
113. GATOR TAILS AND MONKEY RIBS .... Sparts, ABC-Paramount 10585
114. I GUESS I'M CRAZY ............ Jim Reeves, RCA Victor 8383
115. IT HURTS TO BE IN LOVE .......... Betty Everett, Vee Jay 610
116. BABY LET ME TAKE YOU HOME ...... Animals, MGM 13242
117. A TASTE OF HONEY ............ Tony Bennett, Columbia 43073
118. YOU PULLED A FAST ONE ........ V.I.P.'s, Big Top 518
119. (SAY I LOVE YOU) DOO BEE DUM .... Four Evers, Smash 1921
120. MY ADORABLE ONE .............. Joe Simon, Vee Jay 597
121. I'LL FOLLOW THE RAINBOW ...... Terry Stafford, Crusader 109
122. IF YOU WANT THIS LOVE ........ Sonny Knight, Aura 403
123. HAD A TALK WITH MY MAN ...... Mitty Collier, Chess 1907
124. DERN YA .................. Ruby Wright, RIC 126-64
125. BABY, BABY ALL THE TIME ...... Superbs, Dore 715
126. TROUBLE IN MIND ............ Aretha Franklin, Columbia 42746
127. POOR MAN TO DIE .......... Louisiana Red, Glover 3002
128. I COULD CONQUER THE WORLD .... Joe Simon, Vee Jay 597
128. LA DE DA I LOVE YOU .......... Inez & Charlie Foxx, Symbol 201
129. HEARTBREAK ................ Dee Clark, Constellation 132
130. THAT'S WHEN THE CRYING BEGINS ... Kip Anderson, ABC-Paramount 10579
131. IF ..................... Timi Yuro, Mercury 72316
132. I'D RATHER BE RICH ......... Pearl Bailey, Decca 31667
133. OPPORTUNITY ............ Jewels, Dimension 1034
134. FEVER .................. Alvin Robinson, Red Bird 10-010
135. GET MY HANDS ON SOME LOVIN' .... Artistics, Okeh 7193

Compiled from national retail sales and radio station airplay by the Music Popularity Dept. of Record Market Research, Billboard.

Billboard
For Week Ending September 26, 1964

# HOT 100

★ STAR performer—Sides registering greatest proportionate upward progress this week.

Billboard Award

| This Week | 1 Wk. Ago | 2 Wks. Ago | 3 Wks. Ago | Title | Artist, Label & Number | Weeks On Chart |
|---|---|---|---|---|---|---|
| ★1 | 4 | 10 | 27 | OH, PRETTY WOMAN | Roy Orbison, Monument 851 | 5 |
| 2 | 2 | 5 | 6 | BREAD AND BUTTER | Newbeats, Hickory 1269 | 7 |
| 3 | 1 | 1 | 1 | THE HOUSE OF THE RISING SUN | Animals, MGM 13264 | 8 |
| 4 | 5 | 7 | 10 | G.T.O. | Ronny & the Daytonas, Mala 481 | 9 |
| 5 | 7 | 9 | 13 | REMEMBER (Walkin' in the Sand) | Shangri-Las, Red Bird 10-008 | 6 |
| ★6 | 9 | 31 | 58 | DO WAH DIDDY DIDDY | Manfred Mann, Ascot 2157 | 4 |
| 7 | 3 | 2 | 2 | WHERE DID OUR LOVE GO | Supremes, Motown 1060 | 12 |
| 8 | 10 | 25 | 32 | DANCING IN THE STREET | Martha & the Vandellas, Gordy 7033 | 6 |
| ★9 | 16 | 21 | 26 | IT HURTS TO BE IN LOVE | Gene Pitney, Musicor 1040 | 10 |
| ★10 | 18 | 22 | 31 | SAVE IT FOR ME | 4 Seasons, Philips 40225 | 5 |
| 11 | 14 | 16 | 18 | HAUNTED HOUSE | Gene Simmons, Hi 2076 | 8 |
| 12 | 13 | 15 | 17 | MAYBELLINE | Johnny Rivers, Imperial 66056 | 7 |
| 13 | 15 | 24 | 25 | BABY I NEED YOUR LOVING | Four Tops, Motown 1062 | 7 |
| ★14 | 20 | 23 | 24 | WE'LL SING IN THE SUNSHINE | Gale Garnett, RCA Victor 8388 | 8 |
| 15 | 6 | 4 | 3 | EVERYBODY LOVES SOMEBODY | Dean Martin, Reprise 0281 | 13 |
| ★16 | 21 | 28 | 35 | FUNNY | Joe Hinton, Back Beat 541 | 7 |
| 17 | 8 | 3 | 4 | BECAUSE | Dave Clark Five, Epic 9704 | 9 |
| ★18 | 30 | 44 | 60 | A SUMMER SONG | Chad Stuart & Jeremy Clyde, World Artists 1027 | 7 |
| 19 | 12 | 8 | 8 | A HARD DAY'S NIGHT | Beatles, Capitol 5222 | 11 |
| 20 | 11 | 11 | 11 | SELFISH ONE | Jackie Ross, Chess 1903 | 9 |
| ★21 | 34 | 58 | 83 | WHEN I GROW UP TO BE A MAN | Beach Boys, Capitol 5245 | 4 |
| 22 | 25 | 29 | 36 | I'M ON THE OUTSIDE (Looking In) | Little Anthony & the Imperials, DCP 1104 | 6 |
| ★23 | 32 | 42 | 81 | MATCHBOX | Beatles, Capitol 5255 | 4 |
| ★24 | 29 | 35 | 45 | OUT OF SIGHT | James Brown, Smash 1919 | 7 |
| 25 | 19 | 19 | 22 | IN THE MISTY MOONLIGHT | Jerry Wallace, Challenge 59246 | 10 |
| ★26 | 33 | 48 | 67 | YOU MUST BELIEVE ME | Impressions, ABC-Paramount 10581 | 4 |
| ★27 | 40 | 54 | 72 | LET IT BE ME | Betty Everett & Jerry Butler, Vee Jay 613 | 4 |
| ★28 | 39 | 56 | 68 | RHYTHM | Major Lance, Okeh 7203 | 6 |
| ★29 | 42 | 60 | 73 | LAST KISS | J. Frank Wilson & the Cavaliers, Josie 923 | 4 |
| ★30 | 37 | 51 | 64 | FROM A WINDOW | Billy J. Kramer, Imperial 66051 | 6 |
| 31 | 17 | 17 | 19 | CLINGING VINE | Bobby Vinton, Epic 9705 | 8 |
| ★32 | 43 | 67 | 99 | SLOW DOWN | Beatles, Capitol 5255 | 4 |
| 33 | 36 | 39 | 47 | ALWAYS TOGETHER | Al Martino, Capitol 5239 | 7 |
| 34 | 35 | 38 | 46 | SOME DAY WE'RE GONNA LOVE AGAIN | Searchers, Kapp 609 | 7 |
| 35 | 38 | 41 | 52 | YOU'LL NEVER GET TO HEAVEN (If You Break My Heart) | Dionne Warwick, Scepter 1282 | 7 |
| 36 | 23 | 6 | 5 | C'MON AND SWIM | Bobby Freeman, Autumn 2 | 12 |
| 37 | 26 | 27 | 29 | IT'S ALL OVER NOW | Rolling Stones, London 9687 | 10 |
| 38 | 24 | 13 | 7 | UNDER THE BOARDWALK | Drifters, Atlantic 2237 | 14 |
| ★39 | 50 | 65 | — | WHY YOU WANNA MAKE ME BLUE | Temptations, Gordy 7035 | 3 |
| 40 | 45 | 52 | 57 | SAY YOU | Ronnie Dove, Diamond 167 | 11 |
| 41 | 22 | 14 | 16 | MAYBE I KNOW | Lesley Gore, Mercury 72309 | 10 |
| 42 | 44 | 49 | 76 | MICHAEL | Trini Lopez, Reprise 0300 | 6 |
| 43 | 46 | 46 | 48 | HE'S IN TOWN | Tokens, B. T. Puppy 502 | 8 |
| 44 | 27 | 20 | 14 | YOU NEVER CAN TELL | Chuck Berry, Chess 1906 | 9 |
| ★45 | 63 | 78 | 96 | CHUG-A-LUG | Roger Miller, Smash 1926 | 4 |
| ★46 | 56 | 66 | — | ON THE STREET WHERE YOU LIVE | Andy Williams, Columbia 43128 | 3 |
| ★47 | 60 | 84 | — | LITTLE HONDA | Hondells, Mercury 72324 | 3 |
| 48 | 52 | 63 | 82 | 20-75 | Willie Mitchell, Hi 2075 | 5 |
| ★49 | 61 | 77 | 88 | MERCY, MERCY | Don Covay & the Goodtimers, Rosemart 801 | 4 |
| 50 | 54 | 64 | 75 | SHE WANTS T'SWIM | Chubby Checker, Parkway 922 | 5 |
| 51 | 53 | 55 | 63 | (There's) ALWAYS SOMETHING THERE TO REMIND ME | Lou Johnson, Big Hill 552 | 6 |
| ★52 | 81 | — | — | BABY DON'T YOU DO IT | Marvin Gaye, Tamla 54101 | 2 |
| ★53 | 68 | 83 | 90 | SOFTLY, AS I LEAVE YOU | Frank Sinatra, Reprise 0301 | 4 |
| 54 | 47 | 50 | 61 | THERE'S NOTHING I CAN SAY | Rick Nelson, Decca 31656 | 5 |
| ★55 | 71 | 96 | — | FUNNY GIRL | Barbra Streisand, Columbia 43127 | 3 |
| ★56 | 78 | — | — | THAT'S WHAT LOVE IS MADE OF | Miracles, Tamla 54102 | 2 |
| 57 | 65 | 72 | — | GONNA SEND YOU BACK TO WALKER | Animals, MGM 13242 | 3 |
| 58 | 58 | 68 | 79 | CANDY TO ME | Eddie Holland, Motown 1063 | 5 |
| 59 | 55 | 59 | 53 | IF I FELL | Beatles, Capitol 5235 | 9 |
| ★60 | 72 | 90 | — | TOBACCO ROAD | Nashville Teens, London 9689 | 3 |
| ★61 | 90 | — | — | HAVE I THE RIGHT? | Honeycombs, Interphon 7707 | 2 |
| 62 | 74 | 86 | — | COME A LITTLE BIT CLOSER | Jay & the Americans, United Artists 759 | 3 |
| ★63 | 82 | — | — | RIDE THE WILD SURF | Jan & Dean, Liberty 55724 | 2 |
| ★64 | 87 | — | — | DO YOU WANT TO DANCE | Del Shannon, Amy 911 | 2 |
| 65 | 67 | 76 | 91 | THE JAMES BOND THEME | Billy Strange, Crescendo 320 | 6 |
| ★66 | — | — | — | I LIKE IT | Gerry and the Pacemakers, Laurie 3271 | 1 |
| 67 | 73 | 82 | 87 | THE CAT | Jimmy Smith, Verve 10330 | 4 |
| 68 | 64 | 69 | 77 | KNOCK! KNOCK! (Who's There) | Orlons, Cameo 332 | 5 |
| ★69 | 86 | 92 | — | GOOD NIGHT BABY | Butterflys, Red Bird 10-009 | 3 |
| 70 | 70 | 79 | — | PEARLY SHELLS | Burl Ives, Decca 31659 | 3 |
| 71 | 69 | 73 | 70 | I'VE GOT NO TIME TO LOSE | Carla Thomas, Atlantic 2238 | 9 |
| ★72 | — | — | — | I'VE GOT SAND IN MY SHOES | Drifters, Atlantic 2253 | 1 |
| ★73 | — | — | — | COUSIN OF MINE | Sam Cooke, RCA Victor 8426 | 1 |
| 74 | 76 | 91 | — | IT'S ALL OVER | Ben E. King, Atco 6315 | 3 |
| ★75 | — | — | — | ALL CRIED OUT | Dusty Springfield, Philips 40229 | 1 |
| 76 | 80 | 88 | — | I WOULDNT TRADE YOU FOR THE WORLD | Bachelors, London 9693 | 3 |
| ★77 | — | — | — | TRY ME | Jimmy Hughes, Fame 6403 | 1 |
| ★78 | — | — | — | I'M CRYING | Animals, MGM 13274 | 1 |
| 79 | 92 | 98 | — | DEATH OF AN ANGEL | Kingsmen, Wand 164 | 3 |
| 80 | 83 | 85 | — | LA LA LA LA LA | Blendells, Reprise 0291 | 3 |
| 81 | 85 | — | — | I DON'T WANT TO SEE TOMORROW | Nat King Cole, Capitol 5261 | 2 |
| 82 | 84 | — | — | IT'S FOR YOU | Cilla Black, Capitol 5258 | 2 |
| 83 | 77 | 80 | 86 | YET . . . I KNOW (Et Pourtant) | Steve Lawrence, Columbia 43095 | 5 |
| ★84 | — | — | — | THE DOOR IS STILL OPEN TO MY HEART | Dean Martin, Reprise 0307 | 1 |
| 85 | 88 | — | — | TEEN BEAT '65 | Sandy Nelson, Imperial 66060 | 2 |
| 86 | 79 | 70 | 89 | HOLD ME | P. J. Proby, London 9688 | 4 |
| 87 | 98 | — | — | TILL THE END OF TIME | Ray Charles Singers, Command 4049 | 2 |
| ★88 | — | — | — | BABY BE MINE | Jelly Beans, Red Bird 10-011 | 1 |
| ★89 | — | — | — | SMACK DAB IN THE MIDDLE | Ray Charles and His Ork, ABC-Paramount 10588 | 1 |
| ★90 | — | — | — | BEACH GIRL | Pat Boone, Dot 16658 | 1 |
| 91 | 93 | 95 | — | SOCIETY GIRL | Rag Dolls, Parkway 921 | 3 |
| 92 | — | — | — | YOU REALLY GOT ME | Kinks, Reprise 0306 | 1 |
| 93 | 94 | 94 | — | SOON I'LL WED MY LOVE | John Gary, RCA Victor 8413 | 3 |
| 94 | — | — | — | I GUESS I'M CRAZY | Jim Reeves, RCA Victor 8383 | 3 |
| 95 | 95 | — | — | RUNNIN' OUT OF FOOLS | Aretha Franklin, Columbia 43113 | 2 |
| 96 | — | — | — | GATOR TAILS AND MONKEY RIBS | Spats, ABC-Paramount 10585 | 1 |
| 97 | — | — | — | L-O-V-E | Nat King Cole, Capitol 5261 | 1 |
| 98 | — | — | — | BLESS OUR LOVE | Gene Chandler, Constellation 136 | 1 |
| 99 | 99 | — | — | SALLY WAS A GOOD OLD GIRL | Fats Domino, ABC-Paramount 10584 | 2 |
| 100 | — | — | — | I HAD A TALK WITH MY MAN | Mitty Collier, Chess 1907 | 1 |

## HOT 100—A TO Z—(Publisher-Licensee)

All Cried Out (Kingsley, ASCAP) .... 75
Always Together (Damian, ASCAP) .... 33
Baby Be Mine (Trio, BMI) .... 88
Baby Don't You Do It (Jobete, BMI) .... 52
Baby I Need Your Loving (Jobete, BMI) .... 13
Beach Girl (Blackwood-T.M., BMI) .... 90
Because (Ivy, ASCAP) .... 17
Bless Our Love (Jalynne-Curtom, BMI) .... 98
Bread and Butter (Acuff-Rose, BMI) .... 2
Candy to Me (Jobete, BMI) .... 58
Cat, The (Hastings, BMI) .... 67
Chug-A-Lug (Tree, BMI) .... 45
Clinging Vine (Peter Maurice, ASCAP) .... 31
C'mon and Swim (Taracrest, BMI) .... 36
Come a Little Bit Closer (Picturetone, BMI) .... 62
Cousin of Mine (Kags, BMI) .... 73
Dancing in the Street (Jobete, BMI) .... 8
Death of an Angel (Limax, BMI) .... 79
Do Wah Diddy Diddy (Trio, BMI) .... 6
Do You Want to Dance (Clockus, BMI) .... 64
Door Is Still Open to My Heart, The (Berkshire, BMI) .... 84
Everybody Loves Somebody (Sands, ASCAP) .... 15
From a Window (Maclen, BMI) .... 30
Funny (Pamper, BMI) .... 16
Funny Girl (Chappell, ASCAP) .... 55
Gator Tails and Monkey Ribs (Bloor-Hoffman House, BMI) .... 96
G.T.O. (Buckhorn, BMI) .... 4
Gonna Send You Back to Walker (Zann, BMI) .... 57
Good Night Baby (Trio, BMI) .... 69
Hard's Day Night, A (Unart-Maclen, BMI) .... 19
Haunted House (Venice-B Flat, BMI) .... 11
Have I the Right? (Ivy, ASCAP) .... 61
He's in Town (Screen Gems-Columbia, BMI) .... 43
Hold Me (Ross Jungnickel-Robbins-World, ASCAP) .... 86
House of the Rising Sun (Gallico, BMI) .... 3
I Don't Want to See Tomorrow (Sweco, BMI) .... 81
I Guess I'm Crazy (Mallory, BMI) .... 94
I Had a Talk With My Man (Chevis, BMI) .... 100
I Like It (Gil, BMI) .... 66
I Wouldn't Trade You for the World (LeBill, BMI). 76
I'm Crying (Gallico, BMI) .... 78
I'm on the Outside (Looking In) (South Mountain, BMI) .... 22
I've Got No Time to Lose (East, BMI) .... 71
I've Got Sand in My Shoes (T.M., BMI) .... 72
If I Fell (Unart-Maclen, BMI) .... 59
In the Misty Moonlight (Four Star, BMI) .... 25
It Hurts to Be in Love (Screen Gems-Columbia, BMI) .... 9
It's All Over (Keetch, Caesar & Dino, BMI) .... 74
It's All Over Now (Kags, BMI) .... 37
It's for You (Maclen, BMI) .... 82
James Bond Theme, The (Unart, BMI) .... 65
Knock! Knock! (Who's There) (Saturday, ASCAP) .... 68
La La La La La (Jobete, BMI) .... 80
Last Kiss (Boblo, BMI) .... 29
Let It Be Me (Leeds, ASCAP) .... 27
Little Honda (Sea of Tunes, BMI) .... 47
L-O-V-E (Roosevelt, BMI) .... 97
Matchbox (Knox, BMI) .... 23
Maybe I Know (Trio, BMI) .... 41
Maybelline (Arc, BMI) .... 12
Mercy, Mercy (Cotillion-Vonglo, BMI) .... 49
Michael (Unart, BMI) .... 42
Oh, Pretty Woman (Acuff-Rose, BMI) .... 1
On the Street Where You Live (Chappell, ASCAP) .... 46
Out of Sight (Try Me, BMI) .... 24
Pearly Shells (Criterion, ASCAP) .... 70
Remember (Walkin' in the Sand) (Tender Tunes-Trio, BMI) .... 5
Rhythm (Jalynne-Curtom, BMI) .... 28
Ride the Wild Surf (Screen Gems-Columbia, BMI) .... 63
Runnin' Out of Fools (Roosevelt, BMI) .... 95
Sally Was a Good Old Girl (Pamper, BMI) .... 99
Save It for Me (Saturday-Gavadima, ASCAP) .... 10
Say You (T.M., BMI) .... 40
Selfish One (Chevis, BMI) .... 20
She Wants t'Swim (Kalmann-C.C., ASCAP) .... 50
Slow Down (Venice, BMI) .... 32
Smack Dab in the Middle (Roosevelt, BMI) .... 89
Society Girl (Saturday, ASCAP) .... 91
Softly, as I Leave You (Miller, ASCAP) .... 53
Some Day We're Gonna Love Again (McLaughlin, BMI) .... 34
Soon I'll Wed My Love (Laurel, ASCAP) .... 93
Summer Song, A (Unart-Woart, BMI) .... 18
Teen Beat '65 (Drive-In, BMI) .... 85
That's What Love Is Made Of (Jobete, BMI) .... 56
(There's) Always Something There to Remind Me (Ross-Jungnickel & Blue Seas, ASCAP) .... 51
There's Nothing I Can Say (Chappell, ASCAP) .... 54
Till the End of Time (Joy, ASCAP) .... 87
Tobacco Road (Cedarwood, BMI) .... 60
Try Me (Lois, BMI) .... 77
20-75 (Jec, BMI) .... 48
Unde rthe Boardwalk (T.M., BMI) .... 38
We'll Sing in the Sunshine (Lupercalia, ASCAP) .... 14
When I Grow Up to Be a Man (Sea of Tunes, BMI). 21
Where Did Our Love Go (Jobete, BMI) .... 7
Why You Wanna Make Me Blue (Jobete, BMI) .... 39
Yet . . . I Know (Et Pourtant) (Leeds, ASCAP) .... 83
You'll Never Get to Heaven (Jac-Blue Seas, ASCAP). 35
You Must Believe Me (Curtom, BMI) .... 26
You Never Can Tell (Arc, BMI) .... 44
You Really Got Me (Kassner, ASCAP) .... 92

## BUBBLING UNDER THE HOT 100

101. I SEE YOU .... Cathy & Joe, Smash 1929
102. THE ANAHEIM, AZUSA & CUCAMONGA SEWING CIRCLE, BOOK REVIEW AND TIMING ASSOCIATION .... Jan & Dean, Liberty 55724
103. SHE KNOWS ME TOO WELL .... Beach Boys, Capitol 5245
104. LITTLE QUEENIE .... Bill Black's Combo, Hi 2079
105. I COULD CONQUER THE WORLD .... Shevelles, World Artists 1025
106. IF YOU WANT THIS LOVE .... Sonny Knight, Aura 403
107. I DON'T KNOW .... Steve Alaimo, ABC-Paramount 10580
108. DERN YA .... Ruby Wright, Ric 126-64
109. THAT'S HOW STRONG MY LOVE IS .O. V. Wright with the Keys, Goldwax 106
110. IT HURTS TO BE IN LOVE .... Betty Everett, Vee Jay 610
111. THE CLOCK .... Baby Washington, Sue 104
112. SOUL DRESSING .... Booker T. & the MG's, Stax 153
113. THE THINGS IN THIS HOUSE .... Bobby Darin, Capitol 5257
114. SOMEONE, SOMEONE .... Brian Poole, Monument 846
115. TROUBLE IN MIND .... Jimmy Ricks, Atlantic 2246
116. THE DARTELL STOMP .... Mustangs, Providence 401
117. THE END OF A SYMPHONY .... Allan Sherman & Boston Pops Ork (Fiedler), RCA Victor 8412
118. ONE MORE TEAR .... Raindrops, Jubilee 5487
119. FEVER .... Alvin Robinson, Red Bird 10-010
120. SO LONG, DEARIE .... Louis Armstrong, Mercury 72338
121. I WANNA THANK YOU .... Enchanters, Warner Bros. 5460
122. BABY, BABY ALL THE TIME .... Superbs, Dore 715
123. ABSENT MINDED ME .... Barbra Streisand, Columbia 43127
124. LA DE DAH I LOVE YOU .... Inez & Charlie Foxx, Symbol 201
125. I'M TOO POOR TO DIE .... Louisana Red, Glover 3002
126. WHOLE LOTA SHAKIN' GOIN' ON .... Little Richard, Vee Jay 612
127. SCRATCHY .... Travis Wammack, Ara 204
128. GUITARS AND BONGOS .... Lou Christie, Colpix 735
129. HIS LIPS GET IN THE WAY .... Bernadette Castro, Colpix 747
130. CAN'T LIVE WITHOUT HER .... Billy Butler & the Chanters, Okeh 7201
131. GET MY HANDS ON SOME LOVIN' .... Artistics, Okeh 7193
132. LITTLE HONDA (Extended Play) .... Beach Boys, Capitol R 5267
133. I WANNA SWIM WITH HIM .... Daisies, Roulette 4571
134. THE DOG .... Junior & the Classics, Groove 0043
135. SOFTLY AS I LEAVE YOU .... Matt Monroe, Liberty 55725

Compiled from national retail sales and radio station airplay by the Music Popularity Dept. of Record Market Research, Billboard.

Billboard

For Week Ending October 3, 1964

# HOT 100

★ STAR performer—Sides registering greatest proportionate upward progress this week.

Billboard Award

| This Week | 1 Wk. Ago | 2 Wks. Ago | 3 Wks. Ago | TITLE Artist, Label & Number | Weeks On Chart |
|---|---|---|---|---|---|
| 1 | 1 | 4 | 10 | OH, PRETTY WOMAN — Roy Orbison, Monument 851 | 6 |
| ★2 | 6 | 9 | 31 | DO WAH DIDDY DIDDY — Manfred Mann, Ascot 2157 | 5 |
| 3 | 2 | 2 | 5 | BREAD AND BUTTER — Newbeats, Hickory 1269 | 8 |
| ★4 | 8 | 10 | 25 | DANCING IN THE STREET — Martha & the Vandellas, Gordy 7033 | 7 |
| 5 | 5 | 7 | 9 | REMEMBER (Walkin' in the Sand) — Shangri-Las, Red Bird 10-008 | 7 |
| 6 | 4 | 5 | 7 | G.T.O. — Ronny & the Daytonas, Mala 481 | 10 |
| 7 | 9 | 16 | 21 | IT HURTS TO BE IN LOVE — Gene Pitney, Musicor 1040 | 11 |
| 8 | 3 | 1 | 1 | THE HOUSE OF THE RISING SUN — Animals, MGM 13264 | 9 |
| ★9 | 14 | 20 | 23 | WE'LL SING IN THE SUNSHINE — Gale Garnett, RCA Victor 8388 | 9 |
| 10 | 10 | 18 | 22 | SAVE IT FOR ME — 4 Seasons, Philips 40225 | 6 |
| 11 | 13 | 15 | 24 | BABY I NEED YOUR LOVING — Four Tops, Motown 1062 | 8 |
| ★12 | 18 | 30 | 44 | A SUMMER SONG — Chad Stuart & Jeremy Clyde, World Artists 1027 | 8 |
| 13 | 11 | 14 | 16 | HAUNTED HOUSE — Gene Simmons, Hi 2076 | 9 |
| ★14 | 29 | 42 | 60 | LAST KISS — J. Frank Wilson & the Cavaliers, Josie 923 | 5 |
| 15 | 16 | 21 | 28 | FUNNY — Joe Hinton, Back Beat 541 | 8 |
| ★16 | 21 | 34 | 58 | WHEN I GROW UP TO BE A MAN — Beach Boys, Capitol 5245 | 5 |
| ★17 | 22 | 25 | 29 | I'M ON THE OUTSIDE (Looking In) — Little Anthony & the Imperials, DCP 1104 | 7 |
| ★18 | 23 | 32 | 42 | MATCHBOX — Beatles, Capitol 5255 | 5 |
| 19 | 7 | 3 | 2 | WHERE DID OUR LOVE GO — Supremes, Motown 1060 | 13 |
| ★20 | 26 | 33 | 48 | YOU MUST BELIEVE ME — Impressions, ABC-Paramount 10581 | 5 |
| 21 | 12 | 13 | 15 | MAYBELLINE — Johnny Rivers, Imperial 66056 | 8 |
| ★22 | 27 | 40 | 54 | LET IT BE ME — Betty Everett & Jerry Butler, Vee Jay 613 | 5 |
| ★23 | 30 | 37 | 51 | FROM A WINDOW — Billy J. Kramer, Imperial 66051 | 7 |
| 24 | 19 | 12 | 8 | A HARD DAY'S NIGHT — Beatles, Capitol 5222 | 12 |
| 25 | 28 | 39 | 56 | RHYTHM — Major Lance, Okeh 7203 | 7 |
| 26 | 15 | 6 | 4 | EVERYBODY LOVES SOMEBODY — Dean Martin, Reprise 0281 | 14 |
| ★27 | 32 | 43 | 67 | SLOW DOWN — Beatles, Capitol 5255 | 5 |
| 28 | 24 | 29 | 35 | OUT OF SIGHT — James Brown, Smash 1919 | 8 |
| ★29 | 47 | 60 | 84 | LITTLE HONDA — Hondells, Mercury 72324 | 4 |
| ★30 | 39 | 50 | 65 | WHY YOU WANNA MAKE ME BLUE — Temptations, Gordy 7035 | 4 |
| ★31 | 45 | 63 | 78 | CHUG-A-LUG — Roger Miller, Smash 1926 | 5 |
| 32 | 17 | 8 | 3 | BECAUSE — Dave Clark Five, Epic 9704 | 10 |
| 33 | 33 | 36 | 39 | ALWAYS TOGETHER — Al Martino, Capitol 5239 | 8 |
| 34 | 35 | 38 | 41 | YOU'LL NEVER GET TO HEAVEN (If You Break My Heart) — Dionne Warwick, Scepter 1282 | 8 |
| ★35 | 46 | 56 | 66 | ON THE STREET WHERE YOU LIVE — Andy Williams, Columbia 43128 | 4 |
| 36 | 25 | 19 | 19 | IN THE MISTY MOONLIGHT — Jerry Wallace, Challenge 59246 | 11 |
| ★37 | 49 | 61 | 77 | MERCY, MERCY — Don Covay & the Goodtimers, Rosemart 801 | 5 |
| ★38 | 48 | 52 | 63 | 20-75 — Willie Mitchell, Hi 2075 | 6 |
| ★39 | 62 | 74 | 86 | COME A LITTLE BIT CLOSER — Jay & the Americans, United Artists 759 | 4 |
| 40 | 20 | 11 | 11 | SELFISH ONE — Jackie Ross, Chess 1903 | 10 |
| ★41 | 53 | 68 | 83 | SOFTLY, AS I LEAVE YOU — Frank Sinatra, Reprise 0301 | 5 |
| ★42 | 52 | 81 | — | BABY DON'T YOU DO IT — Marvin Gaye, Tamla 54101 | 3 |
| ★43 | 61 | 90 | — | HAVE I THE RIGHT? — Honeycombs, Interphon 7707 | 3 |
| ★44 | 60 | 72 | 90 | TOBACCO ROAD — Nashville Teens, London 9689 | 4 |
| ★45 | 63 | 82 | — | RIDE THE WILD SURF — Jan & Dean, Liberty 55724 | 3 |
| ★46 | 56 | 78 | — | THAT'S WHAT LOVE IS MADE OF — Miracles, Tamla 54102 | 3 |
| 47 | 34 | 35 | 38 | SOME DAY WE'RE GONNA LOVE AGAIN — Searchers, Kapp 609 | 8 |
| ★48 | 66 | — | — | I LIKE IT — Gerry and the Pacemakers, Laurie 3271 | 2 |
| 49 | 51 | 53 | 55 | (There's) ALWAYS SOMETHING THERE TO REMIND ME — Lou Johnson, Big Hill 552 | 7 |
| 50 | 55 | 71 | 96 | FUNNY GIRL — Barbra Streisand, Columbia 43127 | 4 |
| ★51 | — | — | — | BABY LOVE — Supremes, Motown 1066 | 1 |
| ★52 | 72 | — | — | I'VE GOT SAND IN MY SHOES — Drifters, Atlantic 2253 | 2 |
| 53 | 42 | 44 | 49 | MICHAEL — Trini Lopez, Reprise 0300 | 7 |
| ★54 | 64 | 87 | — | DO YOU WANT TO DANCE — Del Shannon, Amy 911 | 3 |
| ★55 | 81 | 85 | — | I DON'T WANT TO SEE TOMORROW — Nat King Cole, Capitol 5261 | 3 |
| 56 | 50 | 54 | 64 | SHE WANTS T'SWIM — Chubby Checker, Parkway 922 | 6 |
| ★57 | 69 | 86 | 92 | GOOD NIGHT BABY — Butterflys, Red Bird 10-009 | 4 |
| 58 | 65 | 67 | 76 | THE JAMES BOND THEME — Billy Strange, Crescendo 320 | 7 |
| ★59 | 75 | — | — | ALL CRIED OUT — Dusty Springfield, Philips 40229 | 2 |
| ★60 | 73 | — | — | COUSIN OF MINE — Sam Cooke, RCA Victor 8426 | 2 |
| ★61 | 78 | — | — | I'M CRYING — Animals, MGM 13274 | 2 |
| ★62 | 84 | — | — | THE DOOR IS STILL OPEN TO MY HEART — Dean Martin, Reprise 0307 | 2 |
| ★63 | 79 | 92 | 98 | DEATH OF AN ANGEL — Kingsmen, Wand 164 | 4 |
| ★64 | 85 | 88 | — | TEEN BEAT '65 — Sandy Nelson, Imperial 66060 | 3 |
| 65 | 70 | 70 | 79 | PEARLY SHELLS — Burl Ives, Decca 31659 | 4 |
| ★66 | — | — | — | EVERYBODY KNOWS — Dave Clark Five, Epic 9722 | 1 |
| 67 | 67 | 73 | 82 | THE CAT — Jimmy Smith, Verve 10330 | 5 |
| ★68 | — | — | — | I WANNA BE WITH YOU — Nancy Wilson, Capitol 5254 | 1 |
| 69 | 58 | 58 | 68 | CANDY TO ME — Eddie Holland, Motown 1063 | 6 |
| ★70 | — | — | — | WHO CAN I TURN TO — Tony Bennett, Columbia 4341 | 1 |
| 71 | 77 | — | — | TRY ME — Jimmy Hughes, Fame 6403 | 2 |
| 72 | 74 | 76 | 91 | IT'S ALL OVER — Ben E. King, Atco 6315 | 4 |
| ★73 | 88 | — | — | BABY BE MINE — Jelly Beans, Red Bird 10-011 | 2 |
| ★74 | 89 | — | — | SMACK DAB IN THE MIDDLE — Ray Charles and His Ork, ABC-Paramount 10588 | 2 |
| 75 | 68 | 64 | 69 | KNOCK! KNOCK! (Who's There) — Orlons, Cameo 332 | 6 |
| 76 | 76 | 80 | 88 | I WOULDN'T TRADE YOU FOR THE WORLD — Bachelors, London 9693 | 4 |
| 77 | 80 | 83 | 85 | LA LA LA LA LA — Blendells, Reprise 0291 | 4 |
| 78 | 83 | 77 | 80 | YET . . . I KNOW (Et Pourtant) — Steve Lawrence, Columbia 43095 | 6 |
| 79 | 82 | 84 | — | IT'S FOR YOU — Cilla Black, Capitol 5258 | 3 |
| ★80 | — | — | — | WHEN YOU'RE YOUNG AND IN LOVE — Ruby & the Romantics, Kapp 615 | 1 |
| 81 | 92 | — | — | YOU REALLY GOT ME — Kinks, Reprise 0306 | 2 |
| 82 | 94 | — | — | I GUESS I'M CRAZY — Jim Reeves, RCA Victor 8383 | 4 |
| 83 | 87 | 98 | — | TILL THE END OF TIME — Ray Charles Singers, Command 4049 | 3 |
| ★84 | — | — | — | I DON'T WANT TO SEE YOU AGAIN — Peter & Gordon, Capitol 5272 | 1 |
| 85 | 97 | — | — | L-O-V-E — Nat King Cole, Capitol 5261 | 2 |
| 86 | 95 | 95 | — | RUNNIN' OUT OF FOOLS — Aretha Franklin, Columbia 43113 | 3 |
| 87 | 90 | — | — | BEACH GIRL — Pat Boone, Dot 16658 | 2 |
| 88 | 98 | — | — | BLESS OUR LOVE — Gene Chandler, Constellation 136 | 2 |
| 89 | 93 | 94 | 94 | SOON I'LL WED MY LOVE — John Gary, RCA Victor 8413 | 4 |
| ★90 | — | — | — | LUMBERJACK — Brook Benton, Mercury 72333 | 1 |
| 91 | — | — | — | BABY, BABY ALL THE TIME — Superbs, Dore 715 | 1 |
| 92 | 100 | — | — | I HAD A TALK WITH MY MAN — Mitty Collier, Chess 1907 | 2 |
| 93 | — | — | — | THE ANAHEIM, AZUSA & CUCAMONGA SEWING CIRCLE, BOOK REVIEW AND TIMING ASSOCIATION — Jan & Dean, Liberty 55724 | 1 |
| 94 | — | — | — | SO LONG, DEARIE — Louis Armstrong, Mercury 72338 | 1 |
| 95 | — | — | — | SOMEBODY NEW — Chuck Jackson, Wand 161 | 1 |
| 96 | — | — | — | DON'T SPREAD IT AROUND — Barbara Lynn, Jamie 1286 | 1 |
| 97 | — | — | — | LITTLE QUEENIE — Bill Black's Combo, Hi 2079 | 1 |
| 98 | — | — | — | I CAN'T BELIEVE WHAT YOU SAY — Ike & Tina Turner, Kent 402 | 1 |
| 99 | — | — | — | THE THINGS IN THIS HOUSE — Bobby Darin, Capitol 5257 | 1 |
| 100 | — | — | — | DARTELL STOMP — Mustangs, Providence 401 | 1 |

## HOT 100—A TO Z—(Publisher-Licensee)

All Cried Out (Kingsley, ASCAP) ... 59
Always Together (Damian, ASCAP) ... 33
Anaheim, Azusa & Cucamonga Sewing Circle, Book Review and Timing Association, The (Screen Gems-Columbia, BMI) ... 93
Baby, Baby All the Time (Embassy, BMI) ... 91
Baby Be Mine (Trio, BMI) ... 73
Baby Don't You Do It (Jogete, BMI) ... 42
Baby I Need Your Loving (Jobete, BMI) ... 11
Baby Love (Jobete, BMI) ... 51
Beach Girl (Blackwood-T.M., BMI) ... 87
Because (Ivy, ASCAP) ... 32
Bless Our Love (Jalynne-Curtom, BMI) ... 88
Bread and Butter (Acuff-Rose, BMI) ... 3
Candy to Me (Jobete, BMI) ... 69
Cat, The (Hastings, BMI) ... 67
Chug-A-Lug (Tree, BMI) ... 31
Come a Little Bit Closer (Picturetone, BMI) ... 39
Cousin of Mine (Kags, BMI) ... 60
Dancing in the Street (Jobete, BMI) ... 4
Dartell Stomp (Goins, BMI) ... 100
Death of an Angel (Limax, BMI) ... 63
Do Wah Diddy Diddy (Trio, BMI) ... 2
Do You Want to Dance (Clockus, BMI) ... 54
Don't Spread It Around (Crazy Cajun, BMI) ... 96
Door Is Still Open to My Heart, The (Berkshire, BMI) ... 62
Everybody Knows (Branston, BMI) ... 66
Everybody Loves Somebody (Sands, ASCAP) ... 26
From a Window (Maclen, BMI) ... 23
Funny (Pamper, BMI) ... 15
Funny Girl (Chappell, ASCAP) ... 50
G.T.O. (Buckhorn, BMI) ... 6
Good Night Baby (Trio, BMI) ... 57
Hard Day's Night, A (Unart-Maclen, BMI) ... 24
Haunted House (Venice-B Flat, BMI) ... 13
Have I the Right? (Duchess, BMI) ... 43
House of the Rising Sun (Gallico, BMI) ... 8
I Can't Believe What You Say (Modern-Placid, BMI) ... 98
I Don't Want to See Tomorrow (Sweco, BMI) ... 55
I Don't Want to See You Again (Maclen, BMI) ... 84
I Guess I'm Crazy (Mallory, BMI) ... 82
I Had a Talk With My Man (Chevis, BMI) ... 92
I Like It (Gil, BMI) ... 48
I Wanna Be With You (Morley, ASCAP) ... 68
I Wouldn't Trade You for the World (LeBill, BMI) 76
I'm Crying (Gallico, BMI) ... 61
I'm on the Outside (Lookin In) (South Mountain, BMI) ... 17
I've Got Sand in My Shoes (T.M., BMI) ... 52
In the Misty Moonlight (Four Star, BMI) ... 36
It Hurts to Be in Love (Screen Gems-Columbia, BMI) ... 7
It's All Over (Keetch, Caesar & Dino, BMI) ... 72
It's for You (Maclen, BMI) ... 79
James Bond Theme, The (Unart, BMI) ... 58
Knock! Knock! (Who's There) Saturday, ASCAP) ... 75
La La La La La (Jobete, BMI) ... 77
Last Kiss (Boblo, BMI) ... 14
Let It Be Me (Leeds, ASCAP) ... 22
Little Hondo (Sea of Tunes, BMI) ... 29
Little Queenie (Arc, BMI) ... 97
L-O-V-E (Roosevelt, BMI) ... 85
Lumberjack (Benday, BMI) ... 90
Matchbox (Knox, BMI) ... 18
Maybelline (Arc, BMI) ... 21
Mercy, Mercy (Cotillion-Vonglo, BMI) ... 37
Michael (Unart, BMI) ... 53
Oh, Pretty Woman (Acuff-Rose, BMI) ... 1
On the Street Where You Live (Chappell, ASCAP) .. 35
Out of Sight (Try Me, BMI) ... 28
Pearly Shells (Criterion, ASCAP) ... 65
Remember (Walkin' in the Sand) (Tender Tunes-Trio, BMI) ... 5
Rhythm (Jalynne-Curtom, BMI) ... 25
Ride the Wild Surf (Screen Gems-Columbia, BMI) .. 45
Runnin' Out of Fools (Roosevelt, BMI) ... 86
Save It for Me (Saturday-Gavadima, ASCAP) ... 10
Selfish One (Chevis, BMI) ... 40
She Wants t'Swim (Kalmann-C.C., ASCAP) ... 56
Slow Down (Venice, BMI) ... 27
Smack Dab in the Middle (Roosevelt, BMI) ... 74
So Long, Dearie (Morris, ASCAP) ... 94
Softly, as I Leave You (Miller, ASCAP) ... 41
Some Day We're Gonna Love Again (McLaughlin, BMI) ... 47
Somebody New (Ludix-Flomarlu, BMI) ... 95
Soon I'll Wed My Love (Laurel, ASCAP) ... 89
Summer Song, A (Unart-Woart, BMI) ... 12
Teen Beat '65 (Drive-In, BMI) ... 64
That's What Love Is Made Of (Jobete, BMI) ... 46
(There's) Always Something There to Remind Me (Ross-Jungnickel & Blue Seas, ASCAP) ... 49
Things in This House, The (T.M., BMI) ... 99
Till the End of Time (Joy, ASCAP) ... 83
Tobacco Road (Cedarwood, BMI) ... 44
Try Me (Lois, BMI) ... 71
20-75 (Jec, BMI) ... 38
We'll Sing in the Sunshine (Lupercalia, ASCAP). 9
When I Grow Up to Be a Man (Sea of Tunes, BMI) 16
When You're Young and in Love (Picturetone, BMI) ... 80
Where Did Our Love Go (Jobete, BMI) ... 19
Who Can I Turn To (Musical Comedy, BMI) ... 70
Why You Wanna Make Me Blue (Jobete, BMI) ... 30
Yet . . . I Know (Et Pourtant) (Leeds, ASCAP)... 78
You'll Never Get to Heaven (Jac-Blue Seas, ASCAP) 34
You Must Believe Me (Curtom, BMI) ... 20
You Really Got Me (Kassner, ASCAP) ... 81

## BUBBLING UNDER THE HOT 100

101. I SEE YOU ... Cathy & Joe, Smash 1929
102. SHAGGY DOG ... Mickey Lee Lane, Swan 4183
103. LETTER FROM ELAINA ... Casey Kasem, Warner Bros. 5474
104. I COULD CONQUER THE WORLD ... Shevelles, World Artists 1025
105. THAT'S WHERE IT'S AT ... Sam Cooke, RCA Victor 8426
106. DERN YA ... Ruby Wright, Ric 126-64
107. I DON'T KNOW ... Steve Alaimo, ABC-Paramount 10580
108. FEVER ... Alvin Robinson, Red Bird 10-010
109. IT HURTS TO BE IN LOVE ... Betty Everett, Vee Jay 610
110. WAIT FOR ME ... Rita Pavone, RCA Victor 8420
111. SOMEONE, SOMEONE ... Brian Poole, Monument 846
112. IF YOU WANT THIS LOVE ... Sonny Knight, Aura 403
113. THE END OF A SYMPHONY ... Allan Sherman & Boston Pops Ork (Fiedler), RCA Victor 8412
114. I SHOULD HAVE KNOWN BETTER ... George Martin & His Ork, United Artists 750
115. GATOR TAILS AND MONKEY RIBS ... Spats, ABC-Paramount 10585
116. SHE'S NOT THERE ... Zombies, Parrot 9695
117. LITTLE HONDA ... Beach Boys, Capitol R 5267 (Extended Play)
118. GET MY HANDS ON SOME LOVIN' ... Artistics, Okeh 7193
119. I WANNA THANK YOU ... Enchanters, Warner Bros. 5460
120. INVASION ... Buchanan & Greenfield, Novel 711
121. SOFTLY AS I LEAVE YOU ... Matt Monro, Liberty 55725
122. A HARD DAY'S NIGHT ... George Martin & His Ork, United Artists 750
123. OH NO NOT MY BABY ... Maxine Brown, Wand 162
124. SCRATCHY ... Travis Wammack, Ara 204
125. GARDEN IN THE RAIN ... Vic Dana, Dolton 99
126. ONCE A DAY ... Connie Smith, RCA Victor 8416
127. HIS LIPS GOT IN THE WAY ... Bernadette Castro, Colpix 747
128. OH NO! ... Ray Peterson, MGM 13269
129. WITHOUT THE ONE YOU LOVE ... Arthur Prysock, Old Town 1170
130. PROMISE YOU'LL TELL HER ... Swinging Blue Jeans, Imperial 66059
131. I'D RATHER BE RICH ... Robert Goulet, Columbia 43131
132. OH, MARIE ... Village Stompers, Epic 9718
133. OVER YOU ... Paul Revere & the Raiders, Columbia 43114
134. GO CAT GO ... Norma Jean, RCA Victor 8433
135. EVERYBODY'S DARLIN', PLUS MINE ... Browns, RCA Victor 8423

Compiled from national retail sales and radio station airplay by the Music Popularity Dept. of Record Market Research, Billboard.

# Billboard

For Week Ending October 10, 1964

# HOT 100

★ STAR performer—Sides registering greatest proportionate upward progress this week.

| This Week | 1 Wk. Ago | 2 Wks. Ago | 3 Wks. Ago | TITLE Artist, Label & Number | Weeks On Chart |
|---|---|---|---|---|---|
| 1 | 1 | 1 | 4 | OH, PRETTY WOMAN — Roy Orbison, Monument 851 | 7 |
| 2 | 2 | 6 | 9 | DO WAH DIDDY DIDDY — Manfred Mann, Ascot 2157 | 6 |
| 3 | 4 | 8 | 10 | DANCING IN THE STREET — Martha & the Vandellas, Gordy 7033 | 8 |
| 4 | 3 | 2 | 2 | BREAD AND BUTTER — Newbeats, Hickory 1269 | 9 |
| 5 | 5 | 5 | 7 | REMEMBER (Walkin' in the Sand) — Shangri-Las, Red Bird 10-008 | 8 |
| ★ 6 | 9 | 14 | 20 | WE'LL SING IN THE SUNSHINE — Gale Garnett, RCA Victor 8388 | 10 |
| 7 | 7 | 9 | 16 | IT HURTS TO BE IN LOVE — Gene Pitney, Musicor 1040 | 12 |
| 8 | 6 | 4 | 5 | G.T.O. — Ronny & the Daytonas, Mala 481 | 11 |
| ★ 9 | 14 | 29 | 42 | LAST KISS — J. Frank Wilson & the Cavaliers, Josie 923 | 6 |
| 10 | 12 | 18 | 30 | A SUMMER SONG — Chad Stuart & Jeremy Clyde, World Artists 1027 | 9 |
| ★ 11 | 16 | 21 | 34 | WHEN I GROW UP TO BE A MAN — Beach Boys, Capitol 5245 | 6 |
| 12 | 11 | 13 | 15 | BABY I NEED YOUR LOVING — Four Tops, Motown 1062 | 9 |
| 13 | 15 | 16 | 21 | FUNNY — Joe Hinton, Back Beat 541 | 9 |
| ★ 14 | 22 | 27 | 40 | LET IT BE ME — Betty Everett & Jerry Butler, Vee Jay 613 | 6 |
| 15 | 17 | 22 | 25 | I'M ON THE OUTSIDE (Looking In) — Little Anthony & the Imperials, DCP 1104 | 8 |
| 16 | 13 | 11 | 14 | HAUNTED HOUSE — Gene Simmons, Hi 2076 | 10 |
| 17 | 20 | 26 | 33 | YOU MUST BELIEVE ME — Impressions, ABC-Paramount 10581 | 6 |
| 18 | 18 | 23 | 32 | MATCHBOX — Beatles, Capitol 5255 | 6 |
| 19 | 8 | 3 | 1 | THE HOUSE OF THE RISING SUN — Animals, MGM 13264 | 10 |
| 20 | 10 | 10 | 18 | SAVE IT FOR ME — 4 Seasons, Philips 40225 | 7 |
| ★ 21 | 29 | 47 | 60 | LITTLE HONDA — Hondells, Mercury 72324 | 5 |
| ★ 22 | 31 | 45 | 63 | CHUG-A-LUG — Roger Miller, Smash 1926 | 6 |
| 23 | 23 | 30 | 37 | FROM A WINDOW — Billy J. Kramer, Imperial 66051 | 8 |
| 24 | 25 | 28 | 39 | RHYTHM — Major Lance, Okeh 7203 | 8 |
| 25 | 27 | 32 | 43 | SLOW DOWN — Beatles, Capitol 5255 | 6 |
| ★ 26 | 51 | — | — | BABY LOVE — Supremes, Motown 1066 | 2 |
| 27 | 30 | 39 | 50 | WHY YOU WANNA MAKE ME BLUE — Temptations, Gordy 7035 | 5 |
| 28 | 28 | 24 | 29 | OUT OF SIGHT — James Brown, Smash 1919 | 9 |
| ★ 29 | 43 | 61 | 90 | HAVE I THE RIGHT? — Honeycombs, Interphon 7707 | 4 |
| ★ 30 | 44 | 60 | 72 | TOBACCO ROAD — Nashville Teens, London 9689 | 5 |
| 31 | 35 | 46 | 56 | ON THE STREET WHERE YOU LIVE — Andy Williams, Columbia 43128 | 5 |
| ★ 32 | 42 | 52 | 81 | BABY DON'T YOU DO IT — Marvin Gaye, Tamla 54101 | 4 |
| ★ 33 | 45 | 63 | 82 | RIDE THE WILD SURF — Jan & Dean, Liberty 55724 | 4 |
| 34 | 38 | 48 | 52 | 20-75 — Willie Mitchell, Hi 2075 | 7 |
| ★ 35 | 46 | 56 | 78 | THAT'S WHAT LOVE IS MADE OF — Miracles, Tamla 54102 | 4 |
| 36 | 37 | 49 | 61 | MERCY, MERCY — Don Covay & the Goodtimers, Rosemart 801 | 6 |
| 37 | 39 | 62 | 74 | COME A LITTLE BIT CLOSER — Jay & the Americans, United Artists 759 | 5 |
| 38 | 19 | 7 | 3 | WHERE DID OUR LOVE GO — Supremes, Motown 1060 | 14 |
| 39 | 41 | 53 | 68 | SOFTLY, AS I LEAVE YOU — Frank Sinatra, Reprise 0301 | 6 |
| ★ 40 | 52 | 72 | — | I'VE GOT SAND IN MY SHOES — Drifters, Atlantic 2253 | 3 |
| 41 | 48 | 66 | — | I LIKE IT — Gerry and the Pacemakers, Laurie 3271 | 3 |
| 42 | 34 | 35 | 38 | YOU'LL NEVER GET TO HEAVEN (If You Break My Heart) — Dionne Warwick, Scepter 1282 | 9 |
| ★ 43 | 61 | 78 | — | I'M CRYING — Animals, MGM 13274 | 3 |
| ★ 44 | 62 | 84 | — | THE DOOR IS STILL OPEN TO MY HEART — Dean Martin, Reprise 0307 | 3 |
| 45 | 50 | 55 | 71 | FUNNY GIRL — Barbra Streisand, Columbia 43127 | 5 |
| 46 | 54 | 64 | 87 | DO YOU WANT TO DANCE — Del Shannon, Amy 911 | 4 |
| ★ 47 | 59 | 75 | — | ALL CRIED OUT — Dusty Springfield, Philips 40229 | 3 |
| ★ 48 | 60 | 73 | — | COUSIN OF MINE — Sam Cooke, RCA Victor 8426 | 3 |
| 49 | 21 | 12 | 13 | MAYBELLINE — Johnny Rivers, Imperial 66056 | 9 |
| 50 | 24 | 19 | 12 | A HARD DAY'S NIGHT — Beatles, Capitol 5222 | 13 |
| 51 | 55 | 81 | 85 | I DON'T WANT TO SEE TOMORROW — Nat King Cole, Capitol 5261 | 4 |
| ★ 52 | 66 | — | — | EVERYBODY KNOWS — Dave Clark Five, Epic 9722 | 2 |
| ★ 53 | 63 | 79 | 92 | DEATH OF AN ANGEL — Kingsmen, Wand 164 | 5 |
| 54 | 57 | 69 | 86 | GOOD NIGHT BABY — Butterflys, Red Bird 10-009 | 5 |
| ★ 55 | 70 | — | — | WHO CAN I TURN TO — Tony Bennett, Columbia 4341 | 2 |
| 56 | 64 | 85 | 88 | TEEN BEAT '65 — Sandy Nelson, Imperial 66060 | 4 |
| ★ 57 | 68 | — | — | I WANNA BE WITH YOU — Nancy Wilson, Capitol 5254 | 2 |
| 58 | 58 | 65 | 67 | THE JAMES BOND THEME — Billy Strange, Crescendo 320 | 8 |
| 59 | 53 | 42 | 44 | MICHAEL — Trini Lopez, Reprise 0300 | 8 |
| 60 | 65 | 70 | 70 | PEARLY SHELLS — Burl Ives, Decca 31659 | 5 |
| ★ 61 | 84 | — | — | I DON'T WANT TO SEE YOU AGAIN — Peter & Gordon, Capitol 5272 | 2 |
| 62 | 73 | 88 | — | BABY BE MINE — Jelly Beans, Red Bird 10-011 | 3 |
| 63 | 74 | 89 | — | SMACK DAB IN THE MIDDLE — Ray Charles and His Ork, ABC-Paramount 10588 | 3 |
| 64 | 56 | 50 | 54 | SHE WANTS T'SWIM — Chubby Checker, Parkway 922 | 7 |
| 65 | 71 | 77 | — | TRY ME — Jimmy Hughes, Fame 6403 | 3 |
| ★ 66 | 81 | 92 | — | YOU REALLY GOT ME — Kinks, Reprise 0306 | 3 |
| ★ 67 | 88 | 98 | — | BLESS OUR LOVE — Gene Chandler, Constellation 136 | 3 |
| ★ 68 | 94 | — | — | SO LONG, DEARIE — Louis Armstrong, Mercury 72338 | 2 |
| 69 | 76 | 76 | 80 | I WOULDN'T TRADE YOU FOR THE WORLD — Bachelors, London 9693 | 5 |
| 70 | 80 | — | — | WHEN YOU'RE YOUNG AND IN LOVE — Ruby & the Romantics, Kapp 615 | 2 |
| ★ 71 | 90 | — | — | LUMBERJACK — Brook Benton, Mercury 72333 | 2 |
| 72 | 77 | 80 | 83 | LA LA LA LA LA — Blendells, Reprise 0291 | 5 |
| 73 | 67 | 67 | 73 | THE CAT — Jimmy Smith, Verve 10330 | 6 |
| 74 | 87 | 90 | — | BEACH GIRL — Pat Boone, Dot 16653 | 3 |
| 75 | 72 | 74 | 76 | IT'S ALL OVER — Ben E. King, Atco 6315 | 5 |
| ★ 76 | — | — | — | AIN'T THAT LOVING YOU BABY — Elvis Presley, RCA Victor 8440 | 1 |
| ★ 77 | 92 | 100 | — | I HAD A TALK WITH MY MAN — Mitty Collier, Chess 1907 | 3 |
| ★ 78 | — | — | — | JUMP BACK — Rufus Thomas, Stax 157 | 1 |
| ★ 79 | 97 | — | — | LITTLE QUEENIE — Bill Black's Combo, Hi 2079 | 2 |
| 80 | 86 | 95 | 95 | RUNNIN' OUT OF FOOLS — Aretha Franklin, Columbia 43113 | 4 |
| 81 | 85 | 97 | — | L-O-V-E — Nat King Cole, Capitol 5261 | 3 |
| 82 | 93 | — | — | THE ANAHEIM, AZUSA & CUCAMONGA SEWING CIRCLE, BOOK REVIEW AND TIMING ASSOCIATION — Jan & Dean, Liberty 55724 | 2 |
| 83 | 91 | — | — | BABY, BABY ALL THE TIME — Superbs, Dore 715 | 2 |
| ★ 84 | — | — | — | OPPORTUNITY — Jewels, Dimension 1034 | 1 |
| ★ 85 | — | — | — | I SEE YOU — Cathy and Joe, Smash 1929 | 1 |
| ★ 86 | — | — | — | LEADER OF THE PACK — Shangri-Las, Red Bird 10-014 | 1 |
| 87 | 99 | — | — | THE THINGS IN THIS HOUSE — Bobby Darin, Capitol 5257 | 2 |
| ★ 88 | — | — | — | ASK ME — Elvis Presley, RCA Victor 8440 | 1 |
| ★ 89 | — | — | — | SOMETHING YOU GOT — Ramsey Lewis Trio, Argo 5481 | 1 |
| ★ 90 | — | — | — | UP ABOVE MY HEAD — Al Hirt, RCA Victor 8439 | 1 |
| 91 | — | — | — | IF YOU WANT THIS LOVE — Sonny Knight, Aura 403 | 1 |
| 92 | 100 | — | — | DARTELL STOMP — Mustangs, Providence 401 | 2 |
| 93 | 95 | — | — | SOMEBODY NEW — Chuck Jackson, Wand 161 | 2 |
| 94 | 96 | — | — | DON'T SPREAD IT AROUND — Barbara Lynn, Jamie 1286 | 2 |
| 95 | — | — | — | SHAGGY DOG — Mickey Lee Lane, Swan 4183 | 1 |
| 96 | 82 | 94 | — | I GUESS I'M CRAZY — Jim Reeves, RCA Victor 8383 | 5 |
| 97 | 98 | — | — | I CAN'T BELIEVE WHAT YOU SAY — Ike & Tina Turner, Kent 402 | 2 |
| 98 | — | — | — | YES I DO — Solomon Burke, Atlantic 2254 | 1 |
| 99 | — | — | — | THAT'S WHERE IT'S AT — Sam Cooke, RCA Victor 8426 | 1 |
| 100 | — | — | — | JUST A MOMENT AGO — Soul Sisters, Sue 111 | 1 |

## HOT 100—A TO Z—*(Publisher-Licensee)*


Ain't That Loving You Baby (Presley, BMI) ...... 76
All Cried Out (Kingsley, ASCAP) ...... 47
Anaheim, Azusa & Cucamonga Sewing Circle, Book Review and Timing Association, The (Screen Gems-Columbia, BMI) ...... 82
Ask Me (Presley, BMI) ...... 88
Baby, Baby All the Time (Embassy, BMI) ...... 83
Baby Be Mine (Trio, BMI) ...... 62
Baby Don't You Do It (Jobete, BMI) ...... 32
Baby I Need Your Loving (Jobete, BMI) ...... 12
Baby Love (Jobete, BMI) ...... 26
Beach Girl (Blackwood-T.M., BMI) ...... 74
Bless Our Love (Jalynne-Curtom, BMI) ...... 67
Bread and Butter (Acuff-Rose, BMI) ...... 4
Cat, The (Hastings, BMI) ...... 73
Chug-a-Lug (Tree, BMI) ...... 22
Come a Little Bit Closer (Picturetone, BMI) ...... 37
Cousin of Mine (Kags, BMI) ...... 48
Dancing in the Street (Jobete, BMI) ...... 3
Dartell Stomp (Goins, BMI) ...... 92
Death of an Angel (Limax, BMI) ...... 53
Do Wah Diddy Diddy (Trio, BMI) ...... 2
Do You Want to Dance (Clockus, BMI) ...... 46
Don't Spread It Around (Crazy Cajun, BMI) ...... 94
Door Is Still Open to My Heart, The (Berkshire, BMI) ...... 44
Everybody Knows (Branston, BMI) ...... 52
From a Window (Maclen, BMI) ...... 23
Funny (Pamper, BMI) ...... 13
Funny Girl (Chappell, ASCAP) ...... 45
G.T.O. (Buckhorn, BMI) ...... 8
Good Night Baby (Trio, BMI) ...... 54
Hard Day's Night, A (Unart-Maclen, BMI) ...... 50
Haunted House (Venice-B Flat, BMI) ...... 16
Have I the Right? (Duchess, BMI) ...... 29
House of the Rising Sun (Gallico, BMI) ...... 19
I Can't Believe What You Say (Modern-Placid, BMI) ...... 97
I Don't Want to See Tomorrow (Sweco, BMI) ...... 51
I Don't Want to See You Again (Maclen, BMI) ...... 61
I Guess I'm Crazy (Mallory, BMI) ...... 96
I Had a Talk With My Man (Chevis, BMI) ...... 77
I Like It (Gil, BMI) ...... 41
I See You (J.D.A., BMI) ...... 85
I Wanna Be With You (Morley, ASCAP) ...... 57
I Wouldn't Trade You for the World (LeBill, BMI). 69
I'm Crying (Gallico, BMI) ...... 43
I'm on the Outside (Looking In) (South Mountain, BMI) ...... 15
I've Got Sand in My Shoes (T.M., BMI) ...... 40
If You Want This Love (Har-Bock, BMI) ...... 91
It Hurts to Be in Love (Screen Gems-Columbia, BMI) ...... 7
It's All Over (Keetch, Caesar & Dino, BMI) ...... 75
James Bond Theme, The (Unart, BMI) ...... 58
Jump Back (East, BMI) ...... 78
Just a Moment Ago (McAllister-Sagittarius, BMI). 100
La La La La La (Jobete, BMI) ...... 72
Last Kiss (Boblo, BMI) ...... 9
Leader of the Pack (Tender Tunes-Trie, BMI) ...... 86
Let It Be Me (Leeds, ASCAP) ...... 14
Little Honda (Sea of Tunes, BMI) ...... 21
Little Queenie (Arc, BMI) ...... 79
L-O-V-E (Roosevelt, BMI) ...... 81
Lumberjack (Benday, BMI) ...... 71
Matchbox (Knox, BMI) ...... 18
Maybelline (Arc, BMI) ...... 49
Mercy, Mercy (Cotillion-Vonglo, BMI) ...... 36
Michael (Unart, BMI) ...... 59
Oh, Pretty Woman (Acuff-Rose, BMI) ...... 1
On the Street Where You Live (Chappell, ASCAP) .. 31
Opportunity (Screen Gems-Columbia, BMI) ...... 84
Out of Sight (Try Me, BMI) ...... 28
Pearly Shells (Criterion, ASCAP) ...... 60
Remember (Walkin' in the Sand) (Tender Tunes-Trio, BMI) ...... 5
Rhythm (Jalynne-Curtom, BMI) ...... 24
Ride the Wild Surf (Screen Gems-Columbia, BMI) .. 33
Runnin' Out of Fools (Roosevelt, BMI) ...... 80
Save It for Me (Saturday-Gavadima, ASCAP) ...... 20
Shaggy Dog (Survey, BMI) ...... 95
She Wants t'Swim (Kalmann-C.C., ASCAP) ...... 64
Slow Down (Venice, BMI) ...... 25
Smack Dab in the Middle (Roosevelt, BMI) ...... 63
So Long, Dearie (Morris, ASCAP) ...... 68
Softly, as I Leave You (Miller, ASCAP) ...... 39
Somebody New (Ludix-Flomarlu, BMI) ...... 93
Something You Got (Tune-Kel, BMI) ...... 89
Summer Song, A (Unart-Woart, BMI) ...... 10
Teen Beat '65 (Drive-In, BMI) ...... 56
That's What Love Is Made Of (Jobete, BMI) ...... 35
That's Where It's At (Kags, BMI) ...... 99
Things in This House, The (T.M., BMI) ...... 87
Tobacco Road (Cedarwood, BMI) ...... 30
Try Me (Lois, BMI) ...... 65
20-75 (Jec, BMI) ...... 34
Up Above My Head (Beechmont, BMI) ...... 90
We'll Sing in the Sunshine (Lupercalia, ASCAP) .. 6
When I Grow Up to Be a Man (Sea of Tunes, BMI). 11
When You're Young and in Love (Picturetone, BMI) ...... 70
Where Did Our Love Go (Jobete, BMI) ...... 38
Who Can I Turn To (Musical Comedy, BMI) ...... 55
Why You Wanna Make Me Blue (Jobete, BMI) ... 27
Yes I Do (Keetch, Caesar & Dino, BMI) ...... 98
You'll Never Get to Heaven (Jac-Blue Seas, ASCAP) 42
You Must Believe Me (Curtom, BMI) ...... 17
You Really Got Me (Kassner, ASCAP) ...... 66


## BUBBLING UNDER THE HOT 100

101. SHE'S NOT THERE ......Zombies, Parrot 9695
102. MY ADORABLE ONE ......Joe Simon, Vee Jay 609
103. IS IT TRUE ......Brenda Lee, Decca 31690
104. WAIT FOR ME ......Rita Pavone, RCA Victor 8420
105. I DON'T KNOW ......Steve Alaimo, ABC-Paramount 10580
106. LISTEN LONELY GIRL ......Johnny Mathis, Mercury 72339
107. I'M INTO SOMETHING GOOD ......Herman's Hermits, MGM 13280
108. SOON I'LL WED MY LOVE ......John Gary, RCA Victor 8413
109. APPLE OF MY EYE ......4 Seasons, Vee Jay 618
110. MAYBE THE LAST TIME ......James Brown, Smash 1919
111. I SHOULD HAVE KNOWN BETTER.George Martin & His Ork, United Artists 750
112. GARDEN IN THE RAIN ......Vic Dana, Dolton 99
113. GATOR TAILS AND MONKEY RIBS ......Spats, ABC-Paramount 10585
114. I WANNA THANK YOU ......Enchanters, Warner Bros. 5460
115. IT'S FOR YOU ......Cilla Black, Capitol 5258
116. TILL THE END OF TIME ......Ray Charles Singers, Command 4049
117. DERN YA ......Ruby Wright, RIC 126-64
118. I COULD CONQUER THE WORLD ......Shevelles, World Artists 1025
119. SCRATCHY ......Travis Wammack, Ara 204
120. THANK YOU FOR LOVING ME ......Sapphires, ABC-Paramount 10590
121. IT HURTS TO BE IN LOVE ......Betty Everett, Vee Jay 610
122. THE CLOCK ......Baby Washington, Sue 104
123. HIS LIPS GET IN THE WAY ......Bernadette Castro, Colpix 747
124. WENDY ......Beach Boys, Capitol R 5267 (Extended Play)
125. NEEDLE IN A HAYSTACK ......Velvelettes, V.I.P. 25007
126. WITHOUT THE ONE YOU LOVE ......Arthur Prysock, Old Town 1170
127. LA DE DA I LOVE YOU ......Inez & Charlie Foxx, Symbol 201
128. OH NO NOT MY BABY ......Maxine Brown, Wand 162
129. FEVER ......Alvin Robinson, Red Bird 10-010
130. LOST LOVE ......Shirelles, Scepter 1284
131. EVERY MINUTE EVERY HOUR ......Dean Martin, Reprise 0307
132. LITTLE HONDA ......Beach Boys, Capitol R 5267 (Extended Play)
133. THAT'S HOW STRONG MY LOVE IS..O. V. Wright With the Keys, Goldwax 106
134. AFTER LAUGHTER COMES TEARS ......Wendy Rene, Stax 154
135. SHE'S ALL RIGHT ......Jackie Wilson, Brunswick 55273

Compiled from national retail sales and radio station airplay by the Music Popularity Dept. of Record Market Research, Billboard.

# Billboard

For Week Ending October 17, 1964

# HOT 100

★ STAR performer—Sides registering greatest proportionate upward progress this week.

| This Week | 1 Wk. Ago | 2 Wks. Ago | 3 Wks. Ago | TITLE Artist, Label & Number | Weeks On Chart |
|---|---|---|---|---|---|
| 1 (Billboard Award) | 2 | 2 | 6 | DO WAH DIDDY DIDDY — Manfred Mann, Ascot 2157 | 7 |
| 2 | 3 | 4 | 8 | DANCING IN THE STREET — Martha & the Vandellas, Gordy 7033 | 9 |
| 3 | 1 | 1 | 1 | OH, PRETTY WOMAN — Roy Orbison, Monument 851 | 8 |
| 4 | 6 | 9 | 14 | WE'LL SING IN THE SUNSHINE — Gale Garnett, RCA Victor 8388 | 11 |
| ★5 | 9 | 14 | 29 | LAST KISS — J. Frank Wilson & the Cavalleers, Josie 923 | 7 |
| 6 | 5 | 5 | 5 | REMEMBER (Walkin' in the Sand) — Shangri-Las, Red Bird 10-008 | 9 |
| ★7 | 10 | 12 | 18 | A SUMMER SONG — Chad Stuart & Jeremy Clyde, World Artists 1027 | 10 |
| 8 | 7 | 7 | 9 | IT HURTS TO BE IN LOVE — Gene Pitney, Musicor 1040 | 13 |
| 9 | 11 | 16 | 21 | WHEN I GROW UP TO BE A MAN — Beach Boys, Capitol 5245 | 7 |
| ★10 | 14 | 22 | 27 | LET IT BE ME — Betty Everett & Jerry Butler, Vee Jay 613 | 7 |
| 11 | 4 | 3 | 2 | BREAD AND BUTTER — Newbeats, Hickory 1269 | 10 |
| ★12 | 26 | 51 | — | BABY LOVE — Supremes, Motown 1066 | 3 |
| ★13 | 21 | 29 | 47 | LITTLE HONDA — Hondells, Mercury 72324 | 6 |
| ★14 | 22 | 31 | 45 | CHUG-A-LUG — Roger Miller, Smash 1926 | 7 |
| 15 | 17 | 20 | 26 | YOU MUST BELIEVE ME — Impressions, ABC-Paramount 10581 | 7 |
| 16 | 12 | 11 | 13 | BABY I NEED YOUR LOVING — Four Tops, Motown 1062 | 10 |
| 17 | 18 | 18 | 23 | MATCHBOX — Beatles, Capitol 5255 | 7 |
| 18 | 13 | 15 | 16 | FUNNY — Joe Hinton, Back Beat 541 | 10 |
| 19 | 8 | 6 | 4 | G.T.O. — Ronny & the Daytonas, Mala 481 | 12 |
| ★20 | 29 | 43 | 61 | HAVE I THE RIGHT? — Honeycombs, Interphon 7707 | 5 |
| 21 | 15 | 17 | 22 | I'M ON THE OUTSIDE (Looking In) — Little Anthony & the Imperials, DCP 1104 | 9 |
| ★22 | 37 | 39 | 62 | COME A LITTLE BIT CLOSER — Jay & the Americans, United Artists 759 | 6 |
| ★23 | 33 | 45 | 63 | RIDE THE WILD SURF — Jan & Dean, Liberty 55724 | 5 |
| ★24 | 44 | 62 | 84 | THE DOOR IS STILL OPEN TO MY HEART — Dean Martin, Reprise 0307 | 4 |
| ★25 | 30 | 44 | 60 | TOBACCO ROAD — Nashville Teens, London 9689 | 6 |
| 26 | 27 | 30 | 39 | WHY YOU WANNA MAKE ME BLUE — Temptations, Gordy 7035 | 6 |
| 27 | 23 | 23 | 30 | FROM A WINDOW — Billy J. Kramer, Imperial 66051 | 9 |
| 28 | 31 | 35 | 46 | ON THE STREET WHERE YOU LIVE — Andy Williams, Columbia 43128 | 6 |
| ★29 | 43 | 61 | 78 | I'M CRYING — Animals, MGM 13274 | 4 |
| ★30 | 39 | 41 | 53 | SOFTLY, AS I LEAVE YOU — Frank Sinatra, Reprise 0301 | 7 |
| ★31 | 41 | 48 | 66 | I LIKE IT — Gerry and the Pacemakers, Laurie 3271 | 4 |
| 32 | 32 | 42 | 52 | BABY DON'T YOU DO IT — Marvin Gaye, Tamla 54101 | 5 |
| 33 | 34 | 38 | 48 | 20-75 — Willie Mitchell, Hi 2075 | 8 |
| 34 | 16 | 13 | 11 | HAUNTED HOUSE — Gene Simmons, Hi 2076 | 11 |
| 35 | 24 | 25 | 28 | RHYTHM — Major Lance, Okeh 7203 | 9 |
| 36 | 36 | 37 | 49 | MERCY, MERCY — Don Covay & the Goodtimers, Rosemart 801 | 7 |
| 37 | 40 | 52 | 72 | I'VE GOT SAND IN MY SHOES — Drifters, Atlantic 2253 | 4 |
| 38 | 19 | 8 | 3 | THE HOUSE OF THE RISING SUN — Animals, MGM 13264 | 11 |
| 39 | 25 | 27 | 32 | SLOW DOWN — Beatles, Capitol 5255 | 7 |
| ★40 | 52 | 66 | — | EVERYBODY KNOWS — Dave Clark Five, Epic 9722 | 3 |
| ★41 | 51 | 55 | 81 | I DON'T WANT TO SEE TOMORROW — Nat King Cole, Capitol 5261 | 5 |
| 42 | 48 | 60 | 73 | COUSIN OF MINE — Sam Cooke, RCA Victor 8426 | 4 |
| 43 | 46 | 54 | 64 | DO YOU WANT TO DANCE — Del Shannon, Amy 911 | 5 |
| 44 | 47 | 59 | 75 | ALL CRIED OUT — Dusty Springfield, Philips 40229 | 4 |
| 45 | 45 | 50 | 55 | FUNNY GIRL — Barbra Streisand, Columbia 43127 | 6 |
| 46 | 35 | 46 | 56 | THAT'S WHAT LOVE IS MADE OF — Miracles, Tamla 54102 | 5 |
| ★47 | 76 | — | — | AIN'T THAT LOVING YOU BABY — Elvis Presley, RCA Victor 8440 | 2 |
| ★48 | 61 | 84 | — | I DON'T WANT TO SEE YOU AGAIN — Peter & Gordon, Capitol 5272 | 3 |
| 49 | 55 | 70 | — | WHO CAN I TURN TO — Tony Bennett, Columbia 4341 | 3 |
| 50 | 20 | 10 | 10 | SAVE IT FOR ME — 4 Seasons, Philips 40225 | 8 |
| 51 | 54 | 57 | 69 | GOOD NIGHT BABY — Butterflys, Red Bird 10-009 | 6 |
| 52 | 56 | 64 | 85 | TEEN BEAT '65 — Sandy Nelson, Imperial 66060 | 5 |
| 53 | 53 | 63 | 79 | DEATH OF AN ANGEL — Kingsmen, Wand 164 | 6 |
| 54 | 62 | 73 | 88 | BABY BE MINE — Jelly Beans, Red Bird 10-011 | 4 |
| 55 | 28 | 28 | 24 | OUT OF SIGHT — James Brown, Smash 1919 | 10 |
| ★56 | 66 | 81 | 92 | YOU REALLY GOT ME — Kinks, Reprise 0306 | 4 |
| 57 | 57 | 68 | — | I WANNA BE WITH YOU — Nancy Wilson, Capitol 5254 | 3 |
| 58 | 58 | 58 | 65 | THE JAMES BOND THEME — Billy Strange, Crescendo 320 | 9 |
| ★59 | 86 | — | — | LEADER OF THE PACK — Shangri-Las, Red Bird 10-014 | 2 |
| 60 | 63 | 74 | 89 | SMACK DAB IN THE MIDDLE — Ray Charles and His Ork, ABC-Paramount 10588 | 4 |
| 61 | 68 | 94 | — | SO LONG, DEARIE — Louis Armstrong, Mercury 72338 | 3 |
| 62 | 72 | 77 | 80 | LA LA LA LA LA — Blendells, Reprise 0291 | 6 |
| 63 | 67 | 88 | 98 | BLESS OUR LOVE — Gene Chandler, Constellation 136 | 4 |
| 64 | 71 | 90 | — | LUMBERJACK — Brook Benton, Mercury 72333 | 3 |
| 65 | 65 | 71 | 77 | TRY ME — Jimmy Hughes, Fame 6403 | 4 |
| 66 | 70 | 80 | — | WHEN YOU'RE YOUNG AND IN LOVE — Ruby & the Romantics, Kapp 615 | 3 |
| 67 | 60 | 65 | 70 | PEARLY SHELLS — Burl Ives, Decca 31659 | 6 |
| ★68 | — | — | — | IS IT TRUE — Brenda Lee, Decca 31690 | 1 |
| 69 | 69 | 76 | 76 | I WOULDN'T TRADE YOU FOR THE WORLD — Bachelors, London 9693 | 6 |
| 70 | 77 | 92 | 100 | I HAD A TALK WITH MY MAN — Mitty Collier, Chess 1907 | 4 |
| ★71 | — | — | — | WENDY — Beach Boys, Capitol R 5267 (EP) | 1 |
| 72 | 74 | 87 | 90 | BEACH GIRL — Pat Boone, Dot 16658 | 4 |
| ★73 | 88 | — | — | ASK ME — Elvis Presley, RCA Victor 8440 | 2 |
| 74 | 78 | — | — | JUMP BACK — Rufus Thomas, Stax 157 | 2 |
| 75 | 79 | 97 | — | LITTLE QUEENIE — Bill Black's Combo, Hi 2079 | 3 |
| ★76 | 89 | — | — | SOMETHING YOU GOT — Ramsey Lewis Trio, Argo 5481 | 2 |
| 77 | 82 | 93 | — | THE ANAHEIM, AZUSA & CUCAMONGA SEWING CIRCLE, BOOK REVIEW AND TIMING ASSOCIATION — Jan & Dean, Liberty 55724 | 3 |
| 78 | 80 | 86 | 95 | RUNNIN' OUT OF FOOLS — Aretha Franklin, Columbia 43113 | 5 |
| ★79 | — | — | — | I'M INTO SOMETHING GOOD — Herman's Hermits, MGM 13280 | 1 |
| ★80 | — | — | — | TIME IS ON MY SIDE — Rolling Stones, London 9708 | 1 |
| 81 | 81 | 85 | 97 | L-O-V-E — Nat King Cole, Capitol 5261 | 4 |
| 82 | 85 | — | — | I SEE YOU — Cathy and Joe, Smash 1929 | 2 |
| 83 | 83 | 91 | — | BABY, BABY ALL THE TIME — Superbs, Dore 715 | 3 |
| 84 | 84 | — | — | OPPORTUNITY — Jewels, Dimension 1034 | 2 |
| ★85 | — | — | — | LITTLE HONDA — Beach Boys, Capitol R 5267 (EP) | 1 |
| 86 | 87 | 99 | — | THE THINGS IN THIS HOUSE — Bobby Darin, Capitol 5257 | 3 |
| ★87 | — | — | — | SHE'S NOT THERE — Zombies, Parrot 9695 | 1 |
| 88 | 90 | — | — | UP ABOVE MY HEAD — Al Hirt, RCA Victor 8439 | 2 |
| ★89 | — | — | — | LOOK AWAY — Garnet Mimms, United Artists 773 | 1 |
| ★90 | — | — | — | NEEDLE IN A HAYSTACK — Velvelettes, V.I.P. 25007 | 1 |
| 91 | 91 | — | — | IF YOU WANT THIS LOVE — Sonny Knight, Aura 403 | 2 |
| 92 | 92 | 100 | — | DARTELL STOMP — Mustangs, Providence 401 | 3 |
| 93 | 94 | 96 | — | DON'T SPREAD IT AROUND — Barbara Lynn, Jamie 1286 | 3 |
| 94 | 95 | — | — | SHAGGY DOG — Mickey Lee Lane, Swan 4183 | 2 |
| 95 | 97 | 98 | — | I CAN'T BELIEVE WHAT YOU SAY — Ike & Tina Turner, Kent 402 | 3 |
| 96 | 98 | — | — | YES I DO — Solomon Burke, Atlantic 2254 | 2 |
| 97 | — | — | — | WHEN YOU WALK IN THE ROOM — Searchers, Kapp 618 | 1 |
| 98 | — | — | — | GONE, GONE, GONE — Everly Brothers, Warner Bros. 5478 | 1 |
| 99 | — | — | — | HEY NOW — Lesley Gore, Mercury 72352 | 1 |
| 100 | — | — | — | GARDEN IN THE RAIN — Vic Dana, Dolton 99 | 1 |

## HOT 100—A TO Z—(Publisher-Licensee)


Ain't That Loving You Baby (Presley, BMI) ..... 47
All Cried Out (Kingsley, ASCAP) ..... 44
Anaheim, Azusa & Cucamonga Sewing Circle, Book Review and Timing Association, The (Screen Gems-Columbia, BMI) ..... 77
Ask Me (Presley, BMI) ..... 73
Baby, Baby All the Time (Embassy, BMI) ..... 83
Baby Be Mine (Trio, BMI) ..... 54
Baby Don't You Do It (Jobete, BMI) ..... 32
Baby I Need Your Loving (Jobete, BMI) ..... 16
Baby Love (Jobete, BMI) ..... 12
Beach Girl (Blackwood-T.M., BMI) ..... 72
Bless Our Love (Jalynne-Curtom, BMI) ..... 63
Bread and Butter (Acuff-Rose, BMI) ..... 11
Chug-a-lug (Tree, BMI) ..... 14
Come a Little Bit Closer (Picturetone, BMI) ..... 22
Cousin of Mine (Kags, BMI) ..... 42
Dancing in the Street (Jobete, BMI) ..... 2
Dartell Stomp (Goins, BMI) ..... 92
Death of an Angel (Limax, BMI) ..... 53
Do Wah Diddy Diddy (Trio, BMI) ..... 1
Do You Want to Dance (Clockus, BMI) ..... 43
Don't Spread It Around (Crazy Cajun, BMI) ..... 93
Door Is Still Open to My Heart, The (Berkshire, BMI) ..... 24
Everybody Knows (Branston, BMI) ..... 40
From a Window (Maclen, BMI) ..... 27
Funny (Pamper, BMI) ..... 18
Funny Girl (Chappell, ASCAP) ..... 45
G.T.O. (Buckhorn, BMI) ..... 19
Garden in the Rain (Campbell-Connelly, ASCAP) ... 100
Gone, Gone, Gone (Acuff-Rose, BMI) ..... 98
Good Night Baby (Trio, BMI) ..... 51
Haunted House (Venice-B Flat, BMI) ..... 34
Have I the Right? (Duchess, BMI) ..... 20
Hey Now (Jenny, ASCAP) ..... 99
House of the Rising Sun (Gallico, BMI) ..... 38
I Can't Believe What You Say (Modern-Placid, BMI) ..... 95
I Don't Want to See Tomorrow (Sweco, BMI) ..... 41
I Don't Want to See You Again (Maclen, BMI) ..... 48
I Had a Talk With My Man (Chevis, BMI) ..... 70
I Like It (Gil, BMI) ..... 31
I See You (J.D.A., BMI) ..... 82
I Wanna Be With You (Morley, ASCAP) ..... 57
I Wouldn't Trade You for the World (LeBill, BMI). 69
I'm Crying (Gallico, BMI) ..... 29
I'm on the Outside (Looking In) (South Mountain, BMI) ..... 21
I'm Into Something Good (Screen Gems-Columbia, BMI) ..... 79
I've Got Sand in My Shoes (T.M., BMI) ..... 37
If You Want This Love (Har-Bock, BMI) ..... 91
Is It True (Southern, ASCAP) ..... 68
It Hurts to Be in Love (Screen Gems-Columbia, BMI) ..... 8
James Bond Theme, The (Unart, BMI) ..... 58
Jump Back (East, BMI) ..... 74
La La La La La (Jobete, BMI) ..... 62
Last Kiss (Boblo, BMI) ..... 5
Leader of the Pack (Tender Tunes-Trio, BMI) ..... 59
Let It Be Me (Leeds, ASCAP) ..... 10
Little Honda—Beach Boys (Sea of Tunes, BMI) ..... 85
Little Honda—Hondells (Sea of Tunes, BMI) ..... 13
Little Queenie (Arc, BMI) ..... 75
Look Away (Rittenhouse-Mellin, BMI) ..... 89
L-O-V-E (Roosevelt, BMI) ..... 81
Lumberjack (Benday, BMI) ..... 64
Matchbox (Knox, BMI) ..... 17
Mercy, Mercy (Cotillion-Vonglo, BMI) ..... 36
Needle in a Haystack (Jobete, BMI) ..... 90
Oh, Pretty Woman (Acuff-Rose, BMI) ..... 3
On the Street Where You Live (Chappell, ASCAP). 28
Opportunity (Screen Gems-Columbia, BMI) ..... 84
Out of Sight (Try Me, BMI) ..... 55
Pearly Shells (Criterion, ASCAP) ..... 67
Remember (Walkin' in the Sand) (Tender Tunes-Trio, BMI) ..... 6
Rhythm (Jalynne-Curtom, BMI) ..... 35
Ride the Wild Surf (Screen Gems-Columbia, BMI). 23
Runnin' Out of Fools (Roosevelt, BMI) ..... 78
Save It for Me (Saturday-Gavadima, ASCAP) ..... 50
Shaggy Dog (Survey, BMI) ..... 94
She's Not There (Gallico, BMI) ..... 87
Slow Down (Venice, BMI) ..... 39
Smack Dab in the Middle (Roosevelt, BMI) ..... 60
So Long, Dearie (Morris, ASCAP) ..... 61
Softly, as I Leave You (Miller, ASCAP) ..... 30
Something You Got (Tune-Kel, BMI) ..... 76
Summer Song, A (Unart-Woart, BMI) ..... 7
Teen Beat '65 (Drive-In, BMI) ..... 52
That's What Love Is Made Of (Jobete, BMI) ..... 46
Things in This House, The (T.M., BMI) ..... 86
Time Is on My Side (Rittenhouse-Maygar, BMI) ... 80
Tobacco Road (Cedarwood, BMI) ..... 25
Try Me (Lois, BMI) ..... 65
20-75 (Jec, BMI) ..... 33
Up Above My Head (Beechmont, BMI) ..... 88
We'll Sing in the Sunshine (Lupercalia, ASCAP) .. 4
Wendy (Sea of Tunes, BMI) ..... 71
When I Grow Up to Be a Man (Sea of Tunes, BMI). 9
When You Walk in the Room (Metric, BMI) ..... 97
When You're Young and in Love (Picturetone, BMI). 66
Who Can I Turn To (Musical Comedy, BMI) ..... 49
Why You Wanna Make Me Blue (Jobete, BMI) .. 26
Yes I Do (Keetch, Caesar & Dino, BMI) ..... 96
You Must Believe Me (Curtom, BMI) ..... 15
You Really Got Me (Kassner, ASCAP) ..... 56


## BUBBLING UNDER THE HOT 100

101. CHAINED AND BOUND ..... Otis Redding, Volt 121
102. MY ADORABLE ONE ..... Joe Simon, Vee Jay 609
103. LISTEN LONELY GIRL ..... Johnny Mathis, Mercury 72339
104. AIN'T DOING TOO BAD ..... Bobby Bland, Duke 383
105. WHAT GOOD AM I WITHOUT YOU .. Marvin Gaye & Kim Weston, Tamla 54104
106. APPLE OF MY EYE ..... 4 Seasons, Vee Jay 618
107. MAYBE THE LAST TIME ..... James Brown, Smash 1919
108. GALE WINDS ..... Egyptian Combo, Norman 549
109. SLAUGHTER ON 10TH AVENUE ..... Ventures, Dolton 300
110. RIGHT OR WRONG ..... Ronnie Dove, Diamond 173
111. THANK YOU FOR LOVING ME ..... Sapphires, ABC-Paramount 10590
112. THAT'S WHERE IT'S AT ..... Sam Cooke, RCA Victor 8426
113. MAYBE TONIGHT ..... Shirelles, Scepter 1284
114. SOON I'LL WED MY LOVE ..... John Gary, RCA Victor 8413
115. EVERYTHING'S ALRIGHT ..... Newbeats, Hickory 12882
116. SCRATCHY ..... Travis Wammack, Ara 204
117. MY LOVE FORGIVE ME (Amore, Scusami) .... Robert Goulet, Columbia 43131
118. SOMEBODY NEW ..... Chuck Jackson, Wand 161
119. WAIT FOR ME ..... Rita Pavone, RCA Victor 8420
120. IT'S FOR ME ..... Cilla Black, Capitol 5258
121. OH NO NOT MY BABY ..... Maxine Brown, Wand 162
122. WHY (Doncha Be My Girl) ..... Chartbusters, Mutual 508
123. EVERY MINUTE EVERY HOUR ..... Dean Martin, Reprise 0307
124. ONCE A DAY ..... Connie Smith, RCA Victor 8416
125. LOST LOVE ..... Shirelles, Scepter 1284
126. GET MY HANDS ON SOME LOVIN' ..... Artistics, Okeh 7193
127. I COULD CONQUER THE WORLD ..... Shevelles, World Artists 1025
128. SHE'S ALL RIGHT ..... Jackie Wilson, Brunswick 55273
129. HIS LIPS GET IN THE WAY ..... Bernadette Castro, Colpix 747
130. LETTER FROM ELAINA ..... Casey Kasem, Warner Bros. 5474
131. THAT'S HOW STRONG MY LOVE IS .. O. V. Wright with the Keys, Goldwax 106
132. SPANISH GUITARS ..... Jerry Wallace, Challenge 59265
133. OH! MARIE ..... Village Stompers, Epic 9718
134. DO ANYTHING YOU WANNA ..... Harold Betters, Gateway 747
135. THAT'S ALL I NEED TO KNOW ..... Bobby Wood, Joy 288

Compiled from national retail sales and radio station airplay by the Music Popularity Dept. of Record Market Research, Billboard.

# Billboard HOT 100

**For Week Ending October 24, 1964**

★ **STAR** performer—Sides registering greatest proportionate upward progress this week.

| This Week | 1 Wk. Ago | 2 Wks. Ago | 3 Wks. Ago | TITLE, Artist, Label & Number | Weeks On Chart |
|---|---|---|---|---|---|
| 1 | 1 | 2 | 2 | DO WAH DIDDY DIDDY — Manfred Mann, Ascot 2157 | 8 |
| 2 | 2 | 3 | 4 | DANCING IN THE STREET — Martha & the Vandellas, Gordy 7033 | 10 |
| 3 | 5 | 9 | 14 | LAST KISS — J. Frank Wilson & the Cavaliers, Josie 923 | 8 |
| 4 | 4 | 6 | 9 | WE'LL SING IN THE SUNSHINE — Gale Garnett, RCA Victor 8388 | 12 |
| 5 | 3 | 1 | 1 | OH, PRETTY WOMAN — Roy Orbison, Monument 851 | 9 |
| ★6 | 12 | 26 | 51 | BABY LOVE — Supremes, Motown 1066 | 4 |
| 7 | 7 | 10 | 12 | A SUMMER SONG — Chad Stuart & Jeremy Clyde, World Artists 1027 | 11 |
| 8 | 10 | 14 | 22 | LET IT BE ME — Betty Everett & Jerry Butler, Vee Jay 613 | 8 |
| 9 | 9 | 11 | 16 | WHEN I GROW UP TO BE A MAN — Beach Boys, Capitol 5245 | 8 |
| 10 | 20 | 29 | 43 | HAVE I THE RIGHT? — Honeycombs, Interphon 7707 | 6 |
| 11 | 13 | 21 | 29 | LITTLE HONDA — Hondells, Mercury 72324 | 7 |
| 12 | 14 | 22 | 31 | CHUG-A-LUG — Roger Miller, Smash 1926 | 8 |
| 13 | 8 | 7 | 7 | IT HURTS TO BE IN LOVE — Gene Pitney, Musicor 1040 | 14 |
| ★14 | 24 | 44 | 62 | THE DOOR IS STILL OPEN TO MY HEART — Dean Martin, Reprise 0307 | 5 |
| 15 | 25 | 30 | 44 | TOBACCO ROAD — Nashville Teens, London 9689 | 7 |
| 16 | 22 | 37 | 39 | COME A LITTLE BIT CLOSER — Jay & the Americans, United Artists 759 | 7 |
| 17 | 23 | 33 | 45 | RIDE THE WILD SURF — Jan & Dean, Liberty 55724 | 6 |
| 18 | 6 | 5 | 5 | REMEMBER (Walkin' in the Sand) — Shangri-Las, Red Bird 10-008 | 10 |
| 19 | 15 | 17 | 20 | YOU MUST BELIEVE ME — Impressions, ABC-Paramount 10581 | 8 |
| ★20 | 59 | 86 | — | LEADER OF THE PACK — Shangri-Las, Red Bird 10-014 | 3 |
| 21 | 16 | 12 | 11 | BABY I NEED YOUR LOVING — Four Tops, Motown 1062 | 11 |
| 22 | 18 | 13 | 15 | FUNNY — Joe Hinton, Back Beat 541 | 11 |
| 23 | 11 | 4 | 3 | BREAD AND BUTTER — Newbeats, Hickory 1269 | 11 |
| ★24 | 29 | 43 | 61 | I'M CRYING — Animals, MGM 13274 | 5 |
| 25 | 40 | 52 | 66 | EVERYBODY KNOWS — Dave Clark Five, Epic 9722 | 4 |
| 26 | 31 | 41 | 48 | I LIKE IT — Gerry and the Pacemakers, Laurie 3271 | 5 |
| ★27 | 48 | 61 | 84 | I DON'T WANT TO SEE YOU AGAIN — Peter & Gordon, Capitol 5272 | 4 |
| 28 | 28 | 31 | 35 | ON THE STREET WHERE YOU LIVE — Andy Williams, Columbia 43128 | 7 |
| 29 | 30 | 39 | 41 | SOFTLY, AS I LEAVE YOU — Frank Sinatra, Reprise 0301 | 8 |
| 30 | 32 | 32 | 42 | BABY DON'T YOU DO IT — Marvin Gaye, Tamla 54101 | 6 |
| 31 | 33 | 34 | 38 | 20-75 — Willie Mitchell, Hi 2075 | 9 |
| ★32 | 47 | 76 | — | AIN'T THAT LOVING YOU BABY — Elvis Presley, RCA Victor 8440 | 3 |
| ★33 | 37 | 40 | 52 | I'VE GOT SAND IN MY SHOES — Drifters, Atlantic 2253 | 5 |
| 34 | 26 | 27 | 30 | WHY YOU WANNA MAKE ME BLUE — Temptations, Gordy 7035 | 7 |
| 35 | 36 | 36 | 37 | MERCY, MERCY — Don Covay & the Goodtimers, Rosemart 801 | 8 |
| 36 | 21 | 15 | 17 | I'M ON THE OUTSIDE (Looking In) — Little Anthony & the Imperials, DCP 1104 | 10 |
| 37 | 42 | 48 | 60 | COUSIN OF MINE — Sam Cooke, RCA Victor 8426 | 5 |
| 38 | 19 | 8 | 6 | G.T.O. — Ronny & the Daytonas, Mala 481 | 13 |
| 39 | 41 | 51 | 55 | I DON'T WANT TO SEE TOMORROW — Nat King Cole, Capitol 5261 | 6 |
| ★40 | 56 | 66 | 81 | YOU REALLY GOT ME — Kinks, Reprise 0306 | 5 |
| 41 | 49 | 55 | 70 | WHO CAN I TURN TO — Tony Bennett, Columbia 4341 | 4 |
| 42 | 44 | 47 | 59 | ALL CRIED OUT — Dusty Springfield, Philips 40229 | 5 |
| 43 | 46 | 35 | 46 | THAT'S WHAT LOVE IS MADE OF — Miracles, Tamla 54102 | 6 |
| 44 | 45 | 45 | 50 | FUNNY GIRL — Barbra Streisand, Columbia 43127 | 7 |
| ★45 | 68 | — | — | IS IT TRUE — Brenda Lee, Decca 31690 | 2 |
| 46 | 52 | 56 | 64 | TEEN BEAT '65 — Sandy Nelson, Imperial 66060 | 6 |
| 47 | 53 | 53 | 63 | DEATH OF AN ANGEL — Kingsmen, Wand 164 | 7 |
| 48 | 35 | 24 | 25 | RHYTHM — Major Lance, Okeh 7203 | 10 |
| 49 | 43 | 46 | 54 | DO YOU WANT TO DANCE — Del Shannon, Amy 911 | 6 |
| 50 | 27 | 23 | 23 | FROM A WINDOW — Billy J. Kramer, Imperial 66051 | 10 |
| 51 | 54 | 62 | 73 | BABY BE MINE — Jelly Beans, Red Bird 10-011 | 5 |
| 52 | 17 | 18 | 18 | MATCHBOX — Beatles, Capitol 5255 | 8 |
| ★53 | 73 | 88 | — | ASK ME — Elvis Presley, RCA Victor 8440 | 3 |
| 54 | 60 | 63 | 74 | SMACK DAB IN THE MIDDLE — Ray Charles and His Ork, ABC-Paramount 10588 | 5 |
| 55 | 51 | 54 | 57 | GOOD NIGHT BABY — Butterflys, Red Bird 10-009 | 7 |
| 56 | 63 | 67 | 88 | BLESS OUR LOVE — Gene Chandler, Constellation 136 | 4 |
| 57 | 64 | 71 | 90 | LUMBERJACK — Brook Benton, Mercury 72333 | 4 |
| 58 | 66 | 70 | 80 | WHEN YOU'RE YOUNG AND IN LOVE — Ruby & the Romantics, Kapp 615 | 4 |
| 59 | 61 | 68 | 94 | SO LONG, DEARIE — Louis Armstrong, Mercury 72338 | 4 |
| 60 | 70 | 77 | 92 | I HAD A TALK WITH MY MAN — Mitty Collier, Chess 1907 | 5 |
| 61 | 87 | — | — | SHE'S NOT THERE — Zombies, Parrot 9695 | 2 |
| 62 | 71 | — | — | WENDY — Beach Boys, Capitol R 5267 (EP) | 3 |
| 63 | 74 | 78 | — | JUMP BACK — Rufus Thomas, Stax 157 | 3 |
| 64 | 79 | — | — | I'M INTO SOMETHING GOOD — Herman's Hermits, MGM 13280 | 2 |
| 65 | 80 | — | — | TIME IS ON MY SIDE — Rolling Stones, London 9708 | 2 |
| 66 | 58 | 58 | 58 | THE JAMES BOND THEME — Billy Strange, Crescendo 320 | 10 |
| 67 | 57 | 57 | 68 | I WANNA BE WITH YOU — Nancy Wilson, Capitol 5254 | 4 |
| 68 | 78 | 80 | 86 | RUNNIN' OUT OF FOOLS — Aretha Franklin, Columbia 43113 | 6 |
| 69 | 62 | 72 | 77 | LA LA LA LA LA — Blendells, Reprise 0291 | 7 |
| 70 | 90 | — | — | NEEDLE IN A HAYSTACK — Velvelettes, V.I.P. 25007 | 2 |
| 71 | 97 | — | — | WHEN YOU WALK IN THE ROOM — Searchers, Kapp 618 | 2 |
| 72 | 72 | 74 | 87 | BEACH GIRL — Pat Boone, Dot 16653 | 5 |
| 73 | 75 | 79 | 97 | LITTLE QUEENIE — Bill Black's Combo, Hi 2079 | 4 |
| 74 | — | — | — | I'M GONNA BE STRONG — Gene Pitney, Musicor 1045 | 1 |
| 75 | 76 | 89 | — | SOMETHING YOU GOT — Ramsey Lewis Trio, Argo 5481 | 3 |
| 76 | 89 | — | — | LOOK AWAY — Garnet Mimms, United Artists 773 | 2 |
| 77 | — | — | — | REACH OUT FOR ME — Dionne Warwick, Scepter 1285 | 1 |
| 78 | 85 | — | — | LITTLE HONDA — Beach Boys, Capitol R 5267 (EP) | 2 |
| 79 | — | — | — | AIN'T DOING TOO BAD — Bobby Bland, Duke 383 | 1 |
| 80 | — | — | — | SLAUGHTER ON 10TH AVE. — Ventures, Dolton 300 | 1 |
| 81 | — | — | — | RIGHT OR WRONG — Ronnie Dove, Diamond 173 | 1 |
| 82 | — | — | — | DON'T EVER LEAVE ME — Connie Francis, MGM 13287 | 1 |
| 83 | 84 | 84 | — | OPPORTUNITY — Jewels, Dimension 1034 | 3 |
| ★84 | — | — | — | WHAT GOOD AM I WITHOUT YOU — Marvin Gaye & Kim Weston, Tamla 54104 | 1 |
| 85 | 98 | — | — | GONE, GONE, GONE — Everly Brothers, Warner Bros. 5478 | 2 |
| 86 | 83 | 83 | 91 | BABY, BABY ALL THE TIME — Superbs, Dore 715 | 4 |
| 87 | 88 | 90 | — | UP ABOVE MY HEAD — Al Hirt, RCA Victor 8439 | 3 |
| 88 | 94 | 95 | — | SHAGGY DOG — Mickey Lee Lane, Swan 4183 | 3 |
| 89 | — | — | — | YOU SHOULD HAVE SEEN THE WAY HE LOOKED AT ME — Dixie Cups, Red Bird 10-012 | 1 |
| 90 | — | — | — | EVERYTHING'S ALRIGHT — Newbeats, Hickory 1282 | 1 |
| 91 | 91 | 91 | — | IF YOU WANT THIS LOVE — Sonny Knight, Aura 403 | 3 |
| 92 | 96 | 98 | — | YES I DO — Solomon Burke, Atlantic 2254 | 3 |
| 93 | — | — | — | LITTLE MARIE — Chuck Berry, Chess 1912 | 1 |
| 94 | 99 | — | — | HEY NOW — Lesley Gore, Mercury 72352 | 2 |
| 95 | — | — | — | WALKING IN THE RAIN — Ronettes, Philles 123 | 1 |
| 96 | — | — | — | OH NO, NOT MY BABY — Maxine Brown, Wand 162 | 1 |
| 97 | — | — | — | CHAINED AND BOUND — Otis Redding, Volt 121 | 1 |
| 98 | 100 | — | — | GARDEN IN THE RAIN — Vic Dana, Dolton 99 | 2 |
| 99 | — | — | — | LISTEN LONELY GIRL — Johnny Mathis, Mercury 72339 | 1 |
| 100 | — | — | — | MY LOVE FORGIVE ME (Amore, Scusami) — Robert Goulet, Columbia 43131 | 1 |

## HOT 100—A TO Z–(Publisher-Licensee)

Ain't Doing Too Bad (Don, BMI) .... 79
Ain't That Loving You Baby (Presley, BMI) ... 32
All Cried Out (Kingsley, ASCAP) .... 42
Ask Me (Presley, BMI) ............. 53
Baby, Baby All the Time (Trio, BMI) .. 86
Baby Be Mine (Trio, BMI) .......... 51
Baby Don't You Do It (Jobete, BMI) .. 30
Baby I Need Your Loving (Jobete, BMI) 21
Baby Love (Jobete, BMI) ........... 6
Beach Girl (Blackwood-T.M., BMI) ... 72
Bless Our Love (Jalynne-Curtom, BMI) . 56
Bread and Butter (Acuff-Rose, BMI) .. 23
Chained and Bound (East-Time, BMI) . 97
Chug-A-Lug (Tree, BMI) ............ 12
Come a Little Bit Closer (Picturetone, BMI) 16
Cousin of Mine (Kags, BMI) ........ 37
Dancing in the Street (Jobete, BMI) . 2
Death of an Angel (Limax, BMI) .... 47
Do Wah Diddy Diddy (Trio, BMI) ... 1
Do You Want to Dance (Clockus, BMI) 49
Don't Ever Leave Me (Trio, BMI) ... 82
Door Is Still Open to My Heart, The (Berkshire, BMI) ... 14
Everybody Knows (Branston, BMI) .. 25
Everything's Alright (Acuff-Rose, BMI) 90
From a Window (Maclen, BMI) .... 50
Funny (Pamper, BMI) ............. 22
Funny Girl (Chappell, ASCAP) ..... 44
G.T.O. (Buckhorn, BMI) ........... 38
Garden in the Rain (Campbell-Connelly, ASCAP) 98
Gone, Gone, Gone (Acuff-Rose, BMI) 85
Good Night Baby (Trio, BMI) ..... 55
Have I the Right? (Duchess, BMI) .. 10
Hey Now (Jenny, BMI) ........... 94
I Don't Want to See Tomorrow (Sweco, BMI) 39
I Don't Want to See Again (Maclen, BMI) 27

I Had a Talk With My Man (Chevis, BMI) 60
I Like It (Gil, BMI) ................. 26
I Wanna Be With You (Morley, ASCAP) 67
I'm Crying (Gallico, BMI) ........... 24
I'm Gonna Be Strong (Screen Gems-Columbia, BMI) ... 74
I'm on the Outside (Looking In) (South Mountain, BMI) 36
I'm Into Something Good (Screen Gems-Columbia, BMI) 64
I've Got Sand in My Shoes (T.M., BMI) 33
If You Want This Love (Har-Rock, BMI) 91
Is It True (Southern, ASCAP) ...... 45
It Hurts to Be in Love (Screen Gems-Columbia, BMI) 13
James Bond Theme, The (Unart, BMI) 66
Jump Back (East, BMI) ............ 63
La La La La La (Jobete, BMI) ..... 69
Last Kiss (Boblo, BMI) ............ 3
Leader of the Pack (Tender Tunes-Trio, BMI) 20
Let It Be Me (Leeds, ASCAP) ...... 8
Listen Lonely Girl (Jenny, ASCAP) . 99
Little Honda (Screen Gems-Columbia, BMI) 95
Little Honda—Beach Boys (Sea of Tunes, BMI) 78
Little Honda—Hondells (Sea of Tunes, BMI) 11
Little Marie (Isalee, BMI) .......... 93
Little Queenie (Arc, BMI) ......... 73
Look Away (Rittenhouse-Mellin, BMI) 76
Lumberjack (Benday, BMI) ........ 57
Matchbox (Knox, BMI) ............ 52
Mercy, Mercy (Collition-Vonglo, BMI) 35
My Love Forgive Me (Amore, Scusami) (Gil, BMI) 100
Needle in a Haystack (Jobete, BMI) . 70
Oh No Not My Baby (Screen Gems-Columbia, BMI) 96
Oh, Pretty Woman (Acuff-Rose, BMI) 5
On the Street Where You Live (Chappell, ASCAP) 28
Opportunity (Screen Gems-Columbia, BMI) 83

Reach Out for Me (Ross Jungnickel-Blue Seas-Jac, BMI) ... 77
Remember (Walkin' in the Sand) (Tender Tunes-Trio, BMI) ... 18
Rhythm (Jalynne-Curtom, BMI) ..... 48
Ride the Wild Surf (Screen Gems-Columbia, BMI) 17
Right or Wrong (Combine, BMI) .... 81
Runnin' Out of Fools (Roosevelt, BMI) 68
Shaggy Dog (Survey, BMI) ........ 88
She's Not There (Gallico, BMI) .... 61
Slaughter on 10th Avenue (Chappell, ASCAP) 80
Smack Dab in the Middle (Roosevelt, BMI) 54
So Long, Dearie (Morris, ASCAP) .. 59
Softly, As I Leave You (Miller, ASCAP) 29
Something You Got (Tune-Kel, BMI) 75
Summer Song, A (Unart-Woart, BMI) 7
Teen Beat '65 (Drive-In, BMI) ..... 46
That's What Love Is Made Of (Jobete, BMI) 43
Time Is on My Side (Rittenhouse-Maygar, BMI) 65
Tobacco Road (Cedarwood, BMI) .. 15
20-75 (Jec, BMI) .................. 31
Up Above My Head (Beechmont, BMI) 87
Walking in the Rain (Screen Gems-Columbia, BMI) 95
We'll Sing in the Sunshine (Lupercalia, ASCAP) 4
Wendy (Sea of Tunes, BMI) ....... 62
What Good Am I Without You (Jobete, BMI) 84
When I Grow Up to Be a Man (Sea of Tunes, BMI) 9
When You Walk in the Room (Metric, BMI) 71
When You're Young and in Love (Picturetone, BMI) 58
Who Can I Turn To (Musical Comedy, BMI) 41
Why You Wanna Make Me Blue (Jobete, BMI) 34
Yes I Do (Keetch, Caesar & Dino, BMI) 92
You Must Believe Me (Jobete, BMI) . 19
You Really Got Me (Kassner, ASCAP) 40
You Should Have Seen the Way He Looked at Me (Trio, BMI) ... 89

## BUBBLING UNDER THE HOT 100

101. SOMETIMES I WISH I WERE A BOY ........... Lesley Gore, Mercury 72352
102. MY ADORABLE ONE ......... Joe Simon, Vee Jay 609
103. TIMES HAVE CHANGED ......... Irma Thomas, Imperial 66069
104. SHE UNDERSTANDS ME ......... Johnny Tillotson, MGM 13284
105. S-W-I-M ......... Bobby Freeman, Autumn 5
106. I SEE YOU ......... Cathy & Joe, Smash 1929
107. GALE WINDS ......... Egyptian Combo, Norman 549
108. MAYBE TONIGHT ......... Shirelles, Scepter 1284
109. THANK YOU FOR LOVING ME ......... Sapphires, ABC-Paramount 10590
110. SCRATCHY ......... Travis Wammack, Ara 204
111. THAT'S WHERE IT'S AT ......... Sam Cooke, RCA Victor 8426
112. APPLE OF MY EYE ......... Four Seasons, Vee Jay 618
113. DON'T SPREAD IT AROUND ......... Barbara Lynn, Jamie 1286
114. THIS LITTLE GIRL OF MINE ......... Righteous Brothers, Moonglow 235
115. FOUR STRONG WINDS ......... Bobby Bare, RCA Victor 8443
116. WHY (DONCHA BE MY GIRL) ......... Lorne Green, RCA Victor 8444
117. RINGO ......... Chartbusters, Mutual 508
118. I'VE GOT THE SKILL ......... Jackie Ross, Chess 1913
119. THE JERK ......... Larks, Money 106
120. THE DODO ......... Lou Johnson, Big Hill 553
121. KENTUCKY BLUEBIRD ......... Connie Smith, RCA Victor 8416
122. ONCE A DAY ......... King Curtis, Capitol 5270
123. HIDE AWAY ......... O. V. Wright with the Keys, Goldwax 106
124. THAT'S HOW STRONG MY LOVE IS ......... Ace Cannon, Hi 2081
125. EMPTY ARMS ......... Volumes, American Arts 6
126. GOTTA GIVE HER LOVE ......... Fats Domino, ABC-Paramount 10596
127. HEARTBREAK HILL ......... Simon Scott, Imperial 66066
128. MOVE IT BABY ......... Terry Black, Tollie 9026
129. THE LONG SHIPS ......... Charles Albertine, Colpix 726
130. DO YOU LOVE ME ......... Harold Betters, Gateway 747
131. SPANISH GUITARS ......... Jerry Wallace, Challenge 59265
132. THAT'S ALL I NEED TO KNOW ......... Bobby Wood, Joy 288
133. DON'T SHUT ME OUT ......... Sammy Davis Jr., Reprise 0322
134. MUMBLES ......... Oscar Peterson Trio, Mercury 72342

Compiled from national retail sales and radio station airplay by the Music Popularity Dept. of Record Market Research, Billboard.

# Billboard HOT 100

*For Week Ending October 31, 1964*

★ STAR performer—Sides registering greatest proportionate upward progress this week.

| This Week | 1 Wk. Ago | 2 Wks. Ago | 3 Wks. Ago | TITLE Artist, Label & Number | Weeks On Chart |
|---|---|---|---|---|---|
| 1 | 6 | 12 | 26 | BABY LOVE — Supremes, Motown 1066 | 5 |
| 2 | 1 | 1 | 2 | DO WAH DIDDY DIDDY — Manfred Mann, Ascot 2157 | 9 |
| 3 | 3 | 5 | 9 | LAST KISS — J. Frank Wilson & the Cavaliers, Josie 923 | 9 |
| 4 | 4 | 4 | 6 | WE'LL SING IN THE SUNSHINE — Gale Garnett, RCA Victor 8388 | 13 |
| 5 | 2 | 2 | 3 | DANCING IN THE STREET — Martha & the Vandellas, Gordy 7033 | 11 |
| 6 | 8 | 10 | 14 | LET IT BE ME — Betty Everett & Jerry Butler, Vee Jay 613 | 9 |
| ★7 | 10 | 20 | 29 | HAVE I THE RIGHT? — Honeycombs, Interphon 7707 | 7 |
| 8 | 5 | 3 | 1 | OH, PRETTY WOMAN — Roy Orbison, Monument 851 | 10 |
| 9 | 11 | 13 | 21 | LITTLE HONDA — Hondells, Mercury 72324 | 8 |
| 10 | 12 | 14 | 22 | CHUG-A-LUG — Roger Miller, Smash 1926 | 9 |
| ★11 | 16 | 22 | 37 | COME A LITTLE BIT CLOSER — Jay & the Americans, United Artists 759 | 8 |
| 12 | 14 | 24 | 44 | THE DOOR IS STILL OPEN TO MY HEART — Dean Martin, Reprise 0307 | 6 |
| 13 | 7 | 7 | 10 | A SUMMER SONG — Chad Stuart & Jeremy Clyde, World Artists 1027 | 12 |
| ★14 | 20 | 59 | 86 | LEADER OF THE PACK — Shangri-Las, Red Bird 10-014 | 4 |
| 15 | 15 | 25 | 30 | TOBACCO ROAD — Nashville Teens, London 9689 | 8 |
| 16 | 17 | 23 | 33 | RIDE THE WILD SURF — Jan & Dean, Liberty 55724 | 7 |
| 17 | 9 | 9 | 11 | WHEN I GROW UP TO BE A MAN — Beach Boys, Capitol 5245 | 9 |
| ★18 | 26 | 31 | 41 | I LIKE IT — Gerry and the Pacemakers, Laurie 3271 | 6 |
| ★19 | 25 | 40 | 52 | EVERYBODY KNOWS — Dave Clark Five, Epic 9722 | 5 |
| ★20 | 27 | 48 | 61 | I DON'T WANT TO SEE YOU AGAIN — Peter & Gordon, Capitol 5272 | 5 |
| 21 | 24 | 29 | 43 | I'M CRYING — Animals, MGM 13274 | 6 |
| 22 | 13 | 8 | 7 | IT HURTS TO BE IN LOVE — Gene Pitney, Musicor 1040 | 15 |
| ★23 | 32 | 47 | 76 | AIN'T THAT LOVING YOU BABY — Elvis Presley, RCA Victor 8440 | 4 |
| 24 | 19 | 15 | 17 | YOU MUST BELIEVE ME — Impressions, ABC-Paramount 10581 | 9 |
| 25 | 21 | 16 | 12 | BABY I NEED YOUR LOVING — Four Tops, Motown 1062 | 12 |
| 26 | 18 | 6 | 5 | REMEMBER (Walkin' in the Sand) — Shangri-Las, Red Bird 10-008 | 11 |
| 27 | 29 | 30 | 39 | SOFTLY, AS I LEAVE YOU — Frank Sinatra, Reprise 0301 | 9 |
| 28 | 23 | 11 | 4 | BREAD AND BUTTER — Newbeats, Hickory 1269 | 12 |
| 29 | 30 | 32 | 32 | BABY DON'T YOU DO IT — Marvin Gaye, Tamla 54101 | 7 |
| ★30 | 45 | 68 | — | IS IT TRUE — Brenda Lee, Decca 31690 | 3 |
| ★31 | 53 | 73 | 88 | ASK ME — Elvis Presley, RCA Victor 8440 | 4 |
| 32 | 40 | 56 | 66 | YOU REALLY GOT ME — Kinks, Reprise 0306 | 6 |
| 33 | 37 | 42 | 48 | COUSIN OF MINE — Sam Cooke, RCA Victor 8426 | 6 |
| 34 | 39 | 41 | 51 | I DON'T WANT TO SEE TOMORROW — Nat King Cole, Capitol 5261 | 7 |
| 35 | 28 | 28 | 31 | ON THE STREET WHERE YOU LIVE — Andy Williams, Columbia 43128 | 8 |
| 36 | 41 | 49 | 55 | WHO CAN I TURN TO — Tony Bennett, Columbia 4341 | 5 |
| 37 | 33 | 37 | 40 | I'VE GOT SAND IN MY SHOES — Drifters, Atlantic 2253 | 6 |
| 38 | 34 | 26 | 27 | WHY YOU WANNA MAKE ME BLUE — Temptations, Gordy 7035 | 8 |
| 39 | 22 | 18 | 13 | FUNNY — Joe Hinton, Back Beat 541 | 12 |
| 40 | 31 | 33 | 34 | 20-75 — Willie Mitchell, Hi 2075 | 10 |
| 41 | 42 | 44 | 47 | ALL CRIED OUT — Dusty Springfield, Philips 40229 | 6 |
| 42 | 47 | 53 | 53 | DEATH OF AN ANGEL — Kingsmen, Wand 164 | 8 |
| 43 | 35 | 36 | 36 | MERCY, MERCY — Don Covay & the Goodtimers, Rosemart 801 | 9 |
| 44 | 46 | 52 | 56 | TEEN BEAT '65 — Sandy Nelson, Imperial 66060 | 7 |
| ★45 | 61 | 87 | — | SHE'S NOT THERE — Zombies, Parrot 9695 | 3 |
| ★46 | 65 | 80 | — | TIME IS ON MY SIDE — Rolling Stones, London 9708 | 3 |
| 47 | 44 | 45 | 45 | FUNNY GIRL — Barbra Streisand, Columbia 43127 | 8 |
| 48 | 56 | 63 | 67 | BLESS OUR LOVE — Gene Chandler, Constellation 136 | 6 |
| 49 | 43 | 46 | — | DO YOU WANT TO DANCE — Del Shannon, Amy 911 | 7 |
| 50 | 58 | 66 | 70 | WHEN YOU'RE YOUNG AND IN LOVE — Ruby & the Romantics, Kapp 615 | 5 |
| ★51 | 74 | — | — | I'M GONNA BE STRONG — Gene Pitney, Musicor 1045 | 2 |
| 52 | 54 | 60 | 63 | SMACK DAB IN THE MIDDLE — Ray Charles and His Ork, ABC-Paramount 10588 | 6 |
| 53 | 57 | 64 | 71 | LUMBERJACK — Brook Benton, Mercury 72333 | 5 |
| 54 | 62 | 71 | — | WENDY — Beach Boys, Capitol R 5267 (EP) | 3 |
| 55 | 60 | 70 | 77 | I HAD A TALK WITH MY MAN — Mitty Collier, Chess 1907 | 6 |
| 56 | 59 | 61 | 68 | SO LONG, DEARIE — Louis Armstrong, Mercury 72338 | 5 |
| 57 | 64 | 79 | — | I'M INTO SOMETHING GOOD — Herman's Hermits, MGM 13280 | 3 |
| ★58 | 71 | 97 | — | WHEN YOU WALK IN THE ROOM — Searchers, Kapp 618 | 3 |
| 59 | 63 | 74 | 78 | JUMP BACK — Rufus Thomas, Stax 157 | 4 |
| 60 | 51 | 54 | 62 | BABY BE MINE — Jelly Beans, Red Bird 10-011 | 6 |
| ★61 | 81 | — | — | RIGHT OR WRONG — Ronnie Dove, Diamond 173 | 2 |
| 62 | — | — | — | RINGO — Lorne Green, RCA Victor 8444 | 1 |
| 63 | 70 | 90 | — | NEEDLE IN A HAYSTACK — Velvelettes, V.I.P. 25007 | 3 |
| ★64 | 89 | — | — | YOU SHOULD HAVE SEEN THE WAY HE LOOKED AT ME — Dixie Cups, Red Bird 10-012 | 2 |
| 65 | 68 | 78 | 80 | RUNNIN' OUT OF FOOLS — Aretha Franklin, Columbia 43113 | 7 |
| 66 | 79 | — | — | AIN'T DOING TOO BAD — Bobby Bland, Duke 383 | 2 |
| 67 | 67 | 57 | 57 | I WANNA BE WITH YOU — Nancy Wilson, Capitol 5254 | 5 |
| 68 | 80 | — | — | SLAUGHTER ON 10TH AVE. — Ventures, Dolton 300 | 2 |
| 69 | 77 | — | — | REACH OUT FOR ME — Dionne Warwick, Scepter 1285 | 2 |
| 70 | — | — | — | MR. LONELY — Bobby Vinton, Epic 9730 | 1 |
| 71 | 88 | 94 | 95 | SHAGGY DOG — Mickey Lee Lane, Swan 4183 | 4 |
| 72 | 75 | 76 | 89 | SOMETHING YOU GOT — Ramsey Lewis Trio, Argo 5481 | 4 |
| 73 | 78 | 85 | — | LITTLE HONDA — Beach Boys, Capitol R 5267 (EP) | 3 |
| 74 | 85 | 98 | — | GONE, GONE, GONE — Everly Brothers, Warner Bros. 5478 | 3 |
| 75 | 82 | — | — | DON'T EVER LEAVE ME — Connie Francis, MGM 13287 | 2 |
| 76 | 76 | 89 | — | LOOK AWAY — Garnet Mimms, United Artists 773 | 3 |
| 77 | 69 | 62 | 72 | LA LA LA LA LA — Blendells, Reprise 0291 | 8 |
| 78 | 90 | — | — | EVERYTHING'S ALRIGHT — Newbeats, Hickory 1282 | 2 |
| 79 | 83 | 84 | 84 | OPPORTUNITY — Jewels, Dimension 1034 | 4 |
| 80 | 95 | — | — | WALKING IN THE RAIN — Ronettes, Philles 123 | 2 |
| 81 | 84 | — | — | WHAT GOOD AM I WITHOUT YOU — Marvin Gaye & Kim Weston, Tamla 54104 | 2 |
| 82 | 99 | — | — | LISTEN LONELY GIRL — Johnny Mathis, Mercury 72339 | 2 |
| 83 | — | — | — | SIDEWALK SURFIN' — Jan & Dean, Liberty 55727 | 1 |
| 84 | 86 | 83 | 83 | BABY, BABY ALL THE TIME — Superbs, Dore 715 | 5 |
| 85 | 87 | 88 | 90 | UP ABOVE MY HEAD — Al Hirt, RCA Victor 8439 | 4 |
| 86 | — | — | — | AIN'T IT THE TRUTH — Mary Wells, 20th Century-Fox 544 | 1 |
| 87 | — | — | — | S-W-I-M — Bobby Freeman, Autumn 5 | 1 |
| 88 | — | — | — | MAYBE TONIGHT — Shirelles, Scepter 1284 | 1 |
| 89 | 94 | 99 | — | HEY NOW — Lesley Gore, Mercury 72352 | 3 |
| 90 | — | — | — | MOUNTAIN OF LOVE — Johnny Rivers, Imperial 66075 | 1 |
| 91 | — | — | — | SHE UNDERSTANDS ME — Johnny Tillotson, MGM 13284 | 1 |
| 92 | 100 | — | — | MY LOVE FORGIVE ME (Amore, Scusami) — Robert Goulet, Columbia 43131 | 2 |
| 93 | 93 | — | — | LITTLE MARIE — Chuck Berry, Chess 1912 | 2 |
| 94 | 96 | — | — | OH NO, NOT MY BABY — Maxine Brown, Wand 162 | 2 |
| 95 | 97 | — | — | CHAINED AND BOUND — Otis Redding, Volt 121 | 2 |
| 96 | — | — | — | SOMETIMES I WISH I WERE A BOY — Lesley Gore, Mercury 72352 | 1 |
| 97 | 98 | 100 | — | GARDEN IN THE RAIN — Vic Dana, Dolton 99 | 3 |
| 98 | — | — | — | FOUR STRONG WINDS — Bobby Bare, RCA Victor 8443 | 1 |
| 99 | — | — | — | HEARTBREAK HILL — Fats Domino, ABC-Paramount 10596 | 1 |
| 100 | — | — | — | IT AIN'T ME, BABE — Johnny Cash, Columbia 43145 | 1 |

## BUBBLING UNDER THE HOT 100

101. CALIFORNIA BOUND — Ronny & the Daytonas, Mala 490
102. STOP TAKIN' ME FOR GRANTED — Mary Wells, 20th Century-Fox 544
103. TIMES HAVE CHANGED — Irma Thomas, Imperial 66049
104. GALE WINDS — Egyptian Combo, Norman 8416
105. IF YOU WANT THIS LOVE — Sonny Knight, Aura 403
106. THANK YOU FOR LOVING ME — Sapphires, ABC-Paramount 10590
107. KENTUCKY BLUEBIRD — Lou Johnson, Big Hill 553
108. I'VE GOT THE SKILLS — Jackie Ross, Chess 1913
109. THE DODO — Jumpin' Gene Simmons, Hi 2080
110. I HOPE HE BREAKS YOUR HEART — Neil Sedaka, RCA Victor 8453
111. I SEE YOU — Cathy & Joe, Smash 1929
112. YES I DO — Solomon Burke, Atlantic 2254
113. BEAUTICIAN BLUES — B. B. King, Kent 403
114. UNLESS YOU CARE — Terry Black, Tollie 9026
115. THE JERK — Larks, Money 106
116. EVEN THE BAD TIMES ARE GOOD — Jerry Wallace, Challenge 59265
117. HIDE AWAY — King Curtis, Capitol 5270
118. SCRATCHY — Travis Wammack, Ara 204
119. ONCE A DAY — Connie Smith, RCA Victor 8416
120. EMPTY ARMS — Ace Cannon, Hi 2081
121. GOTTA GIVE HER LOVE — Volumes, American Arts 8
122. HIGH HEEL SNEAKERS — Jerry Lee Lewis, Smash 1930
123. I LOVE YOU (I JUST LOVE YOU) — Lloyd Price, Monument 856
124. THAT'S WHERE IT'S AT — Sam Cooke, RCA Victor 8426
125. ONE MORE TIME — Ray Charles Singers, Command 4057
126. SLOOP DANCE — Vibrations, Okeh 7205
127. DO ANYTHING YOU WANNA — Harold Betters, Gateway 747
128. A THOUSAND CUPS OF HAPPINESS — Connie Francis, MGM 13287
129. WE HAVE SOMETHING MORE — Joe Henderson, Back Beat 532
130. THAT'S ALL I NEED TO KNOW — Bobby Wood, Joy 288
131. THE LUMBERJACK — Hal Willis, Sims 207
132. DON'T SHUT ME OUT — Sammy Davis Jr., Reprise 0322
133. MUMBLES — Oscar Peterson Trio, Mercury 72342
134. OH! MARIE — Village Stompers, Epic 9718
135. PUSHIN' A GOOD THING TOO FAR — Barbara Lewis, Atlantic 2255

*Compiled from national retail sales and radio station airplay by the Music Popularity Dept. of Record Market Research, Billboard.*

# Billboard HOT 100

*For Week Ending November 7, 1964*

★ STAR performer—Sides registering greatest proportionate upward progress this week.

| This Week | 1 Wk. Ago | 2 Wks. Ago | TITLE, Artist, Label & Number | Weeks On Chart |
|---|---|---|---|---|
| 1 | 1 | 6 | 12 | BABY LOVE — Supremes, Motown 1066 | 6 |
| 2 | 3 | 3 | 5 | LAST KISS — J. Frank Wilson & the Cavaliers, Josie 923 | 10 |
| 3 | 2 | 1 | 1 | DO WAH DIDDY DIDDY — Manfred Mann, Ascot 2157 | 10 |
| ★4 | 14 | 20 | 59 | LEADER OF THE PACK — Shangri-Las, Red Bird 10-014 | |
| 5 | 6 | 8 | 10 | LET IT BE ME — Betty Everett & Jerry Butler, Vee Jay 613 | 10 |
| 6 | 7 | 10 | 20 | HAVE I THE RIGHT? — Honeycombs, Interphon 7707 | 8 |
| ★7 | 11 | 16 | 22 | COME A LITTLE BIT CLOSER — Jay & the Americans, United Artists 759 | 9 |
| ★8 | 12 | 14 | 24 | THE DOOR IS STILL OPEN TO MY HEART — Dean Martin, Reprise 0307 | 7 |
| 9 | 10 | 12 | 14 | CHUG-A-LUG — Roger Miller, Smash 1926 | 10 |
| 10 | 4 | 4 | 4 | WE'LL SING IN THE SUNSHINE — Gale Garnett, RCA Victor 8388 | 14 |
| 11 | 8 | 5 | 3 | OH, PRETTY WOMAN — Roy Orbison, Monument 851 | 11 |
| 12 | 5 | 2 | 2 | DANCING IN THE STREET — Martha & the Vandellas, Gordy 7033 | 12 |
| 13 | 9 | 11 | 13 | LITTLE HONDA — Hondells, Mercury 72324 | 9 |
| 14 | 15 | 15 | 25 | TOBACCO ROAD — Nashville Teens, London 9689 | 7 |
| 15 | 19 | 25 | 40 | EVERYBODY KNOWS — Dave Clark Five, Epic 9722 | 6 |
| 16 | 20 | 27 | 48 | I DON'T WANT TO SEE YOU AGAIN — Peter & Gordon, Capitol 5272 | 6 |
| 17 | 18 | 26 | 31 | I LIKE IT — Gerry and the Pacemakers, Laurie 3271 | 7 |
| ★18 | 23 | 32 | 47 | AIN'T THAT LOVING YOU BABY — Elvis Presley, RCA Victor 8440 | 5 |
| 19 | 21 | 24 | 29 | I'M CRYING — Animals, MGM 13274 | 7 |
| 20 | 32 | 40 | 56 | YOU REALLY GOT ME — Kinks, Reprise 0306 | 7 |
| 21 | 13 | 7 | 7 | A SUMMER SONG — Chad Stuart & Jeremy Clyde, World Artists 1027 | 13 |
| ★22 | 45 | 61 | 87 | SHE'S NOT THERE — Zombies, Parrot 9695 | 4 |
| ★23 | 30 | 45 | 68 | IS IT TRUE — Brenda Lee, Decca 31690 | 4 |
| 24 | 17 | 9 | 9 | WHEN I GROW UP TO BE A MAN — Beach Boys, Capitol 5245 | 10 |
| 25 | 16 | 17 | 23 | RIDE THE WILD SURF — Jan & Dean, Liberty 55724 | 8 |
| 26 | 31 | 53 | 73 | ASK ME — Elvis Presley, RCA Victor 8440 | 5 |
| 27 | 29 | 30 | 32 | BABY DON'T YOU DO IT — Marvin Gaye, Tamla 54101 | 8 |
| ★28 | 62 | — | — | RINGO — Lorne Greene, RCA Victor 8444 | 2 |
| 29 | 24 | 19 | 15 | YOU MUST BELIEVE ME — Impressions, ABC-Paramount 10581 | 10 |
| ★30 | 46 | 65 | 80 | TIME IS ON MY SIDE — Rolling Stones, London 9708 | 4 |
| 31 | 33 | 37 | 42 | COUSIN OF MINE — Sam Cooke, RCA Victor 8426 | 7 |
| 32 | 27 | 29 | 30 | SOFTLY, AS I LEAVE YOU — Frank Sinatra, Reprise 0301 | 10 |
| 33 | 51 | 74 | — | I'M GONNA BE STRONG — Gene Pitney, Musicor 1045 | 3 |
| 34 | 36 | 41 | 49 | WHO CAN I TURN TO — Tony Bennett, Columbia 43141 | 6 |
| ★35 | 70 | — | — | MR. LONELY — Bobby Vinton, Epic 9730 | 2 |
| 36 | 34 | 39 | 41 | I DON'T WANT TO SEE TOMORROW — Nat King Cole, Capitol 5261 | 8 |
| 37 | 37 | 33 | 37 | I'VE GOT SAND IN MY SHOES — Drifters, Atlantic 2253 | 7 |
| 38 | 43 | 35 | 36 | MERCY, MERCY — Don Covay & the Goodtimers, Rosemart 801 | 10 |
| ★39 | 69 | 77 | — | REACH OUT FOR ME — Dionne Warwick, Scepter 1285 | 3 |
| 40 | 78 | 90 | — | EVERYTHING'S ALRIGHT — Newbeats, Hickory 1282 | 3 |
| ★41 | 57 | 64 | 79 | I'M INTO SOMETHING GOOD — Herman's Hermits, MGM 13280 | 4 |
| 42 | 48 | 56 | 63 | BLESS OUR LOVE — Gene Chandler, Constellation 136 | 7 |
| 43 | 41 | 42 | 44 | ALL CRIED OUT — Dusty Springfield, Philips 40229 | 7 |
| ★44 | 58 | 71 | 97 | WHEN YOU WALK IN THE ROOM — Searchers, Kapp 618 | 4 |
| 45 | 42 | 47 | 53 | DEATH OF AN ANGEL — Kingsmen, Wand 164 | 9 |
| ★46 | 61 | 81 | — | RIGHT OR WRONG — Ronnie Dove, Diamond 173 | 3 |
| 47 | 47 | 44 | 45 | FUNNY GIRL — Barbra Streisand, Columbia 43127 | 9 |
| 48 | 50 | 58 | 66 | WHEN YOU'RE YOUNG AND IN LOVE — Ruby & the Romantics, Kapp 615 | 6 |
| 49 | 55 | 60 | 70 | I HAD A TALK WITH MY MAN — Mitty Collier, Chess 1907 | 7 |
| 50 | 54 | 62 | 71 | WENDY — Beach Boys, Capitol R 5267 (EP) | 4 |
| ★51 | 64 | 89 | — | YOU SHOULD HAVE SEEN THE WAY HE LOOKED AT ME — Dixie Cups, Red Bird 10-012 | 3 |
| 52 | 63 | 70 | 90 | NEEDLE IN A HAYSTACK — Velvelettes, V.I.P. 25007 | 4 |
| 53 | 53 | 57 | 64 | LUMBERJACK — Brook Benton, Mercury 72333 | 6 |
| 54 | 44 | 46 | 52 | TEEN BEAT '65 — Sandy Nelson, Imperial 66060 | 8 |
| 55 | 59 | 63 | 74 | JUMP BACK — Rufus Thomas, Stax 157 | 5 |
| 56 | 52 | 54 | 60 | SMACK DAB IN THE MIDDLE — Ray Charles and His Ork, ABC-Paramount 10588 | 7 |
| 57 | 68 | 80 | — | SLAUGHTER ON 10TH AVE. — Ventures, Dolton 300 | 3 |
| 58 | 60 | 51 | 54 | BABY BE MINE — Jelly Beans, Red Bird 10-011 | 7 |
| ★59 | 75 | 82 | — | DON'T EVER LEAVE ME — Connie Francis, MGM 13287 | 3 |
| 60 | 65 | 68 | 78 | RUNNIN' OUT OF FOOLS — Aretha Franklin, Columbia 43113 | 8 |
| ★61 | 90 | — | — | MOUNTAIN OF LOVE — Johnny Rivers, Imperial 66075 | 2 |
| 62 | 66 | 79 | — | AIN'T DOING TOO BAD — Bobby Bland, Duke 383 | 3 |
| 63 | 56 | 59 | 61 | SO LONG, DEARIE — Louis Armstrong, Mercury 72338 | 6 |
| ★64 | 80 | 95 | — | WALKING IN THE RAIN — Ronettes, Philles 123 | 2 |
| 65 | 74 | 85 | 98 | GONE, GONE, GONE — Everly Brothers, Warner Bros. 5478 | 4 |
| 66 | 83 | — | — | SIDEWALK SURFIN' — Jan & Dean, Liberty 55727 | 2 |
| 67 | 71 | 88 | 94 | SHAGGY DOG — Mickey Lee Lane, Swan 4183 | 5 |
| ★68 | 91 | — | — | SHE UNDERSTANDS ME — Johnny Tillotson, MGM 13284 | 2 |
| 69 | 73 | 78 | 85 | LITTLE HONDA — Beach Boys, Capitol R 5267 (EP) | 4 |
| 70 | 72 | 75 | 76 | SOMETHING YOU GOT — Ramsey Lewis Trio, Argo 5481 | 5 |
| ★71 | 86 | — | — | AIN'T IT THE TRUTH — Mary Wells, 20th Century-Fox 544 | 2 |
| 72 | 87 | — | — | S-W-I-M — Bobby Freeman, Autumn 5 | 2 |
| 73 | 76 | 76 | 89 | LOOK AWAY — Garnet Mimms, United Artists 773 | 3 |
| ★74 | 81 | 84 | — | WHAT GOOD AM I WITHOUT YOU — Marvin Gaye & Kim Weston, Tamla 54104 | 3 |
| ★75 | — | — | — | GOIN' OUT OF MY HEAD — Little Anthony & the Imperials, DCP 1119 | 1 |
| ★76 | 93 | 93 | — | LITTLE MARIE — Chuck Berry, Chess 1912 | 2 |
| 77 | 79 | 83 | 84 | OPPORTUNITY — Jewels, Dimension 1034 | 5 |
| 78 | 82 | 99 | — | LISTEN LONELY GIRL — Johnny Mathis, Mercury 72339 | 3 |
| ★79 | — | — | — | DANCE, DANCE, DANCE — Beach Boys, Capitol 5306 | 1 |
| ★80 | — | — | — | BIG MAN IN TOWN — 4 Seasons, Philips 40238 | 1 |
| ★81 | 89 | 94 | 99 | HEY NOW — Lesley Gore, Mercury 72352 | 4 |
| ★82 | — | — | — | TOO MANY FISH IN THE SEA — Marvelettes, Tamla 54105 | 1 |
| ★83 | — | — | — | WE COULD — Al Martino, Capitol 5293 | 1 |
| 84 | 95 | 97 | — | CHAINED AND BOUND — Otis Redding, Volt 121 | 3 |
| 85 | 85 | 87 | 88 | UP ABOVE MY HEAD — Al Hirt, RCA Victor 8439 | 4 |
| 86 | 92 | 100 | — | MY LOVE FORGIVE ME (Amore, Scusami) — Robert Goulet, Columbia 43131 | 3 |
| 87 | 94 | 96 | — | OH NO, NOT MY BABY — Maxine Brown, Wand 162 | 3 |
| 88 | 88 | — | — | MAYBE TONIGHT — Shirelles, Scepter 1284 | 2 |
| ★89 | — | — | — | CALIFORNIA BOUND — Ronny & the Daytonas, Mala 490 | 1 |
| ★90 | — | — | — | THE DODO — Jumpin' Gene Simmons, Hi 2080 | 1 |
| 91 | — | — | — | BEAUTICIAN BLUES — B. B. King, Kent 403 | 1 |
| 92 | 96 | — | — | SOMETIMES I WISH I WERE A BOY — Lesley Gore, Mercury 72352 | 2 |
| 93 | — | — | — | THAT'S WHERE IT'S AT — Sam Cooke, RCA Victor 8426 | 1 |
| 94 | 98 | — | — | FOUR STRONG WINDS — Bobby Bare, RCA Victor 8443 | 2 |
| 95 | — | 91 | 91 | IF YOU WANT THIS LOVE — Sonny Knight, Aura 403 | 4 |
| 96 | — | — | — | NEVER TRUST A WOMAN — B. B. King, ABC-Paramount 10599 | 1 |
| 97 | — | — | — | STOP TAKIN' ME FOR GRANTED — Mary Wells, 20th Century-Fox 544 | 1 |
| 98 | — | 100 | — | IT AIN'T ME, BABE — Johnny Cash, Columbia 43145 | 2 |
| 99 | — | — | — | HEARTBREAK HILL — Fats Domino, ABC-Paramount 10596 | 1 |
| 100 | — | — | — | TIMES HAVE CHANGED — Irma Thomas, Imperial 66069 | 1 |

## BUBBLING UNDER THE HOT 100

101. I'VE GOT THE SKILL — Jackie Ross, Chess 1913
102. SHE'S ALL RIGHT — Jackie Wilson, Brunswick 55273
103. GALE WINDS — Egyptian Combo, Norman 549
104. DO ANYTHING YOU WANNA — Harold Betters, Gateway 747
105. KENTUCKY BLUEBIRD — Lou Johnson, Big Hill 553
106. ALMOST THERE — Andy Williams, Columbia 43128
107. THE JERK — Larks, Money 106
108. MUMBLES — Oscar Peterson Trio, Mercury 72342
109. HIGH HEEL SNEAKERS — Jerry Lee Lewis, Smash 1930
110. I HOPE HE BREAKS YOUR HEART — Neil Sedaka, RCA Victor 8453
111. I DON'T KNOW YOU ANYMORE — Bobby Goldsboro, United Artists 731
112. HIDE AWAY — King Curtis, Capitol 5270
113. UNLESS YOU CARE — Terry Black, Tollie 9026
114. EVEN THE BAD TIMES ARE GOOD — Jerry Wallace, Challenge 59265
115. HE'S JUST A PLAYBOY — Drifters, Atlantic 2253
116. YOU'RE THE ONLY WORLD I KNOW — Sonny James, Capitol 5280
117. ONE MORE TIME — Ray Charles Singers, Command 4057
118. THANK YOU FOR LOVING ME — Sapphires, ABC-Paramount 10590
119. GOTTA GIVE HER LOVE — Volumes, American Arts 6
120. WHY (Doncha Be My Girl) — Chartbusters, Mutual 508
121. SCRATCHY — Travis Wammack, Ara 204
122. EMPTY ARMS — Ace Cannon, Hi 2081
123. WHAT AM I GONNA DO WITH YOU — Skeeter Davis, RCA Victor 8450
124. EITHER WAY I LOSE — Gladys Knight & the Pips, Maxx 331
125. SLOOP DANCE — Vibrations, Okeh 7205
126. SILLY LITTLE GIRL — Tams, ABC-Paramount 10601
127. THE B1 — Candy & the Kisses, Cameo 336
128. HIDE AWAY THE LUMBERJACK — Kai Willis, Sims 207
129. DON'T SHUT ME OUT — Sammy Davis Jr., Reprise 0322
130. RUN, RUN, RUN — Gestures, Soma 1417
131. IT'S ALL OVER — Walter Jackson, Columbia 43128
132. ENDLESS SLEEP — Hank Williams Jr., MGM 13278
133. FIND ANOTHER LOVE — Tams, General American 714
134. ALL MY LOVING — Chipmunks, Liberty 55734
135. LOST WITHOUT YOU — Teddy Randazzo, DCP 1108

*Compiled from national retail sales and radio station airplay by the Music Popularity Dept. of Record Market Research, Billboard.*

# Billboard HOT 100

For Week Ending November 14, 1964

★ STAR performer—Sides registering greatest proportionate upward progress this week.

Ⓡ Record Industry Association of America seal of certification as million selling single.

| This Week | 1 Wk. Ago | 2 Wks. Ago | 3 Wks. Ago | TITLE, Artist, Label & Number | Weeks On Chart |
|---|---|---|---|---|---|
| 1 | 1 | 1 | 6 | **BABY LOVE** — Supremes, Motown 1066 | 7 |
| 2 | 4 | 14 | 20 | **LEADER OF THE PACK** — Shangri-Las, Red Bird 10-014 | 6 |
| 3 | 2 | 3 | 3 | **LAST KISS** — J. Frank Wilson & the Cavaliers, Josie 923 | 11 |
| 4 | 7 | 11 | 16 | **COME A LITTLE BIT CLOSER** — Jay & the Americans, United Artists 759 | 10 |
| 5 | 6 | 7 | 10 | **HAVE I THE RIGHT?** — Honeycombs, Interphon 7707 | 9 |
| 6 | 8 | 12 | 14 | **THE DOOR IS STILL OPEN TO MY HEART** — Dean Martin, Reprise 0307 | 8 |
| 7 | 3 | 2 | 1 | **DO WAH DIDDY DIDDY** — Manfred Mann, Ascot 2157 | 11 |
| 8 | 5 | 6 | 8 | **LET IT BE ME** — Betty Everett & Jerry Butler, Vee Jay 613 | 11 |
| 9 | 22 | 45 | 61 | **SHE'S NOT THERE** — Zombies, Parrot 9695 | 5 |
| 10 | 28 | 62 | — | **RINGO** — Lorne Greene, RCA Victor 8444 | 3 |
| 11 | 11 | 8 | 5 | **OH, PRETTY WOMAN** — Roy Orbison, Monument 851 | 12 |
| 12 | 10 | 4 | 4 | **WE'LL SING IN THE SUNSHINE** — Gale Garnett, RCA Victor 8388 | 15 |
| 13 | 20 | 32 | 40 | **YOU REALLY GOT ME** — Kinks, Reprise 0306 | 8 |
| 14 | 9 | 10 | 12 | **CHUG-A-LUG** — Roger Miller, Smash 1926 | 11 |
| 15 | 14 | 15 | 15 | **TOBACCO ROAD** — Nashville Teens, London 9689 | 10 |
| 16 | 13 | 9 | 11 | **LITTLE HONDA** — Hondells, Mercury 72324 | 10 |
| 17 | 18 | 23 | 32 | **AIN'T THAT LOVING YOU BABY** — Elvis Presley, RCA Victor 8440 | 6 |
| 18 | 30 | 46 | 65 | **TIME IS ON MY SIDE** — Rolling Stones, London 9708 | 5 |
| 19 | 33 | 51 | 74 | **I'M GONNA BE STRONG** — Gene Pitney, Musicor 1045 | 4 |
| 20 | 23 | 30 | 45 | **IS IT TRUE** — Brenda Lee, Decca 31690 | 5 |
| 21 | 35 | 70 | — | **MR. LONELY** — Bobby Vinton, Epic 9730 | 3 |
| 22 | 26 | 31 | 53 | **ASK ME** — Elvis Presley, RCA Victor 8440 | 6 |
| 23 | 15 | 19 | 25 | **EVERYBODY KNOWS** — Dave Clark Five, Epic 9722 | 7 |
| 24 | 16 | 20 | 27 | **I DON'T WANT TO SEE YOU AGAIN** — Peter & Gordon, Capitol 5272 | 7 |
| 25 | 12 | 5 | 2 | **DANCING IN THE STREET** — Martha & the Vandellas, Gordy 7033 | 13 |
| 26 | 17 | 18 | 26 | **I LIKE IT** — Gerry and the Pacemakers, Laurie 3271 | 8 |
| 27 | 19 | 21 | 24 | **I'M CRYING** — Animals, MGM 13274 | 8 |
| 28 | 41 | 57 | 64 | **I'M INTO SOMETHING GOOD** — Herman's Hermits, MGM 13280 | 5 |
| 29 | 40 | 78 | 90 | **EVERYTHING'S ALRIGHT** — Newbeats, Hickory 1282 | 4 |
| 30 | 39 | 69 | 77 | **REACH OUT FOR ME** — Dionne Warwick, Scepter 1285 | 4 |
| 31 | 46 | 61 | 81 | **RIGHT OR WRONG** — Ronnie Dove, Diamond 173 | 4 |
| 32 | 21 | 13 | 7 | **A SUMMER SONG** — Chad Stuart & Jeremy Clyde, World Artists 1027 | 14 |
| 33 | 61 | 90 | — | **MOUNTAIN OF LOVE** — Johnny Rivers, Imperial 66075 | 3 |
| 34 | 34 | 36 | 41 | **WHO CAN I TURN TO** — Tony Bennett, Columbia 43141 | 7 |
| 35 | 27 | 29 | 30 | **BABY DON'T YOU DO IT** — Marvin Gaye, Tamla 54101 | 9 |
| 36 | 32 | 27 | 29 | **SOFTLY, AS I LEAVE YOU** — Frank Sinatra, Reprise 0301 | 11 |
| 37 | 44 | 58 | 71 | **WHEN YOU WALK IN THE ROOM** — Searchers, Kapp 618 | 5 |
| 38 | 31 | 33 | 37 | **COUSIN OF MINE** — Sam Cooke, RCA Victor 8426 | 8 |
| 39 | 42 | 48 | 56 | **BLESS OUR LOVE** — Gene Chandler, Constellation 136 | 8 |
| 40 | 36 | 34 | 39 | **I DON'T WANT TO SEE TOMORROW** — Nat King Cole, Capitol 5261 | 9 |
| 41 | 49 | 55 | 60 | **I HAD A TALK WITH MY MAN** — Mitty Collier, Chess 1907 | 8 |
| 42 | 66 | 83 | — | **SIDEWALK SURFIN'** — Jan & Dean, Liberty 55727 | 3 |
| 43 | 51 | 64 | 89 | **YOU SHOULD HAVE SEEN THE WAY HE LOOKED AT ME** — Dixie Cups, Red Bird 10-012 | 4 |
| 44 | 50 | 54 | 62 | **WENDY** — Beach Boys, Capitol R 5267 (EP) | 5 |
| 45 | 57 | 68 | 80 | **SLAUGHTER ON 10TH AVE.** — Ventures, Dolton 300 | 4 |
| 46 | 52 | 63 | 70 | **NEEDLE IN A HAYSTACK** — Velvelettes, V.I.P. 25007 | 5 |
| 47 | 64 | 80 | 95 | **WALKING IN THE RAIN** — Ronettes, Philles 123 | 4 |
| 48 | 59 | 75 | 82 | **DON'T EVER LEAVE ME** — Connie Francis, MGM 13287 | 4 |
| 49 | 55 | 59 | 63 | **JUMP BACK** — Rufus Thomas, Stax 157 | 6 |
| 50 | 62 | 66 | 79 | **AIN'T DOING TOO BAD** — Bobby Bland, Duke 383 | 4 |
| 51 | 48 | 50 | 58 | **WHEN YOU'RE YOUNG AND IN LOVE** — Ruby & the Romantics, Kapp 615 | 7 |
| 52 | 65 | 74 | 85 | **GONE, GONE, GONE** — Everly Brothers, Warner Bros. 5478 | 5 |
| 53 | 80 | — | — | **BIG MAN IN TOWN** — 4 Seasons, Philips 40238 | 2 |
| 54 | 79 | — | — | **DANCE, DANCE, DANCE** — Beach Boys, Capitol 5306 | 2 |
| 55 | 67 | 71 | 88 | **SHAGGY DOG** — Mickey Lee Lane, Swan 4183 | 6 |
| 56 | 75 | — | — | **GOIN' OUT OF MY HEAD** — Little Anthony & the Imperials, DCP 1119 | 2 |
| 57 | 60 | 65 | 68 | **RUNNIN' OUT OF FOOLS** — Aretha Franklin, Columbia 43113 | 9 |
| 58 | 68 | 91 | — | **SHE UNDERSTANDS ME** — Johnny Tillotson, MGM 13284 | 3 |
| 59 | 83 | — | — | **WE COULD** — Al Martino, Capitol 5293 | 2 |
| 60 | 71 | 86 | — | **AIN'T IT THE TRUTH** — Mary Wells, 20th Century-Fox 544 | 3 |
| 61 | 76 | 93 | 93 | **LITTLE MARIE** — Chuck Berry, Chess 1912 | 4 |
| 62 | 54 | 44 | 46 | **TEEN BEAT '65** — Sandy Nelson, Imperial 66060 | 9 |
| 63 | 70 | 72 | 75 | **SOMETHING YOU GOT** — Ramsey Lewis Trio, Argo 5481 | 6 |
| 64 | 53 | 53 | 57 | **LUMBERJACK** — Brook Benton, Mercury 72333 | 7 |
| 65 | 69 | 73 | 78 | **LITTLE HONDA** — Beach Boys, Capitol R 5267 (EP) | 5 |
| 66 | — | — | — | **COME SEE ABOUT ME** — Supremes, Motown 1068 | 1 |
| 67 | 72 | 87 | — | **S-W-I-M** — Bobby Freeman, Autumn 5 | 3 |
| 68 | 87 | 94 | 96 | **OH NO, NOT MY BABY** — Maxine Brown, Wand 162 | 4 |
| 69 | 74 | 81 | 84 | **WHAT GOOD AM I WITHOUT YOU** — Marvin Gaye & Kim Weston, Tamla 54104 | 4 |
| 70 | 86 | 92 | 100 | **MY LOVE FORGIVE ME (Amore, Scusami)** — Robert Goulet, Columbia 43131 | 4 |
| 71 | — | — | — | **SHA LA LA** — Manfred Mann, Ascot 2165 | 1 |
| 72 | 77 | 79 | 83 | **OPPORTUNITY** — Jewels, Dimension 1034 | 6 |
| 73 | — | — | — | **THE JERKS** — Larks, Money 106 | 1 |
| 74 | 82 | — | — | **TOO MANY FISH IN THE SEA** — Marvelettes, Tamla 54105 | 2 |
| 75 | 78 | 82 | 99 | **LISTEN LONELY GIRL** — Johnny Mathis, Mercury 72339 | 4 |
| 76 | 81 | 89 | 94 | **HEY NOW** — Lesley Gore, Mercury 72352 | 5 |
| 77 | 73 | 76 | 76 | **LOOK AWAY** — Garnet Mimms, United Artists 773 | 5 |
| 78 | — | — | — | **ANY WAY YOU WANT IT** — Dave Clark Five, Epic 9739 | 1 |
| 79 | 98 | 100 | — | **IT AIN'T ME, BABE** — Johnny Cash, Columbia 43145 | 3 |
| 80 | 89 | — | — | **CALIFORNIA BOUND** — Ronny & the Daytonas, Mala 490 | 2 |
| 81 | 94 | 98 | — | **FOUR STRONG WINDS** — Bobby Bare, RCA Victor 8443 | 3 |
| 82 | — | — | — | **SATURDAY NIGHT AT THE MOVIES** — Drifters, Atlantic 2260 | 1 |
| 83 | 95 | — | 91 | **IF YOU WANT THIS LOVE** — Sonny Knight, Aura 403 | 5 |
| 84 | 84 | 95 | 97 | **CHAINED AND BOUND** — Otis Redding, Volt 121 | 4 |
| 85 | 90 | — | — | **THE DODO** — Jumpin' Gene Simmons, Hi 2080 | 2 |
| 86 | 91 | — | — | **BEAUTICIAN BLUES** — B. B. King, Kent 403 | 2 |
| 87 | — | — | — | **COME SEE ABOUT ME** — Nella Dodds, Wand 167 | 1 |
| 88 | 97 | — | — | **STOP TAKIN' ME FOR GRANTED** — Mary Wells, 20th Century-Fox 544 | 2 |
| 89 | — | — | — | **ONE MORE TIME** — Ray Charles Singers, Command 4057 | 1 |
| 90 | — | — | — | **RUN, RUN, RUN** — Gestures, Soma 1417 | 1 |
| 91 | 92 | 96 | — | **SOMETIMES I WISH I WERE A BOY** — Lesley Gore, Mercury 72352 | 3 |
| 92 | — | — | — | **WHY (Doncha Be My Girl)** — Chartbusters, Mutual 508 | 1 |
| 93 | 93 | — | — | **THAT'S WHERE IT'S AT** — Sam Cooke, RCA Victor 8426 | 3 |
| 94 | — | — | — | **WILLOW WEEP FOR ME** — Chad & Jeremy, World Artists 1034 | 1 |
| 95 | 96 | — | — | **NEVER TRUST A WOMAN** — B. B. King, ABC-Paramount 10599 | 2 |
| 96 | — | — | — | **ALMOST THERE** — Andy Williams, Columbia 43128 | 1 |
| 97 | — | — | — | **DO ANYTHING YOU WANNA** — Harold Betters, Gateway 747 | 1 |
| 98 | 100 | — | — | **TIMES HAVE CHANGED** — Irma Thomas, Imperial 66069 | 2 |
| 99 | — | — | — | **SINCE I DON'T HAVE YOU** — Chuck Jackson, Wand 169 | 1 |
| 100 | — | — | — | **I'VE GOT THE SKILL** — Jackie Ross, Chess 1913 | 1 |

## BUBBLING UNDER THE HOT 100

101. ONCE A DAY — Connie Smith, RCA Victor 8416
102. THE WEDDING — Julie Rogers, Mercury 72332
103. UNLESS YOU CARE — Terry Black, Tollie 9026
104. KENTUCKY BLUEBIRD — Lou Johnson, Big Hill 552
105. MUMBLES — Oscar Peterson Trio, Mercury 72342
106. GALE WINDS — Egyptian Combo, Norman 549
107. SCRATCHY — Travis Wammack, Ara 204
108. YOU'RE THE ONLY WORLD I KNOW — Sonny James, Capitol 5280
109. I WON'T FORGET YOU — Jim Reeves, RCA Victor 8461
110. I HOPE HE BREAKS YOUR HEART — Neil Sedaka, RCA Victor 8453
111. I DON'T KNOW YOU ANYMORE — Bobby Goldsboro, United Artists 781
112. THE 81 — Candy & the Kisses, Cameo 336
113. SHE'S ALL RIGHT — Jackie Wilson, Brunswick 55273
114. SHAKE A LADY — Ray Bryant, Sue 108
115. THE PRICE — Solomon Burke, Atlantic 2259
116. SLOOP DANCE — Vibrations, Okeh 7205
117. GOTTA GIVE HER LOVE — Volumes, American Arts 6
118. HIGH HEEL SNEAKERS — Jerry Lee Lewis, Smash 1930
119. A THOUSAND CUPS OF HAPPINESS — Joe Hinton, Back Beat 532
120. THOU SHALT NOT STEAL — Dick & Deedee, Warner Bros. 5482
121. PUSHIN' A GOOD THING TOO FAR — Barbara Lewis, Atlantic 2255
122. SILLY LITTLE GIRL — Tams, ABC-Paramount 10601
123. ONE OF THESE DAYS — Marty Robbins, Columbia 43134
124. DON'T SHUT ME OUT — Sammy Davis Jr., Reprise 0322
125. IT'S ALL OVER — Walter Jackson, Okeh 7204
126. ROSES ARE RED MY LOVE — "You Know Who" Group, 4 Corners 113
127. LUMBERJACK — Hal Willis, Sims 207
128. AS TEARS GO BY — Marianne Faithful, London 9697
129. FIND ANOTHER LOVE — Tams, General American 714
130. LOST WITHOUT YOU — Teddy Randazzo, DCP 1108
131. IT'LL NEVER BE OVER FOR ME — Baby Washington, Sue 114
132. MY ADORABLE ONE — Joe Simon, Vee Jay 549
133. HERE SHE COMES — Tymes, Parkway 924
134. THE BIG JERK — Clyde & the Blue Jays, Loma 2003
135. TOKAPI — Jimmy McGriff, Sue 112

Compiled from national retail sales and radio station airplay by the Music Popularity Dept. of Record Market Research, Billboard.

# Billboard HOT 100

For Week Ending November 21, 1964

★ STAR performer—Sides registering greatest proportionate upward progress this week.

Record Industry Association of America seal of certification as million selling single.

| This Week | 1 Wk. Ago | 2 Wks. Ago | 3 Wks. Ago | TITLE, Artist, Label & Number | Weeks On Chart |
|---|---|---|---|---|---|
| 1 | 1 | 1 | 1 | BABY LOVE — Supremes, Motown 1066 | 8 |
| 2 | 2 | 4 | 14 | LEADER OF THE PACK — Shangri-Las, Red Bird 10-014 | 7 |
| 3 | 4 | 7 | 11 | COME A LITTLE BIT CLOSER — Jay & the Americans, United Artists 759 | 11 |
| 4 | 3 | 2 | 3 | LAST KISS — J. Frank Wilson & the Cavaliers, Josie 923 | 12 |
| ★5 | 9 | 22 | 45 | SHE'S NOT THERE — Zombies, Parrot 9695 | 6 |
| 6 | 10 | 28 | 62 | RINGO — Lorne Greene, RCA Victor 8444 | 4 |
| 7 | 5 | 6 | 7 | HAVE I THE RIGHT? — Honeycombs, Interphon 7707 | 10 |
| 8 | 13 | 20 | 32 | YOU REALLY GOT ME — Kinks, Reprise 0306 | 9 |
| 9 | 6 | 8 | 12 | THE DOOR IS STILL OPEN TO MY HEART — Dean Martin, Reprise 0307 | 9 |
| ★10 | 18 | 30 | 46 | TIME IS ON MY SIDE — Rolling Stones, London 9708 | 6 |
| 11 | 21 | 35 | 70 | MR. LONELY — Bobby Vinton, Epic 9730 | 4 |
| 12 | 19 | 33 | 51 | I'M GONNA BE STRONG — Gene Pitney, Musicor 1045 | 5 |
| 13 | 11 | 11 | 8 | OH, PRETTY WOMAN — Roy Orbison, Monument 851 | 13 |
| 14 | 22 | 26 | 31 | ASK ME — Elvis Presley, RCA Victor 8440 | 7 |
| 15 | 7 | 3 | 2 | DO WAH DIDDY DIDDY — Manfred Mann, Ascot 2157 | 12 |
| 16 | 17 | 18 | 23 | AIN'T THAT LOVING YOU BABY — Elvis Presley, RCA Victor 8440 | 7 |
| 17 | 20 | 23 | 30 | IS IT TRUE — Brenda Lee, Decca 31690 | 6 |
| 18 | 8 | 5 | 6 | LET IT BE ME — Betty Everett & Jerry Butler, Vee Jay 613 | 12 |
| ★19 | 33 | 61 | 90 | MOUNTAIN OF LOVE — Johnny Rivers, Imperial 66075 | 4 |
| 20 | 28 | 41 | 57 | I'M INTO SOMETHING GOOD — Herman's Hermits, MGM 13280 | 6 |
| 21 | 12 | 10 | 4 | WE'LL SING IN THE SUNSHINE — Gale Garnett, RCA Victor 8388 | 16 |
| 22 | 31 | 46 | 61 | RIGHT OR WRONG — Ronnie Dove, Diamond 173 | 5 |
| 23 | 30 | 39 | 69 | REACH OUT FOR ME — Dionne Warwick, Scepter 1285 | 5 |
| 24 | 29 | 40 | 78 | EVERYTHING'S ALRIGHT — Newbeats, Hickory 1282 | 5 |
| 25 | 16 | 13 | 9 | LITTLE HONDA — Hondells, Mercury 72324 | 11 |
| 26 | 24 | 16 | 20 | I DON'T WANT TO SEE YOU AGAIN — Peter & Gordon, Capitol 5272 | 8 |
| 27 | 53 | 80 | — | BIG MAN IN TOWN — 4 Seasons, Philips 40238 | 3 |
| 28 | 26 | 17 | 18 | I LIKE IT — Gerry and the Pacemakers, Laurie 3271 | 9 |
| 29 | 54 | 79 | — | DANCE, DANCE, DANCE — Beach Boys, Capitol 5306 | 3 |
| 30 | 14 | 9 | 10 | CHUG-A-LUG — Roger Miller, Smash 1926 | 12 |
| 31 | 66 | — | — | COME SEE ABOUT ME — Supremes, Motown 1068 | 2 |
| 32 | 42 | 66 | 83 | SIDEWALK SURFIN' — Jan & Dean, Liberty 55727 | 4 |
| 33 | 34 | 34 | 36 | WHO CAN I TURN TO — Tony Bennett, Columbia 43141 | 8 |
| ★34 | 47 | 64 | 80 | WALKING IN THE RAIN — Ronettes, Philles 123 | 5 |
| 35 | 37 | 44 | 58 | WHEN YOU WALK IN THE ROOM — Searchers, Kapp 618 | 6 |
| ★36 | 56 | 75 | — | GOIN' OUT OF MY HEAD — Little Anthony & the Imperials, DCP 1119 | 3 |
| 37 | 23 | 15 | 19 | EVERYBODY KNOWS — Dave Clark Five, Epic 9722 | 8 |
| 38 | 45 | 57 | 68 | SLAUGHTER ON 10TH AVE. — Ventures, Dolton 300 | 5 |
| 39 | 43 | 51 | 64 | YOU SHOULD HAVE SEEN THE WAY HE LOOKED AT ME — Dixie Cups, Red Bird 10-012 | 5 |
| 40 | 27 | 19 | 21 | I'M CRYING — Animals, MGM 13274 | 9 |
| 41 | 15 | 14 | 15 | TOBACCO ROAD — Nashville Teens, London 9689 | 11 |
| 42 | 48 | 59 | 75 | DON'T EVER LEAVE ME — Connie Francis, MGM 13287 | 5 |
| 43 | 25 | 12 | 5 | DANCING IN THE STREET — Martha & the Vandellas, Gordy 7033 | 14 |
| 44 | 55 | 67 | 71 | SHAGGY DOG — Mickey Lee Lane, Swan 4183 | 7 |
| 45 | 46 | 52 | 63 | NEEDLE IN A HAYSTACK — Velvelettes, V.I.P. 25007 | 6 |
| 46 | 58 | 68 | 91 | SHE UNDERSTANDS ME — Johnny Tillotson, MGM 13284 | 4 |
| 47 | 71 | — | — | SHA LA LA — Manfred Mann, Ascot 2165 | 2 |
| 48 | 59 | 83 | — | WE COULD — Al Martino, Capitol 5293 | 3 |
| 49 | 50 | 62 | 66 | AIN'T DOING TOO BAD — Bobby Bland, Duke 383 | 5 |
| 50 | 60 | 71 | 86 | AIN'T IT THE TRUTH — Mary Wells, 20th Century-Fox 544 | 4 |
| 51 | 52 | 65 | 74 | GONE, GONE, GONE — Everly Brothers, Warner Bros. 5478 | 6 |
| 52 | 70 | 86 | 92 | MY LOVE FORGIVE ME (Amore, Scusami) — Robert Goulet, Columbia 43131 | 3 |
| 53 | 68 | 87 | 94 | OH NO, NOT MY BABY — Maxine Brown, Wand 162 | 5 |
| 54 | 39 | 42 | 48 | BLESS OUR LOVE — Gene Chandler, Constellation 136 | 9 |
| 55 | 41 | 49 | 55 | I HAD A TALK WITH MY MAN — Mitty Collier, Chess 1907 | 9 |
| 56 | 44 | 50 | 54 | WENDY — Beach Boys, Capitol R 5267 (EP) | 6 |
| 57 | 57 | 60 | 65 | RUNNIN' OUT OF FOOLS — Aretha Franklin, Columbia 43113 | 10 |
| 58 | 61 | 76 | 93 | LITTLE MARIE — Chuck Berry, Chess 1912 | 5 |
| 59 | 73 | — | — | THE JERK — Larks, Money 106 | 2 |
| 60 | 74 | 82 | — | TOO MANY FISH IN THE SEA — Marvelettes, Tamla 54105 | 3 |
| 61 | 82 | — | — | SATURDAY NIGHT AT THE MOVIES — Drifters, Atlantic 2260 | 2 |
| 62 | 49 | 55 | 59 | JUMP BACK — Rufus Thomas, Stax 157 | 7 |
| 63 | 78 | — | — | ANY WAY YOU WANT IT — Dave Clark Five, Epic 9739 | 2 |
| 64 | 79 | 98 | 100 | IT AIN'T ME, BABE — Johnny Cash, Columbia 43145 | 4 |
| 65 | 62 | 54 | 44 | TEEN BEAT '65 — Sandy Nelson, Imperial 66060 | 10 |
| 66 | 51 | 48 | 50 | WHEN YOU'RE YOUNG AND IN LOVE — Ruby & the Romantics, Kapp 615 | 8 |
| 67 | 72 | 87 | — | S-W-I-M — Bobby Freeman, Autumn 5 | 4 |
| 68 | 69 | 74 | 81 | WHAT GOOD AM I WITHOUT YOU — Marvin Gaye & Kim Weston, Tamla 54104 | 5 |
| 69 | 81 | 94 | 98 | FOUR STRONG WINDS — Bobby Bare, RCA Victor 8443 | 4 |
| 70 | 72 | 77 | 79 | OPPORTUNITY — Jewels, Dimension 1034 | 7 |
| 71 | 90 | — | — | RUN, RUN, RUN — Gestures, Soma 1417 | 2 |
| 72 | 80 | 89 | — | CALIFORNIA BOUND — Ronny & the Daytonas, Mala 490 | 3 |
| 73 | 89 | — | — | ONE MORE TIME — Ray Charles Singers, Command 4057 | 2 |
| 74 | 75 | 78 | 82 | LISTEN LONELY GIRL — Johnny Mathis, Mercury 72339 | 5 |
| 75 | 83 | 95 | — | IF YOU WANT THIS LOVE — Sonny Knight, Aura 403 | 6 |
| 76 | 76 | 81 | 89 | HEY NOW — Lesley Gore, Mercury 72352 | 6 |
| 77 | 96 | — | — | ALMOST THERE — Andy Williams, Columbia 43128 | 2 |
| 78 | 99 | — | — | SINCE I DON'T HAVE YOU — Chuck Jackson, Wand 169 | 2 |
| 79 | 94 | — | — | WILLOW WEEP FOR ME — Chad & Jeremy, World Artists 1034 | 2 |
| 80 | 84 | 84 | 95 | CHAINED AND BOUND — Otis Redding, Volt 121 | 3 |
| 81 | — | — | — | THE WEDDING — Julie Rogers, Mercury 72332 | 1 |
| 82 | 86 | 91 | — | BEAUTICIAN BLUES — B. B. King, Kent 403 | 3 |
| 83 | 85 | 90 | — | THE DODO — Jumpin' Gene Simmons, Hi 2080 | 3 |
| 84 | 87 | — | — | COME SEE ABOUT ME — Nella Dodds, Wand 167 | 2 |
| 85 | 97 | — | — | DO ANYTHING YOU WANNA — Harold Betters, Gateway 747 | 2 |
| 86 | 91 | 92 | 96 | SOMETIMES I WISH I WERE A BOY — Lesley Gore, Mercury 72352 | 4 |
| 87 | — | — | — | KEEP SEARCHIN' — Del Shannon, Amy 916 | 1 |
| 88 | — | — | — | HOW SWEET IT IS — Marvin Gaye, Tamla 54107 | 1 |
| 89 | 100 | — | — | I'VE GOT THE SKILL — Jackie Ross, Chess 1913 | 2 |
| 90 | 95 | 96 | — | NEVER TRUST A WOMAN — B. B. King, ABC-Paramount 10599 | 2 |
| 91 | — | — | — | HIGH HEEL SNEAKERS — Jerry Lee Lewis, Smash 1930 | 1 |
| 92 | — | — | — | WHY (Doncha Be My Girl) — Chartbusters, Mutual 508 | 2 |
| 93 | — | — | — | HERE SHE COMES — Tymes, Parkway 924 | 1 |
| 94 | — | — | — | THOU SHALT NOW STEAL — Dick & Deedee, Warner Bros. 5482 | 1 |
| 95 | — | — | — | SCRATCHY — Travis Wammack, Ara 204 | 1 |
| 96 | — | — | — | AMEN — Impressions, ABC-Paramount 10602 | 1 |
| 97 | — | — | — | THE 81 — Candy & the Kisses, Cameo 336 | 1 |
| 98 | — | — | — | I WON'T FORGET YOU — Jim Reeves, RCA Victor 8461 | 1 |
| 99 | — | — | — | IT'S ALL OVER — Walter Jackson, Okeh 7204 | 1 |
| 100 | — | — | — | UNLESS YOU CARE — Terry Black, Tollie 9026 | 1 |

## BUBBLING UNDER THE HOT 100

101. AS TEARS GO BY — Marianne Faithful, London 9697
102. LOVE POTION NUMBER NINE — Searchers, Kapp Winners Circle 27
103. WALK AWAY — Matt Monro, Liberty 55745
104. I HOPE HE BREAKS YOUR HEART — Neil Sedaka, RCA Victor 8453
105. I DON'T KNOW YOU ANYMORE — Bobby Goldsboro, United Artists 781
106. YOU'RE THE ONLY WORLD I KNOW — Sonny James, Capitol 5280
107. ONCE A DAY — Connie Smith, RCA Victor 8416
108. BIG BROTHER — Dickey Lee, Hall 1924
109. THE PRICE — Solomon Burke, Atlantic 2259
110. WITHOUT THE ONE YOU LOVE — Four Tops, Motown 1069
111. SLOOP DANCE — Vibrations, Okeh 7205
112. PEARLY SHELLS — Burl Ives, Decca 31659
113. SHAKE A LADY — Ray Bryant, Sue 108
114. DON'T SHUT ME OUT — Sammy Davis Jr., Reprise 0322
115. TALK TO ME BABY — Barry Mann, Red Bird 10-015
116. SHE'S ALL RIGHT — Jackie Wilson, Brunswick 55273
117. GOTTA GIVE HER LOVE — Volumes, American Arts 6
118. SILLY LITTLE GIRL — Tams, ABC-Paramount 10601
119. MUMBLES — Oscar Peterson Trio, Mercury 72342
120. ONE OF THESE DAYS — Marty Robbins, Columbia 43134
121. MY ADORABLE ONE — Joe Simon, Vee Jay 609
122. STOP TAKIN' ME FOR GRANTED — Mary Wells, 20th Century-Fox 544
123. GALE WINDS — Egyptian Combo, Norman 549
124. ONCE UPON A TIME — King Curtis, Capitol 5270
125. ROSES ARE RED MY LOVE — "You Know Who" Group, 4 Corners 113
126. LUMBERJACK — Hal Willis, Sims 207
127. THERE'S ALWAYS SOMETHING THERE TO REMIND ME — Sandie Shaw, Reprise 0320
128. I'M THE LOVER MAN — Little Jerry Williams, Loma 2005
129. IT'LL NEVER BE OVER FOR ME — Baby Washington, Sue 114
130. AND SATISFY — Nancy Wilson, Capitol 5319
131. ENDLESS SLEEP — Hank Williams Jr., MGM 13278
132. TOPKAPI — Jimmy Curtis, Coral 62426
133. I DON'T WANT TO WALK WITHOUT YOU — Phillis McGuire, Reprise 0310
134. DON'T FORGET I STILL LOVE YOU — Bobbi Martin, Coral 62426
135. RAP CITY — Ventures, Dolton 300

Compiled from national retail sales and radio station airplay by the Music Popularity Dept. of Record Market Research, Billboard.

# Billboard HOT 100

**For Week Ending November 28, 1964**

★ STAR performer—Sides registering greatest proportionate upward progress this week.

Record Industry Association of America seal of certification as million selling single.

| This Week | Wk. Ago | 2 Wks. Ago | 3 Wks. Ago | TITLE Artist, Label & Number | Weeks On Chart |
|---|---|---|---|---|---|
| 1 | 2 | 2 | 4 | LEADER OF THE PACK — Shangri-Las, Red Bird 10-014 | 8 |
| 2 | 1 | 1 | 1 | BABY LOVE — Supremes, Motown 1066 | 9 |
| 3 | 3 | 4 | 7 | COME A LITTLE BIT CLOSER — Jay & the Americans, United Artists 759 | 12 |
| 4 | 5 | 9 | 22 | SHE'S NOT THERE — Zombies, Parrot 9695 | 7 |
| 5 | 6 | 10 | 28 | RINGO — Lorne Greene, RCA Victor 8444 | 5 |
| 6 | 11 | 21 | 35 | MR. LONELY — Bobby Vinton, Epic 9730 | 5 |
| 7 | 8 | 13 | 20 | YOU REALLY GOT ME — Kinks, Reprise 0306 | 10 |
| 8 | 10 | 18 | 30 | TIME IS ON MY SIDE — Rolling Stones, London 9708 | 7 |
| 9 | 4 | 3 | 2 | LAST KISS — J. Frank Wilson & the Cavaliers, Josie 923 | 13 |
| 10 | 19 | 33 | 61 | MOUNTAIN OF LOVE — Johnny Rivers, Imperial 66075 | 5 |
| 11 | 12 | 19 | 33 | I'M GONNA BE STRONG — Gene Pitney, Musicor 1045 | 6 |
| 12 | 14 | 22 | 26 | ASK ME — Elvis Presley, RCA Victor 8440 | 8 |
| 13 | 31 | 66 | — | COME SEE ABOUT ME — Supremes, Motown 1068 | 3 |
| 14 | 7 | 5 | 6 | HAVE I THE RIGHT? — Honeycombs, Interphon 7707 | 11 |
| 15 | 29 | 54 | 79 | DANCE, DANCE, DANCE — Beach Boys, Capitol 5306 | 4 |
| 16 | 22 | 31 | 46 | RIGHT OR WRONG — Ronnie Dove, Diamond 173 | 6 |
| 17 | 17 | 20 | 23 | IS IT TRUE — Brenda Lee, Decca 31690 | 7 |
| 18 | 24 | 29 | 40 | EVERYTHING'S ALRIGHT — Newbeats, Hickory 1282 | 6 |
| 19 | 20 | 28 | 41 | I'M INTO SOMETHING GOOD — Herman's Hermits, MGM 13280 | 7 |
| 20 | 23 | 30 | 39 | REACH OUT FOR ME — Dionne Warwick, Scepter 1285 | 6 |
| 21 | 13 | 11 | 11 | OH, PRETTY WOMAN — Roy Orbison, Monument 851 | 14 |
| 22 | 27 | 53 | 80 | BIG MAN IN TOWN — 4 Seasons, Philips 40238 | 4 |
| 23 | 9 | 6 | 8 | THE DOOR IS STILL OPEN TO MY HEART — Dean Martin, Reprise 0307 | 10 |
| 24 | 36 | 56 | 75 | GOIN' OUT OF MY HEAD — Little Anthony & the Imperials, DCP 1119 | 4 |
| 25 | 16 | 17 | 18 | AIN'T THAT LOVING YOU BABY — Elvis Presley, RCA Victor 8440 | 8 |
| 26 | 59 | 73 | — | THE JERK — Larks, Money 106 | 3 |
| 27 | 32 | 42 | 66 | SIDEWALK SURFIN' — Jan & Dean, Liberty 55727 | 4 |
| 28 | 47 | 71 | — | SHA LA LA — Manfred Mann, Ascot 2165 | 3 |
| 29 | 34 | 47 | 64 | WALKING IN THE RAIN — Ronettes, Philles 123 | 6 |
| 30 | 61 | 82 | — | SATURDAY NIGHT AT THE MOVIES — Drifters, Atlantic 2260 | 3 |
| 31 | 15 | 7 | 3 | DO WAH DIDDY DIDDY — Manfred Mann, Ascot 2157 | 13 |
| 32 | 18 | 8 | 5 | LET IT BE ME — Betty Everett & Jerry Butler, Vee Jay 613 | 13 |
| 33 | 26 | 24 | 16 | I DON'T WANT TO SEE YOU AGAIN — Peter & Gordon, Capitol 5272 | 9 |
| 34 | 25 | 16 | 13 | LITTLE HONDA — Hondells, Mercury 72324 | 12 |
| 35 | 38 | 45 | 57 | SLAUGHTER ON 10TH AVE. — Ventures, Dolton 300 | 6 |
| 36 | 33 | 34 | 34 | WHO CAN I TURN TO — Tony Bennett, Columbia 43141 | 9 |
| 37 | 21 | 12 | 10 | WE'LL SING IN THE SUNSHINE — Gale Garnett, RCA Victor 8388 | 17 |
| 38 | 44 | 55 | 67 | SHAGGY DOG — Mickey Lee Lane, Swan 4183 | 8 |
| 39 | 46 | 58 | 68 | SHE UNDERSTANDS ME — Johnny Tillotson, MGM 13284 | 5 |
| 40 | 52 | 70 | 86 | MY LOVE FORGIVE ME (Amore, Scusami) — Robert Goulet, Columbia 43131 | 6 |
| 41 | 53 | 68 | 87 | OH NO, NOT MY BABY — Maxine Brown, Wand 162 | 6 |
| 42 | 42 | 48 | 59 | DON'T EVER LEAVE ME — Connie Francis, MGM 13287 | 6 |
| 43 | 48 | 59 | 83 | WE COULD — Al Martino, Capitol 5293 | 4 |
| 44 | 51 | 52 | 65 | GONE, GONE, GONE — Everly Brothers, Warner Bros. 5478 | 7 |
| 45 | 30 | 14 | 9 | CHUG-A-LUG — Roger Miller, Smash 1926 | 13 |
| 46 | 63 | 78 | — | ANY WAY YOU WANT IT — Dave Clark Five, Epic 9739 | 3 |
| 47 | 50 | 60 | 71 | AIN'T IT THE TRUTH — Mary Wells, 20th Century-Fox 544 | 5 |
| 48 | 35 | 37 | 44 | WHEN YOU WALK IN THE ROOM — Searchers, Kapp 618 | 7 |
| 49 | 39 | 43 | 51 | YOU SHOULD HAVE SEEN THE WAY HE LOOKED AT ME — Dixie Cups, Red Bird 10-012 | 6 |
| 50 | 60 | 74 | 82 | TOO MANY FISH IN THE SEA — Marvelettes, Tamla 54105 | 4 |
| 51 | 81 | — | — | THE WEDDING — Julie Rogers, Mercury 72332 | 2 |
| 52 | 49 | 50 | 62 | AIN'T DOING TOO BAD — Bobby Bland, Duke 383 | 6 |
| 53 | 45 | 46 | 52 | NEEDLE IN A HAYSTACK — Velvelettes, V.I.P. 25007 | 7 |
| 54 | 58 | 61 | 76 | LITTLE MARIE — Chuck Berry, Chess 1912 | 6 |
| 55 | 79 | 94 | — | WILLOW WEEP FOR ME — Chad & Jeremy, World Artists 1034 | 3 |
| 56 | 67 | 67 | 72 | S-W-I-M — Bobby Freeman, Autumn 5 | 5 |
| 57 | 55 | 41 | 49 | I HAD A TALK WITH MY MAN — Mitty Collier, Chess 1907 | 10 |
| 58 | 64 | 79 | 98 | IT AIN'T ME, BABE — Johnny Cash, Columbia 43145 | 4 |
| 59 | 96 | — | — | AMEN — Impressions, ABC-Paramount 10602 | 2 |
| 60 | 69 | 81 | 94 | FOUR STRONG WINDS — Bobby Bare, RCA Victor 8443 | 5 |
| 61 | 68 | 69 | 74 | WHAT GOOD AM I WITHOUT YOU — Marvin Gaye & Kim Weston, Tamla 54104 | 6 |
| 62 | 78 | 99 | — | SINCE I DON'T HAVE YOU — Chuck Jackson, Wand 169 | 3 |
| 63 | 71 | 90 | — | RUN, RUN, RUN — Gestures, Soma 1417 | 3 |
| 64 | 73 | 89 | — | ONE MORE TIME — Ray Charles Singers, Command 4057 | 3 |
| 65 | 88 | — | — | HOW SWEET IT IS — Marvin Gaye, Tamla 54107 | 2 |
| 66 | 70 | 72 | 77 | OPPORTUNITY — Jewels, Dimension 1034 | 8 |
| 67 | 77 | 96 | — | ALMOST THERE — Andy Williams, Columbia 43128 | 3 |
| 68 | — | — | — | WITHOUT THE ONE YOU LOVE — Four Tops, Motown 1069 | 1 |
| 69 | 74 | 75 | 78 | LISTEN LONELY GIRL — Johnny Mathis, Mercury 72339 | 6 |
| 70 | 80 | 84 | 84 | CHAINED AND BOUND — Otis Redding, Volt 121 | 6 |
| 71 | 87 | — | — | KEEP SEARCHIN' — Del Shannon, Amy 915 | 2 |
| 72 | 72 | 80 | 89 | CALIFORNIA BOUND — Ronny & the Daytonas, Mala 490 | 4 |
| 73 | 75 | 83 | 95 | IF YOU WANT THIS LOVE — Sonny Knight, Aura 403 | 7 |
| 74 | 84 | 87 | — | COME SEE ABOUT ME — Nella Dodds, Wand 167 | 3 |
| 75 | — | — | — | DEAR HEART — Jack Jones, Kapp 635 | 1 |
| 76 | — | — | — | THE PRICE — Solomon Burke, Atlantic 2259 | 1 |
| 77 | 94 | — | — | THOU SHALT NOT STEAL — Dick & Deedee, Warner Bros. 5482 | 2 |
| 78 | — | — | — | DEAR HEART — Andy Williams, Columbia 43180 | 1 |
| 79 | — | — | — | WALK AWAY — Matt Monro, Liberty 55745 | 1 |
| 80 | 99 | — | — | IT'S ALL OVER — Walter Jackson, Okeh 7204 | 2 |
| 81 | — | — | — | AS TEARS GO BY — Marianne Faithful, London 9697 | 1 |
| 82 | 97 | — | — | THE 81 — Candy & the Kisses, Cameo 336 | 2 |
| 83 | — | — | — | LOVE POTION NUMBER NINE — Searchers, Kapp Winner's Circle 27 | 1 |
| 84 | 85 | 97 | — | DO ANYTHING YOU WANNA — Harold Betters, Gateway 747 | 3 |
| 85 | — | — | — | A WOMAN'S LOVE — Carla Thomas, Atlantic 2258 | 1 |
| 86 | — | — | — | ROSES ARE RED MY LOVE — "You Know Who" Group, 4 Corners 113 | 1 |
| 87 | — | — | — | SILLY LITTLE GIRL — Tams, ABC-Paramount 10601 | 1 |
| 88 | — | — | — | HEY, LITTLE ONE — J. Frank Wilson & the Cavaliers, Josie 926 | 1 |
| 89 | — | — | — | (THERE'S) ALWAYS SOMETHING THERE TO REMIND ME — Sandie Shaw, Reprise 0320 | 1 |
| 90 | — | — | — | I'M GONNA LOVE YOU TOO — Hullabaloos, Roulette 4587 | 1 |
| 91 | — | 88 | 97 | STOP TAKIN' ME FOR GRANTED — Mary Wells, 20th Century-Fox 544 | 3 |
| 92 | — | — | — | DON'T FORGET I STILL LOVE YOU — Bobbi Martin, Coral 62426 | 1 |
| 93 | 93 | — | — | HERE SHE COMES — Tymes, Parkway 924 | 2 |
| 94 | 95 | — | — | SCRATCHY — Travis Wammack, Ara 204 | 2 |
| 95 | 98 | — | — | I WON'T FORGET YOU — Jim Reeves, RCA Victor 8461 | 2 |
| 96 | — | — | — | DO-WACKA-DO — Roger Miller, Smash 1947 | 1 |
| 97 | — | — | — | YOU'RE THE ONLY WORLD I KNOW — Sonny James, Capitol 5280 | 1 |
| 98 | — | — | — | GETTING MIGHTY CROWDED — Betty Everett, Vee Jay 628 | 1 |
| 99 | — | — | — | A HAPPY GUY — Rick Nelson, Decca 31703 | 1 |
| 100 | — | — | — | IT'LL NEVER BE OVER FOR ME — Baby Washington, Sue 114 | 1 |

## BUBBLING UNDER THE HOT 100

101. MUMBLES — Oscar Peterson Trio, Mercury 72342
102. I DON'T WANT TO WALK WITHOUT YOU — Phyllis McGuire, Reprise 0310
103. PEARLY SHELLS — Burl Ives, Decca 31659
104. BIG BROTHER — Dickey Lee, Hall 1924
105. ONE OF THESE DAYS — Marty Robbins, Columbia 43134
106. DON'T SHUT ME OUT — Sammy Davis Jr., Reprise 0322
107. ONCE A DAY — Connie Smith, RCA Victor 8416
108. WHY (Doncha Be My Girl) — Chartbusters, Mutual 508
109. SLOOP DANCE — Vibrations, Okeh 7205
110. I WOULDN'T TRADE YOU FOR THE WORLD — Bachelors, London 9693
111. TALK TO ME BABY — Barry Mann, Red Bird 10-015
112. SHAKE A LADY — Ray Bryant, Sue 108
113. PUSHIN' A GOOD THING TOO FAR — Barbara Lewis, Atlantic 2255
114. I DON'T KNOW YOU ANYMORE — Bobby Goldsboro, United Artists 781
115. DEAR HEART — Henry Mancini's Ork & Chorus, RCA Victor 8458
116. UNLESS YOU CARE — Terry Black, Tollie 9026
117. GOTTA GIVE HER LOVE — Volumes, American Arts 6
118. I'M THE LOVER MAN — Joe Simon, Vee Jay 609
119. MY ADORABLE ONE — Hal Willis, Sims 207
120. THE LUMBERJACK — Hal Willis, Sims 207
121. WATCH OUT, SALLY — Diane Renay, MGM 13296
122. NEVER TRUST A WOMAN — B. B. King, ABC-Paramount 10599
123. THE DODO — Jumpin' Gene Simmons, Hi 2080
124. HIGH HEEL SNEAKERS — Jerry Lee Lewis, Smash 1930
125. ENDLESS SLEEP — Hank Williams Jr., MGM 13272
126. AND SATISFY — Nancy Wilson, Capitol 5319
127. HAWAII TATTOO — Waikikis, Kapp Winners Circle 10
128. I WANT YOU TO HAVE EVERYTHING — Lee Rogers, D-Town 1035
129. FIND ANOTHER LOVE — Tams, Generals America 714
130. IT'S ALRIGHT — Adam Faith, Amy 913
131. CHITTLINS — Gus Jenkins, Tower 107
132. EITHER WAY I LOSE — Gladys Knight & the Pips, Maxx 326
133. A THOUSAND CUPS OF HAPPINESS — Joe Hinton, Back Beat 552
134. ODE TO THE LITTLE BROWN SHACK OUT BACK — Billy Edd Wheeler, Kapp 617
135. THE MONSTER SWIM — Bobby Pickett, RCA Victor 8459

Compiled from national retail sales and radio station airplay by the Music Popularity Dept. of Record Market Research, Billboard.

# Billboard HOT 100

**For Week Ending December 5, 1964**

★ STAR performer—Sides registering greatest proportionate upward progress this week.

Record Industry Association of America seal of certification as million selling single.

| This Week | 1 Wk. Ago | 2 Wks. Ago | 3 Wks. Ago | TITLE Artist, Label & Number | Weeks On Chart |
|---|---|---|---|---|---|
| 1 | 5 | 6 | 10 | RINGO — Lorne Greene, RCA Victor 8444 | 6 |
| 2 | 6 | 11 | 21 | MR. LONELY — Bobby Vinton, Epic 9730 | 7 |
| 3 | 1 | 2 | 2 | LEADER OF THE PACK — Shangri-Las, Red Bird 10-014 | 9 |
| 4 | 4 | 5 | 9 | SHE'S NOT THERE — Zombies, Parrot 9695 | 8 |
| 5 | 2 | 1 | 1 | BABY LOVE — Supremes, Motown 1066 | 10 |
| 6 | 8 | 10 | 18 | TIME IS ON MY SIDE — Rolling Stones, London 9708 | 8 |
| 7 | 7 | 8 | 13 | YOU REALLY GOT ME — Kinks, Reprise 0306 | 11 |
| ★8 | 13 | 31 | 66 | COME SEE ABOUT ME — Supremes, Motown 1068 | 4 |
| 9 | 10 | 19 | 33 | MOUNTAIN OF LOVE — Johnny Rivers, Imperial 66075 | 6 |
| 10 | 11 | 12 | 19 | I'M GONNA BE STRONG — Gene Pitney, Musicor 1045 | 7 |
| 11 | 3 | 3 | 4 | COME A LITTLE BIT CLOSER — Jay & the Americans, United Artists 759 | 13 |
| 12 | 12 | 14 | 22 | ASK ME — Elvis Presley, RCA Victor 8440 | 9 |
| 13 | 15 | 29 | 54 | DANCE, DANCE, DANCE — Beach Boys, Capitol 5306 | 5 |
| 14 | 16 | 22 | 31 | RIGHT OR WRONG — Ronnie Dove, Diamond 173 | 7 |
| 15 | 19 | 20 | 28 | I'M INTO SOMETHING GOOD — Herman's Hermits, MGM 13280 | 8 |
| 16 | 9 | 4 | 3 | LAST KISS — J. Frank Wilson & the Cavaliers, Josie 923 | 14 |
| 17 | 24 | 36 | 56 | GOIN' OUT OF MY HEAD — Little Anthony & the Imperials, DCP 1119 | 5 |
| 18 | 18 | 24 | 29 | EVERYTHING'S ALRIGHT — Newbeats, Hickery 1282 | 7 |
| ★19 | 28 | 47 | 71 | SHA LA LA — Manfred Mann, Ascot 2165 | 4 |
| 20 | 22 | 27 | 53 | BIG MAN IN TOWN — 4 Seasons, Philips 40238 | 5 |
| 21 | 26 | 59 | 73 | THE JERK — Larks, Money 106 | 4 |
| ★22 | — | — | — | I FEEL FINE — Beatles, Capitol 5327 | 1 |
| 23 | 29 | 34 | 47 | WALKING IN THE RAIN — Ronettes, Philles 123 | 7 |
| ★24 | 30 | 61 | 82 | SATURDAY NIGHT AT THE MOVIES — Drifters, Atlantic 2260 | 4 |
| 25 | 27 | 32 | 42 | SIDEWALK SURFIN' — Jan & Dean, Liberty 55727 | 6 |
| 26 | 20 | 23 | 30 | REACH OUT FOR ME — Dionne Warwick, Scepter 1285 | 7 |
| 27 | 25 | 16 | 17 | AIN'T THAT LOVING YOU BABY — Elvis Presley, RCA Victor 8440 | 9 |
| 28 | 14 | 7 | 5 | HAVE I THE RIGHT? — Honeycombs, Interphon 7707 | 12 |
| 29 | 17 | 17 | 20 | IS IT TRUE — Brenda Lee, Decca 31690 | 8 |
| ★30 | 40 | 52 | 70 | MY LOVE FORGIVE ME (Amore, Scusami) — Robert Goulet, Columbia 43131 | 5 |
| 31 | 46 | 63 | 78 | ANY WAY YOU WANT IT — Dave Clark Five, Epic 9739 | 4 |
| 32 | 44 | 51 | 52 | GONE, GONE, GONE — Everly Brothers, Warner Bros. 5478 | 8 |
| 33 | 41 | 53 | 68 | OH NO, NOT MY BABY — Maxine Brown, Wand 162 | 7 |
| 34 | 21 | 13 | 11 | OH, PRETTY WOMAN — Roy Orbison, Monument 851 | 15 |
| 35 | 23 | 9 | 6 | THE DOOR IS STILL OPEN TO MY HEART — Dean Martin, Reprise 0307 | 11 |
| 36 | 39 | 46 | 58 | SHE UNDERSTANDS ME — Johnny Tillotson, MGM 13284 | 5 |
| ★37 | 51 | 81 | — | THE WEDDING — Julie Rogers, Mercury 72332 | 3 |
| ★38 | 50 | 60 | 74 | TOO MANY FISH IN THE SEA — Marvelettes, Tamla 54105 | 5 |
| 39 | 35 | 38 | 45 | SLAUGHTER ON 10TH AVE. — Ventures, Dolton 300 | 7 |
| 40 | 36 | 33 | 34 | WHO CAN I TURN TO — Tony Bennett, Columbia 43141 | 10 |
| 41 | 43 | 48 | 59 | WE COULD — Al Martino, Capitol 5293 | 5 |
| 42 | 38 | 44 | 55 | SHAGGY DOG — Mickey Lee Lane, Swan 4183 | 9 |
| ★43 | 59 | 96 | — | AMEN — Impressions, ABC-Paramount 10602 | 3 |
| 44 | 55 | 79 | 94 | WILLOW WEEP FOR ME — Chad & Jeremy, World Artists 1034 | 4 |
| 45 | 47 | 50 | 60 | AIN'T IT THE TRUTH — Mary Wells, 20th Century-Fox 544 | 6 |
| ★46 | — | — | — | SHE'S A WOMAN — Beatles, Capitol 5327 | 1 |
| 47 | 42 | 42 | 48 | DON'T EVER LEAVE ME — Connie Francis, MGM 13287 | 7 |
| ★48 | 63 | 71 | 90 | RUN, RUN, RUN — Gestures, Soma 1417 | 4 |
| 49 | 65 | 88 | — | HOW SWEET IT IS — Marvin Gaye, Tamla 54107 | 3 |
| ★50 | 81 | — | — | AS TEARS GO BY — Marianne Faithful, London 9697 | 2 |
| ★51 | 68 | — | — | WITHOUT THE ONE YOU LOVE — Four Tops, Motown 1069 | 2 |
| ★52 | 77 | 94 | — | THOU SHALT NOT STEAL — Dick & Deedes, Warner Bros. 5482 | 3 |
| 53 | 78 | — | — | DEAR HEART — Andy Williams, Columbia 43180 | 2 |
| ★54 | 64 | 73 | 89 | ONE MORE TIME — Ray Charles Singers, Command 4057 | 4 |
| ★55 | 71 | 87 | — | KEEP SEARCHIN' — Del Shannon, Amy 915 | 3 |
| 56 | 56 | 67 | 67 | S-W-I-M — Bobby Freeman, Autumn 5 | 6 |
| 57 | 75 | — | — | DEAR HEART — Jack Jones, Kapp 635 | 2 |
| 58 | 58 | 64 | 79 | IT AIN'T ME, BABE — Johnny Cash, Columbia 43145 | 6 |
| 59 | 62 | 78 | 99 | SINCE I DON'T HAVE YOU — Chuck Jackson, Wand 169 | 4 |
| 60 | 53 | 45 | 46 | NEEDLE IN A HAYSTACK — Velvelettes, V.I.P. 25007 | 8 |
| ★61 | 83 | — | — | LOVE POTION NUMBER NINE — Searchers, Kapp Winner's Circle 27 | 2 |
| 62 | 79 | — | — | WALK AWAY — Matt Monro, Liberty 55745 | 2 |
| 63 | — | — | — | WILD ONE — Martha & the Vandellas, Gordy 7036 | 1 |
| 64 | 66 | 70 | 72 | OPPORTUNITY — Jewels, Dimension 1034 | 9 |
| 65 | 69 | 74 | 75 | LISTEN LONELY GIRL — Johnny Mathis, Mercury 72239 | 7 |
| 66 | 60 | 69 | 81 | FOUR STRONG WINDS — Bobby Bare, RCA Victor 8443 | 6 |
| 67 | 67 | 77 | 96 | ALMOST THERE — Andy Williams, Columbia 43128 | 4 |
| 68 | 76 | — | — | THE PRICE — Solomon Burke, Atlantic 2259 | 2 |
| 69 | 82 | 97 | — | THE 81 — Candy & the Kisses, Cameo 336 | 3 |
| ★70 | 86 | — | — | MY LOVE (Roses Are Red) — "You Know Who" Group, 4 Corners 113 | 2 |
| 71 | 96 | — | — | DO-WACKA-DO — Roger Miller, Smash 1947 | 2 |
| 72 | 73 | 75 | 83 | IF YOU WANT THIS LOVE — Sonny Knight, Aura 403 | 8 |
| 73 | 89 | — | — | (There's) ALWAYS SOMETHING THERE TO REMIND ME — Sandie Shaw, Reprise 0320 | 2 |
| ★74 | 90 | — | — | I'M GONNA LOVE YOU TOO — Hullabaloos, Roulette 4587 | 2 |
| 75 | 72 | 72 | 80 | CALIFORNIA BOUND — Ronny & the Daytonas, Mala 490 | 5 |
| ★76 | 92 | — | — | DON'T FORGET I STILL LOVE YOU — Bobbi Martin, Coral 62426 | 2 |
| 77 | 80 | 99 | — | IT'S ALL OVER — Walter Jackson, Okeh 7204 | 3 |
| ★78 | — | — | — | WHAT NOW — Gene Chandler, Constellation 141 | 1 |
| ★79 | — | — | — | SMILE — Betty Everett & Jerry Butler, Vee Jay 633 | 1 |
| ★80 | — | — | — | LEADER OF THE LAUNDROMAT — Detergents, Roulette 4590 | 1 |
| ★81 | — | — | — | HAWAII TATTOO — Waikikis, Kapp Winner's Circle 30 | 1 |
| 82 | 84 | 85 | 97 | DO ANYTHING YOU WANNA — Harold Betters, Gateway 747 | 4 |
| ★83 | 98 | — | — | GETTING MIGHTY CROWDED — Betty Everett, Vee Jay 628 | 2 |
| 84 | 85 | — | — | A WOMAN'S LOVE — Carla Thomas, Atlantic 2258 | 2 |
| 85 | 88 | — | — | HEY, LITTLE ONE — J. Frank Wilson & the Cavaliers, Josie 926 | 2 |
| 86 | 94 | 95 | — | SCRATCHY — Travis Wammack, Ara 204 | 3 |
| ★87 | — | — | — | PARTY GIRL — Tommy Roe, ABC-Paramount 10604 | 1 |
| ★88 | — | — | — | SOMETIMES I WONDER — Major Lance, Okeh 7209 | 1 |
| ★89 | — | — | — | BOOM, BOOM — Animals, MGM 13298 | 1 |
| ★90 | — | — | — | LOVIN' PLACE — Gale Garnett, RCA Victor 8472 | 1 |
| 91 | 99 | — | — | A HAPPY GUY — Rick Nelson, Decca 31703 | 2 |
| 92 | 93 | 93 | — | HERE SHE COMES — Tymes, Parkway 924 | 3 |
| 93 | 95 | 98 | — | I WON'T FORGET YOU — Jim Reeves, RCA Victor 8461 | 3 |
| 94 | — | 97 | — | YOU'RE THE ONLY WORLD I KNOW — Sonny James, Capitol 5280 | 2 |
| 95 | — | — | — | TALK TO ME BABY — Barry Mann, Red Bird 10-015 | 1 |
| 96 | — | — | — | ENDLESS SLEEP — Hank Williams Jr., MGM 13278 | 1 |
| 97 | — | — | — | PRETEND YOU DON'T SEE HER — Bobby Vee, Liberty 55751 | 1 |
| 98 | — | — | — | FIDDLER ON THE ROOF — Village Stompers, Epic 9740 | 1 |
| 99 | — | — | — | ROME WILL NEVER LEAVE YOU — Richard Chamberlain, MGM 12285 | 1 |
| 100 | — | — | — | I DON'T WANT TO WALK WITHOUT YOU — Phyllis McGuire, Reprise 0310 | 1 |

## BUBBLING UNDER THE HOT 100

101. WATCH OUT, SALLY! — Diane Renay, MGM 12296
102. ONCE A DAY — Connie Smith, RCA Victor 8416
103. PEARLY SHELLS — Burl Ives, Decca 31659
104. BIG BROTHER — Dickey Lee, Hall 1924
105. I WOULDN'T TRADE YOU FOR THE WORLD — Bachelors, London 9693
106. MUMBLES — Oscar Peterson Trio, Mercury 72342
107. I DON'T KNOW YOU ANYMORE — Bobby Goldsboro, United Artists 781
108. SHAKE A LADY — Ray Bryant, Sue 108
109. I'M THE LOVER MAN — Little Jerry Williams, Loma 2005
110. DEAR HEART — Henry Mancini's Ork & Chorus, RCA Victor 8458
111. PERCOLATIN' — Willie Mitchell, Hi 2083
112. MY ADORABLE ONE — Joe Simon, Vee Jay 609
113. DON'T SHUT ME OUT — Sammy Davis Jr., Reprise 0322
114. I JUST CAN'T SAY GOODBYE — Bobby Rydell, Capitol 5305
115. I'LL BE THERE — Gerry & the Pacemakers, Laurie 2279
116. WHY (Doncha Be My Girl) — Chartbusters, Mutual 508
117. TOGETHER — P. J. Proby, London 9705
118. MAKIN' WHOOPEE — Ray Charles, ABC-Paramount 10609
119. PLEASE, PLEASE MAKE IT EASY — Brook Benton, Phillies 124
120. MUSTANG 2 + 2 — Casuals, Sound Stage 7 2534
121. NEVERTHELESS — Billy Butler & the Chanters, Okeh 7207
122. UNLESS YOU CARE — Terry Black, Tollie 9026
123. CHITLINS — Soul Jenkins, Tower 147
124. YOU'VE LOST THAT LOVIN' FEELIN' — Righteous Brothers, Phillies 124
125. WOODEN HEART — Elvis Presley, RCA Victor 0720
126. JULIE KNOWS — Randy Sparks, Columbia 43138
127. THE LUMBERJACK — Hal Willis, Sims 207
128. IF I KNEW THEN — Ray Conniff Singers, Columbia 43148
129. GOLDFINGER — Billy Strange, Crescendo 334
130. IT'S ALRIGHT — Adam Faith, Amy 913
131. DON'T LET ME BE MISUNDERSTOOD — Nina Simone, Phillips 40232
132. HASTE MAKES WASTE — Jackie Ross, Chess 1915
133. TELL HER JOHNNY SAID GOODBYE — Jerry Jackson, Columbia 43158
134. PROMISED LAND — Chuck Berry, Chess 1916
135. HAVE YOU EVER BEEN LONELY — Clarence (Frogman) Henry, Parrot 45004

*Compiled from national retail sales and radio station airplay by the Music Popularity Dept. of Record Market Research, Billboard.*

For Week Ending December 12, 1964

# Billboard HOT 100

★ STAR performer—Sides registering greatest proportionate upward progress this week.

Record Industry Association of America seal of certification as million selling single.

Billboard Award

| This Week | 1 Wk. Ago | 2 Wks. Ago | 3 Wks. Ago | TITLE Artist, Label & Number | Weeks On Chart |
|---|---|---|---|---|---|
| 1 | 2 | 6 | 11 | MR. LONELY — Bobby Vinton, Epic 9730 | 7 |
| 2 | 4 | 4 | 5 | SHE'S NOT THERE — Zombies, Parrot 9695 | 9 |
| 3 | 1 | 5 | 6 | RINGO — Lorne Greene, RCA Victor 8444 | 7 |
| 4 | 8 | 13 | 31 | COME SEE ABOUT ME — Supremes, Motown 1068 | 5 |
| 5 | 22 | — | — | I FEEL FINE — Beatles, Capitol 5327 | 2 |
| 6 | 6 | 8 | 10 | TIME IS ON MY SIDE — Rolling Stones, London 9708 | 9 |
| 7 | 7 | 7 | 8 | YOU REALLY GOT ME — Kinks, Reprise 0306 | 12 |
| 8 | 5 | 2 | 1 | BABY LOVE — Supremes, Motown 1066 | 11 |
| 9 | 10 | 11 | 12 | I'M GONNA BE STRONG — Gene Pitney, Musicor 1045 | 8 |
| 10 | 13 | 15 | 29 | DANCE, DANCE, DANCE — Beach Boys, Capitol 5306 | 6 |
| 11 | 3 | 1 | 2 | LEADER OF THE PACK — Shangri-Las, Red Bird 10-014 | 10 |
| 12 | 9 | 10 | 19 | MOUNTAIN OF LOVE — Johnny Rivers, Imperial 66075 | 7 |
| 13 | 15 | 19 | 20 | I'M INTO SOMETHING GOOD — Herman's Hermits, MGM 13280 | 9 |
| 14 | 17 | 24 | 36 | GOIN' OUT OF MY HEAD — Little Anthony & the Imperials, DCP 1119 | 6 |
| 15 | 12 | 12 | 14 | ASK ME — Elvis Presley, RCA Victor 8440 | 10 |
| 16 | 18 | 18 | 24 | EVERYTHING'S ALRIGHT — Newbeats, Hickory 1282 | 8 |
| 17 | 19 | 28 | 47 | SHA LA LA — Manfred Mann, Ascot 2165 | 5 |
| 18 | 14 | 16 | 22 | RIGHT OR WRONG — Ronnie Dove, Diamond 173 | 8 |
| 19 | 24 | 30 | 61 | SATURDAY NIGHT AT THE MOVIES — Drifters, Atlantic 2260 | 5 |
| 20 | 20 | 22 | 27 | BIG MAN IN TOWN — 4 Seasons, Philips 40238 | 6 |
| 21 | 21 | 26 | 59 | THE JERK — Larks, Money 106 | 5 |
| 22 | 11 | 3 | 3 | COME A LITTLE BIT CLOSER — Jay & the Americans, United Artists 759 | 14 |
| 23 | 23 | 29 | 34 | WALKING IN THE RAIN — Ronettes, Philles 123 | 8 |
| 24 | 31 | 46 | 63 | ANY WAY YOU WANT IT — Dave Clark Five, Epic 9739 | 5 |
| 25 | 25 | 27 | 32 | SIDEWALK SURFIN' — Jan & Dean, Liberty 55727 | 7 |
| 26 | 37 | 51 | 81 | THE WEDDING — Julie Rogers, Mercury 72332 | 4 |
| 27 | 33 | 41 | 53 | OH NO, NOT MY BABY — Maxine Brown, Wand 162 | 8 |
| 28 | 30 | 40 | 52 | MY LOVE FORGIVE ME (Amore, Scusami) — Robert Goulet, Columbia 43131 | 8 |
| 29 | 46 | — | — | SHE'S A WOMAN — Beatles, Capitol 5327 | 2 |
| 30 | 43 | 59 | 96 | AMEN — Impressions, ABC-Paramount 10602 | 4 |
| 31 | 32 | 44 | 51 | GONE, GONE, GONE — Everly Brothers, Warner Bros. 5478 | 9 |
| 32 | 26 | 20 | 23 | REACH OUT FOR ME — Dionne Warwick, Scepter 1285 | 8 |
| 33 | 36 | 39 | 46 | SHE UNDERSTANDS ME — Johnny Tillotson, MGM 13284 | 7 |
| 34 | 38 | 50 | 60 | TOO MANY FISH IN THE SEA — Marvelettes, Tamla 54105 | 6 |
| 35 | 16 | 9 | 4 | LAST KISS — J. Frank Wilson & the Cavaliers, Josie 923 | 15 |
| 36 | 44 | 55 | 79 | WILLOW WEEP FOR ME — Chad & Jeremy, World Artists 1034 | 5 |
| 37 | 29 | 17 | 17 | IS IT TRUE — Brenda Lee, Decca 31690 | 9 |
| 38 | 27 | 25 | 16 | AINT THAT LOVING YOU BABY — Elvis Presley, RCA Victor 8440 | 10 |
| 39 | 52 | 77 | 94 | THOU SHALT NOT STEAL — Dick & Deedee, Warner Bros. 5482 | 4 |
| 40 | 49 | 65 | 88 | HOW SWEET IT IS — Marvin Gaye, Tamla 54107 | 4 |
| 41 | 41 | 43 | 48 | WE COULD — Al Martino, Capitol 5293 | 6 |
| 42 | 50 | 81 | — | AS TEARS GO BY — Marianne Faithful, London 9697 | 3 |
| 43 | 54 | 64 | 73 | ONE MORE TIME — Ray Charles Singers, Command 4057 | 5 |
| 44 | 55 | 71 | 87 | KEEP SEARCHIN' — Del Shannon, Amy 915 | 4 |
| 45 | 51 | 68 | — | WITHOUT THE ONE YOU LOVE — Four Tops, Motown 1069 | 3 |
| 46 | 48 | 63 | 71 | RUN, RUN, RUN — Gestures, Soma 1417 | 5 |
| 47 | 59 | 62 | 78 | SINCE I DON'T HAVE YOU — Chuck Jackson, Wand 169 | 5 |
| 48 | 28 | 14 | 7 | HAVE I THE RIGHT? — Honeycombs, Interphon 7707 | 13 |
| 49 | 61 | 83 | — | LOVE POTION NUMBER NINE — Searchers, Kapp Winner's Circle 27 | 3 |
| 50 | 53 | 78 | — | DEAR HEART — Andy Williams, Columbia 43180 | 3 |
| 51 | 63 | — | — | WILD ONE — Martha & the Vandellas, Gordy 7036 | 2 |
| 52 | 45 | 47 | 50 | AIN'T IT THE TRUTH — Mary Wells, 20th Century-Fox 544 | 7 |
| 53 | 57 | 75 | — | DEAR HEART — Jack Jones, Kapp 635 | 3 |
| 54 | 71 | 96 | — | DO-WACKA-DO — Roger Miller, Smash 1947 | 3 |
| 55 | 62 | 79 | — | WALK AWAY — Matt Monro, Liberty 55745 | 3 |
| 56 | 70 | 86 | — | MY LOVE (Roses Are Red) — "You Know Who" Group, 4 Corners 113 | 3 |
| 57 | 69 | 82 | 97 | THE 81 — Candy & the Kisses, Cameo 336 | 4 |
| 58 | 80 | — | — | LEADER OF THE LAUNDROMAT — Detergents, Roulette 4590 | 2 |
| 59 | 78 | — | — | WHAT NOW — Gene Chandler, Constellation 141 | 2 |
| 60 | 68 | 76 | — | THE PRICE — Solomon Burke, Atlantic 2259 | 3 |
| 61 | 58 | 58 | 64 | IT AIN'T ME, BABE — Johnny Cash, Columbia 43145 | 7 |
| 62 | 65 | 69 | 74 | LISTEN LONELY GIRL — Johnny Mathis, Mercury 72339 | 8 |
| 63 | 74 | 90 | — | I'M GONNA LOVE YOU TOO — Hullaballoos, Roulette 4587 | 3 |
| 64 | 76 | 92 | — | DON'T FORGET I STILL LOVE YOU — Bobbi Martin, Coral 62426 | 3 |
| 65 | 73 | 89 | — | (There's) ALWAYS SOMETHING THERE TO REMIND ME — Sandie Shaw, Reprise 0320 | 3 |
| 66 | 64 | 66 | 70 | OPPORTUNITY — Jewels, Dimension 1034 | 10 |
| 67 | 89 | — | — | BOOM BOOM — Animals, MGM 13298 | 2 |
| 68 | 66 | 60 | 69 | FOUR STRONG WINDS — Bobby Bare, RCA Victor 8443 | 7 |
| 69 | 81 | — | — | HAWAII TATTOO — Waikikis, Kapp Winner's Circle 30 | 2 |
| 70 | — | — | — | YOU'RE NOBODY TILL SOMEBODY LOVES YOU — Dean Martin, Reprise 0333 | 1 |
| 71 | 72 | 73 | 75 | IF YOU WANT THIS LOVE — Sonny Knight, Aura 403 | 9 |
| 72 | 83 | 98 | — | GETTING MIGHTY CROWDED — Betty Everett, Vee Jay 628 | 3 |
| 73 | 77 | 80 | 99 | IT'S ALL OVER — Walter Jackson, Okeh 7204 | 4 |
| 74 | 79 | — | — | SMILE — Betty Everett & Jerry Butler, Vee Jay 633 | 2 |
| 75 | 90 | — | — | LOVIN' PLACE — Gale Garnett, RCA Victor 8472 | 2 |
| 76 | 88 | — | — | SOMETIMES I WONDER — Major Lance, Okeh 7209 | 2 |
| 77 | — | — | — | YOU'VE LOST THAT LOVIN' FEELIN' — Righteous Brothers, Philles 124 | 1 |
| 78 | 82 | 84 | 85 | DO ANYTHING YOU WANNA — Harold Betters, Gateway 747 | 5 |
| 79 | 67 | 67 | 77 | ALMOST THERE — Andy Williams, Columbia 43128 | 5 |
| 80 | 84 | 85 | — | A WOMAN'S LOVE — Carla Thomas, Atlantic 2258 | 3 |
| 81 | — | — | — | I'LL BE THERE — Gerry & the Pacemakers, Laurie 3279 | 1 |
| 82 | 100 | — | — | I DON'T WANT TO WALK WITHOUT YOU — Phyllis McGuire, Reprise 0310 | 2 |
| 83 | 86 | 94 | 95 | SCRATCHY — Travis Wammack, Ara 204 | 4 |
| 84 | — | — | — | I FOUND A LOVE, OH WHAT A LOVE — Jo Ann & Troy, Atlantic 2256 | 1 |
| 85 | — | — | — | MAKIN' WHOOPEE — Ray Charles, ABC-Paramount 10609 | 1 |
| 86 | — | — | — | COME ON DO THE JERK — Miracles, Tamla 54109 | 1 |
| 87 | 87 | — | — | PARTY GIRL — Tommy Roe, ABC-Paramount 10604 | 2 |
| 88 | 91 | 99 | — | A HAPPY GUY — Rick Nelson, Decca 31703 | 3 |
| 89 | — | — | — | PROMISED LAND — Chuck Berry, Chess 1916 | 1 |
| 90 | — | — | — | THE NAME GAME — Shirley Ellis, Congress 230 | 1 |
| 91 | — | — | — | DEAR HEART — Henry Mancini's Ork & Chorus, RCA Victor 8458 | 1 |
| 92 | 94 | 97 | — | YOU'RE THE ONLY WORLD I KNOW — Sonny James, Capitol 5280 | 3 |
| 93 | — | — | — | (There'll Come a Day When) EV'RY LITTLE BIT HURTS — Bobby Vee, Liberty 55751 | 1 |
| 94 | 95 | — | — | TALK TO ME BABY — Barry Mann, Red Bird 10-015 | 2 |
| 95 | — | 70 | 80 | CHAINED AND BOUND — Otis Redding, Volt 121 | 7 |
| 96 | 96 | — | — | ENDLESS SLEEP — Hank Williams Jr., MGM 13278 | 2 |
| 97 | 98 | — | — | FIDDLER ON THE ROOF — Village Stompers, Epic 9740 | 2 |
| 98 | — | 100 | — | IT'LL NEVER BE OVER FOR ME — Baby Washington, Sue 114 | 2 |
| 99 | — | — | 100 | UNLESS YOU CARE — Terry Black, Tollie 9026 | 2 |
| 100 | — | — | — | MY BUDDY SEAT — Hondells, Mercury 72366 | 1 |

## HOT 100—A TO Z—(Publisher-Licensee)

Ain't It the Truth (Grand Canyon & Shake-Well, BMI) ........ 52
Ain't That Loving You Baby (Presley, BMI) ........ 38
Almost There (Northern-Barnaby, ASCAP) ........ 79
Amen (Pamco, BMI) ........ 30
Any Way You Want It (Branston, BMI) ........ 24
As Tears Go By (Forward, ASCAP) ........ 42
Ask Me (Presley, BMI) ........ 15
Baby Love (Jobete, BMI) ........ 8
Big Man in Town (Saturday-Gavadima, ASCAP) ........ 20
Boom Boom (Conrad, BMI) ........ 67
Chained and Bound (East-Time, BMI) ........ 95
Come a Little Bit Closer (Picturetone, BMI) ........ 22
Come Do the Jerk (Jobete, BMI) ........ 86
Come See About Me (Jobete, BMI) ........ 4
Dance, Dance, Dance (Sea of Tunes, BMI) ........ 10
Dear Heart—Jones (Northridge-Witmark, ASCAP) ........ 53
Dear Heart—Mancini (Northridge-Witmark, ASCAP) ........ 91
Dear Heart—Williams (Northridge-Witmark, ASCAP) ........ 50
Do Anything You Wanna (Waygate, ASCAP) ........ 78
Do-Wacka-Do (Tree, BMI) ........ 54
Don't Forget I Still Love You (South Mountain, BMI) ........ 64
81, The (Hill & Range, BMI) ........ 57
Endless Sleep (Montei-Elizabeth, BMI) ........ 96
Everything's Alright (Acuff-Rose, BMI) ........ 16
Fiddler on the Roof (Sunbeam, BMI) ........ 97
Four Strong Winds (Witmark, ASCAP) ........ 68
Getting Mighty Crowded (Blackwood, BMI) ........ 72
Goin' Out of My Head (South Mountain, BMI) ........ 14
Gone, Gone, Gone (Acuff-Rose, BMI) ........ 31
Happy Guy, A (Blackwood, BMI) ........ 88
Have I the Right? (Duchess, BMI) ........ 48
Hawaii Tattoo (Zodiac, BMI) ........ 69
How Sweet It Is (Jobete, BMI) ........ 40
I Don't Want to Walk Without You (Paramount, ASCAP) ........ 82
I Feel Fine (Maclen, BMI) ........ 5
I Found a Love, Oh What a Love (Cotillion, BMI) ........ 84
I'll Be There (T.M., BMI) ........ 81
I'm Gonna Be Strong (Screen Gems-Columbia, BMI) ........ 9
I'm Gonna Love You Too (Nor-Va-Jak, BMI) ........ 63
I'm Into Something Good (Screen Gems-Columbia, BMI) ........ 13
If You Want This Love (Har-Bock, BMI) ........ 71
Is It True (Southern, ASCAP) ........ 37
It Ain't Me, Babe (Witmark, ASCAP) ........ 61
It'll Never Be Over for Me (Bourne, ASCAP) ........ 98
It's All Over (Curtom-Jalynne, BMI) ........ 73
Jerk, The (Cash, BMI) ........ 21
Keep Searchin' (Vicki-McLaughlin, BMI) ........ 44
Last Kiss (Boblo, BMI) ........ 35
Leader of the Laundromat (Apt, ASCAP) ........ 58
Leader of the Pack (Tender Tunes-Trio, BMI) ........ 11
Listen Lonely Girl (Jenny, ASCAP) ........ 62
Love Potion Number Nine (Quintet, BMI) ........ 49
Lovin' Place (Leprechaun, BMI) ........ 75
Makin' Whoopee (Bregman, Vocco & Conn-Kahn, ASCAP) ........ 85
Mr. Lonely (Ripley, BMI) ........ 1
Mountain of Love (Trousdale-Vaughn, BMI) ........ 12
My Buddy Seat (New Executive-Beechwood, BMI) ........ 100
My Love Forgive Me (Gil, BMI) ........ 28
My Love (Roses Are Red) (Tiffany, BMI) ........ 56
Name Game, The (Gallico, BMI) ........ 90
Oh No, Not My Baby (Screen Gems-Columbia, BMI) ........ 27
One More Time (January, BMI) ........ 43
Opportunity (Screen Gems-Columbia, BMI) ........ 66
Party Girl (Unart, BMI) ........ 87
Price, The (Cotillion, BMI) ........ 60
Promised Land (Arc, BMI) ........ 89
Reach Out for Me (Ross Jungnickel-Blue Seas-Jac, ASCAP) ........ 32
Right or Wrong (Combine, BMI) ........ 18
Ringo (Robertson, ASCAP) ........ 3
Run, Run, Run (Ringneck, BMI) ........ 46
Saturday Night at the Movies (Screen Gems-Columbia, BMI) ........ 19
Scratchy (Rolando, BMI) ........ 83
Sha La La (Ludix-Flomarlu, BMI) ........ 17
She's a Woman (Maclen, BMI) ........ 29
She's Not There (Gallico, BMI) ........ 2
She Understands Me (Gallico, BMI) ........ 33
Sidewalk Surfin' (Sea of Tunes, BMI) ........ 25
Since I Don't Have You (Circle 7, BMI) ........ 47
Smile (Bourne, ASCAP) ........ 74
Sometimes I Wonder (Camad & Chi-Sound, BMI) ........ 76
Talk to Me Baby (Screen Gems-Columbia, BMI) ........ 94
(There'll Come a Day When) Ev'ry Little Bit Hurts (Blen-Shelby, ASCAP) ........ 93
(There's) Always Something There to Remind Me (Ross Jungnickel-Blue Seas-Jac, ASCAP) ........ 65
Thou Shalt Not Steal (Acuff-Rose, BMI) ........ 39
Time Is on My Side (Rittenhouse-Maygar, BMI) ........ 6
Too Many Fish in the Sea (Jobete, BMI) ........ 34
Unless You Care (Trousdale, BMI) ........ 99
Walk Away (Ardmore-Beechwood, BMI) ........ 55
Walking in the Rain (Screen Gems-Columbia, BMI) ........ 23
We Could (Acuff-Rose, BMI) ........ 41
Wedding, The (Regent, BMI) ........ 26
What Now (Chi-Sound & Camad, BMI) ........ 59
Wild One (Jobete, BMI) ........ 51
Willow Weep for Me (Bourne, ASCAP) ........ 36
Without the One You Love (Jobete, BMI) ........ 45
Woman's Love, A (East, BMI) ........ 80
You Really Got Me (Jay-Boy, BMI) ........ 7
You're Nobody Till Somebody Loves You (Southern, ASCAP) ........ 70
You're the Only World I Knew (Marson, BMI) ........ 92
You've Lost That Lovin' Feelin' (Screen Gems-Columbia, BMI) ........ 77

## BUBBLING UNDER THE HOT 100

101. WATCH OUT, SALLY! ........ Diane Renay, MGM 13296
102. I'M THE LOVER MAN ........ Little Jerry Williams, Loma 2005
103. I WON'T FORGET YOU ........ Jim Reeves, RCA Victor 8461
104. BIG BROTHER ........ Dickey Lee, Hall 1924
105. ROME WILL NEVER LEAVE YOU ........ Richard Chamberlain, MGM 13285
106. AND SATISFY ........ Nancy Wilson, Capitol 5319
107. HERE SHE COMES ........ Tymes, Parkway 924
108. HEY-DA-DA-DOW ........ Dolphins, Fraternity 937
109. PERCOLATIN' ........ Willie Mitchell, Hi 2083
110. DON'T SHUT ME OUT ........ Sammy Davis Jr., Reprise 0322
111. A THOUSAND CUPS OF HAPPINESS ........ Joe Hinton, Back Beat 532
112. I JUST CAN'T SAY GOODBYE ........ Bobby Rydell, Capitol 5305
113. SILLY LITTLE GIRL ........ Tams, ABC-Paramount 10601
114. SEVEN LETTERS ........ Ben E. King, Atco 6328
115. HAVE YOU LOOKED INTO YOUR HEART ........ Jerry Vale, Columbia 43181
116. WHY (Doncha Be My Girl) ........ Chartbusters, Mutual 508
117. MUSTANG 2 + 2 ........ Casuals, Sound Stage 7 2534
118. ONCE A DAY ........ Connie Smith, RCA Victor 8416
119. YOU'LL ALWAYS BE THE ONE I LOVE ........ Dean Martin, Reprise 0333
120. IT'S ALRIGHT ........ Adam Faith, Amy 913
121. THE DODO ........ Jumpin' Gene Simmons, Hi 2080
122. WOODEN HEART ........ Elvis Presley, RCA Victor 0720
123. I WOULDN'T TRADE YOU FOR THE WORLD ........ Bachelors, London 9693
124. ODE TO THE LITTLE BROWN SHACK OUT BACK ........ Billy Edd Wheeler, Kapp 617
125. GOOGLE EYE ........ Nashville Teens, London 9712
126. TELL HER JOHNNY SAID GOODBYE ........ Jerry Jackson, Columbia 43158
127. SHE'S ALL RIGHT ........ Jackie Wilson, Brunswick 55273
128. GOLDFINGER ........ Billy Strange, Crescendo 334
129. EITHER WAY I LOSE ........ Glady's Knight & the Pips, Maxx 331
130. BUCKET "T" ........ Ronny & the Daytonas, Mala 492
131. VOICE YOUR CHOICE ........ Radiants, Chess 1904
132. HAWAII TATTOO ........ Martin Denny, Liberty 55754
133. PAPER TIGER ........ Sue Thompson, Hickory 1284
134. SEND HER TO ME ........ Johnny Thunder, Diamond 175
135. SEND ME NO FLOWERS ........ Doris Day, Columbia 43153

Compiled from national retail sales and radio station airplay by the Music Popularity Dept. of Record Market Research, Billboard.

Billboard — For Week Ending December 19, 1964

# HOT 100

★ **STAR performer—Sides registering greatest proportionate upward progress this week.**

Record Industry Association of America seal of certification as million selling single.

| This Week | 1 Wk. Ago | 2 Wks. Ago | 3 Wks. Ago | TITLE Artist, Label & Number | Weeks On Chart |
|---|---|---|---|---|---|
| ★1 | 4 | 8 | 13 | COME SEE ABOUT ME — Supremes, Motown 1068 | 6 |
| ★2 | 5 | 22 | — | I FEEL FINE — Beatles, Capitol 5327 | 3 |
| 3 | 1 | 2 | 6 | MR. LONELY — Bobby Vinton, Epic 9730 | 8 |
| 4 | 2 | 4 | 4 | SHE'S NOT THERE — Zombies, Parrot 9695 | 10 |
| 5 | 3 | 1 | 5 | RINGO — Lorne Greene, RCA Victor 8444 | 8 |
| 6 | 6 | 6 | 8 | TIME IS ON MY SIDE — Rolling Stones, London 9708 | 10 |
| ★7 | 14 | 17 | 24 | GOIN' OUT OF MY HEAD — Little Anthony & the Imperials, DCP 1119 | 7 |
| 8 | 10 | 13 | 15 | DANCE, DANCE, DANCE — Beach Boys, Capitol 5306 | 7 |
| 9 | 9 | 10 | 11 | I'M GONNA BE STRONG — Gene Pitney, Musicor 1045 | 9 |
| 10 | 7 | 7 | 7 | YOU REALLY GOT ME — Kinks, Reprise 0306 | 13 |
| 11 | 12 | 9 | 10 | MOUNTAIN OF LOVE — Johnny Rivers, Imperial 66075 | 8 |
| ★12 | 21 | 21 | 26 | THE JERK — Larks, Money 106 | 6 |
| 13 | 13 | 15 | 19 | I'M INTO SOMETHING GOOD — Herman's Hermits, MGM 13280 | 10 |
| ★14 | 29 | 46 | — | SHE'S A WOMAN — Beatles, Capitol 5327 | 3 |
| 15 | 8 | 5 | 2 | BABY LOVE — Supremes, Motown 1066 | 12 |
| 16 | 17 | 19 | 28 | SHA LA LA — Manfred Mann, Ascot 2165 | 6 |
| ★17 | 26 | 37 | 51 | THE WEDDING — Julie Rogers, Mercury 72332 | 5 |
| 18 | 19 | 24 | 30 | SATURDAY NIGHT AT THE MOVIES — Drifters, Atlantic 2260 | 6 |
| ★19 | 24 | 31 | 46 | ANY WAY YOU WANT IT — Dave Clark Five, Epic 9739 | 6 |
| 20 | 11 | 3 | 1 | LEADER OF THE PACK — Shangri-Las, Red Bird 10-014 | 11 |
| 21 | 18 | 14 | 16 | RIGHT OR WRONG — Ronnie Dove, Diamond 173 | 9 |
| 22 | 20 | 20 | 22 | BIG MAN IN TOWN — 4 Seasons, Philips 40238 | 7 |
| 23 | 16 | 18 | 18 | EVERYTHING'S ALRIGHT — Newbeats, Hickory 1282 | 9 |
| ★24 | 30 | 43 | 59 | AMEN — Impressions, ABC-Paramount 10602 | 5 |
| 25 | 28 | 30 | 40 | MY LOVE FORGIVE ME (Amore, Scusami) — Robert Goulet, Columbia 4313 | 9 |
| 26 | 27 | 33 | 41 | OH NO, NOT MY BABY — Maxine Brown, Wand 162 | 9 |
| 27 | 15 | 12 | 12 | ASK ME — Elvis Presley, RCA Victor 8440 | 11 |
| ★28 | 36 | 44 | 55 | WILLOW WEEP FOR ME — Chad & Jeremy, World Artists 1034 | 6 |
| ★29 | 34 | 38 | 50 | TOO MANY FISH IN THE SEA — Marvelettes, Tamla 54105 | 7 |
| ★30 | 49 | 61 | 83 | LOVE POTION NUMBER NINE — Searchers, Kapp Winner's Circle 27 | 4 |
| 31 | 33 | 36 | 39 | SHE UNDERSTANDS ME — Johnny Tillotson, MGM 13284 | 8 |
| 32 | 23 | 23 | 29 | WALKING IN THE RAIN — Ronettes, Philles 123 | 9 |
| ★33 | 58 | 80 | — | LEADER OF THE LAUNDROMAT — Detergents, Roulette 4590 | 3 |
| 34 | 40 | 49 | 65 | HOW SWEET IT IS (To Be Loved by You) — Marvin Gaye, Tamla 54107 | 5 |
| 35 | 39 | 52 | 77 | THOU SHALT NOT STEAL — Dick & Deedee, Warner Bros. 5482 | 5 |
| 36 | 42 | 50 | 81 | AS TEARS GO BY — Marianne Faithful, London 9697 | 4 |
| 37 | 25 | 25 | 27 | SIDEWALK SURFIN' — Jan & Dean, Liberty 55727 | 8 |
| ★38 | 50 | 53 | 78 | DEAR HEART — Andy Williams, Columbia 43180 | 4 |
| 39 | 44 | 55 | 71 | KEEP SEARCHIN' — Del Shannon, Amy 915 | 5 |
| 40 | 43 | 54 | 64 | ONE MORE TIME — Ray Charles Singers, Command 4057 | 6 |
| ★41 | 51 | 63 | — | WILD ONE — Martha & the Vandellas, Gordy 7036 | 3 |
| 42 | 22 | 11 | 3 | COME A LITTLE BIT CLOSER — Jay & the Americans, United Artists 759 | 15 |
| 43 | 45 | 51 | 68 | WITHOUT THE ONE YOU LOVE — Four Tops, Motown 1069 | 4 |
| 44 | 46 | 48 | 63 | RUN, RUN, RUN — Gestures, Soma 1417 | 6 |
| ★45 | 55 | 62 | 79 | WALK AWAY — Matt Monro, Liberty 55745 | 4 |
| 46 | 54 | 71 | 96 | DO-WACKA-DO — Roger Miller, Smash 1947 | 4 |
| 47 | 47 | 59 | 62 | SINCE I DON'T HAVE YOU — Chuck Jackson, Wand 169 | 6 |
| 48 | 53 | 57 | 75 | DEAR HEART — Jack Jones, Kapp 635 | 4 |
| 49 | 31 | 32 | 44 | GONE, GONE, GONE — Everly Brothers, Warner Bros. 5478 | 10 |
| ★50 | 74 | 79 | — | SMILE — Betty Everett & Jerry Butler, Vee Jay 633 | 3 |
| 51 | 59 | 78 | — | WHAT NOW — Gene Chandler, Constellation 141 | 3 |
| ★52 | 64 | 76 | 92 | DON'T FORGET I STILL LOVE YOU — Bobbi Martin, Coral 62426 | 4 |
| 53 | 57 | 69 | 82 | THE 81 — Candy & the Kisses, Cameo 336 | 5 |
| ★54 | 65 | 73 | 89 | (There's) ALWAYS SOMETHING THERE TO REMIND ME — Sandie Shaw, Reprise 0320 | 4 |
| ★55 | 67 | 89 | — | BOOM BOOM — Animals, MGM 13298 | 3 |
| 56 | 56 | 70 | 86 | MY LOVE (Roses Are Red) — "You Know Who" Group, 4 Corners 113 | 4 |
| 57 | 60 | 68 | 76 | THE PRICE — Solomon Burke, Atlantic 2259 | 4 |
| ★58 | 69 | 81 | — | HAWAII TATTOO — Waikikis, Kapp Winner's Circle 30 | 3 |
| 59 | 63 | 74 | 90 | I'M GONNA LOVE YOU TOO — Hullaballoos, Roulette 4587 | 4 |
| ★60 | 77 | — | — | YOU'VE LOST THAT LOVIN' FEELIN — Righteous Brothers, Philles 124 | 2 |
| 61 | 52 | 45 | 47 | AIN'T IT THE TRUTH — Mary Wells, 20th Century-Fox 544 | 8 |
| 62 | 75 | 90 | — | LOVIN' PLACE — Gale Garnett, RCA Victor 8472 | 3 |
| ★63 | 81 | — | — | I'LL BE THERE — Gerry & the Pacemakers, Laurie 3279 | 2 |
| 64 | 70 | — | — | YOU'RE NOBODY TILL SOMEBODY LOVES YOU — Dean Martin, Reprise 0333 | 2 |
| ★65 | 89 | — | — | PROMISED LAND — Chuck Berry, Chess 1916 | 2 |
| 66 | 72 | 83 | 98 | GETTING MIGHTY CROWDED — Betty Everett, Vee Jay 628 | 4 |
| 67 | 73 | 77 | 80 | IT'S ALL OVER — Walter Jackson, Okeh 7204 | 5 |
| 68 | 61 | 58 | 58 | IT AIN'T ME, BABE — Johnny Cash, Columbia 43145 | 8 |
| 69 | 76 | 88 | — | SOMETIMES I WONDER — Major Lance, Okeh 7209 | 3 |
| ★70 | 86 | — | — | COME ON DO THE JERK — Miracles, Tamla 54109 | 2 |
| 71 | 80 | 84 | 85 | A WOMAN'S LOVE — Carla Thomas, Atlantic 2258 | 4 |
| 72 | 85 | — | — | MAKIN' WHOOPEE — Ray Charles, ABC-Paramount 10609 | 2 |
| ★73 | 90 | — | — | THE NAME GAME — Shirley Ellis, Congress 230 | 2 |
| 74 | 78 | 82 | 84 | DO ANYTHING YOU WANNA — Harold Betters, Gateway 747 | 6 |
| ★75 | — | — | — | HOLD WHAT YOU'VE GOT — Joe Tex, Dial 4001 | 1 |
| ★76 | — | — | — | HE'S MY GUY — Irma Thomas, Imperial 66080 | 1 |
| ★77 | — | — | — | DO IT RIGHT — Brook Benton, Mercury 72365 | 1 |
| ★78 | — | — | — | SEVEN LETTERS — Ben E. King, Atco 6328 | 1 |
| 79 | 82 | 100 | — | I DON'T WANT TO WALK WITHOUT YOU — Phyllis McGuire, Reprise 0310 | 3 |
| ★80 | — | — | — | CAN YOU JERK LIKE ME — Contours, Gordy 7032 | 1 |
| 81 | 83 | 86 | 94 | SCRATCHY — Travis Wammack, Ara 204 | 5 |
| 82 | 88 | 91 | 99 | A HAPPY GUY — Rick Nelson, Decca 31703 | 4 |
| 83 | 84 | — | — | I FOUND A LOVE OH WHAT A LOVE — Jo Ann & Troy, Atlantic 2256 | 2 |
| ★84 | — | — | — | I CAN'T STOP — Honeycombs, Interphon 7713 | 1 |
| 85 | 87 | 87 | — | PARTY GIRL — Tommy Roe, ABC-Paramount 10604 | 3 |
| 86 | 91 | — | — | DEAR HEART — Henry Mancini's Ork & Chorus, RCA Victor 8458 | 2 |
| ★87 | — | — | — | DOWNTOWN — Petula Clark, Warner Bros. 5494 | 1 |
| ★88 | — | — | — | SOMEWHERE IN YOUR HEART — Frank Sinatra, Reprise 0332 | 1 |
| ★89 | — | — | — | BUCKET "T" — Ronny & the Daytonas, Mala 492 | 1 |
| 90 | 96 | 96 | — | ENDLESS SLEEP — Hank Williams Jr., MGM 13278 | 3 |
| 91 | 92 | 94 | 97 | YOU'RE THE ONLY WORLD I KNOW — Sonny James, Capitol 5280 | 4 |
| 92 | 93 | — | — | (There'll Come a Day When) EV'RY LITTLE BIT HURTS — Bobby Vee, Liberty 55751 | 2 |
| 93 | — | — | — | THE SIDEWINDER — Lee Morgan, Blue Note 1911 | 1 |
| 94 | — | — | — | I JUST CAN'T SAY GOODBYE — Bobby Rydell, Capitol 5305 | 1 |
| 95 | — | — | — | PERCOLATIN' — Willie Mitchell, Hi 2083 | 1 |
| 96 | 100 | — | — | MY BUDDY SEAT — Hondells, Mercury 72366 | 2 |
| 97 | — | — | — | DANNY BOY — Patti LaBelle and Her Bluebells, Parkway 935 | 1 |
| 98 | — | — | — | HAVE YOU LOOKED INTO YOUR HEART — Jerry Vale, Columbia 43181 | 1 |
| 99 | — | — | — | HEY-DA-DA-DOW — Dolphins, Fraternity 937 | 1 |
| 100 | — | — | — | LITTLE BELL — Dixie Cups, Red Bird 10-017 | 1 |

## HOT 100—A TO Z—*(Publisher-Licensee)*


Ain't It the Truth (Grand Canyon & Shake Well, BMI) ... 61
Amen (Pamco, BMI) ... 24
Any Way You Want It (Branston, BMI) ... 19
As Tears Go By (Forward, ASCAP) ... 36
Ask Me (Presley, BMI) ... 27
Baby Love (Jobete, BMI) ... 15
Big Man in Town (Saturday-Gavadima, ASCAP) ... 22
Boom Boom (Conrad, BMI) ... 55
Bucket "T" (Screen Gems-Columbia, BMI) ... 89
Can You Jerk Like Me (Jobete, BMI) ... 80
Come a Little Bit Closer (Picturetone, BMI) ... 42
Come on Do the Jerk (Jobete, BMI) ... 70
Come See About Me (Jobete, BMI) ... 1
Dance, Dance, Dance (Sea of Tunes, BMI) ... 8
Danny Boy (Boosey & Hawkes, ASCAP) ... 97
Dear Heart—Jones (Northridge-Witmark, ASCAP) ... 48
Dear Heart—Mancini (Northridge-Witmark, ASCAP). 86
Dear Heart—Williams (Northridge-Witmark, ASCAP). 38
Do Anything You Wanna (Waygate, ASCAP) ... 74
Do It Right (T.M., BMI) ... 77
Do-Wacka-Do (Tree, BMI) ... 46
Don't Forget I Still Love You (South Mountain, BMI) ... 52
Downtown (Leeds, ASCAP) ... 87
81, The (Hill & Range, BMI) ... 53
Endless Sleep (Montei-Elizabeth, BMI) ... 90
Everything's Alright (Acuff-Rose, BMI) ... 23
Every Little Bit Hurts (Blen-Shelby, ASCAP) ... 92
Getting Mighty Crowded (Blackwood, BMI) ... 66
Goin' Out of My Head (South Mountain, BMI) ... 7
Gone, Gone, Gone (Acuff-Rose, BMI) ... 49
Happy Guy, A (Blackwood, BMI) ... 82
Have You Looked Into Your Heart (South Mountain, BMI) ... 98
Hawaii Tattoo (Zodiac, BMI) ... 58
He's My Guy (Blackwood, BMI) ... 76
Hey-Da-Da-Dow (Edwood, BMI) ... 99
Hold What You've Got (Tree, BMI) ... 75
How Sweet It Is (To Be Loved by You) (Jobete, BMI) ... 34
I Can't Stop (Ivy, ASCAP) ... 84
I Don't Want to Walk Without You (Paramount, ASCAP) ... 79
I Feel Fine (Maclen, BMI) ... 2
I Found a Love Oh What a Love (Cotillion, BMI). 83
I Just Can't Say Goodbye (Screen Gems-Columbia, BMI) ... 94
I'll Be There (T.M., BMI) ... 63
I'm Gonna Be Strong (Screen Gems-Columbia, BMI). 9
I'm Gonna Love You Too (Nor-Va-Jak, BMI) ... 59
I'm Into Something Good (Screen Gems-Columbia, BMI) ... 13
It Ain't Me, Babe (Witmark, ASCAP) ... 68
It's All Over (Curtom-Jalynne, BMI) ... 67
Jerk, The (Cash, BMI) ... 12
Keep Searchin' (Vicki-McLaughlin, BMI) ... 39
Leader of the Laundromat (Apt, ASCAP) ... 33
Leader of the Pack (Tender Tunes-Trio, BMI) ... 20
Little Bell (Trio, BMI) ... 100
Love Portion Number Nine (Quintet, BMI) ... 30
Lovin' Place (Leprechaun, BMI) ... 62
Makin' Whoopee (Bregman, Vocco & Conn-Kahn, ASCAP) ... 72
Mr. Lonely (Ripley, BMI) ... 3
Mountain of Love (Trousdale-Vaughn, BMI) ... 11
My Buddy Seat (New Executive-Beechwood, BMI). 96
My Love Forgive Me (Gil, BMI) ... 25
My Love (Roses Are Red) (Tiffany, BMI) ... 56
Name Game, The (Gallico, BMI) ... 73
Oh No, Not My Baby (Screen Gems-Columbia, BMI). 26
One More Time (January, BMI) ... 40
Party Girl (Unart, BMI) ... 85
Percolatin' (Jec, BMI) ... 95
Price, The (Cotillion, BMI) ... 57
Promised Land (Arc, BMI) ... 65
Right or Wrong (Combine, BMI) ... 21
Ringo (Robertson, ASCAP) ... 5
Run, Run, Run (Ringneck, BMI) ... 44
Saturday Night at the Movies (Screen Gems-Columbia, BMI) ... 18
Scratchy (Rolando, BMI) ... 81
Seven Letters (Milky Way, BMI) ... 78
Sha La La (Ludix-Flomarlu, BMI) ... 16
She's a Woman (Maclen, BMI) ... 14
She's Not There (Gallico, BMI) ... 4
She Understands Me (Gallico, BMI) ... 31
Sidewalk Surfin' (Sea of Tunes, BMI) ... 37
Sidewinder, The (Nom, BMI) ... 93
Since I Don't Have You (Bonneyview-Southern, ASCAP) ... 47
Smile (Bourne, ASCAP) ... 50
Sometimes I Wonder (Camad & Chi-Sound, BMI). 69
Somewhere in Your Heart (Leeds, ASCAP) ... 88
(There's) Always Something There to Remind Me (Ross Jungnickel-Blue Seas-Jac, ASCAP) ... 54
Thou Shalt Not Steal (Acuff-Rose, BMI) ... 35
Time Is on My Side (Rittenhouse-Maygar, BMI) ... 6
Too Many Fish in the Sea (Jobete, BMI) ... 29
Walk Away (Ardmore-Beechwood, BMI) ... 45
Walking in the Rain (Screen Gems-Columbia, BMI). 32
Wedding, The (Regent-Bending, BMI) ... 17
What Now (Chi-Sound & Camad, BMI) ... 51
Wild One (Jobete, BMI) ... 41
Willow Weep for Me (Bourne, ASCAP) ... 28
Without the One You Love (Jobete, BMI) ... 43
Woman's Love, A (East, BMI) ... 71
You Really Got Me (Jay-Boy, BMI) ... 10
You're Nobody Till Somebody Loves You (Southern, ASCAP) ... 64
You're the Only World I Know (Marson, BMI) ... 91
You're Lost That Lovin' Feelin' (Screen Gems-Columbia, BMI) ... 60


## BUBBLING UNDER THE HOT 100

101. BIG BROTHER ... Dickey Lee, Hall 1924
102. NEVERTHELESS ... Billy Butler & the Chanters, Okeh 7207
103. I'M THE LOVER MAN ... Little Jerry Williams, Loma 2005
104. GIVE HIM A GREAT BIG KISS ... Shangri-Las, Red Bird 10-018
105. I WON'T FORGET YOU ... Jim Reeves, RCA Victor 8461
106. TALK TO ME BABY ... Barry Mann, Red Bird 10-015
107. WOODEN HEART ... Elvis Presley, RCA Victor 0720
108. CHAINED AND BOUND ... Otis Redding, Volt 121
109. DON'T SHUT ME OUT ... Sammy Davis Jr., Reprise 0322
110. VOICE YOUR CHOICE ... Radiants, Chess 1904
111. LET'S LOCK THE DOOR (And Throw Away the Key) ... Jay & the Americans, United Artists 805
112. FIDDLER ON THE ROOF ... Village Stompers, Epic 9740
113. IT'S BETTER TO HAVE IT ... Barbara Lynn, Jamie 1292
114. TELL HER JOHNNY SAID GOODBYE ... Jerry Jackson, Columbia 43158
115. CHITTLINS ... Gus Jenkins, Tower 107
116. I WOULDN'T TRADE YOU FOR THE WORLD ... Bachelors, London 9693
117. GOGGLE EYE ... Nashville Teens, London 9712
118. ODE TO THE LITTLE BROWN SHACK OUT BACK. Billy Edd Wheeler, Kapp 617
119. YOU'LL ALWAYS BE THE ONE I LOVE ... Dean Martin, Reprise 0333
120. I WANT YOU TO HAVE EVERYTHING ... Lee Rogers, D-Town 1035
121. GOLDFINGER ... Billy Strange, Crescendo 334
122. LOVE, LOVE (That's All I Want From You) ... Strange Loves, Swan 4192
123. LOOK OF LOVE ... Lesley Gore, Mercury 72372
124. EITHER WAY I LOSE ... Gladys Knight & the Pips, Maxx 331
125. MAYBE ... Shangri-Las, Red Bird 10-019
126. HASTE MAKES WASTE ... Jackie Ross, Chess 1915
127. ONCE A DAY ... Connie Smith, RCA Victor 8416
128. DO WHAT YOU DO DO WELL ... Ned Miller, Fabor 137
129. IT'S ALRIGHT ... Adam Faith, Amy 913
130. LAUGH, LAUGH ... Beau Brummels, Autumn 8
131. THE OTHER RINGO ... Larry Finnegan, Ric 146
132. SEND HER TO ME ... Johnny Thunder, Diamond 175
133. LITTLE STAR ... Randy & the Rainbows, Rust 5091
134. ACROSS THE STREET (Is a Million Miles Away). Ray Peterson, MGM 13299
135. ARE YOU STILL MY BABY ... Shirelles, Scepter 1292

Compiled from national retail sales and radio station airplay by the Music Popularity Dept. of Record Market Research, Billboard.

# Billboard HOT 100

For Week Ending December 26, 1964

★ STAR performer—Sides registering greatest proportionate upward progress this week.

| This Week | Wk. Ago | 2 Wks. Ago | 3 Wks. Ago | TITLE — Artist, Label & Number | Weeks On Chart |
|---|---|---|---|---|---|
| 1 | 2 | 5 | 22 | I FEEL FINE — Beatles, Capitol 5327 | 4 |
| 2 | 1 | 4 | 8 | COME SEE ABOUT ME — Supremes, Motown 1068 | 7 |
| 3 | 3 | 1 | 2 | MR. LONELY — Bobby Vinton, Epic 9730 | 9 |
| ★4 | 14 | 29 | 46 | SHE'S A WOMAN — Beatles, Capitol 5327 | 4 |
| 5 | 4 | 2 | 4 | SHE'S NOT THERE — Zombies, Parrot 9695 | 11 |
| 6 | 7 | 14 | 17 | GOIN' OUT OF MY HEAD — Little Anthony & the Imperials, DCP 1119 | 8 |
| 7 | 5 | 3 | 1 | RINGO — Lorne Greene, RCA Victor 8444 | 9 |
| 8 | 8 | 10 | 13 | DANCE, DANCE, DANCE — Beach Boys, Capitol 5306 | 8 |
| ★9 | 12 | 21 | 21 | THE JERK — Larks, Money 106 | 7 |
| 10 | 6 | 6 | 6 | TIME IS ON MY SIDE — Rolling Stones, London 9708 | 11 |
| 11 | 30 | 49 | 61 | LOVE POTION NUMBER NINE — Searchers, Kapp Winner's Circle 27 | 5 |
| 12 | 24 | 30 | 43 | AMEN — Impressions, ABC-Paramount 10602 | 6 |
| 13 | 16 | 17 | 19 | SHA LA LA — Manfred Mann, Ascot 2165 | 7 |
| 14 | 17 | 26 | 37 | THE WEDDING — Julie Rogers, Mercury 72332 | 6 |
| 15 | 9 | 9 | 10 | I'M GONNA BE STRONG — Gene Pitney, Musicor 1045 | 10 |
| 16 | 11 | 12 | 9 | MOUNTAIN OF LOVE — Johnny Rivers, Imperial 66075 | 9 |
| 17 | 13 | 13 | 15 | I'M INTO SOMETHING GOOD — Herman's Hermits, MGM 13280 | 11 |
| 18 | 10 | 7 | 7 | YOU REALLY GOT ME — Kinks, Reprise 0306 | 14 |
| 19 | 19 | 24 | 31 | ANY WAY YOU WANT IT — Dave Clark Five, Epic 9739 | 7 |
| 20 | 18 | 19 | 24 | SATURDAY NIGHT AT THE MOVIES — Drifters, Atlantic 2260 | 7 |
| 21 | 25 | 28 | 30 | MY LOVE FORGIVE ME (Amore, Scusami) — Robert Goulet, Columbia 43131 | 10 |
| 22 | 20 | 11 | 3 | LEADER OF THE PACK — Shangri-Las, Red Bird 10-014 | 12 |
| ★23 | 39 | 44 | 55 | KEEP SEARCHIN' — Del Shannon, Amy 915 | 6 |
| 24 | 28 | 36 | 44 | WILLOW WEEP FOR ME — Chad & Jeremy, World Artists 1034 | 7 |
| 25 | 26 | 27 | 33 | OH NO, NOT MY BABY — Maxine Brown, Wand 162 | 10 |
| 26 | 36 | 42 | 50 | AS TEARS GO BY — Marianne Faithful, London 9697 | 5 |
| 27 | 34 | 40 | 49 | HOW SWEET IT IS (To Be Loved by You) — Marvin Gaye, Tamla 54107 | 6 |
| ★28 | 33 | 58 | 80 | LEADER OF THE LAUNDROMAT — Detergents, Roulette 4590 | 4 |
| 29 | 29 | 34 | 38 | TOO MANY FISH IN THE SEA — Marvelettes, Tamla 54105 | 8 |
| ★30 | 38 | 50 | 53 | DEAR HEART — Andy Williams, Columbia 43180 | 5 |
| 31 | 31 | 33 | 36 | SHE UNDERSTANDS ME — Johnny Tillotson, MGM 13284 | 5 |
| 32 | 35 | 39 | 52 | THOU SHALT NOT STEAL — Dick & Deedee, Warner Bros. 5482 | 6 |
| 33 | 15 | 8 | 5 | BABY LOVE — Supremes, Motown 1066 | 13 |
| ★34 | 60 | 77 | — | YOU'VE LOST THAT LOVIN' FEELIN' — Righteous Brothers, Philles 124 | 3 |
| 35 | 40 | 43 | 54 | ONE MORE TIME — Ray Charles Singers, Command 4057 | 7 |
| 36 | 21 | 18 | 14 | RIGHT OR WRONG — Ronnie Dove, Diamond 173 | 10 |
| 37 | 48 | 53 | 57 | DEAR HEART — Jack Jones, Kapp 635 | 5 |
| 38 | 32 | 23 | 23 | WALKING IN THE RAIN — Ronettes, Philles 123 | 10 |
| 39 | 41 | 51 | 63 | WILD ONE — Martha & the Vandellas, Gordy 7036 | 4 |
| 40 | 45 | 55 | 62 | WALK AWAY — Matt Monro, Liberty 55745 | 5 |
| 41 | 87 | — | — | DOWNTOWN — Petula Clark, Warner Bros. 5494 | 2 |
| ★42 | 52 | 64 | 76 | DON'T FORGET I STILL LOVE YOU — Bobbi Martin, Coral 62426 | 5 |
| 43 | 46 | 54 | 71 | DO-WACKA-DO — Roger Miller, Smash 1947 | 5 |
| 44 | 44 | 46 | 48 | RUN, RUN, RUN — Gestures, Soma 1417 | 7 |
| 45 | 50 | 74 | 79 | SMILE — Betty Everett & Jerry Butler, Vee Jay 633 | 4 |
| ★46 | 56 | 56 | 70 | MY LOVE (Roses Are Red) — "You Know Who" Group, 4 Corners 113 | 5 |
| 47 | 47 | 47 | 59 | SINCE I DON'T HAVE YOU — Chuck Jackson, Wand 169 | 7 |
| 48 | 51 | 59 | 78 | WHAT NOW — Gene Chandler, Constellation 141 | 4 |
| 49 | 55 | 67 | 89 | BOOM BOOM — Animals, MGM 13298 | 4 |
| 50 | 27 | 15 | 12 | ASK ME — Elvis Presley, RCA Victor 8440 | 12 |
| 51 | 63 | 81 | — | I'LL BE THERE — Gerry & the Pacemakers, Laurie 3279 | 3 |
| 52 | 58 | 69 | 81 | HAWAII TATTOO — Waikikis, Kapp Winner's Circle 30 | 4 |
| 53 | 53 | 57 | 69 | THE 81 — Candy & the Kisses, Cameo 336 | 6 |
| 54 | 54 | 65 | 73 | (There's) ALWAYS SOMETHING THERE TO REMIND ME — Sandie Shaw, Reprise 0320 | 5 |
| 55 | 65 | 89 | — | PROMISED LAND — Chuck Berry, Chess 1916 | 3 |
| 56 | 43 | 45 | 51 | WITHOUT THE ONE YOU LOVE — Four Tops, Motown 1069 | 5 |
| 57 | 64 | 70 | — | YOU'RE NOBODY TILL SOMEBODY LOVES YOU — Dean Martin, Reprise 0333 | 3 |
| 58 | 59 | 63 | 74 | I'M GONNA LOVE YOU TOO — Hullaballoos, Roulette 4587 | 5 |
| 59 | 75 | — | — | HOLD WHAT YOU'VE GOT — Joe Tex, Dial 4001 | 2 |
| 60 | 73 | 90 | — | THE NAME GAME — Shirley Ellis, Congress 230 | 3 |
| 61 | 62 | 75 | 90 | LOVIN' PLACE — Gale Garnett, RCA Victor 8472 | 4 |
| 62 | 72 | 85 | — | MAKIN' WHOOPEE — Ray Charles, ABC-Paramount 10609 | 3 |
| 63 | 78 | — | — | SEVEN LETTERS — Ben E. King, Atco 6328 | 2 |
| 64 | 69 | 76 | 88 | SOMETIMES I WONDER — Major Lance, Okeh 7209 | 4 |
| 65 | 70 | 86 | — | COME ON DO THE JERK — Miracles, Tamla 54109 | 3 |
| 66 | 66 | 72 | 83 | GETTING MIGHTY CROWDED — Betty Everett, Vee Jay 628 | 5 |
| 67 | 57 | 60 | 68 | THE PRICE — Solomon Burke, Atlantic 2259 | 5 |
| 68 | 84 | — | — | I CAN'T STOP — Honeycombs, Interphon 7713 | 2 |
| 69 | — | — | — | ALL DAY AND ALL OF THE NIGHT — Kinks, Reprise 0334 | 1 |
| 70 | 77 | — | — | DO IT RIGHT — Brook Benton, Mercury 72365 | 2 |
| 71 | 76 | — | — | HE'S MY GUY — Irma Thomas, Imperial 66080 | 2 |
| 72 | 67 | 73 | 77 | IT'S ALL OVER — Walter Jackson, Okeh 7204 | 6 |
| 73 | 83 | 84 | — | I FOUND A LOVE OH WHAT A LOVE — Jo Ann & Troy, Atlantic 2256 | 3 |
| 74 | 74 | 78 | 82 | DO ANYTHING YOU WANNA — Harold Betters, Gateway 747 | 7 |
| 75 | 98 | — | — | HAVE YOU LOOKED INTO YOUR HEART — Jerry Vale, Columbia 43181 | 2 |
| 76 | 88 | — | — | SOMEWHERE IN YOUR HEART — Frank Sinatra, Reprise 0332 | 2 |
| 77 | 80 | — | — | CAN YOU JERK LIKE ME — Contours, Gordy 7032 | 2 |
| 78 | 86 | 91 | — | DEAR HEART — Henry Mancini's Ork & Chorus, RCA Victor 8458 | 3 |
| 79 | — | — | — | YOU'LL ALWAYS BE THE ONE I LOVE — Dean Martin, Reprise 0333 | 1 |
| 80 | 81 | 83 | 86 | SCRATCHY — Travis Wammack, Ara 204 | 5 |
| 81 | — | — | — | LET'S LOCK THE DOOR (And Throw Away the Key) — Jay & the Americans, United Artists 805 | 1 |
| 82 | 97 | — | — | DANNY BOY — Patti LaBelle and Her Bluebells, Parkway 935 | 2 |
| 83 | — | — | — | GIVE HIM A GREAT BIG KISS — Shangri-Las, Red Bird 10-018 | 1 |
| 84 | 99 | — | — | HEY-DA-DA-DOW — Dolphins, Fraternity 937 | 2 |
| 85 | 89 | — | — | BUCKET "T" — Ronny & the Daytonas, Mala 492 | 2 |
| 86 | 93 | — | — | THE SIDEWINDER — Lee Morgan, Blue Note 1911 | 2 |
| 87 | 95 | — | — | PERCOLATIN' — Willie Mitchell, Hi 2083 | 2 |
| 88 | 100 | — | — | LITTLE BELL — Dixie Cups, Red Bird 10-017 | 2 |
| 89 | 92 | 93 | — | (There'll Come a Day When) EV'RY LITTLE BIT HURTS — Bobby Vee, Liberty 55751 | 3 |
| 90 | — | — | — | LOOK OF LOVE — Lesley Gore, Mercury 72372 | 1 |
| 91 | 91 | 92 | 94 | YOU'RE THE ONLY WORLD I KNOW — Sonny James, Capitol 5280 | 5 |
| 92 | 96 | 100 | — | MY BUDDY SEAT — Hondells, Mercury 72366 | 3 |
| 93 | — | — | — | MAYBE — Shangri-Las, Red Bird 10-019 | 1 |
| 94 | 90 | 96 | 96 | ENDLESS SLEEP — Hank Williams Jr., MGM 13278 | 4 |
| 95 | — | — | — | HAVE MERCY BABY — James Brown & the Famous Flames, King 5968 | 1 |
| 96 | — | — | — | VOICE YOUR CHOICE — Radiants, Chess 1904 | 1 |
| 97 | — | — | — | TAKE THIS HURT OFF ME — Don Covay, Rosemart 802 | 1 |
| 98 | — | — | — | NO ARMS CAN EVER HOLD YOU — Bachelors, London 9724 | 1 |
| 99 | — | — | — | ARE YOU STILL MY BABY — Shirelles, Scepter 1292 | 1 |
| 100 | — | — | — | DO WHAT YOU DO DO WELL — Ned Miller, Fabor 137 | 1 |

## BUBBLING UNDER THE HOT 100

101. BIG BROTHER — Dickie Lee, Hall 1924
102. WHENEVER A TEENAGER CRIES — Reparata & the Delrons, World Artists 1036
103. I'M THE LOVER MAN — Little Jerry Williams, Loma 2005
104. THE RACE IS ON — George Jones, United Artists 751
105. PAPER TIGER — Sue Thompson, Hickory 1284
106. ACROSS THE STREET (Is a Million Miles Away) — Ray Peterson, MGM 13299
107. WOODEN HEART — Elvis Presley, RCA Victor 0720
108. IT'S BETTER TO HAVE IT — Barbara Lynn, Jamie 1292
109. NEVERTHELESS — Billy Butler & the Chanters, Okeh 7207
110. ODE TO THE LITTLE BROWN SHACK OUT BACK — Billy Ed Wheeler, Kapp 617
111. FIDDLER ON THE ROOF — Village Stompers, Epic 9740
112. TALK TO ME BABY — Barry Mann, Red Bird 10-015
113. CHITLINS — Gus Jenkins, Tower 107
114. GUESS WHO? — Nancy Wilson, Capitol 5319
115. LOVELY, LOVELY (Loverly, Loverly) — Chubby Checker, Parkway 936
116. I WANT YOU TO HAVE EVERYTHING — Lee Rogers, D-Town 1035
117. GOLDFINGER — Billy Strange, Crescendo 334
118. AND SATISFY — Nancy Wilson, Capitol 5319
119. EITHER WAY I LOSE — Gladys Knight & the Pips, Maxx 331
120. THE CRUSHER — Novas, Parrot 9714
121. TRY TO REMEMBER — Ed Ames, RCA Victor 8482
122. TELL HER JOHNNY SAID GOODBYE — Jerry Jackson, Columbia 43158
123. SO WHAT — Bill Black's Combo, Hi 2055
124. AMEN — Lloyd Price, Monument 865
125. CHAINED AND BOUND — Beau Brummels, Autumn 8
126. LAUGH, LAUGH — Beau Brummels, Autumn 8
127. DUSTY — Rag Dolls, Mala 492
128. SEND HER TO ME — Johnny Thunder, Diamond 175
129. A LITTLE BIT OF SOAP — Garnet Mimms, United Artists
130. THE OTHER RINGO — Larry Finnegan, Ric 146
131. I'LL COME RUNNING — Lulu, Parrot 9714
132. HAWAII TATTOO — Martin Denny, Liberty 55754
133. GOOGLE EYE — Nashville Teens, London 9712
134. BABY DON'T GO — Sonny & Cher, Reprise 0309
135. THE "IN" CROWD — Dobie Gray, Charger 105

Compiled from national retail sales and radio station airplay by the Music Popularity Dept. of Record Market Research, Billboard.

# Billboard HOT 100

*For Week Ending January 2, 1965*

★ STAR performer—Sides registering greatest proportionate upward progress this week.

| This Week | Last Week | 2 Wks. Ago | 3 Wks. Ago | TITLE, Artist, Label & Number | Weeks On Chart |
|---|---|---|---|---|---|
| 1 | 1 | 2 | 5 | I FEEL FINE — Beatles, Capitol 5327 | 5 |
| 2 | 2 | 1 | 4 | COME SEE ABOUT ME — Supremes, Motown 1068 | 8 |
| 3 | 3 | 3 | 1 | MR. LONELY — Bobby Vinton, Epic 9730 | 10 |
| 4 | 4 | 14 | 29 | SHE'S A WOMAN — Beatles, Capitol 5327 | 5 |
| ★5 | 11 | 30 | 49 | LOVE POTION NUMBER NINE — Searchers, Kapp Winner's Circle 27 | 6 |
| 6 | 6 | 7 | 14 | GOIN' OUT OF MY HEAD — Little Anthony & the Imperials, DCP 1119 | 9 |
| 7 | 5 | 4 | 2 | SHE'S NOT THERE — Zombies, Parrot 9695 | 12 |
| ★8 | 12 | 24 | 30 | AMEN — Impressions, ABC-Paramount 10602 | 7 |
| 9 | 9 | 12 | 21 | THE JERK — Larks, Money 106 | 8 |
| 10 | 14 | 17 | 26 | THE WEDDING — Julie Rogers, Mercury 72332 | 7 |
| 11 | 7 | 5 | 3 | RINGO — Lorne Greene, RCA Victor 8444 | 10 |
| 12 | 41 | 87 | — | DOWNTOWN — Petula Clark, Warner Bros. 5494 | 3 |
| 13 | 13 | 16 | 17 | SHA LA LA — Manfred Mann, Ascot 2165 | 8 |
| 14 | 34 | 60 | 77 | YOU'VE LOST THAT LOVIN' FEELIN' — Righteous Brothers, Philles 124 | 4 |
| 15 | 23 | 39 | 44 | KEEP SEARCHIN' — Del Shannon, Amy 915 | 7 |
| 16 | 21 | 25 | 28 | MY LOVE FORGIVE ME (Amore, Scusami) — Robert Goulet, Columbia 43131 | 11 |
| 17 | 19 | 19 | 24 | ANY WAY YOU WANT IT — Dave Clark Five, Epic 9739 | 8 |
| 18 | 24 | 28 | 36 | WILLOW WEEP FOR ME — Chad & Jeremy, World Artists 1034 | 8 |
| 19 | 27 | 34 | 40 | HOW SWEET IT IS (To Be Loved by You) — Marvin Gaye, Tamla 54107 | 7 |
| 20 | 10 | 6 | 6 | TIME IS ON MY SIDE — Rolling Stones, London 9708 | 12 |
| 21 | 17 | 13 | 13 | I'M INTO SOMETHING GOOD — Herman's Hermits, MGM 13280 | 12 |
| 22 | 8 | 8 | 10 | DANCE, DANCE, DANCE — Beach Boys, Capitol 5306 | 9 |
| 23 | 28 | 33 | 58 | LEADER OF THE LAUNDROMAT — Detergents, Roulette 4590 | 5 |
| 24 | 25 | 26 | 27 | OH NO, NOT MY BABY — Maxine Brown, Wand 162 | 11 |
| ★25 | 32 | 35 | 39 | THOU SHALT NOT STEAL — Dick & Deedee, Warner Bros. 5482 | 7 |
| 26 | 26 | 36 | 42 | AS TEARS GO BY — Marianne Faithfull, London 9697 | 6 |
| 27 | 30 | 38 | 50 | DEAR HEART — Andy Williams, Columbia 43180 | 6 |
| 28 | 29 | 29 | 34 | TOO MANY FISH IN THE SEA — Marvelettes, Tamla 54105 | 9 |
| 29 | 16 | 11 | 12 | MOUNTAIN OF LOVE — Johnny Rivers, Imperial 66075 | 10 |
| 30 | 20 | 18 | 19 | SATURDAY NIGHT AT THE MOVIES — Drifters, Atlantic 2260 | 8 |
| ★31 | 42 | 52 | 64 | DON'T FORGET I STILL LOVE YOU — Bobbi Martin, Coral 62426 | 6 |
| 32 | 15 | 9 | 9 | I'M GONNA BE STRONG — Gene Pitney, Musicor 1045 | 11 |
| 33 | 37 | 48 | 53 | DEAR HEART — Jack Jones, Kapp 635 | 6 |
| 34 | 35 | 40 | 43 | ONE MORE TIME — Ray Charles Singers, Command 4057 | 8 |
| 35 | 31 | 31 | 33 | SHE UNDERSTANDS ME — Johnny Tillotson, MGM 13284 | 10 |
| 36 | 38 | 32 | 23 | WALKING IN THE RAIN — Ronettes, Philles 123 | 11 |
| 37 | 40 | 45 | 55 | WALK AWAY — Matt Monro, Liberty 55745 | 6 |
| 38 | 39 | 41 | 51 | WILD ONE — Martha & the Vandellas, Gordy 7036 | 5 |
| 39 | 43 | 46 | 54 | DO-WACKA-DO — Roger Miller, Smash 1947 | 6 |
| ★40 | 59 | 75 | — | HOLD WHAT YOU'VE GOT — Joe Tex, Dial 4001 | 3 |
| 41 | 51 | 63 | 81 | I'LL BE THERE — Gerry & the Pacemakers, Laurie 2279 | 4 |
| 42 | 45 | 50 | 74 | SMILE — Betty Everett & Jerry Butler, Vee Jay 633 | 5 |
| 43 | 46 | 56 | 56 | MY LOVE (Roses Are Red) — "You Know Who" Group, 4 Corners 113 | 6 |
| 44 | 18 | 10 | 7 | YOU REALLY GOT ME — Kinks, Reprise 0306 | 15 |
| 45 | 55 | 65 | 89 | PROMISED LAND — Chuck Berry, Chess 1916 | 4 |
| 46 | 48 | 51 | 59 | WHAT NOW — Gene Chandler, Constellation 141 | 5 |
| 47 | 57 | 64 | 70 | YOU'RE NOBODY TILL SOMEBODY LOVES YOU — Dean Martin, Reprise 0333 | 4 |
| 48 | 49 | 55 | 67 | BOOM BOOM — Animals, MGM 13298 | 5 |
| 49 | 52 | 58 | 69 | HAWAII TATTOO — Waikikis, Kapp Winner's Circle 30 | 5 |
| ★50 | 60 | 73 | 90 | THE NAME GAME — Shirley Ellis, Congress 230 | 4 |
| 51 | 53 | 53 | 57 | THE 81 — Candy & the Kisses, Cameo 336 | 7 |
| 52 | 54 | 54 | 65 | (There's) ALWAYS SOMETHING THERE TO REMIND ME — Sandie Shaw, Reprise 0320 | 6 |
| 53 | 47 | 47 | 47 | SINCE I DON'T HAVE YOU — Chuck Jackson, Wand 169 | 8 |
| ★54 | 69 | — | — | ALL DAY AND ALL OF THE NIGHT — Kinks, Reprise 0334 | 2 |
| 55 | 63 | 78 | — | SEVEN LETTERS — Ben E. King, Atco 6328 | 3 |
| 56 | 58 | 59 | 63 | I'M GONNA LOVE YOU TOO — Hullaballoos, Roulette 4587 | 4 |
| 57 | 83 | — | — | GIVE HIM A GREAT BIG KISS — Shangri-Las, Red Bird 10-018 | 2 |
| 58 | 62 | 72 | 85 | MAKIN' WHOOPEE — Ray Charles, ABC-Paramount 10609 | 4 |
| 59 | 61 | 62 | 75 | LOVIN' PLACE — Gale Garnett, RCA Victor 8472 | 4 |
| 60 | 44 | 44 | 46 | RUN, RUN, RUN — Gestures, Soma 1417 | 8 |
| 61 | 68 | 84 | — | I CAN'T STOP — Honeycombs, Interphon 7713 | 3 |
| ★62 | 81 | — | — | LET'S LOCK THE DOOR (And Throw Away the Key) — Jay & the Americans, United Artists 805 | 2 |
| 63 | 65 | 70 | 86 | COME ON DO THE JERK — Miracles, Tamla 54109 | 4 |
| 64 | 64 | 69 | 76 | SOMETIMES I WONDER — Major Lance, Okeh 7209 | 5 |
| 65 | 66 | 66 | 72 | GETTING MIGHTY CROWDED — Betty Everett, Vee Jay 628 | 6 |
| 66 | 75 | 98 | — | HAVE YOU LOOKED INTO YOUR HEART — Jerry Vale, Columbia 43181 | 3 |
| 67 | 70 | 77 | — | DO IT RIGHT — Brook Benton, Mercury 72365 | 3 |
| 68 | 76 | 88 | — | SOMEWHERE IN YOUR HEART — Frank Sinatra, Reprise 0332 | 3 |
| 69 | 71 | 76 | — | HE'S MY GUY — Irma Thomas, Imperial 66080 | 3 |
| 70 | 73 | 83 | 84 | I FOUND A LOVE OH WHAT A LOVE — Jo Ann & Troy, Atlantic 2256 | 4 |
| ★71 | 90 | — | — | LOOK OF LOVE — Lesley Gore, Mercury 72372 | 2 |
| 72 | 79 | — | — | YOU'LL ALWAYS BE THE ONE I LOVE — Dean Martin, Reprise 0333 | 2 |
| 73 | 88 | 100 | — | LITTLE BELL — Dixie Cups, Red Bird 10-017 | 3 |
| 74 | 77 | 80 | — | CAN YOU JERK LIKE ME — Contours, Gordy 7032 | 3 |
| 75 | 85 | 89 | — | BUCKET "T" — Ronny & the Daytonas, Mala 492 | 3 |
| 76 | 82 | 97 | — | DANNY BOY — Patti LaBelle and Her Bluebells, Parkway 935 | 3 |
| 77 | 78 | 86 | 91 | DEAR HEART — Henry Mancini's Ork & Chorus, RCA Victor 8458 | 3 |
| ★78 | — | — | — | PAPER TIGER — Sue Thompson, Hickory 1284 | 1 |
| 79 | 74 | 74 | 78 | DO ANYTHING YOU WANNA — Harold Betters, Gateway 747 | 8 |
| 80 | 98 | — | — | NO ARMS CAN EVER HOLD YOU — Bachelors, London 9724 | 2 |
| 81 | 86 | 93 | — | THE SIDEWINDER — Lee Morgan, Blue Note 1911 | 3 |
| ★82 | — | — | — | LOVELY LOVELY — Chubby Checker, Parkway 936 | 1 |
| 83 | 100 | — | — | DO WHAT YOU DO WELL — Ned Miller, Fabor 137 | 2 |
| 84 | 84 | 99 | — | HEY-DA-DA-DOW — Dolphins, Fraternity 937 | 3 |
| 85 | 87 | 95 | — | PERCOLATIN' — Willie Mitchell, Hi 2083 | 3 |
| 86 | 89 | 92 | 93 | (There'll Come a Day When) EV'RY LITTLE BIT HURTS — Bobby Vee, Liberty 55751 | 4 |
| 87 | 92 | 96 | 100 | MY BUDDY SEAT — Hondells, Mercury 72366 | 4 |
| 88 | — | — | — | BLIND MAN — Little Milton, Checker 1096 | 1 |
| 89 | — | — | — | SO WHAT — Bill Black's Combo, Hi 2055 | 1 |
| 90 | — | — | — | USE YOUR HEAD — Mary Wells, 20th Century-Fox 555 | 1 |
| 91 | 93 | — | — | MAYBE — Shangri-Las, Red Bird 10-019 | 2 |
| 92 | 95 | — | — | HAVE MERCY BABY — James Brown & the Famous Flames, King 5968 | 2 |
| 93 | 99 | — | — | ARE YOU STILL MY BABY — Shirelles, Scepter 1292 | 2 |
| 94 | 96 | — | — | VOICE YOUR CHOICE — Radiants, Chess 1904 | 2 |
| 95 | — | — | — | A LITTLE BIT OF SOAP — Garnet Mimms, United Artists 796 | 1 |
| 96 | — | — | — | LAUGH, LAUGH — Beau Brummels, Autumn 8 | 1 |
| 97 | 97 | — | — | TAKE THIS HURT OFF ME — Don Covay, Rosemart 802 | 2 |
| 98 | — | — | — | ODE TO THE LITTLE BROWN SHACK OUT BACK — Billy Edd Wheeler, Kapp 617 | 1 |
| 99 | — | — | — | BLACK KNIGHT — Bobby Bland, Duke 386 | 1 |
| 100 | — | — | — | TWINE TIME — Alvin Cash & the Crawlers, Mar-V-Lus 6002 | 1 |

## BUBBLING UNDER THE HOT 100

101. THIS DIAMOND RING .......... Gary Lewis & the Playboys, Liberty 55756
102. IT'S BETTER TO HAVE IT .......... Barbara Lynn, Jamie 1292
103. WHENEVER A TEENAGER CRIES .. Reparata & Delrons, World Artists 1036
104. THE RACE IS ON .......... George Jones, United Artists 751
105. NO FAITH, NO LOVE .......... Mitty Collier, Chess 1918
106. I WANT YOU TO BE MY BOY .......... Exciters, Roulette 4591
107. FIDDLER ON THE ROOF .......... Village Stompers, Epic 9740
108. YOU'RE THE ONLY WORLD I KNOW .. Sonny James, Capitol 5280
109. BLIND MAN .......... Bobby Bland, Duke 386
110. ACROSS THE STREET (Is a Million Miles Away) .. Ray Peterson, MGM 12299
111. GOTTA GET A GOIN' .......... New Christy Minstrels, Columbia 43178
112. GUESS WHO? .......... Dusty Springfield, Philips 40245
113. NEVERTHELESS .......... Billy Butler & the Chanters, Okeh 7207
114. I WANT YOU TO HAVE EVERYTHING .. Lee Rogers, D-Town 1035
115. THE CRUSHER .......... Novas, Parrot 45005
116. I'LL COME RUNNING .......... Lulu, Parrot 9714
117. JOLLY GREEN GIANT .......... Kingsmen, Wand 197
118. BIG BROTHER .......... Dickey Lee, Hall 1924
119. TRY TO REMEMBER .......... Ed Ames, RCA Victor 8483
120. PARTY GIRL .......... Tommy Roe, ABC-Paramount 10604
121. SEND HER TO ME .......... Adam Faith, Amy 913
122. DUSTY .......... Rag Dolls, Mala 493
123. IT'S ALRIGHT .......... Adam Faith, Amy 913
124. THE "IN" CROWD .......... Dobie Gray, Charger 105
125. EL PUSSYCAT .......... Mongo Santamaria, Columbia 43171
126. BABY DON'T GO .......... Sonny & Cher, Reprise 0309
127. RINGO BEAT .......... Ella Fitzgerald, Verve 10340
128. IT'S ALRIGHT .......... Adam Faith, Amy 913
129. FINDERS KEEPERS, LOSERS WEEPERS .. Nella Dodds, Wand 171
130. TANYA .......... King Curtis, Capitol 5324
131. SHABBY LITTLE HUT .......... Reflections, Golden World 19
132. POPPIN' POPCORN .......... Dave (Baby) Cortez, Okeh 7206
133. IF I KNEW THEN .......... Ray Conniff Singers, Columbia 43168
134. PEARLY SHELLS .......... Billy Vaughn, Dot 15664
135. I WANT MY BABY BACK .......... Jimmy Cross, Tollie 9039

*Compiled from national retail sales and radio station airplay by the Music Popularity Dept. of Record Market Research, Billboard.*

# Billboard HOT 100

**For Week Ending January 9, 1965**

★ STAR performer—Sides registering greatest proportionate upward progress this week.

| This Week | 1 Wk. Ago | 2 Wks. Ago | TITLE — Artist, Label & Number | Weeks On Chart |
|---|---|---|---|---|
| 1 | 1 | 2 | I FEEL FINE — Beatles, Capitol 5327 | 6 |
| 2 | 2 | 1 | COME SEE ABOUT ME — Supremes, Motown 1068 | 9 |
| 3 | 3 | 3 | MR. LONELY — Bobby Vinton, Epic 9730 | 11 |
| 4 | 5 | 11 | LOVE POTION NUMBER NINE — Searchers, Kapp Winner's Circle 27 | 7 |
| ★5 | 12 | 41 | DOWNTOWN — Petula Clark, Warner Bros. 5494 | 4 |
| 6 | 6 | 7 | GOIN' OUT OF MY HEAD — Little Anthony & the Imperials, DCP 1119 | 10 |
| 7 | 8 | 12 | AMEN — Impressions, ABC-Paramount 10602 | 8 |
| 8 | 9 | 9 | THE JERK — Larks, Money 106 | 9 |
| ★9 | 14 | 34 | YOU'VE LOST THAT LOVIN' FEELIN' — Righteous Brothers, Philles 124 | 5 |
| 10 | 10 | 14 | THE WEDDING — Julie Rogers, Mercury 72332 | 8 |
| 11 | 4 | 4 | SHE'S A WOMAN — Beatles, Capitol 5327 | 9 |
| 12 | 13 | 13 | SHA LA LA — Manfred Mann, Ascot 2165 | 9 |
| 13 | 15 | 23 | KEEP SEARCHIN' — Del Shannon, Amy 915 | 8 |
| ★14 | 17 | 19 | ANY WAY YOU WANT IT — Dave Clark Five, Epic 9739 | 9 |
| 15 | 19 | 27 | HOW SWEET IT IS (To Be Loved by You) — Marvin Gaye, Tamla 54107 | 8 |
| 16 | 7 | 5 | SHE'S NOT THERE — Zombies, Parrot 9695 | 13 |
| 17 | 18 | 24 | WILLOW WEEP FOR ME — Chad & Jeremy, World Artists 1034 | 9 |
| 18 | 16 | 21 | MY LOVE FORGIVE ME (Amore, Scusami) — Robert Goulet, Columbia 43131 | 12 |
| 19 | 23 | 28 | LEADER OF THE LAUNDROMAT — Detergents, Roulette 4590 | 6 |
| 20 | 11 | 7 | RINGO — Lorne Greene, RCA Victor 8444 | 11 |
| 21 | 25 | 32 | THOU SHALT NOT STEAL — Dick & Deedes, Warner Bros. 5482 | 8 |
| 22 | 26 | 26 | AS TEARS GO BY — Marianne Faithful, London 9697 | 7 |
| ★23 | 37 | 40 | WALK AWAY — Matt Monro, Liberty 55745 | 7 |
| ★24 | 31 | 42 | DON'T FORGET I STILL LOVE YOU — Bobbi Martin, Coral 62426 | 7 |
| 25 | 27 | 30 | DEAR HEART — Andy Williams, Columbia 43180 | 7 |
| 26 | 28 | 29 | TOO MANY FISH IN THE SEA — Marvelettes, Tamla 54105 | 10 |
| 27 | 21 | 17 | I'M INTO SOMETHING GOOD — Herman's Hermits, MGM 13280 | 13 |
| ★28 | 40 | 59 | HOLD WHAT YOU'VE GOT — Joe Tex, Dial 4001 | 4 |
| 29 | 41 | 51 | I'LL BE THERE — Gerry & the Pacemakers, Laurie 3279 | 5 |
| 30 | 33 | 37 | DEAR HEART — Jack Jones, Kapp 635 | 7 |
| 31 | 39 | 43 | DO-WACKA-DO — Roger Miller, Smash 1947 | 7 |
| 32 | 34 | 35 | ONE MORE TIME — Ray Charles Singers, Command 4057 | 9 |
| 33 | 22 | 8 | DANCE, DANCE, DANCE — Beach Boys, Capitol 5306 | 10 |
| 34 | 38 | 39 | WILD ONE — Martha & the Vandellas, Gordy 7036 | 6 |
| ★35 | 49 | 52 | HAWAII TATTOO — Waikikis, Kapp Winner's Circle 30 | 6 |
| ★36 | 47 | 57 | YOU'RE NOBODY TILL SOMEBODY LOVES YOU — Dean Martin, Reprise 0333 | 5 |
| 37 | 24 | 25 | OH NO, NOT MY BABY — Maxine Brown, Wand 162 | 12 |
| 38 | 50 | 60 | THE NAME GAME — Shirley Ellis, Congress 230 | 5 |
| 39 | 30 | 20 | SATURDAY NIGHT AT THE MOVIES — Drifters, Atlantic 2260 | 9 |
| 40 | 29 | 16 | MOUNTAIN OF LOVE — Johnny Rivers, Imperial 66075 | 11 |
| 41 | 45 | 55 | PROMISED LAND — Chuck Berry, Chess 1916 | 5 |
| ★42 | 57 | 83 | GIVE HIM A GREAT BIG KISS — Shangri-Las, Red Bird 10-018 | 3 |
| 43 | 48 | 49 | BOOM BOOM — Animals, MGM 13298 | 6 |
| ★44 | 54 | 69 | ALL DAY AND ALL OF THE NIGHT — Kinks, Reprise 0334 | 3 |
| 45 | 46 | 48 | WHAT NOW — Gene Chandler, Constellation 141 | 6 |
| 46 | 35 | 31 | SHE UNDERSTANDS ME — Johnny Tillotson, MGM 13284 | 11 |
| 47 | 43 | 46 | MY LOVE (Roses Are Red) — "You Know Who" Group, 4 Corners 113 | 7 |
| 48 | 32 | 15 | I'M GONNA BE STRONG — Gene Pitney, Musicor 1045 | 12 |
| 49 | 20 | 10 | TIME IS ON MY SIDE — Rolling Stones, London 9708 | 13 |
| ★50 | 62 | 81 | LET'S LOCK THE DOOR (And Throw Away the Key) — Jay & the Americans, United Artists 805 | 3 |
| ★51 | 61 | 68 | I CAN'T STOP — Honeycombs, Interphon 7713 | 4 |
| 52 | 55 | 63 | SEVEN LETTERS — Ben E. King, Atco 6328 | 5 |
| 53 | 42 | 45 | SMILE — Betty Everett & Jerry Butler, Vee Jay 633 | 6 |
| ★54 | 68 | 76 | SOMEWHERE IN YOUR HEART — Frank Sinatra, Reprise 0332 | 4 |
| ★55 | 66 | 75 | HAVE YOU LOOKED INTO YOUR HEART — Jerry Vale, Columbia 43181 | 4 |
| 56 | 59 | 61 | LOVIN' PLACE — Gale Garnett, RCA Victor 8472 | 6 |
| 57 | 71 | 90 | LOOK OF LOVE — Lesley Gore, Mercury 72372 | 3 |
| 58 | 58 | 62 | MAKIN' WHOOPEE — Ray Charles, ABC-Paramount 10609 | 5 |
| 59 | 56 | 58 | I'M GONNA LOVE YOU TOO — Hullaballoos, Roulette 4587 | 7 |
| 60 | 52 | 54 | (There's) ALWAYS SOMETHING THERE TO REMIND ME — Sandie Shaw, Reprise 0320 | 7 |
| 61 | 63 | 65 | COME ON DO THE JERK — Miracles, Tamla 54109 | 5 |
| 62 | 75 | 85 | BUCKET "T" — Ronny & the Daytonas, Mala 492 | 4 |
| 63 | 51 | 53 | THE 81 — Candy & the Kisses, Cameo 336 | 8 |
| 64 | 72 | 79 | YOU'LL ALWAYS BE THE ONE I LOVE — Dean Martin, Reprise 0333 | 3 |
| ★65 | 80 | 98 | NO ARMS CAN EVER HOLD YOU — Bachelors, London 9724 | 3 |
| 66 | 69 | 71 | HE'S MY GUY — Irma Thomas, Imperial 66080 | 4 |
| 67 | 70 | 73 | I FOUND A LOVE OH WHAT A LOVE — Jo Ann & Troy, Atlantic 2256 | 5 |
| 68 | 73 | 88 | LITTLE BELL — Dixie Cups, Red Bird 10-017 | 4 |
| 69 | 78 | — | PAPER TIGER — Sue Thompson, Hickory 1284 | 2 |
| 70 | 74 | 77 | CAN YOU JERK LIKE ME — Contours, Gordy 7032 | 4 |
| ★71 | 90 | — | USE YOUR HEAD — Mary Wells, 20th Century-Fox 555 | 2 |
| 72 | 83 | 100 | DO WHAT YOU DO WELL — Ned Miller, Fabor 137 | 3 |
| 73 | — | — | SHAKE — Sam Cooke, RCA Victor 8486 | 1 |
| 74 | 64 | 64 | SOMETIMES I WONDER — Major Lance, Okeh 7209 | 6 |
| 75 | 67 | 70 | DO IT RIGHT — Brook Benton, Mercury 72365 | 7 |
| 76 | 84 | 84 | HEY-DA-DA-DOW — Dolphins, Fraternity 937 | 4 |
| 77 | — | — | HEART OF STONE — Rolling Stones, London 9725 | 1 |
| 78 | 82 | — | LOVELY, LOVELY — Chubby Checker, Parkway 936 | 2 |
| 79 | — | — | THE "IN" CROWD — Dobie Gray, Charger 105 | 1 |
| 80 | 77 | 78 | DEAR HEART — Henry Mancini's Ork & Chorus, RCA Victor 8458 | 5 |
| 81 | — | — | SHE'S COMING HOME — Zombies, Parrot 9723 | 1 |
| 82 | 76 | 82 | DANNY BOY — Patti LaBelle and Her Bluebells, Parkway 935 | 2 |
| 83 | 96 | — | LAUGH, LAUGH — Beau Brummels, Autumn 8 | 2 |
| 84 | 86 | 89 | (There'll Come a Day When) EV'RY LITTLE BIT HURTS — Bobby Vee, Liberty 55751 | 5 |
| 85 | — | — | I GO TO PIECES — Peter & Gordon, Capitol 5335 | 1 |
| 86 | — | — | BLIND MAN — Bobby Bland, Duke 386 | 1 |
| 87 | 81 | 86 | THE SIDEWINDER — Lee Morgan, Blue Note 1911 | 4 |
| 88 | 88 | — | BLIND MAN — Little Milton, Checker 1096 | 2 |
| ★89 | — | — | THE JOLLY GREEN GIANT — Kingsmen, Wand 172 | 1 |
| 90 | 98 | — | ODE TO THE LITTLE BROWN SHACK OUT BACK — Billy Edd Wheeler, Kapp 617 | 2 |
| 91 | 93 | 99 | ARE YOU STILL MY BABY — Shirelles, Scepter 1292 | 3 |
| 92 | — | — | THE CRUSHER — Novas, Parrot 45005 | 1 |
| 93 | 94 | 96 | VOICE YOUR CHOICE — Radiants, Chess 1904 | 3 |
| 94 | — | — | THE CRYING GAME — Brenda Lee, Decca 31728 | 1 |
| 95 | — | — | IT'S BETTER TO HAVE IT — Barbara Lynn, Jamie 1292 | 1 |
| 96 | 100 | — | TWINE TIME — Alvin Cash and the Crawlers, Mar-V-Lus 6002 | 2 |
| 97 | — | — | WHENEVER A TEENAGER CRIES — Reparata and the Delrons, World Artists 1036 | 1 |
| 98 | — | — | FINDERS KEEPERS, LOSERS WEEPERS — Nella Dodds, Wand 171 | 1 |
| 99 | — | — | NO FAITH, NO LOVE — Mitty Collier, Chess 1918 | 1 |
| 100 | — | — | HELLO PRETTY GIRL — Ronnie Dove, Diamond 176 | 1 |

## BUBBLING UNDER THE HOT 100

101. THIS DIAMOND RING — Gary Lewis & the Playboys, Liberty 55756
102. THE RACE IS ON — George Jones, United Artists 751
103. SO WHAT — Bill Black's Combo, Hi 2055
104. IT'S ALRIGHT — Adam Faith, Amy 913
105. O'BAMBINO — Harry Simeone Chorale, Kapp 628
106. I WANT YOU TO BE MY BOY — Exciters, Roulette 4591
107. FIDDLER ON THE ROOF — Village Stompers, Epic 9739
108. MAYBE — Shangri-Las, Red Bird 10-019
109. GUESS WHO? — Dusty Springfield, Philips 40246
110. ACROSS THE STREET (Is a Million Miles Away) — Ray Peterson, MGM 13299
111. GOTTA GET A GOIN' — New Christy Minstrels, Columbia 43178
112. TRY TO REMEMBER — Ed Ames, RCA Victor 8483
113. I'LL COME RUNNING — Lulu, Parrot 9714
114. BIG BROTHER — Dickey Lee, Hall 1924
115. I WILL WAIT FOR YOU — Steve Lawrence, Columbia 43192
116. PARTY GIRL — Tommy Roe, ABC-Paramount 10604
117. THIS DIAMOND RING — Sammy Ambrose, Musicor 1061
118. PERCOLATIN' — Willie Mitchell, Hi 2062
119. YOU'RE THE ONLY WORLD I KNOW — Sonny James, Capitol 5280
120. THE BOY FROM NEW YORK CITY — Ad Libs, Blue Cat 102
121. DUSTY — Rag Dolls, Mala 493
122. BABY DON'T GO — Sonny & Cher, Reprise 0309
123. BEWITCHED — Steve Lawrence, Columbia 43192
124. LITTLE BROWN JUG — Serendipity Singers, Philips 40246
125. A LITTLE BIT OF SOAP — Garnet Mimms, United Artists 796
126. HAVE MERCY BABY — James Brown and the Famous Flames, King 5968
127. SHABBY LITTLE HUT — Reflections, Golden World 19
128. LIVE IT UP — Dusty Springfield, Philips 40245
129. I WANT MY BABY BACK — Jimmy Cross, Tollie 9039
130. FALL AWAY — Eddie Albert, Hickory 1279
131. SOMEWHERE — Ray Conniff Singers, Columbia 43168
132. IF I KNEW THEN — P. J. Proby, Liberty 55757
133. PEARLY SHELLS — Billy Vaughn, Dot 15664
134. LONG TALL SALLY — Kinks, Cameo 345
135. I DON'T WANT TO TALK WITHOUT YOU — Phyllis McGuire, Reprise 0310

Compiled from national retail sales and radio station airplay by the Music Popularity Dept. of Record Market Research, Billboard.

# Billboard HOT 100

For Week Ending January 16, 1965

★ STAR performer—Sides registering greatest proportionate upward progress this week.

Record Industry Association of America seal of certification as million selling single.

| This Week | 1 Wk. Ago | 2 Wks. Ago | 3 Wks. Ago | TITLE, Artist, Label & Number | Weeks On Chart |
|---|---|---|---|---|---|
| 1 | 2 | 2 | 2 | COME SEE ABOUT ME — Supremes, Motown 1068 | 10 |
| 2 | 1 | 1 | 1 | I FEEL FINE — Beatles, Capitol 5327 | 7 |
| 3 | 4 | 5 | 11 | LOVE POTION NUMBER NINE — Searchers, Kapp Winner's Circle 27 | 8 |
| 4 | 5 | 12 | 41 | DOWNTOWN — Petula Clark, Warner Bros. 5494 | 5 |
| 5 | 9 | 14 | 34 | YOU'VE LOST THAT LOVIN' — Righteous Brothers, Philles 124 | 6 |
| 6 | 3 | 3 | 3 | MR. LONELY — Bobby Vinton, Epic 9730 | 12 |
| 7 | 8 | 9 | 9 | THE JERK — Larks, Money 106 | 10 |
| 8 | 6 | 6 | 6 | GOIN' OUT OF MY HEAD — Little Anthony & the Imperials, DCP 1119 | 11 |
| 9 | 15 | 19 | 27 | HOW SWEET IT IS (To Be Loved by You) — Marvin Gaye, Tamla 54107 | 9 |
| 10 | 13 | 15 | 23 | KEEP SEARCHIN' — Del Shannon, Amy 915 | 9 |
| 11 | 7 | 8 | 12 | AMEN — Impressions, ABC-Paramount 10602 | 9 |
| 12 | 11 | 4 | 4 | SHE'S A WOMAN — Beatles, Capitol 5327 | 7 |
| 13 | 21 | 25 | 32 | THOU SHALT NOT STEAL — Dick & Deedee, Warner Bros. 5482 | 9 |
| 14 | 12 | 13 | 13 | SHA LA LA — Manfred Mann, Ascot 2165 | 6 |
| 15 | 28 | 40 | 59 | HOLD WHAT YOU'VE GOT — Joe Tex, Dial 4001 | 5 |
| 16 | 10 | 10 | 14 | THE WEDDING — Julie Rogers, Mercury 72332 | 9 |
| 17 | 17 | 18 | 24 | WILLOW WEEP FOR ME — Chad & Jeremy, World Artists 1034 | 10 |
| 18 | 14 | 17 | 19 | ANY WAY YOU WANT IT — Dave Clark Five, Epic 9739 | 10 |
| 19 | 24 | 31 | 42 | DON'T FORGET I STILL LOVE YOU — Bobbi Martin, Coral 62426 | 8 |
| 20 | 38 | 50 | 60 | THE NAME GAME — Shirley Ellis, Congress 230 | 6 |
| 21 | 19 | 23 | 28 | LEADER OF THE LAUNDROMAT — Detergents, Roulette 4590 | 7 |
| 22 | 18 | 16 | 21 | MY LOVE FORGIVE ME (Amore, Scusami) — Robert Goulet, Columbia 43131 | 13 |
| 23 | 16 | 7 | 5 | SHE'S NOT THERE — Zombies, Parrot 9695 | 14 |
| 24 | 22 | 26 | 26 | AS TEARS GO BY — Marianne Faithful, London 9697 | 8 |
| 25 | 26 | 28 | 29 | TOO MANY FISH IN THE SEA — Marvelettes, Tamla 54105 | 11 |
| 26 | 29 | 41 | 51 | I'LL BE THERE — Gerry & the Pacemakers, Laurie 3279 | 6 |
| 27 | 25 | 27 | 30 | DEAR HEART — Andy Williams, Columbia 43180 | 8 |
| 28 | 23 | 37 | 40 | WALK AWAY — Matt Monro, Liberty 55745 | 8 |
| 29 | 44 | 54 | 69 | ALL DAY AND ALL OF THE NIGHT — Kinks, Reprise 0334 | 4 |
| 30 | 42 | 57 | 83 | GIVE HIM A GREAT BIG KISS — Shangri-Las, Red Bird 10-018 | 4 |
| 31 | 36 | 47 | 57 | YOU'RE NOBODY TILL SOMEBODY LOVES YOU — Dean Martin, Reprise 0333 | 6 |
| 32 | 30 | 33 | 37 | DEAR HEART — Jack Jones, Kapp 635 | 8 |
| 33 | 35 | 49 | 52 | HAWAII TATTOO — Waikikis, Kapp Winner's Circle 30 | 7 |
| 34 | 50 | 62 | 81 | LET'S LOCK THE DOOR (And Throw Away the Key) — Jay & the Americans, United Artists 805 | 4 |
| 35 | 31 | 39 | 43 | DO-WACKA-DO — Roger Miller, Smash 1947 | 8 |
| 36 | 73 | — | — | SHAKE — Sam Cooke, RCA Victor 8486 | 2 |
| 37 | 34 | 38 | 39 | WILD ONE — Martha & the Vandellas, Gordy 7036 | 7 |
| 38 | 32 | 34 | 35 | ONE MORE TIME — Ray Charles Singers, Command 4057 | 10 |
| 39 | 37 | 24 | 25 | OH NO, NOT MY BABY — Maxine Brown, Wand 162 | 13 |
| 40 | 45 | 46 | 48 | WHAT NOW — Gene Chandler, Constellation 141 | 7 |
| 41 | 33 | 22 | 8 | DANCE, DANCE, DANCE — Beach Boys, Capitol 5306 | 11 |
| 42 | 20 | 11 | 7 | RINGO — Lorne Greene, RCA Victor 8444 | 12 |
| 43 | 55 | 66 | 75 | HAVE YOU LOOKED INTO YOUR HEART — Jerry Vale, Columbia 43181 | 5 |
| 44 | 41 | 45 | 55 | PROMISED LAND — Chuck Berry, Chess 1916 | 6 |
| 45 | 52 | 55 | 63 | SEVEN LETTERS — Ben E. King, Atco 6328 | 5 |
| 46 | 58 | 58 | 62 | MAKIN' WHOOPEE — Ray Charles, ABC-Paramount 10609 | 6 |
| 47 | 57 | 71 | 90 | LOOK OF LOVE — Lesley Gore, Mercury 72372 | 4 |
| 48 | 71 | 90 | — | USE YOUR HEAD — Mary Wells, 20th Century-Fox 555 | 3 |
| 49 | 47 | 43 | 46 | MY LOVE (Roses Are Red) — "You Know Who" Group, 4 Corners 113 | 8 |
| 50 | 79 | — | — | THE "IN" CROWD — Dobie Gray, Charger 105 | 2 |
| 51 | 51 | 61 | 68 | I CAN'T STOP — Honeycombs, Interphon 7713 | 5 |
| 52 | 54 | 68 | 76 | SOMEWHERE IN YOUR HEART — Frank Sinatra, Reprise 0332 | 4 |
| 53 | 63 | 51 | 53 | THE 81 — Candy & the Kisses, Cameo 336 | 9 |
| 54 | 56 | 59 | 61 | LOVIN' PLACE — Gale Garnett, RCA Victor 8472 | 7 |
| 55 | 65 | 80 | 98 | NO ARMS CAN EVER HOLD YOU — Bachelors, London 9724 | 4 |
| 56 | 62 | 75 | 85 | BUCKET "T" — Ronny & the Daytonas, Mala 492 | 5 |
| 57 | 61 | 63 | 65 | COME ON DO THE JERK — Miracles, Tamla 54109 | 6 |
| 58 | 77 | — | — | HEART OF STONE — Rolling Stones, London 9725 | 2 |
| 59 | 70 | 74 | 77 | CAN YOU JERK LIKE ME — Contours, Gordy 7037 | 5 |
| 60 | 68 | 73 | 88 | LITTLE BELL — Dixie Cups, Red Bird 10-017 | 4 |
| 61 | 69 | 78 | — | PAPER TIGER — Sue Thompson, Hickory 1284 | 3 |
| 62 | 85 | — | — | I GO TO PIECES — Peter & Gordon, Capitol 5335 | 2 |
| 63 | 66 | 69 | 71 | HE'S MY GUY — Irma Thomas, Imperial 66080 | 5 |
| 64 | 64 | 72 | 79 | YOU'LL ALWAYS BE THE ONE I LOVE — Dean Martin, Reprise 0333 | 4 |
| 65 | — | — | — | THIS DIAMOND RING — Gary Lewis & the Playboys, Liberty 55756 | 1 |
| 66 | 81 | — | — | TELL HER NO — Zombies, Parrot 9723 | 2 |
| 67 | 59 | 56 | 58 | I'M GONNA LOVE YOU TOO — Hullabaloos, Roulette 4587 | 8 |
| 68 | 83 | 96 | — | LAUGH, LAUGH — Beau Brummels, Autumn 8 | 3 |
| 69 | 43 | 48 | 49 | BOOM BOOM — Animals, MGM 13298 | 7 |
| 70 | 78 | 82 | — | LOVELY, LOVELY — Chubby Checker, Parkway 936 | 3 |
| 71 | 72 | 83 | 100 | DO WHAT YOU DO WELL — Ned Miller, Fabor 137 | 4 |
| 72 | 74 | 64 | 64 | SOMETIMES I WONDER — Major Lance, Okeh 7209 | 7 |
| 73 | 76 | 84 | 84 | HEY-DA-DA-DOW — Dolphins, Fraternity 937 | 5 |
| 74 | 89 | — | — | THE JOLLY GREEN GIANT — Kingsmen, Wand 172 | 2 |
| 75 | 53 | 42 | 45 | SMILE — Betty Everett & Jerry Butler, Vee Jay 633 | 7 |
| 76 | — | — | — | MY GIRL — Temptations, Gordy 7038 | 1 |
| 77 | 96 | 100 | — | TWINE TIME — Alvin Cash & the Crawlers, Mar-V-Lus 6002 | 3 |
| 78 | 86 | — | — | BLIND MAN — Bobby Bland, Duke 386 | 2 |
| 79 | 80 | 77 | 78 | DEAR HEART — Henry Mancini's Ork & Chorus, RCA Victor 8458 | 5 |
| 80 | 93 | 94 | 96 | VOICE YOUR CHOICE — Radiants, Chess 1904 | 4 |
| 81 | — | — | — | COUSIN OF MINE — Sam Cooke, RCA Victor 8426 | 9 |
| 82 | 67 | 70 | 73 | I FOUND A LOVE OH WHAT A LOVE — Jo Ann & Troy, Atlantic 2256 | 6 |
| 83 | — | — | — | THANKS A LOT — Brenda Lee, Decca 31728 | 1 |
| 84 | 97 | — | — | WHENEVER A TEENAGER CRIES — Reparata & the Delrons, World Artists 1036 | 2 |
| 85 | 90 | 98 | — | ODE TO THE LITTLE BROWN SHACK OUT BACK — Billy Edd Wheeler, Kapp 617 | 3 |
| 86 | 88 | 88 | — | BLIND MAN — Little Milton, Checker 1096 | 3 |
| 87 | — | — | — | BYE, BYE, BABY — 4 Seasons, Philips 40260 | 1 |
| 88 | 92 | — | — | THE CRUSHER — Novas, Parrot 45005 | 2 |
| 89 | 100 | — | — | HELLO PRETTY GIRL — Ronnie Dove, Diamond 176 | 2 |
| 90 | — | — | — | THE BOY FROM NEW YORK CITY — Ad Libs, Blue Cat 102 | 1 |
| 91 | 91 | 93 | 99 | ARE YOU STILL MY BABY — Shirelles, Scepter 1292 | 4 |
| 92 | 99 | — | — | NO FAITH, NO LOVE — Mitty Collier, Chess 1918 | 2 |
| 93 | — | — | — | FANCY PANTS — Al Hirt, RCA Victor 8487 | 1 |
| 94 | 94 | — | — | THE CRYING GAME — Brenda Lee, Decca 31728 | 2 |
| 95 | 95 | — | — | IT'S BETTER TO HAVE IT — Barbara Lynn, Jamie 1292 | 2 |
| 96 | 98 | — | — | FINDERS KEEPERS, LOSERS WEEPERS — Nella Dodds, Wand 171 | 2 |
| 97 | — | — | — | IT'S ALRIGHT — Adam Faith, Amy 913 | 1 |
| 98 | — | — | — | I WANT YOU TO BE MY BOY — Exciters, Roulette 4591 | 1 |
| 99 | — | — | — | I WANNA BE (YOUR EVERYTHING) — Manhattans, Carnival 507 | 1 |
| 100 | — | — | — | MY HEART WOULD KNOW — Al Martino, Capitol 5341 | 1 |

## BUBBLING UNDER THE HOT 100

101. THE RACE IS ON ............ George Jones, United Artists 751
102. A LITTLE BIT OF SOAP ...... Garnet Mimms, United Artists 796
103. LEMON TREE ............... Trini Lopez, Reprise 0336
104. I'M GOING HOME ........... Kingston Trio, Decca 31730
105. FIDDLER ON THE ROOF ...... Village Stompers, Epic 9740
106. BY BUDDY SEAT ............ Hondells, Mercury 72366
107. WHOSE HEART ARE YOU BREAKING TONIGHT? .. Connie Francis, MGM 13303
108. TRY TO REMEMBER .......... Ed Ames, RCA Victor 8483
109. ACROSS THE STREET (Is a Million Miles Away) .. Ray Peterson, MGM 13299
110. I'LL COME RUNNING ......... Lulu, Parrot 9714
111. THE SIDEWINDER ........... Lee Morgan, Blue Note 1911
112. YOU'RE THE ONLY WORLD I KNOW .. Sonny James, Capitol 5280
113. PERCOLATIN' .............. Willie Mitchell, Hi 2083
114. PARTY GIRL ............... Tommy Roe, ABC-Paramount 10604
115. DUSTY ................... Billy Strange, Crescendo 334
116. GOLDFINGER ............... Rag Dolls, Mala 493
117. FOR LOVIN' ME ............ Peter, Paul & Mary, Warner Bros. 5496
118. DANNY-BOY ................ Patti LaBelle & Her Bluebells, Parkway 935
119. GOLDFINGER ............... Jack LaForge, Regina 1223
120. SO WHAT .................. Bill Black Combo, Hi 2055
121. SHABBY LITTLE HUT ........ Reflections, Golden World 19
122. BABY DON'T GO ............ Sonny & Cher, Reprise 0309
123. PEARLY SHELLS ............ Billy Vaughn, Dot 13664
124. HAVE MERCY BABY ........ James Brown & the Famous Flames, King 5968
125. SOMEWHERE .............. P. J. Proby, Liberty 55757
126. I'LL WAIT FOR YOU ........ Steve Lawrence, Columbia 43192
127. FALL AWAY ............... Eddie Albert, Hickory 1278
128. GUESS WHO? .............. Dusty Springfield, Philips 40245
129. LONG TALL SALLY .......... Kinks, Cameo 345
130. MAYBE .................... Shangri-Las, Red Bird 10-019
131. RED ROSES FOR A BLUE LADY .. Bert Kaempfert & His Ork, Decca 31722
132. POPPING POPCORN ......... Dave (Baby) Cortez, Okeh 7208
133. TALKIN' FOR YOUR PICTURE .. Tony Martin, Motown 1071
134. THEN AND ONLY THEN ....... Connie Smith, RCA Victor 8489
135. I DON'T WANT TO TALK WITHOUT YOU .. Phyllis McGuire, Reprise 0310

Compiled from national retail sales and radio station airplay by the Music Popularity Dept. of Record Market Research, Billboard.

# Billboard HOT 100

**For Week Ending January 23, 1965**

★ STAR performer—Sides registering greatest proportionate upward progress this week.

| This Week | 1 Wk. Ago | 2 Wks. Ago | 3 Wks. Ago | TITLE — Artist, Label & Number | Weeks On Chart |
|---|---|---|---|---|---|
| 1 | 4 | 5 | 12 | DOWNTOWN — Petula Clark, Warner Bros. 5494 | 6 |
| 2 | 5 | 9 | 14 | YOU'VE LOST THAT LOVIN' FEELIN' — Righteous Brothers, Philles 124 | 7 |
| ★3 | 3 | 4 | 5 | LOVE POTION NUMBER NINE — Searchers, Kapp Winner's Circle 27 | 9 |
| 4 | 2 | 1 | 1 | I FEEL FINE — Beatles, Capitol 5327 | 8 |
| 5 | 1 | 2 | 2 | COME SEE ABOUT ME — Supremes, Motown 1068 | 11 |
| ★6 | 20 | 38 | 50 | THE NAME GAME — Shirley Ellis, Congress 230 | 7 |
| 7 | 6 | 3 | 3 | MR. LONELY — Bobby Vinton, Epic 9730 | 13 |
| 8 | 7 | 8 | 9 | THE JERK — Larks, Money 106 | 11 |
| 9 | 9 | 15 | 19 | HOW SWEET IT IS (To Be Loved by You) — Marvin Gaye, Tamla 54107 | 10 |
| 10 | 10 | 13 | 15 | KEEP SEARCHIN' — Del Shannon, Amy 915 | 10 |
| 11 | 15 | 28 | 40 | HOLD WHAT YOU'VE GOT — Joe Tex, Dial 4001 | 6 |
| 12 | 8 | 6 | 6 | GOIN' OUT OF MY HEAD — Little Anthony & the Imperials, DCP 1119 | 12 |
| 13 | 13 | 21 | 25 | THOU SHALT NOT STEAL — Dick & Deedes, Warner Bros. 5482 | 10 |
| 14 | 12 | 11 | 4 | SHE'S A WOMAN — Beatles, Capitol 5327 | 8 |
| 15 | 17 | 17 | 18 | WILLOW WEEP FOR ME — Chad & Jeremy, World Artists 1034 | 11 |
| ★16 | 26 | 29 | 41 | I'LL BE THERE — Gerry & the Pacemakers, Laurie 3279 | 7 |
| 17 | 11 | 7 | 8 | AMEN — Impressions, ABC-Paramount 10602 | |
| 18 | 34 | 50 | 62 | LET'S LOCK THE DOOR (And Throw Away the Key) — Jay & the Americans, United Artists 805 | 5 |
| 19 | 29 | 44 | 54 | ALL DAY AND ALL OF THE NIGHT — Kinks, Reprise 0334 | 5 |
| 20 | 18 | 14 | 17 | ANY WAY YOU WANT IT — Dave Clark Five, Epic 9739 | 11 |
| 21 | 14 | 12 | 13 | SHA LA LA — Manfred Mann, Ascot 2165 | 11 |
| 22 | 19 | 24 | 31 | DON'T FORGET I STILL LOVE YOU — Bobbi Martin, Coral 62426 | 9 |
| 23 | 30 | 42 | 57 | GIVE HIM A GREAT BIG KISS — Shangri-Las, Red Bird 10-018 | 5 |
| 24 | 27 | 25 | 27 | DEAR HEART — Andy Williams, Columbia 43180 | 9 |
| 25 | 16 | 10 | 10 | THE WEDDING — Julie Rogers, Mercury 72332 | 10 |
| ★26 | 31 | 36 | 47 | YOU'RE NOBODY TILL SOMEBODY LOVES YOU — Dean Martin, Reprise 0333 | 7 |
| ★27 | 36 | 73 | — | SHAKE — Sam Cooke, RCA Victor 8486 | 3 |
| 28 | 22 | 18 | 16 | MY LOVE FORGIVE ME (Amore, Scusami) — Robert Goulet, Columbia 43131 | 14 |
| 29 | 25 | 26 | 28 | TOO MANY FISH IN THE SEA — Marvelettes, Tamla 54105 | 12 |
| 30 | 23 | 16 | 7 | SHE'S NOT THERE — Zombies, Parrot 9695 | 15 |
| 31 | 32 | 30 | 33 | DEAR HEART — Jack Jones, Kapp 635 | 9 |
| 32 | 28 | 23 | 37 | WALK AWAY — Matt Monro, Liberty 55745 | 9 |
| 33 | 62 | 85 | — | I GO TO PIECES — Peter & Gordon, Capitol 5335 | 3 |
| ★34 | 65 | — | — | THIS DIAMOND RING — Gary Lewis & the Playboys, Liberty 55756 | 2 |
| 35 | 33 | 35 | 49 | HAWAII TATTOO — Waikikis, Kapp Winner's Circle 30 | 8 |
| ★36 | 47 | 57 | 71 | LOOK OF LOVE — Lesley Gore, Mercury 72372 | 5 |
| ★37 | 24 | 22 | 26 | AS TEARS GO BY — Marianne Faithful, London 9697 | 9 |
| ★38 | 50 | 79 | — | THE "IN" CROWD — Dobie Gray, Charger 105 | |
| 39 | 43 | 55 | 66 | HAVE YOU LOOKED INTO YOUR HEART — Jerry Vale, Columbia 43181 | 6 |
| 40 | 21 | 19 | 23 | LEADER OF THE LAUNDROMAT — Detergents, Roulette 4590 | 8 |
| ★41 | 76 | — | — | MY GIRL — Temptations, Gordy 7038 | 2 |
| 42 | 66 | 81 | — | TELL HER NO — Zombies, Parrot 9723 | 3 |
| ★43 | 68 | 83 | 96 | LAUGH, LAUGH — Beau Brummels, Autumn 8 | 4 |
| ★44 | 48 | 71 | 90 | USE YOUR HEAD — Mary Wells, 20th Century-Fox 555 | 4 |
| 45 | 55 | 65 | 80 | NO ARMS CAN EVER HOLD YOU — Bachelors, London 9724 | 5 |
| 46 | 52 | 54 | 68 | SOMEWHERE IN YOUR HEART — Frank Sinatra, Reprise 0332 | 6 |
| ★47 | 58 | 77 | — | HEART OF STONE — Rolling Stones, London 9725 | 3 |
| 48 | 51 | 51 | 61 | I CAN'T STOP — Honeycombs, Interphon 7713 | 6 |
| 49 | 44 | 41 | 45 | PROMISED LAND — Chuck Berry, Chess 1916 | |
| ★50 | 74 | 89 | — | THE JOLLY GREEN GIANT — Kingsmen, Wand 172 | 3 |
| 51 | 40 | 45 | 46 | WHAT NOW — Gene Chandler, Constellation 141 | 8 |
| 52 | 45 | 52 | 55 | SEVEN LETTERS — Ben E. King, Atco 6328 | 6 |
| 53 | 49 | 47 | 43 | MY LOVE (Roses Are Red) — "You Know Who" Group, 4 Corners 113 | 9 |
| 54 | 56 | 62 | 75 | BUCKET "T" — Ronny & the Daytonas, Mala 492 | 6 |
| 55 | 59 | 70 | 74 | CAN YOU JERK LIKE ME — Contours, Gordy 7037 | 6 |
| 56 | 61 | 69 | 78 | PAPER TIGER — Sue Thompson, Hickory 1284 | 4 |
| 57 | 57 | 61 | 63 | COME ON DO THE JERK — Miracles, Tamla 54109 | 7 |
| 58 | 77 | 96 | 100 | TWINE TIME — Alvin Cash & the Crawlers, Mar-V-Lus 6002 | 4 |
| 59 | 54 | 56 | 59 | LOVIN' PLACE — Gale Garnett, RCA Victor 8472 | 8 |
| 60 | 60 | 68 | 73 | LITTLE BELL — Dixie Cups, Red Bird 10-017 | 6 |
| ★61 | 87 | — | — | BYE, BYE, BABY — 4 Seasons, Philips 40260 | 2 |
| 62 | 46 | 58 | 58 | MAKIN' WHOOPEE — Ray Charles, ABC-Paramount 10609 | 7 |
| 63 | 71 | 72 | 83 | DO WHAT YOU DO DO WELL — Ned Miller, Fabor 137 | 5 |
| 64 | 53 | 63 | 51 | THE 81 — Candy & the Kisses, Cameo 336 | 10 |
| 65 | 63 | 66 | 69 | HE'S MY GUY — Irma Thomas, Imperial 66080 | 6 |
| ★66 | 90 | — | — | THE BOY FROM NEW YORK CITY — Ad Libs, Blue Cat 102 | 2 |
| ★67 | 85 | 90 | 98 | ODE TO THE LITTLE BROWN SHACK OUT BACK — Billy Edd Wheeler, Kapp 617 | 4 |
| ★68 | 83 | — | — | THANKS A LOT — Brenda Lee, Decca 31728 | 2 |
| 69 | 73 | 76 | 84 | HEY-DA-DA-DOW — Dolphins, Fraternity 937 | 6 |
| 70 | 64 | 64 | 72 | YOU'LL ALWAYS BE THE ONE I LOVE — Dean Martin, Reprise 0333 | 5 |
| 71 | 67 | 59 | 56 | I'M GONNA LOVE YOU TOO — Hullaballoos, Roulette 4587 | 9 |
| 72 | 70 | 78 | 82 | LOVELY, LOVELY — Chubby Checker, Parkway 936 | 4 |
| 73 | 80 | 93 | 94 | VOICE YOUR CHOICE — Radiants, Chess 1904 | 5 |
| ★74 | 89 | 100 | — | HELLO PRETTY GIRL — Ronnie Dove, Diamond 176 | |
| ★75 | — | — | — | LEMON TREE — Trini Lopez, Reprise 0336 | 1 |
| 76 | 84 | 97 | — | WHENEVER A TEENAGER CRIES — Reparata & the Delrons, World Artists 1036 | 3 |
| 77 | 72 | 74 | 64 | SOMETIMES I WONDER — Major Lance, Okeh 7209 | 8 |
| 78 | 78 | 86 | — | BLIND MAN — Bobby Bland, Duke 386 | 3 |
| 79 | 81 | — | — | COUSIN OF MINE — Sam Cooke, RCA Victor 8426 | 10 |
| 80 | — | — | — | BREAK AWAY (FROM THAT BOY) — Newbeats, Hickory 1290 | 1 |
| ★81 | — | — | — | FOR LOVIN' ME — Peter, Paul & Mary, Warner Bros. 5496 | |
| ★82 | 93 | — | — | FANCY PANTS — Al Hirt, RCA Victor 8487 | 2 |
| 83 | 79 | 80 | 77 | DEAR HEART — Henry Mancini's Ork & Chorus, RCA Victor 8458 | 6 |
| 84 | 100 | — | — | MY HEART WOULD KNOW — Al Martino, Capitol 5341 | 2 |
| ★85 | — | — | — | I'VE GOT A TIGER BY THE TAIL — Buck Owens, Capitol 5336 | |
| 86 | — | — | — | RED ROSES FOR A BLUE LADY — Bert Kaempfert & His Ork, Decca 31722 | |
| ★87 | 97 | — | — | IT'S ALRIGHT — Adam Faith, Amy 913 | 2 |
| 88 | 88 | 92 | — | THE CRUSHER — Novas, Parrot 45005 | 3 |
| 89 | 94 | 94 | — | THE CRYING GAME — Brenda Lee, Decca 31728 | |
| ★90 | — | — | — | TRY TO REMEMBER — Ed Ames, RCA Victor 8483 | |
| 91 | — | — | — | LITTLE THINGS — Bobby Goldsboro, United Artist 810 | |
| 92 | — | — | — | WHOSE HEART ARE YOU BREAKING TONIGHT? — Connie Francis, MGM 13303 | |
| 93 | 86 | 88 | 88 | BLIND MAN — Little Milton, Checker 1096 | |
| 94 | — | — | — | DUSTY — Rag Dolls, Mala 493 | |
| 95 | 92 | 99 | — | NO FAITH, NO LOVE — Mitty Collier, Chess 1918 | 3 |
| 96 | — | — | — | THE RACE IS ON — George Jones, United Artists 751 | |
| 97 | — | — | — | YOU'RE THE ONLY WORLD I KNOW — Sonny James, Capitol 5280 | |
| 98 | — | — | — | GOLDFINGER — Billy Strange, Crescendo 334 | |
| 99 | 99 | — | — | I WANNA BE (Your Everything) — Manhattans, Carnival 507 | 2 |
| 100 | — | — | — | THE BIRDS AND THE BEES — Jewel Akens, Era 3141 | |

## BUBBLING UNDER THE HOT 100

101. EVERYDAY — Rogues, Columbia 43190
102. JERK AND TWINE — Jackie Ross, Chess 1920
103. BEWITCHED — Steve Lawrence, Columbia 43192
104. MARRIED MAN — Richard Burton, MGM 13307
105. SOMEWHERE — P. J. Proby, Liberty 55757
106. I WANT YOU TO BE MY BOY — Exciters, Roulette 4591
107. I'LL COME RUNNING — Lulu, Parrot 9714
108. IT'S BETTER TO HAVE IT — Barbara Lynn, Jamie 1292
109. PARTY GIRL — Tommy Roe, ABC-Paramount 10604
110. SIX BOYS — Frank Wilson, Josie 929
111. THE SIDEWINDER — Lee Morgan, Blue Note 1911
112. FIDDLER ON THE ROOF — Village Stompers, Epic 9740
113. A LITTLE BIT OF SOAP — Garnet Mimms, United Artists 796
114. I WILL WAIT FOR YOU — Steve Lawrence, Columbia 43192
115. GOLDFINGER — Jack LaForge, Regina 1323
116. THEN AND ONLY THEN — Connie Smith, RCA Victor 8489
117. FINDERS KEEPERS, LOSERS WEEPERS — Nella Dodds, Wand 171
118. HEL-O-DADDY-O — Newbeats, Hickory 1290
119. FALL AWAY — Eddie Albert, Hickory 1278
120. BABY DON'T GO — Sonny & Cher, Reprise 0309
121. PEARLY SHELLS — Billy Vaughn, Dot 15664
122. PERCOLATIN' — Willie Mitchell, Hi 2083
123. GOLDFINGER — Shirley Bassey, United Artists 790
124. MY GAL SAL — Burl Ives, Decca 31729
125. BIG BROTHER — Dickey Lee, Hall 1924
126. A CHANGE IS GONNA COME — Sam Cooke, RCA Victor 8486
127. I WANT MY BABY BACK — Jimmy Cross, Tollie 9039
128. SOMETHING'S GOT A HOLD ON ME — Sunny & The Sunliners, Tear Drop 3045
129. DIAMOND HEAD — Ventures, Dolton 303
130. THE MAN — Lorne Greene, RCA Victor 8490
131. THE RICHEST MAN ALIVE — Mel Carter, Imperial 66078
132. I WONDER — Butterflys, Tollie 9060
133. TERRY — Twinkle, Tollie 9040
134. CRYING IN THE CHAPEL — Adam Wade, Epic 9752

Compiled from national retail sales and radio station airplay by the Music Popularity Dept. of Record Market Research, Billboard.

**Billboard** For Week Ending January 30, 1965

# HOT 100

★ **STAR performer**—Sides registering greatest proportionate upward progress this week.

Record Industry Association of America seal of certification as million selling single.

| This Week | 1 Wk. Ago | 2 Wks. Ago | 3 Wks. Ago | TITLE Artist, Label & Number | Weeks On Chart |
|---|---|---|---|---|---|
| 1 | 1 | 4 | 5 | **DOWNTOWN** Petula Clark, Warner Bros. 5494 | 7 |
| 2 | 2 | 5 | 9 | **YOU'VE LOST THAT LOVIN' FEELIN'** Righteous Brothers, Philles 124 | 8 |
| ★3 | 6 | 20 | 38 | **THE NAME GAME** Shirley Ellis, Congress 230 | 8 |
| 4 | 3 | 3 | 4 | **LOVE POTION NUMBER NINE** Searchers, Kapp Winner's Circle 27 | 10 |
| ★5 | 11 | 15 | 28 | **HOLD WHAT YOU'VE GOT** Joe Tex, Dial 4001 | 7 |
| ★6 | 9 | 9 | 15 | **HOW SWEET IT IS (To Be Loved by You)** Marvin Gaye, Tamla 54107 | 11 |
| ★7 | 34 | 65 | — | **THIS DIAMOND RING** Gary Lewis & the Playboys, Liberty 55756 | 3 |
| 8 | 5 | 1 | 2 | **COME SEE ABOUT ME** Supremes, Motown 1068 | 12 |
| 9 | 10 | 10 | 13 | **KEEP SEARCHIN'** Del Shannon, Amy 915 | 11 |
| ★10 | 19 | 29 | 44 | **ALL DAY AND ALL OF THE NIGHT** Kinks, Reprise 0334 | 6 |
| 11 | 4 | 2 | 1 | **I FEEL FINE** Beatles, Capitol 5327 | 9 |
| ★12 | 41 | 76 | — | **MY GIRL** Temptations, Gordy 7038 | 3 |
| ★13 | 18 | 34 | 50 | **LET'S LOCK THE DOOR (And Throw Away the Key)** Jay & the Americans, United Artists 805 | 6 |
| 14 | 16 | 26 | 29 | **I'LL BE THERE** Gerry & the Pacemakers, Laurie 3279 | 8 |
| ★15 | 27 | 36 | 73 | **SHAKE** Sam Cooke, RCA Victor 8486 | 4 |
| 16 | 8 | 7 | 8 | **THE JERK** Larks, Money 106 | 12 |
| 17 | 12 | 8 | 6 | **GOIN' OUT OF MY HEAD** Little Anthony & the Imperials, DCP 1119 | 13 |
| ★18 | 23 | 30 | 42 | **GIVE HIM A GREAT BIG KISS** Shangri-Las, Red Bird 10-018 | 6 |
| 19 | 7 | 6 | 3 | **MR. LONELY** Bobby Vinton, Epic 9730 | 14 |
| 20 | 13 | 13 | 21 | **THOU SHALT NOT STEAL** Dick & Deedee, Warner Bros. 5482 | 11 |
| ★21 | 33 | 62 | 85 | **I GO TO PIECES** Peter & Gordon, Capitol 5335 | 4 |
| ★22 | 50 | 74 | 89 | **THE JOLLY GREEN GIANT** Kingsmen, Wand 172 | 4 |
| ★23 | 38 | 50 | 79 | **THE "IN" CROWD** Dobie Gray, Charger 105 | 4 |
| ★24 | 42 | 66 | 81 | **TELL HER NO** Zombies, Parrot 9723 | 4 |
| 25 | 26 | 31 | 36 | **YOU'RE NOBODY TILL SOMEBODY LOVES YOU** Dean Martin, Reprise 0333 | 8 |
| ★26 | 47 | 58 | 77 | **HEART OF STONE** Rolling Stones, London 9725 | 4 |
| 27 | 22 | 19 | 24 | **DON'T FORGET I STILL LOVE YOU** Bobbi Martin, Coral 62426 | 10 |
| ★28 | 39 | 43 | 55 | **HAVE YOU LOOKED INTO YOUR HEART** Jerry Vale, Columbia 43181 | 7 |
| ★29 | 61 | 87 | — | **BYE, BYE, BABY** 4 Seasons, Philips 40260 | 3 |
| ★30 | 36 | 47 | 57 | **LOOK OF LOVE** Lesley Gore, Mercury 72372 | 6 |
| ★31 | 58 | 77 | 96 | **TWINE TIME** Alvin Cash & the Crawlers, Mar-V-Lus 6002 | 5 |
| ★32 | 43 | 68 | 83 | **LAUGH, LAUGH** Beau Brummels, Autumn 8 | 5 |
| ★33 | 45 | 55 | 65 | **NO ARMS CAN EVER HOLD YOU** Bachelors, London 9724 | 6 |
| ★34 | 44 | 48 | 71 | **USE YOUR HEAD** Mary Wells, 20th Century-Fox 555 | 5 |
| 35 | 15 | 17 | 17 | **WILLOW WEEP FOR ME** Chad & Jeremy, World Artists 1034 | 12 |
| ★36 | 46 | 52 | 54 | **SOMEWHERE IN YOUR HEART** Frank Sinatra, Reprise 0332 | 7 |
| 37 | 14 | 12 | 11 | **SHE'S A WOMAN** Beatles, Capitol 5327 | 9 |
| 38 | 24 | 27 | 25 | **DEAR HEART** Andy Williams, Columbia 43180 | 10 |
| 39 | 25 | 16 | 10 | **THE WEDDING** Julie Rogers, Mercury 72332 | 11 |
| 40 | 20 | 18 | 14 | **ANY WAY YOU WANT IT** Dave Clark Five, Epic 9739 | 12 |
| 41 | 28 | 22 | 18 | **MY LOVE FORGIVE ME (Amore, Scusami)** Robert Goulet, Columbia 43131 | 15 |
| 42 | 31 | 32 | 30 | **DEAR HEART** Jack Jones, Kapp 635 | 10 |
| 43 | 17 | 11 | 7 | **AMEN** Impressions, ABC-Paramount 10602 | 11 |
| ★44 | 66 | 90 | — | **THE BOY FROM NEW YORK CITY** Ad Libs, Blue Cat 102 | 3 |
| ★45 | 56 | 61 | 69 | **PAPER TIGER** Sue Thompson, Hickory 1284 | 5 |
| ★46 | 75 | — | — | **LEMON TREE** Trini Lopez, Reprise 0336 | 2 |
| 47 | 55 | 59 | 70 | **CAN YOU JERK LIKE ME** Contours, Gordy 7037 | 7 |
| 48 | 48 | 51 | 51 | **I CAN'T STOP** Honeycombs, Interphon 7713 | 7 |
| 49 | 21 | 14 | 12 | **SHA LA LA** Manfred Mann, Ascot 2165 | 12 |
| 50 | 57 | 57 | 61 | **COME ON DO THE JERK** Miracles, Tamla 54109 | 8 |
| 51 | 35 | 33 | 35 | **HAWAII TATTOO** Waikikis, Kapp Winner's Circle 30 | 9 |
| 52 | 60 | 60 | 68 | **LITTLE BELL** Dixie Cups, Red Bird 10-017 | 7 |
| 53 | 52 | 45 | 52 | **SEVEN LETTERS** Ben E. King, Atco 6328 | 7 |
| 54 | 62 | 46 | 58 | **MAKIN' WHOOPEE** Ray Charles, ABC-Paramount 10609 | 8 |
| 55 | 63 | 71 | 72 | **DO WHAT YOU DO DO WELL** Ned Miller, Fabor 137 | 6 |
| 56 | 54 | 56 | 62 | **BUCKET "T"** Ronny & the Daytonas, Mala 492 | 7 |
| ★57 | 68 | 83 | — | **THANKS A LOT** Brenda Lee, Decca 31728 | 3 |
| 58 | 67 | 85 | 90 | **ODE TO THE LITTLE BROWN SHACK OUT BACK** Billy Edd Wheeler, Kapp 617 | 5 |
| ★59 | 73 | 80 | 93 | **VOICE YOUR CHOICE** Radiants, Chess 1904 | 6 |
| ★60 | 81 | — | — | **FOR LOVIN' ME** Peter, Paul & Mary, Warner Bros. 5496 | 2 |
| ★61 | 82 | 93 | — | **FANCY PANTS** Al Hirt, RCA Victor 8487 | 3 |
| 62 | 74 | 89 | 100 | **HELLO PRETTY GIRL** Ronnie Dove, Diamond 176 | 4 |
| ★63 | — | — | — | **KING OF THE ROAD** Roger Miller, Smash 1965 | 1 |
| ★64 | 36 | — | — | **RED ROSES FOR A BLUE LADY** Bert Kaempfert & His Ork, Decca 31722 | 2 |
| 65 | 65 | 63 | 66 | **HE'S MY GUY** Irma Thomas, Imperial 66080 | 7 |
| 66 | 59 | 54 | 56 | **LOVIN' PLACE** Gale Garnett, RCA Victor 8472 | 9 |
| 67 | 80 | — | — | **BREAK AWAY (From That Boy)** Newbeats, Hickory 1290 | 2 |
| ★68 | 100 | — | — | **THE BIRDS AND THE BEES** Jewel Akens, Era 3141 | 2 |
| 69 | 76 | 84 | 97 | **WHENEVER A TEENAGER CRIES** Reparata & the Delrons, World Artists 1036 | 4 |
| ★70 | — | — | — | **A CHANGE IS GONNA COME** Sam Cooke, RCA Victor 8486 | 1 |
| ★71 | 92 | — | — | **WHOSE HEART ARE YOU BREAKING TONIGHT?** Connie Francis, MGM 13303 | 2 |
| ★72 | — | — | — | **AT THE CLUB** Drifters, Atlantic 2268 | 1 |
| ★73 | — | — | — | **WHAT HAVE THEY DONE TO THE RAIN** Searchers, Kapp 644 | 1 |
| 74 | 79 | 81 | — | **COUSIN OF MINE** Sam Cooke, RCA Victor 8426 | 11 |
| 75 | 85 | — | — | **I'VE GOT A TIGER BY THE TAIL** Buck Owens, Capitol 5336 | 2 |
| 76 | 84 | 100 | — | **MY HEART WOULD KNOW** Al Martino, Capitol 5341 | 3 |
| 77 | 69 | 73 | 76 | **HEY-DA-DA-DOW** Dolphins, Fraternity 937 | 7 |
| 78 | 87 | 97 | — | **IT'S ALRIGHT** Adam Faith, Amy 913 | 3 |
| ★79 | 94 | — | — | **DUSTY** Rag Dolls, Mala 493 | 2 |
| ★80 | — | — | — | **MARRIED MAN** Richard Burton, MGM 13307 | 1 |
| ★81 | — | — | — | **THE MAN** Lorne Greene, RCA Victor 8490 | 1 |
| ★82 | — | — | — | **COMING ON TOO STRONG** Wayne Newton, Capitol 5338 | 1 |
| 83 | 91 | — | — | **LITTLE THINGS** Bobby Goldsboro, United Artist 810 | 2 |
| ★84 | — | — | — | **DON'T COME RUNNING BACK TO ME** Nancy Wilson, Capitol 5340 | 1 |
| ★85 | — | — | — | **CAN'T YOU HEAR MY HEARTBEAT** Herman's Hermits, MGM 13310 | 1 |
| ★86 | — | — | — | **DIAMOND HEAD** Ventures, Dolton 303 | 1 |
| 87 | 89 | 94 | 94 | **THE CRYING GAME** Brenda Lee, Decca 31728 | 4 |
| 88 | 90 | — | — | **TRY TO REMEMBER** Ed Ames, RCA Victor 8483 | 2 |
| 89 | 98 | — | — | **GOLDFINGER** Billy Strange, Crescendo 334 | 2 |
| ★90 | — | — | — | **THAT'S HOW STRONG MY LOVE IS** Otis Redding, Volt 124 | 1 |
| 91 | 95 | 92 | 99 | **NO FAITH, NO LOVE** Mitty Collier, Chess 1918 | 4 |
| 92 | — | — | — | **BRING YOUR LOVE TO ME** Righteous Brothers, Moonglow 238 | 1 |
| 93 | — | — | — | **JERK AND TWINE** Jackie Ross, Chess 1920 | 1 |
| 94 | 99 | 99 | — | **I WANNA BE (Your Everything)** Manhattans, Carnival 507 | 3 |
| 95 | — | — | — | **I WANT MY BABY BACK** Jimmy Cross, Tollie 9039 | 1 |
| 96 | — | — | — | **HE WAS REALLY SAYIN' SOMETHIN'** Velvelettes, V.I.P. 25013 | 1 |
| 97 | — | — | — | **CRYING IN THE CHAPEL** Adam Wade, Epic 9752 | 1 |
| 98 | — | — | — | **GOLDFINGER** Shirley Bassey, United Artists 790 | 1 |
| 99 | — | — | — | **CAN'T YOU JUST SEE ME** Aretha Franklin, Columbia 43203 | 1 |
| 100 | — | — | — | **GOLDFINGER** Jack LaForge, Regina 1323 | 1 |

## HOT 100—A TO Z—*(Publisher-Licensee)*

All Day and All of the Night (Jay Boy, BMI) .... 10
Amen (Pamco, BMI) .... 43
Any Way You Want It (Branston, BMI) .... 40
At the Club (Screen Gems-Columbia, BMI) .... 72
Birds and the Bees, The (Pattern, ASCAP) .... 68
Boy From New York, The (Trio, BMI) .... 44
Break Away (From That Boy) (Acuff-Rose, BMI) .. 67
Bring Your Love to Me (Maxwell, BMI) .... 92
Bucket "T" (Screen Gems-Columbia, BMI) .... 56
Bye, Bye, Baby (Saturday-Seasons Four, BMI) .... 29
Can You Jerk Like Me (Jobete, BMI) .... 47
Can't You Hear My Heartbeat (Southern, ASCAP). 85
Can't You Just See Me (Lily, BMI) .... 99
Change Is Gonna Come, A (Kags, BMI) .... 70
Come on Do the Jerk (Jobete, BMI) .... 50
Come See About Me (Jobete, BMI) .... 8
Coming on Too Strong (Beechwood, BMI) .... 82
Cousin of Mine (Kags, BMI) .... 74
Crying Game, The (Southern, ASCAP) .... 87
Crying in the Chapel (Valley, BMI) .... 97
Dear Heart—Jones (Northridge-Witmark, ASCAP) .. 42
Dear Heart—Williams (Northridge-Witmark, ASCAP). 38
Diamond Head (Election, BMI) .... 86
Do What You Do Do Well (Central Songs, BMI) .. 55
Don't Come Running Back to Me (Leeds, ASCAP) .. 84
Don't Forget I Still Love You (South Mountain, BMI) .... 27
Downtown (Leeds, ASCAP) .... 1
Dusty (Saturday, ASCAP) .... 79
Fancy Pants (Acuff-Rose, BMI) .... 61
For Lovin' Me (Witmark, ASCAP) .... 60
Give Him a Great Big Kiss (Tender Tunes- Trio, BMI) .... 18
Goin' Out of My Head (South Mountain, BMI) ... 17
Goldfinger—Bassey (Unart, BMI) .... 98
Goldfinger—LaForge (Unart, BMI) .... 100
Goldfinger—Strange (Unart, BMI) .... 89
Have You Looked Into Your Heart (South Mountain, BMI) .... 28
Hawaii Tattoo (Zodiac, BMI) .... 51
He Was Really Sayin' Somethin' (Jobete, BMI) .... 96
He's My Guy (Blackwood, BMI) .... 65
Heart of Stone (Immediate, BMI) .... 26
Hello Pretty Girl (Picturetone, BMI) .... 62
Hey-Da-Da-Dow (Edwood, BMI) .... 77
Hold What You've Got (Tree, BMI) .... 5
How Sweet It Is (To Be Loved By You) (Jobete, BMI) .... 6
I Can't Stop (Ivy, ASCAP) .... 48
I Feel Fine (Maclen, BMI) .... 11
I Go to Pieces (Vicki-McLaughlin, BMI) .... 21
I Wanna Be (Your Everything) (Bright Star-Sanavan, BMI) .... 94
I Want My Baby Back (Rock, BMI) .... 95
I'll Be There (T. M., BMI) .... 14
I've Got a Tiger By the Tail (Bluebook, BMI) .. 75
"In" Crowd, The (American, BMI) .... 23
It's Alright (Gil, BMI) .... 78
Jerk, The (Cash, BMI) .... 16
Jerk and Twine (Chevis, BMI) .... 93
Jolly Green Giant, The (Burdette-Flomarlu, BMI) .. 22
Keep Searchin' (Vicki-McLaughlin, BMI) .... 9
King of the Road (Tree, BMI) .... 63
Laugh, Laugh (Taracrest, BMI) .... 32
Lemon Tree (Boulder, ASCAP) .... 46
Let's Lock the Door (Picturetone, BMI) .... 13
Little Bell (Trio, BMI) .... 52
Little Things (Unart, BMI) .... 83
Look of Love (Trio, BMI) .... 30
Love Potion Number Nine (Quintet, BMI) .... 4
Lovin' Place (Leprechaun, BMI) .... 66
Makin' Whoopee (Bregman, Vocco & Conn-Kahn, ASCAP) .... 54
Man, The (Greene, BMI) .... 81
Married Man (Marks, BMI) .... 80
Mr. Lonely (Ripley, BMI) .... 19
My Girl (Jobete, BMI) .... 12
My Heart Would Know (Rose, BMI) .... 76
My Love Forgive Me (Gil, BMI) .... 41
Name Game, The (Gallico, BMI) .... 3
No Arms Can Ever Hold You (Gil, BMI) .... 33
No Faith, No Love (Chevis, BMI) .... 91
Ode to the Little Brown Shack Out Back (Sleepy Hollow, ASCAP) .... 58
Paper Tiger (Acuff-Rose, BMI) .... 45
Red Roses for a Blue Lady (Mills, ASCAP) .... 64
Seven Letters (Milky Way, BMI) .... 53
Sha La La (Ludix-Flomarlu, BMI) .... 49
Shake (Kags, BMI) .... 15
She's a Woman (Maclen, BMI) .... 37
Somewhere in Your Heart (Leeds, ASCAP) .... 36
Tell Her No (Mainstay, BMI) .... 24
Thanks a Lot (Hotpoint, BMI) .... 57
That's How Strong My Love Is (Rise, BMI) .... 90
This Diamond Ring (Sea Lark, BMI) .... 7
Thou Shalt Not Steal (Acuff-Rose, BMI) .... 20
Try to Remember (Chappell, ASCAP) .... 88
Twine Time (Va-Pac, BMI) .... 31
Use Your Head (Conrad-Shakewell, BMI) .... 34
Voice Your Choice (Chevis, BMI) .... 59
Wedding, The (Regent-Bending, BMI) .... 39
What Have They Done to the Rain (Schroder, ASCAP) .... 73
Whenever a Teenager Cries (Schwartz, ASCAP) .. 69
Whose Heart Are You Breaking Tonight? (Francon, ASCAP) .... 71
Willow Weep for Me (Bourne, ASCAP) .... 35
You're Nobody Till Somebody Loves You (Southern, ASCAP) .... 25
You've Lost That Lovin' Feelin' (Screen Gems-Columbia, BMI) .... 2

## BUBBLING UNDER THE HOT 100

101. SIX BOYS .... J. Frank Wilson, Josie 929
102. NEW YORK'S A LONELY TOWN .... Trade Winds, Red Bird 10-020
103. SOMEWHERE .... P. J. Proby, Liberty 55757
104. I WANT YOU TO BE MY BOY .... Exciters, Roulette 4591
105. I'LL COME RUNNING .... Lulu, Parrot 9714
106. IT'S BETTER TO HAVE IT .... Barbara Lynn, Jamie 1292
107. SUDDENLY I'M ALL ALONE .... Walter Jackson, Okeh 7215
108. A LITTLE BIT OF SOAP .... Garnet Mimms, United Artists 796
109. STRAIN ON MY HEART .... Roscoe Shelton, Sims 217
110. I'M OVER YOU .... Jan Bradley, Chess 1919
111. EVERYDAY .... Rogues, Columbia 43190
112. BABY DON'T GO .... Sonny & Cher, Reprise 0309
113. I WILL WAIT FOR YOU .... Steve Lawrence, Columbia 43192
114. YOU'RE THE ONLY WORLD I KNOW .... Sonny James, Capitol 5280
115. TERRY .... Twinkle, Tollie 9040
116. THEN AND ONLY THEN .... Connie Smith, RCA Victor 8489
117. FINDERS KEEPERS, LOSERS WEEPERS .... Nella Dodds, Wand 171
118. PERCOLATIN' .... Willie Mitchell, Hi 2083
119. CROSS MY HEART .... Bobby Vee, Liberty 55761
120. PEARLY SHELLS .... Billy Vaughn, Dot 15664
121. I WONDER .... Butterflys, Red Bird 10-016
122. MY GAL SAL .... Burl Ives, Decca 31729
123. THE RICHEST MAN ALIVE .... Mel Carter, Imperial 66078
124. WHAT A SHAME .... Rolling Stones, London 9725
125. GET OUT .... Harold Melvin, Landa 703
126. IF I KNEW THEN .... Ray Conniff Singers, Columbia 43168
127. RUN MY HEART .... Baby Washington, Sue 119
128. CROSS THE BRAZOS AT WACO .... Billy Walker, Columbia 43120
129. EL PUSSY CAT .... Mongo Santamaria, Columbia 43171
130. LEROY .... Norma Tracey, Day Dell 1005
131. IT'S GOTTA LAST FOREVER .... Billy J. Kramer, Imperial 66085
132. DO-DO DO BAH-AH .... Bert Keyes, Clock 1048
133. WATUSI '64 .... Jay Bentley & the Jet Set, Crescendo 332
134. I WANT TO GET MARRIED .... Delicates, Challenge 59267
135. I LOVE YOU BABY .... Dottie & Ray, LeSage 701

Compiled from national retail sales and radio station airplay by the Music Popularity Dept. of Record Market Research, Billboard.

# Billboard HOT 100

**For Week Ending February 6, 1965**

★ STAR performer—Sides registering greatest proportionate upward progress this week.

| This Week | 1 Wk. Ago | 2 Wks. Ago | 3 Wks. Ago | TITLE Artist, Label & Number | Weeks On Chart |
|---|---|---|---|---|---|
| 1 | 2 | 2 | 5 | YOU'VE LOST THAT LOVIN' FEELIN' — Righteous Brothers, Philles 124 | 9 |
| 2 | 1 | 1 | 4 | DOWNTOWN — Petula Clark, Warner Bros. 5494 | 8 |
| 3 | 3 | 6 | 20 | THE NAME GAME — Shirley Ellis, Congress 230 | 9 |
| 4 | 7 | 34 | 65 | THIS DIAMOND RING — Gary Lewis & the Playboys, Liberty 55756 | 4 |
| 5 | 5 | 11 | 15 | HOLD WHAT YOU'VE GOT — Joe Tex, Dial 4001 | 8 |
| 6 | 4 | 3 | 3 | LOVE POTION NUMBER NINE — Searchers, Kapp Winner's Circle 27 | 11 |
| 7 | 10 | 19 | 29 | ALL DAY AND ALL OF THE NIGHT — Kinks, Reprise 0334 | 7 |
| 8 | 12 | 41 | 76 | MY GIRL — Temptations, Gordy 7038 | 4 |
| 9 | 6 | 9 | 9 | HOW SWEET IT IS (To Be Loved by You) — Marvin Gaye, Tamla 54107 | 12 |
| 10 | 15 | 27 | 36 | SHAKE — Sam Cooke, RCA Victor 8486 | 5 |
| 11 | 13 | 18 | 34 | LET'S LOCK THE DOOR (And Throw Away the Key) — Jay & the Americans, United Artists 805 | 7 |
| 12 | 8 | 5 | 1 | COME SEE ABOUT ME — Supremes, Motown 1068 | 13 |
| 13 | 9 | 10 | 10 | KEEP SEARCHIN' — Del Shannon, Amy 915 | 12 |
| 14 | 22 | 50 | 74 | THE JOLLY GREEN GIANT — Kingsmen, Wand 172 | 5 |
| 15 | 29 | 61 | 87 | BYE, BYE, BABY — 4 Seasons, Philips 40260 | 4 |
| 16 | 21 | 33 | 62 | I GO TO PIECES — Peter & Gordon, Capitol 5335 | 5 |
| 17 | 23 | 38 | 50 | THE "IN" CROWD — Dobie Gray, Charger 105 | 5 |
| 18 | 18 | 23 | 30 | GIVE HIM A GREAT BIG KISS — Shangri-Las, Red Bird 10-018 | 7 |
| 19 | 24 | 42 | 66 | TELL HER NO — Zombies, Parrot 9723 | 5 |
| 20 | 31 | 58 | 77 | TWINE TIME — Alvin Cash & the Crawlers, Mar-V-Lus 6002 | 6 |
| 21 | 14 | 16 | 26 | I'LL BE THERE — Gerry & the Pacemakers, Laurie 3279 | 9 |
| 22 | 11 | 4 | 2 | I FEEL FINE — Beatles, Capitol 5327 | 10 |
| 23 | 26 | 47 | 58 | HEART OF STONE — Rolling Stones, London 9725 | 5 |
| 24 | 28 | 39 | 43 | HAVE YOU LOOKED INTO YOUR HEART — Jerry Vale, Columbia 43181 | 8 |
| 25 | 32 | 43 | 68 | LAUGH, LAUGH — Beau Brummels, Autumn 8 | 6 |
| 26 | 20 | 13 | 13 | THOU SHALT NOT STEAL — Dick & Deedee, Warner Bros. 5482 | 12 |
| 27 | 27 | 22 | 19 | DON'T FORGET I STILL LOVE YOU — Bobbi Martin, Coral 62426 | 11 |
| 28 | 30 | 36 | 47 | LOOK OF LOVE — Lesley Gore, Mercury 72372 | 7 |
| 29 | 44 | 66 | 90 | THE BOY FROM NEW YORK CITY — Ad Libs, Blue Cat 102 | 4 |
| 30 | 33 | 45 | 55 | NO ARMS CAN EVER HOLD YOU! — Bachelors, London 9724 | 7 |
| 31 | 17 | 12 | 8 | GOIN' OUT OF MY HEAD — Little Anthony & the Imperials, DCP 1119 | 14 |
| 32 | 36 | 46 | 52 | SOMEWHERE IN YOUR HEART — Frank Sinatra, Reprise 0332 | 8 |
| 33 | 16 | 8 | 7 | THE JERK — Larks, Money 106 | 13 |
| 34 | 25 | 26 | 31 | YOU'RE NOBODY TILL SOMEBODY LOVES YOU — Dean Martin, Reprise 0333 | 9 |
| 35 | 19 | 7 | 6 | MR. LONELY — Bobby Vinton, Epic 9730 | 15 |
| 36 | 46 | 75 | — | LEMON TREE — Trini Lopez, Reprise 0336 | 3 |
| 37 | 45 | 56 | 61 | PAPER TIGER — Sue Thompson, Hickory 1284 | 6 |
| 38 | 34 | 44 | 48 | USE YOUR HEAD — Mary Wells, 20th Century-Fox 555 | 6 |
| 39 | 63 | — | — | KING OF THE ROAD — Roger Miller, Smash 1965 | 2 |
| 40 | 68 | 100 | — | THE BIRDS AND THE BEES — Jewel Akens, Era 3141 | 3 |
| 41 | 38 | 24 | 27 | DEAR HEART — Andy Williams, Columbia 43180 | 11 |
| 42 | 60 | 81 | — | FOR LOVIN' ME — Peter, Paul & Mary, Warner Bros. 5496 | 3 |
| 43 | 35 | 15 | 17 | WILLOW WEEP FOR ME — Chad & Jeremy, World Artists 1034 | 13 |
| 44 | 42 | 31 | 32 | DEAR HEART — Jack Jones, Kapp 635 | 11 |
| 45 | 64 | 86 | — | RED ROSES FOR A BLUE LADY — Bert Kaempfert & His Ork, Decca 31722 | 3 |
| 46 | 70 | — | — | A CHANGE IS GONNA COME — Sam Cooke, RCA Victor 8486 | 2 |
| 47 | 75 | 85 | — | I'VE GOT A TIGER BY THE TAIL — Buck Owens, Capitol 5336 | 3 |
| 48 | 72 | — | — | AT THE CLUB — Drifters, Atlantic 2268 | 2 |
| 49 | 61 | 82 | 93 | FANCY PANTS — Al Hirt, RCA Victor 8487 | 4 |
| 50 | 58 | 67 | 85 | ODE TO THE LITTLE BROWN SHACK OUT BACK — Billy Edd Wheeler, Kapp 617 | 6 |
| 51 | 52 | 60 | 60 | LITTLE BELL — Dixie Cups, Red Bird 10-017 | 8 |
| 52 | 55 | 63 | 71 | DO WHAT YOU DO DO WELL — Ned Miller, Fabor 137 | 7 |
| 53 | 59 | 73 | 80 | VOICE YOUR CHOICE — Radiants, Chess 1904 | 7 |
| 54 | 57 | 68 | 83 | THANKS A LOT — Brenda Lee, Decca 31728 | 4 |
| 55 | 67 | 80 | — | BREAK AWAY (From That Boy) — Newbeats, Hickory 1290 | 3 |
| 56 | 62 | 74 | 89 | HELLO PRETTY GIRL — Ronnie Dove, Diamond 176 | 5 |
| 57 | 73 | — | — | WHAT HAVE THEY DONE TO THE RAIN — Searchers, Kapp 644 | 2 |
| 58 | 83 | 91 | — | LITTLE THINGS — Bobby Goldsboro, United Artist 810 | 3 |
| 59 | 85 | — | — | CAN'T YOU HEAR MY HEARTBEAT — Herman's Hermits, MGM 13310 | 2 |
| 60 | 71 | 92 | — | WHOSE HEART ARE YOU BREAKING TONIGHT? — Connie Francis, MGM 13303 | 3 |
| 61 | — | — | — | FERRY ACROSS THE MERSEY — Gerry & the Pacemakers, Laurie 3284 | 1 |
| 62 | 69 | 76 | 84 | WHENEVER A TEENAGER CRIES — Reparata & the Delrons, World Artists 1036 | 5 |
| 63 | — | — | — | HURT SO BAD — Little Anthony & the Imperials, DCP 1128 | 1 |
| 64 | 65 | 65 | 63 | HE'S MY GUY — Irma Thomas, Imperial 66080 | 8 |
| 65 | 78 | 87 | 97 | IT'S ALRIGHT — Adam Faith, Amy 913 | 4 |
| 66 | 76 | 84 | 100 | MY HEART WOULD KNOW — Al Martino, Capitol 5341 | 4 |
| 67 | 84 | — | — | DON'T COME RUNNING BACK TO ME — Nancy Wilson, Capitol 5340 | 2 |
| 68 | 79 | 94 | — | DUSTY — Rag Dolls, Mala 493 | 3 |
| 69 | 82 | — | — | COMING ON TOO STRONG — Wayne Newton, Capitol 5338 | 2 |
| 70 | — | — | — | NEW YORK'S A LONELY TOWN — Trade Winds, Red Bird 10-020 | 1 |
| 71 | 80 | — | — | MARRIED MAN — Richard Burton, MGM 13307 | 2 |
| 72 | 81 | — | — | THE MAN — Lorne Greene, RCA Victor 8490 | 2 |
| 73 | 74 | 79 | 81 | COUSIN OF MINE — Sam Cooke, RCA Victor 8426 | 12 |
| 74 | 86 | — | — | DIAMOND HEAD — Ventures, Dolton 303 | 2 |
| 75 | — | — | — | ASK THE LONELY — Four Tops, Motown 1073 | 1 |
| 76 | — | — | — | MIDNIGHT SPECIAL — Johnny Rivers, Imperial 66087 | 1 |
| 77 | — | — | — | COME HOME — Dave Clark Five, Epic 9763 | 1 |
| 78 | — | — | — | BORN TO BE TOGETHER — Ronettes, Philles 126 | 1 |
| 79 | 89 | 98 | — | GOLDFINGER — Billy Strange, Crescendo 334 | 3 |
| 80 | 90 | — | — | THAT'S HOW STRONG MY LOVE IS — Otis Redding, Volt 124 | 2 |
| 81 | 96 | — | — | HE WAS REALLY SAYIN' SOMETHIN' — Velvelettes, V.I.P. 25013 | 2 |
| 82 | 88 | 90 | — | TRY TO REMEMBER — Ed Ames, RCA Victor 8483 | 3 |
| 83 | 92 | — | — | BRING YOUR LOVE TO ME — Righteous Brothers, Moonglow 238 | 2 |
| 84 | — | — | — | HELLO DOLLY! — Bobby Darin, Capitol 5359 | 1 |
| 85 | 98 | — | — | GOLDFINGER — Shirley Bassey, United Artists 790 | 2 |
| 86 | — | — | — | DON'T MESS UP A GOOD THING — Fontella Bass & Bobby McClure, Checker 1097 | 1 |
| 87 | — | — | — | IT'S GOTTA LAST FOREVER — Billy J. Kramer, Imperial 66085 | 1 |
| 88 | 97 | — | — | CRYING IN THE CHAPEL — Adam Wade, Epic 9752 | 2 |
| 89 | — | — | — | DON'T LET ME BE MISUNDERSTOOD — Animals, MGM 13311 | 1 |
| 90 | 93 | — | — | JERK AND TWINE — Jackie Ross, Chess 1920 | 2 |
| 91 | 95 | 92 | — | NO FAITH, NO LOVE — Mitty Collier, Chess 1918 | 5 |
| 92 | 94 | 99 | 99 | I WANNA BE (Your Everything) — Manhattans, Carnival 507 | 4 |
| 93 | 95 | — | — | I WANT MY BABY BACK — Jimmy Cross, Tollie 9039 | 2 |
| 94 | — | — | — | CRY — Ray Charles, ABC-Paramount 10615 | 1 |
| 95 | — | — | — | RED ROSES FOR A BLUE LADY — Vic Dana, Dolton 304 | 1 |
| 96 | 99 | — | — | CAN'T YOU JUST SEE ME — Aretha Franklin, Columbia 43203 | 2 |
| 97 | — | — | — | I'M OVER YOU — Jan Bradley, Chess 1919 | 1 |
| 98 | 100 | — | — | GOLDFINGER — Jack LaForge, Regina 1323 | 2 |
| 99 | — | — | — | CROSS MY HEART — Bobby Vee, Liberty 55761 | 1 |
| 100 | — | — | — | LOVE ME — Sonny Knight, Aura 4505 | 1 |

## BUBBLING UNDER THE HOT 100

101. LIKE A CHILD — Julie Rogers, Mercury 72380
102. THE BOY NEXT DOOR — Standells, Vee Jay 643
103. SOMEWHERE — P. J. Proby, Liberty 55757
104. THE RICHEST MAN ALIVE — Mel Carter, Imperial 66078
105. SUDDENLY I'M ALL ALONE — Walter Jackson, Okeh 7215
106. EVERYDAY — Rogues, Columbia 43190
107. WE CAN'T BELIEVE YOU'RE GONE — Bobby Harris, Atlantic 2270
108. I'LL COME RUNNING — Lulu, Parrot 9714
109. STRAIN ON MY HEART — Roscoe Shelton, Sims 217
110. SIX BOYS — J. Frank Wilson, Josie 929
111. EL PUSSY CAT — Mongo Santamaria, Columbia 43171
112. TEARDROPS FROM MY EYES — Ray Charles, ABC-Paramount 10615
113. TERRY — Twinkle, Tollie 9040
114. I WANT YOU TO BE MY BOY — Exciters, Roulette 4591
115. YOU'RE MY GIRL — Everly Brothers, Warner Bros. 5600
116. REAL LIVE GIRL — Steve Alaimo, ABC-Paramount 10620
117. I WONDER — Butterflys, Red Bird 10-016
118. BABY DON'T GO — Sonny & Cher, Reprise 0309
119. YOU'RE THE ONLY WORLD I KNOW — Sonny James, Capitol 5280
120. MY BABE — Righteous Brothers, Moonglow
121. RUN MY HEART — Baby Washington, Sue 119
122. LEROY — Norma Tracey, Capitol 1005
123. FINDERS KEEPERS, LOSERS WEEPERS — Nella Dodds, Wand 174
124. ANGEL — Johnny Tillotson, MGM 13316
125. I WANT TO GET MARRIED — Delicates, Challenge 59267
126. GOLDFINGER — John Barry & His Ork, United Artists 791
127. RED ROSES FOR A BLUE LADY — Wayne Newton, Capitol 5366
128. COME ON HOME — Bill Black's Combo, Hi 2085
129. I AIN'T COMING BACK — Orlons, Cameo 352
130. WATUSI '64 — Jay Bentley and the Jet Set, Crescendo 332
131. I WONDER — Dottie & Ray, LeSage 701
132. I WANT A LITTLE GIRL — Joe Hinton, Back Beat 545
133. THE HULLABALOO — Bobby Gregg & His Friends, Veep 1207

Compiled from national retail sales and radio station airplay by the Music Popularity Dept. of Record Market Research, Billboard.

# Billboard

For Week Ending February 13, 1965

# HOT 100

★ STAR performer—Sides registering greatest proportionate upward progress this week.

Record Industry Association of America seal of certification as million selling single.

| This Week | 1 Wk. Ago | 2 Wks. Ago | 3 Wks. Ago | TITLE Artist, Label & Number | Weeks On Chart |
|---|---|---|---|---|---|
| 1 | 1 | 2 | 2 | YOU'VE LOST THAT LOVIN' FEELIN' — Righteous Brothers, Philles 124 | 10 |
| 2 | 2 | 1 | 1 | DOWNTOWN — Petula Clark, Warner Bros. 5494 | 9 |
| 3 | 4 | 7 | 34 | THIS DIAMOND RING — Gary Lewis & the Playboys, Liberty 55756 | 5 |
| 4 | 3 | 3 | 6 | THE NAME GAME — Shirley Ellis, Congress 230 | 10 |
| ★ 5 | 8 | 12 | 41 | MY GIRL — Temptations, Gordy 7038 | 5 |
| 6 | 5 | 5 | 11 | HOLD WHAT YOU'VE GOT — Joe Tex, Dial 4001 | 9 |
| 7 | 7 | 10 | 19 | ALL DAY AND ALL OF THE NIGHT — Kinks, Reprise 0334 | 8 |
| 8 | 10 | 15 | 27 | SHAKE — Sam Cooke, RCA Victor 8486 | 6 |
| ★ 9 | 14 | 22 | 50 | THE JOLLY GREEN GIANT — Kingsmen, Wand 172 | 6 |
| ★ 10 | 16 | 21 | 33 | I GO TO PIECES — Peter & Gordon, Capitol 5335 | 6 |
| 11 | 11 | 13 | 18 | LET'S LOCK THE DOOR (And Throw Away the Key) — Jay & the Americans, United Artists 805 | 8 |
| 12 | 15 | 29 | 61 | BYE, BYE BABY — 4 Seasons, Philips 40260 | 5 |
| 13 | 6 | 4 | 3 | LOVE POTION NUMBER NINE — Searchers, Kapp Winner's Circle 27 | 12 |
| 14 | 17 | 23 | 38 | THE "IN" CROWD — Dobie Gray, Charger 105 | 6 |
| ★ 15 | 29 | 44 | 66 | THE BOY FROM NEW YORK CITY — Ad Libs, Blue Cat 102 | 5 |
| 16 | 19 | 24 | 42 | TELL HER NO — Zombies, Parrot 9723 | 6 |
| 17 | 20 | 31 | 58 | TWINE TIME — Alvin Cash & the Crawlers, Mar-V-Lus 6002 | 7 |
| 18 | 9 | 6 | 9 | HOW SWEET IT IS (To Be Loved by You) — Marvin Gaye, Tamla 54107 | 13 |
| 19 | 13 | 9 | 10 | KEEP SEARCHIN' — Del Shannon, Amy 915 | 13 |
| ★ 20 | 25 | 32 | 43 | LAUGH, LAUGH — Beau Brummels, Autumn 8 | 7 |
| 21 | 23 | 26 | 47 | HEART OF STONE — Rolling Stones, London 9725 | 6 |
| ★ 22 | 39 | 63 | — | KING OF THE ROAD — Roger Miller, Smash 1965 | 3 |
| 23 | 12 | 8 | 5 | COME SEE ABOUT ME — Supremes, Motown 1068 | 14 |
| ★ 24 | 36 | 46 | 75 | LEMON TREE — Trini Lopez, Reprise 0336 | 4 |
| 25 | 18 | 18 | 23 | GIVE HIM A GREAT BIG KISS — Shangri-Las, Red Bird 10-018 | 8 |
| ★ 26 | 37 | 45 | 56 | PAPER TIGER — Sue Thompson, Hickory 1284 | 7 |
| 27 | 28 | 30 | 36 | LOOK OF LOVE — Lesley Gore, Mercury 72372 | 8 |
| 28 | 24 | 28 | 39 | HAVE YOU LOOKED INTO YOUR HEART — Jerry Vale, Columbia 43181 | 9 |
| 29 | 30 | 33 | 45 | NO ARMS CAN EVER HOLD YOU! — Bachelors, London 9724 | 8 |
| ★ 30 | 40 | 68 | 100 | THE BIRD'S AND THE BEES — Jewel Akens, Era 3141 | 4 |
| ★ 31 | 45 | 64 | 86 | RED ROSES FOR A BLUE LADY — Bert Kaempfert & His Ork, Decca 31722 | 4 |
| ★ 32 | 42 | 60 | 81 | FOR LOVIN' ME — Peter, Paul & Mary, Warner Bros. 5496 | 4 |
| 33 | 26 | 20 | 13 | THOU SHALT NOT STEAL — Dick & Deedee, Warner Bros. 5482 | 13 |
| 34 | 32 | 36 | 46 | SOMEWHERE IN YOUR HEART — Frank Sinatra, Reprise 0332 | 9 |
| ★ 35 | 47 | 75 | 85 | I'VE GOT A TIGER BY THE TAIL — Buck Owens, Capitol 5336 | 4 |
| ★ 36 | 46 | 70 | — | A CHANGE IS GONNA COME — Sam Cooke, RCA Victor 8486 | 3 |
| 37 | 27 | 27 | 22 | DON'T FORGET I STILL LOVE YOU — Bobbi Martin, Coral 62426 | 12 |
| ★ 38 | 63 | — | — | HURT SO BAD — Little Anthony & the Imperials, DCP 1128 | 2 |
| ★ 39 | 61 | — | — | FERRY ACROSS THE MERSEY — Gerry & the Pacemakers, Laurie 3284 | 2 |
| 40 | 22 | 11 | 4 | I FEEL FINE — Beatles, Capitol 5327 | 11 |
| ★ 41 | 58 | 83 | 91 | LITTLE THINGS — Bobby Goldsboro, United Artist 810 | 4 |
| ★ 42 | 65 | 78 | 87 | IT'S ALRIGHT — Adam Faith, Amy 913 | 5 |
| 43 | 48 | 72 | — | AT THE CLUB — Drifters, Atlantic 2268 | 3 |
| ★ 44 | 55 | 67 | 80 | BREAK AWAY — Newbeats, Hickory 1290 | 4 |
| 45 | 21 | 14 | 16 | I'LL BE THERE — Gerry & the Pacemakers, Laurie 3279 | 10 |
| ★ 46 | 57 | 73 | — | WHAT HAVE THEY DONE TO THE RAIN — Searchers, Kapp 644 | 3 |
| 47 | 49 | 61 | 82 | FANCY PANTS — Al Hirt, RCA Victor 8487 | 5 |
| ★ 48 | 59 | 85 | — | CAN'T YOU HEAR MY HEARTBEAT — Herman's Hermits, MGM 13310 | 3 |
| ★ 49 | 60 | 71 | 92 | WHOSE HEART ARE YOU BREAKING TONIGHT? — Connie Francis, MGM 13303 | 4 |
| 50 | 54 | 57 | 68 | THANKS A LOT — Brenda Lee, Decca 31728 | 5 |
| 51 | 53 | 59 | 73 | VOICE YOUR CHOICE — Radiants, Chess 1904 | 8 |
| 52 | 52 | 55 | 63 | DO WHAT YOU DO DO WELL — Ned Miller, Fabor 137 | 8 |
| ★ 53 | 75 | — | — | ASK THE LONELY — Four Tops, Motown 1073 | 2 |
| 54 | 56 | 62 | 74 | HELLO PRETTY GIRL — Ronnie Dove, Diamond 176 | 6 |
| ★ 55 | 66 | 76 | 84 | MY HEART WOULD KNOW — Al Martino, Capitol 5341 | 5 |
| ★ 56 | 76 | — | — | MIDNIGHT SPECIAL — Johnny Rivers, Imperial 66087 | 2 |
| ★ 57 | 68 | 79 | 94 | DUSTY — Rag Dolls, Mala 493 | 4 |
| ★ 58 | 77 | — | — | COME HOME — Dave Clark Five, Epic 9763 | 2 |
| ★ 59 | 70 | — | — | NEW YORK'S A LONELY TOWN — Trade Winds, Red Bird 10-020 | 2 |
| 60 | 62 | 69 | 76 | WHENEVER A TEENAGER CRIES — Reparata & the Delrons, World Artists 1036 | 6 |
| ★ 61 | — | — | — | GOODNIGHT — Roy Orbison, Monument 873 | 1 |
| 62 | 67 | 84 | — | DON'T COME RUNNING BACK TO ME — Nancy Wilson, Capitol 5340 | 3 |
| ★ 63 | 78 | — | — | BORN TO BE TOGETHER — Ronettes, Philles 126 | 2 |
| ★ 64 | 85 | 98 | — | GOLDFINGER — Shirley Bassey, United Artists 790 | 3 |
| 65 | 69 | 82 | — | COMING ON TOO STRONG — Wayne Newton, Capitol 5338 | 3 |
| 66 | 51 | 52 | 60 | LITTLE BELL — Dixie Cups, Red Bird 10-017 | 9 |
| 67 | 50 | 58 | 67 | ODE TO THE LITTLE BROWN SHACK OUT BACK — Billy Edd Wheeler, Kapp 617 | 7 |
| 68 | 79 | 89 | 98 | GOLDFINGER — Billy Strange, Crescendo 334 | 4 |
| ★ 69 | 95 | — | — | RED ROSES FOR A BLUE LADY — Vic Dana, Dolton 304 | 2 |
| 70 | 74 | 86 | — | DIAMOND HEAD — Ventures, Dolton 303 | 3 |
| 71 | 71 | 80 | — | MARRIED MAN — Richard Burton, MGM 13307 | 3 |
| 72 | 72 | 81 | — | THE MAN — Lorne Greene, RCA Victor 8490 | 3 |
| ★ 73 | 89 | — | — | DON'T LET ME BE MISUNDERSTOOD — Animals, MGM 13311 | 2 |
| 74 | 80 | 90 | — | THAT'S HOW STRONG MY LOVE IS — Otis Redding, Volt 124 | 3 |
| 75 | 86 | — | — | DON'T MESS UP A GOOD THING — Fontella Bass & Bobby McClure, Checker 1097 | 2 |
| 76 | 87 | — | — | IT'S GOTTA LAST FOREVER — Billy J. Kramer, Imperial 66085 | 2 |
| 77 | 82 | 88 | 90 | TRY TO REMEMBER — Ed Ames, RCA Victor 8483 | 4 |
| ★ 78 | — | — | — | YEH, YEH — Georgie Fame, Imperial 66086 | 1 |
| 79 | 81 | 96 | — | HE WAS REALLY SAYIN' SOMETHIN' — Velvelettes, V.I.P. 25013 | 3 |
| ★ 80 | — | — | — | SHOTGUN — Jr. Walker & the All Stars, Soul 35008 | 1 |
| 81 | 84 | — | — | HELLO DOLLY! — Bobby Darin, Capitol 5359 | 2 |
| 82 | 94 | — | — | CRY — Ray Charles, ABC-Paramount 10615 | 2 |
| 83 | 83 | 92 | — | BRING YOUR LOVE TO ME — Righteous Brothers, Moonglow 238 | 3 |
| ★ 84 | — | — | — | PEOPLE GET READY — Impressions, ABC-Paramount 10622 | 1 |
| ★ 85 | — | — | — | FLY ME TO THE MOON — LaVern Baker, Atlantic 2267 | 1 |
| 86 | 90 | 93 | — | JERK AND TWINE — Jackie Ross, Chess 1920 | 3 |
| 87 | 92 | 94 | 99 | I WANNA BE (Your Everything) — Manhattans, Carnival 507 | 5 |
| 88 | 88 | 97 | — | CRYING IN THE CHAPEL — Adam Wade, Epic 9752 | 3 |
| ★ 89 | — | — | — | LIKE A CHILD — Julie Rogers, Mercury 72380 | 1 |
| ★ 90 | — | — | — | APACHE '65 — Arrows, Tower 116 | 1 |
| 91 | — | — | — | SOMEWHERE — P. J. Proby, Liberty 55757 | 1 |
| 92 | 93 | 95 | — | I WANT MY BABY BACK — Jimmy Cross, Tollie 9039 | 3 |
| 93 | 97 | — | — | I'M OVER YOU — Jan Bradley, Chess 1919 | 2 |
| 94 | — | — | — | ANGEL — Johnny Tillotson, MGM 13316 | 1 |
| 95 | — | — | — | ORANGE BLOSSOM SPECIAL — Johnny Cash, Columbia 43206 | 1 |
| 96 | — | — | — | SUDDENLY I'M ALL ALONE — Walter Jackson, Okeh 7215 | 1 |
| 97 | — | — | — | IF I RULED THE WORLD — Tonny Bennett, Columbia 43220 | 1 |
| 98 | — | — | — | DIANA — Bobby Rydell, Capitol 5352 | 1 |
| 99 | — | — | — | IT'S GONNA BE ALRIGHT — Maxine Brown, Wand 173 | 1 |
| 100 | — | — | — | DID YOU EVER — Hullaballoos, Roulette 4593 | 1 |

## HOT 100—A TO Z—*(Publisher-Licensee)*

All Day and All of the Night (Jay Boy, BMI) ... 7
Angel (Disney, ASCAP) ... 94
Apache '65 (Francis, Day & Hunter, PRF, ASCAP). 90
Ask the Lonely (Jobete, BMI) ... 53
At the Club (Screen Gems-Columbia, BMI) ... 43
Birds and the Bees, The (Pattern, ASCAP) ... 30
Born to Be Together (Screen Gems-Columbia, BMI). 63
Boy From New York City, The (Trio, BMI) ... 15
Break Away (From That Boy) (Acuff-Rose, BMI) ... 44
Bring Your Love to Me (Maxwell, BMI) ... 83
Bye, Bye Baby (Saturday-Seasons Four, BMI) ... 12
Can't You Hear My Heartbeat (Southern, ASCAP). 48
Change Is Gonna Come, A (Kags, BMI) ... 36
Come Home (Branston, BMI) ... 58
Come See About Me (Jobete, BMI) ... 23
Coming on Too Strong (Beechwood, BMI) ... 65
Cry (Shapiro-Bernstein, ASCAP) ... 82
Crying in the Chapel (Valley, BMI) ... 88
Diana (Spanka, BMI) ... 98
Diamond Head (Election, BMI) ... 70
Did You Ever (Big Seven, BMI) ... 100
Do What You Do Do Well (Central Songs, BMI) ... 52
Don't Come Running Back to Me (Leeds, ASCAP) .. 62
Don't Forget I Still Love You (South Mountain, BMI) ... 37
Don't Let Me Be Misunderstood (Benjamin, ASCAP). 73
Don't Mess Up a Good Thing (Arc-Saico, BMI) ... 75
Downtown (Leeds, ASCAP) ... 2
Dusty (Saturday, ASCAP) ... 57
Fancy Pants (Acuff-Rose, BMI) ... 47
Ferry Across the Mersey (Unart-Pacer, BMI) ... 39
Fly Me to the Moon (Almanac, ASCAP) ... 85
For Lovin' Me (Witmark, ASCAP) ... 32
Give Him a Great Big Kiss (Tender Tunes-Trio, BMI) ... 25
Goldfinger—Bassey (Unart, BMI) ... 64
Goldfinger—Strange (Unart, BMI) ... 68
Goodnight (Acuff-Rose, BMI) ... 61
Have You Looked Into Your Heart (South Mountain, BMI) ... 28
He Was Really Sayin' Somethin' (Jobete, BMI) ... 79
Heart of Stone (Immediate, BMI) ... 21
Hello, Dolly! (Morris, ASCAP) ... 81
Hello Pretty Girl (Picturetone, BMI) ... 54
Hold What You've Got (Tree, BMI) ... 6
How Sweet It Is (To Be Loved By You) (Jobete, BMI) ... 18
Hurt So Bad (South Mountain, BMI) ... 38
I Feel Fine (Maclen, BMI) ... 40
I Go to Pieces (Vicki-McLaughlin, BMI) ... 10
I Wanna Be (Your Everything) (Bright Star-Sanavan, BMI) ... 87
I Want My Baby Back (Rock, BMI) ... 92
I'll Be There (T.M., BMI) ... 45
I'm Over You (Arc-Jan Jo, BMI) ... 93
I've Got a Tiger By the Tail (Bluebook, BMI) ... 35
If I Ruled the World (Chappell, ASCAP) ... 97
"In" Crowd, The (American, BMI) ... 14
It's Alright (Gil, BMI) ... 42
It's Gonna Be Alright (Screen Gems-Columbia, BMI) ... 99
It's Gotta Last Forever (Lynch-Bigtop, BMI) ... 76
Jerk and Twine (Chevis, BMI) ... 86
Jolly Green Giant, The (Burdette-Flomarlu, BMI) .. 9
Keep Searchin' (Vicki-McLaughlin, BMI) ... 19
King of the Road (Tree, BMI) ... 22
Laugh, Laugh (Taracrest, BMI) ... 20
Lemon Tree (Boulder, ASCAP) ... 24
Let's Lock the Door (Picturetone, BMI) ... 11
Like a Child (Ponderosa, BMI) ... 89
Little Bell (Trio, BMI) ... 66
Little Things (Unart, BMI) ... 41
Look of Love (Trio, BMI) ... 27
Love Potion Number Nine (Quintet, BMI) ... 13
Man, The (Greene, BMI) ... 72
Married Man (Marks, BMI) ... 71
Midnight Special (Trousdale, BMI) ... 56
My Girl (Jobete, BMI) ... 5
My Heart Would Know (Rose, BMI) ... 55
Name Game, The (Gallico, BMI) ... 4
New York's a Lonely Town (Big Top, BMI) ... 59
No Arms Can Ever Hold You (Gil, BMI) ... 29
Ode to the Little Brown Shack Out Back (Sleepy Hollow, ASCAP) ... 67
Orange Blossom Special (Leeds, ASCAP) ... 95
Paper Tiger (Acuff-Rose, BMI) ... 26
People Get Ready (Chi-Sound, BMI) ... 84
Red Roses for a Blue Lady—Dana (Mills, ASCAP). 69
Red Roses for a Blue Lady—Kaempfert (Mills, ASCAP) ... 31
Shake (Kags, BMI) ... 8
Shotgun (Jobete, BMI) ... 80
Somewhere (Schirmer-Chappell, ASCAP) ... 91
Somewhere in Your Heart (Leeds, ASCAP) ... 34
Suddenly I'm All Alone (Blackwood, BMI) ... 96
Tell Her No (Mainstay, BMI) ... 16
Thanks a Lot (Hotpoint, BMI) ... 50
That's How Strong My Love Is (Rise, BMI) ... 74
This Diamond Ring (Sea Lark, BMI) ... 3
Thou Shalt Not Steal (Acuff-Rose, BMI) ... 33
Try to Remember (Chappell, ASCAP) ... 77
Twine Time (Va-Pac, BMI) ... 17
Voice Your Choice (Chevis, BMI) ... 51
What Have They Done to the Rain (Schroder, ASCAP) ... 46
Whenever a Teenager Cries (Schwartz, ASCAP) ... 60
Whose Heart Are You Breaking Tonight? (Francon, ASCAP) ... 49
Yeh, Yeh (Mongo, BMI) ... 78
You've Lost That Lovin' Feelin' (Screen Gems-Columbia, BMI) ... 1

## BUBBLING UNDER THE HOT 100

101. MY BABE ... Righteous Brothers, Moonglow 223
102. THE BOY NEXT DOOR ... Standells, Vee Jay 643
103. GOOD TIMES ... Jerry Butler, Vee Jay 651
104. THE RICHEST MAN ALIVE ... Mel Carter, Imperial 66078
105. EVERYDAY ... Rogues, Columbia 43190
106. LOVE ME ... Sonny Knight, Aura 4505
107. CAMEL WALK ... Ikettes, Modern 1003
108. EL PUSSY CAT ... Mongo Santamaria, Columbia 43171
109. CAN'T YOU JUST SEE ME ... Aretha Franklin, Columbia 43203
110. TERRY ... Twinkle, Tollie 9040
111. GOLDFINGER ... Jack LaForge, Regina 1323
112. YOU'RE MY GIRL ... Everly Brothers, Warner Bros. 5600
113. LEROY ... Norma Tracey, Daydell 1005
114. SIX BOYS ... J. Frank Wilson, Josie 929
115. CROSS MY HEART ... Bobby Vee, Liberty 55761
116. REAL LIVE GIRL ... Steve Alaimo, ABC-Paramount 10620
117. BABY DON'T GO ... Sonny & Cher, Reprise 0309
118. KEEP ON KEEPING ON ... Vibrations, Okeh 7212
119. RED ROSES FOR A BLUE LADY ... Wayne Newton, Capitol 5366
120. I WANT TO GET MARRIED ... Delicates, Challenge 59267
121. STRAIN ON MY HEART ... Roscoe Shelton, Sims 217
122. GOLDFINGER ... John Barry & His Ork, United Artists 791
123. FANNIE MAE ... Righteous Brothers, Moonglow 238
124. MR. PITIFUL ... Otis Redding, Volt 124
125. COME ON HOME ... Bill Black's Combo, Hi 2085
126. PEARLY SHELLS ... Billy Vaughn, Dot 15664
127. THIS IS MY PRAYER ... Ray Charles Singers, Command 4059
128. WATUSI '64 ... Jay Bentley & the Jet Set, Crescendo 332
129. I LOVE YOU BABY ... Dottie & Ray, Le Sage 701
130. GO NOW ... Moody Blues, London 9726
131. YOU'RE NEXT ... Jimmy Witherspoon, Prestige 341
132. DON'T ANSWER THE DOOR ... Jimmy Johnson, Magnum 719
133. CAST YOUR FATE TO THE WIND ... Sounds Orchestral, Parkway 942
134. THIS SPORTING LIFE ... Ian Whitcomb, Tower 120
135. PATCH IT UP ... Linda Scott, Kapp 641

Compiled from national retail sales and radio station airplay by the Music Popularity Dept. of Record Market Research, Billboard.

# Billboard HOT 100

**For Week Ending February 20, 1965**

★ STAR performer—Sides registering greatest proportionate upward progress this week.

| This Week | Wk. Ago | 2 Wks. Ago | 3 Wks. Ago | TITLE — Artist, Label & Number | Weeks On Chart |
|---|---|---|---|---|---|
| 1 | 3 | 4 | 7 | THIS DIAMOND RING — Gary Lewis & the Playboys, Liberty 55756 | 6 |
| 2 | 1 | 1 | 2 | YOU'VE LOST THAT LOVIN' FEELIN' — Righteous Brothers, Philles 124 | 11 |
| 3 | 2 | 2 | 1 | DOWNTOWN — Petula Clark, Warner Bros. 5494 | 10 |
| 4 | 5 | 8 | 12 | MY GIRL — Temptations, Gordy 7038 | 6 |
| 5 | 4 | 3 | 3 | THE NAME GAME — Shirley Ellis, Congress 230 | 11 |
| 6 | 9 | 14 | 22 | THE JOLLY GREEN GIANT — Kingsmen, Wand 172 | 7 |
| 7 | 7 | 7 | 10 | ALL DAY AND ALL OF THE NIGHT — Kinks, Reprise 0334 | 9 |
| 8 | 8 | 10 | 15 | SHAKE — Sam Cooke, RCA Victor 8486 | 7 |
| 9 | 10 | 16 | 21 | I GO TO PIECES — Peter & Gordon, Capitol 5335 | 7 |
| 10 | 15 | 29 | 44 | THE BOY FROM NEW YORK CITY — Ad Libs, Blue Cat 102 | 5 |
| 11 | 16 | 19 | 24 | TELL HER NO — Zombies, Parrot 9723 | 7 |
| 12 | 12 | 15 | 29 | BYE, BYE BABY — 4 Seasons, Philips 40260 | 6 |
| 13 | 14 | 17 | 23 | THE "IN" CROWD — Dobie Gray, Charger 105 | 7 |
| 14 | 17 | 20 | 31 | TWINE TIME — Alvin Cash & the Crawlers, Mar-V-Lus 6002 | 8 |
| 15 | 20 | 25 | 32 | LAUGH, LAUGH — Beau Brummels, Autumn 8 | 8 |
| 16 | 11 | 11 | 13 | LET'S LOCK THE DOOR (And Throw Away the Key) — Jay & the Americans, United Artists 805 | 9 |
| 17 | 22 | 39 | 63 | KING OF THE ROAD — Roger Miller, Smash 1965 | 4 |
| 18 | 6 | 5 | 5 | HOLD WHAT YOU'VE GOT — Joe Tex, Dial 4001 | 10 |
| 19 | 21 | 23 | 26 | HEART OF STONE — Rolling Stones, London 9725 | 7 |
| 20 | 24 | 36 | 46 | LEMON TREE — Trini Lopez, Reprise 0336 | 5 |
| 21 | 39 | 61 | — | FERRY ACROSS THE MERSEY — Gerry & the Pacemakers, Laurie 3284 | 3 |
| 22 | 38 | 63 | — | HURT SO BAD — Little Anthony & the Imperials, DCP 1128 | 3 |
| 23 | 26 | 37 | 45 | PAPER TIGER — Sue Thompson, Hickory 1284 | 8 |
| 24 | 13 | 6 | 4 | LOVE POTION NUMBER NINE — Searchers, Kapp Winner's Circle 27 | 13 |
| 25 | 30 | 40 | 68 | THE BIRDS AND THE BEES — Jewel Akens, Era 3141 | 5 |
| 26 | 31 | 45 | 64 | RED ROSES FOR A BLUE LADY — Bert Kaempfert & His Ork, Decca 31722 | 5 |
| 27 | 29 | 30 | 33 | NO ARMS CAN EVER HOLD YOU! — Bachelors, London 9724 | 9 |
| 28 | 35 | 47 | 75 | I'VE GOT A TIGER BY THE TAIL — Buck Owens, Capitol 5336 | 5 |
| 29 | 19 | 13 | 9 | KEEP SEARCHIN' — Del Shannon, Amy 915 | 14 |
| 30 | 32 | 42 | 60 | FOR LOVIN' ME — Peter, Paul & Mary, Warner Bros. 5496 | 5 |
| 31 | 41 | 58 | 83 | LITTLE THINGS — Bobby Goldsboro, United Artist 810 | 5 |
| 32 | 46 | 57 | 73 | WHAT HAVE THEY DONE TO THE RAIN — Searchers, Kapp 644 | 4 |
| 33 | 36 | 46 | 70 | A CHANGE IS GONNA COME — Sam Cooke, RCA Victor 8486 | 4 |
| 34 | 61 | — | — | GOODNIGHT — Roy Orbison, Monument 873 | 2 |
| 35 | 42 | 65 | 78 | IT'S ALRIGHT — Adam Faith, Amy 913 | 6 |
| 36 | 18 | 9 | 6 | HOW SWEET IT IS (To Be Loved by You) — Marvin Gaye, Tamla 54107 | 14 |
| 37 | 27 | 28 | 30 | LOOK OF LOVE — Lesley Gore, Mercury 72372 | 9 |
| 38 | 48 | 59 | 85 | CAN'T YOU HEAR MY HEARTBEAT — Herman's Hermits, MGM 13310 | 4 |
| 39 | 53 | 75 | — | ASK THE LONELY — Four Tops, Motown 1073 | 3 |
| 40 | 44 | 55 | 67 | BREAK AWAY — Newbeats, Hickory 1290 | 5 |
| 41 | 25 | 18 | 18 | GIVE HIM A GREAT BIG KISS — Shangri-Las, Red Bird 10-018 | 9 |
| 42 | 28 | 24 | 28 | HAVE YOU LOOKED INTO YOUR HEART — Jerry Vale, Columbia 43181 | 10 |
| 43 | 49 | 60 | 71 | WHOSE HEART ARE YOU BREAKING TONIGHT? — Connie Francis, MGM 13303 | 5 |
| 44 | 64 | 85 | 98 | GOLDFINGER — Shirley Bassey, United Artists 790 | 4 |
| 45 | 50 | 54 | 57 | THANKS A LOT — Brenda Lee, Decca 31728 | 6 |
| 46 | 56 | 76 | — | MIDNIGHT SPECIAL — Johnny Rivers, Imperial 66087 | 3 |
| 47 | 47 | 49 | 61 | FANCY PANTS — Al Hirt, RCA Victor 8487 | 6 |
| 48 | 58 | 77 | — | COME HOME — Dave Clark Five, Epic 9763 | 3 |
| 49 | 59 | 70 | — | NEW YORK'S A LONELY TOWN — Trade Winds, Red Bird 10-020 | 3 |
| 50 | 43 | 48 | 72 | AT THE CLUB — Drifters, Atlantic 2268 | 4 |
| 51 | 34 | 32 | 36 | SOMEWHERE IN YOUR HEART — Frank Sinatra, Reprise 0332 | 10 |
| 52 | 55 | 66 | 76 | MY HEART WOULD KNOW — Al Martino, Capitol 5341 | 6 |
| 53 | — | — | — | EIGHT DAYS A WEEK — Beatles, Capitol 5371 | 1 |
| 54 | 78 | — | — | YEH, YEH — Georgie Fame, Imperial 66086 | 2 |
| 55 | 57 | 68 | 79 | DUSTY — Rag Dolls, Mala 493 | 5 |
| 56 | 63 | 78 | — | BORN TO BE TOGETHER — Ronettes, Philles 126 | 3 |
| 57 | 69 | 95 | — | RED ROSES FOR A BLUE LADY — Vic Dana, Dolton 304 | 3 |
| 58 | 62 | 67 | 84 | DON'T COME RUNNING BACK TO ME — Nancy Wilson, Capitol 5340 | 4 |
| 59 | 52 | 52 | 55 | DO WHAT YOU DO DO WELL — Ned Miller, Fabor 137 | 9 |
| 60 | 73 | 89 | — | DON'T LET ME BE MISUNDERSTOOD — Animals, MGM 13311 | 3 |
| 61 | 51 | 53 | 59 | VOICE YOUR CHOICE — Radiants, Chess 1904 | 9 |
| 62 | 68 | 79 | 89 | GOLDFINGER — Billy Strange, Crescendo 334 | 5 |
| 63 | 54 | 56 | 62 | HELLO PRETTY GIRL — Ronnie Dove, Diamond 176 | 7 |
| 64 | 80 | — | — | SHOTGUN — Jr. Walker & the All Stars, Soul 35008 | 2 |
| 65 | 65 | 69 | 82 | COMING ON TOO STRONG — Wayne Newton, Capitol 5338 | 4 |
| 66 | 60 | 62 | 69 | WHENEVER A TEENAGER CRIES — Reparata & the Delrons, World Artists 1036 | 7 |
| 67 | 84 | — | — | PEOPLE GET READY — Impressions, ABC-Paramount 10622 | 2 |
| 68 | — | — | — | SEND ME THE PILLOW YOU DREAM ON — Dean Martin, Reprise 0344 | 1 |
| 69 | 71 | 71 | 80 | MARRIED MAN — Richard Burton, MGM 13307 | 4 |
| 70 | 76 | 87 | — | IT'S GOTTA LAST FOREVER — Billy J. Kramer, Imperial 66085 | 3 |
| 71 | 75 | 86 | — | DON'T MESS UP A GOOD THING — Fontella Bass & Bobby McClure, Checker 1097 | 3 |
| 72 | 82 | 94 | — | CRY — Ray Charles, ABC-Paramount 10615 | 3 |
| 73 | 77 | 82 | 88 | TRY TO REMEMBER — Ed Ames, RCA Victor 8483 | 5 |
| 74 | 74 | 80 | 90 | THAT'S HOW STRONG MY LOVE IS — Otis Redding, Volt 124 | 4 |
| 75 | 79 | 81 | 96 | HE WAS REALLY SAYIN' SOMETHIN' — Velvelettes, V.I.P. 25013 | 4 |
| 76 | 87 | 92 | 94 | I WANNA BE (Your Everything) — Manhattans, Carnival 507 | 6 |
| 77 | — | — | — | IF I LOVED YOU — Chad & Jeremy, World Artists 1041 | 1 |
| 78 | 97 | — | — | IF I RULED THE WORLD — Tony Bennett, Columbia 43220 | 2 |
| 79 | 81 | 84 | — | HELLO DOLLY — Bobby Darin, Capitol 5359 | 3 |
| 80 | — | — | — | STOP! IN THE NAME OF LOVE — Supremes, Motown 1074 | 1 |
| 81 | — | — | — | I DON'T WANT TO SPOIL THE PARTY — Beatles, Capitol 5371 | 1 |
| 82 | 94 | — | — | ANGEL — Johnny Tillotson, MGM 13316 | 2 |
| 83 | — | — | — | YOU BETTER GET IT — Joe Tex, Dial 4003 | 1 |
| 84 | 85 | — | — | FLY ME TO THE MOON — LaVern Baker, Atlantic 2267 | 2 |
| 85 | 86 | 90 | 93 | JERK AND TWINE — Jackie Ross, Chess 1920 | 4 |
| 86 | 90 | — | — | APACHE '65 — Arrows, Tower 116 | 2 |
| 87 | 89 | — | — | LIKE A CHILD — Julie Rogers, Mercury 72380 | 2 |
| 88 | 99 | — | — | IT'S GONNA BE ALRIGHT — Maxine Brown, Wand 173 | 2 |
| 89 | — | — | — | COME TOMORROW — Manfred Mann, Ascot 2170 | 1 |
| 90 | — | — | — | DOES HE REALLY CARE FOR ME — Ruby & the Romantics, Kapp 646 | 1 |
| 91 | 91 | — | — | SOMEWHERE — P. J. Proby, Liberty 55757 | 2 |
| 92 | 95 | — | — | ORANGE BLOSSOM SPECIAL — Johnny Cash, Columbia 43206 | 2 |
| 93 | 93 | 97 | — | I'M OVER YOU — Jan Bradley, Chess 1919 | 3 |
| 94 | — | — | — | CUPID — Johnny Rivers, Imperial 66087 | 1 |
| 95 | — | — | — | MR. PITIFUL — Otis Redding, Volt 124 | 1 |
| 96 | — | — | — | GO NOW — Moody Blues, London 9726 | 1 |
| 97 | — | 98 | 100 | GOLDFINGER — Jack LaForge, Regina 1323 | 3 |
| 98 | 100 | — | — | DID YOU EVER — Hullaballoos, Roulette 4593 | 2 |
| 99 | — | — | — | YOU CAN HAVE HIM — Timi Yuro, Mercury 72391 | 1 |
| 100 | — | — | — | WHIPPED CREAM — Herb Alpert's Tijuana Brass, A&M 760 | 1 |

## BUBBLING UNDER THE HOT 100

101. MY BABE — Righteous Brothers, Moonglow 223
102. THIS IS MY PRAYER — Ray Charles Singers, Command 4059
103. GOOD TIMES — Jerry Butler, Vee Jay 651
104. THE RICHEST MAN ALIVE — Mel Carter, Imperial 66078
105. EVERYDAY — Rogues, Columbia 43171
106. EL PUSSY CAT — Mongo Santamaria, Columbia 43171
107. LEROY — Norma Tracey, Daydell 1005
108. RED ROSES FOR A BLUE LADY — Wayne Newton, Capitol 5366
109. THE BOY NEXT DOOR — Standells, Vee Jay 643
110. YOU'RE NEXT — Everly Brothers, Warner Bros. 5600
111. BRING YOUR LOVE TO ME — Righteous Brothers, Moonglow 238
112. DIANA — Bobby Rydell, Capitol 5352
113. REAL LIVE GIRL — Steve Alaimo, ABC-Paramount 10620
114. SUDDENLY I'M ALL ALONE — Walter Jackson, Okeh 7215
115. CROSS MY HEART — Bobby Vee, Liberty 55761
116. GOLDFINGER — Johny Barry & His Ork, United Artists 791
117. YOU'RE NEXT — Jimmy Witherspoon, Prestige 341
118. DIAMOND HEAD — Ventures, Dolton 303
119. FANNIE MAE — Righteous Brothers, Moonglow 238
120. STRAIN ON MY HEART — Roscoe Shelton, Sims 217
121. CAST YOUR FATE TO THE WIND — Sounds Orchestral, Parkway 942
122. DANNY BOY — Jackie Wilson, Brunswick 55277
123. THIS SPORTING LIFE — Ian Whitcomb, Tower 134
124. COME ON HOME — Bill Black's Combo, Hi 2085
125. NOT TOO LONG AGO — Uniques, Paula 219
126. I LOVE YOU BABY — Dottie & Ray, LeSage 701
127. THE RACE IS ON — George Jones, Kapp 651
128. CAMEL WALK — Ikettes, Modern 1003
129. THE RACE IS ON — Jack Jones, Kapp 651
130. PASS ME BY — Peggy Lee, Capitol 5346
131. I MUST BE SEEING THINGS — Gene Pitney, Musicor 1070
132. STRANGER IN TOWN — Del Shannon, Amy 919
133. I'VE BEEN TRYING — Impressions, ABC-Paramount 10622
134. GIRLS DON'T COME — Sandie Shaw, Reprise 0342
135. IF I RULED THE WORLD — Sammy Davis Jr., Reprise 0345

Compiled from national retail sales and radio station airplay by the Music Popularity Dept. of Record Market Research, Billboard.

# Billboard HOT 100

**For Week Ending February 27, 1965**

★ STAR performer—Sides registering greatest proportionate upward progress this week.

| This Week | Last Week | 2 Wks. Ago | 3 Wks. Ago | TITLE — Artist, Label & Number | Weeks On Chart |
|---|---|---|---|---|---|
| 1 | 1 | 3 | 4 | THIS DIAMOND RING — Gary Lewis & the Playboys, Liberty 55756 | 7 |
| 2 | 2 | 1 | 1 | YOU'VE LOST THAT LOVIN' FEELIN' — Righteous Brothers, Philles 124 | 12 |
| 3 | 4 | 5 | 8 | MY GIRL — Temptations, Gordy 7038 | 7 |
| 4 | 3 | 2 | 2 | DOWNTOWN — Petula Clark, Warner Bros. 5494 | 11 |
| 5 | 6 | 9 | 14 | THE JOLLY GREEN GIANT — Kingsmen, Wand 172 | 8 |
| 6 | 11 | 16 | 19 | TELL HER NO — Zombies, Parrot 9723 | 8 |
| 7 | 8 | 8 | 10 | SHAKE — Sam Cooke, RCA Victor 8486 | 8 |
| 8 | 10 | 15 | 29 | THE BOY FROM NEW YORK CITY — Ad Libs, Blue Cat 102 | 7 |
| 9 | 9 | 10 | 16 | I GO TO PIECES — Peter & Gordon, Capitol 5335 | 8 |
| 10 | 17 | 22 | 39 | KING OF THE ROAD — Roger Miller, Smash 1965 | 5 |
| 11 | 5 | 4 | 3 | THE NAME GAME — Shirley Ellis, Congress 230 | 12 |
| 12 | 21 | 39 | 61 | FERRY CROSS THE MERSEY — Gerry & the Pacemakers, Laurie 3284 | 4 |
| 13 | 25 | 30 | 40 | THE BIRDS AND THE BEES — Jewel Akens, Era 3141 | 6 |
| 14 | 14 | 17 | 20 | TWINE TIME — Alvin Cash & the Crawlers, Mar-V-Lus 6002 | 9 |
| 15 | 15 | 20 | 25 | LAUGH, LAUGH — Beau Brummels, Autumn 8 | 9 |
| 16 | 7 | 7 | 7 | ALL DAY AND ALL OF THE NIGHT — Kinks, Reprise 0334 | 10 |
| 17 | 22 | 38 | 63 | HURT SO BAD — Little Anthony & the Imperials, DCP 1128 | 4 |
| 18 | 26 | 31 | 45 | RED ROSES FOR A BLUE LADY — Bert Kaempfert & His Ork, Decca 31722 | 6 |
| 19 | 53 | — | — | EIGHT DAYS A WEEK — Beatles, Capitol 5371 | 2 |
| 20 | 20 | 24 | 36 | LEMON TREE — Trini Lopez, Reprise 0336 | 6 |
| 21 | 12 | 12 | 15 | BYE, BYE BABY — 4 Seasons, Philips 40260 | 7 |
| 22 | 13 | 14 | 17 | THE "IN" CROWD — Dobie Gray, Charger 105 | 8 |
| 23 | 44 | 64 | 85 | GOLDFINGER — Shirley Bassey, United Artists 790 | 5 |
| 24 | 19 | 21 | 23 | HEART OF STONE — Rolling Stones, London 9725 | 8 |
| 25 | 28 | 35 | 47 | I'VE GOT A TIGER BY THE TAIL — Buck Owens, Capitol 5336 | 6 |
| 26 | 31 | 41 | 58 | LITTLE THINGS — Bobby Goldsboro, United Artist 810 | 6 |
| 27 | 38 | 48 | 59 | CAN'T YOU HEAR MY HEARTBEAT — Herman's Hermits, MGM 13310 | 5 |
| 28 | 34 | 61 | — | GOODNIGHT — Roy Orbison, Monument 873 | 3 |
| 29 | 32 | 45 | 57 | WHAT HAVE THEY DONE TO THE RAIN — Searchers, Kapp 644 | 5 |
| 30 | 30 | 32 | 42 | FOR LOVIN' ME — Peter, Paul & Mary, Warner Bros. 5496 | 6 |
| 31 | 35 | 42 | 65 | IT'S ALRIGHT — Adam Faith, Amy 913 | 7 |
| 32 | 39 | 53 | 75 | ASK THE LONELY — Four Tops, Motown 1073 | 4 |
| 33 | 33 | 36 | 46 | A CHANGE IS GONNA COME — Sam Cooke, RCA Victor 8486 | 5 |
| 34 | 23 | 26 | 37 | PAPER TIGER — Sue Thompson, Hickory 1284 | 9 |
| 35 | 16 | 11 | 11 | LET'S LOCK THE DOOR (And Throw Away the Key) — Jay & the Americans, United Artists 805 | 10 |
| 36 | 24 | 13 | 6 | LOVE POTION NUMBER NINE — Searchers, Kapp Winner's Circle 27 | 14 |
| 37 | 48 | 58 | 77 | COME HOME — Dave Clark Five, Epic 9763 | 4 |
| 38 | 49 | 59 | 70 | NEW YORK'S A LONELY TOWN — Trade Winds, Red Bird 10-020 | 4 |
| 39 | 46 | 56 | 76 | MIDNIGHT SPECIAL — Johnny Rivers, Imperial 66087 | 4 |
| 40 | 54 | 78 | — | YEH, YEH — Georgie Fame, Imperial 66086 | 3 |
| 41 | 80 | — | — | STOP! IN THE NAME OF LOVE — Supremes, Motown 1074 | 2 |
| 42 | 27 | 29 | 30 | NO ARMS CAN EVER HOLD YOU! — Bachelors, London 9724 | 10 |
| 43 | 43 | 49 | 60 | WHOSE HEART ARE YOU BREAKING TONIGHT? — Connie Francis, MGM 13303 | 6 |
| 44 | 18 | 6 | 5 | HOLD WHAT YOU'VE GOT — Joe Tex, Dial 4001 | 11 |
| 45 | 64 | 80 | — | SHOTGUN — Jr. Walker & the All Stars, Soul 35008 | 3 |
| 46 | 57 | 69 | 95 | RED ROSES FOR A BLUE LADY — Vic Dana, Dolton 304 | 4 |
| 47 | 67 | 84 | — | PEOPLE GET READY — Impressions, ABC-Paramount 10622 | 3 |
| 48 | 50 | 43 | 48 | AT THE CLUB — Drifters, Atlantic 2268 | 5 |
| 49 | 60 | 73 | 89 | DON'T LET ME BE MISUNDERSTOOD — Animals, MGM 13311 | 4 |
| 50 | 40 | 44 | 55 | BREAK AWAY — Newbeats, Hickory 1290 | 6 |
| 51 | 45 | 50 | 54 | THANKS A LOT — Brenda Lee, Decca 31728 | 7 |
| 52 | 47 | 47 | 49 | FANCY PANTS — Al Hirt, RCA Victor 8487 | 7 |
| 53 | 77 | — | — | IF I LOVED YOU — Chad & Jeremy, World Artists 1041 | 2 |
| 54 | 68 | — | — | SEND ME THE PILLOW YOU DREAM ON — Dean Martin, Reprise 0344 | 2 |
| 55 | 56 | 63 | 78 | BORN TO BE TOGETHER — Ronettes, Philles 126 | 4 |
| 56 | 52 | 55 | 66 | MY HEART WOULD KNOW — Al Martino, Capitol 5341 | 7 |
| 57 | 55 | 57 | 68 | DUSTY — Rag Dolls, Mala 493 | 6 |
| 58 | 71 | 75 | 86 | DON'T MESS UP A GOOD THING — Fontella Bass & Bobby McClure, Checker 1097 | 4 |
| 59 | 81 | — | — | I DON'T WANT TO SPOIL THE PARTY — Beatles, Capitol 5371 | 2 |
| 60 | 58 | 62 | 67 | DON'T COME RUNNING BACK TO ME — Nancy Wilson, Capitol 5340 | 5 |
| 61 | 62 | 68 | 79 | GOLDFINGER — Billy Strange, Crescendo 334 | 6 |
| 62 | 66 | 60 | 62 | WHENEVER A TEENAGER CRIES — Reparata & the Delrons, World Artists 1036 | 8 |
| 63 | 78 | 97 | — | IF I RULED THE WORLD — Tony Bennett, Columbia 43220 | 3 |
| 64 | 69 | 71 | 71 | MARRIED MAN — Richard Burton, MGM 13307 | 5 |
| 65 | 72 | 82 | 94 | CRY — Ray Charles, ABC-Paramount 10615 | 4 |
| 66 | 82 | 94 | — | ANGEL — Johnny Tillotson, MGM 13316 | 3 |
| 67 | 65 | 65 | 69 | COMING ON TOO STRONG — Wayne Newton, Capitol 5338 | 5 |
| 68 | — | — | — | DO THE CLAM — Elvis Presley, RCA Victor 8500 | 1 |
| 69 | 75 | 79 | 81 | HE WAS REALLY SAYIN' SOMETHIN' — Velvelettes, V.I.P. 25013 | 5 |
| 70 | 70 | 76 | 87 | IT'S GOTTA LAST FOREVER — Billy J. Kramer, Imperial 66085 | 4 |
| 71 | 89 | — | — | COME TOMORROW — Manfred Mann, Ascot 2170 | 2 |
| 72 | 76 | 87 | 92 | I WANNA BE (Your Everything) — Manhattans, Carnival 507 | 7 |
| 73 | — | — | — | NOWHERE TO RUN — Martha & the Vandellas, Gordy 7039 | 1 |
| 74 | — | — | — | STRANGER IN TOWN — Del Shannon, Amy 919 | 1 |
| 75 | 83 | — | — | YOU BETTER GET IT — Joe Tex, Dial 4003 | 2 |
| 76 | — | — | — | RED ROSES FOR A BLUE LADY — Wayne Newton, Capitol 5366 | 1 |
| 77 | 87 | 89 | — | LIKE A CHILD — Julie Rogers, Mercury 72380 | 3 |
| 78 | — | — | — | I MUST BE SEEING THINGS — Gene Pitney, Musicor 1070 | 1 |
| 79 | 73 | 77 | 82 | TRY TO REMEMBER — Ed Ames, RCA Victor 8483 | 6 |
| 80 | 95 | — | — | MR. PITIFUL — Otis Redding, Volt 124 | 2 |
| 81 | — | — | — | FOUR BY THE BEATLES — Beatles, Capitol 5365 (Extended Play) | 1 |
| 82 | — | — | — | YOU GOT WHAT IT TAKES — Joe Tex, Dial 4003 | 1 |
| 83 | 86 | 90 | — | APACHE '65 — Arrows, Tower 116 | 3 |
| 84 | — | — | — | DO YOU WANNA DANCE? — Beach Boys, Capitol 5372 | 1 |
| 85 | 88 | 99 | — | IT'S GONNA BE ALRIGHT — Maxine Brown, Wand 173 | 3 |
| 86 | 96 | — | — | GO NOW — Moody Blues, London 9726 | 2 |
| 87 | 90 | — | — | DOES HE REALLY CARE FOR ME — Ruby & the Romantics, Kapp 646 | 2 |
| 88 | — | — | — | WHO CAN I TURN TO — Dionne Warwick, Scepter 1298 | 1 |
| 89 | — | — | — | THE RACE IS ON — Jack Jones, Kapp 651 | 1 |
| 90 | 92 | 95 | — | ORANGE BLOSSOM SPECIAL — Johnny Cash, Columbia 43206 | 3 |
| 91 | 94 | — | — | CUPID — Johnny Rivers, Imperial 66087 | 2 |
| 92 | 98 | 100 | — | DID YOU EVER — Hullaballoos, Roulette 4593 | 3 |
| 93 | — | — | — | COME AND STAY WITH ME — Marianne Faithfull, London 9731 | 1 |
| 94 | — | — | — | THIS IS MY PRAYER — Ray Charles Singers, Command 4059 | 1 |
| 95 | — | — | — | DANNY BOY — Jackie Wilson, Brunswick 55277 | 1 |
| 96 | 99 | — | — | YOU CAN HAVE HIM — Timi Yuro, Mercury 72391 | 2 |
| 97 | 97 | — | 98 | GOLDFINGER — Jack LaForge, Regina 1323 | 4 |
| 98 | 100 | — | — | WHIPPED CREAM — Herb Alpert's Tijuana Brass, A&M 760 | 2 |
| 99 | — | — | — | PASS ME BY — Peggy Lee, Capitol 5346 | 1 |
| 100 | — | — | — | LAND OF 1000 DANCES — Cannibal & the Headhunters, Rampart 642 | 1 |

## BUBBLING UNDER THE HOT 100

101. THIS SPORTING LIFE ........ Ian Whitcomb, Tower 120
102. GOOD TIMES ........ Jerry Butler, Vee Jay 651
103. THE GREATEST STORY EVER TOLD ........ Ferrante & Teicher, United Artists 816
104. HELLO DOLLY ........ Bobby Darin, Capitol 5359
105. I'M OVER YOU ........ Jan Bradley, Chess 1919
106. REAL LIVE GIRL ........ Steve Alaimo, ABC-Paramount 10620
107. TO LITTLE GIRL ........ LaVerne Baker, Atlantic 2267
108. FLY ME TO THE MOON ........ Joe Harnell, Starday 704
109. MY BABE ........ Righteous Brothers, Moonglow 223
110. TEASIN' YOU ........ Willie Tee, Atlantic 2273
111. DIAMOND HEAD ........ Ventures, Dolton 303
112. DIANA ........ Bobby Rydell, Capitol 5352
113. SUDDENLY I'M ALL ALONE ........ Walter Jackson, Okeh 7215
114. TELL HER I'M NOT HOME ........ Ike & Tina Turner, Loma 2011
115. THAT'S HOW STRONG MY LOVE IS ........ Otis Redding, Volt 124
116. YOU'RE NEXT ........ Jimmy Witherspoon, Prestige 341
117. LET HER LOVE ME ........ Otis Leavill, Blue Rock 4002
118. FANNIE MAE ........ Righteous Brothers, Moonglow 238
119. THIS IS IT ........ Jim Reeves, RCA Victor 8508
120. BEGIN TO LOVE ........ Robert Goulet, Columbia 43224
121. DON'T ANSWER THE DOOR ........ Sandie Shaw, Reprise 0342
121. FOR MAMA ........ Jerry Vale, Columbia 43232
122. FIND MY WAY BACK HOME ........ Nashville Teens, London 9736
123. HERE WE GO AGAIN ........ Bobby Byrd, Smash 1964
124. COME ON HOME ........ Bill Black's Combo, Hi 2085
125. COME SEE ........ Major Lance, Okeh 7216
126. TO LITTLE BOTTLES ........ Johnny Bond, Starday 714
127. FOR MAMA ........ Connie Francis, MGM 13325
128. DON'T ANSWER THE DOOR ........ Jimmy Johnson, Magnum 719
129. BABY, HOLD ME CLOSE ........ Jerry Lee Lewis, Smash 1969
130. I'VE GOT FIVE DOLLARS AND IT'S SATURDAY NIGHT ........ George Jones & Gene Pitney, Musicor 1066
131. SOMEWHERE ........ Brothers Four, Columbia 43211
132. CAN'T YOU JUST SEE ME ........ Aretha Franklin, Columbia 43203
133. FROM ALL OVER THE WORLD ........ Jan & Dean, Liberty 55766
134. LOSING YOU ........ Dusty Springfield, Philips 40270
135. FOR MAMA ........ Matt Monro, Liberty 55763

# Billboard HOT 100

**For Week Ending March 6, 1965**

★ STAR performer—Sides registering greatest proportionate upward progress this week.

Record Industry Association of America seal of certification as million selling single.

| This Week | Wk. Ago | 2 Wks. Ago | 3 Wks. Ago | TITLE, Artist, Label & Number | Weeks On Chart |
|---|---|---|---|---|---|
| 1 | 3 | 4 | 5 | MY GIRL — Temptations, Gordy 7038 | 8 |
| 2 | 1 | 1 | 3 | THIS DIAMOND RING — Gary Lewis & the Playboys, Liberty 55756 | 8 |
| 3 | 2 | 2 | 1 | YOU'VE LOST THAT LOVIN' FEELIN' — Righteous Brothers, Philles 124 | 13 |
| 4 | 5 | 6 | 9 | THE JOLLY GREEN GIANT — Kingsmen, Wand 172 | 9 |
| ★5 | 19 | 53 | — | EIGHT DAYS A WEEK — Beatles, Capitol 5371 | 3 |
| 6 | 6 | 11 | 16 | TELL HER NO — Zombies, Parrot 9723 | 9 |
| ★7 | 10 | 17 | 22 | KING OF THE ROAD — Roger Miller, Smash 1965 | 6 |
| ★8 | 13 | 25 | 30 | THE BIRDS AND THE BEES — Jewel Akens, Era 3141 | 7 |
| 9 | 12 | 21 | 39 | FERRY CROSS THE MERSEY — Gerry & the Pacemakers, Laurie 3284 | 5 |
| 10 | 4 | 3 | 2 | DOWNTOWN — Petula Clark, Warner Bros. 5494 | 12 |
| 11 | 8 | 10 | 15 | THE BOY FROM NEW YORK CITY — Ad Libs, Blue Cat 102 | 8 |
| ★12 | 17 | 22 | 38 | HURT SO BAD — Little Anthony & the Imperials, DCP 1128 | 5 |
| ★13 | 41 | 80 | — | STOP! IN THE NAME OF LOVE — Supremes, Motown 1074 | 3 |
| 14 | 9 | 9 | 10 | I GO TO PIECES — Peter & Gordon, Capitol 5335 | 9 |
| 15 | 18 | 26 | 31 | RED ROSES FOR A BLUE LADY — Bert Kaempfert & His Ork, Decca 31722 | 7 |
| ★16 | 23 | 44 | 64 | GOLDFINGER — Shirley Bassey, United Artists 790 | 6 |
| 17 | 15 | 15 | 20 | LAUGH, LAUGH — Beau Brummels, Autumn 8 | 10 |
| 18 | 11 | 5 | 4 | THE NAME GAME — Shirley Ellis, Congress 230 | 13 |
| ★19 | 27 | 38 | 48 | CAN'T YOU HEAR MY HEARTBEAT — Herman's Hermits, MGM 13310 | 6 |
| 20 | 14 | 14 | 17 | TWINE TIME — Alvin Cash & the Crawlers, Mar-V-Lus 6002 | 10 |
| 21 | 7 | 8 | 8 | SHAKE — Sam Cooke, RCA Victor 8486 | 8 |
| ★22 | 28 | 34 | 61 | GOODNIGHT — Roy Orbison, Monument 873 | 4 |
| 23 | 26 | 31 | 41 | LITTLE THINGS — Bobby Goldsboro, United Artist 810 | 7 |
| ★24 | 39 | 46 | 56 | MIDNIGHT SPECIAL — Johnny Rivers, Imperial 66087 | 5 |
| 25 | 25 | 28 | 35 | I'VE GOT A TIGER BY THE TAIL — Buck Owens, Capitol 5336 | 7 |
| ★26 | 37 | 48 | 58 | COME HOME — Dave Clark Five, Epic 9763 | 4 |
| 27 | 32 | 39 | 53 | ASK THE LONELY — Four Tops, Motown 1073 | 5 |
| 28 | 16 | 7 | 7 | ALL DAY AND ALL OF THE NIGHT — Kinks, Reprise 0334 | 11 |
| 29 | 45 | 64 | 80 | SHOTGUN — Jr. Walker & the All Stars, Soul 35008 | 4 |
| 30 | 40 | 54 | 78 | YEH, YEH — Georgie Fame, Imperial 66086 | 4 |
| 31 | 33 | 33 | 36 | A CHANGE IS GONNA COME — Sam Cooke, RCA Victor 8486 | 6 |
| 32 | 38 | 49 | 59 | NEW YORK'S A LONELY TOWN — Trade Winds, Red Bird 10-020 | 5 |
| 33 | 22 | 13 | 14 | THE "IN" CROWD — Dobie Gray, Charger 105 | 9 |
| 34 | 20 | 20 | 24 | LEMON TREE — Trini Lopez, Reprise 0336 | 7 |
| ★35 | 47 | 67 | 84 | PEOPLE GET READY — Impressions, ABC-Paramount 10622 | 4 |
| 36 | 46 | 57 | 69 | RED ROSES FOR A BLUE LADY — Vic Dana, Dolton 304 | 5 |
| 37 | 29 | 32 | 45 | WHAT HAVE THEY DONE TO THE RAIN — Searchers, Kapp 644 | 6 |
| 38 | 21 | 12 | 12 | BYE, BYE BABY — 4 Seasons, Philips 40260 | 8 |
| ★39 | 49 | 60 | 73 | DON'T LET ME BE MISUNDERSTOOD — Animals, MGM 13311 | 5 |
| 40 | 30 | 30 | 32 | FOR LOVIN' ME — Peter, Paul & Mary, Warner Bros. 5496 | 7 |
| 41 | 34 | 23 | 26 | PAPER TIGER — Sue Thompson, Hickory 1284 | 10 |
| ★42 | 53 | 77 | — | IF I LOVED YOU — Chad & Jeremy, World Artists 1041 | 3 |
| 43 | 24 | 19 | 21 | HEART OF STONE — Rolling Stones, London 9725 | 9 |
| ★44 | 54 | 68 | — | SEND ME THE PILLOW YOU DREAM ON — Dean Martin, Reprise 0344 | 3 |
| 45 | 31 | 35 | 42 | IT'S ALRIGHT — Adam Faith, Amy 913 | 8 |
| ★46 | 73 | — | — | NOWHERE TO RUN — Martha & the Vandellas, Gordy 7039 | 2 |
| ★47 | 59 | 81 | — | I DON'T WANT TO SPOIL THE PARTY — Beatles, Capitol 5371 | 3 |
| ★48 | 74 | — | — | STRANGER IN TOWN — Del Shannon, Amy 919 | 2 |
| ★49 | 68 | — | — | DO THE CLAM — Elvis Presley, RCA Victor 8500 | 2 |
| 50 | 50 | 40 | 44 | BREAK AWAY — Newbeats, Hickory 1290 | 7 |
| 51 | 58 | 71 | 75 | DON'T MESS UP A GOOD THING — Fontella Bass & Bobby McClure, Checker 1097 | 5 |
| 52 | 55 | 56 | 63 | BORN TO BE TOGETHER — Ronettes, Philles 126 | 5 |
| 53 | 48 | 50 | 43 | AT THE CLUB — Drifters, Atlantic 2268 | 6 |
| ★54 | 78 | — | — | I MUST BE SEEING THINGS — Gene Pitney, Musicor 1070 | 2 |
| 55 | 43 | 43 | 49 | WHOSE HEART ARE YOU BREAKING TONIGHT? — Connie Francis, MGM 13303 | 7 |
| 56 | 63 | 78 | 97 | IF I RULED THE WORLD — Tony Bennett, Columbia 43220 | 4 |
| ★57 | 84 | — | — | DO YOU WANNA DANCE? — Beach Boys, Capitol 5372 | 2 |
| ★58 | 89 | — | — | THE RACE IS ON — Jack Jones, Kapp 651 | 2 |
| 59 | 75 | 83 | — | YOU BETTER GET IT — Joe Tex, Dial 4003 | 3 |
| 60 | 66 | 82 | 94 | ANGEL — Johnny Tillotson, MGM 13316 | 4 |
| 61 | 61 | 62 | 68 | GOLDFINGER — Billy Strange, Crescendo 334 | 7 |
| 62 | 62 | 66 | 60 | WHENEVER A TEENAGER CRIES — Reparata & the Delrons, World Artists 1036 | 9 |
| 63 | 65 | 72 | 82 | CRY — Ray Charles, ABC-Paramount 10615 | 5 |
| 64 | 69 | 75 | 79 | HE WAS REALLY SAYIN' SOMETHIN' — Velvelettes, V.I.P. 25013 | 4 |
| 65 | 71 | 89 | — | COME TOMORROW — Manfred Mann, Ascot 2170 | 3 |
| 66 | 76 | — | — | RED ROSES FOR A BLUE LADY — Wayne Newton, Capitol 5366 | 2 |
| 67 | 70 | 70 | 76 | IT'S GOTTA LAST FOREVER — Billy J. Kramer, Imperial 66085 | 5 |
| 68 | 72 | 76 | 87 | I WANNA BE (Your Everything) — Manhattans, Carnival 507 | 8 |
| 69 | 77 | 87 | 89 | LIKE A CHILD — Julie Rogers, Mercury 72380 | 4 |
| 70 | 80 | 95 | — | MR. PITIFUL — Otis Redding, Volt 124 | 3 |
| ★71 | 86 | 96 | — | GO NOW — Moody Blues, London 9726 | 3 |
| 72 | 82 | — | — | YOU GOT WHAT IT TAKES — Joe Tex, Dial 4003 | 2 |
| 73 | 83 | 86 | 90 | APACHE '65 — Arrows, Tower 116 | 4 |
| ★74 | — | — | — | WHEN I'M GONE — Brenda Holloway, Tamla 54111 | 1 |
| 75 | 85 | 88 | 99 | IT'S GONNA BE ALRIGHT — Maxine Brown, Wand 173 | 4 |
| ★76 | — | — | — | GOOD TIMES — Jerry Butler, Vee Jay 651 | 1 |
| 77 | 81 | — | — | FOUR BY THE BEATLES — Beatles, Capitol 5365 (Extended Play) | 2 |
| ★78 | 93 | — | — | COME AND STAY WITH ME — Marianne Faithfull, London 9731 | 2 |
| 79 | 88 | — | — | WHO CAN I TURN TO — Dionne Warwick, Scepter 1298 | 2 |
| ★80 | — | — | — | LONG LONELY NIGHTS — Bobby Vinton, Epic 9768 | 1 |
| 81 | 92 | 98 | 100 | DID YOU EVER — Hullabaloos, Roulette 4593 | 4 |
| 82 | 94 | — | — | THIS IS MY PRAYER — Ray Charles Singers, Command 4059 | 2 |
| 83 | — | — | — | PLEASE LET ME WONDER — Beach Boys, Capitol 5372 | 1 |
| 84 | — | — | — | REAL LIVE GIRL — Steve Alaimo, ABC-Paramount 10620 | 1 |
| 85 | 91 | 94 | — | CUPID — Johnny Rivers, Imperial 66087 | 2 |
| 86 | — | — | — | FOR MAMA — Connie Francis, MGM 13325 | 1 |
| 87 | 87 | 90 | — | DOES HE REALLY CARE FOR ME — Ruby & the Romantics, Kapp 646 | 3 |
| 88 | — | — | — | FOR MAMA — Jerry Vale, Columbia 43232 | 1 |
| 89 | 90 | 92 | 95 | ORANGE BLOSSOM SPECIAL — Johnny Cash, Columbia 43206 | 4 |
| ★90 | — | — | — | GIRL DON'T COME — Sandy Shaw, Reprise 0342 | 1 |
| 91 | — | — | — | GOT TO GET YOU OFF MY MIND — Solomon Burke, Atlantic 2276 | 1 |
| 92 | — | — | — | YOU CAN'T HURT ME NO MORE — Gene Chandler, Constellation 146 | 1 |
| 93 | — | — | — | COME SEE — Major Lance, Okeh 7216 | 1 |
| 94 | 95 | — | — | DANNY BOY — Jackie Wilson, Brunswick 55277 | 2 |
| 95 | 99 | — | — | PASS ME BY — Peggy Lee, Capitol 5346 | 2 |
| 96 | 97 | 97 | — | GOLDFINGER — Jack LaForge, Regina 1323 | 5 |
| 97 | 100 | — | — | LAND OF 1000 DANCES — Cannibal and the Headhunters, Rampart 642 | 2 |
| 98 | — | — | — | YOU'RE NEXT — Jimmy Witherspoon, Prestige 341 | 1 |
| 99 | — | — | — | EL PUSSY CAT — Mongo Santamaria, Columbia 43171 | 1 |
| 100 | — | — | — | GEE BABY (I'm Sorry) — 3 Degrees, Swan 4197 | 1 |

## BUBBLING UNDER THE HOT 100

101. THIS SPORTING LIFE — Ian Whitcomb, Tower 120
102. YOU CAN HAVE HIM — Timi Yuro, Mercury 72391
103. THE GREATEST STORY EVER TOLD — Ferrante & Teicher, United Artists 816
104. WHIPPED CREAM — Herb Alpert's Tijuana Brass, A&M 760
105. TEASIN' YOU — Willie Tee, Atlantic 2273
106. GOLDFINGER — Jimmy Smith, Verve 10346
107. FLY ME TO THE MOON — LaVern Baker, Atlantic 2267
108. I'M OVER YOU — Jan Bradley, Chess 1919
109. TELL HER I'M NOT HOME — Ike & Tina Turner, Loma 2011
110. SUDDENLY I'M ALL ALONE — Walter Jackson, Okeh 1215
111. 10 LITTLE BOTTLES — Johnny Bond, Starday 704
112. HELLO DOLLY — Bobby Darin, Capitol 5359
113. THIS IS IT — Jim Reeves, RCA Victor 8508
114. TIRED OF WAITING FOR YOU — Kinks, Reprise 0347
115. FIND MY WAY BACK HOME — Nashville Teens, London 9736
116. YOU DON'T MISS A GOOD THING — Irma Thomas, Imperial 66095
117. BEGIN TO LOVE — Robert Goulet, Columbia 43224
118. I CAN'T STOP THINKING OF YOU — Bobbi Martin, Coral 62447
119. LOSING YOU — Dusty Springfield, Philips 40270
120. WE ARE IN LOVE — Bobby Byrd, Smash 1964
121. YOU'LL BE GONE — Elvis Presley, RCA Victor 8500
122. IT HURTS ME — Bobby Sherman, Decca 31741
123. ANYTIME AT ALL — Frank Sinatra, Reprise 0350
124. I'VE GOT FIVE DOLLARS AND IT'S SATURDAY NIGHT — George & Gene, Musicor
125. NEVER, NEVER LEAVE ME — Mary Wells, 20th Century-Fox 570
126. FROM ALL OVER THE WORLD — Jan & Dean, Liberty 55766
127. WHY DON'T YOU LET YOURSELF GO — Mary Wells, 20th Century-Fox 570
128. JERK AND TWINE — Jackie Ross, Chess 1920
129. BABY, HOLD ME CLOSE — Jerry Lee Lewis, Smash 1969
130. COME BACK, BABY — Roddie Joy, Red Bird 10-021
131. BE MY BABY — Dick & Dee Dee, Warner Bros. 5608
132. POOR MAN'S SON — Reflections, Golden World 20
133. LAND OF A THOUSAND DANCES — Midnighters, Chattahoochee 666
134. I CAN'T EXPLAIN — The Who, Decca 31725
135. BABY, THE RAIN MUST FALL — Glen Yarbrough, RCA Victor 8498

Compiled from national retail sales and radio station airplay by the Music Popularity Dept. of Record Market Research, Billboard.

# Billboard HOT 100

**For Week Ending March 13, 1965**

★ STAR performer—Sides registering greatest proportionate upward progress this week.

Ⓢ Record Industry Association of America seal of certification as million selling single.

| This Week | Wk. Ago | 2 Wks. Ago | 3 Wks. Ago | TITLE — Artist, Label & Number | Weeks On Chart |
|---|---|---|---|---|---|
| 1 | 5 | 19 | 53 | EIGHT DAYS A WEEK — Beatles, Capitol 5371 | 4 |
| 2 | 1 | 3 | 4 | MY GIRL — Temptations, Gordy 7038 | 9 |
| 3 | 13 | 41 | 80 | STOP! IN THE NAME OF LOVE — Supremes, Motown 1074 | 4 |
| 4 | 2 | 1 | 1 | THIS DIAMOND RING — Gary Lewis & the Playboys, Liberty 55756 | 9 |
| 5 | 8 | 13 | 25 | THE BIRDS AND THE BEES — Jewel Akens, Era 3141 | 8 |
| 6 | 7 | 10 | 17 | KING OF THE ROAD — Roger Miller, Smash 1965 | 7 |
| 7 | 9 | 12 | 21 | FERRY CROSS THE MERSEY — Gerry & the Pacemakers, Laurie 3284 | 6 |
| 8 | 19 | 27 | 38 | CAN'T YOU HEAR MY HEARTBEAT — Herman's Hermits, MGM 13310 | 7 |
| 9 | 4 | 5 | 6 | THE JOLLY GREEN GIANT — Kingsmen, Wand 172 | 10 |
| 10 | 12 | 17 | 22 | HURT SO BAD — Little Anthony & the Imperials, DCP 1128 | 6 |
| 11 | 16 | 23 | 44 | GOLDFINGER — Shirley Bassey, United Artists 790 | 7 |
| 12 | 3 | 2 | 2 | YOU'VE LOST THAT LOVIN' FEELIN' — Righteous Brothers, Philles 124 | 14 |
| 13 | 15 | 18 | 26 | RED ROSES FOR A BLUE LADY — Bert Kaempfert & His Ork, Decca 31722 | 8 |
| 14 | 29 | 45 | 64 | SHOTGUN — Jr. Walker & the All Stars, Soul 35008 | 5 |
| 15 | 10 | 4 | 3 | DOWNTOWN — Petula Clark, Warner Bros. 5494 | 13 |
| 16 | 11 | 8 | 10 | THE BOY FROM NEW YORK CITY — Ad Libs, Blue Cat 102 | 9 |
| 17 | 6 | 6 | 11 | TELL HER NO — Zombies, Parrot 9723 | 10 |
| 18 | 23 | 26 | 31 | LITTLE THINGS — Bobby Goldsboro, United Artist 810 | 8 |
| 19 | 26 | 37 | 48 | COME HOME — Dave Clark Five, Epic 9763 | 6 |
| 20 | 24 | 39 | 46 | MIDNIGHT SPECIAL — Johnny Rivers, Imperial 66087 | 6 |
| 21 | 35 | 47 | 67 | PEOPLE GET READY — Impressions, ABC-Paramount 10622 | 5 |
| 22 | 22 | 28 | 34 | GOODNIGHT — Roy Orbison, Monument 873 | 5 |
| 23 | 36 | 46 | 57 | RED ROSES FOR A BLUE LADY — Vic Dana, Dolton 304 | 5 |
| 24 | 27 | 32 | 39 | ASK THE LONELY — Four Tops, Motown 1073 | 6 |
| 25 | 14 | 9 | 9 | I GO TO PIECES — Peter & Gordon, Capitol 5335 | 10 |
| 26 | 39 | 49 | 60 | DON'T LET ME BE MISUNDERSTOOD — Animals, MGM 13311 | 6 |
| 27 | 30 | 40 | 54 | YEH, YEH — Georgie Fame, Imperial 66086 | 5 |
| 28 | 17 | 15 | 15 | LAUGH, LAUGH — Beau Brummels, Autumn 8 | 11 |
| 29 | 57 | 84 | — | DO YOU WANNA DANCE? — Beach Boys, Capitol 5372 | 3 |
| 30 | 44 | 54 | 68 | SEND ME THE PILLOW YOU DREAM ON — Dean Martin, Reprise 0344 | 4 |
| 31 | 42 | 53 | 77 | IF I LOVED YOU — Chad & Jeremy, World Artists 1041 | 4 |
| 32 | 32 | 38 | 49 | NEW YORK'S A LONELY TOWN — Trade Winds, Red Bird 10-020 | 6 |
| 33 | 20 | 14 | 14 | TWINE TIME — Alvin Cash & the Crawlers, Mar-V-Lus 6002 | 11 |
| 34 | 18 | 11 | 5 | THE NAME GAME — Shirley Ellis, Congress 230 | 14 |
| 35 | 46 | 73 | — | NOWHERE TO RUN — Martha & the Vandellas, Gordy 7039 | 3 |
| 36 | 25 | 25 | 28 | I'VE GOT A TIGER BY THE TAIL — Buck Owens, Capitol 5336 | 8 |
| 37 | 48 | 74 | — | STRANGER IN TOWN — Del Shannon, Amy 919 | 3 |
| 38 | 21 | 7 | 8 | SHAKE — Sam Cooke, RCA Victor 8486 | 10 |
| 39 | 49 | 68 | — | DO THE CLAM — Elvis Presley, RCA Victor 8500 | 3 |
| 40 | 28 | 16 | 7 | ALL DAY AND ALL OF THE NIGHT — Kinks, Reprise 0334 | 12 |
| 41 | 31 | 33 | 33 | A CHANGE IS GONNA COME — Sam Cooke, RCA Victor 8486 | 7 |
| 42 | 37 | 29 | 32 | WHAT HAVE THEY DONE TO THE RAIN — Searchers, Kapp 644 | 7 |
| 43 | 54 | 78 | — | I MUST BE SEEING THINGS — Gene Pitney, Musicor 1070 | 3 |
| 44 | 47 | 59 | 81 | I DON'T WANT TO SPOIL THE PARTY — Beatles, Capitol 5371 | 4 |
| 45 | 51 | 58 | 71 | DON'T MESS UP A GOOD THING — Fontella Bass & Bobby McClure, Checker 1097 | 6 |
| 46 | 38 | 21 | 12 | BYE, BYE BABY — 4 Seasons, Philips 40260 | 9 |
| 47 | 58 | 89 | — | THE RACE IS ON — Jack Jones, Kapp 651 | 3 |
| 48 | 80 | — | — | LONG LONELY NIGHTS — Bobby Vinton, Epic 9768 | 2 |
| 49 | 56 | 63 | 78 | IF I RULED THE WORLD — Tony Bennett, Columbia 43220 | 5 |
| 50 | 66 | 76 | — | RED ROSES FOR A BLUE LADY — Wayne Newton, Capitol 5366 | 3 |
| 51 | 59 | 75 | 83 | YOU BETTER GET IT — Joe Tex, Dial 4003 | 4 |
| 52 | 65 | 71 | 89 | COME TOMORROW — Manfred Mann, Ascot 2170 | 4 |
| 53 | 60 | 66 | 82 | ANGEL — Johnny Tillotson, MGM 13316 | 4 |
| 54 | 52 | 55 | 56 | BORN TO BE TOGETHER — Ronettes, Philles 126 | 6 |
| 55 | 61 | 61 | 62 | GOLDFINGER — Billy Strange, Crescendo 334 | 8 |
| 56 | 71 | 86 | 96 | GO NOW — Moody Blues, London 9726 | 4 |
| 57 | 78 | 93 | — | COME AND STAY WITH ME — Marianne Faithfull, London 9731 | 3 |
| 58 | 63 | 65 | 72 | CRY — Ray Charles, ABC-Paramount 10615 | 6 |
| 59 | 74 | — | — | WHEN I'M GONE — Brenda Holloway, Tamla 54111 | 2 |
| 60 | 72 | 82 | — | YOU GOT WHAT IT TAKES — Joe Tex, Dial 4003 | 3 |
| 61 | 70 | 80 | 95 | MR. PITIFUL — Otis Redding, Volt 124 | 4 |
| 62 | — | — | — | TIRED OF WAITING FOR YOU — Kinks, Reprise 0347 | 1 |
| 63 | 75 | 85 | 88 | IT'S GONNA BE ALRIGHT — Maxine Brown, Wand 173 | 5 |
| 64 | 76 | — | — | GOOD TIMES — Jerry Butler, Vee Jay 651 | 2 |
| 65 | 93 | — | — | COME SEE — Major Lance, Okeh 7216 | 2 |
| 66 | 79 | 88 | — | WHO CAN I TURN TO — Dionne Warwick, Scepter 1298 | 3 |
| 67 | 69 | 77 | 87 | LIKE A CHILD — Julie Rogers, Mercury 72380 | 5 |
| 68 | 86 | — | — | FOR MAMA — Connie Francis, MGM 13325 | 2 |
| 69 | 73 | 83 | 86 | APACHE '65 — Arrows, Tower 116 | 5 |
| 70 | 88 | — | — | FOR MAMA — Jerry Vale, Columbia 43232 | 2 |
| 71 | — | — | — | I'M TELLING YOU NOW — Freddie & the Dreamers, Tower 125 | 1 |
| 72 | 83 | — | — | PLEASE LET ME WONDER — Beach Boys, Capitol 5372 | 2 |
| 73 | 77 | 81 | — | FOUR BY THE BEATLES — Beatles, Capitol 5365 (Extended Play) | 3 |
| 74 | 81 | 92 | 98 | DID YOU EVER — Hullaballoos, Roulette 4593 | 5 |
| 75 | 82 | 94 | — | THIS IS MY PRAYER — Ray Charles Singers, Command 4059 | 3 |
| 76 | 85 | 91 | 94 | CUPID — Johnny Rivers, Imperial 66087 | 4 |
| 77 | 84 | — | — | REAL LIVE GIRL — Steve Alaimo, ABC-Paramount 10620 | 2 |
| 78 | 91 | — | — | GOT TO GET YOU OFF MY MIND — Solomon Burke, Atlantic 2276 | 2 |
| 79 | — | — | — | PEACHES 'N' CREAM — Ikettes, Modern 1005 | 1 |
| 80 | 89 | 90 | 92 | ORANGE BLOSSOM SPECIAL — Johnny Cash, Columbia 43206 | 5 |
| 81 | — | — | — | FROM ALL OVER THE WORLD — Jan & Dean, Liberty 55766 | 1 |
| 82 | 97 | 100 | — | LAND OF 1000 DANCES — Cannibal & the Headhunters, Rampart 642 | 3 |
| 83 | — | — | — | POOR MAN'S SON — Reflections, Golden World 20 | 1 |
| 84 | — | — | — | GOLDFINGER — John Barry & His Ork, United Artists 791 | 1 |
| 85 | — | — | — | I UNDERSTAND — Freddie & the Dreamers, Mercury 72377 | 1 |
| 86 | 90 | — | — | GIRL DON'T COME — Sandy Shaw, Reprise 0342 | 2 |
| 87 | — | — | — | ANYTIME AT ALL — Frank Sinatra, Reprise 0350 | 1 |
| 88 | — | — | — | THIS IS IT — Jim Reeves, RCA Victor 8508 | 1 |
| 89 | — | — | — | LAND OF A THOUSAND DANCES — Midnighters, Chattahoochee 666 | 1 |
| 90 | — | — | — | BE MY BABY — Dick & Dee Dee, Warner Bros. 5608 | 1 |
| 91 | — | — | — | I CAN'T STOP THINKING OF YOU — Bobby Martin, Coral 62447 | 1 |
| 92 | — | — | — | ONE KISS FOR OLD TIMES' SAKE — Ronnie Dove, Diamond 179 | 1 |
| 93 | 95 | 99 | — | PASS ME BY — Peggy Lee, Capitol 5346 | 3 |
| 94 | 94 | 95 | — | DANNY BOY — Jackie Wilson, Brunswick 55277 | 3 |
| 95 | — | — | — | YOU CAN HAVE HIM — Dionne Warwick, Scepter 1294 | 1 |
| 96 | — | — | — | 10 LITTLE BOTTLES — Johnny Bond, Starday 704 | 1 |
| 97 | — | — | — | LOSING YOU — Dusty Springfield, Philips 40270 | 1 |
| 98 | — | — | — | BABY THE RAIN MUST FALL — Glenn Yarbrough, RCA Victor 8498 | 1 |
| 99 | — | — | — | FIND MY WAY BACK HOME — Nashville Teens, London 9736 | 1 |
| 100 | — | — | — | THIS SPORTING LIFE — Ian Whitcomb, Tower 120 | 1 |

## HOT 100—A TO Z–(Publisher-Licensee)

All Day and All of the Night (Jay Boy, BMI) ... 40
Angel (Disney, ASCAP) ... 53
Anytime at All (Duchess, BMI) ... 87
Apache '65 (Francis, Day & Hunter, PRF, ASCAP) 69
Ask the Lonely (Jobete, BMI) ... 24
Baby the Rain Must Fall (Screen Gems-Columbia, BMI) ... 98
Be My Baby (Mother Bertha, ASCAP) ... 90
Birds and the Bees, The (Pattern, ASCAP) ... 5
Born to Be Together (Screen Gems-Columbia, BMI) 54
Boy From New York City, The (Trio, BMI) ... 16
Bye Bye Baby (Saturday-Seasons Four, BMI) ... 46
Can't You Hear My Heartbeat (Southern, ASCAP) 8
Change Is Gonna Come, A (Kags, BMI) ... 41
Come and Stay With Me (Metric, BMI) ... 57
Come Home (Branston, BMI) ... 19
Come See (Camad & Chi-Sound, BMI) ... 65
Come Tomorrow (Noma-Sylvia, BMI) ... 52
Cry (Shapiro-Bernstein, ASCAP) ... 58
Cupid (Kags, BMI) ... 76
Danny Boy (Boosey & Hawkes, ASCAP) ... 94
Did You Ever (Big Seven, BMI) ... 74
Do the Clam (Gladys, ASCAP) ... 39
Do You Wanna Dance? (Clockus, BMI) ... 29
Don't Let Me Be Misunderstood (Benjamin, ASCAP) 26
Don't Mess Up a Good Thing (Arc-Saico, BMI) ... 45
Downtown (Leeds, ASCAP) ... 15
Eight Days a Week (Maclen, BMI) ... 1
Ferry Cross the Mersey (Unart-Pacer, BMI) ... 7
Find My Way Back Home (Fling, BMI) ... 99
For Mama—Francis (Ludlow, BMI) ... 68
For Mama—Vale (Ludlow, BMI) ... 70
Four By the Beatles (Various Publishers) ... 73
From All Over the World (Trousdale, BMI) ... 81

Goldfinger—Barry (Unart, BMI) ... 84
Goldfinger—Bassey (Unart, BMI) ... 11
Goldfinger—Strange (Unart, BMI) ... 55
Good Times (Frost, BMI) ... 64
Goodnight (Acuff-Rose, BMI) ... 22
Got to Get You Off My Mind (Cotillion, BMI) ... 78
Hurt So Bad (South Mountain, BMI) ... 10
I Can't Stop Thinking of You (South Mountain, BMI) ... 91
I Don't Want to Spoil the Party (Maclen, BMI) ... 44
I Go to Pieces (Vicki-McLaughlin, BMI) ... 25
I Must Be Seeing Things (Sea-Lark, BMI) ... 43
I Understand (Jubilee, ASCAP) ... 85
I'm Telling You Now (Bluerock, BMI) ... 71
I've Got a Tiger By the Tail (Bluerock, BMI) ... 36
If I Loved You (Chappell, ASCAP) ... 31
If I Ruled the World (Chappell, ASCAP) ... 49
It's Gonna Be Alright (Screen Gems-Columbia, BMI) 63
Jolly Green Giant, The (Burdette-Flomarlu, BMI) 9
King of the Road (Tree, BMI) ... 6
Land of 1000 Dances (Tune-Kel, BMI) ... 82
Land of a Thousand Dances—Midnighters (Tune-Kel, BMI) ... 89
Laugh, Laugh (Taracrest, BMI) ... 28
Like a Child (Ponderosa, BMI) ... 67
Little Things (Unart, BMI) ... 18
Long Lonely Nights (Arc, BMI) ... 48
Losing You (Springfield, ASCAP) ... 97
Midnight Special (Trousdale, BMI) ... 20
Mr. Pitiful (East-Time, BMI) ... 61
My Girl (Jobete, BMI) ... 2
Name Game, The (Gallico, BMI) ... 34
New York's a Lonely Town (Big Top, BMI) ... 32
Nowhere to Run (Jobete, BMI) ... 35
One Kiss for Old Times' Sake (T. M., BMI) ... 92

Orange Blossom Special (Leeds, ASCAP) ... 80
Pass Me By (Morris, ASCAP) ... 93
Peaches 'N' Cream (Screen Gems-Columbia, BMI) 79
People Get Ready (Chi-Sound, BMI) ... 21
Please Let Me Wonder (Sea of Tunes, BMI) ... 72
Poor Man's Son (Myto, BMI) ... 83
Race Is On (Glad-Acclaim, BMI) ... 47
Real Live Girl (Morris, ASCAP) ... 77
Red Roses for a Blue Lady—Dana (Mills, ASCAP) 23
Red Roses for a Blue Lady—Kaempfert (Mills, ASCAP) ... 13
Red Roses for a Blue Lady—Newton (Mills, ASCAP) 50
Send Me the Pillow You Dream On (Four Star, BMI) ... 30
Shake (Kags, BMI) ... 38
Shotgun (Jobete, BMI) ... 14
Stop! In the Name of Love (Jobete, BMI) ... 3
Stranger in Town (Mainstay, BMI) ... 37
Tell Her No (Mainstay, BMI) ... 17
10 Little Bottles (Red River, BMI) ... 96
This Diamond Ring (Sea-Lark, BMI) ... 4
This Is It (Acclaim, BMI) ... 88
This Is My Prayer (Chappell, ASCAP) ... 75
This Sporting Life (Burdette, BMI) ... 100
Tired of Waiting for You (Jay-Boy, BMI) ... 62
Twine Time (Va-Pac, BMI) ... 33
What Have They Done to the Rain (Schroeder, ASCAP) ... 42
When I'm Gone (Formal-Musical Comedy, BMI) 59
Who Can I Turn To (Musical Comedy, BMI) ... 66
Yeh, Yeh (Mongo, BMI) ... 27
You Better Get It (Tree, BMI) ... 51
You Can Have Him (Harvard-Big Billy, BMI) ... 95
You Got What It Takes (Tree, BMI) ... 60
You've Lost That Lovin' Feelin' (Screen Gems-Columbia, BMI) ... 12

## BUBBLING UNDER THE HOT 100

101. YOU CAN'T HURT ME NO MORE ... Gene Chandler, Constellation 146
102. THE GREATEST STORY EVER TOLD ... Ferrante & Teicher, United Artists 816
103. TEASIN' YOU ... Willie Tee, Atlantic 2273
104. WHIPPED CREAM ... Herb Alpert's Tijuana Brass, A&M 760
105. EL PUSSY CAT ... Mongo Santamaria, Columbia 43171
106. GEE BABY (I'M SORRY) ... 3 Degrees, Swan 4197
107. YOU'RE NEXT ... Jimmy Witherspoon, Prestige 341
108. YOU CAN HAVE HIM ... Timi Yuro, Mercury 72391
109. TELL HER I'M NOT HOME ... Ike & Tina Turner, Loma 2011
110. SUDDENLY I'M ALL ALONE ... Walter Jackson, Okeh 1215
111. I'VE GOT FIVE DOLLARS AND IT'S SATURDAY NIGHT ... George & Gene, Musicor 1066
112. BEGIN TO LOVE ... Robert Goulet, Columbia 43224
113. WHY DON'T YOU LET YOURSELF GO ... Mary Wells, 20th Century-Fox 570
114. YOU DON'T MISS A GOOD THING ... Irma Thomas, Imperial 66095
115. NEVER, NEVER LEAVE ME ... Mary Wells, 20th Century-Fox 570
116. DOES HE REALLY CARE FOR ME ... Ruby & the Romantics, Kapp 646
117. GAME OF LOVE ... Wayne Fontana & the Mindbenders, Fontana 1503
118. SOMEBODY ELSE IS TAKING MY PLACE ... Al Martino, Capitol 5384
119. IT HURTS ME ... Bobby Sherman, Decca 31741
120. MEAN OLD WORLD ... Rick Nelson, Decca 31756
121. HELLO, DOLLY! ... Bobby Darin, Capitol 5359
122. WITH ALL MY HEART ... Al Martino, Capitol 5384
123. LET THE PEOPLE TALK ... Neil Sedaka, RCA Victor 8511
124. DOUBLE-007 ... Detergents, Roulette 4603
125. DEAR JOHN LETTER ... Skeeter Davis & Bobby Bare, RCA Victor 8496
126. STOP AND GET A HOLD OF MYSELF ... Gladys Knight & the Pips, Maxx 334
127. DO IT WITH ALL YOUR HEART ... Dee Dee Warwick, Blue Rock 4008
128. I CAN'T EXPLAIN ... The Who, Decca 31725
129. COME BACK, BABY ... Roddie Joy, Red Bird 10-021
130. I DO LOVE YOU ... Billy Stewart, Chess 1922
131. NOT TOO LONG AGO ... Uniques, Paula 219
132. BABY, PLEASE DON'T GO ... Them, Parrot 9727
133. IS IT LOVE ... Cilla Black, Capitol 5373
134. REACH FOR A STAR ... Sandy Nelson, Imperial 66093
135. APPLES AND BANANAS ... Lawrence Welk, Dot 16697

*Compiled from national retail sales and radio station airplay by the Music Popularity Dept. of Record Market Research, Billboard.*

# Billboard HOT 100

**For Week Ending March 20, 1965**

★ STAR performer—Sides registering greatest proportionate upward progress this week.

| This Week | 1 Wk. Ago | 2 Wks. Ago | TITLE, Artist, Label & Number | Weeks On Chart |
|---|---|---|---|---|
| 1 | 1 | 5 | 19 | EIGHT DAYS A WEEK — Beatles, Capitol 5371 | 5 |
| 2 | 3 | 13 | 41 | STOP! IN THE NAME OF LOVE — Supremes, Motown 1074 | 5 |
| 3 | 5 | 8 | 13 | THE BIRDS AND THE BEES — Jewel Akens, Era 3141 | 9 |
| 4 | 6 | 7 | 10 | KING OF THE ROAD — Roger Miller, Smash 1965 | 8 |
| ★5 | 8 | 19 | 27 | CAN'T YOU HEAR MY HEARTBEAT — Herman's Hermits, MGM 13310 | 8 |
| 6 | 7 | 9 | 12 | FERRY CROSS THE MERSEY — Gerry & the Pacemakers, Laurie 3284 | 7 |
| 7 | 2 | 1 | 3 | MY GIRL — Temptations, Gordy 7038 | 10 |
| 8 | 4 | 2 | 1 | THIS DIAMOND RING — Gary Lewis & the Playboys, Liberty 55756 | 10 |
| 9 | 11 | 16 | 23 | GOLDFINGER — Shirley Bassey, United Artists 790 | 8 |
| 10 | 14 | 29 | 45 | SHOTGUN — Jr. Walker & the All Stars, Soul 35008 | 6 |
| 11 | 13 | 15 | 18 | RED ROSES FOR A BLUE LADY — Bert Kaempfert & His Ork, Decca 31722 | 9 |
| 12 | 10 | 12 | 17 | HURT SO BAD — Little Anthony & the Imperials, DCP 1128 | 7 |
| 13 | 9 | 4 | 5 | THE JOLLY GREEN GIANT — Kingsmen, Wand 172 | 11 |
| 14 | 19 | 26 | 37 | COME HOME — Dave Clark Five, Epic 9763 | 7 |
| 15 | 12 | 3 | 2 | YOU'VE LOST THAT LOVIN' FEELIN' — Righteous Brothers, Philles 124 | 15 |
| ★16 | 21 | 35 | 47 | PEOPLE GET READY — Impressions, ABC-Paramount 10622 | 6 |
| 17 | 23 | 36 | 46 | RED ROSES FOR A BLUE LADY — Vic Dana, Dolton 304 | 7 |
| 18 | 18 | 23 | 26 | LITTLE THINGS — Bobby Goldsboro, United Artists 810 | 9 |
| 19 | 29 | 57 | 84 | DO YOU WANNA DANCE? — Beach Boys, Capitol 5372 | 4 |
| 20 | 20 | 24 | 39 | MIDNIGHT SPECIAL — Johnny Rivers, Imperial 66087 | 7 |
| 21 | 22 | 22 | 28 | GOODNIGHT — Roy Orbison, Monument 873 | 6 |
| 22 | 26 | 39 | 49 | DON'T LET ME BE MISUNDERSTOOD — Animals, MGM 13311 | 7 |
| 23 | 27 | 30 | 40 | YEH, YEH — Georgie Fame, Imperial 66086 | 6 |
| ★24 | 35 | 46 | 73 | NOWHERE TO RUN — Martha & the Vandellas, Gordy 7039 | 4 |
| ★25 | 30 | 44 | 54 | SEND ME THE PILLOW YOU DREAM ON — Dean Martin, Reprise 0344 | 5 |
| 26 | 31 | 42 | 53 | IF I LOVED YOU — Chad & Jeremy, World Artists 1041 | 5 |
| 27 | 15 | 10 | 4 | DOWNTOWN — Petula Clark, Warner Bros. 5494 | 14 |
| 28 | 39 | 49 | 68 | DO THE CLAM — Elvis Presley, RCA Victor 8500 | 4 |
| 29 | 16 | 11 | 8 | THE BOY FROM NEW YORK CITY — Ad Libs, Blue Cat 102 | 10 |
| ★30 | 37 | 48 | 74 | STRANGER IN TOWN — Del Shannon, Amy 919 | 4 |
| 31 | 17 | 6 | 6 | TELL HER NO — Zombies, Parrot 9723 | 11 |
| 32 | 24 | 27 | 32 | ASK THE LONELY — Four Tops, Motown 1073 | 7 |
| 33 | 43 | 54 | 78 | I MUST BE SEEING THINGS — Gene Pitney, Musicor 1070 | 4 |
| 34 | 48 | 80 | — | LONG LONELY NIGHTS — Bobby Vinton, Epic 9768 | 3 |
| 35 | 28 | 17 | 15 | LAUGH, LAUGH — Beau Brummels, Autumn 8 | 12 |
| 36 | 25 | 14 | 9 | I GO TO PIECES — Peter & Gordon, Capitol 5335 | 11 |
| 37 | 32 | 32 | 38 | NEW YORK'S A LONELY TOWN — Trade Winds, Red Bird 10-020 | 7 |
| 38 | 49 | 56 | 63 | IF I RULED THE WORLD — Tony Bennett, Columbia 4320 | 6 |
| 39 | 44 | 47 | 59 | I DON'T WANT TO SPOIL THE PARTY — Beatles, Capitol 5371 | 5 |
| 40 | 47 | 58 | 89 | THE RACE IS ON — Jack Jones, Kapp 651 | 4 |
| 41 | 45 | 51 | 58 | DON'T MESS UP A GOOD THING — Fontella Bass & Bobby McClure, Checker 1097 | 7 |
| 42 | 71 | — | — | I'M TELLING YOU NOW — Freddie & the Dreamers, Tower 125 | 2 |
| 43 | 62 | — | — | TIRED OF WAITING FOR YOU — Kinks, Reprise 0347 | 2 |
| 44 | 59 | 74 | — | WHEN I'M GONE — Brenda Holloway, Tamla 54111 | 3 |
| 45 | 50 | 66 | 76 | RED ROSES FOR A BLUE LADY — Wayne Newton, Capitol 5366 | 4 |
| 46 | 56 | 71 | 86 | GO NOW — Moody Blues, London 9726 | 5 |
| 47 | 38 | 21 | 7 | SHAKE — Sam Cooke, RCA Victor 8486 | 11 |
| 48 | 51 | 59 | 75 | YOU BETTER GET IT — Joe Tex, Dial 4003 | 5 |
| 49 | 57 | 78 | 93 | COME AND STAY WITH ME — Marianne Faithfull, London 9731 | 4 |
| 50 | 52 | 65 | 71 | COME TOMORROW — Manfred Mann, Ascot 2170 | 5 |
| 51 | 53 | 60 | 66 | ANGEL — Johnny Tillotson, MGM 13316 | 6 |
| 52 | 36 | 25 | 25 | I'VE GOT A TIGER BY THE TAIL — Buck Owens, Capitol 5336 | 9 |
| 53 | 65 | 93 | — | COME SEE — Major Lance, Okeh 7216 | 3 |
| 54 | 61 | 70 | 80 | MR. PITIFUL — Otis Redding, Volt 124 | 5 |
| 55 | 78 | 91 | — | GOT TO GET YOU OFF MY MIND — Solomon Burke, Atlantic 2276 | 3 |
| 56 | 63 | 75 | 85 | IT'S GONNA BE ALRIGHT — Maxine Brown, Wand 173 | 6 |
| 57 | 68 | 86 | — | FOR MAMA — Connie Francis, MGM 13325 | 3 |
| 58 | 55 | 61 | 61 | GOLDFINGER — Billy Strange, Crescendo 334 | 9 |
| 59 | 60 | 72 | 82 | YOU GOT WHAT IT TAKES — Joe Tex, Dial 4003 | 4 |
| 60 | 70 | 88 | — | FOR MAMA — Jerry Vale, Columbia 43232 | 3 |
| 61 | 72 | 83 | — | PLEASE LET ME WONDER — Beach Boys, Capitol 5372 | 3 |
| 62 | 79 | — | — | PEACHES 'N' CREAM — Ikettes, Modern 1005 | 2 |
| 63 | — | — | — | GAME OF LOVE — Wayne Fontana & the Mindbenders, Fontana 1503 | 1 |
| 64 | 69 | 73 | 83 | APACHE '65 — Arrows, Tower 116 | 6 |
| 65 | 66 | 79 | 88 | WHO CAN I TURN TO — Dionne Warwick, Scepter 1298 | 4 |
| 66 | 87 | — | — | ANYTIME AT ALL — Frank Sinatra, Reprise 0350 | 2 |
| 67 | 83 | — | — | POOR MAN'S SON — Reflections, Golden World 20 | 2 |
| 68 | 58 | 63 | 65 | CRY — Ray Charles, ABC-Paramount 10615 | 7 |
| 69 | 64 | 76 | — | GOOD TIMES — Jerry Butler, Vee Jay 651 | 3 |
| 70 | 73 | 77 | 81 | FOUR BY THE BEATLES — Beatles, Capitol 5365 (Extended Play) | 4 |
| 71 | 82 | 97 | 100 | LAND OF 1000 DANCES — Cannibal & the Headhunters, Rampart 642 | 4 |
| 72 | 75 | 82 | 94 | THIS IS MY PRAYER — Ray Charles Singers, Command 4059 | 4 |
| 73 | 81 | — | — | FROM ALL OVER THE WORLD — Jan & Dean, Liberty 55766 | 2 |
| 74 | 74 | 81 | 92 | DID YOU EVER — Hullaballoos, Roulette 4593 | 6 |
| ★75 | — | — | — | THE CLAPPING SONG — Shirley Ellis, Congress 234 | 1 |
| 76 | 84 | — | — | GOLDFINGER — John Barry & His Ork, United Artists 791 | 2 |
| 77 | 86 | 90 | — | GIRL DON'T COME — Sandy Shaw, Reprise 0342 | 3 |
| 78 | 85 | — | — | I UNDERSTAND — Freddie & the Dreamers, Mercury 72377 | 2 |
| ★79 | — | — | — | CAST YOUR FATE TO THE WIND — Sounds Orchestral, Parkway 942 | 1 |
| 80 | — | — | — | I'LL BE DOGGONE — Marvin Gaye, Tamla 54112 | 1 |
| 81 | 89 | — | — | LAND OF A THOUSAND DANCES — Midnighters, Chattahoochee 666 | 2 |
| 82 | 92 | — | — | ONE KISS FOR OLD TIMES' SAKE — Ronnie Dove, Diamond 179 | 2 |
| 83 | — | — | — | BUMBLE BEE — Searchers, Kapp Winners Circle 49 | 1 |
| ★84 | — | — | — | NEVER, NEVER LEAVE ME — Mary Wells, 20th Century-Fox 570 | 1 |
| 85 | 96 | — | — | 10 LITTLE BOTTLES — Johnny Bond, Starday 704 | 2 |
| 86 | 80 | 89 | 90 | ORANGE BLOSSOM SPECIAL — Johnny Cash, Columbia 43206 | 6 |
| 87 | 90 | — | — | BE MY BABY — Dick & Dee Dee, Warner Bros. 5608 | 2 |
| 88 | 91 | — | — | I CAN'T STOP THINKING OF YOU — Bobby Martin, Coral 62447 | 2 |
| 89 | 98 | — | — | BABY THE RAIN MUST FALL — Glenn Yarbrough, RCA Victor 8498 | 2 |
| ★90 | — | — | — | COME BACK BABY — Roddie Joy, Red Bird 10-021 | 1 |
| 91 | — | — | — | NOT TOO LONG AGO — Uniques, Paula 219 | 1 |
| 92 | 95 | — | — | YOU CAN HAVE HIM — Dionne Warwick, Scepter 1294 | 2 |
| 93 | — | — | — | DOUBLE-O-SEVEN — Detergents, Roulette 4603 | 1 |
| 94 | — | — | — | I KNOW A PLACE — Petula Clark, Warner Bros. 5612 | 1 |
| 95 | 97 | — | — | LOSING YOU — Dusty Springfield, Philips 40270 | 2 |
| 96 | — | — | — | MEAN OLD WORLD — Rick Nelson, Decca 31756 | 1 |
| 97 | — | 98 | — | WHIPPED CREAM — Herb Alpert's Tijuana Brass, A&M 760 | 1 |
| 98 | 98 | — | — | FIND MY WAY BACK HOME — Nashville Teens, London 9736 | 1 |
| 99 | — | 100 | — | GEE BABY (I'm Sorry) — 3 Degrees, Swan 4197 | 1 |
| 100 | — | — | — | TEASIN' YOU — Willie Tee, Atlantic 2273 | 1 |

## BUBBLING UNDER THE HOT 100

101. THE GREATEST STORY EVER TOLD — Ferrante & Teicher, United Artists 816
102. EL PUSSY CAT — Mongo Santamaria, Columbia 43171
103. THIS IS IT — Jim Reeves, RCA Victor 8508
104. THIS SPORTING LIFE — Ian Whitcomb, Tower 120
105. SOMEBODY ELSE IS TAKING MY PLACE — Al Martino, Capitol 5384
106. I'VE GOT FIVE DOLLARS AND IT'S SATURDAY NIGHT — George & Gene, Musicor 1066
107. WHY DON'T YOU LET YOURSELF GO — Mary Wells, 20th Century-Fox 570
108. TELL HER I'M NOT HOME — Ike & Tina Turner, Loma 2011
109. YOU DON'T MISS A GOOD THING — Irma Thomas, Imperial 66095
110. BABY, PLEASE DON'T GO — Them, Parrot 9727
111. BEGIN TO LOVE — Robert Goulet, Columbia 43224
112. PASS ME BY — Peggy Lee, Capitol 5346
113. LET THE PEOPLE TALK — Neil Sedaka, RCA Victor 8511
114. A DEAR JOHN LETTER — Skeeter Davis & Bobby Bare, RCA Victor 8496
115. CHIM, CHIM, CHEREE — New Christy Minstrels, Columbia 43215
116. I CAN'T EXPLAIN — The Who, Decca 31725
117. APPLES AND BANANAS — Lawrence Welk, Dot 16697
118. IT HURTS ME — Bobby Sherman, Decca 31741
119. YOU CAN'T HURT ME NO MORE — Gene Chandler, Constellation 146
120. YOU ARE NEXT — Jimmy Witherspoon, Prestige 341
121. YOU CAN HAVE HIM — Timi Yuro, Mercury 72391
122. I DO LOVE YOU — Roger Williams, Kapp Winners Circle 48
123. TRY TO REMEMBER — Gladys Knight & the Pips, Maxx 334
124. NOW THAT YOU'RE GONE — Connie Stevens, Warner Bros. 5610
125. STOP AND GET A HOLD OF MYSELF — Jerry Butler, Vee Jay 652
126. DO IT WITH ALL YOUR HEART — Dee Dee Warwick, Blue Rock 4003
127. THAT'LL BE THE DAY — Everly Brothers, Warner Bros.
128. BABY, HOLD ME CLOSE — Peggy Lee, Capitol 5346
129. THE SPECIAL YEARS — Brook Benton, Mercury 72298
130. IT'S NOT UNUSUAL — Tom Jones, Parrot 9737
131. GOLDFINGER — Jerry Lee Lewis, Smash 1969
132. MICKEY'S EAST COAST JERK — Larks, Money 1102
133. REACH FOR A STAR — Sandy Nelson, Imperial 66093
134. (Gary, Please Don't Sell) MY DIAMOND RING — Wendy Hill, Liberty 55771
135. I'LL NEVER FIND ANOTHER YOU — Seekers, Capitol 5383

# Billboard HOT 100

For Week Ending March 27, 1965

★ STAR performer—Sides registering greatest proportionate upward progress this week.

| This Week | Last Week | 2 Wks. Ago | 3 Wks. Ago | TITLE Artist, Label & Number | Weeks On Chart |
|---|---|---|---|---|---|
| 1 | 2 | 3 | 13 | STOP! IN THE NAME OF LOVE — Supremes, Motown 1074 | 6 |
| 2 | 5 | 8 | 19 | CAN'T YOU HEAR MY HEARTBEAT — Herman's Hermits, MGM 13310 | 9 |
| 3 | 3 | 5 | 8 | THE BIRDS AND THE BEES — Jewel Akens, Era 3141 | 10 |
| 4 | 1 | 1 | 5 | EIGHT DAYS A WEEK — Beatles, Capitol 5371 | 6 |
| 5 | 4 | 6 | 7 | KING OF THE ROAD — Roger Miller, Smash 1965 | 9 |
| 6 | 6 | 7 | 9 | FERRY CROSS THE MERSEY — Gerry & the Pacemakers, Laurie 3284 | 8 |
| 7 | 10 | 14 | 29 | SHOTGUN — Jr. Walker & the All Stars, Soul 35008 | 7 |
| 8 | 9 | 11 | 16 | GOLDFINGER — Shirley Bassey, United Artists 790 | 9 |
| 9 | 7 | 2 | 1 | MY GIRL — Temptations, Gordy 7038 | 11 |
| 10 | 8 | 4 | 2 | THIS DIAMOND RING — Gary Lewis & the Playboys, Liberty 55756 | 11 |
| 11 | 11 | 13 | 15 | RED ROSES FOR A BLUE LADY — Bert Kaempfert & His Ork, Decca 31722 | 10 |
| 12 | 24 | 35 | 46 | NOWHERE TO RUN — Martha & the Vandellas, Gordy 7039 | 5 |
| 13 | 18 | 18 | 23 | LITTLE THINGS — Bobby Goldsboro, United Artists 810 | 10 |
| 14 | 16 | 21 | 35 | PEOPLE GET READY — Impressions, ABC-Paramount 10622 | 7 |
| 15 | 17 | 23 | 36 | RED ROSES FOR A BLUE LADY — Vic Dana, Dolton 304 | 8 |
| 16 | 19 | 29 | 57 | DO YOU WANNA DANCE? — Beach Boys, Capitol 5372 | 5 |
| 17 | 22 | 26 | 39 | DON'T LET ME BE MISUNDERSTOOD — Animals, MGM 13311 | 8 |
| 18 | 14 | 19 | 26 | COME HOME — Dave Clark Five, Epic 9763 | 5 |
| 19 | 12 | 10 | 12 | HURT SO BAD — Little Anthony & the Imperials, DCP 1128 | 8 |
| 20 | 42 | 71 | — | I'M TELLING YOU NOW — Freddie & the Dreamers, Tower 125 | 3 |
| 21 | 23 | 27 | 30 | YEH, YEH — Georgie Fame, Imperial 66086 | 7 |
| 22 | 34 | 48 | 80 | LONG LONELY NIGHTS — Bobby Vinton, Epic 9768 | 4 |
| 23 | 28 | 39 | 49 | DO THE CLAM — Elvis Presley, RCA Victor 8500 | 5 |
| 24 | 25 | 30 | 44 | SEND ME THE PILLOW YOU DREAM ON — Dean Martin, Reprise 0344 | 6 |
| 25 | 26 | 31 | 42 | IF I LOVED YOU — Chad & Jeremy, World Artists 1041 | 6 |
| 26 | 43 | 62 | — | TIRED OF WAITING FOR YOU — Kinks, Reprise 0347 | 3 |
| 27 | 46 | 56 | 71 | GO NOW — Moody Blues, London 9726 | 6 |
| 28 | 13 | 9 | 4 | THE JOLLY GREEN GIANT — Kingsmen, Wand 172 | 12 |
| 29 | 40 | 47 | 58 | THE RACE IS ON — Jack Jones, Kapp 651 | 5 |
| 30 | 30 | 37 | 48 | STRANGER IN TOWN — Del Shannon, Amy 919 | 5 |
| 31 | 33 | 43 | 54 | I MUST BE SEEING THINGS — Gene Pitney, Musicor 1070 | 5 |
| 32 | 21 | 22 | 22 | GOODNIGHT — Roy Orbison, Monument 873 | 7 |
| 33 | 41 | 45 | 51 | DON'T MESS UP A GOOD THING — Fontella Bass & Bobby McClure, Checker 1097 | 8 |
| 34 | 32 | 24 | 27 | ASK THE LONELY — Four Tops, Motown 1073 | 8 |
| 35 | 38 | 49 | 56 | IF I RULED THE WORLD — Tony Bennett, Columbia 43220 | 7 |
| 36 | 27 | 15 | 10 | DOWNTOWN — Petula Clark, Warner Bros. 5494 | 15 |
| 37 | 44 | 59 | 74 | WHEN I'M GONE — Brenda Holloway, Tamla 54111 | 4 |
| 38 | 45 | 50 | 66 | RED ROSES FOR A BLUE LADY — Wayne Newton, Capitol 5366 | 5 |
| 39 | 49 | 57 | 78 | COME AND STAY WITH ME — Marianne Faithfull, London 9731 | 5 |
| 40 | 63 | — | — | GAME OF LOVE — Wayne Fontana & the Mindbenders, Fontana 1503 | 2 |
| 41 | 20 | 20 | 24 | MIDNIGHT SPECIAL — Johnny Rivers, Imperial 66087 | 8 |
| 42 | 75 | — | — | THE CLAPPING SONG — Shirley Ellis, Congress 234 | 2 |
| 43 | 15 | 12 | 3 | YOU'VE LOST THAT LOVIN' FEELIN' — Righteous Brothers, Philles 124 | 16 |
| 44 | 39 | 44 | 47 | I DON'T WANT TO SPOIL THE PARTY — Beatles, Capitol 5371 | 6 |
| 45 | 55 | 78 | 91 | GOT TO GET YOU OFF MY MIND — Solomon Burke, Atlantic 2276 | 4 |
| 46 | 48 | 51 | 59 | YOU BETTER GET IT — Joe Tex, Dial 4003 | 6 |
| 47 | 53 | 65 | 93 | COME SEE — Major Lance, Okeh 7216 | 4 |
| 48 | 62 | 79 | — | PEACHES 'N' CREAM — Ikettes, Modern 1005 | 3 |
| 49 | 37 | 32 | 32 | NEW YORK'S A LONELY TOWN — Trade Winds, Red Bird 10-020 | 8 |
| 50 | 94 | — | — | I KNOW A PLACE — Petula Clark, Warner Bros. 5612 | 2 |
| 51 | 54 | 61 | 70 | MR. PITIFUL — Otis Redding, Volt 124 | 6 |
| 52 | 61 | 72 | 83 | PLEASE LET ME WONDER — Beach Boys, Capitol 5372 | 4 |
| 53 | 50 | 52 | 65 | COME TOMORROW — Manfred Mann, Ascot 2170 | 6 |
| 54 | 66 | 87 | — | ANYTIME AT ALL — Frank Sinatra, Reprise 0350 | 3 |
| 55 | 71 | 82 | 97 | LAND OF 1000 DANCES — Cannibal & the Headhunters, Rampart 642 | 5 |
| 56 | 57 | 68 | 86 | FOR MAMA — Connie Francis, MGM 13325 | 4 |
| 57 | 80 | — | — | I'LL BE DOGGONE — Marvin Gaye, Tamla 54112 | 2 |
| 58 | 60 | 70 | 88 | FOR MAMA — Jerry Vale, Columbia 43222 | 4 |
| 59 | 59 | 60 | 72 | YOU GOT WHAT IT TAKES — Joe Tex, Dial 4003 | 5 |
| 60 | 67 | 83 | — | POOR MAN'S SON — Reflections, Golden World 20 | 3 |
| 61 | 82 | 92 | — | ONE KISS FOR OLD TIMES' SAKE — Ronnie Dove, Diamond 179 | 3 |
| 62 | 77 | 86 | 90 | GIRL DON'T COME — Sandie Shaw, Reprise 0342 | 4 |
| 63 | 83 | — | — | BUMBLE BEE — Searchers, Kapp Winners Circle 49 | 2 |
| 64 | 79 | — | — | CAST YOUR FATE TO THE WIND — Sounds Orchestral, Parkway 942 | 2 |
| 65 | 65 | 66 | 79 | WHO CAN I TURN TO — Dionne Warwick, Scepter 1298 | 5 |
| 66 | 51 | 53 | 60 | ANGEL — Johnny Tillotson, MGM 13316 | 7 |
| 67 | 73 | 81 | — | FROM ALL OVER THE WORLD — Jan & Dean, Liberty 55766 | 3 |
| 68 | 70 | 73 | 77 | FOUR BY THE BEATLES — Beatles, Capitol 5365 (Extended Play) | 5 |
| 69 | 78 | 85 | — | I UNDERSTAND — Freddie & the Dreamers, Mercury 72377 | 3 |
| 70 | 85 | 96 | — | 10 LITTLE BOTTLES — Johnny Bond, Starday 704 | 3 |
| 71 | 81 | 89 | — | LAND OF A THOUSAND DANCES — Midnighters, Chattahoochee 666 | 3 |
| 72 | 76 | 84 | — | GOLDFINGER — John Barry & His Ork, United Artists 791 | 3 |
| 73 | 88 | 91 | — | I CAN'T STOP THINKING OF YOU — Bobbi Martin, Coral 62447 | 3 |
| 74 | 89 | 98 | — | BABY THE RAIN MUST FALL — Glenn Yarbrough, RCA Victor 8498 | 3 |
| 75 | 56 | 63 | 75 | IT'S GONNA BE ALRIGHT — Maxine Brown, Wand 173 | 7 |
| 76 | 64 | 69 | 73 | APACHE '65 — Arrows, Tower 116 | 7 |
| 77 | 84 | — | — | NEVER, NEVER LEAVE ME — Mary Wells, 20th Century-Fox 570 | 2 |
| 78 | 69 | 64 | 76 | GOOD TIMES — Jerry Butler, Vee Jay 651 | 4 |
| 79 | — | — | — | THE LAST TIME — Rolling Stones, London 9741 | 1 |
| 80 | — | — | — | THE BARRACUDA — Alvin Cash & the Crawlers, Mar-V-Lus 6005 | 1 |
| 81 | — | — | — | SOMEBODY ELSE IS TAKING MY PLACE — Al Martino, Capitol 5384 | 1 |
| 82 | 97 | — | — | WHIPPED CREAM — Herb Alpert's Tijuana Brass, A&M 760 | 4 |
| 83 | — | — | — | OOO BABY BABY — Miracles, Tamla 54113 | 1 |
| 84 | — | — | — | I'LL NEVER FIND ANOTHER YOU — Seekers, Capitol 5383 | 1 |
| 85 | 91 | — | — | NOT TOO LONG AGO — Uniques, Paula 219 | 2 |
| 86 | 90 | — | — | COME BACK BABY — Roddie Joy, Red Bird 10-021 | 2 |
| 87 | 87 | 90 | — | BE MY BABY — Dick & Dee Dee, Warner Bros. 5608 | 3 |
| 88 | — | — | — | THE ENTERTAINER — Tony Clarke, Chess 1924 | 1 |
| 89 | — | — | — | WE'RE GONNA MAKE IT — Little Milton, Checker 1105 | 1 |
| 90 | — | — | — | CRAZY DOWNTOWN — Allan Sherman, Warner Bros. 5614 | 1 |
| 91 | 95 | 97 | — | LOSING YOU — Dusty Springfield, Philips 40270 | 3 |
| 92 | — | — | — | ALL OF MY LIFE — Lesley Gore, Mercury 72412 | 1 |
| 93 | 93 | — | — | DOUBLE-O-SEVEN — Detergents, Roulette 4603 | 2 |
| 94 | — | — | — | THINK OF THE GOOD TIMES — Jay and the Americans, United Artists 845 | 1 |
| 95 | 99 | — | 100 | GEE BABY (I'm Sorry) — 3 Degrees, Swan 4197 | 2 |
| 96 | 96 | — | — | MEAN OLD WORLD — Rick Nelson, Decca 31756 | 2 |
| 97 | 100 | — | — | TEASIN' YOU — Willie Tee, Atlantic 2273 | 2 |
| 98 | — | — | — | I DO LOVE YOU — Billy Stewart, Chess 1922 | 1 |
| 99 | — | — | — | I CAN'T EXPLAIN — The Who, Decca 31725 | 1 |
| 100 | — | — | 99 | EL PUSSY CAT — Mongo Santamaria, Columbia 43171 | 2 |

## BUBBLING UNDER THE HOT 100

101. THE GREATEST STORY EVER TOLD — Ferrante & Teicher, United Artists 816
102. APPLES AND BANANAS — Lawrence Welk, Dot 16697
103. THIS IS IT — Jim Reeves, RCA Victor 8508
104. THIS SPORTING LIFE — Ian Whitcomb, Tower 120
105. I'VE GOT FIVE DOLLARS AND IT'S SATURDAY NIGHT — George & Gene, Musicor 1066
106. BABY, PLEASE DON'T GO — Them, Parrot 9727
107. LET THE PEOPLE TALK — Neil Sedaka, RCA Victor 8511
108. FIND MY WAY BACK HOME — Nashville Teens, London 9736
109. YOU DON'T MISS A GOOD THING — Irma Thomas, Imperial 66095
110. PASS ME BY — Peggy Lee, Capitol 5346
111. BEGIN TO LOVE — Robert Goulet, Columbia 43224
112. YOU CAN HAVE HIM — Dionne Warwick, Scepter 1294
113. TRY TO REMEMBER — Roger Williams, Kapp Winners Circle 48
114. SHE'S ABOUT A MOVER — Sir Douglas Quintet, Tribe 8308
115. GOLDFINGER — Jimmy Smith, Verve 10346
116. TELL HER I'M NOT HOME — Ike & Tina Turner, Loma 2011
117. SUBTERRANEAN HOMESICK BLUES — Bob Dylan, Columbia 43242
118. THAT'LL BE THE DAY — Everly Brothers, Warner Bros. 5611
119. THE RECORD — Ben E. King, Atco 6343
120. CHIM CHIM CHEREE — New Christy Minstrels, Columbia 43215
121. NOW THAT YOU'VE GONE — Connie Stevens, Warner Bros. 5610
122. STOP AND GET A HOLD OF MYSELF — Gladys Knight & the Pips, Maxx 334
123. DO IT WITH ALL YOUR HEART — Dee Dee Warwick, Blue Rock 4008
124. IT'S NOT UNUSUAL — Tom Jones, Parrot 9737
125. EVERY NIGHT, EVERY DAY — Jimmy McCracklin, Imperial 66094
126. CARMEN — Bruce & Terry, Columbia
127. A DEAR JOHN LETTER — Skeeter Davis & Bobby Bare, RCA Victor 8496
128. CARMEN — Herb Alpert
129. WOOLY BULLY — Sam the Sham and the Pharaohs, MGM 13322
130. TOMORROW NIGHT — Damita Jo, Epic 9768
131. DID I CHOOSE YOU — Barbra Streisand, Columbia 43248
132. SIMON SAYS — Isley Brothers, Atlantic 2277
133. SUDDENLY I'M ALL ALONE — Walter Jackson, Okeh 7215
134. MEXICAN PEARLS — Billy Vaughn, Dot 16705
135. SILVER SPOON — Mary Ann, Federal 12530
136. HAWAII HONEYMOON — Waikikis, Kapp Winners Circle 52

Compiled from national retail sales and radio station airplay by the Music Popularity Dept. of Record Market Research, Billboard.

# Billboard HOT 100

**For Week Ending April 3, 1965**

★ STAR performer—Sides registering greatest proportionate upward progress this week.

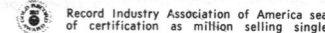

| This Week | 1 Wk. Ago | 2 Wks. Ago | 3 Wks. Ago | TITLE, Artist, Label & Number | Weeks On Chart |
|---|---|---|---|---|---|
| 1 | 1 | 2 | 3 | **STOP! IN THE NAME OF LOVE** — Supremes, Motown 1074 | 7 |
| 2 | 2 | 5 | 8 | **CAN'T YOU HEAR MY HEARTBEAT** — Herman's Hermits, MGM 13310 | 10 |
| ★3 | 20 | 42 | 71 | **I'M TELLING YOU NOW** — Freddie & the Dreamers, Tower 125 | 4 |
| ★4 | 7 | 10 | 14 | **SHOTGUN** — Jr. Walker & the All Stars, Soul 35008 | 8 |
| 5 | 3 | 3 | 5 | **THE BIRDS AND THE BEES** — Jewel Akens, Era 3141 | 11 |
| 6 | 5 | 4 | 6 | **KING OF THE ROAD** — Roger Miller, Smash 1965 | 10 |
| 7 | 4 | 1 | 1 | **EIGHT DAYS A WEEK** — Beatles, Capitol 5371 | 7 |
| 8 | 8 | 9 | 11 | **GOLDFINGER** — Shirley Bassey, United Artists 790 | 10 |
| 9 | 12 | 24 | 35 | **NOWHERE TO RUN** — Martha & the Vandellas, Gordy 7039 | 6 |
| 10 | 15 | 17 | 23 | **RED ROSES FOR A BLUE LADY** — Vic Dana, Dolton 304 | 9 |
| 11 | 6 | 6 | 7 | **FERRY CROSS THE MERSEY** — Gerry & the Pacemakers, Laurie 3284 | 9 |
| 12 | 9 | 7 | 2 | **MY GIRL** — Temptations, Gordy 7038 | 12 |
| 13 | 16 | 19 | 29 | **DO YOU WANNA DANCE?** — Beach Boys, Capitol 5372 | 6 |
| 14 | 11 | 11 | 13 | **RED ROSES FOR A BLUE LADY** — Bert Kaempfert & His Ork, Decca 31722 | 11 |
| 15 | 17 | 22 | 26 | **DON'T LET ME BE MISUNDERSTOOD** — Animals, MGM 13311 | 9 |
| 16 | 13 | 18 | 18 | **LITTLE THINGS** — Bobby Goldsboro, United Artists 810 | 11 |
| ★17 | 40 | 63 | — | **GAME OF LOVE** — Wayne Fontana & the Mindbenders, Fontana 1503 | 3 |
| 18 | 26 | 43 | 62 | **TIRED OF WAITING FOR YOU** — Kinks, Reprise 0347 | 4 |
| 19 | 27 | 46 | 56 | **GO NOW** — Moody Blues, London 9726 | 7 |
| 20 | 22 | 34 | 48 | **LONG LONELY NIGHTS** — Bobby Vinton, Epic 9768 | 5 |
| 21 | 23 | 28 | 39 | **DO THE CLAM** — Elvis Presley, RCA Victor 8500 | 6 |
| 22 | 29 | 40 | 47 | **THE RACE IS ON** — Jack Jones, Kapp 651 | 6 |
| 23 | 10 | 8 | 4 | **THIS DIAMOND RING** — Gary Lewis & the Playboys, Liberty 55756 | 12 |
| 24 | 21 | 23 | 27 | **YEH, YEH** — Georgie Fame, Imperial 66086 | 8 |
| 25 | 25 | 26 | 31 | **IF I LOVED YOU** — Chad & Jeremy, World Artists 1041 | 7 |
| 26 | 24 | 25 | 30 | **SEND ME THE PILLOW YOU DREAM ON** — Dean Martin, Reprise 0344 | 7 |
| 27 | 14 | 16 | 21 | **PEOPLE GET READY** — Impressions, ABC-Paramount 10622 | 8 |
| ★28 | 50 | 94 | — | **I KNOW A PLACE** — Petula Clark, Warner Bros. 5612 | 3 |
| 29 | 38 | 45 | — | **RED ROSES FOR A BLUE LADY** — Wayne Newton, Capitol 5366 | 6 |
| 30 | 39 | 49 | 57 | **COME AND STAY WITH ME** — Marianne Faithfull, London 9731 | 6 |
| 31 | 31 | 33 | 43 | **I MUST BE SEEING THINGS** — Gene Pitney, Musicor 1070 | 6 |
| ★32 | 42 | 75 | — | **THE CLAPPING SONG** — Shirley Ellis, Congress 234 | 3 |
| 33 | 33 | 41 | 45 | **DON'T MESS UP A GOOD THING** — Fontella Bass & Bobby McClure, Checker 1097 | 9 |
| 34 | 35 | 38 | 49 | **IF I RULED THE WORLD** — Tony Bennett, Columbia 43220 | 8 |
| ★35 | 45 | 55 | 78 | **GOT TO GET YOU OFF MY MIND** — Solomon Burke, Atlantic 2276 | 5 |
| 36 | 37 | 44 | 59 | **WHEN I'M GONE** — Brenda Holloway, Tamla 54111 | 5 |
| 37 | 18 | 14 | 19 | **COME HOME** — Dave Clark Five, Epic 9763 | 9 |
| 38 | 19 | 12 | 10 | **HURT SO BAD** — Little Anthony & the Imperials, DCP 1128 | 9 |
| 39 | 30 | 30 | 37 | **STRANGER IN TOWN** — Del Shannon, Amy 919 | 7 |
| 40 | 47 | 53 | 65 | **COME SEE** — Major Lance, Okeh 7216 | 5 |
| 41 | 63 | 83 | — | **BUMBLE BEE** — Searchers, Kapp Winners Circle 49 | 3 |
| 42 | 57 | 80 | — | **I'LL BE DOGGONE** — Marvin Gaye, Tamla 54112 | 3 |
| 43 | 51 | 54 | 61 | **MR. PITIFUL** — Otis Redding, Volt 124 | 7 |
| ★44 | 61 | 82 | 92 | **ONE KISS FOR OLD TIMES' SAKE** — Ronnie Dove, Diamond 179 | 4 |
| 45 | 48 | 62 | 79 | **PEACHES 'N' CREAM** — Ikettes, Modern 1005 | 4 |
| ★46 | 79 | — | — | **THE LAST TIME** — Rolling Stones, London 9741 | 2 |
| 47 | 54 | 66 | 87 | **ANYTIME AT ALL** — Frank Sinatra, Reprise 0350 | 4 |
| 48 | 56 | 57 | 68 | **FOR MAMA** — Connie Francis, MGM 13325 | 5 |
| 49 | 55 | 71 | 82 | **LAND OF 1000 DANCES** — Cannibal & the Headhunters, Rampart 642 | 6 |
| 50 | 46 | 48 | 51 | **YOU BETTER GET IT** — Joe Tex, Dial 4003 | 7 |
| 51 | 59 | 59 | 60 | **YOU GOT WHAT IT TAKES** — Joe Tex, Dial 4003 | 6 |
| 52 | 62 | 77 | 86 | **GIRL DON'T COME** — Sandie Shaw, Reprise 0342 | 5 |
| 53 | 64 | 79 | — | **CAST YOUR FATE TO THE WIND** — Sounds Orchestral, Parkway 942 | 3 |
| 54 | 58 | 60 | 70 | **FOR MAMA** — Jerry Vale, Columbia 43232 | 5 |
| 55 | 60 | 67 | 83 | **POOR MAN'S SON** — Reflections, Golden World 20 | 4 |
| 56 | 67 | 73 | 81 | **FROM ALL OVER THE WORLD** — Jan & Dean, Liberty 55766 | 4 |
| ★57 | 69 | 78 | 85 | **I UNDERSTAND** — Freddie & the Dreamers, Mercury 72377 | 4 |
| 58 | 73 | 89 | 91 | **I CAN'T STOP THINKING OF YOU** — Bobbi Martin, Coral 62447 | 4 |
| 59 | 74 | 89 | 98 | **BABY THE RAIN MUST FALL** — Glenn Yarbrough, RCA Victor 8498 | 4 |
| 60 | 70 | 85 | 96 | **10 LITTLE BOTTLES** — Johnny Bond, Starday 704 | 4 |
| 61 | 84 | — | — | **I'LL NEVER FIND ANOTHER YOU** — Seekers, Capitol 5383 | 2 |
| 62 | 65 | 65 | 66 | **WHO CAN I TURN TO** — Dionne Warwick, Scepter 1298 | 6 |
| 63 | 83 | — | — | **OOO BABY BABY** — Miracles, Tamla 54113 | 2 |
| 64 | 52 | 61 | 72 | **PLEASE LET ME WONDER** — Beach Boys, Capitol 5372 | 5 |
| 65 | 80 | — | — | **THE BARRACUDA** — Alvin Cash & the Crawlers, Mar-V-Lus 6005 | 2 |
| 66 | 77 | 84 | — | **NEVER, NEVER LEAVE ME** — Mary Wells, 20th Century-Fox 570 | 3 |
| 67 | 71 | 81 | 89 | **LAND OF A THOUSAND DANCES** — Midnighters, Chattahoochee 666 | 4 |
| 68 | 90 | — | — | **CRAZY DOWNTOWN** — Allan Sherman, Warner Bros. 5614 | 2 |
| 69 | — | — | — | **SHE'S ABOUT A MOVER** — Sir Douglas Quintet, Tribe 8308 | 1 |
| 70 | 85 | 91 | — | **NOT TOO LONG AGO** — Uniques, Paula 219 | 3 |
| 71 | 81 | — | — | **SOMEBODY ELSE IS TAKING MY PLACE** — Al Martino, Capitol 5384 | 2 |
| 72 | 88 | — | — | **THE ENTERTAINER** — Tony Clarke, Chess 1924 | 2 |
| 73 | 89 | — | — | **WE'RE GONNA MAKE IT** — Little Milton, Checker 1105 | 2 |
| 74 | — | — | — | **THE BIRDS ARE FOR THE BEES** — Newbeats, Hickory 1305 | 1 |
| 75 | 82 | 97 | — | **WHIPPED CREAM** — Herb Alpert's Tijuana Brass, A&M 760 | 5 |
| 76 | — | — | — | **SILHOUETTES** — Herman's Hermits, MGM 13332 | 1 |
| 77 | — | — | — | **IT'S GROWING** — Temptations, Gordy 7043 | 1 |
| 78 | — | — | — | **AND ROSES AND ROSES** — Andy Williams, Columbia 43257 | 1 |
| 79 | — | — | — | **WOMAN'S GOT SOUL** — Impressions, ABC-Paramount 10647 | 1 |
| 80 | 95 | 99 | — | **GEE BABY (I'm Sorry)** — 3 Degrees, Swan 4197 | 4 |
| 81 | 92 | — | — | **ALL OF MY LIFE** — Lesley Gore, Mercury 72412 | 2 |
| 82 | 98 | — | — | **I DO LOVE YOU** — Billy Stewart, Chess 1922 | 2 |
| 83 | — | — | — | **SUBTERRANEAN HOMESICK BLUES** — Bob Dylan, Columbia 43242 | 1 |
| 84 | — | — | — | **GOODBYE MY LOVER GOODBYE** — Searchers, Kapp 658 | 1 |
| 85 | — | — | — | **DO THE FREDDIE** — Chubby Checker, Parkway 949 | 1 |
| 86 | — | — | — | **IKO IKO** — Dixie Cups, Red Bird 60024 | 1 |
| 87 | — | — | — | **WOOLY BULLY** — Sam the Sham and the Pharaohs, MGM 13322 | 1 |
| 88 | — | — | — | **COUNT ME IN** — Gary Lewis and the Playboys, Liberty 55778 | 1 |
| 89 | 93 | 93 | — | **DOUBLE-O-SEVEN** — Detergents, Roulette 4603 | 3 |
| 90 | — | — | — | **TRULY, TRULY, TRUE** — Brenda Lee, Decca 31762 | 1 |
| 91 | 91 | 95 | 97 | **LOSING YOU** — Dusty Springfield, Philips 40270 | 4 |
| 92 | 94 | — | — | **THINK OF THE GOOD TIMES** — Jay and the Americans, United Artists 845 | 2 |
| 93 | 99 | — | — | **I CAN'T EXPLAIN** — The Who, Decca 31725 | 2 |
| 94 | — | — | — | **WHY DID I CHOOSE YOU** — Barbra Streisand, Columbia 43248 | 1 |
| 95 | — | — | — | **SEE YOU AT THE "GO GO"** — Dobie Gray, Charger 107 | 1 |
| 96 | — | — | — | **OUT IN THE STREETS** — Shangri Las, Red Bird 10-025 | 1 |
| 97 | 100 | — | — | **EL PUSSY CAT** — Mongo Santamaria, Columbia 43171 | 2 |
| 98 | — | — | — | **THE RECORD** — Ben E. King, Atco 6343 | 1 |
| 99 | — | — | — | **HAWAII HONEYMOON** — Waikikis, Kapp Winners Circle 52 | 1 |
| 100 | — | — | — | **DEAR DAD** — Chuck Berry, Chess 1926 | 1 |

## BUBBLING UNDER THE HOT 100

101. I'VE GOT FIVE DOLLARS AND IT'S SATURDAY NIGHT — George & Gene, Musicor 1066
102. APPLES AND BANANAS — Lawrence Welk, Dot 16697
103. THIS IS IT — Jim Reeves, RCA Victor 8508
104. BABY, PLEASE DON'T GO — Them, Parrot 9727
105. GOLDFINGER — Jimmy Smith, Verve 10346
106. THE GREATEST STORY EVER TOLD — Ferrante & Teicher, United Artists 816
107. YOU CAN HAVE HIM — Dionne Warwick, Scepter 1294
108. TRY TO REMEMBER — Roger Williams, Kapp Winners Circle 48
109. GOLDFINGER — John Barry & His Ork, United Artist 791
110. BEGIN TO LOVE — Robert Goulet, Columbia 43224
111. MEAN OLD WORLD — Rick Nelson, Decca 31756
112. IT'S NOT UNUSUAL — Tom Jones, Parrot 9737
113. SINCE I DON'T HAVE YOU — Four Seasons, Vee Jay 664
114. TELL HER I'M NOT HOME — Ike & Tina Turner, Loma 2011
115. NOW THAT YOU'VE GONE — Connie Stevens, Warner Bros. 5610
116. A DEAR JOHN LETTER — Skeeter Davis & Bobby Bare, RCA Victor 8496
117. TOY SOLDIER — Four Seasons, Philips 40278
118. COME BACK BABY — Rodie Joy, Red Bird 1
119. THAT'LL BE THE DAY — Everly Brothers, Warner Bros. 5611
120. BE MY BABY — Dick and Dee Dee, Warner Bros. 5608
121. BANANA JUICE — Mar-Keys, Stax 166
122. EVERY NIGHT, EVERY DAY — Jimmy McCracklin, Imperial 66094
123. CARMEN — Bruce & Terry, Columbia 43238
124. THIS SPORTING LIFE — Ian Whitcomb, Tower 134
125. I NEED YOU — Chuck Jackson, Wand 179
126. TEASIN' YOU — Willie Tee, Atlantic 2273
127. TOMORROW NIGHT — Damita Jo, Epic 9766
128. SUPER-CALI-FRAGIL-ISTIC-EXPI-ALI-DOCIOUS — Julie Andrews & Dick Van Dyke, Vista 434
129. I'LL KEEP HOLDING ON — Sonny James, Capitol 5375
130. DREAM ON LITTLE DREAMER — Perry Como, RCA Victor 8533
131. DON'T WAIT TOO LONG — Bettye Swann, Money 108
132. MEXICAN PEARLS — Billy Vaughn, Dot 16706
133. GIRL ON THE BILLBOARD — Del Reeves, United Artists 824
134. MEXICAN PEARLS — Don Randi, Palomar 2203
135. LAND OF A THOUSAND DANCES — Round Robin, Domain 1420

Compiled from national retail sales and radio station airplay by the Music Popularity Dept. of Record Market Research, Billboard.

# Billboard

For Week Ending April 10, 1965

# HOT 100

★ **STAR performer—Sides registering greatest proportionate upward progress this week.**

Record Industry Association of America seal of certification as million selling single.

| This Week | 1 Wk. Ago | 2 Wks. Ago | 3 Wks Ago | TITLE Artist, Label & Number | Weeks On Chart |
|---|---|---|---|---|---|
| 1 | 3 | 20 | 42 | **I'M TELLING YOU NOW** — Freddie & the Dreamers, Tower 125 | 5 |
| 2 | 1 | 1 | 2 | **STOP! IN THE NAME OF LOVE** — Supremes, Motown 1074 | 8 |
| 3 | 2 | 2 | 5 | **CAN'T YOU HEAR MY HEARTBEAT** — Herman's Hermits, MGM 13310 | 11 |
| 4 | 4 | 7 | 10 | **SHOTGUN** — Jr. Walker & the All Stars, Soul 35008 | 9 |
| 5 | 5 | 3 | 3 | **THE BIRDS AND THE BEES** — Jewel Akens, Era 3141 | 12 |
| 6 | 6 | 5 | 4 | **KING OF THE ROAD** — Roger Miller, Smash 1965 | 11 |
| ★7 | 17 | 40 | 63 | **GAME OF LOVE** — Wayne Fontana & the Mindbenders, Fontana 1503 | 4 |
| 8 | 9 | 12 | 24 | **NOWHERE TO RUN** — Martha & the Vandellas, Gordy 7039 | 7 |
| ★9 | 28 | 50 | 94 | **I KNOW A PLACE** — Petula Clark, Warner Bros. 5612 | 4 |
| 10 | 10 | 15 | 17 | **RED ROSES FOR A BLUE LADY** — Vic Dana, Dolton 304 | 10 |
| 11 | 7 | 4 | 1 | **EIGHT DAYS A WEEK** — Beatles, Capitol 5371 | 8 |
| 12 | 13 | 16 | 19 | **DO YOU WANNA DANCE?** — Beach Boys, Capitol 5372 | 7 |
| ★13 | 18 | 26 | 43 | **TIRED OF WAITING FOR YOU** — Kinks, Reprise 0347 | 5 |
| 14 | 8 | 8 | 9 | **GOLDFINGER** — Shirley Bassey, United Artists 790 | 11 |
| 15 | 19 | 27 | 46 | **GO NOW** — Moody Blues, London 9726 | 8 |
| ★16 | 22 | 29 | 40 | **THE RACE IS ON** — Jack Jones, Kapp 651 | 7 |
| 17 | 20 | 22 | 34 | **LONG LONELY NIGHTS** — Bobby Vinton, Epic 9768 | 6 |
| 18 | 11 | 6 | 6 | **FERRY CROSS THE MERSEY** — Gerry & the Pacemakers, Laurie 3284 | 10 |
| ★19 | 32 | 42 | 75 | **THE CLAPPING SONG** — Shirley Ellis, Congress 234 | 4 |
| 20 | 14 | 11 | 11 | **RED ROSES FOR A BLUE LADY** — Bert Kaempfert & His Ork, Decca 31722 | 12 |
| 21 | 21 | 23 | 28 | **DO THE CLAM** — Elvis Presley, RCA Victor 8500 | 7 |
| 22 | 26 | 24 | 25 | **SEND ME THE PILLOW YOU DREAM ON** — Dean Martin, Reprise 0344 | 8 |
| 23 | 25 | 25 | 26 | **IF I LOVED YOU** — Chad & Jeremy, World Artists 1041 | 8 |
| ★24 | 29 | 38 | 45 | **RED ROSES FOR A BLUE LADY** — Wayne Newton, Capitol 5366 | 7 |
| ★25 | 42 | 57 | 80 | **I'LL BE DOGGONE** — Marvin Gaye, Tamla 54112 | 4 |
| 26 | 15 | 17 | 22 | **DON'T LET ME BE MISUNDERSTOOD** — Animals, MGM 13311 | 10 |
| 27 | 30 | 39 | 49 | **COME AND STAY WITH ME** — Marianne Faithfull, London 9731 | 7 |
| ★28 | 41 | 63 | 83 | **BUMBLE BEE** — Searchers, Kapp Winners Circle 49 | 4 |
| 29 | 12 | 9 | 7 | **MY GIRL** — Temptations, Gordy 7038 | 13 |
| ★30 | 36 | 37 | 44 | **WHEN I'M GONE** — Brenda Holloway, Tamla, 54111 | 6 |
| ★31 | 46 | 79 | — | **THE LAST TIME** — Rolling Stones, London 9741 | 3 |
| 32 | 35 | 45 | 55 | **GOT TO GET YOU OFF MY MIND** — Solomon Burke, Atlantic 2276 | 6 |
| 33 | 16 | 13 | 18 | **LITTLE THINGS** — Bobby Goldsboro, United Artists 810 | 12 |
| ★34 | 44 | 61 | 82 | **ONE KISS FOR OLD TIMES' SAKE** — Ronnie Dove, Diamond 179 | 5 |
| ★35 | 53 | 64 | 79 | **CAST YOUR FATE TO THE WIND** — Sounds Orchestral, Parkway 942 | 4 |
| 36 | 33 | 33 | 41 | **DON'T MESS UP A GOOD THING** — Fontella Bass & Bobby McClure, Checker 1097 | 10 |
| ★37 | 61 | 84 | — | **I'LL NEVER FIND ANOTHER YOU** — Seekers, Capitol 5383 | 3 |
| 38 | 34 | 35 | 38 | **IF I RULED THE WORLD** — Tony Bennett, Columbia 43220 | 9 |
| 39 | 45 | 48 | 62 | **PEACHES 'N' CREAM** — Ikettes, Modern 1005 | 5 |
| 40 | 31 | 31 | 33 | **I MUST BE SEEING THINGS** — Gene Pitney, Musicor 1070 | 7 |
| 41 | 43 | 51 | 54 | **MR. PITIFUL** — Otis Redding, Volt 124 | 8 |
| ★42 | 63 | 83 | — | **OOO BABY BABY** — Miracles, Tamla 54113 | 3 |
| 43 | 40 | 47 | 53 | **COME SEE** — Major Lance, Okeh 7216 | 6 |
| ★44 | 76 | — | — | **SILHOUETTES** — Herman's Hermits, MGM 13332 | 2 |
| 45 | 49 | 55 | 71 | **LAND OF 1000 DANCES** — Cannibal & the Headhunters, Rampart 642 | 7 |
| 46 | 47 | 54 | 66 | **ANYTIME AT ALL** — Frank Sinatra, Reprise 0350 | 5 |
| ★47 | 57 | 69 | 78 | **I UNDERSTAND** — Freddie & the Dreamers, Mercury 72377 | 5 |
| ★48 | 77 | — | — | **IT'S GROWING** — Temptations, Gordy 7040 | 2 |
| 49 | 52 | 62 | 77 | **GIRL DON'T COME** — Sandie Shaw, Reprise 0342 | 6 |
| ★50 | 69 | — | — | **SHE'S ABOUT A MOVER** — Sir Douglas Quintet, Tribe 8308 | 2 |
| 51 | 59 | 74 | 89 | **BABY THE RAIN MUST FALL** — Glenn Yarbrough, RCA Victor 8498 | 5 |
| 52 | 58 | 73 | 89 | **I CAN'T STOP THINKING OF YOU** — Bobbi Martin, Coral 62447 | 5 |
| 53 | 48 | 56 | 57 | **FOR MAMA** — Connie Francis, MGM 13325 | 6 |
| ★54 | 68 | 90 | — | **CRAZY DOWNTOWN** — Allan Sherman, Warner Bros. 5614 | 3 |
| 55 | 60 | 70 | 85 | **10 LITTLE BOTTLES** — Johnny Bond, Starday 704 | 5 |
| ★56 | — | — | — | **JUST ONCE IN MY LIFE** — Righteous Brothers, Philles 127 | 1 |
| ★57 | 73 | 89 | — | **WE'RE GONNA MAKE IT** — Little Milton, Checker 1105 | 3 |
| 58 | 66 | 77 | 84 | **NEVER, NEVER LEAVE ME** — Mary Wells, 20th Century-Fox 570 | 4 |
| 59 | 54 | 58 | 60 | **FOR MAMA** — Jerry Vale, Columbia 43232 | 6 |
| ★60 | 71 | 81 | — | **SOMEBODY ELSE IS TAKING MY PLACE** — Al Martino, Capitol 5384 | 3 |
| ★61 | 78 | — | — | **AND ROSES AND ROSES** — Andy Williams, Columbia 43257 | 2 |
| ★62 | 88 | — | — | **COUNT ME IN** — Gary Lewis and the Playboys, Liberty 55778 | 2 |
| ★63 | — | — | — | **IT'S GONNA BE ALRIGHT** — Gerry & the Pacemakers, Laurie 3293 | 1 |
| ★64 | 79 | — | — | **WOMAN'S GOT SOUL** — Impressions, ABC-Paramount 10647 | 2 |
| 65 | 65 | 80 | — | **THE BARRACUDA** — Alvin Cash & the Crawlers, Mar-V-Lus 6005 | 3 |
| 66 | 55 | 60 | 67 | **POOR MAN'S SON** — Reflections, Golden World 20 | 5 |
| 67 | 74 | — | — | **THE BIRDS ARE FOR THE BEES** — Newbeats, Hickory 1305 | 2 |
| 68 | 70 | 85 | 91 | **NOT TOO LONG AGO** — Uniques, Paula 219 | 4 |
| 69 | 72 | 88 | — | **THE ENTERTAINER** — Tony Clarke, Chess 1924 | 3 |
| 70 | 56 | 67 | 73 | **FROM ALL OVER THE WORLD** — Jan & Dean, Liberty 55766 | 5 |
| 71 | 82 | 98 | — | **I DO LOVE YOU** — Billy Stewart, Chess 1922 | 3 |
| ★72 | — | — | — | **IT'S GOT THE WHOLE WORLD SHAKIN'** — Sam Cooke, RCA Victor 8539 | 1 |
| ★73 | 90 | — | — | **TRULY, TRULY, TRUE** — Brenda Lee, Decca 31762 | 2 |
| 74 | 83 | — | — | **SUBTERRANEAN HOMESICK BLUES** — Bob Dylan, Columbia 43242 | 2 |
| 75 | 75 | 82 | 97 | **WHIPPED CREAM** — Herb Alpert's Tijuana Brass, A&M 760 | 6 |
| 76 | 84 | — | — | **GOODBYE MY LOVER GOODBYE** — Searchers, Kapp 658 | 2 |
| 77 | 85 | — | — | **DO THE FREDDIE** — Chubby Checker, Parkway 949 | 2 |
| 78 | 81 | 92 | — | **ALL OF MY LIFE** — Lesley Gore, Mercury 72412 | 3 |
| ★79 | 96 | — | — | **OUT IN THE STREETS** — Shangri Las, Red Bird 10-025 | 2 |
| 80 | 80 | 95 | 99 | **GEE BABY (I'm Sorry)** — 3 Degrees, Swan 4197 | 5 |
| 81 | 86 | — | — | **IKO IKO** — Dixie Cups, Red Bird 10-024 | 2 |
| 82 | 87 | — | — | **WOOLY BULLY** — Sam the Sham and the Pharaohs, MGM 13322 | 2 |
| 83 | 92 | 94 | — | **THINK OF THE GOOD TIMES** — Jay and the Americans, United Artists 845 | 3 |
| ★84 | — | — | — | **TOY SOLDIER** — Four Seasons, Philip 40278 | 1 |
| ★85 | — | — | — | **SHE'S COMING HOME** — Zombies, Parrot 9747 | 1 |
| ★86 | — | — | — | **DREAM ON LITTLE DREAMER** — Perry Como, RCA Victor 8533 | 1 |
| 87 | 98 | — | — | **THE RECORD** — Ben E. King, Atco 6343 | 2 |
| ★88 | — | — | 92 | **YOU CAN HAVE HIM** — Dionne Warwick, Scepter 1294 | 3 |
| ★89 | — | — | — | **APPLES AND BANANAS** — Lawaence Welk, Dot 16697 | 1 |
| ★90 | — | — | — | **IT'S NOT UNUSUAL** — Tom Jones, Parrot 9737 | 1 |
| 91 | — | — | — | **EVERY NIGHT, EVERY DAY** — Jimmy McCracklin, Imperial 66094 | 1 |
| 92 | 95 | — | — | **SEE YOU AT THE "GO GO"** — Dobie Gray, Charger 107 | 2 |
| 93 | 94 | — | — | **WHY DID I CHOOSE YOU** — Barbra Streisand, Columbia 43248 | 2 |
| 94 | 99 | — | — | **HAWAII HONEYMOON** — Waikikis, Kapp Winners Circle 52 | 2 |
| 95 | — | — | — | **DON'T LET YOUR LEFT HAND KNOW** — Joe Tex, Dial 4006 | 1 |
| 96 | — | 86 | 90 | **COME BACK BABY** — Roddie Joy, Red Bird 10-021 | 3 |
| 97 | — | — | — | **WHAT DO YOU WANT WITH ME** — Chad & Jeremy, World Artists 1052 | 1 |
| 98 | 100 | — | — | **DEAR DAD** — Chuck Berry, Chess 1926 | 2 |
| 99 | — | — | — | **TRY TO REMEMBER** — Roger Williams, Kapp Winners Circle 48 | 1 |
| 100 | — | — | — | **A WOMAN CAN CHANGE A MAN** — Joe Tex, Dial 4006 | 1 |

## HOT 100—A TO Z—*(Publisher-Licensee)*

All of My Life (Screen Gems-Columbia, BMI) .. 78
And Roses and Roses (Ipanema, ASCAP) ........ 61
Anytime at All (Duchess, BMI) ........ 46
Apples and Bananas (Von Tilzer, ASCAP) ........ 89
Baby the Rain Must Fall (Screen Gems-Columbia, BMI) ........ 51
Barracuda, The (Va-Pac, BMI) ........ 65
Birds and the Bees, The (Pattern, ASCAP) ........ 5
Birds Are for the Bees, The (Acuff-Rose, BMI) .... 67
Bumble Bee (Malapi, BMI) ........ 28
Can't You Hear My Heartbeat (Southern, ASCAP). 3
Cast Your Fate to the Wind (Friendship, BMI) ... 35
Clapping Song, The (Gallico, BMI) ........ 19
Come and Stay With Me (Metric, BMI) ........ 27
Come Back Baby (Trio-Wemar, BMI) ........ 96
Come See (Camad & Chi-Sound, BMI) ........ 43
Count Me In (Skol, BMI) ........ 62
Crazy Downtown (Leeds, ASCAP) ........ 54
Dear Dad (Isalee, BMI) ........ 98
Do the Clam (Gladys, ASCAP) ........ 21
Do the Freddie (Rumbelero & Cameo-Parkway, BMI) ........ 77
Do You Wanna Dance? (Clockus, BMI) ........ 12
Don't Let Me Be Misunderstood (Benjamin, ASCAP) ........ 26
Don't Let Your Left Hand Know (Tree, BMI) ..... 95
Don't Mess Up a Good Thing (Arc-Saico, BMI) .... 36
Dream on Little Dreamer (Forrest Hills-Cedarwood, BMI) ........ 86
Eight Days a Week (Maclen, BMI) ........ 11
Entertainer, The (Chevis, BMI) ........ 69
Every Night, Every Day (Metric, BMI) ........ 91
Ferry Cross the Mersey (Unart-Pacer, BMI) ...... 18
For Mama—Francis (Ludlow, BMI) ........ 53
For Mama—Vale (Ludlow, BMI) ........ 59
From All Over the World (Trousdale, BMI) ...... 70
Game of Love (Skidmore, ASCAP) ........ 7
Gee Baby (I'm Sorry) (Palmina-Zig Zag, BMI) ... 80
Girl Don't Come (Spectorious, BMI) ........ 49
Goldfinger—Bassey (Unart, BMI) ........ 14
Go Now (Trio, BMI) ........ 15
Goodbye My Lover Goodbye (Sea-Lark, BMI) ..... 76
Got to Get You Off My Mind (Cotillion, BMI) ... 32
Hawaii Honeymoon (Zodiac, BMI) ........ 94
I Can't Stop Thinking of You (South Mountain, BMI) ........ 52
I Do Love You (Chevis, BMI) ........ 71
I Know a Place (Duchess, BMI) ........ 9
I Must Be Seeing Things (Sea-Lark, BMI) ........ 40
I Understand (Jubilee, ASCAP) ........ 47
I'll Be Doggone (Jobete, BMI) ........ 25
I'll Never Find Another You (Chappell, ASCAP) .. 37
I'm Telling You Now (Miller, ASCAP) ........ 1
If I Loved You (Chappell, ASCAP) ........ 23
If I Ruled the World (Chappell, ASCAP) ........ 38
Iko Iko (Trio-Melder, BMI) ........ 81
It's Gonna Be Alright (Pacemaker-Unart, BMI) .. 63
It's Growing (Jobete, BMI) ........ 48
It's Got the Whole World Shakin' (Kags, BMI) ... 72
It's Not Unusual (Duchess, BMI) ........ 90
Just Once in My Life (Screen Gems-Columbia, BMI) ........ 56
King of the Road (Tree, BMI) ........ 6
Land of 1000 Dances—Cannibal & the Headhunters (Tune-Kel, BMI) ........ 45
Last Time, The (Immediate, BMI) ........ 31
Little Things (Unart, BMI) ........ 33
Long Lonely Nights (Arc, BMI) ........ 17
Mr. Pitiful (East-Time, BMI) ........ 41
My Girl (Jobete, BMI) ........ 29
Never, Never Leave Me (Merna, BMI) ........ 58
Not Too Long Ago (Gallico, BMI) ........ 68
Nowhere to Run (Jobete, BMI) ........ 8
One Kiss for Old Times' Sake (T. M., BMI) ..... 34
Ooo Baby Baby (Jobete, BMI) ........ 42
Out in the Streets (Trio-Tender Tunes, BMI) ... 79
Peaches 'N' Cream (Screen Gems-Columbia, BMI). 39
Poor Man's Son (Myto, BMI) ........ 66
Race Is On, The (Glad-Acclaim, BMI) ........ 16
Record, The (T. M., BMI) ........ 87
Red Roses for a Blue Lady—Dana (Mills, ASCAP). 10
Red Roses for a Blue Lady—Kaempfert (Mills, ASCAP) ........ 20
Red Roses for a Blue Lady—Newton (Mills, ASCAP) ........ 24
See You at the "Go-Go" (American, BMI) ...... 92
Send Me the Pillow You Dream On (Four Star, BMI) ........ 22
She's About a Mover (Crazy Cajun, BMI) ...... 50
She's Coming Home (Mainstay, BMI) ........ 85
Shotgun (Jobete, BMI) ........ 4
Silhouettes (Regent, BMI) ........ 44
Somebody Else Is Taking My Place (Shapiro-Bernstein, ASCAP) ........ 60
Stop! In the Name of Love (Jobete, BMI) ...... 2
Subterranean Homesick Blues (Witmark, ASCAP) .. 74
10 Little Bottles (Red River, BMI) ........ 55
Think of the Good Times (Picturctone, BMI) ... 83
Tired of Waiting for You (Jay-Boy, BMI) ...... 13
Toy Soldier (Saturday-4 Seasons, BMI) ........ 84
Truly, Truly, True (Leeds, ASCAP) ........ 73
Try to Remember (Chappell, ASCAP) ........ 99
We're Gonna Make It (Chevis, BMI) ........ 57
What Do You Want With Me (WA-A, BMI) ...... 97
When I'm Gone (Jobete, BMI) ........ 30
Whipped Cream (Jarb, BMI) ........ 75
Why Did I Choose You (Mayfair-Emanuel, ASCAP). 93
Woman Can Change a Man, A (Tree, BMI) ......100
Woman's Got Soul (Curtom, BMI) ........ 64
Wooly Bully (Beckie, BMI) ........ 82
You Can Have Him (Harvard-Big Billy, BMI) .... 88

## BUBBLING UNDER THE HOT 100

101. I'VE GOT FIVE DOLLARS AND IT'S SATURDAY NIGHT ........ George & Gene, Musicor 1066
102. GOLDFINGER ........ John Barry & His Ork, United Artists 791
103. DOUBLE-O-SEVEN ........ Detergents, Roulette 4603
104. BABY, PLEASE DON'T GO ........ Them, Parrot 9727
105. SINCE I DON'T HAVE YOU ........ Four Seasons, Vee Jay 664
106. THE GREATEST STORY EVER TOLD ... Ferrante & Teicher, United Artists 816
107. NOTHING CAN STOP ME ........ Gene Chandler, Constellation 149
108. CARMEN ........ Bruce & Terry, Columbia 43238
109. NOW THAT YOU'VE GONE ........ Connie Stevens, Warner Bros. 5610
110. BEGIN TO LOVE ........ Robert Goulet, Columbia 43224
111. THIS IS IT ........ Jim Reeves, RCA Victor 8508
112. LOSING YOU ........ Dusty Springfield, Philips 40270
113. GOLDFINGER ........ Jimmy Smith, Verve 10346
114. THAT'LL BE THE DAY ........ Everly Brothers, Warner Bros. 5611
115. (Somebody) EASE MY TROUBLIN' MIND ...... Sam Cooke, RCA Victor 8539
116. TRUE LOVE WAYS ........ Peter & Gordon, Capitol 5406
117. TEASIN' YOU ........ Willie Tee, Atlantic 2273
118. CHIM CHIM CHEREE ........ New Christy Minstrels, Columbia 43215
119. EL PUSSY CAT ........ Mongo Santamaria, Columbia 43171
120. CHIM CHIM CHEREE ........ Burl Ives, Disneyland 130
121. MEXICAN PEARLS ........ Billy Vaughn, Dot 16706
122. SUPER-CALI-FRAGIL-ISTIC-EXPI-ALI-DOCIOUS ........ Julie Andrews & Dick Van Dyke, Vista 434
123. SHAKIN' ALL OVER ........ The Guess Who's, Scepter 1295
124. TOMORROW NIGHT ........ Damita Jo, Epic 9766
125. I NEED YOU ........ Chuck Jackson, Wand 179
126. TALK ABOUT LOVE ........ Adam Faith, Amy 922
127. GIRL ON THE BILLBOARD ........ Del Reeves, United Artists 824
128. MEXICAN PEARLS ........ Don Randi, Palomar 2203
129. TOMMY ........ Reparata and the Delrons, World Artists 1051
130. GOOD LOVIN' ........ Olympics, Loma 2013
131. DO I HEAR A WALTZ? ........ Eydie Gorme, Columbia 43225
132. T.C.B. ........ Dee Clark, Constellation 147
133. HUSH, HUSH, SWEET CHARLOTTE ........ Patti Page, Columbia 43251
134. CRY ME A RIVER ........ Marie Knight, Musicor 10176
135. GIRL WITH A LITTLE TIN HEART ........ Lettermen, Capitol 5370

Compiled from national retail sales and radio station airplay by the Music Popularity Dept. of Record Market Research, Billboard.

# Billboard HOT 100

**For Week Ending April 17, 1965**

★ STAR performer—Sides registering greatest proportionate upward progress this week.

| This Week | 1 Wk. Ago | 2 Wks. Ago | 3 Wks. Ago | TITLE, Artist, Label & Number | Weeks On Chart |
|---|---|---|---|---|---|
| 1 | 1 | 3 | 20 | I'M TELLING YOU NOW — Freddie & the Dreamers, Tower 125 | 6 |
| 2 | 2 | 1 | 1 | STOP! IN THE NAME OF LOVE — Supremes, Motown 1074 | 9 |
| 3 | 7 | 17 | 40 | GAME OF LOVE — Wayne Fontana & the Mindbenders, Fontana 1503 | 5 |
| 4 | 9 | 28 | 50 | I KNOW A PLACE — Petula Clark, Warner Bros. 5612 | 5 |
| 5 | 4 | 4 | 7 | SHOTGUN — Jr. Walker & the All Stars, Soul 35008 | 10 |
| 6 | 3 | 2 | 2 | CAN'T YOU HEAR MY HEARTBEAT — Herman's Hermits, MGM 13310 | 12 |
| 7 | 13 | 18 | 26 | TIRED OF WAITING FOR YOU — Kinks, Reprise 0347 | 6 |
| 8 | 8 | 9 | 12 | NOWHERE TO RUN — Martha & the Vandellas, Gordy 7039 | 8 |
| 9 | 19 | 32 | 42 | THE CLAPPING SONG — Shirley Ellis, Congress 234 | 5 |
| 10 | 15 | 19 | 27 | GO NOW — Moody Blues, London 9726 | 9 |
| 11 | 6 | 6 | 5 | KING OF THE ROAD — Roger Miller, Smash 1965 | 12 |
| 12 | — | — | — | MRS. BROWN YOU'VE GOT A LOVELY DAUGHTER — Herman's Hermits, MGM 13341 | 1 |
| 13 | 5 | 5 | 3 | THE BIRDS AND THE BEES — Jewel Akens, Era 3141 | 13 |
| 14 | 37 | 61 | 84 | I'LL NEVER FIND ANOTHER YOU — Seekers, Capitol 5383 | 4 |
| 15 | 16 | 22 | 29 | THE RACE IS ON — Jack Jones, Kapp 651 | 8 |
| 16 | 31 | 46 | 79 | THE LAST TIME — Rolling Stones, London 9741 | 4 |
| 17 | 11 | 7 | 4 | EIGHT DAYS A WEEK — Beatles, Capitol 5371 | 9 |
| 18 | 10 | 10 | 15 | RED ROSES FOR A BLUE LADY — Vic Dana, Dolton 304 | 11 |
| 19 | 44 | 76 | — | SILHOUETTES — Herman's Hermits, MGM 13332 | 3 |
| 20 | 25 | 42 | 57 | I'LL BE DOGGONE — Marvin Gaye, Tamla 54112 | 5 |
| 21 | 12 | 13 | 16 | DO YOU WANNA DANCE? — Beach Boys, Capitol 5372 | 8 |
| 22 | 28 | 41 | 63 | BUMBLE BEE — Searchers, Kapp Winners Circle 49 | 5 |
| 23 | 24 | 29 | 38 | RED ROSES FOR A BLUE LADY — Wayne Newton, Capitol 5366 | 8 |
| 24 | 14 | 8 | 8 | GOLDFINGER — Shirley Bassey, United Artists 790 | 12 |
| 25 | 35 | 53 | 64 | CAST YOUR FATE TO THE WIND — Sounds Orchestral, Parkway 942 | 5 |
| 26 | 27 | 30 | 39 | COME AND STAY WITH ME — Marianne Faithfull, London 9731 | 8 |
| 27 | 34 | 44 | 61 | ONE KISS FOR OLD TIMES' SAKE — Ronnie Dove, Diamond 179 | 6 |
| 28 | 17 | 20 | 22 | LONG LONELY NIGHTS — Bobby Vinton, Epic 9768 | 7 |
| 29 | 62 | 88 | — | COUNT ME IN — Gary Lewis and the Playboys, Liberty 55778 | 3 |
| 30 | 30 | 36 | 37 | WHEN I'M GONE — Brenda Holloway, Tamla 54111 | 7 |
| 31 | 56 | — | — | JUST ONCE IN MY LIFE — Righteous Brothers, Philles 127 | 2 |
| 32 | 32 | 35 | 45 | GOT TO GET YOU OFF MY MIND — Solomon Burke, Atlantic 2276 | 7 |
| 33 | 20 | 14 | 11 | RED ROSES FOR A BLUE LADY — Bert Kaempfert & His Ork, Decca 31722 | 13 |
| 34 | 21 | 21 | 23 | DO THE CLAM — Elvis Presley, RCA Victor 8500 | 8 |
| 35 | 45 | 49 | 55 | LAND OF 1000 DANCES — Cannibal & the Headhunters, Rampart 642 | 8 |
| 36 | 39 | 45 | 48 | PEACHES 'N' CREAM — Ikettes, Modern 1005 | 6 |
| 37 | 48 | 77 | — | IT'S GROWING — Temptations, Gordy 7040 | 3 |
| 38 | 51 | 59 | 74 | BABY THE RAIN MUST FALL — Glenn Yarbrough, RCA Victor 8498 | 3 |
| 39 | 50 | 69 | — | SHE'S ABOUT A MOVER — Sir Douglas Quintet, Tribe 8308 | 3 |
| 40 | 42 | 63 | 83 | OOO BABY BABY — Miracles, Tamla 54113 | 4 |
| 41 | 47 | 57 | 69 | I UNDERSTAND — Freddie & the Dreamers, Mercury 72377 | 6 |
| 42 | 23 | 25 | 25 | IF I LOVED YOU — Chad & Jeremy, World Artists 1041 | 9 |
| 43 | 63 | — | — | IT'S GONNA BE ALRIGHT — Gerry & the Pacemakers, Laurie 3293 | 2 |
| 44 | 18 | 11 | 6 | FERRY CROSS THE MERSEY — Gerry & the Pacemakers, Laurie 3284 | 11 |
| 45 | 55 | 60 | 70 | 10 LITTLE BOTTLES — Johnny Bond, Starday 704 | 6 |
| 46 | 64 | 79 | — | WOMAN'S GOT SOUL — Impressions, ABC-Paramount 10647 | 3 |
| 47 | 49 | 52 | 62 | GIRL DON'T COME — Sandie Shaw, Reprise 0342 | 7 |
| 48 | 52 | 58 | 73 | I CAN'T STOP THINKING OF YOU — Bobbi Martin, Coral 62447 | 5 |
| 49 | 54 | 68 | 90 | CRAZY DOWNTOWN — Allan Sherman, Warner Bros. 5614 | 4 |
| 50 | 61 | 78 | — | AND ROSES AND ROSES — Andy Williams, Columbia 43257 | 3 |
| 51 | 22 | 26 | 24 | SEND ME THE PILLOW YOU DREAM ON — Dean Martin, Reprise 0344 | 9 |
| 52 | 57 | 73 | 89 | WE'RE GONNA MAKE IT — Little Milton, Checker 1105 | 4 |
| 53 | 60 | 71 | 81 | SOMEBODY ELSE IS TAKING MY PLACE — Al Martino, Capitol 5384 | 4 |
| 54 | 58 | 66 | 77 | NEVER, NEVER LEAVE ME — Mary Wells, 20th Century-Fox 570 | 5 |
| 55 | 36 | 33 | 33 | DON'T MESS UP A GOOD THING — Fontella Bass & Bobby McClure, Checker 1097 | 11 |
| 56 | 46 | 47 | 54 | ANYTIME AT ALL — Frank Sinatra, Reprise 0350 | 6 |
| 57 | 67 | 74 | — | THE BIRDS ARE FOR THE BEES — Newbeats, Hickory 1305 | 3 |
| 58 | 43 | 40 | 47 | COME SEE — Major Lance, Okeh 7216 | 7 |
| 59 | 72 | — | — | IT'S GOT THE WHOLE WORLD SHAKIN' — Sam Cooke, RCA Victor 8539 | 2 |
| 60 | 71 | 82 | 98 | I DO LOVE YOU — Billy Stewart, Chess 1922 | 4 |
| 61 | 82 | 87 | — | WOOLY BULLY — Sam the Sham and the Pharaohs, MGM 13322 | 3 |
| 62 | 73 | 90 | — | TRULY, TRULY, TRUE — Brenda Lee, Decca 31762 | 3 |
| 63 | 81 | 86 | — | IKO IKO — Dixie Cups, Red Bird 10-024 | 3 |
| 64 | 65 | 65 | 80 | THE BARRACUDA — Alvin Cash & the Crawlers, Mar-V-Lus 6005 | 4 |
| 65 | 74 | 83 | — | SUBTERRANEAN HOMESICK BLUES — Bob Dylan, Columbia 43242 | 3 |
| 66 | 68 | 70 | 85 | NOT TOO LONG AGO — Uniques, Paula 219 | 5 |
| 67 | 79 | 96 | — | OUT IN THE STREETS — Shangri Las, Red Bird 10-025 | 3 |
| 68 | 85 | — | — | SHE'S COMING HOME — Zombies, Parrot 9747 | 2 |
| 69 | 69 | 72 | 88 | THE ENTERTAINER — Tony Clarke, Chess 1924 | 4 |
| 70 | 76 | 84 | — | GOODBYE MY LOVER GOODBYE — Searchers, Kapp 658 | 3 |
| 71 | 86 | — | — | DREAM ON LITTLE DREAMER — Perry Como, RCA Victor 8533 | 2 |
| 72 | 78 | 81 | 92 | ALL OF MY LIFE — Lesley Gore, Mercury 72412 | 4 |
| 73 | 75 | 75 | 82 | WHIPPED CREAM — Herb Alpert's Tijuana Brass, A&M 760 | 4 |
| 74 | 77 | 85 | — | DO THE FREDDIE — Chubby Checker, Parkway 949 | 3 |
| 75 | 90 | — | — | IT'S NOT UNUSUAL — Tom Jones, Parrot 9737 | 2 |
| 76 | 84 | — | — | TOY SOLDIER — 4 Seasons, Philips 40278 | 2 |
| 77 | 83 | 92 | 94 | THINK OF THE GOOD TIMES — Jay and the Americans, United Artists 845 | 4 |
| 78 | 41 | 43 | 51 | MR. PITIFUL — Otis Redding, Volt 124 | 5 |
| 79 | 100 | — | — | A WOMAN CAN CHANGE A MAN — Joe Tex, Dial 4006 | 2 |
| 80 | — | — | — | HELP ME RHONDA — Beach Boys, Capitol 5395 | 1 |
| 81 | — | — | — | JUST A LITTLE — Beau Brummels, Autumn 10 | 1 |
| 82 | — | — | — | TRUE LOVE WAYS — Peter & Gordon, Capitol 5406 | 1 |
| 83 | — | — | — | REELIN' AND ROCKIN' — Dave Clark Five, Epic 9786 | 1 |
| 84 | 87 | 98 | — | THE RECORD — Ben E. King, Atco 6343 | 3 |
| 85 | 88 | — | — | YOU CAN HAVE HIM — Dionne Warwick, Scepter 1294 | 2 |
| 86 | 89 | — | — | APPLES AND BANANAS — Lawrence Welk, Dot 16697 | 2 |
| 87 | 92 | 95 | — | SEE YOU AT THE "GO GO" — Dobie Gray, Charger 107 | 3 |
| 88 | — | — | — | I GOTTA WOMAN — Ray Charles, ABC-Paramount 10649 | 1 |
| 89 | 97 | — | — | WHAT DO YOU WANT WITH ME — Chad & Jeremy, World Artists 1052 | 2 |
| 90 | — | — | — | AL'S PLACE — Al Hirt, RCA Victor 8542 | 1 |
| 91 | 93 | 94 | — | WHY DID I CHOOSE YOU — Barbra Streisand, Columbia 43248 | 3 |
| 92 | 94 | 99 | — | HAWAII HONEYMOON — Waikikis, Kapp Winners Circle 52 | 3 |
| 93 | 96 | — | 86 | COME BACK BABY — Roddie Joy, Red Bird 10-021 | 4 |
| 94 | — | — | — | MEXICAN PEARLS — Billy Vaughn, Dot 16706 | 1 |
| 95 | 98 | 100 | — | DEAR DAD — Chuck Berry, Chess 1926 | 3 |
| 96 | — | — | — | NOTHING CAN STOP ME — Gene Chandler, Constellation 149 | 1 |
| 97 | 99 | — | — | TRY TO REMEMBER — Roger Williams, Kapp Winners Circle 48 | 2 |
| 98 | — | — | — | TALK ABOUT LOVE — Adam Faith, Amy 922 | 1 |
| 99 | — | — | — | I'VE GOT FIVE DOLLARS AND IT'S SATURDAY NIGHT — George & Gene, Musicor 1066 | 1 |
| 100 | — | — | — | YOU WERE ONLY FOOLING — Vic Damone, Warner Bros. 5616 | 1 |

## BUBBLING UNDER THE HOT 100

101. GOLDFINGER — John Barry & His Ork, United Artists 791
102. GEE BABY (I'm Sorry) — 3 Degrees, Swan 4197
103. BABY PLEASE DON'T GO — Them, Parrot 9727
104. PEANUTS — Sunglows, Sunglow 107
105. NOW THAT YOU'VE GONE — Connie Stevens, Warner Bros. 5610
106. SHAKIN' ALL OVER — Guess Who's, Scepter 1295
107. CARMEN — Bruce & Terry, Columbia 43238
108. I CAN'T EXPLAIN — The Who, Decca 31725
109. EVERY NIGHT, EVERY DAY — Jimmy McCracklin, Imperial 66094
110. GOOD LOVIN' — Olympics, Loma 2013
111. THAT'LL BE THE DAY — Everly Brothers, Warner Bros. 5611
112. BOO-GA-LOO — Tom & Jerrio, ABC-Paramount 10638
113. MEXICAN PEARLS — Don Randi, Palomar 2203
114. THE GREATEST STORY EVER TOLD — Ferrante & Teicher, United Artists 816
115. THE MOUSE — Soupy Sales, ABC-Paramount 10646
116. CHIM CHIM CHEREE — New Christy Minstrels, Columbia 43215
117. TOMMY — Reparata & the Delrons, World Artists 1051
118. TOMORROW NEVER COMES — Glen Campbell, Capitol 5360
119. EL PUSSY CAT — Mongo Santamaria, Columbia 43171
120. DEAR DAD — Burl Ives, Disneyland 130
121. SUPER-CALI-FRAGIL-ISTIC-EXPI-ALI-DOCIOUS — Julie Andrews & Dick Van Dyke, Vista 434
122. SAD TOMORROWS — Trini Lopez, Reprise 0328
123. I NEED YOU — Chuck Jackson, Wand 179
124. IN THE MEANTIME — George Fame, Imperial 66104
125. DO I HEAR A WALTZ — Eydie Gorme, Columbia 43225
126. GIRL ON THE BILLBOARD — Del Reeves, United Artists 824
127. HUSH HUSH SWEET CHARLOTTE — Patti Page, Columbia 43225
128. I'M THINKING — Dave Clark Five, Epic 9786
129. CRY ME A RIVER — Marie Knight, Musicor 1076
130. I'LL KEEP HOLDING ON — Sonny James, Capitol 5375
131. I CAN'T HELP IT — Skeeter Davis, RCA Victor 8543
132. QUEEN OF THE HOUSE — Jody Miller, Capitol 5402
133. POOR BOY — Royalettes, MGM 13327
134. I'LL NEVER FALL IN LOVE AGAIN — Bobby Freeman, Autumn 9
135. SHE'S LOST YOU — Zephyrs, Rotate 5006

Compiled from national retail sales and radio station airplay by the Music Popularity Dept. of Record Market Research, Billboard.

# Billboard HOT 100

For Week Ending April 24, 1965

★ STAR performer—Sides registering greatest proportionate upward progress this week.

| This Week | 1 Wk. Ago | 2 Wks. Ago | 3 Wks. Ago | TITLE, Artist, Label & Number | Weeks on Chart |
|---|---|---|---|---|---|
| 1 | 3 | 7 | 17 | GAME OF LOVE — Wayne Fontana & the Mindbenders, Fontana 1503 | 6 |
| 2 | 12 | — | — | MRS. BROWN YOU'VE GOT A LOVELY DAUGHTER — Herman's Hermits, MGM 13341 | 2 |
| 3 | 1 | 1 | 3 | I'M TELLING YOU NOW — Freddie & the Dreamers, Tower 125 | 7 |
| 4 | 4 | 9 | 28 | I KNOW A PLACE — Petula Clark, Warner Bros. 5612 | 6 |
| 5 | 2 | 2 | 1 | STOP! IN THE NAME OF LOVE — Supremes, Motown 1074 | 10 |
| 6 | 7 | 13 | 18 | TIRED OF WAITING FOR YOU — Kinks, Reprise 0347 | 7 |
| 7 | 14 | 37 | 61 | I'LL NEVER FIND ANOTHER YOU — Seekers, Capitol 5383 | 5 |
| 8 | 9 | 19 | 32 | THE CLAPPING SONG — Shirley Ellis, Congress 234 | 6 |
| 9 | 5 | 4 | 4 | SHOTGUN — Jr. Walker & the All Stars, Soul 35008 | 11 |
| 10 | 19 | 44 | 76 | SILHOUETTES — Herman's Hermits, MGM 13332 | 4 |
| 11 | 29 | 62 | 88 | COUNT ME IN — Gary Lewis and the Playboys, Liberty 55778 | 4 |
| 12 | 16 | 31 | 46 | THE LAST TIME — Rolling Stones, London 9741 | 5 |
| 13 | 10 | 15 | 19 | GO NOW — Moody Blues, London 9726 | 10 |
| 14 | 8 | 8 | 9 | NOWHERE TO RUN — Martha & the Vandellas, Gordy 7039 | 9 |
| 15 | 15 | 16 | 22 | THE RACE IS ON — Jack Jones, Kapp 651 | 9 |
| 16 | 6 | 3 | 2 | CAN'T YOU HEAR MY HEARTBEAT — Herman's Hermits, MGM 13310 | 13 |
| 17 | 25 | 35 | 53 | CAST YOUR FATE TO THE WIND — Sounds Orchestral, Parkway 942 | 6 |
| 18 | 20 | 25 | 42 | I'LL BE DOGGONE — Marvin Gaye, Tamla 54112 | 6 |
| 19 | 27 | 34 | 44 | ONE KISS FOR OLD TIMES' SAKE — Ronnie Dove, Diamond 179 | 7 |
| 20 | 31 | 56 | — | JUST ONCE IN MY LIFE — Righteous Brothers, Philles 127 | 3 |
| 21 | 22 | 28 | 41 | BUMBLE BEE — Searchers, Kapp Winners Circle 49 | 6 |
| 22 | 37 | 48 | 77 | IT'S GROWING — Temptations, Gordy 7040 | 4 |
| 23 | 11 | 6 | 6 | KING OF THE ROAD — Roger Miller, Smash 1965 | 13 |
| 24 | 32 | 32 | 35 | GOT TO GET YOU OFF MY MIND — Solomon Burke, Atlantic 2276 | 8 |
| 25 | 30 | 30 | 36 | WHEN I'M GONE — Brenda Holloway, Tamla 54111 | 8 |
| 26 | 13 | 5 | 5 | THE BIRDS AND THE BEES — Jewel Akens, Era 3141 | 14 |
| 27 | 18 | 10 | 10 | RED ROSES FOR A BLUE LADY — Vic Dana, Dolton 304 | 12 |
| 28 | 38 | 51 | 59 | BABY THE RAIN MUST FALL — Glenn Yarbrough, RCA Victor 8498 | 7 |
| 29 | 40 | 42 | 63 | OOO BABY BABY — Miracles, Tamla 54113 | 5 |
| 30 | 35 | 45 | 49 | LAND OF 1000 DANCES — Cannibal & the Headhunters, Rampart 642 | 9 |
| 31 | 26 | 27 | 30 | COME AND STAY WITH ME — Marianne Faithfull, London 9731 | 9 |
| 32 | 43 | 63 | — | IT'S GONNA BE ALRIGHT — Gerry & the Pacemakers, Laurie 3293 | 3 |
| 33 | 23 | 24 | 29 | RED ROSES FOR A BLUE LADY — Wayne Newton, Capitol 5366 | 9 |
| 34 | 46 | 64 | 79 | WOMAN'S GOT SOUL — Impressions, ABC-Paramount 10647 | 4 |
| 35 | 39 | 50 | 69 | SHE'S ABOUT A MOVER — Sir Douglas Quintet, Tribe 8308 | 4 |
| 36 | 36 | 39 | 45 | PEACHES 'N' CREAM — Ikettes, Modern 1005 | 7 |
| 37 | 52 | 57 | 73 | WE'RE GONNA MAKE IT — Little Milton, Checker 1105 | 5 |
| 38 | 17 | 11 | 7 | EIGHT DAYS A WEEK — Beatles, Capitol 5371 | 10 |
| 39 | 41 | 47 | 57 | I UNDERSTAND — Freddie & the Dreamers, Mercury 72377 | 7 |
| 40 | 50 | 61 | 78 | AND ROSES AND ROSES — Andy Williams, Columbia 43257 | 4 |
| 41 | 60 | 71 | 82 | I DO LOVE YOU — Billy Stewart, Chess 1922 | 5 |
| 42 | 47 | 49 | 52 | GIRL DON'T COME — Sandie Shaw, Reprise 0342 | 8 |
| 43 | 45 | 55 | 60 | 10 LITTLE BOTTLES — Johnny Bond, Starday 704 | 7 |
| 44 | 49 | 54 | 68 | CRAZY DOWNTOWN — Allan Sherman, Warner Bros. 5614 | 5 |
| 45 | 61 | 82 | 87 | WOOLY BULLY — Sam the Sham and the Pharaohs, MGM 13222 | 4 |
| 46 | 48 | 52 | 58 | I CAN'T STOP THINKING OF YOU — Bobbi Martin, Coral 62447 | 7 |
| 47 | 24 | 14 | 8 | GOLDFINGER — Shirley Bassey, United Artists 790 | 13 |
| 48 | 75 | 90 | — | IT'S NOT UNUSUAL — Tom Jones, Parrot 9737 | 3 |
| 49 | 59 | 72 | — | IT'S GOT THE WHOLE WORLD SHAKIN' — Sam Cooke, RCA Victor 8539 | 3 |
| 50 | 63 | 81 | 86 | IKO IKO — Dixie Cups, Red Bird 10-024 | 4 |
| 51 | 71 | 86 | — | DREAM ON LITTLE DREAMER — Perry Como, RCA Victor 8533 | 3 |
| 52 | 69 | 69 | 72 | THE ENTERTAINER — Tony Clarke, Chess 1924 | 5 |
| 53 | 53 | 60 | 71 | SOMEBODY ELSE IS TAKING MY PLACE — Al Martino, Capitol 5384 | 5 |
| 54 | 57 | 67 | 74 | THE BIRDS ARE FOR THE BEES — Newbeats, Hickory 1305 | 4 |
| 55 | 65 | 74 | 83 | SUBTERRANEAN HOMESICK BLUES — Bob Dylan, Columbia 43242 | 4 |
| 56 | 62 | 73 | 90 | TRULY, TRULY, TRUE — Brenda Lee, Decca 31762 | 4 |
| 57 | 67 | 79 | 96 | OUT IN THE STREETS — Shangri Las, Red Bird 10-025 | 4 |
| 58 | 68 | 85 | — | SHE'S COMING HOME — Zombies, Parrot 9747 | 3 |
| 59 | — | — | — | TICKET TO RIDE — Beatles, Capitol 5407 | 1 |
| 60 | 74 | 77 | 85 | DO THE FREDDIE — Chubby Checker, Parkway 949 | 4 |
| 61 | 81 | — | — | JUST A LITTLE — Beau Brummels, Autumn 10 | 2 |
| 62 | 64 | 65 | 65 | THE BARRACUDA — Alvin Cash & the Crawlers, Mar-V-Lus 6005 | 5 |
| 63 | 82 | — | — | TRUE LOVE WAYS — Peter & Gordon, Capitol 5406 | 2 |
| 64 | 79 | 100 | — | A WOMAN CAN CHANGE A MAN — Joe Tex, Dial 4006 | 3 |
| 65 | 80 | — | — | HELP ME RHONDA — Beach Boys, Capitol 5395 | 2 |
| 66 | 70 | 76 | 84 | GOODBYE MY LOVER GOODBYE — Searchers, Kapp 658 | 4 |
| 67 | 83 | — | — | REELIN' AND ROCKIN' — Dave Clark Five, Epic 9786 | 2 |
| 68 | 54 | 58 | 66 | NEVER, NEVER LEAVE ME — Mary Wells, 20th Century-Fox 570 | 6 |
| 69 | 76 | 84 | — | TOY SOLDIER — 4 Seasons, Philips 40278 | 3 |
| 70 | 66 | 68 | 70 | NOT TOO LONG AGO — Uniques, Paula 219 | 6 |
| 71 | 72 | 78 | 81 | ALL OF MY LIFE — Lesley Gore, Mercury 72412 | 5 |
| 72 | 77 | 83 | 92 | THINK OF THE GOOD TIMES — Jay and the Americans, United Artists 845 | 5 |
| 73 | 73 | 75 | 75 | WHIPPED CREAM — Herb Alpert's Tijuana Brass, A&M 760 | 8 |
| 74 | 89 | 97 | — | WHAT DO YOU WANT WITH ME — Chad & Jeremy, World Artists 1052 | 3 |
| 75 | 86 | 89 | — | APPLES AND BANANAS — Lawrence Welk, Dot 16697 | 3 |
| 76 | 87 | 92 | 95 | SEE YOU AT THE "GO GO" — Dobie Gray, Charger 107 | 4 |
| 77 | 85 | 88 | — | YOU CAN HAVE HIM — Dionne Warwick, Scepter 1294 | 5 |
| 78 | — | — | — | DO THE FREDDIE — Freddie & the Dreamers, Mercury 72428 | 1 |
| 79 | — | — | — | CRYING IN THE CHAPEL — Elvis Presley, RCA Victor 0643 | 1 |
| 80 | — | — | — | NOW THAT YOU'VE GONE — Connie Stevens, Warner Bros. 5610 | 1 |
| 81 | 96 | — | — | NOTHING CAN STOP ME — Gene Chandler, Constellation 149 | 2 |
| 82 | 88 | — | — | I GOTTA WOMAN — Ray Charles, ABC-Paramount 10649 | 2 |
| 83 | — | — | — | I NEED YOU — Chuck Jackson, Wand 179 | 1 |
| 84 | 91 | 93 | 94 | WHY DID I CHOOSE YOU — Barbra Streisand, Columbia 43248 | 4 |
| 85 | — | — | — | QUEEN OF THE HOUSE — Jody Miller, Capitol 5402 | 1 |
| 86 | 90 | — | — | AL'S PLACE — Al Hirt, RCA Victor 8542 | 2 |
| 87 | — | — | — | SUPER-CALI-FRAGIL-ISTIC-EXPI-ALI-DOCIOUS — Julie Andrews & Dick Van Dyke, Vista 434 | 1 |
| 88 | — | — | — | CHIM, CHIM, CHEREE — New Christy Minstrels, Columbia 43215 | 1 |
| 89 | — | — | — | SOMETHING YOU GOT — Chuck Jackson & Maxine Brown, Wand 181 | 1 |
| 90 | — | — | — | CHAINS OF LOVE — Drifters, Atlantic 2285 | 1 |
| 91 | 92 | 94 | 99 | HAWAII HONEYMOON — Waikikis, Kapp Winners Circle 52 | 4 |
| 92 | 93 | 96 | — | COME BACK BABY — Roddie Joy, Red Bird 10-021 | 5 |
| 93 | — | — | — | AIN'T NO TELLING — Bobby Bland, Duke 390 | 1 |
| 94 | 94 | — | — | MEXICAN PEARLS — Billy Vaughn, Dot 16706 | 2 |
| 95 | 95 | 98 | 100 | DEAR DAD — Chuck Berry, Chess 1926 | 4 |
| 96 | 100 | — | — | YOU WERE ONLY FOOLING — Vic Damone, Warner Bros. 5616 | 2 |
| 97 | 98 | — | — | TALK ABOUT LOVE — Adam Faith, Amy 922 | 2 |
| 98 | — | — | — | HUSH, HUSH, SWEET CHARLOTTE — Patti Page, Columbia 43251 | 1 |
| 99 | — | — | — | COME ON OVER TO MY PLACE — Drifters, Atlantic 2285 | 1 |
| 100 | — | — | — | THE MOUSE — Soupy Sales, ABC-Paramount 10646 | 1 |

## HOT 100—A TO Z—(Publisher-Licensee)

Ain't No Telling (Don, BMI) .............. 93
Al's Place (Dymor, ASCAP) .............. 86
All of My Life (Screen Gems-Columbia, BMI) .. 71
And Roses and Roses (Ipanema, ASCAP) .... 40
Apples and Bananas (Von Tilzer, ASCAP) ... 75
Baby the Rain Must Fall (Screen Gems-Columbia, BMI) ........................................ 28
Barracuda, The (Va-Pac, BMI) ............ 62
Birds and the Bees, The (Pattern, ASCAP) .. 26
Birds Are for the Bees (Acuff-Rose, BMI) ... 54
Bumble Bee (Malapi, BMI) ................ 21
Can't You Hear My Heartbeat (Southern, ASCAP) .................................. 16
Cast Your Fate to the Wind (Friendship, BMI) 17
Chains of Love (Stillran-Downstairs-Web IV, BMI) 90
Chim, Chim, Cheree (Wonderland, ASCAP) ... 88
Clapping Song, The (Gallico, BMI) ........ 8
Come and Stay With Me (Metric, BMI) ..... 31
Come Back Baby (Trio-Wemar, BMI) ....... 92
Come on Over to My Place (Screen Gems-Columbia, BMI) .................................. 99
Count Me In (Skol, BMI) .................. 11
Crazy Downtown (Leeds, ASCAP) .......... 44
Crying in the Chapel (Valley, BMI) ........ 79
Dear Dad (Isalee, BMI) ................... 95
Do the Freddie (Wumbelero & Cameo-Parkway, BMI) 60
Do the Freddie (Fling-Paoheal, BMI) ....... 78
Dream on Little Dreamer (Forrest Hills-Cedarwood, BMI) .................................. 51
Eight Days a Week (Maclen, BMI) ......... 38
Entertainer, The (Chevis, BMI) ............ 52
Game of Love (Skidmore, ASCAP) .......... 1
Girl Don't Come (Spectorious, BMI) ....... 42
Goldfinger (Unart, BMI) .................. 47
Go Now (Trio, BMI) ...................... 13
Goodbye My Lover Goodbye (Sea-Lark, BMI) 66
Got to Get You Off My Mind (Cotillion, BMI) 24
Hawaii Honeymoon (Zodiac, BMI) .......... 91
Help Me Ronda (Sea of Tunes, BMI) ....... 65
Hush, Hush, Sweet Charlotte (Witmark, ASCAP) 98
I Can't Stop Thinking of You (South Mountain, BMI) .................................. 46
I Do Love You (Chevis, BMI) .............. 41
I Gotta Woman (Progressive, BMI) ........ 82
I Know a Place (Duchess, BMI) ............ 4
I Need You (Screen Gems-Columbia, BMI) .. 83
I Understand (Jubilee, ASCAP) ............ 39
I'll Be Doggone (Jobete, BMI) ............. 18
I'll Never Find Another You (Chappell, ASCAP) 7
I'm Telling You Now (Miller, ASCAP) ....... 3
Iko Iko (Trio-Melder, BMI) ................ 50
It's Gonna Be Alright (Pacemaker-Unart, BMI) 32
It's Growing (Jobete, BMI) ................ 22
It's Got the Whole World Shakin' (Kags, BMI) 49
It's Not Unusual (Duchess, BMI) .......... 48
Just a Little (Taracrest, BMI) ............. 61
Just Once in My Life (Screen Gems-Columbia, BMI) .................................. 20
King of the Road (Tree, BMI) .............. 23
Land of 1000 Dances (Tune-Kel, BMI) ...... 30
Last Time, The (Immediate, BMI) .......... 12
Mexican Pearls (Englewood, BMI) .......... 94
Mouse, The (Starday, BMI) ................ 100
Mrs. Brown You've Got a Lovely Daughter (Bratenbury-Hill & Range, BMI) ............ 2
Never, Never Leave Me (Merna, BMI) ...... 68
Not Too Long Ago (Gallico, BMI) ........... 70
Nothing Can Stop Me (Camad, BMI) ....... 81
Now That You've Gone (Leeds, ASCAP) ..... 80
Nowhere to Run (Jobete, BMI) ............ 14
One Kiss for Old Times' Sake (T.M., BMI) .. 19
Ooo Baby Baby (Jobete, BMI) ............. 29
Out in the Streets (Trio-Tender Tunes, BMI) 57
Peaches 'n' Cream (Screen Gems-Columbia, BMI) 36
Queen of the House (Tree, BMI) ........... 85
Race Is On, The (Glad-Acclaim, BMI) ...... 15
Red Roses for a Blue Lady—Dana (Mills, ASCAP) 27
Red Roses for a Blue Lady—Newton (Mills, ASCAP) 33
Reelin' and Rockin' (Arc, BMI) ............ 67
See You at the "Go-Go" (American, BMI) .. 76
She's About a Mover (Crazy Cajun, BMI) .. 35
She's Coming Home (Mainstay, BMI) ...... 58
Shotgun (Jobete, BMI) .................... 9
Silhouettes (Regent, BMI) ................ 10
Somebody Else Is Taking My Place (Shapiro-Bernstein, ASCAP) ..................... 53
Something You Got (Tune-Kel, BMI) ....... 89
Stop! In the Name of Love (Jobete, BMI) .. 5
Subterranean Homesick Blues (Witmark, ASCAP) 55
Super-Cali-Fragil-Istic-Expi-Ali-Docious (Wonderland, BMI) .................................. 87
Talk About Love (Rose Hill, BMI) .......... 97
10 Little Bottles (Red River, BMI) ......... 43
Think of the Good Times (Picturestone, BMI) 72
Ticket to Ride (Maclen, BMI) .............. 59
Tired of Waiting for You (Jay-Boy, BMI) ... 6
Toy Soldier (Saturday-4 Seasons, BMI) .... 69
True Love Ways (Nor-Va-Jak, BMI) ........ 63
Truly, Truly, True (Leeds, ASCAP) ......... 56
We're Gonna Make It (Chevis, BMI) ........ 37
What Do You Want With Me (WA-A, BMI) .. 74
When I'm Gone (Jobete, BMI) ............. 25
Whipped Cream (Jarb, BMI) ............... 73
Why Did I Choose You (Mayfair-Emanuel, ASCAP) 84
Woman Can Change a Man, A (Tree, BMI) .. 64
Woman's Got Soul (Curtom, BMI) .......... 34
Wooly Bully (Beckie, BMI) ................ 45
You Can Have Him (Harvard-Big Billy, BMI) . 77
You Were Only Fooling (Shapiro-Bernstein, BMI) 96

## BUBBLING UNDER THE HOT 100

101. PEANUTS .......... Sunglows, Sunglow 107
102. BABY, PLEASE DON'T GO .......... Them, Parrot 9727
103. SHAKIN' ALL OVER .......... Guess Who's, Scepter 1295
104. GOOD LOVIN' .......... Olympics, Loma 2013
105. I'VE GOT FIVE DOLLARS AND IT'S SATURDAY NIGHT .......... George & Gene, Musicor 1066
106. BOO-GA-LOO .......... Tom & Jerrio, ABC-Paramount 10638
107. TRY TO REMEMBER .......... Roger Williams, Kapp Winners Circle 48
108. I CAN'T EXPLAIN .......... Who, Decca 31725
109. GOLDFINGER .......... John Barry & His Ork., United Artists 791
110. GEE BABY (I'm Sorry) .......... Three Degrees, Swan 4197
111. TOMMY .......... Reparata & the Delrons, World Artists 1051
112. EVERY NIGHT, EVERY DAY .......... Jimmy McCracklin, Imperial 66094
113. SAD TOMORROWS .......... Trini Lopez, Reprise 0328
114. DEVIL'S HIDEAWAY .......... James Brown, Smash 1975
115. YES IT IS .......... Beatles, Capitol 5407
116. I'LL KEEP HOLDING ON .......... Sonny James, Capitol 5375
117. GOTTA HAVE YOUR LOVE .......... Sapphires, ABC-Paramount 10639
118. IN THE MEANTIME .......... Georgie Fame, Imperial 66104
119. GIRL ON THE BILLBOARD .......... Del Reeves, United Artists 824
120. CHIM CHIM CHEREE .......... Burl Ives, Disneyland 130
121. DO I HEAR A WALTZ .......... Eydie Gorme, Columbia 43225
122. CONCRETE AND CLAY .......... Unit Four Plus Two, London 9751
123. CRY ME A RIVER .......... Marie Knight, Musicor 1076
124. CONCRETE AND CLAY .......... Eddie Rambeau, Dyno Voice 204
125. I CAN'T HELP IT .......... Skeeter Davis, RCA Victor 8543
126. EL PUSSY CAT .......... Mongo Santamaria, Columbia 43171
127. LIPSTICK TRACES .......... O'Jays, Imperial 66102
128. WHO KNOWS .......... Gladys Knight & the Pips, Maxx 334
129. SAD TOMORROWS .......... Betty Everett, Capitol
130. I'LL CRY ALONE .......... Gale Garnett, RCA Victor 8554
131. IT WAS EASIER TO HURT HER .......... Garnet Mimms, United Artists 848
132. I'LL NEVER FALL IN LOVE AGAIN .......... Bobby Freeman, Autumn 9
133. VENICE BLUE .......... Bobby Darin, Capitol 5399
134. I CAN'T REMEMBER .......... Connie Smith, RCA Victor 8551
135. SEA CRUISE .......... Ace Cannon, Hi 2089

Compiled from national retail sales and radio station airplay by the Music Popularity Dept. of Record Market Research, Billboard.

# Billboard HOT 100

**For Week Ending May 1, 1965**

★ STAR performer—Sides registering greatest proportionate upward progress this week.

| This Week | 1 Wk. Ago | 2 Wks. Ago | 3 Wks. Ago | TITLE — Artist, Label & Number | Weeks On Chart |
|---|---|---|---|---|---|
| 1 | 2 | 12 | — | **MRS. BROWN YOU'VE GOT A LOVELY DAUGHTER** — Herman's Hermits, MGM 13341 | 3 |
| 2 | 1 | 3 | 7 | **GAME OF LOVE** — Wayne Fontana & the Mindbenders, Fontana 1503 | 7 |
| 3 | 4 | 4 | 9 | **I KNOW A PLACE** — Petula Clark, Warner Bros. 5612 | 7 |
| 4 | 3 | 1 | 1 | **I'M TELLING YOU NOW** — Freddie & the Dreamers, Tower 125 | 8 |
| 5 | 7 | 14 | 37 | **I'LL NEVER FIND ANOTHER YOU** — Seekers, Capitol 5383 | 6 |
| 6 | 6 | 7 | 13 | **TIRED OF WAITING FOR YOU** — Kinks, Reprise 0347 | 8 |
| ★7 | 11 | 29 | 62 | **COUNT ME IN** — Gary Lewis and the Playboys, Liberty 55778 | 5 |
| 8 | 10 | 19 | 44 | **SILHOUETTES** — Herman's Hermits, MGM 13332 | 5 |
| ★9 | 12 | 16 | 31 | **THE LAST TIME** — Rolling Stones, London 9741 | 6 |
| 10 | 5 | 2 | 2 | **STOP! IN THE NAME OF LOVE** — Supremes, Motown 1074 | 11 |
| 11 | 8 | 9 | 19 | **THE CLAPPING SONG** — Shirley Ellis, Congress 234 | 7 |
| 12 | 17 | 25 | 35 | **CAST YOUR FATE TO THE WIND** — Sounds Orchestral, Parkway 942 | 7 |
| 13 | 13 | 10 | 15 | **GO NOW** — Moody Blues, London 9726 | 11 |
| 14 | 18 | 20 | 25 | **I'LL BE DOGGONE** — Marvin Gaye, Tamla 54112 | 7 |
| 15 | 19 | 27 | 34 | **ONE KISS FOR OLD TIMES' SAKE** — Ronnie Dove, Diamond 179 | 8 |
| 16 | 9 | 5 | 4 | **SHOTGUN** — Jr. Walker & the All Stars, Soul 35008 | 12 |
| 17 | 20 | 31 | 56 | **JUST ONCE IN MY LIFE** — Righteous Brothers, Philles 127 | 4 |
| ★18 | 59 | — | — | **TICKET TO RIDE** — Beatles, Capitol 5407 | 2 |
| ★19 | 29 | 40 | 42 | **OOO BABY BABY** — Miracles, Tamla 54113 | 6 |
| 20 | 22 | 37 | 48 | **IT'S GROWING** — Temptations, Gordy 7040 | 5 |
| 21 | 28 | 38 | 51 | **BABY THE RAIN MUST FALL** — Glenn Yarbrough, RCA Victor 8498 | 8 |
| 22 | 24 | 32 | 32 | **GOT TO GET YOU OFF MY MIND** — Solomon Burke, Atlantic 2276 | 9 |
| 23 | 14 | 8 | 8 | **NOWHERE TO RUN** — Martha & the Vandellas, Gordy 7039 | 10 |
| ★24 | 45 | 61 | 82 | **WOOLY BULLY** — Sam the Sham and the Pharaohs, MGM 13322 | 5 |
| 25 | 16 | 6 | 3 | **CAN'T YOU HEAR MY HEARTBEAT** — Herman's Hermits, MGM 13310 | 14 |
| ★26 | 32 | 43 | 63 | **IT'S GONNA BE ALRIGHT** — Gerry & the Pacemakers, Laurie 3293 | 4 |
| 27 | 15 | 15 | 16 | **THE RACE IS ON** — Jack Jones, Kapp 651 | 10 |
| 28 | 48 | 75 | 90 | **IT'S NOT UNUSUAL** — Tom Jones, Parrot 9737 | 4 |
| 29 | 21 | 22 | 28 | **BUMBLE BEE** — Searchers, Kapp Winners Circle 49 | 7 |
| 30 | 30 | 35 | 45 | **LAND OF 1000 DANCES** — Cannibal & the Headhunters, Rampart 642 | 10 |
| ★31 | 41 | 60 | 71 | **I DO LOVE YOU** — Billy Stewart, Chess 1922 | 6 |
| 32 | 35 | 39 | 50 | **SHE'S ABOUT A MOVER** — Sir Douglas Quintet, Tribe 8308 | 5 |
| 33 | 34 | 46 | 64 | **WOMAN'S GOT SOUL** — Impressions, ABC-Paramount 10647 | 5 |
| 34 | 37 | 52 | 57 | **WE'RE GONNA MAKE IT** — Little Milton, Checker 1105 | 6 |
| ★35 | 65 | 80 | — | **HELP ME RHONDA** — Beach Boys, Capitol 5395 | 3 |
| 36 | 39 | 41 | 47 | **I UNDERSTAND** — Freddie & the Dreamers, Mercury 72377 | 8 |
| 37 | 40 | 50 | 61 | **AND ROSES AND ROSES** — Andy Williams, Columbia 43257 | 5 |
| 38 | 36 | 36 | 39 | **PEACHES 'N' CREAM** — Ikettes, Modern 1005 | 8 |
| ★39 | 50 | 63 | 81 | **IKO IKO** — Dixie Cups, Red Bird 10-024 | 5 |
| ★40 | 51 | 71 | 86 | **DREAM ON LITTLE DREAMER** — Perry Como, RCA Victor 8533 | 4 |
| 41 | 44 | 49 | 54 | **CRAZY DOWNTOWN** — Allan Sherman, Warner Bros. 5614 | 3 |
| 42 | 52 | 69 | 69 | **THE ENTERTAINER** — Tony Clarke, Chess 1924 | 6 |
| ★43 | 67 | 83 | — | **REELIN' AND ROCKIN'** — Dave Clark Five, Epic 9786 | 3 |
| 44 | 55 | 65 | 74 | **SUBTERRANEAN HOMESICK BLUES** — Bob Dylan, Columbia 43242 | 5 |
| 45 | 49 | 59 | 72 | **IT'S GOT THE WHOLE WORLD SHAKIN'** — Sam Cooke, RCA Victor 8539 | 4 |
| 46 | 25 | 30 | 30 | **WHEN I'M GONE** — Brenda Holloway, Tamla 54111 | 9 |
| ★47 | 63 | 82 | — | **TRUE LOVE WAYS** — Peter & Gordon, Capitol 5406 | 3 |
| 48 | 61 | 81 | — | **JUST A LITTLE** — Beau Brummels, Autumn 10 | 3 |
| 49 | 42 | 47 | 49 | **GIRL DON'T COME** — Sandie Shaw, Reprise 0342 | 6 |
| 50 | 60 | 74 | 77 | **DO THE FREDDIE** — Chubby Checker, Parkway 949 | 4 |
| ★51 | 79 | — | — | **CRYING IN THE CHAPEL** — Elvis Presley, RCA Victor 0643 | 2 |
| 52 | 54 | 57 | 67 | **THE BIRDS ARE FOR THE BEES** — Newbeats, Hickory 1305 | 5 |
| 53 | 57 | 67 | 79 | **OUT IN THE STREETS** — Shangri Las, Red Bird 10-025 | 4 |
| 54 | 56 | 62 | 73 | **TRULY, TRULY, TRUE** — Brenda Lee, Decca 31762 | 4 |
| 55 | 66 | 70 | 76 | **GOODBYE MY LOVER GOODBYE** — Searchers, Kapp 658 | 4 |
| 56 | 46 | 48 | 52 | **I CAN'T STOP THINKING OF YOU** — Bobbi Martin, Coral 62447 | 8 |
| 57 | 53 | 53 | 60 | **SOMEBODY ELSE IS TAKING MY PLACE** — Al Martino, Capitol 5384 | 6 |
| 58 | 58 | 68 | 85 | **SHE'S COMING HOME** — Zombies, Parrot 9747 | 4 |
| 59 | 62 | 64 | 65 | **THE BARRACUDA** — Alvin Cash & the Crawlers, Mar-V-Lus 6005 | 4 |
| 60 | 72 | 77 | 83 | **THINK OF THE GOOD TIMES** — Jay and the Americans, United Artists 845 | 6 |
| 61 | 64 | 79 | 100 | **A WOMAN CAN CHANGE A MAN** — Joe Tex, Dial 4006 | 4 |
| 62 | 74 | 89 | 97 | **WHAT DO YOU WANT WITH ME** — Chad & Jeremy, World Artists 1052 | 3 |
| ★63 | 78 | — | — | **DO THE FREDDIE** — Freddie & the Dreamers, Mercury 72428 | 2 |
| 64 | 69 | 76 | 84 | **TOY SOLDIER** — 4 Seasons, Philips 40278 | 4 |
| 65 | 43 | 45 | 55 | **10 LITTLE BOTTLES** — Johnny Bond, Starday 704 | 8 |
| ★66 | — | — | — | **YOU WERE MADE FOR ME** — Freddie & the Dreamers, Tower 127 | 1 |
| ★67 | 85 | — | — | **QUEEN OF THE HOUSE** — Jody Miller, Capitol 5402 | 2 |
| ★68 | — | — | — | **BACK IN MY ARMS AGAIN** — Supremes, Motown 1075 | 1 |
| 69 | 76 | 87 | 92 | **SEE YOU AT THE "GO GO"** — Dobie Gray, Charger 107 | 5 |
| 70 | 73 | 73 | 75 | **WHIPPED CREAM** — Herb Alpert's Tijuana Brass, A&M 760 | 9 |
| ★71 | — | — | — | **YES IT IS** — Beatles, Capitol 5407 | 1 |
| 72 | 81 | 96 | — | **NOTHING CAN STOP ME** — Gene Chandler, Constellation 149 | 3 |
| 73 | 80 | — | — | **NOW THAT YOU'VE GONE** — Connie Stevens, Warner Bros. 5610 | 2 |
| ★74 | 89 | — | — | **SOMETHING YOU GOT** — Chuck Jackson & Maxine Brown, Wand 181 | 2 |
| 75 | 77 | 85 | 88 | **YOU CAN HAVE HIM** — Dionne Warwick, Scepter 1294 | 6 |
| ★76 | 87 | — | — | **SUPER-CALI-FRAGIL-ISTIC-EXPI-ALI-DOCIOUS** — Julie Andrews & Dick Van Dyke, Vista 434 | 2 |
| 77 | 84 | 91 | 93 | **WHY DID I CHOOSE YOU** — Barbra Streisand, Columbia 43248 | 5 |
| 78 | 71 | 72 | 78 | **ALL OF MY LIFE** — Lesley Gore, Mercury 72412 | 6 |
| 79 | 82 | 88 | — | **I GOTTA WOMAN** — Ray Charles, ABC-Paramount 10649 | 3 |
| 80 | 83 | — | — | **I NEED YOU** — Chuck Jackson, Wand 179 | 2 |
| 81 | 96 | 100 | — | **YOU WERE ONLY FOOLING** — Vic Damone, Warner Bros. 5616 | 3 |
| 82 | 86 | 90 | — | **AL'S PLACE** — Al Hirt, RCA Victor 8542 | 3 |
| 83 | 98 | — | — | **HUSH, HUSH, SWEET CHARLOTTE** — Patti Page, Columbia 43251 | 2 |
| ★84 | — | — | — | **THREE O'CLOCK IN THE MORNING** — Bert Kaempfert & His Ork, Decca 31778 | 1 |
| ★85 | 88 | — | — | **CHIM, CHIM, CHEREE** — New Christy Minstrels, Columbia 43215 | 2 |
| ★86 | — | — | — | **BOO-GA-LOO** — Tom & Jerrio, ABC-Paramount 10638 | 1 |
| 87 | 99 | — | — | **COME ON OVER TO MY PLACE** — Drifters, Atlantic 2285 | 2 |
| ★88 | — | — | — | **WISHING IT WAS YOU** — Connie Francis, MGM 13331 | 1 |
| 89 | 100 | — | — | **THE MOUSE** — Soupy Sales, ABC-Paramount 10646 | 2 |
| 90 | 90 | — | — | **CHAINS OF LOVE** — Drifters, Atlantic 2285 | 2 |
| 91 | — | — | — | **GOOD LOVIN'** — Olympics, Loma 2013 | 1 |
| 92 | — | — | — | **GEORGIE PORGIE** — Jewel Akens, Era 3142 | 1 |
| 93 | — | — | — | **GOTTA HAVE YOUR LOVE** — Sapphires, ABC-Paramount 10639 | 1 |
| 94 | — | — | — | **SAD TOMORROWS** — Trini Lopez, Reprise 0328 | 1 |
| 95 | 75 | 86 | 89 | **APPLES AND BANANAS** — Lawrence Welk, Dot 16697 | 3 |
| 96 | — | — | — | **CONCRETE AND CLAY** — Unit Four Plus Two, London 9751 | 1 |
| 97 | — | — | — | **IN THE MEANTIME** — Georgie Fame, Imperial 66104 | 1 |
| 98 | — | — | — | **CONCRETE AND CLAY** — Eddie Rambeau, DynoVoice 204 | 1 |
| 99 | — | — | — | **VOODOO WOMAN** — Bobby Goldsboro, United Artists 862 | 1 |
| 100 | — | — | — | **HE AIN'T NO ANGEL** — Ad Libs, Blue Cat 114 | 1 |

## BUBBLING UNDER THE HOT 100

| # | Title | Artist, Label & Number |
|---|---|---|
| 101 | WITHOUT YOU | Matt Monro, Liberty 55786 |
| 102 | PEANUTS | Sunglows, Sunglow 107 |
| 103 | SHAKIN' ALL OVER | Guess Who's, Scepter 1295 |
| 104 | BABY, PLEASE DON'T GO | Them, Parrot 9727 |
| 105 | A WALK IN THE BLACK FOREST | Horst Jankowski, Mercury 72395 |
| 106 | TOMMY | Reparata & the Delrons, World Artists 1051 |
| 107 | DEAR DAD | Chuck Berry, Chess 1926 |
| 108 | I CAN'T EXPLAIN | The Who, Decca 31725 |
| 109 | LET ME DOWN EASY | Betty Lavette, Calla 102 |
| 110 | WHAT'S HE DOING IN MY WORLD | Eddy Arnold, RCA Victor 8516 |
| 111 | I'LL CRY ALONE | Gale Garnett, RCA Victor 8549 |
| 112 | MEXICAN PEARLS | Billy Vaughn, Dot 16706 |
| 113 | POOR BOY | Royalettes, MGM 13227 |
| 114 | THE CLIMB | Kingsmen, Wand 183 |
| 115 | KEEP ON TRYING | Bobby Vee, Liberty 55790 |
| 116 | SOUL SAUCE | Cal Tjader, Verve 10345 |
| 117 | CRYING WON'T HELP YOU NOW | Clyde McPhatter, Mercury 72407 |
| 118 | CATCH THE WIND | Donovan, Hickory 1309 |
| 119 | WHEN THE SHIP COMES IN | Peter, Paul & Mary, Warner Bros. 5625 |
| 120 | AIN'T NO TELLING | Bobby Bland, Duke 390 |
| 121 | HAWAII HONEYMOON | Waikikis, Kapp Winners Circle 52 |
| 122 | LEARNING THE GAME | Hullaballoos, Roulette 4612 |
| 123 | FOR YOUR LOVE | Yardbirds, Epic 9790 |
| 124 | LIPSTICK TRACES | O'Jays, Imperial 66102 |
| 125 | CHILLY WINDS | Seekers, Marvel 1060 |
| 126 | DARLING TAKE ME BACK | Lenny Welch, Kapp 662 |
| 127 | TIGER-A-GOGO | Buzz and Bucky, Amy 924 |
| 128 | HEY BABY | Hi-Lites, Wassel 701 |
| 129 | THE GIRL FROM GREENWICH VILLAGE | Trade Winds, Red Bird 10-028 |
| 130 | I CAN'T REMEMBER | Connie Smith, RCA Victor 8551 |
| 131 | I'LL NEVER FALL IN LOVE AGAIN | Bobby Freeman, Autumn 9 |
| 132 | YES I'M READY | Freddy Cannon, Warner Bros. 5615 |
| 133 | YES | Barbara Mason, Arctic 105 |
| 134 | OVER THE RAINBOW | Billy Thorpe, Crescendo 340 |
| 135 | BABY I'M YOURS | Barbara Lewis, Atlantic 2283 |

Compiled from national retail sales and radio station airplay by the Music Popularity Dept. of Record Market Research, Billboard.

# Billboard HOT 100

For Week Ending May 8, 1965

★ STAR performer—Sides registering greatest proportionate upward progress this week.

● Record Industry Association of America seal of certification as million selling single.

| This Week | 1 Wk. Ago | 2 Wks. Ago | 3 Wks. Ago | TITLE, Artist, Label & Number | Weeks On Chart |
|---|---|---|---|---|---|
| 1 | 1 | 2 | 12 | MRS. BROWN YOU'VE GOT A LOVELY DAUGHTER — Herman's Hermits, MGM 13341 | 4 |
| 2 | 7 | 11 | 29 | COUNT ME IN — Gary Lewis and the Playboys, Liberty 55778 | 6 |
| 3 | 18 | 59 | — | TICKET TO RIDE — Beatles, Capitol 5407 | 3 |
| 4 | 2 | 1 | 3 | GAME OF LOVE — Wayne Fontana & the Mindbenders, Fontana 1503 | 8 |
| 5 | 5 | 7 | 14 | I'LL NEVER FIND ANOTHER YOU — Seekers, Capitol 5383 | 7 |
| 6 | 3 | 4 | 4 | I KNOW A PLACE — Petula Clark, Warner Bros. 5612 | 8 |
| 7 | 8 | 10 | 19 | SILHOUETTES — Herman's Hermits, MGM 13332 | 6 |
| 8 | 4 | 3 | 1 | I'M TELLING YOU NOW — Freddie & the Dreamers, Tower 125 | 9 |
| 9 | 9 | 12 | 16 | THE LAST TIME — Rolling Stones, London 9741 | 7 |
| 10 | 12 | 17 | 25 | CAST YOUR FATE TO THE WIND — Sounds Orchestral, Parkway 942 | 8 |
| 11 | 14 | 18 | 20 | I'LL BE DOGGONE — Marvin Gaye, Tamla 54112 | 8 |
| 12 | 17 | 20 | 31 | JUST ONCE IN MY LIFE — Righteous Brothers, Philles 127 | 5 |
| 13 | 6 | 6 | 7 | TIRED OF WAITING FOR YOU — Kinks, Reprise 0347 | 9 |
| 14 | 24 | 45 | 61 | WOOLY BULLY — Sam the Sham and the Pharaohs, MGM 13322 | 6 |
| 15 | 15 | 19 | 27 | ONE KISS FOR OLD TIMES' SAKE — Ronnie Dove, Diamond 179 | 9 |
| 16 | 19 | 29 | 40 | OOO BABY BABY — Miracles, Tamla 54113 | 7 |
| 17 | 11 | 8 | 9 | THE CLAPPING SONG — Shirley Ellis, Congress 234 | 8 |
| 18 | 21 | 28 | 38 | BABY THE RAIN MUST FALL — Glenn Yarbrough, RCA Victor 8498 | 9 |
| 19 | 13 | 13 | 10 | GO NOW — Moody Blues, London 9726 | 12 |
| 20 | 20 | 22 | 37 | IT'S GROWING — Temptations, Gordy 7040 | 6 |
| 21 | 35 | 65 | 80 | HELP ME RHONDA — Beach Boys, Capitol 5395 | 4 |
| 22 | 28 | 48 | 75 | IT'S NOT UNUSUAL — Tom Jones, Parrot 9737 | 5 |
| 23 | 26 | 32 | 43 | IT'S GONNA BE ALRIGHT — Gerry & the Pacemakers, Laurie 3293 | 5 |
| 24 | 16 | 9 | 5 | SHOTGUN — Jr. Walker & the All Stars, Soul 35008 | 13 |
| 25 | 39 | 50 | 63 | IKO IKO — Dixie Cups, Red Bird 10-024 | 6 |
| 26 | 31 | 41 | 60 | I DO LOVE YOU — Billy Stewart, Chess 1922 | 7 |
| 27 | 32 | 35 | 39 | SHE'S ABOUT A MOVER — Sir Douglas Quintet, Tribe 8308 | 7 |
| 28 | 34 | 37 | 52 | WE'RE GONNA MAKE IT — Little Milton, Checker 1105 | 7 |
| 29 | 33 | 34 | 46 | WOMAN'S GOT SOUL — Impressions, ABC-Paramount 10647 | 6 |
| 30 | 10 | 5 | 2 | STOP! IN THE NAME OF LOVE — Supremes, Motown 1074 | 12 |
| 31 | 42 | 52 | 69 | THE ENTERTAINER — Tony Clarke, Chess 1924 | 7 |
| 32 | 47 | 63 | 82 | TRUE LOVE WAYS — Peter & Gordon, Capitol 5406 | 4 |
| 33 | 43 | 67 | 83 | REELIN' AND ROCKIN' — Dave Clark Five, Epic 9786 | 4 |
| 34 | 40 | 51 | 71 | DREAM ON LITTLE DREAMER — Perry Como, RCA Victor 8533 | 5 |
| 35 | 48 | 61 | 81 | JUST A LITTLE — Beau Brummels, Autumn 10 | 4 |
| 36 | 37 | 40 | 50 | AND ROSES AND ROSES — Andy Williams, Columbia 43257 | 6 |
| 37 | 30 | 30 | 35 | LAND OF 1000 DANCES — Cannibal & the Headhunters, Rampart 642 | 11 |
| 38 | 66 | — | — | BACK IN MY ARMS AGAIN — Supremes, Motown 1075 | 2 |
| 39 | 51 | 79 | — | CRYING IN THE CHAPEL — Elvis Presley, RCA Victor 0643 | 3 |
| 40 | 41 | 44 | 49 | CRAZY DOWNTOWN — Allan Sherman, Warner Bros. 5614 | 7 |
| 41 | 45 | 49 | 59 | IT'S GOT THE WHOLE WORLD SHAKIN' — Sam Cooke, RCA Victor 8539 | 5 |
| 42 | 23 | 14 | 8 | NOWHERE TO RUN — Martha & the Vandellas, Gordy 7039 | 11 |
| 43 | 25 | 16 | 6 | CAN'T YOU HEAR MY HEARTBEAT — Herman's Hermits, MGM 13310 | 15 |
| 44 | 44 | 55 | 65 | SUBTERRANEAN HOMESICK BLUES — Bob Dylan, Columbia 43242 | 6 |
| 45 | 63 | 78 | — | DO THE FREDDIE — Freddie & the Dreamers, Mercury 72428 | 3 |
| 46 | 67 | 85 | — | QUEEN OF THE HOUSE — Jody Miller, Capitol 5402 | 3 |
| 47 | 66 | — | — | YOU WERE MADE FOR ME — Freddie & the Dreamers, Tower 127 | 2 |
| 48 | 50 | 60 | 74 | DO THE FREDDIE — Chubby Checker, Parkway 949 | 6 |
| 49 | 22 | 24 | 32 | GOT TO GET YOU OFF MY MIND — Solomon Burke, Atlantic 2276 | 10 |
| 50 | 52 | 54 | 57 | THE BIRDS ARE FOR THE BEES — Newbeats, Hickory 1305 | 6 |
| 51 | 29 | 21 | 22 | BUMBLE BEE — Searchers, Kapp Winners Circle 49 | 8 |
| 52 | 55 | 66 | 70 | GOODBYE MY LOVER GOODBYE — Searchers, Kapp 658 | 6 |
| 53 | 36 | 39 | 41 | I UNDERSTAND — Freddie & the Dreamers, Mercury 72377 | 9 |
| 54 | 27 | 15 | 15 | THE RACE IS ON — Jack Jones, Kapp 651 | 11 |
| 55 | 62 | 74 | 89 | WHAT DO YOU WANT WITH ME — Chad & Jeremy, World Artists 1052 | 5 |
| 56 | 61 | 64 | 79 | A WOMAN CAN CHANGE A MAN — Joe Tex, Dial 4006 | 5 |
| 57 | 71 | — | — | YES IT IS — Beatles, Capitol 5407 | 2 |
| 58 | 72 | 81 | 96 | NOTHING CAN STOP ME — Gene Chandler, Constellation 149 | 4 |
| 59 | 53 | 57 | 67 | OUT IN THE STREETS — Shangri Las, Red Bird 10-025 | 6 |
| 60 | 60 | 72 | 77 | THINK OF THE GOOD TIMES — Jay and the Americans, United Artists 845 | 7 |
| 61 | 83 | 98 | — | HUSH, HUSH, SWEET CHARLOTTE — Patti Page, Columbia 43251 | 3 |
| 62 | 73 | 80 | — | NOW THAT YOU'VE GONE — Connie Stevens, Warner Bros. 5610 | 3 |
| 63 | 58 | 58 | 68 | SHE'S COMING HOME — Zombies, Parrot 9747 | 5 |
| 64 | 59 | 62 | 64 | THE BARRACUDA — Alvin Cash & the Crawlers, Mar-V-Lus 6005 | 7 |
| 65 | 54 | 56 | 62 | TRULY, TRULY, TRUE — Brenda Lee, Decca 31762 | 6 |
| 66 | 81 | 96 | 100 | YOU WERE ONLY FOOLING — Vic Damone, Warner Bros. 5616 | 4 |
| 67 | 82 | 86 | 90 | AL'S PLACE — Al Hirt, RCA Victor 8542 | 4 |
| 68 | 70 | 73 | 73 | WHIPPED CREAM — Herb Alpert's Tijuana Brass, A&M 760 | 10 |
| 69 | 69 | 76 | 87 | SEE YOU AT THE "GO GO" — Dobie Gray, Charger 107 | 6 |
| 70 | 64 | 69 | 76 | TOY SOLDIER — 4 Seasons, Phillips 40278 | 5 |
| 71 | 84 | — | — | THREE O'CLOCK IN THE MORNING — Bert Kaempfert & His Ork, Decca 31778 | 2 |
| 72 | 74 | 89 | — | SOMETHING YOU GOT — Chuck Jackson & Maxine Brown, Wand 181 | 3 |
| 73 | — | — | — | LAST CHANCE TO TURN AROUND — Gene Pitney, Musicor 1093 | 1 |
| 74 | 76 | 87 | — | SUPER-CALI-FRAGIL-ISTIC-EXPI-ALI-DOCIOUS — Julie Andrews & Dick Van Dyke, Vista 434 | 3 |
| 75 | 87 | 99 | — | COME ON OVER TO MY PLACE — Drifters, Atlantic 2285 | 3 |
| 76 | — | — | — | L-O-N-E-L-Y — Bobby Vinton, Epic 9791 | 1 |
| 77 | 80 | 83 | — | I NEED YOU — Chuck Jackson, Wand 179 | 3 |
| 78 | — | — | — | ENGINE, ENGINE #9 — Roger Miller, Smash 1983 | 1 |
| 79 | 88 | — | — | WISHING IT WAS YOU — Connie Francis, MGM 13331 | 2 |
| 80 | 96 | — | — | CONCRETE AND CLAY — Unit Four Plus Two, London 9751 | 2 |
| 81 | 85 | 88 | — | CHIM, CHIM, CHEREE — New Christy Minstrels, Columbia 43215 | 3 |
| 82 | 86 | — | — | BOO-GA-LOO — Tom & Jerrio, ABC-Paramount 10638 | 2 |
| 83 | 98 | — | — | CONCRETE AND CLAY — Eddie Rambeau, DynoVoice 204 | 2 |
| 84 | 99 | — | — | VOODOO WOMAN — Bobby Goldsboro, United Artists 862 | 2 |
| 85 | 89 | 100 | — | THE MOUSE — Soupy Sales, ABC-Paramount 10646 | 3 |
| 86 | 92 | — | — | GEORGIE PORGIE — Jewel Akens, Era 3142 | 2 |
| 87 | — | — | — | YOU CAN HAVE HER — Righteous Brothers, Moonglow 239 | 1 |
| 88 | — | — | — | AND I LOVE HIM — Esther Phillips, Atlantic 2281 | 1 |
| 89 | — | — | — | LIPSTICK TRACES — O'Jays, Imperial 66102 | 1 |
| 90 | — | — | — | A WALK IN THE BLACK FOREST — Horst Jankowski, Mercury 72395 | 1 |
| 91 | 91 | — | — | GOOD LOVIN' — Olympics, Loma 2013 | 2 |
| 92 | — | — | — | IT AIN'T NO BIG THING — Radiants, Chess 1925 | 1 |
| 93 | 93 | — | — | GOTTA HAVE YOUR LOVE — Sapphires, ABC-Paramount 10639 | 2 |
| 94 | — | — | — | LOVE IS A 5-LETTER WORD — James Phelps, Argo 5499 | 1 |
| 95 | — | — | — | SHAKIN' ALL OVER — Guess Who's, Scepter 1295 | 1 |
| 96 | — | — | — | THE CLIMB — Kingsmen, Wand 183 | 1 |
| 97 | 97 | — | — | IN THE MEANTIME — Georgie Fame, Imperial 66104 | 2 |
| 98 | — | — | — | KEEP ON TRYING — Bobby Vee, Liberty 55790 | 1 |
| 99 | — | — | — | TOMMY — Reparata and the Delrons, World Artists 1051 | 1 |
| 100 | — | — | — | PEANUTS — Sunglows, Sunglow 107 | 1 |

## BUBBLING UNDER THE HOT 100

101. WITHOUT YOU — Matt Monro, Liberty 55786
102. HE AIN'T NO ANGEL — Ad Libs, Blue Cat 114
103. SAD TOMORROWS — Trini Lopez, Reprise 0328
104. WHAT'S HE DOING IN MY WORLD — Eddy Arnold, RCA Victor 8516
105. SOUL SAUCE — Cal Tjader, Verve 10345
106. CATCH THE WIND — Donovan, Hickory 1309
107. TIGER-A-GO-GO — Buzz & Bucky, Amy 924
108. I'LL CRY ALONE — Gale Garnett, RCA Victor 8549
109. LET ME DOWN EASY — Betty Lavette, Calla 102
110. WHEN THE SHIP COMES IN — Peter, Paul & Mary, Warner Bros. 5625
111. MEXICAN PEARLS — Billy Vaughn, Dot 16706
112. YES, I'M READY — Barbara Mason, Arctic 105
113. GLORIA — Them, Parrot 9727
114. MR. TAMBOURINE MAN — Byrds, Columbia 43271
115. GIRL ON THE BILLBOARD — Del Reeves, United Artists 824
116. FOR YOUR LOVE — Yardbirds, Epic 9790
117. MAGIC TRUMPET — Comparsa Universitaria De La Laguna, RCA Victor F4-6
118. IT'S ALMOST TOMORROW — Jimmy Velvet, Phillips 40285
119. GOTTA TRAVEL ON — Damita Jo, Epic 9797
120. DEVIL'S HIDEAWAY — Scott Bedford Four, Joy 296
121. LEARNING THE GAME — Seekers, Marvel 1060
122. CHILLY WINDS — Nullaballoos, Roulette 4612
123. WELCOME, WELCOME — Gypsies, Old Town 1180
124. IT WAS EASIER TO HURT HER — Garnet Mimms, United Artists 848
125. YOU'VE BEEN CHEATIN' — Wayne Mason, Capitol 5408
126. JERK IT — Gypsies, Old Town 1180
127. APPLE BLOSSOM TIME — Wayne Newton, Capitol 5419
128. TO BE OR NOT TO BE — Otis Leavill, Blue Rock 4015
129. LAST EXIT TO BROOKLYN — Scott Bedford Four, Joy 296
130. OVER THE RAINBOW — Billy Thorpe, Crescendo 340
131. STOP THE MUSIC — Sue Thompson, Hickory 1308
132. YOU GAVE ME SOMEBODY TO LOVE — Dream Lovers, Warner Bros. 5619
133. TEARS KEEP ON FALLING — Jerry Vale, Columbia 43252
134. WELCOME HOME — Walter Jackson, Okeh 7219
135. YOU TURN ME ON — Ian Whitcomb, Tower 127

# Billboard HOT 100

For Week Ending May 15, 1965

★ STAR performer—Sides registering greatest proportionate upward progress this week.

| This Week | Wk. Ago | 2 Wks. Ago | TITLE Artist, Label & Number | Weeks On Chart |
|---|---|---|---|---|
| 1 | 1 | 2 | MRS. BROWN YOU'VE GOT A LOVELY DAUGHTER — Herman's Hermits, MGM 13341 | 5 |
| 2 | 2 | 7 | COUNT ME IN — Gary Lewis and the Playboys, Liberty 55778 | 7 |
| 3 | 3 | 18 | TICKET TO RIDE — Beatles, Capitol 5407 | 4 |
| 4 | 5 | 5 | I'LL NEVER FIND ANOTHER YOU — Seekers, Capitol 5383 | 8 |
| 5 | 7 | 8 | SILHOUETTES — Herman's Hermits, MGM 13332 | 7 |
| 6 | 21 | 35 | HELP ME RHONDA — Beach Boys, Capitol 5395 | 5 |
| 7 | 6 | 3 | I KNOW A PLACE — Petula Clark, Warner Bros. 5612 | 9 |
| 8 | 11 | 14 | I'LL BE DOGGONE — Marvin Gaye, Tamla 54112 | 9 |
| 9 | 12 | 17 | JUST ONCE IN MY LIFE — Righteous Brothers, Philles 127 | 6 |
| 10 | 14 | 24 | WOOLY BULLY — Sam the Sham and the Pharaohs, MGM 13322 | 7 |
| 11 | 4 | 2 | GAME OF LOVE — Wayne Fontana & the Mindbenders, Fontana 1503 | 9 |
| 12 | 10 | 12 | CAST YOUR FATE TO THE WIND — Sounds Orchestral, Parkway 942 | 9 |
| 13 | 18 | 21 | BABY THE RAIN MUST FALL — Glenn Yarbrough, RCA Victor 8498 | 10 |
| 14 | 15 | 15 | ONE KISS FOR OLD TIMES' SAKE — Ronnie Dove, Diamond 179 | 10 |
| 15 | 38 | 66 | BACK IN MY ARMS AGAIN — Supremes, Motown 1075 | 3 |
| 16 | 16 | 19 | OOO BABY BABY — Miracles, Tamla 54113 | 8 |
| 17 | 22 | 28 | IT'S NOT UNUSUAL — Tom Jones, Parrot 9737 | 6 |
| 18 | 20 | 20 | IT'S GROWING — Temptations, Gordy 7040 | 7 |
| 19 | 9 | 9 | THE LAST TIME — Rolling Stones, London 9741 | 8 |
| 20 | 39 | 51 | CRYING IN THE CHAPEL — Elvis Presley, RCA Victor 0643 | 4 |
| 21 | 27 | 32 | SHE'S ABOUT A MOVER — Sir Douglas Quintet, Tribe 8308 | 7 |
| 22 | 25 | 39 | IKO IKO — Dixie Cups, Red Bird 10-024 | 7 |
| 23 | 23 | 26 | IT'S GONNA BE ALRIGHT — Gerry & the Pacemakers, Laurie 3293 | 6 |
| 24 | 35 | 48 | JUST A LITTLE — Beau Brummels, Autumn 10 | 5 |
| 25 | 28 | 34 | WE'RE GONNA MAKE IT — Little Milton, Checker 1105 | 8 |
| 26 | 26 | 31 | I DO LOVE YOU — Billy Stewart, Chess 1922 | 6 |
| 27 | 32 | 47 | TRUE LOVE WAYS — Peter & Gordon, Capitol 5406 | 5 |
| 28 | 33 | 43 | REELIN' AND ROCKIN' — Dave Clark Five, Epic 9786 | 5 |
| 29 | 34 | 40 | DREAM ON LITTLE DREAMER — Perry Como, RCA Victor 8533 | 6 |
| 30 | 46 | 67 | QUEEN OF THE HOUSE — Jody Miller, Capitol 5402 | 4 |
| 31 | 13 | 6 | TIRED OF WAITING FOR YOU — Kinks, Reprise 0347 | 10 |
| 32 | 47 | 66 | YOU WERE MADE FOR ME — Freddie & the Dreamers, Tower 127 | 3 |
| 33 | 37 | 30 | LAND OF 1000 DANCES — Cannibal & the Headhunters, Rampart 642 | 12 |
| 34 | 29 | 33 | WOMAN'S GOT SOUL — Impressions, ABC-Paramount 10647 | 7 |
| 35 | 45 | 63 | DO THE FREDDIE — Freddie & the Dreamers, Mercury 72428 | 4 |
| 36 | 31 | 42 | THE ENTERTAINER — Tony Clarke, Chess 1924 | 8 |
| 37 | 19 | 13 | GO NOW — Moody Blues, London 9726 | 13 |
| 38 | 8 | 4 | I'M TELLING YOU — Freddie & the Dreamers, Tower 125 | 10 |
| 39 | 44 | 44 | SUBTERRANEAN HOMESICK BLUES — Bob Dylan, Columbia 43242 | 7 |
| 40 | 17 | 11 | THE CLAPPING SONG — Shirley Ellis, Congress 234 | 9 |
| 41 | 24 | 16 | SHOTGUN — Jr. Walker & the All Stars, Soul 35008 | 14 |
| 42 | 48 | 50 | DO THE FREDDIE — Chubby Checker, Parkway 949 | 7 |
| 43 | 36 | 37 | AND ROSES AND ROSES — Andy Williams, Columbia 43257 | 7 |
| 44 | 41 | 45 | IT'S GOT THE WHOLE WORLD SHAKIN' — Sam Cooke, RCA Victor 8539 | 6 |
| 45 | 58 | 72 | NOTHING CAN STOP ME — Gene Chandler, Constellation 149 | 5 |
| 46 | 57 | 71 | YES IT IS — Beatles, Capitol 5407 | 3 |
| 47 | 78 | — | ENGINE, ENGINE #9 — Roger Miller, Smash 1983 | 2 |
| 48 | 40 | 41 | CRAZY DOWNTOWN — Allan Sherman, Warner Bros. 5614 | 8 |
| 49 | 73 | — | LAST CHANCE TO TURN AROUND — Gene Pitney, Musicor 1093 | 2 |
| 50 | 76 | — | L-O-N-E-L-Y — Bobby Vinton, Epic 9791 | 2 |
| 51 | 55 | 62 | WHAT DO YOU WANT WITH ME — Chad & Jeremy, World Artists 1052 | 6 |
| 52 | 66 | 81 | YOU WERE ONLY FOOLING — Vic Damone, Warner Bros. 5616 | 5 |
| 53 | 61 | 83 | HUSH, HUSH, SWEET CHARLOTTE — Patti Page, Columbia 43251 | 4 |
| 54 | 62 | 73 | NOW THAT YOU'VE GONE — Connie Stevens, Warner Bros. 5610 | 4 |
| 55 | 52 | 55 | GOODBYE MY LOVER GOODBYE — Searchers, Kapp 658 | 7 |
| 56 | 71 | 84 | THREE O'CLOCK IN THE MORNING — Bert Kaempfert & His Ork, Decca 31778 | 3 |
| 57 | 60 | 60 | THINK OF THE GOOD TIMES — Jay and the Americans, United Artists 845 | 8 |
| 58 | 50 | 52 | THE BIRDS ARE FOR THE BEES — Newbeats, Hickory 1305 | 7 |
| 59 | 56 | 61 | A WOMAN CAN CHANGE A MAN — Joe Tex, Dial 4006 | 6 |
| 60 | 63 | 58 | SHE'S COMING HOME — Zombies, Parrot 9747 | 6 |
| 61 | 80 | 96 | CONCRETE AND CLAY — Unit Four Plus Two, London 9751 | 3 |
| 62 | 67 | 82 | AL'S PLACE — Al Hirt, RCA Victor 8542 | 5 |
| 63 | 83 | 98 | CONCRETE AND CLAY — Eddie Rambeau, DynoVoice 204 | 3 |
| 64 | 72 | 74 | SOMETHING YOU GOT — Chuck Jackson & Maxine Brown, Wand 181 | 4 |
| 65 | — | — | BEFORE AND AFTER — Chad & Jeremy, Columbia 43277 | 1 |
| 66 | — | — | BRING IT ON HOME TO ME — Animals, MGM 13339 | 1 |
| 67 | — | — | I CAN'T HELP MYSELF — Four Tops, Motown 1076 | 1 |
| 68 | 74 | 76 | SUPER-CALI-FRAGIL-ISTIC-EXPI-ALI-DOCIOUS — Julie Andrews & Dick Van Dyke, Vista 434 | 4 |
| 69 | 75 | 87 | COME ON OVER TO MY PLACE — Drifters, Atlantic 2285 | 4 |
| 70 | 90 | — | A WALK IN THE BLACK FOREST — Horst Jankowski, Mercury 72425 | 2 |
| 71 | 79 | 88 | WISHING IT WAS YOU — Connie Francis, MGM 13331 | 3 |
| 72 | 84 | 99 | VOODOO WOMAN — Bobby Goldsboro, United Artists 862 | 3 |
| 73 | 82 | 86 | BOO-GA-LOO — Tom & Jerrio, ABC-Paramount 10638 | 3 |
| 74 | 95 | — | SHAKIN' ALL OVER — Guess Who's, Scepter 1295 | 2 |
| 75 | 77 | 80 | I NEED YOU — Chuck Jackson, Wand 179 | 4 |
| 76 | 100 | — | PEANUTS — Sunglows, Sunglow 107 | 2 |
| 77 | 89 | — | LIPSTICK TRACES — O'Jays, Imperial 66102 | 2 |
| 78 | 85 | 89 | THE MOUSE — Soupy Sales, ABC-Paramount 10646 | 2 |
| 79 | 69 | 69 | SEE YOU AT THE "GO GO" — Dobie Gray, Charger 107 | 7 |
| 80 | 96 | — | THE CLIMB — Kingsmen, Wand 183 | 2 |
| 81 | 87 | — | YOU CAN HAVE HER — Righteous Brothers, Moonglow 239 | 2 |
| 82 | 88 | — | AND I LOVE HIM — Esther Phillips, Atlantic 2281 | 2 |
| 83 | 86 | 92 | GEORGIE PORGIE — Jewel Akens, Era 3142 | 3 |
| 84 | — | — | FOR YOUR LOVE — Yardbirds, Epic 9790 | 1 |
| 85 | — | — | CATCH THE WIND — Donovan, Hickory 1309 | 1 |
| 86 | 91 | 91 | GOOD LOVIN' — Olympics, Loma 2013 | 3 |
| 87 | — | — | MR. TAMBOURINE MAN — Byrds, Columbia 43271 | 1 |
| 88 | 81 | 85 | CHIM, CHIM, CHEREE — New Christy Minstrels, Columbia 43215 | 4 |
| 89 | 93 | 93 | GOTTA HAVE YOUR LOVE — Sapphires, ABC-Paramount 10639 | 3 |
| 90 | — | — | LAURIE — Dickie Lee, Hall 102 | 1 |
| 91 | 92 | — | IT AIN'T NO BIG THING — Radiants, Chess 1925 | 2 |
| 92 | 99 | — | TOMMY — Reparata and the Delrons, World Artists 1051 | 2 |
| 93 | — | — | BEFORE YOU GO — Buck Owens, Capitol 5410 | 1 |
| 94 | 94 | — | LOVE IS A 5-LETTER WORD — James Phelps, Argo 5499 | 2 |
| 95 | 98 | — | KEEP ON TRYING — Bobby Vee, Liberty 55790 | 2 |
| 96 | — | — | I'VE BEEN LOVING YOU TOO LONG — Otis Redding, Volt 126 | 1 |
| 97 | — | — | YES, I'M READY — Barbara Mason, Arctic 105 | 1 |
| 98 | — | — | WHEN THE SHIP COMES IN — Peter, Paul & Mary, Warner Bros. 5625 | 1 |
| 99 | — | — | I DO — Marvelows, ABC-Paramount 10629 | 1 |
| 100 | — | — | WHAT'S HE DOING IN MY WORLD — Eddy Arnold, RCA Victor 8516 | 1 |

## BUBBLING UNDER THE HOT 100

101. GLORIA — Them, Parrot 9727
102. GIRL ON THE BILLBOARD — Del Reeves, United Artists 824
103. RIBBON OF DARKNESS — Marty Robbins, Columbia 43258
104. LET ME DOWN EASY — Betty Lavette, Calla 102
105. IT'S ALMOST TOMORROW — Jimmy Velvet, Philips 40285
106. IN THE MEANTIME — Georgie Fame, Imperial 66104
107. WHAT THE WORLD NEEDS NOW IS LOVE — Jackie DeShannon, Liberty 66110
108. I'LL CRY ALONE — Gale Garnett, RCA Victor 8549
109. TIGER A-GO-GO — Buzz & Bucky, Amy 924
110. SHE'S LOST YOU — Zephyrs, Rotate 5006
111. SOUL SAUCE — Cal Tjader, Verve 10345
112. SAD TOMORROWS — Trini Lopez, Reprise 0328
113. WITHOUT A SONG — Ray Charles, ABC-Paramount 10663
114. HE AIN'T NO ANGEL — Ad Libs, Blue Cat 114
115. MAGIC TRUMPET — Comparsa Universitaria De La Laguna, RCA Victor F4-6
116. MUSTANG SALLY — Sir Mack Rice, Blue Rock 4014
117. STOP THE MUSIC — Sue Thompson, Hickory 1308
118. CRYING WON'T HELP YOU NOW — Clyde McPhatter, Mercury 72407
119. DEVIL'S HIDEAWAY — James Brown, Smash 1975
120. WITHOUT YOU — Matt Monro, Liberty 55786
121. YOU GAVE ME SOMEBODY TO LOVE — Dream Lovers, Mercury 5619
122. TEARS KEEP ON FALLING — Jerry Vale, Columbia 43252
123. HERE COMES THE NIGHT — Them, Parrot 9749
124. DUST ON THE (Turn on Song) — Ian Whitcomb, Tower 127
125. DUST GOT IN DADDY'S EYES — Bobby Bland, Duke 390
126. ONE STEP AHEAD — Aretha Franklin, Columbia 43241
127. I REALLY KNOW HOW TO HURT A GUY — Jan & Dean, Liberty 55792
128. BREAK UP — Del Shannon, Amy 925
129. WELCOME HOME — Walter Jackson, Okeh 7219
130. I'M GONNA CRY TILL MY TEARS RUN DRY — Irma Thomas, Imperial 66106
131. SOMETIMES — Paul Revere & the Raiders, Columbia 43273
132. QUEEN OF THE SENIOR PROM — Vaughn Monroe, Kapp 669
133. THEN I'LL COUNT AGAIN — Johnny Tillotson, MGM 13344
134. BABY I'M YOURS — Barbara Lewis, Atlantic 2283
135. THE PRICE OF LOVE — Everly Brothers, Warner Bros. 5628

Compiled from national retail sales and radio station airplay by the Music Popularity Dept. of Record Market Research, Billboard.

# Billboard HOT 100

For Week Ending May 22, 1965

★ STAR performer—Sides registering greatest proportionate upward progress this week.

Record Industry Association of America seal of certification as million selling single.

| THIS WEEK | Wk. Ago | 2 Wks. Ago | 3 Wks. Ago | TITLE Artist, Label & Number | Weeks On Chart |
|---|---|---|---|---|---|
| 1 | 3 | 3 | 18 | TICKET TO RIDE — Beatles, Capitol 5407 | 5 |
| 2 | 1 | 1 | 1 | MRS. BROWN YOU'VE GOT A LOVELY DAUGHTER — Herman's Hermits, MGM 13341 | 6 |
| 3 | 2 | 2 | 7 | COUNT ME IN — Gary Lewis and the Playboys, Liberty 55778 | 8 |
| 4 | 6 | 21 | 35 | HELP ME RHONDA — Beach Boys, Capitol 5395 | 6 |
| 5 | 4 | 5 | 5 | I'LL NEVER FIND ANOTHER YOU — Seekers, Capitol 5383 | 9 |
| 6 | 15 | 38 | 66 | BACK IN MY ARMS AGAIN — Supremes, Motown 1075 | 4 |
| 7 | 5 | 7 | 8 | SILHOUETTES — Herman's Hermits, MGM 13332 | 7 |
| 8 | 10 | 14 | 24 | WOOLY BULLY — Sam the Sham and the Pharaohs, MGM 13322 | 8 |
| 9 | 9 | 12 | 17 | JUST ONCE IN MY LIFE — Righteous Brothers, Philles 127 | 7 |
| 10 | 20 | 39 | 51 | CRYING IN THE CHAPEL — Elvis Presley, RCA Victor 0643 | 5 |
| 11 | 12 | 10 | 12 | CAST YOUR FATE TO THE WIND — Sounds Orchestral, Parkway 942 | 10 |
| 12 | 13 | 18 | 21 | BABY THE RAIN MUST FALL — Glenn Yarbrough, RCA Victor 8498 | 11 |
| 13 | 7 | 6 | 3 | I KNOW A PLACE — Petula Clark, Warner Bros. 5612 | 10 |
| 14 | 11 | 4 | 2 | GAME OF LOVE — Wayne Fontana & the Mindbenders, Fontana 1503 | 10 |
| 15 | 17 | 22 | 28 | IT'S NOT UNUSUAL — Tom Jones, Parrot 9737 | 7 |
| 16 | 8 | 11 | 14 | I'LL BE DOGGONE — Marvin Gaye, Tamla 54112 | 10 |
| 17 | 27 | 32 | 47 | TRUE LOVE WAYS — Peter & Gordon, Capitol 5406 | 6 |
| 18 | 21 | 27 | 32 | SHE'S ABOUT A MOVER — Sir Douglas Quintet, Tribe 8308 | 8 |
| 19 | 24 | 35 | 48 | JUST A LITTLE — Beau Brummels, Autumn 10 | 7 |
| 20 | 22 | 25 | 39 | IKO IKO — Dixie Cups, Red Bird 10-024 | 8 |
| 21 | 16 | 16 | 19 | OOO BABY BABY — Miracles, Tamla 54113 | 9 |
| 22 | 19 | 9 | 9 | THE LAST TIME — Rolling Stones, London 9741 | 9 |
| 23 | 28 | 33 | 43 | REELIN' AND ROCKIN' — Dave Clark Five, Epic 9786 | 6 |
| 24 | 35 | 45 | 63 | DO THE FREDDIE — Freddie & the Dreamers, Mercury 72428 | 5 |
| 25 | 30 | 46 | 67 | QUEEN OF THE HOUSE — Jody Miller, Capitol 5402 | 5 |
| 26 | 32 | 47 | 66 | YOU WERE MADE FOR ME — Freddie & the Dreamers, Tower 127 | 4 |
| 27 | 29 | 34 | 40 | DREAM ON LITTLE DREAMER — Perry Como, RCA Victor 8533 | 7 |
| 28 | 14 | 15 | 15 | ONE KISS FOR OLD TIMES' SAKE — Ronnie Dove, Diamond 179 | 11 |
| 29 | 25 | 28 | 34 | WE'RE GONNA MAKE IT — Little Milton, Checker 1105 | 9 |
| 30 | 47 | 78 | — | ENGINE, ENGINE #9 — Roger Miller, Smash 1983 | 3 |
| 31 | 18 | 20 | 20 | IT'S GROWING — Temptations, Gordy 7040 | 8 |
| 32 | 67 | — | — | I CAN'T HELP MYSELF — Four Tops, Motown 1076 | 2 |
| 33 | 26 | 26 | 31 | I DO LOVE YOU — Billy Stewart, Chess 1922 | 9 |
| 34 | 45 | 58 | 72 | NOTHING CAN STOP ME — Gene Chandler, Constellation 149 | 6 |
| 35 | 33 | 37 | 30 | LAND OF 1000 DANCES — Cannibal & the Headhunters, Rampart 642 | 13 |
| 36 | 50 | 76 | — | L-O-N-E-L-Y — Bobby Vinton, Epic 9791 | 3 |
| 37 | 23 | 23 | 26 | IT'S GONNA BE ALRIGHT — Gerry & the Pacemakers, Laurie 3293 | 7 |
| 38 | 49 | 73 | — | LAST CHANCE TO TURN AROUND — Gene Pitney, Musicor 1093 | 3 |
| 39 | 53 | 61 | 83 | HUSH, HUSH, SWEET CHARLOTTE — Patti Page, Columbia 43251 | 5 |
| 40 | 42 | 48 | 50 | DO THE FREDDIE — Chubby Checker, Parkway 949 | 8 |
| 41 | 52 | 66 | 81 | YOU WERE ONLY FOOLING — Vic Damone, Warner Bros. 5616 | 6 |
| 42 | 38 | 8 | 4 | I'M TELLING YOU NOW — Freddie & the Dreamers, Tower 125 | 11 |
| 43 | 31 | 13 | 6 | TIRED OF WAITING FOR YOU — Kinks, Reprise 0347 | 11 |
| 44 | 37 | 19 | 13 | GO NOW — Moody Blues, London 9726 | 14 |
| 45 | 56 | 71 | 84 | THREE O'CLOCK IN THE MORNING — Bert Kaempfert & His Ork, Decca 31778 | 4 |
| 46 | 39 | 44 | 44 | SUBTERRANEAN HOMESICK BLUES — Bob Dylan, Columbia 43242 | 8 |
| 47 | 44 | 41 | 45 | IT'S GOT THE WHOLE WORLD SHAKIN' — Sam Cooke, RCA Victor 8539 | 7 |
| 48 | 36 | 31 | 42 | THE ENTERTAINER — Tony Clarke, Chess 1924 | 9 |
| 49 | 61 | 80 | 96 | CONCRETE AND CLAY — Unit Four Plus Two, London 9751 | 4 |
| 50 | 65 | — | — | BEFORE AND AFTER — Chad & Jeremy, Columbia 43277 | 2 |
| 51 | 63 | 83 | 98 | CONCRETE AND CLAY — Eddie Rambeau, DynoVoice 204 | 4 |
| 52 | 66 | — | — | BRING IT ON HOME TO ME — Animals, MGM 13339 | 2 |
| 53 | 54 | 62 | 73 | NOW THAT YOU'VE GONE — Connie Stevens, Warner Bros. 5610 | 5 |
| 54 | 46 | 57 | 71 | YES IT IS — Beatles, Capitol 5407 | 4 |
| 55 | 70 | 90 | — | A WALK IN THE BLACK FOREST — Horst Jankowski, Mercury 72425 | 3 |
| 56 | 72 | 84 | 99 | VOODOO WOMAN — Bobby Goldsboro, United Artists 862 | 4 |
| 57 | 62 | 67 | 82 | AL'S PLACE — Al Hirt, RCA Victor 8542 | 6 |
| 58 | 51 | 55 | 62 | WHAT DO YOU WANT WITH ME — Chad & Jeremy, World Artists 1052 | 7 |
| 59 | 74 | 95 | — | SHAKIN' ALL OVER — Guess Who's, Scepter 1295 | 3 |
| 60 | 69 | 75 | 87 | COME ON OVER TO MY PLACE — Drifters, Atlantic 2285 | 5 |
| 61 | 84 | — | — | FOR YOUR LOVE — Yardbirds, Epic 9790 | 2 |
| 62 | 71 | 79 | 88 | WISHING IT WAS YOU — Connie Francis, MGM 13331 | 4 |
| 63 | 59 | 56 | 61 | A WOMAN CAN CHANGE A MAN — Joe Tex, Dial 4006 | 7 |
| 64 | 76 | 100 | — | PEANUTS — Sunglows, Sunglow 107 | 3 |
| 65 | 73 | 82 | 86 | BOO-GA-LOO — Tom & Jerrio, ABC-Paramount 10638 | 4 |
| 66 | 68 | 74 | 76 | SUPER-CALI-FRAGIL-ISTIC-EXPI-ALI-DOCIOUS — Julie Andrews & Dick Van Dyke, Vista 434 | 5 |
| 67 | 64 | 72 | 74 | SOMETHING YOU GOT — Chuck Jackson & Maxine Brown, Wand 181 | 5 |
| 68 | 77 | 89 | — | LIPSTICK TRACES — O'Jays, Imperial 66102 | 3 |
| 69 | 80 | 96 | — | THE CLIMB — Kingsmen, Wand 183 | 3 |
| 70 | 85 | — | — | CATCH THE WIND — Donovan, Hickory 1309 | 2 |
| 71 | 83 | 86 | 92 | GEORGIE PORGIE — Jewel Akens, Era 3142 | 4 |
| 72 | 87 | — | — | MR. TAMBOURINE MAN — Byrds, Columbia 43271 | 2 |
| 73 | 81 | 87 | — | YOU CAN HAVE HER — Righteous Brothers, Moonglow 239 | 3 |
| 74 | 90 | — | — | LAURIE — Dickie Lee, Hall 102 | 2 |
| 75 | 96 | — | — | I'VE BEEN LOVING YOU TOO LONG — Otis Redding, Volt 126 | 2 |
| 76 | 78 | 85 | 89 | THE MOUSE — Soupy Sales, ABC-Paramount 10646 | 5 |
| 77 | — | — | — | (Remember Me) I'M THE ONE WHO LOVES YOU — Dean Martin, Reprise 0369 | 1 |
| 78 | 82 | 88 | — | AND I LOVE HIM — Esther Phillips, Atlantic 2281 | 3 |
| 79 | 99 | — | — | I DO — Marvelows, ABC-Paramount 10629 | 2 |
| 80 | 89 | 93 | 93 | GOTTA HAVE YOUR LOVE — Sapphires, ABC-Paramount 10639 | 4 |
| 81 | 86 | 91 | 91 | GOOD LOVIN' — Olympics, Loma 2013 | 4 |
| 82 | — | — | — | TELL HER (You Love Her Every Day) — Frank Sinatra, Reprise 0373 | 1 |
| 83 | 93 | — | — | BEFORE YOU GO — Buck Owens, Capitol 5410 | 2 |
| 84 | — | — | — | IT'S WONDERFUL TO BE IN LOVE — Ovations, Goldwax 113 | 1 |
| 85 | 100 | — | — | WHAT'S HE DOING IN MY WORLD — Eddy Arnold, RCA Victor 8516 | 2 |
| 86 | 97 | — | — | YES, I'M READY — Barbara Mason, Arctic 105 | 2 |
| 87 | 88 | 81 | 85 | CHIM, CHIM, CHEREE — New Christy Minstrels, Columbia 43215 | 4 |
| 88 | — | — | — | WHAT THE WORLD NEEDS NOW IS LOVE — Jackie DeShannon, Imperial 66110 | 1 |
| 89 | 94 | 94 | — | LOVE IS A 5-LETTER WORD — James Phelps, Argo 5499 | 3 |
| 90 | — | — | — | APPLE BLOSSOM TIME — Wayne Newton, Capitol 5419 | 1 |
| 91 | — | — | — | YOU REALLY KNOW HOW TO HURT A GUY — Jan & Dean, Liberty 55792 | 1 |
| 92 | 92 | 99 | — | TOMMY — Reparata and the Delrons, World Artists 1051 | 3 |
| 93 | — | — | — | GLORIA — Them, Parrot 9727 | 1 |
| 94 | 98 | — | — | WHEN THE SHIP COMES IN — Peter, Paul & Mary, Warner Bros. 5625 | 2 |
| 95 | 95 | 98 | — | KEEP ON TRYING — Bobby Vee, Liberty 55790 | 3 |
| 96 | — | — | — | PLAY WITH FIRE — Rolling Stones, London 9741 | 1 |
| 97 | — | — | — | BREAK UP — Del Shannon, Amy 925 | 1 |
| 98 | — | — | — | BRING A LITTLE SUNSHINE — Vic Dana, Dolton 305 | 1 |
| 99 | — | — | — | YOU TURN ME ON — Ian Whitcomb, Tower 127 | 1 |
| 100 | — | — | — | TEARS KEEP ON FALLING — Jerry Vale, Columbia 43252 | 1 |

## BUBBLING UNDER THE HOT 100

101. GIRL ON THE BILLBOARD — Del Reeves, United Artists 824
102. IT AIN'T NO BIG THING — Radiants, Chess 3925
103. RIBBON OF DARKNESS — Marty Robbins, Columbia 43158
104. LET ME DOWN EASY — Betty Lavette, Calla 102
105. IT'S ALMOST TOMORROW — Jimmy Velvet, Philips 40285
106. THE PRICE OF LOVE — Everly Brothers, Warner Bros. 5628
107. HERE COMES THE NIGHT — Them, Parrot 9749
108. TIGER A GO-GO — Buzz & Bucky, Amy 924
109. SHE'S LOST YOU — Zephyrs, Parrot 3006
110. MUSTANG SALLY — Sir Mack Rice, Blue Rock 4014
111. MAGIC TRUMPET — Comparsa Universitaria De La Laguna, RCA Victor F4-6
112. WITHOUT A SONG — Ray Charles, ABC-Paramount 10645
113. JERK IT — Gypsies, Old Town 1180
114. CAST YOUR FATE TO THE WIND — Steve Alaimo, ABC-Paramount 10680
115. NO ONE — Brenda Lee, Decca 31792
116. FIRST THING EV'RY MORNING — Jimmy Dean, Columbia 43263
117. STOP THE MUSIC — Sue Thompson, Hickory 1308
118. SOUL SAUCE — Cal Tjader, Verve 10345
119. TOO MANY RIVERS — Brenda Lee, Decca 31792
120. LET THERE BE DRUMS '66 — Sandy Nelson, Imperial 66107
121. NO ONE CAN LIVE FOREVER — Sammy Davis, Reprise 0370
122. CRYING WON'T HELP YOU NOW — Clyde McPhatter, Mercury 72407
123. CHIM CHIM CHEREE — Dick Van Dyke with the Jack-Halloran Singers, Vista 441
124. ONE STEP AHEAD — Aretha Franklin, Columbia 43241
125. DEVILS HIDEAWAY — James Brown, Smash 1975
126. 3 O'CLOCK IN THE MORNING — Lou Rawls, Capitol 5424
127. IT HURTS ME TOO — Elmore James, Enjoy 2015
128. THIS LITTLE BIRD — Marianne Faithfull, London 9759
129. NO ONE ELSE COULD EVER BE — Jay & the Americans, United Artists 881
130. WHEN IT'S ALL OVER — Jay & the Americans, United Artists 881
131. THE REAL THING — Tina Britt, Eastern 604
132. THEN I'LL COUNT AGAIN — Johnny Tillotson, MGM 13344
133. WELCOME HOME — Walter Jackson, Okeh 7219
134. LIP SYNC — Len Barry, Decca 31788
135. SEARCHIN' FOR MY BABY — Manhattans, Carnival 509

Compiled from national retail sales and radio station airplay by the Music Popularity Dept. of Record Market Research, Billboard.

# Billboard HOT 100

For Week Ending May 29, 1965

★ STAR performer—Sides registering greatest proportionate upward progress this week.

Record Industry Association of America seal of certification as million selling single.

| This Week | Wk. Ago | 2 Wks. Ago | 3 Wks. Ago | TITLE, Artist, Label & Number | Weeks On Chart |
|---|---|---|---|---|---|
| 1 | 4 | 6 | 21 | HELP ME RHONDA — Beach Boys, Capitol 5395 | 7 |
| 2 | 1 | 3 | 3 | TICKET TO RIDE — Beatles, Capitol 5407 | 6 |
| 3 | 6 | 15 | 38 | BACK IN MY ARMS AGAIN — Supremes, Motown 1075 | 5 |
| 4 | 2 | 1 | 1 | MRS. BROWN YOU'VE GOT A LOVELY DAUGHTER — Herman's Hermits, MGM 13341 | 7 |
| 5 | 9 | 10 | 14 | WOOLY BULLY — Sam the Sham and the Pharaohs, MGM 13322 | 9 |
| 6 | 10 | 20 | 39 | CRYING IN THE CHAPEL — Elvis Presley, RCA Victor 0643 | 6 |
| 7 | 3 | 2 | 2 | COUNT ME IN — Gary Lewis and the Playboys, Liberty 55778 | 9 |
| 8 | 5 | 4 | 5 | I'LL NEVER FIND ANOTHER YOU — Seekers, Capitol 5383 | 10 |
| 9 | 19 | 24 | 35 | JUST A LITTLE — Beau Brummels, Autumn 10 | 7 |
| 10 | 15 | 17 | 22 | IT'S NOT UNUSUAL — Tom Jones, Parrot 9737 | 8 |
| 11 | 9 | 9 | 12 | JUST ONCE IN MY LIFE — Righteous Brothers, Philles 127 | 8 |
| 12 | 12 | 13 | 18 | BABY THE RAIN MUST FALL — Glenn Yarbrough, RCA Victor 8498 | 12 |
| 13 | 18 | 21 | 27 | SHE'S ABOUT A MOVER — Sir Douglas Quintet, Tribe 8308 | 9 |
| 14 | 7 | 5 | 7 | SILHOUETTES — Herman's Hermits, MGM 13332 | 9 |
| 15 | 11 | 12 | 10 | CAST YOUR FATE TO THE WIND — Sounds Orchestral, Parkway 942 | 11 |
| 16 | 17 | 27 | 32 | TRUE LOVE WAYS — Peter & Gordon, Capitol 5406 | 7 |
| 17 | 32 | 67 | — | I CAN'T HELP MYSELF — Four Tops, Motown 1076 | 3 |
| 18 | 25 | 30 | 46 | QUEEN OF THE HOUSE — Jody Miller, Capitol 5402 | 6 |
| 19 | 30 | 47 | 78 | ENGINE, ENGINE #9 — Roger Miller, Smash 1983 | 4 |
| 20 | 20 | 22 | 25 | IKO IKO — Dixie Cups, Red Bird 10-024 | 9 |
| 21 | 24 | 35 | 45 | DO THE FREDDIE — Freddie & the Dreamers, Mercury 72428 | 6 |
| 22 | 26 | 32 | 47 | YOU WERE MADE FOR ME — Freddie & the Dreamers, Tower 127 | 5 |
| 23 | 23 | 28 | 33 | REELIN' AND ROCKIN' — Dave Clark Five, Epic 9786 | 7 |
| 24 | 21 | 16 | 16 | OOO BABY BABY — Miracles, Tamla 54113 | 10 |
| 25 | 27 | 29 | 34 | DREAM ON LITTLE DREAMER — Perry Como, RCA Victor 8533 | 8 |
| 26 | 29 | 25 | 28 | WE'RE GONNA MAKE IT — Little Milton, Checker 1105 | 10 |
| 27 | 16 | 8 | 11 | I'LL BE DOGGONE — Marvin Gaye, Tamla 54112 | 11 |
| 28 | 36 | 50 | 76 | L-O-N-E-L-Y — Bobby Vinton, Epic 9791 | 4 |
| 29 | 38 | 49 | 73 | LAST CHANCE TO TURN AROUND — Gene Pitney, Musicor 1093 | 4 |
| 30 | 34 | 45 | 58 | NOTHING CAN STOP ME — Gene Chandler, Constellation 149 | 7 |
| 31 | 41 | 52 | 66 | YOU WERE ONLY FOOLING — Vic Damone, Warner Bros. 5616 | 7 |
| 32 | 13 | 7 | 6 | I KNOW A PLACE — Petula Clark, Warner Bros. 5612 | 11 |
| 33 | 14 | 11 | 4 | GAME OF LOVE — Wayne Fontana & the Mindbenders, Fontana 1503 | 11 |
| 34 | 39 | 53 | 61 | HUSH, HUSH, SWEET CHARLOTTE — Patti Page, Columbia 43251 | 6 |
| 35 | 45 | 56 | 71 | THREE O'CLOCK IN THE MORNING — Bert Kaempfert & His Ork, Decca 31778 | 5 |
| 36 | 22 | 19 | 9 | THE LAST TIME — Rolling Stones, London 9741 | 10 |
| 37 | 31 | 18 | 20 | IT'S GROWING — Temptations, Gordy 7040 | 9 |
| 38 | 49 | 61 | 80 | CONCRETE AND CLAY — Unit Four Plus Two, London 9751 | 5 |
| 39 | 50 | 65 | — | BEFORE AND AFTER — Chad & Jeremy, Columbia 43277 | 3 |
| 40 | 52 | 66 | — | BRING IT ON HOME TO ME — Animals, MGM 13339 | 3 |
| 41 | 35 | 33 | 37 | LAND OF 1000 DANCES — Cannibal & the Headhunters, Rampart 642 | 14 |
| 42 | 33 | 26 | 26 | I DO LOVE YOU — Billy Stewart, Chess 1922 | 10 |
| 43 | 37 | 23 | 23 | IT'S GONNA BE ALRIGHT — Gerry & the Pacemakers, Laurie 3293 | 8 |
| 44 | 55 | 70 | 90 | A WALK IN THE BLACK FOREST — Horst Jankowski, Mercury 72425 | 4 |
| 45 | 51 | 63 | 83 | CONCRETE AND CLAY — Eddie Rambeau, DynoVoice 204 | 5 |
| 46 | 56 | 72 | 84 | VOODOO WOMAN — Bobby Goldsboro, United Artists 862 | 5 |
| 47 | 59 | 74 | 95 | SHAKIN' ALL OVER — Guess Who's, Scepter 1295 | 4 |
| 48 | 61 | 84 | — | FOR YOUR LOVE — Yardbirds, Epic 9790 | 3 |
| 49 | 40 | 42 | 48 | DO THE FREDDIE — Chubby Checker, Parkway 949 | 9 |
| 50 | — | — | — | WONDERFUL WORLD — Herman's Hermits, MGM 13354 | 1 |
| 51 | 75 | 96 | — | I'VE BEEN LOVING YOU TOO LONG — Otis Redding, Volt 126 | 3 |
| 52 | 68 | 77 | 89 | LIPSTICK TRACES — O'Jays, Imperial 66102 | 4 |
| 53 | 65 | 73 | 82 | BOO-GA-LOO — Tom & Jerrio, ABC-Paramount 10638 | 5 |
| 54 | 77 | — | — | (Remember Me) I'M THE ONE WHO LOVES YOU — Dean Martin, Reprise 0369 | 2 |
| 55 | 72 | 87 | — | MR. TAMBOURINE MAN — Byrds, Columbia 43271 | 3 |
| 56 | 53 | 54 | 62 | NOW THAT YOU'VE GONE — Connie Stevens, Warner Bros. 5610 | 5 |
| 57 | 62 | 71 | 79 | WISHING IT WAS YOU — Connie Francis, MGM 13331 | 5 |
| 58 | 70 | 85 | — | CATCH THE WIND — Donovan, Hickory 1309 | 3 |
| 59 | 67 | 64 | 72 | (Any Day Now) MY WILD BEAUTIFUL BIRD — Chuck Jackson & Maxine Brown, Wand 181 | 6 |
| 60 | 74 | 90 | — | LAURIE — Dickey Lee, TCF-Hall 102 | 3 |
| 61 | 57 | 62 | 67 | AL'S PLACE — Al Hirt, RCA Victor 8542 | 7 |
| 62 | 58 | 51 | 55 | WHAT DO YOU WANT WITH ME — Chad & Jeremy, World Artists 1052 | 8 |
| 63 | 78 | 82 | 88 | AND I LOVE HIM — Esther Phillips, Atlantic 2281 | 4 |
| 64 | 64 | 76 | 100 | PEANUTS — Sunglows, Sunglow 107 | 4 |
| 65 | 69 | 80 | 96 | THE CLIMB — Kingsmen, Wand 183 | 4 |
| 66 | 79 | 99 | — | I DO — Marvelows, ABC-Paramount 10629 | 3 |
| 67 | 73 | 81 | 87 | YOU CAN HAVE HER — Righteous Brothers, Moonglow 239 | 4 |
| 68 | 71 | 83 | 86 | GEORGIE PORGIE — Jewel Akens, Era 3142 | 5 |
| 69 | 86 | 97 | — | YES, I'M READY — Barbara Mason, Arctic 105 | 3 |
| 70 | 88 | — | — | WHAT THE WORLD NEEDS NOW IS LOVE — Jackie DeShannon, Imperial 66110 | 2 |
| 71 | 82 | — | — | TELL HER (You Love Her Every Day) — Frank Sinatra, Reprise 0373 | 2 |
| 72 | 84 | — | — | IT'S WONDERFUL TO BE IN LOVE — Ovations, Goldwax 113 | 2 |
| 73 | — | — | — | GIVE US YOUR BLESSINGS — Shangri-Las, Red Bird 10-030 | 1 |
| 74 | — | — | — | HERE COMES THE NIGHT — Them, Parrot 9749 | 1 |
| 75 | 90 | — | — | APPLE BLOSSOM TIME — Wayne Newton, Capitol 5419 | 2 |
| 76 | 91 | — | — | YOU REALLY KNOW HOW TO HURT A GUY — Jan & Dean, Liberty 55792 | 2 |
| 77 | 80 | 89 | 93 | GOTTA HAVE YOUR LOVE — Sapphires, ABC-Paramount 10639 | 5 |
| 78 | 85 | 100 | — | WHAT'S HE DOING IN MY WORLD — Eddy Arnold, RCA Victor 8516 | 3 |
| 79 | 89 | 94 | 94 | LOVE IS A 5-LETTER WORD — James Phelps, Argo 5499 | 4 |
| 80 | — | — | — | TONIGHT'S THE NIGHT — Solomon Burke, Atlantic 2288 | 1 |
| 81 | 81 | 86 | 91 | GOOD LOVIN' — Olympics, Loma 2013 | 5 |
| 82 | 99 | — | — | YOU TURN ME ON — Ian Whitcomb, Tower 127 | 2 |
| 83 | 98 | — | — | BRING A LITTLE SUNSHINE — Vic Dana, Dolton 305 | 2 |
| 84 | 76 | 78 | 85 | THE MOUSE — Soupy Sales, ABC-Paramount 10646 | 6 |
| 85 | — | — | — | I'LL KEEP HOLDING ON — Marvelettes, Tamla 54116 | 1 |
| 86 | 95 | 95 | 98 | KEEP ON TRYING — Bobby Vee, Liberty 55790 | 4 |
| 87 | — | — | — | A WORLD OF OUR OWN — Seekers, Capitol 5430 | 1 |
| 88 | — | — | — | IS THIS WHAT I GET FOR LOVING YOU? — Ronettes, Philles 128 | 1 |
| 89 | — | — | — | LITTLE LONELY ONE — Tom Jones, Tower 126 | 1 |
| 90 | — | — | — | LIP SYNC — Len Barry, Decca 31788 | 1 |
| 91 | 94 | 98 | — | WHEN THE SHIP COMES IN — Peter, Paul & Mary, Warner Bros. 5625 | 3 |
| 92 | — | — | — | OO WEE BABY, I LOVE YOU — Fred Hughes, Vee Jay 684 | 1 |
| 93 | — | — | — | YOU'LL MISS ME (When I'm Gone) — Fontella Bass & Bobby McClure, Checker 1111 | 1 |
| 94 | — | — | — | IT'S ALMOST TOMORROW — Jimmy Velvet, Philips 40285 | 1 |
| 95 | 97 | — | — | BREAK UP — Del Shannon, Amy 925 | 2 |
| 96 | — | — | — | TOO MANY RIVERS — Brenda Lee, Decca 31792 | 1 |
| 97 | — | — | — | I LOVE YOU SO — Bobbi Martin, Coral 62452 | 1 |
| 98 | — | — | — | NO ONE — Brenda Lee, Decca 31792 | 1 |
| 99 | — | 91 | 92 | IT AIN'T NO BIG THING — Radiants, Chess 1925 | 3 |
| 100 | — | — | — | THE PUZZLE SONG — Shirley Ellis, Congress 238 | 1 |

## BUBBLING UNDER THE HOT 100

101. SEVENTH SON — Johnny Rivers, Imperial 66112
102. THE FIRST THING EV'RY MORNING — Jimmy Dean, Columbia 43263
103. LET ME DOWN EASY — Betty Lavette, Calla 102
104. THE PRICE OF LOVE — Everly Brothers, Warner Bros. 5628
105. GIRL ON THE BILLBOARD — Del Reeves, United Artists 824
106. IT HURTS ME TOO — Elmore James, Enjoy 2015
107. MAGIC TRUMPET — Comparsa Universitaria De La Laguna, RCA Victor F44
108. MUSTANG SALLY — Sir Mack Rice, Blue Rock 4014
109. TEARS KEEP ON FALLING — Jerry Vale, Columbia 43252
110. SOUL SAUCE — Cal Tjader, Verve 10345
111. JERK IT — Gypsies, Old Town 1180
112. THIS LITTLE BIRD — Marianne Faithfull, London 9759
113. GLORIA — Them, Parrot 9727
114. YOU'LL NEVER WALK ALONE — Gerry & the Pacemakers, Laurie 3302
115. STOP THE MUSIC — Sue Thompson, Hickory 1308
116. AIN'T IT A SHAME — Major Lance, Okeh 7223
117. THE REAL THING — Tina Britt, Eastern 604
118. PLAY WITH FIRE — Rolling Stones, London 9741
119. ONE STEP AHEAD — Aretha Franklin, Columbia 43241
120. 3 O'CLOCK IN THE MORNING — Lou Rawls, Capitol 5424
121. THEN I'LL COUNT AGAIN — Johnny Tillotson, MGM 13344
122. SUMMER SOUNDS — Robert Goulet, Columbia 43301
123. BEFORE YOU GO — Buck Owens, Capitol 5410
124. BABY I'M YOURS — Barbara Lewis, Atlantic 2283
125. WELCOME HOME — Walter Jackson, Okeh 7219
126. (He's Gonna Be) FINE, FINE, FINE — Ikettes, Modern 1008
127. FROM THE BOTTOM OF MY HEART — Moody Blues, London 9764
128. MAE — Herb Alpert's Tijuana Brass, A&M 767
129. LET THERE BE DRUMS '66 — Sandy Nelson, Imperial 66107
130. END UP CRYING — Vibrations, Okeh 7220
131. DO THE BOOMERANG — Jr. Walker & the All Stars, Soul 35012
132. RINDERCELLA — Archie Campbell, RCA Victor 8546
133. YOU TURNED MY BITTER INTO SWEET — Mary Love, Modern 1006
134. LET ME CRY ON YOUR SHOULDER — Georgia Gibbs, Bell 615
135. IT'S ALRIGHT — Bobby Bare, RCA Victor 8571

Compiled from national retail sales and radio station airplay by the Music Popularity Dept. of Record Market Research, Billboard.

# Billboard HOT 100

**For Week Ending June 5, 1965**

★ STAR performer—Sides registering greatest proportionate upward progress this week.

Record Industry Association of America seal of certification as million selling single.

| This Week | 1 Wk. Ago | 2 Wks. Ago | 3 Wks. Ago | TITLE, Artist, Label & Number | Weeks On Chart |
|---|---|---|---|---|---|
| 1 | 1 | 4 | 6 | HELP ME RHONDA — Beach Boys, Capitol 5395 | 8 |
| 2 | 5 | 8 | 10 | WOOLY BULLY — Sam the Sham and the Pharaohs, MGM 13322 | 10 |
| 3 | 3 | 6 | 15 | BACK IN MY ARMS AGAIN — Supremes, Motown 1075 | 6 |
| 4 | 6 | 10 | 20 | CRYING IN THE CHAPEL — Elvis Presley, RCA Victor 0643 | 7 |
| 5 | 2 | 1 | 3 | TICKET TO RIDE — Beatles, Capitol 5407 | 7 |
| 6 | 4 | 2 | 1 | MRS. BROWN YOU'VE GOT A LOVELY DAUGHTER — Herman's Hermits, MGM 13341 | 8 |
| 7 | 17 | 32 | 67 | I CAN'T HELP MYSELF — Four Tops, Motown 1076 | 4 |
| 8 | 9 | 19 | 24 | JUST A LITTLE — Beau Brummels, Autumn 10 | 8 |
| 9 | 19 | 30 | 47 | ENGINE, ENGINE #9 — Roger Miller, Smash 1983 | 5 |
| 10 | 10 | 15 | 17 | IT'S NOT UNUSUAL — Tom Jones, Parrot 9737 | 9 |
| 11 | 8 | 5 | 4 | I'LL NEVER FIND ANOTHER YOU — Seekers, Capitol 5383 | 11 |
| 12 | 18 | 25 | 30 | QUEEN OF THE HOUSE — Jody Miller, Capitol 5402 | 7 |
| 13 | 13 | 18 | 21 | SHE'S ABOUT A MOVER — Sir Douglas Quintet, Tribe 8308 | 10 |
| 14 | 16 | 17 | 27 | TRUE LOVE WAYS — Peter & Gordon, Capitol 5406 | 8 |
| 15 | 11 | 9 | 9 | JUST ONCE IN MY LIFE — Righteous Brothers, Philles 127 | 9 |
| 16 | 14 | 7 | 5 | SILHOUETTES — Herman's Hermits, MGM 13332 | 10 |
| 17 | 55 | 72 | 87 | MR. TAMBOURINE MAN — Byrds, Columbia 43271 | 4 |
| 18 | 21 | 24 | 35 | DO THE FREDDIE — Freddie & the Dreamers, Mercury 72428 | 7 |
| 19 | 7 | 3 | 2 | COUNT ME IN — Gary Lewis and the Playboys, Liberty 55778 | 10 |
| 20 | 12 | 12 | 13 | BABY THE RAIN MUST FALL — Glenn Yarbrough, RCA Victor 8498 | 13 |
| 21 | 22 | 26 | 32 | YOU WERE MADE FOR ME — Freddie & the Dreamers, Tower 127 | 6 |
| 22 | 28 | 36 | 50 | L-O-N-E-L-Y — Bobby Vinton, Epic 9791 | 5 |
| 23 | 15 | 11 | 12 | CAST YOUR FATE TO THE WIND — Sounds Orchestral, Parkway 942 | 12 |
| 24 | 29 | 38 | 49 | LAST CHANCE TO TURN AROUND — Gene Pitney, Musicor 1093 | 5 |
| 25 | 50 | — | — | WONDERFUL WORLD — Herman's Hermits, MGM 13354 | 2 |
| 26 | 30 | 34 | 45 | NOTHING CAN STOP ME — Gene Chandler, Constellation 149 | 8 |
| 27 | 34 | 39 | 53 | HUSH, HUSH, SWEET CHARLOTTE — Patti Page, Columbia 43251 | 7 |
| 28 | 23 | 23 | 28 | REELIN' AND ROCKIN' — Dave Clark Five, Epic 9786 | 8 |
| 29 | 38 | 49 | 61 | CONCRETE AND CLAY — Unit Four Plus Two, London 9751 | 6 |
| 30 | 39 | 50 | 65 | BEFORE AND AFTER — Chad & Jeremy, Columbia 43277 | 4 |
| 31 | 31 | 41 | 52 | YOU WERE ONLY FOOLING — Vic Damone, Warner Bros. 5616 | 8 |
| 32 | 48 | 61 | 84 | FOR YOUR LOVE — Yardbirds, Epic 9790 | 4 |
| 33 | 35 | 45 | 56 | THREE O'CLOCK IN THE MORNING — Bert Kaempfert & His Ork, Decca 31778 | 6 |
| 34 | 25 | 27 | 29 | DREAM ON LITTLE DREAMER — Perry Como, RCA Victor 8533 | 9 |
| 35 | 45 | 51 | 63 | CONCRETE AND CLAY — Eddie Rambeau, DynoVoice 204 | 6 |
| 36 | 47 | 59 | 74 | SHAKIN' ALL OVER — Guess Who's, Scepter 1295 | 5 |
| 37 | 40 | 52 | 66 | BRING IT ON HOME TO ME — Animals, MGM 13339 | 4 |
| 38 | 44 | 55 | 70 | A WALK IN THE BLACK FOREST — Horst Jankowski, Mercury 72425 | 5 |
| 39 | 46 | 56 | 72 | VOODOO WOMAN — Bobby Goldsboro, United Artists 862 | 6 |
| 40 | 26 | 29 | 25 | WE'RE GONNA MAKE IT — Little Milton, Checker 1105 | 11 |
| 41 | 58 | 70 | 85 | CATCH THE WIND — Donovan, Hickory 1309 | 4 |
| 42 | 24 | 21 | 16 | OOO BABY BABY — Miracles, Tamla 54113 | 11 |
| 43 | 20 | 20 | 22 | IKO IKO — Dixie Cups, Red Bird 10-024 | 10 |
| 44 | 54 | 77 | — | (Remember Me) I'M THE ONE WHO LOVES YOU — Dean Martin, Reprise 0369 | 3 |
| 45 | 27 | 16 | 8 | I'LL BE DOGGONE — Marvin Gaye, Tamla 54112 | 12 |
| 46 | 51 | 75 | 96 | I'VE BEEN LOVING YOU TOO LONG — Otis Redding, Volt 126 | 4 |
| 47 | 53 | 65 | 73 | BOO-GA-LOO — Tom & Jerrio, ABC-Paramount 10638 | 6 |
| 48 | 32 | 13 | 7 | I KNOW A PLACE — Petula Clark, Warner Bros. 5612 | 12 |
| 49 | 60 | 74 | 90 | LAURIE — Dickey Lee, TCF-Hall 102 | 4 |
| 50 | 52 | 68 | 77 | LIPSTICK TRACES — O'Jays, Imperial 66102 | 5 |
| 51 | 69 | 86 | 97 | YES, I'M READY — Barbara Mason, Arctic 105 | 4 |
| 52 | 70 | 88 | — | WHAT THE WORLD NEEDS NOW IS LOVE — Jackie DeShannon, Imperial 66110 | 3 |
| 53 | 73 | — | — | GIVE US YOUR BLESSINGS — Shangri-Las, Red Bird 10-030 | 2 |
| 54 | 76 | 91 | — | YOU REALLY KNOW HOW TO HURT A GUY — Jan & Dean, Liberty 55792 | 3 |
| 55 | 92 | — | — | OO WEE BABY, I LOVE YOU — Fred Hughes, Vee Jay 684 | 2 |
| 56 | 56 | 53 | 54 | NOW THAT YOU'VE GONE — Connie Stevens, Warner Bros. 5610 | 7 |
| 57 | 63 | 78 | 82 | AND I LOVE HIM — Esther Phillips, Atlantic 2281 | 5 |
| 58 | 59 | 67 | 64 | SOMETHING YOU GOT — Chuck Jackson & Maxine Brown, Wand 181 | 7 |
| 59 | 57 | 62 | 71 | WISHING IT WAS YOU — Connie Francis, MGM 13331 | 6 |
| 60 | 66 | 79 | 99 | I DO — Marvelows, ABC-Paramount 10629 | 4 |
| 61 | 82 | 99 | — | YOU TURN ME ON — Ian Whitcomb, Tower 127 | 3 |
| 62 | 75 | 90 | — | APPLE BLOSSOM TIME — Wayne Newton, Capitol 5419 | 3 |
| 63 | — | — | — | SEVENTH SON — Johnny Rivers, Imperial 66112 | 1 |
| 64 | 74 | — | — | HERE COMES THE NIGHT — Them, Parrot 9749 | 2 |
| 65 | 65 | 69 | 80 | THE CLIMB — Kingsmen, Wand 183 | 5 |
| 66 | 72 | 84 | — | IT'S WONDERFUL TO BE IN LOVE — Ovations, Goldwax 113 | 3 |
| 67 | 67 | 73 | 81 | YOU CAN HAVE HER — Righteous Brothers, Moonglow 239 | 5 |
| 68 | 71 | 82 | — | TELL HER (You Love Her Every Day) — Frank Sinatra, Reprise 0373 | 3 |
| 69 | 83 | 98 | — | BRING A LITTLE SUNSHINE — Vic Dana, Dolton 305 | 3 |
| 70 | 80 | — | — | TONIGHT'S THE NIGHT — Solomon Burke, Atlantic 2288 | 2 |
| 71 | 87 | — | — | A WORLD OF OUR OWN — Seekers, Capitol 5430 | 2 |
| 72 | 79 | 89 | 94 | LOVE IS A 5-LETTER WORD — James Phelps, Argo 5499 | 5 |
| 73 | — | — | — | THIS LITTLE BIRD — Marianne Faithfull, London 9759 | 1 |
| 74 | 89 | — | — | LITTLE LONELY ONE — Tom Jones, Tower 126 | 2 |
| 75 | 78 | 85 | 100 | WHAT'S HE DOING IN MY WORLD — Eddy Arnold, RCA Victor 8516 | 4 |
| 76 | 85 | — | — | I'LL KEEP HOLDING ON — Marvelettes, Tamla 54116 | 2 |
| 77 | — | — | — | CARA, MIA — Jay & the Americans, United Artists 881 | 1 |
| 78 | 96 | — | — | TOO MANY RIVERS — Brenda Lee, Decca 31792 | 2 |
| 79 | 88 | — | — | IS THIS WHAT I GET FOR LOVING YOU? — Ronettes, Philles 128 | 2 |
| 80 | 100 | — | — | THE PUZZLE SONG — Shirley Ellis, Congress 238 | 2 |
| 81 | — | — | — | YOU'LL NEVER WALK ALONE — Gerry & the Pacemakers, Laurie 3302 | 1 |
| 82 | 97 | — | — | I LOVE YOU SO — Bobbi Martin, Coral 62452 | 2 |
| 83 | — | — | — | 3 O'CLOCK IN THE MORNING — Lou Rawls, Capitol 5424 | 1 |
| 84 | — | — | — | A LITTLE BIT OF HEAVEN — Ronnie Dove, Diamond 184 | 1 |
| 85 | 86 | 95 | 95 | KEEP ON TRYING — Bobby Vee, Liberty 55790 | 5 |
| 86 | 90 | — | — | LIP SYNC — Len Barry, Decca 31788 | 2 |
| 87 | — | — | — | DO THE BOOMERANG — Jr. Walker and the All Stars, Soul 35012 | 1 |
| 88 | — | — | — | SUMMER SOUNDS — Robert Goulet, Columbia 43301 | 1 |
| 89 | — | — | — | WHEN A BOY FALLS IN LOVE — Sam Cooke, RCA Victor 8586 | 1 |
| 90 | — | — | — | BOOT-LEG — Booker T. & MG's, Stax 169 | 1 |
| 91 | 93 | — | — | YOU'LL MISS ME (When I'm Gone) — Fontella Bass & Bobby McClure, Checker 1111 | 2 |
| 92 | — | — | — | THEN I'LL COUNT AGAIN — Johnny Tillotson, MGM 13344 | 1 |
| 93 | 94 | — | — | AIN'T IT A SHAME — Major Lance, Okeh 7223 | 2 |
| 94 | — | — | — | IT'S ALMOST TOMORROW — Jimmy Velvet, Philips 40285 | 1 |
| 95 | 95 | 97 | — | BREAK UP — Del Shannon, Amy 925 | 3 |
| 96 | — | — | — | OPERATOR — Brenda Holloway, Tamla 54115 | 1 |
| 97 | — | — | — | MEETING OVER YONDER — Impressions, ABC-Paramount 10670 | 1 |
| 98 | — | 100 | — | TEARS KEEP ON FALLING — Jerry Vale, Columbia 43252 | 2 |
| 99 | — | — | — | FROM THE BOTTOM OF MY HEART — Moody Blues, London 9764 | 1 |
| 100 | — | — | — | SOUL SAUCE — Cal Tjader, Verve 10345 | 1 |

## BUBBLING UNDER THE HOT 100

101. THE FIRST THING EV'RY MORNING — Jimmy Dean, Columbia 43263
102. TEMPTATION 'BOUT TO GET ME — Knight Brothers, Checker 1107
103. GIRL ON THE BILLBOARD — Del Reeves, United Artists 824
104. LONG LIVE LOVE — Sandie Shaw, Reprise 0375
105. THE REAL THING — Tina Britt, Eastern 604
106. IT HURTS ME TO — Elmore James, Enjoy 2015
107. ARE YOU SINCERE — Trini Lopez, Reprise 0376
108. MARIE — Bachelors, London 9762
109. GOODBYE, SO LONG — Ike & Tina Turner, Modern 1007
110. NEW ORLEANS — Eddie Hodges, Aurora 153
111. NO, NOT MUCH — Vincent Edwards, Colpix 771
112. MY CHERIE — Al Martino, Capitol 5434
113. MUSTANG SALLY — Sir Mack Rice, Blue Rock 4014
114. BEFORE YOU GO — Buck Owens, Capitol 5410
115. WATERMELON MAN — Gloria Lynne, Fontana 1511
116. JERK IT — Gypsies, Old Town 1180
117. GONNA BE READY — Betty Everett, Vee Jay 683
118. STOP THE MUSIC — Sue Thompson, Hickory 1308
119. WELCOME HOME — Walter Jackson, Okeh 7219
120. GEE TO TIGER — Tigers, Colpix 773
121. SEEIN' THE RIGHT LOVE GO WRONG — Jack Jones, Kapp 672
122. BUSTER BROWNE — Willie Mitchell, Hi 2091
123. CAST YOUR FATE TO THE WIND — Steve Alaimo, ABC-Paramount 10680
124. LET THERE BE DRUMS '66 — Sandy Nelson, Imperial 66107
125. (He's Gonna Be) FINE, FINE, FINE — Ikettes, Modern 1008
126. HE'S A LOVER — Mary Wells, 20th Century-Fox 590
127. SWING ME — Nino Tempo & April Stevens, Atco 6350
128. SHE'S GONE AGAIN — Ben E. King, Atco 6357
129. JUST DANCE ON BY — Eydie Gorme, Columbia 43302
130. NO ONE CAN LIVE FOREVER — Sammy Davis Jr., Reprise 0370
131. LAST NIGHT I MADE A LITTLE GIRL CRY — Steve Lawrence, Columbia 43303
132. LET ME CRY ON YOUR SHOULDER — Georgia Gibbs, Bell 615
133. HOLD ME, THRILL ME, KISS ME — Mel Carter, Imperial 66113
134. I CAN'T WORK NO LONGER — Billy Butler, Okeh 7221
135. RIDE YOUR PONY — Lee Dorsey, Amy 927

Compiled from national retail sales and radio station airplay by the Music Popularity Dept. of Record Market Research, Billboard.

# Billboard HOT 100

For Week Ending June 12, 1965

★ STAR performer—Sides registering greatest proportionate upward progress this week.

| This Week | Wk 1 Ago | Wk 2 Ago | Wk 3 Ago | Title, Artist, Label & Number | Weeks On Chart |
|---|---|---|---|---|---|
| 1 | 3 | 3 | 6 | BACK IN MY ARMS AGAIN — Supremes, Motown 1075 | 7 |
| 2 | 2 | 5 | 8 | WOOLY BULLY — Sam the Sham and the Pharaohs, MGM 13322 | 11 |
| 3 | 4 | 6 | 10 | CRYING IN THE CHAPEL — Elvis Presley, RCA Victor 0643 | 8 |
| ★4 | 7 | 17 | 32 | I CAN'T HELP MYSELF — Four Tops, Motown 1076 | 5 |
| 5 | 1 | 1 | 4 | HELP ME RHONDA — Beach Boys, Capitol 5395 | 9 |
| ★6 | 17 | 55 | 72 | MR. TAMBOURINE MAN — Byrds, Columbia 43271 | 5 |
| 7 | 9 | 19 | 30 | ENGINE, ENGINE #9 — Roger Miller, Smash 1983 | 6 |
| ★8 | 25 | 50 | — | WONDERFUL WORLD — Herman's Hermits, MGM 13354 | 3 |
| 9 | 5 | 2 | 1 | TICKET TO RIDE — Beatles, Capitol 5407 | 8 |
| 10 | 8 | 9 | 19 | JUST A LITTLE — Beau Brummels, Autumn 10 | 9 |
| 11 | 6 | 4 | 3 | MRS. BROWN YOU'VE GOT A LOVELY DAUGHTER — Herman's Hermits, MGM 13341 | 9 |
| 12 | 10 | 10 | 15 | IT'S NOT UNUSUAL — Tom Jones, Parrot 9737 | 10 |
| 13 | 32 | 48 | 61 | FOR YOUR LOVE — Yardbirds, Epic 9790 | 5 |
| 14 | 27 | 34 | 39 | HUSH, HUSH, SWEET CHARLOTTE — Patti Page, Columbia 43251 | 8 |
| 15 | 13 | 13 | 18 | SHE'S ABOUT A MOVER — Sir Douglas Quintet, Tribe 8308 | 11 |
| ★16 | 24 | 29 | 38 | LAST CHANCE TO TURN AROUND — Gene Pitney, Musicor 1093 | 6 |
| 17 | 11 | 8 | 5 | I'LL NEVER FIND ANOTHER YOU — Seekers, Capitol 5383 | 12 |
| 18 | 16 | 14 | 7 | SILHOUETTES — Herman's Hermits, MGM 13332 | 11 |
| 19 | 14 | 16 | 17 | TRUE LOVE WAYS — Peter & Gordon, Capitol 5406 | 9 |
| 20 | 12 | 18 | 25 | QUEEN OF THE HOUSE — Jody Miller, Capitol 5402 | 8 |
| 21 | 15 | 11 | 9 | JUST ONCE IN MY LIFE — Righteous Brothers, Philles 127 | 10 |
| 22 | 22 | 28 | 36 | L-O-N-E-L-Y — Bobby Vinton, Epic 9791 | 6 |
| 23 | 20 | 12 | 12 | BABY THE RAIN MUST FALL — Glenn Yarbrough, RCA Victor 8498 | 14 |
| 24 | 26 | 30 | 34 | NOTHING CAN STOP ME — Gene Chandler, Constellation 149 | 9 |
| ★25 | 30 | 39 | 50 | BEFORE AND AFTER — Chad & Jeremy, Columbia 43277 | 5 |
| 26 | 18 | 21 | 24 | DO THE FREDDIE — Freddie & the Dreamers, Mercury 72428 | 8 |
| ★27 | 36 | 47 | 59 | SHAKIN' ALL OVER — Guess Who's, Scepter 1295 | 6 |
| 28 | 29 | 38 | 49 | CONCRETE AND CLAY — Unit Four Plus Two, London 9751 | 7 |
| ★29 | 38 | 44 | 55 | A WALK IN THE BLACK FOREST — Horst Jankowski, Mercury 72425 | 6 |
| 30 | 31 | 31 | 41 | YOU WERE ONLY FOOLING — Vic Damone, Warner Bros. 5616 | 9 |
| 31 | 41 | 58 | 70 | CATCH THE WIND — Donovan, Hickory 1309 | 5 |
| 32 | 37 | 40 | 52 | BRING IT ON HOME TO ME — Animals, MGM 13339 | 5 |
| 33 | 33 | 35 | 45 | THREE O'CLOCK IN THE MORNING — Bert Kaempfert & His Ork, Decca 3177 | 7 |
| ★34 | 44 | 54 | 77 | (Remember Me) I'M THE ONE WHO LOVES YOU — Dean Martin, Reprise 0369 | 4 |
| 35 | 35 | 45 | 51 | CONCRETE AND CLAY — Eddie Rambeau, DynoVoice 204 | 7 |
| 36 | 23 | 15 | 11 | CAST YOUR FATE TO THE WIND — Sounds Orchestral, Parkway 942 | 13 |
| 37 | 39 | 46 | 56 | VOODOO WOMAN — Bobby Goldsboro, United Artists 862 | 7 |
| 38 | 21 | 22 | 26 | YOU WERE MADE FOR ME — Freddie & the Dreamers, Tower 127 | 7 |
| 39 | 19 | 7 | 3 | COUNT ME IN — Gary Lewis and the Playboys, Liberty 55778 | 11 |
| 40 | 51 | 69 | 86 | YES, I'M READY — Barbara Mason, Arctic 105 | 5 |
| 41 | 52 | 70 | 88 | WHAT THE WORLD NEEDS NOW IS LOVE — Jackie DeShannon, Imperial 66110 | 4 |
| ★42 | 53 | 73 | — | GIVE US YOUR BLESSINGS — Shangri-Las, Red Bird 10-030 | 3 |
| ★43 | 63 | — | — | SEVENTH SON — Johnny Rivers, Imperial 66112 | 2 |
| ★44 | 54 | 76 | 91 | YOU REALLY KNOW HOW TO HURT A GUY — Jan & Dean, Liberty 55792 | 4 |
| 45 | 55 | 92 | — | OO WEE BABY, I LOVE YOU — Fred Hughes, Vee Jay 684 | 3 |
| 46 | 46 | 51 | 75 | I'VE BEEN LOVING YOU TOO LONG — Otis Redding, Volt 126 | 5 |
| 47 | 49 | 60 | 74 | LAURIE — Dickey Lee, TCF-Hall 102 | 5 |
| 48 | 50 | 52 | 68 | LIPSTICK TRACES — O'Jays, Imperial 66102 | 6 |
| 49 | 28 | 23 | 23 | REELIN' AND ROCKIN' — Dave Clark Five, Epic 9786 | 9 |
| 50 | 34 | 25 | 27 | DREAM ON LITTLE DREAMER — Perry Como, RCA Victor 8533 | 10 |
| 51 | 61 | 82 | 99 | YOU TURN ME ON — Ian Whitcomb, Tower 127 | 4 |
| 52 | 62 | 75 | 90 | APPLE BLOSSOM TIME — Wayne Newton, Capitol 5419 | 4 |
| 53 | 64 | 74 | — | HERE COMES THE NIGHT — Them, Parrot 9749 | 3 |
| ★54 | 77 | — | — | CARA, MIA — Jay & the Americans, United Artists 881 | 2 |
| 55 | 58 | 59 | 67 | SOMETHING YOU GOT — Chuck Jackson & Maxine Brown, Wand 181 | 8 |
| 56 | 57 | 63 | 78 | AND I LOVE HIM — Esther Phillips, Atlantic 2281 | 6 |
| 57 | 71 | 87 | — | A WORLD OF OUR OWN — Seekers, Capitol 5430 | 3 |
| 58 | 60 | 66 | 79 | I DO — Marvelows, ABC-Paramount 10629 | 5 |
| ★59 | 73 | — | — | THIS LITTLE BIRD — Marianne Faithfull, London 9759 | 2 |
| 60 | 74 | 89 | — | LITTLE LONELY ONE — Tom Jones, Tower 126 | 3 |
| 61 | 76 | 85 | — | I'LL KEEP HOLDING ON — Marvelettes, Tamla 54116 | 3 |
| 62 | 47 | 53 | 65 | BOO-GA-LOO — Tom & Jerrio, ABC-Paramount 10638 | 7 |
| 63 | 78 | 96 | — | TOO MANY RIVERS — Brenda Lee, Decca 31792 | 3 |
| 64 | 68 | 71 | 82 | TELL HER (You Love Her Each Day) — Frank Sinatra, Reprise 0373 | 4 |
| 65 | 59 | 57 | 62 | WISHING IT WAS YOU — Connie Francis, MGM 13331 | 7 |
| 66 | 66 | 72 | 84 | IT'S WONDERFUL TO BE IN LOVE — Ovations, Goldwax 113 | 4 |
| ★67 | — | — | — | (I Can't Get No) SATISFACTION — Rolling Stones, London 9766 | 1 |
| 68 | 84 | — | — | A LITTLE BIT OF HEAVEN — Ronnie Dove, Diamond 184 | 2 |
| 69 | 69 | 83 | 98 | BRING A LITTLE SUNSHINE — Vic Dana, Dolton 305 | 4 |
| 70 | 70 | 80 | — | TONIGHT'S THE NIGHT — Solomon Burke, Atlantic 2288 | 3 |
| 71 | 72 | 79 | 89 | LOVE IS A 5-LETTER WORD — James Phelps, Argo 5499 | 6 |
| 72 | 87 | — | — | DO THE BOOMERANG — Jr. Walker & the All Stars, Soul 35012 | 2 |
| 73 | 75 | 78 | 85 | WHAT'S HE DOING IN MY WORLD — Eddy Arnold, RCA Victor 8516 | 5 |
| ★74 | 89 | — | — | WHEN A BOY FALLS IN LOVE — Sam Cooke, RCA Victor 8586 | 2 |
| 75 | 79 | 88 | — | IS THIS WHAT I GET FOR LOVING YOU? — Ronettes, Philles 128 | 3 |
| 76 | 81 | — | — | YOU'LL NEVER WALK ALONE — Gerry & the Pacemakers, Laurie 3302 | 2 |
| 77 | 82 | 97 | — | I LOVE YOU SO — Bobbi Martin, Coral 62452 | 3 |
| 78 | 88 | — | — | SUMMER SOUNDS — Robert Goulet, Columbia 43301 | 2 |
| 79 | 97 | — | — | MEETING OVER YONDER — Impressions, ABC-Paramount 10670 | 2 |
| 80 | 80 | 100 | — | THE PUZZLE SONG — Shirley Ellis, Congress 238 | 3 |
| 81 | 65 | 65 | 69 | THE CLIMB — Kingsmen, Wand 183 | 6 |
| ★82 | — | — | — | TEMPTATION 'BOUT TO GET ME — Knight Brothers, Checker 1107 | 1 |
| 83 | — | — | — | SET ME FREE — Kinks, Reprise 0379 | 1 |
| ★84 | — | — | — | WHO'S CHEATING WHO? — Little Milton, Checker 1113 | 1 |
| 85 | 90 | — | — | BOOT-LEG — Booker T. & MG's, Stax 169 | 2 |
| 86 | 86 | 90 | — | LIP SYNC — Len Barry, Decca 31788 | 2 |
| 87 | 96 | — | — | OPERATOR — Brenda Holloway, Tamla 54115 | 2 |
| ★88 | — | — | — | IT'S JUST A LITTLE BIT TOO LATE — Wayne Fontana & the Mindbenders, Fontana 1514 | 1 |
| ★89 | — | — | — | MARIE — Bachelors, London 9762 | 1 |
| ★90 | — | — | — | MY CHERIE — Al Martino, Capitol 5434 | 1 |
| 91 | 93 | — | — | AIN'T IT A SHAME — Major Lance, Okeh 7223 | 2 |
| 92 | 92 | — | — | THEN I'LL COUNT AGAIN — Johnny Tillotson, MGM 13344 | 2 |
| 93 | 94 | 94 | — | IT'S ALMOST TOMORROW — Jimmy Velvet, Philips 40285 | 3 |
| 94 | 100 | — | — | SOUL SAUCE — Cal Tjader, Verve 10345 | 2 |
| 95 | — | — | — | SEEIN' THE RIGHT LOVE GO WRONG — Jack Jones, Kapp 672 | 1 |
| 96 | 98 | 100 | — | TEARS KEEP ON FALLING — Jerry Vale, Columbia 43252 | 3 |
| 97 | 99 | — | — | FROM THE BOTTOM OF MY HEART — Moody Blues, London 9764 | 2 |
| 98 | — | — | — | ARE YOU SINCERE — Trini Lopez, Reprise 0376 | 1 |
| 99 | — | — | — | WELCOME HOME — Walter Jackson, Okeh 7219 | 1 |
| 100 | — | — | — | LONG LIVE LOVE — Sandie Shaw, Reprise 0375 | 1 |

## BUBBLING UNDER THE HOT 100

101. 3 O'CLOCK IN THE MORNING .... Lou Rawls, Capitol 5424
102. GIRL ON THE BILLBOARD .... Del Reeves, United Artists 824
103. THE REAL THING .... Tina Britt, Eastern 604
104. FIRST THING EV'RY MORNING .... Jimmy Dean, Columbia 43263
105. TAKE THE TIME .... Johnny Mathis, Mercury 72432
106. IT HURTS ME TOO .... Elmore James, Enjoy 2015
107. NEW ORLEANS .... Eddie Hodges, Aurora 153
108. NO, NOT MUCH .... Vincent Edwards, Colpix 771
109. GOODBYE, SO LONG .... Ike & Tina Turner, Modern 1007
110. YOU'LL MISS ME (When I'm Gone) .... Fontella Bass & Bobby McClure, Checker 1111
111. CAST YOUR FATE TO THE WIND NO LONGER .... Steve Alaimo, ABC-Paramount 10680
112. I CAN'T HELP MYSELF .... Billy Butler, Okeh 7221
113. MUSTANG SALLY .... Sir Mack Rice, Blue Rock 4014
114. WATERMELON MAN .... Gloria Lynne, Fontana 1511
115. NOBODY KNOWS WHAT'S GOIN' ON .... Chiffons, Laurie 3301
116. BABY I'M YOURS .... Barbara Lewis, Atlantic 2283
117. BREAK UP .... Del Shannon, Amy 925
118. WHAT'S NEW PUSSYCAT? .... Tom Jones, Parrot 9765
119. GEETO TIGER .... Tigers, Colpix 773
120. NO ONE CAN LIVE FOREVER .... Sammy Davis Jr., Reprise 0370
121. BUSTER BROWNE .... Willie Mitchell, Hi 2091
122. IT'S ALRIGHT .... Bobby Bare, RCA Victor 8571
123. HE'S A LOVER .... Mary Wells, 20th Century-Fox 590
124. STAY IN MY CORNER .... Dells, Vee Jay 624
125. THE LITTLE BIRD .... Nashville Teens, MGM 13357
126. BORN TO BE WITH YOU .... Capitol Showband, Argo 5502
127. JUST DANCE ON BY .... Eydie Gorme, Columbia 43302
128. TRAINS, BOATS AND PLANES .... Billy J. Kramer & the Dakotas, Imperial 66115
129. HOLD ME, THRILL ME, KISS ME .... Mel Carter, Imperial 66113
130. LAST NIGHT I MADE A LITTLE GIRL CRY .... Steve Lawrence, Columbia 43303
131. I WANT CANDY .... Strangeloves, Bang 501
132. TRAVELIN' ON .... Jack Jones, Kapp 672
133. DARLING TAKE ME BACK .... Lenny Welch, Kapp 662
134. THEME FROM "A SUMMER PLACE" .... Lettermen, Capitol 5437
135. RIDE YOUR PONY .... Lee Dorsey, Amy 927

Compiled from national retail sales and radio station airplay by the Music Popularity Dept. of Record Market Research, Billboard.

# Billboard HOT 100

For Week Ending June 19, 1965

★ STAR performer—Sides registering greatest proportionate upward progress this week.

Record Industry Association of America seal of certification as million selling single.

| This Week | 1 Wk. Ago | 2 Wks. Ago | 3 Wks. Ago | TITLE Artist, Label & Number | Weeks On Chart |
|---|---|---|---|---|---|
| 1 | 4 | 7 | 17 | I CAN'T HELP MYSELF — Four Tops, Motown 1076 | 6 |
| 2 | 6 | 17 | 55 | MR. TAMBOURINE MAN — Byrds, Columbia 43271 | 6 |
| 3 | 2 | 2 | 5 | WOOLY BULLY — Sam the Sham and the Pharaohs, MGM 13322 | 12 |
| 4 | 3 | 4 | 6 | CRYING IN THE CHAPEL — Elvis Presley, RCA Victor 0643 | 9 |
| 5 | 1 | 3 | 3 | BACK IN MY ARMS AGAIN — Supremes, Motown 1075 | 8 |
| 6 | 8 | 25 | 50 | WONDERFUL WORLD — Herman's Hermits, MGM 13354 | 4 |
| 7 | 5 | 1 | 1 | HELP ME RHONDA — Beach Boys, Capitol 5395 | 10 |
| 8 | 7 | 9 | 19 | ENGINE, ENGINE #9 — Roger Miller, Smash 1983 | 7 |
| 9 | 13 | 32 | 48 | FOR YOUR LOVE — Yardbirds, Epic 9790 | 6 |
| 10 | 14 | 27 | 34 | HUSH, HUSH, SWEET CHARLOTTE — Patti Page, Columbia 43251 | 9 |
| 11 | 9 | 5 | 2 | TICKET TO RIDE — Beatles, Capitol 5407 | 9 |
| 12 | 10 | 8 | 9 | JUST A LITTLE — Beau Brummels, Autumn 10 | 10 |
| 13 | 16 | 24 | 29 | LAST CHANCE TO TURN AROUND — Gene Pitney, Musicor 1093 | 7 |
| 14 | 11 | 6 | 4 | MRS. BROWN YOU'VE GOT A LOVELY DAUGHTER — Herman's Hermits, MGM 13341 | 10 |
| 15 | 43 | 63 | — | SEVENTH SON — Johnny Rivers, Imperial 66112 | 3 |
| 16 | 29 | 38 | 44 | A WALK IN THE BLACK FOREST — Horst Jankowski, Mercury 72425 | 7 |
| 17 | 25 | 30 | 39 | BEFORE AND AFTER — Chad & Jeremy, Columbia 43277 | 6 |
| 18 | 24 | 26 | 30 | NOTHING CAN STOP ME — Gene Chandler, Constellation 149 | 10 |
| 19 | 19 | 14 | 16 | TRUE LOVE WAYS — Peter & Gordon, Capitol 5406 | 10 |
| 20 | 12 | 10 | 10 | IT'S NOT UNUSUAL — Tom Jones, Parrot 9737 | 11 |
| 21 | 51 | 61 | 82 | YOU TURN ME ON — Ian Whitcomb, Tower 134 | 5 |
| 22 | 41 | 52 | 70 | WHAT THE WORLD NEEDS NOW IS LOVE — Jackie DeShannon, Imperial 66110 | 5 |
| 23 | 40 | 51 | 69 | YES, I'M READY — Barbara Mason, Arctic 105 | 6 |
| 24 | 27 | 36 | 47 | SHAKIN' ALL OVER — Guess Who's, Scepter 1295 | 7 |
| 25 | 31 | 41 | 58 | CATCH THE WIND — Donovan, Hickory 1309 | 6 |
| 26 | 67 | — | — | (I Can't Get No) SATISFACTION — Rolling Stones, London 9766 | 2 |
| 27 | 22 | 22 | 28 | L-O-N-E-L-Y — Bobby Vinton, Epic 9791 | 6 |
| 28 | 54 | 77 | — | CARA, MIA — Jay & the Americans, United Artists 881 | 3 |
| 29 | 47 | 49 | 60 | LAURIE — Dickey Lee, TCF-Hall 102 | 6 |
| 30 | 37 | 39 | 46 | VOODOO WOMAN — Bobby Goldsboro, United Artists 862 | 8 |
| 31 | 18 | 16 | 14 | SILHOUETTES — Herman's Hermits, MGM 13332 | 12 |
| 32 | 34 | 44 | 54 | (Remember Me) I'M THE ONE WHO LOVES YOU — Dean Martin, Reprise 0369 | 5 |
| 33 | 21 | 15 | 11 | JUST ONCE IN MY LIFE — Righteous Brothers, Philles 127 | 11 |
| 34 | 30 | 31 | 31 | YOU WERE ONLY FOOLING — Vic Damone, Warner Bros. 5616 | 10 |
| 35 | 42 | 53 | 73 | GIVE US YOUR BLESSING — Shangri-Las, Red Bird 10-030 | 4 |
| 36 | 46 | 46 | 51 | I'VE BEEN LOVING YOU TOO LONG — Otis Redding, Volt 126 | 6 |
| 37 | 28 | 29 | 38 | CONCRETE AND CLAY — Unit Four Plus Two, London 9751 | 8 |
| 38 | 45 | 55 | 92 | OO WEE BABY, I LOVE YOU — Fred Hughes, Vee Jay 684 | 4 |
| 39 | 36 | 23 | 15 | CAST YOUR FATE TO THE WIND — Sounds Orchestral, Parkway 942 | 14 |
| 40 | 32 | 37 | 40 | BRING IT ON HOME TO ME — Animals, MGM 13339 | 6 |
| 41 | 44 | 54 | 76 | YOU REALLY KNOW HOW TO HURT A GUY — Jan & Dean, Liberty 55792 | 5 |
| 42 | 33 | 33 | 35 | THREE O'CLOCK IN THE MORNING — Bert Kaempfert & His Ork, Decca 31778 | 8 |
| 43 | 20 | 12 | 18 | QUEEN OF THE HOUSE — Jody Miller, Capitol 5402 | 9 |
| 44 | 57 | 71 | 87 | A WORLD OF OUR OWN — Seekers, Capitol 5430 | 4 |
| 45 | 53 | 64 | 74 | HERE COMES THE NIGHT — Them, Parrot 9749 | 4 |
| 46 | 35 | 35 | 45 | CONCRETE AND CLAY — Eddie Rambeau, DynoVoice 204 | 8 |
| 47 | 68 | 84 | — | A LITTLE BIT OF HEAVEN — Ronnie Dove, Diamond 184 | 3 |
| 48 | 58 | 60 | 66 | I DO — Marvelows, ABC-Paramount 10629 | 6 |
| 49 | 59 | 73 | — | THIS LITTLE BIRD — Marianne Faithfull, London 9759 | 3 |
| 50 | 17 | 11 | 8 | I'LL NEVER FIND ANOTHER YOU — Seekers, Capitol 5383 | 13 |
| 51 | 61 | 76 | 85 | I'LL KEEP HOLDING ON — Marvelettes, Tamla 54116 | 4 |
| 52 | 62 | 75 | — | APPLE BLOSSOM TIME — Wayne Newton, Capitol 5419 | 5 |
| 53 | 63 | 78 | 96 | TOO MANY RIVERS — Brenda Lee, Decca 31792 | 4 |
| 54 | 70 | 70 | 80 | TONIGHT'S THE NIGHT — Solomon Burke, Atlantic 2288 | 4 |
| 55 | 56 | 57 | 63 | AND I LOVE HIM — Esther Phillips, Atlantic 2281 | 7 |
| 56 | 15 | 13 | 13 | SHE'S ABOUT A MOVER — Sir Douglas Quintet, Tribe 8308 | 12 |
| 57 | 48 | 50 | 52 | LIPSTICK TRACES — O'Jays, Imperial 66102 | 7 |
| 58 | 60 | 74 | 89 | LITTLE LONELY ONE — Tom Jones, Tower 126 | 4 |
| 59 | 55 | 58 | 59 | SOMETHING YOU GOT — Chuck Jackson & Maxine Brown, Wand 181 | 9 |
| 60 | 72 | 87 | — | DO THE BOOMERANG — Jr. Walker & the All Stars, Soul 35012 | 3 |
| 61 | 66 | 66 | 72 | IT'S WONDERFUL TO BE IN LOVE — Ovations, Goldwax 113 | 5 |
| 62 | 74 | 89 | — | WHEN A BOY FALLS IN LOVE — Sam Cooke, RCA Victor 8586 | 3 |
| 63 | 76 | 81 | — | YOU'LL NEVER WALK ALONE — Gerry & the Pacemakers, Laurie 3302 | 3 |
| 64 | 64 | 68 | 71 | TELL HER (You Love Her Each Day) — Frank Sinatra, Reprise 0373 | 5 |
| 65 | 62 | 47 | 53 | BOO-GA-LOO — Tom & Jerrio, ABC-Paramount 10638 | 8 |
| 66 | 71 | 72 | 79 | LOVE IS A 5-LETTER WORD — James Phelps, Argo 5499 | 7 |
| 67 | 69 | 69 | 83 | BRING A LITTLE SUNSHINE — Vic Dana, Dolton 305 | 5 |
| 68 | 83 | — | — | SET ME FREE — Kinks, Reprise 0379 | 2 |
| 69 | 73 | 75 | 78 | WHAT'S HE DOING IN MY WORLD — Eddy Arnold, RCA Victor 8516 | 6 |
| 70 | — | — | — | (Such An) EASY QUESTION — Elvis Presley, RCA Victor 8585 | 1 |
| 71 | 89 | — | — | MARIE — Bachelors, London 9762 | 2 |
| 72 | 84 | — | — | WHO'S CHEATING WHO? — Little Milton, Checker 1113 | 2 |
| 73 | 79 | 97 | — | MEETING OVER YONDER — Impressions, ABC-Paramount 10670 | 3 |
| 74 | 77 | 82 | 97 | I LOVE YOU SO — Bobbi Martin, Coral 62452 | 4 |
| 75 | 75 | 79 | 88 | IS THIS WHAT I GET FOR LOVING YOU? — Ronettes, Philles 128 | 4 |
| 76 | 78 | 88 | — | SUMMER SOUNDS — Robert Goulet, Columbia 43301 | 3 |
| 77 | 82 | — | — | TEMPTATION 'BOUT TO GET ME — Knight Brothers, Checker 1107 | 2 |
| 78 | 80 | 80 | 100 | THE PUZZLE SONG — Shirley Ellis, Congress 238 | 4 |
| 79 | — | — | — | WHAT'S NEW PUSSYCAT? — Tom Jones, Parrot 9765 | 1 |
| 80 | 88 | — | — | IT'S JUST A LITTLE BIT TOO LATE — Wayne Fontana & the Mindbenders, Fontana 1514 | 2 |
| 81 | — | — | — | IT FEELS SO RIGHT — Elvis Presley, RCA Victor 8585 | 1 |
| 82 | — | — | — | GIRL COME RUNNING — 4 Seasons, Philips 40305 | 1 |
| 83 | — | — | — | I LIKE IT LIKE THAT — Dave Clark Five, Epic 9811 | 1 |
| 84 | 86 | 86 | 90 | LIP SYNC — Len Barry, Decca 31788 | 4 |
| 85 | 85 | 90 | — | BOOT-LEG — Booker T. & MG's, Stax 169 | 3 |
| 86 | 95 | — | — | SEEIN' THE RIGHT LOVE GO WRONG — Jack Jones, Kapp 672 | 2 |
| 87 | 87 | 96 | — | OPERATOR — Brenda Holloway, Tamla 54115 | 3 |
| 88 | 92 | 92 | — | THEN I'LL COUNT AGAIN — Johnny Tillotson, MGM 13344 | 3 |
| 89 | 90 | — | — | MY CHERIE — Al Martino, Capitol 5434 | 2 |
| 90 | — | — | — | HE'S A LOVER — Mary Wells, 20th Century-Fox 590 | 1 |
| 91 | 91 | 93 | — | AIN'T IT A SHAME — Major Lance, Okeh 7223 | 3 |
| 92 | — | — | — | SITTING IN THE PARK — Billy Stewart, Chess 1932 | 1 |
| 93 | 97 | 99 | — | FROM THE BOTTOM OF MY HEART — Moody Blues, London 9764 | 3 |
| 94 | 94 | 100 | — | SOUL SAUCE — Cal Tjader, Verve 10345 | 3 |
| 95 | 99 | — | — | WELCOME HOME — Walter Jackson, Okeh 7219 | 2 |
| 96 | 98 | — | — | ARE YOU SINCERE — Trini Lopez, Reprise 0376 | 2 |
| 97 | — | — | — | BABY I'M YOURS — Barbara Lewis, Atlantic 2283 | 1 |
| 98 | — | — | — | SUNSHINE, LOLLIPOPS AND RAINBOWS — Lesley Gore, Mercury 72433 | 1 |
| 99 | 100 | — | — | LONG LIVE LOVE — Sandie Shaw, Reprise 0375 | 2 |
| 100 | — | — | — | NOBODY KNOWS WHAT'S GOIN' ON — Chiffons, Laurie 3301 | 1 |

## BUBBLING UNDER THE HOT 100

101. 3 O'CLOCK IN THE MORNING — Lou Rawls, Capitol 5424
102. GIRL ON THE BILLBOARD — Del Reeves, United Artists 824
103. THE REAL THING — Tina Britt, Eastern 604
104. FIRST THING EV'RY MORNING — Jimmy Dean, Columbia 43263
105. TAKE THE TIME — Johnny Mathis, Mercury 72432
106. NEW ORLEANS — Eddie Hodges, Aurora 153
107. WATERMELON MAN — Gloria Lynn, Fontana 1511
108. GOODBYE, SO LONG — Ike & Tina Turner, Modern 1007
109. CAST YOUR FATE TO THE WIND — Steve Alaimo, ABC-Paramount 10680
110. YOU'LL MISS ME (When I'm Gone) — Fontella Bass & Bobby McClure, Checker 1111
111. RIDE YOUR PONY — Lee Dorsey, Amy 927
112. I CAN'T WORK NO LONGER — Billy Butler, Okeh 7221
113. IT'S ALMOST TOMORROW — Jimmy Velvet, Philips 40285
114. DON'T JUST STAND THERE — Patty Duke, United Artists 875
115. NO PITY (In the Naked City) — Jackie Wilson, Brunswick 55280
116. THEME FROM "A SUMMER PLACE" — Lettermen, Capitol 5437
117. TRAINS, BOATS AND PLANES — Billy J. Kramer with the Dakotas, Imperial 66115
118. NO ONE CAN LIVE FOREVER — Sammy Davis Jr., Reprise 0370
119. HOLD ME, THRILL ME, KISS ME — Mel Carter, Imperial 66113
120. BUSTER BROWNE — Willie Mitchell, Hi 2091
121. TEARS KEEP ON FALLING — Jerry Vale, Columbia 43252
122. STAY IN MY CORNER — Dells, Vee Jay 674
123. THE LITTLE BIRD — Nashville Teens, MGM 13357
124. JUST DANCE ON BY — Eydie Gorme, Columbia 43302
125. I WANT CANDY — Strangeloves, Bang 501
126. BORN TO BE WITH YOU — Capitol Showband, Argo 5502
127. SILVER THREADS AND GOLDEN NEEDLES — Jody Miller, Capitol 5429
128. DARLING TAKE ME BACK — Lenny Welch, Kapp 662
129. ONE MONKEY DON'T STOP NO SHOW — Joe Tex, Dial 5011
130. FORGET DOMANI — Connie Francis, MGM 13337
131. MAE — Herb Alpert & His Tijuana Brass, A&M 767
132. SUNRISE, SUNSET — Eddie Fisher, Dot 1712
133. HOLD ON BABY — Sam Hawkins, Blue Cat 112
134. ONE STEP AT A TIME — Maxine Brown, Wand 185
135. FORGET DOMANI — Frank Sinatra, Reprise 0380

# Billboard HOT 100

For Week Ending June 26, 1965

★ STAR performer—Sides registering greatest proportionate upward progress this week.

Record Industry Association of America seal of certification as million selling single.

| This Week | 1 Wk. Ago | 2 Wks. Ago | 3 Wks. Ago | TITLE Artist, Label & Number | Weeks On Chart |
|---|---|---|---|---|---|
| 1 | 2 | 6 | 17 | MR. TAMBOURINE MAN — Byrds, Columbia 43271 | 7 |
| 2 | 1 | 4 | 7 | I CAN'T HELP MYSELF — Four Tops, Motown 1076 | 7 |
| 3 | 3 | 2 | 2 | WOOLY BULLY — Sam the Sham and the Pharaohs, MGM 13322 | 13 |
| 4 | 26 | 67 | — | (I Can't Get No) SATISFACTION — Rolling Stones, London 9766 | 3 |
| 5 | 6 | 8 | 25 | WONDERFUL WORLD — Herman's Hermits, MGM 13354 | 5 |
| 6 | 4 | 3 | 4 | CRYING IN THE CHAPEL — Elvis Presley, RCA Victor 0643 | 10 |
| 7 | 9 | 13 | 32 | FOR YOUR LOVE — Yardbirds, Epic 9790 | 7 |
| 8 | 10 | 14 | 27 | HUSH, HUSH, SWEET CHARLOTTE — Patti Page, Columbia 43251 | 10 |
| 9 | 7 | 5 | 1 | HELP ME RHONDA — Beach Boys, Capitol 5395 | 11 |
| 10 | 15 | 43 | 63 | SEVENTH SON — Johnny Rivers, Imperial 66112 | 4 |
| 11 | 5 | 1 | 3 | BACK IN MY ARMS AGAIN — Supremes, Motown 1075 | 9 |
| 12 | 23 | 40 | 51 | YES, I'M READY — Barbara Mason, Arctic 105 | 7 |
| 13 | 16 | 29 | 38 | A WALK IN THE BLACK FOREST — Horst Jankowski, Mercury 72425 | 8 |
| 14 | 21 | 51 | 61 | YOU TURN ME ON — Ian Whitcomb, Tower 134 | 6 |
| 15 | 22 | 41 | 52 | WHAT THE WORLD NEEDS NOW IS LOVE — Jackie DeShannon, Imperial 66110 | 6 |
| 16 | 28 | 54 | 77 | CARA, MIA — Jay & the Americans, United Artists 881 | 4 |
| 17 | 17 | 25 | 30 | BEFORE AND AFTER — Chad & Jeremy, Columbia 43277 | 7 |
| 18 | 12 | 10 | 8 | JUST A LITTLE — Beau Brummels, Autumn 10 | 11 |
| 19 | 13 | 16 | 24 | LAST CHANCE TO TURN AROUND — Gene Pitney, Musicor 1093 | 8 |
| 20 | 11 | 9 | 5 | TICKET TO RIDE — Beatles, Capitol 5407 | 10 |
| 21 | 8 | 7 | 9 | ENGINE, ENGINE #9 — Roger Miller, Smash 1983 | 8 |
| 22 | 29 | 47 | 49 | LAURIE — Dickey Lee, TCF-Hall 102 | 7 |
| 23 | 14 | 11 | 6 | MRS. BROWN YOU'VE GOT A LOVELY DAUGHTER — Herman's Hermits, MGM 13341 | 11 |
| 24 | 24 | 27 | 36 | SHAKIN' ALL OVER — Guess Who's, Scepter 1295 | 8 |
| 25 | 25 | 31 | 41 | CATCH THE WIND — Donovan, Hickory 1309 | 7 |
| 26 | 19 | 19 | 14 | TRUE LOVE WAYS — Peter & Gordon, Capitol 5406 | 11 |
| 27 | 30 | 37 | 39 | VOODOO WOMAN — Bobby Goldsboro, United Artists 862 | 9 |
| 28 | 36 | 46 | 46 | I'VE BEEN LOVING YOU TOO LONG — Otis Redding, Volt 126 | — |
| 29 | 38 | 45 | 55 | OO WEE BABY, I LOVE YOU — Fred Hughes, Vee Jay 684 | 5 |
| 30 | 35 | 42 | 53 | GIVE US YOUR BLESSING — Shangri-Las, Red Bird 10-030 | 5 |
| 31 | 44 | 57 | 71 | A WORLD OF OUR OWN — Seekers, Capitol 5430 | 5 |
| 32 | 47 | 68 | 84 | A LITTLE BIT OF HEAVEN — Ronnie Dove, Diamond 184 | 4 |
| 33 | 45 | 53 | 64 | HERE COMES THE NIGHT — Them, Parrot 9749 | 5 |
| 34 | 18 | 24 | 26 | NOTHING CAN STOP ME — Gene Chandler, Constellation 149 | 11 |
| 35 | 41 | 44 | 54 | YOU REALLY KNOW HOW TO HURT A GUY — Jan & Dean, Liberty 55792 | 6 |
| 36 | 32 | 34 | 44 | (Remember Me) I'M THE ONE WHO LOVES YOU — Dean Martin, Reprise 0369 | 6 |
| 37 | 20 | 12 | 10 | IT'S NOT UNUSUAL — Tom Jones, Parrot 9737 | 12 |
| 38 | 49 | 59 | 73 | THIS LITTLE BIRD — Marianne Faithfull, London 9759 | 4 |
| 39 | 53 | 63 | 78 | TOO MANY RIVERS — Brenda Lee, Decca 31792 | 5 |
| 40 | 27 | 22 | 22 | L-O-N-E-L-Y — Bobby Vinton, Epic 9791 | 8 |
| 41 | 79 | — | — | WHAT'S NEW PUSSYCAT? — Tom Jones, Parrot 9765 | — |
| 42 | 54 | 70 | 70 | TONIGHT'S THE NIGHT — Solomon Burke, Atlantic 2288 | 5 |
| 43 | 37 | 28 | 29 | CONCRETE AND CLAY — Unit Four Plus Two, London 9751 | 9 |
| 44 | 48 | 58 | 60 | I DO — Marvelows, ABC-Paramount 10629 | 7 |
| 45 | 51 | 61 | 76 | I'LL KEEP HOLDING ON — Marvelettes, Tamla 54116 | 5 |
| 46 | 31 | 18 | 16 | SILHOUETTES — Herman's Hermits, MGM 13332 | 13 |
| 47 | 70 | — | — | (Such An) EASY QUESTION — Elvis Presley, RCA Victor 8585 | 2 |
| 48 | 58 | 60 | 74 | LITTLE LONELY ONE — Tom Jones, Tower 126 | 5 |
| 49 | 60 | 72 | 87 | DO THE BOOMERANG — Jr. Walker & the All Stars, Soul 35012 | 4 |
| 50 | 71 | 89 | — | MARIE — Bachelors, London 9762 | 3 |
| 51 | 68 | 83 | — | SET ME FREE — Kinks, Reprise 0379 | 3 |
| 52 | 62 | 74 | 89 | WHEN A BOY FALLS IN LOVE — Sam Cooke, RCA Victor 8586 | 4 |
| 53 | 63 | 76 | 81 | YOU'LL NEVER WALK ALONE — Gerry & the Pacemakers, Laurie 3302 | 4 |
| 54 | 55 | 56 | 57 | AND I LOVE HIM — Esther Phillips, Atlantic 2281 | 8 |
| 55 | 52 | 52 | 62 | APPLE BLOSSOM TIME — Wayne Newton, Capitol 5419 | 6 |
| 56 | 46 | 35 | 35 | CONCRETE AND CLAY — Eddie Rambeau, DynoVoice 204 | 9 |
| 57 | 64 | 64 | 68 | TELL HER (You Love Her Each Day) — Frank Sinatra, Reprise 0373 | — |
| 58 | 83 | — | — | I LIKE IT LIKE THAT — Dave Clark Five, Epic 9811 | 2 |
| 59 | 82 | — | — | GIRL COME RUNNING — 4 Seasons, Philips 40305 | 2 |
| 60 | 69 | 73 | 75 | WHAT'S HE DOING IN MY WORLD — Eddy Arnold, RCA Victor 8516 | 7 |
| 61 | 86 | 95 | — | SEEIN' THE RIGHT LOVE GO WRONG — Jack Jones, Kapp 672 | 3 |
| 62 | 72 | 84 | — | WHO'S CHEATING WHO? — Little Milton, Checker 1113 | 3 |
| 63 | 73 | 79 | 97 | MEETING OVER YONDER — Impressions, ABC-Paramount 10670 | 4 |
| 64 | 61 | 66 | 66 | IT'S WONDERFUL TO BE IN LOVE — Ovations, Goldwax 113 | 6 |
| 65 | 80 | 88 | — | IT'S JUST A LITTLE BIT TOO LATE — Wayne Fontana & the Mindbenders, Fontana 1514 | 3 |
| 66 | 67 | 69 | 69 | BRING A LITTLE SUNSHINE — Vic Dana, Dolton 305 | 6 |
| 67 | — | — | — | THEME FROM "A SUMMER PLACE" — Lettermen, Capitol 5437 | 1 |
| 68 | 76 | 78 | 88 | SUMMER SOUNDS — Robert Goulet, Columbia 43301 | 4 |
| 69 | — | — | — | I WANT CANDY — Strangeloves, Bang 501 | 1 |
| 70 | 74 | 77 | 82 | I LOVE YOU SO — Bobbi Martin, Coral 62452 | — |
| 71 | 81 | — | — | IT FEELS SO RIGHT — Elvis Presley, RCA Victor 8585 | 2 |
| 72 | 85 | 85 | 90 | BOOT-LEG — Booker T. & MG's, Stax 169 | — |
| 73 | 92 | — | — | SITTING IN THE PARK — Billy Stewart, Chess 1932 | 2 |
| 74 | 97 | — | — | BABY I'M YOURS — Barbara Lewis, Atlantic 2283 | 2 |
| 75 | 98 | — | — | SUNSHINE, LOLLIPOPS AND RAINBOWS — Lesley Gore, Mercury 72433 | — |
| 76 | 77 | 82 | — | TEMPTATION 'BOUT TO GET ME — Knight Brothers, Checker 1107 | 3 |
| 77 | — | — | — | HOLD ME, THRILL ME, KISS ME — Mel Carter, Imperial 66113 | 1 |
| 78 | 78 | 80 | 80 | THE PUZZLE SONG — Shirley Ellis, Congress 238 | 5 |
| 79 | — | — | — | DON'T JUST STAND THERE — Patty Duke, United Artists 875 | 1 |
| 80 | — | — | — | WATERMELON MAN — Gloria Lynne, Fontana 1511 | 1 |
| 81 | — | — | — | TAKE ME BACK — Little Anthony & the Imperials, DCP 1136 | 1 |
| 82 | 90 | — | — | HE'S A LOVER — Mary Wells, 20th Century-Fox 590 | — |
| 83 | 87 | 87 | 96 | OPERATOR — Brenda Holloway, Tamla 54115 | 4 |
| 84 | 100 | — | — | NOBODY KNOWS WHAT'S GOIN' ON — Chiffons, Laurie 3301 | 2 |
| 85 | 96 | 98 | — | ARE YOU SINCERE — Trini Lopez, Reprise 0376 | — |
| 86 | 88 | 92 | 92 | THEN I'LL COUNT AGAIN — Johnny Tillotson, MGM 13344 | — |
| 87 | — | — | — | DARLING TAKE ME BACK — Lenny Welch, Kapp 662 | — |
| 88 | 89 | 90 | — | MY CHERIE — Al Martino, Capitol 5434 | 3 |
| 89 | — | — | — | ONE MONKEY DON'T STOP NO SHOW — Joe Tex, Dial 4011 | — |
| 90 | — | — | — | CAST YOUR FATE TO THE WIND — Steve Alaimo, ABC-Paramount 10680 | 1 |
| 91 | 94 | 94 | 100 | SOUL SAUCE — Cal Tjader, Verve 10345 | 4 |
| 92 | — | — | — | TRAINS AND BOATS AND PLANES — Billy J. Kramer & the Dakotas, Imperial 66115 | 1 |
| 93 | — | — | — | THE FIRST THING EV'RY MORNING — Jimmy Dean, Columbia 43263 | 1 |
| 94 | — | — | — | SILVER THREADS AND GOLDEN NEEDLES — Jody Miller, Capitol 5429 | 1 |
| 95 | — | — | — | FORGET DOMANI — Connie Francis, MGM 13363 | 1 |
| 96 | — | — | — | GIRL ON THE BILLBOARD — Del Reeves, United Artists 824 | 1 |
| 97 | 99 | 100 | — | LONG LIVE LOVE — Sandie Shaw, Reprise 0375 | 3 |
| 98 | — | — | — | I WANT YOU BACK AGAIN — Zombies, Parrot 9769 | 1 |
| 99 | — | — | — | I'M A FOOL — Dino, Desi & Billy, Reprise 0367 | 1 |
| 100 | — | — | — | FORGET DOMANI — Frank Sinatra, Reprise 0380 | 1 |

## BUBBLING UNDER THE HOT 100

101. MY MAN — Barbra Streisand, Columbia 43323
102. ONE STEP AT A TIME — Maxine Brown, Wand 185
103. NEW ORLEANS — Eddie Hodges, Aurora 153
104. TAKE THE TIME — Johnny Mathis, Mercury 13432
105. RIDE YOUR PONY — Lee Dorsey, Amy 927
106. WELCOME HOME — Walter Jackson, Okeh 7219
107. GOODBYE, SO LONG — Ike & Tina Turner, Modern 1007
108. YOUR BABY DOESN'T LOVE YOU ANYMORE
109. THE REAL THING — Ruby & the Romantics, Kapp 665
110. FROM THE BOTTOM OF MY HEART — Moody Blues, London 9764
111. HERE I AM — Dionne Warwick, Scepter 12104
112. YOU'LL MISS ME (When I'm Gone) — Fontella Bass & Bobby McClure, Checker 1111
113. NO PITY (In the Naked City) — Jackie Wilson, Brunswick 55280
114. LIP SYNC — Len Barry, Decca 31788
115. FROM A WINDOW — Chad & Jeremy, World Artists 1056
116. JUSTINE — Righteous Brothers, Moonglow 242
117. NO ONE CAN LIVE FOREVER — Sammy Davis, Reprise 0370
118. I'M A FOOL TO CARE — George & Gene, Musicor 1097
119. THREE O'CLOCK IN THE MORNING — North Alpert's Tijuana Brass, A&M 767
120. JERRY VALE — Jerry Vale, Columbia 43252
121. TEARS KEEP ON FALLING — Pete Fountain, Coral 63464
122. STOP! LOOK WHAT YOU'RE DOING — Carla Thomas, Stax 173
123. THE LITTLE BIRD — Nashville Teens, MGM 13357
124. BLUE SHADOWS — B. B. King, Kent 426
125. BUSTER BROWNE — Willie Mitchell, HI 2091
126. SUNRISE, SUNSET — Eddie Fisher, Dot 16732
127. DOWN IN THE BOONDOCKS — Billy Joe Royal, Columbia 43305
128. LAST NIGHT I MADE A LITTLE GIRL CRY — Steve Lawrence, Columbia 43300
129. MAE — Pete Fountain, Coral 63464
130. BUT I DO — Jewels, Dimension 1048
131. IF YOU REALLY WANT ME TO, I'LL GO — Ron-Dells, Smash 1986
132. I PUT A SPELL ON YOU — Nina Simone, Philips 40286
133. MY LITTLE RED BOOK — Manfred Mann, Ascot 2186
134. NAU NINNY NAU — Cannibal & the Headhunters, Rampert 644
135. YAKETY AXE — Chet Atkins, RCA Victor 8590

Compiled from national retail sales and radio station airplay by the Music Popularity Dept. of Record Market Research, Billboard.

# Billboard HOT 100

**For Week Ending July 3, 1965**

★ STAR performer—Sides registering greatest proportionate upward progress this week.

Record Industry Association of America seal of certification as million selling single.

| This Week | Wk. Ago | 2 Wks. Ago | 3 Wks. Ago | TITLE — Artist, Label & Number | Weeks On Chart |
|---|---|---|---|---|---|
| 1 | 2 | 1 | 4 | I CAN'T HELP MYSELF — Four Tops, Motown 1076 | 8 |
| 2 | 4 | 26 | 67 | (I Can't Get No) SATISFACTION — Rolling Stones, London 9766 | 4 |
| 3 | 1 | 2 | 6 | MR. TAMBOURINE MAN — Byrds, Columbia 43271 | 8 |
| 4 | 3 | 3 | 2 | WOOLY BULLY — Sam the Sham and the Pharaohs, MGM 13322 | 14 |
| 5 | 5 | 6 | 8 | WONDERFUL WORLD — Herman's Hermits, MGM 13354 | 6 |
| 6 | 7 | 9 | 13 | FOR YOUR LOVE — Yardbirds, Epic 9790 | 8 |
| 7 | 10 | 15 | 43 | SEVENTH SON — Johnny Rivers, Imperial 66112 | 5 |
| 8 | 6 | 4 | 3 | CRYING IN THE CHAPEL — Elvis Presley, RCA Victor 0643 | 11 |
| 9 | 12 | 23 | 40 | YES, I'M READY — Barbara Mason, Arctic 105 | 8 |
| 10 | 15 | 22 | 41 | WHAT THE WORLD NEEDS NOW IS LOVE — Jackie DeShannon, Imperial 66110 | 7 |
| 11 | 16 | 28 | 54 | CARA, MIA — Jay & the Americans, United Artists 881 | 5 |
| 12 | 14 | 21 | 51 | YOU TURN ME ON — Ian Whitcomb, Tower 134 | 7 |
| 13 | 13 | 16 | 29 | A WALK IN THE BLACK FOREST — Horst Jankowski, Mercury 72425 | 9 |
| 14 | 8 | 10 | 14 | HUSH, HUSH, SWEET CHARLOTTE — Patti Page, Columbia 43251 | 11 |
| 15 | 11 | 5 | 1 | BACK IN MY ARMS AGAIN — Supremes, Motown 1075 | 10 |
| 16 | 22 | 29 | 47 | LAURIE — Dickey Lee, TCF-Hall 102 | 8 |
| 17 | 17 | 17 | 25 | BEFORE AND AFTER — Chad & Jeremy, Columbia 43277 | 8 |
| 18 | 9 | 7 | 5 | HELP ME RHONDA — Beach Boys, Capitol 5395 | 12 |
| 19 | 19 | 13 | 16 | LAST CHANCE TO TURN AROUND — Gene Pitney, Musicor 1093 | 9 |
| 20 | 32 | 47 | 68 | A LITTLE BIT OF HEAVEN — Ronnie Dove, Diamond 184 | 5 |
| 21 | 28 | 36 | 46 | I'VE BEEN LOVING YOU TOO LONG — Otis Redding, Volt 126 | 6 |
| 22 | 24 | 24 | 27 | SHAKIN' ALL OVER — Guess Who's, Scepter 1295 | 9 |
| 23 | 25 | 25 | 31 | CATCH THE WIND — Donovan, Hickory 1309 | 8 |
| 24 | 29 | 38 | 45 | OO WEE BABY, I LOVE YOU — Fred Hughes, Vee Jay 684 | 6 |
| 25 | 31 | 44 | 57 | A WORLD OF OUR OWN — Seekers, Capitol 5430 | 6 |
| 26 | 41 | 79 | — | WHAT'S NEW PUSSYCAT? — Tom Jones, Parrot 9765 | 3 |
| 27 | 47 | 70 | — | (Such An) EASY QUESTION — Elvis Presley, RCA Victor 8585 | 3 |
| 28 | 33 | 45 | 53 | HERE COMES THE NIGHT — Them, Parrot 9749 | 6 |
| 29 | 30 | 35 | 42 | GIVE US YOUR BLESSING — Shangri-Las, Red Bird 10-030 | 6 |
| 30 | 35 | 41 | 44 | YOU REALLY KNOW HOW TO HURT A GUY — Jan & Dean, Liberty 55792 | 7 |
| 31 | 27 | 30 | 37 | VOODOO WOMAN — Bobby Goldsboro, United Artists 862 | 10 |
| 32 | 42 | 54 | 70 | TONIGHT'S THE NIGHT — Solomon Burke, Atlantic 2288 | 6 |
| 33 | 39 | 53 | 63 | TOO MANY RIVERS — Brenda Lee, Decca 31792 | 6 |
| 34 | 45 | 51 | 61 | I'LL KEEP HOLDING ON — Marvelettes, Tamla 54116 | 6 |
| 35 | 38 | 49 | 59 | THIS LITTLE BIRD — Marianne Faithfull, London 9759 | 5 |
| 36 | 18 | 12 | 10 | JUST A LITTLE — Beau Brummels, Autumn 10 | 12 |
| 37 | 44 | 48 | 58 | I DO — Marvelows, ABC-Paramount 10629 | 8 |
| 38 | 21 | 8 | 7 | ENGINE, ENGINE #9 — Roger Miller, Smash 1983 | 9 |
| 39 | 49 | 60 | 72 | DO THE BOOMERANG — Jr. Walker & the All Stars, Soul 35012 | 5 |
| 40 | 50 | 71 | 89 | MARIE — Bachelors, London 9762 | 4 |
| 41 | 51 | 68 | 83 | SET ME FREE — Kinks, Reprise 0379 | 4 |
| 42 | — | — | — | I'M HENRY VIII, I AM — Herman's Hermits, MGM 13367 | 1 |
| 43 | 58 | 83 | — | I LIKE IT LIKE THAT — Dave Clark Five, Epic 9811 | 3 |
| 44 | 59 | 82 | — | GIRL COME RUNNING — 4 Seasons, Philips 40305 | 3 |
| 45 | 34 | 18 | 24 | NOTHING CAN STOP ME — Gene Chandler, Constellation 149 | 12 |
| 46 | 48 | 58 | 60 | LITTLE LONELY ONE — Tom Jones, Tower 126 | 6 |
| 47 | 20 | 11 | 9 | TICKET TO RIDE — Beatles, Capitol 5407 | 11 |
| 48 | 53 | 63 | 76 | YOU'LL NEVER WALK ALONE — Gerry & the Pacemakers, Laurie 3302 | 5 |
| 49 | 73 | 92 | — | SITTING IN THE PARK — Billy Stewart, Chess 1932 | 3 |
| 50 | 62 | 72 | 84 | WHO'S CHEATING WHO? — Little Milton, Checker 1113 | 4 |
| 51 | 63 | 73 | 79 | MEETING OVER YONDER — Impressions, ABC-Paramount 10670 | 5 |
| 52 | 75 | 98 | — | SUNSHINE, LOLLIPOPS AND RAINBOWS — Lesley Gore, Mercury 72433 | 3 |
| 53 | 61 | 86 | 95 | SEEIN' THE RIGHT LOVE GO WRONG — Jack Jones, Kapp 672 | 4 |
| 54 | 69 | — | — | I WANT CANDY — Strangeloves, Bang 501 | 2 |
| 55 | 65 | 80 | 88 | IT'S JUST A LITTLE BIT TOO LATE — Wayne Fontana & the Mindbenders, Fontana 1514 | 4 |
| 56 | 67 | — | — | THEME FROM "A SUMMER PLACE" — Lettermen, Capitol 5437 | 2 |
| 57 | 79 | — | — | DON'T JUST STAND THERE — Patty Duke, United Artists 875 | 2 |
| 58 | 54 | 55 | 56 | AND I LOVE HIM — Esther Phillips, Atlantic 2281 | 9 |
| 59 | 52 | 62 | 74 | WHEN A BOY FALLS IN LOVE — Sam Cooke, RCA Victor 8586 | 5 |
| 60 | 74 | 97 | — | BABY I'M YOURS — Barbara Lewis, Atlantic 2283 | 3 |
| 61 | 81 | — | — | TAKE ME BACK — Little Anthony & the Imperials, DCP 1136 | 2 |
| 62 | 77 | — | — | HOLD ME, THRILL ME, KISS ME — Mel Carter, Imperials 6113 | 3 |
| 63 | 36 | 32 | 34 | (Remember Me) I'M THE ONE WHO LOVES YOU — Dean Martin, Reprise 0369 | 7 |
| 64 | 68 | 76 | 78 | SUMMER SOUNDS — Robert Goulet, Columbia 43301 | 5 |
| 65 | 71 | 81 | — | IT FEELS SO RIGHT — Elvis Presley, RCA Victor 8585 | 3 |
| 66 | 72 | 85 | 85 | BOOT-LEG — Booker T. & MG's, Stax 169 | 5 |
| 67 | 60 | 69 | 73 | WHAT'S HE DOING IN MY WORLD — Eddy Arnold, RCA Victor 8516 | 8 |
| 68 | 80 | — | — | WATERMELON MAN — Gloria Lynne, Fontana 1511 | 2 |
| 69 | 89 | — | — | ONE MONKEY DON'T STOP NO SHOW — Joe Tex, Dial 4011 | 2 |
| 70 | 76 | 77 | 82 | TEMPTATION 'BOUT TO GET ME — Knight Brothers, Checker 1107 | 4 |
| 71 | 84 | 100 | — | NOBODY KNOWS WHAT'S GOIN' ON — Chiffons, Laurie 3301 | 3 |
| 72 | 94 | — | — | SILVER THREADS AND GOLDEN NEEDLES — Jody Miller, Capitol 5429 | 2 |
| 73 | 92 | — | — | TRAINS AND BOATS AND PLANES — Billy J. Kramer & the Dakotas, Imperial 66115 | 2 |
| 74 | 82 | 90 | — | HE'S A LOVER — Mary Wells, 20th Century-Fox 590 | 3 |
| 75 | 70 | 74 | 77 | I LOVE YOU SO — Bobbi Martin, Coral 62452 | 6 |
| 76 | — | — | — | RIDE YOUR PONY — Lee Dorsey, Amy 927 | 1 |
| 77 | 87 | — | — | DARLING TAKE ME BACK — Lenny Welch, Kapp 662 | 2 |
| 78 | 83 | 87 | 87 | OPERATOR — Brenda Holloway, Tamla 54115 | 5 |
| 79 | 99 | — | — | I'M A FOOL — Dino, Desi & Billy, Reprise 0367 | 2 |
| 80 | — | — | — | SAVE YOUR HEART FOR ME — Gary Lewis & the Playboys, Liberty 55809 | 1 |
| 81 | — | — | — | NO PITY (In the Naked City) — Jackie Wilson, Brunswick 55280 | 1 |
| 82 | — | — | — | I CAN'T WORK NO LONGER — Billy Butler & the Chanters, Okeh 7221 | 1 |
| 83 | — | — | — | ALL I REALLY WANT TO DO — Byrds, Columbia 43332 | 1 |
| 84 | — | — | — | MY MAN — Barbra Streisand, Columbia 43323 | 1 |
| 85 | — | — | — | HERE I AM — Dionne Warwick, Scepter 12104 | 1 |
| 86 | — | — | — | ALL I REALLY WANT TO DO — Cher, Imperial 66114 | 1 |
| 87 | — | — | — | NEW ORLEANS — Eddie Hodges, Aurora 153 | 1 |
| 88 | 91 | 94 | 94 | SOUL SAUCE — Cal Tjader, Verve 10345 | 5 |
| 89 | 90 | — | — | CAST YOUR FATE TO THE WIND — Steve Alaimo, ABC-Paramount 10680 | 2 |
| 90 | — | — | — | JUSTINE — Righteous Brothers, Moonglow 242 | 1 |
| 91 | 93 | — | — | THE FIRST THING EV'RY MORNING — Jimmy Dean, Columbia 43263 | 2 |
| 92 | — | — | — | ONE STEP AT A TIME — Maxine Brown, Wand 185 | 1 |
| 93 | 95 | — | — | FORGET DOMANI — Connie Francis, MGM 13363 | 2 |
| 94 | — | — | — | STOP! LOOK WHAT YOU'RE DOING — Carla Thomas, Stax 172 | 1 |
| 95 | — | — | — | DOWN IN THE BOONDOCKS — Billy Joe Royal, Columbia 43305 | 1 |
| 96 | 98 | — | — | I WANT YOU BACK AGAIN — Zombies, Parrot 9769 | 2 |
| 97 | — | — | — | BLUE SHADOWS — B. B. King, Kent 426 | 1 |
| 98 | — | — | — | FOLLOW ME — Drifters, Atlantic 2292 | 1 |
| 99 | 100 | — | — | FORGET DOMANI — Frank Sinatra, Reprise 0380 | 2 |
| 100 | — | — | — | LOVE ME NOW — Brook Benton, Mercury 72446 | 1 |

## BUBBLING UNDER THE HOT 100

101. TO KNOW YOU IS TO LOVE YOU .............. Peter & Gordon, Capitol 5461
102. AIN'T IT A SHAME .............. Major Lance, Okeh 7223
103. LONG LIVE LOVE .............. Sandie Shaw, Reprise 0375
104. BUSTER BROWNE .............. Willie Mitchell, Hi 2091
105. THE REAL THING .............. Tina Britt, Eastern 604
106. GIRL ON THE BILLBOARD .............. Del Reeves, United Artists 824
107. GOOD BYE, SO LONG .............. Ike & Tina Turner, Modern 1007
108. YAKETY AXE .............. Chet Atkins, RCA Victor 8590
109. FROM THE BOTTOM OF MY HEART .............. Moody Blues, London 9764
110. GEE THE MOON IS SHINING BRIGHT .............. Dixie Cups, Red Bird 032
111. MARCH (You'll Be Sorry) .............. Shirelles, Scepter 12101
112. FROM A WINDOW .............. Chad & Jeremy, World Artists 1056
113. IF YOU REALLY WANT ME TO, I'LL GO .............. Ron-Dells, Smash 1986
114. IT'S TOO LATE BABY, TOO LATE .............. Arthur Prysock, Old Town 1183
115. I'M A FOOL TO CARE .............. George & Gene, Musicor 1097
116. MAE .............. Herb Alpert's Tijuana Brass, A&M 767
117. FRANKFURTER SANDWICHES .............. Streamliners with Joanne, ASCOT 2184
118. YOU'D BETTER COME HOME .............. Petula Clark, Warner Bros. 5643
119. THEME FROM HARLOW (Lonely Girl) .............. Bobby Vinton, Epic 9814
120. I PUT A SPELL ON YOU .............. Nina Simone, Philips 40286
121. YOUR BABY DOESN'T LOVE YOU ANYMORE .............. Ruby & the Romantics, Kapp 665
122. MOON OVER NAPLES .............. Bert Kaempfert & His Ork, Decca 31812
123. SUNRISE, SUNSET .............. Eddie Fisher, Dot 16732
124. MY LITTLE RED BOOK .............. Manfred Mann, ASCOT 2184
125. YOU'VE NEVER BEEN IN LOVE LIKE THIS BEFORE .............. Unit Four Plus Two, London 9761
126. LAST NIGHT I MADE A LITTLE GIRL CRY .............. Steve Lawrence, Columbia 42303
127. STREETS OF LOREDO .............. Johnny Cash, Columbia 43313
128. THE LOSER .............. Skyliner, Jubilee 3506
129. MAE .............. Pete Fountain, Coral 62454
130. COME OUT DANCIN' .............. Rick Nelson, Decca 31800
131. YOU WERE ON MY MIND .............. We Five, A&M 770
132. (LOVE IS LIKE A) RAMBLIN' ROSE .............. Ted Taylor, Okeh 5423
133. NAU NINNY NAU .............. Cannibal & the Headhunters, Rampart 644
134. NEW ORLEANS .............. Chartbusters, Crusader 118
135. IN THE MIDNIGHT HOUR .............. Wilson Pickett, Atlantic 2289

Compiled from national retail sales and radio station airplay by the Music Popularity Dept. of Record Market Research, Billboard.

Billboard

For Week Ending July 10, 1965

# HOT 100

★ **STAR performer—Sides registering greatest proportionate upward progress this week.**

Record Industry Association of America seal of certification as million selling single.

| This Week | 1 Wk. Ago | 2 Wks. Ago | 3 Wks. Ago | TITLE Artist, Label & Number | Weeks On Chart |
|---|---|---|---|---|---|
| 1 | 2 | 4 | 26 | (I Can't Get No) SATISFACTION — Rolling Stones, London 9766 | 5 |
| 2 | 1 | 2 | 1 | I CAN'T HELP MYSELF — Four Tops, Motown 1076 | 9 |
| 3 | 3 | 1 | 2 | MR. TAMBOURINE MAN — Byrds, Columbia 43271 | 9 |
| 4 | 5 | 5 | 6 | WONDERFUL WORLD — Herman's Hermits, MGM 13354 | 7 |
| 5 | 4 | 3 | 3 | WOOLY BULLY — Sam the Sham and the Pharaohs, MGM 13322 | 15 |
| ★ 6 | 9 | 12 | 23 | YES, I'M READY — Barbara Mason, Arctic 105 | 9 |
| 7 | 7 | 10 | 15 | SEVENTH SON — Johnny Rivers, Imperial 66112 | 6 |
| ★ 8 | 11 | 16 | 28 | CARA, MIA — Jay & the Americans, United Artists 881 | 6 |
| ★ 9 | 12 | 14 | 21 | YOU TURN ME ON — Ian Whitcomb, Tower 134 | 8 |
| 10 | 10 | 15 | 22 | WHAT THE WORLD NEEDS NOW IS LOVE — Jackie DeShannon, Imperial 66110 | 8 |
| 11 | 6 | 7 | 9 | FOR YOUR LOVE — Yardbirds, Epic 9790 | 9 |
| 12 | 13 | 13 | 16 | A WALK IN THE BLACK FOREST — Horst Jankowski, Mercury 72425 | 10 |
| ★ 13 | 42 | — | — | I'M HENRY VIII, I AM — Herman's Hermits, MGM 13367 | 2 |
| 14 | 16 | 22 | 29 | LAURIE — Dickey Lee, TCF-Hall 102 | 9 |
| 15 | 8 | 6 | 4 | CRYING IN THE CHAPEL — Elvis Presley, RCA Victor 0643 | 12 |
| 16 | 14 | 8 | 10 | HUSH, HUSH, SWEET CHARLOTTE — Patti Page, Columbia 43251 | 12 |
| ★ 17 | 26 | 41 | 79 | WHAT'S NEW PUSSYCAT? — Tom Jones, Parrot 9765 | 4 |
| 18 | 20 | 32 | 47 | A LITTLE BIT OF HEAVEN — Ronnie Dove, Diamond 184 | 6 |
| ★ 19 | 25 | 31 | 44 | A WORLD OF OUR OWN — Seekers, Capitol 5430 | 7 |
| ★ 20 | 27 | 47 | 70 | (Such An) EASY QUESTION — Elvis Presley, RCA Victor 8585 | 4 |
| 21 | 21 | 28 | 36 | I'VE BEEN LOVING YOU TOO LONG — Otis Redding, Volt 126 | 9 |
| 22 | 22 | 24 | 24 | SHAKIN' ALL OVER — Guess Who's, Scepter 1295 | 10 |
| 23 | 24 | 29 | 38 | OO WEE BABY, I LOVE YOU — Fred Hughes, Vee Jay 684 | 7 |
| ★ 24 | 33 | 39 | 53 | TOO MANY RIVERS — Brenda Lee, Decca 31792 | 7 |
| 25 | 18 | 9 | 7 | HELP ME RHONDA — Beach Boys, Capitol 5395 | 13 |
| 26 | 28 | 33 | 45 | HERE COMES THE NIGHT — Them, Parrot 9749 | 7 |
| 27 | 30 | 35 | 41 | YOU REALLY KNOW HOW TO HURT A GUY — Jan & Dean, Liberty 55792 | 8 |
| ★ 28 | 40 | 50 | 71 | MARIE — Bachelors, London 9762 | 5 |
| 29 | 32 | 42 | 54 | TONIGHT'S THE NIGHT — Solomon Burke, Atlantic 2288 | 7 |
| ★ 30 | 41 | 51 | 68 | SET ME FREE — Kinks, Reprise 0379 | 5 |
| ★ 31 | 43 | 58 | 83 | I LIKE IT LIKE THAT — Dave Clark Five, Epic 9811 | 4 |
| 32 | 23 | 25 | 25 | CATCH THE WIND — Donovan, Hickory 1309 | 9 |
| ★ 33 | 54 | 69 | — | I WANT CANDY — Strangeloves, Bang 501 | 3 |
| ★ 34 | 44 | 59 | 82 | GIRL COME RUNNING — 4 Seasons, Philips 40305 | 4 |
| 35 | 35 | 38 | 49 | THIS LITTLE BIRD — Marianne Faithfull, London 9759 | 6 |
| 36 | 39 | 49 | 60 | DO THE BOOMERANG — Jr. Walker & the All Stars, Soul 35012 | 6 |
| 37 | 15 | 11 | 5 | BACK IN MY ARMS AGAIN — Supremes, Motown 1075 | 11 |
| ★ 38 | 49 | 73 | 92 | SITTING IN THE PARK — Billy Stewart, Chess 1932 | 4 |
| 39 | 29 | 30 | 35 | GIVE US YOUR BLESSING — Shangri-Las, Red Bird 10-030 | 7 |
| 40 | 31 | 27 | 30 | VOODOO WOMAN — Bobby Goldsboro, United Artists 862 | 11 |
| ★ 41 | 52 | 75 | 98 | SUNSHINE, LOLLIPOPS AND RAINBOWS — Lesley Gore, Mercury 72433 | 4 |
| 42 | 17 | 17 | 17 | BEFORE AND AFTER — Chad & Jeremy, Columbia 43277 | 9 |
| 43 | 46 | 48 | 58 | LITTLE LONELY ONE — Tom Jones, Tower 126 | 7 |
| 44 | 19 | 19 | 13 | LAST CHANCE TO TURN AROUND — Gene Pitney, Musicor 1093 | 10 |
| ★ 45 | 57 | 79 | — | DON'T JUST STAND THERE — Patty Duke, United Artists 875 | 3 |
| ★ 46 | 56 | 67 | — | THEME FROM "A SUMMER PLACE" — Lettermen, Capitol 5437 | 3 |
| ★ 47 | 61 | 81 | — | TAKE ME BACK — Little Anthony & the Imperials, DCP 1136 | 3 |
| 48 | 50 | 62 | 72 | WHO'S CHEATING WHO? — Little Milton, Checker 1113 | 5 |
| 49 | 55 | 65 | 80 | IT'S JUST A LITTLE BIT TOO LATE — Wayne Fontana & the Mindbenders, Fontana 1514 | 5 |
| 50 | 53 | 61 | 86 | SEEIN' THE RIGHT LOVE GO WRONG — Jack Jones, Kapp 672 | 5 |
| 51 | 51 | 63 | 73 | MEETING OVER YONDER — Impressions, ABC-Paramount 10670 | 6 |
| ★ 52 | 62 | 77 | — | HOLD ME, THRILL ME, KISS ME — Mel Carter, Imperial 66113 | 3 |
| 53 | 60 | 74 | 97 | BABY I'M YOURS — Barbara Lewis, Atlantic 2283 | 4 |
| 54 | 37 | 44 | 48 | I DO — Marvelows, ABC-Paramount 10629 | 9 |
| 55 | 34 | 45 | 51 | I'LL KEEP HOLDING ON — Marvelettes, Tamla 54116 | 7 |
| ★ 56 | 80 | — | — | SAVE YOUR HEART FOR ME — Gary Lewis & the Playboys, Liberty 55809 | 2 |
| 57 | 48 | 53 | 63 | YOU'LL NEVER WALK ALONE — Gerry & the Pacemakers, Laurie 3302 | 6 |
| 58 | 64 | 68 | 76 | SUMMER SOUNDS — Robert Goulet, Columbia 43301 | 6 |
| 59 | 65 | 71 | 81 | IT FEELS SO RIGHT — Elvis Presley, RCA Victor 8585 | 4 |
| ★ 60 | 79 | 99 | — | I'M A FOOL — Dino, Desi & Billy, Reprise 0367 | 3 |
| ★ 61 | 76 | — | — | RIDE YOUR PONY — Lee Dorsey, Amy 927 | 2 |
| 62 | 73 | 92 | — | TRAINS AND BOATS AND PLANES — Billy J. Kramer & the Dakotas, Imperial 66115 | 3 |
| 63 | 71 | 84 | 100 | NOBODY KNOWS WHAT'S GOIN' ON — Chiffons, Laurie 3301 | 4 |
| 64 | 66 | 72 | 85 | BOOT-LEG — Booker T. & MG's, Stax 169 | 6 |
| 65 | 69 | 89 | — | ONE MONKEY DON'T STOP NO SHOW — Joe Tex, Dial 4011 | 3 |
| ★ 66 | — | — | — | PRETTY LITTLE BABY — Marvin Gaye, Tamla 54117 | 1 |
| 67 | 68 | 80 | — | WATERMELON MAN — Gloria Lynne, Fontana 1511 | 3 |
| 68 | 72 | 94 | — | SILVER THREADS AND GOLDEN NEEDLES — Jody Miller, Capitol 5429 | 3 |
| ★ 69 | — | — | — | TO KNOW YOU IS TO LOVE YOU — Peter & Gordon, Capitol 5461 | 1 |
| 70 | 70 | 76 | 77 | TEMPTATION 'BOUT TO GET ME — Knight Brothers, Checker 1107 | 5 |
| 71 | 67 | 60 | 69 | WHAT'S HE DOING IN MY WORLD — Eddy Arnold, RCA Victor 8516 | 9 |
| 72 | 82 | — | — | I CAN'T WORK NO LONGER — Billy Butler & the Chanters, Okeh 7221 | 2 |
| 73 | 83 | — | — | ALL I REALLY WANT TO DO — Byrds, Columbia 43332 | 2 |
| 74 | 74 | 82 | 90 | HE'S A LOVER — Mary Wells, 20th Century-Fox 590 | 4 |
| 75 | 75 | 70 | 74 | I LOVE YOU SO — Bobbi Martin, Coral 62452 | 7 |
| 76 | 77 | 87 | — | DARLING TAKE ME BACK — Lenny Welch, Kapp 662 | 3 |
| ★ 77 | 95 | — | — | DOWN IN THE BOONDOCKS — Billy Joe Royal, Columbia 43305 | 2 |
| 78 | 81 | — | — | NO PITY (In the Naked City) — Jackie Wilson, Brunswick 55280 | 2 |
| 79 | 84 | — | — | MY MAN — Barbra Streisand, Columbia 43323 | 2 |
| 80 | 85 | — | — | HERE I AM — Dionne Warwick, Scepter 12104 | 2 |
| 81 | 86 | — | — | ALL I REALLY WANT TO DO — Cher, Imperial 66114 | 2 |
| ★ 82 | — | — | — | YOU'D BETTER COME HOME — Petula Clark, Warner Bros. 5643 | 1 |
| ★ 83 | — | — | — | IN THE MIDNIGHT HOUR — Wilson Pickett, Atlantic 2289 | 1 |
| 84 | 87 | — | — | NEW ORLEANS — Eddie Hodges, Aurora 153 | 2 |
| ★ 85 | — | — | — | CANDY — Astors, Stax 170 | 1 |
| ★ 86 | — | — | — | (Say) YOU'RE MY GIRL — Roy Orbison, Monument 891 | 1 |
| 87 | 90 | — | — | JUSTINE — Righteous Brothers, Moonglow 242 | 2 |
| ★ 88 | — | — | — | I GOT YOU BABE — Sonny & Cher, Atco 6359 | 1 |
| 89 | 92 | — | — | ONE STEP AT A TIME — Maxine Brown, Wand 185 | 2 |
| ★ 90 | — | — | — | THEME FROM "HARLOW" (Lonely Girl) — Bobby Vinton, Epic 9814 | 1 |
| 91 | 91 | 93 | — | THE FIRST THING EV'RY MORNING — Jimmy Dean, Columbia 43263 | 3 |
| 92 | 93 | 95 | — | FORGET DOMANI — Connie Francis, MGM 13363 | 3 |
| 93 | 99 | 100 | — | FORGET DOMANI — Frank Sinatra, Reprise 0380 | 3 |
| 94 | 94 | — | — | STOP! LOOK WHAT YOU'RE DOING — Carla Thomas, Stax 172 | 2 |
| 95 | 96 | 98 | — | I WANT YOU BACK AGAIN — Zombies, Parrot 9769 | 3 |
| 96 | 98 | — | — | FOLLOW ME — Drifters, Atlantic 2292 | 2 |
| 97 | — | — | — | MOON OVER NAPLES — Bert Kaempfert & His Ork, Decca 31812 | 1 |
| 98 | — | — | — | "TICKLE ME" — Elvis Presley, RCA Victor EPA 4383 (Extended Play) | 1 |
| 99 | — | — | — | ONE DYIN' AND A BURYIN' — Roger Miller, Smash 1994 | 1 |
| 100 | — | — | — | FROM A WINDOW — Chad & Jeremy, World Artists 1056 | 1 |

## HOT 100—A TO Z—(Publisher-Licensee)

All I Really Want to Do—Byrds (Witmark, ASCAP) 73
All I Really Want to Do—Cher (Witmark, ASCAP) 81
Baby I'm Yours (Blackwood, BMI) 53
Back in My Arms Again (Jobete, BMI) 37
Before and After (Blackwood, BMI) 42
Boot-Leg (East, BMI) 64
Candy (East, BMI) 85
Cara, Mia (Feist, ASCAP) 8
Catch the Wind (Southern, ASCAP) 32
Crying in the Chapel (Valley, BMI) 15
Darling Take Me Back (Murbo, BMI) 76
Do the Boomerang (Jobete, BMI) 36
Don't Just Sand There (Bernice, BMI) 45
Down in the Boondocks (Lowery, BMI) 77
First Thing Ev'ry Morning, The (Plainview, BMI) 91
Follow Me (Hill & Range, BMI) 96
For Your Love (Blackwood, BMI) 11
Forget Domani—Francis (Miller, ASCAP) 92
Forget Domani—Sinatra (Miller, ASCAP) 93
From a Window (Maclen, BMI) 100
Girl Come Running (Saturday, BMI) 34
Give Us Your Blessing (Trio, BMI) 39
He's a Lover (Rual, ASCAP) 74
Help Me Rhonda (Sea of Tunes, BMI) 25
Here Comes the Night (Keetch, Caesar & Dino, BMI) 26
Here I Am (United Artists, ASCAP) 80
Hold Me, Thrill Me, Kiss Me (Mills, ASCAP) 52
Hush, Hush, Sweet Charlotte (Miller, ASCAP) 16
(I Can't Get No) Satisfaction (Immediate, BMI) 1
I Can't Help Myself (Jobete, BMI) 2
I Can't Work No Longer (Curtom, BMI) 72
I Do (Pamco-Yvonne, BMI) 54
I Got You Babe (Five-West-Cotillion, BMI) 88
I Like It Like That (Tune-Kel, BMI) 31
I Love You So (Bark, ASCAP) 75
I Want Candy (Grand Canyon-Webb IV, BMI) 33
I Want You Back Again (Mainstay, BMI) 95
I'll Keep Holding On (Jobete, BMI) 55
I'm a Fool (Atlantic, BMI) 60
I'm Henry VIII, I Am (Miller, ASCAP) 13
I've Been Loving You Too Long (East-Time, BMI) 21
In the Midnight Hour (Cotillion-East, BMI) 83
It Feels So Right (Gladys, ASCAP) 59
It's Just a Little Bit Too Late (Skidmore, ASCAP) 49
Justine (Venice, BMI) 87
Last Chance to Turn Around (Catalog, BMI) 44
Laurie (Long-Gold Dust, BMI) 14
Little Bit of Heaven, A (T.M., BMI) 18
Little Lonely One (We Three, BMI) 43
Marie (Berlin, ASCAP) 28
Meeting Over Yonder (Chi-Sound, BMI) 51
Mr. Tambourine Man (Witmark, ASCAP) 3
Moon Over Naples (Roosevelt, BMI) 97
My Man (Feist, ASCAP) 79
New Orleans (Rockmasters, BMI) 84
No Pity (In the Naked City) (Merrimac, BMI) 78
Nobody Knows What's Goin' On (Bright Tunes, BMI) 63
One Dyin' and a Buryin' (Tree, BMI) 99
One Monkey Don't Stop No Show (Tree, BMI) 65
One Step at a Time (Flomar, BMI) 89
Oo Wee Baby, I Love You (Costoma, BMI) 23
Pretty Little Baby (Jobete, BMI) 66
Ride Your Pony (Jarb, BMI) 61
Save Your Heart for Me (Geld-Udell-Purchase, ASCAP) 56
(Say) You're My Girl (Acuff-Rose, BMI) 86
Seein' the Right Love Go Wrong (Sea-Lark, BMI) 50
Set Me Free (American Metropolitan Ent., BMI) 30
Seventh Son (Arc, BMI) 7
Shakin' All Over (Mills, ASCAP) 22
Silver Threads and Golden Needles (Central Songs, BMI) 68
Sitting in the Park (Chevis, BMI) 38
Stop! Look What You're Doing (East-Falart, BMI) 94
(Such an) Easy Question (Presley, BMI) 20
Summer Sounds (Mills, ASCAP) 58
Sunshine, Lollipops and Rainbows (Hansen, ASCAP 41
Take Me Back (South Mountain, BMI) 47
Temptation 'Bout to Get Me (Chevis-Herco, BMI) 70
Theme From "A Summer Place" (Witmark, ASCAP) 46
Theme From "Harlow" (Lonely Girl) (Consul, ASCAP) 90
This Little Bird (Acuff-Rose, BMI) 35
"Tickle Me" (Various Publishers) 98
To Know You Is to Love You (Hillary, BMI) 69
Tonight's the Night (Cotillion, BMI) 29
Too Many Rivers (Combine, BMI) 24
Trains and Boats and Planes (U. S. Songs, ASCAP) 62
Voodoo Woman (Unart, BMI) 40
Walk in the Black Forest, A (MEC, BMI) 12
Watermelon Man (Hancock, BMI) 67
What the World Needs Now Is Love (Blue Seas-Jac, BMI) 10
What's He Doing in My World (4 Star, BMI) 71
What's New Pussycat? (United Artists, ASCAP) 17
Who's Cheating Who? (Chevis, BMI) 48
Wonderful World (Kags, BMI) 4
Wooly Bully (Beckie, BMI) 5
World of Our Own (Chappell, ASCAP) 19
Yes I'm Ready (Stillran-Dandelion, BMI) 6
You Really Know How to Hurt a Guy (Screen Gems-Columbia, BMI) 27
You Turn Me On (Burdette, BMI) 9
You'd Better Come Home (Duchess, BMI) 82
You'll Never Walk Alone (Williamson, ASCAP) 57

## BUBBLING UNDER THE HOT 100

101. I'LL ALWAYS LOVE YOU — Spinners, Motown 1078
102. UNCHAINED MELODY — Righteous Brothers, Philles 129
103. TRACKS OF MY TEARS — Miracles, Tamla 5418
104. BUSTER BROWNE — Willie Mitchell, Hi 2091
105. GEE THE MOON IS SHINING BRIGHT — Dixie Cups, Red Bird 032
106. YAKETY AXE — Chet Atkins, RCA Victor 8590
107. IF YOU REALLY WANT ME TO, I'LL GO — Ron-Dells, Smash 1986
108. MARCH (YOU'LL BE SORRY) — Shirelles, Scepter 12101
109. IT'S TOO LATE BABY, TOO LATE — Arthur Prysock, Old Town 1183
110. BLUE SHADOWS — B. B. King, Kent 426
111. ONLY THOSE IN LOVE — Baby Washington, Sue 129
112. YOU'RE MY BABY — Vacels, Kama Sutra 200
113. YOU WERE ON MY MIND — We Five, A&M 770
114. LOVE ME NOW — Brook Benton, Mercury 72446
115. GOOD BYE, SO LONG — Ike & Tina Turner, Modern 1007
116. IT'S GONNA BE FINE — Glenn Yarbrough, RCA Victor 8619
117. HALLELUJAH — Invitations, DynoVoice 206
118. HAPPY FEET TIME — Montclairs, Sunburst 106
119. THE LOSER — Skyliners, Jubilee 5506
120. HUNG ON YOU — Righteous Brothers, Philles 129
121. SUNRISE, SUNSET — Eddie Fisher, Dot 16732
122. TIGER WOMAN — Claude King, Columbia 43298
123. YOU'VE NEVER BEEN IN LOVE LIKE THIS BEFORE — Unit 4+2, London 9761
124. IN THE MIDDLE OF NOWHERE — Dusty Springfield, Philips 40303
125. IF I HAD MY LIFE TO LIVE OVER — Lloyd Price, Monument 887
126. STREETS OF LAREDO — Johnny Cash, Columbia 43313
127. AIN'T IT A SHAME — Major Lance, Okeh 7223
128. LAST NIGHT I MADE A LITTLE GIRL CRY — Steve Lawrence, Columbia 43303
129. AROUND THE CORNER — Duprees, Columbia 43336
130. AFTER LOVING YOU — Della Reese, ABC-Paramount 10691
131. I CAN'T STAND TO SEE YOU CRY — Jerry Butler, Vee Jay 651
132. FLY ME TO THE MOON — Tony Bennett, Columbia 43331
133. YOU CAN'T GROW PEACHES ON A CHERRY TREE — Browns, RCA Victor 8603
134. WHY DON'T YOU BELIEVE ME — Vic Damone, Warner Bros. 5644
135. THE LEGEND OF SHENANDOAH — James Stewart, Decca 31795

Compiled from national retail sales and radio station airplay by the Music Popularity Dept. of Record Market Research, Billboard.

For Week Ending July 17, 1965

# Billboard HOT 100

★ STAR performer—Sides registering greatest proportionate upward progress this week.

Record Industry Association of America seal of certification as million selling single.

| This Week | 1 Wk. Ago | 2 Wks. Ago | 3 Wks. Ago | TITLE Artist, Label & Number | Weeks On Chart |
|---|---|---|---|---|---|
| 1 | 1 | 2 | 4 | (I Can't Get No) SATISFACTION — Rolling Stones, London 9766 | 6 |
| 2 | 2 | 1 | 2 | I CAN'T HELP MYSELF — Four Tops, Motown 1076 | 10 |
| ★ 3 | 13 | 42 | — | I'M HENRY VIII, I AM — Herman's Hermits, MGM 13367 | 3 |
| 4 | 3 | 3 | 1 | MR. TAMBOURINE MAN — Byrds, Columbia 43271 | 10 |
| ★ 5 | 8 | 11 | 16 | CARA, MIA — Jay & the Americans, United Artists 881 | 7 |
| 6 | 6 | 9 | 12 | YES, I'M READY — Barbara Mason, Arctic 105 | 10 |
| 7 | 7 | 7 | 10 | SEVENTH SON — Johnny Rivers, Imperial 66112 | 7 |
| 8 | 9 | 12 | 14 | YOU TURN ME ON — Ian Whitcomb, Tower 134 | 9 |
| 9 | 10 | 10 | 15 | WHAT THE WORLD NEEDS NOW IS LOVE — Jackie DeShannon, Imperial 66110 | 9 |
| ★ 10 | 17 | 26 | 41 | WHAT'S NEW PUSSYCAT? — Tom Jones, Parrot 9765 | 5 |
| 11 | 5 | 4 | 3 | WOOLY BULLY — Sam the Sham and the Pharaohs, MGM 13322 | 16 |
| 12 | 4 | 5 | 5 | WONDERFUL WORLD — Herman's Hermits, MGM 13354 | 8 |
| 13 | 11 | 6 | 7 | FOR YOUR LOVE — Yardbirds, Epic 9790 | 10 |
| 14 | 12 | 13 | 13 | A WALK IN THE BLACK FOREST — Horst Jankowski, Mercury 72425 | 11 |
| ★ 15 | 20 | 27 | 47 | (Such An) EASY QUESTION — Elvis Presley, RCA Victor 8585 | 5 |
| 16 | 18 | 20 | 32 | A LITTLE BIT OF HEAVEN — Ronnie Dove, Diamond 184 | 7 |
| 17 | 14 | 16 | 22 | LAURIE — Dickey Lee, TCF-Hall 102 | 10 |
| ★ 18 | 24 | 33 | 39 | TOO MANY RIVERS — Brenda Lee, Decca 31792 | 8 |
| 19 | 19 | 25 | 31 | A WORLD OF OUR OWN — Seekers, Capitol 5430 | 8 |
| 20 | 15 | 8 | 6 | CRYING IN THE CHAPEL — Elvis Presley, RCA Victor 0643 | 13 |
| 21 | 16 | 14 | 8 | HUSH, HUSH, SWEET CHARLOTTE — Patti Page, Columbia 43251 | 13 |
| ★ 22 | 28 | 40 | 50 | MARIE — Bachelors, London 9762 | 6 |
| 23 | 21 | 21 | 28 | I'VE BEEN LOVING YOU TOO LONG — Otis Redding, Volt 126 | 10 |
| 24 | 26 | 28 | 33 | HERE COMES THE NIGHT — Them, Parrot 9749 | 8 |
| ★ 25 | 30 | 41 | 51 | SET ME FREE — Kinks, Reprise 0379 | 6 |
| ★ 26 | 31 | 43 | 58 | I LIKE IT LIKE THAT — Dave Clark Five, Epic 9811 | 5 |
| ★ 27 | 33 | 54 | 69 | I WANT CANDY — Strangeloves, Bang 501 | 4 |
| 28 | 29 | 32 | 42 | TONIGHT'S THE NIGHT — Solomon Burke, Atlantic 2288 | 8 |
| ★ 29 | 38 | 49 | 73 | SITTING IN THE PARK — Billy Stewart, Chess 1932 | 5 |
| 30 | 34 | 44 | 59 | GIRL COME RUNNING — 4 Seasons, Philips 40305 | 5 |
| ★ 31 | 41 | 52 | 75 | SUNSHINE, LOLLIPOPS AND RAINBOWS — Lesley Gore, Mercury 72433 | 5 |
| 32 | 35 | 35 | 38 | THIS LITTLE BIRD — Marianne Faithfull, London 9759 | 7 |
| 33 | 23 | 24 | 29 | OO WEE BABY, I LOVE YOU — Fred Hughes, Vee Jay 684 | 8 |
| ★ 34 | 45 | 57 | 79 | DON'T JUST STAND THERE — Patty Duke, United Artists 875 | 4 |
| ★ 35 | 46 | 56 | 67 | THEME FROM "A SUMMER PLACE" — Lettermen, Capitol 5437 | 4 |
| 36 | 27 | 30 | 35 | YOU REALLY KNOW HOW TO HURT A GUY — Jan & Dean, Liberty 55792 | 9 |
| ★ 37 | 47 | 61 | 81 | TAKE ME BACK — Little Anthony & the Imperials, DCP 1136 | 4 |
| 38 | 22 | 22 | 24 | SHAKIN' ALL OVER — Guess Who's, Scepter 1295 | 11 |
| ★ 39 | 53 | 60 | 74 | BABY I'M YOURS — Barbara Lewis, Atlantic 2283 | 5 |
| ★ 40 | 56 | 80 | — | SAVE YOUR HEART FOR ME — Gary Lewis & the Playboys, Liberty 55809 | 3 |
| ★ 41 | 52 | 62 | 77 | HOLD ME, THRILL ME, KISS ME — Mel Carter, Imperials 66113 | 4 |
| 42 | 43 | 46 | 48 | LITTLE LONELY ONE — Tom Jones, Tower 126 | 8 |
| 43 | 48 | 50 | 62 | WHO'S CHEATING WHO? — Little Milton, Checker 1113 | 6 |
| 44 | 25 | 18 | 9 | HELP ME RHONDA — Beach Boys, Capitol 5395 | 14 |
| 45 | 32 | 23 | 25 | CATCH THE WIND — Donovan, Hickory 1309 | 10 |
| 46 | 49 | 55 | 65 | IT'S JUST A LITTLE BIT TOO LATE — Wayne Fontana & the Mindbenders, Fontana 1514 | 6 |
| 47 | 50 | 53 | 61 | SEEIN' THE RIGHT LOVE GO WRONG — Jack Jones, Kapp 672 | 6 |
| 48 | 51 | 51 | 63 | MEETING OVER YONDER — Impressions, ABC-Paramount 10670 | 7 |
| ★ 49 | 66 | — | — | PRETTY LITTLE BABY — Marvin Gaye, Tamla 54117 | 2 |
| ★ 50 | 60 | 79 | 99 | I'M A FOOL — Dino, Desi & Billy, Reprise 0367 | 4 |
| ★ 51 | 69 | — | — | TO KNOW YOU IS TO LOVE YOU — Peter & Gordon, Capitol 5461 | 2 |
| 52 | 39 | 29 | 30 | GIVE US YOUR BLESSING — Shangri-Las, Red Bird 10-030 | 8 |
| 53 | 36 | 39 | 49 | DO THE BOOMERANG — Jr. Walker & the All Stars, Soul 35012 | 7 |
| 54 | 61 | 76 | — | RIDE YOUR PONY — Lee Dorsey, Amy 927 | 3 |
| 55 | 59 | 65 | 71 | IT FEELS SO RIGHT — Elvis Presley, RCA Victor 8585 | 5 |
| ★ 56 | 68 | 72 | 94 | SILVER THREADS AND GOLDEN NEEDLES — Jody Miller, Capitol 5429 | 4 |
| 57 | 62 | 73 | 92 | TRAINS AND BOATS AND PLANES — Billy J. Kramer & the Dakotas, Imperial 66115 | 4 |
| 58 | 64 | 66 | 72 | BOOT-LEG — Booker T. & MG's, Stax 169 | 7 |
| 59 | 63 | 71 | 84 | NOBODY KNOWS WHAT'S GOIN' ON — Chiffons, Laurie 3301 | 5 |
| ★ 60 | 77 | 95 | — | DOWN IN THE BOONDOCKS — Billy Joe Royal, Columbia 43305 | 3 |
| 61 | 58 | 64 | 68 | SUMMER SOUNDS — Robert Goulet, Columbia 43301 | 7 |
| 62 | 67 | 68 | 80 | WATERMELON MAN — Gloria Lynne, Fontana 1511 | 4 |
| ★ 63 | 86 | — | — | (Say) YOU'RE MY GIRL — Roy Orbison, Monument 891 | 2 |
| 64 | 72 | 82 | — | I CAN'T WORK NO LONGER — Billy Butler & the Chanters, Okeh 7221 | 3 |
| 65 | 65 | 69 | 89 | ONE MONKEY DON'T STOP NO SHOW — Joe Tex, Dial 4011 | 4 |
| ★ 66 | 82 | — | — | YOU'D BETTER COME HOME — Petula Clark, Warner Bros. 5643 | 2 |
| 67 | 73 | 83 | — | ALL I REALLY WANT TO DO — Byrds, Columbia 43332 | 3 |
| ★ 68 | 89 | 92 | — | ONE STEP AT A TIME — Maxine Brown, Wand 185 | 3 |
| 69 | 78 | 81 | — | NO PITY (In the Naked City) — Jackie Wilson, Brunswick 55280 | 3 |
| ★ 70 | 99 | — | — | ONE DYIN' AND A BURYIN' — Roger Miller, Smash 1994 | 2 |
| 71 | 81 | 86 | — | ALL I REALLY WANT TO DO — Cher, Imperial 66114 | 3 |
| ★ 72 | — | — | — | UNCHAINED MELODY — Righteous Brothers, Philles 129 | 1 |
| ★ 73 | 88 | — | — | I GOT YOU BABE — Sonny & Cher, Atco 6359 | 2 |
| 74 | 76 | 77 | 87 | DARLING TAKE ME BACK — Lenny Welch, Kapp 662 | 4 |
| 75 | 84 | 87 | — | NEW ORLEANS — Eddie Hodges, Aurora 153 | 3 |
| 76 | 85 | — | — | CANDY — Astors, Stax 170 | 2 |
| 77 | 80 | 85 | — | HERE I AM — Dionne Warwick, Scepter 12104 | 3 |
| ★ 78 | — | — | — | I'LL ALWAYS LOVE YOU — Spinners, Motown 1078 | 1 |
| 79 | 83 | — | — | IN THE MIDNIGHT HOUR — Wilson Pickett, Atlantic 2289 | 2 |
| ★ 80 | — | — | — | PAPA'S GOT A BRAND NEW BAG — James Brown, King 5999 | 1 |
| ★ 81 | — | — | — | TRACKS OF MY TEARS — Miracles, Tamla 54118 | 1 |
| 82 | 90 | — | — | THEME FROM "HARLOW" (Lonely Girl) — Bobby Vinton, Epic 9814 | 2 |
| ★ 83 | — | — | — | IT'S GONNA TAKE A MIRACLE — Royalettes, MGM 13366 | 1 |
| 84 | 92 | 93 | 95 | FORGET DOMANI — Connie Francis, MGM 13363 | 4 |
| 85 | 87 | 90 | — | JUSTINE — Righteous Brothers, Moonglow 242 | 3 |
| ★ 86 | — | — | — | IT'S TOO LATE BABY, TOO LATE — Arthur Prysock, Old Town 1183 | 1 |
| 87 | 93 | 99 | 100 | FORGET DOMANI — Frank Sinatra, Reprise 0380 | 4 |
| 88 | 98 | — | — | "TICKLE ME" — Elvis Presley, RCA Victor EPA 4383 (Extended Play) | 2 |
| 89 | 79 | 84 | — | MY MAN — Barbra Streisand, Columbia 43323 | 3 |
| ★ 90 | — | — | — | HUNG ON YOU — Righteous Brothers, Philles 129 | 1 |
| 91 | 96 | 98 | — | FOLLOW ME — Drifters, Atlantic 2292 | 3 |
| 92 | 94 | 94 | — | STOP! LOOK WHAT YOU'RE DOING — Carla Thomas, Stax 172 | 3 |
| 93 | — | — | — | THE LOSERS — Skyliners, Jubilee 5506 | 1 |
| 94 | — | — | — | IT'S GONNA BE FINE — Glenn Yarbrough, RCA Victor 8619 | 1 |
| 95 | 97 | — | — | MOON OVER NAPLES — Bert Kaempfert & His Ork, Decca 31812 | 2 |
| 96 | — | — | — | YOU'VE NEVER BEEN IN LOVE LIKE THIS BEFORE — Unit Four Plus Two, London 9761 | 1 |
| 97 | 100 | — | — | FROM A WINDOW — Chad & Jeremy, World Artists 1056 | 2 |
| 98 | — | — | — | YAKETY AXE — Chet Atkins, RCA Victor 8590 | 1 |
| 99 | — | — | — | BUSTER BROWNE — Willie Mitchell, Hi 2091 | 1 |
| 100 | — | — | — | I'M A FOOL TO CARE — Ray Charles, ABC-Paramount 10700 | 1 |

## HOT 100—A TO Z—*(Publisher-Licensee)*

All I Really Want to Do—Byrds (Witmark, ASCAP). 67
All I Really Want to Do—Cher (Witmark, ASCAP). 71

Baby I'm Yours (Blackwood, BMI) 39
Boot-Leg (East, BMI) 58
Buster Browne (Jac, BMI) 99

Candy (East, BMI) 76
Cara, Mia (Feist, ASCAP) 5
Catch the Wind (Southern, ASCAP) 45
Crying in the Chapel (Valley, BMI) 20

Darling Take Me Back (Murbo, BMI) 74
Do the Boomerang (Jobete, BMI) 53
Don't Just Stand There (Bernice, BMI) 34
Down in the Boondocks (Lowery, BMI) 60

Follow Me (Hill & Range, BMI) 91
For Your Love (Blackwood, BMI) 13
Forget Domani—Francis (Miller, ASCAP) 84
Forget Domani—Sinatra (Miller, ASCAP) 87
From a Window (Maclen, BMI) 97

Girl Come Running (Saturday, BMI) 30
Give Us Your Blessing (Trio, BMI) 52

Help Me Rhonda (Sea of Tunes, BMI) 44
Here Comes the Night (Keetch, Caesar & Dino, BMI) 24
Here I Am (United Artists, ASCAP) 77
Hold Me, Thrill Me, Kiss Me (Mills, ASCAP) 41
Hung on You (Screen Gems-Columbia, BMI) 90
Hush, Hush, Sweet Charlotte (Miller, ASCAP) 21

(I Can't Get No) Satisfaction (Immediate, BMI) 1
I Can't Help Myself (Jobete, BMI) 2
I Can't Work No Longer (Curtom, BMI) 64
I Got You Babe (Five-West-Cotillion, BMI) 73
I Like It Like That (Tune-Kel, BMI) 26
I Want Candy (Grand Canyon-Webb IV, BMI) 27
I'll Always Love You (Jobete, BMI) 78
I'm a Fool (Atlantic, BMI) 50
I'm a Fool to Care (Peer Int'l, BMI) 100
I'm Henry VIII, I Am (Miller, ASCAP) 3
I've Been Loving You Too Long (East-Time, BMI) 23
In the Midnight Hour (Cotillion-East, BMI) 79
It Feels So Right (Gladys, ASCAP) 55
It's Gonna Be Fine (Screen Gems-Columbia, BMI) 94
It's Gonna Take a Miracle (South Mountain, BMI). 83
It's Just a Little Bit Too Late (Skidmore, ASCAP) 46
It's Too Late Baby Too Late (Pry-Weiss, BMI) 86

Justine (Venice, BMI) 85

Laurie (Long-Gold Dust, BMI) 17
Little Bit of Heaven, A (T.M., BMI) 16
Little Lonely One (We Three, BMI) 42
Losers, The (Wemar, BMI) 93

Marie (Berlin, ASCAP) 22
Meeting Over Yonder (Chi-Sound, BMI) 48
Mr. Tambourine Man (Witmark, ASCAP) 4
Moon Over Naples (Roosevelt, BMI) 95
My Man (Feist, ASCAP) 89

New Orleans (Rockmasters, BMI) 75
No Pity (In the Naked City) (Merrimac, BMI) 69
Nobody Knows What's Goin' On (Bright Tunes, BMI) 59

One Dyin' and a Buryin' (Tree, BMI) 70
One Monkey Don't Stop No Show (Tree, BMI) 65
One Step at a Time (Flomar, BMI) 68
Oo Wee Baby, I Love You (Costoma, BMI) 33

Papa's Got a Brand New Bag (Lois, BMI) 80
Pretty Little Baby (Jobete, BMI) 49

Ride Your Pony (Jarb, BMI) 54

Save Your Heart for Me (Geld-Udell-Purchase, ASCAP) 40
(Say) You're My Girl (Acuff-Rose, BMI) 63
Seein' the Right Love Go Wrong (Sea-Lark, BMI) 47
Set Me Free (American Metropolitan Ent., BMI) 25
Seventh Son (Arc, BMI) 7
Shakin' All Over (Mills, ASCAP) 38
Silver Threads and Golden Needles (Central Songs, BMI) 56
Sittin' in the Park (Chevis, BMI) 29
Stop! Look What You're Doing (East-Falart, BMI) 92
(Such an) Easy Question (Presley, BMI) 15
Summer Sounds (Mills, ASCAP) 61
Sunshine, Lollipops and Rainbows (Hansen, ASCAP). 31

Take Me Back (South Mountain, BMI) 37
Theme From "A Summer Place" (Witmark, ASCAP). 35
Theme From "Harlow" (Lonely Girl) (Consul, ASCAP) 82
This Little Bird (Acuff-Rose, BMI) 32
"Tickle Me" (Various Publishers) 88
To Know You Is to Love You (Hillary, BMI) 51
Tonight's the Night (Cotillion, BMI) 28
Too Many Rivers (Combine, BMI) 18
Tracks of My Tears (Jobete, BMI) 81
Trains and Boats and Planes (U. S. Songs, ASCAP). 57

Unchained Melody (Frank, ASCAP) 72

Walk in the Black Forest, A (MRC, BMI) 14
Watermelon Man (Hancock, BMI) 62
What the World Needs Now Is Love (Blue Seas-Jac, BMI) 9
What's New Pussycat? (United Artists, ASCAP) 10
Who's Cheating Who? (Chevis, BMI) 43
Wonderful World (Kags, BMI) 12
Wooly Bully (Beckie, BMI) 11
World of Our Own (Chappell, ASCAP) 19

Yakety Axe (Tree, BMI) 98
Yes, I'm Ready (Stillran-Dandelion, BMI) 6
You Really Know How to Hurt a Guy (Screen Gems-Columbia, BMI) 36
You Turn Me On (Burdette, BMI) 8
You'd Better Come Home (Duchess, BMI) 66
You've Never Been in Love Like This Before (Burlington, ASCAP) 96

## BUBBLING UNDER THE HOT 100

101. IF YOU REALLY WANT ME TO, I'LL GO ..... Ron-Dells, Smash 1986
102. YOU WERE ON MY MIND ..... We Five, A&M 770
103. ALIMONY ..... Tommy Tucker, Checker 1112
104. GEE THE MOON IS SHINING BRIGHT ..... Dixie Cups, Red Bird 032
105. YOU BETTER GO ..... Derek Martin, Roulette 4631
106. ONLY THOSE IN LOVE ..... Baby Washington, Sue 129
107. YOU'RE MY BABY ..... Vacels, Kama Sutra 200
108. HAPPY FEET TIME ..... Montclairs, Sunburst 106
109. CALIFORNIA GIRL ..... Beach Boys, Capitol 5464
110. TIGER WOMAN ..... Claude King, Columbia 43293
111. AROUND THE CORNER ..... Duprees, Columbia 43336
112. HALLELUJAH ..... Invitations, DynoVoice 206
113. YOU TELL ME WHY ..... Beau Brummels, Autumn 016
114. MY NAME IS MUD ..... Eddie Rambeau, DynoVoice 207
115. THAT GOES TO SHOW YOU ..... Garnet Mimms, United Artists 887
116. IF I HAD MY LIFE TO LIVE OVER ..... Lloyd Price, Monument 887
117. DO THE 45 ..... Sharpees, One-Derful 4835
118. BLUE SHADOWS ..... B. B. King, Kent 426
119. SUNRISE, SUNSET ..... Eddie Fisher, Dot 16732
120. WE'RE DOING FINE ..... Dee Dee Warwick, Blue Rock 4027
121. AFTER LOVING YOU ..... Della Reese, ABC-Paramount 10691
122. I CAN'T STAND TO SEE YOU CRY ..... Jerry Butler, Vee Jay 696
123. CANADIAN SUNSET ..... Sounds Orchestral, Parkway 958
124. I'M LOSING YOU ..... Aretha Franklin, Columbia 86166
125. FLY ME TO THE MOON ..... Tony Bennett, Columbia 43331
126. LAST NIGHT I MADE A LITTLE GIRL CRY ..... Steve Lawrence, Columbia 43303
127. IN THE MIDDLE OF NOWHERE ..... Dusty Springfield, Philips 40303
128. YOU CAN'T GROW PEACHES ON A CHERRY TREE ..... Browns, RCA Victor 8603
129. STREETS OF LAREDO ..... Johnny Cash, Columbia 43313
130. THOSE MAGNIFICENT MEN IN THEIR FLYING MACHINES ..... Village Stompers, Epic 9824
131. THE SWEETHEART TREE ..... Henry Mancini, RCA Victor 8624
132. WHY DON'T YOU BELIEVE ME ..... Vic Damone, Warner Bros. 5644
133. THE LEGEND OF SHENANDOAH ..... James Stewart, Decca 31795
134. IT HAPPENED JUST THAT WAY ..... Roger Miller, Smash 1994
135. I PUT A SPELL ON YOU ..... Nina Simone, Philips 40286
135. SOUTHERN COUNTRY BOY ..... Carter Brothers, Jewel 745

Compiled from national retail sales and radio station airplay by the Music Popularity Dept. of Record Market Research, Billboard.

For Week Ending July 24, 1965

# Billboard HOT 100

★ STAR performer—Sides registering greatest proportionate upward progress this week.

Record Industry Association of America seal of certification as million selling single.

| This Week | 1 Wk. Ago | 2 Wks. Ago | 3 Wks. Ago | TITLE Artist, Label & Number | Weeks On Chart |
|---|---|---|---|---|---|
| 1 (Billboard Award) | 1 | 1 | 2 | (I Can't Get No) SATISFACTION — Rolling Stones, London 9766 | 7 |
| 2 | 3 | 13 | 42 | I'M HENRY VIII, I AM — Herman's Hermits, MGM 13367 | 4 |
| 3 | 2 | 2 | 1 | I CAN'T HELP MYSELF — Four Tops, Motown 1076 | 11 |
| ★4 | 10 | 17 | 26 | WHAT'S NEW PUSSYCAT? — Tom Jones, Parrot 9765 | 6 |
| 5 | 5 | 8 | 11 | CARA, MIA — Jay & the Americans, United Artists 881 | 8 |
| 6 | 6 | 6 | 9 | YES, I'M READY — Barbara Mason, Arctic 105 | 11 |
| 7 | 9 | 10 | 10 | WHAT THE WORLD NEEDS NOW IS LOVE — Jackie DeShannon, Imperial 66110 | 10 |
| 8 | 7 | 7 | 7 | SEVENTH SON — Johnny Rivers, Imperial 66112 | 8 |
| 9 | 4 | 3 | 3 | MR. TAMBOURINE MAN — Byrds, Columbia 43271 | 11 |
| 10 | 8 | 9 | 12 | YOU TURN ME ON — Ian Whitcomb, Tower 134 | 10 |
| 11 | 15 | 20 | 27 | (Such An) EASY QUESTION — Elvis Presley, RCA Victor 8585 | 6 |
| ★12 | 26 | 31 | 43 | I LIKE IT LIKE THAT — Dave Clark Five, Epic 9811 | 6 |
| ★13 | 40 | 56 | 80 | SAVE YOUR HEART FOR ME — Gary Lewis & the Playboys, Liberty 55809 | 4 |
| 14 | 18 | 24 | 33 | TOO MANY RIVERS — Brenda Lee, Decca 31792 | 9 |
| ★15 | 22 | 24 | 40 | MARIE — Bachelors, London 9762 | 7 |
| 16 | 16 | 18 | 20 | A LITTLE BIT OF HEAVEN — Ronnie Dove, Diamond 184 | 8 |
| 17 | 11 | 5 | 4 | WOOLY BULLY — Sam the Sham and the Pharaohs, MGM 13322 | 17 |
| ★18 | 27 | 33 | 54 | I WANT CANDY — Strangeloves, Bang 501 | 5 |
| ★19 | 31 | 41 | 52 | SUNSHINE, LOLLIPOPS AND RAINBOWS — Lesley Gore, Mercury 72433 | 6 |
| 20 | 13 | 11 | 6 | FOR YOUR LOVE — Yardbirds, Epic 9790 | 11 |
| 21 | 17 | 14 | 16 | LAURIE — Dickey Lee, TCF-Hall 102 | 11 |
| ★22 | 34 | 45 | 57 | DON'T JUST STAND THERE — Patty Duke, United Artists 875 | 5 |
| 23 | 25 | 30 | 41 | SET ME FREE — Kinks, Reprise 0379 | 7 |
| 24 | 24 | 26 | 28 | HERE COMES THE NIGHT — Them, Parrot 9749 | 9 |
| 25 | 12 | 4 | 5 | WONDERFUL WORLD — Herman's Hermits, MGM 13354 | 9 |
| ★26 | 35 | 46 | 56 | THEME FROM A "SUMMER PLACE" — Lettermen, Capitol 5437 | 5 |
| 27 | 29 | 38 | 49 | SITTING IN THE PARK — Billy Stewart, Chess 1932 | 6 |
| 28 | 19 | 19 | 25 | A WORLD OF OUR OWN — Seekers, Capitol 5430 | 9 |
| 29 | 14 | 12 | 13 | A WALK IN THE BLACK FOREST — Horst Jankowski, Mercury 72425 | 12 |
| 30 | 33 | 23 | 24 | OO WEE BABY, I LOVE YOU — Fred Hughes, Vee Jay 684 | 9 |
| ★31 | 41 | 52 | 62 | HOLD ME, THRILL ME, KISS ME — Mel Carter, Imperials 66113 | 5 |
| 32 | 28 | 29 | 32 | TONIGHT'S THE NIGHT — Solomon Burke, Atlantic 2288 | 9 |
| 33 | 39 | 53 | 60 | BABY I'M YOURS — Barbara Lewis, Atlantic 2283 | 6 |
| 34 | 37 | 47 | 61 | TAKE ME BACK — Little Anthony & the Imperials, DCP 1136 | 5 |
| ★35 | 51 | 69 | — | TO KNOW YOU IS TO LOVE YOU — Peter & Gordon, Capitol 5461 | 3 |
| 36 | 23 | 21 | 21 | I'VE BEEN LOVING YOU TOO LONG — Otis Redding, Volt 126 | 11 |
| ★37 | 49 | 66 | — | PRETTY LITTLE BABY — Marvin Gaye, Tamla 54117 | 3 |
| ★38 | 50 | 60 | 79 | I'M A FOOL — Dino, Desi & Billy, Reprise 0367 | 5 |
| 39 | 32 | 35 | 35 | THIS LITTLE BIRD — Marianne Faithfull, London 9759 | 8 |
| 40 | 30 | 34 | 44 | GIRL COME RUNNING — 4 Seasons, Philips 40305 | 6 |
| 41 | 20 | 15 | 8 | CRYING IN THE CHAPEL — Elvis Presley, RCA Victor 0643 | 14 |
| ★42 | 54 | 61 | 76 | RIDE YOUR PONY — Lee Dorsey, Amy 927 | 4 |
| ★43 | 60 | 77 | 95 | DOWN IN THE BOONDOCKS — Billy Joe Royal, Columbia 43305 | 4 |
| ★44 | 66 | 82 | — | YOU'D BETTER COME HOME — Petula Clark, Warner Bros. 5643 | 3 |
| 45 | 46 | 49 | 55 | IT'S JUST A LITTLE BIT TOO LATE — Wayne Fontana & the Mindbenders, Fontana 1514 | 7 |
| 46 | 21 | 16 | 14 | HUSH, HUSH, SWEET CHARLOTTE — Patti Page, Columbia 43251 | 14 |
| 47 | 47 | 50 | 53 | SEEIN' THE RIGHT LOVE GO WRONG — Jack Jones, Kapp 672 | 7 |
| 48 | 57 | 62 | 73 | TRAINS AND BOATS AND PLANES — Billy J. Kramer & the Dakotas, Imperial 66115 | 5 |
| 49 | 43 | 48 | 50 | WHO'S CHEATING WHO? — Little Milton, Checker 1113 | 7 |
| ★50 | 63 | 86 | — | (Say) YOU'RE MY GIRL — Roy Orbison, Monument 891 | 3 |
| 51 | 42 | 43 | 46 | LITTLE LONELY ONE — Tom Jones, Tower 126 | 9 |
| 52 | 59 | 63 | 71 | NOBODY KNOWS WHAT'S GOIN' ON — Chiffons, Laurie 3301 | 6 |
| ★53 | 71 | 81 | 86 | ALL I REALLY WANT TO DO — Cher, Imperial 66114 | 4 |
| 54 | 56 | 68 | 72 | SILVER THREADS AND GOLDEN NEEDLES — Jody Miller, Capitol 5429 | 5 |
| ★55 | 67 | 73 | 83 | ALL I REALLY WANT TO DO — Byrds, Columbia 43332 | 4 |
| ★56 | 72 | — | — | UNCHAINED MELODY — Righteous Brothers, Philles 129 | 2 |
| ★57 | 73 | 88 | — | I GOT YOU BABE — Sonny & Cher, Atco 6359 | 3 |
| 58 | 58 | 64 | 66 | BOOT-LEG — Booker T. & MG's, Stax 169 | 8 |
| ★59 | 70 | 99 | — | ONE DYIN' AND A BURYIN' — Roger Miller, Smash 1994 | 3 |
| ★60 | 78 | — | — | I'LL ALWAYS LOVE YOU — Spinners, Motown 1078 | 2 |
| ★61 | 81 | — | — | TRACKS OF MY TEARS — Miracles, Tamla 54118 | 2 |
| 62 | 48 | 51 | 51 | MEETING OVER YONDER — Impressions, ABC-Paramount 10670 | 8 |
| 63 | 64 | 72 | 82 | I CAN'T WORK NO LONGER — Billy Butler & the Chanters, Okeh 7221 | 4 |
| 64 | 68 | 89 | 92 | ONE STEP AT A TIME — Maxine Brown, Wand 186 | 4 |
| ★65 | 80 | — | — | PAPA'S GOT A BRAND NEW BAG — James Brown, King 5999 | 2 |
| ★66 | 82 | 90 | — | THEME FROM "HARLOW" (Lonely Girl) — Bobby Vinton, Epic 9814 | 3 |
| 67 | 69 | 78 | 81 | NO PITY (In the Naked City) — Jackie Wilson, Brunswick 55280 | 4 |
| ★68 | — | — | — | SINCE I LOST MY BABY — Temptations, Gordy 7043 | 1 |
| 69 | 55 | 59 | 65 | IT FEELS SO RIGHT — Elvis Presley, RCA Victor 8585 | 6 |
| 70 | 75 | 84 | 87 | NEW ORLEANS — Eddie Hodges, Aurora 153 | 4 |
| ★71 | 90 | — | — | HUNG ON YOU — Righteous Brothers, Philles 129 | 2 |
| ★72 | — | — | — | CALIFORNIA GIRLS — Beach Boys, Capitol 5464 | 1 |
| 73 | 76 | 85 | — | CANDY — Astors, Stax 170 | 3 |
| 74 | 74 | 76 | 77 | DARLING TAKE ME BACK — Lenny Welch, Kapp 662 | 5 |
| 75 | 77 | 80 | 85 | HERE I AM — Dionne Warwick, Scepter 12104 | 4 |
| 76 | 83 | — | — | IT'S GONNA TAKE A MIRACLE — Royalettes, MGM 13366 | 2 |
| 77 | 79 | 83 | — | IN THE MIDNIGHT HOUR — Wilson Pickett, Atlantic 2289 | 3 |
| ★78 | — | — | — | YOU WERE ON MY MIND — We Five, A&M 770 | 1 |
| ★79 | 94 | — | — | IT'S GONNA BE FINE — Glenn Yarbrough, RCA Victor 8619 | 2 |
| 80 | 86 | — | — | IT'S TOO LATE BABY, TOO LATE — Arthur Prysock, Old Town 1183 | 2 |
| 81 | 87 | 93 | 99 | FORGET DOMANI — Frank Sinatra, Reprise 0380 | 5 |
| 82 | 62 | 67 | 68 | WATERMELON MAN — Gloria Lynne, Fontana 1511 | 5 |
| 83 | 84 | 92 | 93 | FORGET DOMANI — Connie Francis, MGM 13363 | 5 |
| 84 | 88 | 98 | — | "TICKLE ME" — Elvis Presley, RCA Victor EPA 4383 (Extended Play) | 3 |
| ★85 | — | — | — | YOU TELL ME WHY — Beau Brummels, Autumn 16 | 1 |
| ★86 | — | — | — | LOOKING THROUGH THE EYES OF LOVE — Gene Pitney, Musicor 1103 | 1 |
| 87 | 95 | 97 | — | MOON OVER NAPLES — Bert Kaempfert & His Ork, Decca 31812 | 3 |
| 88 | 93 | — | — | THE LOSERS — Skyliners, Jubilee 5506 | 2 |
| 89 | 89 | 79 | 84 | MY MAN — Barbra Streisand, Columbia 43323 | 4 |
| ★90 | — | — | — | YOU'RE MY BABY — Vacels, Kama Sutra 200 | 1 |
| 91 | — | — | — | LIKE A ROLLING STONE — Bob Dylan, Columbia 43346 | 1 |
| 92 | — | — | — | FLY ME TO THE MOON — Tony Bennett, Columbia 43331 | 1 |
| 93 | — | — | — | AROUND THE CORNER — Duprees, Columbia 43336 | 1 |
| 94 | — | — | — | SUGAR DUMPLING — Sam Cooke, RCA Victor 8631 | 1 |
| 95 | 96 | — | — | YOU'VE NEVER BEEN IN LOVE LIKE THIS BEFORE — Unit Four Plus Two, London 9761 | 2 |
| 96 | 99 | — | — | BUSTER BROWNE — Willie Mitchell, Hi 2091 | 2 |
| 97 | — | — | — | IF YOU REALLY WANT ME TO, I'LL GO — Ron-Dels, Smash 1986 | 1 |
| 98 | 98 | — | — | YAKETY AXE — Chet Atkins, RCA Victor 8590 | 2 |
| 99 | 100 | — | — | I'M A FOOL TO CARE — Ray Charles, ABC-Paramount 10700 | 2 |
| 100 | — | — | — | ONLY THOSE IN LOVE — Baby Washington, Sue 129 | 1 |

## HOT 100—A TO Z—(Publisher-Licensee)


All I Really Want to Do—Byrds (Witmark, ASCAP) . 55
All I Really Want to Do—Cher (Witmark, ASCAP) 53
Around the Corner (South Mountain, BMI) ..... 93

Baby I'm Yours (Blackwood, BMI) ..... 33
Boot-Leg (East, BMI) ..... 58
Buster Browne (Jac, BMI) ..... 96

California Girls (Sea of Tunes, BMI) ..... 72
Candy (East, BMI) ..... 73
Cara, Mia (Feist, ASCAP) ..... 5
Crying in the Chapel (Valley, BMI) ..... 41

Darling Take Me Back (Murbo, BMI) ..... 74
Don't Just Stand There (Bernross, BMI) ..... 22
Down in the Boondocks (Lowery, BMI) ..... 43
Fly Me to the Moon (Almanac, ASCAP) ..... 92
For Your Love (Blackwood, BMI) ..... 20
Forget Domani—Francis (Miller, ASCAP) ..... 83
Forget Domani—Sinatra (Miller, ASCAP) ..... 81
Girl Come Running (Saturday, BMI) ..... 40
Here Comes the Night (Keetch, Caesar & Dino, BMI) 24
Here I Am (United Artists, ASCAP) ..... 75
Hold Me, Thrill Me, Kiss Me (Mills, ASCAP) ... 31
Hung on You (Screen Gems-Columbia, BMI) ..... 71
Hush, Hush, Sweet Charlotte (Miller, ASCAP) .. 46
(I Can't Get No) Satisfaction (Immediate, BMI) ... 1
I Can't Help Myself (Jobete, BMI) ..... 3
I Can't Work No Longer (Curtom, BMI) ..... 63
I Got You Babe (Five-West-Cotillion, BMI) ..... 57
I Like It Like That (Tune-Kel, BMI) ..... 12
I Want Candy (Grand Canyon-Webb IV, BMI) ..... 18
If You Really Want Me To, I'll Go (Billie Fran, BMI) ..... 97
I'll Always Love You (Jobete, BMI) ..... 60
I'm a Fool (Atlantic, BMI) ..... 38
I'm a Fool to Care (Peer Int'l, BMI) ..... 99
I'm Henry VIII, I Am (Miller, ASCAP) ..... 2

I've Been Loving You Too Long (East-Time, BMI). 36
In the Midnight Hour (Cotillion-East, BMI) ..... 77
It Feels So Right (Gladys, ASCAP) ..... 69
It's Gonna Be Fine (Screen Gems-Columbia, BMI) 79
It's Gonna Take a Miracle (South Mountain, BMI).. 76
It's Just a Little Bit Too Late (Skidmore, ASCAP). 45
It's Too Late Baby, Too Late (Pry-Weiss, BMI) ... 80

Laurie (Long-Gold Dust, BMI) ..... 21
Like a Rolling Stone (Witmark, ASCAP) ..... 91
Little Bit of Heaven, A (T. M., BMI) ..... 16
Little Lonely One (We Three, BMI) ..... 51
Looking Through the Eyes of Love (Screen Gems-Columbia, BMI) ..... 86
Losers, The (Wemar, BMI) ..... 88

Marie (Berlin, ASCAP) ..... 15
Meeting Over Yonder (Chi-Sound, BMI) ..... 62
Mr. Tambourine Man (Witmark, ASCAP) ..... 9
Moon Over Naples (Roosevelt, BMI) ..... 87
My Man (Feist, ASCAP) ..... 89

New Orleans (Rockmasters, BMI) ..... 70
No Pity (In the Naked City) (Merrimac, BMI) ... 67
Nobody Knows What's Goin' On (Bright Tunes, BMI) ..... 52

One Dyin' and a Buryin' (Tree, BMI) ..... 59
One Step at a Time (Flomar, BMI) ..... 64
Only Those in Love (Brown, BMI) ..... 100
Oo Wee Baby, I Love You (Costoma, BMI) ..... 30

Papa's Got a Brand New Bag (Lois, BMI) ..... 65
Pretty Little Baby (Jobete, BMI) ..... 37

Ride Your Pony (Jarb, BMI) ..... 42

Save Your Heart for Me (Geld-Udell-Purchase, ASCAP) ..... 13
(Say) You're My Girl (Acuff-Rose, BMI) ..... 50
Seein' the Right Love Go Wrong (Sea-Lark, BMI). 47

Set Me Free (American Metropolitan Ent., BMI) .. 23
Seventh Son (Arc, BMI) ..... 8
Silver Threads and Golden Needles (Central Songs, BMI) ..... 54
Since I Lost My Baby (Jobete, BMI) ..... 68
Sittin' in the Park (Chevis, BMI) ..... 27
(Such an) Easy Question (Presley, BMI) ..... 11
Sugar Dumpling (Kags, BMI) ..... 94
Sunshine, Lollipops and Rainbows (Hanson, ASCAP). 19

Take Me Back (South Mountain, BMI) ..... 34
Theme From "A Summer Place" (Witmark, ASCAP). 26
Theme From "Harlow" (Lonely Girl) (Consul, ASCAP) 66
This Little Bird (Acuff-Rose, BMI) ..... 39
"Tickle Me" (Various Publishers) ..... 84
To Know You Is to Love You (Hillary, BMI) ..... 35
Tonight's the Night (Cotillion, BMI) ..... 32
Too Many Rivers (Combine, BMI) ..... 14
Tracks of My Tears (Jobete, BMI) ..... 61
Trains and Boats and Planes (U. S. Songs, ASCAP). 48
Unchained Melody (Frank, ASCAP) ..... 56
Walk in the Black Forest, A (MRC, BMI) ..... 29
Watermelon Man (Hancock, BMI) ..... 82
What the World Needs Is Love (Blue Seas-Jac, BMI) 7
What's New Pussycat? (United Artists, ASCAP) .. 4
Who's Cheating Who? (Chevis, BMI) ..... 49
Wonderful World (Kags, BMI) ..... 25
Wooly Bully (Beckie, BMI) ..... 17
World of Our Own (Chappell, ASCAP) ..... 28
Yakety Axe (Tree, BMI) ..... 98
Yes, I'm Ready (Stillran-Dandelion, BMI) ..... 6
You Tell Me Why (Taracrest, BMI) ..... 85
You Turn Me On (Burdette, BMI) ..... 10
You Were On My Mind (Witmark, ASCAP) ..... 78
You'd Better Come Home (Duchess, BMI) ..... 44
You're My Baby (Screen Gems-Columbia, BMI) .. 90
You've Never Been in Love Like This Before (Burlington, ASCAP) ..... 95


## BUBBLING UNDER THE HOT 100

101. I'M A HAPPY MAN ..... Jive 5, United Artists 853
102. GEE THE MOON IS SHINING BRIGHT ..... Dixie Cups, Red Bird 032
103. I'LL FEEL A WHOLE LOT BETTER ..... Byrds, Columbia 43332
104. ALIMONY ..... Tommy Tucker, Checker 1112
105. FROM A WINDOW ..... Chad & Jeremy, World Artists 1056
106. IT HAPPENED JUST THAT WAY ..... Roger Miller, Smash 1994
107. JUSTINE ..... Righteous Brothers, Moonglow 242
108. IF I HAD MY LIFE TO LIVE OVER ..... Lloyd Price, Monument 887
109. IN THE MIDDLE OF NOWHERE ..... Dusty Springfield, Philips 40303
110. IT'S THE SAME OLD SONG ..... Four Tops, Motown 1081
111. IT'S A MAN DOWN THERE ..... G. L. Crockett, 4 Brothers 445
112. HALLELUJAH ..... Invitations, DynoVoice 206
113. MY NAME IS MUD ..... Eddie Rambeau, DynoVoice 207
114. WE'RE DOING FINE ..... DeeDee Warwick, Blue Rock 4027
115. YOU'RE GONNA MAKE ME CRY ..... O. V. Wright, Back Beat 548
116. BLUE SHADOWS ..... B. B. King, Kent 426
117. YOU BETTER GO ..... Derek Martin, Roulette 4631
118. THE TRACKER ..... Sir Douglas Quintet, Tribe 8310
119. AIN'T THAT LOVE ..... Four Tops, Columbia 43356
120. YOU CAN'T GROW PEACHES ON A CHERRY TREE..Browns, RCA Victor 8603
121. STOP! LOOK WHAT YOU'RE DOING ..... Carla Thomas, Stax 172
122. I'M LOSING YOU ..... Aretha Franklin, Columbia 86166
123. I PUT A SPELL ON YOU ..... Nina Simone, Philips 40286
124. STREETS OF LAREDO ..... Johnny Cash, Columbia 43313
125. MOONGLOW & THEME FROM PICNIC ..... Esther Phillips, Atlantic 2294
126. THE "IN" CROWD ..... Ramsey Lewis Trio, Argo 5506
127. HAPPY FEET TIME ..... Montclairs, Sunburst 106
128. AFTER LOVING YOU ..... Della Reese, ABC-Paramount 10691
129. TIGER WOMAN ..... Claude King, Columbia 43293
130. CANADIAN SUNSET ..... Sounds Orchestral, Parkway 958
131. DO THE 45 ..... Sharpees, One-Derful 4835
132. ARKANSAS ..... Jimmy McCracklin, Imperial 66116
133. SOUTHERN COUNTRY BOY ..... Carter Brothers, Jewel 745
134. UNWIND THE TWINE ..... Alvin Cash and the Crawlers, Mac-V-Lus 6006
135. I'M THE ONE THAT LOVE FORGOT ..... Manhattan, Carnival 509

Compiled from national retail sales and radio station airplay by the Music Popularity Dept. of Record Market Research, Billboard.

# Billboard HOT 100

**For Week Ending July 31, 1965**

★ STAR performer—Sides registering greatest proportionate upward progress this week.

Record Industry Association of America seal of certification as million selling single.

| This Week | Wks. Ago 1 | Wks. Ago 2 | Wks. Ago 3 | TITLE, Artist, Label & Number | Weeks On Chart |
|---|---|---|---|---|---|
| 1 | 1 | 1 | 1 | (I Can't Get No) SATISFACTION — Rolling Stones, London 9766 | 8 |
| 2 | 2 | 3 | 13 | I'M HENRY VIII, I AM — Herman's Hermits, MGM 13367 | 5 |
| 3 | 4 | 10 | 17 | WHAT'S NEW PUSSYCAT? — Tom Jones, Parrot 9765 | 7 |
| 4 | 5 | 5 | 8 | CARA, MIA — Jay & the Americans, United Artists 881 | 9 |
| 5 | 6 | 6 | 6 | YES, I'M READY — Barbara Mason, Arctic 105 | 12 |
| 6 | 3 | 2 | 2 | I CAN'T HELP MYSELF — Four Tops, Motown 1076 | 12 |
| 7 | 7 | 9 | 10 | WHAT THE WORLD NEEDS NOW IS LOVE — Jackie DeShannon, Imperial 66110 | 11 |
| ★8 | 13 | 40 | 56 | SAVE YOUR HEART FOR ME — Gary Lewis & the Playboys, Liberty 55809 | 4 |
| ★9 | 12 | 26 | 31 | I LIKE IT LIKE THAT — Dave Clark Five, Epic 9811 | 7 |
| 10 | 8 | 7 | 7 | SEVENTH SON — Johnny Rivers, Imperial 66112 | 9 |
| 11 | 11 | 15 | 20 | (Such An) EASY QUESTION — Elvis Presley, RCA Victor 8585 | 7 |
| ★12 | 18 | 27 | 33 | I WANT CANDY — Strangeloves, Bang 501 | 6 |
| 13 | 14 | 18 | 24 | TOO MANY RIVERS — Brenda Lee, Decca 31792 | 10 |
| ★14 | 22 | 34 | 45 | DON'T JUST STAND THERE — Patty Duke, United Artists 875 | 6 |
| 15 | 15 | 22 | 24 | MARIE — Bachelors, London 9762 | 8 |
| 16 | 19 | 31 | 41 | SUNSHINE, LOLLIPOPS AND RAINBOWS — Lesley Gore, Mercury 72433 | 7 |
| 17 | 10 | 8 | 9 | YOU TURN ME ON — Ian Whitcomb, Tower 134 | 11 |
| 18 | 9 | 4 | 3 | MR. TAMBOURINE MAN — Byrds, Columbia 43271 | 12 |
| 19 | 26 | 35 | 46 | THEME FROM "A SUMMER PLACE" — Lettermen, Capitol 5437 | 6 |
| 20 | 16 | 16 | 18 | A LITTLE BIT OF HEAVEN — Ronnie Dove, Diamond 184 | 9 |
| 21 | 21 | 17 | 14 | LAURIE — Dickey Lee, TCF-Hall 102 | 12 |
| ★22 | 57 | 73 | 88 | I GOT YOU BABE — Sonny & Cher, Atco 6359 | 4 |
| 23 | 33 | 39 | 53 | BABY I'M YOURS — Barbara Lewis, Atlantic 2283 | 7 |
| 24 | 27 | 29 | 38 | SITTING IN THE PARK — Billy Stewart, Chess 1932 | 7 |
| 25 | 31 | 41 | 52 | HOLD ME, THRILL ME, KISS ME — Mel Carter, Imperials 66113 | 6 |
| 26 | 34 | 37 | 47 | TAKE ME BACK — Little Anthony & the Imperials, DCP 1136 | 6 |
| 27 | 43 | 60 | 77 | DOWN IN THE BOONDOCKS — Billy Joe Royal, Columbia 43305 | 5 |
| 28 | 38 | 50 | 60 | I'M A FOOL — Dino, Desi & Billy, Reprise 0367 | 6 |
| 29 | 35 | 51 | 69 | TO KNOW YOU IS TO LOVE YOU — Peter & Gordon, Capitol 5461 | 4 |
| 30 | 37 | 49 | 66 | PRETTY LITTLE BABY — Marvin Gaye, Tamla 54117 | 6 |
| 31 | 44 | 66 | 82 | YOU'D BETTER COME HOME — Petula Clark, Warner Bros. 5643 | 4 |
| 32 | 42 | 54 | 61 | RIDE YOUR PONY — Lee Dorsey, Amy 927 | 5 |
| 33 | 24 | 24 | 26 | HERE COMES THE NIGHT — Them, Parrot 9749 | 10 |
| 34 | 23 | 25 | 30 | SET ME FREE — Kinks, Reprise 0379 | 8 |
| 35 | 29 | 14 | 12 | A WALK IN THE BLACK FOREST — Horst Jankowski, Mercury 72425 | 13 |
| 36 | 17 | 11 | 5 | WOOLY BULLY — Sam the Sham and the Pharaohs, MGM 13322 | 18 |
| 37 | 32 | 28 | 29 | TONIGHT'S THE NIGHT — Solomon Burke, Atlantic 2288 | 10 |
| ★38 | 56 | 72 | — | UNCHAINED MELODY — Righteous Brothers, Philles 129 | 3 |
| 39 | 20 | 13 | 11 | FOR YOUR LOVE — Yardbirds, Epic 9790 | 12 |
| 40 | 28 | 19 | 19 | A WORLD OF OUR OWN — Seekers, Capitol 5430 | 10 |
| 41 | 59 | 70 | 99 | ONE DYIN' AND A BURYIN' — Roger Miller, Smash 1994 | 4 |
| ★42 | 53 | 71 | 81 | ALL I REALLY WANT TO DO — Cher, Imperial 66114 | 5 |
| 43 | 50 | 63 | 86 | (Say) YOU'RE MY GIRL — Roy Orbison, Monument 891 | 4 |
| 44 | 65 | 80 | — | PAPA'S GOT A BRAND NEW BAG — James Brown, King 5999 | 3 |
| ★45 | 55 | 67 | 73 | ALL I REALLY WANT TO DO — Byrds, Columbia 43332 | 5 |
| 46 | 47 | 47 | 50 | SEEIN' THE RIGHT LOVE GO WRONG — Jack Jones, Kapp 672 | 8 |
| 47 | 48 | 57 | 62 | TRAINS AND BOATS AND PLANES — Billy J. Kramer & the Dakotas, Imperial 66115 | 7 |
| 48 | 25 | 12 | 4 | WONDERFUL WORLD — Herman's Hermits, MGM 13354 | 10 |
| 49 | 52 | 59 | 63 | NOBODY KNOWS WHAT'S GOIN' ON — Chiffons, Laurie 3301 | 7 |
| 50 | 60 | 78 | — | I'LL ALWAYS LOVE YOU — Spinners, Motown 1078 | 3 |
| 51 | 61 | 81 | — | TRACKS OF MY TEARS — Miracles, Tamla 54118 | 3 |
| 52 | 72 | — | — | CALIFORNIA GIRLS — Beach Boys, Capitol 5464 | 2 |
| 53 | 68 | — | — | SINCE I LOST MY BABY — Temptations, Gordy 7043 | 2 |
| 54 | — | — | — | IT'S THE SAME OLD SONG — Four Tops, Motown 1081 | 1 |
| 55 | 40 | 30 | 34 | GIRL COME RUNNING — 4 Seasons, Philips 40305 | 7 |
| 56 | 30 | 33 | 23 | OO WEE BABY, I LOVE YOU — Fred Hughes, Vee Jay 684 | 10 |
| 57 | 78 | — | — | YOU WERE ON MY MIND — We Five, A&M 770 | 2 |
| 58 | 70 | 75 | 84 | NEW ORLEANS — Eddie Hodges, Aurora 153 | 5 |
| 59 | 45 | 46 | 49 | IT'S JUST A LITTLE BIT TOO LATE — Wayne Fontana & the Mindbenders, Fontana 1514 | 8 |
| 60 | 54 | 56 | 68 | SILVER THREADS AND GOLDEN NEEDLES — Jody Miller, Capitol 5429 | 6 |
| 61 | 63 | 64 | 72 | I CAN'T WORK NO LONGER — Billy Butler & the Chanters, Okeh 7221 | 5 |
| 62 | 77 | 79 | 83 | IN THE MIDNIGHT HOUR — Wilson Pickett, Atlantic 2289 | 4 |
| 63 | 64 | 68 | 89 | ONE STEP AT A TIME — Maxine Brown, Wand 185 | 5 |
| 64 | 66 | 82 | 90 | THEME FROM "HARLOW" (Lonely Girl) — Bobby Vinton, Epic 9814 | 4 |
| 65 | 71 | 90 | — | HUNG ON YOU — Righteous Brothers, Philles 129 | 3 |
| 66 | 67 | 69 | 78 | NO PITY (In the Naked City) — Jackie Wilson, Brunswick 55280 | 5 |
| 67 | 86 | — | — | LOOKING THROUGH THE EYES OF LOVE — Gene Pitney, Musicor 1103 | 2 |
| 68 | 79 | 94 | — | IT'S GONNA BE FINE — Glenn Yarbrough, RCA Victor 8619 | 3 |
| 69 | 76 | 83 | — | IT'S GONNA TAKE A MIRACLE — Royalettes, MGM 13366 | 3 |
| 70 | 85 | — | — | YOU TELL ME WHY — Beau Brummels, Autumn 16 | 2 |
| 71 | 75 | 77 | 80 | HERE I AM — Dionne Warwick, Scepter 12104 | 5 |
| 72 | 74 | 74 | 76 | DARLING TAKE ME BACK — Lenny Welch, Kapp 662 | 6 |
| 73 | 73 | 76 | 85 | CANDY — Astors, Stax 170 | 4 |
| 74 | 58 | 58 | 64 | BOOT-LEG — Booker T. & MG's, Stax 169 | 9 |
| 75 | 80 | 86 | — | IT'S TOO LATE BABY, TOO LATE — Arthur Prysock, Old Town 1183 | 3 |
| 76 | 91 | — | — | LIKE A ROLLING STONE — Bob Dylan, Columbia 43346 | 2 |
| 77 | 94 | — | — | SUGAR DUMPLING — Sam Cooke, RCA Victor 8631 | 2 |
| 78 | 81 | 87 | 93 | FORGET DOMANI — Frank Sinatra, Reprise 0380 | 6 |
| 79 | 83 | 84 | 92 | FORGET DOMANI — Connie Francis, MGM 13363 | 6 |
| 80 | — | — | — | JU JU HAND — Sam the Sham & the Pharaohs, MGM 13364 | 1 |
| 81 | — | — | — | SHAKE AND FINGERPOP — Jr. Walker and the All Stars, Soul 35013 | 1 |
| 82 | 90 | — | — | YOU'RE MY BABY — Vacels, Kama Sutra 200 | 2 |
| 83 | 84 | 88 | 98 | "TICKLE ME" — Elvis Presley, RCA Victor EPA 4383 (Extended Play) | 4 |
| 84 | 87 | 95 | 97 | MOON OVER NAPLES — Bert Kaempfert & His Ork, Decca 31812 | 4 |
| 85 | 88 | 93 | — | THE LOSER — Skyliners, Jubilee 5506 | 3 |
| 86 | — | — | — | HEART FULL OF SOUL — Yardbirds, Epic 9823 | 1 |
| 87 | 89 | 89 | 79 | MY MAN — Barbra Streisand, Columbia 43323 | 5 |
| 88 | — | — | — | NOTHING BUT HEARTACHES — Supremes, Motown 1080 | 1 |
| 89 | 92 | — | — | FLY ME TO THE MOON — Tony Bennett, Columbia 43331 | 2 |
| 90 | — | — | — | A LITTLE YOU — Freddie & the Dreamers, Mercury 72462 | 1 |
| 91 | 93 | — | — | AROUND THE CORNER — Duprees, Columbia 43336 | 2 |
| 92 | — | — | — | CANADIAN SUNSET — Sounds Orchestral, Parkway 958 | 1 |
| 93 | — | — | — | AIN'T THAT LOVE — Four Tops, Columbia 43356 | 1 |
| 94 | 99 | 100 | — | I'M A FOOL TO CARE — Ray Charles, ABC-Paramount 10700 | 3 |
| 95 | — | — | — | HE'S GOT NO LOVE — Searchers, Kapp 686 | 1 |
| 96 | — | — | — | OOWEE, OOWEE — Perry Como, RCA Victor 8636 | 1 |
| 97 | 100 | — | — | ONLY THOSE IN LOVE — Baby Washington, Sue 129 | 2 |
| 98 | — | — | — | YOU BETTER GO — Derek Martin, Roulette 4631 | 1 |
| 99 | — | — | — | AFTER LOVING YOU — Della Reese, ABC-Paramount 10691 | 1 |
| 100 | — | — | — | THE "IN" CROWD — Ramsey Lewis Trio, Argo 5506 | 1 |

## BUBBLING UNDER THE HOT 100

101. WE'RE DOING FINE — Dee Dee Warwick, Blue Rock 4027
102. YAKETY AXE — Chet Atkins, RCA Victor 8590
103. I'LL FEEL A WHOLE LOT BETTER — Byrds, Columbia 43332
104. YOU'RE GONNA MAKE ME CRY — O. V. Wright, Back Beat 548
105. IT HAPPENED JUST THAT WAY — Roger Miller, Smash 1994
106. IF I DIDN'T LOVE YOU — Chuck Jackson, Wand 188
107. IF I HAD MY LIFE TO LIVE OVER — Lloyd Price, Monument 887
108. IN THE MIDDLE OF NOWHERE — Dusty Springfield, Philips 40303
109. I'M A HAPPY MAN — Jive Five, United Artists 853
110. HELP — Beatles, Capitol 5476
111. HALLELUJAH — Invitation, DynoVoice 206
112. MY NAME IS MUD — Eddie Rambeau, DynoVoice 207
113. ALIMONY — Tommy Tucker, Checker 1112
114. THE TRACKER — Sir Douglas Quintet, Tribe 8310
115. I DON'T WANT TO LIVE (Without Your Love) — Bobbi Martin, Coral 62457
116. IT AIN'T ME BABE — Turtles, White Whale 222
117. IF YOU REALLY WANT ME TO, I'LL GO — Ron-Dels, Smash 1986
118. MOONGLOWS & THEME FROM PICNIC — Esther Phillips, Atlantic 2294
119. GEE THE MOON IS SHINING BRIGHT — Dixie Cups, Red Bird 043
120. ONLY YOU — Buck Owens, Capitol 5465
121. COLOURS — Donovan, Hickory 1324
122. BUSTER BROWNE — Willie Mitchell, HI 2091
123. IS IT REALLY OVER? — Jim Reeves, RCA Victor 8625
124. YOU'VE GOT TO EARN IT — Temptations, Gordy 7043
125. SUMMER WIND — Wayne Newton, Capitol 5470
126. YOU'VE NEVER BEEN IN LOVE LIKE THIS BEFORE — Unit Four, Plus Two, London 9761
127. HAPPY FEET TIME — Montclair, Sunburst 106
128. DO THE 45 — Sharpees, One-Derful 4835
129. OUT IN THE SUN (Hey-O) — Beach Nuts, Bang 504
130. IT'S A MAN DOWN THERE — G. L. Crockett, 4 Brothers 445
131. SO MUCH IN LOVE WITH YOU — Ian & the Zodiacs, Philips 40291
132. I'VE CRIED MY LAST TEAR — OJays, Imperial 66121
133. WHY DON'T YOU BELIEVE ME — Vic Damone, Warner Bros. 5644
134. WHERE WERE YOU WHEN I NEEDED YOU — Jerry Vale, Columbia 43337
135. WHAT WE ARE GOING TO DO — David Jones, Colpix 784

Compiled from national retail sales and radio station airplay by the Music Popularity Dept. of Record Market Research, Billboard.

# Billboard

For Week Ending August 7, 1965

# HOT 100

★ STAR performer—Sides registering greatest proportionate upward progress this week.

Record Industry Association of America seal of certification as million selling single.

Billboard Award

| This Week | 1 Wk. Ago | 2 Wks. Ago | 3 Wks. Ago | Title / Artist, Label & Number | Weeks On Chart |
|---|---|---|---|---|---|
| 1 | 2 | 2 | 3 | I'M HENRY VIII, I AM / Herman's Hermits, MGM 13367 | 6 |
| 2 | 1 | 1 | 1 | (I Can't Get No) SATISFACTION / Rolling Stones, London 9766 | 9 |
| 3 | 3 | 4 | 10 | WHAT'S NEW PUSSYCAT? / Tom Jones, Parrot 9765 | 8 |
| ★4 | 8 | 13 | 40 | SAVE YOUR HEART FOR ME / Gary Lewis & the Playboys, Liberty 55809 | 6 |
| ★5 | 22 | 57 | 73 | I GOT YOU BABE / Sonny & Cher, Atco 6359 | 5 |
| 6 | 5 | 6 | 6 | YES, I'M READY / Barbara Mason, Arctic 105 | 13 |
| 7 | 9 | 12 | 26 | I LIKE IT LIKE THAT / Dave Clark Five, Epic 9811 | 8 |
| 8 | 4 | 5 | 5 | CARA, MIA / Jay & the Americans, United Artists 881 | 10 |
| 9 | 6 | 3 | 2 | I CAN'T HELP MYSELF / Four Tops, Motown 1076 | 13 |
| ★10 | 14 | 22 | 34 | DON'T JUST STAND THERE / Patty Duke, United Artists 875 | 7 |
| 11 | 7 | 7 | 9 | WHAT THE WORLD NEEDS NOW IS LOVE / Jackie DeShannon, Imperial 66110 | 12 |
| 12 | 12 | 18 | 27 | I WANT CANDY / Strangeloves, Bang 501 | 7 |
| 13 | 16 | 19 | 31 | SUNSHINE, LOLLIPOPS AND RAINBOWS / Lesley Gore, Mercury 72433 | 8 |
| ★14 | 27 | 43 | 60 | DOWN IN THE BOONDOCKS / Billy Joe Royal, Columbia 43305 | 6 |
| ★15 | 38 | 56 | 72 | UNCHAINED MELODY / Righteous Brothers, Philles 129 | 4 |
| 16 | 19 | 26 | 35 | THEME FROM "A SUMMER PLACE" / Lettermen, Capitol 5437 | 7 |
| ★17 | 54 | — | — | IT'S THE SAME OLD SONG / Four Tops, Motown 1081 | 2 |
| ★18 | 23 | 33 | 39 | BABY I'M YOURS / Barbara Lewis, Atlantic 2283 | 8 |
| ★19 | 26 | 34 | 37 | TAKE ME BACK / Little Anthony & the Imperials, DCP 1136 | 7 |
| ★20 | 25 | 31 | 41 | HOLD ME, THRILL ME, KISS ME / Mel Carter, Imperials 66113 | 7 |
| 21 | 10 | 8 | 7 | SEVENTH SON / Johnny Rivers, Imperial 66112 | 10 |
| ★22 | 28 | 38 | 50 | I'M A FOOL / Dino, Desi & Billy, Reprise 0367 | 7 |
| ★23 | 42 | 53 | 71 | ALL I REALLY WANT TO DO / Cher, Imperial 66114 | 6 |
| ★24 | 29 | 35 | 51 | TO KNOW YOU IS TO LOVE YOU / Peter & Gordon, Capitol 5461 | 5 |
| 25 | 13 | 14 | 18 | TOO MANY RIVERS / Brenda Lee, Decca 31792 | 11 |
| ★26 | 31 | 44 | 66 | YOU'D BETTER COME HOME / Petula Clark, Warner Bros. 5643 | 5 |
| 27 | 30 | 37 | 49 | PRETTY LITTLE BABY / Marvin Gaye, Tamla 54117 | 5 |
| ★28 | 52 | 72 | — | CALIFORNIA GIRLS / Beach Boys, Capitol 5464 | 3 |
| 29 | 32 | 42 | 54 | RIDE YOUR PONY / Lee Dorsey, Amy 927 | 6 |
| ★30 | 44 | 65 | 80 | PAPA'S GOT A BRAND NEW BAG / James Brown, King 5999 | 4 |
| 31 | 15 | 15 | 22 | MARIE / Bachelors, London 9762 | 9 |
| 32 | 24 | 27 | 29 | SITTING IN THE PARK / Billy Stewart, Chess 1932 | 8 |
| ★33 | 57 | 78 | — | YOU WERE ON MY MIND / We Five, A&M 770 | 3 |
| 34 | 17 | 10 | 8 | YOU TURN ME ON / Ian Whitcomb, Tower 134 | 12 |
| 35 | 11 | 11 | 15 | (Such An) EASY QUESTION / Elvis Presley, RCA Victor 8585 | 8 |
| 36 | 41 | 59 | 70 | ONE DYIN' AND A BURYIN' / Roger Miller, Smash 1994 | 5 |
| ★37 | 51 | 61 | 81 | TRACKS OF MY TEARS / Miracles, Tamla 54118 | 4 |
| 38 | 18 | 9 | 4 | MR. TAMBOURINE MAN / Byrds, Columbia 43271 | 13 |
| ★39 | 53 | 68 | — | SINCE I LOST MY BABY / Temptations, Gordy 7043 | 3 |
| 40 | 43 | 50 | 63 | (Say) YOU'RE MY GIRL / Roy Orbison, Monument 891 | 5 |
| ★41 | — | — | — | HELP / Beatles, Capitol 5476 | 1 |
| 42 | 20 | 16 | 16 | A LITTLE BIT OF HEAVEN / Ronnie Dove, Diamond 184 | 10 |
| 43 | 45 | 55 | 67 | ALL I REALLY WANT TO DO / Byrds, Columbia 43332 | 6 |
| ★44 | 76 | 91 | — | LIKE A ROLLING STONE / Bob Dylan, Columbia 43346 | 3 |
| 45 | 50 | 60 | 78 | I'LL ALWAYS LOVE YOU / Spinners, Motown 1078 | 4 |
| 46 | 21 | 21 | 17 | LAURIE / Dickey Lee, TCF-Hall 102 | 13 |
| ★47 | 88 | — | — | NOTHING BUT HEARTACHES / Supremes, Motown 1080 | 2 |
| ★48 | 58 | 70 | 75 | NEW ORLEANS / Eddie Hodges, Aurora 153 | 6 |
| 49 | 49 | 52 | 59 | NOBODY KNOWS WHAT'S GOIN' ON / Chiffons, Laurie 3301 | 8 |
| 50 | 47 | 48 | 57 | TRAINS AND BOATS AND PLANES / Billy J. Kramer & the Dakotas, Imperial 66115 | 7 |
| ★51 | 67 | 86 | — | LOOKING THROUGH THE EYES OF LOVE / Gene Pitney, Musicor 1103 | 3 |
| ★52 | 62 | 77 | 79 | IN THE MIDNIGHT HOUR / Wilson Pickett, Atlantic 2289 | 5 |
| ★53 | 65 | 71 | 90 | HUNG ON YOU / Righteous Brothers, Philles 129 | 4 |
| 54 | 46 | 47 | 47 | SEEIN' THE RIGHT LOVE GO WRONG / Jack Jones, Kapp 672 | 9 |
| ★55 | 68 | 79 | 94 | IT'S GONNA BE FINE / Glenn Yarbrough, RCA Victor 8619 | 4 |
| 56 | 63 | 64 | 68 | ONE STEP AT A TIME / Maxine Brown, Wand 185 | 6 |
| ★57 | 80 | — | — | JU JU HAND / Sam the Sham & the Pharaohs, MGM 13364 | 2 |
| ★58 | 81 | — | — | SHAKE AND FINGERPOP / Jr. Walker & the All Stars, Soul 35013 | 2 |
| ★59 | 70 | 85 | — | YOU TELL ME WHY / Beau Brummels, Autumn 16 | 3 |
| 60 | 61 | 63 | 64 | I CAN'T WORK NO LONGER / Billy Butler & the Chanters, Okeh 7221 | 6 |
| 61 | 64 | 66 | 82 | THEME FROM "HARLOW" (Lonely Girl) / Bobby Vinton, Epic 9814 | 5 |
| 62 | 69 | 76 | 83 | IT'S GONNA TAKE A MIRACLE / Royalettes, MGM 13366 | 4 |
| 63 | 66 | 67 | 69 | NO PITY (In the Naked City) / Jackie Wilson, Brunswick 55280 | 6 |
| 64 | 77 | 94 | — | SUGAR DUMPLING / Sam Cooke, RCA Victor 8631 | 3 |
| 65 | 73 | 73 | 76 | CANDY / Astors, Stax 170 | 5 |
| 66 | 75 | 80 | 86 | IT'S TOO LATE BABY, TOO LATE / Arthur Prysock, Old Town 1183 | 4 |
| 67 | 71 | 75 | 77 | HERE I AM / Dionne Warwick, Scepter 12104 | 6 |
| ★68 | — | — | — | I DON'T WANNA LOSE YOU BABY / Chad & Jeremy, Columbia 43339 | 1 |
| ★69 | 86 | — | — | HEART FULL OF SOUL / Yardbirds, Epic 9823 | 2 |
| 70 | 84 | 87 | 95 | MOON OVER NAPLES / Bert Kaempfert & His Ork, Decca 31812 | 5 |
| ★71 | 90 | — | — | A LITTLE YOU / Freddie & the Dreamers, Mercury 72462 | 2 |
| 72 | 82 | 90 | — | YOU'RE MY BABY / Vacels, Kama Sutra 200 | 3 |
| 73 | 83 | 84 | 88 | "TICKLE ME" / Elvis Presley, RCA Victor EPA 4383 (Extended Play) | 5 |
| 74 | 74 | 58 | 58 | BOOT-LEG / Booker T. & MG's, Stax 169 | 10 |
| 75 | 85 | 88 | 93 | THE LOSER / Skyliners, Jubilee 5506 | 4 |
| ★76 | — | — | — | IT AIN'T ME BABE / Turtles, White Whale 222 | 1 |
| ★77 | 100 | — | — | THE "IN" CROWD / Ramsey Lewis Trio, Argo 5506 | 2 |
| 78 | 78 | 81 | 87 | FORGET DOMANI / Frank Sinatra, Reprise 0380 | 7 |
| ★79 | — | — | — | HOUSTON / Dean Martin, Reprise 0393 | 1 |
| ★80 | — | — | — | IF I DIDN'T LOVE YOU / Chuck Jackson, Wand 188 | 1 |
| 81 | 95 | — | — | HE'S GOT NO LOVE / Searchers, Kapp 686 | 2 |
| 82 | 79 | 83 | 84 | FORGET DOMANI / Connie Francis, MGM 13363 | 7 |
| 83 | 92 | — | — | CANADIAN SUNSET / Sounds Orchestral, Parkway 958 | 2 |
| 84 | 94 | 99 | 100 | I'M A FOOL TO CARE / Ray Charles, ABC-Paramount 10700 | 4 |
| ★85 | — | — | — | AGENT OO-SOUL / Edwin Starr, Ric-Tic 103 | 1 |
| 86 | 87 | 89 | 89 | MY MAN / Barbra Streisand, Columbia 43323 | 6 |
| 87 | 98 | — | — | YOU BETTER GO / Derek Martin, Roulette 4631 | 2 |
| ★88 | — | — | — | IT'S A MAN DOWN THERE / G. L. Crockett, 4 Brothers 445 | 1 |
| 89 | 89 | 92 | — | FLY ME TO THE MOON / Tony Bennett, Columbia 43331 | 3 |
| ★90 | — | — | — | SAD, SAD GIRL / Barbara Mason, Arctic 108 | 1 |
| 91 | — | — | — | YOU'RE GONNA MAKE ME CRY / O. V. Wright, Back Beat 548 | 1 |
| 92 | 96 | — | — | OOWEE, OOWEE / Perry Como, RCA Victor 8636 | 2 |
| 93 | 97 | 100 | — | ONLY THOSE IN LOVE / Baby Washington, Sue 129 | 3 |
| 94 | — | — | — | MOONLIGHT AND ROSES / Vic Dana, Dolton 309 | 1 |
| 95 | 99 | — | — | AFTER LOVING YOU / Della Reese, ABC-Paramount 10691 | 2 |
| 96 | — | — | — | WE'RE DOING FINE / Dee Dee Warwick, Blue Rock 4027 | 1 |
| 97 | — | — | — | ANNIE FANNY / Kingsmen, Wand 189 | 1 |
| 98 | — | — | — | I'VE CRIED MY LAST TEAR / O'Jays, Imperial 66121 | 1 |
| 99 | — | — | — | WHERE WERE YOU WHEN I NEEDED YOU / Jerry Vale, Columbia 43337 | 1 |
| 100 | — | — | — | SUMMER WINDS / Wayne Newton, Capitol 5470 | 1 |

## HOT 100—A TO Z—(Publisher-Licensee)

After Loving You (Red River, BMI) ... 95
Agent 00-Soul (Myto, BMI) ... 85
All I Really Want to Do—Byrds (Witmark, ASCAP). 43
All I Really Want to Do—Cher (Witmark, ASCAP). 23
Annie Fanny (Sharrow & Burdette & Flomar, BMI). 97

Baby I'm Yours (Blackwood, BMI) ... 18
Boot-Leg (East, BMI) ... 74

California Girls (Sea of Tunes, BMI) ... 28
Canadian Sunset (Vogue, BMI) ... 83
Candy (East, BMI) ... 65
Cara, Mia (Feist, ASCAP) ... 8

Don't Just Stand There (Bernross, BMI) ... 10
Down in the Boondocks (Lowery, BMI) ... 14

Fly Me to the Moon (Almanac, ASCAP) ... 89
Forget Domani—Francis (Miller, ASCAP) ... 82
Forget Domani—Sinatra (Miller, ASCAP) ... 78

He's Got No Love (Toby, BMI) ... 81
Heart Full of Soul (Miller, ASCAP) ... 69
Help (Maclen, BMI) ... 41
Here I Am (United Artists, ASCAP) ... 67
Hold Me, Thrill Me, Kiss Me (Mills, ASCAP) ... 20
Houston (Criterion, ASCAP) ... 79
Hung on You (Screen Gems-Columbia, BMI) ... 53

(I Can't Get No) Satisfaction (Immediate, BMI) .. 2
I Can't Help Myself (Jobete, BMI) ... 9
I Can't Work No Longer (Curtom, BMI) ... 60
I Don't Wanna Lose You Baby (Blackwood, BMI) .. 68
I Got You Babe (Five-West-Cotillion, BMI) ... 5
I Like It Like That (Tune-Kel, BMI) ... 7
I Want Candy (Grand Canyon, Webb IV, BMI) .. 12
I'll Always Love You (Jobete, BMI) ... 45
I'm a Fool (Atlantic, BMI) ... 22
I'm a Fool to Care (Peer Int'l, BMI) ... 84
I'm Henry VIII, I Am (Miller, ASCAP) ... 1
I've Cried My Last Tear (Minit, BMI) ... 98
If I Didn't Love You (Metric, BMI) ... 80
"In" Crowd, The (American, BMI) ... 77
In the Midnight Hour (Cotillion-East, BMI) ... 52
It Ain't Me Babe (Witmark, ASCAP) ... 76
It's Gonna Be Fine (Screen Gems-Columbia, BMI). 55
It's Gonna Take a Miracle (South Mountain, BMI). 62
It's a Man Down There (Fairshakes, BMI) ... 88
It's the Same Old Song (Jobete, BMI) ... 17
It's Too Late Baby, Too Late (Pry-Weiss, BMI) ... 66

Ju Ju Hand (Beckie, BMI) ... 57

Laurie (Long-Gold Dust, BMI) ... 46
Like a Rolling Stone (Witmark, ASCAP) ... 44
Little Bit of Heaven, A (T.M., BMI) ... 42
Little You, A (Leeds, ASCAP) ... 71
Looking Through the Eyes of Love (Screen Gems-Columbia, BMI) ... 51
Loser, The (Wemar, BMI) ... 75

Marie (Berlin, ASCAP) ... 31
Mr. Tambourine Man (Witmark, ASCAP) ... 38
Moon Over Naples (Roosevelt, BMI) ... 70
Moonlight and Roses (Daniels, ASCAP) ... 94
My Man (Feist, ASCAP) ... 86

New Orleans (Rockmasters, BMI) ... 48
No Pity (In the Naked City) (Merrimac, BMI) ... 63
Nobody Knows What's Goin' On (Bright Tunes, BMI) 49
Nothing But Heartaches (Jobete, BMI) ... 47

One Dyin' and a Buryin' (Tree, BMI) ... 36
One Step at a Time (Flomar, BMI) ... 56
Only Those in Love (Brown, BMI) ... 93
Oowee, Oowee (Leeds, ASCAP) ... 92
Papa's Got a Brand New Bag (Lois, BMI) ... 30
Pretty Little Baby (Jobete, BMI) ... 27

Ride Your Pony (Jarb, BMI) ... 29

Sad, Sad Girl (Stillran-Dandelion, BMI) ... 90
Save Your Heart for Me (Geld-Udell-Purchase, ASCAP) ... 4
Say You're My Girl (Acuff-Rose, BMI) ... 40
Seein' the Right Love Go Wrong (Sea-Lark, BMI).. 54
Seventh Son (Arc, BMI) ... 21
Shake and Fingerpop (Jobete, BMI) ... 58
Since I Lost My Baby (Jobete, BMI) ... 39
Sittin' in the Park (Chevis, BMI) ... 32
(Such an) Easy Question (Presley, BMI) ... 35
Summer Winds (Witmark, ASCAP) ... 100
Sugar Dumpling (Kags, BMI) ... 64
Sunshine, Lollipops and Rainbows (Hansen, ASCAP). 13

Take Me Back (South Mountain, BMI) ... 19
Theme From "A Summer Place" (Witmark, ASCAP). 16
Theme From "Harlow" (Lonely Girl) (Consul, ASCAP) 61
"Tickle Me" (Various Publishers) ... 73
To Know You Is to Love You (Hillary, BMI) ... 24
Too Many Rivers (Combine, BMI) ... 25
Tracks of My Tears (Jobete, BMI) ... 37
Trains and Boats and Planes (U. S. Songs, ASCAP) 50

Unchained Melody (Frank, ASCAP) ... 15

We're Doing Fine (Leatherneck & Wellmade, BMI).. 96
What the World Needs Now Is Love (Blue Seas-Jac, BMI) ... 11
What's New Pussycat (United Artists, ASCAP) ... 3
Where Were You When I Needed You (Marks, BMI). 99

Yes, I'm Ready (Stillran-Dandelion, BMI) ... 6
You Better Go (South Mountain, BMI) ... 87
You Tell Me Why (Taracrest, BMI) ... 59
You Turn Me On (Burdette, BMI) ... 34
You Were On My Mind (Witmark, ASCAP) ... 33
You'd Better Come Home (Duchess, BMI) ... 26
You're Gonna Make Me Cry (Don, BMI) ... 91
You're My Baby (Screen Gems-Columbia, BMI) ... 72

## BUBBLING UNDER THE HOT 100

101. WHAT ARE WE GOING TO DO ... David Jones, Colpix 784
102. YAKETY AXE ... Chet Atkins, RCA Victor 8590
103. ACTION ... Freddy Cannon, Warner Bros. 5645
104. I'M A HAPPY MAN ... Jive Five, United Artists 853
105. THE TRACKER ... Sir Douglas Quintet, Tribe 8310
106. WHO'LL BE THE NEXT IN LINE ... Kinks, Reprise 0366
107. WE GOTTA GET OUT OF THIS PLACE ... Animals, MGM 13382
108. AROUND THE CORNER ... Duprees, Columbia 43336
109. AIN'T THAT LOVE ... Four Tops, Columbia 43356
110. SUMMER NIGHTS ... Marianne Faithfull, London 8790
111. IS IT REALLY OVER ... Jim Reeves, RCA Victor 8625
112. MY NAME IS MUD ... Eddie Rambeau, DynoVoice 207
113. HALLELUJAH ... Invitations, DynoVoice 206
114. I'LL FEEL A WHOLE LOT BETTER ... Byrds, Columbia 43332
115. MOONGLOW & THEME FROM PICNIC ... Esther Phillips, Atlantic 2294
116. I'LL TAKE YOU WHERE THE MUSIC'S PLAYING ... Drifters, Atlantic 2298
117. DO THE 45 ... Sharpees, One-Derful 4835
118. I'M DOWN ... Beatles, Capitol 5476
119. COLOURS ... Donovan, Hickory 1324
120. HAPPY FEET TIME ... Montclairs, Sunburst 106
121. I'M LOSING YOU ... Aretha Franklin, Columbia 86166
122. OUT IN THE SUN (HEY-O) ... Beach Nuts, Bang 504
123. YOU'VE GOT TO EARN IT ... Temptations, Gordy 7043
124. I DON'T WANT TO LIVE (WITHOUT YOUR LOVE) ... Bobbi Martin, Coral 62457
125. TRUCK DRIVIN' SON-OF-A-GUN ... Dave Dudley, Mercury 72442
126. GOOD TIMES ... Gene Chandler, Constellation 160
127. WHY DON'T YOU BELIEVE ME ... Vic Damone, Warner Bros. 5644
128. TIGER WOMAN ... Claude King, Columbia 43298
129. I'M ALIVE ... Hollie, Imperial 66119
130. THE SWEETHEART TREE ... Johnny Mathis, Mercury 72464
131. LOVE ME NOW ... Brook Benton, Mercury 72446
132. THE SWEETHEART TREE .. Henry Mancini, His Ork & Chorus, RCA Victor 8624
133. LET HER DANCE ... Bobby Fuller Four, Liberty 55812
134. I DON'T NEED ... Ike & Tina Turner, Modern 1012
135. I'M LETTING YOU GO ... Eddy Arnold, RCA Victor 8632

Compiled from national retail sales and radio station airplay by the Music Popularity Dept. of Record Market Research, Billboard.

# Billboard

For Week Ending August 14, 1965

# HOT 100

★ STAR performer—Sides registering greatest proportionate upward progress this week.

Record Industry Association of America seal of certification as million selling single.

| This Week | 1 Wk. Ago | 2 Wks. Ago | 3 Wks. Ago | TITLE | Artist, Label & Number | Weeks On Chart |
|---|---|---|---|---|---|---|
| ★1 | 5 | 22 | 57 | I GOT YOU BABE | Sonny & Cher, Atco 6359 | 6 |
| 2 | 2 | 1 | 1 | (I Can't Get No) SATISFACTION | Rolling Stones, London 9766 | 10 |
| 3 | 4 | 8 | 13 | SAVE YOUR HEART FOR ME | Gary Lewis & the Playboys, Liberty 55809 | 7 |
| 4 | 1 | 2 | 2 | I'M HENRY VIII, I AM | Herman's Hermits, MGM 13367 | 7 |
| 5 | 3 | 3 | 4 | WHAT'S NEW PUSSYCAT? | Tom Jones, Parrot 9765 | 9 |
| ★6 | 15 | 38 | 56 | UNCHAINED MELODY | Righteous Brothers, Philles 129 | 5 |
| ★7 | 17 | 54 | — | IT'S THE SAME OLD SONG | Four Tops, Motown 1081 | 3 |
| 8 | 10 | 14 | 22 | DON'T JUST STAND THERE | Patty Duke, United Artists 875 | 8 |
| ★9 | 28 | 52 | 72 | CALIFORNIA GIRLS | Beach Boys, Capitol 5464 | 4 |
| ★10 | 14 | 27 | 43 | DOWN IN THE BOONDOCKS | Billy Joe Royal, Columbia 43305 | 7 |
| 11 | 12 | 12 | 18 | I WANT CANDY | Strangeloves, Bang 501 | 8 |
| ★12 | 18 | 23 | 33 | BABY I'M YOURS | Barbara Lewis, Atlantic 2283 | 9 |
| 13 | 7 | 9 | 12 | I LIKE IT LIKE THAT | Dave Clark Five, Epic 9811 | 9 |
| ★14 | 41 | — | — | HELP | Beatles, Capitol 5476 | 2 |
| ★15 | 20 | 25 | 31 | HOLD ME, THRILL ME, KISS ME | Mel Carter, Imperial 66113 | 8 |
| 16 | 19 | 26 | 34 | TAKE ME BACK | Little Anthony & the Imperials, DCP 1136 | 8 |
| ★17 | 22 | 28 | 38 | I'M A FOOL | Dino, Desi & Billy, Reprise 0367 | 8 |
| ★18 | 23 | 42 | 53 | ALL I REALLY WANT TO DO | Cher, Imperial 66114 | 7 |
| 19 | 8 | 4 | 5 | CARA, MIA | Jay & the Americans, United Artists 881 | 11 |
| ★20 | 30 | 44 | 65 | PAPA'S GOT A BRAND NEW BAG | James Brown, King 5999 | 5 |
| 21 | 13 | 16 | 19 | SUNSHINE, LOLLIPOPS AND RAINBOWS | Lesley Gore, Mercury 72433 | 9 |
| ★22 | 33 | 57 | 78 | YOU WERE ON MY MIND | We Five, A&M 770 | 4 |
| 23 | 26 | 31 | 44 | YOU'D BETTER COME HOME | Petula Clark, Warner Bros. 5643 | 6 |
| 24 | 24 | 29 | 35 | TO KNOW YOU IS TO LOVE YOU | Peter & Gordon, Capitol 5461 | 6 |
| 25 | 27 | 30 | 37 | PRETTY LITTLE BABY | Marvin Gaye, Tamla 54117 | 6 |
| ★26 | 44 | 76 | 91 | LIKE A ROLLING STONE | Bob Dylan, Columbia 43346 | 4 |
| ★27 | 47 | 88 | — | NOTHING BUT HEARTACHES | Supremes, Motown 1080 | 3 |
| 28 | 29 | 32 | 42 | RIDE YOUR PONY | Lee Dorsey, Amy 927 | 7 |
| ★29 | 39 | 53 | 68 | SINCE I LOST MY BABY | Temptations, Gordy 7043 | 4 |
| ★30 | 37 | 51 | 61 | TRACKS OF MY TEARS | Miracles, Tamla 54118 | 5 |
| 31 | 6 | 5 | 6 | YES, I'M READY | Barbara Mason, Arctic 105 | 14 |
| 32 | 16 | 19 | 26 | THEME FROM "A SUMMER PLACE" | Lettermen, Capitol 5437 | 8 |
| 33 | 11 | 7 | 7 | WHAT THE WORLD NEEDS NOW IS LOVE | Jackie DeShannon, Imperial 66110 | 13 |
| 34 | 36 | 41 | 59 | ONE DYIN' AND A BURYIN' | Roger Miller, Smash 1994 | 6 |
| 35 | 9 | 6 | 3 | I CAN'T HELP MYSELF | Four Tops, Motown 1076 | 14 |
| 36 | 25 | 13 | 14 | TOO MANY RIVERS | Brenda Lee, Decca 31792 | 12 |
| ★37 | 52 | 62 | 77 | IN THE MIDNIGHT HOUR | Wilson Pickett, Atlantic 2289 | 6 |
| 38 | 45 | 50 | 60 | I'LL ALWAYS LOVE YOU | Spinners, Motown 1078 | 5 |
| 39 | 40 | 43 | 50 | (Say) YOU'RE MY GIRL | Roy Orbison, Monument 891 | 6 |
| 40 | 31 | 15 | 15 | MARIE | Bachelors, London 9762 | 10 |
| ★41 | 51 | 67 | 86 | LOOKING THROUGH THE EYES OF LOVE | Gene Pitney, Musicor 1103 | 4 |
| 42 | 43 | 45 | 55 | ALL I REALLY WANT TO DO | Byrds, Columbia 43332 | 7 |
| 43 | 21 | 10 | 8 | SEVENTH SON | Johnny Rivers, Imperial 66112 | 11 |
| 44 | 48 | 58 | 70 | NEW ORLEANS | Eddie Hodges, Aurora 153 | 7 |
| 45 | 34 | 17 | 10 | YOU TURN ME ON | Ian Whitcomb, Tower 134 | 13 |
| ★46 | 59 | 70 | 85 | YOU TELL ME WHY | Beau Brummels, Autumn 16 | 4 |
| ★47 | 57 | 80 | — | JU JU HAND | Sam the Sham & the Pharaohs, MGM 13364 | 3 |
| ★48 | 58 | 81 | — | SHAKE AND FINGERPOP | Jr. Walker & the All Stars, Soul 35013 | 3 |
| ★49 | 69 | 86 | — | HEART FULL OF SOUL | Yardbirds, Epic 9823 | 3 |
| 50 | 53 | 65 | 71 | HUNG ON YOU | Righteous Brothers, Philles 129 | 5 |
| ★51 | 64 | 77 | 94 | SUGAR DUMPLING | Sam Cooke, RCA Victor 8631 | 4 |
| ★52 | 62 | 69 | 76 | IT'S GONNA TAKE A MIRACLE | Royalettes, MGM 13366 | 5 |
| ★53 | 76 | — | — | IT AIN'T ME BABE | Turtles, White Whale 222 | 2 |
| 54 | 55 | 68 | 79 | IT'S GONNA BE FINE | Glenn Yarbrough, RCA Victor 8619 | 5 |
| 55 | 56 | 63 | 64 | ONE STEP AT A TIME | Maxine Brown, Wand 185 | 7 |
| ★56 | 68 | — | — | I DON'T WANNA LOSE YOU BABY | Chad & Jeremy, Columbia 43339 | 2 |
| ★57 | 77 | 100 | — | THE "IN" CROWD | Ramsey Lewis Trio, Argo 5506 | 3 |
| ★58 | 79 | — | — | HOUSTON | Dean Martin, Reprise 0393 | 2 |
| 59 | 63 | 66 | 67 | NO PITY (In the Naked City) | Jackie Wilson, Brunswick 55280 | 7 |
| ★60 | 71 | 90 | — | A LITTLE YOU | Freddie & the Dreamers, Mercury 72462 | 3 |
| 61 | 49 | 49 | 52 | NOBODY KNOWS WHAT'S GOIN' ON | Chiffons, Laurie 3301 | 9 |
| 62 | 66 | 75 | 80 | IT'S TOO LATE BABY, TOO LATE | Arthur Prysock, Old Town 1183 | 5 |
| ★63 | 85 | — | — | AGENT OO-SOUL | Edwin Starr, Ric-Tic 103 | 2 |
| 64 | 70 | 84 | 87 | MOON OVER NAPLES | Bert Kaempfert & His Ork, Decca 31812 | 6 |
| 65 | 72 | 82 | 90 | YOU'RE MY BABY | Vacels, Kama Sutra 200 | 4 |
| 66 | 67 | 71 | 75 | HERE I AM | Dionne Warwick, Scepter 12104 | 7 |
| 67 | 65 | 73 | 73 | CANDY | Astors, Stax 170 | 6 |
| ★68 | 90 | — | — | SAD, SAD GIRL | Barbara Mason, Arctic 108 | 2 |
| 69 | 80 | — | — | IF I DIDN'T LOVE YOU | Chuck Jackson, Wand 188 | 2 |
| 70 | 73 | 83 | 84 | "TICKLE ME" | Elvis Presley, RCA Victor EPA 4383 (Extended Play) | 6 |
| ★71 | — | — | — | ACTION | Freddy Cannon, Warner Bros. 5645 | 1 |
| 72 | 75 | 85 | 88 | THE LOSER | Skyliners, Jubilee 5506 | 5 |
| ★73 | — | — | — | WHO'LL BE THE NEXT IN LINE | Kinks, Reprise 0366 | 1 |
| ★74 | — | — | — | SUMMER NIGHTS | Marianne Faithfull, London 8790 | 1 |
| ★75 | — | — | — | YOU'VE BEEN IN LOVE TOO LONG | Martha & Vandellas, Gordy 7045 | 1 |
| 76 | 83 | 92 | — | CANADIAN SUNSET | Sounds Orchestral, Parkway 958 | 3 |
| ★77 | 97 | — | — | ANNIE FANNY | Kingsmen, Wand 189 | 2 |
| 78 | 88 | — | — | IT'S A MAN DOWN THERE | G. L. Crockett, 4 Brothers 445 | 2 |
| 79 | 81 | 95 | — | HE'S GOT NO LOVE | Searchers, Kapp 686 | 3 |
| ★80 | — | — | — | WE GOTTA GET OUT OF THIS PLACE | Animals, MGM 13382 | 1 |
| ★81 | — | — | — | FIRST I LOOK AT THE PURSE | Contours, Gordy 7044 | 1 |
| 82 | 94 | — | — | MOONLIGHT AND ROSES | Vic Dana, Dolton 309 | 2 |
| 83 | 87 | 98 | — | YOU BETTER GO | Derek Martin, Roulette 4631 | 3 |
| 84 | 89 | 89 | 92 | FLY ME TO THE MOON | Tony Bennett, Columbia 43331 | 4 |
| ★85 | 100 | — | — | SUMMER WIND | Wayne Newton, Capitol 5470 | 2 |
| ★86 | — | — | — | MY GIRL SLOOPY | Little Caesar & Consuls, Mala 512 | 1 |
| ★87 | — | — | — | I'LL TAKE YOU WHERE THE MUSIC'S PLAYING | Drifters, Atlantic 229888 | 1 |
| ★88 | — | — | — | IS IT REALLY OVER? | Jim Reeves, RCA Victor 8625 | 1 |
| 89 | 92 | 96 | — | OOWEE, OOWEE | Perry Como, RCA Victor 8636 | 3 |
| 90 | — | — | — | I'M A HAPPY MAN | Jive Five, United Artists 853 | 1 |
| 91 | 91 | — | — | YOU'RE GONNA MAKE ME CRY | O. V. Wright, Back Beat 548 | 2 |
| 92 | — | — | — | DANGER HEARTBREAK DEAD AHEAD | Marvelettes, Tamla 54120 | 1 |
| 93 | 93 | 97 | 100 | ONLY THOSE IN LOVE | Baby Washington, Sue 129 | 4 |
| 94 | 98 | — | — | I'VE CRIED MY LAST TEAR | O'Jays, Imperial 66121 | 2 |
| 95 | — | — | — | COLOURS | Donovan, Hickory 1324 | 1 |
| 96 | — | — | — | LIAR, LIAR | Castaways, Soma 1433 | 1 |
| 97 | — | — | — | I NEED YOU | Impressions, ABC-Paramount 10710 | 1 |
| 98 | — | — | — | GIVE ALL YOUR LOVE TO ME | Gerry & Pacemakers, Laurie 3313 | 1 |
| 99 | — | — | — | HANG ON SLOOPY | McCoys, Bang 506 | 1 |
| 100 | — | — | — | WHAT ARE WE GOING TO DO | David Jones, Colpix 784 | 1 |

## HOT 100—A TO Z—(Publisher-Licensee)

Action (Screen Gems-Columbia, BMI) .......... 71
Agent OO-Soul (Myto-BMI) .......... 63
All I Really Want to Do—Byrds (Witmark, ASCAP). 42
All I Really Want to Do—Cher (Witmark, ASCAP). 18
Annie Fanny (Sharrow & Burdett & Flomar, BMI).. 77
Baby I'm Yours (Blackwood, BMI) .......... 12
California Girls (Sea of Tunes, BMI) .......... 9
Canadian Sunset (Vogue, BMI) .......... 76
Candy (East, BMI) .......... 67
Cara, Mia (Feist, ASCAP) .......... 19
Colours (Southern, ASCAP) .......... 95
Danger Heartbreak Dead Ahead (Jobete, BMI).... 92
Don't Just Stand There (Bernross, BMI) .......... 8
Down in the Boondocks (Lozery, BMI) .......... 10
First I Look at the Purse (Jobete, BMI) .......... 81
Fly Me to the Moon (Almanac, ASCAP) .......... 84
Give All Your Love to Me (Pacemaker, BMI) .... 98
Hang On Sloopy (Picturetone-Mellin, BMI) ...... 99
He's Got No Love (Toby, BMI) .......... 79
Heart Full of Soul (Miller, ASCAP) .......... 49
Help (Maclen, BMI) .......... 14
Here I Am (United Artists, ASCAP) .......... 66
Hold Me, Thrill Me, Kiss Me (Mills, ASCAP) .... 15
Houston (Criterion, ASCAP) .......... 58
Hung on You (Screen Gems-Columbia, BMI) ...... 50
(I Can't Get No) Satisfaction (Immediate, BMI) ... 2
I Can't Help Myself (Jobete, BMI) .......... 35
I Don't Wanna Lose You Baby (Blackwood, BMI).. 56
I Got You Babe (Five-West-Cotillion, BMI) ...... 1
I Like It Like That (Tune-Kel, BMI) .......... 13
I Need You (Chi-Sound, BMI) .......... 97
I Want Candy (Grand Canyon, Webb IV, BMI)... 11
I'll Always Love You (Jobete, BMI) .......... 38
I'll Take You Where the Music's Playing (Trio, BMI) .......... 87
I'm a Fool (Atlantic, BMI) .......... 17
I'm a Happy Man (Unart, BMI) .......... 90
I'm Henry VIII, I Am (Miller, ASCAP) .......... 4
I've Cried My Last Tear (Minit, BMI) .......... 94
If I Didn't Love You (Metric, BMI) .......... 69
"In" Crowd, The (American, BMI) .......... 57
In the Midnight Hour (Cotillion-East, BMI) .... 37
Is it Really Over? (Tuckahoe, BMI) .......... 88
It Ain't Me Babe (Witmark, ASCAP) .......... 53
It's Gonna Be Fine (Screen Gems-Columbia, BMI).. 54
It's Gonna Take a Miracle (South Mountain, BMI) 52
It's a Man Down There (Fairshakes, BMI) .......... 78
It's the Same Old Song (Jobete, BMI) .......... 7
It's Too Late Baby, Too Late (Pry-Weiss, BMI) .... 62
Ju Ju Hands (Beckie, BMI) .......... 47
Liar, Liar (Celann, BMI) .......... 96
Like a Rolling Stone (Witmark, ASCAP) ..........26
Little You, A (Leeds, ASCAP) .......... 60
Looking Through the Eyes of Love (Screen Gems-Columbia, BMI) .......... 41
Loser, The (Wemar, BMI) .......... 72
Marie (Berlin, ASCAP) .......... 40
Moon Over Naples (Roosevelt, BMI) .......... 64
Moonlight and Roses (Daniels, ASCAP) .......... 82
My Girl Sloopy (Picturetone-Mellin, BMI) ...... 86
New Orleans (Rockmasters, BMI) .......... 44
No Pity (In the Naked City) (Merrimac, BMI) .... 59
Nobody Knows What's Goin' On (Bright Tunes, BMI) .......... 61
Nothing But Heartaches (Jobete, BMI) .......... 27
One Dyin' and a Buryin' (Tree, BMI) .......... 34
One Step at a Time (Flomar, BMI) .......... 55
Only Those in Love (Brown, BMI) .......... 93
Oowee, Oowee (Leeds, ASCAP) .......... 89
Papa's Got a Brand New Bag (Lois, BMI) ...... 20
Pretty Little Baby (Jobete, BMI) .......... 25
Ride Your Pony (Jarb, BMI) .......... 28
Sad, Sad Girl (Stillran-Dandelion, BMI) .......... 68
Save Your Heart for Me (Geld-Udell-Purchase, ASCAP) .......... 3
Say You're My Girl (Acuff-Rose, BMI) .......... 39
Seventh Son (Arc, BMI) .......... 43
Shake and Fingerpop (Jobete, BMI) .......... 48
Since I Lost My Baby (Jobete, BMI) .......... 29
Sugar Dumpling (Kags, BMI) ..........51
Summer Nights (Sea-Lark, BMI) .......... 74
Summer Wind (Witmark, ASCAP) .......... 85
Sunshine, Lollipops and Rainbows (Hansen, ASCAP) 21
Take Me Back (South Mountain, BMI) .......... 16
Theme From "A Summer Place" (Witmark, ASCAP) 32
"Tickle Me" (Various Publishers) .......... 70
To Know You Is to Love You (Hillary, BMI) ...... 24
Too Many Rivers (Combine, BMI) .......... 36
Tracks of My Tears (Jobete, BMI) .......... 30
Unchained Melody (Frank, ASCAP) .......... 6
We Gotta Get Out of This Place (Screen Gems-Columbia, BMI) .......... 80
What Are We Going to Do (Screen Gems-Columbia, BMI) ..........100
What the World Needs Now Is Love (Blue Seas-Jac, BMI) .......... 33
What's New Pussycat (United Artists, ASCAP) .... 5
Who'll Be the Next in Line (Jay Boy, BMI) .... 73
Yes, I'm Ready (Stillran-Dandelion, BMI) ...... 31
You Better Go (South Mountain, BMI) .......... 83
You Tell Me Why (Taracrest, BMI) .......... 46
You Turn Me On (Burdette, BMI) .......... 45
You Were on My Mind (Witmark, ASCAP) ...... 22
You'd Better Come Home (Duchess, BMI) .......... 23
You're Gonna Make Me Cry (Don, BMI) .......... 91
You're My Baby (Screen Gems-Columbia, BMI) .... 65
You've Been in Love Too Long (Jobete, BMI) .... 75

## BUBBLING UNDER THE HOT 100

101. LOUIE LOUIE ..........Kingsmen, Wand 143
102. 99 PLUS 1 ..........J. Gardner, Blue Rock 4026
103. EVE OF DESTRUCTION ..........Barry McGuire, Dunhill 4009
104. I'M ALIVE ..........Hollies, Imperial 66119
105. I'M DOWN ..........Beatles, Capitol 5476
106. WE'RE DOING FINE ..........Dee Dee Warwick, Blue Rock 4027
107. LAUGH AT ME .......... Sonny, Atco 6369
108. OUT IN THE SUN (HEY-O) ..........Beach-Nuts, Bang 504
109. THE TRACKER ..........Sir Douglas Quintet, Tribe 8310
110. AFTER LOVING YOU ..........Della Reese, ABC-Paramount 10691
111. WHERE WERE YOU WHEN I NEEDED YOU....Jerry Vale, Columbia 43337
112. AIN'T THAT LOVE ..........Four Tops, Columbia 43356
113. YOU CAN'T BE TRUE DEAR ..........Patti Page, Columbia 43345
114. I WANT TO (DO EVERYTHING FOR YOU) ..........Joe Tex, Dial 4016
115. I LIVE FOR THE SUN ..........Sunrays, Tower 148
116. YOU'VE GOT YOUR TROUBLES ..........Fortunes, Press 9773
117. IF YOU WAIT FOR LOVE ..........Bobby Goldsboro, United Artists 908
118. THESE HANDS (SMALL BUT MIGHTY) ..........Bobby Bland, Duke 385
119. I'M LOSING YOU ..........Aretha Franklin, Columbia 43333
120. SIMPLE GIMPLE ..........Horst Jankowski, Mercury 72465
121. I DON'T WANT TO LIVE (WITHOUT YOUR LOVE)..Bobby Martin, Coral 62457
122. GOOD TIMES ..........Gene Chandler, Constellation 160
123. GREAT GOO-GA-MOO-GA ..........Tom & Jerrio, ABC-Paramount 10704
124. IT'S THE ONLY WAY TO FLY ..........Jewel Akens, Era 3147
125. TAKE ME FOR A LITTLE WHILE ..........Evie Sands, Blue Cat 118
126. SWEETHEART TREE ..........Johnny Mathis, Mercury 72464
127. TWO DIFFERENT WORLDS ..........Lenny Welch, Kapp 689
128. I'LL STOP AT NOTHING ..........Sandie Shaw, Reprise 0394
129. SWEETHEART TREE ....Henry Mancini, His Ork & Chorus, RCA Victor 8624
130. I CAN'T STAND TO SEE YOU CRY ..........Jerry Butler, Vee Jay 696
131. MOHAIR SAM ..........Charlie Rich, Smash 1993
132. I CAN'T BEGIN TO TELL YOU ..........Buddy Greco, Epic 9817
133. THE WAY OF LOVE ..........Kathy Kirby, Parrot 9775
134. HEY LITTLE GIRL ..........Z. Z. Hill, Kent 427
135. SPOOTIN' ..........Bill Black's Combo, Hi 2094

Compiled from national retail sales and radio station airplay by the Music Popularity Dept. of Record Market Research, Billboard.

# Billboard HOT 100

For Week Ending August 21, 1965

★ STAR performer—Sides registering greatest proportionate upward progress this week.

| This Week | 1 Wk. Ago | 2 Wks. Ago | 3 Wks. Ago | TITLE, Artist, Label & Number | Weeks On Chart |
|---|---|---|---|---|---|
| 1 | 1 | 5 | 22 | I GOT YOU BABE — Sonny & Cher, Atco 6359 | 7 |
| 2 | 3 | 4 | 8 | SAVE YOUR HEART FOR ME — Gary Lewis & the Playboys, Liberty 55809 | 8 |
| ★3 | 14 | 41 | — | HELP — Beatles, Capitol 5476 | 3 |
| 4 | 9 | 28 | 52 | CALIFORNIA GIRLS — Beach Boys, Capitol 5464 | 5 |
| 5 | 6 | 15 | 38 | UNCHAINED MELODY — Righteous Brothers, Philles 129 | 6 |
| 6 | 2 | 2 | 1 | (I Can't Get No) SATISFACTION — Rolling Stones, London 9766 | 11 |
| 7 | 7 | 17 | 54 | IT'S THE SAME OLD SONG — Four Tops, Motown 1081 | 4 |
| 8 | 8 | 10 | 14 | DON'T JUST STAND THERE — Patty Duke, United Artists 875 | 9 |
| 9 | 4 | 1 | 2 | I'M HENRY VIII, I AM — Herman's Hermits, MGM 13367 | 8 |
| 10 | 10 | 14 | 27 | DOWN IN THE BOONDOCKS — Billy Joe Royal, Columbia 43305 | 8 |
| 11 | 12 | 18 | 23 | BABY I'M YOURS — Barbara Lewis, Atlantic 2283 | 10 |
| 12 | 5 | 3 | 3 | WHAT'S NEW PUSSYCAT? — Tom Jones, Parrot 9765 | 10 |
| 13 | 15 | 20 | 25 | HOLD ME, THRILL ME, KISS ME — Mel Carter, Imperial 66113 | 9 |
| ★14 | 20 | 30 | 44 | PAPA'S GOT A BRAND NEW BAG — James Brown, King 5999 | 6 |
| 15 | 18 | 23 | 42 | ALL I REALLY WANT TO DO — Cher, Imperial 66114 | 8 |
| ★16 | 26 | 44 | 76 | LIKE A ROLLING STONE — Bob Dylan, Columbia 43346 | 5 |
| 17 | 22 | 33 | 57 | YOU WERE ON MY MIND — We Five, A&M 770 | 5 |
| ★18 | 27 | 47 | 88 | NOTHING BUT HEARTACHES — Supremes, Motown 1080 | 4 |
| 19 | 16 | 19 | 26 | TAKE ME BACK — Little Anthony & the Imperials, DCP 1136 | 9 |
| 20 | 17 | 22 | 28 | I'M A FOOL — Dino, Desi & Billy, Reprise 0367 | 9 |
| 21 | 11 | 12 | 12 | I WANT CANDY — Strangeloves, Bang 501 | 9 |
| 22 | 23 | 26 | 31 | YOU'D BETTER COME HOME — Petula Clark, Warner Bros. 5643 | 7 |
| 23 | 30 | 37 | 51 | TRACKS OF MY TEARS — Miracles, Tamla 54118 | 6 |
| ★24 | 29 | 39 | 53 | SINCE I LOST MY BABY — Temptations, Gordy 7043 | 5 |
| 25 | 13 | 7 | 9 | I LIKE IT LIKE THAT — Dave Clark Five, Epic 9811 | 10 |
| 26 | 19 | 8 | 4 | CARA, MIA — Jay & the Americans, United Artists 881 | 12 |
| ★27 | 37 | 52 | 62 | IN THE MIDNIGHT HOUR — Wilson Pickett, Atlantic 2289 | 7 |
| 28 | 21 | 13 | 16 | SUNSHINE, LOLLIPOPS AND RAINBOWS — Lesley Gore, Mercury 72433 | 10 |
| ★29 | 47 | 57 | 80 | JU JU HAND — Sam the Sham & the Pharaohs, MGM 13364 | 4 |
| ★30 | 49 | 69 | 86 | HEART FULL OF SOUL — Yardbirds, Epic 9823 | 4 |
| ★31 | 41 | 51 | 67 | LOOKING THROUGH THE EYES OF LOVE — Gene Pitney, Musicor 1103 | 5 |
| ★32 | 53 | 76 | — | IT AIN'T ME BABE — Turtles, White Whale 222 | 3 |
| 33 | 25 | 27 | 30 | PRETTY LITTLE BABY — Marvin Gaye, Tamla 54117 | 7 |
| ★34 | 57 | 77 | 100 | THE "IN" CROWD — Ramsey Lewis Trio, Argo 5506 | 4 |
| 35 | 38 | 45 | 50 | I'LL ALWAYS LOVE YOU — Spinners, Motown 1078 | 6 |
| 36 | 24 | 24 | 29 | TO KNOW YOU IS TO LOVE YOU — Peter & Gordon, Capitol 5461 | 7 |
| ★37 | 48 | 58 | 81 | SHAKE AND FINGERPOP — Jr. Walker & the All Stars, Soul 35013 | 4 |
| 38 | 58 | 79 | — | HOUSTON — Dean Martin, Reprise 0393 | 3 |
| 39 | 28 | 29 | 32 | RIDE YOUR PONY — Lee Dorsey, Amy 927 | 8 |
| 40 | 42 | 43 | 45 | ALL I REALLY WANT TO DO — Byrds, Columbia 43332 | 8 |
| 41 | 46 | 59 | 70 | YOU TELL ME WHY — Beau Brummels, Autumn 16 | 5 |
| 42 | 34 | 36 | 41 | ONE DYIN' AND A BURYIN' — Roger Miller, Smash 1994 | 7 |
| 43 | 32 | 16 | 19 | THEME FROM "A SUMMER PLACE" — Lettermen, Capitol 5437 | 9 |
| 44 | 44 | 48 | 58 | NEW ORLEANS — Eddie Hodges, Aurora 153 | 8 |
| 45 | 51 | 64 | 77 | SUGAR DUMPLING — Sam Cooke, RCA Victor 8631 | 5 |
| 46 | 56 | 68 | — | I DON'T WANNA LOSE YOU BABY — Chad & Jeremy, Columbia 43339 | 3 |
| 47 | 50 | 53 | 65 | HUNG ON YOU — Righteous Brothers, Philles 129 | 6 |
| 48 | 36 | 25 | 13 | TOO MANY RIVERS — Brenda Lee, Decca 31792 | 13 |
| 49 | 52 | 62 | 69 | IT'S GONNA TAKE A MIRACLE — Royalettes, MGM 13366 | 6 |
| 50 | 60 | 71 | 90 | A LITTLE YOU — Freddie & the Dreamers, Mercury 72462 | 4 |
| 51 | — | 63 | 85 | AGENT OO-SOUL — Edwin Starr, Ric-Tic 103 | 3 |
| 52 | 71 | — | — | ACTION — Freddy Cannon, Warner Bros. 5645 | 2 |
| 53 | 73 | — | — | WHO'LL BE THE NEXT IN LINE — Kinks, Reprise 0366 | 2 |
| 54 | 39 | 40 | 43 | (Say) YOU'RE MY GIRL — Roy Orbison, Monument 891 | 7 |
| 55 | 68 | 90 | — | SAD, SAD GIRL — Barbara Mason, Arctic 108 | 3 |
| 56 | 62 | 66 | 75 | IT'S TOO LATE, BABY TOO LATE — Arthur Prysock, Old Town 1183 | 6 |
| 57 | 75 | — | — | YOU'VE BEEN IN LOVE TOO LONG — Martha & Vandellas, Gordy 7045 | 2 |
| 58 | — | — | — | EVE OF DESTRUCTION — Barry McGuire, Dunhill 4009 | 1 |
| 59 | 74 | — | — | SUMMER NIGHTS — Marianne Faithfull, London 8790 | 2 |
| 60 | 69 | 80 | — | IF I DIDN'T LOVE YOU — Chuck Jackson, Wand 188 | 3 |
| 61 | 64 | 70 | 84 | MOON OVER NAPLES — Bert Kaempfert & His Ork, Decca 31812 | 7 |
| 62 | — | — | — | CATCH US IF YOU CAN — Dave Clark Five, Epic 9833 | 1 |
| 63 | 65 | 72 | 82 | YOU'RE MY BABY — Vacels, Kama Sutra 200 | 5 |
| 64 | 67 | 65 | 73 | CANDY — Astors, Stax 170 | |
| 65 | 66 | 67 | 71 | HERE I AM — Dionne Warwick, Scepter 12104 | 8 |
| ★66 | 90 | — | — | I'M A HAPPY MAN — Jive Five, United Artists 853 | 2 |
| ★67 | 99 | — | — | HANG ON SLOOPY — McCoys, Bang 506 | 2 |
| ★68 | 80 | — | — | WE GOTTA GET OUT OF THIS PLACE — Animals, MGM 13382 | 2 |
| ★69 | 87 | — | — | I'LL TAKE YOU WHERE THE MUSIC'S PLAYING — Drifters, Atlantic 229888 | 2 |
| 70 | — | — | — | BABY DON'T GO — Sonny & Cher, Reprise 0309 | 1 |
| 71 | 86 | — | — | MY GIRL SLOOPY — Little Caesar & Consuls, Mala 512 | 2 |
| 72 | 82 | 94 | — | MOONLIGHT AND ROSES — Vic Dana, Dolton 309 | 3 |
| 73 | 77 | 97 | — | ANNIE FANNY — Kingmen, Wand 189 | 3 |
| 74 | 59 | 63 | 66 | NO PITY (In the Naked City) — Jackie Wilson, Brunswick 55280 | 8 |
| 75 | 81 | — | — | FIRST I LOOK AT THE PURSE — Contours, Gordy 7044 | 2 |
| 76 | 54 | 55 | 68 | IT'S GONNA BE FINE — Glenn Yarbrough, RCA Victor 8619 | 6 |
| 77 | 55 | 56 | 63 | ONE STEP AT A TIME — Maxine Brown, Wand 185 | 7 |
| 78 | 78 | 88 | — | IT'S A MAN DOWN THERE — G. L. Crockett, 4 Brothers 445 | 3 |
| 79 | 92 | — | — | DANGER HEARTBREAK DEAD AHEAD — Marvelettes, Tamla 54120 | 2 |
| 80 | 85 | 100 | — | SUMMER WIND — Wayne Newton, Capitol 5470 | 3 |
| 81 | 83 | 87 | 98 | YOU BETTER GO — Derek Martin, Roulette 4631 | 4 |
| 82 | 70 | 73 | 83 | "TICKLE ME" — Elvis Presley, RCA Victor EPA 4383 (Extended Play) | 7 |
| 83 | — | — | — | LAUGH AT ME — Sonny, Atco 6369 | 1 |
| 84 | 95 | — | — | COLOURS — Donovan, Hickory 1324 | 2 |
| 85 | 88 | — | — | IS IT REALLY OVER? — Jim Reeves, RCA Victor 8625 | 2 |
| 86 | 98 | — | — | GIVE ALL YOUR LOVE TO ME — Gerry & Pacemakers, Laurie 3313 | 2 |
| 87 | — | — | — | TWO DIFFERENT WORLDS — Lenny Welch, Kapp 689 | 1 |
| 88 | 89 | 92 | 96 | DOWEE, OOWEE — Perry Como, RCA Victor 8636 | 4 |
| 89 | 93 | 93 | 97 | ONLY THOSE IN LOVE — Baby Washington, Sue 129 | 4 |
| 90 | 97 | — | — | I NEED YOU — Impressions, ABC-Paramount 10710 | 2 |
| 91 | 96 | — | — | LIAR, LIAR — Castaways, Soma 1433 | 2 |
| 92 | 76 | 83 | 92 | CANADIAN SUNSET — Sounds Orchestral, Parkway 958 | 4 |
| 93 | 100 | — | — | WHAT ARE WE GOING TO DO — David Jones, Colpix 784 | 2 |
| 94 | — | — | — | IF YOU WAIT FOR LOVE — Bobby Goldsboro, United Artists 908 | 1 |
| 95 | — | — | — | YOU'VE GOT YOUR TROUBLES — Fortunes, Press 9773 | 1 |
| 96 | — | — | — | DO YOU BELIEVE IN MAGIC — Lovin' Spoonful, Kama Sutra 201 | 1 |
| 97 | — | — | — | GOOD TIMES — Gene Chandler, Constellation 160 | 1 |
| 98 | — | — | — | RIDE AWAY — Roy Orbison, MGM 13386 | 1 |
| 99 | — | — | — | CAN'T LET YOU OUT OF MY SIGHT — Chuck Jackson & Maxine Brown, Wand 191 | 1 |
| 100 | — | — | — | SOMEONE IS WATCHING — Solomon Burke, Atlantic 2299 | 1 |

## BUBBLING UNDER THE HOT 100

101. LOUIE LOUIE ............ Kingsmen, Wand 143
102. 99 PLUS 1 ............. J. Gardner, Jarb, Blue Rock 4026
103. I'M ALIVE ............. Hollies, Imperial 66119
104. WE'RE DOING FINE ..... Dee Dee Warwick, Blue Rock 4027
105. I'M DOWN ............. Beatles, Capitol 5476
106. FLY ME TO THE MOON .. Tony Bennett, Columbia 43331
107. OUT IN THE SUN (Hey-O) .. Beach Nuts, Bang 504
108. WHERE WERE YOU WHEN I NEEDED YOU .. Jerry Vale, Columbia 43337
109. AFTER LOVING YOU .... Della Reese, ABC-Paramount 10691
110. I WANT TO (Do Everything for You) .. Joe Tex, Dial 4016
111. I LIVE FOR THE SUN .. Sunrays, Tower 148
112. YOU CAN'T BE TRUE, DEAR .. Patti Page, Columbia 43345
113. THESE HANDS (Small But Mighty) .. Bobby Bland, Duke 385
114. I'M LOSING YOU ..... Aretha Franklin, Columbia 43333
115. SWEETHEART TREE .... Johnny Mathis, Mercury 72464
116. SIMPLE GIMPEL ...... Horst Jankowski, Mercury 72465
117. SWEETHEART TREE .... Henry Mancini, His Ork. & Chorus, RCA Victor 8624
118. I DON'T WANT TO LIVE (Without Your Love) .. Bobby Martin, Coral 62457
119. SUMMER WIND ...... Roger Williams & the Harry Simeone Chorale & Ork, Kapp 55
120. HEARTACHE BY THE NUMBER .. Johnny Tillotson, MGM 13376
121. IT'S THE ONLY WAY TO FLY .. Jewel Akens, Era 3147
122. YOU'RE GONNA MAKE ME CRY .. O. V. Wright, Back Beat 548
123. TAKE ME FOR A LITTLE WHILE .. Evie Sands, Blue Cat 118
124. N-N-NERVOUS ....... Ian Whitcomb, Tower 155
125. I CAN'T STAND TO SEE YOU CRY .. Jerry Butler, Vee Jay 696
126. I'LL STOP AT NOTHING .. Sandy Shaw, Reprise 0394
127. MOHAIR SAM ....... Charlie Rich, Smash 1993
128. HE'S GOT NO LOVE ... Searchers, Kapp 686
129. THE WAY OF LOVE ... Kathy Kirby, Parrot 9775
130. I'VE CRIED MY LAST TEAR .. O'Jays, Imperial 66131
131. SOUL HEAVEN ....... Dixie Drifter, Roulette 4641
132. YOU'RE THE REASON .. Gerry & the Pacemakers, Laurie 3313
133. THE WORLD THROUGH A TEAR .. Neil Sedaka, RCA Victor 8637
134. TOO HOT TO HOLD ... Major Lance, Okeh 7226
135. LOVE IS STRANGE ... Everly Brothers, Warner Bros. 5649

# Billboard HOT 100

**For Week Ending August 28, 1965**

★ STAR performer—Sides registering greatest proportionate upward progress this week.

| This Week | 2 Wks. Ago | 3 Wks. Ago | TITLE, Artist, Label & Number | Weeks On Chart |
|---|---|---|---|---|
| 1 | 1 | 5 | I GOT YOU BABE — Sonny & Cher, Atco 6359 | 8 |
| 2 | 3 | 14 | HELP — Beatles, Capitol 5476 | 4 |
| 3 | 4 | 9 | CALIFORNIA GIRLS — Beach Boys, Capitol 5464 | 6 |
| 4 | 5 | 6 | UNCHAINED MELODY — Righteous Brothers, Philles 129 | 7 |
| 5 | 7 | 7 | IT'S THE SAME OLD SONG — Four Tops, Motown 1081 | 5 |
| 6 | 16 | 26 | LIKE A ROLLING STONE — Bob Dylan, Columbia 43346 | 6 |
| 7 | 2 | 3 | SAVE YOUR HEART FOR ME — Gary Lewis & the Playboys, Liberty 55809 | 9 |
| 8 | 13 | 15 | HOLD ME, THRILL ME, KISS ME — Mel Carter, Imperial 66113 | 10 |
| 9 | 10 | 10 | DOWN IN THE BOONDOCKS — Billy Joe Royal, Columbia 43305 | 9 |
| 10 | 14 | 20 | PAPA'S GOT A BRAND NEW BAG — James Brown, King 5999 | 7 |
| 11 | 11 | 12 | BABY I'M YOURS — Barbara Lewis, Atlantic 2283 | 11 |
| 12 | 17 | 22 | YOU WERE ON MY MIND — We Five, A&M 770 | 6 |
| 13 | 18 | 27 | NOTHING BUT HEARTACHES — Supremes, Motown 1080 | 5 |
| 14 | 8 | 8 | DON'T JUST STAND THERE — Patty Duke, United Artists 875 | 10 |
| 15 | 15 | 18 | ALL I REALLY WANT TO DO — Cher, Imperial 66114 | 9 |
| 16 | 6 | 2 | (I Can't Get No) SATISFACTION — Rolling Stones, London 9766 | 12 |
| 17 | 24 | 29 | SINCE I LOST MY BABY — Temptations, Gordy 7043 | 6 |
| 18 | 12 | 5 | WHAT'S NEW PUSSYCAT? — Tom Jones, Parrot 9765 | 11 |
| 19 | 23 | 30 | TRACKS OF MY TEARS — Miracles, Tamla 54118 | 7 |
| 20 | 9 | 4 | I'M HENRY VIII, I AM — Herman's Hermits, MGM 13367 | 9 |
| 21 | 32 | 53 | IT AIN'T ME BABE — Turtles, White Whale 222 | 6 |
| 22 | 34 | 57 | THE "IN" CROWD — Ramsey Lewis Trio, Argo 5506 | 5 |
| 23 | 20 | 17 | I'M A FOOL — Dino, Desi & Billy, Reprise 0367 | 10 |
| 24 | 27 | 37 | IN THE MIDNIGHT HOUR — Wilson Pickett, Atlantic 2289 | 7 |
| 25 | 30 | 49 | HEART FULL OF SOUL — Yardbirds, Epic 9823 | 5 |
| 26 | 29 | 47 | JU JU HAND — Sam the Sham & the Pharaohs, MGM 13364 | 5 |
| 27 | 58 | — | EVE OF DESTRUCTION — Barry McGuire, Dunhill 4009 | 2 |
| 28 | 31 | 41 | LOOKING THROUGH THE EYES OF LOVE — Gene Pitney, Musicor 1103 | 6 |
| 29 | 38 | 58 | HOUSTON — Dean Martin, Reprise 0393 | 4 |
| 30 | 19 | 16 | TAKE ME BACK — Little Anthony & the Imperials, DCP 1136 | 10 |
| 31 | 52 | 71 | ACTION — Freddy Cannon, Warner Bros. 5645 | 3 |
| 32 | 37 | 48 | SHAKE AND FINGERPOP — Jr. Walker & the All Stars, Soul 35013 | 5 |
| 33 | 28 | 21 | SUNSHINE, LOLLIPOPS AND RAINBOWS — Lesley Gore, Mercury 72433 | 11 |
| 34 | 22 | 23 | YOU'D BETTER COME HOME — Petula Clark, Warner Bros. 5643 | 8 |
| 35 | 46 | 56 | I DON'T WANNA LOSE YOU BABY — Chad & Jeremy, Columbia 43339 | 4 |
| 36 | 21 | 11 | I WANT CANDY — Strangeloves, Bang 501 | 10 |
| 37 | 45 | 51 | SUGAR DUMPLING — Sam Cooke, RCA Victor 8631 | 6 |
| 38 | 41 | 46 | YOU TELL ME WHY — Beau Brummels, Autumn 16 | 6 |
| 39 | 25 | 13 | I LIKE IT LIKE THAT — Dave Clark Five, Epic 9811 | 11 |
| 40 | 26 | 19 | CARA, MIA — Jay & the Americans, United Artists 881 | 13 |
| 41 | 51 | 63 | AGENT OO-SOUL — Edwin Starr, Ric-Tic 103 | 4 |
| 42 | 62 | — | CATCH US IF YOU CAN — Dave Clark Five, Epic 9833 | 2 |
| 43 | 68 | 80 | WE GOTTA GET OUT OF THIS PLACE — Animals, MGM 13382 | 3 |
| 44 | 55 | 68 | SAD, SAD GIRL — Barbara Mason, Arctic 108 | 4 |
| 45 | 53 | 73 | WHO'LL BE THE NEXT IN LINE — Kinks, Reprise 0366 | 3 |
| 46 | 59 | 74 | SUMMER NIGHTS — Marianne Faithfull, London 8790 | 3 |
| 47 | 40 | 42 | ALL I REALLY WANT TO DO — Byrds, Columbia 43332 | 9 |
| 48 | 50 | 60 | A LITTLE YOU — Freddie & the Dreamers, Mercury 72462 | 5 |
| 49 | 67 | 99 | HANG ON SLOOPY — McCoys, Bang 506 | 3 |
| 50 | 57 | 75 | YOU'VE BEEN IN LOVE TOO LONG — Martha & Vandellas, Gordy 7045 | 3 |
| 51 | 35 | 38 | I'LL ALWAYS LOVE YOU — Spinners, Motown 1078 | 7 |
| 52 | 83 | — | LAUGH AT ME — Sonny, Atco 6369 | 2 |
| 53 | 49 | 52 | IT'S GONNA TAKE A MIRACLE — Royalettes, MGM 13366 | 7 |
| 54 | 60 | 69 | IF I DIDN'T LOVE YOU — Chuck Jackson, Wand 188 | 4 |
| 55 | 66 | 90 | I'M A HAPPY MAN — Jive Five, United Artists 853 | 3 |
| 56 | 69 | 87 | I'LL TAKE YOU WHERE THE MUSIC'S PLAYING — Drifters, Atlantic 2298 | 3 |
| 57 | 39 | 28 | RIDE YOUR PONY — Lee Dorsey, Amy 927 | 9 |
| 58 | 71 | 86 | MY GIRL SLOOPY — Little Caesar & Consuls, Mala 512 | 3 |
| 59 | 61 | 64 | MOON OVER NAPLES — Bert Kaempfert & His Ork, Decca 31812 | 8 |
| 60 | 70 | — | BABY DON'T GO — Sonny & Cher, Reprise 0392 | 2 |
| 61 | 44 | 44 | NEW ORLEANS — Eddie Hodges, Aurora 153 | 9 |
| 62 | 73 | 77 | ANNIE FANNY — Kingsmen, Wand 189 | 4 |
| 63 | 47 | 50 | HUNG ON YOU — Righteous Brothers, Philles 129 | 7 |
| 64 | 64 | 67 | CANDY — Astors, Stax 170 | 8 |
| 65 | 75 | 81 | FIRST I LOOK AT THE PURSE — Contours, Gordy 7044 | 3 |
| 66 | 72 | 82 | MOONLIGHT AND ROSES — Vic Dana, Dolton 309 | 4 |
| 67 | 79 | 92 | DANGER HEARTBREAK DEAD AHEAD — Marvelettes, Tamla 54120 | 3 |
| 68 | 56 | 62 | IT'S TOO LATE, BABY TOO LATE — Arthur Prysock, Old Town 1183 | 7 |
| 69 | 78 | 78 | IT'S A MAN DOWN THERE — G. L. Crockett, 4 Brothers 445 | 4 |
| 70 | — | — | I'LL MAKE ALL YOUR DREAMS COME TRUE — Ronnie Dove, Diamond 188 | 1 |
| 71 | 86 | 98 | GIVE ALL YOUR LOVE TO ME — Gerry & Pacemakers, Laurie 3313 | 3 |
| 72 | — | — | JUST YOU — Sonny & Cher, Atco 6345 | 1 |
| 73 | 98 | — | RIDE AWAY — Roy Orbison, MGM 13386 | 2 |
| 74 | 74 | 59 | NO PITY (In the Naked City) — Jackie Wilson, Brunswick 55280 | 9 |
| 75 | 90 | 97 | I NEED YOU — Impressions, ABC-Paramount 10710 | 3 |
| 76 | 84 | 95 | COLOURS — Donovan, Hickory 1324 | 3 |
| 77 | 95 | — | YOU'VE GOT YOUR TROUBLES — Fortunes, Press 9773 | 2 |
| 78 | 80 | 85 | SUMMER WIND — Wayne Newton, Capitol 5470 | 4 |
| 79 | 96 | — | DO YOU BELIEVE IN MAGIC — Lovin' Spoonful, Kama Sutra 201 | 2 |
| 80 | 81 | 83 | YOU BETTER GO — Derek Martin, Roulette 4631 | 5 |
| 81 | 87 | — | TWO DIFFERENT WORLDS — Lenny Welch, Kapp 689 | 2 |
| 82 | — | — | WITH THESE HANDS — Tom Jones, Parrot 9787 | 1 |
| 83 | — | — | I'M YOURS — Elvis Presley, RCA Victor 8657 | 1 |
| 84 | 85 | 88 | IS IT REALLY OVER? — Jim Reeves, RCA Victor 8625 | 3 |
| 85 | 89 | 93 | ONLY THOSE IN LOVE — Baby Washington, Sue 129 | 6 |
| 86 | — | — | MOHAIR SAM — Charlie Rich, Smash 1993 | 1 |
| 87 | 91 | 96 | LIAR, LIAR — Castaways, Soma 1433 | 3 |
| 88 | 94 | — | IF YOU WAIT FOR LOVE — Bobby Goldsboro, United Artists 908 | 2 |
| 89 | — | — | HOME OF THE BRAVE — Jody Miller, Capitol 5483 | 1 |
| 90 | — | — | HEARTACHES BY THE NUMBER — Johnny Tillotson, MGM 13376 | 1 |
| 91 | 100 | — | SOMEONE IS WATCHING — Solomon Burke, Atlantic 2299 | 2 |
| 92 | — | — | I WANT TO (Do Everything for You) — Joe Tex, Dial 4016 | 1 |
| 93 | 93 | 100 | WHAT ARE WE GOING TO DO — David Jones, Colpix 784 | 3 |
| 94 | — | — | HOME OF THE BRAVE — Bonnie & the Treasures, Phi-Dan 5005 | 1 |
| 95 | 97 | — | GOOD TIMES — Gene Chandler, Constellation 160 | 2 |
| 96 | 99 | — | CAN'T LET YOU OUT OF MY SIGHT — Chuck Jackson & Maxine Brown, Wand 191 | 2 |
| 97 | — | — | TOO HOT TO HOLD — Major Lance, Okeh 7226 | 1 |
| 98 | — | — | THE WORLD THROUGH A TEAR — Neil Sedaka, RCA Victor 8637 | 1 |
| 99 | — | — | HIGH HEEL SNEAKERS — Stevie Wonder, Tamla 54119 | 1 |
| 100 | — | — | THESE HANDS (Small But Mighty) — Bobby Bland, Duke 385 | 1 |

## BUBBLING UNDER THE HOT 100

101. RESPECT — Otis Redding, Volt 128
102. I'M DOWN — Beatles, Capitol 5476
103. LOUIE LOUIE — Kingsmen, Wand 143
104. YOU CAN'T BE TRUE DEAR — Patti Page, Columbia 43345
105. OOWEE, OOWEE — Perry Como, RCA Victor 8636
106. OUT IN THE SUN (Hey-O) — Beach Nuts, Bang 504
107. SIMPLE SIMPLE — Horst Jankowski, Mercury 72465
108. I'M ALIVE — Hollies, Imperial 66119
109. I LIVE FOR THE SUN — Sunrays, Tower 148
110. N-N-NERVOUS — Ian Whitcomb, Tower 155
111. 99 PLUS 1 — J. Gardner, Blue Rock 4026
112. ROUNDABOUT — Connie Francis, MGM 13389
113. SUMMER WIND — Roger Williams & the Harry Simeone Chorale & Or., Kapp 55
114. AIN'T IT TRUE — Andy Williams, Columbia 43358
115. SWEETHEART TREE — Johnny Mathis, Mercury 72464
116. I DON'T WANT TO LIVE (Without Your Love) — Bobbi Martin, Coral 62457
117. THE SILENCE — Al Hirt, RCA Victor 8653
118. (IT'S A) LONG LONELY HIGHWAY — Elvis Presley, RCA Victor 8657
119. BEHIND THE TEAR — Sonny James, Capitol 5454
120. IT'S THE ONLY WAY TO FLY — Jewel Akens, Era 3147
121. YOU'RE GONNA MAKE ME CRY — O. V. Wright, Back Beat 548
122. WE'RE DOING FINE — Dee Dee Warwick, Blue Rock 4027
123. I'LL STOP AT NOTHING — Sandie Shaw, Reprise 0394
124. THE SONGS OF KATIE ELDER — Johnny Cash, Columbia 43342
125. I'M LOSING YOU — Aretha Franklin, Columbia 43333
126. SOUL HEAVEN — Dixie Drifter, Roulette 4641
127. YOU CAN'T TAKE IT AWAY — Fred Hughes, Vee Jay 703
128. WAY OF LOVE — Kathy Kirby, Parrot 9773
129. IT'S ALL OVER — Del Shannon, Amy 937
130. YOU'RE THE REASON — Gerry & the Pacemakers, Laurie 3313
131. SUN GLASSES — Skeeter Davis, RCA Victor 8642
132. MILLIONS OF ROSES — Steve Lawrence, Columbia 43342
133. ROSES AND RAINBOWS — Danny Hutton, HBR 447
134. 1-2-3 — Len Barry, Decca 31827
135. LITTLE MISS SAD — Five Emprees, Freeport 101

Compiled from national retail sales and radio station airplay by the Music Popularity Dept. of Record Market Research, Billboard.

**Billboard** For Week Ending September 4, 1965

# HOT 100

★ STAR performer—Sides registering greatest proportionate upward progress this week.

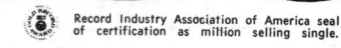

Record Industry Association of America seal of certification as million selling single.

Billboard Award

| This Week | 1 Wk. Ago | 2 Wks. Ago | 3 Wks. Ago | TITLE Artist, Label & Number | Weeks On Chart |
|---|---|---|---|---|---|
| 1 | 2 | 3 | 14 | HELP — Beatles, Capitol 5476 | 5 |
| ★2 | 6 | 16 | 26 | LIKE A ROLLING STONE — Bob Dylan, Columbia 43346 | 7 |
| 3 | 3 | 4 | 9 | CALIFORNIA GIRLS — Beach Boys, Capitol 5464 | 7 |
| 4 | 4 | 5 | 6 | UNCHAINED MELODY — Righteous Brothers, Philles 129 | 8 |
| 5 | 5 | 7 | 7 | IT'S THE SAME OLD SONG — Four Tops, Motown 1081 | 6 |
| 6 | 1 | 1 | 1 | I GOT YOU BABE — Sonny & Cher, Atco 6359 | 9 |
| ★7 | 12 | 17 | 22 | YOU WERE ON MY MIND — We Five, A&M 770 | 7 |
| 8 | 10 | 14 | 20 | PAPA'S GOT A BRAND NEW BAG — James Brown, King 5999 | 8 |
| ★9 | 27 | 58 | — | EVE OF DESTRUCTION — Barry McGuire, Dunhill 4009 | 3 |
| 10 | 8 | 13 | 15 | HOLD ME, THRILL ME, KISS ME — Mel Carter, Imperial 66113 | 11 |
| 11 | 13 | 18 | 27 | NOTHING BUT HEARTACHES — Supremes, Motown 1080 | 6 |
| ★12 | 21 | 32 | 53 | IT AIN'T ME BABE — Turtles, White Whale 222 | 5 |
| 13 | 9 | 10 | 10 | DOWN IN THE BOONDOCKS — Billy Joe Royal, Columbia 43305 | 10 |
| 14 | 11 | 11 | 12 | BABY I'M YOURS — Barbara Lewis, Atlantic 2283 | 12 |
| ★15 | 22 | 34 | 57 | THE "IN" CROWD — Ramsey Lewis Trio, Argo 5506 | 6 |
| 16 | 19 | 23 | 30 | TRACKS OF MY TEARS — Miracles, Tamla 54118 | 8 |
| 17 | 17 | 24 | 29 | SINCE I LOST MY BABY — Temptations, Gordy 7043 | 7 |
| 18 | 15 | 15 | 18 | ALL I REALLY WANT TO DO — Cher, Imperial 66114 | 10 |
| ★19 | 25 | 30 | 49 | HEART FULL OF SOUL — Yardbirds, Epic 9823 | 6 |
| 20 | 7 | 2 | 3 | SAVE YOUR HEART FOR ME — Gary Lewis & the Playboys, Liberty 55809 | 10 |
| 21 | 24 | 27 | 37 | IN THE MIDNIGHT HOUR — Wilson Pickett, Atlantic 2289 | 9 |
| ★22 | 49 | 67 | 99 | HANG ON SLOOPY — McCoys, Bang 506 | 4 |
| ★23 | 31 | 52 | 71 | ACTION — Freddy Cannon, Warner Bros. 5645 | 4 |
| ★24 | 29 | 38 | 58 | HOUSTON — Dean Martin, Reprise 0393 | 5 |
| ★25 | 42 | 62 | — | CATCH US IF YOU CAN — Dave Clark Five, Epic 9833 | 3 |
| 26 | 26 | 29 | 47 | JU JU HAND — Sam the Sham & the Pharaohs, MGM 13364 | 6 |
| ★27 | 52 | 83 | — | LAUGH AT ME — Sonny, Atco 6369 | 3 |
| 28 | 28 | 31 | 41 | LOOKING THROUGH THE EYES OF LOVE — Gene Pitney, Musicor 1103 | 7 |
| 29 | 32 | 37 | 48 | SHAKE AND FINGERPOP — Jr. Walker & the All Stars, Soul 35013 | 6 |
| ★30 | 41 | 51 | 63 | AGENT OO-SOUL — Edwin Starr, Ric-Tic 103 | 5 |
| 31 | 16 | 6 | 2 | (I Can't Get No) SATISFACTION — Rolling Stones, London 9766 (RIAA seal) | 13 |
| 32 | 37 | 45 | 51 | SUGAR DUMPLING — Sam Cooke, RCA Victor 8631 | 7 |
| ★33 | 43 | 68 | 80 | WE GOTTA GET OUT OF THIS PLACE — Animals, MGM 13382 | 4 |
| ★34 | 44 | 55 | 68 | SAD, SAD GIRL — Barbara Mason, Arctic 108 | 5 |
| 35 | 35 | 46 | 56 | I DON'T WANNA LOSE YOU BABY — Chad & Jeremy, Columbia 43339 | 5 |
| 36 | 14 | 8 | 8 | DON'T JUST STAND THERE — Patty Duke, United Artists 875 | 11 |
| 37 | 45 | 53 | 73 | WHO'LL BE THE NEXT IN LINE — Kinks, Reprise 0366 | 4 |
| 38 | 23 | 20 | 17 | I'M A FOOL — Dino, Desi & Billy, Reprise 0367 | 11 |
| 39 | 46 | 59 | 74 | SUMMER NIGHTS — Marianne Faithfull, London 9790 | 4 |
| 40 | 18 | 12 | 5 | WHAT'S NEW PUSSYCAT? — Tom Jones, Parrot 9765 | 12 |
| 41 | 50 | 57 | 75 | YOU'VE BEEN IN LOVE TOO LONG — Martha & Vandellas, Gordy 7045 | 4 |
| 42 | 34 | 22 | 23 | YOU'D BETTER COME HOME — Petula Clark, Warner Bros. 5643 | 9 |
| 43 | 20 | 9 | 4 | I'M HENRY VIII, I AM — Herman's Hermits, MGM 13367 | 10 |
| 44 | 30 | 19 | 16 | TAKE ME BACK — Little Anthony & the Imperials, DCP 1136 | 11 |
| ★45 | 55 | 66 | 90 | I'M A HAPPY MAN — Jive Five, United Artists 853 | 4 |
| 46 | 38 | 41 | 46 | YOU TELL ME WHY — Beau Brummels, Autumn 16 | 7 |
| 47 | 53 | 49 | 52 | IT'S GONNA TAKE A MIRACLE — Royalettes, MGM 13366 | 8 |
| ★48 | 60 | 70 | — | BABY DON'T GO — Sonny & Cher, Reprise 0392 | 3 |
| ★49 | 62 | 73 | 77 | ANNIE FANNY — Kingsmen, Wand 189 | 5 |
| 50 | 54 | 60 | 69 | IF I DIDN'T LOVE YOU — Chuck Jackson, Wand 188 | 5 |
| ★51 | 77 | 95 | — | YOU'VE GOT YOUR TROUBLES — Fortunes, Press 9773 | 3 |
| 52 | 56 | 69 | 87 | I'LL TAKE YOU WHERE THE MUSIC'S PLAYING — Drifters, Atlantic 2298 | 4 |
| 53 | 48 | 50 | 60 | A LITTLE YOU — Freddie & the Dreamers, Mercury 72462 | 6 |
| 54 | 58 | 71 | 86 | MY GIRL SLOOPY — Little Caesar & Consuls, Mala 512 | 4 |
| 55 | 47 | 40 | 42 | ALL I REALLY WANT TO DO — Byrds, Columbia 43332 | 10 |
| ★56 | 66 | 72 | 82 | MOONLIGHT AND ROSES — Vic Dana, Dolton 309 | 5 |
| ★57 | 73 | 98 | — | RIDE AWAY — Roy Orbison, MGM 13386 | 3 |
| ★58 | 70 | — | — | I'LL MAKE ALL YOUR DREAMS COME TRUE — Ronnie Dove, Diamond 188 | 2 |
| 59 | 59 | 61 | 64 | MOON OVER NAPLES — Bert Kaempfert & His Ork, Decca 31812 | 9 |
| ★60 | 72 | — | — | JUST YOU — Sonny & Cher, Atco 6345 | 2 |
| 61 | 65 | 75 | 81 | FIRST I LOOK AT THE PURSE — Contours, Gordy 7044 | 4 |
| ★62 | 82 | — | — | WITH THESE HANDS — Tom Jones, Parrot 9787 | 2 |
| 63 | 64 | 64 | 67 | CANDY — Astors, Stax 170 | 9 |
| ★64 | 79 | 96 | — | DO YOU BELIEVE IN MAGIC — Lovin' Spoonful, Kama Sutra 201 | 3 |
| 65 | 67 | 79 | 92 | DANGER HEARTBREAK DEAD AHEAD — Marvelettes, Tamla 54120 | 4 |
| ★66 | 83 | — | — | I'M YOURS — Elvis Presley, RCA Victor 8657 | 2 |
| 67 | 69 | 78 | 78 | IT'S A MAN DOWN THERE — G. L. Crockett, 4 Brothers 445 | 5 |
| 68 | 76 | 84 | 95 | COLOURS — Donovan, Hickory 1324 | 4 |
| 69 | 71 | 86 | 98 | GIVE ALL YOUR LOVE TO ME — Gerry & Pacemakers, Laurie 3313 | 4 |
| 70 | 75 | 90 | 97 | I NEED YOU — Impressions, ABC-Paramount 10710 | 4 |
| ★71 | 86 | — | — | MOHAIR SAM — Charlie Rich, Smash 1993 | 2 |
| ★72 | 87 | 91 | 96 | LIAR, LIAR — Castaways, Soma 1433 | 4 |
| 73 | 68 | 56 | 62 | IT'S TOO LATE, BABY TOO LATE — Arthur Prysock, Old Town 1183 | 8 |
| ★74 | 89 | — | — | HOME OF THE BRAVE — Jody Miller, Capitol 5483 | 2 |
| 75 | 81 | 87 | — | TWO DIFFERENT WORLDS — Lenny Welch, Kapp 689 | 3 |
| 76 | 74 | 74 | 59 | NO PITY (In the Naked City) — Jackie Wilson, Brunswick 55280 | 10 |
| ★77 | 99 | — | — | HIGH HEEL SNEAKERS — Stevie Wonder, Tamla 54119 | 2 |
| 78 | 80 | 81 | 83 | YOU BETTER GO — Derek Martin, Roulette 4631 | 6 |
| 79 | 90 | — | — | HEARTACHES BY THE NUMBER — Johnny Tillotson, MGM 13376 | 2 |
| ★80 | — | — | — | SOME ENCHANTED EVENING — Jay & the Americans, United Artists 919 | 1 |
| 81 | 85 | 89 | 93 | ONLY THOSE IN LOVE — Baby Washington, Sue 129 | 7 |
| 82 | 84 | 85 | 88 | IS IT REALLY OVER? — Jim Reeves, RCA Victor 8625 | 4 |
| ★83 | — | — | — | TREAT HER RIGHT — Roy Head, Back Beat 546 | 1 |
| 84 | 88 | 94 | — | IF YOU WAIT FOR LOVE — Bobby Goldsboro, United Artists 908 | 3 |
| ★85 | — | — | — | AIN'T IT TRUE — Andy Williams, Columbia 43358 | 1 |
| 86 | 94 | — | — | HOME OF THE BRAVE — Bonnie & the Treasures, Phi-Dan 5005 | 2 |
| ★87 | — | — | — | N-N-NERVOUS — Ian Whitcomb, Tower 155 | 1 |
| 88 | 92 | — | — | I WANT TO (Do Everything for You) — Joe Tex, Dial 4016 | 2 |
| 89 | 91 | 100 | — | SOMEONE IS WATCHING — Solomon Burke, Atlantic 2299 | 3 |
| ★90 | — | — | — | RESPECT — Otis Redding, Volt 128 | 1 |
| 91 | — | — | — | SIMPLE GIMPEL — Horst Jankowski, Mercury 72465 | 1 |
| 92 | 95 | 97 | — | GOOD TIMES — Gene Chandler, Constellation 160 | 3 |
| 93 | 97 | — | — | TOO HOT TO HOLD — Major Lance, Okeh 7226 | 2 |
| 94 | 96 | 99 | — | CAN'T LET YOU OUT OF MY SIGHT — Chuck Jackson & Maxine Brown, Wand 191 | 3 |
| 95 | — | — | — | I LIVE FOR THE SUN — Sunrays, Tower 148 | 1 |
| 96 | 98 | — | — | THE WORLD THROUGH A TEAR — Neil Sedaka, RCA Victor 8637 | 2 |
| 97 | 100 | — | — | THESE HANDS (Small But Mighty) — Bobby Bland, Duke 385 | 2 |
| 98 | — | — | 91 | YOU'RE GONNA MAKE ME CRY — O. V. Wright, Back Beat 548 | 3 |
| 99 | — | — | — | THE GIRL FROM PEYTON PLACE — Dickey Lee, TCF-Hall 111 | 1 |
| 100 | — | — | — | SOUL HEAVEN — Dixie Drifter, Roulette 4641 | 1 |

## HOT 100—A TO Z—*(Publisher-Licensee)*

Action (Screen Gems-Columbia, BMI) .... 23
Agent OO-Soul (Myto, BMI) .... 30
Ain't It True (Wemar & Claudine, BMI) .... 85
All I Really Want to Do—Byrds (Witmark, ASCAP). 55
All I Really Want to Do—Cher (Witmark, ASCAP). 18
Annie Fanny (Sharrow & Burdett & Flomar, BMI) .. 49
Baby Don't Go (Chris-Mark & Ten East, BMI) .... 48
Baby I'm Yours (Blackwood, BMI) .... 14
California Girls (Sea of Tunes, BMI) .... 3
Candy (East, BMI) .... 63
Can't Let You Out of My Sight (Screen Gems-Columbia, BMI) .... 94
Catch Us If You Can (Branston, BMI) .... 25
Colours (Southern, ASCAP) .... 68
Danger Heartbreak Dead Ahead (Jobete, BMI) .... 65
Do You Believe in Magic (Faithful Virtue, BMI) .. 64
Don't Just Stand There (Bernross, BMI) .... 36
Down in the Boondocks (Lowery, BMI) .... 13
Eve of Destruction (Trousdale, BMI) .... 9
First I Look at the Purse (Jobete, BMI) .... 61
Girl From Peyton Place, The (Screen Gems-Columbia, BMI) .... 99
Give All Your Love to Me (Pacemaker, BMI) .... 69
Good Times (Chi-Sound & Jalynne, BMI) .... 92
Hang On Sloopy (Picturetone-Mellin, BMI) .... 22
Heart Full of Soul (Miller, ASCAP) .... 19
Heartaches by the Number (Pamper, BMI) ....79
Help (Maclen, BMI) .... 1
High Heel Sneakers (Medal, BMI) .... 77
Hold Me, Thrill Me, Kiss Me (Mills, ASCAP) .... 10
Home of the Brave—Bonnie & the Treasures (Screen Gems-Columbia, BMI) .... 86
Home of the Brave—Miller (Screen Gems-Columbia, BMI) .... 74
Houston (Criterion, ASCAP) .... 24
(I Can't Get No) Satisfaction (Immediate, BMI) .. 31
I Don't Wanna Lose You, Baby (Blackwood, BMI) .. 35
I Got You Babe (Five-West-Cotillion, BMI) .... 6
I Live for the Sun (Sea of Tunes, BMI) .... 95
I Need You (Chi-Sound, BMI) .... 70
I Want to (Do Everything for You) (Tree, BMI) .. 88
If I Didn't Love You (Metric, BMI) .... 50
If You Wait for Love (Unart, BMI) .... 84
I'll Make All Your Dreams Come True (Picturetone, BMI) .... 58
I'll Take You Where the Music's Playing (Trio, BMI) .... 52
I'm a Fool (Atlantic, BMI) .... 38
I'm a Happy Man (Unart, BMI) .... 45
I'm Henry VIII, I Am (Miller, ASCAP) .... 43
I'm Yours (Glady's, ASCAP) .... 66
"In" Crowd, The (American, BMI) .... 15
In the Midnight Hour (Cotillion-East, BMI) .... 21
Is It Really Over? (Tuckahoe, BMI) .... 82
It Ain't Me Babe (Witmark, ASCAP) .... 12
It's Gonna Take a Miracle (South Mountain, BMI) . 47
It's a Man Down There (Fairshake, BMI) .... 67
It's the Same Old Song (Jobete, BMI) .... 5
It's too Late, Baby Too Late (Pry-Weiss, BMI) . 73
Ju Ju Hand (Beckie, BMI) .... 26
Just You (Five-West-Cotillion, BMI) .... 60
Laugh at Me (Five-West-Cotillion, BMI) .... 27
Liar, Liar (Celann, BMI) .... 72
Like a Rolling Stone (Witmark, ASCAP) .... 2
Little You, A (Leeds, ASCAP) .... 53
Looking Through the Eyes of Love (Screen Gems-Columbia, BMI) .... 28
Mohair Sam (Acclaim, BMI) .... 71
Moon Over Naples (Roosevelt, BMI) .... 59
Moonlight and Roses (Daniels, ASCAP) .... 56
My Girl Sloopy (Picturetone-Mellin, BMI) .... 54
N-N-Nervous (Burdette, BMI) .... 87
No Pity (In the Naked City) (Merrimac, BMI) .... 76
Nothing But Heartaches (Jobete, BMI) .... 11
Only Those in Love (Brown, BMI) .... 81
Papa's Got a Brand New Bag (Lois, BMI) .... 8
Respect (East-Time-Redwal, BMI) .... 90
Ride Away (Acuff-Rose, BMI) .... 57
Sad, Sad Girl (Stillran-Dandelion, BMI) .... 34
Save Your Heart for Me (Geld-Udell-Purchase, ASCAP) .... 20
Shake and Fingerpop (Jobete, BMI) .... 29
Simple Gimpel (MRC, BMI) .... 91
Since I Lost My Baby (Jobete, BMI) .... 17
Some Enchanted Evening (Williamson, ASCAP) .... 80
Someone Is Watching (Webb IV-Falart, BMI) .... 89
Soul Heaven (Unbelievable & Nom, BMI) ....100
Sugar Dumpling (Kags, BMI) .... 32
Summer Nights (Sea-Lark, BMI) .... 39
Take Me Back (South Mountain, BMI) .... 44
These Hands (Small But Mighty) (Don, BMI) .... 97
Too Hot to Hold (Dakar, BMI) .... 93
Tracks of My Tears (Jobete, BMI) .... 16
Treat Her Right (Don, BMI) .... 83
Two Different Worlds (Princess, ASCAP) .... 75
Unchained Melody (Frank, ASCAP) .... 4
We Gotta Get Out of This Place (Screen Gems-Columbia, BMI) .... 33
What's New Pussycat? (United Artists, ASCAP) .. 40
Who'll Be Next in Line" (Jay Boy, BMI) .... 37
With These Hands (Bloom, ASCAP) .... 62
World Through a Tear, The (Bregman, Vocco & Conn, ASCAP) .... 96
You Better Go (South Mountain, BMI) .... 78
You Tell Me Why (Taracrest, BMI) .... 46
You Were on My Mind (Witmark, ASCAP) .... 7
You'd Better Come Home (Duchess, BMI) .... 42
You're Gonna Make Me Cry (Don, BMI) .... 98
You've Been in Love Too Long (Jobete, BMI) .... 41
You've Got Your Troubles (Mills, ASCAP) .... 51

## BUBBLING UNDER THE HOT 100

101. KEEP ON DANCING ....Gentry's, MGM 13379
102. I'M DOWN ....Beatles, Capitol 5476
103. YOU CAN'T TAKE IT AWAY ....Fred Hughes, Vee Jay 703
104. YOU CAN'T BE TRUE DEAR ....Patti Page, Columbia 43345
105. THERE BUT FOR FORTUNE ....Joan Baez, Vanguard 35031
106. 3D MAN THEME ....Herb Alpert & the Tijuana Brass, A&M 775
107. WHAT ARE WE GOING TO DO ....David Jones, Colpix 784
108. (Ive Got a Feeling) YOU'RE GONNA BE SORRY ....Billy Butler, Okeh 7227
109. ROUNDABOUT ....Connie Francis, MGM 13389
110. SUMMER WIND ....Roger Williams, Kapp 55
111. SWEETHEART TREE ....Johnny Mathis, Mercury 72464
112. (It's a) LONG, LONELY HIGHWAY ....Elvis Presley, RCA Victor 8657
113. THE SILENCE ....Al Hirt, RCA Victor 8653
114. TAKE ME FOR A LITTLE WHILE ....Evie Sands, Blue Cat 118
115. WHENEVER YOU'RE READY ....Zombies, Parrot 9786
116. WHOLE LOT OF WOMAN ....Radiants, Chess 1939
117. WHEN SOMEBODY LOVES YOU ....Frank Sinatra, Reprise 0398
118. 99 PLUS 1 ....J. Gardner, Blue Rock 4026
119. BEHIND THE TEAR ....Sonny James, Capitol 5454
120. WE'RE DOING FINE ....Dee Dee Warwick, Blue Rock 4027
121. YOU'RE THE REASON ....Gerry & the Pacemakers, Laurie 3313
122. THE SONS OF KATIE ELDER ....Johnny Cash, Columbia 43342
123. WAY OF LOVE ....Kathy Kirby, Parrot 9775
124. SUN GLASSES ....Skeeter Davis, RCA Victor 8642
125. MILLIONS OF ROSES ....Steve Lawrence, Columbia 43362
126. ROSES AND RAINBOWS ....Danny Hutton, HBR 447
127. LITTLE MISS SAD ....Five Emprees, Freeport 101
128. MOVE IT ON OVER ....Del Shannon, Amy 937
129. DRUMS A GO GO ....Hollywood Persuaders, Original Sound 50
130. 1-2-3 ....Len Barry, Decca 31827
131. ME WITHOUT YOU ....Mary Wells, 20th Century-Fox 606
132. LIVIN' IN A HOUSE FULL OF LOVE ....David Houston, Epic 9831
133. WHITTIER BLVD. ....Midnighters, Chattahooche 684
134. HEY HO WHAT YOU DO TO ME ....Guess Who, Scepter 12108
135. MY TOWN, MY GUY & ME ....Lesley Gore, Mercury 72475

Compiled from national retail sales and radio station airplay by the Music Popularity Dept. of Record Market Research, Billboard.

# Billboard HOT 100

**For Week Ending September 11, 1965**

★ STAR performer—Sides registering greatest proportionate upward progress this week.

| This Week | Wk. Ago | 2 Wk. Ago | 3 Wk. Ago | TITLE Artist, Label & Number | Weeks On Chart |
|---|---|---|---|---|---|
| 1 | 1 | 2 | 3 | HELP — Beatles, Capitol 5476 | 6 |
| 2 | 2 | 6 | 16 | LIKE A ROLLING STONE — Bob Dylan, Columbia 43346 | 8 |
| ★3 | 9 | 27 | 58 | EVE OF DESTRUCTION — Barry McGuire, Dunhill 4009 | 4 |
| 4 | 7 | 12 | 17 | YOU WERE ON MY MIND — We Five, A&M 770 | 8 |
| 5 | 3 | 3 | 4 | CALIFORNIA GIRLS — Beach Boys, Capitol 5464 | 8 |
| 6 | 4 | 4 | 5 | UNCHAINED MELODY — Righteous Brothers, Philles 129 | 9 |
| 7 | 6 | 1 | 1 | I GOT YOU BABE — Sonny & Cher, Atco 6359 | 10 |
| 8 | 8 | 10 | 14 | PAPA'S GOT A BRAND NEW BAG — James Brown, King 5999 | 9 |
| ★9 | 12 | 21 | 32 | IT AIN'T ME BABE — Turtles, White Whale 222 | 6 |
| 10 | 15 | 22 | 34 | THE "IN" CROWD — Ramsey Lewis Trio, Argo 5506 | 7 |
| 11 | 22 | 49 | 67 | HANG ON SLOOPY — McCoys, Bang 506 | 5 |
| 12 | 5 | 5 | 7 | IT'S THE SAME OLD SONG — Four Tops, Motown 1081 | 7 |
| 13 | 25 | 42 | 62 | CATCH US IF YOU CAN — Dave Clark Five, Epic 9833 | 4 |
| 14 | 19 | 25 | 30 | HEART FULL OF SOUL — Yardbirds, Epic 9823 | 7 |
| 15 | 10 | 8 | 13 | HOLD ME, THRILL ME, KISS ME — Mel Carter, Imperial 66113 | 12 |
| 16 | 11 | 13 | 18 | NOTHING BUT HEARTACHES — Supremes, Motown 1080 | 7 |
| 17 | 13 | 9 | 10 | DOWN IN THE BOONDOCKS — Billy Joe Royal, Columbia 43305 | 11 |
| 18 | 23 | 31 | 52 | ACTION — Freddy Cannon, Warner Bros. 5645 | 5 |
| 19 | 27 | 52 | 83 | LAUGH AT ME — Sonny, Atco 6369 | 4 |
| 20 | 16 | 19 | 23 | TRACKS OF MY TEARS — Miracles, Tamla 54118 | 9 |
| 21 | 24 | 29 | 38 | HOUSTON — Dean Martin, Reprise 0393 | 6 |
| 22 | 17 | 17 | 24 | SINCE I LOST MY BABY — Temptations, Gordy 7043 | 8 |
| 23 | 14 | 11 | 11 | BABY I'M YOURS — Barbara Lewis, Atlantic 2283 | 13 |
| 24 | 18 | 15 | 15 | ALL I REALLY WANT TO DO — Cher, Imperial 66114 | 11 |
| 25 | 21 | 24 | 27 | IN THE MIDNIGHT HOUR — Wilson Pickett, Atlantic 2289 | 10 |
| ★26 | 33 | 43 | 68 | WE GOTTA GET OUT OF THIS PLACE — Animals, MGM 13382 | 5 |
| 27 | 30 | 41 | 51 | AGENT OO-SOUL — Edwin Starr, Ric-Tic 103 | 6 |
| ★28 | 39 | 46 | 59 | SUMMER NIGHTS — Marianne Faithfull, London 8790 | 5 |
| 29 | 29 | 32 | 37 | SHAKE AND FINGERPOP — Jr. Walker & the All Stars, Soul 35013 | 7 |
| 30 | 34 | 44 | 55 | SAD SAD GIRL — Barbara Mason, Arctic 108 | 6 |
| 31 | 51 | 77 | 95 | YOU'VE GOT YOUR TROUBLES — Fortunes, Press 9773 | 4 |
| 32 | 48 | 60 | 70 | BABY DON'T GO — Sonny & Cher, Reprise 0392 | 4 |
| 33 | 20 | 7 | 2 | SAVE YOUR HEART FOR ME — Gary Lewis and the Playboys, Liberty 55809 | 11 |
| 34 | 32 | 37 | 45 | SUGAR DUMPLING — Sam Cooke, RCA Victor 8631 | 8 |
| 35 | 37 | 45 | 53 | WHO'LL BE THE NEXT IN LINE — Kinks, Reprise 0366 | 5 |
| 36 | 28 | 28 | 31 | LOOKING THROUGH THE EYES OF LOVE — Gene Pitney, Musicor 1103 | 8 |
| 37 | 35 | 35 | 46 | I DON'T WANNA LOSE YOU BABY — Chad & Jeremy, Columbia 43339 | 6 |
| 38 | 45 | 55 | 66 | I'M A HAPPY MAN — Jive Five, United Artists 853 | 5 |
| 39 | 41 | 50 | 57 | YOU'VE BEEN IN LOVE TOO LONG — Martha & Vandellas, Gordy 7045 | 5 |
| 40 | 26 | 26 | 29 | JU JU HAND — Sam the Sham & the Pharaohs, MGM 13364 | 7 |
| 41 | 31 | 16 | 6 | (I Can't Get No) SATISFACTION — Rolling Stones, London 9766 | 14 |
| ★42 | 64 | 79 | 96 | DO YOU BELIEVE IN MAGIC — Lovin' Spoonful, Kama Sutra 201 | 4 |
| 43 | 47 | 53 | 49 | IT'S GONNA TAKE A MIRACLE — Royalettes, MGM 13366 | 9 |
| ★44 | 58 | 70 | — | I'LL MAKE ALL YOUR DREAMS COME TRUE — Ronnie Dove, Diamond 188 | 3 |
| 45 | 38 | 23 | 20 | I'M A FOOL — Dino, Desi & Billy, Reprise 0367 | 12 |
| ★46 | 57 | 73 | 98 | RIDE AWAY — Roy Orbison, MGM 13386 | 4 |
| 47 | 49 | 62 | 73 | ANNIE FANNY — Kingsmen, Wand 189 | 6 |
| 48 | 50 | 54 | 60 | IF I DIDN'T LOVE YOU — Chuck Jackson, Wand 188 | 6 |
| ★49 | 62 | 82 | — | WITH THESE HANDS — Tom Jones, Parrot 9787 | 3 |
| ★50 | 60 | 72 | — | JUST YOU — Sonny & Cher, Atco 6345 | 3 |
| 51 | 66 | 83 | — | I'M YOURS — Elvis Presley, RCA Victor 8657 | 3 |
| ★52 | 52 | 56 | 69 | I'LL TAKE YOU WHERE THE MUSIC'S PLAYING — Drifters, Atlantic 2298 | — |
| 53 | 54 | 58 | 71 | MY GIRL SLOOPY — Little Caesar & Consuls, Mala 512 | 5 |
| 54 | 56 | 66 | 72 | MOONLIGHT AND ROSES — Vic Dana, Dolton 309 | 6 |
| ★55 | 72 | 87 | 91 | LIAR, LIAR — Castaways, Soma 1433 | 5 |
| 56 | 83 | — | — | TREAT HER RIGHT — Roy Head, Back Beat 546 | 2 |
| 57 | 71 | 86 | — | MOHAIR SAM — Charlie Rich, Smash 1993 | 3 |
| ★58 | 74 | 89 | — | HOME OF THE BRAVE — Jody Miller, Capitol 5483 | 3 |
| 59 | 61 | 65 | 75 | FIRST I LOOK AT THE PURSE — Contours, Gordy 7044 | 5 |
| 60 | 53 | 48 | 50 | A LITTLE YOU — Freddie & the Dreamers, Mercury 72462 | 7 |
| ★61 | 80 | — | — | SOME ENCHANTED EVENING — Jay & the Americans, United Artists 919 | 2 |
| 62 | 65 | 67 | 79 | DANGER HEARTBREAK DEAD AHEAD — Marvelettes, Tamla 54120 | 5 |
| 63 | 68 | 76 | 84 | COLOURS — Donovan, Hickory 1324 | 5 |
| ★64 | 79 | 90 | — | HEARTACHES BY THE NUMBER — Johnny Tillotson, MGM 13376 | — |
| 65 | 77 | 99 | — | HIGH HEEL SNEAKERS — Stevie Wonder, Tamla 54119 | 3 |
| 66 | 59 | 59 | 61 | MOON OVER NAPLES — Bert Kaempfert & His Ork, Decca 31812 | 10 |
| 67 | 70 | 75 | 90 | I NEED YOU — Impressions, ABC-Paramount 10710 | 5 |
| 68 | 69 | 71 | 86 | GIVE ALL YOUR LOVE TO ME — Gerry & Pacemakers, Laurie 3313 | 5 |
| ★69 | 85 | — | — | AIN'T IT TRUE — Andy Williams, Columbia 43358 | 2 |
| 70 | 75 | 81 | 87 | TWO DIFFERENT WORLDS — Lenny Welch, Kapp 689 | 4 |
| 71 | 67 | 69 | 78 | IT'S A MAN DOWN THERE — G. L. Crockett, 4 Brothers 445 | 6 |
| ★72 | — | — | — | KANSAS CITY STAR — Roger Miller, Smash 1998 | 1 |
| 73 | 81 | 85 | 89 | ONLY THOSE IN LOVE — Baby Washington, Sue 129 | 8 |
| 74 | 87 | — | — | N-N-NERVOUS — Ian Whitcomb, Tower 155 | 2 |
| 75 | 88 | 92 | — | I WANT TO (Do Everything for You) — Joe Tex, Dial 4016 | 3 |
| 76 | — | — | — | KEEP ON DANCING — Gentry's, MGM 13379 | 1 |
| 77 | 90 | — | — | RESPECT — Otis Redding, Volt 128 | 2 |
| 78 | 84 | 88 | 94 | IF YOU WAIT FOR LOVE — Bobby Goldsboro, United Artists 908 | 4 |
| 79 | 82 | 84 | 85 | IS IT REALLY OVER? — Jim Reeves, RCA Victor 8625 | 5 |
| 80 | — | — | — | THE 3rd MAN THEME — Herb Alpert & the Tijuana Brass, A&M 775 | 1 |
| 81 | 86 | 94 | — | HOME OF THE BRAVE — Bonnie & the Treasures, Phi-Dan 5005 | 3 |
| 82 | 95 | — | — | I LIVE FOR THE SUN — Sunrays, Tower 148 | 2 |
| 83 | — | — | — | MY TOWN, MY GUY AND ME — Leslie Gore, Mercury 72475 | 1 |
| 84 | 99 | — | — | THE GIRL FROM PEYTON PLACE — Dickey Lee, TCF-Hall 111 | 2 |
| 85 | 97 | 100 | — | THESE HANDS (Small But Mighty) — Bobby Bland, Duke 385 | 3 |
| 86 | — | — | — | ROUNDABOUT — Connie Francis, MGM 13389 | 1 |
| 87 | 98 | — | — | YOU'RE GONNA MAKE ME CRY — O. V. Wright, Back Beat 548 | 4 |
| 88 | 96 | 98 | — | THE WORLD THROUGH A TEAR — Neil Sedaka, RCA Victor 8637 | 3 |
| 89 | 89 | 91 | 100 | SOMEONE IS WATCHING — Solomon Burke, Atlantic 2299 | 4 |
| 90 | — | — | — | THERE BUT FOR FORTUNE — Joan Baez, Vanguard 35031 | 1 |
| 91 | 94 | 96 | 99 | CAN'T LET YOU OUT OF MY SIGHT — Chuck Jackson & Maxine Brown, Wand 191 | 4 |
| 92 | — | — | — | MAKE ME YOUR BABY — Barbara Lewis, Atlantic 2300 | 1 |
| 93 | 93 | 97 | — | TOO HOT TO HOLD — Major Lance, Okeh 7226 | 3 |
| 94 | — | — | — | YOU CAN'T BE TRUE, DEAR — Patti Page, Columbia 43345 | 1 |
| 95 | — | — | — | ME WITHOUT YOU — Mary Wells, 20th Century-Fox 606 | 1 |
| 96 | — | — | — | THE SILENCE — Al Hirt, RCA Victor 8653 | 1 |
| 97 | — | — | — | HUNGRY FOR LOVE — San Remo Golden Strings, Ric-Tic 104 | 1 |
| 98 | — | — | — | A LOVER'S CONCERTO — Toys, DynoVoice 209 | 1 |
| 99 | 100 | — | — | SOUL HEAVEN — Dixie Drifter, Roulette 4641 | 2 |
| 100 | — | — | — | LITTLE MISS SAD — Five Empress, Freeport 1001 | 1 |

## BUBBLING UNDER THE HOT 100

101. I'M DOWN — Beatles, Capitol 5476
102. YOU CAN'T TAKE IT AWAY — Fred Hughes, Vee Jay 703
103. YOU'RE THE ONE — Vogues, Co & Ce 229
104. (I've Got a Feeling) YOU'RE GONNA BE SORRY — Billy Butler, Okeh 7227
105. WHEN SOMEBODY LOVES YOU — Frank Sinatra, Reprise 0398
106. SIMPLE SIMPEL — Horst Jankowski, Mercury 72465
107. I KNEW YOU — Billy Joe Royal, Columbia 43390
108. SWEETHEART TREE — Johnny Mathis, Mercury 72464
109. SUMMER WIND — Roger Williams, Kapp 55
110. WHENEVER YOU'RE READY — Zombies, Parrot 9786
111. CARA-LIN — Strangeloves, Bang 508
112. DAWN OF CORRECTION — Spokesmen, Decca 31844
113. MILLIONS OF ROSES — Steve Lawrence, Columbia 43362
114. DRUMS A GO GO — Hollywood Persuaders, Original Sound 50
115. LET'S MOVE & GROOVE (Together) — Johnny Nash, Joda 102
116. BEHIND THE TEAR — Sonny James, Capitol 5454
117. FOR YOUR LOVE — Sam & Bill, Joda 100
118. WAY OF LOVE — Kathy Kirby, Parrot 9775
119. YOU'RE THE REASON — Gerry & the Pacemakers, Laurie 3313
120. SUN GLASSES — Johnny Cash, Columbia 43342
121. TASTE OF HONEY — Skeeter Davis, RCA Victor 8642
122. SONS OF KATIE ELDER — Herb Alpert & the Tijuana Brass, A&M 775
123. WHAT COLOR (Is a Man) — P. F. Sloan, Dunhill 4007
124. WHAT COLOR (Is a Man) — Bobby Vinton, Epic 9846
125. ROSES AND RAINBOWS — Danny Hutton, HBR 447
126. HEY HO WHAT YOU DO TO ME — Guess Who, Scepter 12108
127. WHITTIER BLVD. — Midnighters, Chattahoochee 684
128. LOVE IS STRANGE — Everly Brothers, Warner Bros. 31827
129. 1-2-3 — Len Barry, Decca 31827
130. LIVIN' IN A HOUSE FULL OF LOVE — David Houston, Epic 9831
131. EVERYONE'S GONE TO THE MOON — Jonathan King, Parrot 9774
132. ARE YOU A BOY OR ARE YOU A GIRL — Barbarians, Laurie 3308
133. SWEETHEART TREE — Henry Mancini, His Ork & Chorus, RCA Victor 8624
134. DO THE 45 — Sharpees, One-Derful 4835
135. I'M SO THANKFUL — Ikettes, Modern 1011

*Compiled from national retail sales and radio station airplay by the Music Popularity Dept. of Record Market Research, Billboard.*

# Billboard HOT 100

**For Week Ending September 18, 1965**

★ STAR performer—Sides registering greatest proportionate upward progress this week.

Record Industry Association of America seal of certification as million selling single.

| This Week | 1 Wk. Ago | 2 Wks. Ago | 3 Wks. Ago | TITLE Artist, Label & Number | Weeks On Chart |
|---|---|---|---|---|---|
| 1 | 1 | 1 | 2 | HELP — Beatles, Capitol 5476 | 7 |
| 2 | 3 | 9 | 27 | EVE OF DESTRUCTION — Barry McGuire, Dunhill 4009 | 5 |
| 3 | 2 | 2 | 6 | LIKE A ROLLING STONE — Bob Dylan, Columbia 43346 | 9 |
| 4 | 4 | 7 | 12 | YOU WERE ON MY MIND — We Five, A&M 770 | 9 |
| 5 | 13 | 25 | 42 | CATCH US IF YOU CAN — Dave Clark Five, Epic 9833 | 5 |
| 6 | 10 | 15 | 22 | THE "IN" CROWD — Ramsey Lewis Trio, Argo 5506 | 8 |
| 7 | 11 | 22 | 49 | HANG ON SLOOPY — McCoys, Bang 506 | 4 |
| 8 | 9 | 12 | 21 | IT AIN'T ME BABE — Turtles, White Whale 222 | 7 |
| 9 | 7 | 6 | 1 | I GOT YOU BABE — Sonny & Cher, Atco 6359 | 11 |
| 10 | 14 | 19 | 25 | HEART FULL OF SOUL — Yardbirds, Epic 9823 | 8 |
| 11 | 6 | 4 | 4 | UNCHAINED MELODY — Righteous Brothers, Philles 129 | 10 |
| 12 | 8 | 8 | 10 | PAPA'S GOT A BRAND NEW BAG — James Brown, King 5999 | 10 |
| 13 | 18 | 23 | 31 | ACTION — Freddy Cannon, Warner Bros. 5645 | 6 |
| 14 | 19 | 27 | 52 | LAUGH AT ME — Sonny, Atco 6369 | 5 |
| 15 | 5 | 3 | 3 | CALIFORNIA GIRLS — Beach Boys, Capitol 5464 | 9 |
| 16 | 31 | 51 | 77 | YOU'VE GOT YOUR TROUBLES — Fortunes, Press 9773 | 5 |
| 17 | 15 | 10 | 8 | HOLD ME, THRILL ME, KISS ME — Mel Carter, Imperial 66113 | 13 |
| 18 | 26 | 33 | 43 | WE GOTTA GET OUT OF THIS PLACE — Animals, MGM 13382 | 6 |
| 19 | 12 | 5 | 5 | IT'S THE SAME OLD SONG — Four Tops, Motown 1081 | 8 |
| 20 | 20 | 16 | 19 | TRACKS OF MY TEARS — Miracles, Tamla 54118 | 10 |
| 21 | 21 | 24 | 29 | HOUSTON — Dean Martin, Reprise 0393 | 7 |
| 22 | 32 | 48 | 60 | BABY DON'T GO — Sonny & Cher, Reprise 0392 | 5 |
| 23 | 16 | 11 | 13 | NOTHING BUT HEARTACHES — Supremes, Motown 1080 | 8 |
| 24 | 27 | 30 | 41 | AGENT OO-SOUL — Edwin Starr, Ric-Tic 103 | 7 |
| 25 | 22 | 17 | 17 | SINCE I LOST MY BABY — Temptations, Gordy 7043 | 9 |
| 26 | 56 | 83 | — | TREAT HER RIGHT — Roy Head, Back Beat 546 | 3 |
| 27 | 28 | 39 | 46 | SUMMER NIGHTS — Marianne Faithfull, London 8790 | 6 |
| 28 | 42 | 64 | 79 | DO YOU BELIEVE IN MAGIC — Lovin' Spoonful, Kama Sutra 201 | 5 |
| 29 | 30 | 34 | 44 | SAD, SAD GIRL — Barbara Mason, Arctic 108 | 7 |
| 30 | 17 | 13 | 9 | DOWN IN THE BOONDOCKS — Billy Joe Royal, Columbia 43305 | 12 |
| 31 | 55 | 72 | 87 | LIAR, LIAR — Castaways, Soma 1433 | 6 |
| 32 | 51 | 66 | 83 | I'M YOURS — Elvis Presley, RCA Victor 8657 | 4 |
| 33 | 44 | 58 | 70 | I'LL MAKE ALL YOUR DREAMS COME TRUE — Ronnie Dove, Diamond 188 | 4 |
| 34 | 35 | 37 | 45 | WHO'LL BE THE NEXT IN LINE — Kinks, Reprise 0366 | 6 |
| 35 | 46 | 57 | 73 | RIDE AWAY — Roy Orbison, MGM 13386 | 5 |
| 36 | 39 | 41 | 50 | YOU'VE BEEN IN LOVE TOO LONG — Martha & Vandellas, Gordy 7045 | 6 |
| 37 | 49 | 62 | 82 | WITH THESE HANDS — Tom Jones, Parrot 9787 | 4 |
| 38 | 38 | 45 | 55 | I'M A HAPPY MAN — Jive Five, United Artists 853 | 6 |
| 39 | 25 | 21 | 24 | IN THE MIDNIGHT HOUR — Wilson Pickett, Atlantic 2289 | 11 |
| 40 | 29 | 29 | 32 | SHAKE AND FINGERPOP — Jr. Walker & the All Stars, Soul 35013 | 8 |
| 41 | 43 | 47 | 53 | IT'S GONNA TAKE A MIRACLE — Royalettes, MGM 13366 | 10 |
| 42 | 50 | 60 | 72 | JUST YOU — Sonny & Cher, Atco 6345 | 4 |
| 43 | 61 | 80 | — | SOME ENCHANTED EVENING — Jay & the Americans, United Artists 919 | 3 |
| 44 | 23 | 14 | 11 | BABY I'M YOURS — Barbara Lewis, Atlantic 2283 | 14 |
| 45 | 57 | 71 | 86 | MOHAIR SAM — Charlie Rich, Smash 1993 | 4 |
| 46 | 48 | 50 | 54 | IF I DIDN'T LOVE YOU — Chuck Jackson, Wand 188 | 7 |
| 47 | 47 | 49 | 62 | ANNIE FANNY — Kingsmen, Wand 189 | 7 |
| 48 | 58 | 74 | 89 | HOME OF THE BRAVE — Jody Miller, Capitol 5483 | 4 |
| 49 | 24 | 18 | 15 | ALL I REALLY WANT TO DO — Cher, Imperial 66114 | 12 |
| 50 | 53 | 54 | 58 | MY GIRL SLOOPY — Little Caesar & Consuls, Mala 512 | 6 |
| 51 | 52 | 52 | 56 | I'LL TAKE YOU WHERE THE MUSIC'S PLAYING — Drifters, Atlantic 2298 | 6 |
| 52 | 64 | 79 | 90 | HEARTACHES BY THE NUMBER — Johnny Tillotson, MGM 13376 | 4 |
| 53 | 54 | 56 | 66 | MOONLIGHT AND ROSES — Vic Dana, Dolton 309 | 7 |
| 54 | 34 | 32 | 37 | SUGAR DUMPLING — Sam Cooke, RCA Victor 8631 | 9 |
| 55 | 37 | 35 | 35 | I DON'T WANNA LOSE YOU BABY — Chad & Jeremy, Columbia 43339 | 7 |
| 56 | 72 | — | — | KANSAS CITY STAR — Roger Miller, Smash 1998 | 2 |
| 57 | 59 | 61 | 65 | FIRST I LOOK AT THE PURSE — Contours, Gordy 7044 | 6 |
| 58 | 69 | 85 | — | AIN'T IT TRUE — Andy Williams, Columbia 43358 | 3 |
| 59 | 76 | — | — | KEEP ON DANCING — Gentrys, MGM 13379 | 2 |
| 60 | 74 | 87 | — | N-N-NERVOUS — Ian Whitcomb, Tower 155 | 3 |
| 61 | 63 | 68 | 76 | COLOURS — Donovan, Hickory 1324 | 6 |
| 62 | 62 | 65 | 67 | DANGER HEARTBREAK DEAD AHEAD — Marvelettes, Tamla 54120 | 6 |
| 63 | 65 | 77 | 99 | HIGH HEEL SNEAKERS — Stevie Wonder, Tamla 54119 | 4 |
| 64 | — | — | — | JUST A LITTLE BIT BETTER — Herman's Hermits, MGM 13398 | 1 |
| 65 | 67 | 70 | 75 | I NEED YOU — Impressions, ABC-Paramount 10710 | 6 |
| 66 | 70 | 75 | 81 | TWO DIFFERENT WORLDS — Lenny Welch, Kapp 689 | 5 |
| 67 | 75 | 88 | 92 | I WANT TO (Do Everything for You) — Joe Tex, Dial 4016 | 4 |
| 68 | 83 | — | — | MY TOWN, MY GUY AND ME — Leslie Gore, Mercury 72475 | 2 |
| 69 | 80 | — | — | THE 3rd MAN THEME — Herb Alpert & the Tijuana Brass, A&M 775 | 2 |
| 70 | 77 | 90 | — | RESPECT — Otis Redding, Volt 128 | 3 |
| 71 | 90 | — | — | THERE BUT FOR FORTUNE — Joan Baez, Vanguard 35031 | 2 |
| 72 | — | — | — | DAWN OF CORRECTION — Spokesmen, Decca 31844 | 1 |
| 73 | 73 | 81 | 85 | ONLY THOSE IN LOVE — Baby Washington, Sue 129 | 9 |
| 74 | 68 | 69 | 71 | GIVE ALL YOUR LOVE TO ME — Gerry & Pacemakers, Laurie 3313 | 6 |
| 75 | 78 | 84 | 88 | IF YOU WAIT FOR LOVE — Bobby Goldsboro, United Artists 908 | 5 |
| 76 | 85 | 97 | 100 | THESE HANDS (Small But Mighty) — Bobby Bland, Duke 385 | 4 |
| 77 | 82 | 95 | — | I LIVE FOR THE SUN — Sunrays, Tower 148 | 3 |
| 78 | 84 | 99 | — | THE GIRL FROM PEYTON PLACE — Dickey Lee, TCF-Hall 111 | 3 |
| 79 | 81 | 86 | 94 | HOME OF THE BRAVE — Bonnie & the Treasures, Phi-Dan 5005 | 4 |
| 80 | 86 | — | — | ROUNDABOUT — Connie Francis, MGM 13389 | 2 |
| 81 | 79 | 82 | 84 | IS IT REALLY OVER? — Jim Reeves, RCA Victor 8625 | 6 |
| 82 | 97 | — | — | HUNGRY FOR LOVE — San Remo Golden Strings, Ric-Tic 104 | 2 |
| 83 | — | — | — | STEPPIN' OUT — Paul Revere & the Raiders, Columbia 43375 | 1 |
| 84 | — | — | — | CARA-LIN — Strangeloves, Bang 508 | 1 |
| 85 | 88 | 96 | 98 | THE WORLD THROUGH A TEAR — Neil Sedaka, RCA Victor 8637 | 4 |
| 86 | 87 | 98 | — | YOU'RE GONNA MAKE ME CRY — O. V. Wright, Back Beat 548 | 5 |
| 87 | — | — | — | WHAT COLOR (Is a Man) — Bobby Vinton, Epic 9846 | 1 |
| 88 | 92 | — | — | MAKE ME YOUR BABY — Barbara Lewis, Atlantic 2300 | 2 |
| 89 | — | — | — | NOT THE LOVIN' KIND — Dino, Desi & Billy, Reprise 0401 | 1 |
| 90 | — | — | — | YOU'RE THE ONE — Vogues, Co & Ce 229 | 1 |
| 91 | 100 | — | — | LITTLE MISS SAD — Five Emprees, Freeport 1001 | 2 |
| 92 | — | — | — | I KNEW YOU WHEN — Billy Joe Royal, Columbia 43390 | 1 |
| 93 | 98 | — | — | A LOVER'S CONCERTO — Toys, DynoVoice 209 | 2 |
| 94 | 94 | — | — | YOU CAN'T BE TRUE, DEAR — Patti Page, Columbia 43345 | 2 |
| 95 | 95 | — | — | ME WITHOUT YOU — Mary Wells, 20th Century-Fox 606 | 2 |
| 96 | 96 | — | — | THE SILENCE — Al Hirt, RCA Victor 8653 | 2 |
| 97 | — | — | — | TOSSING AND TURNING — Ivy League, Cameo 377 | 1 |
| 98 | — | — | — | FOR YOUR LOVE — Sam & Bill, Joda 100 | 1 |
| 99 | — | — | — | THE WAY OF LOVE — Kathy Kirby, Parrot 9775 | 1 |
| 100 | — | — | — | HOW NICE IT IS — Billy Stewart, Chess 1941 | 1 |

## BUBBLING UNDER THE HOT 100

101. A TASTE OF HONEY — Herb Alpert and the Tijuana Brass, A&M 775
102. YOU CAN'T TAKE IT AWAY — Fred Hughes, Vee Jay 703
103. WHEN SOMEBODY LOVES YOU — Frank Sinatra, Reprise 0398
104. (I've Got a Feeling) YOU'RE GONNA BE SORRY — Billy Butler, Okeh 7227
105. LET'S MOVE & GROOVE (Together) — Johnny Nash, Joda 102
106. YESTERDAY — Beatles, Capitol 5498
107. EVERYONE'S GONE TO THE MOON — Jonathan King, Parrot 9774
108. SAY SOMETHING FUNNY — Patty Duke, United Artists 915
109. ACT NATURALLY — Beatles, Capitol 5498
110. IF YOU'VE GOT A HEART — Bobby Goldsboro, United Artists 908
111. MILLIONS OF ROSES — Steve Lawrence, Columbia 43362
112. DRUMS A GO GO — Hollywood Persuaders, Original Sound 50
113. BEHIND THE TEAR — Sonny James, Capitol 5454
114. I'M DOWN — Beatles, Capitol 5476
115. ARE YOU A BOY OR ARE YOU A GIRL — Barbarians, Laurie 3308
116. ROSES & RAINBOWS — Danny Hutton, HBR 447
117. YOU'RE THE REASON — Gerry & the Pacemakers, Laurie 3318
118. FUNNY LITTLE BUTTERFLIES — Patty Duke, United Artists 915
119. SONS OF KATIE ELDER — Johnny Cash, Columbia 43342
120. SUN GLASSES — Skeeter Davis, RCA Victor 8642
121. SINS OF A FAMILY — P. F. Sloan, Dunhill 4007
122. WHENEVER YOU'RE READY — Zombies, Parrot 9786
123. I STILL LOVE YOU — Vejtables, Autumn 15
124. DRUMS A GO GO — Sandy Nelson, Imperial 66137
125. HEY NO WHAT YOU DO TO ME — Guess Who, Scepter 13106
126. ROAD RUNNER — Gants, Liberty 55829
127. LIVIN' IN A HOUSE FULL OF LOVE — David Houston, Epic 9831
128. 1-2-3 — Len Barry, Decca 31827
129. TAKE ME FOR A LITTLE WHILE — Evie Sands, Blue Cat 118
130. I'M SO THANKFUL — Ikettes, Modern 1011
131. HERE COME THE TEARS — Gene Chandler, Constellation 164
132. LOUIE LOUIE — Kingsmen, Wand 143
133. LOVE IS STRANGE — Everly Brothers, Warner Bros. 5649
134. LET HER DANCE — Bobby Fuller Four, Liberty 55812
135. MY LOVE, FORGIVE ME — Ray Charles Singers, Command 4073

Compiled from national retail sales and radio station airplay by the Music Popularity Dept. of Record Market Research, Billboard.

Billboard

For Week Ending September 25, 1965

# HOT 100

★ **STAR performer**—Sides registering greatest proportionate upward progress this week.

(seal) Record Industry Association of America seal of certification as million selling single.

| This Week | 1 Wk. Ago | 2 Wks. Ago | 3 Wks. Ago | TITLE Artist, Label & Number | Weeks On Chart |
|---|---|---|---|---|---|
| 1 | 2 | 3 | 9 | EVE OF DESTRUCTION — Barry McGuire, Dunhill 4009 | 6 |
| ★2 | 7 | 11 | 22 | HANG ON SLOOPY — McCoys, Bang 506 | 7 |
| 3 | 4 | 4 | 7 | YOU WERE ON MY MIND — We Five, A&M 770 | 10 |
| 4 | 5 | 13 | 25 | CATCH US IF YOU CAN — Dave Clark Five, Epic 9833 | 6 |
| 5 | 1 | 1 | 1 | HELP — Beatles, Capitol 5476 (seal) | 8 |
| 6 | 6 | 10 | 15 | THE "IN" CROWD — Ramsey Lewis Trio, Argo 5506 | 9 |
| 7 | 3 | 2 | 2 | LIKE A ROLLING STONE — Bob Dylan, Columbia 43346 | 10 |
| 8 | 8 | 9 | 12 | IT AIN'T ME BABE — Turtles, White Whale 222 | 8 |
| 9 | 10 | 14 | 19 | HEART FULL OF SOUL — Yardbirds, Epic 9823 | 9 |
| ★10 | 14 | 19 | 27 | LAUGH AT ME — Sonny, Atco 6369 | 6 |
| ★11 | 16 | 31 | 51 | YOU'VE GOT YOUR TROUBLES — Fortunes, Press 9773 | 6 |
| ★12 | 26 | 56 | 83 | TREAT HER RIGHT — Roy Head, Back Beat 546 | 4 |
| ★13 | 18 | 26 | 33 | WE GOTTA GET OUT OF THIS PLACE — Animals, MGM 13382 | 7 |
| ★14 | 22 | 32 | 48 | BABY DON'T GO — Sonny & Cher, Reprise 0392 | 6 |
| 15 | 11 | 6 | 4 | UNCHAINED MELODY — Righteous Brothers, Philles 129 | 11 |
| 16 | 9 | 7 | 6 | I GOT YOU BABE — Sonny & Cher, Atco 6359 | 12 |
| ★17 | 28 | 42 | 64 | DO YOU BELIEVE IN MAGIC — Lovin' Spoonful, Kama Sutra 201 | 6 |
| 18 | 13 | 18 | 23 | ACTION — Freddy Cannon, Warner Bros. 5645 | 7 |
| 19 | 15 | 5 | 3 | CALIFORNIA GIRLS — Beach Boys, Capitol 5464 | 10 |
| ★20 | 43 | 61 | 80 | SOME ENCHANTED EVENING — Jay & the Americans, United Artists 919 | 4 |
| ★21 | 32 | 51 | 66 | I'M YOURS — Elvis Presley, RCA Victor 8657 | 5 |
| 22 | 24 | 27 | 30 | AGENT OO-SOUL — Edwin Starr, Ric-Tic 103 | 8 |
| 23 | 17 | 15 | 10 | HOLD ME, THRILL ME, KISS ME — Mel Carter, Imperial 66113 | 14 |
| 24 | 27 | 28 | 39 | SUMMER NIGHTS — Marianne Faithfull, London 8790 | 7 |
| ★25 | 33 | 44 | 58 | I'LL MAKE ALL YOUR DREAMS COME TRUE — Ronnie Dove, Diamond 188 | 5 |
| ★26 | 31 | 55 | 72 | LIAR, LIAR — Castaways, Soma 1433 | 7 |
| 27 | 29 | 30 | 34 | SAD, SAD GIRL — Barbara Mason, Arctic 108 | 8 |
| 28 | 12 | 8 | 8 | PAPA'S GOT A BRAND NEW BAG — James Brown, King 5999 | 11 |
| ★29 | 37 | 49 | 62 | WITH THESE HANDS — Tom Jones, Parrot 9787 | 5 |
| ★30 | 35 | 46 | 57 | RIDE AWAY — Roy Orbison, MGM 13386 | 6 |
| 31 | 20 | 20 | 16 | TRACKS OF MY TEARS — Miracles, Tamla 54118 | 11 |
| ★32 | 42 | 50 | 60 | JUST YOU — Sonny & Cher, Atco 6345 | 5 |
| ★33 | 45 | 57 | 71 | MOHAIR SAM — Charlie Rich, Smash 1993 | 5 |
| ★34 | 59 | 76 | — | KEEP ON DANCING — Gentry's, MGM 13379 | 3 |
| 35 | 21 | 21 | 24 | HOUSTON — Dean Martin, Reprise 0393 | 8 |
| 36 | 38 | 38 | 45 | I'M A HAPPY MAN — Jive Five, United Artists 853 | 7 |
| ★37 | 48 | 58 | 74 | HOME OF THE BRAVE — Jody Miller, Capitol 5483 | 5 |
| 38 | 19 | 12 | 5 | IT'S THE SAME OLD SONG — Four Tops, Motown 1081 | 9 |
| 39 | 23 | 16 | 11 | NOTHING BUT HEARTACHES — Supremes, Motown 1080 | 9 |
| ★40 | 64 | — | — | JUST A LITTLE BIT BETTER — Herman's Hermits, MGM 13398 | 2 |
| 41 | 34 | 35 | 37 | WHO'LL BE THE NEXT IN LINE — Kinks, Reprise 0366 | 7 |
| ★42 | 52 | 64 | 79 | HEARTACHES BY THE NUMBER — Johnny Tillotson, MGM 13376 | 5 |
| 43 | 25 | 22 | 17 | SINCE I LOST MY BABY — Temptations, Gordy 7043 | 10 |
| ★44 | 56 | 72 | — | KANSAS CITY STAR — Roger Miller, Smash 1998 | 3 |
| ★45 | — | — | — | YESTERDAY — Beatles, Capitol 5498 | 1 |
| 46 | 41 | 43 | 47 | IT'S GONNA TAKE A MIRACLE — Royalettes, MGM 13366 | 11 |
| ★47 | 58 | 69 | 85 | AIN'T IT TRUE — Andy Williams, Columbia 43358 | 4 |
| 48 | 39 | 25 | 21 | IN THE MIDNIGHT HOUR — Wilson Pickett, Atlantic 2289 | 12 |
| 49 | 30 | 17 | 13 | DOWN IN THE BOONDOCKS — Billy Joe Royal, Columbia 43305 | 13 |
| 50 | 36 | 39 | 41 | YOU'VE BEEN IN LOVE TOO LONG — Martha & Vandellas, Gordy 7045 | 7 |
| 51 | 53 | 54 | 56 | MOONLIGHT AND ROSES — Vic Dana, Dolton 309 | 8 |
| ★52 | 69 | 80 | — | THE 3rd MAN THEME — Herb Alpert & the Tijuana Brass, A&M 775 | 3 |
| ★53 | 72 | — | — | DAWN OF CORRECTION — Spokesmen, Decca 31884 | 2 |
| ★54 | 68 | 83 | — | MY TOWN, MY GUY AND ME — Lesley Gore, Mercury 72475 | 3 |
| 55 | 50 | 53 | 54 | MY GIRL SLOOPY — Little Caesar & Consuls, Mala 512 | 7 |
| ★56 | 67 | 75 | 88 | I WANT TO (Do Everything for You) — Joe Tex, Dial 4016 | 5 |
| 57 | 57 | 59 | 61 | FIRST I LOOK AT THE PURSE — Contours, Gordy 7044 | 7 |
| 58 | 47 | 47 | 49 | ANNIE FANNY — Kingsmen, Wand 189 | 8 |
| 59 | 60 | 74 | 87 | N-N-NERVOUS — Ian Whitcomb, Tower 155 | 4 |
| ★60 | 88 | 92 | — | MAKE ME YOUR BABY — Barbara Lewis, Atlantic 2300 | 3 |
| 61 | 62 | 62 | 65 | DANGER HEARTBREAK DEAD AHEAD — Marvelettes, Tamla 54120 | 7 |
| 62 | 71 | 90 | — | THERE BUT FOR FORTUNE — Joan Baez, Vanguard 35031 | 3 |
| 63 | 63 | 65 | 77 | HIGH HEEL SNEAKERS — Stevie Wonder, Tamla 54119 | 5 |
| 64 | 65 | 67 | 70 | I NEED YOU — Impressions, ABC-Paramount 10710 | 7 |
| 65 | 66 | 70 | 75 | TWO DIFFERENT WORLDS — Lenny Welch, Kapp 689 | 6 |
| ★66 | 93 | 98 | — | A LOVER'S CONCERTO — Toys, DynoVoice 209 | 3 |
| ★67 | 82 | 97 | — | HUNGRY FOR LOVE — San Remo Golden Strings, Ric-Tic 104 | 3 |
| 68 | 70 | 77 | 90 | RESPECT — Otis Redding, Volt 128 | 4 |
| ★69 | 84 | — | — | CARA-LIN — Strangeloves, Bang 508 | 2 |
| 70 | 77 | 82 | 95 | I LIVE FOR THE SUN — Sunrays, Tower 148 | 4 |
| ★71 | 87 | — | — | WHAT COLOR (Is a Man) — Bobby Vinton, Epic 9846 | 2 |
| ★72 | 90 | — | — | YOU'RE THE ONE — Vogues, Co & Ce 229 | 2 |
| ★73 | 89 | — | — | NOT THE LOVIN' KIND — Dino, Desi & Billy, Reprise 0401 | 2 |
| 74 | 78 | 84 | 99 | THE GIRL FROM PEYTON PLACE — Dickey Lee, TCF-Hall 111 | 4 |
| 75 | 76 | 85 | 97 | THESE HANDS (Small But Mighty) — Bobby Bland, Duke 385 | 5 |
| ★76 | 92 | — | — | I KNEW YOU WHEN — Billy Joe Royal, Columbia 43390 | 2 |
| 77 | 79 | 81 | 86 | HOME OF THE BRAVE — Bonnie & the Treasures, Phi-Dan 5005 | 5 |
| 78 | 83 | — | — | STEPPIN' OUT — Paul Revere & the Raiders, Columbia 43375 | 2 |
| ★79 | — | — | — | EVERYONE'S GONE TO THE MOON — Jonathan King, Parrot 9774 | 1 |
| 80 | 80 | 86 | — | ROUNDABOUT — Connie Francis, MGM 13389 | 3 |
| 81 | 85 | 88 | 96 | THE WORLD THROUGH A TEAR — Neil Sedaka, RCA Victor 8637 | 5 |
| 82 | 91 | 100 | — | LITTLE MISS SAD — Five Emprees, Freeport 1001 | 3 |
| ★83 | — | — | — | ARE YOU A BOY OR ARE YOU A GIRL — Barbarians, Laurie 3308 | 1 |
| ★84 | — | — | — | UNIVERSAL SOLDIER — Donovan, Hickory 1338 | 1 |
| ★85 | — | — | — | EVERYBODY LOVES A CLOWN — Gary Lewis & the Playboys, Liberty 55818 | 1 |
| 86 | 61 | 63 | 68 | COLOURS — Donovan, Hickory 1324 | 7 |
| ★87 | — | — | — | ACT NATURALLY — Beatles, Capitol 5498 | 1 |
| ★88 | — | — | — | FUNNY LITTLE BUTTERFLIES — Patty Duke, United Artists 915 | 1 |
| ★89 | — | — | — | A TASTE OF HONEY — Herb Alpert & the Tijuana Brass, A&M 775 | 1 |
| ★90 | — | — | — | UNIVERSAL SOLDIER — Glen Campbell, Capitol 5504 | 1 |
| 91 | 97 | — | — | TOSSING AND TURNING — Ivy League, Cameo 377 | 2 |
| 92 | — | — | — | IF YOU'VE GOT A HEART — Bobby Goldsboro, United Artists 908 | 1 |
| 93 | — | — | — | 1-2-3 — Len Barry, Decca 31827 | 1 |
| 94 | — | — | — | THE SINS OF A FAMILY — P. F. Sloan, Dunhill 4007 | 1 |
| 95 | 99 | — | — | THE WAY OF LOVE — Kathy Kirby, Parrot 9775 | 2 |
| 96 | 98 | — | — | FOR YOUR LOVE — Sam & Bill, Joda 100 | 2 |
| 97 | 100 | — | — | HOW NICE IT IS — Billy Stewart, Chess 1941 | 2 |
| 98 | — | — | — | ROAD RUNNER — Gants, Liberty 55829 | 1 |
| 99 | — | — | — | YOU CAN'T TAKE IT AWAY — Fred Hughes, Vee Jay 703 | 1 |
| 100 | — | — | — | LET'S MOVE & GROOVE (Together) — Johnny Nash, Joda 102 | 1 |

## HOT 100—A TO Z—*(Publisher-Licensee)*

Act Naturally (Bluebook, BMI) .... 87
Action (Screen Gems-Columbia, BMI) .... 18
Agent OO-Soul (Myto, BMI) .... 22
Ain't It True (Wemar & Claudine, BMI) .... 47
Annie Fanny (Sharrow & Burdette & Flomar, BMI) 58
Are You a Boy or Are You a Girl (Elmwin, BMI) .. 83
Baby, Don't Go (Mother Bertha & Ten East, BMI). 14
California Girls (Sea of Tunes, BMI) .... 19
Cara-lin (Grand Canyon, BMI) .... 69
Catch Us If You Can (Branston, BMI) .... 4
Colours (Southern, ASCAP) .... 86
Danger Heartbreak Dead Ahead (Jobete, BMI) .... 61
Dawn of Correction (Champion & Double Diamond, BMI) .... 53
Do You Believe in Magic (Faithful Virtue, BMI) .. 17
Down in the Boondocks (Lowery, BMI) .... 49
Eve of Destruction (Trousdale, BMI) .... 1
Everybody Loves a Clown (Viva, BMI) .... 85
Everyone's Gone to the Moon (Mainstay, BMI) .. 79
First I Look at the Purse (Jobete, BMI) .... 57
For Your Love (Beechwood, BMI) .... 96
Funny Little Butterflies (Unart, BMI) .... 88
Girl From Peyton Place, The (Screen Gems-Columbia, BMI) .... 74
Hang on Sloopy (Picturetone-Mellin, BMI) .... 2
Heart Full of Soul (Miller, ASCAP) .... 9
Heartaches by the Number (Pamper, BMI) .... 42
Help (Maclen, BMI) .... 5
High Heel Sneakers (Medal, BMI) .... 63
Hold Me, Thrill Me, Kiss Me (Mills, ASCAP) .... 23
Home of the Brave—Bonnie & the Treasures (Screen Gems-Columbia, BMI) .... 77
Home of the Brave—Miller (Screen Gems-Columbia, BMI) .... 37
Houston (Criterion, ASCAP) .... 35
How Nice It Is (Chevis, BMI) .... 97
Hungry for Love (Myto, BMI) .... 67
I Got You Babe (Five-West-Cotillion, BMI) .... 16
I Knew You When (Lowery, BMI) .... 76
I Live for the Sun (Sea of Tunes, BMI) .... 70
I Need You (Chi-Sound, BMI) .... 64
I Want to (Do Everything for You) (Tree, BMI) .... 56
If You've Got a Heart (Unart, BMI) .... 92
I'll Make All Your Dreams Come True (Picturetone, BMI) .... 25
I'm a Happy Man (Unart, BMI) .... 36
I'm Yours (Gladys, ASCAP) .... 21
"In" Crowd, The (American, BMI) .... 6
In the Midnight Hour (Cotillion-East, BMI) .... 48
It Ain't Me Babe (Witmark, ASCAP) .... 8
It's Gonna Take a Miracle (South Mountain, BMI). 46
It's the Same Old Song (Jobete, BMI) .... 38
Just a Little Bit Better (T. M., BMI) .... 40
Just You (Five-West-Cotillion, BMI) .... 32
Kansas City Star (Tree, BMI) .... 44
Keep on Dancing (Arc-Press, BMI) .... 34
Laugh at Me (Five-West-Cotillion, BMI) .... 10
Let's Move & Groove (Together) (And, BMI) ....100
Liar, Liar (Celann, BMI) .... 26
Like a Rolling Stone (Witmark, ASCAP) .... 7
Little Miss Sad (Radford, BMI) .... 82
Lover's Concerto, A (Saturday, BMI) .... 66
Make Me Your Baby (Screen Gems-Columbia, BMI) 60
Mohair Sam (Acclaim, BMI) .... 33
Moonlight and Roses (Daniels, ASCAP) .... 51
My Girl Sloopy (Picturetone-Mellin, BMI) .... 55
My Town, My Guy and Me (Sturossi-Catalog, BMI) 54
N-N-Nervous (Burdette, BMI) .... 59
Not the Lovin' Kind (Criterion, ASCAP) .... 73
Nothing But Heartaches (Jobete, BMI) .... 39
1-2-3 (Champion & Double Diamond, BMI) .... 93
Papa's Got a Brand New Bag (Lois, BMI) .... 28
Respect (East-Time-Redwal, BMI) .... 68
Ride Away (Acuff-Rose, BMI) .... 30
Road Runner (Arc, BMI) .... 98
Roundabout (Leeds, ASCAP) .... 80
Sad, Sad Girl (Stillran-Dandelion, BMI) .... 27
Since I Lost My Baby (Jobete, BMI) ....43
Sins of a Family, The (Trousdale, BMI) .... 94
Some Enchanted Evening (Williamson, ASCAP) .. 20
Steppin' Out (Daywin, BMI) .... 78
Summer Nights (Sea-Lark, BMI) .... 24
Taste of Honey, A (Songfest, ASCAP) .... 89
There But for Fortune (Appleseed, BMI) .... 62
These Hands (Small But Mighty) (Don, BMI) .... 75
3rd Man Theme, The (Chappell, ASCAP) .... 52
Tossing and Turning (Southern, ASCAP) .... 91
Tracks of My Tears (Jobete, BMI) .... 31
Treat Her Right (Don, BMI) .... 12
Two Different Worlds (Princess, ASCAP) .... 65
Unchained Melody (Frank, ASCAP) .... 15
Universal Soldier—Campbell (Woodmere, BMI) .. 90
Universal Soldier—Donovan (Woodmere, BMI) .... 84
Way of Love, The (Chappell, ASCAP) .... 95
We Gotta Get Out of This Place (Screen Gems-Columbia, BMI) .... 13
What Color (Is a Man) (Screen Gems-Columbia, BMI) .... 71
Who'll Be the Next in Line (Jay Boy, BMI) .... 41
With These Hands (Bloom, ASCAP) .... 29
World Through a Tear, The (Bregman, Vocco & Conn, ASCAP) .... 81
Yesterday (Maclen, BMI) .... 45
You Can't Take It Away (Customa, BMI) .... 99
You Were on My Mind (Witmark, ASCAP) .... 3
You're the One (Leeds, ASCAP) .... 72
You've Been in Love Too Long (Jobete, BMI) .... 50
You've Got Your Troubles (Mills, ASCAP) .... 11

## BUBBLING UNDER THE HOT 100

101. A LIFETIME OF LONELINESS ....Jackie DeShannon, Imperial 66132
102. WHEN SOMEBODY LOVES YOU ....Frank Sinatra, Reprise 0398
103. (I've Got a Feeling) YOU'RE GONNA BE SORRY ..Billy Butler, Okeh 7227
104. POSITIVELY 4TH STREET ....Bob Dylan, Columbia 43389
105. ROSES AND RAINBOWS ....Danny Hutton, HBR 447
106. LOUIE LOUIE ....Kingsmen, Wand 143
107. SAY SOMETHING FUNNY ....Patty Duke, United Artists 915
108. YOU CAN'T BE TRUE, DEAR ....Patti Page, Columbia 43345
109. DRUMS A GO-GO ....Hollywood Persuaders, Original Sound 50
110. MILLIONS OF ROSES ....Steve Lawrence, Columbia 43362
111. YOU'RE GONNA MAKE ME CRY ....O. V. Wright, Back Beat 548
112. SOUL HEAVEN ....Dixie Drifter, Roulette 4641
113. ME WITHOUT YOU ....Mary Wells, 20th Century-Fox 606
114. SILENCE ....Al Hirt, RCA Victor 8653
115. I'M SO THANKFUL ....Ikettes, Modern 1011
116. JUST YESTERDAY ....Jack Jones, Kapp 699
117. LIVIN' IN A HOUSE FULL OF LOVE ....David Houston, Epic 9831
118. WHENEVER YOU'RE READY ....Zombies, Parrot 9786
119. RUN, BABY RUN ....Newbeats, Hickory 1332
120. I STILL LOVE YOU ....Vejtables, Autumn 15
121. THE SONS OF KATIE ELDER ....Johnny Cash, Columbia 43342
122. SECRETLY ....Lettermen, Capitol 5499
123. LOOKING WITH ME EYES ....Dionne Warwick, Scepter 12111
124. HERE COME THE TEARS ....Gene Chandler, Constellation 164
125. TAKE ME FOR A LITTLE WHILE ....Evie Sands, Blue Cat 118
126. RUN LIKE THE DEVIL ....Bobby Vee, Liberty 55828
127. THE SPIDER SONG ....Kids Next Door, 4 Corners 129
128. GOT TO FIND A WAY ....Harrold Burrage, M-Pac 7225
129. FORGIVE ME ....Al Martino, Capitol 5506
130. MY LOVE, FORGIVE ME ....Ray Charles Singers, Command 4073
131. TAKE ME IN YOUR ARMS ....Kim Weston, Gordy 7046
132. THE CINCINNATI KID ....Ray Charles, ABC-Paramount 10720
133. YOU CAN CRY ON MY SHOULDER ....Brenda Holloway, Tamla 54121
134. LET'S HANG ON! ....4 Seasons, Philips 40317
135. HONKY TONK '65 ....Lonnie Mack, Fraternity 951

Compiled from national retail sales and radio station airplay by the Music Popularity Dept. of Record Market Research, Billboard.

# Billboard HOT 100

**For Week Ending October 2, 1965**

★ STAR performer—Sides registering greatest proportionate upward progress this week.

Record Industry Association of America seal of certification as million selling single.

| This Week | 1 Wk. Ago | 2 Wks. Ago | TITLE Artist, Label & Number | Weeks On Chart |
|---|---|---|---|---|
| 1 | 2 | 7 11 | HANG ON SLOOPY — McCoys, Bang 506 | 8 |
| 2 | 1 | 2 3 | EVE OF DESTRUCTION — Barry McGuire, Dunhill 4009 | 7 |
| 3 | 45 | — — | YESTERDAY — Beatles, Capitol 5498 | 2 |
| 4 | 4 | 5 13 | CATCH US IF YOU CAN — Dave Clark Five, Epic 9833 | 7 |
| 5 | 3 | 4 4 | YOU WERE ON MY MIND — We Five, A&M 770 | 11 |
| 6 | 6 | 6 10 | THE "IN" CROWD — Ramsey Lewis Trio, Argo 5506 | 10 |
| 7 | 12 | 26 56 | TREAT HER RIGHT — Roy Head, Back Beat 546 | 5 |
| 8 | 11 | 16 31 | YOU'VE GOT YOUR TROUBLES — Fortunes, Press 9773 | 7 |
| 9 | 14 | 22 32 | BABY DON'T GO — Sonny & Cher, Reprise 0392 | 7 |
| 10 | 10 | 14 19 | LAUGH AT ME — Sonny, Atco 6369 | 7 |
| 11 | 5 | 1 1 | HELP — Beatles, Capitol 5476 | 9 |
| 12 | 17 | 28 42 | DO YOU BELIEVE IN MAGIC — Lovin' Spoonful, Kama Sutra 201 | 7 |
| 13 | 13 | 18 26 | WE GOTTA GET OUT OF THIS PLACE — Animals, MGM 13382 | 8 |
| 14 | 9 | 10 14 | HEART FULL OF SOUL — Yardbirds, Epic 9823 | 10 |
| 15 | 20 | 43 61 | SOME ENCHANTED EVENING — Jay & the Americans, United Artists 919 | 5 |
| 16 | 21 | 32 51 | I'M YOURS — Elvis Presley, RCA Victor 8657 | 6 |
| 17 | 8 | 8 9 | IT AIN'T ME BABE — Turtles, White Whale 222 | 9 |
| 18 | 7 | 3 2 | LIKE A ROLLING STONE — Bob Dylan, Columbia 43346 | 11 |
| 19 | 34 | 59 76 | KEEP ON DANCING — Gentry's, MGM 13379 | 4 |
| 20 | 26 | 31 55 | LIAR, LIAR — Castaways, Soma 1433 | 8 |
| 21 | 22 | 24 27 | AGENT OO-SOUL — Edwin Starr, Ric-Tic 103 | 9 |
| 22 | 25 | 33 44 | I'LL MAKE ALL YOUR DREAMS COME TRUE — Ronnie Dove, Diamond 188 | 6 |
| 23 | 15 | 11 6 | UNCHAINED MELODY — Righteous Brothers, Philles 129 | 12 |
| 24 | 32 | 42 50 | JUST YOU — Sonny & Cher, Atco 6345 | 6 |
| 25 | 40 | 64 — | JUST A LITTLE BIT BETTER — Herman's Hermits, MGM 13398 | 3 |
| 26 | 30 | 35 46 | RIDE AWAY — Roy Orbison, MGM 13386 | 7 |
| 27 | 29 | 37 49 | WITH THESE HANDS — Tom Jones, Parrot 9787 | 6 |
| 28 | 33 | 45 57 | MOHAIR SAM — Charlie Rich, Smash 1993 | 6 |
| 29 | 37 | 48 58 | HOME OF THE BRAVE — Jody Miller, Capitol 5483 | 6 |
| 30 | 16 | 9 7 | I GOT YOU BABE — Sonny & Cher, Atco 6359 | 13 |
| 31 | 18 | 13 18 | ACTION — Freddy Cannon, Warner Bros. 5645 | 8 |
| 32 | 19 | 15 5 | CALIFORNIA GIRLS — Beach Boys, Capitol 5464 | 11 |
| 33 | 44 | 56 72 | KANSAS CITY STAR — Roger Miller, Smash 1998 | 4 |
| 34 | 24 | 27 28 | SUMMER NIGHTS — Marianne Faithfull, London 8790 | 8 |
| 35 | 27 | 29 30 | SAD, SAD GIRL — Barbara Mason, Arctic 108 | 9 |
| 36 | 42 | 52 64 | HEARTACHES BY THE NUMBER — Johnny Tillotson, MGM 13376 | 6 |
| 37 | 28 | 12 8 | PAPA'S GOT A BRAND NEW BAG — James Brown, King 5999 | 12 |
| 38 | 66 | 93 98 | A LOVER'S CONCERTO — Toys, DynoVoice 209 | 4 |
| 39 | 23 | 17 15 | HOLD ME, THRILL ME, KISS ME — Mel Carter, Imperial 66113 | 15 |
| 40 | 35 | 21 21 | HOUSTON — Dean Martin, Reprise 0393 | 9 |
| 41 | 72 | 90 — | YOU'RE THE ONE — Vogues, Co & Ce 229 | 3 |
| 42 | 85 | — — | EVERYBODY LOVES A CLOWN — Gary Lewis & the Playboys, Liberty 55818 | 2 |
| 43 | 53 | 72 — | DAWN OF CORRECTION — Spokesmen, Decca 31884 | 3 |
| 44 | 54 | 68 83 | MY TOWN, MY GUY AND ME — Lesley Gore, Mercury 72475 | 4 |
| 45 | 47 | 58 69 | AIN'T IT TRUE — Andy Williams, Columbia 43358 | 5 |
| 46 | 31 | 20 20 | TRACKS OF MY TEARS — Miracles, Tamla 54118 | 12 |
| 47 | 52 | 69 80 | THE 3rd MAN THEME — Herb Alpert & the Tijuana Brass, A&M 775 | 4 |
| 48 | 56 | 67 75 | I WANT TO (Do Everything for You) — Joe Tex, Dial 4016 | 6 |
| 49 | 60 | 88 92 | MAKE ME YOUR BABY — Barbara Lewis, Atlantic 2300 | 4 |
| 50 | 67 | 82 97 | HUNGRY FOR LOVE — San Remo Golden Strings, Ric-Tic 104 | 4 |
| 51 | 71 | 87 — | WHAT COLOR (Is a Man) — Bobby Vinton, Epic 9846 | 3 |
| 52 | 36 | 38 38 | I'M A HAPPY MAN — Jive Five, United Artists 853 | 8 |
| 53 | 62 | 71 90 | THERE BUT FOR FORTUNE — Joan Baez, Vanguard 35031 | 4 |
| 54 | 73 | 89 — | NOT THE LOVIN' KIND — Dino, Desi & Billy, Reprise 0401 | 3 |
| 55 | 76 | 92 — | I KNEW YOU WHEN — Billy Joe Royal, Columbia 43390 | 3 |
| 56 | 69 | 84 — | CARA-LIN — Strangeloves, Bang 508 | 3 |
| 57 | 55 | 50 53 | MY GIRL SLOOPY — Little Caesar & Consuls, Mala 512 | 8 |
| 58 | 51 | 53 54 | MOONLIGHT AND ROSES — Vic Dana, Dolton 309 | 9 |
| 59 | 63 | 63 65 | HIGH HEEL SNEAKERS — Stevie Wonder, Tamla 54119 | 6 |
| 60 | 70 | 77 82 | I LIVE FOR THE SUN — Sunrays, Tower 148 | 5 |
| 61 | 65 | 66 70 | TWO DIFFERENT WORLDS — Lenny Welch, Kapp 689 | 7 |
| 62 | 68 | 70 77 | RESPECT — Otis Redding, Volt 128 | 5 |
| 63 | 78 | 83 — | STEPPIN' OUT — Paul Revere & the Raiders, Columbia 43375 | 3 |
| 64 | 79 | — — | EVERYONE'S GONE TO THE MOON — Jonathan King, Parrot 9774 | 2 |
| 65 | 75 | 76 85 | THESE HANDS (Small But Mighty) — Bobby Bland, Duke 385 | 6 |
| 66 | — | — — | POSITIVELY 4TH STREET — Bob Dylan, Columbia 43389 | 1 |
| 67 | 83 | — — | ARE YOU A BOY OR ARE YOU A GIRL — Barbarians, Laurie 3308 | 2 |
| 68 | 59 | 60 74 | N-N-NERVOUS — Ian Whitcomb, Tower 155 | 5 |
| 69 | 84 | — — | UNIVERSAL SOLDIER — Donovan, Hickory 1338 | 2 |
| 70 | 57 | 57 59 | FIRST I LOOK AT THE PURSE — Contours, Gordy 7044 | 8 |
| 71 | 90 | — — | UNIVERSAL SOLDIER — Glen Campbell, Capitol 5504 | 2 |
| 72 | 87 | — — | ACT NATURALLY — Beatles, Capitol 5498 | 2 |
| 73 | 74 | 78 84 | THE GIRL FROM PEYTON PLACE — Dickey Lee, TCF-Hall 111 | 4 |
| 74 | 89 | — — | A TASTE OF HONEY — Herb Alpert & the Tijuana Brass, A&M 775 | 2 |
| 75 | 61 | 62 62 | DANGER HEARTBREAK DEAD AHEAD — Marvelettes, Tamla 54120 | 8 |
| 76 | — | — — | RESCUE ME — Fontella Bass, Checker 1120 | 1 |
| 77 | 93 | — — | 1-2-3 — Len Barry, Decca 31827 | 2 |
| 78 | 92 | — — | IF YOU'VE GOT A HEART — Bobby Goldsboro, United Artists 908 | 2 |
| 79 | 82 | 91 100 | LITTLE MISS SAD — Five Emprees, Freeport 1001 | 4 |
| 80 | — | — — | TAKE ME IN YOUR ARMS — Kim Weston, Gordy 7046 | 1 |
| 81 | 81 | 85 88 | THE WORLD THROUGH A TEAR — Neil Sedaka, RCA Victor 8637 | 6 |
| 82 | — | — — | SAY SOMETHING FUNNY — Patty Duke, United Artists 915 | 1 |
| 83 | — | — — | I MISS YOU SO — Little Anthony & the Imperials, DCP 1149 | 1 |
| 84 | — | — — | A LIFETIME OF LONELINESS — Jackie DeShannon, Imperial 66132 | 1 |
| 85 | 91 | 97 — | TOSSING AND TURNING — Ivy League, Cameo 377 | 3 |
| 86 | 88 | — — | FUNNY LITTLE BUTTERFLIES — Patty Duke, United Artists 915 | 2 |
| 87 | 94 | — — | THE SINS OF A FAMILY — P. F. Sloan, Dunhill 4007 | 2 |
| 88 | 95 | 99 — | THE WAY OF LOVE — Kathy Kirby, Parrot 9775 | 3 |
| 89 | 80 | 80 86 | ROUNDABOUT — Connie Francis, MGM 13389 | 4 |
| 90 | — | — — | RUN, BABY RUN — Newbeats, Hickory 1332 | 1 |
| 91 | — | — — | JUST ONE KISS FROM YOU — Impressions, ABC-Paramount 10725 | 1 |
| 92 | — | — — | WHERE HAVE ALL THE FLOWERS GONE — Johnny Rivers, Imperial 66133 | 1 |
| 93 | — | — — | SECRETLY — Lettermen, Capitol 5499 | 1 |
| 94 | 98 | — — | ROAD RUNNER — Gants, Liberty 55829 | 2 |
| 95 | 96 | 98 — | FOR YOUR LOVE — Sam & Bill, Joda 100 | 3 |
| 96 | 99 | — — | YOU CAN'T TAKE IT AWAY — Fred Hughes, Vee Jay 703 | 2 |
| 97 | — | — — | LOOKING WITH MY EYES — Dionne Warwick, Scepter 12111 | 1 |
| 98 | 100 | — — | LET'S MOVE & GROOVE (Together) — Johnny Nash, Joda 102 | 2 |
| 99 | — | — — | HE TOUCHED ME — Barbra Streisand, Columbia 43403 | 1 |
| 100 | — | — — | THE ORGAN GRINDER'S SWING — Jimmy Smith, Verve 10363 | 1 |

## BUBBLING UNDER THE HOT 100

101. CLEO'S BACK — Jr. Walker & the All Stars, Soul 35013
102. WHEN SOMEBODY LOVES YOU — Frank Sinatra, Reprise 0398
103. ROSES AND RAINBOWS — Danny Hutton, HBR 447
104. HERE COME THE TEARS — Gene Chandler, Constellation 164
105. JUST YESTERDAY — Jack Jones, Kapp 699
106. MILLIONS OF ROSES — Steve Lawrence, Columbia 43362
107. (I've Got a Feeling) YOU'RE GONNA BE SORRY — Billy Butler, Okeh 7222
108. HOW NICE IT IS — Billy Stewart, Chess 1941
109. I STILL LOVE YOU — Vejtables, Autumn 15
110. ME WITHOUT YOU — Mary Wells, 20th Century-Fox 606
111. LET'S HANG ON — 4 Seasons, Philips 40317
112. LOUIE LOUIE — Kingsmen, Wand 143
113. CHAPEL IN THE MOONLIGHT — Bachelors, London 9793
114. RING DANG DOO — Sam the Sham & the Pharaohs, MGM 13397
115. HAPPY, HAPPY BIRTHDAY BABY — Dolly Parton, Monument 897
116. I FOUND A GIRL — Jan & Dean, Liberty 55833
117. EARLY MORNING RAIN — Peter, Paul & Mary, Warner Bros. 5659
118. FORGIVE ME — Al Martino, Capitol 5506
119. YOU CAN CRY ON MY SHOULDER — Brenda Holloway, Tamla 54121
120. I BELIEVE I'LL LOVE ON — Jackie Wilson, Brunswick 55283
121. COME BACK TO ME MY LOVE — Robert Goulet, Columbia 43394
122. LIVIN' IN A HOUSE FULL OF LOVE — David Houston, Epic 9831
123. SEND A LETTER TO ME — Freddie & the Dreamers, Tower 163
124. RUN LIKE THE DEVIL — Bobby Vee, Liberty 55828
125. RIGHT NOW AND NOT LATER — Shangri-Las, Red Bird 036
126. MY LOVE, FORGIVE ME — Ray Charles Singers, Command 4073
127. THE SPIDER SONG — Kids Next Door, 4 Corners 129
128. CLOSE YOUR EYES — 3 Degrees, Swan 4224
129. HONKY TONK '65 — Lonnie Mack, Fraternity 951
130. THE CINCINNATI KID — Ray Charles, ABC-Paramount 10720
131. STAND BY ME — Earl Grant, Decca 25674
132. FUNNY THING ABOUT IT — Nancy Ames, Epic 9845
133. I'LL KEEP ON TRYING — Walter Jackson, Okeh 7229
134. ONE HAS MY NAME — Barry Young, Dot 16756
135. TWEETIE PIE — Dave (Baby) Cortez, Roulette 4628

Compiled from national retail sales and radio station airplay by the Music Popularity Dept. of Record Market Research, Billboard.

# Billboard HOT 100

**For Week Ending October 9, 1965**

★ STAR performer—Sides registering greatest proportionate upward progress this week.

Record Industry Association of America seal of certification as million selling single.

| This Week | 1 Wk. Ago | 2 Wks. Ago | 3 Wks. Ago | TITLE, Artist, Label & Number | Weeks On Chart |
|---|---|---|---|---|---|
| 1 | 3 | 45 | — | YESTERDAY — Beatles, Capitol 5498 | 3 |
| 2 | 1 | 2 | 7 | HANG ON SLOOPY — McCoys, Bang 506 | 9 |
| ★3 | 7 | 12 | 26 | TREAT HER RIGHT — Roy Head, Back Beat 546 | 6 |
| 4 | 2 | 1 | 2 | EVE OF DESTRUCTION — Barry McGuire, Dunhill 4009 | 8 |
| 5 | 6 | 6 | 6 | THE "IN" CROWD — Ramsey Lewis Trio, Argo 5506 | 11 |
| 6 | 4 | 4 | 5 | CATCH US IF YOU CAN — Dave Clark Five, Epic 9833 | 8 |
| 7 | 8 | 11 | 16 | YOU'VE GOT YOUR TROUBLES — Fortunes, Press 9773 | 8 |
| 8 | 9 | 14 | 22 | BABY DON'T GO — Sonny & Cher, Reprise 0392 | 8 |
| 9 | 5 | 3 | 4 | YOU WERE ON MY MIND — We Five, A&M 770 | 12 |
| 10 | 12 | 17 | 28 | DO YOU BELIEVE IN MAGIC — Lovin' Spoonful, Kama Sutra 201 | 8 |
| 11 | 16 | 21 | 32 | I'M YOURS — Elvis Presley, RCA Victor 8657 | 7 |
| 12 | 25 | 40 | 64 | JUST A LITTLE BIT BETTER — Herman's Hermits, MGM 13398 | 4 |
| 13 | 15 | 20 | 43 | SOME ENCHANTED EVENING — Jay & the Americans, United Artists 919 | 6 |
| 14 | 19 | 34 | 59 | KEEP ON DANCING — Gentry's, MGM 13379 | 5 |
| 15 | 11 | 5 | 1 | HELP — Beatles, Capitol 5476 | 10 |
| 16 | 10 | 10 | 14 | LAUGH AT ME — Sonny, Atco 6369 | 8 |
| 17 | 13 | 13 | 18 | WE GOTTA GET OUT OF THIS PLACE — Animals, MGM 13382 | 9 |
| 18 | 20 | 26 | 31 | LIAR, LIAR — Castaways, Soma 1433 | 9 |
| 19 | 38 | 66 | 93 | A LOVER'S CONCERTO — Toys, DynoVoice 209 | 5 |
| 20 | 24 | 32 | 42 | JUST YOU — Sonny & Cher, Atco 6345 | 7 |
| 21 | 22 | 25 | 33 | I'LL MAKE ALL YOUR DREAMS COME TRUE — Ronnie Dove, Diamond 188 | 7 |
| 22 | 41 | 72 | 90 | YOU'RE THE ONE — Vogues, Co & Ce 229 | 4 |
| 23 | 28 | 33 | 45 | MOHAIR SAM — Charlie Rich, Smash 1993 | 7 |
| ★24 | 42 | 85 | — | EVERYBODY LOVES A CLOWN — Gary Lewis & the Playboys, Liberty 55818 | 3 |
| 25 | 26 | 30 | 35 | RIDE AWAY — Roy Orbison, MGM 13386 | 8 |
| 26 | 14 | 9 | 10 | HEART FULL OF SOUL — Yardbirds, Epic 9823 | 11 |
| 27 | 27 | 29 | 37 | WITH THESE HANDS — Tom Jones, Parrot 9787 | 7 |
| 28 | 29 | 37 | 48 | HOME OF THE BRAVE — Jody Miller, Capitol 5483 | 7 |
| 29 | 17 | 8 | 8 | IT AIN'T ME BABE — Turtles, White Whale 222 | 10 |
| 30 | 21 | 22 | 24 | AGENT OO-SOUL — Edwin Starr, Ric-Tic 103 | 10 |
| 31 | 33 | 44 | 56 | KANSAS CITY STAR — Roger Miller, Smash 1998 | 5 |
| ★32 | 44 | 54 | 68 | MY TOWN, MY GUY AND ME — Lesley Gore, Mercury 72475 | 5 |
| 33 | 18 | 7 | 3 | LIKE A ROLLING STONE — Bob Dylan, Columbia 43346 | 12 |
| ★34 | 66 | — | — | POSITIVELY 4TH STREET — Bob Dylan, Columbia 43389 | 2 |
| 35 | 36 | 42 | 52 | HEARTACHES BY THE NUMBER — Johnny Tillotson, MGM 13376 | 7 |
| ★36 | 55 | 76 | 92 | I KNEW YOU WHEN — Billy Joe Royal, Columbia 43390 | 4 |
| 37 | 49 | 60 | 88 | MAKE ME YOUR BABY — Barbara Lewis, Atlantic 2300 | 5 |
| 38 | 23 | 15 | 11 | UNCHAINED MELODY — Righteous Brothers, Philles 129 | 13 |
| 39 | 43 | 53 | 72 | DAWN OF CORRECTION — Spokesmen, Decca 31844 | 4 |
| 40 | 50 | 67 | 82 | HUNGRY FOR LOVE — San Remo Golden Strings, Ric-Tic 104 | 5 |
| 41 | 30 | 16 | 9 | I GOT YOU BABE — Sonny & Cher, Atco 6359 | 14 |
| 42 | 45 | 47 | 58 | AIN'T IT TRUE — Andy Williams, Columbia 43358 | 6 |
| 43 | 54 | 73 | 89 | NOT THE LOVIN' KIND — Dino, Desi & Billy, Reprise 0401 | 4 |
| 44 | 51 | 71 | 87 | WHAT COLOR (Is a Man) — Bobby Vinton, Epic 9846 | 4 |
| 45 | 74 | 89 | — | A TASTE OF HONEY — Herb Alpert & the Tijuana Brass, A&M 775 | 2 |
| 46 | 48 | 56 | 67 | I WANT TO (Do Everything for You) — Joe Tex, Dial 4016 | 7 |
| 47 | 47 | 52 | 69 | THE 3rd MAN THEME — Herb Alpert & the Tijuana Brass, A&M 775 | 5 |
| 48 | 31 | 18 | 13 | ACTION — Freddy Cannon, Warner Bros. 5645 | 9 |
| 49 | 37 | 28 | 12 | PAPA'S GOT A BRAND NEW BAG — James Brown, King 5999 | 13 |
| 50 | 53 | 62 | 71 | THERE BUT FOR FORTUNE — Joan Baez, Vanguard 35031 | 5 |
| 51 | 72 | 87 | — | ACT NATURALLY — Beatles, Capitol 5498 | 3 |
| 52 | 64 | 79 | — | EVERYONE'S GONE TO THE MOON — Jonathan King, Parrot 9774 | 3 |
| 53 | 56 | 69 | 84 | CARA-LIN — Strangeloves, Bang 508 | 4 |
| 54 | 34 | 24 | 27 | SUMMER NIGHTS — Marianne Faithfull, London 9790 | 9 |
| 55 | 67 | 83 | — | ARE YOU A BOY OR ARE YOU A GIRL — Barbarians, Laurie 3308 | 3 |
| 56 | 62 | 68 | 70 | RESPECT — Otis Redding, Volt 128 | 6 |
| 57 | 63 | 78 | 83 | STEPPIN' OUT — Paul Revere & the Raiders, Columbia 43375 | 4 |
| 58 | 71 | 90 | — | UNIVERSAL SOLDIER — Glen Campbell, Capitol 5504 | 3 |
| 59 | 69 | 84 | — | UNIVERSAL SOLDIER — Donovan, Nickory 1338 | 3 |
| 60 | 60 | 70 | 77 | I LIVE FOR THE SUN — Sunrays, Tower 148 | 6 |
| 61 | 77 | 93 | — | 1-2-3 — Len Barry, Decca 31827 | 3 |
| 62 | 76 | — | — | RESCUE ME — Fontella Bass, Checker 1120 | 2 |
| 63 | 65 | 75 | 76 | THESE HANDS (Small But Mighty) — Bobby Bland, Duke 385 | 7 |
| ★64 | — | — | — | GET OFF OF MY CLOUD — Rolling Stones, London 9792 | 1 |
| ★65 | 80 | — | — | TAKE ME IN YOUR ARMS — Kim Weston, Gordy 7046 | 2 |
| ★66 | 82 | — | — | SAY SOMETHING FUNNY — Patty Duke, United Artists 915 | 2 |
| 67 | 83 | — | — | I MISS YOU SO — Little Anthony & the Imperials, DCP 1149 | 2 |
| ★68 | — | — | — | BUT YOU'RE MINE — Sonny & Cher, Atco 6381 | 1 |
| 69 | 61 | 65 | 66 | TWO DIFFERENT WORLDS — Lenny Welch, Kapp 689 | 8 |
| 70 | 59 | 63 | 63 | HIGH HEEL SNEAKERS — Stevie Wonder, Tamla 54119 | 7 |
| 71 | — | — | — | AIN'T THAT PECULIAR — Marvin Gaye, Tamla 54122 | 1 |
| 72 | — | — | — | LET'S HANG ON — 4 Seasons, Philips 40317 | 1 |
| 73 | 90 | — | — | RUN, BABY RUN — Newbeats, Hickory 1332 | 2 |
| 74 | 79 | 82 | 91 | LITTLE MISS SAD — Five Emprees, Freeport 1001 | 4 |
| 75 | 78 | 92 | — | IF YOU'VE GOT A HEART — Bobby Goldsboro, United Artists 908 | 3 |
| 76 | 84 | — | — | A LIFETIME OF LONELINESS — Jackie DeShannon, Imperial 66132 | 2 |
| 77 | 92 | — | — | WHERE HAVE ALL THE FLOWERS GONE — Johnny Rivers, Imperial 66133 | 2 |
| 78 | 93 | — | — | SECRETLY — Lettermen, Capitol 5499 | 2 |
| 79 | 91 | — | — | JUST ONE KISS FROM YOU — Impressions, ABC-Paramount 10725 | 2 |
| 80 | 81 | 81 | 85 | THE WORLD THROUGH A TEAR — Neil Sedaka, RCA Victor 8637 | 7 |
| 81 | 73 | 74 | 78 | THE GIRL FROM PEYTON PLACE — Dickey Lee, TCF-Hall 111 | 6 |
| 82 | 86 | 88 | — | FUNNY LITTLE BUTTERFLIES — Patty Duke, United Artists 915 | 3 |
| 83 | 85 | 91 | 97 | TOSSING AND TURNING — Ivy League, Cameo 377 | 4 |
| 84 | 94 | 98 | — | ROAD RUNNER — Gants, Liberty 55829 | 3 |
| 85 | — | — | — | ROUND EVERY CORNER — Petula Clark, Warner Bros. 5661 | 1 |
| 86 | 97 | — | — | LOOKING WITH MY EYES — Dionne Warwick, Scepter 12111 | 2 |
| 87 | — | — | — | RING DANG DOO — Sam the Sham and the Pharaohs, MGM 13397 | 1 |
| 88 | — | — | — | CHAPEL IN THE MOONLIGHT — Bachelors, London 9793 | 1 |
| 89 | — | — | — | DON'T TALK TO STRANGERS — Beau Brummels, Autumn 20 | 1 |
| 90 | — | — | — | JUST YESTERDAY — Jack Jones, Kapp 699 | 1 |
| 91 | — | — | — | CLEO'S BACK — Jr. Walker and the All Stars, Soul 35013 | 1 |
| 92 | 100 | — | — | THE ORGAN GRINDER'S SWING — Jimmy Smith, Verve 10363 | 2 |
| 93 | — | — | — | I'M SO THANKFUL — The Ikettes, Modern 1011 | 1 |
| 94 | 99 | — | — | HE TOUCHED ME — Barbra Streisand, Columbia 43403 | 2 |
| 95 | — | — | — | MY GIRL HAS GONE — Miracles, Tamla 54123 | 1 |
| 96 | 96 | 99 | — | YOU CAN'T TAKE IT AWAY — Fred Hughes, Vee Jay 703 | 3 |
| 97 | 98 | 100 | — | LET'S MOVE & GROOVE (Together) — Johnny Nash, Joda 102 | 3 |
| 98 | — | — | — | EARLY MORNING RAIN — Peter, Paul & Mary, Warner Bros. 5659 | 1 |
| 99 | — | — | — | RIGHT NOW AND NOT LATER — Shangri-Las, Red Bird 036 | 1 |
| 100 | — | — | — | RUSTY BELLS — Brenda Lee, Decca 31849 | 1 |

## BUBBLING UNDER THE HOT 100

101. I FOUND A GIRL — Jan & Dean, Liberty 55833
102. HERE COME THE TEARS — Gene Chandler, Constellation 164
103. ROSES AND RAINBOWS — Danny Hutton, HBR 447
104. YOU'VE GOT TO HIDE YOUR LOVE AWAY — The Silkie, Fontana 1525
105. HOW NICE IT IS — Billy Stewart, Chess 1941
106. SINS OF A FAMILY — P.F. Sloan, Dunhill 4014
107. (I've Got a Feeling) YOU'RE GONNA BE SORRY — Bobby Butler, Okeh 7227
108. ME WITHOUT YOU — Mary Wells, 20th Century-Fox 606
109. I STILL LOVE YOU — Vejtables, Autumn 15
110. FOR YOUR LOVE — Sam & Bill, Joda 109
111. WAY OF LOVE — Kathy Kirby, Parrot 9773
112. STAND BY ME — Earl Grant, Decca 25674
113. FORGIVE ME — Al Martino, Capitol 5506
114. THINK — Jimmy McCracklin, Imperial 66129
115. HAPPY HAPPY BIRTHDAY BABY — Dolly Parton, Monument 897
116. YOU CAN CRY ON MY SHOULDER — Brenda Holloway, Tamla 54121
117. I BELIEVE I'LL LOVE ON — Jackie Wilson, Brunswick 55283
118. MISTY — Vibrations, Okeh 7230
119. HONKY TONK '65 — Lonnie Mack, Fraternity 951
120. CINCINNATI KID — Ray Charles, ABC-Paramount 10720
121. WE DIDN'T ASK TO BE BROUGHT HERE — Bobby Darin, Atlantic 2305
122. SINNER MAN — Trini Lopez, Reprise 0405
123. WORK, WORK, WORK — Lee Dorsey, Amy 929
124. MY LOVE FORGIVE ME — Ray Charles Singers, Command 4073
125. SPIDER SONG — Kids Next Door, 4 Corners 129
126. CLOSE YOUR EYES — 3 Degrees, Swan 4224
127. FUNNY THING ABOUT IT — Nancy Ames, Epic 9845
128. I'LL KEEP ON TRYING — Walter Jackson, Okeh 7227
129. AUTUMN LEAVES 1965 — Roger Williams, Kapp 700
130. MAKE IT EASY ON YOURSELF — Walker Bros., Smash 3000
131. ONLY A FOOL BREAKS HIS OWN HEART — Arthur Prysock, Old Town 1185
132. ONE HAS MY NAME — Barry Young, Dot 16756
133. MARK — Unit Four Plus Two, London 9770
134. FOR YOUR LOVE — Righteous Brothers, Moonglow 243
135. PIED PIPER — Changin' Times, Philips 40320

# Billboard HOT 100

For Week Ending October 16, 1965

★ STAR performer—Sides registering greatest proportionate upward progress this week.

Record Industry Association of America seal of certification as million selling single.

| This Week | Wk. 1 Ago | Wk. 2 Ago | Wk. 3 Ago | TITLE Artist, Label & Number | Weeks On Chart |
|---|---|---|---|---|---|
| 1 | 1 | 3 | 45 | YESTERDAY — Beatles, Capitol 5498 | 4 |
| 2 | 3 | 7 | 12 | TREAT HER RIGHT — Roy Head, Back Beat 546 | 7 |
| 3 | 2 | 1 | 2 | HANG ON SLOOPY — McCoys, Bang 506 | 10 |
| 4 | 19 | 38 | 66 | A LOVER'S CONCERTO — Toys, DynoVoice 209 | 6 |
| 5 | 14 | 19 | 34 | KEEP ON DANCING — Gentry's, MGM 13379 | 6 |
| 6 | 5 | 6 | 6 | THE "IN" CROWD — Ramsey Lewis Trio, Argo 5506 | 12 |
| 7 | 12 | 25 | 40 | JUST A LITTLE BIT BETTER — Herman's Hermits, MGM 13398 | 5 |
| 8 | 8 | 9 | 14 | BABY DON'T GO — Sonny & Cher, Reprise 0392 | 9 |
| 9 | 10 | 12 | 17 | DO YOU BELIEVE IN MAGIC — Lovin' Spoonful, Kama Sutra 201 | 9 |
| 10 | 4 | 2 | 1 | EVE OF DESTRUCTION — Barry McGuire, Dunhill 4009 | 9 |
| 11 | 11 | 16 | 21 | I'M YOURS — Elvis Presley, RCA Victor 8657 | 8 |
| 12 | 24 | 42 | 85 | EVERYBODY LOVES A CLOWN — Gary Lewis & the Playboys, Liberty 55818 | 4 |
| 13 | 13 | 15 | 20 | SOME ENCHANTED EVENING — Jay & the Americans, United Artists 919 | 7 |
| 14 | 64 | — | — | GET OFF OF MY CLOUD — Rolling Stones, London 9792 | 2 |
| 15 | 18 | 20 | 26 | LIAR, LIAR — Castaways, Soma 1433 | 10 |
| 16 | 22 | 41 | 72 | YOU'RE THE ONE — Vogues, Co & Ce 229 | 5 |
| 17 | 7 | 8 | 11 | YOU'VE GOT YOUR TROUBLES — Fortunes, Press 9773 | 9 |
| 18 | 34 | 66 | — | POSITIVELY 4TH STREET — Bob Dylan, Columbia 43389 | 3 |
| 19 | 9 | 5 | 3 | YOU WERE ON MY MIND — We Five, A&M 770 | 13 |
| 20 | 6 | 4 | 4 | CATCH US IF YOU CAN — Dave Clark Five, Epic 9833 | 9 |
| 21 | 23 | 28 | 33 | MOHAIR SAM — Charlie Rich, Smash 1993 | 8 |
| 22 | 15 | 11 | 5 | HELP — Beatles, Capitol 5476 | 11 |
| 23 | 17 | 13 | 13 | WE GOTTA GET OUT OF THIS PLACE — Animals, MGM 13382 | 10 |
| 24 | 37 | 49 | 60 | MAKE ME YOUR BABY — Barbara Lewis, Atlantic 2300 | 6 |
| 25 | 28 | 29 | 37 | HOME OF THE BRAVE — Jody Miller, Capitol 5483 | 8 |
| 26 | 16 | 10 | 10 | LAUGH AT ME — Sonny, Atco 6369 | 9 |
| 27 | 21 | 22 | 25 | I'LL MAKE ALL YOUR DREAMS COME TRUE — Ronnie Dove, Diamond 188 | 8 |
| 28 | 36 | 55 | 76 | I KNEW YOU WHEN — Billy Joe Royal, Columbia 43390 | 5 |
| 29 | 20 | 24 | 32 | JUST YOU — Sonny & Cher, Atco 6345 | 8 |
| 30 | 45 | 74 | 89 | A TASTE OF HONEY — Herb Alpert & the Tijuana Brass, A&M 775 | 4 |
| 31 | 31 | 33 | 44 | KANSAS CITY STAR — Roger Miller, Smash 1998 | 5 |
| 32 | 32 | 44 | 54 | MY TOWN, MY GUY AND ME — Lesley Gore, Mercury 72475 | 6 |
| 33 | 43 | 54 | 73 | NOT THE LOVIN' KIND — Dino, Desi & Billy, Reprise 0401 | 5 |
| 34 | 25 | 26 | 30 | RIDE AWAY — Roy Orbison, MGM 13386 | 9 |
| 35 | 46 | 48 | 56 | I WANT TO (Do Everything for You) — Joe Tex, Dial 4016 | 8 |
| 36 | 39 | 43 | 53 | DAWN OF CORRECTION — Spokesmen, Decca 31844 | 5 |
| 37 | 40 | 50 | 67 | HUNGRY FOR LOVE — San Remo Golden Strings, Ric-Tic 104 | 6 |
| 38 | 44 | 51 | 71 | WHAT COLOR (Is a Man) — Bobby Vinton, Epic 9846 | 5 |
| 39 | 27 | 27 | 29 | WITH THESE HANDS — Tom Jones, Parrot 9787 | 8 |
| 40 | 42 | 45 | 47 | AIN'T IT TRUE — Andy Williams, Columbia 43358 | 7 |
| 41 | 35 | 36 | 42 | HEARTACHES BY THE NUMBER — Johnny Tillotson, MGM 13376 | 8 |
| 42 | 52 | 64 | 79 | EVERYONE'S GONE TO THE MOON — Jonathan King, Parrot 9774 | 4 |
| 43 | 53 | 56 | 69 | CARA-LIN — Strangeloves, Bang 508 | 5 |
| 44 | 29 | 17 | 8 | IT AIN'T ME BABE — Turtles, White Whale 222 | 11 |
| 45 | 26 | 14 | 9 | HEART FULL OF SOUL — Yardbirds, Epic 9823 | 12 |
| 46 | 56 | 62 | 68 | RESPECT — Otis Redding, Volt 128 | 7 |
| 47 | 68 | — | — | BUT YOU'RE MINE — Sonny & Cher, Atco 6381 | 2 |
| 48 | 61 | 77 | 93 | 1-2-3 — Len Barry, Decca 31827 | 4 |
| 49 | 51 | 72 | 87 | ACT NATURALLY — Beatles, Capitol 5498 | 4 |
| 50 | 66 | 82 | — | SAY SOMETHING FUNNY — Patty Duke, United Artists 915 | 3 |
| 51 | 62 | 76 | — | RESCUE ME — Fontella Bass, Checker 1120 | 3 |
| 52 | 58 | 71 | 90 | UNIVERSAL SOLDIER — Glen Campbell, Capitol 5504 | 4 |
| 53 | 57 | 63 | 78 | STEPPIN' OUT — Paul Revere & the Raiders, Columbia 43375 | 5 |
| 54 | 59 | 69 | 84 | UNIVERSAL SOLDIER — Donovan, Hickory 1338 | 4 |
| 55 | 55 | 67 | 83 | ARE YOU A BOY OR ARE YOU A GIRL — Barbarians, Laurie 3308 | 4 |
| 56 | 60 | 60 | 70 | I LIVE FOR THE SUN — Sunrays, Tower 148 | 7 |
| 57 | 67 | 83 | — | I MISS YOU SO — Little Anthony & the Imperials, DCP 1149 | 3 |
| 58 | 71 | — | — | AIN'T THAT PECULIAR — Marvin Gaye, Tamla 54122 | 2 |
| 59 | 73 | 90 | — | RUN, BABY RUN — Newbeats, Hickory 1332 | 3 |
| 60 | 72 | — | — | LET'S HANG ON — 4 Seasons, Philips 40317 | 2 |
| 61 | 65 | 80 | — | TAKE ME IN YOUR ARMS — Kim Weston, Gordy 7046 | 3 |
| 62 | 77 | 92 | — | WHERE HAVE ALL THE FLOWERS GONE — Johnny Rivers, Imperial 66133 | 3 |
| 63 | 50 | 53 | 62 | THERE BUT FOR FORTUNE — Joan Baez, Vanguard 35031 | 6 |
| 64 | 75 | 78 | 92 | IF YOU'VE GOT A HEART — Bobby Goldsboro, United Artists 908 | 4 |
| 65 | 85 | — | — | ROUND EVERY CORNER — Petula Clark, Warner Bros. 5661 | 2 |
| 66 | 30 | 21 | 22 | AGENT OO-SOUL — Edwin Starr, Ric-Tic 103 | 11 |
| 67 | 47 | 47 | 52 | THE 3rd MAN THEME — Herb Alpert & the Tijuana Brass, A&M 775 | 6 |
| 68 | 76 | 84 | — | A LIFETIME OF LONELINESS — Jackie DeShannon, Imperial 66122 | 3 |
| 69 | 78 | 93 | — | SECRETLY — Lettermen, Capitol 5499 | 3 |
| 70 | 88 | — | — | CHAPEL IN THE MOONLIGHT — Bachelors, London 9793 | 2 |
| 71 | 87 | — | — | RING DANG DOO — Sam the Sham and the Pharaohs, MGM 13397 | 2 |
| 72 | 89 | — | — | DON'T TALK TO STRANGERS — Beau Brummels, Autumn 20 | 2 |
| 73 | 95 | — | — | MY GIRL HAS GONE — Miracles, Tamla 54123 | 2 |
| 74 | 74 | 79 | 82 | LITTLE MISS SAD — Five Emprees, Freeport 1001 | 6 |
| 75 | 63 | 65 | 75 | THESE HANDS (Small But Mighty) — Bobby Bland, Duke 385 | 8 |
| 76 | 80 | 81 | 81 | THE WORLD THROUGH A TEAR — Neil Sedaka, RCA Victor 8637 | 8 |
| 77 | 82 | 86 | 88 | FUNNY LITTLE BUTTERFLIES — Patty Duke, United Artists 915 | 4 |
| 78 | 84 | 94 | 98 | ROAD RUNNER — Gants, Liberty 55829 | 4 |
| 79 | 79 | 91 | — | JUST ONE KISS FROM YOU — Impressions, ABC-Paramount 10725 | 3 |
| 80 | — | — | — | I FOUND A GIRL — Jan & Dean, Liberty 55833 | 1 |
| 81 | — | — | — | YOU'VE GOT TO HIDE YOUR LOVE AWAY — Silkie, Fontana 1525 | 1 |
| 82 | — | — | — | MAKE THE WORLD GO AWAY — Eddy Arnold, RCA Victor 8679 | 1 |
| 83 | — | — | — | WHERE DO YOU GO — Cher, Imperial 66136 | 1 |
| 84 | 86 | 97 | — | LOOKING WITH MY EYES — Dionne Warwick, Scepter 12111 | 3 |
| 85 | — | — | — | REMEMBER WHEN — Wayne Newton, Capitol 5514 | 1 |
| 86 | 94 | 99 | — | HE TOUCHED ME — Barbra Streisand, Columbia 43403 | 3 |
| 87 | 100 | — | — | RUSTY BELLS — Brenda Lee, Decca 31849 | 2 |
| 88 | 91 | — | — | CLEO'S BACK — Jr. Walker and the All Stars, Soul 35013 | 2 |
| 89 | 90 | — | — | JUST YESTERDAY — Jack Jones, Kapp 699 | 2 |
| 90 | — | — | — | MAY THE BIRD OF PARADISE FLY UP YOUR NOSE — "Little" Jimmy Dickens, Columbia 43388 | 1 |
| 91 | — | — | — | ROSES AND RAINBOWS — Danny Hutton, HBR 447 | 1 |
| 92 | 83 | 85 | 91 | TOSSING AND TURNING — Ivy League, Cameo 377 | 5 |
| 93 | 93 | — | — | I'M SO THANKFUL — The Ikettes, Modern 1011 | 2 |
| 94 | — | — | — | AUTUMN LEAVES—1965 — Roger Williams, Kapp 707 | 1 |
| 95 | — | — | — | FORGIVE ME — Al Martino, Capitol 5506 | 1 |
| 96 | 98 | — | — | EARLY MORNING RAIN — Peter, Paul & Mary, Warner Bros. 5659 | 2 |
| 97 | — | — | — | SINNER MAN — Trini Lopez, Reprise 0405 | 1 |
| 98 | — | — | — | SO LONG BABE — Nancy Sinatra, Reprise 0407 | 1 |
| 99 | 99 | — | — | RIGHT NOW AND NOT LATER — Shangri-Las, Red Bird 036 | 2 |
| 100 | — | — | — | MAKE IT EASY ON YOURSELF — Walker Brothers, Smash 2000 | 1 |

## BUBBLING UNDER THE HOT 100

101. HONKY TONK '65 — Lonnie Mack, Fraternity 951
102. I STILL LOVE YOU — Vejtables, Autumn 15
103. THE ORGAN GRINDER'S SWING — Jimmy Smith, Verve 10363
104. LET ME BE — Turtles, White Whale 224
105. LET'S MOVE & GROOVE (Together) — Johnny Nash, Joda 102
106. HERE COMES THE TEARS — Gene Chandler, Constellation 164
107. IL SILENZIO — Nini Rosso, Columbia 43363
108. HAPPY, HAPPY BIRTHDAY BABY — Dolly Parton, Monument 897
109. FOR YOUR LOVE — Righteous Brothers, Moonglow 243
110. SO LONG BABE — Sam and Bill, Joda 100
111. THE SPIDER SONG — Kids Next Door, 4 Corners 129
112. MISTY — Vibrations, Okeh 7230
113. THINK — Jimmy McCracklin, Imperial 66129
114. LOVE (Makes Me Do Foolish Things) — Martha & The Vandellas, Gordy 7045
115. I HAVE DREAMED — Chad & Jeremy, Columbia 43414
116. SEE MY FRIEND — Kinks, Reprise 0409
117. CINCINNATI KID — Ray Charles, ABC-Paramount 10720
118. WE DIDN'T ASK TO BE BROUGHT HERE — Bobby Darin, Atlantic 2305
119. ON A CLEAR DAY YOU CAN SEE FOREVER — Robert Goulet, Columbia 43394
120. I BELIEVE I'LL LOVE ON — Jackie Wilson, Brunswick 55283
121. WORK, WORK, WORK — Lee Dorsey, Amy 939
122. COME BACK TO ME MY LOVE — Robert Goulet, Columbia 43394
123. FUNNY THING ABOUT IT — Nancy Ames, Epic 9845
124. TRY TO REMEMBER — Brothers Four, Columbia 43404
125. ONLY A FOOL BREAKS HIS OWN HEART — Arthur Prysock, Old Town 1185
126. I'LL KEEP ON TRYING — Walter Jackson, Okeh 7229
127. MY HEART BELONGS TO ONLY YOU — Jerry Vale, Columbia 43413
128. DEEP IN YOUR HEART — Chuck Jackson & Maxine Brown, Wand 179
129. I NEED YOU — Chuck Jackson & Maxine Brown, Wand 179
130. ONE HAS MY NAME — Barry Young, Dot 16756
131. NEVER HAD IT SO GOOD — Ronnie Milsap
132. HARK — Unit Four Plus Two, London 9790
133. DON'T THROW THE ROSES AWAY — John Gary, RCA Victor 8674
134. SEA CRUISE — Hondells, Mercury 72479
135. HARLEM NOCTURNE — Viscounts, Amy 940

Compiled from national retail sales and radio station airplay by the Music Popularity Dept. of Record Market Research, Billboard.

# Billboard HOT 100

**For Week Ending October 23, 1965**

★ STAR performer—Sides registering greatest proportionate upward progress this week.

● Record Industry Association of America seal of certification as million selling single.

| This Week | 1 Wk. Ago | 2 Wks. Ago | 3 Wks. Ago | TITLE Artist, Label & Number | Weeks On Chart |
|---|---|---|---|---|---|
| 1 | 1 | 1 | 3 | YESTERDAY — Beatles, Capitol 5498 | 5 |
| 2 | 2 | 3 | 7 | TREAT HER RIGHT — Roy Head, Back Beat 546 | 8 |
| 3 | 4 | 19 | 38 | A LOVER'S CONCERTO — Toys, DynoVoice 209 | 7 |
| ★4 | 14 | 64 | — | GET OFF OF MY CLOUD — Rolling Stones, London 9792 | 3 |
| 5 | 5 | 14 | 19 | KEEP ON DANCING — Gentry's, MGM 13379 | 7 |
| 6 | 3 | 2 | 1 | HANG ON SLOOPY — McCoys, Bang 506 | 11 |
| 7 | 7 | 12 | 25 | JUST A LITTLE BIT BETTER — Herman's Hermits, MGM 13398 | 6 |
| 8 | 12 | 24 | 42 | EVERYBODY LOVES A CLOWN — Gary Lewis & the Playboys, Liberty 55818 | 5 |
| 9 | 18 | 34 | 66 | POSITIVELY 4TH STREET — Bob Dylan, Columbia 43389 | 4 |
| 10 | 16 | 22 | 41 | YOU'RE THE ONE — Vogues, Co & Ce 229 | 6 |
| 11 | 9 | 10 | 12 | DO YOU BELIEVE IN MAGIC — Lovin' Spoonful, Kama Sutra 201 | 10 |
| 12 | 15 | 18 | 20 | LIAR, LIAR — Castaways, Soma 1433 | 11 |
| 13 | 6 | 5 | 6 | THE "IN" CROWD — Ramsey Lewis Trio, Argo 5506 | 13 |
| 14 | 8 | 8 | 9 | BABY DON'T GO — Sonny & Cher, Reprise 0392 | 10 |
| 15 | 10 | 4 | 2 | EVE OF DESTRUCTION — Barry McGuire, Dunhill 4009 | 10 |
| ★16 | 24 | 37 | 49 | MAKE ME YOUR BABY — Barbara Lewis, Atlantic 2300 | 7 |
| 17 | 11 | 11 | 16 | I'M YOURS — Elvis Presley, RCA Victor 8657 | 9 |
| 18 | 13 | 13 | 15 | SOME ENCHANTED EVENING — Jay & the Americans, United Artists 919 | 8 |
| ★19 | 48 | 61 | 77 | 1-2-3 — Len Barry, Decca 31827 | 5 |
| 20 | 17 | 7 | 8 | YOU'VE GOT YOUR TROUBLES — Fortunes, Press 9773 | 10 |
| 21 | 19 | 9 | 5 | YOU WERE ON MY MIND — We Five, A&M 770 | 14 |
| 22 | 28 | 36 | 55 | I KNEW YOU WHEN — Billy Joe Royal, Columbia 43390 | 6 |
| 23 | 47 | 68 | — | BUT YOU'RE MINE — Sonny & Cher, Atco 6381 | 3 |
| 24 | 21 | 23 | 28 | MOHAIR SAM — Charlie Rich, Smash 1993 | 9 |
| ★25 | 30 | 45 | 74 | A TASTE OF HONEY — Herb Alpert & the Tijuana Brass, A&M 775 | 5 |
| ★26 | 35 | 46 | 48 | I WANT TO (Do Everything for You) — Joe Tex, Dial 4016 | 9 |
| 27 | 33 | 43 | 54 | NOT THE LOVIN' KIND — Dino, Desi & Billy, Reprise 0401 | 6 |
| 28 | 42 | 52 | 64 | EVERYONE'S GONE TO THE MOON — Jonathan King, Parrot 9774 | 5 |
| 29 | 22 | 15 | 11 | HELP — Beatles, Capitol 5476 | 12 |
| 30 | 25 | 28 | 29 | HOME OF THE BRAVE — Jody Miller, Capitol 5483 | 9 |
| 31 | 23 | 17 | 13 | WE GOTTA GET OUT OF THIS PLACE — Animals, MGM 13382 | 11 |
| ★32 | 51 | 62 | 76 | RESCUE ME — Fontella Bass, Checker 1120 | 4 |
| 33 | 20 | 6 | 4 | CATCH US IF YOU CAN — Dave Clark Five, Epic 9833 | 10 |
| 34 | 37 | 40 | 50 | HUNGRY FOR LOVE — San Remo Golden Strings, Ric-Tic 104 | 7 |
| ★35 | 58 | 71 | — | AIN'T THAT PECULIAR — Marvin Gaye, Tamla 54122 | 3 |
| 36 | 32 | 32 | 44 | MY TOWN, MY GUY AND ME — Lesley Gore, Mercury 72475 | 7 |
| 37 | 26 | 16 | 10 | LAUGH AT ME — Sonny, Atco 6369 | 10 |
| 38 | 46 | 56 | 62 | RESPECT — Otis Redding, Volt 128 | 8 |
| 39 | 43 | 53 | 56 | CARA-LIN — Strangeloves, Bang 508 | 6 |
| 40 | 36 | 39 | 43 | DAWN OF CORRECTION — Spokesmen, Decca 31884 | 6 |
| 41 | 60 | 72 | — | LET'S HANG ON — 4 Seasons, Philips 40317 | 3 |
| 42 | 50 | 66 | 82 | SAY SOMETHING FUNNY — Patty Duke, United Artists 915 | 4 |
| 43 | 38 | 44 | 51 | WHAT COLOR (Is a Man) — Bobby Vinton, Epic 9846 | 6 |
| 44 | 29 | 20 | 24 | JUST YOU — Sonny & Cher, Atco 6345 | 9 |
| 45 | 31 | 31 | 33 | KANSAS CITY STAR — Roger Miller, Smash 1998 | 7 |
| ★46 | 57 | 67 | 83 | I MISS YOU SO — Little Anthony & the Imperials, DCP 1149 | 4 |
| 47 | 49 | 51 | 72 | ACT NATURALLY — Beatles, Capitol 5498 | 5 |
| 48 | 52 | 58 | 71 | UNIVERSAL SOLDIER — Glen Campbell, Capitol 5504 | 5 |
| 49 | 59 | 73 | 90 | RUN, BABY RUN — Newbeats, Hickory 1332 | 4 |
| 50 | 53 | 57 | 63 | STEPPIN' OUT — Paul Revere & the Raiders, Columbia 43375 | 6 |
| 51 | 56 | 60 | 60 | I LIVE FOR THE SUN — Sunrays, Tower 148 | 8 |
| 52 | 62 | 77 | 92 | WHERE HAVE ALL THE FLOWERS GONE — Johnny Rivers, Imperial 66133 | 4 |
| 53 | 73 | 95 | — | MY GIRL HAS GONE — Miracles, Tamla 54123 | 3 |
| 54 | 54 | 59 | 69 | UNIVERSAL SOLDIER — Donovan, Hickory 1338 | 4 |
| 55 | 65 | 85 | — | ROUND EVERY CORNER — Petula Clark, Warner Bros. 5661 | 3 |
| 56 | 61 | 65 | 80 | TAKE ME IN YOUR ARMS — Kim Weston, Gordy 7046 | 4 |
| 57 | 27 | 21 | 22 | I'LL MAKE ALL YOUR DREAMS COME TRUE — Ronnie Dove, Diamond 188 | 9 |
| 58 | 34 | 25 | 26 | RIDE AWAY — Roy Orbison, MGM 13386 | 10 |
| 59 | 71 | 87 | — | RING DANG DOO — Sam the Sham and the Pharaohs, MGM 13397 | 3 |
| 60 | 70 | 88 | — | CHAPEL IN THE MOONLIGHT — Bachelors, London 9793 | 3 |
| 61 | 81 | — | — | YOU'VE GOT TO HIDE YOUR LOVE AWAY — Silkie, Fontana 1525 | 2 |
| 62 | 78 | 84 | 94 | ROAD RUNNER — Gants, Liberty 55829 | 5 |
| 63 | 64 | 75 | 78 | IF YOU'VE GOT A HEART — Bobby Goldsboro, United Artists 908 | 5 |
| 64 | 55 | 55 | 67 | ARE YOU A BOY OR ARE YOU A GIRL — Barbarians, Laurie 3308 | 5 |
| 65 | 80 | — | — | I FOUND A GIRL — Jan & Dean, Liberty 55833 | 2 |
| 66 | 68 | 76 | 84 | A LIFETIME OF LONELINESS — Jackie DeShannon, Imperial 66132 | 4 |
| 67 | 69 | 78 | 93 | SECRETLY — Lettermen, Capitol 5499 | 4 |
| ★68 | 83 | — | — | WHERE DO YOU GO — Cher, Imperial 66136 | 2 |
| 69 | 72 | 89 | — | DON'T TALK TO STRANGERS — Beau Brummels, Autumn 20 | 3 |
| 70 | 87 | 100 | — | RUSTY BELLS — Brenda Lee, Decca 31849 | 3 |
| 71 | 63 | 50 | 53 | THERE BUT FOR FORTUNE — Joan Baez, Vanguard 35031 | 7 |
| 72 | 88 | 91 | — | CLEO'S BACK — Jr. Walker and the All Stars, Soul 35013 | 3 |
| 73 | 100 | — | — | MAKE IT EASY ON YOURSELF — Walker Brothers, Smash 2000 | 2 |
| ★74 | — | — | — | MY BABY — Temptations, Gordy 7047 | 1 |
| 75 | 90 | — | — | MAY THE BIRD OF PARADISE FLY UP YOUR NOSE — "Little" Jimmy Dickens, Columbia 43388 | 2 |
| 76 | 76 | 80 | 81 | THE WORLD THROUGH A TEAR — Neil Sedaka, RCA Victor 8637 | 9 |
| 77 | 79 | 79 | 91 | JUST ONE KISS FROM YOU — Impressions, ABC-Paramount 10725 | 4 |
| 78 | 85 | — | — | REMEMBER WHEN — Wayne Newton, Capitol 5514 | 2 |
| 79 | 82 | — | — | MAKE THE WORLD GO AWAY — Eddy Arnold, RCA Victor 8679 | 2 |
| ★80 | — | — | — | TURN! TURN! TURN! — Byrds, Columbia 43424 | 1 |
| 81 | 77 | 82 | 86 | FUNNY LITTLE BUTTERFLIES — Patty Duke, United Artists 915 | 5 |
| 82 | 86 | 94 | 99 | HE TOUCHED ME — Barbra Streisand, Columbia 43403 | 4 |
| 83 | 84 | 86 | 97 | LOOKING WITH MY EYES — Dionne Warwick, Scepter 12111 | 4 |
| 84 | 93 | 93 | — | I'M SO THANKFUL — The Ikettes, Modern 1011 | 3 |
| 85 | 95 | — | — | FORGIVE ME — Al Martino, Capitol 5506 | 2 |
| 86 | 91 | — | — | ROSES AND RAINBOWS — Danny Hutton, HBR 447 | 2 |
| 87 | 89 | 90 | — | JUST YESTERDAY — Jack Jones, Kapp 699 | 3 |
| 88 | — | — | — | I STILL LOVE YOU — Vejtables, Autumn 15 | 1 |
| 89 | — | — | — | THE SPIDER SONG — Kids Next Door, 4 Corners 129 | 1 |
| 90 | 97 | — | — | SINNER MAN — Trini Lopez, Reprise 0405 | 2 |
| 91 | 96 | 98 | — | EARLY MORNING RAIN — Peter, Paul & Mary, Warner Bros. 5659 | 3 |
| 92 | 94 | — | — | AUTUMN LEAVES—1965 — Roger Williams, Kapp 707 | 2 |
| 93 | 98 | — | — | SO LONG BABE — Nancy Sinatra, Reprise 0407 | 2 |
| 94 | — | — | — | DON'T HAVE TO SHOP AROUND — Mad Lads, Volt 127 | 1 |
| 95 | — | — | — | STAND BY ME — Earl Grant, Decca 25674 | 1 |
| 96 | — | — | — | THINK — Jimmy McCracklin, Imperial 66129 | 1 |
| 97 | — | — | — | I BELIEVE I'LL LOVE ON — Jackie Wilson, Brunswick 55283 | 1 |
| 98 | — | — | — | I NEED YOU SO — Chuck Jackson & Maxine Brown, Wand 198 | 1 |
| 99 | — | — | — | MISTY — Vibrations, Okeh 7230 | 1 |
| 100 | — | — | — | THE LETTER — Sonny & Cher, Vault 916 | 1 |

## BUBBLING UNDER THE HOT 100

101. I HEAR A SYMPHONY ............ Supremes, Motown 1083
102. BOYS ................. Beatles, Capitol-Star Line 6066
103. ORGAN GRINDER SWING .......... Jimmy Smith, Verve 10363
104. IL SILENZIO ................. Nini Rosso, Columbia 43368
105. HERE COME THE TEARS ..... Righteous Brothers, Moonglow 243
106. FOR YOUR LOVE ............ Gene Chandler, Constellation 164
107. FOR YOUR LOVE ........................ Sam & Bill, Joda 100
108. RIGHT NOW AND NOT LATER .... Shangri-Las, Red Bird 036
109. ALL OF A SUDDEN MY HEART SINGS ... Mel Carter, Imperial 66138
110. I HAVE DREAMED ......... Chad & Jeremy, Columbia 43414
111. LET'S MOVE AND GROOVE (Together) ... Johnny Nash, Joda 102
112. LOVE (Makes Me Do Foolish Things) .. Martha & the Vandellas, Gordy 7045
113. I'M A MAN .................. Yardbirds, Epic 9857
114. TOSSING AND TURNING .......... Ivy League, Cameo 377
115. CINCINNATI KID ........... Ray Charles, ABC-Paramount 10720
116. SEE MY FRIENDS ................... Kinks, Reprise 0409
117. WE DIDN'T ASK TO BE BROUGHT HERE .... Bobby Darin, Atlantic 2305
118. COME BACK TO ME MY LOVE .... Robert Goulet, Columbia 43394
119. FUNNY THING ABOUT IT ........ Nancy Ames, Epic 9845
120. I'LL KEEP ON TRYING ........ Walter Jackson, Okeh 7229
121. WORK, WORK, WORK .............. Lee Dorsey, Amy 939
122. TRY TO REMEMBER .......... Brothers Four, Columbia 43404
123. DEEP IN YOUR HEART ........ Jerry Vale, Columbia 43413
124. NEVER HAD IT SO GOOD ...... Ronnie Dove, Diamond 191
125. MY HEART BELONGS TO ONLY YOU ... Shirelles, Scepter 12114
126. HARLEM NOCTURNE ........... Viscounts, Amy 940
127. SHE'S WITH HER OTHER LOVE ... Leon Hayward, Imperial 66123
128. SHOULD I .................... Chad & Jeremy, Columbia 43314
129. ONE HAS MY NAME .............. Barry Young, Dot 16756
130. ON A CLEAR DAY YOU CAN SEE FOREVER .. Robert Goulet, Columbia 43394
131. SEA CRUISE ................ Hondells, Mercury 72479
132. DON'T THROW THE ROSES AWAY ... John Gary, RCA Victor 8677
133. STAY TOGETHER YOUNG LOVERS ... Ben Aiken, Roulette 4649
134. TRUE PICTURE ................ Jack Jones, Kapp 699
135. JUST A LITTLE BIT ........... Roy Head, Scepter 12116

Compiled from national retail sales and radio station airplay by the Music Popularity Dept. of Record Market Research, Billboard.

**Billboard** For Week Ending October 30, 1965

# HOT 100

★ **STAR performer**—Sides registering greatest proportionate upward progress this week.

(Seal) Record Industry Association of America seal of certification as million selling single.

Billboard Award

| This Week | 1 Wk. Ago | 2 Wks. Ago | 3 Wks. Ago | Title | Artist, Label & Number | Weeks On Chart |
|---|---|---|---|---|---|---|
| 1 | 1 | 1 | 1 | YESTERDAY (Seal) | Beatles, Capitol 5498 | 6 |
| 2 | 3 | 4 | 19 | A LOVER'S CONCERTO | Toys, DynoVoice 209 | 8 |
| 3 | 4 | 14 | 64 | GET OFF OF MY CLOUD | Rolling Stones, London 9792 | 4 |
| 4 | 5 | 5 | 14 | KEEP ON DANCING | Gentry's, MGM 13379 | 8 |
| ★5 | 8 | 12 | 24 | EVERYBODY LOVES A CLOWN | Gary Lewis & the Playboys, Liberty 55818 | 6 |
| 6 | 2 | 2 | 3 | TREAT HER RIGHT | Roy Head, Back Beat 546 | 9 |
| ★7 | 10 | 16 | 22 | YOU'RE THE ONE | Vogues, Co & Ce 229 | 7 |
| 8 | 9 | 18 | 34 | POSITIVELY 4TH STREET | Bob Dylan, Columbia 43389 | 5 |
| 9 | 6 | 3 | 2 | HANG ON SLOOPY | McCoys, Bang 506 | 12 |
| ★10 | 19 | 48 | 61 | 1-2-3 | Len Barry, Decca 31827 | 6 |
| ★11 | 16 | 24 | 37 | MAKE ME YOUR BABY | Barbara Lewis, Atlantic 2300 | 8 |
| 12 | 12 | 15 | 18 | LIAR, LIAR | Castaways, Soma 1433 | 12 |
| 13 | 7 | 7 | 12 | JUST A LITTLE BIT BETTER | Herman's Hermits, MGM 13398 | 7 |
| ★14 | 32 | 51 | 62 | RESCUE ME | Fontella Bass, Checker 1120 | 5 |
| ★15 | 25 | 30 | 45 | A TASTE OF HONEY | Herb Alpert & the Tijuana Brass, A&M 775 | 6 |
| ★16 | 22 | 28 | 36 | I KNEW YOU WHEN | Billy Joe Royal, Columbia 43390 | 7 |
| ★17 | 23 | 47 | 68 | BUT YOU'RE MINE | Sonny & Cher, Atco 6381 | 4 |
| ★18 | 41 | 60 | 72 | LET'S HANG ON | 4 Seasons, Philips 40317 | 4 |
| ★19 | 35 | 58 | 71 | AIN'T THAT PECULIAR | Marvin Gaye, Tamla 54122 | 4 |
| ★20 | 28 | 42 | 52 | EVERYONE'S GONE TO THE MOON | Jonathan King, Parrot 9774 | 6 |
| 21 | 13 | 6 | 5 | THE "IN" CROWD | Ramsey Lewis Trio, Cadet 5506 | 14 |
| 22 | 11 | 9 | 10 | DO YOU BELIEVE IN MAGIC | Lovin' Spoonful, Kama Sutra 201 | 11 |
| 23 | 26 | 35 | 46 | I WANT TO (Do Everything for You) | Joe Tex, Dial 4016 | 10 |
| 24 | 14 | 8 | 8 | BABY DON'T GO | Sonny & Cher, Reprise 0392 | 11 |
| 25 | 27 | 33 | 43 | NOT THE LOVIN' KIND | Dino, Desi & Billy, Reprise 0401 | 7 |
| 26 | 17 | 11 | 11 | I'M YOURS | Elvis Presley, RCA Victor 8657 | 10 |
| ★27 | 34 | 37 | 40 | HUNGRY FOR LOVE | San Remo Golden Strings, Ric-Tic 104 | 8 |
| 28 | 18 | 13 | 13 | SOME ENCHANTED EVENING | Jay & the Americans, United Artists 919 | 9 |
| 29 | 24 | 21 | 23 | MOHAIR SAM | Charlie Rich, Smash 1993 | 10 |
| ★30 | 42 | 50 | 66 | SAY SOMETHING FUNNY | Patty Duke, United Artists 915 | 5 |
| 31 | 21 | 19 | 9 | YOU WERE ON MY MIND | We Five, A&M 770 | 15 |
| 32 | 29 | 22 | 15 | HELP (Seal) | Beatles, Capitol 5476 | 13 |
| ★33 | 49 | 59 | 73 | RUN, BABY RUN | Newbeats, Hickory 1332 | 5 |
| 34 | 15 | 10 | 4 | EVE OF DESTRUCTION | Barry McGuire, Dunhill 4009 | 11 |
| ★35 | 52 | 62 | 77 | WHERE HAVE ALL THE FLOWERS GONE | Johnny Rivers, Imperial 66133 | 5 |
| 36 | 20 | 17 | 7 | YOU'VE GOT YOUR TROUBLES | Fortunes, Press 9773 | 11 |
| 37 | 38 | 46 | 56 | RESPECT | Otis Redding, Volt 128 | 9 |
| ★38 | 55 | 65 | 85 | ROUND EVERY CORNER | Petula Clark, Warner Bros. 5661 | 4 |
| ★39 | — | — | — | I HEAR A SYMPHONY | Supremes, Motown 1083 | 1 |
| 40 | 33 | 20 | 6 | CATCH US IF YOU CAN | Dave Clark Five, Epic 9833 | 11 |
| 41 | 46 | 57 | 67 | I MISS YOU SO | Little Anthony & the Imperials, DCP 1149 | 5 |
| 42 | 39 | 43 | 53 | CARA-LIN | Strangeloves, Bang 508 | 7 |
| 43 | 36 | 32 | 32 | MY TOWN, MY GUY AND ME | Lesley Gore, Mercury 72475 | 8 |
| ★44 | 68 | 83 | — | WHERE DO YOU GO | Cher, Imperial 66136 | 3 |
| 45 | 48 | 52 | 58 | UNIVERSAL SOLDIER | Glen Campbell, Capitol 5504 | 6 |
| 46 | 50 | 53 | 57 | STEPPIN' OUT | Paul Revere & the Raiders, Columbia 43375 | 7 |
| 47 | 47 | 49 | 51 | ACT NATURALLY | Beatles, Capitol 5498 | 6 |
| ★48 | 60 | 70 | 88 | CHAPEL IN THE MOONLIGHT | Bachelors, London 9793 | 4 |
| 49 | 53 | 73 | 95 | MY GIRL HAS GONE | Miracles, Tamla 54123 | 4 |
| ★50 | 74 | — | — | MY BABY | Temptations, Gordy 7047 | 2 |
| ★51 | 61 | 81 | — | YOU'VE GOT TO HIDE YOUR LOVE AWAY | Silkie, Fontana 1525 | 3 |
| ★52 | 62 | 78 | 84 | ROAD RUNNER | Gants, Liberty 55829 | 6 |
| 53 | 54 | 54 | 59 | UNIVERSAL SOLDIER | Donovan, Hickory 1338 | 6 |
| ★54 | 65 | 80 | — | I FOUND A GIRL | Jan & Dean, Liberty 55833 | 3 |
| 55 | 59 | 71 | 87 | RING DANG DOO | Sam the Sham and the Pharaohs, MGM 13397 | 4 |
| 56 | 56 | 61 | 65 | TAKE ME IN YOUR ARMS | Kim Weston, Gordy 7046 | 5 |
| 57 | 51 | 56 | 60 | I LIVE FOR THE SUN | Sunrays, Tower 148 | 9 |
| ★58 | 73 | 100 | — | MAKE IT EASY ON YOURSELF | Walker Brothers, Smash 2000 | 3 |
| ★59 | 75 | 90 | — | MAY THE BIRD OF PARADISE FLY UP YOUR NOSE | "Little" Jimmy Dickens, Columbia 43388 | 3 |
| ★60 | 70 | 87 | 100 | RUSTY BELLS | Brenda Lee, Decca 31849 | 4 |
| ★61 | 80 | — | — | TURN! TURN! TURN! | Byrds, Columbia 43424 | 2 |
| 62 | 63 | 64 | 75 | IF YOU'VE GOT A HEART | Bobby Goldsboro, United Artists 908 | 6 |
| ★63 | 79 | 82 | — | MAKE THE WORLD GO AWAY | Eddy Arnold, RCA Victor 8679 | 3 |
| 64 | 40 | 36 | 39 | DAWN OF CORRECTION | Spokesmen, Decca 31884 | 7 |
| 65 | 67 | 69 | 78 | SECRETLY | Lettermen, Capitol 5499 | 5 |
| 66 | 66 | 68 | 76 | A LIFETIME OF LONELINESS | Jackie DeShannon, Imperial 66132 | 5 |
| 67 | 72 | 88 | 91 | CLEO'S BACK | Jr. Walker and the All Stars, Soul 35013 | 4 |
| 68 | 69 | 72 | 89 | DON'T TALK TO STRANGERS | Beau Brummels, Autumn 20 | 4 |
| 69 | 43 | 38 | 44 | WHAT COLOR (Is a Man) | Bobby Vinton, Epic 9846 | 7 |
| 70 | 83 | 84 | 86 | LOOKING WITH MY EYES | Dionne Warwick, Scepter 12111 | 5 |
| 71 | 64 | 55 | 55 | ARE YOU A BOY OR ARE YOU A GIRL | Barbarians, Laurie 3308 | 6 |
| 72 | 82 | 86 | 94 | HE TOUCHED ME | Barbra Streisand, Columbia 43403 | 5 |
| 73 | 85 | 95 | — | FORGIVE ME | Al Martino, Capitol 5506 | 3 |
| 74 | 78 | 85 | — | REMEMBER WHEN | Wayne Newton, Capitol 5514 | 3 |
| ★75 | — | — | — | (All of a Sudden) MY HEART SINGS | Mel Carter, Imperial 66138 | 1 |
| 76 | 77 | 79 | 79 | JUST ONE KISS FROM YOU | Impressions, ABC-Paramount 10725 | 5 |
| 77 | 84 | 93 | 93 | I'M SO THANKFUL | The Ikettes, Modern 1011 | 4 |
| 78 | 87 | 89 | 90 | JUST YESTERDAY | Jack Jones, Kapp 699 | 4 |
| 79 | 90 | 97 | — | SINNER MAN | Trini Lopez, Reprise 0405 | 3 |
| ★80 | — | — | — | LET ME BE | Turtles, White Whale 224 | 1 |
| ★81 | 99 | — | — | MISTY | Vibrations, Okeh 7230 | 2 |
| ★82 | — | — | — | JUST A LITTLE BIT | Roy Head, Scepter 12116 | 1 |
| ★83 | — | — | — | I'M A MAN | Yardbirds, Epic 9857 | 1 |
| ★84 | — | — | — | HARLEM NOCTURNE | Viscounts, Amy 940 | 1 |
| 85 | 86 | 91 | — | ROSES AND RAINBOWS | Danny Hutton, HBR 447 | 3 |
| 86 | 89 | — | — | THE SPIDER SONG | Kids Next Door, 4 Corners 129 | 2 |
| 87 | 88 | — | — | I STILL LOVE YOU | Vejtables Autumn 15 | 2 |
| ★88 | — | — | — | I WILL | Dean Martin, Reprise 0415 | 1 |
| ★89 | — | — | — | DANCE WITH ME | Mojo Men, Autumn 19 | 1 |
| 90 | 100 | — | — | THE LETTER | Sonny & Cher, Vault 916 | 2 |
| 91 | 95 | — | — | STAND BY ME | Earl Grant, Decca 25674 | 2 |
| 92 | 93 | 98 | — | SO LONG BABE | Nancy Sinatra, Reprise 0407 | 3 |
| 93 | 94 | — | — | DON'T HAVE TO SHOP AROUND | Mad Lads, Volt 127 | 2 |
| 94 | — | — | — | HONKY TONK '65 | Lonnie Mack, Fraternity 951 | 1 |
| 95 | 96 | — | — | THINK | Jimmy McCracklin, Imperial 66129 | 2 |
| 96 | 97 | — | — | I BELIEVE I'LL LOVE ON | Jackie Wilson, Brunswick 55283 | 2 |
| 97 | — | — | — | MYSTIC EYES | Them, Parrot 9796 | 1 |
| 98 | 92 | 94 | — | AUTUMN LEAVES—1965 | Roger Williams, Kapp 707 | 3 |
| 99 | — | — | 92 | THE ORGAN GRINDER'S SWING | Jimmy Smith, Verve 10363 | 3 |
| 100 | — | — | — | I HAVE DREAMED | Chad & Jeremy, Columbia 43414 | 1 |

## HOT 100—A TO Z—*(Publisher-Licensee)*

Act Naturally (Blue Book, BMI) .... 47
Ain't That Peculiar (Jobete, BMI) .... 19
(All of a Sudden) My Heart Sings (Leeds, ASCAP) 75
Are You a Boy or Are You a Girl (Elmwin, BMI) .. 71
Autumn Leaves—1965 (Moreley, ASCAP) .... 98
Baby Don't Go (Mother Bertha & Ten East, BMI) .. 24
But You're Mine (Five-West-Cotillion, BMI) .... 17
Cara-Lin (Grand Canyon, BMI) .... 42
Catch Us If You Can (Branston, BMI) .... 40
Chapel in the Moonlight (Shapiro-Bernstein, ASCAP) 48
Cleo's Back (Jobete, BMI) .... 67
Dance With Me (Taracrest, BMI) .... 89
Dawn of Correction (Champion & Double Diamond, BMI) .... 64
Do You Believe in Magic (Faithful Virtue, BMI) ... 22
Don't Have to Shop Around (Makmillion, BMI) .. 93
Don't Talk to Strangers (Taracrest, BMI) .... 68
Eve of Destruction (Trousdale, BMI) .... 34
Everybody Loves a Clown (Viva, BMI) .... 5
Everyone's Gone to the Moon (Mainstay, BMI) .. 20
Forgive Me (Advanced, ASCAP) .... 73
Get Off of My Cloud (Gideon, BMI) .... 3
Hang On Sloopy (Picturetone-Mellin, BMI) .... 9
Harlem Nocturne (Shapiro-Bernstein, ASCAP) .... 84
He Touched Me (Morris, ASCAP) .... 72
Help (Maclen, BMI) .... 32
Honky Tonk '65 (W & K-Islip, BMI) .... 94
Hungry for Love (Myto, BMI) .... 27
I Believe I'll Love On (BRC & Ramitary, BMI) ... 96
I Found a Girl (Trousdale, BMI) .... 54
I Have Dreamed (Williamson, ASCAP) ....100
I Hear a Symphony (Jobete, BMI) .... 39
I Knew You When (Lowery, BMI) .... 16
I Live for the Sun (Sea of Tunes, BMI) .... 57
I Miss You So (Leeds, ASCAP) .... 41
I Still Love You (Taracrest, BMI) .... 87
I Want to (Do Everything for You) (Tree, BMI) .. 23
I Will (Camarillo, BMI) .... 88
If You've Got a Heart (Unart, BMI) ....62
I'm a Man (Avalon & Hill & Range, BMI) .... 83
I'm So Thankful (Jobete, BMI) .... 77
I'm Yours (Gladys, ASCAP) .... 26
"In" Crowd, The (American, BMI) .... 21
Just a Little Bit (Tollie, BMI) .... 82
Just a Little Bit Better (T.M., BMI) .... 13
Just One Kiss From You (Chi-Sound, BMI) .... 76
Just Yesterday (Buxton, ASCAP) .... 78
Keep on Dancing (Arc, Press, BMI) .... 4
Let Me Be (Trousdale, BMI) .... 80
Letter, The (Venice, BMI) .... 90
Let's Hang On (Saturday & Seasons Four, BMI) .. 18
Liar, Liar (Celann, BMI) .... 12
Lifetime of Loneliness, A (Blue Seas-Jac, ASCAP) . 66
Looking With My Eyes (Blue Seas-Jac. BMI) .... 70
Lover's Concerto, A (Saturday, BMI) .... 2
Make It Easy on Yourself (Famous, BMI) .... 58
Make Me Your Baby (Screen Gems-Columbia, BMI) . 11
Make the World Go Away (Pamper, BMI) .... 63
May the Bird of Paradise Fly Up Your Nose (Central Songs, BMI) .... 60
Misty (Vernon, ASCAP) .... 81
Mohair Sam (Acclaim, BMI) .... 29
My Baby (Jobete, BMI) .... 50
My Girl Has Gone (Jobete, BMI) .... 49
My Town, My Guy and Me (Sturossi-Catalog, BMI) .... 43
Mystic Eyes (Wemar, BMI) .... 97
Not the Lovin' Kind (Criterion, ASCAP) .... 25
1-2-3 (Champion & Double Diamond, BMI) .... 10
Organ Grinder's Swing, The (Amer. Academy of Music, ASCAP) .... 99
Positively 4th Street (Witmark, ASCAP) .... 8
Remember When (Roosevelt, BMI) .... 74
Rescue Me (Chevis, BMI) .... 14
Respect (East-Time-Redwal, BMI) .... 37
Ring Dang Doo (Valley & Beckie, BMI) .... 55
Road Runner (Arc, BMI) .... 52
Roses and Rainbows (Anihanbar, BMI) ....85
Round Every Corner (Duchess, BMI) .... 38
Rusty Bells (Music City, ASCAP) .... 59
Run, Baby Run (Acuff-Rose, BMI) .... 33
Say Something Funny (Bernross, BMI) .... 30
Secretly (Planetary, ASCAP) .... 65
Sinner Man (Saloon Songs, BMI) .... 79
So Long Babe (Criterion, ASCAP) .... 92
Some Enchanted Evening (Williamson, ASCAP) .... 28
Spider Song, The (Ashland, BMI) .... 86
Stand by Me (Trio & Progressive, BMI) .... 91
Steppin' Out (Daywin, BMI) .... 46
Take Me in Your Arms (Jobete, BMI) .... 56
Taste of Honey, A (Songfest, ASCAP) .... 15
Think (Metric, BMI) .... 95
Treat Her Right (Don, BMI) .... 6
Turn! Turn! Turn! (Melody Trails, BMI) .... 61
Universal Soldier—Campbell (Woodmere, BMI) .... 45
Universal Soldier—Donovan (Woodmere, BMI) .... 53
What Color (Is a Man) (Screen Gems-Columbia, BMI) 69
Where Do You Go (Five-West-Cotillion, BMI) .... 44
Where Have All the Flowers Gone (Fall River, BMI) 35
Yesterday (Maclen, BMI) .... 1
You Were on My Mind (Witmark, ASCAP) .... 31
You're the One (Leeds, ASCAP) .... 7
You've Got to Hide Your Love Away (Maclen, BMI) 51
You've Got Your Troubles (Mills, ASCAP) .... 36

## BUBBLING UNDER THE HOT 100

101. CRAWLING BACK ....Roy Orbison, MGM 13410
102. IL SILENZIO ....Nini Rosso, Columbia 43363
103. FOR YOUR LOVE ....Righteous Brothers, Moonglow 243
104. EARLY MORNING RAIN ....Peter, Paul & Mary, Warner Bros. 5659
105. LET THE GOOD TIMES ROLL ....Roy Orbison, Monument 906
106. FOR YOUR LOVE ....Sam & Bill, Joda 100
107. LET'S MOVE AND GROOVE (Together) ....Johnny Nash, Joda 102
108. LOVE (Makes Me Do Foolish Things) ..Martha & the Vandellas, Gordy 7045
109. I NEED YOU SO ....Chuck Jackson & Maxine Brown, Wand 198
110. FLOWERS ON THE WALL ....Statler Brothers, Columbia 43315
111. KISS AWAY ....Ronnie Dove, Diamond 191
112. ONE HAS MY NAME ....Barry Young, Dot 16756
113. NEVER HAD IT SO GOOD ....Ronnie Milsop, Scepter 12109
114. TOSSING AND TURNING ....Ivy League, Cameo 377
115. SEE MY FRIENDS ....Kinks, Reprise 0409
116. I REALLY LOVE YOU ....Dee Dee Sharp, Cameo 375
117. DON'T FIGHT IT ....Wilson Pickett, Atlantic 2306
118. DEEP IN YOUR HEART ....Jerry Vale, Columbia 43413
119. TRY TO REMEMBER ....Brothers Four, Columbia 43404
120. IF YOU DON'T ....Barbara Mason, Arctic 112
121. UPON A PAINTED OCEAN ....Barry McGuire, Dunhill 4014
122. A BENCH IN THE PARK ....Jive Five, United Artists 936
123. STAY TOGETHER YOUNG LOVERS ....Ben Aiken, Roulette 4649
124. SHE'S WITH HER OTHER LOVE ....Leon Hayward, Imperial 66123
125. MR. JONES ....Grass Roots, Dunhill 4013
126. C. C. RIDER ....Bobby Powell, Whit 714
127. PIED PIPER ....Changin' Times, Philips 40320
128. LOOK THROUGH ANY WINDOW ....Hollies, Imperial 66134
129. LET ME KNOW WHEN IT'S OVER ....Esther Phillips, Atlantic 2304
130. THE SUN AIN'T GONNA SHINE (Anymore) ....Frankie Valli, Smash 1995
131. I WANT TO MEET HIM ....Royalettes, MGM 13405
132. SEESAW ....Don Covey, Atlantic 2301
133. RUN TO MY LOVIN' ARMS ....Lenny Welch, Kapp 712
134. DON'T PITY ME ....Peter & Gordon, Capitol 5532
135. I KNOW YOUR HEART HAS BEEN BROKEN ....Roscoe Shelton, Sound Stage 7 2549

Compiled from national retail sales and radio station airplay by the Music Popularity Dept. of Record Market Research, Billboard.

# Billboard HOT 100

For Week Ending November 6, 1965

★ STAR performer—Sides registering greatest proportionate upward progress this week.

| This Week | 1 Wk. Ago | 2 Wks. Ago | 3 Wks. Ago | TITLE — Artist, Label & Number | Weeks On Chart |
|---|---|---|---|---|---|
| 1 | 3 | 4 | 14 | GET OFF OF MY CLOUD — Rolling Stones, London 9792 | 5 |
| 2 | 2 | 3 | 4 | A LOVER'S CONCERTO — Toys, DynoVoice 209 | 9 |
| 3 | 1 | 1 | 1 | YESTERDAY — Beatles, Capitol 5498 | 7 |
| 4 | 5 | 8 | 12 | EVERYBODY LOVES A CLOWN — Gary Lewis & the Playboys, Liberty 55818 | 7 |
| 5 | 4 | 5 | 5 | KEEP ON DANCING — Gentrys, MGM 13379 | 9 |
| 6 | 7 | 10 | 16 | YOU'RE THE ONE — Vogues, Co & Ce 229 | 8 |
| 7 | 8 | 9 | 18 | POSITIVELY 4TH STREET — Bob Dylan, Columbia 43389 | 6 |
| 8 | 10 | 19 | 48 | 1-2-3 — Len Barry, Decca 31827 | 7 |
| ★9 | 14 | 32 | 51 | RESCUE ME — Fontella Bass, Checker 1120 | 6 |
| 10 | 15 | 25 | 30 | A TASTE OF HONEY — Herb Alpert & the Tijuana Brass, A&M 775 | 7 |
| 11 | 11 | 16 | 24 | MAKE ME YOUR BABY — Barbara Lewis, Atlantic 2300 | 9 |
| 12 | 39 | — | — | I HEAR A SYMPHONY — Supremes, Motown 1083 | 2 |
| 13 | 18 | 41 | 60 | LET'S HANG ON — 4 Seasons, Philips 40317 | 5 |
| 14 | 16 | 22 | 28 | I KNEW YOU WHEN — Billy Joe Royal, Columbia 43390 | 8 |
| 15 | 19 | 35 | 58 | AIN'T THAT PECULIAR — Marvin Gaye, Tamla 54122 | 6 |
| 16 | 17 | 23 | 47 | BUT YOU'RE MINE — Sonny & Cher, Atco 6381 | 5 |
| 17 | 20 | 28 | 42 | EVERYONE'S GONE TO THE MOON — Jonathan King, Parrot 9774 | 7 |
| 18 | 6 | 2 | 2 | TREAT HER RIGHT — Roy Head, Back Beat 546 | 10 |
| 19 | 12 | 12 | 15 | LIAR, LIAR — Castaways, Soma 1433 | 13 |
| 20 | 9 | 6 | 3 | HANG ON SLOOPY — McCoys, Bang 506 | 13 |
| 21 | 33 | 49 | 59 | RUN, BABY RUN — Newbeats, Hickory 1332 | 6 |
| 22 | 13 | 7 | 7 | JUST A LITTLE BIT BETTER — Herman's Hermits, MGM 13398 | 8 |
| 23 | 23 | 26 | 35 | I WANT TO (Do Everything for You) — Joe Tex, Dial 4016 | 11 |
| ★24 | 38 | 55 | 65 | ROUND EVERY CORNER — Petula Clark, Warner Bros. 5661 | 5 |
| ★25 | 30 | 42 | 50 | SAY SOMETHING FUNNY — Patty Duke, United Artists 915 | 6 |
| 26 | 25 | 27 | 33 | NOT THE LOVIN' KIND — Dino, Desi & Billy, Reprise 0401 | 8 |
| 27 | 27 | 34 | 37 | HUNGRY FOR LOVE — San Remo Golden Strings, Ric-Tic 104 | 9 |
| 28 | 22 | 11 | 9 | DO YOU BELIEVE IN MAGIC — Lovin' Spoonful, Kama Sutra 201 | 12 |
| 29 | 21 | 13 | 6 | THE "IN" CROWD — Ramsey Lewis Trio, Cadet 5506 | 15 |
| ★30 | 35 | 52 | 62 | WHERE HAVE ALL THE FLOWERS GONE — Johnny Rivers, Imperial 66133 | 6 |
| ★31 | 61 | 80 | — | TURN! TURN! TURN! — Byrds, Columbia 43424 | 3 |
| ★32 | 44 | 68 | 83 | WHERE DO YOU GO — Cher, Imperial 66136 | 4 |
| 33 | 29 | 24 | 21 | MOHAIR SAM — Charlie Rich, Smash 1993 | 11 |
| 34 | 41 | 46 | 57 | I MISS YOU SO — Little Anthony & the Imperials, DCP 1149 | 6 |
| 35 | 37 | 38 | 46 | RESPECT — Otis Redding, Volt 128 | 10 |
| ★36 | 50 | 74 | — | MY BABY — Temptations, Gordy 7047 | 3 |
| ★37 | 48 | 60 | 70 | CHAPEL IN THE MOONLIGHT — Bachelors, London 9793 | 5 |
| ★38 | 49 | 53 | 73 | MY GIRL HAS GONE — Miracles, Tamla 54123 | 5 |
| ★39 | 51 | 61 | 81 | YOU'VE GOT TO HIDE YOUR LOVE AWAY — Silkie, Fontana 1525 | 4 |
| 40 | 24 | 14 | 8 | BABY DON'T GO — Sonny & Cher, Reprise 3392 | 12 |
| 41 | 28 | 18 | 13 | SOME ENCHANTED EVENING — Jay & the Americans, United Artists 919 | 8 |
| ★42 | 60 | 70 | 87 | RUSTY BELLS — Brenda Lee, Decca 31849 | 5 |
| ★43 | 59 | 75 | 90 | MAY THE BIRD OF PARADISE FLY UP YOUR NOSE — "Little" Jimmy Dickens, Columbia 43388 | 4 |
| ★44 | 54 | 65 | 80 | I FOUND A GIRL — Jan & Dean, Liberty 55833 | 4 |
| 45 | 55 | 59 | 71 | RING DANG DOO — Sam the Sham and the Pharaohs, MGM 13397 | 5 |
| 46 | 46 | 50 | 53 | STEPPIN' OUT — Paul Revere & the Raiders, Columbia 43375 | 8 |
| 47 | 42 | 39 | 43 | CARA-LIN — Strangeloves, Bang 508 | 8 |
| ★48 | 58 | 73 | 100 | MAKE IT EASY ON YOURSELF — Walker Brothers, Smash 2000 | 4 |
| ★49 | 63 | 79 | 82 | MAKE THE WORLD GO AWAY — Eddy Arnold, RCA Victor 8679 | 4 |
| 50 | 26 | 17 | 11 | I'M YOURS — Elvis Presley, RCA Victor 8657 | 11 |
| 51 | 52 | 62 | 78 | ROAD RUNNER — Gants, Liberty 55829 | 7 |
| 52 | 45 | 48 | 52 | UNIVERSAL SOLDIER — Glen Campbell, Capitol 5504 | 7 |
| 53 | 56 | 56 | 61 | TAKE ME IN YOUR ARMS — Kim Weston, Gordy 7046 | 7 |
| 54 | 47 | 47 | 49 | ACT NATURALLY — Beatles, Capitol 5498 | 7 |
| 55 | 53 | 54 | 54 | UNIVERSAL SOLDIER — Donovan, Hickory 1338 | 7 |
| ★56 | 67 | 72 | 88 | CLEO'S BACK — Jr. Walker and the All Stars, Soul 35013 | 5 |
| 57 | 57 | 51 | 56 | I LIVE FOR THE SUN — Sunrays, Tower 148 | 10 |
| ★58 | 88 | — | — | I WILL — Dean Martin, Reprise 0415 | 2 |
| ★59 | 72 | 82 | 86 | HE TOUCHED ME — Barbra Streisand, Columbia 43403 | 6 |
| 60 | 62 | 63 | 64 | IF YOU'VE GOT A HEART — Bobby Goldsboro, United Artists 908 | 7 |
| ★61 | 80 | — | — | LET ME BE — Turtles, White Whale 224 | 2 |
| ★62 | 83 | — | — | I'M A MAN — Yardbirds, Epic 9857 | 2 |
| 63 | 73 | 85 | 95 | FORGIVE ME — Al Martino, Capitol 5506 | 4 |
| 64 | 65 | 67 | 69 | SECRETLY — Lettermen, Capitol 5499 | 6 |
| 65 | 68 | 69 | 72 | DON'T TALK TO STRANGERS — Beau Brummels, Autumn 20 | 5 |
| 66 | 75 | — | — | (All of a Sudden) MY HEART SINGS — Mel Carter, Imperial 66138 | 2 |
| 67 | 82 | — | — | JUST A LITTLE BIT — Roy Head, Scepter 12116 | 2 |
| 68 | 70 | 83 | 84 | LOOKING WITH MY EYES — Dionne Warwick, Scepter 12111 | 6 |
| 69 | 74 | 78 | 85 | REMEMBER WHEN — Wayne Newton, Capitol 5514 | 4 |
| 70 | 79 | 90 | 97 | SINNER MAN — Trini Lopez, Reprise 0405 | 4 |
| 71 | 66 | 66 | 68 | A LIFETIME OF LONELINESS — Jackie DeShannon, Imperial 66132 | 6 |
| ★72 | 97 | — | — | MYSTIC EYES — Them, Parrot 9796 | 2 |
| 73 | 78 | 87 | 89 | JUST YESTERDAY — Jack Jones, Kapp 699 | 5 |
| ★74 | — | — | — | KISS AWAY — Ronnie Dove, Diamond 191 | 1 |
| 75 | 81 | 99 | — | MISTY — Vibrations, Okeh 7230 | 3 |
| 76 | 77 | 84 | 93 | I'M SO THANKFUL — The Ikettes, Modern 1011 | 5 |
| 77 | 84 | — | — | HARLEM NOCTURNE — Viscounts, Amy 940 | 2 |
| 78 | 85 | 86 | 91 | ROSES AND RAINBOWS — Danny Hutton, HBR 447 | 4 |
| 79 | 89 | — | — | DANCE WITH ME — Mojo Men, Autumn 19 | 2 |
| 80 | — | — | — | HERE IT COMES AGAIN — Fortunes, Press 9798 | 1 |
| 81 | — | — | — | ENGLAND SWINGS — Roger Miller, Smash 2010 | 1 |
| 82 | — | — | — | CHILD OF OUR TIMES — Barry McGuire, Dunhill 4014 | 1 |
| 83 | 90 | 100 | — | THE LETTER — Sonny & Cher, Vault 916 | 3 |
| 84 | 86 | 89 | — | THE SPIDER SONG — Kids Next Door, 4 Corners 129 | 3 |
| 85 | 87 | 88 | — | I STILL LOVE YOU — Vejtables Autumn 15 | 3 |
| 86 | 92 | 93 | 98 | SO LONG BABE — Nancy Sinatra, Reprise 0407 | 4 |
| ★87 | — | — | — | IT'S MY LIFE — Animals, MGM 13414 | 1 |
| ★88 | — | — | — | I CAN NEVER GO HOME ANY MORE — Shangri-Las, Red Bird 043 | 1 |
| ★89 | — | — | — | CRAWLING BACK — Roy Orbison, MGM 13410 | 1 |
| ★90 | — | — | — | DON'T THINK TWICE — Wonder Who? Philips 40324 | 1 |
| 91 | 100 | — | — | I HAVE DREAMED — Chad & Jeremy, Columbia 43414 | 2 |
| 92 | — | — | — | ONE HAS MY NAME — Barry Young, Dot 16756 | 1 |
| 93 | 93 | 94 | — | DON'T HAVE TO SHOP AROUND — Mad Lads, Volt 127 | 3 |
| 94 | 94 | — | — | HONKY TONK '65 — Lonnie Mack, Fraternity 951 | 2 |
| 95 | — | — | — | I WANT TO MEET HIM — Royalettes, MGM 13405 | 1 |
| 96 | — | — | — | I REALLY LOVE YOU — Dee Dee Sharp, Cameo 375 | 1 |
| 97 | — | — | — | DON'T FIGHT IT — Wilson Pickett, Atlantic 2306 | 1 |
| 98 | — | — | — | DON'T PITY ME — Peter & Gordon, Capitol 5532 | 1 |
| 99 | — | — | — | IF YOU DON'T — Barbara Mason, Arctic 112 | 1 |
| 100 | — | — | — | TRY TO REMEMBER — Brothers Four, Columbia 43404 | 1 |

## BUBBLING UNDER THE HOT 100

| | | |
|---|---|---|
| 101 | HOLE IN THE WALL | Packers, Pure Soul 1107 |
| 102 | IL SILENZIO | Nini Rosso, Columbia 43363 |
| 103 | LET'S MOVE AND GROOVE (Together) | Johnny Nash, Joda 102 |
| 104 | PIED PIPER | Changin' Times, Philips 40320 |
| 105 | LET THE GOOD TIMES ROLL | Roy Orbison, Monument 906 |
| 106 | NEVER HAD IT SO GOOD | Ronnie Milsap, Scepter 12109 |
| 107 | RUN TO MY LOVIN' ARMS | Lenny Welch, Kapp 712 |
| 108 | LOVE (Makes Me Do Foolish Things) | Martha & the Vandellas, Gordy 7045 |
| 109 | FLOWERS ON THE WALL | Statler Brothers, Columbia 43315 |
| 110 | STAND BY ME | Earl Grant, Decca 25674 |
| 111 | SEE MY FRIENDS | Kinks, Reprise 0409 |
| 112 | FEVER | McCoys, Bang 511 |
| 113 | PUPPET ON A STRING | Elvis Presley, RCA Victor 0650 |
| 114 | THE ORGAN GRINDER'S SWING | Jimmy Smith, Verve 10363 |
| 115 | SHE'S WITH HER OTHER LOVE | Leon Hayward, Imperial 66123 |
| 116 | THINK | Jimmy McCracklin, Imperial 66129 |
| 117 | UPON A PAINTED OCEAN | Barry McGuire, Dunhill 4014 |
| 118 | DEEP IN YOUR HEART | Jerry Vale, Columbia 43413 |
| 119 | AUTUMN LEAVES—1965 | Roger Williams, Kapp 707 |
| 120 | LOOK THROUGH ANY WINDOW | Hollies, Imperial 66134 |
| 121 | MR. JONES | Grass Roots, Dunhill 4013 |
| 122 | STAY TOGETHER YOUNG LOVERS | Ben Aiken, Roulette 4649 |
| 123 | SEESAW | Don Covay, Atlantic 2301 |
| 124 | BUCKAROO | Buck Owens & His Buckaroos, Capitol 5517 |
| 125 | I BELIEVE I'LL LOVE ON | Jackie Wilson, Brunswick 55283 |
| 126 | C. C. RIDER | Bobby Powell, Whit 714 |
| 127 | LET ME SHOW YOU WHERE IT'S AT | Freddy Cannon, Warner Bros. 5666 |
| 128 | THE SUN AIN'T GONNA SHINE (Anymore) | Frankie Valli, Smash 1995 |
| 129 | THE TRAIN | Eddie Rambeau, DynoVoice 211 |
| 130 | MOTHER NATURE, FATHER TIME | Brook Benton, RCA Victor 8693 |
| 131 | EV'RYBODY HAS THE RIGHT TO BE WRONG! | Frank Sinatra, Reprise 0410 |
| 132 | EVERYTHING IS GONNA BE ALRIGHT | P. J. Proby, Liberty 55831 |
| 133 | JUST OUT OF REACH | Zombies, Parrot 9797 |
| 134 | LOVE MINUS ZERO | Eddie Hodges, Aurora 156 |
| 135 | THE TIMES THEY ARE A-CHANGIN' | Peter Antell, Bounty 45103 |

Compiled from national retail sales and radio station airplay by the Music Popularity Dept. of Record Market Research, Billboard.

# Billboard HOT 100

**For Week Ending November 13, 1965**

★ STAR performer—Sides registering greatest proportionate upward progress this week.

Record Industry Association of America seal of certification as million selling single.

| This Week | 1 Wk. Ago | 2 Wk. Ago | 3 Wk. Ago | TITLE, Artist, Label & Number | Weeks On Chart |
|---|---|---|---|---|---|
| 1 | 1 | 3 | 4 | GET OFF OF MY CLOUD — Rolling Stones, London 9792 | 6 |
| 2 | 2 | 2 | 3 | A LOVER'S CONCERTO — Toys, DynoVoice 209 | 10 |
| ★3 | 8 | 10 | 19 | 1-2-3 — Len Barry, Decca 31827 | 8 |
| 4 | 6 | 7 | 10 | YOU'RE THE ONE — Vogues, Co & Ce 229 | 9 |
| ★5 | 12 | 39 | — | I HEAR A SYMPHONY — Supremes, Motown 1083 | 3 |
| 6 | 9 | 14 | 32 | RESCUE ME — Fontella Bass, Checker 1120 | 7 |
| 7 | 4 | 5 | 8 | EVERYBODY LOVES A CLOWN — Gary Lewis & the Playboys, Liberty 55818 | 8 |
| ★8 | 13 | 18 | 41 | LET'S HANG ON — 4 Seasons, Philips 40317 | 6 |
| 9 | 10 | 15 | 25 | A TASTE OF HONEY — Herb Alpert & the Tijuana Brass, A&M 775 | 8 |
| ★10 | 15 | 19 | 35 | AIN'T THAT PECULIAR — Marvin Gaye, Tamla 54122 | 6 |
| 11 | 3 | 1 | 1 | YESTERDAY — Beatles, Capitol 5498 | 8 |
| 12 | 31 | 61 | 80 | TURN! TURN! TURN! — Byrds, Columbia 43424 | 4 |
| 13 | 7 | 8 | 9 | POSITIVELY 4TH STREET — Bob Dylan, Columbia 43389 | 7 |
| 14 | 14 | 16 | 22 | I KNEW YOU WHEN — Billy Joe Royal, Columbia 43390 | 9 |
| 15 | 16 | 17 | 23 | BUT YOU'RE MINE — Sonny & Cher, Atco 6381 | 6 |
| 16 | 21 | 33 | 49 | RUN, BABY RUN — Newbeats, Hickory 1332 | 7 |
| 17 | 17 | 20 | 28 | EVERYONE'S GONE TO THE MOON — Jonathan King, Parrot 9774 | 8 |
| 18 | 5 | 4 | 5 | KEEP ON DANCING — Gentry's, MGM 13379 | 10 |
| 19 | 11 | 11 | 16 | MAKE ME YOUR BABY — Barbara Lewis, Atlantic 2300 | 10 |
| ★20 | 39 | 51 | 61 | YOU'VE GOT TO HIDE YOUR LOVE AWAY — Silkie, Fontana 1525 | 5 |
| 21 | 24 | 38 | 55 | ROUND EVERY CORNER — Petula Clark, Warner Bros. 5661 | 6 |
| 22 | 25 | 30 | 42 | SAY SOMETHING FUNNY — Patty Duke, United Artists 915 | 7 |
| ★23 | 36 | 50 | 74 | MY BABY — Temptations, Gordy 7047 | 4 |
| 24 | 23 | 23 | 26 | I WANT TO (Do Everything for You) — Joe Tex, Dial 4016 | 12 |
| 25 | 32 | 44 | 68 | WHERE DO YOU GO — Cher, Imperial 66136 | 5 |
| 26 | 30 | 35 | 52 | WHERE HAVE ALL THE FLOWERS GONE — Johnny Rivers, Imperial 66133 | 7 |
| ★27 | 38 | 49 | 53 | MY GIRL HAS GONE — Miracles, Tamla 54123 | 6 |
| 28 | 22 | 13 | 7 | JUST A LITTLE BIT BETTER — Herman's Hermits, MGM 13398 | 9 |
| 29 | 43 | 59 | 75 | MAY THE BIRD OF PARADISE FLY UP YOUR NOSE — "Little" Jimmy Dickens, Columbia 43388 | 5 |
| 30 | 18 | 6 | 2 | TREAT HER RIGHT — Roy Head, Back Beat 546 | 11 |
| 31 | 20 | 9 | 6 | HANG ON SLOOPY — McCoys, Bang 506 | 14 |
| 32 | 37 | 48 | 60 | CHAPEL IN THE MOONLIGHT — Bachelors, London 9793 | 6 |
| ★33 | 44 | 54 | 65 | I FOUND A GIRL — Jan & Dean, Liberty 55833 | 5 |
| ★34 | 45 | 55 | 59 | RING DANG DOO — Sam the Sham and the Pharaohs, MGM 13397 | 6 |
| ★35 | 48 | 58 | 73 | MAKE IT EASY ON YOURSELF — Walker Brothers, Smash 2000 | 5 |
| 36 | 42 | 60 | 70 | RUSTY BELLS — Brenda Lee, Decca 31849 | 6 |
| 37 | 19 | 12 | 12 | LIAR, LIAR — Castaways, Soma 1433 | 14 |
| ★38 | 49 | 63 | 79 | MAKE THE WORLD GO AWAY — Eddy Arnold, RCA Victor 8679 | 5 |
| 39 | 58 | 88 | — | I WILL — Dean Martin, Reprise 0415 | 3 |
| 40 | 26 | 25 | 27 | NOT THE LOVIN' KIND — Dino, Desi & Billy, Reprise 0401 | 9 |
| 41 | 35 | 37 | 38 | RESPECT — Otis Redding, Volt 128 | 11 |
| 42 | 29 | 21 | 13 | THE "IN" CROWD — Ramsey Lewis Trio, Cadet 5506 | 16 |
| 43 | 34 | 41 | 46 | I MISS YOU SO — Little Anthony & the Imperials, DCP 1149 | 7 |
| ★44 | 61 | 80 | — | LET ME BE — Turtles, White Whale 224 | 3 |
| ★45 | 62 | 83 | — | I'M A MAN — Yardbirds, Epic 9857 | 3 |
| ★46 | 56 | 67 | 72 | CLEO'S BACK — Jr. Walker and the All Stars, Soul 35013 | 6 |
| 47 | 51 | 52 | 62 | ROAD RUNNER — Gants, Liberty 55829 | 8 |
| 48 | 28 | 22 | 11 | DO YOU BELIEVE IN MAGIC — Lovin' Spoonful, Kama Sutra 201 | 13 |
| 49 | 66 | 75 | — | (All of a Sudden) MY HEART SINGS — Mel Carter, Imperial 66138 | 3 |
| 50 | 53 | 56 | 56 | TAKE ME IN YOUR ARMS — Kim Weston, Gordy 7046 | 7 |
| 51 | 88 | — | — | I CAN NEVER GO HOME ANYMORE — Shangri-Las, Red Bird 043 | 2 |
| 52 | 27 | 27 | 34 | HUNGRY FOR LOVE — San Remo Golden Strings, Ric-Tic 104 | 10 |
| 53 | 74 | — | — | KISS AWAY — Ronnie Dove, Diamond 191 | 2 |
| 54 | 59 | 72 | 82 | HE TOUCHED ME — Barbra Streisand, Columbia 43403 | 7 |
| 55 | 65 | 68 | 69 | DON'T TALK TO STRANGERS — Beau Brummels, Autumn 20 | 6 |
| 56 | 67 | 82 | — | JUST A LITTLE BIT — Roy Head, Scepter 12116 | 3 |
| 57 | 81 | — | — | ENGLAND SWINGS — Roger Miller, Smash 2010 | 2 |
| 58 | — | — | — | SOMETHING ABOUT YOU — Four Tops, Motown 1084 | 1 |
| 59 | 72 | 97 | — | MYSTIC EYES — Them, Parrot 9796 | 3 |
| 60 | 60 | 62 | 63 | IF YOU'VE GOT A HEART — Bobby Goldsboro, United Artists 908 | 8 |
| 61 | 63 | 73 | 85 | FORGIVE ME — Al Martino, Capitol 5506 | 5 |
| 62 | 70 | 79 | 90 | SINNER MAN — Trini Lopez, Reprise 0405 | 5 |
| 63 | — | — | — | OVER AND OVER — Dave Clark Five, Epic 9863 | 1 |
| 64 | 80 | — | — | HERE IT COMES AGAIN — Fortunes, Press 9798 | 2 |
| 65 | 68 | 70 | 83 | LOOKING WITH MY EYES — Dionne Warwick, Scepter 12111 | 7 |
| 66 | 75 | 81 | 99 | MISTY — Vibrations, Okeh 7230 | 4 |
| 67 | 46 | 46 | 50 | STEPPIN' OUT — Paul Revere & the Raiders, Columbia 43375 | 9 |
| 68 | — | — | — | I GOT YOU (I Feel Good) — James Brown, King 6015 | 1 |
| ★69 | 90 | — | — | DON'T THINK TWICE — Wonder Who? Philips 40324 | 2 |
| 70 | 89 | — | — | CRAWLING BACK — Roy Orbison, MGM 13410 | 2 |
| 71 | 77 | 84 | — | HARLEM NOCTURNE — Viscounts, Amy 940 | 3 |
| 72 | — | — | — | FEVER — McCoys, Bang 511 | 1 |
| 73 | 78 | 85 | 86 | ROSES AND RAINBOWS — Danny Hutton, HBR 447 | 5 |
| 74 | 76 | 77 | 84 | I'M SO THANKFUL — The Ikettes, Modern 1011 | 6 |
| 75 | 92 | — | — | ONE HAS MY NAME — Barry Young, Dot 16756 | 2 |
| 76 | 79 | 89 | — | DANCE WITH ME — Mojo Men, Autumn 19 | 3 |
| 77 | 82 | — | — | CHILD OF OUR TIMES — Barry McGuire, Dunhill 4014 | 2 |
| 78 | 87 | — | — | IT'S MY LIFE — Animals, MGM 13414 | 2 |
| 79 | 83 | 90 | 100 | THE LETTER — Sonny & Cher, Vault 916 | 4 |
| 80 | — | — | — | PUPPET ON A STRING — Elvis Presley, RCA Victor 0650 | 1 |
| 81 | — | — | — | A TIME TO LOVE—A TIME TO CRY — Lou Johnson, Big Top 101 | 1 |
| 82 | — | — | — | HOLE IN THE WALL — Packers, Pure Soul 1107 | 1 |
| 83 | — | — | — | MOTHER NATURE, FATHER TIME — Brook Benton, RCA Victor 8693 | 1 |
| 84 | 85 | 87 | 88 | I STILL LOVE YOU — Vejtables, Autumn 15 | 4 |
| 85 | — | — | — | LET THE GOOD TIMES ROLL — Roy Orbison, Monument 906 | 1 |
| 86 | 98 | — | — | DON'T PITY ME — Peter & Gordon, Capitol 5532 | 2 |
| 87 | 95 | — | — | I WANT TO MEET HIM — Royalettes, MGM 13405 | 2 |
| 88 | 94 | 94 | — | HONKY TONK '65 — Lonnie Mack, Fraternity 951 | 3 |
| 89 | 96 | — | — | I REALLY LOVE YOU — Dee Dee Sharp, Cameo 375 | 2 |
| 90 | — | — | — | LET'S GET TOGETHER — We Five, A&M 784 | 1 |
| 91 | 97 | — | — | DON'T FIGHT IT — Wilson Pickett, Atlantic 2306 | 2 |
| 92 | — | — | — | SEESAW — Don Covay, Atlantic 2301 | 1 |
| 93 | — | — | — | PIED PIPER — Changin' Times, Philips 40220 | 1 |
| 94 | 100 | — | — | TRY TO REMEMBER — Brothers Four, Columbia 43404 | 2 |
| 95 | 99 | — | — | IF YOU DON'T — Barbara Mason, Arctic 112 | 2 |
| 96 | — | — | — | FLOWERS ON THE WALL — Statler Brothers, Columbia 43315 | 1 |
| 97 | — | 91 | 95 | STAND BY ME — Earl Grant, Decca 25674 | 3 |
| 98 | — | — | — | LET'S MOVE & GROOVE (Together) — Johnny Nash, Joda 102 | 4 |
| 99 | — | — | — | BUCKAROO — Buck Owens & His Buckaroos, Capitol 5517 | 1 |
| 100 | — | — | — | LOVE THEME FROM THE SANDPIPER — Tony Bennett, Columbia 43431 | 1 |

## BUBBLING UNDER THE HOT 100

101. TRY ME — James Brown, Smash 570
102. SUNDAY AND ME — Jay & the Americans, United Artists 948
103. DON'T HAVE TO SHOP AROUND — Mad Lads, Volt 127
104. ONLY LOVE (Can Save Me Now) — Solomon Burke, Atlantic 2308
105. RUN TO MY LOVIN' ARMS — Lenny Welch, Kapp 714
106. SO LONG BABE — Nancy Sinatra, Reprise 0407
107. REMEMBER WHEN — Wayne Newton, Capitol 5514
108. NEVER HAD IT SO GOOD — Ronnie Milsap, Scepter 12109
109. IL SILENZIO — Nini Rosso, Columbia 43363
110. BACK STREET — Edwin Starr, Ric-Tic
111. SOUNDS OF SILENCE — Simon & Garfunkel, Columbia 43396
112. ORGAN GRINDER'S SWING — Jimmy Smith, Verve 10363
113. THINK — Jimmy McCracklin, Imperial 66129
114. SHE'S WITH HER OTHER LOVE — Leon Haywood, Imperial 66123
115. YOU'VE BEEN CHEATIN' — Impressions, ABC-Paramount 10750
116. THE SPIDER SONG — Kids Next Door, 4 Corners 129
117. OUR WORLD — Johnny Tillotson, MGM 13400
118. I KNOW IT'S ALL RIGHT — Sam Hawkins, Blue Cat 121
119. LOOK THROUGH ANY WINDOW — Hollies, Imperial 66134
120. I HAVE DREAMED — Chad & Jeremy, Columbia 43414
121. STAY TOGETHER YOUNG LOVERS — Ben Aiken, Roulette 4649
122. I'M SATISFIED — San Remo Golden Strings, Ric-Tic
123. C. C. RIDER — Bobby Powell, Whit 714
124. TAKE A LOOK — Irma Thomas, Imperial 66137
125. GOODBYE BABE — Castaways, Soma 1442
126. HANG ON SLOOPY — Ramsey Lewis Trio, Cadet 5522
127. JUST OUT OF REACH — Zombies, Parrot 9797
128. EVERYTHING IS GONNA BE ALRIGHT — Willie Mitchell, Hi 2097
129. THE THREE BELLS — J. Puppy
130. HEARTBEAT — Gloria Jones, Uptown 712
131. LOVE (Makes Me Do Foolish Things) — Martha & the Vandellas, Gordy 7045
132. I BELIEVE I'LL LOVE ON — Jackie Wilson, Brunswick 55283
133. WOODEN HEART — Elvis Presley, RCA Victor 0650
134. EVERYBODY LOVES A GOOD TIME — Major Lance, Okeh 7233
135. A BENCH IN THE PARK — Jive Five, United Artists 936

Compiled from national retail sales and radio station airplay by the Music Popularity Dept. of Record Market Research, Billboard.

# Billboard HOT 100

For Week Ending November 20, 1965

★ STAR performer—Sides registering greatest proportionate upward progress this week.

Record Industry Association of America seal of certification as million selling single.

| This Week | 1 Wk. Ago | 2 Wk. Ago | 3 Wk. Ago | TITLE, Artist, Label & Number | Weeks On Chart |
|---|---|---|---|---|---|
| 1 | 5 | 12 | 39 | I HEAR A SYMPHONY — Supremes, Motown 1083 | 4 |
| 2 | 3 | 8 | 10 | 1-2-3 — Len Barry, Decca 31827 | 9 |
| 3 | 1 | 1 | 3 | GET OFF OF MY CLOUD — Rolling Stones, London 9792 | 7 |
| 4 | 6 | 9 | 14 | RESCUE ME — Fontella Bass, Checker 1120 | 8 |
| 5 | 8 | 13 | 18 | LET'S HANG ON — 4 Seasons, Philips 40317 | 7 |
| 6 | 12 | 31 | 61 | TURN! TURN! TURN! — Byrds, Columbia 43424 | 5 |
| 7 | 2 | 2 | 2 | A LOVER'S CONCERTO — Toys, DynoVoice 209 | 11 |
| 8 | 10 | 15 | 19 | AIN'T THAT PECULIAR — Marvin Gaye, Tamla 54122 | 7 |
| 9 | 9 | 10 | 15 | A TASTE OF HONEY — Herb Alpert & the Tijuana Brass, A&M 775 | 9 |
| 10 | 4 | 6 | 7 | YOU'RE THE ONE — Vogues, Co & Ce 229 | 10 |
| 11 | 7 | 4 | 5 | EVERYBODY LOVES A CLOWN — Gary Lewis & the Playboys, Liberty 55818 | 9 |
| 12 | 20 | 39 | 51 | YOU'VE GOT TO HIDE YOUR LOVE AWAY — Silkie, Fontana 1525 | 6 |
| 13 | 11 | 3 | 1 | YESTERDAY — Beatles, Capitol 5498 | 9 |
| 14 | 68 | — | — | I GOT YOU (I Feel Good) — James Brown, King 6015 | 2 |
| 15 | 16 | 21 | 33 | RUN, BABY RUN — Newbeats, Hickory 1332 | 8 |
| 16 | 27 | 38 | 49 | MY GIRL HAS GONE — Miracles, Tamla 54123 | 7 |
| 17 | 15 | 16 | 17 | BUT YOU'RE MINE — Sonny & Cher, Atco 6381 | 7 |
| 18 | 14 | 14 | 16 | I KNEW YOU WHEN — Billy Joe Royal, Columbia 43390 | 10 |
| 19 | 29 | 43 | 59 | MAY THE BIRD OF PARADISE FLY UP YOUR NOSE — "Little" Jimmy Dickens, Columbia 43388 | 6 |
| 20 | 23 | 36 | 50 | MY BABY — Temptations, Gordy 7047 | 5 |
| 21 | 21 | 24 | 38 | ROUND EVERY CORNER — Petula Clark, Warner Bros. 5661 | 7 |
| 22 | 18 | 5 | 4 | KEEP ON DANCING — Gentry's, MGM 13379 | 11 |
| 23 | 17 | 17 | 20 | EVERYONE'S GONE TO THE MOON — Jonathan King, Parrot 9774 | 9 |
| 24 | 35 | 48 | 58 | MAKE IT EASY ON YOURSELF — Walker Brothers, Smash 2000 | 6 |
| 25 | 25 | 32 | 44 | WHERE DO YOU GO — Cher, Imperial 66136 | 6 |
| 26 | 13 | 7 | 8 | POSITIVELY 4TH STREET — Bob Dylan, Columbia 43389 | 8 |
| 27 | 19 | 11 | 11 | MAKE ME YOUR BABY — Barbara Lewis, Atlantic 2300 | 11 |
| 28 | 38 | 49 | 63 | MAKE THE WORLD GO AWAY — Eddy Arnold, RCA Victor 8679 | 6 |
| 29 | 39 | 58 | 88 | I WILL — Dean Martin, Reprise 0415 | 4 |
| 30 | 33 | 44 | 54 | I FOUND A GIRL — Jan & Dean, Liberty 55833 | 6 |
| 31 | 51 | 88 | — | I CAN NEVER GO HOME ANY MORE — Shangri-Las, Red Bird 043 | 3 |
| 32 | 45 | 62 | 83 | I'M A MAN — Yardbirds, Epic 9857 | 4 |
| 33 | 34 | 45 | 55 | RING DANG DOO — Sam the Sham and the Pharaohs, MGM 13397 | 7 |
| 34 | 44 | 61 | 80 | LET ME BE — Turtles, White Whale 224 | 4 |
| 35 | 22 | 25 | 30 | SAY SOMETHING FUNNY — Patty Duke, United Artists 915 | 8 |
| 36 | 36 | 42 | 60 | RUSTY BELLS — Brenda Lee, Decca 31849 | 7 |
| 37 | 58 | — | — | SOMETHING ABOUT YOU — Four Tops, Motown 1084 | 2 |
| 38 | 63 | — | — | OVER AND OVER — Dave Clark Five, Epic 9863 | 2 |
| 39 | 26 | 30 | 35 | WHERE HAVE ALL THE FLOWERS GONE — Johnny Rivers, Imperial 66133 | 8 |
| 40 | 32 | 37 | 48 | CHAPEL IN THE MOONLIGHT — Bachelors, London 9793 | 7 |
| 41 | 53 | 74 | — | KISS AWAY — Ronnie Dove, Diamond 191 | 3 |
| 42 | 28 | 22 | 13 | JUST A LITTLE BIT BETTER — Herman's Hermits, MGM 13398 | 10 |
| 43 | 46 | 56 | 67 | CLEO'S BACK — Jr. Walker and the All Stars, Soul 35013 | 7 |
| 44 | 57 | 81 | — | ENGLAND SWINGS — Roger Miller, Smash 2010 | 3 |
| 45 | 49 | 66 | 75 | (All of a Sudden) MY HEART SINGS — Mel Carter, Imperial 66138 | 4 |
| 46 | 59 | 72 | 97 | MYSTIC EYES — Them, Parrot 9796 | 4 |
| 47 | 24 | 23 | 23 | I WANT TO (Do Everything for You) — Joe Tex, Dial 4016 | 13 |
| 48 | 47 | 51 | 52 | ROAD RUNNER — Gants, Liberty 55829 | 9 |
| 49 | 64 | 80 | — | HERE IT COMES AGAIN — Fortunes, Press 9798 | 3 |
| 50 | 56 | 67 | 82 | JUST A LITTLE BIT — Roy Head, Scepter 12116 | 4 |
| 51 | 69 | 90 | — | DON'T THINK TWICE — Wonder Who? Philips 40324 | 3 |
| 52 | 55 | 65 | 68 | DON'T TALK TO STRANGERS — Beau Brummels, Autumn 20 | 7 |
| 53 | 54 | 59 | 72 | HE TOUCHED ME — Barbra Streisand, Columbia 43403 | 8 |
| 54 | 62 | 70 | 79 | SINNER MAN — Trini Lopez, Reprise 0405 | 6 |
| 55 | 72 | — | — | FEVER — McCoys, Bang 511 | 2 |
| 56 | 80 | — | — | PUPPET ON A STRING — Elvis Presley, RCA Victor 0650 | 2 |
| 57 | 78 | 87 | — | IT'S MY LIFE — Animals, MGM 13414 | 3 |
| 58 | 71 | 77 | 84 | HARLEM NOCTURNE — Viscounts, Amy 940 | 4 |
| 59 | 50 | 53 | 56 | TAKE ME IN YOUR ARMS — Kim Weston, Gordy 7046 | 8 |
| 60 | 70 | 89 | — | CRAWLING BACK — Roy Orbison, MGM 13410 | 3 |
| 61 | — | — | — | HANG ON SLOOPY — Ramsey Lewis Trio, Cadet 5522 | 1 |
| 62 | 75 | 92 | — | ONE HAS MY NAME — Barry Young, Dot 16756 | 3 |
| 63 | 66 | 75 | 81 | MISTY — Vibrations, Okeh 7230 | 5 |
| 64 | 65 | 68 | 70 | LOOKING WITH MY EYES — Dionne Warwick, Scepter 12111 | 8 |
| 65 | 61 | 63 | 73 | FORGIVE ME — Al Martino, Capitol 5506 | 6 |
| 66 | — | — | — | SUNDAY AND ME — Jay & the Americans, United Artists 948 | 1 |
| 67 | 82 | — | — | HOLE IN THE WALL — Packers, Pure Soul 1107 | 2 |
| 68 | 76 | 79 | 89 | DANCE WITH ME — Mojo Men, Autumn 19 | 4 |
| 69 | 81 | — | — | A TIME TO LOVE—A TIME TO CRY — Lou Johnson, Big Top 101 | 2 |
| 70 | 96 | — | — | FLOWERS ON THE WALL — Statler Brothers, Columbia 43315 | 2 |
| 71 | 83 | — | — | MOTHER NATURE, FATHER TIME — Brook Benton, RCA Victor 8693 | 2 |
| 72 | 77 | 82 | — | CHILD OF OUR TIMES — Barry McGuire, Dunhill 4014 | 3 |
| 73 | 73 | 78 | 85 | ROSES AND RAINBOWS — Danny Hutton, HBR 447 | 6 |
| 74 | 90 | — | — | LET'S GET TOGETHER — We Five, A&M 784 | 2 |
| 75 | 79 | 83 | 90 | THE LETTER — Sonny & Cher, Vault 916 | 5 |
| 76 | 91 | 97 | — | DON'T FIGHT IT — Wilson Pickett, Atlantic 2306 | 3 |
| 77 | — | — | — | APPLE OF MY EYE — Roy Head, Back Beat 555 | 1 |
| 78 | 88 | 94 | 94 | HONKY TONK '65 — Lonnie Mack, Fraternity 951 | 4 |
| 79 | 87 | 95 | — | I WANT TO MEET HIM — Royalettes, MGM 13405 | 3 |
| 80 | — | — | — | SOUNDS OF SILENCE — Simon & Garfunkel, Columbia 43396 | 1 |
| 81 | 85 | — | — | LET THE GOOD TIMES ROLL — Roy Orbison, Monument 906 | 2 |
| 82 | — | — | — | PRINCESS IN RAGS — Gene Pitney, Musicor 1130 | 1 |
| 83 | 99 | — | — | BUCKAROO — Buck Owens & His Buckaroos, Capitol 5517 | 2 |
| 84 | 86 | 98 | — | DON'T PITY ME — Peter & Gordon, Capitol 5532 | 3 |
| 85 | 95 | 99 | — | IF YOU DON'T — Barbara Mason, Arctic 112 | 3 |
| 86 | 92 | — | — | SEESAW — Don Covay, Atlantic 2301 | 2 |
| 87 | 89 | 96 | — | I REALLY LOVE YOU — Dee Dee Sharp, Cameo 375 | 3 |
| 88 | 74 | 76 | 77 | I'M SO THANKFUL — The Ikettes, Modern 1011 | 7 |
| 89 | 93 | — | — | PIED PIPER — Changin' Times, Philips 40320 | 2 |
| 90 | — | — | — | OUR WORLD — Johnny Tillotson, MGM 13408 | 1 |
| 91 | 94 | 100 | — | TRY TO REMEMBER — Brothers Four, Columbia 43404 | 3 |
| 92 | — | — | — | TRY ME — James Brown, Smash 2008 | 1 |
| 93 | 98 | — | — | LET'S MOVE & GROOVE (Together) — Johnny Nash, Joda 102 | 5 |
| 94 | 97 | — | 91 | STAND BY ME — Earl Grant, Decca 25674 | 4 |
| 95 | — | — | — | LOOK THROUGH ANY WINDOW — Hollies, Imperial 66134 | 1 |
| 96 | 100 | — | — | LOVE THEME FROM THE SANDPIPER — Tony Bennett, Columbia 43431 | 2 |
| 97 | — | — | — | YOU'VE BEEN CHEATIN' — Impressions, ABC-Paramount 10750 | 1 |
| 98 | — | — | — | DON'T HAVE TO SHOP AROUND — Mad Lads, Volt 127 | 4 |
| 99 | — | — | — | SHE'S WITH HER OTHER LOVE — Leon Hayward, Imperial 66123 | 1 |
| 100 | — | — | — | THE DUCK — Jackie Lee, Mirwood 5502 | 1 |

## BUBBLING UNDER THE HOT 100

101. ONLY LOVE (Can Save Me Now) — Solomon Burke, Atlantic 2308
102. GOODBYE BABE — Castaways, Soma 1442
103. RUN TO MY-LOVIN' ARMS — Lenny Welch, Kapp 712
104. SO LONG BABE — Nancy Sinatra, Reprise 0407
105. YOU DIDN'T HAVE TO BE SO NICE — Lovin' Spoonful, Kama Sutra 205
106. BACK STREET — Edwin Starr, Ric-Tic 107
107. NEVER HAD IT SO GOOD — Ronnie Milsap, Scepter 12109
108. A BENCH IN THE PARK — Jive Five, United Artists 936
109. IL SILENZIO — Nini Rosso, Columbia 43363
110. WOODEN HEART — Elvis Presley, RCA Victor 0650
111. THE SPIDER SONG — Kids Next Door, 4 Corners 129
112. THINK — Jimmy McCracklin, Imperial 66129
113. JUST OUT OF REACH — Zombies, Parrot 9797
114. ORGAN GRINDER'S SWING — Jimmy Smith, Verve 10363
115. REMEMBER WHEN — Wayne Newton, Capitol 5514
116. I'M SATISFIED — Sam Hawkins, Blue Cat 121
117. I KNOW IT'S ALL RIGHT — Sam Hawkins, Ric-Tic
118. I HAVE DREAMED — Chad & Jeremy, Columbia 43414
119. EVERYBODY LOVES A GOOD TIME — Major Lance, Okeh 7233
120. A YOUNG GIRL — Noel Harrison, London 9795
121. STAY TOGETHER YOUNG LOVERS — Ben Aiken, Roulette 4649
122. TAKE A LOOK — Irma Thomas, Imperial 66137
123. C. C. RIDER — Bobby Powell, Whit 714
124. CARNIVAL IS OVER — Seekers, Capitol 5531
125. SPANISH EYES — Al Martino, Capitol 5542
126. EVERYTHING'S GONNA BE ALL RIGHT — Willie Mitchell, Hi 2097
127. THREE BELLS — Tokens, B. T. Puppy 516
128. HEARTBEAT — Gloria Jones, Uptown 712
129. I BELIEVE I'LL LOVE ON — Jackie Wilson, Brunswick
130. FOR YOU — Spellbinders, Columbia 43386
131. LOVE (Makes Me Do Foolish Things) — Martha & the Vandellas, Gordy 7045
132. EVERYBODY DO THE SLOOPY — Johnny Thunder, Diamond 192
133. CRYSTAL CHANDELIER — Vic Dana, Dolton 313
134. JEALOUS HEART — Connie Francis, MGM 13420
135. WHAT THE NEW BREED SAY — Barbarians, Laurie 3321

Compiled from national retail sales and radio station airplay by the Music Popularity Dept. of Record Market Research, Billboard.

# Billboard HOT 100

**For Week Ending November 27, 1965**

★ STAR performer—Sides registering greatest proportionate upward progress this week.

| This Week | 1 Wk. Ago | 2 Wks. Ago | 3 Wks. Ago | TITLE, Artist, Label & Number | Weeks On Chart |
|---|---|---|---|---|---|
| 1 | 1 | 5 | 12 | I HEAR A SYMPHONY — Supremes, Motown 1083 | 5 |
| 2 | 6 | 12 | 31 | TURN! TURN! TURN! — Byrds, Columbia 43424 | 6 |
| 3 | 2 | 3 | 8 | 1-2-3 — Len Barry, Decca 31827 | 10 |
| 4 | 5 | 8 | 13 | LET'S HANG ON — 4 Seasons, Philips 40317 | 8 |
| 5 | 3 | 1 | 1 | GET OFF OF MY CLOUD — Rolling Stones, London 9792 | 8 |
| 6 | 4 | 6 | 9 | RESCUE ME — Fontella Bass, Checker 1120 | 8 |
| 7 | 9 | 9 | 10 | A TASTE OF HONEY — Herb Alpert & the Tijuana Brass, A&M 775 | 10 |
| 8 | 8 | 10 | 15 | AIN'T THAT PECULIAR — Marvin Gaye, Tamla 54122 | 8 |
| 9 | 14 | 68 | — | I GOT YOU (I Feel Good) — James Brown, King 6015 | 3 |
| 10 | 12 | 20 | 39 | YOU'VE GOT TO HIDE YOUR LOVE AWAY — Silkie, Fontana 1525 | 7 |
| 11 | 7 | 2 | 2 | A LOVER'S CONCERTO — Toys, DynoVoice 209 | 12 |
| 12 | 31 | 51 | 88 | I CAN NEVER GO HOME ANY MORE — Shangri-Las, Red Bird 043 | 4 |
| 13 | 20 | 23 | 36 | MY BABY — Temptations, Gordy 7047 | 6 |
| 14 | 16 | 27 | 38 | MY GIRL HAS GONE — Miracles, Tamla 54123 | 8 |
| 15 | 15 | 16 | 21 | RUN, BABY RUN — Newbeats, Hickory 1332 | 9 |
| 16 | 38 | 63 | — | OVER AND OVER — Dave Clark Five, Epic 9863 | 3 |
| 17 | 19 | 29 | 43 | MAY THE BIRD OF PARADISE FLY UP YOUR NOSE — "Little" Jimmy Dickens, Columbia 43388 | 7 |
| 18 | 29 | 39 | 58 | I WILL — Dean Martin, Reprise 0415 | 5 |
| 19 | 28 | 38 | 49 | MAKE THE WORLD GO AWAY — Eddy Arnold, RCA Victor 8679 | 7 |
| 20 | 37 | 58 | — | SOMETHING ABOUT YOU — Four Tops, Motown 1084 | 3 |
| 21 | 24 | 35 | 48 | MAKE IT EASY ON YOURSELF — Walker Brothers, Smash 2000 | 7 |
| 22 | 10 | 4 | 6 | YOU'RE THE ONE — Vogues, Co & Ce 229 | 11 |
| 23 | 23 | 17 | 17 | EVERYONE'S GONE TO THE MOON — Jonathan King, Parrot 9774 | 10 |
| 24 | 44 | 57 | 81 | ENGLAND SWINGS — Roger Miller, Smash 2010 | 4 |
| 25 | 22 | 18 | 5 | KEEP ON DANCING — Gentry's, MGM 13379 | 12 |
| 26 | 13 | 11 | 3 | YESTERDAY — Beatles, Capitol 5498 | 10 |
| 27 | 32 | 45 | 62 | I'M A MAN — Yardbirds, Epic 9857 | 5 |
| 28 | 61 | — | — | HANG ON SLOOPY — Ramsey Lewis Trio, Cadet 5522 | 2 |
| 29 | 34 | 44 | 61 | LET ME BE — Turtles, White Whale 224 | 5 |
| 30 | 11 | 7 | 4 | EVERYBODY LOVES A CLOWN — Gary Lewis & the Playboys, Liberty 55818 | 10 |
| 31 | 41 | 53 | 74 | KISS AWAY — Ronnie Dove, Diamond 191 | 4 |
| 32 | 51 | 69 | 90 | DON'T THINK TWICE — Wonder Who? Philips 40324 | 4 |
| 33 | 36 | 36 | 42 | RUSTY BELLS — Brenda Lee, Decca 31849 | 8 |
| 34 | 17 | 15 | 16 | BUT YOU'RE MINE — Sonny & Cher, Atco 6381 | 8 |
| 35 | 18 | 14 | 14 | I KNEW YOU WHEN — Billy Joe Royal, Columbia 43390 | 11 |
| 36 | 33 | 34 | 45 | RING DANG DOO — Sam the Sham and the Pharaohs, MGM 13397 | 8 |
| 37 | 55 | 72 | — | FEVER — McCoys, Bang 511 | 3 |
| 38 | 27 | 19 | 11 | MAKE ME YOUR BABY — Barbara Lewis, Atlantic 2300 | 12 |
| 39 | 49 | 64 | 80 | HERE IT COMES AGAIN — Fortunes, Press 9798 | 4 |
| 40 | 45 | 49 | 66 | (All of a Sudden) MY HEART SINGS — Mel Carter, Imperial 66138 | 5 |
| 41 | 30 | 33 | 44 | I FOUND A GIRL — Jan & Dean, Liberty 55833 | 7 |
| 42 | 25 | 25 | 32 | WHERE DO YOU GO — Cher, Imperial 66136 | 7 |
| 43 | 50 | 56 | 67 | JUST A LITTLE BIT — Roy Head, Scepter 12116 | 5 |
| 44 | 21 | 21 | 24 | ROUND EVERY CORNER — Petula Clark, Warner Bros. 5661 | 8 |
| 45 | 46 | 59 | 72 | MYSTIC EYES — Them, Parrot 9796 | 5 |
| 46 | 56 | 80 | — | PUPPET ON A STRING — Elvis Presley, RCA Victor 0650 | 3 |
| 47 | 57 | 78 | 87 | IT'S MY LIFE — Animals, MGM 13414 | 4 |
| 48 | 48 | 47 | 51 | ROAD RUNNER — Gants, Liberty 55829 | 10 |
| 49 | 60 | 70 | 89 | CRAWLING BACK — Roy Orbison, MGM 13410 | 4 |
| 50 | 26 | 13 | 7 | POSITIVELY 4TH STREET — Bob Dylan, Columbia 43389 | 9 |
| 51 | 62 | 75 | 92 | ONE HAS MY NAME — Barry Young, Dot 16756 | 4 |
| 52 | 66 | — | — | SUNDAY AND ME — Jay & the Americans, United Artists 948 | 2 |
| 53 | 53 | 54 | 59 | HE TOUCHED ME — Barbra Streisand, Columbia 43403 | 9 |
| 54 | 43 | 46 | 56 | CLEO'S BACK — Jr. Walker and the All Stars, Soul 35013 | 8 |
| 55 | 58 | 71 | 77 | HARLEM NOCTURNE — Viscounts, Amy 940 | 5 |
| 56 | 54 | 62 | 70 | SINNER MAN — Trini Lopez, Reprise 0405 | 7 |
| 57 | 67 | 82 | — | HOLE IN THE WALL — Packers, Pure Soul 1107 | 2 |
| 58 | 39 | 26 | 30 | WHERE HAVE ALL THE FLOWERS GONE — Johnny Rivers, Imperial 66133 | 9 |
| 59 | 74 | 90 | — | LET'S GET TOGETHER — We Five, A&M 784 | 2 |
| 60 | 70 | 96 | — | FLOWERS ON THE WALL — Statler Brothers, Columbia 43315 | 3 |
| 61 | 77 | — | — | APPLE OF MY EYE — Roy Head, Back Beat 555 | 2 |
| 62 | 52 | 55 | 65 | DON'T TALK TO STRANGERS — Beau Brummels, Autumn 20 | 8 |
| 63 | 63 | 66 | 75 | MISTY — Vibrations, Okeh 7230 | 6 |
| 64 | 82 | — | — | PRINCESS IN RAGS — Gene Pitney, Musicor 1130 | 2 |
| 65 | 80 | — | — | SOUNDS OF SILENCE — Simon & Garfunkel, Columbia 43396 | 2 |
| 66 | 69 | 81 | — | A TIME TO LOVE—A TIME TO CRY — Lou Johnson, Big Top 101 | 3 |
| 67 | 71 | 83 | — | MOTHER NATURE, FATHER TIME — Brook Benton, RCA Victor 8693 | 3 |
| 68 | 68 | 76 | 79 | DANCE WITH ME — Mojo Men, Autumn 19 | 5 |
| 69 | — | — | — | THE LITTLE GIRL I ONCE KNEW — Beach Boys, Capitol 5540 | 1 |
| 70 | 86 | 92 | — | SEESAW — Don Covay, Atlantic 2301 | 3 |
| 71 | 83 | 99 | — | BUCKAROO — Buck Owens & His Buckaroos, Capitol 5517 | 3 |
| 72 | 76 | 91 | 97 | DON'T FIGHT IT — Wilson Pickett, Atlantic 2306 | 4 |
| 73 | 79 | 87 | 95 | I WANT TO MEET HIM — Royalettes, MGM 13405 | 4 |
| 74 | 72 | 77 | 82 | CHILD OF OUR TIMES — Barry McGuire, Dunhill 4014 | 4 |
| 75 | — | — | — | YOU DIDN'T HAVE TO BE SO NICE — Lovin' Spoonful, Kama Sutra 205 | 1 |
| 76 | — | — | — | THE REVOLUTION KIND — Sonny, Atco 6386 | 1 |
| 77 | 100 | — | — | THE DUCK — Jackie Lee, Mirwood 5502 | 2 |
| 78 | 97 | — | — | YOU'VE BEEN CHEATIN' — Impressions, ABC-Paramount 10750 | 2 |
| 79 | 90 | — | — | OUR WORLD — Johnny Tillotson, MGM 13408 | 2 |
| 80 | 78 | 88 | 94 | HONKY TONK '65 — Lonnie Mack, Fraternity 951 | 5 |
| 81 | — | — | — | JEALOUS HEART — Connie Francis, MGM 13420 | 1 |
| 82 | 94 | 97 | — | STAND BY ME — Earl Grant, Decca 25674 | 5 |
| 83 | 84 | 86 | 98 | DON'T PITY ME — Peter & Gordon, Capitol 5532 | 4 |
| 84 | 92 | — | — | TRY ME — James Brown, Smash 2008 | 2 |
| 85 | 87 | 89 | 96 | I REALLY LOVE YOU — Dee Dee Sharp, Cameo 375 | 4 |
| 86 | 95 | — | — | LOOK THROUGH ANY WINDOW — Hollies, Imperial 66134 | 2 |
| 87 | 89 | 93 | — | PIED PIPER — Changin' Times, Philips 40320 | 3 |
| 88 | 81 | 85 | — | LET THE GOOD TIMES ROLL — Roy Orbison, Monument 906 | 3 |
| 89 | — | — | — | RAINBOW '65 — Gene Chandler, Constellation 158 | 1 |
| 90 | — | — | — | EVERYBODY DO THE SLOOPY — Johnny Thunder, Diamond 192 | 1 |
| 91 | 93 | 98 | — | LET'S MOVE & GROOVE (Together) — Johnny Nash, Joda 102 | 6 |
| 92 | — | — | — | I DON'T KNOW WHAT YOU'VE GOT BUT IT'S GOT ME — Little Richard, Vee Jay 698 | 1 |
| 93 | — | — | — | FOR YOU — Spellbinders, Columbia 43384 | 1 |
| 94 | — | — | — | FIVE O'CLOCK WORLD — Vogues, Co & Ce 232 | 1 |
| 95 | 96 | 100 | — | LOVE THEME FROM THE SANDPIPER — Tony Bennett, Columbia 43431 | 3 |
| 96 | 98 | — | — | DON'T HAVE TO SHOP AROUND — Mad Lads, Volt 127 | 2 |
| 97 | — | — | — | ONLY LOVE (Can Save Me Now) — Solomon Burke, Atlantic 2308 | 1 |
| 98 | 99 | — | — | SHE'S WITH HER OTHER LOVE — Leon Hayward, Imperial 66123 | 2 |
| 99 | — | — | — | I'M SATISFIED — San Remo Golden Strings, Ric-Tic 108 | 1 |
| 100 | — | — | — | MICHAEL — C.O.D.'s, Kellmac 1003 | 1 |

## BUBBLING UNDER THE HOT 100

101. GOODBYE BABE — Castaways, Soma 1442
102. EBB TIDE — Righteous Brothers, Philles 130
103. RUN TO MY LOVIN' ARMS — Lenny Welch, Kapp 712
104. BACK STREET — Edwin Starr, Ric-Tic 107
105. THE CARNIVAL IS OVER — Seekers, Capitol 5531
106. BENCH IN THE PARK — Jive Five, United Artists 936
107. IF YOU DON'T — Barbara Mason, Arctic 112
108. TRY TO REMEMBER — Brothers Four, Columbia 43404
109. A WELL RESPECTED MAN — Kinks, Reprise 0420
110. A YOUNG GIRL — Noel Harrison, London 9795
111. C. C. RIDER — Bobby Powell, Whit 714
112. NEVER HAD IT SO GOOD — Ronnie Milsap, Scepter 12109
113. SPANISH EYES — Al Martino, Capitol 5542
114. EVERYBODY LOVES A GOOD TIME — Major Lance, Okeh 7233
115. SO LONG BABE — Nancy Sinatra, Reprise 0407
116. JUST LIKE ME — Paul Revere & the Raiders, Columbia 43461
117. SANDY — Ronny & the Daytonas, Mala 513
118. TAKE A LOOK — Irma Thomas, Imperial 66137
119. THINK — Jimmy McCracklin, Imperial 66129
120. CRYSTAL CHANDELIER — Vic Dana, Dolton 313
121. STAY TOGETHER YOUNG LOVERS — Roulette 4649
122. A DRINKING-MAN'S DIET — Allan Sherman, Warner Bros. 5677
123. RISING SUN — Deep Six, Liberty 55838
124. THREE BELLS — Token, R. T. Puppy 516
125. THE LAST THING ON MY MIND — Vejtables, Autumn 23
126. STAY AWAY FROM MY BABY — Ted Taylor, Okeh 7231
127. LOVE (Makes Me Do Foolish Things) — Martha & the Vandellas, Gordy 7405
128. WHAT THE NEW BREED SAY — Barbarians, Laurie 3321
129. NEW BREED — Jimmy Workman, Diplomacy 339
130. NO TIME FOR PITY — Baby Washington, Sue 137
131. HEARTBEAT — Gloria Jones, Uptown 751
132. IT'S GOOD NEWS WEEK — Hedgehoppers Anonymous, Parrot 9800
133. WHAT'S COME OVER THIS WORLD? — Billy Carr, Colpix 791
134. I WON'T LOVE YOU ANYMORE (Sorry) — Lesley Gore, Mercury 72413
135. GO AWAY FROM MY WORLD — Marianne Faithfull, London 9802

Compiled from national retail sales and radio station airplay by the Music Popularity Dept. of Record Market Research, Billboard.

Billboard

For Week Ending December 4, 1965

# HOT 100

★ **STAR performer—Sides registering greatest proportionate upward progress this week.**

Record Industry Association of America seal of certification as million selling single.

| This Week | 1 Wk. Ago | 2 Wks. Ago | 3 Wks. Ago | TITLE Artist, Label & Number | Weeks On Chart |
|---|---|---|---|---|---|
| 1 | 2 | 6 | 12 | TURN! TURN! TURN! — Byrds, Columbia 43424 | 7 |
| 2 | 1 | 1 | 5 | I HEAR A SYMPHONY — Supremes, Motown 1083 | 6 |
| 3 | 3 | 2 | 3 | 1-2-3 — Len Barry, Decca 31827 | 11 |
| 4 | 4 | 5 | 8 | LET'S HANG ON — 4 Seasons, Philips 40317 | 9 |
| ★5 | 9 | 14 | 68 | I GOT YOU (I Feel Good) — James Brown, King 6015 | 4 |
| 6 | 6 | 4 | 6 | RESCUE ME — Fontella Bass, Checker 1120 | 10 |
| 7 | 7 | 9 | 9 | A TASTE OF HONEY — Herb Alpert & the Tijuana Brass, A&M 775 | 11 |
| 8 | 8 | 8 | 10 | AIN'T THAT PECULIAR — Marvin Gaye, Tamla 54122 | 9 |
| ★9 | 12 | 31 | 51 | I CAN NEVER GO HOME ANY MORE — Shangri-Las, Red Bird 043 | 5 |
| ★10 | 16 | 38 | 63 | OVER AND OVER — Dave Clark Five, Epic 9863 | 4 |
| 11 | 5 | 3 | 1 | GET OFF OF MY CLOUD — Rolling Stones, London 9792 | 9 |
| 12 | 15 | 15 | 16 | RUN, BABY RUN — Newbeats, Hickory 1332 | 10 |
| ★13 | 18 | 29 | 39 | I WILL — Dean Martin, Reprise 0415 | 6 |
| 14 | 10 | 12 | 20 | YOU'VE GOT TO HIDE YOUR LOVE AWAY — Silkie, Fontana 1525 | 8 |
| 15 | 17 | 19 | 29 | MAY THE BIRD OF PARADISE FLY UP YOUR NOSE — "Little" Jimmy Dickens, Columbia 43388 | 8 |
| ★16 | 21 | 24 | 35 | MAKE IT EASY ON YOURSELF — Walker Brothers, Smash 2000 | 8 |
| 17 | 19 | 28 | 38 | MAKE THE WORLD GO AWAY — Eddy Arnold, RCA Victor 8679 | 8 |
| ★18 | 24 | 44 | 57 | ENGLAND SWINGS — Roger Miller, Smash 2010 | 5 |
| 19 | 20 | 37 | 58 | SOMETHING ABOUT YOU — Four Tops, Motown 1084 | 4 |
| ★20 | 37 | 55 | 72 | FEVER — McCoys, Bang 511 | 4 |
| ★21 | 28 | 61 | — | HANG ON SLOOPY — Ramsey Lewis Trio, Cadet 5522 | 3 |
| ★22 | 27 | 32 | 45 | I'M A MAN — Yardbirds, Epic 9857 | 6 |
| 23 | 11 | 7 | 2 | A LOVER'S CONCERTO — Toys, DynoVoice 209 | 13 |
| ★24 | 32 | 51 | 69 | DON'T THINK TWICE — Wonder Who? Philips 40324 | 5 |
| 25 | 13 | 20 | 23 | MY BABY — Temptations, Gordy 7047 | 7 |
| ★26 | 31 | 41 | 53 | KISS AWAY — Ronnie Dove, Diamond 191 | 5 |
| ★27 | 46 | 56 | 80 | PUPPET ON A STRING — Elvis Presley, RCA Victor 0650 | 4 |
| 28 | 14 | 16 | 27 | MY GIRL HAS GONE — Miracles, Tamla 54123 | 9 |
| 29 | 29 | 34 | 44 | LET ME BE — Turtles, White Whale 224 | 6 |
| ★30 | 39 | 49 | 64 | HERE IT COMES AGAIN — Fortunes, Press 9798 | 5 |
| ★31 | 52 | 66 | — | SUNDAY AND ME — Jay & the Americans, United Artists 948 | 3 |
| 32 | 25 | 22 | 18 | KEEP ON DANCING — Gentry's, MGM 13379 | 13 |
| 33 | 22 | 10 | 4 | YOU'RE THE ONE — Vogues, Co & Ce 229 | 12 |
| ★34 | 65 | 80 | — | SOUNDS OF SILENCE — Simon & Garfunkel, Columbia 43396 | 3 |
| ★35 | 45 | 46 | 59 | MYSTIC EYES — Them, Parrot 9796 | 6 |
| ★36 | 47 | 57 | 78 | IT'S MY LIFE — Animals, MGM 13414 | 5 |
| ★37 | 51 | 62 | 75 | ONE HAS MY NAME — Barry Young, Dot 16756 | 5 |
| 38 | 40 | 45 | 49 | (All of a Sudden) MY HEART SINGS — Mel Carter, Imperial 66138 | 6 |
| 39 | 43 | 50 | 56 | JUST A LITTLE BIT — Roy Head, Scepter 12116 | 6 |
| 40 | 23 | 23 | 17 | EVERYONE'S GONE TO THE MOON — Jonathan King, Parrot 9774 | 11 |
| ★41 | — | — | — | EBB TIDE — Righteous Brothers, Philles 130 | 1 |
| ★42 | 69 | — | — | THE LITTLE GIRL I ONCE KNEW — Beach Boys, Capitol 5540 | 2 |
| 43 | 30 | 11 | 7 | EVERYBODY LOVES A CLOWN — Gary Lewis & the Playboys, Liberty 55818 | 11 |
| ★44 | 60 | 70 | 96 | FLOWERS ON THE WALL — Statler Brothers, Columbia 43315 | 4 |
| 45 | 26 | 13 | 11 | YESTERDAY — Beatles, Capitol 5498 | 11 |
| 46 | 48 | 48 | 47 | ROAD RUNNER — Gants, Liberty 55829 | 11 |
| ★47 | 61 | 77 | — | APPLE OF MY EYE — Roy Head, Back Beat 555 | 3 |
| 48 | 49 | 60 | 70 | CRAWLING BACK — Roy Orbison, MGM 13410 | 5 |
| 49 | 36 | 33 | 34 | RING DANG DOO — Sam the Sham and the Pharaohs, MGM 13397 | 9 |
| 50 | 57 | 67 | 82 | HOLE IN THE WALL — Packers, Pure Soul 1107 | 4 |
| 51 | 59 | 74 | 90 | LET'S GET TOGETHER — We Five, A&M 784 | 4 |
| ★52 | 64 | 82 | — | PRINCESS IN RAGS — Gene Pitney, Musicor 1130 | 3 |
| 53 | 55 | 58 | 71 | HARLEM NOCTURNE — Viscounts, Amy 940 | 6 |
| ★54 | 77 | 100 | — | THE DUCK — Jackie Lee, Mirwood 5502 | 3 |
| 55 | 33 | 36 | 36 | RUSTY BELLS — Brenda Lee, Decca 31849 | 9 |
| ★56 | 75 | — | — | YOU DIDN'T HAVE TO BE SO NICE — Lovin' Spoonful, Kama Sutra 205 | 2 |
| ★57 | 67 | 71 | 83 | MOTHER NATURE, FATHER TIME — Brook Benton, RCA Victor 8693 | 4 |
| 58 | 53 | 53 | 54 | HE TOUCHED ME — Barbra Streisand, Columbia 43403 | 10 |
| 59 | 56 | 54 | 62 | SINNER MAN — Trini Lopez, Reprise 0405 | 8 |
| 60 | 66 | 69 | 81 | A TIME TO LOVE—A TIME TO CRY — Lou Johnson, Big Top 101 | 4 |
| 61 | 68 | 68 | 76 | DANCE WITH ME — Mojo Men, Autumn 19 | 6 |
| 62 | 70 | 86 | 92 | SEESAW — Don Covay, Atlantic 2301 | 4 |
| 63 | 72 | 76 | 91 | DON'T FIGHT IT — Wilson Pickett, Atlantic 2306 | 5 |
| 64 | 71 | 83 | 99 | BUCKAROO — Buck Owens & His Buckaroos, Capitol 5517 | 4 |
| 65 | 63 | 63 | 66 | MISTY — Vibrations, Okeh 7230 | 7 |
| ★66 | 84 | 92 | — | TRY ME — James Brown, Smash 2008 | 3 |
| ★67 | 94 | — | — | FIVE O'CLOCK WORLD — Vogues, Co & Ce 232 | 2 |
| ★68 | — | — | — | SPANISH EYES — Al Martino, Capitol 5542 | 1 |
| 69 | 78 | 97 | — | YOU'VE BEEN CHEATIN' — Impressions, ABC-Paramount 10750 | 3 |
| 70 | 76 | — | — | THE REVOLUTION KIND — Sonny, Atco 6386 | 2 |
| ★71 | 90 | — | — | EVERYBODY DO THE SLOOPY — Johnny Thunder, Diamond 192 | 2 |
| 72 | 81 | — | — | JEALOUS HEART — Connie Francis, MGM 13420 | 2 |
| 73 | 79 | 90 | — | OUR WORLD — Johnny Tillotson, MGM 13408 | 3 |
| ★74 | — | — | — | CRYSTAL CHANDELIER — Vic Dana, Dolton 313 | 1 |
| ★75 | — | — | — | A SWEET WOMAN LIKE YOU — Joe Tex, Dial 4022 | 1 |
| 76 | 73 | 79 | 87 | I WANT TO MEET HIM — Royalettes, MGM 13405 | 5 |
| ★77 | — | — | — | SATIN PILLOWS — Bobby Vinton, Epic 9869 | 1 |
| 78 | 86 | 95 | — | LOOK THROUGH ANY WINDOW — Hollies, Imperial 66134 | 3 |
| 79 | 82 | 94 | 97 | STAND BY ME — Earl Grant, Decca 25674 | 6 |
| ★80 | — | — | — | SANDY — Ronny & the Daytonas, Mala 513 | 1 |
| 81 | 85 | 87 | 89 | I REALLY LOVE YOU — Dee Dee Sharp, Cameo 375 | 5 |
| 82 | 89 | — | — | RAINBOW '65 — Gene Chandler, Constellation 158 | 2 |
| ★83 | — | — | — | I'VE GOT TO BE SOMEBODY — Billy Joe Royal, Columbia 43465 | 1 |
| ★84 | — | — | — | A WELL RESPECTED MAN — Kinks, Reprise 0420 | 1 |
| ★85 | — | — | — | JUST LIKE ME — Paul Revere & the Raiders, Columbia 43461 | 1 |
| ★86 | — | — | — | ALL OR NOTHING — Patty LaBelle & the Bluebelles, Atlantic 2311 | 1 |
| ★87 | — | — | — | I WON'T LOVE YOU ANYMORE (Sorry) — Lesley Gore, Mercury 72513 | 1 |
| 88 | 91 | 93 | 98 | LET'S MOVE & GROOVE (Together) — Johnny Nash, Joda 102 | 7 |
| ★89 | — | — | — | C. C. RIDER — Bobby Powell, Whit 714 | 1 |
| 90 | 100 | — | — | MICHAEL — C.O.D.'s, Kellmac 1003 | 2 |
| 91 | 99 | — | — | I'M SATISFIED — San Remo Golden Strings, Ric-Tic 108 | 2 |
| 92 | 98 | 99 | — | SHE'S WITH HER OTHER LOVE — Leon Hayward, Imperial 66123 | 3 |
| 93 | — | — | — | A YOUNG GIRL — Noel Harrison, London 9795 | 1 |
| 94 | 97 | — | — | ONLY LOVE (Can Save Me Now) — Solomon Burke, Atlantic 2308 | 2 |
| 95 | — | — | — | QUIET NIGHTS OF QUIET STARS — Andy Williams, Columbia 43456 | 1 |
| 96 | — | — | — | LIES — Knickerbockers, Challenge 59321 | 1 |
| 97 | — | — | — | RUN TO MY LOVIN' ARMS — Lenny Welch, Kapp 712 | 1 |
| 98 | — | — | — | JUST ONE MORE DAY — Otis Redding, Volt 130 | 1 |
| 99 | — | — | — | STAY AWAY FROM MY BABY — Ted Taylor, Okeh 7231 | 1 |
| 100 | 100 | — | — | IT'S GOODNEWS WEEK — Hedgehoppers Anonymous, Parrot 9800 | 1 |

## HOT 100—A TO Z—*(Publisher-Licensee)*


Ain't That Peculiar (Jobete, BMI) .... 8
(All of a Sudden) My Heart Sings (Leeds, ASCAP). 38
All or Nothing (Big Top-Web IV, BMI) .... 86
Apple of My Eye (Don, BMI) .... 47
Buckaroo (Bluebook, BMI) .... 64
C. C. Rider (Su-Ma, BMI) .... 89
Crawling Back (Acuff-Rose, BMI) .... 48
Crystal Chandelier (Harbot, SESAC) .... 74
Dance With Me (Taracrest, BMI) .... 61
Don't Fight It (East-Web IV, BMI) .... 63
Don't Think Twice (Witmark, ASCAP) .... 24
Duck, The (Keymen-Mirwood, BMI) .... 54
Ebb Tide (Robbins, ASCAP) .... 41
England Swings Me (Tree, BMI) .... 18
Everybody Do the Sloopy (Tobi-Ann-Web IV, BMI). 71
Everybody Loves a Clown (Viva, BMI) .... 43
Everyone's Gone to the Moon (Mainstay, BMI) .. 40
Fever (Lois, BMI) .... 20
Five O'Clock World (Screen Gems-Columbia, BMI).. 67
Flowers on the Wall (Southwind, BMI) .... 44
Get Off of My Cloud (Gideon, BMI) .... 11
Hang on Sloopy (Picturetone, BMI) .... 21
Harlem Nocturne (Shapiro-Bernstein, ASCAP) .... 53
He Touched Me (Morris, ASCAP) .... 58
Here It Comes Again (Miller, ASCAP) .... 30
Hole in the Wall (Pure Soul, BMI) .... 50
I Can Never Go Home Anymore (Trio-Tender Tunes, BMI) .... 9
I Got You (I Feel Good) (Lois-Try Me, BMI) ... 5
I Hear a Symphony (Jobete, BMI) .... 2
I Really Love You (Blockbuster-Downstairs, BMI). 81
I Want to Meet Him (South Mountain, BMI) .... 76
I Will (Camarillo, BMI) .... 13
I Won't Love You Anymore (Buffee, BMI) .... 87
I'm Satisfied (Myto, BMI) .... 91
I'm a Man (Arc, BMI) .... 22
I've Got to Be Somebody (Lowery, BMI) .... 83
It's Good News Week (Mainstay, BMI) ....100
It's My Life (Screen Gems-Columbia, BMI) .... 36
Jealous Heart (Acuff-Rose, BMI) .... 72
Just a Little Bit (Tollie, BMI) .... 39
Just Like Me (Daywin, BMI) .... 85
Just One More Day (East-Redwal-Time, BMI) .... 98
Keep on Dancing (Arc-Press, BMI) .... 32
Kiss Away (Gallico, BMI) .... 26
Let Me Be (Trousdale, BMI) .... 29
Let's Get Together (SFO, BMI) .... 51
Let's Hang On (Saturday & Seasons Four, BMI) .. 4
Let's Move & Groove (Together) (And, BMI) .... 88
Lies (4-Star Sales, BMI) .... 96
Little Girl I Once Knew, The (Sea of Tunes, BMI). 42
Look Through Any Window (Miller, ASCAP) .... 78
Lover's Concerto, A (Saturday, BMI) .... 23
Make It Easy on Yourself (Famous, BMI) .... 16
Make the World Go Away (Pamper, BMI) .... 17
May the Bird of Paradise Fly Up Your Nose (Central Songs, BMI) .... 15
Michael (Chevis, BMI) .... 90
Misty (Vernon, ASCAP) .... 65
Mother Nature, Father Time (Benday & Eden, BMI) .... 57
My Baby (Jobete, BMI) .... 25
My Girl Has Gone (Jobete, BMI) .... 28
Mystic Eyes (Wemar, BMI) .... 35
One Has My Name (Peer Int'l, BMI) .... 37
Only Love (Can Save Me Now) (Pamco, BMI) .... 94
Our World (Natson & Port, ASCAP) .... 73
Over and Over (Recordo, BMI) .... 10
1-2-3 (Champion & Double Diamond, BMI) .... 3
Princess in Rags (Screen Gems-Columbia, BMI) .... 52
Puppet on a String (Gladys, ASCAP) .... 27
Quiet Nights of Quiet Stars (Duchess, BMI) .... 95
Rainbow '65 (Aba-Conrad, BMI) .... 82
Rescue Me (Chevis, BMI) .... 6
Revolution Kind, The (Five-West-Cotillion, BMI) .. 70
Ring Dang Doo (Valley & Beckie, BMI) .... 49
Road Runner (Arc, BMI) .... 46
Run, Baby Run (Acuff-Rose, BMI) .... 12
Run to My Lovin' Arms (Screen Gems-Columbia, BMI) .... 97
Rusty Bells (Music City, ASCAP) .... 55
Sandy (Buckhorn, BMI) .... 80
Satin Pillows (Vintage, BMI) .... 77
Seesaw (East-Cotillion, BMI) .... 62
She's With Her Other Love (Rose, BMI) .... 92
Sinner Man (Saloon Songs, BMI) .... 59
Something About You (Jobete, BMI) .... 19
Sounds of Silence (Eclectic, BMI) .... 34
Spanish Eyes (Roosevelt & G.E.M.A., BMI-ASCAP) .... 68
Stand by Me (Trio-Progressive, BMI) .... 79
Stay Away From My Baby (Lois, BMI) .... 99
Sunday and Me (Tallyrand, BMI) .... 31
Sweet Woman Like You, A (Tree, BMI) .... 75
Taste of Honey, A (Songfest, ASCAP) .... 7
Time to Love—A Time to Cry, A (Hill & Range, BMI) .... 60
Try Me (Try Me, BMI) .... 66
Turn! Turn! Turn! (Melody Trails, BMI) .... 1
Well Respected Man, A (Amer. Met. Ent. of N.Y., BMI) .... 84
Yesterday (Maclen, BMI) .... 45
You Didn't Have to Be So Nice (Faithful Virtue, BMI) .... 56
Young Girl, A (E. B. Marks, BMI) .... 93
You're the One (Leads, ASCAP) .... 33
You've Been Cheatin' (Chi-Sound, BMI) .... 69
You've Got to Hide Your Love Away (Maclen, BMI) .... 14


## BUBBLING UNDER THE HOT 100

101. GOODBYE BABE ....Castaways, Soma 1442
102. BACK STREET ....Edwin Starr, Ric-Tic 107
103. THUNDERBALL ....Tom Jones, Parrot 9801
104. A BOY AND A GIRL ....Sounds Orchestral, Parkway 968
105. THE CARNIVAL IS OVER ....Seekers, Capitol 5531
106. GO AWAY FROM MY WORLD ....Marianne Faithfull, London 9802
107. DON'T HAVE TO SHOP AROUND ....Mad Lads, Volt 127
108. CRYING TIME ....Ray Charles, ABC-Paramount 10739
109. I DON'T KNOW WHAT YOU'VE GOT BUT IT'S GOT ME ....Little Richard, Vee Jay 698
110. EVERYBODY LOVES A GOOD TIME ....Major Lance, Okeh 7233
111. NO MATTER WHAT SHAPE (Your Stomach's In) ....T-Bones, Liberty 55836
112. GOOD THINGS COME TO THOSE WHO WAIT ....Chuck Jackson, Wand 1105
113. WHAT THE NEW BREED SAY ....Barbarians, Laurie 3321
114. THINK ....Jimmy McCracklin, Imperial 66129
115. PIED PIPER ....Changin' Times, Phillips 40320
116. FOR YOU ....Spellbinders, Columbia 43384
117. PRIVATE JOHN Q. ....Glen Campbell, Capitol 5545
118. HONKY TONK '65 ....Lonnie Mack, Fraternity 951
119. DRINKING MAN'S DIET ....Allan Sherman, Warner Bros. 5672
120. PLASTIC ....Serendipity Singers, Philips 40331
121. THE LAST THING ON MY MIND ....Vejtables, Autumn 23
122. RISING SUN ....Deep Six, Liberty 55838
123. LOVE (Makes Me Do Foolish Things) ....Martha & the Vandellas, Gordy 7405
124. THREE BELLS ....Tokens, B. T. Puppy 516
125. MAGIC TOWN ....Jody Miller, Capitol 5541
126. WHAT'S COME OVER THIS WORLD? ....Billy Carr, Colpix 791
127. NEW BREED ....Jimmy Holiday, Diplomacy 339
128. NO TIME FOR PITY ....Baby Washington, Sue 137
129. TAKE A HEART ....Sorrows, Warner Bros. 5662
130. GRAB THIS THING ....Markeys, Stax 181
131. LOVE IS STRANGE ....Caesar & Cleo, Reprise 0419
132. LOVE THEME FROM THE SANDPIPER ....Tony Bennett, Columbia 43431
133. EVERYTHING'S GONNA BE ALRIGHT ....Willie Mitchell, Hi 2097
134. LOOK AT ME ....Three Dimensions, RCA Victor 8709
135. LOVE BUG ....Jack Jones, Kapp 722

Compiled from national retail sales and radio station airplay by the Music Popularity Dept. of Record Market Research, Billboard.

Billboard

For Week Ending December 11, 1965

# HOT 100

★ **STAR performer**—Sides registering greatest proportionate upward progress this week.

● Record Industry Association of America seal of certification as million selling single.

Billboard Award

| This Week | 1 Wk. Ago | 2 Wks. Ago | 3 Wks. Ago | TITLE Artist, Label & Number | Weeks On Chart |
|---|---|---|---|---|---|
| 1 | 1 | 2 | 6 | TURN! TURN! TURN! — Byrds, Columbia 43424 | 8 |
| 2 | 2 | 1 | 1 | I HEAR A SYMPHONY — Supremes, Motown 1083 | 7 |
| 3 | 4 | 4 | 5 | LET'S HANG ON — 4 Seasons, Philips 40317 | 10 |
| 4 | 5 | 9 | 14 | I GOT YOU (I Feel Good) — James Brown, King 6015 | 5 |
| ★5 | 10 | 16 | 38 | OVER AND OVER — Dave Clark Five, Epic 9863 | 5 |
| ★6 | 9 | 12 | 31 | I CAN NEVER GO HOME ANY MORE — Shangri-Las, Red Bird 043 | 6 |
| 7 | 3 | 3 | 2 | 1-2-3 — Len Barry, Decca 31827 | 12 |
| 8 | 7 | 7 | 9 | A TASTE OF HONEY — Herb Alpert & the Tijuana Brass, A&M 775 | 12 |
| 9 | 6 | 6 | 4 | RESCUE ME — Fontella Bass, Checker 1120 | 11 |
| ★10 | 13 | 18 | 29 | I WILL — Dean Martin, Reprise 0415 | 7 |
| ★11 | 21 | 28 | 61 | HANG ON SLOOPY — Ramsey Lewis Trio, Cadet 5522 | 4 |
| ★12 | 18 | 24 | 44 | ENGLAND SWINGS — Roger Miller, Smash 2010 | 6 |
| ★13 | 20 | 37 | 55 | FEVER — McCoys, Bang 511 | 5 |
| 14 | 17 | 19 | 28 | MAKE THE WORLD GO AWAY — Eddy Arnold, RCA Victor 8679 | 9 |
| 15 | 11 | 5 | 3 | GET OFF OF MY CLOUD — Rolling Stones, London 9792 | 10 |
| 16 | 8 | 8 | 8 | AIN'T THAT PECULIAR — Marvin Gaye, Tamla 54122 | 10 |
| ★17 | 22 | 27 | 32 | I'M A MAN — Yardbirds, Epic 9857 | 7 |
| ★18 | 24 | 32 | 51 | DON'T THINK TWICE — Wonder Who? Philips 40324 | 6 |
| 19 | 19 | 20 | 37 | SOMETHING ABOUT YOU — Four Tops, Motown 1084 | 5 |
| 20 | 12 | 15 | 15 | RUN, BABY RUN — Newbeats, Hickory 1332 | 11 |
| ★21 | 41 | — | — | EBB TIDE — Righteous Brothers, Philles 130 | 2 |
| ★22 | 27 | 46 | 56 | PUPPET ON A STRING — Elvis Presley, RCA Victor 0650 | 5 |
| ★23 | 31 | 52 | 66 | SUNDAY AND ME — Jay & the Americans, United Artists 948 | 4 |
| ★24 | 37 | 51 | 62 | ONE HAS MY NAME — Barry Young, Dot 16756 | 6 |
| 25 | 26 | 31 | 41 | KISS AWAY — Ronnie Dove, Diamond 191 | 6 |
| ★26 | 34 | 65 | 80 | SOUNDS OF SILENCE — Simon & Garfunkel, Columbia 43396 | 4 |
| 27 | 14 | 10 | 12 | YOU'VE GOT TO HIDE YOUR LOVE AWAY — Silkie, Fontana 1525 | 9 |
| 28 | 15 | 17 | 19 | MAY THE BIRD OF PARADISE FLY UP YOUR NOSE — "Little" Jimmy Dickens, Columbia 43388 | 9 |
| 29 | 16 | 21 | 24 | MAKE IT EASY ON YOURSELF — Walker Brothers, Smash 2000 | 9 |
| 30 | 30 | 39 | 49 | HERE IT COMES AGAIN — Fortunes, Press 9798 | 6 |
| 31 | 36 | 47 | 57 | IT'S MY LIFE — Animals, MGM 13414 | 6 |
| ★32 | 42 | 69 | — | THE LITTLE GIRL I ONCE KNEW — Beach Boys, Capitol 5540 | 3 |
| 33 | 35 | 45 | 46 | MYSTIC EYES — Them, Parrot 9796 | 7 |
| ★34 | 44 | 60 | 70 | FLOWERS ON THE WALL — Statler Brothers, Columbia 43315 | 5 |
| 35 | 25 | 13 | 20 | MY BABY — Temptations, Gordy 7047 | 7 |
| 36 | 29 | 29 | 34 | LET ME BE — Turtles, White Whale 224 | 7 |
| 37 | 23 | 11 | 7 | A LOVER'S CONCERTO — Toys, DynoVoice 209 | 14 |
| 38 | 28 | 14 | 16 | MY GIRL HAS GONE — Miracles, Tamla 54123 | 10 |
| ★39 | 56 | 75 | — | YOU DIDN'T HAVE TO BE SO NICE — Lovin' Spoonful, Kama Sutra 205 | 3 |
| ★40 | 67 | 94 | — | FIVE O'CLOCK WORLD — Vogues, Co & Ce 232 | 3 |
| 41 | 39 | 43 | 50 | JUST A LITTLE BIT — Roy Head, Scepter 12116 | 7 |
| ★42 | 54 | 77 | 100 | THE DUCK — Jackie Lee, Mirwood 5502 | 4 |
| 43 | 50 | 57 | 67 | HOLE IN THE WALL — Packers, Pure Soul 1107 | 5 |
| 44 | 52 | 64 | 82 | PRINCESS IN RAGS — Gene Pitney, Musicor 1130 | 4 |
| 45 | 47 | 61 | 77 | APPLE OF MY EYE — Roy Head, Back Beat 555 | 4 |
| 46 | 48 | 49 | 60 | CRAWLING BACK — Roy Orbison, MGM 13410 | 6 |
| 47 | 53 | 55 | 58 | HARLEM NOCTURNE — Viscounts, Amy 940 | 7 |
| ★48 | 68 | — | — | SPANISH EYES — Al Martino, Capitol 5542 | 2 |
| 49 | 38 | 40 | 45 | (All of a Sudden) MY HEART SINGS — Mel Carter, Imperial 66138 | 7 |
| 50 | 46 | 48 | 48 | ROAD RUNNER — Gants, Liberty 55829 | 12 |
| 51 | 51 | 59 | 74 | LET'S GET TOGETHER — We Five, A&M 784 | 5 |
| ★52 | 62 | 70 | 86 | SEESAW — Don Covay, Atlantic 2301 | 5 |
| 53 | 57 | 67 | 71 | MOTHER NATURE, FATHER TIME — Brook Benton, RCA Victor 8693 | 5 |
| ★54 | 77 | — | — | SATIN PILLOWS — Bobby Vinton, Epic 9869 | 2 |
| ★55 | 74 | — | — | CRYSTAL CHANDELIER — Vic Dana, Dolton 313 | 2 |
| ★56 | 69 | 78 | 97 | YOU'VE BEEN CHEATIN' — Impressions, ABC-Paramount 10750 | 4 |
| ★57 | — | — | — | SHE'S JUST MY STYLE — Gary Lewis & the Playboys, Liberty 55846 | 1 |
| 58 | 59 | 56 | 54 | SINNER MAN — Trini Lopez, Reprise 0405 | 9 |
| 59 | 60 | 66 | 69 | A TIME TO LOVE—A TIME TO CRY — Lou Johnson, Big Top 101 | 5 |
| ★60 | 75 | — | — | A SWEET WOMAN LIKE YOU — Joe Tex, Dial 4022 | 2 |
| 61 | 63 | 72 | 76 | DON'T FIGHT IT — Wilson Pickett, Atlantic 2306 | 6 |
| ★62 | 78 | 86 | 95 | LOOK THROUGH ANY WINDOW — Hollies, Imperial 66134 | 4 |
| ★63 | — | — | — | THUNDERBALL — Tom Jones, Parrot 9801 | 1 |
| 64 | 64 | 71 | 83 | BUCKAROO — Buck Owens & His Buckaroos, Capitol 5517 | 5 |
| 65 | 72 | 81 | — | JEALOUS HEART — Connie Francis, MGM 13420 | 3 |
| 66 | 66 | 84 | 92 | TRY ME — James Brown, Smash 2008 | 4 |
| 67 | 71 | 90 | — | EVERYBODY DO THE SLOOPY — Johnny Thunder, Diamond 192 | 3 |
| ★68 | 83 | — | — | I'VE GOT TO BE SOMEBODY — Billy Joe Royal, Columbia 43465 | 2 |
| ★69 | 85 | — | — | JUST LIKE ME — Paul Revere & the Raiders, Columbia 43461 | 2 |
| 70 | 70 | 76 | — | THE REVOLUTION KIND — ●Sonny, Atco 6386 | 3 |
| 71 | 73 | 79 | 90 | OUR WORLD — Johnny Tillotson, MGM 13408 | 4 |
| 72 | 76 | 73 | 79 | I WANT TO MEET HIM — Royalettes, MGM 13405 | 6 |
| 73 | 80 | — | — | SANDY — Ronny & the Daytonas, Mala 513 | 2 |
| 74 | 84 | — | — | A WELL RESPECTED MAN — Kinks, Reprise 0420 | 2 |
| 75 | 79 | 82 | 94 | STAND BY ME — Earl Grant, Decca 25674 | 7 |
| 76 | 86 | — | — | ALL OR NOTHING — Patty LaBelle & the Bluebelles, Atlantic 2311 | 2 |
| ★77 | 93 | — | — | A YOUNG GIRL — Noel Harrison, London 9795 | 2 |
| ★78 | — | — | — | NO MATTER WHAT SHAPE (Your Stomach's In) — T-Bones, Liberty 55836 | 1 |
| 79 | 81 | 85 | 87 | I REALLY LOVE YOU — Dee Dee Sharp, Cameo 375 | 6 |
| ★80 | 96 | — | — | LIES — Knickerbockers, Challenge 59321 | 2 |
| ★81 | — | — | — | ARE YOU THERE — Dionne Warwick, Scepter 12122 | 1 |
| 82 | 82 | 89 | — | RAINBOW '65 — Gene Chandler, Constellation 158 | 3 |
| ★83 | — | — | — | LOVE BUG — Jack Jones, Kapp 722 | 1 |
| 84 | 87 | — | — | I WON'T LOVE YOU ANYMORE (Sorry) — Lesley Gore, Mercury 72513 | 2 |
| ★85 | — | — | — | PLEASE DON'T FIGHT IT — Dino, Desi & Billy, Reprise 0426 | 1 |
| 86 | 89 | — | — | C. C. RIDER — Bobby Powell, Whit 714 | 2 |
| 87 | 98 | — | — | JUST ONE MORE DAY — Otis Redding, Volt 130 | 2 |
| 88 | 90 | 100 | — | MICHAEL — C.O.D.'s, Kellmac 1003 | 3 |
| 89 | 91 | 99 | — | I'M SATISFIED — San Remo Golden Strings, Ric-Tic 108 | 3 |
| ★90 | — | — | — | IF YOU GOTTA MAKE A FOOL OF SOMEBODY — Maxine Brown, Wand 1104 | 1 |
| 91 | 100 | — | — | IT'S GOODNEWS WEEK — Hedgehoppers Anonymous, Parrot 9800 | 2 |
| 92 | — | — | — | CRYING TIME — Ray Charles, ABC-Paramount 10739 | 1 |
| 93 | 95 | — | — | QUIET NIGHTS OF QUIET STARS — Andy Williams, Columbia 43456 | 2 |
| 94 | — | — | — | GO AWAY FROM MY WORLD — Marianne Faithfull, London 9802 | 1 |
| 95 | — | — | — | BACK STREET — Edwin Starr, Ric-Tic 107 | 1 |
| 96 | 97 | — | — | RUN TO MY LOVIN' ARMS — Lenny Welch, Kapp 712 | 2 |
| 97 | — | — | — | LOVE THEME FROM THE SANDPIPER — Tony Bennett, Columbia 43431 | 4 |
| 98 | — | — | — | LOVE (Makes Me Do Foolish Things) — Martha & the Vandellas, Gordy 7045 | 1 |
| 99 | 99 | — | — | STAY AWAY FROM MY BABY — Ted Taylor, Okeh 7231 | 2 |
| 100 | — | — | — | JENNY TAKE A RIDE — Mitch Ryder & the Detroit Wheels, New Voices 806 | 1 |

## HOT 100—A TO Z—*(Publisher-Licensee)*

Ain't That Peculiar (Jobete, BMI) ... 16
(All of a Sudden) My Heart Sings (Leeds, ASCAP) ... 49
All or Nothing (Big Top-Web IV, BMI) ... 76
Apple of My Eye (Don, BMI) ... 45
Are You There (Blue Seas-Jac, ASCAP) ... 81
Back Street (Myto, BMI) ... 95
Buckaroo (Bluebook, BMI) ... 64
C. C. Rider (Su-Ma, BMI) ... 86
Crawling Back (Acuff-Rose, BMI) ... 46
Crying Time (Bluebook, BMI) ... 92
Crystal Chandelier (Harbot, SESAC) ... 55
Don't Fight It (East-Web IV, BMI) ... 61
Don't Think Twice (Witmark, ASCAP) ... 18
Duck, The (Keymen-Mirwood, BMI) ... 42
Ebb Tide (Robbins, ASCAP) ... 21
England Swings (Tree, BMI) ... 12
Everybody Do the Sloopy (Tobi-Ann-Web IV, BMI) ... 67
Fever (Lois, BMI) ... 13
Five O'Clock World (Screen Gems-Columbia, BMI) ... 40
Flowers on the Wall (Southwind, BMI) ... 34
Get Off of My Cloud (Gideon, BMI) ... 15
Go Away From My World (Sea Lark, BMI) ... 94
Hang on Sloopy (Picturetone, BMI) ... 11
Harlem Nocturne (Shapiro-Bernstein, ASCAP) ... 47
Here It Comes Again (Miller, ASCAP) ... 30
Hole in the Wall (Pure Soul, BMI) ... 43
I Can Never Go Home Anymore (Trio-Tender Tunes, BMI) ... 6
I Got You (I Feel Good) (Lois-Try Me, BMI) ... 4
I Hear a Symphony (Jobete, BMI) ... 2
I Really Love You (Blockbuster-Downstairs, BMI) ... 79
I Want to Meet Him (South Mountain, BMI) ... 72
I Will (Camarillo, BMI) ... 10
I Won't Love You Anymore (Buffee, BMI) ... 84
I'm Satisfied (Myto, BMI) ... 89
I'm a Man (Arc, BMI) ... 17
I've Got to Be Somebody (Lowery, BMI) ... 68
If You Gotta Make a Fool of Somebody (Good Songs, BMI) ... 90
It's Goodnews Week (Mainstay, BMI) ... 91
It's My Life (Screen Gems-Columbia, BMI) ... 31
Jealous Heart (Acuff-Rose, BMI) ... 65
Jenny Take a Ride (Venus Saturday, BMI) ... 100
Just a Little Bit (Tollie, BMI) ... 41
Just Like Me (Daywin, BMI) ... 69
Just One More Day (East-Redwal-Time, BMI) ... 87
Kiss Away (Gallico, BMI) ... 25
Let Me Be (Trousdale, BMI) ... 36
Let's Get Together (SFO, BMI) ... 51
Let's Hang On (Saturday & Seasons Four, BMI) ... 3
Lies (4-Star Sales, BMI) ... 80
Little Girl I Once Knew, The (Sea of Tunes, BMI) ... 32
Look Through Any Window (Miller, ASCAP) ... 62
Love Bug (Glad, BMI) ... 83
Love (Makes Me Do Foolish Things) (Jobete, BMI) ... 98
Lover's Concerto, A (Saturday, BMI) ... 37
Love Theme From the Sandpiper (Miller, ASCAP) ... 97
Make It Easy on Yourself (Famous, BMI) ... 29
Make the World Go Away (Pamper, BMI) ... 14
May the Bird of Paradise Fly Up Your Nose (Central Songs, BMI) ... 28
Michael (Chevis, BMI) ... 88
Mother Nature, Father Time (Benday & Eden, BMI) ... 53
My Baby (Jobete, BMI) ... 35
My Girl Has Gone (Jobete, BMI) ... 38
Mystic Eyes (Wemar, BMI) ... 33
No Matter What Shape (Your Stomach's In) (C-Hear, BMI) ... 78
One Has My Name (Peer Int'l, BMI) ... 24
Our World (Natson & Port, ASCAP) ... 71
Over and Over (Recordo, BMI) ... 5
1-2-3 (Champion & Double Diamond, BMI) ... 7
Please Don't Fight It (4-Star, BMI) ... 85
Princess in Rags (Screen Gems-Columbia, BMI) ... 44
Puppet on a String (Gladys, ASCAP) ... 22
Quiet Nights of Quiet Stars (Duchess, BMI) ... 93
Rainbow '65 (Aba-Conrad, BMI) ... 82
Rescue Me (Chevis, BMI) ... 9
Revolution Kind, The (Five-West-Cotillion, BMI) ... 70
Road Runner (Arc, BMI) ... 50
Run, Baby Run (Acuff-Rose, BMI) ... 20
Run to My Lovin' Arms (Screen Gems-Columbia, BMI) ... 96
Sandy (Buckhorn, BMI) ... 73
Satin Pillows (Vintage, BMI) ... 54
Seesaw (East-Cotillion, BMI) ... 52
She's Just My Style (Viva, BMI) ... 57
Sinner Man (Saloon Songs, BMI) ... 58
Something About You (Jobete, BMI) ... 19
Sounds of Silence (Eclectic, BMI) ... 26
Spanish Eyes (Roosevelt & G.E.M.A., BMI-ASCAP) 48
Stand By Me (Trio-Progressive, BMI) ... 75
Stay Away From My Baby (Lois, BMI) ... 99
Sunday and Me (Tallyrand, BMI) ... 23
Sweet Woman Like You, A (Tree, BMI) ... 60
Taste of Honey (Songfest, ASCAP) ... 8
Thunderball (Unart, BMI) ... 63
Time to Love-A Time to Cry, A (Hill & Range, BMI) ... 59
Try Me (Try Me, BMI) ... 66
Turn! Turn! Turn! (Melody Trails, BMI) ... 1
Well Respected Man, A (Amer. Met. Ent. of N. Y., BMI) ... 74
You Didn't Have to Be So Nice (Faithful Virtue, BMI) ... 39
Young Girl, A (E. B. Marks, BMI) ... 77
You've Been Cheatin' (Chi-Sound, BMI) ... 56
You've Got to Hide Your Love Away (Maclen, BMI) 27

## BUBBLING UNDER THE HOT 100

101. WE CAN WORK IT OUT ... Beatles, Capitol 5555
102. GOODBYE BABE ... Castaways, Soma 1442
103. DAY TRIPPER ... Beatles, Capitol 5555
104. PIED PIPER ... Changin' Times, Philips 40320
105. DON'T HAVE TO SHOP AROUND ... Mad Lads, Volt 127
106. GOOD THINGS COME TO THOSE WHO WAIT ... Chuck Jackson, Wand 1105
107. ONLY LOVE (Can Save Me Now) ... Solomon Burke, Atlantic 2308
108. I DON'T KNOW WHAT YOU'VE GOT BUT IT'S GOT ME ... Little Richard, Vee Jay 698
109. EVERYBODY LOVES A GOOD TIME ... Major Lance, Okeh 7233
110. THINK ... Jimmy McCracklin, Imperial 66129
111. WHAT THE NEW BREED SAY ... Barbarians, Laurie 3321
112. WALK HAND IN HAND ... Gerry and the Pacemakers, Laurie 3323
113. BROOMSTICK COWBOY ... Bobby Goldsboro, United Artists 952
114. PRIVATE JOHN Q ... Glen Campbell, Capitol 5545
115. NEW BREED ... Jimmy Holiday, Diplomacy 20
116. FOR YOU ... Spellbinders, Columbia 43384
117. LAST THING ON MY MIND ... Vejtables, Autumn 23
118. DRINKING MAN'S DIET ... Allan Sherman, Warner Bros. 5672
119. PLASTIC ... Serendipity Singers, Philips 40331
120. THREE BELLS ... Tokens, B. T. Puppy 516
121. WHAT'S COME OVER THIS WORLD ... Billy Carr, Colpix 791
122. RISING SUN ... Deep Six, Liberty 55838
123. CHILLS AND FEVER ... Paul Kelly, Dial 4021
124. MY GENERATION ... The Who, Decca 31877
125. CHILLS AND FEVER ... Tom Jones, Tower 190
126. I SEE THE LIGHT ... Five Americans, HBR 454
127. NO TIME FOR PITY ... Baby Washington, Sue 137
128. GRAB THIS THING ... Mar-Keys, Stax 181
129. LOOK AT ME ... Three Dimensions, RCA Victor 8709
130. GOOD TIME MUSIC ... Beau Brummels, Autumn 24
131. EVERYTHING'S GONNA BE ALRIGHT ... Willie Mitchell, Hi 2097
132. I CAN'T GO ON ... Charlie Rich, Smash 2012
133. LIGHTNIN' STRIKES ... Lou Christie, MGM 13412
134. PAIN GETS A LITTLE DEEPER ... Darrow Fletcher, Groovy 3001
135. LOOKING BACK ... Nat King Cole, Capitol 5549

Compiled from national retail sales and radio station airplay by the Music Popularity Dept. of Record Market Research, Billboard.

For Week Ending December 18, 1965

# Billboard HOT 100

★ **STAR performer—Sides registering greatest proportionate upward progress this week.**

◉ Record Industry Association of America seal of certification as million selling single.

| This Week | 1 Wk. Ago | 2 Wks. Ago | 3 Wks. Ago | TITLE Artist, Label & Number | Weeks On Chart |
|---|---|---|---|---|---|
| 1 | 1 | 1 | 2 | **TURN! TURN! TURN!** Byrds, Columbia 43424 | 9 |
| ★2 | 5 | 10 | 16 | **OVER AND OVER** Dave Clark Five, Epic 9863 | 6 |
| 3 | 4 | 5 | 9 | **I GOT YOU (I Feel Good)** James Brown, King 6015 | 6 |
| 4 | 3 | 4 | 4 | **LET'S HANG ON** 4 Seasons, Philips 40317 | 11 |
| 5 | 2 | 2 | 1 | **I HEAR A SYMPHONY** Supremes, Motown 1083 | 8 |
| 6 | 6 | 9 | 12 | **I CAN NEVER GO HOME ANY MORE** Shangri-Las, Red Bird 043 | 7 |
| ★7 | 14 | 17 | 19 | **MAKE THE WORLD GO AWAY** Eddy Arnold, RCA Victor 8679 | 10 |
| ★8 | 12 | 18 | 24 | **ENGLAND SWINGS** Roger Miller, Smash 2010 | 7 |
| ★9 | 13 | 20 | 37 | **FEVER** McCoys, Bang 511 | 6 |
| 10 | 10 | 13 | 18 | **I WILL** Dean Martin, Reprise 0415 | 8 |
| 11 | 11 | 21 | 28 | **HANG ON SLOOPY** Ramsey Lewis Trio, Cadet 5522 | 5 |
| ★12 | 21 | 41 | — | **EBB TIDE** Righteous Brothers, Philles 130 | 3 |
| ★13 | 18 | 24 | 32 | **DON'T THINK TWICE** Wonder Who? Philips 40324 | 7 |
| 14 | 8 | 7 | 7 | **A TASTE OF HONEY** Herb Alpert & the Tijuana Brass, A&M 775 | 13 |
| 15 | 7 | 3 | 3 | **1-2-3** Len Barry, Decca 31827 | 13 |
| ★16 | 26 | 34 | 65 | **SOUNDS OF SILENCE** Simon & Garfunkel, Columbia 43396 | 5 |
| ★17 | 24 | 37 | 51 | **ONE HAS MY NAME** Barry Young, Dot 16756 | 7 |
| ★18 | 23 | 31 | 52 | **SUNDAY AND ME** Jay & the Americans, United Artists 948 | 5 |
| 19 | 22 | 27 | 46 | **PUPPET ON A STRING** Elvis Presley, RCA Victor 0650 | 6 |
| 20 | 9 | 6 | 6 | **RESCUE ME** Fontella Bass, Checker 1120 | 12 |
| ★21 | 34 | 44 | 60 | **FLOWERS ON THE WALL** Statler Brothers, Columbia 43315 | 6 |
| 22 | 15 | 11 | 5 | **GET OFF OF MY CLOUD** Rolling Stones, London 9792 | 11 |
| ★23 | 40 | 67 | 94 | **FIVE O'CLOCK WORLD** Vogues, Co & Ce 232 | 4 |
| ★24 | 31 | 36 | 47 | **IT'S MY LIFE** Animals, MGM 13414 | 7 |
| 25 | 17 | 22 | 27 | **I'M A MAN** Yardbirds, Epic 9857 | 8 |
| ★26 | 32 | 42 | 69 | **THE LITTLE GIRL I ONCE KNEW** Beach Boys, Capitol 5540 | 4 |
| 27 | 30 | 30 | 39 | **HERE IT COMES AGAIN** Fortunes, Press 9798 | 7 |
| 28 | 16 | 8 | 8 | **AIN'T THAT PECULIAR** Marvin Gaye, Tamla 54122 | 11 |
| 29 | 19 | 19 | 20 | **SOMETHING ABOUT YOU** Four Tops, Motown 1084 | 6 |
| ★30 | 39 | 56 | 75 | **YOU DIDN'T HAVE TO BE SO NICE** Lovin' Spoonful, Kama Sutra 205 | 4 |
| 31 | 27 | 14 | 10 | **YOU'VE GOT TO HIDE YOUR LOVE AWAY** Silkie, Fontana 1525 | 10 |
| ★32 | 57 | — | — | **SHE'S JUST MY STYLE** Gary Lewis & the Playboys, Liberty 55846 | 2 |
| 33 | 20 | 12 | 15 | **RUN, BABY RUN** Newbeats, Hickory 1332 | 12 |
| 34 | 29 | 16 | 21 | **MAKE IT EASY ON YOURSELF** Walker Brothers, Smash 2000 | 10 |
| ★35 | 45 | 47 | 61 | **APPLE OF MY EYE** Roy Head, Back Beat 555 | 5 |
| ★36 | — | — | — | **WE CAN WORK IT OUT** Beatles, Capitol 5555 | 1 |
| ★37 | 48 | 68 | — | **SPANISH EYES** Al Martino, Capitol 5542 | 3 |
| 38 | 42 | 54 | 77 | **THE DUCK** Jackie Lee, Mirwood 5502 | 5 |
| 39 | 25 | 26 | 31 | **KISS AWAY** Ronnie Dove, Diamond 191 | 7 |
| 40 | 44 | 52 | 64 | **PRINCESS IN RAGS** Gene Pitney, Musicor 1130 | 5 |
| ★41 | 51 | 51 | 59 | **LET'S GET TOGETHER** We Five, A&M 784 | 6 |
| 42 | 33 | 35 | 45 | **MYSTIC EYES** Them, Parrot 9796 | 8 |
| ★43 | 54 | 77 | — | **SATIN PILLOWS** Bobby Vinton, Epic 9869 | 3 |
| 44 | 47 | 53 | 55 | **HARLEM NOCTURNE** Viscounts, Amy 940 | 8 |
| ★45 | 69 | 85 | — | **JUST LIKE ME** Paul Revere & the Raiders, Columbia 43461 | 3 |
| ★46 | 56 | 69 | 78 | **YOU'VE BEEN CHEATIN'** Impressions, ABC-Paramount 10750 | 5 |
| 47 | 28 | 15 | 17 | **MAY THE BIRD OF PARADISE FLY UP YOUR NOSE** "Little" Jimmy Dickens, Columbia 43388 | 10 |
| 48 | 37 | 23 | 11 | **A LOVER'S CONCERTO** Toys, DynoVoice 209 | 15 ◉ |
| 49 | 52 | 62 | 70 | **SEESAW** Don Covay, Atlantic 2301 | 6 |
| ★50 | 60 | 75 | — | **A SWEET WOMAN LIKE YOU** Joe Tex, Dial 4022 | 3 |
| ★51 | 63 | — | — | **THUNDERBALL** Tom Jones, Parrot 9801 | 2 |
| ★52 | 78 | — | — | **NO MATTER WHAT SHAPE (Your Stomach's In)** T-Bones, Liberty 55836 | 2 |
| 53 | 61 | 63 | 72 | **DON'T FIGHT IT** Wilson Pickett, Atlantic 2306 | 7 |
| 54 | 55 | 74 | — | **CRYSTAL CHANDELIER** Vic Dana, Dolton 313 | 3 |
| 55 | 62 | 78 | 86 | **LOOK THROUGH ANY WINDOW** Hollies, Imperial 66134 | 5 |
| ★56 | — | — | — | **DAY TRIPPER** Beatles, Capitol 5555 | 1 |
| 57 | 65 | 72 | 81 | **JEALOUS HEART** Connie Francis, MGM 13420 | 4 |
| ★58 | 68 | 83 | — | **I'VE GOT TO BE SOMEBODY** Billy Joe Royal, Columbia 43465 | 3 |
| 59 | 59 | 60 | 66 | **A TIME TO LOVE—A TIME TO CRY** Lou Johnson, Big Top 101 | 6 |
| 60 | 46 | 48 | 49 | **CRAWLING BACK** Roy Orbison, MGM 13410 | 7 |
| 61 | 64 | 64 | 71 | **BUCKAROO** Buck Owens & His Buckaroos, Capitol 5517 | 6 |
| ★62 | 77 | 93 | — | **A YOUNG GIRL** Noel Harrison, London 9795 | 3 |
| 63 | 73 | 80 | — | **SANDY** Ronny & the Daytonas, Mala 513 | 3 |
| 64 | 66 | 66 | 84 | **TRY ME** James Brown, Smash 2008 | 5 |
| ★65 | 80 | 96 | — | **LIES** Knickerbockers, Challenge 59321 | 3 |
| ★66 | 81 | — | — | **ARE YOU THERE** Dionne Warwick, Scepter 12122 | 2 |
| 67 | 67 | 71 | 90 | **EVERYBODY DO THE SLOOPY** Johnny Thunder, Diamond 192 | 4 |
| 68 | 43 | 50 | 57 | **HOLE IN THE WALL** Packers, Pure Soul 1107 | 6 |
| 69 | 53 | 57 | 67 | **MOTHER NATURE, FATHER TIME** Brook Benton, RCA Victor 8693 | 6 |
| 70 | 71 | 73 | 79 | **OUR WORLD** Johnny Tillotson, MGM 13408 | 5 |
| 71 | 74 | 84 | — | **A WELL RESPECTED MAN** Kinks, Reprise 0420 | 3 |
| 72 | 70 | 70 | 76 | **THE REVOLUTION KIND** Sonny, Atco 6386 | 4 |
| ★73 | 88 | 90 | 100 | **MICHAEL** C.O.D.'s, Kellmac 1003 | 4 |
| 74 | 76 | 86 | — | **ALL OR NOTHING** Patty LaBelle & the Bluebelles, Atlantic 2311 | 3 |
| ★75 | 100 | — | — | **JENNY TAKE A RIDE** Mitch Ryder & the Detroit Wheels, New Voices 806 | 2 |
| ★76 | 91 | 100 | — | **IT'S GOOD NEWS WEEK** Hedgehoppers Anonymous, Parrot 9800 | 3 |
| 77 | 83 | — | — | **LOVE BUG** Jack Jones, Kapp 722 | 2 |
| 78 | 79 | 81 | 85 | **I REALLY LOVE YOU** Dee Dee Sharp, Cameo 375 | 7 |
| 79 | 92 | — | — | **CRYING TIME** Ray Charles, ABC-Paramount 10739 | 2 |
| 80 | 84 | 87 | — | **I WON'T LOVE YOU ANYMORE (Sorry)** Lesley Gore, Mercury 72513 | 3 |
| 81 | 82 | 82 | 89 | **RAINBOW '65** Gene Chandler, Constellation 158 | 4 |
| ★82 | — | — | — | **SECOND HAND ROSE** Barbra Streisand, Columbia 43469 | 1 |
| 83 | 85 | — | — | **PLEASE DON'T FIGHT IT** Dino, Desi & Billy, Reprise 0426 | 2 |
| ★84 | — | — | — | **BROOMSTICK COWBOY** Bobby Goldsboro, United Artists 952 | 1 |
| 85 | 86 | 89 | — | **C. C. RIDER** Bobby Powell, Whit 714 | 3 |
| ★86 | — | — | — | **ATTACK** Toys, DynoVoice 214 | 1 |
| 87 | 87 | 98 | — | **JUST ONE MORE DAY** Otis Redding, Volt 130 | 3 |
| 88 | 90 | — | — | **IF YOU GOTTA MAKE A FOOL OF SOMEBODY** Maxine Brown, Wand 1104 | 2 |
| 89 | 89 | 91 | 99 | **I'M SATISFIED** San Remo Golden Strings, Ric-Tic 108 | 4 |
| ★90 | — | — | — | **UNDER YOUR SPELL AGAIN** Johnny Rivers, Imperial 66144 | 1 |
| 91 | 98 | — | — | **LOVE (Makes Me Do Foolish Things)** Martha & the Vandellas, Gordy 7045 | 2 |
| 92 | 93 | 95 | — | **QUIET NIGHTS OF QUIET STARS** Andy Williams, Columbia 43456 | 3 |
| 93 | — | — | — | **DON'T LOOK BACK** Temptations, Gordy 7047 | 1 |
| 94 | 94 | — | — | **GO AWAY FROM MY WORLD** Marianne Faithfull, London 9802 | 2 |
| 95 | 95 | — | — | **BACK STREET** Edwin Starr, Ric-Tic 107 | 2 |
| 96 | — | — | — | **DO I MAKE MYSELF CLEAR** Etta James & Sugar Pie DeSanto, Cadet 5519 | 1 |
| 97 | 97 | — | — | **LOVE THEME FROM THE SANDPIPER** Tony Bennett, Columbia 43431 | 5 |
| 98 | — | — | — | **THE DRINKING MAN'S DIET** Allan Sherman, Warner Bros. 5672 | 1 |
| 99 | — | — | — | **ON A CLEAR DAY YOU CAN SEE FOREVER** Johnny Mathis, Mercury 72493 | 1 |
| 100 | — | — | — | **UP TIGHT** Stevie Wonder, Tamla 54124 | 1 |

## HOT 100—A TO Z—*(Publisher-Licensee)*


Ain't That Peculiar (Jobete, BMI) .......... 28
All or Nothing (Big Top-Web IV, BMI) .......... 74
Apple of My Eye (Don, BMI) .......... 35
Are You There (Blue Seas-Jac, ASCAP) .......... 66
Attack (Saturday, BMI) .......... 86
Back Street (Myto, BMI) .......... 95
Broomstick Cowboy (Unart, BMI) .......... 84
Buckaroo (Bluebook, BMI) .......... 61
C. C. Rider (Su-Ma, BMI) .......... 85
Crawling Back (Acuff-Rose, BMI) .......... 60
Crying Time (Bluebook, BMI) .......... 79
Crystal Chandelier (Harbot, SESAC) .......... 54
Day Tripper (Maclen, BMI) .......... 56
Do I Make Myself Clear (Chevis, BMI) .......... 96
Don't Fight It (East-Web IV, BMI) .......... 53
Don't Look Back (Jobete, BMI) .......... 93
Don't Think Twice (Witmark, ASCAP) .......... 13
Drinking Man's Diet (Curtain Call, ASCAP) .......... 98
Duck, The (Keymen-Mirwood, BMI) .......... 38
Ebb Tide (Robbins, ASCAP) .......... 12
England Swings (Tree, BMI) .......... 8
Everybody Do the Sloopy (Toby-Ann-Webb IV, BMI) .......... 67
Fever (Lois, BMI) .......... 9
Five o'Clock World (Screen Gems-Columbia, BMI) .. 23
Flowers on the Wall (Southwind, BMI) .......... 21
Get Off of My Cloud (Gideon, BMI) .......... 22
Go Away From My World (Sea Lark, BMI) .......... 94
Hang on Sloopy (Picturetone, BMI) .......... 11
Harlem Nocturne (Shapiro-Bernstein, ASCAP) .... 44
Here It Comes Again (Miller, ASCAP) .......... 27
Hole in the Wall (Pure Soul, BMI) .......... 68
I Can Never Go Home Anymore (Trio-Tender Tunes, BMI) .......... 6
I Got You (I Feel Good) (Lois-Try Me, BMI) ..... 3
I Hear a Symphony (Jobete, BMI) .......... 5
I Really Love You (Blockbuster-Downstairs, BMI).. 78
I Will (Camarillo, BMI) .......... 10
I Won't Love You Anymore (Buffee, BMI) .......... 80
I'm Satisfied (Myto, BMI) .......... 89
I'm a Man (Arc, BMI) .......... 25
I've Got to Be Somebody (Lowery, BMI) .......... 58
If You Gotta Make a Fool of Somebody (Good Songs, BMI) .......... 88
It's Good News Week (Mainstay, BMI) .......... 76
It's My Life (Screen Gems-Columbia, BMI) .......... 24
Jealous Heart (Acuff-Rose, BMI) .......... 57
Jenny Take a Ride (Venus Saturday, BMI) .......... 75
Just Like Me (Daywin, BMI) .......... 45
Just One More Day (East-Redwal-Time, BMI) .......... 87
Kiss Away (Gallico, BMI) .......... 39
Let's Get Together (SFO, BMI) .......... 41
Let's Hang On (Saturday & Seasons Four, BMI) .... 4
Lies (4-Star, BMI) .......... 65
Little Girl I Once Knew, The (Sea of Tunes, BMI).. 26
Look Through Any Window (Miller, ASCAP) .......... 55
Love Bug (Glad, BMI) .......... 77
Love (Makes Me Do Foolish Things) (Jobete, BMI). 91
Lover's Concerto, A (Saturday, BMI) .......... 48
Love Theme From the Sandpiper (Miller, ASCAP).. 97
Make It Easy on Yourself (Famous, BMI) .......... 34
Make the World Go Away (Pamper, BMI) .......... 7
May the Bird of Paradise Fly Up Your Nose (Central Songs, BMI) .......... 47
Michael (Chevis, BMI) .......... 73
Mother Nature, Father Time (Benday & Eden, BMI) 69
Mystic Eyes (Wemar, BMI) .......... 42
No Matter What Shape (Your Stomach's In) (C-Hear, BMI) .......... 52
On a Clear Day You Can See Forever (Chappell, ASCAP) .......... 99
One Has My Name (Peer Int'l, BMI) .......... 17
Our World (Natson & Port, ASCAP) .......... 70
Over and Over (Recordo, BMI) .......... 2
1-2-3 (Champion & Double Diamond, BMI) .......... 15
Please Don't Fight It (4-Star, BMI) .......... 83
Princess in Rags (Screen Gems-Columbia, BMI).... 40
Puppet on a String (Gladys, ASCAP) .......... 19
Quiet Nights of Quiet Stars (Duchess, BMI) .......... 92
Rainbow '65 (Aba-Conrad, BMI) .......... 81
Rescue Me (Chevis, BMI) .......... 20
Revolution Kind, The (Five-West-Cotillion, BMI)... 72
Run, Baby Run (Acuff-Rose, BMI) .......... 33
Sandy (Buckhorn, BMI) .......... 63
Satin Pillows (Vintage, BMI) .......... 43
Second Hand Rose (Fisher-Shapiro-Bernstein, ASCAP) .......... 82
Seesaw (East-Cotillion, BMI) .......... 49
She's Just My Style (Viva, BMI) .......... 32
Something About You (Jobete, BMI) .......... 29
Sounds of Silence (Eclectic, BMI) .......... 16
Spanish Eyes (Roosevelt & G.E.M.A., BMI-ASCAP) 37
Sunday and Me (Tallyrand, BMI) .......... 18
Sweet Woman Like You, A (Tree, BMI) .......... 50
Taste of Honey (Songfest, ASCAP) .......... 14
Thunderball (Unart, BMI) .......... 51
Time to Love-A Time to Cry, A (Hill & Range, BMI) .......... 59
Try Me (Try Me, BMI) .......... 64
Turn! Turn! Turn! (Melody Trails, BMI) .......... 1
Under Your Spell Again (Central Songs, BMI) .... 90
Up Tight (Jobete, BMI) .......... 100
We Can Work It Out (Maclen, BMI) .......... 36
Well Respected Man, A (Amer. Met. Ent. of N. Y., BMI) .......... 71
You Didn't Have to Be So Nice (Faithful Virtue, BMI) .......... 30
Young Girl, A (Marks, BMI) .......... 62
You've Been Cheatin' (Chi-Sound, BMI) .......... 46
You've Got to Hide Your Love Away (Maclen, BMI) 31


## BUBBLING UNDER THE HOT 100

101. GOOD TIME MUSIC .......... Beau Brummels, Autumn 24
102. WHAT THE NEW BREED SAY .......... Barbarians, Laurie 3321
103. WALK HAND IN HAND .......... Gerry & the Pacemakers, Laurie 3323
104. LITTLE BOY (In Grown Up Clothes) .......... Four Seasons, Vee Jay 713
105. RUN TO MY LOVIN' ARMS .......... Lenny Welch, Kapp 712
106. GOOD THINGS COME TO THOSE WHO WAIT .......... Chuck Jackson, Wand 1105
107. STAY AWAY FROM MY BABY .......... Ted Taylor, Okeh 7231
108. I AIN'T GONNA EAT OUT MY HEART ANYMORE .......... Young Rascals, Atlantic 2312
109. YOU MADE ME LOVE YOU .......... Aretha Franklin, Columbia 43442
110. LIGHTNIN' STRIKES .......... Lou Christie, MGM 13412
111. GRAB THIS THING .......... Mar-Keys, Stax 181
112. GOODBYE BABE .......... Castaways, Soma 1442
113. DON'T HAVE TO SHOP AROUND .......... Mad Lads, Volt 127
114. FOR YOU .......... Spellbinders, Columbia 43384
115. THIS HEART OF MINE .......... Artistics, Okeh 7232
116. WHAT'S COME OVER THIS WORLD .......... Billy Carr, Colpix 791
117. GOODNIGHT MY LOVE .......... Ben E. King, Atco 6390
118. PLASTIC .......... Serendipity Singers, Philips 40331
119. TEARS .......... Ken Dodd, Liberty 55835
120. PRIVATE JOHN Q .......... Glen Campbell, Capitol 5545
121. YESTERDAY MAN .......... Chris Andrews, Atco 6385
122. I SEE THE LIGHT .......... Five Americans, HBR 454
123. I FEEL LIKE I'M FALLING IN LOVE .......... Jimmy Beaumont, Bang 510
124. CALL ME .......... Chris Montez, A&M 780
125. NO TIME FOR PITY .......... Baby Washington, Sue 137
126. LOOK AT ME .......... Three Dimensions, RCA Victor 8709
127. WHERE THE SUN HAS NEVER SHONE .......... Jonathan King, Parrot 9804
128. YOUR PEOPLE .......... Little Milton, Checker 1128
129. LOOK IN MY EYES .......... 3 Degrees, Swan 4235
130. PARTY PEOPLE .......... Ray Stevens, Monument 911
131. EVERYTHING'S GONNA BE ALRIGHT .......... Willie Mitchell, Hi 2097
132. SOMETHING I WANT TO TELL YOU .......... Johnny & the Expressions, Josie 946
133. LOOKING BACK .......... Nat King Cole, Capitol 5549
134. PAIN GETS A LITTLE DEEPER .......... Darrow Fletcher, Groovy 3001
135. LITTLE BLACK EGG .......... Nightcrawlers, Kapp 709

Compiled from national retail sales and radio station airplay by the Music Popularity Dept. of Record Market Research, Billboard.

# Billboard HOT 100

*For Week Ending December 25, 1965*

★ STAR performer—Sides registering greatest proportionate upward progress this week.

| This Week | 1 Wk. Ago | 2 Wks. Ago | 3 Wks. Ago | TITLE, Artist, Label & Number | Weeks On Chart |
|---|---|---|---|---|---|
| 1 | 2 | 5 | 10 | OVER AND OVER — Dave Clark Five, Epic 9863 | 7 |
| 2 | 1 | 1 | 1 | TURN! TURN! TURN! — Byrds, Columbia 43424 | 10 |
| 3 | 3 | 4 | 5 | I GOT YOU (I Feel Good) — James Brown, King 6015 | 7 |
| 4 | 4 | 3 | 4 | LET'S HANG ON — 4 Seasons, Philips 40317 | 12 |
| ★5 | 16 | 26 | 34 | SOUNDS OF SILENCE — Simon & Garfunkel, Columbia 43396 | 6 |
| 6 | 7 | 14 | 17 | MAKE THE WORLD GO AWAY — Eddy Arnold, RCA Victor 8679 | 11 |
| 7 | 9 | 13 | 20 | FEVER — McCoys, Bang 511 | 7 |
| 8 | 8 | 12 | 18 | ENGLAND SWINGS — Roger Miller, Smash 2010 | 8 |
| ★9 | 12 | 21 | 41 | EBB TIDE — Righteous Brothers, Philles 130 | 4 |
| 10 | 6 | 6 | 9 | I CAN NEVER GO HOME ANY MORE — Shangri-Las, Red Bird 043 | 8 |
| ★11 | 36 | — | — | WE CAN WORK IT OUT — Beatles, Capitol 5555 | 2 |
| 12 | 13 | 18 | 24 | DON'T THINK TWICE — Wonder Who? Philips 40324 | 8 |
| 13 | 21 | 34 | 44 | FLOWERS ON THE WALL — Statler Brothers, Columbia 43315 | 7 |
| 14 | 19 | 22 | 27 | PUPPET ON A STRING — Elvis Presley, RCA Victor 0650 | 7 |
| 15 | 11 | 11 | 21 | HANG ON SLOOPY — Ramsey Lewis Trio, Cadet 5522 | 6 |
| 16 | 23 | 40 | 67 | FIVE O'CLOCK WORLD — Vogues, Co & Ce 232 | 5 |
| 17 | 17 | 24 | 37 | ONE HAS MY NAME — Barry Young, Dot 16756 | 8 |
| 18 | 18 | 23 | 31 | SUNDAY AND ME — Jay & the Americans, United Artists 948 | 6 |
| 19 | 10 | 10 | 13 | I WILL — Dean Martin, Reprise 0415 | 9 |
| 20 | 5 | 2 | 2 | I HEAR A SYMPHONY — Supremes, Motown 1083 | 9 |
| 21 | 26 | 32 | 42 | THE LITTLE GIRL I ONCE KNEW — Beach Boys, Capitol 5540 | 5 |
| ★22 | 32 | 57 | — | SHE'S JUST MY STYLE — Gary Lewis & the Playboys, Liberty 55846 | 3 |
| ★23 | 30 | 39 | 56 | YOU DIDN'T HAVE TO BE SO NICE — Lovin' Spoonful, Kama Sutra 205 | 5 |
| 24 | 24 | 31 | 36 | IT'S MY LIFE — Animals, MGM 13414 | 8 |
| 25 | 25 | 17 | 22 | I'M A MAN — Yardbirds, Epic 9857 | 9 |
| 26 | 14 | 8 | 7 | A TASTE OF HONEY — Herb Alpert & the Tijuana Brass, A&M 775 | 14 |
| 27 | 15 | 7 | 3 | 1-2-3 — Len Barry, Decca 31827 | 14 |
| ★28 | 56 | — | — | DAY TRIPPER — Beatles, Capitol 5555 | 2 |
| 29 | 38 | 42 | 54 | THE DUCK — Jackie Lee, Mirwood 5502 | 6 |
| 30 | 37 | 48 | 68 | SPANISH EYES — Al Martino, Capitol 5542 | 4 |
| 31 | 41 | 51 | 51 | LET'S GET TOGETHER — We Five, A&M 784 | 7 |
| 32 | 35 | 45 | 47 | APPLE OF MY EYE — Roy Head, Back Beat 555 | 6 |
| 33 | 52 | 78 | — | NO MATTER WHAT SHAPE (Your Stomach's In) — T-Bones, Liberty 55836 | 3 |
| 34 | 29 | 19 | 19 | SOMETHING ABOUT YOU — Four Tops, Motown 1084 | 7 |
| 35 | 43 | 54 | 77 | SATIN PILLOWS — Bobby Vinton, Epic 9869 | 4 |
| 36 | 22 | 15 | 11 | GET OFF OF MY CLOUD — Rolling Stones, London 9792 | 12 |
| 37 | 40 | 44 | 52 | PRINCESS IN RAGS — Gene Pitney, Musicor 1130 | 6 |
| 38 | 45 | 69 | 85 | JUST LIKE ME — Paul Revere & the Raiders, Columbia 43461 | 4 |
| 39 | 33 | 20 | 12 | RUN, BABY RUN — Newbeats, Hickory 1332 | 13 |
| 40 | 20 | 9 | 6 | RESCUE ME — Fontella Bass, Checker 1120 | 13 |
| ★41 | 51 | 63 | — | THUNDERBALL — Tom Jones, Parrot 9801 | 3 |
| 42 | 46 | 56 | 69 | YOU'VE BEEN CHEATIN' — Impressions, ABC-Paramount 10750 | 6 |
| 43 | 44 | 47 | 53 | HARLEM NOCTURNE — Viscounts, Amy 940 | 9 |
| 44 | 49 | 52 | 62 | SEESAW — Don Covay, Atlantic 2301 | 7 |
| 45 | 50 | 60 | 75 | A SWEET WOMAN LIKE YOU — Joe Tex, Dial 4022 | 4 |
| 46 | 28 | 16 | 8 | AIN'T THAT PECULIAR — Marvin Gaye, Tamla 54122 | 12 |
| ★47 | 57 | 65 | 72 | JEALOUS HEART — Connie Francis, MGM 13420 | 5 |
| ★48 | — | — | — | A MUST TO AVOID — Herman's Hermits, MGM 13437 | 1 |
| 49 | 63 | 73 | 80 | SANDY — Ronny & the Daytonas, Mala 513 | 4 |
| 50 | 55 | 62 | 78 | LOOK THROUGH ANY WINDOW — Hollies, Imperial 66134 | 6 |
| 51 | 54 | 55 | 74 | CRYSTAL CHANDELIER — Vic Dana, Dolton 313 | 4 |
| 52 | 27 | 30 | 30 | HERE IT COMES AGAIN — Fortunes, Press 9798 | 8 |
| 53 | 65 | 80 | 96 | LIES — Knickerbockers, Challenge 59321 | 4 |
| 54 | 58 | 68 | 83 | I'VE GOT TO BE SOMEBODY — Billy Joe Royal, Columbia 43465 | 4 |
| 55 | 39 | 25 | 26 | KISS AWAY — Ronnie Dove, Diamond 191 | 8 |
| 56 | 62 | 77 | 93 | A YOUNG GIRL — Noel Harrison, London 9795 | 4 |
| 57 | 71 | 74 | 84 | A WELL RESPECTED MAN — Kinks, Reprise 0420 | 4 |
| 58 | 66 | 81 | — | ARE YOU THERE — Dionne Warwick, Scepter 12122 | 3 |
| ★59 | 86 | — | — | ATTACK — Toys, DynoVoice 214 | 2 |
| 60 | 61 | 64 | 64 | BUCKAROO — Buck Owens & His Buckaroos, Capitol 5517 | 7 |
| ★61 | 79 | 92 | — | CRYING TIME — Ray Charles, ABC-Paramount 10739 | 3 |
| 62 | 68 | 43 | 50 | HOLE IN THE WALL — Packers, Pure Soul 1107 | 7 |
| 63 | 64 | 66 | 66 | TRY ME — James Brown, Smash 2008 | 6 |
| 64 | 53 | 61 | 63 | DON'T FIGHT IT — Wilson Pickett, Atlantic 2306 | 8 |
| ★65 | 75 | 100 | — | JENNY TAKE A RIDE — Mitch Ryder & the Detroit Wheels, New Voices 806 | 3 |
| 66 | 76 | 91 | 100 | IT'S GOOD NEWS WEEK — Hedgehoppers Anonymous, Parrot 9800 | 4 |
| 67 | 83 | 85 | — | PLEASE DON'T FIGHT IT — Dino, Desi & Billy, Reprise 0426 | 3 |
| ★68 | 84 | — | — | BROOMSTICK COWBOY — Bobby Goldsboro, United Artists 982 | 2 |
| 69 | 69 | 53 | 57 | MOTHER NATURE, FATHER TIME — Brook Benton, RCA Victor 8693 | 7 |
| 70 | 59 | 59 | 60 | A TIME TO LOVE—A TIME TO CRY — Lou Johnson, Big Top 101 | 7 |
| 71 | 73 | 88 | 90 | MICHAEL — C.O.D.'s, Kellmac 1003 | 5 |
| 72 | 74 | 76 | 86 | ALL OR NOTHING — Patty LaBelle & the Bluebelles, Atlantic 2311 | 4 |
| 73 | 70 | 71 | 73 | OUR WORLD — Johnny Tillotson, MGM 13408 | 4 |
| ★74 | 90 | — | — | UNDER YOUR SPELL AGAIN — Johnny Rivers, Imperial 66144 | 2 |
| 75 | 77 | 83 | — | LOVE BUG — Jack Jones, Kapp 722 | 3 |
| 76 | 82 | — | — | SECOND HAND ROSE — Barbra Streisand, Columbia 43469 | 2 |
| ★77 | — | — | — | IT WAS A VERY GOOD YEAR — Frank Sinatra, Reprise 0429 | 1 |
| 78 | 85 | 86 | 89 | C. C. RIDER — Bobby Powell, Whit 714 | 4 |
| ★79 | — | — | — | AS TEARS GO BY — Rolling Stones, London 9808 | 1 |
| ★80 | — | — | — | THE MEN IN MY LITTLE GIRL'S LIFE — Mike Douglas, Epic 9876 | 1 |
| 81 | 67 | 67 | 71 | EVERYBODY DO THE SLOOPY — Johnny Thunder, Diamond 192 | 5 |
| ★82 | — | — | — | ZORBA THE GREEK — Herb Alpert & the Tijuana Brass, A&M 787 | 1 |
| 83 | — | — | — | RECOVERY — Fontella Bass, Checker 1131 | 1 |
| ★84 | — | — | — | GOING TO A GO-GO — Miracles, Tamla 54127 | 1 |
| 85 | 87 | 87 | 98 | JUST ONE MORE DAY — Otis Redding, Volt 130 | 4 |
| 86 | — | — | — | TIJUANA TAXI — Herb Alpert & the Tijuana Brass, A&M 787 | 1 |
| 87 | 88 | 90 | — | IF YOU GOTTA MAKE A FOOL OF SOMEBODY — Maxine Brown, Wand 1104 | 3 |
| 88 | — | — | — | LITTLE BOY (In Grown Up Clothes) — 4 Seasons, Vee Jay 713 | 1 |
| 89 | 94 | 94 | — | GO AWAY FROM MY WORLD — Marianne Faithfull, London 9802 | 3 |
| ★90 | — | — | — | MY LOVE — Petula Clark, Warner Bros. 5684 | 1 |
| 91 | 91 | 98 | — | LOVE (Makes Me Do Foolish Things) — Martha & the Vandellas, Gordy 7045 | 3 |
| 92 | 93 | — | — | DON'T LOOK BACK — Temptations, Gordy 7047 | 2 |
| 93 | — | — | — | LIGHTNIN' STRIKES — Lou Christie, MGM 13412 | 1 |
| 94 | — | — | — | I AIN'T GONNA EAT OUT MY HEART ANYMORE — Young Rascals, Atlantic 2312 | 1 |
| 95 | 100 | — | — | UP TIGHT — Stevie Wonder, Tamla 54124 | 2 |
| 96 | — | — | — | BLACK NIGHT — Lowell Fulson, Kent 431 | 1 |
| 97 | — | — | — | GOOD TIME MUSIC — Beau Brummels, Autumn 24 | 1 |
| 98 | 99 | — | — | ON A CLEAR DAY YOU CAN SEE FOREVER — Johnny Mathis, Mercury 72493 | 2 |
| 99 | 97 | 97 | — | LOVE THEME FROM THE SANDPIPER — Tony Bennett, Columbia 43431 | 6 |
| 100 | — | — | — | SPANISH HARLEM — King Curtis, Atco 6387 | 1 |

## BUBBLING UNDER THE HOT 100

101. WHERE THE SUN HAS NEVER SHONE — Jonathan King, Parrot 9804
102. DON'T MESS WITH BILL — Marvelettes, Tamla 54125
103. WALK HAND IN HAND — Gerry & the Pacemakers, Laurie 3323
104. RAINBOW '65 — Gene Chandler, Constellation 158
105. GOOD THINGS COME TO THOSE WHO WAIT — Chuck Jackson, Wand 1105
106. GOODNIGHT MY LOVE — Ben E. King, Atco 6390
107. QUIET NIGHTS OF QUIET STARS — Andy Williams, Columbia 43455
108. THE DRINKING MAN'S DIARY — Allan Sherman, Warner Bros. 5677
109. MY HEART BELONGS TO YOU — Wilson Pickett, Verve 10373
110. I HATE MYSELF CLEAR — (Jim James & Sugar Pie DeSanto), Cadet 5519
111. I WON'T LOVE YOU ANYMORE (Sorry) — Lesley Gore, Mercury 72513
112. CARELESS — Bobby Vinton, Epic 9869
113. TEARS — Ken Dodd, Liberty 55835
114. YESTERDAY MAN — Nini Rosso, Columbia 43363
115. IL SILENZIO — Nini Rosso, Columbia 43363
116. CALIFORNIA DREAMIN' — Mama's & the Papa's, Dunhill 4020
117. WHAT THE NEW BREED SAY — Barbarians, Laurie 3321
118. WHAT'S COME OVER THIS WORLD — Billy Carr, Colpix 791
119. FOR YOU — Spellbinders, Columbia 43384
120. I SEE THE LIGHT — Five Americans, HBR 454
121. CALL ME — Chris Montez, A&M 780
122. (You Get) THE GAMMA GOOCHEE — Kingsmen, Wand 1107
123. PLASTIC — Serendipity Singers, Philips 4033
124. MOMENT TO MOMENT — Frank Sinatra, Reprise 0429
125. LOOK AT ME — Three Dimensions, RCA Victor 8709
126. YOUR PEOPLE — Little Milton, Checker 1128
127. LOOKING BACK — Nat King Cole, Capitol
128. LOOK IN MY EYES — 3 Degrees, Swan 4235
129. FLY ME TO THE MOON — Sam & Bill, Joda 104
130. SOME SUNDAY MORNING — Wayne Newton, Capitol 5552
131. HOW CAN YOU TELL — Sandie Shaw, Reprise 0427
132. PAIN GETS A LITTLE DEEPER — Darrow Fletcher, Groovy 3001
133. HARLEM SHUFFLE — Wayne Cochran, Mercury 72507
134. THIS HEART OF MINE — Artistics, Okeh 7223
135. THE CHEATER — Bob Kuban and the In-Men, Musicland, U.S.A. 21000

# Billboard HOT 100

For Week Ending January 1, 1966

★ STAR performer—Sides registering greatest proportionate upward progress this week.

| This Wk | 1 Wk Ago | 2 Wk Ago | 3 Wk Ago | TITLE Artist, Label & Number | Wks on Chart |
|---|---|---|---|---|---|
| 1 | 5 | 16 | 26 | SOUNDS OF SILENCE — Simon & Garfunkel, Columbia 43396 | 7 |
| 2★ | 11 | 36 | — | WE CAN WORK IT OUT — Beatles, Capitol 5555 | 3 |
| 3 | 3 | 3 | 4 | I GOT YOU (I Feel Good) — James Brown, King 6015 | 8 |
| 4 | 2 | 1 | 1 | TURN! TURN! TURN! — Byrds, Columbia 43424 | 11 |
| 5 | 1 | 2 | 5 | OVER AND OVER — Dave Clark Five, Epic 9863 | 8 |
| 6 | 4 | 4 | 3 | LET'S HANG ON — 4 Seasons, Philips 40317 | 13 |
| 7 | 7 | 9 | 13 | FEVER — McCoys, Bang 511 | 8 |
| 8 | 9 | 12 | 21 | EBB TIDE — Righteous Brothers, Philles 130 | 5 |
| 9 | 8 | 8 | 12 | ENGLAND SWINGS — Roger Miller, Smash 2010 | 9 |
| 10 | 6 | 7 | 14 | MAKE THE WORLD GO AWAY — Eddy Arnold, RCA Victor 8679 | 12 |
| 11 | 16 | 23 | 40 | FIVE O'CLOCK WORLD — Vogues, Co & Ce 232 | 6 |
| 12 | 13 | 21 | 34 | FLOWERS ON THE WALL — Statler Brothers, Columbia 43315 | 8 |
| 13 | 17 | 17 | 24 | ONE HAS MY NAME — Barry Young, Dot 16756 | 9 |
| 14 | 14 | 19 | 22 | PUPPET ON A STRING — Elvis Presley, RCA Victor 0650 | 8 |
| 15 | 10 | 6 | 6 | I CAN NEVER GO HOME ANY MORE — Shangri-Las, Red Bird 043 | 9 |
| 16★ | 22 | 32 | 57 | SHE'S JUST MY STYLE — Gary Lewis & the Playboys, Liberty 55846 | 4 |
| 17 | 12 | 13 | 18 | DON'T THINK TWICE — Wonder Who? Philips 40324 | 9 |
| 18★ | 28 | 56 | — | DAY TRIPPER — Beatles, Capitol 5555 | 3 |
| 19 | 15 | 11 | 11 | HANG ON SLOOPY — Ramsey Lewis Trio, Cadet 5522 | 7 |
| 20 | 21 | 26 | 32 | THE LITTLE GIRL I ONCE KNEW — Beach Boys, Capitol 5540 | 6 |
| 21 | 23 | 30 | 39 | YOU DIDN'T HAVE TO BE SO NICE — Lovin' Spoonful, Kama Sutra 205 | 6 |
| 22★ | 33 | 52 | 78 | NO MATTER WHAT SHAPE (Your Stomach's In) — T-Bones, Liberty 55836 | 4 |
| 23 | 24 | 24 | 31 | IT'S MY LIFE — Animals, MGM 13414 | 9 |
| 24★ | 29 | 38 | 42 | THE DUCK — Jackie Lee, Mirwood 5502 | 7 |
| 25★ | 30 | 37 | 48 | SPANISH EYES — Al Martino, Capitol 5542 | 5 |
| 26 | 18 | 18 | 23 | SUNDAY AND ME — Jay & the Americans, United Artists 948 | 7 |
| 27 | 48 | — | — | A MUST TO AVOID — Herman's Hermits, MGM 13437 | 2 |
| 28 | 38 | 45 | 69 | JUST LIKE ME — Paul Revere & the Raiders, Columbia 43461 | 7 |
| 29 | 35 | 43 | 54 | SATIN PILLOWS — Bobby Vinton, Epic 9869 | 7 |
| 30 | 20 | 5 | 2 | I HEAR A SYMPHONY — Supremes, Motown 1083 | 10 |
| 31 | 26 | 14 | 8 | A TASTE OF HONEY — Herb Alpert & the Tijuana Brass, A&M 775 | 15 |
| 32 | 19 | 10 | 10 | I WILL — Dean Martin, Reprise 0415 | 10 |
| 33 | 59 | 86 | — | ATTACK — Toys, DynoVoice 214 | 3 |
| 34★ | 45 | 50 | 60 | A SWEET WOMAN LIKE YOU — Joe Tex, Dial 4022 | 5 |
| 35 | 25 | 25 | 17 | I'M A MAN — Yardbirds, Epic 9857 | 10 |
| 36 | 41 | 51 | 63 | THUNDERBALL — Tom Jones, Parrot 9801 | 4 |
| 37 | 42 | 46 | 56 | YOU'VE BEEN CHEATIN' — Impressions, ABC-Paramount 10750 | 7 |
| 38 | 31 | 41 | 51 | LET'S GET TOGETHER — We Five, A&M 784 | 8 |
| 39 | 43 | 44 | 47 | HARLEM NOCTURNE — Viscounts, Amy 940 | 10 |
| 40 | 53 | 65 | 80 | LIES — Knickerbockers, Challenge 59321 | 5 |
| 41 | 27 | 15 | 7 | 1-2-3 — Len Barry, Decca 31827 | 15 |
| 42 | 32 | 35 | 45 | APPLE OF MY EYE — Roy Head, Back Beat 555 | 7 |
| 43★ | 65 | 75 | 100 | JENNY TAKE A RIDE — Mitch Ryder & the Detroit Wheels, New Voice 806 | 4 |
| 44★ | 54 | 58 | 68 | I'VE GOT TO BE SOMEBODY — Billy Joe Royal, Columbia 43465 | 5 |
| 45 | 49 | 63 | 73 | SANDY — Ronny & the Daytonas, Mala 513 | 5 |
| 46 | 37 | 40 | 44 | PRINCESS IN RAGS — Gene Pitney, Musicor 1130 | 7 |
| 47 | 47 | 57 | 65 | JEALOUS HEART — Connie Francis, MGM 13420 | 6 |
| 48 | 79 | — | — | AS TEARS GO BY — Rolling Stones, London 9808 | 2 |
| 49 | 50 | 55 | 62 | LOOK THROUGH ANY WINDOW — Hollies, Imperial 66134 | 7 |
| 50 | 57 | 71 | 74 | A WELL RESPECTED MAN — Kinks, Reprise 0420 | 5 |
| 51 | 51 | 54 | 55 | CRYSTAL CHANDELIER — Vic Dana, Dolton 313 | 5 |
| 52 | 58 | 66 | 81 | ARE YOU THERE — Dionne Warwick, Scepter 12122 | 4 |
| 53 | 44 | 49 | 52 | SEESAW — Don Covay, Atlantic 2301 | 8 |
| 54 | 66 | 76 | 91 | IT'S GOOD NEWS WEEK — Hedgehoppers Anonymous, Parrot 9800 | 5 |
| 55 | 56 | 62 | 77 | A YOUNG GIRL — Noel Harrison, London 9795 | 5 |
| 56 | 61 | 79 | 92 | CRYING TIME — Ray Charles, ABC-Paramount 10739 | 4 |
| 57 | 80 | — | — | THE MEN IN MY LITTLE GIRL'S LIFE — Mike Douglas, Epic 9876 | 2 |
| 58★ | 77 | — | — | IT WAS A VERY GOOD YEAR — Frank Sinatra, Reprise 0429 | 2 |
| 59★ | 76 | 82 | — | SECOND HAND ROSE — Barbra Streisand, Columbia 43469 | 3 |
| 60 | 74 | 90 | — | UNDER YOUR SPELL AGAIN — Johnny Rivers, Imperial 66144 | 3 |
| 61 | 62 | 68 | 43 | HOLE IN THE WALL — Packers, Pure Soul 1107 | 8 |
| 62 | 60 | 61 | 64 | BUCKAROO — Buck Owens & His Buckaroos, Capitol 5517 | 8 |
| 63 | 68 | 84 | — | BROOMSTICK COWBOY — Bobby Goldsboro, United Artists 952 | 3 |
| 64 | 67 | 83 | 85 | PLEASE DON'T FIGHT IT — Dino, Desi & Billy, Reprise 0426 | 4 |
| 65 | 71 | 73 | 88 | MICHAEL — C.O.D.'s, Kellmac 1003 | 6 |
| 66 | 63 | 64 | 66 | TRY ME — James Brown, Smash 2008 | 7 |
| 67 | 82 | — | — | ZORBA THE GREEK — Herb Alpert & the Tijuana Brass, A&M 787 | 2 |
| 68 | 72 | 74 | 76 | ALL OR NOTHING — Patty LaBelle & the Bluebelles, Atlantic 2311 | 5 |
| 69 | 84 | — | — | GOING TO A GO-GO — Miracles, Tamla 54127 | 2 |
| 70 | 64 | 53 | 61 | DON'T FIGHT IT — Wilson Pickett, Atlantic 2306 | 9 |
| 71 | 86 | — | — | TIJUANA TAXI — Herb Alpert & the Tijuana Brass, A&M 787 | 2 |
| 72 | 75 | 77 | 83 | LOVE BUG — Jack Jones, Kapp 722 | 4 |
| 73 | 70 | 59 | 59 | A TIME TO LOVE—A TIME TO CRY — Lou Johnson, Big Top 101 | 8 |
| 74 | 90 | — | — | MY LOVE — Petula Clark, Warner Bros. 5684 | 2 |
| 75 | — | — | — | TELL ME WHY — Elvis Presley, RCA Victor 8740 | 1 |
| 76 | 78 | 85 | 86 | C. C. RIDER — Bobby Powell, Whit 714 | 5 |
| 77 | 88 | — | — | LITTLE BOY (In Grown Up Clothes) — 4 Seasons, Vee Jay 713 | 2 |
| 78★ | 95 | 100 | — | UP TIGHT — Stevie Wonder, Tamla 54124 | 3 |
| 79 | 83 | — | — | RECOVERY — Fontella Bass, Checker 1131 | 2 |
| 80 | — | — | — | DON'T MESS WITH BILL — Marvelettes, Tamla 54126 | 1 |
| 81 | — | — | — | BARBARA ANN — Beach Boys, Capitol 5561 | 1 |
| 82 | 93 | — | — | LIGHTNIN' STRIKES — Lou Christie, MGM 13412 | 2 |
| 83 | — | — | — | LIKE A BABY — Len Barry, Decca 31889 | 1 |
| 84 | 87 | 88 | 90 | IF YOU GOTTA MAKE A FOOL OF SOMEBODY — Maxine Brown, Wand 1104 | 4 |
| 85 | — | — | — | SPREAD IT ON THICK — Gentrys, MGM 13432 | 1 |
| 86 | 94 | — | — | I AIN'T GONNA EAT OUT MY HEART ANYMORE — Young Rascals, Atlantic 2312 | 2 |
| 87 | 91 | 91 | 98 | LOVE (Makes Me Do Foolish Things) — Martha & the Vandellas, Gordy 7045 | 4 |
| 88 | 92 | 93 | — | DON'T LOOK BACK — Temptations, Gordy 7047 | 3 |
| 89 | — | — | — | HURT — Little Anthony & the Imperials, DCP 1154 | 1 |
| 90 | 85 | 87 | 87 | JUST ONE MORE DAY — Otis Redding, Volt 130 | 5 |
| 91 | 96 | — | — | BLACK NIGHT — Lowell Folson, Kent 431 | 2 |
| 92 | — | — | — | I SEE THE LIGHT — Five Americans, HBR 454 | 1 |
| 93 | — | — | — | GET OUT OF MY LIFE WOMAN — Lee Dorsey, Amy 945 | 1 |
| 94 | — | — | — | YESTERDAY MAN — Chris Andrews, Atco 6385 | 1 |
| 95 | — | — | — | BLUE RIVER — Elvis Presley, RCA Victor 8740 | 1 |
| 96 | — | — | — | FOLLOW YOUR HEART — Manhattans, Carnival 512 | 1 |
| 97 | — | — | — | LOOK IN MY EYES — 3 Degrees, Swan 4235 | 1 |
| 98 | 100 | — | — | SPANISH HARLEM — King Curtis, Atco 6387 | 2 |
| 99 | — | — | — | CAN YOU PLEASE CRAWL OUT YOUR WINDOW — Bob Dylan, Columbia 43477 | 1 |
| 100 | — | — | — | MOUNTAIN OF LOVE — Billy Stewart, Chess 1948 | 1 |

## BUBBLING UNDER THE HOT 100

101. IL SILENZIO — Nini Rosso, Columbia 43363
102. RAINBOW '65 — Gene Chandler, Constellation 158
103. CALIFORNIA DREAMIN' — Mama's and the Papa's, Dunhill 4020
104. LOVE THEME FROM "THE SANDPIPER" — Tony Bennett, Columbia 43431
105. DO I MAKE MYSELF CLEAR — Etta James & Sugar Pie DeSanto, Cadet 5519
106. YOUR PEOPLE — Little Milton, Checker 1128
107. TEARS — Ken Dodd, Liberty 55835
108. ON A CLEAR DAY YOU CAN SEE FOREVER — Johnny Mathis, Mercury 72493
109. GOODNIGHT MY LOVE — Ben E. King, Atco 6390
110. AS LONG AS THERE IS L-O-V-E LOVE — Tami Terrell, Motown 1086
111. CARELESS — Bobby Vinton, Epic 9869
112. FLY ME TO THE MOON — Sam & Bill, Joda 104
113. GOOD TIME MUSIC — Beau Brummels, Autumn 24
114. GOOD THINGS COME TO THOSE WHO WAIT — Chuck Jackson, Wand 1105
115. MOMENT TO MOMENT — Frank Sinatra, Reprise 0429
116. CALL ME — Chris Montez, A&M 780
117. GO AWAY FROM MY WORLD — Marianne Faithfull, London 9802
118. MY HEART BELONGS TO YOU — Wilson Pickett, Verve 10378
119. THIS HEART OF MINE — Artistics, Okeh 7232
120. LOOK AT ME — Three Dimensions, RCA Victor 8709
121. WALK HAND IN HAND — Gerry & the Pacemakers, Laurie 3323
122. MY GENERATION — Who?, Decca 31877
123. LOOKING BACK — Nat King Cole, Capitol 5549
124. FOR YOU — Spellbinders, Columbia 43384
125. THIS CAN'T BE TRUE — Eddie Holman, Parkway 960
126. A BEGINNING FROM AN END — Jan & Dean, Liberty 55849
127. WHERE THE SUN HAS NEVER SHONE — Jonathan King, Parrot 9804
128. PLEASE DON'T HURT ME — Jackie Wilson & LaVern Baker, Brunswick 55287
129. HARLEM SHUFFLE — Wayne Cochral, Mercury 72507
130. THE PAIN GETS A LITTLE DEEPER — Darrow Fletcher, Groovy 3001
131. THE CHEATER — Bob Kuban & the In-Men, Musicland, U.S.A. 21,000
132. THE NEW BREED — Jimmy Holiday, Diplomacy 20
133. GET BACK — Roy Head, Scepter 12124
134. AS LONG AS THERE IS L-O-V-E LOVE — Jimmy Ruffin, Soul 35016
135. YOU MADE ME LOVE YOU — Aretha Franklin, Columbia 43442

Compiled from national retail sales and radio station airplay by the Music Popularity Dept. of Record Market Research, Billboard.

Billboard
For Week Ending January 8, 1966

# HOT 100

★ STAR performer—Sides registering greatest proportionate upward progress this week.

Record Industry Association of America seal of certification as million selling single.

Billboard Award

| This Week | 1 Wk. Ago | 2 Wks. Ago | 3 Wks. Ago | TITLE Artist, Label & Number | Weeks On Chart |
|---|---|---|---|---|---|
| 1 | 2 | 11 | 36 | WE CAN WORK IT OUT — Beatles, Capitol 5555 | 4 |
| 2 | 1 | 5 | 16 | SOUNDS OF SILENCE — Simon & Garfunkel, Columbia 43396 | 8 |
| ★3 | 16 | 22 | 32 | SHE'S JUST MY STYLE — Gary Lewis & the Playboys, Liberty 55846 | 5 |
| ★4 | 12 | 13 | 21 | FLOWERS ON THE WALL — Statler Brothers, Columbia 43315 | 9 |
| ★5 | 8 | 9 | 12 | EBB TIDE — Righteous Brothers, Philles 130 | 6 |
| 6 | 5 | 1 | 2 | OVER AND OVER — Dave Clark Five, Epic 9863 | 9 |
| 7 | 3 | 3 | 3 | I GOT YOU (I Feel Good) — James Brown, King 6015 | 9 |
| ★8 | 11 | 16 | 23 | FIVE O'CLOCK WORLD — Vogues, Co & Ce 232 | 7 |
| 9 | 4 | 2 | 1 | TURN! TURN! TURN! — Byrds, Columbia 43424 | 12 |
| ★10 | 18 | 28 | 56 | DAY TRIPPER — Beatles, Capitol 5555 | 4 |
| 11 | 6 | 4 | 4 | LET'S HANG ON — 4 Seasons, Philips 40317 | 14 |
| 12 | 7 | 7 | 9 | FEVER — McCoys, Bang 511 | 9 |
| ★13 | 22 | 33 | 52 | NO MATTER WHAT SHAPE (Your Stomach's In) — T-Bones, Liberty 55836 | 5 |
| 14 | 48 | 79 | — | AS TEARS GO BY — Rolling Stones, London 9808 | 3 |
| ★15 | 27 | 48 | — | A MUST TO AVOID — Herman's Hermits, MGM 13437 | 3 |
| ★16 | 21 | 23 | 30 | YOU DIDN'T HAVE TO BE SO NICE — Lovin' Spoonful, Kama Sutra 205 | 7 |
| 17 | 10 | 6 | 7 | MAKE THE WORLD GO AWAY — Eddy Arnold, RCA Victor 8679 | 13 |
| ★18 | 24 | 29 | 38 | THE DUCK — Jackie Lee, Mirwood 5502 | 8 |
| ★19 | 25 | 30 | 37 | SPANISH EYES — Al Martino, Capitol 5542 | 6 |
| 20 | 9 | 8 | 8 | ENGLAND SWINGS — Roger Miller, Smash 2010 | 10 |
| 21 | 14 | 14 | 19 | PUPPET ON A STRING — Elvis Presley, RCA Victor 0650 | 9 |
| 22 | 13 | 17 | 17 | ONE HAS MY NAME — Barry Young, Dot 16756 | 10 |
| ★23 | 28 | 38 | 45 | JUST LIKE ME — Paul Revere & the Raiders, Columbia 43461 | 6 |
| ★24 | 57 | 80 | — | THE MEN IN MY LITTLE GIRL'S LIFE — Mike Douglas, Epic 9876 | 3 |
| 25 | 23 | 24 | 24 | IT'S MY LIFE — Animals, MGM 13414 | 10 |
| 26 | 29 | 35 | 43 | SATIN PILLOWS — Bobby Vinton, Epic 9869 | 6 |
| 27 | 17 | 12 | 13 | DON'T THINK TWICE — Wonder Who? Philips 40324 | 10 |
| ★28 | 33 | 59 | 86 | ATTACK — Toys, DynoVoice 214 | 4 |
| ★29 | 34 | 45 | 50 | A SWEET WOMAN LIKE YOU — Joe Tex, Dial 4022 | 6 |
| ★30 | 36 | 41 | 51 | THUNDERBALL — Tom Jones, Parrot 9801 | 5 |
| 31 | 26 | 18 | 18 | SUNDAY AND ME — Jay & the Americans, United Artists 948 | 8 |
| ★32 | 43 | 65 | 75 | IENNY TAKE A RIDE — Mitch Ryder & the Detroit Wheels, New Voices 806 | 5 |
| 33 | 37 | 42 | 46 | YOU'VE BEEN CHEATIN' — Impressions, ABC-Paramount 10750 | 8 |
| 34 | 20 | 21 | 26 | THE LITTLE GIRL I ONCE KNEW — Beach Boys, Capitol 5540 | 7 |
| 35 | 40 | 53 | 65 | LIES — Knickerbockers, Challenge 59321 | 6 |
| 36 | 15 | 10 | 6 | I CAN NEVER GO HOME ANY MORE — Shangri-Las, Red Bird 043 | 10 |
| ★37 | 45 | 49 | 63 | SANDY — Ronny & the Daytonas, Mala 513 | 6 |
| ★38 | 50 | 57 | 71 | A WELL RESPECTED MAN — Kinks, Reprise 0420 | 6 |
| ★39 | 49 | 50 | 55 | LOOK THROUGH ANY WINDOW — Hollies, Imperial 66134 | 8 |
| 40 | 31 | 26 | 14 | A TASTE OF HONEY — Herb Alpert & the Tijuana Brass, A&M 775 | 16 |
| 41 | 44 | 54 | 58 | I'VE GOT TO BE SOMEBODY — Billy Joe Royal, Columbia 43465 | 6 |
| 42 | 38 | 43 | 44 | HARLEM NOCTURNE — Viscounts, Amy 940 | 11 |
| 43 | 19 | 15 | 11 | HANG ON SLOOPY — Ramsey Lewis Trio, Cadet 5522 | 8 |
| 44 | 42 | 32 | 35 | APPLE OF MY EYE — Roy Head, Back Beat 555 | 8 |
| ★45 | 56 | 61 | 79 | CRYING TIME — Ray Charles, ABC-Paramount 10739 | 5 |
| ★46 | 60 | 74 | 90 | UNDER YOUR SPELL AGAIN — Johnny Rivers, Imperial 66144 | 4 |
| ★47 | 58 | 77 | — | IT WAS A VERY GOOD YEAR — Frank Sinatra, Reprise 0429 | 3 |
| 48 | 52 | 58 | 66 | ARE YOU THERE — Dionne Warwick, Scepter 12122 | 5 |
| ★49 | 59 | 76 | 82 | SECOND HAND ROSE — Barbra Streisand, Columbia 43469 | 4 |
| 50 | 54 | 66 | 76 | IT'S GOOD NEWS WEEK — Hedgehoppers Anonymous, Parrot 9800 | 6 |
| 51 | 55 | 56 | 62 | A YOUNG GIRL — Noel Harrison, London 9795 | 6 |
| ★52 | 74 | 90 | — | MY LOVE — Petula Clark, Warner Bros. 5684 | 3 |
| ★53 | 63 | 68 | 84 | BROOMSTICK COWBOY — Bobby Goldsboro, United Artists 952 | 4 |
| 54 | 47 | 47 | 57 | JEALOUS HEART — Connie Francis, MGM 13420 | 7 |
| 55 | 51 | 51 | 54 | CRYSTAL CHANDELIER — Vic Dana, Dolton 313 | 6 |
| ★56 | 67 | 82 | — | ZORBA THE GREEK — Herb Alpert & the Tijuana Brass, A&M 787 | 3 |
| ★57 | 78 | 95 | 100 | UP TIGHT — Stevie Wonder, Tamla 54124 | 4 |
| ★58 | 81 | — | — | BARBARA ANN — Beach Boys, Capitol 5561 | 2 |
| ★59 | 69 | 84 | — | GOING TO A GO-GO — Miracles, Tamla 54127 | 3 |
| 60 | 64 | 67 | 83 | PLEASE DON'T FIGHT IT — Dino, Desi & Billy, Reprise 0426 | 5 |
| 61 | 65 | 71 | 73 | MICHAEL — C.O.D.'s, Kellmac 1003 | 7 |
| ★62 | 79 | 83 | — | RECOVERY — Fontella Bass, Checker 1131 | 3 |
| 63 | 46 | 37 | 40 | PRINCESS IN RAGS — Gene Pitney, Musicor 1130 | 8 |
| 64 | 75 | — | — | TELL ME WHY — Elvis Presley, RCA Victor 8740 | 2 |
| ★65 | 80 | — | — | DON'T MESS WITH BILL — Marvelettes, Tamla 54126 | 2 |
| ★66 | 82 | 93 | — | LIGHTNIN' STRIKES — Lou Christie, MGM 13412 | 3 |
| ★67 | 83 | — | — | LIKE A BABY — Len Barry, Decca 31889 | 2 |
| 68 | 77 | 88 | — | LITTLE BOY (In Grown Up Clothes) — 4 Seasons, Vee Jay 713 | 3 |
| 69 | 71 | 86 | — | TIJUANA TAXI — Herb Alpert & the Tijuana Brass, A&M 787 | 3 |
| 70 | 61 | 62 | 68 | HOLE IN THE WALL — Packers, Pure Soul 1107 | 9 |
| 71 | 72 | 75 | 77 | LOVE BUG — Jack Jones, Kapp 722 | 5 |
| 72 | 66 | 63 | 64 | TRY ME — James Brown, Smash 2008 | 8 |
| 73 | 70 | 64 | 53 | DON'T FIGHT IT — Wilson Pickett, Atlantic 2306 | 10 |
| 74 | 62 | 60 | 61 | BUCKAROO — Buck Owens & His Buckaroos, Capitol 5517 | 9 |
| 75 | 68 | 72 | 74 | ALL OR NOTHING — Patty LaBelle & the Bluebelles, Atlantic 2311 | 6 |
| 76 | 76 | 78 | 85 | C. C. RIDER — Bobby Powell, Whit 714 | 6 |
| 77 | 85 | — | — | SPREAD IT ON THICK — Gentrys, MGM 13432 | 2 |
| 78 | 53 | 44 | 49 | SEESAW — Don Covay, Atlantic 2301 | 9 |
| 79 | 89 | — | — | HURT — Little Anthony & the Imperials, DCP 1154 | 2 |
| 80 | 92 | — | — | I SEE THE LIGHT — Five Americans, HBR 454 | 2 |
| ★81 | — | — | — | CALL ME — Chris Montez, A&M 780 | 1 |
| 82 | 86 | 94 | — | I AIN'T GONNA EAT OUT MY HEART ANYMORE — Young Rascals, Atlantic 2312 | 3 |
| 83 | 73 | 70 | 59 | A TIME TO LOVE—A TIME TO CRY — Lou Johnson, Big Top 101 | 9 |
| 84 | 84 | 87 | 88 | IF YOU GOTTA MAKE A FOOL OF SOMEBODY — Maxine Brown, Wand 1104 | 5 |
| 85 | 88 | 92 | 93 | DON'T LOOK BACK — Temptations, Gordy 7047 | 4 |
| 86 | 87 | 91 | 91 | LOVE (Makes Me Do Foolish Things) — Martha & the Vandellas, Gordy 7045 | 5 |
| 87 | 99 | — | — | CAN YOU PLEASE CRAWL OUT YOUR WINDOW — Bob Dylan, Columbia 43477 | 2 |
| ★88 | 81 | — | — | RAINBOW '65 — Gene Chandler, Constellation 158 | 5 |
| 89 | 98 | 100 | — | SPANISH HARLEM — King Curtis, Atco 6387 | 3 |
| 90 | 93 | — | — | GET OUT OF MY LIFE WOMAN — Lee Dorsey, Amy 945 | 2 |
| 91 | — | — | — | I'M TOO FAR GONE (To Turn Around) — Bobby Bland, Duke 393 | 1 |
| 92 | 96 | — | — | FOLLOW YOUR HEART — Manhattans, Carnival 512 | 2 |
| 93 | 91 | 96 | — | BLACK NIGHT — Lowell Fulson, Kent 431 | 3 |
| 94 | — | — | — | GIDDYUP GO — Red Sovine, Starday 737 | 1 |
| 95 | — | — | — | GOODNIGHT MY LOVE — Ben E. King, Atco 6390 | 1 |
| 96 | — | — | — | MICHELLE — Billy Vaughn, Dot 16809 | 1 |
| 97 | — | — | — | I CAN'T BELIEVE YOU LOVE ME — Tammi Terrel, Motown 1086 | 1 |
| 98 | — | — | — | MICHELLE — David & Jonathan, Capitol 5563 | 1 |
| 99 | — | — | — | CALIFORNIA DREAMIN' — Mama's and Papa's, Dunhill 4020 | 1 |
| 100 | — | — | — | BABY COME ON HOME — Solomon Burke, Atlantic 2314 | 1 |

## HOT 100—A TO Z—(Publisher-Licensee)

All or Nothing (Big Top-Webb IV, BMI) ........ 75
Apple of My Eye (Don-BMI) ........ 44
Are You There (Blue Seas-Jac, ASCAP) ........ 48
As Tears Go By (Essex, ASCAP) ........ 14
Attack (Saturday, BMI) ........ 28
Baby Come on Home (Keetch, Caesar & Dino, BMI) ........ 100
Barbara Ann (Shoe-String & Cousins, BMI) ........ 58
Black Night (Modern & Little M, BMI) ........ 93
Broomstick Cowboy (Unart, BMI) ........ 53
Buckaroo (Bluebook, BMI) ........ 74
C. C. Rider (Su-Ma, BMI) ........ 76
California Dreamin' (Trousdale, BMI) ........ 99
Call Me (Duchess, BMI) ........ 81
Can You Please Crawl Out Your Window (Witmark, ASCAP) ........ 87
Crying Time (Bluebook, BMI) ........ 45
Crystal Chandelier (Harbot, SESAC) ........ 55
Day Tripper (Maclen, BMI) ........ 10
Don't Fight It (East-Web IV, BMI) ........ 73
Don't Look Back (Jobete, BMI) ........ 85
Don't Mess With Bill (Jobete, BMI) ........ 65
Don't Think Twice (Witmark, ASCAP) ........ 27
Duck, The (Keymen-Mirwood, BMI) ........ 18
Ebb Tide (Robbins, ASCAP) ........ 5
England Swings (Tree, BMI) ........ 20
Fever (Lois, BMI) ........ 12
Five o'Clock World (Screen Gems-Columbia, BMI) ........ 8
Flowers on the Wall (Southwind, BMI) ........ 4
Follow Your Heart (Sanavan, BMI) ........ 92
Get Out of My Life Woman (Marsaint, BMI) ........ 90
Giddyup Go (Starday, BMI) ........ 94
Going to a Go-Go (Jobete, BMI) ........ 59
Goodnight My Love (Quintet-Noma, BMI) ........ 95
Hang on Sloopy (Picturetone, BMI) ........ 43
Harlem Nocturne (Shapiro-Bernstein, ASCAP) ........ 42
Hole in the Wall (Pure Soul, BMI) ........ 70
Hurt (Miller, ASCAP) ........ 79
I Ain't Gonna Eat Out My Heart Anymore (Web IV, BMI) ........ 82
I Can Never Go Home Anymore (Trio-Tender Tunes, BMI) ........ 36
I Can't Believe You Love Me (Jobete, BMI) ........ 97
I Got You (I Feel Good) (Lois-Try Me, BMI) ........ 7
I See the Light (Jetstar, BMI) ........ 80
I'm Too Far Gone (To Turn Around) (M.P.I., BMI) ........ 91
I've Got to Be Somebody (Lowery, BMI) ........ 41
If You Gotta Make a Fool of Somebody (Good Songs, BMI) ........ 84
It Was a Very Good Year (Dolfi, ASCAP) ........ 47
It's Good News Week (Mainstay, BMI) ........ 50
It's My Life (Screen Gems-Columbia, BMI) ........ 25
Jealous Heart (Acuff-Rose, BMI) ........ 54
Jenny Take a Ride (Venice-Saturday, BMI) ........ 32
Just Like Me (Daywin, BMI) ........ 23
Let's Hang On (Saturday & Seasons Four, BMI) ........ 11
Lies (4 Star, BMI) ........ 35
Lightnin' Strikes (Rambed, BMI) ........ 66
Like a Baby (Double Diamond-Champion, BMI) ........ 67
Little Boy (In Grown Up Clothes) (Saturday-Seasons Four, BMI) ........ 68
Little Girl I Once Knew, The (Sea of Tunes, BMI) ........ 34
Look Through Any Window (Miller, ASCAP) ........ 39
Love Bug (Glad, BMI) ........ 71
Love (Makes Me Do Foolish Things) (Jobete, BMI) ........ 86
Make the World Go Away (Pamper, BMI) ........ 17
Men in My Little Girl's Life, The (Jewel, ASCAP) ........ 24
Michael (Chevis, BMI) ........ 61
Michelle—David & Jonathan (Maclen, BMI) ........ 98
Michelle—Vaughn (Maclen, BMI) ........ 96
Must to Avoid, A (Trousdale, BMI) ........ 15
My Love (Duchess, BMI) ........ 52
No Matter What Shape (Your Stomach's In) (C-Hear, BMI) ........ 13
One Has My Name (Peer Int'l, BMI) ........ 22
Over and Over (Recordo, BMI) ........ 6
Please Don't Fight It (4 Star, BMI) ........ 60
Princess in Rags (Screen Gems-Columbia, BMI) ........ 63
Puppet on a String (Gladys, ASCAP) ........ 21
Rainbow '65 (Aba-Conrad, BMI) ........ 88
Recovery (Chevis, BMI) ........ 62
Sandy (Buckhorn, BMI) ........ 37
Satin Pillows (Vintage, BMI) ........ 26
Second Hand Rose (Fisher-Shapiro-Bernstein, ASCAP) ........ 49
Seesaw (East-Cotillion, BMI) ........ 78
She's Just My Style (Viva, BMI) ........ 3
Sounds of Silence, The (Eclectic, BMI) ........ 2
Spanish Eyes (Roosevelt & G.I.M.A., BMI-ASCAP) ........ 19
Spanish Harlem (Progressive-Trio, BMI) ........ 89
Spread It on Thick (Tree, BMI) ........ 77
Sunday and Me (Tallyrand, BMI) ........ 31
Sweet Woman Like You, A (Tree, BMI) ........ 29
Taste of Honey, A (Songfest, ASCAP) ........ 40
Tell Me Why (Brent & Melody Lane, BMI) ........ 64
Thunderball (Unart, BMI) ........ 30
Tijuana Taxi (Irving, BMI) ........ 69
Time to Love—A Time to Cry, A (Hill & Range, BMI) ........ 83
Try Me (Try Me, BMI) ........ 72
Turn! Turn! Turn! (Melody Trails, BMI) ........ 9
Under Your Spell Again (Central Songs, BMI) ........ 46
Up Tight (Jobete, BMI) ........ 57
We Can Work It Out (Maclen, BMI) ........ 1
Well Respected Man, A (Amer. Met. Ent. of N. Y., BMI) ........ 38
You Didn't Have to Be So Nice (Faithful Virtue, BMI) ........ 16
Young Girl, A (Marks, BMI) ........ 51
You've Been Cheatin' (Chi-Sound), BMI) ........ 33
Zorba the Greek (Miller, ASCAP) ........ 56

## BUBBLING UNDER THE HOT 100

101. BROWN PAPER SACK ........ Gentrys, MGM 13432
102. MOUNTAIN OF LOVE ........ Billy Stewart, Chess 1948
103. GET BACK ........ Roy Head, Scepter 12124
104. LOOK IN MY EYES ........ 3 Degrees, Swan 4235
105. GOOD TIME MUSIC ........ Beau Brummels, Autumn 24
106. YOUR PEOPLE ........ Little Milton, Checker 1128
107. ON A CLEAR DAY YOU CAN SEE FOREVER ........ Johnny Mathis, Mercury 72493
108. DO I MAKE MYSELF CLEAR ........ Etta James & Sugar Pie DeSanto, Cadet 5519
109. TEARS ........ Ken Dodd, Liberty 55835
110. LOVE THEME FROM "THE SANDPIPER" ........ Tony Bennett, Columbia 43431
111. (YOU'RE GONNA) HURT YOURSELF ........ Frankie Valli, Smash 2015
112. FLY ME TO THE MOON ........ Sam & Bill, Joda 104
113. GOOD THINGS COME TO THOSE WHO WAIT ........ Chuck Jackson, Wand 1105
114. WHERE THE SUN HAS NEVER SHONE ........ Jonathan King, Parrot 9804
115. IL SILENZIO ........ Nini Rosso, Columbia 43363
116. YESTERDAY MAN ........ Chris Andrews, Atco 6385
117. FOR YOU ........ Spellbinders, Columbia 43384
118. LOOK AT ME ........ Three Dimensions, RCA Victor 8709
119. MY GENERATION ........ The Who, Decca 31877
120. THESE BOOTS ARE MADE FOR WALKIN' ........ Nancy Sinatra, Reprise 0432
121. AS LONG AS THERE IS L-O-V-E LOVE ........ Jimmy Ruffin, Soul 35016
122. SOMETHING I WANT TO TELL YOU ........ Johnny & the Expressions, Josie 946
123. ONCE A DAY ........ Timi Yuro, Mercury 72515
124. A BEGINNING FROM AN END ........ Jan & Dean, Liberty 55849
125. THIS CAN'T BE TRUE ........ Eddie Hollman, Parkway 960
126. THE PAIN GETS A LITTLE DEEPER ........ Darrow Fletcher, Groovey 3001
127. HARLEM SHUFFLE ........ Wayne Cochran, Mercury 72507
128. LOOKING BACK ........ Nat King Cole, Capitol 5549
129. SWEET SEPTEMBER ........ Lettermen, Capitol 5544
130. ELUSIVE BUTTERFLY ........ Bob Lind, World Pacific 77808
131. THE NEW BREED ........ Jimmy Holiday, Diplomacy 20
132. RIB TIPS ........ Andre Williams, Avin 103
133. BIG BRIGHT EYES ........ Danny Hutton, HBR 453
134. YOU MADE ME LOVE YOU ........ Aretha Franklin, Columbia 43442

Compiled from national retail sales and radio station airplay by the Music Popularity Dept. of Record Market Research, Billboard.

# Billboard HOT 100

**For Week Ending January 15, 1966**

★ STAR performer—Sides registering greatest proportionate upward progress this week.

Record Industry Association of America seal of certification as million selling single.

| This Week | 1 Wk. Ago | 2 Wks. Ago | 3 Wks. Ago | TITLE, Artist, Label & Number | Weeks on Chart |
|---|---|---|---|---|---|
| 1 | 1 | 2 | 11 | WE CAN WORK IT OUT — Beatles, Capitol 5555 | 5 |
| 2 | 2 | 1 | 5 | SOUNDS OF SILENCE — Simon & Garfunkel, Columbia 43396 | 9 |
| 3 | 3 | 16 | 22 | SHE'S JUST MY STYLE — Gary Lewis & the Playboys, Liberty 55846 | 6 |
| ★4 | 8 | 11 | 16 | FIVE O'CLOCK WORLD — Vogues, Co & Ce 232 | 8 |
| 5 | 5 | 8 | 9 | EBB TIDE — Righteous Brothers, Philles 130 | 7 |
| 6 | 10 | 18 | 28 | DAY TRIPPER — Beatles, Capitol 5555 | 5 |
| 7 | 4 | 12 | 13 | FLOWERS ON THE WALL — Statler Brothers, Columbia 43315 | 10 |
| 8 | 24 | 57 | 80 | THE MEN IN MY LITTLE GIRL'S LIFE — Mike Douglas, Epic 9876 | 4 |
| 9 | 14 | 48 | 79 | AS TEARS GO BY — Rolling Stones, London 9808 | 4 |
| 10 | 13 | 22 | 33 | NO MATTER WHAT SHAPE (Your Stomach's In) — T-Bones, Liberty 55836 | 6 |
| 11 | 15 | 27 | 48 | A MUST TO AVOID — Herman's Hermits, MGM 13437 | 4 |
| 12 | 16 | 21 | 23 | YOU DIDN'T HAVE TO BE SO NICE — Lovin' Spoonful, Kama Sutra 205 | 8 |
| 13 | 6 | 5 | 1 | OVER AND OVER — Dave Clark Five, Epic 9863 | 10 |
| 14 | 12 | 7 | 7 | FEVER — McCoys, Bang 511 | 10 |
| 15 | 11 | 6 | 4 | LET'S HANG ON — 4 Seasons, Philips 40317 | 15 |
| 16 | 23 | 28 | 38 | JUST LIKE ME — Paul Revere & the Raiders, Columbia 43461 | 7 |
| 17 | 18 | 24 | 29 | THE DUCK — Jackie Lee, Mirwood 5502 | 9 |
| 18 | 19 | 25 | 30 | SPANISH EYES — Al Martino, Capitol 5542 | 7 |
| 19 | 9 | 4 | 2 | TURN! TURN! TURN! — Byrds, Columbia 43424 | 13 |
| 20 | 7 | 3 | 1 | I GOT YOU (I Feel Good) — James Brown, King 6015 | 10 |
| 21 | 32 | 43 | 65 | JENNY TAKE A RIDE — Mitch Ryder & the Detroit Wheels, New Voice 806 | 6 |
| 22 | 28 | 33 | 59 | ATTACK — Toys, DynoVoice 214 | 5 |
| 23 | 26 | 29 | 35 | SATIN PILLOWS — Bobby Vinton, Epic 9869 | 7 |
| 24 | 52 | 74 | 90 | MY LOVE — Petula Clark, Warner Bros. 5684 | 4 |
| 25 | 25 | 23 | 24 | IT'S MY LIFE — Animals, MGM 13414 | 11 |
| 26 | 35 | 40 | 53 | LIES — Knickerbockers, Challenge 59321 | 6 |
| 27 | 30 | 36 | 41 | THUNDERBALL — Tom Jones, Parrot 9801 | 6 |
| 28 | 38 | 50 | 57 | A WELL RESPECTED MAN — Kinks, Reprise 0420 | 7 |
| 29 | 29 | 34 | 45 | A SWEET WOMAN LIKE YOU — Joe Tex, Dial 4022 | 7 |
| 30 | 37 | 45 | 49 | SANDY — Ronny & the Daytonas, Mala 513 | 7 |
| 31 | 58 | 81 | — | BARBARA ANN — Beach Boys, Capitol 5561 | 3 |
| 32 | 17 | 10 | 6 | MAKE THE WORLD GO AWAY — Eddy Arnold, RCA Victor 8679 | 14 |
| ★33 | 45 | 56 | 61 | CRYING TIME — Ray Charles, ABC-Paramount 10739 | 6 |
| 34 | 39 | 49 | 50 | LOOK THROUGH ANY WINDOW — Hollies, Imperial 66134 | 9 |
| ★35 | 46 | 60 | 74 | UNDER YOUR SPELL AGAIN — Johnny Rivers, Imperial 66144 | 5 |
| 36 | 27 | 17 | 12 | DON'T THINK TWICE — Wonder Who? Philips 40324 | 11 |
| ★37 | 47 | 58 | 77 | IT WAS A VERY GOOD YEAR — Frank Sinatra, Reprise 0429 | 4 |
| 38 | 41 | 44 | 54 | I'VE GOT TO BE SOMEBODY — Billy Joe Royal, Columbia 43465 | 7 |
| 39 | 20 | 9 | 8 | ENGLAND SWINGS — Roger Miller, Smash 2010 | 11 |
| 40 | 22 | 13 | 17 | ONE HAS MY NAME — Barry Young, Dot 16756 | 11 |
| 41 | 49 | 59 | 76 | SECOND HAND ROSE — Barbra Streisand, Columbia 43469 | 5 |
| 42 | 42 | 38 | 43 | HARLEM NOCTURNE — Viscounts, Amy 940 | 12 |
| ★43 | 56 | 67 | 82 | ZORBA THE GREEK — Herb Alpert & the Tijuana Brass, A&M 787 | 4 |
| 44 | 21 | 14 | 14 | PUPPET ON A STRING — Elvis Presley, RCA Victor 0650 | 10 |
| 45 | 48 | 52 | 58 | ARE YOU THERE — Dionne Warwick, Scepter 12122 | 6 |
| ★46 | 57 | 78 | 95 | UP TIGHT — Stevie Wonder, Tamla 54124 | 5 |
| ★47 | 64 | 75 | — | TELL ME WHY — Elvis Presley, RCA Victor 8740 | 3 |
| 48 | 59 | 69 | 84 | GOING TO A GO-GO — Miracles, Tamla 54127 | 4 |
| 49 | 36 | 15 | 10 | I CAN NEVER GO HOME ANY MORE — Shangri-Las, Red Bird 043 | 11 |
| 50 | 33 | 37 | 42 | YOU'VE BEEN CHEATIN' — Impressions, ABC-Paramount 10750 | 9 |
| 51 | 51 | 55 | 56 | A YOUNG GIRL — Noel Harrison, London 9795 | 7 |
| ★52 | 66 | 82 | 93 | LIGHTNIN' STRIKES — Lou Christie, MGM 13412 | 4 |
| 53 | 53 | 63 | 68 | BROOMSTICK COWBOY — Bobby Goldsboro, United Artists 932 | 5 |
| 54 | 67 | 83 | — | LIKE A BABY — Len Barry, Decca 31889 | 3 |
| 55 | 65 | 80 | — | DON'T MESS WITH BILL — Marvelettes, Tamla 54126 | 3 |
| 56 | 62 | 79 | 83 | RECOVERY — Fontella Bass, Checker 1131 | 4 |
| 57 | 50 | 54 | 66 | IT'S GOOD NEWS WEEK — Hedgehoppers Anonymous, Parrot 9800 | 7 |
| 58 | 34 | 20 | 21 | THE LITTLE GIRL I ONCE KNEW — Beach Boys, Capitol 5540 | 8 |
| 59 | 54 | 47 | 47 | JEALOUS HEART — Connie Francis, MGM 13420 | 8 |
| 60 | 68 | 77 | 88 | LITTLE BOY (In Grown Up Clothes) — 4 Seasons, Vee Jay 713 | 4 |
| 61 | 61 | 65 | 71 | MICHAEL — C.O.D.'s, Kellmac 1003 | 8 |
| 62 | 55 | 51 | 51 | CRYSTAL CHANDELIER — Vic Dana, Dolton 313 | 7 |
| 63 | 60 | 64 | 67 | PLEASE DON'T FIGHT IT — Dino, Desi & Billy, Reprise 0426 | 6 |
| 64 | 69 | 71 | 86 | TIJUANA TAXI — Herb Alpert & the Tijuana Brass, A&M 787 | 4 |
| 65 | 77 | 85 | — | SPREAD IT ON THICK — Gentrys, MGM 13432 | 3 |
| 66 | 79 | 89 | — | HURT — Little Anthony & the Imperials, DCP 1154 | 3 |
| ★67 | 82 | 86 | 94 | I AIN'T GONNA EAT OUT MY HEART ANYMORE — Young Rascals, Atlantic 2312 | 4 |
| 68 | 81 | — | — | CALL ME — Chris Montez, A&M 780 | 2 |
| 69 | 98 | — | — | MICHELLE — David & Jonathan, Capitol 5563 | 2 |
| 70 | 70 | 61 | 62 | HOLE IN THE WALL — Packers, Pure Soul 1107 | 10 |
| 71 | 80 | 92 | — | I SEE THE LIGHT — Five Americans, HBR 454 | 3 |
| ★72 | 87 | 99 | — | CAN YOU PLEASE CRAWL OUT YOUR WINDOW — Bob Dylan, Columbia 43477 | 3 |
| 73 | 84 | 84 | 87 | IF YOU GOTTA MAKE A FOOL OF SOMEBODY — Maxine Brown, Wand 1104 | 6 |
| 74 | 99 | — | — | CALIFORNIA DREAMIN' — Mama's and Papa's, Dunhill 4020 | 2 |
| 75 | — | — | — | CLEO'S MOOD — Jr. Walker & the All Stars, Soul 35017 | 1 |
| 76 | 76 | 76 | 78 | C. C. RIDER — Bobby Powell, Whit 714 | 7 |
| 77 | 71 | 72 | 75 | LOVE BUG — Jack Jones, Kapp 722 | 6 |
| 78 | — | — | — | MY WORLD IS EMPTY WITHOUT YOU — Supremes, Motown 1089 | 1 |
| 79 | 88 | — | — | RAINBOW '65 — Gene Chandler, Constellation 158 | 6 |
| 80 | 86 | 87 | 91 | LOVE (Makes Me Do Foolish Things) — Martha & the Vandellas, Gordy 7045 | 6 |
| 81 | 90 | 93 | — | GET OUT OF MY LIFE WOMAN — Lee Dorsey, Amy 945 | 3 |
| 82 | 94 | — | — | GIDDYUP GO — Red Sovine, Starday 737 | 2 |
| 83 | 85 | 88 | 92 | DON'T LOOK BACK — Temptations, Gordy 7047 | 5 |
| 84 | 91 | — | — | I'M TOO FAR GONE (To Turn Around) — Bobby Bland, Duke 393 | 2 |
| 85 | — | — | — | NIGHT TIME — Strangeloves, Bang 514 | 1 |
| 86 | — | — | — | (YOU'RE GONNA) HURT YOURSELF — Frankie Valli, Smash 2015 | 1 |
| 87 | 97 | — | — | I CAN'T BELIEVE YOU LOVE ME — Tammi Terrel, Motown 1086 | 2 |
| 88 | — | — | — | SNOW FLAKE — Jim Reeves, RCA Victor 8719 | 1 |
| 89 | 89 | 98 | 100 | SPANISH HARLEM — King Curtis, Atco 6387 | 4 |
| 90 | 96 | — | — | MICHELLE — Billy Vaughn, Dot 16809 | 2 |
| 91 | — | — | — | YOU DON'T KNOW LIKE I KNOW — Sam & Dave, Stax 180 | 1 |
| 92 | — | — | — | TIRED OF BEING LONELY — Sharpees, One-derful 4839 | 1 |
| 93 | — | — | — | THINK TWICE — Jackie Wilson & LaVern Baker, Brunswick 55287 | 1 |
| 94 | — | — | — | THE PAIN GETS A LITTLE DEEPER — Darrow Fletcher, Groovy 3001 | 1 |
| 95 | 95 | — | — | GOODNIGHT MY LOVE — Ben E. King, Atco 6390 | 2 |
| 96 | 100 | — | — | BABY COME ON HOME — Solomon Burke, Atlantic 2314 | 2 |
| 97 | — | — | — | THIS CAN'T BE TRUE — Eddie Holman, Parkway 960 | 1 |
| 98 | — | — | — | MY GENERATION — The Who, Decca 31877 | 1 |
| 99 | — | — | — | GET BACK — Roy Head, Scepter 12124 | 1 |
| 100 | — | — | — | WHERE THE SUN HAS NEVER SHONE — Jonathan King, Parrot 9804 | 1 |

## BUBBLING UNDER THE HOT 100

101. BROWN PAPER SACK — Gentrys, MGM 13432
102. YESTERDAY MAN — Chris Andrews, Atco 6385
103. LOOK IN MY EYES — 3 Degrees, Swan 4235
104. FOLLOW YOUR HEART — Manhattans, Carnival 512
105. THERE WON'T BE ANY SNOW — Derrik Roberts, Roulette 4655
106. ON A CLEAR DAY YOU CAN SEE FOREVER — Johnny Mathis, Mercury 72493
107. GOOD TIME MUSIC — Ken Dodd, Liberty 55835
108. TEARS — Danny Hutton, HBR 453
109. MOUNTAIN OF LOVE — Billy Stewart, Chess 1948
110. FLY ME TO THE MOON — Sam & Bill, Joda 104
111. IL SILENZIO — Nini Rosso, Columbia 43363
112. A BEGINNING FROM AN END — Jan & Dean, Liberty 55849
113. LOOK AT ME — Three Dimensions, RCA Victor 8709
114. SWEET SEPTEMBER — Lettermen, Capitol 5544
115. NO MAN IS AN ISLAND — Van Dykes, Mala 520
116. SOMETHING I WANT TO TELL YOU — Johnny & the Expressions, Josie 946
117. FOR YOU — Spellbinders, Columbia 43384
118. THESE BOOTS ARE MADE FOR WALKIN' — Nancy Sinatra, Reprise 0432
119. GOOD THINGS COME TO THOSE WHO WAIT — Chuck Jackson, Wand 1105
120. AS LONG AS THERE IS L-O-V-E LOVE — Jimmy Ruffin, Soul 35016
121. ONCE A DAY — Timi Yuro, Mercury 72515
122. BABY YOU'RE MY EVERYTHING — Little Jerry Williams, Calla 105
123. SOME SUNDAY MORNING — Wayne Newton, Capitol 5553
124. BIG BRIGHT EYES — Danny Ames, Epic 9885
125. FRIENDS AND LOVERS FOREVER — Nancy Ames, Epic 9885
126. MICHELLE — Bud Shank, World Pacific 77814
127. MICHELLE — Spokesmen, Decca 31895
128. ELUSIVE BUTTERFLY — Bob Lind, World Pacific 77808
129. RIB TIPS — Andre Williams, Avin 103
130. THE LOOP — Savoys, Tower 191
131. ANDREA — Johnny Lytell, Tuba 2004
132. LOVE MAKES THE WORLD GO 'ROUND — Deon Jackson, Carla 2526

Compiled from national retail sales and radio station airplay by the Music Popularity Dept. of Record Market Research, Billboard.

# Billboard

For Week Ending January 22, 1966

# HOT 100

★ STAR performer—Sides registering greatest proportionate upward progress this week.

Record Industry Association of America seal of certification as million selling single.

Billboard Award

| This Week | 1 Wk. Ago | 2 Wks. Ago | 3 Wks. Ago | TITLE Artist, Label & Number | Weeks On Chart |
|---|---|---|---|---|---|
| 1 | 2 | 2 | 1 | SOUNDS OF SILENCE — Simon & Garfunkel, Columbia 43396 | 10 |
| 2 | 1 | 1 | 2 | WE CAN WORK IT OUT — Beatles, Capitol 5555 | 6 |
| 3 | 3 | 3 | 16 | SHE'S JUST MY STYLE — Gary Lewis & the Playboys, Liberty 55846 | 7 |
| 4 | 4 | 8 | 11 | FIVE O'CLOCK WORLD — Vogues, Co & Ce 232 | 9 |
| 5 | 6 | 10 | 18 | DAY TRIPPER — Beatles, Capitol 5555 | 6 |
| ★6 | 10 | 13 | 22 | NO MATTER WHAT SHAPE (Your Stomach's In) — T-Bones, Liberty 55836 | 7 |
| 7 | 8 | 24 | 57 | THE MEN IN MY LITTLE GIRL'S LIFE — Mike Douglas, Epic 9876 | 5 |
| ★8 | 11 | 15 | 27 | A MUST TO AVOID — Herman's Hermits, MGM 13437 | 5 |
| 9 | 9 | 14 | 48 | AS TEARS GO BY — Rolling Stones, London 9808 | 5 |
| 10 | 12 | 16 | 21 | YOU DIDN'T HAVE TO BE SO NICE — Lovin' Spoonful, Kama Sutra 205 | 9 |
| ★11 | 16 | 23 | 28 | JUST LIKE ME — Paul Revere & the Raiders, Columbia 43461 | 8 |
| 12 | 7 | 4 | 12 | FLOWERS ON THE WALL — Statler Brothers, Columbia 43315 | 11 |
| 13 | 5 | 5 | 8 | EBB TIDE — Righteous Brothers, Philles 130 | 8 |
| 14 | 17 | 18 | 24 | THE DUCK — Jackie Lee, Mirwood 5502 | 10 |
| ★15 | 31 | 58 | 81 | BARBARA ANN — Beach Boys, Capitol 5561 | 4 |
| ★16 | 21 | 32 | 43 | JENNY TAKE A RIDE — Mitch Ryder & the Detroit Wheels, New Voices 806 | 7 |
| ★17 | 24 | 52 | 74 | MY LOVE — Petula Clark, Warner Bros. 5684 | 5 |
| 18 | 18 | 19 | 25 | SPANISH EYES — Al Martino, Capitol 5542 | 8 |
| 19 | 22 | 28 | 33 | ATTACK — Toys, DynoVoice 214 | 6 |
| ★20 | 26 | 35 | 40 | LIES — Knickerbockers, Challenge 59321 | 8 |
| ★21 | 33 | 45 | 56 | CRYING TIME — Ray Charles, ABC-Paramount 10739 | 7 |
| 22 | 13 | 6 | 5 | OVER AND OVER — Dave Clark Five, Epic 9863 | 11 |
| 23 | 23 | 26 | 29 | SATIN PILLOWS — Bobby Vinton, Epic 9869 | 8 |
| 24 | 28 | 38 | 50 | A WELL RESPECTED MAN — Kinks, Reprise 0420 | 8 |
| 25 | 27 | 30 | 36 | THUNDERBALL — Tom Jones, Parrot 9801 | 7 |
| ★26 | 46 | 57 | 78 | UP TIGHT — Stevie Wonder, Tamla 54124 | 6 |
| 27 | 30 | 37 | 45 | SANDY — Ronny & the Daytonas, Mala 513 | 8 |
| 28 | 20 | 7 | 3 | I GOT YOU (I Feel Good) — James Brown, King 6015 | 11 |
| ★29 | 48 | 59 | 69 | GOING TO A GO-GO — Miracles, Tamla 54127 | 5 |
| ★30 | 52 | 66 | 82 | LIGHTNIN' STRIKES — Lou Christie, MGM 13412 | 5 |
| 31 | 37 | 47 | 58 | IT WAS A VERY GOOD YEAR — Frank Sinatra, Reprise 0429 | 5 |
| 32 | 34 | 39 | 49 | LOOK THROUGH ANY WINDOW — Hollies, Imperial 66134 | 10 |
| ★33 | 43 | 56 | 67 | ZORBA THE GREEK — Herb Alpert & the Tijuana Brass, A&M 787 | 5 |
| 34 | 25 | 25 | 23 | IT'S MY LIFE — Animals, MGM 13414 | 12 |
| 35 | 35 | 46 | 60 | UNDER YOUR SPELL AGAIN — Johnny Rivers, Imperial 66144 | 6 |
| ★36 | 54 | 67 | 83 | LIKE A BABY — Len Barry, Decca 31889 | 4 |
| ★37 | 47 | 64 | 75 | TELL ME WHY — Elvis Presley, RCA Victor 8740 | 4 |
| 38 | 41 | 49 | 59 | SECOND HAND ROSE — Barbra Streisand, Columbia 43469 | 6 |
| 39 | 45 | 48 | 52 | ARE YOU THERE — Dionne Warwick, Scepter 12122 | 7 |
| 40 | 29 | 29 | 34 | A SWEET WOMAN LIKE YOU — Joe Tex, Dial 4022 | 8 |
| 41 | 14 | 12 | 7 | FEVER — McCoys, Bang 511 | 11 |
| ★42 | 55 | 65 | 80 | DON'T MESS WITH BILL — Marvelettes, Tamla 54126 | 4 |
| 43 | 19 | 9 | 4 | TURN! TURN! TURN! — Byrds, Columbia 43424 | 14 |
| ★44 | 61 | 61 | 65 | MICHAEL — C.O.D.'s, Kellmac 1003 | 9 |
| 45 | 15 | 11 | 6 | LET'S HANG ON — 4 Seasons, Philips 40317 | 16 |
| ★46 | 78 | — | — | MY WORLD IS EMPTY WITHOUT YOU — Supremes, Motown 1089 | 2 |
| ★47 | 69 | 98 | — | MICHELLE — David & Jonathan, Capitol 5563 | 3 |
| 48 | 42 | 42 | 38 | HARLEM NOCTURNE — Viscounts, Amy 940 | 13 |
| 49 | 56 | 62 | 79 | RECOVERY — Fontella Bass, Checker 1131 | 5 |
| 50 | 38 | 41 | 44 | I'VE GOT TO BE SOMEBODY — Billy Joe Royal, Columbia 43465 | 8 |
| ★51 | 64 | 69 | 71 | TIJUANA TAXI — Herb Alpert & the Tijuana Brass, A&M 787 | 5 |
| 52 | 57 | 50 | 54 | IT'S GOOD NEWS WEEK — Hedgehoppers Anonymous, Parrot 9800 | 8 |
| ★53 | 66 | 79 | 89 | HURT — Little Anthony & the Imperials, DCP 1154 | 4 |
| ★54 | 74 | 99 | — | CALIFORNIA DREAMIN' — Mama's and Papa's, Dunhill 4020 | 3 |
| 55 | 51 | 51 | 55 | A YOUNG GIRL — Noel Harrison, London 9795 | 8 |
| 56 | 53 | 53 | 63 | BROOMSTICK COWBOY — Bobby Goldsboro, United Artists 952 | 6 |
| 57 | 65 | 77 | 85 | SPREAD IT ON THICK — Gentrys, MGM 13432 | 4 |
| ★58 | — | — | — | A HARD DAY'S NIGHT — Ramsey Lewis Trio, Cadet 5525 | 1 |
| 59 | 67 | 82 | 86 | I AIN'T GONNA EAT OUT MY HEART ANYMORE — Young Rascals, Atlantic 2312 | 5 |
| ★60 | 71 | 80 | 92 | I SEE THE LIGHT — Five Americans, HBR 454 | 4 |
| 61 | 68 | 81 | — | CALL ME — Chris Montez, A&M 780 | 3 |
| 62 | 75 | — | — | CLEO'S MOOD — Jr. Walker & the All Stars, Soul 35017 | 2 |
| 63 | 73 | 84 | 84 | IF YOU GOTTA MAKE A FOOL OF SOMEBODY — Maxine Brown, Wand 1104 | 7 |
| 64 | 72 | 87 | 99 | CAN YOU PLEASE CRAWL OUT YOUR WINDOW — Bob Dylan, Columbia 43477 | 4 |
| 65 | 60 | 68 | 77 | LITTLE BOY (In Grown Up Clothes) — 4 Seasons, Vee Jay 713 | 5 |
| ★66 | 85 | — | — | NIGHT TIME — Strangeloves, Bang 514 | 2 |
| ★67 | 86 | — | — | (You're Gonna) HURT YOURSELF — Frankie Valli, Smash 2015 | 2 |
| 68 | 81 | 90 | 93 | GET OUT OF MY LIFE WOMAN — Lee Dorsey, Amy 945 | 4 |
| 69 | 79 | 88 | — | RAINBOW '65 — Gene Chandler, Constellation 158 | 7 |
| 70 | 80 | 86 | 87 | LOVE (Makes Me Do Foolish Things) — Martha & the Vandellas, Gordy 7045 | 7 |
| ★71 | — | — | — | WHEN LIKING TURNS TO LOVING — Ronnie Dove, Diamond 195 | 1 |
| 72 | 63 | 60 | 64 | PLEASE DON'T FIGHT IT — Dino, Desi & Billy, Reprise 0426 | 7 |
| 73 | 70 | 70 | 61 | HOLE IN THE WALL — Packers, Pure Soul 1107 | 11 |
| ★74 | — | — | — | THESE BOOTS ARE MADE FOR WALKIN' — Nancy Sinatra, Reprise 0432 | 1 |
| ★75 | — | — | — | MY BABY LOVES ME — Martha & the Vandellas, Gordy 7048 | 1 |
| 76 | 84 | 91 | — | I'M TOO FAR GONE (To Turn Around) — Bobby Bland, Duke 393 | 3 |
| ★77 | 98 | — | — | MY GENERATION — The Who, Decca 31877 | 2 |
| 78 | 90 | 96 | — | MICHELLE — Billy Vaughn, Dot 16809 | 3 |
| 79 | 88 | — | — | SNOW FLAKE — Jim Reeves, RCA Victor 8719 | 2 |
| 80 | 87 | 97 | — | I CAN'T BELIEVE YOU LOVE ME — Tammi Terrel, Motown 1086 | 3 |
| ★81 | — | — | — | BREAKIN' UP IS BREAKIN' MY HEART — Roy Orbison, MGM 13446 | 1 |
| ★82 | — | — | — | ANDREA — Sunrays, Tower 191 | 1 |
| ★83 | — | — | — | ELUSIVE BUTTERFLY — Bob Lind, World-Pacific 77808 | 1 |
| ★84 | — | — | — | LOVE IS ALL WE NEED — Mel Carter, Imperial 66148 | 1 |
| 85 | 82 | 94 | — | GIDDYUP GO — Red Sovine, Starday 737 | 3 |
| ★86 | — | — | — | BYE BYE BLUES — Bert Kaempfert and His Ork, Decca 31882 | 1 |
| 87 | 92 | — | — | TIRED OF BEING LONELY — Sharpees, One-derful 4839 | 2 |
| 88 | 99 | — | — | GET BACK — Roy Head, Scepter 12124 | 2 |
| 89 | 97 | — | — | THIS CAN'T BE TRUE — Eddie Holman, Parkway 960 | 2 |
| 90 | 91 | — | — | YOU DON'T KNOW LIKE I KNOW — Sam & Dave, Stax 180 | 2 |
| 91 | 95 | 95 | — | GOODNIGHT MY LOVE — Ben E. King, Atco 6390 | 3 |
| 92 | — | — | — | MICHELLE — Bud Shank, World-Pacific 77814 | 1 |
| 93 | — | — | — | THE LOOP — Johnny Lytle, Tuba 2004 | 1 |
| 94 | 94 | — | — | THE PAIN GETS A LITTLE DEEPER — Darrow Fletcher, Groovy 3001 | 2 |
| 95 | — | — | — | SOMETHING I WANT TO TELL YOU — Johnny and the Expressions, Josie 946 | 1 |
| 96 | 89 | 89 | 98 | SPANISH HARLEM — King Curtis, Atco 6387 | 5 |
| 97 | 100 | — | — | WHERE THE SUN HAS NEVER SHONE — Jonathan King, Parrot 9804 | 2 |
| 98 | — | — | — | CAN'T YOU SEE — Mary Wells, Atco 6392 | 1 |
| 99 | — | — | — | LOVE MAKES THE WORLD GO ROUND — Deon Jackson, Carla 2526 | 1 |
| 100 | — | — | — | BECAUSE I LOVE YOU — Billy Stewart, Chess 1948 | 1 |

## HOT 100—A TO Z—(Publisher-Licensee)


Andrea (Sea of Tunes, BMI) ... 82
Are You There (Blue Seas-Jac, ASCAP) ... 39
As Tears Go By (Essex, ASCAP) ... 9
Attack (Saturday, BMI) ... 19
Barbara Ann (Shoe-String & Cousins, BMI) ... 15
Because I Love You (Chevis, BMI) ... 100
Breakin' Up Is Breakin' My Heart (Acuff-Rose, BMI) ... 81
Broomstick Cowboy (Unart, BMI) ... 56
Bye Bye Blues (Bourne, ASCAP) ... 86
California Dreamin' (Trousdale, BMI) ... 54
Call Me (Duchess, BMI) ... 61
Can You Please Crawl Out Your Window (Witmark, ASCAP) ... 64
Can't You See (Jalynne, BMI) ... 98
Cleo's Mood (Jobete, BMI) ... 62
Crying Time (Bluebook, BMI) ... 21
Day Tripper (Maclen, BMI) ... 5
Don't Mess With Bill (Jobete, BMI) ... 42
Duck, The (Keymen-Mirwood, BMI) ... 14
Ebb Tide (Robbins, ASCAP) ... 13
Elusive Butterfly (Metric, BMI) ... 83
Fever (Lois, BMI) ... 41
Five O'Clock World (Screen Gems- Columbia, BMI) ... 4
Flowers on the Wall (Southwind, BMI) ... 12
Get Back (Travis, BMI) ... 88
Get Out of My Life Woman (Marsaint, BMI) ... 68
Giddyup Go (Starday, BMI) ... 85
Going to a Go-Go (Jobete, BMI) ... 29
Goodnight My Love (Quintet-Noma, BMI) ... 91
Hard Day's Night, A (Maclen & Unart, BMI) ... 58
Harlem Nocturne (Shapiro-Bernstein, ASCAP) ... 48
Hole in the Wall (Pure Soul, BMI) ... 73
Hurt (Miller, ASCAP) ... 53
I Ain't Gonna Eat Out My Heart Anymore (Web IV, BMI) ... 59
I Can't Believe You Love Me (Jobete, BMI) ... 80
I Got You (I Feel Good) (Lois-Try Me, BMI) ... 28
I See the Light (Jetstar, BMI) ... 60
I'm Too Far Gone (To Turn Around) (M.P.I., BMI) ... 76
I've Got to Be Somebody (Lowery, BMI) ... 50
If You Gotta Make a Fool of Somebody (Good Songs, BMI) ... 63
It Was a Very Good Year (Dolfi, ASCAP) ... 31
It's Good News Week (Mainstay, BMI) ... 52
It's My Life (Screen Gems-Columbia, BMI) ... 34
Jenny Take a Ride (Venice-Saturday, BMI) ... 16
Just Like Me (Daywin, BMI) ... 11
Let's Hang On (Saturday & Seasons Four, BMI) ... 45
Lies (4 Star, BMI) ... 20
Lightnin' Strikes (Rambed, BMI) ... 30
Like a Baby (Double Diamond-Champion, BMI) ... 36
Little Boy (In Grown Up Clothes) (Saturday-Seasons Four, BMI) ... 65
Look Through Any Window (Miller, ASCAP) ... 32
Loop, The (Electra-Vamp, BMI) ... 93
Love Is All We Need (Travis, BMI) ... 84
Love (Makes Me Do Foolish Things) (Jobete, BMI) ... 70
Love Makes the World Go Round (McLaughlin, BMI) ... 99
Men in My Little Girl's Life, The (Jewel, ASCAP) ... 7
Michael (Chevis, BMI) ... 44
Michelle—David & Jonathan (Maclen, BMI) ... 47
Michelle—Shank (Maclen, BMI) ... 92
Michelle—Vaughn (Maclen, BMI) ... 78
Must to Avoid, A (Trousdale, BMI) ... 8
My Baby Loves Me (Jobete, BMI) ... 75
My Generation (Devon, BMI) ... 77
My Love (Duchess, BMI) ... 17
My World Is Empty Without You (Jobete, BMI) ... 46
Night Time (Grand Canyon, BMI) ... 66
No Matter What Shape (Your Stomach's In) (C-Hear, BMI) ... 6
Over and Over (Recordo, BMI) ... 22
Pain Gets a Little Deeper, The (Gesaka & Muriel, BMI) ... 94
Please Don't Fight It (4 Star, BMI) ... 72
Rainbow '65 (Aba-Conrad, BMI) ... 69
Recovery (Chevis, BMI) ... 49
Sandy (Buckhorn, BMI) ... 27
Satin Pillows (Vintage, BMI) ... 23
Second Hand Rose (Fisher-Shapiro-Bernstein, ASCAP) ... 38
She's Just My Style (Viva, BMI) ... 3
Snow Flake (Open Road-Rondo, BMI) ... 79
Something I Want to Tell You (Cranebreak, BMI) ... 95
Sounds of Silence, The (Eclectic, BMI) ... 1
Spanish Eyes (Roosevelt & G.E.M.A., BMI-ASCAP) ... 18
Spanish Harlem (Progressive-Trio, BMI) ... 96
Spread It on Thick (Tree, BMI) ... 57
Sweet Woman Like You, A (Tree, BMI) ... 40
Tell Me Why (Brent & Melody Lane, BMI) ... 37
These Boots Are Made for Walkin' (Criterion, ASCAP) ... 74
This Can't Be True (Cameo-Parkway-Stilran, BMI) ... 89
Thunderball (Unart, BMI) ... 25
Tijuana Taxi (Irving, BMI) ... 51
Tired of Being Lonely (Vapac, BMI) ... 87
Turn! Turn! Turn! (Melody Trails, BMI) ... 43
Under Your Spell Again (Central Songs, BMI) ... 35
Up Tight (Jobete, BMI) ... 26
We Can Work It Out (Maclen, BMI) ... 2
Well Respected Man, A (Amer. Met. Ent. of N. Y., BMI) ... 24
When Liking Turns to Loving (Tobi-Ann & Unart, BMI) ... 71
Where the Sun Has Never Shone (Mainstay, BMI) ... 97
You Didn't Have to Be So Nice (Faithful Virtue, BMI) ... 10
You Don't Know Like I Know (East, BMI) ... 90
Young Girl, A (Marks, BMI) ... 55
(You're Gonna) Hurt Yourself (Saturday & Seasons Four, BMI) ... 67
Zorba the Greek (Miller, ASCAP) ... 33


## BUBBLING UNDER THE HOT 100

101. WAITIN' IN YOUR WELFARE LINE ... Buck Owens, Capitol 5566
102. BROWN PAPER SACK ... Gentrys, MGM 13432
103. THINK TWICE ... Jackie Wilson & LaVern Baker, Brunswick 55287
104. BABY COME ON HOME ... Solomon Burke, Atlantic 2314
105. BLACK NIGHTS ... Lowell Fulson, Kent 431
106. FOLLOW YOUR HEART ... Manhattans, Carnival 512
107. BIG BRIGHT EYES ... Danny Hutton, HBR 453
108. FLY ME TO THE MOON ... Sam & Bill, Joda 104
109. A BEGINNING FROM AN END ... Jan & Dean, Liberty 55849
110. YESTERDAY MAN ... Chris Andrews, Atco 6385
111. I FOUGHT THE LAW ... Bobby Fuller Four, Mustang 3014
112. LOOK IN MY EYES ... Three Degrees, Swan 4235
113. ON A CLEAR DAY YOU CAN SEE FOREVER ... Johnny Mathis, Mercury 72493
114. MICHELLE ... Spokesmen, Decca 31895
115. NO MAN IS AN ISLAND ... Van Dykes, Mala 520
116. WE KNOW WE'RE IN LOVE ... Lesley Gore, Mercury 72530
117. THE RAINS CAME ... Sir Douglas Quintet, Tribe 8314
118. ONCE A DAY ... Timi Yuro, Mercury 72515
119. RIB TIPS ... Andre Williams, Avin 103
120. LOOK AT ME ... Three Dimensions, RCA Victor 8709
121. FOR YOU ... Spellbinders, Columbia 43384
122. STAY AWAY FROM MY BABY ... Ted Taylor, Okeh 7231
123. FRIENDS AND LOVERS FOREVER ... Nancy Ames, Epic 9885
124. WHERE DID SHE GO ... Steff, Epic 9870
125. LONELY FOR YOU ... Ikettes, Modern 1015
126. IS IT ME ... Barbara Mason, Arctic 116
127. A LITTLE BIT OF SOAP ... Exciters, Bang 515
128. BABY SCRATCH MY BACK ... Slim Harpo, Excello 2273
129. I DIG YOU BABY ... Lorraine Ellison, Mercury 72472
130. THE KEYS TO MY SOUL ... Silkie, Fontana 1536
131. WAIT A MINUTE ... Tim Tam & the Turn-Ons, Palmer 5002
132. TIME ... Pozo Seco Singers, Columbia 43437
133. TAKE ME FOR WHAT I'M WORTH ... Searchers, Kapp 729
134. I CAN'T GO ON ... Charlie Rich, Smash 2012
135. THE ANSWER TO MY PRAYER ... Neil Sedaka, RCA Victor 8737

Compiled from national retail sales and radio station airplay by the Music Popularity Dept. of Record Market Research, Billboard.

For Week Ending January 29, 1966

# Billboard HOT 100

★ STAR performer—Sides registering greatest proportionate upward progress this week.

Record Industry Association of America seal of certification as million selling single.

Billboard Award

| This Week | 1 Wk. Ago | 2 Wks. Ago | 3 Wks. Ago | TITLE Artist, Label & Number | Weeks On Chart |
|---|---|---|---|---|---|
| 1 | 2 | 1 | 1 | WE CAN WORK IT OUT — Beatles, Capitol 5555 | 7 |
| ★ 2 | 15 | 31 | 58 | BARBARA ANN — Beach Boys, Capitol 5561 | 5 |
| 3 | 3 | 3 | 3 | SHE'S JUST MY STYLE — Gary Lewis & the Playboys, Liberty 55846 | 8 |
| 4 | 6 | 10 | 13 | NO MATTER WHAT SHAPE (Your Stomach's In) — T-Bones, Liberty 55836 | 8 |
| 5 | 4 | 4 | 8 | FIVE O'CLOCK WORLD — Vogues, Co & Ce 232 | 10 |
| ★ 6 | 9 | 9 | 14 | AS TEARS GO BY — Rolling Stones, London 9808 | 6 |
| 7 | 7 | 8 | 24 | THE MEN IN MY LITTLE GIRL'S LIFE — Mike Douglas, Epic 9876 | 6 |
| 8 | 8 | 11 | 15 | A MUST TO AVOID — Herman's Hermits, MGM 13437 | 6 |
| ★ 9 | 17 | 24 | 52 | MY LOVE — Petula Clark, Warner Bros. 5684 | 6 |
| ★ 10 | 16 | 21 | 32 | JENNY TAKE A RIDE — Mitch Ryder & the Detroit Wheels, New Voices 806 | 8 |
| 11 | 11 | 16 | 23 | JUST LIKE ME — Paul Revere & the Raiders, Columbia 43461 | 9 |
| 12 | 1 | 2 | 2 | SOUNDS OF SILENCE — Simon & Garfunkel, Columbia 43396 | 11 |
| 13 | 5 | 6 | 10 | DAY TRIPPER — Beatles, Capitol 5555 | 7 |
| 14 | 14 | 17 | 18 | THE DUCK — Jackie Lee, Mirwood 5502 | 11 |
| 15 | 18 | 18 | 19 | SPANISH EYES — Al Martino, Capitol 5542 | 9 |
| ★ 16 | 21 | 33 | 45 | CRYING TIME — Ray Charles, ABC-Paramount 10739 | 8 |
| 17 | 10 | 12 | 16 | YOU DIDN'T HAVE TO BE SO NICE — Lovin' Spoonful, Kama Sutra 205 | 10 |
| 18 | 19 | 22 | 28 | ATTACK — Toys, DynoVoice 214 | 7 |
| ★ 19 | 24 | 28 | 38 | A WELL RESPECTED MAN — Kinks, Reprise 0420 | 9 |
| ★ 20 | 30 | 52 | 66 | LIGHTNIN' STRIKES — Lou Christie, MGM 13412 | 6 |
| ★ 21 | 26 | 46 | 57 | UP TIGHT — Stevie Wonder, Tamla 54124 | 7 |
| 22 | 20 | 26 | 35 | LIES — Knickerbockers, Challenge 59321 | 9 |
| ★ 23 | 29 | 48 | 59 | GOING TO A GO-GO — Miracles, Tamla 54127 | 6 |
| ★ 24 | 33 | 43 | 56 | ZORBA THE GREEK — Herb Alpert & the Tijuana Brass, A&M 787 | 6 |
| 25 | 12 | 7 | 4 | FLOWERS ON THE WALL — Statler Brothers, Columbia 43315 | 12 |
| ★ 26 | 46 | 78 | — | MY WORLD IS EMPTY WITHOUT YOU — Supremes, Motown 1089 | 3 |
| 27 | 27 | 30 | 37 | SANDY — Ronny & the Daytonas, Mala 513 | 9 |
| 28 | 31 | 37 | 47 | IT WAS A VERY GOOD YEAR — Frank Sinatra, Reprise 0429 | 6 |
| 29 | 22 | 23 | 26 | SATIN PILLOWS — Bobby Vinton, Epic 9869 | 9 |
| ★ 30 | 36 | 54 | 67 | LIKE A BABY — Len Barry, Decca 31889 | 5 |
| ★ 31 | 42 | 55 | 65 | DON'T MESS WITH BILL — Marvelettes, Tamla 54126 | 5 |
| 32 | 32 | 34 | 39 | LOOK THROUGH ANY WINDOW — Hollies, Imperial 66134 | 11 |
| 33 | 37 | 47 | 64 | TELL ME WHY — Elvis Presley, RCA Victor 8740 | 5 |
| 34 | 38 | 41 | 49 | SECOND HAND ROSE — Barbra Streisand, Columbia 43469 | 7 |
| 35 | 25 | 27 | 30 | THUNDERBALL — Tom Jones, Parrot 9801 | 8 |
| ★ 36 | 47 | 69 | 98 | MICHELLE — David & Jonathan, Capitol 5563 | 4 |
| ★ 37 | 49 | 56 | 62 | RECOVERY — Fontella Bass, Checker 1131 | 6 |
| 38 | 35 | 35 | 46 | UNDER YOUR SPELL AGAIN — Johnny Rivers, Imperial 66144 | 7 |
| 39 | 13 | 5 | 5 | EBB TIDE — Righteous Brothers, Philles 130 | 9 |
| 40 | 22 | 13 | 6 | OVER AND OVER — Dave Clark Five, Epic 9863 | 12 |
| 41 | 44 | 61 | 61 | MICHAEL — C.O.D.'s, Kellmac 1003 | 10 |
| 42 | 28 | 20 | 7 | I GOT YOU (I Feel Good) — James Brown, King 6015 | 12 |
| 43 | 39 | 45 | 48 | ARE YOU THERE — Dionne Warwick, Scepter 12122 | 8 |
| ★ 44 | 54 | 74 | 99 | CALIFORNIA DREAMIN' — Mama's and Papa's, Dunhill 4020 | 4 |
| 45 | 51 | 64 | 69 | TIJUANA TAXI — Herb Alpert & the Tijuana Brass, A&M 787 | 6 |
| ★ 46 | 66 | 85 | — | NIGHT TIME — Strangeloves, Bang 514 | 3 |
| ★ 47 | 58 | — | — | A HARD DAY'S NIGHT — Ramsey Lewis Trio, Cadet 5525 | 2 |
| 48 | 52 | 57 | 50 | IT'S GOOD NEWS WEEK — Hedgehoppers Anonymous, Parrot 9800 | 9 |
| 49 | 40 | 29 | 29 | A SWEET WOMAN LIKE YOU — Joe Tex, Dial 4022 | 9 |
| ★ 50 | 74 | — | — | THESE BOOTS ARE MADE FOR WALKIN' — Nancy Sinatra, Reprise 0432 | 2 |
| 51 | 53 | 66 | 79 | HURT — Little Anthony & the Imperials, DCP 1154 | 5 |
| 52 | 57 | 65 | 77 | SPREAD IT ON THICK — Gentrys, MGM 13432 | 5 |
| 53 | 61 | 68 | 81 | CALL ME — Chris Montez, A&M 780 | 4 |
| 54 | 62 | 75 | — | CLEO'S MOOD — Jr. Walker & the All Stars, Soul 35017 | 3 |
| 55 | 60 | 71 | 80 | I SEE THE LIGHT — Five Americans, HBR 454 | 5 |
| 56 | 59 | 67 | 82 | I AIN'T GONNA EAT OUT MY HEART ANYMORE — Young Rascals, Atlantic 2312 | 6 |
| ★ 57 | 71 | — | — | WHEN LIKING TURNS TO LOVING — Ronnie Dove, Diamond 195 | 2 |
| 58 | 64 | 72 | 87 | CAN YOU PLEASE CRAWL OUT YOUR WINDOW — Bob Dylan, Columbia 43477 | 5 |
| 59 | 56 | 53 | 53 | BROOMSTICK COWBOY — Bobby Goldsboro, United Artists 952 | 7 |
| ★ 60 | 81 | — | — | BREAKIN' UP IS BREAKIN' MY HEART — Roy Orbison, MGM 13446 | 2 |
| 61 | 67 | 86 | — | (You're Gonna) HURT YOURSELF — Frankie Valli, Smash 2015 | 3 |
| 62 | 68 | 81 | 90 | GET OUT OF MY LIFE WOMAN — Lee Dorsey, Amy 945 | 5 |
| ★ 63 | — | — | — | WORKING MY WAY BACK TO YOU — 4 Seasons, Philips 40350 | 1 |
| 64 | 76 | 84 | 91 | I'M TOO FAR GONE (To Turn Around) — Bobby Bland, Duke 393 | 4 |
| 65 | 63 | 73 | 84 | IF YOU GOTTA MAKE A FOOL OF SOMEBODY — Maxine Brown, Wand 1104 | 8 |
| 66 | 75 | — | — | MY BABY LOVES ME — Martha & the Vandellas, Gordy 7048 | 2 |
| 67 | 65 | 60 | 68 | LITTLE BOY (In Grown Up Clothes) — 4 Seasons, Vee Jay 713 | 6 |
| ★ 68 | — | — | — | WHAT NOW MY LOVE — Sonny & Cher, Atco 6395 | 1 |
| 69 | 82 | — | — | ANDREA — Sunrays, Tower 191 | 2 |
| 70 | 83 | — | — | ELUSIVE BUTTERFLY — Bob Lind, World-Pacific 77808 | 2 |
| 71 | 69 | 79 | 88 | RAINBOW '65 — Gene Chandler, Constellation 158 | 8 |
| 72 | 80 | 87 | 97 | I CAN'T BELIEVE YOU LOVE ME — Tammi Terrel, Motown 1086 | 4 |
| 73 | 79 | 88 | — | SNOW FLAKE — Jim Reeves, RCA Victor 8719 | 3 |
| ★ 74 | 89 | 97 | — | THIS CAN'T BE TRUE — Eddie Holman, Parkway 960 | 3 |
| ★ 75 | — | — | — | I FOUGHT THE LAW — Bobby Fuller 4, Mustang 3014 | 1 |
| 76 | 84 | — | — | LOVE IS ALL WE NEED — Mel Carter, Imperial 66148 | 2 |
| 77 | 77 | 98 | — | MY GENERATION — The Who, Decca 31877 | 3 |
| 78 | 78 | 90 | 96 | MICHELLE — Billy Vaughn, Dot 16809 | 4 |
| 79 | 87 | 92 | — | TIRED OF BEING LONELY — Sharpees, One-derful 4839 | 3 |
| 80 | 86 | — | — | BYE BYE BLUES — Bert Kaempfert and His Ork, Decca 31882 | 2 |
| ★ 81 | 99 | — | — | LOVE MAKES THE WORLD GO ROUND — Deon Jackson, Carla 2526 | 2 |
| 82 | 92 | — | — | MICHELLE — Bud Shank, World-Pacific 77814 | 2 |
| 83 | 95 | — | — | SOMETHING I WANT TO TELL YOU — Johnny and the Expressions, Josie 946 | 2 |
| ★ 84 | — | — | — | HIDE & SEEK — Sheep, Boom 60,000 | 1 |
| ★ 85 | — | — | — | A LITTLE BIT OF SOAP — Exciters, Bang 515 | 1 |
| ★ 86 | — | — | — | THE CHEATER — Bob Kuban & the In-Men, Musicland, U.S.A. 20,001 | 1 |
| ★ 87 | — | — | — | MY SHIP IS COMING IN — Walker Brothers, Smash 2016 | 1 |
| 88 | 93 | — | — | THE LOOP — Johnny Lytle, Tuba 2004 | 2 |
| 89 | 94 | 94 | — | THE PAIN GETS A LITTLE DEEPER — Darrow Fletcher, Groovy 3001 | 3 |
| ★ 90 | — | — | — | BABY SCRATCH MY BACK — Slim Harpo, Excello 2273 | 1 |
| 91 | — | — | — | THE RAINS CAME — Sir Douglas Quintet, Tribe 8314 | 1 |
| 92 | — | — | — | MY ANSWER — Jimmy McCracklin, Imperial 66147 | 1 |
| 93 | — | — | — | WAITIN' IN YOUR WELFARE LINE — Buck Owens, Capitol 5566 | 1 |
| 94 | — | — | — | RIB TIPS — Andre Williams, Avin 103 | 1 |
| 95 | 98 | — | — | CAN'T YOU SEE — Mary Wells, Atco 6392 | 2 |
| 96 | 100 | — | — | BECAUSE I LOVE YOU — Billy Stewart, Chess 1948 | 2 |
| 97 | — | — | — | IS IT ME? — Barbara Mason, Arctic 116 | 1 |
| 98 | — | — | — | FLY ME TO THE MOON — Sam & Bill, Joda 104 | 1 |
| 99 | — | — | — | DON'T FORGET ABOUT ME — Barbara Lewis, Atlantic 2316 | 1 |
| 100 | — | — | — | TAKE ME FOR WHAT I'M WORTH — Searchers, Kapp 729 | 1 |

## HOT 100—A TO Z—(Publisher-Licensee)


Andrea (Sea of Tunes, BMI) ... 69
Are You There (Blue Seas-Jac, ASCAP) ... 43
As Tears Go By (Essex, ASCAP) ... 6
Attack (Saturday, BMI) ... 18
Baby Scratch My Back (Excellorec, BMI) ... 90
Barbara Ann (Shoe-String & Cousins, BMI) ... 2
Because I Love You (Chevis, BMI) ... 96
Breakin' Up Is Breakin' My Heart (Acuff-Rose, BMI) 60
Broomstick Cowboy (Unart, BMI) ... 59
Bye Bye Blues (Bourne, ASCAP) ... 80
California Dreamin' (Trousdale, BMI) ... 44
Call Me (Duchess, BMI) ... 53
Can You Please Crawl Out Your Window (Witmark, ASCAP) ... 58
Can't You See (Jalynne, BMI) ... 95
Cheater, The (MAM) ... 86
Cleo's Mood (Jobete, BMI) ... 54
Cryig Time (Bluebook, BMI) ... 16
Day Tripper (Maclen, BMI) ... 13
Don't Forget About Me (Screen Gems-Columbia, BMI) ... 99
Don't Mess With Bill (Jobete, BMI) ... 31
Duck, The (Keymen-Mirwood, BMI) ... 14
Ebb Tide (Robbins, ASCAP) ... 39
Elusive Butterfly (Metric, BMI) ... 70
Five o'Clock World (Screen Gems-Columbia, BMI). 5
Flowers on the Wall (Southwind, BMI) ... 25
Fly Me to the Moon (Almanac, ASCAP) ... 98
Get Out of My Life Woman (Marsaint, BMI) ... 62
Going to a Go-Go (Jobete, BMI) ... 23
Hard Day's Night, A (Maclen & Unart, BMI) ... 47
Hide & Seek (Florentine-Marks, BMI) ... 84
Hurt (Miller, ASCAP) ... 51
I Ain't Gonna Eat Out My Heart Anymore (Web IV, BMI) ... 56
I Can't Believe You Love Me (Jobete, BMI) ... 72
I Fought the Law (Acuff-Rose, BMI) ... 75
I Got You (I Feel Good) (Lois-Try Me, BMI) ... 42
I See the Light (Jetstar, BMI) ... 55
I'm Too Far Gone (To Turn Around) (M.P.I., BMI). 64
If You Gotta Make a Fool of Somebody (Good Songs, BMI) ... 65
Is It Me? (Stilran-Dandelion, BMI) ... 97
It Was a Very Good Year (Dolfi, ASCAP) ... 28
It's Good News Week (Mainstay, BMI) ... 48
Jenny Take a Ride (Venice-Saturday, BMI) ... 10
Just Like Me (Daywin, BMI) ... 11
Lies (4 Star, BMI) ... 22
Lightnin' Strikes (Rambed, BMI) ... 20
Like a Baby (Double Diamond-Champion, BMI) ... 30
Little Bit of Soap, A (Mellin, BMI) ... 85
Little Boy (In Grown Up Clothes) (Saturday-Seasons Four, BMI) ... 67
Look Through Any Window (Miller, ASCAP) ... 32
Loop, The (Electra-Vamp, BMI) ... 88
Love Is All We Need (Travis, BMI) ... 76
Love Makes the World Go Round (McLaughlin, BMI) 81
Men in My Little Girl's Life, The (Jewel, ASCAP). 7
Michael (Chevis, BMI) ... 41
Michelle—David & Jonathan (Maclen, BMI) ... 36
Michelle—Shank (Maclen, BMI) ... 82
Michelle—Vaughn (Maclen, BMI) ... 78
Must to Avoid, A (Trousdale, BMI) ... 8
My Answer (Metric, BMI) ... 92
My Baby Loves Me (Jobete, BMI) ... 66
My Generation (Devon, BMI) ... 77
My Love (Duchess, BMI) ... 9
My Ship Is Coming In (January, BMI) ... 87
My World Is Empty Without You (Jobete, BMI) .. 26
Night Time (Grand Canyon, BMI) ... 45
No Matter What Shape (Your Stomach's In) (C-Hear, BMI) ... 4
Over and Over (Recordo, BMI) ... 40
Pain Gets a Little Deeper, The (Gesaka & Muriel, BMI) ... 89
Rainbow '65 (Aba-Conrad, BMI) ... 71
Rains Came, The (Crazy Cajun & Corrett, BMI) .. 91
Recovery (Chevis, BMI) ... 37
Rib Tips (Celtex, BMI) ... 94
Sandy (Buckhorn, BMI) ... 27
Satin Pillows (Vintage, BMI) ... 29
Second Hand Rose (Fisher-Shapiro-Bernstein, ASCAP) 34
She's Just My Style (Viva, BMI) ... 3
Snow Flake (Open Road-Rondo, BMI) ... 73
Something I Want to Tell You (Cranebreak, BMI). 83
Sounds of Silence, The (Eclectic, BMI) ... 12
Spanish Eyes (Roosevelt & G.E.M.A., BMI-ASCAP) 15
Spread It on Thick (Tree, BMI) ... 52
Sweet Woman Like You, A (Tree, BMI) ... 49
Take Me for What I'm Worth (Trousdale, BMI) ... 100
Tell Me Why (Brent & Melody Lane, BMI) ... 33
These Boots Are Made for Walkin' (Criterion, ASCAP) ... 50
This Can't Be True (Cameo-Parkway-Stilran, BMI) .. 74
Thunderball (Unart, BMI) ... 35
Tijuana Taxi (Irving, BMI) ... 45
Tired of Being Lonely (Vapac, BMI) ... 79
Under Your Spell Again (Central Songs, BMI) ... 38
Up Tight (Jobete, BMI) ... 21
Waitin' in Your Welfare Line (Central Songs, BMI) 93
We Can Work It Out (Maclen, BMI) ... 1
Well Respected Man, A (Amer. Met. Ent. of N. Y., BMI) ... 19
What Now My Love (Remick, ASCAP) ... 68
When Liking Turns to Loving (Tobi-Ann & Unart, BMI) ... 57
Working My Way Back to You (Saturday & Seasons 4, BMI) ... 63
You Didn't Have to Be So Nice (Faithful Virtue, BMI) ... 17
(You're Gonna) Hurt Yourself (Saturday & Seasons 4, BMI) ... 61
Zorba the Greek (Miller, ASCAP) ... 24


## BUBBLING UNDER THE HOT 100

101. AT THE SCENE ... Dave Clark Five, Epic 9882
102. EASY GOING FELLOW ... Roscoe Shelton, Sound Stage 7 2555
103. SINCE I LOST THE ONE I LOVE ... Impressions, ABC-Paramount 10761
104. NO MAN IS AN ISLAND ... Van Dykes, Mala 520
105. GOODNIGHT MY LOVE ... Ben E. King, Atco 6390
106. MICHELLE ... Spokesmen, Decca 31895
107. BIG BRIGHT EYES ... Danny Hutton, HBR 453
108. GET BACK ... Roy Head, Scepter 12124
109. BABY COME ON HOME ... Solomon Burke, Atlantic 2314
110. SET YOU FREE, THIS TIME ... Byrds, Columbia 43501
111. I CONFESS ... New Colony Six, Centaur 1201
112. WE KNOW WE'RE IN LOVE ... Lesley Gore, Mercury 72530
113. THINK TWICE ... Jackie Wilson & LaVern Baker, Brunswick 55287
114. YESTERDAY MAN ... Chris Andrews, Atco 6385
115. FOLLOW YOUR HEART ... Manhattans, Carnival 512
116. STAY AWAY FROM MY BABY ... Ted Taylor, Okeh 7231
117. IN MY ROOM ... Verdelle Smith, Capitol 5567
118. FUNNY ... Walter Jackson, Okeh 7236
119. BLACK NIGHTS ... Lowell Fulson, Kent 431
120. RED HOT ... Sam the Sham & the Pharaohs, MGM 13452
121. I DIG YOU BABY ... Lorraine Ellison, Mercury 72472
122. LOOK IN MY EYES ... Three Degrees, Swan 4325
123. LONELY FOR YOU ... Ikettes, Modern 1015
124. THE KEYS TO MY SOUL ... Silkie, Fontana 1536
125. FRIENDS AND LOVERS FOREVER ... Nancy Ames, Epic 9885
126. PUT YOURSELF IN MY PLACE ... Elgins, V.I.P. 25029
127. ANSWER TO MY PRAYER ... Neil Sedaka, RCA Victor 8737
128. BROWN PAPER SACK ... Gentrys, MGM 13432
129. ONCE A DAY ... Timi Yuro, Mercury 72515
130. WAIT A MINUTE ... Tim Tam & the Turn-Ons, Palmer 5002

Compiled from national retail sales and radio station airplay by the Music Popularity Dept. of Record Market Research, Billboard.

For Week Ending February 5, 1966

# Billboard HOT 100

★ STAR performer—Sides registering greatest proportionate upward progress this week.

Record Industry Association of America seal of certification as million selling single.

Billboard Award

| This Week | 1 Wk. Ago | 2 Wks. Ago | 3 Wks. Ago | TITLE Artist, Label & Number | Weeks On Chart |
|---|---|---|---|---|---|
| ★1 | 9 | 17 | 24 | MY LOVE — Petula Clark, Warner Bros. 5684 | 7 |
| 2 | 2 | 15 | 31 | BARBARA ANN — Beach Boys, Capitol 5561 | 6 |
| 3 | 4 | 6 | 10 | NO MATTER WHAT SHAPE (Your Stomach's In) — T-Bones, Liberty 55836 | 9 |
| 4 | 1 | 2 | 1 | WE CAN WORK IT OUT — Beatles, Capitol 5555 (RIAA seal) | 8 |
| ★5 | 20 | 30 | 52 | LIGHTNIN' STRIKES — Lou Christie, MGM 13412 | 7 |
| 6 | 7 | 7 | 8 | THE MEN IN MY LITTLE GIRL'S LIFE — Mike Douglas, Epic 9876 | 7 |
| 7 | 3 | 3 | 3 | SHE'S JUST MY STYLE — Gary Lewis & the Playboys, Liberty 55846 | 9 |
| 8 | 5 | 4 | 4 | FIVE O'CLOCK WORLD — Vogues, Co & Ce 232 | 11 |
| 9 | 8 | 8 | 11 | A MUST TO AVOID — Herman's Hermits, MGM 13437 | 7 |
| ★10 | 16 | 21 | 33 | CRYING TIME — Ray Charles, ABC-Paramount 10739 | 9 |
| 11 | 10 | 16 | 21 | JENNY TAKE A RIDE — Mitch Ryder & the Detroit Wheels, New Voices 806 | 9 |
| 12 | 6 | 9 | 9 | AS TEARS GO BY — Rolling Stones, London 9808 | 7 |
| ★13 | 26 | 46 | 78 | MY WORLD IS EMPTY WITHOUT YOU — Supremes, Motown 1089 | 4 |
| 14 | 11 | 11 | 16 | JUST LIKE ME — Paul Revere & the Raiders, Columbia 43461 | 10 |
| ★15 | 24 | 33 | 43 | ZORBA THE GREEK — Herb Alpert & the Tijuana Brass, A&M 787 | 7 |
| ★16 | 21 | 26 | 46 | UP TIGHT — Stevie Wonder, Tamla 54124 | 8 |
| 17 | 19 | 24 | 28 | A WELL RESPECTED MAN — Kinks, Reprise 0420 | 10 |
| 18 | 14 | 14 | 17 | THE DUCK — Jackie Lee, Mirwood 5502 | 12 |
| ★19 | 31 | 42 | 55 | DON'T MESS WITH BILL — Marvelettes, Tamla 54126 | 6 |
| 20 | 12 | 1 | 2 | SOUNDS OF SILENCE — Simon & Garfunkel, Columbia 43396 | 12 |
| 21 | 23 | 29 | 48 | GOING TO A GO-GO — Miracles, Tamla 54127 | 7 |
| 22 | 13 | 5 | 6 | DAY TRIPPER — Beatles, Capitol 5555 | 8 |
| 23 | 15 | 18 | 18 | SPANISH EYES — Al Martino, Capitol 5542 | 10 |
| 24 | 22 | 20 | 26 | LIES — Knickerbockers, Challenge 59321 | 10 |
| 25 | 17 | 10 | 12 | YOU DIDN'T HAVE TO BE SO NICE — Lovin' Spoonful, Kama Sutra 205 | 11 |
| ★26 | 36 | 47 | 69 | MICHELLE — David & Jonathan, Capitol 5563 | 5 |
| 27 | 30 | 36 | 54 | LIKE A BABY — Len Barry, Decca 31889 | 6 |
| ★28 | 50 | 74 | — | THESE BOOTS ARE MADE FOR WALKIN' — Nancy Sinatra, Reprise 0432 | 3 |
| 29 | 18 | 19 | 22 | ATTACK — Toys, DynoVoice 214 | 8 |
| 30 | 28 | 31 | 37 | IT WAS A VERY GOOD YEAR — Frank Sinatra, Reprise 0429 | 7 |
| 31 | 25 | 12 | 7 | FLOWERS ON THE WALL — Statler Brothers, Columbia 43315 | 13 |
| 32 | 34 | 38 | 41 | SECOND HAND ROSE — Barbra Streisand, Columbia 43469 | 8 |
| ★33 | 44 | 54 | 74 | CALIFORNIA DREAMIN' — Mama's and Papa's, Dunhill 4020 | 5 |
| ★34 | 57 | 71 | — | WHEN LIKING TURNS TO LOVING — Ronnie Dove, Diamond 195 | 3 |
| 35 | 33 | 37 | 47 | TELL ME WHY — Elvis Presley, RCA Victor 8740 | 6 |
| ★36 | 46 | 66 | 85 | NIGHT TIME — Strangeloves, Bang 514 | 4 |
| ★37 | 47 | 58 | — | A HARD DAY'S NIGHT — Ramsey Lewis Trio, Cadet 5525 | 3 |
| 38 | 45 | 51 | 64 | TIJUANA TAXI — Herb Alpert & the Tijuana Brass, A&M 787 | 7 |
| 39 | 35 | 25 | 27 | THUNDERBALL — Tom Jones, Parrot 9801 | 9 |
| 40 | 27 | 27 | 30 | SANDY — Ronny & the Daytonas, Mala 513 | 10 |
| ★41 | 53 | 61 | 68 | CALL ME — Chris Montez, A&M 780 | 5 |
| 42 | 29 | 23 | 23 | SATIN PILLOWS — Bobby Vinton, Epic 9869 | 10 |
| 43 | 43 | 39 | 45 | ARE YOU THERE — Dionne Warwick, Scepter 12122 | 9 |
| ★44 | 63 | — | — | WORKING MY WAY BACK TO YOU — 4 Seasons, Philips 40350 | 2 |
| ★45 | 55 | 60 | 71 | I SEE THE LIGHT — Five Americans, HBR 454 | 6 |
| 46 | 37 | 49 | 56 | RECOVERY — Fontella Bass, Checker 1131 | 7 |
| ★47 | 68 | — | — | WHAT NOW MY LOVE — Sonny & Cher, Atco 6395 | 2 |
| ★48 | 61 | 67 | 86 | (You're Gonna) HURT YOURSELF — Frankie Valli, Smash 2015 | 4 |
| ★49 | 50 | 81 | — | BREAKIN' UP IS BREAKIN' MY HEART — Roy Orbison, MGM 13446 | 3 |
| 50 | 52 | 57 | 65 | SPREAD IT ON THICK — Gentrys, MGM 13432 | 6 |
| ★51 | 66 | 75 | — | MY BABY LOVES ME — Martha & the Vandellas, Gordy 7048 | 3 |
| 52 | 56 | 59 | 67 | I AIN'T GONNA EAT OUT MY HEART ANYMORE — Young Rascals, Atlantic 2312 | 7 |
| 53 | 54 | 62 | 75 | CLEO'S MOOD — Jr. Walker & the All Stars, Soul 35017 | 4 |
| ★54 | 75 | — | — | I FOUGHT THE LAW — Bobby Fuller 4, Mustang 3014 | 2 |
| 55 | 32 | 32 | 34 | LOOK THROUGH ANY WINDOW — Hollies, Imperial 66134 | 12 |
| 56 | 48 | 52 | 57 | IT'S GOOD NEWS WEEK — Hedgehoppers Anonymous, Parrot 9800 | 10 |
| ★57 | 70 | 83 | — | ELUSIVE BUTTERFLY — Bob Lind, World-Pacific 77808 | 3 |
| 58 | 41 | 44 | 61 | MICHAEL — C.O.D.'s, Kellmac 1003 | 11 |
| 59 | 62 | 68 | 81 | GET OUT OF MY LIFE WOMAN — Lee Dorsey, Amy 945 | 6 |
| 60 | 38 | 35 | 35 | UNDER YOUR SPELL AGAIN — Johnny Rivers, Imperial 66144 | 8 |
| 61 | 69 | 82 | — | ANDREA — Sunrays, Tower 191 | 3 |
| 62 | 51 | 53 | 66 | HURT — Little Anthony & the Imperials, DCP 1154 | 6 |
| 63 | 58 | 64 | 72 | CAN YOU PLEASE CRAWL OUT YOUR WINDOW — Bob Dylan, Columbia 43477 | 6 |
| 64 | 64 | 76 | 84 | I'M TOO FAR GONE (To Turn Around) — Bobby Bland, Duke 393 | 5 |
| ★65 | 80 | 86 | — | BYE BYE BLUES — Bert Kaempfert and His Ork, Decca 31882 | 3 |
| ★66 | 81 | 99 | — | LOVE MAKES THE WORLD GO ROUND — Deon Jackson, Carla 2526 | 3 |
| 67 | 73 | 79 | 88 | SNOW FLAKE — Jim Reeves, RCA Victor 8719 | 4 |
| ★68 | 86 | — | — | THE CHEATER — Bob Kuban & the In-Men, Musicland, U.S.A. 20,001 | 2 |
| 69 | 76 | 84 | — | LOVE IS ALL WE NEED — Mel Carter, Imperial 66148 | 3 |
| ★70 | 85 | — | — | A LITTLE BIT OF SOAP — Exciters, Bang 515 | 2 |
| ★71 | — | — | — | YOU BABY — Turtles, White Whale 227 | 1 |
| 72 | 65 | 63 | 73 | IF YOU GOTTA MAKE A FOOL OF SOMEBODY — Maxine Brown, Wand 1104 | 9 |
| ★73 | — | — | — | AT THE SCENE — Dave Clark Five, Epic 9882 | 1 |
| 74 | 74 | 89 | 97 | THIS CAN'T BE TRUE — Eddie Holman, Parkway 960 | 4 |
| 75 | 77 | 77 | 98 | MY GENERATION — The Who, Decca 31877 | 4 |
| 76 | 87 | — | — | MY SHIP IS COMING IN — Walker Brothers, Smash 2016 | 2 |
| 77 | 78 | 78 | 90 | MICHELLE — Billy Vaughn, Dot 16809 | 5 |
| 78 | 82 | 92 | — | MICHELLE — Bud Shank, World-Pacific 77814 | 3 |
| 79 | 84 | — | — | HIDE & SEEK — Sheep, Boom 60,000 | 2 |
| 80 | 90 | — | — | BABY SCRATCH MY BACK — Slim Harpo, Excello 2273 | 2 |
| ★81 | — | — | — | LONG LIVE OUR LOVE — Shangri-Las, Red Bird 048 | 1 |
| 82 | 91 | — | — | THE RAINS CAME — Sir Douglas Quintet, Tribe 8314 | 2 |
| 83 | 72 | 80 | 87 | I CAN'T BELIEVE YOU LOVE ME — Tammi Terrel, Motown 1086 | 5 |
| 84 | 83 | 95 | — | SOMETHING I WANT TO TELL YOU — Johnny and the Expressions, Josie 946 | 3 |
| ★85 | — | — | — | BATMAN THEME — Marketts, Warner Bros. 5696 | 1 |
| 86 | 88 | 93 | — | THE LOOP — Johnny Lytle, Tuba 2004 | 3 |
| ★87 | — | — | — | THE BALLAD OF THE GREEN BERETS — S/Sgt. Barry Sadler, RCA Victor 8739 | 1 |
| ★88 | — | — | — | WE KNOW WE'RE IN LOVE — Lesley Gore, Mercury 72530 | 1 |
| 89 | 93 | — | — | WAITIN' IN YOUR WELFARE LINE — Buck Owens, Capitol 5566 | 2 |
| ★90 | — | — | — | GEORGIA ON MY MIND — Righteous Brothers, Moonglow 244 | 1 |
| 91 | 100 | — | — | TAKE ME FOR WHAT I'M WORTH — Searchers, Kapp 729 | 2 |
| 92 | — | — | — | SET YOU FREE THIS TIME — Byrds, Columbia 43501 | 1 |
| 93 | — | — | — | IN MY ROOM — Verdelle Smith, Capitol 5567 | 1 |
| 94 | 95 | 98 | — | CAN'T YOU SEE — Mary Wells, Atco 6392 | 3 |
| 95 | — | — | — | LOST SOMEONE — James Brown, King 6020 | 1 |
| 96 | — | — | — | SINCE I LOST THE ONE I LOVE — Impressions, ABC-Paramount 10761 | 1 |
| 97 | — | — | — | RED HOT — Sam the Sham & the Pharaohs, MGM 13452 | 1 |
| 98 | 99 | — | — | DON'T FORGET ABOUT ME — Barbara Lewis, Atlantic 2316 | 2 |
| 99 | — | — | — | I WANT TO GO WITH YOU — Eddy Arnold, RCA Victor 8749 | 1 |
| 100 | — | — | — | THE ANSWER TO MY PRAYER — Neil Sedaka, RCA Victor 8737 | 1 |

## HOT 100—A TO Z—(Publisher-Licensee)

Andrea (Sea of Tunes, BMI) ........ 61
Answer to My Prayer, The (Bregman, Voco & Conn, ASCAP) ........ 100
Are You There (Blue Seas-Jac, ASCAP) ........ 43
As Tears Go By (Essex, ASCAP) ........ 12
At the Scene (Branston, BMI) ........ 73
Attack (Saturday, BMI) ........ 29
Baby Scratch My Back (Excellorec, BMI) ........ 80
Ballad of the Green Berets, The (Music, Music, Music, ASCAP) ........ 87
Barbara Ann (Shoe-String & Cousins, BMI) ........ 2
Batman Theme (Miller, ASCAP) ........ 85
Breakin' Up Is Breakin' My Heart (Acuff-Rose, BMI) ........ 49
Bye Bye Blues (Bourne, ASCAP) ........ 65
California Dreamin' (Trousdale, BMI) ........ 33
Call Me (Duchess, BMI) ........ 41
Can You Please Crawl Out Your Window (Witmark, ASCAP) ........ 63
Can't You See (Jalynne, BMI) ........ 94
Cheater, The (MAM) ........ 68
Cleo's Mood (Jobete, BMI) ........ 53
Crying Time (Bluebook, BMI) ........ 10
Day Tripper (Maclen, BMI) ........ 22
Don't Forget About Me (Screen Gems-Columbia, BMI) ........ 98
Don't Mess With Bill (Jobete, BMI) ........ 19
Duck, The (Keymen-Mirwood, BMI) ........ 18
Elusive Butterfly (Metric, BMI) ........ 57
Five o'Clock World (Screen Gems-Columbia, BMI) ........ 8
Flowers on the Wall (Southwind, BMI) ........ 31
Georgia on My Mind (Peer Int'l, BMI) ........ 90
Get Out of My Life Woman (Marsaint, BMI) ........ 59
Going to a Go-Go (Jobete, BMI) ........ 21
Hard Day's Night, A (Maclen & Unart, BMI) ........ 37
Hide & Seek (Florentine-Marks, BMI) ........ 79
Hurt (Miller, ASCAP) ........ 62
I Ain't Gonna Eat Out My Heart Anymore (Web IV, BMI) ........ 52
I Can't Believe You Love Me (Jobete, BMI) ........ 83
I Fought the Law (Acuff-Rose, BMI) ........ 54
I See the Light (Jetstar, BMI) ........ 45
I Want to Go With You (Pamper, BMI) ........ 99
I'm Too Far Gone (To Turn Around) (M.P.I., BMI) 64
If You Gotta Make a Fool of Somebody (Good Songs, BMI) ........ 72
In My Room (Robbins, ASCAP) ........ 93
It Was a Very Good Year (Dolfi, ASCAP) ........ 30
It's Good News Week (Mainstay, BMI) ........ 56
Jenny Take a Ride (Venice-Saturday, BMI) ........ 11
Just Like Me (Daywin, BMI) ........ 14
Lies (4 Star, BMI) ........ 24
Lightnin' Strikes (Rambed, BMI) ........ 5
Like a Baby (Double Diamond-Champion, BMI)... 27
Little Bit of Soap, A (Mellin, BMI) ........ 70
Long Live Our Love (Trio-Tender Tuner, BMI) .. 81
Look Through Any Window (Miller, ASCAP)..... 55
Loop, The (Electra-Vamp, BMI) ........ 86
Lost Someone (Lois, BMI) ........ 95
Love Is All We Need (Travis, BMI) ........ 69
Love Makes the World Go 'Round (McLaughlin, BMI) ........ 66
Men in My Little Girl's Life, The (Jewel, ASCAP) 6
Michael (Chevis, BMI) ........ 58
Michelle—David & Jonathan (Maclen, BMI) ........ 26
Michelle—Shank (Maclen, BMI) ........ 78
Michelle—Vaughn (Maclen, BMI) ........ 77
Must to Avoid, A (Trousdale, BMI) ........ 9
My Baby Loves Me (Jobete, BMI) ........ 51
My Generation (Devon, BMI) ........ 75
My Love (Duchess, BMI) ........ 1
My Ship Is Coming In (January, BMI) ........ 76
My World Is Empty Without You (Jobete, BMI)... 13
Night Time (Grand Canyon, BMI) ........ 36
No Matter What Shape (Your Stomach's In) (C-Hear, BMI) ........ 3
Rains Came, The (Crazy Cajun & Corrett, BMI)... 82
Recovery (Chevis, BMI) ........ 46
Red Hot (Riverline, BMI) ........ 97
Sandy (Buckhorn, BMI) ........ 40
Satin Pillows (Vintage, BMI) ........ 42
Second Hand Rose (Fisher-Shapiro-Bernstein, ASCAP) ........ 32
Set You Free This Time (Tickson, BMI) ........ 92
She's Just My Style (Viva, BMI) ........ 7
Since I Lost the One I Love (Chi-Sound, BMI)... 96
Snow Flake (Open Road-Rondo, BMI) ........ 67
Something I Want to Tell You (Cranebreak, BMI). 84
Sounds of Silence, The (Eclectic, BMI) ........ 20
Spanish Eyes (Roosevelt & G.E.M.A., BMI-ASCAP) 23
Spread It on Thick (Tree, BMI) ........ 50
Take Me for What I'm Worth (Trousdale, BMI).. 91
Tell Me Why (Brent & Melody Lane, BMI) ........ 35
These Boots Are Made for Walkin' (Criterion, ASCAP) ........ 28
This Can't Be True (Cameo-Parkway-Stilran, BMI) 74
Thunderball (Unart, BMI) ........ 39
Tijuana Taxi (Irving, BMI) ........ 38
Under Your Spell Again (Central Songs, BMI).... 60
Up Tight (Jobete, BMI) ........ 16
Waitin' in Your Welfare Line (Central Songs, BMI) 89
We Can Work It Out (Maclen, BMI) ........ 4
We Know We're in Love (Buffee, BMI) ........ 88
Well Respected Man, A (Amer. Met. Ent. of N. Y., BMI) ........ 17
What Now My Love (Remick, ASCAP) ........ 47
When Liking Turns to Loving (Tobi-Ann & Unart, BMI) ........ 34
Working My Way Back to You (Saturday & Seasons 4, BMI) ........ 44
You Baby (Trousdale, BMI) ........ 71
You Didn't Have to Be So Nice (Faithful Virtue, BMI) ........ 25
(You're Gonna) Hurt Yourself (Saturday & Seasons 4, BMI) ........ 48
Zorba the Greek (Miller, ASCAP) ........ 15

## BUBBLING UNDER THE HOT 100

101. IS IT ME? ........ Barbara Mason, Arctic 116
102. EASY GOING FELLOW ........ Roscoe Shelton, Sound Stage 7 2555
103. MY ANSWER ........ Jimmy McCracklin, Imperial 66147
104. RIB TIPS ........ Andre Williams, Avin 103
105. BIG BRIGHT EYES ........ Danny Hutton, HBR 453
106. HOMEWARD BOUND ........ Simon & Garfunkel, Columbia 43511
107. FLY ME TO THE MOON ........ Sam & Bill, Joda 104
108. THE PAIN GETS A LITTLE DEEPER ........ Darrow Fletcher, Groovy 3001
109. MICHELLE ........ Spokesmen, Decca 31895
110. BECAUSE I LOVE YOU ........ Billy Stewart, Chess 1948
111. WHERE AM I GOING? ........ Barbra Streisand, Columbia 43518
112. BATMAN ........ Jan & Dean, Liberty 55860
113. THIS GOLDEN RING ........ Fortunes, Press 9811
114. BATMAN THEME ........ Neal Hefti, RCA Victor 8755
115. THE ONE ON THE RIGHT IS ON THE LEFT ........ Johnny Cash, Columbia 43496
116. FUNNY ........ Walter Jackson, Okeh 7236
117. I CONFESS ........ New Colony Six, Centaur 1201
118. ANGELS ........ Missionaires of Mary Chorale Group, Kapp 731
119. IT WON'T BE WRONG ........ Byrds, Columbia 43501
120. I DIG YOU BABY ........ Lorraine Ellison, Mercury 72472
121. IF YOU CAN'T BITE, DON'T GROWL ........ Tommy Collins, Columbia 43489
122. LONELY FOR YOU ........ Ikettes, Modern 1015
123. THE WEEKEND ........ Jack Jones, Kapp 736
124. PUT YOURSELF IN MY PLACE ........ Elgins, V.I.P. 25029
125. WAIT A MINUTE ........ Tim Tam & the Turn-Ons, Palmer 5002
126. FEEL IT ........ Sam Cooke, RCA Victor 8751
127. MADE IN PARIS ........ Trini Lopez, Reprise 0435
128. HELLO ENEMY ........ Johnny Tillotson, MGM 13445
129. DON'T TAKE IT OUT ON ME ........ Bobbi Martin, Coral 62475
130. SINCE YOU HAVE GONE FROM ME ........ Barry Young, Dot 16819
131. TEENAGE FAILURE ........ Chad & Jeremy, Columbia 43490
132. YOU BRING ME DOWN ........ Royalettes, MGM 13451
133. FLOWERS ON THE WALL ........ Chet Baker & the Mariachi Brass, World Pacific 77815
134. WE GOT THE WINNING HAND ........ Little Milton, Checker 1132
135. EVER SEE A DIVER KISS HIS WIFE WHILE THE BUBBLES BOUNCE ABOVE THE WATER? ........ Shirley Ellis, Congress 260

Compiled from national retail sales and radio station airplay by the Music Popularity Dept. of Record Market Research, Billboard.

# Billboard HOT 100

For Week Ending February 12, 1966

★ STAR performer—Sides registering greatest proportionate upward progress this week.

Record Industry Association of America seal of certification as million selling single.

| This Wk | Wk. Ago | 2 Wk. Ago | 3 Wk. Ago | TITLE Artist, Label & Number | Weeks On Chart |
|---|---|---|---|---|---|
| 1 | 1 | 9 | 17 | MY LOVE — Petula Clark, Warner Bros. 5684 | 8 |
| 2 | 5 | 20 | 30 | LIGHTNIN' STRIKES — Lou Christie, MGM 13412 | 8 |
| 3 | 16 | 21 | 26 | UP TIGHT — Stevie Wonder, Tamla 54124 | 9 |
| 4 | 2 | 2 | 15 | BARBARA ANN — Beach Boys, Capitol 5561 | 7 |
| 5 | 4 | 1 | 2 | WE CAN WORK IT OUT — Beatles, Capitol 5555 | 9 |
| 6 | 3 | 4 | 6 | NO MATTER WHAT SHAPE (Your Stomach's In) — T-Bones, Liberty 55836 | 10 |
| 7 | 10 | 16 | 21 | CRYING TIME — Ray Charles, ABC-Paramount 10739 | 10 |
| 8 | 13 | 26 | 46 | MY WORLD IS EMPTY WITHOUT YOU — Supremes, Motown 1089 | 5 |
| 9 | 8 | 5 | 4 | FIVE O'CLOCK WORLD — Vogues, Co & Ce 232 | 12 |
| 10 | 19 | 31 | 42 | DON'T MESS WITH BILL — Marvelettes, Tamla 54126 | 7 |
| 11 | 21 | 23 | 29 | GOING TO A GO-GO — Miracles, Tamla 54127 | 8 |
| 12 | 15 | 24 | 33 | ZORBA THE GREEK — Herb Alpert & the Tijuana Brass, A&M 787 | 8 |
| 13 | 17 | 19 | 24 | A WELL RESPECTED MAN — Kinks, Reprise 0420 | 11 |
| 14 | 14 | 11 | 11 | JUST LIKE ME — Paul Revere & the Raiders, Columbia 43461 | 11 |
| 15 | 28 | 50 | 74 | THESE BOOTS ARE MADE FOR WALKIN' — Nancy Sinatra, Reprise 0432 | 4 |
| 16 | 11 | 10 | 16 | JENNY TAKE A RIDE — Mitch Ryder & the Detroit Wheels, New Voices 806 | 10 |
| 17 | 6 | 7 | 7 | THE MEN IN MY LITTLE GIRL'S LIFE — Mike Douglas, Epic 9876 | 8 |
| 18 | 26 | 36 | 47 | MICHELLE — David & Jonathan, Capitol 5563 | 6 |
| 19 | 7 | 3 | 3 | SHE'S JUST MY STYLE — Gary Lewis & the Playboys, Liberty 55846 | 10 |
| 20 | 9 | 8 | 8 | A MUST TO AVOID — Herman's Hermits, MGM 13437 | 8 |
| 21 | 18 | 14 | 14 | THE DUCK — Jackie Lee, Mirwood 5502 | 13 |
| 22 | 44 | 63 | — | WORKING MY WAY BACK TO YOU — 4 Seasons, Philips 40350 | 3 |
| 23 | 33 | 44 | 54 | CALIFORNIA DREAMIN' — Mama's and Papa's, Dunhill 4020 | 6 |
| 24 | 24 | 22 | 20 | LIES — Knickerbockers, Challenge 59321 | 11 |
| 25 | 20 | 12 | 1 | SOUNDS OF SILENCE — Simon & Garfunkel, Columbia 43396 | 13 |
| 26 | 12 | 6 | 9 | AS TEARS GO BY — Rolling Stones, London 9808 | 8 |
| 27 | 27 | 30 | 36 | LIKE A BABY — Len Barry, Decca 31889 | 7 |
| 28 | 47 | 68 | — | WHAT NOW MY LOVE — Sonny & Cher, Atco 6395 | 3 |
| 29 | 34 | 57 | 71 | WHEN LIKING TURNS TO LOVING — Ronnie Dove, Diamond 195 | 4 |
| 30 | 37 | 47 | 58 | A HARD DAY'S NIGHT — Ramsey Lewis Trio, Cadet 5525 | 5 |
| 31 | 41 | 53 | 61 | CALL ME — Chris Montez, A&M 780 | 6 |
| 32 | 57 | 70 | 83 | ELUSIVE BUTTERFLY — Bob Lind, World-Pacific 77808 | 4 |
| 33 | 54 | 75 | — | I FOUGHT THE LAW — Bobby Fuller 4, Mustang 3014 | 3 |
| 34 | 45 | 55 | 60 | I SEE THE LIGHT — Five Americans, HBR 454 | 7 |
| 35 | 36 | 46 | 66 | NIGHT TIME — Strangeloves, Bang 514 | 5 |
| 36 | 22 | 13 | 5 | DAY TRIPPER — Beatles, Capitol 5555 | 9 |
| 37 | 49 | 60 | 81 | BREAKIN' UP IS BREAKIN' MY HEART — Roy Orbison, MGM 13446 | 4 |
| 38 | 23 | 15 | 18 | SPANISH EYES — Al Martino, Capitol 5542 | 11 |
| 39 | 48 | 61 | 67 | (You're Gonna) HURT YOURSELF — Frankie Valli, Smash 2015 | 5 |
| 40 | 38 | 45 | 51 | TIJUANA TAXI — Herb Alpert & the Tijuana Brass, A&M 787 | 8 |
| 41 | 25 | 17 | 10 | YOU DIDN'T HAVE TO BE SO NICE — Lovin' Spoonful, Kama Sutra 205 | 12 |
| 42 | 40 | 27 | 27 | SANDY — Ronny & the Daytonas, Mala 513 | 11 |
| 43 | 73 | — | — | AT THE SCENE — Dave Clark Five, Epic 9882 | 2 |
| 44 | 30 | 28 | 31 | IT WAS A VERY GOOD YEAR — Frank Sinatra, Reprise 0429 | 8 |
| 45 | 29 | 18 | 19 | ATTACK — Toys, DynoVoice 214 | 9 |
| 46 | 51 | 66 | 75 | MY BABY LOVES ME — Martha & the Vandellas, Gordy 7048 | 4 |
| 47 | 35 | 33 | 37 | TELL ME WHY — Elvis Presley, RCA Victor 8740 | 7 |
| 48 | 61 | 69 | 82 | ANDREA — Sunrays, Tower 191 | 4 |
| 49 | 59 | 62 | 68 | GET OUT OF MY LIFE WOMAN — Lee Dorsey, Amy 945 | 7 |
| 50 | 53 | 54 | 62 | CLEO'S MOOD — Jr. Walker & the All Stars, Soul 35017 | 5 |
| 51 | 87 | — | — | THE BALLAD OF THE GREEN BERETS — S/Sgt. Barry Sadler, RCA Victor 8739 | 2 |
| 52 | 68 | 86 | — | THE CHEATER — Bob Kuban & the In-Men, Musicland, U.S.A. 20,001 | 3 |
| 53 | 71 | — | — | YOU BABY — Turtles, White Whale 227 | 2 |
| 54 | 80 | 90 | — | BABY SCRATCH MY BACK — Slim Harpo, Excello 2273 | 3 |
| 55 | 81 | — | — | LONG LIVE OUR LOVE — Shangri-Las, Red Bird 048 | 2 |
| 56 | 66 | 81 | 99 | LOVE MAKES THE WORLD GO ROUND — Deon Jackson, Carla 2526 | 4 |
| 57 | 65 | 80 | 86 | BYE BYE BLUES — Bert Kaempfert and His Ork, Decca 31882 | 4 |
| 58 | 69 | 76 | 84 | LOVE IS ALL WE NEED — Mel Carter, Imperial 66148 | 4 |
| 59 | 43 | 43 | 39 | ARE YOU THERE — Dionne Warwick, Scepter 12122 | 10 |
| 60 | 32 | 34 | 38 | SECOND HAND ROSE — Barbra Streisand, Columbia 43469 | 9 |
| 61 | 58 | 41 | 44 | MICHAEL — C.O.D.'s, Kellmac 1003 | 12 |
| 62 | 64 | 64 | 76 | I'M TOO FAR GONE (To Turn Around) — Bobby Bland, Duke 393 | 6 |
| 63 | 46 | 37 | 49 | RECOVERY — Fontella Bass, Checker 1131 | 8 |
| 64 | 50 | 52 | 57 | SPREAD IT ON THICK — Gentrys, MGM 13432 | 7 |
| 65 | 82 | 91 | — | THE RAINS CAME — Sir Douglas Quintet, Tribe 8314 | 3 |
| 66 | 67 | 73 | 79 | SNOW FLAKE — Jim Reeves, RCA Victor 8719 | 5 |
| 67 | 70 | 85 | — | A LITTLE BIT OF SOAP — Exciters, Bang 515 | 3 |
| 68 | 78 | 82 | 92 | MICHELLE — Bud Shank, World-Pacific 77814 | 4 |
| 69 | 85 | — | — | BATMAN THEME — Marketts, Warner Bros. 5696 | 2 |
| 70 | 52 | 56 | 59 | I AIN'T GONNA EAT OUT MY HEART ANYMORE — Young Rascals, Atlantic 2312 | 8 |
| 71 | 76 | 87 | — | MY SHIP IS COMING IN — Walker Brothers, Smash 2016 | 3 |
| 72 | 79 | 84 | — | HIDE & SEEK — Sheep, Boom 60,000 | 3 |
| 73 | 74 | 74 | 89 | THIS CAN'T BE TRUE — Eddie Holman, Parkway 960 | 6 |
| 74 | 75 | 77 | 77 | MY GENERATION — The Who, Decca 31877 | 5 |
| 75 | 90 | — | — | GEORGIA ON MY MIND — Righteous Brothers, Moonglow 244 | 2 |
| 76 | 88 | — | — | WE KNOW WE'RE IN LOVE — Lesley Gore, Mercury 72530 | 2 |
| 77 | 89 | 93 | — | WAITIN' IN YOUR WELFARE LINE — Buck Owens, Capitol 5566 | 3 |
| 78 | 91 | 100 | — | TAKE ME FOR WHAT I'M WORTH — Searchers, Kapp 729 | 3 |
| 79 | 84 | 83 | 95 | SOMETHING I WANT TO TELL YOU — Johnny and the Expressions, Josie 946 | 4 |
| 80 | 86 | 88 | 93 | THE LOOP — Johnny Lytle, Tuba 2004 | 4 |
| 81 | — | — | 634-5789 | Wilson Pickett, Atlantic 2320 | 1 |
| 82 | 77 | 78 | 78 | MICHELLE — Billy Vaughn, Dot 16809 | 6 |
| 83 | — | — | — | WOMAN — Peter & Gordon, Capitol 5579 | 1 |
| 84 | — | — | — | HOMEWARD BOUND — Simon & Garfunkel, Columbia 43511 | 1 |
| 85 | 93 | — | — | IN MY ROOM — Verdelle Smith, Capitol 5567 | 2 |
| 86 | — | — | — | BATMAN THEME — Neal Hefti, RCA Victor 8755 | 1 |
| 87 | — | — | — | IT WON'T BE WRONG — Byrds, Columbia 43501 | 1 |
| 88 | — | — | — | SOMEWHERE THERE'S A SOMEONE — Dean Martin, Reprise 0443 | 1 |
| 89 | 92 | — | — | SET YOU FREE THIS TIME — Byrds, Columbia 43501 | 2 |
| 90 | 96 | — | — | SINCE I LOST THE ONE I LOVE — Impressions, ABC-Paramount 10761 | 2 |
| 91 | 98 | 99 | — | DON'T FORGET ABOUT ME — Barbara Lewis, Atlantic 2316 | 3 |
| 92 | — | — | — | DEAR LOVER — Mary Wells, Atco 6392 | 1 |
| 93 | 97 | — | — | RED HOT — Sam the Sham & the Pharoahs, MGM 13452 | 2 |
| 94 | 95 | — | — | LOST SOMEONE — James Brown, King 6020 | 2 |
| 95 | — | — | — | BATMAN — Jan & Dean, Liberty 55860 | 1 |
| 96 | 99 | — | — | I WANT TO GO WITH YOU — Eddy Arnold, RCA Victor 8749 | 2 |
| 97 | 100 | — | — | THE ANSWER TO MY PRAYER — Neil Sedaka, RCA Victor 8737 | 2 |
| 98 | — | — | — | UP AND DOWN — McCoys, Bang 516 | 1 |
| 99 | 97 | — | — | IS IT ME? — Barbara Mason, Arctic 116 | 2 |
| 100 | — | — | — | WE GOT THE WINNING HAND — Little Milton, Checker 1132 | 1 |

## BUBBLING UNDER THE HOT 100

101. MY ANSWER — Jimmy McCracklin, Imperial 66147
102. BIG BRIGHT EYES — Danny Hutton, HBR 453
103. I DIG YOU BABY — Lorraine Ellison, Mercury 72472
104. I'M SO LONESOME I COULD CRY — B. J. Thomas, Scepter 12129
105. 634-5789 — Earl-Preate, MMI
106. IT'S TOO LATE — Bobby Goldsboro, United Artists 980
107. I CONFESS — New Colony Six, Centaur 1201
108. TEARS — Bobby Vinton, Epic 9894
109. THIS GOLDEN RING — Fortunes, Press 9811
110. HUSBAND AND WIVES — Roger Miller, Smash 2024
111. WHERE AM I GOING? — Barbra Streisand, Columbia 43518
112. FLY ME TO THE MOON — Sam & Bill, Joda 104
113. I'M SATISFIED — Chuck Jackson & Maxine Brown, Wand 1109
114. YOU DON'T KNOW LIKE I KNOW — Sam & Dave, Stax 180
115. EASY GOIN' FELLOW — Roscoe Shelton, Sound Stage 7 2555
116. PUT YOURSELF IN MY PLACE — Elgins, V.I.P. 25029
117. THE DEDICATION SONG — Freddy Cannon, Warner Bros. 5693
118. ANGELS — Missionaries of Mary Cherrie, Kapp 731
119. THE PAIN GETS A LITTLE DEEPER — Darrow Fletcher, Groovy 3001
120. YOU BRING ME DOWN — Royalettes, MGM 13451
121. FEEL IT — Sam Cooke, RCA Victor 8751
122. FUNNY — Tommy Collins, Columbia 43499
123. CAN'T YOU SEE — Mary Wells, Atco 6392
124. TIME — Pozo-Seco Singers, Columbia 43457
125. MADE IN PARIS — Trini Lopez, Reprise 0435
126. FUNNY — Walter Jackson, Okeh 7236
127. ANGELS — Barbarians, Laurie 3326
128. MOULTY — Moody Blues, London 9810
129. THE ARENA — Al Hirt, RCA Victor 8736
130. STOP! — Edwin Starr, Ric-Tic 109
131. WALKIN' MY CAT NAMED DOG — Norma Tanega, New Voice 807
132. FLOWERS ON THE WALL — Mariachi Brass, World Pacific 77815
133. PROMISE HER ANYTHING — Tom Jones, Parrot 9809
134. FRIENDS AND LOVERS FOREVER — Nancy Ames, Epic 9885
135. WHEN THE SHIP HIT THE SAND — "Little" Jimmy Dickens, Columbia 43514

Compiled from national retail sales and radio station airplay by the Music Popularity Dept. of Record Market Research, Billboard.

# Billboard HOT 100

**For Week Ending February 19, 1966**

★ STAR performer—Sides registering greatest proportionate upward progress this week.

● Record Industry Association of America seal of certification as million selling single.

| This Week | 2 Wks. Ago | 3 Wks. Ago | TITLE Artist, Label & Number | Weeks On Chart |
|---|---|---|---|---|
| ★1 | 2 | 5 | 20 | LIGHTNIN' STRIKES — Lou Christie, MGM 13412 | 9 |
| ★2 | 15 | 28 | 50 | THESE BOOTS ARE MADE FOR WALKIN' — Nancy Sinatra, Reprise 0432 | 5 |
| 3 | 3 | 16 | 21 | UP TIGHT — Stevie Wonder, Tamla 54124 | 10 |
| 4 | 1 | 1 | 9 | MY LOVE — Petula Clark, Warner Bros. 5684 | 9 |
| ★5 | 8 | 13 | 26 | MY WORLD IS EMPTY WITHOUT YOU — Supremes, Motown 1089 | 6 |
| 6 | 7 | 10 | 16 | CRYING TIME — Ray Charles, ABC-Paramount 10739 | 11 |
| 7 | 4 | 2 | 2 | BARBARA ANN — Beach Boys, Capitol 5561 | 8 |
| 8 | 10 | 19 | 31 | DON'T MESS WITH BILL — Marvelettes, Tamla 54126 | 8 |
| 9 | 6 | 3 | 4 | NO MATTER WHAT SHAPE (Your Stomach's In) — T-Bones, Liberty 55836 | 11 |
| ★10 | 51 | 87 | — | THE BALLAD OF THE GREEN BERETS — S/Sgt. Barry Sadler, RCA Victor 8739 | 3 |
| 11 | 11 | 21 | 23 | GOING TO A GO-GO — Miracles, Tamla 54127 | 9 |
| 12 | 12 | 15 | 24 | ZORBA THE GREEK — Herb Alpert & the Tijuana Brass, A&M 787 | 9 |
| 13 | 5 | 4 | 1 | WE CAN WORK IT OUT ● — Beatles, Capitol 5555 | 10 |
| 14 | 9 | 8 | 5 | FIVE O'CLOCK WORLD — Vogues, Co & Ce 232 | 13 |
| ★15 | 22 | 44 | 63 | WORKING MY WAY BACK TO YOU — 4 Seasons, Philips 40350 | 4 |
| 16 | 23 | 33 | 44 | CALIFORNIA DREAMIN' — Mama's and Papa's, Dunhill 4020 | 7 |
| 17 | 13 | 17 | 19 | A WELL RESPECTED MAN — Kinks, Reprise 0420 | 12 |
| 18 | 18 | 26 | 36 | MICHELLE — David & Jonathan, Capitol 5563 | 7 |
| 19 | 28 | 47 | 68 | WHAT NOW MY LOVE — Sonny & Cher, Atco 6395 | 4 |
| 20 | 32 | 57 | 70 | ELUSIVE BUTTERFLY — Bob Lind, World-Pacific 77808 | 5 |
| 21 | 29 | 34 | 57 | WHEN LIKING TURNS TO LOVING — Ronnie Dove, Diamond 195 | 5 |
| 22 | 14 | 14 | 11 | JUST LIKE ME — Paul Revere & the Raiders, Columbia 43461 | 12 |
| 23 | 19 | 7 | 3 | SHE'S JUST MY STYLE — Gary Lewis & the Playboys, Liberty 55846 | 11 |
| ★24 | 43 | 73 | — | AT THE SCENE — Dave Clark Five, Epic 9882 | 3 |
| 25 | 52 | 68 | 86 | THE CHEATER — Bob Kuban & the In-Men, Musicland, U.S.A. 20,001 | 4 |
| 26 | 33 | 54 | 75 | I FOUGHT THE LAW — Bobby Fuller 4, Mustang 3014 | 4 |
| 27 | 16 | 11 | 10 | JENNY TAKE A RIDE — Mitch Ryder & the Detroit Wheels, New Voices 806 | 11 |
| 28 | 31 | 41 | 53 | CALL ME — Chris Montez, A&M 780 | 7 |
| 29 | 30 | 37 | 47 | A HARD DAY'S NIGHT — Ramsey Lewis Trio, Cadet 5525 | 5 |
| ★30 | 35 | 36 | 46 | NIGHT TIME — Strangeloves, Bang 514 | 6 |
| 31 | 17 | 6 | 7 | THE MEN IN MY LITTLE GIRL'S LIFE — Mike Douglas, Epic 9876 | 9 |
| 32 | 24 | 24 | 22 | LIES — Knickerbockers, Challenge 59821 | 12 |
| 33 | 25 | 20 | 12 | SOUNDS OF SILENCE — Simon & Garfunkel, Columbia 43396 | 14 |
| 34 | 34 | 45 | 55 | I SEE THE LIGHT — Five Americans, HBR 454 | 8 |
| ★35 | 53 | 71 | — | YOU BABY — Turtles, White Whale 227 | 3 |
| 36 | 46 | 51 | 66 | MY BABY LOVES ME — Martha & the Vandellas, Gordy 7048 | 5 |
| 37 | 37 | 49 | 60 | BREAKIN' UP IS BREAKIN' MY HEART — Roy Orbison, MGM 13446 | 5 |
| 38 | 56 | 66 | 81 | LOVE MAKES THE WORLD GO ROUND — Deon Jackson, Carla 2526 | 5 |
| 39 | 27 | 27 | 30 | LIKE A BABY — Len Barry, Decca 31889 | 8 |
| 40 | 20 | 9 | 8 | A MUST TO AVOID — Herman's Hermits, MGM 13437 | 9 |
| 41 | — | — | — | LISTEN PEOPLE — Herman's Hermits, MGM 13462 | 1 |
| 42 | 21 | 18 | 14 | THE DUCK — Jackie Lee, Mirwood 5502 | 14 |
| 43 | 48 | 61 | 69 | ANDREA — Sunrays, Tower 191 | 5 |
| ★44 | 55 | 81 | — | LONG LIVE OUR LOVE — Shangri-Las, Red Bird 048 | 3 |
| 45 | 38 | 23 | 15 | SPANISH EYES — Al Martino, Capitol 5542 | 12 |
| 46 | 39 | 48 | 61 | (You're Gonna) HURT YOURSELF — Frankie Valli, Smash 2015 | 6 |
| 47 | 36 | 22 | 13 | DAY TRIPPER — Beatles, Capitol 5555 | 10 |
| 48 | 69 | 85 | — | BATMAN THEME — Marketts, Warner Bros. 5696 | 2 |
| 49 | 49 | 59 | 62 | GET OUT OF MY LIFE WOMAN — Lee Dorsey, Amy 945 | 8 |
| 50 | 26 | 12 | 6 | AS TEARS GO BY — Rolling Stones, London 9808 | 9 |
| 51 | 58 | 69 | 76 | LOVE IS ALL WE NEED — Mel Carter, Imperial 66148 | 4 |
| 52 | — | 86 | — | BATMAN THEME — Neal Hefti, RCA Victor 8755 | 2 |
| 53 | 54 | 80 | 90 | BABY SCRATCH MY BACK — Slim Harpo, Excello 2273 | 4 |
| 54 | — | 84 | — | HOMEWARD BOUND — Simon & Garfunkel, Columbia 43511 | 2 |
| 55 | 50 | 53 | 54 | CLEO'S MOOD — Jr. Walker & the All Stars, Soul 35017 | 4 |
| 56 | 57 | 65 | 80 | BYE BYE BLUES — Bert Kaempfert and His Ork, Decca 31882 | 5 |
| 57 | — | 88 | — | SOMEWHERE THERE'S A SOMEONE — Dean Martin, Reprise 0443 | 2 |
| 58 | — | 81 | — | 634-5789 — Wilson Pickett, Atlantic 2320 | 2 |
| 59 | 65 | 82 | 91 | THE RAINS CAME — Sir Douglas Quintet, Tribe 8314 | 4 |
| 60 | 73 | 74 | 74 | THIS CAN'T BE TRUE — Eddie Holman, Parkway 960 | 6 |
| 61 | — | 83 | — | WOMAN — Peter & Gordon, Capitol 5579 | 2 |
| 62 | 75 | 90 | — | GEORGIA ON MY MIND — Righteous Brothers, Moonglow 244 | 3 |
| 63 | 71 | 76 | 87 | MY SHIP IS COMING IN — Walker Brothers, Smash 2016 | 4 |
| 64 | 64 | 50 | 52 | SPREAD IT ON THICK — Gentrys, MGM 13432 | 8 |
| 65 | 68 | 78 | 82 | MICHELLE — Bud Shank, World-Pacific 77814 | 5 |
| 66 | 67 | 70 | 85 | A LITTLE BIT OF SOAP — Exciters, Bang 515 | 4 |
| 67 | 77 | 89 | 93 | WAITIN' IN YOUR WELFARE LINE — Buck Owens, Capitol 5566 | 4 |
| 68 | 98 | — | — | UP AND DOWN — McCoys, Bang 516 | 2 |
| 69 | 72 | 79 | 84 | HIDE & SEEK — Sheep, Boom 60,000 | 4 |
| 70 | 87 | — | — | IT WON'T BE WRONG — Byrds, Columbia 43501 | 2 |
| 71 | 66 | 67 | 73 | SNOW FLAKE — Jim Reeves, RCA Victor 8719 | 6 |
| 72 | 70 | 52 | 56 | I AIN'T GONNA EAT OUT MY HEART ANYMORE — Young Rascals, Atlantic 2312 | 9 |
| 73 | 85 | 93 | — | IN MY ROOM — Verdelle Smith, Capitol 5567 | 3 |
| 74 | — | — | — | HUSBANDS AND WIVES — Roger Miller, Smash 2024 | 1 |
| 75 | — | — | — | IT'S TOO LATE — Bobby Goldsboro, United Artists 980 | 1 |
| 76 | 76 | 88 | — | WE KNOW WE'RE IN LOVE — Lesley Gore, Mercury 72530 | 3 |
| 77 | 78 | 91 | 100 | TAKE ME FOR WHAT I'M WORTH — Searchers, Kapp 729 | 4 |
| 78 | 95 | — | — | BATMAN — Jan & Dean, Liberty 55860 | 2 |
| 79 | — | — | — | THE DEDICATION SONG — Freddy Cannon, Warner Bros. 5693 | 1 |
| 80 | 80 | 86 | 88 | THE LOOP — Johnny Lytle, Tuba 2004 | 5 |
| 81 | 79 | 84 | 83 | SOMETHING I WANT TO TELL YOU — Johnny and the Expressions, Josie 946 | 5 |
| 82 | 89 | 92 | — | SET YOU FREE THIS TIME — Byrds, Columbia 43501 | 3 |
| 83 | 92 | — | — | DEAR LOVER — Mary Wells, Atco 6392 | 2 |
| 84 | 96 | 99 | — | I WANT TO GO WITH YOU — Eddy Arnold, RCA Victor 8749 | 3 |
| 85 | — | — | — | I'LL GO CRAZY — James Brown, King 6020 | 1 |
| 86 | — | — | — | SHAKE ME, WAKE ME (When It's Over) — Four Tops, Motown 1090 | 1 |
| 87 | — | — | — | I'M SO LONESOME I COULD CRY — B. J. Thomas and the Triumphs, Scepter 12129 | 1 |
| 88 | — | — | — | STOP HER ON SIGHT (S.O.S.) — Edwin Starr, Ric-Tic 109 | 1 |
| 89 | — | — | — | ONE MORE HEARTACHE — Marvin Gaye, Tamla 54129 | 1 |
| 90 | 97 | 100 | — | THE ANSWER TO MY PRAYER — Neil Sedaka, RCA Victor 8737 | 3 |
| 91 | — | — | — | WHY CAN'T YOU BRING ME HOME — Jay and the Americans, United Artists 992 | 1 |
| 92 | 93 | 97 | — | RED HOT — Sam the Sham & the Pharaohs, MGM 13452 | 3 |
| 93 | — | — | — | THIS GOLDEN RING — Fortunes, Press 9811 | 1 |
| 94 | — | — | — | WHERE AM I GOING — Barbra Streisand, Columbia 43518 | 1 |
| 95 | — | — | — | PROMISE HER ANYTHING — Tom Jones, Parrot 9809 | 1 |
| 96 | — | — | — | FEEL IT — Sam Cooke, RCA Victor 8751 | 1 |
| 97 | — | — | — | I CONFESS — New Colony Six, Centaur 1201 | 1 |
| 98 | — | — | — | PUT YOURSELF IN MY PLACE — Elgins, V.I.P. 25029 | 1 |
| 99 | — | — | — | THIS OLD HEART OF MINE — Isley Brothers, Tamla 54128 | 1 |
| 100 | — | — | — | TIME WON'T LET ME — Outsiders, Capitol 5573 | 1 |

## BUBBLING UNDER THE HOT 100

101. S.O.S. (Heart in Distress) — Christine Cooper, Parkway 971
102. TEARS — Bobby Vinton, Epic 9894
103. I DIG YOU BABY — Lorraine Ellison, Mercury 72472
104. I'VE BEEN A LONG TIME LEAVIN' — Roger Miller, Smash 2024
105. LOST SOMEONE — James Brown, King 6020
106. SINCE I LOST THE ONE I LOVE — Impressions, ABC-Paramount 10761
107. DARLING BABY — Elgins, V.I.P. 25029
108. TIME — Pozo-Seco Singers, Columbia 43487
109. BIG BRIGHT EYES — Danny Hutton, HBR 453
110. MOULTY — Barbarians, Laurie 3326
111. WALKIN' MY CAT NAMED DOG — Norma Tanega, New Voice 807
112. MY BABE — Roy Head, Back Beat 560
113. WHENEVER SHE HOLDS YOU — Patty Duke, United Artists 978
114. SECRET AGENT MAN — Ventures, Dolton 316
115. FLOWERS ON THE WALL — Mariachi Brass, World Pacific 77815
116. WE GOT THE WINNING HAND — Little Milton, Checker 1132
117. NIGHT IN PARIS — Trini Lopez, Reprise 0435
118. IF YOU CAN'T BITE, DON'T GROWL — Tommy Collins, Columbia 43489
119. BRING ME DOWN — Royalettes, MGM 13451
120. MY ANSWER — Jimmy McCracklin, Imperial 66147
121. STOP! — Moody Blues, London 9810
122. NIGHT TRAIN — Viscounts, Amy 949
123. BATMAN AND ROBIN — Spotlights, Smash 2026
124. COMMUNICATION — David McCallum, Capitol 5571
125. MR. MOON — Coachmen, MMC 010
126. THE ONE ON THE RIGHT IS ON THE LEFT — Johnny Cash, Columbia 43496
127. FIVE CARD STUD — Lorne Greene, RCA Victor 8757
128. THE WEEKEND — Jack Jones, Kapp 736
129. KEEP ON RUNNING — Spencer Davis Group, Atco 6400
130. THE WEEK-END — Steve Lawrence, Columbia 43515
131. BYE BYE BLUES — Andy Williams, Columbia 43519
132. WHEN THE SHIP HIT THE SAND "Little" — Jimmy Dickens, Columbia 43514
133. ONE OF THOSE SONGS — Ray Charles Singers, Command 4079
134. ONE OF THOSE SONGS — Jimmy Durante, Warner Bros. 5686

Compiled from national retail sales and radio station airplay by the Music Popularity Dept. of Record Market Research, Billboard.

Billboard

For Week Ending February 26, 1966

# HOT 100

★ STAR performer—Sides registering greatest proportionate upward progress this week.

Record Industry Association of America seal of certification as million selling single.

Billboard Award

| This Week | 1 Wk. Ago | 2 Wks. Ago | 3 Wks. Ago | TITLE Artist, Label & Number | Weeks On Chart |
|---|---|---|---|---|---|
| 1 | 2 | 15 | 28 | THESE BOOTS ARE MADE FOR WALKIN' — Nancy Sinatra, Reprise 0432 | 6 |
| 2 | 1 | 2 | 5 | LIGHTNIN' STRIKES — Lou Christie, MGM 13412 | 10 |
| ★3 | 10 | 51 | 87 | THE BALLAD OF THE GREEN BERETS — S/Sgt. Barry Sadler, RCA Victor 8739 | 4 |
| 4 | 3 | 3 | 16 | UP TIGHT — Stevie Wonder, Tamla 54124 | 11 |
| 5 | 5 | 8 | 13 | MY WORLD IS EMPTY WITHOUT YOU — Supremes, Motown 1089 | 7 |
| 6 | 4 | 1 | 1 | MY LOVE — Petula Clark, Warner Bros. 5684 | 10 |
| 7 | 8 | 10 | 19 | DON'T MESS WITH BILL — Marvelettes, Tamla 54126 | 9 |
| ★8 | 16 | 23 | 33 | CALIFORNIA DREAMIN' — Mama's and Papa's, Dunhill 4020 | 8 |
| ★9 | 20 | 32 | 57 | ELUSIVE BUTTERFLY — Bob Lind, World-Pacific 77808 | 6 |
| ★10 | 15 | 22 | 44 | WORKING MY WAY BACK TO YOU — 4 Seasons, Philips 40350 | 5 |
| 11 | 12 | 12 | 15 | ZORBA THE GREEK — Herb Alpert & the Tijuana Brass, A&M 787 | 10 |
| 12 | 6 | 7 | 10 | CRYING TIME — Ray Charles, ABC-Paramount 10739 | 12 |
| ★13 | 41 | — | — | LISTEN PEOPLE — Herman's Hermits, MGM 13462 | 2 |
| ★14 | 26 | 33 | 54 | I FOUGHT THE LAW — Bobby Fuller 4, Mustang 3014 | 5 |
| 15 | 7 | 4 | 2 | BARBARA ANN — Beach Boys, Capitol 5561 | 9 |
| 16 | 19 | 28 | 47 | WHAT NOW MY LOVE — Sonny & Cher, Atco 6395 | 5 |
| 17 | 17 | 13 | 17 | A WELL RESPECTED MAN — Kinks, Reprise 0420 | 13 |
| 18 | 21 | 29 | 34 | WHEN LIKING TURNS TO LOVING — Ronnie Dove, Diamond 195 | 6 |
| 19 | 9 | 6 | 3 | NO MATTER WHAT SHAPE (Your Stomach's In) — T-Bones, Liberty 55836 | 12 |
| ★20 | 25 | 52 | 68 | THE CHEATER — Bob Kuban & the In-Men, Musicland, U.S.A. 20,001 | 5 |
| 21 | 24 | 43 | 73 | AT THE SCENE — Dave Clark Five, Epic 9882 | 4 |
| ★22 | 28 | 31 | 41 | CALL ME — Chris Montez, A&M 780 | 8 |
| 23 | 11 | 11 | 21 | GOING TO A GO-GO — Miracles, Tamla 54127 | 10 |
| 24 | 13 | 5 | 4 | WE CAN WORK IT OUT — Beatles, Capitol 5555 | 11 |
| ★25 | 48 | 69 | 85 | BATMAN THEME — Marketts, Warner Bros. 5696 | 4 |
| 26 | 22 | 14 | 14 | JUST LIKE ME — Paul Revere & the Raiders, Columbia 43461 | 13 |
| ★27 | 34 | 34 | 45 | I SEE THE LIGHT — Five Americans, HBR 454 | 9 |
| ★28 | 35 | 53 | 71 | YOU BABY — Turtles, White Whale 227 | 4 |
| 29 | 18 | 18 | 26 | MICHELLE — David & Jonathan, Capitol 5563 | 8 |
| ★30 | 36 | 46 | 51 | MY BABY LOVES ME — Martha & the Vandellas, Gordy 7048 | 6 |
| ★31 | 54 | 84 | — | HOMEWARD BOUND — Simon & Garfunkel, Columbia 43511 | 3 |
| 32 | 30 | 35 | 36 | NIGHT TIME — Strangeloves, Bang 514 | 7 |
| 33 | 37 | 37 | 49 | BREAKIN' UP IS BREAKIN' MY HEART — Roy Orbison, MGM 13446 | 6 |
| 34 | 32 | 24 | 24 | LIES — Knickerbockers, Challenge 59321 | 13 |
| 35 | 27 | 16 | 11 | JENNY TAKE A RIDE — Mitch Ryder & the Detroit Wheels, New Voices 806 | 12 |
| 36 | 38 | 56 | 66 | LOVE MAKES THE WORLD GO ROUND — Deon Jackson, Carla 2526 | 6 |
| 37 | 44 | 55 | 81 | LONG LIVE OUR LOVE — Shangri-Las, Red Bird 048 | 4 |
| 38 | 29 | 30 | 37 | A HARD DAY'S NIGHT — Ramsey Lewis Trio, Cadet 5525 | 6 |
| 39 | 14 | 9 | 8 | FIVE O'CLOCK WORLD — Vogues, Co & Ce 232 | 14 |
| 40 | 23 | 19 | 7 | SHE'S JUST MY STYLE — Gary Lewis & the Playboys, Liberty 55846 | 12 |
| ★41 | 53 | 54 | 80 | BABY SCRATCH MY BACK — Slim Harpo, Excello 2273 | 5 |
| ★42 | 58 | 81 | — | 634-5789 — Wilson Pickett, Atlantic 2320 | 3 |
| 43 | 43 | 48 | 61 | ANDREA — Sunrays, Tower 191 | 6 |
| 44 | 49 | 49 | 59 | GET OUT OF MY LIFE WOMAN — Lee Dorsey, Amy 945 | 9 |
| 45 | 39 | 27 | 27 | LIKE A BABY — Len Barry, Decca 31889 | 9 |
| ★46 | — | — | — | 19TH NERVOUS BREAKDOWN — Rolling Stones, London 9823 | 1 |
| ★47 | 57 | 88 | — | SOMEWHERE THERE'S A SOMEONE — Dean Martin, Reprise 0443 | 3 |
| 48 | 52 | 86 | — | BATMAN THEME — Neal Hefti, RCA Victor 8755 | 3 |
| ★49 | 59 | 65 | 82 | THE RAINS CAME — Sir Douglas Quintet, Tribe 8314 | 5 |
| ★50 | 74 | — | — | HUSBANDS AND WIVES — Roger Miller, Smash 2024 | 2 |
| 51 | 51 | 58 | 69 | LOVE IS ALL WE NEED — Mel Carter, Imperial 66148 | 6 |
| ★52 | 79 | — | — | THE DEDICATION SONG — Freddy Cannon, Warner Bros. 5693 | 2 |
| 53 | 46 | 39 | 48 | (You're Gonna) HURT YOURSELF — Frankie Valli, Smash 2015 | 7 |
| 54 | 56 | 57 | 65 | BYE BYE BLUES — Bert Kaempfert and His Ork, Decca 31882 | 6 |
| 55 | 61 | 83 | — | WOMAN — Peter & Gordon, Capitol 5579 | 3 |
| ★56 | 75 | — | — | IT'S TOO LATE — Bobby Goldsboro, United Artists 980 | 2 |
| ★57 | 67 | 77 | 89 | WAITIN' IN YOUR WELFARE LINE — Buck Owens, Capitol 5566 | 5 |
| 58 | 66 | 67 | 70 | A LITTLE BIT OF SOAP — Exciters, Bang 515 | 5 |
| ★59 | 84 | 96 | 99 | I WANT TO GO WITH YOU — Eddy Arnold, RCA Victor 8749 | 4 |
| 60 | 60 | 73 | 74 | THIS CAN'T BE TRUE — Eddie Holman, Parkway 960 | 7 |
| 61 | 69 | 72 | 79 | HIDE & SEEK — Sheep, Boom 60,000 | 5 |
| 62 | 68 | 98 | — | UP AND DOWN — McCoys, Bang 516 | 3 |
| 63 | 70 | 87 | — | IT WON'T BE WRONG — Byrds, Columbia 43501 | 3 |
| 64 | 62 | 75 | 90 | GEORGIA ON MY MIND — Righteous Brothers, Moonglow 244 | 4 |
| 65 | 63 | 71 | 76 | MY SHIP IS COMING IN — Walker Brothers, Smash 2016 | 5 |
| 66 | 73 | 85 | 93 | IN MY ROOM — Verdelle Smith, Capitol 5567 | 4 |
| ★67 | 86 | — | — | SHAKE ME, WAKE ME (When It's Over) — Four Tops, Motown 1090 | 2 |
| 68 | 65 | 68 | 78 | MICHELLE — Bud Shank, World-Pacific 77814 | 6 |
| ★69 | 89 | — | — | ONE MORE HEARTACHE — Marvin Gaye, Tamla 54129 | 2 |
| 70 | 78 | 95 | — | BATMAN — Jan & Dean, Liberty 55860 | 3 |
| ★71 | — | — | — | MAGIC TOWN — Vogues, Co & Ce 234 | 1 |
| ★72 | 87 | — | — | I'M SO LONESOME I COULD CRY — B. J. Thomas and the Triumphs, Scepter 12129 | 2 |
| 73 | 85 | — | — | I'LL GO CRAZY — James Brown, King 6020 | 2 |
| 74 | 83 | 92 | — | DEAR LOVER — Mary Wells, Atco 6392 | 3 |
| ★75 | — | — | — | TEARS — Bobby Vinton, Epic 9894 | 1 |
| ★76 | — | — | — | DAYDREAM — Lovin' Spoonful, Kama Sutra 208 | 1 |
| 77 | 77 | 78 | 91 | TAKE ME FOR WHAT I'M WORTH — Searchers, Kapp 729 | 5 |
| 78 | 88 | — | — | STOP HER ON SIGHT (S.O.S.) — Edwin Starr, Ric-Tic 109 | 2 |
| 79 | 82 | 89 | 92 | SET YOU FREE THIS TIME — Byrds, Columbia 43501 | 4 |
| 80 | 91 | — | — | WHY CAN'T YOU BRING ME HOME — Jay and the Americans, United Artists 992 | 2 |
| ★81 | 99 | — | — | THIS OLD HEART OF MINE — Isley Brothers, Tamla 54128 | 2 |
| 82 | 92 | 93 | 97 | RED HOT — Sam the Sham & the Pharaohs, MGM 13452 | 4 |
| ★83 | — | — | — | THE ONE ON THE RIGHT IS ON THE LEFT — Johnny Cash, Columbia 43496 | 1 |
| ★84 | — | — | — | GET READY — Temptations, Gordy 7049 | 1 |
| ★85 | — | — | — | SMOKEY JOE'S LA LA — Googie Rene Combo, Class 1517 | 1 |
| ★86 | — | — | — | WHENEVER SHE HOLDS YOU — Patty Duke, United Artists 978 | 1 |
| ★87 | — | — | — | WALKIN' MY CAT NAMED DOG — Norma Tanega, New Voice 807 | 1 |
| 88 | 97 | — | — | I CONFESS — New Colony Six, Centaur 1201 | 2 |
| 89 | 90 | 97 | 100 | THE ANSWER TO MY PRAYER — Neil Sedaka, RCA Victor 8737 | 4 |
| ★90 | — | — | — | SECRET AGENT MAN — Ventures, Dolton 316 | 1 |
| 91 | — | — | — | TIME — Pozo-Seco Singers, Columbia 43437 | 1 |
| 92 | 93 | — | — | THIS GOLDEN RING — Fortunes, Press 9811 | 2 |
| 93 | 95 | — | — | PROMISE HER ANYTHING — Tom Jones, Parrot 9809 | 2 |
| 94 | 94 | — | — | WHERE AM I GOING — Barbra Streisand, Columbia 43518 | 2 |
| 95 | 96 | — | — | FEEL IT — Sam Cooke, RCA Victor 8751 | 2 |
| 96 | — | — | — | INSIDE-LOOKING OUT — Animals, MGM 13468 | 1 |
| 97 | 100 | — | — | TIME WON'T LET ME — Outsiders, Capitol 5573 | 2 |
| 98 | 98 | — | — | PUT YOURSELF IN MY PLACE — Elgins, V.I.P. 25029 | 2 |
| 99 | — | — | — | SHAKE HANDS — Newbeats, Hickory 1366 | 1 |
| 100 | — | — | — | MOULTY — Barbarians, Laurie 3326 | 1 |

## HOT 100—A TO Z—(Publisher-Licensee)

Andrea (Sea of Tunes, BMI) .......... 43
Answer to My Prayer, The (Bregman, Voco & Conn, ASCAP) .......... 89
At the Scene (Branston, BMI) .......... 21
Baby Sratch My Back (Excellorec, BMI) .......... 41
Ballad of the Green Berets, The (Music, Music, Music, ASCAP) .......... 3
Barbara Ann (Shoe-String & Cousins, BMI) .......... 15
Batman—Jan & Dean (Screen Gems-Columbia, BMI) 70
Batman Theme—Hefti (Miller, ASCAP) .......... 48
Batman Theme—Marketts (Miller, ASCAP) .......... 25
Breakin' Up Is Breakin' My Heart (Acuff-Rose, BMI) .......... 33
Bye Bye Blues (Bourne, ASCAP) .......... 54
California Dreamin' (Trousdale, BMI) .......... 8
Call Me (Duchess, BMI) .......... 22
Cheater, The (MAM) .......... 20
Crying Time (Blue Book, BMI) .......... 12
Daydream (Faithful Virtue, BMI) .......... 76
Dear Lover (Jalynne, BMI) .......... 74
Dedication Song, The (Algrace, BMI) .......... 52
Don't Mess With Bill (Jobete, BMI) .......... 7
Elusive Butterfly (Metric, BMI) .......... 9
Feel It (Kags, BMI) .......... 95
Five o'Clock World (Screen Gems-Columbia, BMI). 39
Georgia on My Mind (Peer Int'l, BMI) .......... 64
Get Out of My Life Woman (Marsaint, BMI) .......... 44
Get Ready (Jobete, BMI) .......... 84
Going to a Go-Go (Jobete, BMI) .......... 23
Hard Day's Night, A (Maclen & Unart, BMI) .......... 38
Hide & Seek (Florentine-Marks, BMI) .......... 61
Homeward Bound (Eclectic, BMI) .......... 31
Husbands and Wives (Tree, BMI) .......... 50
I Confess (New Colony & World Int., BMI) .......... 88
I Fought the Law (Acuff-Rose, BMI) .......... 14
I See the Light (Jetstar, BMI) .......... 27
I Want to Go With You (Pamper, BMI) .......... 59
I'll Go Crazy (Lois, BMI) .......... 73
I'm So Lonesome I Could Cry (Acuff-Rose, BMI). . 72
In My Room (Robbins, ASCAP) .......... 66
Inside—Looking Out (Ludlow, BMI) .......... 96
It Won't Be Wrong (Tickson, BMI) .......... 63
It's Too Late (Unart, BMI) .......... 56
Jenny Take a Ride (Venice-Saturday, BMI) .......... 35
Just Like Me (Daywin, BMI) .......... 26
Lies (4 Star, BMI) .......... 34
Lightnin' Strikes (Rambed, BMI) .......... 2
Like a Baby (Double Diamond-Champion, BMI) .......... 45
Little Bit of Soap, A (Mellin, BMI) .......... 58
Listen People (New World, ASCAP) .......... 13
Long Live Our Love (Trio-Tender Tunes, BMI) .. 37
Love Is All We Need (Travis, BMI) .......... 51
Love Makes the World Go Round (McLaughlin, BMI) .......... 36
Magic Town (Screen Gems-Columbia, BMI) .......... 71
Michelle—David & Jonathan (Maclen, BMI) .......... 29
Michelle—Shank (Maclen, BMI) .......... 68
Moulty (Elmwin, Roznique, BMI) .......... 100
My Baby Loves Me (Jobete, BMI) .......... 30
My Love (Duchess, BMI) .......... 6
My Ship Is Coming In (January, BMI) .......... 65
My World Is Empty Without You (Jobete, BMI) .. 5
Night Time (Grand Cayon, BMI) .......... 32
19th Nervous Breakdown (Gideon, BMI) .......... 46
No Matter What Shape (Your Stomach's In) (C-Hear, BMI) .......... 19
One More Heartache (Jobete, BMI) .......... 69
One on the Right Is on the Left, The (Jack, BMI) 83
Promise Her Anything (Famous, ASCAP) .......... 93
Put Yourself in My Place (Jobete, BMI) .......... 98
Rains Came, The (Crazy Cajun & Corrett, BMI) ... 49
Red Hot (Riverline, BMI) .......... 82
Secret Agent Man (Trousdale, BMI) .......... 90
Set You Free This Time (Tickson, BMI) .......... 79
Shake Hands (Acuff-Rose, BMI) .......... 99
Shake Me, Wake Me (When It's Over) (Jobete, BMI) 67
She's Just My Style (Viva, BMI) .......... 40
634-5789 (East-Pronto, BMI) .......... 42
Smokey Joe's La La (Recordo, BMI) .......... 85
Somewhere There's a Someone (Hill & Range, BMI) 47
Stop Her on Sight (S.O.S.) (Myto, BMI) .......... 78
Take Me for What I'm Worth (Trousdale, BMI) ... 77
Tears (Shapiro-Bernstein, ASCAP) .......... 75
These Boots Are Made for Walkin' (Criterion, ASCAP) .......... 1
This Can't Be True (Cameo-Parkway, Stillran, BMI) 60
This Golden Ring (Mills, ASCAP) .......... 92
This Old Heart of Mine (Jobete, BMI) .......... 81
Time (Regent, BMI) .......... 91
Time Won't Let Me (Beechwood, BMI) .......... 97
Up and Down (Fling, Dayshel-Grand Canyon, BMI) 62
Up Tight (Jobete, BMI) .......... 4
Waitin' in Your Welfare Line (Central Songs, BMI) 57
Walkin' My Cat Named Dog (Starday, BMI) .......... 87
We Can Work It Out (Maclen, BMI) .......... 24
Well Respected Man, A (Amer. Met. Ent. of N.Y., BMI) .......... 17
What Now My Love (Remick, ASCAP) .......... 16
When Liking Turns to Loving (Tobi-Ann & Unart, BMI) .......... 18
Whenever She Holds You (Unart, BMI) .......... 86
Where Am I Going? (Notable, ASCAP) .......... 94
Why Can't You Bring Me Home (Picturetone, BMI) 80
Woman (Maclen, BMI) .......... 55
Working My Way Back to You (Saturday & Seasons 4, BMI) .......... 10
You Baby (Trousdale, BMI) .......... 28
(You're Gonna) Hurt Yourself (Saturday & Seasons 4, BMI) .......... 53
Zorba the Greek (Miller, ASCAP) .......... 11

## BUBBLING UNDER THE HOT 100

101. THINK I'LL GO SOMEWHERE AND CRY MYSELF TO SLEEP .......... Al Martino, Capitol 5598
102. SINCE I LOST THE ONE I LOVE .......... Impressions, ABC-Paramount 10761
103. I'VE BEEN A LONG TIME LEAVIN' .......... Roger Miller, Smash 2024
104. WHEN THE SHIP HITS THE SAND.. "Little" Jimmy Dickens, Columbia 43514
105. AIN'T THAT A GROOVE ..... James Brown & the Famous Flames, King 6025
106. I DIG YOU BABY .......... Lorraine Ellison, Mercury 72472
107. MY BABY .......... Roy Head, Back Beat 560
108. S.O.S. (Heart in Distress) .......... Christine Cooper, Parkway 971
109. IF YOU CAN'T BITE, DON'T GROWL ..... Tommy Collins, Columbia 43489
110. (I'm Just a) FOOL FOR YOU .......... Gene Chandler, Constellation 167
111. BATMAN AND ROBIN .......... Spotlights, Smash 2020
112. KEEP ON RUNNING .......... Spencer Davis Group, Atco 6400
113. MADE IN PARIS .......... Trini Lopez, Reprise 0435
114. SUPERMAN .......... Dino, Desi & Billy, Reprise 0444
115. IT'S A GOOD TIME .......... Billy Joe Royal, Columbia 43538
116. YOU BRING ME DOWN .......... Royalettes, MGM 13451
117. MY DARLING HILDEGARDE .......... Statler Brothers, Columbia 43526
118. FLOWERS ON THE WALL .......... Mariachi Brass, World Pacific 77815
119. DON'T TAKE IT OUT ON ME .......... Bobbi Martin, Coral 62475
120. SHARING YOU .......... Mitty Collier, Chess 1953
121. STOP! .......... Moody Blues, London 9810
122. FIVE CARD STUD .......... Lorne Greene, RCA Victor 8757
123. COMMUNICATION .......... David McCallum, Capitol 5571
124. MR. MOON .......... Coachmen, Bear 1974
125. TOGETHER 'TIL THE END OF TIME .......... Brenda Holloway, Tamla 54125
126. CUSTODY .......... Patti Page, Columbia 43517
127. BYE BYE BLUES .......... Andy Williams, Columbia 43519
128. SONG FROM "THE OSCAR" .......... Tony Bennett, Columbia 43508
129. THAT'S PART OF THE GAME .......... Daytrippers, Karate 525
130. 'ILL YOU COME BACK TO ME .......... Patti Page, Columbia 43517
131. UNNY (How Time Slips Away) .......... Ace Cannon, Hi 2101
132. PUBLIC EXECUTION .......... Mouse, Fraternity 956
133. A GIRL I USED TO KNOW .......... Bobby Vee, Liberty 55854
134. LULLABOY OF LOVE .......... Poppies, Epic 9893
135. JUANITA BANANA .......... Peels, Karate 522

Compiled from national retail sales and radio station airplay by the Music Popularity Dept. of Record Market Research, Billboard.

**Billboard** For Week Ending March 5, 1966

# HOT 100

★ **STAR performer—Sides registering greatest proportionate upward progress this week.**

Record Industry Association of America seal of certification as million selling single. (●)

Billboard Award

| This Week | 1 Wk. Ago | 2 Wks. Ago | 3 Wks. Ago | TITLE Artist, Label & Number | Weeks On Chart |
|---|---|---|---|---|---|
| 1 | 3 | 10 | 51 | THE BALLAD OF THE GREEN BERETS — S/Sgt. Barry Sadler, RCA Victor 8739 ● | 5 |
| 2 | 1 | 2 | 15 | THESE BOOTS ARE MADE FOR WALKIN' — Nancy Sinatra, Reprise 0432 | 7 |
| 3 | 2 | 1 | 2 | LIGHTNIN' STRIKES — Lou Christie, MGM 13412 | 11 |
| ★4 | 13 | 41 | — | LISTEN PEOPLE — Herman's Hermits, MGM 13462 | 3 |
| ★5 | 8 | 16 | 23 | CALIFORNIA DREAMIN' — Mama's and Papa's, Dunhill 4020 | 9 |
| ★6 | 9 | 20 | 32 | ELUSIVE BUTTERFLY — Bob Lind, World-Pacific 77808 | 7 |
| 7 | 6 | 4 | 1 | MY LOVE — Petula Clark, Warner Bros. 5684 | 11 |
| 8 | 4 | 3 | 3 | UP TIGHT — Stevie Wonder, Tamla 54124 | 12 |
| 9 | 10 | 15 | 22 | WORKING MY WAY BACK TO YOU — 4 Seasons, Philips 40350 | 6 |
| 10 | 5 | 5 | 8 | MY WORLD IS EMPTY WITHOUT YOU — Supremes, Motown 1089 | 8 |
| 11 | 14 | 26 | 33 | I FOUGHT THE LAW — Bobby Fuller 4, Mustang 3014 | 6 |
| ★12 | 46 | — | — | 19TH NERVOUS BREAKDOWN — Rolling Stones, London 9823 | 2 |
| 13 | 7 | 8 | 10 | DON'T MESS WITH BILL — Marvelettes, Tamla 54126 | 10 |
| 14 | 16 | 19 | 28 | WHAT NOW MY LOVE — Sonny & Cher, Atco 6395 | 6 |
| 15 | 12 | 6 | 7 | CRYING TIME — Ray Charles, ABC-Paramount 10739 | 13 |
| ★16 | 31 | 54 | 84 | HOMEWARD BOUND — Simon & Garfunkel, Columbia 43511 | 4 |
| 17 | 20 | 25 | 52 | THE CHEATER — Bob Kuban & the In-Men, Musicland, U.S.A. 20,001 | 6 |
| 18 | 18 | 21 | 29 | WHEN LIKING TURNS TO LOVING — Ronnie Dove, Diamond 195 | 7 |
| 19 | 21 | 24 | 43 | AT THE SCENE — Dave Clark Five, Epic 9882 | 5 |
| ★20 | 25 | 48 | 69 | BATMAN THEME — Marketts, Warner Bros. 5696 | 5 |
| 21 | 11 | 12 | 12 | ZORBA THE GREEK — Herb Alpert & the Tijuana Brass, A&M 787 | 11 |
| 22 | 22 | 28 | 31 | CALL ME — Chris Montez, A&M 780 | 9 |
| ★23 | 28 | 35 | 53 | YOU BABY — Turtles, White Whale 227 | 5 |
| 24 | 15 | 7 | 4 | BARBARA ANN — Beach Boys, Capitol 5561 | 10 |
| ★25 | — | — | — | NOWHERE MAN — Beatles, Capitol 5587 | 1 |
| 26 | 27 | 34 | 34 | I SEE THE LIGHT — Five Americans, HBR 454 | 10 |
| ★27 | 36 | 38 | 56 | LOVE MAKES THE WORLD GO ROUND — Deon Jackson, Carla 2526 | 7 |
| ★28 | 41 | 53 | 54 | BABY SCRATCH MY BACK — Slim Harpo, Excello 2273 | 6 |
| 29 | 30 | 36 | 46 | MY BABY LOVES ME — Martha & the Vandellas, Gordy 7048 | 7 |
| 30 | 23 | 11 | 11 | GOING TO A GO-GO — Miracles, Tamla 54127 | 11 |
| 31 | 33 | 37 | 37 | BREAKIN' UP IS BREAKIN' MY HEART — Roy Orbison, MGM 13446 | 7 |
| ★32 | 42 | 58 | 81 | 634-5789 — Wilson Pickett, Atlantic 2320 | 4 |
| 33 | 37 | 44 | 55 | LONG LIVE OUR LOVE — Shangri-Las, Red Bird 048 | 5 |
| 34 | 26 | 22 | 14 | JUST LIKE ME — Paul Revere & the Raiders, Columbia 43461 | 14 |
| 35 | 19 | 9 | 6 | NO MATTER WHAT SHAPE (Your Stomach's In) — T-Bones, Liberty 55836 | 13 |
| ★36 | 47 | 57 | 88 | SOMEWHERE THERE'S A SOMEONE — Dean Martin, Reprise 0443 | 4 |
| ★37 | 48 | 52 | 86 | BATMAN THEME — Neal Hefti, RCA Victor 8755 | 4 |
| 38 | 17 | 17 | 13 | A WELL RESPECTED MAN — Kinks, Reprise 0420 | 14 |
| ★39 | 49 | 59 | 65 | THE RAINS CAME — Sir Douglas Quintet, Tribe 8314 | 6 |
| ★40 | 50 | 74 | — | HUSBANDS AND WIVES — Roger Miller, Smash 2024 | 3 |
| 41 | 43 | 43 | 48 | ANDREA — Sunrays, Tower 191 | 7 |
| 42 | 29 | 18 | 18 | MICHELLE — David & Jonathan, Capitol 5563 | 9 |
| ★43 | 55 | 61 | 83 | WOMAN — Peter & Gordon, Capitol 5579 | 4 |
| ★44 | 56 | 75 | — | ITS TOO LATE — Bobby Goldsboro, United Artists 980 | 3 |
| 45 | 32 | 30 | 35 | NIGHT TIME — Strangeloves, Bang 514 | 8 |
| ★46 | 72 | 87 | — | I'M SO LONESOME I COULD CRY — B. J. Thomas and the Triumphs, Scepter 12129 | 3 |
| 47 | 52 | 79 | — | THE DEDICATION SONG — Freddy Cannon, Warner Bros. 5693 | 3 |
| 48 | 24 | 13 | 5 | WE CAN WORK IT OUT — Beatles, Capitol 5555 ● | 12 |
| ★49 | 59 | 84 | 96 | I WANT TO GO WITH YOU — Eddy Arnold, RCA Victor 8749 | 5 |
| 50 | 51 | 51 | 58 | LOVE IS ALL WE NEED — Mel Carter, Imperial 66148 | 7 |
| ★51 | 69 | 89 | — | ONE MORE HEARTACHE — Marvin Gaye, Tamla 54129 | 3 |
| ★52 | 62 | 68 | 98 | UP AND DOWN — McCoys, Bang 516 | 4 |
| ★53 | 76 | — | — | DAYDREAM — Lovin' Spoonful, Kama Sutra 208 | 2 |
| 54 | 44 | 49 | 49 | GET OUT OF MY LIFE WOMAN — Lee Dorsey, Amy 945 | 10 |
| ★55 | 67 | 86 | — | SHAKE ME, WAKE ME (When It's Over) — Four Tops, Motown 1090 | 3 |
| ★56 | 71 | — | — | MAGIC TOWN — Vogues, Co & Ce 234 | 2 |
| 57 | 57 | 67 | 77 | WAITIN' IN YOUR WELFARE LINE — Buck Owens, Capitol 5566 | 6 |
| 58 | 61 | 69 | 72 | HIDE & SEEK — Sheep, Boom 60,000 | 6 |
| 59 | 60 | 60 | 73 | THIS CAN'T BE TRUE — Eddie Holman, Parkway 960 | 8 |
| 60 | 54 | 56 | 57 | BYE BYE BLUES — Bert Kaempfert and His Ork, Decca 31882 | 7 |
| 61 | 58 | 66 | 67 | A LITTLE BIT OF SOAP — Exciters, Bang 515 | 6 |
| 62 | 66 | 73 | 85 | IN MY ROOM — Verdelle Smith, Capitol 5567 | 5 |
| 63 | 63 | 70 | 87 | IT WON'T BE WRONG — Byrds, Columbia 43501 | 4 |
| ★64 | 81 | 99 | — | THIS OLD HEART OF MINE — Isley Brothers, Tamla 54128 | 3 |
| 65 | 74 | 83 | 92 | DEAR LOVER — Mary Wells, Atco 6392 | 4 |
| 66 | 70 | 78 | 95 | BATMAN — Jan & Dean, Liberty 55860 | 4 |
| ★67 | 84 | — | — | GET READY — Temptations, Gordy 7049 | 2 |
| 68 | 75 | — | — | TEARS — Bobby Vinton, Epic 9894 | 2 |
| ★69 | 87 | — | — | WALKIN' MY CAT NAMED DOG — Norma Tanega, New Voice 807 | 2 |
| 70 | 78 | 88 | — | STOP HER ON SIGHT (S.O.S.) — Edwin Starr, Ric-Tic 109 | 3 |
| 71 | 64 | 62 | 75 | GEORGIA ON MY MIND — Righteous Brothers, Moonglow 244 | 5 |
| ★72 | 96 | — | — | INSIDE-LOOKING OUT — Animals, MGM 13468 | 2 |
| 73 | 83 | — | — | THE ONE ON THE RIGHT IS ON THE LEFT — Johnny Cash, Columbia 43496 | 2 |
| 74 | 80 | 91 | — | WHY CAN'T YOU BRING ME HOME — Jay and the Americans, United Artists 992 | 3 |
| 75 | 86 | — | — | WHENEVER SHE HOLDS YOU — Patty Duke, United Artists 978 | 2 |
| 76 | 77 | 77 | 78 | TAKE ME FOR WHAT I'M WORTH — Searchers, Kapp 729 | 6 |
| 77 | 85 | — | — | SMOKEY JOE'S LA LA — Googie Rene Combo, Class 1517 | 2 |
| ★78 | — | — | — | AIN'T THAT A GROOVE — James Brown & the Famous Flames, King 6025 | 1 |
| ★79 | — | — | — | SATISFACTION — Otis Redding, Volt 132 | 1 |
| 80 | 88 | 97 | — | I CONFESS — New Colony Six, Centaur 1201 | 3 |
| ★81 | 97 | 100 | — | TIME WONT LET ME — Outsiders, Capitol 5573 | 3 |
| 82 | 92 | 93 | — | THIS GOLDEN RING — Fortunes, Press 9811 | 3 |
| ★83 | — | — | — | KEEP ON RUNNING — Spencer Davis Group, Atco 6400 | 1 |
| 84 | 93 | 95 | — | PROMISE HER ANYTHING — Tom Jones, Parrot 9809 | 3 |
| 85 | 82 | 92 | 93 | RED HOT — Sam the Sham & the Pharaohs, MGM 13452 | 5 |
| 86 | 90 | — | — | SECRET AGENT MAN — Ventures, Dolton 316 | 2 |
| ★87 | — | — | — | SURE GONNA MISS HER — Gary Lewis & the Playboys, Liberty 55865 | 1 |
| ★88 | — | — | — | LITTLE LATIN LUPE LU — Mitch Ryder & the Detroit Wheels, New Voice 808 | 1 |
| 89 | 91 | — | — | TIME — Pozo-Seco Singers, Columbia 43437 | 2 |
| ★90 | — | — | — | (You're My) SOUL AND INSPIRATION — Righteous Brothers, Verve 10383 | 1 |
| 91 | — | — | — | WAIT A MINUTE — Tim Tam & the Turn-Ons, Palmer 5002 | 1 |
| 92 | 98 | 98 | — | PUT YOURSELF IN MY PLACE — Elgins, V.I.P. 25029 | 3 |
| 93 | — | — | — | I WANT SOMEONE — Mad Lads, Volt 131 | 1 |
| 94 | — | — | — | LULLABY OF LOVE — Poppies, Epic 9893 | 1 |
| 95 | — | — | — | SUPERMAN — Dino, Desi & Billy, Reprise 0444 | 1 |
| 96 | 100 | — | — | MOULTY — Barbarians, Laurie 3326 | 2 |
| 97 | — | — | — | OUTSIDE THE GATES OF HEAVEN — Lou Christie, Co & Ce 235 | 1 |
| 98 | — | — | — | THE LOVE YOU SAVE — Joe Tex, Dial 4026 | 1 |
| 99 | 99 | — | — | SHAKE HANDS — Newbeats, Hickory 1366 | 2 |
| 100 | — | — | — | PHILLY DOG — Mar-Keys, Stax 185 | 1 |

## HOT 100—A TO Z—(Publisher-Licensee)

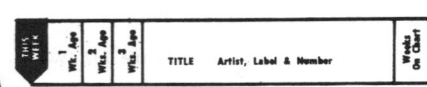

Ain't That a Groove (Dynatone, BMI) .... 78
Andrea (Sea of Tunes, BMI) .... 41
At the Scene (Branston, BMI) .... 19
Baby Scratch My Back (Excellorec, BMI) .... 28
Ballad of the Green Berets, The (Music, Music, Music, ASCAP) .... 1
Barbara Ann (Shoe-String & Cousins, BMI) .... 24
Batman—Jan & Dean (Screen Gems-Columbia, BMI) 66
Batman Theme—Hefti (Miller, ASCAP) .... 37
Batman Theme—Marketts (Miller, ASCAP) .... 20
Breakin' Up Is Breakin' My Heart (Acuff-Rose, BMI) 31
Bye Bye Blues (Bourne, ASCAP) .... 60
California Dreamin' (Trousdale, BMI) .... 5
Call Me (Duchess, BMI) .... 22
Cheater, The (MAM) .... 17
Crying Time (Blue Book, BMI) .... 15
Daydream (Faithful Virtue, BMI) .... 53
Dear Lover (Jalynne, BMI) .... 65
Dedication Song, The (Algrace, BMI) .... 47
Don't Mess With Bill (Jobete, BMI) .... 13
Elusive Butterfly (Metric, BMI) .... 6
Georgia on My Mind (Peer Intl, BMI) .... 71
Get Out of My Life Woman (Marsaint, BMI) .... 54
Get Ready (Jobete, BMI) .... 67
Going to A Go-Go (Jobete, BMI) .... 30
Hide & Seek (Florentine-Marks, BMI) .... 58
Homeward Bound (Eclectic, BMI) .... 16
Husbands and Wives (Tree, BMI) .... 40
I Confess (New Colony & World Int., BMI) .... 80
I Fought the Law (Acuff-Rose, BMI) .... 11
I See the Light (Jetstar, BMI) .... 26
I Want Someone (East, BMI) .... 93
I Want to Go With You (Pamper, BMI) .... 49
I'm So Lonesome I Could Cry (Acuff-Rose, BMI) .. 46
In My Room (Robbins, ASCAP) .... 62
Inside—Looking Out (Ludlow, BMI) .... 72
It Won't Be Wrong (Tickson, BMI) .... 63
It's Too Late (Unart, BMI) .... 44
Just Like Me (Daywin, BMI) .... 34
Keep On Running (Essex, ASCAP) .... 83
Lightin' Strikes (Rambed, BMI) .... 3
Little Bit of Soap, A (Mellin, BMI) .... 61
Little Latin Lupe Lu (Maxwell-Conrad, BMI) .... 88
Listen People (New World, ASCAP) .... 4
Long Live Our Love (Trio-Tender Tunes, BMI) .... 33
Love Is All We Need (Travis, BMI) .... 50
Love Makes the World Go Round (McLaughlin, BMI) 27
Love You Save, The (Tree, BMI) .... 98
Lullaby of Love (Tree, BMI) .... 94
Magic Town (Screen Gems-Columbia, BMI) .... 56
Michelle—David & Jonathan (Maclen, BMI) .... 42
Moulty (Elmwin, Roznique, BMI) .... 96
My Baby Loves Me (Jobete, BMI) .... 29
My Love (Duchess, BMI) .... 7
My World Is Empty Without You (Jobete, BMI) .. 10
Night Time (Grand Canyon, BMI) .... 45
19th Nervous Breakdown (Gideon, BMI) .... 12
No Matter What Shape (Your Stomach's In) (C-Hear, BMI) .... 35
Nowhere Man (Maclen, BMI) .... 25
One More Heartache (Jobete, BMI) .... 51
One on the Right Is on the Left, The (Jack, BMI) 73
Outside the Gates of Heaven (Unart, BMI) .... 97
Philly Dog (East, BMI) .... 100
Promise Her Anything (Famous, ASCAP) .... 84
Put Yourself in My Place (Jobete, BMI) .... 92
Rains Came, The (Crazy Cajun & Corrett, BMI) .. 39
Red Hot (Riverline, BMI) .... 85
Satisfaction (Immediate, BMI) .... 79
Secret Agent Man (Tousdale, BMI) .... 86
Shake Hands (Acuff-Rose, BMI) .... 99
Shake Me, Wake Me (When It's Over) (Jobete, BMI) .... 55
634-5789 (East-Pronto, BMI) .... 32
Smokey Joe's La La (Recordo, BMI) .... 77
Somewhere There's a Someone (Hill & Range, BMI) 36
Stop Her on Sight (S.O.S.) (Myto, BMI) .... 70
Superman (Morris ASCAP) .... 95
Sure Gonna Miss Her (Viva-Tennessee, BMI) .... 87
Take Me For What I'm Worth (Trousdale, BMI) .. 76
Tears (Shapiro-Bernstein, ASCAP) .... 68
These Boots Are Made for Walkin' (Criterion, ASCAP) .... 2
This Can't Be True (Cameo-Parkway, Stillran, BMI) 59
This Golden Ring (Mills, ASCAP) .... 82
This Old Heart of Mine (Jobete, BMI) .... 64
Time (Regent, BMI) .... 89
Time Won't Let Me (Beechwood, BMI) .... 81
Up and Down (Fling, Dayshel-Grand Canyon, BMI) 52
Up Tight (Jobete, BMI) .... 8
Wait a Minute (Palmer, BMI) .... 91
Waitin' in Your Welfare Line (Central Songs, BMI) 57
Walkin' My Cat Named Dog (Stardar, BMI) .... 69
We Can Work It Out (Maclen, BMI) .... 48
Well Respected Man, A (Amer. Met. Ent. of N. Y., BMI) .... 38
What Now My Love (Remick, ASCAP .... 14
When Liking Turns to Loving (Tobi-ann & Unart, BMI) .... 18
Whenever She Holds You (Unart, BMI .... 75
Why Can't You Bring Me Home (Picturetone, BMI) 74
Woman (Maclen, BMI) .... 43
Working My Way Back to You (Saturday & Seasons 4, BMI) .... 9
You Baby (Trousdale, BMI) .... 23
(You're My) Soul and Inspiration (Screen Gems-Columbia, BMI) .... 90
Zorba the Greek (Miller, ASCAP) .... 21

## BUBBLING UNDER THE HOT 100

101. THINK I'LL GO SOMEWHERE AND CRY MYSELF TO SLEEP .... Al Martino, Capitol 5598
102. SINCE I LOST THE ONE I LOVE .... Impressions, ABC-Paramount 10761
103. I DIG YOU BABY .... Lorraine Ellison, Mercury 72472
104. WHEN THE SHIP HITS THE SAND .... Little Jimmy Dickens, Columbia 43514
105. WHERE AM I GOING .... Barbra Streisand, Columbia 43518
106. (I'm Just a) FOOL FOR YOU .... Gene Chandler, Constellation 167
107. THE ANSWER TO MY PRAYER .... Neil Sedaka, RCA Victor 8737
108. S.O.S. (Heart in Distress) .... Christine Cooper, Parkway 971
109. I'VE BEEN A LONG TIME LEAVIN' .... Roger Miller, Smash 2024
110. SONG FROM "THE OSCAR" .... Tony Bennett, Columbia 43508
111. MY BABE .... Roy Head, Back Beat 560
112. HELPLESS .... Kim Weston, Gordy 7050
113. IT'S A GOOD TIME .... Billy Joe Royal, Columbia 43538
114. IF YOU CAN'T BITE, DON'T GROWL .... Tommy Collins, Columbia 43489
115. BATMAN AND ROBIN .... Spotlights, Smash 2020
116. I SPY .... Jamo Thomas & His Party Brothers Ork, Thomas 303
117. MY DARLING HILDEGARDE .... Statler Brothers, Columbia 43526
118. WHAT GOES ON .... Beatles, Capitol 5587
119. MR MOON .... Coachmen, Bear 1974
120. SHARING YOU .... Mitty Collier, Chess 1953
121. FIVE CARD STUD .... Lorne Greene, RCA Victor 8757
122. COMMUNICATION .... Dave McCallum, Capitol 5571
123. YOU BRING ME DOWN .... Royalettes, MGM 13451
124. MADE IN PARIS .... Trini Lopez, Reprise 0435
125. GOOD LOVIN' .... Young Rascals, Atlantic 2321
126. YOUNG LOVE .... Lesley Gore, Mercury 72553
127. YOUR P-E-R-S-O-N-A-L-I-T-Y .... Jackie Lee, Mirwood 5509
128. SHARING YOU .... Carl Henderson, Omen 13
129. FUNNY (How Time Slips Away) .... Ace Cannon, Hi 2101
130. A PUBLIC EXECUTION .... Mouse, Fraternity 956
131. ELVIRA .... Dallas Frazier, Capitol 5560
132. JUANITA BANANA .... Peels, Karate 522
133. THAT'S WHEN THE TEARS START .... Blossoms, Reprise 0436
134. ONLY A GIRL LIKE YOU .... Brook Benton, RCA Victor 8768
135. PHOENIX LOVE THEME .... Brass Ring, Dunhill 4023

Compiled from national retail sales and radio station airplay by the Music Popularity Dept. of Record Market Research, Billboard.

Billboard
For Week Ending March 12, 1966

# HOT 100

★ STAR performer—Sides registering greatest proportionate upward progress this week.

Record Industry Association of America seal of certification as million selling single.

| THIS WEEK | 1 Wk. Ago | 2 Wks. Ago | 3 Wks. Ago | TITLE Artist, Label & Number | Weeks On Chart |
|---|---|---|---|---|---|
| 1 | 1 | 3 | 10 | THE BALLAD OF THE GREEN BERETS — S/Sgt. Barry Sadler (Andy Wiswell), RCA Victor 8739 | 6 |
| 2 | 2 | 1 | 2 | THESE BOOTS ARE MADE FOR WALKIN' — Nancy Sinatra (Lee Hazlewood), Reprise 0432 | 8 |
| 3 | 4 | 13 | 41 | LISTEN PEOPLE — Herman's Hermits (Mickie Most), MGM 13462 | 4 |
| 4 | 5 | 8 | 16 | CALIFORNIA DREAMIN' — Mama's and Papa's (Lou Adler), Dunhill 4020 | 10 |
| 5 | 6 | 9 | 20 | ELUSIVE BUTTERFLY — Bob Lind (Richard Bock), World Pacific 77808 | 8 |
| ★6 | 12 | 46 | — | 19TH NERVOUS BREAKDOWN — Rolling Stones (Andrew Loog Oldham), London 9823 | 3 |
| ★7 | 25 | — | — | NOWHERE MAN — Beatles (George Martin), Capitol 5587 | 2 |
| 8 | 3 | 2 | 1 | LIGHTNIN' STRIKES — Lou Christie (Nick Cenci), MGM 13412 | 12 |
| 9 | 11 | 14 | 26 | I FOUGHT THE LAW — Bobby Fuller 4 (Bob Keene), Mustang 3014 | 7 |
| ★10 | 16 | 31 | 54 | HOMEWARD BOUND — Simon & Garfunkel (Bob Johnston), Columbia 43511 | 5 |
| 11 | 9 | 10 | 15 | WORKING MY WAY BACK TO YOU — 4 Seasons (Bob Crewe), Philips 40350 | 7 |
| ★12 | 17 | 20 | 25 | THE CHEATER — Bob Kuban & the In-Men (Mel Friedman), Musicland, U.S.A. 20,001 | 7 |
| 13 | 8 | 4 | 3 | UP TIGHT — Stevie Wonder (Cosby-Stevenson), Tamla 54124 | 13 |
| 14 | 7 | 6 | 4 | MY LOVE — Petula Clark (Tony Hatch), Warner Bros. 5684 | 12 |
| ★15 | 27 | 36 | 38 | LOVE MAKES THE WORLD GO ROUND — Deon Jackson (Ollie McLaughlin), Carla 2526 | 8 |
| 16 | 10 | 5 | 5 | MY WORLD IS EMPTY WITHOUT YOU — Supremes (Holland & Dozier), Motown 1089 | 9 |
| 17 | 20 | 25 | 48 | BATMAN THEME — Marketts (Dick Glasser), Warner Bros. 5696 | 6 |
| 18 | 19 | 21 | 24 | AT THE SCENE — Dave Clark Five (Dave Clark), Epic 9882 | 6 |
| 19 | 13 | 7 | 8 | DON'T MESS WITH BILL — Marvelettes (Smoky), Tamla 54126 | 11 |
| 20 | 18 | 18 | 21 | WHEN LIKING TURNS TO LOVING — Ronnie Dove (Phil Kahl & Ray Vernon), Diamond 195 | 8 |
| 21 | 14 | 16 | 19 | WHAT NOW MY LOVE — Sonny & Cher (Sonny Bone), Atco 6395 | 7 |
| ★22 | 28 | 41 | 53 | BABY SCRATCH MY BACK — Slim Harpo (Not Available), Excello 2273 | 7 |
| 23 | 23 | 28 | 35 | YOU BABY — Turtles (Banes Howe), White Whale 227 | 6 |
| ★24 | 32 | 42 | 58 | 634-5789 — Wilson Pickett (Jim Stewart & Steve Cropper), Atlantic 2320 | 5 |
| ★25 | 53 | 76 | — | DAYDREAM — Lovin' Spoonful (Erik Jacobson), Kama Sutra 208 | 3 |
| ★26 | 43 | 55 | 61 | WOMAN — Peter & Gordon (Not Available) Capitol 5579 | 5 |
| 27 | 29 | 30 | 36 | MY BABY LOVES ME — Martha & the Vandellas (Hunter & Stevenson), Gordy 7048 | 8 |
| 28 | 15 | 12 | 6 | CRYING TIME — Ray Charles (Not Available) ABC-Paramount 10739 | 14 |
| ★29 | 40 | 50 | 74 | HUSBANDS AND WIVES — Roger Miller (Jerry Kennedy), Smash 2024 | 4 |
| ★30 | 44 | 56 | 75 | IT'S TOO LATE — Bobby Goldsboro (Jack Gold), United Artists 980 | 4 |
| ★31 | 46 | 72 | 87 | I'M SO LONESOME I COULD CRY — B. J. Thomas and the Triumphs (Charlie Booth) Scepter 12129 | 4 |
| 32 | 22 | 22 | 28 | CALL ME — Chris Montez (Herb Alpert), A&M 780 | 10 |
| 33 | 36 | 47 | 57 | SOMEWHERE THERE'S A SOMEONE — Dean Martin (Jimmy Bowen), Reprise 0443 | 5 |
| 34 | 39 | 49 | 59 | THE RAINS CAME — Sir Douglas Quintet (Huey P. Meaux), Tribe 8314 | 7 |
| 35 | 37 | 48 | 52 | BATMAN THEME — Neal Hefti (Neely Plumb), RCA Victor 8755 | 5 |
| ★36 | 55 | 67 | 86 | SHAKE ME, WAKE ME (When It's Over) — Four Tops (Holland & Dozier), Motown 1090 | 4 |
| 37 | 26 | 27 | 34 | I SEE THE LIGHT — Five Americans (Dale Hawkins). HBR 454 | 11 |
| ★38 | 49 | 59 | 84 | I WANT TO GO WITH YOU — Eddy Arnold (Chet Atkins), RCA Victor 8749 | 6 |
| ★39 | 51 | 69 | 89 | ONE MORE HEARTACHE — Marvin Gaye (Smokey), Tamla 54129 | 4 |
| 40 | 24 | 15 | 7 | BARBARA ANN — Beach Boys (Brian Wilson), Capitol 5561 | 11 |
| 41 | 47 | 52 | 79 | THE DEDICATION SONG — Freddy Cannon (Dick Glasser), Warner Bros. 5693 | 4 |
| ★42 | 64 | 81 | 99 | THIS OLD HEART OF MINE — Isley Brothers (Holland & Dozier), Tamla 54128 | 4 |
| 43 | 21 | 11 | 12 | ZORBA THE GREEK — Herb Alpert & the Tijuana Brass (Herb Alpert), A&M 787 | 12 |
| ★44 | 56 | 71 | — | MAGIC TOWN — Vogues (Cenci, Hakim & Mann), Co & Ce 234 | 3 |
| ★45 | 90 | — | — | (You're My) SOUL AND INSPIRATION — Righteous Brothers (Bill Medley), Verve 10383 | 2 |
| 46 | 52 | 62 | 68 | UP AND DOWN — McCoys (Feldman, Goldstein, Gotteher Prod.) Bang 516 | 5 |
| 47 | 34 | 26 | 22 | JUST LIKE ME — Paul Revere & the Raiders (Terry Melcher), Columbia 43461 | 15 |
| 48 | 30 | 23 | 11 | GOING TO A GO-GO — Miracles (Moore-Robinson), Tamla 54127 | 12 |
| 49 | 31 | 33 | 37 | BREAKIN' UP IS BREAKIN' MY HEART — Roy Orbison (Not Available), MGM 13446 | 8 |
| 50 | 33 | 37 | 44 | LONG LIVE OUR LOVE — Shangri-Las (Shadow Morton), Red Bird 048 | 6 |
| ★51 | 69 | 87 | — | WALKIN' MY CAT NAMED DOG — Norma Tanega (Herb Bernstein), New Voice 807 | 3 |
| 52 | 41 | 43 | 43 | ANDREA — Sunrays (Ralke-Wilson Prod.), Tower 191 | 8 |
| ★53 | 67 | 84 | — | GET READY — Temptations (Smokey), Gordy 7049 | 3 |
| ★54 | 78 | — | — | AIN'T THAT A GROOVE — James Brown & the Famous Flames (James Brown Prod.), King 6025 | 2 |
| ★55 | 87 | — | — | SURE GONNA MISS HER — Gary Lewis & the Playboys (Snuff Garrett) Liberty 55865 | 2 |
| ★56 | 72 | 96 | — | INSIDE—LOOKING OUT — Animals (Tom Wilson), MGM 13468 | 3 |
| 57 | 59 | 60 | 60 | THIS CAN'T BE TRUE — Eddie Holman (Harthon Prod.), Parkway 960 | 9 |
| ★58 | 73 | 83 | — | THE ONE ON THE RIGHT IS ON THE LEFT — Johnny Cash (Don Law & Frank Jones), Columbia 43496 | 3 |
| 59 | 50 | 51 | 51 | LOVE IS ALL WE NEED — Mel Carter (Nick De Caro), Imperial 66148 | 8 |
| ★60 | 88 | — | — | LITTLE LATIN LUPE LU — Mitch Ryder & the Detroit Wheels (Bob Crewe), New Voice 808 | 2 |
| 61 | 70 | 78 | 88 | STOP HER ON SIGHT (S.O.S.) — Edwin Starr (Al Kent & Richard Morris), Ric-Tic 109 | 4 |
| 62 | 65 | 74 | 83 | DEAR LOVER — Mary Wells (Carl Davis & Gerald Sims), Atco 6392 | 5 |
| 63 | 68 | 75 | — | TEARS — Bobby Vinton (Bob Morgan), Epic 9894 | 3 |
| ★64 | 79 | — | — | SATISFACTION — Otis Redding (Jim Stewart & Steve Cropper), Volt 132 | 2 |
| ★65 | 81 | 97 | 100 | TIME WON'T LET ME — Outsiders (Tom King), Capitol 5573 | 4 |
| 66 | 66 | 70 | 78 | BATMAN — Jan & Dean (Jan Berry), Liberty 55860 | 5 |
| 67 | 63 | 63 | 70 | IT WON'T BE WRONG — Byrds (Jerry Melcher), Columbia 43501 | 5 |
| 68 | 75 | 86 | — | WHENEVER SHE HOLDS YOU — Patty Duke (Gerry Granahan), United Artists 978 | 3 |
| 69 | 62 | 66 | 73 | IN MY ROOM — Verdelle Smith (Vance/Pockriss Prod.), Capitol 5567 | 6 |
| 70 | 57 | 57 | 67 | WAITIN' IN YOUR WELFARE LINE — Buck Owens (Ken Nelson), Capitol 5566 | 7 |
| 71 | 58 | 61 | 69 | HIDE & SEEK — Sheep (Feldman, Goldstein, Gotteher Prod.), Boom 60,000 | 7 |
| 72 | 74 | 80 | 91 | WHY CAN'T YOU BRING ME HOME — Jay and the Americans (Gerry Granahan), United Artists 992 | 4 |
| ★73 | 89 | 91 | — | TIME — Pozo-Seco Singers (Not Available), Columbia 43437 | 3 |
| 74 | 84 | 93 | 95 | PROMISE HER ANYTHING — Tom Jones (Peter Sullivan), Parrot 9809 | 4 |
| ★75 | — | — | — | BANG BANG — Cher (Sonny Bono), Imperial 66160 | 1 |
| 76 | 83 | — | — | KEEP ON RUNNING — Spencer Davis Group (Chris Blackwell), Atco 6400 | 2 |
| 77 | 77 | 85 | — | SMOKEY JOE'S LA LA — Googie Rene Combo (Studio One), Class 1517 | 3 |
| 78 | 86 | 90 | — | SECRET AGENT MAN — Ventures (Joe Saraceno), Dolton 316 | 3 |
| 79 | 76 | 77 | 77 | TAKE ME FOR WHAT I'M WORTH — Searchers (Pye Records), Kapp 729 | 7 |
| 80 | 80 | 88 | 97 | I CONFESS — New Colony Six (Not Available), Centaur 1201 | 4 |
| ★81 | — | — | — | THINK I'LL GO SOMEWHERE AND CRY MYSELF TO SLEEP — Al Martino (Tom Morgan), Capitol 5598 | 1 |
| 82 | 82 | 92 | 93 | THIS GOLDEN RING — Fortunes (Noel Walker), Press 9811 | 4 |
| 83 | 94 | — | — | LULLABY OF LOVE — Poppies (Billy Sherrill), Epic 9893 | 2 |
| 84 | 91 | — | — | WAIT A MINUTE — Tim Tam & the Turn-Ons (Rick Wiesend & Tom DeAngelo), Palmer 5002 | 2 |
| 85 | 98 | — | — | THE LOVE YOU SAVE — Joe Tex (Buddy Killen), Dial 4026 | 2 |
| ★86 | — | — | — | GOOD LOVIN' — Young Rascals (Tom Dowd, Arif Mardin), Atlantic 2321 | 1 |
| ★87 | — | — | — | HELPLESS — Kim Weston (Holland & Dozier), Gordy 7050 | 1 |
| 88 | 93 | — | — | I WANT SOMEONE — Mad Lads (Jim Stewart & Steve Cropper), Volt 131 | 2 |
| ★89 | — | — | — | WHAT GOES ON — Beatles (George Martin), Capitol 5587 | 1 |
| 90 | 97 | — | — | OUTSIDE THE GATES OF HEAVEN — Lou Christie (Nick Cenci), Co & Ce 235 | 2 |
| 91 | 96 | 100 | — | MOULTY — Barbarians (Not Available), Laurie 3326 | 3 |
| 92 | 99 | 99 | — | SHAKE HANDS — Newbeats (Wesley Rose), Hickory 1366 | 3 |
| 93 | — | — | — | TIPPY TOEING — Harden Trio (Don Law & Frank Jones), Columbia 43463 | 1 |
| 94 | 95 | — | — | SUPERMAN — Dino, Desi & Billy (Lee Hazlewood), Reprise 0444 | 2 |
| 95 | 92 | 98 | 98 | PUT YOURSELF IN MY PLACE — Elgins (Holland & Dozier), V.I.P. 25029 | 4 |
| 96 | — | — | — | I CAN'T GROW PEACHES ON A CHERRY TREE — Just Us (Taylor-Gordoni), Minuteman 203 | 1 |
| 97 | — | — | — | THE PHOENIX LOVE THEME — Brass Ring (Lou Adler), Dunhill 4023 | 1 |
| 98 | 100 | — | — | PHILLY DOG — Mar-Keys (Steve Cropper), Stax 185 | 2 |
| 99 | — | — | — | MY BABE — Roy Head (Roy Head), Back Beat 560 | 1 |
| 100 | — | — | — | JUANITA BANANA — Peels (Howard-Smith), Karate 522 | 1 |

## HOT 100—A TO Z—(Publisher-Licensee)

Ain't That a Groove (Dynatone, BMI) .... 54
Andrea (Sea of Tunes, BMI) .... 52
At the Scene (Branston, BMI) .... 18
Baby Scratch My Back (Excellorec, BMI) .... 22
Ballad of the Green Berets, The (Music, Music, Music, ASCAP) .... 1
Bang Bang (Five-West-Cotillion, BMI) .... 75
Barbara Ann (Shoe-String & Cousins, BMI) .... 40
Batman—Jan & Dean (Screen Gems-Columbia, BMI) 66
Batman Theme—Hefti (Miller, ASCAP) .... 35
Batman Theme—Marketts (Miller, ASCAP) .... 17
Breakin' Up Is Breakin' My Heart (Acuff-Rose, BMI) .... 49
California Dreamin' (Trousdale, BMI) .... 4
Call Me (Duchess, BMI) .... 32
Cheater, The (MAM) .... 12
Crying Time (Blue Book, BMI) .... 28
Daydream (Faithful Virtue, BMI) .... 25
Dear Lover (Jalynne, BMI) .... 62
Dedication Song, The (Algrace, BMI) .... 41
Don't Mess With Bill (Jobete, BMI) .... 19
Elusive Butterfly (Metric, BMI) .... 5
Get Ready (Jobete, BMI) .... 53
Going to a Go-Go (Jobete, BMI) .... 48
Good Lovin' (T.M., BMI) .... 86
Helpless (Jobete, BMI) .... 87
Hide & Seek (Florentine-Marks, BMI) .... 71
Homeward Bound (Eclectic, BMI) .... 10
Husbands and Wives (Tree, BMI) .... 29
I Can't Grow Peaches on a Cherry Tree (April Music, ASCAP) .... 96
I Confess (New Colony & World Int., BMI) .... 80
I Fought the Law (Acuff-Rose, BMI) .... 9
I See the Light (Jetstar, BMI) .... 37
I Want Someone (East, BMI) .... 88
I Want to Go With You (Pamper, BMI) .... 38
I'm So Lonesome I Could Cry (Acuff-Rose, BMI).. 31
In My Room (Robbins, ASCAP) .... 69
Inside—Looking Out (Ludlow, BMI) .... 56
It Won't Be Wrong (Tickson, BMI) .... 67
It's Too Late (Unart, BMI) .... 30
Juanita Banana (Tash, BMI) .... 100
Just Like Me (Daywin, BMI) .... 47
Keep on Running (Essex, ASCAP) .... 76
Lightnin' Strikes (Rambed, BMI) .... 8
Little Latin Lupe Lu (Maxwell-Conrad, BMI) .... 60
Listen People (New World, ASCAP) .... 3
Long Live Our Love (Trio-Tender Tunes, BMI) ... 50
Love Is All We Need (Travis, BMI) .... 59
Loves Makes the World Go Round (McLaughlin, BMI) .... 15
Love You Save, The (Tree, BMI) .... 85
Lullaby of Love (Tree, BMI) .... 83
Magic Town (Screen Gems-Columbia, BMI) .... 44
Moulty (Elmwin, Roznique, BMI) .... 91
My Babe (Arc, BMI) .... 99
My Baby Loves Me (Jobete, BMI) .... 27
My Love (Duchess, BMI) .... 14
My World Is Empty Without You (Jobete, BMI).. 16
19th Nervous Breakdown (Gideon, BMI) .... 6
Nowhere Man (Maclen, BMI) .... 7
One More Heartache (Jobete, BMI) .... 39
One on the Right Is on the Left, The (Jack, BMI) 58
Outside the Gates of Heaven (Unart, BMI) .... 90
Philly Dog (East, BMI) .... 98
Phoenix Love Theme, The (Ludlow, BMI) .... 97
Promise Her Anything (Famous, ASCAP) .... 74
Put Yourself in My Place (Jobete, BMI) .... 95
Rains Came, The (Crazy Cajun & Corrett, BMI) .. 34
Satisfaction (Immediate, BMI) .... 64
Secret Agent Man (Trousdale, BMI) .... 78
Shake Hands (Acuff-Rose, BMI) .... 92
Shake Me, Wake Me (When It's Over) (Jobete, BMI) .... 36
634-5789 (East-Pronto, BMI) .... 24
Smokey Joe's La La (Recordo, BMI) .... 77
Somewhere There's a Someone (Hill & Range, BMI) 33
Stop Her on Sight (S.O.S.) (Myto, BMI) .... 61
Superman (Morris, ASCAP) .... 94
Sure Gonna Miss Her (Viva-Tennessee, BMI) .... 55
Take Me for What I'm Worth (Trousdale, BMI) .. 79
Tears (Shapiro-Bernstein, ASCAP) .... 63
These Boots Are Made for Walkin' (Criterion, ASCAP) .... 2
Think I'll Go Somewhere and Cry Myself to Sleep (Moss Rose, BMI) .... 81
This Can't Be True (Cameo-Parkway, Stillran, BMI) 57
This Golden Ring (Mills, ASCAP) .... 82
This Old Heart of Mine (Jobete, BMI) .... 42
Time (Regent, BMI) .... 73
Time Won't Let Me (Beechwood, BMI) .... 65
Tippy Toeing (Window, BMI) .... 93
Up and Down (Fling, Dayshel-Grand Canyon, BMI). 46
Up Tight (Jobete, BMI) .... 13
Wait a Minute (Palmer, BMI) .... 84
Waitin' in Your Welfare Line (Central Songs, BMI) 70
Walkin' My Cat Named Dog (Starday, BMI) .... 51
What Goes On (Maclen, BMI) .... 89
What Now My Love (Remick, ASCAP) .... 21
When Liking Turns to Loving (Tobi-Ann & Unart, BMI) .... 20
Whenever She Holds You (Unart, BMI) .... 68
Why Can't You Bring Me Home (Picturetone, BMI) 72
Woman (Maclen, BMI) .... 26
Working My Way Back to You (Saturday & Seasons 4, BMI) .... 11
You Baby (Trousdale, BMI) .... 23
(You're My) Soul and Inspiration (Screen Gems-Columbia, BMI) .... 45
Zorba the Greek (Miller, ASCAP) .... 43

## BUBBLING UNDER THE HOT 100

101. SINCE I LOST THE ONE I LOVE ........Impressions, ABC-Paramount 10761
102. FUNNY (How Time Slips Away) ........Ace Cannon, Hi 2101
103. WHEN THE SHIP HIT THE SAND ..."Little" Jimmy Dickens, Columbia 43514
104. WHERE AM I GOING ........Barbra Streisand, Columbia 43518
105. GLORIA ........Shadows of Knight, Dunwich 116
106. SONG FROM "THE OSCAR" ........Tony Bennett, Columbia 43508
107. ANSWER TO MY PRAYER ........Neil Sedaka, RCA Victor 8737
108. (I'm Just a Fool) FOR YOU ........Gene Chandler, Constellation 167
109. SHARING YOU ........Mitty Collier, Chess 1953
110. MY DARLING HILDEGARDE ........Statler Brothers, Columbia 43526
111. I SPY ........Jamo Thomas & His Party Brothers Ork, Thomas 303
112. YOUNG LOVE ........Lesley Gore, Mercury 72553
113. IF YOU CAN'T BITE, DON'T GROWL ........Tommy Collins, Collins 43489
114. BATMAN AND ROBIN ........Spotlights, Smash 2020
115. YOUR P-E-R-S-O-N-A-L-I-T-Y ........Jackie Lee, Mirwood 5509
116. IT'S A GOOD TIME ........Billy Joe Royal, Columbia 43538
117. MR. MOON ........Coachmen, Bear 1974
118. FIVE CARD STUD ........Lorne Greene, RCA Victor 8757
119. COMMUNICATION ........David McCallum, Capitol 5571
120. I HEAR TRUMPETS BLOW ........Tokens, B. T. Puppy 518
121. MY PRAYER ........Johnny Thunder, Diamond 196
122. DARLING BABY ........Elgins, V.I.P. 25029
123. ELVIRA ........Dallas Frazier, Capitol 5560
124. TOO YOUNG ........Tommy Vann, Academy 118
125. WATCHING THE LATE, LATE SHOW ........Don Covan, Atlantic 2323
126. SHARING YOU ........Carl Henderson, Omen 13
127. PUBLIC EXECUTION ........Mouse, Fraternity 956
128. TIME AND TIME AGAIN ........Brenda Lee, Decca 31917
129. BABY I NEED YOU ........Manhattans, Carnival 514
130. SHAPES OF THINGS ........Yardbirds, Epic 9891
131. GIDDYUP GO ........Wink Martindale, Dot 16821
132. LOVE IS ME, LOVE IS YOU ........Connie Francis, MGM 13470
133. HAWG JAW ........Charlie Rich, Smash 2026
134. ONLY A GIRL LIKE YOU ........Brook Benton, RCA Victor 8768
135. RAGS TO RICHES ........Lenny Welch, Kapp 740

Compiled from national retail sales and radio station airplay by the Music Popularity Dept. of Record Market Research, Billboard.

Billboard

For Week Ending March 19, 1966

# HOT 100

★ **STAR performer**—Sides registering greatest proportionate upward progress this week.

Record Industry Association of America seal of certification as million selling single.

Billboard Award

| This Week | 1 Wk. Ago | 2 Wks. Ago | 3 Wks. Ago | TITLE Artist, Label & Number | Weeks On Chart |
|---|---|---|---|---|---|
| 1 | 1 | 1 | 3 | THE BALLAD OF THE GREEN BERETS — S/Sgt. Barry Sadler (Andy Wiswell), RCA Victor 8739 | 7 |
| ★2 | 6 | 12 | 46 | 19TH NERVOUS BREAKDOWN — Rolling Stones (Andrew Loog Oldham), London 9823 | 4 |
| 3 | 2 | 2 | 1 | THESE BOOTS ARE MADE FOR WALKIN' — Nancy Sinatra (Lee Hazlewood), Reprise 0432 | 9 |
| ★4 | 7 | 25 | — | NOWHERE MAN — Beatles (George Martin), Capitol 5587 | 3 |
| 5 | 5 | 6 | 9 | ELUSIVE BUTTERFLY — Bob Lind (Richard Bock), World Pacific 77808 | 9 |
| 6 | 3 | 4 | 13 | LISTEN PEOPLE — Herman's Hermits (Mickie Most), MGM 13462 | 5 |
| 7 | 4 | 5 | 8 | CALIFORNIA DREAMIN' — Mama's and Papa's (Lou Adler), Dunhill 4020 | 11 |
| 8 | 10 | 16 | 31 | HOMEWARD BOUND — Simon & Garfunkel (Bob Johnston), Columbia 43511 | 6 |
| 9 | 9 | 11 | 14 | I FOUGHT THE LAW — Bobby Fuller 4 (Bob Keene), Mustang 3014 | 8 |
| ★10 | 25 | 53 | 76 | DAYDREAM — Lovin' Spoonful (Erik Jacobson), Kama Sutra 208 | 4 |
| 11 | 15 | 27 | 36 | LOVE MAKES THE WORLD GO ROUND — Deon Jackson (Ollie McLaughlin), Carla 2526 | 9 |
| 12 | 12 | 17 | 20 | THE CHEATER — Bob Kuban & the In-Men (Mel Friedman), Musicland, U.S.A. 20,001 | 8 |
| 13 | 8 | 3 | 2 | LIGHTNIN' STRIKES — Lou Christie (RPM Enterprises), MGM13412 | 13 |
| ★14 | 45 | 90 | — | (You're My) SOUL AND INSPIRATION — Righteous Brothers (Bill Medley), Verve 10383 | 3 |
| ★15 | 24 | 32 | 42 | 634-5789 — Wilson Pickett (Jim Stewart & Steve Cropper), Atlantic 2320 | 6 |
| ★16 | 22 | 28 | 41 | BABY SCRATCH MY BACK — Slim Harpo (Not Available), Excello 2273 | 8 |
| 17 | 17 | 20 | 25 | BATMAN THEME — Marketts (Dick Glasser), Warner Bros. 5696 | 7 |
| ★18 | 31 | 46 | 72 | I'M SO LONESOME I COULD CRY — B. J. Thomas and the Triumphs (Charlie Booth), Scepter 12129 | 5 |
| ★19 | 36 | 55 | 67 | SHAKE ME, WAKE ME (When It's Over) — Four Tops (Holland & Dozier), Motown 1090 | 5 |
| ★20 | 26 | 43 | 55 | WOMAN — Peter & Gordon (Not Available), Capitol 5579 | 6 |
| 21 | 23 | 23 | 28 | YOU BABY — Turtles (Banes Howe), White Whale 227 | 7 |
| ★22 | 27 | 29 | 30 | MY BABY LOVES ME — Martha & the Vandellas (Hunter & Stevenson), Gordy 7048 | 9 |
| 23 | 20 | 18 | 18 | WHEN LIKING TURNS TO LOVING — Ronnie Dove (Phil Kahl & Ray Vernon), Diamond 195 | 9 |
| 24 | 19 | 13 | 7 | DON'T MESS WITH BILL — Marvelettes (Smoky), Tamla 54126 | 12 |
| ★25 | 55 | 87 | — | SURE GONNA MISS HER — Gary Lewis & the Playboys (Snuff Garrett), Liberty 55865 | 3 |
| 26 | 29 | 40 | 50 | HUSBANDS AND WIVES — Roger Miller (Jerry Kennedy), Smash 2024 | 5 |
| ★27 | 42 | 64 | 81 | THIS OLD HEART OF MINE — Isley Brothers (Holland & Dozier), Tamla 54128 | 5 |
| 28 | 30 | 44 | 56 | IT'S TOO LATE — Bobby Goldsboro (Jack Gold), United Artists 980 | 5 |
| 29 | 11 | 9 | 10 | WORKING MY WAY BACK TO YOU — 4 Seasons (Bob Crewe), Philips 40350 | 8 |
| 30 | 16 | 10 | 5 | MY WORLD IS EMPTY WITHOUT YOU — Supremes (Holland & Dozier), Motown 1089 | 10 |
| 31 | 34 | 39 | 49 | THE RAINS CAME — Sir Douglas Quintet (Huey P. Meaux), Tribe 8314 | 8 |
| 32 | 33 | 36 | 47 | SOMEWHERE THERE'S A SOMEONE — Dean Martin (Jimmy Bowen), Reprise 0443 | 6 |
| ★33 | 44 | 56 | 71 | MAGIC TOWN — Vogues (Cenci, Hakim & Mann), Co & Ce 234 | 4 |
| 34 | 39 | 51 | 69 | ONE MORE HEARTACHE — Marvin Gaye (Smokey), Tamla 54129 | 5 |
| 35 | 35 | 37 | 48 | BATMAN THEME — Neal Hefti (Neely Plumb), RCA Victor 8755 | 6 |
| 36 | 38 | 49 | 59 | I WANT TO GO WITH YOU — Eddy Arnold (Chet Atkins), RCA Victor 8749 | 7 |
| 37 | 21 | 14 | 16 | WHAT NOW MY LOVE — Sonny & Cher (Sonny Bono), Atco 6395 | 8 |
| ★38 | 51 | 69 | 87 | WALKIN' MY CAT NAMED DOG — Norma Tanega (Herb Bernstein), New Voice 807 | 4 |
| 39 | 18 | 19 | 21 | AT THE SCENE — Dave Clark Five (Dave Clark), Epic 9882 | 7 |
| 40 | 13 | 8 | 4 | UP TIGHT — Stevie Wonder (Cosby-Stevenson), Tamla 54124 | 14 |
| ★41 | 75 | — | — | BANG BANG — Cher (Sonny Bono), Imperial 66160 | 2 |
| ★42 | 53 | 67 | 84 | GET READY — Temptations (Smokey), Gordy 7049 | 4 |
| 43 | 14 | 7 | 6 | MY LOVE — Petula Clark (Tony Hatch), Warner Bros. 5684 | 13 |
| ★44 | 60 | 88 | — | LITTLE LATIN LUPE LU — Mitch Ryder & the Detroit Wheels (Bob Crewe), New Voice 808 | 3 |
| 45 | 41 | 47 | 52 | THE DEDICATION SONG — Freddy Cannon (Dick Glasser), Warner Bros. 5693 | 5 |
| ★46 | 56 | 72 | 96 | INSIDE—LOOKING OUT — Animals (Tom Wilson), MGM 13468 | 4 |
| 47 | 28 | 15 | 12 | CRYING TIME — Ray Charles (Sid Feller), ABC-Paramount 10739 | 15 |
| 48 | 54 | 78 | — | AIN'T THAT A GROOVE — James Brown & the Famous Flames (James Brown Prod.), King 6025 | 3 |
| 49 | 46 | 52 | 62 | UP AND DOWN — McCoys (Feldman, Goldstein, Gottehrer Prod.), Bang 516 | 6 |
| ★50 | 65 | 81 | 97 | TIME WON'T LET ME — Outsiders (Tom King), Capitol 5573 | 5 |
| ★51 | 62 | 65 | 74 | DEAR LOVER — Mary Wells (Carl Davis & Gerald Sims), Atco 6392 | 6 |
| 52 | 58 | 73 | 83 | THE ONE ON THE RIGHT IS ON THE LEFT — Johnny Cash (Don Law & Frank Jones), Columbia 43496 | 4 |
| 53 | 61 | 70 | 78 | STOP HER ON SIGHT (S.O.S.) — Edwin Starr (Al Kent & Richard Morris), Ric-Tic 109 | 5 |
| ★54 | 64 | 79 | — | SATISFACTION — Otis Redding (Jim Stewart & Steve Cropper), Volt 132 | 3 |
| ★55 | 81 | — | — | THINK I'LL GO SOMEWHERE AND CRY MYSELF TO SLEEP — Al Martino (Tom Morgan), Capitol 5598 | 2 |
| ★56 | 73 | 89 | 91 | TIME — Pozo-Seco Singers (Not Available), Columbia 43437 | 4 |
| 57 | 57 | 59 | 60 | THIS CAN'T BE TRUE — Eddie Holman (Harthon Prod.), Parkway 960 | 10 |
| ★58 | 78 | 86 | 90 | SECRET AGENT MAN — Ventures (Joe Saraceno), Dolton 316 | 4 |
| 59 | 63 | 68 | 75 | TEARS — Bobby Vinton (Bob Morgan), Epic 9894 | 4 |
| ★60 | — | — | — | SECRET AGENT MAN — Johnny Rivers (Lou Adler), Imperial 66159 | 1 |
| ★61 | 83 | 94 | — | LULLABY OF LOVE — Poppies (Billy Sherrill), Epic 9893 | 3 |
| ★62 | — | — | — | KICKS — Paul Revere & the Raiders (Terry Melcher), Columbia 43556 | 1 |
| 63 | 72 | 74 | 80 | WHY CAN'T YOU BRING ME HOME — Jay and the Americans (Gerry Granahan), United Artists 992 | 5 |
| 64 | 68 | 75 | 86 | WHENEVER SHE HOLDS YOU — Patty Duke (Gerry Granahan), United Artists 978 | 4 |
| ★65 | 85 | 98 | — | THE LOVE YOU SAVE — Joe Tex (Buddy Killen), Dial 4026 | 3 |
| ★66 | — | — | — | SPANISH FLEA — Herb Alpert & the Tijuana Brass (Herb Alpert), A&M 792 | 1 |
| ★67 | 86 | — | — | GOOD LOVIN' — Young Rascals (Tom Dowd, Arif Mardin), Atlantic 2321 | 2 |
| ★68 | — | — | — | WHAT NOW MY LOVE — Herb Alpert & the Tijuana Brass (Herb Alpert), A&M 792 | 1 |
| 69 | 69 | 62 | 66 | IN MY ROOM — Verdelle Smith (Vance/Pockriss Prod.), Capitol 5567 | 7 |
| ★70 | 100 | — | — | JUANITA BANANA — Peels (Howard-Smith), Karate 522 | 2 |
| ★71 | — | — | — | SOMEWHERE — Len Barry (Madara-White), Decca 31923 | 1 |
| ★72 | — | — | — | SHAPES OF THINGS — Yardbirds (Giorgio Gomelsky), Epic 9891 | 1 |
| ★73 | — | — | — | I HEAR TRUMPETS BLOW — Tokens (Big Time Prod.), B. T. Puppy 518 | 1 |
| ★74 | — | — | — | FRANKIE AND JOHNNY — Elvis Presley (Not Available), RCA Victor 8780 | 1 |
| ★75 | 90 | 97 | — | OUTSIDE THE GATES OF HEAVEN — Lou Christie (Nick Cenci), Co & Ce 235 | 3 |
| 76 | 76 | 83 | — | KEEP ON RUNNING — Spencer Davis Group (Chris Blackwell), Atco 6400 | 3 |
| 77 | 84 | 91 | — | WAIT A MINUTE — Tim Tam & the Turn-Ons (Rick Wiesend & Tom DeAngelo), Palmer 5002 | 3 |
| ★78 | — | — | — | GLORIA — Shadows of Knight (A Dunwich Prod.), Dunwich 116 | 1 |
| 79 | 87 | — | — | HELPLESS — Kim Weston (Holland & Dozier), Gordy 7050 | 2 |
| 80 | 88 | 93 | — | I WANT SOMEONE — Mad Lads (Jim Stewart & Steve Cropper), Volt 131 | 3 |
| 81 | 89 | — | — | WHAT GOES ON — Beatles (George Martin), Capitol 5587 | 2 |
| ★82 | 97 | — | — | THE PHOENIX LOVE THEME — Brass Ring (Lou Adler), Dunhill 4023 | 2 |
| 83 | 93 | — | — | TIPPY TOEING — Harden Trio (Don Law & Frank Jones), Columbia 43463 | 2 |
| ★84 | — | — | — | ONE TRACK MIND — Knickerbockers (Jerry Fuller), Challenge 59326 | 1 |
| ★85 | — | — | — | PLEASE DON'T STOP LOVING ME — Elvis Presley (Not Available), RCA Victor 8780 | 1 |
| 86 | 96 | — | — | I CAN'T GROW PEACHES ON A CHERRY TREE — Just Us (Taylor-Gordoni), Minuteman 203 | 2 |
| ★87 | — | — | — | MEMORIES ARE MADE OF THIS — Drifters (Bert Berns), Atlantic 2325 | 1 |
| ★88 | — | — | — | FOLLOW ME — Lyme & Cybelle (Bones Howe), White Whale 228 | 1 |
| ★89 | — | — | — | SHE BLEW A GOOD THING — Poets (Juggy Prod.), Symbol 214 | 1 |
| 90 | 91 | 96 | 100 | MOULTY — Barbarians (Not Available), Laurie 3326 | 4 |
| 91 | — | — | — | I CAN'T LET GO — Hollies (Ron Richards), Imperial 66158 | 1 |
| 92 | — | — | — | DARLING BABY — Elgins (Holland & Dozier), V.I.P. 25029 | 1 |
| 93 | — | — | — | THE BOOGALOO PARTY — Flamingos (Alice in Wonderland Prods.), Philips 40347 | 1 |
| 94 | — | — | — | (I'm Just a) FOOL FOR YOU — Gene Chandler (Carl Davis), Constellation 167 | 1 |
| 95 | — | — | — | BIG TIME — Lou Christie (Weslu Productions, Inc.), Colpix 799 | 1 |
| 96 | — | — | — | HE WORE THE GREEN BERET — Nancy Ames (Manny Kellem & Billy Sherrill), Epic 10003 | 1 |
| 97 | — | — | — | LOVE IS ME, LOVE IS YOU — Connie Francis (Danny Davis), MGM 13470 | 1 |
| 98 | — | — | — | SHARING YOU — Mitty Collier (Billy Davis), Chess 1953 | 1 |
| 99 | — | — | — | BABY I NEED YOU — Manhattans (Joe Evans), Carnival 514 | 1 |
| 100 | — | — | — | I SPY — Jamo Thomas & His Party Brothers Ork (M. Bland), Thomas 303 | 1 |

## HOT 100—A TO Z—*(Publisher-Licensee)*

Ain't That a Groove (Dynatone, BMI) .......... 48
At the Scene (Branston, BMI) .......... 39
Baby I Need You (Sanavan, BMI) .......... 99
Baby Sratch My Back (Excellorec, BMI) .......... 16
Ballad of the Green Berets, The (Music, Music, Music, ASCAP) .......... 1
Bang Bang (Five-West-Cotillion, BMI) .......... 41
Batman Theme—Hefti (Miller, ASCAP) .......... 35
Batman Theme—Marketts (Miller, ASCAP) .......... 17
Big Time (Weslu Prod., BMI) .......... 95
Boogaloo Party (Ponderosa, BMI) .......... 93
California Dreamin' (Trousdale, BMI) .......... 7
Cheater, The (MAM) .......... 12
Crying Time (Blue Book, BMI) .......... 47
Darling Baby (Jobete, BMI) .......... 92
Daydream (Faithful Virtue, BMI) .......... 10
Dear Lover (Jalynne, BMI) .......... 51
Dedication Song, The (Algrace, BMI) .......... 45
Don't Mess With Bill (Jobete, BMI) .......... 24
Elusive Butterfly (Metric, BMI) .......... 5
Follow Me (Ishmael, BMI) .......... 88
Frankie and Johnny (Gladys, ASCAP) .......... 74
Get Ready (Jobete, BMI) .......... 42
Gloria (Bernice, BMI) .......... 78
Good Lovin' (T. M., BMI) .......... 67
He Wore the Green Beret (Gallico, BMI) .......... 96
Helpless (Jobete, BMI) .......... 79
Homeward Bound (Eclectic, BMI) .......... 8
Husbands and Wives (Tree, BMI) .......... 26
I Can't Grow Peaches on a Cherry Tree (April Music, ASCAP) .......... 86
I Can't Let You Go (Blackwood, BMI) .......... 91
I Fought the Law (Acuff-Rose, BMI) .......... 9
I Hear Trumpets Blow (Bright Tunes, BMI) .......... 73
I Spy (Trio & Bert, BMI) .......... 100
I Want Someone (East, BMI) .......... 80
I Want to Go With You (Pamper, BMI) .......... 36
(I'm Just a) Fool for You (Jalynne, BMI) .......... 94
I'm So Lonesome I Could Cry (Acuff-Rose, BMI) .......... 18
In My Room (Robbins, ASCAP) .......... 69
Inside—Looking Out (Ludlow, BMI) .......... 46
It's Too Late (Unart, BMI) .......... 28
Juanita Banana (Tash, BMI) .......... 70
Keep on Running (Essex, ASCAP) .......... 76
Kicks (Screen Gems-Columbia, BMI) .......... 62
Lightnin' Strikes (Rambed, BMI) .......... 13
Little Latin Lupe Lu (Maxwell-Conrad, BMI) .......... 44
Listen People (New World, ASCAP) .......... 6
Love Is Me, Love Is You (Duchess, BMI) .......... 97
Loves Makes the World Go Round (McLaughlin, BMI) .......... 11
Love You Save, The (Tree, BMI) .......... 65
Lullaby of Love (Tree, BMI) .......... 61
Magic Town (Screen Gems-Columbia, BMI) .......... 33
Memories Are Made of This (Blackwood, BMI) .......... 87
Moulty (Elmwin, Roznique, BMI) .......... 90
My Baby Loves Me (Jobete, BMI) .......... 22
My Love (Duchess, BMI) .......... 43
My World Is Empty Without You (Jobete, BMI) .......... 30
19th Nervous Breakdown (Gideon, BMI) .......... 2
Nowhere Man (Maclen, BMI) .......... 4
One More Heartache (Jobete, BMI) .......... 34
One on the Right Is on the Left, The (Jack, BMI) .......... 52
One Track Mind (4-Star, BMI) .......... 84
Outside the Gates of Heaven (Rambed, BMI) .......... 75
Phoenix Love Theme, The (Ludlow, BMI) .......... 82
Please Don't Stop Loving Me (Presley, BMI) .......... 85
Rains Came, The (Crazy Cajun & Corrett, BMI) .......... 31
Satisfaction (Immediate, BMI) .......... 54
Secret Agent Man—Rivers (Trousdale, BMI) .......... 60
Secret Agent Man—Ventures (Trousdale, BMI) .......... 58
Shake Me, Wake Me (When It's Over) (Jobete, BMI) .......... 19
Shapes of Things (Robbins, ASCAP) .......... 72
She Blew a Good Thing (Sagittarius, BMI) .......... 89
Sharing You (Renfro, BMI) .......... 98
634-5789 (East-Pronto, BMI) .......... 15
Somewhere (Schirmer, ASCAP) .......... 71
Somewhere There's a Someone (Hill & Range, BMI) .......... 32
Spanish Flea (Almo, ASCAP) .......... 66
Stop Her on Sight (S.O.S.) (Myto, BMI) .......... 53
Sure Gonna Miss Her (Viva-Tennessee, BMI) .......... 25
Tears (Shapiro-Bernstein, ASCAP) .......... 59
These Boots Are Made for Walkin' (Criterion, ASCAP) .......... 3
Think I'll Go Somewhere and Cry Myself to Sleep (Moss Rose, BMI) .......... 55
This Can't Be True (Cameo-Parkway, Stillran, BMI) .......... 57
This Old Heart of Mine (Jobete, BMI) .......... 27
Time (Regent, BMI) .......... 56
Time Won't Let Me (Beechwood, BMI) .......... 50
Tippy Toeing (Window, BMI) .......... 83
Up and Down (Fling, Dayshel-Grand Canyon, BMI) .......... 49
Up Tight (Jobete, BMI) .......... 40
Wait a Minute (Palmer, BMI) .......... 77
Walkin' My Cat Named Dog (Starday, BMI) .......... 38
What Goes On (Maclen, BMI) .......... 81
What Now My Love—Alpert (Remick, ASCAP) .......... 68
What Now My Love—Sonny & Cher (Remick, ASCAP) .......... 37
When Liking Turns to Loving (Tobi-Ann & Unart, BMI) .......... 23
Whenever She Holds You (Unart, BMI) .......... 64
Why Can't You Bring Me Home (Picturetone, BMI) .......... 63
Woman (Maclen, BMI) .......... 20
Working My Way Back to You (Saturday & Seasons 4, BMI) .......... 29
You Baby (Trousdale, BMI) .......... 21
(You're My) Soul and Inspiration (Screen Gems-Columbia, BMI) .......... 14

## BUBBLING UNDER THE HOT 100

101. HE WORE THE GREEN BERET ............ Lesley Miller, RCA Victor 8786
102. SHAKE HANDS ............ Newbeats, Hickory 1366
103. MY BABE ............ Roy Head, Back Beat 560
104. IT'S A GOOD TIME ............ Billy Joe Royal, Columbia 43538
105. IF YOU CAN'T BITE, DON'T GROWL ............ Tommy Collins, Columbia 43489
106. SONG FROM "THE OSCAR" ............ Tony Bennett, Columbia 43508
107. YOUNG LOVE ............ Lesley Gore, Mercury 72553
108. CAROLINE, NO ............ Brian Wilson, Capitol 5610
109. WHERE AM I GOING? ............ Barbra Streisand, Columbia 43518
110. RHAPSODY IN THE RAIN ............ Lou Christie, MGM 13473
111. ELVIRA ............ Dallas Frazier, Capitol 5560
112. FIVE CARD STUD ............ Lorne Greene, RCA Victor 8757
113. SIPPIN' 'N' CHIPPIN' ............ T-Bones, Liberty 55867
114. MR. MOON ............ Coachmen, Bear 1974
115. MY PRAYER ............ Johnny Thunder, Diamond 196
116. RAGS TO RICHES ............ Lenny Welch, Kapp 740
117. COMMUNICATION ............ David McCallum, Capitol 5571
118. NESSUNO MI PUO' GUIDCARE ............ Gene Pitney, Musicor 1155
119. FUNNY (Not Much) ............ Walter Jackson, Okeh 7236
120. FUNNY (How Time Slips Away) ............ Ace Cannon, Hi 2101
121. PUBLIC EXECUTION ............ Mouse, Fraternity 956
122. GIDDYUP GO ............ Wink Martindale, Dot 16821
123. WATCHING THE LATE, LATE SHOW ............ Don Covay, Atlantic 2323
124. YOUR P-E-R-S-O-N-A-L-I-T-Y ............ Jackie Lee, Mirwood 5509
125. DON'T MAKE ME OVER ............ Swinging Blue Jeans, Imperial 66154
126. TIME AND TIME AGAIN ............ Brenda Lee, Decca 31917
127. MY DARLING HILDEGARDE ............ Statler Brothers, Columbia 43526
128. THAT'S WHEN THE TEARS START ............ Blossoms, Reprise 0436
129. DON'T PUSH ME ............ Hedgehoppers Anonymous, Parrot 9817
130. STOP! ............ Moody Blues, London 9810
131. IN THE SAME OLD WAY ............ Bobby Bare, RCA Victor 8758
132. HAWG JAW ............ Charlie Rich, Smash 2026
133. IT'S A FUNNY SITUATION ............ Dee Dee Sharp, Cameo 382
134. CHAIN REACTION ............ Spellbinders, Columbia 43522
135. SECOND-HAND MAN ............ Back Porch Majority, Epic 9879

Compiled from national retail sales and radio station airplay by the Music Popularity Dept. of Record Market Research, Billboard.

# Billboard HOT 100

**For Week Ending March 26, 1966**

★ STAR performer—Sides registering greatest proportionate upward progress this week.

● Record Industry Association of America seal of certification as million selling single.

| This Week | 1 Wk. Ago | 2 Wks. Ago | 3 Wks. Ago | TITLE, Artist, Label & Number | Weeks On Chart |
|---|---|---|---|---|---|
| 1 | 1 | 1 | 1 | THE BALLAD OF THE GREEN BERETS — S/Sgt. Barry Sadler (Andy Wiswell), RCA Victor 8739 ● | 8 |
| 2 | 2 | 6 | 12 | 19TH NERVOUS BREAKDOWN — Rolling Stones (Andrew Loog Oldham), London 9823 | 5 |
| 3 | 4 | 7 | 25 | NOWHERE MAN — Beatles (George Martin), Capitol 5587 | 4 |
| 4 | 3 | 2 | 2 | THESE BOOTS ARE MADE FOR WALKIN' — Nancy Sinatra (Lee Hazlewood), Reprise 0432 | 10 |
| ★5 | 8 | 10 | 16 | HOMEWARD BOUND — Simon & Garfunkel (Bob Johnston), Columbia 43511 | 7 |
| ★6 | 10 | 25 | 53 | DAYDREAM — Lovin' Spoonful (Erik Jacobson), Kama Sutra 208 | 5 |
| 7 | 7 | 4 | 5 | CALIFORNIA DREAMIN' — Mama's and Papa's (Lou Adler), Dunhill 4020 | 12 |
| ★8 | 14 | 45 | 90 | (You're My) SOUL AND INSPIRATION — Righteous Brothers (Bill Medley), Verve 10383 | 4 |
| 9 | 5 | 5 | 6 | ELUSIVE BUTTERFLY — Bob Lind (Richard Bock), World Pacific 77808 | 10 |
| 10 | 6 | 3 | 4 | LISTEN PEOPLE — Herman's Hermits (Mickie Most), MGM 13462 | 6 |
| 11 | 11 | 15 | 27 | LOVE MAKES THE WORLD GO ROUND — Deon Jackson (Ollie McLaughlin), Carla 2526 | 10 |
| 12 | 18 | 31 | 46 | I'M SO LONESOME I COULD CRY — B. J. Thomas and the Triumphs (Charlie Booth), Scepter 12129 | 6 |
| 13 | 15 | 24 | 32 | 634-5789 — Wilson Pickett (Jim Stewart & Steve Cropper), Atlantic 2320 | 7 |
| ★14 | 25 | 55 | 87 | SURE GONNA MISS HER — Gary Lewis and the Playboys (Snuff Garrett), Liberty 55865 | 4 |
| 15 | 20 | 26 | 43 | WOMAN — Peter & Gordon (John Burgess), Capitol 5579 | 7 |
| 16 | 16 | 22 | 28 | BABY SCRATCH MY BACK — Slim Harpo (Not Available), Excello 2273 | 8 |
| 17 | 41 | 75 | — | BANG BANG — Cher (Sonny Bono), Imperial 66160 | 3 |
| 18 | 19 | 36 | 55 | SHAKE ME, WAKE ME (When It's Over) — Four Tops (Holland & Dozier), Motown 1090 | 6 |
| 19 | 9 | 9 | 11 | I FOUGHT THE LAW — Bobby Fuller 4 (Bob Keene), Mustang 3014 | 9 |
| 20 | 21 | 23 | 23 | YOU BABY — Turtles (Banes Howe), White Whale 227 | 8 |
| 21 | 50 | 65 | 81 | TIME WON'T LET ME — Outsiders (Tom King), Capitol 5573 | 6 |
| ★22 | 60 | — | — | SECRET AGENT MAN — Johnny Rivers (Lou Adler), Imperial 66159 | 2 |
| 23 | 28 | 30 | 44 | IT'S TOO LATE — Bobby Goldsboro (Bob Montgomery), United Artists 980 | 6 |
| 24 | 22 | 27 | 29 | MY BABY LOVES ME — Martha & the Vandellas (Hunter & Stevenson), Gordy 7048 | 10 |
| 25 | 27 | 42 | 64 | THIS OLD HEART OF MINE — Isley Brothers (Holland & Dozier), Tamla 54128 | 6 |
| 26 | 33 | 44 | 56 | MAGIC TOWN — Vogues (Cenci, Hakim & Mann), Co & Ce 234 | 5 |
| 27 | 44 | 60 | 88 | LITTLE LATIN LUPE LU — Mitch Ryder & the Detroit Wheels (Bob Crewe), New Voice 808 | 4 |
| 28 | 12 | 12 | 17 | THE CHEATER — Bob Kuban & the In-Men (Mel Friedman), Musicland, U.S.A. 20,001 | 9 |
| 29 | 34 | 39 | 51 | ONE MORE HEARTACHE — Marvin Gaye (Smokey Robinson), Tamla 54129 | 6 |
| 30 | 38 | 51 | 69 | WALKIN' MY CAT NAMED DOG — Norma Tanega (Herb Bernstein), New Voice 807 | 5 |
| 31 | 31 | 34 | 39 | THE RAINS CAME — Sir Douglas Quintet (Huey P. Meaux), Tribe 8314 | 9 |
| ★32 | 42 | 53 | 67 | GET READY — Temptations (Smokey Robinson), Gordy 7049 | 5 |
| 33 | 13 | 8 | 3 | LIGHTNIN' STRIKES — Lou Christie (RPM Enterprises), MGM 13412 ● | 14 |
| 34 | 32 | 33 | 36 | SOMEWHERE THERE'S A SOMEONE — Dean Martin (Jimmy Bowen), Reprise 0443 | 7 |
| 35 | 17 | 17 | 20 | BATMAN THEME — Marketts (Dick Glasser), Warner Bros. 5696 | 8 |
| 36 | 36 | 38 | 49 | I WANT TO GO WITH YOU — Eddy Arnold (Chet Atkins), RCA Victor 8749 | 8 |
| 37 | 26 | 29 | 40 | HUSBANDS AND WIVES — Roger Miller (Jerry Kennedy), Smash 2024 | 7 |
| 38 | 35 | 35 | 37 | BATMAN THEME — Neal Hefti (Neely Plumb), RCA Victor 8755 | 7 |
| ★39 | 62 | — | — | KICKS — Paul Revere & the Raiders (Terry Melcher), Columbia 43556 | 2 |
| ★40 | 67 | 86 | — | GOOD LOVIN' — Young Rascals (Tom Dowd, Arif Mardin), Atlantic 2321 | 3 |
| 41 | 46 | 56 | 72 | INSIDE—LOOKING OUT — Animals (Tom Wilson), MGM 13468 | 5 |
| 42 | 29 | 11 | 9 | WORKING MY WAY BACK TO YOU — 4 Seasons (Bob Crewe), Philips 40350 | 9 |
| ★43 | 54 | 64 | 79 | SATISFACTION — Otis Redding (Jim Stewart & Steve Cropper), Volt 132 | 4 |
| 44 | 48 | 54 | 78 | AIN'T THAT A GROOVE — James Brown & the Famous Flames (James Brown Prod.), King 6025 | 4 |
| 45 | 55 | 81 | — | THINK I'LL GO SOMEWHERE AND CRY MYSELF TO SLEEP — Al Martino (Tom Morgan), Capitol 5598 | 3 |
| 46 | 52 | 58 | 73 | THE ONE ON THE RIGHT IS ON THE LEFT — Johnny Cash (Don Law & Frank Jones), Columbia 43496 | 5 |
| 47 | 45 | 41 | 47 | THE DEDICATION SONG — Freddy Cannon (Dick Glasser), Warner Bros. 5693 | 6 |
| 48 | 53 | 61 | 70 | STOP HER ON SIGHT (S.O.S.) — Edwin Starr (Al Kent & Richard Morris), Ric-Tic 109 | 6 |
| 49 | 30 | 16 | 10 | MY WORLD IS EMPTY WITHOUT YOU — Supremes (Holland & Dozier), Motown 1089 | 11 |
| 50 | 56 | 73 | 89 | TIME — Pozo-Seco Singers (Not Available), Columbia 43437 | 5 |
| 51 | 51 | 62 | 65 | DEAR LOVER — Mary Wells (Carl Davis & Gerald Sims), Atco 6392 | 7 |
| 52 | 72 | — | — | SHAPES OF THINGS — Yardbirds (Giorgio Gomelsky), Epic 9891 | 2 |
| 53 | 68 | — | — | WHAT NOW MY LOVE — Herb Alpert & the Tijuana Brass (Herb Alpert), A&M 792 | 2 |
| 54 | 58 | 78 | 86 | SECRET AGENT MAN — Ventures (Joe Saraceno), Dolton 316 | 5 |
| 55 | 66 | — | — | SPANISH FLEA — Herb Alpert & the Tijuana Brass (Herb Alpert), A&M 792 | 2 |
| 56 | 61 | 83 | 94 | LULLABY OF LOVE — Poppies (Billy Sherrill), Epic 9893 | 3 |
| 57 | 75 | 90 | 97 | OUTSIDE THE GATES OF HEAVEN — Lou Christie (Nick Cenci), Co & Ce 235 | 4 |
| 58 | 73 | — | — | I HEAR TRUMPETS BLOW — Tokens (Big Time Prod.), B. T. Puppy 518 | 2 |
| 59 | 71 | — | — | SOMEWHERE — Len Barry (Madara-White), Decca 31923 | 2 |
| 60 | 74 | — | — | FRANKIE AND JOHNNY — Elvis Presley (Not Available), RCA Victor 8780 | 2 |
| 61 | 65 | 85 | 98 | THE LOVE YOU SAVE — Joe Tex (Buddy Killen), Dial 4026 | 4 |
| 62 | 59 | 63 | 68 | TEARS — Bobby Vinton (Bob Morgan), Epic 9894 | 5 |
| 63 | 79 | 87 | — | HELPLESS — Kim Weston (Holland & Dozier), Gordy 7050 | 3 |
| 64 | 82 | 97 | — | THE PHOENIX LOVE THEME — Brass Ring (Phil Bodner), Dunhill 4023 | 3 |
| 65 | 70 | 100 | — | JUANITA BANANA — Peels (Howard-Smith), Karate 522 | 3 |
| 66 | 57 | 57 | 59 | THIS CAN'T BE TRUE — Eddie Holman (Northern Prod.), Parkway 960 | 11 |
| 67 | 84 | — | — | ONE TRACK MIND — Knickerbockers (Jerry Fuller), Challenge 59326 | 2 |
| 68 | 63 | 72 | 74 | WHY CAN'T YOU BRING ME HOME — Jay and the Americans (Gerry Granahan), United Artists 992 | 6 |
| ★69 | 85 | — | — | PLEASE DON'T STOP LOVING ME — Elvis Presley (Not Available), RCA Victor 8780 | 2 |
| 70 | 78 | — | — | A SIGN OF THE TIMES — Petula Clark (Tony Hatch), Warner Bros. 5802 | 2 |
| 71 | 87 | — | — | MEMORIES ARE MADE OF THIS — Drifters (Bert Berns), Atlantic 2325 | 2 |
| 72 | 83 | 93 | — | TIPPY TOEING — Harden Trio (Don Law & Frank Jones), Columbia 43463 | 3 |
| 73 | 88 | — | — | FOLLOW ME — Lyme & Cybelle (Bones Howe), White Whale 228 | 2 |
| 74 | 80 | 88 | 93 | I WANT SOMEONE — Mad Lads (Jim Stewart & Steve Cropper), Volt 131 | 4 |
| 75 | 78 | — | — | GLORIA — Shadows of Knight (A Dunwich Prod.), Dunwich 116 | 1 |
| 76 | 77 | 84 | 91 | WAIT A MINUTE — Tim Tam & the Turn-Ons (Rick Wiesend & Tom DeAngelo), Palmer 5002 | 4 |
| 77 | 64 | 68 | 75 | WHENEVER SHE HOLDS YOU — Patty Duke (Gerry Granahan), United Artists 978 | 5 |
| 78 | — | — | — | YOUNG LOVE — Lesley Gore (Shelby Singleton), Mercury 72553 | 1 |
| 79 | 76 | 76 | 83 | KEEP ON RUNNING — Spencer Davis Group (Chris Blackwell), Atco 6400 | 4 |
| 80 | — | — | — | CAROLINE, NO — Brian Wilson (Brian Wilson), Capitol 5610 | 1 |
| ★81 | 91 | — | — | TILL THE END OF THE DAY — Kinks (Pye Records), Reprise 0454 | 1 |
| 82 | — | — | — | HI HEEL SNEAKERS — Ramsey Lewis Trio (Esmond Edwards), Cadet 5531 | 1 |
| ★83 | — | — | — | RHAPSODY IN THE RAIN — Lou Christie (Charles Calello), MGM 13473 | 1 |
| 84 | — | — | — | I SURRENDER — Fontella Bass (Billy Davis), Checker 14328 | 1 |
| 85 | 86 | 96 | — | I CAN'T GROW PEACHES ON A CHERRY TREE — Just Us (Taylor-Gordoni), Colpix 803 | 3 |
| ★86 | — | — | — | TOGETHER AGAIN — Ray Charles (Sid Feller), ABC-Paramount 10785 | 1 |
| 87 | 92 | — | — | DARLING BABY — Elgins (Holland & Dozier), V.I.P. 25029 | 2 |
| 88 | 94 | — | — | (I'm Just a) FOOL FOR YOU — Gene Chandler (Carl Davis), Constellation 167 | 2 |
| 89 | 89 | — | — | SHE BLEW A GOOD THING — Poets (Juggy Prod.), Symbol 214 | 2 |
| 90 | — | — | — | SIPPIN' 'N' CHIPPIN' — T-Bones (Joe Saraceno), Liberty 55867 | 1 |
| 91 | 91 | — | — | I CAN'T LET GO — Hollies (Ron Richards), Imperial 66158 | 2 |
| 92 | 97 | — | — | LOVE IS ME, LOVE IS YOU — Connie Francis (Danny Davis), MGM 13470 | 2 |
| 93 | 93 | — | — | THE BOOGALOO PARTY — Flamingos (Alice in Wonderland Prods.), Philips 40347 | 2 |
| 94 | — | — | — | I'LL TAKE GOOD CARE OF YOU — Garnet Mimms (Jerry Ragovoy), United Artists 995 | 1 |
| 95 | 96 | — | — | HE WORE THE GREEN BERET — Nancy Ames (Manny Kellem & Billy Sherrill), Epic 10003 | 2 |
| 96 | 99 | — | — | BABY I NEED YOU — Manhattans (Joe Evans), Carnival 514 | 2 |
| 97 | 98 | — | — | SHARING YOU — Mitty Collier (Billy Davis), Chess 1953 | 2 |
| 98 | 100 | — | — | I SPY — Jamo Thomas & His Party Brothers Ork (M. Bland), Thomas 303 | 2 |
| 99 | — | — | — | YOU'RE JUST ABOUT TO LOSE YOUR CLOWN — Ray Charles (Joe Adams), ABC-Paramount 10785 | 1 |
| 100 | — | — | — | FOR YOUR PRECIOUS LOVE — Jerry Butler (Calvin Carter), Vee Jay 715 | 1 |

## HOT 100—A TO Z—(Publisher-Licensee)

Ain't That a Groove (Dynatone, BMI) .......... 44
Baby I Need You (Sanavan, BMI) .............. 96
Baby Scratch My Back (Excellorec, BMI) ...... 16
Ballad of the Green Berets (Music, Music, Music, ASCAP) .......................... 1
Bang Bang (Five-West-Cotillion, BMI) ......... 17
Batman Theme—Hefti (Miller, ASCAP) ......... 38
Batman Theme—Marketts (Miller, ASCAP) ...... 35
Boogaloo Party (Ponderosa, BMI) ............. 93
California Dreamin' (Trousdale, BMI) .......... 7
Caroline, No (Sea of Tunes, BMI) ............. 80
Cheater, The (MAM) ........................... 28
Darling Baby (Jobete, BMI) ................... 87
Daydream (Faithful Virtue, BMI) ............... 6
Dear Lover (Jalynne, BMI) .................... 51
Dedication Song, The (Algrace, BMI) .......... 47
Elusive Butterfly (Metric, BMI) ................ 9
Follow Me (Ishmael, BMI) ..................... 73
For Your Precious Love (Gladstone, ASCAP) ... 100
Frankie and Johnny (Gladys, ASCAP) .......... 60
Get Ready (Jobete, BMI) ...................... 32
Gloria (Bernice, BMI) ......................... 75
Good Lovin' (T. M., BMI) ..................... 40
He Wore the Green Beret (Gallico, BMI) ...... 95
Helpless (Jobete, BMI) ........................ 63
Hi Heel Sneakers (Medal, BMI) ................ 82
Homeward Bound (Eclectic, BMI) .............. 5
Husbands and Wives (Tree, BMI) .............. 37
I Can't Grow Peaches on a Cherry Tree (April Music, ASCAP) .................... 85
I Can't Let Go (Blackwood, BMI) .............. 91
I Fought the Law (Acuff-Rose, BMI) ........... 19
I Hear Trumpets Blow (Bright Tunes, BMI) .... 58
I Spy (Trio & Bert, BMI) ...................... 98
I Surrender (Chevis, BMI) ..................... 84

I Want Someone (East, BMI) .................. 74
I Want to Go With You (Pamper, BMI) ......... 36
I'll Take Good Care of You (Rittenhouse & Web IV, BMI) .......................... 94
(I'm Just a) Fool for You (Jalynne, BMI) ...... 88
I'm So Lonesome I Could Cry (Acuff-Rose, BMI) .......................... 12
Inside—Looking Out (Ludlow, BMI) ............ 41
It's Too Late (Unart, BMI) .................... 23
Juanita Banana (Tash, BMI) ................... 65
Keep on Running (Essex, ASCAP) ............. 79
Kicks (Screen Gems-Columbia, BMI) .......... 39
Lightnin' Strikes (Rambed, BMI) .............. 33
Listen People (Maxwell-Conrad, BMI) .......... 10
Little Latin Lupe Lu (New World, ASCAP) ..... 27
Love Is Me, Love Is You (Duchess, BMI) ...... 92
Love Makes the World Go Round (McLaughlin, BMI) ......................... 11
Love You Save, The (Tree, BMI) ............... 61
Lullaby of Love (Tree, BMI) ................... 56
Magic Town (Screen Gems-Columbia, BMI) .... 26
Memories Are Made of This (Blackwood, BMI) . 71
My Baby Loves Me (Jobete, BMI) ............. 24
My World Is Empty Without You (Jobete, BMI) . 49
19th Nervous Breakdown (Gideon, BMI) ....... 2
Nowhere Man (Maclen, BMI) .................. 3
One More Heartache (Jobete, BMI) ........... 29
One on the Right Is the Left, The (Jack, BMI) .. 46
One Track Mind (4-Star, BMI) ................. 67
Outside the Gates of Heaven (Rambed, BMI) .. 57
Phoenix Love Theme, The (Ludlow, BMI) ...... 64
Please Don't Stop Loving Me (Presley, BMI) ... 69
Rains Came, The (Crazy Cajun & Corrett, BMI) . 31
Rhapsody in the Rain (Rambed, BMI) ......... 83
Satisfaction (Immediate, BMI) ................. 43
Secret Agent Man—Rivers (Trousdale, BMI) .... 22
Secret Agent Man—Ventures (Trousdale, BMI) . 54

Shake Me, Wake Me (When It's Over) (Jobete, BMI) ........................... 18
Shapes of Things (Unart, BMI) ................ 52
She Blew a Good Thing (Sagittarius, BMI) .... 89
Sign of the Times, A (Duchess, BMI) ......... 70
Sippin' 'n' Chippin' (C-Hear, BMI) ............ 90
Somewhere (Schirmer, ASCAP) ................ 59
Somewhere There's a Someone (Hill & Range, BMI) .................................. 34
Spanish Flea (Almo, ASCAP) .................. 55
Stop Her on Sight (S.O.S.) (Myto, BMI) ....... 48
Sure Gonna Miss Her (Viva-Tennessee, BMI) .. 14
These Boots Are Made for Walkin' (Criterion, ASCAP) ............................... 4
Think I'll Go Somewhere and Cry Myself to Sleep (Moss Rose, BMI) ................ 45
This Can't Be True (Cameo-Parkway, Stillran, BMI) ............................. 66
This Old Heart of Mine (Jobete, BMI) ......... 25
Till the End of the Day (Noma, BMI) ......... 81
Time (Regent, BMI) ........................... 50
Time Won't Let Me (Beechwood, BMI) ......... 21
Tippy Toeing (Window, BMI) ................... 72
Together Again (Central, BMI) ................ 86
Wait a Minute (Palmer, BMI) .................. 76
Walkin' My Cat Named Dog (Starday, BMI) .... 30
What Now My Love (Remick, ASCAP) .......... 53
Whenever She Holds You (Unart, BMI) ........ 77
Why Can't You Bring Me Home (Picturetone, BMI) .............................. 68
Woman (Maclen, BMI) ......................... 15
Working My Way Back to You (Saturday & Seasons 4, BMI) ........................ 42
You Baby (Trousdale, BMI) .................... 20
You're Just About to Lose Your Clown (Marks, BMI) .......................... 99
(You're My) Soul and Inspiration (Screen Gems-Columbia, BMI) ........................ 8
634-5789 (East-Pronto, BMI) .................. 13

## BUBBLING UNDER THE HOT 100

101. WATCHING THE LATE, LATE SHOW ........ Don Covay, Atlantic 2323
102. STOP! .......................................... Moody Blues, London 9810
103. FUNNY (How Much) ........................ Walter Jackson, Okeh 7236
104. SONG FROM "THE OSCAR" ............... Tony Bennett, Columbia 43508
105. RAGS TO RICHES ............................ Lenny Welch, Kapp 740
106. A LOVER'S CONCERTO ..................... Sarah Vaughan, Mercury 72543
107. HE WORE THE GREEN BERET ............. Lesley Miller, RCA Victor 8768
108. SHAKE HANDS .............................. Newbeats, Hickory 1366
109. MY PRAYER .................................. Johnny Thunder, Diamond 196
110. BIG TIME .................................... Lou Christie, Colpix 799
111. YOUR P-E-R-S-O-N-A-L-I-T-Y ............... Jackie Lee, Mirwood 5509
112. SLOOP JOHN B ............................. Beach Boys, Capitol 5602
113. I'M LIVING IN TWO WORLDS .............. Bonnie Guitar, Dot 16819
114. REAL HUMDINGER .......................... J. J. Barnes, Ric-Tic 110
115. NESSUNO MI PUO GUIDICARE ............ Gene Pitney, Musicor 1155
116. DON'T MAKE ME OVER ..................... Swinging Blue Jeans, Imperial 66154
117. MAY MY HEART BE CAST INTO STONE ... Toys, DynoVoice 218
118. CHAIN REACTION ........................... Spellbinders, Columbia 43552
119. ONE OF US MUST KNOW .................. Bob Dylan, Columbia 43541
120. GIDDYUP GO ................................ Wink Martindale, Dot 16821
121. SOMEBODY TO LOVE ME ................... Ronny & the Daytonas, Mala 525
122. ONLY A GIRL LIKE YOU .................... Brook Benton, RCA Victor 8768
123. TOO LITTLE TIME ........................... Brenda Lee, Decca 31917
124. DON'T PUSH ME ............................ Hedgehoppers Anonymous, Parrot 9817
125. HAWG JAW ................................... Charlie Rich, Smash 2026
126. A GROOVY KIND OF LOVE .................. Mindbenders, Fontana 1541
127. IT'S A FUNNY SITUATION .................. Dee Dee Sharp, Cameo 382
128. LA LA LA .................................... Gerry & the Pacemakers, Laurie 3337
129. UPTIGHT ..................................... Jazz Crusaders, Pacific Jazz 88125
130. DADDY'S BABY ............................. Ted Taylor, Okeh 7240
131. GREETINGS (This Is Uncle Sam) .......... Monitors, VIP 25032
132. DIRTY WATER ............................... Standells, Tower 185
133. A GIRL I USED TO KNOW .................. Bobby Vee, Liberty 55854
134. DESIREE ..................................... Charts, Wand 1112
135. 3,000 MILES ................................. Brian Hyland, Philips 40354

Compiled from national retail sales and radio station airplay by the Music Popularity Dept. of Record Market Research, Billboard.

Billboard

For Week Ending April 2, 1966

# HOT 100

★ STAR performer—Sides registering greatest proportionate upward progress this week.

Record Industry Association of America seal of certification as million selling single.

| This Week | 1 Wk. Ago | 2 Wks. Ago | 3 Wks. Ago | TITLE Artist, Label & Number | Weeks On Chart |
|---|---|---|---|---|---|
| 1 | 1 | 1 | 1 | THE BALLAD OF THE GREEN BERETS — S/Sgt. Barry Sadler (Andy Wiswell), RCA Victor 8739 | 9 |
| 2 | 2 | 2 | 6 | 19TH NERVOUS BREAKDOWN — Rolling Stones (Andrew Loog Oldham), London 9823 | 6 |
| ★ 3 | 8 | 14 | 45 | (You're My) SOUL AND INSPIRATION — Righteous Brothers (Bill Medley), Verve 10383 | 5 |
| 4 | 6 | 10 | 25 | DAYDREAM — Lovin' Spoonful (Erik Jacobson), Kama Sutra 208 | 6 |
| 5 | 5 | 8 | 10 | HOMEWARD BOUND — Simon & Garfunkel (Bob Johnston), Columbia 43511 | 8 |
| 6 | 3 | 4 | 7 | NOWHERE MAN — Beatles (George Martin), Capitol 5587 | 5 |
| 7 | 7 | 7 | 4 | CALIFORNIA DREAMIN' — Mama's and Papa's (Lou Adler), Dunhill 4020 | 13 |
| 8 | 4 | 3 | 2 | THESE BOOTS ARE MADE FOR WALKIN' — Nancy Sinatra (Lee Hazlewood), Reprise 0432 | 11 |
| ★ 9 | 17 | 41 | 75 | BANG BANG — Cher (Sonny Bono), Imperial 66160 | 4 |
| ★ 10 | 14 | 25 | 55 | SURE GONNA MISS HER — Gary Lewis & the Playboys (Snuff Garrett), Liberty 55865 | 5 |
| 11 | 12 | 18 | 31 | I'M SO LONESOME I COULD CRY — B. J. Thomas and the Triumphs (Music Enterprises Productions), Scepter 12129 | 7 |
| 12 | 11 | 11 | 15 | LOVE MAKES THE WORLD GO ROUND — Deon Jackson (Ollie McLaughlin), Carla 2526 | 11 |
| 13 | 13 | 15 | 24 | 634-5789 — Wilson Pickett (Jim Stewart & Steve Cropper), Atlantic 2320 | 8 |
| 14 | 15 | 20 | 26 | WOMAN — Peter & Gordon (Not Available), Capitol 5579 | 8 |
| ★ 15 | 22 | 60 | — | SECRET AGENT MAN — Johnny Rivers (Lou Adler), Imperial 66159 | 3 |
| ★ 16 | 21 | 50 | 65 | TIME WON'T LET ME — Outsiders (Tom King), Capitol 5573 | 7 |
| 17 | 10 | 6 | 3 | LISTEN PEOPLE — Herman's Hermits (Mickie Most), MGM 13462 | 7 |
| 18 | 9 | 5 | 5 | ELUSIVE BUTTERFLY — Bob Lind (Richard Bock), World Pacific 77808 | 11 |
| 19 | 16 | 16 | 22 | BABY SCRATCH MY BACK — Slim Harpo (Not Available), Excello 2273 | 10 |
| ★ 20 | 25 | 27 | 42 | THIS OLD HEART OF MINE — Isley Brothers (Holland & Dozier), Tamla 54128 | 7 |
| ★ 21 | 26 | 33 | 44 | MAGIC TOWN — Vogues (Cenci, Hakim & Mann), Co & Ce 234 | 6 |
| ★ 22 | 27 | 44 | 60 | LITTLE LATIN LUPE LU — Mitch Ryder & the Detroit Wheels (Bob Crewe), New Voice 808 | 5 |
| 23 | 18 | 19 | 36 | SHAKE ME, WAKE ME (When It's Over) — Four Tops (Holland & Dozier), Motown 1090 | 7 |
| 24 | 20 | 21 | 23 | YOU BABY — Turtles (Banes Howe), White Whale 227 | 9 |
| ★ 25 | 30 | 38 | 51 | WALKIN' MY CAT NAMED DOG — Norma Tanega (Herb B. [illegible]stein), New Voice 807 | 6 |
| 26 | 23 | 28 | 30 | IT'S TOO LATE — Bobby Goldsboro (Jack Gold), United Artists 980 | 7 |
| ★ 27 | 40 | 67 | 86 | GOOD LOVIN' — Young Rascals (Tom Dowd, Arif Mardin), Atlantic 2321 | 4 |
| ★ 28 | 39 | 62 | — | KICKS — Paul Revere & the Raiders (Terry Melcher), Columbia 43556 | 3 |
| 29 | 32 | 42 | 53 | GET READY — Temptations (Smokey Robinson), Gordy 7049 | 6 |
| 30 | 19 | 9 | 9 | I FOUGHT THE LAW — Bobby Fuller 4 (Bob Keene), Mustang 3014 | 10 |
| 31 | 28 | 12 | 12 | THE CHEATER — Bob Kuban & the In-Men (Mel Friedman), Musicland, U.S.A. 20,001 | 10 |
| 32 | 31 | 31 | 34 | THE RAINS CAME — Sir Douglas Quintet (Huey P. Meaux), Tribe 8314 | 10 |
| 33 | 29 | 34 | 39 | ONE MORE HEARTACHE — Marvin Gaye (Smokey Robinson), Tamla 54129 | 7 |
| 34 | 41 | 46 | 56 | INSIDE—LOOKING OUT — Animals (Tom Wilson), MGM 13468 | 6 |
| 35 | 43 | 54 | 64 | SATISFACTION — Otis Redding (Jim Stewart & Steve Cropper), Volt 132 | 5 |
| ★ 36 | 70 | — | — | A SIGN OF THE TIMES — Petula Clark (Tony Hatch), Warner Bros. 5802 | 2 |
| 37 | 45 | 55 | 81 | THINK I'LL GO SOMEWHERE AND CRY MYSELF TO SLEEP — Al Martino (Tom Morgan), Capitol 5598 | 4 |
| 38 | 36 | 36 | 38 | I WANT TO GO WITH YOU — Eddy Arnold (Chet Atkins), RCA Victor 8749 | 9 |
| 39 | 24 | 22 | 27 | MY BABY LOVES ME — Martha & the Vandellas (Hunter & Stevenson), Gordy 7048 | 11 |
| 40 | 37 | 26 | 29 | HUSBANDS AND WIVES — Roger Miller (Jerry Kennedy), Smash 2024 | 7 |
| ★ 41 | 55 | 66 | — | SPANISH FLEA — Herb Alpert & the Tijuana Brass (Herb Alpert), A&M 792 | 3 |
| ★ 42 | 52 | 72 | — | SHAPES OF THINGS — Yardbirds (Giorgio Gomelsky), Epic 9891 | 3 |
| ★ 43 | 53 | 68 | — | WHAT NOW MY LOVE — Herb Alpert & the Tijuana Brass (Herb Alpert), A&M 792 | 3 |
| 44 | 44 | 48 | 54 | AIN'T THAT A GROOVE — James Brown & the Famous Flames (James Brown Prod.), King 6025 | 5 |
| 45 | 34 | 32 | 33 | SOMEWHERE THERE'S A SOMEONE — Dean Martin (Jimmy Bowen), Reprise 0443 | 8 |
| 46 | 33 | 13 | 8 | LIGHTNIN' STRIKES — Lou Christie (RPM Enterprises), MGM13412 | 15 |
| 47 | 50 | 56 | 73 | TIME — Pozo-Seco Singers (Not Available), Columbia 43437 | 6 |
| ★ 48 | 59 | 71 | — | SOMEWHERE — Len Barry (Madara-White), Decca 31923 | 3 |
| 49 | 57 | 75 | 90 | OUTSIDE THE GATES OF HEAVEN — Lou Christie (Nick Cenci), Co & Ce 235 | 5 |
| ★ 50 | 60 | 74 | — | FRANKIE AND JOHNNY — Elvis Presley (Not Available), RCA Victor 8780 | 3 |
| 51 | 58 | 73 | — | I HEAR TRUMPETS BLOW — Tokens (Big Time Prod.), B. T. Puppy 518 | 3 |
| 52 | 35 | 17 | 17 | BATMAN THEME — Marketts (Dick Glasser), Warner Bros. 5696 | 9 |
| 53 | 38 | 35 | 35 | BATMAN THEME — Neal Hefti (Neely Plumb), RCA Victor 8755 | 8 |
| ★ 54 | 64 | 82 | 97 | THE PHOENIX LOVE THEME — Brass Ring (Phil Bodner), Dunhill 4023 | 4 |
| 55 | 46 | 52 | 58 | THE ONE ON THE RIGHT IS ON THE LEFT — Johnny Cash (Don Law & Frank Jones), Columbia 43496 | 6 |
| 56 | 56 | 61 | 83 | LULLABY OF LOVE — Poppies (Billy Sherrill), Epic 9893 | 5 |
| 57 | 63 | 79 | 87 | HELPLESS — Kim Weston (Holland & Dozier), Gordy 7050 | 4 |
| ★ 58 | 69 | 85 | — | PLEASE DON'T STOP LOVING ME — Elvis Presley (Not Available) RCA Victor 8780 | 3 |
| 59 | 65 | 70 | 100 | JUANITA BANANA — Peels (Howard-Smith), Karate 522 | 4 |
| ★ 60 | 75 | 78 | — | GLORIA — Shadows of Knight (A Dunwich Prod.), Dunwich 116 | 3 |
| 61 | 61 | 65 | 85 | THE LOVE YOU SAVE — Joe Tex (Buddy Killen), Dial 4026 | 5 |
| 62 | 67 | 84 | — | ONE TRACK MIND — Knickerbockers (Jerry Fuller), Challenge 59326 | 3 |
| 63 | 54 | 58 | 78 | SECRET AGENT MAN — Ventures (Joe Saraceno), Dolton 316 | 6 |
| 64 | 48 | 53 | 61 | STOP HER ON SIGHT (S.O.S.) — Edwin Starr (Al Kent & Richard Morris), Ric-Tic 109 | 7 |
| ★ 65 | 80 | — | — | CAROLINE, NO — Brian Wilson (Brian Wilson), Capitol 5610 | 2 |
| ★ 66 | 86 | — | — | TOGETHER AGAIN — Ray Charles (Sid Feller), ABC-Paramount 10785 | 2 |
| ★ 67 | 83 | — | — | RHAPSODY IN THE RAIN — Lou Christie (Charles Calello), MGM 13473 | 2 |
| ★ 68 | — | — | — | SLOOP JOHN B — Beach Boys (Brian Wilson), Capitol 5602 | 1 |
| 69 | 78 | — | — | YOUNG LOVE — Lesley Gore (Shelby Singleton), Mercury 72553 | 2 |
| 70 | 71 | 87 | — | MEMORIES ARE MADE OF THIS — Drifters (Bert Berns), Atlantic 2325 | 3 |
| 71 | 72 | 83 | 93 | TIPPY TOEING — Harden Trio (Don Law & Frank Jones), Columbia 43463 | 4 |
| 72 | 51 | 51 | 62 | DEAR LOVER — Mary Wells (Carl Davis & Gerald Sims), Atco 6392 | 8 |
| 73 | 73 | 88 | — | FOLLOW ME — Lyme & Cybelle (Bones Howe), White Whale 228 | 3 |
| 74 | 85 | 86 | 96 | I CAN'T GROW PEACHES ON A CHERRY TREE — Just Us (Taylor-Gordoni), Colpix 803 | 4 |
| 75 | 81 | — | — | TILL THE END OF THE DAY — Kinks (Pye Records), Reprise 0454 | 2 |
| 76 | 82 | — | — | HI HEEL SNEAKERS — Ramsey Lewis Trio (Esmond Edwards), Cadet 5531 | 2 |
| 77 | 74 | 80 | 88 | I WANT SOMEONE — Mad Lads (Jim Stewart & Steve Cropper), Volt 131 | 5 |
| 78 | 76 | 77 | 84 | WAIT A MINUTE — Tim Tam & the Turn-Ons (Rick Wiesend & Tom DeAngelo), Palmer 5002 | 5 |
| ★ 79 | — | — | — | MESSAGE TO MICHAEL — Dionne Warwick (Blue Jac), Scepter 12133 | 1 |
| ★ 80 | — | — | — | GOT MY MOJO WORKING — Jimmy Smith (Creed Taylor), Verve 10393 | 1 |
| 81 | 89 | 89 | — | SHE BLEW A GOOD THING — Poets (Juggy Prod.), Symbol 214 | 3 |
| 82 | 84 | — | — | I SURRENDER — Fontella Bass (Billy Davis), Checker 14328 | 2 |
| 83 | 92 | 97 | — | LOVE IS ME, LOVE IS YOU — Connie Francis (Danny Davis), MGM 13470 | 3 |
| 84 | 91 | 91 | — | I CAN'T LET GO — Hollies (Ron Richards), Imperial 66158 | 3 |
| 85 | 90 | — | — | SIPPIN' 'N' CHIPPIN' — T-Bones (Joe Saraceno), Liberty 55867 | 2 |
| ★ 86 | — | — | — | TRY TOO HARD — Dave Clark Five (Dave Clark), Epic 10004 | 1 |
| ★ 87 | — | — | — | A LOVER'S CONCERTO — Sarah Vaughan (Luchi DeJesus), Mercury 72543 | 1 |
| ★ 88 | — | — | — | KILLER JOE — Kingsmen (Jerden Prod.), Wand 1115 | 1 |
| 89 | 95 | 96 | — | HE WORE THE GREEN BERET — Nancy Ames (Manny Kellem & Billy Sherrill), Epic 10003 | 3 |
| 90 | 94 | — | — | I'LL TAKE GOOD CARE OF YOU — Garnet Mimms (Jerry Ragevoy), United Artists 995 | 2 |
| 91 | 99 | — | — | YOU'RE JUST ABOUT TO LOSE YOUR CLOWN — Ray Charles (Joe Adams), ABC-Paramount 10785 | 2 |
| 92 | — | — | — | LA LA LA — Gerry & the Pacemakers (Not Available), Laurie 3337 | 1 |
| 93 | — | — | — | PHILLY DOG — Mar-Keys (Jim Stewart), Stax 185 | 3 |
| 94 | — | — | — | TOO SLOW — Impressions (Johnny Pate), ABC-Paramount 10789 | 1 |
| 95 | — | — | — | UPTIGHT — Jazz Crusaders (Richard Bock), Pacific Jazz 88125 | 1 |
| 96 | — | — | — | MAY MY HEART BE CAST INTO STONE — Toys (Randel-Linzer Prod.), DynoVoice 218 | 1 |
| 97 | — | — | — | NO MAN IS AN ISLAND — Van Dykes (Charles Stewart), Mala 520 | 1 |
| 98 | — | — | — | STOP! — Moody Blues (Not Available), London 9810 | 1 |
| 99 | 100 | — | — | FOR YOUR PRECIOUS LOVE — Jerry Butler (Calvin Carter), Vee Jay 715 | 2 |
| 100 | — | — | — | I'M LIVING IN TWO WORLDS — Bonnie Guitar (Not Available), Dot 16811 | 1 |

## HOT 100—A TO Z—(Publisher-Licensee)

Ain't That a Groove (Dynatone, BMI) ... 44

Baby Scratch My Back (Excellorec, BMI) ... 19
Ballad of the Green Berets, The (Music, Music, Music, ASCAP) ... 1
Bang Bang (Five-West-Cotillion, BMI) ... 9
Batman Theme—Hefti (Miller, ASCAP) ... 53
Batman Theme—Marketts (Miller, ASCAP) ... 52

California Dreamin' (Trousdale, BMI) ... 7
Caroline, No (Sea of Tunes, BMI) ... 65
Cheater, The (MAM) ... 31

Daydream (Faithful Virtue, BMI) ... 4
Dear Lover (Jalynne, BMI) ... 72

Elusive Butterfly (Metric, BMI) ... 18
Follow Me (Ishmael, BMI) ... 73
For Your Precious Love (Gladstone, ASCAP) ... 99
Frankie and Johnny (Gladys, ASCAP) ... 50

Get Ready (Jobete, BMI) ... 29
Gloria (Bernice, BMI) ... 60
Good Lovin' (T.M., BMI) ... 27
Got My Mojo Working (Arc, BMI) ... 80

He Wore the Green Beret (Gallico, BMI) ... 89
Helpless (Jobete, BMI) ... 57
Hi Heel Sneakers (Medal, BMI) ... 76
Homeward Bound (Eclectic, BMI) ... 5
Husbands and Wives (Tree, BMI) ... 40

I Can't Grow Peaches on a Cherry Tree (April Music, ASCAP) ... 74
I Can't Let Go (Blackwood, BMI) ... 84
I Fought the Law (Acuff-Rose, BMI) ... 30
I Hear Trumpets Blow (Bright Tunes, BMI) ... 51
I Surrender (Chevis, BMI) ... 82
I Want Someone (East, BMI) ... 77
I Want to Go With You (Pamper, BMI) ... 38
I'll Take Good Care of You (Rittenhouse & Web IV, BMI) ... 90

I'm Living in Two Worlds (Forest Hills, BMI) ... 100
I'm So Lonesome I Could Cry (Acuff-Rose, BMI) ... 11
Inside—Looking Out (Ludlow, BMI) ... 34
It's Too Late (Unart, BMI) ... 26

Juanita Banana (Tash, BMI) ... 59

Kicks (Screen Gems-Columbia, BMI) ... 28
Killer Joe (White Castle, BMI) ... 88

La La La (Pacemaker, BMI) ... 92
Lightnin' Strikes (Rambed, BMI) ... 46
Little Latin Lupe Lu (Maxwell-Conrad, BMI) ... 22
Listen People (New World, ASCAP) ... 17
Love Is Me, Love Is You (Duchess, BMI) ... 83
Love Makes the World Go Round (McLaughlin, BMI) 12
Love You Save, The (Tree, BMI) ... 61
Lover's Concerto, A (Saturday, BMI) ... 87
Lullaby of Love (Tree, BMI) ... 56

Magic Town (Screen Gems-Columbia, BMI) ... 21
May My Heart Be Cast Into Stone (Saturday, BMI) 96
Memories Are Made of This (Blackwood, BMI) ... 70
Message to Michael (U. S. Songs, ASCAP) ... 79
My Baby Loves Me (Jobete, BMI) ... 39

19th Nervous Breakdown (Gideon, BMI) ... 2
No Man Is an Island (Cha-Stew, BMI) ... 97
Nowhere Man (Maclen, BMI) ... 6

One More Heartache (Jobete, BMI) ... 33
One on the Right Is on the Left, The (Jack, BMI) 55
One Track Mind (4-Star, BMI) ... 62
Outside the Gates of Heaven (Rambed, BMI) ... 49

Philly Dog (East, BMI) ... 93
Phoenix Love Theme, The (Ludlow, BMI) ... 54
Please Don't Stop Loving Me (Presley, BMI) ... 58

Rains Came, The (Crazy Cajun & Corrett, BMI) ... 32
Rhapsody in the Rain (Rambed, BMI) ... 67

Satisfaction (Immediate, BMI) ... 35
Secret Agent Man—Rivers (Trousdale, BMI) ... 15
Secret Agent Man—Ventures (Trousdale, BMI) ... 63
Shake Me, Wake Me (When It's Over) (Jobete, BMI) 23
Shapes of Things (Unart, BMI) ... 42
She Blew a Good Thing (Sagittarius, BMI) ... 81
Sign of the Times, A (Duchess, BMI) ... 36
Sippin' 'n' Chippin' (C-Hear, BMI) ... 85
634-5789 (East-Pronto, BMI) ... 13
Sloop John B (New Executive, BMI) ... 68
Somewhere (Schirmer, ASCAP) ... 48
Somewhere There's a Someone (Hill & Range, BMI) 45
Spanish Flea (Almo, ASCAP) ... 41
Stop! (Cheshire, BMI) ... 98
Stop Her on Sight (S.O.S.) (Myto, BMI) ... 64
Sure Gonna Miss Her (Viva-Tennessee, BMI) ... 10

These Boots Are Made for Walkin' (Criterion, ASCAP) ... 8
Think I'll Go Somewhere and Cry Myself to Sleep (Moss Rose, BMI) ... 37
This Old Heart of Mine (Jobete, BMI) ... 20
Till the End of the Day (Noma, BMI) ... 75
Time (Regent, BMI) ... 47
Time Won't Let Me (Beechwood, BMI) ... 16
Tippy Toeing (Window, BMI) ... 71
Together Again (Central, BMI) ... 66
Too Slow (Chi-Sound, BMI) ... 94
Try Too Hard (Branston, BMI) ... 86

Uptight (Jobete, BMI) ... 95

Wait a Minute (Palmer, BMI) ... 78
Walkin' My Cat Named Dog (Starday, BMI) ... 25
What Now My Love (Remick, ASCAP) ... 43
Woman (Maclen, BMI) ... 14

You Baby (Trousdale, BMI) ... 24
Young Love (Lowery, BMI) ... 69
You're Just About to Lose Your Clown (Marks, BMI) 91
(You're My) Soul and Inspiration (Screen Gems-Columbia, BMI) ... 3

## BUBBLING UNDER THE HOT 100

101. DARLING BABY ... Elgins, VIP 25029
102. RAGS TO RICHES ... Lenny Welch, Kapp 740
103. FUNNY (Not Much) ... Walter Jackson, Okeh 7236
104. GLORIA ... Them, Parrot 9727
105. HE WORE THE GREEN BERET ... Lesley Miller, RCA Victor 8786
106. MY PRAYER ... Johnny Thunder, Diamond 196
107. REAL HUMDINGER ... J. J. Barnes, Ric-Tic 110
108. I SPY ... Jamo Thomas, Thomas 303
109. FROM A DISTANCE ... P. F. Sloan, Dunhill 4024
110. SHARING YOU ... Mitty Collier, Chess 1953
111. SONG FROM "THE OSCAR" ... Tony Bennett, Columbia 43508
112. A GROOVY KIND OF LOVE ... Mindbenders, Fontana 1541
113. TOO YOUNG ... Tommy Vann, Academy 118
114. GIDDYUP GO ... Wink Martindale, Dot 16821
115. BIG TIME ... Lou Christie, Colpix 799
116. DISTANT DRUMS ... Jim Reeves, RCA Victor 8789
117. BABY I NEED YOU ... Manhattans, Carnival 514
118. SOMEBODY TO LOVE ME ... Ronny & the Daytonas, Mala 525
119. THE BOOGALOO PARTY ... Flamingos, Philips 40347
120. NESSUNO MI PUO' GUIDICARE ... Gene Pitney, Musicor 1155
121. GOOD, GOOD LOVIN' ... Blossoms, Reprise 0436
122. (I'm Just a) FOOL FOR YOU ... Gene Chandler, Constellation 167
123. DON'T PUSH ME ... Hedgehoppers Anonymous, Parrot 9817
124. DIRTY WATER ... Standells, Tower 185
125. GREETING (This Is Uncle Sam) ... Monitors, VIP 25032
126. IT'S A FUNNY SITUATION ... Dee Dee Sharp, Cameo 382
127. LOVE ME WITH ALL YOUR HEART ... Bachelors, London 9828
128. I'M A GOOD GUY ... C.O.D.'s, Kellmac 1005
129. DADDY'S BABY ... Ted Taylor, Okeh 7240
130. 3,000 MILES ... Brian Hyland, Philips 40354
131. VIET NAM BLUES ... Dave Dudley, Mercury 72550
132. DESIREE ... Charts, Wand 1112
133. FROM NASHVILLE WITH LOVE ... Chet Atkins, RCA Victor 8781
134. ELVIRA ... Dallas Frazier, Capitol 5560
135. MY DARLING HILDEGARDE ... Statler Brothers, Columbia 43526

Compiled from national retail sales and radio station airplay by the Music Popularity Dept. of Record Market Research, Billboard.

# Billboard HOT 100

**For Week Ending April 9, 1966**

★ STAR performer—Sides registering greatest proportionate upward progress this week.

Ⓡ Record Industry Association of America seal of certification as million selling single.

| This Week | Wks. Ago 2 | Wks. Ago 3 | TITLE Artist (Producer), Label & Number | Wks. On Chart |
|---|---|---|---|---|
| 1 | 3 | 8 | 14 | (You're My) SOUL AND INSPIRATION — Righteous Brothers (Bill Medley), Verve 10383 | 6 |
| 2 | 4 | 6 | 10 | DAYDREAM — Lovin' Spoonful (Erik Jacobson), Kama Sutra 208 | 7 |
| 3 | 2 | 2 | 2 | 19TH NERVOUS BREAKDOWN — Rolling Stones (Andrew Loog Oldham), London 9823 | 7 |
| 4 | 9 | 17 | 41 | BANG BANG — Cher (Sonny Bono), Imperial 66160 | 5 |
| 5 | 1 | 1 | 1 | THE BALLAD OF THE GREEN BERETS — S/Sgt. Barry Sadler (Andy Wiswell), RCA Victor 8739 | 10 |
| 6 | 6 | 3 | 4 | NOWHERE MAN — Beatles (George Martin), Capitol 5587 | 6 |
| ★7 | 15 | 22 | 60 | SECRET AGENT MAN — Johnny Rivers (Lou Adler), Imperial 66159 | 4 |
| 8 | 11 | 12 | 18 | I'M SO LONESOME I COULD CRY — B. J. Thomas and the Triumphs (Music Enterprises Productions), Scepter 12129 | 8 |
| 9 | 10 | 14 | 25 | SURE GONNA MISS HER — Gary Lewis & the Playboys (Snuff Garrett), Liberty 55865 | 6 |
| 10 | 7 | 7 | 7 | CALIFORNIA DREAMIN' — Mama's and Papa's (Lou Adler), Dunhill 4020 | 14 |
| 11 | 16 | 21 | 50 | TIME WON'T LET ME — Outsiders (Tom King), Capitol 5573 | 8 |
| 12 | 5 | 5 | 8 | HOMEWARD BOUND — Simon & Garfunkel (Bob Johnston), Columbia 43511 | 9 |
| 13 | 13 | 13 | 15 | 634-5789 — Wilson Pickett (Jim Stewart & Steve Cropper), Atlantic 2320 | 9 |
| 14 | 8 | 4 | 3 | THESE BOOTS ARE MADE FOR WALKIN' — Nancy Sinatra (Lee Hazlewood), Reprise 0432 | 12 |
| 15 | 20 | 25 | 27 | THIS OLD HEART OF MINE — Isley Brothers (Holland & Dozier), Tamla 54128 | 8 |
| 16 | 27 | 40 | 67 | GOOD LOVIN' — Young Rascals (Tom Dowd, Arif Mardin), Atlantic 2321 | 5 |
| 17 | 22 | 27 | 44 | LITTLE LATIN LUPE LU — Mitch Ryder & the Detroit Wheels (Bob Crewe), New Voice 808 | 6 |
| 18 | 28 | 29 | 62 | KICKS — Paul Revere & the Raiders (Terry Melcher), Columbia 43556 | 4 |
| 19 | 14 | 15 | 20 | WOMAN — Peter & Gordon, Capitol 5579 | 9 |
| 20 | 12 | 11 | 11 | LOVE MAKES THE WORLD GO ROUND — Deon Jackson (Ollie McLaughlin), Carla 2526 | 12 |
| 21 | 21 | 26 | 33 | MAGIC TOWN — Vogues (Cenci, Hakim & Manni), Co & Ce 234 | 7 |
| 22 | 25 | 30 | 38 | WALKIN' MY CAT NAMED DOG — Norma Tanega (Herb Bernstein), New Voice 807 | 7 |
| 23 | 19 | 16 | 16 | BABY SCRATCH MY BACK — Slim Harpo, Excello 2273 | 11 |
| ★24 | 36 | 70 | — | A SIGN OF THE TIMES — Petula Clark (Tony Hatch), Warner Bros. 5802 | 3 |
| 25 | 24 | 20 | 21 | YOU BABY — Turtles (Banes Howe), White Whale 227 | 10 |
| 26 | 18 | 9 | 5 | ELUSIVE BUTTERFLY — Bob Lind (Richard Bock), World Pacific 77808 | 12 |
| 27 | 23 | 18 | 19 | SHAKE ME, WAKE ME (When It's Over) — Four Tops (Holland & Dozier), Motown 1090 | 8 |
| 28 | 17 | 10 | 6 | LISTEN PEOPLE — Herman's Hermits (Mickie Most), MGM 13462 | 8 |
| 29 | 43 | 53 | 68 | WHAT NOW MY LOVE — Herb Alpert & the Tijuana Brass (Herb Alpert), A&M 792 | 4 |
| ★30 | 37 | 45 | 55 | THINK I'LL GO SOMEWHERE AND CRY MYSELF TO SLEEP — Al Martino (Tom Morgan), Capitol 5598 | 5 |
| 31 | 41 | 55 | 66 | SPANISH FLEA — Herb Alpert & the Tijuana Brass (Herb Alpert), A&M 792 | 4 |
| 32 | 42 | 52 | 72 | SHAPES OF THINGS — Yardbirds (Giorgio Gomelsky), Epic 9891 | 4 |
| 33 | 26 | 23 | 28 | IT'S TOO LATE — Bobby Goldsboro (Jack Gold), United Artists 980 | 8 |
| 34 | 35 | 43 | 54 | SATISFACTION — Otis Redding (Jim Stewart & Steve Cropper), Volt 132 | 6 |
| ★35 | 68 | — | — | SLOOP JOHN B. — Beach Boys (Brian Wilson), Capitol 5602 | 2 |
| 36 | 51 | 58 | 73 | I HEAR TRUMPETS BLOW — Tokens (Big Time Prod.), B. T. Puppy 518 | 4 |
| 37 | 48 | 59 | 71 | SOMEWHERE — Len Barry (Madara-White), Decca 31923 | 4 |
| 38 | 38 | 36 | 36 | I WANT TO GO WITH YOU — Eddy Arnold (Chet Atkins), RCA Victor 8749 | 10 |
| 39 | 50 | 60 | 74 | FRANKIE AND JOHNNY — Elvis Presley, RCA Victor 8780 | 4 |
| 40 | 29 | 32 | 42 | GET READY — Temptations (Smokey Robinson), Gordy 7049 | 7 |
| 41 | 60 | 75 | 78 | GLORIA — Shadows of Knight (A Dunwich Prod.), Dunwich 116 | 4 |
| 42 | 44 | 44 | 48 | AIN'T THAT A GROOVE — James Brown & the Famous Flames (James Brown Prod.), King 6025 | 6 |
| 43 | 54 | 64 | 82 | THE PHOENIX LOVE THEME — Brass Ring (Phil Bodner), Dunhill 4023 | 5 |
| 44 | 34 | 41 | 46 | INSIDE—LOOKING OUT — Animals (Tom Wilson), MGM 13468 | 7 |
| 45 | 33 | 29 | 34 | ONE MORE HEARTACHE — Marvin Gaye (Smokey Robinson), Tamla 54129 | 8 |
| 46 | 30 | 19 | 9 | I FOUGHT THE LAW — Bobby Fuller 4 (Bob Keene), Mustang 3014 | 11 |
| 47 | 31 | 28 | 12 | THE CHEATER — Bob Kuban & the In-Men (Mel Friedman), Musicland, U.S.A. 20,001 | 11 |
| 48 | 58 | 69 | 85 | PLEASE DON'T STOP LOVING ME — Elvis Presley, RCA Victor 8780 | 4 |
| 49 | 49 | 57 | 75 | OUTSIDE THE GATES OF HEAVEN — Lou Christie (Nick Cenci), Co & Ce 235 | 6 |
| 50 | 47 | 50 | 56 | TIME — Pozo-Seco Singers, Columbia 43437 | 7 |
| 51 | 62 | 67 | 84 | ONE TRACK MIND — Knickerbockers (Jerry Fuller), Challenge 59326 | 4 |
| 52 | 32 | 31 | 31 | THE RAINS CAME — Sir Douglas Quintet (Huey P. Meaux), Tribe 8314 | 11 |
| 53 | 66 | 86 | — | TOGETHER AGAIN — Ray Charles (Sid Feller), ABC-Paramount 10785 | 3 |
| 54 | 65 | 80 | — | CAROLINE, NO — Brian Wilson (Brian Wilson), Capitol 5610 | 3 |
| 55 | 67 | 83 | — | RHAPSODY IN THE RAIN — Lou Christie (Charles Calello), MGM 13473 | 3 |
| 56 | 57 | 63 | 79 | HELPLESS — Kim Weston (Holland & Dozier), Gordy 7050 | 5 |
| 57 | 69 | 78 | — | YOUNG LOVE — Lesley Gore (Shelby Singleton), Mercury 72553 | 3 |
| 58 | 70 | 71 | 87 | MEMORIES ARE MADE OF THIS — Drifters (Bert Berns), Atlantic 2325 | 4 |
| 59 | 61 | 61 | 65 | THE LOVE YOU SAVE — Joe Tex (Buddy Killen), Dial 4026 | 6 |
| 60 | 56 | 56 | 61 | LULLABY OF LOVE — Poppies (Billy Sherrill), Epic 9893 | 6 |
| 61 | 86 | — | — | TRY TOO HARD — Dave Clark Five (Dave Clark), Epic 10004 | 2 |
| 62 | 64 | 48 | 53 | STOP HER ON SIGHT (S.O.S.) — Edwin Starr (Al Kent & Richard Morris), Ric-Tic 109 | 8 |
| 63 | 63 | 54 | 58 | SECRET AGENT MAN — Ventures (Joe Saraceno), Dolton 316 | 7 |
| ★64 | 79 | — | — | MESSAGE TO MICHAEL — Dionne Warwick (Blue Jac), Scepter 12133 | 2 |
| ★65 | — | — | — | LEANING ON THE LAMP POST — Herman's Hermits (Mickie Most), MGM 13500 | 1 |
| 66 | 71 | 72 | 83 | TIPPY TOEING — Harden Trio (Don Law & Frank Jones), Columbia 43463 | 5 |
| 67 | 75 | 81 | — | TILL THE END OF THE DAY — Kinks (Pye Records), Reprise 0454 | 3 |
| 68 | 59 | 65 | 70 | JUANITA BANANA — Peels (Howard-Smith), Karate 522 | 5 |
| 69 | 73 | 73 | 88 | FOLLOW ME — Lyme & Cybelle (Bones Howe), White Whale 228 | 4 |
| 70 | 81 | 89 | 89 | SHE BLEW A GOOD THING — Poets (Juggy Prod.), Symbol 214 | 4 |
| 71 | 80 | — | — | GOT MY MOJO WORKING — Jimmy Smith (Creed Taylor), Verve 10393 | 2 |
| 72 | 85 | 90 | — | SIPPIN' 'N' CHIPPIN' — T-Bones (Joe Saraceno), Liberty 55867 | 3 |
| 73 | 76 | 82 | — | HI HEEL SNEAKERS — Ramsey Lewis Trio (Esmond Edwards), Cadet 5531 | 3 |
| 74 | 74 | 85 | 86 | I CAN'T GROW PEACHES ON A CHERRY TREE — Just Us (Taylor-Gordoni), Colpix 803 | 5 |
| 75 | 83 | 92 | 97 | LOVE IS ME, LOVE IS YOU — Connie Francis (Danny Davis), MGM 13470 | 4 |
| 76 | 84 | 91 | 91 | I CAN'T LET GO — Hollies (Ron Richards), Imperial 66158 | 4 |
| 77 | 77 | 74 | 80 | I WANT SOMEONE — Mad Lads (Jim Stewart & Steve Cropper), Volt 131 | 6 |
| 78 | 90 | 94 | — | I'LL TAKE GOOD CARE OF YOU — Garnet Mimms (Jerry Ragovoy), United Artists 995 | 3 |
| ★79 | — | — | — | MONDAY, MONDAY — Mama's and the Papa's (Lou Adler), Dunhill 4026 | 1 |
| 80 | 87 | — | — | A LOVER'S CONCERTO — Sarah Vaughan (Luchi DeJesus), Mercury 72543 | 2 |
| 81 | 88 | — | — | KILLER JOE — Kingsmen (Jerden Prod.), Wand 1115 | 2 |
| 82 | — | — | — | HISTORY REPEATS ITSELF — Buddy Starcher (Chuck Glaser), Boone 1038 | 1 |
| 83 | — | — | — | I'M COMIN' HOME, CINDY — Trini Lopez (Don Costa), Reprise 0455 | 1 |
| 84 | — | — | — | HE CRIED — Shangri-Las (Shadow Morton), Red Bird 10053 | 1 |
| 85 | 96 | — | — | MAY MY HEART BE CAST INTO STONE — Toys (Randel-Linzer Prod.), DynoVoice 218 | 2 |
| 86 | 82 | 84 | — | I SURRENDER — Fontella Bass (Billy Davis), Checker 1137 | 3 |
| 87 | — | — | — | EIGHT MILES HIGH — Byrds (Allen Stanton), Columbia 43578 | 1 |
| 88 | — | — | — | DISTANT DRUMS — Jim Reeves (Chet Atkins), RCA Victor 8789 | 1 |
| 89 | 93 | — | — | PHILLY DOG — Mar-Keys (Jim Stewart), Stax 185 | 4 |
| 90 | — | 87 | 92 | DARLING BABY — Elgins (Holland & Dozier), V.I.P. 25029 | 3 |
| 91 | 92 | — | — | LA LA LA — Gerry & the Pacemakers, Laurie 3337 | 2 |
| 92 | — | — | — | REAL HUMDINGER — J. J. Barnes (Al Kent & Richard Morris), Ric-Tic 110 | 1 |
| 93 | 94 | — | — | TOO SLOW — Impressions (Johnny Pate), ABC-Paramount 10789 | 2 |
| 94 | 97 | — | — | NO MAN IS AN ISLAND — Van Dykes (Charles Stewart), Mala 520 | 2 |
| 95 | — | — | — | YOU'VE GOT MY MIND MESSED UP — James Carr, Goldwax 302 | 1 |
| 96 | — | — | — | BAND OF GOLD — Mel Carter (Nick DeCaro), Imperial 66165 | 1 |
| 97 | — | — | — | (I'm a) ROAD RUNNER — Jr. Walker & the All Stars (Holland-Dozier), Soul 35015 | 1 |
| 98 | — | — | — | I FEEL A SIN COMING ON — Solomon Burke (Jerry Wexler), Atlantic 2327 | 1 |
| 99 | 100 | — | — | I'M LIVING IN TWO WORLDS — Bonnie Guitar, Dot 16811 | 2 |
| 100 | — | — | — | WHEN A MAN LOVES A WOMAN — Percy Sledge (Quin Ivy), Atlantic 2326 | 1 |

## HOT 100—A TO Z–(Publisher-Licensee)

Ain't That a Groove (Dynatone, BMI) .. 42
Baby Scratch My Back (Excellorec, BMI) .. 23
Ballad of the Green Berets, The (Music, Music, Music, ASCAP) .. 5
Band of Gold (Ludlow, BMI) .. 96
Bang Bang (Five-West-Cotillion, BMI) .. 4
California Dreamin' (Trousdale, BMI) .. 10
Caroline, No (Sea of Tunes, BMI) .. 54
Cheater, The (MAM) .. 47
Darling Baby (Jobete, BMI) .. 90
Daydream (Faithful Virtue, BMI) .. 2
Distant Drums (Champion, BMI) .. 88
Eight Miles High (Tickson, BMI) .. 87
Elusive Butterfly (Metric, BMI) .. 26
Follow Me (Ishmael, BMI) .. 69
Frankie and Johnny (Gladys, ASCAP) .. 39
Get Ready (Jobete, BMI) .. 40
Gloria (Bernice, BMI) .. 41
Good Lovin' (T.M., BMI) .. 16
Got My Mojo Working (Arc, BMI) .. 71
Greetings (This Is Uncle Sam) .. 73
Hi Heel Sneakers (Medal, BMI) .. 73
History Repeats Itself (Eclectic, BMI) .. 82
Homeward Bound (Glaser, BMI) .. 12
I Can't Grow Peaches on a Cherry Tree (April, BMI) .. 74
I Can't Let Go (Blackwood, BMI) .. 76
I Feel a Sin Coming On (Painted Desert, BMI) .. 98
I Fought the Law (Acuff-Rose, BMI) .. 46
I Hear Trumpets Blow (Bright Tunes, BMI) .. 36
I Surrender (Chevis, BMI) .. 86
I Want Someone (East, BMI) .. 77
I Want to Go With You (Pamper, BMI) .. 38

I'll Take Good Care of You (Rittenhouse & Web IV, BMI) .. 78
(I'm a) Road Runner (Jobete, BMI) .. 97
I'm Comin' Home, Cindy (Trousdale, BMI) .. 83
I'm Living in Two Worlds (Trousdale, BMI) .. 99
I'm So Lonesome I Could Cry (Acuff-Rose, BMI) .. 8
Inside—Looking Out (Ludlow, BMI) .. 44
It's Too Late (Unart, BMI) .. 33
Juanita Banana (Tash, BMI) .. 68
Kicks (Screen Gems-Columbia, BMI) .. 18
Killer Joe (White Castle, BMI) .. 81
La La La (Pacemaker, BMI) .. 91
Leaning on the Lamp Post (Not Available, BMI) .. 65
Little Latin Lupe Lu (Maxwell-Conrad, BMI) .. 17
Listen People (New World, ASCAP) .. 28
Love Is Me, Love Is You (Duchess, BMI) .. 75
Love Makes the World Go Round (McLaughlin, BMI) .. 20
Love You Save, The (Tree, BMI) .. 59
Lover's Concerto, A (Saturday, BMI) .. 80
Lullaby of Love (Tree, BMI) .. 60
Magic Town (Screen Gems-Columbia, BMI) .. 21
May My Heart Be Cast Into Stone (Saturday, BMI) .. 85
Memories Are Made of This (Blackwood, BMI) .. 58
Message to Michael (U. S. Songs, ASCAP) .. 64
Monday, Monday (Trousdale, BMI) .. 79
19th Nervous Breakdown (Gideon, BMI) .. 3
No Man Is an Island (Cha-Stew, BMI) .. 94
Nowhere Man (Maclen, BMI) .. 6
One More Heartache (Jobete, BMI) .. 45
One Track Mind (4-Star, BMI) .. 51
Outside the Gates of Heaven (Rambed, BMI) .. 49
Philly Dog (East, BMI) .. 89
Phoenix Love Theme, The (Ludlow, BMI) .. 43
Please Don't Stop Loving Me (Presley, BMI) .. 48
Rains Came, The (Crazy Cajun & Corett, BMI) .. 52
Real Humdinger (Myto, BMI) .. 92

Rhapsody in the Rain (Rambed, BMI) .. 55
Satisfaction (Immediate, BMI) .. 34
Secret Agent Man—Rivers (Trousdale, BMI) .. 7
Secret Agent Man—Ventures (Trousdale, BMI) .. 63
Shake Me, Wake Me When It's Over (Jobete, BMI) .. 27
Shapes of Things (Unart, BMI) .. 32
She Blew a Good Thing (Sagittarius, BMI) .. 70
Sign of the Times, A (Duchess, BMI) .. 24
Sippin' 'n' Chippin' (C-Shar, BMI) .. 72
634-5789 (East-Pronto, BMI) .. 13
Sloop John B (New Executive, BMI) .. 35
Somewhere (Schirmer, ASCAP) .. 37
Spanish Flea (Almo, ASCAP) .. 31
Stop Her on Sight (S.O.S.) (Myto, BMI) .. 62
Sure Gonna Miss Her (Viva-Tennessee, BMI) .. 9
These Boots Are Made for Walkin' (Criterion, ASCAP) .. 14
Think I'll Go Somewhere and Cry Myself to Sleep (Mose Rose, BMI) .. 30
This Old Heart of Mine (Jobete, BMI) .. 15
Till the End of the Day (Noma, BMI) .. 67
Time (Regent, BMI) .. 50
Time Won't Let Me (Beechwood, BMI) .. 11
Tippy Toeing (Window, BMI) .. 66
Together Again (Central, BMI) .. 53
Too Slow (Chi-Sound, BMI) .. 93
Try Too Hard (Branston, BMI) .. 61
Walkin' My Cat Named Dog (Starday, BMI) .. 22
What Now My Love (Remick, ASCAP) .. 29
When a Man Loves a Woman (Pronto-Quinvy, BMI) .. 100
Woman (Maclen, BMI) .. 19
You Baby (Trousdale, BMI) .. 25
Young Love (Lowery, BMI) .. 57
(You're My) Soul and Inspiration (Screen Gems-Columbia, BMI) .. 1
You've Got My Mind Messed Up (Rise, BMI) .. 95

## BUBBLING UNDER THE HOT 100

101. GOOD, GOOD LOVIN' .............. Blossoms, Reprise 0436
102. PIN THE TAIL ON THE DONKEY ... Paul Peek, Columbia 43527
103. TOO YOUNG ............................. Tommy Vann, Academy 118
104. STOP! ........................................ Moody Blues, London 9810
105. A GROOVY KIND OF LOVE ..... Mindbenders, Fontana 1541
106. WANG DANG DOODLE .......... Ko Ko Taylor, Checker 1135
107. I SPY ........................................... Jamo Thomas, Thomas 303
108. GLORIA ..................................... Them, Parrot 9727
109. LET'S START ALL OVER AGAIN ... Ronnie Dove, Diamond 198
110. SHARING YOU .......................... Mitty Collier, Chess 1953
111. LOVE ME WITH ALL YOUR HEART ... Bachelors, London 9828
112. BABY I NEED YOU ...................... Manhattans, Carnival 514
113. DOUBLE SHOT (Of My Baby's Love) ... Swingin' Medallions, Smash 2033
114. FOR YOUR PRECIOUS LOVE ... Jerry Butler, Vee Jay 715
115. RAGS TO RICHES ...................... Lenny Welch, Kapp 740
116. EVOL-NOT LOVE ...................... Five Americans, HBR 468
117. THE BIG HURT ........................... Del Shannon, Liberty 55866
118. DON'T PUSH ME ....................... Hedgehoppers Anonymous, Parrot 9817
119. (I'm Just a) FOOL FOR YOU .... Gene Chandler, Constellation 167
120. DIRTY WATER ........................... Standells, Tower 185
121. GREETINGS (This Is Uncle Sam) ... Monitors, VIP 25032
122. 3,000 MILES .............................. Brian Hyland, Philips 40354
123. TOO LITTLE TIME ..................... Brenda Lee, Decca 31917
124. NIGHT TIME GIRL .................... Dallas Frazier, Capitol 5560
125. RAINY DAY WOMEN NO. 12 & 35 ... Bob Dylan, Columbia 43592
126. VIET NAM BLUES ...................... Dave Dudley, Mercury 72550
127. LOUIE LOUIE ............................. Travis Wammack, Atlantic 2322
128. SECOND-HAND MAN ............. Back Porch Majority, Epic 9879
129. HISTORY REPEATS ITSELF ..... Cab Calloway, Boom 60,606
130. WHEN SHE TOUCHES ME ...... Rodge Martin, Bragg 227
131. FROM NASHVILLE WITH LOVE ... Chet Atkins, RCA Victor 8781
132. (You're My) SOUL AND INSPIRATION ... Screen Gems-Columbia, BMI 1
133. DOIN' THE PHILLY DOG ......... Lou Lawton, Capitol 5613
134. BAREFOOTIN' ........................... Robert Parker, Nola 721

Compiled from national retail sales and radio station airplay by the Music Popularity Dept. of Record Market Research, Billboard.

# Billboard HOT 100

**For Week Ending April 16, 1966**

★ STAR performer—Sides registering greatest proportionate upward progress this week.

| TW | LW | 2W | 3W | TITLE – Artist (Producer), Label & Number | WOC |
|---|---|---|---|---|---|
| 1 | 1 | 3 | 8 | (You're My) SOUL AND INSPIRATION – Righteous Brothers (Bill Medley), Verve 10383 | 7 |
| 2 | 2 | 4 | 6 | DAYDREAM – Lovin' Spoonful (Erik Jacobsen), Kama Sutra 208 | 8 |
| 3 | 4 | 9 | 17 | BANG BANG – Cher (Sonny Bono), Imperial 66160 | 6 |
| 4 | 7 | 15 | 22 | SECRET AGENT MAN – Johnny Rivers (Lou Adler), Imperial 66159 | 5 |
| 5 | 11 | 16 | 21 | TIME WON'T LET ME – Outsiders (Tom King), Capitol 5573 | 9 |
| 6 | 3 | 2 | 2 | 19TH NERVOUS BREAKDOWN – Rolling Stones (Andrew Loog Oldham), London 9823 | 8 |
| 7 | 5 | 1 | 1 | THE BALLAD OF THE GREEN BERETS – S/Sgt. Barry Sadler (Andy Wiswell), RCA Victor 8739 | 11 |
| 8 | 8 | 11 | 12 | I'M SO LONESOME I COULD CRY – B.J. Thomas and the Triumphs (Music Enterprises Productions), Scepter 12129 | 9 |
| 9 | 16 | 27 | 40 | GOOD LOVIN' – Young Rascals (Tom Dowd, Arif Mardin), Atlantic 2321 | 6 |
| 10 | 18 | 28 | 29 | KICKS – Paul Revere & the Raiders (Terry Melcher), Columbia 43556 | 5 |
| 11 | 6 | 6 | 3 | NOWHERE MAN – Beatles (George Martin), Capitol 5587 | 7 |
| 12 | 9 | 10 | 14 | SURE GONNA MISS HER – Gary Lewis & the Playboys (Snuff Garrett), Liberty 55865 | 7 |
| 13 | 35 | 68 | — | SLOOP JOHN B – Beach Boys (Brian Wilson), Capitol 5602 | 3 |
| 14 | 24 | 36 | 70 | A SIGN OF THE TIMES – Petula Clark (Tony Hatch), Warner Bros. 5802 | 4 |
| 15 | 15 | 20 | 25 | THIS OLD HEART OF MINE – Isley Brothers (Holland & Dozier), Tamla 54128 | 9 |
| 16 | 10 | 7 | 7 | CALIFORNIA DREAMIN' – Mama's and Papa's (Lou Adler), Dunhill 4020 | 15 |
| 17 | 17 | 22 | 27 | LITTLE LATIN LUPE LU – Mitch Ryder & the Detroit Wheels (Bob Crewe), New Voice 806 | 7 |
| 18 | 19 | 14 | 15 | WOMAN – Peter & Gordon (Peter Asher), Capitol 5579 | 10 |
| 19 | 12 | 5 | 5 | HOMEWARD BOUND – Simon & Garfunkel (Bob Johnston), Columbia 43511 | 10 |
| 20 | 14 | 8 | 4 | THESE BOOTS ARE MADE FOR WALKIN' – Nancy Sinatra (Lee Hazlewood), Reprise 0432 | 13 |
| 21 | 13 | 13 | 13 | 634-5789 – Wilson Pickett (Jim Stewart & Steve Cropper), Atlantic 2320 | 10 |
| 22 | 41 | 60 | 75 | GLORIA – Shadows of Knight (A Dunwich Prod.), Dunwich 116 | 5 |
| 23 | 32 | 42 | 52 | SHAPES OF THINGS – Yardbirds (Giorgio Gomelsky), Epic 9891 | 5 |
| 24 | 22 | 25 | 30 | WALKIN' MY CAT NAMED DOG – Norma Tanega (Herb Bernstein), New Voice 807 | 8 |
| 25 | 29 | 43 | 53 | WHAT NOW MY LOVE – Herb Alpert & the Tijuana Brass (Herb Alpert), A&M 792 | 5 |
| 26 | 37 | 48 | 59 | SOMEWHERE – Len Barry (Madara-White), Decca 31923 | 5 |
| 27 | 31 | 41 | 55 | SPANISH FLEA – Herb Alpert & the Tijuana Brass (Herb Alpert), A&M 792 | 5 |
| 28 | 39 | 50 | 60 | FRANKIE AND JOHNNY – Elvis Presley, RCA Victor 8780 | 5 |
| 29 | 65 | — | — | LEANING ON THE LAMP POST – Herman's Hermits (Mickie Most), MGM 13500 | 2 |
| 30 | 30 | 37 | 45 | THINK I'LL GO SOMEWHERE AND CRY MYSELF TO SLEEP – Al Martino (Tom Morgan), Capitol 5598 | 6 |
| 31 | 34 | 35 | 43 | SATISFACTION – Otis Redding (Jim Stewart & Steve Cropper), Volt 132 | 7 |
| 32 | 21 | 21 | 26 | MAGIC TOWN – Vogues (Cenci, Hakim & Mann), Co & Ce 234 | 8 |
| 33 | 36 | 51 | 58 | I HEAR TRUMPETS BLOW – Tokens (Big Time Prod.), B.T. Puppy 518 | 5 |
| 34 | 79 | — | — | MONDAY, MONDAY – Mama's and the Papa's (Lou Adler), Dunhill 4026 | 2 |
| 35 | 23 | 19 | 16 | BABY SCRATCH MY BACK – Slim Harpo, Excello 2273 | 12 |
| 36 | 20 | 12 | 11 | LOVE MAKES THE WORLD GO ROUND – Deon Jackson (Ollie McLaughlin), Carla 2526 | 13 |
| 37 | 53 | 66 | 86 | TOGETHER AGAIN – Ray Charles (Sid Feller), ABC-Paramount 10785 | 4 |
| 38 | 43 | 54 | 64 | THE PHOENIX LOVE THEME – Brass Ring (Phil Bodner), Dunhill 4023 | 6 |
| 39 | 25 | 24 | 20 | YOU BABY – Turtles (Bones Howe), White Whale 227 | 11 |
| 40 | 27 | 23 | 18 | SHAKE ME, WAKE ME (When It's Over) – Four Tops (Holland & Dozier), Motown 1090 | 9 |
| 41 | 55 | 67 | 83 | RHAPSODY IN THE RAIN – Lou Christie (Charles Calello), MGM 13473 | 4 |
| 42 | 64 | 79 | — | MESSAGE TO MICHAEL – Dionne Warwick (Blue Jac), Scepter 12133 | 3 |
| 43 | 61 | 86 | — | TRY TOO HARD – Dave Clark Five (Dave Clark), Epic 10004 | 3 |
| 44 | 26 | 18 | 9 | ELUSIVE BUTTERFLY – Bob Lind (Richard Bock), World Pacific 77808 | 13 |
| 45 | 49 | 49 | 57 | OUTSIDE THE GATES OF HEAVEN – Lou Christie (Nick Cenci), Co & Ce 229 | 7 |
| 46 | 48 | 58 | 69 | PLEASE DON'T STOP LOVING ME – Elvis Presley, RCA Victor 8780 | 5 |
| 47 | 54 | 65 | 80 | CAROLINE, NO – Brian Wilson (Brian Wilson), Capitol 5610 | 4 |
| 48 | 51 | 62 | 67 | ONE TRACK MIND – Knickerbockers (Jerry Fuller), Challenge 59326 | 5 |
| 49 | 28 | 17 | 10 | LISTEN PEOPLE – Herman's Hermits (Mickie Most), MGM 13462 | 9 |
| 50 | 42 | 44 | 44 | AIN'T THAT A GROOVE – James Brown & the Famous Flames (James Brown Prod.), King 6025 | 4 |
| 51 | 66 | 71 | 72 | TIPPY TOEING – Harden Trio (Don Law & Frank Jones), Columbia 43463 | 6 |
| 52 | 57 | 69 | 78 | YOUNG LOVE – Lesley Gore (Shelby Singleton), Mercury 72553 | 4 |
| 53 | 87 | — | — | EIGHT MILES HIGH – Byrds (Allen Stanton), Columbia 43578 | 2 |
| 54 | 58 | 70 | 71 | MEMORIES ARE MADE OF THIS – Drifters (Bert Berns), Atlantic 2325 | 5 |
| 55 | 38 | 38 | 36 | I WANT TO GO WITH YOU – Eddy Arnold (Chet Atkins), RCA Victor 8749 | 11 |
| 56 | 59 | 61 | 61 | THE LOVE YOU SAVE – Joe Tex (Buddy Killen), Dial 4026 | 4 |
| 57 | 78 | 90 | 94 | I'LL TAKE GOOD CARE OF YOU – Garnet Mimms (Jerry Ragovoy), United Artists 995 | 4 |
| 58 | 56 | 57 | 63 | HELPLESS – Kim Weston (Holland & Dozier), Gordy 7050 | 6 |
| 59 | 74 | 74 | 85 | I CAN'T GROW PEACHES ON A CHERRY TREE – Just Us (Taylor-Gordeal), Colpix 803 | 6 |
| 60 | 76 | 84 | 91 | I CAN'T LET GO – Hollies (Ron Richards), Imperial 66158 | 5 |
| 61 | 67 | 75 | 81 | TILL THE END OF THE DAY – Kinks (Pye Records), Reprise 0454 | 4 |
| 62 | 72 | 85 | 90 | SIPPIN' 'N' CHIPPIN' – T-Bones (Joe Saraceno), Liberty 55867 | 4 |
| 63 | 70 | 81 | 89 | SHE BLEW A GOOD THING – Roots (Juggy Prod.), Symbol 214 | 5 |
| 64 | 83 | — | — | I'M COMIN' HOME, CINDY – Trini Lopez (Don Costa), Reprise 0455 | 2 |
| 65 | 69 | 73 | 73 | FOLLOW ME – Lyme & Cybelle (Bones Howe), White Whale 228 | 4 |
| 66 | 75 | 83 | 92 | LOVE IS ME, LOVE IS YOU – Connie Francis (Danny Davis), MGM 13470 | 5 |
| 67 | 68 | 59 | 65 | JUANITA BANANA – Peels (Howard-Smith), Karate 522 | 6 |
| 68 | 71 | 80 | — | GOT MY MOJO WORKING – Jimmy Smith (Creed Taylor), Verve 10393 | 3 |
| 69 | 82 | — | — | HISTORY REPEATS ITSELF – Buddy Starcher (Chuck Glaser), Boone 1038 | 2 |
| 70 | 73 | 76 | 82 | HI HEEL SNEAKERS – Ramsey Lewis Trio (Esmond Edwards), Cadet 5531 | 4 |
| 71 | — | — | — | RAINY DAY WOMAN #12 & 35 – Bob Dylan (Bob Johnston), Columbia 43592 | 1 |
| 72 | — | — | — | NOTHING'S TOO GOOD FOR MY BABY – Stevie Wonder (Wm. Stevenson), Tamla 54130 | 1 |
| 73 | 100 | — | — | WHEN A MAN LOVES A WOMAN – Percy Sledge (Quin Ivy), Atlantic 2326 | 2 |
| 74 | 80 | 87 | — | A LOVER'S CONCERTO – Sarah Vaughan (Luchi DeJesus), Mercury 72543 | 3 |
| 75 | 84 | — | — | HE CRIED – Shangri-Las (Shadow Morton), Red Bird 10053 | 2 |
| 76 | 88 | — | — | DISTANT DRUMS – Jim Reeves (Chet Atkins), RCA Victor 8789 | 2 |
| 77 | 81 | 88 | — | KILLER JOE – Kingsmen (Jerden Prod.), Wand 1115 | 3 |
| 78 | — | — | — | A GROOVY KIND OF LOVE – Mindbenders, Fontana 1541 | 1 |
| 79 | — | — | — | LOVE ME WITH ALL YOUR HEART – Bachelors, London 9829 | 1 |
| 80 | 96 | — | — | BAND OF GOLD – Mel Carter (Nick DeCaro), Imperial 66165 | 2 |
| 81 | — | — | — | LOVE'S MADE A FOOL OF YOU – Bobby Fuller Four (A Stereo-Fi Prod.), Mustang 816 | 1 |
| 82 | — | — | — | THE BALLAD OF IRVING – Frank Gallop (Booker-Foster), Kapp 45 | 1 |
| 83 | — | — | — | LET'S START ALL OVER AGAIN – Ronnie Dove (Kahl-Vernon), Diamond 198 | 1 |
| 84 | — | — | — | THE SUN AIN'T GONNA SHINE – Walker Brothers, Smash 2032 | 1 |
| 85 | 85 | 96 | — | MAY MY HEART BE CAST INTO STONE – Toys (Randell-Linzer Prod.), DynoVoice 218 | 3 |
| 86 | 86 | 82 | 84 | I SURRENDER – Fontella Bass (Billy Davis), Checker 1137 | 4 |
| 87 | 90 | — | 87 | DARLING BABY – Elgins (Holland & Dozier), V.I.P. 25029 | 4 |
| 88 | 92 | — | — | REAL HUMDINGER – J.J. Barnes (Al Kent & Richard Morris), Ric-Tic 110 | 2 |
| 89 | 89 | 93 | — | PHILLY DOG – Mar-Keys (Jim Stewart), Stax 185 | 3 |
| 90 | 91 | 92 | — | LA LA LA – Gerry & the Pacemakers, Laurie 2237 | 3 |
| 91 | 93 | 94 | — | TOO SLOW – Impressions (Johnny Pate), ABC-Paramount 10789 | 3 |
| 92 | — | — | — | EVOL-NOT LOVE – Five Americans (A Bank Music Prod.), HBR 448 | 1 |
| 93 | — | — | — | PIN THE TAIL ON THE DONKEY – Paul Peek (Joe South), Columbia 43527 | 1 |
| 94 | 97 | — | — | (I'm a) ROAD RUNNER – Jr. Walker and the All Stars (Holland-Dozier), Soul 35015 | 2 |
| 95 | 95 | — | — | YOU'VE GOT MY MIND MESSED UP – James Carr, Goldwax 302 | 2 |
| 96 | — | — | — | HISTORY REPEATS ITSELF – Cab Calloway (Bob Thiele), Boom 60,006 | 1 |
| 97 | 98 | — | — | I FEEL A SIN COMING ON – Solomon Burke (Jerry Wexler), Atlantic 2327 | 2 |
| 98 | — | — | — | THE MORE I SEE YOU – Chris Montez (Herb Alpert), A&M 796 | 1 |
| 99 | — | — | — | 3,000 MILES – Phillips 40254 | 1 |
| 100 | — | — | — | GREETINGS (This Is Uncle Sam) – Monitors (Wm. Stevenson & Henry Cosby), V.I.P. 25032 | 1 |

## BUBBLING UNDER THE HOT 100

101. WANG DANG DOODLE – Koko Taylor, Checker 1135
102. DOUBLE SHOT (Of My Baby's Love) – Swinging Medallions, Smash 2033
103. TOO YOUNG – Tommy Vann, Academy 116
104. COOL JERK – Capitols, Karen 1524
105. GOOD, GOOD LOVIN' – Blossoms, Reprise 0436
106. SHARING YOU – Mitty Collier, Chess 1953
107. GLORIA – Them, Parrot 9727
108. NO MAN IS AN ISLAND – Van Dykes, Mala 530
109. I'M LIVING IN TWO WORLDS – Bonnie Guitar, Dot 16811
110. DON'T PUSH ME – Hedgehoppers Anonymous, Parrot 9815
111. DIRTY WATER – Standells, Tower 185
112. BAD EYE – Willie Mitchell, Hi 2100
113. THE BIG HURT – Del Shannon, Liberty 55866
114. I'M SATISFIED – Otis Clay, One-Derful 3146
115. SOMEBODY TO LOVE ME – Renny & the Daytonas, Mala 525
116. THE TEASER – Bob Kuban & the In-Men, Musicland, U.S.A. 20,006
117. THE CRUEL WAR – Peter, Paul & Mary, Warner Bros. 5809
118. BAREFOOTIN' – Robert Parker, Nola 721
119. COME ON LET'S GO – McCoys, Bang 522
120. THE CRUEL WAR – Chad & Jill Stuart, Columbia 43567
121. I LIE AWAKE – New Colony Six, Centaur 1202
122. NIGHT TIME GIRL – Modern Folk Quintet, Dunhill 4025
123. ELVIRA – Dallas Frazier, Capitol 5560
124. MARBLE BREAKS AND IRON BENDS – Drafi, London 10025
125. BETTER MAN THAN I – Terry Knight and the Pack, Lucky 11 236
126. MARBLE BREAKS AND IRON BENDS – Drafi, London 10025

Compiled from national retail sales and radio station airplay by the Music Popularity Dept. of Record Market Research, Billboard.

# Billboard HOT 100

For Week Ending April 23, 1966

★ STAR performer—Sides registering greatest proportionate upward progress this week.

● Record Industry Association of America seal of certification as million selling single.

| This Week | Wks. Ago 1 | Wks. Ago 2 | Wks. Ago 3 | TITLE Artist (Producer), Label & Number | Weeks On Chart |
|---|---|---|---|---|---|
| 1 | 1 | 1 | 3 | **(You're My) SOUL AND INSPIRATION** — Righteous Brothers (Bill Medley), Verve 10383 | 8 |
| 2 | 3 | 4 | 9 | **BANG BANG** — Cher (Sonny Bono), Imperial 66160 | 7 |
| 3 | 4 | 7 | 15 | **SECRET AGENT MAN** — Johnny Rivers (Lou Adler), Imperial 66159 | 6 |
| 4 | 2 | 2 | 4 | **DAYDREAM** — Lovin' Spoonful (Erik Jacobson), Kama Sutra 208 | 9 |
| 5 | 5 | 11 | 16 | **TIME WON'T LET ME** — Outsiders (Tom King), Capitol 5573 | 10 |
| 6 | 9 | 16 | 27 | **GOOD LOVIN'** — Young Rascals (Tom Dowd, Arif Mardin), Atlantic 2321 | 7 |
| 7 | 10 | 18 | 28 | **KICKS** — Paul Revere & the Raiders (Terry Melcher), Columbia 43556 | 6 |
| 8 | 13 | 35 | 68 | **SLOOP JOHN B** — Beach Boys (Brian Wilson), Capitol 5602 | 4 |
| 9 | 8 | 8 | 11 | **I'M SO LONESOME I COULD CRY** — B. J. Thomas and the Triumphs (Music Enterprises Productions), Scepter 12129 | 10 |
| 10 | 34 | 79 | — | **MONDAY, MONDAY** — Mama's and the Papa's (Lou Adler), Dunhill 4026 | 3 |
| 11 | 14 | 24 | 36 | **A SIGN OF THE TIMES** — Petula Clark (Tony Hatch), Warner Bros. 5802 | 5 |
| 12 | 15 | 15 | 20 | **THIS OLD HEART OF MINE** — Isley Brothers (Holland & Dozier), Tamla 54128 | 10 |
| 13 | 11 | 6 | 6 | **NOWHERE MAN** — Beatles (George Martin), Capitol 5587 | 8 |
| 14 | 6 | 3 | 2 | **19TH NERVOUS BREAKDOWN** — Rolling Stones (Andrew Loog Oldham), London 9823 | 9 |
| 15 | 29 | 65 | — | **LEANING ON THE LAMP POST** — Herman's Hermits (Mickie Most), MGM 13500 | 3 |
| 16 | 22 | 41 | 60 | **GLORIA** — Shadows of Knight (A Dunwich Prod.), Dunwich 116 | 6 |
| 17 | 7 | 5 | 1 | **THE BALLAD OF THE GREEN BERETS** — S/Sgt. Barry Sadler (Andy Wiswell), RCA Victor 8739 | 12 |
| 18 | 23 | 32 | 42 | **SHAPES OF THINGS** — Yardbirds (Giorgio Gomelsky), Epic 9891 | 6 |
| 19 | 16 | 10 | 7 | **CALIFORNIA DREAMIN'** — Mama's and the Papa's (Lou Adler), Dunhill 4020 | 16 |
| 20 | 17 | 17 | 22 | **LITTLE LATIN LUPE LU** — Mitch Ryder and the Detroit Wheels (Bob Crewe), New Voice 808 | 8 |
| 21 | 12 | 9 | 10 | **SURE GONNA MISS HER** — Gary Lewis & the Playboys (Snuff Garrett), Liberty 55865 | 8 |
| 22 | 19 | 12 | 5 | **HOMEWARD BOUND** — Simon & Garfunkel (Bob Johnston), Columbia 43511 | 11 |
| 23 | 18 | 19 | 14 | **WOMAN** — Peter & Gordon, Capitol 5579 | 11 |
| 24 | 25 | 29 | 43 | **WHAT NOW MY LOVE** — Herb Alpert & the Tijuana Brass (Herb Alpert), A&M 792 | 6 |
| 25 | 43 | 61 | 86 | **TRY TOO HARD** — Dave Clark Five (Dave Clark), Epic 10004 | 4 |
| 26 | 26 | 37 | 48 | **SOMEWHERE** — Len Barry (Madara-White), Decca 31923 | 6 |
| 27 | 27 | 31 | 41 | **SPANISH FLEA** — Herb Alpert & the Tijuana Brass (Herb Alpert), A&M 792 | 6 |
| 28 | 28 | 39 | 50 | **FRANKIE AND JOHNNY** — Elvis Presley, RCA Victor 8780 | 6 |
| 29 | 37 | 53 | 66 | **TOGETHER AGAIN** — Ray Charles (Sid Feller), ABC-Paramount 10785 | 5 |
| 30 | 33 | 36 | 51 | **I HEAR TRUMPETS BLOW** — Tokens (Big Time Prod.), B. T. Puppy 518 | 6 |
| 31 | 41 | 55 | 67 | **RHAPSODY IN THE RAIN** — Lou Christie (Charles Calello), MGM 13473 | 5 |
| 32 | 42 | 64 | 79 | **MESSAGE TO MICHAEL** — Dionne Warwick (Blue Jac), Scepter 12133 | 4 |
| 33 | 21 | 13 | 13 | **634-5789** — Wilson Pickett (Jim Stewart & Steve Cropper), Atlantic 2320 | 11 |
| 34 | 20 | 14 | 8 | **THESE BOOTS ARE MADE FOR WALKIN'** — Nancy Sinatra (Lee Hazlewood), Reprise 0432 | 14 |
| 35 | 38 | 43 | 54 | **THE PHOENIX LOVE THEME** — Brass Ring (Phil Bodner), Dunhill 4023 | 7 |
| 36 | 24 | 22 | 25 | **WALKIN' MY CAT NAMED DOG** — Norma Tanega (Herb Bernstein), New Voice 807 | 9 |
| 37 | 47 | 54 | 65 | **CAROLINE, NO** — Brian Wilson (Brian Wilson), Capitol 5610 | 5 |
| 38 | 71 | — | — | **RAINY DAY WOMEN #12 & 35** — Bob Dylan (Bob Johnston), Columbia 43592 | 2 |
| 39 | 32 | 21 | 21 | **MAGIC TOWN** — Vogues (Cenci, Hakim & Mann), Co & Ce 234 | 9 |
| 40 | 30 | 30 | 37 | **THINK I'LL GO SOMEWHERE AND CRY MYSELF TO SLEEP** — Al Martino (Tom Morgan), Capitol 5598 | 7 |
| 41 | 39 | 25 | 24 | **YOU BABY** — Turtles (Banes Howe), White Whale 227 | 12 |
| 42 | 53 | 87 | — | **EIGHT MILES HIGH** — Byrds (Allen Stanton), Columbia 43578 | 3 |
| 43 | 35 | 23 | 19 | **BABY SCRATCH MY BACK** — Slim Harpo, Excello 2273 | 13 |
| 44 | 36 | 20 | 12 | **LOVE MAKES THE WORLD GO ROUND** — Deon Jackson (Ollie McLaughlin), Carla 2526 | 14 |
| 45 | 46 | 48 | 58 | **PLEASE DON'T STOP LOVING ME** — Elvis Presley, RCA Victor 8780 | 6 |
| 46 | 48 | 51 | 62 | **ONE TRACK MIND** — Knickerbockers (Jerry Fuller), Challenge 59326 | 6 |
| 47 | 31 | 34 | 35 | **SATISFACTION** — Otis Redding (Jim Stewart & Steve Cropper), Volt 132 | 8 |
| 48 | 54 | 58 | 70 | **MEMORIES ARE MADE OF THIS** — Drifters (Bert Berns), Atlantic 2325 | 6 |
| 49 | — | — | — | **HOW DOES THAT GRAB YOU DARLIN'** — Nancy Sinatra (Lee Hazelwood), Reprise 0461 | 1 |
| 50 | 52 | 57 | 69 | **YOUNG LOVE** — Lesley Gore (Shelby Singleton), Mercury 72553 | 4 |
| 51 | 51 | 66 | 71 | **TIPPY TOEING** — Harden Trio (Don Law & Frank Jones), Columbia 43463 | 7 |
| 52 | 78 | — | — | **A GROOVY KIND OF LOVE** — Mindbenders, Fontana 1541 | 2 |
| 53 | 73 | 100 | — | **WHEN A MAN LOVES A WOMAN** — Percy Sledge (Quin Ivy), Atlantic 2326 | 3 |
| 54 | 64 | 83 | — | **I'M COMIN' HOME, CINDY** — Trini Lopez (Don Costa), Reprise 0455 | 3 |
| 55 | 59 | 74 | 74 | **I CAN'T GROW PEACHES ON A CHERRY TREE** — Just Us (Taylor-Gordoni), Colpix 803 | 7 |
| 56 | 57 | 78 | 90 | **I'LL TAKE GOOD CARE OF YOU** — Garnet Mimms (Jerry Ragevoy), United Artists 995 | 5 |
| 57 | 63 | 70 | 81 | **SHE BLEW A GOOD THING** — Poets (Juggy Prod.), Symbol 214 | 6 |
| 58 | 60 | 76 | 84 | **I CAN'T LET GO** — Hollies (Ron Richards), Imperial 66158 | 6 |
| 59 | 69 | 82 | — | **HISTORY REPEATS ITSELF** — Buddy Starcher (Chuck Glaser), Boone 1038 | 3 |
| 60 | 72 | — | — | **NOTHING'S TOO GOOD FOR MY BABY** — Stevie Wonder (Wm. Stevenson), Tamla 54130 | 2 |
| 61 | 61 | 67 | 75 | **TILL THE END OF THE DAY** — Kinks (Pye Records), Reprise 0454 | 6 |
| 62 | 81 | — | — | **LOVE'S MADE A FOOL OF YOU** — Bobby Fuller Four (A Stereo-Fi Prod.), Mustang 016 | 2 |
| 63 | 56 | 59 | 61 | **THE LOVE YOU SAVE** — Joe Tex (Buddy Killen), Dial 4026 | 8 |
| 64 | 58 | 56 | 57 | **HELPLESS** — Kim Weston (Holland & Dozier), Gordy 7050 | 7 |
| 65 | 84 | — | — | **THE SUN AIN'T GONNA SHINE** — Walker Brothers, Smash 2032 | 2 |
| 66 | 82 | — | — | **THE BALLAD OF IRVING** — Frank Gallop (Booker-Foster), Kapp 45 | 2 |
| 67 | 68 | 71 | 80 | **GOT MY MOJO WORKING** — Jimmy Smith (Creed Taylor), Verve 10393 | 4 |
| 68 | 83 | — | — | **LET'S START ALL OVER AGAIN** — Ronnie Dove (Kahl-Vernon), Diamond 198 | 2 |
| 69 | 45 | 49 | 49 | **OUTSIDE THE GATES OF HEAVEN** — Lou Christie (Nick Cenci), Co & Ce 235 | 8 |
| 70 | 75 | 84 | — | **HE CRIED** — Shangri-Las (Shadow Morton), Red Bird 10053 | 3 |
| 71 | 80 | 96 | — | **BAND OF GOLD** — Mel Carter (Nick DeCaro), Imperial 66165 | 3 |
| 72 | 79 | — | — | **LOVE ME WITH ALL YOUR HEART** — Bachelors, London 9829 | 2 |
| 73 | 74 | 80 | 87 | **A LOVER'S CONCERTO** — Sarah Vaughan (Luchi DeJesus), Mercury 72543 | 4 |
| 74 | 70 | 73 | 76 | **HI HEEL SNEAKERS** — Ramsey Lewis Trio (Esmond Edwards), Cadet 5531 | 5 |
| 75 | 76 | 88 | — | **DISTANT DRUMS** — Jim Reeves (Chet Atkins), RCA Victor 8789 | 3 |
| 76 | 62 | 72 | 85 | **SIPPIN' 'N' CHIPPIN'** — T-Bones (Joe Saraceno), Liberty 55867 | 4 |
| 77 | 66 | 75 | 83 | **LOVE IS ME, LOVE IS YOU** — Connie Francis (Danny Davis), MGM 13470 | 6 |
| 78 | 86 | 86 | 82 | **I SURRENDER** — Fontella Bass (Billy Davis), Checker 1137 | 5 |
| 79 | — | — | — | **THE "A" TEAM** — S/Sgt. Barry Sadler (Andy Wiswell), RCA Victor 8804 | 1 |
| 80 | 65 | 69 | 73 | **FOLLOW ME** — Lyme & Cybelle (Bones Howe), White Whale 228 | 6 |
| 81 | 94 | 97 | — | **(I'm a) ROAD RUNNER** — Jr. Walker and the All Stars (Holland-Dozier), Soul 35015 | 3 |
| 82 | 92 | — | — | **EVOL-NOT LOVE** — Five Americans (A Bank Music Prod.), HBR 468 | 2 |
| 83 | — | — | — | **REMEMBER THE RAIN** — Bob Lind (Jack Nitzsche), World Pacific 77822 | 1 |
| 84 | 95 | 95 | — | **YOU'VE GOT MY MIND MESSED UP** — James Carr, Goldwax 302 | 3 |
| 85 | 77 | 81 | 88 | **KILLER JOE** — Kingsmen (Jerden Prod.), Wand 1115 | 4 |
| 86 | — | — | — | **BACKSTAGE** — Gene Pitney (Gene Pitney & Stan Kahan), Musicor 1171 | 1 |
| 87 | 87 | 90 | — | **DARLING BABY** — Elgins (Holland & Dozier), V.I.P. 25029 | 5 |
| 88 | 88 | 92 | — | **REAL HUMDINGER** — J. J. Barnes (Al Kent & Richard Morris), Ric-Tic 110 | 3 |
| 89 | — | — | — | **YOU'RE THE ONE** — Marvelettes (Wm. Robinson), Tamla 54131 | 1 |
| 90 | — | — | — | **THE CRUEL WAR** — Peter, Paul & Mary (Albert B. Grossman), Warner Bros. 5809 | 1 |
| 91 | 93 | — | — | **PIN THE TAIL ON THE DONKEY** — Paul Peek (Joe South), Columbia 43527 | 2 |
| 92 | 96 | — | — | **HISTORY REPEATS ITSELF** — Cab Calloway (Bob Thiele), Boom 60,006 | 2 |
| 93 | — | — | — | **THE MORE I SEE YOU** — Chris Montez (Herb Alpert), A&M 796 | 2 |
| 94 | — | — | — | **GLORIA** — Them (Bert Berns), Parrot 9727 | 2 |
| 95 | — | — | — | **HOLD ON! I'M COMIN'** — Sam & Dave (Prod. By Staff), Stax 189 | 1 |
| 96 | — | — | — | **WANG DANG DOODLE** — Ko Ko Taylor (Willie Dixon), Checker 1135 | 1 |
| 97 | — | — | — | **DOUBLE SHOT (Of My Baby's Love)** — Swingin' Medallions (John McElrath), Smash 2033 | 1 |
| 98 | — | — | — | **DIRTY WATER** — Standells (Ed Cobb), Tower 185 | 1 |
| 99 | — | — | — | **COME ON LET'S GO** — McCoys (Feldman, Goldstein, Gottehrer Prod.), Bang 522 | 1 |
| 100 | — | — | — | **BAREFOOTIN'** — Robert Parker (Wherly-Burly Prod.), Nola 721 | 1 |

## BUBBLING UNDER THE HOT 100

101. COOL JERK .................. Capitols, Karen 1524
102. SEARCHING FOR MY LOVE .. Bobby Moore & the Rhythm Aces, Checker 1129
103. TOO YOUNG .................. Tommy Vann, Academy 118
104. GREETINGS (This Is Uncle Sam) ........ Monitors, V.I.P. 25032
105. TWINKLE TOES ............... Roy Orbison, MGM 13498
106. 3,000 MILES ................. Brian Hyland, Philips 40354
107. I FEEL A SIN COMING ON ..... Solomon Burke, Atlantic 2327
108. TOO SLOW .................... Impressions, ABC-Paramount 10789
109. I'M LIVING IN TWO WORLDS ... Bonnie Guitar, Dot 16811
110. BAD EYE ..................... Willie Mitchell, Hi 2103
111. I LOVE YOU FOREVER ......... Del Shannon, Liberty 55866
112. MINE EXCLUSIVELY ........... Olympics, Mirwood 5513
113. DUM-DE-DA .................. Bobby Vinton, Epic 10025
114. DON'T STOP NOW ............. Eddie Holman, Parkway 981
115. THE TEASER ........ Bob Kuban & the In-Men, Musicland, U.S.A. 20,006
116. MARBLE BREAKS AND IRON BENDS ......... Drafi, London 10825
117. CRUEL WAR ................. Chad & Jill Stuart, Columbia 43467
118. STILL ...................... Sunrays, Tower 224
119. I'M SO LONESOME I COULD CRY .. Hank Williams Sr., MGM 13489
120. I LIE AWAKE ............... New Colony Six, Centaur 1202
121. DO SOMETHING FOR YOURSELF .... Bobby Powell, Whit 715
122. ELVIRA .................... Dallas Frazier, Capitol 5560
123. DO THE TEMPTATION WALK .... Jackie Lee, Mirwood 5510
124. I'M SATISFIED .............. Otis Clay, One-Derful 3168
125. I LOVE YOU 1,000 TIMES .... Platters, Musicor 1166
126. LET'S GO STEADY ........... Sam Cooke, RCA Victor 8803
127. I'LL LOVE YOU FOREVER ..... Holidays, Golden World 36
128. SPEAK HER NAME ........... David & Jonathan, Liberty 55866
129. HEADLINE NEWS ............. Edwin Starr, Ric-Tic 114
130. OH HOW HAPPY ............. Shades of Blue, Impact 1007
131. DIDDY WAH DIDDY ........... Remains, Epic 10001
132. CINNAMINT SHUFFLE ........ Johnny Mann Singers, Liberty 55871
133. THAT'S MY STORY .......... Simon & Garfunkel, ABC-Paramount 10788
134. PICK ME UP ON YOUR WAY DOWN ........ Hank Thompson, Capitol 5599
135. IT AIN'T NECESSARY ....... Mamie Galore, St. Lawrence 1012

Compiled from national retail sales and radio station airplay by the Music Popularity Dept. of Record Market Research, Billboard.

# Billboard HOT 100

*For Week Ending April 30, 1966*

★ STAR performer—Sides registering greatest proportionate upward progress this week.

Record Industry Association of America seal of certification as million selling single.

| This Week | Last Week | 2 Wks. Ago | Title, Artist (Producer), Label & Number | Weeks On Chart |
|---|---|---|---|---|
| 1 ★ | 6 | 9 | **GOOD LOVIN'** — Young Rascals (Tom Dowd, Arif Mardin), Atlantic 2321 | 8 |
| 2 | 1 | 1 | (You're My) SOUL AND INSPIRATION — Righteous Brothers (Bill Medley), Verve 10383 | 9 |
| 3 ★ | 10 | 34 | MONDAY, MONDAY — Mama's and the Papa's (Lou Adler), Dunhill 4026 | 4 |
| 4 ★ | 8 | 13 | SLOOP JOHN B — Beach Boys (Brian Wilson), Capitol 5602 | 5 |
| 5 | 3 | 4 | SECRET AGENT MAN — Johnny Rivers (Lou Adler), Imperial 66159 | 7 |
| 6 | 7 | 10 | KICKS — Paul Revere & the Raiders (Terry Melcher), Columbia 43556 | 7 |
| 7 | 5 | 5 | TIME WON'T LET ME — Outsiders (Tom King), Capitol 5573 | 11 |
| 8 | 2 | 3 | BANG BANG — Cher (Sonny Bono), Imperial 66160 | 8 |
| 9 | 4 | 2 | DAYDREAM — Lovin' Spoonful (Erik Jacobsen), Kama Sutra 208 | 10 |
| 10 ★ | 15 | 29 | LEANING ON THE LAMP POST — Herman's Hermits (Mickie Most), MGM 13500 | 4 |
| 11 | 16 | 22 | GLORIA — Shadows of Knight (A Dunwich Prod.), Dunwich 116 | 7 |
| 12 | 9 | 8 | I'M SO LONESOME I COULD CRY — B. J. Thomas and the Triumphs (Music Enterprises Productions), Scepter 12129 | 11 |
| 13 | 11 | 14 | A SIGN OF THE TIMES — Petula Clark (Tony Hatch), Warner Bros. 5802 | 6 |
| 14 ★ | 38 | 71 | RAINY DAY WOMEN #12 & 35 — Bob Dylan (Bob Johnston), Columbia 43592 | 3 |
| 15 | 18 | 23 | SHAPES OF THINGS — Yardbirds (Giorgio Gomelsky), Epic 9891 | 7 |
| 16 ★ | 31 | 41 | RHAPSODY IN THE RAIN — Lou Christie (Charles Calello), MGM 13473 | 6 |
| 17 | 25 | 43 | TRY TOO HARD — Dave Clark Five (Dave Clark), Epic 10004 | 5 |
| 18 ★ | 32 | 42 | MESSAGE TO MICHAEL — Dionne Warwick (Blue Jac), Scepter 12133 | 5 |
| 19 | 29 | 37 | TOGETHER AGAIN — Ray Charles (Sid Feller), ABC-Paramount 10785 | 6 |
| 20 | 17 | 7 | THE BALLAD OF THE GREEN BERETS — S/Sgt. Barry Sadler (Andy Wiswell), RCA Victor 8739 | 13 |
| 21 ★ | 49 | — | HOW DOES THAT GRAB DARLIN' — Nancy Sinatra (Lee Hazelwood), Reprise 0461 | 2 |
| 22 | 42 | 53 | EIGHT MILES HIGH — Byrds (Allen Stanton), Columbia 43578 | 4 |
| 23 ★ | 52 | 78 | A GROOVY KIND OF LOVE — Mindbenders, Fontana 1541 | 3 |
| 24 | 23 | 18 | WOMAN — Peter & Gordon, Capitol 5579 | 12 |
| 25 | 28 | 28 | FRANKIE AND JOHNNY — Elvis Presley, RCA Victor 8780 | 7 |
| 26 | 19 | 16 | CALIFORNIA DREAMIN' — Mama's and the Papa's (Lou Adler), Dunhill 4020 | 17 |
| 27 | 14 | 6 | 19TH NERVOUS BREAKDOWN — Rolling Stones (Andrew Loog Oldham), London 9823 | 10 |
| 28 | 13 | 11 | NOWHERE MAN — Beatles (George Martin), Capitol 5587 | 9 |
| 29 ★ | 53 | 73 | WHEN A MAN LOVES A WOMAN — Percy Sledge (Martin Greene Productions), Atlantic 2326 | 4 |
| 30 | 12 | 15 | THIS OLD HEART OF MINE — Isley Brothers (Holland & Dozier), Tamla 54128 | 11 |
| 31 | 20 | 17 | LITTLE LATIN LUPE LU — Mitch Ryder and the Detroit Wheels (Bob Crewe), New Voice 808 | 9 |
| 32 | 37 | 47 | CAROLINE, NO — Brian Wilson (Brian Wilson), Capitol 5610 | 6 |
| 33 | 35 | 38 | THE PHOENIX LOVE THEME — Brass Ring (Phil Bodner), Dunhill 4023 | 8 |
| 34 | 30 | 33 | I HEAR TRUMPETS BLOW — Tokens (Big Time Prod.), B. T. Puppy 518 | 7 |
| 35 | 24 | 25 | WHAT NOW MY LOVE — Herb Alpert and the Tijuana Brass (Herb Alpert), A&M 792 | 7 |
| 36 | 21 | 12 | SURE GONNA MISS HER — Gary Lewis & the Playboys (Snuff Garrett), Liberty 55865 | 9 |
| 37 | 22 | 19 | HOMEWARD BOUND — Simon & Garfunkel (Bob Johnston), Columbia 43511 | 12 |
| 38 | 26 | 26 | SOMEWHERE — Len Barry (Madara-White), Decca 31923 | 7 |
| 39 ★ | 65 | 84 | THE SUN AIN'T GONNA SHINE — Walker Brothers, Smash 2032 | 3 |
| 40 | 27 | 27 | SPANISH FLEA — Herb Alpert and the Tijuana Brass (Herb Alpert), A&M 792 | 7 |
| 41 ★ | 68 | 83 | LET'S START ALL OVER AGAIN — Ronnie Dove (Kahl-Verna), Diamond 198 | 3 |
| 42 ★ | 60 | 72 | NOTHING'S TOO GOOD FOR MY BABY — Stevie Wonder (Wm. Stevenson), Tamla 54130 | 3 |
| 43 | 40 | 30 | THINK I'LL GO SOMEWHERE AND CRY MYSELF TO SLEEP — Al Martino (Tom Morgan), Capitol 5598 | 8 |
| 44 | 51 | 51 | TIPPY TOEING — Harden Trio (Don Law & Frank Jones), Columbia 43463 | 8 |
| 45 | 45 | 46 | PLEASE DON'T STOP LOVING ME — Elvis Presley, RCA Victor 8780 | 7 |
| 46 | 56 | 57 | I'LL TAKE GOOD CARE OF YOU — Garnet Mimms (Jerry Ragovoy), United Artists 995 | 7 |
| 47 | 55 | 59 | I CAN'T GROW PEACHES ON A CHERRY TREE — Just Us (Taylor-Gorgoni), Colpix 803 | 8 |
| 48 | 59 | 69 | HISTORY REPEATS ITSELF — Buddy Starcher (Chuck Glaser), Boone 1038 | 4 |
| 49 | 46 | 48 | ONE TRACK MIND — Knickerbockers (Jerry Fuller), Challenge 59326 | 6 |
| 50 | 54 | 64 | I'M COMIN' HOME, CINDY — Trini Lopez (Don Costa), Reprise 0455 | 4 |
| 51 | 79 | — | THE "A" TEAM — S/Sgt. Barry Sadler (Andy Wiswell), RCA Victor 8804 | 2 |
| 52 | 58 | 60 | I CAN'T LET GO — Hollies (Ron Richards), Imperial 66158 | 7 |
| 53 | 72 | 79 | LOVE ME WITH ALL YOUR HEART — Bachelors, London 9828 | 3 |
| 54 | 62 | 81 | LOVE'S MADE A FOOL OF YOU — Bobby Fuller Four (A. Stereo-Fi Prod.), Mustang 3016 | 3 |
| 55 | 57 | 63 | SHE BLEW A GOOD THING — Poets (Juggy Pund.), Symbol 214 | 7 |
| 56 | 67 | 68 | GOT MY MOJO WORKING — Jimmy Smith (Creed Taylor), Verve 10393 | 5 |
| 57 | 61 | 61 | TILL THE END OF THE DAY — Kinks (Pye Records), Reprise 0454 | 6 |
| 58 | 66 | 82 | THE BALLAD OF IRVING — Frank Gallop (Booker-Foster), Kapp 745 | 3 |
| 59 | 50 | 52 | YOUNG LOVE — Lesley Gore (Shelby Singleton), Mercury 72553 | 6 |
| 60 | 48 | 54 | MEMORIES ARE MADE OF THIS — Drifters (Bert Berns), Atlantic 2325 | 7 |
| 61 | 71 | 80 | BAND OF GOLD — Mel Carter (Nick DeCaro), Imperial 66165 | 4 |
| 62 | — | — | LOVE IS LIKE AN ITCHING IN MY HEART — Supremes (Holland & Dozier), Motown 1094 | 1 |
| 63 | 73 | 74 | A LOVER'S CONCERTO — Sarah Vaughan (Luchi DeJesus), Mercury 72543 | 5 |
| 64 | 99 | — | COME ON LET'S GO — McCoys (Feldman, Goldstein, Gottehrer Prod.), Bang 522 | 2 |
| 65 | 89 | — | YOU'RE THE ONE — Marvelettes (Wm. Robinson), Tamla 54131 | 2 |
| 66 | 75 | 76 | DISTANT DRUMS — Jim Reeves (Chet Atkins), RCA Victor 8789 | 4 |
| 67 | 70 | 75 | HE CRIED — Shangri-Las (Shadow Morton), Red Bird 10053 | 4 |
| 68 | 83 | — | REMEMBER THE RAIN — Bob Lind (Jack Nitzsche), World Pacific 77822 | 2 |
| 69 | 90 | — | THE CRUEL WAR — Peter, Paul & Mary (Albert B. Grossman), Warner Bros. 5809 | 2 |
| 70 | — | — | IT'S A MAN'S MAN'S MAN'S WORLD — James Brown (James Brown Productions), King 6035 | 1 |
| 71 | 86 | — | BACKSTAGE — Gene Pitney (Gene Pitney & Stan Kahan), Musicor 1171 | 2 |
| 72 | 81 | 94 | (I'm a) ROAD RUNNER — Jr. Walker & the All Stars (Holland-Dozier), Soul 35015 | 4 |
| 73 | — | — | DUM-DE-DA — Bobby Vinton (Bob Morgan), Epic 10014 | 1 |
| 74 | — | — | TWINKLE TOES — Roy Orbison, MGM 13498 | 1 |
| 75 | 84 | 95 | YOU'VE GOT MY MIND MESSED UP — James Carr, Goldwax 302 | 4 |
| 76 | 93 | 98 | THE MORE I SEE YOU — Chris Montez (Herb Alpert), A&M 796 | 3 |
| 77 | 82 | 92 | EVOL-NOT LOVE — Five Americans (A Bank Music Prod.), HBR 468 | 3 |
| 78 | 78 | 86 | I SURRENDER — Fontella Bass (Billy Davis), Checker 1137 | 6 |
| 79 | — | — | MAME — Bobby Darin (Bobby Darin), Atlantic 2329 | 1 |
| 80 | 88 | 88 | REAL HUMDINGER — J. J. Barnes (Al Kent & Richard Morris), Ric-Tic 110 | 4 |
| 81 | — | — | ELVIRA — Dallas Frazier (Marvin Hughes), Capitol 5560 | 1 |
| 82 | — | — | THE TEASER — Bob Kuban and the In-Men (Mel Friedman), Musicland, U.S.A. 20006 | 1 |
| 83 | — | — | I LOVE YOU 1,000 TIMES — The Platters (Luther Dixon), Musicor 1166 | 1 |
| 84 | 87 | 87 | DARLING BABY — Elgins (Holland & Dozier), V.I.P. 25029 | 6 |
| 85 | 100 | — | BAREFOOTIN' — Robert Parker (Wherly-Burly Prod.), Nola 721 | 2 |
| 86 | — | — | COOL JERK — Capitols (Ollie McLaughlin), Karin 1524 | 1 |
| 87 | 95 | — | HOLD ON! I'M COMIN' — Sam & Dave (Prod. By Staff), Stax 189 | 3 |
| 88 | 94 | — | GLORIA — Them (Bert Berns), Parrot 9727 | 3 |
| 89 | 92 | 96 | HISTORY REPEATS ITSELF — Cab Calloway (Bob Thiele), Boom 60,006 | 3 |
| 90 | — | — | LOVE TAKES A LONG TIME GROWING — Dean Jackson (Ollie McLaughlin), Carla 2527 | 1 |
| 91 | — | — | PLEASE DON'T SELL MY DADDY NO MORE WINE — The Greenwoods (Wally Brady), Kapp 742 | 1 |
| 92 | 97 | — | DOUBLE SHOT (Of My Baby's Love) — Swingin' Medallions (John McElrath), Smash 2033 | 2 |
| 93 | 96 | — | WANG DANG DOODLE — Ko Ko Taylor (Willie Dixon), Checker 1135 | 2 |
| 94 | 91 | 93 | PIN THE TAIL ON THE DONKEY — Paul Peek (Joe South), Columbia 43527 | 3 |
| 95 | 98 | — | DIRTY WATER — Standells (Ed Cobb), Tower 185 | 2 |
| 96 | — | — | LET ME BE GOOD TO YOU — Carla Thomas (Prod. by Staff), Stax 188 | 1 |
| 97 | — | — | LET'S GO STEADY — Sam Cooke (Hugo & Luigi), RCA Victor 8803 | 1 |
| 98 | — | — | DOWNTOWN — Mrs. Miller (Alexis De Azevedo), Capitol 5640 | 1 |
| 99 | — | — | MY LITTLE RED BOOK — Love (Jac Holzman & Mark Abramson), Elektra 603 | 1 |
| 100 | — | — | MINE EXCLUSIVELY — Olympics (Fred Smith), Mirwood 5513 | 1 |

## BUBBLING UNDER THE HOT 100

101. LOVER'S CONCERTO — Mrs. Miller, Capitol 5640
102. SEARCHING FOR MY LOVE — Bobby Moore & the Rhythm Aces, Checker 1129
103. GREETINGS (THIS IS UNCLE SAM) — Monitors, V.I.P. 25022
104. THE BIG HURT — Del Shannon, Liberty 55866
105. I'M SATISFIED — Otis Clay, One-Derful 13168
106. 3,000 MILES — Brian Hyland, Philips 40354
107. BAD EYE — Willie Mitchell, Hi 2103
108. DON'T STOP NOW — Eddie Holman, Parkway 961
109. I'M SO LONESOME I COULD CRY — Hank Williams Sr., MGM 13469
110. THE CRUEL WAR — Chad & Jill Stuart, Columbia 43467
111. STILL — Surrays, Tower 234
112. YOU'RE READY NOW — Frankie Valli, Smash 2037
113. I AM A ROCK — Simon & Garfunkel, Columbia 43617
114. MARBLE BREAKS AND IRON BENDS — Drafi, London 10025
115. I'LL LOVE YOU FOREVER — Holidays, Golden World 36
116. YOU WAITED TOO LONG — New Colony Six, Centaur 1202
117. DO IT — Bobby Powell, Whit 715
118. I'M LIVING IN TWO WORLDS — Bonnie Guitar, Dot 16811
119. TWO DROPS — Don Cherry, Monument 920
120. DO SOMETHING FOR YOURSELF — Bobby Powell, Whit 715
121. DO THE TEMPTATION WALK — Jackie Lee, Mirwood 5510
122. I LOVE DROPS — Vic Dana, Dolton 319
123. SWEET TALKIN' GUY — Chiffons, Laurie 3340
124. SPEAK HER NAME — David & Jonathan, Capitol 5635
125. OH HOW HAPPY — Shades of Blue, Impact 1007
126. HEADLINE NEWS — Edwin Starr, Ric-Tic 114
127. THAT'S MY STORY — Simon & Garfunkel, ABC-Paramount 10788
128. TRULY JULIE'S BLUES — Bob Lind, World-Pacific 77822
129. DIDDY WAH DIDDY — Remains, Epic 10001
130. PETER RABBIT — Dee Jay & the Runaways, Smash 2034
131. CHERYL'S GOIN' HOME — Cascades, Arwin 132
132. IT AIN'T NECESSARY — Mamie Galore, St. Lawrence 1012
133. BETTER MAN THAN — Knight & the Pack, Lucky 9 1,6
134. ONCE UPON A TIME — Teddy & the Pandas, Musicor 1176
135. YOU COULDN'T GET MY LOVE BACK — Leroy Van Dyke, Warner Bros. 5807

*Compiled from national retail sales and radio station airplay by the Music Popularity Dept. of Record Market Research, Billboard.*

# Billboard HOT 100

For Week Ending May 7, 1966

★ STAR performer—Sides registering greatest proportionate upward progress this week.

Record Industry Association of America seal of certification as million selling single.

| This Week | 1 Wk. Ago | 2 Wks. Ago | TITLE Artist (Producer), Label & Number | Weeks On Chart |
|---|---|---|---|---|
| 1 ★ | 3 | 10 | MONDAY, MONDAY — Mama's and the Papa's (Lou Adler), Dunhill 4026 | 5 |
| 2 | 1 | 6 | GOOD LOVIN' — Young Rascals (Tom Dowd, Arif Mardin), Atlantic 2321 | 9 |
| 3 | 4 | 8 | SLOOP JOHN B — Beach Boys (Brian Wilson), Capitol 5602 | 6 |
| 4 | 2 | 1 | (You're My) SOUL AND INSPIRATION — Righteous Brothers (Bill Medley), Verve 10383 | 10 |
| 5 | 6 | 7 | KICKS — Paul Revere & the Raiders (Terry Melcher), Columbia 43556 | 8 |
| 6 | 5 | 3 | SECRET AGENT MAN — Johnny Rivers (Lou Adler), Imperial 66159 | 8 |
| 7 ★ | 14 | 38 | RAINY DAY WOMEN #12 & 35 — Bob Dylan (Bob Johnston), Columbia 43592 | 4 |
| 8 | 8 | 2 | BANG BANG — Cher (Sonny Bono), Imperial 66160 | 9 |
| 9 | 10 | 15 | LEANING ON THE LAMP POST — Herman's Hermits (Mickie Most), MGM 13500 | 5 |
| 10 | 11 | 16 | GLORIA — Shadows of Knight (A Dunwich Prod.), Dunwich 116 | 8 |
| 11 | 7 | 5 | TIME WON'T LET ME — Outsiders (Tom King), Capitol 5573 | 12 |
| 12 | 17 | 25 | TRY TOO HARD — Dave Clark Five (Dave Clark), Epic 10004 | 6 |
| 13 | 18 | 32 | MESSAGE TO MICHAEL — Dionne Warwick (Blue Jac), Scepter 12133 | 6 |
| 14 | 15 | 18 | SHAPES OF THINGS — Yardbirds (Giorgio Gomelsky), Epic 9891 | 8 |
| 15 ★ | 21 | 49 | HOW DOES THAT GRAB YOU DARLIN' — Nancy Sinatra (Lee Hazelwood), Reprise 0461 | 3 |
| 16 | 29 | 53 | WHEN A MAN LOVES A WOMAN — Percy Sledge (Marlin Greene Productions), Atlantic 2326 | 5 |
| 17 | 22 | 42 | EIGHT MILES HIGH — Byrds (Allen Stanton), Columbia 43578 | 5 |
| 18 | 23 | 52 | A GROOVY KIND OF LOVE — Mindbenders, Fontana 1541 | 4 |
| 19 | 9 | 4 | DAYDREAM — Lovin' Spoonful (Erik Jacobson), Kama Sutra 208 | 11 |
| 20 | 12 | 9 | I'M SO LONESOME I COULD CRY — B. J. Thomas and the Triumphs (Music Enterprises Productions), Scepter 12129 | 12 |
| 21 | 16 | 31 | RHAPSODY IN THE RAIN — Lou Christie (Charles Calello), MGM 13473 | 7 |
| 22 | 19 | 29 | TOGETHER AGAIN — Ray Charles (Sid Feller), ABC-Paramount 10785 | 7 |
| 23 | 13 | 11 | A SIGN OF THE TIMES — Petula Clark (Tony Hatch), Warner Bros. 5802 | 8 |
| 24 | 39 | 65 | THE SUN AIN'T GONNA SHINE — Walker Brothers (Ivor Raymond), Smash 2032 | 4 |
| 25 | 42 | 60 | NOTHING'S TOO GOOD FOR MY BABY — Stevie Wonder (Wm. Stevenson), Tamla 54130 | 4 |
| 26 | 62 | — | LOVE IS LIKE AN ITCHING IN MY HEART — Supremes (Holland & Dozier), Motown 1094 | 2 |
| 27 | 41 | 68 | LET'S START ALL OVER AGAIN — Ronnie Dove (Kahl-Vernon), Diamond 198 | 4 |
| 28 | 25 | 28 | FRANKIE AND JOHNNY — Elvis Presley, RCA Victor 8780 | 8 |
| 29 | 54 | 62 | LOVE'S MADE A FOOL OF YOU — Bobby Fuller Four (A Stereo-Fi Prod.), Mustang 3016 | 4 |
| 30 | 30 | 12 | THIS OLD HEART OF MINE — Isley Brothers (Holland & Dozier), Tamla 54128 | 12 |
| 31 | 70 | — | IT'S A MAN'S MAN'S MAN'S WORLD — James Brown (James Brown Productions), King 6035 | 2 |
| 32 | 33 | 35 | THE PHOENIX LOVE THEME — Brass Ring (Phil Bodner), Dunhill 4023 | 9 |
| 33 ★ | 46 | 56 | I'LL TAKE GOOD CARE OF YOU — Garnet Mimms (Jerry Ragovoy), United Artists 995 | 7 |
| 34 | 34 | 30 | I HEAR TRUMPETS BLOW — Tokens (Big Time Prod.), B. T. Puppy 518 | 8 |
| 35 | 35 | 24 | WHAT NOW MY LOVE — Herb Alpert and the Tijuana Brass (Herb Alpert), A&M 792 | 7 |
| 36 | 32 | 37 | CAROLINE, NO — Brian Wilson (Brian Wilson), Capitol 5610 | 7 |
| 37 ★ | 58 | 66 | THE BALLAD OF IRVING — Frank Gallop (Booker-Foster), Kapp 745 | 3 |
| 38 | 38 | 26 | SOMEWHERE — Len Barry (Madara-White), Decca 31923 | 8 |
| 39 | 47 | 55 | I CAN'T GROW PEACHES ON A CHERRY TREE — Just Us (Taylor-Gordoni), Colpix 803 | 9 |
| 40 | 50 | 54 | I'M COMIN' HOME, CINDY — Trini Lopez (Don Costa), Reprise 0455 | 5 |
| 41 | 51 | 79 | THE "A" TEAM — S/Sgt. Barry Sadler (Andy Wiswell), RCA Victor 8804 | 3 |
| 42 | 52 | 58 | I CAN'T LET GO — Hollies (Ron Richards), Imperial 66158 | 8 |
| 43 | 53 | 72 | LOVE ME WITH ALL YOUR HEART — Bachelors, London 9828 | 4 |
| 44 | 48 | 59 | HISTORY REPEATS ITSELF — Buddy Starcher (Chuck Glaser), Boone 1038 | 8 |
| 45 | 55 | 57 | SHE BLEW A GOOD THING — Poets (Juggy Prod.), Symbol 214 | 8 |
| 46 | 44 | 51 | TIPPY TOEING — Harden Trio (Don Law & Frank Jones), Columbia 43463 | 9 |
| 47 | 61 | 71 | BAND OF GOLD — Mel Carter (Nick DeCaro), Imperial 66165 | 5 |
| 48 | 64 | 99 | COME ON LET'S GO — McCoys (Feldman, Goldstein, Gottehrer Prod.), Bang 522 | 2 |
| 49 | 71 | 86 | BACKSTAGE — Gene Pitney (Gene Pitney & Stan Green), Musicor 1171 | 3 |
| 50 | 57 | 61 | TILL THE END OF THE DAY — Kinks (Pye Records), Reprise 0454 | 7 |
| 51 | 56 | 67 | GOT MY MOJO WORKING — Jimmy Smith (Creed Taylor), Verve 10393 | 6 |
| 52 | 74 | — | TWINKLE TOES — Roy Orbison, MGM 13498 | 2 |
| 53 | 73 | — | DUM-DE-DA — Bobby Vinton (Bob Morgan), Epic 10014 | 2 |
| 54 | 65 | 89 | YOU'RE THE ONE — Marvelettes (Wm. Robinson), Tamla 54131 | 3 |
| 55 | 66 | 75 | DISTANT DRUMS — Jim Reeves (Chet Atkins), RCA Victor 8789 | 5 |
| 56 | 86 | — | COOL JERK — Capitols (Ollie McLaughlin), Karen 1524 | 2 |
| 57 | 77 | 82 | EVOL-NOT LOVE — Five Americans (A Bank Music Prod.), HBR 468 | 4 |
| 58 | 87 | 95 | HOLD ON! I'M COMIN' — Sam & Dave (Prod. By Staff), Stax 189 | 3 |
| 59 | 69 | 90 | THE CRUEL WAR — Peter, Paul & Mary (Albert B. Grossman), Warner Bros. 5809 | 3 |
| 60 | 72 | 81 | (I'm a) ROAD RUNNER — Jr. Walker & the All Stars (Holland-Dozier), Soul 35015 | 4 |
| 61 | 76 | 93 | THE MORE I SEE YOU — Chris Montez (Herb Alpert), A&M 796 | 3 |
| 62 | — | — | I AM A ROCK — Simon & Garfunkel (Bob Johnston), Columbia 43617 | 1 |
| 63 | 75 | 84 | YOU'VE GOT MY MIND MESSED UP — James Carr, Goldwax 302 | 5 |
| 64 | 68 | 83 | REMEMBER THE RAIN — Bob Lind (Jack Nitzche), World Pacific 77822 | 3 |
| 65 | — | — | DID YOU EVER HAVE TO MAKE UP YOUR MIND? — Lovin' Spoonful (Erik Jacobson), Kama Sutra 209 | 1 |
| 66 | 45 | 45 | PLEASE DON'T STOP LOVING ME — Elvis Presley, RCA Victor 8780 | 8 |
| 67 | 67 | 70 | HE CRIED — Shangri-Las (Shadow Morton), Red Bird 10053 | 5 |
| 68 | 83 | — | I LOVE YOU 1,000 TIMES — The Platters (Luther Dixon), Musicor 1166 | 2 |
| 69 | 95 | 98 | DIRTY WATER — Standells (Ed Cobb), Tower 185 | 3 |
| 70 | 85 | 100 | BAREFOOTIN' — Robert Parker (Wharly-Burly Prod.), Nola 721 | 3 |
| 71 | 63 | 73 | A LOVER'S CONCERTO — Sarah Vaughan (Luchi DeJesus), Mercury 72543 | 6 |
| 72 | 84 | 87 | DARLING BABY — Elgins (Holland & Dozier), V.I.P. 25029 | 7 |
| 73 | 79 | — | MAME — Bobby Darin (Bobby Darin), Atlantic 2329 | 2 |
| 74 | 81 | — | ELVIRA — Dallas Frazier (Marvin Hughes), Capitol 5560 | 2 |
| 75 | 88 | 94 | GLORIA — Them (Bert Burns), Parrot 9727 | 3 |
| 76 | 92 | 97 | DOUBLE SHOT (Of My Baby's Love) — Swingin' Medallions (John McElrath), Smash 2033 | 3 |
| 77 | — | — | I LOVE YOU DROPS — Vic Dana (Bob Reisdorff), Dolton 319 | 1 |
| 78 | 96 | — | LET ME BE GOOD TO YOU — Carla Thomas (Prod. by Staff), Stax 188 | 2 |
| 79 | 82 | — | THE TEASER — Bob Kuban & the In-Men (Mel Friedman), Musicland, U.S.A. 20006 | 2 |
| 80 | — | — | THERE'S NO LIVING WITHOUT YOUR LOVE — Peter & Gordon (John Burgess), Capitol 5650 | 1 |
| 81 | 93 | 96 | WANG DANG DOODLE — Ko Ko Taylor (Willie Dixon), Checker 1135 | 3 |
| 82 | 90 | — | LOVE TAKES A LONG TIME GROWING — Deon Jackson (Ollie McLaughlin), Carla 2527 | 2 |
| 83 | — | — | COME RUNNING BACK — Dean Martin (Jimmy Bowen), Reprise 0466 | 1 |
| 84 | 80 | 88 | REAL HUMDINGER — J. J. Barnes (Al Kent & Richard Morris), Ric-Tic 110 | 5 |
| 85 | 98 | — | DOWNTOWN — Mrs. Miller (Alexis De Azevedo), Capitol 5640 | 2 |
| 86 | — | — | SWEET TALKIN' GUY — Chiffons (Bright Tunes), Laurie 3340 | 1 |
| 87 | — | — | PETER RABBIT — Dee Jay and the Runaways (Iowa Great Lakes Studios), Smash 2034 | 1 |
| 88 | 91 | — | PLEASE DON'T SELL MY DADDY NO MORE WINE — The Greenwoods (Wally Brady), Kapp 742 | 2 |
| 89 | — | — | OH HOW HAPPY — Shades of Blue (John Rhys), Impact 1007 | 1 |
| 90 | — | — | STRANGERS IN THE NIGHT — Frank Sinatra (Jimmy Bowen), Reprise 0470 | 1 |
| 91 | — | — | TRULY JULIE'S BLUES — Bob Lind (Jack Nitzche), World Pacific 77822 | 1 |
| 92 | — | — | BAD EYE — Willie Mitchell (Joe Cuoghi), Hi 2103 | 1 |
| 93 | — | — | STILL — Sunrays (Murry Wilson & Don Ralke), Tower 224 | 1 |
| 94 | 94 | 91 | PIN THE TAIL ON THE DONKEY — Paul Peek (Joe South), Columbia 43527 | 4 |
| 95 | — | — | THE BIG HURT — Del Shannon (Snuff Garrett & Leon Russell), Liberty 55866 | 1 |
| 96 | — | — | A LOVER'S CONCERTO — Mrs. Miller (Alexis DeAzevedo), Capitol 5640 | 1 |
| 97 | 99 | — | MY LITTLE RED BOOK — Love (Jac Holzman & Mark Abramson), Elektra 603 | 2 |
| 98 | — | — | I'LL LOVE YOU FOREVER — Holidays (Davis-Jackson Prod.), Golden World 36 | 1 |
| 99 | 100 | — | MINE EXCLUSIVELY — Olympics (Fred Smith), Mirwood 5513 | 2 |
| 100 | — | — | HEADLINE NEWS — Edwin Starr (Kent & Morris), Ric-Tic 114 | 1 |

## BUBBLING UNDER THE HOT 100

101. SEARCHING FOR MY LOVE ... Bobby Moore & the Rhythm Aces, Checker 1129
102. THE NEW BREED ... James Brown, Smash 2028
103. LOUIE, LOUIE ... Kingsmen, Wand 143
104. DON'T STOP NOW ... Eddie Holman, Parkway 961
105. MARBLE BREAKS AND IRON BENDS ... Drafi, London 10025
106. HISTORY REPEATS ITSELF ... Cab Calloway, Boom 60,006
107. I'M SATISFIED ... Otis Clay, One-Derful 13168
108. THE LAST THING ON MY MIND ... Womenfolk, RCA Victor 8784
109. SECOND-HAND MAN ... Back Porch Majority, Epic 9879
110. 3,000 MILES ... Brian Hyland, Philips 40354
111. I LIE AWAKE ... New Colony Six, Centaur 1202
112. SOLITARY MAN ... Neil Diamond, Bang 519
113. THE TEMPTATION WALK ... Jackie Lee, Mirwood 5510
114. SPEAK HER NAME ... David & Jonathan, Capitol 5625
115. YOU WAITED TOO LONG ... Five Stair-Steps, Windy C 601
116. SWEET PEA ... Tommy Roe, ABC-Paramount 10762
117. I LOVE YOU DROPS ... Don Cherry, Monument 930
118. I'M SO LONESOME I COULD CRY ... Hank Williams Sr., MGM 13489
119. COME ON AND SEE ME ... Tammi Terrell, Motown 1095
120. YOU COULDN'T GET MY LOVE BACK ... Leroy Van Dyke, Warner Bros. 5807
121. TAKE ME BACK TO NEW ORLEANS ... Gary U. S. Bonds, Legrand 1040
122. SILVER SPOON ... Toys, DynoVoice 219
123. GIRL IN LOVE ... Outsiders, Capitol 5646
124. THAT'S MY STORY ... Simon & Garfunkel, Columbia 10738
125. JUST A LITTLE MISUNDERSTANDING ... Contours, Gordy 7052
126. CINNAMINT SHUFFLE ... Mitch Ryder, New Voice 811
127. STRANGERS IN THE NIGHT ... Bert Kaempfert & his Ork., Decca 31945
128. SO MUCH LOVE ... Steve Alaimo, ABC-Paramount 10805
129. BETTER USE YOUR HEAD ... Little Anthony & the Imperials, Veep 1228
130. IT'S OVER ... Jimmie Rodgers, Dot 16861
131. SO MUCH LOVE ... Ben E. King, Atco 6413
132. FUNCTION AT THE JUNCTION ... Shorty Long, Soul 35011
133. I KNOW YOU BETTER THAN THAT ... Bobby Goldsboro, United Artists 50018
134. EVERYDAY I HAVE TO CRY ... Gentrys, MGM 13495
135. I'VE GOT A SECRET ... Sharpees, One-Derful 4843

Compiled from national retail sales and radio station airplay by the Music Popularity Dept. of Record Market Research, Billboard.

# Billboard

For Week Ending May 14, 1966

# HOT 100

★ **STAR performer**—Sides registering greatest proportionate upward progress this week.

Record Industry Association of America seal of certification as million selling single.

| This Week | 1 Wk. Ago | 2 Wks. Ago | 3 Wks. Ago | TITLE Artist (Producer), Label & Number | Weeks On Chart |
|---|---|---|---|---|---|
| 1 (Billboard Award) | 1 | 3 | 10 | **MONDAY, MONDAY** — Mama's and the Papa's (Lou Adler), Dunhill 4026 | 6 |
| 2 | 2 | 1 | 6 | **GOOD LOVIN'** — Young Rascals (Tom Dowd, Arif Mardin), Atlantic 2321 | 10 |
| ★3 | 7 | 14 | 38 | **RAINY DAY WOMEN #12 & 35** — Bob Dylan (Bob Johnston), Columbia 43592 | 5 |
| 4 | 5 | 6 | 7 | **KICKS** — Paul Revere & the Raiders (Terry Melcher), Columbia 43556 | 9 |
| 5 | 3 | 4 | 8 | **SLOOP JOHN B** — Beach Boys (Brian Wilson), Capitol 5602 | 7 |
| 6 | 4 | 2 | 1 | **(You're My) SOUL AND INSPIRATION** — Righteous Brothers (Bill Medley), Verve 10383 | 11 |
| ★7 | 15 | 21 | 49 | **HOW DOES THAT GRAB YOU DARLIN'** — Nancy Sinatra (Lee Hazelwood), Reprise 0461 | 4 |
| ★8 | 13 | 18 | 32 | **MESSAGE TO MICHAEL** — Dionne Warwick (Blue Jac), Scepter 12133 | 7 |
| ★9 | 16 | 29 | 53 | **WHEN A MAN LOVES A WOMAN** — Percy Sledge (Marlin Greene Productions), Atlantic 2326 | 6 |
| 10 | 10 | 11 | 16 | **GLORIA** — Shadows of Knight (A Dunwich Prod.), Dunwich 116 | 9 |
| 11 | 14 | 15 | 18 | **SHAPES OF THINGS** — Yardbirds (Giorgio Gomelsky), Epic 9891 | 9 |
| 12 | 9 | 10 | 15 | **LEANING ON THE LAMP POST** — Herman's Hermits (Mickie Most), MGM 13500 | 6 |
| ★13 | 18 | 23 | 52 | **A GROOVY KIND OF LOVE** — Mindbenders, Fontana 1541 | 5 |
| 14 | 6 | 5 | 3 | **SECRET AGENT MAN** — Johnny Rivers (Lou Adler), Imperial 66159 | 9 |
| ★15 | 26 | 62 | — | **LOVE IS LIKE AN ITCHING IN MY HEART** — Supremes (Holland & Dozier), Motown 1094 | 3 |
| 16 | 17 | 22 | 42 | **EIGHT MILES HIGH** — Byrds (Allen Stanton), Columbia 43578 | 6 |
| 17 | 11 | 7 | 5 | **TIME WON'T LET ME** — Outsiders (Tom King), Capitol 5573 | 13 |
| ★18 | 24 | 39 | 65 | **THE SUN AIN'T GONNA SHINE** — Walker Brothers, Smash 2032 | 5 |
| 19 | 8 | 8 | 2 | **BANG BANG** — Cher (Sonny Bono), Imperial 66160 | 10 |
| ★20 | 25 | 42 | 60 | **NOTHING'S TOO GOOD FOR MY BABY** — Stevie Wonder (Wm. Stevenson), Tamla 54130 | 5 |
| 21 | 12 | 17 | 25 | **TRY TOO HARD** — Dave Clark Five (Dave Clark), Epic 10004 | 7 |
| ★22 | 27 | 41 | 68 | **LET'S START ALL OVER AGAIN** — Ronnie Dove (Kahl-Vernon), Diamond 198 | 5 |
| ★23 | 31 | 70 | — | **IT'S A MAN'S MAN'S MAN'S WORLD** — James Brown (James Brown Productions), King 6035 | 3 |
| ★24 | 62 | — | — | **I AM A ROCK** — Simon & Garfunkel (Bob Johnston), Columbia 43617 | 2 |
| ★25 | 65 | — | — | **DID YOU EVER HAVE TO MAKE UP YOUR MIND?** — Lovin' Spoonful (Erik Jacobsen), Kama Sutra 209 | 2 |
| 26 | 29 | 54 | 62 | **LOVE'S MADE A FOOL OF YOU** — Bobby Fuller Four (A Stereo-Fi Prod.), Mustang 3016 | 5 |
| 27 | 21 | 16 | 31 | **RHAPSODY IN THE RAIN** — Lou Christie (Charles Calello), MGM 13473 | 8 |
| 28 | 20 | 12 | 9 | **I'M SO LONESOME I COULD CRY** — B. J. Thomas and the Triumphs (Music Enterprises Productions), Scepter 12129 | 13 |
| 29 | 19 | 9 | 4 | **DAYDREAM** — Lovin' Spoonful (Erik Jacobson), Kama Sutra 208 | 12 |
| 30 | 22 | 19 | 29 | **TOGETHER AGAIN** — Ray Charles (Sid Feller), ABC-Paramount 10785 | 8 |
| ★31 | 48 | 64 | 99 | **COME ON LET'S GO** — McCoys (Feldman, Goldstein, Gottehrer Prod.) Bang 522 | 4 |
| ★32 | 49 | 71 | 86 | **BACKSTAGE** — Gene Pitney (Gene Pitney & Stan Kahan), Musicor 1171 | 4 |
| 33 | 33 | 46 | 56 | **I'LL TAKE GOOD CARE OF YOU** — Garnet Mimms (Jerry Ragovoy), United Artists 995 | 8 |
| 34 | 39 | 47 | 55 | **I CAN'T GROW PEACHES ON A CHERRY TREE** — Just Us (Taylor-Gordoni), Colpix 803 | 10 |
| 35 | 41 | 51 | 79 | **THE "A" TEAM** — S/Sgt. Barry Sadler (Andy Wiswell), RCA Victor 8804 | 4 |
| 36 | 23 | 13 | 11 | **A SIGN OF THE TIMES** — Petula Clark (Tony Hatch), Warner Bros. 5802 | 8 |
| 37 | 37 | 58 | 66 | **THE BALLAD OF IRVING** — Frank Gallop (Boober-Foster), Kapp 745 | 5 |
| 38 | 43 | 53 | 72 | **LOVE ME WITH ALL OF YOUR HEART** — Bachelors, London 9828 | 5 |
| 39 | 44 | 48 | 59 | **HISTORY REPEATS ITSELF** — Buddy Starcher (Chuck Glaser), Boone 1038 | 6 |
| 40 | 40 | 50 | 54 | **I'M COMIN' HOME, CINDY** — Trini Lopez (Don Costa), Reprise 0455 | 6 |
| 41 | 47 | 61 | 71 | **BAND OF GOLD** — Mel Carter (Nick DeCaro), Imperial 66165 | 6 |
| ★42 | 52 | 74 | — | **TWINKLE TOES** — Roy Orbison, MGM 13498 | 3 |
| ★43 | 60 | 72 | 81 | **(I'm a) ROAD RUNNER** — Jr. Walker & the All Stars (Holland-Dozier), Soul 35015 | 6 |
| 44 | 42 | 52 | 58 | **I CAN'T LET GO** — Hollies (Ron Richards), Imperial 66158 | 9 |
| ★45 | 55 | 66 | 75 | **DISTANT DRUMS** — Jim Reeves (Chet Atkins), RCA Victor 8789 | 6 |
| 46 | 45 | 55 | 57 | **SHE BLEW A GOOD THING** — Poets (Juggy Prod.), Symbol 214 | 9 |
| 47 | 53 | 73 | — | **DUM-DE-DA** — Bobby Vinton (Bob Morgan), Epic 10014 | 3 |
| ★48 | — | — | — | **PAINT IT, BLACK** — Rolling Stones (Andrew Loog Oldham), London 901 | 1 |
| ★49 | — | — | — | **GREEN GRASS** — Gary Lewis & the Playboys (Dave Pell), Liberty 55880 | 1 |
| 50 | 54 | 65 | 89 | **YOU'RE THE ONE** — Marvelettes (Wm. Robinson), Tamla 54131 | 4 |
| 51 | 56 | 86 | — | **COOL JERK** — Capitols (Ollie McLaughlin), Karen 1524 | 3 |
| ★52 | 70 | 85 | 100 | **BAREFOOTIN'** — Robert Parker (Wherly-Burly Prod.), Nola 721 | 4 |
| 53 | 61 | 76 | 93 | **THE MORE I SEE YOU** — Chris Montez (Herb Alpert), A&M 796 | 5 |
| 54 | 59 | 69 | 90 | **THE CRUEL WAR** — Peter, Paul & Mary (Albert B. Grossman), Warner Bros. 5809 | 4 |
| 55 | 58 | 87 | 95 | **HOLD ON! I'M COMIN'** — Sam & Dave (Prod. By Staff), Stax 189 | 4 |
| 56 | 46 | 44 | 51 | **TIPPY TOEING** — Harden Trio (Don Law & Frank Jones), Columbia 43463 | 10 |
| 57 | 57 | 77 | 82 | **EVOL-NOT LOVE** — Five Americans (A Bank Music Prod.), HBR 468 | 5 |
| 58 | 51 | 56 | 67 | **GOT MY MOJO WORKING** — Jimmy Smith (Creed Taylor), Verve 10393 | 7 |
| 59 | 50 | 57 | 61 | **TILL THE END OF THE DAY** — Kinks (Pye Records), Reprise 0454 | 8 |
| 60 | 68 | 83 | — | **I LOVE YOU 1,000 TIMES** — The Platters (Luther Dixon), Musicor 1166 | 3 |
| ★61 | 86 | — | — | **SWEET TALKIN' GUY** — Chiffons (Bright Tunes), Laurie 3340 | 2 |
| ★62 | 83 | — | — | **COME RUNNING BACK** — Dean Martin (Jimmy Bowen), Reprise 0466 | 2 |
| 63 | 69 | 95 | 98 | **DIRTY WATER** — Standells (Ed Cobb), Tower 185 | 4 |
| 64 | 64 | 68 | 83 | **REMEMBER THE RAIN** — Bob Lind (Jack Nitzsche), World Pacific 77822 | 4 |
| 65 | 67 | 67 | 70 | **HE CRIED** — Shangri-Las (Shadow Morton), Red Bird 10053 | 6 |
| 66 | 76 | 92 | 97 | **DOUBLE SHOT (Of My Baby's Love)** — Swingin' Medallions (John McElrath), Smash 2033 | 4 |
| 67 | 77 | — | — | **I LOVE YOU DROPS** — Vic Dana (Bob Reisdorff), Dolton 319 | 2 |
| 68 | 73 | 79 | — | **MAME** — Bobby Darin (Bobby Darin), Atlantic 2329 | 3 |
| 69 | 63 | 75 | 84 | **YOU'VE GOT MY MIND MESSED UP** — James Carr, Goldwax 302 | 6 |
| 70 | 79 | 82 | — | **THE TEASER** — Bob Kuban & the In-Men (Mel Friedman), Musicland, U.S.A. 20006 | 3 |
| ★71 | 90 | — | — | **STRANGERS IN THE NIGHT** — Frank Sinatra (Jimmy Bowen), Reprise 0470 | 2 |
| 72 | 74 | 81 | — | **ELVIRA** — Dallas Frazier (Marvin Hughes), Capitol 5560 | 3 |
| ★73 | 88 | 91 | — | **PLEASE DON'T SELL MY DADDY NO MORE WINE** — The Greenwoods (Wally Brady), Kapp 742 | 3 |
| ★74 | 89 | — | — | **OH HOW HAPPY** — Shades of Blue (John Rhys), Impact 1007 | 2 |
| 75 | 75 | 88 | 94 | **GLORIA** — Them (Bert Burns), Parrot 9727 | 5 |
| 76 | 72 | 84 | 87 | **DARLING BABY** — Elgins (Holland & Dozier), V.I.P. 25029 | 8 |
| 77 | 80 | — | — | **THERE'S NO LIVING WITHOUT YOUR LOVING** — Peter & Gordon (John Burgess), Capitol 5650 | 2 |
| 78 | 78 | 96 | — | **LET ME BE GOOD TO YOU** — Carla Thomas (Prod. by Staff), Stax 188 | 3 |
| 79 | 82 | 90 | — | **LOVE TAKES A LONG TIME GROWING** — Deon Jackson (Ollie McLaughlin), Carla 2527 | 3 |
| 80 | 81 | 93 | 96 | **WANG DANG DOODLE** — Ko Ko Taylor (Willie Dixon), Checker 1135 | 4 |
| 81 | 87 | — | — | **PETER RABBIT** — Dee Jay and the Runaways (Iowa Great Lakes Studios), Smash 2034 | 2 |
| ★82 | — | — | — | **THE LAST WORD IN LONESOME IS ME** — Eddy Arnold (Chet Atkins), RCA Victor 8818 | 1 |
| 83 | 85 | 98 | — | **DOWNTOWN** — Mrs. Miller (Alexis De Azevedo), Capitol 5640 | 3 |
| ★84 | — | — | — | **I KNOW YOU BETTER THAN THAT** — Bobby Goldsboro (Jack Gold), United Artists 50018 | 1 |
| 85 | 91 | — | — | **TRULY JULIE'S BLUES** — Bob Lind (Jack Nitzche), World Pacific 77822 | 2 |
| ★86 | — | — | — | **BETTER USE YOUR HEAD** — Little Anthony & the Imperials (Teddy Randazzo), Veep 1228 | 1 |
| ★87 | — | — | — | **GIRL IN LOVE** — The Outsiders (Tom King), Capitol 5646 | 1 |
| ★88 | — | — | — | **MAMA** — B. J. Thomas (Music Enterprises, Inc.), Scepter 12139 | 1 |
| ★89 | — | — | — | **IT'S OVER** — Jimmie Rodgers (Randy Wood), Dot 16861 | 1 |
| ★90 | — | — | — | **S.Y.S.L.J.F.M. (Letter Song)** — Joe Tex (Buddy Killen), Dial 9902 | 1 |
| 91 | 97 | 99 | — | **MY LITTLE RED BOOK** — Love (Jac Holzman & Mark Abramson), Elektra 603 | 3 |
| 92 | 94 | 94 | 91 | **PIN THE TAIL ON THE DONKEY** — Paul Peek (Joe South), Columbia 43527 | 5 |
| 93 | 93 | — | — | **STILL** — Sunrays (Murry Wilson & Don Ralke), Tower 224 | 2 |
| 94 | 95 | — | — | **THE BIG HURT** — Del Shannon (Snuff Garrett & Leon Russell), Liberty 55866 | 2 |
| 95 | 96 | — | — | **A LOVER'S CONCERTO** — Mrs. Miller (Alexis DeAzevedo), Capitol 5640 | 2 |
| 96 | 100 | — | — | **HEADLINE NEWS** — Edwin Starr (Kent & Morris), Ric-Tic 114 | 2 |
| 97 | 98 | — | — | **I'LL LOVE YOU FOREVER** — Holidays (Davis-Jackson Prod.), Golden World 36 | 2 |
| 98 | — | — | — | **MARBLE BREAKS AND IRON BENDS** — Drafi (Hansa Productions), London 10825 | 1 |
| 99 | — | — | — | **LOUIE, LOUIE** — Kingsmen (Jerden Productions), Wand 143 | 1 |
| 100 | — | — | — | **EVERY DAY I HAVE TO CRY** — Gentrys (Chips Moman), MGM 13495 | 1 |

## HOT 100—A TO Z—*(Publisher-Licensee)*

"A" Team, The (Music, Music, Music, ASCAP)... 35
Backstage (Eden-Catalogue-Primary, BMI) ...... 32
Ballad of Irving, The (Thirteen, ASCAP) ........ 37
Band of Gold (Ludlow, BMI) .................. 41
Bang Bang (Five-West-Cotillion, BMI) .......... 19
Barefootin' (Bonatemp, BMI) .................. 52
Better Use Your Head (South Mountain, BMI) ... 86
Big Hurt, The (Music Productions, ASCAP) ...... 94
Come On Let's Go (Kemo, Figure, Clockus, BMI).. 31
Come Running Back (Richbare-Kita, BMI) ....... 62
Cool Jerk (McLaughlin, BMI) .................. 51
Cruel War, The (Pepamar, ASCAP) ............ 54
Darling Baby (Jobete, BMI) .................. 76
Daydream (Faithful Virtue, BMI) .............. 29
Did You Ever Have to Make Up Your Mind? (Faithful Virtue, BMI) .................. 25
Dirty Water (Equinox, BMI) .................. 63
Distant Drums (Combine, BMI)................. 45
Double Shot (Of My Baby's Love) (Lyresong-Windsong, BMI) ..................... 66
Downtown (Leeds, ASCAP) .................... 83
Dum-De-Da (Gallico, BMI) .................... 47
Eight Miles High (Tickson, BMI) .............. 16
Elvira (Blue Crest, BMI) ..................... 72
Everyday I Have to Cry (Tiki, BMI) ...........100
Evol-Not Love (Jetstar, BMI) ................. 57
Girl in Love (Beechwood, BMI) ............... 87
Gloria—Shadows of Knight (Bernice, BMI) ........ 10
Gloria—Them (Hyde Park, ASCAP) ............ 75
Good Lovin' (T.M., BMI) ..................... 2
Got My Mojo Working (Arc, BMI) .............. 58
Green Grass (Mills, ASCAP) .................. 49
Groovy Kind of Love, A (Screen Gems-Columbia, BMI) ............................ 13
He Cried (Trio, BMI) ........................ 65
Headline News (Myto, BMI) .................. 96
History Repeats Itself (Glaser, BMI) .......... 39
Hold On! I'm Comin' (East-Pronto, BMI) ........ 55
How Does That Grab You Darlin' (Citerion, ASCAP) 7
I Am a Rock (Eclectic, BMI) .................. 24
I Can't Grow Peaches on a Cherry Tree (April, ASCAP) ............................ 34
I Can't Let Go (Blackwood, BMI) .............. 44
I Know You Better Than That (Unart, BMI)........84
I Love You Drops (Moss-Rose, BMI) ............ 67
I Love You 1,000 Times (Ludix, BMI) .......... 60
I'll Love You Forever (Myto, BMI) ............ 97
I'll Take Good Care of You (Rittenhouse & Web IV, BMI) ............................ 33
(I'm a) Road Runner (Jobete, BMI) ............ 43
I'm Comin' Home, Cindy (Tridon, BMI) ........ 40
I'm So Lonesome I Could Cry (Acuff-Rose, BMI).. 28
It's a Man's Man's Man's World (Dynatone, BMI) 23
It's Over (Honeycomb, ASCAP) ................ 89
Kicks (Screen Gems-Columbia, BMI) ........... 4
Last Word in Lonesome Is Me, The (Tree, BMI).. 82
Leaning on the Lamp Post (Mills, ASCAP) ...... 12
Let Me Be Good to You (East, BMI) ........... 78
Let's Start All Over Again (Picturetone, BMI) .... 22
Louie, Louie (Limax, BMI) .................. 99
Love Is Like an Itching in My Heart (Jobete, BMI) 15
Love Me With All of Your Heart (Peer Int'l, BMI). 38
Love Takes a Long Time Growing (Screen Gems-Columbia, BMI) .................. 79
Love's Made a Fool of You (Nor-Va-Jak, BMI) .... 26
Lover's Concerto, A—Mrs. Miller (Saturday, BMI) .. 95
Mama (Flomar, BMI) ......................... 88
Mame (Morris, ASCAP) ....................... 68
Marble Breaks and Iron Bends (Burlington, ASCAP) 98
Message to Michael (U. S. Songs, ASCAP) ...... 8
Monday, Monday (Trousdale, BMI) ............ 1
More I See You, The (Bregman, Vocco & Conn, ASCAP) ............................ 53
My Little Red Book (United Artists, ASCAP) ..... 91
Nothing's Too Good for My Baby (Jobete, BMI) .. 20
Oh How Happy (Myto, BMI) .................. 74
Paint It, Black (Gideon, BMI) ................ 48
Peter Rabbit (Willong, BMI) .................. 81
Pin the Tail on the Donkey (Ahab, BMI) ...... 92
Please Don't Sell My Daddy No More Wine (Third Story, BMI) ............................ 73
Rainy Day Women Nos. 12 & 35 (Dwarf, ASCAP).. 3
Remember the Rain (Metric, BMI) ............ 64
Rhapsody in the Rain (Rambed, BMI) .......... 27
S.Y.S.L.J.F.M. (Letter Song) (Tree, BMI) ......... 90
Secret Agent Man (Trousdale, BMI) ............ 14
Shapes of Things (Unart, BMI) ............... 11
She Blew a Good Thing (Sagittarius, BMI) ...... 46
Sign of the Times, A (Duchess, BMI) .......... 36
Sloop John B (New Executives, BMI) ........... 5
Still (Moss-Rose, BMI) ...................... 93
Strangers in the Night (Roosevelt & Champion, BMI) 71
Sun Ain't Gonna Shine, The (Saturday, BMI) .... 18
Sweet Talkin' Guy (Elmwin, BMI) ............. 61
Teaser, The (Sonkay, BMI) .................. 70
There's No Living Without Your Loving (Catalogue, BMI) ............................ 77
Till the End of the Day (Noma, BMI) .......... 59
Time Won't Let Me (Beechwood, BMI) .......... 17
Tippy Toeing (Window, BMI) .................. 56
Together Again (Central, BMI) ................ 30
Truly Julie's Blues (Metric, BMI) ............. 85
Try Too Hard (Branston, BMI) ................ 21
Twinkle Toes (Acuff-Rose, BMI) .............. 42
Wang Dang Doodle (Arc, BMI) ................ 80
When a Man Loves a Woman (Pronto-Quinvy, BMI) 9
(You're My) Soul and Inspiration (Screen Gems-Columbia, BMI) .......................... 6
You're the One (Jobete, BMI) ................ 50
You've Got My Mind Messed Up (Rose, BMI) .... 69

## BUBBLING UNDER THE HOT 100

101. SEARCHING FOR MY LOVE.Bobby Moore & the Rhythm Aces, Checker 1129
102. BAD EYE ....................Willie Mitchell, Hi 2103
103. SO MUCH LOVE ....................Ben E. King, Atco 6413
104. SOLITARY MAN ....................Neil Diamond, Bang 519
105. SECOND-HAND MAN ..............Back Porch Majority, Epic 9879
106. SO MUCH LOVE ..............Steve Alaimo, ABC-Paramount 10805
107. LAST THING ON MY MIND ..............Womenfolk, RCA Victor 8784
108. DON'T STOP NOW ..............Eddie Holman, Parkway 981
109. SPEAK HER NAME ..............David & Jonathan, Capitol 5625
110. MINE EXCLUSIVELY ..............Olympics, Mirwood 5513
111. SILVER SPOON ....................Toys, DynoVoice 219
112. I LOVE YOU DROPS ..............Don Cherry, Monument 930
113. YOU WAITED TOO LONG ..............Five Stair-Steps, Windy C 601
114. SWEET PEA ..............Tommy Roe, ABC-Paramount 10762
115. DEDICATED FOLLOWER OF FASHION ..............Kinks, Reprise 0471
116. COME ON AND SEE ME ..............Tammi Terrell, Motown 1095
117. TAKE THIS HEART OF MINE ..............Marvin Gaye, Tamla 54132
118. DON'T BRING ME DOWN ..............Animals, MGM 13514
119. JUST A LITTLE MISUNDERSTANDING ..............Contours, Gordy 7052
120. HEY JOE ..............The Leaves, Mira 222
121. YOU'RE READY NOW ..............Frankie Valli, Smash 2037
122. THE IMPOSSIBLE DREAM ..............Jack Jones, Kapp 755
123. THAT'S MY STORY ..........Simon & Garfunkel, ABC-Paramount 10788
124. STRANGERS IN THE NIGHT.....Bert Kaempfert & His Ork, Decca 31945
125. BETTER THAN I..............Terry Knight & the Pack, Lucky 11 226
126. COME AND GET ME ..............Jackie DeShannon, Imperial 66171
127. TAKE ME BACK TO NEW ORLEANS ........Gary (US) Bonds, LeGrand 1040
128. FUNCTION AT THE JUNCTION ..............Shorty Long, Soul 35021
129. SAM, YOU MADE THE PANTS TOO LONG..Barbra Streisand, Columbia 43612
130. STRANGER WITH A BLACK DOVE..........Peter & Gordon, Capitol 5650
131. MAME ..............Louis Armstrong, Mercury 72574
132. YOU COULDN'T GET MY LOVE BACK....Leroy Van Dyke, Warner Bros. 5807
133. I'VE GOT A SECRET ..............Sharpees, One-Derful 4843
134. CHERYL'S GOING HOME ..............Cascades, Arwin 132
135. ONE TOO MANY MORNINGS.........Beau Brummels, Warner Bros. 5813

Compiled from national retail sales and radio station airplay by the Music Popularity Dept. of Record Market Research, Billboard.

For Week Ending May 21, 1966

# Billboard HOT 100

★ STAR performer—Sides registering greatest proportionate upward progress this week.

Record Industry Association of America seal of certification as million selling single.

| This Week | 1 Wk. Ago | 2 Wks. Ago | 3 Wks. Ago | TITLE Artist (Producer), Label & Number | Weeks On Chart |
|---|---|---|---|---|---|
| 1 (Billboard Award) | 1 | 1 | 3 | MONDAY, MONDAY — Mama's and the Papa's (Lou Adler), Dunhill 4026 | 7 |
| 2 | 3 | 7 | 14 | RAINY DAY WOMEN #12 & 35 — Bob Dylan (Bob Johnston), Columbia 43592 | 6 |
| 3 | 2 | 2 | 1 | GOOD LOVIN' — Young Rascals (Tom Dowd, Arif Mardin), Atlantic 2321 | 11 |
| ★4 | 9 | 16 | 29 | WHEN A MAN LOVES A WOMAN — Percy Sledge (Marlin Greene Productions), Atlantic 2326 | 7 |
| ★5 | 13 | 18 | 23 | A GROOVY KIND OF LOVE — Mindbenders, Fontana 1541 | 6 |
| 6 | 4 | 5 | 6 | KICKS — Paul Revere & the Raiders (Terry Melcher), Columbia 43556 | 10 |
| 7 | 7 | 15 | 21 | HOW DOES THAT GRAB YOU DARLIN' — Nancy Sinatra (Lee Hazelwood), Reprise 0461 | 5 |
| 8 | 8 | 13 | 18 | MESSAGE TO MICHAEL — Dionne Warwick (Blue Jac), Scepter 12133 | 8 |
| 9 | 5 | 3 | 4 | SLOOP JOHN B — Beach Boys (Brian Wilson), Capitol 5602 | 8 |
| ★10 | 15 | 26 | 62 | LOVE IS LIKE AN ITCHING IN MY HEART — Supremes (Holland & Dozier), Motown 1094 | 4 |
| 11 | 6 | 4 | 2 | (You're My) SOUL AND INSPIRATION — Righteous Brothers (Bill Medley), Verve 10383 (RIAA seal) | 12 |
| 12 | 10 | 10 | 11 | GLORIA — Shadows of Knight (A Dunwich Prod.), Dunwich 116 | 10 |
| ★13 | 18 | 24 | 39 | THE SUN AIN'T GONNA SHINE (Anymore) — Walker Brothers, Smash 2032 | 6 |
| 14 | 16 | 17 | 22 | EIGHT MILES HIGH — Byrds (Allen Stanton), Columbia 43578 | 7 |
| 15 | 12 | 9 | 10 | LEANING ON THE LAMP POST — Herman's Hermits (Mickie Most), MGM 13500 | 7 |
| ★16 | 25 | 65 | — | DID YOU EVER HAVE TO MAKE UP YOUR MIND? — Lovin' Spoonful (Erik Jacobsen), Kama Sutra 209 | 3 |
| ★17 | 24 | 62 | — | I AM A ROCK — Simon & Garfunkel (Bob Johnston), Columbia 43617 | 3 |
| ★18 | 23 | 31 | 70 | IT'S A MAN'S MAN'S MAN'S WORLD — James Brown (James Brown Productions), King 6035 | 4 |
| ★19 | 48 | — | — | PAINT IT, BLACK — Rolling Stones (Andrew Loog Oldham), London 901 | 2 |
| 20 | 22 | 27 | 41 | LET'S START ALL OVER AGAIN — Ronnie Dove (Kahl-Vernon), Diamond 198 | 6 |
| 21 | 11 | 14 | 15 | SHAPES OF THINGS — Yardbirds (Giorgio Gomelsky), Epic 9891 | 10 |
| 22 | 20 | 25 | 42 | NOTHING'S TOO GOOD FOR MY BABY — Stevie Wonder (Wm. Stevenson), Tamla 54130 | 6 |
| 23 | 17 | 11 | 7 | TIME WON'T LET ME — Outsiders (Tom King), Capitol 5573 | 14 |
| 24 | 14 | 6 | 5 | SECRET AGENT MAN — Johnny Rivers (Lou Adler), Imperial 66159 | 10 |
| ★25 | 49 | — | — | GREEN GRASS — Gary Lewis & the Playboys (Dave Pell), Liberty 55880 | 2 |
| ★26 | 31 | 48 | 64 | COME ON LET'S GO — McCoys (Feldman, Goldstein, Gottehrer Prod.) Bang 522 | 5 |
| ★27 | 32 | 49 | 71 | BACKSTAGE — Gene Pitney (Gene Pitney & Stan Kahan), Musicor 1171 | 5 |
| ★28 | 35 | 41 | 51 | THE "A" TEAM — S/Sgt. Barry Sadler (Andy Wiswell), RCA Victor 8804 | 5 |
| 29 | 26 | 29 | 54 | LOVE'S MADE A FOOL OF YOU — Bobby Fuller Four (A Stereo-Fi Prod.), Mustang 3016 | 6 |
| 30 | 33 | 33 | 46 | I'LL TAKE GOOD CARE OF YOU — Garnet Mimms (Jerry Ragevoy), United Artists 995 | 9 |
| 31 | 19 | 8 | 8 | BANG BANG — Cher (Sonny Bono), Imperial 66160 | 11 |
| 32 | 21 | 12 | 17 | TRY TOO HARD — Dave Clark Five (Dave Clark), Epic 10004 | 8 |
| ★33 | 51 | 56 | 86 | COOL JERK — Capitols (Ollie McLaughlin), Karen 1524 | 4 |
| ★34 | 52 | 70 | 85 | BAREFOOTIN' — Robert Parker (Wherly-Burly Prod.), Nola 721 | 5 |
| 35 | 41 | 47 | 61 | BAND OF GOLD — Mel Carter (Nick DeCaro), Imperial 66165 | 7 |
| 36 | 37 | 37 | 58 | THE BALLAD OF IRVING — Frank Gallop (Booker-Foster), Kapp 745 | 6 |
| 37 | 43 | 60 | 72 | (I'm a) ROAD RUNNER — Jr. Walker & the All Stars (Holland-Dozier), Soul 35015 | 7 |
| 38 | 38 | 43 | 53 | LOVE ME WITH ALL OF YOUR HEART — Bachelors, London 9828 | 6 |
| 39 | 40 | 40 | 50 | I'M COMIN' HOME, CINDY — Trini Lopez (Don Costa), Reprise 0455 | 7 |
| 40 | 42 | 52 | 74 | TWINKLE TOES — Roy Orbison, MGM 13498 | 4 |
| 41 | 47 | 53 | 73 | DUM-DE-DA — Bobby Vinton (Bob Morgan), Epic 10014 | 4 |
| 42 | 34 | 39 | 47 | I CAN'T GROW PEACHES ON A CHERRY TREE — Just Us (Taylor-Gordoni), Colpix 803 | 11 |
| ★43 | 53 | 61 | 76 | THE MORE I SEE YOU — Chris Montez (Herb Alpert), A&M 796 | 6 |
| 44 | 39 | 44 | 48 | HISTORY REPEATS ITSELF — Buddy Starcher (Chuck Glaser), Boone 1038 | 7 |
| ★45 | 55 | 58 | 87 | HOLD ON! I'M COMIN' — Sam & Dave (Prod. By Staff), Stax 189 | 5 |
| 46 | 46 | 45 | 55 | SHE BLEW A GOOD THING — Poets (Juggy Prod.), Symbol 214 | 10 |
| ★47 | 61 | 86 | — | SWEET TALKIN' GUY — Chiffons (Bright Tunes), Laurie 3340 | 3 |
| 48 | 50 | 54 | 65 | YOU'RE THE ONE — Marvelettes (Wm. Robinson), Tamla 54131 | 5 |
| 49 | 45 | 55 | 66 | DISTANT DRUMS — Jim Reeves (Chet Atkins), RCA Victor 8789 | 7 |
| 50 | 44 | 42 | 52 | I CAN'T LET GO — Hollies (Ron Richards), Imperial 66158 | 10 |
| ★51 | 66 | 76 | 92 | DOUBLE SHOT (Of My Baby's Love) — Swingin' Medallions (Karric Prods.), Smash 2033 | 5 |
| 52 | 54 | 59 | 69 | THE CRUEL WAR — Peter, Paul & Mary (Albert B. Grossman), Warner Bros. 5809 | 5 |
| 53 | 57 | 57 | 77 | EVOL-NOT LOVE — Five Americans (Abnak Music Prod.), HBR 465 | 6 |
| ★54 | 71 | 90 | — | STRANGERS IN THE NIGHT — Frank Sinatra (Jimmy Bowen), Reprise 0470 | 3 |
| ★55 | 74 | 89 | — | OH HOW HAPPY — Shades of Blue (John Rhys), Impact 1007 | 3 |
| 56 | 62 | 83 | — | COME RUNNING BACK — Dean Martin (Jimmy Bowen), Reprise 0466 | 3 |
| ★57 | 67 | 77 | — | I LOVE YOU DROPS — Vic Dana (Bob Reisdorff), Dolton 319 | 3 |
| 58 | 60 | 68 | 83 | I LOVE YOU 1,000 TIMES — The Platters (Luther Dixon), Musicor 1166 | 4 |
| ★59 | 88 | — | — | MAMA — B. J. Thomas (Music Enterprises, Inc.), Scepter 12139 | 2 |
| ★60 | 82 | — | — | THE LAST WORD IN LONESOME IS ME — Eddy Arnold (Chet Atkins), RCA Victor 8818 | 2 |
| 61 | 68 | 73 | 79 | MAME — Bobby Darin (Bobby Darin), Atlantic 2329 | 4 |
| 62 | 63 | 69 | 95 | DIRTY WATER — Standells (Ed Cobb), Tower 185 | 5 |
| ★63 | — | — | — | OPUS 17 (Don't Worry 'Bout Me) — 4 Seasons (Bob Crewe), Philips 40370 | 1 |
| 64 | 73 | 88 | 91 | PLEASE DON'T SELL MY DADDY NO MORE WINE — The Greenwoods (Wally Brady), Kapp 742 | 4 |
| 65 | 77 | 80 | — | THERE'S NO LIVING WITHOUT YOUR LOVING — Peter & Gordon (John Burgess), Capitol 5650 | 3 |
| ★66 | 87 | — | — | GIRL IN LOVE — The Outsiders (Tom King), Capitol 5646 | 2 |
| 67 | 64 | 64 | 68 | REMEMBER THE RAIN — Bob Lind (Jack Nitzsche), World Pacific 77822 | 5 |
| 68 | 80 | 81 | 93 | WANG DANG DOODLE — Ko Ko Taylor (Willie Dixon), Checker 1135 | 5 |
| ★69 | 84 | — | — | I KNOW YOU BETTER THAN THAT — Bobby Goldsboro (Jack Gold), United Artists 50018 | 2 |
| 70 | 78 | 78 | 96 | LET ME BE GOOD TO YOU — Carla Thomas (Prod. by Staff), Stax 188 | 4 |
| ★71 | 86 | — | — | BETTER USE YOUR HEAD — Little Anthony & the Imperials (Teddy Randazzo), Veep 1228 | 2 |
| 72 | 81 | 87 | — | PETER RABBIT — Dee Jay and the Runaways (Iowa Great Lakes Studios), Smash 2034 | 3 |
| ★73 | 89 | — | — | IT'S OVER — Jimmie Rodgers (Randy Wood), Dot 16861 | 2 |
| 74 | 72 | 74 | 81 | ELVIRA — Dallas Frazier (Marvin Hughes), Capitol 5560 | 4 |
| ★75 | 90 | — | — | S.Y.S.L.J.F.M. (Letter Song) — Joe Tex (Buddy Killen), Dial 9902 | 2 |
| ★76 | — | — | — | YOU DON'T HAVE TO SAY YOU LOVE ME — Dusty Springfield, Philips 40371 | 1 |
| 77 | 79 | 82 | 90 | LOVE TAKES A LONG TIME GROWING — Deon Jackson (Ollie McLaughlin), Carla 2527 | 4 |
| 78 | 75 | 75 | 88 | GLORIA — Them (Bert Burns), Parrot 9727 | 6 |
| ★79 | — | — | — | DON'T BRING ME DOWN — Animals (Tom Wilson), MGM 13514 | 1 |
| ★80 | — | — | — | DEDICATED FOLLOWER OF FASHION — Kinks (Shel Talmy), Reprise 0471 | 1 |
| 81 | 85 | 91 | — | TRULY JULIE'S BLUES — Bob Lind (Jack Nitzche), World Pacific 77822 | 3 |
| 82 | 83 | 85 | 98 | DOWNTOWN — Mrs. Miller (Alexis De Azevedo), Capitol 5640 | 4 |
| 83 | 91 | 97 | 99 | MY LITTLE RED BOOK — Love (Jac Holzman & Mark Abramson), Elektra 603 | 4 |
| ★84 | — | — | — | HEY JOE — Leaves (Norm Ratner), Mira 222 | 1 |
| ★85 | — | — | — | MAME — Louis Armstrong (Hal Mooney), Mercury 72574 | 1 |
| ★86 | — | — | — | CLOUDY SUMMER AFTERNOON — Barry McGuire (Lou Adler), Dunhill 4028 | 1 |
| ★87 | — | — | — | SOLITARY MAN — Neil Diamond (Barry & Greenwich), Bang 519 | 1 |
| 88 | 98 | — | — | MARBLE BREAKS AND IRON BENDS — Drafi (Hansa Productions), London 10825 | 2 |
| 89 | 96 | 100 | — | HEADLINE NEWS — Edwin Starr (Kent & Morris), Ric-Tic 114 | 3 |
| ★90 | — | — | — | RED RUBBER BALL — Cyrkle (John Simon), Columbia 43589 | 1 |
| 91 | — | — | — | HEART'S DESIRE — Billy Joe Royal (Joe South), Columbia 43622 | 1 |
| 92 | 97 | 98 | — | I'LL LOVE YOU FOREVER — Holidays (Davis-Jackson Prod.), Golden World 36 | 3 |
| 93 | — | — | — | SO MUCH LOVE — Steve Alaimo, ABC-Paramount 10805 | 1 |
| 94 | — | — | — | YOU WAITED TOO LONG — Five Stair-Steps (C. Mayfield), Windy C 601 | 1 |
| 95 | 100 | — | — | EVERYDAY I HAVE TO CRY — Gentrys (Chips Moman), MGM 13495 | 2 |
| 96 | — | — | — | SO MUCH LOVE — Ben E. King, Atco 6413 | 1 |
| 97 | 99 | — | — | LOUIE, LOUIE — Kingsmen (Jerden Productions), Wand 143 | 2 |
| 98 | — | — | — | SAM, YOU MADE THE PANTS TOO LONG — Barbra Streisand (Warren Vincent), Columbia 43612 | 1 |
| 99 | — | — | — | TAKE THIS HEART OF MINE — Marvin Gaye (Robinson-Moore), Tamla 54132 | 1 |
| 100 | — | — | — | GOOD TIME CHARLIE — Bobby Bland, Duke 402 | 1 |

## HOT 100—A TO Z—*(Publisher-Licensee)*


"A" Team, The (Music, Music, Music, ASCAP) .... 28
Backstage (Eden-Catalogue-Primary, BMI) ........ 27
Ballad of Irving, The (Thirteen, ASCAP) ...... 36
Band of Gold (Ludlow, BMI) ........ 35
Bang Bang (Five-West-Cotillion, BMI) ........ 31
Barefootin' (Bonatemp, BMI) ........ 34
Better Use Your Head (South Mountain, BMI) .... 71
Cloudy Summer Afternoon (Metric, BMI) ........ 86
Come On Let's Go (Kemo, Figure, Clockus, BMI) .. 26
Come Running Back (Richbare-Kita, BMI) ...... 56
Cool Jerk (McLaughlin, BMI) ........ 33
Cruel War, The (Pepamar, ASCAP) ........ 52
Dedicated Follower of Fashion (Noma, BMI) .... 80
Did You Ever Have to Make Up Your Mind? (Faithful Virtue, BMI) ........ 16
Dirty Water (Equinox, BMI) ........ 62
Distant Drums (Combine, BMI) ........ 49
Don't Bring Me Down (Screen Gems-Columbia, BMI) ........ 79
Double Shot (Of My Baby's Love) (Lyresong-Windsong, BMI) ........ 51
Downtown (Leeds, ASCAP) ........ 82
Dum-De-Da (Gallico, BMI) ........ 41
Eight Miles High (Tickson, BMI) ........ 14
Elvira (Blue Crest, BMI) ........ 74
Everyday I Have to Cry (Tiki, BMI) ........ 95
Evol-Not Love (Jetstar, BMI) ........ 53
Girl in Love (Beechwood, BMI) ........ 66
Gloria—Shadows of Knight (Bernice, BMI) ........ 12
Gloria—Them (Hyde Park, ASCAP) ........ 78
Good Lovin' (T.M., BMI) ........ 3
Good Time Charlie (Don, BMI) ........ 100
Green Grass (Mills, ASCAP) ........ 25
Groovy Kind of Love, A (Screen Gems-Columbia, BMI) ........ 5
Headline News (Myto, BMI) ........ 89
Heart's Desire (Lowery, BMI) ........ 91
Hey Joe (Third Story, BMI) ........ 84
History Repeats Itself (Glaser, BMI) ........ 44
Hold On! I'm Comin' (East, Pronto, BMI) ........ 45
How Does That Grab You Darlin' (Criterion, ASCAP) ........ 7
I Am a Rock (Eclectic, BMI) ........ 17
I Can't Grow Peaches on a Cherry Tree (April, ASCAP) ........ 42
I Can't Let Go (Blackwood, BMI) ........ 50
I Know You Better Than That (Unart, BMI) ..... 69
I Love You Drops (Moss-Rose, BMI) ........ 57
I Love You 1,000 Times (Ludix, BMI) ........ 58
I'll Love You Forever (Myto, BMI) ........ 92
I'll Take Good Care of You (Rittenhouse & Web IV, BMI) ........ 30
(I'm a) Road Runner (Jobete, BMI) ........ 37
I'm Comin' Home, Cindy (Tridon, BMI) ........ 39
It's a Man's Man's Man's World (Dynatone, BMI) 18
It's Over (Honeycomb, ASCAP) ........ 73
Kicks (Screen Gems-Columbia, BMI) ........ 6
Last Word in Lonesome Is Me, The (Tree, BMI) .. 60
Leaning on the Lamp Post (Mills, ASCAP) ...... 15
Let Me Be Good to You (East, BMI) ........ 70
Let's Start All Over Again (Picturetone, BMI) .. 20
Louie, Louie (Limax, BMI) ........ 97
Love Is Like an Itching in My Heart (Jobete, BMI) 10
Love Me With All of Your Heart (Peer Int'l, BMI) 38
Love Takes a Long Time Growing (Screen Gems-Columbia, BMI) ........ 77
Love's Made a Fool of You (Nor-Va-Jak, BMI) ... 29
Mama (Flomar, BMI) ........ 59
Mame—Armstrong (Morris, ASCAP) ........ 85
Mame—Darin (Morris, ASCAP) ........ 61
Marble Breaks and Iron Bends (Burlington, ASCAP). 88
Message to Michael (U. S. Songs, ASCAP) ........ 8
Monday, Monday (Trousdale, BMI) ........ 1
More I See You, The (Bregman, Vocco & Conn, ASCAP) ........ 43
My Little Red Book (United Artists, ASCAP) ...... 83
Nothing's Too Good for My Baby (Jobete, BMI) .. 22
Oh How Happy (Myto, BMI) ........ 55
Opus 17 (Don't Worry 'Bout Me) (Saturday, BMI). 63
Paint It, Black (Gideon, BMI) ........ 19
Peter Rabbit (Willono, BMI) ........ 72
Please Don't Sell My Daddy No More Wine (Third Story, BMI) ........ 64
Rainy Day Women Nos. 12 & 35 (Dwarf, ASCAP) .. 2
Red Rubber Ball (Eclectic, BMI) ........ 90
Remember the Rain (Metric, BMI) ........ 67
S.Y.S.L.J.F.M. (Letter Song) (Tree, BMI) ........ 75
Sam, You Made the Pants Too Long (Shapiro-Bernstein, ASCAP) ........ 98
Secret Agent Man (Trousdale, BMI) ........ 24
Shapes of Things (Unart, BMI) ........ 21
She Blew a Good Thing (Sagittarius, BMI) ...... 46
Sloop John B (New Executives, BMI) ........ 9
Solitary Man (Tallyrand, BMI) ........ 87
So Much Love—Alaimo (Screen Gems-Columbia, BMI) ........ 93
So Much Love—King (Screen Gems-Columbia, BMI). 96
Strangers in the Night (Champion-Brown, BMI) .. 54
Sun Ain't Gonna Shine, The (Saturday, BMI) ...... 13
Sweet Talkin' Guy (Elmwin, BMI) ........ 47
Take This Heart of Mine (Jobete, BMI) ........ 99
There's No Living Without Your Loving (Catalogue, BMI) ........ 65
Time Won't Let Me (Beechwood, BMI) ........ 23
Truly Julie's Blues (Metric, BMI) ........ 81
Try Too Hard (Branston, BMI) ........ 32
Twinkle Toes (Acuff-Rose, BMI) ........ 40
Wang Dang Doodle (Arc, BMI) ........ 68
When a Man Loves a Woman (Pronto-Quinvy, BMI) 4
You Don't Have to Say You Love Me (Robbins, ASCAP) ........ 76
You Waited Too Long (Camad, BMI) ........ 94
(You're My) Soul and Inspiration (Screen Gems-Columbia, BMI) ........ 11
You're the One (Jobete, BMI) ........ 48


## BUBBLING UNDER THE HOT 100

101. AIN'T TOO PROUD TO BEG ........ Temptations, Gordy 7054
102. BAD EYE ........ Willie Mitchell, Hi 2103
103. YOUNGER GIRL ........ Hondells, Mercury 72563
104. SECOND HAND MAN ........ Back Porch Majority, Epic 9879
105. LAST THING ON MY MIND ........ Womenfolk, RCA Victor 8784
106. BREAK OUT ........ Mitch Ryder & the Detroit Wheels, New Voice 811
107. SEARCHING FOR MY LOVE .. Bobby Moore & the Rhythm Aces, Checker 1129
108. DON'T STOP NOW ........ Eddie Holman, Parkway 981
109. MINE EXCLUSIVELY ........ Olympics, Mirwood 5513
110. SWEET PEA ........ Tommy Roe, ABC-Paramount 10762
111. CRYING ........ Jay & the Americans, United Artists 50016
112. I'LL GO CRAZY ........ Buckinghams, U. S. A. 844
113. LITTLE GIRL ........ Syndicate of Sound, Bell 640
114. COME ON AND SEE ME ........ Tammi Terrell, Motown 1095
115. JUST A LITTLE MISUNDERSTANDING ........ Contours, Gordy 7052
116. SPEAK HER NAME ........ David & Jonathan, Capitol 5625
117. YOU'RE READY NOW ........ Frankie Valli, Smash 2037
118. THE IMPOSSIBLE DREAM ........ Jack Jones, Kapp 755
119. YOUNGER GIRL ........ Critters, Kapp 752
120. WIGGLIN' AND GIGGLIN' ........ Roy Head, Back Beat 563
121. WIEDERSEH'N ........ Al Martino, Capitol 5652
122. ALONG COMES MARY ........ Association, Valiant 741
123. NEIGHBOR, NEIGHBOR ........ Jimmy Hughes, Fame 1003
124. RIVER DEEP—MOUNTAIN HIGH ........ Ike & Tina Turner, Philles 131
125. COME AND GET ME ........ Jackie DeShannon, Imperial 66171
126. TAKE ME BACK TO NEW ORLEANS .... Gary (U.S.) Bonds, Legrand 1040
127. LOVING YOU IS SWEETER THAN EVER ........ Four Tops, Motown 1096
128. SOMEWHERE ........ Johnny Nash, Joda 106
129. QUARTER TO THREE ........ Sir Douglas, Tribe 8317
130. A STREET THAT RHYMES AT SIX A.M. .... Norma Tanega, New Voice 810
131. IT'S AN UPHILL CLIMB TO THE BOTTOM ....... Walter Jackson, Okeh 7247
132. DON'T TOUCH ME ........ Jeannie Seeley, Monument 935
133. TAKE SOME TIME OUT FOR LOVE ........ Isley Brothers, Tamla 54133
134. WHAT'S A NICE KID LIKE YOU DOING IN A PLACE LIKE THIS? ........ Scatman Crothers, HBR 476
135. TRULY YOURS ........ Spinners, Motown 1093


Compiled from national retail sales and radio station airplay by the Music Popularity Dept. of Record Market Research, Billboard.

Billboard

For Week Ending May 28, 1966

# HOT 100

★ STAR performer—Sides registering greatest proportionate upward progress this week.

(Seal) Record Industry Association of America seal of certification as million selling single.

| THIS WEEK | 1 Wk. Ago | 2 Wks. Ago | 3 Wks. Ago | TITLE Artist (Producer), Label & Number | Weeks On Chart |
|---|---|---|---|---|---|
| Billboard Award 1 | 4 | 9 | 16 | WHEN A MAN LOVES A WOMAN — Percy Sledge (Quin Ivy-Marvin Greene) Atlantic 2326 | 8 |
| ★2 | 5 | 13 | 18 | A GROOVY KIND OF LOVE — Mindbenders, Fontana 1541 | 7 |
| 3 | 1 | 1 | 1 | MONDAY, MONDAY — Mama's and the Papa's (Lou Adler), Dunhill 4026 | 8 |
| ★4 | 19 | 48 | — | PAINT IT, BLACK — Rolling Stones (Andrew Loog Oldham), London 901 | 3 |
| 5 | 2 | 3 | 7 | RAINY DAY WOMEN #12 & 35 — Bob Dylan (Bob Johnston), Columbia 43592 | 7 |
| ★6 | 17 | 24 | 62 | I AM A ROCK — Simon & Garfunkel (Bob Johnston), Columbia 43617 | 4 |
| ★7 | 16 | 25 | 65 | DID YOU EVER HAVE TO MAKE UP YOUR MIND? — Lovin' Spoonful (Erik Jacobsen), Kama Sutra 209 | 4 |
| 8 | 3 | 2 | 2 | GOOD LOVIN' — Young Rascals (Tom Dowd, Arif Mardin), Atlantic 2321 | 12 |
| 9 | 10 | 15 | 26 | LOVE IS LIKE AN ITCHING IN MY HEART — Supremes (Holland & Dozier), Motown 1094 | 5 |
| ★10 | 18 | 23 | 31 | IT'S A MAN'S MAN'S MAN'S WORLD — James Brown (James Brown Productions), King 6035 | 5 |
| 11 | 6 | 4 | 5 | KICKS — Paul Revere & the Raiders (Terry Melcher), Columbia 43556 | 11 |
| ★12 | 25 | 49 | — | GREEN GRASS — Gary Lewis & the Playboys (Dave Pell), Liberty 55880 | 3 |
| 13 | 13 | 18 | 24 | THE SUN AIN'T GONNA SHINE (Anymore) — Walker Brothers, Smash 2032 | 7 |
| 14 | 8 | 8 | 13 | MESSAGE TO MICHAEL — Dionne Warwick (Blue Jac), Scepter 12133 | 9 |
| 15 | 9 | 5 | 3 | SLOOP JOHN B — Beach Boys (Brian Wilson), Capitol 5602 | 9 |
| 16 | 7 | 7 | 15 | HOW DOES THAT GRAB YOU DARLIN' — Nancy Sinatra (Lee Hazelwood), Reprise 0461 | 6 |
| ★17 | 34 | 52 | 70 | BAREFOOTIN' — Robert Parker (Wherly-Burly Prod.), Nola 721 | 6 |
| ★18 | 47 | 61 | 86 | SWEET TALKIN' GUY — Chiffons (Bright Tunes), Laurie 3340 | 4 |
| ★19 | 33 | 51 | 56 | COOL JERK — Capitols (Ollie McLaughlin), Karen 1524 | 5 |
| 20 | 12 | 10 | 10 | GLORIA — Shadows of Knight (A Dunwich Prod.), Dunwich 116 | 11 |
| 21 | 14 | 16 | 17 | EIGHT MILES HIGH — Byrds (Allen Stanton), Columbia 43578 | 8 |
| 22 | 20 | 22 | 27 | LET'S START ALL OVER AGAIN — Ronnie Dove (Kahl-Vernon), Diamond 198 | 7 |
| 23 | 26 | 31 | 48 | COME ON LET'S GO — McCoys (Feldman, Goldstein, Gottehrer Prod.) Bang 522 | 6 |
| ★24 | 37 | 43 | 60 | (I'm a) ROAD RUNNER — Jr. Walker & the All Stars (Holland-Dozier), Soul 35015 | 8 |
| 25 | 27 | 32 | 49 | BACKSTAGE — Gene Pitney (Gene Pitney & Stan Kahan), Musicor 1171 | 6 |
| ★26 | 55 | 74 | 89 | OH HOW HAPPY — Shades of Blue (John Rhys), Impact 1007 | 4 |
| ★27 | 54 | 71 | 90 | STRANGERS IN THE NIGHT — Frank Sinatra (Jimmy Bowen), Reprise 0470 | 4 |
| 28 | 28 | 35 | 41 | THE "A" TEAM — S/Sgt. Barry Sadler (Andy Wiswell), RCA Victor 8804 | 6 |
| ★29 | 43 | 53 | 61 | THE MORE I SEE YOU — Chris Montez (Herb Alpert), A&M 796 | 7 |
| 30 | 15 | 12 | 9 | LEANING ON THE LAMP POST — Herman's Hermits (Mickie Most), MGM 13500 | 8 |
| ★31 | 63 | — | — | OPUS 17 (Don't Worry 'Bout Me) — 4 Seasons (Bob Crewe), Philips 40370 | 2 |
| 32 | 35 | 41 | 47 | BAND OF GOLD — Mel Carter (Nick DeCaro), Imperial 66165 | 8 |
| 33 | 11 | 6 | 4 | (You're My) SOUL AND INSPIRATION — Righteous Brothers (Bill Medley), Verve 10383 | 13 (Seal) |
| 34 | 36 | 37 | 37 | THE BALLAD OF IRVING — Frank Gallop (Booker-Foster), Kapp 745 | 7 |
| 35 | 23 | 17 | 11 | TIME WON'T LET ME — Outsiders (Tom King), Capitol 5573 | 15 |
| 36 | 21 | 11 | 14 | SHAPES OF THINGS — Yardbirds (Giorgio Gomelsky), Epic 9891 | 11 |
| 37 | 22 | 20 | 25 | NOTHING'S TOO GOOD FOR MY BABY — Stevie Wonder (Wm. Stevenson), Tamla 54130 | 7 |
| 38 | 24 | 14 | 6 | SECRET AGENT MAN — Johnny Rivers (Lou Adler), Imperial 66159 | 11 |
| 39 | 40 | 42 | 52 | TWINKLE TOES — Roy Orbison, MGM 13498 | 5 |
| 40 | 41 | 47 | 53 | DUM-DE-DA — Bobby Vinton (Bob Morgan), Epic 10014 | 5 |
| ★41 | 51 | 66 | 76 | DOUBLE SHOT (Of My Baby's Love) — Swingin' Medallions (Karric Prods.), Smash 2033 | 6 |
| 42 | 45 | 55 | 58 | HOLD ON! I'M COMIN' — Sam & Dave (Prod. By Staff), Stax 189 | 6 |
| ★43 | 57 | 67 | 77 | I LOVE YOU DROPS — Vic Dana (Bob Reisdorff), Dolton 319 | 4 |
| ★44 | 66 | 87 | — | GIRL IN LOVE — The Outsiders (Tom King), Capitol 5646 | 3 |
| ★45 | 59 | 88 | — | MAMA — B. J. Thomas (Music Enterprises, Inc.), Scepter 12139 | 3 |
| ★46 | 56 | 62 | 83 | COME RUNNING BACK — Dean Martin (Jimmy Bowen), Reprise 0466 | 4 |
| ★47 | 79 | — | — | DON'T BRING ME DOWN — Animals (Tom Wilson), MGM 13514 | 2 |
| 48 | 48 | 50 | 54 | YOU'RE THE ONE — Marvelettes (Wm. Robinson), Tamla 54131 | 6 |
| ★49 | 76 | — | — | YOU DON'T HAVE TO SAY YOU LOVE ME — Dusty Springfield, Philips 40371 | 2 |
| 50 | 58 | 60 | 68 | I LOVE YOU 1,000 TIMES — The Platters (Luther Dixon), Musicor 1166 | 5 |
| ★51 | 75 | 90 | — | S.Y.S.L.J.F.M. (Letter Song) — Joe Tex (Buddy Killen), Dial 9902 | 3 |
| 52 | 60 | 82 | — | THE LAST WORD IN LONESOME IS ME — Eddy Arnold (Chet Atkins), RCA Victor 8818 | 3 |
| 53 | 53 | 57 | 57 | EVOL-NOT LOVE — Five Americans (Abnak Music Prod.), HBR 468 | 7 |
| 54 | 61 | 68 | 73 | MAME — Bobby Darin (Bobby Darin), Atlantic 2329 | 5 |
| ★55 | 65 | 77 | 80 | THERE'S NO LIVING WITHOUT YOUR LOVING — Peter & Gordon (John Burgess), Capitol 5650 | 4 |
| ★56 | 69 | 84 | — | I KNOW YOU BETTER THAN THAT — Bobby Goldsboro (Jack Gold), United Artists 50018 | 3 |
| 57 | 62 | 63 | 69 | DIRTY WATER — Standells (Ed Cobb), Tower 185 | 6 |
| ★58 | 68 | 80 | 81 | WANG DANG DOODLE — Ko Ko Taylor (Willie Dixon), Checker 1135 | 6 |
| ★59 | 73 | 89 | — | IT'S OVER — Jimmie Rodgers (Randy Wood), Dot 16861 | 3 |
| ★60 | 80 | — | — | DEDICATED FOLLOWER OF FASHION — Kinks (Shel Talmy), Reprise 0471 | 2 |
| ★61 | 72 | 81 | 87 | PETER RABBIT — Dee Jay and the Runaways (Iowa Great Lakes Studios), Smash 2034 | 4 |
| 62 | 70 | 78 | 78 | LET ME BE GOOD TO YOU — Carla Thomas (Prod. by Staff), Stax 188 | 5 |
| 63 | 71 | 86 | — | BETTER USE YOUR HEAD — Little Anthony & the Imperials (Teddy Randazzo), Veep 1228 | 3 |
| 64 | 64 | 73 | 88 | PLEASE DON'T SELL MY DADDY NO MORE WINE — The Greenwoods (Wally Buady), Kapp 742 | 5 |
| ★65 | 90 | — | — | RED RUBBER BALL — Cyrkle (John Simon), Columbia 43589 | 2 |
| ★66 | — | — | — | CRYING — Jay & the Americans (Gerry Granahan), United Artists 50016 | 1 |
| ★67 | — | — | — | AIN'T TOO PROUD TO BEG — Temptations (N. Whitfield), Gordy 7054 | 1 |
| ★68 | 83 | 91 | 97 | MY LITTLE RED BOOK — Love (Jac Holzman & Mark Abramson), Elektra 603 | 5 |
| ★69 | 84 | — | — | HEY JOE — Leaves (Norm Ratner), Mira 222 | 2 |
| ★70 | 99 | — | — | TAKE THIS HEART OF MINE — Marvin Gaye (Robinson-Moore), Tamla 54132 | 2 |
| 71 | 78 | 75 | 75 | GLORIA — Them (Bert Burns), Parrot 9727 | 7 |
| 72 | 81 | 85 | 91 | TRULY JULIE'S BLUES — Bob Lind (Jack Nitzche), World Pacific 77822 | 4 |
| ★73 | — | — | — | WIEDERSEH'N — Al Martino (Tom Morgan), Capitol 5652 | 1 |
| ★74 | — | — | — | BREAK OUT — Mitch Ryder and the Detroit Wheels (Bob Crewe), New Voice 811 | 1 |
| ★75 | — | — | — | TAKE SOME TIME OUT FOR LOVE — Isley Brothers (Robert Gordy), Tamla 54133 | 1 |
| ★76 | — | — | — | NINETY-NINE AND A HALF — Wilson Pickett (Steve Cropper), Atlantic 2334 | 1 |
| 77 | 77 | 79 | 82 | LOVE TAKES A LONG TIME GROWING — Deon Jackson (Ollie McLaughlin), Carla 2527 | 5 |
| 78 | 87 | — | — | SOLITARY MAN — Neil Diamond (Barry & Greenwich), Bang 519 | 2 |
| 79 | 86 | — | — | CLOUDY SUMMER AFTERNOON — Barry McGuire (Lou Adler), Dunhill 4028 | 2 |
| 80 | 88 | 98 | — | MARBLE BREAKS AND IRON BENDS — Drafi (Hansa Productions), London 10825 | 3 |
| 81 | 85 | — | — | MAME — Louis Armstrong (Hal Mooney), Mercury 72574 | 2 |
| ★82 | — | — | — | BATMAN & HIS GRANDMOTHER — Dickie Goodman, Red Bird 10-058 | 1 |
| ★83 | — | — | — | LET'S GO GET STONED — Ray Charles (Joe Adams), ABC-Paramount 10808 | 1 |
| 84 | 89 | 96 | 100 | HEADLINE NEWS — Edwin Starr (Kent & Morris), Ric-Tic 114 | 4 |
| ★85 | — | — | — | COME AND GET ME — Jackie DeShannon (Bacharach-David), Imperial 66171 | 1 |
| ★86 | — | — | — | JUST A LITTLE MISUNDERSTANDING — Contours (Paul-Stevenson), Gordy 7052 | 1 |
| 87 | 100 | — | — | GOOD TIME CHARLIE — Bobby Bland, Duke 402 | 2 |
| 88 | 91 | — | — | HEART'S DESIRE — Billy Joe Royal (Joe South), Columbia 43622 | 2 |
| 89 | 95 | 100 | — | EVERYDAY I HAVE TO CRY — Gentrys (Chips Moman), MGM 13495 | 3 |
| ★90 | — | — | — | YOUNGER GIRL — Critters (Artie Ripp), Kapp 752 | 1 |
| 91 | 92 | 97 | 98 | I'LL LOVE YOU FOREVER — Holidays (Davis-Jackson Prod.), Golden World 36 | 4 |
| 92 | 93 | — | — | SO MUCH LOVE — Steve Alaimo, ABC-Paramount 10805 | 2 |
| 93 | — | — | — | YOUNGER GIRL — Hondells (G. P. IV Prod.), Mercury 72563 | 1 |
| 94 | 94 | — | — | YOU WAITED TOO LONG — Five Stair-Steps (C. Mayfield), Windy C 601 | |
| 95 | — | — | — | LOVING YOU IS SWEETER THAN EVER — Four Tops (Ivy Hunter), Motown 1096 | 1 |
| 96 | 96 | — | — | SO MUCH LOVE — Ben E. King, Atco 6413 | 2 |
| 97 | — | — | — | DON'T TOUCH ME — Jeannie Seely (Fred Foster), Monument 9 3 | |
| 98 | — | — | — | RIVER DEEP—MOUNTAIN HIGH — Ike & Tina Turner (Phil Spector), Philles 131 | 1 |
| 99 | — | — | — | THINK OF ME — Buck Owens (Ken Nelson), Capitol 5647 | 1 |
| 100 | — | — | — | COME ON AND SEE ME — Tammi Terrell (Fuqua-Bristol), Motown 1095 | 1 |

## HOT 100—A TO Z—(Publisher-Licensee)

"A" Team, The (Music, Music, Music, ASCAP) .. 28
Ain't Too Proud to Beg (Jobete, BMI) .......... 67
Backstage (Eden-Catalogue-Primary, BMI) ...... 25
Ballad of Irving, The (Thirteen, ASCAP) .......... 34
Band of Gold (Ludlow, BMI) .................. 32
Barefootin' (Bonatemp, BMI) .................. 17
Batman & His Grandmother (Not Available) .... 82
Better Use Your Head (South Mountain, BMI) .... 63
Break Out (Saturday, BMI) .................. 74
Cloudy Summer Afternoon (Metric, BMI) ......... 79
Come and Get Me (Jac, ASCAP) ............. 85
Come On and See Me (Jobete, BMI) ...........100
Come On, Let's Go (Kemo, Figure, Clockus, BMI) .. 23
Come Running Back (Richbare-Kita, BMI) ...... 46
Cool Jerk (McLaughlin, BMI) ............... 19
Crying (Acuff-Rose, BMI) .................. 66
Dedicated Follower of Fashion (Noma, BMI) .... 60
Did You Ever Have to Make Up Your Mind?...... (Faithful Virtue, BMI) .................. 7
Dirty Water (Equinox, BMI) .................. 57
Don't Bring Me Down (Screen Gems-Columbia, BMI) .................. 47
Don't Touch Me (Pamper, BMI) ............... 97
Double Shot (Of My Baby's Love) (Lyricsong-Windsong, BMI) .................. 41
Dum-De-Da (Galllico, BMI) .................. 40
Eight Miles High (Tickson, BMI) ............. 21
Everyday I Have to Cry (Tiki, BMI) ............ 89
Evol-Not Love (Jetstar, BMI) ............... 53
Girl in Love (Beechwood, BMI) ............... 44
Gloria—Shadows of Knight (Bernice, BMI) ...... 20
Gloria—Them (Hyde Park, ASCAP) ............. 71
Good Lovin' (T.M., BMI) .................. 8
Good Time Charlie (Don, BMI) ............... 87
Green Grass (Mills, ASCAP) ............... 12
Groovy Kind of Love, A (Screen Gems-Columbia, BMI) .................. 2
Headline News (Myto, BMI) ............... 84
Heart's Desire (Lowery, BMI) ............... 88
Hey, Joe (Third Story, BMI) ............... 69
Hold On! I'm Comin' (East, Pronto, BMI) ....... 42
How Does That Grab You Darlin' (Criterion, ASCAP) .................. 16
I Am a Rock (Eclectic, BMI) ............... 6
I Know You Better Than That (Unart, BMI) .... 56
I Love You Drops (Moss-Rose, BMI) .......... 43
I Love You 1,000 Times (Ludix, BMI) .......... 50
I'll Love You Forever (Myto, BMI) ............ 91
(I'm a) Road Runner (Jobete, BMI) ............ 24
It's a Man's Man's Man's World (Dynatone, BMI) 10
It's Over (Honeycomb, ASCAP) ............... 59
Just a Little Misunderstanding (Jobete, BMI) .... 86
Kicks (Screen Gems-Columbia, BMI) ............ 11
Last Word in Lonesome Is Me, The (Tree, BMI) .. 52
Leaning on the Lamp Post (Mills, ASCAP) ...... 30
Let Me Be Good to You (East, BMI) .......... 62
Let's Go Get Stoned (Baby Monica, BMI) ........ 83
Let's Start All Over Again (Picturetone, BMI) .... 22
Love Is Like an Itching in My Heart (Jobete, BMI) 9
Love Takes a Long Time Growing (Screen Gems-Columbia, BMI) .................. 77
Loving You Is Sweeter Than Ever (Jobete, BMI) . 95
Mama (Flomar, BMI) .................. 45
Mame—Armstrong (Morris, ASCAP) ............ 81
Mame—Darin (Morris, ASCAP) ............... 54
Marble Breaks and Iron Bends (Burlington, ASCAP) 80
Message to Michael (U. S. Songs, ASCAP) ..... 14
Monday, Monday (Trousdale, BMI) ............ 3
More I See You, The (Bregman, Vocco & Conn, ASCAP) .................. 29
My Little Red Book (United Artists, ASCAP) .... 68
Ninety-Nine and a Half (East-Pronto, BMI) ..... 76
Nothing's Too Good for My Baby (Jobete, BMI) .. 37
Oh How Happy (Myto, BMI) ............... 26
Opus 17 (Don't Worry 'Bout Me) (Saturday, BMI) 31
Paint It, Black (Gideon, BMI) ............... 4
Peter Rabbit (Willong, BMI) ............... 61
Please Don't Sell My Daddy No More Wine (Third Story, BMI) .................. 64
Rainy Day Women Nos. 12 & 35 (Dwarf, ASCAP) .. 5
Red Rubber Ball (Eclectic, BMI) ............ 65
River Deep—Mountain High (Trio, BMI) ......... 98
S.Y.S.L.J.F.M. (Letter Song) (Tree, BMI) ........ 51
Secret Agent Man (Trousdale, BMI) ............ 38
Shapes of Things (Unart, BMI) ............... 36
Sloop John B (New Executives, BMI) .......... 15
Solitary Man (Tallyrand, BMI) ............... 78
So Much Love—Alaimo (Screen Gems-Columbia, BMI) .................. 92
So Much Love—King (Screen Gems-Columbia, BMI). 96
Strangers in the Night (Champion-Brown, BMI) ... 27
Sun Ain't Gonna Shine, The (Anymore) (Saturday, BMI) ..................13
Sweet Talkin' Guy (Elmwin, BMI) ............ 18
Take Some Time Out for Love (Jobete, BMI) ..... 75
Take This Heart of Mine (Jobete, BMI) ........ 70
There's No Living Without Your Loving (Catalogue, BMI) .................. 55
Think of Me (Bluebook, BMI) ............... 99
Time Won't Let Me (Beechwood, BMI) ......... 35
Truly Julie's Blues (Metric, BMI) ............ 72
Twinkle Toes (Acuff-Rose, BMI) ............ 39
Wang Dang Doodle (Arc, BMI) ............... 58
When a Man Loves a Woman (Pronto-Quinvy, BMI) 1
Wiederseh'n (Roosevelt, BMI) ............... 73
You Don't Have to Say You Love Me (Robbins, ASCAP) .................. 49
You Waited Too Long (Camad, BMI) ........... 94
(You're My) Soul and Inspiration (Screen Gems-Columbia, BMI) .................. 33
You're the One (Jobete, BMI) ............... 48
Younger Girl—Critters (Faithful Virtue, BMI) .... 90
Younger Girl—Hondells (Faithful Virtue, BMI) .... 93

## BUBBLING UNDER THE HOT 100

101. NEIGHBOR, NEIGHBOR ....Jimmy Hughes, Fame 1003
102. LOUIE, LOUIE ....Kingsmen, Wand 143
103. IT'S AN UPHILL CLIMB TO THE BOTTOM ....Walter Jackson, Okeh 7247
104. SAM, YOU MADE THE PANTS TOO LONG..Barbra Streisand, Columbia 43612
105. DON'T STOP NOW ....Eddie Holman, Parkway 981
106. SECOND-HAND MAN ....Back Porch Majority, Epic 9879
107. WHEN A WOMAN LOVES A MAN ....Esther Phillips, Atlantic 2335
108. SWEET PEA ....Tommy Roe, ABC-Paramount 10762
109. MINE EXCLUSIVELY ....Olympics, Mirwood 5513
110. WIGGLIN' AND GIGGLIN' ....Roy Head, Back Beat 563
111. THE IMPOSSIBLE DREAM ....Jack Jones, Kapp 755
112. LITTLE GIRL ....Syndicate of Sound, Bell 640
113. ONE TOO MANY MORNINGS ....Beau Brummels, Warner Bros. 5813
114. I'LL GO CRAZY ....Buckinghams, U.S.A. 844
115. YOU'RE READY NOW ....Frankie Valli, Smash 2037
116. ALONG COMES MARY ....Association, Valiant 741
117. GREATEST MOMENTS IN A GIRL'S LIFE ....Tokens, B. T. Puppy 519
118. BAD EYE ....Willie Mitchell, Hi 2103
119. POPSICLE ....Jan & Dean, Liberty 55886
120. SOMEWHERE ....Johnny Nash, Joda 106
121. TRULY YOURS ....Spinners, Motown 1093
122. FUNNY HOW LOVE CAN BE ....Danny Hutton, MGM 13502
123. ALL THESE THINGS ....Uniques, Paula 238
124. FUNCTION AT THE JUNCTION ....Shorty Long, Soul 35021
125. OFF AND RUNNING ....Lesley Gore, Mercury 72580
126. COUNT DOWN ....Dave (Baby) Cortez, Roulette 4679
127. TOO MUCH LOVIN' ....Brook Benton, RCA Victor 8830
128. GOODBYE LITTLE GIRL ....Junior Parker, Duke 398
129. A STREET THAT RHYMES AT 6 A.M. ....Norma Tanega, New Voice 810
130. HE'S READY ....Poppies, Epic 10009
131. YOU DON'T LOVE ME ....Gary Walker, Date 1506
132. THERE STANDS THE DOOR ....We Five, A&M 800
133. I FEEL GOOD ....Sheep, Boom 60007
134. IT'S A DIFFERENT WORLD ....Connie Francis, MGM 13505
135. STAGECOACH TO CHEYENNE ....Wayne Newton, Capitol 5643

Compiled from national retail sales and radio station airplay by the Music Popularity Dept. of Record Market Research, Billboard.

# Billboard

For Week Ending June 4, 1966

# HOT 100

★ STAR performer—Sides registering greatest proportionate upward progress this week.

Record Industry Association of America seal of certification as million selling single.

| This Week | 1 Wk. Ago | 2 Wks. Ago | 3 Wks. Ago | TITLE Artist (Producer), Label & Number | Weeks On Chart |
|---|---|---|---|---|---|
| Billboard Award | 1 | 4 | 9 | WHEN A MAN LOVES A WOMAN — Percy Sledge (Quin Ivy-Marvin Greene) Atlantic 2326 | 9 |
| 2 | 2 | 5 | 13 | A GROOVY KIND OF LOVE — Mindbenders, Fontana 1541 | 8 |
| 3 | 4 | 19 | 48 | PAINT IT, BLACK — Rolling Stones (Andrew Loog Oldham), London 901 | 4 |
| ★ 4 | 7 | 16 | 25 | DID YOU EVER HAVE TO MAKE UP YOUR MIND? — Lovin' Spoonful (Erik Jacobsen), Kama Sutra 209 | 5 |
| 5 | 6 | 17 | 24 | I AM A ROCK — Simon & Garfunkel (Bob Johnston), Columbia 43617 | 5 |
| 6 | 3 | 1 | 1 | MONDAY, MONDAY — Mama's and the Papa's (Lou Adler), Dunhill 4026 | 9 |
| 7 | 5 | 2 | 3 | RAINY DAY WOMEN #12 & 35 — Bob Dylan (Bob Johnston), Columbia 43592 | 8 |
| 8 | 10 | 18 | 23 | IT'S A MAN'S MAN'S MAN'S WORLD — James Brown (James Brown Productions), King 6035 | 6 |
| ★ 9 | 12 | 25 | 49 | GREEN GRASS — Gary Lewis & the Playboys (Dave Pell), Liberty 55880 | 4 |
| ★ 10 | 27 | 54 | 71 | STRANGERS IN THE NIGHT — Frank Sinatra (Jimmy Bowen), Reprise 0470 | 5 |
| 11 | 9 | 10 | 15 | LOVE IS LIKE AN ITCHING IN MY HEART — Supremes (Holland & Dozier), Motown 1094 | 6 |
| ★ 12 | 17 | 34 | 52 | BAREFOOTIN' — Robert Parker (Wherly-Burly Prod.), Nola 721 | 7 |
| ★ 13 | 18 | 47 | 61 | SWEET TALKIN' GUY — Chiffons (Bright Tunes), Laurie 3340 | 5 |
| 14 | 11 | 6 | 4 | KICKS — Paul Revere & the Raiders (Terry Melcher), Columbia 43556 | 12 |
| 15 | 8 | 3 | 2 | GOOD LOVIN' — Young Rascals (Tom Dowd, Arif Mardin), Atlantic 2321 | 13 |
| 16 | 13 | 13 | 18 | THE SUN AIN'T GONNA SHINE (Anymore) — Walker Brothers, Smash 2032 | 8 |
| 17 | 19 | 33 | 51 | COOL JERK — Capitols (Ollie McLaughlin), Karen 1524 | 6 |
| ★ 18 | 26 | 55 | 74 | OH HOW HAPPY — Shades of Blue (John Rhys), Impact 1007 | 5 |
| ★ 19 | 31 | 63 | — | OPUS 17 (Don't You Worry 'Bout Me) — 4 Seasons (Bob Crewe), Philips 40370 | 3 |
| 20 | 14 | 8 | 8 | MESSAGE TO MICHAEL — Dionne Warwick (Blue Jac), Scepter 12133 | 10 |
| ★ 21 | 29 | 43 | 53 | THE MORE I SEE YOU — Chris Montez (Herb Alpert), A&M 796 | 8 |
| 22 | 23 | 26 | 31 | COME ON LET'S GO — McCoys (Feldman, Goldstein, Gottehrer Prod.) Bang 522 | 7 |
| ★ 23 | 49 | 76 | — | YOU DON'T HAVE TO SAY YOU LOVE ME — Dusty Springfield, Philips 40371 | 3 |
| 24 | 24 | 37 | 43 | (I'm a) ROAD RUNNER — Jr. Walker & the All Stars (Holland-Dozier), Soul 35015 | 9 |
| ★ 25 | 45 | 59 | 88 | MAMA — B. J. Thomas (Music Enterprises, Inc.), Scepter 12139 | 4 |
| ★ 26 | 41 | 51 | 66 | DOUBLE SHOT (Of My Baby's Love) — Swingin' Medallions (Karric Prods.), Smash 2033 | 7 |
| 27 | 15 | 9 | 5 | SLOOP JOHN B — Beach Boys (Brian Wilson), Capitol 5602 | 10 |
| 28 | 16 | 7 | 7 | HOW DOES THAT GRAB YOU DARLIN' — Nancy Sinatra (Lee Hazelwood), Reprise 0461 | 7 |
| ★ 29 | 42 | 45 | 55 | HOLD ON! I'M COMIN' — Sam & Dave (Prod. By Staff), Stax 189 | 7 |
| ★ 30 | 47 | 79 | — | DON'T BRING ME DOWN — Animals (Tom Wilson), MGM 13514 | 3 |
| 31 | 20 | 12 | 10 | GLORIA — Shadows of Knight (A Dunwich Prod.), Dunwich 116 | 12 |
| 32 | 21 | 14 | 16 | EIGHT MILES HIGH — Byrds (Allen Stanton), Columbia 43578 | 9 |
| ★ 33 | 44 | 66 | 87 | GIRL IN LOVE — The Outsiders (Tom King), Capitol 5646 | 4 |
| 34 | 25 | 27 | 32 | BACKSTAGE — Gene Pitney (Gene Pitney & Stan Kahan), Musicor 1171 | 7 |
| ★ 35 | 65 | 90 | — | RED RUBBER BALL — Cyrkle (John Simon), Columbia 43589 | 3 |
| 36 | 22 | 20 | 22 | LET'S START ALL OVER AGAIN — Ronnie Dove (Kahl-Vernon), Diamond 198 | 8 |
| 37 | 34 | 36 | 37 | THE BALLAD OF IRVING — Frank Gallop (Booker-Foster), Kapp 745 | 8 |
| 38 | 28 | 28 | 35 | THE "A" TEAM — S/Sgt. Barry Sadler (Andy Wiswell), RCA Victor 8804 | 7 |
| ★ 39 | 50 | 58 | 60 | I LOVE YOU 1,000 TIMES — The Platters (Luther Dixon), Musicor 1166 | 6 |
| 40 | 43 | 57 | 67 | I LOVE YOU DROPS — Vic Dana (Bob Reisdorff), Dolton 319 | 5 |
| 41 | 46 | 56 | 62 | COME RUNNING BACK — Dean Martin (Jimmy Bowen), Reprise 0466 | 5 |
| 42 | 39 | 40 | 42 | TWINKLE TOES — Roy Orbison, MGM 13498 | 6 |
| 43 | 40 | 41 | 47 | DUM-DE-DA — Bobby Vinton (Bob Morgan), Epic 10014 | 6 |
| ★ 44 | 67 | — | — | AIN'T TOO PROUD TO BEG — Temptations (N. Whitfield), Gordy 7054 | 2 |
| ★ 45 | 57 | 62 | 63 | DIRTY WATER — Standells (Ed Cobb), Tower 185 | 7 |
| ★ 46 | 60 | 80 | — | DEDICATED FOLLOWER OF FASHION — Kinks (Shel Talmy), Reprise 0471 | 3 |
| 47 | 52 | 60 | 82 | THE LAST WORD IN LONESOME IS ME — Eddy Arnold (Chet Atkins), RCA Victor 8818 | 4 |
| 48 | 51 | 75 | 90 | S.Y.S.L.J.F.M. (Letter Song) — Joe Tex (Buddy Killen), Dial 9902 | 4 |
| ★ 49 | 59 | 73 | 89 | IT'S OVER — Jimmie Rodgers (Randy Wood), Dot 16861 | 4 |
| ★ 50 | 66 | — | — | CRYING — Jay & the Americans (Gerry Granahan), United Artists 50016 | 2 |
| ★ 51 | 69 | 84 | — | HEY JOE — Leaves (Norm Ratner), Mira 222 | 3 |
| 52 | 53 | 53 | 57 | EVOL-NOT LOVE — Five Americans (Abnak Music Prod.), HBR 468 | 8 |
| 53 | 54 | 61 | 68 | MAME — Bobby Darin (Bobby Darin), Atlantic 2329 | 6 |
| 54 | 55 | 65 | 77 | THERE'S NO LIVING WITHOUT YOUR LOVING — Peter & Gordon (John Burgess), Capitol 5650 | 5 |
| ★ 55 | 70 | 99 | — | TAKE THIS HEART OF MINE — Marvin Gaye (Robinson-Moore), Tamla 54132 | 3 |
| 56 | 56 | 69 | 84 | I KNOW YOU BETTER THAN THAT — Bobby Goldsboro (Jack Gold), United Artists 50018 | 4 |
| ★ 57 | 68 | 83 | 91 | MY LITTLE RED BOOK — Love (Jac Holzman & Mark Abramson), Elektra 603 | 6 |
| 58 | 63 | 71 | 86 | BETTER USE YOUR HEAD — Little Anthony & the Imperials (Teddy Randazzo), Veep 1228 | 4 |
| 59 | 61 | 72 | 81 | PETER RABBIT — Dee Jay and the Runaways (Iowa Great Lakes Studios), Smash 2034 | 5 |
| ★ 60 | 73 | — | — | WIEDERSEH'N — Al Martino (Tom Morgan), Capitol 5652 | 2 |
| 61 | 58 | 68 | 80 | WANG DANG DOODLE — Ko Ko Taylor (Willie Dixon), Checker 1135 | 7 |
| 62 | 62 | 70 | 78 | LET ME BE GOOD TO YOU — Carla Thomas (Prod. by Staff), Stax 188 | 6 |
| 63 | 74 | — | — | BREAK OUT — Mitch Ryder and the Detroit Wheels (Bob Crewe), New Voice 811 | 2 |
| ★ 64 | 83 | — | — | LET'S GO GET STONED — Ray Charles (Joe Adams), ABC-Paramount 10808 | 2 |
| 65 | 72 | 81 | 85 | TRULY JULIE'S BLUES — Bob Lind (Jack Nitzche), World Pacific 77822 | 5 |
| ★ 66 | — | — | — | POPSICLE — Jan & Dean (Jan Berry), Liberty 55886 | 1 |
| 67 | 79 | 86 | — | CLOUDY SUMMER AFTERNOON — Barry McGuire (Lou Adler), Dunhill 4028 | 3 |
| 68 | 76 | — | — | NINETY-NINE AND A HALF — Wilson Pickett (Steve Cropper), Atlantic 2334 | 2 |
| 69 | 75 | — | — | TAKE SOME TIME OUT FOR LOVE — Isley Brothers (Robert Gordy), Tamla 54133 | 2 |
| 70 | 82 | — | — | BATMAN & HIS GRANDMOTHER — Dickie Goodman, Red Bird 10-058 | 2 |
| ★ 71 | 90 | — | — | YOUNGER GIRL — Critters (Artie Ripp), Kapp 752 | 2 |
| ★ 72 | 93 | — | — | YOUNGER GIRL — Hondells (G. P. IV Prod.), Mercury 72563 | 2 |
| 73 | 78 | 87 | — | SOLITARY MAN — Neil Diamond (Barry & Greenwich), Bang 519 | 3 |
| ★ 74 | — | — | — | OH YEAH — Shadows of Knight (Dunwich Prod.), Dunwich 122 | 1 |
| ★ 75 | — | — | — | HANKY PANKY — Tommy James & the Shondells (Jeff Barry & Ellie Greenwich), Roulette 4686 | 1 |
| ★ 76 | — | — | — | THE LAND OF MILK AND HONEY — Vogues (Cenci-Hakim-Moon), Co & Ce 238 | 1 |
| 77 | 89 | 95 | 100 | EVERYDAY I HAVE TO CRY — Gentrys (Chips Moman), MGM 13495 | 4 |
| ★ 78 | — | — | — | LITTLE GIRL — Syndicate of Sound (Gary Thompson), Bell 640 | 1 |
| ★ 79 | — | — | — | ALONG COMES MARY — Association (C. Boettcher), Valiant 741 | 1 |
| ★ 80 | — | — | — | WHEN A WOMAN LOVES A MAN — Esther Phillips (Jerry Wexler), Atlantic 2335 | 1 |
| 81 | 81 | 85 | — | MAME — Louis Armstrong (Hal Mooney), Mercury 72574 | 3 |
| ★ 82 | — | — | — | HAVE I STAYED TOO LONG — Sonny & Cher (Sonny Bono), Atco 6420 | 1 |
| 83 | 85 | — | — | COME AND GET ME — Jackie DeShannon (Bacharach-David), Imperial 66171 | 2 |
| 84 | 87 | 100 | — | GOOD TIME CHARLIE — Bobby Bland, Duke 402 | 3 |
| 85 | 86 | — | — | JUST A LITTLE MISUNDERSTANDING — Contours (Paul-Stevenson), Gordy 7052 | 2 |
| 86 | 95 | — | — | LOVING YOU IS SWEETER THAN EVER — Four Tops (Ivy-Hunter), Motown 1096 | 2 |
| ★ 87 | — | — | — | MY LOVER'S PRAYER — Otis Redding (Prod. by Staff), Volt 136 | 1 |
| 88 | 88 | 91 | — | HEART'S DESIRE — Billy Joe Royal (Joe South), Columbia 43622 | 3 |
| ★ 89 | — | — | — | HE — Righteous Brothers (Bill Medley), Verve 10406 | 1 |
| 90 | 91 | 92 | 97 | I'LL LOVE YOU FOREVER — Holidays (Davis-Jackson Prod.), Golden World 36 | 5 |
| 91 | — | — | — | HE WILL BREAK YOUR HEART — Righteous Brothers (Bill Medley), Verve 10406 | 1 |
| 92 | 99 | — | — | THINK OF ME — Buck Owens (Ken Nelson), Capitol 5647 | 2 |
| 93 | — | — | — | COUNT DOWN — Dave "Baby" Cortez (Henry Glover), Roulette 4679 | 1 |
| 94 | 98 | — | — | RIVER DEEP—MOUNTAIN HIGH — Ike & Tina Turner (Phil Spector), Philles 131 | 2 |
| 95 | 97 | — | — | DON'T TOUCH ME — Jeannie Seely (Fred Foster), Monument 933 | 2 |
| 96 | — | — | — | ONE TOO MANY MORNINGS — Beau Brummels (Autumn Prod.), Warner Bros. 5813 | 1 |
| 97 | 100 | — | — | COME ON AND SEE ME — Tammi Terrell (Fuqua-Bristol), Motown 1095 | 2 |
| 98 | — | — | — | IT'S AN UPHILL CLIMB TO THE BOTTOM — Walter Jackson (Ted Cooper), Okeh 7247 | 1 |
| 99 | — | — | — | NEIGHBOR, NEIGHBOR — Jimmy Hughes (Ric Hall), Fame 1003 | 1 |
| 100 | — | — | — | THE IMPOSSIBLE DREAM — Jack Jones (David Kapp), Kapp 755 | 1 |

## HOT 100—A TO Z—(Publisher-Licensee)


"A" Team, The (Music, Music, Music, ASCAP) .. 38
Ain't Too Proud to Beg (Jobete, BMI) .......... 44
Along Comes Mary (Since & Davon, BMI) ...... 79
Backstage (Eden-Catalogue-Primary, BMI) ...... 34
Ballad of Irving, The (Thirteen, ASCAP) .......... 37
Barefootin' (Bonatemp, BMI) ..................... 12
Batman & His Grandmother (Not Available) ...... 70
Better Use Your Head (South Mountain, BMI) .. 58
Break Out (Saturday, BMI) ....................... 63
Cloudy Summer Afternoon (Metric, BMI) ........ 67
Come and Get Me (Jac, ASCAP) .................. 83
Come On and See Me (Jobete, BMI) .............. 97
Come On, Let's Go (Kemo, Figure, Clockus, BMI) . 22
Come Running Back (Richbare-Kita, BMI) ....... 41
Cool Jerk (McLaughlin, BMI) ..................... 17
Count Down (Frost, BMI) ......................... 93
Crying (Acuff-Rose, BMI) ........................ 50
Dedicated Follower of Fashion (Noma, BMI) .... 46
Did You Ever Have to Make Up Your Mind? (Faithful Virtue, BMI) ........................ 4
Dirty Water (Equinox, BMI) ..................... 45
Don't Bring Me Down (Screen Gems-Columbia, BMI) ........................ 30
Don't Touch Me (Pamper, BMI) .................. 95
Double Shot (Of My Baby's Love) (Lyricsong-Windsong, BMI) ........................ 26
Dum-De-Da (Gallico, BMI) ....................... 43
Eight Miles High (Tickson, BMI) ................ 32
Everyday I Have to Cry (Tiki, BMI) ............ 77
Evol-Not Love (Jetstar, BMI) ................... 52
Girl in Love (Beechwood, BMI) .................. 33
Gloria—Shadows of Knight (Bernice, BMI) ...... 31
Good Lovin' (T. M., BMI) ....................... 15
Good Time Charlie (Don, BMI) .................. 84
Green Grass (Mills, ASCAP) ..................... 9
Groovy Kind of Love, A (Screen Gems-Columbia, BMI) ........................ 2
Hanky Panky (T.M., BMI) ......................... 75
Have I Stayed Too Long (Cotillion-Chrismarc-Five-West, BMI) ........................ 82
He (Avas, ASCAP) ................................ 89
He Will Break Your Heart (Conrad, BMI) ....... 91
Heart's Desire (Lowery, BMI) .................... 88
Hey Joe (Mirwood, BMI) ......................... 51
Hold On! I'm Comin' (East, Pronto, BMI) ...... 29
How Does That Grab You Darlin' (Criterion, ASCAP) ........................ 28
I Am a Rock (Eclectic, BMI) ..................... 5
I Know You Better Than That (Unart, BMI) ..... 56
I Love You Drops (Moss-Rose, BMI) ............ 40
I Love You 1,000 Times (Ludix, BMI) .......... 39
I'll Love You Forever (Myto, BMI) ............. 90
(I'm a) Road Runner (Jobete, BMI) ............ 24
Impossible Dream, The (Fox, ASCAP) ..........100
It's a Man, Man's Man's World (Dynatone, BMI) .. 8
It's an Uphill Climb to the Bottom (Metric, BMI) 98
It's Over (Honey-comb, ASCAP) ................. 49
Just a Little Misunderstanding (Jobete, BMI) .... 85
Kicks (Screen Gems-Columbia, BMI) ............ 14
Land of Milk and Honey, The (Tree, BMI) ...... 76
Last Word in Lonesome Is Me, The (Tree, BMI).. 47
Let Me Be Good to You (East, BMI) ............ 62
Let's Go Get Stoned (Baby Monica, BMI) ...... 64
Let's Start All Over Again (Pictureton, BMI) .... 36
Little Girl (Duane, BMI) ........................ 78
Love Is Like an Itching in My Heart (Jobete, BMI) 11
Loving You Is Sweeter Than Ever (Jobete, BMI) .. 86
Mama (Flomar, BMI) ............................. 25
Mame—Armstrong (Morris, ASCAP) .............. 81
Mame—Darin (Morris, ASCAP) .................. 53
Message to Michael (U. S. Songs, ASCAP) ..... 20
Monday, Monday (Trousdale, BMI) .............. 6
More I See You, The (Bregman, Vocco & Conn, ASCAP) ........................ 21
My Little Red Book (United Artists, ASCAP) .... 57
My Lover's Prayer (East-Time-Redwal, BMI) .... 87
Neighbor, Neighbor (Crazy Cajun, BMI) ........ 99
Ninety-Nine and a Half (East-Pronto, BMI) .... 68
Oh How Happy (Myto, BMI) ...................... 18
Oh Yeah (Arc, BMI) .............................. 74
One Too Many Mornings (Witmark, ASCAP) .... 96
Opus 17 (Don't You Worry 'Bout Me) (Saturday, BMI) ........................ 19
Paint It, Black (Gideon, BMI) .................. 3
Peter Rabbit (Willong, BMI) .................... 59
Popsicle (Lowery, BMI) ......................... 66
Rainy Day Women Nos. 12 & 35 (Dwarf, ASCAP). 7
Red Rubber Ball (Electic, BMI) ................. 35
River Deep—Mountain High (Trio, BMI) ........ 94
S.Y.S.L.J.F.M. (Letter Song) (Tree, BMI) ...... 48
Sloop John B (New Executives, BMI) .......... 27
Solitary Man (Tallyrand, BMI) .................. 73
Strangers in the Night (Champion-Roosevelt, BMI) 10
Sun Ain't Gonna Shine (Anymore), The (Saturday, BMI) ........................ 16
Sweet Talkin' Guy (Elmwin, BMI) .............. 13
Take Some Time Out for Love (Jobete, BMI) .... 69
Take This Heart of Mine (Jobete, BMI) ........ 55
There's No Living Wtihout Your Loving (Catalogue, BMI) ........................ 54
Think of Me (Bluebook, BMI) ................... 92
Truly Julie's Blues (Metric, BMI) .............. 65
Twinkle Toes (Acuff-Rose, BMI) ................ 42
Wang Dang Doodle (Arc, BMI) .................. 61
When a Man Loves a Woman (Pronto-Quinvy, BMI) 1
When a Woman Loves a Man (Pronto-Quinvy, BMI) 80
Wiederseh'n (Roosevelt, BMI) .................. 60
You Don't Have to Say You Love Me (Robbins, ASCAP) ........................ 23
Younger Girl—Critters (Faithful Virtue, BMI) ..... 71
Younger Girl—Hondells (Faithful Virtue, BMI) .... 72


## BUBBLING UNDER THE HOT 100

101. LOOK BEFORE YOU LEAP .............Dave Clark Five, Epic 10031
102. SAM, YOU MADE THE PANTS TOO LONG ..Barbra Streisand, Columbia 43612
103. PLEASE TELL ME WHY .................Dave Clark Five, Epic 10031
104. LOUIE, LOUIE ..............................Kingsmen, Wand 143
105. MINE EXCLUSIVELY .....................Olympics, Mirwood 5513
106. SWEET PEA ...........................Tommy Roe, ABC-Paramount 10762
107. SO MUCH LOVE ..............................Ben E. King, Atco 6413
108. YOU WAITED TOO LONG ................Five Stair-Steps, Windy C 601
109. OFF AND RUNNING .....................Lesley Gore, Mercury 72580
110. SO MUGH LOVE ..................Steve Alaimo, ABC-Paramount 10805
111. I NEED LOVE ..............................Barbara Mason, Arctic 120
112. LIL' RED RIDING HOOD ......Sam the Sham & the Pharaohs, MGM 13452
113. STAGECOACH TO CHEYENNE ..............Wayne Newton, Capitol 5643
114. GREATEST MOMENTS IN A GIRL'S LIFE ........Tokens, B. T. Puppy 519
115. HE'S READY ..................................Poppies, Epic 10009
116. THE PIED PIPER .....................Crispian St. Peters, Jamie 1320
117. BAD EYE ..................................Willie Mitchell, Hi 2103
118. ALL THESE THINGS ..............................Uniques, Paula 238
119. GRIM REAPER OF LOVE ......................Turtles, White Whale 231
120. FUNNY HOW LOVE CAN BE ................Danny Hutton, MGM 13502
121. TRULY YOURS ..............................Spinners, Motown 1093
122. TEEN-AGER'S PRAYER ................Joe Simon, Soundstage 72564
123. HAND JIVE ..................................Strangeloves, Bang 524
124. YOU WOULDN'T LISTEN ......................Ides of March, Parrot 304
125. I ONLY HAVE EYES FOR YOU ................Lettermen, Capitol 5649
126. TOO MUCH GOOD LOVIN' ..............Brook Benton, RCA Victor 8830
127. WHERE WERE YOU WHEN I NEEDED YOU .....Grass Roots, Dunhill 4029
128. GOODBYE LITTLE GIRL ........................Junior Parker, Duke 398
129. YOU DON'T LOVE ME ........................Gary Walker, Date 1506
130. I FEEL GOOD ....................................Sheep, Boom 60007
131. STOP! GET A TICKET ...............Clefs of Lavender Hill, Date 1510
132. THERE STANDS THE DOOR ........................We Five, A&M 800
133. DAY FOR DECISION ....................Johnny Sea, Warner Bros. 5820
134. WE'RE ACTING LIKE LOVERS ..............Spellbinders, Columbia 43611
135. I LOVE ONIONS ......................Susan Christie, Columbia 43595

Compiled from national retail sales and radio station airplay by the Music Popularity Dept. of Record Market Research, Billboard.

For Week Ending June 11, 1966

# Billboard HOT 100

★ **STAR performer**—Sides registering greatest proportionate upward progress this week.

Record Industry Association of America seal of certification as million selling single.

| This Week | 1 Wk. Ago | 2 Wks. Ago | 3 Wks. Ago | TITLE | Artist (Producer), Label & Number | Weeks On Chart |
|---|---|---|---|---|---|---|
| 1 (Billboard Award) | 3 | 4 | 19 | PAINT IT, BLACK | Rolling Stones (Andrew Loog Oldham), London 901 | 5 |
| 2 | 4 | 7 | 16 | DID YOU EVER HAVE TO MAKE UP YOUR MIND? | Lovin' Spoonful (Erik Jacobsen), Kama Sutra 209 | 6 |
| 3 | 5 | 6 | 17 | I AM A ROCK | Simon & Garfunkel (Bob Johnston), Columbia 43617 | 6 |
| 4 | 1 | 1 | 4 | WHEN A MAN LOVES A WOMAN | Percy Sledge (Quin Ivy-Marvin Greene) Atlantic 2326 | 10 |
| 5 | 2 | 2 | 5 | A GROOVY KIND OF LOVE | Mindbenders, Fontana 1541 | 9 |
| ★ 6 | 10 | 27 | 54 | STRANGERS IN THE NIGHT | Frank Sinatra (Jimmy Bowen), Reprise 0470 | 6 |
| 7 | 6 | 3 | 1 | MONDAY, MONDAY | Mama's and the Papa's (Lou Adler), Dunhill 4026 | 10 |
| 8 | 8 | 10 | 18 | IT'S A MAN'S MAN'S MAN'S WORLD | James Brown (James Brown Productions), King 6035 | 7 |
| 9 | 9 | 12 | 25 | GREEN GRASS | Gary Lewis & the Playboys (Dave Pell), Liberty 55880 | 5 |
| 10 | 12 | 17 | 34 | BAREFOOTIN' | Robert Parker (Wherly-Burly Prod.), Nola 721 | 8 |
| 11 | 13 | 18 | 47 | SWEET TALKIN' GUY | Chiffons (Bright Tunes), Laurie 3340 | 6 |
| ★ 12 | 17 | 19 | 33 | COOL JERK | Capitols (Ollie McLaughlin), Karen 1524 | 7 |
| ★ 13 | 18 | 26 | 55 | OH HOW HAPPY | Shades of Blue (John Rhys), Impact 1007 | 6 |
| ★ 14 | 19 | 31 | 63 | OPUS 17 (Don't You Worry 'Bout Me) | 4 Seasons (Bob Crewe), Philips 40370 | 4 |
| 15 | 7 | 5 | 2 | RAINY DAY WOMEN #12 & 35 | Bob Dylan (Bob Johnston), Columbia 43592 | 9 |
| ★ 16 | 21 | 29 | 43 | THE MORE I SEE YOU | Chris Montez (Herb Alpert), A&M 796 | 9 |
| ★ 17 | 23 | 49 | 76 | YOU DON'T HAVE TO SAY YOU LOVE ME | Dusty Springfield, Philips 40371 | 4 |
| 18 | 11 | 9 | 10 | LOVE IS LIKE AN ITCHING IN MY HEART | Supremes (Holland & Dozier), Motown 1094 | 7 |
| ★ 19 | 35 | 65 | 90 | RED RUBBER BALL | Cyrkle (John Simon), Columbia 43589 | 4 |
| 20 | 24 | 24 | 37 | (I'm a) ROAD RUNNER | Jr. Walker & the All Stars (Holland-Dozier), Soul 35015 | 10 |
| ★ 21 | 26 | 41 | 51 | DOUBLE SHOT (Of My Baby's Love) | Swingin' Medallions (Karric Prods.), Smash 2033 | 8 |
| ★ 22 | 30 | 47 | 79 | DON'T BRING ME DOWN | Animals (Tom Wilson), MGM 13514 | 4 |
| ★ 23 | 33 | 44 | 66 | GIRL IN LOVE | The Outsiders (Tom King), Capitol 5646 | 5 |
| 24 | 25 | 45 | 59 | MAMA | B. J. Thomas (Music Enterprises, Inc.), Scepter 12139 | 5 |
| 25 | 22 | 23 | 26 | COME ON LET'S GO | McCoys (Feldman, Goldstein, Gottehrer Prod.) Bang 522 | 8 |
| 26 | 29 | 42 | 45 | HOLD ON! I'M COMIN' | Sam & Dave (Prod. By Staff), Stax 189 | 8 |
| 27 | 14 | 11 | 6 | KICKS | Paul Revere & the Raiders (Terry Melcher), Columbia 43556 | 13 |
| ★ 28 | — | — | — | PAPERBACK WRITER | Beatles (George Martin), Capitol 5651 | 1 |
| 29 | 15 | 8 | 3 | GOOD LOVIN' | Young Rascals (Tom Dowd, Arif Mardin), Atlantic 2321 | 14 |
| 30 | 20 | 14 | 8 | MESSAGE TO MICHAEL | Dionne Warwick (Blue Jac), Scepter 12133 | 11 |
| ★ 31 | 45 | 57 | 62 | DIRTY WATER | Standells (Ed Cobb), Tower 185 | 8 |
| 32 | 16 | 13 | 13 | THE SUN AIN'T GONNA SHINE (Anymore) | Walker Brothers, Smash 2032 | 9 |
| 33 | 27 | 15 | 9 | SLOOP JOHN B | Beach Boys (Brian Wilson), Capitol 5602 | 11 |
| 34 | 40 | 43 | 57 | I LOVE YOU DROPS | Vic Dana (Bob Reisdorff), Dolton 31[illegible] | 6 |
| 35 | 41 | 46 | 56 | COME RUNNING BACK | Dean Martin (Jimmy Bowen), Reprise 0466 | 6 |
| 36 | 44 | 67 | — | AIN'T TOO PROUD TO BEG | Temptations (N. Whitfield), Gordy 7054 | 3 |
| 37 | 28 | 16 | 7 | HOW DOES THAT GRAB YOU DARLIN' | Nancy Sinatra (Lee Hazelwood), Reprise 0461 | 8 |
| ★ 38 | 50 | 66 | — | CRYING | Jay & the Americans (Gerry Granahan), United Artists 50016 | 3 |
| 39 | 39 | 50 | 58 | I LOVE YOU 1,000 TIMES | The Platters (Luther Dixon), Musicor 1166 | 7 |
| 40 | 34 | 25 | 27 | BACKSTAGE | Gene Pitney (Gene Pitney & Stan Kahan), Musicor 1171 | 8 |
| 41 | 46 | 60 | 80 | DEDICATED FOLLOWER OF FASHION | Kinks (Shel Talmy), Reprise 0471 | 4 |
| 42 | 49 | 59 | 73 | IT'S OVER | Jimmie Rodgers (Randy Wood), Dot 16861 | 5 |
| 43 | 51 | 69 | 84 | HEY JOE | Leaves (Norm Ratner), Mira 222 | 4 |
| 44 | 48 | 51 | 75 | S.Y.S.L.J.F.M. (Letter Song) | Joe Tex (Buddy Killen), Dial 9902 | 5 |
| 45 | 37 | 34 | 36 | THE BALLAD OF IRVING | Frank Gallop (Booker-Foster), Kapp 745 | 9 |
| ★ 46 | 66 | — | — | POPSICLE | Jan & Dean (Jan Berry), Liberty 55886 | 2 |
| 47 | 47 | 52 | 60 | THE LAST WORD IN LONESOME IS ME | Eddy Arnold (Chet Atkins), RCA Victor 8818 | 5 |
| ★ 48 | 75 | — | — | HANKY PANKY | Tommy James & the Shondells (Jeff Barry & Ellie Greenwich), Roulette 4686 | 2 |
| ★ 49 | 59 | 61 | 72 | PETER RABBIT | Dee Jay and the Runaways (Iowa Great Lakes Studios), Smash 2034 | 6 |
| 50 | 54 | 55 | 65 | THERE'S NO LIVING WITHOUT YOUR LOVING | Peter & Gordon (John Burgess), Capitol 5650 | 6 |
| ★ 51 | 78 | — | — | LITTLE GIRL | Syndicate of Sound (Gary Thompson), Bell 640 | 2 |
| ★ 52 | 89 | — | — | HE | Righteous Brothers (Bill Medley), Verve 10406 | 2 |
| ★ 53 | 76 | — | — | THE LAND OF MILK AND HONEY | Vogues (Cenci-Hakim-Moon) Co & Ce 238 | 2 |
| 54 | 57 | 68 | 83 | MY LITTLE RED BOOK | Love (Jac Holzman & Mark Abramson), Elektra 603 | 7 |
| 55 | 55 | 70 | 99 | TAKE THIS HEART OF MINE | Marvin Gaye (Robinson-Moore), Tamla 54132 | 4 |
| ★ 56 | 74 | — | — | OH YEAH | Shadows of Knight (Dunwich Prod.), Dunwich 122 | 2 |
| 57 | 60 | 73 | — | WIEDERSEH'N | Al Martino (Tom Morgan), Capitol 5652 | 3 |
| 58 | 58 | 63 | 71 | BETTER USE YOUR HEAD | Little Anthony & the Imperials (Teddy Randazzo), Veep 1228 | 5 |
| 59 | 64 | 83 | — | LET'S GO GET STONED | Ray Charles (Joe Adams), ABC-Paramount 10808 | 3 |
| 60 | 56 | 56 | 69 | I KNOW YOU BETTER THAN THAT | Bobby Goldsboro (Jack Gold), United Artists 50018 | 5 |
| 61 | 61 | 58 | 68 | WANG DANG DOODLE | Ko Ko Taylor (Willie Dixon), Checker 1135 | 8 |
| ★ 62 | 82 | — | — | HAVE I STAYED TOO LONG | Sonny & Cher (Sonny Bono), Atco 6420 | 2 |
| 63 | 63 | 74 | — | BREAK OUT | Mitch Ryder and the Detroit Wheels (Bob Crewe), New Voice 811 | 3 |
| ★ 64 | 79 | — | — | ALONG COMES MARY | Association (C. Boettcher), Valiant 741 | 2 |
| 65 | 67 | 79 | 86 | CLOUDY SUMMER AFTERNOON | Barry McGuire (Lou Adler), Dunhill 4028 | 4 |
| 66 | 69 | 75 | — | TAKE SOME TIME OUT FOR LOVE | Isley Brothers (Robert Gordy), Tamla 54133 | 3 |
| 67 | 71 | 90 | — | YOUNGER GIRL | Critters (Artie Ripp), Kapp 752 | 3 |
| 68 | 68 | 76 | — | NINETY-NINE AND A HALF | Wilson Pickett (Steve Cropper), Atlantic 2334 | 3 |
| 69 | 72 | 93 | — | YOUNGER GIRL | Hondells (G. P. IV Prod.), Mercury 72563 | 3 |
| 70 | 73 | 78 | 87 | SOLITARY MAN | Neil Diamond (Barry & Greenwich), Bang 519 | 4 |
| ★ 71 | 86 | 95 | — | LOVING YOU IS SWEETER THAN EVER | Four Tops (Ivy Hunter), Motown 1096 | 3 |
| ★ 72 | — | — | — | RAIN | Beatles (George Martin), Capitol 5651 | 1 |
| 73 | 70 | 82 | — | BATMAN & HIS GRANDMOTHER | Dickie Goodman, Red Bird 10-058 | 3 |
| 74 | 53 | 54 | 61 | MAME | Bobby Darin (Bobby Darin), Atlantic 2329 | 7 |
| 75 | 52 | 53 | 53 | EVOL-NOT LOVE | Five Americans (Abnak Music Prod.), HBR 468 | 9 |
| 76 | 80 | — | — | WHEN A WOMAN LOVES A MAN | Esther Phillips (Jerry Wexler), Atlantic 2335 | 2 |
| 77 | 77 | 89 | 95 | EVERYDAY I HAVE TO CRY | Gentrys (Chips Moman), MGM 13495 | 5 |
| ★ 78 | — | — | — | DAY FOR DECISION | Johnny Sea (Gene Nash), Warner Bros. 5820 | 1 |
| ★ 79 | — | — | — | PLEASE TELL ME WHY | Dave Clark Five (Dave Clark), Epic 10031 | 1 |
| 80 | 90 | 91 | 92 | I'LL LOVE YOU FOREVER | Holidays (Davis-Jackson Prod.), Golden World 36 | 6 |
| ★ 81 | — | — | — | I WASHED MY HANDS IN MUDDY WATER | Johnny Rivers (Lou Adler), Imperial 66175 | 1 |
| 82 | 84 | 87 | 100 | GOOD TIME CHARLIE | Bobby Bland, Duke 402 | 4 |
| 83 | 83 | 85 | — | COME AND GET ME | Jackie DeShannon (Bacharach-David), Imperial 66171 | 3 |
| ★ 84 | — | — | — | WHAT AM I GOING TO DO WITHOUT YOUR LOVE | Martha & the Vandellas (Wm. Stevenson-I. Hunter), Gordy 7053 | 1 |
| 85 | 97 | 100 | — | COME ON AND SEE ME | Tammi Terrell (Fuqua-Bristol), Motown 1095 | 3 |
| 86 | 87 | — | — | MY LOVER'S PRAYER | Otis Redding (Prod. by Staff), Volt 136 | 2 |
| 87 | 100 | — | — | THE IMPOSSIBLE DREAM | Jack Jones (David Kapp), Kapp 755 | 2 |
| 88 | 92 | 99 | — | THINK OF ME | Righteous Brothers (Bill Medley), Verve 10406; Buck Owens (Ken Nelson), Capitol 5647 | 3 |
| 89 | 81 | 81 | 85 | MAME | Louis Armstrong (Hal Mooney), Mercury 72574 | 4 |
| ★ 90 | — | — | — | SWEET PEA | Tommy Roe, ABC-Paramount 10762 | 1 |
| 91 | 93 | — | — | COUNT DOWN | Dave (Baby) Cortez (Henry Glover), Roulette 4679 | 2 |
| 92 | 95 | 97 | — | DON'T TOUCH ME | Jeannie Seely (Fred Foster), Monument 933 | 3 |
| 93 | 94 | 98 | — | RIVER DEEP—MOUNTAIN HIGH | Ike & Tina Turner (Phil Spector), Philles 131 | 3 |
| 94 | — | — | — | I LOVE ONIONS | Susan Christie (John Hill), Columbia 43595 | 1 |
| 95 | 96 | — | — | ONE TOO MANY MORNINGS | Beau Brummels (Autumn Prod.), Warner Bros. 5813 | 2 |
| 96 | 98 | — | — | IT'S AN UPHILL CLIMB TO THE BOTTOM | Walter Jackson (Ted Cooper), Okeh 7247 | 2 |
| 97 | 99 | — | — | NEIGHBOR, NEIGHBOR | Jimmy Hughes (Ric Hall), Fame 1003 | 2 |
| 98 | — | — | — | THE PIED PIPER | Crispian St. Peters (David Nicolson), Jamie 1320 | 1 |
| 99 | — | — | — | LIL' RED RIDING HOOD | Sam the Sham & the Pharaohs (Stan Kesler), MGM 13506 | 1 |
| 100 | — | — | — | I NEED LOVE | Barbara Mason (Dynodynamics Prod.), Arctic 120 | 1 |

## HOT 100—A TO Z—(Publisher-Licensee)

| | |
|---|---|
| Ain't Too Proud to Beg (Jobete, BMI) | 36 |
| Along Comes Mary (Since & Davon, BMI) | 64 |
| Backstage (Eden-Catalogue-Primary, BMI) | 40 |
| Ballad of Irving, The (Thirteen, ASCAP) | 45 |
| Barefootin' (Bonatemp, BMI) | 10 |
| Batman & His Grandmother (Not Available) | 73 |
| Better Use Your Head (South Mountain, BMI) | 58 |
| Break Out (Saturday, BMI) | 63 |
| Cloudy Summer Afternoon (Metric, BMI) | 65 |
| Come and Get Me (Jac, ASCAP) | 83 |
| Come On and See Me (Jobete, BMI) | 85 |
| Come On, Let's Go (Kemo, Figure, Clockus, BMI) | 25 |
| Come Running Back (Richbare-Kita, BMI) | 35 |
| Cool Jerk (McLaughlin, BMI) | 12 |
| Count Down (Frost, BMI) | 91 |
| Crying (Acuff-Rose, BMI) | 38 |
| Day for Decision (Moss Rose, BMI) | 78 |
| Dedicated Follower of Fashion (Noma, BMI) | 41 |
| Did You Ever Have to Make Up Your Mind? (Faithful Virtue, BMI) | 2 |
| Dirty Water (Equinox, BMI) | 31 |
| Don't Bring Me Down (Screen Gems-Columbia, BMI) | 22 |
| Don't Touch Me (Pamper, BMI) | 92 |
| Double Shot (Of My Baby's Love) (Lyricsong-Windsong, BMI) | 21 |
| Everyday I Have to Cry (Tiki, BMI) | 77 |
| Evol-Not Love (Jetstar, BMI) | 75 |
| Girl in Love (Beechwood, BMI) | 23 |
| Good Lovin' (T. M., BMI) | 29 |
| Good Time Charlie (Don, BMI) | 82 |
| Green Grass (Mills, ASCAP) | 9 |
| Groovy Kind of Love, A (Screen Gems-Columbia, BMI) | 5 |
| Hanky Panky (T. M., BMI) | 48 |
| Have I Stayed Too Long (Cotillion-Chrismarc-Five-West, BMI) | 62 |
| He (Avas, ASCAP) | 52 |
| Hey, Joe (Mirwood, BMI) | 43 |
| Hold On! I'm Comin' (East, Pronto, BMI) | 26 |
| How Does That Grab You Darlin' (Criterion, ASCAP) | 37 |
| I Am a Rock (Eclectic, BMI) | 3 |
| I Know You Better Than That (Unart, BMI) | 60 |
| I Love Onions (Blackwood, BMI) | 94 |
| I Love You Drops (Moss-Rose, BMI) | 34 |
| I Love You 1,000 Times (Ludix, BMI) | 39 |
| I Need Love (Stilran-Dandelion, BMI) | 100 |
| I Washed My Hands in Muddy Water (Maricana, BMI) | 81 |
| I'll Love You Forever (Myto, BMI) | 80 |
| (I'm a) Road Runner (Jobete, BMI) | 20 |
| Impossible Dream, The (Fox, ASCAP) | 87 |
| It's a Man's, Man's, Man's World (Dynatone, BMI) | 8 |
| It's an Uphill Climb to the Bottom (Metric, BMI) | 96 |
| It's Over (Honeycomb, ASCAP) | 42 |
| Kicks (Screen Gems-Columbia, BMI) | 27 |
| Land of Milk and Honey, The (Tree, BMI) | 53 |
| Last Word in Lonesome Is Me, The (Tree, BMI) | 47 |
| Let's Go Get Stoned (Baby Monica, BMI) | 59 |
| Lil' Red Riding Hood (Rose, BMI) | 99 |
| Little Girl (Duane, BMI) | 51 |
| Love Is Like an Itching in My Heart (Jobete, BMI) | 18 |
| Loving You Is Sweeter Than Ever (Jobete, BMI) | 71 |
| Mama (Flomar, BMI) | 24 |
| Mame—Armstrong (Morris, ASCAP) | 89 |
| Mame—Darin (Morris, ASCAP) | 74 |
| Message to Michael (U. S. Songs, ASCAP) | 30 |
| Monday, Monday (Trousdale, BMI) | 7 |
| More I See You, The (Bregman, Vocco & Conn, ASCAP) | 16 |
| My Little Red Book (United Artists, ASCAP) | 54 |
| My Lover's Prayer (East-Time-Redwal, BMI) | 86 |
| Neighbor, Neighbor (Crazy Cajun, BMI) | 97 |
| Ninety-Nine and a Half (East-Pronto, BMI) | 68 |
| Oh How Happy (Myto, BMI) | 13 |
| Oh Yeah (Arc, BMI) | 56 |
| One Too Many Mornings (Witmark ASCAP) | 95 |
| Opus 17 (Don't You Worry 'Bout Me) (Saturday, BMI) | 14 |
| Paint It, Black (Gideon, BMI) | 1 |
| Paperback Writer (Maclen, BMI) | 28 |
| Peter Rabbit (Willong, BMI) | 49 |
| Pied Piper, The (Robbins, ASCAP) | 98 |
| Please Tell Me Why (Branston, BMI) | 79 |
| Popsicle (Lowery, BMI) | 46 |
| Rain (Maclen, BMI) | 72 |
| Rainy Day Women Nos. 12 & 35 (Dwarf, ASCAP) | 15 |
| Red Rubber Ball (Eclectic, BMI) | 19 |
| River Deep—Mountain High (Trio, BMI) | 93 |
| S Y.S.L.J.F.M. (Letter Song) (Tree, BMI) | 44 |
| Sloop John B (New Executives, BMI) | 33 |
| Solitary Man (Tallyrand, BMI) | 70 |
| Strangers in the Night (Champion-Roosevelt, BMI) | 6 |
| Sun Ain't Gonna Shine (Anymore), The (Saturday, BMI) | 32 |
| Sweet Pea (Low Twi, BMI) | 90 |
| Sweet Talkin' Guy (Elmwin, BMI) | 11 |
| Take Some Time Out for Love (Jobete, BMI) | 66 |
| Take This Heart of Mine (Jobete, BMI) | 55 |
| There's No Living Without Your Loving (Catalogue, BMI) | 50 |
| Think of Me (Bluebook, BMI) | 88 |
| Wang Dang Doodle (Arc, BMI) | 61 |
| What Am I Going to Do Without Your Love (Jobete, BMI) | 84 |
| When a Man Loves a Woman (Pronto-Quinvy, BMI) | 4 |
| When a Woman Loves a Man (Pronto-Quinvy, BMI) | 76 |
| Wiederseh'n (Roosevelt, BMI) | 57 |
| You Don't Have to Say You Love Me (Robbins, ASCAP) | 17 |
| Younger Girl—Critters (Faithful Virtue, BMI) | 67 |
| Younger Girl—Hondells (Faithful Virtue, BMI) | 69 |

## BUBBLING UNDER THE HOT 100

101. HE WILL BREAK YOUR HEART ....Righteous Brothers, Verve 10406
102. YOU BETTER RUN ....Young Rascals, Atlantic 2338
103. ALL THESE THINGS ....Uniques, Paula 238
104. GRIM REAPER OF LOVE ....Turtles, White Whale 231
105. DISTANT DRUMS ....Jim Reeves, RCA Victor 8789
106. YOU WAITED TOO LONG ....Five Stair-Steps, Windy C 601
107. GREATEST MOMENTS IN A GIRL'S LIFE ....Tokens, B. T. Puppy 519
108. HE'S READY ....Poppies, Epic 10009
109. OFF AND RUNNING ....Lesley Gore, Mercury 72580
110. TEENAGER'S PRAYER ....Joe Simon, Sound Stage 7 2564
111. TRULY YOURS ....Spinners, Motown 1093
112. AIN'T GONNA CRY NO MORE ....Brenda Lee, Decca 31970
113. SAM, YOU MADE THE PANTS TOO LONG..Barbra Streisand, Columbia 43612
114. SO MUCH LOVE ....Steve Alaimo, ABC-Paramount 10805
115. YOU WOULDN'T LISTEN ....I'des of March, Parrot 304
116. I'LL BE GONE ....Pozo-Seco Singers, Columbia 43646
117. SO MUCH LOVE ....Ben E. King, Atco 6413
118. I ONLY HAVE EYES FOR YOU ....Lettermen, Capitol 5649
119. WHERE WERE YOU WHEN I NEEDED YOU ....Grass Roots, Dunhill 4029
120. NOT RESPONSIBLE ....Tom Jones, Parrot 40006
121. HOW CAN I TELL HER IT'S OVER ....Andy Williams, Columbia 43650
122. BLUE STAR ....Ventures, Dolton 320
123. IT'S YOU ALONE ....Wailers, United Artists 50026
124. THERE STANDS THE DOOR ....We Five, A&M 800
125. HEY GOOD LOOKIN' ....Bill Black's Combo, Hi 2106
126. SWEET DREAMS ....Tommy McLain, MSL 197
127. FIVE MILES FROM HOME ....Pat Boone, Dot 16836
128. COO COO ROO COO COO PALOMA ....Perry Como, RCA Victor 8823
129. MINE EXCLUSIVELY ....Olympics, Mirwood 5513
130. STOP—GET A TICKET ....Clefs of Lavendar Hill, Date 1510
131. TAR AND CEMENT ....Verdelle Smith, Capitol 5632
132. WE'RE ACTING LIKE LOVERS ....Spellbinders, Columbia 43611
133. RACE WITH THE WIND ....Robbs, Mercury 72579
134. IT'S THAT TIME OF THE YEAR ....Len Barry, Decca 31969
135. BOYS ARE MADE TO LOVE ....Karen Small, Venus 1066

Compiled from national retail sales and radio station airplay by the Music Popularity Dept. of Record Market Research, Billboard.

# Billboard HOT 100

**For Week Ending June 18, 1966**

★ STAR performer—Sides registering greatest proportionate upward progress this week.

| This Week | Last Week | 2 Wks. Ago | 3 Wks. Ago | TITLE Artist (Producer), Label & Number | Weeks on Chart |
|---|---|---|---|---|---|
| 1 | 1 | 3 | 4 | **PAINT IT, BLACK** — Rolling Stones (Andrew Loog Oldham), London 901 | 6 |
| 2 | 2 | 4 | 7 | **DID YOU EVER HAVE TO MAKE UP YOUR MIND?** — Lovin' Spoonful (Erik Jacobsen), Kama Sutra 209 | 7 |
| 3 | 3 | 5 | 6 | **I AM A ROCK** — Simon & Garfunkel (Bob Johnston), Columbia 43617 | 7 |
| 4 | 4 | 1 | 1 | **WHEN A MAN LOVES A WOMAN** — Percy Sledge (Quin Ivy-Marvin Greene), Atlantic 2326 | 11 |
| 5 | 6 | 10 | 27 | **STRANGERS IN THE NIGHT** — Frank Sinatra (Jimmy Bowen), Reprise 0470 | 7 |
| 6 | 5 | 2 | 2 | **A GROOVY KIND OF LOVE** — Mindbenders, Fontana 1541 | 10 |
| 7 | 10 | 12 | 17 | **BAREFOOTIN'** — Robert Parker (Wherly-Berly Prod.), Nola 721 | 9 |
| 8 | 9 | 9 | 12 | **GREEN GRASS** — Gary Lewis & the Playboys (Dave Poll), Liberty 55880 | 6 |
| 9 | 12 | 17 | 19 | **COOL JERK** — Capitols (Ollie McLaughlin), Karen 1524 | 8 |
| 10 | 19 | 35 | 65 | **RED RUBBER BALL** — Cyrkle (John Simon), Columbia 43589 | 5 |
| 11 | 11 | 13 | 18 | **SWEET TALKIN' GUY** — Chiffons (Bright Tunes), Laurie 3340 | 7 |
| 12 | 17 | 23 | 49 | **YOU DON'T HAVE TO SAY YOU LOVE ME** — Dusty Springfield, Philips 40371 | 5 |
| 13 | 13 | 18 | 26 | **OH HOW HAPPY** — Shades of Blue (John Rhys), Impact 1007 | 7 |
| 14 | 14 | 19 | 31 | **OPUS 17 (Don't You Worry 'Bout Me)** — 4 Seasons (Bob Crewe), Philips 40370 | 5 |
| 15 | 28 | — | — | **PAPERBACK WRITER** — Beatles (George Martin), Capitol 5651 | 2 |
| 16 | 16 | 21 | 29 | **THE MORE I SEE YOU** — Chris Montez (Herb Alpert), A&M 796 | 10 |
| 17 | 22 | 30 | 47 | **DON'T BRING ME DOWN** — Animals (Tom Wilson), MGM 13514 | 5 |
| 18 | 8 | 8 | 10 | **IT'S A MAN'S MAN'S MAN'S WORLD** — James Brown (James Brown Productions), King 6035 | 8 |
| 19 | 21 | 26 | 41 | **DOUBLE SHOT (Of My Baby's Love)** — Swingin' Medallions (Karric Prods.), Smash 2033 | 9 |
| 20 | 20 | 24 | 24 | **(I'm a) ROAD RUNNER** — Jr. Walker & the All Stars (Holland-Dozier), Soul 35015 | 11 |
| 21 | 26 | 29 | 42 | **HOLD ON! I'M COMIN'** — Sam & Dave (Prod. By Staff), Stax 189 | 9 |
| 22 | 24 | 25 | 45 | **MAMA** — B. J. Thomas (Music Enterprises, Inc), Scepter 12139 | 6 |
| 23 | 23 | 33 | 44 | **GIRL IN LOVE** — Outsiders (Tom King), Capitol 5646 | 6 |
| 24 | 7 | 6 | 3 | **MONDAY, MONDAY** — Mama's and the Papa's (Lou Adler), Dunhill 4026 | 11 |
| 25 | 48 | 75 | — | **HANKY PANKY** — Tommy James & the Shondells (Jeff Barry & Ellie Greenwich), Roulette 4686 | 3 |
| 26 | 31 | 45 | 57 | **DIRTY WATER** — Standells (Ed Cobb), Tower 185 | 6 |
| 27 | 36 | 44 | 67 | **AIN'T TOO PROUD TO BEG** — Temptations (N. Whitfield), Gordy 7054 | 4 |
| 28 | 38 | 50 | 66 | **CRYING** — Jay & the Americans (Gerry Granahan), United Artists 50016 | 4 |
| 29 | 15 | 7 | 5 | **RAINY DAY WOMEN #12 & 35** — Bob Dylan (Bob Johnston), Columbia 43592 | 10 |
| 30 | 34 | 40 | 43 | **I LOVE YOU DROPS** — Vic Dana (Bob Reisdorff), Dolton 319 | 7 |
| 31 | 18 | 11 | 9 | **LOVE IS LIKE AN ITCHING IN MY HEART** — Supremes (Holland & Dozier), Motown 1094 | 8 |
| 32 | 39 | 39 | 50 | **I LOVE YOU 1,000 TIMES** — Platters (Luther Dixon), Musicor 1166 | 8 |
| 33 | 46 | 66 | — | **POPSICLE** — Jan & Dean (Jan Berry), Liberty 55886 | 3 |
| 34 | 52 | 89 | — | **HE** — Righteous Brothers (Bill Medley), Verve 10406 | 3 |
| 35 | 43 | 51 | 69 | **HEY JOE** — Leaves (Norm Ratner), Mira 222 | 5 |
| 36 | 41 | 46 | 60 | **DEDICATED FOLLOWER OF FASHION** — Kinks (Shel Talmy), Reprise 0471 | 5 |
| 37 | 42 | 49 | 59 | **IT'S OVER** — Jimmie Rodgers (Randy Wood), Dot 16861 | 6 |
| 38 | 25 | 22 | 23 | **COME ON LET'S GO** — McCoys (Feldman, Goldstein, Gottehrer Prod.), Bang 522 | 9 |
| 39 | 44 | 48 | 51 | **S.Y.S.L.J.F.M. (Letter Song)** — Joe Tex (Buddy Killen), Dial 9902 | 6 |
| 40 | 47 | 47 | 52 | **THE LAST WORD IN LONESOME IS ME** — Eddy Arnold (Chet Atkins), RCA Victor 8879 | 6 |
| 41 | 51 | 78 | — | **LITTLE GIRL** — Syndicate of Sound (Gary Thompson), Bell 640 | 3 |
| 42 | 72 | — | — | **RAIN** — Beatles (George Martin), Capitol 5651 | 2 |
| 43 | 53 | 76 | — | **THE LAND OF MILK AND HONEY** — Vogues (Conci-Nakim-Moon), Co & Ce 238 | 3 |
| 44 | 64 | 79 | — | **ALONG COMES MARY** — Association (C. Boettcher), Valiant 741 | 3 |
| 45 | 55 | 55 | 70 | **TAKE THIS HEART OF MINE** — Marvin Gaye (Robinson-Moore), Tamla 54132 | 5 |
| 46 | 56 | 74 | — | **OH YEAH** — Shadows of Knight (Dunwich Prod.), Dunwich 122 | 3 |
| 47 | 59 | 64 | 83 | **LET'S GO GET STONED** — Ray Charles (Joe Adams), ABC-Paramount 10808 | 4 |
| 48 | 27 | 14 | 11 | **KICKS** — Paul Revere & the Raiders (Terry Melcher), Columbia 43556 | 14 |
| 49 | 49 | 59 | 61 | **PETER RABBIT** — Dee Jay and the Runaways (Iowa Great Lakes Studios), Smash 2034 | 7 |
| 50 | 30 | 20 | 14 | **MESSAGE TO MICHAEL** — Dionne Warwick (Blue Jac), Scepter 12133 | 12 |
| 51 | 78 | — | — | **DAY FOR DECISION** — Johnny Sea (Gene Nash), Warner Bros. 5820 | 2 |
| 52 | 62 | 82 | — | **HAVE I STAYED TOO LONG** — Sonny & Cher (Sonny Bono), Atco 6420 | 3 |
| 53 | 54 | 57 | 68 | **MY LITTLE RED BOOK** — Love (Jac Holzman & Mark Abramson), Elektra 603 | 8 |
| 54 | 58 | 58 | 63 | **BETTER USE YOUR HEAD** — Little Anthony & the Imperials (Teddy Randazzo), Veep 1228 | 6 |
| 55 | 35 | 41 | 46 | **COME RUNNING BACK** — Dean Martin (Jimmy Bowen), Reprise 0466 | 7 |
| 56 | 67 | 71 | 90 | **YOUNGER GIRL** — Critters (Artie Ripp), Kapp 752 | 4 |
| 57 | 81 | — | — | **I WASHED MY HANDS IN MUDDY WATER** — Johnny Rivers (Lou Adler), Imperial 66175 | 2 |
| 58 | 68 | 68 | 76 | **NINETY-NINE AND A HALF** — Wilson Pickett (Steve Cropper), Atlantic 2334 | 4 |
| 59 | 69 | 72 | 93 | **YOUNGER GIRL** — Hondells (G. P. IV Prod.), Mercury 72563 | 4 |
| 60 | 71 | 86 | 95 | **LOVING YOU IS SWEETER THAN EVER** — Four Tops (Ivy Hunter), Motown 1096 | 4 |
| 61 | 79 | — | — | **PLEASE TELL ME WHY** — Dave Clark Five (Dave Clark), Epic 10031 | 2 |
| 62 | 63 | 63 | 74 | **BREAK OUT** — Mitch Ryder and the Detroit Wheels (Bob Crewe), New Voice 811 | 4 |
| 63 | 57 | 60 | 73 | **WIEDERSEH'N** — Al Martino (Tom Morgan), Capitol 5652 | 4 |
| 64 | 65 | 67 | 79 | **CLOUDY SUMMER AFTERNOON** — Barry McGuire (Lou Adler), Dunhill 4028 | 5 |
| 65 | 80 | 90 | 91 | **I'LL LOVE YOU FOREVER** — Holidays (Davis-Jackson Prod.), Golden World 36 | 7 |
| 66 | 66 | 69 | 75 | **TAKE SOME TIME OUT FOR LOVE** — Isley Brothers (Robert Gordy), Tamla 54133 | 4 |
| 67 | 50 | 54 | 55 | **THERE'S NO LIVING WITHOUT YOUR LOVING** — Peter & Gordon (John Burgess), Capitol 5650 | 7 |
| 68 | 70 | 73 | 78 | **SOLITARY MAN** — Neil Diamond (Barry & Greenwich), Bang 519 | 5 |
| 69 | 97 | 99 | — | **NEIGHBOR, NEIGHBOR** — Jimmy Hughes (Ric Hall), Fame 1003 | 3 |
| 70 | 98 | — | — | **THE PIED PIPER** — Crispian St. Peters (David Nicolson), Jamie 1320 | 2 |
| 71 | 86 | 87 | — | **MY LOVER'S PRAYER** — Otis Redding (Prod. by Staff), Volt 136 | 3 |
| 72 | — | — | — | **YOU BETTER RUN** — Young Rascals (Young Rascals), Atlantic 2338 | 1 |
| 73 | 76 | 80 | — | **WHEN A WOMAN LOVES A MAN** — Esther Phillips (Jerry Wexler), Atlantic 2335 | 3 |
| 74 | 84 | — | — | **WHAT AM I GOING TO DO WITHOUT YOUR LOVE** — Martha & the Vandellas (Wm. Stevenson-I. Hunter), Gordy 7053 | 2 |
| 75 | 82 | 84 | 87 | **GOOD TIME CHARLIE** — Bobby Bland, Duke 402 | 5 |
| 76 | 87 | 100 | — | **THE IMPOSSIBLE DREAM** — Jack Jones (David Kapp), Kapp 755 | 3 |
| 77 | — | — | — | **HAPPY SUMMER DAYS** — Ronnie Dove (Phil Kahl), Diamond 205 | 1 |
| 78 | — | — | — | **SOMEWHERE MY LOVE** — Ray Conniff & the Singers (Ernie Altschuler), Columbia 43626 | 1 |
| 79 | 88 | 92 | 99 | **THINK OF ME** — Buck Owens (Ken Nelson), Capitol 5647 | 4 |
| 80 | 85 | 97 | 100 | **COME ON AND SEE ME** — Tammi Terrell (Fuqua-Bristol), Motown 1095 | 4 |
| 81 | 90 | — | — | **SWEET PEA** — Tommy Roe, ABC-Paramount 10762 | 2 |
| 82 | — | — | — | **HUNGRY** — Paul Revere & the Raiders (Terry Melcher), Columbia 43678 | 1 |
| 83 | — | — | — | **WHOLE LOT OF SHAKIN' IN MY HEART (Since I Met You)** — Miracles (Frank Wilson), Tamla 54134 | 1 |
| 84 | 94 | — | — | **I LOVE ONIONS** — Susan Christie (John Hill), Columbia 43595 | 2 |
| 85 | 92 | 95 | 97 | **DON'T TOUCH ME** — Jeannie Seely (Fred Foster), Monument 933 | 4 |
| 86 | — | — | — | **BILLY AND SUE** — B. J. Thomas, Hickory 1395 | 1 |
| 87 | — | — | — | **I ONLY HAVE EYES FOR YOU** — Lettermen (Steve Douglas), Capitol 5649 | 1 |
| 88 | 93 | 94 | 98 | **RIVER DEEP—MOUNTAIN HIGH** — Ike & Tina Turner (Phil Spector), Philles 131 | 4 |
| 89 | — | — | — | **WHERE WERE YOU WHEN I NEEDED YOU** — Grass Roots (Sloan & Barri), Dunhill 4029 | 1 |
| 90 | — | — | — | **NOT RESPONSIBLE** — Tom Jones (Peter Sullivan), Parrot 40006 | 1 |
| 91 | 91 | 93 | — | **COUNT DOWN** — Dave (Baby) Cortez (Henry Glover), Roulette 4679 | 3 |
| 92 | 96 | 98 | — | **IT'S AN UPHILL CLIMB TO THE BOTTOM** — Walter Jackson (Ted Cooper), Okeh 7247 | 3 |
| 93 | 99 | — | — | **LIL' RED RIDING HOOD** — Sam the Sham & the Pharaohs (Stan Kesler), MGM 13506 | 2 |
| 94 | — | — | — | **IT'S THAT TIME OF THE YEAR** — Len Barry (Madara-White), Decca 31969 | 1 |
| 95 | 95 | 96 | — | **ONE TOO MANY MORNINGS** — Beau Brummels (Autumn Prod.), Warner Bros. 5813 | 3 |
| 96 | — | — | — | **GRIM REAPER OF LOVE** — Turtles (Bones Howe), White Whale 231 | 1 |
| 97 | — | — | — | **TEENAGER'S PRAYER** — Joe Simon (J.R. Enterprises), Sound Stage 7 2564 | 1 |
| 98 | 100 | — | — | **I NEED LOVE** — Barbara Mason (Dynodynamics Prod.), Arctic 120 | 2 |
| 99 | — | — | — | **I'LL BE GONE** — Poso-Seco Singers (Bob Johnston), Columbia 43646 | 1 |
| 100 | — | — | — | **HAND JIVE** — Strangeloves (Feldman, Goldstein, Gottehrer Prod.), Bang 524 | 1 |

## BUBBLING UNDER THE HOT 100

101. MISTY — Groove Holmes, Prestige 401
102. LOOK BEFORE YOU LEAP — Dave Clark Five, Epic 10031
103. ALL THESE THINGS — Uniques, Paula 238
104. MAME — Louis Armstrong, Mercury 72574
105. YOU WAITED TOO LONG — Five Stair-Steps, Windy C 601
106. HE'S READY — Poppies, Epic 10009
107. GREATEST MOMENTS IN A GIRL'S LIFE — Nancy Ames, T. T. Puppy 519
108. OFF AND RUNNING — Lesley Gore, Mercury 72580
109. SEARCHING FOR MY LOVE — Bobby Moore & the Rhythm Aces, Checker 1129
110. SUNNY — Bobby Hebb, Philips 40365
111. AIN'T GONNA CRY NO MORE — Brenda Lee, Decca 31970
112. HE WILL BREAK YOUR HEART — Righteous Brothers, Verve 10406
113. YOU WOULDN'T LISTEN — Ides of March, Parrot 304
114. TRULY YOURS — Spinners, Motown 1093
115. DISTANT DRUMS — Jim Reeves, RCA Victor 8789
116. THERE STANDS THE DOOR — We Five, A&M 800
117. HOW CAN I TELL HER IT'S OVER — Andy Williams, Columbia 43650
118. STAGECOACH TO CHEYENNE — Wayne Newton, Capitol 5643
119. IT'S A MAN-WOMAN'S WORLD — Irma Thomas, Imperials 66178
120. YOU JUST CAN'T QUIT — Rick Nelson, Decca 31965
121. IT'S YOU ALONE — Wailers, United Artists 50026
122. SWEET DREAMS — Tommy McLain, MSL 197
123. GOOD ROCKIN' — Bill Black's Combo, Hi 2106
124. HEY GOOD LOOKIN' — Tommy McLain, MSL 197
125. PAST, PRESENT AND FUTURE — Shangri-Las, Red Bird 10068
126. MINE EXCLUSIVELY — Olympics, Mirwood 5513
127. RACE WITH THE WIND — Robbs, Mercury 72579
128. PAINTER — Lou Christie, MGM 13533
129. BOYS ARE MADE TO LOVE — Karen Small, Venus 1066
130. WE'RE GETTING LIKE LOVERS — SpellBinders, Columbia 43611
131. DAY OF DECISION — Bobby Starcher, Decca 31975
132. INVESTIGATE — Major Lance, Okeh 7245
133. IF HE WALKED INTO MY LIFE — Eydie Gorme, Columbia 43640
134. EVERYBODY LOVES A NUT — Johnny Cash, Columbia 43673
135. 1-2-3 — Jane Morgan, Epic 10032

Compiled from national retail sales and radio station airplay by the Music Popularity Dept. of Record Market Research, Billboard.

# Billboard HOT 100

*For Week Ending June 25, 1966*

★ STAR performer—Sides registering greatest proportionate upward progress this week.

| This Week | 1 Wk. Ago | 2 Wks. Ago | 3 Wks. Ago | TITLE Artist (Producer), Label & Number | Weeks On Chart |
|---|---|---|---|---|---|
| 1 | 15 | 28 | — | **PAPERBACK WRITER** — Beatles (George Martin), Capitol 5651 | 3 |
| 2 | 5 | 6 | 10 | **STRANGERS IN THE NIGHT** — Frank Sinatra (Jimmy Bowen), Reprise 0470 | 8 |
| 3 | 1 | 1 | 3 | **PAINT IT, BLACK** — Rolling Stones (Andrew Loog Oldham), London 901 | 7 |
| 4 | 2 | 2 | 4 | **DID YOU EVER HAVE TO MAKE UP YOUR MIND?** — Lovin' Spoonful (Erik Jacobsen), Kama Sutra 209 | 8 |
| 5 | 3 | 3 | 5 | **I AM A ROCK** — Simon & Garfunkel (Bob Johnston), Columbia 43617 | 8 |
| 6 | 10 | 19 | 35 | **RED RUBBER BALL** — Cyrkle (John Simon), Columbia 43589 | 6 |
| 7 | 7 | 10 | 12 | **BAREFOOTIN'** — Robert Parker (Wherly-Burly Prod.), Nola 721 | 10 |
| 8 | 9 | 12 | 17 | **COOL JERK** — Capitols (Ollie McLaughlin), Karen 1524 | 9 |
| 9 | 12 | 17 | 23 | **YOU DON'T HAVE TO SAY YOU LOVE ME** — Dusty Springfield, Philips 40371 | 6 |
| 10 | 11 | 11 | 13 | **SWEET TALKIN' GUY** — Chiffons (Bright Tunes), Laurie 3340 | 8 |
| 11 | 4 | 4 | 1 | **WHEN A MAN LOVES A WOMAN** — Percy Sledge (Quin Ivy-Marvin Greene), Atlantic 2326 | 12 |
| 12 | 13 | 13 | 18 | **OH HOW HAPPY** — Shades of Blue (John Rhys), Impact 1007 | 8 |
| 13 | 14 | 14 | 19 | **OPUS 17 (Don't You Worry 'Bout Me)** — 4 Seasons (Bob Crewe), Philips 40370 | 6 |
| 14 | 17 | 22 | 30 | **DON'T BRING ME DOWN** — Animals (Tom Wilson), MGM 13514 | 6 |
| 15 | 25 | 48 | 75 | **HANKY PANKY** — Tommy James & the Shondells (Jeff Barry & Ellie Greenwich), Roulette 4686 | 4 |
| 16 | 6 | 5 | 2 | **A GROOVY KIND OF LOVE** — Mindbenders, Fontana 1541 | 11 |
| 17 | 8 | 9 | 9 | **GREEN GRASS** — Gary Lewis & the Playboys (Dave Pell), Liberty 55880 | 7 |
| 18 | 16 | 16 | 21 | **THE MORE I SEE YOU** — Chris Montez (Herb Alpert), A&M 796 | 11 |
| 19 | 19 | 21 | 26 | **DOUBLE SHOT (Of My Baby's Love)** — Swingin' Medallions (Karric Prods.), Smash 2033 | 10 |
| 20 | 27 | 36 | 44 | **AIN'T TOO PROUD TO BEG** — Temptations (N. Whitfield), Gordy 7054 | 5 |
| 21 | 26 | 31 | 45 | **DIRTY WATER** — Standells (Ed Cobb), Tower 185 | 10 |
| 22 | 23 | 23 | 33 | **GIRL IN LOVE** — The Outsiders (Tom King), Capitol 5646 | 7 |
| 23 | 21 | 26 | 29 | **HOLD ON! I'M COMIN'** — Sam & Dave (Prod. By Staff), Stax 189 | 10 |
| 24 | 41 | 51 | 78 | **LITTLE GIRL** — Syndicate of Sound (Gary Thompson), Bell 640 | 4 |
| 25 | 28 | 38 | 50 | **CRYING** — Jay & the Americans (Gerry Granahan), United Artists 50016 | 5 |
| 26 | 34 | 52 | 89 | **HE** — Righteous Brothers (Bill Medley), Verve 10406 | 4 |
| 27 | 33 | 46 | 66 | **POPSICLE** — Jan & Dean (Jan Berry), Liberty 55886 | 4 |
| 28 | 22 | 24 | 25 | **MAMA** — B. J. Thomas (Music Enterprises, Inc.), Scepter 12139 | 7 |
| 29 | 42 | 72 | — | **RAIN** — Beatles (George Martin), Capitol 5651 | 3 |
| 30 | 20 | 20 | 24 | **(I'm a) ROAD RUNNER** — Jr. Walker & the All Stars (Holland-Dozier), Soul 35015 | 12 |
| 31 | 32 | 39 | 39 | **I LOVE YOU 1,000 TIMES** — The Platters (Luther Dixon), Musicor 1166 | 9 |
| 32 | 44 | 64 | 79 | **ALONG COMES MARY** — Association (C. Boettcher), Valiant 741 | 4 |
| 33 | 18 | 8 | 8 | **IT'S A MAN'S MAN'S MAN'S WORLD** — James Brown (James Brown Productions), King 6035 | 9 |
| 34 | 35 | 43 | 51 | **HEY JOE** — Leaves (Norm Ratner), Mira 222 | 6 |
| 35 | 43 | 53 | 76 | **THE LAND OF MILK AND HONEY** — Vogues (Cenci-Hakim-Moen), Co & Ce 238 | 4 |
| 36 | 51 | 78 | — | **DAY FOR DECISION** — Johnny Sea (Gene Nash), Warner Bros. 5820 | 3 |
| 37 | 47 | 59 | 64 | **LET'S GO GET STONED** — Ray Charles (Joe Adams), ABC-Paramount 10808 | 5 |
| 38 | 57 | 81 | — | **I WASHED MY HANDS IN MUDDY WATER** — Johnny Rivers (Lou Adler), Imperial 66175 | 3 |
| 39 | 30 | 34 | 40 | **I LOVE YOU DROPS** — Vic Dana (Bob Reisdorff), Dolton 319 | 8 |
| 40 | 37 | 42 | 49 | **IT'S OVER** — Jimmie Rodgers (Randy Wood), Dot 16861 | 7 |
| 41 | 24 | 7 | 6 | **MONDAY, MONDAY** — Mama's and the Papa's (Lou Adler), Dunhill 4026 | 12 |
| 42 | 46 | 56 | 74 | **OH YEAH** — Shadows of Knight (Dunwich Prod.), Dunwich 122 | 4 |
| 43 | 61 | 79 | — | **PLEASE TELL ME WHY** — Dave Clark Five (Dave Clark), Epic 10031 | 3 |
| 44 | 36 | 41 | 46 | **DEDICATED FOLLOWER OF FASHION** — Kinks (Shel Talmy), Reprise 0471 | 6 |
| 45 | 45 | 55 | 55 | **TAKE THIS HEART OF MINE** — Marvin Gaye (Robinson-Moore), Tamla 54132 | 6 |
| 46 | 49 | 49 | 59 | **PETER RABBIT** — Dee Jay and the Runaways (Iowa Great Lakes Studios), Smash 2034 | 8 |
| 47 | 40 | 47 | 47 | **THE LAST WORD IN LONESOME IS ME** — Eddy Arnold (Chet Atkins), RCA Victor 8818 | 7 |
| 48 | 56 | 67 | 71 | **YOUNGER GIRL** — Critters (Artie Ripp), Kapp 752 | 5 |
| 49 | 52 | 62 | 82 | **HAVE I STAYED TOO LONG** — Sonny & Cher (Sonny Bono), Atco 6420 | 4 |
| 50 | 60 | 71 | 86 | **LOVING YOU IS SWEETER THAN EVER** — Four Tops (Ivy Hunter), Motown 1096 | 5 |
| 51 | 72 | — | — | **YOU BETTER RUN** — Young Rascals (Young Rascals), Atlantic 2338 | 2 |
| 52 | 53 | 54 | 57 | **MY LITTLE RED BOOK** — Love (Jac Holzman & Mark Abramson), Elektra 603 | 9 |
| 53 | 39 | 44 | 48 | **S.Y.S.L.J.F.M. (Letter Song)** — Joe Tex (Buddy Killen), Dial 9902 | 7 |
| 54 | 59 | 69 | 72 | **YOUNGER GIRL** — Hondells (G.P. IV Prod.), Mercury 72563 | 3 |
| 55 | 93 | 99 | — | **LIL' RED RIDING HOOD** — Sam the Sham & the Pharaohs (Stan Kesler), MGM 13506 | 3 |
| 56 | 70 | 98 | — | **THE PIED PIPER** — Crispian St. Peters (David Nicolson), Jamie 1320 | 3 |
| 57 | 58 | 68 | 68 | **NINETY-NINE AND A HALF** — Wilson Pickett (Steve Cropper), Atlantic 2334 | 5 |
| 58 | 81 | 90 | — | **SWEET PEA** — Tommy Roe, ABC-Paramount 10762 | 3 |
| 59 | 78 | — | — | **SOMEWHERE MY LOVE** — Ray Conniff & the Singers (Ernie Altschuler), Columbia 43626 | 2 |
| 60 | 68 | 70 | 73 | **SOLITARY MAN** — Neil Diamond (Barry & Greenwich), Bang 519 | 6 |
| 61 | 77 | — | — | **HAPPY SUMMER DAYS** — Ronnie Dove (Phil Kahl), Diamond 205 | 2 |
| 62 | 64 | 65 | 67 | **CLOUDY SUMMER AFTERNOON** — Barry McGuire (Lou Adler), Dunhill 4028 | 6 |
| 63 | 65 | 80 | 90 | **I'LL LOVE YOU FOREVER** — Holidays (Davis-Jackson Prod.), Golden World 36 | 8 |
| 64 | 76 | 87 | 100 | **THE IMPOSSIBLE DREAM** — Jack Jones (David Kapp), Kapp 755 | 4 |
| 65 | 71 | 86 | 87 | **MY LOVER'S PRAYER** — Otis Redding (Prod. by Staff), Volt 136 | 4 |
| 66 | 69 | 97 | 99 | **NEIGHBOR, NEIGHBOR** — Jimmy Hughes (Ric Hall), Fame 1003 | 4 |
| 67 | 82 | — | — | **HUNGRY** — Paul Revere & the Raiders (Terry Melcher), Columbia 43678 | 2 |
| 68 | 54 | 58 | 58 | **BETTER USE YOUR HEAD** — Little Anthony & the Imperials (Teddy Randazzo), Veep 1228 | 7 |
| 69 | 62 | 63 | 63 | **BREAK OUT** — Mitch Ryder and the Detroit Wheels (Bob Crewe), New Voice 811 | 5 |
| 70 | 89 | — | — | **WHERE WERE YOU WHEN I NEEDED YOU** — Grass Roots (Sloan & Barri), Dunhill 4029 | 2 |
| 71 | 86 | — | — | **BILLY AND SUE** — B. J. Thomas, Hickory 1395 | 2 |
| 72 | 90 | — | — | **NOT RESPONSIBLE** — Tom Jones (Peter Sullivan), Parrot 40006 | 2 |
| 73 | 73 | 76 | 80 | **WHEN A WOMAN LOVES A MAN** — Esther Phillips (Jerry Wexler), Atlantic 2335 | 4 |
| 74 | 79 | 88 | 92 | **THINK OF ME** — Buck Owens (Ken Nelson), Capitol 5647 | 5 |
| 75 | — | — | — | **WILD THING** — Troggs (Page Boy Prod.), Atco 6415-Fontana 1548 | 1 |
| 76 | 75 | 82 | 84 | **GOOD TIME CHARLIE** — Bobby Bland, Duke 402 | 6 |
| 77 | 74 | 84 | — | **WHAT AM I GOING TO DO WITHOUT YOUR LOVE** — Martha & the Vandellas (Wm. Stevenson-J. Hunter), Gordy 7053 | 3 |
| 78 | 84 | 94 | — | **I LOVE ONIONS** — Susan Christie (John Hill), Columbia 43598 | 3 |
| 79 | 83 | — | — | **WHOLE LOT OF SHAKIN' IN MY HEART (Since I Met You)** — Miracles (Frank Wilson), Tamla 54134 | 2 |
| 80 | 97 | — | — | **TEENAGER'S PRAYER** — Joe Simon (J.R. Enterprises), Sound Stage 7 2564 | 2 |
| 81 | 96 | — | — | **GRIM REAPER OF LOVE** — Turtles (Bones Howe), White Whale 231 | 2 |
| 82 | — | — | — | **OVER UNDER SIDEWAYS DOWN** — Yardbirds (Samwell-Smith, Napier-Bell), Epic 10035 | 1 |
| 83 | 80 | 85 | 97 | **COME ON AND SEE ME** — Tammi Terrell (Fuqua-Bristol), Motown 1095 | 5 |
| 84 | 87 | — | — | **I ONLY HAVE EYES FOR YOU** — Lettermen (Steve Douglas), Capitol 5649 | 2 |
| 85 | 85 | 92 | 95 | **DON'T TOUCH ME** — Jeannie Seely (Fred Foster), Monument 933 | 5 |
| 86 | — | — | — | **YOU WOULDN'T LISTEN** — Ides of March (Mike Considine), Parrot 304 | 1 |
| 87 | — | — | — | **SWEET DREAMS** — Tommy McLain (Floyd Soileau & Huey Meaux), MSL 197 | 1 |
| 88 | — | — | — | **SEARCHING FOR MY LOVE** — Bobby Moore & the Rhythm Aces (Rick Hall), Checker 1129 | 1 |
| 89 | 92 | 96 | 98 | **IT'S AN UPHILL CLIMB TO THE BOTTOM** — Walter Jackson (Ted Cooper), Okeh 7247 | 4 |
| 90 | 94 | — | — | **I'M A NUT** — Leroy Pullins (Lissauer-Wheeler), Kapp 758 | 2 |
| 91 | 94 | — | — | **IT'S THAT TIME OF THE YEAR** — Lem Barry (Madara-White), Decca 31969 | 2 |
| 92 | 99 | — | — | **I'LL BE GONE** — Pozo-Seco Singers (Bob Johnston), Columbia 43646 | 2 |
| 93 | — | — | — | **LARA'S THEME FROM "DR. ZHIVAGO"** — Roger Williams, Kapp 738 | 1 |
| 94 | — | — | — | **STOP! GET A TICKET** — Clefs of Lavender Hill (Steven Palmer), Date 1510 | 1 |
| 95 | — | — | — | **SUNNY** — Bobby Hebb (Jerry Ross), Philips 40365 | 1 |
| 96 | — | — | — | **YOU CAN'T ROLLER SKATE IN A BUFFALO HERD** — Roger Miller (Jerry Kennedy), Smash 2043 | 1 |
| 97 | — | — | — | **LA BAMBA** — Trini Lopez (Don Costa Prod.), Reprise 0480 | 1 |
| 98 | — | — | — | **PAINTER** — Lou Christie (Charlie Calello), MGM 13533 | 1 |
| 99 | — | — | — | **PAST, PRESENT AND FUTURE** — Shangri-Las (Shadow Morton), Red Bird 10068 | 1 |
| 100 | — | — | — | **MISTY** — Groove Holmes (Cal Lampley), Prestige 401 | 1 |

## BUBBLING UNDER THE HOT 100

| | | |
|---|---|---|
| 101. | LOOK BEFORE YOU LEAP | Dave Clark Five, Epic 10031 |
| 102. | I NEED YOU | Barbara Mason, Arctic 120 |
| 103. | COUNT DOWN | Dave (Baby) Cortez, Roulette 4679 |
| 104. | YOU WAITED TOO LONG | Five Stair-Steps, Windy C 601 |
| 105. | HAND JIVE | Strangeloves, Bang 524 |
| 106. | HE WILL BREAK YOUR HEART | Righteous Brothers, Verve 10406 |
| 107. | HIGH ON LOVE | Knickerbockers, Challenge 59322 |
| 108. | ALL THESE THINGS | Uniques, Paula 243 |
| 109. | MINE EXCLUSIVELY | Olympics, Mirwood 5513 |
| 110. | TAR AND CEMENT | Verdelle Smith, Capitol 5632 |
| 111. | AIN'T GONNA CRY NO MORE | Brenda Lee, Decca 31970 |
| 112. | OFF AND RUNNING | Lesley Gore, Mercury 72580 |
| 113. | DISTANT DRUMS | Jim Reeves, RCA Victor 8789 |
| 114. | I'VE GOT TO GO ON WITHOUT YOU | Van Dykes, Mala 530 |
| 115. | ON THE GOOD SHIP LOLLIPOP | Wonder Who, Philips 40380 |
| 116. | HOW CAN I TELL HER IT'S OVER | Andy Williams, Columbia 43650 |
| 117. | SUCH A SWEET THING | Mary Wells, Atco 6423 |
| 118. | YOU JUST CAN'T QUIT | Rick Nelson, Decca 31965 |
| 119. | IT'S YOU ALONE | Wailers, United Artists 50026 |
| 120. | BLUE STAR | Ventures, Dolton 320 |
| 121. | SOCK IT TO 'EM, J. B. | Rex Garvin, Mercury 72580 |
| 122. | IT'S A MAN'S—WOMAN'S WORLD | Irma Thomas, Imperial 66178 |
| 123. | BOYS ARE MADE TO LOVE | Karen Small, Venus 1046 |
| 124. | STAGECOACH TO CHEYENNE | Wayne Newton, Capitol 5644 |
| 125. | RACE WITH THE WIND | Mitchell Trio, Mercury 72579 |
| 126. | HEY YOU LITTLE BOO-GA-LOO | Chubby Checker, Parkway 989 |
| 127. | YOU CAN'T LOVE THEM ALL | Drifters, Atlantic 2336 |
| 128. | I WANT YOU | Bob Dylan, Columbia 43683 |
| 129. | GREATEST MOMENTS IN A GIRL'S LIFE | Johnny Cash, Columbia 43673 |
| 130. | EVERYBODY LOVES A NUT | Johnny Cash, Columbia 43673 |
| 131. | IF HE WALKED INTO MY LIFE | Eydie Gorme, Columbia 43644 |

Compiled from national retail sales and radio station airplay by the Music Popularity Dept. of Record Market Research, Billboard.

For Week Ending July 2, 1966

# HOT 100

★ STAR performer—Sides registering greatest proportionate upward progress this week.

Record Industry Association of America seal of certification as million selling single.

| This Week | 1 Wk. Ago | 2 Wks. Ago | 3 Wks. Ago | TITLE Artist (Producer), Label & Number | Weeks On Chart |
|---|---|---|---|---|---|
| 1 (Billboard Award) | 2 | 5 | 6 | STRANGERS IN THE NIGHT — Frank Sinatra (Jimmy Bowen), Reprise 0470 | 9 |
| 2 | 1 | 15 | 28 | PAPERBACK WRITER — Beatles (George Martin), Capitol 5651 | 4 |
| 3 ★ | 6 | 10 | 19 | RED RUBBER BALL — Cyrkle (John Simon), Columbia 43589 | 7 |
| 4 | 3 | 1 | 1 | PAINT IT, BLACK — Rolling Stones (Andrew Loog Oldham), London 901 | 8 |
| 5 ★ | 9 | 12 | 17 | YOU DON'T HAVE TO SAY YOU LOVE ME — Dusty Springfield, Philips 40371 | 7 |
| 6 ★ | 15 | 25 | 48 | HANKY PANKY — Tommy James & the Shondells (Jeff Barry & Ellie Greenwich), Roulette 4686 | 5 |
| 7 | 8 | 9 | 12 | COOL JERK — Capitols (Ollie McLaughlin), Karen 1524 | 10 |
| 8 | 5 | 3 | 3 | I AM A ROCK — Simon & Garfunkel (Bob Johnston), Columbia 43617 | 9 |
| 9 | 4 | 2 | 2 | DID YOU EVER HAVE TO MAKE UP YOUR MIND? — Lovin' Spoonful (Erik Jacobsen), Kama Sutra 209 | 9 |
| 10 | 7 | 7 | 10 | BAREFOOTIN' — Robert Parker (Wherly-Burly Prod.), Nola 721 | 11 |
| 11 ★ | 24 | 41 | 51 | LITTLE GIRL — Syndicate of Sound (Gary Thompson), Bell 640 | 5 |
| 12 | 14 | 17 | 22 | DON'T BRING ME DOWN — Animals (Tom Wilson), MGM 13514 | 7 |
| 13 | 10 | 11 | 11 | SWEET TALKIN' GUY — Chiffons (Bright Tunes), Laurie 3340 | 9 |
| 14 | 12 | 13 | 13 | OH HOW HAPPY — Shades of Blue (John Rhys), Impact 1007 | 9 |
| 15 ★ | 20 | 27 | 36 | AIN'T TOO PROUD TO BEG — Temptations (N. Whitfield), Gordy 7054 | 6 |
| 16 ★ | 21 | 26 | 31 | DIRTY WATER — Standells (Ed Cobb), Tower 185 | 11 |
| 17 | 19 | 19 | 21 | DOUBLE SHOT (Of My Baby's Love) — Swingin' Medallions (Karric Prods.), Smash 2033 | 11 |
| 18 | 13 | 14 | 14 | OPUS 17 (Don't You Worry 'Bout Me) — 4 Seasons (Bob Crewe), Philips 40370 | 7 |
| 19 ★ | 32 | 44 | 64 | ALONG COMES MARY — Association (C. Boettcher), Valiant 741 | 5 |
| 20 ★ | 26 | 34 | 52 | HE — Righteous Brothers (Bill Medley), Verve 10406 | 5 |
| 21 | 22 | 23 | 23 | GIRL IN LOVE — The Outsiders (Tom King), Capitol 5646 | 8 |
| 22 | 23 | 21 | 26 | HOLD ON! I'M COMIN' — Sam & Dave (Prod. By Staff), Stax 189 | 11 |
| 23 | 16 | 6 | 5 | A GROOVY KIND OF LOVE — Mindbenders, Fontana 1541 | 12 |
| 24 ★ | 29 | 42 | 72 | RAIN — Beatles (George Martin), Capitol 5651 | 4 |
| 25 | 18 | 16 | 16 | THE MORE I SEE YOU — Chris Montez (Herb Alpert), A&M 796 | 12 |
| 26 | 27 | 33 | 46 | POPSICLE — Jan & Dean (Jan Berry), Liberty 55886 | 5 |
| 27 | 25 | 28 | 38 | CRYING — Jay & the Americans (Gerry Granahan), United Artists 50016 | 6 |
| 28 | 17 | 8 | 9 | GREEN GRASS — Gary Lewis & the Playboys (Dave Pell), Liberty 55880 | 8 |
| 29 | 11 | 4 | 4 | WHEN A MAN LOVES A WOMAN — Percy Sledge (Quin Ivy-Marvin Greene), Atlantic 2326 | 13 |
| 30 ★ | 38 | 57 | 81 | I WASHED MY HANDS IN MUDDY WATER — Johnny Rivers (Lou Adler), Imperial 66175 | 4 |
| 31 ★ | 55 | 93 | 99 | LIL' RED RIDING HOOD — Sam the Sham & the Pharaohs (Stan Kesler), MGM 13506 | 4 |
| 32 | 34 | 35 | 43 | HEY JOE — Leaves (Norm Ratner), Mira 222 | 7 |
| 33 ★ | 43 | 61 | 79 | PLEASE TELL ME WHY — Dave Clark Five (Dave Clark), Epic 10031 | 4 |
| 34 | 35 | 43 | 53 | THE LAND OF MILK AND HONEY — Vogues (Cenci-Hakim-Moon), Co & Ce 238 | 5 |
| 35 | 36 | 51 | 78 | DAY FOR DECISION — Johnny Sea (Gene Nash), Warner Bros. 5820 | 4 |
| 36 | 37 | 47 | 59 | LET'S GO GET STONED — Ray Charles (Joe Adams), ABC Records 10808 | 6 |
| 37 ★ | 58 | 81 | 90 | SWEET PEA — Tommy Roe, ABC Records 10762 | 4 |
| 38 | 28 | 22 | 24 | MAMA — B. J. Thomas (Music Enterprises, Inc.), Scepter 12139 | 8 |
| 39 | 42 | 46 | 56 | OH YEAH — Shadows of Knight (Dunwich Prod.), Dunwich 122 | 5 |
| 40 | 31 | 32 | 39 | I LOVE YOU 1,000 TIMES — The Platters (Luther Dixon), Musicor 1166 | 10 |
| 41 ★ | 51 | 72 | — | YOU BETTER RUN — Young Rascals (Young Rascals), Atlantic 2338 | 3 |
| 42 ★ | 56 | 70 | 98 | THE PIED PIPER — Crispian St. Peters (David Nicolson), Jamie 1320 | 4 |
| 43 | 48 | 56 | 67 | YOUNGER GIRL — Critters (Artie Ripp), Kapp 752 | 6 |
| 44 | 45 | 45 | 55 | TAKE THIS HEART OF MINE — Marvin Gaye (Robinson-Moore), Tamla 54132 | 7 |
| 45 | 50 | 60 | 71 | LOVING YOU IS SWEETER THAN EVER — Four Tops (Ivy Hunter), Motown 1096 | 6 |
| 46 | 46 | 49 | 49 | PETER RABBIT — Dee Jay and the Runaways (Iowa Great Lakes Studios), Smash 2034 | 9 |
| 47 ★ | 75 | — | — | WILD THING — Troggs (Page One-York Palla), Atco 6415-Fontana 1548 | 2 |
| 48 ★ | 59 | 78 | — | SOMEWHERE MY LOVE — Ray Conniff & the Singers (Ernie Altschuler), Columbia 43626 | 3 |
| 49 | 49 | 52 | 62 | HAVE I STAYED TOO LONG — Sonny & Cher (Sonny Bono), Atco 6420 | 5 |
| 50 ★ | 67 | 82 | — | HUNGRY — Paul Revere & the Raiders (Terry Melcher), Columbia 43678 | 3 |
| 51 ★ | 61 | 77 | — | HAPPY SUMMER DAYS — Ronnie Dove (Phil Kahl), Diamond 205 | 3 |
| 52 | 54 | 59 | 69 | YOUNGER GIRL — Hondells (G. P. IV Prod.), Mercury 72563 | 6 |
| 53 ★ | — | — | — | I SAW HER AGAIN — Mama's & the Papa's (Lou Adler), Dunhill 4031 | 1 |
| 54 | 57 | 58 | 68 | NINETY-NINE AND A HALF — Wilson Pickett (Steve Cropper), Atlantic 2334 | 6 |
| 55 | 60 | 68 | 70 | SOLITARY MAN — Neil Diamond (Barry & Greenwich), Bang 519 | 7 |
| 56 | 52 | 53 | 54 | MY LITTLE RED BOOK — Love (Jac Holzman & Mark Abramson), Elektra 603 | 10 |
| 57 ★ | — | — | — | LOVE LETTERS — Elvis Presley, RCA Victor 8870 | 1 |
| 58 | 64 | 76 | 87 | THE IMPOSSIBLE DREAM — Jack Jones (David Kapp), Kapp 755 | 5 |
| 59 ★ | — | — | — | THE WORK SONG — Herb Alpert & the Tijuana Brass (Herb Alpert), A & M 805 | 1 |
| 60 ★ | 70 | 89 | — | WHERE WERE YOU WHEN I NEEDED YOU — Grass Roots (Sloan & Barri), Dunhill 4029 | 3 |
| 61 | 65 | 71 | 86 | MY LOVER'S PRAYER — Otis Redding (Prod. by Staff), Volt 136 | 5 |
| 62 | 71 | 86 | — | BILLY AND SUE — B. J. Thomas, Hickory 1395 | 3 |
| 63 | 63 | 65 | 80 | I'LL LOVE YOU FOREVER — Holidays (Davis-Jackson Prod.), Golden World 36 | 9 |
| 64 ★ | 79 | 83 | — | WHOLE LOT OF SHAKIN' IN MY HEART (Since I Met You) — Miracles (Frank Wilson), Tamla 54134 | 3 |
| 65 | 66 | 69 | 97 | NEIGHBOR, NEIGHBOR — Jimmy Hughes (Ric Hall), Fame 1003 | 5 |
| 66 ★ | 82 | — | — | OVER UNDER SIDEWAYS DOWN — Yardbirds (Samwell-Smith, Napier-Bell), Epic 10035 | 2 |
| 67 | 62 | 64 | 65 | CLOUDY SUMMER AFTERNOON — Barry McGuire (Lou Adler), Dunhill 402 | 7 |
| 68 ★ | 88 | — | — | SEARCHING FOR MY LOVE — Bobby Moore & the Rhythm Aces (Rick Hall), Checker 1129 | 2 |
| 69 ★ | 96 | — | — | YOU CAN'T ROLLER SKATE IN A BUFFALO HERD — Roger Miller (Jerry Kennedy), Smash [illegible] | 2 |
| 70 | 72 | 90 | — | NOT RESPONSIBLE — Tom Jones (Peter Sullivan), Parrot 40006 | 3 |
| 71 | 77 | 74 | 84 | WHAT AM I GOING TO DO WITHOUT YOUR LOVE — Martha & the Vandellas (Wm. Stevenson-I. Hunter), Gordy 7053 | 4 |
| 72 ★ | — | — | — | PRETTY FLAMINGO — Manfred Mann (John Burgess), United Artists 50040 | 1 |
| 73 | 78 | 84 | 94 | I LOVE ONIONS — Susan Christie (John Hill), Columbia 43595 | 4 |
| 74 | 73 | 73 | 76 | WHEN A WOMAN LOVES A MAN — Esther Phillips (Jerry Wexler), Atlantic 2335 | 5 |
| 75 ★ | 90 | — | — | I'M A NUT — Leroy Pullins (Lissauer-Wheeler), Kapp 759 | 2 |
| 76 | 87 | — | — | SWEET DREAMS — Tommy McLain (Floyd Soileau & Huey Meaux), MSL 197 | 2 |
| 77 | 86 | — | — | YOU WOULDN'T LISTEN — I'des of March (Mike Considine), Parrot 304 | 2 |
| 78 ★ | — | — | — | TRAINS AND BOATS AND PLANES — Dionne Warwick (Bacharach-David), Scepter 12153 | 1 |
| 79 ★ | 95 | — | — | SUNNY — Bobby Hebb (Jerry Ross), Philips 40365 | 2 |
| 80 | 80 | 97 | — | TEENAGER'S PRAYER — Joe Simon (J.R. Enterprises), Sound Stage 7 25 4 | 3 |
| 81 | 81 | 96 | — | GRIM REAPER OF LOVE — Turtles (Bones Howe), White Whale 231 | 3 |
| 82 | 93 | — | — | LARA'S THEME FROM "DR. ZHIVAGO" — Roger Williams, Kapp 738 | 2 |
| 83 | 84 | 87 | — | I ONLY HAVE EYES FOR YOU — Lettermen (Steve Douglas), Capitol 5649 | 3 |
| 84 ★ | 99 | — | — | PAST, PRESENT AND FUTURE — Shangri-Las (Shadow Morton), Red Bird 10068 | 2 |
| 85 ★ | 100 | — | — | MISTY — Groove Holmes (Cal Lampley), Prestige 401 | 2 |
| 86 | 94 | — | — | STOP! GET A TICKET — Clefs of Lavender Hill (Steven Palmer), Date 1510 | 2 |
| 87 ★ | — | — | — | AIN'T GONNA CRY NO MORE — Brenda Lee (Owen Bradley), Decca 31970 | 1 |
| 88 | 89 | 92 | 96 | IT'S AN UPHILL CLIMB TO THE BOTTOM — Walter Jackson (Ted Cooper), Okeh 7247 | 5 |
| 89 ★ | — | — | — | CAN I TRUST YOU? — Bachelors (Dick Rowe), London 20010 | 1 |
| 90 ★ | — | — | — | I WANT YOU — Bob Dylan (Bob Johnston), Columbia 43683 | 1 |
| 91 | 91 | 94 | — | IT'S THAT TIME OF THE YEAR — Len Barry (Madara-White), Decca 31969 | 3 |
| 92 | — | — | — | ON THE GOOD SHIP LOLLIPOP — Wonder Who? (Bob Crewe), Philips 40380 | 1 |
| 93 | 98 | — | — | PAINTER — Lou Christie (Charlie Calello), MGM 13533 | 2 |
| 94 | 97 | — | — | LA BAMBA — Trini Lopez (Don Costa Prod.), Reprise 0480 | 2 |
| 95 | — | — | — | HIGH ON LOVE — Knickerbockers (Jerry Fuller), Challenge 59332 | 1 |
| 96 | — | — | — | HOT SHOT — Buena Vistas (A Magi Prod.), Swan 4255 | 1 |
| 97 | — | — | — | EVERYBODY LOVES A NUT — Johnny Cash (Don Law-Frank Jones), Columbia 43673 | 1 |
| 98 | — | — | — | HEY YOU LITTLE BOO-GA-LOO — Chubby Checker (Dave Appell), Parkway 989 | 1 |
| 99 | — | — | — | ALL THESE THINGS — Uniques, Paula 238 | 1 |
| 100 | — | — | — | SUCH A SWEET THING — Mary Wells (Carl Davis), Atco 6423 | 1 |

## HOT 100—A TO Z—(Publisher-Licensee)

Ain't Gonna Cry No More (Cooga, BMI) ........ 87
Ain't Too Proud to Beg (Jobete, BMI) ........ 15
All These Things (Minit, BMI) ........ 99
Along Comes Mary (Davon, BMI) ........ 19
Barefootin' (Bonatemp, BMI) ........ 10
Billy and Sue (Hernet, BMI) ........ 62
Can I Trust You? (Miller, ASCAP) ........ 89
Cloudy Summer Afternoon (Metric, BMI) ........ 67
Cool Jerk (McLaughlin, BMI) ........ 7
Crying (Acuff-Rose, BMI) ........ 27
Day for Decision (Moss-Rose, BMI) ........ 35
Did You Ever Have to Make Up Your Mind? (Faithful Virtue, BMI) ........ 9
Dirty Water (Equinox, BMI) ........ 16
Don't Bring Me Down (Screen Gems-Columbia, BMI) 12
Double Shot (Of My Baby's Love) (Lyricsong-Windsong, BMI) ........ 17
Everybody Loves a Nut (Jack, BMI) ........ 97
Girl in Love (Beechwood, BMI) ........ 21
Green Grass (Mills, ASCAP) ........ 28
Grim Reaper of Love (Ishmael, BMI) ........ 81
Groovy Kind of Love, A (Screen Gems-Columbia, BMI) ........ 23
Hanky Panky (T. M., BMI) ........ 6
Happy Summer Days (Picturetone, BMI) ........ 51
Have I Stayed Too Long (Cotillion-Chrismarc-Five-West, BMI) ........ 49
He (Avas, ASCAP) ........ 20
Hey, Joe (Third Story, BMI) ........ 32
Hey You Little Boo-Ga-Loo (Double Diamond, Champion, BMI) ........ 98
High on Love (4 Star, BMI) ........ 95
Hold On! I'm Comin' (East, Pronto, BMI) ........ 22
Hot Shot (Palmina-Shan-Todd, BMI) ........ 96
Hungry (Screen Gems-Columbia, BMI) ........ 50
I Am a Rock (Eclectic, BMI) ........ 8
I Love Onions (Blackwood, BMI) ........ 73
I Love You 1,000 Times (Ludix, BMI) ........ 40
I Only Have Eyes for You (Remick, ASCAP) ........ 83
I Saw Her Again (Trousdale, BMI) ........ 53
I Want You (Dwarf, ASCAP) ........ 90
I Washed My Hands in Muddy Water (Maricana, BMI) ........ 30
I'll Love You Forever (Myto, BMI) ........ 63
I'm a Nut (Youmans-Sleepy Hollow, ASCAP) ........ 75
Impossible Dream, The (Fox, ASCAP) ........ 58
It's an Uphill Climb to the Bottom (Metric, BMI) 88
It's That Time of the Year (Double Diamond, BMI) 91
La Bamba (South Mountain, BMI) ........ 94
Land of Milk and Honey, The (Tree, BMI) ........ 34
Lara's Theme From "Dr. Zhivago" (Robbins, ASCAP) ........ 82
Let's Go Get Stoned (Baby Monica, BMI) ........ 36
Lil' Red Riding Hood (Rose, BMI) ........ 31
Little Girl (Duane, BMI) ........ 11
Love Letters (Famous, ASCAP) ........ 57
Loving You is Sweeter Than Ever (Jobete, BMI) .. 45
Mama (Flomar, BMI) ........ 38
Misty (Vernon, ASCAP) ........ 85
More I See You, The (Bregman, Vocco & Conn, ASCAP) ........ 25
My Little Red Book (United Artists, ASCAP) ........ 56
My Lover's Prayer (East-Time-Redwal, BMI) ........ 61
Neighbor, Neighbor (Crazy Cajun, BMI) ........ 65
Ninety-Nine and a Half (East-Pronto, BMI) ........ 54
Not Responsible (Northern, ASCAP) ........ 70
Oh How Happy (Myto, BMI) ........ 14
Oh Yeah (Arc, BMI) ........ 39
On the Good Ship Lollipop (Movietown, ASCAP) .. 92
Opus 17 (Don't You Worry 'Bout Me) (Saturday, BMI) ........ 18
Over, Under, Sideways Down (Feist, ASCAP) ........ 66
Paint It, Black (Gideon, BMI) ........ 4
Painter (Rambed, BMI) ........ 93
Paperback Writer (Maclen, BMI) ........ 2
Past, Present and Future (Tender Tunes, BMI) .. 84
Peter Rabbit (Willong, BMI) ........ 46
Pied Piper, The (Chardon, BMI) ........ 42
Please Tell Me Why (Branston, BMI) ........ 33
Popsicle (Lowery, BMI) ........ 26
Pretty Flamingo (Shapiro-Bernstein, ASCAP) ........ 72
Rain (Maclen, BMI) ........ 24
Red Rubber Ball (Eclectic, BMI) ........ 3
Searching for My Love (Chevis, BMI) ........ 68
Solitary Man (Tallyrand, BMI) ........ 55
Somewhere My Love (Robbins, ASCAP) ........ 48
Stop! Get a Ticket (Gallico, BMI) ........ 86
Strangers in the Night (Champion-Roosevelt, BMI) ........ 1
Such a Sweet Thing (Jalynne-Shakewell, BMI)..100
Sunny (Portable, BMI) ........ 79
Sweet Dreams (Acuff-Rose, BMI) ........ 76
Sweet Pea (Low Twi, BMI) ........ 37
Sweet Talkin' Guy (Elmwin, BMI) ........ 13
Take This Heart of Mine (Jobete, BMI) ........ 44
Teenager's Prayer (Frederick, BMI) ........ 80
Trains and Boats and Planes (U. S. Songs, ASCAP) 78
What Am I Going to Do Without Your Love (Jobete, BMI) ........ 71
When a Man Loves a Woman (Pronto-Quinvy, BMI) 29
When a Woman Loves a Man (Pronto-Quinvy, BMI) ........ 74
Where Were You When I Needed You (Trousdale, BMI) ........ 60
Whole Lot of Shakin' in My Heart (Since I Met You) Jobete, BMI) ........ 64
Wild Thing (Blackwood, BMI) ........ 47
Work Song, The (Upam, BMI) ........ 59
You Better Run (Slacsar, BMI) ........ 41
You Can't Roller Skate in a Buffalo Herd (Tree, BMI) ........ 69
You Don't Have to Say You Love Me (Robbins, ASCAP) ........ 5
You Wouldn't Listen (BMC, BMI) ........ 77
Younger Girl—Critters (Faithful Virtue, BMI) .... 43
Younger Girl—Hondells (Faithful Virtue, BMI) .... 52

## BUBBLING UNDER THE HOT 100

101. TAR AND CEMENT ........ Verdelle Smith, Capitol 5632
102. HE WILL BREAK YOUR HEART ........ Righteous Brothers, Verve 10406
103. I'LL BE GONE ........ Pozo-Seco Singers, Columbia 43646
104. YOU WAITED TOO LONG ........ Five Stair-Steps, Windy C 601
105. BECAUSE OF YOU ........ Rome & Paris, Roulette 4681
106. I NEED LOVE ........ Barbara Mason, Artic 120
107. COUNT DOWN ........ Dave (Baby) Cortez, Roulette 4679
108. HAND JIVE ........ Strangeloves, Bang 524
109. COME WHAT MAY ........ Elvis Presley, RCA Victor 8870
110. HOW CAN I TELL HER IT'S OVER ........ Andy Williams, Columbia 43650
111. LOOK AT ME GIRL ........ Bobby Vee, Liberty 55877
112. LOOK BEFORE YOU LEAP ........ Dave Clark Five, Epic 10031
113. I'VE GOT TO GO ON WITHOUT YOU ........ Van Dykes, Mala 530
114. MINE EXCLUSIVELY ........ Olympics, Mirwood 5513
115. SEE YOU IN SEPTEMBER ........ Happenings, B. T. Puppy 520
116. DISTANT DRUMS ........ Jim Reeves, RCA Victor 8789
117. YOU JUST CAN'T QUIT ........ Rick Nelson, Decca 31965
118. IT'S YOU ALONE ........ Wailers, United Artists 50026
119. RACE WITH THE WIND ........ The Robbs, Mercury 72579
120. IF HE WALKED INTO MY LIFE ........ Eydie Gorme, Columbia 43660
121. SOCK IT TO 'EM J.B. ........ Rex Garvin, Like 301
122. IT'S A MAN'S-WOMAN'S WORLD ........ Irma Thomas, Imperial 66178
123. FARMER JOHN ........ Tidal Waves, HBR 482
124. JUST A LITTLE BIT OF YOU ........ Dallas Frazier, Capitol 5670
125. OFF AND RUNNING ........ Lesley Gore, Mercury 72580
126. YOU'RE NOBODY TILL SOMEBODY LOVES YOU ........ Wonder Who, Philips 40380
127. PRETTY FLAMINGO ........ Tommy Vann, Academy 120
128. GREATEST MOMENTS IN A GIRL'S LIFE ........ Tokens, B. T. Puppy 519
129. THAT'S ENOUGH ........ Roscoe Robinson, Wand 1125
130. LONELY SOLDIER ........ Mike Williams, Atlantic 2339
131. I PUT A SPELL ON YOU ........ Alan Price Set, Parrot 3001
132. WE'LL BE UNITED ........ Intruders, Gamble 201
133. THE STREETS OF BALTIMORE ........ Bobby Bare, RCA Victor 8851
134. LET IT BE ME ........ Arthur Prysock, Old Town 1196
135. FREDDIE FEELGOOD ........ Ray Stevens, Monument 946

Compiled from national retail sales and radio station airplay by the Music Popularity Dept. of Record Market Research, Billboard.

# Billboard HOT 100

For Week Ending July 9, 1966

★ STAR performer—Sides registering greatest proportionate upward progress this week.

| This Week | Last Week | 2 Wks. Ago | TITLE Artist (Producer), Label & Number | Weeks On Chart |
|---|---|---|---|---|
| 1 | 2 | 1 | **PAPERBACK WRITER** — Beatles (George Martin), Capitol 5651 | 5 |
| 2 | 3 | 6 | **RED RUBBER BALL** — Cyrkle (John Simon), Columbia 43589 | 8 |
| 3 | 1 | 2 | **STRANGERS IN THE NIGHT** — Frank Sinatra (Jimmy Bowen), Reprise 0470 | 10 |
| 4 | 6 | 15 | **HANKY PANKY** — Tommy James & the Shondells (Jeff Barry & Ellie Greenwich), Roulette 4686 | 6 |
| 5 | 5 | 9 | **YOU DON'T HAVE TO SAY YOU LOVE ME** — Dusty Springfield, Philips 40371 | 8 |
| ★6 | 47 | 75 | **WILD THING** — Troggs (Page One-York Pala), Atco 6415 / Fontana 1548 | 3 |
| 7 | 7 | 8 | **COOL JERK** — Capitols (Ollie McLaughlin), Karen 1524 | 11 |
| 8 | 11 | 24 | **LITTLE GIRL** — Syndicate of Sound (Gary Thompson), Bell 640 | 6 |
| 9 | 4 | 3 | **PAINT IT, BLACK** — Rolling Stones (Andrew Loog Oldham), London 901 | 9 |
| 10 | 19 | 32 | **ALONG COMES MARY** — Association (C. Boettcher), Valiant 741 | 6 |
| 11 | 16 | 21 | **DIRTY WATER** — Standells (Ed Cobb), Tower 185 | 12 |
| 12 | 31 | 55 | **LIL' RED RIDING HOOD** — Sam the Sham & the Pharaohs (Stan Kesler), MGM 13506 | 5 |
| 13 | 12 | 14 | **DON'T BRING ME DOWN** — Animals (Tom Wilson), MGM 13514 | 8 |
| 14 | 15 | 20 | **AIN'T TOO PROUD TO BEG** — Temptations (N. Whitfield), Gordy 7054 | 7 |
| 15 | 50 | 67 | **HUNGRY** — Paul Revere & the Raiders (Terry Melcher), Columbia 43678 | 4 |
| 16 | 14 | 12 | **OH HOW HAPPY** — Shades of Blue (John Rhys), Impact 1007 | 10 |
| 17 | 8 | 5 | **I AM A ROCK** — Simon & Garfunkel (Bob Johnston), Columbia 43617 | 10 |
| 18 | 20 | 26 | **HE** — Righteous Brothers (Bill Medley), Verve 10406 | 6 |
| ★19 | 53 | — | **I SAW HER AGAIN** — Mama's & the Papa's (Lou Adler), Dunhill 4031 | 2 |
| 20 | 10 | 7 | **BAREFOOTIN'** — Robert Parker (Wherly-Burly Prod.), Nola 721 | 12 |
| 21 | 26 | 27 | **POPSICLE** — Jan & Dean (Jan Berry), Liberty 55886 | 6 |
| 22 | 42 | 56 | **THE PIED PIPER** — Crispian St. Peters (David Nicolson), Jamie 1320 | 5 |
| 23 | 24 | 29 | **RAIN** — Beatles (George Martin), Capitol 5651 | 5 |
| 24 | 37 | 58 | **SWEET PEA** — Tommy Roe, ABC Records 10762 | 5 |
| 25 | 30 | 38 | **I WASHED MY HANDS IN MUDDY WATER** — Johnny Rivers (Lou Adler), Imperial 66175 | 5 |
| 26 | 22 | 23 | **HOLD ON! I'M COMIN'** — Sam & Dave (Prod. By Staff), Stax 189 | 12 |
| 27 | 9 | 4 | **DID YOU EVER HAVE TO MAKE UP YOUR MIND?** — Lovin' Spoonful (Erik Jacobsen), Kama Sutra 209 | 10 |
| ★28 | 33 | 43 | **PLEASE TELL ME WHY** — Dave Clark Five (Dave Clark), Epic 10031 | 5 |
| ★29 | 34 | 35 | **THE LAND OF MILK AND HONEY** — Vogues (Cenci-Hakim-Moon), Co & Ce 238 | 6 |
| ★30 | 41 | 51 | **YOU BETTER RUN** — Young Rascals (Young Rascals), Atlantic 2338 | 4 |
| 31 | 32 | 34 | **HEY JOE** — Leaves (Norm Ratner), Mira 222 | 8 |
| 32 | 36 | 37 | **LET'S GO GET STONED** — Ray Charles (Joe Adams), ABC Records 10808 | 7 |
| 33 | 13 | 10 | **SWEET TALKIN' GUY** — Chiffons (Bright Tunes), Laurie 3340 | 10 |
| 34 | 25 | 18 | **THE MORE I SEE YOU** — Chris Montez (Herb Alpert), A&M 796 | 13 |
| ★35 | 48 | 59 | **SOMEWHERE MY LOVE** — Ray Conniff & the Singers (Ernie Altschuler), Columbia 43626 | 4 |
| 36 | 17 | 19 | **DOUBLE SHOT (Of My Baby's Love)** — Swingin' Medallions (Karric Prods.), Smash 2033 | 12 |
| 37 | 18 | 13 | **OPUS 17 (Don't You Worry 'Bout Me)** — 4 Seasons (Bob Crewe), Philips 40370 | 8 |
| ★38 | 51 | 61 | **HAPPY SUMMER DAYS** — Ronnie Dove (Phil Kahl), Diamond 205 | 4 |
| ★39 | 59 | — | **THE WORK SONG** — Herb Alpert & the Tijuana Brass (Herb Alpert), A&M 805 | 2 |
| 40 | 57 | — | **LOVE LETTERS** — Elvis Presley, RCA Victor 8870 | 2 |
| 41 | 39 | 42 | **OH YEAH** — Shadows of Knight (Dunwich Prod.), Dunwich 122 | 6 |
| 42 | 43 | 48 | **YOUNGER GIRL** — Critters (Artie Ripp), Kapp 752 | 7 |
| 43 | 35 | 36 | **DAY FOR DECISION** — Johnny Sea (Gene Nash), Warner Bros. 5820 | 5 |
| 44 | 23 | 16 | **A GROOVY KIND OF LOVE** — Mindbenders (Fontana 1541) | 13 |
| 45 | 46 | 46 | **PETER RABBIT** — Dee Jay and the Runaways (Iowa Great Lakes Studios), Smash 2034 | 10 |
| 46 | 21 | 22 | **GIRL IN LOVE** — The Outsiders (Tom King), Capitol 5646 | 9 |
| ★47 | 60 | 70 | **WHERE WERE YOU NEEDED YOU** — Grass Roots (Sloan & Barri), Dunhill 4029 | 4 |
| 48 | 58 | 64 | **THE IMPOSSIBLE DREAM** — Jack Jones (David Kapp), Kapp 755 | 6 |
| 49 | 45 | 50 | **LOVING YOU IS SWEETER THAN EVER** — Four Tops (Ivy Hunter), Motown 1096 | 7 |
| ★50 | 62 | 71 | **BILLY AND SUE** — B. J. Thomas, Hickory 1395 | 4 |
| 51 | 90 | — | **I WANT YOU** — Bob Dylan (Bob Johnston), Columbia 43683 | 2 |
| 52 | 52 | 54 | **YOUNGER GIRL** — Hondells (G. P. IV Prod.), Mercury 72563 | 7 |
| 53 | 54 | 57 | **NINETY-NINE AND A HALF** — Wilson Pickett (Steve Cropper), Atlantic 2334 | 7 |
| 54 | 66 | 82 | **OVER UNDER SIDEWAYS DOWN** — Yardbirds (Samwell-Smith, Napier-Bell), Epic 10035 | 3 |
| 55 | 55 | 60 | **SOLITARY MAN** — Neil Diamond (Barry & Greenwich), Bang 519 | 8 |
| 56 | 78 | — | **TRAINS AND BOATS AND PLANES** — Dionne Warwick (Bacharach-David), Scepter 12153 | 2 |
| 57 | 69 | 96 | **YOU CAN'T ROLLER SKATE IN A BUFFALO HERD** — Roger Miller (Jerry Kennedy), Smash 2043 | 3 |
| 58 | 68 | 88 | **SEARCHING FOR MY LOVE** — Bobby Moore & the Rhythm Aces (Rick Hall), Checker 1129 | 3 |
| 59 | 64 | 79 | **WHOLE LOT OF SHAKIN' IN MY HEART (Since I Met You)** — Miracles (Frank Wilson), Tamla 54134 | 4 |
| 60 | 72 | — | **PRETTY FLAMINGO** — Manfred Mann (John Burgess), United Artists 50040 | 2 |
| 61 | 76 | 87 | **SWEET DREAMS** — Tommy McLain (Floyd Soileau & Huey Meaux), MSL 197 | 3 |
| 62 | 77 | 86 | **YOU WOULDN'T LISTEN** — Ides of March (Mike Considine), Parrot 304 | 3 |
| 63 | 44 | 45 | **TAKE THIS HEART OF MINE** — Marvin Gaye (Robinson-Moore), Tamla 54132 | 8 |
| 64 | 79 | 95 | **SUNNY** — Bobby Hebb (Jerry Ross), Philips 40365 | 3 |
| 65 | 75 | 90 | **I'M A NUT** — Leroy Pullins (Lissauer-Wheeler), Kapp 758 | 3 |
| 66 | 49 | 49 | **HAVE I STAYED TOO LONG** — Sonny & Cher (Sonny Bono), Atco 6420 | 6 |
| 67 | 70 | 72 | **NOT RESPONSIBLE** — Tom Jones (Peter Sullivan), Parrot 40006 | 4 |
| 68 | 40 | 31 | **I LOVE YOU 1,000 TIMES** — The Platters (Luther Dixon), Musicor 1166 | 11 |
| ★69 | 84 | 99 | **PAST, PRESENT AND FUTURE** — Shangri-Las (Shadow Morton), Red Bird 10068 | 3 |
| ★70 | — | — | **MOTHER'S LITTLE HELPER** — Rolling Stones (Andrew Loog Oldham), London 902 | 1 |
| 71 | 65 | 66 | **NEIGHBOR, NEIGHBOR** — Jimmy Hughes (Ric Hall), Fame 1003 | 6 |
| 72 | 56 | 52 | **MY LITTLE RED BOOK** — Love (Jac Holzman & Mark Abramson), Elektra 603 | 11 |
| 73 | 73 | 78 | **I LOVE ONIONS** — Susan Christie (John Hill), Columbia 43595 | 5 |
| ★74 | 89 | — | **CAN I TRUST YOU?** — Bachelors (Dick Rowe), London 20010 | 2 |
| 75 | 61 | 65 | **MY LOVER'S PRAYER** — Otis Redding (Prod. by Staff), Volt 136 | 6 |
| 76 | 80 | 80 | **TEENAGER'S PRAYER** — Joe Simon (J.R. Enterprises), Sound Stage 7 2564 | 4 |
| 77 | — | — | **FRIDAY'S CHILD** — Nancy Sinatra (Lee Hazlewood), Reprise 0491 | 1 |
| 78 | — | — | **THIS DOOR SWINGS BOTH WAYS** — Herman's Hermits (Mickie Most), MGM 13548 | 1 |
| 79 | — | — | **TAR AND CEMENT** — Verdelle Smith (Vance-Prokriss Prod.), Capitol 5632 | 1 |
| 80 | 86 | 94 | **STOP! GET A TICKET** — Clefs of Lavender Hill (Steven Palmer), Date 1510 | 3 |
| 81 | 83 | 84 | **I ONLY HAVE EYES FOR YOU** — Lettermen (Steve Douglas), Capitol 5649 | 4 |
| 82 | 82 | 93 | **LARA'S THEME FROM "DR. ZHIVAGO"** — Roger Williams, Kapp 738 | 3 |
| 83 | — | — | **SEE YOU IN SEPTEMBER** — Happenings (Bright Tunes Prod.), B. T. Puppy 520 | 1 |
| 84 | 85 | 100 | **MISTY** — Groove Holmes (Cal Lampley), Prestige 401 | 3 |
| 85 | 71 | 77 | **WHAT AM I GOING TO DO WITHOUT YOUR LOVE** — Martha & the Vandellas (Wm. Stevenson-I. Hunter), Gordy 7053 | 5 |
| 86 | 87 | — | **AIN'T GONNA CRY NO MORE** — Brenda Lee (Owen Bradley), Decca 31970 | 2 |
| 87 | 81 | 81 | **GRIM REAPER OF LOVE** — Turtles (Bones Howe), White Whale 231 | 4 |
| 88 | — | — | **LONELY SOLDIER** — Mike Williams (Prod. by Staff), Atlantic 2339 | 1 |
| 89 | 94 | 97 | **LA BAMBA** — Trini Lopez (Don Costa Prod.), Reprise 0480 | 3 |
| 90 | 92 | — | **ON THE GOOD SHIP LOLLIPOP** — Wonder Who? (Bob Crewe), Philips 40380 | 2 |
| 91 | 93 | 98 | **PAINTER** — Lou Christie (Charlie Calello), MGM 13533 | 3 |
| 92 | 98 | — | **HEY YOU LITTLE BOO-GA-LOO** — Chubby Checker (Dave Appell), Parkway 989 | 2 |
| 93 | — | — | **LOOK AT ME GIRL** — Bobby Vee (Dallas Smith), Liberty 55877 | 1 |
| 94 | 96 | — | **HOT SHOT** — Buena Vistas (A Magi Prod.), Swan 4255 | 2 |
| 95 | 95 | — | **HIGH ON LOVE** — Knickerbockers (Jerry Fuller), Challenge 59332 | 2 |
| 96 | 97 | — | **EVERYBODY LOVES A NUT** — Johnny Cash (Don Law-Frank Jones), Columbia 43673 | 2 |
| 97 | 99 | — | **ALL THESE THINGS** — Uniques, Paula 238 | 2 |
| 98 | — | — | **DISTANT SHORES** — Chad & Jeremy (Larry Marks), Columbia 43682 | 1 |
| 99 | 100 | — | **SUCH A SWEET THING** — Mary Wells (Carl Davis), Atco 6423 | 2 |
| 100 | — | — | **WADE IN THE WATER** — Ramsey Lewis (Esmond Edwards), Cadet 5541 | 1 |

## BUBBLING UNDER THE HOT 100

101. WE'LL BE UNITED — Intruders, Gamble 201
102. HE WILL BREAK YOUR HEART — Righteous Brothers, Verve 10406
103. LADY JANE — Rolling Stones, London 902
104. I'LL BE GONE — Pozo-Seco Singers, Columbia 43646
105. BECAUSE OF YOU — Rome & Paris, Roulette 4631
106. IT'S THAT TIME OF THE YEAR — Len Barry, Decca 31969
107. THE JOKER WENT WILD — Brian Hyland, Philips 40377
108. IT'S AN UPHILL CLIMB TO THE BOTTOM — Walter Jackson, Okeh 7247
109. HOW CAN I TELL HER IT'S OVER — Andy Williams, Columbia 43650
110. FREDDIE FEELGOOD — Ray Stevens, Monument 946
111. 5-D (Fifth Dimension) — Byrds, Columbia 43702
112. YOU JUST CAN'T QUIT — Rick Nelson, Decca 31956
113. I'VE GOT TO GO ON WITHOUT YOU — Van Dykes, Mala 530
114. I GUESS I'LL ALWAYS LOVE YOU — Isley Brothers, Tamla 54135
115. TELL HER — Dean Parrish, Boom 60012
116. RACE WITH THE WIND — Robbs, Mercury 72579
117. A LETTER FROM A SOLDIER — Connie Francis, MGM 13545
118. SUMMER IN THE CITY — Lovin' Spoonful, Kama Sutra 211
119. JUST A LITTLE BIT OF YOU — Dallas Frazier, Capitol 5670
120. GREATEST MOMENTS IN A GIRL'S LIFE — Jelynne-Shakewell, BMI
121. SOCK IT TO 'EM, J. B. — Rex Garvin, Like 321
122. COME-ON HOME — Wayne Fontana, MGM 13546
123. TIDAL WAVES — Ronnie Dove, HBR 482
124. YOU'RE NOBODY TILL SOMEBODY LOVES YOU — Tommy Vann, Academy 120
125. PRETTY FLAMINGO — Tommy Vann, Academy 120
126. DRIVE MY CAR — Bob Kuban and the In-Men, Musicland, U.S.A. 20067
127. THAT'S ENOUGH — Roscoe Robinson, Wand 1125
128. UPTIGHT — Nancy Wilson, Capitol 5672
129. AIN'T THAT PECULIAR — Ramsey Lewis, Cadet 5541
130. THE STREETS OF BALTIMORE — Bobby Bare, RCA Victor 8851
131. SITTIN' ON A FENCE — Twice as Much, HBR 13520
132. LET IT BE ME — Arthur Prysock, Old Town 1196
133. THIS IS MY HOUSE (But Nobody Calls) — Moody Blues, London 1005
134. BORN A WOMAN — Sandy Posey, MGM 13501
135. OPEN THE DOOR TO YOUR HEART — Darrell Banks, Revilot 201

# Billboard

For Week Ending July 16, 1966

# HOT 100

★ **STAR performer**—Sides registering greatest proportionate upward progress this week.

Record Industry Association of America seal of certification as million selling single.

| This Week | 1 Wk. Ago | 2 Wks. Ago | 3 Wks. Ago | TITLE Artist (Producer), Label & Number | Weeks On Chart |
|---|---|---|---|---|---|
| 1 (Billboard Award) | 4 | 6 | 15 | **HANKY PANKY** — Tommy James & the Shondells (Jeff Barry & Ellie Greenwich), Roulette 4686 | 7 |
| ★2 | 6 | 47 | 75 | **WILD THING** — Troggs (Page One-York Palla), Atco 6415-Fontana 1548 | 4 |
| 3 | 2 | 3 | 6 | **RED RUBBER BALL** — Cyrkle (John Simon), Columbia 43589 | 9 |
| 4 | 5 | 5 | 9 | **YOU DON'T HAVE TO SAY YOU LOVE ME** — Dusty Springfield, Philips 40371 | 9 |
| 5 | 1 | 2 | 1 | **PAPERBACK WRITER** — Beatles (George Martin), Capitol 5651 | 6 |
| 6 | 3 | 1 | 2 | **STRANGERS IN THE NIGHT** — Frank Sinatra (Jimmy Bowen), Reprise 0470 | 11 |
| ★7 | 10 | 19 | 32 | **ALONG COMES MARY** — Association (C. Boettcher), Valiant 741 | 7 |
| 8 | 8 | 11 | 24 | **LITTLE GIRL** — Syndicate of Sound (Gary Thompson), Bell 640 | 7 |
| ★9 | 12 | 31 | 55 | **LIL' RED RIDING HOOD** — Sam the Sham & the Pharaohs (Stan Kesler), MGM 13506 | 6 |
| ★10 | 15 | 50 | 67 | **HUNGRY** — Paul Revere & the Raiders (Terry Melcher), Columbia 43678 | 5 |
| 11 | 11 | 16 | 21 | **DIRTY WATER** — Standells (Ed Cobb), Tower 185 | 13 |
| ★12 | 22 | 42 | 56 | **THE PIED PIPER** — Crispian St. Peters (David Nicolson), Jamie 1320 | 6 |
| 13 | 14 | 15 | 20 | **AIN'T TOO PROUD TO BEG** — Temptations (N. Whitfield), Gordy 7054 | 8 |
| ★14 | 19 | 53 | — | **I SAW HER AGAIN** — Mama's & the Papa's (Lou Adler), Dunhill 4031 | 3 |
| ★15 | 24 | 37 | 58 | **SWEET PEA** — Tommy Roe, ABC Records 10762 | 6 |
| 16 | 7 | 7 | 8 | **COOL JERK** — Capitols (Ollie McLaughlin), Karen 1524 | 12 |
| 17 | 9 | 4 | 3 | **PAINT IT, BLACK** — Rolling Stones (Andrew Loog Oldham), London 901 | 10 |
| 18 | 13 | 12 | 14 | **DON'T BRING ME DOWN** — Animals (Tom Wilson), MGM 13514 | 9 |
| ★19 | 25 | 30 | 38 | **I WASHED MY HANDS IN MUDDY WATER** — Johnny Rivers (Lou Adler), Imperial 66175 | 6 |
| ★20 | 30 | 41 | 51 | **YOU BETTER RUN** — Young Rascals (Young Rascals), Atlantic 2338 | 5 |
| ★21 | 35 | 48 | 59 | **SOMEWHERE MY LOVE** — Ray Conniff & the Singers (Ernie Altschuler), Columbia 43626 | 5 |
| 22 | 16 | 14 | 12 | **OH HOW HAPPY** — Shades of Blue (John Rhys), Impact 1007 | 11 |
| 23 | 23 | 24 | 29 | **RAIN** — Beatles (George Martin), Capitol 5651 | 6 |
| 24 | 21 | 26 | 27 | **POPSICLE** — Jan & Dean (Jan Berry), Liberty 55886 | 7 |
| ★25 | 39 | 59 | — | **THE WORK SONG** — Herb Alpert & the Tijuana Brass (Herb Alpert), A & M 805 | 3 |
| ★26 | 40 | 57 | — | **LOVE LETTERS** — Elvis Presley, RCA Victor 8870 | 3 |
| 27 | 18 | 20 | 26 | **HE** — Righteous Brothers (Bill Medley), Verve 10406 | 7 |
| 28 | 28 | 33 | 43 | **PLEASE TELL ME WHY** — Dave Clark Five (Dave Clark), Epic 10031 | 6 |
| 29 | 29 | 34 | 35 | **THE LAND OF MILK AND HONEY** — Vogues (Cenci-Hakim-Moon), Co & Ce 238 | 7 |
| ★30 | 38 | 51 | 61 | **HAPPY SUMMER DAYS** — Ronnie Dove (Phil Kahl), Diamond 205 | 5 |
| 31 | 32 | 36 | 37 | **LET'S GO GET STONED** — Ray Charles (Joe Adams), ABC Records 10808 | 8 |
| ★32 | 47 | 60 | 70 | **WHERE WERE YOU WHEN I NEEDED YOU** — Grass Roots (Sloan & Barri), Dunhill 4029 | 5 |
| 33 | 17 | 8 | 5 | **I AM A ROCK** — Simon & Garfunkel (Bob Johnston), Columbia 43617 | 11 |
| ★34 | 51 | 90 | — | **I WANT YOU** — Bob Dylan (Bob Johnston), Columbia 43683 | 3 |
| ★35 | 56 | 78 | — | **TRAINS AND BOATS AND PLANES** — Dionne Warwick (Bacharach-David), Scepter 12153 | 3 |
| 36 | 20 | 10 | 7 | **BAREFOOTIN'** — Robert Parker (Wherly-Burly Prod.), Nola 721 | 13 |
| 37 | 26 | 22 | 23 | **HOLD ON! I'M COMIN'** — Sam & Dave (Prod. By Staff), Stax 189 | 13 |
| ★38 | 70 | — | — | **MOTHER'S LITTLE HELPER** — Rolling Stones (Andrew Loog Oldham), London 902 | 2 |
| ★39 | 54 | 66 | 82 | **OVER UNDER SIDEWAYS DOWN** — Yardbirds (Samwell-Smith, Napier-Bell), Epic 10035 | 4 |
| 40 | 48 | 58 | 64 | **THE IMPOSSIBLE DREAM** — Jack Jones (David Kapp), Kapp 755 | 7 |
| 41 | 27 | 9 | 4 | **DID YOU EVER HAVE TO MAKE UP YOUR MIND?** — Lovin' Spoonful (Erik Jacobsen), Kama Sutra 209 | 11 |
| 42 | 42 | 43 | 48 | **YOUNGER GIRL** — Critters (Artie Ripp), Kapp 752 | 8 |
| 43 | 50 | 62 | 71 | **BILLY AND SUE** — B. J. Thomas, Hickory 1395 | 5 |
| 44 | 36 | 17 | 19 | **DOUBLE SHOT (Of My Baby's Love)** — Swingin' Medallions (Karric Prods.), Smash 2033 | 13 |
| ★45 | 60 | 72 | — | **PRETTY FLAMINGO** — Manfred Mann (John Burgess), United Artists 50040 | 3 |
| 46 | 34 | 25 | 18 | **THE MORE I SEE YOU** — Chris Montez (Herb Alpert), A&M 796 | 14 |
| ★47 | 57 | 69 | 96 | **YOU CAN'T ROLLER SKATE IN A BUFFALO HERD** — Roger Miller (Jerry Kennedy), Smash 2043 | 4 |
| ★48 | 61 | 76 | 87 | **SWEET DREAMS** — Tommy McLain (Floyd Soileau & Huey Meaux), MSL 197 | 4 |
| ★49 | 59 | 64 | 79 | **WHOLE LOT OF SHAKIN' IN MY HEART (Since I Met You)** — Miracles (Frank Wilson), Tamla 54134 | 5 |
| ★50 | 64 | 79 | 95 | **SUNNY** — Bobby Hebb (Jerry Ross), Philips 40365 | 4 |
| 51 | 49 | 45 | 50 | **LOVING YOU IS SWEETER THAN EVER** — Four Tops (Ivy Hunter), Motown 1096 | 8 |
| ★52 | 62 | 77 | 86 | **YOU WOULDN'T LISTEN** — I'des of March (Mike Considine), Parrot 304 | 4 |
| ★53 | — | — | — | **SUMMER IN THE CITY** — Lovin' Spoonful (Eric-Jacobsen), Kama Sutra 211 | 1 |
| 54 | 31 | 32 | 34 | **HEY JOE** — Leaves (Norm Ratner), Mira 222 | 9 |
| ★55 | 77 | — | — | **FRIDAY'S CHILD** — Nancy Sinatra (Lee Hazlewood), Reprise 0491 | 2 |
| ★56 | 78 | — | — | **THIS DOOR SWINGS BOTH WAYS** — Herman's Hermits (Mickie Most), MGM 13548 | 2 |
| 57 | 55 | 55 | 60 | **SOLITARY MAN** — Neil Diamond (Barry & Greenwich), Bang 519 | 9 |
| 58 | 58 | 68 | 88 | **SEARCHING FOR MY LOVE** — Bobby Moore & the Rhythm Aces (Rick Hall), Checker 1129 | 4 |
| 59 | 52 | 52 | 54 | **YOUNGER GIRL** — Hondells (G. P. IV Prod.), Mercury 72563 | 8 |
| 60 | 43 | 35 | 36 | **DAY FOR DECISION** — Johnny Sea (Gene Nash), Warner Bros. 5820 | 6 |
| 61 | 53 | 54 | 57 | **NINETY-NINE AND A HALF** — Wilson Pickett (Steve Cropper), Atlantic 2334 | 8 |
| 62 | 45 | 46 | 46 | **PETER RABBIT** — Dee Jay and the Runaways (Iowa Great Lakes Studios), Smash 2034 | 11 |
| 63 | 69 | 84 | 99 | **PAST, PRESENT AND FUTURE** — Shangri-Las (Shadow Morton), Red Bird 10068 | 4 |
| 64 | 65 | 75 | 90 | **I'M A NUT** — Leroy Pullins (Lissauer-Wheeler), Kapp 758 | 4 |
| 65 | 67 | 70 | 72 | **NOT RESPONSIBLE** — Tom Jones (Peter Sullivan), Parrot 40006 | 5 |
| 66 | 74 | 89 | — | **CAN I TRUST YOU?** — Bachelors (Dick Rowe), London 20010 | 3 |
| ★67 | 83 | — | — | **SEE YOU IN SEPTEMBER** — Happenings (Bright Tunes Prod.), B. T. Puppy 520 | 2 |
| 68 | 79 | — | — | **TAR AND CEMENT** — Verdelle Smith (Vance-Prokriss Prod.), Capitol 5632 | 2 |
| 69 | 73 | 73 | 78 | **I LOVE ONIONS** — Susan Christie (John Hill), Columbia 43595 | 6 |
| 70 | 76 | 80 | 80 | **TEENAGER'S PRAYER** — Joe Simon (J.R. Enterprises), Sound Stage 7 2564 | 5 |
| 71 | 68 | 40 | 31 | **I LOVE YOU 1,000 TIMES** — The Platters (Luther Dixon), Musicor 1166 | 12 |
| ★72 | — | — | — | **THE JOKER WENT WILD** — Brian Hyland (Snuff Garrett & Leon Russell), Philips 40377 | 1 |
| ★73 | — | — | — | **I COULDN'T LIVE WITHOUT YOUR LOVE** — Petula Clark (Tony Hatch), Warner Bros. 5835 | 1 |
| ★74 | — | — | — | **5 D (Fifth Dimension)** — Byrds (Allen Sherman), Columbia 43702 | 1 |
| 75 | 75 | 61 | 65 | **MY LOVER'S PRAYER** — Otis Redding (Prod. by Staff), Volt 136 | 7 |
| 76 | 82 | 82 | 93 | **LARA'S THEME FROM "DR. ZHIVAGO"** — Roger Williams, Kapp 738 | 4 |
| ★77 | 92 | 98 | — | **HEY YOU LITTLE BOO-GA-LOO** — Chubby Checker (Dave Appell), Parkway 989 | 3 |
| ★78 | 98 | — | — | **DISTANT SHORES** — Chad & Jeremy (Larry Marks), Columbia 43682 | 2 |
| 79 | 81 | 83 | 84 | **I ONLY HAVE EYES FOR YOU** — Lettermen (Steve Douglas), Capitol 5649 | 5 |
| 80 | 86 | 87 | — | **AIN'T GONNA CRY NO MORE** — Brenda Lee (Owen Bradley), Decca 31970 | 3 |
| 81 | 93 | — | — | **LOOK AT ME GIRL** — Bobby Vee (Dallas Smith), Liberty 55877 | 2 |
| 82 | 84 | 85 | 100 | **MISTY** — Groove Holmes (Cal Lampley), Prestige 401 | 4 |
| 83 | 91 | 93 | 98 | **PAINTER** — Lou Christie (Charlie Calello), MGM 13533 | 4 |
| 84 | 80 | 86 | 94 | **STOP! GET A TICKET** — Clefs of Lavender Hill (Steven Palmer), Date 1510 | 4 |
| 85 | 88 | — | — | **LONELY SOLDIER** — Mike Williams (Prod. by Staff), Atlantic 2339 | 2 |
| 86 | 89 | 94 | 97 | **LA BAMBA** — Trini Lopez (Don Costa Prod.), Reprise 0480 | 4 |
| 87 | 90 | 92 | — | **ON THE GOOD SHIP LOLLIPOP** — Wonder Who? (Bob Crewe), Philips 40380 | 3 |
| ★88 | — | — | — | **I GUESS I'LL ALWAYS LOVE YOU** — Isley Brothers (Holland & Dozier), Tamla 54135 | 1 |
| ★89 | — | — | — | **ALMOST PERSUADED** — David Houston (Billy Sherrill), Epic 10025 | 1 |
| ★90 | — | — | — | **YOU YOU YOU** — Mel Carter (Nick De Caro), Imperial 66183 | 1 |
| 91 | — | — | — | **UPTIGHT** — Nancy Wilson (David Cavanaugh), Capitol 5673 | 1 |
| 92 | — | — | — | **FREDDIE FEELGOOD** — Ray Stevens, Monument 946 | 1 |
| 93 | 94 | 96 | — | **HOT SHOT** — Buena Vistas (A Magi Prod.), Swan 4255 | 3 |
| 94 | 95 | 95 | — | **HIGH ON LOVE** — Knickerbockers (Jerry Fuller), Challenge 59332 | 3 |
| 95 | — | — | — | **DRIVE MY CAR** — Bob Kuban & the In-Men (Mel Friedman), Musicland, U.S.A. 20007 | 1 |
| 96 | — | — | — | **YOU'RE NOBODY TILL SOMEBODY LOVES YOU** — Wonder Who? (Bob Crewe), Philips 40380 | 1 |
| 97 | — | — | — | **SUMMERTIME** — Billy Stewart (Billy Davis), Chess 1966 | 1 |
| 98 | — | — | — | **WE'LL BE UNITED** — Intruders, Gamble 201 | 1 |
| 99 | 100 | — | — | **WADE IN THE WATER** — Ramsey Lewis (Esmond Edwards), Cadet 5541 | 2 |
| 100 | — | — | — | **TELL HER** — Dean Parrish (Ritchie Gotteher), Boom 60012 | 1 |

## HOT 100—A TO Z—*(Publisher-Licensee)*

Ain't Gonna Cry No More (Cooga, BMI) .......... 80
Ain't Too Proud to Beg (Jobete, BMI) .......... 13
Almost Persuaded (Gallico, BMI) .......... 89
Along Comes Mary (Davon, BMI) .......... 7
Barefootin' (Bonatemp, BMI) .......... 36
Billy and Sue (Hornet, BMI) .......... 43
Can I Trust You? (Miller, ASCAP) .......... 66
Cool Jerk (McLaughlin, BMI) .......... 16
Day for Decision (Moss-Rose, BMI) .......... 60
Did You Ever Have to Make Up Your Mind? (Faithful Virtue, BMI) .......... 41
Dirty Water (Equinox, BMI) .......... 11
Distant Shores (Chad & Jeremy-Noma, BMI) .......... 78
Don't Bring Me Down (Screen Gems-Columbia, BMI) 18
Double Shot (of My Baby's Love) (Lyricsong-Windsong, BMI) .......... 44
Drive My Car (Maclen, BMI) .......... 95
5 D (Fifth Dimension) (Tickson, BMI) .......... 74
Freddie Feelgood (Ahab, BMI) .......... 92
Friday's Child (Atlantic, BMI) .......... 55
Hanky Panky (T. M., BMI) .......... 1
Happy Summer Days (Picturetone, BMI) .......... 30
He (Avas, ASCAP) .......... 27
Hey, Joe (Third Story, BMI) .......... 54
Hey You Little Boo-Ga-Loo (Double Diamond, Champion, BMI) .......... 77
High on Love (4 Star, BMI) .......... 94
Hold On! I'm Comin' (East, Pronto, BMI) .......... 37
Hot Shot (Palmina-Shan-Todd, BMI) .......... 93
Hungry (Screen Gems-Columbia, BMI) .......... 10
I Am a Rock (Eclectic, BMI) .......... 33
I Couldn't Live Without Your Love (Northern, ASCAP) .......... 73
I Guess I'll Always Love You (Jobete, BMI) .......... 88
I Love Onions (Blackwood, BMI) .......... 69
I Love You 1,000 Times (Ludix, BMI) .......... 71
I Only Have Eyes for You (Remick, ASCAP) .......... 79
I Saw Her Again (Trousdale, BMI) .......... 14
I Want You (Dwarf, ASCAP) .......... 34
I Washed My Hands in Muddy Water (Maricana, BMI) .......... 19
I'm a Nut (Youmans-Sleepy Hollow, ASCAP) .......... 64
Impossible Dream, The (Fox, ASCAP) .......... 40
Joker Went Wild, The (Rising Sons, BMI) .......... 72
La Bamba (South Mountain, BMI) .......... 86
Land of Milk and Honey, The (Tree, BMI) .......... 29
Lara's Theme From "Dr. Zhivago" (Robbins, ASCAP) .......... 76
Let's Go Get Stoned (Baby Monica, BMI) .......... 31
Lil' Red Riding Hood (Rose, BMI) .......... 9
Little Girl (Duane, BMI) .......... 8
Look at Me Girl (Epps, BMI) .......... 81
Lonely Soldier (Pronto-Chevis, BMI) .......... 85
Love Letters (Famous, ASCAP) .......... 26
Loving You Is Sweeter Than Ever (Jobete, BMI) .. 51
Misty (Vernon, ASCAP) .......... 82
More I See You, The (Bregman, Vocco & Conn, ASCAP) .......... 46
Mother's Little Helper (Gideon, BMI) .......... 38
My Lover's Prayer (East-Time-Redwal, BMI) .......... 75
Ninety-Nine and a Half (East-Pronto, BMI) .......... 61
Not Responsible (Northern, ASCAP) .......... 65
Oh How Happy (Myto, BMI) .......... 22
On the Good Ship Lollipop (Movietown, ASCAP) .. 87
Over Under Sideways Down (Feist, ASCAP) .......... 39
Paint It, Black (Gideon, BMI) .......... 17
Painter (Rambed, BMI) .......... 83
Paperback Writer (Maclen, BMI) .......... 5
Past, Present and Future (Tender Tunes, BMI) .......... 63
Peter Rabbit (Willong, BMI) .......... 62
Pied Piper, The (Chardon, BMI) .......... 12
Please Tell Me Why (Branston, BMI) .......... 28
Popsicle (Lowery, BMI) .......... 24
Pretty Flamingo (Shapiro-Bernstein, ASCAP) .......... 45
Rain (Maclen, BMI) .......... 23
Red Rubber Ball (Eclectic, BMI) .......... 3
Searching for My Love (Chevis, BMI) .......... 58
See You in September (Vibar, ASCAP) .......... 67
Solitary Man (Tallyrand, BMI) .......... 57
Somewhere My Love (Robbins, ASCAP) .......... 21
Stop! Get a Ticket (Gallico, BMI) .......... 84
Strangers in the Night (Champion-Roosevelt, BMI) 6
Summer in the City (Faithful Virtue, BMI) .......... 53
Summertime (Gershwin, ASCAP) .......... 97
Sunny (Portable, BMI) .......... 50
Sweet Dreams (Acuff-Rose, BMI) .......... 48
Sweet Pea (Low Twi, BMI) .......... 15
Tar and Cement (Feist, ASCAP) .......... 68
Teenager's Prayer (Frederick, BMI) .......... 70
Tell Her (Mellin, BMI) .......... 100
This Door Swings Both Ways (Blackwood, BMI) .. 56
Trains and Boats and Planes (U. S. Songs, ASCAP) 35
Uptight (Jobete, BMI) .......... 91
Wade in the Water (Ramsel, BMI) .......... 99
We'll Be United (Sharpe, BMI) .......... 98
Where Were You When I Needed You (Trousdale, BMI) .......... 32
Whole Lot of Shakin' in My Heart (Since I Met You) (Jobete, BMI) .......... 49
Wild Thing (Blackwood, BMI) .......... 2
Work Song, The (Upam, BMI) .......... 25
You Better Run (Slacsar, BMI) .......... 20
You Can't Roller Skate in a Buffalo Herd (Tree, BMI) .......... 47
You Don't Have to Say You Love Me (Robbins, ASCAP) .......... 4
You Wouldn't Listen (BMC, BMI) .......... 52
You You You (Mellin, BMI) .......... 90
Younger Girl—Critters (Faithful Virtue, BMI) .......... 42
Younger Girl—Hondells (Faithful Virtue, BMI) ... 59
You're Nobody Till Somebody Loves You (Southern, ASCAP) .......... 96

## BUBBLING UNDER THE HOT 100

101. WARM AND TENDER LOVE .......... Percy Sledge, Atlantic 2342
102. SUCH A SWEET THING .......... Mary Wells, Atco 6423
103. LADY JANE .......... Rolling Stones, London 902
104. BECAUSE OF YOU .......... Rome and Paris, Roulette 4681
105. LETTER FROM A SOLDIER .......... Connie Francis, MGM 13545
106. ALL THESE THINGS .......... Uniques, Paula 238
107. COME SHARE THE GOOD TIMES WITH ME .... Julie Monday, Rainbow 500
108. YOU JUST CAN'T QUIT .......... Rick Nelson, Decca 31965
109. I BELIEVE I'M GONNA MAKE IT .......... Joe Tex, Dial 4033
110. BLOWIN' IN THE WIND .......... Stevie Wonder, Tamla 54136
111. IT'S THAT TIME OF THE YEAR .......... Len Barry, Decca 31969
112. I'VE GOT TO GO ON WITHOUT YOU .......... Van Dykes, Mala 530
113. LAUGHING SONG .......... Freddy Cannon, Warner Bros. 5832
114. RACE WITH THE WIND .......... Robbs, Mercury 72579
115. JUST A LITTLE BIT OF YOU .......... Dallas Frazier, Capitol 5670
116. GREATEST MOMENTS IN A GIRL'S LIFE .......... Tokens, B. T. Puppy 519
117. COME ON HOME .......... Wayne Fontana, MGM 13516
118. SOCK IT TO 'EM J. B. .......... Rex Garvin, Like 301
119. SUGAR AND SPICE .......... Cryan Shames, Destination 624
120. THAT'S ENOUGH .......... Roscoe Robinson, Wand 1125
121. THE MAGIC TOUCH .......... Bobby Fuller Four, Mustang 3018
122. SITTIN' ON A FENCE .......... Twice as Much, MGM 13530
123. I JUST LET IT TAKE ME .......... Bob Lind, World-Pacific 77830
124. THE STREETS OF BALTIMORE .......... Bobby Bare, RCA Victor 8851
125. OPEN THE DOOR TO YOUR HEART .......... Darrell Bank, Revilot 201
126. THIS IS MY HOUSE (But Nobody Calls) .......... Moody Blues, London 1005
127. IT'S BEEN SUCH A LONG WAY HOME .......... Garnet Mimms, Veep 1232
128. BORN A WOMAN .......... Sandy Posey, MGM 13501
129. JUST WALK IN MY SHOES .......... Gladys Knight & the Pipps, Soul 35023
130. BRING BACK THE TIME .......... B. J. Thomas, Scepter 12154
131. WITH A CHILD'S HEART .......... Stevie Wonder, Tamla 54130
132. LET IT BE ME .......... Arthur Prysock, Old Town 1196
133. LOOK AT ME GIRL .......... Playboys of Edinburg, Columbia 43716
134. MOST OF ALL .......... Cowsills, Philips 40382
135. I PUT A SPELL ON YOU .......... Alan Price Set, Parrot 3001

Compiled from national retail sales and radio station airplay by the Music Popularity Dept. of Record Market Research, Billboard.

# Billboard HOT 100

For Week Ending July 23, 1966

★ **STAR** performer—Sides registering greatest proportionate upward progress this week.

Record Industry Association of America seal of certification as million selling single.

| This Week | 1 Wk. Ago | 2 Wks. Ago | 3 Wks. Ago | TITLE  Artist (Producer), Label & Number | Weeks On Chart |
|---|---|---|---|---|---|
| 1 | 1 | 4 | 6 | **HANKY PANKY** — Tommy James & the Shondells (Jeff Barry & Ellie Greenwich), Roulette 4686 (Billboard Award) | 8 |
| 2 | 2 | 6 | 47 | **WILD THING** — Troggs (Page One-York Palla), Atco 6415-Fontana 1548 | 5 |
| 3 | 9 | 12 | 31 | **LIL' RED RIDING HOOD** — Sam the Sham & the Pharaohs (Stan Kesler), MGM 13506 | 5 |
| 4 | 12 | 22 | 42 | **THE PIED PIPER** — Crispian St. Peters (David Nicolson), Jamie 1320 | 5 |
| 5 | 4 | 5 | 5 | **YOU DON'T HAVE TO SAY YOU LOVE ME** — Dusty Springfield, Philips 40371 | 10 |
| 6 | 5 | 1 | 2 | **PAPERBACK WRITER** — Beatles (George Martin), Capitol 5651 | 7 |
| 7 | 10 | 15 | 50 | **HUNGRY** — Paul Revere & the Raiders (Terry Melcher), Columbia 43678 | 6 |
| 8 | 3 | 2 | 3 | **RED RUBBER BALL** — Cyrkle (John Simon), Columbia 43589 | 10 |
| 9 | 14 | 19 | 53 | **I SAW HER AGAIN** — Mama's & the Papa's (Lou Adler), Dunhill 4031 | 4 |
| 10 | 15 | 24 | 37 | **SWEET PEA** — Tommy Roe, ABC Records 10762 | 7 |
| 11 | 7 | 10 | 19 | **ALONG COMES MARY** — Association (C. Boettcher), Valiant 741 | 8 |
| 12 | 6 | 3 | 1 | **STRANGERS IN THE NIGHT** — Frank Sinatra (Jimmy Bowen), Reprise 0470 | 12 |
| 13 | 8 | 8 | 11 | **LITTLE GIRL** — Syndicate of Sound (Gary Thompson), Bell 640 | 8 |
| 14 | 21 | 35 | 48 | **SOMEWHERE MY LOVE** — Ray Conniff & the Singers (Ernie Altschuler), Columbia 43626 | 6 |
| 15 | 13 | 14 | 15 | **AIN'T TOO PROUD TO BEG** — Temptations (N. Whitfield), Gordy 7054 | 9 |
| 16 | 11 | 11 | 16 | **DIRTY WATER** — Standells (Ed Cobb), Tower 185 | 14 |
| 17 | 38 | 70 | — | **MOTHER'S LITTLE HELPER** — Rolling Stones (Andrew Loog Oldham), London 902 | 3 |
| 18 | 25 | 39 | 59 | **THE WORK SONG** — Herb Alpert & the Tijuana Brass (Herb Alpert), A & M 805 | 4 |
| 19 | 26 | 40 | 57 | **LOVE LETTERS** — Elvis Presley, RCA Victor 8870 | 4 |
| 20 | 20 | 30 | 41 | **YOU BETTER RUN** — Young Rascals, Atlantic 2338 | 6 |
| 21 | 53 | — | — | **SUMMER IN THE CITY** — Lovin' Spoonful (Eric-Jacobsen), Kama Sutra 211 | 2 |
| 22 | 19 | 25 | 30 | **I WASHED MY HANDS IN MUDDY WATER** — Johnny Rivers (Lou Adler), Imperial 66175 | 7 |
| 23 | 39 | 54 | 66 | **OVER UNDER SIDEWAYS DOWN** — Yardbirds (Samwell-Smith, Napier-Bell), Epic 10035 | 5 |
| 24 | 34 | 51 | 90 | **I WANT YOU** — Bob Dylan (Bob Johnston), Columbia 43683 | 4 |
| 25 | 50 | 64 | 79 | **SUNNY** — Bobby Hebb (Jerry Ross), Philips 40365 | 5 |
| 26 | 48 | 61 | 76 | **SWEET DREAMS** — Tommy McLain (Floyd Soileau & Huey Meaux), MSL 197 | 5 |
| 27 | 30 | 38 | 51 | **HAPPY SUMMER DAYS** — Ronnie Dove (Phil Kahl), Diamond 205 | 6 |
| 28 | 24 | 21 | 26 | **POPSICLE** — Jan & Dean (Jan Berry), Liberty 55886 | 8 |
| 29 | 32 | 47 | 60 | **WHERE WERE YOU WHEN I NEEDED YOU** — Grass Roots (Sloan & Barri), Dunhill 4029 | 5 |
| 30 | 35 | 56 | 78 | **TRAINS AND BOATS AND PLANES** — Dionne Warwick (Bacharach-David), Scepter 12153 | 4 |
| 31 | 28 | 28 | 33 | **PLEASE TELL ME WHY** — Dave Clark Five (Dave Clark), Epic 10031 | 7 |
| 32 | 56 | 78 | — | **THIS DOOR SWINGS BOTH WAYS** — Herman's Hermits (Mickie Most), MGM 13548 | 3 |
| 33 | 18 | 13 | 12 | **DON'T BRING ME DOWN** — Animals (Tom Wilson), MGM 13514 | 10 |
| 34 | 23 | 23 | 24 | **RAIN** — Beatles (George Martin), Capitol 5651 | 7 |
| 35 | 40 | 48 | 58 | **THE IMPOSSIBLE DREAM** — Jack Jones (David Kapp), Kapp 755 | 8 |
| 36 | 16 | 7 | 7 | **COOL JERK** — Capitols (Ollie McLaughlin), Karen 1524 | 13 |
| 37 | 43 | 50 | 62 | **BILLY AND SUE** — B. J. Thomas, Hickory 1395 | 6 |
| 38 | 45 | 60 | 72 | **PRETTY FLAMINGO** — Manfred Mann (John Burgess), United Artists 50040 | 4 |
| 39 | 17 | 9 | 4 | **PAINT IT, BLACK** — Rolling Stones (Andrew Loog Oldham), London 901 | 11 |
| 40 | 47 | 57 | 69 | **YOU CAN'T ROLLER SKATE IN A BUFFALO HERD** — Roger Miller (Jerry Kennedy), Smash 2043 | 5 |
| 41 | 67 | 83 | — | **SEE YOU IN SEPTEMBER** — Happenings (Bright Tunes Prod.), B. T. Puppy 520 | 3 |
| 42 | 52 | 62 | 77 | **YOU WOULDN'T LISTEN** — I'des of March (Mike Considine), Parrot 304 | 5 |
| 43 | 29 | 29 | 34 | **THE LAND OF MILK AND HONEY** — Vogues (Cenci-Hakim-Moon), Co & Ce 238 | 8 |
| 44 | 31 | 32 | 36 | **LET'S GO GET STONED** — Ray Charles (Joe Adams), ABC Records 10808 | 9 |
| 45 | 22 | 16 | 14 | **OH HOW HAPPY** — Shades of Blue (John Rhys), Impact 1007 | 12 |
| 46 | 73 | — | — | **I COULDN'T LIVE WITHOUT YOUR LOVE** — Petula Clark (Tony Hatch), Warner Bros. 5835 | 2 |
| 47 | 49 | 59 | 64 | **WHOLE LOT OF SHAKIN' IN MY HEART (Since I Met You)** — Miracles (Frank Wilson), Tamla 54134 | 6 |
| 48 | 55 | 77 | — | **FRIDAY'S CHILD** — Nancy Sinatra (Lee Hazlewood), Reprise 0491 | 3 |
| 49 | 36 | 20 | 10 | **BAREFOOTIN'** — Robert Parker (Wherly-Burly Prod.), Nola 721 | 14 |
| 50 | — | — | — | **THEY'RE COMING TO TAKE ME AWAY, HA-HAAA!** — Napoleon XIV (Jepslana Prod.), Warner Bros. 5831 | 1 |
| 51 | 27 | 18 | 20 | **HE** — Righteous Brothers (Bill Medley), Verve 10406 | 8 |
| 52 | 58 | 58 | 68 | **SEARCHING FOR MY LOVE** — Bobby Moore & the Rhythm Aces (Rick Hall), Checker 1129 | 5 |
| 53 | 42 | 42 | 43 | **YOUNGER GIRL** — Critters (Artie Ripp), Kapp 752 | 9 |
| 54 | 74 | — | — | **5 D (Fifth Dimension)** — Byrds (Allen Stanton), Columbia 43702 | 2 |
| 55 | 78 | 98 | — | **DISTANT SHORES** — Chad & Jeremy (Larry Marks), Columbia 43682 | 3 |
| 56 | 66 | 74 | 89 | **CAN I TRUST YOU?** — Bachelors (Dick Rowe), London 20010 | 4 |
| 57 | 64 | 65 | 75 | **I'M A NUT** — Leroy Pullins (Lynn-Wheeler), Kapp 758 | 5 |
| 58 | 65 | 67 | 70 | **NOT RESPONSIBLE** — Tom Jones (Peter Sullivan), Parrot 40006 | 6 |
| 59 | 63 | 69 | 84 | **PAST, PRESENT AND FUTURE** — Shangri-Las (Shadow Morton), Red Bird 10068 | 5 |
| 60 | 57 | 55 | 55 | **SOLITARY MAN** — Neil Diamond (Barry & Greenwich), Bang 519 | 10 |
| 61 | 68 | 79 | — | **TAR AND CEMENT** — Verdelle Smith (Vance-Prokriss Prod.), Capitol 5632 | 3 |
| 62 | 72 | — | — | **THE JOKER WENT WILD** — Brian Hyland (Snuff Garrett & Leon Russell), Philips 40377 | 2 |
| 63 | 69 | 73 | 73 | **I LOVE ONIONS** — Susan Christie (John Hill), Columbia 43595 | 7 |
| 64 | 82 | 84 | 85 | **MISTY** — Groove Holmes (Cal Lampley), Prestige 401 | 3 |
| 65 | 76 | 82 | 82 | **LARA'S THEME FROM "DR. ZHIVAGO"** — Roger Williams, Kapp 738 | 4 |
| 66 | 70 | 76 | 80 | **TEENAGER'S PRAYER** — Joe Simon (J.R. Enterprises), Sound Stage 7 2564 | 6 |
| 67 | 59 | 52 | 52 | **YOUNGER GIRL** — Hondells (G. P. IV Prod.), Mercury 72563 | 9 |
| 68 | — | — | — | **BLOWIN' IN THE WIND** — Stevie Wonder (C. Paul), Tamla 54136 | 1 |
| 69 | 81 | 93 | — | **LOOK AT ME GIRL** — Bobby Vee (Dallas Smith), Liberty 55877 | 3 |
| 70 | 85 | 88 | — | **LONELY SOLDIER** — Mike Williams (Prod. by Staff), Atlantic 2339 | 3 |
| 71 | 71 | 68 | 40 | **I LOVE YOU 1,000 TIMES** — The Platters (Luther Dixon), Musicor 1166 | 13 |
| 72 | 79 | 81 | 83 | **I ONLY HAVE EYES FOR YOU** — Lettermen (Steve Douglass), Capitol 5649 | 6 |
| 73 | 88 | — | — | **I GUESS I'LL ALWAYS LOVE YOU** — Isley Brothers (Holland & Dozier), Tamla 54135 | 2 |
| 74 | 89 | — | — | **ALMOST PERSUADED** — David Houston (Billy Sherrill), Epic 10025 | 2 |
| 75 | 90 | — | — | **YOU YOU YOU** — Mel Carter (Nick De Caro), Imperial 66183 | 2 |
| 76 | 77 | 92 | 98 | **HEY YOU LITTLE BOO-GA-LOO** — Chubby Checker (Dave Appell), Parkway 989 | 4 |
| 77 | 80 | 86 | 87 | **AIN'T GONNA CRY NO MORE** — Brenda Lee (Owen Bradley), Decca 31970 | 4 |
| 78 | — | — | — | **WARM AND TENDER LOVE** — Percy Sledge (Martin Greene & Quin Ivy), Atlantic 2342 | 1 |
| 79 | — | — | — | **THE TIP OF MY FINGER** — Eddy Arnold (Chet Atkins), RCA Victor 8869 | 1 |
| 80 | — | — | — | **MAKE ME BELONG TO YOU** — Barbara Lewis (Jerry Wexler & Ollie McLaughlin), Atlantic 2346 | 1 |
| 81 | 83 | 91 | 93 | **PAINTER** — Lou Christie (Charlie Calello), MGM 13533 | 2 |
| 82 | 97 | — | — | **SUMMERTIME** — Billy Stewart (Billy Davis), Chess 1966 | 2 |
| 83 | — | — | — | **LADY JANE** — Rolling Stones (Andrew Loog Oldham), London 902 | 1 |
| 84 | 84 | 80 | 86 | **STOP! GET A TICKET** — Clefs of Lavender Hill (Steven Palmer), Date 1510 | 5 |
| 85 | 91 | — | — | **UPTIGHT** — Nancy Wilson (David Cavanaugh), Capitol 5673 | 2 |
| 86 | 86 | 89 | 94 | **LA BAMBA** — Trini Lopez (Don Costa Prod.), Reprise 0480 | 5 |
| 87 | 93 | 94 | 96 | **HOT SHOT** — Buena Vistas (A Magi Prod.), Swan 4255 | 4 |
| 88 | — | — | — | **I BELIEVE I'M GONNA MAKE IT** — Joe Tex (Buddy Killen), Dial 4033 | 1 |
| 89 | 99 | 100 | — | **WADE IN THE WATER** — Ramsey Lewis (Esmond Edwards), Cadet 5541 | 3 |
| 90 | — | — | — | **WORKING IN THE COAL MINE** — Lee Dorsey (A. Toussaint-M. Sehorn), Amy 958 | 1 |
| 91 | 92 | — | — | **FREDDIE FEELGOOD** — Ray Stevens, Monument 946 | 2 |
| 92 | — | — | — | **SUGAR AND SPICE** — Cryan Shames (MG Prod.), Destination 624 | 1 |
| 93 | — | — | — | **BORN A WOMAN** — Sandy Posey (Chip Moman), MGM 13501 | 1 |
| 94 | 95 | — | — | **DRIVE MY CAR** — Bob Kuban & the In-Men (Mel Friedman), Musicland, U.S.A. 20007 | 2 |
| 95 | — | — | — | **GEORGIA ROSE** — Tony Bennett (Ernie Altschuler), Columbia 43715 | 1 |
| 96 | 98 | — | — | **WE'LL BE UNITED** — Intruders, Gamble 201 | 2 |
| 97 | 100 | — | — | **TELL HER** — Dean Parrish (Ritchie Gotteher), Boom 60012 | 2 |
| 98 | — | — | — | **BUS STOP** — Hollies (Ron Richardson), Imperial 66186 | 1 |
| 99 | — | — | — | **OPEN THE DOOR TO YOUR HEART** — Darrell Banks, Revilot 201 | 1 |
| 100 | — | — | — | **A MILLION AND ONE** — Dean Martin (Jimmy Bowen), Reprise 0500 | 1 |

## BUBBLING UNDER THE HOT 100

101. COME SHARE THE GOOD TIMES WITH ME — Julie Monday, Rainbow 500
102. GREATEST MOMENTS IN A GIRL'S LIFE — Tokens, B. T. Puppy 519
103. RACE WITH THE WIND — Robbs, Mercury 72579
104. ALL THESE THINGS — Uniques, Paula 238
105. A MILLION AND ONE — Vic Dana, Dolton 322
106. PETTICOAT WHITE (Summer Sky Blue) — Bobby Vinton, Epic 10048
107. (You Make Me Feel) SO GOOD — McCoys, Bang 527
108. LETTER FROM A SOLDIER — Connie Francis, MGM 13545
109. I'VE GOT TO GO ON WITHOUT YOU — Van Dykes, Mala 530
110. JUST A LITTLE BIT OF YOU — Dallas Frazier, Capitol 5670
111. LAUGHING SONG — Freddy Cannon, Warner Bros. 5832
112. JUST YESTERDAY — Al Martino, Capitol 5702
113. LOOK AT ME GIRL — Playboys of Edinburg, Columbia 43716
114. SOCK IT TO 'EM, J. B. — Rex Garvin, Like 301
115. TAKE YOUR LOVE — Bobby Goldsboro, United Artists 50044
116. SHAKE YOUR HIPS — Slim Harpo, Excello 2278
117. THE MAGIC TOUCH — Bobby Fuller Four, Mustang 3018
118. THAT'S ENOUGH — Roscoe Robinson, Wand 1125
119. THIS IS MY HOUSE (But Nobody Calls) — Moody Blues, London 1005
120. I'LL TAKE A LITTLE TIME — Jerry Vale, Columbia 43696
121. WHEN YOU WAKE UP — Cleb McCall, Thomas 8830
122. MOST OF ALL — Cookies, Phillips 40382
123. YOU'RE GONNA MISS ME — Thirteenth Floor Elevators, International Artists 107
124. LET IT BE ME — Arthur Prysock, Old Town 1196
125. IT'S BEEN SUCH A LONG WAY HOME — Garnet Mimms, 3 Veep 1232
126. LET'S CALL IT A DAY, GIRL — Razor's Edge, POW 101
127. BRING BACK THE TIME — B. J. Thomas, Scepter 12154
128. LARA'S THEME — Brass Ring, Dunhill 4036
129. POOR DOG — Little Richard, Okeh 7251
130. I'M A GOOD WOMAN — Barbara Lynn, Tribe 8316
131. LOVE (Oh How Sweet It Is) — Jerry Butler, Mercury 72592
132. I PUT A SPELL ON YOU — Alan Price Set, Parrot 3001
133. WHAT BECOMES OF THE BROKEN HEARTED — Jimmy Ruffin, Soul 35022
134. LOVE ATTACK — James Carr, Goldwax 309
135. WHO DO YOU THINK YOU ARE — Shindogs, Viva 601

Compiled from national retail sales and radio station airplay by the Music Popularity Dept. of Record Market Research, Billboard.

# Billboard

For Week Ending July 30, 1966

# HOT 100

★ STAR performer—Sides registering greatest proportionate upward progress this week.

Record Industry Association of America seal of certification as million selling single.

| This Week | 1 Wk. Ago | 2 Wks. Ago | 3 Wks. Ago | TITLE | Artist (Producer), Label & Number | Weeks On Chart |
|---|---|---|---|---|---|---|
| 1 (Billboard Award) | 2 | 2 | 6 | WILD THING | Troggs (Page One-York Palla), Atco 6415-Fontana 1548 | 6 |
| 2 | 1 | 1 | 4 | HANKY PANKY | Tommy James & the Shondells (Jeff Barry & Ellie Greenwich), Roulette 4686 | 9 |
| 3 | 3 | 9 | 12 | LIL' RED RIDING HOOD | Sam the Sham & the Pharaohs (Stan Kesler), MGM 13506 | 8 |
| 4 | 4 | 12 | 22 | THE PIED PIPER | Crispian St. Peters (David Nicolson), Jamie 1320 | 8 |
| ★5 | 9 | 14 | 19 | I SAW HER AGAIN | Mama's & the Papa's (Lou Adler), Dunhill 4031 | 5 |
| 6 | 7 | 10 | 15 | HUNGRY | Paul Revere & the Raiders (Terry Melcher), Columbia 43678 | 7 |
| ★7 | 21 | 53 | — | SUMMER IN THE CITY | Lovin' Spoonful (Eric-Jacobsen), Kama Sutra 211 | 3 |
| 8 | 10 | 15 | 24 | SWEET PEA | Tommy Roe, ABC Records 10762 | 8 |
| ★9 | 17 | 38 | 70 | MOTHER'S LITTLE HELPER | Rolling Stones (Andrew Loog Oldham), London 902 | 4 |
| ★10 | 14 | 21 | 35 | SOMEWHERE MY LOVE | Ray Conniff & the Singers (Ernie Altschuler), Columbia 43626 | 7 |
| ★11 | 50 | — | — | THEY'RE COMING TO TAKE ME AWAY, HA-HAAA! | Napoleoon XIV (Jepalana Prod.), Warner Bros. 5831 | 2 |
| 12 | 6 | 5 | 1 | PAPERBACK WRITER | Beatles (George Martin), Capitol 5651 | 8 |
| 13 | 8 | 3 | 2 | RED RUBBER BALL | Cyrkle (John Simon), Columbia 43589 | 11 |
| ★14 | 25 | 50 | 64 | SUNNY | Bobby Hebb (Jerry Ross), Philips 40365 | 6 |
| 15 | 5 | 4 | 5 | YOU DON'T HAVE TO SAY YOU LOVE ME | Dusty Springfield, Philips 40371 | 11 |
| ★16 | 32 | 56 | 78 | THIS DOOR SWING BOTH WAYS | Herman's Hermits (Mickie Most), MGM 13548 | 4 |
| ★17 | 23 | 39 | 54 | OVER UNDER SIDEWAYS DOWN | Yardbirds (Samwell-Smith, Napier-Bell), Epic 10035 | 6 |
| 18 | 18 | 25 | 39 | THE WORK SONG | Herb Alpert & the Tijuana Brass (Herb Alpert), A & M 805 | 5 |
| 19 | 19 | 26 | 40 | LOVE LETTERS | Elvis Presley, RCA Victor 8870 | 5 |
| 20 | 24 | 34 | 51 | I WANT YOU | Bob Dylan (Bob Johnston), Columbia 43683 | 5 |
| 21 | 13 | 8 | 8 | LITTLE GIRL | Syndicate of Sound (Gary Thompson), Bell 640 | 9 |
| 22 | 12 | 6 | 3 | STRANGERS IN THE NIGHT | Frank Sinatra (Jimmy Bowen), Reprise 0470 | 13 |
| 23 | 26 | 48 | 61 | SWEET DREAMS | Tommy McLain (Floyd Soileau & Huey Meaux), MSL 197 | 6 |
| 24 | 15 | 13 | 14 | AIN'T TO PROUD TO BEG | Temptations (N. Whitfield), Gordy 7054 | 10 |
| ★25 | 30 | 35 | 56 | TRAINS AND BOATS AND PLANES | Dionne Warwick (Bacharach-David), Scepter 12153 | 5 |
| ★26 | 46 | 73 | — | I COULDN'T LIVE WITHOUT YOUR LOVE | Petula Clark (Tony Hatch), Warner Bros. 5835 | 3 |
| 27 | 27 | 30 | 38 | HAPPY SUMMER DAYS | Ronnie Dove (Phil Kahl), Diamond 205 | 7 |
| 28 | 29 | 32 | 47 | WHERE WERE YOU WHEN I NEEDED YOU | Grass Roots (Sloan & Barri), Dunhill 4029 | 7 |
| 29 | 11 | 7 | 10 | ALONG COMES MARY | Association (C. Boettcher), Valiant 741 | 9 |
| ★30 | 41 | 67 | 83 | SEE YOU IN SEPTEMBER | Happenings (Bright Tunes Prod.), B. T. Puppy 520 | 4 |
| 31 | 16 | 11 | 11 | DIRTY WATER | Standells (Ed Cobb), Tower 185 | 15 |
| 32 | 38 | 45 | 60 | PRETTY FLAMINGO | Manfred Mann (John Burgess), United Artists 50040 | 5 |
| ★33 | 52 | 58 | 58 | SEARCHING FOR MY LOVE | Bobby Moore & the Rhythm Aces (Rick Hall) Checker 1129 | 6 |
| 34 | 37 | 43 | 50 | BILLY AND SUE | B. J. Thomas, Hickory 1395 | 7 |
| 35 | 35 | 40 | 48 | THE IMPOSSIBLE DREAM | Jack Jones (David Kapp), Kapp 755 | 9 |
| ★36 | 48 | 55 | 77 | FRIDAY'S CHILD | Nancy Sinatra (Lee Hazlewood), Reprise 0491 | 4 |
| 37 | 20 | 20 | 30 | YOU BETTER RUN | Young Rascals (Young Rascals), Atlantic 2338 | 7 |
| 38 | 36 | 16 | 7 | COOL JERK | Capitols (Ollie McLaughlin), Karen 1524 | 14 |
| 39 | 22 | 19 | 25 | I WASHED MY HANDS IN MUDDY WATER | Johnny Rivers (Lou Adler), Imperial 66175 | 8 |
| ★40 | 68 | — | — | BLOWIN' IN THE WIND | Stevie Wonder (C. Paul), Tamla 54136 | 2 |
| 41 | 28 | 24 | 21 | POPSICLE | Jan & Dean (Jan Berry), Liberty 55886 | 9 |
| 42 | 42 | 52 | 62 | YOU WOULDN'T LISTEN | I'des of March (Mike Considine), Parrot 304 | 6 |
| 43 | 40 | 47 | 57 | YOU CAN'T ROLLER SKATE IN A BUFFALO HERD | Roger Miller (Jerry Kennedy), Smash 2043 | 6 |
| ★44 | 54 | 74 | — | 5 D (Fifth Dimension) | Byrds (Allen Stanton), Columbia 43702 | 3 |
| ★45 | 55 | 78 | 98 | DISTANT SHORES | Chad & Jeremy (Larry Marks), Columbia 43682 | 4 |
| 46 | 47 | 49 | 59 | WHOLE LOT OF SHAKIN' IN MY HEART (Since I Met You) | Miracles (Frank Wilson), Tamla 54134 | 7 |
| ★47 | 62 | 72 | — | THE JOKER WENT WILD | Brian Hyland (Snuff Garrett & Leon Russell), Philips 40377 | 3 |
| ★48 | 78 | — | — | WARM AND TENDER LOVE | Percy Sledge (Martin Greene & Quin Ivy), Atlantic 2342 | 2 |
| 49 | 56 | 66 | 74 | CAN I TRUST YOU? | Bachelors (Dick Rowe), London 20010 | 5 |
| ★50 | 64 | 82 | 84 | MISTY | Groove Holmes (Cal Lampley), Prestige 401 | 6 |
| ★51 | 83 | — | — | LADY JANE | Rolling Stones (Andrew Loog Oldham), London 902 | 2 |
| ★52 | 69 | 81 | 93 | LOOK AT ME GIRL | Bobby Vee (Dallas Smith), Liberty 55877 | 4 |
| 53 | 61 | 68 | 79 | TAR AND CEMENT | Verdelle Smith (Vance-Prokriss Prod.), Capitol 5632 | 4 |
| ★54 | 4 | 89 | — | ALMOST PERSUADED | David Houston (Billy Sherrill), Epic 10025 | 3 |
| ★55 | 75 | 90 | — | YOU YOU YOU | Mel Carter (Nick De Caro), Imperial 66183 | 3 |
| ★56 | 80 | — | — | MAKE ME BELONG TO YOU | Barbara Lewis (Jerry Wexler & Ollie McLaughlin), Atlantic 2346 | 2 |
| ★57 | 82 | 97 | — | SUMMERTIME | Billy Stewart (Billy Davis), Chess 1966 | 3 |
| 58 | 57 | 64 | 65 | I'M A NUT | Leroy Pullins (Lissauer-Wheeler), Kapp 758 | 6 |
| ★59 | 79 | — | — | THE TIP OF MY FINGER | Eddy Arnold (Chet Atkins), RCA Victor 8869 | 2 |
| 60 | 59 | 63 | 69 | PAST, PRESENT AND FUTURE | Shangri-Las (Shadow Morton), Red Bird 10068 | 6 |
| ★61 | — | — | — | GUANTANAMERA | Sandpipers (Tommy LiPuma), A&M 806 | 1 |
| ★62 | — | — | — | ALFIE | Cher (Sonny Bono), Imperial 66192 | 1 |
| ★63 | 93 | — | — | BORN A WOMAN | Sandy Posey (Chip Moman), MGM 13501 | 2 |
| ★64 | 90 | — | — | WORKING IN THE COAL MINE | Lee Dorsey (A. Toussaint-M. Sehorn), Amy 958 | 2 |
| ★65 | 89 | 99 | 100 | WADE IN THE WATER | Ramsey Lewis (Esmond Edwards), Cadet 5541 | 4 |
| ★66 | 100 | — | — | A MILLION AND ONE | Dean Martin (Jimmy Bowen), Reprise 0500 | 2 |
| 67 | 63 | 69 | 73 | I LOVE ONIONS | Susan Christie (John Hill), Columbia 43595 | 8 |
| 68 | 65 | 76 | 82 | LARA'S THEME FROM "DR. ZHIVAGO" | Roger Williams, Kapp 738 | 6 |
| 69 | 70 | 85 | 88 | LONELY SOLDIER | Mike Williams (Prod. by Staff), Atlantic 2339 | 4 |
| 70 | 73 | 88 | — | I GUESS I'LL ALWAYS LOVE YOU | Isley Brothers (Holland & Dozier), Tamla 54135 | 3 |
| 71 | 66 | 70 | 76 | TEENAGER'S PRAYER | Joe Simon (J.R. Enterprises), Sound Stage 7 2564 | 7 |
| 72 | 71 | 71 | 68 | I LOVE YOU 1,000 TIMES | The Platters (Luther Dixon), Musicor 1166 | 14 |
| ★73 | 98 | — | — | BUS STOP | Hollies (Ron Richardson), Imperial 66186 | 2 |
| ★74 | — | — | — | (YOU MAKE ME FEEL) SO GOOD | McCoys (Feldman, Goldstein, Gottehrer), Bang 527 | 1 |
| ★75 | — | — | — | MY HEART'S SYMPHONY | Gary Lewis & the Playboys (Snuff Barrett), Liberty 55898 | 1 |
| ★76 | — | — | — | LAND OF 1,000 DANCES | Wilson Pickett (Jerry Wexler & Rick Hall) Atlantic 2348 | 1 |
| 77 | 88 | — | — | I BELIEVE I'M GONNA MAKE IT | Joe Tex (Buddy Killen), Dial 4033 | 2 |
| 78 | 76 | 77 | 92 | HEY YOU LITTLE BOO-GA-LOO | Chubby Checker (Dave Appell), Parkway 989 | 5 |
| ★79 | — | — | — | MONEY WON'T CHANGE YOU | James Brown & the Famous Flames (James Brown Prod), King 6048 | 1 |
| 80 | 92 | — | — | SUGAR AND SPICE | Cryan Shames (MG Prod.), Destination 624 | 2 |
| ★81 | 99 | — | — | OPEN THE DOOR TO YOUR HEART | Darrell Banks, Revilot 201 | 2 |
| ★82 | — | — | — | BRING BACK THE TIME | B. J. Thomas (Huey J. Meaux), Scepter 12154 | 1 |
| ★83 | — | — | — | LIVIN' ABOVE YOUR HEAD | Jay & the Americans (Gerry Granaham) United Artists 50046 | 1 |
| ★84 | — | — | — | WOULDN'T IT BE NICE | Beach Boys (Brian Wilson), Capitol 5706 | 1 |
| 85 | 85 | 91 | — | UPTIGHT | Nancy Wilson (David Cavanaugh), Capitol 5673 | 3 |
| ★86 | — | — | — | LONELY SUMMER | Shades of Blue (John Rhys), Impact 1014 | 1 |
| 87 | 84 | 84 | 80 | STOP! GET A TICKET | Clefs of Lavender Hill (Steven Palmer), Date 1510 | 6 |
| ★88 | — | — | — | WIPE OUT | Surfaris, Dot 144 | 17 |
| ★89 | — | — | — | 7 AND 7 IS | Love (Jac Holzman), Elektra 45605 | 1 |
| ★90 | — | — | — | SUNSHINE SUPERMAN | Donovan (Mickey Most), Epic 10045 | 1 |
| 91 | — | — | — | LET'S CALL IT A DAY GIRL | Razor's Edge (Bob Yorey), POW 101 | 1 |
| 92 | — | — | — | I PUT A SPELL ON YOU | Alan Price Set (Alan Price), Parrot 3001 | 1 |
| 93 | 94 | 95 | — | DRIVE MY CAR | Bob Kuban & the In-Men (Mel Friedman), Musicland, U.S.A. 20007 | 3 |
| 94 | 95 | — | — | GEORGIA ROSE | Tony Bennett (Ernie Altschuler), Columbia 43715 | 2 |
| 95 | 96 | 98 | — | (We'll Be) UNITED | Intruders, Gamble 201 | 3 |
| 96 | — | — | — | THE PHILLY FREEZE | Alvin Cash & the Registers, Mar-v-Lus 6012 | 1 |
| 97 | — | — | — | HOW SWEET IT IS | Jr. Walker & the All-Stars (J. Bristol-H. Fuqua), Soul 35024 | 1 |
| 98 | — | — | — | TO SHOW I LOVE YOU | Peter & Gordan (John Burgess), Capitol 5684 | 1 |
| 99 | — | — | — | LOVE ATTACK | James Carr (Q. Claunch), Goldwax 309 | 1 |
| 100 | — | — | — | TAKIN' ALL I CAN GET | Mitch Ryder & the Detroit Wheels (Bob Crewe), New Voice 814 | 1 |

## HOT 100—A TO Z—(Publisher-Licensee)

Ain't Too Proud to Beg (Jobete BMI) .... 24
Alfie (Famous, ASCAP) .... 62
Almost Persuaded (Gallico, BMI) .... 54
Along Comes Mary (Davon, BMI) .... 29
Billy and Sue (Hornet, BMI) .... 34
Blowin' in the Wind (Witmark, ASCAP) .... 40
Born a Woman (Painted Desert, BMI) .... 63
Bring Back the Time (Crazy Cajun-Flomar, BMI). 82
Bus Stop (Manken, BMI) .... 73
Can I Trust You I (Miller, ASCAP) .... 49
Cool Jerk (McLaughlin, BMI) .... 38
Dirty Water (Equinox, BMI) .... 31
Distant Shores (Chad & Jeremy-Norma, BMI) .... 45
Drive My Car (Maclen, BMI) .... 93
5D (Fifth Dimension) (Tickerson, BMI) .... 44
Friday's Child (Atlantic, BMI) .... 36
Georgia Rose (Feist, ASCAP) .... 94
Guantanamera (Fall River, BMI) .... 61
Hanky Panky (T. M., BMI) .... 3
Happy Summer Daqs (Picturetone, BMI) .... 27
Hey You Little Boo-Ga-Loo (Double Diamond, Champion, BMI) .... 78
How Sweet It Is (Jobete, BMI) .... 97
Hungry (Screen Gems-Columbia, BMI) .... 6
I Believe I'm Gonna Make It (Tree, BMI) .... 77
I Couldn't Live Without Your Love (Northern, ASCAP) .... 26
I Guess I'll Always Love You (Jobete, BMI) .... 70
I Love Onions (Blackwood, BMI) .... 67
I Love You 1,000 Times (Ludiz, BMI) .... 72
I Put a Spell on You (Travis, BMI) .... 92
I Saw Her Again (Trousdale, BMI) .... 5
I Want You (Dwarf, ASCAP) .... 20
(I Washed My Hands in) Muddy Water (Maricana, BMI) .... 39
I'm a Nut (Youmans-Sleepy Hollow, ASCAP) .... 58
Impossible Dream, The (Fox, ASCAP) .... 35
Joker Went Wild The (Rising Sons, BMI) .... 47
Lady Jane (Gideon, BMI) .... 51
Land of 1,000 Dances (Tune-Kel-Anatole, BMI) .... 76
Lara's Theme From "Dr. Zhivago" (Robbins, ASCAP) .... 68
Let's Call It a Day Girl (Sea Lark, BMI) .... 91
Lil' Red Riding Hood (Rose, BMI) .... 3
Little Girl (Duane, BMI) .... 21
Livin' Above Your Head (Wippity, BMI) .... 83
Look at Me Girl (Epps, BMI) .... 52
Lonely Soldier (Pronto-Chevis, BMI) .... 69
Lonely Summer (Gamba, BMI) .... 86
Love Attack (Rise-Aim, BMI) .... 99
Love Letters (Famous, ASCAP) .... 19
Make Me Belong to You (Blackwood, BMI) .... 56
Million and One, A (Silver Star, BMI) .... 66
Misty (Vernon, ASCAP) .... 50
Money Won't Change You (Dynatone, BMI) .... 79
Mother's Little Helper (Gideon, BMI) .... 9
My Heart's Symphony (Gringo, BMI) .... 75
Open the Door to Your Heart (T.M. & Parmalier, BMI) .... 81
Over Under Sideways Down (Feist, ASCAP) .... 17
Paperback Writer (Maclen, BMI) .... 12
Past, Present and Future (Tender Tunes, BMI) .... 60
Philly Freeze, The (Vapac, BMI) .... 96
Pied Piper, The (Chardon, BMI) .... 4
Popsicle (Lowery, BMI) .... 41
Pretty Flamingo (Ponderosa, BMI) .... 32
Red Rubber Ball (Eclectic, BMI) .... 13
Searchirn for My Love (Chevis, BMI) .... 33
See You in September (Vibar, ASCAP) .... 30
7 and 7 Is (Grass Roots, BMI) .... 89
Somewhere My Love (Robbins, ASCAP) .... 10
Stop! Get a Ticket (Gallico, BMI) .... 87
Strangers in the Night (Champion-Roosevelt, BMI) .... 22
Sugar and Spice (Duchess, BMI) .... 80
Summer in the City (Faithful Virtue, BMI) .... 7
Summertime (Gershwin, ASCAP) .... 57
Sunny (Portable, BMI) .... 14
Sunshine Superman (Southern, ASCAP) .... 90
Sweet Dreams (Acuff-Rose, BMI) .... 23
Sweet Pea (Low Twi, BMI) .... 8
Takin' All I Can Get (Saturday, BMI) .... 100
Tar and Cement (Feist, ASCAP) .... 53
Teenager's Prayer (Frederick, BMI) .... 71
They're Coming to Take Me Away, Ha-Haaa!! (Japalana, BMI) .... 11
Tip of My Finger, The (Tree & Champion, BMI) .... 59
This Door Swings Both Ways (Blackwood, BMI) .... 16
To Show I Love You (Leeds, ASCAP) .... 98
Trains and Boats and Planes (U. S. Songs, ASCAP) 25
Uptight (Jobete, BMI) .... 85
Wade in the Water (Ramsel, BMI) .... 65
Warm and Tender Love (Pronto-Bob-Dan-Quinvy, BMI) .... 48
(We'll Be) United (Sharpe, BMI) .... 95
Where Were You When I Needed You (Trousdale, BMI) .... 28
Whole Lot of Shakin' in My Heart (Since I Met You) (Jobete, BMI) .... 46
Wild Thing (Blackwood, BMI) .... 1
Wipe Out (Miraleste-Robin Hood, BMI) .... 88
Work Song, The (Upam, BMI) .... 18
Working in the Coal Mine (Marsaint, BMI) .... 64
Wouldn't It Be Nice (Sea of Tunes, BMI) .... 84
You Better Run (Slacsar, BMI) .... 37
You Can't Roller Skate in a Buffalo Herd (Tree, BMI) .... 43
You Don't Have to Say You Love Me (Robbins, ASCAP) .... 15
(You Make Me Feel) So Good (Grand Canyon-Hill & Range, BMI) .... 74
You Wouldn't Listen (BMC, BMI) .... 42
You You You (Mellin, BMI) .... 55

## BUBBLING UNDER THE HOT 100

101. COME SHARE THE GOOD TIMES WITH ME .... Julie Monday, Rainbow 500
102. WITH A GIRL LIKE YOU .... Troggs, Atco 6415-Fontana 1552
103. PETTICOAT WHITE (Summer Sky Blue) .... Bobby Vinton, Epic 10048
104. A MILLION AND ONE .... Vic Dana, Dalton 322
105. GREATEST MOMENTS IN A GIRL'S LIFE .... Tokens, B.T. Puppy 519
106. YOUR GOOD THING (Is About to End) .... Mabel John, Stax 192
107. ALL THESE THINGS .... Uniques, Paula 238
108. JUST A LITTLE BIT OF YOU .... Dallas Frazier, Capitol 5670
109. LET ME TELL YOU, BABE .... Nat King Cole, Capitol 5683
110. FREDDIE FEELGOOD .... Ray Stevens, Monument 946
111. JUST YESTERDAY .... Al Martino, Capitol 5702
112. SAY I AM (What I Am) .... Tommy James & the Shondells, Roulette 4695
113. THAT'S ENOUGH .... Roscoe Robinson, Wand 1125
114. TAKE YOUR LOVE .... Bobby Goldsboro, United Artists 50044
115. LOOK AT ME GIRL .... Playboys of Edinburg, Columbia 43716
116. SOCK IT TO 'EM, J.B. .... Rex Garvin, Like 301
117. TELL HER .... Dean Parrish, Boom 60012
118. MOST OF ALL .... Cowsills, Philips 40382
119. TOO SOON TO KNOW .... Roy Orbison, MGM 13549
120. RESPECTABLE .... Outsiders, Capitol 5701
121. WHEN YOU WAKE UP .... Cash McCall, Thomas 8830
122. IN THE BASEMENT .... Etta James & Sugar Pie DeSanto, Cadet 5539
123. YOU'RE GONNA MISS ME. Thirteenth Floor Elevators, International Artists 107
124. OUT OF THIS WORLD .... Chiffons, Laurie 3350
125. ANGELICA .... Barry Mann, Capitol 5695
126. LARA'S THEME .... Brass Ring, Dunhill 4036
127. POOR DOG .... Little Richard Okeh 7251
128. WHO DO YOU THINK YOU ARE .... Shindogs, Viva 601
129. I'M A GOOD WOMAN .... Barbara Lynn, Tribe 8316
130. WORLD OF FANTASY .... Five Stair-Steps, Windy C 602
131. SUSPICIONS .... Sidekicks, RCA Victor 8864
132. WHAT BECOMES OF THE BROKEN HEARTS .... Jimmy Ruffin, Soul 35022
133. IT'S BEEN SUCH A LONG WAY HOME .... Garnet Mimms, Veep 1232
134. CAST YOUR FATE TO THE WIND .... Shelby Flint, Valiant 743
135. DIRTY WORK GOING ON .... Little Joe Blue, Checker 1141

Compiled from national retail sales and radio station airplay by the Music Popularity Dept. of Record Market Research, Billboard.

Billboard

For Week Ending August 6, 1966

# HOT 100

★ STAR performer—Sides registering greatest proportionate upward progress this week.

Ⓡ Record Industry Association of America seal of certification as million selling single.

| THIS WEEK | 1 Wk. Ago | 2 Wks. Ago | 3 Wks. Ago | TITLE Artist (Producer), Label & Number | Weeks On Chart |
|---|---|---|---|---|---|
| 1 (Billboard Award) | 2 | 2 | | WILD THING — Troggs (Page One-York Palla), Atco 6415-Fontana 1548 | 7 |
| 2 | 3 | 3 | 9 | LIL' RED RIDING HOOD — Sam the Sham & the Pharaohs (Stan Kesler), MGM 13506 | 9 |
| ★ 3 | 7 | 21 | 53 | SUMMER IN THE CITY — Lovin' Spoonful (Eric-Jacobsen), Kama Sutra 211 | 4 |
| 4 | 4 | 4 | 12 | THE PIED PIPER — Crispian St. Peters (David Nicolson), Jamie 1320 | 9 |
| ★ 5 | 11 | 50 | — | THEY'RE COMING TO TAKE ME AWAY, HA-HAA! — Napoloeon XIV (Jepalana Prod.), Warner Bros. 5831 | 3 |
| 6 | 5 | 9 | 14 | I SAW HER AGAIN — Mama's & the Papa's (Lou Adler), Dunhill 4031 | 6 |
| 7 | 2 | 1 | 1 | HANKY PANKY — Tommy James & the Shondells (Jeff Barry & Ellie Greenwich), Roulette 4686 | 10 |
| 8 | 8 | 10 | 15 | SWEET PEA — Tommy Roe, ABC Records 10762 | 9 |
| 9 | 9 | 17 | 38 | MOTHER'S LITTLE HELPER — Rolling Stones (Andrew Loog Oldham), London 902 | 5 |
| 10 | 10 | 14 | 21 | SOMEWHERE MY LOVE — Ray Conniff & the Singers (Ernie Altschuler), Columbia 43626 | 8 |
| 11 | 14 | 25 | 50 | SUNNY — Bobby Hebb (Jerry Ross), Philips 40365 | 7 |
| 12 | 6 | 7 | 10 | HUNGRY — Paul Revere & the Raiders (Terry Melcher), Columbia 43678 | 8 |
| 13 | 16 | 32 | 56 | THIS DOOR SWINGS BOTH WAYS — Herman's Hermits (Mickie Most), MGM 13548 | 5 |
| 14 | 17 | 23 | 39 | OVER UNDER SIDEWAYS DOWN — Yardbirds (Samwell-Smith, Napier-Bell), Epic 10035 | 7 |
| ★ 15 | 30 | 41 | 67 | SEE YOU IN SEPTEMBER — Happenings (Bright Tunes Prod.), B. T. Puppy 520 | 5 |
| ★ 16 | 26 | 46 | 73 | I COULDN'T LIVE WITHOUT YOUR LOVE — Petula Clark (Tony Hatch), Warner Bros. 5835 | 4 |
| ★ 17 | 23 | 26 | 48 | SWEET DREAMS — Tommy McLain (Floyd Soileau & Huey Meaux), MSL 197 | 7 |
| 18 | 12 | 6 | 5 | PAPERBACK WRITER — Beatles (George Martin), Capitol 5651 | 9 Ⓡ |
| 19 | 18 | 18 | 25 | THE WORK SONG — Herb Alpert & the Tijuana Brass (Herb Alpert), A & M 805 | 6 |
| 20 | 20 | 24 | 34 | I WANT YOU — Bob Dylan (Bob Johnston), Columbia 43683 | 6 |
| 21 | 19 | 19 | 26 | LOVE LETTERS — Elvis Presley, RCA Victor 8870 | 6 |
| 22 | 25 | 30 | 35 | TRAINS AND BOATS AND PLANES — Dionne Warwick (Bacharach-David), Scepter 12153 | 6 |
| 23 | 13 | 8 | 3 | RED RUBBER BALL — Cyrkle (John Simon), Columbia 43589 | 12 |
| ★ 24 | 40 | 68 | — | BLOWIN' IN THE WIND — Stevie Wonder (C. Paul), Tamla 54136 | 3 |
| 25 | 24 | 15 | 13 | AIN'T TOO PROUD TO BEG — Temptations (N. Whitfield), Gordy 7054 | 11 |
| 26 | 15 | 5 | 4 | YOU DON'T HAVE TO SAY YOU LOVE ME — Dusty Springfield, Philips 40371 | 12 |
| 27 | 22 | 12 | 6 | STRANGERS IN THE NIGHT — Frank Sinatra (Jimmy Bowen), Reprise 0470 | 14 |
| ★ 28 | 33 | 52 | 58 | SEARCHING FOR MY LOVE — Bobby Moore & the Rhythm Aces (Rick Hall), Checker 1129 | 7 |
| 29 | 32 | 38 | 45 | PRETTY FLAMINGO — Manfred Mann (John Burgess), United Artists 50040 | 6 |
| 30 | 28 | 29 | 32 | WHERE WERE YOU WHEN I NEEDED YOU — Grass Roots (Sloan & Barri), Dunhill 4029 | 8 |
| 31 | 31 | 16 | 11 | DIRTY WATER — Standells (Ed Cobb), Tower 185 | 16 |
| 32 | 29 | 11 | 7 | ALONG COMES MARY — Association (C. Boettcher), Valiant 741 | 10 |
| ★ 33 | 57 | 82 | 97 | SUMMERTIME — Billy Stewart (Billy Davis), Chess 1966 | 4 |
| 34 | 34 | 37 | 43 | BILLY AND SUE — B. J. Thomas, Hickory 1395 | 8 |
| ★ 35 | 48 | 78 | — | WARM AND TENDER LOVE — Percy Sledge (Martin Greene & Quin Ivy), Atlantic 2342 | 3 |
| 36 | 36 | 48 | 55 | FRIDAY'S CHILD — Nancy Sinatra (Lee Hazlewood), Reprise 0491 | 5 |
| ★ 37 | 47 | 62 | 72 | THE JOKER WENT WILD — Brian Hyland (Snuff Garrett & Leon Russell), Philips 40377 | 4 |
| ★ 38 | 63 | 93 | — | BORN A WOMAN — Sandy Posey (Chip Moman), MGM 13501 | 3 |
| ★ 39 | 51 | 83 | — | LADY JANE — Rolling Stones (Andrew Loog Oldham), London 902 | 3 |
| 40 | 35 | 35 | 40 | THE IMPOSSIBLE DREAM — Jack Jones (David Kapp), Kapp 755 | 10 |
| 41 | 45 | 55 | 78 | DISTANT SHORES — Chad & Jeremy (Larry Marks), Columbia 43682 | 5 |
| ★ 42 | 53 | 61 | 68 | TAR AND CEMENT — Verdelle Smith (Vance-Prokriss Prod.), Capitol 5632 | 5 |
| ★ 43 | 76 | — | — | LAND OF 1,000 DANCES — Wilson Pickett (Jerry Wexler & Rick Hall), Atlantic 2348 | 2 |
| 44 | 44 | 54 | 74 | 5 D (Fifth Dimension) — Byrds (Allen Stanton), Columbia 43702 | 4 |
| ★ 45 | 64 | 90 | — | WORKING IN THE COAL MINE — Lee Dorsey (A. Toussaint-M. Sehorn), Amy 958 | 3 |
| ★ 46 | 56 | 80 | — | MAKE ME BELONG TO YOU — Barbara Lewis (Jerry Wexler & Ollie McLaughlin), Atlantic 2346 | 3 |
| 47 | 50 | 64 | 82 | MISTY — Groove Holmes (Cal Lampley), Prestige 401 | 7 |
| ★ 48 | 59 | 79 | — | THE TIP OF MY FINGER — Eddy Arnold (Chet Atkins), RCA Victor 8869 | 3 |
| 49 | 21 | 13 | 8 | LITTLE GIRL — Syndicate of Sound (Gary Thompson), Bell 640 | 10 |
| 50 | 55 | 75 | 90 | YOU YOU YOU — Mel Carter (Nick De Caro), Imperial 66183 | 4 |
| ★ 51 | 61 | — | — | GUANTANAMERA — Sandpipers (Tommy LiPuma), A&M 806 | 2 |
| ★ 52 | 62 | — | — | ALFIE — Cher (Sonny Bono), Imperial 66192 | 2 |
| 53 | 54 | 4 | 89 | ALMOST PERSUADED — David Houston (Billy Sherrill), Epic 10025 | 4 |
| 54 | 27 | 27 | 30 | HAPPY SUMMER DAYS — Ronnie Dove (Phil Kahl), Diamond 205 | 8 |
| ★ 55 | 65 | 89 | 99 | WADE IN THE WATER — Ramsey Lewis (Esmond Edwards), Cadet 5541 | 5 |
| ★ 56 | 66 | 100 | — | A MILLION AND ONE — Dean Martin (Jimmy Bowen), Reprise 0500 | 3 |
| ★ 57 | 75 | — | — | MY HEART'S SYMPHONY — Gary Lewis & the Playboys (Snuff Garrett), Liberty 55898 | 2 |
| ★ 58 | 73 | 98 | — | BUS STOP — Hollies (Ron Richardson), Imperial 66186 | 3 |
| ★ 59 | 74 | — | — | (You Make Me Feel) SO GOOD — McCoys (Feldman, Goldstein, Gottehrer), Bang 527 | 2 |
| 60 | 42 | 42 | 52 | YOU WOULDN'T LISTEN — I'des of March (Mike Considine), Parrot 304 | 7 |
| ★ 61 | 90 | — | — | SUNSHINE SUPERMAN — Donovan (Mickey Most), Epic 10045 | 2 |
| ★ 62 | 84 | — | — | WOULDN'T IT BE NICE — Beach Boys (Brian Wilson), Capitol 5706 | 2 |
| 63 | 52 | 69 | 81 | LOOK AT ME GIRL — Bobby Vee (Dallas Smith), Liberty 55877 | 5 |
| ★ 64 | 79 | — | — | MONEY WON'T CHANGE YOU — James Brown & the Famous Flames (James Brown Prod), King 6048 | 2 |
| 65 | 70 | 73 | 88 | I GUESS I'LL ALWAYS LOVE YOU — Isley Brothers (Holland & Dozier), Tamla 54135 | 4 |
| ★ 66 | 81 | 99 | — | OPEN THE DOOR TO YOUR HEART — Darrell Banks, Revilot 201 | 3 |
| 67 | 49 | 56 | 66 | CAN I TRUST YOU? — Bachelors (Dick Rowe), London 20010 | 6 |
| 68 | 77 | 88 | — | I BELIEVE I'M GONNA MAKE IT — Joe Tex (Buddy Killen), Dial 4033 | 3 |
| 69 | 46 | 47 | 49 | WHOLE LOT OF SHAKIN' IN MY HEART (Since I Met You) — Miracles (Frank Wilson), Tamla 54134 | 8 |
| ★ 70 | — | — | — | RESPECTABLE — Outsiders (Tom King), Capitol 5701 | 1 |
| ★ 71 | — | — | — | SAY I AM (What I Am) — Tommy Jones and the Shondells (Bob Mack), Roulette 4695 | 1 |
| ★ 72 | — | — | — | GO AHEAD AND CRY — Righteous Brothers (Bill Medley), Verve 10430 | 1 |
| 73 | 69 | 70 | 85 | LONELY SOLDIER — Mike Williams (Prod. by Staff), Atlantic 2339 | 5 |
| 74 | 80 | 92 | — | SUGAR AND SPICE — Cryan Shames (MG Prod.), Destination 624 | 3 |
| ★ 75 | — | — | — | WITH A GIRL LIKE YOU — Troggs (Page One-York-Pala), Atco 6415-Fontana 1552 | 1 |
| 76 | 88 | — | — | WIPE OUT — Surfaris, Dot 144 | 18 |
| ★ 77 | — | — | — | TOO SOON TO KNOW — Roy Orbison (Rose & Venneau), MGM 13549 | 1 |
| 78 | 82 | — | — | BRING BACK THE TIME — B. J. Thomas (Huey J. Meaux), Scepter 12154 | 2 |
| 79 | 89 | — | — | 7 AND 7 IS — Love (Jac Holzman), Elektra 45605 | 2 |
| 80 | 86 | — | — | LONELY SUMMER — Shades of Blue (John Rhys), Impact 1014 | 2 |
| ★ 81 | — | — | — | A MILLION AND ONE — Vic Dana (Bob Reisdorff), Dolton 322 | 1 |
| 82 | 95 | 96 | 98 | (We'll Be) UNITED — Intruders, Gamble 201 | 4 |
| 83 | 83 | — | — | LIVIN' ABOVE YOUR HEAD — Jay & the Americans (Gerry Granaham), United Artists 50046 | 2 |
| 84 | 85 | 85 | 91 | UPTIGHT — Nancy Wilson (David Cavanaugh), Capitol 5673 | 4 |
| ★ 85 | — | — | — | PETTICOAT WHITE (Summer Sky Blue) — Bobby Vinton (Bob Morgan), Epic 10048 | 1 |
| ★ 86 | — | — | — | OUT OF THIS WORLD — Chiffons (Bright Tunes), Laurie 3350 | 1 |
| 87 | 91 | — | — | LET'S CALL IT A DAY GIRL — Razor's Edge (Bob Yorey), POW 101 | 2 |
| 88 | 92 | — | — | I PUT A SPELL ON YOU — Alan Price Set (Alan Price), Parrot 3001 | 2 |
| 89 | 94 | 95 | — | GEORGIA ROSE — Tony Bennett (Ernie Altschuler), Columbia 43715 | 3 |
| ★ 90 | — | — | — | SUNNY AFTERNOON — Kinks (Shel Talmy), Reprise 0497 | 1 |
| 91 | — | — | — | LET ME TELL YOU, BABE — Nat King Cole (Lee Gillette & David Cavanaugh), Capitol 5683 | 1 |
| 92 | — | — | — | THE DANGLING CONVERSATION — Simon & Garfunkel (Bob Johnston), Columbia 43728 | 1 |
| 93 | — | — | — | WORLD OF FANTASY — Five Stair-Steps (C. Mayfield), Windy C 602 | 1 |
| 94 | 96 | — | — | THE PHILLY FREEZE — Alvin Cash & the Registers, Mar-v-Lus 6012 | 2 |
| 95 | 97 | — | — | HOW SWEET IT IS — Jr. Walker & the All-Stars (J. Bristol-H. Fuqua), Soul 35024 | 2 |
| 96 | — | — | — | YOUR GOOD THING (Is About to End) — Mable John (Prod. By Staff), Stax 192 | 1 |
| 97 | — | — | — | JUST YESTERDAY — Al Martino (Tom Morgan), Capitol 5702 | 1 |
| 98 | 98 | — | — | TO SHOW I LOVE YOU — Peter & Gordan (John Burgess), Capitol 5684 | 2 |
| 99 | — | — | — | SUSPICIONS — Sidekicks, RCA Victor 8864 | 1 |
| 100 | — | — | — | THAT'S ENOUGH — Roscoe Robinson (Roscoe Robinson), Wand 1125 | 1 |

## HOT 100—A TO Z—(Publisher-Licensee)


Ain't Too Proud to Beg (Jobete, BMI) .......... 25
Alfie (Famous, ASCAP) .......... 52
Almost Persuaded (Galico, BMI) .......... 53
Along Comes Mary (Davon, BMI) .......... 32
Billy and Sue (Hornet, BMI) .......... 34
Blowin' in the Wind (Witmark, ASCAP) .......... 24
Born a Woman (Painted Desert, BMI) .......... 38
Bring Back the Time (Crazy Cajun, Flomar, BMI). 78
Bus Stop (Manken, BMI) .......... 58
Can I Trust You? (Miller, ASCAP) .......... 67
Dangling Conversation, The (Charing Cross, BMI).. 92
Dirty Water (Equinox, BMI) .......... 31
Distant Shores (Chad & Jeremy-Noma, BMI) .......... 41
5 D (Fifth Dimension) (Tickson, BMI) .......... 44
Friday's Child (Atlantic, BMI) .......... 36
Georgia Rose (Feist, BMI) .......... 89
Go Ahead and Cry (Righteous Bros., BMI) .......... 72
Guantanamera (Fall River, BMI) .......... 51
Hanky Panky (T. M., BMI) .......... 7
Happy Summer Days (Picturetone, BMI) .......... 54
How Sweet It Is (Jobete, BMI) .......... 95
Hungry (Screen Gems-Columbia, BMI) .......... 12
I Believe I'm Gonna Make It (Tree, BMI) .......... 68
I Couldn't Live Without Your Love (Northern, ASCAP) .......... 16
I Guess I'll Always Love You (Jobete, BMI) .......... 65
I Put a Spell on You (Travis, BMI) .......... 88
I Saw Her Again (Trousdale, BMI) .......... 6
I Want You (Dwarf, ASCAP) .......... 20
Impossible Dream, The (Fox, ASCAP) .......... 40
Joker Went Wild, The (Rising Sons, BMI) .......... 37
Just Yesterday (Damian, ASCAP) .......... 97
Lady Jane (Gideon, BMI) .......... 39
Land of 1,000 Dances (Tune-Kel-Anatole, BMI) .. 43
Let's Call It a Day Girl (Sea Lark, BMI) .......... 87
Let Me Tell You, Babe (Comet, ASCAP) .......... 91
Lil' Red Riding Hood (Rose, BMI) .......... 2
Little Girl (Duane, BMI) .......... 49
Livin' Above Your Head (Wippity, BMI) .......... 83
Look at Me Girl (Epps, BMI) .......... 63
Lonely Soldier (Pronto-Chevis, BMI) .......... 73
Lonely Summer (Gamba, BMI) .......... 80
Love Letters (Famous, ASCAP) .......... 21
Make Me Belong to You (Blackwood, BMI) .......... 46
Million and One, A—Martin (Silver Star, BMI) ... 56
Million and One, A—Dana (Silver Star, BMI) .......... 81
Misty (Vernon, ASCAP) .......... 47
Money Won't Change You (Dynatone, BMI) .......... 64
Mother's Little Helper (Gideon, BMI) .......... 9
My Heart's Symphony (Gringol, BMI) .......... 57
Open the Door to Your Heart (T.M. & Parmalier, BMI) .......... 66
Out of This World (Roznique-Elmwin, BMI) .......... 86
Over Under Sideways Down (Feist, ASCAP) .......... 14
Paperback Writer (Maclen, BMI) .......... 18
Petticoat White (Summer Sky Blue) (Noma-Feather-Hi Count, BMI) .......... 85
Philly Freeze, The (Vapac, BMI) .......... 94
Pied Piper, The (Chardon, BMI) .......... 4
Pretty Flamingo (Ponderosa, BMI) .......... 29
Red Rubber Ball (Eclectric, BMI) .......... 23
Respectable (Wemar, BMI) .......... 70
Say I Am (What I Am) (Dundee, BMI) .......... 71
Searching for My Love (Chevis, BMI) .......... 28
See You in September (Vibar, ASCAP) .......... 15
7 and 7 Is (Grass Roots, BMI) .......... 79
Somewhere My Love (Robbins, ASCAP) .......... 10
Strangers in the Night (Champion-Roosevelt, BMI). 27
Sugar and Spice (Duchess, BMI) .......... 74
Summer in the City (Faithful Virtue, BMI) .......... 3
Summertime (Gershwin, ASCAP) .......... 33
Sunny (Portable, BMI) .......... 11
Sunny Afternoon (Norma, BMI) .......... 90
Sunshine Superman (Southern, ASCAP) .......... 61
Suspicions (Ricemill & R&S, BMI) .......... 99
Sweet Dreams (Acuff-Rose, BMI) .......... 17
Sweet Pea (Low Twi, BMI) .......... 8
Tar and Cement (Feist, ASCAP) .......... 42
That's Enough (Kapa, BMI) ..........100
They're Coming to Take Me Away, Ha-Haaa! (XIV, SESAC) .......... 5
This Door Swings Both Ways (Blackwood, BMI) ... 13
Tip of My Finger, The (Tree & Champion, BMI) ... 48
To Show I Love You (Leeds, ASCAP) .......... 98
Too Soon to Know (Acuff-Rose, BMI) .......... 77
Trains and Boats and Planes (U. S. Songs, ASCAP) 22
Uptight (Jobete, BMI) .......... 84
Wade in the Water (Ramsel, BMI) .......... 55
Warm and Tender Love (Pronto-Bob-Dan-Quinvy, BMI) .......... 35
(We'll Be) United (Sharpe, BMI) .......... 82
Where Were You When I Needed You (Trousdale, BMI) .......... 30
Whole Lot of Shakin' in My Heart (Since I Met You) (Jobete, BMI) .......... 69
Wild Thing (Blackwood, BMI) .......... 1
Wipe Out (Miraleste-Robin Hood, BMI) .......... 76
With a Girl Like You (James, BMI) .......... 75
Work Song, The (Upam, BMI) .......... 19
Working in the Coal Mine (Marsaint, BMI) .......... 45
World of Fantasy (Camad, BMI) .......... 93
Wouldn't It Be Nice (Sea of Tunes, BMI) .......... 62
You Don't Have to Say You Love Me (Robbins, ASCAP) .......... 26
(You Make Me Feel) So Good (Grand Canyon-Hill & Range, BMI) .......... 59
You Wouldn't Listen (BMC, BMI) .......... 60
You You You (Mellin, BMI) .......... 50
Your Good Thing (Is About to End) (East, BMI) .. 96


## BUBBLING UNDER THE HOT 100

101. OPEN UP YOUR DOOR ..........Richard & the Young Lions, Philips 40381
102. WHEN YOU WAKE UP ..........Cash McCall, Thomas 8830
103. LOVE (Oh How Sweet It Is) ..........Jerry Butler, Mercury 72592
104. LARA'S THEME FROM "DR. ZHIVAGO" ..........Roger Williams, Kapp 738
105. COME SHARE THE GOOD TIMES WITH ME ......Julie Monday, Rainbow 500
106. LOVE ATTACK ..........James Carr, Goldwax 309
107. I WANT TO BE WITH YOU ..........Dee Dee Warwick, Mercury 72584
108. SATISFIED WITH YOU ..........Dave Clark Five, Epic 10053
109. GOD ONLY KNOWS ..........Beach Boys, Capitol 5706
110. SOCK IT TO 'EM, J.B. ..........Rex Garvin, Like 301
111. DIRTY WORK GOING ON ..........Little Joe Blue, Checker 1141
112. IN THE BASEMENT ..........Etta James & Sugar Pie DeSanto, Cadet 5539
113. LOOK AT ME GIRL ..........Playboys of Edinburg, Columbia 43716
114. TAKE YOUR LOVE ..........Bobby Goldsboro, United Artists 50044
115. YOU'RE GONNA MISS ME ....13th Floor Elevators, International Artists 107
116. EL PITO ..........Joe Cuba, Tico 470
117. ANGELICA ..........Barry Mann, Capitol 5695
118. MOST OF ALL ..........Cowsills, Philips 40382
119. WHO-DUN-IT? ..........Monk Higgins, St. Lawrence 1013
120. TAKIN' ALL I CAN GET ..Mitch Ryder & the Detroit Wheels, New Voice 814
121. POOR DOG ..........Little Richard, Okeh 7251
122. TURN-DOWN DAY ..........Cryrkle, Columbia 43729
123. WHO DO YOU THINK YOU ARE ..........Shindogs, Viva 601
124. CAST YOUR FATE TO THE WIND ..........Shelby Flint, Valiant 743
125. DIANNE, DIANNE ..........Ronny & the Daytonas, RCA Victor 8896
126. YOU CAN'T HURRY LOVE ..........Supremes, Motown 1099
127. WE CAN MAKE IT ..........Ruby & the Romantics, Kapp 759
128. FUNCTION AT THE JUNCTION ..........Shorty Long, Soul 35021
129. WITHOUT A SONG ..........James Cleveland, Savoy 4269
130. SOMETIMES GOOD GUYS DON'T WEAR WHITE ........Standells, Tower 257
131. PUT IT BACK ..........Sue Thompson, Hickory 1403
132. INVESTIGATE ..........Major Lance, Okeh 7250
133. BORN TO BE WITH YOU ..........Silkie, Fontana 1551
134. ASHES TO ASHES ..........Mindbenders, Fontana 1555
135. ALFIE ..........Cilla Black, Capitol 5674

Compiled from national retail sales and radio station airplay by the Music Popularity Dept. of Record Market Research, Billboard.

# Billboard HOT 100

**For Week Ending August 13, 1966**

★ STAR performer—Sides registering greatest proportionate upward progress this week.

● Record Industry Association of America seal of certification as million selling single.

| This Week | 1 Wk. Ago | 2 Wks. Ago | 3 Wks. Ago | TITLE  Artist (Producer), Label & Number | Weeks On Chart |
|---|---|---|---|---|---|
| 1 ★ Billboard Award | 3 | 7 | 21 | SUMMER IN THE CITY  Lovin' Spoonful (Eric Jacobsen), Kama Sutra 211 | 5 |
| 2 | 2 | 3 | 1 | LIL' RED RIDING HOOD  Sam the Sham & the Pharaohs (Stan Kesler), MGM 13506 | 10 |
| 3 | 5 | 11 | 50 | THEY'RE GOING TO TAKE ME AWAY, HA-HAAA!  Napoleon XIV (Jepalana Prod.), Warner Bros. 5831 | 4 |
| 4 | 1 | 1 | 2 | WILD THING  Troggs (Page One-York Pala), Atco 6415-Fontana 1548 | 8 |
| 5 | 4 | 4 | 4 | THE PIED PIPER  Crispian St. Peters (David Nicolson), Jamie 1320 | 10 |
| 6 | 6 | 5 | 9 | I SAW HER AGAIN  Mama's & the Papa's (Lou Adler), Dunhill 4031 | 7 |
| 7 ★ | 11 | 14 | 25 | SUNNY  Bobby Hebb (Jerry Ross), Philips 40365 | 8 |
| 8 | 9 | 9 | 17 | MOTHER'S LITTLE HELPER  Rolling Stones (Andrew Loog Oldham), London 902 | 6 |
| 9 | 10 | 10 | 14 | SOMEWHERE MY LOVE  Ray Conniff & the Singers (Ernie Altschuler), Columbia 43626 | 9 |
| 10 | 8 | 8 | 10 | SWEET PEA  Tommy Roe, ABC Records 10762 | 10 |
| 11 ★ | 16 | 26 | 46 | I COULDN'T LIVE WITHOUT YOUR LOVE  Petula Clark (Tony Hatch), Warner Bros. 5835 | 5 |
| 12 | 13 | 16 | 32 | THIS DOOR SWINGS BOTH WAYS  Herman's Hermits (Mickie Most), MGM 13548 | 6 |
| 13 | 14 | 17 | 23 | OVER UNDER SIDEWAYS DOWN  Yardbirds (Samwell-Smith, Napier-Bell), Epic 10035 | 8 |
| 14 | 15 | 30 | 41 | SEE YOU IN SEPTEMBER  Happenings (Bright Tunes Prod.), B. T. Puppy 520 | 6 |
| 15 | 7 | 2 | 1 | HANKY PANKY  Tommy James & the Shondells (Jeff Barry & Ellie Greenwich), Roulette 4686 | 11 |
| 16 | 17 | 23 | 26 | SWEET DREAMS  Tommy McLain (Floyd Soileau & Huey Meaux), MSL 197 | 8 |
| 17 | 12 | 6 | 7 | HUNGRY  Paul Revere & the Raiders (Terry Melcher), Columbia 43678 | 9 |
| 18 ★ | 24 | 40 | 68 | BLOWIN' IN THE WIND  Stevie Wonder (C. Paul), Tamla 54136 | 4 |
| 19 | 57 | 75 | — | MY HEART'S SYMPHONY  Gary Lewis & the Playboys (Snuff Garrett), Liberty 55898 | 3 |
| 20 | 51 | 90 | — | SUNSHINE SUPERMAN  Donovan (Mickey Most), Epic 10045 | 3 |
| 21 | 33 | 57 | 82 | SUMMERTIME  Billy Stewart (Billy Davis), Chess 1966 | 5 |
| 22 ★ | 45 | 64 | 90 | WORKING IN THE COAL MINE  Lee Dorsey (A. Toussaint-M. Sehorn), Amy 958 | 4 |
| 23 | 35 | 48 | 78 | WARM AND TENDER LOVE  Percy Sledge (Marlin Greene & Quin Ivy), Atlantic 2342 | 4 |
| 24 | 39 | 51 | 83 | LADY JANE  Rolling Stones (Andrew Loog Oldham), London 902 | 4 |
| 25 ★ | 43 | 76 | — | LAND OF 1,000 DANCES  Wilson Pickett (Jerry Wexler & Rick Hall), Atlantic 2348 | 3 |
| 26 | 37 | 47 | 62 | THE JOKER WENT WILD  Brian Hyland (Snuff Garrett & Leon Russell), Philips 40377 | 5 |
| 27 | 28 | 33 | 52 | SEARCHING FOR MY LOVE  Bobby Moore & the Rhythm Aces (Rick Hall), Checker 1129 | 8 |
| 28 ★ | 38 | 63 | 93 | BORN A WOMAN  Sandy Posey (Chip Moman), MGM 13501 | 6 |
| 29 | 29 | 32 | 38 | PRETTY FLAMINGO  Manfred Mann (John Burgess), United Artists 50040 | 7 |
| 30 | 19 | 18 | 18 | THE WORK SONG  Herb Alpert & the Tijuana Brass (Herb Alpert), A & M 805 | 7 |
| 31 | 41 | 45 | 55 | DISTANT SHORES  Chad & Jeremy (Larry Marks), Columbia 43682 | 6 |
| 32 | 22 | 25 | 30 | TRAINS AND BOATS AND PLANES  Dionne Warwick (Bacharach-David), Scepter 12153 | 7 |
| 33 ★ | 51 | 61 | — | GUANTANAMERA  Sandpipers (Tommy LiPuma), A&M 806 | 3 |
| 34 | 25 | 24 | 15 | AIN'T TOO PROUD TO BEG  Temptations (N. Whitfield), Gordy 7054 | 12 |
| 35 | 46 | 56 | 80 | MAKE ME BELONG TO YOU  Barbara Lewis (Jerry Wexler & Ollie McLaughlin), Atlantic 2346 | 4 |
| 36 | 23 | 13 | 8 | RED RUBBER BALL  Cyrkle (John Simon), Columbia 43589 | 13 |
| 37 | 18 | 12 | 6 | PAPERBACK WRITER  Beatles (George Martin), Capitol 5651 | 10 |
| 38 | 32 | 29 | 11 | ALONG COMES MARY  Association (C. Boettcher), Valiant 741 | 11 |
| 39 | 42 | 53 | 61 | TAR AND CEMENT  Verdelle Smith (Vance-Prokriss Prod.), Capitol 5632 | 6 |
| 40 | 34 | 34 | 37 | BILLY AND SUE  B. J. Thomas, Hickory 1395 | 9 |
| 41 | 52 | 62 | — | ALFIE  Cher (Sonny Bono), Imperial 66192 | 3 |
| 42 | 26 | 15 | 5 | YOU DON'T HAVE TO SAY YOU LOVE ME  Dusty Springfield (Johnny Franz), Philips 40371 | 13 |
| 43 | 55 | 65 | 89 | WADE IN THE WATER  Ramsey Lewis (Esmond Edwards), Cadet 5541 | 4 |
| 44 | 27 | 22 | 12 | STRANGERS IN THE NIGHT  Frank Sinatra (Jimmy Bowen), Reprise 0470 | 15 |
| 45 | 56 | 66 | 100 | A MILLION AND ONE  Dean Martin (Jimmy Bowen), Reprise 0500 | 4 |
| 46 | 47 | 50 | 64 | MISTY  Groove Holmes (Cal Lampley), Prestige 401 | 8 |
| 47 ★ | 58 | 73 | 98 | BUS STOP  Hollies (Ron Richardson), Imperial 66186 | 4 |
| 48 | 48 | 59 | 79 | THE TIP OF MY FINGER  Eddy Arnold (Chet Atkins), RCA Victor 8869 | 4 |
| 49 | 53 | 54 | 4 | ALMOST PERSUADED  David Houston (Billy Sherrill), Epic 10025 | 5 |
| 50 | 50 | 55 | 75 | YOU YOU YOU  Mel Carter (Nick De Caro), Imperial 66183 | 4 |
| 51 | 62 | 84 | — | WOULDN'T IT BE NICE  Beach Boys (Brian Wilson), Capitol 5706 | 3 |
| 52 | 20 | 20 | 24 | I WANT YOU  Bob Dylan (Bob Johnston), Columbia 43683 | 7 |
| 53 | 59 | 74 | — | (You Make Me Feel) SO GOOD  McCoys (Feldman, Goldstein, Gottehrer), Bang 527 | 3 |
| 54 | 64 | 79 | — | MONEY WON'T CHANGE YOU  James Brown & the Famous Flames (James Brown Prod.), King 6048 | 3 |
| 55 | 21 | 19 | 19 | LOVE LETTERS  Elvis Presley, RCA Victor 8870 | 7 |
| 56 | 30 | 28 | 29 | WHERE WERE YOU WHEN I NEEDED YOU  Grass Roots (Sloan & Barri), Dunhill 4029 | 9 |
| 57 | 70 | — | — | RESPECTABLE  Outsiders (Tom King), Capitol 5701 | 2 |
| 58 | 71 | — | — | SAY I AM (What I Am)  Tommy James and the Shondells (Bob Mack), Roulette 4695 | 2 |
| 59 | 72 | — | — | GO AHEAD AND CRY  Righteous Brothers (Bill Medley), Verve 10430 | 2 |
| 60 | 75 | — | — | WITH A GIRL LIKE YOU  Troggs (Page One-York-Pala), Atco 6415-Fontana 1552 | 2 |
| 61 | 76 | 88 | — | WIPE OUT  Surfaris, Dot 144 | 19 |
| 62 | 65 | 70 | 73 | I GUESS I'LL ALWAYS LOVE YOU  Isley Brothers (Holland & Dozier), Tamla 54135 | 5 |
| 63 | 66 | 81 | 99 | OPEN THE DOOR TO YOUR HEART  Darrell Banks, Revilot 201 | 4 |
| 64 | 74 | 80 | 92 | SUGAR AND SPICE  Cryan Shames (MG Prod.), Destination 624 | 4 |
| 65 | 63 | 52 | 69 | LOOK AT ME GIRL  Bobby Vee (Dallas Smith), Liberty 55877 | 4 |
| 66 | — | — | — | YOU CAN'T HURRY LOVE  Supremes (Holland & Dozier), Motown 1097 | 1 |
| 67 | 68 | 77 | 88 | I BELIEVE I'M GONNA MAKE IT  Joe Tex (Buddy Killen), Dial 4033 | 4 |
| 68 ★ | 90 | — | — | SUNNY AFTERNOON  Kinks (Shel Talmy), Reprise 0497 | 2 |
| 69 | 44 | 44 | 54 | 5 D (Fifth Dimension)  Byrds (Allen Stanton), Columbia 43702 | 5 |
| 70 ★ | 92 | — | — | THE DANGLING CONVERSATION  Simon & Garfunkel (Bob Johnston), Columbia 43728 | 2 |
| 71 | 79 | 89 | — | 7 AND 7 IS  Love (Jac Holzman), Elektra 45605 | 2 |
| 72 | 77 | — | — | TOO SOON TO KNOW  Roy Orbison (Rose & Vanneau), MGM 13549 | 2 |
| 73 | 80 | 86 | — | LONELY SUMMER  Shades of Blue (John Rhys), Impact 1014 | 3 |
| 74 | 86 | — | — | OUT OF THIS WORLD  Chiffons (Bright Tunes), Laurie 3350 | 2 |
| 75 | — | — | — | TURN-DOWN DAY  Cyrkle (John Simon), Columbia 43729 | 1 |
| 76 | 81 | — | — | A MILLION AND ONE  Vic Dana (Bob Reisdorff), Dolton 322 | 2 |
| 77 | 83 | 83 | — | LIVIN' ABOVE YOUR HEAD  Jay & the Americans (Gerry Granaham), United Artists 50046 | 3 |
| 78 | 78 | 82 | — | BRING BACK THE TIME  B. J. Thomas (Huey J. Meaux), Scepter 12154 | 3 |
| 79 | 95 | 97 | — | HOW SWEET IT IS  Jr. Walker & the All-Stars (J. Bristol-H. Fuqua), Soul 35024 | 3 |
| 80 | 88 | 92 | — | I PUT A SPELL ON YOU  Alan Price Set (Alan Price), Parrot 3001 | 4 |
| 81 | — | — | — | GOD ONLY KNOWS  Beach Boys (Brian Wilson), Capitol 5706 | 1 |
| 82 | 82 | 95 | 96 | (We'll Be) UNITED  Intruders, Gamble 201 | 5 |
| 83 | 87 | 91 | — | LET'S CALL IT A DAY GIRL  Razor's Edge (Bob Yorey), POW 101 | 3 |
| 84 | — | — | 99 | SUSPICIONS  Sidekicks, RCA Victor 8864 | 2 |
| 85 | 85 | — | — | PETTICOAT WHITE (Summer Sky Blue)  Bobby Vinton (Bob Morgan), Epic 10048 | 2 |
| 86 | — | — | — | MR. DIEINGLY SAID  Critters (Artie Ripp), Kapp 769 | 1 |
| 87 | 97 | — | — | JUST YESTERDAY  Al Martino (Tom Morgan), Capitol 5702 | 2 |
| 88 | — | — | — | SATISFIED WITH YOU  Dave Clark Five (Dave Clark), Epic 10053 | 1 |
| 89 | 94 | 96 | — | THE PHILLY FREEZE  Alvin Cash & the Registers, Mar-v-Lus 6012 | 3 |
| 90 | — | — | — | THERE WILL NEVER BE ANOTHER YOU  Chris Montez (Tommy Li Puma), A&M 810 | 1 |
| 91 | 91 | — | — | LET ME TELL YOU, BABE  Nat King Cole (Lee Gillette & David Cavanaugh), Capitol 5683 | 2 |
| 92 | 93 | — | — | WORLD OF FANTASY  Five Stair-Steps (C. Mayfield), Windy C 602 | 2 |
| 93 | 89 | 94 | 95 | GEORGIA ROSE  Tony Bennett (Ernie Altschuler), Columbia 43715 | 4 |
| 94 | — | — | — | CAST YOUR FATE TO THE WIND  Shelby Flint, Valiant 743 | 1 |
| 95 | 96 | — | — | YOUR GOOD THING (Is About to End)  Mable John (Prod. By Staff), Stax 192 | 2 |
| 96 | — | — | — | SOMETIMES GOOD GUYS DON'T WEAR WHITE  Standells (Ed Cobb), Tower 257 | 1 |
| 97 | 100 | — | — | THAT'S ENOUGH  Roscoe Robinson (Roscoe Robinson), Wand 1125 | 2 |
| 98 | — | — | — | IN THE BASEMENT  Etta James & Sugar Pie DeSanto (Davis, Smith, Miner), Cadet 5539 | 1 |
| 99 | — | — | — | ASHES TO ASHES  Mindbenders (Jack Baverstock), Fontana 1555 | 1 |
| 100 | — | — | — | BLACK IS BLACK  Los Bravos (Ivor Raymonde), Press 60002 | 1 |

## BUBBLING UNDER THE HOT 100

101. OPEN UP YOUR DOOR ......... Richard & the Young Lions, Philips 40381
102. WHEN YOU WAKE UP ......... Cash McCall, Thomas 307
103. LARA'S THEME FROM "DR. ZHIVAGO" ......... Roger Williams, Kapp 738
104. LOVE ATTACK ......... James Carr, Goldwax 309
105. COME SHARE THE GOOD TIMES WITH ME ......... Julie Monday, Rainbow 500
106. TO SHOW I LOVE YOU ......... Peter & Gordon, Capitol 5684
107. I WANT TO BE WITH YOU ......... Dee Dee Warwick, Mercury 72584
108. CHAPEL IN THE FIELDS ......... Knickerbockers, Challenge 59335
109. YOU'RE GONNA MISS ME ......... Thirteenth Floor Elevators, International Artists 107
110. LOOK AT ME, GIRL ......... Playboys of Edinburg, Columbia 43716
111. LOVE (Oh How Sweet It Is) ......... Jerry Butler, Mercury 72592
112. DIANNE, DIANNE ......... Dynatones, HBR 494
113. ANGELICA ......... Cilla Black, Capitol 5674
114. ALFIE ......... Joe Cobb, Tice 470
115. EL PITO ......... Joe Cuba, Tico 470
116. I'M YOUR HOOCHIE COOCHIE MAN ......... Jimmy Smith, Verve 10426
117. THE KIDS ARE ALRIGHT ......... The Who, Decca 31988
118. WHO-DUN-IT? ......... Monk Higgins, St. Lawrence 1013
119. DEAR MRS. APPLEBEE ......... Flip Cartridge, Parrot 306
120. WHO DO YOU THINK YOU ARE ......... Shindogs, Viva 605
121. DIANNE, DIANNE ......... Ronny & the Daytonas, RCA Victor 8896
122. A CHANGE ON THE WAY ......... Terry Knight & the Pack, Lucky 11229
123. SHE DRIVES ME OUT OF MY MIND ......... Swingin' Medallions, Smash 2033
124. GET AWAY ......... Georgie Fame, Imperial 66189
125. WE CAN MAKE IT ......... Ruby & the Romantics, Kapp 759
126. RUMORS ......... Syndicate of Sou-I, Bell 646
127. AIN'T NOBODY HOME ......... Howard Tate, Verve 10420
128. LITTLE DARLING (I Need You) ......... Marvin Gaye, Tamla 54138
129. CAMPFIRE GIRLS ......... Billy Joe Royal, Columbia 43740
130. BABY ......... Jimmy Holiday, Minit 32002
131. CHERRY, CHERRY ......... Neil Diamond, Bang 528
132. B-A-B-Y ......... Carla Thomas, Stax 195
133. KISSIN' MY LIFE AWAY ......... Mondellos, Warner 72605
134. MIND EXCURSION ......... Trade Winds, Kama Sutra 212
135. MAN LOVES TWO ......... Little Milton, Checker 1149

Compiled from national retail sales and radio station airplay by the Music Popularity Dept. of Record Market Research, Billboard.

# Billboard HOT 100

**For Week Ending August 20, 1966**

★ STAR performer—Sides registering greatest proportionate upward progress this week.

Record Industry Association of America seal of certification as million selling single.

| # | Last Wk | 2 Wks Ago | 3 Wks Ago | TITLE, Artist (Producer), Label & Number | Weeks On Chart |
|---|---|---|---|---|---|
| 1 | 1 | 3 | 7 | SUMMER IN THE CITY — Lovin' Spoonful (Erik Jacobsen), Kama Sutra 211 (Billboard Award) | 6 |
| 2 | 7 | 11 | 14 | SUNNY — Bobby Hebb (Jerry Ross), Philips 40365 | 9 |
| 3 | 2 | 2 | 3 | LIL' RED RIDING HOOD — Sam the Sham & the Pharaohs (Stan Kesler), MGM 13506 | 11 |
| 4 | 4 | 1 | 1 | WILD THING — Troggs (Page One-York, Palla), Atco 6415-Fontana 1548 | 9 |
| 5 | 3 | 5 | 11 | THEY'RE GOING TO TAKE ME AWAY, HA-HAAA! — Napoleon XIV (Jepalana Prod.), Warner Bros. 5831 | 5 |
| 6 | 14 | 15 | 30 | SEE YOU IN SEPTEMBER — Happenings (Bright Tunes Prod.), B.T. Puppy 520 | 7 |
| 7 | 5 | 4 | 4 | THE PIED PIPER — Crispian St. Peters (David Nicolson), Jamie 1320 | 11 |
| 8 | 8 | 9 | 9 | MOTHER'S LITTLE HELPER — Rolling Stones (Andrew Loog Oldham), London 902 | 7 |
| 9 | 11 | 16 | 26 | I COULDN'T LIVE WITHOUT YOUR LOVE — Petula Clark (Tony Hatch), Warner Bros. 5835 | 6 |
| 10 | 20 | 61 | 90 | SUNSHINE SUPERMAN — Donovan (Mickey Most), Epic 10045 | 4 |
| 11 | 18 | 24 | 40 | BLOWIN' IN THE WIND — Stevie Wonder (C. Paul), Tamla 54136 | 5 |
| 12 | 10 | 8 | 8 | SWEET PEA — Tommy Roe, ABC 10762 | 11 |
| 13 | 13 | 14 | 17 | OVER UNDER SIDEWAYS DOWN — Yardbirds (Samwell-Smith, Napier-Bell), Epic 10035 | 9 |
| 14 | 19 | 57 | 75 | MY HEART'S SYMPHONY — Gary Lewis & the Playboys (Snuff Garrett), Liberty 55898 | 4 |
| 15 | 16 | 17 | 23 | SWEET DREAMS — Tommy McLain (Floyd Soileau & Huey Meaux), MSL 197 | 9 |
| 16 | 21 | 33 | 57 | SUMMERTIME — Billy Stewart (Billy Davis), Chess 1966 | 6 |
| 17 | 22 | 45 | 64 | WORKING IN THE COAL MINE — Lee Dorsey (A. Toussaint-M. Sehorn), Amy 958 | 5 |
| 18 | 12 | 13 | 16 | THIS DOOR SWINGS BOTH WAYS — Herman's Hermits (Mickie Most), MGM 13548 | 7 |
| 19 | 9 | 10 | 10 | SOMEWHERE MY LOVE — Ray Conniff & the Singers (Ernie Altschuler), Columbia 43626 | 10 |
| 20 | 25 | 43 | 76 | LAND OF 1,000 DANCES — Wilson Pickett (Jerry Wexler & Rick Hall), Atlantic 2348 | 4 |
| 21 | 26 | 37 | 47 | THE JOKER WENT WILD — Brian Hyland (Snuff Garrett & Leon Russell), Philips 40377 | 6 |
| 22 | 28 | 38 | 63 | BORN A WOMAN — Sandy Posey (Chip Moman), MGM 13501 | 5 |
| 23 | 23 | 35 | 48 | WARM AND TENDER LOVE — Percy Sledge (Marlin Greene & Quin Ivy), Atlantic 2342 | 5 |
| 24 | 6 | 6 | 5 | I SAW HER AGAIN — Mama's & the Papa's (Lou Adler), Dunhill 4031 | 8 |
| 25 | 17 | 12 | 6 | HUNGRY — Paul Revere & the Raiders (Terry Melcher), Columbia 43678 | 10 |
| 26 | 51 | 62 | 84 | WOULDN'T IT BE NICE — Beach Boys (Brian Wilson), Capitol 5706 | 4 |
| 27 | 33 | 51 | 61 | GUANTANAMERA — Sandpipers (Tommy LiPuma), A&M 806 | 4 |
| 28 | 66 | — | — | YOU CAN'T HURRY LOVE — Supremes (Holland & Dozier), Motown 1097 | 2 |
| 29 | 35 | 46 | 56 | MAKE ME BELONG TO YOU — Barbara Lewis (Jerry Wexler & Ollie McLaughlin), Atlantic 2346 | 5 |
| 30 | 31 | 41 | 45 | DISTANT SHORES — Chad & Jeremy (Larry Marks), Columbia 43682 | 7 |
| 31 | 47 | 58 | 73 | BUS STOP — Hollies (Ron Richardson), Imperial 66186 | 5 |
| 32 | 43 | 55 | 65 | WADE IN THE WATER — Ramsey Lewis (Esmond Edwards), Cadet 5541 | 7 |
| 33 | 15 | 7 | 2 | HANKY PANKY — Tommy James & the Shondells (Jeff Barry & Ellie Greenwich), Roulette 4686 | 12 |
| 34 | 57 | 70 | — | RESPECTABLE — Outsiders (Tom King), Capitol 5701 | 3 |
| 35 | 41 | 52 | 62 | ALFIE — Cher (Sonny Bono), Imperial 66192 | 5 |
| 36 | 24 | 39 | 51 | LADY JANE — Rolling Stones (Andrew Loog Oldham), London 902 | 5 |
| 37 | 58 | 71 | — | SAY I AM (What I Am) — Tommy Jones and the Shondells (Bob Mack), Roulette 4695 | 3 |
| 38 | 39 | 42 | 53 | TAR AND CEMENT — Verdelle Smith (Vance-Prokriss Prod.), Capitol 5632 | 7 |
| 39 | 27 | 28 | 33 | SEARCHING FOR MY LOVE — Bobby Moore & the Rhythm Aces (Rick Hall), Checker 1129 | 9 |
| 40 | 29 | 29 | 32 | PRETTY FLAMINGO — Manfred Mann (John Burgess), United Artists 50040 | 8 |
| 41 | 45 | 56 | 66 | A MILLION AND ONE — Dean Martin (Jimmy Bowen), Reprise 0500 | 5 |
| 42 | 34 | 25 | 24 | AIN'T TOO PROUD TO BEG — Temptations (N. Whitfield), Gordy 7054 | 13 |
| 43 | 40 | 34 | 34 | BILLY AND SUE — B.J. Thomas, Hickory 1395 | 10 |
| 44 | 46 | 47 | 50 | MISTY — Groove Holmes (Cal Lampley), Prestige 401 | 9 |
| 45 | 48 | 48 | 59 | THE TIP OF MY FINGERS — Eddy Arnold (Chet Atkins), RCA Victor 8869 | 5 |
| 46 | 49 | 53 | 54 | ALMOST PERSUADED — David Houston (Billy Sherrill), Epic 10025 | 6 |
| 47 | 60 | 75 | — | WITH A GIRL LIKE YOU — Troggs (Page One-York-Pala), Atco 6415-Fontana 1552 | 3 |
| 48 | 59 | 72 | — | GO AHEAD AND CRY — Righteous Brothers (Bill Medley), Verve 10430 | 3 |
| 49 | 50 | 50 | 55 | YOU YOU YOU — Mel Carter (Nick De Caro), Imperial 66183 | 6 |
| 50 | 30 | 19 | 18 | THE WORK SONG — Herb Alpert & the Tijuana Brass (Herb Alpert), A&M 805 | 8 |
| 51 | 61 | 76 | 88 | WIPE OUT — Surfaris, Dot 144 | 20 |
| 52 | — | — | — | YELLOW SUBMARINE — Beatles (Martin), Capitol 5715 | 1 |
| 53 | 54 | 64 | 79 | MONEY WON'T CHANGE YOU — James Brown & the Famous Flames (James Brown Prod), King 6048 | 4 |
| 54 | 64 | 74 | 80 | SUGAR AND SPICE — Cryan Shames (MG Prod.), Destination 624 | 5 |
| 55 | 68 | 90 | — | SUNNY AFTERNOON — Kinks (Shel Talmy), Reprise 0497 | 3 |
| 56 | 53 | 59 | 74 | (You Make Me Feel) SO GOOD — McCoys (Feldman, Goldstein, Gottehrer), Bang 527 | 4 |
| 57 | 70 | 92 | — | THE DANGLING CONVERSATION — Simon & Garfunkel (Bob Johnston), Columbia 43728 | 2 |
| 58 | 75 | — | — | TURN-DOWN DAY — Cyrkle (Jim Simon), Columbia 43729 | 2 |
| 59 | 63 | 66 | 81 | OPEN THE DOOR TO YOUR HEART — Darrell Banks (Revilot Prod.), Revilot 201 | 5 |
| 60 | 79 | 95 | 97 | HOW SWEET IT IS — Jr. Walker & the All-Stars (H. Bristol-H. Fuqua), Soul 35024 | 4 |
| 61 | 62 | 65 | 70 | I GUESS I'LL ALWAYS LOVE YOU — Isley Brothers (Holland & Dozier), Tamla 54135 | 6 |
| 62 | 65 | 63 | 52 | LOOK AT ME GIRL — Bobby Vee (Dallas Smith), Liberty 55877 | 7 |
| 63 | 71 | 79 | 89 | 7 AND 7 IS — Love (Jac Holzman), Elektra 45605 | 4 |
| 64 | 81 | — | — | GOD ONLY KNOWS — Beach Boys (Brian Wilson), Capitol 5706 | 2 |
| 65 | 86 | — | — | MR. DIEINGLY SAD — Critters (Artie Ripp), Kapp 769 | 2 |
| 66 | 92 | 93 | — | WORLD OF FANTASY — Five Stair-Steps (C. Mayfield), Windy C 602 | 3 |
| 67 | 67 | 68 | 77 | I BELIEVE I'M GONNA MAKE IT — Joe Tex (Buddy Killen), Dial 4033 | 5 |
| 68 | 72 | 77 | — | TOO SOON TO KNOW — Roy Orbison (Rose & Venneau), MGM 13549 | 3 |
| 69 | 88 | — | — | SATISFIED WITH YOU — Dave Clark Five (Dave Clark), Epic 10053 | 2 |
| 70 | 74 | 86 | — | OUT OF THIS WORLD — Chiffons (Bright Tunes), Laurie 3350 | 3 |
| 71 | 76 | 81 | — | A MILLION AND ONE — Vic Dana (Bob Reisdorff), Dolton 322 | 3 |
| 72 | 73 | 80 | 86 | LONELY SUMMER — Shades of Blue (John Rhys), Impact 1014 | 4 |
| 73 | 89 | 94 | 96 | THE PHILLY FREEZE — Alvin Cash & the Registers, Mar-v-Lus 6012 | 4 |
| 74 | 90 | — | — | THERE WILL NEVER BE ANOTHER YOU — Chris Montez (Tommy Li Puma), A&M 810 | 2 |
| 75 | 78 | 78 | 82 | BRING BACK THE TIME — B.J. Thomas (Huey J. Meaux), Scepter 12154 | 4 |
| 76 | 77 | 83 | 83 | LIVIN' ABOVE YOUR HEAD — Jay & the Americans (Gerry Granaham), United Artists 50046 | 4 |
| 77 | 84 | 99 | — | SUSPICIONS — Sidekicks, RCA Victor 8864 | 3 |
| 78 | 82 | 82 | 95 | (We'll Be) UNITED — Intruders, Gamble 201 | 6 |
| 79 | 94 | — | — | CAST YOUR FATE TO THE WIND — Shelby Flint, Valiant 743 | 2 |
| 80 | — | — | — | BEAUTY IS ONLY SKIN DEEP — Temptations (Norman Whitfield), Gordy 7055 | 1 |
| 81 | 85 | 85 | — | PETTICOAT WHITE (Summer Sky Blue) — Bobby Vinton (Bob Morgan), Epic 10048 | 3 |
| 82 | 100 | — | — | BLACK IS BLACK — Los Bravos (Ivor Raymondo), Press 66002 | 2 |
| 83 | 83 | 87 | 91 | LET'S CALL IT A DAY GIRL — Razor's Edge (Bob Yorey), POW 101 | 4 |
| 84 | 87 | 97 | — | JUST YESTERDAY — Al Martino (Tom Morgan), Capitol 5702 | 3 |
| 85 | 97 | 100 | — | THAT'S ENOUGH — Roscoe Robinson (Roscoe Robinson), Wand 1125 | 3 |
| 86 | 96 | — | — | SOMETIMES GOOD GUYS DON'T WEAR WHITE — Standells (Ed Cobb), Tower 257 | 2 |
| 87 | — | — | — | WHAT BECOMES OF THE BROKEN HEARTED — Jimmy Ruffin (William Stevenson), Soul 35022 | 1 |
| 88 | — | — | — | CHERRY, CHERRY — Neil Diamond (Jeff Barry & Ellie Greenwich), Bang 528 | 1 |
| 89 | — | — | — | B-A-B-Y — Carla Thomas (Staff), Stax 195 | 1 |
| 90 | — | — | — | LITTLE DARLING (I Need You) — Marvin Gaye, (Holland & Dozier), Tamla 54138 | 1 |
| 91 | 99 | — | — | ASHES TO ASHES — Mindbenders (Jack Baverstock), Fontana 1555 | 2 |
| 92 | 91 | 91 | — | LET ME TELL YOU, BABE — Nat King Cole (Lee Gillette & David Cavanaugh), Capitol 5683 | 3 |
| 93 | — | — | — | AIN'T NOBODY HOME — Howard Tate (Jerry Ragovoy), Verve 10420 | 1 |
| 94 | — | — | — | DEAR MRS. APPLEBEE — Flip Cartridge (Hugo & Luigi), Parrot 306 | 1 |
| 95 | — | — | — | YOU'RE GONNA MISS ME — Thirteenth Floor Elevators (Gorbyn Prod.), International Artists 107 | 1 |
| 96 | — | — | — | SHE DRIVES ME OUT OF MY MIND — Swingin' Medallions (Karric Prod.), Smash 2050 | 1 |
| 97 | 98 | — | — | IN THE BASEMENT — Etta James & Sugar Pie DeSanto (Davis, Smith & Miner), Cadet 5539 | 2 |
| 98 | — | — | — | COME SHARE THE GOOD TIMES WITH ME — Julie Monday (Joey Brooks), Rainbow 500 | 1 |
| 99 | — | — | — | GET AWAY — Georgie Fame (Denny Cordell), Imperial 66189 | 1 |
| 100 | — | — | — | RUMORS — Syndicate of Sound (Garrie Thompson), Bell 646 | 1 |

## BUBBLING UNDER THE HOT 100

101. ELEANOR RIGBY .......... Beatles, Capitol 5715
102. WHEN YOU WAKE UP .......... Cash McCall, Thomas 307
103. TO SHOW I LOVE YOU .......... Peter & Gordon, Capitol 5684
104. I WANT TO BE WITH YOU .......... Dee Dee Warwick, Mercury 72584
105. OPEN UP YOUR DOOR .......... Richard & the Young Lions, Philips 40389
106. CHAPEL IN THE FIELDS .......... Knickerbockers, Challenge 59325
107. THE KIDS ARE ALRIGHT .......... The Who, Decca 31988
108. LOOK AT ME, GIRL .......... Playboys of Edinburg, Columbia 43716
109. FIFE PIPER .......... Dynatones, HBR 494
110. ALFIE .......... Cilla Black, Capitol 5674
111. ANGELICA .......... Barry Mann, Capitol 5695
112. YOUR GOOD THING (Is About to End) .......... Mabel John, Stax 192
113. I PUT A SPELL ON YOU .......... Alan Price Set, Parrot 3001
114. DIANNE .......... Ronny & the Daytonas, RCA Victor 8896
115. A CHANGE ON THE WAY .......... Terry Knight & the Pack, Lucky 11 329
116. WHO DO YOU THINK YOU ARE .......... Shindogs, Viva 601
117. WHO-DUN-IT? .......... Monk Higgins, St. Lawrence 1013
118. CAMPFIRE GIRLS .......... Billy Joe Royal, Columbia 43740
119. GEORGIA ROSE .......... Tony Bennett, Columbia 43715
120. WE CAN HOLD ON .......... Ruby & the Romantics, Kapp 759
121. WE CAN'T GO ON THIS WAY .......... Teddy and the Pandas, Musicor 1190
122. BLUE SIDE OF LONESOME .......... Jim Reeves, RCA Victor 8902
123. KISSIN' MY LIFE AWAY .......... Shondells, Mercury 77605
124. COME ON SUNSHINE .......... Gil & Johnny, World-Pacific 77823
125. YOU BETTER TAKE IT EASY BABY .......... Anthony & the Imperials, Veep 1233
126. EL PITO .......... Joe Cuba, Tico 475
127. BABY, I LOVE YOU .......... Jimmy Holliday, Minit 32002
128. BORN FREE .......... Roger Williams, Kapp 767
129. MIND EXCURSION .......... Trade Winds, Kama Sutra 212
130. NOWADAYS CLANCY CAN'T EVEN SING .......... Buffalo Springfield, Atco 6428
131. I'M YOUR HOOCHIE COOCHE MAN .......... Jimmy Smith, Verve 10426
132. LOVE (Oh How Sweet It Is) .......... Jerry Butler, Mercury 72597
133. MAN LOVES TWO .......... Little Milton, Checker 1149
134. JUST LIKE A WOMAN .......... Manfred Mann, Mercury 72607
135. MELODY FOR AN UNKNOWN GIRL .......... Unknowns, Parrot 307

Compiled from national retail sales and radio station airplay by the Music Popularity Dept. of Record Market Research, Billboard.

# Billboard HOT 100

**For Week Ending August 27, 1966**

★ STAR performer—Sides registering greatest proportionate upward progress this week.

Record Industry Association of America seal of certification as million selling single.

| This Week | 1 Wk. Ago | 2 Wks. Ago | 3 Wks. Ago | TITLE — Artist (Producer), Label & Number | Weeks On Chart |
|---|---|---|---|---|---|
| 1 | 1 | 1 | 3 | SUMMER IN THE CITY — Lovin' Spoonful (Erik Jacobsen), Kama Sutra 211 | 7 |
| 2 | 2 | 7 | 11 | SUNNY — Bobby Hebb (Jerry Ross), Philips 40365 | 10 |
| 3 | 6 | 14 | 15 | SEE YOU IN SEPTEMBER — Happenings (Bright Tunes Prod.), B. T. Puppy 520 | 8 |
| 4 | 3 | 2 | 2 | LIL' RED RIDING HOOD — Sam the Sham & the Pharaohs (Stan Kesler), MGM 13506 | 12 |
| 5 | 10 | 20 | 61 | SUNSHINE SUPERMAN — Donovan (Mickey Most), Epic 10045 | 5 |
| 6 | 4 | 4 | 1 | WILD THING — Troggs (Page One-York-Palla), Atco 6415-Fontana 1548 | 10 |
| 7 | 28 | 66 | — | YOU CAN'T HURRY LOVE — Supremes (Holland & Dozier), Motown 1097 | 3 |
| 8 | 52 | — | — | YELLOW SUBMARINE — Beatles (Martin), Capitol 5715 | 2 |
| 9 | 9 | 11 | 16 | I COULDN'T LIVE WITHOUT YOUR LOVE — Petula Clark (Tony Hatch), Warner Bros. 5835 | 7 |
| 10 | 16 | 21 | 33 | SUMMERTIME — Billy Stewart (Billy Davis), Chess 1966 | 7 |
| 11 | 11 | 18 | 24 | BLOWIN' IN THE WIND — Stevie Wonder (C. Paul), Tamla 54136 | 6 |
| 12 | 17 | 22 | 45 | WORKING IN THE COAL MINE — Lee Dorsey (A. Toussaint-M. Sehorn), Amy 958 | 6 |
| 13 | 8 | 8 | 9 | MOTHER'S LITTLE HELPER — Rolling Stones (Andrew Loog Oldham), London 902 | 8 |
| 14 | 14 | 19 | 57 | MY HEART'S SYMPHONY — Gary Lewis & the Playboys (Snuff Barrett), Liberty 55898 | 5 |
| 15 | 20 | 25 | 43 | LAND OF 1,000 DANCES — Wilson Pickett (Jerry Wexler & Rick Hall), Atlantic 2348 | 6 |
| 16 | 26 | 51 | 62 | WOULDN'T IT BE NICE — Beach Boys (Brian Wilson), Capitol 5706 | 5 |
| 17 | 15 | 16 | 17 | SWEET DREAMS — Tommy McLain (Floyd Soileau & Huey Meaux), MSL 197 | 10 |
| 18 | 23 | 23 | 35 | WARM AND TENDER LOVE — Percy Sledge (Marlin Greene & Quin Ivy), Atlantic 2342 | 6 |
| 19 | 12 | 10 | 8 | SWEET PEA — Tommy Roe, ABC 10762 | 12 |
| 20 | 22 | 28 | 38 | BORN A WOMAN — Sandy Posey (Chip Moman), MGM 13501 | 6 |
| 21 | 21 | 26 | 37 | THE JOKER WENT WILD — Brian Hyland (Snuff Garrett & Leon Russell), Philips 40377 | 7 |
| 22 | 27 | 33 | 51 | GUANTANAMERA — Sandpipers (Tommy LiPuma), A&M 806 | 5 |
| 23 | 31 | 47 | 58 | BUS STOP — Hollies (Ron Richardson), Imperial 66186 | 6 |
| 24 | 19 | 9 | 10 | SOMEWHERE MY LOVE — Ray Conniff & the Singers (Ernie Altschuler), Columbia 43626 | 11 |
| 25 | 13 | 13 | 14 | OVER UNDER SIDEWAYS DOWN — Yardbirds (Samwell-Smith, Napier-Bell), Epic 10035 | 10 |
| 26 | 37 | 58 | 71 | SAY I AM (What I Am) — Tommy Jones and the Shondells (Bob Mack), Roulette 4695 | 4 |
| 27 | 32 | 43 | 55 | WADE IN THE WATER — Ramsey Lewis (Esmond Edwards), Cadet 5541 | 8 |
| 28 | 29 | 35 | 46 | MAKE ME BELONG TO YOU — Barbara Lewis (Jerry Wexler & Ollie McLaughlin), Atlantic 2346 | 6 |
| 29 | 34 | 57 | 70 | RESPECTABLE — Outsiders (Tom King), Capitol 5701 | 4 |
| 30 | 7 | 5 | 4 | THE PIED PIPER — Crispian St. Peters (David Nicolson), Jamie 1320 | 12 |
| 31 | 58 | 75 | — | TURN-DOWN DAY — Cyrkle (John Simon), Columbia 43729 | 3 |
| 32 | 35 | 41 | 52 | ALFIE — Cher (Sonny Bono), Imperial 66192 | 5 |
| 33 | 24 | 6 | 6 | I SAW HER AGAIN — Mama's & the Papa's (Lou Adler), Dunhill 4031 | 9 |
| 34 | 57 | 70 | 92 | THE DANGLING CONVERSATION — Simon & Garfunkel (Bob Johnston), Columbia 43728 | 4 |
| 35 | 55 | 68 | 90 | SUNNY AFTERNOON — Kinks (Shel Talmy), Reprise 0497 | 4 |
| 36 | 36 | 24 | 39 | LADY JANE — Rolling Stones (Andrew Loog Oldham), London 902 | 6 |
| 37 | 5 | 3 | 5 | THEY'RE GOING TO TAKE ME AWAY, HA-HAAA! — Napoleon XIV (Jepalana Prod.), Warner Bros. 5831 | 6 |
| 38 | 48 | 59 | 72 | GO AHEAD AND CRY — Righteous Brothers (Bill Medley), Verve 10430 | 4 |
| 39 | 51 | 61 | 76 | WIPE OUT — Surfaris, Dot 144 | 21 |
| 40 | 46 | 49 | 53 | ALMOST PERSUADED — David Houston (Billy Sherrill), Epic 10025 | 7 |
| 41 | 41 | 45 | 56 | A MILLION AND ONE — Dean Martin (Jimmy Bowen), Reprise 0500 | 6 |
| 42 | 47 | 60 | 75 | WITH A GIRL LIKE YOU — Troggs (Page One-York-Pala), Atco 6415-Fontana 1552 | 4 |
| 43 | 45 | 48 | 48 | THE TIP OF MY FINGERS — Eddy Arnold (Chet Atkins), RCA Victor 8869 | 6 |
| 44 | 39 | 27 | 28 | SEARCHING FOR MY LOVE — Bobby Moore & the Rhythm Aces (Rick Hall), Checker 1129 | 10 |
| 45 | 25 | 17 | 12 | HUNGRY — Paul Revere and the Raiders (Terry Melcher), Columbia 43678 | 11 |
| 46 | 18 | 12 | 13 | THIS DOOR SWINGS BOTH WAYS — Herman's Hermits (Mickie Most), MGM 13548 | 8 |
| 47 | 60 | 79 | 95 | HOW SWEET IT IS — Jr. Walker & the All-Stars (J. Bristol-H. Fuqua), Soul 35024 | 3 |
| 48 | 44 | 46 | 47 | MISTY — Groove Holmes (Cal Lampley), Prestige 401 | 10 |
| 49 | 30 | 31 | 41 | DISTANT SHORES — Chad & Jeremy (Larry Marks), Columbia 43682 | 8 |
| 50 | 43 | 40 | 34 | BILLY AND SUE — B. J. Thomas, Hickory 1395 | 11 |
| 51 | 64 | 81 | — | GOD ONLY KNOWS — Beach Boys (Brian Wilson), Capitol 5706 | 3 |
| 52 | 54 | 64 | 74 | SUGAR AND SPICE — Cryan Shames (MG Prod.), Destination 624 | 6 |
| 53 | 63 | 71 | 79 | 7 AND 7 IS — Love (Jac Holzman), Elektra 45605 | 5 |
| 54 | 65 | 86 | — | MR. DIEINGLY SAD — Critters (Artie Ripp), Kapp 769 | 3 |
| 55 | 69 | 88 | — | SATISFIED WITH YOU — Dave Clark Five (Dave Clark), Epic 10053 | 3 |
| 56 | 38 | 39 | 42 | TAR AND CEMENT — Verdelle Smith (Vance-Prokriss Prod.), Capitol 5632 | 7 |
| 57 | 53 | 54 | 64 | MONEY WON'T CHANGE YOU — James Brown & the Famous Flames (James Brown Prod), King 6048 | 5 |
| 58 | 59 | 63 | 66 | OPEN THE DOOR TO YOUR HEART — Darrell Banks, Revilot 201 | 6 |
| 59 | 74 | 90 | — | THERE WILL NEVER BE ANOTHER YOU — Chris Montez (Tommy Li Puma), A&M 810 | 3 |
| 60 | 49 | 50 | 50 | YOU YOU YOU — Mel Carter (Nick De Caro), Imperial 66183 | 7 |
| 61 | 66 | 92 | 93 | WORLD OF FANTASY — Five Stair-Steps (C. Mayfield), Windy C 602 | 4 |
| 62 | 80 | — | — | BEAUTY IS ONLY SKIN DEEP — Temptations (Norman Whitfield), Gordy 7055 | 2 |
| 63 | 82 | 100 | — | BLACK IS BLACK — Los Bravos (Ivor Raymonde), Press 66002 | 3 |
| 64 | 73 | 89 | 94 | THE PHILLY FREEZE — Alvin Cash & the Registers, Mar-v-Lus 6012 | 5 |
| 65 | — | — | — | ELEANOR RIGBY — Beatles (George Martin), Capitol 5715 | 1 |
| 66 | — | — | — | CHERISH — Association (C. Boettcher), Valiant 747 | 1 |
| 67 | 70 | 74 | 86 | OUT OF THIS WORLD — Chiffons (Bright Tunes), Laurie 3350 | 4 |
| 68 | 86 | 96 | — | SOMETIMES GOOD GUYS DON'T WEAR WHITE — Standells (Ed Cobb), Tower 257 | 3 |
| 69 | 87 | — | — | WHAT BECOMES OF THE BROKEN HEARTED — Jimmy Ruffin (William Stevenson), Soul 35022 | 2 |
| 70 | 68 | 72 | 77 | TOO SOON TO KNOW — Roy Orbison (Rose & Venneau), MGM 13549 | 4 |
| 71 | 77 | 84 | 99 | SUSPICIONS — Sidekicks, RCA Victor 8864 | 4 |
| 72 | 88 | — | — | CHERRY, CHERRY — Neil Diamond (Jeff Barry & Ellie Greenwich), Bang 528 | 2 |
| 73 | 90 | — | — | LITTLE DARLING (I Need You) — Marvin Gaye (Holland & Dozier), Tamla 54138 | 2 |
| 74 | 79 | 94 | — | CAST YOUR FATE TO THE WIND — Barry Devrazon, Valiant 747 | 3 |
| 75 | 91 | 99 | — | ASHES TO ASHES — Mindbenders (Jack Baverstock), Fontana 1555 | 3 |
| 76 | 76 | 77 | 83 | LIVIN' ABOVE YOUR HEAD — Jay & the Americans (Gerry Granaham), United Artists 50046 | 5 |
| 77 | 84 | 87 | 97 | JUST YESTERDAY — Al Martino (Tom Morgan), Capitol 5702 | 4 |
| 78 | 61 | 62 | 65 | I GUESS I'LL ALWAYS LOVE YOU — Isley Brothers (Holland & Dozier), Tamla 54135 | 7 |
| 79 | 85 | 97 | 100 | THAT'S ENOUGH — Roscoe Robinson (Roscoe Robinson), Wand 1125 | 4 |
| 80 | 62 | 65 | 63 | LOOK AT ME GIRL — Bobby Vee (Dallas Smith), Liberty 55877 | 8 |
| 81 | 99 | — | — | GET AWAY — Georgie Fame (Denny Cordell), Imperial 66189 | 2 |
| 82 | 93 | 83 | 87 | LET'S CALL IT A DAY GIRL — Razor's Edge (Bob Yorey), POW 101 | 5 |
| 83 | 89 | — | — | B-A-B-Y — Carla Thomas (Staff), Stax 195 | 2 |
| 84 | 95 | — | — | YOU'RE GONNA MISS ME — Thirteenth Floor Elevators (Gorbyn Prod.), International Artists 107 | 2 |
| 85 | 72 | 73 | 80 | LONELY SUMMER — Shades of Blue (John Rhys), Impact 1014 | 5 |
| 86 | — | — | — | IN THE ARMS OF LOVE — Andy Williams (Robert Mersey), Columbia 43737 | 1 |
| 87 | — | — | — | I GOT TO HANDLE IT — Capitols (Ollie McLaughlin), Karen 1525 | 1 |
| 88 | — | — | — | BLUE SIDE OF LONESOME — Jim Reeves (Chet Atkins), RCA Victor 8902 | 1 |
| 89 | — | — | — | SUMMER SAMBA — Walter Wanderley (Creed Taylor), Verve 10421 | 1 |
| 90 | 92 | 91 | 91 | LET ME TELL YOU, BABE — Nat King Cole (Lee Gillette & David Cavanaugh), Capitol 5683 | 4 |
| 91 | 94 | — | — | DEAR MRS. APPLEBEE — Flip Cartridge (Hugo & Luigi), Parrot 306 | 2 |
| 92 | 93 | — | — | AIN'T NOBODY HOME — Howard Tate (Jerry Ragovoy), Verve 10420 | 2 |
| 93 | 96 | — | — | SHE DRIVES ME OUT OF MY MIND — Swingin' Medallions (Karric Prod.), Smash 2050 | 2 |
| 94 | — | — | — | I'M YOUR HOOCHIE COOCHE MAN — Jimmy Smith (Creed Taylor), Verve 10426 | 1 |
| 95 | — | — | — | I WANT TO BE WITH YOU — Dee Dee Warwick, Mercury 72584 | 1 |
| 96 | 98 | — | — | COME SHARE THE GOOD TIMES WITH ME — Julie Monday (Joey Brooks), Rainbow 500 | 2 |
| 97 | 100 | — | — | RUMORS — Syndicate of Sound (Garrie Thompson), Bell 646 | 2 |
| 98 | — | — | — | ALFIE — Cilla Black (George Martin), Capitol 5674 | 1 |
| 99 | — | — | — | BORN FREE — Roger Williams (Hy Grill), Kapp 767 | 1 |
| 100 | — | — | — | SAFE AND SOUND — Fontella Bass (Davis & Sain), Checker 1147 | 1 |

## BUBBLING UNDER THE HOT 100

101. I CHOSE TO SING THE BLUES — Ray Charles, ABC 10840
102. FUNCTION AT THE JUNCTION — Shorty Long, Soul 35021
103. OPEN UP YOUR DOOR — Richard & the Young Lions, Philips 40381
104. PETTICOAT WHITE (Summer Sky Blue) — Bobby Vinton, Epic 10048
105. CAN'T GO ON TH'S WAY — Teddy & the Pandas, Musicor 1190
106. THE KIDS ARE ALRIGHT — The Who, Decca 31988
107. TO SHOW I LOVE YOU — Peter & Gordon, Capitol 5684
108. DIANNE, DIANNE — Ronny & the Daytonas, RCA Victor 8896
109. FIFE PIPER — Dynatones, HBR 494
110. WHO DO YOU THINK YOU ARE — Shindogs, Viva 601
111. CAMPFIRE GIRLS — Billy Joe Royal, Columbia 43740
112. 96 TEARS — (Question Mark) and the Mysterians, Cameo 423
113. LOOK AT ME GIRL — Playboys of Edinburg, Columbia 43716
114. A CHANGE ON THE WAY — Terry Knight & the Pack, Lucky 11 229
115. BABY, I LOVE YOU — Jimmy Holiday, Minit 32002
116. MY SWEET POTATO — Booker T. & the M.G.'s, Stax 196
117. COME ON, SUNSHINE — Gil & Johnny, World-Pacific 77833
118. OPEN THE DOOR — Trade Winds, Kama Sutra 212
119. MIND EXCURSION — Tradewinds, Kama Sutra 212
119. IN THE BASEMENT — Etta James & Sugar Pie DeSanto, Cadet Sutra 5539
120. BRING BACK THE TIME — B. J. Thomas, Scepter 12154
121. KISSIN' MY LIFE AWAY — Hondells, Mercury 72605
122. WALK AWAY, RENEE — The Left Banke, Smash 2041
123. JUST LIKE A WOMAN — Manfred Mann, Mercury 72607
124. NOWADAYS CLANCY CAN'T EVEN SING — Buffalo Springfield, Atco 6428
125. KEEP LOOKING — Solomon Burke, Atlantic 2349
126. PSYCHOTIC REACTION — Count Five, Double Shot 104
127. ANGELICA — Barry Mann, Capitol 5695
128. MELODY FOR AN UNKNOWN GIRL — Parrot 307
129. DEEP INSIDE — Jagged Edge, RCA Victor 8880
130. SHE AIN'T LOVIN' YOU — Distant Cousins, Date 1514
131. BABY TOYS — DynoVoice 222
132. THE BEAT — Major Lance, Ok-h 7755
133. THE BEST OF LUCK TO YOU — Earl Gains, HBR 481
134. MAN LOVES TWO — Little Milton, Checker 1149
135. BATMAN TO THE RESCUE — LaVern Baker, Brunswick 55297

Compiled from national retail sales and radio station airplay by the Music Popularity Dept. of Record Market Research, Billboard.

For Week Ending September 3, 1966

# Billboard HOT 100

★ STAR performer—Sides registering greatest proportionate upward progress this week.

Record Industry Association of America seal of certification as million selling single.

| This Week | 1 Wk. Ago | 2 Wks. Ago | 3 Wks. Ago | TITLE Artist (Producer), Label & Number | Weeks On Chart |
|---|---|---|---|---|---|
| 1 (Billboard Award) | 5 | 10 | 20 | **SUNSHINE SUPERMAN** Donovan (Mickey Most), Epic 10045 | 6 |
| 2 | 1 | 1 | 1 | **SUMMER IN THE CITY** Lovin' Spoonful (Eric-Jacobsen), Kama Sutra 211 | 8 |
| 3 | 3 | 6 | 14 | **SEE YOU IN SEPTEMBER** Happenings (Bright Tunes Prod.), B. T. Puppy 520 | 9 |
| ★ 4 | 7 | 28 | 66 | **YOU CAN'T HURRY LOVE** Supremes (Holland & Dozier), Motown 1097 | 4 |
| ★ 5 | 8 | 52 | — | **YELLOW SUBMARINE** Beatles (Martin), Capitol 5715 | 3 |
| 6 | 2 | 2 | 7 | **SUNNY** Bobby Hebb (Jerry Ross), Philips 40365 | 11 |
| ★ 7 | 15 | 20 | 25 | **LAND OF 1,000 DANCES** Wilson Pickett (Jerry Wexler & Rick Hall) Atlantic 2348 | 6 |
| ★ 8 | 12 | 17 | 22 | **WORKING IN THE COAL MINE** Lee Dorsey (A. Toussaint-M. Sehorn), Amy 958 | 7 |
| 9 | 11 | 11 | 18 | **BLOWIN' IN THE WIND** Stevie Wonder (C. Paul), Tamla 54136 | 7 |
| 10 | 10 | 16 | 21 | **SUMMERTIME** Billy Stewart (Billy Davis), Chess 1966 | 8 |
| ★ 11 | 16 | 26 | 51 | **WOULDN'T IT BE NICE** Beach Boys (Brian Wilson), Capitol 5706 | 6 |
| 12 | 4 | 3 | 2 | **LIL' RED RIDING HOOD** Sam the Sham & the Pharaohs (Stan Kesler), MGM 13506 | 13 |
| 13 | 14 | 14 | 19 | **MY HEART'S SYMPHONY** Gary Lewis & the Playboys (Snuff Barrett), Liberty 55898 | 6 |
| 14 | 9 | 9 | 11 | **I COULDN'T LIVE WITHOUT YOUR LOVE** Petula Clark (Tony Hatch), Warner Bros. 5835 | 8 |
| ★ 15 | 29 | 34 | 57 | **RESPECTABLE** Outsiders (Tom King), Capitol 5701 | 5 |
| ★ 16 | 22 | 27 | 33 | **GUANTANAMERA** Sandpipers (Tommy LiPuma), A&M 806 | 6 |
| 17 | 18 | 23 | 23 | **WARM AND TENDER LOVE** Percy Sledge (Marlin Greene & Quin Ivy), Atlantic 2342 | 7 |
| ★ 18 | 23 | 31 | 47 | **BUS STOP** Hollies (Ron Richardson), Imperial 66186 | 7 |
| 19 | 20 | 22 | 28 | **BORN A WOMAN** Sandy Posey (Chip Moman), MGM 13501 | 7 |
| 20 | 21 | 21 | 26 | **THE JOKER WENT WILD** Brian Hyland (Snuff Garrett & Leon Russell), Philips 40377 | 8 |
| ★ 21 | 26 | 37 | 58 | **SAY I AM (What I Am)** Tommy James and the Shondells (Bob Mack), Roulette 4695 | 5 |
| ★ 22 | 35 | 55 | 68 | **SUNNY AFTERNOON** Kinks (Shel Talmy), Reprise 0497 | 5 |
| ★ 23 | 31 | 58 | 75 | **TURN-DOWN DAY** Cyrkle (John Simon), Columbia 43729 | 4 |
| 24 | 27 | 32 | 43 | **WADE IN THE WATER** Ramsey Lewis (Esmond Edwards), Cadet 5541 | 9 |
| ★ 25 | 34 | 57 | 70 | **THE DANGLING CONVERSATION** Simon & Garfunkel (Bob Johnston), Columbia 43728 | 5 |
| ★ 26 | 62 | 80 | — | **BEAUTY IS ONLY SKIN DEEP** Temptations (Norman Whitfield), Gordy 7055 | 3 |
| ★ 27 | 66 | — | — | **CHERISH** Association (C. Boettcher), Valiant 747 | 2 |
| ★ 28 | 39 | 51 | 61 | **WIPE OUT** Surfaris, Dot 144 | 22 |
| ★ 29 | 47 | 60 | 79 | **HOW SWEET IT IS** Jr. Walker & the All-Stars (J. Bristol-H. Fuqua), Soul 35024 | 6 |
| ★ 30 | 38 | 48 | 59 | **GO AHEAD AND CRY** Righteous Brothers (Bill Medley), Verve 10430 | 5 |
| 31 | 6 | 4 | 4 | **WILD THING** Troggs (Page One-York Palla), Atco 6415-Fontana 1548 | 11 |
| ★ 32 | 42 | 47 | 60 | **WITH A GIRL LIKE YOU** Troggs (Page One-York-Pala), Atco 6415-Fontana 1552 | 5 |
| 33 | 28 | 29 | 35 | **MAKE ME BELONG TO YOU** Barbara Lewis (Jerry Wexler & Ollie McLaughlin), Atlantic 2346 | 7 |
| 34 | 24 | 19 | 9 | **SOMEWHERE MY LOVE** Ray Conniff & the Singers (Ernie Altschuler), Columbia 43626 | 12 |
| 35 | 19 | 12 | 10 | **SWEET PEA** Tommy Roe, ABC 10762 | 13 |
| 36 | 40 | 46 | 49 | **ALMOST PERSUADED** David Houston (Billy Sherrill), Epic 10025 | 8 |
| 37 | 32 | 35 | 41 | **ALFIE** Cher (Sonny Bono), Imperial 66192 | 6 |
| ★ 38 | 54 | 65 | 86 | **DIEINGLY SAD** Critters (Artie Ripp), Kapp 769 | 4 |
| 39 | 17 | 15 | 16 | **SWEET DREAMS** Tommy McLain (Floyd Soileau & Huey Meaux), MSL 197 | 11 |
| 40 | 13 | 8 | 8 | **MOTHER'S LITTLE HELPER** Rolling Stones (Andrew Loog Oldham), London 902 | 9 |
| ★ 41 | 63 | 82 | 100 | **BLACK IS BLACK** Los Bravos (Ivor Raymonde), Press 66002 | 4 |
| ★ 42 | 53 | 63 | 71 | **7 AND 7 IS** Love (Jac Holzman), Elektra 45605 | 6 |
| ★ 43 | 59 | 74 | 90 | **THERE WILL NEVER BE ANOTHER YOU** Chris Montez (Tommy Li Puma), A&M 810 | 4 |
| 44 | 41 | 41 | 45 | **A MILLION AND ONE** Dean Martin (Jimmy Bowen), Reprise 0500 | 7 |
| 45 | 51 | 64 | 81 | **GOD ONLY KNOWS** Beach Boys (Brian Wilson), Capitol 5706 | 4 |
| 46 | 25 | 13 | 13 | **OVER UNDER SIDEWAYS DOWN** Yardbirds (Samwell-Smith, Napier-Bell), Epic 10035 | 11 |
| ★ 47 | 65 | — | — | **ELEANOR RIGBY** Beatles (George Martin), Capitol 5715 | 2 |
| ★ 48 | 58 | 59 | 63 | **OPEN THE DOOR TO YOUR HEART** Darrell Banks, Revilot 201 | 7 |
| 49 | 52 | 54 | 64 | **SUGAR AND SPICE** Cryan Shames (MG Prod.), Destination 624 | 7 |
| 50 | 55 | 69 | 88 | **SATISFIED WITH YOU** Dave Clark Five (Dave Clark), Epic 10053 | 4 |
| 51 | 43 | 45 | 48 | **THE TIP OF MY FINGERS** Eddy Arnold (Chet Atkins), RCA Victor 8869 | 7 |
| ★ 52 | 69 | 87 | — | **WHAT BECOMES OF THE BROKENHEARTED** Jimmy Ruffin (William Stevenson), Soul 35022 | 3 |
| ★ 53 | 64 | 73 | 89 | **THE PHILLY FREEZE** Alvin Cash & the Registers, Mar-v-Lus 6012 | 6 |
| ★ 54 | 72 | 88 | — | **CHERRY, CHERRY** Neil Diamond (Jeff Barry & Ellie Greenwich), Bang 528 | 3 |
| ★ 55 | 73 | 90 | — | **LITTLE DARLING (I Need You)** Marvin Gaye, (Holland & Dozier), Tamla 54138 | 3 |
| ★ 56 | 75 | 91 | 99 | **ASHES TO ASHES** Mindbenders (Jack Baverstock), Fontana 1555 | 4 |
| 57 | 57 | 53 | 54 | **MONEY WON'T CHANGE YOU** James Brown & the Famous Flames (James Brown Prod), King 6048 | 6 |
| 58 | 48 | 44 | 46 | **MISTY** Groove Holmes (Cal Lampley), Prestige 401 | 11 |
| 59 | 49 | 30 | 31 | **DISTANT SHORES** Chad & Jeremy (Larry Marks), Columbia 43682 | 9 |
| 60 | 61 | 66 | 92 | **WORLD OF FANTASY** Five Stair-Steps (C. Mayfield), Windy C 602 | 5 |
| 61 | 68 | 86 | 96 | **SOMETIMES GOOD GUYS DON'T WEAR WHITE** Standells (Ed Cobb), Tower 257 | 4 |
| 62 | 71 | 77 | 84 | **SUSPICIONS** Sidekicks, RCA Victor 8864 | 5 |
| 63 | 74 | 79 | 94 | **CAST YOUR FATE TO THE WIND** Barry Devorzon, Valient 747 | 4 |
| ★ 64 | 86 | — | — | **IN THE ARMS OF LOVE** Andy Williams (Robert Mersey), Columbia 43737 | 2 |
| ★ 65 | 83 | 89 | — | **B-A-B-Y** Carla Thomas (Staff), Stax 195 | 3 |
| ★ 66 | 97 | 100 | — | **RUMORS** Syndicate of Sound (Garrie Thompson), Bell 646 | 3 |
| ★ 67 | 88 | — | — | **BLUE SIDE OF LONESOME** Jim Reeves (Chet Atkins), RCA Victor 8902 | 2 |
| ★ 68 | 84 | 95 | — | **YOU'RE GONNA MISS ME** Thirteenth Floor Elevators (Gorbyn Prod.), International Artists 107 | 3 |
| 69 | 79 | 85 | 97 | **THAT'S ENOUGH** Roscoe Robinson (Roscoe Robinson), Wand 1125 | 5 |
| 70 | 70 | 68 | 72 | **TOO SOON TO KNOW** Roy Orbison (Rose & Venneau), MGM 13549 | 5 |
| ★ 71 | — | — | — | **I CHOSE TO SING THE BLUES** Ray Charles, (Tangerine Records), ABC 10840 | 1 |
| ★ 72 | — | — | — | **FLAMINGO** Herb Alpert & the Tijuana Brass (Herb Alpert), A&M 813 | 1 |
| 73 | 81 | 99 | — | **GET AWAY** Georgie Fame (Denny Cordell), Imperial 66189 | 3 |
| ★ 74 | — | — | — | **SUMMER WIND** Frank Sinatra (Sonny Burke), Reprise 0509 | 1 |
| ★ 75 | — | — | — | **96 TEARS** (Question Mark) & the Mysterians (Question Marks), Cameo 428 | 1 |
| ★ 76 | 93 | 96 | — | **SHE DRIVES ME OUT OF MY MIND** Swingin' Medallions (Karric Prod.), Smash 2050 | 3 |
| 77 | 82 | 83 | 83 | **LET'S CALL IT A DAY GIRL** Razor's Edge (Bob Yorey), POW 101 | 6 |
| 78 | 87 | — | — | **I GOT TO HANDLE IT** Capitols (Ollie McLaughlin), Karen 1525 | 2 |
| ★ 79 | — | — | — | **I REALLY DON'T WANT TO KNOW** Ronnie Dove (Phil Kahl), Diamond 208 | 1 |
| ★ 80 | 95 | — | — | **I WANT TO BE WITH YOU** Dee Dee Warwick, Mercury 72584 | 2 |
| 81 | 89 | — | — | **SUMMER SAMBA** Walter Wanderley (Creed Taylor), Verve 10421 | 2 |
| ★ 82 | — | — | — | **REACH OUT I'LL BE THERE** Four Tops (Holland & Dozier), Motown 1098 | 1 |
| ★ 83 | — | — | — | **I'VE GOT YOU UNDER MY SKIN** 4 Seasons (Bob Crewe), Philips 40393 | 1 |
| 84 | 92 | 93 | — | **AIN'T NOBODY HOME** Howard Tate (Jerry Ragovoy), Verve 10420 | 3 |
| 85 | 85 | 72 | 73 | **LONELY SUMMER** Shades of Blue (John Rhys), Impact 1014 | 6 |
| 86 | 99 | — | — | **BORN FREE** Roger Williams (Hy Grill), Kapp 767 | 2 |
| ★ 87 | — | — | — | **DIANNE, DIANNE** Ronny & the Daytonas, (Bucky Wilkin), RCA Victor 8896 | 1 |
| ★ 88 | — | — | — | **BABY TOYS** Toys (Randell & Linzer), DynoVoice 222 | 1 |
| ★ 89 | — | — | — | **CAN'T SATISFY** Impressions (Johnny Tate), ABC 10831 | 1 |
| ★ 90 | — | — | — | **MY SWEET POTATO** Booker T. & the M.G.'s, (Prod. by Staff), Stax 196 | 1 |
| 91 | — | — | — | **WHO DO YOU THINK YOU ARE** Shindogs (Leon Russell), Viva 601 | 1 |
| 92 | — | — | — | **THE FIFE PIPER** Dynatones (J. J. Jules), HBR 494 | 1 |
| 93 | — | — | — | **CAMPFIRE GIRLS** Billy Joe Royal (Joe South), Columbia 43740 | 1 |
| 94 | 94 | — | — | **I'M YOUR HOOCHIE COOCHE MAN** Jimmy Smith (Creed Taylor), Verve 10426 | 2 |
| 95 | — | — | — | **IT HURTS ME** Bobby Goldsboro (Jack Gold), United Artists 50056 | 1 |
| 96 | — | — | — | **MIND EXCURSION** Trade Winds (Anders-Poncia), Kama Sutra 212 | 1 |
| 97 | 98 | — | — | **ALFIE** Cilla Black (George Martin), Capitol 5674 | 2 |
| 98 | — | — | — | **BABY I LOVE YOU** Jimmy Holiday (Cal Carter & Hal Pickens), Minit 32002 | 1 |
| 99 | — | — | — | **FIDDLE AROUND** Jan & Dean (Jan Berry), Liberty 5905 | 1 |
| 100 | — | — | — | **DAY TRIPPER** Vontastics (Higins & Gardner), St. Lawrence 1014 | 1 |

## HOT 100—A TO Z—(Publisher-Licensee)

| | |
|---|---|
| Ain't Nobody Home (Rittenhouse, BMI) | 84 |
| Alfie (Black) (Famous, ASCAP) | 97 |
| Alfie (Chere) (Famous, ASCAP) | 37 |
| Almost Persuaded (Gallico, BMI) | 36 |
| Ashes to Ashes (Screen Gems-Columbia, BMI) | 56 |
| B-A-B-Y (East, BMI) | 65 |
| Baby I Love You (Metric, BMI) | 98 |
| Baby Toys (Saturday-My Songs, BMI) | 88 |
| Beauty Is Only Skin Deep (Jobete, BMI) | 26 |
| Black Is Black (Elmwin, BMI) | 41 |
| Blowin' in the Wind (Witmark, ASCAP) | 9 |
| Blue Side of Lonesome (Glad, BMI) | 67 |
| Born a Woman (Painted Desert, BMI) | 19 |
| Born Free (Columbia, BMI) | 86 |
| Bus Stop (Manken, BMI) | 18 |
| Campfire Girls (Lowery, BMI) | 93 |
| Can't Satisfy (Chi-Sound, BMI) | 89 |
| Cast Your Fate to the Wind (Friendship, BMI) | 63 |
| Cherish (Beechwood, BMI) | 27 |
| Cherry, Cherry (Tallyrand, BMI) | 54 |
| Dangling Conversation, The (Charing Cross, BMI) | 25 |
| Day Tripper (Maclen, BMI) | 100 |
| Dianne, Dianne (Buckhorn & Gallico, BMI) | 87 |
| Distant Shores (Chad & Jeremy-Noma, BMI) | 59 |
| Eleanor Rigby (Maclen, BMI) | 47 |
| Fiddle Around (Bourne, ASCAP) | 99 |
| Fife Piper (Jules-Tone, BMI) | 92 |
| Flamingo (Tempo, ASCAP) | 72 |
| Get Away (Noma-Gunnell, BMI) | 73 |
| Go Ahead and Cry (Righteous Brothers, BMI) | 30 |
| God Only Knows (Sea of Tunes, BMI) | 45 |
| Guantanamera (Fall River, BMI) | 16 |
| How Sweet It Is (Jobete, BMI) | 29 |
| I Chose to Sing the Blues (Metric, BMI) | 71 |
| I Couldn't Live Without Your Love (Northern, ASCAP) | 14 |
| I Got to Handle It (McLaughlin-Gomba, BMI) | 78 |
| I Really Don't Want to Know (Hill & Range, BMI) | 79 |
| I Want to Be With You (Moreley, ASCAP) | 80 |
| I'm Your Hoochie Cooche Man (Arc, BMI) | 94 |
| I've Got You Under My Skin (Chappell, ASCAP) | 83 |
| In the Arms of Love (Twin-Chris, ASCAP) | 64 |
| It Hurts Me (Unart, BMI) | 95 |
| Joker Went Wild, The (Rising Sons, BMI) | 20 |
| Land of 1,000 Dances (Tune-Kel-Anatole, BMI) | 7 |
| Let's Call It a Day Girl (Sea Lark, BMI) | 77 |
| Lil' Red Riding Hood (Rose, BMI) | 12 |
| Little Darling (I Need You) (Jobete, BMI) | 55 |
| Lonely Summer (Gamba, BMI) | 85 |
| Make Me Belong to You (Blackwood, BMI) | 33 |
| Million and One, A (Martin) (Silver Star, BMI) | 44 |
| Mind Excursion (Tender Tunes, BMI) | 96 |
| Mr. Dieingly Sad (Tender Tunes-Elmwin, BMI) | 38 |
| Misty (Vernon, ASCAP) | 58 |
| Money Won't Change You (Dynatone, BMI) | 57 |
| Mother's Little Helper (Gideon, BMI) | 40 |
| My Heart's Symphony (Gringol, BMI) | 13 |
| My Sweet Potato (Instrumental, BMI) | 90 |
| 96 Tears (Arguello, BMI) | 75 |
| Open the Door to Your Heart (T.M. & Parmalier, BMI) | 48 |
| Over Under Sideways Down (Feist, ASCAP) | 46 |
| Philly Freeze, The (Vapac, BMI) | 53 |
| Reach Out I'll Be There (Jobete, BMI) | 82 |
| Respectable (Wemar, BMI) | 15 |
| Rumors (Duane-Aim, BMI) | 66 |
| Satisfied With You (Branston, BMI) | 50 |
| Say I Am (What I Am) (Dundee, BMI) | 21 |
| See You in September (Vibar, ASCAP) | 3 |
| 7 and 7 Is (Grass Roots, BMI) | 42 |
| She Drives Me Out of My Mind (Lowery, BMI) | 76 |
| Sometimes Good Guys Don't Wear White (Equinox, BMI) | 61 |
| Somewhere My Love (Robbins, ASCAP) | 34 |
| Sugar and Spice (Duchess, BMI) | 49 |
| Summer in the City (Faithful Virtue, BMI) | 2 |
| Summer Samba (Duchess, BMI) | 81 |
| Summer Wind (Witmark, ASCAP) | 74 |
| Summertime (Gershwin, ASCAP) | 10 |
| Sunny (Portable, BMI) | 6 |
| Sunny Afternoon (Norma, BMI) | 22 |
| Sunshine Superman (Southern, ASCAP) | 1 |
| Suspicions (Ricemill-R & S, BMI) | 62 |
| Sweet Dreams (Acuff-Rose, BMI) | 39 |
| Sweet Pea (Low Twi, BMI) | 35 |
| That's Enough (Kapa, BMI) | 69 |
| There Will Never Be Another You (Morris, ASCAP) | 43 |
| Tip of My Fingers, The (Tree & Champion, BMI) | 51 |
| Too Soon to Know (Acuff-Rose, BMI) | 70 |
| Turndown Day (Northern, ASCAP) | 23 |
| Wade in the Water (Ramsel, BMI) | 24 |
| Warm and Tender Love (Pronto-Bob-Dan-Quinvy, BMI) | 17 |
| What Becomes of the Brokenhearted (Jobete, BMI) | 52 |
| Who Do You Think You Are (Criterion, ASCAP) | 91 |
| Wild Thing (Blackwood, BMI) | 31 |
| Wipe Out (Miraleste-Robin Hood, BMI) | 28 |
| With a Girl Like You (James, BMI) | 32 |
| Working in the Coal Mine (Marsaint, BMI) | 8 |
| World of Fantasy (Camad, BMI) | 60 |
| Wouldn't It Be Nice (Sea of Tunes, BMI) | 11 |
| Yellow Submarine (Maclen, BMI) | 5 |
| You Can't Hurry Love (Jobete, Bobete, BMI) | 4 |
| You're Gonna Miss Me (Acquire, BMI) | 68 |

## BUBBLING UNDER THE HOT 100

| | | |
|---|---|---|
| 101. | LAST TRAIN TO CLARKSVILLE | Monkees, Colgems 1001 |
| 102. | ALL STRUNG OUT | Nino Tempo & April Stevens, White Whale 236 |
| 103. | JUST LIKE A WOMAN | Bob Dylan, Columbia 43792 |
| 104. | WE CAN'T GO ON THIS WAY | Teddy & the Pandas, Musicor 1190 |
| 105. | FUNCTION AT THE JUNCTION | Shorty Long, Soul 35021 |
| 106. | JUST LIKE A WOMAN | Manfred Mann, Mercury 72607 |
| 107. | LET ME TELL YOU, BABE | Nat King Cole, Capitol 5638 |
| 108. | BOA CONSTRICTOR | Johnny Cash, Columbia 43763 |
| 109. | KEEP LOOKING | Solomon Burke, Atlantic 2349 |
| 110. | LAND OF 1,000 DANCES | Cannibal & the Headhunters, Date 1525 |
| 111. | A CHANGE ON THE WAY | Terry Knight & the Pack, Lucky 11229 |
| 112. | COME ON, SUNSHINE | Gil & Johnny, World-Pacific 77833 |
| 113. | STICKY, STICKY | Bobby Harris, Shout 203 |
| 114. | WALK AWAY, RENEE | Left Banke, Smash 2041 |
| 115. | COME SHARE THE GOOD TIMES WITH ME | Julie Monday, Rainbow 500 |
| 116. | SAFE AND SOUND | Fontella Bass, Checker 1147 |
| 117. | I CAN MAKE IT WITH YOU | Pozo-Seco Singers, Columbia 43784 |
| 118. | KISSIN' MY LIFE AWAY | Hondells, Mercury 72605 |
| 119. | MELODY FOR AN UNKNOWN GIRL | Unknowns, Parrot 307 |
| 120. | I CAN MAKE IT WITH YOU | Jackie DeShannon, Imperial 66202 |
| 121. | PSYCHOTIC REACTION | Count Five, Double Shot 104 |
| 122. | A WOMAN OF THE WORLD | Gentrys, MGM 13561 |
| 123. | NOWADAYS CLANCY CAN'T EVEN SING | Buffalo Springfield, Atco 6428 |
| 124. | CRY SOFTLY | Nancy Ames, Epic 10056 |
| 125. | I'M GONNA LOVE YOU ANYWAY | Birdwatchers, Mala 536 |
| 126. | SHE AIN'T LOVING YOU | Distant Cousins, Date 1514 |
| 127. | MAN LOVES TWO | Little Milton, Checker 1149 |
| 128. | THE BEAT | Major Lance, Okeh 7255 |
| 129. | IMPRESSIONS | Jones Boys, Atco 6426 |
| 130. | JUG BAND MUSIC | Mugwumps, Sidewalk 900 |
| 131. | WHO-DUN-IT? | Monk Higgins, St. Lawrence 1013 |
| 132. | GREEN HORNET THEME | Ventures, Dolton 323 |
| 133. | AIN'T GONNA LIE | Keith, Mercury 72596 |
| 134. | OH, LONESOME ME | Bobbi Martin, Coral 62488 |
| 135. | AFTER YOU THERE CAN BE NOTHING | Walter Jackson, Okeh 7256 |

Compiled from national retail sales and radio station airplay by the Music Popularity Dept. of Record Market Research, Billboard.

Billboard — For Week Ending September 10, 1966

# HOT 100

★ STAR performer—Sides registering greatest proportionate upward progress this week.

Record Industry Association of America seal of certification as million selling single.

| THIS WEEK | 1 Wk. Ago | 2 Wks. Ago | 3 Wks. Ago | TITLE — Artist (Producer), Label & Number | Weeks On Chart |
|---|---|---|---|---|---|
| 1 (Billboard Award) | 4 | 7 | 28 | YOU CAN'T HURRY LOVE — Supremes (Holland & Dozier), Motown 1097 | 5 |
| 2 | 1 | 5 | 10 | SUNSHINE SUPERMAN — Donovan (Mickey Most), Epic 10045 | 7 |
| 3 | 5 | 8 | 52 | YELLOW SUBMARINE — Beatles (Martin), Capitol 5715 | 4 |
| 4 | 3 | 3 | 6 | SEE YOU IN SEPTEMBER — Happenings (Bright Tunes Prod.), B. T. Puppy 520 | 10 |
| 5 | 2 | 1 | 1 | SUMMER IN THE CITY — Lovin' Spoonful (Eric-Jacobsen), Kama Sutra 211 | 9 |
| 6 | 7 | 15 | 20 | LAND OF 1,000 DANCES — Wilson Pickett (Jerry Wexler & Rick Hall) Atlantic 2348 | 7 |
| 7 | 6 | 2 | 2 | SUNNY — Bobby Hebb (Jerry Ross), Philips 40365 | 12 |
| 8 | 8 | 12 | 17 | WORKING IN THE COAL MINE — Lee Dorsey (A. Toussaint-M. Sehorn), Amy 958 | 8 |
| ★ 9 | 18 | 23 | 31 | BUS STOP — Hollies (Ron Richardson), Imperial 66186 | 8 |
| ★ 10 | 16 | 22 | 27 | GUANTANAMERA — Sandpipers (Tommy LiPuma), A&M 806 | 7 |
| 11 | 11 | 16 | 26 | WOULDN'T IT BE NICE — Beach Boys (Brian Wilson), Capitol 5706 | 7 |
| 12 | 10 | 10 | 16 | SUMMERTIME — Billy Stewart (Billy Davis), Chess 1966 | 9 |
| ★ 13 | 19 | 20 | 22 | BORN A WOMAN — Sandy Posey (Chip Moman), MGM 13501 | 8 |
| ★ 14 | 27 | 66 | — | CHERISH — Association (C. Boettcher), Valiant 747 | 3 |
| 15 | 15 | 29 | 34 | RESPECTABLE — Outsiders (Tom King), Capitol 5701 | 6 |
| ★ 16 | 26 | 62 | 80 | BEAUTY IS ONLY SKIN DEEP — Temptations (Norman Whitfield), Gordy 7055 | 4 |
| 17 | 9 | 11 | 11 | BLOWIN' IN THE WIND — Stevie Wonder (C. Paul), Tamla 54136 | 8 |
| ★ 18 | 23 | 31 | 58 | TURN-DOWN DAY — Cyrkle (John Simon), Columbia 43729 | 5 |
| ★ 19 | 24 | 27 | 32 | WADE IN THE WATER — Ramsey Lewis (Esmond Edwards), Cadet 5541 | 10 |
| 20 | 22 | 35 | 55 | SUNNY AFTERNOON — Kinks (Shel Talmy), Reprise 0497 | 6 |
| 21 | 21 | 26 | 37 | SAY I AM (What I Am) — Tommy James and the Shondells (Bob Mack), Roulette 4695 | 6 |
| 22 | 17 | 18 | 23 | WARM AND TENDER LOVE — Percy Sledge (Marlin Greene & Quin Ivy), Atlantic 2342 | 8 |
| ★ 23 | 28 | 39 | 51 | WIPE OUT — Surfaris, Dot 144 | 23 |
| ★ 24 | 29 | 47 | 60 | HOW SWEET IT IS — Jr. Walker & the All-Stars (J. Bristol-H. Fuqua), Soul 35024 | 7 |
| 25 | 25 | 34 | 57 | THE DANGLING CONVERSATION — Simon & Garfunkel (Bob Johnston), Columbia 43728 | 6 |
| ★ 26 | 47 | 65 | — | ELEANOR RIGBY — Beatles (George Martin), Capitol 5715 | 3 |
| ★ 27 | 41 | 63 | 82 | BLACK IS BLACK — Los Bravos (Ivor Raymonde), Press 66002 | 5 |
| 28 | 20 | 21 | 21 | THE JOKER WENT WILD — Brian Hyland (Snuff Garrett & Leon Russell), Philips 40377 | 9 |
| 29 | 32 | 42 | 47 | WITH A GIRL LIKE YOU — Troggs (Page One-York-Pala), Atco 6415-Fontana 1552 | 6 |
| 30 | 12 | 4 | 3 | LIL' RED RIDING HOOD — Sam the Sham & the Pharaohs (Stan Kesler), MGM 13506 | 14 (RIAA seal) |
| ★ 31 | 48 | 58 | 59 | OPEN THE DOOR TO YOUR HEART — Darrell Banks, Revilot 201 | 8 |
| 32 | 38 | 54 | 65 | MR. DIEINGLY SAD — Critters (Artie Ripp), Kapp 769 | 5 |
| 33 | 14 | 9 | 9 | I COULDN'T LIVE WITHOUT YOUR LOVE — Petula Clark (Tony Hatch), Warner Bros. 5835 | 9 |
| 34 | 13 | 14 | 14 | MY HEART'S SYMPHONY — Gary Lewis & the Playboys (Snuff Barrett), Liberty 55898 | 7 |
| 35 | 43 | 59 | 74 | THERE WILL NEVER BE ANOTHER YOU — Chris Montez (Tommy LiPuma), A&M 810 | 5 |
| 36 | 36 | 40 | 46 | ALMOST PERSUADED — David Houston (Billy Sherrill), Epic 10025 | 9 |
| ★ 37 | 52 | 69 | 87 | WHAT BECOMES OF THE BROKENHEARTED — Jimmy Ruffin (William Stevenson), Soul 35022 | 4 |
| 38 | 42 | 53 | 63 | 7 AND 7 IS — Love (Jac Holzman), Elektra 45605 | 7 |
| ★ 39 | 54 | 72 | 88 | CHERRY, CHERRY — Neil Diamond (Jeff Barry & Ellie Greenwich), Bang 528 | 4 |
| 40 | 30 | 38 | 48 | GO AHEAD AND CRY — Righteous Brothers (Bill Medley), Verve 10430 | 6 |
| ★ 41 | 83 | — | — | I'VE GOT YOU UNDER MY SKIN — 4 Seasons (Bob Crewe), Philips 40393 | 2 |
| 42 | 45 | 51 | 64 | GOD ONLY KNOWS — Beach Boys (Brian Wilson), Capitol 5706 | 5 |
| 43 | 35 | 19 | 12 | SWEET PEA — Tommy Roe, ABC 10762 | 14 |
| 44 | 33 | 28 | 29 | MAKE ME BELONG TO YOU — Barbara Lewis (Jerry Wexler & Ollie McLaughlin), Atlantic 2346 | 8 |
| ★ 45 | 75 | — | — | 96 TEARS — ? (Question Mark) & the Mysterians, Cameo 428 | 2 |
| ★ 46 | 72 | — | — | FLAMINGO — Herb Alpert & the Tijuana Brass (Herb Alpert), A&M 813 | 2 |
| 47 | 55 | 73 | 90 | LITTLE DARLING (I Need You) — Marvin Gaye, (Holland & Dozier), Tamla 54138 | 4 |
| ★ 48 | 74 | — | — | SUMMER WIND — Frank Sinatra (Sonny Burke), Reprise 0509 | 2 |
| 49 | 53 | 64 | 73 | THE PHILLY FREEZE — Alvin Cash & the Registers, Mar-v-Lus 6012 | 7 |
| 50 | 50 | 55 | 69 | SATISFIED WITH YOU — Dave Clark Five (Dave Clark), Epic 10053 | 5 |
| 51 | 49 | 52 | 54 | SUGAR AND SPICE — Cryan Shames (MG Prod.), Destination 624 | 8 |
| 52 | 60 | 61 | 66 | WORLD OF FANTASY — Five Stair-Steps (C. Mayfield), Windy C 602 | 6 |
| 53 | 61 | 68 | 86 | SOMETIMES GOOD GUYS DON'T WEAR WHITE — Standells (Ed Cobb), Tower 257 | 5 |
| ★ 54 | 65 | 83 | 89 | B-A-B-Y — Carla Thomas (Staff), Stax 195 | 4 |
| 55 | 56 | 75 | 91 | ASHES TO ASHES — Mindbenders (Jack Baverstock), Fontana 1555 | 5 |
| ★ 56 | 79 | — | — | I REALLY DON'T WANT TO KNOW — Ronnie Dove (Phil Kahl); Diamond 208 | 2 |
| ★ 57 | 82 | — | — | REACH OUT I'LL BE THERE — Four Tops (Holland & Dozier), Motown 1098 | 2 |
| 58 | 57 | 57 | 53 | MONEY WON'T CHANGE YOU — James Brown & the Famous Flames (James Brown Prod.), King 6048 | 7 |
| 59 | 66 | 97 | 100 | RUMORS — Syndicate of Sound (Garrie Thompson), Bell 646 | 4 |
| 60 | 62 | 71 | 77 | SUSPICIONS — Sidekicks, RCA Victor 8864 | 6 |
| 61 | 64 | 86 | — | IN THE ARMS OF LOVE — Andy Williams (Robert Mersey), Columbia 43737 | 3 |
| 62 | 69 | 79 | 85 | THAT'S ENOUGH — Roscoe Robinson (Roscoe Robinson), Wand 1125 | 6 |
| 63 | 63 | 74 | 79 | CAST YOUR FATE TO THE WIND — Shelby Flint (Barry Devorzon), Valient 747 | 5 |
| 64 | 67 | 88 | — | BLUE SIDE OF LONESOME — Jim Reeves (Chet Atkins), RCA Victor 8902 | 3 |
| 65 | 71 | — | — | I CHOSE TO SING THE BLUES — Ray Charles, (Tangerine Records), ABC 10840 | 2 |
| 66 | 68 | 84 | 95 | YOU'RE GONNA MISS ME — Thirteenth Floor Elevators (Gorbyn Prod.), International Artists 107 | 4 |
| ★ 67 | — | — | — | LAST TRAIN TO CLARKSVILLE — Monkees (Tommy Boyce & Bobby Hart), Colgems 1001 | 1 |
| 68 | 80 | 95 | — | I WANT TO BE WITH YOU — Dee Dee Warwick, Mercury 72584 | 3 |
| ★ 69 | — | — | — | WALK AWAY RENEE — Left Banke (World United Prod. Inc.), Smash 2041 | 1 |
| 70 | 73 | 81 | 99 | GET AWAY — Georgie Fame (Denny Cordell), Imperial 66189 | 4 |
| 71 | 76 | 93 | 96 | SHE DRIVES ME OUT OF MY MIND — Swingin' Medallions (Karric Prod.), Smash 2050 | 4 |
| 72 | 84 | 92 | 93 | AIN'T NOBODY HOME — Howard Tate (Jerry Ragovoy), Verve 10420 | 4 |
| 73 | 86 | 99 | — | BORN FREE — Roger Williams (Hy Grill), Kapp 767 | 3 |
| 74 | 78 | 87 | — | I GOT TO HANDLE IT — Capitols (Ollie McLaughlin), Karen 1525 | 3 |
| 75 | 87 | — | — | DIANNE, DIANNE — Ronny & the Daytonas, (Rucky Wilkin), RCA Victor 8896 | 2 |
| 76 | 81 | 89 | — | SUMMER SAMBA — Walter Wanderley (Creed Taylor), Verve 10421 | 3 |
| 77 | 77 | 82 | 83 | LET'S CALL IT A DAY GIRL — Razor's Edge (Bob Yorey), POW 101 | 7 |
| 78 | 88 | — | — | BABY TOYS — Toys (Randell & Linzer), DynoVoice 222 | 2 |
| ★ 79 | — | — | — | PSYCHOTIC REACTION — Count Five, Double Shot 104 | 1 |
| ★ 80 | — | — | — | ALL STRUNG OUT — Nino Tempo & April Stevens (Nino Tempo-Jerry Riopell), White Whale 236 | 1 |
| ★ 81 | — | — | — | JUST LIKE A WOMAN — Bob Dylan (Bob Johnston), Columbia 43792 | 1 |
| 82 | 89 | — | — | CAN'T SATISFY — Impressions (Johnny Tate), ABC 10831 | 2 |
| ★ 83 | — | — | — | SAID I WASN'T GONNA TELL NOBODY — Sam & Dave (Prod. by Staff), Stax 198 | 1 |
| 84 | 96 | — | — | MIND EXCURSION — Trade Winds (Anders-Poncia), Kama Sutra 212 | 2 |
| ★ 85 | — | — | — | GIRL ON A SWING — Gerry & the Pacemakers, Laurie 3354 | 1 |
| ★ 86 | — | — | — | I CAN MAKE IT WITH YOU — Jackie DeShannon (Calvin Carter), Imperial 66202 | 1 |
| ★ 87 | — | — | — | I CAN MAKE IT WITH YOU — Pozo-Seco Singers (Bob Johnston), Columbia 43784 | 1 |
| 88 | 92 | — | — | THE FIFE PIPER — Dynatones (J. J. Jules), HBR 494 | 2 |
| 89 | 90 | — | — | MY SWEET POTATO — Booker T. & the M.G.'s, (Prod. by Staff), Stax 196 | 2 |
| 90 | 95 | — | — | IT HURTS ME — Bobby Goldsboro (Jack Gold), United Artists 50056 | 2 |
| 91 | 93 | — | — | CAMPFIRE GIRLS — Billy Joe Royal (Joe South), Columbia 43740 | 2 |
| 92 | — | — | — | ROLLER COASTER — Ides of March (Mike Considine), Parrot 310 | 1 |
| 93 | — | — | — | TOMORROW NEVER COMES — B. J. Thomas (Huey P. Meaux), Scepter 12165 | 1 |
| 94 | 99 | — | — | FIDDLE AROUND — Jan & Dean (Jan Berry), Liberty 5905 | 2 |
| 95 | 97 | 98 | — | ALFIE — Cilla Black (George Martin), Capitol 5674 | 3 |
| 96 | — | — | — | BAD LITTLE WOMAN — Shadows of Knight (Bill Traut), Dunwich 128 | 1 |
| 97 | — | — | — | KNOCK ON WOOD — Eddie Floyd (Prod. by Staff), Stax 194 | 1 |
| 98 | — | — | — | ONLY WHEN YOU'RE LONELY — Grass Roots (Sloan & Barri), Dunhill 4043 | 1 |
| 99 | — | — | — | LOVE IS A HURTIN' THING — Lou Rawls (David Axelrod), Capitol 5709 | 1 |
| 100 | — | — | — | IT WAS A VERY GOOD YEAR — Della Reese (Lee Magid), ABC 10841 | 1 |

## HOT 100—A TO Z—(Publisher-Licensee)


Ain't Nobody Home (Rittenhouse, BMI) .......... 72
Alfie (Famous, ASCAP) .......... 95
All Strong Out (Daddy Sam-Jerell, BMI) .......... 80
Almost Persuaded (Gallico, BMI) .......... 36
Ashes to Ashes (Screen Gems-Columbia, BMI) .......... 55
B-A-B-Y (East, BMI) .......... 54
Baby Toys (Starday-My Songs, BMI) .......... 78
Bad Little Woman (Bernice, BMI) .......... 96
Beauty Is Only Skin Deep (Jobete, BMI) .......... 16
Black Is Black (Elmwin, BMI) .......... 27
Blowin' in the Wind (Witmark, ASCAP) .......... 17
Blue Side of Lonesome (Glad, BMI) .......... 64
Born a Woman (Painted Desert, BMI) .......... 13
Born Free (Columbia, BMI) .......... 73
Bus Stop (Manken, BMI) .......... 9
Campfire Girls (Lowery, BMI) .......... 91
Can't Satisfy (Chi-Sound, BMI) .......... 82
Cast Your Fate to the Wind (Friendship, BMI) .......... 63
Cherish (Beechwood, BMI) .......... 14
Cherry, Cherry (Tallyrand, BMI) .......... 39
Dangling Conversation, The (Charing Cross, BMI) .......... 25
Dianne, Dianne (Buckhorn & Gallico, BMI) .......... 75
Eleanor Rigby (Maclen, BMI) .......... 26
Fiddle Around (Bourne, ASCAP) .......... 94
Fife Piper (Jules-Tone, BMI) .......... 88
Flamingo (Tempo, ASCAP) .......... 46
Get Away (Noma-Gunnell, BMI) .......... 70
Girl on a Swing (Bright Tunes, BMI) .......... 85
Go Ahead and Cry (Righteous Brothers, BMI) .......... 40
God Only Knows (Sea of Tunes, BMI) .......... 42
Guantanamera (Fall River, BMI) .......... 10
How Sweet It Is (Jobete, BMI) .......... 24
I Can Make It With You (DeShannon) (Blackwood, BMI) .......... 86
I Can Make It With You (Pozo Seco Singers) (Blackwood, BMI) .......... 87
I Chose to Sing the Blues (Metric, BMI) .......... 65
I Couldn't Live Without Your Love (Northern, ASCAP) .......... 33
I Got to Handle It (McLaughlin-Gomba, BMI) .......... 74
I Really Don't Want to Know (Hill & Range, BMI) .......... 56
I Want to Be With You (Moreley, ASCAP) .......... 68
I've Got You Under My Skin (Chappell, ASCAP) .......... 41
In the Arms of Love (Twin-Chris, ASCAP) .......... 61
It Hurts Me (Unart, BMI) .......... 90
It Was a Very Good Year (Dolfi, ASCAP) .......... 100
Joker Went Wild, The (Rising Sons, BMI) .......... 28
Just Like a Woman (Dwarf, ASCAP) .......... 81
Knock on Wood (East, BMI) .......... 97
Land of 1,000 Dances (Tune-Kel-Anatole, BMI) .......... 6
Last Train to Clarksville (Screen Gems-Columbia, BMI) .......... 67
Let's Call It a Day Girl (Sea Lark, BMI) .......... 77
Lil' Red Riding Hood (Rose, BMI) .......... 30
Little Darling (I Need You) (Jobete, BMI) .......... 47
Love Is a Hurtin' Thing (Rawlou, BMI) .......... 99
Make Me Belong to You (Blackwood, BMI) .......... 44
Mind Excursion (Tender Tunes, BMI) .......... 84
Mr. Dieingly Sad (Tender Tunes-Elmwin, BMI) .......... 32
Money Won't Change You (Dynatone, BMI) .......... 58
My Heart's Symphony (Gringol, BMI) .......... 34
My Sweet Potato (Instrumental, BMI) .......... 89
96 Tears (Arguello, BMI) .......... 45
Only When You're Lonely (Trousdale, BMI) .......... 98
Open the Door to Your Heart (T.M. & Parmalier, BMI) .......... 31
Philly Freeze, The (Vapac, BMI) .......... 49
Psychotic Reaction (Hot Shot, BMI) .......... 79
Reach Out I'll Be There (Jobete, BMI) .......... 57
Respectable (Wemar, BMI) .......... 15
Roller Coaster (Junik, BMI) .......... 92
Rumors (Duane-Aim, BMI) .......... 59
Said I Wasn't Gonna Tell Nobody (East-Pronto, BMI) .......... 83
Satisfied With You (Branston, BMI) .......... 50
Say I Am (What I Am) (Dundee, BMI) .......... 21
See You in September (Vibar, ASCAP) .......... 4
7 and 7 Is (Grass Roots, BMI) .......... 38
She Drives Me Out of My Mind (Lowery, BMI) .......... 71
Sometimes Good Guys Don't Wear White (Equinox, BMI) .......... 53
Sugar and Spice (Duchess, BMI) .......... 51
Summer in the City (Faithful Virtue, BMI) .......... 5
Summer Samba (Duchess, BMI) .......... 76
Summer Wind (Witmark, ASCAP) .......... 48
Summertime (Gershwin, ASCAP) .......... 12
Sunny (Portable, BMI) .......... 7
Sunny Afternoon (Norma, BMI) .......... 20
Sunshine Superman (Southern, ASCAP) .......... 2
Suspicions (Ricemill-R & S, BMI) .......... 60
Sweet Pea (Low Twi, BMI) .......... 43
That's Enough (Kapa, BMI) .......... 62
There Will Never Be Another You (Morris, ASCAP) .......... 35
Tomorrow Never Comes (Noma, BMI) .......... 93
Turn-Down Day (Northern, ASCAP) .......... 18
Wade in the Water (Ramsel, BMI) .......... 19
Walk Away Renee (Twin Tone, BMI) .......... 69
Warm and Tendes Love (Pronto-Bob-Dan-Quinvy, BMI) .......... 22
What Becomes of the Brokenhearted (Jobete, BMI) 37
Wipe Out (Miraleste-Robin Hood, BMI) .......... 23
With a Girl Like You (James, BMI) .......... 29
Working in the Coal Mine (Marsaint, BMI) .......... 8
World of Fantasy (Camad, BMI) .......... 52
Wouldn't It Be Nice (Sea of Tunes, BMI) .......... 11
Yellow Submarine (Maclen, BMI) .......... 3
You Can't Hurry Love (Jobete, Bobete, BMI) .......... 1
You're Gonna Miss Me (Acquire, BMI) .......... 66


## BUBBLING UNDER THE HOT 100

| | | |
|---|---|---|
| 101. | STICKY, STICKY | Bobby Harris, Shout 203 |
| 102. | JUST LIKE A WOMAN | Manfred Mann, Mercury 72607 |
| 103. | WE CAN'T GO ON THIS WAY | Teddy & the Pandas, Musicor 1190 |
| 104. | BABY, I LOVE YOU | Jimmy Holiday, Minit 32002 |
| 105. | I'M YOUR HOOCHIE COOCHE MAN | Jimmy Smith, Verve 10426 |
| 106. | LAND OF 1,000 DANCES | Cannibal & Headhunters, Date 1525 |
| 107. | BOA CONSTRICTOR | Johnny Cash, Columbia 43763 |
| 108. | FUNCTION AT THE JUNCTION | Shorty Long, Soul 35021 |
| 109. | KEEP LOOKING | Solomon Burke, Atlantic 2349 |
| 110. | NOWADAYS CLANCY CAN'T EVEN SING | Buffalo Springfield, Atco 6428 |
| 111. | DEVRI | Platters, Musicor 1195 |
| 112. | ALL I SEE IS YOU | Dusty Springfield, Philips 40396 |
| 113. | A WOMAN OF THE WORLD | Gentrys, MGM 13561 |
| 114. | SEE SEE RIDER | Eric Burdon & the Animals, MGM 13582 |
| 115. | SAFE AND SOUND | Fontella Bass, Checker 1147 |
| 116. | HE'LL BE BACK | Players, Minit 32001 |
| 117. | GREEN HORNET THEME | Ventures, Dolton 323 |
| 118. | MELODY FOR AN UNKNOWN GIRL | Unknowns, Parrot 307 |
| 119. | COLD LIGHT OF DAY | Gene Pitney, Musicor 1200 |
| 120. | WHAT A PARTY | Tom Jones, Parrot 40008 |
| 121. | CRY SOFTLY | Nancy Ames, Epic 10056 |
| 122. | IMPRESSIONS | Jones Boys, Atco 6426 |
| 123. | HOORAY FOR HAZEL | Tommy Roe, ABC 10852 |
| 124. | I STRUCK IT RICH | Len Barry, Decca 32011 |
| 125. | SHE AIN'T LOVING YOU | Distant Cousins, Date 1514 |
| 126. | SECRET LOVE | Richard (Groove) Holmes, Pacific Jazz 88130 |
| 127. | JUG BAND MUSIC | Mugwumps, Sidewalk 900 |
| 128. | GREEN HORNET THEME | Al Hirt, RCA Victor 8925 |
| 129. | AIN'T GONNA LIE | Keith, Mercury 72596 |
| 130. | TO MAKE A BIG MAN CRY | Roy Head, Back Beat 571 |
| 131. | AFTER YOU THERE CAN BE NOTHING | Walter Jackson, Okeh 7256 |
| 132. | SUNDAY, THE DAY BEFORE MONDAY | Tommy Boyce, A&M 809 |
| 133. | HOLD ON, I'M COMIN' | Billy Larkin & the Delegates, World-Pacific 77844 |
| 134. | UNDER MY THUMB | Del Shannon, Liberty 55904 |
| 135. | SAN FRANCISCO WOMAN | Bob Lind, World-Pacific 77839 |

Compiled from national retail sales and radio station airplay by the Music Popularity Dept. of Record Market Research, Billboard.

Billboard

For Week Ending September 17, 1966

# HOT 100

★ **STAR performer**—Sides registering greatest proportionate upward progress this week.

Record Industry Association of America seal of certification as million selling single.

| This Week | 1 Wk. Ago | 2 Wks. Ago | 3 Wks. Ago | TITLE Artist (Producer), Label & Number | Weeks On Chart |
|---|---|---|---|---|---|
| 1 (Billboard Award) | 1 | 4 | 7 | **YOU CAN'T HURRY LOVE** Supremes (Holland & Dozier), Motown 1097 | 6 |
| 2 | 3 | 5 | 8 | **YELLOW SUBMARINE** Beatles (Martin), Capitol 5715 | 5 |
| 3 | 2 | 1 | 5 | **SUNSHINE SUPERMAN** Donovan (Mickey Most), Epic 10045 | 8 |
| ★4 | 14 | 27 | 66 | **CHERISH** Association (C. Boettcher), Valiant 747 | 4 |
| ★5 | 9 | 18 | 23 | **BUS STOP** Hollies (Ron Richardson), Imperial 66186 | 9 |
| 6 | 4 | 3 | 3 | **SEE YOU IN SEPTEMBER** Happenings (Bright Tunes Prod.), B. T. Puppy 520 | 11 |
| 7 | 6 | 7 | 15 | **LAND OF 1,000 DANCES** Wilson Pickett (Jerry Wexler & Rick Hall) Atlantic 2348 | 8 |
| ★8 | 11 | 11 | 16 | **WOULDN'T IT BE NICE** Beach Boys (Brian Wilson), Capitol 5706 | 8 |
| 9 | 10 | 16 | 22 | **GUANTANAMERA** Sandpipers (Tommy LiPuma), A&M 806 | 8 |
| 10 | 7 | 6 | 2 | **SUNNY** Bobby Hebb (Jerry Ross), Philips 40365 | 13 |
| ★11 | 16 | 26 | 62 | **BEAUTY IS ONLY SKIN DEEP** Temptations (Norman Whitfield), Gordy 7055 | 5 |
| 12 | 13 | 19 | 20 | **BORN A WOMAN** Sandy Posey (Chip Moman), MGM 13501 | 9 |
| 13 | 8 | 8 | 12 | **WORKING IN THE COAL MINE** Lee Dorsey (A. Toussaint-M. Sehorn), Amy 958 | 9 |
| ★14 | 26 | 47 | 65 | **ELEANOR RIGBY** Beatles (George Martin), Capitol 5715 | 4 |
| ★15 | 20 | 22 | 35 | **SUNNY AFTERNOON** Kinks (Shel Talmy), Reprise 0497 | 7 |
| 16 | 18 | 23 | 31 | **TURN-DOWN DAY** Cyrkle (John Simon), Columbia 43729 | 6 |
| 17 | 5 | 2 | 1 | **SUMMER IN THE CITY** Lovin' Spoonful (Eric-Jacobsen), Kama Sutra 211 | 10 |
| ★18 | 27 | 41 | 63 | **BLACK IS BLACK** Los Bravos (Ivor Raymonde), Press 60002 | 6 |
| 19 | 19 | 24 | 27 | **WADE IN THE WATER** Ramsey Lewis (Esmond Edwards), Cadet 5541 | 11 |
| 20 | 23 | 28 | 39 | **WIPE OUT** Surfaris, Dot 144 | 24 |
| 21 | 21 | 21 | 26 | **SAY I AM (What I Am)** Tommy James and the Shondells (Bob Mack), Roulette 4695 | 7 |
| 22 | 15 | 15 | 29 | **RESPECTABLE** Outsiders (Tom King), Capitol 5701 | 7 |
| 23 | 24 | 29 | 47 | **HOW SWEET IT IS** Jr. Walker & the All-Stars (J. Bristol-H. Fuqua), Soul 35024 | 8 |
| ★24 | 39 | 54 | 72 | **CHERRY, CHERRY** Neil Diamond (Jeff Barry & Ellie Greenwich), Bang 528 | 5 |
| ★25 | 45 | 75 | — | **96 TEARS** ? (Question Mark) & the Mysterians, Cameo 428 | 3 |
| ★26 | 57 | 82 | — | **REACH OUT I'LL BE THERE** Four Tops (Holland & Dozier), Motown 1098 | 3 |
| ★27 | 32 | 38 | 54 | **MR. DIEINGLY SAD** Critters (Artie Ripp), Kapp 769 | 6 |
| ★28 | 41 | 83 | — | **I'VE GOT YOU UNDER MY SKIN** 4 Seasons (Bob Crewe), Philips 40393 | 3 |
| ★29 | 37 | 52 | 69 | **WHAT BECOMES OF THE BROKENHEARTED** Jimmy Ruffin (William Stevenson), Soul 35022 | 5 |
| ★30 | 36 | 36 | 40 | **ALMOST PERSUADED** David Houston (Billy Sherrill), Epic 10025 | 10 |
| 31 | 31 | 48 | 58 | **OPEN THE DOOR TO YOUR HEART** Darrell Banks, Revilot 201 | 9 |
| 32 | 25 | 25 | 34 | **THE DANGLING CONVERSATION** Simon & Garfunkel (Bob Johnston), Columbia 43728 | 7 |
| 33 | 35 | 43 | 59 | **THERE WILL NEVER BE ANOTHER YOU** Chris Montez (Tommy LiPuma), A&M 810 | 6 |
| 34 | 28 | 20 | 21 | **THE JOKER WENT WILD** Brian Hyland (Snuff Garrett & Leon Russell), Philips 40377 | 10 |
| 35 | 17 | 9 | 11 | **BLOWIN' IN THE WIND** Stevie Wonder (C. Paul), Tamla 54136 | 9 |
| ★36 | 46 | 72 | — | **FLAMINGO** Herb Alpert & the Tijuana Brass (Herb Alpert), A&M 813 | 3 |
| ★37 | 48 | 74 | — | **SUMMER WIND** Frank Sinatra (Sonny Burke), Reprise 0509 | 3 |
| 38 | 38 | 42 | 53 | **7 AND 7 IS** Love (Jac Holzman), Elektra 45605 | 8 |
| 39 | 12 | 10 | 10 | **SUMMERTIME** Billy Stewart (Billy Davis), Chess 1966 | 10 |
| 40 | 42 | 45 | 51 | **GOD ONLY KNOWS** Beach Boys (Brian Wilson), Capitol 5706 | 6 |
| 41 | 22 | 17 | 18 | **WARM AND TENDER LOVE** Percy Sledge (Marlin Greene & Quin Ivy), Atlantic 2342 | 9 |
| ★42 | 79 | — | — | **PSYCHOTIC REACTION** Count Five (Hooven-Winn), Double Shot 104 | 2 |
| ★43 | 67 | — | — | **LAST TRAIN TO CLARKSVILLE** Monkees (Tommy Boyce & Bobby Hart), Colgems 1001 | 2 |
| ★44 | 54 | 65 | 83 | **B-A-B-Y** Carla Thomas (Staff), Stax 195 | 5 |
| 45 | 29 | 32 | 42 | **WITH A GIRL LIKE YOU** Troggs (Page One-York-Pala), Atco 6415-Fontana 1552 | 7 |
| ★46 | 56 | 79 | — | **I REALLY DON'T WANT TO KNOW** Ronnie Dove (Phil Kahl), Diamond 208 | 3 |
| 47 | 47 | 55 | 73 | **LITTLE DARLING (I Need You)** Marvin Gaye, (Holland & Dozier), Tamla 54138 | 5 |
| 48 | 53 | 61 | 68 | **SOMETIMES GOOD GUYS DON'T WEAR WHITE** Standells (Ed Cobb), Tower 257 | 6 |
| 49 | 52 | 60 | 61 | **WORLD OF FANTASY** Five Stair-Steps (C. Mayfield), Windy C 602 | 7 |
| 50 | 49 | 53 | 64 | **THE PHILLY FREEZE** Alvin Cash & the Registers, Mar-v-Lus 6012 | 8 |
| 51 | 51 | 49 | 52 | **SUGAR AND SPICE** Cryan Shames (MG Prod.), Destination 624 | 9 |
| ★52 | 80 | — | — | **ALL STRUNG OUT** Nino Tempo & April Stevens (Nino Tempo-Jerry Riopell), White Whale 236 | 2 |
| 53 | 50 | 50 | 55 | **SATISFIED WITH YOU** Dave Clark Five (Dave Clark), Epic 10053 | 6 |
| ★54 | 81 | — | — | **JUST LIKE A WOMAN** Bob Dylan (Bob Johnston), Columbia 43792 | 2 |
| ★55 | 65 | 71 | — | **I CHOSE TO SING THE BLUES** Ray Charles, (Tangerine Records), ABC 10840 | 3 |
| ★56 | 76 | 81 | 89 | **SUMMER SAMBA** Walter Wanderley (Creed Taylor), Verve 10421 | 4 |
| 57 | 61 | 64 | 86 | **IN THE ARMS OF LOVE** Andy Williams (Robert Mersey), Columbia 43737 | 4 |
| ★58 | 69 | — | — | **WALK AWAY RENEE** Left Banke (World United Prod. Inc.), Smash 2041 | 2 |
| 59 | 60 | 62 | 71 | **SUSPICIONS** Sidekicks, RCA Victor 8864 | 7 |
| 60 | 66 | 68 | 84 | **YOU'RE GONNA MISS ME** Thirteenth Floor Elevators (Gorbyn Prod.), International Artists 107 | 5 |
| 61 | 63 | 63 | 74 | **CAST YOUR FATE TO THE WIND** Shelby Flint (Barry Devorzon), Valient 747 | 6 |
| 62 | 55 | 56 | 75 | **ASHES TO ASHES** Mindbenders (Jack Baverstock), Fontana 1555 | 6 |
| 63 | 59 | 66 | 97 | **RUMORS** Syndicate of Sound (Garrie Thompson), Bell 646 | 5 |
| 64 | 64 | 67 | 88 | **BLUE SIDE OF LONESOME** Jim Reeves (Chet Atkins), RCA Victor 8902 | 4 |
| 65 | 68 | 80 | 95 | **I WANT TO BE WITH YOU** Dee Dee Warwick, Mercury 72584 | 4 |
| 66 | 58 | 57 | 57 | **MONEY WON'T CHANGE YOU** James Brown & the Famous Flames (James Brown Prod.), King 6048 | 8 |
| ★67 | 82 | 89 | — | **CAN'T SATISFY** Impressions (Johnny Tate), ABC 10831 | 3 |
| 68 | 73 | 86 | 99 | **BORN FREE** Roger Williams (Hy Grill), Kapp 767 | 4 |
| 69 | 75 | 87 | — | **DIANNE, DIANNE** Ronny & the Daytonas, (Bucky Wilkin), RCA Victor 8896 | 3 |
| 70 | 72 | 84 | 92 | **AIN'T NOBODY HOME** Howard Tate (Jerry Ragovoy), Verve 10420 | 5 |
| 71 | 71 | 76 | 93 | **SHE DRIVES ME OUT OF MY MIND** Swingin' Medallions (Karric Prod.), Smash 2050 | 5 |
| ★72 | 87 | — | — | **I CAN MAKE IT WITH YOU** Pozo-Seco Singers (Bob Johnston), Columbia 43784 | 2 |
| 73 | 62 | 69 | 79 | **THAT'S ENOUGH** Roscoe Robinson (Roscoe Robinson), Wand 1125 | 7 |
| 74 | 74 | 78 | 87 | **I GOT TO HANDLE IT** Capitols (Ollie McLaughlin), Karen 1525 | 4 |
| ★75 | — | — | — | **HOORAY FOR HAZEL** Tommy Roe (Our Prods.), ABC 10852 | 1 |
| 76 | 78 | 88 | — | **BABY TOYS** Toys (Randell & Linzer), DynoVoice 222 | 3 |
| 77 | 70 | 73 | 81 | **GET AWAY** Georgie Fame (Denny Cordell), Imperial 66189 | 5 |
| 78 | 88 | 92 | — | **THE FIFE PIPER** Dynatones (J. J. Jules), HBR 494 | 3 |
| 79 | 85 | — | — | **GIRL ON A SWING** Gerry & the Pacemakers, Laurie 3354 | 2 |
| 80 | 90 | 95 | — | **IT HURTS ME** Bobby Goldsboro (Jack Gold), United Artists 50056 | 3 |
| ★81 | — | — | — | **ALL I SEE IS YOU** Dusty Springfield, Philips 40396 | 1 |
| ★82 | — | — | — | **MY UNCLE USED TO LOVE ME BUT SHE DIED** Roger Miller (Jerry Kennedy), Smash 2055 | 1 |
| 83 | 83 | — | — | **SAID I WASN'T GONNA TELL NOBODY** Sam & Dave (Prod. by Staff), Stax 198 | 2 |
| 84 | 86 | — | — | **I CAN MAKE IT WITH YOU** Jackie DeShannon (Calvin Carter), Imperial 66202 | 2 |
| ★85 | — | — | — | **SEE SEE RIDER** Eric Burdon & the Animals (Tom Wilson), MGM 13582 | 1 |
| ★86 | — | — | — | **POVERTY** Bobby Bland, Duke 407 | 1 |
| 87 | 89 | 90 | — | **MY SWEET POTATO** Booker T. & the M.G.'s, (Prod. by Staff), Stax 196 | 3 |
| ★88 | — | — | — | **IN OUR TIME** Nancy Sinatra (Lee Hazlewood), Reprise 0514 | 1 |
| 89 | 99 | — | — | **LOVE IS A HURTIN' THING** Lou Rawls (David Axelrod), Capitol 5709 | 2 |
| ★90 | — | — | — | **POOR SIDE OF TOWN** Johnny Rivers (Lou Adler), Imperial 66205 | 1 |
| 91 | 96 | — | — | **BAD LITTLE WOMAN** Shadows of Knight (Bill Traut), Dunwich 128 | 2 |
| 92 | 93 | — | — | **TOMORROW NEVER COMES** B. J. Thomas (Huey P. Meaux), Scepter 12165 | 2 |
| 93 | 94 | 99 | — | **FIDDLE AROUND** Jan & Dean (Jan Berry), Liberty 5905 | 3 |
| 94 | — | — | — | **AIN'T GONNA LIE** Keith (Jerry Ross), Mercury 72596 | 1 |
| 95 | — | — | — | **CHANGES** Crispian St. Peters (David Nicolson), Jamie 1324 | 1 |
| 96 | 98 | — | — | **ONLY WHEN YOU'RE LONELY** Grass Roots (Sloan & Barri), Dunhill 4043 | 2 |
| 97 | 97 | — | — | **KNOCK ON WOOD** Eddie Floyd (Prod. by Staff), Stax 194 | 2 |
| 98 | — | — | — | **TO MAKE A BIG MAN CRY** Roy Head, Back Beat 571 | 1 |
| 99 | 100 | — | — | **IT WAS A VERY GOOD YEAR** Della Reese (Lee Magid), ABC 10841 | 2 |
| 100 | — | — | — | **I STRUCK IT RICH** Len Barry (Madera-White), Decca 32011 | 1 |

## HOT 100—A TO Z—(Publisher-Licensee)

Ain't Gonna Lie (Screen Gems-Columbia) ........ 94
Ain't Nobody Home (Rittenhouse, BMI) ........ 70
All I See Is You (Anne-Rachel, ASCAP) ........ 81
All Strung Out (Daddy Sam-Jerell, BMI) ........ 52
Almost Persuaded (Gallico, BMI) ........ 30
Ashes to Ashes (Screen Gems-Columbia, BMI) .... 62

B-A-B-Y (East, BMI) ........ 44
Baby Toys (Saturday-My Songs, BMI) ........ 76
Bad Little Woman (Bernice, BMI) ........ 91
Beauty Is Only Skin Deep (Jobete, BMI) ........ 11
Black Is Black (Elmwin, BMI) ........ 18
Blowin' in the Wind (Witmark, ASCAP) ........ 35
Blue Side of Lonesome (Glad, BMI) ........ 64
Born a Woman (Painted Desert, BMI) ........ 12
Born Free (Columbia, BMI) ........ 68
Bus Stop (Manken, BMI) ........ 5

Can't Satisfy (Chi-Sound, BMI) ........ 67
Cast Your Fate to the Wind (Friendship, BMI) ... 61
Changes (Barricade, ASCAP) ........ 95
Cherish (Beechwood, BMI) ........ 4
Cherry, Cherry (Tallyrand, BMI) ........ 24

Dangling Conversation, The (Charing Cross, BMI). 32
Dianne, Dianne (Buckhorn & Gallico, BMI) .... 69

Eleanor Rigby (Maclen, BMI) ........ 14

Fiddle Around (Bourne, ASCAP) ........ 93
Fife Piper (Jules-Tone, BMI) ........ 78
Flamingo (Tempo, ASCAP) ........ 36

Get Away (Noma-Gunnel, BMI) ........ 77
Girl on a Swing (Bright Tunes, BMI) ........ 79
God Only Knows (Sea of Tunes, BMI) ........ 40
Guantanamera (Fall River, BMI) ........ 9

Hooray for Hazel (Low Twi, BMI) ........ 75
How Sweet It Is (Jobete, BMI) ........ 23
I Can Make It With You (DeShannon) (Blackwood, BMI) ........ 84
I Can Make It With You (Pozo Seco Singers) (Blackwood, BMI) ........ 72
I Chose to Sing the Blues (Metric, BMI) ........ 55
I Got to Handle It (McLaughlin-Gomba, BMI) .... 74
I Really Don't Want to Know (Hill & Range, BMI) 46
I Struck It Rich (Champion-Double Diamond, BMI) 100
I Want to Be With You (Moreley, ASCAP) ........ 65
I've Got You Under My Skin (Chappell, ASCAP) .. 28
In Our Time (Criterion, ASCAP) ........ 88
In the Arms of Love (Twin-Chris, ASCAP) ........ 57
It Hurts Me (Unart, BMI) ........ 80
It Was a Very Good Year (Dolfi, ASCAP) ........ 99

Joker Went Wild, The (Rising Sons, BMI) ........ 34
Just Like a Woman (Dwarf, ASCAP) ........ 54

Knock on Wood (East, BMI) ........ 97

Land of 1,000 Dances (Tune-Kel-Anatole, BMI) .. 7
Last Train to Clarksville (Screen Gems-Columbia, BMI) ........ 43
Little Darlin' (I Need You) (Jobete, BMI) ........ 47
Love Is a Hurtin' Thing (Rawlou, BMI) ........ 89

Mr. Dieingly Sad (Tender Tunes-Elmwin, BMI) .. 27
Money Won't Change You (Dynatone, BMI) .... 66
My Sweet Potato (Instrumental, BMI) ........ 87
My Uncle Used to Love Me But She Died (Tree, BMI) ........ 82

96 Tears (Arguello, BMI) ........ 25

Only When You're Lonely (Trousdale, BMI) .... 96
Open the Door to Your Heart (T. M. & Parmalier, BMI) ........ 31

Philly Freeze, The (Vapac, BMI) ........ 50
Poor Side of Town (Rivers, BMI) ........ 90
Poverty (Don, BMI) ........ 86
Psychotic Reaction (Hot Shot, BMI) ........ 42

Reach Out I'll Be There (Jobete, BMI) ........ 26
Respectable (Wemar, BMI) ........ 22
Rumors (Duane-Aim, BMI) ........ 63
Said I Wasn't Gonna Tell Nobody (East-Pronto, BMI) ........ 83
Satisfied With You (Branston, BMI) ........ 53
Say I Am (What I Am) (Dundee, BMI) ........ 21
See See Rider (Leeds, ASCAP) ........ 85
See You in September (Vibar, ASCAP) ........ 6
7 and 7 Is (Grass Roots, BMI) ........ 38
She Drives Me Out of My Mind (Lowery, BMI) .. 71
Sometimes Good Guys Don't Wear White (Equinox, BMI) ........ 48
Sugar and Spice (Duchess, BMI) ........ 51
Summer in the City (Faithful Virtue, BMI) ...... 17
Summer Samba (Duchess, BMI) ........ 56
Summer Wind (Witmark, ASCAP) ........ 37
Summertime (Gershwin, ASCAP) ........ 39
Sunny (Portable, BMI) ........ 10
Sunny Afternoon (Norma, BMI) ........ 15
Sunshine Superman (Southern, ASCAP) ........ 3
Suspicions (Ricemill-R & S, BMI) ........ 59
That's Enough (Kapa, BMI) ........ 73
There Will Never Be Another You (Morris, ASCAP) 33
To Make a Big Man Cry (Regent, BMI) ........ 98
Tomorrow Never Comes (Noma, BMI) ........ 92
Turn-Down Day (Northern, ASCAP) ........ 16
Wade in the Water (Ramsel, BMI) ........ 19
Walk Away Renee (Twin Tone, BMI) ........ 58
Warm and Tender Love (Pronto-Bob-Dan-Quinvy, BMI) ........ 41
What Becomes of the Brokenhearted (Jobete, BMI) 29
Wipe Out (Miraleste-Robin Hood, BMI) ........ 20
With a Girl Like You (James, BMI) ........ 45
Working in the Coal Mine (Marsaint, BMI) ...... 13
World of Fantasy (Camad, BMI) ........ 49
Wouldn't It Be Nice (Sea of Tunes, BMI) ...... 8
Yellow Submarine (Maclen, BMI) ........ 2
You Can't Hurry Love (Jobete, BMI) ........ 1
You're Gonna Miss Me (Acquire, BMI) ........ 60

## BUBBLING UNDER THE HOT 100

101. JUST LIKE A WOMAN ........ Manfred Mann, Mercury 72607
102. OPEN UP YOUR DOOR ........ Richard & the Young Lions, Philips 40381
103. WE CAN'T GO ON THIS WAY ........ Teddy & the Pandas, Musicor 1190
104. CAMPFIRE GIRLS ........ Billy Joe Royal, Columbia 43740
105. STICKY, STICKY ........ Bobby Harris, Shout 203
106. BABY I LOVE YOU ........ Jimmy Holiday, Minit 32002
107. HE'LL BE BACK ........ Players, Minit 32001
108. OFF TO DUBLIN IN THE GREEN ........ Abbey Tavern Singers, HBR 498
109. THE WHEEL OF HURT ........ Margaret Whiting, London 101
110. LOVE IS A WONDERFUL THING ........ Isley Brothers, Veep 1230
111. DOMMAGE, DOMMAGE ........ Jerry Vale, Columbia 43774
112. A WOMAN OF THE WORLD ........ Gentrys, MGM 13561
113. MIND EXCURSION ........ Trade Winds, Kama Sutra 212
114. ROLLER COASTER ........ I'des of March, Parrot 310
115. TREAT ME LIKE A LADY ........ Lesley Gore, Mercury 72611
116. GREEN HORNET THEME ........ Ventures, Dolton 323
117. COLD LIGHT OF DAY ........ Gene Pitney, Musicor 1200
118. CRY SOFTLY ........ Nancy Ames, Epic 10056
119. SHE AIN'T LOVING YOU ........ Distant Cousins, Date 1514
120. WHAT A PARTY ........ Tom Jones, Parrot 40008
121. PLEASE MR. SUN ........ Vogues, Co & Ce 240
122. IF MY CAR COULD ONLY TALK ........ Lou Christie, MGM 13576
123. A TIME FOR LOVE ........ Tony Bennett, Columbia 43768
124. SECRET LOVE ........ Richard (Groove) Holmes, Pacific Jazz 88130
125. POLLYANNA ........ Classics, Capitol 5710
126. GREEN HORNET THEME ........ Al Hirt, RCA Victor 8925
127. GLORIA'S DREAM ........ Belfast Gypsies, Loma 2051
128. DOMAGE, DOMAGE ........ Paul Vance, Scepter 12164
129. THE SCRATCH ........ Robert Parker, Nola 726
130. HOLD ON I'M COMIN' ........ Billy Larkin & the Delegates, World-Pacific 77844
131. COMING ON STRONG ........ Brenda Lee, Decca 32018
132. WISH YOU WERE HERE, BUDDY ........ Pat Boone, Dot 16933
133. THE OTHER SIDE OF THIS LIFE ........ Peter, Paul & Mary, Warner Bros. 5849
134. I REMEMBER YOU ........ Slim Whitman, Imperial 66181
135. I COVER THE WATERFRONT ........ Jimmy McGriff Trio, Solid State 250-

Compiled from national retail sales and radio station airplay by the Music Popularity Dept. of Record Market Research, Billboard.

# Billboard

For Week Ending September 24, 1966

# HOT 100

★ STAR performer—Sides registering greatest proportionate upward progress this week.

Record Industry Association of America seal of certification as million selling single.

| THIS WEEK | 1 Wk. Ago | 2 Wks. Ago | 3 Wks. Ago | TITLE Artist (Producer), Label & Number | Weeks On Chart |
|---|---|---|---|---|---|
| Billboard Award | 4 | 14 | 27 | CHERISH — Association (C. Boettcher), Valiant 747 | 5 |
| 2 | 1 | 1 | 4 | YOU CAN'T HURRY LOVE — Supremes (Holland & Dozier), Motown 1097 | 7 |
| 3 | 3 | 2 | 1 | SUNSHINE SUPERMAN — Donovan (Mickey Most), Epic 10045 | 9 |
| 4 | 2 | 3 | 5 | YELLOW SUBMARINE — Beatles (Martin), Capitol 5715 | 6 |
| 5 | 5 | 9 | 18 | BUS STOP — Hollies (Ron Richardson), Imperial 66186 | 10 |
| ★ 6 | 11 | 16 | 26 | BEAUTY IS ONLY SKIN DEEP — Temptations (Norman Whitfield), Gordy 7055 | 6 |
| ★ 7 | 18 | 27 | 41 | BLACK IS BLACK — Los Bravos (Ivor Raymonde), Press 60002 | 7 |
| ★ 8 | 25 | 45 | 75 | 96 TEARS — ? (Question Mark) & the Mysterians, Cameo 428 | 4 |
| 9 | 8 | 11 | 11 | WOULDN'T IT BE NICE — Beach Boys (Brian Wilson), Capitol 5706 | 9 |
| ★ 10 | 26 | 57 | 82 | REACH OUT I'LL BE THERE — Four Tops (Holland & Dozier), Motown 1098 | 4 |
| 11 | 14 | 26 | 47 | ELEANOR RIGBY — Beatles (George Martin), Capitol 5715 | 5 |
| 12 | 6 | 4 | 3 | SEE YOU IN SEPTEMBER — Happenings (Bright Tunes Prod.), B. T. Puppy 520 | 12 |
| 13 | 9 | 10 | 16 | GUANTANAMERA — Sandpipers (Tommy LiPuma), A&M 806 | 9 |
| ★ 14 | 24 | 39 | 54 | CHERRY, CHERRY — Neil Diamond (Jeff Barry & Ellie Greenwich), Bang 528 | 6 |
| 15 | 15 | 20 | 22 | SUNNY AFTERNOON — Kinks (Shel Talmy), Reprise 0497 | 8 |
| 16 | 12 | 13 | 19 | BORN A WOMAN — Sandy Posey (Chip Moman), MGM 13501 | 10 |
| 17 | 20 | 23 | 28 | WIPE OUT — Surfaris, Dot 144 | 25 |
| ★ 18 | 23 | 24 | 29 | HOW SWEET IT IS — Jr. Walker & the All-Stars (J. Bristol-H. Fuqua), Soul 35024 | 9 |
| ★ 19 | 28 | 41 | 83 | I'VE GOT YOU UNDER MY SKIN — 4 Seasons (Bob Crewe), Philips 40393 | 4 |
| ★ 20 | 27 | 32 | 38 | MR. DIEINGLY SAD — Critters (Artie Ripp), Kapp 769 | 7 |
| 21 | 10 | 7 | 6 | SUNNY — Bobby Hebb (Jerry Ross), Philips 40365 | 14 |
| 22 | 16 | 18 | 23 | TURN-DOWN DAY — Cyrkle (John Simon), Columbia 43729 | 7 |
| ★ 23 | 29 | 37 | 52 | WHAT BECOMES OF THE BROKENHEARTED — Jimmy Ruffin (William Stevenson), Soul 35022 | 6 |
| 24 | 7 | 6 | 7 | LAND OF 1,000 DANCES — Wilson Pickett (Jerry Wexler & Rick Hall) Atlantic 2348 | 9 |
| ★ 25 | 42 | 79 | — | PSYCHOTIC REACTION — Count Five (Hooven-Winn), Double Shot 104 | 3 |
| ★ 26 | 43 | 67 | — | LAST TRAIN TO CLARKSVILLE — Monkees (Tommy Boyce & Bobby Hart), Colgems 1001 | 3 |
| 27 | 13 | 8 | 8 | WORKING IN THE COAL MINE — Lee Dorsey (A. Toussaint-M. Sehorn), Amy 958 | 10 |
| 28 | 31 | 31 | 48 | OPEN THE DOOR TO YOUR HEART — Darrell Banks, Revilot 201 | 10 |
| 29 | 30 | 36 | 36 | ALMOST PERSUADED — David Houston (Billy Sherrill), Epic 10025 | 11 |
| ★ 30 | 36 | 46 | 72 | FLAMINGO — Herb Alpert & the Tijuana Brass (Herb Alpert), A&M 813 | 4 |
| 31 | 22 | 15 | 15 | RESPECTABLE — Outsiders (Tom King), Capitol 5701 | 8 |
| 32 | 37 | 48 | 74 | SUMMER WIND — Frank Sinatra (Sonny Burke), Reprise 0509 | 4 |
| 33 | 38 | 38 | 42 | 7 AND 7 IS — Love (Jac Holzman), Elektra 45605 | 9 |
| 34 | 34 | 28 | 20 | THE JOKER WENT WILD — Brian Hyland (Snuff Garrett & Leon Russell), Philips 40377 | 11 |
| 35 | 19 | 19 | 24 | WADE IN THE WATER — Ramsey Lewis (Esmond Edwards), Cadet 5541 | 12 |
| ★ 36 | 46 | 56 | 79 | I REALLY DON'T WANT TO KNOW — Ronnie Dove (Phil Kahl), Diamond 208 | 4 |
| 37 | 17 | 5 | 2 | SUMMER IN THE CITY — Lovin' Spoonful (Eric-Jacobsen), Kama Sutra 211 | 11 |
| 38 | 44 | 54 | 65 | B-A-B-Y — Carla Thomas (Staff), Stax 195 | 6 |
| 39 | 40 | 42 | 45 | GOD ONLY KNOWS — Beach Boys (Brian Wilson), Capitol 5706 | 7 |
| ★ 40 | 58 | 69 | — | WALK AWAY RENEE — Left Banke (World United Prod. Inc.), Smash 2041 | 3 |
| ★ 41 | 54 | 81 | — | JUST LIKE A WOMAN — Bob Dylan (Bob Johnston), Columbia 43792 | 3 |
| ★ 42 | 52 | 80 | — | ALL STRUNG OUT — Nino Tempo & April Stevens (Nino Tempo-Jerry Riopell), White Whale 236 | 3 |
| 43 | 48 | 53 | 61 | SOMETIMES GOOD GUYS DON'T WEAR WHITE — Standells (Ed Cobb), Tower 257 | 7 |
| ★ 44 | 56 | 76 | 81 | SUMMER SAMBA — Walter Wanderley (Creed Taylor), Verve 10421 | 5 |
| ★ 45 | 55 | 65 | 71 | I CHOSE TO SING THE BLUES — Ray Charles, (Tangerine Records), ABC 10840 | 4 |
| 46 | 33 | 35 | 43 | THERE WILL NEVER BE ANOTHER YOU — Chris Montez (Tommy LiPuma), A&M 810 | 7 |
| 47 | 35 | 17 | 9 | BLOWIN' IN THE WIND — Stevie Wonder (C. Paul); Tamla 54136 | 10 |
| 48 | 21 | 21 | 21 | SAY I AM (What I Am) — Tommy James and the Shondells (Bob Mack), Roulette 4695 | 8 |
| 49 | 57 | 61 | 64 | IN THE ARMS OF LOVE — Andy Williams (Robert Mersey), Columbia 43737 | 5 |
| 50 | 45 | 29 | 32 | WITH A GIRL LIKE YOU — Troggs (Page One-York-Pala), Atco 6415-Fontana 1552 | 8 |
| ★ 51 | 81 | — | — | ALL I SEE IS YOU — Dusty Springfield, Philips 40396 | 2 |
| 52 | 49 | 52 | 60 | WORLD OF FANTASY — Five Stair-Steps (C. Mayfield), Windy C 602 | 8 |
| ★ 53 | 85 | — | — | SEE SEE RIDER — Eric Burdon & the Animals (Tom Wilson), MGM 13582 | 2 |
| ★ 54 | 68 | 73 | 86 | BORN FREE — Roger Williams (Hy Grill), Kapp 767 | 5 |
| 55 | 59 | 60 | 62 | SUSPICIONS — Sidekicks, RCA Victor 8864 | 8 |
| 56 | 60 | 66 | 68 | YOU'RE GONNA MISS ME — Thirteenth Floor Elevators (Gorbyn Prod.), International Artists 107 | 6 |
| 57 | 47 | 47 | 55 | LITTLE DARLING (I Need You) — Marvin Gaye, (Holland & Dozier), Tamla 54138 | 6 |
| ★ 58 | 72 | 87 | — | I CAN MAKE IT WITH YOU — Pozo-Seco Singers (Bob Johnston), Columbia 43784 | 3 |
| ★ 59 | 75 | — | — | HOORAY FOR HAZEL — Tommy Roe (Our Prods.), ABC 10852 | 2 |
| 60 | 64 | 64 | 67 | BLUE SIDE OF LONESOME — Jim Reeves (Chet Atkins), RCA Victor 8902 | 5 |
| 61 | 63 | 59 | 66 | RUMORS — Syndicate of Sound (Garrie Thompson), Bell 646 | 6 |
| 62 | 65 | 68 | 80 | I WANT TO BE WITH YOU — Dee Dee Warwick; Mercury 72584 | 5 |
| 63 | 61 | 63 | 63 | CAST YOUR FATE TO THE WIND — Shelby Flint (Barry Devorzon), Valient 747 | 7 |
| ★ 64 | 79 | 85 | — | GIRL ON A SWING — Gerry & the Pacemakers, Laurie 3354 | 3 |
| 65 | 78 | 88 | 92 | THE FIFE PIPER — Dynatones (J. J. Jules), HBR 494 | 4 |
| ★ 66 | 82 | — | — | MY UNCLE USED TO LOVE ME BUT SHE DIED — Roger Miller (Jerry Kennedy), Smash 2055 | 2 |
| 67 | 67 | 82 | 89 | CAN'T SATISFY — Impressions (Johnny Tate), ABC 10831 | 4 |
| 68 | 70 | 72 | 84 | AIN'T NOBODY HOME — Howard Tate (Jerry Ragevoy), Verve 10420 | 6 |
| 69 | 50 | 49 | 53 | THE PHILLY FREEZE — Alvin Cash & the Registers, Mar-v-Lus 6012 | 9 |
| 70 | 66 | 58 | 57 | MONEY WON'T CHANGE YOU — James Brown & the Famous Flames (James Brown Prod.), King 6048 | 9 |
| 71 | 69 | 75 | 87 | DIANNE, DIANNE — Ronny & the Daytonas, (Bucky Wilkin), RCA Victor 8896 | 4 |
| ★ 72 | 90 | — | — | POOR SIDE OF TOWN — Johnny Rivers (Lou Adler), Imperial 66205 | 2 |
| ★ 73 | 89 | 99 | — | LOVE IS A HURTIN' THING — Lou Rawls (David Axelrod), Capitol 5709 | 3 |
| 74 | 86 | — | — | POVERTY — Bobby Bland, Duke 407 | 2 |
| 75 | 88 | — | — | IN OUR TIME — Nancy Sinatra (Lee Hazlewood), Reprise 0514 | 2 |
| 76 | 76 | 78 | 78 | BABY TOYS — Toys (Randell & Linzer), DynoVoice 222 | 4 |
| 77 | 77 | 70 | 73 | GET AWAY — Georgie Fame (Denny Cordell), Imperial 66189 | 6 |
| 78 | 80 | 90 | 95 | IT HURTS ME — Bobby Goldsboro (Jack Gold), United Artists 50056 | 4 |
| 79 | 84 | 86 | — | I CAN MAKE IT WITH YOU — Jackie DeShannon (Calvin Carter), Imperial 66202 | 3 |
| 80 | 73 | 62 | 69 | THAT'S ENOUGH — Roscoe Robinson (Roscoe Robinson), Wand 1125 | 8 |
| ★ 81 | — | — | — | IF I WERE A CARPENTER — Bobby Darin (Koppleman-Rubin), Atlantic 2350 | 1 |
| 82 | 83 | 83 | — | SAID I WASN'T GONNA TELL NOBODY — Sam & Dave (Prod. by Staff), Stax 198 | 3 |
| ★ 83 | — | — | — | MIND EXCURSION — The Trade Winds (Anders-Poncia), Kama Sutra 212 | 3 |
| ★ 84 | — | — | — | MELODY FOR AN UNKNOWN GIRL — Unknowns (Steve Alaimo), Parrot 307 | 1 |
| ★ 85 | — | — | — | MAS QUE NADA — Sergio Mendes & Brazil '66 (Herb Alpert), A&M 807 | 1 |
| ★ 86 | — | — | — | COME ON UP — Young Rascals (Young Rascals), Atlantic 2353 | 1 |
| 87 | 87 | 89 | 90 | MY SWEET POTATO — Booker T. & the M.G.'s, (Prod. by Staff), Stax 196 | 4 |
| 88 | 95 | — | — | CHANGES — Crispian St. Peters (David Nicolson), Jamie 1324 | 2 |
| 89 | 97 | 97 | — | KNOCK ON WOOD — Eddie Floyd (Prod. by Staff), Stax 194 | 3 |
| ★ 90 | — | — | — | MR. SPACEMAN — Byrds (Allen Stanton), Columbia 43766 | 1 |
| 91 | 94 | — | — | AIN'T GONNA LIE — Keith (Jerry Ross), Mercury 72596 | 2 |
| 92 | — | — | — | PLEASE MR. SUN — Vogues (Cenci-Moon-Hakim), Co & Ce 240 | 1 |
| 93 | 93 | 94 | 99 | FIDDLE AROUND — Jan & Dean (Jan Berry), Liberty 5905 | 4 |
| 94 | — | — | — | OFF TO DUBLIN IN THE GREEN — Abbey Tavern Singers (Hanna Barbera Prod.), HBR 498 | 1 |
| 95 | 98 | — | — | TO MAKE A BIG MAN CRY — Roy Head, Back Beat 571 | 2 |
| 96 | — | — | — | I'M YOUR PUPPET — James & Bobby Purify (Don Schroeder), Bell 648 | 1 |
| 97 | — | — | — | FUNCTION AT THE JUNCTION — Shorty Long (Holland, Dozier & Holland), Soul 35021 | 1 |
| 98 | 100 | — | — | I STRUCK IT RICH — Len Barry (Madera-White), Decca 32011 | 2 |
| 99 | — | — | — | OPEN UP YOUR DOOR — Richard & The Young Lions (L. Brown-R. Bloodworth), Philips 40381 | 1 |
| 100 | — | — | — | THE OTHER SIDE OF THIS LIFE — Peter, Paul & Mary (Albert B. Grossman), Warner Bros. 5849 | 1 |

## HOT 100—A TO Z—(Publisher-Licensee)

Ain't Gonna Lie (Screen Gems-Columbia, BMI) ..... 91
Ain't Nobody Home (Rittenhouse, BMI) ..... 68
All I See Is You (Anne-Rachel, ASCAP) ..... 51
All Strung Out (Daddy Sam-Jerell, BMI) ..... 42
Almost Persuaded (Gallico, BMI) ..... 29

B-A-B-Y (East, BMI) ..... 38
Baby Toys (Saturday-My Songs, BMI) ..... 76
Beauty Is Only Skin Deep (Jobete, BMI) ..... 6
Black Is Black (Elmwin, BMI) ..... 7
Blowin' in the Wind (Witmark, ASCAP) ..... 47
Blue Side of Lonesome (Glad, BMI) ..... 60
Born a Woman (Painted Desert, BMI) ..... 16
Born Free (Columbia, BMI) ..... 54
Bus Stop (Manken, BMI) ..... 5

Can't Satisfy (Chi-Sound, BMI) ..... 67
Cast Your Fate to the Wind (Friendship, BMI) ..... 63
Changes (Barricade, ASCAP) ..... 88
Cherish (Beechwood, BMI) ..... 1
Cherry, Cherry (Tallyrand, BMI) ..... 14
Come On Up (Slacsar, BMI) ..... 86

Dianne, Dianne (Buckhorn & Gallico, BMI) ..... 71

Eleanor Rigby (Maclen, BMI) ..... 11

Fiddle Around (Bourne, ASCAP) ..... 93
Fife Piper (Jules-Tone, BMI) ..... 65
Flamingo (Tempo, ASCAP) ..... 30
Function at the Junction (Jobete, BMI) ..... 97

Get Away (Noma-Gunnel, BMI) ..... 77
Girl on a Swing (Bright Tunes, BMI) ..... 64
God Only Knows (Sea of Tunes, BMI) ..... 39
Guantanamera (Fall River, BMI) ..... 13

Hooray for Hazel (Low Twi, BMI) ..... 59
How Sweet It Is (Jobete, BMI) ..... 18

I Can Make It With You (De Shannon) (Blackwood, BMI) ..... 79
I Can Make It With You (Pozo Seco Singers) Blackwood, BMI) ..... 58
I Chose to Sing the Blues (Metric, BMI) ..... 45
I Really Don't Want to Know (Hill & Range, BMI) ..... 36
I Struck It Rich (Champion-Double Diamond, BMI) ..... 98
I Want to Be With You (Moreley, ASCAP) ..... 62
I'm Your Puppet (Fame, BMI) ..... 96
I've Got You Under My Skin (Chappell, ASCAP) ..... 19
If I Were a Carpenter (Faithful Virtue, BMI) ..... 81
In Our Time (Criterion, ASCAP) ..... 75
In the Arms of Love (Twin-Chris, ASCAP) ..... 49
It Hurts Me (Unart, BMI) ..... 78

Joker Went Wild, The (Rising Sons, BMI) ..... 34
Just Like a Woman (Dwarf, ASCAP) ..... 41

Knock on Wood (East, BMI) ..... 89
Land of 1,000 Dances (Tune-Kel-Anatole, BMI) ..... 24
Last Train to Clarksville (Screen Gems-Columbia, BMI) ..... 26
Little Darlin' (I Need You) (Jobete, BMI) ..... 57
Love Is a Hurtin' Thing (Rawlou, BMI) ..... 73

Mas Que Nada (Peer Int'l., BMI) ..... 85
Melody for an Unknown Girl (Daywin, BMI) ..... 84
Mind Excursion (Tender Tunes, BMI) ..... 83
Mr. Dieingly Sad (Tender Tunes-Elmwin, BMI) ..... 20
Mr. Spaceman (Tickson, BMI) ..... 90
Money Won't Change You (Dynatone, BMI) ..... 70
My Sweet Potato (Instrumental, BMI) ..... 87
My Uncle Used to Love Me But She Died (Tree, BMI) ..... 66

96 Tears (Arquello, BMI) ..... 8

Off to Dublin in the Green (Melody Trails, BMI) ..... 94
Open the Door to Your Heart (T. M. & Parmalier, BMI) ..... 28
Open Up Your Door (Saturday, BMI) ..... 99
Other Side of This Life, The (Third Story, BMI) ..... 100

Philly Freeze, The (Vapac, BMI) ..... 69
Please Mr. Sun (Weiss-Barry, BMI) ..... 92
Poor Side of Town (Rivers, BMI) ..... 72
Poverty (Don, BMI) ..... 74
Psychotic Reaction (Hot Shot, BMI) ..... 25
Reach Out I'll Be There (Jobete, BMI) ..... 10
Respectable (Wemar, BMI) ..... 31
Rumors (Duane-Aim, BMI) ..... 61

Said I Wasn't Gonna Tell Nobody (East-Pronto, BMI) ..... 82
Say I Am (What I Said) (Dunde, BMI) ..... 48
See See Rider (Leeds, ASCAP) ..... 53
See You in September (Vibar, ASCAP) ..... 12
7 and 7 Is (Grass Roots, BMI) ..... 33
Sometimes Good Guys Don't Wear White (Equinox, BMI) ..... 43
Summer in the City (Faithful Virtue, BMI) ..... 37
Summer Samba (Duchess, BMI) ..... 44
Summer Wind (Witmark, ASCAP) ..... 32
Sunny (Portable, BMI) ..... 21
Sunny Afternoon (Norma, BMI) ..... 15
Sunshine Superman (Southern, ASCAP) ..... 3
Suspicions (Ricemill-R & S, BMI) ..... 55

That's Enough (Kapa, BMI) ..... 80
There Will Never Be Another You (Morris, ASCAP) ..... 46
To Make a Big Man Cry (Regent, BMI) ..... 95
Turn-Down Day (Northern, ASCAP) ..... 22

Wade in the Water (Ramsel, BMI) ..... 35
Walk Away Renee (Twin Tone, BMI) ..... 40
What Becomes of the Brokenhearted (Jobete, BMI) ..... 23
Wipe Out (Miraleste-Robin Hood, BMI) ..... 17
With a Girl Like You (James, BMI) ..... 50
Working in the Coal Mine (Marsaint, BMI) ..... 27
World of Fantasy (Camad, BMI) ..... 52
Wouldn't It Be Nice (Sea of Tunes, BMI) ..... 9

Yellow Submarine (Maclen, BMI) ..... 4
You Can't Hurry Love (Jobete, BMI) ..... 2
You're Gonna Miss Me (Acquire, BMI) ..... 56

## BUBBLING UNDER THE HOT 100

101. IMPRESSIONS ..... The Jones Boys, Atco 6426
102. HAPPINESS ..... Shades of Blue, Impact 1015
103. DON'T WORRY MOTHER, YOUR SON'S HEART IS PURE ..... McCoys, Bang 532
104. BAD LITTLE WOMAN ..... Shadows of Knight, Dunwich 128
105. ONLY WHEN YOU'RE LONELY ..... Grass Roots, Dunhill 1043
106. POLLYANNA ..... Classics, Capitol 5710
107. TOMORROW NEVER COMES ..... B. J. Thomas, Scepter 12165
108. SHE DRIVES ME OUT OF MY MIND ..... Swingin' Medallions, Smash 2050
109. THE WHEEL OF HURT ..... Margaret Whiting, London 101
110. DOMMAGE, DOMMAGE ..... Jerry Vale, Columbia 43774
111. CRY SOFTLY ..... Nancy Ames, Epic 10056
112. A WOMAN OF THE WORLD ..... Gentrys, MGM 13561
113. ROLLER COASTER ..... I'des of March, Parrot 310
114. ASHES TO ASHES ..... Mindbenders, Fontana 1555
115. COLD LIGHT OF DAY ..... Gene Pitney, Musicor 1200
116. IT WAS A VERY GOOD YEAR ..... Della Reese, ABC 10841
117. SHE AIN'T LOVIN' YOU ..... Distant Cousins, Date 1514
118. IF MY CAR COULD ONLY TALK ..... Lou Christie, MGM 13576
119. A TIME FOR LOVE ..... Tony Bennett, Columbia 43768
120. JUST LIKE A WOMAN ..... Manfred Mann, Mercury 72607
121. HE'LL BE BACK ..... Players, Minit 32001
122. SECRET LOVE ..... Richard "Groove" Holmes, Pacific Jazz 88130
123. COMING ON STRONG ..... Brenda Lee, Decca 32018
124. GLORIA'S DREAM ..... Belfast Gypsies, Loma 2051
125. DOMAGE, DOMAGE ..... Paul Vance, Scepter 12164
126. HERE, THERE AND EVERYWHERE ..... Fourmost, Capitol 5738
127. STOP LOOK AND LISTEN ..... Chiffons, Laurie 3357
128. THE SCRATCH ..... Robert Parker, Nola 726
129. BABY, DO THE PHILLY DOG ..... Olympics, Mirwood 5523
130. ROSEANNA ..... Capreez, Sound 126
131. SHAKE SHERRY ..... Harvey Russell & the Rogues, Roulette 4697
132. FA-FA-FA-FA-FA ..... Otis Redding, Volt 138
133. FANNIE MAE ..... Mighty Sam, Amy 963
134. HEAVEN MUST HAVE SENT YOU ..... Elgins, V.I.P. 25037
135. LOOKIN' FOR LOVE ..... Ray Conniff Singers, Columbia 43814

Compiled from national retail sales and radio station airplay by the Music Popularity Dept. of Record Market Research, Billboard.

# Billboard HOT 100

For Week Ending October 1, 1966

★ STAR performer—Sides registering greatest proportionate upward progress this week.

Record Industry Association of America seal of certification as million selling single.

| This Week | 1 Wk. Ago | 2 Wks. Ago | 3 Wks. Ago | TITLE — Artist (Producer), Label & Number | Weeks on Chart |
|---|---|---|---|---|---|
| 1 | 1 | 4 | 14 | **CHERISH** — Association (C. Boettcher), Valiant 747 [Billboard Award] | 6 |
| 2 | 2 | 1 | 1 | YOU CAN'T HURRY LOVE — Supremes (Holland & Dozier), Motown 1097 | 8 |
| 3 | 6 | 11 | 16 | BEAUTY IS ONLY SKIN DEEP — Temptations (Norman Whitfield), Gordy 7055 | 7 |
| 4 | 7 | 18 | 27 | BLACK IS BLACK — Los Bravos (Ivor Raymonde), Press 60002 | 8 |
| 5 | 5 | 5 | 9 | BUS STOP — Hollies (Ron Richardson), Imperial 66186 | 11 |
| 6 | 8 | 25 | 45 | 96 TEARS — ? (Question Mark) & the Mysterians, Cameo 428 | 5 |
| 7 | 10 | 26 | 57 | REACH OUT I'LL BE THERE — Four Tops (Holland & Dozier), Motown 1098 | 5 |
| 8 | 4 | 2 | 3 | YELLOW SUBMARINE — Beatles (Martin), Capitol 5715 | 7 |
| 9 | 3 | 3 | 2 | SUNSHINE SUPERMAN — Donovan (Mickey Most), Epic 10045 | 10 |
| 10 | 14 | 24 | 39 | CHERRY, CHERRY — Neil Diamond (Jeff Barry & Ellie Greenwich), Bang 528 | 7 |
| 11 | 11 | 14 | 26 | ELEANOR RIGBY — Beatles (George Martin), Capitol 5715 | 6 |
| 12 | 19 | 28 | 41 | I'VE GOT YOU UNDER MY SKIN — 4 Seasons (Bob Crewe), Philips 40393 | 5 |
| 13 | 16 | 12 | 13 | BORN A WOMAN — Sandy Posey (Chip Moman), MGM 1350 | 11 |
| 14 | 15 | 15 | 20 | SUNNY AFTERNOON — Kinks (Shel Talmy), Reprise 0497 | 9 |
| 15 | 25 | 42 | 79 | PSYCHOTIC REACTION — Count Five (Hooven-Winn), Double Shot 104 | 4 |
| 16 | 17 | 20 | 23 | WIPE OUT — Surfaris, Dot 144 | 26 |
| 17 | 13 | 9 | 10 | GUANTANAMERA — Sandpipers (Tommy LiPuma), A&M 806 | 10 |
| 18 | 26 | 43 | 67 | LAST TRAIN TO CLARKSVILLE — Monkees (Tommy Boyce & Bobby Hart), Colgems 1001 | 4 |
| 19 | 23 | 29 | 37 | WHAT BECOMES OF THE BROKENHEARTED — Jimmy Ruffin (William Stevenson), Soul 35022 | 7 |
| 20 | 20 | 27 | 32 | MR. DIEINGLY SAD — Critters (Artie Ripp), Kapp 769 | 8 |
| 21 | 18 | 23 | 24 | HOW SWEET IT IS — Jr. Walker & the All-Stars (J. Bristol-H. Fuqua), Soul 35024 | 10 |
| 22 | 12 | 6 | 4 | SEE YOU IN SEPTEMBER — Happenings (Bright Tunes Prod.), B. T. Puppy 520 | 13 |
| 23 | 9 | 8 | 11 | WOULDN'T IT BE NICE — Beach Boys (Brian Wilson), Capitol 5706 | 10 |
| 24 | 29 | 30 | 36 | ALMOST PERSUADED — David Houston (Billy Sherrill), Epic 10025 | 12 |
| 25 | 32 | 37 | 48 | SUMMER WIND — Frank Sinatra (Sonny Burke), Reprise 0509 | 5 |
| 26 | 24 | 7 | 6 | LAND OF 1,000 DANCES — Wilson Pickett (Jerry Wexler & Rick Hall), Atlantic 2348 | 10 |
| 27 | 28 | 31 | 31 | OPEN THE DOOR TO YOUR HEART — Darrell Banks (Bright Tunes Prod.), Revilot 201 | 11 |
| 28 | 30 | 36 | 46 | FLAMINGO — Herb Alpert & the Tijuana Brass (Herb Alpert), A&M 813 | 5 |
| 29 | 44 | 56 | 76 | SUMMER SAMBA — Walter Wanderley (Creed Taylor), Verve 10421 | 6 |
| 30 | 40 | 58 | 69 | WALK AWAY RENEE — Left Banke (World United Prod. Inc.), Smash 2041 | 4 |
| 31 | 38 | 44 | 54 | B-A-B-Y — Carla Thomas (Staff), Stax 195 | 7 |
| 32 | 27 | 13 | 8 | WORKING IN THE COAL MINE — Lee Dorsey (A. Toussaint-M. Sehorn), Amy 958 | 11 |
| 33 | 21 | 10 | 7 | SUNNY — Bobby Hebb (Jerry Ross), Philips 40365 | 15 |
| 34 | 45 | 55 | 65 | I CHOSE TO SING THE BLUES — Ray Charles (Tangerine Records), ABC 10840 | 5 |
| 35 | 41 | 54 | 81 | JUST LIKE A WOMAN — Bob Dylan (Bob Johnston), Columbia 43792 | 4 |
| 36 | 36 | 46 | 56 | I REALLY DON'T WANT TO KNOW — Ronnie Dove (Phil Kahl), Diamond 208 | 6 |
| 37 | 53 | 85 | — | SEE SEE RIDER — Eric Burdon & the Animals (Tom Wilson), MGM 13582 | 3 |
| 38 | 42 | 52 | 80 | ALL STRUNG OUT — Nino Tempo & April Stevens (Nino Tempo-Jerry Riopelle), White Whale 236 | 4 |
| 39 | 59 | 75 | — | HOORAY FOR HAZEL — Tommy Roe (Our Prods.), ABC 10852 | 3 |
| 40 | 51 | 81 | — | ALL I SEE IS YOU — Dusty Springfield (Johnny Franz), Philips 40396 | 3 |
| 41 | 22 | 16 | 18 | TURN-DOWN DAY — Cyrkle (John Simon), Columbia 43729 | 8 |
| 42 | 72 | 90 | — | POOR SIDE OF TOWN — Johnny Rivers (Lou Adler), Imperial 66205 | 3 |
| 43 | 33 | 38 | 38 | 7 AND 7 IS — Love (Jac Holzman), Elektra 45605 / Philips 40377 | 10 |
| 44 | 35 | 19 | 19 | WADE IN THE WATER — Ramsey Lewis (Esmond Edwards), Cadet 5541 | 13 |
| 45 | 39 | 40 | 42 | GOD ONLY KNOWS — Beach Boys (Brian Wilson), Capitol 5706 | 8 |
| 46 | 46 | 33 | 35 | THERE WILL NEVER BE ANOTHER YOU — Chris Montez (Tommy LiPuma), A&M 810 | 8 |
| 47 | 54 | 68 | 73 | BORN FREE — Roger Williams (Hy Grill), Kapp 767 | 6 |
| 48 | 58 | 72 | 87 | I CAN MAKE IT WITH YOU — Pozo-Seco Singers (Bob Johnston), Columbia 43784 | 4 |
| 49 | 49 | 57 | 61 | IN THE ARMS OF LOVE — Andy Williams (Robert Mersey), Columbia 43737 | 6 |
| 50 | 43 | 48 | 53 | SOMETIMES GOOD GUYS DON'T WEAR WHITE — Standells (Ed Cobb), Tower 257 | 8 |
| 51 | 81 | — | — | IF I WERE A CARPENTER — Bobby Darin (Koppleman-Rubin), Atlantic 2350 | 2 |
| 52 | 64 | 79 | 85 | GIRL ON A SWING — Gerry & the Pacemakers, Laurie 3354 | 4 |
| 53 | 65 | 78 | 88 | THE FIFE PIPER — Dynatones (J. J. Jules), HBR 494 | 5 |
| 54 | 62 | 65 | 68 | I WANT TO BE WITH YOU — Dee Dee Warwick, Mercury 72584 | 6 |
| 55 | 61 | 63 | 59 | RUMORS — Syndicate of Sound (Garrie Thompson), Bell 646 | 7 |
| 56 | 56 | 60 | 66 | YOU'RE GONNA MISS ME — Thirteenth Floor Elevators (Gorbyn Prod.), International Artists 107 | 6 |
| 57 | 55 | 59 | 60 | SUSPICIONS — Sidekicks, RCA Victor 8864 | 5 |
| 58 | 66 | 82 | — | MY UNCLE USED TO LOVE ME BUT SHE DIED — Roger Miller (Jerry Kennedy), Smash 2055 | 3 |
| 59 | 60 | 64 | 64 | BLUE SIDE OF LONESOME — Jim Reeves (Chet Atkins), RCA Victor 8902 | 6 |
| 60 | 75 | 88 | — | IN OUR TIME — Nancy Sinatra (Lee Hazlewood), Reprise 0514 | 3 |
| 61 | 73 | 89 | 99 | LOVE IS A HURTIN' THING — Lou Rawls (David Axelrod), Capitol 5709 | 4 |
| 62 | 57 | 47 | 47 | LITTLE DARLIN' (I Need You) — Marvin Gaye (Holland & Dozier), Tamla 54138 | 7 |
| 63 | 68 | 70 | 72 | AIN'T NOBODY HOME — Howard Tate (Jerry Ragovoy), Verve 10420 | 7 |
| 64 | 82 | 83 | 83 | SAID I WASN'T GONNA TELL NOBODY — Sam & Dave (Prod. by Staff), Stax 198 | 3 |
| 65 | 74 | 86 | — | POVERTY — Bobby Bland, Duke 407 | 3 |
| 66 | 67 | 67 | 82 | CAN'T SATISFY — Impressions (Johnny Pate), ABC 10831 | 5 |
| 67 | 86 | — | — | COME ON UP — Young Rascals (Young Rascals), Atlantic 2353 | 2 |
| 68 | 79 | 84 | 86 | I CAN MAKE IT WITH YOU — Jackie DeShannon (Calvin Carter), Imperial 66202 | 4 |
| 69 | 90 | — | — | MR. SPACEMAN — Byrds (Allen Stanton), Columbia 43766 | 2 |
| 70 | 78 | 80 | 90 | IT HURTS ME — Bobby Goldsboro (Jack Gold), United Artists 50056 | 5 |
| 71 | 71 | 69 | 75 | DIANNE, DIANNE — Ronny & the Daytonas (Bucky Wilkin), RCA Victor 8896 | 5 |
| 72 | — | — | — | LITTLE MAN — Sonny & Cher (Sonny Bono), Atco 6440 | 1 |
| 73 | 92 | — | — | PLEASE MR. SUN — Vogues (Cenci-Moon-Hakim), Co & Ce 240 | 2 |
| 74 | 84 | — | — | MELODY FOR AN UNKNOWN GIRL — Unknowns (Steve Alaimo), Parrot 307 | 2 |
| 75 | 84 | — | — | MIND EXCURSION — The Trade Winds (Anders-Poncia), Kama Sutra 212 | 4 |
| 76 | 91 | 94 | — | AIN'T GONNA LIE — Keith (Jerry Ross), Mercury 72596 | 3 |
| 77 | 85 | — | — | MAS QUE NADA — Sergio Mendes & Brazil '66 (Herb Alpert), A&M 807 | 2 |
| 78 | 77 | 77 | 70 | GET AWAY — Georgie Fame (Denny Cordell), Imperial 66189 | 7 |
| 79 | 96 | — | — | I'M YOUR PUPPET — James & Bobby Purify (Don Schroeder), Bell 648 | 2 |
| 80 | — | — | — | GO AWAY LITTLE GIRL — Happenings (Tokens), B. T. Puppy 522 | 1 |
| 81 | — | — | — | THE HAIR ON MY CHINNY CHIN CHIN — Sam the Sham & the Pharaohs (Stan Kesler), MGM 13581 | 1 |
| 82 | — | — | — | FA-FA-FA-FA-FA — Otis Redding, Volt. 138 | 1 |
| 83 | — | — | — | GOING ON STRONG — Brenda Lee (Owen Bradley), Decca 32018 | 1 |
| 84 | — | — | — | I JUST DON'T KNOW WHAT TO DO WITH MYSELF — Dionne Warwick (Bacharach-David), Scepter 12167 | 1 |
| 85 | 87 | 87 | 89 | MY SWEET POTATO — Booker T. & the M.G.'s (Prod. by Staff), Stax 196 | 5 |
| 86 | 89 | 97 | 97 | KNOCK ON WOOD — Eddie Floyd (Prod. by Staff), Stax 194 | 4 |
| 87 | 88 | 95 | — | CHANGES — Crispian St. Peters (David Nicolson), Jamie 1324 | 3 |
| 88 | — | — | — | THE GREAT AIRPLANE STRIKE — Paul Revere & the Raiders (Terry Melcher), Columbia 43810 | 1 |
| 89 | — | — | — | DANDY — Herman's Hermits (Mickie Most), MGM 13603 | 1 |
| 90 | — | — | — | BABY, DO THE PHILLY DOG — Olympics (Smith), Mirwood 5523 | 1 |
| 91 | — | — | — | BUT IT'S ALRIGHT — J. J. Jackson (Lew Futterman), Calla 119 | 1 |
| 92 | — | — | — | DON'T WORRY MOTHER, YOUR SON'S HEART IS PURE — McCoys (Feldman-Goldstein-Gottehrers), Bang 532 | 1 |
| 93 | — | — | — | PHILLY DOG — Herbie Mann, Atlantic 5074 | 1 |
| 94 | 94 | — | — | OFF TO DUBLIN IN THE GREEN — Abbey Tavern Singers (Hanna Barbera Prod.), HBR 498 | 2 |
| 95 | — | — | — | ALMOST PERSUADED NO. 2 — Ben Colder (Jack Clement), MGM 13590 | 1 |
| 96 | — | — | — | HAPPINESS — Shades of Blue (John Phys), Impact 1015 | 1 |
| 97 | — | — | — | STOP LOOK AND LISTEN — Chiffons (Bright Tunes Prod.), Laurie 3357 | 1 |
| 98 | — | — | — | WHAT NOW, MY LOVE — "Groove" Holmes (Cal Lampley), Prestige 427 | 1 |
| 99 | — | — | — | TAKE GOOD CARE OF HER — Mel Carter (Nick DeCaro), Imperial 66208 | 1 |
| 100 | — | — | — | SECRET LOVE — Richard "Groove" Holmes (Richard Bock), Pacific Jazz 88130 | 1 |

## BUBBLING UNDER THE HOT 100

101. SPINOUT — Elvis Presley, RCA Victor 8941
102. I STRUCK IT RICH — Len Barry, Decca 32011
103. DOMMAGE, DOMMAGE — Jerry Vale, Columbia 43774
104. BAD LITTLE WOMAN — Shadows of Knight, Dunwich 128
105. TO MAKE A BIG MAN CRY — Roy Head, Back Beat 571
106. TOMORROW NEVER COMES — B. J. Thomas, Scepter 12165
107. SHE AIN'T LOVING YOU — Distant Cousins, Date 1514
108. THE WHEEL OF HURT — Margaret Whiting, London 101
109. FUNCTION AT THE JUNCTION — Shorty Long, Soul 35021
110. POLLYANNA — Classics, Musicor 5710
111. CRY SOFTLY — Nancy Ames, Epic 10056
112. ASHES TO ASHES — Mindbenders, Fontana 1555
113. DOMMAGE, DOMMAGE — Paul Vance, Scepter 12164
114. A WOMAN OF THE WORLD — Gentrys, MGM 13561
115. WISH YOU WERE HERE, BUDDY — Pat Boone, Dot 16933
116. IMPRESSIONS — Jones Boys, Atco 6426
117. FIDDLE AROUND — Jan & Dean, Liberty 55905
118. OPEN UP YOUR DOOR — Richard & the Young Lions, Phillips 40381
119. PIPELINE — Chantays, Dot 145
120. FANNIE MAE — Mighty Sam, Amy 963
121. HERE THERE AND EVERYWHERE — Fourmost, Capitol 5738
122. HEAVEN MUST HAVE SENT YOU — Elgins, V.I.P. 25031
123. TREAT ME LIKE A LADY — Lesley Gore, Mercury 72611
124. THE OTHER SIDE OF THIS LIFE — Peter, Paul & Mary, Warner Bros. 5849
125. ROSEANNA — Capreez, Sound 126
126. NOBODY'S BABY AGAIN — Dean Martin, Reprise 0516
127. WHISPERS — Jackie Wilson, Brunswick 55300
128. UNDER MY THUMB — Del Shannon, Liberty 55904
129. I CAN'T DO WITHOUT YOU — Dean Jackson, Carla 2530
130. AFTER YOU, THERE CAN BE NOTHING — Walter Jackson, Okeh 7256
131. HOLD ON! I'M A COMIN' — Billy Larkin & the Delegates, World-Pacific 77844
132. MY BABY — Garnet Mimms, Veep 1234
133. LOVE'S GONE BAD — Chris Clark, V.I.P. 25028
134. LOOKIN' FOR LOVE — Ray Conniff Singers, Columbia 43814
135. THESE THINGS WILL KEEP ME LOVING YOU — Velvelettes, Soul 35025

Compiled from national retail sales and radio station airplay by the Music Popularity Dept. of Record Market Research, Billboard.

# Billboard HOT 100

**For Week Ending October 8, 1966**

★ STAR performer—Sides registering greatest proportionate upward progress this week.

Record Industry Association of America seal of certification as million selling single.

| This Week | 1 Wk. Ago | 2 Wks. Ago | 3 Wks. Ago | TITLE — Artist (Producer), Label & Number | Weeks On Chart |
|---|---|---|---|---|---|
| 1 ★ | 1 | 1 | 4 | CHERISH — Association (C. Boettcher), Valiant 747 | 7 |
| 2 | 7 | 10 | 26 | REACH OUT I'LL BE THERE — Four Tops (Holland & Dozier), Motown 1098 | 6 |
| 3 | 6 | 8 | 25 | TEARS — ? (Question Mark) & the Mysterians, Cameo 428 | 6 |
| 4 | 4 | 7 | 18 | BLACK IS BLACK — Los Bravos (Ivor Raymonde), Press 60002 | 9 |
| 5 | 3 | 6 | 11 | BEAUTY IS ONLY SKIN DEEP — Temptations (Norman Whitfield), Gordy 7055 | 8 |
| 6 | 18 | 26 | 43 | LAST TRAIN TO CLARKSVILLE — Monkees (Tommy Boyce & Bobby Hart), Colgems 1001 | 5 |
| 7 | 10 | 14 | 24 | CHERRY, CHERRY — Neil Diamond (Jeff Barry & Ellie Greenwich), Bang 528 | 8 |
| 8 | 2 | 2 | 1 | YOU CAN'T HURRY LOVE — Supremes (Holland & Dozier), Motown 1097 | 7 |
| 9 | 15 | 25 | 42 | PSYCHOTIC REACTION — Count Five (Hooven-Winn), Double Shot 104 | 5 |
| 10 | 12 | 19 | 28 | I'VE GOT YOU UNDER MY SKIN — 4 Seasons (Bob Crewe), Philips 40393 | 6 |
| 11 | 19 | 23 | 29 | WHAT BECOMES OF THE BROKENHEARTED — Jimmy Ruffin (William Stevenson), Soul 35022 | 8 |
| 12 | 9 | 3 | 3 | SUNSHINE SUPERMAN — Donovan (Mickey Most), Epic 10045 | 11 |
| 13 | 13 | 16 | 12 | BORN A WOMAN — Sandy Posey (Chip Moman), MGM 13501 | 12 |
| 14 | 30 | 40 | 58 | WALK AWAY RENEE — cft Banke (World United Prod. Inc.), Smash 2041 | 5 |
| 15 | 5 | 5 | 5 | BUS STOP — Hollies (Ron Richardson), Imperial 66186 | 12 |
| 16 | 8 | 4 | 2 | YELLOW SUBMARINE — Beatles (Martin), Capitol 5715 | 8 |
| 17 | 20 | 20 | 27 | MR. DIEINGLY SAD — Critters (Artie Ripp), Kapp 769 | 9 |
| 18 | 16 | 17 | 20 | WIPE OUT — Surfaris, Dot 144 | 27 |
| 19 | 37 | 53 | 85 | SEE SEE RIDER — Eric Burdon & the Animals (Tom Wilson), MGM 13582 | 4 |
| 20 | 42 | 72 | 90 | POOR SIDE OF TOWN — Johnny Rivers (Lou Adler), Imperial 66205 | 3 |
| 21 | 11 | 11 | 14 | ELEANOR RIGBY — Beatles (George Martin), Capitol 5715 | 7 |
| 22 | 51 | 81 | — | IF I WERE A CARPENTER — Bobby Darin (Koppleman-Rubin), Atlantic 2350 | 3 |
| 23 | 39 | 59 | 75 | HOORAY FOR HAZEL — Tommy Roe (Our Prods.), ABC 10852 | 4 |
| 24 | 36 | 36 | 46 | I REALLY DON'T WANT TO KNOW — Ronnie Dove (Phil Kahl), Diamond 208 | 6 |
| 25 | 31 | 38 | 44 | B-A-B-Y — Carla Thomas (Staff), Stax 195 | 8 |
| 26 | 40 | 51 | 81 | ALL I SEE IS YOU — Dusty Springfield, Philips 40396 | 4 |
| 27 | 14 | 15 | 15 | SUNNY AFTERNOON — Kinks (Shel Talmy), Reprise 0497 | 10 |
| 28 | 29 | 44 | 56 | SUMMER SAMBA — Walter Wanderley (Creed Taylor), Verve 10421 | 7 |
| 29 ★ | 38 | 42 | 52 | ALL STRUNG OUT — Nino Tempo & April Stevens (Nino Tempo-Jerry Riopell), White Whale 236 | 5 |
| 30 | 28 | 30 | 36 | FLAMINGO — Herb Alpert & the Tijuana Brass (Herb Alpert), A&M 813 | 6 |
| 31 | 24 | 29 | 30 | ALMOST PERSUADED — David Houston (Billy Sherrill), Epic 10025 | 13 |
| 32 | 34 | 45 | 55 | I CHOSE TO SING THE BLUES — Ray Charles (Tangerine Records), ABC 10840 | 6 |
| 33 | 35 | 41 | 54 | JUST LIKE A WOMAN — Bob Dylan (Bob Johnston), Columbia 43792 | 5 |
| 34 | 25 | 32 | 37 | SUMMER WIND — Frank Sinatra (Sonny Burke), Reprise 0509 | 6 |
| 35 | 17 | 13 | 9 | GUANTANAMERA — Sandpipers (Tommy LiPuma), A&M 806 | 11 |
| 36 | 22 | 12 | 6 | SEE YOU IN SEPTEMBER — Happenings (Bright Tunes Prod.), B. T. Puppy 520 | 14 |
| 37 | 52 | 64 | 79 | GIRL ON A SWING — Gerry & the Pacemakers, Laurie 3354 | 5 |
| 38 | 48 | 58 | 72 | I CAN MAKE IT WITH YOU — Pozo-Seco Singers (Bob Johnston), Columbia 43784 | 5 |
| 39 | 32 | 27 | 13 | WORKING IN THE COAL MINE — Lee Dorsey (A. Toussaint-M. Sehorn), Amy 958 | 12 |
| 40 ★ | — | — | — | HAVE YOU SEEN YOUR MOTHER, BABY, STANDING IN THE SHADOW? — Rolling Stones (Andrew Oldham), London 903 | 1 |
| 41 | 47 | 54 | 68 | BORN FREE — Roger Williams (Hy Grill), Kapp 767 | 7 |
| 42 | 27 | 28 | 31 | OPEN THE DOOR TO YOUR HEART — Darrell Banks, Revilot 201 | 12 |
| 43 | 72 | — | — | LITTLE MAN — Sonny & Cher (Sonny Bono), Atco 6440 | 2 |
| 44 | 61 | 73 | 89 | LOVE IS A HURTIN' THING — Lou Rawls (David Axelrod), Capitol 5709 | 5 |
| 45 | 23 | 9 | 8 | WOULDN'T IT BE NICE — Beach Boys (Brian Wilson), Capitol 5706 | 11 |
| 46 | 26 | 24 | 7 | LAND OF 1,000 DANCES — Wilson Pickett (Jerry Wexler & Rick Hall), Atlantic 2348 | 11 |
| 47 | 21 | 18 | 23 | HOW SWEET IT IS — Jr. Walker & the All-Stars (J. Bristol-H. Fuqua), Soul 35024 | 11 |
| 48 ★ | 89 | — | — | DANDY — Herman's Hermits (Mickie Most), MGM 13603 | 2 |
| 49 | 60 | 75 | 88 | IN OUR TIME — Nancy Sinatra (Lee Hazlewood), Reprise 0514 | 4 |
| 50 | 49 | 49 | 57 | IN THE ARMS OF LOVE — Andy Williams (Robert Mersey), Columbia 43737 | 7 |
| 51 | 81 | — | — | THE HAIR ON MY CHINNY CHIN CHIN — Sam the Sham & the Pharaohs (Stan Kesler), MGM 13581 | 2 |
| 52 | 88 | — | — | THE GREAT AIRPLANE STRIKE — Paul Revere & the Raiders (Terry Melcher), Columbia 43810 | 2 |
| 53 | 53 | 65 | 78 | THE FIFE PIPER — Dynatones (J. J. Jules), HBR 494 | 6 |
| 54 | 54 | 62 | 65 | I WANT TO BE WITH YOU — Dee Dee Warwick (Jerry Ragavoy), Mercury 72584 | 7 |
| 55 | 56 | 56 | 60 | YOU'RE GONNA MISS ME — Thirteenth Floor Elevators (Gorbyn Prod.), International Artists. 107 | 8 |
| 56 | 69 | 90 | — | MR. SPACEMAN — Byrds (Allen Stanton), Columbia 43766 | 3 |
| 57 | 67 | 86 | — | COME ON UP — Young Rascals (Young Rascals), Atlantic 2353 | 3 |
| 58 | 75 | 84 | — | MIND EXCURSION — The Trade Winds (Anders-Poncia), Kama Sutra 212 | 3 |
| 59 | 59 | 60 | 64 | BLUE SIDE OF LONESOME — Jim Reeves (Chet Atkins), RCA Victor 8902 | 7 |
| 60 | 73 | 92 | — | PLEASE MR. SUN — Vogues (Cenci-Moon-Hakim), Co & Ce 240 | 3 |
| 61 | 58 | 66 | 82 | MY UNCLE USED TO LOVE ME BUT SHE DIED — Roger Miller (Jerry Kennedy), Smash 2055 | 4 |
| 62 | 77 | 85 | — | MAS QUE NADA — Sergio Mendes & Brazil '66 (Herb Alpert), A&M 807 | 3 |
| 63 | 80 | — | — | GO AWAY LITTLE GIRL — Happenings (Tokens), B. T. Puppy 522 | 2 |
| 64 | 64 | 82 | 83 | SAID I WASN'T GONNA TELL NOBODY — Sam & Dave (Prod. by Staff), Stax 198 | 5 |
| 65 | 66 | 67 | 67 | CAN'T SATISFY — Impressions (Johnny Pate), ABC 10831 | 6 |
| 66 | 83 | — | — | GOING ON STRONG — Brenda Lee (Owen Bradley), Decca 32018 | 2 |
| 67 | 82 | — | — | FA-FA-FA-FA-FA — Otis Redding, Volt 138 | 2 |
| 68 | 68 | 79 | 84 | I CAN MAKE IT WITH YOU — Jackie DeShannon (Calvin Carter), Imperial 66202 | 5 |
| 69 ★ | 84 | — | — | I JUST DON'T KNOW WHAT TO DO WITH MYSELF — Dionne Warwick (Bacharach-David), Scepter 12167 | 2 |
| 70 | 92 | — | — | DON'T WORRY MOTHER, YOUR SON'S HEART IS PURE — McCoys (Feldman-Goldstein-Gottehrers), Bang 532 | 2 |
| 71 | 79 | 96 | — | I'M YOUR PUPPET — James & Bobby Purify (Don Schroeder), Bell 648 | 4 |
| 72 | 87 | 88 | 95 | CHANGES — Crispian St. Peters (David Nicolson), Jamie 1324 | 4 |
| 73 | — | — | — | (YOU DON'T HAVE TO) PAINT ME A PICTURE — Gary Lewis & the Playboys, (Snuff Garrett), Liberty 55914 | 1 |
| 74 | 74 | 84 | — | MELODY FOR AN UNKNOWN GIRL — Unknowns (Steve Alaimo), Parrot 307 | 3 |
| 75 | 76 | 91 | 94 | AIN'T GONNA LIE — Keith (Jerry Ross), Mercury 72596 | 4 |
| 76 | 91 | — | — | BUT IT'S ALRIGHT — J. J. Jackson (Lew Futterman), Calla 119 | 2 |
| 77 | 86 | 89 | 97 | KNOCK ON WOOD — Eddie Floyd (Prod. by Staff), Stax 194 | 5 |
| 78 | — | — | — | SPINOUT — Elvis Presley (Joe Pasternak), RCA Victor 8941 | 1 |
| 79 ★ | — | — | — | DEVIL WITH A BLUE DRESS ON & GOOD GOLLY MISS MOLLY — Mitch Ryder & the Detroit Wheels, New Voice 817 (Bob Crew) | 1 |
| 80 | 95 | — | — | ALMOST PERSUADED NO. 2 — Ben Colder (Jack Clement), MGM 13590 | 2 |
| 81 | 96 | — | — | HAPPINESS — Shades of Blue (John Rhys), Impact 1015 | 2 |
| 82 | — | — | — | ALL THAT I AM — Elvis Presley (Joe Pasternark), RCA Victor 8941 | 1 |
| 83 | — | — | — | A SATISFIED MIND — Bobby Hebb (Jerry Ross), Philips 40400 | 1 |
| 84 | 99 | — | — | TAKE GOOD CARE OF HER — Mel Carter (Nick DeCaro), Imperial 66208 | 2 |
| 85 | 97 | — | — | STOP LOOK AND LISTEN — Chiffons (Bright Tunes Prod.), Laurie 3357 | 2 |
| 86 | 90 | — | — | BABY, DO THE PHILLY DOG — Olympics (Smith), Mirwood 5523 | 2 |
| 87 | — | — | — | I'VE GOT TO DO A LITTLE BIT BETTER — Joe Tex (Buddy Killen), Dial 4045 | 1 |
| 88 | — | — | — | NOBODY'S BABY AGAIN — Dean Martin (Jimmy Bowen), Reprise 0516 | 1 |
| 89 | — | 92 | — | TOMORROW NEVER COMES — B. J. Thomas (Huey Meaux), Scepter 12165 | 3 |
| 90 | — | — | — | LADY GODIVA — Peter & Gordon (John Burgess), Capitol 5740 | 1 |
| 91 | — | — | — | YOU ARE SHE — Mark Columbia 43807 | 1 |
| 92 | — | — | — | STAY WITH ME — Lorraine Ellison (Jerry Ragavoy), Warner Bros. 5850 | 1 |
| 93 | — | — | — | DON'T BE A DROP-OUT — James Brown & His Famous Flames (James Brown Prod.), King 6056 | 1 |
| 94 | — | — | — | LOOKIN' FOR LOVE — Ray Conniff Singers (Ernie Altschuler), Columbia 43814 | 1 |
| 95 | — | — | — | THE WHEEL OF HURT — Margaret Whiting (Arnold Goland), London 101 | 1 |
| 96 | — | — | — | DOMMAGE, DOMMAGE — Jerry Vale (Mike Berniker), Columbia 43774 | 1 |
| 97 | — | — | — | DOMMAGE, DOMMAGE — Paul Vance (Vance-Pockriss), Scepter 12164 | 1 |
| 98 | 98 | — | — | WHAT NOW, MY LOVE — "Groove" Holmes (Cal Lampley), Prestige 427 | 2 |
| 99 | 99 | 100 | — | SECRET LOVE — Richard "Groove" Holmes (Richard Bock), Pacific Jazz 88130 | 2 |
| 100 | — | — | — | CRY SOFTLY — Nancy Ames (Kellem), Epic 10056 | 1 |

## BUBBLING UNDER THE HOT 100

101. FREE AGAIN — Barbra Streisand, Columbia 43808
102. SHE AIN'T LOVING YOU — Distant Cousins, Date 1514
103. BAD LITTLE WOMAN — Shadows of Knight, Dunwich 128
104. TO MAKE A BIG MAN CRY — Roy Head, Backbeat 571
105. OPEN UP YOUR DOOR — Richard & Young Lions, Philips 40381
106. MY SWEET POTATO — Booker T. & the M.G.'s, Stax 196
107. WISH YOU WERE HERE, BUDDY — Pat Boone, Dot 16933
108. FUNCTION AT THE JUNCTION — Shorty Long, Soul 35021
109. A DAY IN THE LIFE OF A FOOL — Jack Jones, Kapp 781
110. POLLYANNA — Classics, Capitol 5710
111. OFF TO DUBLIN IN THE GREEN — Abbey Tavern Singers, HBR 498
112. RESPECT — Rationals, Cameo 437
113. HEAVEN MUST HAVE SENT YOU — Elgins, V.I.P. 25031
114. ONE MORE TIME — Clefs of Lavender Hill, Date 1530
115. ROSANNA — Capreez, Sound 126
116. BANG BANG — Joe Cuba Sextette, Tico 475
117. PIPELINE — Chantays, Dot 145
118. THE WILLY — The Willies, Co & Ce 240
119. THE OTHER SIDE OF THIS LIFE — Peter, Paul and Mary, Warner Bros. 5849
120. THERE HERE AND EVERYWHERE — Fourmost, Capitol 5738
121. TREAT ME LIKE A LADY — Leslie Gore, Mercury 72611
122. STICKY STICKY — Bobby Harris, Shout 203
123. HURTIN' — Gary Stites, Epic 10064
124. WHISPERS — Jackie Wilson, Brunswick 55300
125. HEART — Two of Clubs, Fraternity 972
126. RUN AND HIDE — Uniques, Paula 245
127. JUG BAND MUSIC — Mugwumps, Sidewalk 900
128. YOU LEFT THE WATER RUNNING — Barbara Lynn, Tribe 8319
129. A DAY IN THE LIFE OF A FOOL — Jack Jones, Kapp 781
130. POURING WATER ON A DROWNING MAN — James Carr, Goldwax 311
131. ALMOST PERSUADED — Patti Page, Columbia 43794
132. SOMEBODY (SOMEWHERE) NEEDS YOU — Darrell Banks, Revilot 203
133. SHADES OF BLUE — Shirelles, Scepter 12162
134. MY WAY OF LIFE — Sonny Curtis, Viva 6082
135. SHAKE SHERRY — Harvey Russell, Roulette 4697

Compiled from national retail sales and radio station airplay by the Music Popularity Dept. of Record Market Research, Billboard.

# Billboard HOT 100

For Week Ending October 15, 1966

★ STAR performer—Sides registering greatest proportionate upward progress this week.

Ⓡ Record Industry Association of America seal of certification as million selling single.

| This Week | Wk. Ago | 2 Wks. Ago | 3 Wks. Ago | TITLE Artist (Producer), Label & Number | Weeks On Chart |
|---|---|---|---|---|---|
| 1 ★ | 2 | 7 | 10 | **REACH OUT I'LL BE THERE** — Four Tops (Holland & Dozier), Motown 1098 | 7 |
| 2 | 1 | 1 | 1 | **CHERISH** — Association (C. Boettcher), Valiant 747 | 8 |
| 3 | 3 | 6 | 8 | **96 TEARS** — ? (Question Mark) & the Mysterians, Cameo 428 | 7 |
| 4 | 6 | 18 | 26 | **LAST TRAIN TO CLARKSVILLE** — Monkees (Tommy Boyce & Bobby Hart), Colgems 1001 | 6 |
| 5 | 9 | 15 | 25 | **PSYCHOTIC REACTION** — Count Five (Hooven-Winn), Double Shot 104 | 6 |
| 6 | 7 | 10 | 14 | **CHERRY, CHERRY** — Neil Diamond (Jeff Barry & Ellie Greenwich), Bang 528 | 9 |
| 7 | 14 | 30 | 40 | **WALK AWAY RENEE** — Left Banke (World United Prod. Inc.), Smash 2041 | 6 |
| 8 | 11 | 19 | 23 | **WHAT BECOMES OF THE BROKENHEARTED** — Jimmy Ruffin (William Stevenson), Soul 35022 | 9 |
| 9 | 10 | 12 | 19 | **I'VE GOT YOU UNDER MY SKIN** — 4 Seasons (Bob Crewe), Philips 40393 | 7 |
| 10 | 8 | 2 | 2 | **YOU CAN'T HURRY LOVE** — Supremes (Holland & Dozier), Motown 1097 | 10 |
| 11 | 20 | 42 | 72 | **POOR SIDE OF TOWN** — Johnny Rivers (Lou Adler), Imperial 66205 | 5 |
| 12 | 5 | 3 | 6 | **BEAUTY IS ONLY SKIN DEEP** — Temptations (Norman Whitfield), Gordy 7055 | 9 |
| 13 | 4 | 4 | 7 | **BLACK IS BLACK** — Los Bravos (Ivor Raymonds), Press 60002 | 10 |
| 14 | 19 | 37 | 53 | **SEE SEE RIDER** — Eric Burdon and the Animals (Tom Wilson), MGM 13582 | 5 |
| 15 | 48 | 89 | — | **DANDY** — Herman's Hermits (Mickie Most), MGM 13603 | 3 |
| 16 | 23 | 39 | 59 | **HOORAY FOR HAZEL** — Tommy Roe (Our Prods.), ABC 10852 | 5 |
| 17 | 22 | 51 | 81 | **IF I WERE A CARPENTER** — Bobby Darin (Koppleman-Rubin), Atlantic 2350 | 4 |
| 18 | 40 | — | — | **HAVE YOU SEEN YOUR MOTHER, BABY, STANDING IN THE SHADOW?** — Rolling Stones (Andrew Oldham), London 903 | 2 |
| 19 | 25 | 31 | 38 | **B-A-B-Y** — Carla Thomas (Staff), Stax 195 | 9 |
| 20 | 17 | 20 | 20 | **MR. DIEINGLY SAD** — Critters (Artie Ripp), Kapp 769 | 10 |
| 21 | 26 | 40 | 51 | **ALL I SEE IS YOU** — Dusty Springfield, Philips 40396 | 5 |
| 22 | 24 | 36 | 36 | **I REALLY DON'T WANT TO KNOW** — Ronnie Dove (Phil Kahl), Diamond 208 | 7 |
| 23 | 15 | 5 | 5 | **BUS STOP** — Hollies (Ron Richardson), Imperial 66186 | 13 |
| 24 | 13 | 13 | 16 | **BORN A WOMAN** — Sandy Posey (Chip Moman), MGM 13501 | 13 |
| 25 | 18 | 16 | 17 | **WIPE OUT** — Surfaris, Dot 144 | 28 |
| 26 | 28 | 29 | 44 | **SUMMER SAMBA** — Walter Wanderley (Creed Taylor), Verve 10421 | 8 |
| 27 | 29 | 38 | 42 | **ALL STRUNG OUT** — Nino Tempo & April Stevens (Nino Tempo-Jerry Riopol), White Whale 236 | 6 |
| 28 ★ | 43 | 72 | — | **LITTLE MAN** — Sonny & Cher (Sonny Bono), Atco 6440 | 3 |
| 29 | 12 | 9 | 3 | **SUNSHINE SUPERMAN** — Donovan (Mickey Most), Epic 10045 | 12 |
| 30 | 37 | 52 | 64 | **GIRL ON A SWING** — Gerry & the Pacemakers, Laurie 3354 | 6 |
| 31 | 41 | 47 | 54 | **BORN FREE** — Roger Williams (Hy Grill), Kapp 767 | 8 |
| 32 | 16 | 8 | 4 | **YELLOW SUBMARINE** — Beatles (Martin), Capitol 5715 | 9 |
| 33 | 31 | 24 | 29 | **ALMOST PERSUADED** — David Houston (Billy Sherrill), Epic 10025 | 14 |
| 34 | 38 | 48 | 58 | **I CAN MAKE IT WITH YOU** — Pozo-Seco Singers (Bob Johnston), Columbia 43784 | 6 |
| 35 | 52 | 88 | — | **THE GREAT AIRPLANE STRIKE** — Paul Revere & the Raiders (Terry Melcher), Columbia 43810 | 3 |
| 36 | 51 | 81 | — | **THE HAIR ON MY CHINNY CHIN CHIN** — Sam the Sham & the Pharaohs (Stan Kesler), MGM 13581 | 3 |
| 37 | 21 | 11 | 11 | **ELEANOR RIGBY** — Beatles (George Martin), Capitol 5715 | 8 |
| 38 | 44 | 61 | 73 | **LOVE IS A HURTIN' THING** — Lou Rawls (David Axelrod), Capitol 5709 | 6 |
| 39 | 33 | 35 | 41 | **JUST LIKE A WOMAN** — Bob Dylan (Bob Johnston), Columbia 43792 | 6 |
| 40 | 34 | 25 | 32 | **SUMMER WIND** — Frank Sinatra (Sonny Burke), Reprise 0509 | 7 |
| 41 | 32 | 34 | 45 | **I CHOSE TO SING THE BLUES** — Ray Charles (Tangerine Records), ABC 10840 | 7 |
| 42 | 63 | 80 | — | **GO AWAY LITTLE GIRL** — Happenings (Tokens), B.T. Puppy 522 | 3 |
| 43 | 56 | 69 | 90 | **MR. SPACEMAN** — Byrds (Allen Stanton), Columbia 43766 | 4 |
| 44 | 57 | 67 | 86 | **COME ON UP** — Young Rascals (Young Rascals), Atlantic 2353 | 4 |
| 45 ★ | 69 | 84 | — | **I JUST DON'T KNOW WHAT TO DO WITH MYSELF** — Dionne Warwick (Bacharach-David), Scepter 12167 | 3 |
| 46 | 49 | 60 | 75 | **IN OUR TIME** — Nancy Sinatra (Lee Hazlewood), Reprise 0514 | 5 |
| 47 | 54 | 54 | 62 | **I WANT TO BE WITH YOU** — Dee Dee Warwick, Mercury 72584 | 8 |
| 48 | 27 | 14 | 15 | **SUNNY AFTERNOON** — Kinks (Shel Talmy), Reprise 0497 | 11 |
| 49 | 71 | 79 | 96 | **I'M YOUR PUPPET** — James & Bobby Purify (Don Schroeder), Bell 648 | 4 |
| 50 | 73 | — | — | **(You Don't Have To) PAINT ME A PICTURE** — Gary Lewis & the Playboys (Snuff Garrett), Liberty 55914 | 2 |
| 51 | 62 | 77 | 85 | **MAS QUE NADA** — Sergio Mendes & Brazil '66 (Herb Alpert), A&M 807 | 4 |
| 52 | 58 | 75 | 84 | **MIND EXCURSION** — The Trade Winds (Anders-Poncia), Kama Sutra 212 | 4 |
| 53 | 66 | 83 | — | **COMING ON STRONG** — Brenda Lee (Owen Bradley), Decca 32018 | 3 |
| 54 | 50 | 49 | 49 | **IN THE ARMS OF LOVE** — Andy Williams (Robert Mersey), Columbia 43737 | 8 |
| 55 | 67 | 82 | — | **FA-FA-FA-FA-FA** — Otis Redding, Volt 138 | 3 |
| 56 | 53 | 53 | 65 | **THE FIFE PIPER** — Dynatones (B.J. Jules), HBR 494 | 7 |
| 57 | 78 | — | — | **SPINOUT** — Elvis Presley (Joe Pasternak), RCA Victor 8941 | 2 |
| 58 | 60 | 73 | 92 | **PLEASE MR. SUN** — Vogues (Cenci-Moon-Hakim), Co & Ce 240 | 4 |
| 59 | 79 | — | — | **DEVIL WITH A BLUE DRESS ON & GOOD GOLLY MISS MOLLY** — Mitch Ryder & the Detroit Wheels, New Voice 817 | 2 |
| 60 | 80 | 95 | — | **ALMOST PERSUADED NO. 2** — Ben Colder (Jack Clement), MGM 13590 | 3 |
| 61 | 61 | 58 | 66 | **MY UNCLE USED TO LOVE ME BUT SHE DIED** — Roger Miller (Jerry Kennedy), Smash 2055 | 5 |
| 62 | 82 | — | — | **ALL THAT I AM** — Elvis Presley (Joe Pasternak), RCA Victor 8941 | 2 |
| 63 | 59 | 59 | 60 | **BLUE SIDE OF LONESOME** — Jim Reeves (Chet Atkins), RCA Victor 8902 | 5 |
| 64 | 72 | 87 | 88 | **CHANGES** — Crispian St. Peters (David Nicolson), Jamie 1324 | 5 |
| 65 | 65 | 66 | 67 | **CAN'T SATISFY** — Impressions (Johnny Pate), ABC 10831 | 5 |
| 66 | 75 | 76 | 91 | **AIN'T GONNA LIE** — Keith (Jerry Ross), Mercury 72596 | 5 |
| 67 ★ | 83 | — | — | **A SATISFIED MIND** — Bobby Hebb (Jerry Ross), Philips 40400 | 2 |
| 68 | 76 | 91 | — | **BUT IT'S ALRIGHT** — J.J. Jackson (Lew Futterman), Calla 119 | 3 |
| 69 | 64 | 64 | 82 | **SAID I WASN'T GONNA TELL NOBODY** — Sam & Dave (Prod. by Staff), Stax 198 | 6 |
| 70 | 70 | 92 | — | **DON'T WORRY MOTHER, YOUR SON'S HEART IS PURE** — McCoys (Feldman-Goldstein-Gottehrers), Bang 532 | 3 |
| 71 | 68 | 68 | 79 | **I CAN MAKE IT WITH YOU** — Jackie DeShannon (Calvin Carter), Imperial 66202 | 6 |
| 72 | 77 | 86 | 89 | **KNOCK ON WOOD** — Eddie Floyd (Prod. by Staff), Stax 194 | 6 |
| 73 | — | — | — | **SECRET LOVE** — Billy Stewart (Dave & Caston), Chess 1978 | 1 |
| 74 | — | — | — | **UP TIGHT** — Ramsey Lewis (E. Edwards), Cadet 5547 | 1 |
| 75 | 90 | — | — | **LADY GODIVA** — Peter & Gordon (John Burgess), Capitol 5740 | 2 |
| 76 | — | — | — | **RAIN ON THE ROOF** — Lovin' Spoonful (Erik Jacobson), Kama Sutra 216 | 1 |
| 77 | 74 | 74 | 84 | **MELODY FOR AN UNKNOWN GIRL** — Unknowns (Steve Alaimo), Parrot 307 | 4 |
| 78 | 81 | 96 | — | **HAPPINESS** — Shades of Blue (John Rhys), Impact 1015 | 3 |
| 79 | 95 | — | — | **THE WHEEL OF HURT** — Margaret Whiting (Arnold Goland), London 101 | 2 |
| 80 | 89 | — | — | **TOMORROW NEVER COMES** — B.J. Thomas (Huey Meaux), Scepter 12165 | 4 |
| 81 | 87 | — | — | **I'VE GOT TO DO A LITTLE BIT BETTER** — Joe Tex (Buddy Killen), Dial 4045 | 2 |
| 82 | 93 | — | — | **DON'T BE A DROP-OUT** — James Brown & His Famous Flames (James Brown Prod.), King 6056 | 2 |
| 83 | — | — | — | **SOMEBODY (Somewhere) NEEDS YOU** — Darrell Banks (Solid Hitbound Prod., Inc.), Revilot 203 | 1 |
| 84 | 84 | 99 | — | **TAKE GOOD CARE OF HER** — Mel Carter (Nick DeCaro), Imperial 66208 | 3 |
| 85 | — | — | — | **I CAN'T CONTROL MYSELF** — Troggs (Larry Page), Fontana 1557, Atco 6444 | 1 |
| 86 | 86 | 90 | — | **BABY, DO THE PHILLY DOG** — Olympics (Smith), Mirwood 5523 | 3 |
| 87 | 88 | — | — | **NOBODY'S BABY AGAIN** — Dean Martin (Jimmy Bowen), Reprise 0516 | 2 |
| 88 | — | — | — | **SOMEBODY LIKE ME** — Eddy Arnold (Chet Atkins), RCA Victor 8965 | 1 |
| 89 | — | — | — | **FREE AGAIN** — Barbra Streisand (Ettore Stratta), Columbia 43808 | 1 |
| 90 | — | — | — | **WHISPERS** — Jackie Wilson (Carl Davis), Brunswick 55300 | 1 |
| 91 | — | — | — | **YOU ARE SHE** — Chad & Jeremy (Mark), Columbia 43807 | 2 |
| 92 | — | — | — | **STAY WITH ME** — Lorraine Ellison (Jerry Ragavoy), Warner Bros. 5850 | 2 |
| 93 | 96 | — | — | **DOMMAGE, DOMMAGE** — Jerry Vale (Mike Berniker), Columbia 43774 | 2 |
| 94 | 94 | — | — | **LOOKIN' FOR LOVE** — Ray Conniff Singers (Ernie Altschuler), Columbia 43814 | 2 |
| 95 | — | — | — | **A SYMPHONY FOR SUSAN** — Arbors, (Richard Carney), Date 1529 | 1 |
| 96 | 98 | 98 | — | **WHAT NOW, MY LOVE** — "Groove" Holmes (Cal Lampley), Prestige 427 | 3 |
| 97 | 97 | — | — | **DOMMAGE, DOMMAGE** — Paul Vance (Vance-Pockriss), Scepter 12164 | 2 |
| 98 | 100 | — | — | **CRY SOFTLY** — Nancy Ames (Kellem), Epic 10056 | 2 |
| 99 | — | — | — | **THE WHEEL OF HURT** — Al Martino (T. Morgan), Capitol 5741 | 1 |
| 100 | — | — | — | **I CAN'T GIVE YOU ANYTHING BUT LOVE** — Bert Kaempfert & His Ork (Milt Gabler), Decca 32006 | 1 |

## BUBBLING UNDER THE HOT 100

101. HEAVEN MUST HAVE SENT YOU ... Elgins, V.I.P. 25031
102. WISH YOU WERE HERE, BUDDY ... Pat Boone, Dot 16933
103. SECRET LOVE ... Richard (Groove) Holmes, Pacific-Jazz 88130
104. OPEN UP YOUR DOOR ... Richard & the Young Lions, Philips 40381
105. STOP, LOOK AND LISTEN ... Chiffons, Laurie 3357
106. STAND IN FOR LOVE ... O'Jays, Imperial 66197
107. POLLYANNA ... Classics, Capitol 5710
108. DON'T OPEN THE DOOR ... B.B. King, ABC 10856
109. PHILLY DOG ... Herbie Mann, Atlantic 5047
110. NINETEEN DAYS ... Dave Clark Five, Epic 10076
111. I CAN'T DO WITHOUT YOU ... Deon Jackson, Carla 2530
112. RESPECT ... Rationals, Cameo 437
113. SHE AIN'T LOVING YOU ... Distant Cousins, Date 1514
114. ONE MORE TIME ... Clefs of Lavender Hill, Date 1530
115. BANG, BANG ... Joe Cuba Sextet, Tico 475
116. GAMES THAT LOVERS PLAY ... Wayne Newton, Capitol 5754
117. ROSANNA ... Caprees, Sound 126
118. THE WHITE CLIFFS OF DOVER ... Righteous Brothers, Phillies 132
119. THE OTHER SIDE OF THIS LIFE ... Peter, Paul & Mary, Warner Bros. 5849
120. PIPELINE ... Chantays, Dot 145
121. TREAT ME LIKE A LADY ... Lesley Gore, Mercury 72611
122. (In The) COLD LIGHT OF DAY ... Gene Pitney, Musicor 1200
123. YOU LEFT THE WATER RUNNING ... Barbara Lynn, Tribe 8319
124. A DAY IN THE LIFE OF A FOOL ... Jack Jones, Kapp 781
125. HEART ... 2 of Clubs, Fraternity 972
126. EVERY DAY AND EVERY NIGHT ... Troys, ABC 10823
127. MERCY ... Willie Mitchell, Hi 2112
128. POURING WATER ON A DROWNING MAN ... James Carr, Goldwax 211
129. SHE'S MY GIRL ... Coastliners, Back Beat 566
130. ALMOST PERSUADED ... Patti Page, Columbia 43794
131. AND I LOVE HER ... Vibrations, Okeh 7257
132. SHADES OF BLUE ... Shadows, Scepter 12162
133. I WANNA MEET YOU ... Cryan Shames, Columbia 43836
134. HOLY COW ... Lee Dorsey, Amy 965
135. RUN, RUN, LOOK AND SEE ... Brian Hyland, Philips 40405

Compiled from national retail sales and radio station airplay by the Music Popularity Dept. of Record Market Research, Billboard.

For Week Ending October 22, 1966

# HOT 100

★ STAR performer—Sides registering greatest proportionate upward progress this week.

Record Industry Association of America seal of certification as million selling single.

| THIS WEEK | 1 Wk. Ago | 2 Wks. Ago | 3 Wks. Ago | TITLE | Artist (Producer), Label & Number | Weeks On Chart |
|---|---|---|---|---|---|---|
| 1 (Billboard Award) | 1 | 2 | 7 | REACH OUT I'LL BE THERE | Four Tops (Holland & Dozier), Motown 1098 | 8 |
| 2 | 3 | 3 | 6 | 96 TEARS | ? (Question Mark) & the Mysterians, Cameo 428 | 8 |
| 3 | 4 | 6 | 18 | LAST TRAIN TO CLARKSVILLE | Monkees (Tommy Boyce & Bobby Hart), Colgems 1001 | 7 |
| 4 | 2 | 1 | 1 | CHERISH | Association (C. Boettcher), Valiant 747 | 9 |
| 5 | 5 | 9 | 15 | PSYCHOTIC REACTION | Count Five (Hooven-Winn), Double Shot 104 | 7 |
| 6 | 7 | 14 | 30 | WALK AWAY RENEE | Left Banke (World United Prod. Inc.), Smash 2041 | 7 |
| ★ 7 | 11 | 20 | 42 | POOR SIDE OF TOWN | Johnny Rivers (Lou Adler), Imperial 66205 | 6 |
| 8 | 8 | 11 | 19 | WHAT BECOMES OF THE BROKENHEARTED | Jimmy Ruffin (William Stevenson), Soul 35022 | 10 |
| ★ 9 | 15 | 48 | 89 | DANDY | Herman's Hermits (Mickie Most), MGM 13603 | 4 |
| ★ 10 | 14 | 19 | 37 | SEE SEE RIDER | Eric Burdon & the Animals (Tom Wilson), MGM 13582 | 6 |
| ★ 11 | 16 | 23 | 39 | HOORAY FOR HAZEL | Tommy Roe (Our Prods.), ABC 10852 | 6 |
| ★ 12 | 17 | 22 | 51 | IF I WERE A CARPENTER | Bobby Darin (Koppleman-Rubin), Atlantic 2350 | 5 |
| ★ 13 | 18 | 40 | — | HAVE YOU SEEN YOUR MOTHER, BABY, STANDING IN THE SHADOW? | Rolling Stones (Andrew Oldham), London 903 | 3 |
| 14 | 6 | 7 | 10 | CHERRY, CHERRY | Neil Diamond (Jeff Barry & Ellie Greenwich), Bang 528 | 10 |
| 15 | 9 | 10 | 12 | I'VE GOT YOU UNDER MY SKIN | 4 Seasons (Bob Crewe), Philips 40393 | 8 |
| 16 | 19 | 25 | 31 | B-A-B-Y | Carla Thomas (Staff), Stax 195 | 10 |
| ★ 17 | 42 | 63 | 80 | GO AWAY LITTLE GIRL | Happenings (Tokens), B. T. Puppy 522 | 4 |
| 18 | 10 | 8 | 2 | YOU CAN'T HURRY LOVE | Supremes (Holland & Dozier), Motown 1097 | 11 |
| 19 | 13 | 4 | 4 | BLACK IS BLACK | Los Bravos (Ivor Raymonde), Press 60002 | 11 |
| 20 | 21 | 26 | 40 | ALL I SEE IS YOU | Dusty Springfield, Philips 40396 | 6 |
| ★ 21 | 35 | 52 | 88 | THE GREAT AIRPLANE STRIKE | Paul Revere & the Raiders (Terry Melcher), Columbia 43810 | 4 |
| 22 | 12 | 5 | 3 | BEAUTY IS ONLY SKIN DEEP | Temptations (Norman Whitfield), Gordy 7055 | 10 |
| ★ 23 | 28 | 43 | 72 | LITTLE MAN | Sonny & Cher (Sonny Bono), Atco 6440 | 4 |
| ★ 24 | 38 | 44 | 61 | LOVE IS A HURTIN' THING | Lou Rawls (David Axelrod), Capitol 5709 | 7 |
| ★ 25 | 31 | 41 | 47 | BORN FREE | Roger Williams (Hy Grill), Kapp 767 | 9 |
| 26 | 27 | 29 | 38 | ALL STRUNG OUT | Nino Tempo & April Stevens (Nino Tempo-Jerry Riopelli), White Whale 236 | 7 |
| ★ 27 | 36 | 51 | 81 | THE HAIR ON MY CHINNY CHIN CHIN | Sam the Sham & the Pharaohs (Stan Kesler), MGM 13581 | 4 |
| 28 | 30 | 37 | 52 | GIRL ON A SWING | Gerry & the Pacemakers, Laurie 3354 | 7 |
| 29 | 22 | 24 | 36 | I REALLY DON'T WANT TO KNOW | Ronnie Dove (Phil Kahl), Diamond 208 | 8 |
| 30 | 25 | 18 | 16 | WIPE OUT | Surfaris, Dot 144 | 29 |
| 31 | 24 | 13 | 13 | BORN A WOMAN | Sandy Posey (Chip Moman), MGM 13501 | 14 |
| 32 | 34 | 38 | 48 | I CAN MAKE IT WITH YOU | Pozo-Seco Singers (Bob Johnston), Columbia 43784 | 7 |
| ★ 33 | 49 | 71 | 79 | I'M YOUR PUPPET | James & Bobby Purify (Don Schroeder), Bell 648 | 5 |
| ★ 34 | 59 | 79 | — | DEVIL WITH A BLUE DRESS ON & GOOD GOLLY MISS MOLLY | Mitch Ryder & the Detroit Wheels (Bob Crew), New Voice 817 | 3 |
| ★ 35 | 45 | 69 | 84 | I JUST DON'T KNOW WHAT TO DO WITH MYSELF | Dionne Warwick (Bacharach-David), Scepter 12167 | 4 |
| 36 | 20 | 17 | 20 | MR. DIEINGLY SAD | Critters (Artie Ripp), Kapp 769 | 11 |
| ★ 37 | 50 | 73 | — | (You Don't Have To) PAINT ME A PICTURE | Gary Lewis & the Playboys, (Snuff Garrett), Liberty 55914 | 3 |
| 38 | 43 | 56 | 69 | MR. SPACEMAN | Byrds (Allen Stanton), Columbia 43766 | 5 |
| 39 | 26 | 28 | 29 | SUMMER SAMBA | Walter Wanderley (Creed Taylor), Verve 10421 | 9 |
| ★ 40 | 76 | — | — | RAIN ON THE ROOF | Lovin' Spoonful (Erik Jacobson), Kama Sutra 216 | 2 |
| 41 | 23 | 15 | 5 | BUS STOP | Hollies (Ron Richardson), Imperial 66186 | 14 |
| ★ 42 | 53 | 66 | 83 | COMING ON STRONG | Brenda Lee (Owen Bradley), Decca 32018 | 4 |
| 43 | 33 | 31 | 24 | ALMOST PERSUADED | David Houston (Billy Sherrill), Epic 10025 | 15 |
| 44 | 44 | 57 | 67 | COME ON UP | Young Rascals (Young Rascals), Atlantic 2353 | 5 |
| ★ 45 | 55 | 67 | 82 | FA-FA-FA-FA-FA | Otis Redding, Volt 138 | 4 |
| 46 | 47 | 54 | 54 | I WANT TO BE WITH YOU | Dee Dee Warwick, Mercury 72584 | 9 |
| ★ 47 | 57 | 78 | — | SPINOUT | Elvis Presley (Joe Pasternak), RCA Victor 8941 | 3 |
| ★ 48 | 58 | 60 | 73 | PLEASE MR. SUN | Vogues (Cenci-Moon-Hakim), Co & Ce 240 | 5 |
| 49 | 51 | 62 | 77 | MAS QUE NADA | Sergio Mendes & Brazil '66 (Herb Alpert), A&M 807 | 5 |
| 50 | 29 | 12 | 9 | SUNSHINE SUPERMAN | Donovan (Mickey Most), Epic 10045 | 13 |
| 51 | 52 | 58 | 75 | MIND EXCURSION | The Trade Winds (Anders-Poncia), Kama Sutra 212 | 7 |
| ★ 52 | 62 | 82 | — | ALL THAT I AM | Elvis Presley (Joe Pasternark), RCA Victor 8941 | 3 |
| 53 | 46 | 49 | 60 | IN OUR TIME | Nancy Sinatra (Lee Hazlewood), Reprise 0514 | 6 |
| ★ 54 | 66 | 75 | 76 | AIN'T GONNA LIE | Keith (Jerry Ross), Mercury 72596 | 6 |
| ★ 55 | 67 | 83 | — | A SATISFIED MIND | Bobby Hebb, (Jerry Ross), Philips 40400 | 3 |
| ★ 56 | 68 | 76 | 91 | BUT IT'S ALRIGHT | J. J. Jackson (Lew Futterman), Calla 119 | 4 |
| ★ 57 | 75 | 90 | — | LADY GODIVA | Peter & Gordon (John Burgess), Capitol 5740 | 3 |
| ★ 58 | 74 | — | — | UP TIGHT | Ramsey Lewis, (E. Edwards), Cadet 5547 | 2 |
| ★ 59 | 73 | — | — | SECRET LOVE | Billy Stewart, (Dave & Caston), Chess 1978 | 2 |
| 60 | 60 | 80 | 95 | ALMOST PERSUADED NO. 2 | Ben Colder (Jack Clement), MGM 13590 | 4 |
| 61 | 56 | 53 | 53 | THE FIFE PIPER | Dynatones (J. J. Jules), HBR 494 | 8 |
| 62 | 72 | 77 | 86 | KNOCK ON WOOD | Eddie Floyd (Prod. by Staff), Stax 194 | 7 |
| 63 | 64 | 72 | 87 | CHANGES | Crispian St. Peters (David Nicolson), Jamie 1324 | 6 |
| ★ 64 | 86 | 86 | 90 | BABY, DO THE PHILLY DOG | Olympics (Smith), Mirwood 5523 | 4 |
| ★ 65 | — | — | — | LOOK THROUGH MY WINDOW | Mama's and the Papa's, (Lou Adler), Dunhill 4050 | 1 |
| ★ 66 | 85 | — | — | I CAN'T CONTROL MYSELF | Troggs (Larry Page), Fontana 1557, Atco 6444 | 2 |
| 67 | 70 | 70 | 92 | DON'T WORRY MOTHER YOUR SON'S HEART IS PURE | McCoys (Feldman-Goldstein-Gottehrers), Bang 532 | 4 |
| 68 | 79 | 95 | — | THE WHEEL OF HURT | Margaret Whiting (Arnold Goland), London 101 | 3 |
| 69 | 82 | 93 | — | DON'T BE A DROP-OUT | James Brown & His Famous Flames (James Brown Prod.) King 6056 | 3 |
| ★ 70 | — | — | — | WHO AM I | Petula Clark, (Tony Hatch), Warner Bros. 5863 | 1 |
| 71 | 81 | 87 | — | I'VE GOT TO DO A LITTLE BIT BETTER | Joe Tex (Buddy Killen), Dial 4045 | 3 |
| ★ 72 | 87 | 88 | — | NOBODY'S BABY AGAIN | Dean Martin (Jimmy Bowen), Reprise 0516 | 3 |
| ★ 73 | 92 | 92 | — | STAY WITH ME | Lorraine Ellison (Jerry Ragavoy), Warner Bros. 5850 | 3 |
| ★ 74 | — | — | — | LOUIE, LOUIE | Sandpipers (Tommy LaPuma), A&M 819 | 1 |
| 75 | 83 | — | — | SOMEBODY (Somewhere) NEEDS YOU | Darrell Banks (Solid Hitbound Prod., Inc.), Revilot 203 | 2 |
| 76 | 88 | — | — | SOMEBODY LIKE ME | Eddy Arnold (Chet Atkins), RCA Victor 8965 | 2 |
| ★ 77 | 99 | — | — | THE WHEEL OF HURT | Al Martino (T. Morgan), Capitol 5741 | 2 |
| 78 | 78 | 81 | 96 | HAPPINESS | Shades of Blue (John Rhys), Impact 1015 | 4 |
| 79 | 84 | 84 | 99 | TAKE GOOD CARE OF HER | Mel Carter (Nick DeCaro), Imperial 66208 | 4 |
| 80 | 80 | 89 | — | TOMORROW NEVER COMES | B. J. Thomas (Huey Meaux), Scepter 12165 | 5 |
| ★ 81 | — | — | — | GOOD VIBRATIONS | Beach Boys (Brian Wilson), Capitol 5676 | 1 |
| ★ 82 | — | — | — | HEAVEN MUST HAVE SENT YOU | Elgins (Holland-Dozier), V.I.P. 25037 | 1 |
| ★ 83 | — | — | — | WISH YOU WERE HERE, BUDDY | Pat Boone (Nick Venet and Randy Wood), Dot 16933 | 1 |
| ★ 84 | — | — | — | NINETEEN DAYS | Dave Clark Five (Dave Clark), Epic 10076 | 1 |
| ★ 85 | — | — | — | HOLY COW | Lee Dorsey (A. Toussaint-M. Sehorn), Amy 965 | 1 |
| 86 | 95 | — | — | A SYMPHONY FOR SUSAN | Arbors, (Richard Carney), Date 1529 | 2 |
| 87 | 90 | — | — | WHISPERS | Jackie Wilson (Carl Davis), Brunswick 55300 | 2 |
| 88 | 89 | — | — | FREE AGAIN | Barbra Streisand (Ettore Stratta), Columbia 43808 | 2 |
| 89 | 91 | 91 | — | YOU ARE SHE | Chad & Jeremy (Mark), Columbia 43807 | 3 |
| ★ 90 | — | — | — | RUN, RUN, LOOK AND SEE | Brian Hyland (Snuff Garrett), Philips 40405 | 1 |
| 91 | — | — | — | POURING WATER ON A DROWNING MAN | James Carr (Quinton Claunche and Doc Russell), Goldwax 311 | 1 |
| 92 | — | — | — | IT TEARS ME UP | Percy Sledge (Martin Greene-Quin Ivy), Atlantic 2358 | 1 |
| 93 | — | — | — | WHY PICK ON ME | Standells (Ed Cobb), Tower 282 | 1 |
| 94 | — | — | — | BANG! BANG! | Joe Cuba Sextet (Pancho Cristal), Tico 475 | 1 |
| 95 | 98 | 100 | — | CRY SOFTLY | Nancy Ames (Kellem), Epic 10056 | 3 |
| 96 | — | — | — | EVERY DAY, EVERY NIGHT | Trolls (Johnny Pate), ABC 10823 | 1 |
| 97 | — | — | 65 | POVERTY | Bobby Bland, Duke 407 | 4 |
| 98 | — | — | — | STAND IN FOR LOVE | O'Jays (Wri-Hand Prod.), Imperial 66197 | 1 |
| 99 | — | — | — | DON'T ANSWER THE DOOR | B. B. King (Johnny Pate), ABC 10856 | 1 |
| 100 | — | — | — | GAMES THAT LOVERS PLAY | Wayne Newton (Steve Douglas), Capitol 5754 | 1 |

## HOT 100—A TO Z—(Publisher-Licensee)

Ain't Gonna Lie (Screen Gems-Columbia, BMI) ... 54
All I See Is You (Anne-Rachel, ASCAP) ... 20
All Strung Out (Daddy Sam-Jerel, BMI) ... 26
All That I Am (Gladys, ASCAP) ... 52
Almost Persuaded (Gallico, BMI) ... 43
Almost Persuaded No. 2 (Gallico, BMI) ... 60

B-A-B-Y (East, BMI) ... 16
Baby, Do the Philly Dog (Keymen, Mirwood, BMI) ... 64
Bang! Bang! (Cordon, BMI) ... 94
Beauty Is Only Skin Deep (Jobete, BMI) ... 22
Black Is Black (Elmwin, BMI) ... 19
Born a Woman (Painted Desert, BMI) ... 31
Born Free (Screen Gems-Columbia, BMI) ... 25
Bus Stop (Manken, BMI) ... 41
But It's Alright (Pamelarosa, BMI) ... 56

Changes (Barricade, ASCAP) ... 63
Cherish (Beechwood, BMI) ... 4
Cherry, Cherry (Tallyrand, BMI) ... 14
Come On Up (Slacsar, BMI) ... 44
Coming On Strong (Moss-Rose, BMI) ... 42
Cry Softly (Tree, BMI) ... 95

Dandy (Noma, BMI) ... 9
Devil With a Blue Dress On & Good Golly Miss Molly (Jobete-Venus, BMI) ... 34
Don't Answer the Door (Mercedes, BMI) ... 99
Don't Be a Drop-Out (Dynatone, BMI) ... 69
Don't Worry Mother, Your Son's Heart Is Pure (Grand Canyon, BMI) ... 67

Every Day, Every Night (Pamco-Yvonne, BMI) ... 96
Fa-Fa-Fa-Fa-Fa (East-Redwal, BMI) ... 45
Fife Piper, The (Jules-Tone, BMI) ... 61
Free Again (Emanuel-Beaujolais, ASCAP) ... 88

Girl on a Swing (Bright Tunes, BMI) ... 28
Go Away Little Girl (Screen Gems-Columbia, BMI) . 17
Games That Lovers Play (Miller, ASCAP) ... 100
Good Vibrations (Sea of Tunes, BMI) ... 81
Great Airplane Strike, The (Daywin, BMI) ... 21

Hair on My Chinny Chin Chin, The (Rose, BMI) .. 27
Happiness (Gomba, BMI) ... 72
Heaven Must Have Sent You (Jobete, BMI) ... 82
Holy Cow (Marsaint, BMI) ... 85
Hooray for Hazel (Low Twi, BMI) ... 11
Have You Seen Your Mother, Baby, Standing in the Shadow? (Gideon, BMI) ... 13

I Can Make It With You (Blackwood, BMI) ... 32
I Can't Control Myself (James, BMI) ... 66
I Just Don't Know What to Do With Myself (U. S. Songs, ASCAP) ... 35
I Really Don't Want to Know (Hill & Range, BMI) 29
I Want to Be With You (Moreley, ASCAP) ... 46
I'm Your Puppet (Fame, BMI) ... 33
I've Got to Do a Little Bit Better (Tree, BMI) .. 71
I've Got You Under My Skin (Chappell, ASCAP) .. 15
If I Were a Carpenter (Faithful Virtue, BMI) ... 12
In Our Time (Criterion, ASCAP) ... 53
It Tears Me Up (Fame, BMI) ... 92

Knock on Wood (East, BMI) ... 62

Lady Godiva (Regent, BMI) ... 57
Last Train to Clarksville (Screen Gems-Columbia, BMI) ... 3
Little Man (Cotillion-Chris-Marc, BMI) ... 23
Look Through My Window (Trousdale, BMI) ... 65
Louie, Louie (Limax, BMI) ... 74
Love Is a Hurtin' Thing (Rawlou, BMI) ... 24

Mas Que Nada (Peer Int'l., BMI) ... 49
Mind Excursion (Kama Sutra, BMI) ... 51
Mr. Dieingly Sad (Tender Tunes-Elmwin, BMI) .. 36
Mr. Spaceman (Tickson, BMI) ... 38

Nineteen Days (Branston, BMI) ... 84
96 Tears (Arguello, BMI) ... 2
Nobody's Baby Again (Smooth-Noma, BMI) ... 72

Paint Me a Picture (Viva, BMI) ... 37
Please Mr. Sun (Weiss-Barry, BMI) ... 48
Poor Side of Town (Rivers, BMI) ... 7
Poverty (Don, BMI) ... 97
Pouring Water on a Drowning Man (Pronto-Quinvy, BMI) ... 91
Psychotic Reaction (Hot Shot, BMI) ... 5

Rain on the Roof (Faithful Virtue, BMI) ... 40
Reach Out I'll Be There (Jobete, BMI) ... 1
Run, Run, Look and See (Little Darlin'-Low Twi, BMI) ... 90

Satisfied Mind, A (Starday, BMI) ... 55
Secret Love (Remick, ASCAP) ... 59
See See Rider (Leeds, ASCAP) ... 10
Somebody Like Me (Barton, BMI) ... 76
Somebody (Somewhere) Needs You (Jobete, BMI) .. 75
Spinout (Gladys, ASCAP) ... 47
Stand in for Love (Metric-Bar-New, BMI) ... 98
Stay With Me (Ragmar-Crenshaw, BMI) ... 73
Summer Samba (Duchess, BMI) ... 39
Sunshine Superman (Southern, ASCAP) ... 50
Symphony for Susan, A (Kris, ASCAP) ... 86

Take Good Care of Her (Paxton-Recherche, ASCAP) 79
Tomorrow Never Comes (Noma, BMI) ... 80

Up Tight (Jobete, BMI) ... 58

Walk Away Renee (Twin Tone, BMI) ... 6
What Becomes of the Brokenhearted (Jobete, BMI) 8
Wheel of Hurt, The (Martino) (Roosevelt, BMI) .. 77
Wheel of Hurt, The (Whiting) (Roosevelt, BMI) .. 68
Whispers (Jalynne, BRC, BMI) ... 87
Who Am I (Duchess, BMI) ... 70
Wish You Were Here, Buddy (Roosevelt, BMI) ... 83
Why Pick oh Me (Equinox, BMI) ... 93
Wipe Out (Miraleste-Robin Hood, BMI) ... 30

You Are She (Chad and Jeremy, BMI) ... 89
You Can't Hurry Love (Jobete, BMI) ... 18

## BUBBLING UNDER THE HOT 100

101. (When She Wants Good Lovin') SHE COMES TO ME ... Chicago Loop, DynoVoice 226
102. SECRET LOVE ... Richard (Groove) Holmes, Pacific-Jazz 88130
103. DOMMAGE, DOMMAGE ... Paul Vance, Scepter 12164
104. WHAT NOW MY LOVE ... (Groove) Holmes, Prestige 427
105. I CAN'T GIVE YOU ANYTHING BUT LOVE ... Bert Kaempfert & his Ork, Decca 32008
106. POLLYANNA ... Classics, Capitol 571
107. DOMMAGE, DOMMAGE ... Jerry Vale, Columbia 43774
108. LOOKIN' FOR LOVE ... Ray Conniff Singers, Columbia 43814
109. RESPECT ... Rationals, Cameo 437
110. YOU LEFT THE WATER RUNNING ... Barbara Lynn, Tribe 8319
111. I CAN'T DO WITHOUT YOU ... Deon Jackson, Carla 2530
112. A DAY IN THE LIFE OF A FOOL ... Jack Jones, Kapp 781
113. ALMOST PERSUADED ... Patti Page, Columbia 43794
114. STOP, LOOK & LISTEN ... Chiffons, Laurie 3357
115. STOP, STOP, STOP ... Hollies, Imperial 66214
116. GAMES THAT LOVERS PLAY ... Eddie Fisher, RCA Victor 8956
117. PIPELINE ... Chantays, Dot 145
118. WHITE CLIFFS OF DOVER ... Righteous Brothers, Phillies 132
119. SOCIETY'S CHILD ... Janis Ian, Verve Folkway 5027
120. I HEAR MUSIC ... Ronettes, Phillies 133
121. SHE'S MY GIRL ... Coastliners, Back Beat 566
122. SHADES OF BLUE ... Shirelles, Scepter 12162
123. LAVENDER BLUE ... Finders Keepers, Challenge 59338
124. FORTUNE TELLER ... Hardtimes, World-Pacific 77851
125. DISTANT DRUMS ... Vic Dana, Dolton 324
126. PORTUGUESE WASHERWOMEN ... Baja Marimba Band, A & M 816
127. SOMEBODY'S GOT TO LOVE YOU ... Don Covay, Atlantic 2357
128. I (Who Have Nothing) ... Terry Knight & the Pack, Lucky 11 230
129. WEDDING BELL BLUES ... Laura Nyro, Verve Folkways 5024
130. UNDER MY THUMB ... Del Shannon, Liberty 55904
131. CAN I GET TO KNOW YOU BETTER ... Turtles, White Whale 238
132. I WANNA MEET YOU ... Cryan Shames, Columbia 43836
133. LOVE IS A BIRD ... Knickerbockers, Challenge 59341
134. THE WILLY ... Williees, Co & C E 239
135. CLOCK ... Eddie Rambeau, DynoVoice 225

Compiled from national retail sales and radio station airplay by the Music Popularity Dept. of Record Market Research, Billboard.

# Billboard HOT 100

**For Week Ending October 29, 1966**

★ STAR performer—Sides registering greatest proportionate upward progress this week.

Record Industry Association of America seal of certification as million selling single.

| This Week | 2 Wks. Ago | 3 Wks. Ago | TITLE Artist (Producer), Label & Number | Weeks On Chart |
|---|---|---|---|---|
| 1 | 2 | 3 | **96 TEARS** — ? (Question Mark) & the Mysterians, Cameo 428 (Billboard Award) | 9 |
| 2 | 3 | 4 | **LAST TRAIN TO CLARKSVILLE** — Monkees (Tommy Boyce & Bobby Hart), Colgems 1001 | 8 |
| 3 | 1 | 1 | **REACH OUT I'LL BE THERE** — Four Tops (Holland & Dozier), Motown 1098 | 9 |
| 4 | 7 | 11 | **POOR SIDE OF TOWN** — Johnny Rivers (Lou Adler), Imperial 66205 | 7 |
| 5 | 6 | 7 | **WALK AWAY RENEE** — Left Banke (World United Prod. Inc.), Smash 2041 | 8 |
| 6 | 9 | 15 | **DANDY** — Herman's Hermits (Mickie Most), MGM 13603 | 5 |
| 7 | 8 | 8 | **WHAT BECOMES OF THE BROKENHEARTED** — Jimmy Ruffin (William Stevenson), Soul 35022 | 11 |
| 8 | 11 | 16 | **HOORAY FOR HAZEL** — Tommy Roe (Our Prods.), ABC 10852 | 7 |
| 9 | 13 | 18 | **HAVE YOU SEEN YOUR MOTHER, BABY, STANDING IN THE SHADOW?** — Rolling Stones (Andrew Oldham), London 903 | 4 |
| 10 | 10 | 14 | **SEE SEE RIDER** — Eric Burdon & the Animals (Tom Wilson), MGM 13582 | 7 |
| 11 | 12 | 17 | **IF I WERE A CARPENTER** — Bobby Darin (Koppleman-Rubin), Atlantic 2350 | 6 |
| 12 | 17 | 42 | **GO AWAY LITTLE GIRL** — Happenings (Tokens), B. T. Puppy 522 | 5 |
| 13 | 4 | 2 | **CHERISH** — Association (C. Boettcher), Valiant 747 | 10 |
| 14 | 5 | 5 | **PSYCHOTIC REACTION** — Count Five (Hooven-Winn), Double Shot 104 | 8 |
| 15 | 16 | 19 | **B-A-B-Y** — Carla Thomas (Staff), Stax 195 | 11 |
| 16 | 33 | 49 | **I'M YOUR PUPPET** — James & Bobby Purify (Don Schroeder), Bell 648 | 6 |
| 17 | 14 | 6 | **CHERRY, CHERRY** — Neil Diamond (Jeff Barry & Ellie Greenwich), Bang 528 | 11 |
| 18 | 37 | 50 | **(You Don't Have To) PAINT ME A PICTURE** — Gary Lewis & the Playboys (Snuff Garrett), Liberty 55914 | 4 |
| 19 | 24 | 38 | **LOVE IS A HURTIN' THING** — Lou Rawls (David Axelrod), Capitol 5709 | 8 |
| 20 | 21 | 35 | **THE GREAT AIRPLANE STRIKE** — Paul Revere & the Raiders (Terry Melcher), Columbia 43810 | 5 |
| 21 | 23 | 28 | **LITTLE MAN** — Sonny & Cher (Sonny Bono), Atco 6440 | 5 |
| 22 | 27 | 36 | **THE HAIR ON MY CHINNY CHIN CHIN** — Sam the Sham and the Pharaohs (Stan Kesler), MGM 13581 | 5 |
| 23 | 15 | 9 | **I'VE GOT YOU UNDER MY SKIN** — 4 Seasons (Bob Crewe), Philips 40393 | 9 |
| 24 | 25 | 31 | **BORN FREE** — Roger Williams (Hy Grill), Kapp 767 | 9 |
| 25 | 18 | 10 | **YOU CAN'T HURRY LOVE** — Supremes (Holland & Dozier), Motown 1097 | 12 |
| 26 | 40 | 76 | **RAIN ON THE ROOF** — Lovin' Spoonful (Erik Jacobson), Kama Sutra 216 | 3 |
| 27 | 34 | 59 | **DEVIL WITH A BLUE DRESS ON & GOOD GOLLY MISS MOLLY** — Mitch Ryder & the Detroit Wheels (Bob Crew), New Voice 817 | 4 |
| 28 | 19 | 13 | **BLACK IS BLACK** — Los Bravos (Ivor Raymonde), Press 60002 | 12 |
| 29 | 20 | 21 | **ALL I SEE IS YOU** — Dusty Springfield, Philips 40396 | 7 |
| 30 | 35 | 45 | **I JUST DON'T KNOW WHAT TO DO WITH MYSELF** — Dionne Warwick (Bacharach-David), Scepter 12167 | 6 |
| 31 | 42 | 53 | **COMING ON STRONG** — Brenda Lee (Owen Bradley), Decca 32018 | 5 |
| 32 | 28 | 30 | **GIRL ON A SWING** — Gerry & the Pacemakers, Laurie 3354 | 8 |
| 33 | 32 | 34 | **I CAN MAKE IT WITH YOU** — Pozo-Seco Singers (Bob Johnston), Columbia 43784 | 8 |
| 34 | 45 | 55 | **FA-FA-FA-FA-FA** — Otis Redding, Volt 138 | 5 |
| 35 | 30 | 25 | **WIPE OUT** — Surfaris, Dot 144 | 30 |
| 36 | 38 | 43 | **MR. SPACEMAN** — Byrds (Allen Stanton), Columbia 43766 | 6 |
| 37 | 22 | 12 | **BEAUTY IS ONLY SKIN DEEP** — Temptations (Norman Whitfield), Gordy 7055 | 11 |
| 38 | 81 | — | **GOOD VIBRATIONS** — Beach Boys (Brian Wilson), Capitol 5676 | 2 |
| 39 | 70 | — | **WHO AM I** — Petula Clark (Tony Hatch), Warner Bros. 5863 | 2 |
| 40 | 26 | 27 | **ALL STRUNG OUT** — Nino Tempo & April Stevens (Nino Tempo-Jerry Riopelle), White Whale 236 | 8 |
| 41 | 46 | 47 | **I WANT TO BE WITH YOU** — Dee Dee Warwick (Ed Townsend), Mercury 72584 | 10 |
| 42 | 52 | 62 | **ALL THAT I AM** — Elvis Presley (Joe Pasternak), RCA Victor 8941 | 4 |
| 43 | 44 | 44 | **COME ON UP** — Young Rascals (Young Rascals), Atlantic 2353 | 6 |
| 44 | 47 | 57 | **SPINOUT** — Elvis Presley (Joe Pasternak), RCA Victor 8941 | 4 |
| 45 | 55 | 67 | **A SATISFIED MIND** — Bobby Hebb (Jerry Ross), Philips 40400 | 4 |
| 46 | 57 | 75 | **LADY GODIVA** — Peter & Gordon (John Burgess), Capitol 5740 | 4 |
| 47 | 49 | 51 | **MAS QUE NADA** — Sergio Mendes & Brazil '66 (Herb Alpert), A&M 807 | 6 |
| 48 | 48 | 58 | **PLEASE MR. SUN** — Vogues (Cenci-Moon-Hakim), Co & Ce 240 | 6 |
| 49 | 59 | 73 | **SECRET LOVE** — Billy Stewart (Dave & Caston), Chess 1978 | 3 |
| 50 | 58 | 74 | **UP TIGHT** — Ramsey Lewis (E. Edwards), Cadet 5547 | 3 |
| 51 | 65 | — | **LOOK THROUGH MY WINDOW** — Mama's and the Papa's (Lou Adler), Dunhill 4050 | 2 |
| 52 | 54 | 66 | **AIN'T GONNA LIE** — Keith (Jerry Ross), Mercury 72596 | 7 |
| 53 | 29 | 22 | **I REALLY DON'T WANT TO KNOW** — Ronnie Dove (Phil Kahl), Diamond 208 | 8 |
| 54 | 56 | 68 | **BUT IT'S ALRIGHT** — J. J. Jackson (Lew Futterman), Calla 119 | 5 |
| 55 | 66 | 85 | **I CAN'T CONTROL MYSELF** — Troggs (Larry Page), Fontana 1557, Atco 6444 | 3 |
| 56 | 69 | 82 | **DON'T BE A DROP-OUT** — James Brown & His Famous Flames (James Brown Prod.), King 6054 | 3 |
| 57 | 63 | 64 | **CHANGES** — Crispian St. Peters (David Nicolson), Jamie 1324 | 7 |
| 58 | 60 | 60 | **ALMOST PERSUADED NO. 2** — Ben Colder (Jack Clement), MGM 13590 | 5 |
| 59 | 74 | — | **LOUIE, LOUIE** — Sandpipers (Tommy LaPuma), A&M 819 | 2 |
| 60 | 72 | 87 | **NOBODY'S BABY AGAIN** — Dean Martin (Jimmy Bowen), Reprise 0516 | 4 |
| 61 | 76 | 88 | **SOMEBODY LIKE ME** — Eddy Arnold (Chet Atkins), RCA Victor 8965 | 3 |
| 62 | 62 | 72 | **KNOCK ON WOOD** — Eddie Floyd (Proc. by Staff), Stax 194 | 7 |
| 63 | 64 | 86 | **BABY, DO THE PHILLY DOG** — Olympics (Smith), Mirwood 5523 | 4 |
| 64 | 71 | 81 | **I'VE GOT TO DO A LITTLE BIT BETTER** — Joe Tex (Buddy Killen), Dial 4045 | 4 |
| 65 | 51 | 52 | **MIND EXCURSION** — The Trade Winds (Anders-Poncia), Kama Sutra 212 | 8 |
| 66 | — | — | **WINCHESTER CATHEDRAL** — New Vaudeville Band (Geoff Stephens), Fontana 1562 | 1 |
| 67 | 68 | 79 | **THE WHEEL OF HURT** — Margaret Whiting (Arnold Goland), London 101 | 4 |
| 68 | — | — | **YOU KEEP ME HANGIN' ON** — Supremes (Holland-Dozier), Motown 1101 | 1 |
| 69 | 84 | — | **NINETEEN DAYS** — Dave Clark Five (Dave Clark), Epic 10076 | 2 |
| 70 | — | — | **I'M READY FOR LOVE** — Martha & the Vandellas (Holland-Dozier), Gordy 7056 | 1 |
| 71 | 73 | 92 | **STAY WITH ME** — Lorraine Ellison (Jerry Ragavoy), Warner Bros. 5850 | 4 |
| 72 | 82 | — | **HEAVEN MUST HAVE SENT YOU** — Elgins (Holland-Dozier), V.I.P. 25037 | 2 |
| 73 | 67 | 70 | **DON'T WORRY MOTHER YOUR SON'S HEART IS PURE** — McCoys (Feldman-Goldstein-Gottehrers), Bang 532 | 5 |
| 74 | 77 | 99 | **THE WHEEL OF HURT** — Al Martino (T. Morgan), Capitol 5741 | 3 |
| 75 | 75 | 83 | **SOMEBODY (Somewhere) NEEDS YOU** — Darrell Banks (Solid Hitbound Prod., Inc.), Revilot 203 | 3 |
| 76 | — | — | **STOP STOP STOP** — Hollies (Ron Richards), Imperial 66214 | 1 |
| 77 | — | — | **ON THIS SIDE OF GOODBYE** — Righteous Brothers (Bill Medley), Verve 10449 | 1 |
| 78 | 79 | 84 | **TAKE GOOD CARE OF HER** — Mel Carter (Nick DeCaro), Imperial 66208 | 5 |
| 79 | 92 | — | **IT TEARS ME UP** — Percy Sledge (Martin Greene-Quin Ivy), Atlantic 2358 | 2 |
| 80 | 86 | 95 | **A SYMPHONY FOR SUSAN** — Arbors (Richard Carney), Date 1529 | 3 |
| 81 | 83 | — | **WISH YOU WERE HERE, BUDDY** — Pat Boone (Nick Venet and Randy Wood), Dot 16933 | 2 |
| 82 | 85 | — | **HOLY COW** — Lee Dorsey (A. Toussaint-M. Sehorn), Amy 965 | 2 |
| 83 | 90 | — | **RUN, RUN, LOOK AND SEE** — Brian Hyland (Snuff Garrett), Philips 40405 | 2 |
| 84 | 88 | 89 | **FREE AGAIN** — Barbra Streisand (Ettore Stratta), Columbia 43808 | 3 |
| 85 | — | — | **A DAY IN THE LIFE OF A FOOL** — Jack Jones (David Kapp), Kapp 781 | 1 |
| 86 | — | — | **BABY, WHAT DO YOU WANT ME TO DO?** — Barbara Lewis (Ollie McLaughlin), Atlantic 2361 | 1 |
| 87 | 89 | 91 | **YOU ARE SHE** — Chad & Jeremy (Mark), Columbia 43807 | 4 |
| 88 | 94 | — | **BANG! BANG!** — Joe Cuba Sextet (Pancho Cristal), Tico 475 | 2 |
| 89 | 93 | — | **WHY PICK ON ME** — Standells (Ed Cobb), Tower 282 | 2 |
| 90 | — | — | **HELP ME GIRL** — Outsiders (Roger Karshner), Capitol 5759 | 1 |
| 91 | 91 | — | **POURING WATER ON A DROWNING MAN** — James Carr (Quinton Claunche and Doc Russell), Goldwax 311 | 2 |
| 92 | — | — | **GAMES THAT LOVERS PLAY** — Eddie Fisher (Al Schmitt), RCA Victor 8956 | 1 |
| 93 | — | — | **TIME AFTER TIME** — Chris Montez (Tommy LiPuma-Herb Alpert), A&M 822 | 1 |
| 94 | — | 100 | **GAMES THAT LOVERS PLAY** — Wayne Newton (Steve Douglas), Capitol 5754 | 3 |
| 95 | 95 | 98 100 | **CRY SOFTLY** — Nancy Ames (Kellem), Epic 10056 | 4 |
| 96 | 98 | — | **STAND IN FOR LOVE** — O'Jays (Wri-Hand Prod.), Imperial 66197 | 2 |
| 97 | 97 | — | **POVERTY** — Bobby Bland, Duke 407 | 5 |
| 98 | 99 | — | **DON'T ANSWER THE DOOR** — B. B. King (Johnny Pate), ABC 10856 | 2 |
| 99 | — | — | **CAN I GET TO KNOW YOU BETTER** — Turtles (Bones Howe), White Whale 238 | 1 |
| 100 | — | — | **I CAN HEAR MUSIC** — Ronettes (Jeff Barry), Philles 133 | 1 |

## BUBBLING UNDER THE HOT 100

101. (When She Needs Good Loving) SHE COMES TO ME ... Chicago Loop, DynoVoice 226
102. COME BACK ... Five Stair-Steps, Windy C 603
103. WHISPERS ... Jackie Wilson, Brunswick 55300
104. TOMORROW NEVER COMES ... B. J. Thomas, Scepter 12165
105. WE GOT A THING THAT'S IN THE GROOVE ... Capitols, Karen 1526
106. PIPELINE ... Chantays, Dot 145
107. LOOKIN' FOR LOVE ... Ray Conniff & the Singers, Columbia 43814
108. RESPECT ... Rationals, Cameo 437
109. WHAT NOW MY LOVE ... Richard "Groove" Holmes, Prestige 427
110. WINDOWS AND DOORS ... Jackie DeShannon, Imperial 66196
111. EVERY DAY, EVERY NIGHT ... Trolls, ABC 10822
112. MEDITATION ... Claudine Longet, A&M 817
113. FORTUNE TELLER ... Hardtimes, World-Pacific 77851
114. WILD ANGELS THEME ... Davie Allen & the Arrows, Tower 267
115. SOCIETY'S CHILD ... Janis Ian, Verve Folkways 5027
116. WILD THING ... Ventures, Dolton 325
117. DISTANT DRUMS ... Vic Dana, Dolton 324
118. WHITE CLIFFS OF DOVER ... Righteous Brothers, Philles 134
119. FIFI THE FLEA ... Sidekicks, RCA Victor 8969
120. I (Who Have Nothing) ... Terry Knight & the Pack, Lucky 11, 230
121. TALK TALK ... Music Machine, Original Sound 61
122. SHADES OF BLUE ... Shirelles, Scepter 12162
123. I WANNA MEET YOU ... Cryan' Shames, Columbia 43836
124. WINCHESTER CATHEDRAL ... New Happiness, Columbia 43851
125. WINCHESTER CATHEDRAL ... Dana Rollin, Tower 283
126. CLOCK ... Eddie Rambeau, Dynovoice 225
127. WEDDING BELL BLUES ... Laura Nyro, Verve Folkways 502
128. HI HI HAZEL ... Gary & Hornets, Smash 2061
129. PORTUGUESE WASHERWOMEN ... Baja Marimba Band, A&M 812
130. MUSIC ... Festivals, Smash 2056
131. I'M A LOSER ... Eddie Holman, Parkway 106
132. SHE DIGS MY LOVE ... Sir Douglas, Tribe 8321
133. CABARET ... Mike Douglas, Epic 10076
134. THE WILLY ... Willies, Co & Ce 229
135. A MAN AND A WOMAN ... Tomika Jones and Herbie Mann, Atlantic 2362

Compiled from national retail sales and radio station airplay by the Music Popularity Dept. of Record Market Research, Billboard.

Billboard

For Week Ending November 5, 1966

# HOT 100

★ STAR performer—Sides registering greatest proportionate upward progress this week.

(Seal) Record Industry Association of America seal of certification as million selling single.

| THIS WEEK | 1 Wk. Ago | 2 Wks. Ago | 3 Wks. Ago | TITLE | Artist (Producer), Label & Number | Weeks On Chart |
|---|---|---|---|---|---|---|
| 1 (Billboard Award) | 2 | 3 | 4 | LAST TRAIN TO CLARKSVILLE (Seal) | Monkees (Tommy Boyce & Bobby Hart), Colgems 1001 | 9 |
| 2 | 1 | 2 | 3 | 96 TEARS | ? (Question Mark) & the Mysterians, Cameo 428 | 10 |
| 3 | 4 | 7 | 11 | POOR SIDE OF TOWN | Johnny Rivers (Lou Adler), Imperial 66205 | 8 |
| 4 | 3 | 1 | 1 | REACH OUT I'LL BE THERE | Four Tops (Holland & Dozier), Motown 1098 | 10 |
| 5 | 6 | 9 | 15 | DANDY | Herman's Hermits (Mickie Most), MGM 13603 | 6 |
| 6 | 8 | 11 | 16 | HOORAY FOR HAZEL | Tommy Roe (Our Prods.), ABC 10852 | 8 |
| 7 | 7 | 8 | 8 | WHAT BECOMES OF THE BROKENHEARTED | Jimmy Ruffin (William Stevenson), Soul 35022 | 11 |
| ★8 | 11 | 12 | 17 | IF I WERE A CARPENTER | Bobby Darin (Koppleman-Rubin), Atlantic 2350 | 7 |
| 9 | 9 | 13 | 18 | HAVE YOU SEEN YOUR MOTHER, BABY, STANDING IN THE SHADOW? | Rolling Stones (Andrew Oldham), London 903 | 5 |
| 10 | 5 | 6 | 7 | WALK AWAY RENEE | Left Banke (World United Prod. Inc.), Smash 2041 | 9 |
| ★11 | 16 | 33 | 49 | I'M YOUR PUPPET | James & Bobby Purify (Don Schroeder), Bell 648 | 7 |
| 12 | 12 | 17 | 42 | GO AWAY LITTLE GIRL | Happenings (Tokens), B. T. Puppy 522 | 6 |
| ★13 | 19 | 24 | 38 | LOVE IS A HURTIN' THING | Lou Rawls (David Axelrod), Capitol 5709 | 9 |
| 14 | 15 | 16 | 19 | B-A-B-Y | Carla Thomas (Staff), Stax 195 | 12 |
| 15 | 18 | 37 | 50 | (You Don't Have To) PAINT ME A PICTURE | Gary Lewis & the Playboys, (Snuff Garrett), Liberty 55914 | 5 |
| 16 | 10 | 10 | 14 | SEE SEE RIDER | Eric Burdon & the Animals (Tom Wilson), MGM 13582 | 8 |
| ★17 | 38 | 81 | — | GOOD VIBRATIONS | Beach Boys (Brian Wilson), Capitol 5676 | 3 |
| ★18 | 27 | 34 | 59 | DEVIL WITH A BLUE DRESS ON & GOOD GOLLY MISS MOLLY | Mitch Ryder & the Detroit Wheels (Bob Crew), New Voice 817 | 5 |
| ★19 | 24 | 25 | 31 | BORN FREE | Roger Williams (Hy Grill), Kapp 767 | 10 |
| ★20 | 26 | 40 | 76 | RAIN ON THE ROOF | Lovin' Spoonful (Erik Jacobson), Kama Sutra 216 | 4 |
| 21 | 13 | 4 | 2 | CHERISH (Seal) | Association (C. Boettcher), Valiant 747 | 11 |
| 22 | 22 | 27 | 36 | THE HAIR ON MY CHINNY CHIN CHIN | Sam the Sham & the Pharaohs (Stan Kesler), MGM 13581 | 6 |
| 23 | 14 | 5 | 5 | PSYCHOTIC REACTION | Count Five (Hooven-Winn), Double Shot 104 | 9 |
| ★24 | 66 | — | — | WINCHESTER CATHEDRAL | New Vaudeville Band, (Geoff Stephens), Fontana 1562 | 2 |
| ★25 | 31 | 42 | 53 | COMING ON STRONG | Brenda Lee (Owen Bradley), Decca 32018 | 6 |
| 26 | 20 | 21 | 35 | THE GREAT AIRPLANE STRIKE | Paul Revere & the Raiders (Terry Melcher), Columbia 43810 | 6 |
| ★27 | 68 | — | — | YOU KEEP ME HANGIN' ON | Supremes (Holland-Dozier), Motown 1101 | 2 |
| 28 | 30 | 35 | 45 | I JUST DON'T KNOW WHAT TO DO WITH MYSELF | Dionne Warwick (Bacharach-David), Scepter 12167 | 6 |
| ★29 | 46 | 57 | 75 | LADY GODIVA | Peter & Gordon (John Burgess), Capitol 5740 | 5 |
| ★30 | 39 | 70 | — | WHO AM I | Petula Clark. (Tony Hatch), Warner Bros. 5863 | 3 |
| 31 | 17 | 14 | 6 | CHERRY, CHERRY | Neil Diamond (Jeff Barry & Ellie Greenwich), Bang 528 | 12 |
| 32 | 35 | 30 | 25 | WIPE OUT | Surfaris, Dot 144 | 31 |
| 33 | 34 | 45 | 55 | FA-FA-FA-FA-FA | Otis Redding, Volt 138 | 6 |
| ★34 | 51 | 65 | — | LOOK THROUGH MY WINDOW | Mama's and the Papa's, (Lou Adler), Dunhill 4050 | 3 |
| 35 | 21 | 23 | 28 | LITTLE MAN | Sonny & Cher (Sonny Bono), Atco 6440 | 6 |
| 36 | 23 | 15 | 9 | I'VE GOT YOU UNDER MY SKIN | 4 Seasons (Bob Crewe), Philips 40393 | 10 |
| ★37 | 49 | 59 | 73 | SECRET LOVE | Billy Stewart, (Dave & Caston), Chess 1978 | 4 |
| ★38 | 54 | 56 | 68 | BUT IT'S ALRIGHT | J. J. Jackson (Lew Futterman), Calla 119 | 6 |
| 39 | 45 | 55 | 67 | A SATISFIED MIND | Bobby Hebb, (Jerry Ross), Philips 40400 | 5 |
| 40 | 44 | 47 | 57 | SPIN OUT | Elvis Presley (Joe Pasternak), RCA Victor 8941 | 5 |
| ★41 | 52 | 54 | 66 | AIN'T GONNA LIE | Keith (Jerry Ross), Mercury 72596 | 8 |
| 42 | 42 | 52 | 62 | ALL THAT I AM | Elvis Presley (Joe Pasternark), RCA Victor 8941 | 5 |
| ★43 | 76 | — | — | STOP STOP STOP | Hollies, (Ron Richards), Imperial 66214 | 2 |
| 44 | 32 | 28 | 30 | GIRL ON A SWING | Gerry & the Pacemakers, Laurie 3354 | 9 |
| ★45 | 55 | 66 | 85 | I CAN'T CONTROL MYSELF | Troggs (Larry Page), Fontana 1557, Atco 6444 | 4 |
| ★46 | 59 | 74 | — | LOUIE, LOUIE | Sandpipers (Tommy LaPuma), A&M 819 | 3 |
| 47 | 47 | 49 | 51 | MAS QUE NADA | Sergio Mendes & Brazil '66 (Herb Alpert), A&M 807 | 7 |
| 48 | 37 | 22 | 12 | BEAUTY IS ONLY SKIN DEEP | Temptations (Norman Whitfield), Gordy 7055 | 12 |
| 49 | 50 | 58 | 74 | UP TIGHT | Ramsey Lewis, (E. Edwards), Cadet 5547 | 4 |
| 50 | 25 | 18 | 10 | YOU CAN'T HURRY LOVE | Supremes (Holland & Dozier), Motown 1097 | 13 |
| 51 | 43 | 44 | 44 | COME ON UP | Young Rascals (Young Rascals), Atlantic 2353 | 7 |
| 52 | 48 | 48 | 58 | PLEASE MR. SUN | Vogues (Cenci-Moon-Hakim), Co & Ce 240 | 7 |
| 53 | 56 | 69 | 82 | DON'T BE A DROP-OUT | James Brown & His Famous Flames (James Brown Prod.) King 6056 | 5 |
| 54 | 29 | 20 | 21 | ALL I SEE IS YOU | Dusty Springfield, Philips 40396 | 8 |
| 55 | 36 | 38 | 43 | MR. SPACEMAN | Byrds (Allen Stanton), Columbia 43766 | 7 |
| ★56 | 67 | 68 | 79 | THE WHEEL OF HURT | Margaret Whiting (Arnold Goland), London 101 | 5 |
| ★57 | 70 | — | — | I'M READY FOR LOVE | Martha & the Vandellas, (Holland-Dozier), Gordy 7056 | 2 |
| 58 | 62 | 62 | 72 | KNOCK ON WOOD | Eddie Floyd (Prod. by Staff), Stax 194 | 9 |
| ★59 | 69 | 84 | — | NINETEEN DAYS | Dave Clark Five (Dave Clark), Epic 10076 | 3 |
| 60 | 60 | 72 | 87 | NOBODY'S BABY AGAIN | Dean Martin (Jimmy Bowen), Reprise 0516 | 5 |
| 61 | 61 | 76 | 88 | SOMEBODY LIKE ME | Eddy Arnold (Chet Atkins), RCA Victor 8965 | 4 |
| ★62 | 79 | 92 | — | IT TEARS ME UP | Percy Sledge (Martin Greene-Quin Ivy), Atlantic 2358 | 3 |
| 63 | 41 | 46 | 47 | I WANT TO BE WITH YOU | Dee Dee Warwick (Ed Townsend), Mercury 72584 | 11 |
| 64 | 72 | 82 | — | HEAVEN MUST HAVE SENT YOU | Elgins (Holland-Dozier), V.I.P. 25037 | 3 |
| ★65 | 82 | 85 | — | HOLY COW | Lee Dorsey (A. Toussaint-M. Sehorn), Amy 965 | 3 |
| 66 | 58 | 60 | 60 | ALMOST PERSUADED NO. 2 | Ben Colder (Jack Clement), MGM 13590 | 6 |
| 67 | 64 | 71 | 81 | I'VE GOT TO DO A LITTLE BIT BETTER | Joe Tex (Buddy Killen), Dial 4045 | 5 |
| 68 | 77 | — | — | ON THIS SIDE OF GOODBYE | Righteous Brothers, (Bill Medley), Verve 10449 | 2 |
| 69 | 65 | 51 | 52 | MIND EXCURSION | The Trade Winds (Anders-Poncia), Kama Sutra 212 | 9 |
| 70 | 63 | 64 | 86 | BABY, DO THE PHILLY DOG | Olympics (Smith), Mirwood 5523 | 6 |
| 71 | 71 | 73 | 92 | STAY WITH ME | Lorraine Ellison (Jerry Ragavoy), Warner Bros. 5850 | 5 |
| ★72 | 89 | 93 | — | WHY PICK ON ME | Standells (Ed Cobb), Tower 282 | 3 |
| 73 | 74 | 77 | 99 | THE WHEEL OF HURT | Al Martino (T. Morgan), Capitol 5741 | 4 |
| 74 | 75 | 75 | 83 | SOMEBODY (Somewhere) NEEDS YOU | Darrell Banks (Solid Hitbound Prod., Inc.), Revilot 203 | 4 |
| 75 | 88 | 94 | — | BANG! BANG! | Joe Cuba Sextet (Pancho Cristal), Tico 475 | 3 |
| 76 | 81 | 83 | — | WISH YOU WERE HERE, BUDDY | Pat Boone (Nick Venet and Randy Wood), Dot 16933 | 3 |
| 77 | 83 | 90 | — | RUN, RUN, LOOK AND SEE | Brian Hyland (Snuff Garrett), Philips 40405 | 3 |
| ★78 | — | 87 | 90 | WHISPERS | Jackie Wilson (Carl Davis), Brunswick 55300 | 3 |
| 79 | 86 | — | — | BABY, WHAT DO YOU WANT ME TO DO? | Barbara Lewis, (Ollie McLaughlin), Atlantic 2361 | 2 |
| 80 | 80 | 86 | 95 | A SYMPHONY FOR SUSAN | Arbors, (Richard Carney), Date 1529 | 4 |
| ★81 | — | — | — | A HAZY SHADE OF WINTER | Simon & Garfunkel (Bob Johnston), Columbia 43873 | 1 |
| ★82 | — | — | — | (When She Needs Good Lovin') SHE COMES TO ME | Chicago Loop (Bob Crewe) DynoVoice 226 | 1 |
| 83 | 84 | 88 | 89 | FREE AGAIN | Barbra Streisand (Ettore Stratta), Columbia 43808 | 4 |
| 84 | 85 | — | — | A DAY IN THE LIFE OF A FOOL | Jack Jones, (David Kapp), Kapp 781 | 2 |
| 85 | 93 | — | — | TIME AFTER TIME | Chris Montez, (Tommy LiPuma-Herb Alpert), A&M 822 | 2 |
| ★86 | — | — | — | COME BACK | Five Stairsteps, Windy C 603 | 1 |
| 87 | 98 | 99 | — | DON'T ANSWER THE DOOR | B. B. King (Johnny Pate), ABC 10856 | 3 |
| 88 | 90 | — | — | HELP ME GIRL | Outsiders, (Roger Karshner), Capitol 5759 | 2 |
| 89 | 91 | 91 | — | POURING WATER ON A DROWNING MAN | James Carr (Quinton Claunche and Doc Russell), Goldwax 311 | 3 |
| ★90 | — | — | — | (Come 'Round Here) I'M THE ONE YOU NEED | Miracles (Holland & Dozier) Tamla 54140 | 1 |
| 91 | 92 | — | — | GAMES THAT LOVERS PLAY | Eddie Fisher, (Al Schmitt), RCA Victor 8956 | 2 |
| 92 | — | — | — | HEARTBREAK HOTEL | Roger Miller (Jerry Kennedy) Smash 2066 | 1 |
| 93 | 94 | 100 | — | GAMES THAT LOVERS PLAY | Wayne Newton (Steve Douglas), Capitol 5754 | 3 |
| 94 | — | — | — | A CORNER IN THE SUN | Walter Jackson (Ted Cooper) Okeh 7260 | 1 |
| 95 | 96 | 98 | — | STAND IN FOR LOVE | O'Jays (Wri-Hand Prod.), Imperial 66197 | 3 |
| 96 | — | — | — | IT'S ONLY LOVE | Tommy James & the Shondells, Roulette 4710 | 1 |
| 97 | 99 | — | — | CAN I GET TO KNOW YOU BETTER | Turtles, (Bones Howe), White Whale 238 | 2 |
| 98 | — | — | — | WINCHESTER CATHEDRAL | Dana Rolin, Tower 283 | 1 |
| 99 | — | — | — | SPANISH NIGHTS AND YOU | Connie Francis (Lorber-Spargo) MGM 13610 | 1 |
| 100 | — | — | — | MEDITATION | Claudine Longet (Tommy LiPuma) A&M 817 | 1 |

## HOT 100—A TO Z—*(Publisher-Licensee)*


Ain't Gonna Lie (Screen Gems-Columbia, BMI) .. 41
All I See Is You (Anne-Rachel, ASCAP) .......... 54
All That I Am (Gladys, ASCAP) .......... 42
Almost Persuaded No. 2 (Gallico, BMI) .......... 66
B-A-B-Y (East, BMI) .......... 14
Baby, Do the Philly Dog (Keymen, Mirwood, BMI) 70
Baby What Do You Want Me to Do (McLaughlin, BMI) .......... 79
Bang! Bang! (Cordon, BMI) .......... 75
Beauty Is Only Skin Deep (Jobete, BMI) .......... 48
Born Free (Screen Gems-Columbia, BMI) .......... 19
But It's Alright (Pamelarosa, BMI) .......... 38
Can I Get to Know You Better (Trousdale, BMI) .. 97
Cherish (Beechwood, BMI) .......... 21
Cherry, Cherry (Tallyrand, BMI) .......... 31
Come Back (Camad, BMI) .......... 86
Come On Up (Slacsar, BMI) .......... 51
(Come 'Round Here) I'm the One You Need (Jobete, BMI) .......... 90
Coming On Strong (Moss-Rose, BMI) .......... 25
Corner in the Sun, A (Blackwood, Blue Chip, BMI) 94
Dandy (Noma, BMI) .......... 5
Day in the Life of a Fool, A (Jungnickel, ASCAP) .......... 84
Devil With a Blue Dress On & Good Molly Miss Molly (Jobete-Venice, BMI) .......... 18
Don't Answer the Door (Mercedes, BMI) .......... 87
Don't Be a Drop-Out (Dynatone, BMI) .......... 53
Fa-Fa-Fa-Fa-Fa (East-Redwal, BMI) .......... 32
Free Again (Emanuel-Beaujolais, ASCAP) .......... 83
Games That Lovers Play (Fisher) (Miller, ASCAP) 91
Games That Lovers Play (Newton) (Miller, ASCAP) 93
Girl on a Swing (Bright Tunes, BMI) .......... 44
Go Away Little Girl (Screen Gems-Columbia, BMI) 12
Good Vibrations (Sea of Tunes, BMI) .......... 17
Great Airplane Strike, The (Daywin, BMI) .......... 26
Hair on My Chinny Chin Chin, The (Rose, BMI).. 22
Have You Seen Your Mother, Baby, Standing in the Shadow? (Gideon, BMI) .......... 9
Hazy Shade of Winter, A (Charing Cross, BMI) .. 81
Heartbreak Hotel (Tree, BMI) .......... 92
Heaven Must Have Sent You (Jobete, BMI) .......... 64
Help Me, Girl (Helios, BMI) .......... 88
Holy Cow (Marsaint, BMI) .......... 65
Hooray for Hazel (Low Twi, BMI) .......... 6
I Can Make It With You (Blackwood, BMI) .......... 33
I Can't Control Myself (James, BMI) .......... 45
I Just Don't Know What to Do With Myself (U. S. Songs, ASCAP) .......... 28
I Want to Be With You (Moreley, ASCAP) .......... 63
I'm Ready for Love (Jobete, BMI) .......... 57
I'm Your Puppet (Fame, BMI) .......... 11
It's Only Love (Tender Tunes, BMI) .......... 96
I've Got to Do a Little Bit Better (Tree, BMI) .... 67
I've Got You Under My Skin (Chappell, ASCAP) .. 36
If I Were a Carpenter (Faithful Virtue, BMI) .... 8
It Tears Me Up (Fame, BMI) .......... 62
Knock on Wood (East, BMI) .......... 58
Lady Godiva (Regent, BMI) .......... 29
Last Train to Clarksville (Screen Gems-Columbia, BMI) .......... 1
Little Man (Cotillion-Chris-Marc, BMI) .......... 35
Look Through My Window (Trousdale, BMI) .... 34
Louie, Louie (Limax, BMI) .......... 46
Love Is a Hurtin' Thing (Rawlou, BMI) .......... 13
Mas Que Nada (Peer Int'l., BMI) .......... 47
Meditation (Duchess, BMI) ..........100
Mind Excursion (Kama Sutra, BMI) .......... 69
Mr. Spaceman (Tickson, BMI) .......... 55
Nineteen Days (Branston, BMI) .......... 59
96 Tears (Arguello, BMI) .......... 2
Nobody's Baby Again (Smooth-Noma, BMI) .......... 60
On This Side of Goodbye (Screen Gems-Columbia, BMI) .......... 68
Paint Me a Picture (Viva, BMI) .......... 15
Please Mr. Sun (Weiss-Barry, BMI) .......... 52
Poor Side of Town (Rivers, BMI) .......... 3
Pouring Water on a Drowning Man (Pronto-Quinvy, BMI) .......... 89
Psychotic Reaction (Hot Shot, BMI) .......... 23
Rain on the Roof (Faithful Virtue, BMI) .......... 20
Reach Out I'll Be There (Jobete, BMI) .......... 4
Run, Run, Look and See (Little Darlin'-Low Twi, BMI) .......... 77
Satisfied Mind, A (Starday, BMI) .......... 39
Secret Love (Remick, ASCAP) .......... 37
See See Rider (Leeds, ASCAP) .......... 16
Somebody Like Me (Barton, BMI) .......... 61
Somebody (Somewhere) Needs You (Jobete, BMI) .. 74
Spanish Nights and You (Wanessa, Brookings, BMI) 99
Spinout (Gladys, ASCAP) .......... 40
Stand in for Love (Metric-Bar-New, BMI) .......... 95
Stay With Me (Ragmar-Crenshaw, BMI) .......... 71
Stop Stop Stop (Maribus, BMI) .......... 43
Symphony for Susan, A (Kris, ASCAP) .......... 80
Time After Time (Sands, ASCAP) .......... 85
Up Tight (Jobete, BMI) .......... 49
Walk Away Renee (Twin Tone, BMI) .......... 10
What Becomes of the Brokenhearted (Jobete, BMI) 7
Wheel of Hurt, The (Martino) (Roosevelt, BMI) .. 73
Wheel of Hurt, The (Whiting) (Roosevelt, BMI) .. 56
Whispers (Jalynne,-BRC, BMI) .......... 78
(When She Needs Good Lovin') She Comes to Me (Tiger, BMI) .......... 82
Who Am I (Duchess, BMI) .......... 30
Why Pick On Me (Equinox, BMI) .......... 72
Winchester Cathedral (Rollin) (Southern, ASCAP) .. 98
Winchester Cathedral (Vaudeville Band) (Southern, ASCAP) ..........24
Wish You Were Here, Buddy (Roosevelt, BMI) ... 76
You Can't Hurry Love (Jobete, BMI) .......... 50
You Keep Me Hangin' On (Jobete, BMI) .......... 27


## BUBBLING UNDER THE HOT 100

101. I WANNA MEET YOU ..........Cryin' Shames, Columbia 43836
102. THESE THINGS WILL KEEP ME LOVING YOU ....Velvelettes, Soul 35025
103. WE GOT A THING THAT'S IN THE GROOVE ..........Capitols, Karen 1526
104. LOOKIN' FOR LOVE ........Ray Conniff & the Singers, Columbia 43814
105. POVERTY ..........Bobby Bland, Duke 407
106. PIPELINE ..........Chantays, Dot 145
107. I GOT THE FEELIN' "OH, NO NO NO" ..........Neil Diamond, Bang 536
108. RESPECT .......... Rationals, Cameo 437
109. WILD ANGELS THEME ..........Davie Allen & the Arrows, Tower 267
110. WINDOWS AND DOORS ..........Jackie DeShannon, Imperial 66196
111. EGGPLANT THAT ATE CHICAGO .......... ..Dr. West's Medicine Show & Junk Band, Go Go 100
112. FORTUNE TELLER ..........Hardtimes, World Pacific 77851
113. I CAN HEAR MUSIC ..........Ronnettes, Philles 133
114. DISTANT DRUMS ..........Vic Dana, Dolton 324
115. SOCIETY'S CHILD ..........Janis Ian, Verve Folkways 5027
116. WILD THING ..........Ventures, Dolton 325
117. FIFI THE FLEA ..........Sidekicks, RCA Victor 8969
118. TALK TALK ..........Music Machine, Original Sound 61
119. I (Who Have Nothing) ..........Terry Knight & the Pack, Lucky 11 230
120. WINCHESTER CATHEDRAL ..........The Happiness, Columbia 43851
121. CHANSON D'AMOUR ..........Lettermen, Capitol 5749
122. CLOCK ..........Eddie Rambeau, DynoVoice 225
123. AS I A LOSER ..........Eddie Holman, Parkway 106
124. WEDDING BELL BLUES ..........Laura Nyro, Verve-Folkways 502
125. COMING HOME SOLDIER ..........Bobby Vinton, Epic 10090
126. IT'S NOT THE SAME ..........Anthony & the Imperials, Veep 1248
127. HI HI HAZEL ..........Gary & the Hornets, Smash 2061
128. MAN AND A WOMAN ........Tomika Jones & Herbie Mann, Atlantic 2362
129. STANDING ON GUARD ..........Falcons, Big Wheel 1967
130. THE WILLY ..........Willies, Co & Ce 239
131. TINY BUBBLES ..........Billy Vaughn, Dot 16987
132. CABARET ..........Mike Douglas, Epic 10078
133. PLEASE SAY YOU'RE FOOLING ..........Ray Charles, ABC 10065
134. IT'S A HAPPENING ..........Magic Mushrooms, A&M 815
135. LONG HAIR MUSIC ..........Guise, Musicland, U.S.A. 20.001

Compiled from national retail sales and radio station airplay by the Music Popularity Dept. of Record Market Research, Billboard.

# HOT 100

★ STAR performer—Sides registering greatest proportionate upward progress this week.

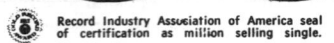

Record Industry Association of America seal of certification as million selling single.

| This Week | 1 Wk. Ago | 2 Wks. Ago | 3 Wks. Ago | TITLE Artist (Producer), Label & Number | Weeks On Chart |
|---|---|---|---|---|---|
| Billboard Award | 3 | 4 | 7 | POOR SIDE OF TOWN — Johnny Rivers (Lou Adler), Imperial 66205 | 9 |
| 2 | 1 | 2 | 3 | LAST TRAIN TO CLARKSVILLE — Monkees (Tommy Boyce & Bobby Hart), Colgems 1001 | 10 |
| 3 | 2 | 1 | 2 | 96 TEARS — ? (Question Mark) & the Mysterians, Cameo 428 | 11 |
| ★ 4 | 17 | 38 | 81 | GOOD VIBRATIONS — Beach Boys (Brian Wilson), Capitol 5676 | 4 |
| 5 | 5 | 6 | 9 | DANDY — Herman's Hermits (Mickie Most), MGM 13603 | 7 |
| ★ 6 | 24 | 66 | — | WINCHESTER CATHEDRAL — New Vaudeville Band, (Geoff Stephens), Fontana 1562 | 3 |
| ★ 7 | 27 | 68 | — | YOU KEEP ME HANGIN' ON — Supremes (Holland-Dozier), Motown 1101 | 3 |
| 8 | 8 | 11 | 12 | IF I WERE A CARPENTER — Bobby Darin (Koppleman-Rubin), Atlantic 2350 | 8 |
| ★ 9 | 18 | 27 | 34 | DEVIL WITH A BLUE DRESS ON & GOOD GOLLY MISS MOLLY — Mitch Ryder & the Detroit Wheels (Bob Crew), New Voice 817 | 5 |
| 10 | 11 | 16 | 33 | I'M YOUR PUPPET — James & Bobby Purify (Don Schroeder), Bell 648 | 8 |
| 11 | 4 | 3 | 1 | REACH OUT I'LL BE THERE — Four Tops (Holland & Dozier), Motown 1098 | 11 |
| 12 | 10 | 5 | 6 | WALK AWAY RENEE — Left Banke (World United Prod. Inc.), Smash 2041 | 10 |
| 13 | 13 | 19 | 24 | LOVE IS A HURTIN' THING — Lou Rawls (David Axelrod), Capitol 5709 | 10 |
| 14 | 6 | 8 | 11 | HOORAY FOR HAZEL — Tommy Roe (Our Prods.), ABC 10852 | 9 |
| ★ 15 | 20 | 26 | 40 | RAIN ON THE ROOF — Lovin' Spoonful (Erik Jacobson), Kama Sutra 216 | 5 |
| 16 | 9 | 9 | 13 | HAVE YOU SEEN YOUR MOTHER, BABY, STANDING IN THE SHADOWS? — Rolling Stones (Andrew Oldham), London 903 | 6 |
| 17 | 19 | 24 | 25 | BORN FREE — Roger Williams (Hy Grill), Kapp 767 | 11 |
| 18 | 7 | 7 | 8 | WHAT BECOMES OF THE BROKENHEARTED — Jimmy Ruffin (William Stevenson), Soul 35022 | 12 |
| 19 | 12 | 12 | 17 | GO AWAY LITTLE GIRL — Happenings (Tokens), B. T. Puppy 522 | 7 |
| ★ 20 | 25 | 31 | 42 | COMING ON STRONG — Brenda Lee (Owen Bradley), Decca 32018 | 7 |
| ★ 21 | 29 | 46 | 57 | LADY GODIVA — Peter & Gordon (John Burgess), Capitol 5740 | 6 |
| ★ 22 | 30 | 39 | 70 | WHO AM I — Petula Clark, (Tony Hatch), Warner Bros. 5863 | 4 |
| 23 | 16 | 10 | 10 | SEE SEE RIDER — Eric Burdon & the Animals (Tom Wilson), MGM 13582 | 9 |
| 24 | 15 | 18 | 37 | (You Don't Have To) PAINT ME A PICTURE — Gary Lewis & the Playboys, (Snuff Garrett), Liberty 55914 | 6 |
| ★ 25 | 34 | 51 | 65 | LOOK THROUGH MY WINDOW — Mama's and the Papa's, (Lou Adler), Dunhill 4050 | 4 |
| 26 | 28 | 30 | 35 | I JUST DON'T KNOW WHAT TO DO WITH MYSELF — Dionne Warwick (Bacharach-David), Scepter 12167 | 7 |
| 27 | 14 | 15 | 16 | B-A-B-Y — Carla Thomas (Staff), Stax 195 | 13 |
| 28 | 22 | 22 | 27 | THE HAIR ON MY CHINNY CHIN CHIN — Sam the Sham & the Pharaohs (Stan Kesler), MGM 13581 | 7 |
| 29 | 32 | 34 | 45 | FA-FA-FA-FA-FA — Otis Redding, Volt 138 | 7 |
| ★ 30 | 38 | 54 | 56 | BUT IT'S ALRIGHT — J. J. Jackson (Lew Futterman), Calla 119 | 7 |
| ★ 31 | 43 | 76 | — | STOP STOP STOP — Hollies, (Ron Richards), Imperial 66214 | 3 |
| 32 | 21 | 13 | 4 | CHERISH — Association (C. Boettcher), Valiant 747 | 12 |
| 33 | 23 | 14 | 5 | PSYCHOTIC REACTION — Count Five (Hooven-Winn), Double Shot 104 | 10 |
| ★ 34 | 57 | 70 | — | I'M READY FOR LOVE — Martha & the Vandellas, (Holland-Dozier), Gordy 7056 | 3 |
| 35 | 33 | 33 | 32 | I CAN MAKE IT WITH YOU — Pozo-Seco Singers, (Bob Johnston) Columbia 43784 | 10 |
| 36 | 26 | 20 | 21 | THE GREAT AIRPLANE STRIKE — Paul Revere & the Raiders (Terry Melcher), Columbia 43810 | 7 |
| 37 | 37 | 49 | 59 | SECRET LOVE — Billy Stewart, (Dave & Caston), Chess 1978 | 5 |
| 38 | 46 | 59 | 74 | LOUIE, LOUIE — Sandpipers (Tommy LaPuma), A&M 819 | 4 |
| 39 | 41 | 52 | 54 | AIN'T GONNA LIE — Keith (Jerry Ross), Mercury 72596 | 9 |
| 40 | 40 | 44 | 47 | SPIN OUT — Elvis Presley (Joe Pasternak), RCA Victor 8941 | 6 |
| 41 | 39 | 45 | 55 | A SATISFIED MIND — Bobby Hebb, (Jerry Ross), Philips 40400 | 6 |
| 42 | 42 | 42 | 52 | ALL THAT I AM — Elvis Presley (Joe Pasternak), RCA Victor 8941 | 6 |
| 43 | 45 | 55 | 66 | I CAN'T CONTROL MYSELF — Troggs (Larry Page), Fontana 1557, Atco 6444 | 5 |
| 44 | 35 | 21 | 23 | LITTLE MAN — Sonny & Cher (Sonny Bono), Atco 6440 | 7 |
| ★ 45 | 58 | 62 | 62 | KNOCK ON WOOD — Eddie Floyd (Prod. by Staff), Stax 194 | 10 |
| ★ 46 | 65 | 82 | 85 | HOLY COW — Lee Dorsey (A. Toussaint-M. Sehorn), Amy 965 | 4 |
| ★ 47 | 81 | — | — | A HAZY SHADE OF WINTER — Simon & Garfunkel (Bob Johnston), Columbia 43873 | 2 |
| 48 | 47 | 47 | 49 | MAS QUE NADA — Sergio Mendes & Brazil '66 (Herb Alpert), A&M 807 | 8 |
| 49 | 56 | 67 | 68 | THE WHEEL OF HURT — Margaret Whiting (Arnold Goland), London 101 | 6 |
| 50 | 53 | 56 | 69 | DON'T BE A DROP-OUT — James Brown & His Famous Flames (James Brown Prod.) King 6056 | 6 |
| ★ 51 | 62 | 79 | 92 | IT TEARS ME UP — Percy Sledge (Martin Greene-Quin Ivy), Atlantic 2358 | 4 |
| 52 | 49 | 50 | 58 | UP TIGHT — Ramsey Lewis, (E. Edwards), Cadet 5547 | 5 |
| 53 | 61 | 61 | 76 | SOMEBODY LIKE ME — Eddy Arnold (Chet Atkins), RCA Victor 8965 | 5 |
| 54 | 59 | 69 | 84 | NINETEEN DAYS — Dave Clark Five (Dave Clark), Epic 10076 | 4 |
| ★ 55 | 78 | — | 87 | WHISPERS — Jackie Wilson (Carl Davis), Brunswick 55300 | 4 |
| 56 | 64 | 72 | 82 | HEAVEN MUST HAVE SENT YOU — Elgins (Holland-Dozier), V.I.P. 25037 | 4 |
| ★ 57 | 77 | 83 | 90 | RUN, RUN, LOOK AND SEE — Brian Hyland (Snuff Garrett), Philips 40405 | 4 |
| ★ 58 | 68 | 77 | — | ON THIS SIDE OF GOODBYE — Righteous Brothers, (Bill Medley), Verve 10449 | 3 |
| 59 | 52 | 48 | 48 | PLEASE MR. SUN — Vogues (Cenci-Moon-Hakim), Co & Ce 240 | 8 |
| ★ 60 | 74 | 75 | 75 | SOMEBODY (Somewhere) NEEDS YOU — Darrell Banks (Solid Hitbound Prod., Inc.), Revilot 203 | 5 |
| 61 | 72 | 89 | 93 | WHY PICK ON ME — Standells (Ed Cobb), Tower 282 | 4 |
| 62 | 60 | 60 | 72 | NOBODY'S BABY AGAIN — Dean Martin (Jimmy Bowen), Reprise 0516 | 6 |
| 63 | 73 | 74 | 77 | THE WHEEL OF HURT — Al Martino (T. Morgan), Capitol 5741 | 5 |
| 64 | 71 | 71 | 73 | STAY WITH ME — Lorraine Ellison (Jerry Ragavey), Warner Bros. 5850 | 6 |
| ★ 65 | — | — | — | MELLOW YELLOW — Donovan, (Mickie Most), Epic 10098 | 1 |
| 66 | 63 | 41 | 46 | I WANT TO BE WITH YOU — Dee Dee Warwick (Ed Townsend), Mercury 72584 | 12 |
| ★ 67 | 82 | — | — | (When She Needs Good Lovin') SHE COMES TO ME — Chicago Loop (Bob Crewe & Al Kasha), DynoVoice 226 | 2 |
| 68 | 76 | 81 | 83 | WISH YOU WERE HERE, BUDDY — Pat Boone (Nick Venet and Randy Wood), Dot 16933 | 4 |
| ★ 69 | — | — | — | I GOT THE FEELIN' "OH NO NO" — Neil Diamond, (Jeff Barry-Ellie Greenwich), Bang 536 | 1 |
| 70 | 80 | 80 | 86 | A SYMPHONY FOR SUSAN — Arbors, (Richard Carney), Date 1529 | 5 |
| ★ 71 | 86 | — | — | COME BACK — Five Stairsteps, Windy C 603 | 2 |
| 72 | 75 | 88 | 94 | BANG! BANG! — Joe Cuba Sextet (Pancho Cristal), Tico 475 | 4 |
| ★ 73 | 90 | — | — | (Come 'Round Here) I'M THE ONE YOU NEED — Miracles (Holland & Dozier) Tamla 54140 | 2 |
| 74 | 84 | 85 | — | A DAY IN THE LIFE OF A FOOL — Jack Jones, (David Kapp), Kapp 781 | 3 |
| 75 | 85 | 93 | — | TIME AFTER TIME — Chris Montez, (Tommy LiPuma-Herb Alpert), A&M 822 | 3 |
| 76 | 88 | 90 | — | HELP ME GIRL — Outsiders, (Roger Karshner), Capitol 5759 | 3 |
| 77 | 79 | 86 | — | BABY, WHAT DO YOU WANT ME TO DO? — Barbara Lewis, (Jerry Wexler & Ollie McLaughlin), Atlantic 2361 | 3 |
| ★ 78 | 98 | — | — | WINCHESTER CATHEDRAL — Dana Rollin, Tower 283 | 2 |
| ★ 79 | — | — | — | WE GOT A THING THAT'S IN THE GROOVE — Capitols, (Ollie McLaughlin), Karen 1526 | 1 |
| 80 | 87 | 98 | 99 | DON'T ANSWER THE DOOR — B. B. King (Johnny Pate), ABC 10856 | 4 |
| ★ 81 | 96 | — | — | IT'S ONLY LOVE — Tommy James & the Shondells, Roulette 4710 | 2 |
| ★ 82 | — | — | — | PLEASE SAY YOU'RE FOOLING — Ray Charles (TRC), ABC 10865 | 1 |
| ★ 83 | — | — | — | A PLACE IN THE SUN — Stevie Wonder, (C. Paul), Tamla 54139 | 1 |
| 84 | 91 | 92 | — | GAMES THAT LOVERS PLAY — Eddie Fisher, (Al Schmitt), RCA Victor 8956 | 3 |
| 85 | 89 | 91 | 91 | POURING WATER ON A DROWNING MAN — James Carr (Quinton Claunche and Doc Russell), Goldwax 311 | 4 |
| 86 | 94 | — | — | A CORNER IN THE SUN — Walter Jackson (Ted Cooper) Okeh 7260 | 2 |
| ★ 87 | — | — | — | THE PROUD ONE — Frankie Valli, (Bob Crew), Philips 40407 | 1 |
| ★ 88 | — | — | — | A MAN AND A WOMAN — Tamiko Jones & Herbie Mann, Atlantic 2362 | 1 |
| 89 | 93 | 94 | 100 | GAMES THAT LOVERS PLAY — Wayne Newton (Steve Douglas), Capitol 5754 | 4 |
| 90 | 92 | — | — | HEARTBREAK HOTEL — Roger Miller (Jerry Kennedy) Smash 2066 | 2 |
| 91 | 97 | 99 | — | CAN I GET TO KNOW YOU BETTER — Turtles, (Bones Howe), White Whale 238 | 3 |
| 92 | — | — | — | IT'S NOT THE SAME — Anthony & the Imperials, (Teddy Randazzo), Veep 1248 | 1 |
| 93 | — | — | — | IT'S-A-HAPPENING — Magic Mushrooms, (Sonny Casella), A&M 815 | 1 |
| 94 | — | — | — | HARLEM SHUFFLE — Traits, (Huey F. Meaux), Sceptor 12169 | 1 |
| 95 | — | — | — | RESPECT — Rationals, (Jeep Holland), Cameo 437 | 1 |
| 96 | — | — | — | TALK TALK — Music Machine, (Maurice Bercov), Original Sound 61 | 1 |
| 97 | — | — | — | I (WHO HAVE NOTHING) — Tery Knight & the Pack, (Terry Knight), Lucky 11 230 | 1 |
| 98 | 100 | — | — | MEDITATION — Claudine Longet (Tommy LiPuma) A&M 817 | 2 |
| 99 | 99 | — | — | SPANISH NIGHTS AND YOU — Connie Francis (Lorber-Spargo) MGM 13610 | 2 |
| 100 | — | — | — | WILD ANGELS THEME — Davie Allen & the Arrows, (Mike Curb) Tower 267 | 1 |

## HOT 100—A TO Z—*(Publisher-Licensee)*


A Man and A Woman (Northern, ASCAP) ........ 88
A Place In The Sun (Stein-Vanstock, ASCAP) .... 83
Ain't Gonna Lie (Screen Gems-Columbia, BMI) .... 39
All That I Am (Gladys, ASCAP) ........ 42
B-A-B-Y (East, BMI) ........ 27
Baby What Do You Want Me to Do (McLaughlin, BMI) ........ 77
Bang! Bang! (Cordon, BMI) ........ 72
Born Free (Screen Gems-Columbia, BMI) ........ 17
But It's Alright (Pamelarosa, BMI) ........ 30
Can I Get to Know You Better (Trousdale, BMI) .. 91
Cherish (Beechwood, BMI) ........ 32
Come Back (Camad, BMI) ........ 71
(Come 'Round Here) I'm the One You Need (Jobete, BMI) ........ 73
Coming On Strong (Moss-Rose, BMI) ........ 20
Corner in the Sun, A (Blackwood, Blue Chip, BMI) 86
Dandy (Noma, BMI) ........ 5
Day in the Life of a Fool, A (Jungnickel, ASCAP) 74
Devil With a Blue Dress On & Good Golly Miss Molly (Jobete-Vanice, BMI) ........ 9
Don't Answer the Door (Mercedes, BMI) ........ 80
Don't Be a Drop-Out (Dynatone, BMI) ........ 50
Fa-Fa-Fa-Fa-Fa (East-Redwal, BMI) ........ 29
Games That Lovers Play (Fisher) (Miller, ASCAP) 84
Games That Lovers Play (Newton) (Miller, ASCAP) 89
Go Away Little Girl (Screen Gems-Columbia, BMI) 19
Good Vibrations (Sea of Tunes, BMI) ........ 4
Great Airplane Strike, The (Daywin, BMI) ........ 36
Hair on My Chinny Chin Chin, The (Rose, BMI) .. 28
Harlem Shuffle (Keyman, BMI) ........ 94
Have You Seen Your Mother, Baby, Standing in the Shadow? (Gideon, BMI) ........ 16
Hazy Shade of Winter, A (Charing Cross, BMI) .. 47
Heartbreak Hotel (Tree, BMI) ........ 90
Heaven Must Have Sent You (Jobete, BMI) ........ 56
Help Me, Girl (Helios, BMI) ........ 76
Holy Cow (Marsaint, BMI) ........ 46
Hooray for Hazel (Low Twi, BMI) ........ 14
I Can Make It With You (Blackwood, BMI) .... 35
I Can't Control Myself (James, BMI) ........ 43
I Got The Feelin' "Oh No No" (Tallyrand, BMI) .. 69
I Just Don't Know What to Do With Myself (U. S. Songs, ASCAP) ........ 26
I (Who Have Nothing) (Milky Way-Trio-Catillio, BMI) ........ 97
I Want to Be With You (Moreley, ASCAP) ........ 66
If I Were a Carpenter (Faithful Virtue, BMI) .. 8
It Tears Me Up (Fame, BMI) ........ 51
I'm Ready for Love (Jobete, BMI) ........ 34
I'm Your Puppet (Fame, BMI) ........ 10
It's Not The Same (South Mountain, BMI) ........ 92
It's-A-Happening (Back Rome, BMI) ........ 93
It's Only Love (Tender Tunes, BMI) ........ 81
Knock on Wood (East, BMI) ........ 45
Lady Godiva (Regent, BMI) ........ 21
Last Train to Clarksville (Screen Gems-Columbia, BMI) ........ 2
Little Man (Cotillion-Chris-Marc, BMI) ........ 44
Look Through My Window (Trousdale, BMI) .... 25
Louie, Louie (Limax, BMI) ........ 38
Love Is a Hurtin' Thing (Rawlou, BMI) ........ 13
Mas Que Nada (Peer Int'l., BMI) ........ 48
Meditation (Duchess, BMI) ........ 98
Mellow Yellow (Donovan Ltd., BMI) ........ 65
Nineteen Days (Branston, BMI) ........ 54
96 Tears (Arguello, BMI) ........ 3
Nobody's Baby Again (Smooth-Noma, BMI) ........ 62
On This Side of Goodbye (Screen Gems-Columbia, BMI) ........ 58
Paint Me a Picture (Vive, BMI) ........ 24
Please Mr. Sun (Weiss-Barry, BMI) ........ 59
Please Say You're Fooling (Eden, BMI) ........ 82
Poor Side of Town (Rivers, BMI) ........ 1
Pouring Water on a Drowning Man (Pronto-Quinvy, BMI) ........ 85
Psychotic Reaction (Hot Shot, BMI) ........ 33
Rain on the Roof (Faithful Virtue, BMI) ........ 15
Reach Out I'll Be There (Jobete BMI) ........ 11
Respect (East-Time-Walco, BMI) ........ 95
Run, Run, Look and See (Little Darlin'-Low Twi, BMI) ........ 57
Satisfied Mind, A (Starday, BMI) ........ 41
Secret Love (Remick, ASCAP) ........ 37
See See Rider (Leeds, ASCAP) ........ 23
Somebody Like Me (Barton, BMI) ........ 53
Somebody (Somewhere) Needs You (Jobete, BMI) .. 60
Spanish Nights and You (Wanessa, Brookings, BMI) 99
Spin Out (Gladys, ASCAP) ........ 40
Stay With Me (Ragmar-Crenshaw, BMI) ........ 64
Stop Stop Stop (Maribus, BMI) ........ 31
Symphony for Susan, A (Kris, ASCAP) ........ 70
Talk Talk (Thrush, BMI) ........ 96
The Proud One (Saturday & Seasons' Four, BMI) .. 87
Time After Time (Sands, ASCAP) ........ 75
Up Tight (Jobete, BMI) ........ 52
Walk Away Renee (Twin Tone, BMI) ........ 12
We Got A Thing That's In The Groove (McLaughlin, BMI) ........ 79
What Becomes of the Brokenhearted (Jobete, BMI) 18
Wheel of Hurt, The (Martino) (Roosevelt, BMI) .. 63
Wheel of Hurt, The (Whiting) (Roosevelt, BMI) .. 49
Whispers (Jalynne,-BRC, BMI) ........ 55
(When She Needs Good Lovin') She Comes to Me (Tiger, BMI) ........ 67
Who Am I (Duchess, BMI) ........ 22
Why Pick On Me (Equinox, BMI) ........ 61
Wild Angels Theme (Dijon, BMI) ........ 100
Winchester Cathedral (Rollin) (Southern, ASCAP) .. 78
Winchester Cathedral (Vaudeville Band) (Southern, ASCAP) ........ 6
Wish You Were Here, Buddy (Roosevelt, BMI) .... 68
You Keep Me Hangin' On (Jobete, BMI) ........ 7


## BUBBLING UNDER THE HOT 100

101. I NEED SOMEONE ........ ?(Question Mark) & the Mysterians, Cameo 441
102. STAND IN FOR LOVE ........ O'Jays, Imperial 66197
103. COMING HOME SOLDIER ........ Bobby Vinton, Epic 10090
104. I WANNA MEET YOU ........ Cryin' Shames, Columbia 43836
105. BEHIND THE DOOR ........ Cher, Imperial 66217
106. THE EGGPLANT THAT ATE CHICAGO ........ Dr. West's Medicine Show & Junk Band, GoGo 100
107. QUESTIONS AND ANSWERS ........ The In-Crowd, Viva 604
108. WINDOWS AND DOORS ........ Jackie DeShannon, Imperial 66196
109. FORTUNE TELLER ........ Hardtimes, World Pacific 77851
110. HAVE YOU EVER LOVED SOMEBODY ........ The Searchers, Kapp 783
111. I'LL BE HOME ........ Platters, Musicor 1211
112. CHANSON D'AMOUR ........ Lettermen, Capitol 5749
113. THE WILLY ........ Willies, Co & Ce 239
114. SOCIETY'S CHILD ........ Janis Ian, Verve Folkways 5027
115. PUSHING TOO HARD ........ Seeds, GNP Crescendo 372
116. AM I A LOSER ........ Eddie Holman, Parkway 106
117. FIFI THE FLEA ........ Sidekicks, RCA Victor 8969
118. WINCHESTER CATHEDRAL ........ New Happiness, Columbia 43851
119. WEDDING BELL BLUES ........ Laura Nyro, Verve Folkways 502
120. HI HI HAZEL ........ Gary & the Hornets, Smash 2061
121. STANDING ON GUARD ........ Falcons, Big Wheel 1967
122. OUT OF TIME ........ Chris Farlowe, MGM 13567
123. LONG HAIR MUSIC ........ Guise, Musicland, USS. A. 20001
124. LOVE'S GONE DAD ........ Chris Clark, V.I.P. 25038
125. HOW MUCH PRESSURE (DO YOU THINK I CAN STAND) ........ Roscoe Robinson, Wand 1143
126. HELP ME ........ Spellbinders, Columbia 43830
127. I'M GONNA MISS YOU ........ Artistics, Brunswick 55301
128. SUGAR TOWN ........ Nancy Sinatra, Reprise 0527
129. CABARET ........ Mike Douglas, Epic 10078
130. GAMES THAT LOVERS PLAY ........ Mantovani, London 20015
131. I CAN'T MAKE IT ALONE ........ P. J. Proby, Liberty 55915

Compiled from national retail sales and radio station airplay by the Music Popularity Dept. of Record Market Research, Billboard.

# Billboard HOT 100

**For Week Ending November 19, 1966**

★ STAR performer—Sides registering greatest proportionate upward progress this week.

Record Industry Association of America seal of certification as million selling single.

| This Week | Wk. Ago | 2 Wks. Ago | 3 Wks. Ago | TITLE, Artist (Producer), Label & Number | Weeks On Chart |
|---|---|---|---|---|---|
| 1 | 7 | 27 | 68 | YOU KEEP ME HANGIN' ON — Supremes (Holland-Dozier), Motown 1101 | 4 |
| 2 | 4 | 17 | 38 | GOOD VIBRATIONS — Beach Boys (Brian Wilson), Capitol 5676 | 5 |
| 3 | 6 | 24 | 66 | WINCHESTER CATHEDRAL — New Vaudeville Band, (Geoff Stephens), Fontana 1562 | 4 |
| 4 | 2 | 1 | 2 | LAST TRAIN TO CLARKSVILLE — Monkees (Tommy Boyce & Bobby Hart), Colgems 1001 | 11 |
| 5 | 1 | 3 | 4 | POOR SIDE OF TOWN — Johnny Rivers (Lou Adler), Imperial 66205 | 10 |
| 6 | 9 | 18 | 27 | DEVIL WITH A BLUE DRESS ON & GOOD GOLLY MISS MOLLY — Mitch Ryder & the Detroit Wheels (Bob Crewe), New Voice 817 | 6 |
| 7 | 10 | 11 | 16 | I'M YOUR PUPPET — James & Bobby Purify (Dan Schroeder), Bell 648 | 9 |
| 8 | 3 | 2 | 1 | 96 TEARS — ? (Question Mark) & the Mysterians, Cameo 428 | 12 |
| 9 | 8 | 8 | 11 | IF I WERE A CARPENTER — Bobby Darin (Koppleman-Rubin), Atlantic 2350 | 9 |
| 10 | 15 | 20 | 26 | RAIN ON THE ROOF — Lovin' Spoonful (Erik Jacobson), Kama Sutra 216 | 6 |
| 11 | 21 | 29 | 46 | LADY GODIVA — Peter & Gordon (John Burgess), Capitol 5740 | 7 |
| 12 | 17 | 19 | 24 | BORN FREE — Roger Williams (Hy Grill), Kapp 767 | 12 |
| 13 | 13 | 13 | 19 | LOVE IS A HURTIN' THING — Lou Rawls (David Axelrod), Capitol 5709 | 11 |
| 14 | 11 | 4 | 3 | REACH OUT I'LL BE THERE — Four Tops (Holland & Dozier), Motown 1098 | 12 |
| 15 | 14 | 6 | 8 | HOORAY FOR HAZEL — Tommy Roe (Our Prods.), ABC 10852 | 10 |
| 16 | 12 | 10 | 5 | WALK AWAY RENEE — Left Banke (World United Prod. Inc.), Smash 2041 | 11 |
| 17 | 20 | 25 | 31 | COMING ON STRONG — Brenda Lee (Owen Bradley), Decca 32018 | 8 |
| 18 | 18 | 7 | 7 | WHAT BECOMES OF THE BROKENHEARTED — Jimmy Ruffin (William Stevenson), Soul 35022 | 13 |
| 19 | 5 | 5 | 6 | DANDY — Herman's Hermits (Mickie Most), MGM 13603 | 8 |
| 20 | 31 | 43 | 76 | STOP STOP STOP — Hollies (Ron Richards), Imperial 66214 | 4 |
| 21 | 34 | 57 | 70 | I'M READY FOR LOVE — Martha & the Vandellas, (Holland-Dozier), Gordy 7056 | 4 |
| 22 | 22 | 30 | 39 | WHO AM I — Petula Clark (Tony Hatch), Warner Bros. 5863 | 5 |
| 23 | 47 | 81 | — | A HAZY SHADE OF WINTER — Simon & Garfunkel (Bob Johnston), Columbia 43873 | 3 |
| 24 | 65 | — | — | MELLOW YELLOW — Donovan, (Mickie Most), Epic 10098 | 2 |
| 25 | 25 | 34 | 51 | LOOK THROUGH MY WINDOW — Mama's and the Papa's, (Lou Adler), Dunhill 4050 | 5 |
| 26 | 30 | 38 | 54 | BUT IT'S ALRIGHT — J. J. Jackson (Lew Futterman), Calla 119 | 8 |
| 27 | 27 | 14 | 15 | B-A-B-Y — Carla Thomas (Staff), Stax 195 | 14 |
| 28 | 24 | 15 | 18 | (You Don't Have To) PAINT ME A PICTURE — Gary Lewis & the Playboys, (Snuff Garrett), Liberty 55914 | 7 |
| 29 | 37 | 37 | 49 | SECRET LOVE — Billy Stewart, (Dave & Casten), Chess 1978 | 6 |
| 30 | 19 | 12 | 12 | GO AWAY LITTLE GIRL — Happenings (Tokens), B. T. Puppy 522 | 8 |
| 31 | 26 | 28 | 30 | I JUST DON'T KNOW WHAT TO DO WITH MYSELF — Dionne Warwick (Bacharach-David), Scepter 12167 | 8 |
| 32 | 38 | 46 | 59 | LOUIE, LOUIE — Sandpipers (Tommy LaPuma), A&M 819 | 5 |
| 33 | 49 | 56 | 67 | THE WHEEL OF HURT — Margaret Whiting (Arnold Goland), London 101 | 7 |
| 34 | 46 | 65 | 82 | HOLY COW — Lee Dorsey (A. Toussaint-M. Sehorn), Amy 965 | 5 |
| 35 | 33 | 23 | 14 | PSYCHOTIC REACTION — Count Five (Hooven-Winn), Double Shot 104 | 11 |
| 36 | 32 | 21 | 13 | CHERISH — Association (C. Boettcher), Valiant 747 | 13 |
| 37 | 45 | 58 | 62 | KNOCK ON WOOD — Eddie Floyd (Prod. by Staff), Stax 194 | 11 |
| 38 | 29 | 32 | 34 | FA-FA-FA-FA-FA — Otis Redding, Volt 138 | 8 |
| 39 | 55 | 78 | — | WHISPERS — Jackie Wilson (Carl Davis), Brunswick 55300 | 5 |
| 40 | 51 | 62 | 79 | IT TEARS ME UP — Percy Sledge (Martin Greene-Quin Ivy), Atlantic 2358 | 5 |
| 41 | 42 | 42 | 42 | ALL THAT I AM — Elvis Presley (Joe Pasternark), RCA Victor 8941 | 7 |
| 42 | 39 | 41 | 52 | AIN'T GONNA LIE — Keith (Jerry Ross), Mercury 72596 | 10 |
| 43 | 57 | 77 | 83 | RUN, RUN, LOOK AND SEE — Brian Hyland (Snuff Garrett), Philips 40405 | 5 |
| 44 | 36 | 26 | 20 | THE GREAT AIRPLANE STRIKE — Paul Revere & the Raiders (Terry Melcher), Columbia 43810 | 8 |
| 45 | 23 | 16 | 10 | SEE SEE RIDER — Eric Burden & the Animals (Tom Wilson), MGM 13582 | 10 |
| 46 | 16 | 9 | 9 | HAVE YOU SEEN YOUR MOTHER, BABY, STANDING IN THE SHADOWS? — Rolling Stones (Andrew Oldham), London 903 | 7 |
| 47 | 58 | 68 | 77 | ON THIS SIDE OF GOODBYE — Righteous Brothers, (Bill Medley), Verve 10449 | 4 |
| 48 | 54 | 59 | 69 | NINETEEN DAYS — Dave Clark Five (Dave Clark), Epic 10076 | 5 |
| 49 | 35 | 33 | 33 | I CAN MAKE IT WITH YOU — Pozo-Seco Singers, (Bob Johnston) Columbia 43784 | 11 |
| 50 | 28 | 22 | 22 | THE HAIR ON MY CHINNY CHIN CHIN — Sam the Sham & the Pharaohs (Stan Kesler), MGM 13581 | 8 |
| 51 | 43 | 45 | 55 | I CAN'T CONTROL MYSELF — Troggs (Larry Page), Fontana 1557, Atco 6444 | 5 |
| 52 | 56 | 64 | 72 | HEAVEN MUST HAVE SENT YOU — Elgins (Holland-Dozier), V.I.P. 25037 | 5 |
| 53 | 83 | — | — | A PLACE IN THE SUN — Stevie Wonder, (C. Paul), Tamla 54139 | 2 |
| 54 | 75 | 85 | 93 | TIME AFTER TIME — Chris Montez (Tommy LiPuma-Herb Alpert), A&M 822 | 4 |
| 55 | 73 | 90 | — | (Come 'Round Here) I'M THE ONE YOU NEED — Miracles (Holland & Dozier) Tamla 54140 | 3 |
| 56 | 68 | 76 | 81 | WISH YOU WERE HERE, BUDDY — Pat Boone (Nick Venet and Randy Wood), Dot T6933 | 5 |
| 57 | 67 | 82 | — | (When She Needs Good Lovin') SHE COMES TO ME — Chicago Loop (Bob Crewe & Al Kasha), DynoVoice 226 | 3 |
| 58 | 69 | — | — | I GOT THE FEELIN' "OH NO NO" — Neil Diamond, (Jeff Barry-Ellie Greenwich), Bang 536 | 2 |
| 59 | 60 | 74 | 75 | SOMEBODY (Somewhere) NEEDS YOU — Darrell Banks (Solid Hitbound Prod., Inc.), Revilot 203 | 6 |
| 60 | 76 | 88 | 90 | HELP ME GIRL — Outsiders, (Roger Karshner), Capitol 5759 | 4 |
| 61 | 61 | 72 | 89 | WHY PICK ON ME — Standells (Ed Cobb), Tower 282 | 5 |
| 62 | 63 | 73 | 74 | THE WHEEL OF HURT — Al Martino (T. Morgan), Capitol 5741 | 6 |
| 63 | 71 | 86 | — | COME BACK — Five Stairsteps, Windy C 603 | 3 |
| 64 | 64 | 71 | 71 | STAY WITH ME — Lorraine Ellison (Jerry Ragavoy), Warner Bros. 5850 | 7 |
| 65 | 70 | 80 | 80 | A SYMPHONY FOR SUSAN — Arbors, (Richard Carney), Date 1529 | 6 |
| 66 | 81 | 96 | — | IT'S ONLY LOVE — Tommy James & the Shondells, Roulette 4710 | 3 |
| 67 | 84 | 91 | 92 | GAMES THAT LOVERS PLAY — Eddie Fisher, (Al Schmitt), RCA Victor 8956 | 4 |
| 68 | 40 | 40 | 44 | SPIN OUT — Elvis Presley (Joe Pasternak), RCA Victor 8941 | 8 |
| 69 | 50 | 53 | 56 | DON'T BE A DROP-OUT — James Brown & His Famous Flames (James Brown Prod.) King 6056 | 7 |
| 70 | 53 | 61 | 61 | SOMEBODY LIKE ME — Eddy Arnold (Chet Atkins), RCA Victor 8965 | 6 |
| 71 | 72 | 75 | 88 | BANG! BANG! — Joe Cuba Sextet (Pancho Cristal), Tico 475 | 5 |
| 72 | 78 | 98 | — | WINCHESTER CATHEDRAL — Dana Rollin (Steve Douglas), Tower 283 | 3 |
| 73 | 74 | 84 | 85 | A DAY IN THE LIFE OF A FOOL — Jack Jones, (David Kapp), Kapp 781 | 4 |
| 74 | 77 | 79 | 86 | BABY, WHAT DO YOU WANT ME TO DO? — Barbara Lewis, (Jerry Wexler & Ollie McLaughlin), Atlantic 2361 | 4 |
| 75 | — | — | — | THAT'S LIFE — Frank Sinatra (Jimmy Bowen), Reprise 0531 | 1 |
| 76 | 80 | 87 | 98 | DON'T ANSWER THE DOOR — B. B. King (Johnny Pate), ABC 10856 | 5 |
| 77 | 79 | — | — | WE GOT A THING THAT'S IN THE GROOVE — Capitols, (Ollie McLaughlin), Karen 1526 | 2 |
| 78 | 82 | — | — | PLEASE SAY YOU'RE FOOLING — Ray Charles (TRC), ABC 10865 | 2 |
| 79 | — | — | — | (I Know) I'M LOSING YOU — Temptations, (N. Whitfield), Gordy 7057 | 1 |
| 80 | 87 | — | — | THE PROUD ONE — Frankie Valli (Bob Crewe), Philips 40407 | 2 |
| 81 | 96 | — | — | TALK TALK — Music Machine, (Maurice Bercov), Original Sound 61 | 2 |
| 82 | — | — | — | MAME — Herb Alpert & the Tijuana Brass, (Herb Alpert), A&M 823 | 1 |
| 83 | — | — | — | SUGAR TOWN — Nancy Sinatra, (Lee Haselwood), Reprise 0527 | 1 |
| 84 | — | — | — | COMING HOME SOLDIER — Bobby Vinton (Robert Mersey), Epic 10090 | 1 |
| 85 | 90 | 92 | — | HEARTBREAK HOTEL — Roger Miller (Jerry Kennedy) Smash 2066 | 3 |
| 86 | 86 | 94 | — | A CORNER IN THE SUN — Walter Jackson (Ted Cooper) Okeh 7260 | 3 |
| 87 | 89 | 93 | 94 | GAMES THAT LOVERS PLAY — Wayne Newton (Steve Douglas), Capitol 5754 | 5 |
| 88 | 88 | — | — | A MAN AND A WOMAN — Tamiko Jones & Herbie Mann, Atlantic 2362 | 2 |
| 89 | — | — | — | MONEY (That's What I Want) — Jr. Walker & the All Stars, (B. Gordy, Jr.-L. Horn) Soul 35026 | 1 |
| 90 | — | — | — | I NEED SOMEBODY — ? (Question Mark) & the Mysterians, Cameo 441 | 1 |
| 91 | 91 | 97 | 99 | CAN I GET TO KNOW YOU BETTER — Turtles, (Bones Howe), White Whale 238 | 4 |
| 92 | 92 | — | — | IT'S NOT THE SAME — Anthony & the Imperials, (Teddy Randazzo), Veep 1248 | 2 |
| 93 | 97 | — | — | I (Who Have Nothing) — Tory Knight & the Pack, (Terry Knight), Lucky 11 230 | 2 |
| 94 | 94 | — | — | HARLEM SHUFFLE — Traits, (Huey F. Meaux), Sceptor 12169 | 2 |
| 95 | 95 | — | — | RESPECT — Rationals, (Jeep Holland), Cameo 437 | 2 |
| 96 | — | — | — | SINGLE GIRL — Sandy Posey (Chips Moman), MGM 13612 | 1 |
| 97 | — | — | — | LIVING FOR YOU — Sonny & Cher, (Sonny Bono), Atco 6449 | 1 |
| 98 | — | — | — | HI HI HAZEL — Gary & the Hornets, (Lou Beizner), Smash 2061 | 1 |
| 99 | 100 | — | — | WILD ANGELS THEME — Davie Allen & the Arrows, (Mike Curb) Tower 267 | 2 |
| 100 | — | — | — | HELP ME — Spellbinders, (Kaprelit-McCoy), Columbia 43830 | 1 |

## BUBBLING UNDER THE HOT 100

101. MUSTANG SALLY — Wilson Pickett, Atlantic 2365
102. BEHIND THE DOOR — Cher, Imperial 66217
103. EGGPLANT THAT ATE CHICAGO — Dr. West's Medicine Show & Junk Band, Go Go 100
104. I WANNA MEET YOU — Cryan' Shames, Columbia 43836
105. QUESTIONS AND ANSWERS — The In Crowd, Viva 604
106. WEDDING BELL BLUES — Laura Nyro, Verve Folkways 502
107. MEDITATION — Glendine Longet, A&M 817
108. (HE'S) RAINING IN MY SUNSHINE — Jay & the Americans, United Artists 50094
109. I'LL BE HOME — Platters, Musicor 1211
110. HAVE YOU EVER LOVED SOMEBODY — Searchers, Kapp 783
111. IF YOU GO AWAY — Damita Jo, Epic 10061
112. WINCHESTER CATHEDRAL — New Happiness, Columbia 43851
113. PLEASE DON'T EVER LEAVE ME — Cyrkle, Columbia 43871
114. PEAK OF LOVE — Bobby McClure, Checker 1152
115. FIFI THE FLEA — Sidekicks, RCA Victor 8969
116. AM I A LOSER — Eddie Holman, Parkway 104
117. IT'S A HAPPENING — Dee Dee Warwick, Mercury 72628
118. STANDING ON GUARD — Magic Mushrooms, A&M 815
119. CRY LIKE A BABY — Aretha Franklin, Columbia 43827
120. LOVE'S GONE BAD — Chris Clark, V.I.P. 25038
121. STANDING ON GUARD — Falcons, Big Wheel 1967
122. GAMES THAT LOVERS PLAY — Mantovani, London 20015
123. BUZZZZZZ — Jimmy Gordon, Challenge 59194
124. I DON'T NEED NO DOCTOR — Ray Charles, ABC 10865
125. I'M GONNA MISS YOU — Artistics, Brunswick 55301
126. TINY BUBBLES — Don Ho & Alifa, Reprise 0509
127. FOOLED TO THIS TIME — Gene Chandler, Checker 1155
128. HYMN NO. 5 — Mighty Hannibal, Josie 964
129. SPANISH NIGHTS AND YOU — Connie Francis, MGM 13610
130. LET'S FALL IN LOVE — Peaches & Herb, Date 1522
131. THERE'S GOT TO BE A WORD — Innocence, Kama Sutra 214
132. TELL IT LIKE IT IS — Aaron Neville, Par-Lo 101
133. I'LL THINK OF SUMMER — Ronny & the Daytonas, Mala 542
134. AND I LOVE HER — Vibrations, Okeh 7257
135. I BET'CHA (COULDN'T LOVE ME) — Manhattans, Carnival 522

Compiled from national retail sales and radio station airplay by the Music Popularity Dept. of Record Market Research, Billboard.

Billboard

For Week Ending November 26, 1966

# HOT 100

★ STAR performer—Sides registering greatest proportionate upward progress this week.

Record Industry Association of America seal of certification as million selling single.

| THIS WEEK | 1 Wk. Ago | 2 Wks. Ago | 3 Wks. Ago | TITLE Artist (Producer), Label & Number | Weeks On Chart |
|---|---|---|---|---|---|
| 1 (Billboard Award) | 1 | 7 | 27 | YOU KEEP ME HANGIN' ON — Supremes (Holland-Dozier), Motown 1101 | 5 |
| 2 | 2 | 4 | 17 | GOOD VIBRATIONS — Beach Boys (Brian Wilson), Capitol 5676 | 6 |
| 3 | 3 | 6 | 24 | WINCHESTER CATHEDRAL — New Vaudeville Band, (Geoff Stephens), Fontana 1562 | 5 |
| 4 | 6 | 9 | 18 | DEVIL WITH A BLUE DRESS ON & GOOD GOLLY MISS MOLLY — Mitch Ryder & the Detroit Wheels (Bob Crew), New Voice 817 | 7 |
| 5 | 5 | 1 | 3 | POOR SIDE OF TOWN — Johnny Rivers (Lou Adler), Imperial 66205 | 11 |
| 6 | 7 | 10 | 11 | I'M YOUR PUPPET — James & Bobby Purify (Don Schroeder), Bell 648 | 10 |
| 7 | 4 | 2 | 1 | LAST TRAIN TO CLARKSVILLE — Monkees (Tommy Boyce & Bobby Hart), Colgems 1001 | 12 (RIAA seal) |
| ★ 8 | 11 | 21 | 29 | LADY GODIVA — Peter & Gordon (John Burgess), Capitol 5740 | 8 |
| ★ 9 | 24 | 65 | — | MELLOW YELLOW — Donovan, (Mickie Most), Epic 10098 | 3 |
| 10 | 12 | 17 | 19 | BORN FREE — Roger Williams (Hy Grill), Kapp 767 | 13 |
| 11 | 8 | 3 | 2 | 96 TEARS — ? (Question Mark) & the Mysterians, Cameo 428 | 13 |
| ★ 12 | 17 | 20 | 25 | COMING ON STRONG — Brenda Lee (Owen Bradley), Decca 32018 | 9 |
| ★ 13 | 20 | 31 | 43 | STOP STOP STOP — Hollies, (Ron Richards), Imperial 66214 | 5 |
| 14 | 10 | 15 | 20 | RAIN ON THE ROOF — Lovin' Spoonful (Erik Jacobson), Kama Sutra 216 | 7 |
| 15 | 9 | 8 | 8 | IF I WERE A CARPENTER — Bobby Darin (Koppleman-Rubin), Atlantic 2350 | 10 |
| ★ 16 | 21 | 34 | 57 | I'M READY FOR LOVE — Martha & the Vandellas, (Holland-Dozier), Gordy 7056 | 5 |
| ★ 17 | 23 | 47 | 81 | A HAZY SHADE OF WINTER — Simon & Garfunkel (Bob Johnston), Columbia 43873 | 4 |
| 18 | 13 | 13 | 13 | LOVE IS A HURTIN' THING — Lou Rawls (David Axelrod), Capitol 5709 | 12 |
| 19 | 15 | 14 | 6 | HOORAY FOR HAZEL — Tommy Roe (Our Prods.), ABC 10852 | 11 |
| 20 | 18 | 18 | 7 | WHAT BECOMES OF THE BROKENHEARTED — Jimmy Ruffin (William Stevenson), Soul 35022 | 14 |
| 21 | 22 | 22 | 30 | WHO AM I — Petula Clark (Tony Hatch), Warner Bros. 5863 | 6 |
| 22 | 14 | 11 | 4 | REACH OUT I'LL BE THERE — Four Tops (Holland & Dozier), Motown 1098 | 13 |
| 23 | 16 | 12 | 10 | WALK AWAY RENEE — Left Banke (World United Prod. Inc.), Smash 2041 | 12 |
| 24 | 25 | 25 | 34 | LOOK THROUGH MY WINDOW — Mama's and the Papa's, (Lou Adler), Dunhill 4050 | 6 |
| 25 | 19 | 5 | 5 | DANDY — Herman's Hermits (Mickie Most), MGM 13603 | 9 |
| ★ 26 | 39 | 55 | 78 | WHISPERS — Jackie Wilson (Carl Davis), Brunswick 55300 | 6 |
| 27 | 58 | 69 | — | I GOT THE FEELIN' "OH NO NO" — Neil Diamond, (Jeff Barry-Ellie Greenwich), Bang 536 | 3 |
| 28 | 26 | 30 | 38 | BUT IT'S ALRIGHT — J. J. Jackson (Lew Futterman), Calla 119 | 9 |
| 29 | 29 | 37 | 37 | SECRET LOVE — Billy Stewart, (Dave & Caston), Chess 1978 | 7 |
| 30 | 32 | 38 | 46 | LOUIE, LOUIE — Sandpipers (Tommy LaPuma), A&M 819 | 6 |
| 31 | 33 | 49 | 56 | THE WHEEL OF HURT — Margaret Whiting (Arnold Goland), London 101 | 8 |
| 32 | 34 | 46 | 65 | HOLY COW — Lee Dorsey (A. Toussaint-M. Sehorn), Amy 965 | 6 |
| ★ 33 | 43 | 57 | 77 | RUN, RUN, LOOK AND SEE — Brian Hyland (Snuff Garrett), Philips 40405 | 6 |
| 34 | 40 | 51 | 62 | IT TEARS ME UP — Percy Sledge (Marlin Greene-Quin Ivy), Atlantic 2358 | 6 |
| 35 | 37 | 45 | 58 | KNOCK ON WOOD — Eddie Floyd (Prod. by Staff), Stax 194 | 12 |
| ★ 36 | 55 | 73 | 90 | (Come 'Round Here) I'M THE ONE YOU NEED — Miracles (Holland & Dozier) Tamla 54140 | 4 |
| ★ 37 | 53 | 83 | — | A PLACE IN THE SUN — Stevie Wonder, (C. Paul), Tamla 54139 | 3 |
| 38 | 27 | 27 | 14 | B-A-B-Y — Carla Thomas (Staff), Stax 195 | 15 |
| ★ 39 | 57 | 67 | 82 | (When She Needs Good Lovin') SHE COMES TO ME — Chicago Loop (Bob Crewe & Al Kasha), DynoVoice 226 | 4 |
| 40 | 28 | 24 | 15 | (You Don't Have To) PAINT ME A PICTURE — Gary Lewis & the Playboys, (Snuff Garrett), Liberty 55914 | 8 |
| 41 | 35 | 33 | 23 | PSYCHOTIC REACTION — Count Five (Hooven-Winn), Double Shot 104 | 12 |
| ★ 42 | 75 | — | — | THAT'S LIFE — Frank Sinatra (Jimmy Bowen), Reprise 0531 | 2 |
| ★ 43 | 79 | — | — | (I Know) I'M LOSING YOU — Temptations, (N. Whitfield), Gordy 7057 | 2 |
| 44 | 36 | 32 | 21 | CHERISH — Association (C. Boettcher), Valiant 747 | 14 (RIAA seal) |
| ★ 45 | 82 | — | — | MAME — Herb Alpert & the Tijuana Brass, (Herb Alpert), A&M 823 | 2 |
| 46 | 54 | 75 | 85 | TIME AFTER TIME — Chris Montez, (Tommy LiPuma-Herb Alpert), A&M 822 | 5 |
| 47 | 47 | 58 | 68 | ON THIS SIDE OF GOODBYE — Righteous Brothers, (Bill Medley), Verve 10449 | 5 |
| 48 | 30 | 19 | 12 | GO AWAY LITTLE GIRL — Happenings (Tokens), B. T. Puppy 522 | 9 |
| 49 | 48 | 54 | 59 | NINETEEN DAYS — Dave Clark Five (Dave Clark), Epic 10076 | 6 |
| ★ 50 | 60 | 76 | 88 | HELP ME GIRL — Outsiders, (Roger Karshner), Capitol 5759 | 5 |
| ★ 51 | 65 | 70 | 80 | A SYMPHONY FOR SUSAN — Arbors, (Richard Carney), Date 1529 | 7 |
| 52 | 52 | 56 | 64 | HEAVEN MUST HAVE SENT YOU — Elgins (Holland-Dozier), V.I.P. 25037 | 6 |
| 53 | 56 | 68 | 76 | WISH YOU WERE HERE, BUDDY — Pat Boone (Nick Venet and Randy Wood), Dot 16933 | 6 |
| 54 | 61 | 61 | 72 | WHY PICK ON ME — Standells (Ed Cobb), Tower 282 | 6 |
| 55 | 59 | 60 | 74 | SOMEBODY (Somewhere) NEEDS YOU — Darrell Banks (Solid Hitbound Prod., Inc.), Revilot 203 | 7 |
| ★ 56 | 66 | 81 | 96 | IT'S ONLY LOVE — Tommy James & the Shondells, Roulette 4710 | 4 |
| ★ 57 | 67 | 84 | 91 | GAMES THAT LOVERS PLAY — Eddie Fisher, (Al Schmitt), RCA Victor 8956 | 5 |
| ★ 58 | 81 | 96 | — | TALK TALK — Music Machine, (Maurice Bercov), Original Sound 61 | 3 |
| 59 | 62 | 63 | 73 | THE WHEEL OF HURT — Al Martino (T. Morgan), Capitol 5741 | 7 |
| 60 | 41 | 42 | 42 | ALL THAT I AM — Elvis Presley (Joe Pasternak), RCA Victor 8941 | 8 |
| 61 | 63 | 71 | 86 | COME BACK — Five Stairsteps, Windy C 603 | 4 |
| ★ 62 | 83 | — | — | SUGAR TOWN — Nancy Sinatra, (Lee Hazelwood), Reprise 0527 | 2 |
| 63 | 71 | 72 | 75 | BANG! BANG! — Joe Cuba Sextet (Pancho Cristal), Tico 475 | 6 |
| 64 | 73 | 74 | 84 | A DAY IN THE LIFE OF A FOOL — Jack Jones, (David Kapp), Kapp 781 | 5 |
| 65 | 64 | 64 | 71 | STAY WITH ME — Lorraine Ellison (Jerry Ragavoy), Warner Bros. 5850 | 8 |
| ★ 66 | — | — | — | MUSTANG SALLY — Wilson Pickett, (Jerry Wexler-Rick Hall), Atlantic 2365 | 1 |
| 67 | 77 | 79 | — | WE GOT A THING THAT'S IN THE GROOVE — Capitols (Ollie McLaughlin), Karen 1526 | 3 |
| 68 | 78 | 82 | — | PLEASE SAY YOU'RE FOOLING — Ray Charles (TRC), ABC 10865 | 3 |
| ★ 69 | 96 | — | — | SINGLE GIRL — Sandy Posey, (Chips Moman), MGM 13612 | 2 |
| 70 | 80 | 87 | — | THE PROUD ONE — Frankie Valli, (Bob Crew), Philips 40407 | 3 |
| ★ 71 | 90 | — | — | I NEED SOMEBODY — ? (Question Mark) & the Mysterians, Cameo 441 | 2 |
| 72 | 72 | 78 | 98 | WINCHESTER CATHEDRAL — Dana Rollin, Tower 283 | 4 |
| 73 | 84 | — | — | COMING HOME SOLDIER — Bobby Vinton, (Robert Mersey), Epic 10090 | 2 |
| ★ 74 | 89 | — | — | MONEY (That's What I Want) — Jr. Walker & the All Stars, (B. Gordy, Jr.-L. Horn) Soul 35026 | 2 |
| 75 | 76 | 80 | 87 | DON'T ANSWER THE DOOR — B. B. King (Johnny Pate), ABC 10856 | 6 |
| 76 | 74 | 77 | 79 | BABY, WHAT DO YOU WANT ME TO DO? — Barbara Lewis, (Jerry Wexler & Ollie McLaughlin), Atlantic 2361 | 5 |
| ★ 77 | — | — | — | PANDORA'S GOLDEN HEEBIE JEEBIES — Association, (J. Yestar), Valiant 755 | 1 |
| ★ 78 | — | — | — | I FOOLED YOU THIS TIME — Gene Chandler, (Carl Davis), Checker 1155 | 1 |
| 79 | 93 | 97 | — | I (Who Have Nothing) — Terry Knight & the Pack (Terry Knight), Lucky 11 230 | 3 |
| ★ 80 | — | — | — | I DON'T NEED NO DOCTOR — Ray Charles (TRC), ABC 10865 | 1 |
| ★ 81 | — | — | — | ALVIN'S BOO-GA-LOO — Alvin Cash & the Registers, (J. Jones), Mar-V-Lus 6014 | 1 |
| ★ 82 | — | — | — | GHOST RIDERS IN THE SKY — Baja Marimba Band, (Herb Alpert & Jerry Moss), A&M 824 | 1 |
| 83 | 86 | 86 | 94 | A CORNER IN THE SUN — Walter Jackson (Ted Cooper) Okeh 7260 | 4 |
| 84 | 85 | 90 | 92 | HEARTBREAK HOTEL — Roger Miller (Jerry Kennedy) Smash 2056 | 4 |
| ★ 85 | — | — | — | THE EGGPLANT THAT ATE CHICAGO — Dr. West's Medicine Show & Junk Band, (T. Marer), Go Go 100 | 1 |
| 86 | 87 | 89 | 93 | GAMES THAT LOVERS PLAY — Wayne Newton (Steve Douglas), Capitol 5754 | 6 |
| 87 | 97 | — | — | LIVING FOR YOU — Sonny & Cher, (Sonny Bono), Atco 6449 | 2 |
| ★ 88 | — | — | — | YOU CAN BRING ME ALL YOUR HEARTACHES — Lou Rawls, (David Axelrod), Capitol 5790 | 1 |
| 89 | 91 | 91 | 97 | CAN I GET TO KNOW YOU BETTER — Turtles, (Bones Howe), White Whale 238 | 5 |
| ★ 90 | — | — | — | I WANNA MEET YOU — Cryin' Shames, (Jim Golden), Columbia 43836 | 1 |
| 91 | — | — | — | HELP ME, GIRL — Eric Burdon & the Animals (Tom Wilson), MGM 13636 | 1 |
| 92 | 95 | 95 | — | RESPECT — Rationals, (Jeep Holland), Cameo 437 | 3 |
| 93 | — | — | — | TINY BUBBLES — Don Ho & the Aliis, (Burke), Reprise 0507 | 1 |
| 94 | — | — | — | I'M GONNA MAKE YOU LOVE ME — Dee Dee Warwick, (Jerry Ross), Mercury 72638 | 1 |
| 95 | — | — | — | (He's) RAINING IN MY SUNSHINE — Jay & the Americans, (Bob Feldman), United Artists 50094 | 1 |
| 96 | 98 | — | — | HI HI HAZEL — Gary & the Hornets, (Lou Reizner), Smash 2061 | 2 |
| 97 | — | — | — | BEHIND THE DOOR — Cher (Sonny Bono), Imperial 66217 | 1 |
| 98 | — | — | — | HAVE YOU EVER LOVED SOMEBODY — Searchers, Kapp 783 | 1 |
| 99 | — | — | — | HAPPENINGS TEN YEARS TIME AGO — Yardbirds, (Simon Napier-Bell), Epic 10094 | 1 |
| 100 | — | — | — | CRY — Ronnie Dove, (Phil Kahl), Diamond 214 | 1 |

## HOT 100—A TO Z—*(Publisher-Licensee)*

All That I Am (Gladys, ASCAP) .... 60
Alvin's Boo-Ga-Loo (Vapac, BMI) .... 81
B-A-B-Y (East, BMI) .... 38
Baby What Do You Want Me to Do (McLaughlin, BMI) .... 76
Bang! Bang! (Cordon, BMI) .... 63
Behind The Door (Man-Ken, Ltd.-Equinox, BMI) .... 97
Born Free (Screen Gems-Columbia, BMI) .... 10
But It's Alright (Pamelaross, BMI) .... 28
Can I Get to Know You Better (Trousdale, BMI) .... 89
Cherish (Beachwood, BMI) .... 44
Come Back (Camad, BMI) .... 61
(Come 'Round Here) I'm the One You Need (Jobete, BMI) .... 36
Coming Home Soldier (Feather, BMI) .... 73
Coming On Strong (Moss-Rose, BMI) .... 12
Corner in the Sun, A (Blackwood, Blue-Chip, BMI) .... 83
Cry (Shapiro-Bernstein, ASCAP) .... 100
Dandy (Nome, BMI) .... 25
Day in the Life of a Fool, A (Jungnickel, ASCAP) .... 64
Devil With a Blue Dress On & Good Golly Miss Molly (Jobete-Vanice, BMI) .... 4
Don't Answer the Door (Mercedes, BMI) .... 75
Eggplant That Ate Chicago, The (Borscht, BMI) .... 85
Games That Lovers Play (Fisher) (Miller, ASCAP) .... 57
Games That Lovers Play (Newton) (Miller, ASCAP) .... 86
Ghost Riders in the Sky (Morris, ASCAP) .... 82
Go Away Little Girl (Screen Gems-Columbia, BMI) .... 48
Good Vibrations (Sea of Tunes, BMI) .... 2
Happenings Ten Years Time Ago (Yardbirds-Feist, ASCAP) .... 99
Have You Ever Loved Somebody (Maribus, BMI) .... 98
Hazy Shadow of Winter, A (Charing Cross, BMI) .... 17
Heartbreak Hotel (Tree, BMI) .... 84
Heaven Must Have Sent You (Jobete, BMI) .... 52
Help Me, Girl (Burdon) (Helios, BMI) .... 91
Help Me, Girl (Outsiders) (Helios, BMI) .... 50
(He's) Raining in My Sunshine (Greenlight, BMI) .... 95
Hi Hi Hazel (Gallico, BMI) .... 96
Holy Cow (Marsaint, BMI) .... 32
Hooray for Hazel (Low Twi, BMI) .... 19
I Don't Need No Doctor (Flomar-Baby Monica, BMI) .... 80
I Fooled You This Time (Cachand-Jalynee, BMI) .... 78
I Got The Feelin' "Oh No No" (Tallyrand, BMI) .... 27
(I Know), I'm Losing You (Jobete, BMI) .... 43
I (Who Have Nothing) (Milky Way-Trio-Catillio, BMI) .... 79
I Need Somebody (Cameo-Parkway, BMI) .... 71
If I Were a Carpenter (Faithful Virtue, BMI) .... 15
I'm Gonna Make You Love Me (Act Three, BMI) .... 96
I'm Ready for Love (Jobete, BMI) .... 16
I'm Your Puppet (Fame, BMI) .... 6
It Tears Me Up (Fame, BMI) .... 34
It's Only Love (Tender Tunes, BMI) .... 56
I Wanna Meet You (Destination, BMI) .... 90
Knock on Wood (East, BMI) .... 35
Lady Godiva (Regent, BMI) .... 8
Last Train to Clarksville (Screen Gems-Columbia, BMI) .... 7
Living For You (Cotillion-Chris-Marc, BMI) .... 87
Look Through My Window (Trousdale, BMI) .... 24
Louie, Louie (Limax, BMI) .... 30
Love Is a Hurtin' Thing (Rawlou, BMI) .... 18
Mame (Morris, ASCAP) .... 45
Mellow Yellow (Donovan Ltd., BMI) .... 9
Mustang Sally (Fourteen Hour, BMI) .... 66
Nineteen Days (Branston, BMI) .... 49
Money (That's What I Want) (Jobete, BMI) .... 74
96 Tears (Arguello, BMI) .... 11
On This Side of Goodbye (Screen Gems-Columbia, BMI) .... 47
Paint Me a Picture (Vive, BMI) .... 40
Pandora's Golden Heebie Jeebies (Beechwood, BMI) 77
Place in the Sun, A (Stein-Vanstock, ASCAP) .... 37
Please Say You're Fooling (Eden, BMI) .... 68
Poor Side of Town (Rivers, BMI) .... 5
Proud One, The (Saturday & Season's Four, BMI) 70
Psychotic Reaction (Hot Shot, BMI) .... 41
Rain on the Roof (Faithful Virtue, BMI) .... 14
Reach Out I'll Be There (Jobete, BMI) .... 22
Respect (East-Time-Walco, BMI) .... 92
Run, Run, Look and See (Little Darlin'-Low Twi, BMI) .... 33
Secret Love (Remick, ASCAP) .... 29
Single Girl (Combine, BMI) .... 69
Somebody (Somewhere) Needs You (Jobete, BMI) . 55
Stay With Me (Ragmar-Crenshaw, BMI) .... 65
Stop Stop Stop (Maribus, BMI) .... 13
Sugar Town (Criterion, ASCAP) .... 62
Symphony for Susan, A (Kris, ASCAP) .... 51
Talk Talk (Thrush, BMI) .... 58
That's Life (Four Star Television) .... 42
Time After Time (Sands, ASCAP) .... 46
Tiny Bubbles (Granite, ASCAP) .... 93
Walk Away Renee (Twin Tone, BMI) .... 23
We Got a Thing That's in the Groove (McLaughlin, BMI) .... 67
What Becomes of the Brokenhearted (Jobete, BMI) 20
Wheel of Hurt, The (Martino) (Roosevelt, BMI) .. 59
Wheel of Hurt, The (Whiting) (Roosevelt, BMI) .. 31
Whispers (Jalynne-BRC, BMI) .... 26
(When She Needs Good Lovin') She Comes to Me (Tiger, BMI) .... 39
Who Am I (Duchess, BMI) .... 21
Why Pick On Me (Equinox, BMI) .... 54
Winchester Cathedral (Rollin) (Southern, ASCAP) .. 72
Winchester Cathedral (Vaudeville Band), (Southern, ASCAP) .... 3
Wish You Were Here, Buddy (Roosevelt, BMI) .... 53
You Can Bring Me All Your Heartaches (Raw Lou, BMI) .... 88
You Keep Me Hangin' On (Jobete, BMI) .... 1

## BUBBLING UNDER THE HOT 100

101. WHERE DID ROBINSON CRUSOE GO WITH FRIDAY ON SATURDAY NIGHT .... Ian Whitcomb, Tower 274
102. PLEASE DON'T EVER LEAVE ME .... The Cyrkle, Columbia 43871
103. QUESTIONS AND ANSWERS .... The In Crowd, Viva 604
104. A MAN AND A WOMAN .... Tamiko Jones & Herbie Mann, Atlantic 2362
105. LOVE'S GONE BAD .... Chris Clark, V.I.P. 25038
106. WEDDING BELL BLUES .... Laura Nyro, Verve Folkways 5024
107. MEDITATION .... Claudine Longet, A&M 817
108. IT'S NOT THE SAME .... Anthony & the Imperials, Veep 1248
109. IF YOU GO AWAY .... Damita Jo, Epic 10061
110. WILD ANGELS THEME .... Davie Allen & the Arrows, Tower 267
111. YOUR EVER CHANGIN' MIND .... Crispian St. Peters, Janie 1328
112. I'LL BE HOME .... Platters, Musicor 1211
113. PEAK OF LOVE .... Bobby McClure, Checker 1152
114. THERE'S GOT TO BE A WORD .... Innocence, Kama Sutra 214
115. HYMN No. 5 .... Mighty Hannibal, Josie 964
116. I'M GONNA MISS YOU .... Artistics, Brunswick 55301
117. STANDING ON GUARD .... Falcons, Big Wheel 1967
118. TELL IT LIKE IT IS .... Aaron Neville, Parlo 101
119. LET'S GET LOST ON A COUNTRY ROAD .... The Kit Kats, Jamie 1326
120. (WE AIN'T GOT) NOTHIN' YET .... Blues Magoos, Mercury 72622
121. BLUE AUTUMN .... Bobby Goldsboro, United Artists 50087
122. BAD MISUNDERSTANDING .... The Critters, Kapp 793
123. BUZZZZZZ .... Jimmy Gordon, Challenge 59194
124. PUSHING TOO HARD .... The Seeds, GNP Crescendo 372
125. WE'RE GONNA BRING THE COUNTRY TO THE CITY .... Tony Mason, RCA Victor 8938
126. BORN FREE .... Matt Monro, Capitol 5623
127. SPANISH NIGHTS AND YOU .... Connie Francis, MGM 13610
128. KARATE .... The Emperors, Mala 543
129. REVERBERATION (DOUBT) .... 13th Floor Elevators, International Artists 111
130. WINDOWS AND DOORS .... Jackie DeShannon, Imperial 66169
131. GEORGY GIRL .... The Seekers, Capitol 5756
132. SOMETHING ON YOUR MIND .... Baby Ray, Imperial 66216
133. THE BEARS .... The Fastest Group Alive, Valiant 784

Compiled from national retail sales and radio station airplay by the Music Popularity Dept. of Record Market Research, Billboard.

# Billboard HOT 100

For Week Ending December 3, 1966

★ STAR performer—Sides registering greatest proportionate upward progress this week.

| This Week | 1 Wk. Ago | 2 Wks. Ago | 3 Wks. Ago | TITLE Artist (Producer), Label & Number | Weeks On Chart |
|---|---|---|---|---|---|
| 1 | 3 | 3 | 6 | WINCHESTER CATHEDRAL — New Vaudeville Band, (Geoff Stephens), Fontana 1562 | 6 |
| 2 | 2 | 2 | 4 | GOOD VIBRATIONS — Beach Boys (Brian Wilson), Capitol 5676 | 7 |
| 3 | 1 | 1 | 7 | YOU KEEP ME HANGIN' ON — Supremes (Holland-Dozier), Motown 1101 | 6 |
| 4 | 4 | 6 | 9 | DEVIL WITH A BLUE DRESS ON & GOOD GOLLY MISS MOLLY — Mitch Ryder & the Detroit Wheels (Bob Crew), New Voice 817 | 8 |
| ★5 | 9 | 24 | 65 | MELLOW YELLOW — Donovan, (Mickie Most), Epic 10098 | 4 |
| 6 | 6 | 7 | 10 | I'M YOUR PUPPET — James & Bobby Purify (Don Schroeder), Bell 648 | 11 |
| 7 | 8 | 11 | 21 | LADY GODIVA — Peter & Gordon (John Burgess), Capitol 5740 | 9 |
| 8 | 10 | 12 | 17 | BORN FREE — Roger Williams (Hy Grill), Kapp 767 | 14 |
| 9 | 5 | 5 | 1 | POOR SIDE OF TOWN — Johnny Rivers (Lou Adler), Imperial 66205 | 12 |
| 10 | 7 | 4 | 2 | LAST TRAIN TO CLARKSVILLE — Monkees (Tommy Boyce & Bobby Hart), Colgems 1001 | 13 |
| 11 | 12 | 17 | 20 | COMING ON STRONG — Brenda Lee (Owen Bradley), Decca 32018 | 10 |
| 12 | 16 | 21 | 34 | I'M READY FOR LOVE — Martha & the Vandellas, (Holland-Dozier), Gordy 7056 | 6 |
| 13 | 13 | 20 | 31 | STOP STOP STOP — Hollies, (Ron Richards), Imperial 66214 | 6 |
| 14 | 17 | 23 | 47 | A HAZY SHADE OF WINTER — Simon & Garfunkel (Bob Johnston), Columbia 43873 | 5 |
| 15 | 42 | 75 | — | THAT'S LIFE — Frank Sinatra (Jimmy Bowen), Reprise 0531 | 3 |
| 16 | 26 | 39 | 55 | WHISPERS — Jackie Wilson (Carl Davis), Brunswick 55300 | 7 |
| 17 | 27 | 58 | 69 | I GOT THE FEELIN' "OH NO NO" — Neil Diamond, (Jeff Barry-Ellie Greenwich), Bang 536 | 4 |
| 18 | 11 | 8 | 3 | 96 TEARS — ? (Question Mark) & the Mysterians, Cameo 428 | 14 |
| 19 | 14 | 10 | 15 | RAIN ON THE ROOF — Lovin' Spoonful (Erik Jacobson), Kama Sutra 216 | 8 |
| ★20 | 36 | 55 | 73 | (Come 'Round Here) I'M THE ONE YOU NEED — Miracles (Holland & Dozier), Tamla 54140 | 5 |
| 21 | 19 | 15 | 14 | HOORAY FOR HAZEL — Tommy Roe (Our Prods.), ABC 10852 | 12 |
| 22 | 34 | 40 | 51 | IT TEARS ME UP — Percy Sledge (Martin Greene-Quin Ivy), Atlantic 2358 | 7 |
| 23 | 37 | 53 | 83 | A PLACE IN THE SUN — Stevie Wonder, (C. Paul), Tamla 54139 | 4 |
| 24 | 21 | 22 | 22 | WHO AM I — Petula Clark (Tony Hatch), Warner Bros. 5863 | 7 |
| 25 | 20 | 18 | 18 | WHAT BECOMES OF THE BROKENHEARTED — Jimmy Ruffin (William Stevenson), Soul 35022 | 15 |
| 26 | 31 | 33 | 49 | THE WHEEL OF HURT — Margaret Whiting (Arnold Geland), London 101 | 9 |
| 27 | 28 | 26 | 30 | BUT IT'S ALRIGHT — J. J. Jackson (Lew Futterman), Calla 119 | 10 |
| 28 | 33 | 43 | 57 | RUN, RUN, LOOK AND SEE — Brian Hyland (Snuff Garrett), Philips 40405 | 7 |
| 29 | 35 | 37 | 45 | KNOCK ON WOOD — Eddie Floyd (Prod. by Staff), Stax 194 | 13 |
| 30 | 18 | 13 | 13 | LOVE IS A HURTIN' THING — Lou Rawls (David Axelrod), Capitol 5709 | 13 |
| 31 | 45 | 82 | — | MAME — Herb Alpert & the Tijuana Brass, (Herb Alpert), A&M 823 | 3 |
| 32 | 43 | 79 | — | (I Know) I'M LOSING YOU — Temptations, (N. Whitfield), Grady 7057 | 3 |
| 33 | 15 | 9 | 8 | IF I WERE A CARPENTER — Bobby Darin (Koppleman-Rubin), Atlantic 2350 | 11 |
| 34 | 32 | 34 | 46 | HOLY COW — Lee Dorsey (A. Toussaint-M. Sehorn), Amy 965 | 7 |
| 35 | 30 | 32 | 38 | LOUIE, LOUIE — Sandpipers (Tommy LaPuma), A&M 819 | 7 |
| 36 | 46 | 54 | 75 | TIME AFTER TIME — Chris Montez, (Tommy LiPuma-Herb Alpert), A&M 822 | 6 |
| 37 | 39 | 57 | 67 | (When She Needs Good Lovin') SHE COMES TO ME — Chicago Loop (Bob Crewe & Al Kasha), DynoVoice 226 | 5 |
| 38 | 22 | 14 | 11 | REACH OUT I'LL BE THERE — Four Tops (Holland & Dozier), Motown 1098 | 14 |
| 39 | 25 | 19 | 5 | DANDY — Herman's Hermits (Mickie Most), MGM 13603 | 10 |
| 40 | 29 | 29 | 37 | SECRET LOVE — Billy Stewart, (Dave & Caston), Chess 1978 | 8 |
| 41 | 24 | 25 | 25 | LOOK THROUGH MY WINDOW — Mama's and the Papa's (Lou Adler), Dunhill 4050 | 7 |
| 42 | 56 | 66 | 81 | IT'S ONLY LOVE — Tommy James & the Shondells, Roulette 4710 | 5 |
| 43 | 23 | 16 | 12 | WALK AWAY RENEE — Left Banke (World United Prod., Inc.), Smash 2041 | 13 |
| 44 | 62 | 83 | — | SUGAR TOWN — Nancy Sinatra, (Lee Hazelwood), Reprise 0527 | 3 |
| 45 | 38 | 27 | 28 | B-A-B-Y — Carla Thomas (Staff), Stax 195 | 16 |
| 46 | 57 | 67 | 84 | GAMES THAT LOVERS PLAY — Eddie Fisher, (Al Schmitt), RCA Victor 8956 | 4 |
| 47 | 58 | 81 | 96 | TALK TALK — Music Machine, (Maurice Bercov), Original Sound 61 | 4 |
| 48 | 50 | 60 | 76 | HELP ME GIRL — Outsiders, (Roger Karshner), Capitol 5759 | 6 |
| 49 | 53 | 56 | 68 | WISH YOU WERE HERE, BUDDY — Pat Boone (Nick Venet and Randy Wood), Dot 16933 | 7 |
| 50 | 52 | 52 | 56 | HEAVEN MUST HAVE SENT YOU — Elgins (Holland-Dozier), V.I.P. 25037 | 7 |
| 51 | 51 | 65 | 70 | A SYMPHONY FOR SUSAN — Arbors, (Richard Carney), Date 1529 | 8 |
| 52 | 66 | — | — | MUSTANG SALLY — Wilson Pickett, (Jerry Wexler-Rick Hall), Atlantic 2365 | 2 |
| 53 | 69 | 96 | — | SINGLE GIRL — Sandy Posey, (Chips Moman), MGM 13612 | 3 |
| 54 | 47 | 47 | 58 | ON THIS SIDE OF GOODBYE — Righteous Brothers, (Bill Medley), Verve 10449 | 6 |
| 55 | 73 | 84 | — | COMING HOME SOLDIER — Bobby Vinton, (Robert Mersey), Epic 10090 | 3 |
| 56 | 71 | 90 | — | I NEED SOMEBODY — ? (Question Mark) & the Mysterians, Cameo 441 | 3 |
| 57 | 100 | — | — | CRY — Ronnie Dove, (Phil Kahl), Diamond 214 | 2 |
| 58 | 77 | — | — | PANDORA'S GOLDEN HEEBIE JEEBIES — Association, (J. Yester), Valiant 755 | 2 |
| 59 | 54 | 61 | 61 | WHY PICK ON ME — Standells (Ed Cobb), Tower 282 | 7 |
| 60 | 74 | 89 | — | MONEY (That's What I Want) — Jr. Walker & the All Stars, (B. Gordy, Jr.-L. Horn), Soul 35026 | 3 |
| 61 | 79 | 93 | 97 | I (Who Have Nothing) — Terry Knight & the Pack (Terry Knight), Lucky 11 230 | 4 |
| 62 | 64 | 73 | 74 | A DAY IN THE LIFE OF A FOOL — Jack Jones, (David Kapp), Kapp 781 | 6 |
| 63 | 63 | 71 | 72 | BANG! BANG! — Joe Cuba Sextet (Pancho Cristal), Tico 475 | 7 |
| 64 | 55 | 59 | 60 | SOMEBODY (Somewhere) NEEDS YOU — Sam & Dave, (Pro. by Staff), Stax 204 | 8 |
| 65 | 67 | 77 | 79 | WE GOT A THING THAT'S IN THE GROOVE — Capitols (Ollie McLaughlin), Karem 1526 | 4 |
| 66 | 68 | 78 | 82 | PLEASE SAY YOU'RE FOOLING — Ray Charles (TRC), ABC 10865 | 4 |
| 67 | 78 | — | — | I FOOLED YOU THIS TIME — Gene Chandler, (Carl Davis), Checker 1155 | 2 |
| 68 | 70 | 80 | 87 | THE PROUD ONE — Frankie Valli, (Bob Crew), Philips 40407 | 4 |
| 69 | 61 | 63 | 71 | COME BACK — Five Stairsteps, Windy C 603 | 5 |
| ★70 | 85 | — | — | THE EGGPLANT THAT ATE CHICAGO — Dr. West's Medicine Show & Junk Band, (T. Marer), Go Go 100 | 2 |
| 71 | 72 | 72 | 78 | WINCHESTER CATHEDRAL — Dana Rollin, Tower 283 | 5 |
| 72 | 59 | 62 | 63 | THE WHEEL OF HURT — Al Martino (T. Morgan), Capitol 5741 | 8 |
| 73 | 88 | — | — | YOU CAN BRING ME ALL YOUR HEARTACHES — Lou Rawls, (David Axelrod), Capitol 5790 | 2 |
| 74 | 82 | — | — | GHOST RIDERS IN THE SKY — Baja Marimba Band, (Herb Alpert & Jerry Moss), A&M 824 | 2 |
| 75 | 75 | 76 | 80 | DON'T ANSWER THE DOOR — B. B. King (Johnny Pate), ABC 10856 | 7 |
| 76 | 76 | 74 | 77 | BABY, WHAT DO YOU WANT ME TO DO? — Barbara Lewis, (Jerry Wexler & Ollie McLaughlin), Atlantic 2361 | 6 |
| ★77 | 99 | — | — | HAPPENINGS TEN YEARS TIME AGO — Yardbirds (Simon Napier-Bell), Epic 10094 | 2 |
| 78 | — | — | — | TELL IT LIKE IT IS — Aaron Neville, Parlo 101 | 1 |
| 79 | 80 | — | — | I DON'T NEED NO DOCTOR — Ray Charles (TRC), ABC 10865 | 2 |
| 80 | 81 | — | — | ALVIN'S BOO-GA-LOO — Alvin Cash & the Registers, (J. Jones), Mar-V-Lus 6014 | 2 |
| 81 | — | — | — | WORDS OF LOVE — Mama's & the Papa's (Lou Adler), Dunhill 4037 | 1 |
| 82 | — | — | — | GEORGY GIRL — Seekers, (W. H. Miller), Capitol 5756 | 1 |
| 83 | — | — | — | EAST WEST — Herman's Hermits, (Mickie Most), MGM 13639 | 1 |
| 84 | — | — | — | I'VE PASSED THIS WAY BEFORE — Jimmy Ruffin, (J. Dean & W. Weatherspoon), Soul 35027 | 1 |
| 85 | — | — | — | TRY A LITTLE TENDERNESS — Otis Redding (Prod. by Staff), Volt 141 | 1 |
| 86 | — | — | — | PLEASE DON'T EVER LEAVE ME — Cyrkle, (John Simon), Columbia 43871 | 1 |
| 87 | 90 | — | — | I WANNA MEET YOU — Cryin' Shames, (Jim Golden), Columbia 43836 | 2 |
| 88 | — | — | — | GOOD THING — Paul Revere & the Raiders, (Terry Melcher), Columbia 43907 | 1 |
| 89 | 91 | — | — | HELP ME, GIRL — Eric Burdon & the Animals (Tom Wilson), MGM 13636 | 2 |
| 90 | — | — | — | THERE'S GOT TO BE A WORD — Innocence, (Ripp-Anders-Poncia), Kama Sutra 214 | 1 |
| 91 | 95 | — | — | (He's) RAINING IN MY SUNSHINE — Jay & the Americans, (Bob Feldman), United Artists 50094 | 2 |
| 92 | 93 | — | — | TINY BUBBLES — Don Ho & the Allis, (Burke), Reprise 0507 | 2 |
| 93 | 94 | — | — | I'M GONNA MAKE YOU LOVE ME — Dee Dee Warwick, (Jerry Ross), Mercury 72638 | 2 |
| 94 | — | — | — | THERE'S SOMETHING ON YOUR MIND — Baby Ray, (Scott Turner), Imperial 66216 | 1 |
| 95 | — | — | — | KARATE — Emperor's, (George Wilson & Phil Gaber), Male 543 | 1 |
| 96 | — | — | — | YOU GOT ME HUMMIN' — Sam & Dave, (Pro. by Staff), Stax 204 | 1 |
| 97 | 98 | — | — | HAVE YOU EVER LOVED SOMEBODY — Searchers, Kapp 783 | 2 |
| 98 | — | — | — | BABY WHAT I MEAN — Drifters, (Bob Gallo & Tom Dowd), Atlantic 2366 | 1 |
| 99 | — | — | — | I'LL BE HOME — Platters, (Luther Dixon), Musicor 1211 | 1 |
| 100 | — | — | — | BAD MISUNDERSTANDING — Critters, (Ripp-Anders-Poncia), Kapp 793 | 1 |

## BUBBLING UNDER THE HOT 100

101. AM I A LOSER — Eddie Holman, Parkway 106
102. QUESTIONS & ANSWERS — In Crowd, Viva 604
103. IF YOU GO AWAY — Damita Jo, Epic 10061
104. WHERE DID ROBINSON CRUSOE GO WITH FRIDAY ON SATURDAY NIGHT — Ian Whitcomb, Tower 274
105. COMMUNICATION BREAKDOWN — Roy Orbison, MGM 13634
106. YOUR EVER CHANGIN' MIND — Crispian St. Peters, Jamie 1328
107. STANDING ON GUARD — Falcons, Big Wheel 1967
108. BLUE AUTUMN — Bobby Goldsboro, United Artists 50067
109. CORNER IN THE SUN — Walter Jackson, Okeh 7260
110. GIRL THAT STOOD BESIDE ME — Bobby Darin, Atlantic 2367
111. CAN I GET TO KNOW YOU BETTER — Turtles, White Whale 238
112. PEAK OF LOVE — Bobby McClure, Checker 1152
113. PUSHING TOO HARD — Seeds, GMP Crescendo 372
114. HI NI HAZEL — Gary & the Hornets, Smash 2051
115. I'M GONNA MISS YOU — Artistics, Brunswick 55301
116. HEARTBREAK HOTEL — Roger Miller, Smash 2066
117. MY BOYFRIENDS BACK — Chiffons, Laurie 3564
118. AND I LOVE HER — Vibrations, Okeh 7257
119. (WE AIN'T GOT) NOTHING YET — Blues Magoos, Mercury 72622
120. LIVING FOR YOU — Sonny & Cher, Atco 6449
121. BUZZZZZZ — Jimmy Gordon, Challenge 59194
122. RESPECT — Rationals, Cameo 437
123. GOODNIGHT MY LOVE — Happenings, B. T. Puppy 523
124. I HAD TOO MUCH TO DREAM (LAST NIGHT) — Electric Prunes, Reprise 0532
125. 98.6 — Keith, Mercury 72639
126. SPANISH NIGHTS AND YOU — Connie Francis, MGM 13610
127. I'M GONNA MAKE YOU MINE — Shadows of Knight, Dunwich 141
128. BACK IN THE SAME OLD BAG — Bobby Bland, Duke 412
129. WISH ME A RAINBOW — Gunther Kallmann Chorus, Four Corners of the World 138
130. I BETCHA COULDN'T LOVE ME — Carnival 527
131. CRY LIKE A BABY — Aretha Franklin, Columbia 43827
132. LOOK WHAT YOU'VE DONE — Pozo-Seco Singers, Columbia 43927
133. HARLEM SHUFFLE — Traits, Scepter 12169
134. DANCING IN THE STREET — Mama's & Papa's, Dunhill 4057
135. SINCE I DON'T HAVE YOU — Lou Christie, MGM 13623

Compiled from national retail sales and radio station airplay by the Music Popularity Dept. of Record Market Research, Billboard.

# Billboard HOT 100

For Week Ending December 10, 1966

★ STAR performer—Sides registering greatest proportionate upward progress this week.

(seal) Record Industry Association of America seal of certification as million selling single.

| This Week | 1 Wk. Ago | 2 Wks. Ago | 3 Wks. Ago | TITLE | Artist (Producer), Label & Number | Weeks On Chart |
|---|---|---|---|---|---|---|
| 1 (Billboard Award) | 2 | 2 | 2 | GOOD VIBRATIONS | Beach Boys (Brian Wilson), Capitol 5676 | 8 |
| ★2 | 5 | 9 | 24 | MELLOW YELLOW | Donovan, (Mickie Most), Epic 10098 | 5 |
| 3 | 1 | 3 | 3 | WINCHESTER CATHEDRAL | New Vaudeville Band, (Geoff Stephens), Fontana 1562 | 7 (seal) |
| 4 | 4 | 4 | 6 | DEVIL WITH A BLUE DRESS ON & GOOD GOLLY MISS MOLLY | Mitch Ryder & the Detroit Wheels (Bob Crew), New Voice 817 | 9 |
| 5 | 3 | 1 | 1 | YOU KEEP ME HANGIN' ON | Supremes (Holland-Dozier), Motown 1101 | 7 |
| 6 | 7 | 8 | 11 | LADY GODIVA | Peter & Gordon (John Burgess), Capitol 5740 | 10 |
| ★7 | 13 | 13 | 20 | STOP STOP STOP | Hollies, (Ron Richards), Imperial 66214 | 7 |
| 8 | 8 | 10 | 12 | BORN FREE | Roger Williams (Hy Grill), Kapp 767 | 15 |
| ★9 | 12 | 16 | 21 | I'M READY FOR LOVE | Martha & the Vandellas, (Holland-Dozier), Gordy 7056 | 7 |
| ★10 | 15 | 42 | 75 | THAT'S LIFE | Frank Sinatra (Jimmy Bowen), Reprise 0531 | 4 |
| ★11 | 16 | 26 | 39 | WHISPERS | Jackie Wilson (Carl Davis), Brunswick 55300 | 8 |
| 12 | 6 | 6 | 7 | I'M YOUR PUPPET | James & Bobby Purify (Don Schroeder), Bell 648 | 12 |
| 13 | 14 | 17 | 23 | A HAZY SHADE OF WINTER | Simon & Garfunkel (Bob Johnston), Columbia 43873 | 6 |
| ★14 | 23 | 37 | 53 | A PLACE IN THE SUN | Stevie Wonder, (C. Paul), Tamla 54139 | 5 |
| 15 | 9 | 5 | 5 | POOR SIDE OF TOWN | Johnny Rivers (Lou Adler), Imperial 66205 | 13 |
| ★16 | 44 | 62 | 83 | SUGAR TOWN | Nancy Sinatra, (Lee Hazelwood), Reprise 0527 | 4 |
| 17 | 17 | 27 | 58 | I GOT THE FEELIN' "OH NO NO" | Neil Diamond, (Jeff Barry-Ellie Greenwich), Bang 536 | 5 |
| 18 | 20 | 36 | 55 | (Come 'Round Here) I'M THE ONE YOU NEED | Miracles (Holland & Dozier) Tamla 54140 | 6 |
| ★19 | 32 | 43 | 79 | (I Know) I'M LOSING YOU | Tmptations, (N. Whitfield, Grady 7057 | 4 |
| 20 | 11 | 12 | 17 | COMING ON STRONG | Brenda Lee (Owen Bradley), Decca 32018 | 11 |
| 21 | 22 | 34 | 40 | IT TEARS ME UP | Percy Sledge (Marlin Greene-Quin Ivy), Atlantic 2358 | 8 |
| ★22 | 27 | 28 | 26 | BUT IT'S ALRIGHT | J. J. Jackson (Lew Futterman), Calla 119 | 11 |
| 23 | 24 | 32 | 34 | HOLY COW | Lee Dorsey (A. Toussaint-M. Sehorn), Amy 965 | 8 |
| ★24 | 31 | 45 | 82 | MAME | Herb Alpert & the Tijuana Brass, (Herb Alpert) A&M 823 | 4 |
| 25 | 28 | 33 | 43 | RUN, RUN, LOOK AND SEE | Brian Hyland (Snuff Garrett), Philips 40405 | 8 |
| 26 | 26 | 31 | 33 | THE WHEEL OF HURT | Margaret Whiting (Arnold Goland), London 101 | 10 |
| 27 | 10 | 7 | 4 | LAST TRAIN TO CLARKSVILLE | Monkees (Tommy Boyce & Bobby Hart), Colgems 1001 | 14 (seal) |
| 28 | 29 | 35 | 37 | KNOCK ON WOOD | Eddie Floyd (Prod. by Staff), Stax 194 | 14 |
| 29 | 25 | 20 | 18 | WHAT BECOMES OF THE BROKENHEARTED | Jimmy Ruffin (William Stevenson), Soul 35022 | 16 |
| 30 | 19 | 14 | 10 | RAIN ON THE ROOF | Lovin' Spoonful (Erik Jacobson), Kama Sutra 216 | 9 |
| ★31 | 53 | 69 | 96 | SINGLE GIRL | Sandy Posey, (Chips Moman), MGM 13612 | 4 |
| ★32 | 42 | 56 | 66 | IT'S ONLY LOVE | Tommy James & the Shondells, Roulette 4710 | 6 |
| ★33 | 56 | 71 | 90 | I NEED SOMEBODY | ? (Question Mark) & the Mysterians, Cameo 441 | 4 |
| ★34 | 52 | 66 | — | MUSTANG SALLY | Wilson Pickett, (Jerry Wexler-Rick Hall), Atlantic 2365 | 3 |
| ★35 | 57 | 100 | — | CRY | Ronnie Dove, (Phil Kahl), Diamond 214 | 3 |
| 36 | 36 | 46 | 54 | TIME AFTER TIME | Chris Montez, (Tommy LiPuma-Herb Alpert), A&M 822 | 7 |
| ★37 | 47 | 58 | 81 | TALK TALK | Music Machine, (Maurice Bercov), Original Sound 61 | 5 |
| ★38 | 48 | 50 | 60 | HELP ME GIRL | Outsiders, (Roger Karshner), Capitol 5759 | 7 |
| 39 | 37 | 39 | 57 | (When She Needs Good Lovin') SHE COMES TO ME | Chicago Loop (Bob Crewe & Al Kasha), DynoVoice 226 | 6 |
| 40 | 21 | 19 | 15 | HOORAY FOR HAZEL | Tommy Roe (Our Prods.), ABC 10852 | 13 |
| 41 | 18 | 11 | 8 | 96 TEARS | ? (Question Mark) & the Mysterians, Cameo 428 | 15 (seal) |
| ★42 | 55 | 73 | 84 | COMING HOME SOLDIER | Bobby Vinton, (Robert Mersey), Epic 10090 | 4 |
| ★43 | 58 | 77 | — | PANDORA'S GOLDEN HEEBIE JEEBIES | Association, (J. Yester), Valiant 755 | 3 |
| ★44 | — | — | — | I'M A BELIEVER | Monkees (Jeff Barry), Colgems 1002 | 1 (seal) |
| 45 | 46 | 57 | 67 | GAMES THAT LOVERS PLAY | Eddie Fisher, (Al Schmitt), RCA Victor 8956 | 7 |
| ★46 | 81 | — | — | WORDS OF LOVE | Mama's & the Papa's (Lou Adler), Dunhill 4037 | 2 |
| 47 | 38 | 22 | 14 | REACH OUT I'LL BE THERE | Four Tops (Holland & Dozier), Motown 1098 | 15 |
| 48 | 30 | 18 | 13 | LOVE IS A HURTIN' THING | Lou Rawls (David Axelrod), Capitol 5709 | 14 |
| 49 | 39 | 25 | 19 | DANDY | Herman's Hermits (Mickie Most), MGM 13603 | 11 |
| ★50 | 67 | 78 | — | I FOOLED YOU THIS TIME | Gene Chandler, (Carl Davis), Checker 1155 | 3 |
| ★51 | 78 | — | — | TELL IT LIKE IT IS | Aaron Neville, Parlo 101 | 2 |
| 52 | 49 | 53 | 56 | WISH YOU WERE HERE, BUDDY | Pat Boone (Nick Venet and Randy Wood), Dot 16933 | 8 |
| 53 | 60 | 74 | 89 | MONEY (That's What I Want) | Jr. Walker & the All Stars, (B. Gordy, Jr.-L. Horn) Soul 35026 | 4 |
| 54 | 50 | 52 | 52 | HEAVEN MUST HAVE SENT YOU | Elgins (Holland-Dozier), V.I.P. 25037 | 8 |
| 55 | 51 | 51 | 65 | A SYMPHONY FOR SUSAN | Arbors, (Richard Carney), Date 1529 | 9 |
| 56 | 61 | 79 | 93 | I (Who Have Nothing) | Terry Knight & the Pack (Terry Knight), Lucky 11 230 | 5 |
| ★57 | 77 | 99 | — | HAPPENINGS TEN YEARS TIME AGO | Yardbirds, (Simon Napier-Bell), Epic 10094 | 3 |
| ★58 | 84 | — | — | I'VE PASSED THIS WAY BEFORE | Jimmy Ruffin, (J. Dean & W. Weatherspoon), Soul 35027 | 2 |
| ★59 | 89 | 91 | — | HELP ME GIRL | Eric Burdon & the Animals (Tom Wilson), MGM 13636 | 3 |
| ★60 | 83 | — | — | EAST WEST | Herman's Hermits, (Mickie Most), MGM 13639 | 2 |
| ★61 | 86 | — | — | PLEASE DON'T EVER LEAVE ME | Cyrkle, (John Simon) Columbia 43871 | 2 |
| 62 | 62 | 64 | 73 | A DAY IN THE LIFE OF A FOOL | Jack Jones, (David Kapp), Kapp 781 | 7 |
| 63 | 70 | 85 | — | THE EGGPLANT THAT ATE CHICAGO | Dr. West's Medicine Show & Junk Band, (T. Marer), Go Go 100 | 3 |
| 64 | 66 | 68 | 78 | PLEASE SAY YOU'RE FOOLING | Ray Charles (TRC), ABC 10865 | 5 |
| 65 | 63 | 63 | 71 | BANG! BANG! | Joe Cuba Sextet (Pancho Cristal), Tico 475 | 8 |
| ★66 | 88 | — | — | GOOD THING | Paul Revere & the Raiders, (Terry Melcher), Columbia 43907 | 2 |
| 67 | 65 | 67 | 77 | WE GOT A THING THAT'S IN THE GROOVE | Capitols (Ollie McLaughlin), Karen 1526 | 5 |
| 68 | 68 | 70 | 80 | THE PROUD ONE | Frankie Valli (Bob Crewe), Philips 40407 | 5 |
| ★69 | 90 | — | — | THERE'S GOT TO BE A WORD | Innocence, (Ripp-Anders-Poncia), Kama Sutra 214 | 2 |
| ★70 | 85 | — | — | TRY A LITTLE TENDERNESS | Otis Redding (Prod. by Staff), Volt 141 | 2 |
| 71 | 71 | 72 | 72 | WINCHESTER CATHEDRAL | Dana Rollin, Tower 283 | 6 |
| 72 | 75 | 75 | 76 | DON'T ANSWER THE DOOR | B. B. King (Johnny Pate), ABC 10856 | 8 |
| 73 | 73 | 88 | — | YOU CAN BRING ME ALL YOUR HEARTACHES | Lou Rawls, (David Axelrod), Capitol 5790 | 3 |
| 74 | 74 | 82 | — | GHOST RIDERS IN THE SKY | Baja Marimba Band, (Herb Alpert & Jerry Moss), A&M 824 | 3 |
| 75 | 69 | 61 | 63 | COME BACK | Five Stairsteps, Windy C 603 | 6 |
| 76 | 79 | 80 | — | I DON'T NEED NO DOCTOR | Ray Charles (TRC), ABC 10865 | 3 |
| ★77 | 100 | — | — | BAD MISUNDERSTANDING | Critters, (Ripp-Anders-Poncia), Kapp 793 | 2 |
| 78 | 80 | 81 | — | ALVIN'S BOO-GA-LOO | Alvin Cash & the Registers, (J. Jones), Mar-V-Lus 6014 | 3 |
| 79 | 82 | — | — | GEORGY GIRL | Seekers, (W. H. Miller), Capitol 5756 | 2 |
| ★80 | — | — | — | BLUE AUTUMN | Bobby Goldsboro (Jack Gold), United Artists 50087 | 1 |
| ★81 | — | — | — | GOODNIGHT MY LOVE | Happenings (Tokens), B. T. Puppy 523 | 1 |
| ★82 | — | — | — | COMMUNICATION BREAKDOWN | Roy Orbison (Rose & Vienneau), MGM 13634 | 1 |
| ★83 | 98 | — | — | BABY WHAT I MEAN | Drifters, (Bob Gallo & Tom Dowd), Atlantic 2366 | 2 |
| ★84 | — | — | — | THE GIRL THAT STOOD BESIDE ME | Bobby Darin (Koppleman-Rubin), Atlantic 2367 | 1 |
| 85 | 87 | 90 | — | I WANNA MEET YOU | Cryin' Shames, (Jim Golden), Columbia 43836 | 3 |
| 86 | 94 | — | — | THERE'S SOMETHING ON YOUR MIND | Baby Ray, (Scott Turner), Imperial 66216 | 2 |
| 87 | 92 | 93 | — | TINY BUBBLES | Don Ho & the Allis, (Burke), Reprise 0507 | 3 |
| 88 | 93 | 94 | — | I'M GONNA MAKE YOU LOVE ME | Dee Dee Warwick, (Jerry Ross), Mercury 72638 | 3 |
| ★89 | — | — | — | (We Ain't Got) NOTHIN' YET | Blues Magoos (Wyld & Polhamus), Mercury 72622 | 1 |
| ★90 | — | — | — | 98.6 | Keith (Jerry Ross), Mercury 72639 | 1 |
| 91 | 91 | 95 | — | (He's) RAINING IN MY SUNSHINE | Jay & the Americans, (Bob Feldman), United Artists 50094 | 3 |
| 92 | — | — | — | TELL IT TO THE RAIN | 4 Seasons (Bob Crewe), Philips 40412 | 1 |
| 93 | 95 | — | — | KARATE | Emperor's, (George Wilson & Phil Gaber), Mala 543 | 2 |
| 94 | 97 | 98 | — | HAVE YOU EVER LOVED SOMEBODY | Searchers, Kapp 783 | 3 |
| 95 | 96 | — | — | YOU GOT ME HUMMIN' | Sam & Dave, (Pro. by Staff), Stax 204 | 2 |
| 96 | — | — | — | QUESTIONS AND ANSWERS | In Crowd (Snuff Carrett), Viva 604 | 1 |
| 97 | 99 | — | — | I'LL BE HOME | Platters, (Luther Dixon), Musicor 1211 | 2 |
| 98 | — | — | — | I HAD TOO MUCH TO DREAM (Last Night) | Electric Prunes (Damo Prod.), Reprise 0532 | 1 |
| 99 | — | — | — | IF YOU GO AWAY | Damite Jo (Bob Morgan-Ted Cooper), Epic 10061 | 1 |
| 100 | — | — | — | PEAK OF LOVE | Bobby McClure (Billy Davis), Checker 1152 | 1 |

## HOT 100—A TO Z—(Publisher-Licensee)

Alvin's Boo-Ga-Loo (Vapac, BMI) ... 78
Baby What I Mean (Unart, BMI) ... 83
Bad Misunderstanding (Kama Sutra, BMI) ... 77
Bang! Bang! (Cordon, BMI) ... 65
Blue Autumn (Unart, BMI) ... 80
Born Free (Screen Gems-Columbia, BMI) ... 8
But It's Alright (Pamelarosa, BMI) ... 22
Come Back (Camad, BMI) ... 75
(Come 'Round Here) I'm the One You Need (Jobete, BMI) ... 18
Coming Home Soldier (Feather, BMI) ... 42
Coming On Strong (Moss-Rose, BMI) ... 20
Communication Breakdown (Acuff-Rose, BMI) ... 82
Cry (Shapiro-Bernstein, ASCAP) ... 35
Dandy (Noma, BMI) ... 49
Day in the Life of a Fool, A (Jungnickel, ASCAP) 62
Devil With a Blue Dress On & Good Golly Miss Molly (Jobete-Vanice, BMI) ... 4
Don't Answer the Door (Mercedes, BMI) ... 72
East West (Man-Ken, BMI) ... 60
Eggplant That Ate Chicago, The (Borscht, BMI) .. 63
Games That Lovers Play (Fisher) (Miller, ASCAP) .. 43
Georgy Girl (Chappell, ASCAP) ... 79
Ghost Riders in the Sky (Morris, ASCAP) ... 74
Goodnight My Love (Captain Marble, BMI) ... 81
Good Thing (Daywin, BMI) ... 66
Good Vibrations (Sea of Tunes, BMI) ... 1
Happenings Ten Years Time Ago (Yardbirds-Feist, ASCAP) ... 57
Have You Ever Loved Somebody (Maribus, BMI) .. 94
Hazy Shadow of Winter, A (Charing Cross, BMI) .. 13
Heaven Must Have Sent You (Jobete, BMI) ... 54
Help Me, Girl (Burdon) (Helios, BMI) ... 59
Help Me, Girl (Outsiders) (Helios, BMI) ... 38
(He's) Raining In My Sunshine (Greenlight, BMI) .. 91
Holy Cow (Marsaint, BMI) ... 23
Hooray for Hazel (Low Twi, BMI) ... 40
I Don't Need No Doctor (Flomar-Baby Monica, BMI) 76
I Fooled You This Time (Cachand-Jalynes, BMI) .. 50
I Got The Feelin' "Oh No No" (Tallyrand, BMI) .. 17
I Had Too Much To Dream (Last Night) (Star, BMI) 98
I'll Be Home (Arc, BMI) ... 97
(I Know), I'm Losing You (Jobete, BMI) ... 19
I (Who Have Nothing) (Milky Way-Trio-Catillio, BMI) ... 56
I Need Somebody (Cameo-Parkway, BMI) ... 33
If You Go Away (Marks, BMI) ... 99
I'm a Believer (Screen Gems-Columbia, BMI) ... 44
I'm Gonna Make You Love Me (Act Three, BMI) .. 88
I'm Ready for Love (Jobete, BMI) ... 9
I'm Your Puppet (Fame, BMI) ... 12
It Tears Me Up (Fame, BMI) ... 21
It's Only Love (Tender Tunes, BMI) ... 32
I Wanna Meet You (Destination, BMI) ... 85
I've Passed This Way Before (Jobete, BMI) ... 58
Karate (Wilson, BMI) ... 93
Knock on Wood (East, BMI) ... 28
Lady Godiva (Regent, BMI) ... 6
Last Train to Clarksville (Screen Gems-Columbia, BMI) ... 27
Love Is a Hurtin' Thing (Rawlou, BMI) ... 48
Mame (Morris, ASCAP) ... 24
Mellow Yellow (Donovan Ltd., BMI) ... 2
Mustang Sally (Fourteen Hour, BMI) ... 34
Money (That's What I Want) (Jobete, BMI) ... 53
98.6 (Screen Gems-Columbia, BMI) ... 90
96 Tears (Arguello, BMI) ... 41
Pandora's Golden Heebie Jeebie (Beachwood, BMI) 43
Peak Of Love (Chevis, BMI) ...100
Place in the Sun, A (Stein-Vanstock, ASCAP) ... 14
Please Don't Ever Leave Me (Chappell, BMI) ... 61
Please Say You're Fooling (Eden, BMI) ... 64
Poor Side of Town (Rivers, BMI) ... 15
Proud One, The (Saturday & Season's Four, BMI) 68
Questions And Answers (Arch, ASCAP) ... 96
Rain on the Roof (Faithful Virute, BMI) ... 30
Reach Out I'll Be There (Jobete, BMI) ... 47
Run, Run, Look and See (Little Darlin'-Low Twi, BMI) ... 25
Single Girl (Combine, BMI) ... 31
Stop Stop Stop (Maribus, BMI) ... 7
Sugar Town (Criterion, ASCAP) ... 16
Symphony for Susan, A (Kris, ASCAP) ... 55
Talk Talk (Thrush, BMI) ... 37
Tell It Like It Is (Olrap, BMI) ... 51
Tell It To The Rain (Saturday/Seasons Four, BMI) 92
That's Life (Four Star Television) ... 10
The Girl That Stood Beside Me (Chardon, BMI) .. 84
There's Got To Be A Word (Kama Sutra, BMI) .. 69
There's Something On Your Mind (Mercedes, BMI) 86
Time After Time (Sands, ASCAP) ... 36
Tiny Bubbles (Granite, ASCAP) ... 87
Try A Little Tenderness (Campbell/Connelly/Robbins, ASCAP) ... 70
(We Ain't Got) Nothin' Yet (Ananga-Ranga, BMI) 89
We Got a Thing That's in the Groove (McLaughlin, BMI) ... 67
What Becomes of the Brokenhearted (Jobete, BMI) 29
Wheel of Hurt, The (Whiting) (Roosevelt, BMI) .. 26
Whispers (Jalynna-BRC, BMI) ... 11
(When She Needs Good Lovin') She Comes to Me (Tiger, BMI) ... 39
Winchester Cathedral (Rollin) (Southern, ASCAP) 71
Winchester Cathedral (Vaudeville Band) (Southern, ASCAP) ... 3
Wish You Were Here, Buddy (Roosevelt, BMI) .. 52
Words of Love (Trousdale, BMI) ... 46
You Can Bring Me All Your Heartaches (Raw Lou, BMI) ... 73
You Got Me Hummin' (Pronto/East, BMI) ... 95
You Keep Me Hangin' On (Jobete, BMI) ... 5

## BUBBLING UNDER THE HOT 100

101. DANCING IN THE STREET ... Mamas & the Papas, Dunhill 4057
102. GOING NOWHERE ... Los Bravos, Press 60003
103. I'M GONNA MISS YOU ... Artistics, Brunswick 55301
104. BACK IN THE SAME OLD BAG AGAIN ... Bobby Bland, Duke 412
105. A CORNER IN THE SUN ... Walter Jackson, Okeh 7260
106. YOUR EVER CHANGIN' MIND ... Crispian St. Peters, Jamie 1328
107. SUNSHINE SUPERMAN ... Willie Bobo, Verve 10448
108. I'LL MAKE IT EASY ... Incredibles, Audio Arts, 60002
109. AM I A LOSER ... Eddie Holman, Parkway 106
110. NASHVILLE CATS ... Lovin' Spoonful, Kama Sutra 219
111. PUSHING TOO HARD ... Seeds, GNP Crescendo 372
112. HI HI HAZEL ... Gary & the Hornets, Smash 2051
113. CRY LIKE A BABY ... Aretha Franklin, Columbia 43827
114. SPANISH NIGHTS AND YOU ... Connie Frances, MGM 13610
115. WACK WACK ... Young Holt Trio, Brunswick 55305
116. OPEN UP THE DOOR LET THE GOOD TIMES IN ... Dean Martin, Reprise 0538
117. JUST ONE SMILE ... Gene Pitney, Musicor 1219
118. YO YO ... Billy Joe Royal, Columbia 43883
119. PAP WAS TOO ... Joe Tex, Dial 4051
120. STEPPIN' STONE ... Monkees, Colgems 1002
121. HARLEM SHUFFLE ... Traits, Scepter 12169
122. SNOOPY VS. THE RED BARON ... Royal Guardsmen, Laurie 3366
123. WISH ME A RAINBOW ... Gunther Kallmann Chorus, Four Corners of the World 138
124. SINCE I DON'T HAVE YOU ... Lou Christie, MGM 13623
125. PEACE OF MIND ... Count Five, Double Shot 106
126. LOOK WHAT YOU'VE DONE ... Pozo Seco Singers, Columbia 43927
127. I'M GONNA MAKE YOU MINE ... Shadows of Knight, Dunwich 141
128. WEDDING BELL BLUES ... Laura Nyro, Verve Folkways 5024
129. I DON'T NEED ANYTHING ... Maxine Brown, Wand 1145
130. I BET'CHA COULDN'T LOVE ME ... Manhattans, Carnival 522
131. I'M GLAD I WAITED ... Players, Minit 32012
132. FORGET ABOUT ME ... Prince Harold, Mercury 72621
133. WHERE COULD I GO ... David Houston, Epic 10102
134. GRISSLEY BEAR ... The Youngbloods, RCA Victor 479015
135. HELLO HELLO ... Sop With Camel, Kama Sutra 217

Compiled from national retail sales and radio station airplay by the Music Popularity Dept. of Record Market Research, Billboard.

# Billboard

For Week Ending December 17, 1966

# HOT 100

★ **STAR performer—Sides registering greatest proportionate upward progress this week.**

Record Industry Association of America seal of certification as million selling single.

| THIS WEEK | 1 Wk. Ago | 2 Wks. Ago | 3 Wks. Ago | TITLE Artist (Producer), Label & Number | Weeks On Chart |
|---|---|---|---|---|---|
| 1 (Billboard Award) | 3 | 1 | 3 | **WINCHESTER CATHEDRAL** — New Vaudeville Band, (Geoff Stephens), Fontana 1562 | 8 |
| 2 | 2 | 5 | 9 | **MELLOW YELLOW** — Donovan, (Mickie Most), Epic 10098 | 6 |
| 3 | 1 | 2 | 2 | **GOOD VIBRATIONS** — Beach Boys (Brian Wilson), Capitol 5676 | 9 |
| 4 | 4 | 4 | 4 | **DEVIL WITH A BLUE DRESS ON & GOOD GOLLY MISS MOLLY** — Mitch Ryder & the Detroit Wheels (Bob Crew), New Voice 817 | 10 |
| 5 | 5 | 3 | 1 | **YOU KEEP ME HANGIN' ON** — Supremes (Holland-Dozier), Motown 1101 | 8 |
| ★6 | 10 | 15 | 42 | **THAT'S LIFE** — Frank Sinatra (Jimmy Bowen), Reprise 0531 | 5 |
| 7 | 8 | 8 | 10 | **BORN FREE** — Roger Williams (Hy Grill), Kapp 767 | 16 |
| ★8 | 44 | — | — | **I'M A BELIEVER** — Monkees (Jeff Barry), Colgems 1002 | 2 |
| ★9 | 16 | 44 | 62 | **SUGAR TOWN** — Nancy Sinatra, (Lee Hazelwood), Reprise 0527 | 5 |
| ★10 | 14 | 23 | 37 | **A PLACE IN THE SUN** — Stevie Wonder, (C. Paul), Tamla 54139 | 6 |
| 11 | 11 | 16 | 26 | **WHISPERS** — Jackie Wilson (Carl Davis), Brunswick 55300 | 9 |
| ★12 | 19 | 32 | 43 | **(I Know) I'M LOSING YOU** — Temptations (N. Whitfield), Grady 7057 | 5 |
| 13 | 6 | 7 | 8 | **LADY GODIVA** — Peter & Gordon (John Burgess), Capitol 5740 | 11 |
| 14 | 9 | 12 | 16 | **I'M READY FOR LOVE** — Martha & the Vandellas, (Holland-Dozier), Gordy 7056 | 8 |
| 15 | 13 | 14 | 17 | **A HAZY SHADE OF WINTER** — Simon & Garfunkel (Bob Johnston), Columbia 43873 | 7 |
| 16 | 17 | 17 | 27 | **I GOT THE FEELIN' "OH NO NO"** — Neil Diamond, (Jeff Barry-Ellie Greenwich), Bang 536 | 6 |
| 17 | 18 | 20 | 36 | **(Come 'Round Here) I'M THE ONE YOU NEED** — Miracles (Holland & Dozier) Tamla 54140 | 7 |
| 18 | 7 | 13 | 13 | **STOP STOP STOP** — Hollies, (Ron Richards), Imperial 66214 | 8 |
| ★19 | 24 | 31 | 45 | **MAME** — Herb Alpert & the Tijuana Brass, (Herb Alpert) A&M 823 | 5 |
| 20 | 21 | 22 | 34 | **IT TEARS ME UP** — Percy Sledge (Marlin Greene-Quin Ivy), Atlantic 2358 | 9 |
| 21 | 12 | 6 | 6 | **I'M YOUR PUPPET** — James & Bobby Purify (Don Schroeder), Bell 648 | 13 |
| 22 | 15 | 9 | 5 | **POOR SIDE OF TOWN** — Johnny Rivers (Lou Adler), Imperial 66205 | 14 |
| ★23 | 31 | 53 | 69 | **SINGLE GIRL** — Sandy Posey, (Chips Moman), MGM 13612 | 5 |
| ★24 | 37 | 47 | 58 | **TALK TALK** — Music Machine, (Maurice Bercov), Original Sound 61 | 6 |
| ★25 | 51 | 78 | — | **TELL IT LIKE IT IS** — Aaron Neville, Parlo 101 | 3 |
| ★26 | 35 | 57 | 100 | **CRY** — Ronnie Dove, (Phil Kahl), Diamond 214 | 4 |
| ★27 | 33 | 56 | 71 | **I NEED SOMEBODY** — ? (Question Mark) & the Mysterians, Cameo 441 | 5 |
| 28 | 28 | 29 | 35 | **KNOCK ON WOOD** — Eddie Floyd (Frod. by Staff), Stax 194 | 15 |
| ★29 | 34 | 52 | 66 | **MUSTANG SALLY** — Wilson Pickett, (Jerry Wexler-Rick Hall), Atlantic 2365 | 4 |
| ★30 | — | — | — | **SNOOPY VS. THE RED BARON** — Royal Guardsmen (Phil Gernhard), Laurie 3366 | 1 |
| 31 | 32 | 42 | 56 | **IT'S ONLY LOVE** — Tommy James & the Shondells, Roulette 4710 | 7 |
| ★32 | 42 | 55 | 73 | **COMING HOME SOLDIER** — Bobby Vinton, (Robert Mersey), Epic 10090 | 5 |
| 33 | 20 | 11 | 12 | **COMING ON STRONG** — Brenda Lee (Owen Bradley), Decca 32018 | 12 |
| 34 | 22 | 27 | 28 | **BUT IT'S ALRIGHT** — J. J. Jackson (Lew Futterman), Calla 119 | 12 |
| ★35 | 66 | 88 | — | **GOOD THING** — Paul Revere & the Raiders, (Terry Melcher), Columbia 43907 | 3 |
| ★36 | 46 | 81 | — | **WORDS OF LOVE** — Mama's & the Papa's (Lou Adler), Dunhill 4037 | 3 |
| 37 | 38 | 48 | 50 | **HELP ME GIRL** — Outsiders, (Roger Karshner), Capitol 5759 | 8 |
| 38 | 23 | 24 | 32 | **HOLY COW** — Lee Dorsey (A. Toussaint-M. Sehorn), Amy 965 | 9 |
| 39 | 43 | 58 | 77 | **PANDORA'S GOLDEN HEEBIE JEEBIES** — Association, (J. Yestar), Valiant 755 | 4 |
| 40 | 26 | 26 | 31 | **THE WHEEL OF HURT** — Margaret Whiting (Arnold Goland), London 101 | 11 |
| ★41 | 60 | 83 | — | **EAST-WEST** — Herman's Hermits, (Mickie Most), MGM 13639 | 3 |
| 42 | 25 | 28 | 33 | **RUN, RUN, LOOK AND SEE** — Brian Hyland (Snuff Garrett), Philips 40405 | 9 |
| 43 | 27 | 10 | 7 | **LAST TRAIN TO CLARKSVILLE** — Monkees (Tommy Boyce & Bobby Hart), Colgems 1001 | 15 |
| 44 | 30 | 19 | 14 | **RAIN ON THE ROOF** — Lovin' Spoonful (Erik Jacobson), Kama Sutra 216 | 10 |
| 45 | 45 | 46 | 57 | **GAMES THAT LOVERS PLAY** — Eddie Fisher, (Al Schmitt), RCA Victor 8956 | 8 |
| ★46 | 58 | 84 | — | **I'VE PASSED THIS WAY BEFORE** — Jimmy Ruffin, (J. Dean & W. Weatherspoon), Soul 35027 | 3 |
| ★47 | 57 | 77 | 99 | **HAPPENINGS TEN YEARS TIME AGO** — Yardbirds, (Simon Napier-Bell), Epic 10094 | 4 |
| 48 | 50 | 67 | 78 | **I FOOLED YOU THIS TIME** — Gene Chandler, (Carl Davis), Checker 1155 | 4 |
| ★49 | 59 | 89 | 91 | **HELP ME GIRL** — Eric Burdon & the Animals (Tom Wilson), MGM 13636 | 4 |
| 50 | 36 | 36 | 46 | **TIME AFTER TIME** — Chris Montez, (Tommy LiPuma-Herb Alpert), A&M 822 | 8 |
| 51 | 56 | 61 | 79 | **I (Who Have Nothing)** — Terry Knight & the Pack (Terry Knight), Lucky 11 230 | 6 |
| 52 | 53 | 60 | 74 | **MONEY (That's What I Want)** — Jr. Walker & the All Stars, (B. Gordy, Jr.-L. Horn) Soul 35026 | 5 |
| ★53 | 63 | 70 | 85 | **THE EGGPLANT THAT ATE CHICAGO** — Dr. West's Medicine Show & Junk Band, (T. Marer), Go Go 100 | 4 |
| 54 | 39 | 37 | 39 | **(When She Needs Good Lovin') SHE COMES TO ME** — Chicago Loop (Bob Crewe & Al Kasha), DynoVoice 226 | 7 |
| ★55 | 69 | 90 | — | **THERE'S GOT TO BE A WORD** — Innocence, (Ripp-Anders-Poncia), Kama Sutra 214 | 3 |
| ★56 | 70 | 85 | — | **TRY A LITTLE TENDERNESS** — Otis Redding (Prod. by Staff), Volt 141 | 3 |
| ★57 | 74 | 74 | 82 | **GHOST RIDERS IN THE SKY** — Baja Marimba Band, (Herb Alpert & Jerry Moss), A&M 824 | 4 |
| ★58 | 92 | — | — | **TELL IT TO THE RAIN** — 4 Seasons (Bob Crewe), Philips 40412 | 2 |
| ★59 | 79 | 82 | — | **GEORGY GIRL** — Seekers, (W. H. Miller), Capitol 5756 | 3 |
| 60 | 55 | 51 | 51 | **A SYMPHONY FOR SUSAN** — Arbors, (Richard Carney), Date 1529 | 10 |
| 61 | 61 | 86 | — | **PLEASE DON'T EVER LEAVE ME** — Cyrkle, (John Simon), Columbia 43871 | 3 |
| ★62 | — | — | — | **STANDING IN THE SHADOWS OF LOVE** — Four Tops (Holland & Dosier), Motown 1102 | 1 |
| ★63 | 80 | — | — | **BLUE AUTUMN** — Bobby Goldsboro (Jack Gold), United Artists 50087 | 2 |
| 64 | 77 | 100 | — | **BAD MISUNDERSTANDING** — Critters, (Ripp-Anders-Poncia), Kapp 793 | 3 |
| 65 | 62 | 62 | 64 | **A DAY IN THE LIFE OF A FOOL** — Jack Jones, (David Kapp), Kapp 781 | 8 |
| ★66 | 81 | — | — | **GOODNIGHT MY LOVE** — Happenings (Tokens), B. T. Puppy 523 | 2 |
| 67 | 64 | 66 | 68 | **PLEASE SAY YOU'RE FOOLING** — Ray Charles (TRC), ABC 10865 | 6 |
| 68 | 73 | 73 | 88 | **YOU CAN BRING ME ALL YOUR HEARTACHES** — Lou Rawls, (David Axelrod), Capitol 5790 | 4 |
| 69 | 68 | 68 | 70 | **THE PROUD ONE** — Frankie Valli (Bob Crewe), Philips 40407 | 6 |
| 70 | 67 | 65 | 67 | **WE GOT A THING THAT'S IN THE GROOVE** — Capitols (Ollie McLaughlin), Karen 1526 | 6 |
| 71 | 83 | 98 | — | **BABY WHAT I MEAN** — Drifters, (Bob Gallo & Tom Dowd), Atlantic 2366 | 3 |
| 72 | 76 | 79 | 80 | **I DON'T NEED NO DOCTOR** — Ray Charles (TRC), ABC 10865 | 4 |
| ★73 | 90 | — | — | **98.6** — Keith (Jerry Ross), Mercury 72639 | 2 |
| ★74 | 89 | — | — | **(We Ain't Got) NOTHIN' YET** — Blues Magoos (Wyld & Polhamus), Mercury 72622 | 2 |
| 75 | 84 | — | — | **THE GIRL THAT STOOD BESIDE ME** — Bobby Darin (Koppleman-Rubin), Atlantic 2367 | 2 |
| 76 | 78 | 80 | 81 | **ALVIN'S BOO-GA-LOO** — Alvin Cash & the Registers, (J. Jones), Mar-V-Lus 6014 | 4 |
| ★77 | — | — | — | **(I'm Not Your) STEPPIN' STONE** — Monkees (Tommy Boyce & Bobby Hart), Colgems 1002 | 1 |
| 78 | 86 | 94 | — | **THERE'S SOMETHING ON YOUR MIND** — Baby Ray, (Scott Turner), Imperial 66216 | 3 |
| 79 | 82 | — | — | **COMMUNICATION BREAKDOWN** — Roy Orbison (Rose & Vienneau), MGM 13634 | 2 |
| 80 | 72 | 75 | 75 | **DON'T ANSWER THE DOOR** — B. B. King (Johnny Pate), ABC 10856 | 9 |
| 81 | 98 | — | — | **I HAD TOO MUCH TO DREAM (Last Night)** — Electric Prunes (Damo Prod.), Reprise 0532 | 2 |
| 82 | 95 | 96 | — | **YOU GOT ME HUMMIN'** — Sam & Dave, (Pro. by Staff), Stax 204 | 3 |
| ★83 | — | — | — | **PAPA WAS TOO** — Joe Tex (Buddy Killen), Dial 4051 | 1 |
| 84 | 93 | 95 | — | **KARATE** — Emperor's, (George Wilson & Phil Gaber), Mala 543 | 3 |
| 85 | 85 | 87 | 90 | **I WANNA MEET YOU** — Cryin' Shames, (Jim Golden), Columbia 43836 | 4 |
| ★86 | — | — | — | **NASHVILLE CATS** — Lovin' Spoonful (Brik Jacobsen), Kama Sutra 219 | 1 |
| ★87 | — | — | — | **WHERE WILL THE WORDS COME FROM** — Gary Lewis & the Playboys (Snuff Garrett), Liberty 5933 | 1 |
| ★88 | — | — | — | **I'M GONNA MISS YOU** — Artistics (Carl Davis), Brunswick 55301 | 1 |
| 89 | 99 | — | — | **IF YOU GO AWAY** — Damite Jo (Bob Morgan-Ted Cooper), Epic 10061 | 2 |
| 90 | 91 | 91 | 95 | **(He's) RAINING IN MY SUNSHINE** — Jay & the Americans, (Bob Feldman), United Artists 50094 | 4 |
| 91 | — | — | — | **WACK WACK** — Young-Holt Trio (Carl Davis), Brunswick 55305 | 1 |
| 92 | 96 | — | — | **QUESTIONS AND ANSWERS** — In Crowd (Snuff Carrett), Viva 604 | 2 |
| 93 | — | — | — | **(Open Up the Door) LET THE GOOD TIMES IN** — Dean Martin (Jimmy Bowen), Reprise 0538 | 1 |
| 94 | — | — | — | **DANCING IN THE STREETS** — Mamas & the Papas (Lou Adler), Dunhill 4057 | 1 |
| 95 | — | — | — | **GRIZZLY BEAR** — Youngbloods (Felix Pappalardi), RCA Victor 9015 | 1 |
| 96 | — | — | — | **GOING NOWHERE** — Los Bravos (Ivor Raymonde), Press 60003 | 1 |
| 97 | 100 | — | — | **PEAK OF LOVE** — Bobby McClure (Billy Davis), Checker 1152 | 2 |
| 98 | — | — | — | **LOOK WHAT YOU'VE DONE** — Pozo Seco Singers (Bob Johnston), Columbia 43927 | 1 |
| 99 | — | — | — | **STAND BY ME** — Spyder Turner (Arnold Geller), MGM 13617 | 1 |
| 100 | — | — | — | **TRY MY LOVE AGAIN** — Bobby Moore's Rhythm Aces (M. Higgins), Checker 1156 | 1 |

## HOT 100—A TO Z—*(Publisher-Licensee)*

Alvin's Boo-Ga-Loo (Vapac, BMI) .......... 76
Baby What I Mean (United Artists, ASCAP) .... 71
Bad Misunderstanding (Kama Sutra, BMI) ...... 64
Blue Autumn (Unart, BMI) .......... 63
Born Free (Screen Gems-Coulmbia, BMI) ........ 7
But It's Alright (Pamelarosa, BMI) .......... 34
(Come 'Round Here) I'm the One You Need (Jobete, BMI) .......... 17
Coming Home Soldier (Feather, BMI) .......... 32
Coming On Strong (Moss-Rose, BMI) .......... 33
Communication Breakdown (Acuff-Rose, BMI) .... 79
Cry (Shapiro-Bernstein, ASCAP) .......... 26
Dancing In The Streets (Jobete, BMI) .......... 94
Day in the Life of a Fool, A (Jungnickel, ASCAP) 65
Devil With a Blue Dress On & Good Golly Miss Molly (Jobete-Vanice, BMI) .......... 4
Don't Answer the Door (Mercedes, BMI) ........ 80
East-West (Man-Ken, BMI) .......... 41
Eggplant That Ate Chicago, The (Borscht, BMI) .. 53
Games That Lovers Play (Miller, ASCAP) ...... 45
Georgy Girl (Chappell, ASCAP) .......... 59
Ghost Riders in the Sky (Morris, ASCAP) ...... 57
Girl That Stood Beside Me, The (Chardon, BMI) .. 75
Going Nowhere (April, ASCAP) .......... 96
Goodnight My Love (Captain Marble, BMI) .... 66
Good Thing (Daywin, BMI) .......... 35
Good Vibrations (Sea of Tunes, BMI) .......... 3
Grizzly Bear (Whitfield, BMI) .......... 95
Happenings Ten Years Time Ago (Yardbirds-Feist, ASCAP) .......... 47
Hazy Shadow of Winter, A (Charing Cross, BMI) .. 15
Help Me, Girl (Bardon) (Helios, BMI) .......... 49
Help Me, Girl (Outsiders) (Helios, BMI) ........ 37
(He's) Raining In My Sunshine (Greenlight, BMI) 90
Holy Cow (Marsaint, BMI) .......... 38
I Don't Need No Doctor (Flomar-Baby Monica, BMI) 72
I Fooled You This Time (Cachand-Jalynee, BMI) .. 48
I Got The Feelin' "Oh No No" (Tallyrand, BMI) .. 16
I Had Too Much To Dream (Last Night) (Star, BMI) 81
(I Know), I'm Losing You (Jobete, BMI) ........ 12
I Wanna Meet You (Destination, BMI) .......... 85
I (Who Have Nothing) (Milky Way-Trio-Catillio, BMI) .......... 51
I Need Somebody (Cameo-Parkway, BMI) ........ 27
If You Go Away (Marks, BMI) .......... 89
I'm a Believer (Screen Gems-Columbia, BMI) .... 8
I'm Gonna Miss You (Jalynne-BRC, BMI) ........ 88
(I'm Not Your) Steppin' Stone (Screen Gems-Columbia, BMI) .......... 77
I'm Ready for Love (Jobete, BMI) .......... 14
I'm Your Puppet (Fame, BMI) .......... 21
I've Passed This Way Before (Jobete, BMI) ...... 46
It Tears Me Up (Fame, BMI) .......... 20
It's Only Love (Tender Tunes, BMI) .......... 31
Karate (Wilson, BMI) .......... 84
Knock on Wood (East, BMI) .......... 28
Lady Godiva (Regent, BMI) .......... 13
Last Train to Clarksville (Screen Gems-Columbia, BMI) .......... 43
Look What You've Done (Pocketful of Fames/Noma, BMI) .......... 98
Mame (Morris, ASCAP) .......... 19
Mellow Yellow (Donovan Ltd., BMI) .......... 2
Mustang Sally (Fourteen Hour, BMI) .......... 29
Money (That's What I Want) (Jobete, BMI) ...... 52
Nashville Cats (Faithful Virtue, BMI) .......... 86
98.6 (Screen Gems-Columbia, BMI) .......... 73
(Open Up the Door) Let the Good Times In (Smooth, BMI) .......... 93
Pandora's Golden Heebie Jeebies (Beachwood, BMI) 39
Papa Was Too (Tree, BMI) .......... 83
Peak Of Love (Chevis, BMI) .......... 97
Place in the Sun, A (Stein-Vanstock, ASCAP) .... 10
Please Don't Ever Leave Me (Chappell, BMI) .... 61
Please Say You're Fooling (Eden, BMI) ........ 67
Poor Side of Town (Rivers, BMI) .......... 22
Proud One, The (Saturday & Season's Four, BMI) 69
Questions And Answers (Arch, ASCAP) ........ 92
Run, Run, Look and See (Little Darlin'-Low Twi,
Rain On The Roof (Faithful Virtue, BMI) ...... 44
BMI) .......... 42
Single Girl (Combine, BMI) .......... 23
Snoopy vs. The Red Baron (Fuller/Samphil/Windsong, BMI) .......... 30
Stand By Me (Progressive/Trio/A.B.T. Tet, BMI) .. 99
Standing In The Shadows Of Love (Jobete, BMI) .. 62
Stop Stop Stop (Maribus, BMI) .......... 18
Sugar Town (Criterion, ASCAP) .......... 9
Symphony for Susan, A (Kris, ASCAP) ........ 60
Talk Talk (Thrush, BMI) .......... 24
Tell It Like It Is (Olrap, BMI) .......... 25
Tell It To The Rain (Saturday/Seasons Four, BMI) 58
That's Life (Four Star Television) .......... 6
There's Got To Be A Word (Kama Sutra, BMI) .. 55
There's Something On Your Mind (Mercedes, BMI) 78
Time After Time (Sands, ASCAP) .......... 50
Try A Little Tenderness (Campbell/Connelly/Robbins, ASCAP) .......... 56
Try My Love Again (Arc, BMI) .......... 100
Wack Wack (Yo Yo, BMI) .......... 91
(We Ain't Got) Nothin' Yet (Anange-Range, BMI) 74
We Got a Thing That's in the Groove (McLaughlin, BMI) .......... 70
Wheel of Hurt, The (Roosevelt, BMI) .......... 40
(When She Needs Good Lovin') She Comes to Me (Tiger, BMI) .......... 54
Where Will The Words Come From (Viva, BMI) .. 87
Whispers (Jalynne-BRC, BMI) .......... 11
Winchester Cathedral (Southern, ASCAP) ........ 1
Words of Love (Trousdale, BMI) .......... 36
You Can Bring Me All Your Heartaches (Raw Lou, BMI) .......... 68
You Got Me Hummin' (Pronto/East, BMI) ...... 82
You Keep Me Hangin' On (Jobete, BMI) ...... 5

## BUBBLING UNDER THE HOT 100

101. GALLANT MEN ............Senator Everett McKinley Dirksen, Capitol 5805
102. SINCE I DON'T HAVE YOU ....................Lou Christie, MGM 13623
103. HELLO HELLO ................The Sopwith "Camel", Kama Sutra 217
104. BACK IN THE SAME OLD BAG AGAIN ............Bobby Bland, Duke 412
105. WEDDING BELL BLUES ................Laura Myro, Verve Folkways 5024
106. GREEN, GREEN GRASS OF HOME ................Tom Jones, Parrot 40009
107. HAVE YOU EVER LOVED SOMEBODY ............The Searchers, Kapp 283
108. I'M GONNA MAKE YOU LOVE ME ........Dee Dee Warwick, Mercury 72638
109. PUSHIN' TOO HARD ....................Seeds, GNP Crescendo 372
110. TINY BUBBLES ....................Don Ho & the Allis, Reprise 0507
111. HI HI HAZEL ....................Gary & the Hornets, Smash 2061
112. SPANISH NIGHTS AND YOU ................Connie Francis, MGM 13610
113. CRY LIKE A BABY ................Aretha Franklin, Columbia 43827
114. FORGET ABOUT ME ....................Prince Harold, Mercury 72621
115. WHERE DID ROBINSON CRUSOE GO WITH FRIDAY ON SATURDAY NIGHT? ....................Ian Whitcomb, Tower 274
116. I'LL BE HOME ....................Platters, Musicor 1211
117. YO-YO ....................Billy Joe Royal, Columbia 43883
118. WISH ME A RAINBOW ....................Gunter Kallmann Chorus, 4 Corners of the World 188
119. ARE YOU LONELY FOR ME ....................Freddie Scott, Shant 207
120. SUNSHINE SUPERMAN ....................Willie Bobo, Verve 10448
121. ANOTHER NIGHT ....................Dionne Warwick, Scepter 12181
122. I'LL MAKE IT EASY (IF YOU'LL COME ON HOME) ....................Incredibles, Amdio Artal 80001
123. KING OF A DRAG ....................Buckingham, U.S.A. 8968
124. ANY WAY THAT YOU WANT ME ........Liverpool Five, RCA Victor 8968
125. THE SHADOW OF YOUR SMILE ..........Boots Randolph, Monument 976
126. I'M GONNA MAKE YOU MINE ........Shadows of Knight, Dunwich 141
127. LET'S FALL IN LOVE ....................Peaches & Herb, Date 1523
128. I BET'CHA (COULDN'T LOVE ME) ............Manhattans, Carnival 522
129. CONSTANT RAIN ..............Sergio Mendes & Brasil '66, A&M 825
130. I'M GLAD I WAITED ....................Players, Minit 32012
131. THE MORE I SEE YOU ..............Groove Holmes, Prestige 45-428
132. I LOVE MY DOG ....................Cat Stevens, Deram 7501
133. MAMA (WHEN MY DOLLIES HAVE BABIES) ..........Cher, Imperial 66223
134. PLAIN JANE ....................B. J. Thomas, Scepter 12179
135. FORTUNE TELLER ....................Hardtimes, Andition 77851

Compiled from national retail sales and radio station airplay by the Music Popularity Dept. of Record Market Research, Billboard.

# Billboard HOT 100

For Week Ending December 24, 1966

★ STAR performer—Sides registering greatest proportionate upward progress this week.

Record Industry Association of America seal of certification as million selling single.

| This Week | Wk. Ago | 2 Wks. Ago | 3 Wks. Ago | TITLE Artist (Producer), Label & Number | Weeks On Chart |
|---|---|---|---|---|---|
| 1 | 1 | 3 | 1 | **WINCHESTER CATHEDRAL** — New Vaudeville Band, (Geoff Stephens), Fontana 1562 | 9 |
| 2 | 2 | 2 | 5 | **MELLOW YELLOW** — Donovan, (Mickie Most), Epic 10098 | 7 |
| 3 | 8 | 44 | — | **I'M A BELIEVER** — Monkees (Jeff Barry), Colgems 1002 | 3 |
| 4 | 6 | 10 | 15 | **THAT'S LIFE** — Frank Sinatra (Jimmy Bowen), Reprise 0531 | 6 |
| 5 | 4 | 4 | 4 | **DEVIL WITH A BLUE DRESS ON & GOOD GOLLY MISS MOLLY** — Mitch Ryder & the Detroit Wheels (Bob Crewe), New Voice 817 | 11 |
| 6 | 9 | 16 | 44 | **SUGAR TOWN** — Nancy Sinatra, (Lee Hazelwood), Reprise 0527 | 6 |
| 7 | 30 | — | — | **SNOOPY VS. THE RED BARON** — Royal Guardsmen (Phil Gernhard), Laurie 3366 | 2 |
| 8 | 3 | 1 | 2 | **GOOD VIBRATIONS** — Beach Boys (Brian Wilson), Capitol 5676 | 10 |
| 9 | 10 | 14 | 23 | **A PLACE IN THE SUN** — Stevie Wonder, (C. Paul), Tamla 54139 | 7 |
| 10 | 12 | 19 | 32 | **(I Know) I'M LOSING YOU** — Temptations, (N. Whitfield), Grady 7057 | 6 |
| 11 | 5 | 5 | 3 | **YOU KEEP ME HANGIN' ON** — Supremes (Holland-Dozier), Motown 1101 | 9 |
| 12 | 7 | 8 | — | **BORN FREE** — Roger Williams (Hy Grill), Kapp 767 | 17 |
| 13 | 11 | 11 | 16 | **WHISPERS** — Jackie Wilson (Carl Davis), Brunswick 55300 | 10 |
| 14 | 25 | 51 | 78 | **TELL IT LIKE IT IS** — Aaron Neville, Parlo 101 | 4 |
| 15 | 13 | 6 | 7 | **LADY GODIVA** — Peter & Gordon (John Burgess), Capitol 5740 | 12 |
| 16 | 16 | 17 | 17 | **I GOT THE FEELIN' "OH NO NO"** — Neil Diamond, (Jeff Barry-Ellie Greenwich), Bang 536 | 7 |
| 17 | 23 | 31 | 53 | **SINGLE GIRL** — Sandy Posey (Chips Moman), MGM 13612 | 6 |
| 18 | 26 | 35 | 57 | **CRY** — Ronnie Dove, (Phil Kahl), Diamond 214 | 5 |
| 19 | 19 | 24 | 31 | **MAME** — Herb Alpert & the Tijuana Brass, (Herb Alpert), A&M 823 | 6 |
| 20 | 32 | 42 | 55 | **COMING HOME SOLDIER** — Bobby Vinton, (Robert Mersey), Epic 10090 | 6 |
| 21 | 24 | 37 | 47 | **TALK TALK** — Music Machine (Brian Ross-API), Original Sound 61 | 7 |
| 22 | 27 | 33 | 56 | **I NEED SOMEBODY** — ? (Question Mark) & the Mysterians, Cameo 441 | 6 |
| 23 | 29 | 34 | 52 | **MUSTANG SALLY** — Wilson Pickett, (Jerry Wexler-Rick Hall), Atlantic 2365 | 5 |
| 24 | 36 | 46 | 81 | **WORDS OF LOVE** — Mama's & the Papa's (Lou Adler), Dunhill 4037 | 4 |
| 25 | 14 | 9 | 12 | **I'M READY FOR LOVE** — Martha & the Vandellas, (Holland-Dozier), Gordy 7056 | 9 |
| 26 | 18 | 7 | 13 | **STOP STOP STOP** — Hollies, (Ron Richards), Imperial 66214 | 9 |
| 27 | 35 | 66 | 88 | **GOOD THING** — Paul Revere & the Raiders, (Terry Melcher), Columbia 43907 | 4 |
| 28 | 15 | 13 | 14 | **A HAZY SHADE OF WINTER** — Simon & Garfunkel (Bob Johnston), Columbia 43873 | 8 |
| 29 | 41 | 60 | 83 | **EAST-WEST** — Herman's Hermits, (Mickie Most), MGM 13639 | 4 |
| 30 | 17 | 18 | 20 | **(Come 'Round Here) I'M THE ONE YOU NEED** — Miracles (Holland & Dozier), Tamla 54140 | 8 |
| 31 | 58 | 92 | — | **TELL IT TO THE RAIN** — 4 Seasons (Bob Crewe), Philips 40412 | 3 |
| 32 | 31 | 32 | 42 | **IT'S ONLY LOVE** — Tommy James & the Shondells, Roulette 4710 | 8 |

| 33 | 46 | 58 | 84 | **I'VE PASSED THIS WAY BEFORE** — Jimmy Ruffin, (J. Dean & W. Weatherspoon), Soul 35027 | 4 |
| 34 | 28 | 28 | 29 | **KNOCK ON WOOD** — Eddie Floyd- (Prod. by Staff), Stax 194 | 16 |
| 35 | 39 | 43 | 58 | **PANDORA'S GOLDEN HEEBIE JEEBIES** — Association, (J. Yester), Valiant 755 | 5 |
| 36 | 21 | 12 | 6 | **I'M YOUR PUPPET** — James & Bobby Purify (Don Schroeder), Bell 648 | 14 |
| 37 | 20 | 21 | 22 | **IT TEARS ME UP** — Percy Sledge (Marlin Greene-Quin Ivy), Atlantic 2358 | 10 |
| 38 | 62 | — | — | **STANDING IN THE SHADOWS OF LOVE** — Four Tops (Holland & Desier), Motown 1102 | 2 |
| 39 | 22 | 15 | 9 | **POOR SIDE OF TOWN** — Johnny Rivers (Lou Adler), Imperial 66205 | 15 |
| 40 | 47 | 57 | 77 | **HAPPENINGS TEN YEARS TIME AGO** — Yardbirds, (Simon Napier-Bell), Epic 10094 | 5 |
| 41 | 49 | 59 | 89 | **HELP ME GIRL** — Eric Burdon & the Animals (Tom Wilson), MGM 13636 | 4 |
| 42 | 34 | 22 | 27 | **BUT IT'S ALRIGHT** — J. J. Jackson (Lew Futterman), Calla 119 | 13 |
| 43 | 37 | 38 | 48 | **HELP ME GIRL** — Outsiders, (Roger Karsimer), Capitol 5759 | 6 |
| 44 | 33 | 20 | 11 | **COMING ON STRONG** — Brenda Lee (Owen Bradley), Decca 32018 | 13 |
| 45 | 86 | — | — | **NASHVILLE CATS** — Lovin' Spoonful (Erik Jacobsen), Kama Sutra 219 | 2 |
| 46 | 56 | 70 | 85 | **TRY A LITTLE TENDERNESS** — Otis Redding (Prod. by Staff), Volt 141 | 4 |
| 47 | 45 | 45 | 46 | **GAMES THAT LOVERS PLAY** — Eddie Fisher, (Al Schmitt), RCA Victor 8956 | 9 |
| 48 | 77 | — | — | **(I'm Not Your) STEPPIN' STONE** — Monkees (Tommy Boyce & Bobby Hart), Colgems | 2 |
| 49 | 48 | 50 | 67 | **I FOOLED YOU THIS TIME** — Gene Chandler, (Carl Davis), Checker 1155 | 5 |
| 50 | 59 | 79 | 82 | **GEORGY GIRL** — Seekers (Jack Gold / Springfield), Capitol 5756 | 4 |
| 51 | 51 | 56 | 61 | **I (Who Have Nothing)** — Terry Knight & the Pack (Terry Knight), Lucky 11 230 | 7 |
| 52 | 57 | 74 | 74 | **GHOST RIDERS IN THE SKY** — Baja Marimba Band, (Herb Alpert & Jerry Moss), A&M 824 | 5 |
| 53 | 53 | 63 | 70 | **THE EGGPLANT THAT ATE CHICAGO** — Dr. West's Medicine Show & Junk Band, (T. Marer), Go Go 100 | 5 |
| 54 | 63 | 80 | — | **BLUE AUTUMN** — Bobby Goldsboro (Jack Gold), United Artists 50087 | 3 |
| 55 | 55 | 69 | 90 | **THERE'S GOT TO BE A WORD** — Innocence, (Ripp-Anders-Poncia), Kama Sutra 214 | 4 |
| 56 | 66 | 81 | — | **GOODNIGHT MY LOVE** — Happenings (Tokens), B. T. Puppy 523 | 3 |
| 57 | 73 | 90 | — | **98.6** — Keith (Jerry Ross), Mercury 72639 | 3 |
| 58 | 64 | 77 | 100 | **BAD MISUNDERSTANDING** — Critters, (Ripp-Anders-Poncia), Kapp 793 | 4 |
| 59 | 61 | 61 | 86 | **PLEASE DON'T EVER LEAVE ME** — Cyrkle, (John Simon), Columbia 43871 | 4 |
| 60 | 74 | 89 | — | **(We Ain't Got) NOTHIN' YET** — Blues Magoos (Wyld & Polhamus), Mercury 72622 | 3 |
| 61 | 87 | — | — | **WHERE WILL THE WORDS COME FROM** — Gary Lewis & the Playboys (Snuff Garrett), Liberty 5933 | 2 |
| 62 | 68 | 73 | 73 | **YOU CAN BRING ME ALL YOUR HEARTACHES** — Lou Rawls, (David Axelrod), Capitol 5790 | 5 |
| 63 | 84 | 93 | 95 | **KARATE** — Emperor's, (George Wilson & Phil Gaber), Mala 543 | 4 |
| 64 | 71 | 83 | 98 | **BABY WHAT I MEAN** — Drifters, (Bob Gallo & Tom Dowd), Atlantic 2366 | 4 |
| 65 | — | — | — | **GALLANT MEN** — Senator Everett McKinley Dirksen (Arch Lustberg), Capitol 5805 | 1 |

| 66 | 75 | 84 | — | **THE GIRL THAT STOOD BESIDE ME** — Bobby Darin (Koppleman-Rubin), Atlantic 2367 | 3 |
| 67 | 52 | 53 | 60 | **MONEY (That's What I Want)** — Jr. Walker & the All Stars, (B. Gordy, Jr.-L. Horn), Soul 35026 | 6 |
| 68 | 81 | 98 | — | **I HAD TOO MUCH TO DREAM (Last Night)** — Electric Prunes (Dave Prod.), Reprise 0532 | 3 |
| 69 | — | — | — | **COLOR MY WORLD** — Petula Clark (Tony Hatch), Warner Bros. 5882 | 1 |
| 70 | 83 | — | — | **PAPA WAS TOO** — Joe Tex (Buddy Killen), Dial 4051 | 2 |
| 71 | 93 | — | — | **(Open Up the Door) LET THE GOOD TIMES IN** — Dean Martin (Jimmy Bowen), Reprise 0528 | 2 |
| 72 | 79 | 82 | — | **COMMUNICATION BREAKDOWN** — Roy Orbison (Rose & Vienneau), MGM 13634 | 3 |
| 73 | 78 | 86 | 94 | **THERE'S SOMETHING ON YOUR MIND** — Baby Ray, (Scott Turner), Imperial 66216 | 4 |
| 74 | 76 | 78 | 80 | **ALVIN'S BOO-GA-LOO** — Alvin Cash & the Registers, (J. Jones), Mar-V-Lus 6014 | 5 |
| 75 | — | — | — | **ANOTHER NIGHT** — Dionne Warwick (Burt Bacharach), Scepter 12181 | 1 |
| 76 | — | — | — | **GREEN, GREEN GRASS OF HOME** — Tom Jones (Peter Sullivan), Parrot 40009 | 1 |
| 77 | 94 | — | — | **DANCING IN THE STREETS** — Mamas & the Papas (Lou Adler), Dunhill 4057 | 2 |
| 78 | — | — | — | **HOW DO YOU CATCH A GIRL** — Sam The Sham & the Pharaohs (Stan Kesler), MGM 13649 | 1 |
| 79 | 98 | — | — | **LOOK WHAT YOU'VE DONE** — Pozo Seco Singers (Bob Johnston), Columbia 43927 | 2 |
| 80 | — | — | — | **DAY TRIPPER** — Ramsey Lewis (E. Edwards), Cadet 5553 | 1 |
| 81 | 91 | — | — | **WACK WACK** — Young-Holt Trio (Carl Davis), Brunswick 55305 | 2 |
| 82 | 99 | — | — | **STAND BY ME** — Spyder Turner (Arnold Geller), MGM 13617 | 2 |
| 83 | 88 | — | — | **I'M GONNA MISS YOU** — Artistics (Carl Davis), Brunswick 55301 | 2 |
| 84 | 89 | 99 | — | **IF YOU GO AWAY** — Damite Jo (Bob Morgan-Ted Cooper), Epic 10061 | 3 |
| 85 | 95 | — | — | **GRIZZLY BEAR** — Youngbloods (Felix Pappalardi), RCA Victor 9015 | 2 |
| 86 | — | — | — | **KNIGHT IN RUSTY ARMOUR** — Peter & Gordon (W. H. Miller), Capitol 5808 | 1 |
| 87 | — | — | — | **IT'S NOW WINTER'S DAY** — Tommy Roe (Our Prod.), ABC 10888 | 1 |
| 88 | — | — | — | **JUST ONE SMILE** — Gene Pitney (Gene Pitney), Musicor 1219 | 1 |
| 89 | — | — | — | **CONSTANT RAIN** — Sergio Mendes & Brasil '66 (Herb Alpert), A&M 825 | 1 |
| 90 | — | — | — | **I'M GONNA MAKE YOU MINE** — Shadows of Knight (Dunwich Prod.), Dunwich 141 | 1 |
| 91 | 96 | — | — | **GOING NOWHERE** — Los Bravos (Ivor Raymonds), Press 60003 | 2 |
| 92 | — | — | — | **LOOK AT GRANNY RUN RUN** — Howard Tate (M. Ragavoy), Verve 10464 | 1 |
| 93 | — | — | — | **ARE YOU LONELY FOR ME** — Freddy Scott (Bert Berns), Shout 207 | 1 |
| 94 | — | — | — | **THE SHADOW OF YOUR SMILE** — Boots Randolph (Fred Foster), Monument 976 | 1 |
| 95 | — | — | — | **PUSHIN' TOO HARD** — Seeds (Marcus Tybalt), GNP Crescendo 372 | 1 |
| 96 | — | — | — | **WISH ME A RAINBOW** — Gunther Kallmann Chorus, 4 Corners of the World 138 | 1 |
| 97 | 100 | — | — | **TRY MY LOVE AGAIN** — Bobby Moore's Rhythm Aces (M. Higgins), Checker 1156 | 2 |
| 98 | — | — | — | **ANY WAY THAT YOU WANT ME** — Liverpool Five (Al Schmitt), RCA Victor 8968 | 1 |
| 99 | — | — | — | **THAT'S THE TUNE** — Vogues (Nick Cenci-Jack Hakin), Co & Co 242 | 1 |
| 100 | — | — | — | **HELLO HELLO** — Sopwith "Camel" (Erik Jacobsen), Kama Sutra 217 | 1 |

## BUBBLING UNDER THE HOT 100

101. I DON'T NEED NO DOCTOR .... Ray Charles, ABC 10865
102. BACK IN THE SAME OLD BAG AGAIN .... Bobby Bland, Duke 412
103. YOU GOT ME HUMMIN' .... Sam & Dave, Stax 204
104. WEDDING BELL BLUES .... Laura Nyro, Verve Folkways 5024
105. I WANNA MEET YOU .... Cryan Shames, Columbia 43836
106. HAVE YOU EVER LOVED SOMEBODY .... Searchers, Kapp 283
107. SINCE I DON'T HAVE YOU .... Lou Christie, MGM 13623
108. I'M GONNA MAKE YOU LOVE ME .... Dee Dee Warwick, Mercury 72606
109. TINY BUBBLES .... Don Ho & The Aliis, Reprise 6507
110. SPANISH NIGHTS & YOU .... Connie Francis, MGM 13610
111. I GOT TO GO BACK .... McCoys, Bang 538
112. (HE'S) RAINING IN MY SUNSHINE Jay & the Americans, United Artists 50094
113. DEAD END STREET .... Kinks, Reprise 0540
114. LOVE ME .... Bobby McClure, Phillips 40421
115. LOVE ME .... Peaches & Herb, Date 1523
116. QUESTIONS AND ANSWERS .... Jon Crowd, Viva 604
117. PRETTY BALLERINA .... Left Banke, Smash 2074
118. LOVE MY LIFE .... Cat Stevens, Dream 7501
119. LETTER FULL OF TEARS .... Drifters, Atlantic 2366
120. I'M GONNA SIT RIGHT DOWN AND WRITE MYSELF A LETTER .... Palm Beach Blues Band Boys, RCA Victor 9026
121. KING OF A DRAG .... Buckinghams, USA 860
122. WALK WITH FAITH IN YOUR HEART .... Bachelors, London 20018
123. FORTUNE TELLER .... Hard Times, World Pacific 77851
124. JAMES DARREN STORY .... Mr. Crier, Capitol 66223
125. IT TAKES TWO .... Marvin Gaye & Kim Weston, Tamla 54141
126. LET'S FALL IN LOVE .... Peaches & Herb, Date 1523
127. HEY LEROY! YOUR MOM IS CALLING .... Jerry Castor, Smash 2069
128. TAKE ME FOR A LITTLE WHILE .... Patti LaBelle & the Bluebelles, Atlantic 2373
129. WILD ANGELS .... Ventures, Dolton 319
130. FULL MEASURE .... Lovin' Spoonful, Kama Sutra 219
131. I CAN'T PLEASE YOU .... Jimmy Robbins, Jeehart 20721
132. CATCH ME IN THE MEADOW .... Tradewinds, Kama Sutra 218
133. PLAIN JANE .... B. J. Thomas, Scepter 12179
134. MY BABY LIKES TO BOOGALOO .... Don Gardner, Tru-Glo-Town 1002
135. SKATE NOW .... Lou Courtney, Riverside 4588

# Billboard

For Week Ending December 31, 1966

# HOT 100

★ STAR performer—Sides registering greatest proportionate upward progress this week.

Record Industry Association of America seal of certification as million selling single.

| This Week | 1 Wk. Ago | 2 Wks. Ago | 3 Wks. Ago | TITLE Artist (Producer), Label & Number | Weeks On Chart |
|---|---|---|---|---|---|
| 1 (Billboard Award) | 3 | 8 | 44 | I'M A BELIEVER — Monkees (Jeff Barry), Colgems 1002 | 4 |
| ★2 | 7 | 30 | — | SNOOPY VS. THE RED BARON — Royal Guardsmen (Phil Gernhard), Laurie 3366 | 3 |
| 3 | 1 | 1 | 3 | WINCHESTER CATHEDRAL — New Vaudeville Band, (Geoff Stephens), Fontana 1562 | 10 |
| 4 | 4 | 6 | 10 | THAT'S LIFE — Frank Sinatra (Jimmy Bowen), Reprise 0531 | 7 |
| 5 | 6 | 9 | 16 | SUGAR TOWN — Nancy Sinatra, (Lee Hazelwood), Reprise 0527 | 7 |
| 6 | 2 | 2 | 2 | MELLOW YELLOW — Donovan, (Mickie Most), Epic 10098 | 8 |
| ★7 | 14 | 25 | 51 | TELL IT LIKE IT IS — Aaron Neville, Parlo 101 | 5 |
| 8 | 10 | 12 | 19 | (I Know) I'M LOSING YOU — Temptations (N. Whitfield), Gordy 7057 | 7 |
| 9 | 9 | 10 | 14 | A PLACE IN THE SUN — Stevie Wonder, (C. Paul), Tamla 54139 | 8 |
| ★10 | 27 | 35 | 66 | GOOD THING — Paul Revere & the Raiders, (Terry Melcher), Columbia 43907 | 5 |
| 11 | 5 | 4 | 4 | DEVIL WITH A BLUE DRESS ON & GOOD GOLLY MISS MOLLY — Mitch Ryder & the Detroit Wheels (Bob Crew), New Voice 817 | 12 |
| ★12 | 17 | 23 | 31 | SINGLE GIRL — Sandy Posey, (Chips Moman), MGM 13612 | 7 |
| 13 | 8 | 3 | 1 | GOOD VIBRATIONS — Beach Boys (Brian Wilson), Capitol 5676 | 11 |
| 14 | 11 | 5 | 5 | YOU KEEP ME HANGIN' ON — Supremes (Holland-Dozier), Motown 1101 | 10 |
| ★15 | 38 | 62 | — | STANDING IN THE SHADOWS OF LOVE — Four Tops (Holland & Dozier), Motown 1102 | 3 |
| ★16 | 21 | 24 | 37 | TALK TALK — Music Machine (Brian Ross-API), Original Sound 61 | 8 |
| 17 | 20 | 32 | 42 | COMING HOME SOLDIER — Bobby Vinton, (Robert Mersey), Epic 10090 | 7 |
| 18 | 18 | 26 | 35 | CRY — Ronnie Dove, (Phil Kahl), Diamond 214 | 6 |
| ★19 | 24 | 36 | 46 | WORDS OF LOVE — Mama's & the Papa's (Lou Adler), Dunhill 4037 | 5 |
| 20 | 12 | 7 | 6 | BORN FREE — Roger Williams (Hy Grill), Kapp 767 | 18 |
| 21 | 13 | 11 | 11 | WHISPERS — Jackie Wilson (Carl Davis), Brunswick 55300 | 11 |
| 22 | 22 | 27 | 33 | I NEED SOMEBODY — ? (Question Mark) & the Mysterians, Cameo 441 | 7 |
| ★23 | 31 | 58 | 92 | TELL IT TO THE RAIN — 4 Seasons (Bob Crewe), Philips 40412 | 4 |
| 24 | 19 | 19 | 24 | MAME — Herb Alpert & the Tijuana Brass, (Herb Alpert) A&M 823 | 7 |
| 25 | 15 | 13 | 6 | LADY GODIVA — Peter & Gordon (John Burgess), Capitol 5740 | 13 |
| 26 | 23 | 29 | 34 | MUSTANG SALLY — Wilson Pickett, (Jerry Wexler-Rick Hall), Atlantic 2365 | 6 |
| 27 | 29 | 41 | 60 | EAST-WEST — Herman's Hermits, (Mickie Most), MGM 13639 | 5 |
| ★28 | 33 | 46 | 58 | I'VE PASSED THIS WAY BEFORE — Jimmy Ruffin, (J. Dean & W. Weatherspoon), Soul 35027 | 5 |
| ★29 | 41 | 49 | 59 | HELP ME GIRL — Eric Burdon & the Animals (Tom Wilson), MGM 13636 | 6 |
| ★30 | 40 | 47 | 57 | HAPPENINGS TEN YEARS TIME AGO — Yardbirds, (Simon Napier-Bell), Epic 10094 | 6 |
| 31 | 16 | 16 | 17 | I GOT THE FEELIN' "OH NO NO" — Neil Diamond, (Jeff Barry-Ellie Greenwich), Bang 536 | 8 |
| ★32 | 48 | 77 | — | (I'm Not Your) STEPPIN' STONE — Monkees (Tommy Boyce & Bobby Hart), Colgems 1002 | 3 |
| ★33 | 45 | 86 | — | NASHVILLE CATS — Lovin' Spoonful (Erik Jacobsen), Kama Sutra 219 | 3 |
| 34 | 30 | 17 | 18 | (Come 'Round Here) I'M THE ONE YOU NEED — Miracles (Holland & Dozier) Tamla 54140 | 9 |
| 35 | 35 | 39 | 43 | PANDORA'S GOLDEN HEEBIE JEEBIES — Association, (J. Yestar), Valiant 755 | 6 |
| ★36 | 46 | 56 | 70 | TRY A LITTLE TENDERNESS — Otis Redding (Prod. by Staff), Volt 141 | 5 |
| ★37 | 50 | 59 | 79 | GEORGY GIRL — Seekers (Tom Springfield), Capitol 5756 | 5 |
| ★38 | 69 | — | — | COLOR MY WORLD — Petula Clark (Tony Hatch), Warner Bros. 5882 | 2 |
| 39 | 32 | 31 | 32 | IT'S ONLY LOVE — Tommy James & the Shondells, Roulette 4710 | 9 |
| 40 | 37 | 20 | 21 | IT TEARS ME UP — Percy Sledge (Marlin Greene-Quin Ivy), Atlantic 2358 | 11 |
| ★41 | 60 | 74 | 89 | (We Ain't Got) NOTHIN' YET — Blues Magoos (Wyld & Polhamus), Mercury 72622 | 4 |
| ★42 | 55 | 55 | 69 | THERE'S GOT TO BE A WORD — Innocence, (Ripp-Anders-Poncia), Kama Sutra 214 | 5 |
| ★43 | 65 | — | — | GALLANT MEN — Senator Everett McKinley Dirksen (Arch Lustberg), Capitol 5805 | 2 |
| ★44 | 54 | 63 | 80 | BLUE AUTUMN — Bobby Goldsboro (Jack Gold), United Artists 50087 | 4 |
| 45 | 25 | 14 | 9 | I'M READY FOR LOVE — Martha & the Vandellas, (Holland-Dozier), Gordy 7056 | 10 |
| 46 | 28 | 15 | 13 | A HAZY SHADE OF WINTER — Simon & Garfunkel (Bob Johnston), Columbia 43873 | 9 |
| ★47 | 57 | 73 | 90 | 98.6 — Keith (Jerry Ross), Mercury 72639 | 4 |
| 48 | 51 | 51 | 56 | I (Who Have Nothing) — Terry Knight & the Pack (Terry Knight), Lucky 11 230 | 8 |
| 49 | 49 | 48 | 50 | I FOOLED YOU THIS TIME — Gene Chandler, (Carl Davis), Checker 1155 | 6 |
| 50 | 26 | 18 | 7 | STOP STOP STOP — Hollies, (Ron Richards), Imperial 66214 | 10 |
| ★51 | 61 | 87 | — | WHERE WILL THE WORDS COME FROM — Gary Lewis & the Playboys (Snuff Garrett), Liberty 5933 | 3 |
| 52 | 53 | 53 | 63 | THE EGGPLANT THAT ATE CHICAGO — Dr. West's Medicine Show & Junk Band, (T. Marer), Go Go 100 | 6 |
| 53 | 34 | 28 | 28 | KNOCK ON WOOD — Eddie Floyd (Prod. by Staff), Stax 194 | 17 |
| ★54 | 68 | 81 | 98 | I HAD TOO MUCH TO DREAM (Last Night) — Electric Prunes (Damo Prod.), Reprise 0532 | 4 |
| 55 | 58 | 64 | 77 | BAD MISUNDERSTANDING — Critters, (Ripp-Anders-Poncia), Kapp 793 | 5 |
| 56 | 56 | 66 | 81 | GOODNIGHT MY LOVE — Happenings (Tokens), B. T. Puppy 523 | 4 |
| 57 | 52 | 57 | 74 | GHOST RIDERS IN THE SKY — Baja Marimba Band, (Herb Alpert & Jerry Moss), A&M 824 | 6 |
| ★58 | 82 | 99 | — | STAND BY ME — Spyder Turner (Arnold Geller), MGM 13617 | 3 |
| ★59 | 70 | 83 | — | PAPA WAS TOO — Joe Tex (Buddy Killen), Dial 4051 | 3 |
| 60 | 62 | 68 | 73 | YOU CAN BRING ME ALL YOUR HEARTACHES — Lou Rawls, (David Axelrod), Capitol 5790 | 6 |
| ★61 | 78 | — | — | HOW DO YOU CATCH A GIRL — Sam The Sham & the Pharaohs (Stan Kesler), MGM 13649 | 2 |
| 62 | 64 | 71 | 83 | BABY WHAT I MEAN — Drifters, (Bob Gallo & Tom Dowd), Atlantic 2366 | 5 |
| 63 | 63 | 84 | 93 | KARATE — Emperor's, (George Wilson & Phil Gaber), Mala 543 | 5 |
| ★64 | 79 | 98 | — | LOOK WHAT YOU'VE DONE — Pozo Seco Singers (Bob Johnston), Columbia 43927 | 3 |
| 65 | 43 | 37 | 38 | HELP ME GIRL — Outsiders, (Roger Karshner), Capitol 5759 | 10 |
| 66 | 66 | 75 | 84 | THE GAL THAT STOOD BESIDE ME — Bobby Darin (Koppleman-Rubin), Atlantic 2367 | 4 |
| 67 | 71 | 93 | — | (Open Up the Door) LET THE GOOD TIMES IN — Dean Martin (Jimmy Bowen), Reprise 0538 | 3 |
| 68 | 81 | 91 | — | WACK WACK — Young-Holt Trio (Carl Davis), Brunswick 55305 | 3 |
| 69 | 73 | 78 | 86 | THERE'S SOMETHING ON YOUR MIND — Baby Ray, (Scott Turner), Imperial 66216 | 5 |
| ★70 | 85 | 95 | — | GRIZZLY BEAR — Youngbloods (Felix Pappalardi), RCA Victor 9015 | 3 |
| ★71 | 86 | — | — | KNIGHT IN RUSTY ARMOUR — Peter & Gordon (W. H. Miller), Capitol 5808 | 2 |
| 72 | 72 | 79 | 82 | COMMUNICATION BREAKDOWN — Roy Orbison (Rose & Vienneau), MGM 13634 | 4 |
| 73 | 75 | — | — | ANOTHER NIGHT — Dionne Warwick (Burt Bacharach), Scepter 12181 | 2 |
| 74 | 76 | — | — | GREEN, GREEN GRASS OF HOME — Tom Jones (Peter Sullivan), Parrot 40009 | 2 |
| 75 | 88 | — | — | JUST ONE SMILE — Gene Pitney (Gene Pitney), Musicor 1219 | 2 |
| 76 | 74 | 76 | 78 | ALVIN'S BOO-GA-LOO — Alvin Cash & the Registers, (J. Jones), Mar-V-Lus 6014 | 6 |
| 77 | 77 | 94 | — | DANCING IN THE STREETS — Mamas & the Papas (Lou Adler), Dunhill 4057 | 3 |
| 78 | 80 | — | — | DAY TRIPPER — Ramsey Lewis (E. Edwards), Cadet 5553 | 2 |
| 79 | 84 | 89 | 99 | IF YOU GO AWAY — Damita Jo (Bob Morgan-Ted Cooper), Epic 10061 | 4 |
| 80 | 83 | 88 | — | I'M GONNA MISS YOU — Artistics (Carl Davis), Brunswick 55301 | 3 |
| ★81 | 96 | — | — | WISH ME A RAINBOW — Gunther Kallmann Chorus, 4 Corners of the World 138 | 2 |
| 82 | 59 | 61 | 61 | PLEASE DON'T EVER LEAVE ME — Cyrkle, (John Simon), Columbia 43871 | 5 |
| 83 | 89 | — | — | CONSTANT RAIN — Sergio Mendes & Brasil '66 (Herb Alpert), A&M 825 | 2 |
| 84 | 87 | — | — | IT'S NOW WINTER'S DAY — Tommy Roe (Our Prod.), ABC 10888 | 2 |
| 85 | 95 | — | — | PUSHIN' TOO HARD — Seeds (Marcus Tybalt), GNP Crescendo 372 | 2 |
| 86 | — | — | — | MUSIC TO WATCH GIRLS BY — Bob Crewe Generation (Bob Crewe), DynoVoice 229 | 1 |
| 87 | 92 | — | — | LOOK AT GRANNY RUN RUN — Howard Tate (M. Ragavoy), Verve 10464 | 2 |
| 88 | 93 | — | — | ARE YOU LONELY FOR ME — Freddy Scott (Bert Berns), Shout 207 | 2 |
| 89 | — | — | — | I DIG GIRLS — J. J. Jackson (Lem Futterman), Calla 125 | 1 |
| ★90 | — | — | — | KIND OF A DRAG — Buckinghams (Carl Bonafede & Dan Bellock), U.S.A. 860 | 1 |
| 91 | 100 | — | — | HELLO HELLO — Sopwith "Camel" (Erik Jacobsen), Kama Sutra 217 | 2 |
| 92 | — | — | — | LET'S FALL IN LOVE — Peaches & Herb (Kapralik-McCoy), Date 1523 | 1 |
| 93 | — | — | — | TAKE ME FOR A LITTLE WHILE — Patti LaBelle & the Bluebelles (Bob Gallo & Tom Dowd), Atlantic 2373 | 1 |
| 94 | 94 | — | — | THE SHADOW OF YOUR SMILE — Boots Randolph (Fred Foster), Monument 976 | 2 |
| 95 | — | — | — | HEY, LEROY, YOUR MAMA'S CALLING YOU — Jimmy Castor (Johnny Brantly), Smash 2069 | 1 |
| 96 | — | — | — | LOVE ME — Bobby Hebb (Jerry Ross), Philips 40421 | 1 |
| 97 | — | 82 | 95 | YOU GOT ME HUMMIN' — Sam & Dave (Prod. by Staff), Stax 204 | 4 |
| 98 | — | — | 87 | TINY BUBBLES — Don Ho & Allis (Burke), Reprise 0507 | 4 |
| 99 | — | — | — | FORTUNE TELLER — Hardtimes (Richard Bock), World-Pacific 77851 | 1 |
| 100 | — | — | — | GIMME SOME LOVIN' — Spencer Davis Group (Chris Blackwell & Jimmy Miller), United Artists 50108 | 1 |

## HOT 100—A TO Z—(Publisher-Licensee)


Alvin's Boo-Ga-Loo (Vapac, BMI) 76
Another Night (Blue Seas/Jac, ASCAP) 73
Are You Lonely For Me (Web IV, BMI) 88
Baby What I Mean (United Artists, ASCAP) 62
Bad Misunderstanding (Kama Sutra, BMI) 55
Blue Autumn (Unart, BMI) 44
Born Free (Screen Gems-Columbia, BMI) 20
Color My World (Northern, ASCAP) 38
(Come 'Round Here) I'm the One You Need (Jobete, BMI) 34
Coming Home Soldier (Feather, BMI) 17
Communication Breakdown (Acuff-Rose, BMI) 72
Constant Rain (Peer Int'l, BMI) 83
Cry (Shapiro-Bernstein, ASCAP) 18
Dancing In The Streets, (Jobete, BMI) 77
Day Tripper (Maclen, BMI) 78
Devil With a Blue Dress On & Good Golly Miss Molly (Jobete-Venice, BMI) 11
East-West (Man-Ken, BMI) 27
Eggplant That Ate Chicago, The (Borscht, BMI) 52
Fortune Teller (Minit, BMI) 99
Gallant Men (Chappell, ASCAP) 43
Georgy Girl (Chappell, ASCAP) 37
Ghost Riders in the Sky (Morris, ASCAP) 57
Gimme Some Lovin' (Essex, ASCAP) 100
Girl That Stood Beside Me, The (Chardon, BMI) 66
Goodnight My Love (Captain Marble, BMI) 56
Good Thing (Daywin, BMI) 10
Good Vibrations (Sea of Tunes, BMI) 13
Green, Green Grass Of Home (Tree, BMI) 74
Grizzly Bear (Whitfield, BMI) 70
Happenings Ten Years Time Ago (Yardbirds-Feist, ASCAP) 30
Hazy Shadow of Winter, A (Charing Cross, BMI) 46
Hello Hello (Great Honesty, BMI) 91
Help Me, Girl (Burdon) (Helios, BMI) 29
Help Me, Girl (Outsiders) (Helios, BMI) 65
Hey, Leroy, Your Mama's Callin' You (Bozart, BMI) 95
How Do You Catch A Girl (Rose, BMI) 61
I Dig Girls (Meager, BMI) 89
I Fooled You This Time (Cachand-Jalynne, BMI) 49
I Got The Feelin' "Oh No No" (Tallyrand, BMI) 31
I Had Too Much To Dream (Last Night) (Star, BMI) 54
(I Know) I'm Losing You (Jobete, BMI) 8
I (Who Have Nothing) (Milky Way-Trio-Catillio, BMI) 48
I Need Somebody (Cameo-Parkway, BMI) 22
I'm a Believer (Screen Gems-Columbia, BMI) 1
I'm Gonna Miss You (Jalynne-BRC, BMI) 80
(I'm Not Your) Steppin' Stone (Screen Gems-Columbia, BMI) 32
I'm Ready for Love (Jobete, BMI) 45
If You Go Away (Marks, BMI) 79
It Tears Me Up (Fame, BMI) 40
It's Now Winter's Day (Low Twi, BMI) 84
It's Only Love (Tender Tunes, BMI) 39
I've Passed This Way Before (Jobete, BMI) 28
Just One Smile (January, BMI) 75
Karate (Wilson, BMI) 63
Kind of a Drag (Maryon, ASCAP) 90
Knight In Rusty Armour (Barricade, ASCAP) 71
Knock on Wood (East, BMI) 53
Lady Godiva (Regent, BMI) 25
Let's Fall In Love (Bourne, ASCAP) 92
Look At Granny Run Run (Ragmar/Rumbalero, BMI) 87
Look What You've Done (Pocketful of Fames/Noma, BMI) 64
Love Me (Act Three-Downstairs, BMI) 96
Mame (Morris, ASCAP) 24
Mellow Yellow (Donovan Ltd., BMI) 6
Music To Watch Girls By (SCP, ASCAP) 86
Mustang Sally (Fourteen Hour, BMI) 26
Nashville Cats (Faithful Virtue, BMI) 33
98.6 (Screen Gems-Columbia, BMI) 47
(Open Up the Door) Let the Good Times In (Smooth, BMI) 67
Pandora's Golden Heebie Jeebies (Beachwood, BMI) 35
Papa Was Too (Tree, BMI) 59
Place in the Sun, A (Stein-Vanstock, ASCAP) 9
Please Don't Ever Leave Me (Chappell, BMI) 82
Pushin' Too Hard (Neil-Seeds, BMI) 85
Shadow Of Your Smile, The (Miller, ASCAP) 94
Single Girl (Combine, BMI) 12
Snoopy vs. The Red Baron (Fuller/Samphil/Windsong, BMI) 2
Stand By Me (Progressive/Trio/A.B.T. Tet, BMI) 58
Standing In The Shadows Of Love (Jobete, BMI) 15
Stop Stop Stop (Maribus, BMI) 50
Sugar Town (Criterion, ASCAP) 5
Take Me for a Little While (Lollipop, BMI) 93
Talk Talk (Thrush, BMI) 16
Tell It Like It Is (Olrap, BMI) 7
Tell It To The Rain (Saturday/Seasons Four, BMI) 23
That's Life (Four Star Television) 4
There's Got To Be A Word (Kama Sutra, BMI) 42
There's Something On Your Mind (Mercedes, BMI) 69
Tiny Bubbles (Granite, ASCAP) 98
Try A Little Tenderness (Campbell/Connelly/Robbins, ASCAP) 36
Wack Wack (Yo Yo, BMI) 68
(We Ain't Got) Nothin' Yet (Anange-Range, BMI) 41
Where Will The Words Come From (Viva, BMI) 51
Whispers (Jalynne-BRC, BMI) 21
Winchester Cathedral (Southern, ASCAP) 3
Wish Me A Rainbow (Famous, ASCAP) 81
Words of Love (Trousdale, BMI) 19
You Can Bring Me All Your Heartaches (Raw Lou, BMI) 60
You Got Me Hummin' (Pronto-East, BMI) 97
You Keep Me Hangin' On (Jobete, BMI) 14


## BUBBLING UNDER THE HOT 100

101. FULL MEASURE ... Lovin' Spoonful, Kama Sutra 219
102. SMASHED! BLOCKED! ... John's Children, White Whale 239
103. I WANNA MEET YOU ... Cryan Shames, Columbia 43836
104. WEDDING BELL BLUES ... Laura Nyro, Verve Folkways 5024
105. THAT'S THE TUNE ... The Vogues, Co & Ce 242
106. I'VE GOT TO HAVE A REASON ... Dave Clark Five, Epic 10114
107. DEAD END STREET ... Kinks, Reprise 0540
108. BACK IN THE SAME OLD BAG AGAIN ... Bobby Bland, Duke 412
109. TRY MY LOVE AGAIN ... Bobby Moore's Rhythm Aces, Checker 1156
110. I GOT TO GO BACK ... McCoys, Bang 538
111. PEAK OF LOVE ... Bobby McClure, Checker 1152
112. QUESTIONS AND ANSWERS ... In Crowd, Viva 604
113. PRETTY BALLERINA ... Left Banke, Smash 2074
114. SPANISH NIGHTS AND YOU ... Connie Francis, MGM 13610
115. ANY WAY THAT YOU WANT ME ... Liverpool Five, RCA Victor 8968
116. LITTLE BLACK EGG ... Nightcrawlers, Kapp 709
117. I'M GONNA SIT RIGHT DOWN AND WRITE MYSELF A LETTER ... Palm Beach Band Boys, RCA Victor 9026
118. I'M YOUR BREAD MAKER, BABY ... Slim Harpo, Excello 2282
119. ALL ... James Darren, Warner Bros. 5874
120. WALK WITH FAITH IN YOUR HEART ... Bachelors, London 20018
121. IT TAKES TWO ... Marvin Gaye & Kim Weston, Tamla 54141
122. BEND IT ... Dave Dee, Dozy, Beaky, Mick, Tich, Fontana 1559
123. AT THE PARTY ... Hector Rivera, Barry 1011
124. WALK TALL ... 2 Of Clubs, Fraternity 975
125. SWEETEST ONE ... Metros, RCA Victor 8994
126. HARD LOVIN' LOSER ... Judy Collins, Elektra 45610
127. OH YEAH ... Joe Cuba Sextet, Tico 490
128. I'M GONNA MAKE YOU MINE ... Shadows of Night, Dunwich 141
129. PLAIN JANE ... B. J. Thomas, Scepter 12179
130. MY BABY LIKES TO BOOGALOO ... Don Gardner, Tru-Glo-Town, 1002
131. A GOOD LOVE ... Lorraine Ellison, Warner Bros. 5879
132. THE CHILDREN OF ST. MONICA ... Don Grady, Canterbury 501
133. SOUL SISTER ... Four Gents, HBR 509
134. SKATE NOW ... Lou Courtney, Riverside 4588
135. LOSERS CATHEDRAL ... David Houston, Epic 10102

Compiled from national retail sales and radio station airplay by the Music Popularity Dept. of Record Market Research, Billboard.

# Billboard HOT 100

**For Week Ending January 7, 1967**

★ STAR performer—Sides registering greatest proportionate upward progress this week.

Record Industry Association of America seal of certification as million selling single.

| This Week | Wk. Ago | 2 Wks. Ago | 3 Wks. Ago | TITLE — Artist (Producer), Label & Number | Weeks On Chart |
|---|---|---|---|---|---|
| 1 | 3 | 8 | — | **I'M A BELIEVER** — Monkees (Jeff Barry), Colgems 1002 | 5 |
| 2 | 2 | 7 | 30 | **SNOOPY VS. THE RED BARON** — Royal Guardsmen (Phil Gernhard), Laurie 3366 | 4 |
| 3 | 7 | 14 | 25 | **TELL IT LIKE IT IS** — Aaron Neville, Parlo 101 | 6 |
| 4 | 3 | 1 | 1 | **WINCHESTER CATHEDRAL** — New Vaudeville Band, (Geoff Stephens), Fontana 1562 | 11 |
| 5 | 5 | 6 | 9 | **SUGAR TOWN** — Nancy Sinatra, (Lee Hazelwood), Reprise 0527 | 8 |
| 6 | 4 | 4 | 6 | **THAT'S LIFE** — Frank Sinatra (Jimmy Bowen), Reprise 0531 | 8 |
| 7 | 10 | 27 | 35 | **GOOD THING** — Paul Revere & the Raiders (Terry Melcher), Columbia 43907 | 6 |
| 8 | 19 | 24 | 36 | **WORDS OF LOVE** — Mamas & the Papa's (Lou Adler), Dunhill 4037 | 6 |
| 9 | 15 | 38 | 62 | **STANDING IN THE SHADOWS OF LOVE** — Four Tops (Holland & Dozier), Motown 1102 | 4 |
| 10 | 6 | 2 | 2 | **MELLOW YELLOW** — Donovan (Mickie Most), Epic 10098 | 9 |
| 11 | 17 | 20 | 32 | **COMING HOME SOLDIER** — Bobby Vinton (Robert Mersey), Epic 10090 | 8 |
| 12 | 12 | 17 | 23 | **SINGLE GIRL** — Sandy Posey (Chips Moman), MGM 13612 | 8 |
| 13 | 8 | 10 | 12 | **(I Know) I'M LOSING YOU** — Temptations (N. Whitfield), Gordy 7057 | 8 |
| 14 | 11 | 5 | 4 | **DEVIL WITH A BLUE DRESS ON & GOOD GOLLY MISS MOLLY** — Mitch Ryder & the Detroit Wheels (Bob Crewe), New Voice 817 | 13 |
| 15 | 23 | 31 | 58 | **TELL IT TO THE RAIN** — 4 Seasons (Bob Crewe), Philips 40412 | 5 |
| 16 | 16 | 21 | 24 | **TALK TALK** — Music Machine (Brian Ross-API), Original Sound 61 | 9 |
| 17 | 13 | 8 | 3 | **GOOD VIBRATIONS** — Beach Boys (Brian Wilson), Capitol 5676 | 12 |
| 18 | 18 | 18 | 26 | **CRY** — Ronnie Dove (Phil Kahl), Diamond 214 | 7 |
| 19 | 9 | 9 | 10 | **A PLACE IN THE SUN** — Stevie Wonder, (C. Paul), Tamla 54139 | 9 |
| 20 | 37 | 50 | 59 | **GEORGY GIRL** — Seekers (Tom Springfield), Capitol 5756 | 6 |
| 21 | 14 | 11 | 5 | **YOU KEEP ME HANGIN' ON** — Supremes (Holland-Dozier), Motown 1101 | 11 |
| 22 | 20 | 12 | 7 | **BORN FREE** — Roger Williams (Hy Grill), Kapp 767 | 19 |
| 23 | 28 | 33 | 46 | **I'VE PASSED THIS WAY BEFORE** — Jimmy Ruffin, (J. Dean & W. Weatherspoon), Soul 35027 | 6 |
| 24 | 33 | 45 | 86 | **NASHVILLE CATS** — Lovin' Spoonful (Erik Jacobsen), Kama Sutra 219 | 4 |
| 25 | 22 | 22 | 27 | **I NEED SOMEBODY** — ? (Question Mark) & the Mysterians, Cameo 441 | 8 |
| 26 | 26 | 23 | 29 | **MUSTANG SALLY** — Wilson Pickett, (Jerry Wexler-Rick Hall), Atlantic 2365 | 7 |
| 27 | 27 | 29 | 41 | **EAST-WEST** — Herman's Hermits, (Mickie Most), MGM 13639 | 7 |
| 28 | 38 | 69 | — | **COLOR MY WORLD** — Petula Clark (Tony Hatch), Warner Bros. 5882 | 3 |
| 29 | 29 | 41 | 49 | **HELP ME GIRL** — Eric Burdon and the Animals (Tom Wilson), MGM 13636 | 6 |
| 30 | 30 | 40 | 47 | **HAPPENINGS TEN YEARS TIME AGO** — Yardbirds, (Simon Napier-Bell), Epic 10094 | 7 |
| 31 | 41 | 60 | 74 | **(We Ain't Got) NOTHIN' YET** — Blues Magoos (Wyld & Polhamus), Mercury 72622 | 5 |
| 32 | 32 | 48 | 77 | **(I'm Not Your) STEPPIN' STONE** — Monkees (Tommy Boyce & Bobby Hart), Colgems 1002 | 4 |
| 33 | 43 | 65 | — | **GALLANT MEN** — Senator Everett McKinley Dirksen (Arch Lustberg), Capitol 5805 | 3 |
| 34 | 36 | 46 | 56 | **TRY A LITTLE TENDERNESS** — Otis Redding (Prod. by Staff), Volt 141 | 6 |
| 35 | 25 | 15 | 13 | **LADY GODIVA** — Peter & Gordon (John Burgess), Capitol 5740 | 14 |
| 36 | 42 | 55 | 55 | **THERE'S GOT TO BE A WORD** — Innocence, (Ripp-Anders-Poncia), Kama Sutra 214 | 6 |
| 37 | 47 | 57 | 73 | **98.6** — Keith (Jerry Ross), Mercury 72639 | 5 |
| 38 | 21 | 13 | 11 | **WHISPERS** — Jackie Wilson (Carl Davis), Brunswick 55300 | 12 |
| 39 | 51 | 61 | 87 | **WHERE WILL THE WORDS COME FROM** — Gary Lewis & the Playboys (Snuff Garrett), Liberty 5933 | 4 |
| 40 | 24 | 19 | 19 | **MAME** — Herb Alpert & the Tijuana Brass, (Herb Alpert) A&M 823 | 8 |
| 41 | 71 | 86 | — | **KNIGHT IN RUSTY ARMOUR** — Peter & Gordon (W. H. Miller), Capitol 5808 | 3 |
| 42 | 44 | 54 | 63 | **BLUE AUTUMN** — Bobby Goldsboro (Jack Gold), United Artists 50087 | 5 |
| 43 | 58 | 82 | 99 | **STAND BY ME** — Spyder Turner (Arnold Geller), MGM 13617 | 4 |
| 44 | 35 | 35 | 39 | **PANDORA'S GOLDEN HEEBIE JEEBIES** — Association, (J. Yester), Valiant 755 | 7 |
| 45 | 49 | 49 | 48 | **I FOOLED YOU THIS TIME** — Gene Chandler, (Carl Davis), Checker 1155 | 7 |
| 46 | 48 | 51 | 51 | **I (Who Have Nothing)** — Terry Knight and the Pack (Terry Knight), Lucky 11 230 | 9 |
| 47 | 54 | 68 | 81 | **I HAD TOO MUCH TO DREAM (Last Night)** — Electric Prunes (Damo Prod.), Reprise 0532 | 5 |
| 48 | 64 | 79 | 98 | **LOOK WHAT YOU'VE DONE** — Pozo Seco Singers (Bob Johnston), Columbia 43927 | 4 |
| 49 | 59 | 70 | 83 | **PAPA WAS TOO** — Joe Tex (Buddy Killen), Dial 4051 | 4 |
| 50 | 61 | 78 | — | **HOW DO YOU CATCH A GIRL** — Sam The Sham & the Pharaohs (Stan Kesler), MGM 13649 | 3 |
| 51 | 74 | 76 | — | **GREEN, GREEN GRASS OF HOME** — Tom Jones (Peter Sullivan), Parrot 40009 | 3 |
| 52 | 56 | 56 | 66 | **GOODNIGHT MY LOVE** — Happenings (Tokens), B. T. Puppy 522 | 5 |
| 53 | 68 | 81 | 91 | **WACK WACK** — Young-Holt Trio (Carl Davis), Brunswick 55305 | 4 |
| 54 | 52 | 53 | 53 | **THE EGGPLANT THAT ATE CHICAGO** — Dr. West's Medicine Show & Junk Band, (T. Marer), Go Go 100 | 7 |
| 55 | 60 | 62 | 68 | **YOU CAN BRING ME ALL YOUR HEARTACHES** — Lou Rawls, (David Axelrod), Capitol 5790 | 7 |
| 56 | 55 | 58 | 64 | **BAD MISUNDERSTANDING** — Critters, (Ripp-Anders-Poncia), Kapp 792 | 6 |
| 57 | 63 | 63 | 84 | **KARATE** — Emperor's, (George Wilson & Phil Gaber), Mala 543 | 6 |
| 58 | 86 | — | — | **MUSIC TO WATCH GIRLS BY** — Bob Crewe Generation (Bob Crewe), DynoVoice 229 | 2 |
| 59 | 73 | 75 | — | **ANOTHER NIGHT** — Dionne Warwick (Burt Bacharach), Scepter 12181 | 3 |
| 60 | 72 | 72 | 79 | **COMMUNICATION BREAKDOWN** — Roy Orbison (Ross & Vienneau), MGM 13634 | 5 |
| 61 | 70 | 85 | 95 | **GRIZZLY BEAR** — Youngbloods (Felix Pappalardi), RCA Victor 9015 | 4 |
| 62 | 62 | 64 | 71 | **BABY WHAT I MEAN** — Drifters, (Bob Gallo & Tom Dowd), Atlantic 2366 | 6 |
| 63 | 67 | 71 | 93 | **(Open Up the Door) LET THE GOOD TIMES IN** — Dean Martin (Jimmy Bowen), Reprise 0528 | 4 |
| 64 | 84 | 87 | — | **IT'S NOW WINTER'S DAY** — Tommy Roe (Our Prod.), ABC 10888 | 3 |
| 65 | 91 | 100 | — | **HELLO HELLO** — Sopwith "Camel" (Erik Jacobsen), Kama Sutra 217 | 3 |
| 66 | 90 | — | — | **KIND OF A DRAG** — Buckinghams (Carl Bonafede & Dan Bellock), U.S.A. 860 | 2 |
| 67 | 95 | — | — | **HEY, LEROY, YOUR MAMA'S CALLING YOU** — Jimmy Castor (Johnny Brantly), Smash 2069 | 2 |
| 68 | 66 | 66 | 75 | **THE GIRL THAT STOOD BESIDE ME** — Bobby Darin (Koppleman-Rubin), Atlantic 2367 | 6 |
| 69 | 69 | 73 | 78 | **THERE'S SOMETHING ON YOUR MIND** — Baby Ray, (Scott Turner), Imperial 66216 | 6 |
| 70 | 75 | 88 | — | **JUST ONE SMILE** — Gene Pitney (Gene Pitney & Stanley Kahan), Musicor 1219 | 3 |
| 71 | 80 | 83 | 88 | **I'M GONNA MISS YOU** — Artistics (Carl Davis), Brunswick 55301 | 4 |
| 72 | 81 | 96 | — | **WISH ME A RAINBOW** — Gunther Kallmann Chorus, 4 Corners of the World 138 | 3 |
| 73 | 79 | 84 | 89 | **IF YOU GO AWAY** — Damite Jo (Bob Morgan-Ted Cooper), Epic 10061 | 5 |
| 74 | 78 | 80 | — | **DAY TRIPPER** — Ramsey Lewis (E. Edwards), Cadet 5553 | 3 |
| 75 | 77 | 77 | 94 | **DANCING IN THE STREETS** — Mamas & the Papas (Lou Adler), Dunhill 4057 | 3 |
| 76 | 85 | 95 | — | **PUSHIN' TOO HARD** — Seeds (Marcus Tybalt), GNP Crescendo 372 | 3 |
| 77 | — | — | — | **WILD THING** — Senator Bobby (C & D Prod.), Parkway 127 | 1 |
| 78 | — | — | — | **BRING IT UP** — James Brown & The Famous Flames (James Brown), King 6071 | 1 |
| 79 | 88 | 93 | — | **ARE YOU LONELY FOR ME** — Freddy Scott (Bert Berns), Shout 207 | 3 |
| 80 | 100 | — | — | **GIMME SOME LOVIN'** — Spencer Davis Group (Chris Blackwell & Jimmy Miller), United Artists 50108 | 2 |
| 81 | 83 | 89 | — | **CONSTANT RAIN** — Sergio Mendes & Brasil '66 (Herb Alpert), A&M 825 | 3 |
| 82 | — | — | — | **MERCY, MERCY, MERCY** — "Cannonball" Adderley (David Axelrod), Capitol 5798 | 1 |
| 83 | 89 | — | — | **I DIG GIRLS** — J. J. Jackson (Lem Futterman), Calla 125 | 2 |
| 84 | — | — | — | **I'VE GOT TO HAVE A REASON** — Dave Clark Five (Dave Clark), Epic 10114 | 1 |
| 85 | — | — | — | **OH YEAH!** — Joe Cuba Sextet (Pancho Cristal), Tico 490 | 1 |
| 86 | 97 | 82 | — | **YOU GOT ME HUMMIN'** — Sam & Dave (Prod. by Staff), Stax 204 | 5 |
| 87 | 87 | 92 | — | **LOOK AT GRANNY RUN RUN** — Howard Tate (M. Ragavoy), Verve 10464 | 3 |
| 88 | — | — | — | **IT TAKES TWO** — Marvin Gaye & Kim Weston (Wm. Stevenson-H. Cosby), Tamla 54141 | 1 |
| 89 | 93 | — | — | **TAKE ME FOR A LITTLE WHILE** — Patti LaBelle & the Bluebelles (Bob Gallo & Tom Dowd), Atlantic 2373 | 2 |
| 90 | 92 | — | — | **LET'S FALL IN LOVE** — Peaches & Herb (Kapralik-McCoy), Date 1523 | 2 |
| 91 | — | — | — | **I GOT TO GO BACK** — McCoys (Berns & Barry Prod.), Bang 538 | 1 |
| 92 | 96 | — | — | **LOVE ME** — Bobby Hebb (Jerry Ross), Philips 40421 | 2 |
| 93 | 94 | 94 | — | **THE SHADOW OF YOUR SMILE** — Boots Randolph (Fred Foster), Monument 976 | 3 |
| 94 | — | — | — | **WALK WITH FAITH IN YOUR HEART** — Bachelors (Dick Rowe), London 20018 | 1 |
| 95 | 98 | — | — | **TINY BUBBLES** — Don Ho & Allis (Burke), Reprise 0507 | 2 |
| 96 | — | — | — | **PRETTY BALLERINA** — Left Banke (Harry Lookofsky), Smash 2074 | 1 |
| 97 | 99 | — | — | **FORTUNE TELLER** — Hardtimes (Richard Bock), World-Pacific 77851 | 2 |
| 98 | — | — | — | **DEADEND STREET** — Kinks (Shel Talmy), Reprise 0540 | 1 |
| 99 | — | — | — | **FULL MEASURE** — Lovin' Spoonful (Erik Jacobsen), Kama Sutra 219 | 1 |
| 100 | — | — | — | **THERE GOES MY EVERYTHING** — Jack Greene, Decca 32023 | 1 |

## BUBBLING UNDER THE HOT 100

101. I WANNA MEET YOU — Cryan Shames, Columbia 43836
102. SMASHED! BLOCKED! — John's Children, White Whale 239
103. WEDDING BELL BLUES — Laura Nyro, Verve-Folkways 5024
104. ALL — James Darren, Warner Bros. 5875
105. THAT'S THE TUNE — Vogues, Co & Ce 242
106. TRAMP — Lowell Fulson, Kent 456
107. PEAK OF LOVE — Bobby McClure, Checker 1152
108. I WISH YOU COULD BE HERE — Cyrkle, Columbia 43965
109. SWEETEST ONE — Metros, RCA Victor 8994
110. SKATE NOW — Lou Courtney, Riverside 4588
111. OUR WINTER LOVE — Lettermen, Capitol 5813
112. IT MAY BE WINTER OUTSIDE — Felice Taylor, Mustang 3024
113. THERE GOES MY EVERYTHING — Don Cherry, Monument 989
114. LITTLE BLACK EGG — Nightcrawlers, Kapp 709
115. THEME FROM "THE WILD ANGELS" — Ventures, Dolton 327
116. I'M YOUR BREAD MAKER, BABY — Slim Harpo, Excello 2282
117. DANGER! SHE'S A STRANGER — Meteor Rivera, Barry 1011
118. AT THE PARTY — Al Hirt, RCA Victor 9060
119. MUSIC TO WATCH GIRLS BY — Mike Sharpe, Liberty 55922
120. SPOOKY — Mike Sharpe, Liberty 55922
121. WE CAN MAKE IT IF WE TRY — RCA Victor 9004
122. BEND IT — Dave Dee, Dozy, Beaky, Mick & Tick, Fontana 1559
123. THE SWEET SOUNDS OF SUMMER — Shangri-Las, Mercury 72645
124. HERE COMES MY BABY — Perry Como, RCA Victor 0618
125. HURT-Y SUNDOWN — Peter, Paul & Mary, Warner Bros. 5882
126. I'M GONNA MAKE YOU MINE — Shadows of Knight, Dunwich 141
127. SIT DOWN, I THINK I LOVE YOU — Mojo Men, Reprise 0539
128. I'LL TAKE CARE OF YOUR CARES — Frankie Laine, ABC 10891
129. THEN YOU CAN TELL ME GOODBYE — Casinos, Fraternity 977
130. BY BABY LIKES TO BOOGALOO — Don Gardner, Tru-Glo-Town 501
131. HARD LOVIN' LOSER — Judy Collins, Elektra 45610
132. I'VE LOST MY HEART AGAIN — Jerry Vale, Columbia 43895

For Week Ending January 14, 1967

# Billboard HOT 100

★ **STAR performer**—Sides registering greatest proportionate upward progress this week.

(seal) Record Industry Association of America seal of certification as million selling single.

| THIS WEEK | 1 Wk. Ago | 2 Wks. Ago | 3 Wks. Ago | TITLE Artist (Producer), Label & Number | Weeks On Chart |
|---|---|---|---|---|---|
| 1 (Billboard Award) | 1 | 1 | 3 | I'M A BELIEVER — Monkees (Jeff Barry), Colgems 1002 (seal) | 6 |
| 2 | 2 | 2 | 7 | SNOOPY VS. THE RED BARON — Royal Guardsmen (Phil Gernhard), Laurie 3366 | 5 |
| 3 | 3 | 7 | 14 | TELL IT LIKE IT IS — Aaron Neville, Parlo 101 | 7 |
| ★4 | 7 | 10 | 27 | GOOD THING — Paul Revere & the Raiders, (Terry Melcher), Columbia 43907 | 7 |
| 5 | 5 | 5 | 6 | SUGAR TOWN — Nancy Sinatra, (Lee Hazelwood), Reprise 0527 | 9 |
| 6 | 8 | 19 | 24 | WORDS OF LOVE — Mama's & the Papa's (Lou Adler), Dunhill 4037 | 7 |
| 7 | 9 | 15 | 38 | STANDING IN THE SHADOWS OF LOVE — Four Tops (Holland & Dosier), Motown 1102 | 5 |
| 8 | 4 | 3 | 1 | WINCHESTER CATHEDRAL — New Vaudeville Band, (Geoff Stephens), Fontana 1562 (seal) | 12 |
| 9 | 6 | 4 | 4 | THAT'S LIFE — Frank Sinatra (Jimmy Bowen), Reprise 0531 | 9 |
| ★10 | 20 | 37 | 50 | GEORGY GIRL — Seekers (Tom Springfield), Capitol 5756 | 7 |
| 11 | 11 | 17 | 20 | COMING HOME SOLDIER — Bobby Vinton, (Robert Mersey), Epic 10090 | 9 |
| 12 | 15 | 23 | 31 | TELL IT TO THE RAIN — 4 Seasons (Bob Crewe), Philips 40412 | 6 |
| 13 | 10 | 6 | 2 | MELLOW YELLOW — Donovan, (Mickie Most), Epic 10098 | 10 |
| 14 | 12 | 12 | 17 | SINGLE GIRL — Sandy Posey, (Chips Moman), MGM 13612 | 9 |
| 15 | 16 | 16 | 21 | TALK TALK — Music Machine (Brian Ross-API), Original Sound 61 | 10 |
| ★16 | 24 | 33 | 45 | NASHVILLE CATS — Lovin' Spoonful (Brik Jacobsen), Kama Sutra 219 | 5 |
| 17 | 14 | 11 | 5 | DEVIL WITH A BLUE DRESS ON & GOOD GOLLY MISS MOLLY — Mitch Ryder & the Detroit Wheels (Bob Crew), New Voice 817 | 14 |
| ★18 | 23 | 28 | 33 | I'E PASSED THIS WAY BEFORE — Jimmy Ruffin, (J. Dean & W. Weatherspoon), Soul 35027 | 7 |
| 19 | 13 | 8 | 10 | (I Know) I'M LOSING YOU — Temptations (N. Whitfield), Gordy 7057 | 9 |
| 20 | 32 | 32 | 48 | (I'm Not Your) STEPPIN' STONE — Monkees (Tommy Boyce & Bobby Hart), Colgems 1002 | 5 |
| 21 | 17 | 13 | 8 | GOOD VIBRATIONS — Beach Boys (Brian Wilson), Capitol 5676 (seal) | 13 |
| 22 | 18 | 18 | 18 | CRY — Ronnie Dove, (Phil Kahl), Diamond 214 | 8 |
| ★23 | 28 | 38 | 69 | COLOR MY WORLD — Petula Clark (Tony Hatch), Warner Bros. 5882 | 4 |
| ★24 | 31 | 41 | 60 | (We Ain't Got) NOTHIN' YET — Blues Magoos (Wyld & Polhemus), Mercury 72622 | 6 |
| ★25 | 37 | 47 | 57 | 98.6 — Keith (Jerry Ress), Mercury 72639 | 6 |
| ★26 | 43 | 58 | 82 | STAND BY ME — Spyder Turner (Arnold Geller), MGM 13617 | 5 |
| 27 | 27 | 27 | 29 | EAST-WEST — Herman's Hermits, (Mickie Most), MGM 13639 | 7 |
| ★28 | 39 | 51 | 61 | WHERE WILL THE WORDS COME FROM — Gary Lewis & the Playboys (Snuff Garrett), Liberty 5933 | 5 |
| ★29 | 34 | 36 | 46 | TRY A LITTLE TENDERNESS — Otis Reding (Prod. by Staff), Volt 141 | 7 |
| 30 | 33 | 43 | 65 | GALLANT MEN — Senator Everett McKinley Dirksen (Arch Lustberg), | 4 |
| ★31 | 41 | 71 | 86 | KNIGHT IN RUSTY ARMOUR — Peter & Gordon (W. H. Miller), Capitol 5808 | 4 |
| 32 | 26 | 26 | 23 | MUSTANG SALLY — Wilson Pickett, (Jerry Wexler-Rick Hall), Atlantic 2365 | 8 |
| 33 | 19 | 9 | 9 | A PLACE IN THE SUN — Stevie Wonder, (C. Paul), Tamla 54139 | 10 |
| 34 | 36 | 42 | 55 | THERE'S GOT TO BE A WORD — Innocence, (Ripp-Anders-Poncia), Kama Sutra 214 | 7 |
| 35 | 29 | 29 | 41 | HELP ME GIRL — Eric Burdon & the Animals (Tom Wilson), MGM 13636 | 8 |
| 36 | 25 | 22 | 22 | I NEED SOMEBODY — ? (Question Mark) & the Mysterians, Cameo 441 | 9 |
| 37 | 42 | 44 | 54 | BLUE AUTUMN — Bobby Goldsboro (Jack Gold), United Artists 50087 | 6 |
| 38 | 30 | 30 | 40 | HAPPENINGS TEN YEARS TIME AGO — Yardbirds, (Simon Napier-Bell), Epic 10094 | 8 |
| 39 | 22 | 20 | 12 | BORN FREE — Roger Williams (Hy Grill), Kapp 767 | 20 |
| 40 | 48 | 64 | 79 | LOOK WHAT YOU'VE DONE — Pozo Seco Singers (Bob Johnston), Columbia 43927 | 5 |
| ★41 | 51 | 74 | 76 | GREEN, GREEN GRASS OF HOME — Tom Jones (Peter Sullivan), Parrot 40009 | 4 |
| ★42 | 66 | 90 | — | KIND OF A DRAG — Buckinghams (Carl Bonafede & Dan Bellock), U.S.A. 860 | 3 |
| 43 | 50 | 61 | 78 | HOW DO YOU CATCH A GIRL — Sam The Sham & the Pharaohs (Stan Kesler), MGM 13649 | 4 |
| 44 | 47 | 54 | 68 | I HAD TOO MUCH TO DREAM (Last Night) — Electric Prunes (Damo Prod.), Reprise 0532 | 6 |
| 45 | 45 | 49 | 49 | I FOOLED YOU THIS TIME — Gene Chandler, (Carl Davis), Checker 1155 | 8 |
| 46 | 53 | 68 | 81 | WACK WACK — Young-Holt Trio (Carl Davis), Brunswick 55305 | 5 |
| ★47 | 58 | 86 | — | MUSIC TO WATCH GIRLS BY — Bob Crewe Generation (Bob Crewe), DynoVoice 229 | 3 |
| 48 | 49 | 59 | 70 | PAPA WAS TOO — Joe Tex (Buddy Killen), Dial 4051 | 5 |
| ★49 | 59 | 73 | 75 | ANOTHER NIGHT — Dionne Warwick (Burt Bacharach), Scepter 12181 | 4 |
| 50 | 21 | 14 | 11 | YOU KEEP ME HANGIN' ON — Supremes (Holland-Dozier), Motown 1101 | 12 |
| 51 | 52 | 56 | 56 | GOODNIGHT MY LOVE — Happenings (Tokens), B. T. Puppy 523 | 6 |
| ★52 | 77 | — | — | WILD THING — Senator Bobby (C & D Prod.), Parkway 127 | 2 |
| ★53 | 64 | 84 | 87 | IT'S NOW WINTER'S DAY — Tommy Roe (Our Prod.), ABC 10888 | 4 |
| 54 | 46 | 48 | 51 | I (Who Have Nothing) — Terry Knight & the Pack (Terry Knight), Lucky 11 230 | 10 |
| 55 | 63 | 67 | 71 | (Open Up the Door) LET THE GOOD TIMES IN — Dean Martin (Jimmy Bowen), Reprise 0538 | 5 |
| 56 | 61 | 70 | 85 | GRIZZLY BEAR — Youngbloods (Felix Pappalardi), RCA Victor 9015 | 5 |
| 57 | 57 | 63 | 63 | KARATE — Emperor's, (George Wilson & Phil Gaber), Mala 543 | 7 |
| 58 | 65 | 91 | 100 | HELLO HELLO — Sopwith "Camel" (Erik Jacobsen), Kama Sutra 217 | 4 |
| ★59 | 78 | — | — | BRING IT UP — James Brown & The Famous Flames (James Brown), King 6071 | 2 |
| 60 | 60 | 72 | 72 | COMMUNICATION BREAKDOWN — Roy Orbison (Rose & Vienneau), MGM 13634 | 6 |
| 61 | 55 | 60 | 62 | YOU CAN BRING ME ALL YOUR HEARTACHES — Lou Rawls, (David Axelrod), Capitol 5790 | 8 |
| 62 | 71 | 80 | 83 | I'M GONNA MISS YOU — Artistics (Carl Davis), Brunswick 55301 | 5 |
| ★63 | 80 | 100 | — | GIMME SOME LOVIN' — Spencer Davis Group (Chris Blackwell & Jimmy Miller), United Artists 50108 | 3 |
| 64 | 67 | 95 | — | HEY, LEROY, YOUR MAMA'S CALLING YOU — Jimmy Castor (Johnny Brantly), Smash 2069 | 3 |
| 65 | 76 | 85 | 95 | PUSHIN' TOO HARD — Seeds (Marcus Tybalt), GNP Crescendo 372 | 4 |
| 66 | 72 | 81 | 96 | WISH ME A RAINBOW — Gunther Kallmann Chorus, 4 Corners of the World 138 | 4 |
| ★67 | 82 | — | — | MERCY, MERCY, MERCY — "Cannonball" Adderley (David Axelrod), Capitol 5798 | 2 |
| ★68 | 88 | — | — | IT TAKES TWO — Marvin Gaye & Kim Weston (Wm. Stevenson-H. Cosby), Tamla 54141 | 2 |
| 69 | 79 | 88 | 93 | ARE YOU LONELY FOR ME — Freddy Scott (Bert Berns), Shout 207 | 4 |
| 70 | 70 | 75 | 88 | JUST ONE SMILE — Gene Pitney (Gene Pitney & Stanley Kahan), Musicor 1219 | 4 |
| 71 | 62 | 62 | 64 | BABY WHAT I MEAN — Drifters, (Bob Gallo & Tom Dowd), Atlantic 2366 | 7 |
| ★72 | — | — | — | THE BEAT GOES ON — Sonny & Cher (Sonny Bono), Atco 6461 | 1 |
| 73 | 75 | 77 | 77 | DANCING IN THE STREETS — Mamas & the Papas (Lou Adler), Dunhill 4057 | 5 |
| 74 | 74 | 78 | 80 | DAY TRIPPER — Ramsey Lewis (E. Edwards), Cadet 5553 | 4 |
| 75 | 73 | 79 | 84 | IF YOU GO AWAY — Damite Jo (Bob Morgan-Ted Cooper), Epic 10061 | 6 |
| 76 | 84 | — | — | I'VE GOT TO HAVE A REASON — Dave Clark Five (Dave Clark), Epic 10114 | 2 |
| 77 | 86 | 97 | — | YOU GOT ME HUMMIN' — Sam & Dave (Prod. by Staff), Stax 204 | 6 |
| 78 | 81 | 83 | 89 | CONSTANT RAIN — Sergio Mendes & Brasil-'66 (Herb Alpert), A&M 825 | 4 |
| ★79 | — | — | — | TRAMP — Lowell Fulsom, Kent 456 | 1 |
| 80 | 87 | 87 | 92 | LOOK AT GRANNY RUN RUN — Howard Tate (M. Ragavoy), Verve 10464 | 4 |
| ★81 | 96 | — | — | PRETTY BALLERINA — Left Banke (World United Prod.), Smash 2074 | 2 |
| 82 | 85 | — | — | OH YEAH! — Joe Cuba Sextet (Pancho Cristal), Tico 490 | 2 |
| 83 | 83 | 89 | — | I DIG GIRLS — J. J. Jackson (Lem Futterman), Calla 125 | 3 |
| 84 | 92 | 96 | — | LOVE ME — Bobby Hebb (Jerry Ross), Philips 40421 | 3 |
| 85 | 98 | — | — | DEADEND STREET — Kinks (Shel Talmy), Reprise 0540 | 2 |
| ★86 | — | — | — | LOVIN' YOU — Bobby Darin (Charles Koppelman & Don Rubin), Atlantic 2376 | 1 |
| ★87 | — | — | — | RIDE, RIDE, RIDE — Brenda Lee (Owen Bradley), Decca 32079 | 1 |
| 88 | 91 | — | — | I GOT TO GO BACK — McCoys (Berns & Barry Prod.), Bang 538 | 2 |
| 89 | 99 | — | — | FULL MEASURE — Lovin' Spoonful (Erik Jacobsen), Kama Sutra 219 | 2 |
| 90 | 95 | 98 | — | TINY BUBBLES — Don Ho & Allis (Burke), Reprise 0507 | 6 |
| 91 | — | — | — | IT MAY BE WINTER OUTSIDE — Felice Taylor (Keene-White Prod.), Mustang 3024 | 1 |
| 92 | 100 | — | — | THERE GOES MY EVERYTHING — Jack Greene, Decca 32023 | 2 |
| 93 | 94 | — | — | WALK WITH FAITH IN YOUR HEART — Bachelors (Dick Rowe), London 20018 | 2 |
| 94 | — | — | — | THEN YOU CAN TELL ME GOODBYE — Casinos (Gene Hughes), Fraternity 977 | 1 |
| 95 | — | — | — | GO WHERE YOU WANNA GO — 5th Dimension (Johnny Rivers & Marc Gordon), Soul City 753 | 1 |
| 96 | — | — | — | SWEETEST ONE — Metros (Pied Piper Prod.), RCA Victor 8994 | 1 |
| 97 | — | — | — | DANGER! SHE'S A STRANGER — Five Stairsteps (Curtis Mayfiled), Windy C 604 | 1 |
| 98 | — | — | — | 96 TEARS — Big Maybelle (Taylor-Gallo Prod.), Rojac 112 | 1 |
| 99 | — | — | — | SOMETHING GOOD — Carla Thomas (Prod. by Satff), Stax 207 | 1 |
| 100 | — | — | — | ALL — James Darren (Dick Glasser), Warner Bros., 5874 | 1 |

## HOT 100—A TO Z—*(Publisher-Licensee)*

| | |
|---|---|
| All (Marks, BMI) | 100 |
| Another Night (Blue Seas/Jac, ASCAP) | 49 |
| Are You Lonely For Me (Web IV, BMI) | 69 |
| Baby What I Mean (United Artists, ASCAP) | 71 |
| Beat Goes On, The (Chris Marc/Cotillion, BMI) | 72 |
| Blue Autumn (Unart, BMI) | 37 |
| Born Free (Screen Gems-Columbia, BMI) | 39 |
| Bring It Up (Dynatone, BMI) | 59 |
| Color My World (Northern, ASCAP) | 23 |
| Coming Home Soldier (Feather, BMI) | 11 |
| Communication Breakdown (Acuff-Rose, BMI) | 60 |
| Constant Rain (Peer Int'l, BMI) | 78 |
| Cry (Shapiro-Bernstein, ASCAP) | 22 |
| Dancing In The Streets (Jobete, BMI) | 73 |
| Danger! She's A Stranger (Camad, BMI) | 97 |
| Day Tripper (Maclen, BMI) | 74 |
| Deadend Street (Mondvies/Noma, BMI) | 85 |
| Devil With a Blue Dress On & Good Golly Miss Molly (Jobete-Venice, BMI) | 17 |
| East-West (Man-Ken, BMI) | 27 |
| Full Measure (Faithful Virtue, BMI) | 89 |
| Gallant Men (Chappell, ASCAP) | 30 |
| Georgy Girl (Chappell, ASCAP) | 10 |
| Gimme Some Lovin' (Essex, ASCAP) | 63 |
| Go Where You Wanna Go (Trousdale, BMI) | 95 |
| Goodnight My Love (Captain Marble, BMI) | 51 |
| Good Thing (Daywin, BMI) | 4 |
| Good Vibrations (Sea of Tunes, BMI) | 21 |
| Green, Green Grass Of Home (Tree, BMI) | 41 |
| Grizzly Bear (Whitfield, BMI) | 56 |
| Happenings Ten Years Time Ago (Yardbirds-Feist, ASCAP) | 38 |
| Hello Hello (Great Honesty, BMI) | 58 |
| Help Me, Girl (Burdon) (Helios, BMI) | 35 |
| Hey, Leroy, Your Mama's Callin' You (Bozart, BMI) | 64 |
| How Do You Catch A Girl (Rose, BMI) | 43 |
| I Dig Girls (Meager, BMI) | 83 |
| I Fooled You This Time (Cachand-Jalynne, BMI) | 45 |
| I Got To Go Back (Web IV/Trio, BMI) | 88 |
| I Had Too Much To Dream (Last Night) (Star, BMI) | 44 |
| (I Know) I'm Losing You (Jobete, BMI) | 19 |
| I Need Somebody (Cameo-Parkway, BMI) | 36 |
| I (Who Have Nothing) (Milky Way-Trio-Catillio, BMI) | 54 |
| I'm a Believer (Screen Gems-Columbia, BMI) | 1 |
| I'm Gonna Miss You (Jalynne-BRC, BMI) | 62 |
| (I'm Not Your) Steppin' Stone (Screen Gems-Columbia, BMI) | 20 |
| I've Got To Have A Reason (Branston, BMI) | 76 |
| I've Passed This Way Before (Jobete, BMI) | 18 |
| If You Go Away (Marks, BMI) | 75 |
| It May Be Winter Outside (Maravilla, BMI) | 91 |
| It Takes Two (Jobete, BMI) | 68 |
| It's Now Winter's Day (Low Twi, BMI) | 53 |
| Just One Smile (January, BMI) | 70 |
| Karate (Wilson, BMI) | 57 |
| Kind of a Drag (Maryon, ASCAP) | 42 |
| Knight In Rusty Armour (Dean Street/Feist, ASCAP) | 31 |
| Look At Granny Run Run (Ragmar/Rumbalero, BMI) | 80 |
| Look What You've Done (Pocketful of Fames/Noma, BMI) | 40 |
| Love Me (Act Three-Downstairs, BMI) | 84 |
| Lovin' You (Faithful Virtue, BMI) | 86 |
| Mellow Yellow (Donovan Ltd., BMI) | 13 |
| Mercy, Mrecy, Mercy (Zawinul, BMI) | 67 |
| Music To Watch Girls By (SCP, ASCAP) | 47 |
| Mustang Sally (Fourteen Hour, BMI) | 32 |
| Nashville Cats (Faithful Virtue, BMI) | 16 |
| 98.6 (Screen Gems-Columbia, BMI) | 25 |
| 96 Tears (Arguello, BMI) | 98 |
| (Open Up the Door) Let the Good Times In (Smooth, BMI) | 55 |
| Oh Yeah! (Cordon, BMI) | 82 |
| Papa Was Too (Tree, BMI) | 48 |
| Place in the Sun, A (Stein-Vanstock, ASCAP) | 33 |
| Pretty Ballerina (Last Day, BMI) | 81 |
| Pushin' Too Hard (Neil-Seeds, BMI) | 65 |
| Ride, Ride, Ride (Yonah, BMI) | 87 |
| Single Girl (Combine, BMI) | 14 |
| Snoopy vs. The Red Baron (Fuller/Samphil/Windsong, BMI) | 2 |
| Something Good (East, BMI) | 99 |
| Stand By Me (Progressive/Trio/A.B.T. Tet, BMI) | 26 |
| Standing In The Shadows Of Love (Jobete, BMI) | 7 |
| Sugar Town (Criterion, ASCAP) | 5 |
| Sweetest One (Polaris-Millbridge, BMI) | 96 |
| Talk Talk (Thrush, BMI) | 15 |
| Tell It Like It Is (Olrap, BMI) | 3 |
| Tell It To The Rain (Saturday/Seasons Four, BMI) | 12 |
| That's Life (Four Star Television) | 9 |
| Then You Can Tell Me Goodbye (Acuff-Rose, BMI) | 94 |
| There Goes My Everything (Blue Crest-Husky, BMI) | 92 |
| There's Got To Be A Word (Kama Sutra, BMI) | 34 |
| Tiny Bubbles (Granite, ASCAP) | 90 |
| Tramp (Modern, BMI) | 79 |
| Try A Little Tenderness (Campbell/Connelly/Robbins, ASCAP) | 29 |
| Wack Wack (McLaughlin/Yo Ho, BMI) | 46 |
| Walk With Faith In Your Heart ,Tee Pee, ASCAP) | 93 |
| (We Ain't Got) Nothin' Yet (Anange-Range, BMI) | 24 |
| Where Will The Words Come From (Viva, BMI) | 28 |
| Wild Thing (Blackwood, BMI) | 52 |
| Winchester Cathedral (Southern, ASCAP) | 8 |
| Wish Me A Rainbow (Famous, ASCAP) | 66 |
| Words of Love (Trousdale, BMI) | 6 |
| You Can Bring Me All Your Heartaches (Raw Lou, BMI) | 61 |
| You Got Me Hummin' (Pronto-East, BMI) | 77 |
| You Keep Me Hangin' On (Jobete, BMI) | 50 |

## BUBBLING UNDER THE HOT 100

101. LITTLE BLACK EGG ..... Nightcrawlers, Kapp 709
102. SMASHED! BLOCKED! ..... John's Children, White Whale 239
103. I WISH YOU COUD BE HERE ..... Cyrkle, Columbia 43965
104. OUR WINTER LOVE ..... Lettermen, Capitol 5813
105. THAT'S THE TUNE ..... Vogues, Co & Ce 242
106. OOH BABY ..... Bo Diddley, Checker 1158
107. THE SHADOW OF YOUR SMILE ..... Boots Randolph, Monument 976
108. TAKE ME FOR A LITTLE WHILE ..... Patti LaBelle and the Bluebelles, Atlantic 2373
109. SKATE NOW ..... Lou Courtney, Riverside 4588
110. BEND IT ..... Dave Dee, Dozy, Beaky, Mick and Tich, Fontana 1559
111. LET'S FALL IN LOVE ..... Peaches & Herb, Date 1523
112. WEDDING BELL BLUES ..... Laura Nyro, Verve Folkways 5024
113. AT THE PARTY ..... Hector Rivera, Barry 1011
114. WAITIN' ON YOU ..... B. B. King, ABC 10889
115. FOR WHAT IT'S WORTH ..... Buffalo Springfield, Atco 6459
116. I'LL TAKE CARE OF YOUR CARES ..... Frankie Laine, ABC 10891
117. HARD LOVIN' LOSER ..... Judy Collins, Elektra 45610
118. SPOOKY ..... Mike Sharpe, Liberty 55922
119. GRITS 'N CORNBREAD ..... Soul Runners, MoSoul 101
120. MY SPECIAL PRAYER ..... Joe Simon, Sound Stage 7, 2577
121. NIKI HOEKY ..... P. J. Proby, Liberty 55936
122. SIT DOWN, I THINK I LOVE YOU ..... Mojo Men, Reprise 0539
123. THE SWEET SOUNDS OF SUMMER ..... Shangri-Las, Mercury 72645
124. HURRY SUNDOWN ..... Peter, Paul & Mary, Warner Bros. 5883
125. TWO WAYS TO SKIN A CAT ..... Jimmy Reed, ABC 10887
126. MY BABY LIKES TO BOOGALOO ..... Don Gardner, Tru-Glo-Town 501
127. LOVE YOU SO MUCH ..... New Colony Six, Sencar 1205

Compiled from national retail sales and radio station airplay by the Music Popularity Dept. of Record Market Research, Billboard.

# Billboard HOT 100

For Week Ending January 21, 1967

★ STAR performer—Sides registering greatest proportionate upward progress this week.

● Record Industry Association of America seal of certification as million selling single.

| This Week | 1 Wk. Ago | 2 Wks. Ago | 3 Wks. Ago | TITLE Artist (Producer), Label & Number | Weeks On Chart |
|---|---|---|---|---|---|
| 1 | 1 | 1 | 1 | **I'M A BELIEVER** — Monkees (Jeff Barry), Colgems 1002 | 7 |
| 2 | 2 | 2 | 2 | **SNOOPY VS. THE RED BARON** — Royal Guardsmen (Phil Gernhard), Laurie 3366 | 6 |
| 3 | 3 | 3 | 7 | **TELL IT LIKE IT IS** — Aaron Neville, Parlo 101 | 8 |
| 4 | 4 | 7 | 10 | **GOOD THING** — Paul Revere & the Raiders (Terry Melcher), Columbia 43907 | 8 |
| 5 | 6 | 8 | 19 | **WORDS OF LOVE** — Mama's & the Papa's (Lou Adler), Dunhill 4037 | 8 |
| 6 | 7 | 9 | 15 | **STANDING IN THE SHADOWS OF LOVE** — Four Tops (Holland & Dozier), Motown 1102 | 6 |
| 7 | 10 | 20 | 37 | **GEORGY GIRL** — Seekers (Tom Springfield), Capitol 5756 | 8 |
| 8 | 5 | 5 | 5 | **SUGAR TOWN** — Nancy Sinatra (Lee Hazelwood), Reprise 0527 | 10 |
| 9 | 16 | 24 | 34 | **NASHVILLE CATS** — Lovin' Spoonful (Erik Jacobsen), Kama Sutra 219 | 6 |
| 10 | 12 | 15 | 23 | **TELL IT TO THE RAIN** — 4 Seasons (Bob Crewe), Philips 40412 | 7 |
| 11 | 11 | 11 | 17 | **COMING HOME SOLDIER** — Bobby Vinton (Robert Mersey), Epic 10090 | 10 |
| 12 | 8 | 4 | 3 | **WINCHESTER CATHEDRAL** — New Vaudeville Band (Geoff Stephens), Fontana 1562 | 13 ● |
| 13 | 24 | 31 | 41 | **(We Ain't Got) NOTHIN' YET** — Blues Magoos (Wyld & Polhemus), Mercury 72622 | 7 |
| 14 | 25 | 37 | 47 | **98.6** — Keith (Jerry Ross), Mercury 72639 | 7 |
| 15 | 42 | 66 | 90 | **KIND OF A DRAG** — Buckinghams (Carl Bonafede & Dan Belloc), U.S.A. 860 | 4 |
| 16 | 23 | 28 | 38 | **COLOR MY WORLD** — Petula Clark (Tony Hatch), Warner Bros. 5882 | 5 |
| 17 | 15 | 16 | 16 | **TALK TALK** — Music Machine (Brian Ross-API), Original Sound 61 | 11 |
| 18 | 18 | 23 | 28 | **I'VE PASSED THIS WAY BEFORE** — Jimmy Ruffin, (J. Dean & W. Weatherspoon), Soul 35027 | 8 |
| 19 | 9 | 6 | 4 | **THAT'S LIFE** — Frank Sinatra (Jimmy Bowen), Reprise 0531 | 10 |
| 20 | 31 | 41 | 71 | **KNIGHT IN RUSTY ARMOUR** — Peter and Gordon (W. H. Miller), Capitol 5808 | 5 |
| 21 | 26 | 43 | 52 | **STAND BY ME** — Spyder Turner (Arnold Geller), MGM 13617 | 6 |
| 22 | 17 | 14 | 11 | **DEVIL WITH A BLUE DRESS ON & GOOD GOLLY MISS MOLLY** — Mitch Ryder & the Detroit Wheels (Bob Crew), New Voice 817 | 15 |
| 23 | 14 | 12 | 12 | **SINGLE GIRL** — Sandy Posey (Chips Moman), MGM 13612 | 10 |
| 24 | 44 | 47 | 54 | **I HAD TOO MUCH TO DREAM (Last Night)** — Electric Prunes (Damo Prod.), Reprise 0532 | 7 |
| 25 | 28 | 39 | 51 | **WHERE WILL THE WORDS COME FROM** — Gary Lewis & the Playboys (Snuff Garrett), Liberty 5933 | 6 |
| 26 | 29 | 34 | 36 | **TRY A LITTLE TENDERNESS** — Otis Redding (Prod. by Staff), Volt 141 | 8 |
| 27 | 13 | 10 | 6 | **MELLOW YELLOW** — Donovan, (Mickie Most), Epic 10098 | 11 |
| 28 | 20 | 32 | 32 | **(I'm Not Your) STEPPIN' STONE** — Monkees (Tommy Boyce & Bobby Hart), Colgems 1002 | 6 |
| 29 | 30 | 33 | 43 | **GALLANT MEN** — Senator Everett McKinley Dirksen (Arch Lustberg), Capitol | 5 |
| 30 | 52 | 77 | — | **WILD THING** — Senator Bobby (C & D Prod.), Parkway 127 | 3 |
| 31 | 41 | 51 | 74 | **GREEN, GREEN GRASS OF HOME** — Tom Jones (Peter Sullivan), Parrot 40009 | 5 |
| 32 | 47 | 58 | 86 | **MUSIC TO WATCH GIRLS BY** — Bob Crewe Generation (Bob Crewe), DynoVoice 229 | 4 |
| 33 | 43 | 50 | 61 | **HOW DO YOU CATCH A GIRL** — Sam The Sham & the Pharaohs (Stan Kesler), MGM 13649 | 5 |
| 34 | 27 | 27 | 27 | **EAST-WEST** — Herman's Hermits, (Mickie Most), MGM 13639 | 8 |
| 35 | 35 | 29 | 29 | **HELP ME GIRL** — Eric Burdon & the Animals (Tom Wilson), MGM 13636 | 9 |
| 36 | 40 | 45 | 64 | **LOOK WHAT YOU'VE DONE** — Pozo Seco Singers (Bob Johnston), Columbia 43927 | 5 |
| 37 | 37 | 42 | 44 | **BLUE AUTUMN** — Bobby Goldsboro (Jack Gold), United Artists 50087 | 7 |
| 38 | 19 | 13 | 8 | **(I Know) I'M LOSING YOU** — Temptations (N. Whitfield), Gordy 7057 | 10 |
| 39 | 34 | 36 | 42 | **THERE'S GOT TO BE A WORD** — Innocence, (Ripp-Anders-Poucia), Kama Sutra 214 | 8 |
| 40 | 46 | 53 | 68 | **WACK WACK** — Young-Holt Trio (Carl Davis), Brunswick 55305 | 6 |
| 41 | 36 | 25 | 22 | **I NEED SOMEBODY** — ? (Question Mark) & the Mysterians, Cameo 441 | 10 |
| 42 | 53 | 64 | 84 | **IT'S NOW WINTER'S DAY** — Tommy Roe (Our Prod.), ABC 10888 | 5 |
| 43 | 58 | 65 | 91 | **HELLO HELLO** — Sopwith "Camel" (Erik Jacobsen), Kama Sutra 217 | 5 |
| 44 | 38 | 30 | 30 | **HAPPENINGS TEN YEARS TIME AGO** — Yardbirds, (Simon Napier-Bell), Epic 10094 | 9 |
| 45 | 33 | 19 | 9 | **A PLACE IN THE SUN** — Stevie Wonder, (C. Paul), Tamla 54139 | 9 |
| 46 | 48 | 49 | 59 | **PAPA WAS TOO** — Joe Tex (Buddy Killen), Dial 4051 | 6 |
| 47 | 32 | 26 | 26 | **MUSTANG SALLY** — Wilson Pickett, (Jerry Wexler-Rick Hall), Atlantic 2365 | 9 |
| 48 | 59 | 78 | — | **BRING IT UP** — James Brown & the Famous Flames (James Brown), King 6071 | 3 |
| 49 | 49 | 59 | 73 | **ANOTHER NIGHT** — Dionne Warwick (Burt Bacharach), Scepter 12181 | 5 |
| 50 | 21 | 17 | 13 | **GOOD VIBRATIONS** — Beach Boys (Brian Wilson), Capitol 5676 | 14 ● |
| 51 | 65 | 76 | 85 | **PUSHIN' TOO HARD** — Seeds (Marcus Tybalt), GNP Crescendo 372 | 5 |
| 52 | 63 | 80 | 100 | **GIMME SOME LOVIN'** — Spencer Davis Group (Chris Blackwell & Jimmy Miller), United Artists 50108 | 5 |
| 53 | 54 | 67 | 95 | **HEY, LEROY, YOUR MAMA'S CALLING YOU** — Jimmy Castor (Johnny Brantly), Smash 2069 | 4 |
| 54 | 56 | 61 | 70 | **GRIZZLY BEAR** — Youngbloods (Felix Pappalardi), RCA Victor 9015 | 6 |
| 55 | 55 | 63 | 67 | **(Open Up the Door) LET THE GOOD TIMES IN** — Dean Martin (Jimmy Bowen), Reprise 0528 | 6 |
| 56 | 57 | 57 | 63 | **KARATE** — Emperor's, (George Wilson & Phil Gaber), Mala 543 | 8 |
| 57 | 67 | 82 | — | **MERCY, MERCY, MERCY** — "Cannonball" Adderley (David Axelrod), Capitol 5798 | 3 |
| 58 | 72 | — | — | **THE BEAT GOES ON** — Sonny & Cher (Sonny Bono), Atco 6461 | 2 |
| 59 | 62 | 71 | 80 | **I'M GONNA MISS YOU** — Artistics (Carl Davis), Brunswick 55301 | 6 |
| 60 | 69 | 79 | 88 | **ARE YOU LONELY FOR ME** — Freddy Scott (Bert Berns), Shout 207 | 5 |
| 61 | 68 | 88 | — | **IT TAKES TWO** — Marvin Gaye & Kim Weston (Wm. Stevenson-H. Cosby), Tamla 54141 | 4 |
| 62 | 81 | 96 | — | **PRETTY BALLERINA** — Left Banke (World United Prod.), Smash 2074 | 3 |
| 63 | 66 | 72 | 81 | **WISH ME A RAINBOW** — Gunther Kallmann Chorus, 4 Corners of the World 138 | 5 |
| 64 | 22 | 18 | 18 | **CRY** — Ronnie Dove (Phil Kahl), Diamond 214 | 9 |
| 65 | 60 | 60 | 72 | **COMMUNICATION BREAKDOWN** — Roy Orbison (Rose & Vienneau), MGM 13634 | 7 |
| 66 | 76 | 84 | — | **I'VE GOT TO HAVE A REASON** — Dave Clark Five (Dave Clark), Epic 10114 | 3 |
| 67 | 79 | — | — | **TRAMP** — Lowell Fulsom, Kent 456 | 2 |
| 68 | 70 | 70 | 75 | **JUST ONE SMILE** — Gene Pitney (Gene Pitney & Stanley Kahan), Musicor 1219 | 5 |
| 69 | 94 | — | — | **THEN YOU CAN TELL ME GOODBYE** — Casinos (Gene Hughes), Fraternity 977 | 2 |
| 70 | 87 | — | — | **RIDE, RIDE RIDE** — Brenda Lee (Owen Bradley), Decca 32079 | 2 |
| 71 | 95 | — | — | **GO WHERE YOU WANNA GO** — 5th Dimension (Johnny Rivers & Marc Gordon), Soul City 753 | 2 |
| 72 | 91 | — | — | **IT MAY BE WINTER OUTSIDE** — Felice Taylor (Keene-White Prod.), Mustang 3024 | 2 |
| 73 | 73 | 75 | 77 | **DANCING IN THE STREETS** — Mamas & the Papas (Lou Adler), Dunhill 4057 | 6 |
| 74 | 82 | 85 | — | **OH YEAH!** — Joe Cuba Sextet (Pancho Cristal), Tico 490 | 3 |
| 75 | 75 | 73 | 79 | **IF YOU GO AWAY** — Damita Jo (Bob Morgan-Ted Cooper), Epic 10061 | 7 |
| 76 | 86 | — | — | **LOVIN' YOU** — Bobby Darin (Charles Koppelman & Don Rubin), Atlantic 2376 | 2 |
| 77 | 78 | 81 | 83 | **CONSTANT RAIN** — Sergio Mendes & Brasil '66 (Herb Alpert), A&M 825 | 5 |
| 78 | — | — | — | **RUBY TUESDAY** — Rolling Stones (Andrew Loog Oldham), London 904 | 1 |
| 79 | 80 | 87 | 87 | **LOOK AT GRANNY RUN RUN** — Howard Tate (M. Ragavoy), Verve 10464 | 5 |
| 80 | 90 | 95 | 98 | **TINY BUBBLES** — Don Ho & Allis (Burke), Reprise 0507 | 7 |
| 81 | 85 | 98 | — | **DEADEND STREET** — Kinks (Shel Talmy), Reprise 0540 | 3 |
| 82 | — | — | — | **MY CUP RUNNETH OVER** — Ed Ames (Jim Foglesong & Joe Reisman), RCA Victor 9002 | 1 |
| 83 | 93 | 94 | — | **WALK WITH FAITH IN YOUR HEART** — Bachelors (Dick Rowe), London 20018 | 3 |
| 84 | 100 | — | — | **ALL** — James Darren (Dick Glasser), Warner Bros. 5874 | 2 |
| 85 | — | — | — | **LET'S SPEND THE NIGHT TOGETHER** — Rolling Stones (Andrew Loog Oldham), London 904 | 1 |
| 86 | 88 | 91 | — | **I GOT TO GO BACK** — McCoys (Berns & Barry Prod.), Bang 538 | 3 |
| 87 | 89 | 99 | — | **FULL MEASURE** — Lovin' Spoonful (Erik Jacobsen), Kama Sutra 219 | 3 |
| 88 | 92 | 100 | — | **THERE GOES MY EVERYTHING** — Jack Greene, Decca 32023 | 3 |
| 89 | 99 | — | — | **SOMETHING GOOD** — Carla Thomas (Prod. by Seiff), Stax 207 | 2 |
| 90 | — | — | — | **LITTLE BLACK EGG** — Nightcrawlers, Kapp 709 | 1 |
| 91 | 96 | — | — | **SWEETEST ONE** — Metros (Pied Piper Prod.), RCA Victor 8994 | 2 |
| 92 | — | — | — | **OOH BABY** — Bo Diddley (M. Chess-E. Edwards), Checker 1158 | 1 |
| 93 | 97 | — | — | **DANGER! SHE'S A STRANGER** — Five Stairsteps (Curtis Mayfield), Windy C 604 | 2 |
| 94 | — | — | — | **I DIG YOU BABY** — Jerry Butler (Jerry Ross), Mercury 72648 | 1 |
| 95 | — | — | — | **TIP TOE** — Robert Parker, Nola 729 | 1 |
| 96 | — | — | — | **I'LL TAKE CARE OF YOUR CARES** — Frankie Laine (Bob Thiele), ABC 10891 | 1 |
| 97 | — | — | — | **THE HUNTER GETS CAPTURED BY THE GAME** — Marvelettes (William Robinson), Tamla 54143 | 1 |
| 98 | 98 | — | — | **96 TEARS** — Big Maybelle (Taylor-Gallo Prod.), Rojac 112 | 2 |
| 99 | — | — | — | **HARD LOVIN' LOSER** — Judy Collins (Mark Abramson), Elektra 45610 | 1 |
| 100 | — | — | — | **LADY** — Jack Jones, Kapp 800 | 1 |

## BUBBLING UNDER THE HOT 100

101. FOR WHAT IT'S WORTH — Buffalo Springfield, Atco 6459
102. I WISH YOU COULD BE HERE — Cyrkle, Columbia 43965
103. OUR WINTER LOVE — Lettermen, Capitol 5813
104. THAT'S THE TUNE — Vogues, Co & Ce 242
105. SPOOKY — Mike Sharpe, Liberty 55922
106. LOVE YOU SO MUCH — New Colony Six, Sentar 1205
107. SIT DOWN, I THINK I LOVE YOU — Mojo Men, Reprise 0539
108. SKATE NOW — Lou Courtney, Riverside 4588
109. LET'S FALL IN LOVE — Peaches & Herb, Date 1523
110. SMASHED! BLOCKED! — John's Children, White Whale 239
111. AT THE PARTY — Hector Rivera, Barry 1011
112. YOU GOT ME HUMMIN' — Sam & Dave, Stax 204
113. WAITIN' ON YOU — B. B. King, ABC 10869
114. BEND IT — Dave Dee, Dozy, Beaky, Mich & Tich, Fontana 1559
115. MY SPECIAL PRAYER — Joe Simon, Sound Stage 7, 2577
116. GRITS 'N' CORNBREAD — Soul Runners, Mo Soul 101
117. DAY TRIPPER — Ramsey Lewis, Cadet 5553
118. FORTUNE TELLER — Hardtimes, World Pacific 77851
119. NIKI HOEKY — P. J. Proby, Liberty 55936
120. DIG GIRLS — P. J. Jackson, Calla 135
121. LOVE ME — Bobby Hebb, Philips 40421
122. I WON'T COME IN WHILE HE'S THERE — Jim Reeves, RCA Victor 9057
123. HURRY SUNDOWN — Peter, Paul & Mary, Warner Bros. 5883
124. SUNRISE, SUNSET — Roger Williams, Kapp 801
125. TWO WAYS TO SKIN A CAT — Jimmy Reed, Arc 10887
126. WILD ANGELS — Ventures, Dolton 307
127. THAT'S LIFE — D. C. Smith, Columbia 43525
128. TEN COMMANDMENTS — Prince Buster, Philips 40427
129. WISH YOU DIDN'T HAVE TO GO — James Bobby Purify, Bell 666
130. GIMME SOME LOVIN' — Jordan Brothers, Philips 40415
131. MIDNIGHT HOUR — B. B. King, Kent 461
132. MUSIC TO WATCH GIRLS BY — Kit & the Outlaws, Philips 40419
133. CHILDREN OF ST. MONICA — Al Hirt, RCA Victor 9060
134. YOU'LL BE NEEDING ME HOME — Don Crady, Canterbury 501
135. THAT'S HOW STRONG MY LOVE IS — Nino Tempo & April Stevens, White Whale 241 / Mattie Moultrie, Columbia 43857

Compiled from national retail sales and radio station airplay by the Music Popularity Dept. of Record Market Research, Billboard.

# Billboard HOT 100

*For Week Ending January 28, 1967*

★ STAR performer—Sides registering greatest proportionate upward progress this week.

Record Industry Association of America seal of certification as million selling single.

| This Wk | Last Wk | 2 Wks Ago | 3 Wks Ago | TITLE—Artist (Producer), Label & Number | Wks on Chart |
|---|---|---|---|---|---|
| 1 | 1 | 1 | 1 | **I'M A BELIEVER** — Monkees (Jeff Barry), Colgems 1002 | 8 |
| 2 | 3 | 3 | 3 | **TELL IT LIKE IT IS** — Aaron Neville, Parlo 101 | 9 |
| 3 | 2 | 2 | 2 | **SNOOPY VS. THE RED BARON** — Royal Guardsmen (Phil Gernhard), Laurie 3366 | 7 |
| 4 | 7 | 10 | 20 | **GEORGY GIRL** — Seekers (Tom Springfield), Capitol 5756 | 9 |
| 5 | 5 | 6 | 8 | **WORDS OF LOVE** — Mama's & the Papa's (Lou Adler), Dunhill 4057 | 9 |
| 6 | 6 | 7 | 9 | **STANDING IN THE SHADOWS OF LOVE** — Four Tops (Holland & Dozier), Motown 1102 | 7 |
| 7 | 4 | 4 | 7 | **GOOD THING** — Paul Revere & the Raiders (Terry Melcher), Columbia 43907 | 9 |
| 8 | 9 | 16 | 24 | **NASHVILLE CATS** — Lovin' Spoonful (Erik Jacobsen), Kama Sutra 219 | 7 |
| 9 | 15 | 42 | 66 | **KIND OF A DRAG** — Buckinghams (Carl Bonafede & Dan Bellock), U.S.A. 860 | 5 |
| 10 | 13 | 24 | 31 | **(We Ain't Got) NOTHIN' YET** — Blues Magoos (Wyld & Polhemus), Mercury 72622 | 8 |
| 11 | 14 | 25 | 37 | **98.6** — Keith (Jerry Ross), Mercury 72639 | 8 |
| 12 | 8 | 5 | 5 | **SUGAR TOWN** — Nancy Sinatra (Lee Hazelwood), Reprise 0527 | 11 |
| 13 | 10 | 12 | 15 | **TELL IT TO THE RAIN** — 4 Seasons (Bob Crewe), Philips 40412 | 8 |
| 14 | 21 | 26 | 43 | **STAND BY ME** — Spyder Turner (Arnold Geller), MGM 13617 | 7 |
| 15 | 20 | 31 | 41 | **KNIGHT IN RUSTY ARMOUR** — Peter & Gordon (W. H. Miller), Capitol 5808 | 6 |
| 16 | 16 | 23 | 28 | **COLOR MY WORLD** — Petula Clark (Tony Hatch), Warner Bros. 5882 | 6 |
| 17 | 18 | 18 | 23 | **I'VE PASSED THIS WAY BEFORE** — Jimmy Ruffin (J. Dean & W. Weatherspoon), Soul 35027 | 9 |
| 18 | 11 | 11 | 11 | **COMING HOME SOLDIER** — Bobby Vinton (Robert Mersey), Epic 10090 | 11 |
| 19 | 31 | 41 | 51 | **GREEN, GREEN GRASS OF HOME** — Tom Jones (Peter Sullivan), Parrot 40009 | 6 |
| 20 | 24 | 44 | 47 | **I HAD TOO MUCH TO DREAM (Last Night)** — Electric Prunes (Damo Prod.), Reprise 0532 | 8 |
| 21 | 25 | 28 | 39 | **WHERE WILL THE WORDS COME FROM** — Gary Lewis & the Playboys (Snuff Garrett), Liberty 55933 | 7 |
| 22 | 12 | 8 | 4 | **WINCHESTER CATHEDRAL** — New Vaudeville Band (Geoff Stephens), Fontana 1562 | 14 |
| 23 | 30 | 52 | 77 | **WILD THING** — Senator Bobby (C & D Prod.), Parkway 127 | 4 |
| 24 | 32 | 47 | 58 | **MUSIC TO WATCH GIRLS BY** — Bob Crewe Generation (Bob Crewe), DynoVoice 229 | 5 |
| 25 | 26 | 29 | 34 | **TRY A LITTLE TENDERNESS** — Otis Redding (Prod. by Staff), Volt 141 | 9 |
| 26 | 23 | 14 | 12 | **SINGLE GIRL** — Sandy Posey (Chips Moman), MGM 13612 | 11 |
| 27 | 33 | 43 | 50 | **HOW DO YOU CATCH A GIRL** — Sam The Sham & the Pharaohs (Stan Kesler), MGM 13649 | 6 |
| 28 | 28 | 20 | 32 | **(I'm Not Your) STEPPIN' STONE** — Monkees (Tommy Boyce & Bobby Hart), Colgems 1002 | 7 |
| 29 | 42 | 53 | 62 | **IT'S NOW WINTER'S DAY** — Tommy Roe (Our Prod.), ABC 10888 | 6 |
| 30 | 17 | 15 | 16 | **TALK TALK** — Music Machine (Brian Ross-API), Original Sound 61 | 12 |
| 31 | 43 | 58 | 65 | **HELLO HELLO** — Sopwith "Camel" (Erik Jacobsen), Kama Sutra 217 | 6 |
| 32 | 19 | 9 | 6 | **THAT'S LIFE** — Frank Sinatra (Jimmy Bowen), Reprise 0531 | 11 |
| 33 | 36 | 40 | 45 | **LOOK WHAT YOU'VE DONE** — Pozo Seco Singers (Bob Johnston), Columbia 43927 | 7 |
| 34 | 58 | 72 | — | **THE BEAT GOES ON** — Sonny & Cher (Sonny Bono), Atco 6461 | 2 |
| 35 | 37 | 37 | 42 | **BLUE AUTUMN** — Bobby Goldsboro (Jack Gold), United Artists 50087 | 8 |
| 36 | 69 | 94 | — | **THEN YOU CAN TELL ME GOODBYE** — Casinos (Gene Hughes), Fraternity 977 | 3 |
| 37 | 48 | 59 | 78 | **BRING IT UP** — James Brown & The Famous Flames (James Brown), King 6071 | 4 |
| 38 | 57 | 67 | 82 | **MERCY, MERCY, MERCY** — "Cannonball" Adderley (David Axelrod), Capitol 5798 | 4 |
| 39 | 52 | 63 | 80 | **GIMME SOME LOVIN'** — Spencer Davis Group (Chris Blackwell & Jimmy Miller), United Artists 50108 | 5 |
| 40 | 40 | 46 | 53 | **WACK WACK** — Young-Holt Trio (Carl Davis), Brunswick 55305 | 7 |
| 41 | 29 | 30 | 33 | **GALLANT MEN** — Senator Everett McKinley Dirksen (Arch Lustberg), Capitol | 6 |
| 42 | 27 | 13 | 10 | **MELLOW YELLOW** — Donovan (Mickie Most), Epic 10098 | 12 |
| 43 | 78 | — | — | **RUBY TUESDAY** — Rolling Stones (Andrew Loog Oldham), London 904 | 2 |
| 44 | 46 | 48 | 49 | **PAPA WAS TOO** — Joe Tex (Buddy Killen), Dial 4051 | 7 |
| 45 | 53 | 64 | 67 | **HEY, LEROY, YOUR MAMA'S CALLING YOU** — Jimmy Castor (Johnny Brantly), Smash 2069 | 5 |
| 46 | 61 | 68 | 88 | **IT TAKES TWO** — Marvin Gaye & Kim Weston (Wm. Stevenson-H. Cosby), Tamla 54141 | 4 |
| 47 | — | — | — | **LOVE IS HERE AND NOW YOU'RE GONE** — Supremes (Holland-Dozier), Motown 1103 | 1 |
| 48 | 72 | 91 | — | **IT MAY BE WINTER OUTSIDE** — Felice Taylor (Keene-White Prod.), Mustang 3024 | 3 |
| 49 | 49 | 49 | 59 | **ANOTHER NIGHT** — Dionne Warwick (Burt Bacharach), Scepter 12181 | 6 |
| 50 | 62 | 81 | 96 | **PRETTY BALLERINA** — Left Banke (World United Prod.), Smash 2074 | 4 |
| 51 | 51 | 65 | 76 | **PUSHIN' TOO HARD** — Seeds (Marcus Tybalt), GNP Crescendo 372 | 6 |
| 52 | 71 | 95 | — | **GO WHERE YOU WANNA GO** — 5th Dimension (Johnny Rivers & Marc Gordon), Soul City 753 | 3 |
| 53 | 54 | 56 | 61 | **GRIZZLY BEAR** — Youngbloods (Felix Pappalardi), RCA Victor 9015 | 7 |
| 54 | 70 | 87 | — | **RIDE, RIDE, RIDE** — Brenda Lee (Owen Bradley), Decca 32079 | 3 |
| 55 | 56 | 57 | 57 | **KARATE** — Emperor's (George Wilson & Phil Gaber), Mala 543 | 9 |
| 56 | 66 | 76 | 84 | **I'VE GOT TO HAVE A REASON** — Dave Clark Five (Dave Clark), Epic 10114 | 4 |
| 57 | 60 | 69 | 79 | **ARE YOU LONELY FOR ME** — Freddy Scott (Bert Berns), Shout 207 | 6 |
| 58 | 59 | 62 | 71 | **I'M GONNA MISS YOU** — Artistics (Carl Davis), Brunswick 55301 | 7 |
| 59 | 84 | 100 | — | **ALL** — James Darren (Dick Glasser), Warner Bros. 5874 | 3 |
| 60 | 76 | 86 | — | **LOVIN' YOU** — Bobby Darin (Charles Koppelman & Don Rubin), Atlantic 2376 | 3 |
| 61 | 82 | — | — | **MY CUP RUNNETH OVER** — Ed Ames (Jim Foglesong & Joe Reisman), RCA Victor 9002 | 2 |
| 62 | 74 | 82 | 85 | **OH YEAH!** — Joe Cuba Sextet (Pancho Cristal), Tico 490 | 4 |
| 63 | 67 | 79 | — | **TRAMP** — Lowell Fulsom, Kent 456 | 3 |
| 64 | 68 | 70 | 70 | **JUST ONE SMILE** — Gene Pitney (Gene Pitney & Stanley Kahan), Musicor 1219 | 6 |
| 65 | 63 | 66 | 72 | **WISH ME A RAINBOW** — Gunther Kallmann Chorus, 4 Corners of the World 138 | 6 |
| 66 | — | — | — | **YOU GOT TO ME** — Neil Diamond (Jeff Barry & Ellie Greenwich), Bang 540 | 1 |
| 67 | 97 | — | — | **THE HUNTER GETS CAPTURED BY THE GAME** — Marvelettes (William Robinson), Tamla 54143 | 2 |
| 68 | — | — | — | **WISH YOU DIDN'T HAVE TO GO** — James & Bobby Purify (Papa Don Easy), Bell 660 | 1 |
| 69 | 79 | 80 | 87 | **LOOK AT GRANNY RUN RUN** — Howard Tate (M. Ragavoy), Verve 10464 | 6 |
| 70 | 86 | 88 | 91 | **I GOT TO GO BACK** — McCoys (Berns & Barry Prod.), Bang 538 | 4 |
| 71 | 77 | 78 | 81 | **CONSTANT RAIN** — Sergio Mendes & Brasil '66 (Herb Alpert), A&M 825 | 6 |
| 72 | 75 | 75 | 73 | **IF YOU GO AWAY** — Damite Jo (Bob Morgan-Ted Cooper), Epic 10061 | 8 |
| 73 | 81 | 85 | 98 | **DEADEND STREET** — Kinks (Shel Talmy), Reprise 0540 | 4 |
| 74 | — | — | — | **NIKI HOEKY** — P. J. Proby (Calvin Carter), Liberty 55936 | 1 |
| 75 | 85 | — | — | **LET'S SPEND THE NIGHT TOGETHER** — Rolling Stones (Andrew Loog Oldham), London 904 | 2 |
| 76 | — | — | — | **SO YOU WANT TO BE A ROCK 'N' ROLL STAR** — Byrds (Gary Usher), Columbia 43987 | 1 |
| 77 | — | — | — | **INDESCRIBABLY BLUE** — Elvis Presley, RCA Victor 9056 | 1 |
| 78 | — | — | — | **SPOOKY** — Mike Sharpe (Harry Middlebrooks), Liberty 55922 | 1 |
| 79 | — | — | — | **I'VE BEEN LONELY TOO LONG** — Young Rascals (Young Rascals), Atlantic 2377 | 1 |
| 80 | 80 | 90 | 95 | **TINY BUBBLES** — Don Ho & Allis (Burke), Reprise 0507 | 8 |
| 81 | 96 | — | — | **I'LL TAKE CARE OF YOUR CARES** — Frankie Laine (Bob Thiele), ABC 10891 | 2 |
| 82 | — | — | — | **OUR WINTER LOVE** — Lettermen (Steve Douglas), Capitol 5813 | 1 |
| 83 | 89 | 99 | — | **SOMETHING GOOD** — Carla Thomas (Prod. by Satff), Stax 207 | 3 |
| 84 | 95 | — | — | **TIP TOE** — Robert Parker, Nola 729 | 2 |
| 85 | 88 | 92 | 100 | **THERE GOES MY EVERYTHING** — Jack Greene, Decca 32023 | 4 |
| 86 | 94 | — | — | **I DIG YOU BABY** — Jerry Butler (Jerry Ross), Mercury 72648 | 2 |
| 87 | 100 | — | — | **LADY** — Jack Jones, Kapp 800 | 2 |
| 88 | 90 | — | — | **LITTLE BLACK EGG** — Nightcrawlers, Kapp 709 | 2 |
| 89 | 91 | 96 | — | **SWEETEST ONE** — Metros (Pied Piper Prod.), RCA Victor 8994 | 3 |
| 90 | — | — | — | **FOR WHAT IT'S WORTH** — Buffalo Springfield (Greene & Stone), Atco 6459 | 1 |
| 91 | 92 | — | — | **OOH BABY** — Bo Diddley (M. Chess-E. Edwards), Checker 1158 | 2 |
| 92 | 93 | 97 | — | **DANGER! SHE'S A STRANGER** — Five Stairsteps (Curtis Mayfield), Windy C 604 | 3 |
| 93 | — | — | 90 | **LET'S FALL IN LOVE** — Peaches & Herb (Kapralik-McCoy), Date 1523 | 2 |
| 94 | — | — | — | **TROUBLE DOWN HERE BELOW** — Lou Rawls (David Axelrod), Capitol 5824 | 1 |
| 95 | — | — | — | **SUNRISE, SUNSET** — Roger Williams (Hy Grill), Kapp 801 | 1 |
| 96 | 98 | 98 | — | **96 TEARS** — Big Maybelle (Taylor-Gallo Prod.), Rojac 112 | 2 |
| 97 | 99 | — | — | **HARD LOVIN' LOSER** — Judy Collins (Mark Abramson), Elektra 45610 | 2 |
| 98 | — | — | — | **SKATE NOW** — Lou Courtney (Funk Bros. Prod.), Riverside 4588 | 1 |
| 99 | — | — | — | **DADDY'S LITTLE GIRL** — Al Martino (Tom Morgan), Capitol 5825 | 1 |
| 100 | — | — | — | **THE PEOPLE IN ME** — Music Machine (Brian Ross), Original Sound 67 | 1 |

## HOT 100—A TO Z—(Publisher-Licensee)

All (Marks, BMI) ........ 59
Another Night (Blue Seas/Jac, ASCAP) ........ 49
Are You Lonely For Me (Web IV, BMI) ........ 57
Beat Goes On, The (Chris Marc/Cotillion, BMI) ........ 34
Blue Autumn (Unart, BMI) ........ 35
Bring It Up (Dynatone, BMI) ........ 37
Color My World (Northern, ASCAP) ........ 16
Coming Home Soldier (Feather, BMI) ........ 18
Constant Rain (Peer Int'l, BMI) ........ 71
Daddy's Little Girl (Cherio, BMI) ........ 99
Danger! She's A Stranger (Camad, BMI) ........ 92
Deadend Street (Mondvies/Norma, BMI) ........ 73
For What It's Worth (Ten East/Springalo, BMI) ........ 90
Gallant Men (Chappell, ASCAP) ........ 41
Georgy Girl (Chappell, ASCAP) ........ 4
Gimme Some Lovin' (Essex, ASCAP) ........ 39
Go Where You Wanna Go (Trousdale, BMI) ........ 52
Good Thing (Daywin, BMI) ........ 7
Green, Green Grass Of Home (Tree, BMI) ........ 19
Grizzly Bear (Whitfield, BMI) ........ 53
Hard Lovin' Loser (Wittmark, ASCAP) ........ 97
Hello Hello (Great Honesty, BMI) ........ 31
Hey, Leroy, Your Mama's Callin' You (Bozart, BMI) ........ 45
How Do You Catch A Girl (Rose, BMI) ........ 27
Hunter Gets Captured by the Game, The (Jobete, BMI) ........ 67

I've Passed This Way Before (Jobete, BMI) ........ 17
If You Go Away (Marks, BMI) ........ 72
Indescribably Blue (Elvis Presley, BMI) ........ 77
It May Be Winter Outside (Maravilla, BMI) ........ 48
It Takes Two (Jobete, BMI) ........ 46
It's Now Winter's Day (Low Twi, BMI) ........ 29
Just One Smile (January, BMI) ........ 64
Karate (Wilson, BMI) ........ 55
Kind of a Drag (Maryon, ASCAP) ........ 9
Knight in Rusty Armour (Dean Street/Feist, BMI) ........ 15
Lady (Roosevelt, BMI) ........ 87
Let's Fall In Love (Bourne, ASCAP) ........ 93
Let's Spend The Night Together (Gideon, BMI) ........ 75
Little Black Egg (Alison, ASCAP) ........ 88
Look What You've Done (Pocketful of Fames/Home, BMI) ........ 33
Love Is Here and Now You're Gone (Jobete, BMI) ........ 47
Lovin' You (Faithful Virtue, BMI) ........ 60
Mellow Yellow (Donovan Ltd, BMI) ........ 42
Mercy, Mercy, Mercy (Zawinul, BMI) ........ 38
Music To Watch Girls By (SCP, ASCAP) ........ 24
My Cup Runneth Over (Chappell, ASCAP) ........ 61
Nashville Cats (Faithful Virtue, BMI) ........ 8
Niki Hoeky (Novalene, BMI) ........ 74
98.6 (Screen Gems-Columbia, BMI) ........ 11
96 Tears (Cameo-Parkway, BMI) ........ 96
Oh Yeah! (Comedian, BMI) ........ 62
Ooh Baby (Arc, BMI) ........ 91
Our Winter Love (Cramart, BMI) ........ 82
Papa Was Too (Tree, BMI) ........ 44
People In Me, The (Thrush, BMI) ........ 100
Pretty Ballerina (Last Day, BMI) ........ 50
Pushin' Too Hard (Neil/Purple Bottle, BMI) ........ 51

Ride, Ride, Ride (Yonah, BMI) ........ 54
Ruby Tuesday (Gideon, BMI) ........ 43
Single Girl (Combine, BMI) ........ 26
Skate Now (3 Track, BMI) ........ 98
Snoopy Vs. The Red Baron (Fuller/Samphill/Windsong, BMI) ........ 3
So You Want To Be A Rock 'n' Roll Star (Tickson, BMI) ........ 76
Something Good (East, BMI) ........ 83
Spooky (Lowery, BMI) ........ 78
Stand By Me (Progressive/Trio/A.B.T. BMI) ........ 14
Standing In The Shadow Of Love (Jobete, BMI) ........ 6
Sugar Town (Criterion, ASCAP) ........ 12
Sunrise, Sunset (Sunbeam, BMI) ........ 95
Sweetest One (Polaris-Millbridge, BMI) ........ 89
Talk Talk (Thrush, BMI) ........ 30
Tell It Like It Is (Olrap, BMI) ........ 2
Tell It To The Rain (Saturday/Seasons Four, BMI) ........ 13
Then You Can Tell Me Goodbye (Acuff-Rose, BMI) ........ 36
There Goes My Everything (Blue Crest-Husky, BMI) ........ 85
Tiny Bubbles (Granite, BMI) ........ 80
Tip Top (Bonatemp, BMI) ........ 84
Tramp (Modern, BMI) ........ 63
Trouble Down Here Below (Raw Lou, BMI) ........ 94
Try A Little Tenderness (Campbell/Connelly/Robbins, ASCAP) ........ 25
Wack Wack (McLaughlin/Yo Ho, BMI) ........ 40
(We Ain't Got) Nothin' Yet (Ananga-Ranga, BMI) ........ 10
Where Will The Words Come From (Viva, BMI) ........ 21
Wild Thing (Blackwood, BMI) ........ 23
Winchester Cathedral (Southern, ASCAP) ........ 22
Wish Me A Rainbow (Famous, ASCAP) ........ 65
Wish You Didn't Have To Go (Fame, BMI) ........ 68
Words of Love (Trousdale, BMI) ........ 5
You Got Me To (Tallyrand, BMI) ........ 66

## BUBBLING UNDER THE HOT 100

101. LOVING YOU SO MUCH ........ New Colony Six, Senter 1205
102. I WISH YOU COULD BE HERE ........ Cyrkle, Columbia 43965
103. SIT DOWN, I THINK I LOVE YOU ........ Mojo Men, Reprise 0539
104. FOOLS FALL IN LOVE ........ Elvis Presley, RCA Victor 9056
105. AT THE PARTY ........ Hector Rivera, Barry 1011
106. FULL MEASURE ........ Lovin' Spoonful, Kama Sutra 219
107. CALIFORNIA NIGHTS ........ Lesley Gore, Mercury 72649
108. THAT'S THE TUNE ........ Vogues, Co & Ce 242
109. MY SPECIAL PRAYER ........ Joe Simon, Sound Stage 7 2577
110. LIFE IS GROOVY ........ United States Double Quartet (The Tokens Kirby Stone Four), B. T. Puppy 524
111. YOU GOT ME HUMMIN' ........ Sam & Dave, Stax 204
112. WAITIN' ON YOU ........ B. B. King, ABC 10889
113. LOOKING GLASS ........ Association, Valiant 758
114. SWEET MARIA ........ Billy Vaughn Singers, Dot 16985
115. HEY 'N' CORN BREAD ........ Soul Runners, MoSoul 101
116. I WON'T COME IN WHILE HE'S HERE ........ Jim Reeves, RCA Victor 9057
117. SOFTLY, AS I LEAVE YOU ........ Eydie Gorme, Columbia 43971
118. DON'T GO HOME (My Little Darlin') ........ Shirelles, Scepter 12185
119. DIG DIGS ........ J. Jackson, Calla 125
120. YOU DON'T HAVE TO SAY YOU LOVE ME ........ Arthur Prysock, Verve 10470
121. LOVE ME AT ALL ........ Association, Valiant 758
122. WILD ANGELS ........ Ventures, Dolton 322
123. TEN COMMANDMENTS ........ Prince Buster, Philips 40427
124. SHE'S LOOKING GOOD ........ Roger Collins, Galaxy 750
125. TWO WAYS TO SKIN A CAT ........ Lainie Kazan, MGM 13657
126. KISS TOMORROW GOODBYE ........ Lainie Kazan, MGM 10032
127. KISS TOMORROW GOODBYE ........ Jane Morgan, Epic
128. GIMME SOME LOVIN' ........ Jordan Brothers, Philips 40415
129. MUSIC TO WATCH GIRLS BY ........ Al Hirt, RCA Victor 9060
130. SNOW QUEEN ........ Roger Nichols Trio, A&M 830
131. THAT'S HOW STRONG MY LOVE IS ........ Mattie Moultrie, Columbia 43857
132. YOU'LL BE NEEDING ME NEXT ........ Nino Tempo & April Stevens, White Whale 241
133. I CAN'T PLEASE YOU ........ Jimmy Robins, Jerhart 207
134. FUNKY BROADWAY ........ Dyke & the Blazers, Original Sound 64

*Compiled from national retail sales and radio station airplay by the Music Popularity Dept. of Record Market Research, Billboard.*

For Week Ending February 4, 1967

# Billboard HOT 100

★ STAR performer—Sides registering greatest proportionate upward progress this week.

(Seal) Record Industry Association of America seal of certification as million selling single.

| This Week | 1 Wk. Ago | 2 Wks. Ago | 3 Wks. Ago | TITLE Artist (Producer), Label & Number | Weeks On Chart |
|---|---|---|---|---|---|
| 1 (Billboard Award) | 1 | 1 | 1 | I'M A BELIEVER — Monkees (Jeff Barry), Colgems 1002 (RIAA seal) | 9 |
| 2 | 4 | 7 | 10 | GEORGY GIRL — Seekers (Tom Springfield), Capitol 5756 | 10 |
| 3 | 3 | 2 | 2 | SNOOPY VS. THE RED BARON — Royal Guardsmen (Phil Gernhard), Laurie 3366 (RIAA seal) | 8 |
| 4 | 2 | 3 | 3 | TELL IT LIKE IT IS — Aaron Neville, Parlo 101 | 10 |
| ★ 5 | 9 | 15 | 42 | KIND OF A DRAG — Buckinghams (Carl Bonafede & Dan Bellock), U.S.A. 860 | 6 |
| 6 | 5 | 5 | 6 | WORDS OF LOVE — Mama's & the Papa's (Lou Adler), Dunhill 4057 | 10 |
| ★ 7 | 10 | 13 | 24 | (We Ain't Got) NOTHIN' YET — Blues Magoos (Wyld & Polhemus), Mercury 72622 | 9 |
| ★ 8 | 11 | 14 | 25 | 98.6 — Keith (Jerry Ross), Mercury 72639 | 9 |
| 9 | 7 | 4 | 4 | GOOD THING — Paul Revere & the Raiders, (Terry Melcher), Columbia 43907 | 10 |
| 10 | 6 | 6 | 7 | STANDING IN THE SHADOWS OF LOVE — Four Tops (Holland & Dozier), Motown 1102 | 8 |
| ★ 11 | 43 | 78 | — | RUBY TUESDAY — Rolling Stones (Andrew Loog Oldham), London 904 | 3 |
| 12 | 8 | 9 | 16 | NASHVILLE CATS — Lovin' Spoonful (Erik Jacobsen), Kama Sutra 219 | 8 |
| ★ 13 | 19 | 31 | 41 | GREEN, GREEN GRASS OF HOME — Tom Jones (Peter Sullivan), Parrot 40009 | 7 |
| 14 | 14 | 21 | 26 | STAND BY ME — Spyder Turner (Arnold Geller), MGM 13617 | 8 |
| 15 | 15 | 20 | 31 | KNIGHT IN RUSTY ARMOUR — Peter & Gordon (W. H. Miller), Capitol 5808 | 7 |
| ★ 16 | 34 | 58 | 72 | THE BEAT GOES ON — Sonny & Cher (Sonny Bono), Atco 6461 | 4 |
| ★ 17 | 24 | 32 | 47 | MUSIC TO WATCH GIRLS BY — Bob Crewe Generation (Bob Crewe), DynoVoice 229 | 6 |
| 18 | 20 | 24 | 44 | I HAD TOO MUCH TO DREAM (Last Night) — Electric Prunes (Damo Prod.), Reprise 0532 | 9 |
| 19 | 16 | 16 | 23 | COLOR MY WORLD — Petula Clark (Tony Hatch), Warner Bros. 5882 | 7 |
| 20 | 23 | 30 | 52 | WILD THING — Senator Bobby (C & D Prod.), Parkway 127 | 5 |
| 21 | 13 | 10 | 12 | TELL IT TO THE RAIN — 4 Seasons (Bob Crewe), Philips 40412 | 9 |
| 22 | 12 | 8 | 5 | SUGAR TOWN — Nancy Sinatra, (Lee Hazelwood), Reprise 0527 | 12 |
| ★ 23 | 36 | 69 | 94 | THEN YOU CAN TELL ME GOODBYE — Casinos (Gene Hughes), Fraternity 977 | 4 |
| ★ 24 | 29 | 42 | 53 | IT'S NOW WINTER'S DAY — Tommy Roe (Our Prod.), ABC 10888 | 7 |
| 25 | 21 | 25 | 28 | WHERE WILL THE WORDS COME FROM — Gary Lewis & the Playboys (Snuff Garrett), Liberty 5933 | 8 |
| ★ 26 | 39 | 52 | 63 | GIMME SOME LOVIN' — Spencer Davis Group (Chris Blackwell & Jimmy Miller), United Artists 50108 | 6 |
| ★ 27 | 47 | — | — | LOVE IS HERE AND NOW YOU'RE GONE — Supremes (Holland-Dozier), Motown 1103 | 2 |
| 28 | 17 | 18 | 18 | I'VE PASSED THIS WAY BEFORE — Jimmy Ruffin, (J. Dean & W. Weatherspoon), Soul 35027 | 10 |
| ★ 29 | 38 | 57 | 67 | MERCY, MERCY, MERCY — "Cannonball" Adderley (David Axelrod), Capitol 5798 | 5 |
| ★ 30 | 37 | 48 | 59 | BRING IT UP — James Brown & The Famous Flames (James Brown), King 6071 | 5 |
| 31 | 31 | 43 | 58 | HELLO HELLO — Sopwith "Camel" (Erik Jacobsen), Kama Sutra 217 | 7 |
| 32 | 33 | 36 | 40 | LOOK WHAT YOU'VE DONE — Pozo Seco Singers (Bob Johnston), Columbia 43927 | 8 |
| 33 | 27 | 33 | 43 | HOW DO YOU CATCH A GIRL — Sam The Sham & the Pharaohs (Stan Kesler), MGM 13649 | 7 |
| ★ 34 | 50 | 62 | 81 | PRETTY BALLERINA — Left Banke (World United Prod.), Smash 2074 | 5 |
| ★ 35 | 46 | 61 | 68 | IT TAKES TWO — Marvin Gaye & Kim Weston (Wm. Stevenson-H. Cosby), Tamla 54141 | 5 |
| ★ 36 | 52 | 71 | 95 | GO WHERE YOU WANNA GO — 5th Dimension (Johnny Rivers & Marc Gordon), Soul City 753 | 4 |
| 37 | 18 | 11 | 11 | COMING HOME SOLDIER — Bobby Vinton, (Robert Mersey), Epic 10090 | 12 |
| 38 | 45 | 53 | 64 | HEY, LEROY, YOUR MAMA'S CALLING YOU — Jimmy Castor (Johnny Brantly), Smash 2069 | 6 |
| 39 | 25 | 26 | 29 | TRY A LITTLE TENDERNESS — Otis Redding (Prod. by Staff), Volt 141 | 10 |
| 40 | 28 | 28 | 20 | (I'm Not Your) STEPPIN' STONE — Monkees (Tommy Boyce & Bobby Hart), Colgems 1002 | 8 |
| ★ 41 | 51 | 51 | 65 | PUSHIN' TOO HARD — Seeds (Marcus Tybalt), GNP Crescendo 372 | 7 |
| 42 | 48 | 72 | 91 | IT MAY BE WINTER OUTSIDE — Felice Taylor (Keene-White Prod.), Mustang 3024 | 4 |
| ★ 43 | 54 | 70 | 87 | RIDE, RIDE, RIDE — Brenda Lee (Owen Bradley), Decca 32079 | 4 |
| 44 | 22 | 12 | 8 | WINCHESTER CATHEDRAL — New Vaudeville Band, (Geoff Stephens), Fontana 1562 (RIAA seal) | 15 |
| ★ 45 | 56 | 66 | 76 | I'VE GOT TO HAVE A REASON — Dave Clark Five (Dave Clark), Epic 10114 | 5 |
| ★ 46 | 57 | 60 | 69 | ARE YOU LONELY FOR ME — Freddy Scott (Bert Berns), Shout 207 | 7 |
| 47 | 26 | 23 | 14 | SINGLE GIRL — Sandy Posey, (Chips Moman), MGM 13612 | 12 |
| ★ 48 | 60 | 76 | 86 | LOVIN' YOU — Bobby Darin (Charles Koppelman & Don Rubin), Atlantic 2376 | 4 |
| ★ 49 | 59 | 84 | 100 | ALL — James Darren (Dick Glasser), Warner Bros., 5874 | 4 |
| ★ 50 | 61 | 82 | — | MY CUP RUNNETH OVER — Ed Ames (Jim Foglesong & Joe Reisman), RCA Victor 9002 | 3 |
| ★ 51 | 68 | — | — | WISH YOU DIDN'T HAVE TO GO — James & Bobby Purify (Papa Don Easy), Bell 660 | 2 |
| 52 | 40 | 40 | 46 | WACK WACK — Young-Holt Trio (Carl Davis), Brunswick 55305 | 8 |
| 53 | 53 | 54 | 56 | GRIZZLY BEAR — Youngbloods (Felix Pappalardi), RCA Victor 9015 | 8 |
| ★ 54 | 66 | — | — | YOU GOT TO ME — Neil Diamond (Jeff Barry & Ellie Greenwich), Bang 540 | 2 |
| 55 | 58 | 59 | 62 | I'M GONNA MISS YOU — Artistics (Carl Davis), Brunswick 55301 | 8 |
| ★ 56 | 67 | 97 | — | THE HUNTERS GET CAPTURED BY THE GAME — Marvelettes (William Robinson), Tamla 54143 | 3 |
| 57 | 35 | 37 | 37 | BLUE AUTUMN — Bobby Goldsboro (Jack Gold), United Artists 50087 | 9 |
| ★ 58 | 77 | — | — | INDESCRIBABLY BLUE — Elvis Presley, RCA Victor 9056 | 2 |
| ★ 59 | 75 | 85 | — | LET'S SPEND THE NIGHT TOGETHER — Rolling Stones (Andrew Loog Oldham), London 904 | 3 |
| 60 | 63 | 67 | 79 | TRAMP — Lowell Fulsom, Kent 456 | 4 |
| ★ 61 | 76 | — | — | SO YOU WANT TO BE A ROCK 'N' ROLL STAR — Byrds (Gary Usher), Columbia 43987 | 2 |
| 62 | 62 | 74 | 82 | OH YEAH! — Joe Cuba Sextet (Pancho Cristal), Tico 490 | 5 |
| ★ 63 | 79 | — | — | I'VE BEEN LONELY TOO LONG — Young Rascals (Young Rascals), Atlantic 2377 | 2 |
| 64 | 65 | 63 | 66 | WISH ME A RAINBOW — Gunther Kallmann Chorus, 4 Corners of the World 138 | 7 |
| 65 | 74 | — | — | NIKI HOEKY — P. J. Proby (Calvin Carter), Liberty 55936 | 2 |
| ★ 66 | 81 | 96 | — | I'LL TAKE CARE OF YOUR CARES — Frankie Laine (Bob Thiele), ABC 10891 | 3 |
| 67 | 69 | 79 | 80 | LOOK AT GRANNY RUN RUN — Howard Tate (M. Ragavoy), Verve 10464 | 7 |
| 68 | 72 | 75 | 75 | IF YOU GO AWAY — Damita Jo (Bob Morgan-Ted Cooper), Epic 10061 | 9 |
| 69 | 70 | 86 | 88 | I GOT TO GO BACK — McCoys (Berns & Barry Prod.), Bang 538 | 5 |
| ★ 70 | 90 | — | — | FOR WHAT IT'S WORTH — Buffalo Springfield (Greene & Stone), Atco 6459 | 2 |
| ★ 71 | 93 | — | — | LET'S FALL IN LOVE — Peaches & Herb (Kapralik-McCoy), Date 1523 | 4 |
| ★ 72 | 87 | 100 | — | LADY — Jack Jones, Kapp 800 | 3 |
| 73 | 78 | — | — | SPOOKY — Mike Sharpe (Harry Middlebrooks), Liberty 55922 | 2 |
| 74 | 85 | 88 | 92 | THERE GOES MY EVERYTHING — Jack Greene, Decca 32023 | 5 |
| 75 | 80 | 80 | 90 | TINY BUBBLES — Don Ho & Allis (Burke), Reprise 0507 | 9 |
| 76 | 82 | — | — | OUR WINTER LOVE — Lettermen (Steve Douglas), Capitol 5813 | 2 |
| ★ 77 | — | — | — | EVERYBODY NEEDS SOMEBODY TO LOVE — Wilson Pickett (Jerry Wexler & Rick Hall), Atlantic 2381 | 1 |
| 78 | 83 | 89 | 99 | SOMETHING GOOD — Carla Thomas (Prod. by Staff), Stax 207 | 4 |
| ★ 79 | — | — | — | DIS-ADVANTAGES OF YOU — Brass Ring (Steve Barri), Dunhill 4065 | 1 |
| ★ 80 | — | — | — | NO FAIR AT ALL — Association (Jerry Yester), Valiant 758 | 1 |
| ★ 81 | — | — | — | BABY, I NEED YOUR LOVIN' — Johnny Rivers (Lou Adler), Imperial 66227 | 1 |
| ★ 82 | — | — | — | SOCK IT TO ME—BABY! — Mitch Ryder & the Detroit Wheels (Bob Crewe), New Voice 820 | 1 |
| 83 | 84 | 95 | — | TIP TOE — Robert Parker, Nola 729 | 3 |
| ★ 84 | 99 | — | — | DADDY'S LITTLE GIRL — Al Martino (Tom Morgan), Capitol 5825 | 2 |
| 85 | 88 | 90 | — | LITTLE BLACK EGG — Nightcrawlers, Kapp 709 | 3 |
| 86 | 86 | 94 | — | I DIG YOU BABY — Jerry Butler (Jerry Ross), Mercury 72648 | 3 |
| 87 | 98 | — | — | SKATE NOW — Lou Courtney (Funk Bros. Prod.), Riverside 4588 | 2 |
| 88 | 89 | 91 | 96 | SWEETEST ONE — Metros (Pied Piper Prod.), RCA Victor 8994 | 4 |
| 89 | 91 | 92 | — | OOH BABY — Bo Diddley (M. Chess-E. Edwards), Checker 1158 | 3 |
| ★ 90 | — | — | — | SIT DOWN, I THINK I LOVE YOU — Mojo Men (Lenny Waronker), Reprise 0539 | 1 |
| 91 | 92 | 93 | 97 | DANGER! SHE'S A STRANGER — Five Stairsteps (Curtis Mayfield), Windy C 604 | 4 |
| 92 | 95 | — | — | SUNRISE, SUNSET — Roger Williams (Hy Grill), Kapp 801 | 2 |
| 93 | 94 | — | — | TROUBLE DOWN HERE BELOW — Lou Rawls (David Axelrod), Capitol 5824 | 2 |
| 94 | — | — | — | CALIFORNIA NIGHTS — Lesley Gore (Bob Crewe), Mercury 72649 | 1 |
| 95 | — | — | — | I WISH YOU COULD BE HERE — Cyrkle (John Simon), Columbia 43965 | 1 |
| 96 | — | — | — | MY SPECIAL PRAYER — Joe Simon (J. R. Ent.), Sound Stage 72577 | 1 |
| 97 | — | — | — | FEEL SO BAD — Little Milton, Checker 1162 | 1 |
| 98 | 100 | — | — | THE PEOPLE IN ME — Music Machine (Brian Ross), Original Sound 67 | 2 |
| 99 | — | — | — | TEN COMMANDMENTS — Prince Buster (Buster-East Prod.), Philips 40427 | 1 |
| 100 | — | — | — | RAISE YOUR HAND — Eddie Floyd (Prod. by Staff), Stax 208 | 1 |

## HOT 100—A TO Z—(Publisher-Licensee)


All (Marks, BMI) .... 49
Are You Lonely for Me (Web IV, BMI) .... 46
Baby, I Need Your Lovin' (Jobete, BMI) .... 81
Beat Goes On, The (Chris Marc/Cotillion, BMI) .. 16
Blue Autumn (Unart, BMI) .... 57
Bring It Up (Dynatone, BMI) .... 30
California Nights (Genius/Enchanted, ASCAP) .... 94
Color My World (Northern, ASCAP) .... 19
Coming Home Soldier (Feather, BMI) .... 37
Daddy's Little Girl (Cherio, BMI) .... 84
Danger! She's a Stranger (Camad, BMI) .... 91
Dis-Advantages of You (Scott, ASCAP) .... 79
Everybody Needs Somebody to Love (Reetch, Caesar & Dino, BMI) .... 77
Feel So Bad (Travis, BMI) .... 97
For What It's Worth (Ten East/Springalo, BMI) .. 70
Georgy Girl (Chappell, ASCAP) .... 2
Gimme Some Lovin' (Essex, ASCAP) .... 26
Go Where You Wanna Go (Trousdale, BMI) .... 36
Good Thing (Daywin, BMI) .... 9
Green, Green Grass of Home (Tree, BMI) .... 13
Grizzly Bear (Whitfield, BMI) .... 63
Hello Hello (Great Honesty, BMI) .... 31
Hey, Leroy, Your Mama's Callin' You (Bozart, BMI) .... 38
How Do You Catch a Girl (Rose, BMI) .... 33
Hunter Gets Captured by the Game, The (Jobete, BMI) .... 56
I Dig You Baby (Morpine, BMI) .... 86
I Got to Go Back (Web IV/Trio, BMI) .... 69
I Had Too Much to Dream (Last Night) (Star, BMI) .... 18
I Wish You Could Be Here (Charing Cross, BMI) .. 95
I'll Take Care of Your Cares (Remick, ASCAP) .. 66
I'm a Believer (Screen Gems-Columbia, BMI) .... 1
I'm Gonna Miss You (Jalynne-BRC, BMI) .... 55
(I'm Not Your) Steppin' Stone (Screen Gems-Columbia, BMI) .... 40
I've Been Lonely Too Long (Slacsar, BMI) .... 63
I've Got to Have a Reason (Branstor, BMI) .... 45
I've Passed This Way Before (Jobete, BMI) .... 28
If You Go Away (Marks, BMI) .... 68
Indescribably Blue (Elvis Presley, BMI) .... 58
It May Be Winter Outside (Maravilla, BMI) .... 42
It Takes Two (Jobete, BMI) .... 35
It's Now Winter's Day (Low Twi, BMI) .... 24
Kind of a Drag (Maryon, ASCAP) .... 5
Knight in Rusty Armour (Dean Street/Feist, ASCAP) .... 15
Lady (Roosevelt, BMI) .... 72
Let's Fall in Love (Bourne, ASCAP) .... 71
Let's Spend the Night Together (Gideon, BMI) 59
Little Black Egg (Alison, ASCAP) .... 85
Look at Granny Run Run (Ragmar/Rumbalero, BMI) .... 67
Look What You've Done (Pocketful of Fames/Noma, BMI) .... 32
Love Is Here and Now You're Gone (Jobete, BMI) 27
Lovin' You (Faithful Virtue, BMI) .... 48
Mercy, Mercy, Mercy (Zawinul, BMI) .... 29
Music to Watch Girls By (SCP, ASCAP) .... 17
My Cup Runneth Over (Chappell, ASCAP) .... 50
My Special Prayer (Maureen, BMI) .... 96
Nashville Cats (Faithful Virtue, BMI) .... 12
Niki Hoeky (Novalene, BMI) .... 65
98.6 (Screen Gems-Columbia, BMI) .... 8
No Fair at All (Beechwood, BMI) .... 80
Oh Yeah! (Cordon, BMI) .... 62
Ooh Baby (Arc, BMI) .... 89
Our Winter Love (Cramart, BMI) .... 76
People in Me, The (Thrush, BMI) .... 98
Pretty Ballerina (Last Day, BMI) .... 34
Pushin' Too Hard (Neil/Purple Bottle, BMI) .. 41
Raise Your Hand (East, BMI) ....100
Ride, Ride, Ride (Yonah, BMI) .... 43
Ruby Tuesday (Gideon, BMI) .... 11
Single Girl (Combine, BMI) .... 47
Sit Down, I Think I Love You (Screen Gems-Columbia) .... 90
Skate Now (3 Track, BMI) .... 87
Snoopy vs. the Red Baron (Fuller/Samphil/Windsong, BMI) .... 3
So You Want to Be a Rock 'n' Roll Star (Tickson, BMI) .... 61
Sock It to Me—Baby! (Saturday, BMI) .... 82
Something Good (East, BMI) .... 78
Spooky (Lowery, BMI) .... 73
Stand By Me (Progressive/Trio/A.B.T. Tet, BMI) .. 14
Standing in the Shadows of Love (Jobete, BMI) .. 10
Sugar Town (Criterion, ASCAP) .... 22
Sunrise, Sunset (Sunbeam, BMI) .... 92
Sweetest One (Polaris-Millbridge, BMI) .... 88
Tell It Like It Is (Olrap, BMI) .... 4
Tell It to the Rain (Saturday/Seasons Four, BMI) 21
Ten Commandments (Carab, BMI) .... 99
Then You Can Tell Me Goodbye (Acuff-Rose, BMI) 23
There Goes My Everything (Blue Crest-Husky, BMI) 74
Tiny Bubbles (Granite, ASCAP) .... 75
Tip Toe (Bonatemp, BMI) .... 83
Tramp (Modern, BMI) .... 60
Trouble Down Here Below (Raw Lou, BMI) .... 93
Try a Little Tenderness (Campbell/Connelly/Robbins, ASCAP) .... 39
Wack Wack (McLaughlin/Yo Ho, BMI) .... 52
(We Ain't Got) Nothin' Yet (Anange-Range, BMI) 7
Where Will the Words Come From (Viva, BMI) .. 25
Wild Thing (Blackwood, BMI) .... 20
Winchester Cathedral (Southern, ASCAP) .... 44
Wish Me a Rainbow (Famous, ASCAP) .... 64
Wish You Didn't Have to Go (Fame, BMI) .... 51
Words of Love (Trousdale, BMI) .... 6
You Got to Me (Tallyrand, BMI) .... 54


## BUBBLING UNDER THE HOT 100

101. LOVE YOU SO MUCH ....New Colony Six, Sentar 1205
102. FOOLS FALL IN LOVE ....Elvis Presley, RCA Victor 9056
103. HARD LOVIN' LOSER ....Judy Collins, Elektra 45610
104. EPISTLE TO DIPPY ....Donovan, Epic 10127
105. RAIN, RAIN GO AWAY ....Lee Dorsey, Amy 974
106. THAT'S THE TUNE ....Vogues, Co & Ce 242
107. DARK END OF THE STREET ....James Carr, Goldwax 317
108. AT THE PARTY ....Hector Rivera, Barry 1011
109. SWEET MARIA ....Billy Vaughn Singers, Dot 16985
110. LIFE IS GROOVY .... United States Double Quartet (The Tokens Kirby Stone Four, B. T. Puppy 524
111. DON'T GO HOME (MY LITTLE DARLIN') ....Shirelles, Scepter 12185
112. I THINK WE'RE ALONE NOW ....Tommy James & Shondells, Roulette 4720
113. JUST LET IT HAPPEN ....Arbors, Date 1546
114. MY BEST FRIEND ....Jefferson Airplane, RCA Victor 9063
115. I WON'T COME IN WHILE HE'S HERE ....Jim Reeves, RCA Victor 9057
116. 96 TEARS ....Bib Maybelle, Rojac 112
117. I DIG GIRLS ....J. J. Jackson, Calla 125
118. WILD ANGELS ....Ventures, Dolton 327
119. PUCKER UP BUTTER CUP ....Jr. Walker and the All Stars, Soul 35030
120. YOU DON'T HAVE TO SAY YOU LOVE ME ....Arthur Prysock, Verve 10470
121. KISS TOMORROW GOODBYE ....Jane Morgan, Epic 10032
122. GIRLS ARE OUT TO GET YOU ....Fascinations, Hayfield 7714
123. KISS TOMORROW GOODBYE ....Lainie Kazan, MGM 13657
124. ONE TWO THREE ....Ramsey Lewis, Cadet 5356
125. SHE'S LOOKING GOOD ....Roger Collins, Galaxy 750
126. LOVE'S GONE BAD ....Underdogs, V.I.P. 25040
127. WALK TALL ....2 of Clubs, Fraternity 975
128. WAITIN' ON YOU ....B.B. King, ABC 10889
129. SNOW QUEEN ....Roger Nichols Trio, A & M 830
130. MUSIC TO WATCH GIRLS BY ....Al Hirt, RCA Victor 9060
131. BALLAD OF WALTER WART ....Thorndike Pickeldish Choir, MTA 114
132. SHADOW OF YOUR SMILE ....Boots Randolph, Monument 1976
133. MR. FARMER ....Seeds, CNP Crescendo 383
134. HAPPY TOGETHER ....Turtles, White Whale 244
135. ANOTHER PAGE ....Connie Francis, MGM 13665

Compiled from national retail sales and radio station airplay by the Music Popularity Dept. of Record Market Research, Billboard.

For Week Ending February 11, 1967

# Billboard HOT 100

★ **STAR performer**—Sides registering greatest proportionate upward progress this week.

Record Industry Association of America seal of certification as million selling single.

| This Week | 1 Wk. Ago | 2 Wks. Ago | 3 Wks. Ago | TITLE Artist (Producer), Label & Number | Weeks On Chart |
|---|---|---|---|---|---|
| 1 (Billboard Award) | 1 | 1 | 1 | **I'M A BELIEVER** — Monkees (Jeff Barry), Colgems 1002 (RIAA seal) | 10 |
| 2 | 2 | 4 | 7 | **GEORGY GIRL** — Seekers (Tom Springfield), Capitol 5756 | 11 |
| 3 | 5 | 9 | 15 | **KIND OF A DRAG** — Buckinghams (Carl Bonafede & Dan Bellock), U.S.A. 860 | 7 |
| ★4 | 11 | 43 | 78 | **RUBY TUESDAY** — Rolling Stones (Andrew Loog Oldham), London 904 | 4 |
| 5 | 7 | 10 | 13 | **(We Ain't Got) NOTHIN YET** — Blues Magoos (Wyld & Polhemus), Mercury 72622 | 10 |
| 6 | 4 | 2 | 3 | **TELL IT LIKE IT IS** — Aaron Neville, Parlo 101 | 11 |
| 7 | 8 | 11 | 14 | **98.6** — Keith (Jerry Ross), Mercury 72639 | 10 |
| 8 | 3 | 3 | 2 | **SNOOPY VS. THE RED BARON** — Royal Guardsmen (Phil Gernhard), Laurie 3366 (RIAA seal) | 9 |
| ★9 | 27 | 47 | — | **LOVE IS HERE AND NOW YOU'RE GONE** — Supremes (Holland-Dozier), Motown 1103 | 3 |
| ★10 | 16 | 34 | 58 | **THE BEAT GOES ON** — Sonny & Cher (Sonny Bono), Atco 6461 | 5 |
| ★11 | 18 | 20 | 24 | **I HAD TOO MUCH TO DREAM (Last Night)** — Electric Prunes (Dave Prod.), Reprise 0532 | 10 |
| 12 | 14 | 14 | 21 | **STAND BY ME** — Spyder Turner (Arnold Geller), MGM 13617 | 9 |
| 13 | 13 | 19 | 31 | **GREEN, GREEN GRASS OF HOME** — Tom Jones (Peter Sullivan), Parrot 40009 | 8 |
| 14 | 6 | 5 | 5 | **WORDS OF LOVE** — Mama's & the Papa's (Lou Adler), Dunhill 4037 | 11 |
| 15 | 17 | 24 | 32 | **MUSIC TO WATCH GIRLS BY** — Bob Crewe Generation (Bob Crewe), DynoVoice 229 | 7 |
| ★16 | 23 | 36 | 69 | **THEN YOU CAN TELL ME GOODBYE** — Casinos (Gene Hughes), Fraternity 977 | 5 |
| ★17 | 26 | 39 | 52 | **GIMME SOME LOVIN'** — Spencer Davis Group (Chris Blackwell & Jimmy Miller), United Artists 50108 | 7 |
| 18 | 10 | 6 | 6 | **STANDING IN THE SHADOWS OF LOVE** — Four Tops (Holland & Dozier), Motown 1102 | 9 |
| 19 | 9 | 7 | 4 | **GOOD THING** — Paul Revere & the Raiders, (Terry Melcher), Columbia 43907 | 11 |
| 20 | 20 | 23 | 30 | **WILD THING** — Senator Bobby (C & D Prod.), Parkway 127 | 6 |
| ★21 | 29 | 38 | 57 | **MERCY, MERCY, MERCY** — "Cannonball" Adderley (David Axelrod), Capitol 5798 | 6 |
| 22 | 12 | 8 | 9 | **NASHVILLE CATS** — Lovin' Spoonful (Erik Jacobsen), Kama Sutra 219 | 9 |
| 23 | 15 | 15 | 20 | **KNIGHT IN RUSTY ARMOUR** — Peter & Gordon (John Burgess), Capitol 5808 | 8 |
| 24 | 24 | 29 | 42 | **IT'S NOW WINTER'S DAY** — Tommy Roe (Our Prod.), ABC 10888 | 8 |
| ★25 | 34 | 50 | 62 | **PRETTY BALLERINA** — Left Banke (World United Prod.), Smash 2074 | 6 |
| ★26 | 31 | 31 | 43 | **HELLO HELLO** — Sopwith "Camel" (Erik Jacobsen), Kama Sutra 217 | 8 |
| ★27 | 36 | 52 | 71 | **GO WHERE YOU WANNA GO** — 5th Dimension (Johnny Rivers & Marc Gordon), Soul City 753 | 5 |
| 28 | 19 | 16 | 16 | **COLOR MY WORLD** — Petula Clark (Tony Hatch), Warner Bros. 5882 | 8 |
| ★29 | 35 | 46 | 61 | **IT TAKES TWO** — Marvin Gaye & Kim Weston (Wm. Stevenson-H. Cosby), Tamla 54141 | 6 |
| 30 | 30 | 37 | 48 | **BRING IT UP** — James Brown & The Famous Flames (James Brown), King 6071 | 6 |
| 31 | 21 | 13 | 10 | **TELL IT TO THE RAIN** — 4 Seasons (Bob Crewe), Philips 40412 | 10 |
| ★32 | 54 | 66 | — | **YOU GOT TO ME** — Neil Diamond (Jeff Barry & Ellie Greenwich), Bang 540 | 3 |
| 33 | 28 | 17 | 18 | **I'VE PASSED THIS WAY BEFORE** — Jimmy Ruffin, (J. Dean & W. Weatherspoon), Soul 35027 | 11 |
| 34 | 25 | 21 | 25 | **WHERE WILL THE WORDS COME FROM** — Gary Lewis & the Playboys (Snuff Garrett), Liberty 5933 | 9 |
| ★35 | 48 | 60 | 76 | **LOVIN' YOU** — Bobby Darin (Charles Koppelman & Don Rubin), Atlantic 2376 | 5 |
| ★36 | 50 | 61 | 82 | **MY CUP RUNNETH OVER** — Ed Ames (Jim Foglesong & Joe Reisman), RCA Victor 9002 | 4 |
| 37 | 43 | 54 | 70 | **RIDE, RIDE, RIDE** — Brenda Lee (Owen Bradley), Decca 32079 | 5 |
| 38 | 38 | 45 | 53 | **HEY, LEROY, YOUR MAMA'S CALLING YOU** — Jimmy Castor (Johnny Brantly), Smash 2069 | 7 |
| 39 | 33 | 27 | 33 | **HOW DO YOU CATCH A GIRL** — Sam The Sham & the Pharaohs (Stan Kesler), MGM 13649 | 8 |
| 40 | 41 | 51 | 51 | **PUSHIN' TOO HARD** — Seeds (Marcus Tybalt), GNP Crescendo 372 | 8 |
| 41 | 22 | 12 | 8 | **SUGAR TOWN** — Nancy Sinatra, (Lee Hazelwood), Reprise 0527 | 13 |
| 42 | 42 | 48 | 72 | **IT MAY BE WINTER OUTSIDE** — Felice Taylor (Keene-White Prod.), Mustang 3024 | 5 |
| 43 | 49 | 59 | 84 | **ALL** — James Darren (Dick Glasser), Warner Bros., 5874 | 5 |
| 44 | 45 | 56 | 66 | **I'VE GOT TO HAVE A REASON** — Dave Clark Five (Dave Clark), Epic 10114 | 6 |
| 45 | 46 | 57 | 60 | **ARE YOU LONELY FOR ME** — Freddy Scott (Bert Berns), Shout 207 | 8 |
| ★46 | 56 | 67 | 97 | **THE HUNTER GETS CAPTURED BY THE GAME** — Marvelettes (William Robinson), Tamla 54143 | 4 |
| ★47 | 58 | 77 | — | **INDESCRIBABLY BLUE** — Elvis Presley, RCA Victor 9056 | 3 |
| 48 | 51 | 68 | — | **WISH YOU DIDN'T HAVE TO GO** — James & Bobby Purify (Papa Don Easy), Bell 660 | 3 |
| ★49 | 81 | — | — | **BABY, I NEED YOUR LOVIN'** — Johnny Rivers (Lou Adler), Imperial 66227 | 2 |
| 50 | 32 | 33 | 36 | **LOOK WHAT YOU'VE DONE** — Pozo Seco Singers (Bob Johnston), Columbia 43927 | 9 |
| ★51 | 61 | 76 | — | **SO YOU WANT TO BE A ROCK 'N' ROLL STAR** — Byrds (Gary Usher), Columbia 43987 | 3 |
| 52 | 53 | 53 | 54 | **GRIZZLY BEAR** — Youngbloods (Felix Pappalardi), RCA Victor 9015 | 9 |
| ★53 | 63 | 79 | — | **I'VE BEEN LONELY TOO LONG** — Young Rascals (Young Rascals), Atlantic 2377 | 3 |
| 54 | 60 | 63 | 67 | **TRAMP** — Lowell Fulsom, Kent 456 | 5 |
| ★55 | 65 | 74 | — | **NIKI HOEKY** — P. J. Proby (Calvin Carter), Liberty 55936 | 3 |
| ★56 | 70 | 90 | — | **FOR WHAT IT'S WORTH** — Buffalo Springfield (Greene & Stone), Atco 6459 | 3 |
| 57 | 59 | 75 | 85 | **LET'S SPEND THE NIGHT TOGETHER** — Rolling Stones (Andrew Loog Oldham), London 904 | 4 |
| ★58 | 82 | — | — | **SOCK IT TO ME—BABY!** — Mitch Ryder & the Detroit Wheels (Bob Crewe), New Voice 820 | 2 |
| ★59 | 77 | — | — | **EVERYBODY NEEDS SOMEBODY TO LOVE** — Wilson Pickett (Jerry Wexler & Rick Hall), Atlantic 2381 | 2 |
| ★60 | 71 | 93 | — | **LET'S FALL IN LOVE** — Peaches & Herb (Kapralik-McCoy), Date 1523 | 5 |
| 61 | 66 | 81 | 96 | **I'LL TAKE CARE OF YOUR CARES** — Frankie Laine (Bob Thiele), ABC 10891 | 4 |
| 62 | 55 | 58 | 59 | **I'M GONNA MISS YOU** — Artistics (Carl Davis), Brunswick 55301 | 9 |
| 63 | 64 | 65 | 63 | **WISH ME A RAINBOW** — Gunther Kallmann Chorus, 4 Corners of the World 138 | 8 |
| ★64 | 79 | — | — | **DIS-ADVANTAGES OF YOU** — Brass Ring (Phil Bodner), Dunhill 4065 | 2 |
| ★65 | 80 | — | — | **NO FAIR AT ALL** — Association (Jerry Yester), Valiant 758 | 2 |
| ★66 | 84 | 99 | — | **DADDY'S LITTLE GIRL** — Al Martino (Tom Morgan), Capitol 5825 | 3 |
| 67 | 72 | 87 | 100 | **LADY** — Jack Jones, Kapp 800 | 4 |
| 68 | 68 | 72 | 75 | **IF YOU GO AWAY** — Damita Jo (Bob Morgan-Ted Cooper), Epic 10061 | 10 |
| ★69 | — | — | — | **EPISTLE TO DIPPY** — Donovan (Mickie Most), Epic 10127 | 1 |
| 70 | 75 | 80 | 80 | **TINY BUBBLES** — Don Ho & Allis (Burke), Reprise 0507 | 10 |
| ★71 | 94 | — | — | **CALIFORNIA NIGHTS** — Lesley Gore (Bob Crewe), Mercury 72649 | 2 |
| 72 | 74 | 85 | 88 | **THERE GOES MY EVERYTHING** — Jack Greene, Decca 32023 | 6 |
| 73 | 73 | 78 | — | **SPOOKY** — Mike Sharpe (Harry Middlebrooks), Liberty 55922 | 3 |
| 74 | 76 | 82 | — | **OUR WINTER LOVE** — Lettermen (Steve Douglas), Capitol 5813 | 3 |
| ★75 | — | — | — | **PUCKER UP BUTTERCUP** — Jr. Walker & the All Stars, (H. Fuqua-J. Bristol), Soul 35030 | 1 |
| 76 | 86 | 86 | 94 | **I DIG YOU BABY** — Jerry Butler (Jerry Ross), Mercury 72648 | 4 |
| ★77 | 95 | — | — | **I WISH YOU COULD BE HERE** — Cyrkle (John Simon), Columbia 43965 | 2 |
| 78 | 78 | 83 | 89 | **SOMETHING GOOD** — Carla Thomas (Prod. by Satff), Stax 207 | 5 |
| ★79 | — | — | — | **HAPPY TOGETHER** — Turtles (Joe Wissert), White Whale 244 | 1 |
| 80 | 90 | — | — | **SIT DOWN, I THINK I LOVE YOU** — Mojo Men (Lenny Waronker), Reprise 0539 | 2 |
| ★81 | — | — | — | **KEEP A LIGHT IN THE WINDOW TILL I COME HOME** — Solomon Burke (Bob Gallo), Atlantic 2378 | 1 |
| ★82 | — | — | — | **I THINK WE'RE ALONE NOW** — Tommy James and the Shondells (Cordell-Gentry), Roulette 4720 | 1 |
| ★83 | 98 | 100 | — | **THE PEOPLE IN ME** — Music Machine (Brian Ross), Original Sound 67 | 3 |
| ★84 | — | — | — | **DARLIN' BE HOME SOON** — Lovin' Spoonful (Erik Jacobsen), Kama Sutra 220 | 1 |
| 85 | 85 | 88 | 90 | **LITTLE BLACK EGG** — Nightcrawlers, Kapp 709 | 4 |
| 86 | 87 | 98 | — | **SKATE NOW** — Lou Courtney (Funk Bros. Prod.), Riverside 4588 | 3 |
| 87 | 92 | 95 | — | **SUNRISE, SUNSET** — Roger Williams (Hy Grill), Kapp 801 | 3 |
| 88 | 89 | 91 | 92 | **OOH BABY** — Bo Diddley (M. Chess-E. Edwards), Checker 1158 | 4 |
| 89 | 91 | 92 | 93 | **DANGER! SHE'S A STRANGER** — Five Stairsteps (Curtis Mayfiled), Windy C 604 | 5 |
| ★90 | — | — | — | **THERE'S A KIND OF A HUSH** — Herman's Hermits (Mickie Most), MGM 13681 | 1 |
| 91 | 97 | — | — | **FEEL SO BAD** — Little Milton, Checker 1162 | 2 |
| 92 | 93 | 94 | — | **TROUBLE DOWN HERE BELOW** — Lou Rawls (David Axelrod), Capitol 5824 | 3 |
| 93 | — | — | — | **JUST BE SINCERE** — Jackie Wilson (Carl Davis), Brunswick 55309 | 1 |
| 94 | 96 | — | — | **MY SPECIAL PRAYER** — Joe Simon (J. R. Ent.), Sound Stage 72577 | 2 |
| 95 | — | — | — | **ONE, TWO, THREE** — Ramsey Lewis (E. Edwards), Cadet 5556 | 1 |
| 96 | — | — | — | **EVERYDAY I HAVE THE BLUES** — Billy Stewart (Billy Davis), Chess 1991 | 1 |
| 97 | 99 | — | — | **TEN COMMANDMENTS** — Prince Buster (Buster-East Prod.), Philips 40427 | 2 |
| 98 | 100 | — | — | **RAISE YOUR HAND** — Eddie Floyd (Prod. by Staff), Stax 208 | 2 |
| 99 | — | — | — | **PEOPLE LIKE YOU** — Eddie Fisher (Al Schmitt), RCA Victor 9070 | 1 |
| 100 | — | — | — | **GIRLS ARE OUT TO GET YOU** — Fascinations, Mayfield 7714 | 1 |

## HOT 100—A TO Z—*(Publisher-Licensee)*

All (Marks, BMI) .......... 43
Are You Lonely for Me (Web IV, BMI) .......... 45
Baby, I Need Your Lovin' (Jobete, BMI) .......... 49
Beat Goes On, The (Chris Marc/Cotillion, BMI) .. 10
Bring It Up (Dynatone, BMI) .......... 30
California Nights (Genius/Enchanted, ASCAP) .... 71
Color My World (Northern, ASCAP) .......... 28
Daddy's Little Girl (Cherio, BMI) .......... 66
Danger! She's a Stranger (Camad, BMI) .......... 89
Darlin' Be Home Soon (Faithful Virtue, BMI) .... 84
Dis-Advantages of You (Scott, ASCAP) .......... 64
Epistle To Dippy (Peer Int'l., BMI) .......... 69
Everybody Needs Somebody to Love (Reetch, Caesar & Dino, BMI) .......... 59
Everyday I Have the Blues (Arc, BMI) .......... 96
Feel So Bad (Travis, BMI) .......... 91
For What It's Worth (Ten East/Springalo, BMI) .. 56
Georgy Girl (Chappell, ASCAP) .......... 2
Gimme Some Lovin' (Essex, ASCAP) .......... 17
Girls are Out to Get You (Camad, BMI) .......... 100
Go Where You Wanna Go (Trousdale, BMI) .......... 27
Good Thing (Daywin, BMI) .......... 19
Green, Green Grass of Home (Tree, BMI) .......... 13
Grizzly Bear (Whitfield, BMI) .......... 52
Happy Together (Chardon, BMI) .......... 79
Hello Hello (Great Honesty, BMI) .......... 31
Hey, Leroy, Your Mama's Callin' You (Bozart, BMI) .......... 38
How Do You Catch a Girl (Rose, BMI) .......... 39
Hunter Gets Captured by the Game, The (Jobete, BMI) .......... 46
I Dig You Baby (Morpine, BMI) .......... 76
I Had Too Much to Dream (Last Night) (Star, BMI) .......... 11
I Think We're Alone Now (Patricia, BMI) .......... 82
I Wish You Could Be Here (Charing Cross, BMI) .. 77
I'll Take Care of Your Cares (Remick, ASCAP) .... 61
I'm a Believer (Screen Gems-Columbia, BMI) .... 1
I'm Gonna Miss You (Jalynne-BRC, BMI) .......... 62
I've Been Lonely Too Long (Slacsar, BMI) .......... 53
I've Got to Have a Reason (Branstor, BMI) .... 44
I've Passed This Way Before (Jobete, BMI) .... 33
If You Go Away (Marks, BMI) .......... 68
Indescribably Blue (Elvis Presley, BMI) .......... 47
It May Be Winter Outside (Maravilla, BMI) .... 42
It Takes Two (Jobete, BMI) .......... 29
It's Now Winter's Day (Low Twi, BMI) .......... 24
Just Be Sincere (Jalynne-BRC, BMI) .......... 93
Keep a Light in the Window Till I Come Home (Rags, BMI) .......... 81
Kind of a Drag (Maryon, ASCAP) .......... 3
Knight in Rusty Armour (Dean Street/Feist, ASCAP) .......... 23
Lady (Roosevelt, BMI) .......... 67
Let's Fall in Love (Bourne, ASCAP) .......... 60
Let's Spend the Night Together (Gideon, BMI) ... 57
Little Black Egg (Alison, ASCAP) .......... 85
Look What You've Done (Pocketful of Fames/Noma, BMI) .......... 50
Love Is Here and Now You're Gone (Jobete, BMI) 9
Lovin' You (Faithful Virtue, BMI) .......... 35
Mercy, Mercy, Mercy (Zawinul, BMI) .......... 21
Music to Watch Girls By (SCP, ASCAP) .......... 15
My Cup Runneth Over (Chappell, ASCAP) .......... 36
My Special Prayer (Maureen, BMI) .......... 94
Nashville Cats (Faithful Virtue, BMI) .......... 22
Niki Hoeky (Novalene, BMI) .......... 55
98.6 (Screen Gems-Columbia, BMI) .......... 7
No Fair at All (Beechwood, BMI) .......... 65
One, Two, Three (Double Diamond, BMI) .......... 95
Ooh Baby (Arc, BMI) .......... 88
Our Winter Love (Cramart, BMI) .......... 74
People in Me, The (Thrush, BMI) .......... 83
People Like You (Feist, ASCAP) .......... 99
Pretty Ballerina (Last Day, BMI) .......... 25
Pucker Up Buttercup (Jobete, BMI) .......... 75
Pushin' Too Hard (Neil/Purple Bottle, BMI) .... 40
Raise Your Hand (East, BMI) .......... 98
Ride, Ride, Ride (Yonah, BMI) .......... 37
Ruby Tuesday (Gideon, BMI) .......... 4
Sit Down, I Think I Love You (Screen Gems-Columbia) .......... 80
Skate Now (3 Track, BMI) .......... 86
Snoopy vs. the Red Baron (Fuller/Samphil/Windsong, BMI) .......... 8
So You Want to Be a Rock 'n' Roll Star (Tickson, BMI) .......... 51
Sock It to Me—Baby! (Saturday, BMI) .......... 58
Something Good (East, BMI) .......... 78
Spooky (Lowery, BMI) .......... 73
Stand By Me (Progressive/Trio/A.B.T. Tet, BMI) .. 12
Standing in the Shadows of Love (Jobete, BMI) .. 18
Sugar Town (Criterion, ASCAP) .......... 41
Sunrise, Sunset (Sunbeam, BMI) .......... 87
Tell It Like It Is (Olrap, BMI) .......... 6
Tell It to the Rain (Saturday/Seasons Four, BMI) 31
Ten Commandments (Carab, BMI) .......... 97
Then You Can Tell Me Goodbye (Acuff-Rose, BMI) 16
There Goes My Everything (Blue Crest-Husky, BMI) 72
There's a Kind of a Hush (Feist, ASCAP) .......... 90
Tiny Bubbles (Granite, ASCAP) .......... 70
Tramp (Modern, BMI) .......... 54
Trouble Down Here Below (Raw Lou, BMI) .......... 92
(We Ain't Got) Nothin' Yet (Anange-Range, BMI) 5
Where Will the Words Come From (Viva, BMI) .. 34
Wild Thing (Blackwood, BMI) .......... 20
Wish Me a Rainbow (Famous, ASCAP) .......... 63
Wish You Didn't Have to Go (Fame, BMI) .......... 48
Words of Love (Trousdale, BMI) .......... 14
You Got to Me (Tallyrand, BMI) .......... 32

## BUBBLING UNDER THE HOT 100

101. DARK END OF THE STREET .......... James Carr, Goldwax 317
102. FOOLS FALL IN LOVE .......... Elvis Presley, RCA Victor 9056
103. LOVE YOU SO MUCH .......... New Colony Six, Sentar 1205
104. AT THE PARTY .......... Hèctor Riviera, Barry 101
105. THAT'S THE TUNE .......... Vogues, Co & Ce 242
106. SWEET MARIA .......... Billy Vaughan Singers, Dot 16985
107. TIP TOE .......... Robert Parker, Nola 729
108. WALK TALL .......... 2 of Clubs, Fraternity 975
109. SHE'S LOOKING GOOD .......... Roger Collins, Galaxy 750
110. DON'T GO HOME (My Little Darlin') .......... Shirelles, Scepter 12185
111. LOOK AT GRANNY RUN RUN .......... Howard Tate, Verve 10464
112. I WON'T COME IN WHILE HE'S THERE .......... Jim Reeves, RCA Victor 9057
113. MY BEST FRIEND .......... Jefferson Airplane, RCA Victor 9063
114. SWEETEST ONE .......... Metros, RCA Victor 8994
115. HARD LOVIN' LOSER .......... Judy Collins, Elektra 45610
116. FUNKY BROADWAY .......... Dyke & the Blazers, Original Sound 64
117. MORNINGTOWN RIDE .......... Seekers, Capitol 5787
118. CABARET .......... Ray Conniff, Columbia 43975
119. RAIN, RAIN GO AWAY .......... Lee Dorsey, Amy 974
120. THIS PRECIOUS TIME .......... Terry Knight & the Pack, Lucky 11 235
121. GONNA GET ALONG WITHOUT YA' NOW .......... Trini Lopez, Reprise 0547
122. THE 59TH STREET BRIDGE SONG .......... Harpers Bizarre, Warner Bros. 5890
123. LOVE'S GONE BAD .......... Underdogs, V.I.P. 25040
124. ALONG CAME JONES .......... Righteous Brothers, Verve 10479
125. PEEK-A-BOO .......... New Vaudeville Band, Fontana 1573
126. ANOTHER PAGE .......... Connie Francis, MGM 13665
127. MUSIC TO WATCH GIRLS BY .......... Al Hirt, RCA Victor 9060
128. SHADOW OF YOUR SMILE .......... Boots Randolph, Monument 1976
129. SNOW QUEEN .......... Roger Nichols Trio, A&M 830
130. GRITS 'N' CORN BREAD .......... Soul Runners, MoSoul 101
131. KIND OF A HUSH .......... Gary and the Hornets, Smash 2078
132. SHE .......... Del Shannon, Liberty 55939
133. SHINGALING '67 .......... Don Covay, Atlantic 2375
134. SINCE I LOST YOU GIRL .......... Monitors, V.I.P. 25039
135. HOLD ON, I'M COMING .......... Chuck Jackson & Maxine Brown, Wand 1148

Compiled from national retail sales and radio station airplay by the Music Popularity Dept. of Record Market Research, Billboard.

# Billboard HOT 100

For Week Ending February 18, 1967

★ STAR performer—Sides registering greatest proportionate upward progress this week.

Record Industry Association of America seal of certification as million selling single.

| This Week | 1 Wk. Ago | 2 Wks. Ago | 3 Wks. Ago | TITLE Artist (Producer), Label & Number | Weeks On Chart |
|---|---|---|---|---|---|
| 1 | 3 | 5 | 9 | **KIND OF A DRAG** — Buckinghams (Carl Bonafede & Dan Belloch), U.S.A. 860 (Billboard Award) | 8 |
| 2 | 1 | 1 | 1 | **I'M A BELIEVER** — Monkees (Jeff Barry), Colgems 1002 | 11 |
| 3 | 4 | 11 | 43 | **RUBY TUESDAY** — Rolling Stones (Andrew Loog Oldham), London 904 | 5 |
| 4 | 2 | 2 | 2 | **GEORGY GIRL** — Seekers (Tom Springfield), Capitol 5756 | 12 |
| 5 | 5 | 7 | 10 | **(We Ain't Got) NOTHIN' YET** — Blues Magoos (Wyld & Polhemus), Mercury 72622 | 11 |
| 6 | 9 | 27 | 47 | **LOVE IS HERE AND NOW YOU'RE GONE** — Supremes (Holland-Dozier), Motown 1103 | 4 |
| 7 | 7 | 8 | 11 | **98.6** — Keith (Jerry Ross), Mercury 72639 | 11 |
| 8 | 6 | 4 | 2 | **TELL IT LIKE IT IS** — Aaron Neville, Parlo 101 | 12 |
| 9 | 10 | 16 | 34 | **THE BEAT GOES ON** — Sonny & Cher (Sonny Bono), Atco 6461 | 6 |
| 10 | 17 | 26 | 39 | **GIMME SOME LOVIN'** — Spencer Davis Group (Chris Blackwell & Jimmy Miller), United Artists 50106 | 8 |
| 11 | 13 | 13 | 19 | **GREEN, GREEN GRASS OF HOME** — Tom Jones (Peter Sullivan), Parrot 40009 | 9 |
| 12 | 12 | 14 | 14 | **STAND BY ME** — Spyder Turner (Arnold Geller), MGM 13617 | 10 |
| 13 | 16 | 23 | 36 | **THEN YOU CAN TELL ME GOODBYE** — Casinos (Gene Hughes), Fraternity 977 | 6 |
| 14 | 11 | 18 | 20 | **I HAD TOO MUCH TO DREAM (Last Night)** — Electric Prunes (Damo Prod.), Reprise 0532 | 11 |
| 15 | 8 | 3 | 3 | **SNOOPY VS. THE RED BARON** — Royal Guardsmen (Phil Gernhard), Laurie 3366 | 10 |
| 16 | 21 | 29 | 38 | **MERCY, MERCY, MERCY** — "Cannonball" Adderley (David-Axelrod), Capitol 5798 | 7 |
| 17 | 25 | 34 | 50 | **PRETTY BALLERINA** — Left Banke (World United Prod.), Smash 2074 | 7 |
| 18 | 15 | 17 | 24 | **MUSIC TO WATCH GIRLS BY** — Bob Crewe Generation (Bob Crewe), DynoVoice 229 | 8 |
| 19 | 49 | 81 | — | **BABY, I NEED YOUR LOVIN'** — Johnny Rivers (Lou Adler), Imperial 66227 | 3 |
| 20 | 29 | 35 | 46 | **IT TAKES TWO** — Marvin Gaye & Kim Weston (Wm. Stevenson-H. Cosby), Tamla 54141 | 7 |
| 21 | 27 | 36 | 52 | **GO WHERE YOU WANNA GO** — 5th Dimension (Johnny Rivers & Marc Gordon), Soul City 753 | 6 |
| 22 | 19 | 9 | 7 | **GOOD THING** — Paul Revere & the Raiders (Terry Melcher), Columbia 43907 | 12 |
| 23 | 24 | 24 | 29 | **IT'S NOW WINTER'S DAY** — Tommy Roe (Our Prod.), ABC 10888 | 9 |
| 24 | 36 | 50 | 61 | **MY CUP RUNNETH OVER** — Ed Ames (Jim Foglesong & Joe Reisman), RCA Victor 9002 | 5 |
| 25 | 32 | 54 | 66 | **YOU GOT TO ME** — Neil Diamond (Jeff Barry & Ellie Greenwich), Bang 540 | 4 |
| 26 | 18 | 10 | 6 | **STANDING IN THE SHADOWS OF LOVE** — Four Tops (Holland & Dozier), Motown 1102 | 10 |
| 27 | 58 | 82 | — | **SOCK IT TO ME—BABY!** — Mitch Ryder & the Detroit Wheels (Bob Crewe), New Voice 820 | 3 |
| 28 | 26 | 31 | 31 | **HELLO HELLO** — Sopwith "Camel" (Erik Jacobsen), Kama Sutra 217 | 9 |
| 29 | 30 | 30 | 37 | **BRING IT UP** — James Brown & the Famous Flames (James Brown), King 6071 | 7 |
| 30 | 22 | 12 | 8 | **NASHVILLE CATS** — Lovin' Spoonful (Erik Jacobsen), Kama Sutra 219 | 10 |
| 31 | 38 | 35 | 45 | **HEY, LEROY, YOUR MAMA'S CALLING YOU** — Jimmy Castor (Johnny Brantly), Smash 2069 | 8 |
| 32 | 35 | 48 | 60 | **LOVIN' YOU** — Bobby Darin (Charles Koppelman & Don Rubin), Atlantic 2376 | 6 |
| 33 | 46 | 56 | 67 | **THE HUNTER GETS CAPTURED BY THE GAME** — Marvelettes (William Robinson), Tamla 54143 | 5 |
| 34 | 51 | 61 | 76 | **SO YOU WANT TO BE A ROCK 'N' ROLL STAR** — Byrds (Gary Usher), Columbia 43987 | 4 |
| 35 | 47 | 58 | 77 | **INDESCRIBABLY BLUE** — Elvis Presley, RCA Victor 9056 | 4 |
| 36 | 43 | 49 | 59 | **ALL** — James Darren (Dick Glasser), Warner Bros. 5874 | 6 |
| 37 | 37 | 43 | 54 | **RIDE, RIDE, RIDE** — Brenda Lee (Owen Bradley), Decca 32079 | 6 |
| 38 | 40 | 41 | 51 | **PUSHIN' TOO HARD** — Seeds (Marcus Tybalt), GNP Crescendo 372 | 9 |
| 39 | 56 | 70 | 90 | **FOR WHAT IT'S WORTH** — Buffalo Springfield (Greene & Stone), Atco 6459 | 4 |
| 40 | 45 | 46 | 57 | **ARE YOU LONELY FOR ME** — Freddy Scott (Bert Berns), Shout 207 | 9 |
| 41 | 53 | 63 | 79 | **I'VE BEEN LONELY TOO LONG** — Young Rascals (Young Rascals), Atlantic 2377 | 4 |
| 42 | 48 | 51 | 68 | **WISH YOU DIDN'T HAVE TO GO** — James & Bobby Purify (Papa Don Easy), Bell 660 | 5 |
| 43 | 69 | — | — | **EPISTLE TO DIPPY** — Donovan (Mickie Most), Epic 10127 | 2 |
| 44 | 55 | 65 | 74 | **NIKI HOEKY** — P. J. Proby (Calvin Carter), Liberty 55936 | 5 |
| 45 | 14 | 6 | 5 | **WORDS OF LOVE** — Mama's & the Papa's (Lou Adler), Dunhill 4057 | 12 |
| 46 | 59 | 77 | — | **EVERYBODY NEEDS SOMEBODY TO LOVE** — Wilson Pickett (Jerry Wexler & Rick Hall), Atlantic 2381 | 3 |
| 47 | 60 | 71 | 93 | **LET'S FALL IN LOVE** — Peaches & Herb (Kapralik-McCoy), Date 1523 | 6 |
| 48 | 23 | 15 | 15 | **KNIGHT IN RUSTY ARMOUR** — Peter & Gordon (John Burgess), Capitol 5808 | 9 |
| 49 | 42 | 42 | 48 | **IT MAY BE WINTER OUTSIDE** — Felice Taylor (Keene-White Prod.), Mustang 3024 | 7 |
| 50 | 28 | 19 | 16 | **COLOR MY WORLD** — Petula Clark (Tony Hatch), Warner Bros. 5882 | 9 |
| 51 | 61 | 66 | 81 | **I'LL TAKE CARE OF YOUR CARES** — Frankie Laine (Bob Thiele), ABC 10891 | 5 |
| 52 | 54 | 60 | 63 | **TRAMP** — Lowel Fulsom, Kent 456 | 6 |
| 53 | 20 | 20 | 23 | **WILD THING** — Senator Bobby (C & D Prod.), Parkway 127 | 7 |
| 54 | 90 | — | — | **THERE'S A KIND OF A HUSH** — Herman's Hermits (Mickie Most), MGM 13681 | 2 |
| 55 | 67 | 72 | 87 | **LADY** — Jack Jones, Kapp 800 | 4 |
| 56 | 66 | 84 | 99 | **DADDY'S LITTLE GIRL** — Al Martino (Tom Morgan), Capitol 5825 | 4 |
| 57 | 57 | 59 | 75 | **LET'S SPEND THE NIGHT TOGETHER** — Rolling Stones (Andrew Loog Oldham), London 904 | 5 |
| 58 | 71 | 94 | — | **CALIFORNIA NIGHTS** — Lesley Gore (Bob Crewe), Mercury 72649 | 3 |
| 59 | 84 | — | — | **DARLIN' BE HOME SOON** — Lovin' Spoonful (Erik Jacobsen), Kama Sutra 220 | 2 |
| 60 | 64 | 79 | — | **DIS-ADVANTAGES OF YOU** — Brass Ring (Steve Barri), Dunhill 4065 | 3 |
| 61 | 65 | 80 | — | **NO FAIR AT ALL** — Association (Jerry Yester), Valiant 758 | 3 |
| 62 | 79 | — | — | **HAPPY TOGETHER** — Turtles (Joe Wissert), White Whale 244 | 2 |
| 63 | 52 | 53 | 53 | **GRIZZLY BEAR** — Youngbloods (Felix Pappalardi), RCA Victor 9015 | 10 |
| 64 | 62 | 55 | 58 | **I'M GONNA MISS YOU** — Artistics (Carl Davis), Brunswick 55301 | 10 |
| 65 | 82 | — | — | **I THINK WE'RE ALONE NOW** — Tommy James and the Shondells (Cordell-Gentry), Roulette 4720 | 1 |
| 66 | 44 | 45 | 56 | **I'VE GOT TO HAVE A REASON** — Dave Clark Five (Dave Clark), Epic 10114 | 7 |
| 67 | 73 | 73 | 78 | **SPOOKY** — Mike Sharpe (Harry Middlebrooks), Liberty 55922 | 4 |
| 68 | 83 | 98 | 100 | **THE PEOPLE IN ME** — Music Machine (Brian Ross), Original Sound 67 | 4 |
| 69 | 75 | — | — | **PUCKER UP BUTTERCUP** — Jr. Walker and the All Stars, (H. Fuqua-J. Bristol), Soul 35030 | 2 |
| 70 | 70 | 75 | 80 | **TINY BUBBLES** — Don Ho & Allis Burke, Reprise 0507 | 11 |
| 71 | 80 | 90 | — | **SIT DOWN, I THINK I LOVE YOU** — Mojo Men (Lenny Waronker), Reprise 0539 | 3 |
| 72 | 74 | 76 | 82 | **OUR WINTER LOVE** — Lettermen (Steve Douglas), Capitol 5813 | 4 |
| 73 | 72 | 74 | 85 | **THERE GOES MY EVERYTHING** — Jack Greene, Decca 32023 | 7 |
| 74 | 78 | 78 | 83 | **SOMETHING GOOD** — Carla Thomas (Prod. by Satff), Stax 207 | 6 |
| 75 | 76 | 86 | 86 | **I DIG YOU BABY** — Jerry Butler (Jerry Ross), Mercury 72648 | 5 |
| 76 | 77 | 95 | — | **I WISH YOU COULD BE HERE** — Cyrkle (John Simon), Columbia 43965 | 3 |
| 77 | — | — | — | **UPS AND DOWNS** — Paul Revere & the Raiders (Terry Melchers), Columbia 44018 | 1 |
| 78 | 81 | — | — | **KEEP A LIGHT IN THE WINDOW TILL I COME HOME** — Solomon Burks (Bob Gallo), Atlantic 2378 | 2 |
| 79 | — | — | — | **ONE MORE MOUNTAIN TO CLIMB** — Ronnie Dove (Phil Kahl), Diamond 217 | 1 |
| 80 | 95 | — | — | **ONE, TWO, THREE** — Ramsey Lewis (E. Edwards), Cadet 5556 | 2 |
| 81 | — | — | — | **HUNG IN YOUR EYES** — Brian Hyland (Snuff Garrett), Philips 40424 | 1 |
| 82 | — | — | — | **PEEK-A-BOO** — New Vaudeville Band (Geoff Stephens), Fontana 1573 | 1 |
| 83 | 98 | 100 | — | **RAISE YOUR HAND** — Eddie Floyd (Prod. by Staff), Stax 208 | 3 |
| 84 | 86 | 87 | 98 | **SKATE NOW** — Lou Courtney (Funk Bros. Prod.), Riverside 4588 | 4 |
| 85 | 97 | 99 | — | **TEN COMMANDMENTS** — Prince Buster (Buster-East Prod.), Philips 40427 | 3 |
| 86 | 87 | 92 | 95 | **SUNRISE, SUNSET** — Roger Williams (Hy Grill), Kapp 801 | 4 |
| 87 | — | — | — | **MORNINGTOWN RIDE** — Seekers (Tom Springfield), Capitol 5787 | 1 |
| 88 | — | — | — | **THE 59TH STREET BRIDGE SONG** — Harpers Bizarre (Lenny Waronker), Warner Bros. 5890 | 1 |
| 89 | 96 | — | — | **EVERYDAY I HAVE THE BLUES** — Billy Stewart (Billy Davis), Chess 1991 | 2 |
| 90 | — | — | — | **LOVE YOU SO MUCH** — New Colony Six (Ron Malo), Sentar 1205 | 1 |
| 91 | 91 | 97 | — | **FEEL SO BAD** — Little Milton, Checker 1162 | 3 |
| 92 | 94 | 96 | — | **MY SPECIAL PRAYER** — Joe Simon (J. R. Ent.), Sound Stage 72577 | 3 |
| 93 | 93 | — | — | **JUST BE SINCERE** — Jackie Wilson (Carl Davis), Brunswick 55309 | 2 |
| 94 | — | — | — | **NO MILK TODAY** — Herman's Hermits (Mickie Most), MGM 13681 | 1 |
| 95 | — | — | — | **THE LOVE I SAW IN YOU WAS JUST A MIRAGE** — Smokey Robinson and the Miracles (Wm. Robinson-W. Moore), Tamla 54145 | 1 |
| 96 | — | — | — | **HOLD ON, I'M COMING** — Chuck Jackson and Maxine Brown, Wand 1148 | 1 |
| 97 | 99 | — | — | **PEOPLE LIKE YOU** — Eddie Fisher (Al Schmitt), RCA Victor 9070 | 2 |
| 98 | 100 | — | — | **GIRLS ARE OUT TO GET YOU** — Fascinations, Mayfield 7714 | 2 |
| 99 | — | — | — | **BABY, HELP ME** — Percy Sledge (Quin Ivy and Marlin Greene), Atlantic 2383 | 1 |
| 100 | — | — | — | **GONNA GET ALONG WITHOUT YA' NOW** — Trini Lopez (Don Costa Prod.), Reprise 0547 | 1 |

## BUBBLING UNDER THE HOT 100

101. DARK END OF THE STREET ............ James Carr, Goldwax 317
102. FOOLS FALL IN LOVE ............ Elvis Presley, RCA Victor 9056
103. MY BEST FRIEND ............ Jefferson Airplane, RCA Victor 9063
104. WALK TALL ............ 2 of Clubs, Fraternity 975
105. SWEET MARIA ............ Billy Vaughn Singers, Dot 16985
106. TIP TOE ............ Robert Parker, Nola 729
107. SHE'S LOOKING GOOD ............ Roger Collins, Galaxy 750
108. TROUBLE DOWN HERE BELOW ............ Lou Rawls, Capitol 5824
109. DANGER! SHE'S A STRANGER ............ Five Stairsteps, Windy C 604
110. ALONG COMES JONES ............ Righteous Bros., Verve 10479
111. OOH BABY ............ Bo Diddley, Checker 1158
112. SOUL TIME ............ Shirley Ellis, Columbia 44021
113. WHO DO YOU LOVE ............ Woolies, Dunhill 4052
114. FUNKY BROADWAY ............ Dyke & the Blazers, Original Sound 64
115. WHERE DOES THE GOOD TIMES GO ............ Buck Owens, Capitol 5811
116. PENNY LANE ............ Beatles, Capitol 5810
117. SINCE I LOST YOU GIRL ............ Monitors, V.I.P. 25039
118. STRAWBERRY FIELDS FOREVER ............ Beatles, Capitol 5810
119. RAIN RAIN GO AWAY ............ Lee Dorsey, AMI 974
120. CABARET ............ Ray Conniff, Columbia 43975
121. ANOTHER PAGE ............ Connie Francis, MGM 13665
122. LOVE'S GONE BAD ............ Underdogs, V.I.P. 25040
123. MARRYIN' KIND OF LOVE ............ Critters, Kapp 805
124. GRITS 'N' CORN BREAD ............ Soul Runners, MoSoul 101
125. WHY NOT TONIGHT ............ Jimmy Hughes, Fame 1011
126. WITH THIS RING ............ Platters, Musicor 1229
127. KIND OF A HUSH ............ Gary & the Hornets, Smash 2078
128. THEME FROM THE WILD ANGELS ............ Davie Allan, Tower 295
129. SPEAK HER NAME ............ Walter Jackson, Okeh 7272
130. LONELY AGAIN ............ Eddy Arnold, RCA Victor 9080
131. SHE ............ Del Shannon, Liberty 55939
132. BIGGEST MAN ............ Jimmy Hunt, Dynamo 101
133. CRY OF THE WILD GOOSE ............ Baja Marimba Band, A&M 833
134. MAIRZY DOATS ............ Innocence, Kama Sutra 221
135. COME ON DOWN ............ Jackie DeShannon, Imperial 66224

Compiled from national retail sales and radio station airplay by the Music Popularity Dept. of Record Market Research, Billboard.

# Billboard HOT 100

**For Week Ending February 25, 1967**

★ STAR performer—Sides registering greatest proportionate upward progress this week.

Record Industry Association of America seal of certification as million selling single.

| TW | 2W | 3W | TITLE Artist (Producer), Label & Number | WoC |
|---|---|---|---|---|
| 1 | 1 | 3 | 5 | KIND OF A DRAG — Buckinghams (Carl Bonafede & Dan Belleck), U.S.A. 860 | 9 |
| 2 | 6 | 9 | 27 | LOVE IS HERE AND NOW YOU'RE GONE — Supremes (Holland-Dozier), Motown 1103 | 5 |
| 3 | 3 | 4 | 11 | RUBY TUESDAY — Rolling Stones (Andrew Loog Oldham), London 904 | 6 |
| 4 | 2 | 1 | 1 | I'M A BELIEVER — Monkees (Jeff Barry), Colgems 1002 | 12 |
| 5 | 4 | 2 | 2 | GEORGY GIRL — Seekers (Tom Springfield), Capitol 5756 | 13 |
| 6 | 9 | 10 | 16 | THE BEAT GOES ON — Sonny & Cher (Sonny Bono), Atco 6461 | 7 |
| 7 | 10 | 17 | 26 | GIMME SOME LOVIN' — Spencer Davis Group (Chris Blackwell & Jimmy Miller), United Artists 50108 | 9 |
| 8 | 13 | 16 | 23 | THEN YOU CAN TELL ME GOODBYE — Casinos (Gene Hughes), Fraternity 977 | 7 |
| 9 | 5 | 5 | 7 | (We Ain't Got) NOTHIN' YET — Blues Magoos (Wyld & Polhemus), Mercury 72622 | 12 |
| 10 | 19 | 49 | 81 | BABY, I NEED YOUR LOVIN' — Johnny Rivers (Lou Adler), Imperial 66227 | 4 |
| 11 | 16 | 21 | 29 | MERCY, MERCY, MERCY — "Cannonball" Adderley (David Axelrod), Capitol 5798 | 8 |
| 12 | 7 | 7 | 8 | 98.6 — Keith (Jerry Ross), Mercury 72639 | 12 |
| 13 | 11 | 13 | 13 | GREEN, GREEN GRASS OF HOME — Tom Jones (Peter Sullivan), Parrot 40009 | 10 |
| 14 | 27 | 58 | 82 | SOCK IT TO ME—BABY! — Mitch Ryder & the Detroit Wheels (Bob Crewe), New Voice 820 | 4 |
| 15 | 17 | 25 | 34 | PRETTY BALLERINA — Left Banke (World United Prod.), Smash 2074 | 8 |
| 16 | 21 | 27 | 36 | GO WHERE YOU WANNA GO — 5th Dimension (Johnny Rivers & Marc Gordon), Soul City 753 | 7 |
| 17 | 14 | 11 | 18 | I HAD TOO MUCH TO DREAM (Last Night) — Electric Prunes (Dave Prod.), Reprise 0532 | 12 |
| 18 | 20 | 29 | 35 | IT TAKES TWO — Marvin Gaye & Kim Weston (Wm. Stevenson-H. Cosby), Tamla 54141 | 8 |
| 19 | 24 | 36 | 50 | MY CUP RUNNETH OVER — Ed Ames (Jim Foglesong & Joe Reisman), RCA Victor 9002 | 6 |
| 20 | 12 | 12 | 14 | STAND BY ME — Spyder Turner (Arnold Geller), MGM 13617 | 11 |
| 21 | 25 | 32 | 54 | YOU GOT TO ME — Neil Diamond (Jeff Barry & Ellie Greenwich), Bang 540 | 5 |
| 22 | 8 | 6 | 4 | TELL IT LIKE IT IS — Aaron Neville, Parlo 101 | 13 |
| 23 | 23 | 24 | 24 | IT'S NOW WINTER'S DAY — Tommy Roe (Our Prod.), ABC 10888 | 10 |
| 24 | 18 | 15 | 17 | MUSIC TO WATCH GIRLS BY — Bob Crewe Generation (Bob Crewe), DynoVoice 229 | 9 |
| 25 | 39 | 56 | 70 | FOR WHAT IT'S WORTH — Buffalo Springfield (Greene & Stone), Atco 6459 | 5 |
| 26 | 33 | 46 | 56 | THE HUNTER GETS CAPTURED BY THE GAME — Marvelettes (William Robinson), Tamla 54143 | 6 |
| 27 | 59 | 84 | — | DARLIN' BE HOME SOON — Lovin' Spoonful (Erik Jacobsen), Kama Sutra 220 | 3 |
| 28 | 15 | 8 | 3 | SNOOPY VS. THE RED BARON — Royal Guardsmen (Phil Gernhard), Laurie 3366 | 11 |
| 29 | 43 | 69 | — | EPISTLE TO DIPPY — Donovan (Mickie Most), Epic 10127 | 3 |
| 30 | 34 | 51 | 61 | SO YOU WANT TO BE A ROCK 'N' ROLL STAR — Byrds (Gary Usher), Columbia 43987 | 5 |
| 31 | 41 | 53 | 63 | I'VE BEEN LONELY TOO LONG — Young Rascals (Young Rascals), Atlantic 2377 | 5 |
| 32 | 32 | 35 | 48 | LOVIN' YOU — Bobby Darin (Charles Koppelman & Don Rubin), Atlantic 2376 | 7 |
| 33 | 35 | 47 | 58 | INDESCRIBABLY BLUE — Elvis Presley, RCA Victor 9056 | 5 |
| 34 | 44 | 55 | 65 | NIKI HOEKY — P. J. Proby (Calvin Carter), Liberty 55936 | 5 |
| 35 | 36 | 43 | 49 | ALL — James Darren (Dick Glasser), Warner Bros. 5874 | 7 |
| 36 | 38 | 40 | 41 | PUSHIN' TOO HARD — Seeds (Marcus Tybalt), GNP Crescendo 372 | 10 |
| 37 | 47 | 60 | 71 | LET'S FALL IN LOVE — Peaches & Herb (Kapralik-McCoy), Date 1523 | 7 |
| 38 | 42 | 48 | 51 | WISH YOU DIDN'T HAVE TO GO — James & Bobby Purify (Papa Don Easy), Bell 660 | 5 |
| 39 | 40 | 45 | 46 | ARE YOU LONELY FOR ME — Freddy Scott (Bert Berns), Shout 207 | 10 |
| 40 | 46 | 59 | 77 | EVERYBODY NEEDS SOMEBODY TO LOVE — Wilson Pickett (Jerry Wexler & Rick Hall), Atlantic 2381 | 4 |
| 41 | 62 | 79 | — | HAPPY TOGETHER — Turtles (Joe Wissert), White Whale 244 | 3 |
| 42 | 54 | 90 | — | THERE'S A KIND OF A HUSH — Herman's Hermits (Mickie Most), MGM 13681 | 3 |
| 43 | 58 | 71 | 94 | CALIFORNIA NIGHTS — Lesley Gore (Bob Crewe), Mercury 72649 | 4 |
| 44 | 29 | 30 | 30 | BRING IT UP — James Brown & The Famous Flames (James Brown), King 6071 | 8 |
| 45 | 56 | 66 | 84 | DADDY'S LITTLE GIRL — Al Martino (Tom Morgan), Capitol 5825 | 5 |
| 46 | 28 | 26 | 31 | HELLO HELLO — Sopwith "Camel" (Erik Jacobsen), Kama Sutra 217 | 10 |
| 47 | 31 | 38 | 35 | HEY, LEROY, YOUR MAMA'S CALLING YOU — Jimmy Castor (Johnny Brantly), Smash 2069 | 9 |
| 48 | 37 | 37 | 43 | RIDE, RIDE, RIDE — Brenda Lee (Owen Bradley), Decca 32079 | 7 |
| 49 | 51 | 61 | 66 | I'LL TAKE CARE OF YOUR CARES — Frankie Laine (Bob Thiele), ABC 10891 | 6 |
| 50 | 60 | 64 | 79 | DIS-ADVANTAGES OF YOU — Brass Ring (Steve Barri), Dunhill 4065 | 4 |
| 51 | 61 | 65 | 80 | NO FAIR AT ALL — Association (Jerry Yester), Valiant 758 | 4 |
| 52 | 65 | 82 | — | I THINK WE'RE ALONE NOW — Tommy James and the Shondells (Cordell-Gentry), Roulette 4720 | 3 |
| 53 | 55 | 67 | 72 | LADY — Jack Jones, Kapp 800 | 5 |
| 54 | 77 | — | — | UPS AND DOWNS — Paul Revere & the Raiders (Terry Melchers), Columbia 44018 | 2 |
| 55 | 69 | 75 | — | PUCKER UP BUTTERCUP — Jr. Walker & the All Stars, (H. Fuqua-J. Bristol), Soul 35030 | 3 |
| 56 | 57 | 57 | 59 | LET'S SPEND THE NIGHT TOGETHER — Rolling Stones (Andrew Loog Oldham), London 904 | 8 |
| 57 | — | — | — | DEDICATED TO THE ONE I LOVE — Mama's and the Papa's (Lou Adler), Dunhill 4077 | 1 |
| 58 | 52 | 54 | 60 | TRAMP — Lowell Fulsom, Kent 456 | 7 |
| 59 | 67 | 73 | 73 | SPOOKY — Mike Sharpe (Harry Middlebrooks), Liberty 55922 | 4 |
| 60 | 71 | 80 | 90 | SIT DOWN, I THINK I LOVE YOU — Mojo Men (Lenny Waronker), Reprise 0539 | 4 |
| 61 | — | 79 | — | ONE MORE MOUNTAIN TO CLIMB — Ronnie Dove (Phil Kahl), Diamond 217 | 2 |
| 62 | — | — | 95 | THE LOVE I SAW IN YOU WAS JUST A MIRAGE — Smokey Robinson and the Miracles (Wm. Robinson-W. Moore), Tamla 54145 | 2 |
| 63 | 75 | 76 | 86 | I DIG YOU BABY — Jerry Butler (Jerry Ross), Mercury 72648 | 6 |
| 64 | — | 78 | 81 | KEEP A LIGHT IN THE WINDOW TILL I COME HOME — Solomon Burke (Bob Gallo), Atlantic 2378 | 3 |
| 65 | 73 | 72 | 74 | THERE GOES MY EVERYTHING — Jack Greene, Decca 32023 | 8 |
| 66 | 70 | 70 | 75 | TINY BUBBLES — Don Ho & Allis (Burke), Reprise 0507 | 12 |
| 67 | 94 | — | — | NO MILK TODAY — Herman's Hermits (Mickie Most), MGM 13681 | 2 |
| 68 | 68 | 83 | 98 | THE PEOPLE IN ME — Music Machine (Brian Ross), Original Sound 67 | 5 |
| 69 | 88 | — | — | THE 59TH STREET BRIDGE SONG — Harpers Bizarre (Lenny Waronker), Warner Bros. 5890 | 2 |
| 70 | 76 | 77 | 95 | I WISH YOU COULD BE HERE — Cyrkle (John Simon), Columbia 43965 | 4 |
| 71 | 84 | 86 | 87 | SKATE NOW — Lou Courtney (Funk Bros. Prod.), Riverside 4588 | 5 |
| 72 | 87 | — | — | MORNINGTOWN RIDE — Seekers (Tom Springfield), Capitol 5787 | 2 |
| 73 | 81 | — | — | HUNG UP IN YOUR EYES — Brian Hyland (Snuff Garrett), Philips 40424 | 2 |
| 74 | 89 | 96 | — | EVERYDAY I HAVE THE BLUES — Billy Stewart (Billy Davis), Chess 1991 | 3 |
| 75 | 80 | 95 | — | ONE, TWO, THREE — Ramsey Lewis (E. Edwards), Cadet 5556 | 3 |
| 76 | 82 | — | — | PEEK-A-BOO — New Vaudeville Band (Geoff Stephens), Fontana 1573 | 2 |
| 77 | 74 | 78 | 78 | SOMETHING GOOD — Carla Thomas (Prod. by Satff), Stax 207 | 7 |
| 78 | — | — | — | WHEN SOMETHING IS WRONG WITH MY BABY — Sam and Dave (Prod. by Staff), Stax 210 | 1 |
| 79 | — | — | — | RETURN OF THE RED BARON — Royal Guardsmen (Gernhard Ent.), Laurie 3379 | 1 |
| 80 | 83 | 98 | 100 | RAISE YOUR HAND — Eddie Floyd (Prod. by Staff), Stax 208 | 4 |
| 81 | 85 | 97 | 99 | TEN COMMANDMENTS — Prince Buster (Buster-East Prod.), Philips 40427 | 4 |
| 82 | — | — | — | DRY YOUR EYES — Brenda & the Tabulations (Bob Finz), Dionn 500 | 1 |
| 83 | — | — | — | STRAWBERRY FIELDS FOREVER — Beatles (George Martin), Capitol 5810 | 1 |
| 84 | 86 | 87 | 92 | SUNRISE, SUNSET — Roger Williams (My Grill), Kapp 801 | 5 |
| 85 | — | — | — | PENNY LANE — Beatles (George Martin), Capitol 5810 | 1 |
| 86 | 90 | — | — | LOVE YOU SO MUCH — New Colony Six (Ron Malo), Sentar 1205 | 2 |
| 87 | — | — | — | SOUL TIME — Shirley Ellis (Charlie Calello), Columbia 44021 | 1 |
| 88 | 92 | 94 | 96 | MY SPECIAL PRAYER — Joe Simon (J. R. Ent.), Sound Stage 72577 | 4 |
| 89 | — | — | — | JIMMY MACK — Martha and the Vandellas (Holland-Dozier), Gordy 7058 | 1 |
| 90 | — | — | — | WITH THIS RING — Platters (Luther Dixon), Musicor 1229 | 1 |
| 91 | 93 | 93 | — | JUST BE SINCERE — Jackie Wilson (Carl Davis), Brunswick 55309 | 3 |
| 92 | 98 | 100 | — | GIRLS ARE OUT TO GET YOU — Fascinations, Mayfield 7714 | 3 |
| 93 | — | 100 | — | GONNA GET ALONG WITHOUT YA' NOW — Trini Lopez (Don Costa Prod.), Reprise 0547 | 2 |
| 94 | 96 | — | — | HOLD ON, I'M COMING — Chuck Jackson and Maxine Brown, Wand 1148 | 2 |
| 95 | 99 | — | — | BABY, HELP ME — Percy Sledge (Quin Ivy and Marlin Greene), Atlantic 2383 | 2 |
| 96 | — | 88 | 89 | OOH BABY — Bo Diddley (M. Chess-E. Edwards), Checker 1156 | 5 |
| 97 | 97 | 99 | — | PEOPLE LIKE YOU — Eddie Fisher (Al Schmitt), RCA Victor 9070 | 3 |
| 98 | — | — | — | THE DARK END OF THE STREET — James Carr (Quinton Claunch and Randolph Russell), Goldwax 317 | 1 |
| 99 | — | — | — | GIRL DON'T CARE — Gene Chandler (Carl Davis), Brunswick 55312 | 1 |
| 100 | — | — | — | MERCY, MERCY, MERCY — Larry Williams and Johnny Watson (Larry Williams and Johnny Watson), Okeh 7274 | 1 |

## HOT 100—A TO Z—(Publisher-Licensee)

## BUBBLING UNDER THE HOT 100

101. FEEL SO BAD ... Little Milton, Checker 1162
102. WALK TALL ... 2 of Clubs, Fraternity 975
103. MY BEST FRIEND ... Jefferson Airplane, RCA Victor 9063
104. WHO DO YOU LOVE ... Woolies, Dunhill 4052
105. FOOLS FALL IN LOVE ... Elvis Presley, RCA Victor 9056
106. SHE'S LOOKING GOOD ... Roger Collins, Galaxy 750
107. TROUBLE DOWN HERE BELOW ... Lou Rawls, Capitol 5824
108. SUMMER WINE ... Nancy Sinatra, Reprise 0527
109. MAIRZY DOATS ... Innocence, Kama Sutra 222
110. ALONG COMES JONES ... Righteous Brothers, Verve 10479
111. SPEAK HER NAME ... Walter Jackson, Okeh 7272
112. RAIN RAIN GO AWAY ... Lee Dorsey, AMY 974
113. SWEET MARIA ... Billy Vaughn, Dot 16985
114. TIP TOE ... Robert Parker, Nola 729
115. DANGER! SHE'S A STRANGER ... Five Stairsteps, Windy C 604
116. FUNKY BROADWAY ... Dyke and the Blazers, Original Sound 64
117. WILD ANGELS ... Ventures, Dolton 327
118. YOU ALWAYS HURT ME ... Impressions, ABC 10900
119. WHY NOT TONIGHT ... Jimmy Hughes, Fame 1011
120. WHERE DOES THE GOOD TIMES GO ... Buck Owens, Capitol 5811
121. SHOW ME ... Joe Tex, Dial 4055
122. MARVIN' KIND OF LOVE ... Critters, Kapp 805
123. GRITS 'N' CORNBREAD ... Soul Runners, McSoul 101
124. I DON'T WANT TO LOSE YOU ... Jackie Wilson, Brunswick 55309
125. LOVES GONE BAD ... Underdogs, V.I.P. 25040
126. LONELY AGAIN ... Eddy Arnold, RCA Victor 9080
127. KIND OF A HUSH ... Gary and the Hornets, Smash 2078
128. IF YOU'RE THINKIN' WHAT I'M THINKIN' ... Jackie DeShannon, Imperial 66224
129. COME ON DOWN ... Every Mother's Son, MGM 13683
130. BIGGEST MAN ... Tommy Hunt, Dynamo 101
131. WESTERN UNION ... Five Americans, Abnak 118
132. STORMY WEATHER ... Magnificent Men, Capitol 5812
133. MR. FARMER ... Seeds, GNP-Crescendo 383
134. I WON'T COME IN WHILE HE'S THERE ... Jim Reeves, RCA Victor 9057
135. IT'S A HAPPENING THING ... Peanut Butter Conspiracy, Columbia 43985

Compiled from national retail sales and radio station airplay by the Music Popularity Dept. of Record Market Research, Billboard.

# Billboard HOT 100

For Week Ending March 4, 1967

★ STAR performer—Sides registering greatest proportionate upward progress this week.

| This Week | Last Week | 2 Wks. Ago | 3 Wks. Ago | TITLE Artist (Producer), Label & Number | Weeks on Chart |
|---|---|---|---|---|---|
| 1 | 3 | 3 | 4 | **RUBY TUESDAY** — Rolling Stones (Andrew Loog Oldham), London 904 | 7 |
| 2 | 2 | 6 | 9 | **LOVE IS HERE AND NOW YOU'RE GONE** — Supremes (Holland-Dozier), Motown 1103 | 6 |
| 3 | 1 | 1 | 3 | **KIND OF A DRAG** — Buckinghams (Carl Bonafede & Dan Bellock), U.S.A. 860 | 10 |
| 4 | 10 | 19 | 49 | **BABY, I NEED YOUR LOVIN'** — Johnny Rivers (Lou Adler), Imperial 66227 | 5 |
| 5 | 5 | 4 | 2 | **GEORGY GIRL** — Seekers (Tom Springfield), Capitol 5756 | 14 |
| 6 | 6 | 9 | 10 | **THE BEAT GOES ON** — Sonny & Cher (Sonny Bono), Atco 6461 | 8 |
| 7 | 7 | 10 | 17 | **GIMME SOME LOVIN'** — Spencer Davis Group (Chris Blackwell & Jimmy Miller), United Artists 50108 | 10 |
| 8 | 8 | 13 | 16 | **THEN YOU CAN TELL ME GOODBYE** — Casinos (Gene Hughes), Fraternity 977 | 8 |
| 9 | 14 | 27 | 58 | **SOCK IT TO ME—BABY!** — Mitch Ryder & the Detroit Wheels (Bob Crewe), New Voice 820 | 5 |
| 10 | 4 | 2 | 1 | **I'M A BELIEVER** — Monkees (Jeff Barry), Colgems 1002 | 13 |
| 11 | 11 | 16 | 21 | **MERCY, MERCY, MERCY** — "Cannonball" Adderley (David Axelrod), Capitol 5798 | 9 |
| 12 | 9 | 5 | 5 | **(We Ain't Got) NOTHIN' YET** — Blues Magoos (Wyld & Polhemus), Mercury 72622 | 13 |
| 13 | 19 | 24 | 36 | **MY CUP RUNNETH OVER** — Ed Ames (Jim Foglesong & Joe Reisman), RCA Victor 9002 | 7 |
| 14 | 18 | 20 | 29 | **IT TAKES TWO** — Marvin Gaye & Kim Weston (Wm. Stevenson-H. Cosby), Tamla 54141 | 9 |
| 15 | 15 | 17 | 25 | **PRETTY BALLERINA** — Left Banke (World United Prod.), Smash 2074 | 9 |
| 16 | 16 | 21 | 27 | **GO WHERE YOU WANNA GO** — 5th Dimension (Johnny Rivers & Marc Gordon), Soul City 753 | 8 |
| 17 | 17 | 14 | 11 | **I HAD TOO MUCH TO DREAM (Last Night)** — Electric Prunes (Damo Prod.), Reprise 0532 | 13 |
| 18 | 21 | 25 | 32 | **YOU GOT TO ME** — Neil Diamond (Jeff Barry & Ellie Greenwich), Bang 540 | 6 |
| 19 | 26 | 33 | 46 | **THE HUNTER GETS CAPTURED BY THE GAME** — Marvelettes (William Robinson), Tamla 54143 | 7 |
| 20 | 25 | 39 | 56 | **FOR WHAT IT'S WORTH** — Buffalo Springfield (Greene & Stone), Atco 6459 | 4 |
| 21 | 41 | 62 | 79 | **HAPPY TOGETHER** — Turtles (Joe Wissert), White Whale 244 | 4 |
| 22 | 27 | 59 | 84 | **DARLIN' BE HOME SOON** — Lovin' Spoonful (Erik Jacobsen), Kama Sutra 220 | 4 |
| 23 | 42 | 54 | 90 | **THERE'S A KIND OF A HUSH** — Herman's Hermits (Mickie Most), MGM 13681 | 4 |
| 24 | 29 | 43 | 69 | **EPISTLE TO DIPPY** — Donovan (Mickie Most), Epic 10127 | 4 |
| 25 | 57 | — | — | **DEDICATED TO THE ONE I LOVE** — Mama's and the Papa's (Lou Adler), Dunhill 4077 | 2 |
| 26 | 12 | 7 | 7 | **98.6** — Keith (Jerry Ross), Mercury 72639 | 13 |
| 27 | 37 | 47 | 60 | **LET'S FALL IN LOVE** — Peaches & Herb (Kapralik-McCoy), Date 1523 | 8 |
| 28 | 31 | 41 | 53 | **I'VE BEEN LONELY TOO LONG** — Young Rascals (Young Rascals), Atlantic 2377 | 6 |
| 29 | 30 | 34 | 51 | **SO YOU WANT TO BE A ROCK 'N' ROLL STAR** — Byrds (Gary Usher), Columbia 43987 | 6 |
| 30 | 34 | 44 | 55 | **NIKI HOEKY** — P. J. Proby (Calvin Carter), Liberty 55936 | 6 |
| 31 | 13 | 11 | 13 | **GREEN, GREEN GRASS OF HOME** — Tom Jones (Peter Sullivan), Parrot 40009 | 11 |
| 32 | 43 | 58 | 71 | **CALIFORNIA NIGHTS** — Lesley Gore (Bob Crewe), Mercury 72649 | 5 |
| 33 | 33 | 35 | 47 | **INDESCRIBABLY BLUE** — Elvis Presley, RCA Victor 9056 | 6 |
| 34 | 40 | 46 | 59 | **EVERYBODY NEEDS SOMEBODY TO LOVE** — Wilson Pickett (Jerry Wexler & Rick Hall), Atlantic 2381 | 5 |
| 35 | 24 | 18 | 15 | **MUSIC TO WATCH GIRLS BY** — Bob Crewe Generation (Bob Crewe), DynoVoice 229 | 10 |
| 36 | 85 | — | — | **PENNY LANE** — Beatles (George Martin), Capitol 5810 | 2 |
| 37 | 54 | 77 | — | **UPS AND DOWNS** — Paul Revere & the Raiders (Terry Melchers), Columbia 44018 | 3 |
| 38 | 20 | 12 | 12 | **STAND BY ME** — Spyder Turner (Arnold Geller), MGM 13617 | 12 |
| 39 | 49 | 51 | 61 | **I'LL TAKE CARE OF YOUR CARES** — Frankie Laine (Bob Thiele), ABC 10891 | 7 |
| 40 | 50 | 60 | 64 | **DIS-ADVANTAGES OF YOU** — Brass Ring (Steve Barri), Dunhill 4065 | 6 |
| 41 | 52 | 65 | 82 | **I THINK WE'RE ALONE NOW** — Tommy James and the Shondells (Cordell-Gentry), Roulette 4720 | 4 |
| 42 | 22 | 8 | 6 | **TELL IT LIKE IT IS** — Aaron Neville, Parlo 101 | 14 |
| 43 | 45 | 56 | 66 | **DADDY'S LITTLE GIRL** — Al Martino (Tom Morgan), Capitol 5825 | 6 |
| 44 | 55 | 69 | 75 | **PUCKER UP BUTTERCUP** — Jr. Walker & the All Stars (H. Fuqua-J. Bristol), Soul 35030 | 4 |
| 45 | 83 | — | — | **STRAWBERRY FIELDS FOREVER** — Beatles (George Martin), Capitol 5810 | 2 |
| 46 | 36 | 38 | 40 | **PUSHIN' TOO HARD** — Seeds (Marcus Tybalt), GNP Crescendo 372 | 11 |
| 47 | 67 | 94 | — | **NO MILK TODAY** — Herman's Hermits (Mickie Most), MGM 13681 | 3 |
| 48 | 60 | 71 | 80 | **SIT DOWN, I THINK I LOVE YOU** — Mojo Men (Lenny Waronker), Reprise 0539 | 5 |
| 49 | 28 | 15 | 8 | **SNOOPY VS. THE RED BARON** — Royal Guardsmen (Phil Gernhard), Laurie 3366 | 12 |
| 50 | 62 | 95 | — | **THE LOVE I SAW IN YOU WAS JUST A MIRAGE** — Smokey Robinson and the Miracles (Wm. Robinson-W. Moore), Tamla 54145 | 3 |
| 51 | 61 | 79 | — | **ONE MORE MOUNTAIN TO CLIMB** — Ronnie Dove (Phil Kahl), Diamond 217 | 3 |
| 52 | 53 | 55 | 67 | **LADY** — Jack Jones, Kapp 800 | 7 |
| 53 | 51 | 61 | 65 | **NO FAIR AT ALL** — Association (Jerry Yester), Valiant 758 | 5 |
| 54 | 69 | 88 | — | **THE 59TH STREET BRIDGE SONG** — Harpers Bizarre (Lenny Waronker), Warner Bros. 5890 | 3 |
| 55 | 56 | 57 | 57 | **LET'S SPEND THE NIGHT TOGETHER** — Rolling Stones (Andrew Loog Oldham), London 904 | 7 |
| 56 | 38 | 42 | 48 | **WISH YOU DIDN'T HAVE TO GO** — James & Bobby Purify (Papa Don Easy), Bell 660 | 6 |
| 57 | 59 | 67 | 73 | **SPOOKY** — Mike Sharpe (Harry Middlebrooks), Liberty 55922 | 6 |
| 58 | 79 | — | — | **RETURN OF THE RED BARON** — Royal Guardsmen (Gernhard Ent.), Laurie 3379 | 2 |
| 59 | 32 | 32 | 35 | **LOVIN' YOU** — Bobby Darin (Charles Koppelman & Don Rubin), Atlantic 2376 | 8 |
| 60 | 72 | 87 | — | **MORNINGTOWN RIDE** — Seekers (Tom Springfield), Capitol 5787 | 3 |
| 61 | 63 | 75 | 76 | **I DIG YOU BABY** — Jerry Butler (Jerry Ross), Mercury 72648 | 7 |
| 62 | 39 | 40 | 45 | **ARE YOU LONELY FOR ME** — Freddy Scott (Bert Berns), Shout 207 | 11 |
| 63 | 35 | 46 | 43 | **ALL** — James Darren (Dick Glasser), Warner Bros. 5874 | 8 |
| 64 | 64 | 78 | 81 | **KEEP A LIGHT IN THE WINDOW TILL I COME HOME** — Solomon Burke (Bob Gallo), Atlantic 2378 | 4 |
| 65 | 23 | 23 | 24 | **IT'S NOW WINTER'S DAY** — Tommy Roe (Our Prod.), ABC 10888 | 11 |
| 66 | 66 | 70 | 70 | **TINY BUBBLES** — Don Ho & Allis (Burke), Reprise 0507 | 13 |
| 67 | 68 | 68 | 83 | **THE PEOPLE IN ME** — Music Machine (Brian Ross), Original Sound 67 | 6 |
| 68 | 89 | — | — | **JIMMY MACK** — Martha and the Vandellas (Holland-Dozier), Gordy 7058 | 2 |
| 69 | 73 | 81 | — | **HUNG UP IN YOUR EYES** — Brian Hyland (Snuff Garrett), Philips 40424 | 3 |
| 70 | 78 | — | — | **WHEN SOMETHING IS WRONG WITH MY BABY** — Sam and Dave (Prod. by Staff), Stax 210 | 2 |
| 71 | 71 | 84 | 86 | **SKATE NOW** — Lou Courtney (Funk Bros. Prod.), Riverside 4588 | 6 |
| 72 | 76 | 82 | — | **PEEK-A-BOO** — New Vaudeville Band (Geoff Stephens), Fontana 1573 | 3 |
| 73 | 75 | 80 | 95 | **ONE, TWO, THREE** — Ramsey Lewis (E. Edwards), Cadet 5556 | 4 |
| 74 | 74 | 89 | 96 | **EVERYDAY I HAVE THE BLUES** — Billy Stewart (Billy Davis), Chess 1991 | 4 |
| 75 | 86 | 90 | — | **LOVE YOU SO MUCH** — New Colony Six (Ron Malo), Sentar 1205 | 3 |
| 76 | 65 | 73 | 72 | **THERE GOES MY EVERYTHING** — Jack Greene, Decca 32023 | 9 |
| 77 | 82 | — | — | **DRY YOUR EYES** — Brenda and the Tabulations (Bob Finz), Dionn 500 | 2 |
| 78 | 87 | — | — | **SOUL TIME** — Shirley Ellis (Charlie Calello), Columbia 44021 | 2 |
| 79 | 80 | 83 | 98 | **RAISE YOUR HAND** — Eddie Floyd (Prod. by Staff), Stax 208 | 5 |
| 80 | — | — | — | **I NEVER LOVED A MAN THE WAY I LOVED YOU** — Aretha Franklin (Jerry Wexler), Atlantic 2386 | 1 |
| 81 | — | — | — | **WESTERN UNION** — Five Americans (Dale Hawkins), Abnak 118 | 1 |
| 82 | — | — | — | **MAIRZY DOATS** — Innocence (Ripp-Amders-Poncia), Kama Sutra 222 | 1 |
| 83 | — | — | — | **BEGGIN'** — 4 Seasons (Bob Crewe), Philips 40433 | 1 |
| 84 | — | — | — | **DON'T DO IT** — Micky Dolenz (Sepe/Brooks Prod.), Challenge 59353 | 1 |
| 85 | 90 | — | — | **WITH THIS RING** — Platters (Luther Dixon), Musicor 1229 | 1 |
| 86 | — | — | — | **KANSAS CITY** — James Brown & The Famous Flames (James Brown), King 6086 | 1 |
| 87 | 88 | 92 | 94 | **MY SPECIAL PRAYER** — Joe Simon (J. R. Ent.), Sound Stage 72577 | 5 |
| 88 | — | — | — | **SHOW ME** — Joe Tex (Buddy Killen), Dial 4055 | 1 |
| 89 | — | — | — | **TRAVLIN' MAN** — Stevie Wonder (Clarence Paul), Tamla 54147 | 1 |
| 90 | — | — | — | **THIS IS MY SONG** — Petula Clark (Sonny Burke), Warner Bros. 7002 | 1 |
| 91 | 98 | — | — | **THE DARK END OF THE STREET** — James Carr (Quinton Claunch and Randolph Russell), Goldwax 317 | 3 |
| 92 | 95 | 99 | — | **BABY, HELP ME** — Percy Sledge (Quin Ivy and Marlin Greene), Atlantic 2383 | 3 |
| 93 | 93 | 100 | — | **GONNA GET ALONG WITHOUT YA' NOW** — Trini Lopez (Don Costa Prod.), Reprise 0547 | 3 |
| 94 | — | — | — | **BECAUSE OF YOU** — Chris Montez (Herb Alpert), A&M 839 | 1 |
| 95 | 96 | — | 88 | **OOH BABY** — Bo Diddley (M. Chess-E. Edwards), Checker 1158 | 6 |
| 96 | — | — | — | **I DON'T WANT TO LOSE YOU** — Jackie Wilson (Carl Davis), Brunswick 55309 | 1 |
| 97 | — | — | — | **YOU ALWAYS HURT ME** — Impressions (Johnny Pate), ABC 10900 | 1 |
| 98 | — | — | — | **SUMMER WINE** — Nancy Sinatra and Lee Hazlewood (Lee Hazlewood), Reprise 0527 | 1 |
| 99 | 99 | — | — | **GIRL DON'T CARE** — Gene Chandler (Carl Davis), Brunswick 55312 | 2 |
| 100 | 100 | — | — | **MERCY, MERCY, MERCY** — Larry Williams and Johnny Watson (Larry Williams and Johnny Watson), Okeh 7274 | 1 |

## BUBBLING UNDER THE HOT 100

101. WALK TALL — 2 of Clubs, Fraternity 975
102. GIRLS ARE OUT TO GET YOU — Fascinations, Mayfield 7714
103. SHE'S LOOKING GOOD — Roger Collins, Galaxy 750
104. WHO DO YOU LOVE — Woolies, Dunhill 4052
105. FEEL SO BAD — Little Milton, Checker 1162
106. TEN COMMANDMENTS — Prince Buster, Philips 40427
107. MY BEST FRIEND — Jefferson Airplane, RCA Victor 9063
108. ALONG COMES JONES — Righteous Brothers, Verve 10479
109. PEOPLE LIKE YOU — Eddie Fisher, RCA Victor 9070
110. HOLD ON, I'M COMING — Chuck Jackson and Maxine Brown, Wand 1148
111. AS TIME GOES BY — Mel Carter, Imperial 66228
112. SWEETMARIA — Billy Vaughn, Dot 16985
113. WHY NOT TONIGHT — Jimmy Hughes, Fame 1011
114. WHERE DOES THE GOOD TIMES GO — Buck Owens, Capitol 5811
115. SUNRISE FROM THE WILD ANGELS — Ventures, Dolton 327
116. SUNRISE, SUNSET — Roger Williams, Kapp 801
117. LONELY AGAIN — Eddy Arnold, RCA Victor 9080
118. GRITS 'N' CORNBREAD — Soul Runners, McSoul 101
119. MARTYIN' KIND OF LOVE — Robert Parker, Nola 729
120. TIP TOP — Critters, Kapp 805
121. ICE MELTS IN THE SUN — Gary Lewis & the Playboys, Liberty 55949
122. COME ON DOWN — Jackie DeShannon, Imperial 66229
123. THE LOSER — Peter Courtney, Viva 609
124. I'LL GIVE YOU TIME TO THINK IT OVER — Outsiders, Capitol 5843
125. THE LOSER (With a Broken Heart) — Gary Lewis & the Playboys, Liberty 55949
126. DETROIT CITY — Tom Jones, Parrot 40012
127. IT'S A HAPPENING THING — Peanut Butter Conspiracy, Columbia 43985
128. MELLOW YELLOW — Senator Bobby & Senator McKinley, Parkway 127
129. BIGGEST MAN — Tommy Hunt, Dynamo 101
130. HERE, THERE AND EVERYWHERE — Claudine Longet, A&M 832
131. MR. ARMER — Seeds, GNP Crescendo 383
132. JUST LIKE A MAN — Margaret Whiting, London 106
133. DON'T TIE ME DOWN — Anthony & the Imperials, Veep 1255
134. THAT ACAPULCO GOLD — Rainy Daze, Uni 55001
135. WADE IN THE WATER — Herb Alpert & the Tijuana Brass, A&M 840

Compiled from national retail sales and radio station airplay by the Music Popularity Dept. of Record Market Research, Billboard.

# Billboard HOT 100

For Week Ending March 11, 1967

★ STAR performer—Sides registering greatest proportionate upward progress this week.

Record Industry Association of America seal of certification as million selling single.

| This Week | 1 Wk. Ago | 2 Wks. Ago | 3 Wks. Ago | TITLE Artist (Producer), Label & Number | Weeks On Chart |
|---|---|---|---|---|---|
| 1 ★ | 2 | 2 | 6 | LOVE IS HERE AND NOW YOU'RE GONE — Supremes (Holland-Dozier), Motown 1103 | 7 |
| 2 | 1 | 3 | 3 | RUBY TUESDAY — Rolling Stones (Andrew Loog Oldham), London 904 | 8 |
| 3 | 4 | 10 | 19 | BABY, I NEED YOUR LOVIN' — Johnny Rivers (Lou Adler), Imperial 66227 | 6 |
| 4 | 3 | 1 | 1 | KIND OF A DRAG — Buckinghams (Carl Bonafede & Dan Belleck), U.S.A. 860 | 11 |
| 5 | 36 | 85 | — | PENNY LANE — Beatles (George Martin), Capitol 5810 | 3 |
| 6 | 8 | 8 | 13 | THEN YOU CAN TELL ME GOODBYE — Casinos (Gene Hughes), Fraternity 977 | 9 |
| 7 | 9 | 14 | 27 | SOCK IT TO ME—BABY! — Mitch Ryder and the Detroit Wheels (Bob Crewe), New Voice 820 | 6 |
| 8 | 21 | 41 | 62 | HAPPY TOGETHER — Turtles (Joe Wissert), White Whale 244 | 5 |
| 9 | 13 | 19 | 24 | MY CUP RUNNETH OVER — Ed Ames (Jim Foglesong & Joe Reisman), RCA Victor 9002 | 6 |
| 10 | 26 | 57 | — | DEDICATED TO THE ONE I LOVE — Mama's and the Papa's (Lou Adler), Dunhill 4077 | 3 |
| 11 | 7 | 7 | 10 | GIMME SOME LOVIN' — Spencer Davis Group (Chris Blackwell & Jimmy Miller), United Artists 50108 | 11 |
| 12 | 23 | 42 | 54 | THERE'S A KIND OF A HUSH — Herman's Hermits (Mickie Most), MGM 13681 | 5 |
| 13 | 11 | 11 | 16 | MERCY, MERCY, MERCY — "Cannonball" Adderley (David Axelrod), Capitol 5798 | 10 |
| 14 | 19 | 26 | 33 | THE HUNTER GETS CAPTURED BY THE GAME — Marvelettes (William Robinson), Tamla 54143 | 8 |
| 15 ★ | 20 | 25 | 39 | FOR WHAT IT'S WORTH — Buffalo Springfield (Greene & Stone), Atco 6459 | 7 |
| 16 ★ | 45 | 83 | — | STRAWBERRY FIELDS FOREVER — Beatles (George Martin), Capitol 5810 | 3 |
| 17 | 22 | 27 | 59 | DARLIN' BE HOME SOON — Lovin' Spoonful (Erik Jacobsen), Kama Sutra 220 | 5 |
| 18 | 6 | 6 | 9 | THE BEAT GOES ON — Sonny & Cher (Sonny Bono), Atco 6461 | 9 |
| 19 | 24 | 29 | 43 | EPISTLE TO DIPPY — Donovan (Mickie Most), Epic 10127 | 5 |
| 20 | 5 | 5 | 4 | GEORGY GIRL — Seekers (Tom Springfield), Capitol 5756 | 15 |
| 21 | 10 | 4 | 2 | I'M A BELIEVER — Monkees (Jeff Barry), Colgems 1002 | 14 |
| 22 | 28 | 31 | 41 | I'VE BEEN LONELY TOO LONG — Young Rascals (Young Rascals), Atlantic 2377 | 7 |
| 23 | 18 | 21 | 25 | YOU GOT TO ME — Neil Diamond (Jeff Barry & Ellie Greenwich), Bang 540 | 7 |
| 24 | 37 | 54 | 77 | UPS AND DOWNS — Paul Revere and the Raiders (Terry Melchers), Columbia 44018 | 4 |
| 25 | 30 | 34 | 44 | NIKI HOEKY — P. J. Proby (Calvin Carter), Liberty 55936 | 7 |
| 26 | 27 | 37 | 47 | LET'S FALL IN LOVE — Peaches & Herb (Kapralik-McCoy), Date 1523 | 9 |
| 27 | 32 | 43 | 58 | CALIFORNIA NIGHTS — Lesley Gore (Bob Crewe), Mercury 72649 | 6 |
| 28 | 16 | 16 | 21 | GO WHERE YOU WANNA GO — 5th Dimension (Johnny Rivers & Marc Gordon), Soul City 753 | 9 |
| 29 | 34 | 40 | 46 | EVERYBODY NEEDS SOMEBODY TO LOVE — Wilson Pickett (Jerry Wexler & Rick Hall), Atlantic 2381 | 6 |
| 30 | 15 | 15 | 17 | PRETTY BALLERINA — Left Banke (World United Prod.), Smash 2074 | 10 |
| 31 | 41 | 52 | 65 | I THINK WE'RE ALONE NOW — Tommy James and the Shondells (Cordell-Gentry), Roulette 4720 | 5 |
| 32 | 14 | 18 | 20 | IT TAKES TWO — Marvin Gaye & Kim Weston (Wm. Stevenson-H. Cosby), Tamla 54141 | 10 |
| 33 | 17 | 17 | 14 | I HAD TOO MUCH TO DREAM (Last Night) — Electric Prunes (Damo Prod.), Reprise 0532 | 14 |
| 34 ★ | 44 | 55 | 69 | PUCKER UP BUTTERCUP — Jr. Walker & the All Stars (H. Fuqua-J. Bristol), Soul 35030 | 5 |
| 35 | 12 | 9 | 5 | (We Ain't Got) NOTHIN' YET — Blues Magoos (Wyld & Polhemus), Mercury 72622 | 14 |
| 36 | 40 | 50 | 60 | DIS-ADVANTAGES OF YOU — Brass Ring (Steve Barri), Dunhill 4065 | 6 |
| 37 | 58 | 79 | — | RETURN OF THE RED BARON — Royal Guardsmen (Gernhard Ent.), Laurie 3379 | 3 |
| 38 | 33 | 33 | 35 | INDESCRIBABLY BLUE — Elvis Presley, RCA Victor 9056 | 7 |
| 39 | 39 | 49 | 51 | I'LL TAKE CARE OF YOUR CARES — Frankie Laine (Bob Thiele), ABC 10891 | 8 |
| 40 ★ | 50 | 62 | 95 | THE LOVE I SAW IN YOU WAS JUST A MIRAGE — Smokey Robinson and the Miracles (Wm. Robinson-W. Moore), Tamla 54145 | 4 |
| 41 | 31 | 13 | 11 | GREEN, GREEN GRASS OF HOME — Tom Jones (Peter Sullivan), Parrot 40009 | 12 |
| 42 | 54 | 69 | 88 | THE 59TH STREET BRIDGE SONG — Harpers Bizarre (Lenny Waronker), Warner Bros. 5890 | 4 |
| 43 | 43 | 45 | 56 | DADDY'S LITTLE GIRL — Al Martino (Tom Morgan), Capitol 5825 | 7 |
| 44 | 29 | 30 | 34 | SO YOU WANT TO BE A ROCK 'N' ROLL STAR — Byrds (Gary Usher), Columbia 43987 | 7 |
| 45 | 47 | 67 | 94 | NO MILK TODAY — Herman's Hermits (Mickie Most), MGM 13681 | 4 |
| 46 | 48 | 60 | 71 | SIT DOWN, I THINK I LOVE YOU — Mojo Men (Lenny Waronker), Reprise 0539 | 6 |
| 47 | 52 | 53 | 55 | LADY — Jack Jones, Kapp 800 | 8 |
| 48 | 51 | 61 | 79 | ONE MORE MOUNTAIN TO CLIMB — Ronnie Dove (Phil Kahl), Diamond 217 | 4 |
| 49 | 25 | 12 | 7 | 98.6 — Keith (Jerry Ross), Mercury 72639 | 14 |
| 50 | 68 | 89 | — | JIMMY MACK — Martha and the Vandellas (Holland-Dozier), Gordy 7058 | 3 |
| 51 | 77 | 82 | — | DRY YOUR EYES — Brenda and the Tabulations (Bob Finiz), Dionn 500 | 2 |
| 52 | 80 | — | — | I NEVER LOVED A MAN THE WAY I LOVED YOU — Eddie Floyd (Prod. by Staff), Stax 208 | 2 |
| 53 | 60 | 72 | 87 | MORNINGTOWN RIDE — Seekers (Tom Springfield), Capitol 5787 | 4 |
| 54 | 53 | 51 | 61 | NO FAIR AT ALL — Association (Jerry Yester), Valiant 758 | 4 |
| 55 | 70 | 78 | — | WHEN SOMETHING IS WRONG WITH MY BABY — Sam and Dave (Prod. by Staff), Stax 210 | 3 |
| 56 | 83 | — | — | BEGGIN' — 4 Seasons (Bob Crewe), Philips 40433 | 2 |
| 57 | 90 | — | — | THIS IS MY SONG — Petula Clark (Sonny Burke), Warner Bros. 7002 | 2 |
| 58 | 81 | — | — | WESTERN UNION — Five Americans (Dale Hawkins), Abnak 118 | 2 |
| 59 | 57 | 59 | 67 | SPOOKY — Mike Sharpe (Harry Middlebrooks), Liberty 55922 | 6 |
| 60 | 61 | 63 | 75 | I DIG YOU BABY — Jerry Butler (Jerry Ross), Mercury 72648 | 8 |
| 61 | 55 | 56 | 57 | LET'S SPEND THE NIGHT TOGETHER — Rolling Stones (Andrew Loog Oldham), London 904 | 8 |
| 62 | 69 | 73 | 81 | HUNG UP IN YOUR EYES — Brian Hyland (Snuff Garrett), Philips 40424 | 4 |
| 63 | 66 | 66 | 70 | TINY BUBBLES — Don Ho & Allis (Burke), Reprise 0507 | 14 |
| 64 ★ | 89 | — | — | TRAVLIN' MAN — Stevie Wonder (Clarence Paul), Tamla 54147 | 2 |
| 65 | — | — | — | BERNADETTE — Four Tops (Holland and Dozier), Motown 1104 | 1 |
| 66 | 67 | 68 | 68 | THE PEOPLE IN ME — Music Machine (Brian Ross), Original Sound 67 | 7 |
| 67 | 62 | 39 | 40 | ARE YOU LONELY FOR ME — Freddy Scott (Bert Berns), Shout 207 | 12 |
| 68 | 85 | 90 | — | WITH THIS RING — Platters (Luther Dixon), Musicor 1229 | 3 |
| 69 | 64 | 64 | 78 | KEEP A LIGHT IN THE WINDOW TILL I COME HOME — Solomon Burke (Bob Galla), Atlantic 2378 | 5 |
| 70 | 73 | 75 | 80 | ONE, TWO, THREE — Ramsey Lewis (E. Edwards), Cadet 5556 | 5 |
| 71 | — | — | — | WALK IN THE WATER — Herb Alpert and the Tijuana Brass, A&M 840 | 1 |
| 72 ★ | — | — | — | THE LOSER (With a Broken Heart) — Gary Lewis and the Playboys (Snuff Garrett), Liberty 55949 | 1 |
| 73 | 78 | 87 | — | SOUL TIME — Shirley Ellis (Charlie Calello), Columbia 44021 | 3 |
| 74 | 86 | — | — | KANSAS CITY — James Brown & The Famous Flames (James Brown), King 6086 | 2 |
| 75 | 75 | 86 | 90 | LOVE YOU SO MUCH — New Colony Six (Ron Malo), Sentar 1205 | 4 |
| 76 | — | — | — | WHAT A WOMAN IN LOVE WON'T DO — Sandy Posey (Chips Moman), MGM 13702 | 1 |
| 77 | 74 | 74 | 89 | EVERYDAY I HAVE THE BLUES — Billy Stewart (Billy Davis), Chess 1991 | 5 |
| 78 | 72 | 76 | 82 | PEEK-A-BOO — New Vaudeville Band (Geoff Stephens), Fontana 1573 | 4 |
| 79 | 82 | — | — | MAIRZY DOATS — Innocence (Ripp-Amders-Poncia), Kama Sutra 222 | 2 |
| 80 | 88 | — | — | SHOW ME — Joe Tex (Buddy Killen), Dial 4055 | 2 |
| 81 | — | — | — | SWEET SOUL MUSIC — Arthur Conley (Otis Redding), Atco 6463 | 1 |
| 82 | 84 | — | — | DON'T DO IT — Micky Dolenz (Sepe/Brooks Prod.), Challenge 59353 | 2 |
| 83 | 98 | — | — | SUMMER WINE — Nancy Sinatra and Lee Hazlewood (Lee Hazlewood), Reprise 0527 | 2 |
| 84 | — | — | — | DETROIT CITY — Tom Jones (Peter Sullivan), Parrot 40012 | 1 |
| 85 | — | — | — | MERCY, MERCY, MERCY — Marlena Shaw (Billy Davis), Cadet 5557 | 1 |
| 86 | 96 | — | — | I DON'T WANT TO LOSE YOU — Jackie Wilson (Carl Davis), Brunswick 55309 | 2 |
| 87 | 92 | 95 | 99 | BABY, HELP ME — Percy Sledge (Quin Ivy and Marlin Greene), Atlantic 2383 | 4 |
| 88 | 94 | — | — | BECAUSE OF YOU — Chris Montez (Herb Alpert), A&M 839 | 2 |
| 89 | 79 | 80 | 83 | RAISE YOUR HAND — Aretha Franklin (Jerry Wexler), Atlantic 2386 | 6 |
| 90 ★ | — | — | — | MR. FARMER — Seeds (Marcus Tybelt), GNP Crescendo 383 | 1 |
| 91 | 91 | 98 | — | THE DARK END OF THE STREET — James Carr (Quinton Claunch and Randolph Russell), Goldwax 317 | 3 |
| 92 | 99 | 99 | — | GIRL DON'T CARE — Gene Chandler (Carl Davis), Brunswick 55312 | 3 |
| 93 | — | — | — | THAT ACAPULCO GOLD — Rainy Davis (Frank Slay), BMI 55002 | 1 |
| 94 | — | — | — | IT'S A HAPPENING THING — Peanut Butter Conspiracy (Gary Usher), Columbia 43985 | 1 |
| 95 | 95 | 96 | — | OOH BABY — Bo Diddley (M. Chess-E. Edwards), Checker 1156 | 7 |
| 96 | 97 | — | — | YOU ALWAYS HURT ME — Impressions (Johnny Pate), ABC 10900 | 2 |
| 97 | — | — | — | WHO DO YOU LOVE — Woolies (Jill Gibson-Don Altfield), Dunhill 4052 | 1 |
| 98 | — | — | — | LAWDY MISS CLAWDY — Buckinghams (Carl Bonafide, Dan Belleck), U.S.A. 869 | 1 |
| 99 | — | — | — | MELLOW YELLOW — Senator Bobby & Senator McKinley (Chip Taylor-Dennis Wholey), Parkway 137 | 1 |
| 100 | — | — | — | DON'T YOU CARE — Buckinghams (Jim Guercio), Columbia 44053 | 1 |

## BUBBLING UNDER THE HOT 100

101. WALK TALL ................... Two of Clubs, Fraternity 975
102. GIRLS ARE OUT TO GET YOU ... Fascinations, Mayfield 7714
103. HOLD ON, I'M COMING ... Chuck Jackson & Maxine Brown, Wand 1148
104. TEN COMMANDMENTS ....... Prince Buster, Philips 40427
105. SHE'S LOOKING GOOD ........ Roger Collins, Galaxy 750
106. ANIMAL CRACKERS (IN CELLOPHANE BAGS) ... Gene Pitney, Musicor 1235
107. FEEL SO BAD ............... Little Milton, Checker 1162
108. GRITS 'N' CORNBREAD ....... Soultremers, MoGowl 101
109. ALONG CAME JONES ......... Righteous Brothers, Verve 10479
110. THEME FROM THE WILD ANGELS ... Ventures, Dolton 327
111. RESCUE ME, DEAR MARTHA ... Pozo-Seco Singers, Columbia 44041
112. AS TIME GOES BY ........... Mel Carter, Imperial 66224
113. CRY ON THE WILD GOOSE ..... Baja Marimba Band, A&M 833
114. MERCY, MERCY, MERCY ....... Larry Williams & Johnny Watson, Okeh 7274
115. MARTYIN' KIND OF LOVE ..... Critters, Kapp 805
116. WHY NOT TONIGHT .......... Jimmy Hughes, Fame 1011
117. PEOPLE LIKE YOU ........... Eddie Fisher, RCA Victor 9070
118. TIP TOE ................... Robert Parker, Nola 729
119. LONELY AGAIN .............. Eddy Arnold, RCA Victor 9080
120. I'LL GIVE YOU TIME TO THINK IT OVER ...... Outsiders, Capitol 5843
121. I WANT TO TALK ABOUT YOU ... Ray Charles, ABC 10901
122. BIGGEST MAN .............. Peter Courtney, Viva 609
123. THE LOSER ................. Tommy Hunt, Dynamo 101
124. BEGINNING OF LONELINESS .... Dionne Warwick, Scepter 12187
125. IS THIS WHAT I GET FOR LOVING YOU ... Marianne Faithfull, London 20020
126. HERE, THERE, AND EVERYWHERE .. Claudine Longet, A&M 822
127. ON A CAROUSEL ............ Hollies, Imperial 66231
128. I'LL LOVE YOU FOREVER ...... Holidays, Golden World 43
129. SING ALONG WITH ME ........ Tommy Roe, ABC 10908
130. FRIDAY ON MY MIND ......... Easybeats, United Artists 50106
131. FOR HE'S A JOLLY GOOD FELLOW ... Bobby Vinton, Epic 10136
132. KANSAS CITY .............. Cat Stevens, Deram 7905
133. MATHEW AND SON ........... Cat Stevens, Deram 7905
134. ICE MELTS IN THE SUN ...... Gary Lewis and the Playboys, Liberty 55949
135. SHE TOOK YOU FOR A RIDE ... Aaron Neville, Parlo 103

Compiled from national retail sales and radio station airplay by the Music Popularity Dept. of Record Market Research, Billboard.

For Week Ending March 18, 1967

# Billboard HOT 100

★ STAR performer—Sides registering greatest proportionate upward progress this week.

Record Industry Association of America seal of certification as million selling single.

| This Week | 1 Wk. Ago | 2 Wks. Ago | 3 Wks. Ago | TITLE Artist (Producer), Label & Number | Weeks On Chart |
|---|---|---|---|---|---|
| 1 (Billboard Award) | 5 | 36 | 85 | PENNY LANE — Beatles (George Martin), Capitol 5810 | 4 |
| ★ 2 | 8 | 21 | 41 | HAPPY TOGETHER — Turtles (Joe Wissert), White Whale 244 | 6 |
| 3 | 3 | 4 | 10 | BABY, I NEED YOUR LOVIN' — Johnny Rivers (Lou Adler), Imperial 66227 | 7 |
| 4 | 1 | 2 | 2 | LOVE IS HERE AND NOW YOU'RE GONE — Supremes (Holland-Dozier), Motown 1103 | 8 |
| 5 | 2 | 1 | 3 | RUBY TUESDAY — Rolling Stones (Andrew Loog Oldham), London 904 | 9 |
| ★ 6 | 10 | 26 | 57 | DEDICATED TO THE ONE I LOVE — Mama's and the Papa's (Lou Adler), Dunhill 4077 | 4 |
| 7 | 7 | 9 | 14 | SOCK IT TO ME—BABY! — Mitch Ryder & the Detroit Wheels (Bob Crewe), New Voice 820 | 7 |
| ★ 8 | 12 | 23 | 42 | THERE'S A KIND OF A HUSH — Herman's Hermits (Mickie Most), MGM 13681 | 6 |
| 9 | 9 | 13 | 19 | MY CUP RUNNETH OVER — Ed Ames (Jim Foglesong & Joe Reisman), RCA Victor 9002 | 9 |
| 10 | 6 | 8 | 8 | THEN YOU CAN TELL ME GOODBYE — Casinos (Gene Hughes), Fraternity 977 | 10 |
| ★ 11 | 16 | 45 | 83 | STRAWBERRY FIELDS FOREVER — Beatles (George Martin), Capitol 5810 | 4 |
| 12 | 15 | 20 | 25 | FOR WHAT IT'S WORTH — Buffalo Springfield (Greene & Stone), Atco 6459 | 8 |
| 13 | 14 | 19 | 26 | THE HUNTER GETS CAPTURED BY THE GAME — Marvelettes (William Robinson), Tamla 54143 | 9 |
| 14 | 4 | 3 | 1 | KIND OF A DRAG — Buckinghams (Carl Bonafede & Dan Bellock), U.S.A. 860 | 12 |
| 15 | 17 | 22 | 27 | DARLIN' BE HOME SOON — Lovin' Spoonful (Erik Jacobsen), Kama Sutra 220 | 6 |
| ★ 16 | 27 | 32 | 43 | CALIFORNIA NIGHTS — Lesley Gore (Bob Crewe), Mercury 72649 | 7 |
| ★ 17 | 22 | 28 | 31 | I'VE BEEN LONELY TOO LONG — Young Rascals (Young Rascals), Atlantic 2377 | 8 |
| ★ 18 | 31 | 41 | 52 | I THINK WE'RE ALONE NOW — Tommy James and The Shondells (Cordell-Gentry), Roulette 4720 | 6 |
| 19 | 19 | 24 | 29 | EPISTLE TO DIPPY — Donovan (Mickie Most), Epic 10127 | 6 |
| 20 | 11 | 7 | 7 | GIMME SOME LOVIN' — Spencer Davis Group (Chris Blackwell & Jimmy Miller), United Artists 50108 | 12 |
| ★ 21 | 26 | 27 | 37 | LET'S FALL IN LOVE — Peaches & Herb (Kapralik-McCoy), Date 1523 | 10 |
| 22 | 24 | 37 | 54 | UPS AND DOWNS — Paul Revere & the Raiders (Terry Melchers), Columbia 44018 | 5 |
| ★ 23 | 65 | — | — | BERNADETTE — Four Tops (Holland and Dozier), Motown 1104 | 2 |
| 24 | 25 | 30 | 34 | NIKI HOEKY — P. J. Proby (Calvin Carter), Liberty 55936 | 8 |
| ★ 25 | 52 | 80 | — | I NEVER LOVED A MAN THE WAY I LOVED YOU — Eddie Floyd (Prod. by Staff), Stax 208 | 3 |
| ★ 26 | 42 | 54 | 69 | THE 59TH STREET BRIDGE SONG — Harpers Bizarre (Lenny Waronker), Warner Bros. 5890 | 5 |
| ★ 27 | 37 | 58 | 79 | RETURN OF THE RED BARON — Royal Guardsmen (Gernhard Ent.), Laurie 3379 | 4 |
| ★ 28 | 57 | 90 | — | THIS IS MY SONG — Petula Clark (Sonny Burke), Warner Bros. 7002 | 3 |
| 29 | 50 | 68 | 89 | JIMMY MACK — Martha and the Vandellas (Holland-Dozier), Gordy 7058 | 4 |
| ★ 30 | 40 | 50 | 62 | THE LOVE I SAW IN YOU WAS JUST A MIRAGE — Smokey Robinson and the Miracles (Wm. Robinson-W. Moore), Tamla 54145 | 5 |
| 31 | 34 | 44 | 55 | PUCKER UP BUTTERCUP — Jr. Walker & the All Stars, (H. Fuqua-J. Bristol), Soul 35030 | 6 |
| 32 | 32 | 14 | 18 | IT TAKES TWO — Marvin Gaye & Kim Weston (Wm. Stevenson-H. Cosby), Tamla 54141 | 11 |
| 33 | 13 | 11 | 11 | MERCY, MERCY, MERCY — "Cannonball" Adderley (David Axelrod), Capitol 5798 | 11 |
| 34 | 18 | 6 | 6 | THE BEAT GOES ON — Sonny & Cher (Sonny Bono), Atco 6461 | 10 |
| ★ 35 | 58 | 81 | — | WESTERN UNION — Five Americans (Dale Hawkins), Abnak 118 | 3 |
| ★ 36 | 46 | 48 | 60 | SIT DOWN, I THINK I LOVE YOU — Mojo Men (Lenny Waronker), Reprise 0539 | 7 |
| ★ 37 | 56 | 83 | — | BEGGIN' — 4 Seasons (Bob Crewe), Philips 40433 | 3 |
| 38 | 28 | 16 | 16 | GO WHERE YOU WANNA GO — 5th Dimension (Johnny Rivers & Marc Gordon), Soul City 753 | 10 |
| 39 | 20 | 5 | 5 | GEORGY GIRL — Seekers (Tom Springfield), Capitol 5756 | 16 |
| 40 | 45 | 47 | 67 | NO MILK TODAY — Herman's Hermits (Mickie Most), MGM 13681 | 5 |
| ★ 41 | 51 | 77 | 82 | DRY YOUR EYES — Brenda and the Tabulations (Bob Finiz), Dionn 500 | 4 |
| 42 | 43 | 43 | 45 | DADDY'S LITTLE GIRL — Al Martino (Tom Morgan), Capitol 5825 | 8 |
| 43 | 21 | 10 | 4 | I'M A BELIEVER — Monkees (Jeff Barry), Colgems 1002 | 15 (RIAA seal) |
| 44 | 47 | 52 | 53 | LADY — Jack Jones, Kapp 800 | 9 |
| 45 | 48 | 51 | 61 | ONE MORE MOUNTAIN TO CLIMB — Ronnie Dove (Phil Kahl), Diamond 217 | 5 |
| 46 | 53 | 60 | 72 | MORNINGTOWN RIDE — Seekers (Tom Springfield), Capitol 5787 | 5 |
| 47 | 39 | 39 | 49 | I'LL TAKE CARE OF YOUR CARES — Frankie Laine (Bob Thiele), ABC 10891 | 9 |
| 48 | 23 | 18 | 21 | YOU GOT TO ME — Neil Diamond (Jeff Barry & Ellie Greenwich), Bang 540 | 8 |
| 49 | 29 | 34 | 40 | EVERYBODY NEEDS SOMEBODY TO LOVE — Wilson Pickett (Jerry Wexler & Rick Hall), Atlantic 2381 | 7 |
| ★ 50 | — | — | — | SOMETHIN' STUPID — Nancy Sinatra & Frank Sinatra (Jimmy Bowen & Lee Hazlewood), Reprise 0561 | 1 |
| ★ 51 | 68 | 85 | 90 | WITH THIS RING — Platters (Luther Dixon), Musicor 1229 | 4 |
| 52 | 55 | 70 | 78 | WHEN SOMETHING IS WRONG WITH MY BABY — Sam and Dave (Prod. by Staff), Stax 210 | 4 |
| ★ 53 | 64 | 89 | — | TRAVLIN' MAN — Stevie Wonder (Clarence Paul), Tamla 54147 | 3 |
| 54 | 38 | 33 | 33 | INDESCRIBABLY BLUE — Elvis Presley, RCA Victor 9056 | 8 |
| ★ 55 | 81 | — | — | SWEET SOUL MUSIC — Arthur Conley (Otis Redding), Atco 6463 | 2 |
| 56 | 36 | 40 | 50 | DIS-ADVANTAGES OF YOU — Brass Ring (Steve Barri), Dunhill 4065 | 7 |
| ★ 57 | 72 | — | — | THE LOSER (With a Broken Heart) — Gary Lewis and the Playboys (Snuff Garrett), Liberty 55949 | 2 |
| 58 | 62 | 69 | 73 | HUNG UP IN YOUR EYES — Brian Hyland (Snuff Garrett), Philips 40424 | 5 |
| ★ 59 | 74 | 86 | — | KANSAS CITY — James Brown & The Famous Flames (James Brown), King 6086 | 3 |
| 60 | 60 | 61 | 63 | I DIG YOU BABY — Jerry Butler (Jerry Ross), Mercury 72648 | 9 |
| 61 | 71 | — | — | WALK IN THE WATER — Herb Alpert and the Tijuana Brass, A&M 840 | 2 |
| 62 | 54 | 53 | 51 | NO FAIR AT ALL — Association (Jerry Yester), Valiant 758 | 7 |
| ★ 63 | 80 | 88 | — | SHOW ME — Joe Tex (Buddy Killen), Dial 4055 | 3 |
| ★ 64 | 84 | — | — | DETROIT CITY — Tom Jones (Peter Sullivan), Parrot 40012 | 2 |
| 65 | 76 | — | — | WHAT A WOMAN IN LOVE WON'T DO — Sandy Posey (Chips Moman), MGM 13702 | 2 |
| 66 | 63 | 66 | 66 | TINY BUBBLES — Don Ho & Aliis (Burke), Reprise 0507 | 15 |
| 67 | 70 | 73 | 75 | ONE, TWO, THREE — Ramsey Lewis (E. Edwards), Cadet 5556 | 6 |
| 68 | 66 | 67 | 68 | THE PEOPLE IN ME — Music Machine (Brian Ross), Original Sound 67 | 8 |
| 69 | 75 | 75 | 86 | LOVE YOU SO MUCH — New Colony Six (Ron Malo), Sentar 1205 | 5 |
| ★ 70 | 85 | — | — | MERCY, MERCY, MERCY — Marlena Shaw (Billy Davis), Cadet 5557 | 2 |
| 71 | 83 | 98 | — | SUMMER WINE — Nancy Sinatra and Lee Hazlewood (Lee Hazlewood), Reprise 0527 | 3 |
| 72 | 73 | 78 | 87 | SOUL TIME — Shirley Ellis (Charlie Calello), Columbia 44021 | 4 |
| ★ 73 | 88 | 94 | — | BECAUSE OF YOU — Chris Montez (Herb Alpert), A&M 839 | 3 |
| ★ 74 | — | — | — | GONNA GIVE HER ALL THE LOVE I'VE GOT — Jimmy Ruffin (N. Whitfield), Soul 35032 | 1 |
| 75 | 79 | 82 | — | MAIRZY DOATS — Innocence (Ripp-Anders-Poncia), Kama Sutra 222 | 3 |
| ★ 76 | 92 | 99 | 99 | GIRL DON'T CARE — Gene Chandler (Carl Davis), Brunswick 55312 | 4 |
| ★ 77 | — | — | — | TELL ME TO MY FACE — Keith (Jerry Ross), Mercury 72652 | 1 |
| ★ 78 | 93 | — | — | THAT ACAPULCO GOLD — Rainy Daze (Frank Slay), UNI 55002 | 2 |
| ★ 79 | 91 | 91 | 98 | THE DARK END OF THE STREET — James Carr (Quinton Claunch and Randolph Russell), Goldwax 317 | 4 |
| 80 | 82 | 84 | — | DON'T DO IT — Micky Dolenz (Sepe/Brooks Prod.), Challenge 59353 | 3 |
| ★ 81 | — | — | — | PIPE DREAM — Blues Magoos (Bob Wyld & Art Polhemus), Mercury 72660 | 1 |
| ★ 82 | — | — | — | FOR HE'S A JOLLY GOOD FELLOW — Bobby Vinton (Robert Mersey), Epic 10136 | 1 |
| ★ 83 | 98 | — | — | LAWDY MISS CLAWDY — Buckinghams (Carl Bonafide, Dan Bellock), U.S.A. 869 | 2 |
| 84 | 86 | 96 | — | I DON'T WANT TO LOSE YOU — Jackie Wilson (Carl Davis), Brunswick 55309 | 3 |
| ★ 85 | 100 | — | — | DON'T YOU CARE — Buckinghams (Jim Guercio), Columbia 44053 | 2 |
| 86 | 90 | — | — | MR. FARMER — Seeds (Marcus Tybelt), GNP Crescendo 383 | 2 |
| 87 | 87 | 92 | 95 | BABY, HELP ME — Percy Sledge (Quin Ivy and Marlin Greene), Atlantic 2383 | 5 |
| ★ 88 | — | — | — | LONELY AGAIN — Eddy Arnold (Chet Atkins), RCA Victor 9080 | 1 |
| ★ 89 | — | — | — | AT THE ZOO — Simon & Garfunkel (Bob Johnston), Columbia 44046 | 1 |
| ★ 90 | — | — | — | I'LL TRY ANYTHING — Dusty Springfield (Tri-Parte Prod.), Philips 40439 | 1 |
| 91 | — | — | — | WHY NOT TONIGHT — Jimmy Hughes (Rick Hall & Staff), Fame 1011 | 1 |
| 92 | — | — | — | GIRL I NEED YOU — Artistics (Carl Davis), Brunswick 5531[illegible] | 1 |
| 93 | 94 | — | — | IT'S A HAPPENING THING — Peanut Butter Conspiracy (Gary Usher), Columbia 4398[illegible] | 2 |
| 94 | — | — | — | THE BEGINNING OF LONELINESS — Dionne Warwick (Bacharach-David), Scepter 1218[illegible] | 1 |
| 95 | — | — | — | WALK TALL — 2 of Clubs (Carl Edmondson), Fraternity 9[illegible]5 | 1 |
| 96 | — | — | — | OH THAT'S GOOD, NO THAT'S BAD — Sam the Sham & the Pharaohs (Stan Kesler), MGM 13713 | 1 |
| 97 | 97 | — | — | WHO DO YOU LOVE — Woolies (Jill Gibson-Don Altfield), Dunhill 4052 | 2 |
| 98 | — | — | — | I WANT TO TALK ABOUT YOU — Ray Charles (TRC), ABC 10901 | 1 |
| 99 | — | — | — | ON A CAROUSEL — Hollies (Ron Richards), Imperial 66231 | 1 |
| 100 | — | — | — | FRIDAY ON MY MIND — Easybeats, The (Shell Talmy) United Artists 50106 | 1 |

## HOT 100—A TO Z—(Publisher-Licensee)


At The Zoo (Charing Cross, BMI) ... 89
Baby, Help Me (Pronto/Quinvy, BMI) ... 87
Baby, I Need Your Lovin' (Jobete, BMI) ... 3
Beat Goes On, The (Chris Marc/Cotillion, BMI) ... 34
Because of You (Gower, BMI) ... 73
Beggin' (Saturday/Season's Four, BMI) ... 37
Beginning of Loneliness, The (Blue Seas/Jac, ASCAP) ... 94
Bernadette (Jobete, BMI) ... 23
California Nights (Genius/Enchanted, ASCAP) ... 16
Daddy's Little Girl (Cherie, BMI) ... 42
Dark End of the Street, The (Press, BMI) ... 79
Darlin' Be Home Soon (Faithful Virtue, BMI) ... 15
Dedicated to the One I Love (Trousdale, BMI) ... 6
Detroit City (Cedarwood, BMI) ... 64
Dry Your Eyes (Bee Cool, BMI) ... 41
Dis-Advantages of You (Scott, ASCAP) ... 56
Don't Do It (4. Star/Popcorn/Corn, BMI) ... 80
Don't You Care (Beechwood/Macbeth, BMI) ... 85
Epistle To Dippy (Peer Int'l, BMI) ... 19
Everybody Needs Somebody to Love (Reetch, Caesar & Dino, BMI) ... 49
59th Street Bridge Song, The (Charing Cross, BMI) ... 26
For He's a Jolly Good Fellow (Arab, BMI) ... 82
For What It's Worth (Ten East/Springalo, BMI) ... 12
Friday on My Mind (Unart, BMI) ... 100
Georgy Girl (Chappell, ASCAP) ... 39
Gimme Some Lovni' (Essex, ASCAP) ... 20
Girl Don't Care (Jalynne/Cachand/BRC, BMI) ... 76
Girl I Need You (Jalynne/BRC, BMI) ... 92
Gonna Give Her All the Love I've Got (Jobete, BMI) 74
Go Where You Wanna Go (Trousdale, BMI) ... 38
Happy Together (Chardon, BMI) ... 2
Hung Up in Your Eyes (Viva, BMI) ... 58
Hunter Gets Captured by the Game, The (Jobete, BMI) ... 13
I Dig You Baby (Morpine, BMI) ... 60
I Don't Want to Lose You (Jalynne/BRC, BMI) ... 84
I Never Loved a Man the Way I Loved You (14th Hour, BMI) ... 25
I Think We're Alone Now (Patricia, BMI) ... 18
I Want to Talk About You (St. Louis, BMI) ... 98
I'll Take Care of Your Cares (Remick, ASCAP) ... 47
I'll Try Anything (Pambar, BMI) ... 90
I'm a Believer (Screen Gems-Columbia, BMI) ... 43
I've Been Lonely Too Long (Slacsar, BMI) ... 17
Indescribably Blue (Elvis Presley, BMI) ... 54
It Takes Two (Jobete, BMI) ... 32
It's a Happening Thing (Four Star, BMI) ... 93
Jimmy Mack (Jobete, BMI) ... 29
Kansas City (Arno, BMI) ... 59
Kind of a Drag (Maryon, ASCAP) ... 14
Lady (Roosevelt, BMI) ... 44
Lawdy Miss Clawdy (Venice, BMI) ... 83
Let's Fall In Love (Bourne, ASCAP) ... 21
Lonely Again (4 Star, BMI) ... 88
Loser (With a Broken Heart), The (Skyhill, BMI) ... 57
Love I Saw in You Was Just a Mirage, The (Jobete, BMI) ... 30
Love Is Here and Now You're Gone (Jobete, BMI) 4
Love You So Much (T. M./Colony, BMI) ... 69
Mairzy Doats (Miller, ASCAP) ... 75
Mercy, Mercy, Mercy (Adderley) (Zawinul, BMI) ... 33
Mercy, Mercy, Mercy (Zawinul, BMI) ... 70
Morningtown Ride (Amadeo, BMI) ... 46
Mr. Farmer (Neil/Purple Bottle, BMI) ... 86
My Cup Runneth Over (Chappell, ASCAP) ... 9
Niki Hoeky (Novalene, BMI) ... 24
No Fair at All (Beechwood, BMI) ... 62
No Milk Today (Man-Ken Ltd., BMI) ... 40
Oh That's Good, No That's Bad (Fred Rose, BMI) 96
On a Carousel (Maribus, BMI) ... 99
One, Two, Three (Double Diamond-Champion, BMI) 67
One More Mountain to Climb (Tobi-Ann, BMI) ... 45
Penny Lane (Maclen, BMI) ... 1
People in Me, The (Thrush, BMI) ... 68
Pipe Dream (Amanga-Bunga, BMI) ... 81
Pucker Up Buttercup (Jobete, BMI) ... 31
Return of the Red Baron (Samphil, BMI) ... 27
Ruby Tuesday (Gideon, BMI) ... 5
Show Me (Tree, BMI) ... 63
Sit Down, I Think I Love You (Screen Gems-Columbia, BMI) ... 36
Sock It to Me—Baby! (Saturday, BMI) ... 7
Somethin' Stupid (Green Wood, BMI) ... 50
Soul Time (Gallico, BMI) ... 72
Strawberry Fields Forever (Maclen, BMI) ... 11
Summer Wine (Criterion, ASCAP) ... 71
Sweet Soul Music (Bedwal, BMI) ... 55
Tell Me to My Face (Maribus, BMI) ... 77
That Acapulco Gold (Claridge, ASCAP) ... 78
Then You Can Tell Me Goodbye (Acuff-Rose, BMI) 10
There's a Kind of a Hush (F., D. & M., ASCAP) ... 8
This Is My Song (Shawley, ASCAP) ... 28
Tiny Bubbles (Granite, ASCAP) ... 66
Travlin' Man (Stein, Van Stock, ASCAP) ... 53
Ups and Downs (Daywin, BMI) ... 22
Wade in the Water (Almo, ASCAP) ... 61
Walk Tall (Miller, ASCAP) ... 95
Western Union (Jetstar, BMI) ... 35
What a Woman in Love Won't Do (Windward Side, BMI) ... 65
Why Not Tonight (Fame, BMI) ... 91
When Something Is Wrong With My Baby (East/Pronto, BMI) ... 52
Who Do You Love (Arc, BMI) ... 97
With This Ring (Vee Vee, BMI) ... 51
You Got to Me (Tallyrand, BMI) ... 48


## BUBBLING UNDER THE HOT 100

101. GIRLS ARE OUT TO GET YOU ... Fascinations, Mayfield 7714
102. SHE'S LOOKING GOOD ... Roger Collins, Galaxy 750
103. GRITS 'N' CORNBREAD ... Soulrunners, Mo Soul 101
104. HIP HUG HER ... Booker T & the M. G.'s, Stax 211
105. EXCUSE ME, DEAR MARTHA ... Pozo-Seco Singers, Columbia 44041
106. HOLD ON, I'M COMING ... Chuck Jackson & Maxine Brown, Wand 1148
107. NOTHING TAKES THE PLACE OF YOU ... Toussaint McCall, Ronn 3
108. MERCY, MERCY, MERCY ... Larry Williams & Johnny Watson, Okeh 7274
109. CRY TO ME ... Freddy Scott, Shout 211
110. OOH BABY ... Bo Diddley, Checker 1156
111. MARRYIN' KIND OF LOVE ... Critters, Kapp 805
112. SOMETHING INSIDE ME ... Ray Charles, ABC 10901
113. WHOLE WORLD IS A STAGE ... Fantastic Four, Ric-Tic 122
114. YELLOW BALLOON ... Yellow Balloon, Canterbury 508
115. ANIMAL CRACKERS (IN CELLOPHANE BAGS) ... Gene Pitney, Musicor 1235
116. SPEAK HER NAME ... Walter Jackson, Okeh 7272
117. YELLOW BALLOON ... Jan & Dean, Columbia 44036
118. I'LL GIVE YOU TIME TO THINK IT OVER ... Outsiders, Capitol 5843
119. MAKE A LITTLE LOVE ... Lowell Fulsom, Kent 463
120. MATTHEW & SON ... Cat Stevens, Deran 7905
121. THE LOSER ... Peter Courtney, Viva 609
122. MAKE LOVE TO ME ... Johnny Thunder & Ruby Winter, Diamond 218
123. YOU ALWAYS HURT ME ... Impressions, ABC 10900
124. WALKIN' IN THE SUNSHINE ... Roger Miller, Smash 2081
125. IS THIS WHAT I GET FOR LOVING YOU ... Marianne Faithfull, London 20020
126. HERE, THERE, AND EVERYWHERE ... Claudine Longet, A&M 832
127. SING ALONG WITH ME ... Tommy Roe, ABC 10908
128. AFTER THE BALL ... Bob Crewe, DynoVoice 231
129. SHE TOOK YOU FOR A RIDE ... Arron Neville, Parlo 103
130. ICE MELTS IN THE SUN ... Gary Lewis & the Playboys, Liberty 55949
131. CAN'T GET ENOUGH OF YOU BABY ... ? (Question Mark) & the Mysterians, Cameo 457
132. WHAT'S THAT GOT TO DO WITH ME ... Jim & Jean, Verve Folkways 5035
133. YOU MAKE ME FEEL SO GOOD ... Gentrys, MGM 13690
134. SINCE I FELL FOR YOU ... Lenny Welch, Columbia 44007
135. FOR ME ... Sergio Mendes, A&M 836

Compiled from national retail sales and radio station airplay by the Music Popularity Dept. of Record Market Research, Billboard.

# Billboard

For Week Ending March 25, 1967

# HOT 100

★ STAR performer—Sides registering greatest proportionate upward progress this week.

Record Industry Association of America seal of certification as million selling single.

| This Week | 1 Wk. Ago | 2 Wks. Ago | 3 Wks. Ago | TITLE Artist (Producer), Label & Number | Weeks On Chart |
|---|---|---|---|---|---|
| 1 (Billboard Award) | 2 | 8 | 21 | HAPPY TOGETHER — Turtles (Joe Wissert), White Whale 244 | 7 |
| ★ 2 | 6 | 10 | 26 | DEDICATED TO THE ONE I LOVE — Mama's and the Papa's (Lou Adler), Dunhill 4077 | 5 |
| 3 | 1 | 5 | 36 | PENNY LANE — Beatles (George Martin), Capitol 5810 | 5 |
| ★ 4 | 8 | 12 | 23 | THERE'S A KIND OF A HUSH — Herman's Hermits (Mickie Most), MGM 13681 | 7 |
| 5 | 3 | 3 | 4 | BABY, I NEED YOUR LOVIN' — Johnny Rivers (Lou Adler), Imperial 66227 | 8 |
| 6 | 7 | 7 | 9 | SOCK IT TO ME—BABY! — Mitch Ryder & the Detroit Wheels (Bob Crewe), New Voice 820 | 8 |
| ★ 7 | 12 | 15 | 20 | FOR WHAT IT'S WORTH — Buffalo Springfield (Greene & Stone), Atco 6459 | 9 |
| 8 | 9 | 9 | 13 | MY CUP RUNNETH OVER — Ed Ames (Jim Foglesong & Joe Reisman), RCA Victor 9002 | 10 |
| 9 | 4 | 1 | 2 | LOVE IS HERE AND NOW YOU'RE GONE — Supremes (Holland-Dozier), Motown 1103 | 9 |
| 10 | 5 | 2 | 1 | RUBY TUESDAY — Rolling Stones (Andrew Loog Oldham), London 904 | 10 |
| 11 | 11 | 16 | 45 | STRAWBERRY FIELDS FOREVER — Beatles (George Martin), Capitol 5810 | 5 |
| 12 | 10 | 6 | 8 | THEN YOU CAN TELL ME GOODBYE — Casinos (Gene Hughes), Fraternity 977 | 11 |
| ★ 13 | 18 | 31 | 41 | I THINK WE'RE ALONE NOW — Tommy James and the Shondells (Cordell-Gentry), Roulette 4720 | 7 |
| ★ 14 | 26 | 42 | 54 | THE 59TH STREET BRIDGE SONG — Harpers Bizarre (Lenny Waronker), Warner Bros. 5890 | 6 |
| ★ 15 | 27 | 37 | 58 | RETURN OF THE RED BARON — Royal Guardsmen (Gernhard Ent.), Laurie 3379 | 5 |
| 16 | 16 | 27 | 32 | CALIFORNIA NIGHTS — Lesley Gore (Bob Crewe), Mercury 72649 | 8 |
| 17 | 17 | 22 | 28 | I'VE BEEN LONELY TOO LONG — Young Rascals (Young Rascals), Atlantic 2377 | 9 |
| ★ 18 | 23 | 65 | — | BERNADETTE — Four Tops (Holland and Dozier), Motown 1104 | 3 |
| ★ 19 | 28 | 57 | 90 | THIS IS MY SONG — Petula Clark (Sonny Burke), Warner Bros. 7002 | 4 |
| ★ 20 | 25 | 52 | 80 | I NEVER LOVED A MAN THE WAY I LOVED YOU — Eddie Floyd (Prod. by Staff), Stax 208 / Aretha Franklin (Jerry Wexler), Atlantic 2386 | 4 |
| 21 | 15 | 17 | 22 | DARLIN' BE HOME SOON — Lovin' Spoonful (Erik Jacobsen), Kama Sutra 220 | 7 |
| 22 | 22 | 24 | 37 | UPS AND DOWNS — Paul Revere & the Raiders (Terry Melchers), Columbia 44018 | 6 |
| 23 | 24 | 25 | 30 | NIKI HOEKY — P. J. Proby (Calvin Carter), Liberty 55936 | 9 |
| ★ 24 | 29 | 50 | 68 | JIMMY MACK — Martha and the Vandellas (Holland-Dozier), Gordy 7058 | 5 |
| 25 | 21 | 26 | 27 | LET'S FALL IN LOVE — Peaches & Herb (Kapralik-McCoy), Date 1523 | 11 |
| 26 | 13 | 14 | 19 | THE HUNTER GETS CAPTURED BY THE GAME — Marvelettes (William Robinson), Tamla 54143 | 10 |
| 27 | 30 | 40 | 50 | THE LOVE I SAW IN YOU WAS JUST A MIRAGE — Smokey Robinson and the Miracles (Wm. Robinson-W. Moore), Tamla 54145 | 6 |
| ★ 28 | 35 | 58 | 81 | WESTERN UNION — Five Americans (Dale Hawkins), Abnak 118 | 4 |
| ★ 29 | 50 | — | — | SOMETHIN' STUPID — Nancy Sinatra & Frank Sinatra (Jimmy Bowen & Lee Hazlewood), Reprise 0561 | 2 |
| ★ 30 | 37 | 56 | 83 | BEGGIN' — 4 Seasons (Bob Crewe), Philips 40433 | 4 |
| ★ 31 | 41 | 51 | 77 | DRY YOUR EYES — Brenda and the Tabulations (Bob Finiz), Dionn 500 | 5 |
| ★ 32 | — | — | — | A LITTLE BIT YOU, A LITTLE BIT ME — Monkees (Jeff Barry), Colgems 1004 | 1 |
| 33 | 20 | 11 | 7 | GIMME SOME LOVIN' — Spencer Davis Group (Chris Blackwell & Jimmy Miller), United Artists 50108 | 13 |
| 34 | 14 | 4 | 3 | KIND OF A DRAG — Buckinghams (Carl Bonafede & Dan Bellock), U.S.A. 860 | 13 |
| 35 | 31 | 34 | 44 | PUCKER UP BUTTERCUP — Jr. Walker & the All Stars, (H. Fuqua-J. Bristol), Soul 35030 | 7 |
| 36 | 36 | 46 | 48 | SIT DOWN, I THINK I LOVE YOU — Mojo Men (Lenny Waronker), Reprise 0539 | 8 |
| ★ 37 | 51 | 68 | 85 | WITH THIS RING — Platters (Luther Dixon), Musicor 1229 | 5 |
| 38 | 40 | 45 | 47 | NO MILK TODAY — Herman's Hermits (Mickie Most), MGM 13681 | 6 |
| 39 | 44 | 47 | 52 | LADY — Jack Jones, Kapp 800 | 10 |
| 40 | 19 | 19 | 24 | EPISTLE TO DIPPY — Donovan (Mickie Most), Epic 10127 | 7 |
| 41 | 32 | 32 | 14 | IT TAKES TWO — Marvin Gaye & Kim Weston (Wm. Stevenson-H. Cosby), Tamla 54141 | 12 |
| 42 | 34 | 18 | 6 | THE BEAT GOES ON — Sonny & Cher (Sonny Bono), Atco 6461 | 11 |
| ★ 43 | 53 | 64 | 89 | TRAVELIN' MAN — Stevie Wonder (Clarence Paul), Tamla 54147 | 4 |
| 44 | 46 | 53 | 60 | MORNINGTOWN RIDE — Seekers (Tom Springfield), Capitol 5787 | 6 |
| ★ 45 | 55 | 81 | — | SWEET SOUL MUSIC — Arthur Conley (Otis Redding), Atco 6463 | 3 |
| 46 | 52 | 55 | 70 | WHEN SOMETHING IS WRONG WITH MY BABY — Sam and Dave (Prod. by Staff), Stax 210 | 5 |
| ★ 47 | 61 | 71 | — | WADE IN THE WATER — Herb Alpert and the Tijuana Brass, A&M 840 | 3 |
| 48 | 45 | 48 | 51 | ONE MORE MOUNTAIN TO CLIMB — Ronnie Dove (Phil Kahl), Diamond 217 | 6 |
| 49 | 42 | 43 | 43 | DADDY'S LITTLE GIRL — Al Martino (Tom Morgan), Capitol 5825 | 9 |
| 50 | 57 | 72 | — | THE LOSER (With a Broken Heart) — Gary Lewis and the Playboys (Snuff Garrett), Liberty 55949 | 3 |
| ★ 51 | 64 | 84 | — | DETROIT CITY — Tom Jones (Peter Sullivan), Parrot 40012 | 3 |
| ★ 52 | 65 | 76 | — | WHAT A WOMAN IN LOVE WON'T DO — Sandy Posey (Chips Moman), MGM 13702 | 3 |
| ★ 53 | 63 | 80 | 88 | SHOW ME — Joe Tex (Buddy Killen), Dial 4055 | 4 |
| ★ 54 | 77 | — | — | TELL ME TO MY FACE — Keith (Jerry Ross), Mercury 72652 | 2 |
| 55 | 59 | 74 | 86 | KANSAS CITY — James Brown & The Famous Flames (James Brown), King 6086 | 4 |
| ★ 56 | 83 | 98 | — | LAWDY MISS CLAWDY — Buckinghams (Carl Bonafide, Dan Bellock), U.S.A. 869 | 3 |
| 57 | 66 | 63 | 66 | TINY BUBBLES — Don Ho & Allis (Burke), Reprise 0507 | 16 |
| ★ 58 | 89 | — | — | AT THE ZOO — Simon & Garfunkel (Bob Johnston), Columbia 44046 | 2 |
| ★ 59 | 85 | 100 | — | DON'T YOU CARE — Buckinghams (Jim Guercio), Columbia 44053 | 3 |
| ★ 60 | 71 | 83 | 98 | SUMMER WINE — Nancy Sinatra and. Lee Hazlewood (Lee Hazlewood), Reprise 0527 | 4 |
| 61 | 69 | 75 | 75 | LOVE YOU SO MUCH — New Colony Six (Ron Malo), Sentar 1205 | 6 |
| 62 | 70 | 85 | — | MERCY, MERCY, MERCY — Marlena Shaw (Billy Davis), Cadet 5557 | 3 |
| 63 | 74 | — | — | GONNA GIVE HER ALL THE LOVE I'VE GOT — Jimmy Ruffin (N. Whitfield), Soul 350322 | 2 |
| ★ 64 | 99 | — | — | ON A CAROUSEL — Hollies (Ron Richards), Imperial 66231 | 2 |
| ★ 65 | — | — | — | THE GIRL I KNEW SOMEWHERE — Monkees (Douglas Farthing Hafelid), Colgems 1004 | 1 |
| ★ 66 | — | — | — | SUNDAY FOR TEA — Peter & Gordon (John Burgess), Capitol 5864 | 1 |
| 67 | 72 | 73 | 78 | SOUL TIME — Shirley Ellis (Charlie Calello), Columbia 44021 | 5 |
| 68 | 76 | 92 | 99 | GIRL DON'T CARE — Gene Chandler (Carl Davis), Brunswick 55312 | 5 |
| 69 | 82 | — | — | FOR HE'S A JOLLY GOOD FELLOW — Bobby Vinton (Robert Mersey), Epic 10136 | 2 |
| 70 | 78 | 93 | — | THAT ACAPULCO GOLD — Rainy Daze (Frank Slay), BMI 55002 | 3 |
| ★ 71 | — | — | — | I'M A MAN — Spencer Davis Group (Jimmy Miller), United Artists 50144 | 1 |
| ★ 72 | 90 | — | — | I'LL TRY ANYTHING — Dusty Springfield (Herb Bernstein), Philips 40439 | 2 |
| 73 | 73 | 88 | 94 | BECAUSE OF YOU — Chris Montez (Herb Alpert), A&M 839 | 4 |
| ★ 74 | 92 | — | — | GIRL I NEED YOU — Artistics (Carl Davis), Brunswick 55315 | 2 |
| ★ 75 | 96 | — | — | OH THAT'S GOOD, NO THAT'S BAD — Sam the Sham & the Pharaohs (Stan Kesler), MGM 13713 | 2 |
| 76 | 80 | 82 | 84 | DON'T DO IT — Micky Dolenz (Sepe/Brooks Prod.), Challenge 59353 | 4 |
| ★ 77 | — | — | — | CAN'T GET ENOUGH OF YOU, BABY — ? (Question Mark) & the Mysterians (Neil Bogart, Pa-Go-Go Prod.), Cameo 467 | 1 |
| 78 | 79 | 91 | 91 | THE DARK END OF THE STREET — James Carr (Quinton Claunch and Randolph Russell), Goldwax 317 | 5 |
| 79 | 81 | — | — | PIPE DREAM — Blues Magoos (Bob Wyld & Art Polhemus), Mercury 72660 | 2 |
| ★ 80 | — | — | — | MUSIC TO WATCH GIRLS BY — Andy Williams (Nick De Caro), Columbia 44065 | 1 |
| ★ 81 | — | — | — | WALKIN' IN THE SUNSHINE — Roger Miller (Jerry Kennedy), Smash 2081 | 1 |
| ★ 82 | — | — | — | LOVE EYES — Nancy Sinatra (Lee Hazlewood), Reprise 0559 | 1 |
| ★ 83 | — | — | — | DANNY BOY — Ray Price (Don Law & Frank Jones), Columbia 44042 | 1 |
| ★ 84 | 100 | — | — | FRIDAY ON MY MIND — Easybeats, The (Shell Talmy) United Artists 50106 | 2 |
| ★ 85 | — | — | — | CRY TO ME — Freddie Scott (Bert Bruns), Shout 211 | 1 |
| ★ 86 | — | — | — | CLOSE YOUR EYES — Peaches & Herb (Dave Kapralik-Ken Williams), Date 1549 | 1 |
| 87 | 88 | — | — | LONELY AGAIN — Eddy Arnold (Chet Atkins), RCA Victor 9080 | 2 |
| 88 | 94 | — | — | THE BEGINNING OF LONELINESS — Dionne Warwick (Bacharach-David), Scepter 12187 | 2 |
| ★ 89 | — | — | — | DEAD END STREET — Lou Rawls (David Axlerod), Capitol 5869 | 1 |
| 90 | 91 | — | — | WHY NOT TONIGHT — Jimmy Hughes (Rick Hall & Staff), Fame 1011 | 2 |
| 91 | — | — | — | HOLD ON, I'M COMING — Chuck Jackson & Maxine Brown, Wand 1148 | 3 |
| 92 | 95 | — | — | WALK TALL — 2 of Clubs (Carl Edmondson), Fraternity 975 | 2 |
| 93 | 93 | 94 | — | IT'S A HAPPENING THING — Peanut Butter Conspiracy (Gary Usher), Columbia 43985 | 3 |
| 94 | — | — | — | HIP HUG-HER — Booker T. & the M. G.'s (Prod. By Staff), Stax 211 | 1 |
| 95 | 97 | 97 | — | WHO DO YOU LOVE — Woolies (Jill Gibson-Don Altfield), Dunhill 4052 | 3 |
| 96 | — | — | — | I CAN'T MAKE IT ANYMORE — Snyder Turner (Arnold Geller Prod.), MGM 13692 | 1 |
| 97 | — | — | 100 | MERCY, MERCY, MERCY — Larry William & Johnny Watson (Larry Williams & Johnny Watson), Okeh 7274 | 3 |
| 98 | — | — | — | SHE TOOK YOU FOR A RIDE — Arron Neville (Par-Lo Prod.), Parlo 103 | 1 |
| 99 | — | — | — | THE WHOLE WORLD IS A STAGE — Fantastic Four (Al Kent & E. Wingate), Ric Tic 122 | 1 |
| 100 | — | — | — | NOTHING TAKES THE PLACE OF YOU — Toussaint McCall (Jewel Productions), Ronn 3 | 1 |

## HOT 100—A TO Z—(Publisher-Licensee)

| | |
|---|---|
| At The Zoo (Charing Cross, BMI) | 58 |
| Baby, I Need Your Lovin' (Jobete, BMI) | 5 |
| Beat Goes On, The (Chris Marc/Cotillion, BMI) | 42 |
| Because of You (Gower, BMI) | 73 |
| Beggin' (Saturday/Season's Four, BMI) | 30 |
| Beginning of Loneliness; The (Blue Seas/Jac, ASCAP) | 88 |
| Bernadette (Jobete, BMI) | 18 |
| California Nights (Genius/Enchanted, ASCAP) | 16 |
| Can't Get Enough of You, Baby (Saturday, BMI) | 77 |
| Close Your Eyes (Tideland, BMI) | 86 |
| Cry To Me (Progressive, BMI) | 85 |
| Daddy's Little Girl (Cherie, BMI) | 49 |
| Dark End of the Street, The (Press, BMI) | 78 |
| Danny Boy (Boosey & Hawkes, ASCAP) | 83 |
| Darlin' Be Home Soon (Faithful Virtue, BMI) | 21 |
| Dead End Street (Raw Lou/Beechwood, BMI) | 89 |
| Dedicated to the One I Love (Trousdale, BMI) | 2 |
| Detroit City (Cedarwood, BMI) | 51 |
| Don't Do It (4 Star/Popcorn/Corn, BMI) | 76 |
| Don't You Care (Beechwood/Macbeth, BMI) | 59 |
| Dry Your Eyes (Bee Cool, BMI) | 31 |
| Epistle To Dippy (Peer Int'l., BMI) | 40 |
| 59th Street Bridge Song, The (Charing Cross, BMI) | 14 |
| For He's a Jolly Good Fellow (Arab, BMI) | 62 |
| For What It's Worth (Ten East/Springalo, BMI) | 7 |
| Friday on My Mind (Unart, BMI) | 84 |
| Gimme Some Lovin' (Essex, ASCAP) | 33 |
| Girl Don't Care (Jalynne/Cachand/BRC, BMI) | 68 |
| Girl I Need You (Jalynne/BRC, BMI) | 74 |
| Girl I Knew Somewhere, The (Screen Gems-Columbia, BMI) | 65 |
| Gonna Give Her All the Love I've Got (Jobete, BMI) | 63 |
| Happy Together (Chardon, BMI) | 1 |
| Hip Hug-Her (East, BMI) | 94 |
| Hold On, I'm Coming (Pronto/East, BMI) | 91 |
| Hunter Gets Captured by the Game, The (Jobete, BMI) | 26 |
| I Can't Make It Anymore (Witmark, ASCAP) | 96 |
| I Never Loved a Man the Way I Loved You (14th Hour, BMI) | 20 |
| I Think We're Alone Now (Patricia, BMI) | 13 |
| I'll Try Anything (Pambar, BMI) | 72 |
| I'm a Man (Essex, ASCAP) | 71 |
| I've Been Lonely Too Long (Slacsar, BMI) | 17 |
| It Takes Two (Jobete, BMI) | 41 |
| It's a Happening Thing (Four Star, BMI) | 93 |
| Jimmy Mack (Jobete, BMI) | 24 |
| Kansas City (Arno, BMI) | 55 |
| Kind of a Drag (Maryon, ASCAP) | 34 |
| Lady (Roosevelt, BMI) | 39 |
| Lawdy Miss Clawdy (Venice, BMI) | 56 |
| Let's Fall In Love (Bourne, ASCAP) | 25 |
| Little Bit You, A Little Bit Me, A (Screen Gems-Columbia, BMI) | 32 |
| Lonely Again (4 Star, BMI) | 87 |
| Loser (With a Broken Heart), The (Skyhill, BMI) | 50 |
| Love Eyes (Criterion, ASCAP) | 82 |
| Love I Saw in You Was Just a Mirage, The (Jobete, BMI) | 27 |
| Love Is Here and Now You're Gone (Jobete, BMI) | 9 |
| Love You So Much (T. M./Colony, BMI) | 61 |
| Mercy, Mercy, Mercy (Zawinul, BMI) (Shaw) | 62 |
| Mercy, Mercy, Mercy (Zawinul, BMI) | 97 |
| Morningtown Ride (Amadeo, BMI) | 44 |
| Music To Watch Girls By (S.C.P., ASCAP) | 80 |
| My Cup Runneth Over (Chappell, ASCAP) | 8 |
| Niki Hoeky (Novalene, BMI) | 23 |
| No Milk Today (Man-Ken Ltd., BMI) | 38 |
| Nothing Takes The Place of You (Su-Ma, BMI) | 100 |
| Oh That's Good, No That's Bad (Fred Rose, BMI) | 75 |
| On a Carousel (Maribus, BMI) | 64 |
| One More Mountain to Climb (Tobi-Ann, BMI) | 48 |
| Penny Lane (Maclen, BMI) | 3 |
| Pipe Dream (Amanga-Bunga, BMI) | 79 |
| Pucker Up Buttercup (Jobete, BMI) | 35 |
| Return of the Red Baron (Samphil, BMI) | 15 |
| Ruby Tuesday (Gideon, BMI) | 10 |
| She Took You For A Ride (Olrap, BMI) | 98 |
| Show Me (Tree, BMI) | 53 |
| Sit Down, I Think I Love You (Screen Gems-Columbia, BMI) | 36 |
| Sock It to Me—Baby! (Saturday, BMI) | 6 |
| Somethin' Stupid (Green Wood, BMI) | 29 |
| Soul Time (Gallico, BMI) | 67 |
| Strawberry Fields Forever (Maclen, BMI) | 11 |
| Summer Wine (Criterion, ASCAP) | 60 |
| Sweet Soul Music (Bedwal, BMI) | 45 |
| Tell Me to My Face (Maribus, BMI) | 54 |
| That Acapulco Gold (Claridge, ASCAP) | 70 |
| Then You Can Tell Me Goodbye (Acuff-Rose, BMI) | 12 |
| There's a Kin dof a Hush (F., D. & M., ASCAP) | 4 |
| This Is My Song (Shawley, ASCAP) | 19 |
| Tiny Bubbles (Granite, ASCAP) | 57 |
| Travelin' Man (Stein, Van Stock, ASCAP) | 43 |
| Ups and Downs (Daywin, BMI) | 22 |
| Wade in the Water (Almo, ASCAP) | 47 |
| Walk Tall (Miller, ASCAP) | 92 |
| Walkin' In the Sunshine (Tree, BMI) | 81 |
| Western Union (Jetstar, BMI) | 28 |
| What a Woman in Love Won't Do (Windward Side, BMI) | 52 |
| Why Not Tonight (Fame, BMI) | 90 |
| When Something Is Wrong With My Baby (East/Pronto, BMI) | 46 |
| Who Do You Love (Arc, BMI) | 95 |
| Whole World Is A Stage, The (Myto, BMI) | 99 |
| With This Ring (Vee Vee, BMI) | 37 |

## BUBBLING UNDER THE HOT 100

101. SHE'S LOOKING GOOD ..... Roger Collins, Galaxy 750
102. YELLOW BALLOON ..... Yellow Ballons, Canterbury 508
103. EXCUSE ME, DEAR MARTHA ..... Pozo Seco Singers, Columbia 44041
104. ONE, TWO, THREE ..... Ramsey Lewis, Cadet 5556
105. THERE'S A CHANCE WE CAN MAKE IT ..... Blues Magoos, Mercury 72660
106. GET ME TO THE WORLD ON TIME ..... Electric Prunes, Reprise 0564
107. MAIRZY DOATS ..... Innocence, Kama Sutra 222
108. POSTCARD FROM JAMAICA ..... Sopwith "Camel," Kama Sutra 224
109. MR. FARMER ..... Seeds, GNP Crescendo 383
110. I DON'T WANT TO LOSE YOU ..... Jackie Wilson, Brunswick 55309
111. YELLOW BALLOON ..... Jan & Dean, Columbia 44036
112. I WANT TO TALK ABOUT YOU ..... Ray Charles, ABC 10901
113. GO GO RADIO MOSCOW ..... Nikita The K, Warner Bros. 7005
114. BABY HELP ME ..... Percy Sledge, Atlantic 2383
115. SPEAK HER NAME ..... Walter Jackson, Okeh 7272
116. MARRYIN' KIND OF LOVE ..... Critters, Kapp 805
117. ANIMAL CRACKERS (IN CELLOPHANE BAGS) ..... Gene Pitney, Musicor 1235
118. I WON'T COME IN WHILE HE'S THERE ..... Jim Reeves, RCA Victor 9057
119. MATTHEW & SON ..... Cat Stevens, Deran 7905
120. MY BACK PAGES ..... Byrds, Columbia 44054
121. MAKE LOVE TO ME ..... Johnny Thunder & Ruby Winters, Diamond 218
122. SING ALONG WITH ME ..... Tommy Ros, ABC 10908
123. WHAT'S THAT GOT TO DO WITH ME ..... Jim & Jean, Verve Folkways 5035
124. SOMEBODY TO LOVE ..... Jefferson Airplane, RCA Victor 9140
125. MAKE A LITTLE LOVE ..... Lowell Fulsom, Kent 463
126. AFTER THE BALL ..... Bob Crewe, Dyno Voice 231
127. PRECIOUS MEMORIES ..... Romeos, Mark II J-1
128. RIGHT TO CRY ..... Lenny Welch, Kapp 808
129. MR. UNRELIABLE ..... Cryan' Shames, Columbia 44037
130. YOU MAKE ME FEEL SO GOOD ..... Gentrys, MGM 13690
131. DON'T TIE ME DOWN ..... Anthony & the Imperials, Veep 1255
132. SO GOOD ..... Roy Orbison, MGM 13685
133. RIOT ON SUNSET STRIP ..... Standells, Tower 314
134. LIVE ..... Merry-Go-Round, A&M 834
135. FOR ME ..... Sergio Mendes & Brasil '66, A&M 836

Compiled from national retail sales and radio station airplay by the Music Popularity Dept. of Record Market Research, Billboard.

For Week Ending April 1, 1967

# Billboard HOT 100

★ STAR performer—Sides registering greatest proportionate upward progress this week.

Record Industry Association of America seal of certification as million selling single.

| This Week | 1 Wk. Ago | 2 Wks. Ago | 3 Wks. Ago | TITLE Artist (Producer), Label & Number | Weeks On Chart |
|---|---|---|---|---|---|
| 1 (Billboard Award) | 1 | 2 | 8 | **HAPPY TOGETHER** Turtles (Joe Wissert), White Whale 244 | 8 |
| 2 | 2 | 6 | 10 | **DEDICATED TO THE ONE I LOVE** Mama's and the Papa's (Lou Adler), Dunhill 4077 | 6 |
| 3 | 3 | 1 | 5 | **PENNY LANE** Beatles (George Martin), Capitol 5810 | 6 |
| 4 | 4 | 8 | 12 | **THERE'S A KIND OF A HUSH** Herman's Hermits (Mickie Most), MGM 13681 | 8 |
| ★ 5 | 18 | 23 | 65 | **BERNADETTE** Four Tops (Holland and Dozier), Motown 1104 | 4 |
| ★ 6 | 19 | 28 | 57 | **THIS IS MY SONG** Petula Clark (Sonny Burke), Warner Bros. 7002 | 5 |
| 7 | 7 | 12 | 15 | **FOR WHAT IT'S WORTH** Buffalo Springfield (Greene & Stone), Atco 6459 | 10 |
| ★ 8 | 11 | 11 | 16 | **STRAWBERRY FIELDS FOREVER** Beatles (George Martin), Capitol 5810 | 6 |
| ★ 9 | 29 | 50 | — | **SOMETHIN' STUPID** Nancy Sinatra & Frank Sinatra (Jimmy Bowen & Lee Hazlewood), Reprise 0561 | 3 |
| ★ 10 | 28 | 35 | 58 | **WESTERN UNION** Five Americans (Dale Hawkins), Abnak 118 | 5 |
| 11 | 8 | 9 | 9 | **MY CUP RUNNETH OVER** Ed Ames (Jim Foglesong & Joe Reisman), RCA Victor 9002 | 11 |
| 12 | 13 | 18 | 31 | **I THINK WE'RE ALONE NOW** Tommy James and the Shondells (Cordell-Gentry), Roulette 4720 | 8 |
| 13 | 14 | 26 | 42 | **THE 59TH STREET BRIDGE SONG** Harpers Bizarre (Lenny Waronker), Warner Bros. 5890 | 7 |
| ★ 14 | 20 | 25 | 52 | **I NEVER LOVED A MAN THE WAY I LOVE YOU** Aretha Franklin (Jerry Wexler), Atlantic 2386 | 5 |
| 15 | 5 | 3 | 3 | **BABY, I NEED YOUR LOVIN'** Johnny Rivers (Lou Adler), Imperial 66227 | 9 |
| 16 | 17 | 17 | 22 | **I'VE BEEN LONELY TOO LONG** Young Rascals (Young Rascals), Atlantic 2377 | 10 |
| 17 | 6 | 7 | 7 | **SOCK IT TO ME—BABY!** Mitch Ryder & the Detroit Wheels (Bob Crewe), New Voice 820 | 9 |
| ★ 18 | 24 | 29 | 50 | **JIMMY MACK** Martha and the Vandellas (Holland-Dozier), Gordy 7058 | 6 |
| ★ 19 | 32 | — | — | **A LITTLE BIT YOU, A LITTLE BIT ME** Monkees (Jeff Barry), Colgems 1004 | 2 |
| 20 | 9 | 4 | 1 | **LOVE IS HERE AND NOW YOU'RE GONE** Supremes (Holland-Dozier), Motown 1103 | 10 |
| 21 | 15 | 27 | 37 | **RETURN OF THE RED BARON** Royal Guardsmen (Gernhard Ent.), Laurie 3379 | 6 |
| 22 | 16 | 16 | 27 | **CALIFORNIA NIGHTS** Lesley Gore (Bob Crewe), Mercury 72649 | 9 |
| 23 | 10 | 5 | 2 | **RUBY TUESDAY** Rolling Stones (Andrew Loog Oldham), London 904 | 11 |
| 24 | 27 | 30 | 40 | **THE LOVE I SAW IN YOU WAS JUST A MIRAGE** Smokey Robinson and the Miracles (Wm. Robinson-W. Moore), Tamla 54145 | 7 |
| ★ 25 | 30 | 37 | 56 | **BEGGIN'** 4 Seasons (Bob Crewe), Philips 40433 | 5 |
| ★ 26 | 31 | 41 | 51 | **DRY YOUR EYES** Brenda and the Tabulations (Bob Finiz), Dionn 500 | 6 |
| 27 | 12 | 10 | 6 | **THEN YOU CAN TELL ME GOODBYE** Casinos (Gene Hughes), Fraternity 977 | 12 |
| ★ 28 | 37 | 51 | 68 | **WITH THIS RING** Platters (Luther Dixon), Musicor 1229 | 6 |
| 29 | 22 | 22 | 24 | **UPS AND DOWNS** Paul Revere & the Raiders (Terry Melchers), Columbia 44018 | 7 |
| ★ 30 | 45 | 55 | 81 | **SWEET SOUL MUSIC** Arthur Conley (Otis Redding), Atco 6463 | 4 |
| 31 | 26 | 13 | 14 | **THE HUNTER GETS CAPTURED BY THE GAME** Marvelettes (William Robinson), Tamla 54143 | 11 |
| ★ 32 | 43 | 53 | 64 | **TRAVELIN' MAN** Stevie Wonder (Clarence Paul), Tamla 54147 | 5 |
| 33 | 25 | 21 | 26 | **LET'S FALL IN LOVE** Peaches & Herb (Kapralik-McCoy), Date 1523 | 12 |
| ★ 34 | 58 | 89 | — | **AT THE ZOO** Simon & Garfunkel (Bob Johnston), Columbia 44046 | 3 |
| 35 | 35 | 31 | 34 | **PUCKER UP BUTTERCUP** Jr. Walker & the All Stars, (H. Fuqua-J. Bristol), Soul 35030 | 8 |
| 36 | 38 | 40 | 45 | **NO MILK TODAY** Herman's Hermits (Mickie Most), MGM 13681 | 7 |
| ★ 37 | 47 | 61 | 71 | **WADE IN THE WATER** Herb Alpert and the Tijuana Brass, A&M 840 | 4 |
| ★ 38 | 51 | 64 | 84 | **DETROIT CITY** Tom Jones (Peter Sullivan), Parrot 40012 | 4 |
| 39 | 39 | 44 | 47 | **LADY** Jack Jones, Kapp 800 | 11 |
| 40 | 36 | 36 | 46 | **SIT DOWN, I THINK I LOVE YOU** Mojo Men (Lenny Waronker), Reprise 0539 | 9 |
| ★ 41 | 52 | 65 | 76 | **WHAT A WOMAN IN LOVE WON'T DO** Sandy Posey (Chips Moman), MGM 13702 | 4 |
| 42 | 46 | 52 | 55 | **WHEN SOMETHING IS WRONG WITH MY BABY** Sam and Dave (Prod. by Staff), Stax 210 | 6 |
| ★ 43 | 53 | 63 | 80 | **SHOW ME** Joe Tex (Buddy Killen), Dial 4055 | 5 |
| ★ 44 | 54 | 77 | — | **TELL ME TO MY FACE** Keith (Jerry Ross), Mercury 72652 | 3 |
| 45 | 50 | 57 | 72 | **THE LOSER (With a Broken Heart)** Gary Lewis and the Playboys (Leon Russell Liberty 55949 | 4 |
| 46 | 21 | 15 | 17 | **DARLIN' BE HOME SOON** Lovin' Spoonful (Erik Jacobsen), Kama Sutra 220 | 8 |
| 47 | 23 | 24 | 25 | **NIKI HOEKY** P. J. Proby (Calvin Carter), Liberty 55936 | 10 |
| ★ 48 | 59 | 85 | 100 | **DON'T YOU CARE** Buckinghams (Jim Guercio), Columbia 44053 | 4 |
| ★ 49 | 71 | — | — | **I'M A MAN** Spencer Davis Group (Jimmy Miller), United Artists 50144 | 2 |
| 50 | 44 | 46 | 53 | **MORNINGTOWN RIDE** Seekers (Tom Springfield), Capitol 5787 | 7 |
| ★ 51 | 65 | — | — | **THE GIRL I KNEW SOMEWHERE** Monkees (Douglas Farthing Hatelid), Colgems 1004 | 2 |
| ★ 52 | 63 | 74 | — | **GONNA GIVE HER ALL THE LOVE I'VE GOT** Jimmy Ruffin (N. Whitfield), Soul 350322 | 3 |
| 53 | 56 | 83 | 98 | **LAWDY MISS CLAWDY** Buckinghams (Carl Bonafide, Dan Bellock), U.S.A. 869 | 4 |
| 54 | 60 | 71 | 83 | **SUMMER WINE** Nancy Sinatra and Lee Hazlewood (Lee Hazlewood), Reprise 0527 | 5 |
| 55 | 64 | 99 | — | **ON A CAROUSEL** Hollies (Ron Richards), Imperial 66231 | 3 |
| ★ 56 | 66 | — | — | **SUNDAY FOR TEA** Peter & Gordon (John Burgess), Capitol 5864 | 2 |
| ★ 57 | 75 | 96 | — | **OH THAT'S GOOD, NO THAT'S BAD** Sam the Sham & the Pharaohs (Stan Kesler), MGM 13713 | 3 |
| 58 | 62 | 70 | 85 | **MERCY, MERCY, MERCY** Marlena Shaw (Billy Davis), Cadet 5557 | 4 |
| 59 | 55 | 59 | 74 | **KANSAS CITY** James Brown & The Famous Flames (James Brown), King 6086 | 5 |
| 60 | 57 | 66 | 63 | **TINY BUBBLES** Don Ho & Allis (Burke), Reprise 0507 | 17 |
| ★ 61 | 82 | — | — | **LOVE EYES** Nancy Sinatra (Lee Hazlewood), Reprise 0559 | 2 |
| ★ 62 | 80 | — | — | **MUSIC TO WATCH GIRLS BY** Andy Williams (Nick De Caro), Columbia 44065 | 2 |
| 63 | 72 | 90 | — | **I'LL TRY ANYTHING** Dusty Springfield (Herb Bernstein), Philips 40439 | 3 |
| ★ 64 | 86 | — | — | **CLOSE YOUR EYES** Peaches & Herb (Dave Kapralik-Ken Williams), Date 1549 | 2 |
| ★ 65 | — | — | — | **GET ME TO THE WORLD ON TIME** Electric Prunes (Dave Hassinger), Reprise 0564 | 1 |
| 66 | 69 | 82 | — | **FOR HE'S A JOLLY GOOD FELLOW** Bobby Vinton (Robert Mersey), Epic 10136 | 3 |
| 67 | 68 | 76 | 92 | **GIRL DON'T CARE** Gene Chandler (Carl Davis), Brunswick 55312 | 5 |
| 68 | 77 | — | — | **CAN'T GET ENOUGH OF YOU, BABY** ? (Question Mark) & the Mysterians (Neil Bogart, Pa-Go-Go Prod.), Cameo 467 | 2 |
| 69 | 67 | 72 | 73 | **SOUL TIME** Shirley Ellis (Charlie Calello), Columbia 44021 | 6 |
| 70 | 70 | 78 | 93 | **THAT ACAPULCO GOLD** Rainy Daze (Frank Slay), BMI 55002 | 4 |
| 71 | 73 | 73 | 88 | **BECAUSE OF YOU** Chris Montez (Herb Alpert), A&M 839 | 5 |
| 72 | 84 | 100 | — | **FRIDAY ON MY MIND** Easybeats, The (Shell Talmy) United Artists 50106 | 3 |
| 73 | 74 | 92 | — | **GIRL I NEED YOU** Artistics (Carl Davis), Brunswick 55315 | 3 |
| 74 | 85 | — | — | **CRY TO ME** Freddie Scott (Bert Bruns), Shout 211 | 2 |
| 75 | 76 | 80 | 82 | **DON'T DO IT** Micky Dolenz (Sepe/Brooks Prod.), Challenge 59353 | 5 |
| 76 | 81 | — | — | **WALKIN' IN THE SUNSHINE** Roger Miller (Jerry Kennedy), Smash 2081 | 2 |
| 77 | 78 | 79 | 91 | **THE DARK END OF THE STREET** James Carr (Quinton Claunch and Randolph Russell), Goldwax 317 | 6 |
| 78 | 79 | 81 | — | **PIPE DREAM** Blues Magoos (Bob Wyld & Art Polhemus), Mercury 72660 | 3 |
| 79 | 88 | 94 | — | **THE BEGINNING OF LONELINESS** Dionne Warwick (Bacharach-David), Scepter 1218[illegible] | 3 |
| 80 | 83 | — | — | **DANNY BOY** Ray Price (Don Law & Frank Jones), Columbia 4404[illegible] | 2 |
| 81 | 89 | — | — | **DEAD END STREET** Lou Rawls (David Axlerod), Capitol 5869 | 2 |
| ★ 82 | — | — | — | **I FOUND A LOVE** Wilson Pickett (Jerry Wexler), Atlantic 2394 | 1 |
| ★ 83 | — | — | — | **YOU GOT WHAT IT TAKES** Dave Clark Five (Dave Clark), Epic 101[illegible]4 | 1 |
| ★ 84 | 99 | — | — | **THE WHOLE WORLD IS A STAGE** Fantastic Four (Al Kent & E. Wingate), Ric Tic 122 | 2 |
| ★ 85 | 100 | — | — | **NOTHING TAKES THE PLACE OF YOU** Toussaint McCall (Jewel Productions), Ronn 3 | 2 |
| ★ 86 | — | — | — | **MY BACK PAGES** Byrds (Gary Usher), Columbia 44054 | 1 |
| 87 | 94 | — | — | **HIP HUG-HER** Booker T. & the M. G.'s (Prod. By Staff), Stax 211 | 2 |
| 88 | — | — | — | **SOMEBODY TO LOVE** Jefferson Airplane (Rick Jarrard), RCA Victor 9140 | 1 |
| ★ 89 | — | — | — | **YELLOW BALLOON** Yellow Balloon (Ken Handler & Yoder Critch), Canterbury 508 | 1 |
| ★ 90 | — | — | — | **POSTCARD FROM JAMAICA** Sopwith "Camel" (E. Jacobsen Sweet Reliable Prod.) Kama Sutra 224 | 1 |
| 91 | 91 | — | — | **HOLD ON, I'M COMING** Chuck Jackson & Maxine Brown, Wand 1148 | 4 |
| 92 | 92 | 95 | — | **WALK TALL** 2 of Clubs (Carl Edmondson), Fraternity 975 | 3 |
| 93 | 98 | — | — | **SHE TOOK YOU FOR A RIDE** Arron Neville (Par-Lo Prod.), Parlo 103 | 2 |
| 94 | — | — | — | **THE JUNGLE** B. B. King, Kent 462 | 1 |
| 95 | 96 | — | — | **I CAN'T MAKE IT ANYMORE** Snyder Turner (Arnold Geller Prod.), MGM 13692 | 2 |
| 96 | 97 | — | — | **MERCY, MERCY, MERCY** Larry William & Johnny Watson (Larry Williams & Johnny Watson), Okeh 7274 | 4 |
| 97 | — | — | — | **MAKE A LITTLE LOVE** Lowell Fulsom, Kent 463 | 1 |
| 98 | — | — | — | **FOR ME** Sergio Mendes & Brasil '66 (Herb Alpert), A&M 836 | 1 |
| 99 | — | — | — | **PRECIOUS MEMORIES** Romeos, Mark II J-1 | 1 |
| 100 | — | — | — | **NO TIME LIKE THE RIGHT TIME** Blues Project (Tom Wilson), Verve Folkways 5040 | 1 |

## HOT 100—A TO Z—(Publisher-Licensee)

At The Zoo (Charing Cross, BMI) ... 34
Baby, I Need Your Lovin' (Jobete, BMI) ... 15
Because of You (Gower, BMI) ... 71
Beggin' (Saturday/Season's Four, BMI) ... 25
Beginning of Loneliness, The (Blue Seas/Jac, ASCAP) ... 79
Bernadette (Jobete, BMI) ... 5
California Nights (Genius/Enchanted, ASCAP) ... 22
Can't Get Enough of You, Baby (Saturday, BMI) ... 68
Close Your Eyes (Tideland, BMI) ... 64
Cry To Me (Progressive, BMI) ... 74
Dark End of the Street, The (Press, BMI) ... 77
Danny Boy (Boosey & Hawkes, ASCAP) ... 80
Darlin' Be Home Soon (Faithful Virtue, BMI) ... 46
Dead End Street (Raw Lou/Beechwood, BMI) ... 81
Dedicated to the One I Love (Trousdale, BMI) ... 2
Detroit City (Cedarwood, BMI) ... 38
Don't Do It (4 Star/Popcorn/Corn, BMI) ... 75
Don't You Care (Beechwood/Macbeth, BMI) ... 48
Dry Your Eyes (Bee Cool, BMI) ... 26
59th Street Bridge Song, The (Charing Cross, BMI) 13
For He's a Jolly Good Fellow (Arab, BMI) ... 66
For Me (Butterfield, BMI) ... 98
For What It's Worth (Ten East/Springalo, BMI) ... 7
Friday on My Mind (Unart, BMI) ... 72
Get Me to the World on Time (Pomona, BMI) ... 65
Girl Don't Care (Jalynne/Cachand/BRC, BMI) ... 67
Girl I Need You (Jalynne/BRC, BMI) ... 73
Girl I Knew Somewhere, The (Screen Gems-Columbia, BMI) ... 51
Gonna Give Her All the Love I've Got (Jobete, BMI) ... 52
Happy Together (Chardon, BMI) ... 1
Hip Hug-Her (East, BMI) ... 87
Hold On, I'm Coming (Pronto/East, BMI) ... 91
Hunter Gets Captured by the Game, The (Jobete, BMI) ... 31
I Can't Make It Anymore (Witmark, ASCAP) ... 95
I Found A Love (Progressive/Lupine-Alibre, BMI) . 82
I Never Loved a Man the Way I Love You (14th Hour, BMI) ... 14
I Think We're Alone Now (Patricia, BMI) ... 12
I'll Try Anything (Pambar, BMI) ... 63
I'm a Man (Essex, ASCAP) ... 49
I've Been Lonely Too Long (Slacsar, BMI) ... 16
Jimmy Mack (Jobete, BMI) ... 18
The Jungle (Modern, BMI) ... 94
Kansas City (Arno, BMI) ... 59
Lady (Roosevelt, BMI) ... 39
Lawdy Miss Clawdy (Venice, BMI) ... 53
Let's Fall In Love (Bourne, ASCAP) ... 33
Little Bit You, A Little Bit Me, A (Screen Gems-Columbia, BMI) ... 19
Loser (With a Broken Heart), The (Skyhill, BMI) .. 45
Love Eyes (Criterion, ASCAP) ... 61
Love I Saw in You Was Just a Mirage, The (Jobete, BMI) ... 24
Love Is Here and Now You're Gone (Jobete, BMI) 20
Make A Little Love (Metric, BMI) ... 97
Mercy, Mercy, Mercy (Zawinul, BMI) (Shaw) ... 58
Mercy, Mercy, Mercy (Zawinul, BMI) ... 96
Morningtown Ride (Amadeo, BMI) ... 50
Music To Watch Girls By (S.C.P., ASCAP) ... 62
My Back Pages (Witmark, ASCAP) ... 86
My Cup Runneth Over (Chappell, ASCAP) ... 11
Niki Hoeky (Novalene, BMI) ... 47
No Milk Today (Man-Ken Ltd., BMI) ... 36
No Time Like The Right Time (Sealark, BMI) ... 100
Nothing Takes The Place of You (Su-Ma, BMI) ... 85
Oh That's Good, No That's Bad (Fred Rose, BMI) .. 57
On a Carousel (Maribus, BMI) ... 55
Penny Lane (Maclen, BMI) ... 3
Pipe Dream (Amanga-Bunga, BMI) ... 78
Precious Memories (Naro, ASCAP) ... 99
Postcard From Jamaica (Great Honesty, BMI) ... 90
Pucker Up Buttercup (Jobete, BMI) ... 35
Return of the Red Baron (Samphil, BMI) ... 21
Ruby Tuesday (Gideon, BMI) ... 23
She Took You For A Ride (Olrap, BMI) ... 93
Show Me (Tree, BMI) ... 43
Sit Down, I Think I Love You (Screen Gems-Columbia, BMI) ... 40
Sock It to Me—Baby! (Saturday, BMI) ... 17
Somebody To Love (Copper Penny, BMI) ... 88
Somethin' Stupid (Green Wood, BMI) ... 9
Soul Time (Gallico, BMI) ... 69
Strawberry Fields Forever (Maclen, BMI) ... 8
Summer Wine (Criterion, ASCAP) ... 54
Sunday For Tea (Southern, ASCAP) ... 56
Sweet Soul Music (Bedwal, BMI) ... 30
Tell Me to My Face (Maribus, BMI) ... 44
That Acapulco Gold (Claridge, ASCAP) ... 70
Then You Can Tell Me Goodbye (Acuff-Rose, BMI) 27
There's a Kind of a Hush (F., D. & M., ASCAP) .. 4
This Is My Song (Shawley, ASCAP) ... 6
Tiny Bubbles (Granite, ASCAP) ... 60
Travelin' Man (Stein, Van Stock, ASCAP) ... 32
Ups and Downs (Daywin, BMI) ... 29
Wade in the Water (Almo, ASCAP) ... 37
Walk Tall (Miller, ASCAP) ... 92
Walkin' in the Sunshine (Tree, BMI) ... 76
Western Union (Jetstar, BMI) ... 10
What a Woman in Love Won't Do (Windward Side, BMI) ... 41
When Something Is Wrong With My Baby (East/Pronto, BMI) ... 42
Whole World Is A Stage, The (Myto, BMI) ... 84
With This Ring (Vee Vee, BMI) ... 28
Yellow Balloon (Teeny Bopper, ASCAP) ... 89
You Got What It Takes (Fidelity, BMI) ... 83

## BUBBLING UNDER THE HOT 100

101. SHE'S LOOKING GOOD ... Roger Collins, Galaxy 750
102. EXCUSE ME, DEAR MARTHA ... Pozo Seco Singers, Columbia 44041
103. ONE, TWO, THREE ... Ramsey Lewis, Cadet 5556
104. THERE'S A CHANCE WE CAN MAKE IT ... Blues Magoos, Mercury 72660
105. GO GO RADIO MOSCOW ... Nikita The K, Warner Bros. 7005
106. LONELY AGAIN ... Eddy Arnold, RCA Victor 9080
107. MAKE LOVE TO ME ... Johnny Thunder & Ruby Winters, Diamond 218
108. SPEAK HER NAME ... Walter Jackson, Okeh 7272
109. WHO DO YOU LOVE ... Woolies, Dunhill 4052
110. I DON'T WANT TO LOSE YOU ... Jackie Wilson, Brunswick 55309
111. THINK ... James Brown & Vickie Anderson, King 6091
112. THE HAPPENING ... Supremes, Motown 1107
113. YELLOW BALLOON ... Jan & Dean, Columbia 44036
114. WHY NOT TONIGHT ... Jimmy Hughes, Fame 1011
115. WHEN I WAS YOUNG ... Eric Burdon & the Animals, MGM 13721
116. ANIMAL CRACKERS ... Gene Pitney, Musicor 1235
117. MATTHEW & SON ... Cat Stevens, Deram 7905
118. EVERYBODY NEEDS HELP ... Jimmy Holiday, Minit 232016
119. RELEASE ME ... Engelbert Humperdinck, Parrot 40011
120. EVERYBODY LOVES A WINNER ... William Bell, Stax 212
121. AIN'T GONNA REST TILL I GET YOU ... Five Stair Steps, Windy C 605
122. (HEY YOU) SET MY SOUL ON FIRE ... Mary Wells, Atco 6459
123. DON'T TIE ME DOWN ... Anthony & the Imperials, Veep 1255
124. HERE COME THE TEARS ... Darrell Banks, Atco 6471
125. ALWAYS SOMETHING THERE TO REMIND ME ... Patti LaBelle & the Bluebells, Atlantic 2390
126. AFTER THE BALL ... Bob Crewe, Dyno Voice 231
127. WHAT'S THAT GOT TO DO WITH ME ... Jim & Jean, Verve Folkways 5053
128. MR. UNRELIABLE ... Cryan' Shames, Columbia 44037
129. LIVE ... Merry Go Round, A&M 834
130. I GOT RHYTHM ... Happenings, B. T. Puppy 527
131. HERE COMES MY BABY ... Tremeloes, Epic 10139
132. ONE HURT DESERVES ANOTHER ... Raelets, Tangerine 296
133. GIRL YOU'LL BE A WOMAN SOON ... Neil Diamond, Bang 542
134. TEARS TEARS TEARS ... Ben E. King, Atco 6472
135. BUY FOR ME THE RAIN ... Nitty Gritty Dirt Band, Liberty 55948

Compiled from national retail sales and radio station airplay by the Music Popularity Dept. of Record Market Research, Billboard.

# Billboard HOT 100

For Week Ending April 8, 1967

★ STAR performer—Sides registering greatest proportionate upward progress this week.

Record Industry Association of America seal of certification as million selling single.

| This Week | 1 Wk. Ago | 2 Wks. Ago | 3 Wks. Ago | TITLE Artist (Producer), Label & Number | Weeks On Chart |
|---|---|---|---|---|---|
| 1 | 1 | 1 | 2 | HAPPY TOGETHER — Turtles (Joe Wissert), White Whale 244 | 9 |
| 2 | 2 | 2 | 6 | DEDICATED TO THE ONE I LOVE — Mama's and the Papa's (Lou Adler), Dunhill 4077 | 7 |
| 3 | 9 | 29 | 50 | SOMETHIN' STUPID — Nancy Sinatra & Frank Sinatra (Jimmy Bowen & Lee Hazlewood), Reprise 0561 | 4 |
| 4 | 5 | 18 | 23 | BERNADETTE — Four Tops (Holland and Dozier), Motown 1104 | 5 |
| 5 | 6 | 19 | 28 | THIS IS MY SONG — Petula Clark (Sonny Burke), Warner Bros. 7002 | 6 |
| 6 | 3 | 3 | 1 | PENNY LANE — Beatles (George Martin), Capitol 5810 | 7 |
| 7 | 10 | 28 | 35 | WESTERN UNION — Five Americans (Dale Hawkins), Abnak 118 | 6 |
| 8 | 12 | 13 | 18 | I THINK WE'RE ALONE NOW — Tommy James and the Shondells (Cordell-Gentry), Roulette 4720 | 9 |
| 9 | 19 | 32 | — | A LITTLE BIT YOU, A LITTLE BIT ME — Monkees (Jeff Barry), Colgems 1004 | 3 |
| 10 | 4 | 4 | 8 | THERE'S A KIND OF A HUSH — Herman's Hermits (Mickie Most), MGM 13681 | 9 |
| 11 | 18 | 24 | 29 | JIMMY MACK — Martha and the Vandellas (Holland-Dozier), Gordy 7058 | 7 |
| 12 | 14 | 20 | 25 | I NEVER LOVED A MAN THE WAY I LOVE YOU — Aretha Franklin (Jerry Wexler), Atlantic 2386 | 6 |
| 13 | 13 | 14 | 26 | THE 59TH STREET BRIDGE SONG — Harpers Bizarre (Lenny Waronker), Warner Bros. 5890 | 8 |
| 14 | 7 | 7 | 12 | FOR WHAT IT'S WORTH — Buffalo Springfield (Greene & Stone), Atco 6459 | 11 |
| 15 | 8 | 11 | 11 | STRAWBERRY FIELDS FOREVER — Beatles (George Martin), Capitol 5810 | 7 |
| 16 | 25 | 30 | 37 | BEGGIN' — 4 Seasons (Bob Crewe), Philips 40433 | 6 |
| 17 | 15 | 5 | 3 | BABY, I NEED YOUR LOVIN' — Johnny Rivers (Lou Adler), Imperial 66227 | 10 |
| 18 | 30 | 45 | 55 | SWEET SOUL MUSIC — Arthur Conley (Otis Redding), Atco 6463 | 5 |
| 19 | 17 | 6 | 7 | SOCK IT TO ME—BABY! — Mitch Ryder & the Detroit Wheels (Bob Crewe), New Voice 820 | 10 |
| 20 | 24 | 27 | 30 | THE LOVE I SAW IN YOU WAS JUST A MIRAGE — Smokey Robinson and the Miracles (Wm. Robinson-W. Moore), Tamla 54145 | 8 |
| 21 | 26 | 31 | 41 | DRY YOUR EYES — Brenda and the Tabulations (Bob Finiz), Dionn 500 | 7 |
| 22 | 16 | 17 | 17 | I'VE BEEN LONELY TOO LONG — Young Rascals (Young Rascals), Atlantic 2377 | 11 |
| 23 | 11 | 8 | 9 | MY CUP RUNNETH OVER — Ed Ames (Jim Foglesong & Joe Reisman), RCA Victor 9002 | 12 |
| 24 | 21 | 15 | 27 | RETURN OF THE RED BARON — Royal Guardsmen (Gernhard Ent.), Laurie 3379 | 7 |
| 25 | 22 | 16 | 16 | CALIFORNIA NIGHTS — Lesley Gore (Bob Crewe), Mercury 72649 | 10 |
| 26 | 28 | 37 | 51 | WITH THIS RING — Platters (Luther Dixon), Musicor 1229 | 7 |
| 27 | 34 | 58 | 89 | AT THE ZOO — Simon & Garfunkel (Bob Johnston), Columbia 44046 | 4 |
| 28 | 48 | 59 | 85 | DON'T YOU CARE — Buckinghams (Jim Guercio), Columbia 44053 | 5 |
| 29 | 20 | 9 | 4 | LOVE IS HERE AND NOW YOU'RE GONE — Supremes (Holland-Dozier), Motown 1103 | 11 |
| 30 | 38 | 51 | 64 | DETROIT CITY — Tom Jones (Peter Sullivan), Parrot 40012 | 5 |
| 31 | 41 | 52 | 65 | WHAT A WOMAN IN LOVE WON'T DO — Sandy Posey (Chips Moman), MGM 13702 | 5 |
| 32 | 32 | 43 | 53 | TRAVELIN' MAN — Stevie Wonder (Clarence Paul), Tamla 54147 | 4 |
| 33 | 49 | 71 | — | I'M A MAN — Spencer Davis Group (Jimmy Miller), United Artists 50144 | 3 |
| 34 | 29 | 22 | 22 | UPS AND DOWNS — Paul Revere & the Raiders (Terry Melchers), Columbia 44018 | 8 |
| 35 | 36 | 38 | 40 | NO MILK TODAY — Herman's Hermits (Mickie Most), MGM 13681 | 8 |
| 36 | 43 | 53 | 63 | SHOW ME — Joe Tex (Buddy Killen), Dial 4055 | 6 |
| 37 | 37 | 47 | 61 | WADE IN THE WATER — Herb Alpert and the Tijuana Brass, A&M 840 | 5 |
| 38 | 61 | 82 | — | LOVE EYES — Nancy Sinatra (Lee Hazlewood), Reprise 0559 | 3 |
| 39 | 52 | 63 | 74 | GONNA GIVE HER ALL THE LOVE I'VE GOT — Jimmy Ruffin (N. Whitfield), Soul 350322 | 4 |
| 40 | 44 | 54 | 77 | TELL ME TO MY FACE — Keith (Jerry Ross), Mercury 72652 | 4 |
| 41 | 53 | 56 | 83 | LAWDY MISS CLAWDY — Buckinghams (Carl Bonafide, Dan Belleck), U.S.A. 869 | 5 |
| 42 | 27 | 12 | 10 | THEN YOU CAN TELL ME GOODBYE — Casinos (Gene Hughes), Fraternity 977 | 13 |
| 43 | 45 | 50 | 57 | THE LOSER (With a Broken Heart) — Gary Lewis and the Playboys (Leon Russell), Liberty 55949 | 5 |
| 44 | 42 | 46 | 52 | WHEN SOMETHING IS WRONG WITH MY BABY — Sam and Dave (Prod. by Staff), Stax 210 | 7 |
| 45 | 56 | 66 | — | SUNDAY FOR TEA — Peter & Gordon (John Burgess), Capitol 5864 | 3 |
| 46 | 51 | 65 | — | THE GIRL I KNEW SOMEWHERE — Monkees (Douglas Farthing Hatelid), Colgems 1004 | 3 |
| 47 | 23 | 10 | 5 | RUBY TUESDAY — Rolling Stones (Andrew Loog Oldham), London 904 | 12 |
| 48 | 83 | — | — | YOU GOT WHAT IT TAKES — Dave Clark Five (Dave Clark), Epic 10144 | 2 |
| 49 | 54 | 60 | 71 | SUMMER WINE — Nancy Sinatra and Lee Hazlewood (Lee Hazlewood), Reprise 0527 | 6 |
| 50 | 55 | 64 | 99 | ON A CAROUSEL — Hollies (Ron Richards), Imperial 66231 | 4 |
| 51 | 64 | 86 | — | CLOSE YOUR EYES — Peaches & Herb (Dave Kapralik-Ken Williams), Date 1549 | 3 |
| 52 | 62 | 80 | — | MUSIC TO WATCH GIRLS BY — Andy Williams (Nick De Caro), Columbia 44065 | 3 |
| 53 | 63 | 72 | 90 | I'LL TRY ANYTHING — Dusty Springfield (Herb Bernstein), Philips 40439 | 4 |
| 54 | 57 | 75 | 96 | OH THAT'S GOOD, NO THAT'S BAD — Sam the Sham & the Pharaohs (Stan Kesler), MGM 13713 | 4 |
| 55 | 65 | — | — | GET ME TO THE WORLD ON TIME — Electric Prunes (Dave Hassinger), Reprise 0564 | 2 |
| 56 | 72 | 84 | 100 | FRIDAY ON MY MIND — Easybeats, The (Shell Talmy) United Artists 50106 | 4 |
| 57 | — | — | — | THE HAPPENING — Supremes (Holland & Dozier), Motown 1107 | 1 |
| 58 | 40 | 36 | 36 | SIT DOWN, I THINK I LOVE YOU — Mojo Men (Lenny Waronker), Reprise 0539 | 10 |
| 59 | 82 | — | — | I FOUND A LOVE — Wilson Pickett (Jerry Wexler), Atlantic 2394 | 2 |
| 60 | 68 | 77 | — | CAN'T GET ENOUGH OF YOU, BABY — ? (Question Mark) & the Mysterians (Neil Bogart, Pa-Go-Go Prod.), Cameo 467 | 3 |
| 61 | 76 | 81 | — | WALKIN' IN THE SUNSHINE — Roger Miller (Jerry Kennedy), Smash 2081 | 3 |
| 62 | 86 | — | — | MY BACK PAGES — Byrds (Gary Usher), Columbia 44054 | 2 |
| 63 | 58 | 62 | 70 | MERCY, MERCY, MERCY — Marlena Shaw (Billy Davis), Cadet 5557 | 5 |
| 64 | 80 | 83 | — | DANNY BOY — Ray Price (Don Law & Frank Jones), Columbia 44042 | 3 |
| 65 | 81 | 89 | — | DEAD END STREET — Lou Rawls (David Axelrod), Capitol 5869 | 3 |
| 66 | 66 | 69 | 82 | FOR HE'S A JOLLY GOOD FELLOW — Bobby Vinton (Robert Mersey), Epic 10136 | 4 |
| 67 | 67 | 68 | 76 | GIRL DON'T CARE — Gene Chandler (Carl Davis), Brunswick 55312 | 7 |
| 68 | — | — | — | GIRL, YOU'LL BE A WOMAN SOON — Neil Diamond (Jeff Barry & Ellie Greenwich), Bang 542 | 1 |
| 69 | 78 | 79 | 81 | PIPE DREAM — Blues Magoos (Bob Wyld & Art Polhemus) | 4 |
| 70 | 73 | 74 | 92 | GIRL I NEED YOU — Artistics (Carl Davis), Brunswick 55315 | 4 |
| 71 | 89 | — | — | YELLOW BALLOON — Yellow Balloon (Ken Handler & Yoder Critch), Canterbury 508 | 2 |
| 72 | 74 | 85 | — | CRY TO ME — Freddie Scott (Bert Bruns), Shout 211 | 3 |
| 73 | — | — | — | I GOT RHYTHM — Happenings (The Tokens) B.T. Puppy 527 | 1 |
| 74 | 87 | 94 | — | HIP HUG-HER — Booker T. and the M.G.'s (Prod. By Staff), Stax 211 | 3 |
| 75 | 75 | 76 | 80 | DON'T DO IT — Micky Dolenz (Sepe/Brooks Prod.), Challenge 59353 | 6 |
| 76 | 88 | — | — | SOMEBODY TO LOVE — Jefferson Airplane (Rick Jarrard), RCA Victor 9140 | 2 |
| 77 | — | — | — | WHEN I WAS YOUNG — Eric Burdon and the Animals (Tom Wilson), MGM 13721 | 1 |
| 78 | 84 | 99 | — | THE WHOLE WORLD IS A STAGE — Fantastic Four (Al Kent & E. Wingate), Ric Tic 122 | 3 |
| 79 | — | — | — | OUT OF LEFT FIELD — Percy Sledge (Quin Ivy & Marlin Greene), Atlantic 2396 | 1 |
| 80 | — | — | — | CASINO ROYALE — Herb Alpert & the Tijuana Brass (Herb Alpert & Jerry Moss), A&M 850 | 1 |
| 81 | — | — | — | I LOVE YOU MORE THAN WORDS CAN SAY — Otis Redding (Prod. by Staff), Volt 146 | 1 |
| 82 | — | — | — | BUY FOR ME THE RAIN — Nitty Gritty Dirt Band (Dallas Smith), Liberty 55948 | 1 |
| 83 | — | — | — | THERE'S A CHANCE WE CAN MAKE IT — Blues Magoos (Bob Wyld & Art Polhemus), Mercury 72660 | 1 |
| 84 | — | — | — | HERE COMES MY BABY — Tremeloes, Epic 10139 | 1 |
| 85 | 85 | 100 | — | NOTHING TAKES THE PLACE OF YOU — Toussaint McCall (Jewel Productions), Ronn 3 | 3 |
| 86 | — | — | — | THE LADY COMES FROM BALTIMORE — Bobby Darin (Charles Koppelman & Don Rubin), Atlantic 2395 | 1 |
| 87 | — | — | — | DO THE THING — Lou Courtney (Robert Bateman), Riverside 7589 | 1 |
| 88 | 90 | — | — | POSTCARD FROM JAMAICA — Sopwith "Camel" (E. Jacobsen Sweet Reliable Prod.), Kama Sutra 224 | 2 |
| 89 | 99 | — | — | PRECIOUS MEMORIES — Romeos, Mark II J-1 | 2 |
| 90 | — | — | — | WHY? (Am I Treated So Bad) — Cannonball Adderley (David Axelrod), Capitol 5877 | 1 |
| 91 | — | — | — | SING ALONG WITH ME — Tommy Roe (Steve Clark), ABC 10908 | 1 |
| 92 | 93 | 98 | — | SHE TOOK YOU FOR A RIDE — Arron Neville (Par-Lo Prod.), Parlo 103 | 3 |
| 93 | — | — | — | MAKING MEMORIES — Frankie Laine (Bob Thiele), ABC 10924 | 1 |
| 94 | 94 | — | — | THE JUNGLE — B.B. King, Kent 462 | 2 |
| 95 | — | — | — | ALFIE — Dionne Warwick (Bacharach-David), Scepter 12187 | 1 |
| 96 | 100 | — | — | NO TIME LIKE THE RIGHT TIME — Blues Project (Tom Wilson), Verve Folkways 5040 | 2 |
| 97 | 97 | — | — | MAKE A LITTLE LOVE — Lowell Fulsom, Kent 463 | 2 |
| 98 | 98 | — | — | FOR ME — Sergio Mendes & Brasil '66 (Herb Alpert), A&M 836 | 2 |
| 99 | — | — | — | RELEASE ME (And Let Me Love Again) — Engelbert Humperdinck, Parrot 40011 | 1 |
| 100 | — | — | — | THINK — Vicki Anderson & James Brown (James Brown Prod.), King 12315 | 1 |

## BUBBLING UNDER THE HOT 100

101. LONELY AGAIN — Eddy Arnold, RCA Victor 9080
102. TEARS TEARS TEARS — Ben E. King, Atco 6472
103. CAN'T SEEM TO MAKE YOU MINE — Seeds, GNP Crescendo 354
104. PORTRAIT OF MY LIFE — Tokens, Warner Bros. 5900
105. SHE'S LOOKING GOOD — Roger Collins, Galaxy 750
106. BLUES THEME — The Arrows, Tower 295
107. MAKE LOVE TO ME — Johnny Thunder & Ruby Winters, Diamond 218
108. EXCUSE ME DEAR MARTHA — Pozo-Seco Singers, Columbia 44041
109. I CAN'T MAKE IT ANYMORE — Spyder Turner, MGM 13692
110. GO GO RADIO MOSCOW — Nikita The K, Warner Bros. 7005
111. WHY NOT TONIGHT — Jimmy Hughes, Fame 1011
112. MERCY, MERCY, MERCY — Larry Williams & Johnny Watson, Okeh 7274
113. BEAT GOES ON — Lawrence Welk, Dot 17001
114. JUST LOOK WHAT YOU'VE DONE — Brenda Holloway, Tamla 54148
115. CALIFORNIA ON MY MIND — Coastliners, Dear 1300
116. EIGHT MEN—FOUR WOMEN — O.V. Wright, Back Beat 580
117. MATTHEW AND SON — Cat Stevens, Deram 7905
118. IN THE MIDNIGHT HOUR — Wanted, A&M 834
119. THAT ACAPULCO GOLD — Rainy Daze, Uni 55005
120. EVERYBODY NEEDS HELP — Jimmy Holiday, Minit 232016
121. YOU'RE GONNA BE MINE — New Colony Six, Sentar 1206
122. I WANT TO GO BACK THERE AGAIN — Chris Clark, VIP 2504
123. SHAKE HANDS & WALK AWAY CRYING — Lou Christie, Columbia 44062
124. IN THE MIDNIGHT HOUR — Wanted, A&M 844
125. GOODBYE TO ALL YOU WOMEN — Bobby Goldsboro, United Artists 50138
126. BREAK ON THROUGH — Doors, Elektra 45611
127. MR. UNRELIABLE — Cryan' Shames, Columbia 44037
128. SUNSHINE GIRL — Parade, A&M 841
129. TAKE ME — Brenda Lee, Decca 32119
130. IT'S SO HARD BEING A LOSER — Contours, Gordy 7059
131. SHAKE — British Walkers, Cameo 460
132. WHEN LOVE SLIPS AWAY — Dee Dee Warwick, Mercury 72667
133. HAPPY JACK — Who, Decca 32114
134. GET WHILE YOU CAN — Howard Tate, Verve 10496
135. SHE'S GOT THE TIME, SHE'S GOT THE CHANGES — Poor, York 402

Compiled from national retail sales and radio station airplay by the Music Popularity Dept. of Record Market Research, Billboard.

For Week Ending April 15, 1967

# Billboard HOT 100

★ STAR performer—Sides registering greatest proportionate upward progress this week.

(Seal) Record Industry Association of America seal of certification as million selling single.

| This Week | 1 Wk. Ago | 2 Wks. Ago | 3 Wks. Ago | TITLE Artist (Producer), Label & Number | Weeks On Chart |
|---|---|---|---|---|---|
| 1 (Billboard Award) | 3 | 9 | 29 | SOMETHIN' STUPID — Nancy Sinatra & Frank Sinatra (Jimmy Bowen & Lee Hazlewood), Reprise 0561 | 5 |
| 2 | 1 | 1 | 1 | HAPPY TOGETHER — Turtles (Joe Wissert), White Whale 244 | 10 |
| 3 | 5 | 6 | 19 | THIS IS MY SONG — Petula Clark (Sonny Burke), Warner Bros. 7002 | 7 |
| 4 | 4 | 5 | 18 | BERNADETTE — Four Tops (Holland and Dozier), Motown 1104 | 6 |
| ★5 | 9 | 19 | 32 | A LITTLE BIT YOU, A LITTLE BIT ME — Monkees (Jeff Barry), Colgems 1004 (RIAA seal) | 4 |
| 6 | 7 | 10 | 28 | WESTERN UNION — Five Americans (Dale Hawkins), Abnak 118 | 7 |
| 7 | 8 | 12 | 13 | I THINK WE'RE ALONE NOW — Tommy James and the Shondells (Cordell-Gentry), Roulette 4720 | 10 |
| 8 | 2 | 2 | 2 | DEDICATED TO THE ONE I LOVE — Mama's and the Papa's (Lou Adler), Dunhill 4077 | 8 |
| ★9 | 12 | 14 | 20 | I NEVER LOVED A MAN THE WAY I LOVE YOU — Aretha Franklin (Jerry Wexler), Atlantic 2386 | 7 |
| 10 | 11 | 18 | 24 | JIMMY MACK — Martha and the Vandellas (Holland-Dozier), Gordy 7058 | 8 |
| ★11 | 18 | 30 | 45 | SWEET SOUL MUSIC — Arthur Conley (Otis Redding), Atco 6463 | 6 |
| 12 | 6 | 3 | 3 | PENNY LANE — Beatles (George Martin), Capitol 5810 (RIAA seal) | 8 |
| 13 | 10 | 4 | 4 | THERE'S A KIND OF A HUSH — Herman's Hermits (Mickie Most), MGM 13681 | 10 |
| 14 | 13 | 13 | 14 | THE 59TH STREET BRIDGE SONG — Harpers Bizarre (Lenny Waronker), Warner Bros. 5890 | 9 |
| 15 | 14 | 7 | 7 | FOR WHAT IT'S WORTH — Buffalo Springfield (Greene & Stone), Atco 6459 | 12 |
| 16 | 16 | 25 | 30 | BEGGIN' — 4 Seasons (Bob Crewe), Philips 40433 | 7 |
| ★17 | 27 | 34 | 58 | AT THE ZOO — Simon & Garfunkel (Bob Johnston), Columbia 44046 | 5 |
| ★18 | 26 | 28 | 37 | WITH THIS RING — Platters (Luther Dixon), Musicor 1229 | 8 |
| ★19 | 57 | — | — | THE HAPPENING — Supremes (Holland & Dozier), Motown 1107 | 2 |
| 20 | 21 | 26 | 31 | DRY YOUR EYES — Brenda and the Tabulations (Bob Finiz), Dionn 500 | 8 |
| 21 | 15 | 8 | 11 | STRAWBERRY FIELDS FOREVER — Beatles (George Martin), Capitol 5810 | 8 |
| ★22 | 33 | 49 | 71 | I'M A MAN — Spencer Davis Group (Jimmy Miller), United Artists 50144 | 4 |
| ★23 | 28 | 48 | 59 | DON'T YOU CARE — Buckinghams (Jim Guercio), Columbia 44053 | 6 |
| 24 | 22 | 16 | 17 | I'VE BEEN LONELY TOO LONG — Young Rascals (Young Rascals), Atlantic 2377 | 12 |
| 25 | 20 | 24 | 27 | THE LOVE I SAW IN YOU WAS JUST A MIRAGE — Smokey Robinson and the Miracles (Wm. Robinson-W. Moore), Tamla 54145 | 9 |
| 26 | 19 | 17 | 6 | SOCK IT TO ME—BABY! — Mitch Ryder & the Detroit Wheels (Bob Crewe), New Voice 820 | 11 |
| 27 | 25 | 22 | 16 | CALIFORNIA NIGHTS — Lesley Gore (Bob Crewe), Mercury 72649 | 11 |
| 28 | 30 | 38 | 51 | DETROIT CITY — Tom Jones (Peter Sullivan), Parrot 40012 | 6 |
| ★29 | 38 | 61 | 82 | LOVE EYES — Nancy Sinatra (Lee Hazlewood), Reprise 0559 | 4 |
| ★30 | 39 | 52 | 63 | GONNA GIVE HER ALL THE LOVE I'VE GOT — Jimmy Ruffin (N. Whitfield), Soul 350322 | 5 |
| 31 | 31 | 41 | 52 | WHAT A WOMAN IN LOVE WON'T DO — Sandy Posey (Chips Moman), MGM 13702 | 6 |
| 32 | 23 | 11 | 8 | MY CUP RUNNETH OVER — Ed Ames (Jim Foglesong & Joe Reisman), RCA Victor 9002 | 13 |
| ★33 | 51 | 64 | 86 | CLOSE YOUR EYES — Peaches & Herb (Dave Kapralik-Ken Williams), Date 1549 | 4 |
| ★34 | 45 | 56 | 66 | SUNDAY FOR TEA — Peter & Gordon (John Burgess), Capitol 5864 | 4 |
| 35 | 36 | 43 | 53 | SHOW ME — Joe Tex (Buddy Killen), Dial 4055 | 7 |
| ★36 | 50 | 55 | 64 | ON A CAROUSEL — Hollies (Ron Richards), Imperial 66231 | 5 |
| 37 | 40 | 44 | 54 | TELL ME TO MY FACE — Keith (Jerry Ross), Mercury 72652 | 5 |
| ★38 | 48 | 83 | — | YOU GOT WHAT IT TAKES — Dave Clark Five (Dave Clark), Epic 10144 | 3 |
| 39 | 46 | 51 | 65 | THE GIRL I KNEW SOMEWHERE — Monkees (Douglas Farthing Hatelid), Colgems 1004 | 4 |
| 40 | 32 | 32 | 43 | TRAVELIN' MAN — Stevie Wonder (Clarence Paul), Tamla 54147 | 7 |
| 41 | 41 | 53 | 56 | LAWDY MISS CLAWDY — Buckinghams (Carl Bonafide, Dan Bellock), U.S.A. 869 | 6 |
| 42 | 35 | 36 | 38 | NO MILK TODAY — Herman's Hermits (Mickie Most), MGM 13681 | 9 |
| ★43 | 59 | 82 | — | I FOUND A LOVE — Wilson Pickett (Jerry Wexler), Atlantic 2394 | 3 |
| 44 | 44 | 42 | 46 | WHEN SOMETHING IS WRONG WITH MY BABY — Sam and Dave (Prod. by Staff), Stax 210 | 8 |
| ★45 | 55 | 65 | — | GET ME TO THE WORLD ON TIME — Electric Prunes (Dave Hassinger), Reprise 0564 | 3 |
| ★46 | 56 | 72 | 84 | FRIDAY ON MY MIND — Easybeats, The (Shell Talmy) United Artists 50106 | 5 |
| 47 | 52 | 62 | 80 | MUSIC TO WATCH GIRLS BY — Andy Williams (Nick De Caro), Columbia 44065 | 4 |
| 48 | 17 | 15 | 5 | BABY, I NEED YOUR LOVIN' — Johnny Rivers (Lou Adler), Imperial 66227 | 11 |
| 49 | 49 | 54 | 60 | SUMMER WINE — Nancy Sinatra and Lee Hazlewood (Lee Hazlewood), Reprise 0527 | 7 |
| 50 | 53 | 63 | 72 | I'LL TRY ANYTHING — Dusty Springfield (Herb Bernstein), Philips 40439 | 5 |
| ★51 | 61 | 76 | 81 | WALKIN' IN THE SUNSHINE — Roger Miller (Jerry Kennedy), Smash 2081 | 4 |
| ★52 | 62 | 86 | — | MY BACK PAGES — Byrds (Gary Usher), Columbia 44054 | 3 |
| ★53 | 68 | — | — | GIRL, YOU'LL BE A WOMAN SOON — Neil Diamond (Jeff Barry & Ellie Greenwich), Bang 542 | 2 |
| 54 | 54 | 57 | 75 | OH THAT'S GOOD, NO THAT'S BAD — Sam the Sham & the Pharaohs (Stan Kesler), MGM 13713 | 5 |
| ★55 | 65 | 81 | 89 | DEAD END STREET — Lou Rawls (David Axlerod), Capitol 5869 | 4 |
| 56 | 43 | 45 | 50 | THE LOSER (With a Broken Heart) — Gary Lewis and the Playboys (Leon Russell Liberty 55949 | 6 |
| ★57 | 71 | 89 | — | YELLOW BALLOON — Yellow Balloon (Ken Handler & Yoder Critch), Canterbury 508 | 3 |
| 58 | 58 | 40 | 36 | SIT DOWN, I THINK I LOVE YOU — Mojo Men (Lenny Waronker), Reprise 0539 | 11 |
| ★59 | 73 | — | — | I GOT RHYTHM — Happenings (The Tokens) B. T. Puppy 527 | 2 |
| 60 | 60 | 68 | 77 | CAN'T GET ENOUGH OF YOU, BABY — ? (Question Mark) & the Mysterians (Neil Bogart, Pa-Go-Go Prod.), Cameo 467 | 4 |
| ★61 | 77 | — | — | WHEN I WAS YOUNG — Eric Burdon & the Animals (Tom Wilson), MGM 13721 | 2 |
| 62 | 64 | 80 | 83 | DANNY BOY — Ray Price (Don Law & Frank Jones), Columbia 44042 | 4 |
| 63 | 74 | 87 | 94 | HIP HUG-HER — Booker T. & the M. G.'s (Prod. By Staff), Stax 211 | 4 |
| 64 | 69 | 78 | 79 | PIPE DREAM — Blues Magoos (Bob Wyld & Art Polhemus), | 5 |
| ★65 | 80 | — | — | CASINO ROYALE — Herb Alpert & the Tijuana Brass (Herb Alpert & Jerry Moss), A&M 850 | 2 |
| 66 | 67 | 67 | 68 | GIRL DON'T CARE — Gene Chandler (Carl Davis), Brunswick 55312 | 8 |
| ★67 | 82 | — | — | BUY FOR ME THE RAIN — Nitty Gritty Dirt Band (Dallas Smith), Liberty 55948 | 2 |
| 68 | 76 | 88 | — | SOMEBODY TO LOVE — Jefferson Airplane (Rick Jarrard), RCA Victor 9140 | 3 |
| 69 | 70 | 73 | 74 | GIRL I NEED YOU — Artistics (Carl Davis), Brunswick 55315 | 5 |
| 70 | 72 | 74 | 85 | CRY TO ME — Freddie Scott (Bert Bruns), Shout 211 | 4 |
| ★71 | 99 | — | — | RELEASE ME (And Let Me Love Again) — Engelbert Humperdinck, Parrot 40011 | 2 |
| 72 | 84 | — | — | HERE COMES MY BABY — Tremeloes, Epic 10139 | 2 |
| 73 | 79 | — | — | OUT OF LEFT FIELD — Percy Sledge (Quin Ivy & Marlin Greene), Atlantic 2396 | 2 |
| 74 | 85 | 85 | 100 | NOTHING TAKES THE PLACE OF YOU — Toussaint McCall (Jewel Productions), Ronn 3 | 4 |
| ★75 | 93 | — | — | MAKING MEMORIES — Frankie Laine (Bob Thiele), ABC 10924 | 2 |
| 76 | 89 | 99 | — | PRECIOUS MEMORIES — Romeos, Mark II J-1 | 3 |
| 77 | 78 | 84 | 99 | THE WHOLE WORLD IS A STAGE — Fantastic Four (Al Kent & E. Wingate), Ric Tic 122 | 4 |
| 78 | 86 | — | — | THE LADY CAME FROM BALTIMORE — Bobby Darin (Charles Koppelman & Don Rubin), Atlantic 2395 | 2 |
| 79 | 90 | — | — | WHY? (Am I Treated So Bad) — Cannonball Adderley (David Axelrod), Capitol 5877 | 2 |
| 80 | 81 | — | — | I LOVE YOU MORE THAN WORDS CAN SAY — Otis Redding (Prod. by Staff) Volt 14[illegible] | 2 |
| 81 | 83 | — | — | THERE'S A CHANCE WE CAN MAKE IT — Blues Magoos (Bob Wyld & Art Polhemus), Mercury 726[illegible] | 2 |
| ★82 | — | — | — | SHAKE A TAIL FEATHER — James & Bobby Purify (Papa Don, Cogbill, Young, Emmons & Chrisman), Bell 6[illegible]9 | 1 |
| 83 | 87 | — | — | DO THE THING — Lou Courtney (Robert Bateman), Riverside 7[illegible]9 | 2 |
| ★84 | — | — | — | SUNSHINE GIRL — Parade (Jerry Riopelle), A&M [illegible]41 | 1 |
| ★85 | — | — | — | IT'S SO HARD BEING A LOSER — Contours (W. Weatherspoon & J. Dean), Gordy 7[illegible]59 | 1 |
| ★86 | — | — | — | PORTRAIT OF MY LOVE — Tokens (Bright Tunes Prod.), Warner Bros. [illegible]00 | 1 |
| 87 | — | — | — | MY GIRL JOSEPHINE — Jerry Jaye, Hi [illegible]120 | 1 |
| 88 | 95 | — | — | ALFIE — Dionne Warwick (Bacharach-David), Scepter 1[illegible]187 | 2 |
| ★89 | — | — | — | AIN'T GONNA REST (Till I Get You) — Five Stairsteps (Curtis Mayfield), Windy C 605 | 1 |
| ★90 | — | — | — | SPEAK HER NAME — Walter Jackson (Ted Cooper), Okeh 7272 | 1 |
| 91 | — | — | — | FUNKY BROADWAY — Dyke & the Blazers (Coleman & Barrett), Original Sound 64 | 1 |
| 92 | 92 | 93 | 98 | SHE TOOK YOU FOR A RIDE — Arron Neville (Par-Lo Prod.), Parlo 103 | 4 |
| 93 | — | — | — | ONE HURT DESERVES ANOTHER — Raelets (Ray Charles), Tangerine 296 | 1 |
| 94 | — | — | — | TIME ALONE WILL TELL — Connie Francis (Bob Morgan), MGM 13718 | 1 |
| 95 | — | — | — | EVERYBODY LOVES A WINNER — William Bell (Prod. By Staff), Stax 212 | 1 |
| 96 | — | — | — | MAKE LOVE TO ME — Johnny Thunder & Ruby Winters (Budey Killen & Phila Kahl), Diamond 218 | 1 |
| 97 | — | — | — | SAM'S PLACE — Buck Owens (Ken Nelson), Capitol 5865 | 1 |
| 98 | — | — | — | THE OOGUM BOOGUM SONG — Brenton Wood (Hooven-Winn), Double Shot 111 | 1 |
| 99 | — | — | — | HAPPY JACK — Who, Decca 32114 | 1 |
| 100 | — | — | — | I'M INDESTRUCTIBLE — Jack Jones (Hy Grill), Kapp 818 | 1 |

## HOT 100—A TO Z—(Publisher-Licensee)


Ain't Gonna Rest (Till I Get You) (Camad, BMI) .. 89
Alfie (Famous, ASCAP) .......... 88
At The Zoo (Charing Cross, BMI) .......... 17
Baby, I Need Your Lovin' (Jobete, BMI) .......... 48
Beggin' (Saturday/Season's Four, BMI) .......... 16
Bernadette (Jobete, BMI) .......... 4
Buy for Me the Rain (Nina, BMI) .......... 67
California Nights (Genius/Enchanted, ASCAP) .... 27
Can't Get Enough of You, Baby (Saturday, BMI) .. 60
Casino Royale (Colgems, ASCAP) .......... 65
Close Your Eyes (Tideland, BMI) .......... 33
Cry To Me (Progressive, BMI) .......... 70
Danny Boy (Boosey & Hawkes, ASCAP) .......... 62
Dead End Street (Raw Lou/Beechwood, BMI) .... 55
Dedicated to the One I Love (Trousdale, BMI) .. 8
Detroit City (Cedarwood, BMI) .......... 28
Do the Thing (Bold, BMI) .......... 83
Don't You Care (Beechwood/Macbeth, BMI) .......... 23
Dry Your Eyes (Bee Cool, BMI) .......... 20
Everybody Loves A Winner (East, BMI) .......... 95
59th Street Bridge Song, The (Charing Cross, BMI) 14
For What It's Worth (Ten East/Springalo, BMI) .. 15
Friday on My Mind (Unart, BMI) .......... 46
Funky Broadway (Drive-In/Routeen, BMI) .......... 91
Get Me to the World on Time (Pomona, BMI) .. 45
Girl Don't Care (Jalynee/Cachand/BRC, BMI) .... 66
Girl I Need You (Jalynne/BRC, BMI) .......... 69
Girl I Knew Somewhere, The (Screen Gems-Columbia, BMI) .......... 39
Girl, You'll Be a Woman Soon (Tallyrand, BMI) .. 53
Gonna Give Her All the Love I've Got (Jobete, BMI) .......... 30
Happening, The (Jobete, BMI) .......... 19
Happy Jack (Essex, ASCAP) .......... 99
Happy Together (Chardon, BMI) .......... 2
Here Comes My Baby (Mainstay, BMI) .......... 72
Hip Hug-Her (East, BMI) .......... 63
I Found A Love (Progressive/Lupine-Alibre, BMI) 43
I Got Rhythm (New World, ASCAP) .......... 59
I Love You More Than Words Can Say (East-Time-Redwal, BMI) .......... 80
I Never Loved a Man the Way I Love You (14th Hour, BMI) .......... 9
I Think We're Alone Now (Patricia, BMI) .......... 7
I'll Try Anything (Pambar, BMI) .......... 50
I'm a Man (Essex, ASCAP) .......... 22
I'm Indestructible (Ensign, BMI) ..........100
It's So Hard Being A Loser (Jobete, BMI) .......... 85
I've Been Lonely Too Long (Slacsar, BMI) .......... 24
Jimmy Mack (Jobete, BMI) .......... 10
Lady Came From Baltimore, The (Faithful Virtue, BMI) .......... 78
Lawdy Miss Clawdy (Venice, BMI) .......... 41
Little Bit You, A Little Bit Me, A (Screen Gems-Columbia, BMI) .......... 5
Loser (With a Broken Heart), The (Skyhill, BMI) 56
Love Eyes (Criterion, ASCAP) .......... 29
Love I Saw in You Was Just a Mirage, The (Jobete, BMI) .......... 25
Make Love To Me (Melrose, ASCAP) .......... 96
Making Memories (Feist, ASCAP) .......... 75
Music To Watch Girls By (S.C.P., ASCAP) .......... 47
My Back Pages (Witmark, ASCAP) .......... 52
My Cup Runneth Over (Chappel, ASCAP) .......... 32
My Girl Josephine (Travis, BMI) .......... 87
No Milk Today (Man-Ken Ltd., BMI) .......... 42
Nothing Takes The Place of You (Su-Ma, BMI) .. 74
Oh That's Good, No That's Bad (Fred Rose, BMI) 54
On a Carousel (Maribus, BMI) .......... 36
One Hurt Deserves Another (Hastings, BMI) .......... 93
Oogum Boogum Song, The (Big Shot, ASCAP) .... 98
Out of Left Field (Press, BMI) .......... 73
Penny Lane (Maclen, BMI) .......... 12
Pipe Dream (Amanga-Bunga, BMI) .......... 64
Portrait of My Love (Piccadilly, BMI) .......... 86
Precious Memories (Naro, ASCAP) .......... 76
Release Me (And Let Me Love Again) (Four Star, BMI) .......... 71
Sam's Place (Blue Book, BMI) .......... 97
Shake A Tail Feather (Va-Pac, BMI) .......... 82
She Took You For A Ride (Olrap, BMI) .......... 92
Show Me (Tree, BMI) .......... 35
Sit Down, I Think I Love You (Screen Gems-Columbia, BMI) .......... 58
Sock It to Me—Baby! (Saturday, BMI) .......... 26
Somebody To Love (Copper Penny, BMI) .......... 68
Somethin' Stupid (Green Wood, BMI) .......... 1
Speak Her Name (Skidmore, ASCAP) .......... 90
Strawberry Fields Forever (Maclen, BMI) .......... 21
Summer Wine (Criterion, ASCAP) .......... 49
Sunday For Tea (Southern, ASCAP) .......... 34
Sunshine Girl (Inevitable/Good Sam, BMI) .......... 84
Sweet Soul Music (Bedwal, BMI) .......... 11
Tell Me to My Face (Maribus, BMI) .......... 37
There's a Chance We Can Make It (Ananga-Ranga, BMI) .......... 81
There's a Kind of a Hush (F., D. & M., ASCAP) .. 13
This Is My Song (Shawley, ASCAP) .......... 3
Time Alone Will Tell (Chappell, ASCAP) .......... 94
Travelin' Man (Stein, Van Stock, ASCAP) .......... 40
Walkin' In the Sunshine (Tree, BMI) .......... 51
Western Union (Jetstar, BMI) .......... 6
What a Woman In Love Won't Do (Windward Side, BMI) .......... 31
When I Was Young (Yamata, BMI) .......... 61
When Something Is Wrong With My Baby (East/Pronto, BMI) .......... 44
Whole World Is A Stage, The (Myto, BMI) .......... 77
Why? (Am I Treated So Bad) (Staple, BMI) .......... 79
With This Ring (Vee Vee, BMI) .......... 18
Yellow Balloon (Teeny Bopper, ASCAP) .......... 57
You Got What It Takes (Fidelity, BMI) .......... 38


## BUBBLING UNDER THE HOT 100

101. LONELY AGAIN ....Eddy Arnold, RCA Victor 9080
102. TEARS, TEARS, TEARS ....Ben E. King, Atco 6472
103. CAN'T SEEM TO MAKE YOU MINE ....Seeds, GNP Crescendo 354
104. BLUES THEME ....The Arrows, Tower 295
105. SHE'S LOOKING GOOD ....Roger Collins, Galaxy 750
106. MELANCHOLY MUSIC MAN ....Righteous Bros., Verve 10507
107. SING ALONG WITH ME ....Tommy Roe, ABC 10905
108. DON'T DO IT ....Mickey Dolenz, Challenge 59353
109. MERCY, MERCY, MERCY ....Marlena Shaw, Cadet 5557
110. SHAKE HANDS & WALK AWAY CRYIN' ....Lou Christie, Columbia 44062
111. BEAT GOES ON ....Lawrence Welk, Dot 17001
112. MERCY, MERCY, MERCY ....Larry Williams & Johnny Watson, Okeh 7274
113. THE JUNGLE ....B. B. King, Kent 462
114. EIGHT MEN—FOUR WOMEN ....O. V. Wright, Back Beat 580
115. MATTHEW & SON ....Cat Stevens, Deram 7905
116. JUST LOOK WHAT YOU'VE DONE ....Brenda Holloway, Tamla 54146
117. POSTCARD FROM JAMAICA ....Sopwith "Camel", Kama Sutra 224
118. LIVE ....Merry Go Round, A&M 834
119. I WANNA GO BACK THERE AGAIN ....Chris Clark, VIP 2504
120. EVERYBODY NEEDS HELP ....Jimmy Holiday, Minit 32016
121. MAKE A LITTLE LOVE ....Lowell Fulson, Kent 463
122. LATER FOR TOMORROW ....Ernie K. Doe, Duke 411
123. IN THE MIDNIGHT HOUR ....Wanted, A&M 844
124. GOODBYE TO ALL YOU WOMEN ....Bobby Goldsboro, United Artists 50135
125. NO TIME LIKE THE RIGHT TIME ....Blues Project, Verve Folkways 5040
126. TAKE ME ....Brenda Lee, Decca 32119
127. THINK ....Vicki Anderson & James Brown, King 12315
128. WHEN TOMORROW COMES ....Carla Thomas, Stax 214
129. IF YOU'RE THINKIN' WHAT I'M THINKIN' ..Dino, Desi & Billy, Reprise 0544
130. WHEN LOVE SLIPS AWAY ....Dee Dee Warwick, Mercury 72667
131. SHAKE ....British Walker, Cameo 466
132. MY OLD FLAME ....April Stevens & Nino Tempo, White Whale 246
133. DO IT AGAIN A LITTLE BIT SLOWER Jon & Robin & the In Crowd, Abnak 119
134. LITTLE GAMES ....Yardbirds, Epic 10156
135. MY BABE ....Ronnie Dove, Diamond 221

Compiled from national retail sales and radio station airplay by the Music Popularity Dept. of Record Market Research, Billboard.

# Billboard HOT 100

For Week Ending April 22, 1967

★ STAR performer—Sides registering greatest proportionate upward progress this week.

Record Industry Association of America seal of certification as million selling single.

| This Week | Last Week | 2 Wks. Ago | 3 Wks. Ago | TITLE Artist (Producer), Label & Number | Weeks On Chart |
|---|---|---|---|---|---|
| 1 | 1 | 3 | 9 | SOMETHIN' STUPID — Nancy Sinatra & Frank Sinatra (Jimmy Bowen & Lee Hazlewood), Reprise 0561 | 6 |
| 2 | 2 | 1 | 1 | HAPPY TOGETHER — Turtles (Joe Wissert), White Whale 244 | 11 |
| 3 | 5 | 9 | 19 | A LITTLE BIT YOU, A LITTLE BIT ME — Monkees (Jeff Barry), Colgems 1004 | 5 |
| 4 | 7 | 8 | 12 | I THINK WE'RE ALONE NOW — Tommy James and the Shondells (Cordell-Gentry), Roulette 4720 | 11 |
| 5 | 6 | 7 | 10 | WESTERN UNION — Five Americans (Dale Hawkins), Abnak 118 | 8 |
| 6 | 3 | 5 | 6 | THIS IS MY SONG — Petula Clark (Sonny Burke), Warner Bros. 7002 | 8 |
| 7 | 11 | 18 | 30 | SWEET SOUL MUSIC — Arthur Conley (Otis Redding), Atco 6463 | 7 |
| 8 | 4 | 4 | 5 | BERNADETTE — Four Tops (Holland and Dozier), Motown 1104 | 7 |
| 9 | 9 | 12 | 14 | I NEVER LOVED A MAN THE WAY I LOVE YOU — Aretha Franklin (Jerry Wexler), Atlantic 2386 | 8 |
| 10 | 10 | 11 | 18 | JIMMY MACK — Martha and the Vandellas (Holland-Dozier), Gordy 7058 | 9 |
| 11 | 19 | 57 | — | THE HAPPENING — Supremes (Holland & Dozier), Motown 1107 | 3 |
| 12 | 8 | 2 | 2 | DEDICATED TO THE ONE I LOVE — Mama's and the Papa's (Lou Adler), Dunhill 4077 | 9 |
| 13 | 22 | 33 | 49 | I'M A MAN — Spencer Davis Group (Jimmy Miller), United Artists 50144 | 5 |
| 14 | 18 | 26 | 28 | WITH THIS RING — Platters (Luther Dixon), Musicor 1229 | 9 |
| 15 | 29 | 38 | 61 | LOVE EYES — Nancy Sinatra (Lee Hazlewood), Reprise 0559 | 5 |
| 16 | 17 | 27 | 34 | AT THE ZOO — Simon & Garfunkel (Bob Johnston), Columbia 44046 | 6 |
| 17 | 23 | 28 | 48 | DON'T YOU CARE — Buckinghams (Jim Guercio), Columbia 44053 | 7 |
| 18 | 38 | 48 | 83 | YOU GOT WHAT IT TAKES — Dave Clark Five (Dave Clark), Epic 10144 | 4 |
| 19 | 15 | 14 | 7 | FOR WHAT IT'S WORTH — Buffalo Springfield (Greene & Stone), Atco 6459 | 13 |
| 20 | 20 | 21 | 26 | DRY YOUR EYES — Brenda and the Tabulations (Bob Finiz), Dionn 500 | 9 |
| 21 | 12 | 6 | 3 | PENNY LANE — Beatles (George Martin), Capitol 5810 | 9 |
| 22 | 13 | 10 | 4 | THERE'S A KIND OF A HUSH — Herman's Hermits (Mickie Most), MGM 13681 | 11 |
| 23 | 14 | 13 | 13 | THE 59TH STREET BRIDGE SONG — Harpers Bizarre (Lenny Waronker), Warner Bros. 5890 | 10 |
| 24 | 36 | 50 | 55 | ON A CAROUSEL — Hollies (Ron Richards), Imperial 66231 | 6 |
| 25 | 16 | 16 | 25 | BEGGIN' — 4 Seasons (Bob Crewe), Philips 40433 | 8 |
| 26 | 33 | 51 | 64 | CLOSE YOUR EYES — Peaches & Herb (Dave Kapralik-Ken Williams), Date 1549 | 5 |
| 27 | 28 | 30 | 38 | DETROIT CITY — Tom Jones (Peter Sullivan), Parrot 40012 | 7 |
| 28 | 21 | 15 | 8 | STRAWBERRY FIELDS FOREVER — Beatles (George Martin), Capitol 5810 | 9 |
| 29 | 30 | 39 | 52 | GONNA GIVE HER ALL THE LOVE I'VE GOT — Jimmy Ruffin (N. Whitfield), Soul 350222 | 6 |
| 30 | 46 | 56 | 72 | FRIDAY ON MY MIND — Easybeats, The (Shell Talmy) United Artists 50136 | 4 |
| 31 | 34 | 45 | 56 | SUNDAY FOR TEA — Peter & Gordon (John Burgess), Capitol 5864 | 5 |
| 32 | 43 | 59 | 82 | I FOUND A LOVE — Wilson Pickett (Jerry Wexler), Atlantic 2354 | 4 |
| 33 | 27 | 25 | 22 | CALIFORNIA NIGHTS — Lesley Gore (Bob Crewe), Mercury 72649 | 12 |
| 34 | 45 | 55 | 65 | GET ME TO THE WORLD ON TIME — Electric Prunes (Dave Hassinger), Reprise 0564 | 4 |
| 35 | 47 | 52 | 62 | MUSIC TO WATCH GIRLS BY — Andy Williams (Nick De Caro), Columbia 44065 | 5 |
| 36 | 25 | 20 | 24 | THE LOVE I SAW IN YOU WAS JUST A MIRAGE — Smokey Robinson and the Miracles (Wm. Robinson–W. Moore), Tamla 54145 | 10 |
| 37 | 35 | 36 | 43 | SHOW ME — Joe Tex (Buddy Killen), Dial 4055 | 8 |
| 38 | 61 | 77 | — | WHEN I WAS YOUNG — Eric Burdon & the Animals (Tom Wilson), MGM 13721 | 3 |
| 39 | 24 | 22 | 16 | I'VE BEEN LONELY TOO LONG — Young Rascals (Young Rascals), Atlantic 2377 | 7 |
| 40 | 50 | 53 | 63 | I'LL TRY ANYTHING — Dusty Springfield (Herb Bernstein), Philips 40439 | 5 |
| 41 | 51 | 61 | 76 | WALKIN' IN THE SUNSHINE — Roger Miller (Jerry Kennedy), Smash 2081 | 4 |
| 42 | 52 | 62 | 86 | MY BACK PAGES — Byrds (Gary Usher), Columbia 44054 | 4 |
| 43 | 53 | 68 | — | GIRL, YOU'LL BE A WOMAN SOON — Neil Diamond (Jeff Barry & Ellie Greenwich), Bang 542 | 3 |
| 44 | 31 | 31 | 41 | WHAT A WOMAN IN LOVE WON'T DO — Sandy Posey (Chips Moman), MGM 13702 | 7 |
| 45 | 42 | 35 | 36 | NO MILK TODAY — Herman's Hermits (Mickie Most), MGM 13681 | 10 |
| 46 | 59 | 73 | — | I GOT RHYTHM — Happenings (The Tokens) B. T. Puppy 527 | 3 |
| 47 | 57 | 71 | 89 | YELLOW BALLOON — Yellow Balloon (Ken Handler & Yoder Critch), Canterbury 508 | 4 |
| 48 | 39 | 46 | 51 | THE GIRL I KNEW SOMEWHERE — Monkees (Douglas Farthing Hatelid), Colgems 1004 | 5 |
| 49 | 37 | 40 | 44 | TELL ME TO MY FACE — Keith (Jerry Ross), Mercury 72652 | 6 |
| 50 | 65 | 80 | — | CASINO ROYALE — Herb Alpert & the Tijuana Brass (Herb Alpert & Jerry Moss), A&M 850 | 3 |
| 51 | 49 | 49 | 54 | SUMMER WINE — Nancy Sinatra and Lee Hazlewood (Lee Hazlewood), Reprise 0527 | 8 |
| 52 | 55 | 65 | 81 | DEAD END STREET — Lou Rawls (David Axelrod), Capitol 5869 | 5 |
| 53 | 72 | 84 | — | HERE COMES MY BABY — Tremeloes (Peter Walsh), Epic 10139 | 3 |
| 54 | 71 | 99 | — | RELEASE ME (And Let Me Love Again) — Engelbert Humperdinck (Peter Sullivan), Parrot 40011 | 3 |
| 55 | 63 | 74 | 87 | HIP HUG-HER — Booker T. & the M. G.'s (Prod. by Staff), Stax 211 | 5 |
| 56 | 60 | 60 | 68 | CAN'T GET ENOUGH OF YOU, BABY — ? (Question Mark) & the Mysterians (Neil Bogart, Pa-Go-Go Prod.), Cameo 467 | 5 |
| 57 | 67 | 82 | — | BUY FOR ME THE RAIN — Nitty Gritty Dirt Band (Dallas Smith), Liberty 55948 | 3 |
| 58 | 68 | 76 | 88 | SOMEBODY TO LOVE — Jefferson Airplane (Rick Jarrard), RCA Victor 9140 | 4 |
| 59 | 75 | 93 | — | MAKING MEMORIES — Frankie Laine (Bob Thiele), ABC 10924 | 3 |
| 60 | 64 | 69 | 78 | PIPE DREAM — Blues Magoos (Bob Wyld & Art Polhemus), Mercury 72660 | 6 |
| 61 | 62 | 64 | 80 | DANNY BOY — Ray Price (Don Law & Frank Jones), Columbia 44042 | 5 |
| 62 | 54 | 54 | 57 | OH THAT'S GOOD, NO THAT'S BAD — Sam the Sham & the Pharaohs (Stan Kesler), MGM 13713 | 6 |
| 63 | 78 | 86 | — | THE LADY CAME FROM BALTIMORE — Bobby Darin (Charles Koppelman & Don Rubin), Atlantic 2395 | 3 |
| 64 | 74 | 85 | 85 | NOTHING TAKES THE PLACE OF YOU — Toussaint McCall (Jewel Productions), Ronn 3 | 4 |
| 65 | 82 | — | — | SHAKE A TAIL FEATHER — James & Bobby Purify (Papa Don, Cogbill, Young, Emmons & Chrisman), Bell 669 | 2 |
| 66 | 66 | 67 | 67 | GIRL DON'T CARE — Gene Chandler (Carl Davis), Brunswick 55312 | 9 |
| 67 | 73 | 79 | — | OUT OF LEFT FIELD — Percy Sledge (Quin Ivy & Marlin Greene), Atlantic 2396 | 3 |
| 68 | 76 | 89 | 99 | PRECIOUS MEMORIES — Romeos, Mark II J-1 | 4 |
| 69 | 84 | — | — | SUNSHINE GIRL — Parade (Jerry Riopelle), A&M 841 | 2 |
| 70 | 70 | 72 | 74 | CRY TO ME — Freddie Scott (Bert Bruns), Shout 211 | 5 |
| 71 | 86 | — | — | PORTRAIT OF MY LOVE — Tokens (Bright Tunes Prod.), Warner Bros. 5900 | 2 |
| 72 | 69 | 70 | 73 | GIRL I NEED YOU — Artistics (Carl Davis), Brunswick 55315 | 6 |
| 73 | 79 | 90 | — | WHY? (Am I Treated So Bad) — Cannonball Adderley (David Axelrod), Capitol 5877 | 3 |
| 74 | 77 | 78 | 84 | THE WHOLE WORLD IS A STAGE — Fantastic Four (Al Kent & E. Wingate), Ric Tic 122 | 4 |
| 75 | 87 | — | — | MY GIRL JOSEPHINE — Jerry Jaye, Hi 2120 | 2 |
| 76 | — | — | — | MELANCHOLY MUSIC MAN — Righteous Bros. (Koppelman-Rubin), Verve 10507 | 1 |
| 77 | 88 | 95 | — | ALFIE — Dionne Warwick (Bacharach-David), Scepter 12187 | 3 |
| 78 | 80 | 81 | — | I LOVE YOU MORE THAN WORDS CAN SAY — Otis Redding (Prod. by Staff), Volt 146 | 3 |
| 79 | — | — | — | GROOVIN' — Young Rascals (Young Rascals), Atlantic 2401 | 1 |
| 80 | 83 | 87 | — | DO THE THING — Lou Courtney (Robert Bateman), Riverside 7589 | 3 |
| 81 | — | — | — | LITTLE GAMES — Yardbirds (Mickie Most), Epic 10156 | 1 |
| 82 | — | — | — | I'LL MAKE HIM LOVE ME — Barbara Lewis (Bob Gallo & Ollie McLaughlin), Atlantic 2400 | 1 |
| 83 | 99 | — | — | HAPPY JACK — Who, Decca 32114 | 2 |
| 84 | 85 | — | — | IT'S SO HARD BEING A LOSER — Contours (W. Weatherspoon & J. Dean), Gordy 7059 | 2 |
| 85 | — | — | — | JUST LOOK WHAT YOU'VE DONE — Brenda Holloway (Frank Wilson), Tamla 54148 | 1 |
| 86 | — | — | — | WHEN YOU'RE YOUNG AND IN LOVE — Marvelettes (J. Dean & William Weatherspoon), Tamla 54150 | 1 |
| 87 | 89 | — | — | AIN'T GONNA REST (Till I Get You) — Five Stairsteps (Curtis Mayfield), Windy C 605 | 2 |
| 88 | — | — | — | YOU'RE ALL I NEED — Bobby Bland, Duke 416 | 1 |
| 89 | 90 | — | — | SPEAK HER NAME — Walter Jackson (Ted Cooper), Okeh 7272 | 2 |
| 90 | — | — | — | MY BABE — Ronnie Dove (Neil Diamond), Diamond 221 | 1 |
| 91 | — | — | — | FUNKY BROADWAY — Dyke & the Blazers (Coleman & Barrett), Original Sound 64 | 1 |
| 92 | 97 | — | — | SAM'S PLACE — Buck Owens (Ken Nelson), Capitol 5865 | 2 |
| 93 | 93 | — | — | ONE HURT DESERVES ANOTHER — Raelets (Ray Charles), Tangerine 296 | 2 |
| 94 | 98 | — | — | THE OOGUM BOOGUM SONG — Brenton Wood (Hooven-Winn), Double Shot 111 | 2 |
| 95 | 95 | — | — | EVERYBODY LOVES A WINNER — William Bell (Prod. by Staff), Stax 212 | 2 |
| 96 | 100 | — | — | I'M INDESTRUCTIBLE — Jack Jones (Hy Grill), Kapp 818 | 2 |
| 97 | — | — | — | BLUES THEME — Arrows (Mike Curb), Tower 295 | 1 |
| 98 | — | — | — | I COULD BE SO GOOD TO YOU — Don & the Goodtimes (Jack Nitzche), Epic 10145 | 1 |
| 99 | — | — | — | TEARS, TEARS, TEARS — Ben E. King (Bob Gallo), Atco 6472 | 1 |
| 100 | — | — | — | HEY LOVE — Stevie Wonder (Clarence Paul), Tamla 54147 | 1 |

## BUBBLING UNDER THE HOT 100

101. CAN'T SEEM TO MAKE YOU MINE ... Seeds, GNP Crescendo 354
102. I WAS KAISER BILL'S BATMAN ... Whistling Jack Smith, Deram 850
103. SHE'S LOOKING GOOD ... Roger Collins, Galaxy 750
104. LIVE ... Merry Go Round, A&M 834
105. SHAKE HANDS AND WALK AWAY CRYING ... Lou Christie, Columbia 44063
106. EIGHT MEN—FOUR WOMEN ... O. V. Wright, Back Beat 580
107. GOODBYE TO ALL YOU WOMEN ... Bobby Goldsboro, United Artist 50153
108. MY OLD FLAME ... Nino Tempo & April Stevens, White Whale 246
109. NO TIME LIKE THE RIGHT TIME ... Blues Project, Verve Folkways 5040
110. BEAT GOES ON ... Lawrence Welk, Dot 17001
111. IT'S ALL OVER ... Casinos, Fraternity 985
112. DO IT AGAIN A LITTLE BIT SLOWER ... Jon & Robin & the In Crowd, Abnak 119
113. MAKE LOVE TO ME ... Johnny Thunder & Ruby Winters, Diamond 218
114. I WANT TO GO BACK THERE AGAIN ... Chris Clark, VIP 2504
115. TIME ALONE WILL TELL ... Connie Francis, MGM 13718
116. TOGETHER ... Intruders, Gamble 214
117. WHEN TOMORROW COMES ... Carla Thomas, Stax 214
118. TAKE ME IN YOUR ARMS AND LOVE ME ... Gladys Knight & the Pips, Soul 35035
119. HIM OR ME—WHAT'S IT GONNA BE? ... Paul Revere & Raiders, Columbia 44094
120. LOVE SOME HAPPINESS ON ME ... Dean Martin, Reprise 0571
121. WHEN LOVE SLIPS AWAY ... Dee Dee Warwick, Mercury 7266
122. LATER FOR TOMORROW ... Ernie K Doe, Duke 411
123. POSTCARD FROM JAMAICA ... Sopwith "Camel," Kama Sutra 224
124. EDELWEISS ... Vince Hill, Warner Bros. 70
125. SINCE I DON'T HAVE YOU ... Lonnie Brooks, Warner Bros. 7
126. YOU'RE GONNA BE MINE ... New Colony Six, Sentar 1206
127. I GOT WHAT YOU NEED ... Kim Weston, MGM 13720
128. IT'S YOU THINKIN' WHAT I'M THINKIN' ... Dino, Desi & Billy, Reprise 0544
129. SHAKE ... British Walkers, Canco 466
130. HERE COME THE TEARS ... Darrell Banks, Atco 6471
131. MIDNIGHT HOUR ... Michael & the Messengers, USA 866
132. FLOWER CHILDREN ... Marcia Strassman, UNI 55006
133. SHE'S GOT THE TIME (SHE'S GOT THE CHANGES) ... Poor, York 402
134. BORN TO BE BY YOUR SIDE ... Brenda Lee, Decca 32119
135. TIME ALONE WILL TELL ... Jerry Vale, Columbia 44087

Compiled from national retail sales and radio station airplay by the Music Popularity Dept. of Record Market Research, Billboard.

For Week Ending April 29, 1967

# Billboard HOT 100

★ **STAR performer—Sides registering greatest proportionate upward progress this week.**

(seal) Record Industry Association of America seal of certification as million selling single.

| This Week | 1 Wk. Ago | 2 Wks. Ago | 3 Wks. Ago | TITLE Artist (Producer), Label & Number | Weeks On Chart |
|---|---|---|---|---|---|
| 1 (Billboard Award) | 1 | 1 | 3 | SOMETHIN' STUPID — Nancy Sinatra & Frank Sinatra (Jimmy Bowen & Lee Hazlewood), Reprise 0561 (RIAA seal) | 7 |
| 2 | 3 | 5 | 9 | A LITTLE BIT YOU, A LITTLE BIT ME — Monkees (Jeff Barry), Colgems 1004 (RIAA seal) | 6 |
| 3 | 2 | 2 | 1 | HAPPY TOGETHER — Turtles (Joe Wissert), White Whale 244 | 12 |
| ★4 | 7 | 11 | 18 | SWEET SOUL MUSIC — Arthur Conley (Otis Redding), Atco 6463 | 8 |
| 5 | 4 | 7 | 8 | I THINK WE'RE ALONE NOW — Tommy James and the Shondells (Cordell-Gentry), Roulette 4720 | 12 |
| 6 | 5 | 6 | 7 | WESTERN UNION — Five Americans (Dale Hawkins), Abnak 118 | 9 |
| 7 | 6 | 3 | 5 | THIS IS MY SONG — Petula Clark (Sonny Burke), Warner Bros. 7002 | 9 |
| ★8 | 11 | 19 | 57 | THE HAPPENING — Supremes (Holland & Dozier), Motown 1107 | 4 |
| 9 | 8 | 4 | 4 | BERNADETTE — Four Tops (Holland and Dozier), Motown 1104 | 8 |
| 10 | 10 | 10 | 11 | JIMMY MACK — Martha and the Vandellas (Holland-Dozier), Gordy 7058 | 10 |
| ★11 | 17 | 23 | 28 | DON'T YOU CARE — Buckinghams (Jim Guercio), Columbia 44053 | 8 |
| ★12 | 18 | 38 | 48 | YOU GOT WHAT IT TAKES — Dave Clark Five (Dave Clark), Epic 10144 | 5 |
| 13 | 13 | 22 | 33 | I'M A MAN — Spencer Davis Group (Jimmy Miller), United Artists 50144 | 6 |
| 14 | 9 | 9 | 12 | I NEVER LOVED A MAN THE WAY I LOVE YOU — Aretha Franklin (Jerry Wexler), Atlantic 2386 | 9 |
| 15 | 15 | 29 | 38 | LOVE EYES — Nancy Sinatra (Lee Hazlewood), Reprise 0559 | 6 |
| 16 | 16 | 17 | 27 | AT THE ZOO — Simon & Garfunkel (Bob Johnston), Columbia 44046 | 7 |
| ★17 | 24 | 36 | 50 | ON A CAROUSEL — Hollies (Ron Richards), Imperial 66231 | 7 |
| ★18 | 26 | 33 | 51 | CLOSE YOUR EYES — Peaches & Herb (Dave Kapralik-Ken Williams), Date 1549 | 6 |
| 19 | 14 | 18 | 26 | WITH THIS RING — Platters (Luther Dixon), Musicor 1229 | 10 |
| 20 | 12 | 8 | 2 | DEDICATED TO THE ONE I LOVE — Mama's and the Papa's (Lou Adler), Dunhill 4077 | 10 |
| ★21 | 38 | 61 | 77 | WHEN I WAS YOUNG — Eric Burdon & the Animals (Tom Wilson), MGM 13721 | 4 |
| 22 | 20 | 20 | 21 | DRY YOUR EYES — Brenda and the Tabulations (Bob Finlz), Dionn 500 | 10 |
| ★23 | 30 | 46 | 56 | FRIDAY ON MY MIND — Easybeats, The (Shell Talmy) United Artists 50106 | 7 |
| 24 | 23 | 14 | 13 | THE 59TH STREET BRIDGE SONG — Harpers Bizarre (Lenny Waronker), Warner Bros. 5890 | 11 |
| 25 | 21 | 12 | 6 | PENNY LANE — Beatles (George Martin), Capitol 5810 (RIAA seal) | 10 |
| 26 | 22 | 13 | 10 | THERE'S A KIND OF A HUSH — Herman's Hermits (Mickie Most), MGM 13681 | 12 |
| 27 | 19 | 15 | 14 | FOR WHAT IT'S WORTH — Buffalo Springfield (Greene & Stone), Atco 6459 | 14 |
| ★28 | 34 | 45 | 55 | GET ME TO THE WORLD ON TIME — Electric Prunes (Dave Hassinger), Reprise 0564 | 5 |
| ★29 | 46 | 59 | 73 | I GOT RHYTHM — Happenings (The Tokens) B. T. Puppy 527 | 4 |
| 30 | 25 | 16 | 16 | BEGGIN' — 4 Seasons (Bob Crewe), Philips 40433 | 9 |
| ★31 | 42 | 52 | 62 | MY BACK PAGES — Byrds (Gary Usher), Columbia 44054 | 5 |
| 32 | 32 | 43 | 59 | I FOUND A LOVE — Wilson Pickett (Jerry Wexler), Atlantic 2394 | 5 |
| ★33 | 43 | 53 | 68 | GIRL, YOU'LL BE A WOMAN SOON — Neil Diamond (Jeff Barry & Ellie Greenwich), Bang 542 | 4 |
| 34 | 35 | 47 | 52 | MUSIC TO WATCH GIRLS BY — Andy Williams (Nick De Caro), Columbia 44065 | 6 |
| 35 | 33 | 27 | 25 | CALIFORNIA NIGHTS — Lesley Gore (Bob Crewe), Mercury 72649 | 13 |
| ★36 | 54 | 71 | 99 | RELEASE ME (And Let Me Love Again) — Engelbert Humperdinck, Parrot 40011 | 4 |
| ★37 | 47 | 57 | 71 | YELLOW BALLOON — Yellow Balloon (Ken Handler & Yoder Critch), Canterbury 508 | 5 |
| 38 | 31 | 34 | 45 | SUNDAY FOR TEA — Peter & Gordon (John Burgess), Capitol 5864 | 6 |
| ★39 | 50 | 65 | 80 | CASINO ROYALE — Herb Alpert & the Tijuana Brass (Herb Alpert & Jerry Moss), A&M 850 | 4 |
| 40 | 40 | 50 | 53 | I'LL TRY ANYTHING — Dusty Springfield (Herb Bernstein), Philips 40439 | 7 |
| 41 | 41 | 51 | 61 | WALKIN' IN THE SUNSHINE — Roger Miller (Jerry Kennedy), Smash 2081 | 6 |
| ★42 | 52 | 55 | 65 | DEAD END STREET — Lou Rawls (David Axlerod), Capitol 5869 | 6 |
| ★43 | 53 | 72 | 84 | HERE COMES MY BABY — Tremeloes, Epic 10139 | 4 |
| ★44 | 58 | 68 | 76 | SOMEBODY TO LOVE — Jefferson Airplane (Rick Jarrard), RCA Victor 9140 | 5 |
| 45 | 39 | 24 | 22 | I'VE BEEN LONELY TOO LONG — Young Rascals (Young Rascals), Atlantic 2377 | 14 |
| 46 | 29 | 30 | 39 | GONNA GIVE HER ALL THE LOVE I'VE GOT — Jimmy Ruffin (N. Whitfield), Soul 350322 | 7 |
| 47 | 27 | 28 | 30 | DETROIT CITY — Tom Jones (Peter Sullivan), Parrot 40012 | 8 |
| ★48 | 59 | 75 | 93 | MAKING MEMORIES — Frankie Laine (Bob Thiele), ABC 10924 | 4 |
| ★49 | 79 | — | — | GROOVIN' — Young Rascals (Young Rascals), Atlantic 2401 | 2 |
| ★50 | — | — | — | RESPECT — Aretha Franklin (Jerry Wexler), Atlantic 2403 | 1 |
| ★51 | 65 | 82 | — | SHAKE A TAIL FEATHER — James & Bobby Purify (Papa Don, Cogbill, Young, Emmons & Chrisman), Bell 669 | 3 |
| 52 | 55 | 63 | 74 | HIP HUG-HER — Booker T. & the M. G.'s (Prod. By Staff), Stax 211 | 6 |
| ★53 | 71 | 86 | — | PORTRAIT OF MY LOVE — Tokens (Bright Tunes Prod.), Warner Bros. 5900 | 3 |
| 54 | 51 | 49 | 49 | SUMMER WINE — Nancy Sinatra and Lee Hazlewood (Lee Hazlewood), Reprise 0527 | 9 |
| 55 | 57 | 67 | 82 | BUY FOR ME THE RAIN — Nitty Gritty Dirt Band (Dallas Smith), Liberty 55948 | 4 |
| ★56 | 69 | 84 | — | SUNSHINE GIRL — Parade (Jerry Riopelle), A&M 841 | 3 |
| ★57 | 76 | — | — | MELANCHOLY MUSIC MAN — Righteous Bros. (Koppelman-Rubin), Verve 10507 | 2 |
| 58 | 56 | 60 | 60 | CAN'T GET ENOUGH OF YOU, BABY — ? (Question Mark) & the Mysterians (Neil Bogart, Pa-Go-Go Prod.), Cameo 467 | 6 |
| 59 | 64 | 74 | 85 | NOTHING TAKES THE PLACE OF YOU — Toussaint McCall (Jewel Productions), Ronn 3 | 6 |
| ★60 | 75 | 87 | — | MY GIRL JOSEPHINE — Jerry Jaye, Hi 2120 | 3 |
| 61 | 61 | 62 | 64 | DANNY BOY — Ray Price (Don Law & Frank Jones), Columbia 44042 | 6 |
| 62 | 63 | 78 | 86 | THE LADY CAME FROM BALTIMORE — Bobby Darin (Charles Koppelman & Don Rubin), Atlantic 2395 | 4 |
| 63 | 67 | 73 | 79 | OUT OF LEFT FIELD — Percy Sledge (Quin Ivy & Marlin Greene), Atlantic 2396 | 4 |
| ★64 | — | — | — | I WAS KAISER BILL'S BATMAN — Whistling Jack Smith, Deram 85003 | 1 |
| ★65 | — | — | — | HIM OR ME—WHAT'S IT GONNA BE? — Paul Revere & the Raiders (Terry Melcher), Columbia 44094 | 1 |
| ★66 | 81 | — | — | LITTLE GAMES — Yardbirds (Mickie Most), Epic 10156 | 2 |
| 67 | 68 | 76 | 89 | PRECIOUS MEMORIES — Romeos, Mark II J-1 | 5 |
| ★68 | 83 | 99 | — | HAPPY JACK — Who, Decca 32114 | 3 |
| ★69 | — | — | — | MIRAGE — Tommy James & the Shondells (Bo Gentry & Ritchie Cordell), Roulette 4736 | 1 |
| 70 | 77 | 88 | 95 | ALFIE — Dionne Warwick (Bacharach-David), Scepter 12187 | 4 |
| ★71 | 86 | — | — | WHEN YOU'RE YOUNG AND IN LOVE — Marvelettes (J. Dean & William Weatherspoon), Tamla 54150 | 2 |
| 72 | 74 | 77 | 78 | THE WHOLE WORLD IS A STAGE — Fantastic Four (Al Kent & E. Wingate), Ric Tic 122 | 6 |
| 73 | 73 | 79 | 90 | WHY? (Am I Treated So Bad) — Cannonball Adderley (David Axelrod), Capitol 5877 | 4 |
| ★74 | 90 | — | — | MY BABE — Ronnie Dove (Neil Diamond), Diamond 221 | 2 |
| 75 | 85 | — | — | JUST LOOK WHAT YOU'VE DONE — Brenda Holloway (Frank Wilson), Tamla 54148 | 2 |
| ★76 | — | — | — | TOO MANY FISH IN THE SEA & THREE LITTLE FISHES — Mitch Ryder & the Detroit Wheels (Bob Crewe), New Voice 822 | 1 |
| ★77 | 94 | 98 | — | THE OOGUM BOOGUM SONG — Brenton Wood (Hooven-Winn), Double Shot 111 | 3 |
| ★78 | 93 | 93 | — | ONE HURT DESERVES ANOTHER — Raelets (Ray Charles), Tangerine 296 | 3 |
| 79 | 84 | 85 | — | IT'S SO HARD BEING A LOSER — Contours (W. Weatherspoon & J. Dean), Gordy 7059 | 3 |
| ★80 | — | — | — | LAY SOME HAPPINESS ON ME — Dean Martin (Jimmy Bowen), Reprise 0571 | 1 |
| ★81 | — | — | — | ALL I NEED IS YOU — Temptations (F. Wilson), Gordy 7061 | 1 |
| 82 | 82 | — | — | I'LL MAKE HIM LOVE ME — Barbara Lewis (Bob Gallo & Ollie McLaughlin), Atlantic 2400 | 2 |
| ★83 | — | — | — | CREEQUE ALLEY — Mamas & the Papas (Lou Adler), Dunhill 4083 | 1 |
| ★84 | — | — | — | IT'S ALL OVER — Casinos (Gene Hughes), Fraternity 985 | 1 |
| ★85 | — | — | — | CAN'T SEEM TO MAKE YOU MINE — Seeds (Marcus Tybalt), GNP Crescendo 354 | 1 |
| ★86 | — | — | — | A BEAUTIFUL STORY — Sonny & Cher (Bill Rinehart), Atco 6480 | 1 |
| ★87 | — | — | — | ANOTHER DAY, ANOTHER HEARTACHE — 5th Dimension (Johnny Rivers & Marc Gordon), Soul City 755 | 1 |
| 88 | — | — | — | YOU'RE ALL I NEED — Bobby Bland, Duke 416 | 1 |
| 89 | 91 | 91 | — | FUNKY BROADWAY — Dyke & the Blazers (Coleman & Barrett), Original Sound 64 | 3 |
| ★90 | — | — | — | SIX O'CLOCK — Lovin' Spoonful (Erik Jacobsen), Kama Sutra 225 | 1 |
| 91 | 98 | — | — | I COULD BE SO GOOD TO YOU — Don & the Goodtimes (Jack Nitzche), Epic 10145 | 2 |
| 92 | 96 | 100 | — | I'M INDESTRUCTIBLE — Jack Jones (Hy Grill), Kapp 818 | 3 |
| 93 | 99 | — | — | TEARS, TEARS, TEARS — Ben E. King (Bob Gallo), Atco 6472 | 2 |
| 94 | — | — | — | LIVE — Merry-Go-Round (Larry Marks), A&M 834 | 1 |
| 95 | 97 | — | — | BLUES THEME — Arrows (Mike Curb), Tower 295 | 2 |
| 96 | — | — | — | SHAKE HANDS AND WALK AWAY CRYING — Lou Christie (Charles Calello), Columbia 44062 | 1 |
| 97 | 100 | — | — | HEY LOVE — Stevie Wonder (Clarence Paul), Tamla 54147 | 2 |
| 98 | — | — | — | GEORGY GIRL — Baja Marimba Band (Herb Alpert & Jerry Moss), A&M 843 | 1 |
| 99 | — | — | — | I GOT WHAT YOU NEED — Kim Weston (Mickey Stevenson), MGM 13720 | 1 |
| 100 | — | — | — | TOGETHER — Intruders, Gamble 205 | 1 |

## HOT 100—A TO Z—(Publisher-Licensee)

Alfie (Famous, ASCAP) .... 70
All I Need Is You (Jobete, BMI) .... 81
Another Day, Another Heartache (Trousdale, BMI) .... 87
At the Zoo (Charing Cross, BMI) .... 16
Beautiful Story, A (Chris Marc-Cotillion, BMI) .... 86
Beggin' (Saturday/Season's Four, BMI) .... 30
Bernadette (Jobete, BMI) .... 9
Blues Theme (Dijon, BMI) .... 95
Buy for Me the Rain (Nina, BMI) .... 55
California Nights (Genius/Enchanted, ASCAP) .... 35
Can't Get Enough of You, Baby (Saturday, BMI) .... 58
Can't Seem to Make You Mine (Neil-Purple Bottle, BMI) .... 85
Casino Royale (Colgems, ASCAP) .... 39
Close Your Eyes (Tideland, BMI) .... 18
Creeque Alley (Trousdale, BMI) .... 83
Danny Boy (Boosey & Hawkes, ASCAP) .... 61
Dead-End Street (Raw Lou/Beechwood, BMI) .... 42
Dedicated to the One I Love (Trousdale, BMI) .... 20
Detroit City (Cedarwood, BMI) .... 47
Don't You Care (Beechwood, BMI) .... 11
Dry Your Eyes (Bee Cool, BMI) .... 22
59th Street Bridge Song, The (Charing Cross, BMI) 24
For What It's Worth (Ten East/Springalo, BMI) .... 27
Friday on My Mind (Unart, BMI) .... 23
Funky Broadway (Drive-In/Routeen, BMI) .... 89
Georgy Girl (Chappell, ASCAP) .... 98
Get Me to the World on Time (Pomona, BMI) .... 28
Girl, You'll Be a Woman Soon (Tallyrand, BMI) .... 33
Gonna Give Her All the Love I've Got (Jobete, BMI) 46
Groovin' (Slacsar, BMI) .... 49
Happening, The (Jobete, BMI) .... 8
Happy Jack (Essex, ASCAP) .... 68
Happy Together (Chardon, BMI) .... 3
Here Comes My Baby (Mainstay, BMI) .... 43
Hey, Love (Jobete, BMI) .... 97
Him or Me—What's It Gonna Be? (Daywin, BMI) .... 65
Hip Hug-Her (East, BMI) .... 52
I Could Be So Good to You (Stoutworthy & Sona, BMI) .... 91
I Found a Love (Progressive/Lupine-Alibre, BMI) .... 32
I Got Rhythm (New World, ASCAP) .... 29
I Got What You Need (Mikim, BMI) .... 99
I Never Loved a Man the Way I Love You (14th Hour, BMI) .... 14
I Think We're Alone Now (Patricia, BMI) .... 5
I Was Kaiser Bill's Batman (Mills, ASCAP) .... 64
I'll Make Him Love Me (Screen Gems-Columbia, BMI) .... 82
I'll Try Anything (Pambar, BMI) .... 40
I'm a Man (Essex, ASCAP) .... 13
I'm Indestructable (Ensign, BMI) .... 92
It's All Over (Acuff-Rose, BMI) .... 84
It's So Hard Being a Loser (Jobete, BMI) .... 79
I've Been Lonely too Long (Slacsar, BMI) .... 45
Jimmy Mack (Jobete, BMI) .... 10
Just Look What You've Done (Jobete, BMI) .... 75
Lady Came From Baltimore, The (Faithful Virtue, BMI) .... 62
Lay Some Happiness on Me (Four Star Music, BMI) 80
Little Bit You, a Little Bit Me, A (Screen Gems-Columbia, BMI) .... 2
Little Games (Mills, ASCAP) .... 66
Live (Thirty-four/LaBrea, ASCAP) .... 94
Love Eyes (Criterion, ASCAP) .... 15
Making Memories (Feist, ASCAP) .... 48
Melancholy Music Man (Chardon, BMI) .... 57
Mirage (Patricia, BMI) .... 69
Music to Watch Girls By (S.C.P., ASCAP) .... 34
My Babe (Tallyrand, BMI) .... 74
My Back Pages (Witmark, ASCAP) .... 31
My Girl Josephine (Travis, BMI) .... 60
Nothing Takes the Place of You (Su-Ma, BMI) .... 59
On a Carousel (Maribus, BMI) .... 17
One Hurt Deserves Another (Hastings, BMI) .... 78
Ooogum Boogum Song, The (Big Shot, ASCAP) .... 77
Out of Left Field (Press, BMI) .... 63
Penny Lane (Maclen, BMI) .... 25
Portrait of My Love (Piccadilly, BMI) .... 53
Precious Memories (Naro, ASCAP) .... 67
Release Me (And Let Me Love Again) (Four Star, BMI) .... 36
Respect (East-Time-Walco, BMI) .... 50
Shake a Tail Feather (Va-Pac, BMI) .... 51
Shake Hands and Walk Away Crying (Rambed, BMI) 96
Six o'Clock (Faithful Virtue, BMI) .... 90
Somebody to Love (Copper Penny, BMI) .... 44
Somethin' Stupid (Green Wood, BMI) .... 1
Summer Wine (Criterion, ASCAP) .... 54
Sunday for Tea (Southcrn, ASCAP) .... 38
Sunshine Girl (Inevitable/Good Sam, BMI) .... 56
Sweet Soul Music (Bedwal, BMI) .... 4
Tears, Tears, Tears (Pronto-Sue, BMI) .... 93
There's a Kind of a Hush (F., D. & M., ASCAP) .... 26
This Is My Song (Shawley, ASCAP) .... 7
Together (Razor Sharp, BMI) .... 100
Too Many Fish in the Sea & Three Little Fishes (Jobete/Joy, BMI) .... 76
Walkin' in the Sunshine (Tree, BMI) .... 41
Western Union (Jetstar, BMI) .... 6
When I Was Young (Yamata, BMI) .... 21
When You're Young and in Love (Picturetoan, BMI) 71
Whole Worll Is a Stage, The (Myto, BMI) .... 72
Why? (Am I Treated So Bad) (Staple, BMI) .... 73
With This Ring (Vee Vee, BMI) .... 19
Yellow Balloon (Teeny Bopper, ASCAP) .... 37
You Got What It Takes (Fidelity, BMI) .... 12
You're All I Need (Don, BMI) .... 88

## BUBBLING UNDER THE HOT 100

101. MY OLD FLAME....Nino Tempo & April Stevens, White Whale 246
102. GOODBYE TO ALL YOU WOMEN....Bobby Goldsboro, United Artists 50153
103. EIGHT MEN, FOUR WOMEN....O. V. Wright, Back Beat 580
104. THE BEAT GOES ON....Lawrence Welk, Dot 17001
105. WHEN TOMORROW COMES....Carla Thomas, Stax 214
106. PIPE DREAM....Blues Magoos, Mercury 72660
107. DO IT AGAIN A LITTLE BIT SLOWER..Jon & Robin & the In Crowd, Abak 179
108. YOU'RE GONNA BE MINE....New Colony Six, Sentar 1206
109. MAKE LOVE TO ME....Johnny Thunder & Ruby Winters, Diamond 218
110. BEAT THE CLOCK....McCoys, Bang 543
111. I FOUND A RAINBOW....Swingin' Medallions, Smash 2084
112. SHAKE....British Walkers, Cameo 466
113. TIME ALONE WILL TELL....Connie Francis, MGM 13718
114. JUMP BACK....King Curtis, Atco 6476
115. LOVE ME FOREVER....Roger Williams, Kapp 821
116. TAKE ME IN YOUR ARMS & LOVE ME..Gladys Knight & the Pips, Soul 35033
117. AIN'T GONNA REST (TILL I GET YOU)....Five Stairsteps, Windy C 605
118. WHEN LOVE SLIPS AWAY....Dee Dee Warwick, Mercury 7266
119. EDELWEISS....Vince Hill, Tower 323
120. STOP! AND THINK IT OVER....Perry Como, RCA Victor 9165
121. MIDNIGHT HOUR....Michael & the Messengers, U.S.A. 866
122. GOT TO HAVE YOU BACK....Isley Bros., Tamla 54146
123. SAM'S PLACE....Buck Owens, Capitol 5865
124. SINCE I DON'T HAVE YOU....James Darren, Warner Bros. 7013
125. SPEAK HER NAME....Walter Jackson, Okah 7272
126. PATTY CAKE....Capitols, Karen 1534
127. FLOWER CHILDREN....Marcia Strassman, UNI 55006
128. IN THE MIDNIGHT HOUR....Wanted, A&M 844
129. DO THE THING....Lou Courtney, Riverside 7589
130. DADDY'S HOME....Chuck Jackson & Maxine Brown, Wand 1155
131. MOVING FINGER WRITES....Len Barry, RCA Victor 9150
132. TIME ALONE WILL TELL....Jerry Vale, Columbia 44087
133. I WANT YOU TO BE MY BABY....Ellis Greenwich, United Artists 50151
134. I CAN'T HELP IT....B. J. Thomas, Scepter 12194
135. TAKE ME....Brenda Lee, Decca 32119

Compiled from national retail sales and radio station airplay by the Music Popularity Dept. of Record Market Research, Billboard.

# Billboard HOT 100

For Week Ending May 6, 1967

★ STAR performer—Sides registering greatest proportionate upward progress this week.
Ⓡ Record Industry Association of America seal of certification as million selling single.

| This Week | 1 Wk. Ago | 2 Wks. Ago | 3 Wks. Ago | TITLE Artist (Producer), Label & Number | Weeks On Chart |
|---|---|---|---|---|---|
| 1 | 1 | 1 | 1 | SOMETHIN' STUPID — Nancy Sinatra & Frank Sinatra (Jimmy Bowen & Lee Hazlewood), Reprise 0561 | 8 |
| 2 | 8 | 11 | 19 | THE HAPPENING — Supremes (Holland & Dozier), Motown 1107 | 5 |
| 3 | 4 | 7 | 11 | SWEET SOUL MUSIC — Arthur Conley (Otis Redding), Atco 6463 | 9 |
| 4 | 2 | 3 | 5 | A LITTLE BIT YOU, A LITTLE BIT ME — Monkees (Jeff Barry), Colgems 1004 | 7 |
| 5 | 3 | 2 | 2 | HAPPY TOGETHER — Turtles (Joe Wissert), White Whale 244 | 13 |
| 6 | 5 | 4 | 7 | I THINK WE'RE ALONE NOW — Tommy James and the Shondells (Cordell-Gentry), Roulette 4720 | 13 |
| 7 | 11 | 17 | 23 | DON'T YOU CARE — Buckinghams (Jim Guercio), Columbia 44053 | 9 |
| 8 | 18 | 26 | 33 | CLOSE YOUR EYES — Peaches & Herb (Dave Kapralik-Ken Williams), Date 1549 | 7 |
| 9 | 12 | 18 | 38 | YOU GOT WHAT IT TAKES — Dave Clark Five (Dave Clark), Epic 10144 | 6 |
| 10 | 13 | 13 | 22 | I'M A MAN — Spencer Davis Group (Jimmy Miller), United Artists 50144 | 7 |
| 11 | 10 | 10 | 10 | JIMMY MACK — Martha and the Vandellas (Holland-Dozier), Gordy 7058 | 11 |
| 12 | 17 | 24 | 36 | ON A CAROUSEL — Hollies (Ron Richards), Imperial 66231 | 8 |
| 13 | 7 | 6 | 3 | THIS IS MY SONG — Petula Clark (Sonny Burke), Warner Bros. 7002 | 10 |
| 14 | 6 | 5 | 6 | WESTERN UNION — Five Americans (Dale Hawkins), Abnak 118 | 10 |
| 15 | 21 | 38 | 61 | WHEN I WAS YOUNG — Eric Burdon and the Animals (Tom Wilson), MGM 13721 | 5 |
| 16 | 14 | 9 | 9 | I NEVER LOVED A MAN THE WAY I LOVE YOU — Aretha Franklin (Jerry Wexler), Atlantic 2386 | 10 |
| 17 | 29 | 46 | 59 | I GOT RHYTHM — Happenings (The Tokens) B. T. Puppy 527 | 5 |
| 18 | 23 | 30 | 46 | FRIDAY ON MY MIND — Easybeats, The (Shel Talmy) United Artists 50106 | 8 |
| 19 | 49 | 79 | — | GROOVIN' — Young Rascals (Young Rascals), Atlantic 2401 | 3 |
| 20 | 36 | 54 | 71 | RELEASE ME (And Let Me Love Again) — Engelbert Humperdinck, Parrot 40011 | 5 |
| 21 | 33 | 43 | 53 | GIRL, YOU'LL BE A WOMAN SOON — Neil Diamond (Jeff Barry & Ellie Greenwich), Bang 542 | 5 |
| 22 | 15 | 15 | 29 | LOVE EYES — Nancy Sinatra (Lee Hazlewood), Reprise 0559 | 7 |
| 23 | 16 | 16 | 17 | AT THE ZOO — Simon & Garfunkel (Bob Johnston), Columbia 44046 | 8 |
| 24 | 9 | 8 | 4 | BERNADETTE — Four Tops (Holland and Dozier), Motown 1104 | 9 |
| 25 | 43 | 53 | 72 | HERE COMES MY BABY — Tremeloes, Epic 10139 | 5 |
| 26 | 50 | — | — | RESPECT — Aretha Franklin (Jerry Wexler), Atlantic 2403 | 2 |
| 27 | 19 | 14 | 18 | WITH THIS RING — Platters (Luther Dixon), Musicor 1229 | 11 |
| 28 | 28 | 34 | 45 | GET ME TO THE WORLD ON TIME — Electric Prunes (Dave Hassinger), Reprise 0564 | 6 |
| 29 | 37 | 47 | 57 | YELLOW BALLOON — Yellow Balloon (Ken Handler & Yoder Critch), Canterbury 508 | 6 |
| 30 | 31 | 42 | 52 | MY BACK PAGES — Byrds (Gary Usher), Columbia 44054 | 6 |
| 31 | 44 | 58 | 68 | SOMEBODY TO LOVE — Jefferson Airplane (Rick Jarrard), RCA Victor 9140 | 4 |
| 32 | 42 | 52 | 55 | DEAD END STREET — Lou Rawls (David Axelrod), Capitol 5869 | 7 |
| 33 | 65 | — | — | HIM OR ME—WHAT'S IT GONNA BE? — Paul Revere & the Raiders (Terry Melcher), Columbia 44094 | 2 |
| 34 | 34 | 35 | 47 | MUSIC TO WATCH GIRLS BY — Andy Williams (Nick De Caro), Columbia 44065 | 7 |
| 35 | 56 | 69 | 84 | SUNSHINE GIRL — Parade (Jerry Riopelle), A&M 841 | 4 |
| 36 | 48 | 59 | 75 | MAKING MEMORIES — Frankie Laine (Bob Thiele), ABC 10924 | 5 |
| 37 | 41 | 41 | 51 | WALKIN' IN THE SUNSHINE — Roger Miller (Jerry Kennedy), Smash 2081 | 7 |
| 38 | 60 | 75 | 87 | MY GIRL JOSEPHINE — Jerry Jaye, Hi 2120 | 4 |
| 39 | 39 | 50 | 65 | CASINO ROYALE — Herb Alpert & the Tijuana Brass (Herb Alpert & Jerry Moss), A&M 850 | 4 |
| 40 | 69 | — | — | MIRAGE — Tommy James & the Shondells (Bo Gentry & Ritchie Cordell), Roulette 4736 | 2 |
| 41 | 51 | 65 | 82 | SHAKE A TAIL FEATHER — James & Bobby Purify (Papa Don, Cogbill, Young, Emmons & Chrisman), Bell 669 | 4 |
| 42 | 81 | — | — | ALL I NEED IS YOU — Temptations (F. Wilson), Gordy 7061 | 2 |
| 43 | 35 | 33 | 27 | CALIFORNIA NIGHTS — Lesley Gore (Bob Crewe), Mercury 72649 | 14 |
| 44 | 83 | — | — | CREEQUE ALLEY — Mamas & the Papas (Lou Adler), Dunhill 4083 | 2 |
| 45 | 55 | 57 | 67 | BUY FOR ME THE RAIN — Nitty Gritty Dirt Band (Dallas Smith), Liberty 55948 | 5 |
| 46 | 64 | — | — | I WAS KAISER BILL'S BATMAN — Whistling Jack Smith, Deram 85003 | 3 |
| 47 | 57 | 76 | — | MELANCHOLY MUSIC MAN — Righteous Brothers (Joe Wissert), Verve 10507 | 3 |
| 48 | 53 | 71 | 86 | PORTRAIT OF MY LOVE — Tokens (Bright Tunes Prod.), Warner Bros. 5900 | 4 |
| 49 | 52 | 55 | 63 | HIP HUG-HER — Booker T. & the M. G.'s (Prod. By Staff), Stax 211 | 7 |
| 50 | 27 | 19 | 15 | FOR WHAT IT'S WORTH — Buffalo Springfield (Greene & Stone), Atco 6459 | 15 |
| 51 | 68 | 83 | 99 | HAPPY JACK — Who, Decca 32114 | 4 |
| 52 | 22 | 20 | 20 | DRY YOUR EYES — Brenda and the Tabulations (Bob Finiz), Dionn 500 | 11 |
| 53 | 32 | 32 | 43 | I FOUND A LOVE — Wilson Pickett (Jerry Wexler), Atlantic 2394 | 6 |
| 54 | 40 | 40 | 50 | I'LL TRY ANYTHING — Dusty Springfield (Herb Bernstein), Philips 40439 | 8 |
| 55 | 74 | 90 | — | MY BABE — Ronnie Dove (Neil Diamond), Diamond 221 | 3 |
| 56 | 66 | 81 | — | LITTLE GAMES — Yardbirds (Mickie Most), Epic 10156 | 3 |
| 57 | 76 | — | — | TOO MANY FISH IN THE SEA & THREE LITTLE FISHES — Mitch Ryder & the Detroit Wheels (Bob Crewe), New Voice 822 | 2 |
| 58 | 59 | 64 | 74 | NOTHING TAKES THE PLACE OF YOU — Toussaint McCall (Jewel Productions), Ronn 3 | 7 |
| 59 | 71 | 86 | — | WHEN YOU'RE YOUNG AND IN LOVE — Marvelettes (J. Dean & William Weatherspoon), Tamla 54150 | 3 |
| 60 | 61 | 61 | 62 | DANNY BOY — Ray Price (Don Law & Frank Jones), Columbia 44042 | 7 |
| 61 | 63 | 67 | 73 | OUT OF LEFT FIELD — Percy Sledge (Quin Ivy & Marlin Greene), Atlantic 2396 | 5 |
| 62 | 62 | 63 | 78 | THE LADY CAME FROM BALTIMORE — Bobby Darin (Charles Koppelman & Don Rubin), Atlantic 2395 | 5 |
| 63 | 85 | — | — | CAN'T SEEM TO MAKE YOU MINE — Seeds (Marcus Tybalt), GNP Crescendo 354 | 2 |
| 64 | 90 | — | — | SIX O'CLOCK — Lovin' Spoonful (Erik Jacobsen), Kama Sutra 225 | 2 |
| 65 | 80 | — | — | LAY SOME HAPPINESS ON ME — Dean Martin (Jimmy Bowen), Reprise 0571 | 2 |
| 66 | 77 | 94 | 98 | THE OOGUM BOOGUM SONG — Brenton Wood (Hooven-Winn), Double Shot 111 | 4 |
| 67 | 67 | 68 | 76 | PRECIOUS MEMORIES — Romeos, Mark II J-1 | 6 |
| 68 | 70 | 77 | 88 | ALFIE — Dionne Warwick (Bacharach-David), Scepter 12187 | 5 |
| 69 | 94 | — | — | LIVE — Merry-Go-Round (Larry Marks), A&M 834 | 2 |
| 70 | 72 | 74 | 77 | THE WHOLE WORLD IS A STAGE — Fantastic Four (Al Kent & E. Wingate), Ric Tic 122 | 7 |
| 71 | 86 | — | — | A BEAUTIFUL STORY — Sonny & Cher (Bill Rinehart), Atco 6480 | 3 |
| 72 | 91 | 98 | — | I COULD BE SO GOOD TO YOU — Don & the Goodtimes (Jack Nitzche), Epic 10145 | 3 |
| 73 | 75 | 85 | — | JUST LOOK WHAT YOU'VE DONE — Brenda Holloway (Frank Wilson), Tamla 54148 | 3 |
| 74 | 82 | 82 | — | I'LL MAKE HIM LOVE ME — Barbara Lewis (Bob Gallo & Ollie McLaughlin), Atlantic 2400 | 3 |
| 75 | 87 | — | — | ANOTHER DAY, ANOTHER HEARTACHE — 5th Dimension (Johnny Rivers & Marc Gordon), Soul City 755 | 2 |
| 76 | 84 | — | — | IT'S ALL OVER — Casinos (Gene Hughes), Fraternity 985 | 2 |
| 77 | 73 | 73 | 79 | WHY? (Am I Treated So Bad) — Cannonball Adderley (David Axelrod), Capitol 5877 | 5 |
| 78 | 78 | 93 | 93 | ONE HURT DESERVES ANOTHER — Raelets (Ray Charles), Tangerine 296 | 4 |
| 79 | — | — | — | TRAMP — Otis & Carla (Prod. by Staff), Stax 216 | 1 |
| 80 | — | — | — | TIME, TIME — Ed Ames (Jim Foglesong), RCA Victor 9178 | 1 |
| 81 | 92 | 96 | 100 | I'M INDESTRUCTIBLE — Jack Jones (Hy Grill), Kapp 818 | 3 |
| 82 | — | — | — | MISTY BLUE — Eddy Arnold (Chet Atkins), RCA Victor 9182 | 1 |
| 83 | — | — | — | LOVE ME FOREVER — Roger Williams (Hy Grill), Kapp 821 | 2 |
| 84 | 100 | — | — | TOGETHER — Intruders, Gamble 205 | 2 |
| 85 | — | — | — | COME ON DOWN TO MY BOAT — Every Mothers' Son (Coral Rock Prod.), MGM 13733 | 1 |
| 86 | — | — | — | DO IT AGAIN A LITTLE BIT SLOWER — Jon & Robin & the In Crowd (Dale Hawkins), Abram 119 | 1 |
| 87 | 89 | 91 | 91 | FUNKY BROADWAY — Dyke & the Blazers (Coleman & Barrett), Original Sound 64 | 4 |
| 88 | — | — | — | I WANT YOU TO BE MY BABY — Ellie Greenwich (Bob Crewe), United Artists 50151 | 1 |
| 89 | — | — | — | I'VE LOST YOU — Jackie Wilson (Carl Davis), Brunswick 55321 | 1 |
| 90 | — | — | — | LET YOURSELF GO — James Brown and the Famous Flames (James Brown), King 6100 | 1 |
| 91 | — | — | — | DADDY'S HOME — Chuck Jackson & Maxine Brown (Stan Green & Neil Galligan), Wand 1155 | 1 |
| 92 | — | — | — | WHEN LOVE SLIPS AWAY — Dee Dee Warwick (Jerry Ross), Mercury 72667 | 1 |
| 93 | — | — | — | GOT TO HAVE YOU BACK — Isley Brothers (Ivy Hunter), Tamla 54146 | 1 |
| 94 | 95 | 97 | — | BLUES THEME — Arrows (Mike Curb), Tower 295 | 3 |
| 95 | 96 | — | — | SHAKE HANDS AND WALK AWAY CRYING — Lou Christie (Charles Calello), Columbia 44062 | 2 |
| 96 | — | — | — | I BELIEVED IT ALL — Pozo-Seco Singers (Bob Johnston), Columbia 44041 | 1 |
| 97 | 97 | 100 | — | HEY LOVE — Stevie Wonder (Clarence Paul), Tamla 54147 | 3 |
| 98 | — | — | — | TAKE ME IN YOUR ARMS AND LOVE ME — Gladys Knight & the Pips (Norman Whitfield), Soul 35033 | 1 |
| 99 | — | — | — | WHEN TOMORROW COMES — Carla Thomas (Prod. by Staff), Stax 214 | 1 |
| 100 | — | — | — | SHE SHOT A HOLE IN MY SOUL — Clifford Curry (Buzz Cason), Elf 90002 | 1 |

## BUBBLING UNDER THE HOT 100

101. MY OLD FLAME — Nino Tempo & April Stevens, White Whale 246
102. SHE'D RATHER BE WITH ME — The Turtles, White Whale 249
103. EIGHT MEN, FOUR WOMEN — O. V. Wright, Back Beat 580
104. JUMP BACK — King Curtis, Atco 6476
105. GOODBYE TO ALL YOU WOMEN — Bobby Goldsboro, United Artists 50138
106. PIPE DREAM — Blues Magoos, Mercury 72660
107. GEORGY GIRL — Baja Marimba Band, A&M 843
108. YOU'RE GONNA BE MINE — New Colony Six, Sentar 1206
109. SHAKE — British Walkers, Cameo 466
110. TIME ALONE WILL TELL — Connie Francis, MGM 13718
111. I FOUND A RAINBOW — Swingin' Medallions, Smash 2084
112. BEAT THE CLOCK — McCoys, Bang 543
113. GIRL IN LOVE — Gary Lewis & the Playboys, Liberty 55971
114. STOP AND THINK IT OVER — Perry Como, RCA Victor 9165
115. AIN'T GONNA REST TILL I GET YOU — Five Stairsteps, Windy C 605
116. MIDNIGHT HOUR — Messengers, U.S.A. 806
117. HOLIDAY FOR CLOWNS — Brian Hyland, Philips 40444
118. TEARS, TEARS, TEARS — Ben E. King, Atco 6472
119. SPEAK HER NAME — Walter Jackson, Okeh 7272
120. FLOWER CHILDREN — Marcia Strassman, Uni 55006
121. DO THE FLOWER — Lou Courtney, Riverside 7589
122. MAKE ME YOURS — Betty Swann, Money 126
123. I LOVE YOU, I DON'T HAVE YOU — James Darren, Warner Bros. 7013
124. MOVING FINGER WRITES — Len Barry, RCA Victor 9150
125. PATTY CAKE — Capitols, Karen 1534
126. TAKE ME — Brenda Lee, Decca 32119
127. I CAN'T HELP IT (IF I'M STILL IN LOVE WITH YOU) — B. J. Thomas, Scepter 12194
128. TIME WILL TELL — Jerry Vale, Columbia 44087
129. ONLY LOVE CAN BREAK A HEART — Margaret Whiting, London 108
130. I LOVE YOU MORE THAN WORDS CAN SAY — Otis Redding, Volt 146
131. RAPID TRANSIT — Robbs, Mercury 72678
132. BOWLING GREEN — Everly Brothers, Warner Bros. 2020
133. IVY, IVY — Left Banke, Smash 2089
134. GOTTA LEAVE US ALONE — Outsiders, Capitol 5892
135. MINISKIRTS IN MOSCOW — Bob Crewe Generation, New Voice 233

Compiled from national retail sales and radio station airplay by the Music Popularity Dept. of Record Market Research, Billboard.

For Week Ending May 13, 1967

# Billboard

# HOT 100

★ **STAR performer—Sides registering greatest proportionate upward progress this week.**

Record Industry Association of America seal of certification as million selling single.

| This Week | 1 Wk. Ago | 2 Wks. Ago | 3 Wks. Ago | TITLE Artist (Producer), Label & Number | Weeks On Chart |
|---|---|---|---|---|---|
| Billboard Award | 2 | 8 | 11 | THE HAPPENING — Supremes (Holland & Dozier), Motown 1107 | 6 |
| 2 | 3 | 4 | 7 | SWEET SOUL MUSIC — Arthur Conley (Otis Redding), Atco 6463 | 10 |
| 3 | 1 | 1 | 1 | SOMETHIN' STUPID — Nancy Sinatra & Frank Sinatra (Jimmy Bowen & Lee Hazlewood), Reprise 0561 | 9 |
| ★4 | 19 | 49 | 79 | GROOVIN' — Young Rascals (Young Rascals), Atlantic 2401 | 4 |
| 5 | 4 | 2 | 3 | A LITTLE BIT YOU, A LITTLE BIT ME — Monkees (Jeff Barry), Colgems 1004 | 8 |
| 6 | 7 | 11 | 17 | DON'T YOU CARE — Buckinghams (Jim Guercio), Columbia 44053 | 10 |
| 7 | 9 | 12 | 18 | YOU GOT WHAT IT TAKES — Dave Clark Five (Dave Clark), Epic 10144 | 7 |
| 8 | 8 | 18 | 26 | CLOSE YOUR EYES — Peaches & Herb (Dave Kapralik-Ken Williams), Date 1549 | 8 |
| ★9 | 17 | 29 | 46 | I GOT RHYTHM — Happenings (The Tokens) B. T. Puppy 527 | 6 |
| 10 | 6 | 5 | 4 | I THINK WE'RE ALONE NOW — Tommy James and the Shondells (Cordell-Gentry), Roulette 4720 | 14 |
| ★11 | 21 | 33 | 43 | GIRL, YOU'LL BE A WOMAN SOON — Neil Diamond (Jeff Barry & Ellie Greenwich), Bang 542 | 6 |
| 12 | 12 | 17 | 24 | ON A CAROUSEL — Hollies (Ron Richards), Imperial 66231 | 9 |
| ★13 | 20 | 36 | 54 | RELEASE ME (And Let Me Love Again) — Engelbert Humperdinck, Parrot 40011 | 6 |
| ★14 | 26 | 50 | — | RESPECT — Aretha Franklin (Jerry Wexler), Atlantic 2403 | 3 |
| 15 | 15 | 21 | 38 | WHEN I WAS YOUNG — Eric Burdon & the Animals (Tom Wilson), MGM 13721 | 6 |
| 16 | 5 | 3 | 2 | HAPPY TOGETHER — Turtles (Joe Wissert), White Whale 244 | 14 |
| 17 | 10 | 13 | 13 | I'M A MAN — Spencer Davis Group (Jimmy Miller), United Artists 50144 | 8 |
| 18 | 18 | 23 | 30 | FRIDAY ON MY MIND — Easybeats, (Shell Talmy) United Artists 50106 | 9 |
| ★19 | 25 | 43 | 53 | HERE COMES MY BABY — Tremeloes, Epic 10139 | 6 |
| 20 | 11 | 10 | 10 | JIMMY MACK — Martha and the Vandellas (Holland-Dozier), Gordy 7058 | 12 |
| ★21 | 33 | 65 | — | HIM OR ME—WHAT'S IT GONNA BE? — Paul Revere & the Raiders (Terry Melcher), Columbia 44094 | 3 |
| ★22 | 44 | 83 | — | CREEQUE ALLEY — Mamas & the Papas (Lou Adler), Dunhill 4083 | 3 |
| 23 | 13 | 7 | 6 | THIS IS MY SONG — Petula Clark (Sonny Burke), Warner Bros. 7002 | 11 |
| ★24 | 40 | 69 | — | MIRAGE — Tommy James & the Shondells (Bo Gentry & Ritchie Cordell), Roulette 4736 | 3 |
| ★25 | 35 | 56 | 69 | SUNSHINE GIRL — Parade (Jerry Riopelle), A&M 841 | 5 |
| 26 | 29 | 37 | 47 | YELLOW BALLOON — Yellow Balloon (Ken Handler & Yoder Critch), Canterbury 508 | 7 |
| 27 | 28 | 28 | 34 | GET ME TO THE WORLD ON TIME — Electric Prunes (Dave Hassinger), Reprise 0564 | 7 |
| ★28 | 42 | 81 | — | ALL I NEED IS YOU — Temptations (F. Wilson), Gordy 7061 | 3 |
| 29 | 32 | 42 | 52 | DEAD END STREET — Lou Rawls (David Axlerod), Capitol 5869 | 8 |
| ★30 | 41 | 51 | 65 | SHAKE A TAIL FEATHER — James & Bobby Purify (Papa Don, Cogbill, Young, Emmons & Chrisman), Bell 669 | 5 |
| 31 | 31 | 44 | 58 | SOMEBODY TO LOVE — Jefferson Airplane (Rick Jarrard), RCA Victor 9140 | 7 |
| 32 | 16 | 14 | 9 | I NEVER LOVED A MAN THE WAY I LOVE YOU — Aretha Franklin (Jerry Wexler), Atlantic 2386 | 11 |
| 33 | 23 | 16 | 16 | AT THE ZOO — Simon & Garfunkel (Bob Johnston), Columbia 44046 | 9 |
| ★34 | 46 | 64 | — | I WAS KAISER BILL'S BATMAN — Whistling Jack Smith, Deram 85003 | 3 |
| 35 | 38 | 60 | 75 | MY GIRL JOSEPHINE — Jerry Jaye, Hi 2120 | 5 |
| 36 | 36 | 48 | 59 | MAKING MEMORIES — Frankie Laine (Bob Thiele), ABC 10924 | 6 |
| 37 | 39 | 39 | 50 | CASINO ROYALE — Herb Alpert & the Tijuana Brass (Herb Alpert & Jerry Moss), A&M 850 | 6 |
| 38 | 14 | 6 | 5 | WESTERN UNION — Five Americans (Dale Hawkins), Abnak 118 | 11 |
| 39 | 30 | 31 | 42 | MY BACK PAGES — Byrds (Gary Usher), Columbia 44054 | 7 |
| ★40 | 57 | 76 | — | TOO MANY FISH IN THE SEA & THREE LITTLE FISHES — Mitch Ryder & the Detroit Wheels (Bob Crewe), New Voice 822 | 3 |
| ★41 | 51 | 68 | 83 | HAPPY JACK — Who, Decca 32114 | 5 |
| 42 | 49 | 52 | 55 | HIP HUG-HER — Booker T. & the M. G.'s (Prod. By Staff), Stax 211 | 8 |
| 43 | 27 | 19 | 14 | WITH THIS RING — Platters (Luther Dixon), Musicor 1229 | 12 |
| 44 | 48 | 53 | 71 | PORTRAIT OF MY LOVE — Tokens (Bright Tunes Prod.), Warner Bros. 5900 | 5 |
| 45 | 45 | 55 | 57 | BUY FOR ME THE RAIN — Nitty Gritty Dirt Band (Dallas Smith), Liberty 55948 | 6 |
| 46 | 22 | 15 | 15 | LOVE EYES — Nancy Sinatra (Lee Hazlewood), Reprise 0559 | 8 |
| 47 | 47 | 57 | 76 | MELANCHOLY MUSIC MAN — Righteous Brothers (Joe Wissert), Verve 10507 | 4 |
| ★48 | 64 | 90 | — | SIX O'CLOCK — Lovin' Spoonful (Erik Jacobsen), Kama Sutra 225 | 3 |
| ★49 | 59 | 71 | 86 | WHEN YOU'RE YOUNG AND IN LOVE — Marvelettes (J. Dean & William Weatherspoon), Tamla 54150 | 4 |
| 50 | 24 | 9 | 8 | BERNADETTE — Four Tops (Holland and Dozier), Motown 1104 | 10 |
| 51 | 55 | 74 | 90 | MY BABE — Ronnie Dove (Neil Diamond), Diamond 221 | 4 |
| 52 | 58 | 59 | 64 | NOTHING TAKES THE PLACE OF YOU — Toussaint McCall (Jewel Productions), Ronn 3 | 8 |
| 53 | 56 | 66 | 81 | LITTLE GAMES — Yardbirds (Mickie Most), Epic 10156 | 4 |
| 54 | 34 | 34 | 35 | MUSIC TO WATCH GIRLS BY — Andy Williams (Nick De Caro), Columbia 44065 | 8 |
| ★55 | 65 | 80 | — | LAY SOME HAPPINESS ON ME — Dean Martin (Jimmy Bowen), Reprise 0571 | 3 |
| ★56 | 66 | 77 | 94 | THE OOGUM BOOGUM SONG — Brenton Wood (Hooven-Winn), Double Shot 111 | 5 |
| 57 | 63 | 85 | — | CAN'T SEEM TO MAKE YOU MINE — Seeds (Marcus Tybalt), GNP Crescendo 354 | 3 |
| ★58 | 71 | 86 | — | A BEAUTIFUL STORY — Sonny & Cher (Bill Rinehart), Atco 6480 | 3 |
| 59 | 61 | 63 | 67 | OUT OF LEFT FIELD — Percy Sledge (Quin Ivy & Marlin Greene), Atlantic 2396 | 6 |
| ★60 | 75 | 87 | — | ANOTHER DAY, ANOTHER HEARTACHE — 5th Dimension (Johnny Rivers & Marc Gordon), Soul City 755 | 3 |
| 61 | 68 | 70 | 77 | ALFIE — Dionne Warwick (Bacharach-David), Scepter 12187 | 6 |
| 62 | 72 | 91 | 98 | I COULD BE SO GOOD TO YOU — Don & the Goodtimes (Jack Nitzche), Epic 10145 | 4 |
| 63 | 69 | 94 | — | LIVE — Merry-Go-Round (Larry Marks), A&M 834 | 3 |
| ★64 | 79 | — | — | TRAMP — Otis & Carla (Prod. by Staff), Stax 216 | 2 |
| 65 | 76 | 84 | — | IT'S ALL OVER — Casinos (Gene Hughes), Fraternity 985 | 3 |
| 66 | 70 | 72 | 74 | THE WHOLE WORLD IS A STAGE — Fantastic Four (Al Kent & E. Wingate), Ric Tic 122 | 8 |
| 67 | 67 | 67 | 68 | PRECIOUS MEMORIES — Romeos, Mark II J-1 | 7 |
| ★68 | 86 | — | — | DO IT AGAIN A LITTLE BIT SLOWER — Jon & Robin & the In Crowd (Dale Hawkins), Abram 119 | 2 |
| 69 | 73 | 75 | 85 | JUST LOOK WHAT YOU'VE DONE — Brenda Holloway (Frank Wilson), Tamla 54148 | 4 |
| 70 | 82 | — | — | MISTY BLUE — Eddy Arnold (Chet Atkins), RCA Victor 9182 | 2 |
| 71 | 60 | 61 | 61 | DANNY BOY — Ray Price (Don Law & Frank Jones), Columbia 44042 | 8 |
| 72 | 85 | — | — | COME ON DOWN TO MY BOAT — Every Mother's Son (Wes Farrell), MGM 13733 | 2 |
| 73 | 74 | 82 | 82 | I'LL MAKE HIM LOVE ME — Barbara Lewis (Bob Gallo & Ollie McLaughlin), Atlantic 2400 | 4 |
| 74 | 83 | — | — | LOVE ME FOREVER — Roger Williams (Hy Grill), Kapp 821 | 2 |
| ★75 | 90 | — | — | LET YOURSELF GO — James Brown & the Famous Flames (James Brown), King 6100 | 2 |
| 76 | 80 | — | — | TIME, TIME — Ed Ames (Jim Foglesong), RCA Victor 9178 | 2 |
| 77 | 78 | 78 | 93 | ONE HURT DESERVES ANOTHER — Raelets (Ray Charles), Tangerine 296 | 5 |
| ★78 | — | — | — | JUMP BACK — King Curtis (Jerry Wexler), Atco 6476 | 1 |
| ★79 | — | — | — | AIN'T NO MOUNTAIN HIGH ENOUGH — Marvin Gaye & Tammi Terrell (H. Fuqua & J. Bristol), Tamla 54149 | 1 |
| ★80 | — | — | — | GIRLS IN LOVE — Gary Lewis & the Playboys (Koppelman-Rubin-Klein), Liberty 55971 | 1 |
| 81 | 81 | 92 | 96 | I'M INDESTRUCTIBLE — Jack Jones (Hy Grill), Kapp 818 | 5 |
| 82 | 84 | 100 | — | TOGETHER — Intruders, Gamble 205 | 3 |
| 83 | 88 | — | — | I WANT YOU TO BE MY BABY — Ellie Greenwich (Bob Crewe), United Artists 50151 | 2 |
| ★84 | — | — | — | EIGHT MEN, FOUR WOMEN — O. V. Wright (Willie Mitchell), Back Beat 580 | 1 |
| 85 | 89 | — | — | I'VE LOST YOU — Jackie Wilson (Carl Davis), Brunswick 55321 | 2 |
| 86 | 87 | 89 | 91 | FUNKY BROADWAY — Dyke & the Blazers (Coleman & Barrett), Original Sound 64 | 5 |
| ★87 | — | — | — | LET'S LIVE FOR TODAY — Grass Roots (Steve Barri & P. F. Sloan), Dunhill 4084 | 1 |
| ★88 | — | — | — | SHE'D RATHER BE WITH ME — Turtles (Joe Wissert), White Whale 249 | 1 |
| ★89 | — | — | — | AM I GROOVING YOU — Freddie Scott (Bert Berns), Shout 212 | 1 |
| ★90 | — | — | — | LITTLE BIT O' SOUL — Music Explosion (J. Katz-J. Kasenentz & E. Chiprut) Laurie 3380 | 1 |
| 91 | 97 | 97 | 100 | HEY LOVE — Stevie Wonder (Clarence Paul), Tamla 54147 | 4 |
| 92 | 94 | 95 | 97 | BLUES THEME — Arrows (Mike Curb), Tower 295 | 4 |
| 93 | 93 | — | — | GOT TO HAVE YOU BACK — Isley Brothers (Ivy Hunter), Tamla 54146 | 2 |
| 94 | — | — | — | I CAN'T HELP IT IF I'M STILL IN LOVE WITH YOU — B. J. Thomas (Huey P. Meaux), Scepter 12194 | 1 |
| 95 | 100 | — | — | SHE SHOT A HOLE IN MY SOUL — Clifford Curry (Buzz Cason), Elf 90002 | 2 |
| 96 | — | — | — | MAKE ME YOURS — Bettye Swann, Money 126 | 1 |
| 97 | — | — | — | MY OLD CAR — Lee Dorsey (A. Toussaint & M. E. Sehorn), Amy 987 | 1 |
| 98 | 98 | — | — | TAKE ME IN YOUR ARMS AND LOVE ME — Gladys Knight & the Pips (Norman Whitfield), Soul 35033 | 2 |
| 99 | — | — | — | BEAT THE CLOCK — McCoys (F.G.G. Prod.), Bang 543 | 1 |
| 100 | — | — | — | WE HAD A GOOD THING GOIN' — Cyrkle (John Simon), Columbia 44108 | 1 |

## HOT 100—A TO Z—*(Publisher-Licensee)*

Ain't No Mountain High Enough (Jobete, BMI).... 79
Alfie (Famous, ASCAP).... 61
All I Need Is You (Jobete, BMI).... 28
Am I Grooving You (Web IV, BMI).... 89
Another Day, Another Heartache (Trousdale, BMI).. 60
At the Zoo (Charing Cross, BMI).... 33
Beat the Clock (Doraflo, BMI).... 99
Beautiful Story, A (Chris Marc-Cotillion, BMI).... 58
Bernadette (Jobete, BMI).... 50
Blues Theme (Dijon, BMI).... 92
Buy for Me the Rain (Nina, BMI).... 45
Can't Seem to Make You Mine (Neil-Purple Bottle, BMI).... 57
Casino Royale (Colgems, ASCAP).... 37
Close Your Eyes (Tideland, BMI).... 8
Come on Down to My Boat (Picturetone-Goldstein, BMI).... 72
Creeque Alley (Trousdale, BMI).... 22
Danny Boy (Boosey & Hawkes, ASCAP).... 71
Dead-End Street (Raw Lou/Beechwood, BMI).... 29
Do It Again a Little Bit Slower (Barton, BMI).... 68
Don't You Care (Beechwood, BMI).... 6
Eight Men, Four Women (Don, BMI).... 84
Friday on My Mind (Unart, BMI).... 18
Funky Broadway (Drive-In/Routeen, BMI).... 86
Get Me to the World on Time (Pamona, BMI).... 27
Girl, You'll Be a Woman Soon (Tallyrand, BMI).... 11
Girls in Love (Chardon, BMI).... 80
Got to Have You Back (Jobete, BMI).... 93
Groovin' (Slacsar, BMI).... 4
Happening, The (Jobete, BMI).... 1
Happy Jack (Essex, ASCAP).... 41
Happy Together (Chardon, BMI).... 16
Here Comes My Baby (Mainstay, BMI).... 19
Hey, Love (Jobete, BMI).... 91
Him or Me—What's It Gonna Be? (Daywin, BMI).. 21
Hip Hug-Her (East, BMI).... 42
I Can't Help It if I'm Still in Love With You (Rose, BMI).... 94
I Could Be So Good to You (Stoutworthy & Sona, BMI).... 62
I Got Rhythm (New World, ASCAP).... 9
I Never Loved a Man the Way I Love You (14th Hour, BMI).... 32
I Think We're Alone Now (Patricia, BMI).... 10
I Want You to Be My Baby (Hendricks, BMI).... 83
I Was Kaiser Bill's Batman (Mills, ASCAP).... 34
I'll Make Him Love Me (Screen Gems-Columbia, BMI).... 73
I'm a Man (Essex, ASCAP).... 17
I'm Indestructible (Ensign, BMI).... 81
It's All Over (Acuff-Rose, BMI).... 65
I've Lost You (Blackwood, BMI).... 85
Jimmy Mack (Jobete, BMI).... 20
Jump Back (East, BMI).... 78
Just Look What You've Done (Jobete, BMI).... 69
Lay Some Happiness on Me (Four Star Music, BMI) 55
Let Yourself Go (Dynatone, BMI).... 75
Let's Live for Today (James, BMI).... 87
Little Bit o'Soul (Southern, ASCAP).... 90
Little Bit You, a Little Bit Me, A (Screen Gems-Columbia, BMI).... 5
Little Games (Mills, ASCAP).... 53
Live (Thirty-four/LaBrea, ASCAP).... 63
Love Eyes (Criterion, ASCAP).... 46
Love Me Forever (Rogelle, BMI).... 74
Make Me Yours (Cash Songs, BMI).... 96
Making Memories (Feist, ASCAP).... 36
Melancholy Music Man (Chardon, BMI).... 47
Mirage (Patricia, BMI).... 24
Misty Blue (Talmount, BMI).... 70
Music to Watch Girls By (S.C.P., ASCAP).... 54
My Babe (Tallyrand, BMI).... 51
My Back Pages (Witmark, ASCAP).... 39
My Girl Josephine (Travis, BMI).... 35
My Old Car (Marsaint, BMI).... 97
Nothing Takes the Place of You (Su-Ma, BMI).... 52
On a Carousel (Maribus, BMI).... 12
One Hurt Deserves Another (Hastings, BMI).... 77
Ooogum Boogum Song, The (Big Shot, ASCAP).... 56
Out of Left Field (Press, BMI).... 59
Portrait of My Love (Piccadilly, BMI).... 44
Precious Memories (Naro, ASCAP).... 67
Release Me (And Let Me Love Again) (Four Star, BMI).... 13
Respect (East-Time-Walco, BMI).... 14
Shake a Tail Feather (Va-Pac, BMI).... 30
She Shot a Hole in My Soul (Morrowood Music, BMI).... 95
She'd Rather Be With Me (Chardon, BMI).... 88
Six o'Clock (Faithful Virtue, BMI).... 48
Somebody to Love (Copper Penny, BMI).... 31
Somethin' Stupid (Green Wood, BMI).... 3
Sunshine Girl (Inevitable/Good Sam, BMI).... 25
Sweet Soul Music (Bedwal, BMI).... 2
Take Me in Your Arms and Love Me (Jobete, BMI) 98
This Is My Song (Shawley, ASCAP).... 23
Time, Time (April, ASCAP).... 76
Together (Razor Sharp, BMI).... 82
Too Many Fish in the Sea & Three Little Fishes (Jobete/Joy, BMI).... 40
Tramp (Modern, BMI).... 64
We Had a Good Thing Goin' (Screen Gems-Columbia, BMI)....100
Western Union (Jetstar, BMI).... 38
When I Was Young (Sea Lark/Slamina, BMI).... 15
When You're Young and in Love (Picturetoan, BMI) 49
Whole World Is a Stage, The (Myto, BMI).... 66
With This Ring (Vee Vee, BMI).... 43
Yellow Balloon (Teeny Bopper, ASCAP).... 26
You Got What It Takes (Fidelity, BMI).... 7

## BUBBLING UNDER THE HOT 100

101. LONG-LEGGED GIRL....Elvis Presley, RCA Victor 9115
102. SUNDAY WILL NEVER BE THE SAME....Spanky & Our Gang, Mercury 72679
103. SHAKE HANDS AND WALK AWAY CRYING....Lou Christie, Columbia 44062
104. MY OLD FLAME....Nino Tempo & April Stevens, White Whale 246
105. SOMEBODY OUGHT TO WRITE A BOOK....Ray Charles, ABC 10938
106. CAN'T TAKE MY EYES OFF YOU....Frankie Valli, Philips 40446
107. I FOUND A RAINBOW....Swinging Medallions, Smash 2087
108. IT'S COLD OUTSIDE....Choir, Roulette 4738
109. SHAKE....British Walkers, Cameo 466
110. ONLY LOVE CAN BREAK A HEART....Margaret Whiting, London 108
111. WHEN LOVE SLIPS AWAY....Dee Dee Warwick, Mercury 72667
112. STOP! AND THINK IT OVER....Perry Como, RCA Victor 9165
113. DADDY'S HOME....Chuck Jackson & Maxine Brown, Wand 115
114. I BELIEVED IT ALL....Pozo-Seco Singers, Columbia 44041
115. DING DONG THE WITCH IS DEAD....Fifth Estate, Jubilee 5573
116. HOLIDAY FOR CLOWNS....Brian Hyland, Philips 40444
117. FLOWER CHILDREN....Marcia Strassman, Uni 55006
118. FUNNY FAMILIAR FORGOTTEN FEELINGS....Tom Jones, Parrot 40014
119. SHAKE....Otis Redding, Volt 149
120. SOUND OF LOVE....Five Americans, Abnak 120
121. CREATORS OF RAIN....Smokey & His Sister, Columbia 43995
122. NO GOOD TO CRY....Wildweeds, Cadet 5561
123. RAPID TRANSIT....Robbs, Mercury 72678
124. DOUBLE YELLOW LINE....Music Machine, Original Sound 71
125. HERE I AM, BABY....Barbara McNair, Motown 1106
126. TIME ALONE WILL TELL....Jerry Vale, Columbia 44087
127. SOUL FINGER....Bar-Kays, Volt 148
128. EVERYBODY NEEDS HELP....Jimmy Holiday, Minit 32016
129. THAT SOMEONE YOU'LL NEVER FORGET....Elvis Presley, RCA Victor 9115
130. ROUND, ROUND....Jonathan King, Parrot 3011
131. EVERYBODY LOVES MY BABY....King Richard's Fluegel Knights, MTA 120
132. MINISKIRTS IN MOSCOW....Bob Crewe Generation, DynoVoice 233
133. GOTTA LEAVE US ALONE....Outsiders, Capitol 5892
134. BOWLING GREEN....Everly Brothers, Warner Bros. 7020
135. IVY, IVY....Left Banke, Smash 2089

Compiled from national retail sales and radio station airplay by the Music Popularity Dept. of Record Market Research, Billboard.

For Week Ending May 20, 1967

# Billboard HOT 100

★ STAR performer—Sides registering greatest proportionate upward progress this week.

Record Industry Association of America seal of certification as million selling single.

| THIS WEEK | 1 Wk. Ago | 2 Wks. Ago | 3 Wks. Ago | TITLE Artist (Producer), Label & Number | Weeks On Chart |
|---|---|---|---|---|---|
| 1 (Billboard Award) | 4 | 19 | 49 | **GROOVIN'** Young Rascals (Young Rascals), Atlantic 2401 | 5 |
| 2 | 1 | 2 | 8 | **THE HAPPENING** Supremes (Holland & Dozier), Motown 1107 | 7 |
| 3 | 2 | 3 | 4 | **SWEET SOUL MUSIC** Arthur Conley (Otis Redding), Atco 6463 | 11 |
| 4 | 3 | 1 | 1 | **SOMETHIN' STUPID** Nancy Sinatra & Frank Sinatra (Jimmy Bowen & Lee Hazlewood), Reprise 0561 | 10 |
| ★5 | 14 | 26 | 50 | **RESPECT** Aretha Franklin (Jerry Wexler), Atlantic 2403 | 4 |
| ★6 | 9 | 17 | 29 | **I GOT RHYTHM** Happenings (The Tokens) B. T. Puppy 527 | 7 |
| ★7 | 13 | 20 | 36 | **RELEASE ME (And Let Me Love Again)** Engelbert Humperdinck, Parrot 40011 | 7 |
| 8 | 8 | 8 | 18 | **CLOSE YOUR EYES** Peaches & Herb (Dave Kapralik-Ken Williams), Date 1549 | 9 |
| 9 | 6 | 7 | 11 | **DON'T YOU CARE** Buckinghams (Jim Guercio), Columbia 44053 | 11 |
| 10 | 7 | 9 | 12 | **YOU GOT WHAT IT TAKES** Dave Clark Five (Dave Clark), Epic 10144 | 8 |
| 11 | 11 | 21 | 33 | **GIRL, YOU'LL BE A WOMAN SOON** Neil Diamond (Jeff Barry & Ellie Greenwich), Bang 542 | 7 |
| 12 | 12 | 12 | 17 | **ON A CAROUSEL** Hollies (Ron Richards), Imperial 66231 | 10 |
| ★13 | 22 | 44 | 83 | **CREEQUE ALLEY** Mamas & the Papas (Lou Adler), Dunhill 4083 | 4 |
| ★14 | 21 | 33 | 65 | **HIM OR ME—WHAT'S IT GONNA BE?** Paul Revere & the Raiders (Terry Melcher), Columbia 44094 | 4 |
| 15 | 15 | 15 | 21 | **WHEN I WAS YOUNG** Eric Burdon & the Animals (Tom Wilson), MGM 13721 | 7 |
| 16 | 18 | 18 | 23 | **FRIDAY ON MY MIND** Easybeats, (Shell Talmy) United Artists 50106 | 10 |
| 17 | 10 | 6 | 5 | **I THINK WE'RE ALONE NOW** Tommy James and the Shondells (Cordell-Gentry), Roulette 4720 | 15 |
| 18 | 19 | 25 | 43 | **HERE COMES MY BABY** Tremeloes, Epic 10139 | 7 |
| ★19 | 24 | 40 | 69 | **MIRAGE** Tommy James & the Shondells (Bo Gentry & Ritchie Cordell), Roulette 4736 | 4 |
| 20 | 5 | 4 | 2 | **A LITTLE BIT YOU, A LITTLE BIT ME** Monkees (Jeff Barry), Colgems 1004 | 9 |
| ★21 | 28 | 42 | 81 | **ALL I NEED IS YOU** Temptations (F. Wilson), Gordy 7061 | 4 |
| ★22 | 31 | 31 | 44 | **SOMEBODY TO LOVE** Jefferson Airplane (Rick Jarrard), RCA Victor 9140 | 8 |
| 23 | 25 | 35 | 56 | **SUNSHINE GIRL** Parade (Jerry Riopelle), A&M 841 | 6 |
| 24 | 17 | 10 | 13 | **I'M A MAN** Spencer Davis Group (Jimmy Miller), United Artists 50144 | 9 |
| 25 | 26 | 29 | 37 | **YELLOW BALLOON** Yellow Balloon (Ken Handler & Yoder Critch), Canterbury 508 | 8 |
| ★26 | 34 | 46 | 64 | **I WAS KAISER BILL'S BATMAN** Whistling Jack Smith, Deram 85003 | 4 |
| ★27 | 40 | 57 | 76 | **TOO MANY FISH IN THE SEA & THREE LITTLE FISHES** Mitch Ryder & the Detroit Wheels (Bob Crewe), New Voice 822 | 4 |
| 28 | 30 | 41 | 51 | **SHAKE A TAIL FEATHER** James & Bobby Purify (Papa Don, Cogbill, Young, Emmons & Chrisman), Bell 669 | 6 |
| 29 | 29 | 32 | 42 | **DEAD END STREET** Lou Rawls (David Axlerod), Capitol 5869 | 9 |
| ★30 | 37 | 39 | 39 | **CASINO ROYALE** Herb Alpert & the Tijuana Brass (Herb Alpert & Jerry Moss), A&M 850 | 7 |
| ★31 | 41 | 51 | 68 | **HAPPY JACK** Who, Decca 32114 | 6 |
| ★32 | 48 | 64 | 90 | **SIX O'CLOCK** Lovin' Spoonful (Erik Jacobsen), Kama Sutra 225 | 4 |
| 33 | 16 | 5 | 3 | **HAPPY TOGETHER** Turtles (Joe Wissert), White Whale 244 | 15 |
| 34 | 35 | 38 | 60 | **MY GIRL JOSEPHINE** Jerry Jaye, Hi 2120 | 6 |
| 35 | 36 | 36 | 48 | **MAKING MEMORIES** Frankie Laine (Bob Thiele), ABC 10924 | 7 |
| 36 | 20 | 11 | 10 | **JIMMY MACK** Martha and the Vandellas (Holland-Dozier), Gordy 7058 | 13 |
| 37 | 44 | 48 | 53 | **PORTRAIT OF MY LOVE** Tokens (Bright Tunes Prod.), Warner Bros. 5900 | 6 |
| 38 | 42 | 49 | 52 | **HIP HUG-HER** Booker T. & the M. G.'s (Prod. By Staff), Stax 211 | 9 |
| ★39 | 49 | 59 | 71 | **WHEN YOU'RE YOUNG AND IN LOVE** Marvelettes (J. Dean & William Weatherspoon), Tamla 54150 | 5 |
| 40 | 27 | 28 | 28 | **GET ME TO THE WORLD ON TIME** Electric Prunes (Dave Hassinger), Reprise 0564 | 8 |
| 41 | 38 | 14 | 6 | **WESTERN UNION** Five Americans (Dale Hawkins), Abnak 118 | 12 |
| 42 | 23 | 13 | 7 | **THIS IS MY SONG** Petula Clark (Sonny Burke), Warner Bros. 7002 | 12 |
| 43 | 47 | 47 | 57 | **MELANCHOLY MUSIC MAN** Righteous Brothers (Joe Wissert), Verve 10507 | 5 |
| ★44 | 72 | 85 | — | **COME ON DOWN TO MY BOAT** Every Mother's Son (Wes Farrell), MGM 13733 | 3 |
| 45 | 45 | 45 | 55 | **BUY FOR ME THE RAIN** Nitty Gritty Dirt Band (Dallas Smith), Liberty 55948 | 7 |
| ★46 | 68 | 86 | — | **DO IT AGAIN A LITTLE BIT SLOWER** Jon & Robin & the In Crowd (Dale Hawkins), Abnak 119 | 3 |
| ★47 | 61 | 68 | 70 | **ALFIE** Dionne Warwick (Bacharach-David), Scepter 12187 | 7 |
| ★48 | 60 | 75 | 87 | **ANOTHER DAY, ANOTHER HEARTACHE** 5th Dimension (Johnny Rivers & Marc Gordon), Soul City 755 | 4 |
| 49 | 57 | 63 | 85 | **CAN'T SEEM TO MAKE YOU MINE** Seeds (Marcus Tybalt), GNP Crescendo 354 | 4 |
| 50 | 51 | 55 | 74 | **MY BABE** Ronnie Dove (Neil Diamond), Diamond 221 | 5 |
| 51 | 53 | 56 | 66 | **LITTLE GAMES** Yardbirds (Mickie Most), Epic 10156 | 5 |
| 52 | 52 | 58 | 59 | **NOTHING TAKES THE PLACE OF YOU** Toussaint McCall (Jewel Productions), Ronn 3 | 9 |
| 53 | 58 | 71 | 86 | **A BEAUTIFUL STORY** Sonny & Cher (Bill Rinehart), Atco 6480 | 4 |
| ★54 | 64 | 79 | — | **TRAMP** Otis & Carla (Prod. by Staff), Stax 216 | 3 |
| 55 | 55 | 65 | 80 | **LAY SOME HAPPINESS ON ME** Dean Martin (Jimmy Bowen), Reprise 0571 | 4 |
| 56 | 56 | 66 | 77 | **THE OOGUM BOOGUM SONG** Brenton Wood (Hooven-Winn), Double Shot 111 | 6 |
| 57 | 62 | 72 | 91 | **I COULD BE SO GOOD TO YOU** Don & the Goodtimes (Jack Nitzche), Epic 10145 | 5 |
| ★58 | 88 | — | — | **SHE'D RATHER BE WITH ME** Turtles (Joe Wissert), White Whale 249 | 2 |
| ★59 | 75 | 90 | — | **LET YOURSELF GO** James Brown & the Famous Flames (James Brown), King 6100 | 3 |
| ★60 | 70 | 82 | — | **MISTY BLUE** Eddy Arnold (Chet Atkins), RCA Victor 9182 | 3 |
| ★61 | 76 | 80 | — | **TIME, TIME** Ed Ames (Jim Foglesong), RCA Victor 9178 | 3 |
| ★62 | 79 | — | — | **AIN'T NO MOUNTAIN HIGH ENOUGH** Marvin Gaye & Tammi Terrell (H. Fuqua & J. Bristol), Tamla 54149 | 2 |
| 63 | 66 | 70 | 72 | **THE WHOLE WORLD IS A STAGE** Fantastic Four (Al Kent & E. Wingate), Ric Tic 122 | 9 |
| 64 | 74 | 83 | — | **LOVE ME FOREVER** Roger Williams (Hy Grill), Kapp 821 | 3 |
| ★65 | 80 | — | — | **GIRLS IN LOVE** Gary Lewis & the Playboys (Koppelman-Rubin-Klein), Liberty 55971 | 2 |
| ★66 | 87 | — | — | **LET'S LIVE FOR TODAY** Grass Roots (Steve Barri & P. F. Sloan), Dunhill 4084 | 2 |
| ★67 | 82 | 84 | 100 | **TOGETHER** Intruders, Gamble 205 | 4 |
| 68 | 63 | 69 | 94 | **LIVE** Merry-Go-Round (Larry Marks), A&M 834 | 4 |
| 69 | 69 | 73 | 75 | **JUST LOOK WHAT YOU'VE DONE** Brenda Holloway (Frank Wilson), Tamla 54148 | 5 |
| 70 | 59 | 61 | 63 | **OUT OF LEFT FIELD** Percy Sledge (Quin Ivy & Marlin Greene), Atlantic 2396 | 7 |
| 71 | 65 | 76 | 84 | **IT'S ALL OVER** Casinos (Gene Hughes), Fraternity 985 | 4 |
| 72 | 73 | 74 | 82 | **I'LL MAKE HIM LOVE ME** Barbara Lewis (Bob Gallo & Ollie McLaughlin), Atlantic 2400 | 5 |
| ★73 | 90 | — | — | **LITTLE BIT O' SOUL** Music Explosion (J. Katz-J. Kasenentz & E. Chiprut) Laurie 3380 | 2 |
| ★74 | — | — | — | **CAN'T TAKE MY EYES OFF YOU** Frankie Valli (Bob Crewe), Philips 40486 | 1 |
| 75 | 78 | — | — | **JUMP BACK** King Curtis (Jerry Wexler), Atco 6476 | 2 |
| 76 | 77 | 78 | 78 | **ONE HURT DESERVES ANOTHER** Raelets (Ray Charles), Tangerine 296 | 6 |
| ★77 | — | — | — | **FUNNY FAMILIAR FORGOTTEN FEELINGS** Tom Jones (Peter Sullivan), Parrot 40014 | 1 |
| ★78 | — | — | — | **SHAKE** Otis Redding, Volt 149 | 1 |
| ★79 | — | — | — | **HERE WE GO AGAIN** Ray Charles (TRC), ABC 10938 | 1 |
| 80 | 89 | — | — | **AM I GROOVING YOU** Freddie Scott (Bert Berns), Shout 212 | 2 |
| 81 | 86 | 87 | 89 | **FUNKY BROADWAY** Dyke & the Blazers (Coleman & Barrett), Original Sound 64 | 6 |
| 82 | 85 | 89 | — | **I'VE LOST YOU** Jackie Wilson (Carl Davis), Brunswick 55321 | 3 |
| 83 | 84 | — | — | **EIGHT MEN, FOUR WOMEN** O. V. Wright (Willie Mitchell), Back Beat 580 | 2 |
| ★84 | — | — | — | **DING DONG THE WITCH IS DEAD** Fifth Estate (Steve & Bill Jerome), Jubilee 5573 | 1 |
| ★85 | 100 | — | — | **WE HAD A GOOD THING GOIN'** Cyrkle (John Simon), Columbia 44108 | 2 |
| ★86 | — | — | — | **LONG LEGGED GIRL (With the Short Dress On)** Elvis Presley, RCA Victor 9115 | 1 |
| ★87 | — | — | — | **SEVEN ROOMS OF GLOOM** Four Tops (Holland & Dozier), Motown 1110 | 1 |
| ★88 | — | — | — | **SOUND OF LOVE** Five Americans (Dale Hawkins), Abnak 120 | 1 |
| ★89 | — | — | — | **COME TO THE SUNSHINE** Harpers Bizarre (Lenny Waconker), Warner Bros. 7028 | 1 |
| ★90 | — | — | — | **LEOPARD-SKIN PILL-BOX HAT** Bob Dylan (Bob Johnston), Columbia 44069 | 1 |
| 91 | 91 | 97 | 97 | **HEY LOVE** Stevie Wonder (Clarence Paul), Tamla 54147 | 5 |
| 92 | 99 | — | — | **BEAT THE CLOCK** McCoys (F.G.G. Prod.), Bang 543 | 2 |
| 93 | — | — | — | **STOP! AND THINK IT OVER** Perry Como (Andy Wisewell), RCA Victor 9165 | 1 |
| 94 | — | — | — | **STAY TOGETHER YOUNG LOVERS** Brenda & the Tabulations (Bob Finiz), Dionn 501 | 1 |
| 95 | 95 | 100 | — | **SHE SHOT A HOLE IN MY SOUL** Clifford Curry (Buzz Cason), Elf 90002 | 3 |
| 96 | 96 | — | — | **MAKE ME YOURS** Bettye Swann, Money 126 | 2 |
| 97 | — | — | — | **RED ROSES FOR MOM** Bobby Vinton (Robert Mersey), Epic 10168 | 1 |
| 98 | — | — | — | **SUNDAY WILL NEVER BE THE SAME** Spanky and Our Gang (Jerry Ross), Mercury 72679 | 1 |
| 99 | — | — | — | **BABY PLEASE COME BACK HOME** J. J. Barnes (Davis-Barnes), Groovesville 1006 | 1 |
| 100 | — | — | — | **SOUL FINGER** Bar-Kays (Produced by Staff), Volt 148 | 1 |

## HOT 100—A TO Z—(Publisher-Licensee)

Ain't No Mountain High Enough (Jobete, BMI) .... 62
Alfie (Famous, ASCAP) .... 47
All I Need Is You (Jobete, BMI) .... 21
Am I Grooving You? (Web IV, BMI) .... 80
Another Day, Another Heartache (Trousdale, BMI) .. 48
Baby, Please Come Back Home (Groovesville, BMI) 99
Beat the Clock (Doraflo, BMI) .... 92
Beautiful Story, A (Chris Marc-Cotillion, BMI) .... 53
Buy for Me the Rain (Nina, BMI) .... 45
Can't Seem to Make You Mine (Neil-Purple Bottle, BMI) .... 49
Can't Take My Eyes Off You (Saturday/Seasons' Four, BMI) .... 74
Casino Royale (Colgems, ASCAP) .... 30
Close Your Eyes (Tideland, BMI) .... 8
Come on Down to My Boat (Picturetone-Goldstein, BMI) .... 44
Come to the Sunshine (Vantim, BMI) .... 89
Creeque Alley (Trousdale, BMI) .... 13
Dead-End Street (Raw Lou/ Beechwood, BMI) .... 29
Ding Dong the Witch Is Dead (Feist, ASCAP) .... 84
Do It Again a Little Bit Slower (Barton, BMI) .... 46
Don't You Care (Beechwood, BMI) .... 9
Eight Men, Four Women (Don, BMI) .... 83
Friday on My Mind (Unart, BMI) .... 16
Funky Broadway (Drive-In/Routeen, BMI) .... 81
Funny Familiar Forgotten Feelings (Acuff-Rose, BMI) 77
Get Me to the World on Time (Pamona, BMI) .... 40
Girl, You'll Be a Woman Soon (Tallyrand, BMI) .... 11
Girls in Love (Chardon, BMI) .... 65
Groovin' (Slacsar, BMI) .... 1
Happening, The (Jobete, BMI) .... 2
Happy Jack (Essex, ASCAP) .... 31
Happy Together (Chardon, BMI) .... 33
Here Comes My Baby (Mainstay, BMI) .... 18
Here We Go Again (Dirk, BMI) .... 79
Hey, Love (Jobete, BMI) .... 91
Him or Me—What's It Gonne Be? (Daywin, BMI) .. 14
Hip Hug-Her (East, BMI) .... 38
I Could Be So Good to You (Stoutworthy & Sona, BMI) .... 57
I Got Rhythm (New World, ASCAP) .... 6
I Think We're Alone Now (Patricia, BMI) .... 17
I Was Kaiser Bill's Batman (Mills, ASCAP) .... 26
I'll Make Him Love Me (Screen Gems-Columbia, BMI) .... 72
I'm a Man (Essex, ASCAP) .... 24
It's All Over (Acuff-Rose, BMI) .... 71
I've Lost You (Blackwood, BMI) .... 82
Jimmy Mack (Jobete, BMI) .... 36
Jump Back (East, BMI) .... 75
Just Look What You've Done (Jobete, BMI) .... 69
Lay Some Happiness on Me (Four Star Music, BMI) 55
Let Yourself Go (Dynatone, BMI) .... 59
Let's Live for Today (James, BMI) .... 67
Leopard-Skin Pill-Box Hat (Dwarf, ASCAP) .... 90
Little Bit o'Soul (Southern, ASCAP) .... 73
Little Bit You, a Little Bit Me, A (Screen Gems-Columbia, BMI) .... 20
Little Games (Mills, ASCAP) .... 51
Live (Thirty-four/LaBrea, ASCAP) .... 68
Long-Legged Girl (With the Short Dress On) (Presley, BMI) .... 86
Love Me Forever (Rogelle, BMI) .... 64
Make Me Yours (Cash Songs, BMI) .... 96
Making Memories (Feist, ASCAP) .... 35
Melancholy Music Man (Chardon, BMI) .... 43
Mirage (Patricia, BMI) .... 19
Misty Blue (Talmount, BMI) .... 60
My Babe (Tallyrand, BMI) .... 50
My Girl Josephine (Travis, BMI) .... 34
Nothing Takes the Place of You (Su-Ma, BMI) .... 52
On a Carousel (Maribus, BMI) .... 12
One Hurt Deserves Another (Hastings, BMI) .... 76
Ooogum Boogum Song, The (Big Shot, ASCAP) .... 56
Out of Left Field (Press, BMI) .... 70
Portrait of My Love (Piccadilly, BMI) .... 37
Red Roses for Mom (Feather, BMI) .... 97
Release Me (And Let Me Love Again) (Four Star, BMI) .... 7
Respect (East-Time-Walco, BMI) .... 5
Seven Rooms of Gloom (Jobete, BMI) .... 87
Shake (Kags, BMI) .... 78
Shake a Tail Feather (Va-Pac, BMI) .... 28
She Shot a Hole in My Soul (Morrowwood Music, BMI) .... 95
She'd Rather Be With Me (Chardon, BMI) .... 58
Six o'Clock (Faithful Virtue, BMI) .... 32
Somebody to Love (Copper Penny, BMI) .... 22
Somethin' Stupid (Green Wood, BMI) .... 4
Soul Finger (East, BMI) .... 100
Sound of Love (Jetstar, BMI) .... 88
Stay Together Young Lovers (Missile/Rittenhouse, BMI) .... 94
Stop! And Think It Over (Northern, ASCAP) .... 93
Sunshine Girl (Inevitable/Good Sam, BMI) .... 23
Sweet Soul Music (Bedwal, BMI) .... 3
This Is My Song (Shawley, ASCAP) .... 42
Time, Time (April, ASCAP) .... 61
Together (Razor Sharp, BMI) .... 67
Too Many Fish in the Sea & Three Little Fishes (Jobete/Joy, BMI) .... 27
Tramp (Modern, BMI) .... 54
We Had a Good Thing Goin' (Screen Gems-Columbia, BMI) .... 85
Western Union (Jetstar, BMI) .... 41
When I Was Young (Sea Lark/Slamina, BMI) .... 15
When You're Young and in Love (Picturetone, BMI) 39
Whole World Is a Stage, The (Myto, BMI) .... 63
Yellow Balloon (Teeny Bopper, ASCAP) .... 25
You Got What It Takes (Fidelity, BMI) .... 1

## BUBBLING UNDER THE HOT 100

101. NO GOOD TO CRY .... Wildweeds, Cadet 5561
102. FOR YOUR PRECIOUS LOVE .... Oscar Toney Jr., Bell 672
103. SHAKE HANDS AND WALK AWAY CRYING .... Lou Christie, Columbia 44062
104. IT'S COLD OUTSIDE .... Choir, Roulette 4738
105. THAT'S SOMEONE YOU'LL NEVER FORGET .. Elvis Presley, RCA Victor 9115
106. SHAKE .... British Walkers, Cameo 466
107. I FOUND A RAINBOW .... Swingin' Medallions, Smash 2087
108. GOT TO HAVE YOU BACK .... Isley Brothers, Tamla 54146
109. BLUES THEME .... Arrows, Tower 295
110. ONLY LOVE CAN BREAK A HEART .... Margaret Whiting, London 108
111. DOUBLE YELLOW LINE .... Music Machine, Original Sound 71
112. HOLIDAY FOR CLOWNS .... Brian Hyland, Philips 40444
113. I BELIEVE IT ALL .... Pozo-Seco Singers, Columbia 44041
114. MARY IN THE MORNING .... Al Martino, Capitol 5904
115. I WANT YOU TO BE MY BABY .... Ellie Greenwich, United Artists 50151
116. EVERYBODY NEEDS HELP .... Jimmy Holiday, Minit 32016
117. FLOWER CHILDREN .... Marcia Strassman, Uni 55006
118. I CAN'T HELP IT IF I'M STILL IN LOVE WITH YOU .. B. J. Thomas, Sceptor 12194
119. GLASS .... Sandpipers, A&M 851
120. IVY, IVY .... Left Banke, Smash 2089
121. TAKE ME IN YOUR ARMS AND LOVE ME .. Gladys Knight & the Pips, Soul 35033
122. GOTTA LEAVE US ALONE .... Outsiders, Capitol 5892
123. ROUND, ROUND .... Jonathan King, Parrot 3011
124. I'M INDESTRUCTIBLE .... Jack Jones, Kapp 818
125. HERE I AM, BABY .... Barbara McNair, Motown 1106
126. MY OLD CAR .... Lee Dorsey, Amy 987
127. EVERYBODY LOVES A WINNER .... William Bell, Stax 212
128. ME ABOUT YOU .... Mojo Men, Reprise 0580
129. LOVE SONG .... Artistics, Brunswick 55326
130. EVERYBODY LOVES MY BABY ... King Richard's Fluegel Knights, MTA 120
131. HI HO SILVER LINING .... Jeff Beck, Epic 10157
123. ROUND, ROUND .... Jonathan King, Parrot 3011
133. YOU'RE ALL I NEED .... Bobby Bland, Duke 416
134. I CAN'T GET NO SATISFACTION .... Jimmy McGriff, Solid State 2510
135. WHY? (AM I TREATED SO BAD) .... Staple Singers, Epic 10158

Compiled from national retail sales and radio station airplay by the Music Popularity Dept. of Record Market Research, Billboard.

# Billboard HOT 100

For Week Ending May 27, 1967

★ STAR performer—Sides registering greatest proportionate upward progress this week.

Ⓡ Record Industry Association of America seal of certification as million selling single.

| This Week | 1 Wk. Ago | 2 Wks. Ago | 3 Wks. Ago | TITLE Artist (Producer), Label & Number | Weeks On Chart |
|---|---|---|---|---|---|
| 1 | 1 | 4 | 19 | **GROOVIN'** — Young Rascals (Young Rascals), Atlantic 2401 | 6 |
| 2 | 5 | 14 | 26 | **RESPECT** — Aretha Franklin (Jerry Wexler), Atlantic 2403 | 5 |
| 3 | 6 | 9 | 17 | **I GOT RHYTHM** — Happenings (The Tokens), B. T. Puppy 527 | 8 |
| 4 | 7 | 13 | 20 | **RELEASE ME (And Let Me Love Again)** — Engelbert Humperdinck, Parrot 40011 | 8 |
| 5 | 5 | 1 | 2 | **THE HAPPENING** — Supremes (Holland & Dozier), Motown 1107 | 8 |
| 6 | 3 | 2 | 3 | **SWEET SOUL MUSIC** — Arthur Conley (Otis Redding), Atco 6463 | 12 |
| 7 | 14 | 21 | 33 | **HIM OR ME—WHAT'S IT GONNA BE?** — Paul Revere & the Raiders (Terry Melcher), Columbia 44094 | 5 |
| 8 | 13 | 22 | 44 | **CREEQUE ALLEY** — Mamas & the Papas (Lou Adler), Dunhill 4083 | 5 |
| 9 | 4 | 3 | 1 | **SOMETHIN' STUPID** — Nancy Sinatra & Frank Sinatra (Jimmy Bowen & Lee Hazlewood), Reprise 0561 | 11 |
| 10 | 11 | 11 | 21 | **GIRL, YOU'LL BE A WOMAN SOON** — Neil Diamond (Jeff Barry & Ellie Greenwich), Bang 542 | 8 |
| 11 | 12 | 12 | 12 | **ON A CAROUSEL** — Hollies (Ron Richards), Imperial 66231 | 12 |
| 12 | 9 | 6 | 7 | **DON'T YOU CARE** — Buckinghams (Jim Guercio), Columbia 44053 | 12 |
| 13 | 18 | 19 | 25 | **HERE COMES MY BABY** — Tremeloes, Epic 10139 | 8 |
| 14 | 19 | 24 | 40 | **MIRAGE** — Tommy James & the Shondells (Bo Gentry & Ritchie Cordell), Roulette 4736 | 5 |
| 15 | 21 | 28 | 42 | **ALL I NEED IS YOU** — Temptations (F. Wilson), Gordy 7061 | 5 |
| 16 | 16 | 18 | 18 | **FRIDAY ON MY MIND** — Easybeats (Shell Talmy), United Artists 50106 | 11 |
| 17 | 22 | 31 | 31 | **SOMEBODY TO LOVE** — Jefferson Airplane (Rick Jarrard), RCA Victor 9140 | 9 |
| 18 | 8 | 8 | 8 | **CLOSE YOUR EYES** — Peaches & Herb (Dave Kapralik-Ken Williams), Date 1549 | 10 |
| 19 | 10 | 7 | 9 | **YOU GOT WHAT IT TAKES** — Dave Clark Five (Dave Clark), Epic 10144 | 9 |
| 20 | 23 | 25 | 35 | **SUNSHINE GIRL** — Parade (Jerry Riopelle), A&M 841 | 7 |
| 21 | 26 | 34 | 46 | **I WAS KAISER BILL'S BATMAN** — Whistling Jack Smith, Deram 85003 | 5 |
| 22 | 15 | 15 | 15 | **WHEN I WAS YOUNG** — Eric Burdon & the Animals (Tom Wilson), MGM 13721 | 8 |
| 23 | 17 | 10 | 6 | **I THINK WE'RE ALONE NOW** — Tommy James and the Shondells (Cordell-Gentry), Roulette 4720 | 16 |
| 24 | 27 | 40 | 57 | **TOO MANY FISH IN THE SEA & THREE LITTLE FISHES** — Mitch Ryder & the Detroit Wheels (Bob Crewe), New Voice 822 | 5 |
| 25 | 28 | 30 | 41 | **SHAKE A TAIL FEATHER** — James & Bobby Purify (Papa Don, Cogbill, Young, Emmons & Chrisman), Bell 669 | 7 |
| 26 | 31 | 41 | 51 | **HAPPY JACK** — Who, Decca 32114 | 7 |
| 27 | 30 | 37 | 39 | **CASINO ROYALE** — Herb Alpert & the Tijuana Brass (Herb Alpert & Jerry Moss), A&M 850 | 8 |
| 28 | 39 | 49 | 59 | **WHEN YOU'RE YOUNG AND IN LOVE** — Marvelettes (J. Dean & William Weatherspoon), Tamla 54150 | 6 |
| 29 | 34 | 35 | 38 | **MY GIRL JOSEPHINE** — Jerry Jaye, Hi 2120 | 7 |
| 30 | 32 | 48 | 64 | **SIX O'CLOCK** — Lovin' Spoonful (Erik Jacobsen), Kama Sutra 225 | 4 |
| 31 | 25 | 26 | 29 | **YELLOW BALLOON** — Yellow Balloon (Ken Handler & Yoder Critch), Canterbury 508 | 9 |
| 32 | 29 | 29 | 32 | **DEAD END STREET** — Lou Rawls (David Axelrod), Capitol 5869 | 10 |
| 33 | 20 | 5 | 4 | **A LITTLE BIT YOU, A LITTLE BIT ME** — Monkees (Jeff Barry), Colgems 1004 | 10 |
| 34 | 44 | 72 | 85 | **COME ON DOWN TO MY BOAT** — Every Mother's Son (Wes Farrell), MGM 13733 | 4 |
| 35 | 46 | 68 | 86 | **DO IT AGAIN A LITTLE BIT SLOWER** — Jon & Robin & the In Crowd (Dale Hawkins), Abram 119 | 4 |
| 36 | 37 | 44 | 48 | **PORTRAIT OF MY LOVE** — Tokens (Bright Tunes Prod.), Warner Bros. 5900 | 7 |
| 37 | 47 | 61 | 68 | **ALFIE** — Dionne Warwick (Bacharach-David), Scepter 12187 | 8 |
| 38 | 38 | 42 | 49 | **HIP HUG-HER** — Booker T. & the M. G.'s (Prod. By Staff), Stax 211 | 10 |
| 39 | 58 | 88 | — | **SHE'D RATHER BE WITH ME** — Turtles (Joe Wissert), White Whale 249 | 3 |
| 40 | 73 | 90 | — | **LITTLE BIT O' SOUL** — Music Explosion (J. Katz-J. Kasenentz & E. Chiprut), Laurie 3380 | 3 |
| 41 | 49 | 57 | 63 | **CAN'T SEEM TO MAKE YOU MINE** — Seeds (Marcus Tybalt), GNP Crescendo 354 | 5 |
| 42 | 54 | 64 | 79 | **TRAMP** — Otis & Carla (Prod. by Staff), Stax 216 | 4 |
| 43 | 65 | 80 | — | **GIRLS IN LOVE** — Gary Lewis & the Playboys (Koppelman-Rubin-Klein), Liberty 55971 | 3 |
| 44 | 35 | 36 | 36 | **MAKING MEMORIES** — Frankie Laine (Bob Thiele), ABC 10924 | 8 |
| 45 | 48 | 60 | 75 | **ANOTHER DAY, ANOTHER HEARTACHE** — 5th Dimension (Johnny Rivers & Marc Gordon), Soul City 755 | 5 |
| 46 | 66 | 87 | — | **LET'S LIVE FOR TODAY** — Grass Roots (Steve Barri & P. F. Sloan), Dunhill 4084 | 3 |
| 47 | 62 | 79 | — | **AIN'T NO MOUNTAIN HIGH ENOUGH** — Marvin Gaye & Tammi Terrell (H. Fuqua & J. Bristol), Tamla 54149 | 3 |
| 48 | 36 | 20 | 11 | **JIMMY MACK** — Martha and the Vandellas (Holland-Dozier), Gordy 7058 | 14 |
| 49 | 98 | — | — | **SUNDAY WILL NEVER BE THE SAME** — Spanky and Our Gang (Jerry Ross), Mercury 72679 | 2 |
| 50 | 87 | — | — | **7 ROOMS OF GLOOM** — Four Tops (Holland & Dozier), Motown 1110 | 2 |
| 51 | 51 | 53 | 56 | **LITTLE GAMES** — Yardbirds (Mickie Most), Epic 10156 | 6 |
| 52 | — | — | — | **WINDY** — The Association (Bones Howe), Warner Bros. 7041 | 1 |
| 53 | 74 | — | — | **CAN'T TAKE MY EYES OFF YOU** — Frankie Valli (Bob Crewe), Philips 40446 | 2 |
| 54 | 56 | 56 | 66 | **THE OOGUM BOOGUM SONG** — Brenton Wood (Hooven-Winn), Double Shot 111 | 7 |
| 55 | 55 | 55 | 65 | **LAY SOME HAPPINESS ON ME** — Dean Martin (Jimmy Bowen), Reprise 0571 | 7 |
| 56 | 59 | 75 | 90 | **LET YOURSELF GO** — James Brown & the Famous Flames (James Brown), King 6100 | 4 |
| 57 | 57 | 62 | 72 | **I COULD BE SO GOOD TO YOU** — Don & the Goodtimes (Jack Nitzche), Epic 10145 | 6 |
| 58 | 84 | — | — | **DING DONG THE WITCH IS DEAD** — Fifth Estate (Steve & Bill Jerome), Jubilee 5573 | 2 |
| 59 | 60 | 70 | 82 | **MISTY BLUE** — Eddy Arnold (Chet Atkins), RCA Victor 9182 | 4 |
| 60 | 64 | 74 | 83 | **LOVE ME FOREVER** — Roger Williams (Hy Grill), Kapp 821 | 4 |
| 61 | 61 | 76 | 80 | **TIME, TIME** — Ed Ames (Jim Foglesong), RCA Victor 9178 | 4 |
| 62 | 78 | — | — | **SHAKE** — Otis Redding, Volt 149 | 2 |
| 63 | 52 | 52 | 58 | **NOTHING TAKES THE PLACE OF YOU** — Toussaint McCall (Jewel Productions), Ronn 3 | 10 |
| 64 | 79 | — | — | **HERE WE GO AGAIN** — Ray Charles (TRC), ABC 10938 | 2 |
| 65 | 53 | 58 | 71 | **A BEAUTIFUL STORY** — Sonny & Cher (Bill Rinehart), Atco 6480 | 5 |
| 66 | 88 | — | — | **SOUND OF LOVE** — Five Americans (Dale Hawkins), Abnak 120 | 2 |
| 67 | 67 | 82 | 84 | **TOGETHER** — Intruders, Gamble 205 | 5 |
| 68 | 50 | 51 | 55 | **MY BABE** — Ronnie Dove (Neil Diamond), Diamond 221 | 6 |
| 69 | 43 | 47 | 47 | **MELANCHOLY MUSIC MAN** — Righteous Brothers (Joe Wissert), Verve 10507 | 6 |
| 70 | 77 | — | — | **FUNNY FAMILIAR FORGOTTEN FEELINGS** — Tom Jones (Peter Sullivan), Parrot 40014 | 2 |
| 71 | 86 | — | — | **LONG LEGGED GIRL (With the Short Dress On)** — Elvis Presley, RCA Victor 9115 | 2 |
| 72 | 85 | 100 | — | **WE HAD A GOOD THING GOIN'** — Cyrkle (John Simon), Columbia 44108 | 3 |
| 73 | 80 | 89 | — | **AM I GROOVING YOU** — Freddie Scott (Bert Berns), Shout 212 | 3 |
| 74 | 89 | — | — | **COME TO THE SUNSHINE** — Harpers Bizarre (Lenny Waconker), Warner Bros. 7028 | 2 |
| 75 | 75 | 78 | — | **JUMP BACK** — King Curtis (Jerry Wexler), Atco 6476 | 3 |
| 76 | — | — | — | **DON'T BLAME THE CHILDREN** — Sammy Davis Jr. (Jimmy Bowen), Reprise 0566 | 1 |
| 77 | — | — | — | **MARY IN THE MORNING** — Al Martino (Tom Morgan & Arvin Holtzman), Capitol 5904 | 1 |
| 78 | — | — | — | **FOR YOUR PRECIOUS LOVE** — Oscar Toney Jr. (Papa Don, Coghill, Emmons, Chrisman & Young), Bell 672 | 1 |
| 79 | — | — | — | **NEW YORK MINING DISASTER 1941 (Have You Seen My Wife Mr. Jones)** — The Bee Gees (Ossie Byrne), Atco 6487 | 1 |
| 80 | 83 | 84 | — | **EIGHT MEN, FOUR WOMEN** — O. V. Wright (Willie Mitchell), Back Beat 580 | 3 |
| 81 | — | — | — | **SOCIETY'S CHILD** — Janis Ian (Shadow Morton), Verve 5027 | 1 |
| 82 | 82 | 85 | 89 | **I'VE LOST YOU** — Jackie Wilson (Carl Davis), Brunswick 55321 | 4 |
| 83 | — | — | — | **OOH BABY BABY** — Five Stairsteps (Curtis Mayfield), Windy C 607 | 1 |
| 84 | 94 | — | — | **STAY TOGETHER YOUNG LOVERS** — Brenda & the Tabulations (Bob Finiz), Dionn 501 | 2 |
| 85 | 90 | — | — | **LEOPARD-SKIN PILL-BOX HAT** — Bob Dylan (Bob Johnston), Columbia 44069 | 2 |
| 86 | — | — | — | **YOU CAN'T STAND ALONE** — Wilson Picket (Jerry Wexler), Atlantic 2412 | 1 |
| 87 | — | — | — | **YOU GAVE ME SOMETHING (And Everything Is All Right)** — Fantastic Four (Kent, Wingate, Weems), Ric Tic 128 | 1 |
| 88 | — | — | — | **ME ABOUT YOU** — The Mojo Men (Lenny Waronker), Reprise 0580 | 1 |
| 89 | — | — | — | **BOWLING GREEN** — The Everly Brothers (Dick Glasser), Warner Bros. 7020 | 1 |
| 90 | 91 | 91 | 97 | **HEY LOVE** — Stevie Wonder (Clarence Paul), Tamla 54147 | 6 |
| 91 | — | — | — | **HELLO, HELLO** — Claudine Longet (Tommy LiPuma), A&M 846 | 1 |
| 92 | — | — | — | **THAT'S SOMEONE YOU NEVER FORGET** — Elvis Presley, RCA Victor 9115 | 1 |
| 93 | 93 | — | — | **STOP! AND THINK IT OVER** — Perry Como (Andy Wiswell), RCA Victor 9165 | 2 |
| 94 | 100 | — | — | **SOUL FINGER** — Bar-Kays (Produced by Staff), Volt 148 | 2 |
| 95 | 97 | — | — | **RED ROSES FOR MOM** — Bobby Vinton (Robert Mersey), Epic 10168 | 2 |
| 96 | 99 | — | — | **BABY, PLEASE COME BACK HOME** — J. J. Barnes (Davis-Barnes), Groovesville 1006 | 2 |
| 97 | — | — | — | **I WANT YOU TO BE MY BABY** — Ellie Greenwich (Bob Crewe), United Artists 50151 | 3 |
| 98 | — | — | — | **SAN FRANCISCO "WEAR SOME FLOWERS IN YOUR HAIR"** — Scott McKenzie (John Phillips & Lou Adler), Ode 103 | 1 |
| 99 | — | — | — | **HOLIDAY FOR CLOWNS** — Brian Hyland (Snuff Garrett), Philips 40444 | 1 |
| 100 | — | — | — | **NO GOOD TO CRY** — The Wildweeds (J. Greenberg & Trod Nossel), Cadet 5561 | 1 |

## HOT 100—A TO Z—(Publisher-Licensee)

Ain't No Mountain High Enough (Jobete, BMI) ... 47
Alfie (Famous, ASCAP) ... 37
All I Need Is You (Jobete, BMI) ... 15
Am I Grooving You? (Unart & Web IV, BMI) ... 73
Another Day, Another Heartache (Trousdale, BMI) ... 45
Baby, Please Come Back Home (Groovesville, BMI) ... 96
Beautiful Story, A (Chris Marc-Cotillion, BMI) ... 65
Bowling Green (Rook, BMI) ... 89
Can't Seem to Make You Mine (Neil-Purple Bottle, BMI) ... 41
Can't Take My Eyes Off You (Saturday/Seasons' Four, BMI) ... 53
Casino Royale (Colgems, ASCAP) ... 27
Close Your Eyes (Tideland, BMI) ... 18
Come on Down to My Boat (Picturetone-Goldstein, BMI) ... 34
Come to the Sunshine (Vantim, BMI) ... 74
Creeque Alley (Trousdale, BMI) ... 8
Dead-End Street (Raw Lou/Beechwood, BMI) ... 32
Ding Dong the Witch Is Dead (Feist, ASCAP) ... 58
Do It Again a Little Bit Slower (Barton, BMI) ... 35
Don't Blame the Children (Saloon Songs, BMI) ... 76
Don't You Care (Beechwood, BMI) ... 12
Eight Men, Four Women (Don, BMI) ... 80
For Your Precious Love (Sunflower, BMI) ... 78
Friday on My Mind (Unart, BMI) ... 16
Funny Familiar Forgotten Feelings (Acuff-Rose, BMI) ... 70
Girl, You'll Be a Wonma Soon (Tallyrand, BMI) ... 10
Girls in Love (Chardon, BMI) ... 43
Groovin' (Slacsar, BMI) ... 1
Happening, The (Jobete, BMI) ... 5
Happy Jack (Essex, ASCAP) ... 26
Hello, Hello (Great Honesty, BMI) ... 91
Here Comes My Baby (Mainstay, BMI) ... 13
Here We Go Again (Dirk, BMI) ... 64
Hey, Love (Jobete, BMI) ... 90
Him or Me—What's It Gonna Be? (Daywin, BMI) ... 7

Hip Hug-Her (East, BMI) ... 38
Holiday for Clowns (Viva Music, BMI) ... 99
I Could Be So Good to You (Strousworthy & Sona, BMI) ... 57
I Got Rhythm (New World, ASCAP) ... 3
I Think We're Alone Now (Patricia, BMI) ... 23
I Want You to be My Baby (Hendricks, ASCAP) ... 97
I've Lost You (Blackwood, BMI) ... 82
I Was Kaiser Bill's Batman (Mills, ASCAP) ... 21
Jimmy Mack (Jobete, BMI) ... 48
Jump Back (East, BMI) ... 75
Lay Some Happiness on Me (Four Star Music, BMI) ... 55
Let Yourself Go (Dynatone, BMI) ... 56
Let's Live for Today (James, BMI) ... 46
Leopard-Skin Pill-Box Hat (Dwarf, ASCAP) ... 85
Little Bit o' Soul (Southern, ASCAP) ... 40
Little Bit You, a Little Bit Me, A (Missile/Rittenhouse, BMI) ... 33
Little Games (Mills, ASCAP) ... 51
Long-Legged Girl (With the Short Dress On) (Presley, BMI) ... 71
Love Me Forever (Rogelle, BMI) ... 60
Making Memories (Feist, ASCAP) ... 44
Mary in the Morning (Pamco, BMI) ... 77
Me About You (Chardon, BMI) ... 88
Melancholy Music Man (Chardon, BMI) ... 69
Mirage (Patricia, BMI) ... 14
Misty Blue (Talmount, BMI) ... 59
My Babe (Tallyrand, BMI) ... 68
My Girl Josephine (Travis, BMI) ... 29
Nothing Takes the Place of You (Su-Ma, BMI) ... 63
New York Mining Disaster 1941 (Have You Seen My Wife Mr. Jones) (Abigail, BMI) ... 79
No Good to Cry (Abigail, BMI) ... 100
On a Carousel (Maribus, BMI) ... 11
Ooh Baby, Baby (Jobete, BMI) ... 83
Ooogum Boogum Song, The (Big Shot, ASCAP) ... 54
Portrait of My Love (Piccadilly, BMI) ... 36

Red Roses for Mom (Feather, BMI) ... 95
Release Me (And Let Me Love Again) (Four Star, BMI) ... 4
Respect (East-Time-Walco, BMI) ... 2
San Francisco "Wear Some Flowers in Your Hair" (Trousdale, BMI) ... 98
7 Rooms of Gloom (Jobete, BMI) ... 50
Shake (Kags, BMI) ... 62
Shake a Tail Feather (Va-Pac, BMI) ... 25
She'd Rather Be With Me (Chardon, BMI) ... 39
Six-o'Clock (Faithful Virtue, BMI) ... 30
Society's Child (Wabatuck, BMI) ... 81
Somebody to Love (Cooper Penny, BMI) ... 17
Somethin' Stupid (Green Wood, BMI) ... 9
Soul Finger (East, BMI) ... 94
Sound of Love (Jetstar, BMI) ... 66
Stay Together Young Lovers (Screen Gems-Columbia, BMI) ... 84
Stop! And Think It Over (Northern, ASCAP) ... 93
Sunday Will Never Be the Same (Pamco, BMI) ... 49
Sunshine Girl (Inevitable/Good Sam, BMI) ... 20
Sweet Soul Music (Redwal, BMI) ... 6
That's Someone You Never Forget (Presley, BMI) ... 92
Time, Time (April, ASCAP) ... 61
Together (Razor Sharp, BMI) ... 67
Too Many Fish in the Sea & Three Little Fishes (Jobete/Joy, BMI) ... 24
Tramp (Modern, BMI) ... 42
We Had a Good Thing Goin' (Screen Gems-Columbia, BMI) ... 72
When I Was Young (Sea Lark/Slamina, BMI) ... 22
When You're Young and in Love (Picturetone, BMI) ... 28
Yellow Balloon (Teeny Bopper, ASCAP) ... 31
You Can't Stand Alone (T.M., BMI) ... 86
You Gave Me Something (And Everything Is All Right) (Myto, BMI) ... 87

## BUBBLING UNDER THE HOT 100

101. IT'S COLD OUTSIDE ............ Choir, Roulette 4738
102. BEAT THE CLOCK ............ McCoys, Bang 543
103. SHAKE HANDS & WALK AWAY CRYING .... Lou Christie, Columbia 44062
104. MAKE ME YOURS ............ Bettye Swann, Money 126
105. BLUES THEME ............ Arrows, Tower 295
106. PAY YOU BACK WITH INTEREST ........ Hollies, Imperial 66240
107. SHE SHOT A WHOLE IN MY SOUL ...... Clifford Curry, Elf 90002
108. FUNKY BROADWAY ........ Dyke & the Blazers, Original Sound 64
109. ONLY LOVE CAN BREAK A HEART ...... Margaret Whiting, London 108
110. I'LL MAKE HIM LOVE ME .......... Barbara Lewis, Atlantic 2400
111. LOVE SONG ............ Artistics, Brunswick 55326
112. GLASS ............ Sandpipers, A&M 851
113. MY OLD CAR ............ Lee Dorsey, Amy 987
114. I BELIEVED IT ALL ........ Pozo Seco Singers, Columbia 44041
115. FLOWER CHILDREN ........ Marcia Strassman, Uni 55006
116. UP, UP AND AWAY ........ 5th Dimension, Soul City 756
117. LOVE, LOVE, LOVE, LOVE, LOVE ...... Terry Knight and the Pack, Lucky Eleven 235
118. AIN'T NOTHIN' BUT A HOUSE PARTY .... Show Stoppers, Showtime 101
119. IVY, IVY ............ Lee Banke, Smash 2089
120. WHY? (AM I TREATED SO BAD) ....... Sweet Inspirations, Atlantic 2410
121. GOTTA LEAVE US ALONE ........ Outsiders, Capitol 5892
122. ROUND, ROUND ............ Jonathan King, Parrot 3011
123. HI NO SILVER LINING ........ Jeff Beck, Epic 10157
124. UP TO NOW ............ Trini Lopez, Reprise 0574
125. UP, UP AND AWAY ............ Johnny Mann, Liberty 55972
126. I STAND ACCUSED ............ Glories, Date 1553
127. EVERYBODY LOVES A WINNER ........ William Bell, Atlantic 2400
128. EVERYBODY LOVES MY BABY ....... King Richard's Fluegel Knights, MTA 120
129. MINISKIRTS IN MOSCOW OR OOH LA LA ... Bob Crewe Generation, Dyno Voice 233
130. I CAN'T GET NO SATISFACTION ...... Otis McGriff, Solid State 2510
131. LIGHT MY FIRE ............ Doors, Elektra 45615
132. YOU'RE ALL I NEED ............ Bobby Bland, Duke 416
133. WHY? (AM I TREATED SO BAD) ........ Staple Singers, Epic 10158
134. ALL THE TIME ............ Jack Greene, Decca 32123
135. THEY'RE HERE ............ Boots Walker, Rust 5115

*Compiled from national retail sales and radio station airplay by the Music Popularity Dept. of Record Market Research, Billboard*

# Billboard HOT 100

For Week Ending June 3, 1967

★ STAR performer—Sides registering greatest proportionate upward progress this week.

● Record Industry Association of America seal of certification as million selling single.

| This Week | 1 Wk. Ago | 2 Wks. Ago | 3 Wks. Ago | TITLE Artist (Producer), Label & Number | Weeks On Chart |
|---|---|---|---|---|---|
| 1★ | 2 | 5 | 14 | RESPECT — Aretha Franklin (Jerry Wexler), Atlantic 2403 | 6 |
| 2 | 1 | 1 | 4 | GROOVIN' — Young Rascals (Young Rascals), Atlantic 2401 | 7 |
| 3 | 3 | 6 | 9 | I GOT RHYTHM — Happenings (The Tokens) B.T. Puppy 527 | 9 |
| 4 | 4 | 7 | 13 | RELEASE ME (And Let Me Love Again) — Engelbert Humperdinck, Parrot 40011 | 9 |
| 5★ | 8 | 13 | 22 | CREEQUE ALLEY — Mamas & the Papas (Lou Adler), Dunhill 4083 | 6 |
| 6 | 7 | 14 | 21 | HIM OR ME—WHAT'S IT GONNA BE? — Paul Revere & the Raiders (Terry Melcher), Columbia 44094 | 6 |
| 7 | 5 | 5 | 1 | THE HAPPENING — Supremes (Holland & Dozier), Motown 1107 | 9 |
| 8 | 6 | 3 | 2 | SWEET SOUL MUSIC — Arthur Conley (Otis Redding), Atco 6463 | 13 |
| 9★ | 17 | 22 | 31 | SOMEBODY TO LOVE — Jefferson Airplane (Rick Jarrard), RCA Victor 9140 | 10 |
| 10 | 15 | 21 | 28 | ALL I NEED IS YOU — Temptations (F. Wilson), Gordy 7061 | 6 |
| 11 | 14 | 19 | 24 | MIRAGE — Tommy James & the Shondells (Bo Gentry & Ritchie Cordell), Roulette 4736 | 6 |
| 12 | 10 | 11 | 11 | GIRL, YOU'LL BE A WOMAN SOON — Neil Diamond (Jeff Barry & Ellie Greenwich), Bang 542 | 9 |
| 13 | 13 | 18 | 19 | HERE COMES MY BABY — Tremeloes, Epic 10139 | 9 |
| 14★ | 39 | 58 | 88 | SHE'D RATHER BE WITH ME — Turtles (Joe Wissert), White Whale 249 | 4 |
| 15 | 11 | 12 | 12 | ON A CAROUSEL — Hollies (Ron Richards), Imperial 66231 | 12 |
| 16 | 9 | 4 | 3 | SOMETHIN' STUPID — Nancy Sinatra & Frank Sinatra (Jimmy Bowen & Lee Hazlewood), Reprise 0561 | 12 |
| 17★ | 40 | 73 | 90 | LITTLE BIT O' SOUL — Music Explosion (J. Katz-J. Kasenetz & E. Chiprut), Laurie 3380 | 4 |
| 18 | 16 | 16 | 18 | FRIDAY ON MY MIND — Easybeats (Shell Talmy) United Artists 50106 | 12 |
| 19★ | 30 | 32 | 48 | SIX O'CLOCK — Lovin' Spoonful (Erik Jacobsen), Kama Sutra 225 | 5 |
| 20 | 21 | 26 | 34 | I WAS KAISER BILL'S BATMAN — Whistling Jack Smith, Deram 85003 | 7 |
| 21 | 18 | 8 | 8 | CLOSE YOUR EYES — Peaches & Herb (Dave Kapralik-Ken Williams), Date 1549 | 11 |
| 22 | 12 | 9 | 7 | DON'T YOU CARE — Buckinghams (Jim Guercio), Columbia 44053 | 13 |
| 23★ | 28 | 39 | 49 | WHEN YOU'RE YOUNG AND IN LOVE — Marvelettes (J. Dean & William Weatherspoon), Tamla 54150 | 7 |
| 24 | 26 | 31 | 41 | HAPPY JACK — Who, Decca 32114 | 6 |
| 25 | 25 | 28 | 30 | SHAKE A TAIL FEATHER — James & Bobby Purify (Papa Don, Coghill, Young, Emmons & Chrisman), Bell 669 | 8 |
| 26★ | 35 | 46 | 68 | DO IT AGAIN A LITTLE BIT SLOWER — Jon & Robin & the In Crowd (Dale Hawkins), Abnak 119 | 5 |
| 27 | 49 | 98 | — | SUNDAY WILL NEVER BE THE SAME — Spanky and Our Gang (Jerry Ross), Mercury 72679 | 3 |
| 28★ | 52 | — | — | WINDY — The Association (Bones Howe), Warner Bros. 7041 | 2 |
| 29 | 34 | 44 | 72 | COME ON DOWN TO MY BOAT — Every Mother's Son (Wes Farrell), MGM 13733 | 5 |
| 30★ | 50 | 87 | — | 7 ROOMS OF GLOOM — Four Tops (Holland & Dozier), Motown 1110 | 3 |
| 31 | 20 | 23 | 25 | SUNSHINE GIRL — Parade (Jerry Riopelle), A&M 841 | 8 |
| 32 | 24 | 27 | 40 | TOO MANY FISH IN THE SEA & THREE LITTLE FISHES — Mitch Ryder & the Detroit Wheels (Bob Crewe), New Voice 822 | 6 |
| 33★ | 53 | 74 | — | CAN'T TAKE MY EYES OFF YOU — Frankie Valli (Bob Crewe), Philips 40446 | 3 |
| 34 | 29 | 34 | 35 | MY GIRL JOSEPHINE — Jerry Jaye, Hi 2120 | 8 |
| 35 | 37 | 47 | 61 | ALFIE — Dionne Warwick (Bacharach-David), Scepter 12187 | 9 |
| 36★ | 46 | 66 | 87 | LET'S LIVE FOR TODAY — Grass Roots (Steve Barri & P.F. Sloan), Dunhill 4084 | 4 |
| 37 | 38 | 38 | 42 | HIP HUG-HER — Booker T. & the M.G.'s (Prod. By Staff), Stax 211 | 11 |
| 38 | 27 | 30 | 37 | CASINO ROYALE — Herb Alpert & the Tijuana Brass (Herb Alpert & Jerry Moss), A&M 850 | 9 |
| 39 | 47 | 62 | 79 | AIN'T NO MOUNTAIN HIGH ENOUGH — Marvin Gaye & Tammi Terrell (H. Fuqua & J. Bristol), Tamla 54149 | 4 |
| 40 | 42 | 54 | 64 | TRAMP — Otis & Carla (Prod. by Staff), Stax 216 | 5 |
| 41 | 41 | 49 | 57 | CAN'T SEEM TO MAKE YOU MINE — Seeds (Marcus Tybalt), GNP Crescendo 354 | 6 |
| 42 | 43 | 65 | 80 | GIRLS IN LOVE — Gary Lewis & the Playboys (Koppelman-Rubin-Klein), Liberty 55971 | 4 |
| 43 | 19 | 10 | 7 | YOU GOT WHAT IT TAKES — Dave Clark Five (Dave Clark), Epic 10144 | 10 |
| 44 | 54 | 56 | 56 | THE OOGUM BOOGUM SONG — Brenton Wood (Hooven-Winn), Double Shot 111 | 8 |
| 45 | 58 | 84 | — | DING DONG THE WITCH IS DEAD — Fifth Estate (Steve & Bill Jerome), Jubilee 5573 | 3 |
| 46 | 23 | 17 | 10 | I THINK WE'RE ALONE NOW — Tommy James and the Shondells (Cordell-Gentry), Roulette 4720 | 17 |
| 47 | 22 | 15 | 15 | WHEN I WAS YOUNG — Eric Burdon & the Animals (Tom Wilson), MGM 13721 | 9 |
| 48 | 32 | 29 | 29 | DEAD END STREET — Lou Rawls (David Axelrod), Capitol 5869 | 11 |
| 49★ | 79 | — | — | NEW YORK MINING DISASTER 1941 (Have You Seen My Wife Mr. Jones) — The Bee Gees (Ossie Byrne), Atco 6487 | 2 |
| 50 | 36 | 37 | 44 | PORTRAIT OF MY LOVE — Tokens (Bright Tunes Prod.), Warner Bros. 5900 | 8 |
| 51 | 56 | 59 | 75 | LET YOURSELF GO — James Brown & the Famous Flames (James Brown), King 6100 | 5 |
| 52 | 66 | 88 | — | SOUND OF LOVE — Five Americans (Dale Hawkins), Abnak 120 | 3 |
| 53 | 64 | 79 | — | HERE WE GO AGAIN — Ray Charles (TRC), ABC 10938 | 3 |
| 54 | 31 | 25 | 26 | YELLOW BALLOON — Yellow Balloon (Ken Handler & Yoder Critch), Canterbury 508 | 10 |
| 55★ | 98 | — | — | SAN FRANCISCO "WEAR SOME FLOWERS IN YOUR HAIR" — Scott McKenzie (John Phillips & Lou Adler), Ode 103 | 2 |
| 56 | 57 | 57 | 62 | I COULD BE SO GOOD TO YOU — Don & the Goodtimes (Jack Nitzche), Epic 10145 | 7 |
| 57 | 70 | 77 | — | FUNNY FAMILIAR FORGOTTEN FEELINGS — Tom Jones (Peter Sullivan), Parrot 40014 | 3 |
| 58 | 62 | 78 | — | SHAKE — Otis Redding, Volt 149 | 3 |
| 59 | 59 | 60 | 70 | MISTY BLUE — Eddy Arnold (Chet Atkins), RCA Victor 9182 | 5 |
| 60 | 74 | 89 | — | COME TO THE SUNSHINE — Harpers Bizarre (Lenny Waconker), Warner Bros. 7028 | 3 |
| 61 | 76 | — | — | DON'T BLAME THE CHILDREN — Sammy Davis Jr. (Jimmy Bowen), Reprise 0566 | 2 |
| 62 | 77 | — | — | MARY IN THE MORNING — Al Martino (Tom Morgan & Arvin Holtzman), Capitol 5904 | 2 |
| 63 | 78 | — | — | FOR YOUR PRECIOUS LOVE — Oscar Toney Jr. (Papa Don, Coghill, Emmons, Chrisman & Young), Bell 672 | 2 |
| 64 | 67 | 67 | 82 | TOGETHER — Intruders, Gamble 205 | 6 |
| 65 | 60 | 64 | 74 | LOVE ME FOREVER — Roger Williams (Hy Grill), Kapp 821 | 5 |
| 66 | 81 | — | — | SOCIETY'S CHILD — Janis Ian (Shadow Morton), Verve 5027 | 2 |
| 67 | 45 | 48 | 60 | ANOTHER DAY, ANOTHER HEARTACHE — 5th Dimension (Johnny Rivers & Marc Gordon), Soul City 755 | 6 |
| 68★ | 71 | 86 | — | LONG LEGGED GIRL (With the Short Dress On) — Elvis Presley, RCA Victor 9115 | 3 |
| 69 | 61 | 61 | 76 | TIME, TIME — Ed Ames (Jim Foglesong), RCA Victor 9178 | 5 |
| 70 | — | — | — | THE TRACKS OF MY TEARS — Johnny Rivers (Lou Adler), Imperial 66244 | 1 |
| 71 | 63 | 52 | 52 | NOTHING TAKES THE PLACE OF YOU — Toussaint McCall (Jewel Productions), Ronn 3 | 11 |
| 72 | 72 | 85 | 100 | WE HAD A GOOD THING GOIN' — Cyrkle (John Simon), Columbia 44108 | 4 |
| 73 | 73 | 80 | 89 | AM I GROOVING YOU — Freddie Scott (Bert Berns), Shout 212 | 4 |
| 74 | 75 | 75 | 78 | JUMP BACK — King Curtis (Jerry Wexler), Atco 6476 | 4 |
| 75 | — | — | — | PAY YOU BACK WITH INTEREST — Hollies, Imperial 66240 | 1 |
| 76★ | — | — | — | DON'T SLEEP IN THE SUBWAY — Petula Clark (Tony Hatch), Warner Bros. 7049 | 1 |
| 77 | 89 | — | — | BOWLING GREEN — The Everly Brothers (Dick Glasser), Warner Bros. 7020 | 2 |
| 78 | 86 | — | — | YOU CAN'T STAND ALONE — Wilson Pickett (Jerry Wexler), Atlantic 2412 | 2 |
| 79 | 84 | 94 | — | STAY TOGETHER YOUNG LOVERS — Brenda & the Tabulations (Bob Finiz), Dionn 501 | 3 |
| 80 | 83 | — | — | OOH BABY BABY — Five Stairsteps (Curtis Mayfield), Windy C 607 | 2 |
| 81 | 85 | 90 | — | LEOPARD-SKIN PILL-BOX HAT — Bob Dylan (Bob Johnston), Columbia 44069 | 3 |
| 82★ | — | — | — | WHY (Am I Treated So Bad) — Sweet Inspirations (Jerry Wexler), Atlantic 2410 | 1 |
| 83 | — | — | — | UP—UP AND AWAY — 5th Dimension (Johnny Rivers & Marc Gordon), Soul City 756 | 1 |
| 84 | 88 | — | — | ME ABOUT YOU — The Mojo Men (Lenny Waronker), Reprise 0580 | 2 |
| 85★ | — | — | — | WOMAN LIKE THAT, YEAH — Joe Tex (Buddy Killen), Dial 4059 | 1 |
| 86 | 87 | — | — | YOU GAVE ME SOMETHING (And Everything Is All Right) — Fantastic Four (Wingate, Weems), Ric Tic 128 | 2 |
| 87★ | — | — | — | NIGHT AND DAY — Sergio Mendes & Brasil '66 (Herb Alpert), A&M 853 | 1 |
| 88 | 94 | 100 | — | SOUL FINGER — Bar-Kays (Produced by Staff), Volt 148 | 3 |
| 89★ | — | — | — | IT'S COLD OUTSIDE — Choir (Najweb Hedafy), Roulette 4738 | 1 |
| 90★ | — | — | — | STEP OUT OF YOUR MIND — American Breed, Acta 804 | 1 |
| 91 | 100 | — | — | NO GOOD TO CRY — The Wildweeds (J. Greenberg & Trod Nossel), Cadet 5561 | 2 |
| 92 | 93 | 93 | — | STOP! AND THINK IT OVER — Perry Como (Andy Wiswell), RCA Victor 9165 | 3 |
| 93 | 96 | 99 | — | BABY, PLEASE COME BACK HOME — J.J. Barnes (Davis-Barnes), Groovesville 1006 | 3 |
| 94 | — | — | — | RELEASE ME — Esther Phillips, Atlantic 2411 | 1 |
| 95 | — | — | — | WHY (Am I Treated So Bad) — Staple Singers (Larry Williams & Manny Kellem), Epic 10158 | 1 |
| 96 | — | — | — | ONLY LOVE CAN BREAK A HEART — Margaret Whiting (Jack Gold), London 108 | 1 |
| 97 | 99 | — | — | HOLIDAY FOR CLOWNS — Brian Hyland (Snuff Garrett), Philips 40444 | 2 |
| 98 | — | — | — | LIGHT MY FIRE — Doors (Paul A. Rothchild), Elektra 45615 | 1 |
| 99 | — | 96 | 96 | MAKE ME YOURS — Bettye Swann, Money 126 | 3 |
| 100 | — | — | — | WHEN THE GOOD SUN SHINES — Elmo & Almo (Gary Klein), Daddy Best Presents 2501 | 1 |

## BUBBLING UNDER THE HOT 100

101. THAT'S SOMEONE YOU'LL NEVER FORGET....Elvis Presley, RCA Victor 9115
102. I TAKE IT BACK....Sandy Posey, MGM 13744
103. ALL THE TIME....Jack Greene, Decca 32123
104. SUMMER & SANDY....Lesley Gore, Mercury 72683
105. FINCHLEY CENTRAL....New Vaudville Band, Fontana 1589
106. GIANT SUNFLOWER....Giant Sunflower, Ode 25 7102
107. HEY LOVE....Stevie Wonder, Tamla 54147
108. I'VE LOST YOU....Jackie Wilson, Brunswick 55321
109. HELLO, HELLO....Claudine Longet, A&M 846
110. THEY'RE HERE....Boots Walker, Rust 5115
111. RED ROSES FOR MOM....Bobby Vinton, Epic 10168
112. I BELIEVED IT ALL....Poco Seco Singers, Columbia 44041
113. THESE ARE NOT MY PEOPLE....Billy Joe Royal, Columbia 44103
114. TONIGHT CARMEN....Marty Robbins, Columbia 44128
115. CALIFORNIA SUNSHINE GIRL....Shackelfords, Liberty 17006
116. I STAND ACCUSED....Glories, Date 1553
117. LOVE, LOVE, LOVE, LOVE....Terry Knight & the Pack, Lucky Eleven 238
118. YOU MUST HAVE BEEN A BEAUTIFUL BABY....Dave Clark Five, Epic 10179
119. FLOWER CHILDREN....Marcia Strassman, Uni 55006
120. TWO IN THE AFTERNOON....Dino, Desi & Billy, Reprise 0579
121. UP—UP AND AWAY....Johnny Mann Singers, Liberty 55972
122. ROUND, ROUND....Johnnie Mann King, Parrot 3011
123. UP TO NOW....Trini Lopez, Reprise 0587
124. SING ME A RAINBOW....Sons of Champlain, Verve 10500
125. GIRL (You Captivate Me)....7 Mack & the Mysterians, Cameo 479
126. EVERYBODY LOVES MY BABY....King Richard's Fleugel Knights, MTA 120
127. LIFE TURNED HER THAT WAY....Mel Tillis, Kapp 804
128. I STAND ACCUSED....Charles & Inez Foxx, Dynamo 104
129. LOVE, LOVE, LOVE....Al Hirt, RCA Victor 9198
130. BROWN EYED GIRL....Van Morrison, Bang 545
131. HERE I AM....Barbara Mechel, Motown 1106
132. LOVE, LOVE, LOVE....Delmonicos, Kapp 833
133. NOW I KNOW....Eddie Fisher, RCA Victor 9204
134. THREAD THE NEEDLE....Clarence Carter, Fame 1013
135. LITTLE BY LITTLE & BIT BY BIT....Ray Charles Singers, Command 4096

Compiled from national retail sales and radio station airplay by the Music Popularity Dept. of Record Market Research, Billboard.

For Week Ending June 10, 1967

# Billboard HOT 100

★ STAR performer—Sides registering greatest proportionate upward progress this week.

Record Industry Association of America seal of certification as million selling single.

| THIS WEEK | 1 Wk. Ago | 2 Wks. Ago | 3 Wks. Ago | TITLE Artist (Producer), Label & Number | Weeks On Chart |
|---|---|---|---|---|---|
| Billboard Award | 1 | 2 | 5 | RESPECT — Aretha Franklin (Jerry Wexler), Atlantic 2403 | 7 |
| 2 | 2 | 1 | 1 | GROOVIN' — Young Rascals (Young Rascals), Atlantic 2401 | 8 |
| 3 | 3 | 3 | 6 | I GOT RHYTHM — Happenings (The Tokens) B. T. Puppy 527 | 10 |
| 4 | 4 | 4 | 7 | RELEASE ME (And Let Me Love Again) — Engelbert Humperdinck, Parrot 40011 | 10 |
| 5 | 6 | 7 | 14 | HIM OR ME—WHAT'S IT GONNA BE? — Paul Revere & the Raiders (Terry Melcher), Columbia 44094 | 7 |
| ★6 | 9 | 17 | 22 | SOMEBODY TO LOVE — Jefferson Airplane (Rick Jarrard), RCA Victor 9140 | 11 |
| ★7 | 14 | 39 | 58 | SHE'D RATHER BE WITH ME — Turtles (Joe Wissert), White Whale 249 | 5 |
| ★8 | 17 | 40 | 73 | LITTLE BIT O' SOUL — Music Explosion (J. Katz-J. Kasenentz & E. Chiprut) Laurie 3380 | 5 |
| 9 | 10 | 15 | 21 | ALL I NEED IS YOU — Temptations (F. Wilson), Gordy 7061 | 7 |
| 10 | 5 | 8 | 13 | CREEQUE ALLEY — Mamas & the Papas (Lou Adler), Dunhill 4083 | 7 |
| 11 | 11 | 14 | 19 | MIRAGE — Tommy James & the Shondells (Bo Gentry & Ritchie Cordell), Roulette 4736 | 7 |
| ★12 | 28 | 52 | — | WINDY — The Association, (Bones Howe), Warner Bros. 7041 | 3 |
| 13 | 13 | 13 | 18 | HERE COMES MY BABY — Tremeloes, Epic 10139 | 10 |
| ★14 | 27 | 49 | 98 | SUNDAY WILL NEVER BE THE SAME — Spanky and Our Gang (Jerry Ross), Mercury 72679 | 4 |
| ★15 | 36 | 46 | 66 | LET'S LIVE FOR TODAY — Grass Roots (Steve Barri & P. F. Sloan), Dunhill 4084 | 5 |
| ★16 | 29 | 34 | 44 | COME ON DOWN TO MY BOAT — Every Mother's Son (Wes Farrell), MGM 13733 | 6 |
| ★17 | 33 | 53 | 74 | CAN'T TAKE MY EYES OFF YOU — Frankie Valli (Bob Crewe), Philips 40446 | 4 |
| 18 | 19 | 30 | 32 | SIX O'CLOCK — Lovin' Spoonful (Erik Jacobsen), Kama Sutra 225 | 7 |
| ★19 | 30 | 50 | 87 | 7 ROOMS OF GLOOM — Four Tops (Holland & Dozier), Motown 1110 | 4 |
| 20 | 15 | 11 | 12 | ON A CAROUSEL — Hollies (Ron Richards), Imperial 66231 | 13 |
| ★21 | 26 | 35 | 46 | DO IT AGAIN A LITTLE BIT SLOWER — Jon & Robin & the In Crowd (Dale Hawkins), Abnak 119 | 6 |
| 22 | 18 | 16 | 16 | FRIDAY ON MY MIND — Easybeats, (Shell Talmy) United Artists 50106 | 13 |
| 23 | 23 | 28 | 39 | WHEN YOU'RE YOUNG AND IN LOVE — Marvelettes (J. Dean & William Weatherspoon), Tamla 54150 | 8 |
| 24 | 12 | 10 | 11 | GIRL, YOU'LL BE A WOMAN SOON — Neil Diamond (Jeff Barry & Ellie Greenwich), Bang 542 | 10 |
| 25 | 7 | 5 | 5 | THE HAPPENING — Supremes (Holland & Dozier), Motown 1107 | 10 |
| ★26 | 49 | 79 | — | NEW YORK MINING DISASTER 1941 (Have You Seen My Wife Mr. Jones) — The Bee Gees (Ossie Byrne), Atco 6487 | 3 |
| 27 | 8 | 6 | 3 | SWEET SOUL MUSIC — Arthur Conley (Otis Redding), Atco 6463 | 14 |
| ★28 | 35 | 37 | 47 | ALFIE — Dionne Warwick (Bacharach-David), Scepter 12187 | 10 |
| ★29 | 39 | 47 | 62 | AIN'T NO MOUNTAIN HIGH ENOUGH — Marvin Gaye & Tammi Terrell (H. Fuqua & J. Bristol), Tamla 54149 | 5 |
| ★30 | 40 | 42 | 54 | TRAMP — Otis & Carla (Prod. by Staff), Stax 216 | 6 |
| 31 | 20 | 21 | 26 | I WAS KAISER BILL'S BATMAN — Whistling Jack Smith, Deram 85003 | 7 |
| ★32 | 55 | 98 | — | SAN FRANCISCO "WEAR SOME FLOWERS IN YOUR HAIR" — Scott McKenzie (John Phillips & Lou Adler), Ode 103 | 3 |
| ★33 | 45 | 58 | 84 | DING DONG THE WITCH IS DEAD — Fifth Estate (Steve & Bill Jerome), Jubilee 5573 | 4 |
| 34 | 22 | 12 | 9 | DON'T YOU CARE — Buckinghams (Jim Guercio), Columbia 44053 | 14 |
| 35 | 21 | 18 | 8 | CLOSE YOUR EYES — Peaches & Herb (Dave Kapralik-Ken Williams), Date 1549 | 12 |
| 36 | 25 | 25 | 28 | SHAKE A TAIL FEATHER — James & Bobby Purify (Papa Don, Cogbill, Young, Emmons & Chrisman), Bell 669 | 9 |
| ★37 | 53 | 64 | 79 | HERE WE GO AGAIN — Ray Charles (TRC), ABC 10938 | 4 |
| 38 | 24 | 26 | 31 | HAPPY JACK — Who, Decca 32114 | 9 |
| 39 | 34 | 29 | 34 | MY GIRL JOSEPHINE — Jerry Jaye, Hi 2120 | 9 |
| 40 | 42 | 43 | 65 | GIRLS IN LOVE — Gary Lewis & the Playboys (Koppelman-Rubin-Klein), Liberty 55971 | 5 |
| 41 | 16 | 9 | 4 | SOMETHIN' STUPID — Nancy Sinatra & Frank Sinatra (Jimmy Bowen & Lee Hazlewood), Reprise 0561 | 13 |
| ★42 | 52 | 66 | 88 | SOUND OF LOVE — Five Americans (Dale Hawkins), Abnak 120 | 4 |
| 43 | 44 | 54 | 56 | THE OOGUM BOOGUM SONG — Brenton Wood (Hooven-Winn), Double Shot 111 | 9 |
| ★44 | 83 | — | — | UP—UP AND AWAY — 5th Dimension (Johnny Rivers & Marc Gordon), Soul City 756 | 2 |
| ★45 | 70 | — | — | THE TRACKS OF MY TEARS — Johnny Rivers (Lou Adler), Imperial 66244 | 2 |
| 46 | 51 | 56 | 59 | LET YOURSELF GO — James Brown & the Famous Flames (James Brown), King 6100 | 6 |
| ★47 | 60 | 74 | 89 | COME TO THE SUNSHINE — Harpers Bizarre (Lenny Waconker), Warner Bros. 7028 | 4 |
| ★48 | 66 | 81 | — | SOCIETY'S CHILD — Janis Ian (Shadow Morton), Verve 5027 | 3 |
| ★49 | 76 | — | — | DON'T SLEEP IN THE SUBWAY — Petula Clark (Tony Hatch), Warner Bros. 7049 | 2 |
| 50 | 41 | 41 | 49 | CAN'T SEEM TO MAKE YOU MINE — Seeds (Marcus Tybalt), GNP Crescendo 354 | 7 |
| 51 | 37 | 38 | 38 | HIP HUG-HER — Booker T. & the M. G.'s (Prod. By Staff), Stax 211 | 12 |
| ★52 | 62 | 77 | — | MARY IN THE MORNING — Al Martino (Tom Morgan & Marvin Holtzman), Capitol 5904 | 3 |
| ★53 | 63 | 78 | — | FOR YOUR PRECIOUS LOVE — Oscar Toney Jr. (Papa Don, Coghill, Emmons, Chrisman & Young), Bell 672 | 3 |
| 54 | 58 | 62 | 78 | SHAKE — Otis Redding, Volt 149 | 4 |
| 55 | 57 | 70 | 77 | FUNNY FAMILIAR FORGOTTEN FEELINGS — Tom Jones (Peter Sullivan), Parrot 40014 | 4 |
| ★56 | 75 | — | — | PAY YOU BACK WITH INTEREST — Hollies, Imperial 66240 | 2 |
| 57 | 59 | 59 | 60 | MISTY BLUE — Eddy Arnold (Chet Atkins), RCA Victor 9182 | 6 |
| 58 | 61 | 76 | — | DON'T BLAME THE CHILDREN — Sammy Davis Jr. (Jimmy Bowen), Reprise 0566 | 3 |
| 59 | 64 | 67 | 67 | TOGETHER — Intruders, Gamble 205 | 7 |
| ★60 | 77 | 89 | — | BOWLING GREEN — The Everly Brothers (Dick Glasser), Warner Bros. 7020 | 3 |
| ★61 | 98 | — | — | LIGHT MY FIRE — Doors (Paul A. Rothchild), Elektra 45615 | 2 |
| 62 | 69 | 61 | 61 | TIME, TIME — Ed Ames (Jim Foglesong), RCA Victor 9178 | 6 |
| 63 | 68 | 71 | 86 | LONG LEGGED GIRL (With the Short Dresss On) — Elvis Presley, RCA Victor 9115 | 4 |
| 64 | 74 | 75 | 75 | JUMP BACK — King Curtis (Jerry Wexler), Atco 6476 | 5 |
| ★65 | 86 | 87 | — | YOU GAVE ME SOMETHING (And Everything Is All Right) — Fantastic Four (Kent, Wingate, Weems), Ric Tic 128 | 3 |
| ★66 | — | — | — | C'MON MARIANNE — Four Seasons (Bob Crewe), Philips 40460 | 1 |
| ★67 | — | — | — | YOU MUST HAVE BEEN A BEAUTIFUL BABY — Dave Clark Five (Dave Clark), Epic 10179 | 1 |
| ★68 | — | — | — | I WAS MADE TO LOVE HER — Stevie Wonder (H. Cosby), Tamla 54151 | 1 |
| 69 | 79 | 84 | 94 | STAY TOGETHER YOUNG LOVERS — Brenda & the Tabulations (Bob Finiz), Dionn 501 | 4 |
| ★70 | 88 | 94 | 100 | SOUL FINGER — Bar-Kays (Produced by Staff), Volt 148 | 4 |
| 71 | 73 | 73 | 80 | AM I GROOVING YOU — Freddie Scott (Bert Berns), Shout 212 | 5 |
| 72 | 82 | — | — | WHY (Am I Treated So Bad) — Sweet Inspirations (Jerry Wexler), Atlantic 2410 | 2 |
| 73 | 80 | 83 | — | OOH BABY BABY — Five Stairsteps, (Curtis Mayfield), Windy C 607 | 3 |
| 74 | 78 | 86 | — | YOU CAN'T STAND ALONE — Wilson Picket (Jerry Wexler), Atlantic 2412 | 3 |
| 75 | 72 | 72 | 85 | WE HAD A GOOD THING GOIN' — Cyrkle (John Simon), Columbia 44108 | 5 |
| ★76 | — | — | — | PLASTIC MAN — Sonny & Cher (Sonny Bono), Atco 6486 | 1 |
| ★77 | — | — | — | THEY'RE HERE — Boots Walker (Ernie Maresca), Rust 5115 | 1 |
| ★78 | 93 | 96 | 99 | BABY, PLEASE COME BACK HOME — J. J. Barnes (Davis-Barnes), Groovesville 1006 | 4 |
| 79 | 89 | — | — | IT'S COLD OUTSIDE — Choir (Najweb Hedafy), Roulette 4738 | 2 |
| ★80 | — | — | — | ONE BY ONE — Blues Magoos (Art Polhemus & Bob Wyld), Mercury 72692 | 1 |
| 81 | 81 | 85 | 90 | LEOPARD-SKIN PILL-BOX HAT — Bob Dylan (Bob Johnston), Columbia 44069 | 4 |
| ★82 | — | — | — | SHAKE, RATTLE AND ROLL — Arthur Conley (Otis Redding), Atco 6494 | 1 |
| 83 | 84 | 88 | — | ME ABOUT YOU — The Mojo Men (Lenny Waronker), Reprise 0580 | 3 |
| ★84 | 99 | — | 96 | MAKE ME YOURS — Bettye Swann, Money 126 | 4 |
| 85 | 85 | — | — | WOMAN LIKE THAT, YEAH — Joe Tex (Buddy Killen), Dial 4059 | 2 |
| 86 | 90 | — | — | STEP OUT OF YOUR MIND — American Breed, Acta 804 | 2 |
| 87 | 87 | — | — | NIGHT AND DAY — Sergio Mendes & Brasil '66 (Herb Alpert), A&M 853 | 2 |
| ★88 | — | — | — | NOW I KNOW — Jack Jones, Kapp 833 | 1 |
| ★89 | — | — | — | I TAKE IT BACK — Sandy Posey (Chips Moman), MGM 13744 | 1 |
| ★90 | — | — | — | SUMMER AND SANDY — Lesley Gore (Bob Crewe), Mercury 72683 | 1 |
| 91 | 91 | 100 | — | NO GOOD TO CRY — The Wildweeds (J. Greenberg & Trod Nossel), Cadet 5561 | 3 |
| 92 | 92 | 93 | 93 | STOP! AND THINK IT OVER — Perry Como (Andy Wisewell), RCA Victor 9165 | 4 |
| 93 | 94 | — | — | RELEASE ME — Esther Phillips, Atlantic 2411 | 2 |
| 94 | 97 | 99 | — | HOLIDAY FOR CLOWNS — Brian Hyland (Snuff Garrett), Philips 40444 | 3 |
| 95 | — | — | — | WHO'S LOVIN' YOU — Brenda & the Tabulations (Bob Finiz) Dionn 501 | 1 |
| 96 | — | — | — | TO BE A LOVER — Gene Chandler (Carl Davis), Checker 1165 | 1 |
| 97 | — | — | — | HAVE YOU SEEN HER FACE — Byrds (Gary Usher), Columbia 44157 | 1 |
| 98 | 100 | — | — | WHEN THE GOOD SUN SHINES — Elmo & Almo (Gary Klein), Daddy Best Presents 2501 | 2 |
| 99 | — | — | — | LITTLE MISS SUNSHINE — Tommy Roe (Steve Clark), ABC 10945 | 1 |
| 100 | — | — | — | GIRL (You Captivate Me) — ? & the Mysterians (Neil Bogart), Cameo 479 | 1 |

## HOT 100—A TO Z—(Publisher-Licensee)


Ain't No Mountain High Enough (Jobete, BMI).... 29
Alfie (Famous, ASCAP).... 28
All I Need Is You (Jobete, BMI).... 9
Am I Grooving You? (Unart & Web IV, BMI).... 71
Baby, Please Come Back Home (Groovesville, BMI).... 78
Bowling Green (Rook, BMI).... 60
Can't Seem to Make You Mine (Neil-Purple Bottle, BMI).... 50
Can't Take My Eyes Off You (Saturday/Seasons' Four, BMI).... 17
Close Your Eyes (Tideland, BMI).... 35
C'Mon Marianne (Saturday/Seasons' Four, BMI).... 66
Come on Down to My Boat (Picturetone-Goldstein, BMI).... 16
Come to the Sunshine (Vantim, BMI).... 47
Creeque Alley (Trousdale, BMI).... 10
Ding Dong the Witch Is Dead (Feist, ASCAP).... 33
Do It Again a Little Bit Slower (Barton, BMI).... 21
Don't Blame the Children (Saloon Songs, BMI).... 58
Don't Sleep in the Subway (Duchess, BMI).... 49
Don't You Care (Beechwood, BMI).... 34
For Your Precious Love (Sunflower, ASCAP).... 53
Friday on My Mind (Unart, BMI).... 22
Funny Familiar Forgotten Feelings (Acuff-Rose, BMI).... 55
Girl (You Captivate Me) (S&J, BMI).... 100
Girl, You'll Be a Woman Soon (Tallyrand, BMI).... 24
Girls in Love (Chardon, BMI).... 40
Groovin' (Slacsar, BMI).... 2
Happening, The (Jobete, BMI).... 25
Happy Jack (Essex, ASCAP).... 38
Have You Seen Her Face (Tickson, BMI).... 97
Here Comes My Baby (Mainstay, BMI).... 13
Here We Go Again (Dirk, BMI).... 37
Him or Me—What's It Gonna Be? (Daywin, BMI).... 5
Hip Hug-Her (East, BMI).... 51
Holiday for Clowns (Viva Music, BMI).... 94
I Got Rhythm (New World, ASCAP).... 3
I Take It Back (Low-Sal, BMI).... 89
I Was Kaiser Bill's Batman (Mills, ASCAP).... 31
I Was Made to Love Her (Jobete, BMI).... 68
It's Cold Outside (R.G.D., BMI).... 79
Jump Back (East, BMI).... 64
Let Yourself Go (Dynatone, BMI).... 46
Let's Live for Today (James, BMI).... 18
Leopard-Skin Pill-Box Hat (Dwarf, ASCAP).... 81
Light My Fire (Nipper, ASCAP).... 61
Little Bit o' Soul (Southern, ASCAP).... 8
Little Miss Sunshine (Low Twi, BMI).... 99
Long-Legged Girl (With the Short Dress On) (Presley, BMI).... 63
Make Me Yours (Cash Songs, BMI).... 99
Mary in the Morning (Pamco, BMI).... 52
Me About You (Chardon, BMI).... 83
Mirage (Patricia, BMI).... 11
Misty Blue (Talmount, BMI).... 57
My Girl Josephine (Travis, BMI).... 39
New York Mining Disaster 1941 (Have You Seen My Wife Mr. Jones) (Abigail, BMI).... 26
Night and Day (Harms, ASCAP).... 87
No Good to Cry (Linesider-Barrisue, BMI).... 91
Now I Know (Helios, BMI).... 88
On a Carousel (Maribus, BMI).... 20
Ooh Baby, Baby (Jobete, BMI).... 73
One By One (Ananga-Ranga, BMI).... 80
Ooogum Boogum Song, The (Big Shot, ASCAP).... 43
Pay You Back With Interest (Maribus, BMI).... 56
Plastic Man (Chris-Marc-Cotillion, BMI).... 76
Release Me (And Let Me Love Again) (Four Star, BMI).... 4
Release Me (Four-Star Sales, BMI).... 93
Respect (East-Time-Walco, BMI).... 1
San Francisco "Wear Some Flowers in Your Hair" (Trousdale, BMI).... 32
7 Rooms of Gloom (Jobete, BMI).... 19
Shake (Kags, BMI).... 54
Shake, Rattle and Roll (Progressive, BMI).... 82
Shake a Tail Feather (Va-Pac, BMI).... 36
She'd Rather Be With Me (Chardon, BMI).... 7
Six-o'Clock (Faithful Virtue, BMI).... 18
Society's Child (Webatuck, BMI).... 48
Somebody to Love (Cooper Penny, BMI).... 6
Somethin' Stupid (Green Wood, BMI).... 41
Soul Finger (East, BMI).... 70
Sound of Love (Jetstar, BMI).... 42
Stay Together Young Lovers (Missile/Rittenhouse, BMI).... 69
Step Out of Your Mind (Blackwood, BMI).... 86
Stop! And Think It Over (Northern, ASCAP).... 92
Summer and Sandy (Saturday, BMI).... 90
Sunday Will Never Be the Same (Pamco, BMI).... 14
Sweet Soul Music (Bedwal, BMI).... 27
They're Here (Maresca, ASCAP).... 77
Time, Time (April, ASCAP).... 62
Together (Razor Sharp, BMI).... 59
To Be a Lover (Cachand/Jalynne, BMI).... 96
The Tracks of My Tears (Jobete, BMI).... 45
Tramp (Modern, BMI).... 30
Up-Up and Away (Rivers, BMI).... 44
We Had a Good Thing Goin' (Screen Gems-Columbia, BMI).... 75
When the Good Sun Shines (Chardon, BMI).... 98
When You're Young and in Love (Picturetone, BMI).... 23
Who's Lovin' You (Jobete, BMI).... 95
Why? (Am I Treated So Bad) (Staples, BMI).... 72
Windy (Almo, BMI).... 12
Woman Like That, Yeah (Tree, BMI).... 15
You Can't Stand Alone (T.M., BMI).... 24
You Gave Me Something (And Everything Is All Right (Myto, BMI).... 65
You Must Have Been a Beautiful Baby (Remick, ASCAP).... 67


## BUBBLING UNDER THE HOT 100

101. THAT'S SOMEONE YOU'LL NEVER FORGET....Elvis Presley, RCA Victor 9115
102. FINCHLEY CENTRAL....New Vaudeville Band, Fontana 1589
103. ONLY LOVE CAN BREAK A HEART....Margaret Whiting, London 108
104. WHY? (AM I TREATED SO BAD)....Staple Singers, Epic 10158
105. ALL THE TIME....Jack Greene, Decca 32123
106. I'VE LOST YOU....Jackie Wilson, Brunswick 55321
107. HEY LOVE....Stevie Wonder, Tamla 54147
108. HELLO, HELLO....Claudine Longet, A&M 846
109. RED ROSES FOR MOM....Bobby Vinton, Epic 10168
110. GRADUATION DAY....Arbors, Date 1561
111. FLOWER CHILDREN....Marcia Strassman, Uni 55006
112. I STAND ACCUSED....Glories, Date 1553
113. CARRIE ANN....Hollies, Epic 10180
114. WHY? (AM I TREATED SO BAD)....Bobby Powell, Whit 730
115. DAYLIGHT SAVING TIME....Keith, Mercury 72695
116. SOMEBODY OUGHT TO WRITE A BOOK ABOUT IT....Ray Charles, ABC 10938
117. TWO IN THE AFTERNOON....Dino, Desi & Billy, Reprise 0579
118. LET IT HAPPEN....James Carr, Goldwax 323
119. GREATEST LOVE....Billy J. Royal, Columbia 44103
120. ALL'S QUIET ON WEST 23RD ST....Jetstream, Smash 2095
121. GROOVY SUMMERTIME....Love Generation, Imperial 66243
122. THREAD THE NEEDLE....Clarence Carter, Fame 1013
123. WORK WITH ME ANNIE....P. J. Proby, Liberty 55974
124. LONELY DRIFTER....Pieces of Eight, A&M 854
125. AIRPLANE SONG....Royal Guardsmen, Laurie 3391
126. NO MORE RUNNING AROUND....Lamp of Childhood, Dunhill 4089
127. TONIGHT CARMEN....Marty Robbins, Columbia 44128
128. I STAND ACCUSED....Inez & Charlie Foxx, Dynamo 104
129. UP, UP & AWAY....Johnny Mann Singers, Liberty 55972
130. HERE I AM....Barbara McNair, Motown 1106

Compiled from national retail sales and radio station airplay by the Music Popularity Dept. of Record Market Research, Billboard.

For Week Ending June 17, 1967

# Billboard HOT 100

★ STAR performer—Sides registering greatest proportionate upward progress this week.

Record Industry Association of America seal of certification as million selling single.

| This Week | 1 Wk. Ago | 2 Wks. Ago | 3 Wks. Ago | TITLE Artist (Producer), Label & Number | Weeks On Chart |
|---|---|---|---|---|---|
| 1 (Billboard Award) | 2 | 2 | 1 | GROOVIN' — Young Rascals (Young Rascals), Atlantic 2401 | 9 |
| 2 | 1 | 1 | 2 | RESPECT — Aretha Franklin (Jerry Wexler), Atlantic 2403 | 8 |
| ★3 | 7 | 14 | 39 | SHE'D RATHER BE WITH ME — Turtles (Joe Wissert), White Whale 249 | 6 |
| 4 | 4 | 4 | 4 | RELEASE ME (And Let Me Love Again) — Engelbert Humperdinck, Parrot 40011 | 11 |
| 5 | 6 | 9 | 17 | SOMEBODY TO LOVE — Jefferson Airplane (Rick Jarrard), RCA Victor 9140 | 12 |
| 6 | 8 | 17 | 40 | LITTLE BIT O' SOUL — Music Explosion (J. Katz-J. Kasenentz & E. Chiprut) Laurie 3380 | 6 |
| ★7 | 12 | 28 | 52 | WINDY — The Association, (Bones Howe), Warner Bros. 7041 | 4 |
| 8 | 9 | 10 | 15 | ALL I NEED IS YOU — Temptations (F. Wilson), Gordy 7061 | 8 |
| 9 | 3 | 3 | 3 | I GOT RHYTHM — Happenings (The Tokens) B. T. Puppy 527 | 11 |
| 10 | 11 | 11 | 14 | MIRAGE — Tommy James & the Shondells (Bo Gentry & Ritchie Cordell), Roulette 4736 | 8 |
| ★11 | 17 | 33 | 53 | CAN'T TAKE MY EYES OFF YOU — Frankie Valli (Bob Crewe), Philips 40446 | 5 |
| 12 | 14 | 27 | 49 | SUNDAY WILL NEVER BE THE SAME — Spanky and Our Gang (Jerry Ross), Mercury 72679 | 5 |
| 13 | 16 | 29 | 34 | COME ON DOWN TO MY BOAT — Every Mother's Son (Wes Farrell), MGM 13733 | 7 |
| ★14 | 19 | 30 | 50 | 7 ROOMS OF GLOOM — Four Tops (Holland & Dozier), Motown 1110 | 5 |
| 15 | 15 | 36 | 46 | LET'S LIVE FOR TODAY — Grass Roots (Steve Barri & P. F. Sloan), Dunhill 4084 | 6 |
| 16 | 5 | 6 | 7 | HIM OR ME—WHAT'S IT GONNA BE? — Paul Revere & the Raiders (Terry Melcher), Columbia 44094 | 8 |
| ★17 | 33 | 45 | 58 | DING DONG THE WITCH IS DEAD — Fifth Estate (Steve & Bill Jerome), Jubilee 5573 | 5 |
| ★18 | 26 | 49 | 79 | NEW YORK MINING DISASTER 1941 (Have You Seen My Wife Mr. Jones) — The Bee Gees (Ossie Byrne), Atco 6487 | 4 |
| 19 | 21 | 26 | 35 | DO IT AGAIN A LITTLE BIT SLOWER — Jon & Robin & the In Crowd (Dale Hawkins), Abnak 119 | 7 |
| ★20 | 32 | 55 | 98 | SAN FRANCISCO "WEAR SOME FLOWERS IN YOUR HAIR" — Scott McKenzie (John Phillips & Lou Adler), Ode 103 | 4 |
| 21 | 10 | 5 | 8 | CREEQUE ALLEY — Mamas & the Papas (Lou Adler), Dunhill 4083 | 7 |
| ★22 | 28 | 35 | 37 | ALFIE — Dionne Warwick (Bacharach-David), Scepter 12187 | 11 |
| 23 | 13 | 13 | 13 | HERE COMES MY BABY — Tremeloes, Epic 10139 | 11 |
| ★24 | 45 | 70 | — | THE TRACKS OF MY TEARS — Johnny Rivers (Lou Adler), Imperial 66244 | 3 |
| 25 | 18 | 19 | 30 | SIX O'CLOCK — Lovin' Spoonful (Erik Jacobsen), Kama Sutra 225 | 8 |
| ★26 | 49 | 76 | — | DON'T SLEEP IN THE SUBWAY — Petula Clark (Tony Hatch), Warner Bros. 7049 | 3 |
| 27 | 29 | 39 | 47 | AIN'T NO MOUNTAIN HIGH ENOUGH — Marvin Gaye & Tammi Terrell (H. Fuqua & J. Bristol), Tamla 54149 | 6 |
| ★28 | 37 | 53 | 64 | HERE WE GO AGAIN — Ray Charles (TRC), ABC 10938 | 5 |
| 29 | 30 | 40 | 42 | TRAMP — Otis & Carla (Prod. by Staff), Stax 216 | 7 |
| ★30 | 48 | 66 | 81 | SOCIETY'S CHILD — Janis Ian (Shadow Morton), Verve 5027 | 4 |
| ★31 | 44 | 83 | — | UP—UP AND AWAY — 5th Dimension (Johnny Rivers & Marc Gordon), Soul City 756 | 3 |
| 32 | 23 | 23 | 28 | WHEN YOU'RE YOUNG AND IN LOVE — Marvelettes (J. Dean & William Weatherspoon), Tamla 54150 | 9 |
| ★33 | 66 | — | — | C'MON MARIANNE — Four Seasons (Bob Crewe), Philips 40460 | 2 |
| ★34 | 53 | 63 | 78 | FOR YOUR PRECIOUS LOVE — Oscar Toney Jr. (Papa Don, Coghill, Emmons, Chrisman & Young), Bell 672 | 4 |
| 35 | 24 | 12 | 10 | GIRL, YOU'LL BE A WOMAN SOON — Neil Diamond (Jeff Barry & Ellie Greenwich), Bang 542 | 11 |
| 36 | 42 | 52 | 66 | SOUND OF LOVE — Five Americans (Dale Hawkins), Abnak 120 | 5 |
| ★37 | 47 | 60 | 74 | COME TO THE SUNSHINE — Harpers Bizarre (Lenny Waconker), Warner Bros. 7028 | 5 |
| ★38 | 52 | 62 | 77 | MARY IN THE MORNING — Al Martino (Tom Morgan & Marvin Holtzman), Capitol 5904 | 4 |
| 39 | 40 | 42 | 43 | GIRLS IN LOVE — Gary Lewis & the Playboys (Koppelman-Rubin-Klein), Liberty 55971 | 6 |
| 40 | 25 | 7 | 5 | THE HAPPENING — Supremes (Holland & Dozier), Motown 1107 | 11 |
| 41 | 20 | 15 | 11 | ON A CAROUSEL — Hollies (Ron Richards), Imperial 66231 | 13 |
| 42 | 43 | 44 | 54 | THE OOGUM BOOGUM SONG — Brenton Wood (Hooven-Winn), Double Shot 111 | 10 |
| ★43 | 68 | — | — | I WAS MADE TO LOVE HER — Stevie Wonder (H. Cosby), Tamla 54151 | 2 |
| 44 | 27 | 8 | 6 | SWEET SOUL MUSIC — Arthur Conley (Otis Redding), Atco 6463 | 15 |
| 45 | 22 | 18 | 16 | FRIDAY ON MY MIND — Easybeats, (Shell Talmy) United Artists 50106 | 14 |
| ★46 | 56 | 75 | — | PAY YOU BACK WITH INTEREST — Hollies, Imperial 66240 | 3 |
| 47 | 54 | 58 | 62 | SHAKE — Otis Redding, Volt 149 | 5 |
| ★48 | 58 | 61 | 76 | DON'T BLAME THE CHILDREN — Sammy Davis Jr. (Jimmy Bowen), Reprise 0566 | 4 |
| 49 | 55 | 57 | 70 | FUNNY FAMILIAR FORGOTTEN FEELINGS — Tom Jones (Peter Sullivan), Parrot 40014 | 5 |
| ★50 | 61 | 98 | — | LIGHT MY FIRE — Doors (Paul A. Rothchild), Elektra 45615 | 3 |
| 51 | 51 | 37 | 38 | HIP HUG-HER — Booker T. & the M. G.'s (Prod. By Staff), Stax 211 | 13 |
| 52 | 46 | 51 | 56 | LET YOURSELF GO — James Brown & the Famous Flames (James Brown), King 6100 | 7 |
| ★53 | 84 | 99 | — | MAKE ME YOURS — Bettye Swann, Money 126 | 5 |
| ★54 | 70 | 88 | 94 | SOUL FINGER — Bar-Kays (Produced by Staff), Volt 148 | 5 |
| ★55 | 67 | — | — | YOU MUST HAVE BEEN A BEAUTIFUL BABY — Dave Clark Five (Dave Clark), Epic 10179 | 2 |
| 56 | 59 | 64 | 67 | TOGETHER — Intruders, Gamble 205 | 8 |
| 57 | 57 | 59 | 59 | MISTY BLUE — Eddv Arnold (Chet Atkins), RCA Victor 9182 | 7 |
| ★58 | 72 | 82 | — | WHY (Am I Treated So Bad) — Sweet Inspirations (Jerry Wexler), Atlantic 2410 | 3 |
| 59 | 65 | 86 | 87 | YOU GAVE ME SOMETHING (And Everything Is All Right) — Fantastic Four (Kent, Wingate, Weems), Ric Tic 128 | 4 |
| 60 | 60 | 77 | 89 | BOWLING GREEN — The Everly Brothers (Dick Glasser), Warner Bros. 7020 | 4 |
| ★61 | 82 | — | — | SHAKE, RATTLE AND ROLL — Arthur Conley (Otis Redding), Atco 6494 | 2 |
| ★62 | 89 | — | — | I TAKE IT BACK — Sandy Posey (Chips Moman), MGM 13744 | 2 |
| 63 | 64 | 74 | 75 | JUMP BACK — King Curtis (Jerry Wexler), Atco 6476 | 6 |
| 64 | 73 | 80 | 83 | OOH BABY BABY — Five Stairsteps, (Curtis Mayfield), Windy C 607 | 4 |
| ★65 | 85 | 85 | — | WOMAN LIKE THAT, YEAH — Joe Tex (Buddy Killen), Dial 4059 | 3 |
| 66 | 69 | 79 | 84 | STAY TOGETHER YOUNG LOVERS — Brenda & the Tabulations (Bob Finiz), Dionn 501 | 5 |
| 67 | 63 | 68 | 71 | LONG LEGGED GIRL (With the Short Dress On) — Elvis Presley, RCA Victor 9115 | 5 |
| 68 | 62 | 69 | 61 | TIME, TIME — Ed Ames (Jim Foglesong), RCA Victor 9178 | 7 |
| 69 | 79 | 89 | — | IT'S COLD OUTSIDE — Choir (Najweb Hedafy), Roulette 4738 | 3 |
| 70 | 74 | 78 | 86 | YOU CAN'T STAND ALONE — Wilson Picket (Jerry Wexler), Atlantic 2412 | 4 |
| ★71 | 86 | 90 | — | STEP OUT OF YOUR MIND — American Breed, Acta 804 | 3 |
| 72 | 78 | 93 | 96 | BABY, PLEASE COME BACK HOME — J. J. Barnes (Davis-Barnes), Groovesville 1006 | 5 |
| ★73 | — | — | — | CARRIE ANN — Hollies (Ron Richards), Epic 10180 | 1 |
| 74 | 76 | — | — | PLASTIC MAN — Sonny & Cher (Sonny Bono), Atco 6486 | 2 |
| ★75 | 90 | — | — | SUMMER AND SANDY — Lesley Gore (Bob Crewe), Mercury 72683 | 2 |
| ★76 | — | — | — | MORE LOVE — Smokey Robinson & the Miracles ("Smokey") Tamla 54152 | 1 |
| 77 | 77 | — | — | THEY'RE HERE — Boots Walker (Ernie Maresca), Rust 5115 | 2 |
| 78 | 88 | — | — | NOW I KNOW — Jack Jones, Kapp 833 | 2 |
| ★79 | 95 | — | — | WHO'S LOVIN' YOU — Brenda & the Tabulations (Bob Finiz) Dionn 501 | 2 |
| 80 | 80 | — | — | ONE BY ONE — Blues Magoos (Art Polhemus & Bob Wyld), Mercury 72692 | 2 |
| ★81 | — | — | — | MERCY, MERCY, MERCY — Buckinghams (James William Guercio), Columbia 44162 | 1 |
| ★82 | — | — | — | SOMEBODY HELP ME — Spencer Davis Group (Chris Blackwell & Jimmy Miller). United Artists 50162 | 1 |
| ★83 | — | — | — | YOU WANTED SOMEONE TO PLAY WITH (I Wanted Someone to Love) — Frankie Laine (Bob Thiele), ABC 10946 | 1 |
| ★84 | — | — | — | LOVE ME TENDER — Percy Sledge (Quin Ivy & Marlin Greene), Atlantic 2414 | 1 |
| ★85 | — | — | — | GRADUATION DAY — Arbors (Richard E. Carney), Date 1561 | 1 |
| 86 | 87 | 87 | — | NIGHT AND DAY — Sergio Mendes & Brasil '66 (Herb Alpert), A&M 853 | 3 |
| ★87 | — | — | — | AIRPLANE SONG — Royal Guardsmen (Gernhard Ent.), Laurie 3391 | 1 |
| 88 | 91 | 91 | 100 | NO GOOD TO CRY — The Wildweeds (J. Greenberg & Trod Nossel), Cadet 5561 | 3 |
| ★89 | — | — | — | SOOTHE ME — Sam & Dave (Prod. by Staff), Stax 218 | 1 |
| ★90 | — | — | — | DAYLIGHT SAVIN' TIME — Keith (Jerry Ross), Mercury 72695 | 1 |
| 91 | — | — | — | SILENCE IS GOLDEN — Tremeloes (Mike Smith), Epic 10184 | 1 |
| 92 | — | — | — | SOUL DANCE NUMBER THREE — Wilson Pickett (Jerry Wexler), Atlantic 2412 | 1 |
| 93 | — | — | — | WHY (Am I Treated So Bad) — Bobby Powell (Lionel Whitfield), Whit 730 | 1 |
| 94 | — | — | — | I'LL ALWAYS HAVE FAITH IN YOU — Carla Thomas (David Porter & Isaac Hayes), Stax 222 | 1 |
| 95 | 96 | — | — | TO BE A LOVER — Gene Chandler (Carl Davis), Checker 1165 | 2 |
| 96 | 97 | — | — | HAVE YOU SEEN HER FACE — Byrds (Gary Usher), Columbia 44157 | 2 |
| 97 | — | — | — | I STAND ACCUSED (Of Loving You) — Glories (Bob Yorey), Date 1553 | 1 |
| 98 | 100 | — | — | GIRL (You Captivate Me) — ? (Question Mark) & the Mysterians (Neil Bogart), Cameo 479 | 2 |
| 99 | — | — | — | TWO IN THE AFTERNOON — Dino, Desi & Billy (Gary Klein), Reprise 0579 | 1 |
| 100 | — | — | — | BLACK SHEEP — Sam the Sham & the Pharaohs (Stan Kesler) MGM 13747 | 1 |

## HOT 100—A TO Z—(Publisher-Licensee)


Ain't No Mountain High Enough (Jobete, BMI) .... 27
Airplane Song (My Airplane) (Hastings, BMI) .... 87
Alfie (Famous, ASCAP) .... 22
All I Need Is You (Jobete, BMI) .... 8
Baby, Please Come Back Home (Groovesville, BMI) .... 72
Black Sheep (Il-Gato, BMI) .... 100
Bowling Green (Rook, BMI) .... 60
Can't Take My Eyes Off You (Saturday/Seasons' Four, BMI) .... 11
Carrie Ann (Maribus, BMI) .... 73
C'Mon Marianne (Saturday/Seasons' Four, BMI) .... 33
Come on Down to My Boat (Picturetone-Goldstein, BMI) .... 13
Come to the Sunshine (Vantim, BMI) .... 37
Creeque Alley (Trousdale, BMI) .... 21
Daylight Savin' Time (Rumbalero, BMI) .... 90
Ding Dong the Witch Is Dead (Feist, ASCAP) .... 17
Do It Again a Little Bit Slower (Barton, BMI) .... 19
Don't Blame the Children (Saloon Songs, BMI) .... 48
Don't Sleep in the Subway (Duchess, BMI) .... 26
For Your Precious Love (Sunflower, ASCAP) .... 34
Friday on My Mind (Unart, BMI) .... 45
Funny Familiar Forgotten Feelings (Acuff-Rose, BMI) .... 49
Girl (You Captivate Me) (S&J, BMI) .... 98
Girl, You'll Be a Woman Soon (Tallyrand, BMI) .... 35
Girls in Love (Chardon, BMI) .... 39
Graduation Day (Travis, BMI) .... 85
Groovin' (Slacsar, BMI) .... 1
Happening, The (Jobete, BMI) .... 40
Have You Seen Her Face (Tickson, BMI) .... 96
Here Comes My Baby (Mainstay, BMI) .... 23
Here We Go Again (Dirk, BMI) .... 28
Him or Me—What's It Gonna Be? (Daywin, BMI) .... 16
Hig Hug-Her (East, BMI) .... 51
I Got Rhythm (New World, ASCAP) .... 9
I Stand Accused (Of Loving You) (Yorey-Piote, BMI) .... 97
I Take It Back (Low-Sal, BMI) .... 62
I Was Made to Love Her (Jobete, BMI) .... 43
I'll Always Have Faith in You (Falart/Champion, BMI) .... 94
It's Cold Outside (R.G.D., BMI) .... 63
Jump Back (East, BMI) .... 63
Let Yourself Go (Dynatone, BMI) .... 52
Let's Live for Today (James, BMI) .... 15
Light My Fire (Nipper, ASCAP) .... 50
Little Bit o' Soul (Southern, ASCAP) .... 6
Long-Legged Girl (With the Short Dress On) (Presley, BMI) .... 67
Love Me Tender (Presley, BMI) .... 84
Make Me Yours (Cash Songs, BMI) .... 53
Mary in the Morning (Pamco, BMI) .... 38
Mercy, Mercy, Mercy (Zawinal, BMI) .... 81
Mirage (Patricia, BMI) .... 10
Misty Blue (Talmount, BMI) .... 57
More Love (Jobete, BMI) .... 76
New York Mining Disaster 1941 (Have You Seen My Wife Mr. Jones) (Abigail, BMI) .... 18
Night and Day (Harms, ASCAP) .... 86
No Good to Cry (Linesider-Barrisue, BMI) .... 88
Now I Know (Helios, BMI) .... 78
On a Carousel (Maribus, BMI) .... 41
Ooh Baby, Baby (Jobete, BMI) .... 64
One By One (Ananga-Ranga, BMI) .... 80
Ooogum Boogum Song, The (Big Shot, ASCAP) .... 42
Pay You Back With Interest (Maribus, BMI) .... 46
Plastic Man (Chris-Marc-Cotillion, BMI) .... 74
Release Me (And Let Me Love Again) (Four Star, BMI) .... 4
Respect (East-Time-Walco, BMI) .... 2
San Francisco "Wear Some Flowers in Your Hair" (Trousdale, BMI) .... 20
7 Rooms of Gloom (Jobete, BMI) .... 14
Shake (Kags, BMI) .... 47
Shake, Rattle and Roll (Progressive, BMI) .... 61
She'd Rather Be With Me (Chardon, BMI) .... 3
Silence Is Golden (Saturday/Gevadium, BMI) .... 91
Six-o'Clock (Faithful Virtue, BMI) .... 25
Society's Child (Webatuck, BMI) .... 30
Somebody Help Me (Essex, ASCAP) .... 82
Somebody to Love (Cooper Penny, BMI) .... 5
Soothe Me (Kags, BMI) .... 89
Soul Dance Number Three (Pronto, BMI) .... 92
Soul Finger (East, BMI) .... 54
Sound of Love (Jetstar, BMI) .... 36
Stay Together Young Lovers (Missile/Rittenhouse, BMI) .... 66
Step Out of Your Mind (Blackwood, BMI) .... 71
Summer and Sandy (Saturday, BMI) .... 75
Sunday Will Never Be the Same (Pamco, BMI) .... 12
Sweet Soul Music (Bedwal, BMI) .... 44
They're Here (Maresca, ASCAP) .... 77
Time, Time (April, ASCAP) .... 68
Together (Razor Sharp, BMI) .... 56
To Be a Lover (Cachand/Jalynne, BMI) .... 95
Tracks of My Tears, The (Jobete, BMI) .... 24
Tramp (Modern, BMI) .... 29
Two in the Afternoon (Chardon, BMI) .... 99
Up-Up and Away (Rivers, BMI) .... 31
When You're Young and in Love (Picturetone, BMI) .... 32
Who's Lovin' You (Jobete, BMI) .... 79
Why? (Am I Treated So Bad) (Powell) (Staples, BMI) .... 93
Why? (Am I Treated So Bad) (Sweet Inspirations) (Staples, BMI) .... 58
Windy (Irving, BMI) .... 7
Woman Like That, Yeah (Tree, BMI) .... 65
You Can't Stand Alone (T.M., BMI) .... 70
You Gave Me Something (And Everything Is All Right (Myto, BMI) .... 59
You Must Have Been a Beautiful Baby (Remick, ASCAP) .... 55
You Wanted Someone to Play With (I Wanted Someone to Love) (Morris, ASCAP) .... 83


## BUBBLING UNDER THE HOT 100

101. ONLY LOVE CAN BREAK A HEART .... Margaret Whiting, London 108
102. FINCHLEY CENTRAL .... New Vaudeville Band, Fontana 1589
103. LITTLE MISS SUNSHINE .... Tommy Roe, ABC 10945
104. WHY? (AM I TREATED SO BAD) .... Staple Singers, Epic 10158
105. FLOWER CHILDREN .... Marcia Strassman, Uni 55006
106. HEY LOVE .... Stevie Wonder, Tamla 54151
107. WHEN THE GOOD SUN SHINES .... Elmo & Almo, Daddy Best Presents 2501
108. ME ABOUT YOU .... Mojo Men, Reprise 0380
109. AM I GROOVING YOU .... Freddie Scott, Shout 212
110. I CAN'T HELP IT (IF I'M STILL IN LOVE WITH YOU) .... B. J. Thomas, Scepter 12194
111 JACKSON .... Nancy Sinatra & Lee Hazelwood, Reprise 0595
112. LET IT HAPPEN .... James Carr, Goldwax 323
113. YOU ONLY LIVE TWICE .... Nancy Sinatra, Reprise 0595
114. ALL'S QUIET ON WEST 23RD STREET .... Jetstream, Smash 2095
115. LONELY DRIFTER .... Pieces of Eight, 854
116. NO MORE HUNTING AROUND .... Lamp of Childhood, Dunhill 4089
117 GREATEST LOVE .... Billy Joe Royal, Columbia 44103
118. THREAD THE NEEDLE .... Clarence Carter, Fame 1013
119. WORK WITH ME ANNIE .... P. J. Proby, Liberty 55974
120. GROOVY SUMMERTIME .... Love Generation, Imperial 66243
121. HOW LONG HAS IT BEEN .... Casinos, Fraternity 987
122. DON'T ROCK THE BOAT .... Eddie Floyd, Stax 219
123. TONIGHT CARMEN .... Marty Robbins, Columbia 44128
124. HYPNOTISED .... Linda Jones, Lema 2070
125. SOME KIND OF WONDERFUL .... Soul Brother 6, Atlantic 2406
126. HERE I AM .... Barbara McNair, Motown 1106
127. LOSIN' BOY .... Eddy Giles, Marco 1031
128. APPLES, PEACHES & PUMPKIN PIE .... Jay & the Techniques, Smash 2086
129 GLAD I COULD BE SO HAPPY .... Magnificent Men, Capitol 5005
130. 39-21-46 .... The Showmen, Minit 32007
131. NOW I KNOW .... Eddie Fisher, RCA Victor 9204
132. SO SHARP .... Dyke & the Blazers, Original Sound 69
133. A WHITER SHADE OF PALE .... Procol Harum, Deram 7607
134. MORE, MORE OF YOUR LOVE .... Bob Brady & the Concords, Chariot 101
135. MR. PLEASANT .... Kinks, Reprise 0587

Compiled from national retail sales and radio station airplay by the Music Popularity Dept. of Record Market Research, Billboard.

# Billboard HOT 100

**For Week Ending June 24, 1967**

★ STAR performer—Sides registering greatest proportionate upward progress this week.

® Record Industry Association of America seal of certification as million selling single.

| This Week | Wk. Ago | 2 Wks. Ago | TITLE Artist (Producer), Label & Number | Weeks On Chart |
|---|---|---|---|---|
| 1 | 1 | 2 | **GROOVIN'** — Young Rascals (Young Rascals), Atlantic 2401 | 10 |
| 2 | 2 | 1 | **RESPECT** — Aretha Franklin (Jerry Wexler), Atlantic 2403 | 9 |
| 3 | 3 | 7 | **SHE'D RATHER BE WITH ME** — Turtles (Joe Wissert), White Whale 249 | 7 |
| 4 | 7 | 12 | **WINDY** — The Association (Bones Howe), Warner Bros. 7041 | 5 |
| 5 | 6 | 8 | **LITTLE BIT O' SOUL** — Music Explosion (J. Katz-J. Kasenetz & E. Chiprut), Laurie 3380 | 7 |
| 6 | 20 | 32 | **SAN FRANCISCO "WEAR SOME FLOWERS IN YOUR HAIR"** — Scott McKenzie (John Phillips & Lou Adler), Ode 103 | 5 |
| 7 | 5 | 6 | **SOMEBODY TO LOVE** — Jefferson Airplane (Rick Jarrard), RCA Victor 9140 | 13 |
| 8 | 11 | 17 | **CAN'T TAKE MY EYES OFF YOU** — Frankie Valli (Bob Crewe), Philips 40446 | 6 |
| 9 | 12 | 14 | **SUNDAY WILL NEVER BE THE SAME** — Spanky and Our Gang (Jerry Ross), Mercury 72679 | 6 |
| 10 | 15 | 15 | **LET'S LIVE FOR TODAY** — Grass Roots (Steve Barri & P. F. Sloan), Dunhill 4084 | 7 |
| 11 | 13 | 16 | **COME ON DOWN TO MY BOAT** — Every Mother's Son (Wes Farrell), MGM 13733 | 8 |
| 12 | 4 | 4 | **RELEASE ME (And Let Me Love Again)** — Engelbert Humperdinck, Parrot 40011 | 12 |
| 13 | 24 | 45 | **THE TRACKS OF MY TEARS** — Johnny Rivers (Lou Adler), Imperial 66244 | 4 |
| 14 | 14 | 19 | **7 ROOMS OF GLOOM** — Four Tops (Holland & Dozier), Motown 1110 | 6 |
| 15 | 17 | 33 | **DING DONG THE WITCH IS DEAD** — Fifth Estate (Steve & Bill Jerome), Jubilee 5573 | 6 |
| 16 | 18 | 26 | **NEW YORK MINING DISASTER 1951 (Have You Seen My Wife Mr. Jones)** — The Bee Gees (Ossie Byrne), Atco 6487 | 5 |
| 17 | 22 | 28 | **ALFIE** — Dionne Warwick (Bacharach-David), Scepter 12187 | 12 |
| 18 | 19 | 21 | **DO IT AGAIN A LITTLE BIT SLOWER** — Jon & Robin & the In Crowd (Dale Hawkins), Abnak 119 | 8 |
| 19 | 8 | 9 | **ALL I NEED IS YOU** — Temptations (F. Wilson), Gordy 7061 | 9 |
| 20 | 26 | 49 | **DON'T SLEEP IN THE SUBWAY** — Petula Clark (Tony Hatch), Warner Bros. 7049 | 4 |
| 21 | 31 | 44 | **UP—UP AND AWAY** — 5th Dimension (Johnny Rivers & Marc Gordon), Soul City 756 | 4 |
| 22 | 27 | 29 | **AIN'T NO MOUNTAIN HIGH ENOUGH** — Marvin Gaye & Tammi Terrell (H. Fuqua & J. Bristol), Tamla 54149 | 7 |
| 23 | 28 | 37 | **HERE WE GO AGAIN** — Ray Charles (TRC), ABC 10938 | 6 |
| 24 | 50 | 61 | **LIGHT MY FIRE** — Doors (Paul A. Rothchild), Elektra 45615 | 4 |
| 25 | 30 | 48 | **SOCIETY'S CHILD** — Janis Ian (Shadow Morton), Verve 5027 | 8 |
| 26 | 29 | 30 | **TRAMP** — Otis & Carla (Prod. by Staff), Stax 216 | 9 |
| 27 | 10 | 11 | **MIRAGE** — Tommy James and the Shondells (Bo Gentry & Ritchie Cordell), Roulette 4736 | 8 |
| 28 | 33 | 66 | **C'MON MARIANNE** — Four Seasons (Bob Crewe), Philips 40460 | 3 |
| 29 | 9 | 3 | **I GOT RHYTHM** — Happenings (The Tokens & B. T. Puppy 527) | 12 |
| 30 | 38 | 52 | **MARY IN THE MORNING** — Al Martino (Tom Morgan & Marvin Holtzman), Capitol 5904 | 5 |
| 31 | 34 | 53 | **FOR YOUR PRECIOUS LOVE** — Oscar Toney Jr. (Papa Don, Coghill, Emmons, Chrisman & Young), Bell 672 | 5 |
| 32 | 16 | 5 | **HIM OR ME—WHAT'S IT GONNA BE?** — Paul Revere & the Raiders (Terry Melcher), Columbia 44094 | 9 |
| 33 | 43 | 68 | **I WAS MADE TO LOVE HER** — Stevie Wonder (H. Cosby), Tamla 54151 | 3 |
| 34 | 42 | 43 | **THE OOGUM BOOGUM SONG** — Brenton Wood (Hooven-Winn), Double Shot 111 | 11 |
| 35 | 46 | 56 | **PAY YOU BACK WITH INTEREST** — Hollies, Imperial 66240 | 4 |
| 36 | 36 | 42 | **SOUND OF LOVE** — Five Americans (Dale Hawkins), Abnak 120 | 6 |
| 37 | 37 | 47 | **COME TO THE SUNSHINE** — Harpers Bizarre (Lenny Waronker), Warner Bros. 7028 | 6 |
| 38 | 48 | 58 | **DON'T BLAME THE CHILDREN** — Sammy Davis Jr. (Jimmy Bowen), Reprise 0565 | 3 |
| 39 | 23 | 13 | **HERE COMES MY BABY** — Tremeloes, Epic 10139 | 12 |
| 40 | 21 | 10 | **CREEQUE ALLEY** — Mamas & the Papas (Lou Adler), Dunhill 4083 | 8 |
| 41 | 54 | 70 | **SOUL FINGER** — Bar-Kays (Produced by Staff), Volt 148 | 6 |
| 42 | 32 | 23 | **WHEN YOU'RE YOUNG AND IN LOVE** — Marvelettes (J. Dean & William Weatherspoon), Tamla 54150 | 10 |
| 43 | 60 | 60 | **BOWLING GREEN** — The Everly Brothers (Dick Glasser), Warner Bros. 7020 | 4 |
| 44 | 61 | 82 | **SHAKE, RATTLE AND ROLL** — Arthur Conley (Otis Redding), Atco 6494 | 3 |
| 45 | 55 | 67 | **YOU MUST HAVE BEEN A BEAUTIFUL BABY** — Dave Clark Five (Dave Clark), Epic 10179 | 3 |
| 46 | 53 | 84 | **MAKE ME YOURS** — Bettye Swann, Money 126 | 6 |
| 47 | 47 | 54 | **SHAKE** — Otis Redding, Volt 149 | 6 |
| 48 | 56 | 59 | **TOGETHER** — Intruders, Gamble 205 | 6 |
| 49 | 81 | — | **MERCY, MERCY, MERCY** — Buckinghams (James William Guercio), Columbia 44162 | 2 |
| 50 | — | — | **WHITE RABBIT** — Jefferson Airplane (Rick Jarrard), RCA Victor 9248 | 1 |
| 51 | 62 | 89 | **I TAKE IT BACK** — Sandy Posey (Chips Moman), MGM 13744 | 3 |
| 52 | 76 | — | **MORE LOVE** — Smokey Robinson & the Miracles ("Smokey"), Tamla 54152 | 2 |
| 53 | 71 | 86 | **STEP OUT OF YOUR MIND** — American Breed (Acta 804) | 4 |
| 54 | 49 | 55 | **FUNNY FAMILIAR FORGOTTEN FEELINGS** — Tom Jones (Peter Sullivan), Parrot 40014 | 6 |
| 55 | 73 | — | **CARRIE ANN** — Hollies (Ron Richards), Epic 10180 | 2 |
| 56 | — | — | **FOR YOUR LOVE** — Peaches & Herb (Bert Kaprelik & Ken Williams), Date 1563 | 1 |
| 57 | 65 | 85 | **WOMAN LIKE THAT, YEAH** — Joe Tex (Buddy Killen), Dial 4059 | 4 |
| 58 | 58 | 72 | **WHY (Am I Treated So Bad)** — Sweet Inspirations (Jerry Wexler), Atlantic 2410 | 4 |
| 59 | 59 | 65 | **YOU GAVE ME SOMETHING (And Everything Is All Right)** — Fantastic Four (Kent, Wingate, Weems), Ric Tic 128 | 5 |
| 60 | 57 | 57 | **MISTY BLUE** — Eddy Arnold (Chet Atkins), RCA Victor 9182 | 8 |
| 61 | 72 | 78 | **BABY, PLEASE COME BACK HOME** — J. J. Barnes (Davis-Barnes), Groovesville 1006 | 6 |
| 62 | 85 | — | **GRADUATION DAY** — Arbors (Richard E. Carney), Date 1561 | 2 |
| 63 | 64 | 73 | **OOH BABY BABY** — Five Stairsteps (Curtis Mayfield), Windy C 607 | 5 |
| 64 | 83 | — | **YOU WANTED SOMEONE TO PLAY WITH (I Wanted Someone to Love)** — Frankie Laine (Bob Thiele), ABC 10946 | 2 |
| 65 | 84 | — | **LOVE ME TENDER** — Percy Sledge (Quin Ivy & Marlin Greene), Atlantic 2414 | 2 |
| 66 | 66 | 69 | **STAY TOGETHER YOUNG LOVERS** — Brenda & the Tabulations (Bob Finiz), Dionn 501 | 6 |
| 67 | 79 | 95 | **WHO'S LOVIN' YOU** — Brenda & the Tabulations (Bob Finiz), Dionn 501 | 3 |
| 68 | 69 | 79 | **IT'S COLD OUTSIDE** — Choir (Najweb Hedafy), Roulette 4738 | 4 |
| 69 | 75 | 90 | **SUMMER AND SANDY** — Lesley Gore (Bob Crewe), Mercury 72683 | 3 |
| 70 | 82 | — | **SOMEBODY HELP ME** — Spencer Davis Group (Chris Blackwell & Jimmy Miller), United Artists 50162 | 2 |
| 71 | 92 | — | **SOUL DANCE NUMBER THREE** — Wilson Pickett (Jerry Wexler), Atlantic 2412 | 2 |
| 72 | 87 | — | **AIRPLANE SONG** — Royal Guardsmen (Gernhard Ent.), Laurie 3391 | 2 |
| 73 | 70 | 74 | **YOU CAN'T STAND ALONE** — Wilson Picket (Jerry Wexler), Atlantic 2412 | 5 |
| 74 | 74 | 76 | **PLASTIC MAN** — Sonny & Cher (Sonny Bono), Atco 6486 | 3 |
| 75 | 100 | — | **BLACK SHEEP** — Sam the Sham & the Pharaohs (Stan Kesler), MGM 13747 | 2 |
| 76 | 91 | — | **SILENCE IS GOLDEN** — Tremeloes (Mike Smith), Epic 10134 | 2 |
| 77 | 78 | 88 | **NOW I KNOW** — Jack Jones, Kapp 833 | 3 |
| 78 | 80 | 80 | **ONE BY ONE** — Blues Magoos (Art Polhemus & Bob Wyld), Mercury 72692 | 3 |
| 79 | — | — | **JACKSON** — Nancy Sinatra & Lee Hazlewood (Lee Hazlewood), Reprise 0595 | 1 |
| 80 | — | — | **A WHITER SHADE OF PALE** — Procol Harum (Denny Cordell), Deram 7507 | 1 |
| 81 | — | — | **DON'T GO OUT INTO THE RAIN (You're Going to Melt)** — Herman's Hermits (Mickie Most), MGM 13761 | 1 |
| 82 | — | — | **YOU ONLY LIVE TWICE** — Nancy Sinatra (Lee Hazlewood), Reprise 0595 | 1 |
| 83 | 96 | 97 | **HAVE YOU SEEN HER FACE** — Byrds (Gary Usher), Columbia 44157 | 3 |
| 84 | 86 | 87 | **NIGHT AND DAY** — Sergio Mendes & Brasil '66 (Herb Alpert), A&M 853 | 3 |
| 85 | 97 | — | **I STAND ACCUSED (Of Loving You)** — Glories (Bob Yorey), Date 1553 | 2 |
| 86 | 94 | — | **I'LL ALWAYS HAVE FAITH IN YOU** — Carla Thomas (David Porter & Isaac Hayes), Stax 222 | 2 |
| 87 | 89 | — | **SOOTHE ME** — Sam & Dave (Prod. by Staff), Stax 218 | 2 |
| 88 | — | — | **THERE GOES MY EVERYTHING** — Engelbert Humperdinck (Peter Sullivan), Parrot 40015 | 1 |
| 89 | 90 | — | **DAYLIGHT SAVIN' TIME** — Keith (Jerry Ross), Mercury 72695 | 2 |
| 90 | — | — | **LONELY DRIFTER** — Pieces of Eight, A&M 854 | 1 |
| 91 | — | — | **SOME KIND OF WONDERFUL** — Soul Brothers Six, Atlantic 2406 | 1 |
| 92 | — | — | **UP, UP AND AWAY** — Johnny Mann Singers (Jack Tracy), Liberty 55972 | 1 |
| 93 | 93 | — | **WHY (Am I Treated So Bad)** — Bobby Powell (Lionel Whitfield), Whit 730 | 2 |
| 94 | — | — | **MY WORLD FELL DOWN** — Sagittarius (Gary Usher), Columbia 44163 | 1 |
| 95 | 95 | 96 | **TO BE A LOVER** — Gene Chandler (Carl Davis), Checker 1165 | 3 |
| 96 | — | — | **HYPNOTIZED** — Linda Jones (George Kerr), Loma 2070 | 1 |
| 97 | — | — | **THE JOKERS** — Peter & Gordon (John Burgess), Capitol 5919 | 1 |
| 98 | — | — | **THREAD THE NEEDLE** — Clarence Carter (Rick Hall & Staff), Fame 1013 | 1 |
| 99 | — | — | **LET THE GOOD TIMES ROLL & FEEL SO GOOD** — Bunny Sigler (Madara-White-Huff), Parkway 153 | 1 |
| 100 | — | — | **GROOVY SUMMERTIME** — Love Generation (Tommy Oliver), Imperial 66243 | 1 |

## BUBBLING UNDER THE HOT 100

101. 39-21-40 SHAPE ... Snowmen, Minit 32007
102. NO GOOD TO CRY ... Wildweeds, Cadet 5581
103. LITTLE MISS SUNSHINE ... Tommy Roe, ABC 10945
104. ALL'S QUIET ON WEST 23RD STREET ... Jet Stream, Smash 2095
105. TWO IN THE AFTERNOON ... Dino, Desi & Billy, Reprise 0579
106. ME ABOUT YOU ... Mojo Men, Reprise 0580
107. WHEN THE GOOD SUN SHINES ... Elmo & Almo, Buddy Best Presents 2501
108. IT'S THE LITTLE THINGS ... Sonny & Cher, Atco 6486
109. GIRL (YOU CAPTIVATE ME) ... ? (Question Mark) & the Mysterians, Cameo 479
110. I LIKE IT THAT WAY ... Tommy James & the Shondells, Roulette 4756
111. GIVE ME TIME ... Dusty Springfield, Philips 40465
112. LET IT HAPPEN ... James Carr, Goldwax 323
113. DON'T ROCK THE BOAT ... Eddie Floyd, Stax 219
114. HEY LOVE ... Stevie Wonder, Tamla 54151
115. FUNNY BROADWAY ... Dyke & the Blazers, Original Sound 64
116. ONLY LOVE CAN BREAK A HEART ... Margaret Whiting, London 108
117. DEEP IN THE HEART OF HARLEM ... Walter Jackson, Okeh 7285
118. WHEN LOVE SLIPS AWAY ... Dee Dee Warwick, Blue Rock 4041
119. JUST LOOK WHAT YOU'VE DONE ... Brenda Holloway, Tamla 54148
120. SHE MAY CALL YOU UP TONIGHT ... Left Banke, Smash 2097
121. OMAHA ... Moby Grape, Columbia 44173
122. (I WANNA) TESTIFY ... Parliaments, Revilot 207
123. JUST ONE LOOK ... Soul Twins, Karen 1535
124. SHE'S LEAVIN' TIME ... Davis & Jonathan, Capitol 5934
125. I'LL GO TO YOU ... Yellow Balloon, Canterbury 513
126. GOOD FEELIN' TIME ... Toussaint McCall, Ronn 9
127. SWEET SWEET LOVIN' ... Paul Kelly, Philips 40457
128. WOMAN WITH THE BLUES ... Helene Smith, Phil-L-A of Soul 300
129. YOU WERE ON MY MIND ... Crispian St. Peters, Jamie 1310
130. SO SHARP ... Dyke & the Blazers, Original Sound 64
131. MR. PLEASANT ... Kinks, Reprise 0587
132. MORE, MORE, MORE OF YOUR LOVE ... Bob Brady & Concords, Chariot 101
133. BLUES THEME ... Arrows, Tower 295
134. NOT SO SWEET MARTHA LORRAINE ... Country Joe & the Fish, Vanguard 35052
135. TEMPTATION ... Boots Randolph, Monument 1009

# Billboard HOT 100

For Week Ending July 1, 1967

★ STAR performer—Sides registering greatest proportionate upward progress this week.

● Record Industry Association of America seal of certification as million selling single.

| This Week | 1 Wk. Ago | 2 Wk. Ago | 3 Wk. Ago | TITLE, Artist (Producer), Label & Number | Weeks on Chart |
|---|---|---|---|---|---|
| 1 | 4 | 7 | 12 | WINDY — The Association (Bones Howe), Warner Bros. 7041 | 6 |
| 2 | 1 | 1 | 2 | GROOVIN' — Young Rascals (Young Rascals), Atlantic 2401 | 11 |
| 3 | 5 | 6 | 8 | LITTLE BIT O' SOUL — Music Explosion (J. Katz-J. Kasenetz & E. Chiprut), Laurie 3380 | 8 |
| 4 | 6 | 20 | 32 | SAN FRANCISCO "WEAR SOME FLOWERS IN YOUR HAIR" — Scott McKenzie (John Phillips & Lou Adler), Ode 103 | 4 |
| 5 | 3 | 3 | 7 | SHE'D RATHER BE WITH ME — Turtles (Joe Wissert), White Whale 249 | 8 |
| 6 | 2 | 2 | 1 | RESPECT — Aretha Franklin (Jerry Wexler), Atlantic 2403 | 10 |
| 7 | 8 | 11 | 17 | CAN'T TAKE MY EYES OFF YOU — Frankie Valli (Bob Crewe), Philips 40446 | 7 |
| 8 | 10 | 15 | 15 | LET'S LIVE FOR TODAY — Grass Roots (Steve Barri & P. F. Sloan), Dunhill 4084 | 8 |
| 9 | 11 | 13 | 16 | COME ON DOWN TO MY BOAT — Every Mother's Son (Wes Farrell), MGM 13733 | 9 |
| 10 | 20 | 26 | 49 | DON'T SLEEP IN THE SUBWAY — Petula Clark (Tony Hatch), Warner Bros. 7049 | 5 |
| 11 | 15 | 17 | 33 | DING DONG THE WITCH IS DEAD — Fifth Estate (Steve & Bill Jerome), Jubilee 5573 | 7 |
| 12 | 21 | 31 | 44 | UP—UP AND AWAY — 5th Dimension (Johnny Rivers & Marc Gordon), Soul City 756 | 5 |
| 13 | 13 | 24 | 45 | THE TRACKS OF MY TEARS — Johnny Rivers (Lou Adler), Imperial 66244 | 5 |
| 14 | 16 | 18 | 26 | NEW YORK MINING DISASTER 1941 (Have You Seen My Wife Mr. Jones) — The Bee Gees (Ossie Byrne), Atco 6487 | 6 |
| 15 | 17 | 22 | 28 | ALFIE — Dionne Warwick (Bacharach-David), Scepter 12187 | 13 |
| 16 | 9 | 12 | 14 | SUNDAY WILL NEVER BE THE SAME — Spanky and Our Gang (Jerry Ross), Mercury 72679 | 7 |
| 17 | 7 | 5 | 6 | SOMEBODY TO LOVE — Jefferson Airplane (Rick Jarrard), RCA Victor 9140 | 14 |
| 18 | 28 | 33 | 66 | C'MON MARIANNE — Four Seasons (Bob Crewe), Philips 40460 | 4 |
| 19 | 24 | 50 | 61 | LIGHT MY FIRE — Doors (Paul A. Rothchild), Elektra 45615 | 5 |
| 20 | 14 | 14 | 19 | 7 ROOMS OF GLOOM — Four Tops (Holland & Dozier), Motown 1110 | 7 |
| 21 | 22 | 27 | 29 | AIN'T NO MOUNTAIN HIGH ENOUGH — Marvin Gaye & Tammi Terrell (N. Fuqua & J. Bristol), Tamla 54149 | 8 |
| 22 | 25 | 30 | 48 | SOCIETY'S CHILD — Janis Ian (Shadow Morton), Verve 5027 | 6 |
| 23 | 23 | 28 | 37 | HERE WE GO AGAIN — Ray Charles (TRC), ABC 10938 | 7 |
| 24 | 18 | 19 | 21 | DO IT AGAIN A LITTLE BIT SLOWER — Jon & Robin & the In Crowd (Dale Hawkins), Abnak 119 | 9 |
| 25 | 33 | 43 | 68 | I WAS MADE TO LOVE HER — Stevie Wonder (H. Cosby), Tamla 54151 | 4 |
| 26 | 31 | 34 | 53 | FOR YOUR PRECIOUS LOVE — Oscar Toney Jr. (Papa Don, Coghill, Emmons, Chrisman & Young), Bell 672 | 6 |
| 27 | 12 | 4 | 4 | RELEASE ME (And Let Me Love Again) — Engelbert Humperdinck (Peter Sullivan), Parrot 40011 | 13 |
| 28 | 80 | — | — | A WHITER SHADE OF PALE — Procol Harum (Denny Cordell), Deram 7507 | 2 |
| 29 | 35 | 46 | 56 | PAY YOU BACK WITH INTEREST — Hollies, Imperial 66240 | 5 |
| 30 | 30 | 38 | 52 | MARY IN THE MORNING — Al Martino (Tom Morgan & Marvin Holtzman), Capitol 5904 | 6 |
| 31 | 41 | 54 | 70 | SOUL FINGER — Bar-Kays (Produced by Staff), Volt 148 | 7 |
| 32 | 46 | 53 | 84 | MAKE ME YOURS — Bettye Swann, Money 126 | 7 |
| 33 | 50 | — | — | WHITE RABBIT — Jefferson Airplane (Rick Jarrard), RCA Victor 9248 | 2 |
| 34 | 44 | 61 | 82 | SHAKE, RATTLE AND ROLL — Arthur Conley (Otis Redding), Atco 6494 | 4 |
| 35 | 45 | 55 | 67 | YOU MUST HAVE BEEN A BEAUTIFUL BABY — Dave Clark Five (Dave Clark), Epic 10179 | 4 |
| 36 | 49 | 81 | — | MERCY, MERCY, MERCY — Buckinghams (James William Guercio), Columbia 44162 | 3 |
| 37 | 37 | 37 | 47 | COME TO THE SUNSHINE — Harpers Bizarre (Lenny Waconker), Warner Bros. 7028 | 4 |
| 38 | 38 | 48 | 58 | DON'T BLAME THE CHILDREN — Sammy Davis Jr. (Jimmy Bowen), Reprise 0566 | 6 |
| 39 | 51 | 62 | 89 | I TAKE IT BACK — Sandy Posey (Chips Moman), MGM 13744 | 4 |
| 40 | 19 | 8 | 9 | ALL I NEED IS YOU — Temptations (F. Wilson), Gordy 7061 | 10 |
| 41 | 53 | 71 | 86 | STEP OUT OF YOUR MIND — American Breed, Acta 804 | 5 |
| 42 | 52 | 76 | — | MORE LOVE — Smokey Robinson & the Miracles ("Smokey"), Tamla 54152 | 3 |
| 43 | 43 | 60 | 60 | BOWLING GREEN — The Everly Brothers (Dick Glasser) | 9 |
| 44 | 26 | 29 | 30 | TRAMP — Otis & Carla (Prod. by Staff), Stax 216 | 9 |
| 45 | 55 | 73 | — | CARRIE ANN — Hollies (Ron Richards), Epic 10180 | 3 |
| 46 | 56 | — | — | FOR YOUR LOVE — Peaches & Herb (Bert Kapralik & Ken Williams), Date 1563 | 2 |
| 47 | 27 | 10 | 11 | MIRAGE — Tommy James & the Shondells (Bo Gentry & Ritchie Cordell), Roulette 4736 | 10 |
| 48 | 29 | 9 | 3 | I GOT RHYTHM — Happenings (The Tokens), B. T. Puppy 527 | 13 |
| 49 | 81 | — | — | DON'T GO OUT INTO THE RAIN (You're Going to Melt) — Herman's Hermits (Mickie Most), MGM 13761 | 2 |
| 50 | 79 | — | — | JACKSON — Nancy Sinatra & Lee Hazlewood (Lee Hazlewood), Reprise 0595 | 2 |
| 51 | 36 | 36 | 42 | SOUND OF LOVE — Five Americans (Dale Hawkins), Abnak 120 | 7 |
| 52 | 34 | 42 | 43 | THE OOGUM BOOGUM SONG — Brenton Wood (Hooven-Winn), Double Shot 111 | 12 |
| 53 | 65 | 84 | — | LOVE ME TENDER — Percy Sledge (Quin Ivy & Marlin Greene), Atlantic 2414 | 3 |
| 54 | 72 | 87 | — | AIRPLANE SONG — Royal Guardsmen (Gernhard Ent.), Laurie 3391 | 3 |
| 55 | 59 | 59 | 65 | YOU GAVE ME SOMETHING (And Everything Is All Right) — Fantastic Four (Kent, Wingate, Weems), Ric Tic 128 | 6 |
| 56 | 57 | 85 | — | WOMAN LIKE THAT, YEAH — Joe Tex (Buddy Killen), Dial 4059 | 3 |
| 57 | 58 | 58 | 72 | WHY (Am I Treated So Bad) — Sweet Inspirations (Jerry Wexler), Atlantic 2410 | 5 |
| 58 | 76 | 91 | — | SILENCE IS GOLDEN — Tremeloes (Mike Smith), Epic 10184 | 3 |
| 59 | 62 | 85 | — | GRADUATION DAY — Arbors (Richard E. Carney), Date 1561 | 3 |
| 60 | 71 | 92 | — | SOUL DANCE NUMBER THREE — Wilson Pickett (Jerry Wexler), Atlantic 2412 | 3 |
| 61 | 61 | 72 | 78 | BABY, PLEASE COME BACK HOME — J. J. Barnes (Davis-Barnes), Groovesville 1006 | 7 |
| 62 | 64 | 83 | — | YOU WANTED SOMEONE TO PLAY WITH (I Wanted Someone to Love) — Frankie Laine (Bob Thiele), ABC 10946 | 3 |
| 63 | 88 | — | — | THERE GOES MY EVERYTHING — Engelbert Humperdinck (Peter Sullivan), Parrot 40015 | 2 |
| 64 | 70 | 82 | — | SOMEBODY HELP ME — Spencer Davis Group (Chris Blackwell & Jimmy Miller), United Artists 50162 | 3 |
| 65 | 63 | 64 | 73 | OOH BABY BABY — Five Stairsteps (Curtis Mayfield), Windy C 607 | 6 |
| 66 | 69 | 75 | 90 | SUMMER AND SANDY — Lesley Gore (Bob Crewe), Mercury 72683 | 4 |
| 67 | 67 | 79 | 95 | WHO'S LOVIN' YOU — Brenda & the Tabulations (Bob Finiz), Dionn 501 | 4 |
| 68 | 68 | 69 | 79 | IT'S COLD OUTSIDE — Choir (Najweb Hedafy), Roulette 4738 | 5 |
| 69 | 87 | 89 | — | SOOTHE ME — Sam & Dave (Prod. by Staff), Stax 218 | 3 |
| 70 | 66 | 66 | 69 | STAY TOGETHER YOUNG LOVERS — Brenda & the Tabulations (Bob Finiz), Dionn 501 | 7 |
| 71 | 78 | 80 | 80 | ONE BY ONE — Blues Magoos (Art Polhemus & Bob Wyld), Mercury 72692 | 4 |
| 72 | 82 | — | — | YOU ONLY LIVE TWICE — Nancy Sinatra (Lee Hazlewood), Reprise 0595 | 2 |
| 73 | 77 | 78 | 88 | NOW I KNOW — Jack Jones, Kapp 833 | 4 |
| 74 | 83 | 96 | 97 | HAVE YOU SEEN HER FACE — Byrds (Gary Usher), Columbia 44157 | 4 |
| 75 | 75 | 100 | — | BLACK SHEEP — Sam the Sham & the Pharaohs (Stan Kesler), MGM 13747 | 3 |
| 76 | 96 | — | — | HYPNOTIZED — Linda Jones (George Kerr), Loma 2070 | 2 |
| 77 | — | — | — | I LIKE THE WAY — Tommy James & the Shondells (Bo Gentry & Ritchie Cordell), Roulette 4756 | 1 |
| 78 | — | — | — | SHOW BUSINESS — Lou Rawls (David Axelrod), Capitol 3941 | 1 |
| 79 | — | — | — | YOU WERE ON MY MIND — Crispian St. Peters, Jamie 1310 | 1 |
| 80 | 89 | 90 | — | DAYLIGHT SAVIN' TIME — Keith (Jerry Ross), Mercury 72695 | 3 |
| 81 | — | — | — | I'LL DO IT FOR YOU — Toussaint McCall (Scotty Moore), Room 9 | 1 |
| 82 | 84 | 86 | 87 | NIGHT AND DAY — Sergio Mendes & Brasil '66 (Herb Alpert), A&M 853 | 5 |
| 83 | 85 | 97 | — | I STAND ACCUSED (Of Loving You) — Glories (Bob Yorey), Date 1553 | 3 |
| 84 | 99 | — | — | LET THE GOOD TIMES ROLL & FEEL SO GOOD — Bunny Sigler (Madara-White-Huff), Parkway 153 | 2 |
| 85 | 100 | — | — | GROOVY SUMMERTIME — Love Generation (Tommy Oliver), Imperial 66243 | 2 |
| 86 | 86 | 94 | — | I'LL ALWAYS HAVE FAITH IN YOU — Carla Thomas (David Porter & Isaac Hayes), Stax 222 | 3 |
| 87 | — | — | — | TAKE ME (Just As I Am) — Solomon Burke (Chips Moman & Dan Penn), Atlantic 2416 | 1 |
| 88 | 90 | — | — | LONELY DRIFTER — Pieces of Eight, A&M 854 | 2 |
| 89 | — | — | — | GIVE ME TIME — Dusty Springfield, Philips 40465 | 1 |
| 90 | — | — | — | PICTURES OF LILY — Who (Kit Lambert), Decca 32156 | 1 |
| 91 | 93 | 93 | — | WHY (Am I Treated So Bad) — Bobby Powell (Lionel Whitfield), Whit 730 | 3 |
| 92 | 92 | — | — | UP, UP AND AWAY — Johnny Mann Singers (Jack Tracy), Liberty 55972 | 2 |
| 93 | 94 | — | — | MY WORLD FELL DOWN — Sagittarius (Gary Usher), Columbia 44163 | 2 |
| 94 | 95 | 95 | 96 | TO BE A LOVER — Gene Chandler (Carl Davis), Checker 1165 | 4 |
| 95 | — | — | — | (I Wanna) TESTIFY — Parliaments (Leon Ware), Revilot 207 | 1 |
| 96 | — | — | — | YOUR UNCHANGING LOVE — Marvin Gaye (Holland & Dozier), Tamla 54153 | 1 |
| 97 | — | — | — | WASHED ASHORE (On a Lonely Island in the Sea) — Platters (Richard Popcorn Wylie), Musicor 1251 | 1 |
| 98 | — | — | — | DON'T ROCK THE BOAT — Eddie Floyd, Stax 219 | 1 |
| 99 | — | — | — | MR. PLEASANT — Kinks (Shel Talmy), Reprise 0587 | 1 |
| 100 | — | — | — | JOY — Mitch Ryder (Bob Crewe), New Voice 824 | 1 |

## BUBBLING UNDER THE HOT 100

101. ALL'S QUIET ON WEST 23RD STREET — Jet Stream, Smash 2095
102. GOOD FEELIN' TIME — Yellow Balloon, Canterbury 513
103. PLASTIC MAN — Sonny & Cher, Atco 6486
104. SOME KIND OF WONDERFUL — Soul Brothers 6, Atlantic 2406
105. TWO IN THE AFTERNOON — Dino, Desi & Billy, Reprise 0579
106. 39-21-40 SHAPE — Wildweeds, Cadet 5561
107. NO GOOD TO CRY — Sonny & Cher, Atco 6486
108. IT'S THE LITTLE THINGS — Sonny & Cher, Atco 6486
109. THREAD THE NEEDLE — Clarence Carter, Fame 1013
110. LET IT HAPPEN — Jimmy Carr Jazz, Goldwax 323
111. FUNKY BROADWAY — Dyke & the Blazers, Original Sound 64
112. THE DOG — Jimmy McCracklin, Minit 32022
113. THE JOKERS — Peter & Gordon, Capitol 3919
114. YOU DON'T MISS YOUR WATER — King Curtis, Atco 6496
115. EVERYBODY NEEDS LOVE — Gladys Knight & the Pips, Soul 35034
116. LOOK OF LOVE — Dusty Springfield, Philips 40465
117. DEEP IN THE HEART OF HARLEM — Walter Jackson, Okeh 7285
118. I'LL NEVER NEED MORE THAN THIS — Ike & Tina Turner, Philles 135
119. OUT & ABOUT — Tommy Boyce & Bobby Hart, A&M 858
120. OMAHA — Moby Grape, Columbia 44173
121. BOAT THAT I ROW — Lulu, Epic 10187
122. MORE & MORE — Andy Williams, Columbia 44207
123. SHE'S LEAVING HOME — David & Jonathan, Capitol 5934
124. TEMPTATION — Boots Randolph, Monument 1017
125. YOU KEEP ME HANGIN' ON — Vanilla Fudge, Atco 6495
126. SWEET SWEET LOVIN' — Paul Kelly, Philips 40457
127. HAPPY — Sunshine Company, Imperial 66247
128. I CAN'T SEE NOBODY — Bee Gees, Atco 6487
129. MORE, MORE, MORE OF YOUR LOVE — Bob Brady & Concords, Chariot 101
130. I'LL NEVER FALL IN LOVE AGAIN — Tom Jones, Parrot 40018
131. BLUES THEME — Arrows, Tower 295
132. NOT SO SWEET MARTHA LORRAINE — Country Joe & the Fish, Vanguard 35052
133. OUT OF NOWHERE — Frank Ifield, Hickory 1454
134. DE DO DOO — Electric Prunes, Reprise 0594
135. ENDLESS SUMMER — Ventures, Liberty 55977
136. CITY OF WINDOWS — Stephen Monahan, Kapp 825

Compiled from national retail sales and radio station airplay by the Music Popularity Dept. of Record Market Research, Billboard.

# Billboard HOT 100

**For Week Ending July 8, 1967**

★ STAR performer—Sides registering greatest proportionate upward progress this week.

Record Industry Association of America seal of certification as million selling single.

| This Week | 1 Wk. Ago | 2 Wks. Ago | 3 Wks. Ago | TITLE — Artist (Producer), Label & Number | Weeks On Chart |
|---|---|---|---|---|---|
| 1 | 1 | 4 | 7 | **WINDY** — The Association, (Bones Howe), Warner Bros. 7041 | 7 |
| 2 | 3 | 5 | 6 | **LITTLE BIT O' SOUL** — Music Explosion (J. Katz-J. Kasenetz & E. Chiprut), Laurie 3380 | 9 |
| 3 | 7 | 8 | 11 | **CAN'T TAKE MY EYES OFF YOU** — Frankie Valli (Bob Crewe), Philips 40446 | 8 |
| 4 | 4 | 6 | 20 | **SAN FRANCISCO "WEAR SOME FLOWERS IN YOUR HAIR"** — Scott McKenzie (John Phillips & Lou Adler), Ode 103 | 7 |
| 5 | 10 | 20 | 26 | **DON'T SLEEP IN THE SUBWAY** — Petula Clark (Tony Hatch), Warner Bros. 7049 | 6 |
| 6 | 9 | 11 | 13 | **COME ON DOWN TO MY BOAT** — Every Mother's Son (Wes Farrell), MGM 13733 | 10 |
| 7 | 12 | 21 | 31 | **UP—UP AND AWAY** — 5th Dimension (Johnny Rivers & Marc Gordon), Soul City 756 | 6 |
| 8 | 8 | 10 | 15 | **LET'S LIVE FOR TODAY** — Grass Roots (Steve Barri & P. F. Sloan), Dunhill 4084 | 9 |
| 9 | 2 | 1 | 1 | **GROOVIN'** — Young Rascals (Young Rascals), Atlantic 2401 | 12 |
| 10 | 13 | 13 | 24 | **THE TRACKS OF MY TEARS** — Johnny Rivers (Lou Adler), Imperial 66244 | 6 |
| 11 | 5 | 3 | 3 | **SHE'D RATHER BE WITH ME** — Turtles (Bones Howe), White Whale 249 | 9 |
| 12 | 19 | 24 | 50 | **LIGHT MY FIRE** — Doors (Paul A. Rothchild), Elektra 45615 | 6 |
| 13 | 28 | 80 | — | **A WHITER SHADE OF PALE** — Procol Harum (Denny Cordell), Deram 7507 | 3 |
| 14 | 6 | 2 | 2 | **RESPECT** — Aretha Franklin (Jerry Wexler), Atlantic 2403 | 11 |
| 15 | 15 | 17 | 22 | **ALFIE** — Dionne Warwick (Bacharach-David), Scepter 12187 | 14 |
| 16 | 18 | 28 | 33 | **C'MON MARIANNE** — Four Seasons (Bob Crewe), Philips 40460 | 5 |
| 17 | 22 | 25 | 30 | **SOCIETY'S CHILD** — Janis Ian (Shadow Morton), Verve 5027 | 7 |
| 18 | 11 | 15 | 17 | **DING DONG THE WITCH IS DEAD** — Fifth Estate (Steve & Bill Jerome), Jubilee 5573 | 8 |
| 19 | 25 | 33 | 43 | **I WAS MADE TO LOVE HER** — Stevie Wonder (H. Cosby), Tamla 54151 | 5 |
| 20 | 23 | 23 | 28 | **HERE WE GO AGAIN** — Ray Charles (TRC), ABC 10938 | 8 |
| 21 | 21 | 22 | 27 | **AIN'T NO MOUNTAIN HIGH ENOUGH** — Marvin Gaye & Tammi Terrell (H. Fuqua & J. Bristol), Tamla 54149 | 9 |
| 22 | 33 | 50 | — | **WHITE RABBIT** — Jefferson Airplane (Rick Jarrard), RCA Victor 9248 | 3 |
| 23 | 26 | 31 | 54 | **FOR YOUR PRECIOUS LOVE** — Oscar Toney Jr. (Papa Don, Coghill, Emmons, Chrisman & Young), Bell 672 | 7 |
| 24 | 31 | 41 | 54 | **SOUL FINGER** — Bar-Kays (Produced by Staff), Volt 148 | 7 |
| 25 | 39 | 51 | 62 | **I TAKE IT BACK** — Sandy Posey (Chips Moman), MGM 13744 | 6 |
| 26 | 32 | 46 | 53 | **MAKE ME YOURS** — Bettye Swann, Money 126 | 8 |
| 27 | 30 | 30 | 38 | **MARY IN THE MORNING** — Al Martino (Tom Morgan & Marvin Holtzman), Capitol 5904 | 7 |
| 28 | 29 | 35 | 46 | **PAY YOU BACK WITH INTEREST** — Hollies, Imperial 66240 | 6 |
| 29 | 36 | 49 | 81 | **MERCY, MERCY, MERCY** — Buckinghams (James William Guercio), Columbia 44162 | 4 |
| 30 | 42 | 52 | 76 | **MORE LOVE** — Smokey Robinson & the Miracles ("Smokey"), Tamla 54152 | 4 |
| 31 | 34 | 44 | 61 | **SHAKE, RATTLE AND ROLL** — Arthur Conley (Otis Redding), Atco 6494 | 5 |
| 32 | 46 | 56 | — | **FOR YOUR LOVE** — Peaches & Herb (Bert Kaprolik & Ken Williams), Date 1563 | 3 |
| 33 | 50 | 79 | — | **JACKSON** — Nancy Sinatra & Lee Hazlewood (Lee Hazlewood), Reprise 0595 | 3 |
| 34 | 45 | 55 | 73 | **CARRIE ANN** — Hollies (Ron Richards), Epic 10180 | 4 |
| 35 | 35 | 45 | 55 | **YOU MUST HAVE BEEN A BEAUTIFUL BABY** — Dave Clark Five (Dave Clark), Epic 10179 | 5 |
| 36 | 41 | 53 | 71 | **STEP OUT OF YOUR MIND** — American Breed (Mickie Most), Acta 804 | 6 |
| 37 | 49 | 81 | — | **DON'T GO OUT INTO THE RAIN (You're Going to Melt)** — Herman's Hermits (Mickie Most), MGM 13761 | 3 |
| 38 | 38 | 38 | 38 | **DON'T BLAME THE CHILDREN** — Sammy Davis Jr. (Jimmy Bowen), Reprise 0566 | 7 |
| 39 | 20 | 14 | 14 | **7 ROOMS OF GLOOM** — Four Tops (Holland & Dozier), Motown 1110 | 8 |
| 40 | 43 | 43 | 60 | **BOWLING GREEN** — The Everly Brothers (Dick Glasser), Warner Bros. 7020 | 7 |
| 41 | 17 | 7 | 5 | **SOMEBODY TO LOVE** — Jefferson Airplane (Rick Jarrard), RCA Victor 9140 | 15 |
| 42 | 14 | 16 | 18 | **NEW YORK MINING DISASTER 1941 (Have You Seen My Wife Mr. Jones)** — The Bee Gees (Ossie Byrne), Atco 6487 | 7 |
| 43 | 53 | 65 | 84 | **LOVE ME TENDER** — Percy Sledge (Quin Ivy & Marlin Greene), Atlantic 2414 | 4 |
| 44 | 16 | 9 | 12 | **SUNDAY WILL NEVER BE THE SAME** — Spanky and Our Gang (Jerry Ross), Mercury 72679 | 8 |
| 45 | 63 | 88 | — | **THERE GOES MY EVERYTHING** — Engelbert Humperdinck (Peter Sullivan), Parrot 40015 | 3 |
| 46 | 24 | 18 | 19 | **DO IT AGAIN A LITTLE BIT SLOWER** — Jon & Robin & the In Crowd (Dale Hawkins), Abnak 119 | 10 |
| 47 | 58 | 76 | 91 | **SILENCE IS GOLDEN** — Tremeloes (Mike Smith), Epic 10184 | 4 |
| 48 | 54 | 72 | 87 | **AIRPLANE SONG** — Royal Guardsmen (Gernhard Ent.), Laurie 3391 | 4 |
| 49 | 27 | 12 | 4 | **RELEASE ME (And Let Me Love Again)** — Engelbert Humperdinck (Parrot 40011) | 14 |
| 50 | 77 | — | — | **I LIKE THE WAY** — Tommy James and the Shondells (Bo Gentry & Ritchie Cordell), Roulette 4756 | 2 |
| 51 | 76 | 96 | — | **HYPNOTIZED** — Linda Jones (George Kerr), Loma 2070 | 3 |
| 52 | 62 | 64 | 83 | **YOU WANTED SOMEONE TO PLAY WITH (I Wanted Someone to Love)** — Frankie Laine (Bob Thiele), ABC 10946 | 4 |
| 53 | 51 | 36 | 36 | **SOUND OF LOVE** — Five Americans (Dale Hawkins), Abnak 120 | 8 |
| 54 | 56 | 57 | 65 | **WOMAN LIKE THAT, YEAH** — Joe Tex (Buddy Killen), Dial 4059 | 6 |
| 55 | 60 | 71 | 92 | **SOUL DANCE NUMBER THREE** — Wilson Pickett (Jerry Wexler), Atlantic 2412 | 4 |
| 56 | 72 | 82 | — | **YOU ONLY LIVE TWICE** — Nancy Sinatra (Lee Hazlewood), Reprise 0595 | 3 |
| 57 | 69 | 87 | 89 | **SOOTHE ME** — Sam & Dave (Prod. by Staff), Stax 218 | 4 |
| 58 | 78 | — | — | **SHOW BUSINESS** — Lou Rawls (David Axelrod), Capitol 5941 | 2 |
| 59 | 55 | 59 | 59 | **YOU GAVE ME SOMETHING (And Everything Is All Right)** — Fantastic Four (Kent, Wingate, Weems), Ric Tic 128 | 7 |
| 60 | — | — | — | **IN THE CHAPEL IN THE MOONLIGHT** — Dean Martin (Jimmy Bowen), Reprise 0601 | 1 |
| 61 | 84 | 99 | — | **LET THE GOOD TIMES ROLL & FEEL SO GOOD** — Bunny Sigler (Madara-White-Huff), Parkway 153 | 3 |
| 62 | 96 | — | — | **YOUR UNCHANGING LOVE** — Marvin Gaye (Holland & Dozier), Tamla 54153 | 2 |
| 63 | 87 | — | — | **TAKE ME (Just as I Am)** — Solomon Burke (Chips Moman & Dan Penn), Atlantic 2416 | 2 |
| 64 | 64 | 70 | 82 | **SOMEBODY HELP ME** — Spencer Davis Group (Chris Blackwell & Jimmy Miller), United Artists 50162 | 4 |
| 65 | 66 | 69 | 75 | **SUMMER AND SANDY** — Lesley Gore (Bob Crewe), Mercury 72683 | 5 |
| 66 | 67 | 67 | 79 | **WHO'S LOVIN' YOU** — Brenda & the Tabulations (Bob Finiz), Dionn 501 | 5 |
| 67 | 79 | — | — | **YOU WERE ON MY MIND** — Crispian St. Peters, Jamie 1310 | 2 |
| 68 | 75 | 75 | 100 | **BLACK SHEEP** — Sam the Sham & the Pharaohs (Stan Kesler), MGM 13747 | 4 |
| 69 | 61 | 61 | 72 | **BABY, PLEASE COME BACK HOME** — J. J. Barnes (Davis-Barnes), Groovesville 1006 | 8 |
| 70 | 59 | 62 | 85 | **GRADUATION DAY** — Arbors (Richard E. Carney), Date 1561 | 4 |
| 71 | 71 | 78 | 80 | **ONE BY ONE** — Blues Magoos (Art Polhemus & Bob Wyld), Mercury 72692 | 5 |
| 72 | 95 | — | — | **(I Wanna) TESTIFY** — Parliaments (Leon Ware), Revilot 207 | 2 |
| 73 | 73 | 77 | 78 | **NOW I KNOW** — Jack Jones, Kapp 833 | 5 |
| 74 | 83 | 85 | 97 | **I STAND ACCUSED (Of Loving You)** — Glories (Bob Yorey), Date 1553 | 4 |
| 75 | 68 | 68 | 69 | **IT'S COLD OUTSIDE** — Choir (Najweb Hedafy), Roulette 4738 | 6 |
| 76 | — | — | — | **THE HAPPENING** — Herb Alpert & The Tijuana Brass (Herb Alpert & Jerry Moss), A&M 860 | 1 |
| 77 | 88 | 90 | — | **LONELY DRIFTER** — Pieces of Eight, A&M 854 | 3 |
| 78 | 85 | 100 | — | **GROOVY SUMMERTIME** — Love Generation (Tommy Oliver), Imperial 66243 | 3 |
| 79 | 80 | 89 | 90 | **DAYLIGHT SAVIN' TIME** — Keith (Jerry Ross), Mercury 72695 | 4 |
| 80 | 81 | — | — | **I'LL DO IT FOR YOU** — Toussaint McCall (Scotty Moore), Room 9 | 2 |
| 81 | 100 | — | — | **JOY** — Mitch Ryder (Bob Crewe), New Voice 824 | 2 |
| 82 | 90 | — | — | **PICTURES OF LILY** — Who (Kit Lambert), Decca 32156 | 2 |
| 83 | 89 | — | — | **GIVE ME TIME** — Dusty Springfield, Philips 40465 | 2 |
| 84 | — | — | — | **DON'T LET THE RAIN FALL ON ME** — Critters (Anders-Poncia), Kapp 838 | 1 |
| 85 | 86 | 86 | 94 | **I'LL ALWAYS HAVE FAITH IN YOU** — Carla Thomas (David Porter & Isaac Hayes), Stax 222 | 4 |
| 86 | — | — | — | **YOU KEEP ME HANGING ON** — Vanilla Fudge (Shadow Morton), Atco 6495 | 1 |
| 87 | — | — | — | **EVERYBODY NEEDS LOVE** — Gladys Knight & The Pips (Norman Whitfield), Soul 35034 | 1 |
| 88 | — | — | — | **RIVER IS WIDE** — Forum (Norm Hatnar), Mira 3065 | 1 |
| 89 | 93 | 94 | — | **MY WORLD FELL DOWN** — Sagittarius (Gary Usher), Columbia 44163 | 3 |
| 90 | 99 | — | — | **MR. PLEASANT** — Kinks (Shel Talmy), Reprise 0587 | 2 |
| 91 | 92 | 92 | — | **UP, UP AND AWAY** — Johnny Mann Singers (Jack Tracy), Liberty 55972 | 3 |
| 92 | — | — | — | **FUNKY BROADWAY** — Dyke & the Blazers (Coleman & Barrett), Original Sound 64 | 7 |
| 93 | — | — | — | **TEMPTATION** — Boots Randolph (Fred Foster), Monument 1009 | 1 |
| 94 | — | — | — | **WHAT AM I LIVING FOR** — Percy Sledge (Quin Ivy & Marlin Greene), Atlantic 2414 | 1 |
| 95 | — | — | — | **MORE AND MORE** — Andy Williams (Nick DeCarlo), Columbia 44202 | 1 |
| 96 | 97 | — | — | **MY ELUSIVE DREAMS** — David Houston & Tommy Wynette (Billy Sherrill), Epic 10190 | 2 |
| 97 | — | — | — | **WASHED ASHORE (On a Lonely Island in the Sea)** — Platters (Richard Popcorn Wylie), Musicor 1251 | 1 |
| 98 | — | — | — | **OMAHA** — Moby Grape (David Rubinson), Columbia 44173 | 1 |
| 99 | — | — | — | **BLUES THEME** — Arrows (Mike Curb), Tower 295 | 5 |
| 100 | — | — | — | **GENTLE ON MY MIND** — Glen Campbell (Al de lory), Capitol 5939 | 1 |

## BUBBLING UNDER THE HOT 100

101. GOOD FEELIN' TIME — Yellow Balloon, Canterbury 513
102. 39-21-46 — Showmen, Minit 32007
103. SOME KIND OF WONDERFUL — Soul Brothers 6, Atlantic 2406
104. MORE, MORE, MORE OF YOUR LOVE — Bob Brady and the Conchords, Chariot 101
105. THREAD THE NEEDLE — Clarence Carter, Fame 1013
106. LET IT HAPPEN — James Carr, Goldwax 323
107. YOU DON'T MISS YOUR WATER — King Curtis, Atco 6496
108. ALL'S QUIET ON WEST 23rd STREET — Jet Stream, Smash 2095
109. LOOK OF LOVE — Dusty Springfield, Philips 40465
110. OUT & ABOUT — Tommy Boyce & Bobby Hart A&M 858
111. MY MAMMY — Happenings, BT Puppy 530
112. APPLES, PEACHES AND PUMPKIN PIE — Jay & the Techniques, Smash 2086
113. BROWN EYED GIRL — Van Morrison, Bang 545
114. DEEP IN THE HEART OF HARLEM — Walter Jackson, Okeh 7285
115. I'LL TURN TO STONE — Four Tops, Motown 1110
116. TOGETHER — Intruders, Gamble 205
117. BOAT THAT I ROW — Lulu, Epic 10187
118. I'LL NEVER NEED MORE THAN THIS — Ike & Tina Turner, Phillies 135
119. NOT SO SWEET MARTHA LORAINE — Country Joe & the Fish, Vanguard 35052
120. HAPPY — Blades of Grass, Jubilee
121. DON'T LOSE YOUR GOOD THING — Jimmy Hughes, Fame 1011
122. YOU MAKE ME FEEL LIKE SOMEONE — Gary Russell, Dunhill 4085
123. IT'S SUCH A PRETTY WORLD TODAY — Stephan Monahan, Kapp 823
124. BLUEBIRD — Buffalo Springfield, Atco 6499
125. CITY OF WINDOWS — Stephen Monahan, Kapp 823
126. HAPPY — Sunshine Company, Imperial 66247
127. ENDLESS SUMMER — Ventures, Liberty 55977
128. DO, DO, DO GOOD — Electric Prune, Reprise 0594
129. THOUSAND SHADOWS — Sir Douglas Quintet, Tribe 8314
130. THERE MUST BE A WAY — Jimmy Roselli, United Artists 51029
131. LOVIN' SOUND — Ian & Sylvia, MGM 13686
132. OUT OF NOWHERE — Frank Ifield, Hickory 1454
133. SO SO HAPPY — Magnificent Men, Capitol 5945
134. DEVIL'S ANGELS — Davie Allen & the Arrows, Tower 341
135. MY ELUSIVE DREAMS — Curley Putman, ABC 10934

Compiled from national retail sales and radio station airplay by the Music Popularity Dept. of Record Market Research, Billboard.

# Billboard HOT 100

For Week Ending July 15, 1967

★ STAR performer—Sides registering greatest proportionate upward progress this week.

● Record Industry Association of America seal of certification as million selling single.

| This Week | 1 Wk. Ago | 2 Wk. Ago | 3 Wk. Ago | TITLE, Artist (Producer), Label & Number | Weeks On Chart |
|---|---|---|---|---|---|
| 1 | 1 | 1 | 4 | **WINDY** — The Association, (Bones Howe), Warner Bros. 7041 | 8 |
| 2 | 2 | 3 | 5 | **LITTLE BIT O' SOUL** — Music Explosion (J. Katz-J. Kasenentz & E. Chiprut), Laurie 3380 | 10 |
| 3 | 3 | 7 | 8 | **CAN'T TAKE MY EYES OFF YOU** — Frankie Valli (Bob Crewe), Philips 40446 | 9 |
| 4 | 4 | 4 | 6 | **SAN FRANCISCO "WEAR SOME FLOWERS IN YOUR HAIR"** — Scott McKenzie (John Phillips & Lou Adler), Ode 103 | 6 |
| 5 | 5 | 10 | 20 | **DON'T SLEEP IN THE SUBWAY** — Petula Clark (Tony Hatch), Warner Bros. 7049 | 7 |
| 6 | 6 | 9 | 11 | **COME ON DOWN TO MY BOAT** — Every Mother's Son (Wes Farrell), MGM 13733 | 11 |
| 7 | 7 | 12 | 21 | **UP— UP AND AWAY** — 5th Dimension (Johnny Rivers & Marc Gordon), Soul City 756 | 7 |
| 8 | 12 | 19 | 24 | **LIGHT MY FIRE** — Doors (Paul A. Rothchild), Elektra 45615 | 7 |
| 9 | 16 | 18 | 28 | **C'MON MARIANNE** — Four Seasons (Bob Crewe), Philips 40460 | 6 |
| 10 | 13 | 28 | 80 | **A WHITER SHADE OF PALE** — Procol Harum (Denny Cordell), Deram 7507 | 4 |
| 11 | 19 | 25 | 33 | **I WAS MADE TO LOVE HER** — Stevie Wonder (H. Cosby), Tamla 54151 | 6 |
| 12 | 22 | 33 | 50 | **WHITE RABBIT** — Jefferson Airplane (Rick Jarrard), RCA Victor 9248 | 4 |
| 13 | 10 | 13 | 13 | **THE TRACKS OF MY TEARS** — Johnny Rivers (Lou Adler), Imperial 66244 | 7 |
| 14 | 17 | 22 | 25 | **SOCIETY'S CHILD** — Janis Ian (Shadow Morton), Verve 5027 | 8 |
| 15 | 20 | 23 | 23 | **HERE WE GO AGAIN** — Ray Charles (TRC), ABC 10938 | 9 |
| 16 | 8 | 8 | 10 | **LET'S LIVE FOR TODAY** — Grass Roots (Steve Barri & P. F. Sloan), Dunhill 4084 | 10 |
| 17 | 29 | 36 | 49 | **MERCY, MERCY, MERCY** — Buckinghams (James William Guercio), Columbia 44182 | 5 |
| 18 | 15 | 15 | 17 | **ALFIE** — Dionne Warwick (Bacharach-David), Scepter 12187 | 15 |
| 19 | 21 | 21 | 22 | **AIN'T NO MOUNTAIN HIGH ENOUGH** — Marvin Gaye & Tammi Terrell (H. Fuqua & J. Bristol), Tamla 54149 | 10 |
| 20 | 25 | 39 | 51 | **I TAKE IT BACK** — Sandy Posey (Chips Moman), MGM 13744 | 6 |
| 21 | 33 | 50 | 79 | **JACKSON** — Nancy Sinatra & Lee Hazlewood (Lee Hazlewood), Reprise 0595 | 4 |
| 22 | 24 | 31 | 41 | **SOUL FINGER** — Bar-Kays (Produced by Staff), Volt 148 | 9 |
| 23 | 37 | 49 | 81 | **DON'T GO OUT INTO THE RAIN (You're Going to Melt)** — Herman's Hermits (Mickie Most), MGM 13761 | 4 |
| 24 | 36 | 41 | 53 | **STEP OUT OF YOUR MIND** — American Breed, Acta 804 | 7 |
| 25 | 30 | 42 | 52 | **MORE LOVE** — Smokey Robinson & the Miracles ("Smokey"), Tamla 54152 | 5 |
| 26 | 26 | 32 | 46 | **MAKE ME YOURS** — Bettye Swann, Money 126 | 9 |
| 27 | 32 | 46 | 56 | **FOR YOUR LOVE** — Peaches & Herb (Bert Kapralik & Ken Williams), Date 1563 | 4 |
| 28 | 34 | 45 | 55 | **CARRIE ANN** — Hollies (Ron Richards), Epic 10180 | 5 |
| 29 | 18 | 11 | 15 | **DING DONG THE WITCH IS DEAD** — Fifth Estate (Steve & Bill Jerome), Jubilee 5573 | 9 |
| 30 | 45 | 63 | 88 | **THERE GOES MY EVERYTHING** — Engelbert Humperdinck (Peter Sullivan), Parrot 40015 | 4 |
| 31 | 31 | 34 | 44 | **SHAKE, RATTLE AND ROLL** — Arthur Conley (Otis Redding), Atco 6494 | 6 |
| 32 | 47 | 58 | 76 | **SILENCE IS GOLDEN** — Tremeloes (Mike Smith), Epic 10184 | 5 |
| 33 | 11 | 5 | 3 | **SHE'D RATHER BE WITH ME** — Turtles (Joe Wissert), White Whale 249 | 10 |
| 34 | 23 | 26 | 31 | **FOR YOUR PRECIOUS LOVE** — Oscar Toney Jr. (Papa Don, Coghill, Emmons, Chrisman & Young), Bell 672 | 8 |
| 35 | 50 | 77 | — | **I LIKE THE WAY** — Tommy James & the Shondells (Bo Gentry & Ritchie Cordell), Roulette 4756 | 3 |
| 36 | 14 | 6 | 2 | **RESPECT** — Aretha Franklin (Jerry Wexler), Atlantic 2403 | 12 ● |
| 37 | 38 | 38 | 38 | **DON'T BLAME THE CHILDREN** — Sammy Davis Jr. (Jimmy Bowen), Reprise 0566 | 8 |
| 38 | 9 | 2 | 1 | **GROOVIN'** — Young Rascals (Young Rascals), Atlantic 2401 | 13 ● |
| 39 | 27 | 30 | 30 | **MARY IN THE MORNING** — Al Martino (Tom Morgan & Marvin Holtzman), Capitol 5904 | 8 |
| 40 | 40 | 43 | 43 | **BOWLING GREEN** — The Everly Brothers (Dick Glasser), Warner Bros. 7020 | 8 |
| 41 | 43 | 53 | 65 | **LOVE ME TENDER** — Percy Sledge (Quin Ivy & Marlin Greene), Atlantic 2414 | 5 |
| 42 | — | 60 | — | **IN THE CHAPEL IN THE MOONLIGHT** — Dean Martin (Jimmy Bowen), Reprise 0601 | 2 |
| 43 | 28 | 29 | 35 | **PAY YOU BACK WITH INTEREST** — Hollies, Imperial 66240 | 7 |
| 44 | 35 | 35 | 45 | **YOU MUST HAVE BEEN A BEAUTIFUL BABY** — Dave Clark Five (Dave Clark), Epic 10179 | 6 |
| 45 | 51 | 76 | 96 | **HYPNOTIZED** — Linda Jones (George Kerr), Loma 2070 | 4 |
| 46 | 48 | 54 | 72 | **AIRPLANE SONG** — Royal Guardsmen (Gernhard Ent.), Laurie 3391 | 5 |
| 47 | 61 | 84 | 99 | **LET THE GOOD TIMES ROLL & FEEL SO GOOD** — Bunny Sigler (Madara-White-Huff), Parkway 153 | 4 |
| 48 | 58 | 78 | — | **SHOW BUSINESS** — Lou Rawls (David Axelrod), Capitol 5941 | 3 |
| 49 | 62 | 96 | — | **YOUR UNCHANGING LOVE** — Marvin Gaye (Holland & Dozier), Tamla 54153 | 3 |
| 50 | 63 | 87 | — | **TAKE ME (Just as I Am)** — Solomon Burke (Chips Moman & Dan Penn), Atlantic 2416 | 3 |
| 51 | 52 | 62 | 64 | **YOU WANTED SOMEONE TO PLAY WITH (I Wanted Someone to Love)** — Frankie Laine (Bob Thiele), ABC 10946 | 5 |
| 52 | — | — | — | **MY MAMMY** — Happenings (Tokens), B.T. Puppy 530 | 1 |
| 53 | — | 76 | — | **THE HAPPENING** — Herb Alpert & The Tijuana Brass (Herb Alpert & Jerry Moss), A&M 860 | 2 |
| 54 | 64 | 64 | 70 | **SOMEBODY HELP ME** — Spencer Davis Group (Chris Blackwell & Jimmy Miller), United Artists 50162 | 5 |
| 55 | 56 | 72 | 82 | **YOU ONLY LIVE TWICE** — Nancy Sinatra (Lee Hazlewood), Reprise 0595 | 4 |
| 56 | 57 | 69 | 87 | **SOOTHE ME** — Sam & Dave (Prod. by Staff), Stax 218 | 5 |
| 57 | 67 | 79 | — | **YOU WERE ON MY MIND** — Crispian St. Peters, Jamie 1310 | 3 |
| 58 | 81 | 100 | — | **JOY** — Mitch Ryder (Bob Crewe), New Voice 824 | 3 |
| 59 | 55 | 60 | 71 | **SOUL DANCE NUMBER THREE** — Wilson Pickett (Jerry Wexler), Atlantic 2412 | 5 |
| 60 | 72 | 95 | — | **(I Wanna) TESTIFY** — Parliaments (Leon Ware), Revilot 207 | 3 |
| 61 | — | — | — | **A GIRL LIKE YOU** — Young Rascals (Young Rascals), Atlantic 2424 | 1 |
| 62 | 77 | 88 | 90 | **LONELY DRIFTER** — Pieces of Eight, A&M 854 | 4 |
| 63 | 54 | 56 | 57 | **WOMAN LIKE THAT, YEAH** — Joe Tex (Buddy Killen), Dial 4059 | 7 |
| 64 | 88 | — | — | **RIVER IS WIDE** — Forum (Norm Hatner), Mira 3065 | 2 |
| 65 | 82 | 90 | — | **PICTURES OF LILY** — Who (Kit Lambert), Decca 32156 | 3 |
| 66 | 65 | 66 | 69 | **SUMMER AND SANDY** — Lesley Gore (Bob Crewe), Mercury 72683 | 6 |
| 67 | 66 | 67 | 67 | **WHO'S LOVIN' YOU** — Brenda & the Tabulations (Bob Finiz), Dionn 501 | 6 |
| 68 | 68 | 75 | 75 | **BLACK SHEEP** — Sam the Sham & the Pharaohs (Stan Kesler), MGM 13747 | 5 |
| 69 | 69 | 61 | 61 | **BABY, PLEASE COME BACK HOME** — J. J. Barnes (Davis-Barnes), Groovesville 1006 | 9 |
| 70 | 86 | — | — | **YOU KEEP ME HANGING ON** — Vanilla Fudge (Shadow Morton), Atco 6495 | 2 |
| 71 | 89 | 93 | 94 | **MY WORLD FELL DOWN** — Sagittarius (Gary Usher), Columbia 44163 | 4 |
| 72 | 84 | — | — | **DON'T LET THE RAIN FALL ON ME** — Critters (Anders-Poncia), Kapp 838 | 2 |
| 73 | 73 | 73 | 77 | **NOW I KNOW** — Jack Jones, Kapp 833 | 6 |
| 74 | 74 | 83 | 85 | **I STAND ACCUSED (Of Loving You)** — Glories (Bob Yorey), Date 1553 | 6 |
| 75 | 78 | 85 | 100 | **GROOVY SUMMERTIME** — Love Generation (Tommy Oliver), Imperial 66243 | 4 |
| 76 | 83 | 89 | — | **GIVE ME TIME** — Dusty Springfield, Philips 40465 | 3 |
| 77 | 80 | 81 | — | **I'LL DO IT FOR YOU** — Toussaint McCall (Scotty Moore), Room 9 | 3 |
| 78 | — | — | — | **BLUEBIRD** — Buffalo Springfield, Atco 6499 | 1 |
| 79 | — | — | — | **TO LOVE SOMEBODY** — Bee Gees (Robert Stigwood), Atco 6503 | 1 |
| 80 | 90 | 99 | — | **MR. PLEASANT** — Kinks (Shel Talmy), Reprise 0587 | 2 |
| 81 | — | — | — | **OUT AND ABOUT** — Tommy Boyce & Bobby Hart (Tommy Boyce & Bobby Hart), A&M 858 | 1 |
| 82 | 97 | 97 | — | **WASHED ASHORE (On a Lonely Island in the Sea)** — Platters (Richard Popcorn Wylie), Musicor 1251 | 2 |
| 83 | — | — | — | **I'LL TURN TO STONE** — Four Tops (Holland & Dozier), Motown 1110 | 1 |
| 84 | 87 | — | — | **EVERYBODY NEEDS LOVE** — Gladys Knight & The Pips (Norman Whitfield), Soul 35034 | 2 |
| 85 | 100 | — | — | **GENTLE ON MY MIND** — Glen Campbell (Al de Iory), Capitol 5939 | 2 |
| 86 | — | — | — | **THANK THE LORD FOR THE NIGHT TIME** — Neil Diamond (Jeff Barry & Ellie Greenwich), Bang 547 | 1 |
| 87 | — | — | — | **I TAKE WHAT I WANT** — James & Bobby Purify (Papa Don), Bell 680 | 1 |
| 88 | 98 | — | — | **OMAHA** — Moby Grape (David Rubinson), Columbia 44173 | 2 |
| 89 | 92 | — | — | **FUNKY BROADWAY** — Dyke & the Blazers (Coleman & Barrett), Original Sound 64 | 6 |
| 90 | 99 | — | — | **BLUES THEME** — Arrows (Mike Curb), Tower 295 | 6 |
| 91 | 94 | — | — | **WHAT AM I LIVING FOR** — Percy Sledge (Quin Ivy & Marlin Greene), Atlantic 2414 | 2 |
| 92 | — | — | — | **COLD SWEAT** — James Brown & the Famous Flames (James Brown), King 6110 | 1 |
| 93 | — | — | — | **I COULD BE SO HAPPY** — Magnificent Men (Marvin Holtzman), Capitol 5905 | 1 |
| 94 | 96 | — | — | **MY ELUSIVE DREAMS** — David Houston & Tommy Wynette (Billy Sherrill), Epic 10094 | 2 |
| 95 | 95 | — | — | **MORE AND MORE** — Andy Williams (Nick DeCarlo), Columbia 44202 | 2 |
| 96 | — | — | — | **HAPPY** — Blades of Grass (Bill & Steve Jerome), Jubilee 5582 | 1 |
| 97 | — | — | — | **HAPPY** — Sunshine Company (Joe Saracenno), Imperial 66247 | 1 |
| 98 | — | — | — | **APPLES, PEACHES, PUMPKIN PIE** — Jay & the Techniques (Jerry Ross), Smash 2086 | 1 |
| 99 | — | — | — | **BROWN-EYED GIRL** — Van Morrison (Bert Berns), Bang 545 | 1 |
| 100 | — | — | — | **THOUSAND SHADOWS** — Seeds (Marcus Tybalt), GNP Crescendo 394 | 1 |

## HOT 100—A TO Z—(Publisher-Licensee)

Ain't No Mountain High Enough (Jobete, BMI) .... 19
Airplane Song (My Airplane) (Hastings, BMI) ... 46
Alfie (Famous, ASCAP) ... 18
Apples, Peaches, Pumpkin Pie (Philstox/Act Three, BMI) ... 98
Baby, Please Come Back Home (Groovesville, BMI) ... 69
Black Sheep (Il-Gato, BMI) ... 68
Blues Theme (Dijon, BMI) ... 90
Bluebird (Ten-East/Springalo/Cotillion, BMI) ... 78
Bowling Green (Rook, BMI) ... 40
Brown Eyed Girl (Web IV, BMI) ... 99
Can't Take My Eyes Off You (Saturday/Seasons' Four, BMI) ... 3
Carrie Ann (Maribus, BMI) ... 28
C'Mon Marianne (Saturday/Seasons' Four, BMI) ... 9
Cold Sweat (Dynatone, BMI) ... 92
Come on Down to My Boat (Picturetone-Goldstein, BMI) ... 6
Ding Dong the Witch Is Dead (James, ASCAP) ... 29
Don't Blame the Children (Saloon Songs, BMI) ... 37
Don't Go Out Into the Rain (You're Going to Melt) (Unart, BMI) ... 23
Don't Let the Rain Fall Down on Me (Uganda, BMI) ... 72
Don't Sleep in the Subway (Duchess, BMI) ... 5
Everybody Needs Love (Jobete, BMI) ... 84
For Your Love (Beechwood, BMI) ... 27
For Your Precious Love (Sunflower, ASCAP) ... 34
Funky Broadway (Drive-In/Routeen, BMI) ... 89
Gentle on My Mind (Glazer, BMI) ... 85
Girl Like You (Slacsar, BMI) ... 61
Give Me Time (Ponderosa, BMI) ... 76
Groovin' (Slacsar, BMI) ... 38
Groovy Summertime (4 Star, BMI) ... 75
Happening, The (Jobete, BMI) ... 53
Happy (Blades of Grass) (Unart, BMI) ... 96
Happy (Sunshine Company) (Unart, BMI) ... 97
Here We Go Again (Dirk, BMI) ... 15

Hypnotized (Zira/Floteca, BMI) ... 45
I Could Be So Happy (Sid-Lee, ASCAP) ... 93
I Like the Way (Patricia, BMI) ... 35
I Stand Accused (Of Loving You) (Yorey-Plote, BMI) ... 74
I Take It Back (Low-Sal, BMI) ... 20
I Take What I Want (East/Cotillion, BMI) ... 87
I Was Made to Love Her (Jobete, BMI) ... 11
I'll Do It for You (Su-Ma, BMI) ... 77
I'll Turn to Stone (Jobete, BMI) ... 83
In the Chapel in the Moonlight (Shapiro/Bernstein, ASCAP) ... 42
I Wanna Testify (Groovesville, BMI) ... 60
Jackson (Bexhill Quartet, ASCAP) ... 21
Joy (Saturday, BMI) ... 58
Let's Live for Today (James, BMI) ... 16
Let the Good Times Roll & Feel So Good (Travis, BMI) ... 47
Light My Fire (Nipper, ASCAP) ... 8
Little Bit o' Soul (Southern, BMI) ... 2
Lonely Drifter (Bidle, BMI) ... 62
Love Me Tender (Presley, BMI) ... 41
Make Me Yours (Cash Songs, BMI) ... 26
Mary in the Morning (Pamco, BMI) ... 39
Mercy, Mercy, Mercy (Zawinul, BMI) ... 17
Mr. Pleasant (Noma-Hi-Count, BMI) ... 80
More and More (Sunbeam, BMI) ... 95
More Love (Jobete, BMI) ... 25
My Elusive Dreams (Tree, BMI) ... 94
My Mammy (Bourne/Donaldson/Warock) ... 52
My World Fell Down (Southern, ASCAP) ... 71
Now I Know (Helion, BMI) ... 73
Omaha (After You, BMI) ... 88
Out and About (Screen Gems-Columbia, BMI) ... 81
Pay You Back With Interest (Maribus, BMI) ... 43
Pictures of Lily (Essex, ASCAP) ... 65
Respect (East-Time-Walco, BMI) ... 36

River Is Wide, The (Saturday, BMI) ... 64
San Francisco "Wear Some Flowers in Your Hair" (Trousdale, BMI) ... 4
Shake, Rattle and Roll (Progressive, BMI) ... 31
She'd Rather Be With Me (Chardon, BMI) ... 33
Show Business (Raw Lou-Hidle, BMI) ... 48
Silence Is Golden (Saturday/Gevadium, BMI) ... 32
Society's Child (Dialogue, BMI) ... 14
Somebody Help Me (Essex, ASCAP) ... 54
Soothe Me (Kags, BMI) ... 56
Soul Dance Number Three (Pronto, BMI) ... 59
Soul Finger (East, BMI) ... 22
Step Out of Your Mind (Blackwood, BMI) ... 24
Summer and Sandy (Fame, BMI) ... 66
Take Me (Just As I Am) (Fame, BMI) ... 50
Thank the Lord for the Night Time (Tallyrand, BMI) ... 86
There Goes My Everything (Blue Crest, BMI) ... 30
Thousand Shadows (Neil/Purple Bottle, BMI) ... 100
To Love Somebody (Nemperor, BMI) ... 79
Tracks of My Tears, The (Jobete, BMI) ... 13
Up, Up and Away (5th Dimension) (Rivers, BMI) ... 7
Washed Ashore (On a Lonely Island in the Sea) (Catalogue-La King, BMI) ... 82
What Am I Living For (Progressive/Tideland, BMI) ... 91
White Rabbit (Cooper Penny, BMI) ... 12
Whiter Shade of Pale (Jobete, BMI) ... 10
Who's Lovin' You (Jobete, BMI) ... 67
Windy (Irving, BMI) ... 1
Woman Like That, Yeah (Tree, BMI) ... 63
You Keep Me Hanging On (Jobete, BMI) ... 70
You Must Have Been a Beautiful Baby (Remick, ASCAP) ... 44
You Only Live Twice (Unart, BMI) ... 55
You Wanted Someone to Play With (I Wanted Someone to Love) (Morris, ASCAP) ... 51
You Were on My Mind (Witmark, ASCAP) ... 57
Your Unchanging Love (Jobete, BMI) ... 49

## BUBBLING UNDER THE HOT 100

101. GOOD FEELIN' TIME ... Yellow Balloon, Canterbury 513
102. 36-21-40 SHAPE ... Showmen, Minit 32007
103. SOME KIND OF WONDERFUL ... Soul Brothers 6, Atlantic 2406
104. COME BACK WHEN YOU GROW UP ... Bobby Vee, Liberty 55964
105. CITY OF WINDOWS ... Stephen Monahan, Kapp 835
106. THE LOOK OF LOVE ... Dusty Springfield, Philips 40466
107. YOU DON'T MISS YOUR WATER ... King Curtis, Atco 6496
108. SLIPPIN' & SLIDING ... Willie Mitchell, Hi 2125
109. ENDLESS SUMMER ... Ventures, Liberty 55977
110. SUMMER ... Johnny Mann Singers, Liberty 55972
111. DEEP IN THE HEART OF HARLEM ... Walter Jackson, Okeh 7282
112. DEVIL'S ANGELS ... Davie Allan & the Arrows, Tower 341
113. SHOOT YOUR SHOT ... Jr. Walker & the All Stars, Soul 35036
114. NOT SO SWEET, MARTHA LORRAINE ... Country Joe & the Fish, Vanguard 35052
115. BOAT THAT I ROW ... Lulu, Epic 10187
116. COLD SWEAT ... Carla Thomas, Stax 222
117. TEMPTATION ... Boots Randolph, Monument 1009
118. NEARER TO YOU ... Betty Harris, Sansu 466
119. I'LL NEVER NEED MORE THAN THIS ... Ike & Tina Turner, Phillies 135
120. HEY BABY (They're Playing Our Song) ... Blues Magoos, Mercury 72692
121. HAPPY ... Nancy Ames, Epic 10191
122. LET IT BE ME ... Sweet Inspirations, Atlantic 2418
123. LAST MINUTE MIRACLE ... Shirelles, Scepter 12198
124. IT'S SUCH A PRETTY WORLD TODAY ... Andy Russell, Capitol 5917
125. LOVIN' SOUND ... Ian & Sylvia, MGM 13686
126. TOGETHER ... Intruders, Gamble 205
127. HEY GRANDMA ... Moby Grapes, Columbia 44174
128. DR. DO GOOD ... Electric Prunes, Reprise 0594
129. IT COULD BE IN LOVE ... Cryan' Shames, Columbia 44191
130. I CAN'T GO ON LIVIN' WITHOUT YOU, BABY ... Nino Tempo & April Stevens, White Whale 252
131. FOUR WALLS ... J.J. Jackson, Calla 133
132. IT'S BEEN A LONG, LONG TIME ... Elgins, VIP 25043
133. RUN RUN RUN ... Third Rail, Epic 10191
134. THE SWEETEST THING THIS SIDE OF HEAVEN ... Chris Bartley, Vando 101
135. I'LL NEVER FIND ANOTHER YOU ... Sonny James, Capitol 5914

Compiled from national retail sales and radio station airplay by the Music Popularity Dept. of Record Market Research, Billboard.

# Billboard HOT 100

**For Week Ending July 22, 1967**

★ STAR performer—Sides registering greatest proportionate upward progress this week.

🅡 Record Industry Association of America seal of certification as million selling single.

| This Week | 1 Wk. Ago | 2 Wks. Ago | 3 Wks. Ago | TITLE Artist (Producer), Label & Number | Weeks On Chart |
|---|---|---|---|---|---|
| 1 | 1 | 1 | 1 | **WINDY** — The Association, (Bones Howe), Warner Bros. 7041 | 9 |
| 2 | 3 | 3 | 7 | **CAN'T TAKE MY EYES OFF YOU** — Frankie Valli (Bob Crewe), Philips 40446 | 10 |
| ★3 | 8 | 12 | 19 | **LIGHT MY FIRE** — Doors (Paul A. Rothchild), Elektra 45615 | 8 |
| 4 | 4 | 4 | 4 | **SAN FRANCISCO "WEAR SOME FLOWERS IN YOUR HAIR"** — Scott McKenzie (John Phillips & Lou Adler), Ode 103 | 9 |
| 5 | 2 | 2 | 3 | **LITTLE BIT O' SOUL** — Music Explosion (J. Katz-J. Kasenentz & E. Chiprut), Laurie 3380 | 11 |
| ★6 | 11 | 19 | 25 | **I WAS MADE TO LOVE HER** — Stevie Wonder (H. Cosby), Tamla 54151 | 7 |
| 7 | 7 | 7 | 12 | **UP, UP AND AWAY** — 5th Dimension (Johnny Rivers & Marc Gordon), Soul City 756 | 8 |
| 8 | 10 | 13 | 28 | **A WHITER SHADE OF PALE** — Procol Harum (Denny Cordell), Deram 7507 | 5 |
| 9 | 9 | 16 | 18 | **C'MON MARIANNE** — Four Seasons (Bob Crewe), Philips 40460 | 7 |
| 10 | 6 | 6 | 9 | **COME ON DOWN TO MY BOAT** — Every Mother's Son (Wes Farrell), MGM 13733 | 12 |
| ★11 | 17 | 29 | 36 | **MERCY, MERCY, MERCY** — Buckinghams (James William Guercio), Columbia 44162 | 6 |
| 12 | 12 | 22 | 33 | **WHITE RABBIT** — Jefferson Airplane (Rick Jarrard), RCA Victor 9248 | 5 |
| 13 | 5 | 5 | 10 | **DON'T SLEEP IN THE SUBWAY** — Petula Clark (Tony Hatch), Warner Bros. 7049 | 8 |
| 14 | 14 | 17 | 22 | **SOCIETY'S CHILD** — Janis Ian (Shadow Morton), Verve 5027 | 9 |
| 15 | 15 | 20 | 23 | **HERE WE GO AGAIN** — Ray Charles (TRC), ABC 10938 | 10 |
| 16 | 21 | 33 | 50 | **JACKSON** — Nancy Sinatra & Lee Hazlewood (Lee Hazlewood), Reprise 0595 | 5 |
| 17 | 20 | 25 | 39 | **I TAKE IT BACK** — Sandy Posey (Chips Moman), MGM 13744 | 7 |
| 18 | 23 | 37 | 49 | **DON'T GO OUT INTO THE RAIN (You're Going to Melt)** — Herman's Hermits (Mickie Most), MGM 13761 | 5 |
| 19 | 19 | 21 | 21 | **AIN'T NO MOUNTAIN HIGH ENOUGH** — Marvin Gaye & Tammi Terrell (H. Fuqua & J. Bristol), Tamla 54149 | 11 |
| 20 | 22 | 24 | 31 | **SOUL FINGER** — Bar-Kays (Produced by Staff), Volt 148 | 10 |
| 21 | 26 | 26 | 32 | **MAKE ME YOURS** — Bettye Swann (Money 126) | 10 |
| ★22 | 27 | 32 | 46 | **FOR YOUR LOVE** — Peaches & Herb (Bert Kapralik & Ken Williams), Date 1563 | 5 |
| ★23 | 28 | 34 | 45 | **CARRIE ANN** — Hollies (Ron Richards), Epic 10180 | 6 |
| 24 | 24 | 36 | 41 | **STEP OUT OF YOUR MIND** — American Breed, Acta 804 | 8 |
| 25 | 25 | 30 | 42 | **MORE LOVE** — Smokey Robinson & the Miracles ("Smokey"), Tamla 54152 | 6 |
| ★26 | 32 | 47 | 58 | **SILENCE IS GOLDEN** — Tremeloes (Mike Smith), Epic 10184 | 6 |
| 27 | 30 | 45 | 63 | **THERE GOES MY EVERYTHING** — Engelbert Humperdinck (Peter Sullivan), Parrot 40015 | 4 |
| 28 | 16 | 8 | 8 | **LET'S LIVE FOR TODAY** — Grass Roots (Steve Barri & P. F. Sloan), Dunhill 4084 | 11 |
| 29 | 13 | 10 | 13 | **THE TRACKS OF MY TEARS** — Johnny Rivers (Lou Adler), Imperial 66244 | 8 |
| 30 | 35 | 50 | 77 | **I LIKE THE WAY** — Tommy James & the Shondells (Bo Gentry & Ritchie Cordell), Roulette 4756 | 4 |
| 31 | 61 | — | — | **A GIRL LIKE YOU** — Young Rascals (Young Rascals), Atlantic 2424 | 6 |
| 32 | 42 | 60 | — | **IN THE CHAPEL IN THE MOONLIGHT** — Dean Martin (Jimmy Bowen), Reprise 0601 | 3 |
| 33 | 52 | — | — | **MY MAMMY** — Happenings (Tokens), B. T. Puppy 530 | 2 |
| ★34 | 53 | 76 | — | **THE HAPPENING** — Herb Alpert & The Tijuana Brass (Herb Alpert & Jerry Moss), A&M 860 | 3 |
| ★35 | 45 | 51 | 76 | **HYPNOTIZED** — Linda Jones (George Kerr), Loma 2070 | 6 |
| 36 | 57 | 67 | 79 | **YOU WERE ON MY MIND** — Crispian St. Peters, Jamie 1310 | 4 |
| ★37 | 47 | 61 | 84 | **LET THE GOOD TIMES ROLL & FEEL SO GOOD** — Bunny Sigler (Madara-White-Huff), Parkway 153 | 5 |
| 38 | 18 | 15 | 15 | **ALFIE** — Dionne Warwick (Bacharach-David), Scepter 12187 | 16 |
| ★39 | 49 | 62 | 96 | **YOUR UNCHANGING LOVE** — Marvin Gaye (Holland & Dozier), Tamla 54153 | 4 |
| 40 | 41 | 43 | 53 | **LOVE ME TENDER** — Percy Sledge (Quin Ivy & Marlin Greene), Atlantic 2414 | 6 |
| ★41 | 58 | 81 | 100 | **JOY** — Mitch Ryder (Bob Crewe), New Voice 824 | 4 |
| ★42 | 79 | — | — | **TO LOVE SOMEBODY** — Bee Gees (Robert Stigwood), Atco 6503 | 2 |
| 43 | 29 | 18 | 11 | **DING DONG THE WITCH IS DEAD** — Fifth Estate (Steve & Bill Jerome), Jubilee 5573 | 10 |
| 44 | 33 | 11 | 5 | **SHE'D RATHER BE WITH ME** — Turtles (Joe Wissert), White Whale 249 | 11 |
| 45 | 48 | 58 | 78 | **SHOW BUSINESS** — Lou Rawls (David Axelrod), Capitol 5941 | 4 |
| 46 | 46 | 48 | 54 | **AIRPLANE SONG** — Royal Guardsmen (Gernhard Ent.), Laurie 3391 | 6 |
| 47 | 54 | 64 | 64 | **SOMEBODY HELP ME** — Spencer Davis Group (Chris Blackwell & Jimmy Miller), United Artists 50162 | 6 |
| 48 | 51 | 52 | 62 | **YOU WANTED SOMEONE TO PLAY WITH (I Wanted Someone to Love)** — Frankie Laine (Bob Thiele), ABC 10946 | 6 |
| 49 | 50 | 63 | 87 | **TAKE ME (Just as I Am)** — Solomon Burke (Chips Moman & Dan Penn), Atlantic 2416 | 4 |
| 50 | 55 | 56 | 72 | **YOU ONLY LIVE TWICE** — Nancy Sinatra (Lee Hazlewood), Reprise 0595 | 5 |
| ★51 | — | — | — | **PLEASANT VALLEY SUNDAY** — Monkees (Douglas Farthing Hatfield), Colgems 1007 | 1 |
| 52 | 65 | 82 | 90 | **PICTURES OF LILY** — Who (Kit Lambert), Decca 32156 | 4 |
| ★53 | 64 | 88 | — | **RIVER IS WIDE** — Forum (Norm Ratner), Mira 232 | 3 |
| 54 | 60 | 72 | 95 | **(I Wanna) TESTIFY** — Parliaments (George Clinton), Revilot 207 | 6 |
| 55 | 34 | 23 | 26 | **FOR YOUR PRECIOUS LOVE** — Oscar Toney Jr. (Papa Don, Coghill, Emmons, Chrisman & Young), Bell 672 | 9 |
| 56 | 56 | 57 | 69 | **SOOTHE ME** — Sam & Dave (Prod. by Staff), Stax 218 | 6 |
| ★57 | 81 | — | — | **OUT AND ABOUT** — Tommy Boyce & Bobby Hart (Tommy Boyce & Bobby Hart), A&M 858 | 2 |
| ★58 | 72 | 84 | — | **DON'T LET THE RAIN FALL ON ME** — Critters (Anders-Poncia), Kapp 838 | 3 |
| 59 | 37 | 38 | 38 | **DON'T BLAME THE CHILDREN** — Sammy Davis Jr. (Jimmy Bowen), Reprise 0566 | 9 |
| 60 | 31 | 31 | 34 | **SHAKE, RATTLE AND ROLL** — Arthur Conley (Otis Redding), Atco 6494 | 7 |
| 61 | 62 | 77 | 88 | **LONELY DRIFTER** — Pieces of Eight, A&M 854 | 5 |
| ★62 | 86 | — | — | **THANK THE LORD FOR THE NIGHT TIME** — Neil Diamond (Jeff Barry & Ellie Greenwich), Bang 547 | 2 |
| ★63 | 78 | — | — | **BLUEBIRD** — Buffalo Springfield (York-Pala), Atco 6499 | 2 |
| ★64 | 87 | — | — | **I TAKE WHAT I WANT** — James & Bobby Purify (Papa Don), Bell 680 | 2 |
| ★65 | — | — | — | **BABY I LOVE YOU** — Aretha Franklin (Jerry Wexler), Atlantic 2427 | 1 |
| 66 | 82 | 97 | 97 | **WASHED ASHORE (On a Lonely Island in the Sea)** — Platters (Richard Popcorn Wylie), Musicor 1251 | 4 |
| 67 | 70 | 86 | — | **YOU KEEP ME HANGING ON** — Vanilla Fudge (Shadow Morton), Atco 6495 | 3 |
| ★68 | 85 | 100 | — | **GENTLE ON MY MIND** — Glen Campbell (Al de lory), Capitol 5939 | 3 |
| 69 | 84 | 87 | — | **EVERYBODY NEEDS LOVE** — Gladys Knight & The Pips (Norman Whitfield), Soul 35034 | 3 |
| 70 | 71 | 89 | 93 | **MY WORLD FELL DOWN** — Sagittarius (Gary Usher), Columbia 44163 | 5 |
| ★71 | — | — | — | **ALL YOU NEED IS LOVE** — Beatles (George Martin), Capitol 5964 | 1 |
| 72 | 69 | 69 | 61 | **BABY, PLEASE COME BACK HOME** — J. J. Barnes (Davis-Barnes), Groovesville 1006 | 10 |
| ★73 | — | — | — | **IT'S A HAPPENING WORLD** — Tokens (Tokens), Warner Bros. 7056 | 1 |
| 74 | 75 | 78 | 85 | **GROOVY SUMMERTIME** — Love Generation (Tommy Oliver), Imperial 66243 | 5 |
| ★75 | 92 | — | — | **COLD SWEAT** — James Brown & the Famous Flames (James Brown), King 6110 | 2 |
| 76 | 76 | 83 | 89 | **GIVE ME TIME** — Dusty Springfield (Johnny Franz), Philips 40465 | 4 |
| ★77 | 77 | 80 | 81 | **I'LL DO IT FOR YOU** — Toussaint McCall (Scotty Moore), Room 9 | 4 |
| ★78 | — | — | — | **WORDS** — Monkees (Douglas Farthing Hatfield), Colgems 1007 | 1 |
| 79 | 90 | 99 | — | **BLUES THEME** — Arrows (Mike Curb), Tower 295 | 7 |
| 80 | 80 | 90 | 99 | **MR. PLEASANT** — Kinks (Shel Talmy), Reprise 6587 | 4 |
| 81 | 83 | — | — | **I'LL TURN TO STONE** — Four Tops (Holland & Dozier), Motown 1110 | 2 |
| 82 | 100 | — | — | **THOUSAND SHADOWS** — Seeds (Marcus Tybalt), GNP Crescendo 394 | 2 |
| 83 | 68 | 68 | 75 | **BLACK SHEEP** — Sam the Sham & the Pharaohs (Stan Kesler), MGM 13747 | 6 |
| ★84 | — | — | — | **SHOOT YOUR SHOT** — Jr. Walker & the All Stars (Gordy Jr.-J. Horn), Soul 35036 | 1 |
| ★85 | — | — | — | **THE SWEETEST THING THIS SIDE OF HEAVEN** — Chris Bartley (Van McCoy), Vando 101 | 1 |
| 86 | 66 | 65 | 66 | **SUMMER AND SANDY** — Lesley Gore (Bob Crewe), Mercury 72683 | 7 |
| ★87 | — | — | — | **I CAN'T GO ON LIVIN' WITHOUT YOU, BABY** — Nino Tempo & April Stevens (Nino Tempo & Jerry Ripoell), White Wale 252 | 1 |
| 88 | 88 | 98 | — | **OMAHA** — Moby Grape (David Rubinson), Columbia 44173 | 3 |
| 89 | 89 | 92 | — | **FUNKY BROADWAY** — Dyke & the Blazers (Coleman & Barrett), Original Sound 64 | 7 |
| 90 | 97 | — | — | **HAPPY** — Sunshine Company (Joe Saracerno), Imperial 66247 | 2 |
| 91 | 94 | 96 | — | **MY ELUSIVE DREAMS** — David Houston & Tammy Wynette (Billy Sherrill), Epic 10094 | 3 |
| 92 | 96 | — | — | **HAPPY** — Blades of Grass (Bill & Steve Jerome), Jubilee 5582 | 2 |
| ★93 | — | — | — | **DON'T YOU MISS ME A LITTLE BIT, BABY** — Jimmy Ruffin (Norman Whitfield), Soul 35035 | 1 |
| 94 | — | — | — | **COME BACK WHEN YOU GROW UP** — Bobby Vee & the Strangers (Dallas Smith), Liberty 55964 | 1 |
| ★95 | — | — | — | **LET IT BE ME** — Sweet Inspirations (Jerry Wexler), Atlantic 2418 | 1 |
| 96 | 98 | — | — | **APPLES, PEACHES, PUMPKIN PIE** — Jay & the Techniques (Jerry Ross), Smash 2086 | 2 |
| 97 | 99 | — | — | **BROWN-EYED GIRL** — Van Morrison (Bert Berns), Bang 545 | 2 |
| 98 | — | — | — | **THE LOOK OF LOVE** — Dusty Springfield (Johnny Franz), Philips 40465 | 1 |
| 99 | — | — | — | **SLIPPIN' & SLIDIN'** — Willie Mitchell (Willie Mitchell), Hi 2125 | 1 |
| 100 | — | — | — | **I'LL NEVER FIND ANOTHER YOU** — Sonny James (Marvin Hughes), Capitol 5914 | 1 |

## BUBBLING UNDER THE HOT 100

101. 36-21-40 SHAPE — Showmen, Minit 32008
102. SOME KIND OF WONDERFUL — Soul Brothers 6, Atlantic 2405
103. GOOD FEELIN' TIME — Yellow Balloon, Canterbury 513
104. CITY OF WINDOWS — Stephen Monahan, Kapp 825
105. NEARER TO YOU — Betty Harris, Sansu 466
106. YOU DON'T MISS YOUR WATER — King Curtis, Atco 6496
107. GLORY OF LOVE — Otis Redding, Volt 152
108. ENDLESS SUMMER — Ventures, Liberty 55977
109. UP, UP & AWAY — Johnny Mann Singers, Liberty 55972
110. DEEP IN THE HEART OF HARLEM — Walter Jackson, Okeh 7285
111. DEVIL'S ANGELS — Davie Allen & the Arrows, Tower 341
112. MORE & MORE — Andy Williams, Columbia 44203
113. NOT SO SWEET MARTHA LORRAINE — Country Joe & the Fish, Vanguard 35052
114. WOMAN LIKE THAT, YEAH — Joe Tex, Dial 4059
115. BABY, YOU'RE A RICH MAN — Beatles, Capitol 5964
116. I'LL NEVER NEED MORE THAN THIS — Ike & Tina Turner, Philles 135
117. TEMPTATION — Boots Randolph, Monument 1009
118. THERE MUST BE A WAY — Jimmy Rosselli, United Artists 1079
119. IT'S SUCH A PRETTY WORLD TODAY — Andy Russell, Capitol 5917
120. LOVIN' SOUND — Ian & Sylvia, MGM 13686
121. IT'S BEEN A LONG, LONG TIME — Elgins, VIP 25043
122. LAST MINUTE MIRACLE — Shirelles, Scepter 12198
123. IT COULD BE WE'RE IN LOVE — Cryan' Shames, Columbia 44191
124. I COULD BE SO HAPPY — Magnificent Men, Capitol 5905
125. LONESOME ROAD — Wonder Who, Philips 40471
126. RUN, RUN, RUN — Third Rail, Epic 10191
127. DARLING BE HOME SOON — Bobby Darin, Atlantic 2420
128. TOGETHER — Intruders, Gamble 205
129. FOUR WALLS — Jackson 5, Calla 133
130. I'M JUST WAITIN' — New Colony Six, Senter 1207
131. ROMEO & JULIET — Michael & the Messengers, USA 874
132. PURPLE HAZE — Jimi Hendrix Experience, Reprise 0597
133. CRY SOFTLY LONELY ONE — Roy Orbison, MGM 13764
134. MORNING GLORY DAYS — Pleasure Fair, Uni 55016
135. MY ELUSIVE DREAMS — Curly Putnam, ABC 10934

Compiled from national retail sales and radio station airplay by the Music Popularity Dept. of Record Market Research, Billboard.

For Week Ending July 29, 1967

# Billboard HOT 100

★ STAR performer—Sides registering greatest proportionate upward progress this week.

Record Industry Association of America seal of certification as million selling single.

| This Week | 1 Wk. Ago | 2 Wks. Ago | 3 Wks. Ago | TITLE Artist (Producer), Label & Number | Weeks On Chart |
|---|---|---|---|---|---|
| 1 (Billboard Award) | 3 | 8 | 12 | LIGHT MY FIRE — Doors (Paul A. Rothchild), Elektra 45615 | 9 |
| ★2 | 6 | 11 | 19 | I WAS MADE TO LOVE HER — Stevie Wonder (H. Cosby), Tamla 54151 | 8 |
| 3 | 1 | 1 | 1 | WINDY — The Association, (Bones Howe), Warner Bros. 7041 | 10 |
| 4 | 2 | 3 | 3 | CAN'T TAKE MY EYES OFF YOU — Frankie Valli (Bob Crewe), Philips 40446 | 11 |
| ★5 | 8 | 10 | 13 | A WHITER SHADE OF PALE — Procol Harum (Denny Cordell), Deram 7507 | 6 |
| 6 | 5 | 2 | 2 | LITTLE BIT O' SOUL — Music Explosion (J. Katz-J. Kasenentz & E. Chiprut) Laurie 3380 | 12 |
| ★7 | 11 | 17 | 29 | MERCY, MERCY, MERCY — Buckinghams (James William Guercio), Columbia 44162 | 7 |
| ★8 | 12 | 12 | 22 | WHITE RABBIT — Jefferson Airplane (Rick Jarrard), RCA Victor 9248 | 6 |
| 9 | 7 | 7 | 7 | UP, UP AND AWAY — 5th Dimension (Johnny Rivers & Marc Gordon), Soul City 756 | 9 |
| 10 | 9 | 9 | 16 | C'MON MARIANNE — Four Seasons (Bob Crewe), Philips 40460 | 8 |
| 11 | 4 | 4 | 4 | SAN FRANCISCO "WEAR SOME FLOWERS IN YOUR HAIR" — Scott McKenzie (John Phillips & Lou Adler), Ode 103 | 10 |
| ★12 | 17 | 20 | 25 | I TAKE IT BACK — Sandy Posey (Chips Moman), MGM 13744 | 8 |
| 13 | 10 | 6 | 6 | COME ON DOWN TO MY BOAT — Every Mother's Son (Wes Farrell), MGM 13733 | 13 |
| 14 | 16 | 21 | 33 | JACKSON — Nancy Sinatra & Lee Hazlewood (Lee Hazlewood), Reprise 0595 | 6 |
| 15 | 15 | 15 | 20 | HERE WE GO AGAIN — Ray Charles (TRC), ABC 10938 | 11 |
| ★16 | 23 | 28 | 34 | CARRIE ANN — Hollies (Ron Richards), Epic 10180 | 7 |
| ★17 | 26 | 32 | 47 | SILENCE IS GOLDEN — Tremeloes (Mike Smith), Epic 10184 | 7 |
| 18 | 20 | 22 | 24 | SOUL FINGER — Bar-Kays (Produced by Staff), Volt 148 | 11 |
| ★19 | 31 | 61 | — | A GIRL LIKE YOU — Young Rascals (Young Rascals), Atlantic 2424 | 7 |
| ★20 | 27 | 30 | 45 | THERE GOES MY EVERYTHING — Engelbert Humperdinck (Peter Sullivan), Parrot 40015 | 5 |
| 21 | 21 | 26 | 26 | MAKE ME YOURS — Bettye Swann, Money 126 | 11 |
| 22 | 22 | 27 | 32 | FOR YOUR LOVE — Peaches & Herb (Bert Kapralik & Ken Williams), Date 1563 | 6 |
| 23 | 25 | 25 | 30 | MORE LOVE — Smokey Robinson & the Miracles ("Smokey") Tamla 54152 | 7 |
| ★24 | 51 | — | — | PLEASANT VALLEY SUNDAY — Monkees (Douglas Farthing Hatlelie), Colgems 1007 | 2 |
| ★25 | 30 | 35 | 50 | I LIKE THE WAY — Tommy James & the Shondells (Bo Gentry & Ritchie Cordell), Roulette 4756 | 5 |
| 26 | 14 | 14 | 17 | SOCIETY'S CHILD — Janis Ian (Shadow Morton), Verve 5027 | 10 |
| 27 | 13 | 5 | 5 | DON'T SLEEP IN THE SUBWAY — Petula Clark (Tony Hatch), Warner Bros. 7049 | 9 |
| ★28 | 33 | 52 | — | MY MAMMY — Happenings (Tokens), B. T. Puppy 530 | 3 |
| ★29 | 71 | — | — | ALL YOU NEED IS LOVE — Beatles (George Martin), Capitol 5964 | 2 |
| ★30 | 35 | 45 | 51 | HYPNOTIZED — Linda Jones (George Kerr), Loma 2070 | 6 |
| 31 | 32 | 42 | 60 | IN THE CHAPEL IN THE MOONLIGHT — Dean Martin (Jimmy Bowen), Reprise 0601 | 4 |
| ★32 | 42 | 79 | — | TO LOVE SOMEBODY — Bee Gees (Robert Stigwood), Atco 6503 | 3 |
| 33 | 34 | 53 | 76 | THE HAPPENING — Herb Alpert & The Tijuana Brass (Herb Alpert & Jerry Moss), A&M 860 | 4 |
| 34 | 18 | 23 | 37 | DON'T GO OUT INTO THE RAIN (You're Going to Melt) — Herman's Hermits (Mickie Most), MGM 13761 | 6 |
| 35 | 37 | 47 | 61 | LET THE GOOD TIMES ROLL & FEEL SO GOOD — Bunny Sigler (Madara-White-Huff), Parkway 153 | 6 |
| 36 | 36 | 57 | 67 | YOU WERE ON MY MIND — Crispian St. Peters, Jamie 1310 | 5 |
| 37 | 39 | 49 | 62 | YOUR UNCHANGING LOVE — Marvin Gaye (Holland & Dozier), Tamla 54153 | 5 |
| 38 | 19 | 19 | 21 | AIN'T NO MOUNTAIN HIGH ENOUGH — Marvin Gaye & Tammi Terrell (H. Fuqua & J. Bristol), Tamla 54149 | 12 |
| 39 | 24 | 24 | 36 | STEP OUT OF YOUR MIND — American Breed, Acta 804 | 9 |
| 40 | 28 | 16 | 8 | LET'S LIVE FOR TODAY — Grass Roots (Steve Barri & P. F. Sloan), Dunhill 4084 | 12 |
| 41 | 41 | 58 | 81 | JOY — Mitch Ryder (Bob Crewe), New Voice 824 | 5 |
| 42 | 38 | 18 | 15 | ALFIE — Dionne Warwick (Bacharach-David), Scepter 12187 | 17 |
| ★43 | 54 | 60 | 72 | (I Wanna) TESTIFY — Parliaments (George Clinton), Revilot 207 | 5 |
| 44 | 50 | 55 | 56 | YOU ONLY LIVE TWICE — Nancy Sinatra (Lee Hazlewood), Reprise 0595 | 6 |
| 45 | 45 | 48 | 58 | SHOW BUSINESS — Lou Rawls (David Axelrod), Capitol 5941 | 5 |
| ★46 | 78 | — | — | WORDS — Monkees (Douglas Farthing Hatlelid), Colgems 1007 | 2 |
| ★47 | 65 | — | — | BABY I LOVE YOU — Aretha Franklin (Jerry Wexler), Atlantic 2427 | 2 |
| ★48 | 62 | 86 | — | THANK THE LORD FOR THE NIGHT TIME — Neil Diamond (Jeff Barry & Ellie Greenwich), Bang 547 | 3 |
| 49 | 29 | 13 | 10 | THE TRACKS OF MY TEARS — Johnny Rivers (Lou Adler), Imperial 66244 | 9 |
| 50 | 58 | 72 | 84 | DON'T LET THE RAIN FALL ON ME — Critters (Anders-Poncia), Kapp 838 | 4 |
| 51 | 53 | 64 | 88 | RIVER IS WIDE — Forum (Norm Ratner), Mira 232 | 4 |
| 52 | 52 | 65 | 82 | PICTURES OF LILY — Who (Kit Lambert), Decca 32156 | 5 |
| 53 | 49 | 50 | 63 | TAKE ME (Just as I Am) — Solomon Burke (Chips Moman & Dan Penn), Atlantic 2416 | 5 |
| ★54 | 64 | 87 | — | I TAKE WHAT I WANT — James & Bobby Purify (Papa Don), Bell 680 | 3 |
| 55 | 57 | 81 | — | OUT AND ABOUT — Tommy Boyce & Bobby Hart (Tommy Boyce & Bobby Hart), A&M 858 | 3 |
| 56 | 56 | 56 | 57 | SOOTHE ME — Sam & Dave (Prod. by Staff), Stax 218 | 7 |
| 57 | 47 | 54 | 64 | SOMEBODY HELP ME — Spencer Davis Group (Chris Blackwell & Jimmy Miller), United Artists 50162 | 7 |
| ★58 | 75 | 92 | — | COLD SWEAT — James Brown & the Famous Flames (James Brown), King 6110 | 3 |
| ★59 | 69 | 84 | 87 | EVERYBODY NEEDS LOVE — Gladys Knight & The Pips (Norman Whitfield) Soul 35034 | 4 |
| 60 | 63 | 78 | — | BLUEBIRD — Buffalo Springfield (York-Pala), Atco 6499 | 3 |
| 61 | 61 | 62 | 77 | LONELY DRIFTER — Pieces of Eight, A&M 854 | 6 |
| 62 | 66 | 82 | 97 | WASHED ASHORE (On a Lonely Island in the Sea) — Platters (Richard Popcorn Wylie), Musicor 1251 | 5 |
| 63 | 48 | 51 | 52 | YOU WANTED SOMEONE TO PLAY WITH (I Wanted Someone to Love) — Frankie Laine (Bob Thiele), ABC 10946 | 7 |
| ★64 | — | — | — | BABY YOU'RE A RICH MAN NOW — Beatles (George Martin), Capitol 5964 | 1 |
| 65 | 68 | 85 | 100 | GENTLE ON MY MIND — Glen Campbell (Al de Lory), Capitol 5939 | 4 |
| ★66 | 85 | — | — | THE SWEETEST THING THIS SIDE OF HEAVEN — Chris Bartley (Van McCoy), Vando 101 | 2 |
| 67 | 67 | 70 | 86 | YOU KEEP ME HANGING ON — Vanilla Fudge (Shadow Morton), Atco 6495 | 4 |
| ★68 | 84 | — | — | SHOOT YOUR SHOT — Jr. Walker & the All Stars (Gordy Jr.-L. Horn), Soul 35036 | 2 |
| 69 | 79 | 90 | 99 | BLUES THEME — Arrows (Mike Curb), Tower 295 | 8 |
| 70 | 73 | — | — | IT'S A HAPPENING WORLD — Tokens (Tokens), Warner Bros. 7056 | 2 |
| ★71 | 94 | — | — | COME BACK WHEN YOU GROW UP — Bobby Vee & the Strangers (Dallas Smith), Liberty 55964 | 2 |
| 72 | 82 | 100 | — | THOUSAND SHADOWS — Seeds (Marcus Tybalt), GNP Crescendo 394 | 3 |
| ★73 | 93 | — | — | DON'T YOU MISS ME A LITTLE BIT, BABY — Jimmy Ruffin (Norman Whitfield), Soul 35035 | 2 |
| ★74 | — | — | — | YOU'RE MY EVERYTHING — Temptations (Norman Whitfield), Gordy 7063 | 1 |
| ★75 | — | — | — | GLORY OF LOVE — Otis Redding (Steve Cropper), Volt 152 | 1 |
| ★76 | — | — | — | SLIM JENKIN'S PLACE — Booker T. & the M.G.'s (Staff), Stax 224 | 1 |
| 77 | 81 | 83 | — | I'LL TURN TO STONE — Four Tops (Holland & Dozier), Motown 1110 | 3 |
| ★78 | 97 | 99 | — | BROWN-EYED GIRL — Van Morrison (Bert Berns), Bang 545 | 3 |
| ★79 | — | — | — | THE WINDOWS OF THE WORLD — Dionne Warwick (Bacharach-David), Scepter 12196 | 1 |
| ★80 | — | — | — | CRY SOFTLY LONELY ONE — Roy Orbison (Rose & Vienneau), MGM 13764 | 1 |
| ★81 | — | — | — | FAKIN' IT — Simon & Garfunkel (John Simon), Columbia 44232 | 1 |
| 82 | 89 | 89 | 92 | FUNKY BROADWAY — Dyke & the Blazers (Coleman & Barrett), Original Sound 64 | 8 |
| 83 | 96 | 98 | — | APPLES, PEACHES, PUMPKIN PIE — Jay & the Techniques (Jerry Ross), Smash 2086 | 3 |
| 84 | 74 | 75 | 78 | GROOVY SUMMERTIME — Love Generation (Tommy Oliver), Imperial 66243 | 6 |
| ★85 | — | — | — | NEARER TO YOU — Berry Harris (A. Toussaint-M. Sehorn), Sansu 466 | 1 |
| 86 | 87 | — | — | I CAN'T GO ON LIVIN' WITHOUT YOU, BABY — Nino Tempo & April Stevens (Nino Tempo & Jerry Ripoell), White Wale 252 | 2 |
| 87 | 92 | 96 | — | HAPPY — Blades of Grass (Bill & Steve Jerome), Jubilee 5582 | 3 |
| 88 | 90 | 97 | — | HAPPY — Sunshine Company (Joe Saraceno), Imperial 66247 | 3 |
| 89 | 91 | 94 | 96 | MY ELUSIVE DREAMS — David Houston & Tammy Wynette (Billy Sherrill), Epic 10094 | 4 |
| ★90 | — | — | — | PEARL TIME — Andre Williams (Super Sonic Sound), Sport 105 | 1 |
| 91 | — | 95 | 95 | MORE AND MORE — Andy Williams (Nick DeCaro), Columbia 44202 | 3 |
| 92 | — | — | — | IT'S BEEN A LONG, LONG TIME — Elgins (H. Fuqua-J. Bristol), V.I.P 25043 | 1 |
| 93 | — | — | — | DARLING BE HOME SOON — Bobby Darin (Koppleman & Rubin), Atlantic 2420 | 1 |
| 94 | 95 | — | — | LET IT BE ME — Sweet Inspirations (Jerry Wexler), Atlantic 2418 | 2 |
| 95 | 98 | — | — | THE LOOK OF LOVE — Dusty Springfield (Johnny Franz), Philips 40465 | 2 |
| 96 | 99 | — | — | SLIPPIN' & SLIDIN' — Willie Mitchell (Willie Mitchell), Hi 2125 | 2 |
| 97 | — | — | — | DEVIL'S ANGELS — Davie Allan (Mike Curb), Tower 341 | 1 |
| 98 | — | — | — | HAPPY AND ME — Don & the Goodtimes (Jerry Fuller), Epic 10199 | 1 |
| 99 | — | — | — | LONESOME ROAD — Wonder Who? (Bob Crewe), Philips 40471 | 1 |
| 100 | 100 | — | — | I'LL NEVER FIND ANOTHER YOU — Sonny James (Marvin Hughes), Capitol 5914 | 2 |

## HOT 100—A TO Z—(Publisher-Licensee)


Ain't No Mountain High Enough (Jobete, BMI)... 38
Alfie (Famous, ASCAP)... 42
All You Need Is Love (Maclen, BMI)... 29
Apples, Peaches, Pumpkin Pie (Philstox/Act Three, BMI)... 83
Baby, I Love You (14th Hour/Pronto, BMI)... 47
Baby, You're a Rich Man Now (Maclen, BMI)... 64
Blues Theme (Dijon, BMI)... 69
Bluebird (Ten-East/Springalo/Cotillion, BMI)... 60
Brown-Eyed Girl (Web IV, BMI)... 78
Can't Take My Eyes Off You (Saturday/Seasons' Four, BMI)... 4
Carrie Ann (Maribus, BMI)... 16
C'Mon Marianne (Saturday/Seasons' Four, BMI)... 10
Cold Sweat (Dynatone, BMI)... 58
Come Back When You Grow Up (Painted Desert, BMI)... 71
Come on Down to My Boat (Picturetone-Goldstein, BMI)... 13
Cry Softly Lonely One (Rose & Vinneau, BMI)... 80
Darling Be Home Soon (Faithful Virtue, BMI)... 93
Devil's Angels (Dijon, BMI)... 97
Don't Go Out Into the Rain (You're Going to Melt) (Unart, BMI)... 34
Don't Let the Rain Fall Down on Me (Ugenda, BMI) 50
Don't Sleep in the Subway (Duchess, BMI)... 27
Don't You Miss Me a Little Bit, Baby (Jobete, BMI) 73
Everybody Needs Love (Jobete, BMI)... 59
Fakin' It (Charing Cross, BMI)... 81
For Your Love (Beechwood, BMI)... 22
Funky Broadway (Drive-In/Routeen, BMI)... 82
Gentle on My Mind (Glazier, BMI)... 65
Girl Like You (Slacsar, BMI)... 19
Glory of Love (Shapiro-Bernstein, ASCAP)... 75
Groovy Summertime (4 Star, BMI)... 84
Happening, The (Jobete, BMI)... 33
Happy and Me (Burdette/Shingle, BMI)... 98
Happy (Blades of Grass) (Unart, BMI)... 87
Happy (Sunshine Company) (Unart, BMI)... 88
Here We Go Again (Dirk, BMI)... 15
Hypnotized (Zira/Floreca, BMI)... 30
I Can't Go on Livin' Without You, Baby (Daddy San/Jerell, BMI)... 86
I Like the Way (Patricia, BMI)... 25
I Take It Back (Low-Sal, BMI)... 12
I Take What I Want (East/Cotillion, BMI)... 54
I Was Made to Love Her (Jobete, BMI)... 2
I'll Never Find Another You (Chappell, ASCAP)... 100
I'll Turn to Stone (Jobete, BMI)... 77
In the Chapel in the Moonlight (Shapiro-Bernstein, ASCAP)... 31
It's a Happening World (Screen Gems-Columbia, BMI)... 70
It's Been a Long, Long Time (Jobete, BMI)... 92
(I Wanna) Testify (Groovesville, BMI)... 43
Jackson (Bexhill Quartet, ASCAP)... 14
Joy (Saturday, BMI)... 41
Let's Live for Today (James, BMI)... 40
Let the Good Times Roll & Feel So Good (Travis, BMI)... 35
Let It Be Me (Music Corp. of America, ASCAP)... 94
Light My Fire (Nipper, ASCAP)... 1
Little Bit o' Soul (Southern, ASCAP)... 6
Lonely Drifter (Bidle, BMI)... 61
Lonesome Road (Shilkret/Paramount, ASCAP)... 99
Look of Love, The (Colgems, ASCAP)... 95
Make Me Yours (Cash Songs, BMI)... 21
Mercy, Mercy, Mercy (Zawinal, BMI)... 7
More and More (Sunbeam, BMI)... 91
More Love (Jobete, BMI)... 23
My Elusive Dreams (Tree, BMI)... 89
My Mammy (Bourne/Donaldson/Warock, BMI)... 28
Nearer to You (Marsaint, BMI)... 85
Out and About (Screen Gems-Columbia, BMI)... 55
Pearl Time (Polaris/John L, BMI)... 90
Pictures of Lily (Essex, ASCAP)... 52
Pleasant Valley Sunday (Screen Gems-Columbia, BMI)... 24
River Is Wide, The (Saturday, BMI)... 51
San Francisco "Wear Some Flowers in Your Hair" (Trousdale, BMI)... 11
Shoot Your Shot (Jobete, BMI)... 68
Show Business (Raw Lou-Hidle, BMI)... 45
Silence Is Golden (Saturday/Gevadium, BMI)... 17
Slippin' & Slidin' (Venice, BMI)... 96
Slim Jenkin's Place (East, BMI)... 76
Society's Child (Dialogue, BMI)... 26
Somebody Help Me (Essex, ASCAP)... 57
Soothe Me (Kags, BMI)... 56
Soul Finger (East, BMI)... 18
Step Out of Your Mind (Blackwood, BMI)... 39
Sweetest Thing This Side of Heaven, The (Blackwood, BMI)... 48
Take Me (Just As I Am) (Fame, BMI)... 53
Thank the Lord for the Night Time (Tallyrand, BMI)... 48
The Windows of the World (Jac/Blue Seas, ASCAP) 79
There Goes My Everything (Blue Crest, BMI)... 20
Thousand Shadows (Neil/Purple Bottle, BMI)... 72
To Love Somebody (Nemperor, BMI)... 32
Tracks of My Tears, The (Jobete, BMI)... 49
Up, Up and Away (5th Dimension) (Rivers, BMI)... 9
Washed Ashore (On a Lonely Island in the Sea) (Catalogue-A La King, BMI)... 62
White Rabbit (Copper Penny, BMI)... 8
Whiter Shade of Pale (Essex, ASCAP)... 5
Windy (Irving, BMI)... 3
Words (Screen Gems-Columbia, BMI)... 46
You Keep Me Hanging On (Jobete, BMI)... 67
You Ony Live Twice (Unart, BMI)... 44
You Wanted Someone to Play With (I Wanted Someone to Love) (Morris, ASCAP)... 63
You Were on My Mind (Whitmark, ASCAP)... 36
You're My Everything (Jobete, BMI)... 74
Your Unchanging Love (Jobete, BMI)... 37


## BUBBLING UNDER THE HOT 100

101. CITY OF WINDOWS... Stephen Monahan, Kapp 835
102. SOME KIND OF WONDERFUL... Soul Brothers Six, Atlantic 2406
103. GOOD FEELIN' TIME... Yellow Balloon, Canterbury 513
104. 39-21-40... Showmen, Minit 32007
105. YOU DON'T MISS YOUR WATER... King Curtis, Atco 6496
106. ENDLESS SUMMER... Ventures, Liberty 55977
107. CASONOVA (Your Playing Days Are Over)... Ruby Andrews, Zodiac 1004
108. LET THE FOUR WINDS BLOW... Jerry Jaye, Hi 21218
109. UP, UP & AWAY... Johnny Mann Singers, Liberty 55972
110. NOT SO SWEET MARTHA LORRAINE.. Country Joe & the Fish, Vanguard 35052
111. RUN, RUN, RUN... Third Rail, Epic 10191
112. LAST MINUTE MIRACLE... Shirelles, Scepter 12198
113. OMAHA... Moby Grape, Columbia 44173
114. I'LL NEVER NEED MORE THAN THIS... Ike & Tina Turner, Philles 135
115. ROLLIN' AND TUMBLIN'... Canned Heat, Liberty 55979
116. LOVIN' SOUND... Ian & Sylvia, MGM 13686
117. THERE MUST BE A WAY... Jimmy Roselli, United Artists 51079
118. ODE TO BILLY JOE... Bobbie Gentry, Capitol 6950
119. IT COULD BE WE'RE IN LOVE... Cryan' Shames, Columbia 44191
120. IT'S SUCH A PRETTY WORLD TODAY... Andy Russell, Capitol 5917
121. HA, HA SAID THE CLOWN... Yardbirds, Epic 10204
122. ALONG COMES MARY... Baja Marimba Band, A&M 862
123. SUNNY GOOOGE STREET... Tom Northcott, Warner Bros. 7051
124. HEART & SOUL... Incredibles, Audio Arts 60007
125. AGNES ENGLISH... John Fred & the Playboys, Paula 273
126. GET THE MESSAGE... Brian Hyland, Philips 40472
127. CRYING LIKE A BABY... Jive Five, Musicor 1250
128. I'M JUST WAITIN'... New Colony 6, Sentar 1207
129. ROMEO & JULIET... Michael & the Messengers, U.S.A. 874
130. PURPLE HAZE... Jimi Hendrix Experience, Reprise 0597
131. HOLD ON... Mauds, Mercury 72694
132. I WANNA HURRY MY BROTHERS HOME... Jimmy Holiday, Minit 32023
133. I WANT TO LOVE YOU FOR WHAT YOU ARE... Ronnie Dove, Diamond 227
134. MY ELUSIVE DREAMS... Curly Putnam, ABC 10934
135. FOOLIN' AROUND... Chris Montez, A&M 855

Compiled from national retail sales and radio station airplay by the Music Popularity Dept. of Record Market Research, Billboard.

# Billboard HOT 100

For Week Ending August 5, 1967

★ STAR performer—Sides registering greatest proportionate upward progress this week.

Record Industry Association of America seal of certification as million selling single.

| This Week | 1 Wk. Ago | 2 Wks. Ago | TITLE Artist (Producer), Label & Number | Weeks On Chart |
|---|---|---|---|---|
| 1 | 1 | 3 | **LIGHT MY FIRE** — Doors (Paul A. Rothchild), Elektra 45615 | 8 |
| 2 | 2 | 6 | **I WAS MADE TO LOVE HER** — Stevie Wonder (H. Cosby), Tamla 54151 | 9 |
| 3 | 29 | 71 | **ALL YOU NEED IS LOVE** — Beatles (George Martin), Capitol 5964 | 3 |
| 4 | 3 | 1 | **WINDY** — The Association (Bones Howe), Warner Bros. 7041 | 11 |
| 5 | 5 | 8 | **A WHITER SHADE OF PALE** — Procol Harum (Denny Cordell), Deram 7507 | 7 |
| 6 | 4 | 2 | **CAN'T TAKE MY EYES OFF YOU** — Frankie Valli (Bob Crewe), Philips 40446 | 12 |
| 7 | 7 | 11 | **MERCY, MERCY, MERCY** — Buckinghams (James William Guercio), Columbia 44182 | 8 |
| 8 | 8 | 12 | **WHITE RABBIT** — Jefferson Airplane (Rick Jarrard), RCA Victor 9248 | 7 |
| 9 | 24 | 51 | **PLEASANT VALLEY SUNDAY** — Monkees (Douglas Farthing Hatlelid), Colgems 1007 | 3 |
| 10 | 6 | 5 | **LITTLE BIT O' SOUL** — Music Explosion (J. Katz-J. Kasenetz & E. Chiprut), Laurie 3380 | 13 |
| 11 | 19 | 31 | **A GIRL LIKE YOU** — Young Rascals (Young Rascals), Atlantic 2424 | 4 |
| 12 | 12 | 17 | **I TAKE IT BACK** — Sandy Posey (Chips Moman), MGM 13744 | 9 |
| 13 | 17 | 26 | **SILENCE IS GOLDEN** — Tremeloes (Mike Smith), Epic 10184 | 8 |
| 14 | 14 | 16 | **JACKSON** — Nancy Sinatra & Lee Hazlewood (Lee Hazlewood), Reprise 0595 | 7 |
| 15 | 28 | 33 | **MY MAMMY** — Happenings (Tokens), B. T. Puppy 530 | 4 |
| 16 | 16 | 23 | **CARRIE ANN** — Hollies (Ron Richards), Epic 10180 | 8 |
| 17 | 11 | 4 | **SAN FRANCISCO "WEAR SOME FLOWERS IN YOUR HAIR"** — Scott McKenzie (John Phillips & Lou Adler), Ode 103 | 11 |
| 18 | 18 | 20 | **SOUL FINGER** — Bar-Kays (Produced by Staff), Volt 148 | 12 |
| 19 | 9 | 7 | **UP, UP AND AWAY** — 5th Dimension (Johnny Rivers & Marc Gordon), Soul City 756 | 10 |
| 20 | 22 | 22 | **FOR YOUR LOVE** — Peaches & Herb (Bert Kapralik & Ken Williams), Date 1563 | 7 |
| 21 | 21 | 21 | **MAKE ME YOURS** — Bettye Swann, Money 126 | 12 |
| 22 | 47 | 65 | **BABY I LOVE YOU** — Aretha Franklin (Jerry Wexler), Atlantic 2427 | 3 |
| 23 | 23 | 25 | **MORE LOVE** — Smokey Robinson & the Miracles ("Smokey"), Tamla 54152 | 8 |
| 24 | 48 | 62 | **THANK THE LORD FOR THE NIGHT TIME** — Neil Diamond (Jeff Barry & Ellie Greenwich), Bang 547 | 4 |
| 25 | 25 | 30 | **I LIKE THE WAY** — Tommy James & the Shondells (Bo Gentry & Ritchie Cordell), Roulette 4756 | 6 |
| 26 | 31 | 32 | **IN THE CHAPEL IN THE MOONLIGHT** — Dean Martin (Jimmy Bowen), Reprise 0601 | 5 |
| 27 | 32 | 42 | **TO LOVE SOMEBODY** — Bee Gees (Robert Stigwood), Atco 6503 | 4 |
| 28 | 30 | 35 | **HYPNOTIZED** — Linda Jones (George Kerr), Loma 2070 | 7 |
| 29 | 13 | 10 | **COME ON DOWN TO MY BOAT** — Every Mother's Son (Wes Farrell), MGM 13733 | 14 |
| 30 | 35 | 37 | **LET THE GOOD TIMES ROLL & FEEL SO GOOD** — Bunny Sigler (Madara-White-Huff), Parkway 153 | 7 |
| 31 | 20 | 27 | **THERE GOES MY EVERYTHING** — Engelbert Humperdinck (Peter Sullivan), Parrot 40015 | 6 |
| 32 | 33 | 34 | **THE HAPPENING** — Herb Alpert & The Tijuana Brass (Herb Alpert & Jerry Moss), A&M 860 | 5 |
| 33 | 37 | 39 | **YOUR UNCHANGING LOVE** — Marvin Gaye (Holland & Dozier), Tamla 54153 | 6 |
| 34 | 46 | 78 | **WORDS** — Monkees (Douglas Farthing Hatlelid), Colgems 1007 | 3 |
| 35 | 10 | 9 | **C'MON MARIANNE** — Four Seasons (Bob Crewe), Philips 40460 | 9 |
| 36 | 26 | 14 | **SOCIETY'S CHILD** — Janis Ian (Shadow Morton), Verve 5027 | 11 |
| 37 | 43 | 54 | **(I Wanna) TESTIFY** — Parliaments (George Clinton), Revilot 207 | 6 |
| 38 | 15 | 15 | **HERE WE GO AGAIN** — Ray Charles (TRC), ABC 10938 | 12 |
| 39 | 55 | 57 | **OUT AND ABOUT** — Tommy Boyce & Bobby Hart (Tommy Boyce & Bobby Hart), A&M 858 | 4 |
| 40 | 50 | 58 | **DON'T LET THE RAIN FALL ON ME** — Critters (Anders-Poncia), Kapp 838 | 5 |
| 41 | 64 | — | **BABY YOU'RE A RICH MAN NOW** — Beatles (George Martin), Capitol 5964 | 2 |
| 42 | 27 | 13 | **DON'T SLEEP IN THE SUBWAY** — Petula Clark (Tony Hatch), Warner Bros. 7049 | 10 |
| 43 | 54 | 64 | **I TAKE WHAT I WANT** — James & Bobby Purify (Papa Don), Bell 680 | 4 |
| 44 | 44 | 50 | **YOU ONLY LIVE TWICE** — Nancy Sinatra (Lee Hazlewood), Reprise 0595 | 7 |
| 45 | 45 | 45 | **SHOW BUSINESS** — Lou Rawls (David Axelrod), Capitol 5941 | 6 |
| 46 | 51 | 53 | **RIVER IS WIDE** — Forum (Norm Hatner), Mira 232 | 5 |
| 47 | 58 | 75 | **COLD SWEAT** — James Brown & the Famous Flames (James Brown), King 6110 | 4 |
| 48 | 34 | 18 | **DON'T GO OUT INTO THE RAIN (You're Going to Melt)** — Herman's Hermits (Mickie Most), MGM 13761 | 7 |
| 49 | 36 | 36 | **YOU WERE ON MY MIND** — Crispian St. Peters, Jamie 1310 | 5 |
| 50 | 66 | 85 | **THE SWEETEST THING THIS SIDE OF HEAVEN** — Chris Bartley (Van McCoy), Vando 101 | 3 |
| 51 | 52 | 52 | **PICTURES OF LILY** — Who (Kit Lambert), Decca 32156 | 5 |
| 52 | 74 | — | **YOU'RE MY EVERYTHING** — Temptations (Norman Whitfield), Gordy 7063 | 2 |
| 53 | 81 | — | **FAKIN' IT** — Simon & Garfunkel (John Simon), Columbia 44232 | 2 |
| 54 | 68 | 84 | **SHOOT YOUR SHOT** — Jr. Walker and All Stars (Gordy Jr.-L. Horn), Soul 35036 | 3 |
| 55 | 71 | 94 | **COME BACK WHEN YOU GROW UP** — Bobby Vee & the Strangers (Dallas Smith), Liberty 55964 | 3 |
| 56 | 59 | 69 | **EVERYBODY NEEDS LOVE** — Gladys Knight & The Pips (Norman Whitfield), Soul 35034 | 5 |
| 57 | 62 | 66 | **WASHED ASHORE (On a Lonely Island in the Sea)** — Platters (Richard Popcorn Wylie), Musicor 1251 | 6 |
| 58 | 60 | 63 | **BLUEBIRD** — Buffalo Springfield (York-Pala), Atco 6499 | 4 |
| 59 | 61 | 61 | **LONELY DRIFTER** — Pieces of Eight, A&M 854 | 7 |
| 60 | 75 | — | **GLORY OF LOVE** — Otis Redding (Steve Cropper), Volt 152 | 2 |
| 61 | — | — | **HEROES AND VILLAINS** — Beach Boys (Beach Boys), Brother records 1001 | 1 |
| 62 | 65 | 68 | **GENTLE ON MY MIND** — Glen Campbell (Al de lory), Capitol 5939 | 5 |
| 63 | 41 | 41 | **JOY** — Mitch Ryder (Bob Crewe), New Voice 824 | 6 |
| 64 | — | 79 | **THE WINDOWS OF THE WORLD** — Dionne Warwick (Bacharach-David), Scepter 12196 | 4 |
| 65 | 80 | — | **CRY SOFTLY LONELY ONE** — Roy Orbison (Rose & Vienneau), MGM 13764 | 2 |
| 66 | 78 | 97 | **BROWN-EYED GIRL** — Van Morrison (Bert Berns), Bang 545 | 4 |
| 67 | 69 | 79 | **BLUES THEME** — Arrows (Mike Curb), Tower 295 | 9 |
| 68 | 83 | 96 | **APPLES, PEACHES, PUMPKIN PIE** — Jay & the Techniques (Jerry Ross), Smash 2086 | 4 |
| 69 | 70 | 73 | **IT'S A HAPPENING WORLD** — Tokens (Tokens), Warner Bros. 7056 | 3 |
| 70 | 73 | 93 | **DON'T YOU MISS ME A LITTLE BIT, BABY** — Jimmy Ruffin (Norman Whitfield), Soul 35035 | 3 |
| 71 | — | — | **ODE TO BILLIE JOE** — Bobbie Gentry (Kelly Gordon & Bobby Paris), Capitol 5950 | 1 |
| 72 | 72 | 82 | **THOUSAND ROSES** — Seeds (Marcus Tybalt), GNP Crescendo 394 | 4 |
| 73 | — | — | **SAN FRANCISCO NIGHTS** — Eric Burdon and the Animals (Tom Wilson), MGM 13769 | 1 |
| 74 | 67 | 67 | **YOU KEEP ME HANGING ON** — Vanilla Fudge (Shadow Morton), Atco 6495 | 5 |
| 75 | — | — | **YOU KNOW WHAT I MEAN** — Turtles (Joe Wissert), White Whale 254 | 1 |
| 76 | 76 | — | **SLIM JENKIN'S PLACE** — Booker T. & the M.G.'s (Staff), Stax 224 | 2 |
| 77 | 77 | 81 | **I'LL TURN TO STONE** — Four Tops (Holland & Dozier), Motown 1110 | 4 |
| 78 | — | — | **THE WORLD WE KNEW (Over and Over)** — Frank Sinatra (Jimmy Bowen), Reprise 0610 | 1 |
| 79 | 88 | 90 | **HAPPY** — Sunshine Company (Joe Saraceno), Imperial 66247 | 4 |
| 80 | — | — | **HA HA SAID THE CLOWN** — Yardbirds (Mickie Most), Epic 10204 | 1 |
| 81 | 82 | 89 | **FUNKY BROADWAY** — Dyke & the Blazers (Coleman & Barrett), Original Sound 64 | 4 |
| 82 | — | — | **I WANT TO LOVE YOU FOR WHAT YOU ARE** — Ronnie Dove (Phil Kahl), Diamond 227 | 1 |
| 83 | — | — | **A WOMAN'S HANDS** — Joe Tex (Buddy Killen), Dial 4061 | 1 |
| 84 | 84 | 74 | **GROOVY SUMMERTIME** — Love Generation (Tommy Oliver), Imperial 66243 | 7 |
| 85 | 85 | — | **NEARER TO YOU** — Betty Harris (A. Toussaint-M. Sehorn), Sansu 466 | 2 |
| 86 | — | — | **GROOVIN'** — Booker T. and the M.G.'s (Staff), Stax 224 | 1 |
| 87 | 87 | 92 | **HAPPY** — Blades of Grass (Bill & Steve Jerome), Jubilee 5582 | 4 |
| 88 | 91 | — | **MORE AND MORE** — Andy Williams (Nick DeCaro), Columbia 44202 | 4 |
| 89 | 89 | 91 | **MY ELUSIVE DREAMS** — David Houston & Tammy Wynette (Billy Sherrill), Epic 10094 | 5 |
| 90 | 90 | — | **PEARL TIME** — Andre Williams (Super Sonic Sound), Sport 105 | 2 |
| 91 | 99 | — | **LONESOME ROAD** — Wonder Who? (Bob Crewe), Philips 40471 | 2 |
| 92 | — | — | **FUNKY BROADWAY** — Wilson Pickett (Jerry Wexler), Atlantic 2430 | 1 |
| 93 | 93 | — | **DARLING BE HOME SOON** — Bobby Darin (Koppleman & Rubin), Atlantic 2420 | 2 |
| 94 | 95 | 98 | **THE LOOK OF LOVE** — Dusty Springfield (Johnny Franz), Philips 40465 | 3 |
| 95 | — | — | **NOT SO SWEET MARTHA LORRAINE** — Country Joe and the Fish (Sam Charters), Vanguard 35052 | 1 |
| 96 | — | — | **ALONG COMES MARY** — Baja Marimba Band (Jerry Moss), A&M 862 | 1 |
| 97 | 100 | 100 | **I'LL NEVER FIND ANOTHER YOU** — Sonny James (Marvin Hughes), Capitol 5914 | 3 |
| 98 | — | — | **RUN, RUN, RUN** — Third Rail (Levine/Resnick/Cooper), Epic 10191 | 1 |
| 99 | — | — | **IT COULD BE WE'RE IN LOVE** — Cryan' Shames (Jim Golden), Columbia 44191 | 1 |
| 100 | — | — | **GOOD DAY SUNSHINE** — Claudine Longet (Tommy Li Puma), A&M 864 | 1 |

## BUBBLING UNDER THE HOT 100

101. PENNY ARCADE ............ Cyrkle, Columbia 44224
102. GIMME LITTLE SIGN ........ Brenton Wood, Double Shot 116
103. DEVIL'S ANGELS ............ Davie Allen, Tower 341
104. CASANOVA (Your Playing Days Are Over) ... Ruby Andrews, Zodiac 1004
105. LOVIN' SOUND ............ Ian & Sylvia, MGM 13686
106. LET IT BE ME ............ Sweet Inspirations, Atlantic 2413
107. LET THE FOUR WINDS BLOW ... Jerry Jaye, Hi 21218
108. ENDLESS SUMMER .......... Ventures, Liberty 55977
109. DRUMS .................... Jon & Robin, Abnak 122
110. OMAHA .................... Moby Grape, Columbia 44173
111. IT'S BEEN A LONG, LONG TIME ... Eddie Floyd, Stax V.I.P. 25043
112. PURPLE HAZE .............. Jimi Hendrix Experience, Reprise 0597
113. SLIPPIN' AND SLIDIN' ...... Willie Mitchell, Hi 2125
114. IT'S THE LITTLE THINGS .... Sonny & Cher, Atco 6486
115. I CAN'T GO ON LIVING WITHOUT YOU ... Nino Tempo & April Stevens, White Whale 252
116. THERE MUST BE A WAY ...... Jimmy Russelll, United Artists 51079
117. SLIPPIN' AND SLIDIN' ...... Willie Mitchell, Hi 2125
118. HOLD ON ................... Mauds, Mercury 72694
119. IT'S SUCH A PRETTY WORLD TODAY ... Andy Russell, Capitol 5912
120. LOOK IN YOUR EYES ........ Scott McKenzie, Capitol 5961
121. THINGS WE SHOULD HAVE SAID ... Little Milton, Checker 596
122. HEART & SOUL ............. Incredibles, Audio Arts 6000
123. LADY FRIEND .............. Byrds, Columbia 44230
124. I'VE BEEN GOOD TO YOU ..... Temptations, Gordy 7065
125. JILL ...................... Gary Lewis and the Playboys, Liberty 55985
126. FOUR WALLS ................ J. Jackson, Calla 132
127. THAT'S THE WAY LOVE IS .... Isley Brothers, Tamla 54154
128. A LITTLE BIT NOW .......... Dave Clark Five, Epic 10209
129. LOVE IS A DOGGONE GOOD THING ... Eddie Floyd, Stax 597
130. WOULD YOU BELIEVE ........ Tempests, Smash 2084
131. PUT YOUR TRUST IN ME ...... Joe Simon, Sound Stage 7 452583
132. LITTLE OLD WINE DRINKER ME ... Robert Mitchum, Monument 1026
133. YOU'RE A VERY LOVELY WOMAN ... Merry Go Round, A&M 868
134. 16 TONS ................... Tom Jones, Parrot 40016
135. SUMMER DAY REFLECTION SONG ... Donovan, Hickory 1-70

# Billboard HOT 100

*For Week Ending August 12, 1967*

★ STAR performer—Sides registering greatest proportionate upward progress this week.
● Record Industry Association of America seal of certification as million selling single.

| This Week | 1 Wk. Ago | 2 Wks. Ago | 3 Wks. Ago | TITLE Artist (Producer), Label & Number | Weeks on Chart |
|---|---|---|---|---|---|
| 1 | 1 | 1 | 3 | **LIGHT MY FIRE** — Doors (Paul A. Rothch1d), Elektra 45615 | 11 |
| 2 | 3 | 29 | 71 | **ALL YOU NEED IS LOVE** — Beatles (George Martin), Capitol 5964 | 4 |
| 3 | 2 | 2 | 6 | **I WAS MADE TO LOVE HER** — Stevie Wonder (H. Cosby), Tamla 54151 | 10 |
| 4 | 9 | 24 | 51 | **PLEASANT VALLEY SUNDAY** — Monkees (Douglas Farthing Hatfield), Colgems 1007 | 4 |
| 5 | 7 | 7 | 11 | **MERCY, MERCY, MERCY** — Buckinghams (James William Guercio), Columbia 44162 | 9 |
| 6 | 6 | 4 | 2 | **CAN'T TAKE MY EYES OFF YOU** — Frankie Valli (Bob Crewe), Philips 40446 | 13 |
| 7 | 5 | 5 | 8 | **A WHITER SHADE OF PALE** — Procol Harum (Denny Cordell), Deram 7507 | 8 |
| 8 | 4 | 3 | 1 | **WINDY** — The Association (Jones Howe), Warner Bros. 7041 | 12 |
| 9 | 16 | 16 | 23 | **CARRIE ANN** — Hollies (Ron Richards), Epic 10180 | 9 |
| 10 | 11 | 19 | 31 | **A GIRL LIKE YOU** — Young Rascals (Young Rascals), Atlantic 2424 | 5 |
| 11 | 22 | 47 | 65 | **BABY I LOVE YOU** — Aretha Franklin (Jerry Wexler), Atlantic 2427 | 4 |
| 12 | 13 | 17 | 26 | **SILENCE IS GOLDEN** — Tremeloes (Mike Smith), Epic 10184 | 9 |
| 13 | 15 | 28 | 33 | **MY MAMMY** — Happenings (Tokens), B.T. Puppy 530 | 5 |
| 14 | 14 | 14 | 16 | **JACKSON** — Nancy Sinatra & Lee Hazlewood (Lee Hazlewood), Reprise 0595 | 8 |
| 15 | 8 | 8 | 12 | **WHITE RABBIT** — Jefferson Airplane (Rick Jarrard), RCA Victor 9248 | 8 |
| 16 | 10 | 6 | 5 | **LITTLE BIT O' SOUL** — Music Explosion (J. Katz-J. Kasenentz & E Chiprut), Laurie 3380 | 14 |
| 17 | 18 | 18 | 20 | **SOUL FINGER** — Bar-Kays (Produced by Staff), Volt 148 | 13 |
| 18 | 12 | 12 | 17 | **I TAKE IT BACK** — Sandy Posey (Chips Moman), MGM 13744 | 10 |
| 19 | 24 | 48 | 62 | **THANK THE LORD FOR THE NIGHT TIME** — Neil Diamond (Jeff Barry & Ellie Greenwich), Bang 547 | 5 |
| 20 | 47 | 58 | 75 | **COLD SWEAT** — James Brown and the Famous Flames (James Brown), King 6110 | 5 |
| 21 | 71 | — | — | **ODE TO BILLIE JOE** — Bobbie Gentry (Kelly Gordon & Bobby Paris), Capitol 5950 | 2 |
| 22 | 27 | 32 | 42 | **TO LOVE SOMEBODY** — Bee Gees (Robert Stigwood), Atco 6503 | 5 |
| 23 | 28 | 30 | 35 | **HYPNOTIZED** — Linda Jones (George Kerr), Loma 2070 | 8 |
| 24 | 34 | 46 | 78 | **WORDS** — Monkees (Douglas Farthing Hatfield), Colgems 1007 | 4 |
| 25 | 26 | 31 | 32 | **IN THE CHAPEL IN THE MOONLIGHT** — Dean Martin (Jimmy Bowen), Reprise 0601 | 6 |
| 26 | 19 | 9 | 7 | **UP, UP AND AWAY** — 5th Dimension (Johnny Rivers & Marc Gordon), Soul City 756 | 11 |
| 27 | 30 | 35 | 37 | **LET THE GOOD TIMES ROLL & FEEL SO GOOD** — Bunny Sigler (Madara-White-Huff), Parkway 153 | 8 |
| 28 | 17 | 11 | 4 | **SAN FRANCISCO "WEAR SOME FLOWERS IN YOUR HAIR"** — Scott McKenzie (John Phillips & Lou Adler), Ode 103 | 12 |
| 29 | 23 | 23 | 25 | **MORE LOVE** — Smokey Robinson & the Miracles ("Smokey"), Tamla 54152 | 9 |
| 30 | 21 | 21 | 21 | **MAKE ME YOURS** — Bettye Swann, Money 126 | 13 |
| 31 | 29 | 13 | 10 | **COME ON DOWN TO MY BOAT** — Every Mother's Son (Wes Farrell), MGM 13733 | 15 |
| 32 | 25 | 25 | 30 | **I LIKE THE WAY** — Tommy James & the Shondells (Bo Gentry & Ritchie Cordell), Roulette 4756 | 7 |
| 33 | 61 | — | — | **HEROES AND VILLAINS** — Beach Boys (Beach Boys), Brother records 1001 | 2 |
| 34 | 41 | 64 | — | **BABY YOU'RE A RICH MAN NOW** — Beatles (George Martin), Capitol 5964 | 3 |
| 35 | 52 | 74 | — | **YOU'RE MY EVERYTHING** — Temptations (Norman Whitfield), Gordy 7063 | 3 |
| 36 | 55 | 71 | 94 | **COME BACK WHEN YOU GROW UP** — Bobby Vee & the Strangers (Dallas Smith), Liberty 55964 | 3 |
| 37 | 37 | 43 | 54 | **(I Wanna) TESTIFY** — Parliaments (George Clinton), Revilot 207 | 7 |
| 38 | 53 | 81 | — | **FAKIN' IT** — Simon & Garfunkel (John Simon), Columbia 44232 | 3 |
| 39 | 39 | 55 | 57 | **OUT AND ABOUT** — Tommy Boyce & Bobby Hart (Tommy Boyce & Bobby Hart), A&M 858 | 5 |
| 40 | 40 | 50 | 58 | **DON'T LET THE RAIN FALL ON ME** — Critters (Anders-Poncia), Kapp 838 | 6 |
| 41 | 36 | 26 | 14 | **SOCIETY'S CHILD** — Janis Ian (Shadow Morton), Verve 5027 | 12 |
| 42 | 50 | 66 | 85 | **THE SWEETEST THING THIS SIDE OF HEAVEN** — Chris Bartley (Van McCoy), Vando 101 | 4 |
| 43 | 43 | 54 | 64 | **I TAKE WHAT I WANT** — James & Bobby Purify (Papa Don), Bell 680 | 5 |
| 44 | 54 | 68 | 84 | **SHOOT YOUR SHOT** — Jr. Walker and the All Stars (Gordy Jr.-L. Horn), Soul 35036 | 4 |
| 45 | 35 | 10 | 9 | **C'MON MARIANNE** — Four Seasons (Bob Crewe), Philips 40460 | 10 |
| 46 | 46 | 51 | 53 | **RIVER IS WIDE** — Forum (Norm Hatner), Mira 232 | 6 |
| 47 | 68 | 83 | 96 | **APPLES, PEACHES, PUMPKIN PIE** — Jay & the Techniques (Jerry Ross), Smash 2086 | 5 |
| 48 | 73 | — | — | **SAN FRANCISCAN NIGHTS** — Eric Burdon and the Animals (Tom Wilson), MGM 13769 | 2 |
| 49 | 20 | 22 | 22 | **FOR YOUR LOVE** — Peaches & Herb (Bert Kapralik & Ken Williams), Date 1563 | 8 |
| 50 | 56 | 59 | 69 | **EVERYBODY NEEDS LOVE** — Gladys Knight & The Pips (Norman Whitfield), Soul 35034 | 6 |
| 51 | 33 | 37 | 39 | **YOUR UNCHANGING LOVE** — Marvin Gaye (Holland & Dozier), Tamla 54153 | 7 |
| 52 | 65 | 80 | — | **CRY SOFTLY LONELY ONE** — Roy Orbison (Rose & Vienneau), MGM 13764 | 3 |
| 53 | 44 | 44 | 50 | **YOU ONLY LIVE TWICE** — Nancy Sinatra (Lee Hazlewood), Reprise 0595 | 8 |
| 54 | 64 | 79 | — | **THE WINDOWS OF THE WORLD** — Dionne Warwick (Bacharach-David), Scepter 12196 | 3 |
| 55 | 66 | 78 | 97 | **BROWN-EYED GIRL** — Van Morrison (Bert Berns), Bang 545 | 5 |
| 56 | 57 | 62 | 66 | **WASHED ASHORE (On a Lonely Island in the Sea)** — Platters (Richard Popcorn Wylie), Musicor 1251 | 7 |
| 57 | 67 | 69 | 79 | **BLUES THEME** — Arrows (Mike Curb), Tower 295 | 10 |
| 58 | 78 | — | — | **THE WORLD WE KNEW (Over and Over)** — Frank Sinatra (Jimmy Bowen), Reprise 0610 | 2 |
| 59 | 75 | — | — | **YOU KNOW WHAT I MEAN** — Turtles (Joe Wissert), White Whale 254 | 2 |
| 60 | 60 | 75 | — | **GLORY OF LOVE** — Otis Redding (Steve Cropper), Volt 152 | 3 |
| 61 | — | — | — | **REFLECTIONS** — Diana Ross & the Supremes (Holland & Dozier), Motown 1111 | 1 |
| 62 | 62 | 65 | 68 | **GENTLE ON MY MIND** — Glen Campbell (Al de Iory), Capitol 5939 | 6 |
| 63 | 58 | 60 | 63 | **BLUEBIRD** — Buffalo Springfield (York-Pala), Atco 6499 | 5 |
| 64 | 79 | 88 | 90 | **HAPPY** — Sunshine Company (Joe Saraceno), Imperial 66247 | 5 |
| 65 | 45 | 45 | 45 | **SHOW BUSINESS** — Lou Rawls (David Axelrod), Capitol 5941 | 7 |
| 66 | 59 | 61 | 61 | **LONELY DRIFTER** — Pieces of Eight, A&M 854 | 8 |
| 67 | 82 | — | — | **I WANT TO LOVE YOU FOR WHAT YOU ARE** — Ronnie Dove (Phil Kahl), Diamond 227 | 2 |
| 68 | 70 | 73 | 93 | **DON'T YOU MISS ME A LITTLE BIT, BABY** — Jimmy Ruffin (Norman Whitfield), Soul 35035 | 4 |
| 69 | 69 | 70 | 73 | **IT'S A HAPPENING WORLD** — Tokens (Tokens), Warner Bros. 7056 | 4 |
| 70 | — | — | — | **IT'S THE LITTLE THINGS** — Sonny & Cher (Sonny Bono), Atco 6507 | 1 |
| 71 | — | — | — | **(Your Love Keeps Lifting Me) HIGHER AND HIGHER** — Jackie Wilson (Carl Davis), Brunswick 55336 | 1 |
| 72 | 81 | 82 | 89 | **FUNKY BROADWAY** — Dyke & the Blazers (Coleman & Barrett), Original Sound 64 | 10 |
| 73 | 86 | — | — | **GROOVIN'** — Booker T. and the M.G.'s (Staff), Stax 224 | 2 |
| 74 | 76 | 76 | — | **SLIM JENKIN'S PLACE** — Booker T. & the M.G.'s (Staff), Stax 224 | 3 |
| 75 | 80 | — | — | **HA HA SAID THE CLOWN** — Yardbirds (Mickie Most), Epic 10204 | 2 |
| 76 | 77 | 77 | 81 | **I'LL TURN TO STONE** — Four Tops (Holland & Dozier), Motown 1110 | 5 |
| 77 | 92 | — | — | **FUNKY BROADWAY** — Wilson Pickett (Jerry Wexler), Atlantic 2430 | 2 |
| 78 | 83 | — | — | **A WOMAN'S HANDS** — Joe Tex (Buddy Killen), Dial 4061 | 2 |
| 79 | 98 | — | — | **RUN, RUN, RUN** — Third Rail (Levine/Resnick/Cooper), Epic 10191 | 2 |
| 80 | — | — | — | **THINGS I SHOULD HAVE SAID** — Grass Roots (Steve Harris & P.F. Dloan), Dunhill 4094 | 1 |
| 81 | — | — | — | **THE LETTER** — Box Tops (Dan Penn), Mala 565 | 1 |
| 82 | — | — | — | **JILL** — Gary Lewis & the Playboys (Koppelman/Rubin), Liberty 55985 | 1 |
| 83 | — | — | — | **GIMME LITTLE SIGN** — Brenton Wood (Hooven-Winn), Double Shot 116 | 1 |
| 84 | — | — | — | **THERE IS A MOUNTAIN** — Donovan (Mickie Most), Epic 10212 | 1 |
| 85 | — | — | — | **ZIP CODE** — Five Americans (Dale Hawkins), Abnak 123 | 1 |
| 86 | — | — | — | **TURN ON YOUR LOVE LIGHT** — Oscar Toney, Jr. (Papa Don), Bell 681 | 1 |
| 87 | — | — | — | **SIXTEEN TONS** — Tom Jones (Peter Sullivan), Parrot 40016 | 1 |
| 88 | — | — | — | **LAURA, WHAT'S HE GOT THAT I AIN'T GOT** — Frankie Laine (Bob Thiele), ABC 10967 | 1 |
| 89 | 91 | 99 | — | **LONESOME ROAD** — Wonder Who? (Bob Crewe), Philips 40471 | 3 |
| 90 | — | — | — | **A LITTLE BIT NOW** — Dave Clark Five (Dave Clark), Epic 10209 | 1 |
| 91 | — | — | — | **GET THE MESSAGE** — Brian Hyland (Snuff Garrett), Philips 40472 | 1 |
| 92 | — | — | — | **KNOCK ON WOOD** — Otis & Carla (Staff), Stax 228 | 1 |
| 93 | — | — | — | **THERE MUST BE A WAY** — Jimmy Roselli (Henry Jerome), United Artists 50179 | 1 |
| 94 | — | — | — | **IT'S GOT TO BE MELLOW** — Leon Haywood (Leon Haywood), Decca 32164 | 1 |
| 95 | 95 | — | — | **NOT SO SWEET MARTHA LORRAINE** — Country Joe and the Fish (San Charters), Vanguard 35052 | 2 |
| 96 | 96 | — | — | **ALONG COMES MARY** — Baja Marimba Band (Jerry Moss), A&M 862 | 2 |
| 97 | 99 | — | — | **IT COULD BE WE'RE IN LOVE** — Cryan' Shames (Jim Golden), Columbia 44191 | 2 |
| 98 | — | — | — | **LITTLE OLD WINE DRINKER ME** — Robert Mitchum (Fred Foster), Monument 1006 | 1 |
| 99 | — | — | — | **JUST ONCE IN A LIFETIME** — Brenda & the Tabulations (Bob Finiz), Dionn 503 | 1 |
| 100 | 100 | — | — | **GOOD DAY SUNSHINE** — Claudine Longet (Tommy Li Puma), A&M 864 | 1 |

## BUBBLING UNDER THE HOT 100

101. PENNY ARCADE ........ Cyrkle, Columbia 44224
102. THOUSAND SHADOWS ........ Seeds, GNP Crescendo 394
103. LADY FRIEND ........ Byrds, Columbia 44230
104. NEARER TO YOU ........ Betty Harris, Sansu 466
105. LOVIN' SOUND ........ Ian & Sylvia, MGM 13686
106. MORE & MORE ........ Andy Williams, Columbia 44200
107. HAPPY ........ Blades of Grass, Jubilee 5582
108. CASONOVA ........ Ruby Andrews, Zodiac 1004
109. DRUMS ........ Jon & Robin & the In Crowd, Abnak 122
110. OMAHA ........ Moby Grape, Columbia 44173
111. PURPLE HAZE ........ Jimi Hendrix Experience, Reprise 0597
112. PEARL TIME ........ Andre Williams, Sport 105
113. LOOK IN YOUR EYES ........ Scott McKenzie, Capitol 5961
114. HOLD ON ........ Mauds, Mercury 72694
115. IT'S BEEN A LONG, LONG TIME ........ Elgins, V.I.P. 25043
116. SLIPPIN' & SLIDIN' ........ Willie Mitchell, Hi 2125
117. YOU DON'T KNOW YOUR WATER ........ King Curtis, Atco 6496
118. MY HEART CRIES FOR YOU ........ Connie Francis, MGM 13972
119. DON'T FORGET ABOUT ME ........ American Breed, Acta 808
120. I'LL NEVER FIND ANOTHER YOU ........ Sonny James, Capitol 5914
121. HE WILL BREAK YOUR HEART ........ Freddie Scott, Shout 216
122. TRY TRY TRY ........ Jim Valley, Dunhill 4096
123. YOU'VE GOT TO PAY THE PRICE ........ Al Kent, Ric Tic 127
124. ANYTHING GOES ........ Harpers Bizarre, Warner Bros. 7063
125. FOUR WALLS ........ J.J. Jackson, Calla 133
126. THAT'S THE WAY LOVE IS ........ Isley Brothers, Tamla 54154
127. TIP ON IN ........ Slim Harpo, Excello 2285
128. LAST MINUTE MIRACLE ........ Shirelles, Scepter 12198
129. LOVE IS A DOGGONE GOOD THING ........ Eddie Floyd, Stax 223
130. PUT YOUR TRUST IN ME ........ Joe Simon, Sound Stage 7 2583
131. PAPER SUN ........ Traffic, United Artists 50195
132. A VERY LOVELY WOMAN ........ Merry-Go-Round, A&M 863
133. AGNES ENGLISH ........ John Fred & His Playboys, Paula 273
134. I FEEL GOOD (I FEEL BAD) ........ Lewis & Clark Expedition, Colgems 1006
135. WHERE LOVE IS ........ Brenda Lee, Decca 32161

*Compiled from national retail sales and radio station airplay by the Music Popularity Dept. of Record Market Research, Billboard.*

For Week Ending August 19, 1967

# Billboard HOT 100

★ STAR performer—Sides registering greatest proportionate upward progress this week.

Record Industry Association of America seal of certification as million selling single.

| This Week | 1 Wk. Ago | 2 Wks. Ago | 3 Wks. Ago | TITLE Artist (Producer), Label & Number | Weeks On Chart |
|---|---|---|---|---|---|
| 1 (Billboard Award) | 2 | 3 | 29 | ALL YOU NEED IS LOVE — Beatles (George Martin), Capitol 5964 | 5 |
| 2 | 1 | 1 | 1 | LIGHT MY FIRE — Doors (Paul A. Rothchild), Elektra 45615 | 12 |
| 3 | 4 | 9 | 24 | PLEASANT VALLEY SUNDAY — Monkees (Douglas Farthing Hatlelid), Colgems 1007 | 5 (RIAA seal) |
| 4 | 3 | 2 | 2 | I WAS MADE TO LOVE HER — Stevie Wonder (H. Cosby), Tamla 54151 | 11 |
| ★5 | 11 | 22 | 47 | BABY I LOVE YOU — Aretha Franklin (Jerry Wexler), Atlantic 2427 | 5 |
| 6 | 5 | 7 | 7 | MERCY, MERCY, MERCY — Buckinghams (James William Guercio), Columbia 44162 | 10 |
| ★7 | 21 | 71 | — | ODE TO BILLIE JOE — Bobbie Gentry (Kelly Gordon & Bobby Paris), Capitol 5950 | 3 |
| ★8 | 20 | 47 | 58 | COLD SWEAT — James Brown & the Famous Flames (James Brown), King 6110 | 6 |
| 9 | 7 | 5 | 5 | A WHITER SHADE OF PALE — Procol Harum (Denny Cordell), Deram 7507 | 9 |
| 10 | 10 | 11 | 19 | A GIRL LIKE YOU — Young Rascals (Young Rascals), Atlantic 2424 | 6 |
| 11 | 12 | 13 | 17 | SILENCE IS GOLDEN — Tremeloes (Mike Smith), Epic 10184 | 10 |
| 12 | 9 | 16 | 16 | CARRIE ANN — Hollies (Ron Richards), Epic 10180 | 10 |
| 13 | 13 | 15 | 28 | MY MAMMY — Happenings (Tokens), B. T. Puppy 530 | 6 |
| 14 | 6 | 6 | 4 | CAN'T TAKE MY EYES OFF YOU — Frankie Valli (Bob Crewe), Philips 40446 | 14 |
| ★15 | 24 | 34 | 46 | WORDS — Monkees (Douglas Farthing Hatlelid), Colgems 1007 | 5 |
| 16 | 8 | 4 | 3 | WINDY — The Association, (Bones Howe), Warner Bros. 7041 | 13 (RIAA seal) |
| ★17 | 33 | 61 | — | HEROES AND VILLAINS — Beach Boys (Beach Boys), Brother records 1001 | 3 |
| 18 | 22 | 27 | 32 | TO LOVE SOMEBODY — Bee Gees (Robert Stigwood), Atco 6503 | 6 |
| 19 | 19 | 24 | 48 | THANK THE LORD FOR THE NIGHT TIME — Neil Diamond (Jeff Barry & Ellie Greenwich), Bang 547 | 6 |
| ★20 | 61 | — | — | REFLECTIONS — Dianna Ross & the Supremes (Holland & Dozier), Motown 1111 | 2 |
| ★21 | 35 | 52 | 74 | YOU'RE MY EVERYTHING — Temptations (Norman Whitfield), Gordy 7063 | 4 |
| ★22 | 27 | 30 | 35 | LET THE GOOD TIMES ROLL & FEEL SO GOOD — Bunny Sigler (Madara-White-Huff), Parkway 153 | 9 |
| 23 | 23 | 28 | 30 | HYNOTIZED — Linda Jones (George Kerr), Loma 2070 | 9 |
| ★24 | 47 | 68 | 83 | APPLES, PEACHES, PUMPKIN PIE — Jay & the Techniques (Jerry Ross), Smash 2086 | 6 |
| 25 | 15 | 8 | 8 | WHITE RABBIT — Jefferson Airplane (Rick Jarrard), RCA Victor 9248 | 9 |
| 26 | 16 | 10 | 6 | LITTLE BIT O' SOUL — Music Explosion (J. Katz-J. Kasenentz & E. Chiprut) Laurie 3380 | 15 (RIAA seal) |
| ★27 | 36 | 55 | 71 | COME BACK WHEN YOU GROW UP — Bobby Vee & the Strangers (Dallas Smith), Liberty 55964 | 5 |
| ★28 | 38 | 53 | 81 | FAKIN' IT — Simon & Garfunkel (John Simon), Columbia 44232 | 4 |
| 29 | 29 | 23 | 23 | MORE LOVE — Smokey Robinson & the Miracles ("Smokey") Tamla 54152 | 10 |
| ★30 | 37 | 37 | 43 | (I Wanna) TESTIFY — Parliaments (George Clinton), Revilot 207 | 8 |
| ★31 | 48 | 73 | — | SAN FRANCISCAN NIGHTS — Eric Burdon and the Animals (Tom Wilson), MGM 13769 | 3 |
| ★32 | 42 | 50 | 66 | THE SWEETEST THING THIS SIDE OF HEAVEN — Chris Bartley (Van McCoy), Vando 101 | 5 |
| 33 | 17 | 18 | 18 | SOUL FINGER — Bar-Kays (Produced by Staff), Volt 148 | 14 |
| ★34 | 55 | 66 | 78 | BROWN-EYED GIRL — Van Morrison (Bert Berns), Bang 545 | 6 |
| 35 | 26 | 19 | 9 | UP, UP AND AWAY — 5th Dimension (Johnny Rivers & Marc Gordon), Soul City 756 | 12 |
| 36 | 14 | 14 | 14 | JACKSON — Nancy Sinatra & Lee Hazlewood (Lee Hazlewood), Reprise 0595 | 9 |
| 37 | 18 | 12 | 12 | I TAKE IT BACK — Sandy Posey (Chips Moman), MGM 13744 | 11 |
| 38 | 34 | 41 | 64 | BABY YOU'RE A RICH MAN NOW — Beatles (George Martin), Capitol 5964 | 4 |
| 39 | 40 | 40 | 50 | DON'T LET THE RAIN FALL ON ME — Critters (Anders-Poncia), Kapp 838 | 7 |
| ★40 | 50 | 56 | 59 | EVERYBODY NEEDS LOVE — Gladys Knight & The Pips (Norman Whitfield) Soul 35034 | 7 |
| 41 | 43 | 43 | 54 | I TAKE WHAT I WANT — James & Bobby Purify (Papa Don) Bell 680 | 6 |
| ★42 | 58 | 78 | — | THE WORLD WE KNEW (Over and Over) — Frank Sinatra (Jimmy Bowen), Reprise 0610 | 3 |
| ★43 | 54 | 64 | 79 | THE WINDOWS OF THE WORLD — Dionne Warwick (Bacharach-David), Scepter 12196 | 4 |
| 44 | 44 | 54 | 68 | SHOOT YOUR SHOT — Jr. Walker & the All Stars (Gordy Jr.-L. Horn), Soul 35036 | 5 |
| 45 | 46 | 46 | 51 | RIVER IS WIDE — Forum (Norm Hatner), Mira 232 | 7 |
| ★46 | 77 | 92 | — | FUNKY BROADWAY — Wilson Pickett (Jerry Wexler), Atlantic 2430 | 3 |
| 47 | 30 | 21 | 21 | MAKE ME YOURS — Bettye Swann, Money 126 | 14 |
| ★48 | 59 | 75 | — | YOU KNOW WHAT I MEAN — Turtles (Joe Wissert), White Whale 254 | 3 |
| 49 | 39 | 39 | 55 | OUT AND ABOUT — Tommy Boyce & Bobby Hart (Tommy Boyce & Bobby Hart), A&M 858 | 6 |
| 50 | 25 | 26 | 31 | IN THE CHAPEL IN THE MOONLIGHT — Dean Martin (Jimmy Bowen), Reprise 0601 | 7 |
| 51 | 57 | 67 | 69 | BLUES THEME — Arrows (Mike Curb), Tower 295 | 11 |
| 52 | 52 | 65 | 80 | CRY SOFTLY LONELY ONE — Roy Orbison (Rose & Vienneau), MGM 13764 | 4 |
| 53 | 53 | 44 | 44 | YOU ONLY LIVE TWICE — Nancy Sinatra (Lee Hazlewood), Reprise 0595 | 9 |
| ★54 | 84 | — | — | THERE IS A MOUNTAIN — Donovan (Mickie Most), Epic 10212 | 2 |
| ★55 | 71 | — | — | (Your Love Keeps Lifting Me) HIGHER AND HIGHER — Jackie Wilson (Carl Davis), Brunswick 55336 | 2 |
| ★56 | 73 | 86 | — | GROOVIN' — Booker T. and the M.G.'s (Staff), Stax 224 | 3 |
| ★57 | 67 | 82 | — | I WANT TO LOVE YOU FOR WHAT YOU ARE — Ronnie Dove (Phil Kahl), Diamond 227 | 3 |
| ★58 | 81 | — | — | THE LETTER — Box Tops (Dan Penn), Mala 565 | 2 |
| ★59 | 80 | — | — | THINGS I SHOULD HAVE SAID — Grass Roots (Steve Harris & P. F. Dloan), Dunhill 4094 | 2 |
| ★60 | 75 | 80 | — | HA HA SAID THE CLOWN — Yardbirds (Mickie Most), Epic 10204 | 3 |
| 61 | 64 | 79 | 88 | HAPPY — Sunshine Company (Joe Saraceno), Imperial 66247 | 6 |
| 62 | 63 | 58 | 60 | BLUEBIRD — Buffalo Springfield (York-Pala), Atco 6499 | 6 |
| ★63 | 78 | 83 | — | A WOMAN'S HANDS — Joe Tex (Buddy Killen), Dial 4061 | 3 |
| 64 | 70 | — | — | IT'S THE LITTLE THINGS — Sonny & Cher (Sonny Bono), Atco 6507 | 2 |
| ★65 | 85 | — | — | ZIP CODE — Five Americans (Dale Hawkins), Abnak 123 | 2 |
| ★66 | 83 | — | — | GIMME LITTLE SIGN — Brenton Wood (Hooven-Winn), Double Shot 116 | 2 |
| ★67 | 82 | — | — | JILL — Gary Lewis & the Playboys (Koppelman/Rubin), Liberty 55985 | 2 |
| 68 | 68 | 70 | 73 | DON'T YOU MISS ME A LITTLE BIT, BABY — Jimmy Ruffin (Norman Whitfield), Soul 35035 | 5 |
| 69 | 56 | 57 | 62 | WASHED ASHORE (On a Lonely Island in the Sea) — Platters (Richard Popcorn Wylie), Musicor 1251 | 8 |
| 70 | 60 | 60 | 75 | GLORY OF LOVE — Otis Redding (Steve Cropper), Volt 152 | 4 |
| 71 | 72 | 81 | 82 | FUNKY BROADWAY — Dyke & the Blazers (Coleman & Barrett), Original Sound 64 | 11 |
| 72 | 79 | 98 | — | RUN, RUN, RUN — Third Rail (Levine/Resnick/Cooper), Epic 10191 | 3 |
| 73 | 74 | 76 | 76 | SLIM JENKIN'S PLACE — Booker T. & the M.G.'s (Staff), Stax 224 | 4 |
| 74 | 62 | 62 | 65 | GENTLE ON MY MIND — Glen Campbell (Al de lory), Capitol 5939 | 7 |
| ★75 | 90 | — | — | A LITTLE BIT NOW — Dave Clark Five (Dave Clark), Epic 10209 | 2 |
| ★76 | — | — | — | I DIG ROCK AND ROLL MUSIC — Peter, Paul & Mary (Albert B. Grossman & Milt Okun), Warner Bros. 7067 | 1 |
| 77 | 87 | — | — | SIXTEEN TONS — Tom Jones (Peter Sullivan), Parrot 40016 | 2 |
| ★78 | — | — | — | LITTLE OLD WINE DRINKER, ME — Dean Martin (Jimmy Bowen), Reprise 0608 | 1 |
| 79 | 86 | — | — | TURN ON YOUR LOVE LIGHT — Oscar Toney, Jr. (Papa Don), Bell 681 | 2 |
| ★80 | — | — | — | I HAD A DREAM — Paul Revere & the Raiders with Mark Lindsay (Terry Melcher), Columbia 44227 | 1 |
| ★81 | — | — | — | YOU'VE GOT TO PAY THE PRICE — Al Kent (Ed Wingate, Al Kent, H. Weems), Ric Tic 127 | 1 |
| ★82 | — | — | — | LADY FRIEND — Byrds (Gary Usher), Columbia 44230 | 1 |
| 83 | 88 | — | — | LAURA, WHAT'S HE GOT THAT I AIN'T GOT — Frankie Laine (Bob Thiele), ABC 10967 | 2 |
| ★84 | — | — | — | MAKING EVERY MINUTE COUNT — Spanky & Our Gang (Jerry Ross), Mercury 72714 | 1 |
| ★85 | — | — | — | ANYTHING GOES — Harpers Bizarre (Lenny Waronker), Warner Bros. 7063 | 1 |
| 86 | 94 | — | — | IT'S GOT TO BE MELLOW — Leon Haywood (Leon Haywood), Decca 32164 | 2 |
| 87 | 97 | 99 | — | IT COULD BE WE'RE IN LOVE — Cryan' Shames (Jim Golden), Columbia 44191 | 3 |
| 88 | 92 | — | — | KNOCK ON WOOD — Otis & Carla (Staff), Stax 228 | 2 |
| 89 | 89 | 91 | 99 | LONESOME ROAD — Wonder Who? (Bob Crewe), Philips 40471 | 4 |
| ★90 | — | — | — | LAURA (What's He Got That I Ain't Got?) — Brook Benton (Jimmy Bowen), Reprise 0611 | 1 |
| 91 | 91 | — | — | GET THE MESSAGE — Brian Hyland (Snuff Garrett), Philips 40472 | 2 |
| 92 | — | — | — | GET ON UP — Esquires (Bill Sheppard), Bunky 7750 | 1 |
| 93 | 93 | — | — | THERE MUST BE A WAY — Jimmy Roselli (Henry Jerome), United Artists 50179 | 2 |
| 94 | — | — | — | LOVE BUG LEAVE MY HEART ALONE — Martha & the Vandellas (Richard Morris), Gordy 7062 | 1 |
| 95 | — | — | — | TURN THE WORLD AROUND — Eddy Arnold (Chet Atkins), RCA Victor 9265 | [illegible] |
| 96 | 98 | — | — | LITTLE OLD WINE DRINKER ME — Robert Mitchum (Fred Foster), Monument 1006 | 2 |
| 97 | 99 | — | — | JUST ONCE IN A LIFETIME — Brenda & the Tabulations (Bob Finiz), Dionn 503 | 2 |
| 98 | — | — | — | COME ON SOCK IT TO ME — Syl Johnson, Twilight 100 | 1 |
| 99 | — | — | — | LAST MINUTE MIRACLE — Shirelles, Scepter 12198 | 1 |
| 100 | — | — | — | DRUMS — Jon & Robin (Dale Hawkins), Abnak 122 | 1 |

## HOT 100—A TO Z—(Publisher-Licensee)


All You Need Is Love (Maclen, BMI) .......... 1
Anything Goes (Harms, ASCAP) .......... 85
Apples, Peaches, Pumpkin Pie (Philstox/Act Three, BMI) .......... 24
Baby, I Love You (14th Hour/Pronto, BMI) .......... 5
Baby, You're a Rich Man Now (Maclen, BMI) .......... 38
Blues Theme (Dijon, BMI) .......... 51
Bluebird (Ten-East/Springalo/Cotillion, BMI) .......... 62
Brown-Eyed Girl (Web IV, BMI) .......... 34
Can't Take My Eyes Off You (Saturday/Seasons' Four, BMI) .......... 14
Carrie Ann (Maribus, BMI) .......... 12
Cold Sweat (Dynatone, BMI) .......... 8
Come Back When You Grow Up (Painted Desert, BMI) .......... 27
Come On Sock It To Me (Caforn, BMI) .......... 98
Cry Softly Lonely One (Rose & Vinneau, BMI) .......... 52
Don't Let the Rain Fall Down on Me (Ugenda, BMI) .......... 39
Don't You Miss Me a Little Bit, Baby (Jobete, BMI) 68
Drums (Barton, BMI) .......... 100
Everybody Needs Love (Jobete, BMI) .......... 40
Fakin' It (Charing Cross, BMI) .......... 28
Funky Broadway (Drive-In/Routeen, BMI) .......... 71
Funky Broadway (Routine/Drive-In, BMI) .......... 46
Gentle on My Mind (Glazier, BMI) .......... 74
Get on Up (Hi-Mi, BMI) .......... 92
Get the Message (Stone Canyon, BMI) .......... 91
Gimme Little Sign (Big Shot, ASCAP) .......... 66
Girl Like You (Slacsar, BMI) .......... 10
Glory of Love (Shapiro-Bernstein, ASCAP) .......... 70
Groovin' (Slacsar, BMI) .......... 56
Ha Ha Said the Clown (Ponderosa, BMI) .......... 60
Happy (Sunshine Company) (Unart, BMI) .......... 61
Heroes and Villains (Sea of Tunes, BMI) .......... 17
Hypnotized (Zira/Floteca, BMI) .......... 23
I Dig Rock and Roll Music (Pepamar, ASCAP) .......... 76
I Had a Dream (Daywin, BMI) .......... 80
I Take It Back (Low-Sal, BMI) .......... 37
I Take What I Want (East/Cotillion, BMI) .......... 41
I Want to Love You for What You Are (Irwin, ASCAP) .......... 57
I Was Made to Love Her (Jobete, BMI) .......... 4
In the Chapel in the Moonlight (Shapiro-Bernstein, ASCAP) .......... 50
It Could Be We're in Love (Destination, BMI) .......... 87
It's Got to Be Mellow (Jim-Edd, BMI) .......... 86
It's the Little Things (Chris Marc/Cotillion, BMI) 64
(I Wanna) Testify (Groovesville, BMI) .......... 30
Jackson (Bexhill Quartet, ASCAP) .......... 36
Jill (Chardon, BMI) .......... 67
Just Once in a Lifetime (Bee Cool, BMI) .......... 97
Knock on Wood (East, BMI) .......... 88
Lady Friend (Tickson, BMI) .......... 82
Last Minute Miracle (Flomar-Floteca, BMI) .......... 99
Laura (Tell Me What He's Got That I Ain't Got) (Ashmar, BMI) .......... 90
Laura, What's He Got That I Ain't Got? (Gallico, BMI) .......... 83
Letter, The (Barton, BMI) .......... 58
Let the Good Times Roll & Feel So Good (Travis, BMI) .......... 22
Light My Fire (Nipper, ASCAP) .......... 2
Little Bit Now, A (Travis/Rittenhouse, BMI) .......... 75
Little Bit o' Soul (Southern, ASCAP) .......... 26
Little Old Wine Drinker, Me (Moss-Rose, BMI) .......... 96
Little Old Wine Drinker, Me (Moss Rose, BMI) .......... 78
Lonesome Road (Shilkret/Paramount, ASCAP) .......... 89
Love Bug Leave My Heart Alone (Jobete, BMI) .......... 94
Make Me Yours (Cash Songs, BMI) .......... 47
Making Every Minute Count (Akbesteo, BMI) .......... 84
Mercy, Mercy, Mercy (Zawinal, BMI) .......... 6
More Love (Jobete, BMI) .......... 29
My Mammy (Bourne/Donaldson/Warock, ASCAP) .......... 13
Ode to Billie Joe (Shayne, ASCAP) .......... 7
Out and About (Screen Gems-Columbia, BMI) .......... 49
Pleasant Valley Sunday (Screen Gems-Columbia, BMI) .......... 3
Reflections (Jobete, BMI .......... 20
River Is Wide, The (Saturday, BMI) .......... 45
Run, Run, Run (T.M., BMI) .......... 72
San Franciscan Nights (Sealark/Slamine, BMI) .......... 31
Shoot Your Shot (Jobete, BMI) .......... 44
Silence Is Golden (Saturday/Gevadium, BMI) .......... 11
Sixteen Tons (Noma/Presley, BMI) .......... 77
Slim Jenkin's Place (East, BMI) .......... 73
Soul Finger (East, BMI) .......... 33
Sweetest Thing This Side of Heaven, The (Blackwood, BMI) .......... 32
Thank the Lord for the Night Time (Tallyrand, BMI) .......... 19
There Is a Mountain (Peer Int'l/Hi-Count, BMI) .......... 54
There Must Be a Way (Laurel, ASCAP) .......... 93
Things I Should Have Said (Trousdale, BMI) .......... 59
To Love Somebody (Nemperor, BMI) .......... 18
Turn on Your Love Light (Don, BMI) .......... 76
Turn the World Around (Fingerlake, BMI) .......... 95
Up, Up and Away (5th Dimension) (Rivers, BMI) .......... 35
Washed Ashore (On a Lonely Island in the Sea) (Catalogue-A La King, BMI) .......... 69
White Rabbit (Copper Penny, BMI) .......... 25
Whiter Shade of Pale (Essex, ASCAP) .......... 9
Windows of the World, The (Jac/Blue Seas, ASCAP) 43
Windy (Irving, BMI) .......... 16
Woman's Hands, A (Tree, BMI) .......... 63
Words (Screen Gems-Columbia, BMI) .......... 15
World We Knew, The (Over and Over) (Roosevelt, BMI) .......... 42
You Know What I Mean (Chardon, BMI) .......... 48
You Only Live Twice (Unart, BMI) .......... 53
(Your Love Keeps Lifting Me) Higher and Higher Jalynne/HRC, BMI) .......... 55
You're My Everything (Jobete, BMI) .......... 21
You've Got to Pay the Price (Myto, BMI) .......... 81
Zip Code (Jetstar, BMI) .......... 65


## BUBBLING UNDER THE HOT 100

101. PENNY ARCADE ..........Cyrkle, Columbia 44224
102. A THOUSAND SHADOWS ..........Seeds, GNP Crescendo 394
103. NEARER TO YOU ..........Betty Harris, Sansu 466
104. LOVIN' SOUND ..........Ian & Sylvia, MGM 13686
105. HAPPY ..........Blades of Grass, Jubilee 5582
106. CASONOVA ..........Ruby Andrews, Zodiac 1004
107. NOT SO SWEET MARTHA LORRAINE..Country Joe & the Fish, Vanguard 35052
108. GOOD DAY SUNSHINE ..........Claudine Longet, A&M 864
109. PURPLE HAZE ..........Jimi Hendrix Experience, Reprise 0997
110. PEARL TIME ..........Andre Williams, Sport 105
111. I'LL TURN TO STONE ..........Four Tops, Motown 1110
112. IT'S BEEN A LONG, LONG TIME ..........Elgins, VIP 25043
113. LOOK IN YOUR EYES ..........Scott McKenzie, Capitol 5961
114. DON'T FORGET ABOUT ME ..........American Breed, Acta 808
115. HOLD ON ..........Mauds, Mercury 72694
116. SLIPPIN' & SLIDIN' ..........Willie Mitchell, Hi 2125
117. PAPER SUN ..........Traffic, United Artists 50195
118. MY HEART CRIES FOR YOU ..........Connie Francis, MGM 13973
119. I'LL NEVER FIND ANOTHER YOU ..........Sonny James, Capitol 5914
120. HE WILL BREAK YOUR HEART ..........Freddie Scott, Shout 216
121. YOU'RE A VERY LOVERLY WOMAN ..........Merry-Go-Round, A&M 863
122. TRY, TRY, TRY ..........Jim Valley, Dunhill 4096
123. FOUR WALLS ..........J. J. Jackson, Calla 133
124. I FEEL GOOD ..........Lewis & Clark Expedition, Colgems 1006
125. THAT'S THE WAY LOVE IS ..........Isley Brothers, Tamla 54154
126. AGNES ENGLISH ..........John Fred & the Playboys, Paula 273
127. TIP ON IN ..........Slim Harpo, Excello 2285
128. LOVE IS A DOGGONE GOOD THING ..........Eddie Floyd, Stax 223
129. PUT YOUR TRUST IN ME ..........Joe Simon, Sound Stage 7 452483
130. MUSEUM ..........Herman's Hermits, MGM 13787
131. (WE'LL MEET IN THE) YELLOW FOREST ..........Jay & the Americans, United Artists 50196
132. GET TOGETHER ..........Youngbloods, RCA Victor 9264
133. SALLY SAYIN' SOMETHING ..........Billy Harper, Kama Sutra 226
134. WHERE LOVE IS ..........Brenda Lee, Decca 32161
135. HEART & SOUL ..........Incredibles, Audio Arts 60.007

Compiled from national retail sales and radio station airplay by the Music Popularity Dept. of Record Market Research, Billboard.

# Billboard HOT 100

**For Week Ending August 26, 1967**

★ STAR performer—Sides registering greatest proportionate upward progress this week.

Record Industry Association of America seal of certification as million selling single.

| This Week | Wk. Ago | 2 Wks. Ago | 3 Wks. Ago | TITLE — Artist (Producer), Label & Number | Weeks on Chart |
|---|---|---|---|---|---|
| 1 | 7 | 21 | 71 | ODE TO BILLIE JOE — Bobbie Gentry (Kelly Gordon & Bobby Paris), Capitol 5950 | 4 |
| 2 | 1 | 2 | 3 | ALL YOU NEED IS LOVE — Beatles (George Martin), Capitol 5964 | 6 |
| 3 | 3 | 4 | 9 | PLEASANT VALLEY SUNDAY — Monkees (Douglas Farthing Hatfield), Colgems 1007 | 6 |
| 4 | 2 | 1 | 1 | LIGHT MY FIRE — Doors (Paul A. Rothchild), Elektra 45615 | 13 |
| 5 | 5 | 11 | 22 | BABY I LOVE YOU — Aretha Franklin (Jerry Wexler), Atlantic 2427 | 6 |
| 6 | 4 | 3 | 2 | I WAS MADE TO LOVE HER — Stevie Wonder (H. Cosby), Tamla 54151 | 12 |
| 7 | 8 | 20 | 47 | COLD SWEAT — James Brown & the Famous Flames (James Brown), King 6110 | 7 |
| 8 | 20 | 61 | — | REFLECTIONS — Diana Ross & the Supremes (Holland & Dozier), Motown 1111 | 3 |
| 9 | 21 | 35 | 52 | YOU'RE MY EVERYTHING — Temptations (Norman Whitfield), Gordy 7063 | 5 |
| 10 | 9 | 7 | 5 | A WHITER SHADE OF PALE — Procol Harum (Denny Cordell), Deram 7507 | 10 |
| 11 | 10 | 10 | 11 | A GIRL LIKE YOU — Young Rascals (Young Rascals), Atlantic 2424 | 7 |
| 12 | 17 | 33 | 61 | HEROES AND VILLAINS — Beach Boys (Beach Boys), Brother records 1001 | 4 |
| 13 | 19 | 19 | 24 | THANK THE LORD FOR THE NIGHT TIME — Neil Diamond (Jeff Barry & Ellie Greenwich), Bang 547 | 7 |
| 14 | 27 | 36 | 55 | COME BACK WHEN YOU GROW UP — Bobby Vee & the Strangers (Dallas Smith), Liberty 55964 | 6 |
| 15 | 15 | 24 | 34 | WORDS — Monkees (Douglas Farthing Hatfield), Colgems 1007 | 6 |
| 16 | 11 | 12 | 13 | SILENCE IS GOLDEN — Tremeloes (Mike Smith), Epic 10184 | 11 |
| 17 | 18 | 22 | 27 | TO LOVE SOMEBODY — Bee Gees (Robert Stigwood), Atco 6503 | 7 |
| 18 | 12 | 9 | 16 | CARRIE ANN — Hollies (Ron Richards), Epic 10180 | 11 |
| 19 | 24 | 47 | 68 | APPLES, PEACHES, PUMPKIN PIE — Jay & the Techniques (Jerry Ross), Smash 2086 | 7 |
| 20 | 13 | 13 | 15 | MY MAMMY — Happenings (Tokens), B. T. Puppy 530 | 7 |
| 21 | 23 | 23 | 28 | HYPNOTIZED — Linda Jones (George Kerr), Loma 2070 | 10 |
| 22 | 6 | 5 | 7 | MERCY, MERCY, MERCY — Buckinghams (James William Guercio), Columbia 44162 | 11 |
| 23 | 28 | 38 | 53 | FAKIN' IT — Simon & Garfunkel (John Simon), Columbia 44232 | 5 |
| 24 | 14 | 6 | 6 | CAN'T TAKE MY EYES OFF YOU — Frankie Valli (Bob Crewe), Philips 40446 | 15 |
| 25 | 58 | 81 | — | THE LETTER — Box Tops (Dan Penn), Mala 565 | 3 |
| 26 | 31 | 48 | 73 | SAN FRANCISCAN NIGHTS — Eric Burdon and the Animals (Tom Wilson), MGM 13769 | 4 |
| 27 | 34 | 55 | 66 | BROWN-EYED GIRL — van Morrison (Bert Berns), Bang 545 | 7 |
| 28 | 30 | 37 | 37 | (I Wanna) TESTIFY — Parliaments (George Clinton), Revilot 207 | 9 |
| 29 | 46 | 77 | 92 | FUNKY BROADWAY — Wilson Pickett (Jerry Wexler), Atlantic 2430 | 4 |
| 30 | 22 | 27 | 30 | LET THE GOOD TIMES ROLL & FEEL SO GOOD — Bunny Sigler (Madara-White-Huff), Parkway 153 | 10 |
| 31 | 42 | 58 | 78 | THE WORLD WE KNEW (Over and Over) — Frank Sinatra (Jimmy Bowen), Reprise 0610 | 4 |
| 32 | 32 | 42 | 50 | THE SWEETEST THING THIS SIDE OF HEAVEN — Chris Bartley (Van McCoy), Vando 101 | 6 |
| 33 | 43 | 54 | 64 | THE WINDOWS OF THE WORLD — Dionne Warwick (Bacharach-David), Scepter 12196 | 5 |
| 34 | 16 | 8 | 4 | WINDY — The Association (Bones Howe), Warner Bros. 7041 | 14 |
| 35 | 29 | 29 | 23 | MORE LOVE — Smokey Robinson & the Miracles ("Smokey"), Tamla 54152 | 11 |
| 36 | 54 | 84 | — | THERE IS A MOUNTAIN — Donovan (Mickie Most), Epic 10212 | 3 |
| 37 | 48 | 59 | 75 | YOU KNOW WHAT I MEAN — Turtles (Joe Wissert), White Whale 254 | 4 |
| 38 | 33 | 17 | 18 | SOUL FINGER — Bar-Kays (Produced by Staff), Volt 148 | 15 |
| 39 | 40 | 50 | 56 | EVERYBODY NEEDS LOVE — Gladys Knight & The Pips (Norman Whitfield), Soul 35034 | 8 |
| 40 | 25 | 15 | 8 | WHITE RABBIT — Jefferson Airplane (Rick Jarrard), RCA Victor 9248 | 10 |
| 41 | 38 | 34 | 41 | BABY YOU'RE A RICH MAN NOW — Beatles (George Martin), Capitol 5964 | 5 |
| 42 | 37 | 18 | 12 | I TAKE IT BACK — Sandy Posey (Chips Moman), MGM 13744 | 12 |
| 43 | 56 | 73 | 86 | GROOVIN' — Booker T. and the M.G.'s (Staff), Stax 224 | 4 |
| 44 | 44 | 44 | 54 | SHOOT YOUR SHOT — Jr. Walker & the All Stars (Gordy Jr.-L. Horn), Soul 35036 | 6 |
| 45 | 55 | 71 | — | (Your Love Keeps Lifting Me) HIGHER AND HIGHER — Jackie Wilson (Carl Davis), Brunswick 55336 | 4 |
| 46 | 26 | 16 | 10 | LITTLE BIT O' SOUL — Music Explosion (J. Katz-J. Kasenentz & E. Chiprut), Laurie 3380 | 16 |
| 47 | 59 | 80 | — | THINGS I SHOULD HAVE SAID — Grass Roots (Steve Harris & P. F. Sloan), Dunhill 4094 | 3 |
| 48 | 76 | — | — | I DIG ROCK AND ROLL MUSIC — Peter, Paul & Mary (Albert B. Grossman & Milt Okun), Warner Bros. 7067 | 2 |
| 49 | 39 | 40 | 40 | DON'T LET THE RAIN FALL DOWN ON ME — Critters (Anders-Poncia), Kapp 838 | 8 |
| 50 | 60 | 75 | 80 | HA HA SAID THE CLOWN — Yardbirds (Mickie Most), Epic 10204 | 4 |
| 51 | 51 | 57 | 67 | BLUES THEME — Arrows (Mike Curb), Tower 295 | 12 |
| 52 | 65 | 85 | — | ZIP CODE — Five Americans (Dale Hawkins), Abnak 123 | 3 |
| 53 | 52 | 52 | 65 | CRY SOFTLY LONELY ONE — Roy Orbison (Rose & Vienneau), MGM 13764 | 5 |
| 54 | 80 | — | — | I HAD A DREAM — Paul Revere & the Raiders with Mark Lindsay (Terry Melcher), Columbia 44227 | 2 |
| 55 | 57 | 67 | 82 | I WANT TO LOVE YOU FOR WHAT YOU ARE — Ronnie Dove (Phil Kahl), Diamond 227 | 4 |
| 56 | 66 | 83 | — | GIMME LITTLE SIGN — Brenton Wood (Hooven-Winn), Double Shot 116 | 3 |
| 57 | 67 | 82 | — | JILL — Gary Lewis & the Playboys (Koppelman/Rubin), Liberty 55985 | 3 |
| 58 | 61 | 64 | 79 | HAPPY — Sunshine Company (Joe Saracena), Imperial 66247 | 5 |
| 59 | 78 | — | — | LITTLE OLD WINE DRINKER, ME — Dean Martin (Jimmy Bowen), Reprise 0608 | 2 |
| 60 | 64 | 70 | — | IT'S THE LITTLE THINGS — Sonny & Cher (Sonny Bono), Atco 6507 | 3 |
| 61 | 62 | 63 | 58 | BLUEBIRD — Buffalo Springfield (York-Pala), Atco 6499 | 7 |
| 62 | 49 | 39 | 39 | OUT AND ABOUT — Tommy Boyce & Bobby Hart (Tommy Boyce & Bobby Hart), A&M 858 | 7 |
| 63 | 63 | 78 | 83 | A WOMAN'S HANDS — Joe Tex (Buddy Killen), Dial 4061 | 4 |
| 64 | 45 | 46 | 46 | RIVER IS WIDE — Forum (Norm Hatner), Mira 232 | 8 |
| 65 | 71 | 72 | 81 | FUNKY BROADWAY — Dyke & the Blazers (Coleman & Barrett), Original Sound 64 | 12 |
| 66 | 72 | 79 | 98 | RUN, RUN, RUN — Third Rail (Levine/Resnick/Cooper), Epic 10191 | 4 |
| 67 | 75 | 90 | — | A LITTLE BIT NOW — Dave Clark Five (Dave Clark), Epic 10209 | 3 |
| 68 | 77 | 87 | — | SIXTEEN TONS — Tom Jones (Peter Sullivan), Parrot 40016 | 3 |
| 69 | 84 | — | — | MAKING EVERY MINUTE COUNT — Spanky & Our Gang (Jerry Ross), Mercury 72714 | 2 |
| 70 | 73 | 74 | 76 | SLIM JENKIN'S PLACE — Booker T. & the M.G.'s (Staff), Stax 224 | 5 |
| 71 | 81 | — | — | YOU'VE GOT TO PAY THE PRICE — Al Kent (Ed Wingate, Al Kent, H. Weems), Ric Tic 127 | 2 |
| 72 | — | — | — | TWELVE THIRTY — Mamas & the Papas (Lou Adler), Dunhill 4099 | 1 |
| 73 | 88 | 92 | — | KNOCK ON WOOD — Otis & Carla (Staff), Stax 228 | 3 |
| 74 | 83 | 88 | — | LAURA, WHAT'S HE GOT THAT I AIN'T GOT — Frankie Laine (Bob Thiele), ABC 10967 | 3 |
| 75 | — | — | — | GETTIN' TOGETHER — Tommy James & the Shondells (Bo Gentry/Ritchie Cordell), Roulette 4762 | 1 |
| 76 | 79 | 86 | — | TURN ON YOUR LOVE LIGHT — Oscar Toney, Jr. (Papa Don), Bell 681 | 3 |
| 77 | 85 | — | — | ANYTHING GOES — Harpers Bizarre (Lenny Waronker), Warner Bros. 7063 | 2 |
| 78 | — | — | — | MUSEUM — Herman's Hermits (Mickie Most), MGM 13787 | 1 |
| 79 | 94 | — | — | LOVE BUG LEAVE MY HEART ALONE — Martha & the Vandellas (Richard Morris), Gordy 7062 | 2 |
| 80 | 92 | — | — | GET ON UP — Esquires (Bill Sheppard), Bunky 7750 | 2 |
| 81 | — | — | — | I FEEL GOOD (I Feel Bad) — Lewis & Clarke Expedition (Jack Keller), Colgems 1006 | 1 |
| 82 | 82 | — | — | LADY FRIEND — Byrds (Gary Usher), Columbia 44230 | 2 |
| 83 | — | — | — | NEVER MY LOVE — Association (Bones Howe), Warner Bros. 7074 | 1 |
| 84 | — | — | — | PUT YOUR MIND AT EASE — Every Mother's Son (Wes Farrell), MGM 13788 | 1 |
| 85 | 90 | — | — | LAURA (Tell Me What He's Got That I Ain't Got — Brook Benton (Jimmy Bowen), Reprise 0611 | 2 |
| 86 | 95 | — | — | TURN THE WORLD AROUND — Eddy Arnold (Chet Atkins), RCA Victor 9265 | 2 |
| 87 | 87 | 97 | 99 | IT COULD BE WE'RE IN LOVE — Cryan' Shames (Jim Golden), Columbia 44191 | 4 |
| 88 | — | — | — | MEMPHIS SOUL STEW — King Curtis (Tommy Cogbill), Atco 6511 | 1 |
| 89 | — | — | — | IN THE HEART OF THE NIGHT — Ray Charles (TRC), ABC 10970 | 1 |
| 90 | — | — | — | THERE'S ALWAYS ME — Elvis Presley, RCA Victor 9287 | 1 |
| 91 | — | — | — | TELL HIM — Patti Drew (Carone), Capitol 5861 | 1 |
| 92 | — | — | — | STOUT-HEARTED MEN — Barbra Streisand (Howard A. Roberts & Jack Gold), Columbia 44225 | 1 |
| 93 | — | — | — | I MAKE A FOOL OF MYSELF — Frankie Valli (Bob Crewe), Philips 40484 | 1 |
| 94 | — | — | — | PURPLE HAZE — Jimi Hendrix Experience (Yameta), Reprise 0597 | 1 |
| 95 | — | — | — | CASONOVA (Your Playing Days Are Over) — Ruby Andrews (McGregor & Terry), Zodiac 1004 | 1 |
| 96 | — | — | — | HOW CAN YOU MISTREAT THE ONE YOU LOVE — Jean & the Darlings (Isaac Hayes & David Porter), Volt 151 | 1 |
| 97 | — | — | — | LOVE IS A DOGGONE GOOD THING — Eddie Floyd (Staff), Stax 223 | 1 |
| 98 | 98 | — | — | COME ON SOCK IT TO ME — Syl Johnson, Twilight 100 | 2 |
| 99 | 99 | — | — | LAST MINUTE MIRACLE — Shirelles, Scepter 12198 | 2 |
| 100 | 100 | — | — | DRUMS — Jon & Robin (Dale Hawkins), Abnak 122 | 2 |

## BUBBLING UNDER THE HOT 100

101. LOVIN' SOUND — Ian & Sylvia, MGM 13686
102. JUST ONCE IN A LIFETIME — Brenda & the Tabulations, Dionn 503
103. PENNY ARCADE — Cyrkle, Columbia 44224
104. YOU'RE A VERY LOVELY WOMAN — Merry-Go-Round, A&M 863
105. HAPPY — Blades of Grass, Jubilee 5582
106. TRY, TRY, TRY — Jim Valley, Dunhill 4096
107. PEARL TIME — Andre Williams, Sport 105
108. LITTLE OLD WINE DRINKER ME — Robert Mitchum, Monument 1006
109. IT'S GOT TO BE MELLOW — Leon Haywood, Decca 32164
110. GET THE MESSAGE — Brian Hyland, Philips 40472
111. LOOK IN YOUR EYES — Scott MacKenzie, Capitol 5961
112. DON'T FORGET ABOUT ME — American Breed, Acta 808
113. PAPER SUN — Traffic, United Artists 50195
114. THERE MUST BE A WAY — Jimmy Roselli, United Artists 50179
115. DO SOMETHING TO ME — ? (Question Mark) & the Mysterians, Cameo 496
116. JUST OUT OF REACH — Percy Sledge, Atlantic 2434
117. GET TOGETHER — Youngbloods, RCA Victor 9264
118. UNDER THE STREET LAMP — Exits, Gemini 1004
119. WEDNESDAY — Royal Guardsmen, Laurie 3397
120. THERE GOES THE LOVER — Gene Chandler, Brunswick 55339
121. OUR SONG — Jack Jones, Kapp 846
122. SALLY SAYIN' SOMETHING — Billy Harner, Kama Sutra 226
123. LITTLE OLE MAN (UPTIGHT-EVERYTHING'S ALRIGHT) — Bill Cosby, Warner Bros. 7072
124. ON THE OTHER SIDE — Seekers, Capitol 5974
125. CAN'T STOP LOVIN' YOU — Last Word, Atco 6498
126. AGNES ENGLISH — John Fred & His Playboys, Paula 273
127. YOU CAN'T DO THAT — Nilsson, RCA Victor 9298
128. TO SIR WITH LOVE — Lulu, Epic 10187
129. WHAT DOES IT TAKE TO KEEP A MAN LIKE YOU SATISFIED — Skeeter Davis, RCA Victor 9242
130. BELIEVE IN ME BABY — Jessie James, 20th-Century Fox 6694
131. (WE'LL MEET IN THE) YELLOW FOREST — Jay & the Americans, United Artists 50196
132. IT MUST BE HIM — Vikki Carr, Liberty 55986
133. ROLLIN' & TUMBLIN' — Canned Heat, Liberty 55979
134. I WANNA BE THERE — Blues Magoos, Mercury 72707
135. LAURA (WHAT'S HE GOT THAT I AIN'T GOT) — Leon Ashley, Ashley 2003

Compiled from national retail sales and radio station airplay by the Music Popularity Dept. of Record Market Research, Billboard.

# Billboard HOT 100

For Week Ending September 2, 1967

★ STAR performer—Sides registering greatest proportionate upward progress this week.

Record Industry Association of America seal of certification as million selling single.

| This Week | 2 Wks. Ago | 3 Wks. Ago | TITLE Artist (Producer), Label & Number | Weeks On Chart |
|---|---|---|---|---|
| 1 | 1 | 7 | 21 | ODE TO BILLIE JOE — Bobbie Gentry (Kelly Gordon & Bobby Paris), Capitol 5950 | 5 |
| 2 | 2 | 1 | 2 | ALL YOU NEED IS LOVE — Beatles (George Martin), Capitol 5964 | 7 |
| 3 | 8 | 20 | 61 | REFLECTIONS — Diana Ross & the Supremes (Holland & Dozier), Motown 1111 | 4 |
| 4 | 4 | 2 | 1 | LIGHT MY FIRE — Doors (Paul A. Rothchild), Elektra 45615 | 14 |
| 5 | 5 | 5 | 11 | BABY I LOVE YOU — Aretha Franklin (Jerry Wexler), Atlantic 2427 | 7 |
| 6 | 14 | 27 | 36 | COME BACK WHEN YOU GROW UP — Bobby Vee & the Strangers (Dallas Smith), Liberty 55964 | 7 |
| 7 | 7 | 8 | 20 | COLD SWEAT — James Brown & the Famous Flames (James Brown), King 6110 | 8 |
| 8 | 3 | 3 | 4 | PLEASANT VALLEY SUNDAY — Monkees (Douglas Farthing Hatfield), Colgems 1007 | 7 |
| 9 | 9 | 21 | 35 | YOU'RE MY EVERYTHING — Temptations (Norman Whitfield), Gordy 7063 | 6 |
| 10 | 6 | 4 | 3 | I WAS MADE TO LOVE HER — Stevie Wonder (H. Cosby), Tamla 54151 | 13 |
| 11 | 15 | 15 | 24 | WORDS — Monkees (Douglas Farthing Hatfield), Colgems 1007 | 7 |
| 12 | 12 | 17 | 33 | HEROES AND VILLAINS — Beach Boys (Beach Boys), Brother records 1001 | 5 |
| 13 | 13 | 19 | 19 | THANK THE LORD FOR THE NIGHT TIME — Neil Diamond (Jeff Barry & Ellie Greenwich), Bang 547 | 8 |
| 14 | 19 | 24 | 47 | APPLES, PEACHES, PUMPKIN PIE — Jay & the Techniques (Jerry Ross), Smash 2086 | 8 |
| 15 | 25 | 58 | 81 | THE LETTER — Box Tops (Dan Penn), Mala 565 | 4 |
| 16 | 10 | 9 | 7 | A WHITER SHADE OF PALE — Procol Harum (Denny Cordell), Deram 7507 | 11 |
| 17 | 11 | 10 | 10 | A GIRL LIKE YOU — Young Rascals (Young Rascals), Atlantic 2424 | 8 |
| 18 | 18 | 12 | 9 | CARRIE ANN — Hollies (Ron Richards), Epic 10180 | 12 |
| 19 | 29 | 46 | 77 | FUNKY BROADWAY — Wilson Pickett (Jerry Wexler), Atlantic 2430 | 5 |
| 20 | 28 | 30 | 37 | (I Wanna) TESTIFY — Parliaments (George Clinton), Revilot 207 | 10 |
| 21 | 16 | 11 | 12 | SILENCE IS GOLDEN — Tremeloes (Mike Smith), Epic 10184 | 12 |
| 22 | 27 | 34 | 55 | BROWN-EYED GIRL — Van Morrison (Bert Berns), Bang 545 | 8 |
| 23 | 23 | 28 | 38 | FAKIN' IT — Simon & Garfunkel (John Simon), Columbia 44232 | 6 |
| 24 | 36 | 54 | 84 | THERE IS A MOUNTAIN — Donovan (Mickie Most), Epic 10212 | 4 |
| 25 | 26 | 31 | 48 | SAN FRANCISCAN NIGHTS — Eric Burdon and the Animals (Tom Wilson), MGM 13769 | 5 |
| 26 | 17 | 18 | 22 | TO LOVE SOMEBODY — Bee Gees (Robert Stigwood), Atco 6503 | 8 |
| 27 | 45 | 55 | 71 | (Your Love Keeps Lifting Me) HIGHER AND HIGHER — Jackie Wilson (Carl Davis), Brunswick 55336 | 4 |
| 28 | 37 | 48 | 59 | YOU KNOW WHAT I MEAN — Turtles (Joe Wissert), White Whale 254 | 5 |
| 29 | 54 | 80 | — | I HAD A DREAM — Paul Revere & the Raiders with Mark Lindsay (Terry Melcher), Columbia 44227 | 3 |
| 30 | 31 | 42 | 58 | THE WORLD WE KNEW (Over and Over) — Frank Sinatra (Jimmy Bowen), Reprise 0610 | 5 |
| 31 | 22 | 6 | 5 | MERCY, MERCY, MERCY — Buckinghams (James William Guercio), Columbia 44182 | 12 |
| 32 | 33 | 43 | 54 | THE WINDOWS OF THE WORLD — Dionne Warwick (Bacharach-David), Scepter 12196 | |
| 33 | 43 | 56 | 73 | GROOVIN' — Booker T. and the M.G.'s (Staff), Stax 224 | 5 |
| 34 | 30 | 22 | 27 | LET THE GOOD TIMES ROLL & FEEL SO GOOD — Bunny Sigler (Madara-White-Huff), Parkway 153 | 11 |
| 35 | 24 | 14 | 6 | CAN'T TAKE MY EYES OFF YOU — Frankie Valli (Bob Crewe), Philips 40446 | 16 |
| 36 | 72 | — | — | TWELVE THIRTY — Mamas & the Papas (Lou Adler), Dunhill 4099 | 2 |
| 37 | 47 | 59 | 80 | THINGS I SHOULD HAVE SAID — Grass Roots (Barri Harris & P. F. Sloan), Dunhill 4094 | 4 |
| 38 | 48 | 76 | — | I DIG ROCK AND ROLL MUSIC — Peter, Paul & Mary (Albert B. Grossman & Milt Okun), Warner Bros. 7067 | 3 |
| 39 | 21 | 23 | 23 | HYPNOTIZED — Linda Jones (George Kerr), Loma 2070 | 11 |
| 40 | 75 | — | — | GETTIN' TOGETHER — Tommy James & the Shondells (Bo Gentry/Ritchie Cordell), Roulette 4762 | 2 |
| 41 | 51 | 51 | 57 | BLUES THEME — Arrows (Mike Curb), Tower 295 | 13 |
| 42 | 52 | 65 | 85 | ZIP CODE — Five Americans (Dale Hawkins), Abnak 123 | 4 |
| 43 | 32 | 32 | 42 | THE SWEETEST THING THIS SIDE OF HEAVEN — Chris Bartley (Van McCoy), Vando 101 | 7 |
| 44 | 44 | 44 | 44 | SHOOT YOUR SHOT — Jr. Walker & the All Stars (Gordy Jr./A. Horn), Soul 35036 | |
| 45 | 50 | 60 | 75 | HA HA SAID THE CLOWN — Yardbirds (Mickie Most), Epic 10204 | 5 |
| 46 | 56 | 66 | 83 | GIMME LITTLE SIGN — Brenton Wood (Hooven-Winn), Double Shot 116 | 4 |
| 47 | 20 | 13 | 13 | MY MAMMY — Happenings (Tokens), B. T. Puppy 530 | 8 |
| 48 | 39 | 40 | 50 | EVERYBODY NEEDS LOVE — Gladys Knight & The Pips (Norman Whitfield), Soul 35034 | |
| 49 | 59 | 78 | — | LITTLE OLD WINE DRINKER, ME — Dean Martin (Jimmy Bowen), Reprise 0608 | 3 |
| 50 | 60 | 64 | 70 | IT'S THE LITTLE THINGS — Sonny & Cher (Sonny Bono), Atco 6507 | 4 |
| 51 | 69 | 84 | — | MAKING EVERY MINUTE COUNT — Spanky & Our Gang (Jerry Ross), Mercury 72714 | 3 |
| 52 | 58 | 61 | 64 | HAPPY — Sunshine Company (Joe Saracone), Imperial 66247 | |
| 53 | 53 | 52 | 52 | CRY SOFTLY LONELY ONE — Roy Orbison (Rose & Vienneau), MGM 13764 | 6 |
| 54 | 55 | 57 | 67 | I WANT TO LOVE YOU FOR WHAT YOU ARE — Ronnie Dove (Phil Kahl), Diamond 227 | 5 |
| 55 | 73 | 88 | 92 | KNOCK ON WOOD — Otis & Carla (Staff), Stax 228 | 4 |
| 56 | 57 | 67 | 82 | JILL — Gary Lewis & the Playboys (Koppelman/Rubin), Liberty 55985 | |
| 57 | 80 | 92 | — | GET ON UP — Esquires (Bill Sheppard), Bunky 7750 | 3 |
| 58 | 79 | 94 | — | LOVE BUG LEAVE MY HEART ALONE — Martha & the Vandellas (Richard Morris), Gordy 7062 | 3 |
| 59 | 83 | — | — | NEVER MY LOVE — Association (B—s Howe), Warner Bros. 7074 | 2 |
| 60 | 71 | 81 | — | YOU'VE GOT TO PAY THE PRICE — Al Kent (Ed Wingate, Al Kent, H. Weems), Ric Tic 127 | 3 |
| 61 | 77 | 85 | — | ANYTHING GOES — Harpers Bizarre (Lenny Waronker), Warner Bros. 7063 | |
| 62 | 78 | — | — | MUSEUM — Herman's Hermits (Mickie Most), MGM 13787 | |
| 63 | 66 | 72 | 79 | RUN, RUN, RUN — Third Rail (Levine/Resnick/Cooper), Epic 10191 | 5 |
| 64 | 84 | — | — | PUT YOUR MIND AT EASE — Every Mother's Son (Wes Farrell), MGM 13788 | 2 |
| 65 | 76 | 79 | 86 | TURN ON YOUR LOVE LIGHT — Oscar Toney, Jr. (Papa Don), Bell 681 | 4 |
| 66 | 65 | 71 | 72 | FUNKY BROADWAY — Dyke & the Blazers (Coleman & Barrett), Original Sound 64 | 13 |
| 67 | 67 | 75 | 90 | A LITTLE BIT NOW — Dave Clark Five (Dave Clark), Epic 10209 | 4 |
| 68 | 74 | 83 | 88 | LAURA (What's He Got That I Ain't Got) — Frankie Laine (Bob Thiele), ABC 10967 | 4 |
| 69 | 63 | 63 | 78 | A WOMAN'S HANDS — Joe Tex (Buddy Killen), Dial 4061 | 5 |
| 70 | 93 | — | — | I MAKE A FOOL OF MYSELF — Frankie Valli (Bob Crewe), Philips 40484 | 2 |
| 71 | — | — | — | LITTLE OLE MAN (Uptight—Everything's Alright) — Bill Cosby (Fred Smith), Warner Bros. 7072 | 1 |
| 72 | — | — | — | THE CAT IN THE WINDOW (The Bird in the Sky) — Petula Clark (Charles Koppelman & Don Rubin), Warner Bros. 7073 | 1 |
| 73 | 68 | 77 | 87 | SIXTEEN TONS — Tom Jones (Peter Sullivan), Parrot 40016 | 4 |
| 74 | 90 | — | — | THERE'S ALWAYS ME — Elvis Presley, RCA Victor 9287 | 2 |
| 75 | 88 | — | — | MEMPHIS SOUL STEW — King Curtis (Tommy Cogbill & King Curtis), Atco 6511 | 2 |
| 76 | 89 | — | — | IN THE HEAT OF THE NIGHT — Ray Charles (TRC), ABC 10970 | 2 |
| 77 | 81 | — | — | I FEEL GOOD (I Feel Bad) — Lewis & Clarke Expedition (Jack Keller), Colgems 1006 | 2 |
| 78 | 95 | — | — | CASONOVA (Your Playing Days Are Over) — Ruby Andrews (McGregor & Terry), Zodiac 1004 | 2 |
| 79 | — | — | — | JUST OUT OF REACH (Of My Two Empty Arms) — Percy Sledge, Atlantic 2434 | 1 |
| 80 | — | — | — | IT MUST BE HIM — Vikki Carr (Dave Pell), Liberty 55986 | 1 |
| 81 | 85 | 90 | — | LAURA (What's He Got That I Ain't Got) — Brook Benton (Jimmy Bowen), Reprise 0611 | 3 |
| 82 | — | — | — | TAKE A LOOK — Aretha Franklin (Clyde Otis), Columbia 44270 | 1 |
| 83 | — | — | — | EXPRESSWAY TO YOUR HEART — Soul Survivors (Gamble-Huff), Crimson 1010 | 1 |
| 84 | — | — | — | BALLAD OF YOU & ME & POONEIL — Jefferson Airplane (Al Schmitt), RCA Victor 9297 | 1 |
| 85 | 86 | 95 | — | TURN THE WORLD AROUND — Eddy Arnold (Chet Atkins), RCA Victor 9265 | 3 |
| 86 | 87 | 87 | 97 | IT COULD BE WE'RE IN LOVE — Cryan' Shames (Jim Golden), Columbia 44191 | 5 |
| 87 | — | — | — | KNUCKLEHEAD — Bar-Kays (Staff), Volt 148 | 1 |
| 88 | — | — | — | GET TOGETHER — Youngbloods (Felix Pappalardi), RCA Victor 9264 | 1 |
| 89 | — | 86 | 94 | IT'S GOT TO BE MELLOW — Leon Haywood (Leon Haywood), Decca 32164 | 3 |
| 90 | — | — | — | I CAN'T STAY AWAY FROM YOU — Impressions (Johnny Pate), ABC 10964 | 1 |
| 91 | 91 | — | — | TELL HIM — Patti Drew (Carone), Capitol 5861 | 2 |
| 92 | 92 | — | — | STOUT-HEARTED MEN — Barbra Streisand (Howard A. Roberts & Jack Gold), Columbia 44225 | 2 |
| 93 | 94 | — | — | PURPLE HAZE — Jimi Hendrix Experience (Yameta), Reprise 0597 | 1 |
| 94 | — | — | — | PAPER SUN — Traffic Featuring Stevie Winwood (Jimmy Miller), United Artists 50195 | 1 |
| 95 | — | — | — | PENNY ARCADE — Cyrkle Charlie Calello), Columbia 44224 | 1 |
| 96 | — | — | — | THE LOOK OF LOVE — Dusty Springfield (Johnny Prenz), Philips 40465 | 4 |
| 97 | 98 | 98 | — | COME ON SOCK IT TO ME — Syl Johnson, Twilight 100 | 3 |
| 98 | — | — | — | THERE GOES THE LOVER — Gene Chandler (Carl Davis), Brunswick 55339 | 1 |
| 99 | — | — | — | NEARER TO YOU — Betty Harris (A. Toussaint-M. Sehorn), Sansu 466 | 3 |
| 100 | — | — | — | REQUIEM FOR THE MASSES — Association (Bones Howe), Warner Bros. 7074 | 1 |

## BUBBLING UNDER THE HOT 100

101. ABANDA — Herb Alpert & the Tijuana Brass, A&M 870
102. JUST ONCE IN MY LIFE — Brenda & the Tabulations, Dionn 503
103. LAST MINUTE MIRACLE — Shirelles, Scepter 12198
104. DRUMS — Jon & Robin, Abnak 126
105. LOVIN' SOUND — Ian & Sylvia, MGM 13686
106. YOU'RE A VERY LOVERLY WOMAN — Merry-Go-Round, A&M 863
107. DON'T FORGET ABOUT ME — American Breed, Acta 808
108. GET THE MESSAGE — Brian Hyland, Philips 40472
109. PEARL TIME — Andre Williams, Sport 105
110. DO SOMETHING TO ME — ? (Question Mark) & the Mysterians, Cameo 496
111. LITTLE OLD WINE DRINKER ME — Robert Mitchum, Monument 1006
112. THERE MUST BE A WAY — Jimmy Roselli, United Artists 50179
113. TRY, TRY, TRY — Jim Valley, Dunhill 4096
114. LOVE IS DOGGONE GOOD THING — Eddie Floyd, Stax 223
115. WEDNESDAY — Royal Guardsmen, Laurie 3397
116. CAN'T STOP LOVING YOU — Last Word, Atco 6498
117. UNDER THE STREET LAMP — Exits, Gemini 1004
118. SALLY SAYIN' SOMETHING — Billy Harper, Kama-Sutra 226
119. HOW CAN YOU MISTREAT THE ONE YOU LOVE — Jean & the Darlings, Volt 151
120. OUR SONG — Jack Jones, Kapp 846
121. WHAT DOES IT TAKE (To Keep a Man Like You Satisfied) — Skeeter Davis, RCA Victor 9242
122. YOU CAN'T DO THAT — Nilsson, RCA Victor 9298
123. BELIEVE IN ME BABY — Jessie James, 20th Century-Fox 6684
124. ON THE OTHER SIDE — Seekers, Capitol 5974
125. AGNES ENGLISH — John Fred & His Playboys, Paula 273
126. SUNSHINE GAMES — Music Explosion, Laurie 3400
127. TO SIR WITH LOVE — Lulu, Epic 10187
128. SOME KIND OF WONDERFUL — Soul Brothers 6, Atlantic 2406
129. LAURA (What's He Got That I Ain't Got) — Lean Ashley, Ashley 2003
130. THAT'S HOW IT IS (When You're In Love) — Otis Clay, One-Derful 4846
131. ROLLIN' & TUMBLIN' — Canned Heat, Liberty 55979
132. I WANNA BE THERE — Blues Magoos, Mercury 72729
133. LOVE IS LOVE — Verve Forecast 5058
134. LET IT OUT — Hombres, Verve Forecast 5058
135. STRAIGHT SHOOTER — Mamas & Papas, Dunhill 4099

For Week Ending September 9, 1967

# Billboard HOT 100

★ STAR performer—Sides registering greatest proportionate upward progress this week.

Record Industry Association of America seal of certification as million selling single.

| This Week | 1 Wk. Ago | 2 Wks. Ago | 3 Wks. Ago | TITLE Artist (Producer), Label & Number | Weeks On Chart |
|---|---|---|---|---|---|
| Billboard Award | 1 | 1 | 7 | ODE TO BILLIE JOE — Bobbie Gentry (Kelly Gordon & Bobby Paris), Capitol 5950 | 6 |
| 2 | 3 | 8 | 20 | REFLECTIONS — Dianna Ross & the Supremes (Holland & Dozier), Motown 1111 | 5 |
| ★3 | 6 | 14 | 27 | COME BACK WHEN YOU GROW UP — Bobby Vee & the Strangers (Dallas Smith), Liberty 55964 | 8 |
| 4 | 5 | 5 | 5 | BABY I LOVE YOU — Aretha Franklin (Jerry Wexler), Atlantic 2427 | 8 |
| ★5 | 15 | 25 | 58 | THE LETTER — Box Tops (Dan Penn), Mala 565 | 5 |
| 6 | 2 | 2 | 1 | ALL YOU NEED IS LOVE — Beatles (George Martin), Capitol 5964 | 8 |
| 7 | 9 | 9 | 21 | YOU'RE MY EVERYTHING — Temptations (Norman Whitfield), Gordy 7063 | 7 |
| 8 | 4 | 4 | 2 | LIGHT MY FIRE — Doors (Paul A. Rothchild), Elektra 45615 | 15 |
| ★9 | 14 | 19 | 24 | APPLES, PEACHES, PUMPKIN PIE — Jay & the Techniques (Jerry Ross), Smash 2086 | 9 |
| ★10 | 25 | 26 | 31 | SAN FRANCISCAN NIGHTS — Eric Burdon and the Animals (Tom Wilson), MGM 13769 | 6 |
| 11 | 7 | 7 | 8 | COLD SWEAT — James Brown & the Famous Flames (James Brown), King 6110 | 9 |
| 12 | 11 | 15 | 15 | WORDS — Monkees (Douglas Farthing Hatlelid), Colgems 1007 | 8 |
| 13 | 8 | 3 | 3 | PLEASANT VALLEY SUNDAY — Monkees (Douglas Farthing Hatlelid), Colgems 1007 | 8 |
| ★14 | 22 | 27 | 34 | BROWN-EYED GIRL — Van Morrison (Bert Berns), Bang 545 | 9 |
| 15 | 13 | 13 | 19 | THANK THE LORD FOR THE NIGHT TIME — Neil Diamond (Jeff Barry & Ellie Greenwich), Bang 547 | 9 |
| ★16 | 28 | 37 | 48 | YOU KNOW WHAT I MEAN — Turtles (Joe Wissert), White Whale 254 | 6 |
| ★17 | 24 | 36 | 54 | THERE IS A MOUNTAIN — Donovan (Mickie Most), Epic 10212 | 5 |
| 18 | 19 | 29 | 46 | FUNKY BROADWAY — Wilson Pickett (Jerry Wexler), Atlantic 2430 | 6 |
| ★19 | 27 | 45 | 55 | (Your Love Keeps Lifting Me) HIGHER AND HIGHER — Jackie Wilson (Carl Davis), Brunswick 55336 | 5 |
| 20 | 20 | 28 | 30 | (I Wanna) TESTIFY — Parliaments (George Clinton), Revilot 207 | 11 |
| 21 | 12 | 12 | 17 | HEROES AND VILLAINS — Beach Boys (Beach Boys), Brother Records 1001 | 6 |
| 22 | 10 | 6 | 4 | I WAS MADE TO LOVE HER — Stevie Wonder (H. Cosby), Tamla 54151 | 14 |
| 23 | 21 | 16 | 11 | SILENCE IS GOLDEN — Tremeloes (Mike Smith), Epic 10184 | 13 |
| ★24 | 29 | 54 | 80 | I HAD A DREAM — Paul Revere & the Raiders with Mark Lindsay (Terry Melcher), Columbia 44227 | 4 |
| ★25 | 59 | 83 | — | NEVER MY LOVE — Association (Bones Howe), Warner Bros. 7074 | 3 |
| ★26 | 38 | 48 | 76 | I DIG ROCK AND ROLL MUSIC — Peter, Paul & Mary (Albert B. Grossman & Milt Okun), Warner Bros. 7067 | 4 |
| ★27 | 36 | 72 | — | TWELVE THIRTY — Mamas & the Papas (Lou Adler), Dunhill 4099 | 3 |
| ★28 | 37 | 47 | 59 | THINGS I SHOULD HAVE SAID — Grass Roots (Barri Harris & P. F. Dloan), Dunhill 4094 | 5 |
| ★29 | 40 | 75 | — | GETTIN' TOGETHER — Tommy James & the Shondelles (Bo Gentry/Ritchie Cordell) Roulette 4762 | 3 |
| 30 | 30 | 31 | 42 | THE WORLD WE KNEW (Over and Over) — Frank Sinatra (Jimmy Bowen), Reprise 0610 | 6 |
| 31 | 33 | 43 | 56 | GROOVIN' — Booker T. and the M.G.'s (Staff), Stax 224 | 6 |
| 32 | 32 | 33 | 43 | THE WINDOWS OF THE WORLD — Dionne Warwick (Bacharach-David), Scepter 12196 | 7 |
| ★33 | 46 | 56 | 66 | GIMME LITTLE SIGN — Brenton Wood (Hooven-Winn), Double Shot 116 | 5 |
| 34 | 17 | 11 | 10 | A GIRL LIKE YOU — Young Rascals (Young Rascals), Atlantic 2424 | 9 |
| 35 | 23 | 23 | 28 | FAKIN' IT — Simon & Garfunkel (John Simon), Columbia 44232 | 7 |
| 36 | 18 | 18 | 12 | CARRIE ANN — Hollies (Ron Richards), Epic 10180 | 13 |
| 37 | 26 | 17 | 18 | TO LOVE SOMEBODY — Bee Gees (Robert Stigwood), Atco 6503 | 9 |
| ★38 | 49 | 59 | 78 | LITTLE OLD WINE DRINKER, ME — Dean Martin (Jimmy Bowen), Reprise 0608 | 4 |
| ★39 | 58 | 79 | 94 | LOVE BUG LEAVE MY HEART ALONE — Martha Reeves & the Vandellas (Richard Morris), Gordy 7062 | 4 |
| 40 | 41 | 51 | 51 | BLUES THEME — Arrows (Mike Curb), Tower 295 | 14 |
| ★41 | 51 | 69 | 84 | MAKING EVERY MINUTE COUNT — Spanky & Our Gang (Jerry Ross), Mercury 72714 | 4 |
| 42 | 42 | 52 | 65 | ZIP CODE — Five Americans (Dale Hawkins), Abnak 123 | 5 |
| ★43 | 70 | 93 | — | I MAKE A FOOL OF MYSELF — Frankie Valli (Bob Crewe), Philips 40484 | 3 |
| 44 | 16 | 10 | 9 | A WHITER SHADE OF PALE — Procol Harum (Denny Cordell), Deram 7507 | 12 |
| 45 | 45 | 50 | 60 | HA HA SAID THE CLOWN — Yardbirds (Mickie Most), Epic 10204 | 6 |
| 46 | 39 | 21 | 23 | HYPNOTIZED — Linda Jones (George Kerr), Loma 2070 | 12 |
| ★47 | 57 | 80 | 92 | GET ON UP — Esquires (Bill Sheppard), Bunky 7750 | 4 |
| ★48 | 72 | — | — | THE CAT IN THE WINDOW (The Bird in the Sky) — Petula Clark (Charles Koppelman & Don Rubin), Warner Bros. 7073 | 2 |
| ★49 | 62 | 78 | — | MUSEUM — Herman's Hermits (Mickie Most), MGM 13787 | 3 |
| 50 | 50 | 60 | 64 | IT'S THE LITTLE THINGS — Sonny & Cher (Sonny Bono), Atco 6507 | 5 |
| 51 | 55 | 73 | 88 | KNOCK ON WOOD — Otis & Carla (Staff), Stax 228 | 5 |
| 52 | 52 | 58 | 61 | HAPPY — Sunshine Company (Joe Saraceno), Imperial 66247 | 9 |
| 53 | 60 | 71 | 81 | YOU'VE GOT TO PAY THE PRICE — Al Kent (Ed Wingate, Al Kent, H. Weems), Ric Tic 127 | 4 |
| 54 | 56 | 57 | 67 | JILL — Gary Lewis & the Playboys (Koppelman/Rubin), Liberty 55985 | 5 |
| ★55 | 71 | — | — | LITTLE OLE MAN (Uptight—Everything's Alright) — Bill Cosby (Fred Smith), Warner Bros. 7072 | 2 |
| 56 | 64 | 84 | — | PUT YOUR MIND AT EASE — Every Mother's Son (Wes Farrell), MGM 13788 | 3 |
| ★57 | 75 | 88 | — | MEMPHIS SOUL STEW — King Curtis (Tommy Cogbill & King Curtis), Atco 6511 | 3 |
| ★58 | 74 | 90 | — | THERE'S ALWAYS ME — Elvis Presley, RCA Victor 9287 | 3 |
| ★59 | 76 | 89 | — | IN THE HEAT OF THE NIGHT — Ray Charles (TRC), ABC 10970 | 3 |
| 60 | 61 | 77 | 85 | ANYTHING GOES — Harpers Bizarre (Lenny Waronker), Warner Bros. 7063 | 4 |
| ★61 | 83 | — | — | EXPRESSWAY TO YOUR HEART — Soul Survivors (Gemble-Huff), Crimson 1010 | 2 |
| ★62 | 78 | 95 | — | CASONOVA (Your Playing Days Are Over) — Ruby Andrews (McGregor & Terry), Zodiac 1004 | 3 |
| 63 | 63 | 66 | 72 | RUN, RUN, RUN — Third Rail (Levine/Resnick/Cooper), Epic 10191 | 6 |
| ★64 | 84 | — | — | BALLAD OF YOU & ME & POONEIL — Jefferson Airplane (Al Schmitt), RCA Victor 9297 | 2 |
| 65 | 65 | 76 | 79 | TURN ON YOUR LOVE LIGHT — Oscar Toney, Jr. (Papa Don), Bell 681 | 5 |
| 66 | 68 | 74 | 83 | LAURA (What's He Got That I Ain't Got) — Frankie Laine (Bob Thiele), ABC 10967 | 5 |
| 67 | 79 | — | — | JUST OUT OF REACH (Of My Two Empty Arms) — Percy Sledge, Atlantic 2434 | 2 |
| ★68 | 96 | — | — | THE LOOK OF LOVE — Dusty Springfield (Johnny Prenz), Philips 40465 | 5 |
| 69 | 77 | 81 | — | I FEEL GOOD (I Feel Bad) — Lewis & Clarke Expedition (Jack Keller), Colgems 1006 | 3 |
| ★70 | 85 | 86 | 95 | TURN THE WORLD AROUND — Eddy Arnold (Chet Atkins), RCA Victor 9265 | 4 |
| 71 | 82 | — | — | TAKE A LOOK — Aretha Franklin (Clyde Otis), Columbia 44270 | 2 |
| 72 | 80 | — | — | IT MUST BE HIM — Vikki Carr (Dave Pell), Liberty 55986 | 2 |
| ★73 | — | — | — | YOUR PRECIOUS LOVE — Marvin Gaye & Tammy Terrell (H. Fuqua-J. Bristol), Tamla 54156 | 1 |
| ★74 | — | — | — | TO SIR WITH LOVE — Lulu (Mickie Most), Epic 10187 | 1 |
| ★75 | — | — | — | DANDELION — Rolling Stones (Andrew Loog Oldham), London 905 | 1 |
| ★76 | — | — | — | A BANDA — Herb Alpert & the Tijuana Brass (Herb Alpert & Jerry Moss), A&M 870 | 1 |
| ★77 | — | — | — | LET LOVE COME BETWEEN US — James & Bobby Purify (Papa Don), Bell 685 | 1 |
| 78 | 81 | 85 | 90 | LAURA (What's He Got That I Ain't Got) — Brook Benton (Jimmy Bowen), Reprise 0611 | 4 |
| ★79 | — | — | — | SOUL MAN — Sam & Dave (Isaac Hayes & David Porter), Stax 231 | 1 |
| ★80 | — | — | — | HOW CAN I BE SURE — Young Rascals (Young Rascals), Atlantic 2438 | 1 |
| ★81 | — | — | — | YOU'VE MADE ME SO VERY HAPPY — Brenda Holloway (Berry Gordy Jr.), Tamla 54155 | 1 |
| ★82 | — | — | — | WHAT NOW MY LOVE — Mitch Ryder (Bob Crewe), DynoVoice 901 | 1 |
| ★83 | — | — | — | HEY BABY (They're Playing Our Song) — Buckinghams (James William Guercio), Columbia 44254 | 1 |
| ★84 | — | — | — | I'LL NEVER FALL IN LOVE AGAIN — Tom Jones (Peter Sullivan), Parrot 40018 | 1 |
| 85 | 88 | — | — | GET TOGETHER — Youngbloods (Felix Pappalardi), RCA Victor 9264 | 2 |
| 86 | 89 | — | 86 | IT'S GOT TO BE MELLOW — Leon Haywood (Leon Haywood), Decca 32164 | 4 |
| 87 | 87 | — | — | KNUCKLEHEAD — Bar-Kays (Staff), Volt 148 | 2 |
| 88 | 90 | — | — | I CAN'T STAY AWAY FROM YOU — Impressions (Johnny Pate), ABC 10964 | 2 |
| ★89 | — | — | — | JUDY — Elvis Presley, RCA Victor 9287 | 1 |
| 90 | 91 | 91 | — | TELL HIM — Patti Drew (Carone), Capitol 5861 | 3 |
| 91 | — | — | — | SWEET SOUL MEDLEY — Magnificent Man (Marvin Holtmann), Capitol 5975 | 1 |
| 92 | — | — | — | OUR SONG — Jack Jones (Kapp), Kapp 847 | 1 |
| 93 | — | — | — | SUNSHINE GAMES — Music Explosion (J. Kassemern-Kate-Chiperut), Laurie 3400 | 1 |
| 94 | — | — | — | HEY JOE — Cher (Sonny Bono), Imperial 66252 | 1 |
| 95 | — | — | — | SPREADIN' HONEY — Watts 103rd St. Rhythm Band (Fred Smith), Keynen 103 | 1 |
| 96 | — | — | — | FORGET IT — Sandpebbles (Teddy Vann), Cella 134 | 1 |
| 97 | 99 | — | — | NEARER TO YOU — Betty Harris (A. Toussaint-M. Sehorn), Sensu 466 | 4 |
| 98 | — | — | — | WEDNESDAY — Royal Guardsmen (Gernhard), Laurie 3397 | 1 |
| 99 | — | — | — | YOU'RE A VERY LOVELY WOMAN — Merry-Go-Round (Larry Marks), A&M 863 | 1 |
| 100 | 100 | — | — | REQUIEM FOR THE MASSES — Association (Bones Howe), Warner Bros. 7074 | 2 |

## HOT 100—A TO Z—(Publisher-Licensee)


A Banda (Permata, ASCAP) .... 76
All You Need Is Love (Maclen, BMI) .... 6
Anything Goes (Harms, ASCAP) .... 60
Apples, Peaches, Pumpkin Pie (Akbestal/Act Three, BMI) .... 9
Baby, I Love You (14th Hour/Pronto, BMI) .... 4
Ballad of You & Me & Pooneil (Jefferson Airplane, BMI) .... 64
Blues Theme (Dijon, BMI) .... 40
Brown-Eyed Girl (Web IV, BMI) .... 14
Carrie Ann (Maribus, BMI) .... 36
Casonova (Your Playing Days Are Over) (RicWil/Colfam, BMI) .... 62
Cat In the Window, The (The Bird in the Sky) Chardon, BMI) .... 48
Cold Sweat (Dynatone, BMI) .... 11
Come Back When You Grow Up (Painted Desert, BMI) .... 3
Dandelion (Gideon, BMI) .... 75
Expressway to Your Heart (Double Diamond/Downstairs, BMI) .... 61
Fakin' It (Charing Cross, BMI) .... 35
Forget It (Unbelievable, BMI) .... 96
Funky Broadway (Pickett) (Drive-In/Routeen, BMI) .... 18
Get On Up (Hi-Mi, BMI) .... 47
Gettin' Together (Patricia, BMI) .... 29
Get Together (S.F.O., BMI) .... 85
Gimme Little Sign (Big Shot, ASCAP) .... 33
Girl Like You (Slacsar, BMI) .... 34
Groovin' (Slacsar, BMI) .... 31
Ha Ha Said the Clown (Ponderosa, BMI) .... 45
Happy (Sunshine Company) (Unart, BMI) .... 52
Heroes and Villians (Sea of Tunes, BMI) .... 21
Hey Baby They're Playing Our Song) (Diogenes/Bag O'Tunes, BMI) .... 83
Hey Joe (Third Story, BMI) .... 94
How Can I Be Sure (Slacsar, BMI) .... 80
Hypnotized (Zira/Floteca, BMI) .... 46
I Can't Stay Away From You (Chi-Sound, BMI) .... 88
I Dig Rock and Roll Music (Pepamar, ASCAP) .... 26
I Feel Good (I Feel Bad) Screen Gems-Columbia, BMI) .... 69
I Had a Dream (Daywin, BMI) .... 24
I Make a Fool of Myself (Saturday/Seasons Four, BMI) .... 43
(I Wanna) Testify (Groovesville, BMI) .... 20
I Was Made to Love Her (Jobete, BMI) .... 22
I'll Never Fall In Love Again (Hollis, BMI) .... 84
In the Heat of the Night (United Artists, ASCAP) .... 59
It Must Be Him (Asa, ASCAP) .... 72
It's Got to Be Mellow (Jim-Edd, BMI) .... 89
It's the Little Things (Chris Marc/Cotillion, BMI) .... 50
Jill (Chardon, BMI) .... 54
Judy (Progressive/Presley/McDaniel, BMI) .... 89
Just Out of Reach Of My Two Empty Arms) (Four Star, BMI) .... 67
Knock on Wood (East, BMI) .... 54
Knucklehead (East, BMI) .... 87
Laura (What's He Got That I Ain't Got?) (Laine) (Gallico, BMI) .... 66
Let Love Come Between Us (Gallico, BMI) .... 77
Letter, The (Barton, BMI) .... 5
Light My Fire (Nipper, ASCAP) .... 8
Little Old Wine Drinker, Me (Moss-Rose, BMI) .... 38
Little Ole Man (Uptight-Everything's Alright) (Jobete, BMI) .... 55
Lock of Love, The (Ponderosa, BMI) .... 68
Love Bug Leave My Heart Alone (Jobete, BMI) .... 39
Making Every Minute Count (Akbestal, BMI) .... 41
Memphis Soul Stew (Pronto/K lynn, BMI) .... 57
Museum (Peer Int'l, BMI) .... 49
Nearer to You (Marsaint, BMI) .... 97
Never My Love (Temerlene, BMI) .... 25
Ode to Billie Joe (Shayne, ASCAP) .... 1
Our Song (Senta Cecilia, BMI) .... 92
Pleasant Valley Sunday (Screen Gems-Columbia, BMI) .... 13
Put Your Mind at Ease (Pocket Full of Tunes/Tobifun, BMI) .... 56
Reflections (Jobete, BMI) .... 2
Requiem for the Masses (Beechwood, BMI) .... 100
Run, Run, Run (T. M., BMI) .... 63
San Francisican Nights (Sealark/Slamine, BMI) .... 10
Silence Is Golden (Saturday/Geradium, BMI) .... 23
Soul Man (East/Pronto, BMI) .... 79
Spreadin' Honey (Neymen/Pure Soul, BMI) .... 95
Sunshine Games (Southern, ASCAP) .... 93
Sweet Soul Medley (Redwal/Jobete, BMI) .... 91
Take a Look (Eden, BMI) .... 71
Tell Him (Beechwood/Edgewater, BMI) .... 90
Thank the Lord for the Night Time (Tallyrand, BMI) .... 15
There Is a Mountain (Peer Int'l/Hi-Count, BMI) .... 17
There's Always Me (Gladys, ASCAP) .... 58
Things I Should Have Said (Trousdale, BMI) .... 28
To Love Somebody (Namperer, BMI) .... 37
To Sir With Love (Screen Gems-Columbia, BMI) .... 74
Turn on Your Love Light (Don, BMI) .... 65
Turn the World Around (Fingerlake, BMI) .... 70
Twelve Thirty (Wingate, ASCAP) .... 27
Wednesday (Senjhil/Ronnigua, BMI) .... 98
What Now My Love (Remick, ASCAP) .... 82
Whiter Shade of Pale (Essex, ASCAP) .... 44
Windows of the World, The (Jac/Blue Seas, ASCAP) .... 32
Words (Screen Gems-Columbia, BMI) .... 12
World We Knew, The (Over and Over) (Roosevelt, BMI) .... 30
You Know What I Mean (Chardon, BMI) .... 16
(Your Love Keeps Lifting Me) Higher and Higher (Jalynne/BRC, BMI) .... 19
Your Precious Love (Jobete, BMI) .... 73
You're a Very Lovely Woman (Thirty Four/LaBres, ASCAP) .... 99
You're My Everything (Jobete, BMI) .... 7
You've Got to Pay the Price (Myto, BMI) .... 53
You've Made Me So Very Happy (Jobete, BMI) .... 81
Zip Code (Jetstar, BMI) .... 42


## BUBBLING UNDER THE HOT 100

101. JUST ONCE IN A LIFETIME .... Brenda & the Tabulations, Dioan 503
102. YOU KEEP RUNNING AWAY .... Four Tops, Motown 1113
103. COME ON SOCK IT TO ME .... Syl Johnson, Twilight 100
104. IT COULD BE WE'RE IN LOVE .... Cryan' Shames, Columbia 44191
105. DEVIL'S ANGELS .... Devie Allan, Tower 341
106. PENNY ARCADE .... Cyrkle, Columbia 44224
107. DRUMS .... Jon & Robin, Abnak 122
108. CHILD OF CLAY .... Jimmie Rodgers, A&M 871
109. FOR ONCE IN MY LIFE .... Tony Bennett, Columbia 44258
110. PURPLE HAZE .... Jimi Hendrix Experience, Reprise 0597
111. PAPER SUN .... Traffic Featuring Stevie Winwood, United Artists 50135
112. CAN'T STOP LOVING YOU .... Last Word, Atco 6498
113. THERE MUST BE A WAY .... Jimmy Roselli, United Artists 50179
114. SHE KNOWS .... Bobby Darin, Atlantic 2433
115. ON THE OTHER SIDE .... Seekers, Capitol 5974
116. UNDER THE STREET LAMP .... Exits, Gemini 1004
117. BLINDMAN .... Big Brother & the Holding Company, Mainstream 657
118. SALLY SAYIN' SOMETHING .... Billy Warner, Kama Sutra 226
119. PEAS 'N' RICE .... Freddie McCoy, Prestige 450
120. LAURA (What's He Got That I Ain't Got?) .... Leon Ashley, Ashley 2003
121. I'LL RELEASE YOU .... Joann and the Coquettes, MCA 129
122. BYE, BYE BABY .... Big Brother & the Holding Company, Mainstream 666
123. THAT'S HOW STRONG MY LOVE IS .... Sweet Inspirations, Atlantic 2436
124. EVERLASTING LOVE .... Robert Knight, Rising Sons 705
125. NINE POUND STEEL .... Joe Simon, Sound Stage 7 2589
126. TIME SELLER .... Spencer Davis Group, United Artists 50202
127. SOULSATION .... Capreez, Sound 149
128. FOR WHAT IT'S WORTH .... Staple Singers, Epic 10220
129. SOME KIND OF WONDERFUL .... Soul Brothers Six, Atlantic 2406
130. STRAIGHT SHOOTER .... Mamas & the Papas, Dunhill 4099
131. LET IT ALL OUT .... Hombres, Verve Forecast 5058
132. RUNAWAY .... Del Shannon, Liberty 55993
133. WE LOVE YOU .... Rolling Stones, Lenion 905
134. HEAVY MUSIC .... Bob Seeger, Cameo 494
135. BEG, BORROW & STEAL .... Ohio Express, Cameo 483

Compiled from national retail sales and radio station airplay by the Music Popularity Dept. of Record Market Research, Billboard.

For Week Ending September 16, 1967

# Billboard HOT 100

★ **STAR performer—Sides registering greatest proportionate upward progress this week.**

Record Industry Association of America seal of certification as million selling single.

| This Week | 1 Wk. Ago | 2 Wks. Ago | 3 Wks. Ago | TITLE Artist (Producer), Label & Number | Weeks On Chart |
|---|---|---|---|---|---|
| 1 (Billboard Award) | 1 | 1 | 1 | **ODE TO BILLIE JOE** — Bobbie Gentry (Kelly Gordon & Bobby Paris), Capitol 5950 | 7 |
| 2 | 2 | 3 | 8 | **REFLECTIONS** — Dianna Ross & the Supremes (Holland & Dozier), Motown 1111 | 6 |
| 3 | 3 | 6 | 14 | **COME BACK WHEN YOU GROW UP** — Bobby Vee & the Strangers (Dallas Smith), Liberty 55964 | 9 |
| 4 | 5 | 15 | 25 | **THE LETTER** — Box Tops (Dan Penn), Mala 565 | 6 |
| 5 | 4 | 5 | 5 | **BABY I LOVE YOU** — Aretha Franklin (Jerry Wexler), Atlantic 2427 | 9 (RIAA seal) |
| 6 | 7 | 9 | 9 | **YOU'RE MY EVERYTHING** — Temptations (Norman Whitfield), Gordy 7063 | 8 |
| 7 | 9 | 14 | 19 | **APPLES, PEACHES, PUMPKIN PIE** — Jay & the Techniques (Jerry Ross), Smash 2086 | 10 |
| 8 | 6 | 2 | 2 | **ALL YOU NEED IS LOVE** — Beatles (George Martin), Capitol 5964 | 9 |
| 9 | 10 | 25 | 26 | **SAN FRANCISCAN NIGHTS** — Eric Burdon and the Animals (Tom Wilson), MGM 13769 | 7 |
| ★10 | 18 | 19 | 29 | **FUNKY BROADWAY** — Wilson Pickett (Jerry Wexler), Atlantic 2430 | 7 |
| ★11 | 17 | 24 | 36 | **THERE IS A MOUNTAIN** — Donovan (Mickie Most), Epic 10212 | 6 |
| ★12 | 19 | 27 | 45 | **(Your Love Keeps Lifting Me) HIGHER AND HIGHER** — Jackie Wilson (Carl Davis), Brunswick 55336 | 6 |
| 13 | 16 | 28 | 37 | **YOU KNOW WHAT I MEAN** — Turtles (Joe Wissert), White Whale 254 | 7 |
| 14 | 14 | 22 | 27 | **BROWN-EYED GIRL** — Van Morrison (Bert Berns), Bang 545 | 10 |
| ★15 | 25 | 59 | 83 | **NEVER MY LOVE** — Association (Bones Howe), Warner Bros. 7074 | 4 |
| ★16 | 26 | 38 | 48 | **I DIG ROCK AND ROLL MUSIC** — Peter, Paul & Mary (Albert B. Grossman & Milt Okun), Warner Bros. 7067 | 5 |
| 17 | 11 | 7 | 7 | **COLD SWEAT** — James Brown & the Famous Flames (James Brown), King 6110 | 10 |
| 18 | 8 | 4 | 4 | **LIGHT MY FIRE** — Doors (Paul A. Rothchild), Elektra 45615 | 16 |
| ★19 | 24 | 29 | 54 | **I HAD A DREAM** — Paul Revere & the Raiders with Mark Lindsay (Terry Melcher), Columbia 44227 | 5 |
| ★20 | 27 | 36 | 72 | **TWELVE THIRTY** — Mamas & the Papas (Lou Adler), Dunhill 4099 | 4 |
| ★21 | 33 | 46 | 56 | **GIMME LITTLE SIGN** — Brenton Wood (Hooven-Winn), Double Shot 116 | 8 |
| 22 | 20 | 20 | 28 | **(I Wanna) TESTIFY** — Parliaments (George Clinton), Revilot 207 | 12 |
| ★23 | 28 | 37 | 47 | **THINGS I SHOULD HAVE SAID** — Grass Roots (Steve Barri & P. F. Sloan), Dunhill 4094 | 6 |
| ★24 | 29 | 40 | 75 | **GETTIN' TOGETHER** — Tommy James & the Shondelles (Bo Gentry/Ritchie Cordell) Roulette 4762 | 4 |
| 25 | 13 | 8 | 3 | **PLEASANT VALLEY SUNDAY** — Monkees (Douglas Farthing Hatlelid), Colgems 1007 | 9 (RIAA seal) |
| ★26 | 31 | 33 | 43 | **GROOVIN'** — Booker T. and the M.G.'s (Staff), Stax 224 | 7 |
| 27 | 15 | 13 | 13 | **THANK THE LORD FOR THE NIGHT TIME** — Neil Diamond (Jeff Barry & Ellie Greenwich), Bang 547 | 10 |
| ★28 | 43 | 70 | 93 | **I MAKE A FOOL OF MYSELF** — Frankie Valli (Bob Crewe), Philips 40484 | 4 |
| 29 | 12 | 11 | 15 | **WORDS** — Monkees (Douglas Farthing Hatlelid), Colgems 1007 | 9 |
| ★30 | 39 | 58 | 79 | **LOVE BUG LEAVE MY HEART ALONE** — Martha Reeves & the Vandellas (Richard Morris), Gordy 7062 | 5 |
| ★31 | 41 | 51 | 69 | **MAKING EVERY MINUTE COUNT** — Spanky & Our Gang (Jerry Ross), Mercury 72714 | 6 |
| ★32 | 55 | 71 | — | **LITTLE OLE MAN (Uptight—Everything's Alright)** — Bill Cosby (Fred Smith), Warner Bros. 7072 | 3 |
| 33 | 23 | 21 | 16 | **SILENCE IS GOLDEN** — Tremeloes (Mike Smith), Epic 10184 | 14 |
| ★34 | 48 | 72 | — | **THE CAT IN THE WINDOW (The Bird in the Sky)** — Petula Clark (Charles Koppelman & Don Rubin), Warner Bros. 7073 | 3 |
| ★35 | 47 | 57 | 80 | **GET ON UP** — Esquires (Bill Sheppard), Bunky 7750 | 5 |
| 36 | 42 | 42 | 52 | **ZIP CODE** — Five Americans (Dale Hawkins), Abnak 123 | 6 |
| 37 | 30 | 30 | 31 | **THE WORLD WE KNEW (Over and Over)** — Frank Sinatra (Jimmy Bowen), Reprise 0610 | 7 |
| 38 | 38 | 49 | 59 | **LITTLE OLD WINE DRINKER, ME** — Dean Martin (Jimmy Bowen), Reprise 0608 | 5 |
| ★39 | 49 | 62 | 78 | **MUSEUM** — Herman's Hermits (Mickie Most), MGM 13787 | 3 |
| 40 | 40 | 41 | 51 | **BLUES THEME** — Arrows (Mike Curb), Tower 295 | 15 |
| ★41 | 51 | 55 | 73 | **KNOCK ON WOOD** — Otis & Carla (Staff), Stax 228 | 6 |
| ★42 | 75 | — | — | **DANDELION** — Rolling Stones (Andrew Loog Oldham), London 905 | 2 |
| ★43 | 80 | — | — | **HOW CAN I BE SURE** — Young Rascals (Young Rascals), Atlantic 2438 | 2 |
| 44 | 22 | 10 | 6 | **I WAS MADE TO LOVE HER** — Stevie Wonder (H. Cosby), Tamla 54151 | 15 |
| ★45 | 61 | 83 | — | **EXPRESSWAY TO YOUR HEART** — Soul Survivors (Gemble-Huff), Crimson 1010 | 3 |
| ★46 | 56 | 64 | 84 | **PUT YOUR MIND AT EASE** — Every Mother's Son (Wes Farrell), MGM 13788 | 4 |
| ★47 | 57 | 75 | 88 | **MEMPHIS SOUL STEW** — King Curtis (Tommy Cogbill & King Curtis), Atco 6511 | 4 |
| ★48 | 60 | 61 | 77 | **ANYTHING GOES** — Harpers Bizarre (Lenny Waronker), Warner Bros. 7063 | 5 |
| ★49 | 59 | 76 | 89 | **IN THE HEAT OF THE NIGHT** — Ray Charles (TRC), ABC 10970 | 4 |
| 50 | 52 | 52 | 58 | **HAPPY** — Sunshine Company (Joe Saraceno), Imperial 66247 | 10 |
| 51 | 53 | 60 | 71 | **YOU'VE GOT TO PAY THE PRICE** — Al Kent (Ed Wingate, Al Kent, H. Weems), Ric Tic 127 | 5 |
| 52 | 54 | 56 | 57 | **JILL** — Gary Lewis & the Playboys (Koppelman/Rubin), Liberty 55985 | 6 |
| ★53 | 63 | 63 | 66 | **RUN, RUN, RUN** — Third Rail (Levine/Resnick/Cooper), Epic 10191 | 7 |
| ★54 | 64 | 84 | — | **BALLAD OF YOU & ME & POONEIL** — Jefferson Airplane (Al Schmitt), RCA Victor 9297 | 3 |
| 55 | 21 | 12 | 12 | **HEROES AND VILLAINS** — Beach Boys (Beach Boys), Brother Records 1001 | 7 |
| 56 | 58 | 74 | 90 | **THERE'S ALWAYS ME** — Elvis Presley, RCA Victor 9287 | 4 |
| ★57 | 76 | — | — | **A BANDA** — Herb Alpert & the Tijuana Brass (Herb Alpert & Jerry Moss), A&M 870 | 2 |
| ★58 | 74 | — | — | **TO SIR WITH LOVE** — Lulu (Mickie Most), Epic 10187 | 2 |
| ★59 | 73 | — | — | **YOUR PRECIOUS LOVE** — Marvin Gaye & Tammy Terrell (H. Fuqua-J. Bristol), Tamla 54156 | 2 |
| ★60 | 72 | 80 | — | **IT MUST BE HIM** — Vikki Carr (Dave Pell), Liberty 55986 | 3 |
| 61 | 62 | 78 | 95 | **CASONOVA (Your Playing Days Are Over)** — Ruby Andrews (McGregor & Terry), Zodiac 1004 | 4 |
| ★62 | 77 | — | — | **LET LOVE COME BETWEEN US** — James & Bobby Purify (Papa Don), Bell 685 | 2 |
| 63 | 68 | 96 | — | **THE LOOK OF LOVE** — Dusty Springfield (Johnny Prenz), Philips 40465 | 6 |
| 64 | 69 | 77 | 81 | **I FEEL GOOD (I Feel Bad)** — Lewis & Clarke Expedition (Jack Keller), Colgems 1006 | 4 |
| 65 | 35 | 23 | 23 | **FAKIN' IT** — Simon & Garfunkel (John Simon), Columbia 44232 | 8 |
| 66 | 67 | 79 | — | **JUST OUT OF REACH (Of My Two Empty Arms)** — Percy Sledge, Atlantic 2434 | 3 |
| ★67 | 82 | — | — | **WHAT NOW MY LOVE** — Mitch Ryder (Bob Crewe), DynoVoice 901 | 2 |
| ★68 | 83 | — | — | **HEY BABY (They're Playing Our Song)** — Buckinghams (James William Guercio), Columbia 44254 | 2 |
| 69 | 70 | 85 | 86 | **TURN THE WORLD AROUND** — Eddy Arnold (Chet Atkins), RCA Victor 9265 | 5 |
| ★70 | 85 | 88 | — | **GET TOGETHER** — Youngbloods (Felix Pappalardi), RCA Victor 9264 | 3 |
| 71 | 71 | 82 | — | **TAKE A LOOK** — Aretha Franklin (Clyde Otis), Columbia 44270 | 3 |
| 72 | 32 | 32 | 33 | **THE WINDOWS OF THE WORLD** — Dionne Warwick (Bacharach-David), Scepter 12196 | 8 |
| 73 | 79 | — | — | **SOUL MAN** — Sam & Dave (Isaac Hayes & David Porter), Stax 231 | 2 |
| 74 | 50 | 50 | 60 | **IT'S THE LITTLE THINGS** — Sonny & Cher (Sonny Bono), Atco 6507 | 5 |
| ★75 | — | — | — | **YOU KEEP RUNNING AWAY** — Four Tops (Holland & Dozier), Motown 1113 | 1 |
| 76 | 45 | 45 | 50 | **HA HA SAID THE CLOWN** — Yardbirds (Mickie Most), Epic 10204 | 7 |
| 77 | 84 | — | — | **I'LL NEVER FALL IN LOVE AGAIN** — Tom Jones (Peter Sullivan), Parrot 40018 | 2 |
| ★78 | 93 | — | — | **SUNSHINE GAMES** — Music Explosion (J. Kassemern-Kate-Chiperut), Laurie 3400 | 2 |
| 79 | 66 | 68 | 74 | **LAURA (What's He Got That I Ain't Got?)** — Frankie Laine (Bob Thiele), ABC 10967 | 6 |
| 80 | 81 | — | — | **YOU'VE MADE ME SO VERY HAPPY** — Brenda Holloway (Berry Gordy Jr.), Tamla 54155 | 2 |
| ★81 | 96 | — | — | **FORGET IT** — Sandpebbles (Teddy Vann), Cella 134 | 2 |
| 82 | 86 | 89 | — | **IT'S GOT TO BE MELLOW** — Leon Haywood (Leon Haywood), Decca 32164 | 5 |
| 83 | 88 | 90 | — | **I CAN'T STAY AWAY FROM YOU** — Impressions (Johnny Pate), ABC 10964 | 3 |
| 84 | 87 | 87 | — | **KNUCKLEHEAD** — Bar-Kays (Staff), Volt 148 | 3 |
| 85 | 65 | 65 | 76 | **TURN ON YOUR LOVE LIGHT** — Oscar Toney, Jr. (Papa Don), Bell 681 | 6 |
| ★86 | — | — | — | **WE LOVE YOU** — Rolling Stones (Andrew Loog Oldham), London 905 | 1 |
| ★87 | — | — | — | **BABY, I'M LONELY** — Intruders (Gamble-Huff), Gamble 207 | 1 |
| 88 | 89 | — | — | **JUDY** — Elvis Presley, RCA Victor 9287 | 2 |
| 89 | 90 | 91 | 91 | **TELL HIM** — Patti Drew (Carone), Capitol 5861 | 4 |
| 90 | 91 | — | — | **SWEET SOUL MEDLEY** — Magnificent Man (Marvin Holtmann), Capitol 5976 | 2 |
| 91 | — | 86 | 87 | **IT COULD BE WE'RE IN LOVE** — Cryan' Shames (Jim Golden), Columbia 44191 | 6 |
| 92 | 92 | — | — | **OUR SONG** — Jack Jones (Kapp), Kapp 847 | 2 |
| 93 | 95 | — | — | **SPREADIN' HONEY** — Watts 103rd St. Rhythm Band (Fred Smith), Keynen 103 | 2 |
| 94 | 94 | — | — | **HEY JOE** — Cher (Sonny Bono), Imperial 66252 | 2 |
| 95 | — | — | — | **LET IT OUT** — Hombres (Huey P. Meaux), Verve Forecast 5058 | 1 |
| 96 | 99 | — | — | **YOU'RE A VERY LOVELY WOMAN** — Merry-Go-Round (Larry Marks), A&M 863 | 2 |
| 97 | 98 | — | — | **WEDNESDAY** — Royal Guardsmen (Gernhard), Laurie 3397 | 2 |
| 98 | — | — | — | **LOUISIANA MAN** — Pozo Seco Singers (Bob Johnston), Columbia 44263 | 1 |
| 99 | — | — | — | **KARATE-BOO-GA-LOO** — Jerry O (Jerry Murray), Shout 217 | 1 |
| 100 | — | — | — | **TIME SELLER** — Spencer Davis Group (Ron Richards), United Artists 50202 | 1 |

## HOT 100—A TO Z—(Publisher-Licensee)

A Banda (Permata, ASCAP) .... 57
All You Need Is Love (Maclen, BMI) .... 8
Anything Goes (Harms, ASCAP) .... 48
Apples, Peaches, Pumpkin Pie (Akbestal/Act Three, BMI) .... 7
Baby, I Love You (14th Hour/Pronto, BMI) .... 5
Baby, I'm Lonely (Razor Sharp, BMI) .... 87
Ballad of You & Me & Poonell (Jefferson Airplane, BMI) .... 54
Blues Theme (Dijon, BMI) .... 40
Brown-Eyed Girl (Web IV, BMI) .... 14
Casonova (Your Playing Days Are Over) (RicWil/Colfam, BMI) .... 61
Cat in the Window, The (The Bird in the Sky) (Chardon, BMI) .... 34
Cold Sweat (Dynatone, BMI) .... 17
Come Back When You Grow Up (Painted Desert, BMI) .... 3
Dandelion (Gideon, BMI) .... 42
Expressway to Your Heart (Double Diamond/Downstairs, BMI) .... 45
Fakin' It (Charing Cross, BMI) .... 65
Forget It (Unbelievable, BMI) .... 81
Funky Broadway (Drive-In/Routeen, BMI) .... 10
Get on Up (Hi-Mi, BMI) .... 35
Gettin' Together (Patricia, BMI) .... 24
Get Together (S.F.O., BMI) .... 70
Gimme Little Sign (Big Shot, ASCAP) .... 21
Groovin' (Slacsar, BMI) .... 26
Ha Ha Said the Clown (Ponderosa, BMI) .... 76
Happy (Unart, BMI) .... 50
Heroes and Villians (Sea of Tunes, BMI) .... 55
Hey Baby (They're Playing Our Song) (Diogenes/Bag of Tunes, BMI) .... 68
Hey Joe (Third Story, BMI) .... 94
How Can I Be Sure (Slacsar, BMI) .... 43
I Can't Stay Away From You (Chi-Sound, BMI) .... 83
I Dig Rock and Roll Music (Pepamar, ASCAP) .... 16
I Feel Good (I Feel Bad) (Screen Gems-Columbia, BMI) .... 64
I Had a Dream (Daywin, BMI) .... 19
I Make a Fool of Myself (Saturday/Seasons Four, BMI) .... 28
(I Wanna) Testify (Groovesville, BMI) .... 22
I Was Made to Love Her (Jobete, BMI) .... 44
I'll Never Fall in Love Again (Hollis, BMI) .... 77
In the Heat of the Night (United Artists, ASCAP) .... 49
It Could Be We're in Love (Destination, BMI) .... 91
It Must Be Him (Asa, ASCAP) .... 60
It's Got to Be Mellow (Jim-Edd, BMI) .... 82
It's the Little Things (Chris Marc/Cotillion, BMI) .... 74
Jill (Chardon, BMI) .... 52
Judy (Progressive/Presley/McDaniel, BMI) .... 88
Just Out of Reach (Of My Two Empty Arms) (Four Star, BMI) .... 66
Karate-Boo-Ga-Loo (Boogaloo/Love Lane, BMI) .... 99
Knock on Wood (East, BMI) .... 41
Knucklehead (East, BMI) .... 84
Laura (What's He Got That I Ain't Got?) (Gallico, BMI) .... 79
Let It Out (Crazy Cajun, BMI) .... 95
Let Love Come Between Us (Gallico, BMI) .... 62
Letter, The (Barton, BMI) .... 4
Light My Fire (Nipper, ASCAP) .... 18
Little Old Wine Drinker, Me (Moss-Rose, BMI) .... 38
Little Ole Man (Uptight-Everything's Alright) (Jobete, BMI) .... 32
Look of Love, The (Ponderosa, BMI) .... 63
Louisiana Man (Acuff-Rose, BMI) .... 98
Love Bug Leave My Heart Alone (Jobete, BMI) .... 30
Making Every Minute Count (Akbestal, BMI) .... 31
Memphis Soul Stew (Pronto/Kilynn, BMI) .... 47
Museum (Peer Int'l, BMI) .... 39
Never My Love (Temerlene, BMI) .... 15
Ode to Billie Joe (Shayne, ASCAP) .... 1
Our Song (Senta Cecilia, BMI) .... 92
Pleasant Valley Sunday (Screen Gems-Columbia, BMI) .... 25
Put Your Mind at Ease (Pocket Full of Tunes/Tobifun, BMI) .... 46
Reflections (Jobete, BMI) .... 2
Run, Run, Run (T. M., BMI) .... 53
San Franciscan Nights (Sealark/Slamine, BMI) .... 9
Silence Is Golden (Saturday/Geradium, BMI) .... 33
Soul Man (East/Pronto, BMI) .... 73
Spreadin' Honey (Neymen/Pure Soul, BMI) .... 93
Sunshine Games (Southern, ASCAP) .... 78
Sweet Soul Medley (Redwal/Jobete, BMI) .... 90
Take a Look (Eden, BMI) .... 71
Tell Him (Beechwood/Edgewater, BMI) .... 89
Thank the Lord for the Night Time (Tallyrand, BMI) .... 27
There Is a Mountain (Peer Int'l/Hi-Count, BMI) .... 11
There's Always Me (Gladys, ASCAP) .... 56
Things I Should Have Said (Trousdale, BMI) .... 23
Time Seller (Maribus, BMI) .... 100
To Sir With Love (Screen Gems-Columbia, BMI) .... 58
Turn on Your Love Light (Don, BMI) .... 85
Turn the World Around (Fingerlake, BMI) .... 69
Twelve Thirty (Wingate, ASCAP) .... 20
We Love You (Gideon, BMI) .... 86
Wednesday (Senjhil/Ronnigua, BMI) .... 97
What Now My Love (Remick, ASCAP) .... 67
Windows of the World, The (Jac/Blue Seas, ASCAP) .... 72
Words (Screen Gems-Columbia, BMI) .... 29
World We Knew, The (Over and Over) (Roosevelt, BMI) .... 37
You Keep Running (Jobete, BMI) .... 75
You Know What I Mean (Chardon, BMI) .... 13
(Your Love Keeps Lifting Me) Higher and Higher (Jalynne/BRC, BMI) .... 12
Your Precious Love (Jobete, BMI) .... 59
You're a Very Lovely Woman (Thirty Four/LaBres, ASCAP) .... 96
You're My Everything (Jobete, BMI) .... 6
You've Got to Pay the Price (Myto, BMI) .... 51
You've Made Me So Very Happy (Jobete, BMI) .... 80
Zip Code (Jetstar, BMI) .... 36

## BUBBLING UNDER THE HOT 100

101. WHY DO FOOLS FALL IN LOVE .... Happenings, B.T. Puppy 532
102. PEOPLE ARE STRANGE .... Doors, Elektra 45621
103. CHILD OF CLAY .... Jimmie Rodgers, A&M 871
104. HEAVY MUSIC .... Bob Seegar & Doug Brown, Cameo 494
105. SHE KNOWS .... Bobby Darin, Atlantic 2433
106. CAN'T STOP LOVING YOU .... Last Word, Atco 6498
107. DEVIL'S ANGELS .... Davis Allen, Tower 341
108. FOR ONCE IN MY LIFE .... Tony Bennett, Columbia 44258
109. PAPER SUN .... Traffic, Featuring Stevie Winwood, United Artists 50135
110. PURPLE HAZE .... Jimi Hendrix Experience, Reprise 0597
111. LAURA (What's He Got That I Ain't Got?) .... Brook Benton, Reprise 0611
112. DO SOMETHING TO ME .... ? (Question Mark) & the Mysterians, Cameo 496
113. I'LL RELEASE YOU .... Joann Bon & the Coquettes, MTA 129
114. EVERLASTING LOVE .... Robert Knight, Rising Sons 705
115. BLINDMAN .... Big Brother & the Holding Company, Mainstream 657
116. THE LAST WALTZ .... Engelbert Humperdinck, Parrot 40019
117. HUSH .... Billy Joe Royal, Columbia 44277
118. FOR WHAT IT'S WORTH .... Staple Singers, Epic 10220
119. NINE POUND STEEL .... Joe Simon, Sound Stage 7 2589
120. PEAS 'N' RICE .... Freddie McCoy, Prestige 450
121. BYE, BYE BABY .... Big Brother & the Holding Company, Mainstream 666
122. ON THE OTHER SIDE .... Seekers, Capitol 5974
123. THAT'S HOW STRONG MY LOVE IS .... Sweet Inspirations, Atlantic 2436
124. (I Love You Babe But) GIVE ME MY FREEDOM .... Glories, Date 1571
125. SOULSATION .... Capreez, Sound 149
126. I'M A FOOL FOR YOU .... James Carr, Coldwax 328
127. NEW ORLEANS .... Steve Alaimo, Atco 6512
128. RUNAWAY .... Del Shannon, Liberty 55993
129. BEG, BORROW & STEAL .... Ohio Express, Cameo 483
130. FUNKY DONKEY .... Pretty Purdie, Date 1568
131. KITTY DOYLE .... Dino, Desi & Billy, Reprise 0619
132. MORE THAN THE EYE CAN SEE .... Al Martino, Capitol 5989
133. YOU ONLY LIVE TWICE .... Nancy Sinatra, Reprise 0595
134. SEE EMILY PLAY .... Pink Floyd, Tower 356
135. THERE GOES THE LOVER .... Gene Chandler, Brunswick 55339

Compiled from national retail sales and radio station airplay by the Music Popularity Dept. of Record Market Research, Billboard.

# Billboard HOT 100

For Week Ending September 23, 1967

★ STAR performer—Sides registering greatest proportionate upward progress this week.

● Record Industry Association of America seal of certification as million selling single.

| This Week | 1 Wk. Ago | 2 Wks. Ago | 3 Wks. Ago | TITLE Artist (Producer), Label & Number | Weeks on Chart |
|---|---|---|---|---|---|
| ★1 | 4 | 5 | 15 | THE LETTER — Box Tops (Dan Penn), Mala 565 | 7 |
| 2 | 1 | 1 | 1 | ODE TO BILLIE JOE — Bobbie Gentry (Kelly Gordon & Bobby Paris), Capitol 5950 | 8 |
| 3 | 3 | 3 | 6 | COME BACK WHEN YOU GROW UP — Bobby Vee & the Strangers (Dallas Smith), Liberty 55964 | 10 |
| 4 | 2 | 2 | 3 | REFLECTIONS — Diana Ross & the Supremes (Holland & Dozier), Motown 1111 | 7 |
| ★5 | 15 | 25 | 59 | NEVER MY LOVE — Association (Bones Howe), Warner Bros. 7074 | 5 |
| 6 | 7 | 9 | 14 | APPLES, PEACHES, PUMPKIN PIE — Jay & the Techniques (Jerry Ross), Smash 2086 | 11 |
| ★7 | 12 | 19 | 27 | (Your Love Keeps Lifting Me) HIGHER AND HIGHER — Jackie Wilson (Carl Davis), Brunswick 55336 | 7 |
| 8 | 6 | 7 | 9 | YOU'RE MY EVERYTHING — Temptations (Norman Whitfield), Gordy 7063 | 9 |
| 9 | 16 | 26 | 38 | I DIG ROCK AND ROLL MUSIC — Peter, Paul & Mary (Albert B. Grossman & Milt Okun), Warner Bros. 7067 | 6 |
| 10 | 10 | 18 | 19 | FUNKY BROADWAY — Wilson Pickett (Jerry Wexler), Atlantic 2430 | 8 |
| 11 | 11 | 17 | 24 | THERE IS A MOUNTAIN — Donovan (Mickie Most), Epic 10212 | 7 |
| 12 | 5 | 4 | 5 | BABY I LOVE YOU — Aretha Franklin (Jerry Wexler), Atlantic 2427 | 10 |
| 13 | 13 | 16 | 28 | YOU KNOW WHAT I MEAN — Turtles (Joe Wissert), White Whale 254 | 8 |
| 14 | 14 | 14 | 22 | BROWN-EYED GIRL — Van Morrison (Bert Berns), Bang 545 | 11 |
| 15 | 9 | 10 | 25 | SAN FRANCISCAN NIGHTS — Eric Burdon and the Animals (Tom Wilson), MGM 13769 | 8 |
| 16 | 21 | 33 | 46 | GIMME LITTLE SIGN — Brenton Wood (Hooven-Winn), Double Shot 116 | 9 |
| 17 | 19 | 24 | 29 | I HAD A DREAM — Paul Revere & the Raiders with Mark Lindsay (Terry Melcher), Columbia 44227 | 6 |
| 18 | 32 | 55 | 71 | LITTLE OLE MAN (Uptight—Everything's Alright) — Bill Cosby (Fred Smith), Warner Bros. 7072 | 4 |
| 19 | 24 | 29 | 40 | GETTIN' TOGETHER — Tommy James & the Shondells (Bo Gentry / Ritchie Cordell), Roulette 4762 | 5 |
| 20 | 20 | 27 | 36 | TWELVE THIRTY — Mamas & the Papas (Lou Adler), Dunhill 4099 | 5 |
| 21 | 26 | 31 | 33 | GROOVIN' — Booker T. and the M.G.'s (Staff), Stax 224 | 8 |
| 22 | 28 | 43 | 70 | I MAKE A FOOL OF MYSELF — Frankie Valli (Bob Crewe), Philips 40484 | 4 |
| 23 | 23 | 28 | 37 | THINGS I SHOULD HAVE SAID — Grass Roots (Steve Barri & P. F. Sloan), Dunhill 4094 | 7 |
| 24 | 8 | 6 | 2 | ALL YOU NEED IS LOVE — Beatles (George Martin), Capitol 5964 | 10 |
| 25 | 30 | 39 | 58 | LOVE BUG LEAVE MY HEART ALONE — Martha Reeves & the Vandellas (Richard Morris), Gordy 7062 | 6 |
| 26 | 43 | 80 | — | HOW CAN I BE SURE — Young Rascals (Young Rascals), Atlantic 2438 | 3 |
| 27 | 34 | 48 | 72 | THE CAT IN THE WINDOW (The Bird in the Sky) — Petula Clark (Charles Koppelman & Don Rubin), Warner Bros. 7073 | 4 |
| 28 | 17 | 11 | 7 | COLD SWEAT — James Brown & the Famous Flames (James Brown), King 6110 | 11 |
| 29 | 42 | 75 | — | DANDELION — Rolling Stones (Andrew Loog Oldham), London 905 | 3 |
| 30 | 41 | 51 | 55 | KNOCK ON WOOD — Otis & Carla (Staff), Stax 228 | 7 |
| 31 | 31 | 41 | 51 | MAKING EVERY MINUTE COUNT — Spanky & Our Gang (Jerry Ross), Mercury 72714 | 7 |
| 32 | 18 | 8 | 4 | LIGHT MY FIRE — Doors (Paul A. Rothchild), Elektra 45615 | 17 |
| 33 | 35 | 47 | 57 | GET ON UP — Esquires (Bill Sheppard), Bunky 7750 | 6 |
| 34 | 45 | 61 | 83 | EXPRESSWAY TO YOUR HEART — Soul Survivors (Gamble-Huff), Crimson 1010 | 4 |
| 35 | 58 | 74 | — | TO SIR WITH LOVE — Lulu (Mickie Most), Epic 10187 | 3 |
| 36 | 47 | 57 | 75 | MEMPHIS SOUL STEW — King Curtis (Tommy Cogbill & King Curtis), Atco 6511 | 5 |
| 37 | 40 | 40 | 41 | BLUES THEME — Arrows (Mike Curb), Tower 295 | 16 |
| 38 | 49 | 59 | 76 | IN THE HEAT OF THE NIGHT — Ray Charles (TRC), ABC 10970 | 5 |
| 39 | 39 | 49 | 62 | MUSEUM — Herman's Hermits (Mickie Most), MGM 13787 | 4 |
| 40 | 25 | 13 | 8 | PLEASANT VALLEY SUNDAY — Monkees (Douglas Farthing Hatfield), Colgems 1007 | 10 |
| 41 | 27 | 13 | 13 | THANK THE LORD FOR THE NIGHT TIME — Neil Diamond (Jeff Barry & Ellie Greenwich), Bang 547 | 11 |
| 42 | 54 | 64 | 84 | BALLAD OF YOU & ME & POONEIL — Jefferson Airplane (Al Schmitt), RCA Victor 9297 | 4 |
| 43 | 48 | 60 | 61 | ANYTHING GOES — Harpers Bizarre (Lenny Waronker), Warner Bros. 7063 | 6 |
| 44 | 68 | 83 | — | HEY BABY (They're Playing Our Song) — Buckinghams (James William Guercio), Columbia 44254 | 3 |
| 45 | 75 | — | — | YOU KEEP RUNNING AWAY — Four Tops (Holland & Dozier), Motown 1113 | 2 |
| 46 | 46 | 56 | 64 | PUT YOUR MIND AT EASE — Every Mother's Son (Wes Farrell), MGM 13788 | 5 |
| 47 | 57 | 76 | — | A BANDA — Herb Alpert & the Tijuana Brass (Herb Alpert & Jerry Moss), A&M 870 | 3 |
| 48 | 59 | 73 | — | YOUR PRECIOUS LOVE — Marvin Gaye & Tammy Terrell (H. Fuqua-J. Bristol), Tamla 54156 | 3 |
| 49 | 60 | 72 | 80 | IT MUST BE HIM — Vikki Carr (Ed Silvers), Liberty 55986 | 4 |
| 50 | 51 | 53 | 60 | YOU'VE GOT TO PAY THE PRICE — Al Kent (Ed Wingate, Al Kent, H. Weems), Ric Tic 127 | 6 |
| 51 | 61 | 62 | 78 | CASONOVA (Your Playing Days Are Over) — Ruby Andrews (McGregor & Terry), Zodiac 1004 | 5 |
| 52 | 62 | 77 | — | LET LOVE COME BETWEEN US — James & Bobby Purify (Papa Don), Bell 685 | 3 |
| 53 | 53 | 63 | 63 | RUN, RUN, RUN — Third Rail (Levine/Resnick/Cooper), Epic 10191 | 8 |
| 54 | 67 | 82 | — | WHAT NOW MY LOVE — Mitch Ryder (Bob Crewe), DynoVoice 901 | 3 |
| 55 | 22 | 20 | 20 | (I Wanna) TESTIFY — Parliaments (George Clinton), Revilot 207 | 13 |
| 56 | 56 | 58 | 74 | THERE'S ALWAYS ME — Elvis Presley, RCA Victor 9287 | 5 |
| 57 | 38 | 38 | 49 | LITTLE OLD WINE DRINKER, ME — Dean Martin (Jimmy Bowen), Reprise 0608 | 6 |
| 58 | 36 | 42 | 42 | ZIP CODE — Five Americans (Dale Hawkins), Abnak 123 | 7 |
| 59 | 73 | 79 | — | SOUL MAN — Sam & Dave (Isaac Hayes & David Porter), Stax 231 | 3 |
| 60 | 71 | 71 | 82 | TAKE A LOOK — Aretha Franklin (Clyde Otis), Columbia 44270 | 4 |
| 61 | 77 | 84 | — | I'LL NEVER FALL IN LOVE AGAIN — Tom Jones (Peter Sullivan), Parrot 40018 | 3 |
| 62 | 63 | 68 | 96 | THE LOOK OF LOVE — Dusty Springfield (Johnny Franz), Philips 40465 | 7 |
| 63 | 52 | 54 | 56 | JILL — Gary Lewis & the Playboys (Koppelman/Rubin), Liberty 55985 | 7 |
| 64 | 86 | — | — | WE LOVE YOU — Rolling Stones (Andrew Loog Oldham), London 905 | 2 |
| 65 | — | — | — | PEOPLE ARE STRANGE — Doors (Paul Rothchild), Elektra 45621 | 1 |
| 66 | 66 | 67 | 79 | JUST OUT OF REACH (Of My Two Empty Arms) — Percy Sledge, Atlantic 2434 | 4 |
| 67 | — | — | — | CHILD OF CLAY — Jimmie Rodgers (Allen Stanton), A&M 871 | 1 |
| 68 | 69 | 70 | 85 | TURN THE WORLD AROUND — Eddy Arnold (Chet Atkins), RCA Victor 9265 | 6 |
| 69 | — | — | — | LIGHTNING'S GIRL — Nancy Sinatra (Lee Hazlewood), Reprise 0620 | 1 |
| 70 | 70 | 85 | 88 | GET TOGETHER — Youngbloods (Felix Pappalardi), RCA Victor 9264 | 4 |
| 71 | 82 | 86 | 89 | IT'S GOT TO BE MELLOW — Leon Haywood (Leon Haywood), Decca 32164 | 6 |
| 72 | 72 | 32 | 32 | THE WINDOWS OF THE WORLD — Dionne Warwick (Bacharach-David), Scepter 12196 | 9 |
| 73 | 78 | 93 | — | SUNSHINE GAMES — Music Explosion (Kasenetz/Katz/Chiprut), Laurie 3400 | 3 |
| 74 | 74 | 50 | 50 | IT'S THE LITTLE THINGS — Sonny & Cher (Sonny Bono), Atco 6507 | 6 |
| 75 | 80 | 81 | — | YOU'VE MADE ME SO VERY HAPPY — Brenda Holloway (Barry Gordy Jr.), Tamla 54155 | 3 |
| 76 | 84 | 87 | 87 | KNUCKLEHEAD — Bar-Kays (Staff), Volt 148 | 4 |
| 77 | — | — | — | ODE TO BILLIE JOE — Kingpins (Cogbill & Dowd), Atco 6516 | 1 |
| 78 | — | — | — | THE LAST WALTZ — Engelbert Humperdinck (Peter Sullivan), Parrot 40019 | 1 |
| 79 | — | — | — | WHY DO FOOLS FALL IN LOVE — Happenings (Tokens), B.T. Puppy 532 | 1 |
| 80 | 83 | 88 | 90 | I CAN'T STAY AWAY FROM YOU — Impressions (Johnny Pate), ABC 10964 | 3 |
| 81 | 81 | 96 | — | FORGET IT — Sandpebbles (Teddy Vann), Calla 134 | 3 |
| 82 | 88 | 89 | — | JUDY — Elvis Presley, RCA Victor 9287 | 3 |
| 83 | — | — | — | TO SHARE YOUR LOVE — Fantastic Four (Ed Wyngate & Al Kent), Ric Tic 130 | 1 |
| 84 | 87 | — | — | BABY, I'M LONELY — Intruders (Gamble-Huff), Gamble 207 | 2 |
| 85 | 91 | — | 86 | IT COULD BE WE'RE IN LOVE — Cryan' Shames (Jim Golden), Columbia 44191 | 7 |
| 86 | — | — | — | FOR WHAT IT'S WORTH — Staple Singers (Larry Williams), Epic 10220 | 1 |
| 87 | 89 | 90 | 91 | TELL HIM — Patti Drew (Carone), Capitol 5861 | 5 |
| 88 | — | — | — | MORE THAN THE EYE CAN SEE — Al Martino (Tom Morgan & Marvin Holtzman), Capitol 5989 | 1 |
| 89 | — | — | — | FALL IN LOVE WITH ME — Bettye Swann (Malynn), Money 129 | 1 |
| 90 | 95 | — | — | LET IT OUT — Hombres (Huey P. Meaux), Verve Forecast 5058 | 2 |
| 91 | 93 | 95 | — | SPREADIN' HONEY — Watts 103rd St. Rhythm Band (Fred Smith), Keymen 103 | 3 |
| 92 | — | — | — | DANCING IN THE STREET — Ramsey Lewis (Esmond Edwards), Cadet 5572 | 1 |
| 93 | — | — | — | DIRTY MAN — Laura Lee (Rick Hall), Chess 2013 | 1 |
| 94 | 96 | 99 | — | YOU'RE A VERY LOVELY WOMAN — Merry-Go-Round (Larry Marks), A&M 863 | 3 |
| 95 | — | — | 93 | PURPLE HAZE — Jimi Hendrix Experience (Yameta), Reprise 0597 | 3 |
| 96 | — | — | — | FUNKY DONKEY — Pretty Purdie (Dave Kapralik & Ken Williams), Date 1568 | 1 |
| 97 | 99 | — | — | KARATE-BOO-GA-LOO — Jerry O (Jerry Murray), Shout 217 | 2 |
| 98 | 98 | — | — | LOUISIANA MAN — Poso Seco Singers (Bob Johnston), Columbia 44263 | 2 |
| 99 | — | — | — | NINE POUND STEEL — Joe Simon (J.R. Enterprises, Inc.) Sound Stage 7 2589 | 1 |
| 100 | — | — | — | I'M A FOOL FOR YOU — James Carr (Quinton M. Claunch & Rudolph V. Russell), Goldwax 325 | 1 |

## BUBBLING UNDER THE HOT 100

101. INCENSE AND PEPPERMINTS — Strawberry Alarm Clock, Uni 55018
102. PLEASE LOVE ME FOREVER — Bobby Vinton, Epic 10228
103. HEAVY MUSIC — Bob Seeger & Doug Brown, Cameo 494
104. OUR SONG — Jack Jones, Kapp 847
105. TIME SELLER — Spencer Davis Group, United Artists 50202
106. CAN'T STOP LOVING YOU — Last Word, Atco 6498
107. I FEEL GOOD (I Feel Bad) — Lewis & Clark Expedition, Colgems 1006
108. FOR ONCE IN MY LIFE — Tony Bennett, Columbia 44258
109. LAURA (What's He Got That I Ain't Got) — Brook Benton, Reprise 0611
110. EVERLASTING LOVE — Robert Knight, Rising Sons 705
111. SWEET SOUL MEDLEY — Magnificent Men, Capitol 5976
112. I'LL RELEASE YOU — Joann Bon & the Coquettes, MTA 129
113. BLIND MAN — Big Brother & the Holding Company, Mainstream 657
114. BOOGALOO DOWN BROADWAY — The Fantastic Johnny C., Phil-L.A. of Soul 305
115. HUSH — Billy Joe Royal, Columbia 44277
116. WHAT'VE I DONE — Linda Jones, Loma 2077
117. EVEN THE BAD TIMES ARE GOOD — Tremeloes, Epic 10233
118. YOU MEAN THE WORLD TO ME — David Houston, Epic 10224
119. BANNED IN BOSTON — Sam the Sham & the Pharaohs, MGM 13803
120. PEAS 'N' RICE — Freddie McCoy, Prestige 450
121. ROCK 'N' ROLL WOMAN — Buffalo Springfield, Atco 6519
122. HARLEM SHUFFLE — Hollies, Imperial 66258
123. BEG, BORROW & STEAL — Ohio Express, Cameo 483
124. TEARS OF JOY — Glories, Date 1571
125. I LOVE YOU BABE BUT GIVE ME MY FREEDOM — Nancy Wilson, Capitol 5976
126. YOU ONLY LIVE TWICE — Nancy Sinatra, Reprise 0595
127. NEW ORLEANS — Steve Alaimo, Atco 6513
128. ODE TO BILLIE JOE — Ray Bryant, Cadet 5575
129. KITTY DOYLE — Dino, Desi & Billy, Reprise 0619
130. SEVEN DAYS TOO LONG — Chuck Wood, Roulette 4754
131. THE FROG — Sergio Mendes & Brasil '66, A&M 872
132. VISIT TO A SAD PLANET — Leonard Nimoy, Dot 17038
133. TEARS OF JOY — Glories, Date 16109
134. JUST HOLDING ON — P. J. Proby, Liberty 55990
135. WOULD YOU BELIEVE — Tempest, Smash 2094

# Billboard HOT 100

**For Week Ending September 30, 1967**

★ STAR performer—Sides registering greatest proportionate upward progress this week.

Record Industry Association of America seal of certification as million selling single.

| This Week | Last Week | 2 Wks. Ago | 3 Wks. Ago | TITLE, Artist (Producer), Label & Number | Weeks on Chart |
|---|---|---|---|---|---|
| 1 | 1 | 4 | 5 | THE LETTER — Box Tops (Dan Penn), Mala 565 | 8 |
| 2 | 2 | 1 | 1 | ODE TO BILLIE JOE — Bobbie Gentry (Kelly Gordon & Bobby Paris), Capitol 5950 | 9 |
| 3 | 5 | 15 | 25 | NEVER MY LOVE — Association (Bones Howe), Warner Bros. 7074 | 6 |
| 4 | 3 | 3 | 3 | COME BACK WHEN YOU GROW UP — Bobby Vee & the Strangers (Dallas Smith), Liberty 55964 | 11 |
| 5 | 4 | 2 | 2 | REFLECTIONS — Diana Ross & the Supremes (Holland & Dozier), Motown 1111 | 8 |
| 6 | 6 | 7 | 9 | APPLES, PEACHES, PUMPKIN PIE — Jay & the Techniques (Jerry Ross), Smash 2086 | 12 |
| 7 | 7 | 12 | 19 | (Your Love Keeps Lifting Me) HIGHER AND HIGHER — Jackie Wilson (Carl Davis), Brunswick 55336 | 8 |
| 8 | 10 | 10 | 18 | FUNKY BROADWAY — Wilson Pickett (Jerry Wexler), Atlantic 2430 | 9 |
| 9 | 9 | 16 | 26 | I DIG ROCK AND ROLL MUSIC — Peter, Paul & Mary (Albert B. Grossman & Milt Okun), Warner Bros. 7067 | 7 |
| 10 | 14 | 14 | 14 | BROWN-EYED GIRL — Van Morrison (Bert Berns), Bang 545 | 12 |
| 11 | 16 | 21 | 33 | GIMME LITTLE SIGN — Brenton Wood (Hooven-Winn), Double Shot 116 | 10 |
| 12 | 13 | 13 | 16 | YOU KNOW WHAT I MEAN — Turtles (Joe Wissert), White Whale 254 | 9 |
| 13 | 18 | 32 | 55 | LITTLE OLE MAN (Uptight—Everything's Alright) — Bill Cosby (Fred Smith), Warner Bros. 7072 | 5 |
| 14 | 26 | 43 | 80 | HOW CAN I BE SURE — Young Rascals (Young Rascals), Atlantic 2438 | 4 |
| 15 | 8 | 6 | 7 | YOU'RE MY EVERYTHING — Temptations (Norman Whitfield), Gordy 7063 | 10 |
| 16 | 11 | 11 | 17 | THERE IS A MOUNTAIN — Donovan (Mickie Most), Epic 10212 | 8 |
| 17 | 17 | 19 | 24 | I HAD A DREAM — Paul Revere & the Raiders with Mark Lindsay (Terry Melcher), Columbia 44227 | 7 |
| 18 | 19 | 24 | 29 | GETTIN' TOGETHER — Tommy James & the Shondells (Bo Gentry/Ritchie Cordell), Roulette 4762 | 7 |
| 19 | 22 | 28 | 43 | I MAKE A FOOL OF MYSELF — Frankie Valli (Bob Crewe), Philips 40484 | 5 |
| 20 | 29 | 42 | 75 | DANDELION — Rolling Stones (Andrew Loog Oldham), London 905 | 4 |
| 21 | 21 | 26 | 31 | GROOVIN' — Booker T. and the M.G.'s (Staff), Stax 224 | 9 |
| 22 | 35 | 58 | 74 | TO SIR WITH LOVE — Lulu (Mickie Most), Epic 10187 | 4 |
| 23 | 20 | 20 | 27 | TWELVE THIRTY — Mamas & the Papas (Lou Adler), Dunhill 4099 | 6 |
| 24 | 44 | 68 | 83 | HEY BABY (They're Playing Our Song) — Buckinghams (James William Guercio), Columbia 44254 | 4 |
| 25 | 25 | 30 | 39 | LOVE BUG LEAVE MY HEART ALONE — Martha Reeves & the Vandellas (Richard Morris), Gordy 7062 | 7 |
| 26 | 27 | 34 | 48 | THE CAT IN THE WINDOW (The Bird in the Sky) — Petula Clark (Charles Koppelman & Don Rubin), Warner Bros. 7073 | 5 |
| 27 | 33 | 35 | 47 | GET ON UP — Esquires (Bill Sheppard), Bunky 7750 | 7 |
| 28 | 34 | 45 | 61 | EXPRESSWAY TO YOUR HEART — Soul Survivors (Gamble-Huff), Crimson 1010 | 5 |
| 29 | 15 | 9 | 10 | SAN FRANCISCAN NIGHTS — Eric Burdon and the Animals (Tom Wilson), MGM 13769 | 7 |
| 30 | 30 | 41 | 51 | KNOCK ON WOOD — Otis & Carla (Staff), Stax 228 | 8 |
| 31 | 48 | 59 | 73 | YOUR PRECIOUS LOVE — Marvin Gaye & Tammy Terrell (H. Fuqua-J. Bristol), Tamla 54156 | 4 |
| 32 | 45 | 75 | — | YOU KEEP RUNNING AWAY — Four Tops (Holland & Dozier), Motown 1113 | 3 |
| 33 | 38 | 49 | 59 | IN THE HEAT OF THE NIGHT — Ray Charles (TRC), ABC 10970 | 6 |
| 34 | 28 | 17 | 11 | COLD SWEAT — James Brown & the Famous Flames (James Brown), King 6110 | 12 |
| 35 | 36 | 47 | 57 | MEMPHIS SOUL STEW — King Curtis (Tommy Coghill & King Curtis), Atco 6511 | 6 |
| 36 | 47 | 57 | 76 | A BANDA — Herb Alpert & the Tijuana Brass (Herb Alpert & Jerry Moss), A&M 870 | 4 |
| 37 | 54 | 67 | 82 | WHAT NOW MY LOVE — Mitch Ryder (Bob Crewe), DynoVoice 901 | 4 |
| 38 | 49 | 60 | 72 | IT MUST BE HIM — Vikki Carr (Dave Pell), Liberty 55986 | 5 |
| 39 | 31 | 31 | 41 | MAKING EVERY MINUTE COUNT — Spanky & Our Gang (Jerry Ross), Mercury 72714 | 8 |
| 40 | 59 | 73 | 79 | SOUL MAN — Sam & Dave (Isaac Hayes & David Porter), Stax 231 | 4 |
| 41 | 52 | 62 | 77 | LET LOVE COME BETWEEN US — James & Bobby Purify (Papa Don), Bell 685 | 4 |
| 42 | 42 | 54 | 64 | BALLAD OF YOU & ME & POONEIL — Jefferson Airplane (Al Schmitt), RCA Victor 9297 | 5 |
| 43 | 43 | 48 | 60 | ANYTHING GOES — Harpers Bizarre (Lenny Waronker), Warner Bros. 7063 | 7 |
| 44 | 65 | — | — | PEOPLE ARE STRANGE — Doors (Paul Rothchild), Elektra 45621 | 2 |
| 45 | 69 | — | — | LIGHTNING'S GIRL — Nancy Sinatra (Lee Hazlewood), Reprise 0620 | 2 |
| 46 | 46 | 46 | 56 | PUT YOUR MIND AT EASE — Every Mother's Son (Wes Farrell), MGM 13788 | 6 |
| 47 | 12 | 5 | 4 | BABY I LOVE YOU — Aretha Franklin (Jerry Wexler), Atlantic 2427 | 11 |
| 48 | 24 | 8 | 6 | ALL YOU NEED IS LOVE — Beatles (George Martin), Capitol 5964 | 11 |
| 49 | 50 | 51 | 53 | YOU'VE GOT TO PAY THE PRICE — Al Kent (Ed Wingate, Al Kent, H. Weems), Ric Tic 127 | 7 |
| 50 | 23 | 23 | 28 | THINGS I SHOULD HAVE SAID — Grass Roots (Steve Barri & P.F. Sloan), Dunhill 4094 | 8 |
| 51 | 64 | 86 | — | WE LOVE YOU — Rolling Stones (Andrew Loog Oldham), London 905 | 3 |
| 52 | 62 | 63 | 68 | THE LOOK OF LOVE — Dusty Springfield (Johnny Prenz), Philips 40465 | 8 |
| 53 | 51 | 61 | 62 | CASONOVA (Your Playing Days Are Over) — Ruby Andrews (McGregor & Terry), Zodiac 1004 | 6 |
| 54 | 37 | 40 | 40 | BLUES THEME — Arrows (Mike Curb), Tower 295 | 17 |
| 55 | 53 | 53 | 63 | RUN, RUN, RUN — Third Rail (Levine/Resnick/Cooper), Epic 10191 | 9 |
| 56 | 67 | — | — | CHILD OF CLAY — Jimmie Rodgers (Allen Stanton), A&M 871 | 2 |
| 57 | 77 | — | — | ODE TO BILLIE JOE — King Curtis & His Kingpins (Coghill & Dowd), Atco 6516 | 2 |
| 58 | 39 | 39 | 49 | MUSEUM — Herman's Hermits (Mickie Most), MGM 13787 | 6 |
| 59 | 78 | — | — | THE LAST WALTZ — Englebert Humperdinck (Peter Sullivan), Parrot 40019 | 2 |
| 60 | 60 | 71 | 71 | TAKE A LOOK — Aretha Franklin (Clyde Otis), Columbia 44270 | 5 |
| 61 | 61 | 77 | 84 | I'LL NEVER FALL IN LOVE AGAIN — Tom Jones (Peter Sullivan), Parrot 40018 | 4 |
| 62 | 56 | 56 | 58 | THERE'S ALWAYS ME — Elvis Presley, RCA Victor 9287 | 6 |
| 63 | 90 | 95 | — | LET IT OUT — Hombres (Huey P. Meaux), Verve Forecast 5058 | 3 |
| 64 | 79 | — | — | WHY DO FOOLS FALL IN LOVE — Happenings (Tokens), B.T. Puppy 532 | 2 |
| 65 | 73 | 78 | 93 | SUNSHINE GAMES — Music Explosion (Kasenetz/Katz/Chiprut), Laurie 3400 | 4 |
| 66 | 68 | 69 | 70 | TURN THE WORLD AROUND — Eddy Arnold (Chet Atkins), RCA Victor 9265 | 7 |
| 67 | 71 | 82 | 86 | IT'S GOT TO BE MELLOW — Leon Haywood (Stephen Haywood), Decca 32164 | 7 |
| 68 | 70 | 70 | 85 | GET TOGETHER — Youngbloods (Felix Pappalardi), RCA Victor 9264 | 5 |
| 69 | — | — | — | LOVE IS STRANGE — Peaches & Herb (David Kapralik & Ken Williams), Date 1574 | 1 |
| 70 | — | — | — | A NATURAL WOMAN — Aretha Franklin (Jerry Wexler), Atlantic 2441 | 1 |
| 71 | — | — | — | ROCK 'N' ROLL WOMAN — Buffalo Springfield (Stephen Stills & Neil Young), Atco 6519 | 1 |
| 72 | — | — | — | PLEASE LOVE ME FOREVER — Bobby Vinton (Billy Sherrill), Epic 10228 | 1 |
| 73 | 88 | — | — | MORE THAN THE EYE CAN SEE — Al Martino (Tom Morgan & Marvin Holtzman), Capitol 5989 | 2 |
| 74 | 75 | 80 | 81 | YOU'VE MADE ME SO VERY HAPPY — Brenda Holloway (Berry Gordy Jr.), Tamla 54155 | 4 |
| 75 | 84 | 87 | — | BABY, I'M LONELY — Intruders (Gamble-Huff), Gamble 237 | 3 |
| 76 | 95 | — | — | PURPLE HAZE — Jimi Hendrix Experience (Yameta), Reprise 0597 | 4 |
| 77 | 89 | — | — | FALL IN LOVE WITH ME — Bettye Swann (Malynn), Money 129 | 2 |
| 78 | 82 | 88 | 89 | JUDY — Elvis Presley, RCA Victor 9287 | 4 |
| 79 | 86 | — | — | FOR WHAT IT'S WORTH — Staple Singers (Larry Williams), Epic 10220 | 2 |
| 80 | 83 | — | — | TO SHARE YOUR LOVE — Fantastic Four (Ed Wyngate & Al Kent), Ric Tic 130 | 2 |
| 81 | — | — | — | EVEN THE BAD TIMES ARE GOOD — Tremeloes (Mike Smith), Epic 10233 | 1 |
| 82 | — | — | — | JUST ONE LOOK — Hollies, Imperial 56258 | 1 |
| 83 | — | — | — | EVERLASTING LOVE — Robert Knight (Buzz Cason & Mac Gayden), Rising Sons 117 | 1 |
| 84 | — | — | — | HOLIDAY — Bee Gees (Robert Stigwood), Atco 6521 | 1 |
| 85 | 85 | 91 | — | IT COULD BE WE'RE IN LOVE — Cryan' Shames (Jim Golden), Columbia 44191 | 8 |
| 86 | 92 | — | — | DANCING IN THE STREET — Ramsey Lewis (Esmond Edwards), Cadet 5572 | 2 |
| 87 | 87 | 89 | 90 | TELL HIM — Patti Drew (Carone), Capitol 5861 | 6 |
| 88 | — | — | — | INCENSE AND PEPPERMINTS — Strawberry Alarm Clock (Frank Slay), Uni 55018 | 1 |
| 89 | 91 | 93 | 95 | SPREADIN' HONEY — Watts 103rd St. Rhythm Band (Fred Smith), Keymen 103 | 4 |
| 90 | — | — | — | THE RAIN, THE PARK & OTHER THINGS — Cowsills (Artie Kornfeld), MGM 13810 | 1 |
| 91 | — | — | — | HUSH — Billy Joe Royal (Joe South), Columbia 44277 | 1 |
| 92 | 93 | — | — | DIRTY MAN — Laura Lee (Rick Hall), Chess 2013 | 2 |
| 93 | — | — | — | WHAT'VE I DONE (To Make You Mad) — Linda Jones (George Kerr), Loma 2077 | 1 |
| 94 | — | — | — | ODE TO BILLIE JOE — Ray Bryant (R. Evans), Cadet 5575 | 1 |
| 95 | — | — | — | STRANDED IN THE MIDDLE OF NO PLACE — Righteous Brothers (Mickey Stevenson), Verve 10551 | 1 |
| 96 | 96 | — | — | FUNKY DONKEY — Pretty Purdie (Dave Kapralik & Ken Williams), Date 1568 | 2 |
| 97 | 98 | 98 | — | LOUISIANA MAN — Peso Seco Singers (Bob Johnston), Columbia 44263 | 3 |
| 98 | 99 | — | — | NINE POUND STEEL — Joe Simon (J.R. Enterprises, Inc.), Sound Stage 7 2509 | 2 |
| 99 | 100 | — | — | I'M A FOOL FOR YOU — James Carr (Quinton M. Claunch & Rudolph V. Russell), Goldwax 328 | 2 |
| 100 | — | — | — | WHEN THE SNOW IS ON THE ROSES — Ed Ames (Jim Foglesong), RCA Victor 9319 | 1 |

## HOT 100—A TO Z—(Publisher-Licensee)

A Banda (Permata, ASCAP)............36
All You Need Is Love (Maclen, BMI)...48
Anything Goes (Harms, ASCAP)......43
Apples, Peaches, Pumpkin Pie (Akbestal/Act Three, BMI)...6
Baby I Love You (Pronto, BMI)........47
Baby, I'm Lonely (Razor Sharp, BMI)..75
Ballad of You & Me & Pooneil (Jefferson Airplane, BMI)...42
Blues Theme (Dijon, BMI)................54
Brown-Eyed Girl (Web IV, BMI)........10
Casanova (Your Playing Days Are Over) (RicWil/Colfam, BMI)...53
Cat in the Window, The (The Bird in the Sky) (Chardon, BMI)...26
Child of Clay (Maresca, ASCAP).......56
Cold Sweat (Dynatone, BMI)............34
Come Back When You Grow Up (Painted Desert, BMI)....4
Dancing in the Street (Jobete, BMI)...86
Dandelion (Gideon, BMI)....................20
Dirty Man (Chevis, BMI).....................92
Even the Bad Times Are Good (Ponderosa, BMI)...81
Everlasting Love (Rising Sons, BMI)...83
Expressway to Your Heart (Double Diamond/Downstairs, BMI)...28
Fall in Love With Me (Money, BMI)...77
For What It's Worth (Ten East/Cotillion)...79
Funky Broadway (Drive-In/Routeen, BMI)...8
Funky Donkey (Purdie, BMI)..............96
Get on Up (Hi-Mi, BMI)......................27
Get Together (S.F.O., BMI)................68
Gettin' Together (Patricia, BMI).........18
Gimme Little Sign (Big Shot, ASCAP)..11
Groovin' (Slacsar, BMI)......................21
Hey Baby (They're Playing Our Song) (Diogenes, BMI)...24
Holiday (Nemperor, BMI)...................84

How Can I Be Sure (Slacsar, BMI)...14
Hush (Lowery, BMI)............................91
I Dig Rock and Roll Music (Pepamar, ASCAP)...9
I Had a Dream (Daywin, BMI)..........17
I Make a Fool of Myself (Saturday/Seasons Four, BMI)...19
I'll Never Fall in Love Again (Hollis, ASCAP)...61
I'm a Fool for You (Rise/Aim, BMI)..99
In the Heat of the Night (United Artists, ASCAP)...33
Incense and Peppermints (Claridge, ASCAP)...88
It Could Be We're in Love (Destination, BMI)...85
It Must Be Him (Asa, ASCAP)..........38
It's Got to Be Mellow (Jim-Edd, BMI)...67
Judy (Progressive/Presley/McDaniel, BMI)...78
Just One Look (Premier Albums, BMI)...82
Knock on Wood (East, BMI)..............30
Last Waltz, The (Donna, ASCAP)......59
Let It Out (Crazy Cajun, BMI)..........63
Let Love Come Between Us (Gallico, BMI)...41
Letter, The (Barton, BMI)..................1
Lightning's Girl (Hazlewood, ASCAP)...45
Little Ole Man (Uptight-Everything's Alright) (Jobete, BMI)...13
Look of Love, The (Ponderosa, BMI)..52
Louisiana Man (Acuff-Rose, BMI)....97
Love Bug Leave My Heart Alone (Jobete, BMI)...25
Love Is Strange (Ben Ghazi, BMI)...69
Making Every Minute Count (Akbestal, BMI)...39
Memphis Soul Stew (Pronto/Kilynn, BMI)...35
More Than the Eye Can See (Pronto, BMI)...73
Museum (Peer Int'l, BMI)..................58
Natural Woman, A (Screen Gems-Columbia, BMI)...70
Never My Love (Tamerlane, BMI)...3
Nine Pound Steel (Cape Ann, BMI)...98
Ode to Billie Joe (Shayne, BMI)......2
Ode to Billie Joe (Ray Bryant) (Shayne, BMI)...94
Ode to Billie Joe (Kingpins) (Shayne, BMI)...57
People Are Strange (Nipper, ASCAP)..44

Please Love Me Forever (Selma, BMI)...72
Purple Haze (Sea-Lark, BMI)............76
Put Your Mind at Ease (Pocket Full of Tunes/Tobitun, BMI)...46
Rain, the Park & Other Things, The (Akbestal/Luvlin, BMI)...90
Reflections (Jobete, BMI)...................5
Rock 'n' Roll Woman (Ten-East/Springalo/Cotillion, BMI)...71
Run, Run, Run (T. M., BMI)..............55
San Franciscan Nights (Sealark/Slamina, BMI)...29
Soul Man (East/Pronto, BMI).............40
Spreadin' Honey (Neymen/Pure Soul, BMI)...89
Stranded in the Middle of No Place (Mikim, BMI)...95
Sunshine Games (Southern, ASCAP)...65
Take a Look (Eden, BMI)...................60
Tell Him (Beechwood/Edgewater, BMI)...87
There Is a Mountain (Peer Int'l/Hi-Count, BMI)...16
There's Always Me (Gladys, ASCAP)..62
Things I Should Have Said (Trousdale, BMI)...50
To Share Your Love (Jobete, BMI)...80
To Sir With Love (Screen Gems-Columbia, BMI)...22
Turn the World Around (Fingerlake, BMI)...66
Twelve Thirty (Wingate, ASCAP)......23
We Love You (Gideon, BMI)..............51
What Now My Love (Remick, ASCAP)..37
What've I Done (To Make You Mad) (Ziro/Flotron, BMI)...93
When the Snow Is on the Roses (Miller, ASCAP)...100
Why Do Fools Fall in Love (Patricia, BMI)...64
You Keep Running Away (Jobete, BMI)...32
You Know What I Mean (Chardon, BMI)...12
(Your Love Keeps Lifting Me) Higher and Higher (Jalynne/BRC, BMI)...7
Your Precious Love (Jobete, BMI).....31
You're My Everything (Jobete, BMI)..15
You've Got to Pay the Price (Myto, BMI)...49
You've Made Me So Very Happy (Jobete, BMI)...74

## BUBBLING UNDER THE HOT 100

101. WALKIN' PROUD...........Pete Klint Quintet, Mercury 72709
102. TIME SELLER..............Spencer Davis Group, United Artists 50202
103. OUR SONG..................Jack Jones, Kapp 847
104. CAN'T STOP LOVING YOU........Last Word, Atco 6498
105. YOU MEAN THE WORLD TO ME.....David Houston, Epic 10224
106. HEAVY MUSIC.............Bob Seeger & Doug Brown, Cameo 494
107. YOU'RE A VERY LOVELY WOMAN...Merry-Go-Round, A&M 863
108. LAURA (WHAT'S HE GOT THAT I AIN'T GOT)..Brook Benton, Reprise 0611
109. SWEET SOUL MEDLEY.........Magnificent Men, Capitol 5976
110. BOOGALOO DOWN BROADWAY....Johnny C. Phil-L.A. of Soul 305
111. IF THIS IS LOVE (I'D RATHER BE LONELY)..Precisions, Drew 1003
112. I'LL RELEASE YOU.........Joann Bon & the Coquettes, MTA 129
113. BLIND MAN...............Big Brother & the Holding Company, Mainstream 657
114. SOMETIMES SHE'S A LITTLE GIRL...Tommy Boyce & Bobby Hart, A&M 874
115. KITTY DOYLE..............Dino, Desi & Billy, Reprise 0619
116. NEXT PLANE TO LONDON.....Rose Garden, Atco 6510
117. BANNED IN BOSTON.........Sam the Sham & the Pharaohs, MGM 13803
118. YOU, NO ONE BUT YOU....Frankie Laine, ABC 10983
119. PEAS 'N' RICE............Freddie McCoy, Prestige 450
120. BYE, BYE BABY...........Big Brother & the Holding Company, Mainstream 666
121. BEG, BORROW & STEAL.....Ohio Express, Cameo 483
122. PATA PATA................Miriam Makeba, Reprise 0606
123. RUNAWAY..................Del Shannon, Shout 217
124. KARATE BO-GA-LOO........Jerry O, Shout 217
125. SUZANNE..................Noel Harrison, Reprise 0615
126. SEVEN DAYS TOO LONG....Noel Harrison, Reprise 0615
127. WOULD YOU BELIEVE......Tempest, Smash 2094
128. THE FROG................Gean & Debbe, TRX 5002
129. JUST HOLDING ON........Sergio Mendes & Brasil '66, A&M 872
130. GO WITH ME..............P.J. Proby, Liberty 55989
131. TEARS OF JOY............Vikki Anderson, King 16109
132. HEART BE STILL..........Lorraine Ellison, Loma 2074
133. TWO HEADS...............Jefferson Airplane, RCA Victor 9297
134. IT'S ALL IN THE GAME....Jackie De Shannon, Imperial 66251
135. BEEN SO NICE............Righteous Brothers, Verve 10551

*Compiled from national retail sales and radio station airplay by the Music Popularity Dept. of Record Market Research, Billboard.*

# Billboard HOT 100

For Week Ending October 7, 1967

★ STAR performer—Sides registering greatest proportionate upward progress this week.

● Record Industry Association of America seal of certification as million selling single.

| This Week | Wk. Ago | 2 Wks. Ago | 3 Wks. Ago | TITLE Artist (Producer), Label & Number | Weeks On Chart |
|---|---|---|---|---|---|
| 1 | 1 | 1 | 4 | **THE LETTER** — Box Tops (Dan Penn), Mala 565 | 9 ● |
| 2 ★ | 3 | 5 | 15 | **NEVER MY LOVE** — Association (Bones Howe), Warner Bros. 7074 | 7 |
| 3 ● | 2 | 2 | 1 | **ODE TO BILLIE JOE** — Bobbie Gentry (Kelly Gordon & Bobby Paris), Capitol 5950 | 10 ● |
| 4 | 4 | 3 | 3 | **COME BACK WHEN YOU GROW UP** — Bobby Vee & the Strangers (Dallas Smith), Liberty 55964 | 12 |
| 5 ★ | 13 | 18 | 32 | **LITTLE OLE MAN (Uptight—Everything's Alright)** — Bill Cosby (Fred Smith), Warner Bros. 7072 | 6 |
| 6 | 7 | 7 | 12 | **(Your Love Keeps Lifting Me) HIGHER AND HIGHER** — Jackie Wilson (Carl Davis), Brunswick 55336 | 9 |
| 7 | 5 | 4 | 2 | **REFLECTIONS** — Diana Ross & the Supremes (Holland & Dozier), Motown 1111 | 9 |
| 8 | 6 | 6 | 7 | **APPLES, PEACHES, PUMPKIN PIE** — Jay & the Techniques (Jerry Ross), Smash 2086 | 13 |
| 9 ★ | 14 | 26 | 43 | **HOW CAN I BE SURE** — Young Rascals (Young Rascals), Atlantic 2438 | 5 |
| 10 | 11 | 16 | 21 | **GIMME LITTLE SIGN** — Brenton Wood (Hooven-Winn), Double Shot 116 | 11 |
| 11 ★ | 22 | 35 | 58 | **TO SIR, WITH LOVE** — Lulu (Mickie Most), Epic 10187 | 5 |
| 12 | 9 | 9 | 16 | **I DIG ROCK AND ROLL MUSIC** — Peter, Paul & Mary (Albert B. Grossman & Milt Okun), Warner Bros. 7067 | 8 |
| 13 | 10 | 14 | 14 | **BROWN-EYED GIRL** — Van Morrison (Bert Berns), Bang 545 | 13 |
| 14 | 8 | 10 | 10 | **FUNKY BROADWAY** — Wilson Pickett (Jerry Wexler), Atlantic 2430 | 10 |
| 15 | 20 | 29 | 42 | **DANDELION** — Rolling Stones (Andrew Loog Oldham), London 905 | 5 |
| 16 ★ | 27 | 33 | 35 | **GET ON UP** — Esquires (Bill Sheppard), Bunky 7750 | 8 |
| 17 | 28 | 34 | 45 | **EXPRESSWAY TO YOUR HEART** — Soul Survivors (Gamble-Huff), Crimson 1010 | 6 |
| 18 | 19 | 22 | 28 | **I MAKE A FOOL OF MYSELF** — Frankie Valli (Bob Crewe), Philips 40484 | 7 |
| 19 | 24 | 44 | 68 | **HEY BABY (They're Playing Our Song)** — Buckinghams (James William Guercio), Columbia 44254 | 5 |
| 20 ★ | 40 | 59 | 73 | **SOUL MAN** — Sam & Dave (Isaac Hayes & David Porter), Stax 231 | |
| 21 | 21 | 21 | 26 | **GROOVIN'** — Booker T. and the M.G.'s (Staff), Stax 224 | 10 |
| 22 | 12 | 13 | 13 | **YOU KNOW WHAT I MEAN** — Turtles (Joe Wissert), White Whale 254 | 10 |
| 23 | 31 | 48 | 59 | **YOUR PRECIOUS LOVE** — Marvin Gaye & Tammy Terrell (H. Fuqua-J. Bristol), Tamla 54156 | 5 |
| 24 ★ | 32 | 45 | 75 | **YOU KEEP RUNNING AWAY** — Four Tops (Holland & Dozier), Motown 1113 | 4 |
| 25 | 25 | 25 | 30 | **LOVE BUG LEAVE MY HEART ALONE** — Martha Reeves & the Vandellas (Richard Morris), Gordy 7062 | 8 |
| 26 | 26 | 27 | 34 | **THE CAT IN THE WINDOW (The Bird in the Sky)** — Petula Clark (Charles Koppelman & Don Rubin), Warner Bros. 7073 | 6 |
| 27 | 15 | 8 | 6 | **YOU'RE MY EVERYTHING** — Temptations (Norman Whitfield), Gordy 7063 | 11 |
| 28 | 18 | 19 | 24 | **GETTIN' TOGETHER** — Tommy James & the Shondells (Bo Gentry/Ritchie Cordell), Roulette 4762 | 7 |
| 29 | 38 | 49 | 60 | **IT MUST BE HIM** — Vikki Carr (Dave Pell), Liberty 55986 | 6 |
| 30 | 37 | 54 | 67 | **WHAT NOW MY LOVE** — Mitch Ryder (Bob Crewe), DynoVoice 901 | 5 |
| 31 ★ | 41 | 52 | 62 | **LET LOVE COME BETWEEN US** — James & Bobby Purify (Papa Don), Bell 685 | 5 |
| 32 ★ | 44 | 65 | — | **PEOPLE ARE STRANGE** — Doors (Paul Rothchild), Elektra 45621 | 3 |
| 33 ★ | 45 | 69 | — | **LIGHTNING'S GIRL** — Nancy Sinatra (Lee Hazlewood), Reprise 0620 | 3 |
| 34 | 35 | 36 | 47 | **MEMPHIS SOUL STEW** — King Curtis (Tommy Cogbill & King Curtis), Atco 6511 | 7 |
| 35 | 33 | 38 | 49 | **IN THE HEAT OF THE NIGHT** — Ray Charles (TRC), ABC 10970 | 7 |
| 36 | 36 | 47 | 57 | **A BANDA** — Herb Alpert & the Tijuana Brass (Herb Alpert & Jerry Moss), A&M 870 | 6 |
| 37 | 29 | 15 | 9 | **SAN FRANCISCAN NIGHTS** — Eric Burdon and the Animals (Tom Wilson), MGM 13769 | 10 |
| 38 ★ | 70 | — | — | **NATURAL WOMAN** — Aretha Franklin (Jerry Wexler), Atlantic 2441 | 2 |
| 39 | 57 | 77 | — | **ODE TO BILLIE JOE** — King Curtis & his Kingpins (Cogbill & Dowd), Atco 6516 | 3 |
| 40 ★ | 63 | 90 | 95 | **LET IT OUT** — Hombres (Huey P. Meaux), Verve Forecast 5058 | 4 |
| 41 | 52 | 62 | 63 | **THE LOOK OF LOVE** — Dusty Springfield (Johnny Prenz), Philips 40465 | 9 |
| 42 ★ | 56 | 67 | — | **CHILD OF CLAY** — Jimmie Rodgers (Allen Stanton), A&M 871 | 3 |
| 43 | 43 | 43 | 48 | **ANYTHING GOES** — Harpers Bizarre (Lenny Waronker), Warner Bros. 7063 | 8 |
| 44 | 17 | 17 | 19 | **I HAD A DREAM** — Paul Revere & the Raiders with Mark Lindsay (Terry Melcher), Columbia 44227 | 8 |
| 45 | 16 | 11 | 11 | **THERE IS A MOUNTAIN** — Donovan (Mickie Most), Epic 10212 | 9 |
| 46 | 30 | 30 | 41 | **KNOCK ON WOOD** — Otis & Carla (Staff), Stax 228 | |
| 47 | 42 | 42 | 54 | **BALLAD OF YOU & ME & POONEIL** — Jefferson Airplane (Al Schmitt), RCA Victor 9297 | 6 |
| 48 ★ | 59 | 78 | — | **THE LAST WALTZ** — Englebert Humperdinck (Peter Sullivan), Parrot 40019 | 3 |
| 49 | 49 | 50 | 51 | **YOU'VE GOT TO PAY THE PRICE** — Al Kent (Ed Wingate, Al Kent, H. Weems), Ric Tic 127 | 8 |
| 50 | 51 | 64 | 86 | **WE LOVE YOU** — Rolling Stones (Andrew Loog Oldham), London 905 | 4 |
| 51 ★ | 72 | — | — | **PLEASE LOVE ME FOREVER** — Bobby Vinton (Billy Sherrill), Epic 10228 | 2 |
| 52 | 69 | — | — | **LOVE IS STRANGE** — Peaches & Herb (David Kapralik & Ken Williams), Date 1574 | 2 |
| 53 | 53 | 51 | 61 | **CASONOVA (Your Playing Days Are Over)** — Ruby Andrews (McGregor & Terry), Zodiac 1004 | 7 |
| 54 ★ | 64 | 79 | — | **WHY DO FOOLS FALL IN LOVE** — Happenings (Tokens), B.T. Puppy 532 | 3 |
| 55 | 46 | 46 | 46 | **PUT YOUR MIND AT EASE** — Every Mother's Son (Wes Farrell), MGM 13788 | 7 |
| 56 | 61 | 61 | 77 | **I'LL NEVER FALL IN LOVE AGAIN** — Tom Jones (Peter Sullivan), Parrot 40018 | 6 |
| 57 | 60 | 60 | 71 | **TAKE A LOOK** — Aretha Franklin (Clyde Otis), Columbia 44270 | 6 |
| 58 ★ | 84 | — | — | **HOLIDAY** — Bee Gees (Robert Stigwood), Atco 6521 | 2 |
| 59 ★ | 88 | — | — | **INCENSE AND PEPPERMINTS** — Strawberry Alarm Clock (Frank Slay), Uni 55018 | 2 |
| 60 ★ | 81 | — | — | **EVEN THE BAD TIMES ARE GOOD** — Tremeloes (Mike Smith), Epic 10233 | |
| 61 | — | — | — | **I'M WONDERING** — Stevie Wonder (Henry Cosby), Tamla 54157 | 1 |
| 62 | 90 | — | — | **THE RAIN, THE PARK & OTHER THINGS** — Cowsills (Artie Kornfeld), MGM 13810 | 2 |
| 63 | 65 | 73 | 78 | **SUNSHINE GAMES** — Music Explosion (Kasenetz/Katz/Chiprut), Laurie 3400 | 5 |
| 64 | 67 | 71 | 82 | **IT'S GOT TO BE MELLOW** — Leon Haywood (Leon Haywood), Decca 32164 | 8 |
| 65 | 73 | 88 | — | **MORE THAN THE EYE CAN SEE** — Al Martino (Tom Morgan & Marvin Holtzman), Capitol 5989 | |
| 66 | 79 | 86 | — | **FOR WHAT IT'S WORTH** — Staple Singers (Larry Williams), Epic 10220 | 3 |
| 67 | 68 | 70 | 70 | **GET TOGETHER** — Youngbloods (Felix Pappalardi), RCA Victor 9264 | 6 |
| 68 ★ | 83 | — | — | **EVERLASTING LOVE** — Robert Knight (Buzz Cason & King Curtis), Rising Sons 117 | |
| 69 | 71 | — | — | **ROCK 'N' ROLL WOMAN** — Buffalo Springfield (Stephen Stills & Neil Young), Atco 6519 | 2 |
| 70 | 66 | 68 | 69 | **TURN THE WORLD AROUND** — Eddy Arnold (Chet Atkins), RCA Victor 9265 | 8 |
| 71 | 74 | 75 | 80 | **YOU'VE MADE ME SO VERY HAPPY** — Brenda Holloway (Berry Gordy Jr.), Tamla 54155 | 5 |
| 72 | 76 | 95 | — | **PURPLE HAZE** — Jimi Hendrix Experience (Yameta), Reprise 0597 | 5 |
| 73 ★ | — | — | — | **KING MIDAS IN REVERSE** — Hollies (Ron Richards), Epic 10234 | 1 |
| 74 | 77 | 89 | — | **FALL IN LOVE WITH ME** — Bettye Swann (Malynn), Money 129 | 3 |
| 75 | 75 | 84 | 87 | **BABY, I'M LONELY** — Intruders (Gamble-Huff), Gamble 207 | 4 |
| 76 | 80 | 83 | — | **TO SHARE YOUR LOVE** — Fantastic Four (Ed Wyngate & Al Kent), Ric Tic 130 | |
| 77 ★ | 95 | — | — | **STRANDED IN THE MIDDLE OF NO PLACE** — Righteous Brothers (Mickey Stevenson), Verve 10551 | 2 |
| 78 | 78 | 82 | 88 | **JUDY** — Elvis Presley, RCA Victor 9287 | 5 |
| 79 | — | — | — | **IF THIS IS LOVE (I'd Rather Be Lonely)** — Precisions (Coleman-Bassoline-Val Vale), Drew 1003 | 1 |
| 80 | 82 | — | — | **JUST ONE LOOK** — Hollies, Imperial 66258 | 2 |
| 81 | — | — | — | **SHOUT BAMALAMA** — Mickey Murray (Bobby Smith), 555715 | 1 |
| 82 | 91 | — | — | **HUSH** — Billy Joe Royal (Joe South), Columbia 44277 | 2 |
| 83 | 89 | 91 | 93 | **SPREADIN' HONEY** — Watts 103rd St. Rhythm Band (Fred Smith), Keymen 103 | 5 |
| 84 | 92 | 93 | — | **DIRTY MAN** — Laura Lee (Rick Hall), Chess 2013 | |
| 85 | 86 | 92 | — | **DANCING IN THE STREET** — Ramsey Lewis (Esmond Edwards), Cadet 5572 | 3 |
| 86 | 87 | 87 | 89 | **TELL HIM** — Patti Drew (Carone), Capitol 5861 | 7 |
| 87 | 96 | 96 | — | **FUNKY DONKEY** — Pretty Purdie (Dave Kapralik & Ken Williams), Date 1568 | |
| 88 | 98 | 99 | — | **NINE POUND STEEL** — Joe Simon (J.R. Enterprises, Inc.), Sound Stage 7 2589 | |
| 89 | 94 | — | — | **ODE TO BILLIE JOE** — Ray Bryant (R. Evans), Cadet 5575 | 2 |
| 90 | 93 | — | — | **WHAT'VE I DONE (To Make You Mad)** — Linda Jones (George Kerr), Loma 2077 | 2 |
| 91 | — | — | — | **HEART BE STILL** — Lorraine Ellison (Jerry Racovey), Loma 2074 | 1 |
| 92 | — | — | — | **PEAS 'N' RICE** — Freddie McCoy (Cal Lampley), Prestige 450 | 1 |
| 93 | — | — | — | **PATA PATA** — Miriam Makeba (Jerry Ragovoy), Reprise 0606 | 1 |
| 94 | — | — | — | **BOOGALOO DOWN BROADWAY** — Fantastic Johnny C. (Jesse James), Phil-L.A. of Soul 305 | |
| 95 | — | — | — | **YOU, NO ONE BUT YOU** — Frankie Laine (Bob Thiele), ABC 10983 | |
| 96 | — | — | — | **BEG, BORROW AND STEAL** — Ohio Express (J. Katz & J. Kasemetz), Cameo 483 | |
| 97 | 99 | 100 | — | **I'M A FOOL FOR YOU** — James Carr (Quinton M. Clauch & Rudolph V. Russell), Goldwax 328 | 3 |
| 98 | 100 | — | — | **WHEN THE SNOW IS ON THE ROSES** — Ed Ames (Jim Foglesong), RCA Victor 9319 | 2 |
| 99 | — | — | — | **WALKIN' PROUD** — Pete Klint Quintet, Mercury 72709 | 1 |
| 100 | — | — | — | **YOU MEAN THE WORLD TO ME** — David Houston (Billy Sherrill), Epic 10224 | |

## BUBBLING UNDER THE HOT 100

101. (LONELINESS MADE ME REALIZE) IT'S YOU THAT I NEED .......... Temptations, Gordy 7065
102. THE SELLER .......... Spencer Davis Group, United Artists 50202
103. CAN'T STOP LOVING YOU .......... Last Word, Atco 6498
104. LOUISIANA MAN .......... Pozo Seco Singers, Columbia 44263
105. I'LL RELEASE YOU .......... Joann Bon & the Coquettes, MTA 129
106. AS LONG AS YOU'RE HERE .......... Zal Yanowsky (Zally), Kama Sutra 239
107. KARATE BOO-GA-LOO .......... Jerry O., Shout 217
108. I CAN SEE FOR MILES .......... Who, Decca 32206
109. KITTY DOYLE .......... Dino, Desi & Billy, Reprise 0619
110. BLIND MEN .......... Big Brother & the Holding Company, Mainstream 657
111. REFLECTIONS OF CHARLES BROWN .......... Rupert's People, Bell 654
112. SOMETIMES SHE'S A LITTLE GIRL .......... Tommy Boyce & Bobby Hart, A&M 874
113. GET DOWN .......... Harvey Scales & the Seven Sounds, Magic Touch 2007
114. LOVEY DOVEY/YOU'RE SO FINE .......... Bunny Sigler, Parkway 6000
115. NEXT PLANE TO LONDON .......... Rose Garden, Atco 6510
116. GO WITH ME .......... John Davidson, Columbia 44283
117. SUZANNE .......... Noel Harrison, Warner Bros. 7062
118. BYE, BYE, BABY .......... Big Brother & the Holding Company, Mainstream 666
119. SEVEN DAYS TOO LONG .......... Chuck Wood, Roulette 4741
120. SPLASH .......... Clique, Scepter 12202
121. I'M A DRIFTER .......... Lowell Fulsom, Kent 474
122. RUNAWAY .......... Del Shannon, Liberty 55993
123. LAPLAND .......... Baltimore & Ohio Marching Band, Jubilee 5592
124. BRINK OF DISASTER .......... Lesley Gore, Mercury 72726
125. TWO HEADS .......... Jefferson Airplane, RCA Victor 9297
126. MYSTERY OF TALLAHATCHIE BRIDGE .......... Sergio Mendes & Brasil '66, A&M 872
127. THE FROG .......... Sandy Nelson, Imperial 66260
128. REALLY, REALLY LOVE YOU .......... Ronnie Walker, Phillis 40470
129. BEEN SO NICE .......... Righteous Brothers, Verve 10551
130. IT'S ALL IN THE GAME .......... Jackie DeShannon, Imperial 66251
131. SOMETHING'S GOTTEN HOLD OF MY HEART .......... Gene Pitney, Musicor 1252
132. TURN AROUND AND TAKE A LOOK .......... Lemon Pipers, Buddah 10
133. SEA OF LOVE .......... Kit Kats, Jamie 1343
134. IT CAN'T HAPPEN WITHOUT YOU .......... Power Plant, Diamond 229
135. A HUNK OF FUNK .......... Gene Dozier & the Brotherhood, Minit 32026

Compiled from national retail sales and radio station airplay by the Music Popularity Dept. of Record Market Research, Billboard.

For Week Ending October 14, 1967

# Billboard HOT 100

★ STAR performer—Sides registering greatest proportionate upward progress this week.

Record Industry Association of America seal of certification as million selling single.

| This Week | 1 Wk. Ago | 2 Wks. Ago | 3 Wks. Ago | TITLE Artist (Producer), Label & Number | Weeks On Chart |
|---|---|---|---|---|---|
| Billboard Award 1 | 1 | 1 | 1 | THE LETTER — Box Tops (Dan Penn), Mala 565 | 10 |
| 2 | 2 | 3 | 5 | NEVER MY LOVE — Association (Bones Howe), Warner Bros. 7074 | 8 |
| ★3 | 11 | 22 | 35 | TO SIR, WITH LOVE — Lulu (Mickie Most), Epic 10187 | 6 |
| 4 | 5 | 13 | 18 | LITTLE OLE MAN (Uptight—Everything's Alright) — Bill Cosby (Fred Smith), Warner Bros. 7072 | 7 |
| 5 | 3 | 2 | 2 | ODE TO BILLIE JOE — Bobbie Gentry (Kelly Gordon & Bobby Paris), Capitol 5950 | 11 |
| 6 | 6 | 7 | 7 | (Your Love Keeps Lifting Me) HIGHER AND HIGHER — Jackie Wilson (Carl Davis), Brunswick 55336 | 10 |
| 7 | 4 | 4 | 3 | COME BACK WHEN YOU GROW UP — Bobby Vee & the Strangers (Dallas Smith), Liberty 55964 | 13 |
| 8 | 9 | 14 | 26 | HOW CAN I BE SURE — Young Rascals (Young Rascals), Atlantic 2438 | 6 |
| 9 | 10 | 11 | 16 | GIMME LITTLE SIGN — Brenton Wood (Hooven-Winn), Double Shot 116 | 12 |
| ★10 | 20 | 40 | 59 | SOUL MAN — Sam & Dave (Isaac Hayes & David Porter), Stax 231 | 6 |
| 11 | 8 | 6 | 6 | APPLES, PEACHES, PUMPKIN PIE — Jay & the Techniques (Jerry Ross), Smash 2086 | 14 |
| ★12 | 19 | 24 | 44 | HEY BABY (They're Playing Our Song) — Buckinghams (James William Guercio), Columbia 44254 | 6 |
| ★13 | 23 | 31 | 48 | YOUR PRECIOUS LOVE — Marvin Gaye & Tammy Terrell (H. Fuqua-J. Bristol), Tamla 54156 | 6 |
| 14 | 15 | 20 | 29 | DANDELION — Rolling Stones (Andrew Loog Oldham), London 905 | 6 |
| 15 | 17 | 28 | 34 | EXPRESSWAY TO YOUR HEART — Soul Survivors (Gemble-Huff), Crimson 1010 | 7 |
| 16 | 16 | 27 | 33 | GET ON UP — Esquires (Bill Sheppard), Bunky 7750 | 9 |
| 17 | 12 | 9 | 9 | I DIG ROCK AND ROLL MUSIC — Peter, Paul & Mary (Albert B. Grossman & Milt Okun), Warner Bros. 7067 | 9 |
| ★18 | 38 | 70 | — | A NATURAL WOMAN — Aretha Franklin (Jerry Wexler), Atlantic 2441 | 3 |
| ★19 | 24 | 32 | 45 | YOU KEEP RUNNING AWAY — Four Tops (Holland & Dozier), Motown 1113 | 5 |
| 20 | 13 | 10 | 14 | BROWN-EYED GIRL — Van Morrison (Bert Berns), Bang 545 | 14 |
| 21 | 14 | 8 | 10 | FUNKY BROADWAY — Wilson Pickett (Jerry Wexler), Atlantic 2430 | 11 |
| 22 | 7 | 5 | 4 | REFLECTIONS — Dianna Ross & the Supremes (Holland & Dozier), Motown 1111 | 10 |
| ★23 | 32 | 44 | 65 | PEOPLE ARE STRANGE — Doors (Paul Rothchild), Elektra 45621 | 4 |
| ★24 | 29 | 38 | 49 | IT MUST BE HIM — Vikki Carr (Dave Pell), Liberty 55986 | 7 |
| ★25 | 33 | 45 | 69 | LIGHTNING'S GIRL — Nancy Sinatra (Lee Hazlewood), Reprise 0620 | 4 |
| 26 | 21 | 21 | 21 | GROOVIN' — Booker T. and the M.G.'s (Staff), Stax 224 | 11 |
| ★27 | 40 | 63 | 90 | LET IT OUT — Hombres (Huey P. Meaux), Verve Forecast 5058 | 5 |
| 28 | 31 | 41 | 52 | LET LOVE COME BETWEEN US — James & Bobby Purify (Papa Don), Bell 685 | 6 |
| ★29 | 39 | 57 | 77 | ODE TO BILLIE JOE — King Curtis & His Kingpins (Cogbil & Dowd), Atco 6516 | 4 |
| 30 | 30 | 37 | 54 | WHAT NOW MY LOVE — Mitch Ryder (Bob Crewe), DynoVoice 901 | 6 |
| ★31 | 41 | 52 | 62 | THE LOOK OF LOVE — Dusty Springfield (Johnny Prenz), Philips 40465 | 10 |
| ★32 | 42 | 56 | 67 | CHILD OF CLAY — Jimmie Rodgers (Allen Stanton), A&M 871 | 4 |
| 33 | 34 | 35 | 36 | MEMPHIS SOUL STEW — King Curtis (Tommy Cogbill & King Curtis), Atco 6511 | 8 |
| ★34 | 59 | 88 | — | INCENSE AND PEPPERMINTS — Strawberry Alarm Clock (Frank Slay), Uni 55018 | 3 |
| 35 | 36 | 36 | 47 | A BANDA — Herb Alpert & the Tijuana Brass (Herb Alpert & Jerry Moss), A&M 870 | 6 |
| ★36 | 48 | 59 | 78 | THE LAST WALTZ — Englebert Humperdinck (Peter Sullivan), Parrot 40019 | 4 |
| ★37 | 51 | 72 | — | PLEASE LOVE ME FOREVER — Bobby Vinton (Billy Sherrill), Epic 10228 | 3 |
| ★38 | 52 | 69 | — | LOVE IS STRANGE — Peaches & Herb (David Kapralik & Ken Williams), Date 1574 | 3 |
| 39 | 18 | 19 | 22 | I MAKE A FOOL OF MYSELF — Frankie Valli (Bob Crewe), Philips 40484 | 8 |
| 40 | 25 | 25 | 25 | LOVE BUG LEAVE MY HEART ALONE — Martha Reeves & the Vandellas (Richard Morris), Gordy 7062 | 9 |
| ★41 | 61 | — | — | I'M WONDERING — Stevie Wonder (Henry Cosby), Tamla 54157 | 2 |
| 42 | 28 | 18 | 19 | GETTIN' TOGETHER — Tommy James & the Shondelles (Big Kahoona Prod.) Ritchie Cordell) Roulette 4762 | 8 |
| 43 | 27 | 15 | 8 | YOU'RE MY EVERYTHING — Temptations (Norman Whitfield), Gordy 7063 | 12 |
| ★44 | 54 | 64 | 79 | WHY DO FOOLS FALL IN LOVE — Happenings (Tokens), B.T. Puppy 532 | 4 |
| 45 | 22 | 12 | 13 | YOU KNOW WHAT I MEAN — Turtles (Joe Wissert), White Whale 254 | 11 |
| ★46 | 58 | 84 | — | HOLIDAY — Bee Gees (Robert Stigwood), Atco 6521 | 3 |
| 47 | 44 | 17 | 17 | I HAD A DREAM — Paul Revere & the Raiders with Mark Lindsay (Terry Melcher), Columbia 44227 | 9 |
| ★48 | 62 | 90 | — | THE RAIN, THE PARK & OTHER THINGS — Cowsills (Artie Kornfeld), MGM 13810 | 3 |
| ★49 | 60 | 81 | — | EVEN THE BAD TIMES ARE GOOD — Tremeloes (Mike Smith), Epic 10233 | 3 |
| 50 | 26 | 26 | 27 | THE CAT IN THE WINDOW (The Bird in the Sky) — Petula Clark (Charles Koppelman & Don Rubin), Warner Bros. 7073 | 7 |
| 51 | 56 | 61 | 61 | I'LL NEVER FALL IN LOVE AGAIN — Tom Jones (Peter Sullivan), Parrot 40018 | 6 |
| 52 | 49 | 49 | 50 | YOU'VE GOT TO PAY THE PRICE — Al Kent (Ed Wingate, Al Kent, H. Weems), Ric Tic 127 | 9 |
| 53 | 53 | 53 | 51 | CASONOVA (Your Playing Days Are Over) — Ruby Andrews (McGregor & Terry), Zodiac 1004 | 8 |
| 54 | 50 | 51 | 64 | WE LOVE YOU — Rolling Stones (Andrew Loog Oldham), London 905 | 5 |
| ★55 | 65 | 73 | 88 | MORE THAN THE EYE CAN SEE — Al Martino (Tom Morgan & Marvin Holtzman), Capitol 5989 | 4 |
| 56 | 57 | 60 | 60 | TAKE A LOOK — Aretha Franklin (Clyde Otis), Columbia 44270 | 7 |
| ★57 | 68 | 83 | — | EVERLASTING LOVE — Robert Knight (Buzz Cason & Mac Gayden), Rising Sons 117 | 3 |
| ★58 | 73 | — | — | KING MIDAS IN REVERSE — Hollies (Ron Richards), Epic 10234 | 2 |
| ★59 | 69 | 71 | — | ROCK 'N' ROLL WOMAN — Buffalo Springfield (Stephen Stills & Neil Young), Atco 6519 | 3 |
| ★60 | 71 | 74 | 75 | YOU'VE MADE ME SO VERY HAPPY — Brenda Holloway (Berry Gordy Jr.), Tamla 54155 | 6 |
| ★61 | — | — | — | (Loneliness Made Me Realize) IT'S YOU THAT I NEED — Temptations (N. Whitfield), Gordy 7065 | 1 |
| 62 | 67 | 68 | 70 | GET TOGETHER — Youngbloods (Felix Pappalardi), RCA Victor 9264 | 7 |
| ★63 | 80 | 82 | — | JUST ONE LOOK — Hollies, Imperial 66258 | 3 |
| 64 | 64 | 67 | 71 | IT'S GOT TO BE MELLOW — Leon Haywood (Leon Haywood), Decca 32164 | 9 |
| 65 | 72 | 76 | 95 | PURPLE HAZE — Jimi Hendrix Experience (Yameta), Reprise 0597 | 6 |
| 66 | 66 | 79 | 86 | FOR WHAT IT'S WORTH — Staple Singers (Larry Williams), Epic 10220 | 4 |
| 67 | 74 | 77 | 89 | FALL IN LOVE WITH ME — Bettye Swann (Malynn), Money 129 | 4 |
| 68 | 76 | 80 | 83 | TO SHARE YOUR LOVE — Fantastic Four (Ed Wyngate & Al Kent), Ric Tic 130 | 4 |
| 69 | 81 | — | — | SHOUT BAMALAMA — Mickey Murray (Bobby Smith), 555715 | 2 |
| 70 | 75 | 75 | 84 | BABY, I'M LONELY — Intruders (Gamble-Huff), Gamble 207 | 5 |
| ★71 | — | — | — | BIG BOSS MAN — Elvis Presley, RCA Victor 9341 | 1 |
| ★72 | — | — | — | I CAN SEE FOR MILES — Who (Kit Lambert), Decca 32206 | 1 |
| ★73 | 93 | — | — | PATA PATA — Miriam Makeba (Jerry Ragovoy), Reprise 0606 | 2 |
| 74 | 77 | 95 | — | STRANDED IN THE MIDDLE OF NO PLACE — Righteous Brothers (Mickey Stevenson), Verve 10551 | 3 |
| ★75 | 90 | 93 | — | WHAT'VE I DONE (To Make You Mad) — Linda Jones (George Kerr), Loma 2077 | 3 |
| 76 | 82 | 91 | — | HUSH — Billy Joe Royal (Joe South), Columbia 44277 | 3 |
| 77 | 79 | — | — | IF THIS IS LOVE (I'd Rather Be Lonely) — Precisions (Coleman-Basseline-Val Valo), Drew 1003 | 2 |
| ★78 | 100 | — | — | YOU MEAN THE WORLD TO ME — David Houston (Billy Sherrill), Epic 10224 | 2 |
| 79 | 83 | 89 | 91 | SPREADIN' HONEY — Watts 103rd St. Rhythm Band (Fred Smith), Keymen 103 | 6 |
| 80 | 84 | 92 | 93 | DIRTY MAN — Laura Lee (Rick Hall), Chess 2013 | 4 |
| ★81 | — | — | 97 | KARATE-BOO-GA-LOO — Jerry O (Jerry Murray), Shout 217 | 3 |
| ★82 | — | — | — | KENTUCKY WOMAN — Neil Diamond (Jeff Barry & Ellie Greenwich), Bang 551 | 1 |
| 83 | 94 | — | — | BOOGALOO DOWN BROADWAY — Fantastic Johnny C. (Jesse James), Phil-L.A. of Soul 305 | 2 |
| 84 | 85 | 86 | 92 | DANCING IN THE STREET — Ramsey Lewis (Esmond Edwards), Cadet 5572 | 4 |
| 85 | 86 | 87 | 87 | TELL HIM — Patti Drew (Carone), Capitol 5861 | 8 |
| 86 | 88 | 98 | 99 | NINE POUND STEEL — Joe Simon (J.R. Enterprises, Inc.) Sound Stage 7 2589 | 4 |
| 87 | 95 | — | — | YOU, NO ONE BUT YOU — Frankie Laine (Bob Thiele), ABC 10983 | 2 |
| ★88 | — | — | — | LAZY DAY — Spanky & Our Gang (Jerry Ross), Mercury 72732 | 1 |
| 89 | 91 | — | — | HEART BE STILL — Lorraine Ellison (Jerry Racovey), Loma 2074 | 2 |
| ★90 | — | — | — | GO WITH ME — Gene & Debbe (Troy Caldwell), TRK 5002 | 1 |
| 91 | — | — | — | GET DOWN — Harvey Scales & the Seven Sounds (Lennie LaCour), Magic Touch 2007 | 1 |
| 92 | 92 | — | — | PEAS 'N' RICE — Freddie McCoy (Cal Lampley), Prestige 450 | 2 |
| 93 | 96 | — | — | BEG, BORROW AND STEAL — Ohio Express (Big Kahoona Prod.), Cameo 483 | 2 |
| 94 | — | — | — | YOU DON'T KNOW ME — Elvis Presley, RCA Victor 9341 | 1 |
| 95 | — | — | — | DIFFERENT STROKES — Syl Johnson (3 J's), Twilight 103 | 1 |
| 96 | — | — | — | GIVE EVERYBODY SOME — Bar-Kays (David Porter & Isaac Hayes), Volt 154 | 1 |
| 97 | — | — | — | ALL YOUR GOODIES ARE GONE — Parliaments (Clinton & Taylor), Revilot 211 | 1 |
| 98 | — | — | — | LOVEY DOVEY/YOU'RE SO FINE — Bunny Sigler (John Madara & Leon Huff), Parkway 6000 | 1 |
| 99 | 99 | — | — | WALKIN' PROUD — Pete Klint Quintet, Mercury 72709 | 2 |
| 100 | — | — | — | SHAME ON ME — Chuck Jackson (Don Schroeder), Vend 1166 | 1 |

## HOT 100—A TO Z—(Publisher-Licensee)

A Banda (Permata, ASCAP) ... 35
All Your Goodies Are Gone (Groovesville, BMI) ... 97
Apples, Peaches, Pumpkin Pie (Akbestal/Act Three, BMI) ... 11
Baby, I'm Lonely (Razor Sharp, BMI) ... 70
Beg, Borrow and Steal (S&J, ASCAP) ... 93
Big Boss Man (Conrad, BMI) ... 71
Boogaloo Down Broadway (Dandelion/James Boy, BMI) ... 83
Brown-Eyed Girl (Web IV, BMI) ... 20
Casonova (Your Playing Days Are Over) (RicWil/Colfam, BMI) ... 53
Cat in the Window, The (The Bird in the Sky) (Chardon, BMI) ... 50
Child of Clay (Maresca, ASCAP) ... 32
Come Back When You Grow Up (Painted Desert, BMI) ... 7
Dancing in the Street (Jobete, BMI) ... 84
Dandelion (Gideon, BMI) ... 14
Different Strokes (Zachron/Edgewater, BMI) ... 95
Dirty Man (Chervis, BMI) ... 80
Even the Bad Times Are Good (Ponderosa, BMI) ... 49
Everlasting Love (Rising Sons, BMI) ... 57
Expressway to Your Heart (Double Diamond/Downstairs, BMI) ... 15
Fall in Love With Me (Money, BMI) ... 67
For What It's Worth (Ten East/Cotillion) ... 66
Funky Broadway (Drive-In Routeen, BMI) ... 21
Get Down (LaCour/East, BMI) ... 91
Get on Up (Mi-Mi, BMI) ... 16
Gettin' Together (Patricia, BMI) ... 42
Get Together (S.F.O., BMI) ... 62
Gimme Little Sign (Big Shot, ASCAP) ... 9
Give Everybody Some (East, BMI) ... 96
Go With Me (Acuff-Rose, BMI) ... 90
Groovin' (Slacsar, BMI) ... 12
Heart Be Still (Raemar/Web IV, BMI) ... 89
Hey Baby (They're Playing Our Song) (Diogenes/Bag of Tunes, BMI) ... 12
Holiday (Nemperor, BMI) ... 46
How Can I Be Sure (Slacsar, BMI) ... 8
Hush (Lowery, BMI) ... 76
I Can See for Miles (Devon, BMI) ... 72
I Dig Rock and Roll Music (Pepamar, ASCAP) ... 17
I Had a Dream (Daywin, BMI) ... 47
I Make a Fool of Myself (Saturday/Seasons Four, BMI) ... 39
If This Is Love (I'd Rather Be Lonely) (In-The-Pocket/Sidrian, BMI) ... 77
I'll Never Fall in Love Again (Hollis, BMI) ... 51
I'm Wondering (Jobete, BMI) ... 41
Incense and Peppermints (Claridge, ASCAP) ... 34
It Must Be Him (Asa, ASCAP) ... 24
It's Got to Be Mellow (Jim-Edd, BMI) ... 64
Just One Look (Premier Albums, BMI) ... 63
Karate-Boo-Ga-Loo (Boogaloo/Love Lane, BMI) ... 81
Kentucky Woman (Tallyrand, BMI) ... 82
King Midas in Reverse (Maribus, BMI) ... 58
Knock on Wood (East, BMI) ... 68
Last Waltz, The (Donna, ASCAP) ... 36
Lazy Day (Screen Gems-Columbia, BMI) ... 88
Let It Out (Crazy Cajun, BMI) ... 27
Let Love Come Between Us (Gallico, BMI) ... 28
Letter, The (Barton, BMI) ... 1
Lightning's Girl (Hazlewood, ASCAP) ... 25
Little Ole Man (Uptight-Everything's Alright) (Jobete, BMI) ... 4
Look of Love, The (Colgems, ASCAP) ... 31
(Loneliness Made Me Realize) It's You That I Need (Jobete, BMI) ... 61
Love Bug Leave My Heart Alone (Jobete, BMI) ... 40
Love Is Strange (Chazi, BMI) ... 38
Lovey Dovey/You're So Fine (Progressive/West Higgin, BMI) ... 98
Making Every Minute Count (Akbestal, BMI) ... 13
Memphis Soul Stew (Pronto/Kilynn, BMI) ... 33
More Than the Eye Can See (Saturday, BMI) ... 55
Natural Woman, A (Screen Gems-Columbia, BMI) ... 18
Never My Love (Tamerlane, BMI) ... 2
Nine Pound Steel (Press, BMI) ... 86
Ode to Billie Joe (Bobbie Gentry) (Shayne, ASCAP) ... 5
Ode to Billie Joe (Kingpins) (Shayne, ASCAP) ... 29
Pata Pata (Xima, ASCAP) ... 73
Peas 'n' Rice (Prestige, BMI) ... 92
People Are Strange (Nipper, ASCAP) ... 23
Please Love Me Forever (Selma, BMI) ... 37
Rain, the Park & Other Things, The (Akbestal/Luvlin, BMI) ... 48
Reflections (Jobete, BMI) ... 22
Rock 'n' Roll Woman (Ten-East/Springalo/Cotillion, BMI) ... 59
Shame on Me (Lois, BMI) ... 100
Shout Bamalama (Macon, BMI) ... 69
Soul Man (East/Pronto, BMI) ... 10
Spreadin' Honey (Keymen/Pure Soul, BMI) ... 79
Stranded in the Middle of No Place (Mikim, BMI) ... 74
Take a Look (Eden, BMI) ... 56
Tell Hill (Beechwood/Edgewater, BMI) ... 85
To Share Your Love (Don, BMI) ... 68
To Sir, With Love (Screen Gems-Columbia, BMI) ... 3
Walkin' Proud (AnPeter/Fantastic, BMI) ... 99
We Love You (Gideon, BMI) ... 54
What Now My Love (Remick, ASCAP) ... 30
What've I Done (To Make You Mad) (Zira/Floteca, BMI) ... 75
Why Do Fools Fall in Love (Patricia, BMI) ... 44
You Don't Know Me (Hill & Range, BMI) ... 94
You Keep Running (Jobete, BMI) ... 19
You Know What I Mean (Chardon, BMI) ... 45
You Mean the World to Me (Gallico, BMI) ... 78
You, No One But You (Damian/Sawyer, ASCAP) ... 87
(Your Love Keeps Lifting Me) Higher and Higher (Jalvane/BRC, BMI) ... 6
Your Precious Love (Jobete, BMI) ... 13
You're My Everything (Jobete, BMI) ... 43
You've Got to Pay the Price (Myto, BMI) ... 52
You've Made Me So Very Happy (Jobete, BMI) ... 60

## BUBBLING UNDER THE HOT 100

101. LIKE AN OLD-TIME MOVIE ... Scott McKenzie, Ode 105
102. CAN'T STOP LOVING YOU ... Last Word, Atco 6498
103. AS LONG AS YOU'RE HERE ... Zal Yanowsky (Zally), Buddah 12
104. WHEN THE SNOW IS ON THE ROSES ... Ed Ames, RCA Victor 5319
105. FUNKY DONKEY ... Pretty Purdie, Date 1568
106. ODE TO BILLIE JOE ... Ray Bryant, Cadet 5575
107. WAKE UP, WAKE UP ... Grass Roots, Dunhill 4105
108. KITTY DOYLE ... Dino, Desi & Billy, Reprise 0619
109. GO, GO GIRL ... Lee Dorsey, Amy 998
110. SOMETIMES SHE'S A LITTLE GIRL ... Tommy Boyce & Bobby Hart, A&M 874
111. I HEARD IT FROM THE GRAPEVINE ... Gladys Knight & the Pips, Soul 35039
112. SUZANNE ... Noel Harrison, Warner Bros. 0615
113. BRINK OF DISASTER ... Lesley Gore, Mercury 72726
114. SPLASH 1 ... Clique, Scepter 12202
115. NEXT PLANE TO LONDON ... Rose Garden, Atco 6510
116. WHAT'S SO GOOD ABOUT GOODBYE ... Giant Sunflower, Ode 104
117. BY THE TIME I GET TO PHOENIX ... Glen Campbell, Capitol 2015
118. I'M A DRIFTER ... Lowell Fulson, Kent 474
119. I GOT A FEELING ... Barbara Randolph, Soul 35038
120. LAPLAND ... Baltimore & Ohio Marching Band, Jubilee 5592
121. RUNAWAY ... Del Shannon, Liberty 55993
122. YOU CAN LEAD YOUR WOMAN TO THE ALTAR ... Oscar Toney Jr., Bell 688
123. WE GOTTA GO HOME ... Music Explosion, Laurie 3414
124. TWO HEADS ... Jefferson Airplane, RCA Victor 9297
125. MYSTERY OF TALLAHATCHIE BRIDGE ... Roger White, Big A 103
126. THE FROG ... Sergio Mendes & Brasil '66, A&M 872
127. ALLIGATOR BOOGALOO ... Lou Donaldson, Blue Note 1934
128. IT'S ALL IN THE GAME ... Jackie DeShannon, Imperial 66251
129. BEEN SO NICE ... Righteous Brothers, Verve 10551
130. SOMETHING'S GOT A HOLD OF MY HEART ... Gene Pitney, Musicor 1252
131. SEA OF LOVE ... Kit Kats, Jamie 1343
132. HUNK OF FUNK ... Gene Dozier & the Brotherhood, Minit 32026
133. WINDOW SHOPPING ... Messengers, Soul 35037
134. MORE THAN A MIRACLE ... Roger Williams, Kapp 843
135. ARE YOU NEVER COMING HOME? ... Sandy Posey, MGM, 13824

Compiled from national retail sales and radio station airplay by the Music Popularity Dept. of Record Market Research, Billboard.

For Week Ending October 21, 1967

# Billboard HOT 100

★ STAR performer—Sides registering greatest proportionate upward progress this week.

Record Industry Association of America seal of certification as million selling single.

| This Week | 1 Wk. Ago | 2 Wks. Ago | 3 Wks. Ago | TITLE Artist (Producer), Label & Number | Weeks On Chart |
|---|---|---|---|---|---|
| 1 (Billboard Award) | 3 | 11 | 22 | TO SIR, WITH LOVE — Lulu (Mickie Most), Epic 10187 | 7 |
| 2 | 1 | 1 | 1 | THE LETTER — Box Tops (Dan Penn), Mala 565 | 11 |
| 3 | 2 | 2 | 3 | NEVER MY LOVE — Association (Bones Howe), Warner Bros. 7074 | 9 |
| ★4 | 8 | 9 | 14 | HOW CAN I BE SURE — Young Rascals (Young Rascals), Atlantic 2438 | 7 |
| ★5 | 15 | 17 | 28 | EXPRESSWAY TO YOUR HEART — Soul Survivors (Gemble-Huff), Crimson 1010 | 8 |
| ★6 | 24 | 29 | 38 | IT MUST BE HIM — Vikki Carr (Dave Pell), Liberty 55986 | 8 |
| ★7 | 10 | 20 | 40 | SOUL MAN — Sam & Dave (Isaac Hayes & David Porter), Stax 231 | 7 |
| 8 | 4 | 5 | 13 | LITTLE OLE MAN (Uptight—Everything's Alright) — Bill Cosby (Fred Smith), Warner Bros. 7072 | 8 |
| 9 | 9 | 10 | 11 | GIMME LITTLE SIGN — Brenton Wood (Hooven-Winn), Double Shot 116 | 13 |
| ★10 | 13 | 23 | 31 | YOUR PRECIOUS LOVE — Marvin Gaye & Tammy Terrell (H. Fuqua-J. Bristol), Tamla 54156 | 7 |
| ★11 | 16 | 16 | 27 | GET ON UP — Esquires (Bill Sheppard), Bunky 7750 | 10 |
| 12 | 12 | 19 | 24 | HEY BABY (They're Playing Our Song) — Buckinghams (James William Guercio), Columbia 44254 | 7 |
| ★13 | 18 | 38 | 70 | A NATURAL WOMAN — Aretha Franklin (Jerry Wexler), Atlantic 2441 | 4 |
| 14 | 5 | 3 | 2 | ODE TO BILLIE JOE — Bobbie Gentry (Kelly Gordon & Bobby Paris), Capitol 5950 | 12 |
| 15 | 6 | 6 | 7 | (Your Love Keeps Lifting Me) HIGHER AND HIGHER — Jackie Wilson (Carl Davis), Brunswick 55336 | 11 |
| 16 | 7 | 4 | 4 | COME BACK WHEN YOU GROW UP — Bobby Vee & the Strangers (Dallas Smith), Liberty 55964 | 14 |
| ★17 | 23 | 32 | 44 | PEOPLE ARE STRANGE — Doors (Paul Rothchild), Elektra 45621 | 5 |
| 18 | 11 | 8 | 6 | APPLES, PEACHES, PUMPKIN PIE — Jay & the Techniques (Jerry Ross), Smash 2086 | 15 |
| ★19 | 34 | 59 | 88 | INCENSE AND PEPPERMINTS — Strawberry Alarm Clock (Frank Slay & Bill Holmes), Uni 55018 | 4 |
| ★20 | 37 | 51 | 72 | PLEASE LOVE ME FOREVER — Bobby Vinton (Billy Sherrill), Epic 10228 | 4 |
| ★21 | 27 | 40 | 63 | LET IT OUT — Hombres (Huey P. Meaux), Verve Forecast 5058 | 6 |
| 22 | 19 | 24 | 32 | YOU KEEP RUNNING AWAY — Four Tops (Holland & Dozier), Motown 1113 | 6 |
| ★23 | 28 | 31 | 41 | LET LOVE COME BETWEEN US — James & Bobby Purify (Papa Don), Bell 685 | 7 |
| 24 | 25 | 33 | 45 | LIGHTNING'S GIRL — Nancy Sinatra (Lee Hazlewood), Reprise 0620 | 5 |
| 25 | 14 | 15 | 20 | DANDELION — Rolling Stones (Andrew Loog Oldham), London 905 | 7 |
| ★26 | 41 | 61 | — | I'M WONDERING — Stevie Wonder (Henry Cosby), Tamla 54157 | 3 |
| 27 | 20 | 13 | 10 | BROWN-EYED GIRL — Van Morrison (Bert Berns), Bang 545 | 15 |
| 28 | 29 | 39 | 57 | ODE TO BILLIE JOE — King Curtis & His Kingpins (Cogbil & Dowd), Atco 6516 | 5 |
| ★29 | 38 | 52 | 69 | LOVE IS STRANGE — Peaches & Herb (David Kapralik & Ken Williams), Date 1574 | 4 |
| 30 | 31 | 41 | 52 | THE LOOK OF LOVE — Dusty Springfield (Johnny Prenz), Philips 40465 | 11 |
| 31 | 36 | 48 | 59 | THE LAST WALTZ — Englebert Humperdinck (Peter Sullivan), Parrot 40019 | 5 |
| 32 | 32 | 42 | 56 | CHILD OF CLAY — Jimmie Rodgers (Allen Stanton), A&M 871 | 5 |
| ★33 | 46 | 58 | 84 | HOLIDAY — Bee Gees (Robert Stigwood), Atco 6521 | 4 |
| 34 | 17 | 12 | 9 | I DIG ROCK AND ROLL MUSIC — Peter, Paul & Mary (Albert B. Grossman & Milt Okun), Warner Bros. 7067 | 10 |
| ★35 | 48 | 62 | 90 | THE RAIN, THE PARK & OTHER THINGS — Cowsills (Artie Kornfeld), MGM 13810 | 4 |
| 36 | 30 | 30 | 37 | WHAT NOW MY LOVE — Mitch Ryder (Bob Crewe), DynoVoice 901 | 7 |
| ★37 | 49 | 60 | 81 | EVEN THE BAD TIMES ARE GOOD — Tremeloes (Mike Smith), Epic 10233 | 4 |
| 38 | 21 | 14 | 8 | FUNKY BROADWAY — Wilson Pickett (Jerry Wexler), Atlantic 2430 | 12 |
| 39 | 22 | 7 | 5 | REFLECTIONS — Dianna Ross & the Supremes (Holland & Dozier), Motown 1111 | 11 |
| ★40 | 61 | — | — | (Loneliness Made Me Realize) IT'S YOU THAT I NEED — Temptations (N. Whitfield), Gordy 7065 | 2 |
| 41 | 44 | 54 | 64 | WHY DO FOOLS FALL IN LOVE — Happenings (Tokens), B.T. Puppy 532 | 5 |
| 42 | 33 | 34 | 35 | MEMPHIS SOUL STEW — King Curtis (Tommy Cogbill & King Curtis), Atco 6511 | 9 |
| 43 | 26 | 21 | 21 | GROOVIN' — Booker T. and the M.G.'s (Staff), Stax 224 | 12 |
| ★44 | 59 | 69 | 71 | ROCK 'N' ROLL WOMAN — Buffalo Springfield (Stephen Stills & Neil Young), Atco 6519 | 4 |
| ★45 | 57 | 68 | 83 | EVERLASTING LOVE — Robert Knight (Buzz Cason & Mac Gayden), Rising Sons 117 | 4 |
| ★46 | 73 | 93 | — | PATA PATA — Miriam Makeba (Jerry Ragovoy), Reprise 0606 | 3 |
| ★47 | 82 | — | — | KENTUCKY WOMAN — Neil Diamond (Jeff Barry & Ellie Greenwich), Bang 551 | 2 |
| ★48 | 72 | — | — | I CAN SEE FOR MILES — Who (Kit Lambert), Decca 32206 | 2 |
| 49 | 51 | 56 | 61 | I'LL NEVER FALL IN LOVE AGAIN — Tom Jones (Peter Sullivan), Parrot 40018 | 7 |
| ★50 | 88 | — | — | LAZY DAY — Spanky & Our Gang (Jerry Ross), Mercury 72732 | 2 |
| ★51 | 63 | 80 | 82 | JUST ONE LOOK — Hollies, Imperial 66258 | 4 |
| 52 | 58 | 73 | — | KING MIDAS IN REVERSE — Hollies (Ron Richards), Epic 10234 | 3 |
| 53 | 60 | 71 | 74 | YOU'VE MADE ME SO VERY HAPPY — Brenda Holloway (Berry Gordy Jr.), Tamla 54155 | 7 |
| 54 | 55 | 65 | 73 | MORE THAN THE EYE CAN SEE — Al Martino (Tom Morgan & Marvin Holtzman), Capitol 5989 | 5 |
| ★55 | 71 | — | — | BIG BOSS MAN — Elvis Presley, RCA Victor 9341 | 2 |
| ★56 | 76 | 82 | 91 | HUSH — Billy Joe Royal (Joe South), Columbia 44277 | 4 |
| ★57 | 94 | — | — | YOU DON'T KNOW ME — Elvis Presley, RCA Victor 9341 | 2 |
| ★58 | 81 | — | — | KARATE-BOO-GA-LOO — Jerry O (Jerry Murray), Shout 217 | 4 |
| 59 | 54 | 50 | 51 | WE LOVE YOU — Rolling Stones (Andrew Loog Oldham), London 905 | 6 |
| 60 | 56 | 57 | 60 | TAKE A LOOK — Aretha Franklin (Clyde Otis), Columbia 44270 | 8 |
| 61 | 69 | 81 | — | SHOUT BAMALAMA — Mickey Murray (Bobby Smith), 555715 | 3 |
| 62 | 53 | 53 | 53 | CASONOVA (Your Playing Days Are Over) — Ruby Andrews (McGregor & Terry), Zodiac 1004 | 9 |
| 63 | 64 | 64 | 67 | IT'S GOT TO BE MELLOW — Leon Haywood (Leon Haywood), Decca 32164 | 10 |
| 64 | 77 | 79 | — | IF THIS IS LOVE (I'd Rather Be Lonely) — Precisions (Coleman-Bassoline-Val Valo), Drew 1003 | 3 |
| 65 | 65 | 72 | 76 | PURPLE HAZE — Jimi Hendrix Experience (Yameta), Reprise 0597 | 7 |
| 66 | 75 | 90 | 93 | WHAT'VE I DONE (To Make You Mad) — Linda Jones (George Kerr), Loma 2077 | 4 |
| 67 | 67 | 74 | 77 | FALL IN LOVE WITH ME — Bettye Swann (Malynn), Money 129 | 5 |
| 68 | 68 | 76 | 80 | TO SHARE YOUR LOVE — Fantastic Four (Ed Wyngate & Al Kent), Ric Tic 130 | 5 |
| 69 | 62 | 67 | 68 | GET TOGETHER — Youngbloods (Felix Pappalardi), RCA Victor 9264 | 8 |
| 70 | 80 | 84 | 92 | DIRTY MAN — Laura Lee (Rick Hall), Chess 2013 | 5 |
| 71 | 83 | 94 | — | BOOGALOO DOWN BROADWAY — Fantastic Johnny C. (Jesse James), Phil-L.A. of Soul 305 | 3 |
| 72 | 74 | 77 | 95 | STRANDED IN THE MIDDLE OF NO PLACE — Righteous Brothers (Mickey Stevenson), Verve 10551 | 4 |
| 73 | 79 | 83 | 89 | SPREADIN' HONEY — Watts 103rd St. Rhythm Band (Fred Smith), Keymen 103 | 7 |
| ★74 | — | — | — | I HEARD IT THROUGH THE GRAPEVINE — Gladys Knight & the Pips (N. Whitfield), Soul 35039 | 1 |
| ★75 | — | — | — | I SAY A LITTLE PRAYER — Dionne Warwick (Bacharach-David), Scepter 12203 | 1 |
| ★76 | — | — | — | LADY BIRD — Nancy Sinatra & Lee Hazlewood (Lee Hazlewood), Reprise 0629 | 1 |
| ★77 | 93 | 96 | — | BEG, BORROW AND STEAL — Ohio Express (Big Kahoona Prod.), Cameo 483 | 3 |
| 78 | 78 | 100 | — | YOU MEAN THE WORLD TO ME — David Houston (Billy Sherrill), Epic 10224 | 3 |
| ★79 | — | — | — | MR. DREAM MERCHANT — Jerry Butler (Jerry Ross), Mercury 72721 | 1 |
| ★80 | — | — | — | LIKE AN OLD TIME MOVIE — Scott McKenzie (John Phillips & Lou Adler), Ode 105 | 1 |
| ★81 | — | — | — | ARE YOU NEVER COMING HOME — Sandy Posey (Chips Moman), MGM 13824 | 1 |
| 82 | 86 | 88 | 98 | NINE POUND STEEL — Joe Simon (J.R. Enterprises, Inc.) Sound Stage 7 2589 | 5 |
| 83 | 87 | 95 | — | YOU, NO ONE BUT YOU — Frankie Laine (Bob Thiele), ABC 10983 | 3 |
| ★84 | — | — | — | CAN'T STOP LOVING YOU — Last Word (Brad Shapiro & Steve Alaimo), Atco 6498 | 1 |
| 85 | 91 | — | — | GET DOWN — Harvey Scales & the Seven Sounds (Lennie LaCour), Magic Touch 2007 | 2 |
| ★86 | — | — | — | BRINK OF DISASTER — Lesley Gore (Steve Douglas), Mercury 72726 | 1 |
| ★87 | — | — | — | GO-GO GIRL — Lee Dorsey (Allen R. Toussaint & Marshall E. Schorn), Amy 998 | 1 |
| 88 | 90 | — | — | GO WITH ME — Gene & Debbe (Troy Caldwell), TRX 5002 | 2 |
| 89 | 98 | — | — | LOVEY DOVEY/YOU'RE SO FINE — Bunny Sigler (John Madare & Leon Huff), Parkway 6000 | 2 |
| ★90 | — | — | — | KEEP THE BALL ROLLIN' — Jay & the Techniques (Jerry Ross), Smash 2124 | 1 |
| 91 | — | — | — | NEXT PLANE TO LONDON — Rose Garden (Greene/Stone), Atco 6510 | 1 |
| 92 | — | — | — | BELIEVE IN ME BABY — Jesse James (Jesse Mason), 20th Century-Fox 6684 | 1 |
| 93 | — | — | — | TO SIR, WITH LOVE — Herbie Mann (Tom Dowd), Atlantic 2444 | 1 |
| 94 | 97 | — | — | ALL YOUR GOODIES ARE GONE — Parliaments (Clinton & Taylor), Revilot 211 | 2 |
| 95 | 95 | — | — | DIFFERENT STROKES — Syl Johnson (3 J's), Twilight 103 | 2 |
| 96 | 96 | — | — | GIVE EVERYBODY SOME — Bar-Kays (David Porter & Isaac Hayes), Volt 154 | 2 |
| 97 | 100 | — | — | SHAME ON ME — Chuck Jackson (Don Schroeder), Vend 1166 | 2 |
| 98 | 99 | 99 | — | WALKIN' PROUD — Pete Klint Quintet, Mercury 72709 | 3 |
| 99 | — | — | — | SWEET, SWEET LOVIN' — Platters (Richard "Popcorn" Wylie), Musicor 1275 | 1 |
| 100 | — | — | — | BACK ON THE STREET AGAIN — Sunshine Company (Joe Saraceno), Imperial 66260 | 1 |

## HOT 100—A TO Z—(Publisher-Licensee)

All Your Goodies Are Gone (Groovesville, BMI)... 94
Apples, Peaches, Pumpkin Pie (Akbestal/Act Three, BMI)... 18
Are You Never Coming Home (Press, BMI)... 81
Back on the Street Again (Cherry Lane, ASCAP)..100
Beg, Borrow and Steal (S&J, ASCAP)... 77
Believe in Me Baby (Je-Ma/Checis, BMI)... 92
Big Boss Man (Conrad, BMI)... 55
Boogaloo Down Broadway (Dandelion/James Boy, BMI)... 71
Brink of Disaster (Stone Canyon, BMI)... 86
Brown-Eyed Girl (Web IV, BMI)... 27
Can't Stop Loving You (Sherlyn, BMI)... 84
Casonova (Your Playing Days Are Over (RicWil/Colfam, BMI)... 62
Child of Clay (Maresca, ASCAP)... 32
Come Back When You Grow Up (Painted Desert, BMI)... 16
Dandelion (Gideon, BMI)... 25
Different Strokes (Zachron/Edgewater, BMI)... 95
Dirty Man (Chervis, BMI)... 70
Even the Bad Times Are Good (Ponderosa, BMI).. 37
Everlasting Love (Rising Sons, BMI)... 45
Expressway to Your Heart (Double Diamond/Downstairs, BMI)... 5
Fall in Love With Me (Money, BMI)... 67
Funky Broadway (Drive-In Routeen, BMI)... 38
Get Down (LaCour/East, BMI)... 85
Get on Up (Hi-Mi, BMI)... 11
Get Together (S.F.O., BMI)... 69
Gimme Little Sign (Big Shot, ASCAP)... 9
Give Everybody Some (East, BMI)... 96
Go-Go Girl (Marsaint, BMI)... 87
Go With Me (Acuff-Rose, BMI)... 88
Groovin' (Slacsar, BMI)... 43
Hey Baby (They're Playing Our Song) (Diogenes/Bag of Tunes, BMI)... 12
Holiday (Nemperor, BMI)... 33
How Can I Be Sure (Slacsar, BMI)... 4
Hush (Lowery, BMI)... 56
I Can See for Miles (Essex, ASCAP)... 48
I Dig Rock and Roll Music (Pepemar, ASCAP)... 34
I Heard It Through the Grapevine (Jobete, BMI).. 74
I Say a Little Prayer (Blue Seas/Jac, ASCAP)... 75
If This Is Love (I'd Rather Be Lonely) (In-The Pocket/Sidrian, BMI)... 64
I'll Never Fall in Love Again (Hollis, BMI)... 49
I'm Wondering (Jobete, BMI)... 26
Incense and Peppermints (Claridge, ASCAP)... 19
It Must Be Him (Asa, ASCAP)... 6
It's Got to Be Mellow (Jim-Edd, BMI)... 63
Just One Look (Premier Albums, BMI)... 51
Karate-Boo-Ga-Loo (Boogaloo/Love Lane, BMI)... 58
Keep the Ball Rollin' (Screen Gems-Columbia, BMI)... 90
Kentucky Woman (Tallyrand, BMI)... 47
King Midas in Reverse (Maribus, BMI)... 52
Lady Bird (Hazlewood, ASCAP)... 76
Last Waltz, The (Donna, ASCAP)... 31
Lazy Day (Screen Gems-Columbia, BMI)... 50
Let It Out (Crazy Cajun, BMI)... 21
Let Love Come Between Us (Gallico, BMI)... 23
Letter, The (Barton, BMI)... 2
Like an Old-Time Movie (Wingate, ASCAP)... 80
Lightning's Girl (Hazlewood, ASCAP)... 24
Little Ole Man (Uptight-Everything's Alright) (Jobete, BMI)... 8
Look of Love, The (Colgems, ASCAP)... 30
(Loneliness Made Me Realize) It's You That I Need (Jobete, BMI)... 40
Love Is Strange (Ghazi, BMI)... 29
Lovey Dovey/You're So Fine (Progressive/West Higgin, BMI)... 89
Memphis Soul Stew (Pronto/Kilynn, BMI)... 42
More Than the Eye Can See (Saturday, BMI)... 54
Mr. Dream Merchant (Saturday, BMI)... 79
Natural Woman, A (Screen Gems-Columbia, BMI).. 13
Never My Love (Tamerlane, BMI)... 3
Next Plane to London (Myrwood/Antlers, BMI)... 91
Nine Pound Steel (Press, BMI)... 82
Ode to Billie Joe (Bobbie Gentry) (Shayne, ASCAP) 14
Ode to Billie Joe (Kingpins) (Shayne, ASCAP)... 28
Pata Pata (Xima, ASCAP)... 46
People Are Strange (Nipper, ASCAP)... 17
Please Love Me Forever (Selma, BMI)... 20
Purple Haze (Sea-Lark, BMI)... 65
Rain, the Park & Other Things, The (Akbestal/Luvlin, BMI)... 35
Reflections (Jobete, BMI)... 39
Rock 'n' Roll Woman (Ten-East/Springalo/Cotillion, BMI)... 44
Shame on Me (Lois, BMI)... 97
Shout Bamalama (Macon, BMI)... 61
Soul Man (East/Pronto, BMI)... 7
Spreadin' Honey (Keymen/Pure Soul, BMI)... 73
Stranded in the Middle of No Place (Mikim, BMI)... 72
Sweet, Sweet Lovin' (Catalogue, BMI)... 99
Take a Look (Eden, BMI)... 60
To Share Your Love (Don, BMI)... 68
To Sir, With Love (Lulu) (Screen Gems-Columbia, BMI)... 1
To Sir, With Love (Mann) (Screen Gems-Columbia, BMI)... 93
Walkin' Proud (AnPeter/Fantastic, BMI)... 98
We Love You (Gideon, BMI)... 59
What Now My Love (Remick, ASCAP)... 36
What've I Done (To Make You Mad) (Zira/Floteca, BMI)... 66
Why Do Fools Fall in Love (Patricia, BMI)... 41
You Don't Know Me (Hill & Range, BMI)... 57
You Keep Running (Jobete, BMI)... 22
You Mean the World to Me (Gallico, BMI)... 78
You, No One But You (Damian/Sawyer, ASCAP).. 83
(Your Love Keeps Lifting Me) Higher and Higher (Jalynne/BRC, BMI)... 15
Your Precious Love (Jobete, BMI)... 10
You've Made Me So Very Happy (Jobete, BMI)... 53

## BUBBLING UNDER THE HOT 100

101. AS LONG AS YOU'RE HERE ... Zalman Yanovsky (Zally), Buddah 12
102. WAKE UP, WAKE UP ... Grass Roots, Dunhill 4105
103. BY THE TIME I GET TO PHOENIX ... Glen Campbell, Capitol 2015
104. SUZANNE ... Noel Harrison, Warner Bros. 0615
105. WE GOTTA GO HOME ... Music Explosion, Laurie 3414
106. WHEN THE SNOW IS ON THE ROSES ... Ed Ames, RCA Victor 9319
107. FUNKY DONKEY ... Pretty Purdie, Date 1568
108. FOR ONCE IN MY LIFE ... Tony Bennett, Columbia 44258
109. LAPLAND ... Baltimore & Ohio Marching Band, Jubilee 5592
110. IT'S ALL IN THE GAME ... Jackie DeShannon, Imperial 66251
111. PIECE OF MY HEART ... Erma Franklin, Shout 221
112. RUNAWAY ... Del Shannon, Liberty 55993
113. SPLASH 1 ... Clique, Scepter 12202
114. HEAVY MUSIC ... Bob Seegar & Doug Brown, Cameo 494
115. NOBODY BUT ME ... Human Beinz, Capitol 5990
116. LITTLE GIRL ... Critters, Kapp 858
117. EXCERPT FROM A TEENAGE OPERA ... Keith West, New Voice 825
118. HOMBURG ... Procol Harum, A&M 885
119. I GOT A FEELIN' ... Barbara Randolph, Soul 35038
120. YOU CAN LEAD YOUR WOMAN TO THE ALTAR ... Oscar Toney Jr., Bell 688
121. VISIT TO A SAD PLANET ... Leonard Nimoy, Dot 17038
122. BALLAD OF WATERHOLE #3 ... Roger Miller, Smash 2121
123. MYSTERY OF TALLAHATCHIE BRIDGE ... Roger White, Big A 103
124. RICHARD & ME ... Gene & Tommy, ABC 10981
125. (THEME FROM) VALLEY OF THE DOLLS ... Dionne Warwick, Scepter 12203
126. I ALMOST CALLED YOUR NAME ... Margaret Whiting, London 115
127. ALLIGATOR BOOGALOO ... Lou Donaldson, Blue Note 1934
128. BEEN SO NICE ... Righteous Brothers, Verve 10551
129. WHERE IS THE PARTY ... Helena Ferguson, Compass 7009
130. SEA OF LOVE ... Kit Kats, Jamie 1343
131. HUNK OF FUNK ... Gene Dozier and the Brotherhood, Minit 32026
132. WINDOW SHOPPING ... Messengers, Soul 35037
133. BE MY LOVE ... Mel Carter, Liberty 56000
134. MY SHIP IS COMING IN ... Walter Jackson, Okeh 7295
135. BO DIDDLEY BACH ... Kingsmen, Wand 1164

Compiled from national retail sales and radio station airplay by the Music Popularity Dept. of Record Market Research, Billboard.

# Billboard

For Week Ending October 28, 1967

# HOT 100

★ **STAR performer**—Sides registering greatest proportionate upward progress this week.

(seal) Record Industry Association of America seal of certification as million selling single.

| This Week | 1 Wk. Ago | 2 Wks. Ago | 3 Wks. Ago | TITLE Artist (Producer), Label & Number | Weeks On Chart |
|---|---|---|---|---|---|
| 1 (Billboard Award) | 1 | 3 | 11 | **TO SIR, WITH LOVE** — Lulu (Mickie Most), Epic 10187 | 8 |
| 2 | 2 | 1 | 1 | **THE LETTER** — Box Tops (Dan Penn), Mala 565 | 12 (seal) |
| 3 | 3 | 2 | 2 | **NEVER MY LOVE** — Association (Bones Howe), Warner Bros. 7074 | 10 |
| 4 | 4 | 8 | 9 | **HOW CAN I BE SURE** — Young Rascals (Young Rascals), Atlantic 2438 | 8 |
| 5 | 5 | 15 | 17 | **EXPRESSWAY TO YOUR HEART** — Soul Survivors (Gamble-Huff), Crimson 1010 | 9 |
| 6 | 6 | 24 | 29 | **IT MUST BE HIM** — Vikki Carr (Dave Pell), Liberty 55986 | 9 |
| 7 | 7 | 10 | 20 | **SOUL MAN** — Sam & Dave (Isaac Hayes & David Porter), Stax 231 | 8 |
| 8 | 10 | 13 | 23 | **YOUR PRECIOUS LOVE** — Marvin Gaye & Tammy Terrell (H. Fuqua-J. Bristol), Tamla 54156 | 8 |
| ★ 9 | 13 | 18 | 38 | **A NATURAL WOMAN** — Aretha Franklin (Jerry Wexler), Atlantic 2441 | 5 |
| ★ 10 | 19 | 34 | 59 | **INCENSE AND PEPPERMINTS** — Strawberry Alarm Clock (Frank Slay & Bill Holmes), Uni 55018 | 5 |
| 11 | 11 | 16 | 16 | **GET ON UP** — Esquires (Bill Sheppard), Bunky 7750 | 11 |
| ★ 12 | 17 | 23 | 32 | **PEOPLE ARE STRANGE** — Doors (Paul Rothchild), Elektra 45621 | 6 |
| 13 | 9 | 9 | 10 | **GIMME LITTLE SIGN** — Brenton Wood (Hooven-Winn), Double Shot 116 | 14 |
| 14 | 12 | 12 | 19 | **HEY BABY (They're Playing Our Song)** — Buckinghams (James William Guercio), Columbia 44254 | 8 |
| ★ 15 | 20 | 37 | 51 | **PLEASE LOVE ME FOREVER** — Bobby Vinton (Billy Sherrill), Epic 10228 | 5 |
| ★ 16 | 21 | 27 | 40 | **LET IT OUT** — Hombres (Huey P. Meaux), Verve Forecast 5058 | 7 |
| ★ 17 | 26 | 41 | 61 | **I'M WONDERING** — Stevie Wonder (Henry Cosby), Tamla 54157 | 4 |
| 18 | 8 | 4 | 5 | **LITTLE OLE MAN (Uptight—Everything's Alright)** — Bill Cosby (Fred Smith), Warner Bros. 7072 | 9 |
| ★ 19 | 35 | 48 | 62 | **THE RAIN, THE PARK & OTHER THINGS** — Cowsills (Artie Kornfeld), MGM 13810 | 5 |
| ★ 20 | 40 | 61 | — | **(Loneliness Made Me Realize) IT'S YOU THAT I NEED** — Temptations (N. Whitfield), Gordy 7065 | 3 |
| 21 | 16 | 7 | 4 | **COME BACK WHEN YOU GROW UP** — Bobby Vee & the Strangers (Dallas Smith), Liberty 55964 | 15 (seal) |
| 22 | 22 | 19 | 24 | **YOU KEEP RUNNING AWAY** — Four Tops (Holland & Dozier), Motown 1113 | 7 |
| 23 | 23 | 28 | 31 | **LET LOVE COME BETWEEN US** — James & Bobby Purify (Papa Don), Bell 685 | 8 |
| ★ 24 | 29 | 38 | 52 | **LOVE IS STRANGE** — Peaches & Herb (David Kapralik & Ken Williams), Date 1574 | 5 |
| ★ 25 | 30 | 31 | 41 | **THE LOOK OF LOVE** — Dusty Springfield (Jonnny rrenz), Philips 40465 | 12 |
| 26 | 33 | 46 | 58 | **HOLIDAY** — Bee Gees (Robert Stigwood), Atco 6521 | 5 |
| 27 | 18 | 11 | 8 | **APPLES, PEACHES, PUMPKIN PIE** — Jay & the Techniques (Jerry Ross), Smash 2086 | 16 |
| 28 | 31 | 36 | 48 | **THE LAST WALTZ** — Englebert Humperdinck (Peter Sullivan), Parrot 40019 | 6 |
| 29 | 14 | 5 | 3 | **ODE TO BILLIE JOE** — Bobbie Gentry (Kelly Gordon & Bobby Paris), Capitol 5950 | 13 (seal) |
| 30 | 15 | 6 | 6 | **(Your Love Keeps Lifting Me) HIGHER AND HIGHER** — Jackie Wilson (Carl Davis), Brunswick 55336 | 12 |
| 31 | 32 | 32 | 42 | **CHILD OF CLAY** — Jimmie Rodgers (Allen Stanton), A&M 871 | 6 |
| 32 | 24 | 25 | 33 | **LIGHTNING'S GIRL** — Nancy Sinatra (Lee Hazlewood), Reprise 0620 | 6 |
| 33 | 28 | 29 | 39 | **ODE TO BILLIE JOE** — King Curtis & His Kingpins (Cogbil & Dowd), Atco 6516 | 6 |
| ★ 34 | 47 | 82 | — | **KENTUCKY WOMAN** — Neil Diamond (Jeff Barry & Ellie Greenwich), Bang 551 | 3 |
| ★ 35 | 45 | 57 | 68 | **EVERLASTING LOVE** — Robert Knight (Buzz Cason & Mac Gayden), Rising Sons 117 | 5 |
| ★ 36 | 46 | 73 | 93 | **PATA PATA** — Miriam Makeba (Jerry Ragovoy), Reprise 0606 | 4 |
| 37 | 37 | 49 | 60 | **EVEN THE BAD TIMES ARE GOOD** — Tremeloes (Mike Smith), Epic 10233 | 5 |
| 38 | 48 | 72 | — | **I CAN SEE FOR MILES** — Who (Kit Lambert), Decca 32206 | 3 |
| 39 | 25 | 14 | 15 | **DANDELION** — Rolling Stones (Andrew Loog Oldham), London 905 | 8 |
| ★ 40 | 50 | 88 | — | **LAZY DAY** — Spanky & Our Gang (Jerry Ross), Mercury 72732 | 3 |
| 41 | 27 | 20 | 13 | **BROWN-EYED GIRL** — Van Morrison (Bert Berns), Bang 545 | 16 |
| ★ 42 | 75 | — | — | **I SAY A LITTLE PRAYER** — Dionne Warwick (Bacharach-David), Scepter 12203 | 2 |
| | 53 | 60 | 71 | Brenda Holloway (Berry Gordy Jr.), Tamla 54155 | 8 |
| 44 | 44 | 59 | 69 | **ROCK 'N' ROLL WOMAN** — Buffalo Springfield (Stephen Stills & Neil Young), Atco 6519 | 5 |
| 45 | 41 | 44 | 54 | **WHY DO FOOLS FALL IN LOVE** — Happenings (Tokens), B.T. Puppy 532 | 6 |
| ★ 46 | 76 | — | — | **LADY BIRD** — Nancy Sinatra & Lee Hazlewood (Lee Hazlewood), Reprise 0629 | 2 |
| 47 | 51 | 63 | 80 | **JUST ONE LOOK** — Hollies, Imperial 66258 | 5 |
| 48 | 55 | 71 | — | **BIG BOSS MAN** — Elvis Presley, RCA Victor 9341 | 3 |
| 49 | 34 | 17 | 12 | **I DIG ROCK AND ROLL MUSIC** — Peter, Paul & Mary (Albert B. Grossman & Milt Okun), Warner Bros. 7067 | 11 |
| ★ 50 | 71 | 83 | 94 | **BOOGALOO DOWN BROADWAY** — Fantastic Johnny C. (Jesse James), Phil-L.A. of Soul 305 | 4 |
| 51 | 52 | 58 | 73 | **KING MIDAS IN REVERSE** — Hollies (Ron Richards), Epic 10234 | 4 |
| 52 | 56 | 76 | 82 | **HUSH** — Billy Joe Royal (Joe South), Columbia 44277 | 5 |
| 53 | 58 | 81 | — | **KARATE-BOO-GA-LOO** — Jerry O (Jerry Murray), Shout 217 | 5 |
| ★ 54 | 74 | — | — | **I HEARD IT THROUGH THE GRAPEVINE** — Gladys Knight & the Pips (N. Whitfield), Soul 35039 | 2 |
| 55 | 54 | 55 | 65 | **MORE THAN THE EYE CAN SEE** — Al Martino (Tom Morgan & Marvin Holtzman), Capitol 5989 | 6 |
| 56 | 57 | 94 | — | **YOU DON'T KNOW ME** — Elvis Presley, RCA Victor 9341 | 3 |
| ★ 57 | 90 | — | — | **KEEP THE BALL ROLLIN'** — Jay & the Techniques (Jerry Ross), Smash 2124 | 2 |
| 58 | 61 | 69 | 81 | **SHOUT BAMALAMA** — Mickey Murray (Bobby Smith), 555715 | 4 |
| ★ 59 | 80 | — | — | **LIKE AN OLD TIME MOVIE** — Scott McKenzie (John Phillips & Lou Adler), Ode 105 | 2 |
| 60 | 64 | 77 | 79 | **IF THIS IS LOVE (I'd Rather Be Lonely)** — Precisions (Coleman-Basseline-Val Vale), Drew 1003 | 4 |
| 61 | 66 | 75 | 90 | **WHAT'VE I DONE (To Make You Mad)** — Linda Jones (George Kerr), Loma 2077 | 5 |
| ★ 62 | — | — | — | **GLAD TO BE UNHAPPY** — Mamas & the Papas (Lou Adler), Dunhill 4107 | 1 |
| ★ 63 | — | — | — | **SHE IS STILL A MYSTERY** — Lovin' Spoonful (Joe Wissert), Kama Sutra 239 | 1 |
| ★ 64 | 100 | — | — | **BACK ON THE STREET AGAIN** — Sunshine Company (Joe Saraceno), Imperial 66260 | 2 |
| ★ 65 | — | — | — | **GET IT TOGETHER** — James Brown & the Famous Flames (James Brown), King 6122 | 1 |
| ★ 66 | — | — | — | **HOMBURG** — Procol Harum (Denny Cordell), A&M 885 | 1 |
| 67 | 63 | 64 | 64 | **IT'S GOT TO BE MELLOW** — Leon Haywood (Leon Haywood), Decca 32164 | 11 |
| 68 | 70 | 80 | 84 | **DIRTY MAN** — Laura Lee (Rick Hall), Chess 2013 | 6 |
| 69 | 79 | — | — | **MR. DREAM MERCHANT** — Jerry Butler (Jerry Ross), Mercury 72721 | 2 |
| 70 | 81 | — | — | **ARE YOU NEVER COMING HOME** — Sandy Posey (Chips Moman), MGM 13824 | 2 |
| 71 | 82 | 86 | 88 | **NINE POUND STEEL** — Joe Simon (J.R. Enterprises, Inc.) Sound Stage 7 2589 | 6 |
| 72 | 77 | 93 | 96 | **BEG, BORROW AND STEAL** — Ohio Express (Big Kahoona Prod.), Cameo 483 | 4 |
| 73 | 73 | 79 | 83 | **SPREADIN' HONEY** — Watts 103rd St. Rhythm Band (Fred Smith), Keymen 103 | 8 |
| 74 | 65 | 65 | 72 | **PURPLE HAZE** — Jimi Hendrix Experience (Yameta), Reprise 0597 | 8 |
| ★ 75 | — | — | — | **WAKE UP, WAKE UP** — Grass Roots (Steve Barri & P. F. Sloan), Dunhill 4105 | 1 |
| ★ 76 | — | — | — | **WATCH THE FLOWERS GROW** — 4 Seasons (Bob Crewe), Philips 40490 | 1 |
| 77 | 78 | 78 | 100 | **YOU MEAN THE WORLD TO ME** — David Houston (Billy Sherrill), Epic 10224 | 4 |
| ★ 78 | — | — | — | **THIS TOWN** — Frank Sinatra (Jimmy Bowen), Reprise 0631 | 1 |
| ★ 79 | — | — | — | **YOU BETTER SIT DOWN KIDS** — Cher (Sonny Bond), Imperial 66261 | 1 |
| 80 | 87 | — | — | **GO-GO GIRL** — Lee Dorsey (Allen R. Toussaint & Marshall E. Sehorn), Amy 998 | 2 |
| 81 | 84 | — | — | **CAN'T STOP LOVING YOU** — Last Word (Brad Shapiro & Steve Alaimo), Atco 6498 | 2 |
| 82 | 86 | — | — | **BRINK OF DISASTER** — Lesley Gore (Steve Douglas), Mercury 72726 | 2 |
| 83 | 88 | 90 | — | **GO WITH ME** — Gene & Debbe (Troy Caldwell), TRX 5002 | 3 |
| 84 | 85 | 91 | — | **GET DOWN** — Harvey Scales & the Seven Sounds (Lonnie LaCour), Magic Touch 2007 | 3 |
| ★ 85 | — | — | — | **OUT OF THE BLUE** — Tommy James & the Shondells (Big Kahoona Prod.) Roulette 4775 | 1 |
| ★ 86 | — | — | — | **SUZANNE** — Noel Harrison (Jimmy Bowen), Reprise 0615 | 1 |
| ★ 87 | — | — | — | **BY THE TIME I GET TO PHOENIX** — Glen Campbell (Al De Lory), Capitol 2015 | 1 |
| 88 | 89 | 98 | — | **LOVEY DOVEY/YOU'RE SO FINE** — Bunny Sigler (John Madara & Leon Huff), Parkway 6000 | 3 |
| 89 | 94 | 97 | — | **ALL YOUR GOODIES ARE GONE** — Parliaments (Clinton & Taylor), Revilot 211 | 3 |
| 90 | 91 | — | — | **NEXT PLANE TO LONDON** — Rose Garden (Greene/Stone), Atco 6510 | 2 |
| 91 | 96 | 96 | — | **GIVE EVERYBODY SOME** — Bar-Kays (David Porter & Isaac Hayes), Volt 154 | 3 |
| 92 | — | — | — | **FOR ONCE IN MY LIFE** — Tony Bennett (Howard A. Roberts), Columbia 44258 | 1 |
| 93 | — | — | — | **SKINNY LEGS AND ALL** — Joe Tex (Buddy Killen), Dial 4063 | 1 |
| 94 | — | — | — | **YOU ARE MY SUNSHINE** — Mitch Ryder (Bob Crewe), New Voice 826 | 1 |
| 95 | — | — | — | **BIRDS OF BRITAIN** — Bob Crewe Generation (Bob Crewe), DynoVoice 902 | 1 |
| 96 | 99 | — | — | **SWEET, SWEET LOVIN'** — Platters (Richard "Popcorn" Wylie), Musicor 1275 | 2 |
| 97 | 97 | 100 | — | **SHAME ON ME** — Chuck Jackson (Don Schroeder), Wand 1166 | 3 |
| 98 | — | — | — | **LAPLAND** — Baltimore & Ohio Marching Band (Mouse House), Jubilee 5592 | 1 |
| 99 | — | — | — | **DESIREE'** — Left Banke (Mike Brown), Smash 2119 | 1 |
| 100 | — | — | — | **ON A SATURDAY NIGHT** — Eddie Floyd (Steve Grapper), Stax 233 | 1 |

## HOT 100—A TO Z—(Publisher-Licensee)

All Your Goodies Are Gone (Groovesville, BMI) .. 89
Apples, Peaches, Pumpkin Pie (Akbestal/Act Three, BMI) .... 27
Are You Never Coming Home (Press, BMI) ..... 70
Back on the Street Again (Cherry Lane, ASCAP) .. 64
Beg, Borrow and Steal (S&J, ASCAP) .......... 72
Big Boss Man (Conrad, BMI) .......... 48
Birds of Britain (Saturday, BMI) .......... 95
Boogaloo Down Broadway (Dandelion/James Boy, BMI) .......... 50
Brink of Disaster (Stone Canyon, BMI) .......... 82
Brown-Eyed Girl (Web IV, BMI) .......... 41
By the Time I Get to Phoenix (Rivers, BMI) ..... 87
Can't Stop Loving You (Sherlyn, BMI) .......... 81
Child of Clay (Maresca, ASCAP).......... 31
Come Back When You Grow Up (Painted Desert, BMI) .......... 21
Dandelion (Gideon, BMI) .......... 39
Desiree' (Minuet, ASCAP) .......... 99
Dirty Man (Chervis, BMI) .......... 68
Even the Bad Times Are Good (Ponderosa, BMI) .. 37
Everlasting Love (Rising Sons, BMI) .......... 35
Expressway to Your Heart (Double Diamond/Downstairs, BMI) .......... 5
For Once In My Life (Stein & Van Stock, ASCAP) 92
Get Down (LaCour/East, BMI).......... 84
Get It Together (Dynatone, BMI) .......... 65
Get on Up (Hi-Mi, BMI) .......... 11
Gimme Little Sign (Big Shot, ASCAP) .......... 13
Give Everybody Some (East, BMI) .......... 91
Glad To Be Unhappy (Chappell, ASCAP) .......... 62
Go-Go Girl (Marsaint, BMI).......... 80
Go With Me (Acuff-Rose, BMI) .......... 83
Hey Baby (They're Playing Our Song) (Diogenes/Bag of Tunes, BMI) .......... 14
Holiday (Nemperor, BMI) .......... 26
Homburg (Total, BMI) .......... 66
How Can I Be Sure (Slacsar, BMI) .......... 4
Hush (Lowery, BMI) .......... 52
I Can See for Miles (Essex, ASCAP) .......... 38
I Dig Rock and Roll Music (Pepamar, ASCAP) ... 49
I Heard It Through the Grapevine (Jobete, BMI) .. 54
I Say a Little Prayer (Blue Seas/Jac, ASCAP) .... 42
I'm Wondering (Jobete, BMI) .......... 17
If This Is Love (I'd Rather Be Lonely) (In-The Pocket/Sidrian, BMI) .......... 60
Incense and Peppermints (Claridge, ASCAP) ...... 10
It Must Be Him (Asa, ASCAP) .......... 6
It's Got to Be Mellow (Jim-Edd, BMI) .......... 67
Just One Look (Premier Albums, BMI) .......... 47
Karate-Boo-Ga-Loo (Boogaloo/Love Lane, BMI) ... 53
Keep the Ball Rollin' (Screen Gems-Columbia, BMI) .......... 57
Kentucky Woman (Tallyrand, BMI) .......... 34
King Midas in Reverse (Maribus, BMI) .......... 51
Lady Bird (Hazlewood, ASCAP) .......... 46
Lapland (Just Music, BMI) .......... 98
Last Waltz, The (Donna, ASCAP) .......... 28
Lazy Day (Screen Gems-Columbia, BMI) .......... 40
Let It Out (Crazy Cajun, BMI) .......... 16
Let Love Come Between Us (Gallico, BMI) ...... 23
Letter, The (Barton, BMI) .......... 2
Like an Old-Time Movie (Wingate, ASCAP) ...... 59
Lightning's Girl (Hazlewood, ASCAP) .......... 32
Little Ole Man (Uptight-Everything's Alright) (Jobete, BMI) .......... 18
Look of Love, The (Colgems, ASCAP) .......... 25
(Loneliness Made Me Realize) It's You That I Need (Jobete, BMI) .......... 20
Love Is Strange (Chazi, BMI) .......... 24
Lovey Dovey/You're So Fine (Progressive/West Higgins, BMI) .......... 88
More Than the Eye Can See (Saturday, BMI) .... 55
Mr. Dream Merchant (Saturday, BMI) .......... 69
Natural Woman, A (Screen Gems-Columbia, BMI) 9
Never My Love (Tamerlane, BMI) .......... 3
Next Plane to London (Myrwood/Antlers, BMI) ... 90
Nine Pound Steel (Press, BMI) .......... 71
Ode to Billie Joe (Bobbie Gentry) (Shayne, ASCAP) 29
Ode to Billie Joe (Kingpins) (Shayne, ASCAP) .... 33
On a Saturday Night (East, BMI) ..........100
Out of the Blue (Patricia, BMI) .......... 85
Pata Pata (Xima, ASCAP).......... 36
People Are Strange (Nipper, ASCAP) .......... 12
Please Love Me Forever (Selma, BMI) .......... 15
Purple Haze (Sea-Lark, BMI) .......... 74
Rain, the Park & Other Thing, The (Akbestal/Luvlin, BMI) .......... 19
Rock 'n' Roll Woman (Ten-East/Springalo/Cotillion, BMI) .......... 44
Shame on Me (Lois, BMI) .......... 97
She Is Still a Mystery (Faithful Virtue, BMI) .... 63
Shout Bamalama (Macon, BMI) .......... 58
Skinny Legs and All (Tree, BMI) .......... 93
Soul Man (East/Pronto, BMI) .......... 7
Spreadin' Honey (Keymen/Pure Soul, BMI) ...... 73
Suzanne (Project 7, BMI) .......... 86
Sweet, Sweet Lovin' (Catalogue, BMI) .......... 96
This Town (Remick, ASCAP) .......... 78
To Sir, With Love (Lulu) (Screen Gems-Columbia, BMI) .......... 1
Wake Up, Wake Up (Trousdale, BMI) .......... 75
Watch The Flowers Grow (Saturday/Seasons' Four, BMI) .......... 76
What've I Done (To Make You Mad) (Zira/Floteca, BMI) .......... 61
Why Do Fools Fall in Love (Patricia, BMI) ...... 45
You Are My Sunshine (Peer Int'l., BMI).......... 94
You Better Sit Down Kids (Chrismarc/Cotillion, BMI) .......... 79
You Don't Know Me (Hill & Range, BMI) ....... 56
You Keep Running (Jobete, BMI) .......... 22
You Mean the World to Me (Gallico, BMI) ...... 77
(Your Love Keeps Lifting Me) Higher and Higher (Jalynne/BRC, BMI) .......... 30
Your Precious Love (Jobete, BMI) .......... 8
You've Made Me So Very Happy (Jobete, BMI) ... 43

## BUBBLING UNDER THE HOT 100

101. AS LONG AS YOU'RE HERE..........Zal Yanovsky (Zally), Buddah 12
102. WILD HONEY..........Beach Boys, Capitol 2028
103. WE GOTTA GO HOME..........Music Explosion, Laurie 3414
104. STAG-O-LEE..........Wilson Pickett, Atlantic 2448
105. PIECE OF MY HEART..........Erma Franklin, Shout 221
106. WHEN THE SNOW IS ON THE ROSES..........Ed Ames, RCA Victor 9319
107. SAND..........Nancy Sinatra & Lee Hazlewood, Reprise 0629
108. BALLAD OF WATERHOLE #3..........Roger Miller, Smash 2121
109. YOU, NO ONE BUT YOU..........Frankie Laine, ABC 10983
110. CALIFORNIA MY WAY..........Committee, White Whale 257
111. TO SIR, WITH LOVE..........Herbie Mann, Atlantic 2444
112. EXCERPT FROM A TEENAGE OPERA..........Keith West, New Voice 825
113. NOBODY BUT ME..........Human Beinz, Capitol 5990
114. LITTLE GIRL..........Critters, Kapp 853
115. LOVE OF THE COMMON PEOPLE..........Wayne Newton, Capitol 2016
116. ITCHYCOO PARK..........Small Faces, Immediate 501
117. I GOT A FEELIN'..........Barbara Randolph, Soul 35038
118. PONY WITH A GOLDEN MANE..........Every Mothers' Son, MGM 13844
119. (THEME FROM) VALLEY OF THE DOLLS..........Dionne Warwick, Scepter 12203
120. YOU CAN LEAD YOUR WOMAN TO THE ALTAR..........Oscar Toney Jr., Bell 688
121. SHE..........Roy Orbison, MGM 13817
122. RICHARD & ME..........Gene & Tommy, ABC 10981
123. MYSTERY OF TALLAHATCHIE BRIDGE..........Roger White, Big A 103
124. I ALMOST CALLED YOUR NAME..........Margaret Whiting, London 115
125. WHOLE LOTTA WOMEN..........Arthur Conley, Atco 6529
126. ALLIGATOR BOOGALOO..........Lou Donaldson, Blue Note 1934
127. IT TAKES PEOPLE LIKE YOU..........Buck Owens, Capitol 2001
128. WHERE IS THE PARTY..........Helena Ferguson, Compass 7009
129. MY SHIP IS COMING IN..........Walter Jackson, Okeh 7295
130. OPEN FOR BUSINESS..........Jack Jones, Kapp 860
131. HUNK OF FUNK..........Gene Dozier & the Brotherhood, Minit 32026
132. BE MY LOVE..........Mel Carter, Liberty 56000
133. I WANT ACTION..........Ruby Winters, Diamond 230
134. HEY GIRL..........Mamas & Papas, Dunhill 4107
135. BO DIDDLEY BACH..........Kingsmen, Wand 1164

Compiled from national retail sales and radio station airplay by the Music Popularity Dept. of Record Market Research, Billboard.

# Billboard HOT 100

For Week Ending November 4, 1967

★ STAR performer—Sides registering greatest proportionate upward progress this week.

Record Industry Association of America seal of certification as million selling single.

| This Week | Last Week | 2 Wks. Ago | 3 Wks. Ago | TITLE Artist (Producer), Label & Number | Weeks on Chart |
|---|---|---|---|---|---|
| 1 | 1 | 1 | 3 | TO SIR, WITH LOVE — Lulu (Mickie Most), Epic 10187 | 9 |
| 2 | 7 | 7 | 10 | SOUL MAN — Sam & Dave (Isaac Hayes & David Porter), Stax 231 | 9 |
| 3 | 6 | 6 | 24 | IT MUST BE HIM — Vikki Carr (Dave Pell), Liberty 55986 | 10 |
| 4 | 5 | 5 | 15 | EXPRESSWAY TO YOUR HEART — Soul Survivors (Gamble-Huff), Crimson 1010 | 10 |
| 5 | 8 | 10 | 13 | YOUR PRECIOUS LOVE — Marvin Gaye & Tammy Terrell (H. Fuqua-J. Bristol), Tamla 54156 | 9 |
| 6 | 3 | 3 | 2 | NEVER MY LOVE — Association (Bones Howe), Warner Bros. 7074 | 11 |
| 7 | 10 | 19 | 34 | INCENSE AND PEPPERMINTS — Strawberry Alarm Clock (Frank Slay & Bill Holmes), Uni 55018 | 6 |
| 8 | 9 | 13 | 18 | A NATURAL WOMAN — Aretha Franklin (Jerry Wexler), Atlantic 2441 | 6 |
| 9 | 19 | 35 | 48 | THE RAIN, THE PARK & OTHER THINGS — Cowsills (Artie Kornfeld), MGM 13810 | 6 |
| 10 | 15 | 20 | 37 | PLEASE LOVE ME FOREVER — Bobby Vinton (Billy Sherrill), Epic 10228 | 6 |
| 11 | 11 | 11 | 16 | GET ON UP — Esquires (Bill Sheppard), Bunky 7750 | 12 |
| 12 | 17 | 26 | 41 | I'M WONDERING — Stevie Wonder (Henry Cosby), Tamla 54157 | 5 |
| 13 | 4 | 4 | 8 | HOW CAN I BE SURE — Young Rascals (Young Rascals), Atlantic 2438 | 9 |
| 14 | 12 | 17 | 23 | PEOPLE ARE STRANGE — Doors (Paul Rothchild), Elektra 45621 | 7 |
| 15 | 20 | 40 | 61 | (Loneliness Made Me Realize) IT'S YOU THAT I NEED — Temptations (N. Whitfield), Gordy 7065 | 4 |
| 16 | 16 | 21 | 27 | LET IT OUT — Hombres (Huey P. Meaux), Verve Forecast 5058 | 8 |
| 17 | 2 | 2 | 1 | THE LETTER — Box Tops (Dan Penn), Mala 565 | 13 |
| 18 | 24 | 29 | 38 | LOVE IS STRANGE — Peaches & Herb (David Kapralik & Ken Williams), Date 1574 | 6 |
| 19 | 13 | 9 | 9 | GIMME LITTLE SIGN — Brenton Wood (Hooven-Winn), Double Shot 116 | 15 |
| 20 | 14 | 12 | 12 | HEY BABY (They're Playing Our Song) — Buckinghams (James William Guercio), Columbia 44254 | 9 |
| 21 | 26 | 33 | 46 | HOLIDAY — Bee Gees (Robert Stigwood), Atco 6521 | 6 |
| 22 | 25 | 30 | 31 | THE LOOK OF LOVE — Dusty Springfield (Johnny Prenz), Philips 40465 | 13 |
| 23 | 38 | 48 | 72 | I CAN SEE FOR MILES — Who (Kit Lambert), Decca 32206 | 4 |
| 24 | 35 | 45 | 57 | EVERLASTING LOVE — Robert Knight (Buzz Cason & Mac Gayden), Rising Sons 117 | 6 |
| 25 | 28 | 31 | 36 | THE LAST WALTZ — Englebert Humperdinck (Peter Sullivan), Parrot 40019 | 7 |
| 26 | 36 | 46 | 73 | PATA PATA — Miriam Makeba (Jerry Ragovoy), Reprise 0606 | 5 |
| 27 | 42 | 75 | — | I SAY A LITTLE PRAYER — Dionne Warwick (Bacharach-David), Scepter 12203 | 3 |
| 28 | 34 | 47 | 82 | KENTUCKY WOMAN — Neil Diamond (Jeff Barry & Ellie Greenwich), Bang 551 | 4 |
| 29 | 40 | 50 | 88 | LAZY DAY — Spanky & Our Gang (Jerry Ross), Mercury 72732 | 4 |
| 30 | 46 | 76 | — | LADY BIRD — Nancy Sinatra & Lee Hazlewood (Lee Hazlewood), Reprise 0629 | 3 |
| 31 | 31 | 32 | 32 | CHILD OF CLAY — Jimmie Rodgers (Allen Stanton), A&M 871 | 7 |
| 32 | 54 | 74 | — | I HEARD IT THROUGH THE GRAPEVINE — Gladys Knight & the Pips (N. Whitfield), Soul 35039 | 3 |
| 33 | 23 | 23 | 28 | LET LOVE COME BETWEEN US — James & Bobby Purify (Papa Don), Bell 685 | 9 |
| 34 | 21 | 16 | 7 | COME BACK WHEN YOU GROW UP — Bobby Vee & the Strangers (Dallas Smith), Liberty 55964 | 16 |
| 35 | 18 | 8 | 4 | LITTLE OLE MAN (Uptight—Everything's Alright) — Bill Cosby (Fred Smith), Warner Bros. 7072 | 10 |
| 36 | 37 | 37 | 49 | EVEN THE BAD TIMES ARE GOOD — Tremeloes (Mike Smith), Epic 10233 | 6 |
| 37 | 62 | — | — | GLAD TO BE UNHAPPY — Mamas & the Papas (Lou Adler), Dunhill 4107 | 2 |
| 38 | 48 | 55 | 71 | BIG BOSS MAN — Elvis Presley, RCA Victor 9341 | 4 |
| 39 | 43 | 53 | 60 | YOU'VE MADE ME SO VERY HAPPY — Brenda Holloway (Berry Gordy Jr.), Tamla 54155 | 9 |
| 40 | 50 | 71 | 83 | BOOGALOO DOWN BROADWAY — Fantastic Johnny C. (Jesse James), Phil-L.A. of Soul 305 | 4 |
| 41 | 59 | 80 | — | LIKE AN OLD TIME MOVIE — Scott McKenzie (John Phillips & Lou Adler), Ode 105 | 3 |
| 42 | 63 | — | — | SHE IS STILL A MYSTERY — Lovin' Spoonful (Joe Wissert), Kama Sutra 239 | 2 |
| 43 | 29 | 14 | 5 | ODE TO BILLIE JOE — Bobbie Gentry (Kelly Gordon & Bobby Paris), Capitol 5950 | 14 |
| 44 | 47 | 51 | 63 | JUST ONE LOOK — Hollies, Imperial 66258 | 5 |
| 45 | 56 | 57 | 94 | YOU DON'T KNOW ME — Elvis Presley, RCA Victor 9341 | 4 |
| 46 | 57 | 90 | — | KEEP THE BALL ROLLIN' — Jay & the Techniques (Jerry Ross), Smash 2124 | 3 |
| 47 | 66 | — | — | HOMBURG — Procol Harum (Denny Cordell), A&M 885 | 2 |
| 48 | 27 | 18 | 11 | APPLES, PEACHES, PUMPKIN PIE — Jay & the Techniques (Jerry Ross), Smash 2086 | 17 |
| 49 | 32 | 24 | 25 | LIGHTNING'S GIRL — Nancy Sinatra (Lee Hazlewood), Reprise 0620 | 7 |
| 50 | 22 | 22 | 19 | YOU KEEP RUNNING AWAY — Four Tops (Holland & Dozier), Motown 1113 | 8 |
| 51 | 53 | 58 | 81 | KARATE-BOO-GA-LOO — Jerry O (Jerry Murray), Shout 217 | 6 |
| 52 | 52 | 56 | 76 | HUSH — Billy Joe Royal (Joe South), Columbia 44277 | 2 |
| 53 | 65 | — | — | GET IT TOGETHER — James Brown & the Famous Flames (James Brown), King 6122 | 2 |
| 54 | 64 | 100 | — | BACK ON THE STREET AGAIN — Sunshine Company (Joe Saraceno), Imperial 66260 | 3 |
| 55 | 69 | 79 | — | MR. DREAM MERCHANT — Jerry Butler (Jerry Ross), Mercury 72721 | 3 |
| 56 | 58 | 61 | 69 | SHOUT BAMALAMA — Mickey Murray (Bobby Smith), SSS715 | 6 |
| 57 | — | — | — | STAG-O-LEE — Wilson Pickett (Tom Dowd & Tommy Cogbill), Atlantic 2448 | 1 |
| 58 | 72 | 77 | 93 | BEG, BORROW AND STEAL — Ohio Express (Jeff Katy & Jerry Kasenetz), Cameo 483 | 4 |
| 59 | 70 | 81 | — | ARE YOU NEVER COMING HOME — Sandy Posey (Chips Moman), MGM 13824 | 3 |
| 60 | 60 | 64 | 77 | IF THIS IS LOVE (I'd Rather Be Lonely) — Precisions (Coleman-Bassoline-Val King), Drew 1003 | 5 |
| 61 | 76 | — | — | WATCH THE FLOWERS GROW — 4 Seasons (Bob Crewe), Philips 40490 | 2 |
| 62 | 79 | — | — | YOU BETTER SIT DOWN KIDS — Cher (Sonny Bond), Imperial 66261 | 2 |
| 63 | 78 | — | — | THIS TOWN — Frank Sinatra (Jimmy Bowen), Reprise 0631 | 2 |
| 64 | 51 | 52 | 58 | KING MIDAS IN REVERSE — Hollies (Ron Richards), Epic 10234 | 4 |
| 65 | 80 | 87 | — | GO-GO GIRL — Lee Dorsey (Allen R. Toussaint & Marshall E. Schorn), Amy 998 | 3 |
| 66 | 44 | 44 | 59 | ROCK 'N' ROLL WOMAN — Buffalo Springfield (Stephen Stills & Neil Young), Atco 6519 | 6 |
| 67 | — | — | — | WILD HONEY — Beach Boys (Beach Boys), Capitol 2028 | 1 |
| 68 | 85 | — | — | OUT OF THE BLUE — Tommy James & the Shondells (Big Kahoona Prod.), Roulette 4775 | 2 |
| 69 | 93 | — | — | SKINNY LEGS AND ALL — Joe Tex (Buddy Killen), Dial 4063 | 2 |
| 70 | 86 | — | — | SUZANNE — Noel Harrison (Jimmy Bowen), Reprise 0615 | 2 |
| 71 | 71 | 82 | 86 | NINE POUND STEEL — Joe Simon (J.R. Enterprises, Inc.), Sound Stage 7 2589 | 7 |
| 72 | 75 | — | — | WAKE UP, WAKE UP — Grass Roots (Steve Barri & P.P. Sloan), Dunhill 4105 | 2 |
| 73 | 73 | 73 | 79 | SPREADIN' HONEY — Watts 103rd St. Rhythm Band (Fred Smith), Keymen 103 | 9 |
| 74 | 61 | 66 | 75 | WHAT'VE I DONE (To Make You Mad) — Linda Jones (George Kerr), Loma 2077 | 6 |
| 75 | 90 | 91 | — | NEXT PLANE TO LONDON — Rose Garden (Greene/Stone), Atco 6510 | 3 |
| 76 | 87 | — | — | BY THE TIME I GET TO PHOENIX — Glen Campbell (Al De Lory), Capitol 2015 | 2 |
| 77 | 77 | 78 | 78 | YOU MEAN THE WORLD TO ME — David Houston (Billy Sherrill), Epic 10224 | 5 |
| 78 | 68 | 70 | 80 | DIRTY MAN — Laura Lee (Rick Hall), Chess 2013 | 7 |
| 79 | 81 | 84 | — | CAN'T STOP LOVING YOU — Last Word (Brad Shapiro & Steve Alaimo), Atco 6498 | 4 |
| 80 | 83 | 88 | 90 | GO WITH ME — Gene & Debbe (Troy Caldwell), TRX 5002 | 4 |
| 81 | 84 | 85 | 91 | GET DOWN — Harvey Scales & the Seven Sounds (Lennie LaCour), Magic Touch 2007 | 4 |
| 82 | 82 | 96 | — | BRINK OF DISASTER — Lesley Gore (Steve Douglas), Mercury 72726 | 3 |
| 83 | — | — | — | WHOLE LOTTA WOMAN — Arthur Conley (Otis Redding), Atco 6529 | 1 |
| 84 | — | — | — | WHEN YOU'RE GONE — Brenda & Tabulations (Bob Finis), Dicon 504 | 1 |
| 85 | — | — | — | I SECOND THAT EMOTION — Smokey Robinson & Miracles ("Smokey" A. Cleveland), Tamla 54159 | 1 |
| 86 | 88 | 89 | 98 | LOVEY DOVEY/YOU'RE SO FINE — Bunny Sigler (John Madare & Leon Huff), Parkway 6000 | 4 |
| 87 | 97 | 97 | 100 | SHAME ON ME — Chuck Jackson (Don Schroeder), Wand 1166 | 4 |
| 88 | 89 | 94 | 97 | ALL YOUR GOODIES ARE GONE — Parliaments (Clinton & Taylor), Revilot 211 | 3 |
| 89 | 95 | — | — | BIRDS OF BRITAIN — Bob Crewe Generation (Bob Crewe), DynoVoice 902 | 2 |
| 90 | — | — | — | PAPER CUP — 5th Dimension (Bones Howe), Soul City 760 | 1 |
| 91 | 91 | 96 | 96 | GIVE EVERYBODY SOME — Bar-Kays (David Porter & Isaac Hayes), Volt 154 | 4 |
| 92 | — | — | — | FOR ONCE IN MY LIFE — Tony Bennett (Howard A. Roberts), Columbia 44258 | 2 |
| 93 | 94 | — | — | YOU ARE MY SUNSHINE — Mitch Ryder (Bob Crewe), New Voice 826 | 2 |
| 94 | 96 | 99 | — | SWEET, SWEET LOVIN' — Platters (Richard "Popcorn" Wylie), Musicor 1275 | 3 |
| 95 | — | — | — | O-O, I LOVE YOU — Dells (B. Miller), Cadet 5574 | 1 |
| 96 | 98 | — | — | LAPLAND — Baltimore & Ohio Marching Band (Mouse House), Jubilee 5592 | 2 |
| 97 | 100 | — | — | ON A SATURDAY NIGHT — Eddie Floyd (Steve Grapper), Stax 233 | 2 |
| 98 | 99 | — | — | DESIREE' — Left Banke (Mike Brown), Smash 2119 | 2 |
| 99 | — | — | — | ALLIGATOR BOOGALOO — Lou Donaldson (Alfred Lion), Blue Note 1934 | 1 |
| 100 | — | — | — | PIECE OF MY HEART — Erma Franklin (Bert Berns), Shout 221 | 1 |

## BUBBLING UNDER THE HOT 100

101. ITCHYCOO PARK ..... Small Faces, Immediate 501
102. BALLAD OF WATERHOLE #3 ..... Roger Miller, Smash 2121
103. WE GOTTA GO HOME ..... Music Explosion, Laurie 3414
104. PONY WITH THE GOLDEN MANE ..... Every Mother's Son, MGM 13864
105. FOR A FEW DOLLARS MORE ..... Hugo Montenegro, RCA Victor 9224
106. WHEN THE LOVE IS ON THE ROSES ..... Ed Ames, RCA Victor 9319
107. NO, NO, ROSEY ..... Van Morrison, Bang 552
108. YOU, NO ONE BUT YOU ..... Frankie Laine, ABC 10983
109. EXCERPT FROM A TEENAGE OPERA ..... Keith West, New Voice 2000
110. BELIEVE IN ME BABY ..... Jesse James, 20th Century-Fox 6684
111. I WANT ACTION ..... Ruby Winters, Diamond 230
112. AS LONG AS YOU'RE HERE ..... Zalman Yanovsky (Zally), Buddah 12
113. LITTLE GIRL ..... Critters, Kapp 858
114. LOVE OF THE COMMON PEOPLE ..... Wayne Newton, Capitol 2016
115. LOVE OF THE COMMON PEOPLE ..... Everly Brothers, Warner Bros. 7088
116. I GOT A FEELING ..... Barbara Randolph, Soul 35038
117. I ALMOST CALLED YOUR NAME ..... Margaret Whiting, London 115
118. IT TAKES PEOPLE LIKE YOU ..... Buck Owens, Capitol 2001
119. SHE ..... Roy Orbison, MGM 13817
120. JUST LOVIN' YOU ..... Anita Harris, Columbia 44236
121. GEORGIA PINES ..... Candymen, ABC 10995
122. DIFFERENT DRUM ..... Stone Poneys, Capitol 2004
123. CROSS MY HEART ..... Billy Stewart, Chess 2002
124. MY SHIP IS COMIN' IN ..... Walter Jackson, Okeh 7295
125. HUNK OF FUNK ..... Gene Dozier & the Brotherhood, Minit 32026
126. BABY IT'S WONDERFUL ..... Chris Bartley, Vando 4005
127. BEAUTIFUL PEOPLE ..... Kenny O'Dell, Vegas 718
128. BO DIDDLEY BACH ..... Wingsmen, Bang 1164
129. I WANT MY BABY BACK ..... Edwin Starr, Gordy 7066
130. OPEN FOR BUSINESS ..... Jack Jones, Kapp 860
131. WHERE IS THE MELODY ..... Stone Poneys, Decca 22213
132. I WANT SOME MORE ..... Jon & Robin & the In Crowd, Abnak 124
133. YOU'LL GO TO HELL ..... Nina Simone, RCA Victor 9286
134. SHE'S MY GIRL ..... Turtles, White Whale 264
135. A LOVE THAT'S REAL ..... Intruders, Gamble 209

Compiled from national retail sales and radio station airplay by the Music Popularity Dept. of Record Market Research, Billboard.

# Billboard HOT 100

For Week Ending November 11, 1967

★ STAR performer—Sides registering greatest proportionate upward progress this week.

Record Industry Association of America seal of certification as million selling single.

| This Week | 1 Wk. Ago | 2 Wks. Ago | 3 Wks. Ago | TITLE Artist (Producer), Label & Number | Weeks On Chart |
|---|---|---|---|---|---|
| 1 ★ | 1 | 1 | 1 | **TO SIR, WITH LOVE**<br>Lulu (Mickie Most), Epic 10187 | 10 |
| 2 | 2 | 7 | 7 | **SOUL MAN**<br>Sam & Dave (Isaac Hayes & David Porter), Stax 231 | 10 |
| 3 | 3 | 6 | 6 | **IT MUST BE HIM**<br>Vikki Carr (Dave Pell), Liberty 55986 | 11 |
| 4 | 7 | 10 | 19 | **INCENSE AND PEPPERMINTS**<br>Strawberry Alarm Clock (Frank Slay & Bill Holmes), Uni 55018 | 7 |
| 5 | 5 | 8 | 10 | **YOUR PRECIOUS LOVE**<br>Marvin Gaye & Tammy Terrell (H. Fuqua-J. Bristol), Tamla 54156 | 10 |
| 6 | 9 | 19 | 35 | **THE RAIN, THE PARK & OTHER THINGS**<br>Cowsills (Artie Kornfeld), MGM 13810 | 7 |
| 7 | 10 | 15 | 20 | **PLEASE LOVE ME FOREVER**<br>Bobby Vinton (Billy Sherrill), Epic 10228 | 7 |
| 8 | 8 | 9 | 13 | **A NATURAL WOMAN**<br>Aretha Franklin (Jerry Wexler), Atlantic 2441 | 7 |
| 9 | 4 | 5 | 5 | **EXPRESSWAY TO YOUR HEART**<br>Soul Survivors (Gamble-Huff), Crimson 1010 | 11 |
| 10 | 6 | 3 | 3 | **NEVER MY LOVE**<br>Association (Bones Howe), Warner Bros. 7074 | 12 |
| 11 ★ | 23 | 38 | 48 | **I CAN SEE FOR MILES**<br>Who (Kit Lambert), Decca 32206 | 4 |
| 12 | 12 | 17 | 26 | **I'M WONDERING**<br>Stevie Wonder (Henry Cosby), Tamla 54157 | 6 |
| 13 | 18 | 24 | 29 | **LOVE IS STRANGE**<br>Peaches & Herb (David Kapralik & Ken Williams), Date 1574 | 7 |
| 14 | 15 | 20 | 40 | **(Loneliness Made Me Realize) IT'S YOU THAT I NEED**<br>Temptations (N. Whitfield), Gordy 7065 | 5 |
| 15 | 16 | 16 | 21 | **LET IT OUT**<br>Hombres (Huey P. Meaux), Verve Forecast 5058 | 9 |
| 16 | 21 | 26 | 33 | **HOLIDAY**<br>Bee Gees (Robert Stigwood), Atco 6521 | 7 |
| 17 | 13 | 4 | 4 | **HOW CAN I BE SURE**<br>Young Rascals (Young Rascals), Atlantic 2438 | 10 |
| 18 | 14 | 12 | 17 | **PEOPLE ARE STRANGE**<br>Doors (Paul Rothchild), Elektra 45621 | 8 |
| 19 | 24 | 35 | 45 | **EVERLASTING LOVE**<br>Robert Knight (Buzz Cason & Mac Gayden), Rising Sons 117 | 7 |
| 20 | 11 | 11 | 11 | **GET ON UP**<br>Esquires (Bill Sheppard), Bunky 7750 | 13 |
| 21 ★ | 26 | 36 | 46 | **PATA PATA**<br>Miriam Makeba (Jerry Ragovoy), Reprise 0606 | 5 |
| 22 | 27 | 42 | 75 | **I SAY A LITTLE PRAYER**<br>Dionne Warwick (Bacharach-David), Scepter 12203 | 4 |
| 23 | 28 | 34 | 47 | **KENTUCKY WOMAN**<br>Neil Diamond (Jeff Barry & Ellie Greenwich), Bang 551 | 5 |
| 24 | 29 | 40 | 50 | **LAZY DAY**<br>Spanky & Our Gang (Jerry Ross), Mercury 72732 | 5 |
| 25 | 30 | 46 | 76 | **LADY BIRD**<br>Nancy Sinatra & Lee Hazlewood (Lee Hazlewood), Reprise 0629 | 4 |
| 26 | 17 | 2 | 2 | **THE LETTER**<br>Box Tops (Dan Penn), Mala 565 | 14 |
| 27 | 32 | 54 | 74 | **I HEARD IT THROUGH THE GRAPEVINE**<br>Gladys Knight & the Pips (N. Whitfield), Soul 35039 | 4 |
| 28 | 19 | 13 | 9 | **GIMME LITTLE SIGN**<br>Brenton Wood (Hooven-Winn), Double Shot 116 | 16 |
| 29 | 37 | 62 | — | **GLAD TO BE UNHAPPY**<br>Mamas & the Papas (Lou Adler), Dunhill 4107 | 3 |
| 30 | 40 | 50 | 71 | **BOOGALOO DOWN BROADWAY**<br>Fantastic Johnny C. (Jesse James), Phil-L.A. of Soul 305 | 6 |
| 31 | 41 | 59 | 80 | **LIKE AN OLD TIME MOVIE**<br>Scott McKenzie (John Phillips & Lou Adler), Ode 105 | 4 |
| 32 | 42 | 63 | — | **SHE IS STILL A MYSTERY**<br>Lovin' Spoonful (Joe Wissert), Kama Sutra 239 | 3 |
| 33 | 25 | 28 | 31 | **THE LAST WALTZ**<br>Engelbert Humperdinck (Peter Sullivan), Parrot 40019 | 8 |
| 34 | 22 | 25 | 30 | **THE LOOK OF LOVE**<br>Dusty Springfield (Johnny Prenz), Philips 40465 | 14 |
| 35 ★ | 46 | 57 | 90 | **KEEP THE BALL ROLLIN'**<br>Jay & the Techniques (Jerry Ross), Smash 2124 | 4 |
| 36 | 20 | 14 | 12 | **HEY BABY (They're Playing Our Song)**<br>Buckinghams (James William Guercio), Columbia 44254 | 10 |
| 37 | 47 | 66 | — | **HOMBURG**<br>Procol Harum (Denny Cordell), A&M 885 | 3 |
| 38 | 38 | 48 | 55 | **BIG BOSS MAN**<br>Elvis Presley, RCA Victor 9341 | 5 |
| 39 | 57 | — | — | **STAG-O-LEE**<br>Wilson Pickett (Tom Dowd & Tommy Cogbill), Atlantic 2448 | 2 |
| 40 | 36 | 37 | 37 | **EVEN THE BAD TIMES ARE GOOD**<br>Tremeloes (Mike Smith), Epic 10233 | 7 |
| 41 ★ | 62 | 79 | — | **YOU BETTER SIT DOWN KIDS**<br>Cher (Sonny Bono), Imperial 66261 | 3 |
| 42 | 53 | 65 | — | **GET IT TOGETHER**<br>James Brown & the Famous Flames (James Brown), King 6122 | 3 |
| 43 ★ | 54 | 64 | 100 | **BACK ON THE STREET AGAIN**<br>Sunshine Company (Joe Saraceno), Imperial 66260 | 4 |
| 44 ★ | 55 | 69 | 79 | **MR. DREAM MERCHANT**<br>Jerry Butler (Jerry Ross), Mercury 72721 | 4 |
| 45 | 45 | 56 | 57 | **YOU DON'T KNOW ME**<br>Elvis Presley, RCA Victor 9341 | 5 |
| 46 | 67 | — | — | **WILD HONEY**<br>Beach Boys (Beach Boys), Capitol 2028 | 2 |
| 47 | 35 | 18 | 8 | **LITTLE OLE MAN (Uptight—Everything's Alright)**<br>Bill Cosby (Fred Smith), Warner Bros. 7072 | 11 |
| 48 | 58 | 72 | 77 | **BEG, BORROW AND STEAL**<br>Ohio Express (Jeff Katz & Jerry Kasenetz), Cameo 483 | 6 |
| 49 | 61 | 76 | — | **WATCH THE FLOWERS GROW**<br>4 Seasons (Bob Crewe), Philips 40490 | 3 |
| 50 | 31 | 31 | 32 | **CHILD OF CLAY**<br>Jimmie Rodgers (Allen Stanton), A&M 871 | 8 |
| 51 ★ | 76 | 87 | — | **BY THE TIME I GET TO PHOENIX**<br>Glen Campbell (Al De Lory), Capitol 2015 | 3 |
| 52 | 52 | 52 | 56 | **HUSH**<br>Billy Joe Royal (Joe South), Columbia 44277 | 7 |
| 53 | 63 | 78 | — | **THIS TOWN**<br>Frank Sinatra (Jimmy Bowen), Reprise 0631 | 3 |
| 54 | 56 | 58 | 61 | **SHOUT BAMALAMA**<br>Mickey Murray (Bobby Smith), 555715 | 6 |
| 55 | 39 | 43 | 53 | **YOU'VE MADE ME SO VERY HAPPY**<br>Brenda Holloway (Berry Gordy Jr.), Tamla 54155 | 10 |
| 56 | 68 | 85 | — | **OUT OF THE BLUE**<br>Tommy James & the Shondells (Big Kahoona Prod.), Roulette 4775 | 3 |
| 57 | 85 | — | — | **I SECOND THAT EMOTION**<br>Smokey Robinson & Miracles ("Smokey" A. Cleveland), Tamla 54159 | 2 |
| 58 | 69 | 93 | — | **SKINNY LEGS AND ALL**<br>Joe Tex (Buddy Killen), Dial 4063 | 3 |
| 59 | 59 | 70 | 81 | **ARE YOU NEVER COMING HOME**<br>Sandy Posey (Chips Moman), MGM 13824 | 4 |
| 60 | 70 | 86 | — | **SUZANNE**<br>Noel Harrison (Jimmy Bowen), Reprise 0615 | 3 |
| 61 | 51 | 53 | 58 | **KARATE-BOO-GA-LOO**<br>Jerry O (Jerry Murray), Shout 217 | 7 |
| 62 | — | — | — | **YESTERDAY**<br>Ray Charles (TRC), ABC 11009 | 1 |
| 63 | 60 | 60 | 64 | **IF THIS IS LOVE (I'd Rather Be Lonely)**<br>Precisions (Coleman-Bassoline-Val Valo), Drew 1003 | 6 |
| 64 | 65 | 80 | 87 | **GO-GO GIRL**<br>Lee Dorsey (Allen R. Toussaint & Marshall E. Schorn), Amy 998 | 4 |
| 65 | — | — | — | **IN AND OUT OF LOVE**<br>Diana Ross & the Supremes (Holland, Dozier), Motown 1116 | 1 |
| 66 | 75 | 90 | 91 | **NEXT PLANE TO LONDON**<br>Rose Garden (Greene/Stone), Atco 6510 | 4 |
| 67 | — | — | — | **SHE'S MY GIRL**<br>Turtles (Joe Wissert), White Whale 260 | 1 |
| 68 | 66 | 44 | 44 | **ROCK 'N' ROLL WOMAN**<br>Buffalo Springfield (Stephen Stills & Neil Young), Atco 6519 | 7 |
| 69 | 44 | 47 | 51 | **JUST ONE LOOK**<br>Hollies, Imperial 66258 | 7 |
| 70 | 72 | 75 | — | **WAKE UP, WAKE UP**<br>Grass Roots (Steve Barri & P. F. Sloan), Dunhill 4105 | 3 |
| 71 | 71 | 71 | 82 | **NINE POUND STEEL**<br>Joe Simon (J.R. Enterprises, Inc.) Sound Stage 7 2589 | 8 |
| 72 | 90 | — | — | **PAPER CUP**<br>5th Dimension (Bones Howe), Soul City 760 | 2 |
| 73 | 83 | — | — | **WHOLE LOTTA WOMAN**<br>Arthur Conley (Otis Redding), Atco 6529 | 2 |
| 74 | — | — | — | **(The Lights Went Out In) MASSACHUSETTS**<br>Bee Gees (Robert Stigwood), Atco 6532 | 1 |
| 75 | 77 | 77 | 78 | **YOU MEAN THE WORLD TO ME**<br>David Houston (Billy Sherrill), Epic 10224 | 6 |
| 76 | 73 | 73 | 73 | **SPREADIN' HONEY**<br>Watts 103rd St. Rhythm Band (Fred Smith), Keymen 103 | 10 |
| 77 | 94 | 96 | 99 | **SWEET, SWEET LOVIN'**<br>Platters (Richard "Popcorn" Wylie), Musicor 1275 | 4 |
| 78 | 80 | 83 | 88 | **GO WITH ME**<br>Gene & Debbe (Troy Caldwell), TRX 5002 | 5 |
| 79 | 79 | 81 | 84 | **CAN'T STOP LOVING YOU**<br>Last Word (Brad Shapiro & Steve Alaimo), Atco 6498 | 4 |
| 80 | 81 | 84 | 85 | **GET DOWN**<br>Harvey Scales & the Seven Sounds (Lennie LaCour), Magic Touch 2007 | 5 |
| 81 | — | — | — | **SOUL MAN**<br>Ramsey Lewis (Richard Evans), Cadet 5583 | 1 |
| 82 | 82 | 82 | 86 | **BRINK OF DISASTER**<br>Lesley Gore (Steve Douglas), Mercury 72726 | 4 |
| 83 | 84 | — | — | **WHEN YOU'RE GONE**<br>Brenda & Tabulations (Bob Finis), Dicon 504 | 3 |
| 84 | — | — | — | **AN OPEN LETTER TO MY TEENAGE SON**<br>Victor Lundberg, Liberty 55996 | 1 |
| 85 | 87 | 97 | 97 | **SHAME ON ME**<br>Chuck Jackson (Don Schroeder), Wand 1166 | 4 |
| 86 | 88 | 89 | 94 | **ALL YOUR GOODIES ARE GONE**<br>Parliaments (Clinton & Taylor), Revilot 211 | 5 |
| 87 | — | — | — | **NEON RAINBOW**<br>Box Tops (Dan Penn), Mala 580 | 1 |
| 88 | 93 | 94 | — | **YOU ARE MY SUNSHINE**<br>Mitch Ryder (Bob Crewe), New Voice 826 | 3 |
| 89 | 95 | — | — | **O-O, I LOVE YOU**<br>Dells (B. Miller), Cadet 5574 | 2 |
| 90 | — | — | — | **DIFFERENT DRUM**<br>Stone Poneys (Nick Venet), Capitol 2004 | 1 |
| 91 | 92 | 92 | — | **FOR ONCE IN MY LIFE**<br>Tony Bennett (Howard A. Roberts), Columbia 44258 | 3 |
| 92 | — | — | — | **ITCHYCOO PARK**<br>Small Faces (Steve Marriott & Ronnie Lane), Immediate 501 | 1 |
| 93 | — | — | — | **WHERE IS THE PARTY**<br>Helena Ferguson (Lincoln Kilpatrick), Compass 7009 | 1 |
| 94 | 96 | 98 | — | **LAPLAND**<br>Baltimore & Ohio Marching Band (Mouse House), Jubilee 5592 | 3 |
| 95 | — | 99 | — | **ALLIGATOR BOOGALOO**<br>Lou Donaldson (Alfred Lion), Blue Note 1934 | 2 |
| 96 | — | — | — | **PONY WITH THE GOLDEN MANE**<br>Every Mother's Son (Wes Farrell), MGM 13844 | 1 |
| 97 | 97 | 100 | — | **ON A SATURDAY NIGHT**<br>Eddie Floyd (Steve Grapper), Stax 233 | 3 |
| 98 | — | — | — | **TELL MAMA**<br>Etta James (Rick Hall), Cadet 5578 | 1 |
| 99 | 100 | — | — | **PIECE OF MY HEART**<br>Erma Franklin (Bert Berns), Shout 221 | 2 |
| 100 | — | — | — | **HE AIN'T GIVE YOU NONE**<br>Freddie Scott (Bert Berns), Shout 220 | 1 |

## HOT 100—A TO Z—(Publisher-Licensee)

All Your Goodies Are Gone (Grooveville, BMI) .. 86
Alligator Boogaloo (Blue Horizon, BMI) ........ 95
An Open Letter to My Teenage Son (Asa, ASCAP) 84
Are You Never Coming Home (Press, BMI) ..... 59
Back on the Street Again (Cherry Lane, ASCAP) 43
Beg, Borrow and Steal (S&J, ASCAP) .......... 48
Big Boss Man (Conrad, BMI) .................. 38
Boogaloo Down Broadway (Dandelion/James Boy, BMI) ...................................... 30
Brink of Disaster (Stone Canyon, BMI) ........ 82
By the Time I Get to Phoenix (Rivers, BMI) ... 51
Can't Stop Loving You (Sherlyn, BMI) ......... 79
Child of Clay (Screen Gems-Columbia, BMI) ... 50
Different Drum (Screen Gems-Columbia, BMI) . 90
Even the Bad Times Are Good (Ponderosa, BMI) 40
Everlasting Love (Rising Sons, BMI) ........... 19
Expressway to Your Heart (Double Diamond/Downstairs, BMI) .............................. 9
For Once in My Life (Stein & Van Stock, ASCAP) 91
Get Down (LaCour/East, BMI) ................. 80
Get It Together (Dynatone, BMI) ............... 42
Get on Up (Hi-Mi, BMI) ........................ 20
Gimme Little Sign (Big Shot, ASCAP) .......... 28
Glad to Be Unhappy (Chappell, ASCAP) ....... 29
Go-Go Girl (Marsaint, BMI) .................... 64
Go With Me (Acuff-Rose, BMI) ................ 78
He Ain't Give You None (Web IV, BMI) ........ 100
Hey Baby (They're Playing Our Song) (Diogenes/Bag of Tunes, BMI) .......................... 36
Holiday (Nemperor, BMI) ...................... 16
Homburg (Total, BMI) ......................... 37
How Can I Be Sure (Slacsar, BMI) ............. 17
Hush (Lowery, BMI) ........................... 52
I Can See for Miles (Essex, ASCAP) ............ 11
I Heard It Through the Grapevine (Jobete, BMI) 27
I Say a Little Prayer (Blue Seas/Jac, ASCAP) ... 22
I Second That Emotion (Jobete, BMI) .......... 57

If This Is Love (I'd Rather Be Lonely) (In-The-Pocket/Sidrian, BMI) ........................... 63
I'm Wondering (Jobete, BMI) ................... 12
In and Out of Love (Jobete, BMI) .............. 65
Incense and Peppermints (Claridge, ASCAP) ... 4
Itchycoo Park (Nice Songs, BMI) ............... 92
It Must Be Him (Asa, ASCAP) .................. 3
Just One Look (Premier Albums, BMI) .......... 69
Karate-Boo-Ga-Loo (Boogaloo/Love Lane, BMI) . 61
Keep the Ball Rollin' (Screen Gems-Columbia, BMI) ........................................ 35
Kentucky Woman (Tallyrand, BMI) .............. 23
Lady Bird (Hazlewood, ASCAP) ................. 25
Lapland (Screen Gems-Columbia, BMI) ........ 94
Last Waltz, The (Donna, ASCAP) ............... 33
Lazy Day (Screen Gems-Columbia, BMI) ....... 24
Let It Out (Crazy Cajun, BMI) .................. 15
Letter, The (Barton, BMI) ...................... 26
Like an Old-Time Movie (Wingate, ASCAP) .... 31
Little Ole Man (Uptight-Everything's Alright) (Jobete, BMI) .................................. 47
Look of Love, The (Colgems, ASCAP) .......... 34
(Loneliness Made Me Realize) It's You That I Need (Jobete, BMI) ............................. 14
Love Is Strange (Chazi, BMI) ................... 13
Mr. Dream Merchant (Saturday, BMI) .......... 44
Natural Woman, A (Screen Gems-Columbia, BMI) 8
Neon Rainbow (Barton, BMI) ................... 87
Never My Love (Tamerlane, BMI) ............... 10
Next Plane to London (Myrwood/Antlers, BMI) . 66
O-O, I Love You (Chevris, BMI) ................. 89
On a Saturday Night (East, BMI) ............... 97
Out of the Blue (Patricia, BMI) ................. 56
Paper Cup (Rivers, BMI) ....................... 72
Pata Pata (Xina, ASCAP) ....................... 21
People Are Strange (Nipper, ASCAP) ........... 18
Piece of My Heart (Web IV/Ragmar, BMI) ...... 99

Please Love Me Forever (Selma, BMI) .......... 7
Pony With the Golden Mane (Pocket Full of Tunes/TobiAnn, BMI) ........................... 96
Rain, the Park & Other Things, The (Akbestal/Lucalon, BMI) ......................... 6
Rock 'n' Roll Woman (Ten-East/Springale/Cotillion, BMI) ................................. 68
Shame on Me (Lois, BMI) ...................... 85
She Is Still a Mystery (Faithful Virtue, BMI) ... 32
She's My Girl (Screen Gems-Columbia, BMI) .. 67
Shout Bamalama (Press-East/Pronto, BMI) ..... 54
Skinny Legs and All (Tree, BMI) ................ 58
Soul Man (East/Pronto, BMI) ................... 2
Soul Man (Public Domain) ...................... 81
Spreadin' Honey (Kaymen/Pure Soul, BMI) .... 76
Stag-O-Lee (Public Domain) .................... 39
Suzanne (Project 7, BMI) ...................... 60
Sweet, Sweet Lovin' (Catalogue, BMI) ......... 77
Tell Mama (Fame, BMI) ........................ 98
(The Lights Went Out In) Massachusetts (Nemperor, BMI) ............................... 74
This Town (Remick, ASCAP) .................... 53
To Sir, With Love (Screen Gems-Columbia, BMI) 1
Wake Up, Wake Up (Trousdale, BMI) ........... 70
Watch the Flowers Grow (Saturday/Seasons Four, BMI) ...................................... 49
When You're Gone (Dandelion, BMI) ........... 83
Where Is the Party (Frabob/Palo Alto/Dakar, BMI) ........................................... 93
Whole Lotta Woman (Kags, BMI) ............... 73
Wild Honey (Sea of Tunes, BMI) ................ 46
Yesterday (Maclen, BMI) ....................... 62
You Are My Sunshine (Peer Int'l., BMI) ........ 88
You Better Sit Down Kids (Chrismarc/Cotillion, BMI) ........................................... 41
You Don't Know Me (Hill & Range, BMI) ...... 45
You Mean the World to Me (G-Illico, BMI) ..... 75
Your Precious Love (Jobete, BMI) .............. 5
You've Made Me So Very Happy (Jobete, BMI) . 55

## BUBBLING UNDER THE HOT 100

101. DAYDREAM BELIEVER ............. Monkees, Colgems 1012
102. BALLAD OF WATERHOLE #3 .... Roger Miller, Smash 2121
103. WE GOTTA GO HOME ............ Music Explosion, Laurie 3414
104. DESIREE ............................. The Left Banke, Smash 2119
105. FOR A FEW DOLLARS MORE ... Hugo Montenegro, RCA Victor 9224
106. GIVE EVERYBODY SOME ........ Bar-Cays, Volt 154
107. RO RO ROSEY ...................... Van Morrison, Bang 552
108. BIRDS OF BRITAIN ............... Bob Crewe Generation, Dyno Voice 902
109. I WANT ACTION ................... Ruby Winters, Diamond 230
110. RED & BLUE ......................... Dave Clark Five, Epic 10244
111. GEORGIA PINES .................... Candymen, ABC 10995
112. LOVE OF THE COMMON PEOPLE ... Wayne Newton, Capitol 2016
113. WHEN THE SNOW IS ON THE ROSES ... Ed Ames, RCA Victor 9319
114. LOVE OF THE COMMON PEOPLE ... Everly Brothers, Warner Bros. 7088
115. BEAUTIFUL PEOPLE ............... Kenny O'Dell, Vegas 718
116. BEAUTIFUL PEOPLE ............... Bobby Vee, Liberty 56009
117. CHATTANOOGA CHOO CHOO ... Harpers Bizarre, Warner Bros. 7090
118. IT TAKES PEOPLE LIKE YOU ... Buck Owens, Capitol 2001
119. WHERE IS THE MELODY .......... Brenda Lee, Decca 32213
120. BEAUTIFUL PEOPLE ............... Margaret Whiting, London 115
121. WHAT'S IT GONNA BE ............. Dusty Springfield, Philips 40498
122. CROSS MY HEART .................. Billy Stewart, Chess 2002
123. I WANT SOME MORE ............. Jon & Robin & the In Crowd, Abnak 124
124. HUNK OF FUNK ..................... Gene Dozier & the Brotherhood, Minit 32026
125. BABY, IT'S WONDERFUL ......... Chris Bartley, Vando 3000
126. MY SHIP IS COMING IN ........... Walter Jackson, Okeh 7295
127. I WANT MY BABY BACK ......... Edwin Starr, Gordy 7064
128. WOMAN, WOMAN .................. Union Gap, Featuring Gary Puckett, Columbia 44297
129. MEND ME, SHAPE ME .............. American Breed, Acta 811
130. A LOVE THAT'S REAL ............. Intruders, Gamble 209
131. TEN LITTLE INDIANS .............. Yardbirds, Epic 10248
132. STOP LIGHT ........................ Five Americans, Abnak 125
133. JUDY IN DISGUISE (With Glasses) ... John Fred & His Playboy Band, Paula 282
134. SAND ................................. Nancy Sinatra & Lee Hazlewood, Reprise 0629
135. I'M SO PROUD ..................... Keith, Mercury 72746

Compiled from national retail sales and radio station airplay by the Music Popularity Dept. of Record Market Research, Billboard.

# Billboard HOT 100

For Week Ending November 18, 1967

★ STAR performer—Sides registering greatest proportionate upward progress this week.

Record Industry Association of America seal of certification as million selling single.

| This Week | 1 Wk. Ago | 2 Wks. Ago | 3 Wks. Ago | TITLE Artist (Producer), Label & Number | Weeks On Chart |
|---|---|---|---|---|---|
| 1 ★ | 1 | 1 | 1 | **TO SIR, WITH LOVE** — Lulu (Mickie Most), Epic 10187 | 11 |
| 2 | 2 | 2 | 7 | **SOUL MAN** — Sam & Dave (Isaac Hayes & David Porter), Stax 231 | 11 |
| 3 | 4 | 7 | 10 | **INCENSE AND PEPPERMINTS** — Strawberry Alarm Clock (Frank Slay & Bill Holmes), Uni 55018 | 8 |
| 4 | 6 | 9 | 19 | **THE RAIN, THE PARK & OTHER THINGS** — Cowsills (Artie Kornfeld), MGM 13810 | 8 |
| 5 | 3 | 3 | 6 | **IT MUST BE HIM** — Vikki Carr (Dave Pell), Liberty 55986 | 12 |
| 6 | 7 | 10 | 15 | **PLEASE LOVE ME FOREVER** — Bobby Vinton (Billy Sherrill), Epic 10228 | 8 |
| 7 | 5 | 5 | 8 | **YOUR PRECIOUS LOVE** — Marvin Gaye & Tammy Terrell (H. Fuqua-J. Bristol), Tamla 54156 | 11 |
| 8 ★ | 22 | 27 | 42 | **I SAY A LITTLE PRAYER** — Dionne Warwick (Bacharach-David), Scepter 12203 | 5 |
| 9 | 9 | 4 | 5 | **EXPRESSWAY TO YOUR HEART** — Soul Survivors (Gamble-Huff), Crimson 1010 | 12 |
| 10 | 11 | 23 | 38 | **I CAN SEE FOR MILES** — Who (Kit Lambert), Decca 32206 | 6 |
| 11 | 8 | 8 | 9 | **A NATURAL WOMAN** — Aretha Franklin (Jerry Wexler), Atlantic 2441 | 8 |
| 12 | 15 | 16 | 16 | **LET IT OUT** — Hombres (Huey P. Meaux), Verve Forecast 5058 | 10 |
| 13 ★ | 19 | 24 | 35 | **EVERLASTING LOVE** — Robert Knight (Buzz Cason & Mac Gayden), Rising Sons 117 | 8 |
| 14 | 14 | 15 | 20 | **(Loneliness Made Me Realize) IT'S YOU THAT I NEED** — Temptations (N. Whitfield), Gordy 7065 | 6 |
| 15 | 10 | 6 | 3 | **NEVER MY LOVE** — Association (Bones Howe), Warner Bros. 7074 | 13 |
| 16 | 16 | 21 | 26 | **HOLIDAY** — Bee Gees (Robert Stigwood), Atco 6521 | 8 |
| 17 | 13 | 18 | 24 | **LOVE IS STRANGE** — Peaches & Herb (David Kapralik & Ken Williams), Date 1574 | 8 |
| 18 | 21 | 26 | 36 | **PATA PATA** — Miriam Makeba (Jerry Ragovoy), Reprise 0606 | 7 |
| 19 | 24 | 29 | 40 | **LAZY DAY** — Spanky & Our Gang (Jerry Ross), Mercury 72732 | 6 |
| 20 | 25 | 30 | 46 | **LADY BIRD** — Nancy Sinatra & Lee Hazlewood (Lee Hazlewood), Reprise 0629 | 5 |
| 21 ★ | 27 | 32 | 54 | **I HEARD IT THROUGH THE GRAPEVINE** — Gladys Knight & the Pips (N. Whitfield), Soul 35039 | 5 |
| 22 | 23 | 28 | 34 | **KENTUCKY WOMAN** — Neil Diamond (Jeff Barry & Ellie Greenwich), Bang 551 | 6 |
| 23 | 12 | 12 | 17 | **I'M WONDERING** — Stevie Wonder (Henry Cosby), Tamla 54157 | 7 |
| 24 | 31 | 41 | 59 | **LIKE AN OLD TIME MOVIE** — Scott McKenzie (John Phillips & Lou Adler), Ode 105 | 5 |
| 25 | 30 | 40 | 50 | **BOOGALOO DOWN BROADWAY** — Fantastic Johnny C. (Jesse James), Phil-L.A. of Soul 305 | 7 |
| 26 | 35 | 46 | 57 | **KEEP THE BALL ROLLIN'** — Jay & the Techniques (Jerry Ross), Smash 2124 | 5 |
| 27 | 32 | 42 | 63 | **SHE IS STILL A MYSTERY** — Lovin' Spoonful (Joe Wissert), Kama Sutra 239 | 4 |
| 28 | 29 | 37 | 62 | **GLAD TO BE UNHAPPY** — Mamas & the Papas (Lou Adler), Dunhill 4107 | 4 |
| 29 | 39 | 57 | — | **STAGGER-LEE** — Wilson Pickett (Tom Dowd & Tommy Cogbill), Atlantic 2448 | 3 |
| 30 | 20 | 11 | 11 | **GET ON UP** — Esquires (Bill Sheppard), Bunky 7750 | 14 |
| 31 | 41 | 62 | 79 | **YOU BETTER SIT DOWN KIDS** — Cher (Sonny Bono), Imperial 66261 | 4 |
| 32 | 17 | 13 | 4 | **HOW CAN I BE SURE** — Young Rascals (Young Rascals), Atlantic 2438 | 11 |
| 33 | — | — | — | **DAYDREAM BELIEVER** — Monkees (Chip Douglas), Colgems 1012 | 1 |
| 34 | 37 | 47 | 66 | **HOMBURG** — Procol Harum (Denny Cordell), A&M 885 | 4 |
| 35 | 46 | 67 | — | **WILD HONEY** — Beach Boys (Beach Boys), Capitol 2028 | 3 |
| 36 ★ | 48 | 58 | 72 | **BEG, BORROW AND STEAL** — Ohio Express (Jeff Katz & Jerry Kasenetz), Cameo 483 | 7 |
| 37 | 26 | 17 | 2 | **THE LETTER** — Box Tops (Dan Penn), Mala 565 | 15 |
| 38 | 43 | 54 | 64 | **BACK ON THE STREET AGAIN** — Sunshine Company (Joe Saracento), Imperial 66260 | 5 |
| 39 | 49 | 61 | 76 | **WATCH THE FLOWERS GROW** — 4 Seasons (Bob Crewe), Philips 40490 | 4 |
| 40 | 18 | 14 | 12 | **PEOPLE ARE STRANGE** — Doors (Paul Rothchild), Elektra 45621 | 9 |
| 41 | 42 | 53 | 65 | **GET IT TOGETHER** — James Brown & the Famous Flames (James Brown), King 6122 | 4 |
| 42 | 44 | 55 | 69 | **MR. DREAM MERCHANT** — Jerry Butler (Jerry Ross), Mercury 72721 | 5 |
| 43 ★ | 57 | 85 | — | **I SECOND THAT EMOTION** — Smokey Robinson & Miracles ("Smokey" A. Cleveland), Tamla 54159 | 3 |
| 44 | 45 | 45 | 56 | **YOU DON'T KNOW ME** — Elvis Presley, RCA Victor 9341 | 6 |
| 45 | 58 | 69 | 93 | **SKINNY LEGS AND ALL** — Joe Tex (Buddy Killen), Dial 4063 | 4 |
| 46 | 56 | 68 | 85 | **OUT OF THE BLUE** — Tommy James & the Shondells (Big Kahoona Prod.), Roulette 4775 | 4 |
| 47 ★ | 65 | — | — | **IN AND OUT OF LOVE** — Diana Ross & the Supremes (Holland, Dozier), Motown 1116 | 2 |
| 48 | 38 | 38 | 48 | **BIG BOSS MAN** — Elvis Presley, RCA Victor 9341 | 6 |
| 49 | 51 | 76 | 87 | **BY THE TIME I GET TO PHOENIX** — Glen Campbell (Al De Lory), Capitol 2015 | 4 |
| 50 | 28 | 19 | 13 | **GIMME LITTLE SIGN** — Brenton Wood (Hooven-Winn), Double Shot 116 | 17 |
| 51 | 62 | — | — | **YESTERDAY** — Ray Charles (TRC), ABC 11009 | 2 |
| 52 | 74 | — | — | **(The Lights Went Out In) MASSACHUSETTS** — Bee Gees (Robert Stigwood), Atco 6532 | 2 |
| 53 | 53 | 63 | 78 | **THIS TOWN** — Frank Sinatra (Jimmy Bowen), Reprise 0631 | 4 |
| 54 | 54 | 56 | 58 | **SHOUT BAMALAMA** — Mickey Murray (Bobby Smith), 555715 | 7 |
| 55 | 67 | — | — | **SHE'S MY GIRL** — Turtles (Joe Wissert), White Whale 260 | 2 |
| 56 | 33 | 25 | 28 | **THE LAST WALTZ** — Englebert Humperdinck (Peter Sullivan), Parrot 40019 | 9 |
| 57 | 60 | 70 | 86 | **SUZANNE** — Noel Harrison (Jimmy Bowen), Reprise 0615 | 4 |
| 58 | 84 | — | — | **AN OPEN LETTER TO MY TEENAGE SON** — Victor Lundberg, Liberty 55996 | 2 |
| 59 | 59 | 59 | 70 | **ARE YOU NEVER COMING HOME** — Sandy Posey (Chips Moman), MGM 13824 | 5 |
| 60 | 72 | 90 | — | **PAPER CUP** — 5th Dimension (Bones Howe), Soul City 760 | 3 |
| 61 | 52 | 52 | 52 | **HUSH** — Billy Joe Royal (Joe South), Columbia 44277 | 8 |
| 62 | 87 | — | — | **NEON RAINBOW** — Box Tops (Dan Penn), Mala 580 | 2 |
| 63 | 81 | — | — | **SOUL MAN** — Ramsey Lewis (Richard Evans), Cadet 5583 | 2 |
| 64 | 66 | 75 | 90 | **NEXT PLANE TO LONDON** — Rose Garden (Greene/Stone), Atco 6510 | 5 |
| 65 | — | — | — | **HONEY CHILE** — Martha Reeves & the Vandellas (R. Morris), Gordy 7067 | 1 |
| 66 | 64 | 65 | 80 | **GO-GO GIRL** — Lee Dorsey (Allen R. Toussaint & Marshall E. Schorn), Amy 998 | 5 |
| 67 | 34 | 22 | 25 | **THE LOOK OF LOVE** — Dusty Springfield (Johnny Franz), Philips 40465 | 15 |
| 68 | 61 | 51 | 53 | **KARATE-BOO-GA-LOO** — Jerry O (Jerry Murray), Shout 217 | 8 |
| 69 | 70 | 72 | 75 | **WAKE UP, WAKE UP** — Grass Roots (Steve Barri & P. F. Sloan), Dunhill 4105 | 4 |
| 70 | 71 | 71 | 71 | **NINE POUND STEEL** — Joe Simon (Jr. Enterprises, Inc.), Sound Stage 7 2589 | 9 |
| 71 | — | — | — | **BEAUTIFUL PEOPLE** — Kenny O'Dell, Vegas 718 | 1 |
| 72 | 77 | 94 | 96 | **SWEET, SWEET LOVIN'** — Platters (Richard "Popcorn" Wylie), Musicor 1275 | 5 |
| 73 | 73 | 83 | — | **WHOLE LOTTA WOMAN** — Arthur Conley (Otis Redding), Atco 6529 | 3 |
| 74 | 89 | 95 | — | **O-O, I LOVE YOU** — Dells (B. Miller), Cadet 5574 | 3 |
| 75 | 83 | 84 | — | **WHEN YOU'RE GONE** — Brenda & Tabulations (Bob Finis), Dicon 504 | 3 |
| 76 | — | — | — | **BEAUTIFUL PEOPLE** — Bobby Vee (Dallas Smith), Liberty 56009 | 1 |
| 77 | 75 | 77 | 77 | **YOU MEAN THE WORLD TO ME** — David Houston (Billy Sherrill), Epic 10224 | 7 |
| 78 | 79 | 79 | 81 | **CAN'T STOP LOVING YOU** — Last Word (Brad Shapiro & Steve Alaimo), Atco 6498 | 5 |
| 79 | 80 | 81 | 84 | **GET DOWN** — Harvey Scales & the Seven Sounds (Lennie LaCour), Magic Touch 2007 | 6 |
| 80 | 85 | 87 | 97 | **SHAME ON ME** — Chuck Jackson (Don Schroeder), Wand 1166 | 6 |
| 81 | — | — | — | **SUMMER RAIN** — Johnny Rivers (Work), Imperial 66267 | 1 |
| 82 | — | — | — | **WOMAN, WOMAN** — Union Gap (Jerry Fuller), Columbia 44297 | 1 |
| 83 | 86 | 88 | 89 | **ALL YOUR GOODIES ARE GONE** — Parliaments (Clinton & Taylor), Revilot 211 | 6 |
| 84 | 78 | 80 | 83 | **GO WITH ME** — Gene & Debbe (Troy Caldwell), TRX 5002 | 6 |
| 85 | — | — | — | **PEACE OF MIND** — Paul Revere & the Raiders (Terry Helcher), Columbia 44335 | 1 |
| 86 | — | — | — | **GEORGIA PINES** — Candymen (Buddy Buie), ABC 10995 | 1 |
| 87 | 90 | — | — | **DIFFERENT DRUM** — Stone Poneys (Nick Venet), Capitol 2004 | 2 |
| 88 | 92 | — | — | **ITCHYCOO PARK** — Small Faces (Steve Marriott & Ronnie Lane), Immediate 501 | 2 |
| 89 | — | — | — | **WHAT'S IT GONNA BE** — Dusty Springfield, Philips 40498 | 1 |
| 90 | — | — | — | **RED AND BLUE** — Dave Clark Five (Dave Clark), Epic 10244 | 1 |
| 91 | 91 | 92 | 92 | **FOR ONCE IN MY LIFE** — Tony Bennett (Howard A. Roberts), Columbia 44258 | 4 |
| 92 | 93 | — | — | **WHERE IS THE PARTY** — Helena Ferguson (Lincoln Kilpatrick), Compass 7009 | 2 |
| 93 | 96 | — | — | **PONY WITH THE GOLDEN MANE** — Every Mother's Son (Wes Farrell), MGM 13844 | 2 |
| 94 | — | — | — | **GOIN' BACK** — Byrds (Gary Usher), Columbia 44362 | 1 |
| 95 | 98 | — | — | **TELL MAMA** — Etta James (Rick Hall), Cadet 5578 | 2 |
| 96 | — | — | — | **TEN LITTLE INDIANS** — Yardbirds (Mickie Most), Epic 10248 | 1 |
| 97 | 99 | 100 | — | **PIECE OF MY HEART** — Erma Franklin (Bert Berns), Shout 221 | 3 |
| 98 | — | — | — | **CHATTANOOGA CHOO CHOO** — Harpers Bizarre (Lenny Waronker), Warner Bros. 7090 | 1 |
| 99 | — | — | — | **OOH BABY** — Deon Jackson (Ollie McLaughlin), Carla 2537 | 1 |
| 100 | — | — | — | **FELICIDAD** — Sally Field (Jack Keller), Colgems 1008 | 1 |

## BUBBLING UNDER THE HOT 100

101. NOBODY BUT ME ............ Human Beinz, Capitol 5990
102. BEND ME, SHAPE ME ............ American Breed, Acta 811
103. WE GOTTA GO HOME ............ Music Explosion, Laurie 3414
104. FOR A FEW DOLLARS MORE ............ Hugo Montenegro, RCA Victor 9224
105. WHERE IS THE MELODY ............ Brenda Lee, Decca 32213
106. ALLIGATOR BOOGALOO ............ Lou Donaldson, Blue Note 1934
107. WINDY ............ Wes Montgomery, A&M 883
108. HE AIN'T GIVE YOU NONE ............ Freddie Scott, Shout 220
109. LOVE OF THE COMMON PEOPLE ............ Wayne Newton, Capitol 2016
110. GOIN' DOWN ............ Monkees, Colgems 1012
111. I ALMOST CALLED YOUR NAME ............ Margaret Whiting, London 115
112. GIVE EVERYBODY SOME ............ Bar-Kays, Volt 154
113. LAPLAND ............ Baltimore & Ohio Marching Band, Jubilee 5592
114. IT TAKES PEOPLE LIKE YOU (To Make People Like Me) ............ Buck Owens, Capitol 2001
115. BALLAD OF WATERHOLE #3 ............ Roger Miller, Smash 2121
116. WHEN THE SNOW IS ON THE ROSES ............ Ed Ames, RCA Victor 9319
117. YOU ARE MY SUNSHINE ............ Mitch Ryder, New Voice 826
118. CAN'T HELP BUT LOVE YOU ............ Standells, Tower 348
119. BABY YOU GOT IT ............ Brenton Wood, Double Shot 121
120. I WANT MY BABY BACK ............ Edwin Starr, Gordy 7066
121. HUNK OF FUNK ............ Gene Dozier & the Brotherhood, Minit 32026
122. CROSS MY HEART ............ Billy Stewart, Chess 2002
123. JUDY IN DISGUISE (With Glasses) ............ John Freed & His Playboy Band, Paula 282
124. WILD HONEY (Sea of Tunes, BMI) ............ Jack Jones, RCA Victor 9365
125. LIVE FOR LIFE ............ Carmen McRae & Herbie Mann, Atlantic 2451
126. UPTOWN ............ Chambers Brothers, Columbia 44296
127. MOLLY ............ Andy Williams, Columbia 44325
128. A LOVE THAT'S REAL ............ Intruders, Gamble 209
129. ON A SATURDAY NIGHT ............ Eddie Floyd, Stax 233

Compiled from national retail sales and radio station airplay by the Music Popularity Dept. of Record Market Research, Billboard.

# Billboard HOT 100

FOR WEEK ENDING NOVEMBER 25, 1967

★ STAR PERFORMER—Sides registering greatest proportionate upward progress this week.

Record Industry Association of America seal of certification as million selling single.

| This Week | 1 Wk. Ago | 2 Wks. Ago | 3 Wks. Ago | TITLE Artist (Producer), Label & Number | Weeks On Chart |
|---|---|---|---|---|---|
| 1 (Billboard Award) | 3 | 4 | 7 | INCENSE AND PEPPERMINTS — Strawberry Alarm Clock (Frank Slay & Bill Holmes), Uni 55018 | 9 |
| 2 | 1 | 1 | 1 | TO SIR, WITH LOVE — Lulu (Mickie Most), Epic 10187 | 12 |
| 3 | 4 | 6 | 9 | THE RAIN, THE PARK & OTHER THINGS — Cowsills (Artie Kornfeld), MGM 13810 | 9 |
| 4 | 2 | 2 | 2 | SOUL MAN — Sam & Dave (Isaac Hayes & David Porter), Stax 231 | 12 |
| ★ 5 | 33 | — | — | DAYDREAM BELIEVER — Monkees (Chip Douglas), Colgems 1012 | 2 |
| 6 | 6 | 7 | 10 | PLEASE LOVE ME FOREVER — Bobby Vinton (Billy Sherrill), Epic 10228 | 9 |
| 7 | 8 | 22 | 27 | I SAY A LITTLE PRAYER — Dionne Warwick (Bacharach-David), Scepter 12203 | 6 |
| 8 | 5 | 3 | 3 | IT MUST BE HIM — Vikki Carr (Dave Pell), Liberty 55986 | 13 |
| 9 | 10 | 11 | 23 | I CAN SEE FOR MILES — Who (Kit Lambert), Decca 32206 | 7 |
| 10 | 9 | 9 | 4 | EXPRESSWAY TO YOUR HEART — Soul Survivors (Gemble-Huff), Crimson 1010 | 13 |
| 11 | 7 | 5 | 5 | YOUR PRECIOUS LOVE — Marvin Gaye & Tammy Terrell (H. Fuqua-J. Bristol), Tamla 54156 | 12 |
| ★ 12 | 18 | 21 | 26 | PATA PATA — Miriam Makeba (Jerry Ragovoy), Reprise 0606 | 8 |
| 13 | 13 | 19 | 24 | EVERLASTING LOVE — Robert Knight (Buzz Cason & Mac Gayden), Rising Sons 117 | 9 |
| 14 | 14 | 14 | 15 | (Loneliness Made Me Realize) IT'S YOU THAT I NEED — Temptations (N. Whitfield), Gordy 7065 | 7 |
| 15 | 12 | 15 | 16 | LET IT OUT — Hombres (Huey P. Meaux), Verve Forecast 5058 | 11 |
| ★ 16 | 21 | 27 | 32 | I HEARD IT THROUGH THE GRAPEVINE — Gladys Knight & the Pips (N. Whitfield), Soul 35039 | 6 |
| ★ 17 | 31 | 41 | 62 | YOU BETTER SIT DOWN KIDS — Cher (Sonny Bond), Imperial 66261 | 5 |
| ★ 18 | 58 | 84 | — | AN OPEN LETTER TO MY TEENAGE SON — Victor Lundberg (Jack Tracy), Liberty 55996 | 3 |
| 19 | 19 | 24 | 29 | LAZY DAY — Spanky & Our Gang (Jerry Ross), Mercury 72732 | 7 |
| ★ 20 | 25 | 30 | 40 | BOOGALOO DOWN BROADWAY — Fantastic Johnny C. (Jesse James), Phil-L.A. of Soul 305 | 8 |
| ★ 21 | 26 | 35 | 46 | KEEP THE BALL ROLLIN' — Jay & the Techniques (Jerry Ross), Smash 2124 | 6 |
| 22 | 22 | 23 | 28 | KENTUCKY WOMAN — Neil Diamond (Jeff Barry & Ellie Greenwich), Bang 551 | 7 |
| ★ 23 | 29 | 39 | 57 | STAGGER-LEE — Wilson Pickett (Tom Dowd & Tommy Cogbill), Atlantic 2448 | 4 |
| 24 | 24 | 31 | 41 | LIKE AN OLD TIME MOVIE — Scott McKenzie (John Phillips & Lou Adler), Ode 105 | 6 |
| 25 | 20 | 25 | 30 | LADY BIRD — Nancy Sinatra & Lee Hazlewood (Lee Hazlewood), Reprise 0629 | 6 |
| 26 | 28 | 29 | 37 | GLAD TO BE UNHAPPY — Mamas & the Papas (Lou Adler), Dunhill 4107 | 5 |
| 27 | 27 | 32 | 42 | SHE IS STILL A MYSTERY — Lovin' Spoonful (Joe Wissert), Kama Sutra 239 | 5 |
| ★ 28 | 43 | 57 | 85 | I SECOND THAT EMOTION — Smokey Robinson & Miracles ("Smokey" A. Cleveland), Tamla 54159 | 4 |
| ★ 29 | 47 | 65 | — | IN AND OUT OF LOVE — Diana Ross & the Supremes (Holland, Dozier), Motown 1116 | 3 |
| ★ 30 | 39 | 49 | 61 | WATCH THE FLOWERS GROW — 4 Seasons (Bob Crewe), Philips 40490 | 5 |
| 31 | 17 | 13 | 18 | LOVE IS STRANGE — Peaches & Herb (David Kapralik & Ken Williams), Date 1574 | 9 |
| 32 | 35 | 46 | 67 | WILD HONEY — Beach Boys (Beach Boys), Capitol 2028 | 4 |
| 33 | 11 | 8 | 8 | A NATURAL WOMAN — Aretha Franklin (Jerry Wexler), Atlantic 2441 | 9 |
| ★ 34 | 45 | 58 | 69 | SKINNY LEGS AND ALL — Joe Tex (Buddy Killen), Dial 4063 | 5 |
| 35 | 36 | 48 | 58 | BEG, BORROW AND STEAL — Ohio Express (Jeff Katy & Jerry Kasenetz), Cameo 483 | 8 |
| 36 | 38 | 43 | 54 | BACK ON THE STREET AGAIN — Sunshine Company (Joe Saraceno), Imperial 66260 | 6 |
| ★ 37 | 52 | 74 | — | (The Lights Went Out In) MASSACHUSETTS — Bee Gees (Robert Stigwood), Atco 6532 | 3 |
| 38 | 42 | 44 | 55 | MR. DREAM MERCHANT — Jerry Butler (Jerry Ross), Mercury 72721 | 6 |
| ★ 39 | 49 | 51 | 76 | BY THE TIME I GET TO PHOENIX — Glen Campbell (Al De Lory), Capitol 2015 | 5 |
| 40 | 41 | 42 | 53 | GET IT TOGETHER — James Brown & the Famous Flames (James Brown), King 6122 | 5 |
| ★ 41 | 51 | 62 | — | YESTERDAY — Ray Charles (TRC), ABC 11009 | 3 |
| 42 | 30 | 20 | 11 | GET ON UP — Esquires (Bill Sheppard), Bunky 7750 | 15 |
| 43 | 46 | 56 | 68 | OUT OF THE BLUE — Tommy James & the Shondells (Big Kahoona Prod.) Roulette 4775 | 5 |
| ★ 44 | 55 | 67 | — | SHE'S MY GIRL — Turtles (Joe Wissert), White Whale 260 | 3 |
| 45 | 16 | 16 | 21 | HOLIDAY — Bee Gees (Robert Stigwood), Atco 6521 | 9 |
| 46 | 37 | 26 | 17 | THE LETTER — Box Tops (Dan Penn), Mala 565 | 16 |
| ★ 47 | 62 | 87 | — | NEON RAINBOW — Box Tops (Dan Penn), Mala 580 | 3 |
| ★ 48 | 60 | 72 | 90 | PAPER CUP — 5th Dimension (Bones Howe), Soul City 760 | 4 |
| 49 | 23 | 12 | 12 | I'M WONDERING — Stevie Wonder (Henry Cosby), Tamla 54157 | 8 |
| 50 | 15 | 10 | 6 | NEVER MY LOVE — Association (Bones Howe), Warner Bros. 7074 | 14 |
| 51 | 34 | 37 | 47 | HOMBURG — Procol Harum (Denny Cordell), A&M 885 | 5 |
| ★ 52 | 63 | 81 | — | SOUL MAN — Ramsey Lewis (Richard Evans), Cadet 5583 | 3 |
| 53 | 53 | 53 | 63 | THIS TOWN — Frank Sinatra (Jimmy Bowen), Reprise 0631 | 5 |
| ★ 54 | 87 | 90 | — | DIFFERENT DRUM — Stone Poneys (Nick Venet), Capitol 2004 | 3 |
| ★ 55 | 65 | — | — | HONEY CHILE — Martha Reeves & the Vandellas (R. Morris) Gordy 7067 | 2 |
| 56 | 57 | 60 | 70 | SUZANNE — Noel Harrison (Jimmy Bowen), Reprise 0615 | 5 |
| 57 | 64 | 66 | 75 | NEXT PLANE TO LONDON — Rose Garden (Greene/Stone), Atco 6510 | 6 |
| ★ 58 | 81 | — | — | SUMMER RAIN — Johnny Rivers (Work), Imperial 66267 | 2 |
| ★ 59 | 82 | — | — | WOMAN, WOMAN — Union Gap (Jerry Fuller), Columbia 44297 | 2 |
| ★ 60 | 71 | — | — | BEAUTIFUL PEOPLE — Kenny O'Dell, Vegas 718 | 2 |
| ★ 61 | 76 | — | — | BEAUTIFUL PEOPLE — Bobby Vee (Dallas Smith), Liberty 56009 | 2 |
| 62 | 66 | 64 | 65 | GO-GO GIRL — Lee Dorsey (Allen R. Toussaint & Marshall E. Schorn), Amy 998 | 6 |
| ★ 63 | 85 | — | — | PEACE OF MIND — Paul Revere & the Raiders (Terry Melcher), (Columbia 44335 | 2 |
| 64 | 54 | 54 | 56 | SHOUT BAMALAMA — Mickey Murray (Bobby Smith), 555715 | 8 |
| ★ 65 | 98 | — | — | CHATTANOOGA CHOO CHOO — Harpers Bizarre (Lenny Waronker), Warner Bros. 7090 | 2 |
| 66 | 74 | 89 | 95 | O-O, I LOVE YOU — Della (B. Miller), Cadet 5574 | 4 |
| 67 | 68 | 61 | 51 | KARATE-BOO-GA-LOO — Jerry O (Jerry Murray), Shout 217 | 9 |
| 68 | 69 | 70 | 72 | WAKE UP, WAKE UP — Grass Roots (Steve Barri & P. P. Sloan), Dunhill 4105 | 5 |
| 69 | 75 | 83 | 84 | WHEN YOU'RE GONE — Brenda & Tabulations (Bob Finis), Dicon 504 | 4 |
| 70 | 72 | 77 | 94 | SWEET, SWEET LOVIN' — Platters (Richard "Popcorn" Wylie), Musicor 1275 | 6 |
| ★ 71 | — | — | — | AND GET AWAY — Esquires (Bill Sheppard), Bunky 7752 | 1 |
| ★ 72 | — | — | — | SINCE YOU SHOWED ME HOW TO BE HAPPY — Jackie Wilson (Carl Davis), Brunswick 55354 | 1 |
| ★ 73 | — | — | — | LOVE POWER — Sandpebbles (Teddy Vann), Calla 141 | 1 |
| ★ 74 | — | — | — | WEAR YOUR LOVE LIKE HEAVEN — Donovan (Mickie Most), Epic 10253 | 1 |
| ★ 75 | 95 | 98 | — | TELL MAMA — Etta James (Rick Hall), Cadet 5578 | 3 |
| ★ 76 | — | — | — | COVER ME — Percy Sledge (Quin Ivy & Marlin Greene), Atlantic 2453 | 1 |
| 77 | 80 | 85 | 87 | SHAME ON ME — Chuck Jackson (Don Schroeder), Wand 1166 | 7 |
| 78 | 88 | 92 | — | ITCHYCOO PARK — Small Faces (Steve Marriott & Ronnie Lane), Immediate 501 | 3 |
| ★ 79 | 89 | — | — | WHAT'S IT GONNA BE — Dusty Springfield, Philips 40498 | 2 |
| 80 | 83 | 86 | 88 | ALL YOUR GOODIES ARE GONE — Parliaments (Clinton & Taylor), Revilot 211 | 7 |
| ★ 81 | — | — | — | BABY YOU GOT IT — Brenton Wood (Hooven-Winn), Double Shot 121 | 1 |
| ★ 82 | — | — | — | OKOLONA RIVER BOTTOM BAND — Bobbie Gentry (Kelly Gordon), Capitol 2044 | 1 |
| 83 | 86 | — | — | GEORGIA PINES — Candymen (Buddy Buie), ABC 10995 | 2 |
| ★ 84 | 99 | — | — | OOH BABY — Deon Jackson (Ollie McLaughlin), Carla 2537 | 2 |
| ★ 85 | — | — | — | WINDY — Wes Montgomery (Creed Taylor), A&M 883 | 1 |
| ★ 86 | — | — | — | COME SEE ABOUT ME — Jr. Walker & the All Stars (Holland & Dozier), Soul 3501 | 1 |
| ★ 87 | — | — | — | TOO MUCH OF NOTHING — Peter, Paul & Mary (Albert B. Grossman & Milt Okun), Warner Bros. 7092 | 1 |
| ★ 88 | — | — | — | CAN'T HELP BUT LOVE YOU — Standells (Ed Cobb), Tower 348 | 1 |
| 89 | 90 | — | — | RED AND BLUE — Dave Clark Five (Dave Clark), Epic 10244 | 2 |
| 90 | 97 | 99 | 100 | PIECE OF MY HEART — Erma Franklin (Bert Berns), Shout 221 | 4 |
| 91 | 91 | 91 | 92 | FOR ONCE IN MY LIFE — Tony Bennett (Howard A. Roberts), Columbia 44258 | 5 |
| 92 | 92 | 93 | — | WHERE IS THE PARTY — Helena Ferguson (Lincoln Kilpatrick), Compass 7009 | 3 |
| 93 | — | — | — | ALLIGATOR BOOGALOO — Lou Donaldson (Alfred Lion), Blue Note 1934 | 1 |
| 94 | 94 | — | — | GOIN' BACK — Byrds (Gary Usher), Columbia 44362 | 2 |
| 95 | 100 | — | — | FELICIDAD — Sally Field (Jack Keller), Colgems 1008 | 2 |
| 96 | 96 | — | — | TEN LITTLE INDIANS — Yardbirds (Mickie Most), Epic 10248 | 2 |
| 97 | — | — | — | I'LL BE SWEETER TOMORROW — O'Jays (George Kerr), Bell 691 | 1 |
| 98 | — | — | — | LETTER TO DAD, A — Every Father's Teenage Son (Inherit Prod.), Buddah 25 | 1 |
| 99 | — | — | — | JUDY IN DISGUISE (With Glasses) — John Fred & His Playboy Band (J. Fred & A. Bernard), Paula 282 | 1 |
| 100 | — | — | — | FOR WHAT IT'S WORTH — King Curtis & Kingpins (Tom Dowd & Tommy Cogbill), Atco 6534 | 1 |

## HOT 100—A TO Z—(Publisher-Licensee)


Alligator Bogaloo (Blue Horizon, BMI) ... 93
All Your Goodies Are Gone (Groovesville, BMI) ... 80
An Open Letter to My Teenage Son (Asa, ASCAP) ... 18
And Get Away (Hi-Mi/Flomar, BMI) ... 71
Baby You Got It (Big Shot, ASCAP) ... 81
Back on the Street Again (Cherry Lane, ASCAP) ... 36
Beautiful People (O'Dell) (Mirwood Antlers, BMI) ... 60
Beautiful People (Vee) (Mirwood Antlers, BMI) ... 61
Beg, Borrow and Steal (S&J, ASCAP) ... 35
Boogaloo Down Broadway (Dandelion/James Boys, BMI) ... 20
By the Time I Get to Phoenix (Rivers, BMI) ... 39
Can't Help But Love You (Equinux, BMI) ... 88
Chattanooga Choo Choo (Feist, ASCAP) ... 65
Come See About Me (Jobete, BMI) ... 86
Cover Me (Pronto/Quiney, BMI) ... 76
Daydream Believer (Screen Gems-Columbia, BMI) ... 5
Different Drum (Screen Gems-Columbia, BMI) ... 54
Everlasting Love (Rising Sons, BMI) ... 13
Expressway to Your Heart (Double Diamond/Downstairs, BMI) ... 10
Felicidad (Screen Gems-Columbia, BMI) ... 95
For Once in My Life (Stein & Van Stock, ASCAP) ... 91
For What It's Worth (Cotillion/Ten East/Springalo, BMI) ... 100
Georgia Pines (Unart, BMI) ... 83
Get It Together (Dynatone, BMI) ... 40
Get on Up (Hi-Mi, BMI) ... 42
Glad to Be Unhappy (Chappell, ASCAP) ... 26
Goin' Back (Screen Gems-Columbia, BMI) ... 94
Go-Go Girl (Marsaint, BMI) ... 62
Holiday (Nemperor, BMI) ... 45
Homburg (Total, BMI) ... 51
Honey Chile (Jobete, BMI) ... 55
I Can See for Miles (Essex, ASCAP) ... 9
I Heard It Through the Grapevine (Jobete, BMI) ... 16
I Say a Little Prayer (Blue Seas/Jac, ASCAP) ... 7
I Second That Emotion (Jobete, BMI) ... 28
I'll Be Sweeter Tomorrow (Zira/Floteca/Mia, BMI) ... 97
I'm Wondering (Jobete, BMI) ... 49
In and Out of Love (Jobete, BMI) ... 29
Incense and Peppermints (Claridge, ASCAP) ... 1
Itchycoo Park (Nice Songs, BMI) ... 78
It Must Be Him (Asa, ASCAP) ... 8
Judy In Disguise (With Glasses) (Su-Ma, BMI) ... 99
Karate-Boo-Ga-Loo (Boogaloo/Love Lane, BMI) ... 67
Keep the Ball Rollin' (Screen Gems-Columbia, BMI) ... 21
Kentucky Woman (Tallyrand, BMI) ... 22
Lady Bird (Hazlewood, ASCAP) ... 25
Lazy Day (Screen Gems-Columbia, BMI) ... 19
Let It Out (Crazy Cajun, BMI) ... 15
Letter, The (Barton, BMI) ... 46
Letter To Dad, A (Bob-Len, BMI) ... 98
(Lights Went Out In) Massachusetts, The (Nemperor, BMI) ... 37
Like an Old-Time Movie (Wingate, ASCAP) ... 24
(Loneliness Made Me Realize) It's You That I Need (Jobete, BMI) ... 14
Love Is Strange (Chazi, BMI) ... 31
Love Power (Unbelievable, BMI) ... 73
Mr. Dream Merchant (Saturday, BMI) ... 38
Natural Woman, A (Screen Gems-Columbia, BMI) ... 33
Neon Rainbow (Barton, BMI) ... 47
Never My Love (Tamerlane, BMI) ... 50
Next Plane to London (Mirwood Antlers, BMI) ... 57
Okolona River Bottom Band (Shayne, ASCAP) ... 82
O-O, I Love You (Chervis, BMI) ... 66
Ooh Baby (Gencho/McLaughlin, BMI) ... 84
Out of the Blue (Patricia, BMI) ... 43
Paper Cup (Rivers, BMI) ... 48
Pata Pata (Xina, ASCAP) ... 12
Peace of Mind (Daywin, BMI) ... 63
Piece of My Heart (Web IV/Ragmar, BMI) ... 90
Please Love Me Forever (Selma, BMI) ... 6
Rain, the Park & Other Things, The (Akbestal/Luvlin, BMI) ... 3
Red and Blue (Branston, BMI) ... 89
Shame on Me (Lois, BMI) ... 77
She Is Still a Mystery (Faithful Virtue, BMI) ... 27
She's My Girl (Chardon, BMI) ... 44
Shout Bamalama (Macon, BMI) ... 64
Since You Showed Me How to Be Happy (Jalynne/BRC, BMI) ... 72
Skinny Legs and All (Tree, BMI) ... 34
Soul Man (Sam & Dave) (East/Pronto, BMI) ... 4
Soul Man (Lewis) (East/Pronto, BMI) ... 52
Stagger-Lee (Travis, BMI) ... 23
Summer Rain (Rivers, BMI) ... 58
Suzanne (Project 7, BMI) ... 56
Sweet, Sweet Lovin' (Catalogue, BMI) ... 70
Tell Mama (Fame, BMI) ... 75
Ten Little Indians (Donber, BMI) ... 96
This Town (Remick, ASCAP) ... 53
Too Much of Nothing (Dwarf, ASCAP) ... 87
To Sir, With Love (Screen Gems-Columbia, BMI) ... 2
Wake Up, Wake Up (Trousdale, BMI) ... 68
Watch the Flowers Grow (Saturday/Seasons' Four, BMI) ... 30
Wear Your Love Like Heaven (Peer Int'l., BMI) ... 74
What's It Gonna Be (Rumbalero/Ragmar, BMI) ... 79
When You're Gone (Dandelion, BMI) ... 69
Where Is the Party (Frabob/Palo, Alto/Dakar, BMI) ... 92
Wild Honey (Sea of Tunes, BMI) ... 32
Windy (Almo, BMI) ... 85
Woman, Woman (Glaser, BMI) ... 59
Yesterday (Maclen, BMI) ... 41
You Better Sit Down Kids (Chrismarc/Cotillion, BMI) ... 17
Your Precious Love (Jobete, BMI) ... 11


## BUBBLING UNDER THE HOT 100

101. BEND ME, SHAPE ME ... American Breed, Acta 811
102. FOR A FEW DOLLARS MORE ... Hugo Montenegro, RCA Victor 9224
103. NOBODY BUT ME ... Human Beinz, Capitol 5990
104. GOIN' DOWN ... Monkees, Colgems 1012
105. STORYBOOK CHILDREN ... Billy Vera & Judy Clay, Atlantic 2445
106. WHERE IS THE MELODY ... Brenda Lee, Decca 32213
107. MR. BUS DRIVER ... Bruce Channel, Mala 579
108. I ALMOST CALLED YOUR NAME ... Margaret Whiting, London 115
109. I WANT SOME MORE ... Jon & Robin & the In Crowd, Abnak 124
110. WHEN THE SNOW IS ON THE ROSES ... Ed Ames, RCA Victor 9319
111. JO-JO'S PLACE ... Bobby Goldsboro, United Artists 50224
112. YOU GOT ME HUMMIN' ... Hassels, United Artists 50215
113. DEAR ELOISE ... Hollies, Epic 10251
114. SOMETHING'S MISSING ... Five Stairsteps & Cubie, Buddah 20
115. YOU ARE MY SUNSHINE ... Mitch Ryder, New Voice 826
116. HOLLY ... Andy Williams, Columbia 44325
117. ON A SATURDAY NIGHT ... Eddie Floyd, Stax 233
118. CROSS MY HEART ... Billy Stewart, Chess 2002
119. LIVE FOR LIFE ... Jack Jones, RCA Victor 9365
120. LIVE FOR LIFE ... Carmen McRae & Herbie Mann, Atlantic 2451

Compiled from national retail sales and radio station airplay by the Music Popularity Dept. of Record Market Research, Billboard.

# Billboard HOT 100

FOR WEEK ENDING DECEMBER 2, 1967

★ STAR PERFORMER—Sides registering greatest proportionate upward progress this week.

Record Industry Association of America seal of certification as million selling single.

| THIS WEEK | 1 Wk. Ago | 2 Wks. Ago | 3 Wks. Ago | TITLE Artist (Producer), Label & Number | Weeks On Chart |
|---|---|---|---|---|---|
| Billboard Award 1 | 5 | 33 | — | **DAYDREAM BELIEVER** Monkees (Chip Douglas), Colgems 1012 | 3 |
| 2 | 3 | 4 | 6 | **THE RAIN, THE PARK & OTHER THINGS** Cowsills (Artie Kornfeld), MGM 13810 | 10 |
| 3 | 1 | 3 | 4 | **INCENSE AND PEPPERMINTS** Strawberry Alarm Clock (Frank Slay & Bill Holmes), Uni 55018 | 10 |
| 4 | 2 | 1 | 1 | **TO SIR, WITH LOVE** Lulu (Mickie Most), Epic 10187 | 13 |
| 5 | 7 | 8 | 22 | **I SAY A LITTLE PRAYER** Dionne Warwick (Bacharach-David), Scepter 12203 | 7 |
| 6 | 6 | 6 | 7 | **PLEASE LOVE ME FOREVER** Bobby Vinton (Billy Sherrill), Epic 10228 | 10 |
| 7 | 4 | 2 | 2 | **SOUL MAN** Sam & Dave (Isaac Hayes & David Porter), Stax 231 | 13 |
| ★8 | 16 | 21 | 27 | **I HEARD IT THROUGH THE GRAPEVINE** Gladys Knight & the Pips (N. Whitfield), Soul 35039 | 7 |
| 9 | 9 | 10 | 11 | **I CAN SEE FOR MILES** Who (Kit Lambert), Decca 32206 | 8 |
| ★10 | 18 | 54 | 84 | **AN OPEN LETTER TO MY TEENAGE SON** Victor Lundberg (Jack Tracy), Liberty 55996 | 4 |
| ★11 | 28 | 43 | 57 | **I SECOND THAT EMOTION** Smokey Robinson & Miracles ("Smokey" A. Cleveland), Tamla 54159 | 5 |
| ★12 | 17 | 31 | 41 | **YOU BETTER SIT DOWN KIDS** Cher (Sonny Bond), Imperial 66261 | 6 |
| ★13 | 29 | 47 | 65 | **IN AND OUT OF LOVE** Diana Ross & the Supremes (Holland, Dozier), Motown 1116 | 4 |
| ★14 | 19 | 19 | 24 | **LAZY DAY** Spanky & Our Gang (Jerry Ross), Mercury 72732 | 8 |
| ★15 | 20 | 25 | 30 | **BOOGALOO DOWN BROADWAY** Fantastic Johnny C. (Jesse James), Phil-L.A. of Soul 305 | 9 |
| ★16 | 21 | 26 | 35 | **KEEP THE BALL ROLLIN'** Jay & the Techniques (Jerry Ross), Smash 2124 | 7 |
| 17 | 13 | 13 | 19 | **EVERLASTING LOVE** Robert Knight (Buzz Casen & Mac Gayden), Rising Sons 117 | 10 |
| 18 | 10 | 9 | 9 | **EXPRESSWAY TO YOUR HEART** Soul Survivors (Gemble-Huff), Crimson 1010 | 14 |
| 19 | 12 | 18 | 21 | **PATA PATA** Miriam Makeba (Jerry Ragovoy), Reprise 0606 | 9 |
| ★20 | 37 | 52 | 74 | **(The Lights Went Out In) MASSACHUSETTS** Bee Gees (Robert Stigwood), Atco 6532 | 4 |
| 21 | 8 | 5 | 3 | **IT MUST BE HIM** Vikki Carr (Dave Pell), Liberty 55986 | 14 |
| 22 | 23 | 29 | 39 | **STAGGER-LEE** Wilson Pickett (Tom Dowd & Tommy Cogbill), Atlantic 2448 | 5 |
| 23 | 15 | 12 | 15 | **LET IT OUT** Hombres (Huey P. Meaux), Verve Forecast 5058 | 12 |
| ★24 | 44 | 55 | 67 | **SHE'S MY GIRL** Turtles (Joe Wissert), White Whale 260 | 4 |
| ★25 | 41 | 51 | 62 | **YESTERDAY** Ray Charles (TRC), ABC 11009 | 4 |
| ★26 | 34 | 45 | 58 | **SKINNY LEGS AND ALL** Joe Tex (Buddy Killen), Dial 4063 | 6 |
| 27 | 14 | 14 | 14 | **(Loneliness Made Me Realize) IT'S YOU THAT I NEED** Temptations (N. Whitfield), Gordy 7065 | 8 |
| ★28 | 39 | 49 | 51 | **BY THE TIME I GET TO PHOENIX** Glen Campbell (Al De Lory), Capitol 2015 | 6 |
| ★29 | 35 | 36 | 48 | **BEG, BORROW AND STEAL** Ohio Express (Jeff Katz & Jerry Kasenetz), Cameo 483 | 9 |
| 30 | 30 | 39 | 49 | **WATCH THE FLOWERS GROW** 4 Seasons (Bob Crewe), Philips 40490 | 6 |
| 31 | 32 | 35 | 46 | **WILD HONEY** Beach Boys (Beach Boys), Capitol 2028 | 5 |
| ★32 | 59 | 82 | — | **WOMAN, WOMAN** Union Gap (Jerry Fuller), Columbia 44297 | 3 |
| 33 | 22 | 22 | 23 | **KENTUCKY WOMAN** Neil Diamond (Jeff Barry & Ellie Greenwich), Bang 551 | 8 |
| 34 | 26 | 28 | 29 | **GLAD TO BE UNHAPPY** Mamas & the Papas (Lou Adler), Dunhill 4107 | 6 |
| ★35 | 55 | 65 | — | **HONEY CHILE** Martha Reeves & the Vandellas (R. Morris) Gordy 7067 | 3 |
| 36 | 36 | 38 | 43 | **BACK ON THE STREET AGAIN** Sunshine Company (Joe Saraceno), Imperial 66260 | 7 |
| ★37 | 47 | 62 | 87 | **NEON RAINBOW** Box Tops (Dan Penn), Mala 580 | 4 |
| 38 | 38 | 42 | 44 | **MR. DREAM MERCHANT** Jerry Butler (Jerry Ross), Mercury 72721 | 7 |
| 39 | 11 | 7 | 5 | **YOUR PRECIOUS LOVE** Marvin Gaye & Tammy Terrell (H. Fuqua-J. Bristol), Tamla 54156 | 13 |
| ★40 | 58 | 81 | — | **SUMMER RAIN** Johnny Rivers (Work), Imperial 66267 | 3 |
| 41 | 27 | 27 | 32 | **SHE IS STILL A MYSTERY** Lovin' Spoonful (Joe Wissert), Kama Sutra 239 | 6 |
| 42 | 24 | 24 | 31 | **LIKE AN OLD TIME MOVIE** Scott McKenzie (John Phillips & Lou Adler), Ode 105 Reprise 0629 | 7 |
| ★43 | 54 | 87 | 90 | **DIFFERENT DRUM** Stone Poneys (Nick Venet), Capitol 2004 | 4 |
| 44 | 48 | 60 | 72 | **PAPER CUP** 5th Dimension (Bones Howe), Soul City 760 | 5 |
| ★45 | — | — | — | **HELLO GOODBYE** Beatles (George Martin), Capitol 2056 | 1 |
| ★46 | 74 | — | — | **WEAR YOUR LOVE LIKE HEAVEN** Donovan (Mickie Most), Epic 10253 | 2 |
| ★47 | 57 | 64 | 66 | **NEXT PLANE TO LONDON** Rose Garden (Greene/Stone), Atco 6510 | 7 |
| ★48 | 61 | 76 | — | **BEAUTIFUL PEOPLE** Bobby Vee (Dallas Smith), Liberty 56009 Schorn), Amy 998 | 3 |
| 49 | 52 | 63 | 81 | **SOUL MAN** Ramsey Lewis (Richard Evans), Cadet 5583 | 4 |
| ★50 | 60 | 71 | — | **BEAUTIFUL PEOPLE** Kenny O'Dell, Vegas 718 | 3 |
| 51 | 43 | 46 | 56 | **OUT OF THE BLUE** Tommy James & the Shondells (Big Kahoona Prod.) Roulette 4775 | 6 |
| ★52 | 65 | 98 | — | **CHATTANOOGA CHOO CHOO** Harpers Bizarre (Lenny Waronker), Warner Bros. 7090 | 3 |
| ★53 | 63 | 85 | — | **PEACE OF MIND** Paul Revere & the Raiders (Terry Helcher), (Columbia 44335 | 3 |
| 54 | 40 | 41 | 42 | **GET IT TOGETHER** James Brown & the Famous Flames (James Brown), King 6122 | 6 |
| ★55 | 71 | — | — | **AND GET AWAY** Esquires (Bill Sheppard), Bunky 7752 | 2 |
| 56 | 56 | 57 | 60 | **SUZANNE** Noel Harrison (Jimmy Bowen), Reprise 0615 | 6 |
| ★57 | 79 | 89 | — | **WHAT'S IT GONNA BE** Dusty Springfield, Philips 40498 | 3 |
| ★58 | 72 | — | — | **SINCE YOU SHOWED ME HOW TO BE HAPPY** Jackie Wilson (Carl Davis), Brunswick 55354 | 2 |
| ★59 | 82 | — | — | **OKOLONA RIVER BOTTOM BAND** Bobbie Gentry (Kelly Gordon), Capitol 2044 | 2 |
| 60 | 69 | 75 | 83 | **WHEN YOU'RE GONE** Brenda & Tabulations (Bob Finis), Dicon 504 | 5 |
| ★61 | 81 | — | — | **BABY YOU GOT IT** Brenton Wood (Hooven-Winn), Double Shot 121 | 2 |
| ★62 | 87 | — | — | **TOO MUCH OF NOTHING** Peter, Paul & Mary (Albert B. Grossman & Milt Okun), Warner Bros. 7092 | 2 |
| ★63 | 86 | — | — | **COME SEE ABOUT ME** Jr. Walker & the All Stars (Holland & Dozier), Soul 3501 | 2 |
| 64 | 66 | 74 | 89 | **O-O, I LOVE YOU** Della (B. Miller), Cadet 5574 Dunhill 4105 | 5 |
| ★65 | — | — | — | **IF I COULD BUILD MY WHOLE WORLD AROUND YOU** Marvin Gaye & Tammi Terrell (Fuqus, Bristol), Tamla 54161 | 1 |
| ★66 | 85 | — | — | **WINDY** Wes Montgomery (Creed Taylor), A&M 883 | 2 |
| 67 | 73 | — | — | **LOVE POWER** Sandpebbles (Teddy Vann), Calla 141 | 2 |
| ★68 | 84 | 99 | — | **OOH BABY** Deon Jackson (Ollie McLaughlin), Carla 2537 | 3 |
| 69 | 75 | 95 | 98 | **TELL MAMA** Etta James (Rick Hall), Cadet 5578 | 4 |
| 70 | 70 | 72 | 77 | **SWEET, SWEET LOVIN'** Platters (Richard "Popcorn" Wylie), Musicor 1275 | 7 |
| 71 | 76 | — | — | **COVER ME** Percy Sledge (Quin Ivy & Marlin Greene), Atlantic 2453 | 2 |
| 72 | 78 | 88 | 92 | **ITCHYCOO PARK** Small Faces (Steve Marriott & Ronnie Lane), Immediate 501 | 4 |
| ★73 | — | — | — | **BEND ME, SHAPE ME** American Breed (Bill Trant), Acta 811 | 1 |
| ★74 | 99 | — | — | **JUDY IN DISGUISE (With Glasses)** John Fred & His Playboy Band (J. Fred & A. Bernard), Paula 282 | 2 |
| ★75 | 90 | 97 | 99 | **PIECE OF MY HEART** Erma Franklin (Bert Berns), Shout 221 | 5 |
| 76 | 77 | 80 | 85 | **SHAME ON ME** Chuck Jackson (Don Schroeder), Wand 1166 | 8 |
| ★77 | — | — | — | **THE OTHER MAN'S GRASS IS ALWAYS GREENER** Petula Clark (Tony Hatch), Warner Bros. 7097 | 1 |
| ★78 | — | — | — | **HOORAY FOR THE SALVATION ARMY BAND** Bill Cosby (Fred Smith), Warner Bros. 7096 | 1 |
| ★79 | 97 | — | — | **I'LL BE SWEETER TOMORROW** O'Jays (George Kerr), Bell 691 | 2 |
| ★80 | — | — | — | **SOCKIN' 1-2-3-4** John Roberts (Bob Garner), Duke 425 | 1 |
| ★81 | — | — | — | **STORYBOOK CHILDREN** Billy Vera & Judy Clay (Chip Taylor & Ted Deryll), Atlantic 2445 | 1 |
| ★82 | — | — | — | **I'M IN LOVE** Wilson Pickett (Tom Dowd & Tommy Cogbill), Atlantic 2448 | 1 |
| 83 | 83 | 86 | — | **GEORGIA PINES** Candymen (Buddy Buie), ABC 10995 | 3 |
| ★84 | — | — | — | **WANTED: LOVER, NO EXPERIENCE NECESSARY** Laura Lee (Rick Hall), Chess 2030 | 1 |
| ★85 | — | — | — | **TONY ROME** Nancy Sinatra (Lee Kezlewood), Reprise 0636 | 1 |
| ★86 | — | — | — | **DEAR ELOISE** Gallics (Ron Richards), Epic 10251 | 1 |
| ★87 | — | — | — | **IN THE MISTY MOONLIGHT** Dean Martin (Jimmy Bowen), Reprise 0640 | 1 |
| 88 | 88 | — | — | **CAN'T HELP BUT LOVE YOU** Standells (Ed Cobb), Tower 348 | 2 |
| 89 | 94 | 94 | — | **GOIN' BACK** Byrds (Gary Usher), Columbia 44362 | 3 |
| 90 | 92 | 92 | 93 | **WHERE IS THE PARTY** Helena Ferguson (Lincoln Kilpatrick), Compass 7009 | 4 |
| 91 | — | — | — | **HERE COMES HEAVEN** Eddy Arnold (Chet Atkins), RCA Victor 9368 | 1 |
| 92 | — | — | 97 | **ON A SATURDAY NIGHT** Eddie Floyd (Steve Cropper), Stax 233 | 4 |
| 93 | 93 | — | — | **ALLIGATOR BOOGALOO** Lou Donaldson (Alfred Lion), Blue Note 1934 | 2 |
| 94 | — | — | — | **A LOVE THAT'S REAL** Intruders (Joe Benzetti), Gamble 209 | 1 |
| 95 | 95 | 100 | — | **FELICIDAD** Sally Field (Jack Keller), Colgems 1008 | 3 |
| 96 | — | — | — | **SOMETHING'S MISSING** 5 Stairsteps & Cubie (Clarence Burke, Jr.), Buddah 20 | 1 |
| 97 | 98 | — | — | **LETTER TO DAD, A** Every Father's Teenage Son (Inherit Prod.), Buddah 25 | 2 |
| 98 | 100 | — | — | **FOR WHAT IT'S WORTH** King Curtis & Kingpins (Tom Dowd & Tommy Cogbill), Atco 6534 | 2 |
| 99 | — | — | — | **CROSS MY HEART** Billy Stewart (Davis & Caston), Chess 2002 | 1 |
| 100 | — | — | — | **LIVE FOR LIFE** Jack Jones (Ernie Altschuler), RCA Victor 9365 | 1 |

## HOT 100—A TO Z—*(Publisher-Licensee)*


Alligator Boogaloo (Blue Horizon, BMI) .......... 93
An Open Letter to My Teenage Son (Asa, ASCAP) 10
And Get Away (Hi-Mi/Flomar, BMI) .......... 55
Baby You Got It (Big Shot, ASCAP) .......... 61
Back on the Street Again (Cherry Lane, ASCAP) .. 36
Beautiful People (O'Dell) (Mirwood Antlers, BMI) 50
Beautiful People (Vee) (Mirwood Antlers, BMI) .. 48
Beg, Borrow and Steal (S&J, ASCAP) .......... 29
Bend Me, Shape Me (Helios, BMI) .......... 73
Boogalo Down Broadway (Dandelion/James Boys, BMI) .......... 15
By the Time I Get to Phoenix (Rivers, BMI) .... 28
Can't Help But Love You (Equinux, BMI) .......... 88
Chattanooga Choo Choo (Feist, ASCAP) .......... 52
Come See About Me (Jobete, BMI) .......... 63
Cover Me (Pronto/Quiney, BMI) .......... 71
Cross My Heart (Chevis, BMI) .......... 99
Daydream Believer (Screen Gems-Columbia, BMI) .. 1
Dear Eloise (Marthus, BMI) .......... 86
Different Drum (Screen Gems-Columbia, BMI) .... 43
Everlasting Love (Rising Sons, BMI) .......... 17
Expressway to Your Heart (Double Diamond/Downstairs, BMI) .......... 18
Felicidad (Screen Gems-Columbia, BMI) .......... 95
For What It's Worth (Cotillion/Ten East/Springalo, BMI) .......... 98
Georgia Pines (Unart, BMI) .......... 83
Get It Together (Dynatone, BMI) .......... 54
Glad to Be Unhappy (Chappell, ASCAP) .......... 34
Goin' Back (Screen Gems-Columbia, BMI) .......... 89
Hello Goodbye (Maclen, BMI) .......... 45
Hooray for the Salvation Army Band (Monger/Keymen, BMI) .......... 78
Honey Chile (Jobete, BMI) .......... 35
Here Comes Heaven (Hill & Range, BMI) .......... 91
I Can See for Miles (Essex, ASCAP) .......... 9
I Heard It Through the Grapevine (Jobete, BMI) 8
I Say a Little Prayer (Blue Seas/Jac, ASCAP) .... 5
I Second That Emotion (Jobete, BMI) .......... 11
If I Could Build My Whole World Around You (Jobete, BMI) .......... 65
I'll Be Sweeter Tomorrow (Zira/Floteca/Mia, BMI) 79
I'm In Love (Pronto/Trecebob, BMI) .......... 82
In and Out of Love (Jobete, BMI) .......... 13
In the Misty Moonlight (4 Star, BMI) .......... 87
Incense and Peppermints (Claridge, ASCAP) ...... 3
Itchycoo Park (Nice Songs, BMI) .......... 72
It Must Be Him (Asa, ASCAP) .......... 21
Judy In Disguise (With Glasses) (Su-Ma, BMI) .... 74
Keep the Ball Rollin' (Screen Gems-Columbia, BMI) 16
Kentucky Woman (Tallyrand, BMI) .......... 33
Lazy Day (Screen Gems-Columbia, BMI) .......... 14
Let It Out (Crazy Cajun, BMI) .......... 23
Letter To Dad, A (Bob-Len, BMI) .......... 97
(Lights Went Out In) Massachusetts, The (Nemperor, BMI) .......... 20
Like an Old-Time Movie (Wingate, ASCAP) ...... 42
Live for Life (Unart, BMI) .......... 100
(Loneliness Made Me Realize) It's You That I Need (Jobete, BMI) .......... 27
Love Power (Unbelievable, BMI) .......... 67
Love That's Real, A (Razor Sharp, BMI) .......... 94
Mr. Dream Merchant (Saturday, BMI) .......... 38
Neon Rainbow (Barton, BMI) .......... 37
Next Plane to London (Mirwood Antlers, BMI) .... 47
Okolona River Bottom (Shayne, ASCAP) .......... 59
On a Saturday Night (East, BMI) .......... 92
O-O, I Love You (Chervis, BMI) .......... 64
Ooh Baby (Goncho/McLaughlin, BMI) .......... 68
Other Man's Grass Is Always Greenier, The (Northern, ASCAP) .......... 77
Out of the Blue (Patricia, BMI) .......... 51
Paper Cup (Rivers, BMI) .......... 44
Pata Pata (Xina, ASCAP) .......... 19
Peace of Mind (Daywin, BMI) .......... 53
Piece of My Heart (Web IV/Ragmar, BMI) ...... 75
Please Love Me Forever (Selma, BMI) .......... 6
Rain, the Park & Other Things, The (Akbestal/Luvlin, BMI) .......... 2
Shame on Me (Lois, BMI) .......... 76
She Is Still a Mystery (Faithful Virtue, BMI) .... 41
She's My Girl (Chardon, BMI) .......... 24
Since You Showed Me How to Be Happy (Jalynne/BRC, BMI) .......... 58
Skinny Legs and All (Tree, BMI) .......... 26
Sockin' 1-2-3-4 (Don, BMI) .......... 80
Something's Missing (Kama Sutra/Burke Family, BMI) .......... 96
Soul Man (Sam & Dave) (East/Pronto, BMI) .... 7
Soul Man (Lewis) (East/Pronto, BMI) .......... 49
Stagger-Lee (Travis, BMI) .......... 22
Storybook Children (Blackwood, BMI) .......... 81
Summer Rain (Rivers, BMI) .......... 40
Suzanne (Project 7, BMI) .......... 56
Sweet, Sweet Lovin' (Catalogue, BMI) .......... 70
Tell Mama (Fame, BMI) .......... 69
Too Much of Nothing (Dwarf, ASCAP) .......... 62
Tony Rome (Sergeant, ASCAP) .......... 85
To Sir, With Love (Screen Gems-Columbia, BMI) .. 4
Wanted: Lover, No Experience Necessary (Chevis, BMI) .......... 84
Watch the Flowers Grow (Saturday/Seasons' Four, BMI) .......... 30
Wear Your Love Like Heaven (Peer Int'l, BMI) .... 46
What's It Gonna Be (Rumbalero/Ragmar, BMI) .. 57
When You're Gone (Dandelion, BMI) .......... 60
Where Is the Party (Frabob/Palo, Alto/Dakar, BMI) .......... 90
Wild Honey (Sea of Tunes, BMI) .......... 31
Windy (Almo, BMI) .......... 66
Woman, Woman (Glaser, BMI) .......... 32
Yesterday (Maclen, BMI) .......... 25
You Better Sit Down Kids (Chrismarc/Cotillion, BMI) .......... 12
Your Precious Love (Jobete, BMI) .......... 39


## BUBBLING UNDER THE HOT 100

101. LIVE FOR LIFE ..........Carmen McRae & Herbie Mann, Atlantic 2451
102. I AM A WALRUS ..........Beatles, Capitol 2056
103. NOBODY BUT ME ..........Human Beins, Capitol 5990
104. FOR ONCE IN MY LIFE ..........Tony Bennett, Columbia 44258
105. DANCIN' OUT OF MY HEART ..........Ronnie Dove, Diamond 233
106. LOVE OF THE COMMON PEOPLE ..........Wayne Newton, Capitol 2016
107. MR. BUS DRIVER ..........Bruce Channel, Mala 579
108. I WANT SOME MORE ..........Jon & Robin & the In Crowd, Abnak 124
109. TEN LITTLE INDIANS ..........Yardbirds, Epic 10248
110. SAND ..........Nancy Sinatra & Lee Hazlewood, Reprise 0629
111. THIS THING CALLED LOVE ..........Webs, Pop-Side 4593
112. MORE THAN A MIRACE ..........Roger Williams, Kapp 843
113. HOLLY ..........Andy Williams, Columbia 44325
114. FOR A FEW DOLLARS MORE ..........Hugo Montonegro, RCA Victor 9224
115. BACK UP TRAIN ..........Al Greene & Soul Mate's, Hot Line 15000
116. GREEN TAMBOURINE ..........Lemon Pipers, Buddah 23
117. DO UNTO OTHERS ..........Paul Revere & the Raiders, Columbia 44335
118. DETROIT CITY ..........Solomon Burke, Atlantic 2459

Compiled from national retail sales and radio station airplay by the Music Popularity Dept. of Record Market Research, Billboard.

HOT 100

HOT 100

# Billboard HOT 100

**FOR WEEK ENDING DECEMBER 9, 1967**

★ STAR PERFORMER—Sides registering greatest proportionate upward progress this week.   ● Record Industry Association of America seal of certification as million selling single.

| This Week | 2 Wks. Ago | 3 Wks. Ago | TITLE — Artist (Producer), Label & Number | Weeks on Chart |
|---|---|---|---|---|
| 1 | 1 | 5 | 33 | DAYDREAM BELIEVER — Monkees (Chip Douglas), Colgems 1012 | 4 |
| 2 | 2 | 3 | 4 | THE RAIN, THE PARK & OTHER THINGS — Cowsills (Artie Kornfeld), MGM 13810 | 11 |
| 3 | 3 | 1 | 3 | INCENSE AND PEPPERMINTS — Strawberry Alarm Clock (Frank Slay & Bill Holmes), Uni 55018 | 11 |
| 4 | 5 | 7 | 8 | I SAY A LITTLE PRAYER — Dionne Warwick (Bacharach-David), Scepter 12203 | 8 |
| ★5 | 8 | 16 | 21 | I HEARD IT THROUGH THE GRAPEVINE — Gladys Knight & the Pips (N. Whitfield), Soul 35039 | 8 |
| 6 | 4 | 2 | 1 | TO SIR, WITH LOVE — Lulu (Mickie Most), Epic 10187 | 14 |
| 7 | 11 | 28 | 43 | I SECOND THAT EMOTION — Smokey Robinson & Miracles ("Smokey" A. Cleveland), Tamla 54159 | 6 |
| 8 | 45 | — | — | HELLO GOODBYE — Beatles (George Martin), Capitol 2056 | 2 |
| 9 | 13 | 29 | 47 | IN AND OUT OF LOVE — Diana Ross & the Supremes (Holland, Dozier), Motown 1116 | 5 |
| 10 | 10 | 18 | 54 | AN OPEN LETTER TO MY TEENAGE SON — Victor Lundberg (Jack Tracy), Liberty 55996 | 5 |
| 11 | 20 | 37 | 52 | (The Lights Went Out In) MASSACHUSETTS — Bee Gees (Robert Stigwood), Atco 6532 | 5 |
| 12 | 12 | 17 | 31 | YOU BETTER SIT DOWN KIDS — Cher (Sonny Bond), Imperial 66261 | 7 |
| 13 | 15 | 20 | 25 | BOOGALOO DOWN BROADWAY — Fantastic Johnny C. (Jesse James), Phil-L.A. of Soul 305 | 10 |
| 14 | 9 | 9 | 10 | I CAN SEE FOR MILES — Who (Kit Lambert), Decca 32206 | 9 |
| 15 | 16 | 21 | 26 | KEEP THE BALL ROLLIN' — Jay & the Techniques (Jerry Ross), Smash 2124 | 8 |
| 16 | 6 | 6 | 6 | PLEASE LOVE ME FOREVER — Bobby Vinton (Billy Sherrill), Epic 10228 | 11 |
| 17 | 7 | 4 | 2 | SOUL MAN — Sam & Dave (Isaac Hayes & David Porter), Stax 231 | 14 |
| 18 | 14 | 19 | 19 | LAZY DAY — Spanky & Our Gang (Jerry Ross), Mercury 72732 | 8 |
| 19 | 19 | 12 | 18 | PATA PATA — Miriam Makeba (Jerry Ragovoy), Reprise 0606 | 10 |
| ★20 | 26 | 34 | 45 | SKINNY LEGS AND ALL — Joe Tex (Buddy Killen), Dial 4063 | 7 |
| 21 | 24 | 44 | 55 | SHE'S MY GIRL — Turtles (Joe Wissert), White Whale 260 | 5 |
| 22 | 32 | 59 | 82 | WOMAN, WOMAN — Union Gap (Jerry Fuller), Columbia 44297 | 4 |
| 23 | 17 | 13 | 13 | EVERLASTING LOVE — Robert Knight (Buzz Cason & Mac Gayden), Rising Sons 117 | 11 |
| ★24 | 37 | 47 | 62 | NEON RAINBOW — Box Tops (Dan Penn), Mala 580 | 4 |
| 25 | 25 | 41 | 51 | YESTERDAY — Ray Charles (TRC), ABC 11009 | 5 |
| ★26 | 40 | 58 | 81 | SUMMER RAIN — Johnny Rivers (Work), Imperial 66267 | 4 |
| 27 | 28 | 39 | 49 | BY THE TIME I GET TO PHOENIX — Glen Campbell (Al De Lory), Capitol 2015 | 7 |
| 28 | 18 | 10 | 9 | EXPRESSWAY TO YOUR HEART — Soul Survivors (Gamble-Huff), Crimson 1010 | 15 |
| 29 | 29 | 35 | 36 | BEG, BORROW AND STEAL — Ohio Express (Jeff Katz & Jerry Kasenetz), Cameo 483 | 10 |
| ★30 | 35 | 55 | 65 | HONEY CHILE — Martha Reeves & the Vandellas (R. Morris), Gordy 7067 | 4 |
| 31 | 31 | 32 | 35 | WILD HONEY — Beach Boys (Beach Boys), Capitol 2028 | 5 |
| 32 | 30 | 30 | 39 | WATCH THE FLOWERS GROW — 4 Seasons (Bob Crewe), Philips 40490 | 7 |
| 33 | 43 | 54 | 87 | DIFFERENT DRUM — Stone Poneys (Nick Venet), Capitol 2004 | 5 |
| 34 | 44 | 48 | 60 | PAPER CUP — 5th Dimension (Bones Howe), Soul City 760 | 6 |
| 35 | 27 | 14 | 14 | (Loneliness Made Me Realize) IT'S YOU THAT I NEED — Temptations (N. Whitfield), Gordy 7065 | 9 |
| ★36 | 46 | 74 | — | WEAR YOUR LOVE LIKE HEAVEN — Donovan (Mickie Most), Epic 10253 | 3 |
| 37 | 47 | 57 | 64 | NEXT PLANE TO LONDON — Rose Garden (Greene/Stone), Atco 6510 | 8 |
| 38 | 22 | 23 | 29 | STAGGER-LEE — Wilson Pickett (Tom Dowd & Tommy Cogbill), Atlantic 2448 | 6 |
| 39 | 23 | 15 | 12 | LET IT OUT — Hombres (Huey P. Meaux), Verve Forecast 5058 | 13 |
| 40 | 21 | 8 | 5 | IT MUST BE HIM — Vikki Carr (Dave Pell), Liberty 55986 | 15 |
| ★41 | 73 | — | — | BEND ME, SHAPE ME — American Breed (Bill Traut), Acta 811 | 2 |
| 42 | 53 | 63 | 85 | PEACE OF MIND — Paul Revere & the Raiders (Terry Helcher), Columbia 44335 | 4 |
| 43 | 48 | 61 | 76 | BEAUTIFUL PEOPLE — Bobby Vee (Dallas Smith), Liberty 56009 | 4 |
| 44 | 50 | 60 | 71 | BEAUTIFUL PEOPLE — Kenny O'Dell (Porter & O'Dell), Vegas 718 | 4 |
| 45 | 55 | 71 | — | AND GET AWAY — Esquires (Bill Sheppard), Bunky 7752 | 3 |
| 46 | 58 | 72 | — | SINCE YOU SHOWED ME HOW TO BE HAPPY — Jackie Wilson (Carl Davis), Brunswick 55354 | 3 |
| ★47 | 65 | — | — | IF I COULD BUILD MY WHOLE WORLD AROUND YOU — Marvin Gaye & Tammi Terrell (Fuqua, Bristol), Tamla 54161 | 2 |
| 48 | 52 | 65 | 98 | CHATTANOOGA CHOO CHOO — Harpers Bizarre (Lenny Waronker), Warner Bros. 7090 | 4 |
| 49 | 49 | 52 | 63 | SOUL MAN — Ramsey Lewis (Richard Evans), Cadet 5583 | 5 |
| 50 | 57 | 79 | 89 | WHAT'S IT GONNA BE — Dusty Springfield, Philips 40498 | 4 |
| 51 | 61 | 81 | — | BABY YOU GOT IT — Brenton Wood (Hooven-Winn), Double Shot 121 | 3 |
| 52 | 62 | 87 | — | TOO MUCH OF NOTHING — Peter, Paul & Mary (Albert B. Grossman & Milt Okun), Warner Bros. 7092 | 3 |
| 53 | 63 | 86 | — | COME SEE ABOUT ME — Jr. Walker & the All Stars (Holland & Dozier), Soul 3501 | 3 |
| 54 | 59 | 82 | — | OKOLONA RIVER BOTTOM BAND — Bobbie Gentry (Kelly Gordon), Capitol 2044 | 3 |
| 55 | 74 | 99 | — | JUDY IN DISGUISE (With Glasses) — John Fred & His Playboy Band (J. Fred & A. Bernard), Paula 282 | 3 |
| 56 | 66 | 85 | — | WINDY — Wes Montgomery (Creed Taylor), A&M 883 | 3 |
| 57 | 69 | 75 | 95 | TELL MAMA — Etta James (Rick Hall), Cadet 5578 | 5 |
| 58 | 60 | 69 | 75 | WHEN YOU'RE GONE — Brenda & Tabulations (Bob Finis), Dionn 504 | 6 |
| 59 | 87 | — | — | IN THE MISTY MOONLIGHT — Dean Martin (Jimmy Bowen), Reprise 0640 | 2 |
| 60 | 71 | 76 | — | COVER ME — Percy Sledge (Quin Ivy & Marlin Greene), Atlantic 2453 | 3 |
| 61 | 64 | 66 | 74 | O-O, I LOVE YOU — Della (B. Miller), Cadet 5574 | 6 |
| 62 | 77 | — | — | THE OTHER MAN'S GRASS IS ALWAYS GREENER — Petula Clark (Tony Hatch), Warner Bros. 7097 | 2 |
| 63 | 34 | 26 | 28 | GLAD TO BE UNHAPPY — Mamas & the Papas (Lou Adler), Dunhill 4107 | 7 |
| 64 | — | — | — | I AM THE WALRUS — Beatles (George Martin), Capitol 2096 | 1 |
| 65 | 68 | 84 | 99 | OOH BABY — Deon Jackson (Ollie McLaughlin), Carla 2537 | 4 |
| ★66 | — | — | — | CHAIN OF FOOLS — Aretha Franklin (Jerry Wexler), Atlantic 2464 | 1 |
| 67 | 67 | 73 | — | LOVE POWER — Sandpebbles (Teddy Vann), Calla 141 | 3 |
| ★68 | — | — | — | IT'S WONDERFUL — Young Rascals (Young Rascals), Atlantic 2463 | 1 |
| 69 | 72 | 78 | 88 | ITCHYCOO PARK — Small Faces (Steve Marriott & Ronnie Lane), Immediate 501 | 5 |
| 70 | 75 | 90 | 97 | PIECE OF MY HEART — Erma Franklin (Bert Berns), Shout 221 | 6 |
| ★71 | 86 | — | — | DEAR ELOISE — Hollies (Ron Richards), Epic 10251 | 2 |
| 72 | 81 | — | — | STORYBOOK CHILDREN — Billy Vera & Judy Clay (Chip Taylor & Ted Deryll), Atlantic 2445 | 2 |
| 73 | 78 | — | — | HOORAY FOR THE SALVATION ARMY BAND — Bill Cosby (Fred Smith), Warner Bros. 7096 | 2 |
| ★74 | — | — | — | SUSAN — Buckinghams (James William Guercio), Columbia 44378 | 1 |
| 75 | — | — | — | LOVE ME TWO TIMES — Doors (Paul A. Rothchild), Elektra 45624 | 1 |
| 76 | 76 | 77 | 80 | SHAME ON ME — Chuck Jackson (Bob Schroeder), Wand 1166 | 9 |
| 77 | 80 | — | — | SOCKIN' 1-2-3-4 — John Roberts (Bob Garner), Duke 425 | 2 |
| 78 | 88 | 88 | — | CAN'T HELP BUT LOVE YOU — Standells (Ed Cobb), Tower 348 | 3 |
| 79 | 79 | 97 | — | I'LL BE SWEETER TOMORROW — O'Jays (George Kerr), Bell 691 | 3 |
| 80 | 82 | — | — | I'M IN LOVE — Wilson Pickett (Tom Dowd & Tommy Cogbill), Atlantic 2448 | 2 |
| 81 | 83 | 83 | 86 | GEORGIA PINES — Candymen (Buddy Buie), ABC 10995 | 4 |
| 82 | 94 | — | — | A LOVE THAT'S REAL — Intruders (Joe Benzetti), Gamble 209 | 2 |
| 83 | 85 | — | — | TONY ROME — Nancy Sinatra (Lee Hazlewood), Reprise 0636 | 2 |
| 84 | 84 | — | — | WANTED: LOVER, NO EXPERIENCE NECESSARY — Laura Lee (Rick Hall), Chess 2030 | 2 |
| 85 | — | — | — | I CAN'T STAND MYSELF (When You Touch Me) — James Brown & His Famous Flames (James Brown), King 6144 | 1 |
| 86 | — | — | — | UP-UP AND AWAY — Hugh Masakela (Stewart Lovine), Uni 55037 | 1 |
| 87 | — | — | — | GOIN' OUT OF MY HEAD / CAN'T TAKE MY EYES OFF YOU — Lettermen (Kelly Gordon), Capitol 2054 | 1 |
| 88 | 98 | 100 | — | FOR WHAT IT'S WORTH — King Curtis & Kingpins (Tom Dowd & Tommy Cogbill), Atco 6534 | 3 |
| 89 | — | — | — | BACK UP TRAIN — Al Greene & Soul Mate's (Rodgers & James), Hot Line 15000 | 1 |
| 90 | 90 | 92 | 92 | WHERE IS THE PARTY — Helena Ferguson (Lincoln Kilpatrick), Compass 7009 | 5 |
| 91 | 91 | — | — | HERE COMES HEAVEN — Eddy Arnold (Chet Atkins), RCA Victor 9368 | 2 |
| 92 | 96 | — | — | SOMETHING'S MISSING — 5 Stairsteps & Cubie (Clarence Burke, Jr.), Buddah 20 | 2 |
| 93 | 97 | 98 | — | LETTER TO DAD, A — Every Father's Teenage Son (Inherit Prod.), Buddah 25 | 3 |
| 94 | 95 | 95 | 100 | FELICIDAD — Sally Field (Jack Keller), Colgems 1008 | 4 |
| 95 | 99 | — | — | CROSS MY HEART — Billy Stewart (Davis & Caston), Chess 2002 | 2 |
| 96 | — | — | — | DANCING BEAR — Mamas & Papas (Lou Adler), Dunhill 4113 | 1 |
| 97 | — | — | — | SHOUT — Lulu (Dick Rowe), Parrot 40021 | 1 |
| 98 | — | — | — | NOBODY BUT ME — Human Beinz (Alexis de Azevado), Capitol 5990 | 1 |
| 99 | 100 | — | — | LIVE FOR LIFE — Jack Jones (Ernie Altschuler), RCA Victor 9365 | 2 |
| 100 | — | — | — | A VOICE IN THE CHOIR — Al Martino (Tom Morgan & Marvin Holtzman), Capitol 2053 | 1 |

## BUBBLING UNDER THE HOT 100

101. LIVE FOR LIFE .............. Carmen McRae & Herbie Mann, Atlantic 2451
102. DANCIN' OUT OF MY HEART .............. Ronnie Dove, Diamond 233
103. I WONDER WHAT SHE'S DOING TONIGHT .............. Tommy Boyce & Bobby Hart, A&M 893
104. MR. BUS DRIVER .............. Bruce Channel, Mala 579
105. DETROIT CITY .............. Solomon Burke, Atlantic 2459
106. BABY NOW THAT I FOUND YOU .............. Foundations, Uni 55035
107. GREEN TAMBOURINE .............. Lemon Pipers, Buddah 23
108. A LITTLE RAIN MUST FALL .............. Epic Splendor, Hot Biscuit 1450
109. MORE THAN A MIRACLE .............. Roger Williams, Kapp 843
110. IN ANOTHER LAND .............. Bill Wyman, London 907
111. THIS THING CALLED LOVE .............. Webs, Pop-Side 4593
112. TURN OF THE CENTURY .............. Cyrkle, Columbia 44366
113. SPOOKY .............. Classics Four, Imperial 66259
114. MELLOW MOONLIGHT .............. Leon Haywood, Decca 32230
115. DO UNTO OTHERS .............. Paul Revere & the Raiders, Columbia 44335
116. INSANITY COMES QUIETLY TO THE STRUCTURED MIND .............. Janis Ian, Verve Forecast 5072
117. LITTLE BIT OF LOVIN' .............. Outsiders, Capitol 2055
118. WATCH HER RIDE .............. Jefferson Airplane, RCA Victor 9389
119. MONTEREY .............. Eric Burdon & the Animals, MGM 13868
120. SKIP A ROPE .............. Henson Cargill, Monument 1041

*Compiled from national retail sales and radio station airplay by the Music Popularity Dept. of Record Market Research, Billboard.*

# Billboard HOT 100

FOR WEEK ENDING DECEMBER 16, 1967

★ STAR PERFORMER—Sides registering greatest proportionate upward progress this week.

Record Industry Association of America seal of certification as million selling single.

| This Week | 1 Wk. Ago | 2 Wks. Ago | 3 Wks. Ago | TITLE Artist (Producer), Label & Number | Weeks On Chart |
|---|---|---|---|---|---|
| 1 (Billboard Award) | 1 | 1 | 5 | DAYDREAM BELIEVER — Monkees (Chip Douglas), Colgems 1012 (RIAA seal) | 5 |
| ★2 | 5 | 8 | 16 | I HEARD IT THROUGH THE GRAPEVINE — Gladys Knight & the Pips (N. Whitfield), Soul 35039 | 8 |
| ★3 | 8 | 45 | — | HELLO GOODBYE — Beatles (George Martin), Capitol 2056 | 3 |
| ★4 | 7 | 11 | 28 | I SECOND THAT EMOTION — Smokey Robinson & Miracles ("Smokey" A. Cleveland), Tamla 54159 | 7 |
| 5 | 2 | 2 | 3 | THE RAIN, THE PARK & OTHER THINGS — Cowsills (Artie Kornfeld), MGM 13810 | 12 |
| 6 | 3 | 3 | 1 | INCENSE AND PEPPERMINTS — Strawberry Alarm Clock (Frank Slay & Bill Holmes), Uni 55018 | 12 |
| 7 | 4 | 5 | 7 | I SAY A LITTLE PRAYER — Dionne Warwick (Bacharach-David), Scepter 12203 | 9 |
| ★8 | 13 | 15 | 20 | BOOGALOO DOWN BROADWAY — Fantastic Johnny C. (Jesse James), Phil-L.A. of Soul 305 | 11 |
| 9 | 9 | 13 | 29 | IN AND OUT OF LOVE — Diana Ross & the Supremes (Holland, Dozier), Motown 1116 | 6 |
| 10 | 12 | 12 | 17 | YOU BETTER SIT DOWN KIDS — Cher (Sonny Bond), Imperial 66261 | 8 |
| 11 | 11 | 20 | 37 | (The Lights Went Out In) MASSACHUSETTS — Bee Gees (Robert Stigwood), Atco 6532 | 6 |
| ★12 | 22 | 32 | 59 | WOMAN, WOMAN — Union Gap (Jerry Fuller), Columbia 44297 | 5 |
| 13 | 6 | 4 | 2 | TO SIR, WITH LOVE — Lulu (Mickie Most), Epic 10187 (RIAA seal) | 15 |
| 14 | 15 | 16 | 21 | KEEP THE BALL ROLLIN' — Jay & the Techniques (Jerry Ross), Smash 2124 | 9 |
| ★15 | 20 | 26 | 34 | SKINNY LEGS AND ALL — Joe Tex (Buddy Killen), Dial 4063 | 8 |
| ★16 | 21 | 24 | 44 | SHE'S MY GIRL — Turtles (Joe Wissert), White Whale 260 | 6 |
| ★17 | 30 | 35 | 55 | HONEY CHILE — Martha Reeves & the Vandellas (R. Morris), Gordy 7067 | 5 |
| 18 | 18 | 14 | 19 | LAZY DAY — Spanky & Our Gang (Jerry Ross), Mercury 72732 | 10 |
| ★19 | 26 | 40 | 58 | SUMMER RAIN — Johnny Rivers (Werk), Imperial 66267 | 5 |
| 20 | 16 | 6 | 6 | PLEASE LOVE ME FOREVER — Bobby Vinton (Billy Sherrill), Epic 10228 | 12 |
| 21 | 14 | 9 | 9 | I CAN SEE FOR MILES — Who (Kit Lambert), Decca 32206 | 10 |
| 22 | 10 | 10 | 18 | AN OPEN LETTER TO MY TEENAGE SON — Victor Lundberg (Jack Tracy), Liberty 55996 | 6 |
| ★23 | 41 | 73 | — | BEND ME, SHAPE ME — American Breed (Bill Traut), Acta 811 | 3 |
| 24 | 24 | 37 | 47 | NEON RAINBOW — Box Tops (Dan Penn), Mala 580 | 6 |
| 25 | 25 | 25 | 41 | YESTERDAY — Ray Charles (TRC), ABC 11009 | 6 |
| 26 | 27 | 28 | 39 | BY THE TIME I GET TO PHOENIX — Glen Campbell (Al De Lory), Capitol 2015 | 8 |
| ★27 | 55 | 74 | 99 | JUDY IN DISGUISE (With Glasses) — John Fred & His Playboy Band (J. Fred & A. Bernard), Paula 282 | 4 |
| ★28 | 33 | 43 | 54 | DIFFERENT DRUM — Stone Poneys (Nick Venet), Capitol 2004 | 6 |
| ★29 | 66 | — | — | CHAIN OF FOOLS — Aretha Franklin (Jerry Wexler), Atlantic 2464 | 2 |
| ★30 | 37 | 47 | 57 | NEXT PLANE TO LONDON — Rose Garden (Greene/Stone), Atco 6510 | 9 |
| 31 | 29 | 29 | 35 | BEG, BORROW AND STEAL — Ohio Express (Jeff Katz & Jerry Kasenetz), Cameo 483 | 11 |
| 32 | 19 | 19 | 12 | PATA PATA — Miriam Makeba (Jerry Ragovoy), Reprise 0606 | 11 |
| ★33 | 47 | 65 | — | IF I COULD BUILD MY WHOLE WORLD AROUND YOU — Marvin Gaye & Tammi Terrell (Fugua, Bristol), Tamla 54161 | 3 |
| ★34 | 45 | 55 | 71 | AND GET AWAY — Esquires (Bill Sheppard), Bunky 7752 | 4 |
| ★35 | 46 | 58 | 72 | SINCE YOU SHOWED ME HOW TO BE HAPPY — Jackie Wilson (Carl Davis), Brunswick 55354 | 4 |
| 36 | 36 | 46 | 74 | WEAR YOUR LOVE LIKE HEAVEN — Donovan (Mickie Most), Epic 10253 | 4 |
| 37 | 43 | 48 | 61 | BEAUTIFUL PEOPLE — Bobby Vee (Dallas Smith), Liberty 56009 | 5 |
| 38 | 44 | 50 | 60 | BEAUTIFUL PEOPLE — Kenny O'Dell (Porter & O'Dell), Vegas 718 | 5 |
| 39 | 23 | 17 | 13 | EVERLASTING LOVE — Robert Knight (Buzz Cason & Mac Gayden), Rising Sons 117 | 12 |
| ★40 | 51 | 61 | 81 | BABY YOU GOT IT — Brenton Wood (Hooven-Winn), Double Shot 121 | 4 |
| ★41 | 52 | 62 | 87 | TOO MUCH OF NOTHING — Peter, Paul & Mary (Albert B. Grossman & Milt Okun), Warner Bros. 7092 | 4 |
| 42 | 42 | 53 | 63 | PEACE OF MIND — Paul Revere & the Raiders (Terry Melcher), Columbia 44335 | 5 |
| ★43 | 68 | — | — | IT'S WONDERFUL — Young Rascals (Young Rascals), Atlantic 2463 | 2 |
| 44 | 34 | 44 | 48 | PAPER CUP — 5th Dimension (Bones Howe), Soul City 760 | 7 |
| 45 | 48 | 52 | 65 | CHATTANOOGA CHOO CHOO — Harpers Bizarre (Lenny Waronker), Warner Bros. 7090 | 5 |
| 46 | 53 | 63 | 86 | COME SEE ABOUT ME — Jr. Walker & the All Stars (Holland & Dozier), Soul 3501 | 4 |
| 47 | 17 | 7 | 4 | SOUL MAN — Sam & Dave (Isaac Hayes & David Porter), Stax 231 (RIAA seal) | 15 |
| ★48 | 74 | — | — | SUSAN — Buckinghams (James William Guercio), Columbia 44378 | 2 |
| ★49 | 60 | 71 | 76 | COVER ME — Percy Sledge (Quin Ivy & Marlin Greene), Atlantic 2453 | 4 |
| 50 | 50 | 57 | 79 | WHAT'S IT GONNA BE — Dusty Springfield, Philips 40498 | 5 |
| 51 | 57 | 69 | 75 | TELL MAMA — Etta James (Rick Hall), Cadet 5578 | 6 |
| ★52 | 62 | 77 | — | THE OTHER MAN'S GRASS IS ALWAYS GREENER — Petula Clark (Tony Hatch), Warner Bros. 7097 | 3 |
| ★53 | 67 | 67 | 73 | LOVE POWER — Sandpebbles (Teddy Vann), Calla 141 | 4 |
| 54 | 54 | 59 | 82 | OKOLONA RIVER BOTTOM BAND — Bobbie Gentry (Kelly Gordon), Capitol 2044 | 4 |
| 55 | 56 | 66 | 85 | WINDY — Wes Montgomery (Creed Taylor), A&M 883 | 4 |
| 56 | 59 | 87 | — | IN THE MISTY MOONLIGHT — Dean Martin (Jimmy Bowen), Reprise 0640 | 3 |
| 57 | 64 | — | — | I AM THE WALRUS — Beatles (George Martin), Capitol 2096 | 2 |
| 58 | 58 | 60 | 69 | WHEN YOU'RE GONE — Brenda & Tabulations (Bob Finis), Dionn 504 | 7 |
| ★59 | 75 | — | — | LOVE ME TWO TIMES — Doors (Paul A. Rothchild), Elektra 45624 | 2 |
| ★60 | 71 | 86 | — | DEAR ELOISE — Hollies (Ron Richards), Epic 10251 | 3 |
| 61 | 61 | 64 | 66 | O-O, I LOVE YOU — Della (B. Miller), Cadet 5574 | 7 |
| 62 | 70 | 75 | 90 | PIECE OF MY HEART — Erma Franklin (Bert Berns), Shout 221 | 7 |
| 63 | 49 | 49 | 52 | SOUL MAN — Ramsey Lewis (Richard Evans), Cadet 5583 | 6 |
| ★64 | 80 | 82 | — | I'M IN LOVE — Wilson Pickett (Tom Dowd & Tommy Cogbill), Atlantic 2448 | 3 |
| 65 | 65 | 68 | 84 | OOH BABY — Deon Jackson (Ollie McLaughlin), Carla 2537 | 5 |
| 66 | 69 | 72 | 78 | ITCHYCOO PARK — Small Faces (Steve Marriott & Ronnie Lane), Immediate 501 | 6 |
| 67 | 72 | 81 | — | STORYBOOK CHILDREN — Billy Vera & Judy Clay (Chip Taylor & Ted Daryll), Atlantic 2445 | 3 |
| ★68 | — | — | — | GREEN TAMBOURINE — Lemon Pipers (Paul Leka), Buddah 23 | 1 |
| ★69 | 87 | — | — | GOIN' OUT OF MY HEAD/CAN'T TAKE MY EYES OFF YOU — Lettermen (Kelly Gordon), Capitol 2054 | 2 |
| 70 | 79 | 79 | 97 | I'LL BE SWEETER TOMORROW — O'Jays (George Kerr), Bell 691 | 4 |
| 71 | 77 | 80 | — | SOCKIN' 1-2-3-4 — John Roberts (Bob Garner), Duke 425 | 3 |
| 72 | 85 | — | — | I CAN'T STAND MYSELF (When You Touch Me) — James Brown & His Famous Flames (James Brown), King 6144 | 2 |
| 73 | 73 | 78 | — | HOORAY FOR THE SALVATION ARMY BAND — Bill Cosby (Fred Smith), Warner Bros. 7096 | 3 |
| ★74 | — | — | — | WHO WILL ANSWER — Ed Ames (Jim Foglesong), RCA Victor 9400 | 1 |
| ★75 | — | — | — | BEST OF BOTH WORLDS — Lulu (Mickie Most), Epic 10260 | 1 |
| ★76 | — | — | — | WATCH HER RIDE — Jefferson Airplane (Al Schmitt), RCA Victor 9389 | 1 |
| ★77 | 96 | — | — | DANCING BEAR — Mamas & Papas (Lou Adler), Dunhill 4113 | 2 |
| ★78 | — | — | — | MY BABY MUST BE A MAGICIAN — Marvelettes ("Smokey"), Tamla 54158 | 1 |
| ★79 | — | — | — | GOOD COMBINATION — Sonny & Cher (Sonny Bono), Atco 6541 | 1 |
| 80 | 89 | — | — | BACK UP TRAIN — Al Greene & Soul Mate's (Rodgers & James), Hot Line 15000 | 2 |
| 81 | 81 | 83 | 83 | GEORGIA PINES — Candymen (Buddy Buie), ABC 10995 | 5 |
| 82 | 82 | 94 | — | A LOVE THAT'S REAL — Intruders (Joe Renzetti), Gamble 209 | 3 |
| 83 | 83 | 85 | — | TONY ROME — Nancy Sinatra (Lee Hazlewood), Reprise 0636 | 3 |
| 84 | 86 | — | — | UP-UP AND AWAY — Hugh Masakela (Stewart Levine), Uni 55037 | 2 |
| ★85 | — | — | — | MONTEREY — Eric Burdon & the Animals (Tom Wilson), MGM 13868 | 1 |
| ★86 | — | — | — | EVERYBODY KNOWS — Dave Clark Five (Dave Clark), Epic 10265 | 1 |
| 87 | 88 | 98 | 100 | FOR WHAT IT'S WORTH — King Curtis & Kingpins (Tom Dowd & Tommy Cogbill), Atco 6534 | 4 |
| 88 | 98 | — | — | NOBODY BUT ME — Human Beinz (Alexis de Azevedo), Capitol 5990 | 2 |
| ★89 | — | — | — | AM I THAT EASY TO FORGET — Engelbert Humperdinck (Peter Sullivan), Parrot 40023 | 1 |
| ★90 | — | — | — | TWO LITTLE KIDS — Peaches & Herb (David Kapralik & Ken Williams), Date 1586 | 1 |
| 91 | 91 | 91 | — | HERE COMES HEAVEN — Eddy Arnold (Chet Atkins), RCA Victor 9368 | 3 |
| 92 | 92 | 96 | — | SOMETHING'S MISSING — 5 Stairsteps & Cubie (Clarence Burke, Jr.), Buddah 20 | 3 |
| 93 | 93 | 97 | 98 | LETTER TO DAD, A — Every Father's Teenage Son (Inherit Prod.), Buddah 25 | 4 |
| 94 | 95 | 99 | — | CROSS MY HEART — Billy Stewart (Davis & Caston), Chess 2002 | 3 |
| 95 | — | — | — | SOMEBODY'S SLEEPING IN MY BED — Johnnie Taylor (Al Jackson), Stax 235 | 1 |
| 96 | 96 | — | — | A VOICE IN THE CHOIR — Al Martino (Tom Morgan & Marvin Holtzman), Capitol 2053 | 2 |
| 97 | 97 | — | — | SHOUT — Lulu (Dick Rowe), Parrot 40021 | 2 |
| 98 | — | — | — | IN ANOTHER LAND — Bill Wyman (Rolling Stones), London 907 | 1 |
| 99 | — | — | — | DANCIN' OUT OF MY HEART — Ronnie Dove (Phil Kahl), Diamond 233 | 1 |
| 100 | — | — | — | A LITTLE RAIN MUST FALL — Epic Splendor (John Boylan), Hot Biscuit 1450 | 1 |

## HOT 100—A TO Z—(Publisher-Licensee)

Am I That Easy to Forget (Four Star, BMI) .... 89
An Open Letter to My Teenage Son (Asa, ASCAP) .... 22
And Get Away (Hi-Mi/Flomar, BMI) .... 34

Baby You Got It (Big Shot, ASCAP) .... 40
Back Up Train (Tosted, BMI) .... 80
Beautiful People (O'Dell) (Mirwood Antlers, BMI) .... 38
Beautiful People (Vee) (Mirwood Antlers, BMI) .... 37
Beg, Borrow and Steal (S&J, ASCAP) .... 31
Bend Me, Shape Me (Helios, BMI) .... 23
Best of Both Worlds (James, BMI) .... 75
Boogaloo Down Broadway (Dandelion/James Boys, BMI) .... 8
By the Time I Get to Phoenix (Rivers, BMI) .... 26

Chain of Fools (14th Hour/Pronto, BMI) .... 29
Chattanooga Choo Choo (Feist, ASCAP) .... 45
Come See About Me (Jobete, BMI) .... 46
Cover Me (Pronto/Quiney, BMI) .... 49
Cross My Heart (Chevis, BMI) .... 94

Dancing Bear (Wingate, ASCAP) .... 77
Dancin' Out of My Heart (Irwin, ASCAP) .... 99
Daydream Believer (Screen Gems-Columbia, BMI) .... 1
Dear Eloise (Marthus, BMI) .... 60
Different Drum (Screen Gems-Columbia, BMI) .... 28

Everybody Knows (Francis, Day & Hunter, ASCAP) 86
Everlasting Love (Rising Sons, BMI) .... 39
For What It's Worth (Cotillion/Ten East/Springalo, BMI) .... 87

Georgia Pines (Unart, BMI) .... 81
Goin' Out of My Head/Can't Take My Eyes Off You (Vogue/Saturday/Seasons' Four, BMI) .... 69
Good Combination (Triparte/Pamper/D-K, BMI) .... 79
Green Tambourine (Kama Sutra, BMI) .... 68

Hello Goodbye (Maclen, BMI) .... 3
Here Comes Heaven (Hill & Range, BMI) .... 91
Honey Chile (Jobete, BMI) .... 17
Hooray for the Salvation Army Band (Monger/Kaymen, BMI) .... 73

I Am the Walrus (Maclen, BMI) .... 57
I Can See for Miles (Essex, ASCAP) .... 21
I Can't Stand Myself (When You Touch Me) (Taccon/Soil, BMI) .... 72
I Heard It Through the Grapevine (Jobete, BMI) .... 2
I Say a Little Prayer (Blue Seas/Jac, ASCAP) .... 7
I Second That Emotion (Jobete, BMI) .... 4
If I Could Build My Whole World Around You (Jobete, BMI) .... 33
I'll Be Sweeter Tomorrow (Zira/Floteca, Mia, BMI) 70
I'm in Love (Pronto/Trecebob, BMI) .... 64
In and Out of Love (Jobete, BMI) .... 9
In Another Land (Gideon, BMI) .... 98
In the Misty Moonlight (4 Star, BMI) .... 56
Incense and Peppermints (Claridge, ASCAP) .... 6
Itchycoo Park (Nice Songs, BMI) .... 66
It's Wonderful (Slacsar, BMI) .... 43

Judy in Disguise (With Glasses) (Su-Ma, BMI) .... 27

Keep the Ball Rollin' (Screen Gems-Columbia, BMI) 14

Lazy Day (Screen Gems-Columbia, BMI) .... 18
Letter to Dad, A (Bob-Len, BMI) .... 93
(Lights Went Out In) Massachusetts, The (Nemperor, BMI) .... 11
Little Rain Must Fall, A (Chardon, BMI) .... 100
Love Me Two Times (Nipper, ASCAP) .... 59
Love Power (Unbelievable, BMI) .... 53
Love That's Real, A (Razor Sharp, BMI) .... 82

Monterey (Slamina/Sea-Lark, BMI) .... 85
Neon Rainbow (Earl Barton, BMI) .... 24
Next Plane to London (Mirwood Antlers, BMI) .... 30
Nobody But Be (Wemar, BMI) .... 88

Okolona River Bottom Band (Shayne, ASCAP) .... 54
O-O, I Love You (Chervis, BMI) .... 61
Ooh Baby (Goncho/McLaughlin, BMI) .... 65
Other Man's Grass Is Always Greener, The (Northern, ASCAP) .... 52

Paper Cup (Rivers, BMI) .... 44
Pata Pata (Xina, ASCAP) .... 32
Peace of Mind (Daywin, BMI) .... 42
Piece of My Heart (Web IV/Ragmar, BMI) .... 62
Please Love Me Forever (Selma, BMI) .... 20

Rain, the Park & Other Things, The (Akbestal/Luvlin, BMI) .... 5

She's My Girl (Chardon, BMI) .... 16
Shout (Wemar/Nom, BMI) .... 97
Since You Showed Me How to Be Happy (Jalynne/BRC, BMI) .... 35
Skinny Legs and All (Tree, BMI) .... 15
Sockin' 1-2-3-4 (Don, BMI) .... 71
Somebody's Sleeping in My Bed (East, BMI) .... 95
Something's Missing (Kama Sutra/Burke Family, BMI) .... 92
Soul Man (Sam & Dave) (East/Pronto, BMI) .... 47
Soul Man (Lewis) (East/Pronto, BMI) .... 63
Storybook Children (Blackwood, BMI) .... 67
Summer Rain (Rivers, BMI) .... 19
Susan (Diongenes/Beg O'Tunes, BMI) .... 48

Tell Mama (Fame, BMI) .... 51
Too Much of Nothing (Dwarf, ASCAP) .... 41
To Sir, With Love (Screen Gems-Columbia, BMI) .... 13
Tony Rome (Sergeant, ASCAP) .... 83
Two Little Kids (Jalynne, BMI) .... 90

Up-Up and Away (Rivers, BMI) .... 84

Watch Her Ride .... 76
Wear Your Love Like Heaven (Peer Int'l, BMI) .... 36
What's It Gonna Be (Rumbalero/Ragmar, BMI) .... 50
When You're Gone (Dandelion, BMI) .... 58
Who Will Answer (Sunbary, ASCAP) .... 74
Windy (Almo, BMI) .... 55
Woman, Woman (Glaser, BMI) .... 12

Yesterday (Maclen, BMI) .... 26
You Better Sit Down Kids (Chrismarc/Cotillion, BMI) .... 10

## BUBBLING UNDER THE HOT 100

101. SPOOKY .... Classics IV, Imperial 66259
102. I WONDER WHAT SHE'S DOING TONIGHT .... Tommy Boyce & Bobby Hart, MGM 893
103. MR. BUS DRIVER .... Bruce Channel, Mala 579
104. DETROIT CITY .... Solomon Burke, Atlantic 2499
105. BABY NOW THAT I FOUND YOU .... Foundations, Uni 55038
106. THIS THING CALLED LOVE .... Webs, Pop Side 4593
107. FELICIDAD .... Sally Fields, Colgems 1008
108. MORE THAN A MIRACLE .... Roger Williams, Kapp 843
109. INSANITY COMES QUIETLY TO THE STRUCTURED MIND .... Janis Ian, Verve Forecast 5072
110. MELLOW MOONLIGHT .... Leon Haywood, Decca 32230
111. WHERE IS THE PARTY .... Helena Ferguson, Compass 7009
112. UPTIGHT GOOD MAN .... Laura Lee, Chess 2030
113. SKIP A ROPE .... Henson Cargill, Monument 1041
114. DO UNTO OTHERS .... Paul Revere & the Raiders, Columbia 44335
115. GOOD, GOOD LOVIN' .... Blossoms, Reprise 0639
116. I FEEL FREE .... Cream, Atco 6462
117. FOXEY LADY .... Jimi Hendrix, Reprise 0641
118. COME SEE ABOUT ME ... Mitch Ryder & the Detroit Wheels, New Voice 828
119. YAKETY YAK .... Sam the Sham, MGM 13863
120. LETTER FROM A TEEN-AGE SON .... Brandon Wade, Philips 40503
121. LOST .... Jerry Butler, Mercury 72764
122. (1-2-3-4-5-6-7) COUNT THE DAYS .... Inez & Charlie Foxx, Dynamo 112

Compiled from national retail sales and radio station airplay by the Music Popularity Dept. of Record Market Research, Billboard.

HOT 100

HOT 100

# Billboard HOT 100

**For Week Ending December 23, 1967**

★ STAR PERFORMER—Sides registering greatest proportionate upward progress this week.
● Record Industry Association of America seal of certification as million selling single.

| This Week | 1 Wk. Ago | 2 Wk. Ago | 3 Wk. Ago | TITLE – Artist (Producer), Label & Number | Weeks On Chart |
|---|---|---|---|---|---|
| 1 | 1 | 1 | 1 | **DAYDREAM BELIEVER** — Monkees (Chip Douglas), Colgems 1012 ● | 6 |
| 2 | 2 | 5 | 8 | I HEARD IT THROUGH THE GRAPEVINE — Gladys Knight & the Pips (N. Whitfield), Soul 35039 | 9 |
| 3 | 3 | 8 | 45 | HELLO GOODBYE — Beatles (George Martin), Capitol 2056 | 4 |
| 4 | 4 | 7 | 11 | I SECOND THAT EMOTION — Smokey Robinson & Miracles ("Smokey" A. Cleveland), Tamla 54159 | 8 |
| ★5 | 12 | 22 | 32 | WOMAN, WOMAN — Union Gap (Jerry Fuller), Columbia 44297 | 6 |
| 6 | 5 | 2 | 2 | THE RAIN, THE PARK & OTHER THINGS — Cowsills (Artie Kornfeld), MGM 13810 | 13 |
| 7 | 8 | 13 | 15 | BOOGALOO DOWN BROADWAY — Fantastic Johnny C. (Jesse James), Phil-L.A. of Soul 305 | 12 |
| 8 | 6 | 3 | 3 | INCENSE AND PEPPERMINTS — Strawberry Alarm Clock (Frank Slay & Bill Holmes), Uni 55018 | 13 |
| 9 | 10 | 12 | 12 | YOU BETTER SIT DOWN KIDS — Cher (Sonny Bond), Imperial 66261 | 9 |
| 10 | 7 | 4 | 5 | I SAY A LITTLE PRAYER — Dionne Warwick (Bacharach-David), Scepter 12203 | 10 |
| 11 | 27 | 55 | 74 | JUDY IN DISGUISE (With Glasses) — John Fred & His Playboy Band (J. Fred & A. Bernard), Paula 282 | 5 |
| 12 | 9 | 9 | 13 | IN AND OUT OF LOVE — Diana Ross & the Supremes (Holland, Dozier), Motown 1116 | 7 |
| ★13 | 23 | 41 | 73 | BEND ME, SHAPE ME — American Breed (Bill Traut), Acta 811 | 4 |
| 14 | 16 | 21 | 24 | SHE'S MY GIRL — Turtles (Joe Wissert), White Whale 260 | 7 |
| 15 | 15 | 20 | 26 | SKINNY LEGS AND ALL — Joe Tex (Buddy Killen), Dial 4063 | 9 |
| 16 | 17 | 30 | 35 | HONEY CHILE — Martha Reeves & the Vandellas (R. Morris), Gordy 7067 | 6 |
| ★17 | 29 | 66 | — | CHAIN OF FOOLS — Aretha Franklin (Jerry Wexler), Atlantic 2464 | 3 |
| 18 | 19 | 26 | 40 | SUMMER RAIN — Johnny Rivers (Work), Imperial 66267 | 6 |
| 19 | 14 | 15 | 16 | KEEP THE BALL ROLLIN' — Jay & the Techniques (Jerry Ross), Smash 2124 | 10 |
| 20 | 11 | 11 | 20 | (The Lights Went Out In) MASSACHUSETTS — Bee Gees (Robert Stigwood), Atco 6532 | 7 |
| 21 | 13 | 6 | 4 | TO SIR, WITH LOVE — Lulu (Mickie Most), Epic 10187 ● | 16 |
| 22 | 30 | 37 | 47 | NEXT PLANE TO LONDON — Rose Garden (Greene/Stone), Atco 6510 | 10 |
| ★23 | 33 | 47 | 65 | IF I COULD BUILD MY WHOLE WORLD AROUND YOU — Marvin Gaye & Tammi Terrell (Fuqus, Bristol), Tamla 54161 | 4 |
| 24 | 24 | 24 | 37 | NEON RAINBOW — Box Tops (Dan Penn), Mala 580 | 6 |
| 25 | 21 | 14 | 9 | I CAN SEE FOR MILES — Who (Kit Lambert), Decca 32206 | 11 |
| 26 | 28 | 33 | 43 | DIFFERENT DRUM — Stone Poneys (Nick Venet), Capitol 2004 | 7 |
| 27 | 20 | 16 | 6 | PLEASE LOVE ME FOREVER — Bobby Vinton (Billy Sherrill), Epic 10228 | 13 |
| 28 | 36 | 36 | 46 | WEAR YOUR LOVE LIKE HEAVEN — Donovan (Mickie Most), Epic 10253 | 5 |
| 29 | 34 | 45 | 55 | AND GET AWAY — Esquires (Bill Sheppard), Bunky 7752 | 6 |
| 30 | 26 | 27 | 28 | BY THE TIME I GET TO PHOENIX — Glen Campbell (Al De Lory), Capitol 2015 | 9 |
| ★31 | 43 | 68 | — | IT'S WONDERFUL — Young Rascals (Young Rascals), Atlantic 2463 | 3 |
| 32 | 35 | 46 | 58 | SINCE YOU SHOWED ME HOW TO BE HAPPY — Jackie Wilson (Carl Davis), Brunswick 55354 | 5 |
| ★33 | 68 | — | — | GREEN TAMBOURINE — Lemon Pipers (Paul Leka), Buddah 23 | 2 |
| ★34 | 48 | 74 | — | SUSAN — Buckinghams (James William Guercio), Columbia 44378 | 3 |
| 35 | 40 | 51 | 61 | BABY YOU GOT IT — Brenton Wood (Hooven-Winn), Double Shot 121 | 5 |
| 36 | 46 | 53 | 63 | COME SEE ABOUT ME — Jr. Walker & the All Stars (Holland & Dozier), Soul 3501 | 5 |
| 37 | 37 | 43 | 48 | BEAUTIFUL PEOPLE — Bobby Vee (Dallas Smith), Liberty 56009 | 6 |
| 38 | 38 | 44 | 50 | BEAUTIFUL PEOPLE — Kenny O'Dell (Porter & O'Dell), Vegas 718 | 6 |
| 39 | 41 | 52 | 62 | TOO MUCH OF NOTHING — Peter, Paul & Mary (Albert B. Grossman & Milt Okun), Warner Bros. 7092 | 5 |
| 40 | 18 | 18 | 14 | LAZY DAY — Spanky & Our Gang (Jerry Ross), Mercury 72732 | 11 |
| ★41 | 52 | 62 | 77 | THE OTHER MAN'S GRASS IS ALWAYS GREENER — Petula Clark (Tony Hatch), Warner Bros. 7097 | 4 |
| 42 | 42 | 42 | 53 | PEACE OF MIND — Paul Revere & the Raiders (Terry Helcher), Columbia 44335 | 6 |
| 43 | 31 | 29 | 29 | BEG, BORROW AND STEAL — Ohio Express (Jeff Katz & Jerry Kasenetz), Cameo 483 | 12 |
| 44 | 55 | 56 | 66 | WINDY — Wes Montgomery (Creed Taylor), A&M 883 | 5 |
| 45 | 45 | 48 | 52 | CHATTANOOGA CHOO CHOO — Harpers Bizarre (Lenny Waronker), Warner Bros. 7090 | 6 |
| 46 | 56 | 59 | 87 | IN THE MISTY MOONLIGHT — Dean Martin (Jimmy Bowen), Reprise 0640 | 4 |
| 47 | 49 | 60 | 71 | COVER ME — Percy Sledge (Quin Ivy & Marlin Greene), Atlantic 2453 | 5 |
| ★48 | 59 | 75 | — | LOVE ME TWO TIMES — Doors (Paul A. Rothchild), Elektra 45624 | 3 |
| 49 | 50 | 50 | 57 | WHAT'S IT GONNA BE — Dusty Springfield (Johnny Franz), Philips 40498 | 6 |
| 50 | 51 | 57 | 69 | TELL MAMA — Etta James (Rick Hall), Cadet 5578 | 7 |
| ★51 | 74 | — | — | WHO WILL ANSWER — Ed Ames (Jim Foglesong), RCA Victor 9400 | 2 |
| 52 | 53 | 67 | 67 | LOVE POWER — Sandpebbles (Teddy Vann), Calla 141 | 5 |
| 53 | 66 | 69 | 72 | ITCHYCOO PARK — Small Faces (Steve Marriott & Ronnie Lane), Immediate 501 | 7 |
| 54 | 25 | 25 | 25 | YESTERDAY — Ray Charles (TRC), ABC 11009 | 7 |
| ★55 | 72 | 85 | — | I CAN'T STAND MYSELF (When You Touch Me) — James Brown & His Famous Flames (James Brown), King 6144 | 3 |
| 56 | 57 | 64 | — | I AM THE WALRUS — Beatles (George Martin), Capitol 2096 | 3 |
| 57 | 64 | 80 | 82 | I'M IN LOVE — Wilson Pickett (Tom Dowd & Tommy Cogbill), Atlantic 2448 | 4 |
| ★58 | 75 | — | — | BEST OF BOTH WORLDS — Lulu (Mickie Most), Epic 10260 | 2 |
| 59 | 69 | 87 | — | GOIN' OUT OF MY HEAD/CAN'T TAKE MY EYES OFF YOU — Lettermen (Kelly Gordon), Capitol 2054 | 3 |
| 60 | 60 | 71 | 86 | DEAR ELOISE — Hollies (Ron Richards), Epic 10251 | 4 |
| ★61 | 76 | — | — | WATCH HER RIDE — Jefferson Airplane (Al Schmitt), RCA Victor 9389 | 2 |
| 62 | 77 | 96 | — | DANCING BEAR — Mamas & Papas (Lou Adler), Dunhill 4113 | 3 |
| ★63 | 78 | — | — | MY BABY MUST BE A MAGICIAN — Marvelettes ("Smokey"), Tamla 54158 | 2 |
| ★64 | 85 | — | — | MONTEREY — Eric Burdon & the Animals (Tom Wilson), MGM 13868 | 2 |
| 65 | 67 | 72 | 81 | STORYBOOK CHILDREN — Billy Vera & Judy Clay (Chip Taylor & Ted Deryll), Atlantic 2445 | 4 |
| 66 | 61 | 61 | 64 | O-O, I LOVE YOU — Della (B. Miller), Cadet 5574 | 8 |
| 67 | 65 | 65 | 68 | OOH BABY — Deon Jackson (Ollie McLaughlin), Carla 2537 | 6 |
| 68 | 70 | 79 | 79 | I'LL BE SWEETER TOMORROW — O'Jays (George Kerr), Bell 691 | 5 |
| ★69 | 89 | — | — | AM I THAT EASY TO FORGET — Engelbert Humperdinck (Peter Sullivan), Parrot 40023 | 2 |
| 70 | 86 | — | — | EVERYBODY KNOWS — Dave Clark Five (Dave Clark), Epic 10265 | 2 |
| 71 | 71 | 77 | 80 | SOCKIN' 1-2-3-4 — John Roberts (Bob Garner), Duke 425 | 4 |
| 72 | 73 | 73 | 78 | HOORAY FOR THE SALVATION ARMY BAND — Bill Cosby (Fred Smith), Warner Bros. 7096 | 4 |
| 73 | 62 | 70 | 75 | PIECE OF MY HEART — Erma Franklin (Bert Berns), Shout 221 | 8 |
| ★74 | 90 | — | — | TWO LITTLE KIDS — Peaches & Herb (David Kapralik & Ken Williams), Date 1586 | 2 |
| 75 | 84 | 86 | — | UP-UP AND AWAY — Hugh Masakela (Stewart Lovine), Uni 55037 | 3 |
| 76 | 79 | — | — | GOOD COMBINATION — Sonny & Cher (Sonny Bono), Atco 6541 | 2 |
| 77 | 88 | 98 | — | NOBODY BUT ME — Human Beinz (Alexis de Azevado), Capitol 5990 | 3 |
| 78 | 80 | 89 | — | BACK UP TRAIN — Al Greene & Soul Mate's (Rodgers & James), Hot Line 15000 | 3 |
| 79 | — | — | — | EXPLOSION IN MY SOUL — Soul Survivors (Gamble-Huff), Crimson 1012 | 1 |
| 80 | — | — | — | FOXEY LADY — Jimi Hendrix (Yameta), Reprise 0641 | 1 |
| 81 | — | — | — | BABY, NOW THAT I'VE FOUND YOU — Foundations (Tony Macaulay), UNI 55038 | 1 |
| 82 | — | — | — | DARLIN' — Beach Boys (Beach Boys), Capitol 2968 | 1 |
| 83 | — | — | — | SKIP A ROPE — Henson Cargill (Don Law), Monument 1041 | 1 |
| 84 | — | — | — | THE LESSON — Vikki Carr (Tommy Oliver), Liberty 56012 | 1 |
| 85 | — | — | — | SPOOKY — Classics IV (Buddy Buie), Imperial 66259 | 1 |
| 86 | 96 | 96 | — | A VOICE IN THE CHOIR — Al Martino (Tom Morgan & Marvin Holtzman), Capitol 2053 | 3 |
| 87 | — | — | — | I WONDER WHAT SHE'S DOING TONIGHT — Tommy Boyce & Bobby Hart (Tommy Boyce & Bobby Hart), A&M 893 | 1 |
| 88 | 98 | — | — | IN ANOTHER LAND — Bill Wyman (Rolling Stones), London 907 | 2 |
| 89 | 99 | — | — | DANCIN' OUT OF MY HEART — Ronnie Dove (Phil Kahl), Diamond 233 | 2 |
| 90 | — | — | — | MR. BUS DRIVER — Bruce Channel (Dale Hawkins), Mala 579 | 1 |
| 91 | 91 | 91 | 91 | HERE COMES HEAVEN — Eddy Arnold (Chet Atkins), RCA Victor 9368 | 4 |
| 92 | 92 | 96 | 96 | SOMETHING MISSING — 5 Stairsteps & Cubie (Clarence Burke, Jr.), Buddah 20 | 4 |
| 93 | 94 | 95 | 99 | CROSS MY HEART — Billy Stewart (Davis & Caston), Chess 2002 | 4 |
| 94 | — | — | — | MOCKINGBIRD — Aretha Franklin (Clyde Otis, Howard A. Roberts & Brad Baker), Columbia 44381 | 1 |
| 95 | 95 | — | — | SOMEBODY'S SLEEPING IN MY BED — Johnnie Taylor (Al Jackson), Stax 235 | 2 |
| 96 | 97 | 97 | — | SHOUT — Lulu (Dick Rowe), Parrot 40021 | 3 |
| 97 | — | — | — | I CALL IT LOVE — Manhattans (Joe Evans), Carnival 533 | 1 |
| 98 | — | — | — | OH, HOW IT HURTS — Barbara Mason (J. Bishop), Arctic 137 | 1 |
| 99 | — | — | — | UP TIGHT GOOD MAN — Laura Lee (Rick Hall), Chess 2030 | 1 |
| 100 | 100 | — | — | A LITTLE RAIN MUST FALL — Epic Splendor (John Boylan), Hot Biscuit 1450 | 2 |

## BUBBLING UNDER THE HOT 100

| | | |
|---|---|---|
| 101 | I'M COMING HOME | Tom Jones, Parrot 40024 |
| 102 | DO UNTO OTHERS | Paul Revere & the Raiders, Columbia 44335 |
| 103 | THIS THING CALLED LOVE | Webs, Pop Side 4593 |
| 104 | DETROIT CITY | Solomon Burke, Atlantic 2499 |
| 105 | WE'RE A WINNER | Impressions, ABC 11022 |
| 106 | FELICIDAD | Sally Field, Colgems 1008 |
| 107 | UNITED | Music Makers, Gamble 210 |
| 108 | GIVE MY LOVE A TRY | Linda Jones, Loma 5907 |
| 109 | MELLOW MOONLIGHT | Leon Haywood, Decca 32230 |
| 110 | LOVE LOTS OF LOVIN' | Lee Dorsey & Betty Harris, Sansu 474 |
| 111 | HEY BOY | Ruby Andrews, Zodiac 1006 |
| 112 | YAKETY YAK | Sam the Sham, MGM 13863 |
| 113 | COME SEE ABOUT ME | Mitch Ryder and the Detroit Wheels, New Voice 828 |
| 114 | BOTTLE OF WINE | Fireballs, Atco 6491 |
| 115 | KITES ARE FUN | Free Design, Project 3 1324 |
| 116 | LIVING IN A WORLD OF MAKE BELIEVE | Good & Plenty, Senate 2105 |
| 117 | (1-2-3-4-5-6-7) COUNT THE DAYS | Inez & Charlie Foxx, Dynamo 114 |
| 118 | LOST | Jerry Butler, Mercury 72764 |
| 119 | LOVE IS BLUE | Paul Mauriat, Philips 40495 |
| 120 | 7:30 GUIDED TOUR | Five Americans, Abnak 126 |
| 121 | TO GIVE (The Reason I Live) | Frankie Valli, Philips 40510 |
| 122 | PLEDGE OF LOVE | Bobby Goldsboro, United Artists 50224 |
| 123 | EXPECTING TO FLY | Buffalo Springfield, Atco 6545 |

Compiled from national retail sales and radio station airplay by the Music Popularity Dept. of Record Market Research, Billboard.

# Billboard HOT 100
## For Week Ending December 30, 1967

**STAR PERFORMER** — Sides registering greatest proportionate upward progress this week.

🅁 Record Industry Association of America seal of certification as million selling single.

| This Week | Wk. Ago | 2 Wks. Ago | 3 Wks. Ago | TITLE Artist (Producer), Label & Number | Weeks On Chart |
|---|---|---|---|---|---|
| 1 (Billboard Award) | 3 | 3 | 8 | HELLO GOODBYE — Beatles (George Martin), Capitol 2056 | 5 |
| 2 | 2 | 2 | 5 | I HEARD IT THROUGH THE GRAPEVINE — Gladys Knight & the Pips (N. Whitfield), Soul 35039 | 10 |
| 3 | 1 | 1 | 1 | DAYDREAM BELIEVER — Monkees (Chip Douglas), Colgems 1012 | 7 🅁 |
| 4 | 4 | 4 | 7 | I SECOND THAT EMOTION — Smokey Robinson & Miracles ("Smokey" A. Cleveland), Tamla 54159 | 9 |
| 5 | 5 | 12 | 22 | WOMAN, WOMAN — Union Gap (Jerry Fuller), Columbia 44297 | 7 |
| 6 | 11 | 27 | 55 | JUDY IN DISGUISE (With Glasses) — John Fred & His Playboy Band (J. Fred & A. Bernard), Paula 282 | 6 |
| 7 | 17 | 29 | 66 | CHAIN OF FOOLS — Aretha Franklin (Jerry Wexler), Atlantic 2464 | 4 |
| 8 | 13 | 23 | 41 | BEND ME, SHAPE ME — American Breed (Bill Traut), Acta 811 | 5 |
| 9 | 7 | 8 | 13 | BOOGALOO DOWN BROADWAY — Fantastic Johnny C. (Jesse James), Phil-L.A. of Soul 305 | 13 |
| 10 | 15 | 15 | 20 | SKINNY LEGS AND ALL — Joe Tex (Buddy Killen), Dial 4063 | 10 |
| 11 | 16 | 17 | 30 | HONEY CHILE — Martha Reeves & the Vandellas (R. Morris), Gordy 7067 | 7 |
| 12 | 9 | 10 | 12 | YOU BETTER SIT DOWN KIDS — Cher (Sonny Bond), Imperial 66261 | 10 |
| 13 | 8 | 6 | 3 | INCENSE AND PEPPERMINTS — Strawberry Alarm Clock (Frank Slay & Bill Holmes), Uni 55018 | 14 |
| 14 | 6 | 5 | 2 | THE RAIN, THE PARK & OTHER THINGS — Cowsills (Artie Kornfeld), MGM 13810 | 14 |
| 15 | 18 | 19 | 26 | SUMMER RAIN — Johnny Rivers (Work), Imperial 66267 | 7 |
| 16 | 10 | 7 | 4 | I SAY A LITTLE PRAYER — Dionne Warwick (Bacharach-David), Scepter 12203 | 8 |
| 17 | 22 | 30 | 37 | NEXT PLANE TO LONDON — Rose Garden (Greene/Stone), Atco 6510 | 11 |
| 18 | 23 | 33 | 47 | IF I COULD BUILD MY WHOLE WORLD AROUND YOU — Marvin Gaye & Tammi Terrell (Fuqua, Bristol), Tamla 54161 | 7 |
| 19 | 26 | 28 | 33 | DIFFERENT DRUM — Stone Poneys (Nick Venet), Capitol 2004 | 8 |
| 20 | 14 | 16 | 21 | SHE'S MY GIRL — Turtles (Joe Wissert), White Whale 260 | 8 |
| 21 | 12 | 9 | 9 | IN AND OUT OF LOVE — Diana Ross & the Supremes (Holland, Dozier), Motown 1116 | 8 |
| 22 | 29 | 34 | 45 | AND GET AWAY — Esquires (Bill Sheppard), Bunky 7752 | 6 |
| 23 | 28 | 36 | 36 | WEAR YOUR LOVE LIKE HEAVEN — Donovan (Mickie Most), Epic 10253 | 6 |
| 24 | 24 | 24 | 24 | NEON RAINBOW — Box Tops (Dan Penn), Mala 580 | 8 |
| 25 | 33 | 68 | — | GREEN TAMBOURINE — Lemon Pipers (Paul Leka), Buddah 23 | 3 |
| 26 | 31 | 43 | 68 | IT'S WONDERFUL — Young Rascals (Young Rascals), Atlantic 2463 | 4 |
| 27 | 20 | 11 | 11 | (The Lights Went Out In) MASSACHUSETTS — Bee Gees (Robert Stigwood), Atco 6532 | 8 |
| 28 | 19 | 14 | 15 | KEEP THE BALL ROLLIN' — Jay & the Techniques (Jerry Ross), Smash 2124 | 11 |
| 29 | 34 | 48 | 74 | SUSAN — Buckinghams (James William Guercio), Columbia 44378 | 4 |
| 30 | 36 | 46 | 53 | COME SEE ABOUT ME — Jr. Walker & the All Stars (Holland & Dozier), Soul 3501 | 6 |
| 31 | 41 | 52 | 62 | THE OTHER MAN'S GRASS IS ALWAYS GREENER — Petula Clark (Tony Hatch), Warner Bros. 7097 | 5 |
| 32 | 64 | 85 | — | MONTEREY — Eric Burdon & the Animals (Tom Wilson), MGM 13868 | 3 |
| 33 | 30 | 26 | 27 | BY THE TIME I GET TO PHOENIX — Glen Campbell (Al De Lory), Capitol 2015 | 10 |
| 34 | 35 | 40 | 51 | BABY YOU GOT IT — Brenton Wood (Hooven-Winn), Double Shot 121 | 6 |
| 35 | 39 | 41 | 52 | TOO MUCH OF NOTHING — Peter, Paul & Mary (Albert B. Grossman & Milt Okun), Warner Bros. 7092 | 6 |
| 36 | 51 | 74 | — | WHO WILL ANSWER — Ed Ames (Jim Foglesong), RCA Victor 9400 | 3 |
| 37 | 55 | 72 | 85 | I CAN'T STAND MYSELF (When You Touch Me) — James Brown & His Famous Flames (James Brown), King 6144 | 4 |
| 38 | 48 | 59 | 75 | LOVE ME TWO TIMES — Doors (Paul A. Rothchild), Elektra 45624 | 4 |
| 39 | 21 | 13 | 6 | TO SIR, WITH LOVE — Lulu (Mickie Most), Epic 10187 | 17 🅁 |
| 40 | 50 | 51 | 57 | TELL MAMA — Etta James (Rick Hall), Cadet 5578 | 8 |
| 41 | 32 | 35 | 46 | SINCE YOU SHOWED ME HOW TO BE HAPPY — Jackie Wilson (Carl Davis), Brunswick 55354 | 6 |
| 42 | 52 | 53 | 67 | LOVE POWER — Sandpebbles (Teddy Vann), Calla 141 | 6 |
| 43 | 47 | 49 | 60 | COVER ME — Percy Sledge (Quin Ivy & Marlin Greene), Atlantic 2453 | 6 |
| 44 | 44 | 55 | 56 | WINDY — Wes Montgomery (Creed Taylor), A&M 883 | 6 |
| 45 | 57 | 64 | 80 | I'M IN LOVE — Wilson Pickett (Tom Dowd & Tommy Cogbill), Atlantic 2448 | 5 |
| 46 | 46 | 56 | 59 | IN THE MISTY MOONLIGHT — Dean Martin (Jimmy Bowen), Reprise 0640 | 5 |
| 47 | 58 | 75 | — | BEST OF BOTH WORLDS — Lulu (Mickie Most), Epic 10260 | 3 |
| 48 | 59 | 69 | 87 | GOIN' OUT OF MY HEAD / CAN'T TAKE MY EYES OFF YOU — Lettermen (Kelly Gordon), Capitol 2054 | 4 |
| 49 | 49 | 50 | 50 | WHAT'S IT GONNA BE — Dusty Springfield, Philips 40498 | 7 |
| 50 | 60 | 60 | 71 | DEAR ELOISE — Hollies (Ron Richards), Epic 10251 | 5 |
| 51 | 63 | 78 | — | MY BABY MUST BE A MAGICIAN — Marvelettes ("Smokey"), Tamla 54158 | 3 |
| 52 | 62 | 77 | 96 | DANCING BEAR — Mamas & Papas (Lou Adler), Dunhill 4113 | 4 |
| 53 | 53 | 66 | 69 | ITCHYCOO PARK — Small Faces (Steve Marriott & Ronnie Lane), Immediate 501 | 8 |
| 54 | 69 | 89 | — | AM I THAT EASY TO FORGET — Engelbert Humperdinck (Peter Sullivan), Parrot 40023 | 3 |
| 55 | 38 | 38 | 44 | BEAUTIFUL PEOPLE — Kenny O'Dell (Porter & O'Dell), Vegas 718 | 7 |
| 56 | 74 | 90 | — | TWO LITTLE KIDS — Peaches & Herb (David Kaprelik & Ken Williams), Date 1586 | 3 |
| 57 | 37 | 37 | 43 | BEAUTIFUL PEOPLE — Bobby Vee (Dallas Smith), Liberty 56009 | 7 |
| 58 | 65 | 67 | 72 | STORYBOOK CHILDREN — Billy Vera & Judy Clay (Chip Taylor & Ted Deryll), Atlantic 2445 | 5 |
| 59 | 76 | 79 | — | GOOD COMBINATION — Sonny & Cher (Sonny Bono), Atco 6541 | 3 |
| 60 | 70 | 86 | — | EVERYBODY KNOWS — Dave Clark Five (Dave Clark), Epic 10265 | 3 |
| 61 | 61 | 76 | — | WATCH HER RIDE — Jefferson Airplane (Al Schmitt), RCA Victor 9389 | 3 |
| 62 | 77 | 88 | 98 | NOBODY BUT ME — Human Beinz (Alexis de Azevado), Capitol 5990 | 4 |
| 63 | 82 | — | — | DARLIN' — Beach Boys (Beach Boys), Capitol 2068 | 2 |
| 64 | 79 | — | — | EXPLOSION IN MY SOUL — Soul Survivors (Gamble-Huff), Crimson 1012 | 2 |
| 65 | 66 | 61 | 61 | O-O, I LOVE YOU — Della (B. Miller), Cadet 5574 | 9 |
| 66 | 81 | — | — | BABY, NOW THAT I'VE FOUND YOU — Foundations (Tony Macaulay), UNI 55038 | 2 |
| 67 | 68 | 70 | 79 | I'LL BE SWEETER TOMORROW — O'Jays (George Kerr), Bell 691 | 6 |
| 68 | 83 | — | — | SKIP A ROPE — Henson Cargill (Don Law), Monument 1041 | 2 |
| 69 | 84 | — | — | THE LESSON — Vikki Carr (Tommy Oliver), Liberty 56012 | 2 |
| 70 | 85 | — | — | SPOOKY — Classics IV (Buddy Buie), Imperial 66259 | 2 |
| 71 | 72 | 73 | 73 | HOORAY FOR THE SALVATION ARMY BAND — Bill Cosby (Fred Smith), Warner Bros. 7096 | 5 |
| 72 | 87 | — | — | I WONDER WHAT SHE'S DOING TONIGHT — Tommy Boyce & Bobby Hart (Tommy Boyce & Bobby Hart), A&M 893 | 2 |
| 73 | 78 | 80 | 89 | BACK UP TRAIN — Al Greene & Soul Mate's (Rodgers & James), Hot Line 15000 | 4 |
| 74 | 75 | 84 | 86 | UP-UP AND AWAY — Hugh Masakela (Stewart Lovine), Uni 55037 | 4 |
| 75 | 56 | 57 | 64 | I AM THE WALRUS — Beatles (George Martin), Capitol 2096 | 4 |
| 76 | 45 | 45 | 48 | CHATTANOOGA CHOO CHOO — Harpers Bizarre (Lenny Waronker), Warner Bros. 7090 | 7 |
| 77 | — | — | — | SHE'S A RAINBOW — Rolling Stones (Andrew Long Oldham), London 906 | 1 |
| 78 | — | — | — | TO GIVE (The Reason I Live) — Frankie Valli (Bob Crewe), Philips 40510 | 1 |
| 79 | 80 | — | — | FOXEY LADY — Jimi Hendrix (Yameta), Reprise 0641 | 2 |
| 80 | — | — | — | TOMORROW — Strawberry Alarm Clock (Frank Slay & Bill Holmes), Uni 55046 | 1 |
| 81 | — | — | — | I'M COMING HOME — Tom Jones (Peter Sullivan), Parrot 40024 | 1 |
| 82 | — | — | — | PICK UP THE PIECES — Carla Thomas (Bell & Don Davis), Stax 239 | 1 |
| 83 | — | — | — | JUST AS MUCH AS EVER — Bobby Vinton (Billy Sherrill), Epic 10266 | 1 |
| 84 | — | — | — | LOST — Jerry Butler (Gamble & Huff), Mercury 72764 | 1 |
| 85 | 86 | 96 | 96 | A VOICE IN THE CHOIR — Al Martino (Tom Morgan & Marvin Holtzman), Capitol 2053 | 4 |
| 86 | — | — | — | I WAS MADE TO LOVE HER — King Curtis & His Kingpins (Tom Dowd & Tommy Cogbill), Atco 6547 | 1 |
| 87 | 89 | 99 | — | DANCIN' OUT OF MY HEART — Ronnie Dove (Phil Kahl), Diamond 233 | 3 |
| 88 | 88 | 98 | — | IN ANOTHER LAND — Bill Wyman (Rolling Stones), London 907 | 3 |
| 89 | 92 | 92 | 96 | SOMETHING'S MISSING — 5 Stairsteps & Cubie (Clarence Burke, Jr.), Buddah 20 | 5 |
| 90 | 90 | — | — | MR. BUS DRIVER — Bruce Channel (Dale Hawkins), Mala 579 | 2 |
| 91 | 93 | 94 | 95 | CROSS MY HEART — Billy Stewart (Davis & Caston), Chess 2002 | 4 |
| 92 | — | — | — | UNITED — Music Makers (Gamble-Huff), Gamble 210 | 1 |
| 93 | — | — | — | MELLOW MOONLIGHT — Leon Baywood (Leon Baywood), Decca 32230 | 1 |
| 94 | 94 | — | — | MOCKINGBIRD — Aretha Franklin (Clyde Otis, Howard A. Roberts & Brad Baker), Columbia 44381 | 2 |
| 95 | 98 | — | — | OH, HOW IT HURTS — Barbara Mason (J. Bishop), Arctic 137 | 2 |
| 96 | 100 | 100 | — | A LITTLE RAIN MUST FALL — Epic Splendor (John Boylan), Hot Biscuit 1450 | 3 |
| 97 | 97 | — | — | I CALL IT LOVE — Manhattans (Joe Evans), Carnival 533 | 2 |
| 98 | 99 | — | — | UP TIGHT GOOD MAN — Laura Lee (Rick Hall), Chess 2030 | 2 |
| 99 | — | — | — | WE'RE A WINNER — Impressions (Johnny Pate), ABC 11022 | 1 |
| 100 | — | — | — | BOTTLE OF WINE — Fireballs (Norman Petty), Atco 6491 | 1 |

## BUBBLING UNDER THE HOT 100

101. HERE COMES HEAVEN ............ Eddy Arnold, RCA Victor 9368
102. THIS THING CALLED LOVE ............ Webs, Popside 4593
103. GIVE MY LOVE A TRY ............ Linda Jones, Loma 5907
104. DETROIT CITY ............ Solomon Burke, Atlantic 2499
105. NO SAD SONGS ............ Joe Simon, Sound Stage 7 2602
106. SOMEBODY'S SLEEPING IN MY BED ............ Johnnie Taylor, Stax 235
107. A WORKING MAN'S PRAYER ............ Arthur Prysock, Verve 10574
108. BIG DADDY ............ Boots Randolph, Monument 1038
109. LOVE IS BLUE ............ Paul Mauriat, Philips 40495
110. HEY BOY ............ Ruby Andrews, Zodiac 1006
111. ZABADAK ............ Dave Dee, Dozy, Beaky, Mick & Tich, Imperial 66270
112. YAKETY YAX ............ Sam the Sham, MGM 13863
113. 7:30 GUIDED TOUR ............ Five Americans, Abnak 126
114. KITES ARE FUN ............ Free Design, Project 3 1324
115. (1-2-3-4-5-6-7) COUNT THE DAYS ............ Inez & Charlie Fox, Dynamo 112
116. LIVING IN A WORLD OF MAKE BELIEVE ............ Good & Plenty, Senate 2105
117. I WISH I HAD TIME ............ Last Words, Atco 6542
118. LET THE HEARTACHES BEGIN ............ Long John Baldry, Warner Bros. 7098
119. EXPECTING TO FLY ............ Buffalo Springfield, Atco 6545
120. PLEDGE OF LOVE ............ Bobby Goldsboro, United Artists 50224

Compiled from national retail sales and radio station airplay by the Music Popularity Dept. of Record Market Research, Billboard.

# Billboard HOT 100

FOR WEEK ENDING JANUARY 6, 1968

★ STAR PERFORMER—Sides registering greatest proportionate upward progress this week.

Record Industry Association of America seal of certification as million selling single.

| This Week | 1 Wk. Ago | 2 Wks. Ago | 3 Wks. Ago | TITLE Artist (Producer), Label & Number | Weeks On Chart |
|---|---|---|---|---|---|
| 1 (Billboard Award) | 1 | 3 | 3 | HELLO GOODBYE — Beatles (George Martin), Capitol 2056 | 6 |
| 2 | 3 | 1 | 1 | DAYDREAM BELIEVER — Monkees (Chip Douglas), Colgems 1012 | 8 |
| ★ 3 | 6 | 11 | 27 | JUDY IN DISGUISE (With Glasses) — John Fred & His Playboy Band (J. Fred & A. Bernard), Paula 282 | 7 |
| 4 | 2 | 2 | 2 | I HEARD IT THROUGH THE GRAPEVINE — Gladys Knight & the Pips (N. Whitfield), Soul 35039 | 11 |
| 5 | 5 | 5 | 12 | WOMAN, WOMAN — Union Gap (Jerry Fuller), Columbia 44297 | 8 |
| 6 | 4 | 4 | 4 | I SECOND THAT EMOTION — Smokey Robinson & Miracles ("Smokey" A. Cleveland), Tamla 54159 | 10 |
| 7 | 7 | 17 | 29 | CHAIN OF FOOLS — Aretha Franklin (Jerry Wexler), Atlantic 2464 | 5 |
| 8 | 8 | 13 | 23 | BEND ME, SHAPE ME — American Breed (Bill Traut), Acta 811 | 6 |
| 9 | 9 | 7 | 8 | BOOGALOO DOWN BROADWAY — Fantastic Johnny C. (Jesse James), Phil-L.A. of Soul 305 | 14 |
| 10 | 10 | 15 | 15 | SKINNY LEGS AND ALL — Joe Tex (Buddy Killen), Dial 4063 | 11 |
| 11 | 11 | 16 | 17 | HONEY CHILE — Martha Reeves & the Vandellas (R. Morris) Gordy 7067 | 8 |
| ★ 12 | 25 | 33 | 68 | GREEN TAMBOURINE — Lemon Pipers (Paul Leka), Buddah 23 | 4 |
| ★ 13 | 18 | 23 | 33 | IF I COULD BUILD MY WHOLE WORLD AROUND YOU — Marvin Gaye & Tammi Terrell (Fuqus, Bristol), Tamla 54161 | 5 |
| 14 | 15 | 18 | 19 | SUMMER RAIN — Johnny Rivers (Work), Imperial 66267 | 8 |
| 15 | 13 | 8 | 6 | INCENSE AND PEPPERMINTS — Strawberry Alarm Clock (Frank Slay & Bill Holmes), Uni 55018 | 15 |
| 16 | 12 | 9 | 10 | YOU BETTER SIT DOWN KIDS — Cher (Sonny Bond), Imperial 66261 | 11 |
| 17 | 17 | 22 | 30 | NEXT PLANE TO LONDON — Rose Garden (Greene/Stone), Atco 6510 | 12 |
| 18 | 19 | 26 | 28 | DIFFERENT DRUM — Stone Poneys (Nick Venet), Capitol 2004 | 9 |
| 19 | 14 | 6 | 5 | THE RAIN, THE PARK & OTHER THINGS — Cowsills (Artie Kornfeld), MGM 13810 | 15 |
| 20 | 16 | 10 | 7 | I SAY A LITTLE PRAYER — Dionne Warwick (Bacharach-David), Scepter 12203 | 12 |
| ★ 21 | 29 | 34 | 48 | SUSAN — Buckinghams (James William Guercio), Columbia 44378 | 5 |
| 22 | 22 | 29 | 34 | AND GET AWAY — Esquires (Bill Sheppard), Bunky 7752 | 7 |
| 23 | 23 | 28 | 36 | WEAR YOUR LOVE LIKE HEAVEN — Donovan (Mickie Most), Epic 10253 | 7 |
| ★ 24 | 32 | 64 | 85 | MONTEREY — Eric Burdon & the Animals (Tom Wilson), MGM 13868 | 4 |
| 25 | 26 | 31 | 43 | IT'S WONDERFUL — Young Rascals (Young Rascals), Atlantic 2463 | 5 |
| 26 | 20 | 14 | 16 | SHE'S MY GIRL — Turtles (Joe Wissert), White Whale 260 | 9 |
| ★ 27 | 36 | 51 | 74 | WHO WILL ANSWER — Ed Ames (Jim Foglesong), RCA Victor 9400 | 4 |
| ★ 28 | 40 | 50 | 51 | TELL MAMA — Etta James (Rick Hall), Cadet 5578 | 9 |
| 29 | 30 | 36 | 46 | COME SEE ABOUT ME — Jr. Walker & the All Stars (Holland & Dozier), Soul 3501 | 7 |
| ★ 30 | 38 | 48 | 59 | LOVE ME TWO TIMES — Doors (Paul A. Rothchild), Elektra 45624 | 5 |
| 31 | 31 | 41 | 52 | THE OTHER MAN'S GRASS IS ALWAYS GREENER — Petula Clark (Tony Hatch), Warner Bros. 7097 | 6 |
| ★ 32 | 42 | 52 | 53 | LOVE POWER — Sandpebbles (Teddy Vann), Calla 141 | 7 |
| 33 | 37 | 55 | 72 | I CAN'T STAND MYSELF (When You Touch Me) — James Brown & His Famous Flames (James Brown), King 6144 | 5 |
| 34 | 28 | 19 | 14 | KEEP THE BALL ROLLIN' — Jay & the Techniques (Jerry Ross), Smash 2124 | 12 |
| ★ 35 | 62 | 77 | 88 | NOBODY BUT ME — Human Beinz (Alexis de Azevado), Capitol 5990 | 5 |
| 36 | 33 | 30 | 26 | BY THE TIME I GET TO PHOENIX — Glen Campbell (Al De Lory), Capitol 2015 | 11 |
| ★ 37 | 47 | 58 | 75 | BEST OF BOTH WORLDS — Lulu (Mickie Most), Epic 10260 | 4 |
| ★ 38 | 48 | 59 | 69 | GOIN' OUT OF MY HEAD/CAN'T TAKE MY EYES OFF YOU — Lettermen (Kelly Gordon), Capitol 2054 | 5 |
| ★ 39 | 54 | 69 | 89 | AM I THAT EASY TO FORGET — Engelbert Humperdinck (Peter Sullivan), Parrot 40023 | 4 |
| ★ 40 | 51 | 63 | 78 | MY BABY MUST BE A MAGICIAN — Marvelettes ("Smokey"), Tamla 54158 | 4 |
| ★ 41 | 56 | 74 | 90 | TWO LITTLE KIDS — Peaches & Herb (David Kaprelik & Ken Williams), Date 1586 | 4 |
| 42 | 43 | 47 | 49 | COVER ME — Percy Sledge (Quin Ivy & Marlin Greene), Atlantic 2453 | 7 |
| ★ 43 | 53 | 53 | 66 | ITCHYCOO PARK — Small Faces (Steve Marriott & Ronnie Lane), Immediate 501 | 9 |
| 44 | 44 | 44 | 55 | WINDY — Wes Montgomery (Creed Taylor), A&M 883 | 7 |
| 45 | 45 | 57 | 64 | I'M IN LOVE — Wilson Pickett (Tom Dowd & Tommy Cogbill), Atlantic 2448 | 6 |
| 46 | 46 | 46 | 56 | IN THE MISTY MOONLIGHT — Dean Martin (Jimmy Bowen), Reprise 0640 | 6 |
| ★ 47 | 70 | 85 | — | SPOOKY — Classics IV (Buddy Buie), Imperial 66259 | 3 |
| ★ 48 | 77 | — | — | SHE'S A RAINBOW — Rolling Stones (Andrew Long Oldham), London 906 | 2 |
| ★ 49 | 60 | 70 | 86 | EVERYBODY KNOWS — Dave Clark Five (Dave Clark), Epic 10265 | 4 |
| 50 | 50 | 60 | 60 | DEAR ELOISE — Hollies (Ron Richards), Epic 10251 | 6 |
| 51 | 52 | 62 | 77 | DANCING BEAR — Mamas & Papas (Lou Adler), Dunhill 4113 | 5 |
| ★ 52 | 66 | 81 | — | BABY, NOW THAT I'VE FOUND YOU — Foundations (Tony Macaulay), UNI 55038 | 3 |
| ★ 53 | 63 | 82 | — | DARLIN' — Beach Boys (Beach Boys), Capitol 2968 | 2 |
| ★ 54 | 64 | 79 | — | EXPLOSION IN MY SOUL — Soul Survivors (Gamble-Huff), Crimson 1012 | 3 |
| 55 | 24 | 24 | 24 | NEON RAINBOW — Box Tops (Dan Penn), Mala 580 | 9 |
| 56 | 58 | 65 | 67 | STORYBOOK CHILDREN — Billy Vera & Judy Clay (Chip Taylor & Ted Deryll), Atlantic 2445 | 6 |
| ★ 57 | 68 | 83 | — | SKIP A ROPE — Henson Cargill (Don Law), Monument 1041 | 3 |
| 58 | 59 | 76 | 79 | GOOD COMBINATION — Sonny & Cher (Sonny Bono), Atco 6541 | 4 |
| ★ 59 | 69 | 84 | — | THE LESSON — Vikki Carr (Tommy Oliver), Liberty 56012 | 3 |
| ★ 60 | 72 | 87 | — | I WONDER WHAT SHE'S DOING TONIGHT — Tommy Boyce & Bobby Hart (Tommy Boyce & Bobby Hart), A&M 893 | 3 |
| 61 | 35 | 39 | 41 | TOO MUCH OF NOTHING — Peter, Paul & Mary (Albert B. Grossman & Milt Okun), Warner Bros. 7092 | 7 |
| ★ 62 | 78 | — | — | TO GIVE (The Reason I Live) — Frankie Valli (Bob Crewe), Philips 40510 | 2 |
| ★ 63 | 80 | — | — | TOMORROW — Strawberry Alarm Clock (Frank Slay & Bill Holmes), Uni 55046 | 2 |
| ★ 64 | 81 | — | — | I'M COMING HOME — Tom Jones (Peter Sullivan), Parrot 40024 | 2 |
| 65 | 65 | 66 | 61 | O-O, I LOVE YOU — Della (B. Miller), Cadet 5574 | 10 |
| 66 | 67 | 68 | 70 | I'LL BE SWEETER TOMORROW — O'Jays (George Kerr), Bell 691 | 7 |
| ★ 67 | 83 | — | — | JUST AS MUCH AS EVER — Bobby Vinton (Billy Sherrill), Epic 10266 | 2 |
| 68 | 34 | 35 | 40 | BABY YOU GOT IT — Brenton Wood (Hooven-Winn), Double Shot 121 | 7 |
| 69 | 49 | 49 | 50 | WHAT'S IT GONNA BE — Dusty Springfield, Philips 40498 | 8 |
| 70 | 61 | 61 | 76 | WATCH HER RIDE — Jefferson Airplane (Al Schmitt), RCA Victor 9389 | 4 |
| 71 | 71 | 72 | 73 | HOORAY FOR THE SALVATION ARMY BAND — Bill Cosby (Fred Smith), Warner Bros. 7096 | 6 |
| ★ 72 | — | — | — | SOME VELVET MORNING — Nancy Sinatra & Lee Hazlewood (Lee Hazlewood), Reprise 0651 | 1 |
| 73 | 73 | 78 | 80 | BACK UP TRAIN — Al Greene & Soul Mate's (Rodgers & James), Hot Line 15000 | 5 |
| 74 | 74 | 75 | 84 | UP-UP AND AWAY — Hugh Masakela (Stewart Lovine), Uni 55037 | 5 |
| 75 | 79 | 80 | — | FOXEY LADY — Jimi Hendrix (Yameta), Reprise 0641 | 3 |
| 76 | 82 | — | — | PICK UP THE PIECES — Carla Thomas (A) (Bell & Don Davis, Stax 239 | 2 |
| 77 | 86 | — | — | I WAS MADE TO LOVE HER — King Curtis & His Kingpins (Tom Dowd & Tommy Cogbill), Atco 6547 | 2 |
| 78 | 84 | — | — | LOST — Jerry Butler (Gamble & Huff), Mercury 72764 | 2 |
| ★ 79 | 100 | — | — | BOTTLE OF WINE — Fireballs (Norman Petty), Atco 6491 | 2 |
| 80 | 85 | 86 | 96 | A VOICE IN THE CHOIR — Al Martino (Tom Morgan & Marvin Holtzman), Capitol 2053 | 5 |
| ★ 81 | — | — | — | WORKING MAN'S PRAYER — Arthur Prysock (Hy Weiss), Verve 10574 | 1 |
| ★ 82 | — | — | — | NO SAD SONGS — Joe Simon (J. R. Ent.), Sound Stage 7 2602 | 1 |
| ★ 83 | — | — | — | ZABADAK — Dave Dee, Dozy, Beaky, Mick & Tich (Jack Baverstock), Imperial 66270 | 1 |
| ★ 84 | 99 | — | — | WE'RE A WINNER — Impressions (Johnny Pate), ABC 11022 | 2 |
| ★ 85 | — | — | — | MONEY — Lovin' Spoonful (Lovin' Spoonful & Joe Wissert), Kama Sutra 241 | 1 |
| ★ 86 | — | — | — | SUNDAY MORNIN' — Spanky & Our Gang (Scharf-Dorough), Mercury 72765 | 1 |
| 87 | 88 | 88 | 98 | IN ANOTHER LAND — Bill Wyman (Rolling Stones), London 907 | 4 |
| 88 | 89 | 92 | 92 | SOMETHING'S MISSING — 5 Stairsteps & Cubie (Clarence Burke, Jr.), Buddah 20 | 6 |
| 89 | 91 | 93 | 94 | CROSS MY HEART — Billy Stewart (Davis & Caston), Chess 2002 | 6 |
| ★ 90 | — | — | — | MISSION: IMPOSSIBLE — Lalo Schifrin (Tom Mack), Dot 17059 | 1 |
| 91 | 92 | — | — | UNITED — Music Makers (Gamble-Huff), Gamble 210 | 2 |
| 92 | 93 | — | — | MELLOW MOONLIGHT — Leon Baywood (Leon Baywood), Decca 32230 | 2 |
| 93 | 96 | 100 | 100 | A LITTLE RAIN MUST FALL — Epic Splendor (John Boylan), Hot Biscuit 1450 | 4 |
| 94 | 95 | 98 | — | OH, HOW IT HURTS — Barbara Mason (J. Bishop), Arctic 137 | 3 |
| 95 | 98 | 99 | — | UP TIGHT GOOD MAN — Laura Lee (Rick Hall), Chess 2030 | 3 |
| 96 | 97 | 97 | — | I CALL IT LOVE — Manhattans (Joe Evans), Carnival 533 | 3 |
| 97 | — | — | — | MAN NEEDS A WOMAN — James Carr (Quinton Claunch & Rudolph Russell), Goldwax 332 | 1 |
| 98 | — | — | — | NEW ORLEANS — Neil Diamond (Jeff Barry & Ellie Greenwich), Bang 554 | 1 |
| 99 | — | — | — | LOVE IS BLUE — Paul Mauriat, Philips 40495 | 1 |
| 100 | — | — | — | BORN FREE — Hesitations (GWP), Kapp 878 | 1 |

## HOT 100—A TO Z—(Publisher-Licensee)

Am I That Easy to Forget (Four Star, BMI)...... 39
And Get Away (Hi-Mi/Flomar, BMI)............ 22
Baby, Now That I've Found You (January/ Nelbeck, BMI)............ 52
Baby You Got It (Big Shot, ASCAP)............ 68
Back Up Train (Tosted, BMI)............ 73
Bend Me, Shape Me (Helios, BMI)............ 8
Best of Both Worlds (James, BMI)............ 37
Boogaloo Down Broadway (Dandelion/James Boys, BMI)............ 9
Born Free (Screen Gems-Columbia, BMI)..........100
Bottle of Wine (Deep Fork, BMI)............ 79
By the Time I Get to Phoenix (Rivers, BMI)..... 36
Chain of Fools (14th Hour/Pronto, BMI)........ 7
Come See About Me (Jobete, BMI)............ 29
Cover Me (Pronto/Quiney, BMI)............ 42
Cross My Heart (Chevis, BMI)............ 89
Dancing Bear (Wingate, ASCAP)............ 51
Darlin' (Sea of Tunes, BMI)............ 53
Daydream Believer (Screen Gems-Columbia, BMI).. 2
Dear Eloise (Marthus, BMI)............ 50
Different Drum (Screen Gems-Columbia, BMI).... 18
Everybody Knows (Francis, Day & Hunter, ASCAP) 49
Explosion in My Soul (Double Diamond/Downstairs, BMI)............ 54
Foxey Lady (Sea Lark/Yaneta, BMI) ............ 75
Goin' Out of My Head/Can't Take My Eyes Off You (Vogue/Saturday/Season's Four, BMI)........ 38
Good Combination (Triparte/Pamper/D-K, BMI)... 58
Green Tambourine (Kama Sutra, BMI)............ 12
Hello Goodbye (Maclen, BMI)............ 1
Honey Chile (Jobete, BMI)............ 11
Hooray for the Salvation Army Band (Monger/Kaymen, BMI) ............ 71
I Call It Love (Sanavan, BMI)............ 96
I Can't Stand Myself (When You Touch Me) (Taccon/Soil, BMI) ............ 33
I Heard It Through the Grapevine (Jobete, BMI).. 4
I Say a Little Prayer (Blue Seas/Jac, ASCAP)..... 20
I Second That Emotion (Jobete, BMI)............ 6
I Was Made to Love Her (Jobete, BMI) ............ 77
I Wonder What She's Doing Tonight (Screen Gems-Columbia, BMI)............ 60
If I Could Build My Whole World Around You (Jobete, BMI) ............ 13
I'll Be Sweeter Tomorrow (Zira/Floteca/Mia, BMI) 66
I'm Coming Home (Morris, ASCAP)............ 64
I'm in Love (Pronto/Trecebob, BMI) ............ 45
In Another Land (Gideon, BMI)............ 87
In the Misty Moonlight (4 Star, BMI)............ 46
Incense and Peppermints (Claridge, ASCAP)....... 15
Itchycoo Park (Nice Songs, BMI)............ 43
It's Wonderful (Slacsar, BMI)............ 25
Judy in Disguise (With Glasses) (Su-Ma, BMI).... 3
Just as Much as Ever (Roosevelt, BMI)............ 67
Keep the Ball Rollin' (Screen Gems-Columbia, BMI) 34
Lesson, The (Alta, ASCAP)............ 59
Little Rain Must Fall, A (Chardon, BMI)......... 93
Lost (Double Diamond/Downstairs/Perabut, BMI).. 78
Love Is Blue (Crown, ASCAP)............ 99
Love Me Two Times (Nipper, ASCAP)............ 30
Love Power (Unbelievable, BMI)............ 32
Man Needs a Woman, A (Rise/Aim, BMI)......... 97
Mellow Moonlight (Evejim, BMI)............ 92
Mission: Impossible (Bruin, BMI)............ 90
Money (Faithful Virtue, BMI)............ 85
Monterey (Slamina/Sea-Lark, BMI)............ 24
My Baby Must Be a Magician (Jobete, BMI).... 40
Neon Rainbow (Earl Barton, BMI)............ 55
New Orleans (Rock Masters, BMI)............ 98
Next Plane to London (Mirwood Antlers, BMI).... 17
Nobody But Me (Wemar, BMI)............ 35
No Sad Songs (Press, BMI)............ 82
Oh, How It Hurts (Blockbuster, BMI)............ 94
O-O, I Love You (Chervis, BMI)............ 65
Other Man's Grass Is Always Greener, The (Northern, ASCAP) ............ 31
Pick Up the Pieces (East/Groovesville, BMI)..... 76
Rain, the Park & Other Things, The (Akbestal/Luvlin, BMI) ............ 19
She's a Rainbow (Gideon, BMI)............ 48
She's My Girl (Chardon, BMI)............ 26
Skinny Legs and All (Tree, BMI)............ 10
Skip a Rope (Tree, BMI)............ 57
Something's Missing (Kama Sutra/Burke Family, BMI)............ 88
Some Velvet Morning (Hazlewood, ASCAP)....... 72
Spooky (Lowery, BMI)............ 47
Storybook Children (Blackwood, BMI)............ 56
Summer Rain (Rivers, BMI)............ 14
Sunday Mornin' (Blackwood, BMI)............ 86
Susan (Diongenes/Beg O'Tunes, BMI)............ 21
Tell Mama (Fame, BMI)............ 28
To Give (The Reason I Live) (Saturday/Seasons' Four, BMI)............ 62
Tomorrow (Alarm Clock, ASCAP)............ 63
Too Much of Nothing (Dwarf, ASCAP)............ 61
Two Little Kids (Jalynne, BMI)............ 41
United (Razor Sharp/Blockbuster, BMI)......... 91
Up, Up and Away (Rivers, BMI)............ 74
Up Tight Good Man (Chevis, BMI)............ 95
Voice in the Choir, A (Case, ASCAP)............ 80
Watch Her Ride............ 70
We're a Winner (Chi-Sound, BMI)............ 84
Wear Your Love Like Heaven (Peer Int'l, BMI)... 23
What's It Gonna Be (Rumbalero/Ragmar, BMI) .... 69
Who Will Answer (Sunbary, ASCAP)............ 27
Windy (Almo, BMI)............ 44
Woman, Woman (Glaser, BMI)............ 5
Working Man's Prayer, A (Flower/Sark, BMI).... 81
You Better Sit Down Kids (Chrismarc/Cotillion, BMI) ............ 16
Zabadak (Callico, BMI)............ 83

## BUBBLING UNDER THE HOT 100

101. GIVE MY LOVE A TRY ............Linda Jones, Loma 5907
102. DANCIN' OUT OF MY HEART ............Ronnie Dove, Diamond 233
103. MR. BUS DRIVER ............Bruce Channel, Mala 579
104. DETROIT CITY ............Solomon Burke, Atlantic 2499
105. BIG DADDY ............Boots Randolph, Monument 1038
106. WITHOUT LOVE (There Is Nothing) ............Oscar Toney Jr., Bell 699
107. MOCKINGBIRD ............Aretha Franklin, Columbia 44381
108. HEY BOY ............Ruby Andrews, Zodiac 1006
109. (1-2-3-4-5-6-7) COUNT THE DAYS ........Inez & Charlie Foxx, Dynamo 112
110. YAKETY YAK ............Sam the Sham, MGM 13863
111. 7:30 GUIDED TOUR ............Five Americans, Abnak 126
112. LIVING IN A WORLD OF MAKE BELIEVE ......Good & Plenty, Senate 2105
113. I WISH I HAD TIME ............Last Words, Atco 6542
114. SUNSHINE OF YOUR LOVE ............Cream, Atco 6544
115. EXPECTING TO FLY ............Buffalo Springfield, Atco 6545
116. LET THE HEARTACHES BEGIN ........Long John Baldry, Warner Bros. 7098
117. BREAK MY MIND ............Bobby Wood, MGM 13797
118. BLESSED ARE THE LONELY ............Robert Knight, Rising Sons 707
119. PLEDGE OF LOVE ............Bobby Goldsboro, United Artists 50224
120. COME RAIN OR COME SHINE ............Ray Charles, Atlantic 2470
121. DO WHAT YOU GOTTA DO ............Al Wilson, Soul City 761
122. DO UNTO ME ............James & Bobby Purify, Bell 700
123. STILL BURNING IN MY HEART ............Drifters, Atlantic 2471
124. TO EACH HIS OWN ............Frankie Laine, ABC 11032

Compiled from national retail sales and radio station airplay by the Music Popularity Dept. of Record Market Research, Billboard.

# Billboard HOT 100

**For Week Ending January 13, 1968**

★ STAR PERFORMER—Sides registering greatest proportionate upward progress this week.
Ⓡ Record Industry Association of America seal of certification as million selling single.

| This Wk | Last Wk | 2 Wk Ago | TITLE, Artist (Producer), Label & Number | Wks on Chart |
|---|---|---|---|---|
| 1 | 1 | 3 | HELLO GOODBYE — Beatles (George Martin), Capitol 2056 ★ Billboard Award | 7 |
| 2 | 3 | 6 | JUDY IN DISGUISE (With Glasses) — John Fred & His Playboy Band (J. Fred & A. Bernard), Paula 282 | 8 |
| 3 | 2 | 3 | DAYDREAM BELIEVER — Monkees (Chip Douglas), Colgems 1012 | 9 |
| 4 | 5 | 5 | WOMAN, WOMAN — Union Gap (Jerry Fuller), Columbia 44297 | 9 |
| 5 | 4 | 2 | I HEARD IT THROUGH THE GRAPEVINE — Gladys Knight & the Pips (N. Whitfield), Soul 35039 | 12 |
| 6 | 7 | 17 | CHAIN OF FOOLS — Aretha Franklin (Jerry Wexler), Atlantic 2464 | 6 |
| 7 | 8 | 13 | BEND ME, SHAPE ME — American Breed (Bill Traut), Acta 811 | 7 |
| 8 | 6 | 4 | I SECOND THAT EMOTION — Smokey Robinson & Miracles ("Smokey" A. Cleveland), Tamla 54159 | 11 |
| 9 | 12 | 25 | GREEN TAMBOURINE — Lemon Pipers (Paul Leka), Buddah 23 | 5 |
| 10 | 10 | 10 | SKINNY LEGS AND ALL — Joe Tex (Buddy Killen), Dial 4063 | 12 |
| 11 | 11 | 11 | HONEY CHILE — Martha Reeves & the Vandellas (R. Morris), Gordy 7067 | 9 |
| 12 | 9 | 9 | BOOGALOO DOWN BROADWAY — Fantastic Johnny C. (Jesse James), Phil-L.A. of Soul 305 | 15 |
| 13 | 13 | 18 | IF I COULD BUILD MY WHOLE WORLD AROUND YOU — Marvin Gaye & Tammi Terrell (Fuqua, Bristol), Tamla 54161 | 6 |
| 14 | 18 | 19 | DIFFERENT DRUM — Stone Poneys (Nick Venet), Capitol 2004 | 10 |
| 15 | 24 | 32 | MONTEREY — Eric Burdon & the Animals (Tom Wilson), MGM 13868 | 5 |
| 16 | 21 | 29 | SUSAN — Buckinghams (James William Guercio), Columbia 44378 | 6 |
| 17 | 14 | 15 | SUMMER RAIN — Johnny Rivers (Work), Imperial 66267 | 9 |
| 18 | 35 | 62 | NOBODY BUT ME — Human Beinz (Alexis de Azevedo), Capitol 5990 | 6 |
| 19 | 27 | 36 | WHO WILL ANSWER — Ed Ames (Jim Foglesong), RCA Victor 9400 | 5 |
| 20 | 25 | 26 | IT'S WONDERFUL — Young Rascals (Young Rascals), Atlantic 2463 | 6 |
| 21 | 16 | 12 | YOU BETTER SIT DOWN KIDS — Cher (Sonny Bono), Imperial 66261 | 12 |
| 22 | 17 | 17 | NEXT PLANE TO LONDON — Rose Garden (Greene/Stone), Atco 6510 | 13 |
| 23 | 47 | 70 | SPOOKY — Classics IV (Buddy Buie), Imperial 66259 | 4 |
| 24 | 29 | 30 | COME SEE ABOUT ME — Jr. Walker & the All Stars (Holland & Dozier), Soul 35041 | 8 |
| 25 | 30 | 38 | LOVE ME TWO TIMES — Doors (Paul A. Rothchild), Elektra 45624 | 6 |
| 26 | 40 | 51 | MY BABY MUST BE A MAGICIAN — Marvelettes ("Smokey"), Tamla 54158 | 5 |
| 27 | 32 | 42 | LOVE POWER — Sandpebbles (Teddy Vann), Calla 141 | 8 |
| 28 | 28 | 40 | TELL MAMA — Etta James (Rick Hall), Cadet 5578 | 10 |
| 29 | 38 | 48 | GOIN' OUT OF MY HEAD/CAN'T TAKE MY EYES OFF YOU — Lettermen (Kelly Gordon), Capitol 2054 | 6 |
| 30 | 39 | 54 | AM I THAT EASY TO FORGET — Engelbert Humperdinck (Peter Sullivan), Parrot 40023 | 5 |
| 31 | 41 | 56 | TWO LITTLE KIDS — Peaches & Herb (David Kapralik & Ken Williams), Date 1586 | 5 |
| 32 | 43 | 53 | ITCHYCOO PARK — Small Faces (Steve Marriott & Ronnie Lane), Immediate 501 | 10 |
| 33 | 33 | 37 | I CAN'T STAND MYSELF (When You Touch Me) — James Brown & His Famous Flames (James Brown), King 6144 | 6 |
| 34 | 37 | 47 | BEST OF BOTH WORLDS — Lulu (Mickie Most), Epic 10260 | 5 |
| 35 | 26 | 20 | SHE'S MY GIRL — Turtles (Joe Wissert), White Whale 260 | 10 |
| 36 | 48 | 77 | SHE'S A RAINBOW — Rolling Stones (Andrew Loog Oldham), London 906 | 3 |
| 37 | 15 | 13 | INCENSE AND PEPPERMINTS — Strawberry Alarm Clock (Frank Slay & Bill Holmes), Uni 55018 | 16 |
| 38 | 52 | 66 | BABY, NOW THAT I'VE FOUND YOU — Foundations (Tony Macaulay), UNI 55038 | 8 |
| 39 | 53 | 63 | DARLIN' — Beach Boys (Beach Boys), Capitol 2068 | 5 |
| 40 | 22 | 22 | AND GET AWAY — Esquires (Bill Sheppard), Bunky 7752 | 8 |
| 41 | 19 | 14 | THE RAIN, THE PARK & OTHER THINGS — Cowsills (Artie Kornfeld), MGM 13810 | 16 |
| 42 | 20 | 16 | I SAY A LITTLE PRAYER — Dionne Warwick (Bacharach-David), Scepter 12203 | 13 |
| 43 | 54 | 64 | EXPLOSION IN MY SOUL — Soul Survivors (Gamble-Huff), Crimson 1012 | 4 |
| 44 | 49 | 60 | EVERYBODY KNOWS — Dave Clark Five (Dave Clark), Epic 10265 | 5 |
| 45 | 31 | 31 | THE OTHER MAN'S GRASS IS ALWAYS GREENER — Petula Clark (Tony Hatch), Warner Bros. 7097 | 7 |
| 46 | 60 | 72 | I WONDER WHAT SHE'S DOING TONIGHT — Tommy Boyce & Bobby Hart (Tommy Boyce & Bobby Hart), A&M 893 | 4 |
| 47 | 57 | 68 | SKIP A ROPE — Henson Cargill (Don Law), Monument 1041 | 4 |
| 48 | 59 | 69 | THE LESSON — Vikki Carr (Tommy Oliver), Liberty 56012 | 4 |
| 49 | 62 | 78 | TO GIVE (The Reason I Live) — Frankie Valli (Bob Crewe), Philips 40510 | 3 |
| 50 | 50 | 50 | DEAR ELOISE — Hollies (Ron Richards), Epic 10251 | 7 |
| 51 | 63 | 80 | TOMORROW — Strawberry Alarm Clock (Frank Slay & Bill Holmes), Uni 55046 | 3 |
| 52 | 67 | 83 | JUST AS MUCH AS EVER — Bobby Vinton (Billy Sherrill), Epic 10266 | 3 |
| 53 | 45 | 45 | I'M IN LOVE — Wilson Pickett (Tom Dowd & Tommy Cogbill), Atlantic 2448 | 7 |
| 54 | 56 | 58 | STORYBOOK CHILDREN — Billy Vera & Judy Clay (Chip Taylor & Ted Daryll), Atlantic 2445 | 7 |
| 55 | 44 | 44 | WINDY — Wes Montgomery (Creed Taylor), A&M 883 | 8 |
| 56 | — | — | I WISH IT WOULD RAIN — Temptations (Norman Whitfield), Gordy 7068 | 1 |
| 57 | 58 | 59 | GOOD COMBINATION — Sonny & Cher (Sonny Bono), Atco 6541 | 5 |
| 58 | 64 | 81 | I'M COMING HOME — Tom Jones (Peter Sullivan), Parrot 40024 | 3 |
| 59 | 46 | 46 | IN THE MISTY MOONLIGHT — Dean Martin (Jimmy Bowen), Reprise 0640 | 7 |
| 60 | 72 | — | SOME VELVET MORNING — Nancy Sinatra & Lee Hazlewood (Lee Hazlewood), Reprise 0651 | 2 |
| 61 | 79 | 100 | BOTTLE OF WINE — Fireballs (Norman Petty), Atco 6491 | 3 |
| 62 | 51 | 52 | DANCING BEAR — Mamas & Papas (Lou Adler), Dunhill 4113 | 6 |
| 63 | 78 | 84 | LOST — Jerry Butler (Gamble & Huff), Mercury 72764 | 3 |
| 64 | 82 | — | NO SAD SONGS — Joe Simon (J. R. Ent.), Sound Stage 7 2602 | 2 |
| 65 | 83 | — | ZABADAK — Dave Dee, Dozy, Beaky, Mick & Tich (Jack Baverstock), Imperial 66270 | 2 |
| 66 | 86 | — | SUNDAY MORNIN' — Spanky & Our Gang (Scharf-Dorough), Mercury 72765 | 2 |
| 67 | 75 | 79 | FOXEY LADY — Jimi Hendrix (Yameta), Reprise 0641 | 4 |
| 68 | 76 | 82 | PICK UP THE PIECES — Carla Thomas (A) (Bell & Don Davis), Stax 239 | 3 |
| 69 | 84 | 99 | WE'RE A WINNER — Impressions (Johnny Pate), ABC 11022 | 3 |
| 70 | 85 | — | MONEY — Lovin' Spoonful (Lovin' Spoonful & Joe Wissert), Kama Sutra 241 | 2 |
| 71 | 74 | 74 | UP-UP AND AWAY — Hugh Masekela (Stewart Levine), Uni 55027 | 6 |
| 72 | 94 | 95 | OH, HOW IT HURTS — Barbara Mason (J. Bishop), Arctic 137 | 4 |
| 73 | 73 | 73 | BACK UP TRAIN — Al Greene & Soul Mate's (Rodgers & James), Hot Line 15000 | 6 |
| 74 | — | — | SUNSHINE OF YOUR LOVE — Cream (Felix Pappalardi), Atco 6544 | 1 |
| 75 | 66 | 67 | I'LL BE SWEETER TOMORROW — O'Jays (George Kerr), Bell 691 | 8 |
| 76 | 81 | — | WORKING MAN'S PRAYER — Arthur Prysock (Hy Weiss), Verve 10574 | 2 |
| 77 | 77 | 86 | I WAS MADE TO LOVE HER — King Curtis & His Kingpins (Tom Dowd & Tommy Cogbill), Atco 6547 | 3 |
| 78 | 42 | 43 | COVER ME — Percy Sledge (Quin Ivy & Marlin Greene), Atlantic 2453 | 8 |
| 79 | 98 | — | NEW ORLEANS — Neil Diamond (Jeff Barry & Ellie Greenwich), Bang 554 | 2 |
| 80 | 80 | 85 | A VOICE IN THE CHOIR — Al Martino (Tom Morgan & Marvin Holtzman), Capitol 2053 | 6 |
| 81 | — | — | WE CAN FLY — Cowsills (Bill & Bob Cowsill), MGM 13886 | 1 |
| 82 | — | — | I CAN TAKE OR LEAVE YOUR LOVING — Herman's Hermits (Mickie Most), MGM 13885 | 1 |
| 83 | — | — | YOU — Marvin Gaye (I. Hunter), Tamla 54160 | 1 |
| 84 | 99 | — | LOVE IS BLUE — Paul Mauriat, Philips 40495 | 2 |
| 85 | — | — | DO UNTO ME — James & Bobby Purify (Papa Don), Bell 700 | 1 |
| 86 | — | — | CARMEN — Herb Alpert and the Tijuana Brass, A&M 890 | 1 |
| 87 | 87 | 88 | IN ANOTHER LAND — Bill Wyman (Rolling Stones), London 907 | 5 |
| 88 | 90 | — | MISSION: IMPOSSIBLE — Lalo Schifrin (Tom Mack), Dot 17059 | 2 |
| 89 | 89 | 91 | CROSS MY HEART — Billy Stewart (Davis & Cason), Chess 2002 | 7 |
| 90 | 97 | — | MAN NEEDS A WOMAN — James Carr (Quinton Claunch & Rudolph Russell), Goldwax 332 | 2 |
| 91 | 91 | 92 | UNITED — Music Makers (Gamble-Huff), Gamble 210 | 3 |
| 92 | 92 | 93 | MELLOW MOONLIGHT — Leon Haywood (Leon Haywood), Decca 32230 | 3 |
| 93 | 93 | 96 | A LITTLE RAIN MUST FALL — Epic Splendor (John Boylan), Hot Biscuit 1450 | 5 |
| 94 | 100 | — | BORN FREE — Hesitations (GWP), Kapp 878 | 2 |
| 95 | 95 | 98 | UP TIGHT GOOD MAN — Laura Lee (Rick Hall), Chess 2030 | 4 |
| 96 | — | — | WITHOUT LOVE (There Is Nothing) — Oscar Toney Jr. (Papa Don), Bell 699 | 1 |
| 97 | — | — | (1-2-3-4-5-6-7) COUNT THE DAYS — Inez & Charlie Foxx (Charlie Foxx), Dynamo 112 | 1 |
| 98 | — | — | LET THE HEARTACHES BEGIN — Long John Baldry, Warner Bros. 7098 | 1 |
| 99 | — | — | EXPECTING TO FLY — Buffalo Springfield (York/Pala), Atco 6545 | 1 |
| 100 | 100 | — | FUNKY WAY — Calvin Arnold (Cooper, Paul & Shelby), Venture 605 | 2 |

## BUBBLING UNDER THE HOT 100

101. SOMETHING'S MISSING ............ 5 Stairsteps & Cubie, Buddah 20
102. BLESSED ARE THE LONELY ............ Robert Knight, Rising Sons 707
103. I CALL IT LOVE ............ Manhattans, Carnival 533
104. GIVE MY LOVE A TRY ............ Linda Jones, Loma 2007
105. BIG DADDY ............ Boots Randolph, Monument 1028
106. 7:30 GUIDED TOUR ............ 5 Americans, Abnak 126
107. I WISH I HAD TIME ............ Last Words, Atco 6542
108. THERE IS ............ Dells, Cadet 5574
109. HEY BOY ............ Ruby Andrews, Zodiac 1006
110. YAKETY YAK ............ Sam the Sham, MGM 13863
111. LIVING IN A WORLD OF MAKE BELIEVE ............ Good & Plenty, Smate 2105
112. STILL BURNING IN MY HEART ............ Drifters, Atlantic 2471
113. DETROIT CITY ............ Solomon Burke, Atlantic 2499
114. IT'S A GAS ............ Hombres, Verve Forecast 5076
115. BIRDS OF A FEATHER ............ Joe South, Capitol 2060
116. BREAK MY MIND ............ Bobby Wood, MGM 13797
117. IT'S NOT EASY ............ Will-O-Bees, Date 1583
118. PLEDGE OF LOVE ............ Bobby Goldsboro, United Artists 50224
119. TO EACH HIS OWN ............ Frankie Laine, ABC 11032
120. CAMELOT ............ King Richard's Fluegel Knights, MTA 136

*Compiled from national retail sales and radio station airplay by the Music Popularity Dept. of Record Market Research, Billboard.*

# Billboard HOT 100

**For Week Ending January 20, 1968**

★ STAR PERFORMER—Sides registering greatest proportionate upward progress this week.
● Record Industry Association of America seal of certification as million selling single.

| This Week | 1 Wk. Ago | 2 Wks. Ago | 3 Wks. Ago | TITLE, Artist (Producer), Label & Number | Weeks On Chart |
|---|---|---|---|---|---|
| 1 | 2 | 3 | 6 | **JUDY IN DISGUISE (With Glasses)** — John Fred & His Playboy Band (J. Fred & A. Bernard), Paula 282 | 9 |
| 2 | 6 | 7 | 7 | **CHAIN OF FOOLS** — Aretha Franklin (Jerry Wexler), Atlantic 2464 ● | 7 |
| 3 | 1 | 1 | 1 | **HELLO GOODBYE** — Beatles (George Martin), Capitol 2056 | 8 |
| 4 | 4 | 5 | 5 | **WOMAN, WOMAN** — Union Gap (Jerry Fuller), Columbia 44297 | 10 |
| 5 | 9 | 12 | 25 | **GREEN TAMBOURINE** — Lemon Pipers (Paul Leka), Buddah 23 | 6 |
| 6 | 3 | 2 | 3 | **DAYDREAM BELIEVER** — Monkees (Chip Douglas), Colgems 1012 ● | 10 |
| 7 | 7 | 8 | 8 | **BEND ME, SHAPE ME** — American Breed (Bill Traut), Acta 811 | 8 |
| 8 | 8 | 6 | 4 | **I SECOND THAT EMOTION** — Smokey Robinson & Miracles ("Smokey" A. Cleveland), Tamla 54159 | 12 |
| 9 | 5 | 4 | 2 | **I HEARD IT THROUGH THE GRAPEVINE** — Gladys Knight & the Pips (N. Whitfield), Soul 35039 | 13 |
| 10 | 13 | 13 | 18 | **IF I COULD BUILD MY WHOLE WORLD AROUND YOU** — Marvin Gaye & Tammi Terrell (Fuqua, Bristol), Tamla 54161 | 7 |
| 11 | 11 | 11 | 11 | **HONEY CHILE** — Martha Reeves & the Vandellas (R. Morris), Gordy 7067 | 10 |
| 12 | 10 | 10 | 10 | **SKINNY LEGS AND ALL** — Joe Tex (Buddy Killen), Dial 4063 | 13 |
| 13 | 16 | 21 | 29 | **SUSAN** — Buckinghams (James William Guercio), Columbia 44378 | 7 |
| 14 | 14 | 18 | 19 | **DIFFERENT DRUM** — Stone Poneys (Nick Venet), Capitol 2004 | 11 |
| 15 | 15 | 24 | 32 | **MONTEREY** — Eric Burdon & the Animals (Tom Wilson), MGM 13868 | 6 |
| 16 | 23 | 47 | 70 | **SPOOKY** — Classics IV (Buddy Buie), Imperial 66259 | 5 |
| 17 | 18 | 35 | 62 | **NOBODY BUT ME** — Human Beinz (Alexis de Azedozo), Capitol 5990 | 7 |
| 18 | 12 | 9 | 9 | **BOOGALOO DOWN BROADWAY** — Fantastic Johnny C. (Jesse James), Phil-L.A. of Soul 305 | 16 |
| 19 | 19 | 27 | 36 | **WHO WILL ANSWER** — Ed Ames (Jim Foglesong), RCA Victor 9400 | 6 |
| 20 | 38 | 52 | 66 | **BABY, NOW THAT I'VE FOUND YOU** — Foundations (Tony Macaulay), Uni 55038 | 5 |
| 21 | 32 | 43 | 53 | **ITCHYCOO PARK** — Small Faces (Steve Marriott & Ronnie Lane), Immediate 501 | 11 |
| 22 | 29 | 38 | 48 | **GOIN' OUT OF MY HEAD/CAN'T TAKE MY EYES OFF YOU** — Lettermen (Kelly Gordon), Capitol 2054 | 7 |
| 23 | 28 | 28 | 40 | **TELL MAMA** — Etta James (Rick Hall), Cadet 5578 | 11 |
| 24 | 24 | 29 | 30 | **COME SEE ABOUT ME** — Jr. Walker and the All Stars (Holland & Dozier), Soul 3501 | 9 |
| 25 | 30 | 39 | 54 | **AM I THAT EASY TO FORGET** — Engelbert Humperdinck (Peter Sullivan), Parrot 40023 | 6 |
| 26 | 26 | 40 | 51 | **MY BABY MUST BE A MAGICIAN** — Marvelettes ("Smokey"), Tamla 54158 | 6 |
| 27 | 27 | 32 | 42 | **LOVE POWER** — Sandpebbles (Teddy Vann), Calla 141 | 9 |
| 28 | 33 | 33 | 37 | **I CAN'T STAND MYSELF (When You Touch Me)** — James Brown & His Famous Flames (James Brown), King 6144 | 7 |
| 29 | 39 | 53 | 63 | **DARLIN'** — Beach Boys (Beach Boys), Capitol 2068 | 4 |
| 30 | 36 | 48 | 77 | **SHE'S A RAINBOW** — Rolling Stones (Rolling Stones), London 906 | 4 |
| 31 | 41 | 56 | — | **TWO LITTLE KIDS** — Peaches & Herb (David Kapralik & Ken Williams), Date 1586 | 6 |
| 32 | 34 | 37 | 47 | **BEST OF BOTH WORLDS** — Lulu (Mickie Most), Epic 10260 | 6 |
| 33 | 43 | 54 | 64 | **EXPLOSION IN MY SOUL** — Soul Survivors (Gamble-Huff), Crimson 1012 | 5 |
| 34 | 20 | 25 | 26 | **IT'S WONDERFUL** — Young Rascals (Young Rascals), Atlantic 2463 | 7 |
| 35 | 22 | 17 | 17 | **NEXT PLANE TO LONDON** — Rose Garden (Greene/Stone), Atco 6510 | 14 |
| 36 | 17 | 14 | 15 | **SUMMER RAIN** — Johnny Rivers (Work), Imperial 66267 | 10 |
| 37 | 47 | 57 | 68 | **SKIP A ROPE** — Henson Cargill (Don Law), Monument 1041 | 5 |
| 38 | 46 | 60 | 72 | **I WONDER WHAT SHE'S DOING TONIGHT** — Tommy Boyce & Bobby Hart (Tommy Boyce & Bobby Hart), A&M 893 | 5 |
| 39 | 49 | 62 | 78 | **TO GIVE (The Reason I Live)** — Frankie Valli (Bob Crewe), Philips 40510 | 4 |
| 40 | 25 | 30 | 38 | **LOVE ME TWO TIMES** — Doors (Paul A. Rothchild), Elektra 45624 | 7 |
| 41 | 51 | 63 | 80 | **TOMORROW** — Strawberry Alarm Clock (Frank Slay & Bill Holmes), Uni 55046 | 4 |
| 42 | 52 | 67 | 83 | **JUST AS MUCH AS EVER** — Bobby Vinton (Billy Sherrill), Epic 10266 | 4 |
| 43 | 44 | 49 | 60 | **EVERYBODY KNOWS** — Dave Clark Five (Dave Clark), Epic 10265 | 6 |
| 44 | 48 | 59 | 69 | **THE LESSON** — Vikki Carr (Tommy Oliver), Liberty 56012 | 5 |
| 45 | 56 | — | — | **I WISH IT WOULD RAIN** — Temptations (Norman Whitfield), Gordy 7068 | 2 |
| 46 | 21 | 16 | 12 | **YOU BETTER SIT DOWN KIDS** — Cher (Sonny Bono), Imperial 66261 | 13 |
| 47 | 84 | 99 | — | **LOVE IS BLUE** — Paul Mauriat, Philips 40495 | 3 |
| 48 | 61 | 79 | 100 | **BOTTLE OF WINE** — Fireballs (Normaa Petty), Atco 6491 | 4 |
| 49 | 60 | 72 | — | **SOME VELVET MORNING** — Nancy Sinatra & Lee Hazlewood (Lee Hazlewood), Reprise 0651 | 3 |
| 50 | 53 | 45 | 45 | **I'M IN LOVE** — Wilson Pickett (Tom Dowd & Tommy Cogbill), Atlantic 2448 | 8 |
| 51 | 66 | 86 | — | **SUNDAY MORNIN'** — Spanky & Our Gang (Scharf-Dorough), Mercury 72765 | 3 |
| 52 | 50 | 50 | 50 | **DEAR ELOISE** — Hollies (Ron Richards), Epic 10251 | 8 |
| 53 | 55 | 44 | 44 | **WINDY** — Wes Montgomery (Creed Taylor), A&M 883 | 9 |
| 54 | 81 | — | — | **WE CAN FLY** — Cowsills (Bill & Bob Gowsill), MGM 13886 | 2 |
| 55 | 83 | — | — | **YOU** — Marvin Gaye (J. Hunter), Tamla 54160 | 2 |
| 56 | 57 | 58 | 59 | **GOOD COMBINATION** — Sonny & Cher (Sonny Bono), Atco 6541 | 6 |
| 57 | 58 | 64 | 81 | **I'M COMING HOME** — Tom Jones (Peter Sullivan), Parrot 40024 | 4 |
| 58 | 73 | 73 | 73 | **BACK UP TRAIN** — Al Greene & Soul Mate's (Rodgers & James), Hot Line 15000 | 7 |
| 59 | 70 | 85 | — | **MONEY** — Lovin' Spoonful (Lovin' Spoonful & Joe Wissert), Kama Sutra 241 | 3 |
| 60 | 64 | 82 | — | **NO SAD SONGS** — Joe Simon (J. R. Ent.), Sound Stage 7 2602 | 4 |
| 61 | 54 | 56 | 58 | **STORYBOOK CHILDREN** — Billy Vera & Judy Clay (Chip Taylor & Ted Daryll), Atlantic 2445 | 8 |
| 62 | 69 | 84 | 99 | **WE'RE A WINNER** — Impressions (Johnny Pate), ABC 11022 | 4 |
| 63 | 63 | 78 | 84 | **LOST** — Jerry Butler (Gamble & Huff), Mercury 72764 | 4 |
| 64 | 79 | 98 | — | **NEW ORLEANS** — Neil Diamond (Jeff Barry & Ellie Greenwich), Bang 554 | 3 |
| 65 | 65 | 83 | — | **ZABADAK** — Dave Dee, Dozy Beaky, Mick & Tich (Steve Rowland), Imperial 66270 | 3 |
| 66 | 82 | — | — | **I CAN TAKE OR LEAVE YOUR LOVING** — Herman's Hermits (Mickie Most), MGM 13885 | 2 |
| 67 | 94 | 100 | — | **BORN FREE** — Hesitations (GWP), Kapp 878 | 3 |
| 68 | 68 | 76 | 82 | **PICK UP THE PIECES** — Carla Thomas (A) (Bell & Don Davis), Stax 239 | 4 |
| 69 | 86 | — | — | **CARMEN** — Herb Alpert & the Tijuana Brass, A&M 890 | 2 |
| 70 | 72 | 94 | 95 | **OH, HOW IT HURTS** — Barbara Mason (J. Bishop), Arctic 137 | 5 |
| 71 | 71 | 74 | 74 | **UP-UP AND AWAY** — Hugh Masakela (Stewart Lovine), Uni 55037 | 7 |
| 72 | 62 | 51 | 52 | **DANCING BEAR** — Mamas & Papas (Lou Adler), Dunhill 4113 | 7 |
| 73 | 74 | — | — | **SUNSHINE OF YOUR LOVE** — Cream (Felix Pappalardi), Atco 6544 | 2 |
| 74 | 76 | 81 | — | **WORKING MAN'S PRAYER** — Arthur Prysock (Hy Weiss), Verve 10574 | 3 |
| 75 | 85 | — | — | **DO UNTO ME** — James & Bobby Purify (Papa Don), Bell 700 | 2 |
| 76 | 77 | 77 | 86 | **I WAS MADE TO LOVE HER** — King Curtis & His Kingpins (Tom Dowd & Tommy Cogbill), Atco 6547 | 4 |
| 77 | — | — | — | **(Theme From) VALLEY OF THE DOLLS** — Dionne Warwick (Bacharach-David), Scepter 12203 | 1 |
| 78 | 88 | 90 | — | **MISSION: IMPOSSIBLE** — Lalo Schifrin (Tom Mack), Dot 17059 | 3 |
| 79 | — | — | — | **WORDS** — Bee Gees (Robert Stigwood & the Bee Gees), Atco 6548 | 1 |
| 80 | — | — | — | **STRAWBERRY SHORTCAKE** — Jay & The Techniques (Jerry Ross), Smash 2142 | 1 |
| 81 | — | — | — | **THERE WAS A TIME** — James Brown & His Famous Flames (James Brown), King 6144 | 1 |
| 82 | — | — | — | **THERE IS** — Dells (B. Miller), Cadet 5574 | 1 |
| 83 | 90 | 97 | — | **MAN NEEDS A WOMAN** — James Carr (Quinton Claunch & Rudolph Russell), Goldwax 332 | 3 |
| 84 | 97 | — | — | **(1-2-3-4-5-6-7) COUNT THE DAYS** — Inez & Charlie Foxx (Charlie Foxx), Dynamo 112 | 2 |
| 85 | — | — | — | **HEY LITTLE ONE** — Glen Campbell (Al De Lory), Capitol 2076 | 1 |
| 86 | 75 | 66 | 67 | **I'LL BE SWEETER TOMORROW** — O'Jays (George Kerr), Bell 691 | 9 |
| 87 | 93 | 93 | 96 | **A LITTLE RAIN MUST FALL** — Epic Splendor (John Boylan), Hot Biscuit 1450 | 6 |
| 88 | 98 | — | — | **LET THE HEARTACHES BEGIN** — Long John Baldry, Warner Bros. 7098 | 2 |
| 89 | 89 | 89 | 91 | **CROSS MY HEART** — Billy Stewart (Davis & Caston), Chess 2002 | 8 |
| 90 | 91 | 91 | 92 | **UNITED** — Music Makers (Gamble-Huff), Gamble 210 | 4 |
| 91 | — | — | — | **LOOKING FOR A FOX** — Clarence Carter (Rick Hall), Atlantic 2461 | 1 |
| 92 | — | — | — | **HEY BOY (Take a Chance on Love)** — Ruby Andrews (Terry Bridges & Eaton), Zodiac 1006 | 1 |
| 93 | 96 | — | — | **WITHOUT LOVE (There Is Nothing)** — Oscar Toney Jr. (Papa Don), Bell 699 | 2 |
| 94 | — | — | — | **GIVE MY LOVE A TRY** — Linda Jones (George Kerr), Loma 2085 | 1 |
| 95 | 95 | 95 | 98 | **UP TIGHT GOOD MAN** — Laura Lee (Rick Hall), Chess 2030 | 5 |
| 96 | — | — | — | **TO EACH HIS OWN** — Frankie Laine (Bob Thiele), ABC 11032 | 1 |
| 97 | — | — | — | **BLESSED ARE THE LONELY** — Robert Knight (Buzz Cason & Mac Gayden), Rising Sons 707 | 1 |
| 98 | 99 | — | — | **EXPECTING TO FLY** — Buffalo Springfield (York/Pala), Atco 6545 | 2 |
| 99 | 100 | 100 | — | **FUNKY WAY** — Calvin Arnold (Cooper, Paul & Shelby), Venture 605 | 2 |
| 100 | — | — | — | **COME RAIN OR COME SHINE** — Ray Charles, Atlantic 2470 | 1 |

## BUBBLING UNDER THE HOT 100

101. SOMETHING'S MISSING ............ 5 Stairsteps & Cubie, Buddah 20
102. MELLOW MOONLIGHT ............ Leon Haywood, Decca 32230
103. I CALL IT LOVE ............ Manhattans, Carnival 533
104. 7:30 GUIDED TOUR ............ Five Americans, Abnak 126
105. I WISH I HAD TIME ............ Last Words, Atco 6542
106. BIG DADDY ............ Boots Randolph, Monument 1038
107. CAMELOT ............ King Richard's Fluegel Knights, MTA 138
108. MALAYISHA ............ Miriam Makeba, Reprise 0654
109. BIRDS OF A FEATHER ............ Joe South, Capitol 2060
110. LOVE EXPLOSION ............ Troy Keyes, ABC 11027
111. STILL BURNING IN MY HEART ............ Drifters, Atlantic 2471
112. BREAK MY MIND ............ Bobby Wood, MGM 13797
113. IT'S A GAS ............ Hombres, Verve Forecast 5076
114. IT'S NOT EASY ............ Will-O-Bees, Date 1583
115. SIMON SAYS ............ 1910 Fruitgum Company, Buddah 24

*Compiled from national retail sales and radio station airplay by the Music Popularity Dept. of Record Market Research, Billboard.*

# Billboard HOT 100

**FOR WEEK ENDING JANUARY 27, 1968**

★ STAR PERFORMER—Sides registering greatest proportionate upward progress this week.
Ⓡ Record Industry Association of America seal of certification as million selling single.

| This Week | Last Week | 2 Wks. Ago | 3 Wks. Ago | TITLE, Artist (Producer), Label & Number | Weeks on Chart |
|---|---|---|---|---|---|
| 1 (Billboard Award) | 1 | 2 | 3 | JUDY IN DISGUISE (With Glasses) — John Fred & His Playboy Band (J. Fred & A. A. Bernard), Paula 282 | 10 |
| 2 | 2 | 6 | 7 | CHAIN OF FOOLS — Aretha Franklin (Jerry Wexler), Atlantic 2464 | 8 |
| 3 | 5 | 9 | 12 | GREEN TAMBOURINE — Lemon Pipers (Paul Leka), Buddah 23 | 7 |
| 4 | 4 | 4 | 5 | WOMAN, WOMAN — Union Gap (Jerry Fuller), Columbia 44297 | 11 |
| 5 | 7 | 7 | 8 | BEND ME, SHAPE ME — American Breed (Bill Traut), Acta 811 | 9 |
| 6 | 3 | 1 | 1 | HELLO GOODBYE — Beatles (George Martin), Capitol 2056 | 9 |
| 7 | 16 | 23 | 47 | SPOOKY — Classics IV (Buddy Buie), Imperial 66259 | 6 |
| 8 | 6 | 3 | 2 | DAYDREAM BELIEVER — Monkees (Chip Douglas), Colgems 1012 | 11 |
| 9 | 9 | 5 | 4 | I HEARD IT THROUGH THE GRAPEVINE — Gladys Knight & the Pips (N. Whitfield), Soul 35039 | 15 |
| 10 | 10 | 13 | 13 | IF I COULD BUILD MY WHOLE WORLD AROUND YOU — Marvin Gaye & Tammi Terrell (Fuqua, Bristol), Tamla 54161 | 8 |
| 11 | 13 | 16 | 21 | SUSAN — Buckinghams (James William Guercio), Columbia 44378 | 8 |
| 12 | 17 | 18 | 35 | NOBODY BUT ME — Human Beinz (Alexis de Azevedo), Capitol 5990 | 8 |
| 13 | 14 | 14 | 18 | DIFFERENT DRUM — Stone Poneys (Nick Venet), Capitol 2004 | 12 |
| 14 | 8 | 8 | 6 | I SECOND THAT EMOTION — Smokey Robinson & Miracles ("Smokey" A. Cleveland), Tamla 54159 | 13 |
| 15 | 45 | 56 | — | I WISH IT WOULD RAIN — Temptations (Norman Whitfield), Gordy 7068 | 3 |
| 16 | 21 | 32 | 43 | ITCHYCOO PARK — Small Faces (Steve Marriott & Ronnie Lane), Immediate 501 | 12 |
| 17 | 22 | 29 | 38 | GOIN' OUT OF MY HEAD/CAN'T TAKE MY EYES OFF YOU — Lettermen (Kelly Gordon), Capitol 2054 | 7 |
| 18 | 47 | 84 | 99 | LOVE IS BLUE — Paul Mauriat, Philips 40495 | 4 |
| 19 | 25 | 30 | 39 | AM I THAT EASY TO FORGET — Engelbert Humperdinck (Peter Sullivan), Parrot 40023 | 7 |
| 20 | 20 | 38 | 52 | BABY, NOW THAT I'VE FOUND YOU — Foundations (Tony Macaulay), Uni 55038 | 8 |
| 21 | 26 | 26 | 40 | MY BABY MUST BE A MAGICIAN — Marvelettes ("Smokey"), Tamla 54158 | 7 |
| 22 | 27 | 27 | 32 | LOVE POWER — Sandpebbles (Teddy Vann), Calla 141 | 10 |
| 23 | 23 | 28 | 25 | TELL MAMA — Etta James (Rick Hall), Cadet 5578 | 12 |
| 24 | 29 | 39 | 53 | DARLIN' — Beach Boys (Beach Boys), Capitol 2068 | 5 |
| 25 | 30 | 36 | 48 | SHE'S A RAINBOW — Rolling Stones (Rolling Stones), London 906 | 5 |
| 26 | 38 | 46 | 60 | I WONDER WHAT SHE'S DOING TONIGHT — Tommy Boyce & Bobby Hart (Tommy Boyce & Bobby Hart), A&M 893 | 6 |
| 27 | 24 | 24 | 29 | COME SEE ABOUT ME — Jr. Walker and the All Stars (Holland & Dozier), Soul 3501 | 10 |
| 28 | 48 | 61 | 79 | BOTTLE OF WINE — Fireballs (Norman Petty), Atco 6491 | 5 |
| 29 | 41 | 51 | 63 | TOMORROW — Strawberry Alarm Clock (Frank Slay & Bill Holmes), Uni 55046 | 5 |
| 30 | 39 | 49 | 62 | TO GIVE (The Reason I Live) — Frankie Valli (Bob Crewe), Philips 40510 | 5 |
| 31 | 31 | 31 | 41 | TWO LITTLE KIDS — Peaches & Herb (David Kapralik & Ken Williams), Date 1586 | 7 |
| 32 | 42 | 52 | 67 | JUST AS MUCH AS EVER — Bobby Vinton (Billy Sherrill), Epic 10266 | 5 |
| 33 | 33 | 43 | 54 | EXPLOSION IN MY SOUL — Soul Survivors (Gamble-Huff), Crimson 1012 | 6 |
| 34 | 44 | 48 | 59 | THE LESSON — Vikki Carr (Tommy Oliver), Liberty 56012 | 6 |
| 35 | 37 | 47 | 57 | SKIP A ROPE — Henson Cargill (Don Law), Monument 1041 | 6 |
| 36 | 28 | 33 | 33 | I CAN'T STAND MYSELF (When You Touch Me) — James Brown & His Famous Flames (James Brown), King 6144 | 8 |
| 37 | 15 | 15 | 24 | MONTEREY — Eric Burdon & the Animals (Tom Wilson), MGM 13868 | 7 |
| 38 | 11 | 11 | 11 | HONEY CHILE — Martha Reeves & the Vandellas (R. Morris), Gordy 7067 | 11 |
| 39 | 49 | 60 | 72 | SOME VELVET MORNING — Nancy Sinatra & Lee Hazlewood (Lee Hazlewood), Reprise 0651 | 4 |
| 40 | 12 | 10 | 10 | SKINNY LEGS AND ALL — Joe Tex (Buddy Killen), Dial 4063 | 14 |
| 41 | 51 | 66 | 86 | SUNDAY MORNIN' — Spanky & Our Gang (Scharf-Dorough), Mercury 72765 | 4 |
| 42 | 18 | 12 | 9 | BOOGALOO DOWN BROADWAY — Fantastic Johnny C. (Jesse James), Phil-L.A. of Soul 305 | 17 |
| 43 | 43 | 44 | 49 | EVERYBODY KNOWS — Dave Clark Five (Dave Clark), Epic 10265 | 7 |
| 44 | 54 | 81 | — | WE CAN FLY — Cowsills (Bill & Bob Cowsill), MGM 13886 | 3 |
| 45 | 55 | 83 | — | YOU — Marvin Gaye (I. Hunter), Tamla 54160 | 3 |
| 46 | 19 | 19 | 27 | WHO WILL ANSWER — Ed Ames (Jim Foglesong), RCA Victor 9400 | 7 |
| 47 | 62 | 69 | 84 | WE'RE A WINNER — Impressions (Johnny Pate), ABC 11022 | 5 |
| 48 | 66 | 82 | — | I CAN TAKE OR LEAVE YOUR LOVING — Herman's Hermits (Mickie Most), MGM 13885 | 3 |
| 49 | 59 | 70 | 85 | MONEY — Lovin' Spoonful (Lovin' Spoonful & Joe Wissert), Kama Sutra 241 | 4 |
| 50 | 60 | 64 | 82 | NO SAD SONGS — Joe Simon (J. R. Ent.), Sound Stage 7 2602 | 4 |
| 51 | 58 | 73 | 73 | BACK UP TRAIN — Al Greene & Soul Mate's (Rodgers & James), Hot Line 15000 | 8 |
| 52 | 64 | 79 | 98 | NEW ORLEANS — Neil Diamond (Jeff Barry & Ellie Greenwich), Bang 554 | 4 |
| 53 | 53 | 55 | 44 | WINDY — Wes Montgomery (Creed Taylor), A&M 883 | 10 |
| 54 | 32 | 34 | 37 | BEST OF BOTH WORLDS — Lulu (Mickie Most), Epic 10260 | 7 |
| 55 | 65 | 65 | 83 | ZABADAK — Dave Dee, Dozy, Beaky, Mick & Tich (Steve Rowland), Imperial 66270 | 4 |
| 56 | 67 | 94 | 100 | BORN FREE — Hesitations (GWP), Kapp 878 | 4 |
| 57 | 57 | 58 | 64 | I'M COMING HOME — Tom Jones (Peter Sullivan), Parrot 40024 | 5 |
| 58 | 50 | 53 | 45 | I'M IN LOVE — Wilson Pickett (Tom Dowd & Tommy Cogbill), Atlantic 2448 | 9 |
| 59 | 70 | 72 | 94 | OH, HOW IT HURTS — Barbara Mason (J. Bishop), Arctic 137 | 6 |
| 60 | — | — | — | STRAWBERRY SHORTCAKE — Jay & The Techniques (Jerry Ross), Smash 2142 | 1 |
| 61 | 77 | — | — | (Theme From) VALLEY OF THE DOLLS — Dionne Warwick (Bacharach-David), Scepter 12203 | 2 |
| 62 | 63 | 63 | 78 | LOST — Jerry Butler (Gamble & Huff), Mercury 72764 | 5 |
| 63 | 69 | 86 | — | CARMEN — Herb Alpert & the Tijuana Brass, A&M 890 | 3 |
| 64 | 79 | — | — | WORDS — Bee Gees (Robert Stigwood & the Bee Gees), Atco 6548 | 2 |
| 65 | 81 | — | — | THERE WAS A TIME — James Brown & His Famous Flames (James Brown), King 6144 | 2 |
| 66 | 82 | — | — | THERE IS — Dells (B. Miller), Cadet 5590 | 2 |
| 67 | — | — | — | (Sittin' On) THE DOCK OF THE BAY — Otis Redding (Steve Cropper), Volt 157 | 1 |
| 68 | 68 | 68 | 76 | PICK UP THE PIECES — Carla Thomas (A) (Bell & Don Davis), Stax 239 | 5 |
| 69 | 73 | 74 | — | SUNSHINE OF YOUR LOVE — Cream (Felix Pappalardi), Atco 6544 | 3 |
| 70 | 85 | — | — | HEY LITTLE ONE — Glen Campbell (Al De Lory), Capitol 2076 | 2 |
| 71 | 61 | 54 | 56 | STORYBOOK CHILDREN — Billy Vera & Judy Clay (Chip Taylor & Ted Deryll), Atlantic 2445 | 9 |
| 72 | — | — | — | I THANK YOU — Sam & Dave (Isaac Hayes & David Porter), Stax 242 | 1 |
| 73 | 75 | 85 | — | DO UNTO ME — James & Bobby Purify (Papa Don), Bell 700 | 3 |
| 74 | 74 | 76 | 81 | WORKING MAN'S PRAYER — Arthur Prysock (Hy Weiss), Verve 10574 | 4 |
| 75 | 71 | 71 | 74 | UP-UP AND AWAY — Hugh Masakela (Stewart Lovine), Uni 55037 | 4 |
| 76 | 84 | 97 | — | (1-2-3-4-5-6-7) COUNT THE DAYS — Inez & Charlie Foxx (Charlie Foxx), Dynamo 112 | 3 |
| 77 | — | — | — | SIMON SAYS — 1910 Fruitgum Co. (J. Katz/J. Kasenetz/E. Chiprut), Buddah 24 | 1 |
| 78 | 78 | 88 | 90 | MISSION: IMPOSSIBLE — Lalo Schifrin (Tom Mack), Dot 17059 | 4 |
| 79 | 90 | 91 | 91 | UNITED — Music Makers (Gamble-Huff), Gamble 210 | 5 |
| 80 | 83 | 90 | 97 | MAN NEEDS A WOMAN — James Carr (Quinton Claunch & Rudolph Russell), Goldwax 332 | 4 |
| 81 | — | — | — | GET OUT NOW — Tommy James & the Shondells (Kaboona), Roulette 7000 | 1 |
| 82 | — | — | — | STOP — Howard Tate (Jerry Ragovoy), Verve 10573 | 1 |
| 83 | — | — | — | GUITAR MAN — Elvis Presley, RCA Victor 47-9425 | 1 |
| 84 | — | — | — | A MILLION TO ONE — Five Stairsteps & Cubie (Clarence Burke, Jr.), Buddah 26 | 1 |
| 85 | — | — | — | MALAYISHA — Miriam Makeba (Jerry Ragovoy), Reprise 0654 | 1 |
| 86 | 89 | 89 | 89 | CROSS MY HEART — Billy Stewart (Davis & Caston), Chess 2002 | 9 |
| 87 | 87 | 93 | 93 | A LITTLE RAIN MUST FALL — Epic Splendor (John Boylan), Big Biscuit 1450 | 7 |
| 88 | 91 | — | — | LOOKING FOR A FOX — Clarence Carter (Rick Hall), Atlantic 2461 | 2 |
| 89 | 99 | 100 | 100 | FUNKY WAY — Calvin Arnold (Cooper, Paul & Shelby), Venture 605 | 3 |
| 90 | 93 | 96 | — | WITHOUT LOVE (There Is Nothing) — Oscar Toney Jr. (Papa Don), Bell 699 | 3 |
| 91 | — | — | — | ROSANNA'S GOING WILD — Johnny Cash (Bob Johnston), Columbia 44373 | 1 |
| 92 | — | — | — | CAB DRIVER — Mills Brothers (Charles R. Grean & Tom Mack), Dot 17041 | 1 |
| 93 | 95 | 95 | 95 | UP TIGHT GOOD MAN — Laura Lee (Rick Hall), Chess 2030 | 6 |
| 94 | 94 | — | — | GIVE MY LOVE A TRY — Linda Jones (George Kerr), Loma 2085 | 2 |
| 95 | 96 | — | — | TO EACH HIS OWN — Frankie Laine (Bob Thiele), ABC 11032 | 2 |
| 96 | — | — | — | 7:30 GUIDED TOUR — Five Americans (Abnak Music), Abnak 126 | 1 |
| 97 | 97 | — | — | BLESSED ARE THE LONELY — Robert Knight (Buzz Cason & Mac Gayden), Rising Sons 707 | 2 |
| 98 | 100 | — | — | COME RAIN OR COME SHINE — Ray Charles, Atlantic 2470 | 2 |
| 99 | — | — | — | NO ONE KNOWS — Every Mother's Son (Wes Farrell), MGM 13887 | 1 |
| 100 | — | — | — | KEEP THE BALL ROLLIN' — Al Hirt (Paul Robinson), RCA Victor 47-9417 | 1 |

## BUBBLING UNDER THE HOT 100

101. I WAS TO LOVE HER ............ King Curtis & His Kingpins, Atco 6547
102. MELLOW MOONLIGHT ............ Leon Haywood, Decca 32230
103. LET THE HEARTACHES BEGIN .... Long John Baldry, Warner Bros. 7098
104. EVERYTHING THAT TOUCHES YOU ... Association, Warner Bros. 7163
105. CARPET MAN ............ 5th Dimension, Soul City 762
106. SOMETHING'S MISSING ....... 5 Stairsteps & Cubie, Buddah 20
107. WHAT CAN YOU DO WHEN YOU AIN'T GOT NOBODY ........ Soul Brothers Six, Atlantic 2456
108. BIRDS OF A FEATHER ............ Joe South, Capitol 2060
109. LOVE EXPLOSION ............ Troy Keyes, ABC 11027
110. IT'S NOT EASY ............ Will-O-Bees, Date 1583
111. BREAK MY MIND ............ Bobby Wood, MGM 13797
112. GREEN GREEN GRASS OF HOME ... Skitch Henderson & His Ork, Columbia 44333
113. DANCE TO THE MUSIC ............ Sly & Family Stone, Epic 10256
114. GET TOGETHER ............ Jimmy McCracklin, Minit 32033
115. (YOU'VE GOT) PERSONALITY & CHANTILLY LACE ........ Mitch Ryder, Dyno Voice 905
116. I SAY A LITTLE PRAYER ............ Sergio Mendes, Atlantic 2472
117. RED, GREEN, YELLOW & BLUE ... Dickie Lee, Atco 6546
118. THAT'S ALL RIGHT ............ Brenda Lee, Decca 32248
119. WORLD OF OUR OWN ............ Sonny James, Capitol 2067

Compiled from national retail sales and radio station airplay by the Music Popularity Dept. of Record Market Research, Billboard.

# Billboard HOT 100

FOR WEEK ENDING FEBRUARY 3, 1968

★ STAR PERFORMER—Sides registering greatest proportionate upward progress this week.

Record Industry Association of America seal of certification as million selling single.

| This Week | 1 Wk. Ago | 2 Wks. Ago | 3 Wks. Ago | TITLE Artist (Producer), Label & Number | Weeks On Chart |
|---|---|---|---|---|---|
| 1 (Billboard Award) | 3 | 5 | 9 | GREEN TAMBOURINE — Lemon Pipers (Paul Leka), Buddah 23 | 8 |
| 2 | 1 | 1 | 2 | JUDY IN DISGUISE (With Glasses) — John Fred & His Playboy Band (J. Fred & A. Bernard), Paula 282 | 11 |
| 3 | 2 | 2 | 6 | CHAIN OF FOOLS — Aretha Franklin (Jerry Wexler), Atlantic 2464 | 9 |
| ★ 4 | 7 | 16 | 23 | SPOOKY — Classics IV (Buddy Buie), Imperial 66259 | 7 |
| 5 | 5 | 7 | 7 | BEND ME, SHAPE ME — American Breed (Bill Traut), Acta 811 | 10 |
| 6 | 4 | 4 | 4 | WOMAN, WOMAN — Union Gap (Jerry Fuller), Columbia 44297 | 12 |
| ★ 7 | 18 | 47 | 84 | LOVE IS BLUE — Paul Mauriat, Philips 40495 | 5 |
| ★ 8 | 12 | 17 | 18 | NOBODY BUT ME — Human Beinz (Alexis de Azevedo), Capitol 5990 | 9 |
| ★ 9 | 17 | 22 | 29 | GOIN' OUT OF MY HEAD/ CAN'T TAKE MY EYES OFF YOU — Lettermen (Kelly Gordon), Capitol 2054 | 9 |
| ★ 10 | 15 | 45 | 56 | I WISH IT WOULD RAIN — Temptations (Norman Whitfield), Gordy 7068 | 4 |
| 11 | 11 | 13 | 16 | SUSAN — Buckinghams (James William Guercio), Columbia 44378 | 9 |
| 12 | 6 | 3 | 1 | HELLO GOODBYE — Beatles (George Martin), Capitol 2056 | 10 |
| ★ 13 | 20 | 20 | 38 | BABY, NOW THAT I'VE FOUND YOU — Foundations (Tony Macaulay), Uni 55038 | 7 |
| 14 | 13 | 14 | 14 | DIFFERENT DRUM — Stone Poneys (Nick Venet), Capitol 2004 | 13 |
| 15 | 9 | 9 | 5 | I HEARD IT THROUGH THE GRAPEVINE — Gladys Knight & the Pips (N. Whitfield), Soul 35039 | 16 |
| 16 | 16 | 21 | 32 | ITCHYCOO PARK — Small Faces (Steve Marriott & Ronnie Lane), Immediate 501 | 13 |
| 17 | 14 | 8 | 8 | I SECOND THAT EMOTION — Smokey Robinson & Miracles ("Smokey" A. Cleveland), Tamla 54159 | 14 |
| 18 | 19 | 25 | 30 | AM I THAT EASY TO FORGET — Engelbert Humperdinck (Peter Sullivan), Parrot 40023 | 8 |
| ★ 19 | 24 | 29 | 39 | DARLIN' — Beach Boys (Beach Boys), Capitol 2968 | 6 |
| ★ 20 | 26 | 38 | 46 | I WONDER WHAT SHE'S DOING TONIGHT — Tommy Boyce & Bobby Hart (Tommy Boyce & Bobby Hart), A&M 893 | 7 |
| 21 | 21 | 26 | 26 | MY BABY MUST BE A MAGICIAN — Marvelettes ("Smokey"), Tamla 54158 | 8 |
| ★ 22 | 28 | 48 | 61 | BOTTLE OF WINE — Fireballs (Norman Petty), Atco 6491 | 6 |
| 23 | 23 | 23 | 28 | TELL MAMA — Etta James (Rick Hall), Cadet 5578 | 13 |
| 24 | 8 | 6 | 3 | DAYDREAM BELIEVER — Monkees (Chip Douglas), Colgems 1012 | 12 |
| 25 | 22 | 27 | 27 | LOVE POWER — Sandpebbles (Teddy Vann), Calla 141 | 11 |
| ★ 26 | 35 | 37 | 47 | SKIP A ROPE — Henson Cargill (Don Law), Monument 1041 | 7 |
| ★ 27 | 32 | 42 | 52 | JUST AS MUCH AS EVER — Bobby Vinton (Billy Sherrill), Epic 10266 | 6 |
| 28 | 29 | 41 | 51 | TOMORROW — Strawberry Alarm Clock (Frank Slay & Bill Holmes), Uni 55046 | 6 |
| 29 | 10 | 10 | 13 | IF I COULD BUILD MY WHOLE WORLD AROUND YOU — Marvin Gaye & Tammi Terrell (Fuqus, Bristol), Tamla 54161 | 9 |
| 30 | 30 | 39 | 49 | TO GIVE (The Reason I Live) — Frankie Valli (Bob Crewe), Philips 40510 | 6 |
| ★ 31 | 41 | 51 | 66 | SUNDAY MORNIN' — Spanky & Our Gang (Scharf-Dorough), Mercury 72765 | 5 |
| 32 | 39 | 49 | 60 | SOME VELVET MORNING — Nancy Sinatra & Lee Hazlewood (Lee Hazlewood), Reprise 0651 | 5 |
| ★ 33 | 61 | 77 | — | (Theme From) VALLEY OF THE DOLLS — Dionne Warwick (Bacharach-David), Scepter 12203 | 3 |
| ★ 34 | 44 | 54 | 81 | WE CAN FLY — Cowsills (Bill & Bob Cowsill), MGM 13886 | 4 |
| ★ 35 | 45 | 55 | 83 | YOU — Marvin Gaye (I. Hunter), Tamla 54160 | 4 |
| ★ 36 | 47 | 62 | 69 | WE'RE A WINNER — Impressions (Johnny Pate), ABC 11022 | 6 |
| 37 | 25 | 30 | 36 | SHE'S A RAINBOW — Rolling Stones (Rolling Stones) London 906 | 6 |
| ★ 38 | 48 | 66 | 82 | I CAN TAKE OR LEAVE YOUR LOVING — Herman's Hermits (Mickie Most), MGM 13885 | 4 |
| 39 | 37 | 15 | 15 | MONTEREY — Eric Burdon & the Animals (Tom Wilson), MGM 13868 | 8 |
| 40 | 33 | 33 | 43 | EXPLOSION IN MY SOUL — Soul Survivors (Gamble-Huff), Crimson 1012 | 7 |
| ★ 41 | 51 | 58 | 73 | BACK UP TRAIN — Al Greene & Soul Mate's (Rodgers & James), Hot Line 15000 | 9 |
| 42 | 40 | 12 | 10 | SKINNY LEGS AND ALL — Joe Tex (Buddy Killen), Dial 4063 | 15 |
| 43 | 31 | 31 | 31 | TWO LITTLE KIDS — Peaches & Herb (David Kaprelik & Ken Williams), Date 1586 | 8 |
| 44 | 34 | 44 | 48 | THE LESSON — Vikki Carr (Tommy Oliver), Liberty 56012 | 7 |
| 45 | 42 | 18 | 12 | BOOGALOO DOWN BROADWAY — Fantastic Johnny C. (Jesse James), Phil-L.A. of Soul 305 | 18 |
| ★ 46 | 64 | 79 | — | WORDS — Bee Gees (Robert Stigwood & the Bee Gees), Atco 6548 | 3 |
| ★ 47 | 67 | — | — | (Sittin' On) THE DOCK OF THE BAY — Otis Redding (Steve Cropper), Volt 157 | 2 |
| 48 | 49 | 59 | 70 | MONEY — Lovin' Spoonful (Lovin' Spoonful & Joe Wissert), Kama Sutra 241 | 5 |
| 49 | 50 | 60 | 64 | NO SAD SONGS — Joe Simon (J. R. Ent.), Sound Stage 7 2602 | 5 |
| ★ 50 | 60 | 80 | — | STRAWBERRY SHORTCAKE — Jay & The Techniques (Jerry Ross), Smash 2142 | 3 |
| 51 | 52 | 64 | 79 | NEW ORLEANS — Neil Diamond (Jeff Barry & Ellie Greenwich), Bang 554 | 5 |
| 52 | 55 | 65 | 65 | ZABADAK — Dave Dee, Dozy, Beaky, Mick & Tich (Steve Rowland), Imperial 66270 | 5 |
| ★ 53 | 63 | 69 | 86 | CARMEN — Herb Alpert & the Tijuana Brass, A&M 890 | 4 |
| 54 | 54 | 32 | 34 | BEST OF BOTH WORLDS — Lulu (Mickie Most), Epic 10260 | 8 |
| 55 | 56 | 67 | 94 | BORN FREE — Hesitations (GWP), Kapp 878 | 5 |
| ★ 56 | 66 | 82 | — | THERE IS — Dells (B. Miller), Cadet 5590 | 3 |
| 57 | 36 | 28 | 33 | I CAN'T STAND MYSELF (When You Touch Me) — James Brown & His Famous Flames (James Brown), King 6144 | 9 |
| ★ 58 | 77 | — | — | SIMON SAYS — 1910 Fruitgum Co. (J. Katz/J. Kasenete/ E. Chiprut), Buddah 24 | 2 |
| 59 | 59 | 70 | 72 | OH, HOW IT HURTS — Barbara Mason (J. Bishop), Arctic 137 | 7 |
| ★ 60 | 72 | — | — | I THANK YOU — Sam & Dave (Isaac Hayes & David Porter), Stax 242 | 2 |
| 61 | 65 | 81 | — | THERE WAS A TIME — James Brown & His Famous Flames (James Brown), King 6144 | 3 |
| ★ 62 | — | — | — | EVERYTHING THAT TOUCHES YOU — Association (Bones Bowe), Warner Bros. 7163 | 1 |
| ★ 63 | 78 | 78 | 88 | MISSION: IMPOSSIBLE — Lalo Schifrin (Tom Mack), Dot 17059 | 5 |
| 64 | 69 | 73 | 74 | SUNSHINE OF YOUR LOVE — Cream (Felix Pappalardi), Atco 6544 | 4 |
| 65 | 38 | 11 | 11 | HONEY CHILE — Martha Reeves & the Vandellas (R. Morris) Gordy 7067 | 12 |
| ★ 66 | 81 | — | — | GET OUT NOW — Tommy James & the Shondells (Big Kaboona), Roulette 7000 | 2 |
| ★ 67 | 83 | — | — | GUITAR MAN — Elvis Presley, RCA Victor 47-9425 | 2 |
| 68 | 70 | 85 | — | HEY LITTLE ONE — Glen Campbell (Al De Lory), Capitol 2076 | 3 |
| 69 | 46 | 19 | 19 | WHO WILL ANSWER — Ed Ames (Jim Foglesong), RCA Victor 9400 | 8 |
| 70 | 58 | 50 | 53 | I'M IN LOVE — Wilson Pickett (Tom Dowd & Tommy Cogbill), Atlantic 2448 | 10 |
| ★ 71 | — | — | — | WALK AWAY RENEE — Four Tops (Rolland & Dozier), Motown 1119 | 1 |
| 72 | 43 | 43 | 44 | EVERYBODY KNOWS — Dave Clark Five (Dave Clark), Epic 10265 | 8 |
| 73 | 73 | 75 | 85 | DO UNTO ME — James & Bobby Purify (Papa Don), Bell 700 | 4 |
| 74 | 74 | 74 | 76 | WORKING MAN'S PRAYER — Arthur Prysock (Hy Weiss), Verve 10574 | 5 |
| 75 | 27 | 24 | 24 | COME SEE ABOUT ME — Jr. Walker & the All Stars (Holland & Dozier), Soul 3501 | 11 |
| 76 | 53 | 53 | 55 | WINDY — Wes Montgomery (Creed Taylor), A&M 883 | 11 |
| 77 | 68 | 68 | 68 | PICK UP THE PIECES — Carla Thomas (A) (Bell & Don Davis), Stax 239 | 6 |
| 78 | 79 | 90 | 91 | UNITED — Music Makers (Gamble-Huff), Gamble 210 | 6 |
| 79 | 62 | 63 | 63 | LOST — Jerry Butler (Gamble & Huff), Mercury 72764 | 6 |
| 80 | 80 | 83 | 90 | MAN NEEDS A WOMAN — James Carr (Quinton Claunch & Rudolph Russell), Goldwax 332 | 5 |
| 81 | 84 | — | — | A MILLION TO ONE — Five Stairsteps & Cubie (Clarence Burke, Jr.), Buddah 26 | 2 |
| 82 | 82 | — | — | STOP — Howard Tate (Jerry Ragovoy), Verve 10573 | 2 |
| 83 | 88 | 91 | — | LOOKING FOR A FOX — Clarence Carter (Rick Hall), Atlantic 2461 | 3 |
| 84 | 92 | — | — | CAB DRIVER — Mills Brothers (Charles R. Grean & Tom Mack), Dot 17041 | 2 |
| 85 | 85 | — | — | MALAYISHA — Miriam Makeba (Jerry Ragovoy), Reprise 0654 | 2 |
| 86 | 76 | 84 | 97 | (1-2-3-4-5-6-7) COUNT THE DAYS — Inez & Charlie Foxx (Charlie Foxx), Dynamo 112 | 4 |
| ★ 87 | — | — | — | COLD FEET — Albert King (Al Jackson Jr.), Stax 241 | 1 |
| ★ 88 | — | — | — | BURNING SPEAR — Soulful Strings (Esmond Edwards), Cadet 5576 | 1 |
| 89 | 89 | 99 | 100 | FUNKY WAY — Calvin Arnold (Cooper, Paul & Shelby), Venture 605 | 4 |
| ★ 90 | — | — | — | TRY IT — Ohio Express (J. Katz & J. Kasenetz), Cameo 2001 | 1 |
| 91 | 91 | — | — | ROSANNA'S GOING WILD — Johnny Cash (Bob Johnston), Columbia 44373 | 2 |
| 92 | — | — | — | LA-LA MEANS I LOVE YOU — Delfonica (Stan & Bell), Philly Groove 150 | 1 |
| 93 | 94 | 94 | — | GIVE MY LOVE A TRY — Linda Jones (George Kerr), Loma 2085 | 3 |
| 94 | 95 | 96 | — | TO EACH HIS OWN — Frankie Laine (Bob Thiele), ABC 11032 | 3 |
| 95 | — | — | — | PEOPLE WORLD — Jim & Jean (Jimmy Wisner), Verve Forecast 5073 | 1 |
| 96 | 96 | — | — | 7:30 GUIDED TOUR — Five Americans (Abnak Music), Abnak 126 | 2 |
| 97 | — | — | — | CARPET MAN — 5th Dimension (Bones Bowe), Soul City 762 | 1 |
| 98 | — | — | — | IT'S NOT EASY — Will-O-Bees (Bill Traut), Date 1583 | 1 |
| 99 | 99 | — | — | NO ONE KNOWS — Every Mother's Son (Wes Farrell), MGM 13887 | 2 |
| 100 | — | — | — | (You've Got) PERSONALITY & CHANTILLY LACE — Mitch Ryder (Bob Crewe), Dynovoice 905 | 1 |

## HOT 100—A TO Z—(Publisher-Licensee)


Am I That Easy to Forget (Four Star, BMI) ..... 18
Baby, Now That I've Found You (January/Welbeck, BMI) ..... 13
Back Up Train (Tosted, BMI) ..... 41
Bend Me, Shape Me (Helios, BMI) ..... 5
Best of Both Worlds (James, BMI) ..... 54
Boogaloo Down Broadway (Dandelion/James Boys, BMI) ..... 45
Born Free (Screen Gems-Columbia, BMI) ..... 55
Bottle of Wine (Deep Fork, ASCAP) ..... 22
Burning Spear (Discus, BMI) ..... 88
Cab Driver (Blackhawk, BMI) ..... 84
Carmen (Irving, BMI) ..... 53
Carpet Man (Rivers, BMI) ..... 97
Chain of Fools (14th Hour/Pronto, BMI) ..... 3
Cold Feet (East, BMI) ..... 87
Come See About Me (Jobete, BMI) ..... 75
Darlin' (Sea of Tunes, BMI) ..... 19
Daydream Believer (Screen Gems-Columbia, BMI) ..... 24
Different Drum (Screen Gems-Columbia, BMI) ..... 14
Do Unto Me (Big Seven, BMI) ..... 73
Everybody Knows (Francis, Day & Hunter, ASCAP) ..... 72
Everything That Touches You (Beechwood, BMI) ..... 62
Explosion in My Soul (Double Diamond/Downstairs, BMI) ..... 40
Funky Way (Mikim, BMI) ..... 89
Get Out Now (Patricia, BMI) ..... 66
Give My Love a Try (Zira/Twilight, BMI) ..... 93
Goin' Out of My Head/Can't Take My Eyes Off You (Vogue/Saturday/Season's Four, BMI) ..... 9
Green Tambourine (Kama Sutra, BMI) ..... 1
Guitar Man (Vector, BMI) ..... 67
Hello, Goodbye (Maclen, BMI) ..... 12
Hey Little One (Sherman & De Vorzon, BMI) ..... 68
Honey Chile (Jobete, BMI) ..... 65
I Can Take or Leave Your Loving (Miller, ASCAP) ..... 38
I Can't Stand Myself (When You Touch Me) (Taccon/Soil, BMI) ..... 57
I Heard it Through the Grapevine (Jobete, BMI) ..... 15
I Second That Emotion (Jobete, BMI) ..... 17
I Thank You (East/Pronto, BMI) ..... 60
I Wish It Would Rain (Jobete, BMI) ..... 10
I Wonder What She's Doing Tonight (Screen Gems-Columbia, BMI) ..... 20
If I Could Build My Whole World Around You (Jobete, BMI) ..... 29
I'm in Love (Pronto/Tracebob, BMI) ..... 70
Itchycoo Park (Nice Songs, BMI) ..... 16
It's Not Easy (Screen Gems-Columbia, BMI) ..... 98
Judy in Disguise (With Glasses) (Su-Ma, BMI) ..... 2
Just as Much as Ever (Roosevelt, BMI) ..... 27
La-La Means I Love You (Nickel Shoe, BMI) ..... 92
Lesson, The (Alta, ASCAP) ..... 44
Looking for a Fox (Fame, BMI) ..... 83
Lost (Double Diamond/Downstairs/Parabut, BMI) ..... 79
Love Is Blue (Croma, ASCAP) ..... 7
Love Power (Unbelievable, BMI) ..... 25
Malayisha (Raj Kumar, BMI) ..... 85
Man Needs a Woman, A (Rise/Aim, BMI) ..... 80
Million To One, A (Jobete, BMI) ..... 81
Mission: Impossible (Bruin, BMI) ..... 63
Money (Faithful Virtue, BMI) ..... 48
Monterey (Slamina/Sea-Lark, BMI) ..... 39
My Baby Must Be a Magician (Jobete, BMI) ..... 21
New Orleans (Rock Masters, BMI) ..... 51
Nobody But Me (Wemar, BMI) ..... 8
No One Knows (Pocket Full of Tunes, Tobi-Ann, BMI) ..... 99
No Sad Songs (Press, BMI) ..... 49
Oh, How It Hurts (Blockbuster, BMI) ..... 59
(1-2-3-4-5-6-7) Count the Days (Catlogue/Cee & Eye, BMI) ..... 86
People World (Akbestal ,BMI) ..... 95
Pick Up the Pieces (East/Groovesville, BMI) ..... 77
Rosanna's Going Wild (Melody Lane/ Copper Creek, BMI) ..... 91
7:30 Guided Tour (Sunnybrook, BMI) ..... 96
She's a Rainbow (Gideon, BMI) ..... 37
(Sittin' On) The Dock of the Bay (East/Pine/Radwal, BMI) ..... 47
Skinny Legs and All (Tree, BMI) ..... 42
Skip a Rope (Tree, BMI) ..... 26
Simon Says (Maskat, BMI) ..... 58
Some Velvet Morning (Hazlewood, ASCAP) ..... 32
Spooky (Lowery, BMI) ..... 4
Stop (Ragmar/Rumbalero, BMI) ..... 82
Strawberry Shortcake (Bradley, BMI) ..... 50
Sunday Mornin' (Blackwood, BMI) ..... 31
Sunshine of Your Love (Dratleaf, BMI) ..... 64
Susan (Diogenes/Bag of Tunes, BMI) ..... 11
Tell Mama (Fame, BMI) ..... 23
(Theme From) Valley of the Dolls (Feist, ASCAP) ..... 33
There Is (Chevis, BMI) ..... 56
There Was a Time (Galo, BMI) ..... 61
To Each His Own (Paramount, ASCAP) ..... 94
To Give (The Reason I Live) (Saturday/Seasons' Four, BMI) ..... 30
Tomorrow (Alarm Clock, ASCAP) ..... 28
Try It (Blackwood, BMI) ..... 90
Two Little Kids (Jalynne, BMI) ..... 43
United (Razor Sharp/Blockbuster, BMI) ..... 78
Walk Away Renee (Twin Tone, BMI) ..... 71
We Can Fly (Akbestal/Luvlin, BMI) ..... 34
We're a Winner (Camad, BMI) ..... 36
Who Will Answer (Sunbary, ASCAP) ..... 69
Windy (Almo, BMI) ..... 76
Woman, Woman (Glaser, BMI) ..... 6
Words (Nemperor, BMI) ..... 46
Working Man's Prayer, A (Flower/Sark, BMI) ..... 74
You (Jobete, BMI) ..... 35
(You've Got) Personality & Chantilly Lace (Lloyd & Logan/Glad, BMI) ..... 100
Zabadak (Gallico, BMI) ..... 52


## BUBBLING UNDER THE HOT 100

101. I WAS MADE TO LOVE HER ........ King Curtis & His Kingpins, Atco 6547
102. BLESSED ARE THE LONELY ........ Robert Knight, Rising Sons 707
103. DO WHAT YOU GOTTA DO ........ Al Wilson, Soul City 761
104. JUST DROPPED IN ........ First Edition, Reprise 0655
105. WITHOUT LOVE (There Is Nothing) ........ Oscar Toney Jr., Bell 699
106. I SAY A LITTLE PRAYER ........ Sergio Mendes, Atlantic 2472
107. BIRDS OF A FEATHER ........ Joe South, Capitol 2060
108. LOVE EXPLOSION ........ Troy Keyes, ABC 11027
109. HERE COMES THE RAIN, BABY ........ Eddy Arnold, RCA Victor 47-9437
110. BREAK MY MIND ........ Bobby Wood, MGM 13797
111. KEEP THE BALL ROLLIN' ........ Al Hirt, RCA Victor 47-9417
112. GREEN GREEN GRASS OF HOME. Skitch Henderson & His Ork, Columbia 44333
113. DANCE TO THE MUSIC ........ Sly & Family Stone, Epic 10256
114. LOVE IS BLUE ........ Manny Kellem, His Ork & Chorus, Epic 10282
115. UNCHAIN MY HEART ........ Herbie Mann, A&M 896
116. RED, GREEN, YELLOW & BLUE ........ Dickie Lee, Atco 6546
117. WHAT CAN YOU DO WHEN YOU AIN'T GOT NOBODY ........ Soul Brothers Six, Atlantic 2456
118. WORLD OF OUR OWN ........ Sonny James, Capitol 2067
119. THANK YOU VERY MUCH ........ Scaffold, Bell 701
120. LOVE IS BLUE ........ Al Martino, Capitol 2102
121. HERE I AM ........ Righteous Brothers, Verve 10577
122. ODE TO OTIS REDDING ........ Mark Johnson, Diamond 237
123. A QUESTION OF TEMPERATURE ........ Balloon Farm, Laurie 3405
124. MR. SOUL SATISFACTION ........ Timmy Willis, Veep 1279
125. WHO AM I ........ Country Joe & the Fish, Vanguard 35061
126. DEAR DELILAH ........ Grapefruit, Equinox 70000
127. CAPTAIN OF YOUR SHIP ........ Reparata & the Delrons, Mala 589

Compiled from national retail sales and radio station airplay by the Music Popularity Dept. of Record Market Research, Billboard.

# Billboard HOT 100

**For Week Ending February 10, 1968**

★ STAR PERFORMER—Sides registering greatest proportionate upward progress this week.
● Record Industry Association of America seal of certification as million selling single.

| This Week | 1 Wk. Ago | 2 Wk. Ago | 3 Wk. Ago | TITLE Artist (Producer), Label & Number | Weeks On Chart |
|---|---|---|---|---|---|
| 1 (Billboard Award) | 7 | 18 | 47 | **LOVE IS BLUE** — Paul Mauriat, Philips 40495 | 6 |
| 2 | 1 | 3 | 5 | **GREEN TAMBOURINE** — Lemon Pipers (Paul Leka), Buddah 23 | |
| 3 | 4 | 7 | 16 | **SPOOKY** — Classics IV (Buddy Buie), Imperial 66259 | 8 |
| 4 | 2 | 1 | 1 | **JUDY IN DISGUISE (With Glasses)** — John Fred & His Playboy Band (J. Fred & A. Bernard), Paula 282 | 12 |
| 5 | 3 | 2 | 2 | **CHAIN OF FOOLS** — Aretha Franklin (Jerry Wexler), Atlantic 2464 | 10 |
| ★6 | 10 | 15 | 45 | **I WISH IT WOULD RAIN** — Temptations (Norman Whitfield), Gordy 7068 | 5 |
| ★7 | 9 | 17 | 22 | **GOIN' OUT OF MY HEAD/CAN'T TAKE MY EYES OFF YOU** — Lettermen (Kelly Gordon), Capitol 2054 | |
| 8 | 8 | 12 | 17 | **NOBODY BUT ME** — Human Beinz (Alexis de Azevedo), Capitol 5990 | 10 |
| 9 | 6 | 4 | 4 | **WOMAN, WOMAN** — Union Gap (Jerry Fuller), Columbia 44297 | 13 |
| 10 | 5 | 5 | 7 | **BEND ME, SHAPE ME** — American Breed (Bill Traut), Acta 811 | 11 |
| 11 | 11 | 11 | 13 | **SUSAN** — Buckinghams (James William Guercio), Columbia 44378 | 10 |
| 12 | 13 | 20 | 20 | **BABY, NOW THAT I'VE FOUND YOU** — Foundations (Tony Macauley), Uni 55038 | 8 |
| ★13 | 20 | 26 | 38 | **I WONDER WHAT SHE'S DOING TONIGHT** — Tommy Boyce & Bobby Hart (Tommy Boyce & Bobby Hart), A&M 893 | 8 |
| ★14 | 22 | 28 | 48 | **BOTTLE OF WINE** — Fireballs (Norman Petty), Atco 6491 | 7 |
| ★15 | 33 | 61 | 77 | **(Theme From) VALLEY OF THE DOLLS** — Dionne Warwick (Bacharach-David), Scepter 12203 | 4 |
| 16 | 16 | 16 | 21 | **ITCHYCOO PARK** — Small Faces (Steve Marriott & Ronnie Lane), Immediate 501 | 14 |
| 17 | 21 | 21 | 26 | **MY BABY MUST BE A MAGICIAN** — Marvelettes ("Smokey"), Tamla 54158 | 9 |
| 18 | 18 | 19 | 25 | **AM I THAT EASY TO FORGET** — Engelbert Humperdinck (Peter Sullivan), Parrot 40023 | 9 |
| 19 | 19 | 24 | 29 | **DARLIN'** — Beach Boys (Beach Boys), Capitol 2068 | 7 |
| 20 | 14 | 13 | 14 | **DIFFERENT DRUM** — Stone Poneys (Nick Venet), Capitol 2004 | 14 |
| 21 | 34 | 44 | 54 | **WE CAN FLY** — Cowsills (Bill & Bob Cowsill), MGM 13886 | 5 |
| 22 | 38 | 48 | 66 | **I CAN TAKE OR LEAVE YOUR LOVING** — Herman's Hermits (Mickie Most), MGM 13885 | 5 |
| ★23 | 28 | 29 | 41 | **TOMORROW** — Strawberry Alarm Clock (Frank Slay & Bill Holmes), Uni 55046 | 7 |
| 24 | 27 | 32 | 42 | **JUST AS MUCH AS EVER** — Bobby Vinton (Billy Sherrill), Epic 10266 | 7 |
| 25 | 26 | 35 | 37 | **SKIP A ROPE** — Henson Cargill (Don Law), Monument 1041 | 8 |
| ★26 | 32 | 39 | 49 | **SOME VELVET MORNING** — Nancy Sinatra & Lee Hazlewood (Lee Hazlewood), Reprise 0651 | |
| 27 | 36 | 47 | 62 | **WE'RE A WINNER** — Impressions (Johnny Pate), ABC 11022 | 7 |
| ★28 | 47 | 67 | — | **(Sittin' On) THE DOCK OF THE BAY** — Otis Redding (Steve Cropper), Volt 157 | 3 |
| 29 | 30 | 30 | 39 | **TO GIVE (The Reason I Live)** — Frankie Valli (Bob Crewe), Philips 40510 | 7 |
| 30 | 31 | 41 | 51 | **SUNDAY MORNIN'** — Spanky & Our Gang (Scharf-Dorough), Mercury 72765 | 6 |
| 31 | 12 | 6 | 3 | **HELLO GOODBYE** — Beatles (George Martin), Capitol 2056 | 11 |
| ★32 | 46 | 64 | 79 | **WORDS** — Bee Gees (Robert Stigwood & the Bee Gees), Atco 6548 | 4 |
| 33 | 25 | 22 | 27 | **LOVE POWER** — Sandpebbles (Teddy Vann), Calla 141 | 12 |
| 34 | 17 | 14 | 8 | **I SECOND THAT EMOTION** — Smokey Robinson & Miracles ("Smokey" A. Cleveland), Tamla 54159 | 15 |
| 35 | 35 | 45 | 55 | **YOU** — Marvin Gaye (I. Hunter), Tamla 54160 | 5 |
| 36 | 29 | 10 | 10 | **IF I COULD BUILD MY WHOLE WORLD AROUND YOU** — Marvin Gaye & Tammi Terrell (Fuqua, Bristol), Tamla 54161 | 10 |
| ★37 | 58 | 77 | — | **SIMON SAYS** — 1910 Fruitgum Co. (J. Katz/J. Kasenetz/E. Chiprut), Buddah 24 | |
| ★38 | 62 | — | — | **EVERYTHING THAT TOUCHES YOU** — Association (Bones Howe), Warner Bros. 7163 | |
| 39 | 23 | 23 | 23 | **TELL MAMA** — Etta James (Rick Hall), Cadet 5578 | 14 |
| ★40 | 50 | 60 | 80 | **STRAWBERRY SHORTCAKE** — Jay & The Techniques (Jerry Ross), Smash 2142 | 4 |
| 41 | 41 | 51 | 58 | **BACK UP TRAIN** — Al Greene & Soul Mates (Rodgers & James), Hot Line 15000 | 10 |
| 42 | 39 | 37 | 15 | **MONTEREY** — Eric Burdon & the Animals (Tom Wilson), MGM 13868 | 9 |
| 43 | 15 | 9 | 9 | **I HEARD IT THROUGH THE GRAPEVINE** — Gladys Knight & the Pips (N. Whitfield), Soul 35039 | 17 |
| 44 | 60 | 72 | — | **I THANK YOU** — Sam & Dave (Isaac Hayes & David Porter), Stax 242 | 3 |
| 45 | 55 | 56 | 67 | **BORN FREE** — Hesitations (GWP), Kapp 878 | 6 |
| ★46 | 71 | — | — | **WALK AWAY RENEE** — Four Tops (Holland & Dozier), Motown 1119 | 2 |
| 47 | 61 | 65 | 81 | **THERE WAS A TIME** — James Brown & His Famous Flames (James Brown), King 6144 | |
| 48 | 56 | 66 | 82 | **THERE IS** — Dells (B. Miller), Cadet 5590 | 4 |
| 49 | 49 | 50 | 60 | **NO SAD SONGS** — Joe Simon (J. R. Ent.), Sound Stage 7 2602 | 6 |
| 50 | 67 | 83 | — | **GUITAR MAN** — Elvis Presley, RCA Victor 47-9425 | |
| 51 | 53 | 63 | 69 | **CARMEN** — Herb Alpert & the Tijuana Brass, A&M 890 | 5 |
| 52 | 52 | 55 | 65 | **ZABADAK** — Dave Dee, Dozy, Beaky, Mick & Tich (Steve Rowland), Imperial 66270 | 6 |
| 53 | 64 | 69 | 73 | **SUNSHINE OF YOUR LOVE** — Cream (Felix Pappalardi), Atco 6544 | |
| 54 | 63 | 78 | 78 | **MISSION: IMPOSSIBLE** — Lalo Schifrin (Tom Mack), Dot 17059 | 6 |
| 55 | 54 | 54 | 32 | **BEST OF BOTH WORLDS** — Lulu (Mickie Most), Epic 10260 | 9 |
| 56 | 97 | — | — | **CARPET MAN** — 5th Dimension (Bones Howe), Soul City 762 | 2 |
| 57 | 48 | 49 | 59 | **MONEY** — Lovin' Spoonful (Lovin' Spoonful & Joe Wissert), Kama Sutra 241 | |
| 58 | 66 | 81 | — | **GET OUT NOW** — Tommy James & the Shondells (Big Kabanna), Roulette 7000 | 3 |
| 59 | 68 | 70 | 85 | **HEY LITTLE ONE** — Glen Campbell (Al De Lory), Capitol 2076 | 4 |
| 60 | 40 | 33 | 33 | **EXPLOSION IN MY SOUL** — Soul Survivors (Gamble-Huff), Crimson 1012 | 8 |
| 61 | 59 | 59 | 70 | **OH, HOW IT HURTS** — Barbara Mason (J. Bishop), Arctic 137 | 8 |
| 62 | 51 | 52 | 64 | **NEW ORLEANS** — Neil Diamond (Jeff Barry & Ellie Greenwich), Bang 554 | 6 |
| ★63 | — | — | — | **JUST DROPPED IN (To See What Condition My Condition Was In)** — First Edition (Mike Post), Reprise 0655 | 1 |
| 64 | 37 | 25 | 30 | **SHE'S A RAINBOW** — Rolling Stones (Rolling Stones), London 906 | 7 |
| 65 | 44 | 34 | 44 | **THE LESSON** — Vikki Carr (Tommy Oliver), Liberty 56012 | 8 |
| ★66 | 92 | — | — | **LA-LA MEANS I LOVE YOU** — Delfonics (Stan & Bell), Philly Groove 150 | 2 |
| ★67 | — | — | — | **LOOK, HERE COMES THE SUN** — Sunshine Company (Joe Saraceno), Imperial 66280 | 1 |
| ★68 | — | — | — | **THE END OF OUR ROAD** — Gladys Knight & the Pips (M. Whitfield), Soul 35042 | 1 |
| 69 | 84 | 92 | — | **CAB DRIVER** — Mills Brothers (Charles R. Grean & Tom Mack), Dot 17041 | 3 |
| 70 | 80 | 80 | 83 | **MAN NEEDS A WOMAN** — James Carr (Quinton Claunch & Rudolph Russell), Goldwax 332 | 6 |
| 71 | 88 | — | — | **BURNING SPEAR** — Soulful Strings (Esmond Edwards), Cadet 5576 | 2 |
| ★72 | — | — | — | **DANCE TO THE MUSIC** — Sly & the Family Stone (Sly Stone), Epic 10256 | 1 |
| 73 | — | — | — | **LOVE IS BLUE** — Al Martino (Voyle Gilmore), Capitol 2102 | 1 |
| 74 | 74 | 74 | 74 | **WORKING MAN'S PRAYER** — Arthur Prysock (Hy Weiss), Verve 10574 | |
| 75 | 73 | 73 | 75 | **DO UNTO ME** — James & Bobby Purify (Papa Don), Bell 700 | 5 |
| 76 | — | — | — | **TOO MUCH TALK** — Paul Revere & the Raiders (Mark Lindsay), Columbia 44444 | 1 |
| 77 | 83 | 88 | 91 | **LOOKING FOR A FOX** — Clarence Carter (Rick Hall), Atlantic 2461 | 4 |
| 78 | 78 | 79 | 90 | **UNITED** — Music Makers (Gamble-Huff), Gamble 210 | 7 |
| 79 | 89 | 89 | 99 | **FUNKY WAY** — Calvin Arnold (Cooper, Paul & Shelby), Venture 605 | 5 |
| 80 | 81 | 84 | — | **A MILLION TO ONE** — Five Stairsteps & Cubie (Clarence Burke, Jr.), Buddah 26 | |
| 81 | 82 | 82 | — | **STOP** — Howard Tate (Jerry Ragovoy), Verve 10573 | 3 |
| 82 | 90 | — | — | **HERE COMES THE RAIN, BABY** — Eddy Arnold (Chet Atkins), RCA Victor 47-9437 | |
| 83 | 90 | — | — | **TRY IT** — Ohio Express (J. Katz & J. Kasenetz), Cameo 2001 | 2 |
| 84 | — | — | — | **THANK U VERY MUCH** — Scaffold (Tony Palmer), Bell 701 | 1 |
| 85 | 85 | 85 | — | **MALAYISHA** — Miriam Makeba (Jerry Ragovoy), Reprise 0654 | 3 |
| 86 | 87 | — | — | **COLD FEET** — Albert King (Al Jackson Jr.), Stax 241 | 2 |
| 87 | 100 | — | — | **(You've Got) PERSONALITY & CHANTILLY LACE** — Mitch Ryder (Bob Crewe), Dynovoice 905 | 2 |
| ★88 | 94 | 95 | 96 | **TO EACH HIS OWN** — Frankie Laine (Bob Thiele), ABC 11032 | 4 |
| 89 | — | — | — | **I'M GONNA MAKE YOU LOVE ME** — Madeline Bell (Johnny Franz), Philips 40517 | 1 |
| 90 | — | — | — | **MAYBE JUST TODAY** — Bobby Vee & the Strangers (Dallas Smith), Liberty 56014 | 1 |
| 91 | — | 76 | — | **I WAS MADE TO LOVE HER** — King Curtis & His Kingpins (Tom Dowd & Tommy Coghill), Atco 6547 | 5 |
| 92 | — | — | — | **WHERE IS MY MIND** — Vanilla Fudge (Shadow Morton), Atco 6554 | 1 |
| 93 | — | — | — | **YOU DON'T HAVE TO SAY YOU LOVE ME** — Four Sonics (Shelley Haims), Sport 110 | 1 |
| 94 | — | — | — | **LOVEY DOVEY** — Otis & Carla (Prod. by Staff), Stax 244 | 1 |
| 95 | 95 | — | — | **PEOPLE WORLD** — Jim & Jean (Jimmy Wisner), Verve Forecast 5073 | 2 |
| 96 | 99 | 99 | — | **NO ONE KNOWS** — Every Mother's Son (Wes Farrell), MGM 13887 | 3 |
| 97 | 98 | — | — | **IT'S NOT EASY** — Will-O-Bees (Bill Traut), Date 1583 | |
| 98 | — | — | — | **MEN ARE GETTIN' SCARCE** — Joe Tex (Buddy Killen), Dial 4069 | 1 |
| 99 | — | — | — | **GOT WHAT YOU NEED** — Fantastic Johnny C (Jesse James), Phil L.A. of Soul 309 | |
| 100 | — | — | — | **GENTLE ON MY MIND** — Patti Page (Jack Gold), Columbia 44353 | 1 |

## BUBBLING UNDER THE HOT 100

101. LOVE IS BLUE .......... Manny Kellem, His Ork & Chorus, Epic 10282
102. BALLAD OF BONNIE & CLYDE .......... Georgie Fame, Epic 10283
103. DO WHAT YOU GOTTA DO .......... Al Wilson, Soul City 707
105. FOGGY MOUNTAIN BREAKDOWN .......... Flatt & Scruggs, Columbia 44380/Mercury 72739
105. FOGGY MOUNTAIN BREAKDOWN .......... Flatt & Scruggs, Mercury 72739
106. BIRDS OF A FEATHER .......... Joe South, Capitol 2060
107. KEEP THE BALL ROLLING .......... Al Hirt, RCA Victor 47-9417
108. LOVE EXPLOSION .......... Troy Keyes, ABC 11027
109. A QUESTION OF TEMPERATURE .......... Balloon Farm, Laurie 3405
110. RED, GREEN, YELLOW & BLUE .......... Dickie Lee, Atco 6546
111. GREEN GREEN GRASS OF HOME .......... Skitch Henderson & His Ork, Columbia 44333
112. 1941 .......... Tom Northcott, Warner Bros. 7160
113. DEAR DELILAH .......... Grapefruit, Equinox 70000
114. UNCHAIN MY HEART .......... Herbie Mann, A&M 896
115. LIFE IS BUT A MOMENT .......... Eydie Gorme, Columbia 44299
116. WHO AM I .......... Country Joe & the Fish, Vanguard 35061
117. YOU HAVEN'T SEEN MY LOVE .......... Ones, Motown 1117
118. LESSON, The (Alfa, ASCAP) .......... 
119. YOU'VE GOT TO BE LOVED .......... Montanas, Independence 83
120. MR. SOUL SATISFACTION .......... Timmy Willis, Veep 1279
121. MUSIC, MUSIC, MUSIC .......... Happenings, B.T. Puppy 538
122. NIGHTS IN WHITE SATIN .......... Moody Blues, Deram 85023
123. WHAT YOU WANT .......... Music Explosion, Laurie 3429
124. I SAY LOVE .......... Royal Guardsmen, Laurie 3428
125. DOTTIE I LIKE IT .......... Tommy Roe, ABC 11039

Compiled from national retail sales and radio station airplay by the Music Popularity Dept. of Record Market Research, Billboard.

# Billboard HOT 100

**FOR WEEK ENDING FEBRUARY 17, 1968**

★ STAR PERFORMER—Sides registering greatest proportionate upward progress this week.
⓼ Record Industry Association of America seal of certification as million selling single.

| This Week | Wk. Ago | 2 Wks. Ago | 3 Wks. Ago | TITLE, Artist (Producer), Label & Number | Weeks On Chart |
|---|---|---|---|---|---|
| 1 | 1 | 7 | 18 | **LOVE IS BLUE** — Paul Mauriat, Philips 40495 (Billboard Award) | 7 |
| 2 | 2 | 1 | 3 | **GREEN TAMBOURINE** — Lemon Pipers (Paul Leka), Buddah 23 | 10 |
| 3 | 3 | 4 | 7 | **SPOOKY** — Classics IV (Buddy Buie), Imperial 66259 | 9 |
| 4 | 6 | 10 | 15 | **I WISH IT WOULD RAIN** — Temptations (Norman Whitfield), Gordy 7068 | 6 |
| 5 | 15 | 33 | 61 | **(Theme From) THE VALLEY OF THE DOLLS** — Dionne Warwick (Bacharach-David), Scepter 12203 | 4 |
| 6 | 28 | 47 | 67 | **(Sittin' On) THE DOCK OF THE BAY** — Otis Redding (Steve Cropper), Volt 157 | 4 |
| 7 | 7 | 9 | 17 | **GOIN' OUT OF MY HEAD / CAN'T TAKE MY EYES OFF YOU** — Lettermen (Kelly Gordon), Capitol 2054 | 11 |
| 8 | 8 | 8 | 12 | **NOBODY BUT ME** — Human Beinz (Alexis de Azevedo), Capitol 5990 | 11 |
| 9 | 4 | 2 | 1 | **JUDY IN DISGUISE (With Glasses)** — John Fred & His Playboy Band (J. Fred & A. Bernard), Paula 282 | 13 |
| 10 | 13 | 20 | 26 | **I WONDER WHAT SHE'S DOING TONIGHT** — Tommy Boyce & Bobby Hart (Tommy Boyce & Bobby Hart), A&M 893 | 9 |
| 11 | 12 | 13 | 20 | **BABY, NOW THAT I'VE FOUND YOU** — Foundations (Tony Macaulay), Uni 55038 | 9 |
| 12 | 9 | 6 | 4 | **WOMAN, WOMAN** — Union Gap (Jerry Fuller), Columbia 44297 | 14 |
| 13 | 10 | 5 | 5 | **BEND ME, SHAPE ME** — American Breed (Bill Traut), Acta 811 | 12 |
| 14 | 14 | 22 | 28 | **BOTTLE OF WINE** — Fireballs (Norman Petty), Atco 6491 | 8 |
| 15 | 27 | 36 | 47 | **WE'RE A WINNER** — Impressions (Johnny Pate), ABC 11022 | 5 |
| 16 | 5 | 3 | 2 | **CHAIN OF FOOLS** — Aretha Franklin (Jerry Wexler), Atlantic 2464 | 11 |
| 17 | 37 | 58 | 77 | **SIMON SAYS** — 1910 Fruitgum Co. (J. Katz/J. Kasenetz/E. Chiprut), Buddah 24 | 4 |
| 18 | 11 | 11 | 11 | **SUSAN** — Buckinghams (James William Guercio), Columbia 44378 | 8 |
| 19 | 17 | 21 | 21 | **MY BABY MUST BE A MAGICIAN** — Marvelettes ("Smokey"), Tamla 54158 | 10 |
| 20 | 48 | 56 | 66 | **THERE IS** — Dells (B. Miller), Cadet 5590 | 5 |
| 21 | 21 | 34 | 44 | **WE CAN FLY** — Cowsills (Bill & Bob Cowsill), MGM 13886 | 6 |
| 22 | 22 | 38 | 48 | **I CAN TAKE OR LEAVE YOUR LOVING** — Herman's Hermits (Mickie Most), MGM 13885 | 6 |
| 23 | 23 | 28 | 29 | **TOMORROW** — Strawberry Alarm Clock (Frank Slay & Bill Holmes), Uni 55046 | 8 |
| 24 | 20 | 14 | 13 | **DIFFERENT DRUM** — Stone Poneys (Nick Venet), Capitol 2004 | 15 |
| 25 | 25 | 26 | 35 | **SKIP A ROPE** — Henson Cargill (Don Law), Monument 1041 | 9 |
| 26 | 26 | 32 | 39 | **SOME VELVET MORNING** — Nancy Sinatra & Lee Hazlewood (Lee Hazlewood), Reprise 0651 | 7 |
| 27 | 16 | 16 | 16 | **ITCHYCOO PARK** — Small Faces (Steve Marriott & Ronnie Lane), Immediate 501 | 15 |
| 28 | 18 | 18 | 19 | **AM I THAT EASY TO FORGET** — Engelbert Humperdinck (Peter Sullivan), Parrot 40023 | 10 |
| 29 | 44 | 60 | 72 | **I THANK YOU** — Sam & Dave (Isaac Hayes & David Porter), Stax 242 | 4 |
| 30 | 30 | 31 | 41 | **SUNDAY MORNIN'** — Spanky & Our Gang (Scharf-Dorough), Mercury 72765 | 7 |
| 31 | 38 | 62 | — | **EVERYTHING THAT TOUCHES YOU** — Association (Bones Howe), Warner Bros. 7163 | 3 |
| 32 | 32 | 46 | 64 | **WORDS** — Bee Gees (Robert Stigwood & the Bee Gees), Atco 6548 | 5 |
| 33 | 19 | 19 | 24 | **DARLIN'** — Beach Boys (Beach Boys), Capitol 2068 | 8 |
| 34 | 35 | 35 | 45 | **YOU** — Marvin Gaye (I. Hunter), Tamla 54160 | 6 |
| 35 | 24 | 27 | 32 | **JUST AS MUCH AS EVER** — Bobby Vinton (Billy Sherrill), Epic 10266 | 8 |
| 36 | 47 | 61 | 65 | **THERE WAS A TIME** — James Brown & His Famous Flames (James Brown), King 6144 | 4 |
| 37 | 46 | 71 | — | **WALK AWAY RENEE** — Four Tops (Holland & Dozier), Motown 1119 | 3 |
| 38 | 45 | 55 | 56 | **BORN FREE** — Hesitations (GWP), Kapp 878 | 7 |
| 39 | 40 | 50 | 60 | **STRAWBERRY SHORTCAKE** — Jay & The Techniques (Jerry Ross), Smash 2142 | 5 |
| 40 | 68 | — | — | **THE END OF OUR ROAD** — Gladys Knight and the Pips (N. Whitfield), Soul 35042 | 2 |
| 41 | 41 | 41 | 51 | **BACK UP TRAIN** — Al Greene & Soul Mate's (Rodgers & James), Hot Line 15000 | 11 |
| 42 | 29 | 30 | 30 | **TO GIVE (The Reason I Live)** — Frankie Valli (Bob Crewe), Philips 40510 | 8 |
| 43 | 63 | — | — | **JUST DROPPED IN (To See What Condition My Condition Was In)** — First Edition (Mike Post), Reprise 0655 | 2 |
| 44 | 50 | 67 | 83 | **GUITAR MAN** — Elvis Presley, RCA Victor 47-9425 | 4 |
| 45 | 53 | 64 | 69 | **SUNSHINE OF YOUR LOVE** — Cream (Felix Pappalardi), Atco 6544 | 6 |
| 46 | 54 | 63 | 78 | **MISSION: IMPOSSIBLE** — Lalo Schifrin (Tom Mack), Dot 17059 | 7 |
| 47 | 56 | 97 | — | **CARPET MAN** — 5th Dimension (Bones Howe), Soul City 762 | 3 |
| 48 | 58 | 66 | 81 | **GET OUT NOW** — Tommy James & the Shondells (Big Kahoona), Roulette 7000 | 4 |
| 49 | 76 | — | — | **TOO MUCH TALK** — Paul Revere & the Raiders (Mark Lindsay), Columbia 44444 | 2 |
| 50 | 66 | 92 | — | **LA-LA MEANS I LOVE YOU** — Delfonics (Stan & Bell), Philly Groove 150 | 3 |
| 51 | 69 | 84 | 92 | **CAB DRIVER** — Mills Brothers (Charles R. Grean & Paul Cohen), Dot 17041 | 4 |
| 52 | 49 | 49 | 50 | **NO SAD SONGS** — Joe Simon (J. R. Ent.), Sound Stage 7 2602 | 7 |
| 53 | 98 | — | — | **MEN ARE GETTIN' SCARCE** — Joe Tex (Buddy Killen), Dial 4069 | 2 |
| 54 | 51 | 53 | 63 | **CARMEN** — Herb Alpert & the Tijuana Brass, A&M 890 | 6 |
| 55 | 55 | 54 | 54 | **BEST OF BOTH WORLDS** — Lulu (Mickie Most), Epic 10260 | 10 |
| 56 | 67 | — | — | **LOOK, HERE COMES THE SUN** — Sunshine Company (Joe Saraceno), Imperial 66280 | 2 |
| 57 | 59 | 68 | 70 | **HEY LITTLE ONE** — Glen Campbell (Al De Lory), Capitol 2076 | 5 |
| 58 | 72 | — | — | **DANCE TO THE MUSIC** — Sly & the Family Stone (Sly Stone), Epic 10256 | 2 |
| 59 | 99 | — | — | **GOT WHAT YOU NEED** — Fantastic Johnny C (Jesse James), Phil L.A. of Soul 309 | 2 |
| 60 | 89 | — | — | **I'M GONNA MAKE YOU LOVE ME** — Madeline Bell (Johnny Franz), Philips 40517 | 2 |
| 61 | 61 | 59 | 59 | **OH, HOW IT HURTS** — Barbara Mason (J. Hill), Arctic 137 | 9 |
| 62 | — | — | — | **COUNTRY GIRL—CITY MAN** — Billy Vera & Judy Clay (Chip Taylor & Daryll), Atlantic 2480 | 1 |
| 63 | — | — | — | **THE BALLAD OF BONNIE AND CLYDE** — Georgie Fame (Mannoy Kellem), Epic 10283 | 1 |
| 64 | 71 | 88 | — | **BURNING SPEAR** — Soulful Strings (Esmond Edwards), Cadet 5576 | 3 |
| 65 | 70 | 80 | 80 | **MAN NEEDS A WOMAN** — James Carr (Quinton Claunch & Rudolph Russell), Goldwax 332 | 7 |
| 66 | 77 | 83 | 88 | **LOOKING FOR A FOX** — Clarence Carter (Rick Hall), Atlantic 2461 | 5 |
| 67 | 86 | 87 | — | **COLD FEET** — Albert King (Al Jackson Jr.), Stax 241 | 3 |
| 68 | 90 | — | — | **MAYBE JUST TODAY** — Bobby Vee & the Strangers (Dallas Smith), Liberty 56014 | 2 |
| 69 | 73 | — | — | **LOVE IS BLUE** — Al Martino (Voyle Gilmore), Capitol 2102 | 2 |
| 70 | 80 | 81 | 84 | **A MILLION TO ONE** — Five Stairsteps & Cubie (Clarence Burke, Jr.), Buddah 26 | 4 |
| 71 | — | — | — | **FOR YOUR PRECIOUS LOVE** — Jackie Wilson & Count Basie, (Nat Tarnopo & Teddy Reig), Brunswick | 1 |
| 72 | 79 | 89 | 89 | **FUNKY WAY** — Calvin Arnold (Cooper, Paul & Shelby), Venture 605 | 6 |
| 73 | — | — | — | **IN THE MIDNIGHT HOUR** — Mirettes (Jerry Goldstein), Revue 11004 | 1 |
| 74 | — | — | — | **THIS IS THE THANKS I GET** — Bartons Lynn (Huey P. Meaux), Atlantic 2450 | 1 |
| 75 | 75 | 73 | 73 | **DO UNTO ME** — James & Bobby Purify (Papa Don), Bell 700 | 6 |
| 76 | 81 | 82 | 82 | **STOP** — Howard Tate (Jerry Ragovoy), Verve 10573 | 4 |
| 77 | 82 | — | — | **HERE COMES THE RAIN, BABY** — Eddy Arnold (Chet Atkins), RCA Victor 47-9437 | 2 |
| 78 | — | — | — | **JEALOUS LOVE** — Wilson Pickett (Tom Dowd & Tommy Cogbill), Atlantic 2484 | 1 |
| 79 | — | — | — | **NIGHT FO' LAST** — Shorty Long (Holland & Dozier), Soul 35040 | 1 |
| 80 | — | — | — | **I SAY LOVE** — Royal Guardsmen (Gernhard Ent.), Laurie 3428 | 1 |
| 81 | — | — | — | **UNCHAIN MY HEART** — Herbie Mann (Creed Taylor), A&M 896 | 1 |
| 82 | — | — | — | **KISS ME GOODBYE** — Petula Clark (Tony Hatch), Warner Bros. 7170 | 1 |
| 83 | 84 | — | — | **THANK U VERY MUCH** — Scaffold (Tony Palmer), Bell 701 | 2 |
| 84 | — | — | — | **PLAYBOY** — Gene & Debbe (Don Gantry), 5006 | 1 |
| 85 | 88 | 94 | 95 | **TO EACH HIS OWN** — Frankie Laine (Bob Thiele), ABC 11032 | 5 |
| 86 | 91 | — | — | **I WAS MADE TO LOVE HER** — King Curtis & His Kingpins (Tom Dowd & Tommy Cogbill), Atco 6547 | 6 |
| 87 | 87 | 100 | — | **(You've Got) PERSONALITY & CHANTILLY LACE** — Mitch Ryder (Bob Crewe), Dynovoice 905 | 3 |
| 88 | 94 | — | — | **LOVEY DOVEY** — Otis & Carla (Prod. by Staff), Stax 244 | 2 |
| 89 | 93 | — | — | **YOU DON'T HAVE TO SAY YOU LOVE ME** — Four Sonics (Shelley Haims), Sport 110 | 2 |
| 90 | 92 | — | — | **WHERE IS MY MIND** — Vanilla Fudge (Shadow Morton), Atco 6554 | 2 |
| 91 | — | — | — | **LICKIN' STICK** — George Torrence & Naturals (T.M.S.), Shout 224 | 1 |
| 92 | — | — | — | **IF YOU EVER LEAVE ME** — Jack Jones (Ernie Altschuler), RCA Victor 47-9441 | 1 |
| 93 | — | — | — | **LOVE EXPLOSIONS** — Troy Keyes (George Kerr), ABC 11027 | 1 |
| 94 | 95 | 95 | — | **PEOPLE WORLD** — Jim & Jean (Jimmy Wisner), Verve/Forecast 5073 | 3 |
| 95 | 97 | 98 | — | **IT'S NOT EASY** — Will-O-Bees (Bill Traut), Date 1583 | 3 |
| 96 | 100 | — | — | **GENTLE ON MY MIND** — Patti Page (Jack Gold), Columbia 44353 | 2 |
| 97 | — | — | — | **THE GOOD, THE BAD AND THE UGLY** — Hugo Montenegro, His Ork and Chorus (Neely Plumb), RCA Victor 9423 | 1 |
| 98 | — | — | — | **I'M HYPNOTIZED** — Anthony & the Imperials (Teddy Randazzo), Veep 1278 | 1 |
| 99 | — | — | — | **MUSIC, MUSIC, MUSIC** — Happenings (Tokens), B. T. Puppy 538 | 1 |
| 100 | — | — | — | **SUDDENLY YOU LOVE ME** — Tremeloes (Mike Smith), Epic 10293 | 1 |

## BUBBLING UNDER THE HOT 100

101. LOVE IS BLUE — Manny Kellem, His Ork & Chorus, Epic 10282
102. DO WHAT YOU GOTTA DO — Al Wilson, Soul City 707
103. SOMETHING I'LL REMEMBER — Sandy Posey, MGM 13892
104. NIGHTS IN WHITE SATIN — Moody Blues, Deram 85023
105. FOGGY MOUNTAIN BREAKDOWN — Flatt & Scruggs, Columbia 44380/Mercury 72739
106. BIRDS OF A FEATHER — Joe South, Capitol 2060
107. KEEP THE BALL ROLLIN' — Al Hirt, RCA Victor 9-9417
108. RED, GREEN, YELLOW & BLUE — Dickie Lee, Atco 6545
109. QUESTION OF TEMPERATURE — Balloon Farm, Laurie 3405
110. GREEN, GREEN GRASS OF HOME — Skitch Henderson, Columbia 44353
111. 1941 — Tom Northcott, Warner Bros. 7160
112. DARLING TAKE ME BACK — Lenny Welch, Mercury 72777
113. DEAR DELILAH — Grapefruit, Equinox 70800
114. WHO AM I — Country Joe & the Fish, Vanguard 35061
115. DOTTIE I LIKE IT — Tommy Roe, ABC 11039
116. LOVE IS ALL AROUND — Troggs, Fontana 1607
117. YOU'VE GOT TO BE LOVED — Montanas, Independence 84
118. SOUL COAXIN' (Ame Caline) — Raymond LeFevre, 4 Corners of the World 141
119. WHAT YOU WANT — Music Explosion, Laurie 3429
120. MR. SOUL SATISFACTION — Timmy Willie, Veep 1279
121. SON OF HICKORY HOLLER'S TRAMP — O. C. Smith, Columbia 44425
122. MY ANCESTORS — Lou Rawls, Capitol 2064
123. SUMMERTIME BLUES — Blue Cheer, Philips 40516

# Billboard HOT 100

FOR WEEK ENDING FEBRUARY 24, 1968

★ STAR PERFORMER—Sides registering greatest proportionate upward progress this week.

Record Industry Association of America seal of certification as million selling single.

| This Week | 1 Wk. Ago | 2 Wks. Ago | 3 Wks. Ago | TITLE | Artist (Producer), Label & Number | Weeks On Chart |
|---|---|---|---|---|---|---|
| 1 (Billboard Award) | 1 | 1 | 7 | LOVE IS BLUE | Paul Mauriat, Philips 40495 | 8 |
| ★2 | 5 | 15 | 33 | (Theme From) THE VALLEY OF THE DOLLS | Dionne Warwick (Bacharach-David), Scepter 12203 | 6 |
| 3 | 3 | 3 | 4 | SPOOKY | Classics IV (Buddy Buie), Imperial 66259 | 10 |
| 4 | 4 | 6 | 10 | I WISH IT WOULD RAIN | Temptations (Norman Whitfield), Gordy 7068 | 7 |
| ★5 | 6 | 28 | 47 | (Sittin' On) THE DOCK OF THE BAY | Otis Redding (Steve Cropper), Volt 157 | 5 |
| ★6 | 17 | 37 | 58 | SIMON SAYS | 1910 Fruitgum Co. (J. Katz/J. Kasenetz/E. Chiprut), Buddah 24 | 5 |
| 7 | 2 | 2 | 1 | GREEN TAMBOURINE | Lemon Pipers (Paul Leka), Buddah 23 | 11 |
| ★8 | 10 | 13 | 20 | I WONDER WHAT SHE'S DOING TONIGHT | Tommy Boyce & Bobby Hart (Tommy Boyce & Bobby Hart), A&M 893 | 10 |
| 9 | 7 | 7 | 9 | GOIN' OUT OF MY HEAD/CAN'T TAKE MY EYES OFF YOU | Lettermen (Kelly Gordon), Capitol 2054 | 12 |
| 10 | 8 | 8 | 8 | NOBODY BUT ME | Human Beinz (Alexis de Azevedo), Capitol 5990 | 12 |
| 11 | 11 | 12 | 13 | BABY, NOW THAT I'VE FOUND YOU | Foundations (Tony Macaulay), Uni 55038 | 10 |
| ★12 | 14 | 14 | 22 | BOTTLE OF WINE | Fireballs (Norman Petty), Atco 6491 | 9 |
| 13 | 9 | 4 | 2 | JUDY IN DISGUISE (With Glasses) | John Fred & His Playboy Band (J. Fred & A. Bernard), Paula 282 | 14 |
| ★14 | 15 | 27 | 36 | WE'RE A WINNER | Impressions (Johnny Pate), ABC 11022 | 9 |
| ★15 | 31 | 38 | 62 | EVERYTHING THAT TOUCHES YOU | Association (Bones Howe), Warner Bros. 7163 | 4 |
| ★16 | 32 | 32 | 46 | WORDS | Bee Gees (Robert Stigwood & the Bee Gees), Atco 6548 | 6 |
| 17 | 12 | 9 | 6 | WOMAN, WOMAN | Union Gap (Jerry Fuller), Columbia 44297 | 15 |
| 18 | 13 | 10 | 5 | BEND ME, SHAPE ME | American Breed (Bill Traut), Acta 811 | 13 |
| ★19 | 37 | 46 | 71 | WALK AWAY RENEE | Four Tops (Holland & Dozier), Motown 1119 | 4 |
| ★20 | 20 | 48 | 56 | THERE IS | Dells (B. Miller), Cadet 5590 | 6 |
| ★21 | 43 | 63 | — | JUST DROPPED IN (To See What Condition My Condition Was In) | First Edition (Mike Post), Reprise 0655 | 3 |
| 22 | 22 | 22 | 38 | I CAN TAKE OR LEAVE YOUR LOVING | Herman's Hermits (Mickie Most), MGM 13885 | 7 |
| 23 | 21 | 21 | 34 | WE CAN FLY | Cowsills (Bill & Bob Cowsill), MGM 13886 | 7 |
| ★24 | 29 | 44 | 60 | I THANK YOU | Sam & Dave (Isaac Hayes & David Porter), Stax 242 | 5 |
| 25 | 18 | 11 | 11 | SUSAN | Buckinghams (James William Guercio), Columbia 44378 | 12 |
| 26 | 25 | 25 | 26 | SKIP A ROPE | Henson Cargill (Don Law), Monument 1041 | 10 |
| 27 | 27 | 16 | 16 | ITCHYCOO PARK | Small Faces (Steve Marriott & Ronnie Lane), Immediate 501 | 16 |
| 28 | 16 | 5 | 3 | CHAIN OF FOOLS | Aretha Franklin (Jerry Wexler), Atlantic 2464 | 12 |
| 29 | 24 | 20 | 14 | DIFFERENT DRUM | Stone Poneys (Nick Venet), Capitol 2004 | 16 |
| ★30 | 40 | 68 | — | THE END OF OUR ROAD | Gladys Knight & the Pips (M. Whitfield), Soul 35042 | 3 |
| 31 | 30 | 30 | 31 | SUNDAY MORNIN' | Spanky & Our Gang (Scharf-Dorough), Mercury 72765 | 8 |
| 32 | 23 | 23 | 28 | TOMORROW | Strawberry Alarm Clock (Frank Slay & Bill Holmes), Uni 55046 | 9 |
| 33 | 19 | 17 | 21 | MY BABY MUST BE A MAGICIAN | Marvelettes ("Smokey"), Tamla 54158 | 11 |
| ★34 | 49 | 76 | — | TOO MUCH TALK | Paul Revere & the Raiders (Mark Lindsay), Columbia 44444 | 3 |
| ★35 | 50 | 66 | 92 | LA-LA MEANS I LOVE YOU | Delfonics (Stan & Bell), Philly Groove 150 | 4 |
| 36 | 36 | 47 | 61 | THERE WAS A TIME | James Brown & His Famous Flames (James Brown), King 6144 | 6 |
| ★37 | 45 | 53 | 64 | SUNSHINE OF YOUR LOVE | Cream (Felix Pappalardi), Atco 6544 | 7 |
| 38 | 38 | 45 | 55 | BORN FREE | Hesitations (GWP), Kapp 878 | 8 |
| 39 | 26 | 26 | 32 | SOME VELVET MORNING | Nancy Sinatra & Lee Hazlewood (Lee Hazlewood), Reprise 0651 | 8 |
| 40 | 47 | 56 | 97 | CARPET MAN | 5th Dimension (Bones Howe), Soul City 762 | 4 |
| ★41 | 58 | 72 | — | DANCE TO THE MUSIC | Sly & the Family Stone (Sly Stone), Epic 10256 | 3 |
| ★42 | 46 | 54 | 63 | MISSION: IMPOSSIBLE | Lalo Schifrin (Tom Mack), Dot 17059 | 8 |
| 43 | 44 | 50 | 67 | GUITAR MAN | Elvis Presley, RCA Victor 47-9425 | 5 |
| ★44 | 53 | 98 | — | MEN ARE GETTIN' SCARCE | Joe Tex (Buddy Killen), Dial 4069 | 3 |
| 45 | 39 | 40 | 50 | STRAWBERRY SHORTCAKE | Jay & the Techniques (Jerry Ross), Smash 2142 | 6 |
| 46 | 41 | 41 | 41 | BACK UP TRAIN | Al Greene & Soul Mates (Rodgers & James), Hot Line 15000 | 12 |
| 47 | 34 | 35 | 35 | YOU | Marvin Gaye (I. Hunter), Tamla 54160 | 7 |
| 48 | 48 | 58 | 66 | GET OUT NOW | Tommy James & the Shondells (Big Kahoona), Roulette 7000 | 5 |
| ★49 | 63 | — | — | THE BALLAD OF BONNIE AND CLYDE | Georgie Fame (Manny Kellem), Epic 10283 | 2 |
| ★50 | 51 | 69 | 84 | CAB DRIVER | Mills Brothers (Charles R. Grean & Tom Mack), Dot 17041 | 5 |
| ★51 | 60 | 89 | — | I'M GONNA MAKE YOU LOVE ME | Madeline Bell (Johnny Franz), Philips 40517 | 3 |
| ★52 | 82 | — | — | KISS ME GOODBYE | Petula Clark (Tony Hatch), Warner Bros. 7170 | 2 |
| ★53 | 68 | 90 | — | MAYBE JUST TODAY | Bobby Vee & the Strangers (Dallas Smith), Liberty 56014 | 3 |
| 54 | 57 | 59 | 68 | HEY LITTLE ONE | Glen Campbell (Al De Lory), Capitol 2076 | 6 |
| ★55 | 62 | — | — | COUNTRY GIRL—CITY MAN | Billy Vera & Judy Clay (Chip Taylor & Daryll), Atlantic 2480 | 2 |
| 56 | 56 | 67 | — | LOOK, HERE COMES THE SUN | Sunshine Company (Joe Seraceno), Imperial 66280 | 3 |
| ★57 | 69 | 73 | — | LOVE IS BLUE | Al Martino (Voyle Gilmore), Capitol 2102 | 3 |
| 58 | 59 | 99 | — | GOT WHAT YOU NEED | Fantastic Johnny C (Jesse James), Phil L.A. of Soul 309 | 3 |
| ★59 | 78 | — | — | JEALOUS LOVE | Wilson Pickett (Tom Dowd & Tommy Cogbill), Atlantic 2484 | 2 |
| ★60 | 84 | — | — | PLAYBOY | Gene & Debbie (Don Gant), TRX 5006 | 2 |
| 61 | 73 | — | — | IN THE MIDNIGHT HOUR | Mirettes (Jerry Goldstein), Revue 11004 | 2 |
| 62 | 66 | 77 | 83 | LOOKING FOR A FOX | Clarence Carter (Rick Hall), Atlantic 2461 | 6 |
| 63 | 65 | 70 | 80 | MAN NEEDS A WOMAN | James Carr (Quinton Claunch & Rudolph Russell), Goldwax 332 | 8 |
| ★64 | 71 | — | — | FOR YOUR PRECIOUS LOVE | Jackie Wilson & Count Basie (Nat Tarnepo & Teddy Reig), Brunswick 55365 | 2 |
| 65 | 74 | — | — | THIS IS THE THANKS I GET | Barbara Lynn (Huey P. Meaux), Atlantic 2450 | 2 |
| ★66 | — | — | — | A QUESTION OF TEMPERATURE | Balloon Farm (Laurie Prod. & Peter Shekeryk), Laurie 3405 | 1 |
| 67 | 67 | 86 | 87 | COLD FEET | Albert King (Al Jackson Jr.), Stax 241 | 4 |
| 68 | 70 | 80 | 81 | A MILLION TO ONE | Five Stairsteps & Cubie (Clarence Burke Jr.), Buddah 26 | 5 |
| 69 | 64 | 71 | 88 | BURNING SPEAR | Soulful Strings (Esmond Edwards), Cadet 5576 | 4 |
| ★70 | 83 | 84 | — | THANK U VERY MUCH | Scaffold (Tony Palmer), Bell 701 | 3 |
| ★71 | 100 | — | — | SUDDENLY YOU LOVE ME | Tremeloes (Mike Smith), Epic 10293 | 2 |
| 72 | 72 | 79 | 89 | FUNKY WAY | Calvin Arnold (Cooper, Paul & Shelby), Venture 605 | 7 |
| 73 | 80 | — | — | I SAY LOVE | Royal Guardsmen (GernHard Ent.), Laurie 3428 | 2 |
| 74 | 88 | 94 | — | LOVEY DOVEY | Otis & Carla (Prod. by Staff), Stax 244 | 3 |
| 75 | 77 | 82 | — | HERE COMES THE RAIN, BABY | Eddy Arnold (Chet Atkins), RCA Victor 47-9437 | 3 |
| 76 | 76 | 81 | 82 | STOP | Howard Tate (Jerry Ragovoy), Verve 10573 | 5 |
| ★77 | 97 | — | — | THE GOOD, THE BAD AND THE UGLY | Hugo Montenegro, His Ork and Chorus (Neely Plumb), RCA Victor 9423 | 2 |
| ★78 | — | — | — | WILL YOU LOVE ME TOMORROW? | 4 Seasons (Bob Crewe), Philips 40523 | 1 |
| 79 | 79 | — | — | NIGHT FO' LAST | Shorty Long (Holland & Dozier), Soul 35040 | 2 |
| ★80 | — | — | — | THE TEN COMMANDMENTS OF LOVE | Peaches & Herb (David Kapralik & Ken Williams), Date 1592 | 1 |
| 81 | 81 | — | — | UNCHAIN MY HEART | Herbie Mann (Creed Taylor), A&M 896 | 2 |
| 82 | 85 | 88 | 94 | TO EACH HIS OWN | Frankie Laine (Bob Thiele), ABC 11032 | 6 |
| 83 | 90 | 92 | — | WHERE IS MY MIND | Vanilla Fudge (Shadow Morton), Atco 6554 | 3 |
| ★84 | — | — | — | SOULVILLE | Aretha Franklin (Robert Mersey), Columbia 44441 | 1 |
| ★85 | — | — | — | IF YOU CAN WANT | Smokey Robinson and the Miracles ("Smokey" Cleveland), Tamla 54162 | 1 |
| ★86 | — | — | — | THAT'S A LIE | Ray Charles (Ray Charles), ABC 11045 | 1 |
| 87 | 87 | 87 | 100 | (You've Got) PERSONALITY & CHANTILLY LACE | Mitch Ryder (Bob Crewe), DynoVoice 905 | 4 |
| ★88 | — | — | — | THE SON OF HICKORY HOLLER'S TRAMP | O. C. Smith (Jerry Fuller), Columbia 44425 | 1 |
| ★89 | — | — | — | HEY, HEY BUNNY | John Fred & His Playboy Band (John Fred & Andrew Bernard), Paula 294 | 1 |
| ★90 | — | — | — | GREEN LIGHT | American Breed (Bill Traut), Acta 821 | 1 |
| 91 | 91 | — | — | LICKIN' STICK | George Torrence & Naturals (T.M.S.), Shout 224 | 2 |
| 92 | 92 | — | — | IF YOU EVER LEAVE ME | Jack Jones (Ernie Altschuler), RCA Victor 47-9441 | 2 |
| 93 | 93 | — | — | LOVE EXPLOSIONS | Troy Keyes (George Kerr), ABC 11027 | 2 |
| 94 | — | — | — | SPRINGFIELD PLANE | Kenny O'Dell (Kenny O'Dell & Bill Porter), Vegas 722 | 1 |
| 95 | 96 | 100 | — | GENTLE ON MY MIND | Patti Page (Jack Gold), Columbia 44353 | 3 |
| 96 | 99 | — | — | MUSIC, MUSIC, MUSIC | Happenings (Tokens), B. T. Puppy 538 | 2 |
| 97 | — | — | — | LOVE IS BLUE | Claudine Longet (Tommy LiPuma), A&M 909 | 1 |
| 98 | — | — | — | LOVE IS ALL AROUND | Troggs (Page One), Fontana 1607 | 1 |
| 99 | — | — | — | SOUL COAXIN' (Ame Caline) | Raymond LeFevre, 4 Corners of the World 141 | 1 |
| 100 | — | — | — | LOVE IS BLUE | Manny Kellem, His Ork & Chorus (Manny Kellem), Epic 10282 | 1 |

## HOT 100—A TO Z—(Publisher-Licensee)


Baby, Now That I've Found You (January/Welbeck, BMI) ... 11
Back Up Train (Tosted, BMI) ... 46
Ballad of Bonnie and Clyde, The (Peer Int'l, BMI) ... 49
Bend Me, Shape Me (Helios, BMI) ... 18
Born Free (Screen Gems-Columbia, BMI) ... 38
Bottle of Wine (Deep Fork, ASCAP) ... 12
Burning Spear (Discus, BMI) ... 69

Cab Driver (Blackhawk, BMI) ... 50
Carpet Man (Rivers, BMI) ... 40
Chain of Fools (13th Hour/Pronto, BMI) ... 28
Cold Feet (East, BMI) ... 67
Country Girl—City Man (Blackwood, BMI) ... 55

Dance to the Music (Daly City, BMI) ... 41
Different Drum (Screen Gems-Columbia, BMI) ... 29

End of Our Road, The (Jobete, BMI) ... 30
Everything That Touches You (Beechwood, BMI) ... 15

For Your Precious Love (Sunflower, BMI) ... 64
Funky Way (Mikim, BMI) ... 72

Gentle on My Mind (Sherman-DeVorzan, BMI) ... 95
Get Out Now (Patricia, BMI) ... 48
Goin' Out of My Head/Can't Take My Eyes Off You (Vogue/Saturday/Season's Four, BMI) ... 9
Good, the Bad and the Ugly, The (Unart, BMI) ... 77
Got What You Need (Dandelion/James Boy, BMI) ... 58
Green Light (Four Star, BMI) ... 90
Green Tambourine (Kama Sutra, BMI) ... 7
Guitar Man (Vector, BMI) ... 43

Here Comes the Rain, Baby (Acuff-Rose, BMI) ... 75
Hey Little One (Sherman-DeVorzan, BMI) ... 54
Hey, Hey Bunny (Su-Ma/Bengal, BMI) ... 89

I Can Take or Leave Your Loving (Miller, ASCAP) ... 22
I Say Love (Roanique, BMI) ... 73
I Thank You (East/Pronto, BMI) ... 24
I Wish It Would Rain (Jobete, BMI) ... 4
I Wonder What She's Doing Tonight (Screen Gems-Columbia, BMI) ... 8
If You Ever Leave Me (Northern, ASCAP) ... 92
If You Can Want (Jobete, BMI) ... 85
I'm Gonna Make You Love Me (Act Three, BMI) ... 51
In the Midnight Hour (East/Cotillion, BMI) ... 61
Itchycoo Park (Nice Songs, BMI) ... 27

Jealous Love (Cotillion/Tracebob, BMI) ... 59
Judy in Disguise (With Glasses) (Su-Ma, BMI) ... 13
Just Dropped In (To See What Condition My Condition Was In) (Acuff-Rose, BMI) ... 21

Kiss Me Goodbye (Donna, ASCAP) ... 52

La-La Means I Love You (Nickel Shoe, BMI) ... 35
Lickin' Stick (Web IV, BMI) ... 91
Look, Here Comes the Sun (Chardon, BMI) ... 56
Looking for a Fox (Fame, BMI) ... 62
Love Explosions (Zira/Floteca/Mia, BMI) ... 93
Love Is All Around (James, BMI) ... 98
Love Is Blue (Croma, ASCAP) (Paul Mauriat) ... 1
Love Is Blue (Croma, ASCAP) (Al Martino) ... 57
Love Is Blue (Claudine Longet) (Croma, ASCAP) ... 97
Love Is Blue (Manny Kellem) (Croma, ASCAP) ... 100
Lovey Dovey (Progressive, BMI) ... 74

Man Needs a Woman, A (Rise/Aim, BMI) ... 63
Maybe Just Today (Screen Gems-Columbia, BMI) ... 53
Men Are Gettin' Scarce (Tree, BMI) ... 44
Million to One, A (Jobete, BMI) ... 68
Mission: Impossible (Bruin, BMI) ... 42
Music, Music, Music (Creewell, ASCAP) ... 96
My Baby Must Be a Magician (Jobete, BMI) ... 33

Nobody But Me (Wemar, BMI) ... 10
Night fo' Last (Jobete, BMI) ... 79

Playboy (Acuff-Rose, BMI) ... 60

Question of Temperature (H & L, BMI) ... 66

(Sittin' On) The Dock of the Bay (East/Fine/Redwal, BMI) ... 5
Skip a Rope (Tree, BMI) ... 26
Simon Says (Maskat, BMI) ... 6
Some Velvet Morning (Hazlewood, ASCAP) ... 39
Son of Hickory Holler's Tramp, The (Blue Crest, BMI) ... 88
Soulville (Nom/DeLarue, BMI) ... 84
Soul Coaxin' (Ame Caline) (Southern, ASCAP) ... 99
Spooky (Lowery, BMI) ... 3
Springfield Plane (Beautiful Music, BMI) ... 94
Stop (Ragmar/Rumbalero, BMI) ... 76
Strawberry Shortcake (Bradley, BMI) ... 45
Suddenly You Love Me (Ponderosa, BMI) ... 71
Sunday Mornin' (Blackwood, BMI) ... 31
Sunshine of Your Love (Dratleaf, BMI) ... 37
Susan (Diogenes/Bag of Tunes, BMI) ... 25

Thank U Very Much (Felicia, BMI) ... 70
That's a Lie (Tangerine, BMI) ... 86
(Theme From) Valley of the Dolls (Feist, ASCAP) ... 2
There Is (Chevis, BMI) ... 20
There Was a Time (Galo, BMI) ... 36
This Is the Thanks I Get (Crazy Cajun/Pronto, BMI) ... 65
Ten Commandments of Love, The (Arc, BMI) ... 80
To Each His Own (Paramount, ASCAP) ... 82
Tomorrow (Alarm Clock, ASCAP) ... 32
Too Much Talk (Boom, BMI) ... 34

Unchain My Heart (Teepee, ASCAP) ... 81

Walk Away Renee (Twin Tone, BMI) ... 19
We Can Fly (Akbestal/Luvlin, BMI) ... 23
We're a Winner (Camad, BMI) ... 14
Where Is My Mind? (Cotillion/Vanilla Fudge, BMI) ... 83
Will You Love Me Tomorrow (Screen Gems-Columbia, BMI) ... 78
Woman, Woman (Glaser, BMI) ... 17
Words (Nemperor, BMI) ... 16

You (Jobete, BMI) ... 47
(You've Got) Personality & Chantilly Lace (Lloyd & Logan/Glad, BMI) ... 87


## BUBBLING UNDER THE HOT 100

101. SCARBOROUGH FAIR (Canticle) ... Simon & Garfunkel, Columbia 44465
102. L. DAVID SLOANE ... Michele Lee, Columbia 44413
103. SOMETHING I'LL REMEMBER ... Sandy Posey, MGM 13892
104. NIGHTS IN WHITE SATIN ... Moody Blues, Deram 85023
105. FOGGY MOUNTAIN BREAKDOWN ... Flatt & Scruggs, Columbia 44380/Mercury 72739
106. SWEET INSPIRATION ... Sweet Inspirations, Atlantic 2476
107. PEOPLE WORLD ... Jim & Jean, Verve Forecast 5073
108. RED, GREEN, YELLOW & BLUE ... Dickie Lee, Atco 6546
109. YOU'VE GOT TO BE LOVED ... Montanas, Independence 83
110. 1941 ... Tom Northcott, Warner Bros.-Seven Arts 7160
111. SUMMERTIME BLUES ... Blue Cheer, Philips 40516
112. LITTLE GREEN APPLES ... Roger Miller, Smash 2148
113. DEAR DELILAH ... Grapefruit, Equinox 70000
114. DOTTIE I LIKE IT ... Tommy Roe, ABC 11039
115. SOUL SERENADE ... Willie Mitchell, Hi 2140
116. I'M HYPNOTIZED ... Anthony & the Imperials, Veep 1278
117. (1-2-3-4-5-6-7) COUNT THE DAYS ... Inez & Charlie Foxx, Dynamo 285
118. YOUNG GIRL ... Union Gap, Columbia 44450
119. SALLY WAS A GOOD OLD GIRL ... Trini Lopez, Reprise 0659
120. MY ANCESTORS ... Lou Rawls, Capitol 2084
121. MIGHTY QUINN ... Manfred Mann, Mercury 72770
122. I CANNOT STOP YOU ... Cherry Slush, U.S.A. 895
123. IT KEEPS RIGHT ON A HURTIN' ... Margaret Whiting, London 119
124. BEAR MASH ... Ramsey Lewis, Cadet 5593
125. DR. JON (The Medicine Man) ... Jon & Robin & the In Crowd, Abnak 127
126. MELODY FOR YOU ... Grassroots, Dunhill 4122
127. THE RADIO SONG ... Parade, A&M 904
128. CRY LIKE A BABY ... Box Tops, Mala 593
129. OUTSIDE OF A SMALL CIRCLE OF FRIENDS ... Phil Ochs, A&M 891
130. FUNKY NORTH PHILLY ... Bill Cosby, Warner Bros.-Seven Arts 7171

Compiled from national retail sales and radio station airplay by the Music Popularity Dept. of Record Market Research, Billboard.

# Billboard HOT 100

FOR WEEK ENDING MARCH 2, 1968

★ STAR PERFORMER—Sides registering greatest proportionate upward progress this week.

(Seal) Record Industry Association of America seal of certification as million selling single.

| This Week | 1 Wk. Ago | 2 Wks. Ago | 3 Wks. Ago | TITLE Artist (Producer), Label & Number | Weeks On Chart |
|---|---|---|---|---|---|
| 1 (Billboard Award) | 1 | 1 | 1 | LOVE IS BLUE — Paul Mauriat, Philips 40495 | 9 |
| ★2 (RIAA seal) | 2 | 5 | 15 | (Theme From) THE VALLEY OF THE DOLLS — Dionne Warwick (Bacharach-David), Scepter 12203 | 7 |
| ★3 | 5 | 6 | 28 | (Sittin' On) THE DOCK OF THE BAY — Otis Redding (Steve Cropper), Volt 157 | 6 |
| 4 | 4 | 4 | 6 | I WISH IT WOULD RAIN — Temptations (Norman Whitfield), Gordy 7068 | 8 |
| ★5 | 6 | 17 | 37 | SIMON SAYS — 1910 Fruitgum Co. (J. Katz/J. Kasenetz/E. Chiprut), Buddah 24 | 6 |
| 6 | 3 | 3 | 3 | SPOOKY — Classics IV (Buddy Buie), Imperial 66259 | 11 |
| ★7 | 21 | 43 | 63 | JUST DROPPED IN (To See What Condition My Condition Was In) — First Edition (Mike Post), Reprise 0655 | 4 |
| 8 | 8 | 10 | 13 | I WONDER WHAT SHE'S DOING TONIGHT — Tommy Boyce & Bobby Hart (Tommy Boyce & Bobby Hart), A&M 893 | 11 |
| 9 | 12 | 14 | 14 | BOTTLE OF WINE — Fireballs (Norman Petty), Atco 6491 | 10 |
| ★10 | 15 | 31 | 38 | EVERYTHING THAT TOUCHES YOU — Association (Bones Howe), Warner Bros. 7163 | 5 |
| 11 | 11 | 11 | 12 | BABY, NOW THAT I'VE FOUND YOU — Foundations (Tony Macaulay), Uni 55038 | 11 |
| 12 | 10 | 8 | 8 | NOBODY BUT ME — Human Beinz (Alexis de Azevedo), Capitol 5990 | 13 |
| 13 | 9 | 7 | 7 | GOIN' OUT OF MY HEAD/CAN'T TAKE MY EYES OFF YOU — Lettermen (Kelly Gordon), Capitol 2054 | 13 |
| 14 (RIAA seal) | 7 | 2 | 2 | GREEN TAMBOURINE — Lemon Pipers (Paul Leka), Buddah 23 | 12 |
| 15 | 16 | 32 | 32 | WORDS — Bee Gees (Robert Stigwood & the Bee Gees), Atco 6548 | 7 |
| 16 | 14 | 15 | 27 | WE'RE A WINNER — Impressions (Johnny Pate), ABC 11022 | 10 |
| 17 | 19 | 37 | 46 | WALK AWAY RENEE — Four Tops (Holland & Dozier), Motown 1119 | 5 |
| 18 (RIAA seal) | 13 | 9 | 4 | JUDY IN DISGUISE (With Glasses) — John Fred & His Playboy Band (J. Fred & A. Bernard), Paula 282 | 15 |
| ★19 | 35 | 50 | 66 | LA-LA MEANS I LOVE YOU — DelfonicS (Stan & Bell), Philly Groove 150 | 5 |
| 20 | 20 | 20 | 48 | THERE IS — Dells (B. Miller), Cadet 5590 | 7 |
| ★21 | 24 | 29 | 44 | I THANK YOU — Sam & Dave (Isaac Hayes & David Porter), Stax 242 | 6 |
| 22 (RIAA seal) | 18 | 13 | 10 | BEND ME, SHAPE ME — American Breed (Bill Traut), Acta 811 | 14 |
| 23 | 22 | 22 | 22 | I CAN TAKE OR LEAVE YOUR LOVING — Herman's Hermits (Mickie Most), MGM 13885 | 8 |
| 24 (RIAA seal) | 17 | 12 | 9 | WOMAN, WOMAN — Union Gap (Jerry Fuller), Columbia 44297 | 16 |
| ★25 | 34 | 49 | 76 | TOO MUCH TALK — Paul Revere & the Raiders (Mark Lindsay), Columbia 44444 | 4 |
| ★26 | 30 | 40 | 68 | THE END OF OUR ROAD — Gladys Knight & the Pips (M. Whitfield), Soul 35042 | 4 |
| 27 | 23 | 21 | 21 | WE CAN FLY — Cowsills (Bill & Bob Cowsill), MGM 13886 | 8 |
| 28 | 27 | 27 | 16 | ITCHYCOO PARK — Small Faces (Steve Marriott & Ronnie Lane), Immediate 501 | 17 |
| 29 | 26 | 25 | 25 | SKIP A ROPE — Henson Cargill (Don Law), Monument 1041 | 11 |
| ★30 | 49 | 63 | — | THE BALLAD OF BONNIE AND CLYDE — Georgie Fame (Manny Kellem), Epic 10283 | 3 |
| ★31 | — | — | — | (Sweet Sweet Baby) SINCE YOU'VE BEEN GONE — Aretha Franklin (Jerry Wexler), Atlantic 2486 | 1 |
| 32 | 29 | 24 | 20 | DIFFERENT DRUM — Stone Poneys (Nick Venet), Capitol 2004 | 17 |
| 33 | 32 | 23 | 23 | TOMORROW — Strawberry Alarm Clock (Frank Slay & Bill Holmes), Uni 55046 | 10 |
| ★34 | 41 | 58 | 72 | DANCE TO THE MUSIC — Sly & the Family Stone (Sly Stone), Epic 10256 | 4 |
| ★35 | 52 | 82 | — | KISS ME GOODBYE — Petula Clark (Tony Hatch), Warner Bros. 7170 | 3 |
| 36 | 37 | 45 | 53 | SUNSHINE OF YOUR LOVE — Cream (Felix Pappalardi), Atco 6544 | 8 |
| ★37 | 40 | 47 | 56 | CARPET MAN — 5th Dimension (Bones Howe), Soul City 762 | 5 |
| ★38 | 50 | 51 | 69 | CAB DRIVER — Mills Brothers (Charles R. Grean & Tom Mack), Dot 17041 | 6 |
| 39 | 36 | 36 | 47 | THERE WAS A TIME — James Brown & His Famous Flames (James Brown), King 6144 | 7 |
| ★40 | 44 | 53 | 98 | MEN ARE GETTIN' SCARCE — Joe Tex (Buddy Killen), Dial 4069 | 4 |
| 41 | 42 | 46 | 54 | MISSION: IMPOSSIBLE — Lalo Schifrin (Tom Mack), Dot 17059 | 9 |
| 42 | 38 | 38 | 45 | BORN FREE — Hesitations (GWP), Kapp 878 | 9 |
| 43 | 43 | 44 | 50 | GUITAR MAN — Elvis Presley, RCA Victor 47-9425 | 6 |
| ★44 | 78 | — | — | WILL YOU LOVE ME TOMORROW? — 4 Seasons (Bob Crewe), Philips 40523 | 2 |
| ★45 | 60 | 84 | — | PLAYBOY — Gene & Debbie (Don Gant), TRX 5006 | 3 |
| 46 | 51 | 60 | 89 | I'M GONNA MAKE YOU LOVE ME — Madeline Bell (Johnny Franz), Philips 40517 | 4 |
| ★47 | 85 | — | — | IF YOU CAN WANT — Smokey Robinson and the Miracles ("Smokey" Cleveland), Tamla 54162 | 2 |
| ★48 | 55 | 62 | — | COUNTRY GIRL—CITY MAN — Billy Vera & Judy Clay (Chip Taylor & Daryll), Atlantic 2480 | 3 |
| 49 | 48 | 48 | 58 | GET OUT NOW — Tommy James & the Shondells (Big Kahoona), Roulette 7000 | 6 |
| ★50 | 59 | 78 | — | JEALOUS LOVE — Wilson Pickett (Tom Dowd & Tommy Cogbill), Atlantic 2484 | 3 |
| ★51 | 71 | 100 | — | SUDDENLY YOU LOVE ME — Tremeloes (Mike Smith), Epic 10293 | 3 |
| ★52 | 64 | 71 | — | FOR YOUR PRECIOUS LOVE — Jackie Wilson & Count Basie (Nat Tarnepo & Teddy Reig), Brunswick 55365 | 3 |
| 53 | 53 | 68 | 90 | MAYBE JUST TODAY — Bobby Vee & the Strangers (Dallas Smith), Liberty 56014 | 4 |
| 54 | 66 | — | — | A QUESTION OF TEMPERATURE — Balloon Farm (Laurie Prod. & Peter Shekeryk), Laurie 3405 | 2 |
| 55 | 61 | 73 | — | IN THE MIDNIGHT HOUR — Mirettes (Jerry Goldstein), Revue 11004 | 3 |
| 56 | 56 | 56 | 67 | LOOK, HERE COMES THE SUN — Sunshine Company (Joe Seraceno), Imperial 66280 | 4 |
| 57 | 57 | 69 | 73 | LOVE IS BLUE — Al Martino (Voyle Gilmore), Capitol 2102 | 4 |
| 58 | 58 | 59 | 99 | GOT WHAT YOU NEED — Fantastic Johnny C (Jesse James), Phil L.A. of Soul 309 | 4 |
| 59 | 54 | 57 | 59 | HEY LITTLE ONE — Glen Campbell (Al De Lory), Capitol 2076 | 7 |
| ★60 | — | — | — | CRY LIKE A BABY — Box Tops (Dan Penn), Mala 593 | 1 |
| ★61 | — | — | — | SCARBOROUGH FAIR (/Canticle) — Simon & Garfunkel (Bob Johnston), Columbia 44465 | 1 |
| 62 | 62 | 66 | 77 | LOOKING FOR A FOX — Clarence Carter (Rick Hall), Atlantic 2461 | 7 |
| 63 | 63 | 65 | 70 | MAN NEEDS A WOMAN — James Carr (Quinton Claunch & Rudolph Russell), Goldwax 332 | 9 |
| ★64 | 90 | — | — | GREEN LIGHT — American Breed (Bill Traut), Acta 821 | 2 |
| ★65 | — | — | — | LITTLE GREEN APPLES — Roger Miller (Jerry Kennedy), Smash 2148 | 1 |
| ★66 | 77 | 97 | — | THE GOOD, THE BAD AND THE UGLY — Hugo Montenegro, His Ork and Chorus (Neely Plumb), RCA Victor 9423 | 3 |
| 67 | 74 | 88 | 94 | LOVEY DOVEY — Otis & Carla (Prod. by Staff), Stax 244 | 4 |
| ★68 | — | — | — | THE MIGHTY QUINN — Manfred Mann, Mercury 72770 | 1 |
| 69 | 70 | 83 | 84 | THANK U VERY MUCH — Scaffold (Tony Palmer), Bell 701 | 4 |
| ★70 | 80 | — | — | THE TEN COMMANDMENTS OF LOVE — Peaches & Herb (David Kapralik & Ken Williams), Date 1592 | 2 |
| 71 | 68 | 70 | 80 | A MILLION TO ONE — Five Stairsteps & Cubie (Clarence Burke Jr.), Buddah 26 | 6 |
| 72 | 73 | 80 | — | I SAY LOVE — Royal Guardsmen (GernHard Ent.), Laurie 3428 | 3 |
| ★73 | 83 | 90 | 92 | WHERE IS MY MIND — Vanilla Fudge (Shadow Morton), Atco 6554 | 4 |
| 74 | 75 | 77 | 82 | HERE COMES THE RAIN, BABY — Eddy Arnold (Chet Atkins), RCA Victor 47-9437 | 4 |
| 75 | 69 | 64 | 71 | BURNING SPEAR — Soulful Strings (Esmond Edwards), Cadet 5576 | 5 |
| 76 | 72 | 72 | 79 | FUNKY WAY — Calvin Arnold (Cooper, Paul & Shelby), Venture 605 | 8 |
| 77 | 86 | — | — | THAT'S A LIE — Ray Charles (Ray Charles), ABC 11045 | 2 |
| 78 | 79 | 79 | — | NIGHT FO' LAST — Shorty Long (Holland & Dozier), Soul 35040 | 3 |
| ★79 | 89 | — | — | HEY, HEY BUNNY — John Fred & His Playboy Band (John Fred & Andrew Bernard), Paula 294 | 2 |
| 80 | 88 | — | — | THE SON OF HICKORY HOLLER'S TRAMP — O. C. Smith (Jerry Fuller), Columbia 44425 | 2 |
| ★81 | — | — | — | IF THIS WORLD WERE MINE — Marvin Gaye & Tammi Terrell (Fugua, Bristol), Tamla 54161 | 1 |
| ★82 | 99 | — | — | SOUL COAXIN' (Ame Caline) — Raymond Lefevre, 4 Corners of the World 141 | 2 |
| 83 | 84 | — | — | SOULSVILLE — Aretha Franklin (Robert Mersey), Columbia 44441 | 2 |
| ★84 | — | — | — | SECURITY — Etta James (Rick Hall & Staff), Cadet 5594 | 1 |
| ★85 | 98 | — | — | LOVE IS ALL AROUND — Troggs (Page One), Fontana 1607 | 2 |
| ★86 | — | — | — | L. DAVID SLOANE — Michele Lee (Jack Gold), Columbia 44413 | 1 |
| ★87 | — | — | — | YOUNG GIRL — Union Gap Featuring Gary Puckett (Jerry Fuller), Columbia 44450 | 1 |
| ★88 | — | — | — | SWEET INSPIRATION — Sweet Inspirations (Tom Dowd & Tommy Cogbill), Atlantic 2476 | 1 |
| ★89 | — | — | — | SUMMERTIME BLUES — Blue Cheer (Abe "Voce" Kesh), Philips 40516 | 1 |
| ★90 | — | — | — | SOUND ASLEEP — Turtles (Turtles & Blimp), White Whale 264 | 1 |
| 91 | — | — | — | FUNKY NORTH PHILLY — Bill Cosby (Fred Smith), Warner Bros.-Seven Arts 7171 | 1 |
| 92 | 93 | 93 | — | LOVE EXPLOSIONS — Troy Keyes (George Kerr), ABC 11027 | 3 |
| 93 | 95 | 96 | 100 | GENTLE ON MY MIND — Patti Page (Jack Gold), Columbia 44353 | 4 |
| 94 | 94 | — | — | SPRINGFIELD PLANE — Kenny O'Dell (Kenny O'Dell & Bill Porter), Vegas 722 | 2 |
| 95 | — | — | — | FOGGY MOUNTAIN BREAKDOWN — Flatt & Scruggs (Bob Johnston), Columbia 44380/Mercury 72739 | 1 |
| 96 | 100 | — | — | LOVE IS BLUE — Manny Kellem, His Ork & Chorus (Manny Kellem), Epic 10282 | 2 |
| 97 | 97 | — | — | LOVE IS BLUE — Claudine Longet (Tommy LiPuma), A&M 909 | 2 |
| 98 | — | — | — | DEAR DELILAH — Grapefruit (Terry Melcher), Equinox 70000 | 1 |
| 99 | — | — | — | SALLY WAS A GOOD OLD GIRL — Trini Lopez (Don Costa Prod.), Reprise 0659 | 1 |
| 100 | — | — | — | YOU'VE GOT TO BE LOVED — Montanas (Tony Hatch), Independence 83 | 1 |

## HOT 100—A TO Z—(Publisher-Licensee)

Baby, Now That I've Found You (January/Welbeck, BMI) .... 11
Ballad of Bonnie and Clyde, The (Peer Int'l, BMI) 30
Bend Me, Shape Me (Helios, BMI) .... 22
Born Free (Screen Gems-Columbia, BMI) .... 42
Bottle of Wine (Deep Fork, ASCAP) .... 9
Burning Spear (Discus, BMI) .... 75

Cab Driver (Blackhawk, BMI) .... 38
Carpet Man (Rivers, BMI) .... 37
Country Girl—City Man (Blackwood, BMI) .... 48
Cry Like a Baby (Press, BMI) .... 60

Dance to the Music (Daly City, BMI) .... 34
Dear Delilah (Egg Music, Prom England, BMI) .... 98
Different Drum (Screen Gems-Columbia, BMI) .... 32

End of Our Road, The (Jobete, BMI) .... 26
Everything That Touches You (Beechwood, BMI) .. 10

Foggy Mountain Breakdown (Peer International, BMI) .... 95
For Your Precious Love (Sunflower, BMI) .... 52
Funky North Philly (Manger/Keymen, BMI) .... 91
Funky Way (Mikim, BMI) .... 76

Gentle on My Mind (Sherman-DeVorzan, BMI) .... 93
Get Out Now (Patricia, BMI) .... 49
Goin' Out of My Head/Can't Take My Eyes Off You (Vogue/Starday/Season's Four, BMI) .... 13
Good, the Bad and the Ugly, The (Unart, BMI) .. 66
Got What You Need (Dandelion/James Boy, BMI) .. 58
Green Light (Four Star, BMI) .... 64
Green Tambourine (Kama Sutra, BMI) .... 14
Guitar Man (Vector, BMI) .... 43

Here Comes the Rain, Baby (Acuff-Rose,, BMI) .. 74
Hey Little One (Sherman-DeVorzan, BMI) .... 59
Hey, Hey Bunny (Su-Ma/Bengal, BMI) .... 79

I Can Take or Leave Your Loving (Miller, ASCAP) 23
I Say Love (Roanique, BMI) .... 72
I Thank You (East/Pronto, BMI) .... 21
I Wish It Would Rain (Jobete, BMI) .... 4
I Wonder What She's Doing Tonight (Screen Gems-Columbia, BMI) .... 8
If This World Were Mine (Jobete, BMI) .... 81
If You Can Want (Jobete, BMI) .... 47
I'm Gonna Make You Love Me (Act Three, BMI) .. 46
In the Midnight Hour (East/Cotillion, BMI) .... 55
Itchycoo Park (Nice Songs, BMI) .... 28

Jealous Love (Cotillion/Tracebob, BMI) .... 50
Judy in Disguise (With Glasses) (Su-Ma, BMI) .... 18
Just Dropped In (To See What Condition My Condition Was In) (Acuff-Rose, BMI) .... 7

Kiss Me Goodbye (Donna, ASCAP) .... 35

L. David Sloane (Meager, BMI) .... 86
La-La Means I Love You (Nickel Shoe, BMI) .... 19
Little Green Apples (Russell-Cason, ASCAP) .... 65
Look, Here Comes the Sun (Chardon, BMI) .... 56
Looking for a Fox (Fame, BMI) .... 62
Love Explosions (Zira/Floteca/Mia, BMI) .... 92
Love Is All Around (James, BMI) .... 85
Love Is Blue (Croma, ASCAP) (Paul Mauriat) .... 1
Love Is Blue (Croma, ASCAP) (Al Martino) .... 57
Love Is Blue (Claudine Longet) (Croma, ASCAP) .. 97
Love Is Blue (Manny Kellem) (Croma, ASCAP) .... 96
Lovey Dovey (Progressive, BMI) .... 67

Man Needs a Woman, A (Rise/Aim, BMI) .... 63
Maybe Just Today (Screen Gems-Columbia, BMI) .. 53
Men Are Gettin' Scarce (Tree, BMI) .... 40
Mighty Quinn, The (Dwarf, ASCAP) .... 68
Million to One, A (Jobete, BMI) .... 71
Mission: Impossible (Bruin, BMI) .... 41

Nobody But Me (Wemar, BMI) .... 12
Night fo' Last (Jobete, BMI) .... 78
Playboy (Acuff-Rose, BMI) .... 45
Question of Temperature (H&L, BMI) .... 54
(Sittin' On) The Dock of the Bay (East/Pine/Redwal, BMI) .... 3

Sally Was a Good Old Girl (Pamper, BMI) .... 99
Scarborough Fair (/Canticle) (Charing Cross, BMI) .. 61
Security (East, BMI) .... 84
Skip a Rope (Tree, BMI) .... 29
Simon Says (Maskat, BMI) .... 5
Son of Hickory Holler's Tramp, The (Blue Crest, BMI) .... 80
Soulsville (Nom/DeLarue, BMI) .... 83
Soul Coaxin' (Ame Caline) (Southern, ASCAP) .... 82
Sound Asleep (Ishmael, BMI) .... 90
Spooky (Lowery, BMI) .... 6
Springfield Plane (Beautiful Music, BMI) .... 94
Suddenly You Love Me (Ponderosa, BMI) .... 51
Summertime Blues (American Music, BMI) .... 89
Sunshine of Your Love (Dratleaf, BMI) .... 36
Sweet Inspiration (Press, BMI) .... 88
(Sweet Sweet Baby) Since You've Been Gone (14th Hour/Cotillion, BMI) .... 31

Thank U Very Much (Felicia, BMI) .... 69
That's a Lie (Tangerine, BMI) .... 77
(Theme From) Valley of the Dolls (Feist, ASCAP) .. 2
There Is (Chevis, BMI) .... 20
There Was a Time (Galo, BMI) .... 39
Ten Commandments of Love, The (Arc, BMI) .... 70
Tomorrow (Alarm Clock, ASCAP) .... 33
Too Much Talk (Boom, BMI) .... 26

Walk Away Renee (Twin Tone, BMI) .... 17
We Can Fly (Akbestal/Luvlin, BMI) .... 27
We're a Winner (Camad, BMI) .... 16
Where Is My Mind? (Cotillion/Vanilla Fudge, BMI) 73
Will You Love Me Tomorrow? (Screen Gems-Columbia, BMI) .... 44
Woman, Woman (Glaser, BMI) .... 24
Words (Nemperor, BMI) .... 15

Young Girl (Viva, BMI) .... 87
You've Got to Be Loved (Duchess, BMI) .... 100

## BUBBLING UNDER THE HOT 100

101. UNCHAIN MY HEART .... Herbie Mann, A&M 896
102. SOMETHING I'LL REMEMBER .... Sandy Posey, MGM 13892
103. NIGHTS IN WHITE SATIN .... Moody Blues, Deram 85023
104. (You've Got) PERSONALITY & CHANTILLY LACE .. Mitch Ryder, DynoVoice 905
105. SOUL SERENADE .... Willie Mitchell, Hi 2140
106. PEOPLE WORLD .... Jim & Jean, Verve Forecast 5073
107. 1941 .... Tom Northcott, Warner Bros.-Seven Arts 7160
108. RED, GREEN, YELLOW & BLUE .... Dickie Lee, Atco 6546
109. THIS IS THE THANKS I GET .... Barbara Lynn, Atlantic 2450
110. BABY PLEASE DON'T GO .... Amboy Dukes, Mainstream 676
111. COME TO ME SOFTLY .... Jimmy James & the Vagabonds, Atco 6551
112. BABY, WHAT I MEAN .... Spiral Staircase, Columbia 44442
113. TURN ON YOUR LOVELIGHT .... Human Beinz, Capitol 2119
114. DOTTIE I LIKE IT .... Tommy Roe, ABC 11039
115. UP ON THE ROOF .... Cryan' Shames, Columbia 44457
116. MY ANCESTORS .... Lou Rawls, Capitol 2084
117. (1-2-3-4-5-6-7) COUNT THE DAYS .... Inez & Charlie Foxx, Dynamo 285
118. IT KEEPS RIGHT ON A HURTIN' .... Margaret Whiting, London 119
119. OUTSIDE OF A SMALL CIRCLE OF FRIENDS .... Phil Ochs, A&M 891
120. I CANNOT STOP YOU .... Cherry Slush, USA 895
121. DRIFTIN' BLUES .... Bobby Bland, Duke 432
122. ATLANTA, GEORGIA, STRAY .... Sonny Curtis, Viva 626
123. BEAR MASH .... Ramsey Lewis, Cadet 5593
124. DR. JON (Medicine Man) .... Jon & Robin & the In-Crowd, Abnak 127
125. MELODY FOR YOU .... Grassroots, Dunhill 4122
126. AT THE TOP OF THE STAIRS .... Formations, MGM 13899
127. (You Can't Let the Boy Overpower) THE MAN IN YOU .... Chuck Jackson, Motown 1118
128. IF THE WHOLE WORLD STOPPED LOVING .... Val Doonican, Decca 32252
129. I WILL ALWAYS THINK ABOUT YOU .... New Colony Six, Mercury 72775
130. WE GOT A THING GOING ON .... Ben E. King & Dee Dee Sharp, Atco 6557

Compiled from national retail sales and radio station airplay by the Music Popularity Dept. of Record Market Research, Billboard.

# Billboard HOT 100

FOR WEEK ENDING MARCH 9, 1968

★ STAR PERFORMER—Sides registering greatest proportionate upward progress this week.

Record Industry Association of America seal of certification as million selling single.

| This Week | 1 Wk. Ago | 2 Wks. Ago | 3 Wks. Ago | TITLE Artist (Producer), Label & Number | Weeks On Chart |
|---|---|---|---|---|---|
| 1 (Billboard Award) | 1 | 1 | 1 | LOVE IS BLUE — Paul Mauriat, Philips 40495 | 10 |
| 2 | 2 | 2 | 5 | (Theme From) THE VALLEY OF THE DOLLS — Dionne Warwick (Bacharach-David), Scepter 12203 | 8 |
| ★3 | 3 | 5 | 6 | (Sittin' On) THE DOCK OF THE BAY — Otis Redding (Steve Cropper), Volt 157 | 7 |
| 4 | 5 | 6 | 17 | SIMON SAYS — 1910 Fruitgum Co. (J. Katz/J. Kasenetz/E. Chiprut), Buddah 24 | 7 |
| 5 | 4 | 4 | 4 | I WISH IT WOULD RAIN — Temptations (Norman Whitfield), Gordy 7068 | 9 |
| ★6 | 7 | 21 | 43 | JUST DROPPED IN (To See What Condition My Condition Was In) — First Edition (Mike Post), Reprise 0655 | 4 |
| 7 | 6 | 3 | 3 | SPOOKY — Classics IV (Buddy Buie), Imperial 66259 | 12 |
| 8 | 8 | 8 | 10 | I WONDER WHAT SHE'S DOING TONIGHT — Tommy Boyce & Bobby Hart (Tommy Boyce & Bobby Hart), A&M 893 | 12 |
| ★9 | 19 | 35 | 50 | LA-LA MEANS I LOVE YOU — Delfonics (Stan & Bell), Philly Groove 150 | 6 |
| 10 | 10 | 15 | 31 | EVERYTHING THAT TOUCHES YOU — Association (Bones Howe), Warner Bros. 7163 | 6 |
| ★11 | 21 | 24 | 29 | I THANK YOU — Sam & Dave (Isaac Hayes & David Porter), Stax 242 | 7 |
| 12 | 11 | 11 | 11 | BABY, NOW THAT I'VE FOUND YOU — Foundations (Tony Macaulay), Uni 55038 | 12 |
| 13 | 9 | 12 | 14 | BOTTLE OF WINE — Fireballs (Norman Petty), Atco 6491 | 11 |
| 14 | 17 | 19 | 37 | WALK AWAY RENEE — Four Tops (Holland & Dozier), Motown 1119 | 6 |
| ★15 | 26 | 30 | 40 | THE END OF OUR ROAD — Gladys Knight & the Pips (N. Whitfield), Soul 35042 | 5 |
| 16 | 16 | 14 | 15 | WE'RE A WINNER — Impressions (Johnny Pate), ABC 11022 | 11 |
| ★17 | 31 | — | — | (Sweet Sweet Baby) SINCE YOU'VE BEEN GONE — Aretha Franklin (Jerry Wexler), Atlantic 2486 | 2 |
| 18 | 15 | 16 | 32 | WORDS — Bee Gees (Robert Stigwood & the Bee Gees), Atco 6548 | 8 |
| ★19 | 34 | 41 | 58 | DANCE TO THE MUSIC — Sly & the Family Stone (Sly Stone), Epic 10256 | 5 |
| ★20 | 25 | 34 | 49 | TOO MUCH TALK — Paul Revere & the Raiders (Mark Lindsay), Columbia 44444 | 5 |
| 21 | 13 | 9 | 7 | GOIN' OUT OF MY HEAD/CAN'T TAKE MY EYES OFF YOU — Lettermen (Kelly Gordon), Capitol 2054 | 14 |
| 22 | 12 | 10 | 8 | NOBODY BUT ME — Human Beinz (Alexis de Azevedo), Capitol 5990 | 14 |
| 23 | 20 | 20 | 20 | THERE IS — Dells (B. Miller), Cadet 5590 | 8 |
| ★24 | — | — | — | VALLERI — Monkees (Monkees), Colgems 66-1019 | 1 |
| 25 | 14 | 7 | 2 | GREEN TAMBOURINE — Lemon Pipers (Paul Leka), Buddah 23 | 13 |
| ★26 | 30 | 49 | 63 | THE BALLAD OF BONNIE AND CLYDE — Georgie Fame (Manny Kellem), Epic 10283 | 4 |
| ★27 | 35 | 52 | 82 | KISS ME GOODBYE — Petula Clark (Tony Hatch), Warner Bros. 7170 | 4 |
| ★28 | 44 | 78 | — | WILL YOU LOVE ME TOMORROW? — 4 Seasons (Bob Crewe), Philips 40523 | 3 |
| ★29 | 37 | 40 | 47 | CARPET MAN — 5th Dimension (Bones Howe), Soul City 762 | 6 |
| 30 | 18 | 13 | 9 | JUDY IN DISGUISE (With Glasses) — John Fred & His Playboy Band (J. Fred & A. Bernard), Paula 282 | 16 |
| ★31 | 47 | 85 | — | IF YOU CAN WANT — Smokey Robinson and the Miracles ("Smokey" Cleveland), Tamla 54162 | 3 |
| 32 | 27 | 23 | 21 | WE CAN FLY — Cowsills (Bill & Bob Cowsill), MGM 13886 | 9 |
| ★33 | 40 | 44 | 53 | MEN ARE GETTIN' SCARCE — Joe Tex (Buddy Killen), Dial 4069 | 5 |
| ★34 | 46 | 51 | 60 | I'M GONNA MAKE YOU LOVE ME — Madeline Bell (Johnny Franz), Philips 40517 | 5 |
| ★35 | 68 | — | — | THE MIGHTY QUINN — Manfred Mann, Mercury 72770 | 2 |
| 36 | 24 | 17 | 12 | WOMAN, WOMAN — Union Gap (Jerry Fuller), Columbia 44297 | 17 |
| 37 | 38 | 50 | 51 | CAB DRIVER — Mills Brothers (Charles R. Green & Tom Mack), Dot 17041 | 7 |
| 38 | 39 | 36 | 36 | THERE WAS A TIME — James Brown & His Famous Flames (James Brown), King 6144 | 8 |
| 39 | 23 | 22 | 22 | I CAN TAKE OR LEAVE YOUR LOVING — Herman's Hermits (Mickie Most), MGM 13885 | 9 |
| ★40 | 45 | 60 | 84 | PLAYBOY — Gene & Debbie (Don Gant), TRX 5006 | 4 |
| 41 | 41 | 42 | 46 | MISSION: IMPOSSIBLE — Lalo Schifrin (Tom Mack), Dot 17059 | 10 |
| ★42 | 61 | — | — | SCARBOROUGH FAIR (/Canticle) — Simon & Garfunkel (Bob Johnston), Columbia 44465 | 2 |
| 43 | 36 | 37 | 45 | SUNSHINE OF YOUR LOVE — Cream (Felix Pappalardi), Atco 6544 | 9 |
| ★44 | 54 | 66 | — | A QUESTION OF TEMPERATURE — Balloon Farm (Laurie Prod. & Peter Shekeryk), Laurie 3405 | 3 |
| 45 | 48 | 55 | 62 | COUNTRY GIRL—CITY MAN — Billy Vera & Judy Clay (Chip Taylor & Darryll), Atlantic 2480 | 4 |
| 46 | 29 | 26 | 25 | SKIP A ROPE — Henson Cargill (Don Law), Monument 1041 | 12 |
| ★47 | 55 | 61 | 73 | IN THE MIDNIGHT HOUR — Mirettes (Jerry Goldstein), Revue 11004 | 4 |
| ★48 | 53 | 53 | 68 | MAYBE JUST TODAY — Bobby Vee & the Strangers (Dallas Smith), Liberty 56014 | 5 |
| 49 | 52 | 64 | 71 | FOR YOUR PRECIOUS LOVE — Jackie Wilson & Count Basie (Nat Tarnopol & Teddy Reig), Brunswick 55365 | 4 |
| 50 | 50 | 59 | 78 | JEALOUS LOVE — Wilson Pickett (Tom Dowd & Tommy Cogbill), Atlantic 2484 | 4 |
| 51 | 51 | 71 | 100 | SUDDENLY YOU LOVE ME — Tremeloes (Mike Smith), Epic 10293 | 4 |
| ★52 | 87 | — | — | YOUNG GIRL — Union Gap Featuring Gary Puckett (Jerry Fuller), Columbia 44450 | 2 |
| 53 | 60 | — | — | CRY LIKE A BABY — Box Tops (Dan Penn), Mala 593 | 2 |
| 54 | 42 | 38 | 38 | BORN FREE — Hesitations (GWP), Kapp 878 | 10 |
| ★55 | 64 | 90 | — | GREEN LIGHT — American Breed (Bill Traut), Acta 821 | 3 |
| ★56 | 58 | 58 | 59 | GOT WHAT YOU NEED — Fantastic Johnny C (Jesse James), Phil L.A. of Soul 309 | 5 |
| 57 | 57 | 57 | 69 | LOVE IS BLUE — Al Martino (Voyle Gilmore), Capitol 2102 | 5 |
| 58 | 70 | 80 | — | THE TEN COMMANDMENTS OF LOVE — Peaches & Herb (David Kapralik & Ken Williams), Date 1592 | 3 |
| 59 | 65 | — | — | LITTLE GREEN APPLES — Roger Miller (Jerry Kennedy), Smash 2148 | 2 |
| ★60 | 67 | 74 | 88 | LOVEY DOVEY — Otis & Carla (Prod. by Staff), Stax 244 | 5 |
| 61 | 56 | 56 | 56 | LOOK, HERE COMES THE SUN — Sunshine Company (Joe Saraceno), Imperial 66280 | 5 |
| 62 | 62 | 62 | 66 | LOOKING FOR A FOX — Clarence Carter (Rick Hall), Atlantic 2461 | 8 |
| 63 | 63 | 63 | 65 | MAN NEEDS A WOMAN — James Carr (Quinton Claunch & Rudolph Russell), Goldwax 332 | 10 |
| 64 | 66 | 77 | 97 | THE GOOD, THE BAD AND THE UGLY — Hugo Montenegro, His Ork and Chorus (Neely Plumb), RCA Victor 9423 | 4 |
| 65 | 49 | 48 | 48 | GET OUT NOW — Tommy James & the Shondells (Big Kahoona), Roulette 7000 | 7 |
| ★66 | 89 | — | — | SUMMERTIME BLUES — Blue Cheer (Abe "Voco" Kesh), Philips 40516 | 2 |
| ★67 | 85 | 98 | — | LOVE IS ALL AROUND — Troggs (Page One), Fontana 1607 | 3 |
| ★68 | 80 | 88 | — | THE SON OF HICKORY HOLLER'S TRAMP — O. C. Smith (Jerry Fuller), Columbia 44425 | 3 |
| 69 | 69 | 70 | 83 | THANK U VERY MUCH — Scaffold (Tony Palmer), Bell 701 | 5 |
| ★70 | 84 | — | — | SECURITY — Etta James (Rick Hall & Staff), Cadet 5594 | 2 |
| ★71 | 77 | 86 | — | THAT'S A LIE — Ray Charles (Ray Charles), ABC 11045 | 3 |
| 72 | 72 | 73 | 80 | I SAY LOVE — Royal Guardsmen (Gernhard Ent.), Laurie 3428 | 4 |
| ★73 | — | — | — | TAPIOCA TUNDRA — Monkees (Monkees), Colgems 66-1019 | 1 |
| ★74 | — | — | — | SOUL SERENADE — Willie Mitchell (Willie Mitchell/Joe Cuoghi), Hi 2140 | 1 |
| 75 | 78 | 79 | 79 | NIGHT FO' LAST — Shorty Long (Holland & Dozier), Soul 35040 | 4 |
| 76 | 79 | 89 | — | HEY, HEY BUNNY — John Fred & His Playboy Band (John Fred & Andrew Bernard), Paula 294 | 3 |
| ★77 | 82 | 99 | — | SOUL COAXIN' (Ame Caline) — Raymond Lefevre, 4 Corners of the World 141 | 3 |
| 78 | 88 | — | — | SWEET INSPIRATION — Sweet Inspirations (Tom Dowd & Tommy Cogbill), Atlantic 2476 | 2 |
| ★79 | 100 | — | — | YOU'VE GOT TO BE LOVED — Montanas (Tony Hatch), Independence 83 | 2 |
| 80 | 81 | — | — | IF THIS WORLD WERE MINE — Marvin Gaye & Tammi Terrell (Fuqua, Bristol), Tamla 54161 | 2 |
| ★81 | 90 | — | — | SOUND ASLEEP — Turtles (Turtles & Blimp), White Whale 264 | 2 |
| 82 | 73 | 83 | 90 | WHERE IS MY MIND — Vanilla Fudge (Shadow Morton), Atco 6554 | 5 |
| 83 | 83 | 84 | — | SOULSVILLE — Aretha Franklin (Robert Mersey), Columbia 44441 | 2 |
| ★84 | — | — | — | RICE IS NICE — Lemon Pipers (Paul Leka), Buddah 31 | 1 |
| ★85 | — | — | — | I'LL SAY FOREVER MY LOVE — Jimmy Ruffin (Dean & Weatherspoon), Soul 35043 | 1 |
| 86 | 86 | — | — | L. DAVID SLOANE — Michele Lee (Jack Gold), Columbia 44413 | 2 |
| 87 | 97 | 97 | — | LOVE IS BLUE — Claudine Longet (Tommy LiPuma), A&M 909 | 3 |
| ★88 | — | — | — | JENNIFER JUNIPER — Donovan (Mickie Most), Epic 10300 | 1 |
| ★89 | — | — | — | (Sittin' On) THE DOCK OF THE BAY — King Curtis & His Kingpins (Tom Dowd), Atco 6562 | 1 |
| ★90 | — | — | — | BACK ON MY FEET AGAIN — Foundations (Tony Macaulay), Uni 55058 | 1 |
| 91 | 91 | — | — | FUNKY NORTH PHILLY — Bill Cosby (Fred Smith), Warner Bros.-Seven Arts 7171 | 2 |
| 92 | — | — | — | TURN ON YOUR LOVELIGHT — Human Beinz (Lex de Asavedo), Capitol 2119 | 1 |
| 93 | 93 | 95 | 96 | GENTLE ON MY MIND — Patti Page (Jack Gold), Columbia 44353 | 5 |
| 94 | — | — | — | (You Can't Let the Boy Overpower) THE MAN IN YOU — Chuck Jackson ("Smokey" A. Cleveland), Motown 1118 | 1 |
| 95 | 95 | — | — | FOGGY MOUNTAIN BREAKDOWN — Flatt & Scruggs (Bob Johnston), Columbia 44380/Mercury 72739 | 2 |
| 96 | — | — | — | DRIFTIN' BLUES — Bobby Bland (Joe Scott), Duke 432 | 1 |
| 97 | — | — | — | (1-2-3-4-5-6-7) COUNT THE DAYS — Inez & Charlie Foxx (Charlie Foxx), Dynamo 112 | 5 |
| 98 | — | — | — | HAVE A LITTLE FAITH — David Houston (Billy Sherrill), Epic 10291 | 1 |
| 99 | 99 | — | — | SALLY WAS A GOOD OLD GIRL — Trini Lopez (Don Costa Prod.), Reprise 0659 | 2 |
| 100 | — | — | — | LOVEY DOVEY KINDA LOVIN' — Brenton Wood (Hooven-Winn), Double Shot 126 | 1 |

## HOT 100—A TO Z—(Publisher-Licensee)

Baby, Now That I've Found You (January/Welbeck, BMI) .... 12
Back on My Feet Again (January/Welbeck, BMI) .... 90
Ballad of Bonnie and Clyde, The (Peer Int'l, BMI) .... 26
Born Free (Screen Gems-Columbia, BMI) .... 54
Bottle of Wine (Deep Fork, ASCAP) .... 13
Cab Driver (Blackhawk, BMI) .... 37
Carpet Man (Rivers, BMI) .... 29
Country Girl—City Man (Blackwood, BMI) .... 45
Cry Like a Baby (Press, BMI) .... 53
Dance to the Music (Daly City, BMI) .... 19
Driftin' Blues (Travis, BMI) .... 96
End of Our Road, The (Jobete, BMI) .... 15
Everything That Touches You (Beechwood, BMI) .... 10
Foggy Mountain Breakdown (Peer International, BMI) .... 85
For Your Precious Love (Sunflower, BMI) .... 49
Funky North Philly (Manger/Keymen, BMI) .... 91
Gentle on My Mind (Sherman-DeVorzan, BMI) .... 93
Get Out Now (Patricia, BMI) .... 65
Goin' Out of My Head/Can't Take My Eyes Off You (Vogue/Starday/Season's Four, BMI) .... 21
Good, the Bad and the Ugly, The (Unart, BMI) .... 64
Got What You Need (Dandelion/James Boy, BMI) .... 56
Green Light (Four Star, BMI) .... 55
Green Tambourine (Kama Sutra, BMI) .... 25
Have a Little Faith (Gallico, BMI) .... 98
Hey, Hey Bunny (Su-Ma/Bengal, BMI) .... 76
I Can Take or Leave Your Loving (Miller, ASCAP) .... 39
I Say Love (Roanique, BMI) .... 72
I Thank You (East/Pronto, BMI) .... 11
I Wish It Would Rain (Jobete, BMI) .... 5
I Wonder What She's Doing Tonight (Screen Gems-Columbia, BMI) .... 8
If This World Were Mine (Jobete, BMI) .... 80
If You Can Want (Jobete, BMI) .... 31
I'll Say Forever My Love (Jobete, BMI) .... 85
I'm Gonna Make You Love Me (Act Three, BMI) .... 34
In the Midnight Hour (East/Cotillion, BMI) .... 47
Jealous Love (Cotillion/Tracebob, BMI) .... 50
Jennifer Juniper (Peer International, BMI) .... 88
Judy in Disguise (With Glasses) (Su-Ma, BMI) .... 30
Just Dropped In (To See What Condition My Condition Was In) (Acuff-Rose, BMI) .... 6
Kiss Me Goodbye (Donna, ASCAP) .... 27
L. David Sloane (Meager, BMI) .... 86
La-La Means I Love You (Nickel Shoe, BMI) .... 9
Little Green Apples (Russell-Cason, ASCAP) .... 59
Look, Here Comes the Sun (Chardon, BMI) .... 61
Looking for a Fox (Fame, BMI) .... 62
Love Is All Around (James, BMI) .... 67
Love Is Blue (Croma, ASCAP) (Paul Mauriat) .... 1
Love Is Blue (Croma, ASCAP) (Al Martino) .... 57
Love Is Blue (Croma, ASCAP) (Claudine Longet) .... 87
Lovey Dovey (Progressive, BMI) .... 60
Lovey Dovey Kinda Lovin' (Big Shot, BMI) .... 100
Man Needs a Woman, A (Rise/Aim, BMI) .... 63
Maybe Just Today (Screen Gems-Columbia, BMI) .... 48
Men Are Gettin' Scarce (Tree, BMI) .... 33
Mighty Quinn, The (Dwarf, ASCAP) .... 35
Mission: Impossible (Bruin, BMI) .... 41
Nobody But Me (Wemar, BMI) .... 22
Night fo' Last (Jobete, BMI) .... 75
(1-2-3-4-5-6-7) Count the Days (Catalogue/Cee & Eye, BMI) .... 97
Playboy (Acuff-Rose, BMI) .... 40
Question of Temperature (H&L, BMI) .... 44
Rice Is Nice (Kama Sutra, BMI) .... 84
Sally Was a Good Old Girl (Pamper, BMI) .... 99
Scarborough Fair (/Canticle) (Charing Cross, BMI) .... 42
Security (East, BMI) .... 70
(Sittin' On) The Dock of the Bay (East/Pine/Redwal, BMI) (King Curtis) .... 89
(Sittin' On) The Dock of the Bay (East/Pine/Redwal, BMI) (Otis Redding) .... 3
Skip a Rope (Tree, BMI) .... 46
Simon Says (Maskat, BMI) .... 4
Son of Hickory Holler's Tramp, The (Blue Crest, BMI) .... 68
Soulsville (Nom/DeLarue, BMI) .... 83
Soul Coaxin' (Ame Caline) (Southern, ASCAP) .... 77
Soul Serenade (Kilyn, BMI) .... 74
Sound Asleep (Ishmael, BMI) .... 81
Spooky (Lowery, BMI) .... 7
Suddenly You Love Me (Ponderosa, BMI) .... 51
Summertime Blues (American Music, BMI) .... 66
Sunshine of Your Love (Dratleaf, BMI) .... 43
Sweet Inspiration (Press, BMI) .... 78
(Sweet Sweet Baby) Since You've Been Gone (14th Hour/Cotillion, BMI) .... 17
Tapioca Tundra (Screen Gems-Columbia, BMI) .... 73
Thank U Very Much (Felicia, BMI) .... 69
That's a Lie (Tangerine, BMI) .... 75
(Theme From) Valley of the Dolls (Feist, ASCAP) .... 2
There Is (Chevis, BMI) .... 23
There Was a Time (Galo, BMI) .... 38
Ten Commandments of Love, The (Arc, BMI) .... 58
Too Much Talk (Boom, BMI) .... 20
Turn On Your Lovelight (Lion, BMI) .... 92
Valleri (Screen Gems-Columbia, BMI) .... 24
Walk Away Renee (Twin Tone, BMI) .... 14
We Can Fly (Akbestal/Luvlin, BMI) .... 32
We're a Winner (Camad, BMI) .... 16
Where Is My Mind? (Cotillion/Vanilla Fudge, BMI) .... 82
Will You Love Me Tomorrow? (Screen Gems-Columbia, BMI) .... 28
Woman, Woman (Glaser, BMI) .... 36
Words (Nemperor, BMI) .... 18
Young Girl (Viva, BMI) .... 52
(You Can't Let the Boy Overpower) The Man in You (Jobete, BMI) .... 94
You've Got to Be Loved (Duchess, BMI) .... 79

## BUBBLING UNDER THE HOT 100

101. UNCHAIN MY HEART .... Herbie Mann, A&M 896
102. SOMETHING I'LL REMEMBER .... Sandy Posey, MGM 13892
103. HERE COMES THE RAIN BABY .... Eddy Arnold, RCA Victor 47-9437
104. BURNING SPEAR .... Soulful Strings, Cadet 5576
105. 1941 .... Tom Northcott, Warner Bros.-Seven Arts 7160
106. PEOPLE WORLD .... Jim & Jean, Verve Forecast 5073
107. RED, GREEN, YELLOW & BLUE .... Dickie Lee, Atco 6546
108. BABY, PLEASE DON'T GO .... Amboy Dukes, Mainstream 676
109. THIS IS THE THANKS I GET .... Barbara Lynn, Atlantic 2450
110. COME TO ME SOFTLY .... Jimmy James & Vagabonds, Atco 6551
111. BABY, WHAT I MEAN .... Spiral Staircase, Columbia 44442
112. UP ON THE ROOF .... Cryan' Shames, Columbia 44457
113. MY ANCESTORS .... Lou Rawls, Capitol 2084
114. DR. JON (MEDICINE MAN) .... Jon & Robin & the In Crowd, Abnak 127
115. IT KEEPS RIGHT ON A HURTIN' .... Margaret Whiting, London 119
116. LOVE IS BLUE .... Manny Kellem, His Ork, Chorus, Epic 10282
117. SPRINGFIELD PLANE .... Kenny O'Dell, Vegas 722
118. OUTSIDE OF A SMALL CIRCLE OF FRIENDS .... Phil Ochs, A&M 891
119. I CANNOT STOP YOU .... Cherry Slush, USA 895
120. JENNIFER ECCLES .... Hollies, Epic 10298
121. ATLANTA GEORGIA STRAY .... Sonny Curtis, Viva 626
122. SHOWTIME .... Detroit Emeralds, Ric Tic 135
123. MELODY FOR YOU .... Grassroots, Dunhill 4122
124. CAN'T FIND THE TIME .... Orpheus, MGM 13882
125. AT THE TOP OF THE STAIRS .... Formations, MGM 13899
126. UP FROM THE SKIES .... Jimi Hendrix Experience, Reprise 0665
127. WE GOT A THING GOING ON .... Ben E. King & Dee Dee Sharp, Atco 6557
128. I HATE TO SEE ME GO .... Margaret Whiting, London 119
129. I WILL ALWAYS THINK ABOUT YOU .... New Colony Six, Mercury 72775
130. ME ABOUT YOU .... Jackie De Shannon, Imperial 66281
131. MUSIC, MUSIC, MUSIC .... Happenings, B.T. Puppy 538
132. BIG BIRD .... Eddie Floyd, Stax 246
133. UP TO MY NECK IN HIGH MUDDY WATER .... Linda Ronstadt & the Stone Poneys, Capitol 2110
134. IN THE HEAT OF THE NIGHT .... Dick Hyman & the Group, Command 4114
135. YOU SAY .... Esquires, Bunky 7753

Compiled from national retail sales and radio station airplay by the Music Popularity Dept. of Record Market Research, Billboard.

# Billboard HOT 100

FOR WEEK ENDING MARCH 16, 1968

★ STAR PERFORMER—Sides registering greatest proportionate upward progress this week.

● Record Industry Association of America seal of certification as million selling single.

| This Week | 1 Wk. Ago | 2 Wks. Ago | 3 Wks. Ago | TITLE Artist (Producer), Label & Number | Weeks On Chart |
|---|---|---|---|---|---|
| Billboard Award | 3 | 3 | 5 | (Sittin' On) THE DOCK OF THE BAY — Otis Redding (Steve Cropper), Volt 157 | 8 |
| 2 | 2 | 2 | 2 | (Theme From) THE VALLEY OF THE DOLLS — Dionne Warwick (Bacharach-David), Scepter 12203 | 9 |
| ● 3 | 1 | 1 | 1 | LOVE IS BLUE — Paul Mauriat, Philips 40495 | 11 |
| ● ★ 4 | 4 | 5 | 6 | SIMON SAYS — 1910 Fruitgum Co. (J. Katz/J. Kasenetz/E. Chiprut), Buddah 24 | 8 |
| 5 | 6 | 7 | 21 | JUST DROPPED IN (To See What Condition My Condition Was In) — First Edition (Mike Post), Reprise 0655 | 5 |
| 6 | 5 | 4 | 4 | I WISH IT WOULD RAIN — Temptations (Norman Whitfield), Gordy 7068 | 10 |
| ★ 7 | 9 | 19 | 35 | LA-LA MEANS I LOVE YOU — Delfonics (Stan & Bell), Philly Groove 150 | 7 |
| ● ★ 8 | 24 | — | — | VALLERI — Monkees (Monkees), Colgems 66-1019 | 2 |
| ★ 9 | 17 | 31 | — | (Sweet Sweet Baby) SINCE YOU'VE BEEN GONE — Aretha Franklin (Jerry Wexler), Atlantic 2486 | 3 |
| 10 | 11 | 21 | 24 | I THANK YOU — Sam & Dave (Isaac Hayes & David Porter), Stax 242 | 8 |
| 11 | 7 | 6 | 3 | SPOOKY — Classics IV (Buddy Buie), Imperial 66259 | 13 |
| 12 | 10 | 10 | 15 | EVERYTHING THAT TOUCHES YOU — Association (Bones Howe), Warner Bros.-Seven Arts 7163 | 7 |
| 13 | 13 | 9 | 12 | BOTTLE OF WINE — Fireballs (Norman Petty), Atco 6491 | 12 |
| 14 | 14 | 17 | 19 | WALK AWAY RENEE — Four Tops (Holland & Dozier), Motown 1119 | 7 |
| 15 | 15 | 26 | 30 | THE END OF OUR ROAD — Gladys Knight & the Pips (M. Whitfield), Soul 35042 | 6 |
| ★ 16 | 19 | 34 | 41 | DANCE TO THE MUSIC — Sly & the Family Stone (Sly Stone), Epic 10256 | 6 |
| ★ 17 | 26 | 30 | 49 | THE BALLAD OF BONNIE AND CLYDE — Georgie Fame (Manny Kellem), Epic 10283 | 5 |
| 18 | 18 | 15 | 16 | WORDS — Bee Gees (Robert Stigwood & the Bee Gees), Atco 6548 | 9 |
| 19 | 20 | 25 | 34 | TOO MUCH TALK — Paul Revere & the Raiders (Mark Lindsay), Columbia 44444 | 6 |
| 20 | 8 | 8 | 8 | I WONDER WHAT SHE'S DOING TONIGHT — Tommy Boyce & Bobby Hart (Tommy Boyce & Bobby Hart), A&M 893 | 13 |
| 21 | 16 | 16 | 14 | WE'RE A WINNER — Impressions (Johnny Pate), ABC 11022 | 12 |
| ★ 22 | 27 | 35 | 52 | KISS ME GOODBYE — Petula Clark (Tony Hatch), Warner Bros.-Seven Arts 7170 | 5 |
| 23 | 23 | 20 | 20 | THERE IS — Dells (B. Miller), Cadet 5590 | 9 |
| ★ 24 | 52 | 87 | — | YOUNG GIRL — Union Gap Featuring Gary Puckett (Jerry Fuller), Columbia 44450 | 3 |
| ★ 25 | 35 | 68 | — | THE MIGHTY QUINN — Manfred Mann, Mercury 72770 | 3 |
| 26 | 12 | 11 | 11 | BABY, NOW THAT I'VE FOUND YOU — Foundations (Tony Macaulay), Uni 55038 | 13 |
| ★ 27 | 28 | 44 | 78 | WILL YOU LOVE ME TOMORROW? — 4 Seasons (Bob Crewe), Philips 40523 | 4 |
| ★ 28 | 53 | 60 | — | CRY LIKE A BABY — Box Tops (Dan Penn), Mala 593 | 3 |
| ★ 29 | 42 | 61 | — | SCARBOROUGH FAIR (/Canticle) — Simon & Garfunkel (Bob Johnston), Columbia 44465 | 3 |
| 30 | 31 | 47 | 85 | IF YOU CAN WANT — Smokey Robinson and the Miracles ("Smokey" Cleveland), Tamla 54162 | 4 |
| 31 | 22 | 12 | 10 | NOBODY BUT ME — Human Beinz (Alexis de Azevedo), Capitol 5990 | 15 |
| 32 | 21 | 13 | 9 | GOIN' OUT OF MY HEAD/CAN'T TAKE MY EYES OFF YOU — Lettermen (Kelly Gordon), Capitol 2054 | 15 |
| 33 | 33 | 40 | 44 | MEN ARE GETTIN' SCARCE — Joe Tex (Buddy Killen), Dial 4069 | 6 |
| 34 | 34 | 46 | 51 | I'M GONNA MAKE YOU LOVE ME — Madeline Bell (Johnny Franz), Philips 40517 | 6 |
| ★ 35 | 37 | 38 | 50 | CAB DRIVER — Mills Brothers (Charles R. Grean & Tom Mack), Dot 17041 | 8 |
| 36 | 29 | 37 | 40 | CARPET MAN — 5th Dimension (Bones Howe), Soul City 762 | 7 |
| ★ 37 | 40 | 45 | 60 | PLAYBOY — Gene & Debbie (Don Gant), TRX 5006 | 5 |
| 38 | 44 | 54 | 66 | A QUESTION OF TEMPERATURE — Balloon Farm (Laurie Prod. & Peter Shekeryk), Laurie 3405 | 4 |
| ★ 39 | 55 | 64 | 90 | GREEN LIGHT — American Breed (Bill Traut), Acta 821 | 4 |
| ★ 40 | 59 | 65 | — | LITTLE GREEN APPLES — Roger Miller (Jerry Kennedy), Smash 2148 | 3 |
| 41 | 43 | 36 | 37 | SUNSHINE OF YOUR LOVE — Cream (Felix Pappalardi), Atco 6544 | 10 |
| ★ 42 | 67 | 85 | 98 | LOVE IS ALL AROUND — Troggs (Page One), Fontana 1607 | 4 |
| 43 | 45 | 48 | 55 | COUNTRY GIRL — CITY MAN — Billy Vera & Judy Clay (Chip Taylor & Daryll), Atlantic 2480 | 5 |
| 44 | 39 | 23 | 22 | I CAN TAKE OR LEAVE YOUR LOVING — Herman's Hermits (Mickie Most), MGM 13885 | 10 |
| 45 | 51 | 51 | 71 | SUDDENLY YOU LOVE ME — Tremeloes (Mike Smith), Epic 10293 | 5 |
| 46 | 48 | 53 | 53 | MAYBE JUST TODAY — Bobby Vee & the Strangers (Dallas Smith), Liberty 56014 | 6 |
| 47 | 47 | 55 | 61 | IN THE MIDNIGHT HOUR — Mirettes (Jerry Goldstein), Revue 11004 | 5 |
| 48 | 41 | 41 | 42 | MISSION: IMPOSSIBLE — Lalo Schifrin (Tom Mack), Dot 17059 | 11 |
| ★ 49 | 73 | — | — | TAPIOCA TUNDRA — Monkees (Monkees), Colgems 66-1019 | 2 |
| ★ 50 | 77 | 82 | 99 | SOUL COAXING (Ame Caline) — Raymond Lefevre, 4 Corners of the World 147 | 4 |
| ★ 51 | 66 | 89 | — | SUMMERTIME BLUES — Blue Cheer (Abe "Voce" Kesh), Philips 40516 | 3 |
| ★ 52 | 68 | 80 | 88 | THE SON OF HICKORY HOLLER'S TRAMP — O. C. Smith (Jerry Fuller), Columbia 44425 | 4 |
| ★ 53 | 64 | 66 | 67 | THE GOOD, THE BAD AND THE UGLY — Hugo Montenegro, His Ork and Chorus (Neely Plumb), RCA Victor 9423 | 5 |
| 54 | 49 | 52 | 64 | FOR YOUR PRECIOUS LOVE — Jackie Wilson & Count Basie (Nat Tarnepo & Teddy Reig), Brunswick 55365 | 5 |
| 55 | 58 | 70 | 80 | THE TEN COMMANDMENTS OF LOVE — Peaches & Herb (David Kapralik & Ken Williams), Date 1592 | 4 |
| 56 | 50 | 50 | 59 | JEALOUS LOVE — Wilson Pickett (Tom Dowd & Tommy Cogbill), Atlantic 2484 | 5 |
| 57 | 57 | 57 | 57 | LOVE IS BLUE — Al Martino (Voyle Gilmore), Capitol 2102 | 6 |
| ★ 58 | 76 | 79 | 89 | HEY, HEY BUNNY — John Fred & His Playboy Band (John Fred & Andrew Bernard), Paula 294 | 4 |
| ★ 59 | 81 | 90 | — | SOUND ASLEEP — Turtles (Turtles & Blimp), White Whale 264 | 3 |
| ★ 60 | 79 | 100 | — | YOU'VE GOT TO BE LOVED — Montanas (Tony Hatch), Independence 83 | 3 |
| ★ 61 | 88 | — | — | JENNIFER JUNIPER — Donovan (Mickie Most), Epic 10300 | 2 |
| 62 | 56 | 58 | 58 | GOT WHAT YOU NEED — Fantastic Johnny C (Jesse James), Phil L.A. of Soul 309 | 6 |
| ★ 63 | — | — | — | I GOT THE FEELIN' — James Brown & the Famous Flames (James Brown), King 6155 | 1 |
| 64 | 60 | 67 | 74 | LOVEY DOVEY — Otis & Carla (Prod. by Staff), Stax 244 | 6 |
| ★ 65 | 84 | — | — | RICE IS NICE — Lemon Pipers (Paul Leka), Buddah 31 | 2 |
| ★ 66 | 71 | 77 | 86 | THAT'S A LIE — Ray Charles (Ray Charles), ABC 11045 | 4 |
| 67 | 70 | 84 | — | SECURITY — Etta James (Rick Hall & Staff), Cadet 5594 | 3 |
| 68 | 74 | — | — | SOUL SERENADE — Willie Mitchell (Willie Mitchell/Joe Cuoghi), Hi 2140 | 2 |
| ★ 69 | 90 | — | — | BACK ON MY FEET AGAIN — Foundations (Tony Macaulay), Uni 55058 | 2 |
| ★ 70 | — | — | — | FOREVER CAME TODAY — Diana Ross & the Supremes (Holland & Dozier), Motown 1122 | 1 |
| 71 | 80 | 81 | — | IF THIS WORLD WERE MINE — Marvin Gaye & Tammi Terrell (Fugua, Bristol), Tamla 54161 | 3 |
| 72 | 78 | 88 | — | SWEET INSPIRATION — Sweet Inspirations (Tom Dowd & Tommy Cogbill), Atlantic 2476 | 3 |
| ★ 73 | 86 | 86 | — | L. DAVID SLOANE — Michele Lee (Jack Gold), Columbia 44413 | 3 |
| ★ 74 | — | — | — | TAKE TIME TO KNOW HER — Percy Sledge (Quin Ivy & Marlin Greene), Atlantic 2490 | 1 |
| ★ 75 | — | — | — | SIT WITH THE GURU — Strawberry Alarm Clock (Frank Slay & Bill Holmes), Uni 55055 | 1 |
| ★ 76 | — | — | — | JENNIFER ECCLES — Hollies (Ron Richards), Epic 10298 | 1 |
| ★ 77 | — | — | — | FUNKY STREET — Arthur Conley (Tom Dowd), Atco 6563 | 1 |
| ★ 78 | — | — | — | TIN SOLDIER — Small Faces (Steve Marriott & Ronnie Lane), Immediate 5003 | 1 |
| 79 | 87 | 97 | 97 | LOVE IS BLUE — Claudine Longet (Tommy LiPuma), A&M 909 | 4 |
| ★ 80 | 95 | 95 | — | FOGGY MOUNTAIN BREAKDOWN — Flatt & Scruggs (Bob Johnston), Columbia 44380/Mercury 72739 | 3 |
| 81 | 85 | — | — | I'LL SAY FOREVER MY LOVE — Jimmy Ruffin (Dean & Weatherspoon), Soul 35043 | 2 |
| 82 | 82 | 73 | 83 | WHERE IS MY MIND — Vanilla Fudge (Shadow Morton), Atco 6554 | 6 |
| ★ 83 | — | — | — | STAY AWAY — Elvis Presley, RCA Victor 47-9465 | 1 |
| ★ 84 | — | — | — | IN NEED OF A FRIEND — Cowsills (Bill & Bob Cowsill), MGM 13909 | 1 |
| 85 | 92 | — | — | TURN ON YOUR LOVELIGHT — Human Beinz (Lex de Asavedo), Capitol 2119 | 2 |
| 86 | 89 | — | — | (Sittin' On) THE DOCK OF THE BAY — King Curtis & His Kingpins (Tom Dowd), Atco 6562 | 2 |
| ★ 87 | — | — | — | BABY YOU'RE SO RIGHT — Brenda & the Tabulations (Bob Finiz), Dionn 507 | 1 |
| ★ 88 | — | — | — | 1941 — Tom Northcott (Lenny Waronker & Leon Russell), Warner Bros.-Seven Arts 7160 | 1 |
| ★ 89 | — | — | — | AT THE TOP OF THE STAIRS — Formations (Leon Huff), MGM 13899 | 1 |
| ★ 90 | — | — | — | THE IMPOSSIBLE DREAM — Hesitations (Wiltshire-Banks-Victor), Kapp 899 | 1 |
| 91 | 91 | 91 | — | FUNKY NORTH PHILLY — Bill Cosby (Fred Smith), Warner Bros.-Seven Arts 7171 | 3 |
| 92 | — | — | — | FATHER OF GIRLS — Perry Como (Andy Wisewell), RCA Victor 47-9448 | 1 |
| 93 | 93 | 93 | 95 | GENTLE ON MY MIND — Patti Page (Jack Gold), Columbia 44353 | 6 |
| 94 | — | — | — | UP FROM THE SKIES — Jimi Hendrix Experience (Charles Chandler), Reprise 0665 | 1 |
| 95 | — | — | — | DR. JON (The Medicine Man) — Jon & Robin & the In Crowd (Abnak Music), Abnak 127 | 1 |
| 96 | 96 | — | — | DRIFTIN' BLUES — Bobby Bland (Joe Scott), Duke 432 | 2 |
| 97 | — | — | — | DELILAH — Tom Jones (Peter Sullivan), Parrot 40025 | 1 |
| 98 | 98 | — | — | HAVE A LITTLE FAITH — David Houston (Billy Sherrill), Epic 10291 | 2 |
| 99 | 100 | — | — | LOVEY DOVEY KINDA LOVIN' — Brenton Wood (Hoeven-Winn), Double Shot 126 | 2 |
| 100 | — | — | — | IN SOME TIME — Ronnie Dove (Lee Hazlewood), Diamond 240 | 1 |

## HOT 100—A TO Z—(Publisher-Licensee)



## BUBBLING UNDER THE HOT 100

101. UNCHAIN MY HEART ... Herbie Mann, A&M 896
102. SOULSVILLE ... Aretha Franklin, Columbia 44441
103. HERE COMES THE RAIN, BABY ... Eddy Arnold, RCA Victor 47-9437
104. BURNING SPEAR ... Soulful Strings, Cadet 5576
105. SALLY WAS A GOOD GIRL ... Trini Lopez, Reprise 0659
106. BABY, PLEASE DON'T GO ... Amboy Dukes, Mainstream 676
107. (You Can't Let the Boy Overpower) THE MAN IN YOU ... Chuck Jackson, Motown 1118
108. THIS IS THE THANKS I GET ... Barbara Lynn, Atlantic 2450
109. COME TO ME SOFTLY ... Jimmy James & the Vagabonds, Atco 6551
110. I SAY LOVE ... Royal Guardsmen, Laurie 3428
111. UP ON THE ROOF ... Cryan' Shames, Columbia 44457
112. SHE'LL BE THERE ... Vikki Carr, Liberty 56026
113. IT'S TIME TO SAY GOODBYE ... Third Rail, Epic 10285
114. NO OTHER LOVE ... Jay & the Americans, United Artists 50282
115. ME, THE PEACEFUL HEART ... Lulu, Epic 10302
116. OUR CORNER OF THE NIGHT ... Barbra Streisand, Columbia 44474
117. UNWIND ... Ray Stevens, Monument 1048
118. CINDERELLA ROCKEFELLA ... Esther & Abi Ofarim, Philips 40526
119. FOOL OF FOOLS ... Tony Bennett, Columbia 44443
120. ATLANTA GEORGIA STRAY ... Sonny Curtis, Viva 626
121. SHOWTIME ... Detroit Emeralds, Ric Tic 135
122. DO DROP INN ... Fifth Estate, Jubilee 5617
123. CAN'T FIND THE TIME ... Orpheus, MGM 13882
124. SMALL TALK ... Lesley Gore, Mercury 72787
125. YOU'VE GOT TO CHANGE YOUR MIND ... Bobby Byrd & James Brown, King 6151
126. COME LIVE WITH ME ... Tony Scotti, Liberty 56006
127. I HATE TO SEE ME GO ... Margaret Whiting, London 119
128. I WILL ALWAYS THINK ABOUT YOU ... New Colony Six, Mercury 72775
129. ME ABOUT YOU ... Jackie DeShannon, Imperial 66281
130. UP TO MY NECK IN HIGH MUDDY WATER ... Linda Ronstadt & the Stone Poneys, Capitol 2110
131. MUSIC, MUSIC, MUSIC ... Happenings, B. T. Puppy 538
132. YOU SAY ... Esquires, Bunky 7753
133. IN THE HEAT OF THE NIGHT ... Dick Hyman & the Group, Command 4114
134. UNICORN ... Irish Rovers, Decca 42254
135. LOVE IS KIND, LOVE IS WINE ... Seekers, Capitol 2122

Compiled from national retail sales and radio station airplay by the Music Popularity Dept. of Record Market Research, Billboard.

# Billboard HOT 100

FOR WEEK ENDING MARCH 23, 1968

★ STAR PERFORMER—Sides registering greatest proportionate upward progress this week.

Record Industry Association of America seal of certification as million selling single.

| This Week | 1 Wk. Ago | 2 Wks. Ago | 3 Wks. Ago | TITLE Artist (Producer), Label & Number | Weeks On Chart |
|---|---|---|---|---|---|
| Billboard Award | | 3 | 3 | (Sittin' On) THE DOCK OF THE BAY — Otis Redding (Steve Cropper), Volt 157 | 9 |
| 2 | 3 | 1 | 1 | LOVE IS BLUE — Paul Mauriat, Philips 40495 | 12 |
| 3 | 2 | 2 | 2 | (Theme From) THE VALLEY OF THE DOLLS — Dionne Warwick (Bacharach-David), Scepter 12203 | 10 |
| 4 | 4 | 4 | 5 | SIMON SAYS — 1910 Fruitgum Co. (J. Katz/J. Kasenetz/E. Chiprut), Buddah 24 | 9 |
| 5 | 5 | 6 | 7 | JUST DROPPED IN (To See What Condition My Condition Was In) — First Edition (Mike Post), Reprise 0655 | 6 |
| ★ 6 | 7 | 9 | 19 | LA-LA MEANS I LOVE YOU — Delfonics (Stan & Bell), Philly Groove 150 | 8 |
| ★ 7 | 8 | 24 | — | VALLERI — Monkees (Monkees), Colgems 66-1019 | 3 |
| ★ 8 | 9 | 17 | 31 | (Sweet Sweet Baby) SINCE YOU'VE BEEN GONE — Aretha Franklin (Jerry Wexler), Atlantic 2486 | 4 |
| ★ 9 | 10 | 11 | 21 | I THANK YOU — Sam & Dave (Isaac Hayes & David Porter), Stax 242 | 9 |
| ★ 10 | 17 | 26 | 30 | THE BALLAD OF BONNIE AND CLYDE — Georgie Fame (Manny Kellem), Epic 10283 | 6 |
| ★ 11 | 25 | 35 | 68 | THE MIGHTY QUINN — Manfred Mann, Mercury 72770 | 4 |
| ★ 12 | 24 | 52 | 87 | YOUNG GIRL — Union Gap Featuring Gary Puckett (Jerry Fuller), Columbia 44450 | 4 |
| ★ 13 | 29 | 42 | 61 | SCARBOROUGH FAIR (/Canticle) — Simon & Garfunkel (Bob Johnston), Columbia 44465 | 4 |
| 14 | 16 | 19 | 34 | DANCE TO THE MUSIC — Sly & the Family Stone (Sly Stone), Epic 10256 | 7 |
| 15 | 15 | 15 | 26 | THE END OF OUR ROAD — Gladys Knight & the Pips (M. Whitfield), Soul 35042 | 7 |
| ★ 16 | 22 | 27 | 35 | KISS ME GOODBYE — Petula Clark (Tony Hatch), Warner Bros.-Seven Arts 7170 | 6 |
| ★ 17 | 28 | 53 | 60 | CRY LIKE A BABY — Box Tops (Dan Penn), Mala 593 | 4 |
| 18 | 12 | 10 | 10 | EVERYTHING THAT TOUCHES YOU — Association (Bones Howe), Warner Bros.-Seven Arts 7163 | 8 |
| 19 | 19 | 20 | 25 | TOO MUCH TALK — Paul Revere & the Raiders (Mark Lindsay), Columbia 44444 | 7 |
| 20 | 6 | 5 | 4 | I WISH IT WOULD RAIN — Temptations (Norman Whitfield), Gordy 7068 | 11 |
| ★ 21 | 37 | 40 | 45 | PLAYBOY — Gene & Debbie (Don Gant), TRX 5006 | 6 |
| 22 | 18 | 18 | 15 | WORDS — Bee Gees (Robert Stigwood & the Bee Gees), Atco 6548 | 10 |
| ★ 23 | — | — | — | LADY MADONNA — Beatles (George Martin), Capitol 2138 | 1 |
| ★ 24 | 27 | 28 | 44 | WILL YOU LOVE ME TOMORROW? — 4 Seasons (Bob Crewe), Philips 40523 | 5 |
| ★ 25 | 30 | 31 | 47 | IF YOU CAN WANT — Smokey Robinson and the Miracles ("Smokey" Cleveland), Tamla 54162 | 5 |
| ★ 26 | 34 | 34 | 46 | I'M GONNA MAKE YOU LOVE ME — Madeline Bell (Johnny Franz), Philips 40517 | 7 |
| 27 | 11 | 7 | 6 | SPOOKY — Classics IV (Buddy Buie), Imperial 66259 | 14 |
| 28 | 13 | 13 | 9 | BOTTLE OF WINE — Fireballs (Norman Petty), Atco 6491 | 13 |
| ★ 29 | 35 | 37 | 38 | CAB DRIVER — Mills Brothers (Charles R. Grean & Tom Mack), Dot 17041 | 9 |
| 30 | 14 | 14 | 17 | WALK AWAY RENEE — Four Tops (Holland & Dozier), Motown 1119 | 8 |
| 31 | 21 | 16 | 16 | WE'RE A WINNER — Impressions (Johnny Pate), ABC 11022 | 13 |
| 32 | 23 | 23 | 20 | THERE IS — Dells (B. Miller), Cadet 5590 | 10 |
| ★ 33 | 63 | — | — | I GOT THE FEELIN' — James Brown & the Famous Flames (James Brown), King 6155 | 2 |
| 34 | 42 | 67 | 85 | LOVE IS ALL AROUND — Troggs (Page One), Fontana 1607 | 5 |
| 35 | 36 | 29 | 37 | CARPET MAN — 5th Dimension (Bones Howe), Soul City 762 | 8 |
| 36 | 43 | 45 | 48 | COUNTRY GIRL—CITY MAN — Billy Vera & Judy Clay (Chip Taylor & Daryll), Atlantic 2480 | 6 |
| 37 | 38 | 44 | 54 | A QUESTION OF TEMPERATURE — Balloon Farm (Laurie Prod. & Peter Shekeryk), Laurie 3405 | 5 |
| ★ 38 | 51 | 66 | 89 | SUMMERTIME BLUES — Blue Cheer (Abe "Voce" Kesh), Philips 40516 | 4 |
| 39 | 39 | 55 | 64 | GREEN LIGHT — American Breed (Bill Traut), Acta 821 | 5 |
| 40 | 40 | 59 | 65 | LITTLE GREEN APPLES — Roger Miller (Jerry Kennedy), Smash 2148 | 4 |
| 41 | 20 | 8 | 8 | I WONDER WHAT SHE'S DOING TONIGHT — Tommy Boyce & Bobby Hart (Tommy Boyce & Bobby Hart), A&M 893 | 14 |
| ★ 42 | 61 | 88 | — | JENNIFER JUNIPER — Donovan (Mickie Most), Epic 10300 | 3 |
| 43 | 50 | 77 | 82 | SOUL COAXING (Ame Caline) — Raymond Lefevre, 4 Corners of the World 147 | 5 |
| ★ 44 | 45 | 51 | 51 | SUDDENLY YOU LOVE ME — Tremeloes (Mike Smith), Epic 10293 | 6 |
| 45 | 47 | 47 | 55 | IN THE MIDNIGHT HOUR — Mirettes (Jerry Goldstein), Revue 11004 | 6 |
| 46 | 33 | 33 | 40 | MEN ARE GETTIN' SCARCE — Joe Tex (Buddy Killen), Dial 4069 | 7 |
| 47 | 44 | 39 | 23 | I CAN TAKE OR LEAVE YOUR LOVING — Herman's Hermits (Mickie Most), MGM 13885 | 11 |
| 48 | 48 | 41 | 41 | MISSION: IMPOSSIBLE — Lalo Schifrin (Tom Mack), Dot 17059 | 12 |
| 49 | 49 | 73 | — | TAPIOCA TUNDRA — Monkees (Monkees), Colgems 66-1019 | 3 |
| ★ 50 | 68 | 74 | — | SOUL SERENADE — Willie Mitchell (Willie Mitchell/Joe Cuoghi), Hi 2140 | 3 |
| 51 | 52 | 68 | 80 | THE SON OF HICKORY HOLLER'S TRAMP — O. C. Smith (Jerry Fuller), Columbia 44425 | 5 |
| ★ 52 | 53 | 64 | 66 | THE GOOD, THE BAD AND THE UGLY — Hugo Montenegro, His Ork and Chorus (Neely Plumb), RCA Victor 9423 | 6 |
| ★ 53 | 70 | — | — | FOREVER CAME TODAY — Diana Ross & the Supremes (Holland & Dozier), Motown 1122 | 2 |
| 54 | 54 | 49 | 52 | FOR YOUR PRECIOUS LOVE — Jackie Wilson & Count Basie (Nat Tarnepo & Teddy Reig), Brunswick 55365 | 6 |
| ★ 55 | 72 | 78 | 88 | SWEET INSPIRATION — Sweet Inspirations (Tom Dowd & Tommy Cogbill), Atlantic 2476 | 4 |
| ★ 56 | 67 | 70 | 84 | SECURITY — Etta James (Rick Hall & Staff), Cadet 5594 | 4 |
| 57 | 58 | 76 | 79 | HEY, HEY BUNNY — John Fred & His Playboy Band (John Fred & Andrew Bernard), Paula 294 | 5 |
| 58 | 59 | 81 | 90 | SOUND ASLEEP — Turtles (Turtles & Blimp), White Whale 264 | 4 |
| ★ 59 | 60 | 79 | 100 | YOU'VE GOT TO BE LOVED — Montanas (Tony Hatch), Independence 83 | 4 |
| 60 | 41 | 43 | 36 | SUNSHINE OF YOUR LOVE — Cream (Felix Pappalardi), Atco 6544 | 11 |
| ★ 61 | 65 | 84 | — | RICE IS NICE — Lemon Pipers (Paul Leka), Buddah 31 | 3 |
| ★ 62 | 69 | 90 | — | BACK ON MY FEET AGAIN — Foundations (Tony Macaulay), Uni 55058 | 3 |
| ★ 63 | 77 | — | — | FUNKY STREET — Arthur Conley (Tom Dowd), Atco 6563 | 2 |
| ★ 64 | — | — | — | HONEY — Bobby Goldsboro (Bob Montgomery & Bobby Goldsboro), United Artists 50283 | 1 |
| ★ 65 | 66 | 71 | 77 | THAT'S A LIE — Ray Charles (Ray Charles), ABC 11045 | 5 |
| ★ 66 | 74 | — | — | TAKE TIME TO KNOW HER — Percy Sledge (Quin Ivy & Marlin Greene), Atlantic 2490 | 2 |
| 67 | 57 | 57 | 57 | LOVE IS BLUE — Al Martino (Voyle Gilmore), Capitol 2102 | 7 |
| 68 | 55 | 58 | 70 | THE TEN COMMANDMENTS OF LOVE — Peaches & Herb (David Kapralik & Ken Williams), Date 1592 | 5 |
| ★ 69 | 73 | 86 | 86 | L. DAVID SLOANE — Michele Lee (Jack Gold), Columbia 44413 | 4 |
| 70 | 71 | 80 | 81 | IF THIS WORLD WERE MINE — Marvin Gaye & Tammi Terrell (Fugua, Bristol), Tamla 54161 | 4 |
| ★ 71 | 76 | — | — | JENNIFER ECCLES — Hollies (Ron Richards), Epic 10298 | 2 |
| 72 | 75 | — | — | SIT WITH THE GURU — Strawberry Alarm Clock (Frank Slay & Bill Holmes), Uni 55055 | 2 |
| ★ 73 | 90 | — | — | THE IMPOSSIBLE DREAM — Hesitations (Wiltshire-Banks-Victor), Kapp 899 | 2 |
| ★ 74 | 97 | — | — | DELILAH — Tom Jones (Peter Sullivan), Parrot 40025 | 2 |
| ★ 75 | — | — | — | U. S. MALE — Elvis Presley, RCA Victor 47-9465 | 1 |
| ★ 76 | 84 | — | — | IN NEED OF A FRIEND — Cowsills (Bill & Bob Cowsill), MGM 13909 | 2 |
| ★ 77 | — | — | — | THE UNICORN — Irish Rovers (Charles Bud Dant), Decca 32254 | 1 |
| 78 | 78 | — | — | TIN SOLDIER — Small Faces (Steve Marriott & Ronnie Lane), Immediate 5003 | 2 |
| 79 | 81 | 85 | -- | I'LL SAY FOREVER MY LOVE — Jimmy Ruffin (Dean & Weatherspoon), Soul 35043 | 3 |
| 80 | 80 | 95 | 95 | FOGGY MOUNTAIN BREAKDOWN — Flatt & Scruggs (Bob Johnston), Columbia 44380/Mercury 72739 | 4 |
| 81 | 83 | — | — | STAY AWAY — Elvis Presley, RCA Victor 47-9465 | 2 |
| 82 | 79 | 87 | 97 | LOVE IS BLUE — Claudine Longet (Tommy LiPuma), A&M 909 | 5 |
| 83 | 85 | 92 | — | TURN ON YOUR LOVELIGHT — Human Beinz (Lex de Asavedo), Capitol 2119 | 3 |
| ★ 84 | — | — | — | COME TO ME SOFTLY — Jimmy James & the Vagabonds (Jimmy James & Peter Meaden), Atco 6851 | 1 |
| 85 | 86 | 89 | — | (Sittin' On) THE DOCK OF THE BAY — King Curtis & His Kingpins (Tom Dowd), Atco 6562 | 3 |
| 86 | 87 | — | — | BABY YOU'RE SO RIGHT — Brenda & the Tabulations (Bob Finiz), Dionn 507 | 2 |
| ★ 87 | — | — | — | COWBOYS TO GIRLS — Intruders (Gamble-Huff), Gamble 214 | 1 |
| 88 | 88 | — | — | 1941 — Tom Northcott (Lenny Waronker & Leon Russell), Warner Bros.-Seven Arts 7160 | 2 |
| 89 | 89 | — | — | AT THE TOP OF THE STAIRS — Formations (Leon Huff), MGM 13899 | 2 |
| ★ 90 | — | — | — | YOU'VE STILL GOT A PLACE IN MY HEART — Dean Martin (Jimmy Bowen), Reprise 0672 | 1 |
| 91 | — | — | — | ME, THE PEACEFUL HEART — Lulu (Mickie Most), Epic 10302 | 1 |
| 92 | 92 | — | — | FATHER OF GIRLS — Perry Como (Andy Wisewell), RCA Victor 47-9448 | 2 |
| 93 | 93 | 93 | 93 | GENTLE ON MY MIND — Patti Page (Jack Gold), Columbia 44353 | 7 |
| 94 | 94 | — | — | UP FROM THE SKIES — Jimi Hendrix Experience (Charles Chandler), Reprise 0665 | 2 |
| 95 | 95 | — | — | DR. JON (The Medicine Man) — Jon & Robin & the In Crowd (Abnak Music), Abnak 127 | 2 |
| 96 | 96 | 96 | — | DRIFTIN' BLUES — Bobby Bland (Joe Scott), Duke 432 | 3 |
| 97 | — | — | — | 100 YEARS — Nancy Sinatra (Lee Hazlewood), Reprise 0670 | 1 |
| 98 | — | — | — | SHERRY DON'T GO — Lettermen (Kelly Gordon), Capitol 2132 | 1 |
| 99 | 100 | — | — | IN SOME TIME — Ronnie Dove (Lee Hazlewood), Diamond 240 | 2 |
| 100 | — | — | — | SHE'LL BE THERE — Vikki Carr (Dave Pell & Bob Bledsoe), Liberty 56026 | 1 |

## HOT 100—A TO Z—(Publisher-Licensee)



## BUBBLING UNDER THE HOT 100

101. I'VE COME A LONG WAY ... Wilson Pickett, Atlantic 2484
102. SOULSVILLE ... Aretha Franklin, Columbia 44441
103. SHOWTIME ... Detroit Emeralds, Ric Tic 135
104. UP ON THE ROOF ... Cryan' Shames, Columbia 44457
105. CINDERELLA ROCKEFELLA ... Esther & Abi Ofarim, Philips 40526
106. BABY, PLEASE DON'T GO ... Amboy Dukes, Mainstream 676
107. (You Can't Let the Boy Overpower) THE MAN IN YOU ... Chuck Jackson, Motown 1118
108. IN THE HEAT OF THE NIGHT ... Dick Hyman & The Group, Command 4114
109. LOVEY DOVEY KINDA LOVIN' ... Brenton Wood, Double Shot 126
110. CHAIN OF FOOLS ... Jimmy Smith, Verve 10583
111. YOU'VE GOT TO CHANGE YOUR MIND ... Bobby Byrd & James Brown, King 6151
112. PARTY PEOPLE ... Solomon Burke, Atlantic 2483
113. IT'S TIME TO SAY GOODBYE ... Third Rail, Epic 10285
114. HONEY ... Bob Shane, Decca 32275
115. OUR CORNER OF THE NIGHT ... Barbra Streisand, Columbia 44474
116. UNWIND ... Ray Stevens, Monument 1048
117. THE INNER LIGHT ... Beatles, Capitol 2138
118. CAN'T FIND THE TIME ... Orpheus, MGM 13882
119. DENVER ... Steve Alaimo, Atco 6561
120. I WILL ALWAYS THINK ABOUT YOU ... New Colony Six, Mercury 72775
121. ME ABOUT YOU ... Jackie DeShannon, Imperial 66281
122. CALL ME LIGHTNING ... The Who, Decca 32288
123. HERE'S TO YOU ... Hamilton Camp, Warner Bros.-Seven Arts 7165
124. WHAT IS LOVE ... Miriam Makeba, Reprise 0671
125. UP TO MY NECK IN HIGH MUDDY WATER ... Linda Ronstadt & Stone Poneys, Capitol 2110
126. YOU SAY ... Esquires, Bunky 7753
127. HAVE A LITTLE FAITH ... David Houston, Epic 10291
128. NIGHTS IN WHITE SATIN ... Moody Blues, Deram 85023
129. I LOVE YOU ... People, Capitol 2078
130. IF YOU DON'T WANT MY LOVE ... Robert John, Columbia 44435
131. AFRICAN BOO-GA-LOO ... Jackie Lee, Keymen 114

Compiled from national retail sales and radio station airplay by the Music Popularity Dept. of Record Market Research, Billboard.

# Billboard HOT 100

**For Week Ending March 30, 1968**

★ STAR PERFORMER—Sides registering greatest proportionate upward progress this week.
® Record Industry Association of America seal of certification as million selling single.

| This Week | Last Week | 2 Wks. Ago | 3 Wks. Ago | Title — Artist (Producer), Label & Number | Wks. on Chart |
|---|---|---|---|---|---|
| 1 | 1 | 1 | 3 | (Sittin' On) THE DOCK OF THE BAY — Otis Redding (Steve Cropper), Volt 157 | 10 |
| 2 | 2 | 3 | 1 | LOVE IS BLUE — Paul Mauriat, Philips 40495 | 13 |
| 3 | 7 | 8 | — | VALLERI — Monkees (Monkees), Colgems 66-1019 | 4 |
| 4 | 4 | 4 | 4 | SIMON SAYS — 1910 Fruitgum Co. (J. Katz/J. Kasenetz/E. Chiprut), Buddah 24 | 10 |
| 5 | 8 | 9 | 17 | (Sweet Sweet Baby) SINCE YOU'VE BEEN GONE — Aretha Franklin (Jerry Wexler), Atlantic 2486 | 5 |
| 6 | 6 | 7 | 9 | LA-LA MEANS I LOVE YOU — Delfonics (Stan & Bell), Philly Groove 150 | 9 |
| 7 | 12 | 24 | 52 | YOUNG GIRL — Union Gap Featuring Gary Puckett (Jerry Fuller), Columbia 44450 | 4 |
| 8 | 10 | 17 | 26 | THE BALLAD OF BONNIE AND CLYDE — Georgie Fame (Manny Kellem), Epic 10283 | 7 |
| 9 | 23 | — | — | LADY MADONNA — Beatles (George Martin), Capitol 2138 | 2 |
| 10 | 3 | 2 | 2 | (Theme From) THE VALLEY OF THE DOLLS — Dionne Warwick (Bacharach-David), Scepter 12203 | 11 |
| 11 | 11 | 25 | 35 | THE MIGHTY QUINN — Manfred Mann, Mercury 72770 | 5 |
| 12 | 5 | 5 | 6 | JUST DROPPED IN (To See What Condition My Condition Was In) — First Edition (Mike Post), Reprise 0655 | 7 |
| 13 | 13 | 29 | 42 | SCARBOROUGH FAIR (/Canticle) — Simon & Garfunkel (Bob Johnston), Columbia 44465 | 5 |
| 14 | 14 | 16 | 19 | DANCE TO THE MUSIC — Sly & the Family Stone (Sly Stone), Epic 10256 | 8 |
| 15 | 17 | 28 | 63 | CRY LIKE A BABY — Box Tops (Dan Penn), Mala 593 | 5 |
| 16 | 16 | 22 | 27 | KISS ME GOODBYE — Petula Clark (Tony Hatch), Warner Bros.-Seven Arts 7170 | 7 |
| 17 | 9 | 10 | 11 | I THANK YOU — Sam & Dave (Isaac Hayes & David Porter), Stax 242 | 10 |
| 18 | 25 | 30 | 31 | IF YOU CAN WANT — Smokey Robinson and the Miracles ("Smokey" Cleveland), Tamla 54162 | 6 |
| 19 | 33 | 63 | — | I GOT THE FEELIN' — James Brown & the Famous Flames (James Brown), King 6155 | 3 |
| 20 | 15 | 15 | 15 | THE END OF OUR ROAD — Gladys Knight & the Pips (M. Whitfield), Soul 35042 | 8 |
| 21 | 21 | 37 | 40 | PLAYBOY — Gene & Debbie (Don Gant), TRX 5006 | 7 |
| 22 | 20 | 6 | 5 | I WISH IT WOULD RAIN — Temptations (Norman Whitfield), Gordy 7068 | 12 |
| 23 | 64 | — | — | HONEY — Bobby Goldsboro (Bob Montgomery & Bobby Goldsboro), United Artists 50283 | 3 |
| 24 | 24 | 27 | 28 | WILL YOU LOVE ME TOMORROW? — 4 Seasons (Bob Crewe), Philips 40523 | 6 |
| 25 | 29 | 35 | 37 | CAB DRIVER — Mills Brothers (Charles R. Grean & Tom Mack), Dot 17041 | 10 |
| 26 | 18 | 12 | 10 | EVERYTHING THAT TOUCHES YOU — Association (Bones Howe), Warner Bros.-Seven Arts 7163 | 7 |
| 27 | 55 | 72 | 78 | SWEET INSPIRATION — Sweet Inspirations (Tom Dowd & Tommy Cogbill), Atlantic 2476 | 5 |
| 28 | 34 | 42 | 67 | LOVE IS ALL AROUND — Troggs (Page One), Fontana 1607 | 6 |
| 29 | 28 | 13 | 13 | BOTTLE OF WINE — Fireballs (Norman Petty), Atco 6491 | 8 |
| 30 | 42 | 61 | 88 | JENNIFER JUNIPER — Donovan (Mickie Most), Epic 10300 | 4 |
| 31 | 27 | 11 | 7 | SPOOKY — Classics IV (Buddy Buie), Imperial 66259 | 15 |
| 32 | 26 | 34 | 34 | I'M GONNA MAKE YOU LOVE ME — Madeline Bell (Johnny Franz), Philips 40517 | 8 |
| 33 | 19 | 19 | 20 | TOO MUCH TALK — Paul Revere and the Raiders (Mark Lindsay), Columbia 44444 | 8 |
| 34 | 49 | 49 | 73 | TAPIOCA TUNDRA — Monkees (Monkees), Colgems 66-1019 | 4 |
| 35 | 22 | 18 | 18 | WORDS — Bee Gees (Robert Stigwood & the Bee Gees), Atco 6548 | 11 |
| 36 | 32 | 23 | 23 | THERE IS — Dells (B. Miller), Cadet 5590 | 11 |
| 37 | 37 | 38 | 44 | A QUESTION OF TEMPERATURE — Balloon Farm (Laurie Prod. & Peter Shekeryk), Laurie 3405 | 6 |
| 38 | 38 | 51 | 66 | SUMMERTIME BLUES — Blue Cheer (Abe "Voco" Kesh), Philips 40516 | 5 |
| 39 | 39 | 39 | 55 | GREEN LIGHT — American Breed (Bill Traut), Acta 821 | 6 |
| 40 | 40 | 40 | 59 | LITTLE GREEN APPLES — Roger Miller (Jerry Kennedy), Smash 2148 | 6 |
| 41 | 50 | 68 | 74 | SOUL SERENADE — Willie Mitchell (Willie Mitchell/Joe Cuoghi), Hi 2140 | 4 |
| 42 | 87 | — | — | COWBOYS TO GIRLS — Intruders (Gamble-Huff), Gamble 214 | 3 |
| 43 | 43 | 50 | 77 | SOUL COAXING (Ame Caline) — Raymond Lefevre, 4 Corners of the World 147 | 6 |
| 44 | 53 | 70 | — | FOREVER CAME TODAY — Diana Ross & the Supremes (Holland & Dozier), Motown 1122 | 3 |
| 45 | 51 | 52 | 68 | THE SON OF HICKORY HOLLER'S TRAMP — O. C. Smith (Jerry Fuller), Columbia 44425 | 6 |
| 46 | 35 | 36 | 29 | CARPET MAN — 5th Dimension (Bones Howe), Soul City 762 | 9 |
| 47 | 52 | 53 | 64 | THE GOOD, THE BAD AND THE UGLY — Hugo Montenegro, His Ork and Chorus | 5 |
| 48 | 66 | 74 | — | TAKE TIME TO KNOW HER — Percy Sledge (Quin Ivy & Marlin Greene), Atlantic 2490 | 2 |
| 49 | 77 | — | — | THE UNICORN — Irish Rovers (Charles Bud Dant), Decca 32254 | 2 |
| 50 | 48 | 48 | 41 | MISSION: IMPOSSIBLE — Lalo Schifrin (Tom Mack), Dot 17059 | 13 |
| 51 | 61 | 65 | 84 | RICE IS NICE — Lemon Pipers (Paul Leka), Buddah 31 | 4 |
| 52 | 56 | 67 | 70 | SECURITY — Etta James (Rick Hall & Staff), Cadet 5594 | 5 |
| 53 | 63 | 77 | — | FUNKY STREET — Arthur Conley (Tom Dowd), Atco 6563 | 3 |
| 54 | 54 | 54 | 49 | FOR YOUR PRECIOUS LOVE — Jackie Wilson & Count Basie (Nat Tarnepo & Teddy Reig), Brunswick 55365 | 7 |
| 55 | 45 | 47 | 47 | IN THE MIDNIGHT HOUR — Mirettes (Jerry Goldstein), Revue 11004 | 4 |
| 56 | 44 | 45 | 51 | SUDDENLY YOU LOVE ME — Tremeloes (Mike Smith), Epic 10293 | 7 |
| 57 | 58 | 59 | 81 | SOUND ASLEEP — Turtles (Turtles & Blimp), White Whale 264 | 5 |
| 58 | 59 | 60 | 79 | YOU'VE GOT TO BE LOVED — Montanas (Tony Hatch), Independence 83 | 5 |
| 59 | 57 | 58 | 76 | HEY, HEY BUNNY — John Fred & His Playboy Band (John Fred & Andrew Bernard), Paula 294 | 5 |
| 60 | 60 | 41 | 43 | SUNSHINE OF YOUR LOVE — Cream (Felix Pappalardi), Atco 6544 | 12 |
| 61 | 69 | 73 | 86 | L. DAVID SLOANE — Michele Lee (Jack Gold), Columbia 44413 | 4 |
| 62 | 62 | 69 | 90 | BACK ON MY FEET AGAIN — Foundations (Tony Macaulay), Uni 55058 | 4 |
| 63 | 75 | — | — | U. S. MALE — Elvis Presley, RCA Victor 47-9465 | 2 |
| 64 | 65 | 66 | 71 | THAT'S A LIE — Ray Charles (Ray Charles), ABC 11045 | 4 |
| 65 | 72 | 75 | — | SIT WITH THE GURU — Strawberry Alarm Clock (Frank Slay & Bill Holmes), Uni 55055 | 3 |
| 66 | 76 | 84 | — | IN NEED OF A FRIEND — Cowsills (Bill & Bob Cowsill), MGM 13909 | 3 |
| 67 | 74 | 97 | — | DELILAH — Tom Jones (Peter Sullivan), Parrot 40025 | 3 |
| 68 | 70 | 71 | 80 | IF THIS WORLD WERE MINE — Marvin Gaye & Tammi Terrell (Fuqua, Bristol), Tamla 54161 | 5 |
| 69 | 73 | 90 | — | THE IMPOSSIBLE DREAM — Hesitations (Wiltshire-Banks-Victor), Kapp 899 | 3 |
| 70 | 71 | 76 | — | JENNIFER ECCLES — Hollies (Ron Richards), Epic 10298 / Uni 55055 | 3 |
| 71 | 82 | 79 | 87 | LOVE IS BLUE — Claudine Longet (Tommy LiPuma), A&M 909 | 6 |
| 72 | 91 | — | — | ME, THE PEACEFUL HEART — Lulu (Mickie Most), Epic 10302 | 2 |
| 73 | 81 | 83 | — | STAY AWAY — Elvis Presley, RCA Victor 47-9465 | 3 |
| 74 | 80 | 80 | 95 | FOGGY MOUNTAIN BREAKDOWN — Flatt & Scruggs (Bob Johnston), Columbia 44380 / Mercury 72739 | 5 |
| 75 | 90 | — | — | YOU'VE STILL GOT A PLACE IN MY HEART — Dean Martin (Jimmy Bowen), Reprise 0672 | 2 |
| 76 | 84 | — | — | COME TO ME SOFTLY — Jimmy James & the Vagabonds (Jimmy James & Peter Meaden), Atco 6851 | 2 |
| 77 | 78 | 78 | — | TIN SOLDIER — Small Faces (Steve Marriott & Ronnie Lane), Immediate 5003 | 4 |
| 78 | 79 | 81 | 85 | I'LL SAY FOREVER MY LOVE — Jimmy Ruffin (Dean & Weatherspoon), Soul 35043 | 4 |
| 79 | — | — | — | UNKNOWN SOLDIER — Doors (Paul A. Rothchild), Elektra 45628 | 1 |
| 80 | — | — | — | CALL ME LIGHTNING — The Who (Kit Lambert), Decca 32288 | 1 |
| 81 | — | — | — | TIGHTEN UP — Archie Bell & the Drells (L.J.F. Production), Atlantic 2478 | 1 |
| 82 | 94 | 94 | — | UP FROM THE SKIES — Jimi Hendrix Experience (Charles Chandler), Reprise 0665 | 3 |
| 83 | 83 | 85 | 92 | TURN ON YOUR LOVELIGHT — Human Beinz (Lex de Azevedo), Capitol 2119 | 4 |
| 84 | — | — | — | TAKE GOOD CARE OF MY BABY — Bobby Vinton (Billy Sherrill), Epic 10305 | 1 |
| 85 | 85 | 86 | 89 | (Sittin' On) THE DOCK OF THE BAY — King Curtis & His Kingpins (Tom Dowd), Atco 6562 | 3 |
| 86 | 89 | 89 | — | AT THE TOP OF THE STAIRS — Formations (Leon Huff), MGM 13899 | 3 |
| 87 | 93 | 93 | 93 | GENTLE ON MY MIND — Patti Page (Jack Gold), Columbia 44353 | 8 |
| 88 | 95 | 95 | — | DR. JON (The Medicine Man) — Jon & Robin & the In Crowd (Abnak Music), Abnak 127 | 3 |
| 89 | 98 | — | — | SHERRY DON'T GO — Lettermen (Kelly Gordon), Capitol 2132 | 2 |
| 90 | — | — | — | CINDERELLA ROCKEFELLA — Esther & Abi Ofarim (Philips 40526) | 1 |
| 91 | — | — | — | SHOWTIME — Detroit Emeralds (Kent-Weems & Garrett), Ric Tic 135 | 1 |
| 92 | — | — | — | YOUR HEART IS FREE JUST LIKE THE WIND — Vikki Carr (Dave Pell & Rob Bledsoe), Liberty 56026 | 1 |
| 93 | — | — | — | UP TO MY NECK IN HIGH MUDDY WATER — Linda Ronstadt & the Stone Poneys (Nick Venet), Capitol 2110 | 1 |
| 94 | — | — | — | MASTER JACK — Four Jacks & A Jill, RCA Victor 47-9473 | 1 |
| 95 | — | — | — | I WILL ALWAYS THINK ABOUT YOU — New Colony Six (Senator Records Corp./Mercury 72773) | 1 |
| 96 | — | — | — | THE INNER LIGHT — Beatles (George Martin), Capitol 2138 | 1 |
| 97 | 97 | — | — | 100 YEARS — Nancy Sinatra (Lee Hazlewood), Reprise 0670 | 2 |
| 98 | — | — | — | ANOTHER PLACE, ANOTHER TIME — Jerry Lee Lewis (Jerry Kennedy), Smash 2146 | 1 |
| 99 | 99 | 100 | — | IN SOME TIME — Ronnie Dove (Lee Hazlewood), Diamond 240 | 2 |
| 100 | 100 | — | — | SHE'LL BE THERE — Vikki Carr (Dave Pell & Bob Bledsoe), Liberty 56026 | 1 |

## BUBBLING UNDER THE HOT 100

101. I'VE COME A LONG WAY ................ Wilson Pickett, Atlantic 2484
102. GOODBYE BABY (I Don't Want to See You Cry) ........ Tommy Boyce & Bobby Hart, A&M 919
103. (You Keep Me) HANGIN' ON ........ Joe Simon, Sound Stage 7 2608
104. BABY YOU'RE SO RIGHT ........ Brenda & the Tabulations, Dionn 507
105. HONEY ........ Bob Shane, Decca 32275
106. UP ON THE ROOF ........ Cryan' Shames, Columbia 44457
107. YOU'VE GOT TO CHANGE YOUR MIND ........ Bobby Byrd & James Brown, King 6151
108. IN THE HEAT OF THE NIGHT ........ Dick Hyman & the Group, Command 4114
109. LOVEY DOVEY KINDA LOVIN' ........ Brenton Wood, Double Shot 126
110. CHAIN OF FOOLS ........ Jimmy Smith, Verve 10583
111. IN THE MORNING ........ Mighty Marvelows, ABC 11071
112. RED RED WINE ........ Neil Diamond, Bang 556
113. OUR CORNER OF THE NIGHT ........ Barbra Streisand, Columbia 44474
114. UNWIND ........ Ray Stevens, Monument 1048
115. WIND SONG ........ Wes Montgomery, A&M 916
116. I TRULY, TRULY BELIEVE ........ Temptations, Gordy 7068
117. CAN'T FIND THE TIME ........ Orpheus, MGM 13882
118. DENVER ........ Steve Alaimo, Atco 6561
119. ME ABOUT YOU ........ Jackie DeShannon, Imperial 66281
120. HERE'S TO YOU ........ Hamilton Camp, Warner Bros.-Seven Arts 7165
121. FOOL OF FOOLS ........ Tony Bennett, Columbia 44443
122. AIN'T NO WAY ........ Aretha Franklin, Atlantic 2486
123. THE LAST GOODBYE ........ Dick Miles, Capitol 2113
124. WHAT IS LOVE ........ Miriam Makeba, Reprise 0671
125. I LOVE YOU ........ People, Bunky 7753
126. YOU SAY ........ Esquires, Bunky
127. HAVE A LITTLE FAITH ........ David Houston, Epic 1029
128. AFRICAN BOO-GA-LOO ........ Jackie Lee, Keymen 114
129. IF YOU DON'T WANT MY LOVE ........ Robert John, Columbia 44435
130. SO FINE ........ Ike & Tina & Ikettes, Innis 6667

Compiled from national retail sales and radio station airplay by the Music Popularity Dept. of Record Market Research, Billboard.

# Billboard HOT 100

FOR WEEK ENDING APRIL 6, 1968

★ STAR PERFORMER—Sides registering greatest proportionate upward progress this week.

(seal) Record Industry Association of America seal of certification as million selling single.

| This Week | 1 Wk. Ago | 2 Wks. Ago | 3 Wks. Ago | TITLE Artist (Producer), Label & Number | Weeks On Chart |
|---|---|---|---|---|---|
| 1 (Billboard Award) | 1 | 1 | 1 | (Sittin' On) THE DOCK OF THE BAY — Otis Redding (Steve Cropper), Volt 157 | 11 |
| ★2 | 7 | 12 | 24 | YOUNG GIRL — Union Gap Featuring Gary Puckett (Jerry Fuller), Columbia 44450 | 6 |
| 3 (seal) | 3 | 7 | 8 | VALLERI — Monkees (Monkees), Colgems 66-1019 | 5 |
| 4 | 6 | 6 | 7 | LA-LA MEANS I LOVE YOU — Delfonics (Stan & Bell), Philly Groove 150 | 10 |
| 5 | 5 | 8 | 9 | (Sweet Sweet Baby) SINCE YOU'VE BEEN GONE — Aretha Franklin (Jerry Wexler), Atlantic 2486 | 6 |
| ★6 | 15 | 17 | 28 | CRY LIKE A BABY — Box Tops (Dan Penn), Mala 593 | 6 |
| ★7 | 9 | 23 | — | LADY MADONNA — Beatles (George Martin), Capitol 2138 | 3 |
| 8 | 8 | 10 | 17 | THE BALLAD OF BONNIE AND CLYDE — Georgie Fame (Manny Kellem), Epic 10283 | 8 |
| 9 (seal) | 2 | 2 | 3 | LOVE IS BLUE — Paul Mauriat, Philips 40495 | 14 |
| ★10 | 23 | 64 | — | HONEY — Bobby Goldsboro (Bob Montgomery & Bobby Goldsboro), United Artists 50283 | 3 |
| 11 | 11 | 11 | 25 | THE MIGHTY QUINN — Manfred Mann, Mercury 72770 | 6 |
| 12 (seal) | 4 | 4 | 4 | SIMON SAYS — 1910 Fruitgum Co. (J. Katz/J. Kasenetz/E. Chiprut), Buddah 24 | 11 |
| ★13 | 13 | 13 | 29 | SCARBOROUGH FAIR (/Canticle) — Simon & Garfunkel (Bob Johnston), Columbia 44465 | 6 |
| ★14 | 14 | 14 | 16 | DANCE TO THE MUSIC — Sly & the Family Stone (Sly Stone), Epic 10256 | 9 |
| ★15 | 16 | 16 | 22 | KISS ME GOODBYE — Petula Clark (Tony Hatch), Warner Bros.-Seven Arts 7170 | 8 |
| ★16 | 18 | 25 | 30 | IF YOU CAN WANT — Smokey Robinson and the Miracles ("Smokey" Cleveland), Tamla 54162 | 7 |
| 17 | 10 | 3 | 2 | (Theme From) THE VALLEY OF THE DOLLS — Dionne Warwick (Bacharach-David), Scepter 12203 | 12 |
| ★18 | 19 | 33 | 63 | I GOT THE FEELIN' — James Brown & the Famous Flames (James Brown), King 6155 | 4 |
| 19 | 12 | 5 | 5 | JUST DROPPED IN (To See What Condition My Condition Was In) — First Edition (Mike Post), Reprise 0655 | 8 |
| 20 | 17 | 9 | 10 | I THANK YOU — Sam & Dave (Isaac Hayes & David Porter), Stax 242 | 11 |
| 21 | 21 | 21 | 37 | PLAYBOY — Gene & Debbie (Don Gant), TRX 5006 | 8 |
| ★22 | 38 | 38 | 51 | SUMMERTIME BLUES — Blue Cheer (Abe "Voce" Kesh), Philips 40516 | 6 |
| 23 | 25 | 29 | 35 | CAB DRIVER — Mills Brothers (Charles R. Grean & Tom Mack), Dot 17041 | 11 |
| 24 | 24 | 24 | 27 | WILL YOU LOVE ME TOMORROW? — 4 Seasons (Bob Crewe), Philips 40523 | 7 |
| 25 | 28 | 34 | 42 | LOVE IS ALL AROUND — Troggs (Page One), Fontana 1607 | 7 |
| 26 | 27 | 55 | 72 | SWEET INSPIRATION — Sweet Inspirations (Tom Dowd & Tommy Cogbill), Atlantic 2476 | 6 |
| ★27 | 49 | 77 | — | THE UNICORN — Irish Rovers (Charles Bud Dant), Decca 32254 | 3 |
| ★28 | 42 | 87 | — | COWBOYS TO GIRLS — Intruders (Gamble-Huff), Gamble 214 | 3 |
| 29 | 30 | 42 | 61 | JENNIFER JUNIPER — Donovan (Mickie Most), Epic 10300 | 5 |
| ★30 | 48 | 66 | 74 | TAKE TIME TO KNOW HER — Percy Sledge (Quin Ivy & Marlin Greene), Atlantic 2490 | 4 |
| ★31 | 44 | 53 | 70 | FOREVER CAME TODAY — Diana Ross & the Supremes (Holland & Dozier), Motown 1122 | 4 |
| 32 | 20 | 15 | 15 | THE END OF OUR ROAD — Gladys Knight & the Pips (M. Whitfield), Soul 35042 | 9 |
| 33 | 22 | 20 | 6 | I WISH IT WOULD RAIN — Temptations (Norman Whitfield), Gordy 7068 | 13 |
| ★34 | 47 | 52 | 53 | THE GOOD, THE BAD AND THE UGLY — Hugo Montenegro, His Ork and Chorus | 8 |
| ★35 | 53 | 63 | 77 | FUNKY STREET — Arthur Conley (Tom Dowd), Atco 6563 | 4 |
| 36 | 32 | 26 | 34 | I'M GONNA MAKE YOU LOVE ME — Madeline Bell (Johnny Franz), Philips 40517 | 9 |
| 37 | 37 | 37 | 38 | A QUESTION OF TEMPERATURE — Balloon Farm (Laurie Prod. & Peter Shekeryk), Laurie 3405 | 7 |
| ★38 | 52 | 56 | 67 | SECURITY — Etta James (Rick Hall & Staff), Cadet 5594 | 6 |
| 39 | 40 | 40 | 40 | LITTLE GREEN APPLES — Roger Miller (Jerry Kennedy), Smash 2148 | 6 |
| ★40 | 43 | 43 | 50 | SOUL COAXING (Ame Caline) — Raymond Lefevre, 4 Corners of the World 147 | 7 |
| 41 | 41 | 50 | 68 | SOUL SERENADE — Willie Mitchell (Willie Mitchell/Joe Cuoghi), Hi 2140 | 5 |
| 42 | 39 | 39 | 39 | GREEN LIGHT — American Breed (Bill Traut), Acta 821 | 7 |
| 43 | 45 | 51 | 52 | THE SON OF HICKORY HOLLER'S TRAMP — O. C. Smith (Jerry Fuller), Columbia 44425 | 7 |
| ★44 | 69 | 73 | 90 | THE IMPOSSIBLE DREAM — Hesitations (Wiltshire-Banks-Victor), Kapp 899 | 4 |
| 45 | 34 | 49 | 49 | TAPIOCA TUNDRA — Monkees (Monkees), Colgems 66-1019 | 5 |
| ★46 | 81 | — | — | TIGHTEN UP — Archie Bell & the Drells (L.J.F. Production), Atlantic 2478 | 2 |
| ★47 | 63 | 75 | — | U. S. MALE — Elvis Presley, RCA Victor 47-9465 | 3 |
| ★48 | 95 | — | — | I WILL ALWAYS THINK ABOUT YOU — New Colony Six (Senator Records Corp.), Mercury 72775 | 2 |
| 49 | 51 | 61 | 65 | RICE IS NICE — Lemon Pipers (Paul Leka), Buddah 31 | 5 |
| 50 | 50 | 48 | 48 | MISSION: IMPOSSIBLE — Lalo Schifrin (Tom Mack), Dot 17059 | 14 |
| ★51 | 84 | — | — | TAKE GOOD CARE OF MY BABY — Bobby Vinton (Billy Sherrill), Epic 10305 | 2 |
| 52 | 61 | 69 | 73 | L. DAVID SLOANE — Michele Lee (Jack Gold), Columbia 44413 | 6 |
| ★53 | 67 | 74 | 97 | DELILAH — Tom Jones (Peter Sullivan), Parrot 40025 | 4 |
| ★54 | 70 | 71 | 76 | JENNIFER ECCLES — Hollies (Ron Richards), Epic 10298 Uni 55055 | 4 |
| ★55 | 66 | 76 | 84 | IN NEED OF A FRIEND — Cowsills (Bill & Bob Cowsill), MGM 13909 | 4 |
| 56 | 56 | 44 | 45 | SUDDENLY YOU LOVE ME — Tremeloes (Mike Smith), Epic 10293 | 8 |
| ★57 | 80 | — | — | CALL ME LIGHTNING — The Who (Kit Lambert), Decca 32288 | 2 |
| 58 | 58 | 59 | 60 | YOU'VE GOT TO BE LOVED — Montanas (Tony Hatch), Independence 83 | 6 |
| 59 | 62 | 62 | 69 | BACK ON MY FEET AGAIN — Foundations (Tony Macaclay), Uni 55058 | 5 |
| 60 | 60 | 60 | 41 | SUNSHINE OF YOUR LOVE — Cream (Felix Pappalardi), Atco 6544 | 13 |
| 61 | 57 | 58 | 59 | SOUND ASLEEP — Turtles (Turtles & Blimp), White Whale 264 | 6 |
| ★62 | 79 | — | — | UNKNOWN SOLDIER — Doors (Paul A. Rothchild), Elektra 45628 | 2 |
| ★63 | 89 | 98 | — | SHERRY DON'T GO — Lettermen (Kelly Gordon), Capitol 2132 | 3 |
| 64 | 64 | 65 | 66 | THAT'S A LIE — Ray Charles (Ray Charles), ABC 11045 | 7 |
| 65 | 65 | 72 | 75 | SIT WITH THE GURU — Strawberry Alarm Clock (Frank Slay & Bill Holmes), Uni 55055 | 4 |
| ★66 | 75 | 90 | — | YOU'VE STILL GOT A PLACE IN MY HEART — Dean Martin (Jimmy Bowen), Reprise 0672 | 3 |
| 67 | 73 | 81 | 83 | STAY AWAY — Elvis Presley, RCA Victor 47-9465 | 4 |
| 68 | 68 | 70 | 71 | IF THIS WORLD WERE MINE — Marvin Gaye & Tammi Terrell (Fugua, Bristol), Tamla 54161 | 6 |
| 69 | 72 | 91 | — | ME, THE PEACEFUL HEART — Lulu (Mickie Most), Epic 10302 | 3 |
| ★70 | — | — | — | GOODBYE BABY (I Don't Want to See You Cry) — Tommy Boyce & Bobby Hart (Boyce-Hart), A&M 919 | 1 |
| 71 | 71 | 82 | 79 | LOVE IS BLUE — Claudine Longet (Tommy LiPuma), A&M 909 | 7 |
| 72 | 74 | 80 | 80 | FOGGY MOUNTAIN BREAKDOWN — Flatt & Scruggs (Bob Johnston), Columbia 44380/Mercury 72739 | 6 |
| 73 | 77 | 78 | 78 | TIN SOLDIER — Small Faces (Steve Marriott & Ronnie Lane), Immediate 5003 | 4 |
| ★74 | — | — | — | SHOO-BE-DOO-BE-DOO-DA-DAY — Stevie Wonder (H. Cosby), Tamla 54165 | 1 |
| ★75 | — | — | — | LOOK TO YOUR SOUL — Johnny Rivers (Work), Imperial 66286 | 1 |
| 76 | 76 | 84 | — | COME TO ME SOFTLY — Jimmy James & the Vagabonds (Jimmy James & Peter Meaden), Atco 6851 | 3 |
| 77 | 78 | 79 | 81 | I'LL SAY FOREVER MY LOVE — Jimmy Ruffin (Dean & Weatherspoon), Soul 35043 | 5 |
| ★78 | — | — | — | AIN'T NO WAY — Aretha Franklin (Jerry Wexler), Atlantic 2486 | 1 |
| 79 | 87 | 93 | 93 | GENTLE ON MY MIND — Patti Page (Jack Gold), Columbia 44353 | 9 |
| 80 | 83 | 83 | 85 | TURN ON YOUR LOVELIGHT — Human Beinz (Lex de Asavedo), Capitol 2119 | 5 |
| ★81 | 97 | 97 | — | 100 YEARS — Nancy Sinatra (Lee Hazlewood), Reprise 0670 | 3 |
| 82 | 82 | 94 | 94 | UP FROM THE SKIES — Jimi Hendrix Experience (Charles Chandler), Reprise 0665 | 4 |
| ★83 | — | — | — | I GOT A SURE THING — Ollie & the Nightingales (Booker T. Jones), Stax 245 | 1 |
| 84 | 85 | 85 | 86 | (Sittin' On) THE DOCK OF THE BAY — King Curtis & His Kingpins (Tom Dowd), Atco 6562 | 4 |
| 85 | 86 | 89 | 89 | AT THE TOP OF THE STAIRS — Formations (Leon Huff), MGM 13899 | 4 |
| ★86 | — | — | — | UP ON THE ROOF — Cryan' Shames (Jim Golden & Bob Monaco), Columbia 44457 | 1 |
| 87 | 88 | 95 | 95 | DR. JON (The Medicine Man) — Jon & Robin & the In Crowd (Abnak Music), Abnak 127 | 4 |
| ★88 | — | — | — | I WANNA LIVE — Glen Campbell (Alyde Lory), Capitol 2146 | 1 |
| 89 | 90 | — | — | CINDERELLA ROCKEFELLA — Esther & Abi Ofarim, Philips 40526 | 2 |
| ★90 | — | — | — | JUMBO — Bee Gees (Robert Stigwood & Bee Gees), Atco 6570 | 1 |
| 91 | 91 | — | — | SHOWTIME — Detroit Emeralds (Kent-Weems & Garrett), Ric Tic 135 | 2 |
| 92 | 92 | — | — | YOUR HEART IS FREE JUST LIKE THE WIND — Vikki Carr (Dave Pell & Rob Bledsoe), Liberty 56026 | 2 |
| 93 | 93 | — | — | UP TO MY NECK IN HIGH MUDDY WATER — Linda Ronstadt & the Stone Poneys (Nick Venet), Capitol 2110 | 2 |
| 94 | 94 | — | — | MASTER JACK — Four Jacks & A Jill, RCA Victor 47-9473 | 2 |
| 95 | — | — | — | MONY MONY — Tommy James & Shondells (Bo Gentry & Ritchie Cordell), Roulette 7008 | 1 |
| 96 | — | — | — | I LOVE YOU — People (Mikel Hunter), Capitol 2078 | 1 |
| 97 | 98 | — | — | ANOTHER PLACE, ANOTHER TIME — Jerry Lee Lewis (Jerry Kennedy), Smash 2146 | 2 |
| 98 | — | 86 | 87 | BABY YOU'RE SO RIGHT FOR ME — Brenda & Tabulations (Bob Finiz), Dionn 507 | 3 |
| 99 | 100 | 100 | — | SHE'LL BE THERE — Vikki Carr (Dave Pell & Bob Bledsoe), Liberty 56026 | 3 |
| 100 | — | — | — | CHAIN OF FOOLS — Jimmy Smith (Esmond Edwards), Verve 10583 | 1 |

## HOT 100—A TO Z—*(Publisher-Licensee)*


Ain't No Way (14th Hour/Cotillion, BMI) ...... 78
Another Place, Another Time (Passkey, BMI) ..... 97
At the Top of the Stairs (Double Diamond/Mured, BMI) ...... 85
Baby You're So Right for Me (Chardon, BMI) ..... 98
Back on My Feet Again (January/Welbeck, BMI) .. 59
Ballad of Bonnie and Clyde, The (Peer Int'l, BMI). 8
Cab Driver (Blackhawk, BMI) ...... 23
Call Me Lightning (Fabulous, ASCAP) ...... 57
Chain of Fools (14th Hour/Pronto, BMI) ......100
Cinderella Rockefella (Irving, BMI) ...... 89
Come to Me Softly (Regent, BMI) ...... 76
Cowboys to Girls (Razor Sharp, BMI) ...... 28
Cry Like a Baby (Press, BMI) ...... 6
Dance to the Music (Daly City, BMI) ...... 14
Delilah (Francis, Day & Hunter, ASCAP) ...... 53
Dr. Jon (The Medicine Man) (Barton, BMI) ..... 87
End of Our Road, The (Jobete, BMI) ...... 32
Foggy Mountain Breakdown (Peer Int'l, BMI) ... 72
Forever Came Today (Jobete, BMI) ...... 31
Funky Street (Redwal, BMI) ...... 35
Gentle on My Mind (Sherman-DeVorzan, BMI) ... 79
Good, the Bad and the Ugly, The (Unart, BMI) ... 34
Goodbye Baby (I Don't Want to See You Cry) (Screen Gems-Columbia, BMI) ...... 70
Green Light (Four Star, BMI) ...... 42
Honey (Rnssell-Cason, ASCAP) ...... 10
I Got a Sure Thing (East, BMI) ...... 83
I Got the Feelin' (Toccoa-Lois, BMI) ...... 18
I Love You (Mainstay, BMI) ...... 96
I Thank You (East/Pronto, BMI) ...... 20
I Wanna Live (Windward Side, BMI) ...... 88
I Will Always Think About You (New Colony, BMI) 48
I Wish It Would Rain (Jobete, BMI) ...... 33
If This World Were Mine (Jobete, BMI) ...... 68
If You Can Want (Jobete, BMI) ...... 16
I'll Say Forever My Love (Jobete, BMI) ...... 77
Impossible Dream (Fox, ASCAP) ...... 44
I'm Gonna Make You Love Me (Act Three, BMI) .. 36
In Need of a Friend (Akbestal, BMI) ...... 55
Jennifer Eccles (Maribus, BMI) ...... 54
Jennifer Juniper (Peer Int'l, BMI) ...... 29
Jumbo (Nemperor, BMI) ...... 90
Just Dropped In (To See What Condition My Condition Was In) (Acuff-Rose, BMI) ...... 19
Kiss Me Goodbye (Donna, ASCAP) ...... 15
L. David Sloane (Meager, BMI) ...... 52
Lady Madonna (Maclen, BMI) ...... 7
La-La Means I Love You (Nickel Shoe, BMI) .... 4
Little Green Apples (Russell-Cason, ASCAP) ...... 39
Look to Your Soul (Rivers, BMI) ...... 75
Love Is All Around (James, BMI) ...... 25
Love Is Blue (Croma, ASCAP) (Paul Mauriat) ... 9
Love Is Blue (Croma, ASCAP) (Claudine Longet) .. 71
Master Jack (Milene, ASCAP) ...... 94
Me, the Peaceful Heart (James, BMI) ...... 69
Mighty Quinn, The (Dwarf, ASCAP) ...... 11
Mission: Impossible (Bruin, BMI) ...... 50
Mony Mony (Patricia, BMI) ...... 95
100 Years (Hazlewood, ASCAP) ...... 81
Playboy (Acuff-Rose, BMI) ...... 21
Question of Temperature (H&L, BMI) ...... 37
Rice Is Nice (Kama Sutra, BMI) ...... 49
Scarborough Fair (/Canticle) (Charing Cross, BMI). 13
Security (East, BMI) ...... 38
She'll Be There (Alta, ASCAP) ...... 99
Sherry Don't Go (Grey Fox, BMI) ...... 63
Shoo-Be-Doo-Be-Doo-Da-Day (Jobete, BMI) ...... 74
Showtime (Wingate, BMI) ...... 91
Simon Says (Maskat, BMI) ...... 12
(Sittin' On) The Dock of the Bay (East/Pine/Redwal, BMI) (King Curtis) ...... 84
(Sittin' On) The Dock of the Bay (East/Pine/Redwal, BMI) (Otis Redding) ...... 1
Sit With the Guru (Alarm Clock/Claridge, ASCAP).. 65
Son of Hickory Holler's Tramp, The (Blue Crest, BMI) ...... 43
Soul Coaxing (Ame Caline) (Southern, ASCAP) ... 40
Soul Serenade (Kilyn, BMI) ...... 41
Sound Asleep (Ishmael, BMI) ...... 61
Stay Away (Gladys, ASCAP) ...... 67
Suddenly You Love Me (Ponderosa, BMI) ...... 56
Summertime Blues (Sea Chest, BMI) ...... 22
Sunshine of Your Love (Dratleaf, BMI) ...... 60
Sweet Inspiration (Press, BMI) ...... 26
(Sweet Sweet Baby) Since You've Been Gone (14th Hour/Cotillion, BMI) ...... 5
Take Good Care of My Baby (Screen Gems-Columbia, BMI) ...... 51
Take Time to Know Her (Gallico, BMI) ...... 30
Tapioca Tundra (Screen Gems-Columbia, BMI) ... 45
That's a Lie (Tangerine, BMI) ...... 64
(Theme From) Valley of the Dolls (Feist, ASCAP) . 17
Tighten Up (Cotillion/Orellis, BMI) ...... 46
Tin Soldier (Nice Songs, BMI) ...... 73
Turn on Your Lovelight (Lion, BMI) ...... 80
Unicorn, The (Hollis, BMI) ...... 27
Unkown Soldier (Nipper, ASCAP) ...... 62
Up From the Skies (Sea-Lark Ent., BMI) ...... 82
Up on the Roof (Screen Gems-Columbia, BMI) .. 86
Up to My Neck in High Muddy Water (Ryerson, BMI) ...... 93
U. S. Male (Vector, BMI) ...... 47
Valleri (Screen Gems-Columbia, BMI) ...... 3
Will You Love Me Tomorrow? (Screen Gems-Columbia, BMI) ...... 24
Young Girl (Viva, BMI) ...... 2
Your Heart Is Free Just Like the Wind (MRC, BMI). 92
You've Got to Be Loved (Duchess, BMI) ...... 58
You've Still Got a Place in My Heart (Acuff-Rose, BMI) ...... 66


## BUBBLING UNDER THE HOT 100

101. I'VE COME A LONG WAY ......Wilson Pickett, Atlantic 2484
102. (You Keep Me) HANGIN' ON ......Joe Simon, Sound Stage 7 2608
103. IN SOME TIME ......Ronnie Dove, Diamond 240
104. HONEY ......Bob Shane, Decca 32275
105. YOU'VE GOT TO CHANGE YOUR MIND.Bobby Byrd & James Brown, King 6151
106. IN THE HEAT OF THE NIGHT ....Dick Hyman & the Group, Command 4114
107. INNER LIGHT ......Beatles, Capitol 2138
108. IN THE MORNING ......Mighty Marvelows, ABC 11011
109. WIND SONG ......Wes Montgomery, A&M 916
110. OUR CORNER OF THE NIGHT ......Barbra Streisand, Columbia 44474
111. RED RED WINE ......Neil Diamond, Bang 556
112. CAN'T FIND THE TIME ......Orpheus, MGM 13882
113. UNWIND ......Roy Stevens, Monument 1048
114. LAST GOODBYE ......Dick Miles, Capitol 2113
115. EVERY MAN OUGHTA HAVE A WOMAN ......William Bell, Stax 248
116. I TRULY, TRULY BELIEVE ......Temptations, Gordy 7068
117. SHE WEARS MY RING ......Solomon King, Capitol 2114
118. HERE'S TO YOU ......Hamilton Camp, Warner Bros.-Seven Arts 7165
119. ME ABOUT YOU ......Jackie DeShannon, Imperial 66281
120. HAVE A LITTLE FAITH ......David Houston, Epic 10291
121. AFRICAN BOO-GA-LOO ......Jackie Lee, Keymen 114
122. IF YOU DIDN'T HEAR ME THE FIRST TIME (I'll Say It Again) ......Sandpebbles, Calla 148
123. WHAT IS LOVE ......Miriam Makeba, Reprise 0671
124. IF YOU DON'T WANT MY LOVE ......Robert John, Columbia 44435
125. SO FINE ......Ike & Tina Iketts, Innis 6667
126. GREASY HEART ......Jefferson Airplane, RCA Victor 47-9496
127. DOES YOUR MAMA KNOW ABOUT ME ......Bobby Taylor & the Vancouvers, Gordy 7069
128. I FOUND YOU ......Frankie Laine, ABC 11057
129. I DON'T KNOW ......Violinaires, Checker 5043
130. BONNIE & CLYDE ......New Vaudeville Band, Fontana 1612
131. LOVING YOU HAS MADE ME BANANAS ......Guy Marks, ABC 11055
132. GOIN' AWAY ......Fireballs, Atco 6569
133. ANYTHING ......Eric Burdon & the Animals, MGM 13917

Compiled from national retail sales and radio station airplay by the Music Popularity Dept. of Record Market Research, Billboard.

# Billboard HOT 100

FOR WEEK ENDING APRIL 13, 1968

★ STAR PERFORMER—Sides registering greatest proportionate upward progress this week.

● Record Industry Association of America seal of certification as million selling single.

| THIS WEEK | 1 Wk. Ago | 2 Wks. Ago | 3 Wks. Ago | TITLE Artist (Producer), Label & Number | Weeks On Chart |
|---|---|---|---|---|---|
| 1 (Billboard Award) ● | 10 | 23 | 64 | HONEY — Bobby Goldsboro (Bob Montgomery & Bobby Goldsboro), United Artists 50283 | 4 |
| ★ 2 | 2 | 7 | 12 | YOUNG GIRL — Union Gap Featuring Gary Puckett (Jerry Fuller), Columbia 44450 | 7 |
| ● 3 | 1 | 1 | 1 | (Sittin' On) THE DOCK OF THE BAY — Otis Redding (Steve Cropper), Volt 157 | 12 |
| ★ 4 | 6 | 15 | 17 | CRY LIKE A BABY — Box Tops (Dan Penn), Mala 593 | 7 |
| ● 5 | 5 | 5 | 8 | (Sweet Sweet Baby) SINCE YOU'VE BEEN GONE — Aretha Franklin (Jerry Wexler), Atlantic 2486 | 7 |
| ★ 6 | 7 | 9 | 23 | LADY MADONNA — Beatles (George Martin), Capitol 2138 | 4 |
| 7 | 8 | 8 | 10 | THE BALLAD OF BONNIE AND CLYDE — Georgie Fame (Manny Kellem), Epic 10283 | 9 |
| 8 | 4 | 6 | 6 | LA-LA MEANS I LOVE YOU — Delfonics (Stan & Bell), Philly Groove 150 | 11 |
| ● 9 | 3 | 3 | 7 | VALLERI — Monkees (Monkees), Colgems 66-1019 | 6 |
| 10 | 11 | 11 | 11 | THE MIGHTY QUINN — Manfred Mann, Mercury 72770 | 7 |
| ★ 11 | 18 | 19 | 33 | I GOT THE FEELIN' — James Brown & the Famous Flames (James Brown), King 6155 | 5 |
| ● 12 | 9 | 2 | 2 | LOVE IS BLUE — Paul Mauriat, Philips 40495 | 15 |
| 13 | 13 | 13 | 13 | SCARBOROUGH FAIR (/Canticle) — Simon & Garfunkel (Bob Johnston), Columbia 44465 | 7 |
| 14 | 14 | 14 | 14 | DANCE TO THE MUSIC — Sly & the Family Stone (Sly Stone), Epic 10256 | 10 |
| ● 15 | 12 | 4 | 4 | SIMON SAYS — 1910 Fruitgum Co. (J. Katz/J. Kasenetz/E. Chiprut), Buddah 24 | 12 |
| 16 | 16 | 18 | 25 | IF YOU CAN WANT — Smokey Robinson and the Miracles ("Smokey" Cleveland), Tamla 54162 | 8 |
| ★ 17 | 21 | 21 | 21 | PLAYBOY — Gene & Debbie (Don Gant), TRX 5006 | 9 |
| ★ 18 | 28 | 42 | 87 | COWBOYS TO GIRLS — Intruders (Gamble-Huff), Gamble 214 | 4 |
| ★ 19 | 22 | 38 | 38 | SUMMERTIME BLUES — Blue Cheer (Abe "Voce" Kesh), Philips 40516 | 7 |
| 20 | 15 | 16 | 16 | KISS ME GOODBYE — Petula Clark (Tony Hatch), Warner Bros.-Seven Arts 7170 | 9 |
| ★ 21 | 78 | — | — | AIN'T NO WAY — Aretha Franklin (Jerry Wexler), Atlantic 2486 | 2 |
| 22 | 17 | 10 | 3 | (Theme From) THE VALLEY OF THE DOLLS — Dionne Warwick (Bacharach-David), Scepter 12203 | 13 |
| 23 | 23 | 25 | 29 | CAB DRIVER — Mills Brothers (Charles R. Grean & Tom Mack), Dot 17041 | 12 |
| ★ 24 | 26 | 27 | 55 | SWEET INSPIRATION — Sweet Inspirations (Tom Dowd & Tommy Cogbill), Atlantic 2476 | 7 |
| 25 | 25 | 28 | 34 | LOVE IS ALL AROUND — Troggs (Page One), Fontana 1607 | 8 |
| ★ 26 | 27 | 49 | 77 | THE UNICORN — Irish Rovers (Charles Bud Dant), Decca 32254 | 4 |
| 27 | 20 | 17 | 9 | I THANK YOU — Sam & Dave (Isaac Hayes & David Porter), Stax 242 | 12 |
| ★ 28 | 29 | 30 | 42 | JENNIFER JUNIPER — Donovan (Mickie Most), Epic 10300 | 6 |
| ★ 29 | 31 | 44 | 53 | FOREVER CAME TODAY — Diana Ross & the Supremes (Holland & Dozier), Motown 1122 | 5 |
| 30 | 30 | 48 | 66 | TAKE TIME TO KNOW HER — Percy Sledge (Quin Ivy & Marlin Greene), Atlantic 2490 | 5 |
| ★ 31 | 35 | 53 | 63 | FUNKY STREET — Arthur Conley (Tom Dowd), Atco 6563 | 5 |
| 32 | 34 | 47 | 52 | THE GOOD, THE BAD AND THE UGLY — Hugo Montenegro, His Ork and Chorus (Neely Plumb), RCA Victor 9423 | 9 |
| 33 | 19 | 12 | 5 | JUST DROPPED IN (To See What Condition My Condition Was In) — First Edition (Mike Post), Reprise 0655 | 9 |
| ★ 34 | 53 | 67 | 74 | DELILAH — Tom Jones (Peter Sullivan), Parrot 40025 | 5 |
| ★ 35 | 38 | 52 | 56 | SECURITY — Etta James (Rick Hall & Staff), Cadet 5594 | 7 |
| ★ 36 | 51 | 84 | — | TAKE GOOD CARE OF MY BABY — Bobby Vinton (Billy Sherrill), Epic 10305 | 3 |
| ★ 37 | 46 | 81 | — | TIGHTEN UP — Archie Bell & the Drells (L.J.F. Production), Atlantic 2478 | 3 |
| ★ 38 | 41 | 41 | 50 | SOUL SERENADE — Willie Mitchell (Willie Mitchell/Joe Cuoghi), Hi 2140 | 6 |
| 39 | 39 | 40 | 40 | LITTLE GREEN APPLES — Roger Miller (Jerry Kennedy), Smash 2148 | 7 |
| 40 | 40 | 43 | 43 | SOUL COAXING (Ame Caline) — Raymond Lefevre, 4 Corners of the World 147 | 8 |
| 41 | 24 | 24 | 24 | WILL YOU LOVE ME TOMORROW? — 4 Seasons (Bob Crewe), Philips 40523 | 8 |
| ★ 42 | 47 | 63 | 75 | U. S. MALE — Elvis Presley, RCA Victor 47-9465 | 4 |
| 43 | 43 | 45 | 51 | THE SON OF HICKORY HOLLER'S TRAMP — O. C. Smith (Jerry Fuller), Columbia 44425 | 8 |
| 44 | 44 | 69 | 73 | THE IMPOSSIBLE DREAM — Hesitations (Wiltshire-Banks-Victor), Kapp 899 | 5 |
| 45 | 45 | 34 | 49 | TAPIOCA TUNDRA — Monkees (Monkees), Colgems 66-1019 | 6 |
| ★ 46 | 48 | 95 | — | I WILL ALWAYS THINK ABOUT YOU — New Colony Six (Senator Records Corp.), Mercury 72775 | 3 |
| ★ 47 | 54 | 70 | 71 | JENNIFER ECCLES — Hollies (Ron Richards), Epic 10298 Uni 55055 | 5 |
| 48 | 32 | 20 | 15 | THE END OF OUR ROAD — Gladys Knight & the Pips (M. Whitfield), Soul 35042 | 10 |
| 49 | 49 | 51 | 61 | RICE IS NICE — Lemon Pipers (Paul Leka), Buddah 31 | 6 |
| 50 | 33 | 22 | 20 | I WISH IT WOULD RAIN — Temptations (Norman Whitfield), Gordy 7068 | 14 |
| 51 | 37 | 37 | 37 | A QUESTION OF TEMPERATURE — Balloon Farm (Laurie Prod. & Peter Shekeryk), Laurie 3405 | 8 |
| 52 | 52 | 61 | 69 | L. DAVID SLOANE — Michele Lee (Jack Gold), Columbia 44413 | 7 |
| ★ 53 | 57 | 80 | — | CALL ME LIGHTNING — The Who (Kit Lambert), Decca 32288 | 3 |
| 54 | 56 | 56 | 44 | SUDDENLY YOU LOVE ME — Tremeloes (Mike Smith), Epic 10293 | 9 |
| 55 | 55 | 66 | 76 | IN NEED OF A FRIEND — Cowsills (Bill & Bob Cowsill), MGM 13909 | 5 |
| ★ 56 | — | — | — | BEAUTIFUL MORNING — Rascals (Rascals), Atlantic 2493 | 1 |
| ★ 57 | 74 | — | — | SHOO-BE-DOO-BE-DOO-DA-DAY — Stevie Wonder (H. Cosby), Tamla 54165 | 2 |
| ★ 58 | 62 | 79 | — | UNKNOWN SOLDIER — Doors (Paul A. Rothchild), Elektra 45628 | 3 |
| 59 | 60 | 60 | 60 | SUNSHINE OF YOUR LOVE — Cream (Felix Pappalardi), Atco 6544 | 14 |
| ★ 60 | 63 | 89 | 98 | SHERRY DON'T GO — Lettermen (Kelly Gordon), Capitol 2132 | 4 |
| 61 | 69 | 72 | 91 | ME, THE PEACEFUL HEART — Lulu (Mickie Most), Epic 10302 | 4 |
| ★ 62 | 75 | — | — | LOOK TO YOUR SOUL — Johnny Rivers (Work), Imperial 66286 | 2 |
| ★ 63 | 66 | 75 | 90 | YOU'VE STILL GOT A PLACE IN MY HEART — Dean Martin (Jimmy Bowen), Reprise 0672 | 4 |
| ★ 64 | 70 | — | — | GOODBYE BABY (I Don't Want to See You Cry) — Tommy Boyce & Bobby Hart (Boyce-Hart), A&M 919 | 2 |
| ★ 65 | 72 | 74 | 80 | FOGGY MOUNTAIN BREAKDOWN — Flatt & Scruggs (Bob Johnston), Columbia 44380/Mercury 72739 | 7 |
| ★ 66 | — | — | — | SHE'S LOOKIN' GOOD — Wilson Pickett (Tom Dowd & Tommy Cogbill), Atlantic 2504 | 1 |
| 67 | 58 | 58 | 59 | YOU'VE GOT TO BE LOVED — Montanas (Tony Hatch), Independence 83 | 7 |
| 68 | 64 | 64 | 65 | THAT'S A LIE — Ray Charles (Ray Charles), ABC 11045 | 8 |
| 69 | 79 | 87 | 93 | GENTLE ON MY MIND — Patti Page (Jack Gold), Columbia 44353 | 10 |
| 70 | 59 | 62 | 62 | BACK ON MY FEET AGAIN — Foundations (Tony Macaulay), Uni 55058 | 6 |
| ★ 71 | 90 | — | — | JUMBO — Bee Gees (Robert Stigwood & Bee Gees), Atco 6570 | 2 |
| ★ 72 | 95 | — | — | MONY MONY — Tommy James & Shondells (Bo Gentry & Ritchie Cordell), Roulette 7008 | 2 |
| ★ 73 | — | — | — | RED RED WINE — Neil Diamond (Jeff Barry & Ellie Greenwich), Bang 556 | 1 |
| 74 | 65 | 65 | 72 | SIT WITH THE GURU — Strawberry Alarm Clock (Frank Slay & Bill Holmes), Uni 55055 | 5 |
| ★ 75 | — | — | — | AIN'T NOTHING LIKE THE REAL THING — Marvin Gaye & Tammi Terrell (Ashford-Simpson), Tamla 54163 | 1 |
| 76 | 81 | 97 | 97 | 100 YEARS — Nancy Sinatra (Lee Hazlewood), Reprise 0670 | 4 |
| 77 | 67 | 73 | 81 | STAY AWAY — Elvis Presley, RCA Victor 47-9465 | 5 |
| 78 | 73 | 77 | 78 | TIN SOLDIER — Small Faces (Steve Marriott & Ronnie Lane), Immediate 5003 | 5 |
| 79 | 71 | 71 | 82 | LOVE IS BLUE — Claudine Longet (Tommy LiPuma), A&M 909 | 8 |
| 80 | 88 | — | — | I WANNA LIVE — Glen Campbell (Alyde Lory), Capitol 2146 | 2 |
| 81 | 83 | — | — | I GOT A SURE THING — Ollie & the Nightingales (Booker T. Jones), Stax 245 | 2 |
| ★ 82 | — | — | — | WEAR IT ON OUR FACE — Dells (Bobby Miller), Cadet 5599 | 1 |
| 83 | 85 | 86 | 89 | AT THE TOP OF THE STAIRS — Formations (Leon Huff), MGM 13899 | 5 |
| ★ 84 | — | — | — | DO YOU KNOW THE WAY TO SAN JOSE — Dionne Warwick (Bacharach-David), Scepter 12216 | 1 |
| 85 | 86 | — | — | UP ON THE ROOF — Cryan' Shames (Jim Golden & Bob Monaco), Columbia 44457 | 2 |
| 86 | 89 | 90 | — | CINDERELLA ROCKEFELLA — Esther & Abi Ofarim, Philips 40526 | 3 |
| ★ 87 | — | — | — | I CAN'T BELIEVE I'M LOSING YOU — Frank Sinatra (Sonny Burks), Reprise 0677 | 1 |
| ★ 88 | — | — | — | (You Keep Me) HANGIN' ON — Joe Simon (J.R. Enterprises), Sound Stage 7 2608 | 1 |
| ★ 89 | — | — | — | FUNKY WALK, Part 1 — Dyke & the Blazers (East/Art Barrett), Original Sound 79 | 1 |
| ★ 90 | — | — | — | LOVING YOU HAS MADE ME BANANAS — Guy Marks (Peter De Angelis), ABC 11055 | 1 |
| 91 | 91 | 91 | — | SHOWTIME — Detroit Emeralds (Kent-Weems & Garrett), Ric Tic 13[illegible] | 3 |
| 92 | 92 | 92 | — | YOUR HEART IS FREE JUST LIKE THE WIND — Vikki Carr (Dave Pell & Rob Bledsoe), Liberty 5602[illegible] | 3 |
| 93 | 94 | 94 | — | MASTER JACK — Four Jacks & A Jill, RCA Victor 47-94[illegible] | 3 |
| 94 | — | — | — | IF YOU DON'T WANT MY LOVE — Robert John (David Rubinson), Columbia 444[illegible]5 | 1 |
| 95 | 96 | — | — | I LOVE YOU — People (Mikel Hunter), Capitol 2078 | 2 |
| 96 | — | — | — | ANYTHING — Eric Burdon & the Animals (Tom Wilson), MGM 13917 | 1 |
| 97 | 98 | — | 86 | BABY YOU'RE SO RIGHT FOR ME — Brenda & Tabulations (Bob Finiz), Dionn 507 | 4 |
| 98 | — | — | — | GOIN' AWAY — Fireballs (Norman Petty), Atco 6569 | 1 |
| 99 | — | — | — | BABY MAKE YOUR OWN SWEET MUSIC — Jay & the Techniques (Jerry Ross), Smash 2154 | 1 |
| 100 | 100 | — | — | CHAIN OF FOOLS — Jimmy Smith (Esmond Edwards), Verve 10583 | 2 |

## HOT 100—A TO Z —(Publisher-Licensee)

| Title (Publisher-Licensee) | Position |
|---|---|
| Ain't Nothing Like the Real Thing (Jobete, BMI) | 75 |
| Ain't No Way (14th Hour/Cotillion, BMI) | 21 |
| Anything (Sea-Lark/Slamina, BMI) | 96 |
| At the Top of the Stairs (Double Diamond/Mured, BMI) | 83 |
| Baby Make Your Own Sweet Music (Screen Gems-Columbia, BMI) | 99 |
| Baby You're So Right for Me (Chardon, BMI) | 97 |
| Back on My Feet Again (January/Welbeck, BMI) | 70 |
| Ballad of Bonnie and Clyde, The (Peer Int'l, BMI) | 7 |
| Beautiful Morning, A (Slacsar, BMI) | 56 |
| Cab Driver (Blackhawk, BMI) | 23 |
| Call Me Lightning (Fabulous, ASCAP) | 53 |
| Chain of Fools (14th Hour/Pronto, BMI) | 100 |
| Cinderella Rockefella (Irving, BMI) | 86 |
| Cowboys to Girls (Razor Sharp, BMI) | 18 |
| Cry Like a Baby (Press, BMI) | 4 |
| Dance to the Music (Daly City, BMI) | 14 |
| Delilah (Francis, Day & Hunter, ASCAP) | 34 |
| Do You Know the Way to San Jose (Jac/Blue Seas, ASCAP) | 84 |
| End of Our Road, The (Jobete, BMI) | 48 |
| Foggy Mountain Breakdown (Peer Int'l, BMI) | 65 |
| Forever Came Today (Jobete, BMI) | 29 |
| Funky Street (Redwal, BMI) | 31 |
| Funky Walk, Part 1 (Drive-In/Westward, BMI) | 89 |
| Gentle on My Mind (Sherman-DeVorzan, BMI) | 69 |
| Goin' Away (Dundee, BMI) | 98 |
| Good, the Bad and the Ugly, The (Unart, BMI) | 32 |
| Goodbye Baby (I Don't Want to See You Cry) (Screen Gems-Columbia, BMI) | 64 |
| Honey (Russel-Cason, ASCAP) | 1 |
| I Can't Believe I'm Losing You (Vogue/Hollyland, BMI) | 87 |
| I Got a Sure Thing (East, BMI) | 81 |
| I Got the Feelin' (Toccoa-Lois, BMI) | 11 |
| I Love You (Mainstay, BMI) | 95 |
| I Thank You (East/Pronto, BMI) | 27 |
| I Wanna Live (Windward Side, BMI) | 80 |
| I Will Always Think About You (New Colony/T.M., BMI) | 46 |
| I Wish It Would Rain (Jobete, BMI) | 50 |
| If You Can Want (Jobete, BMI) | 16 |
| If You Don't Want My Love (Bornwin, BMI) | 94 |
| Impossible Dream (Fox, ASCAP) | 44 |
| In Need of a Friend (Akbestal, BMI) | 55 |
| Jennifer Eccles (Maribus, BMI) | 47 |
| Jennifer Juniper (Peer Int'l, BMI) | 28 |
| Jumbo (Nemperor, BMI) | 71 |
| Just Dropped In (To See What Condition My Condition Was In) (Acuff-Rose, BMI) | 33 |
| Kiss Me Goodbye (Donna, ASCAP) | 20 |
| L. David Sloane (Meager, BMI) | 52 |
| Lady Madonna (Maclen, BMI) | 6 |
| La-La Means I Love You (Nickel Shoe, BMI) | 8 |
| Little Green Apples (Russell-Cason, ASCAP) | 39 |
| Look to Your Soul (Rivers, BMI) | 62 |
| Loving You Has Made Me Bananas (Curtis, ASCAP) | 90 |
| Love Is All Around (James, BMI) | 25 |
| Love Is Blue (Croma, ASCAP) (Paul Mauriat) | 12 |
| Love Is Blue (Croma, ASCAP) (Claudine Longet) | 79 |
| Master Jack (Milene, ASCAP) | 93 |
| Me, the Peaceful Heart (James, BMI) | 61 |
| Mighty Quinn, The (Dwarf, ASCAP) | 10 |
| Mony Mony (Patricia, BMI) | 72 |
| 100 Years (Hazlewood, ASCAP) | 76 |
| Playboy (Acuff-Rose, BMI) | 17 |
| Question of Temperature (H&L, BMI) | 51 |
| Red Red Wine (Tallyrand, BMI) | 73 |
| Rice Is Nice (Kama Sutra, BMI) | 49 |
| Scarborough Fair (/Canticle) (Charing Cross, BMI) | 13 |
| Security (East, BMI) | 35 |
| She's Lookin' Good (Veytig, BMI) | 66 |
| Sherry Don't Go (Grey Fox, BMI) | 60 |
| Shoo-Be-Doo-Be-Doo-Da-Day (Jobete, BMI) | 57 |
| Showtime (Wingate, BMI) | 91 |
| Simon Says (Maskat, BMI) | 15 |
| (Sittin' On) The Dock of the Bay (East/Pine/Redwal, BMI) | 3 |
| Sit With the Guru (Alarm Clock/Claridge, ASCAP) | 74 |
| Son of Hickory Holler's Tramp, The (Blue Crest, BMI) | 43 |
| Soul Coaxing (Ame Caline) (Southern, ASCAP) | 40 |
| Soul Serenade (Kilyn, BMI) | 38 |
| Stay Away (Gladys, ASCAP) | 77 |
| Suddenly You Love Me (Ponderosa, BMI) | 54 |
| Summertime Blues (Sea Chest, BMI) | 19 |
| Sunshine of Your Love (Dratleaf, BMI) | 59 |
| Sweet Inspiration (Press, BMI) | 24 |
| (Sweet Sweet Baby) Since You've Been Gone (14th Hour/Cotillion, BMI) | 5 |
| Take Good Care of My Baby (Screen Gems-Columbia, BMI) | 36 |
| Take Time to Know Her (Gallico, BMI) | 30 |
| Tapioca Tundra (Screen Gems-Columbia, BMI) | 45 |
| That's a Lie (Tangerine, BMI) | 68 |
| (Theme From) Valley of the Dolls (Feist, ASCAP) | 22 |
| Tighten Up (Cotillion/Orellis, BMI) | 37 |
| Tin Soldier (Nice Songs, BMI) | 78 |
| Unicorn, The (Hollis, BMI) | 26 |
| Unknown Soldier (Nipper, ASCAP) | 58 |
| Up on the Roof (Screen Gems-Columbia, BMI) | 85 |
| U. S. Male (Vector, BMI) | 42 |
| Valleri (Screen Gems-Columbia, BMI) | 9 |
| Wear It on Our Face (Chevis, BMI) | 82 |
| Will You Love Me Tomorrow? (Screen Gems-Columbia, BMI) | 41 |
| (You Keep Me) Hangin' On (Garpex/Alambo, BMI) | 88 |
| Young Girl (Viva, BMI) | 2 |
| Your Heart Is Free Just Like the Wind (MRC, BMI) | 92 |
| You've Got to Be Loved (Duchess, BMI) | 67 |
| You've Still Got a Place in My Heart (Acuff-Rose, BMI) | 63 |

## BUBBLING UNDER THE HOT 100

101. DOES YOUR MAMA KNOW ABOUT ME....Bobby Taylor & the Vancouvers, Gordy 7069
102. YOU'VE GOT TO CHANGE YOUR MIND..James Brown & Bobby Byrd, King 6151
103. IN SOME TIME....Ronnie Dove, Diamond 240
104. HONEY....Bob Shane, Decca 32275
105. WIND SONG....Wes Montgomery, A&M 91[illegible]
106. IN THE HEAT OF THE NIGHT....Dick Hyman & the Group, Command 4114
107. OUR CORNER OF THE NIGHT....Barbra Streisand, Columbia 44474
108. IN THE MORNING....Mighty Marvelows, ABC 11011
109. UNWIND....Ray Stevens, Monument 1048
110. HERE'S TO YOU....Hamilton Camp, Warner Bros.-Seven Arts 7165
111. CAN'T FIND THE TIME....Orpheus, MGM 13882
112. COME TO ME SOFTLY....Jimmy James & the Vagabonds, Atco 6851
113. (Sittin' On) THE DOCK OF THE BAY....King Curtis & His Kingpins, Atco 6562
114. CABARET....Herb Alpert & the Tijuana Brass, A&M 925
115. UP FROM THE SKIES....Jimi Hendrix Experience, Reprise 0665
116. DR. JON (The Medicine Man)....Jon & Robin & the In Crowd, Abnak 127
117. ANOTHER PLACE, ANOTHER TIME....Jerry Lee Lewis, Smash 2146
118. UP TO MY NECK IN HIGH MUDDY WATER....Linda Ronstadt & Stone Poneys, Capitol 2110
119. SO FINE....Ike & Tina Iketts, Innis 6667
120. I FOUND YOU....Frankie Laine, ABC 11057
121. GREASY HEART....Jefferson Airplane, RCA Victor 47-9496
122. LOUISIANA MAN....Bobbie Gentry, Capitol 2147
123. WHAT A DAY....Contrasts, Featuring Bob Morrison, Monument 1058
124. SOUL TRAIN....Classics IV, Imperial 66293
125. LEGEND OF XANADU..Dave Dee, Dozy, Beaky, Mick & Tich, Imperial 66287
126. HEY GIRL, MY GIRL....Bobby Vee, Liberty 56033
127. I DON'T KNOW....Violinaires, Checker 5043
128. LIKE TO GET TO KNOW YOU....Spanky & Our Gang, Mercury 72795
129. THE BONNIE & CLYDE....New Vaudeville Band, Fontana 1612
130. TAKE ME IN YOUR ARMS....Isley Brothers, Tamla 54164
131. LOOK AT WHAT I ALMOST MISSED....Parliaments, Revilot 217
132. HOUSE THAT JACK BUILT....Thelma Jones, Barry 1023
133. SHADOW OF YOUR LOVE....5 Stairsteps & Cubie, Buddah 35
134. GET-E-UP....Preparations, Heart & Soul 201

Compiled from national retail sales and radio station airplay by the Music Popularity Dept. of Record Market Research, Billboard.

# Billboard HOT 100

FOR WEEK ENDING APRIL 20, 1968

★ STAR PERFORMER—Sides registering greatest proportionate upward progress this week.

Ⓢ Record Industry Association of America seal of certification as million selling single.

| This Week | 1 Wk. Ago | 2 Wks. Ago | 3 Wks. Ago | TITLE | Artist (Producer), Label & Number | Weeks On Chart |
|---|---|---|---|---|---|---|
| 1 (Billboard Award) | 1 | 10 | 23 | HONEY | Bobby Goldsboro (Bob Montgomery & Bobby Goldsboro), United Artists 50283 | 5 |
| 2 | 2 | 2 | 7 | YOUNG GIRL | Union Gap Featuring Gary Puckett (Jerry Fuller), Columbia 44450 | 8 |
| ★3 | 4 | 6 | 15 | CRY LIKE A BABY | Box Tops (Dan Penn), Mala 593 | 8 |
| ★4 Ⓢ | 6 | 7 | 9 | LADY MADONNA | Beatles (George Martin), Capitol 2138 | 5 |
| 5 Ⓢ | 5 | 5 | 5 | (Sweet Sweet Baby) SINCE YOU'VE BEEN GONE | Aretha Franklin (Jerry Wexler), Atlantic 2486 | 8 |
| 6 Ⓢ | 3 | 1 | 1 | (Sittin' On) THE DOCK OF THE BAY | Otis Redding (Steve Cropper), Volt 157 | 13 |
| 7 | 7 | 8 | 8 | THE BALLAD OF BONNIE AND CLYDE | Georgie Fame (Manny Kellem), Epic 10283 | 10 |
| ★8 | 14 | 14 | 14 | DANCE TO THE MUSIC | Sly & the Family Stone (Sly Stone), Epic 10256 | 11 |
| 9 | 11 | 18 | 19 | I GOT THE FEELIN' | James Brown & the Famous Flames (James Brown), King 6155 | 6 |
| 10 | 10 | 11 | 11 | THE MIGHTY QUINN | Manfred Mann, Mercury 72770 | 8 |
| ★11 | 13 | 13 | 13 | SCARBOROUGH FAIR (/Canticle) | Simon & Garfunkel (Bob Johnston), Columbia 44465 | 8 |
| 12 | 8 | 4 | 6 | LA-LA MEANS I LOVE YOU | Delfonics (Stan & Bell), Philly Groove 150 | 12 |
| 13 Ⓢ | 9 | 3 | 3 | VALLERI | Monkees (Monkees), Colgems 66-1019 | 7 |
| ★14 | 16 | 16 | 18 | IF YOU CAN WANT | Smokey Robinson and the Miracles ("Smokey" Cleveland), Tamla 54162 | 9 |
| 15 Ⓢ | 12 | 9 | 2 | LOVE IS BLUE | Paul Mauriat, Philips 40495 | 16 |
| ★16 | 19 | 22 | 38 | SUMMERTIME BLUES | Blue Cheer (Abe "Voco" Kesh), Philips 40516 | 8 |
| 17 | 17 | 21 | 21 | PLAYBOY | Gene & Debbie (Don Gant), TRX 5006 | 10 |
| 18 | 18 | 28 | 42 | COWBOYS TO GIRLS | Intruders (Gamble-Huff), Gamble 214 | 5 |
| ★19 | 32 | 34 | 47 | THE GOOD, THE BAD AND THE UGLY | Hugo Montenegro, His Ork and Chorus (Neely Plumb), RCA Victor 9423 | 10 |
| ★20 | 26 | 27 | 49 | THE UNICORN | Irish Rovers (Charles Bud Dant), Decca 32254 | 5 |
| 21 | 21 | 78 | — | AIN'T NO WAY | Aretha Franklin (Jerry Wexler), Atlantic 2486 | 3 |
| ★22 | 25 | 25 | 28 | LOVE IS ALL AROUND | Troggs (Page One), Fontana 1607 | 9 |
| 23 | 24 | 26 | 27 | SWEET INSPIRATION | Sweet Inspirations (Tom Dowd & Tommy Cogbill), Atlantic 2476 | 8 |
| 24 | 20 | 15 | 16 | KISS ME GOODBYE | Petula Clark (Tony Hatch), Warner Bros.-Seven Arts 7170 | 10 |
| ★25 | 37 | 46 | 81 | TIGHTEN UP | Archie Bell & the Drells (L.J.F. Production), Atlantic 2478 | 4 |
| ★26 | 28 | 29 | 30 | JENNIFER JUNIPER | Donovan (Mickie Most), Epic 10300 | 7 |
| 27 | 23 | 23 | 25 | CAB DRIVER | Mills Brothers (Charles R. Grean & Tom Mack), Dot 17041 | 13 |
| ★28 | 30 | 30 | 48 | TAKE TIME TO KNOW HER | Percy Sledge (Quin Ivy & Marlin Greene), Atlantic 2490 | 6 |
| 29 | 29 | 31 | 44 | FOREVER CAME TODAY | Diana Ross & the Supremes (Holland & Dozier), Motown 1122 | 6 |
| 30 | 31 | 35 | 53 | FUNKY STREET | Arthur Conley (Tom Dowd), Atco 6563 | 6 |
| ★31 | 56 | — | — | BEAUTIFUL MORNING | Rascals (Rascals), Atlantic 2493 | 2 |
| ★32 | 42 | 47 | 63 | U. S. MALE | Elvis Presley, RCA Victor 47-9465 | 5 |
| ★33 | 36 | 51 | 84 | TAKE GOOD CARE OF MY BABY | Bobby Vinton (Billy Sherrill), Epic 10305 | 4 |
| 34 | 34 | 53 | 67 | DELILAH | Tom Jones (Peter Sullivan), Parrot 40025 | 6 |
| 35 | 35 | 38 | 52 | SECURITY | Etta James (Rick Hall & Staff), Cadet 5594 | 8 |
| 36 Ⓢ | 15 | 12 | 4 | SIMON SAYS | 1910 Fruitgum Co. (J. Katz/J. Kasenetz/E. Chiprut), Buddah 24 | 13 |
| 37 | 40 | 40 | 43 | SOUL COAXING (Ame Caline) | Raymond Lefevre, 4 Corners of the World 147 | 9 |
| 38 | 38 | 41 | 41 | SOUL SERENADE | Willie Mitchell (Willie Mitchell/Joe Cuoghi), Hi 2140 | 7 |
| 39 | 39 | 39 | 40 | LITTLE GREEN APPLES | Roger Miller (Jerry Kennedy), Smash 2148 | 8 |
| ★40 | 43 | 43 | 45 | THE SON OF HICKORY HOLLER'S TRAMP | O. C. Smith (Jerry Fuller), Columbia 44425 | 9 |
| 41 | 27 | 20 | 17 | I THANK YOU | Sam & Dave (Isaac Hayes & David Porter), Stax 242 | 13 |
| 42 | 44 | 44 | 69 | THE IMPOSSIBLE DREAM | Hesitations (Wiltshire-Banks-Victor), Kapp 899 | 6 |
| ★43 | 47 | 54 | 70 | JENNIFER ECCLES | Hollies (Ron Richards), Epic 10298 Uni 55055 | 6 |
| ★44 | 46 | 48 | 95 | I WILL ALWAYS THINK ABOUT YOU | New Colony Six (Senator Records Corp.), Mercury 72775 | 4 |
| ★45 | 66 | — | — | SHE'S LOOKIN' GOOD | Wilson Pickett (Tom Dowd & Tommy Cogbill), Atlantic 2504 | 2 |
| ★46 | 49 | 49 | 51 | RICE IS NICE | Lemon Pipers (Paul Leka), Buddah 31 | 7 |
| ★47 | 57 | 74 | — | SHOO-BE-DOO-BE-DOO-DA-DAY | Stevie Wonder (H. Cosby), Tamla 54165 | 3 |
| ★48 | 58 | 67 | 79 | UNKNOWN SOLDIER | Doors (Paul A. Rothchild), Elektra 45628 | 4 |
| ★49 | 53 | 57 | 80 | CALL ME LIGHTNING | The Who (Kit Lambert), Decca 32288 | 4 |
| ★50 | 72 | 95 | — | MONY MONY | Tommy James & Shondells (Bo Gentry & Ritchie Cordell), Roulette 7008 | 3 |
| ★51 | 62 | 75 | — | LOOK TO YOUR SOUL | Johnny Rivers (Work), Imperial 66286 | 3 |
| 52 | 52 | 52 | 61 | L. DAVID SLOANE | Michele Lee (Jack Gold), Columbia 44413 | 8 |
| ★53 | 61 | 69 | 72 | ME, THE PEACEFUL HEART | Lulu (Mickie Most), Epic 10302 | 5 |
| 54 | 55 | 55 | 66 | IN NEED OF A FRIEND | Cowsills (Bill & Bob Cowsill), MGM 13909 | 6 |
| ★55 | 65 | 72 | 74 | FOGGY MOUNTAIN BREAKDOWN | Flatt & Scruggs (Bob Johnston), Columbia 44380/Mercury 72739 | 8 |
| ★56 | 75 | — | — | AIN'T NOTHING LIKE THE REAL THING | Marvin Gaye & Tammi Terrell (Ashford-Simpson), Tamla 54163 | 2 |
| ★57 | 71 | 90 | — | JUMBO | Bee Gees (Robert Stigwood & Bee Gees), Atco 6570 | 3 |
| ★58 | 64 | 70 | — | GOODBYE BABY (I Don't Want to See You Cry) | Tommy Boyce & Bobby Hart (Boyce-Hart), A&M 919 | 3 |
| ★59 | 60 | 63 | 89 | SHERRY DON'T GO | Lettermen (Kelly Gordon), Capitol 2132 | 5 |
| ★60 | 63 | 66 | 75 | YOU'VE STILL GOT A PLACE IN MY HEART | Dean Martin (Jimmy Bowen), Reprise 0672 | 5 |
| ★61 | 84 | — | — | DO YOU KNOW THE WAY TO SAN JOSE | Dionne Warwick (Bacharach-David), Scepter 12216 | 2 |
| ★62 | 73 | — | — | RED RED WINE | Neil Diamond (Jeff Barry & Ellie Greenwich), Bang 556 | 2 |
| ★63 | 80 | 88 | — | I WANNA LIVE | Glen Campbell (Alyde Lory), Capitol [illegible] | 3 |
| 64 | 54 | 56 | 56 | SUDDENLY YOU LOVE ME | Tremeloes (Mike Smith), Epic 10293 | 10 |
| ★65 | 87 | — | — | I CAN'T BELIEVE I'M LOSING YOU | Frank Sinatra (Sonny Burks), Reprise 0677 | 2 |
| 66 | 69 | 79 | 87 | GENTLE ON MY MIND | Patti Page (Jack Gold), Columbia 44353 | 11 |
| ★67 | 90 | — | — | LOVING YOU HAS MADE ME BANANAS | Guy Marks (Peter De Angelis), ABC 11055 | 2 |
| ★68 | 86 | 89 | 90 | CINDERELLA ROCKEFELLA | Esther & Abi Ofarim, Philips 40526 | 4 |
| ★69 | 76 | 81 | 97 | 100 YEARS | Nancy Sinatra (Lee Hazlewood), Reprise 0670 | 5 |
| ★70 | 82 | — | — | WEAR IT ON OUR FACE | Dells (Bobby Miller), Cadet 5599 | 2 |
| ★71 | — | — | — | LIKE TO GET TO KNOW YOU | Spanky & Our Gang (Scharf-Dorough), Mercury 72795 | 1 |
| ★72 | — | — | — | IMPOSSIBLE MISSION (Mission Impossible) | Soul Survivors (Gamble-Huff), Crimson 1016 | 1 |
| ★73 | — | — | — | PAYING THE COST TO BE THE BOSS | B.B. King (Lou Zito & Johnny Pate), Bluesway 61015 | 1 |
| ★74 | 89 | — | — | FUNKY WALK, Part 1 | Dyke & the Blazers (East/Art Barrett), Original Sound 79 | 2 |
| 75 | 81 | 83 | — | I GOT A SURE THING | Ollie & the Nightingales (Booker T. Jones), Stax 245 | 3 |
| ★76 | 93 | 94 | 94 | MASTER JACK | Four Jacks & A Jill, RCA Victor 47-9473 | 4 |
| ★77 | 94 | — | — | IF YOU DON'T WANT MY LOVE | Robert John (David Rubinson), Columbia 44435 | 2 |
| ★78 | — | — | — | WE'RE ROLLING ON | Impressions (Curtis Mayfield & Johnny Pate), ABC 11076 | 1 |
| 79 | 79 | 71 | 71 | LOVE IS BLUE | Claudine Longet (Tommy LiPuma), A&M 909 | 9 |
| ★80 | 98 | — | — | GOIN' AWAY | Fireballs (Norman Petty), Atco 6569 | 2 |
| ★81 | 96 | — | — | ANYTHING | Eric Burdon & the Animals (Tom Wilson), MGM 13917 | 2 |
| ★82 | — | — | — | MEDLEY: MY GIRL, HEY GIRL | Bobby Vee (Dallas Smith), Liberty 56033 | 1 |
| ★83 | — | — | — | CABARET | Herb Alpert & the Tijuana Brass (Herb Alpert & Jerry Moss), A&M 925 | 1 |
| ★84 | — | — | — | I PROMISE TO WAIT MY LOVE | Martha Reeves & Vandellas (Cosby & Brown), Gordy 7070 | 1 |
| 85 | 88 | — | — | (You Keep Me) HANGIN' ON | Joe Simon (J.R. Enterprises), Sound Stage 7 2608 | 2 |
| ★86 | — | — | — | MAY I TAKE A GIANT STEP | 1910 Fruitgum Co. (J. Katz/E. Chiprut/J. Kasenetz), Buddah 39 | 1 |
| 87 | 95 | 96 | — | I LOVE YOU | People (Mikel Hunter), Capitol 2078 | 3 |
| 88 | 85 | 86 | — | UP ON THE ROOF | Cryan' Shames (Jim Golden & Bob Monaco), Columbia 44457 | 3 |
| 89 | 91 | 91 | 91 | SHOWTIME | Detroit Emeralds (Kent-Weems & Garrett), Ric Tic 135 | 4 |
| ★90 | — | — | — | YOU'LL NEVER WALK ALONE | Elvis Presley, RCA Victor 47-9600 | 1 |
| 91 | 92 | 92 | 92 | YOUR HEART IS FREE JUST LIKE THE WIND | Vikki Carr (Dave Pell & Rob Bledsoe), Liberty 56026 | 4 |
| 92 | 99 | — | — | BABY MAKE OUR OWN SWEET MUSIC | Jay & the Techniques (Jerry Ross), Smash 2154 | 2 |
| 93 | — | — | — | LOVE IN THEM THERE HILLS | Vibrations (Gamble-Huff), Okeh 7311 | 1 |
| 94 | — | — | — | THE SHADOW OF YOUR LOVE | 5 Stairsteps & Cubie (Clarence Burke Jr.), Buddah 35 | 1 |
| 95 | — | — | — | NEVER GET ENOUGH OF YOUR LOVE | Oscar Toney Jr. (Papa Don), Bell 714 | 1 |
| 96 | — | — | — | FRIENDS | Beach Boys (Beach Boys), Capitol 2160 | 1 |
| 97 | — | — | — | DOES YOUR MAMA KNOW ABOUT ME | Bobby Taylor & Vancouvers (B. Gordy Jr.), Gordy 7069 | 1 |
| 98 | — | — | — | GREASY HEART | Jefferson Airplane (Al Schmitt), RCA Victor 47-9496 | 1 |
| 99 | — | — | — | UNWIND | Ray Stevens (Fred Foster & Ray Stevens), Monument 1048 | 1 |
| 100 | — | — | — | LOUISIANA MAN | Bobbie Gentry (Kelly Gordon), Capitol 2147 | 1 |

## HOT 100—A TO Z—(Publisher-Licensee)


Ain't Nothing Like the Real Thing (Jobete, BMI).. 56
Ain't No Way (14th Hour/Cotillion, BMI)........ 21
Anything (Sea-Lark/Slamina, BMI)............ 81
Baby Make Your Own Sweet Music (Screen Gems-Columbia, BMI)............ 92
Ballad of Bonnie and Clyde, The (Peer Int'l, BMI) 7
Beautiful Morning, A (Slacsar, BMI)............ 31
Cab Driver (Blackhawk, BMI)............ 27
Cabaret (Sunbeam, BMI)............ 83
Call Me Lightning (Fabulous, ASCAP)............ 49
Cinderella Rockefella (Irving, BMI)............ 68
Cowboys to Girls (Razor Sharp, BMI)............ 18
Cry Like a Baby (Press, BMI)............ 3
Dance to the Music (Daly City, BMI)............ 8
Delilah (Francis, Day & Hunter, ASCAP)............ 34
Do You Know the Way to San Jose (Jac/Blue Seas, ASCAP)............ 61
Does Your Mama Know About Me (Stein & Van Stock, ASCAP)............ 97
Foggy Mountain Breakdown (Peer Int'l, BMI)..... 55
Forever Came Today (Jobete, BMI)............ 29
Friends (Sea of Tunes, BMI)............ 96
Funky Street (Redwal, BMI)............ 30
Funky Walk, Part 1 (Drive-In/Westward, BMI).... 74
Gentle on My Mind (Sherman-DeVorzan, BMI).... 66
Goin' Away (Dundee, BMI)............ 80
Good, the Bad and the Ugly, The (Unart, BMI).... 19
Goodbye Baby (I Don't Want to See You Cry) (Screen Gems-Columbia, BMI)............ 58
Greasy Heart (Icebag, BMI)............ 98
Honey (Russell-Cason, ASCAP)............ 1
I Can't Believe I'm Losing You (Vogue/Hollyland, BMI)............ 65
I Got a Sure Thing (East, BMI)............ 75
I Got the Feelin' (Toccoa-Lois, BMI)............ 9
I Love You (Mainstay, BMI)............ 87
I Promise to Wait My Love (Jobete, BMI)............ 84
I Thank You (East/Pronto, BMI)............ 41
I Wanna Live (Windward Side, BMI)............ 63
I Will Always Think About You (New Colony/T.M., BMI)............ 44
If You Can Want (Jobete, BMI)............ 14
If You Don't Want My Love (Bornwin, BMI)...... 77
Impossible Dream (Fox, ASCAP)............ 42
Impossible Mission (Mission Impossible) (Double Diamond/Downstairs, BMI)............ 72
In Need of a Friend (Akbestal, BMI)............ 54
Jennifer Eccles (Maribus, BMI)............ 43
Jennifer Juniper (Peer Int'l, BMI)............ 26
Jumbo (Nemperor, BMI)............ 57
Kiss Me Goodbye (Donna, ASCAP)............ 24
L. David Sloane (Meager, BMI)............ 52
Lady Madonna (Maclen, BMI)............ 4
La-La Means I Love You (Nickel Shoe, BMI)...... 12
Like to Get to Know You (Takya, ASCAP)........ 71
Little Green Apples (Russell-Cason, ASCAP)....... 39
Look to Your Soul (Rivers, BMI)............ 51
Louisiana Man (Acuff-Rose, BMI)............ 100
Loving You Has Made Me Bananas (Curtis, ASCAP) 67
Love in Them There Hills (Downstairs/Double Diamond, BMI)............ 93
Love Is All Around (James, BMI)............ 22
Love Is Blue (Croma, ASCAP) (Paul Mauriat)..... 15
Love Is Blue (Croma, ASCAP) (Claudine Longet)... 79
Master Jack (Milene, ASCAP)............ 76
May I Take a Giant Step (Kaskat, BMI)............ 86
Me, the Peaceful Heart (James, BMI)............ 53
Medley: My Girl, Hey Girl (Jobete/Screen Gems-Columbia, BMI)............ 82
Mighty Quinn, The (Dwarf, ASCAP)............ 10
Mony, Mony (Patricia, BMI)............ 50
Never Get Enough of Your Love (East, BMI)..... 95
100 Years (Hazlewood, ASCAP)............ 69
Paying the Cost to Be the Boss (Panco/LZMC, BMI) 73
Playboy (Acuff-Rose, BMI)............ 17
Red Red Wine (Tallyrand, BMI)............ 62
Rice Is Nice (Kama Sutra, BMI)............ 46
Scarborough Fair (/Canticle) (Charing Cross, BMI).. 11
Security (East, BMI)............ 35
Shadow of Your Love, The (Chardon, BMI) ....... 94
She's Lookin' Good (Veytig, BMI)............ 45
Sherry Don't Go (Grey Fox, BMI)............ 59
Shoo-Be-Doo-Be-Doo-Da-Day (Jobete, BMI)......... 47
Showtime (Wingate, BMI)............ 89
Simon Says (Maskat, BMI)............ 36
(Sittin' On) The Dock of the Bay (East/Pine/Redwal, BMI)............ 6
Son of Hickory Holler's Tramp, The (Blue Crest, BMI)............ 40
Soul Coaxing (Ame Caline) (Southern, ASCAP).... 37
Soul Serenade (Kilyn, BMI)............ 38
Suddenly You Love Me (Ponderosa, BMI)......... 64
Summertime Blues (Sea Chest, BMI)............ 16
Sweet Inspiration (Press, BMI)............ 23
(Sweet Sweet Baby) Since You've Been Gone (14th Hour/Cotillion, BMI)............ 5
Take Good Care of My Baby (Screen Gems-Columbia, BMI)............ 33
Take Time to Know Her (Gallico, BMI)............ 28
Tighten Up (Cotillion/Orellis, BMI)............ 25
Unicorn, The (Hollis, BMI)............ 20
Unknown Soldier (Nipper, ASCAP)............ 48
Unwind (Ahab, BMI)............ 99
Up on the Roof (Screen Gems-Columbia, BMI).... 88
U. S. Male (Vector, BMI)............ 32
Valleri (Screen Gems-Columbia, BMI)............ 13
We're Rolling On (Caman, BMI)............ 78
Wear It on Our Face (Chevis, BMI)............ 70
(You Keep Me) Hangin' On (Garpex/Alambo, BMI).. 85
Young Girl (Viva, BMI)............ 2
Your Heart Is Free Just Like the Wind (MRC, BMI) 91
You'll Never Walk Alone (Williamson, ASCAP).... 90
You've Still Got a Place in My Heart (Acuff-Rose, BMI)............ 60


## BUBBLING UNDER THE HOT 100

101. BABY, YOU'RE SO RIGHT FOR ME....Brenda & the Tabulations, Dionn 507
102. AT THE TOP OF THE STAIRS....Formations, MGM 13899
103. HERE'S TO YOU....Hamilton Camp, Warner Bros.-Seven Arts 7165
104. HONEY....Bob Shane, Decca 32275
105. WIND SONG....Wes Montgomery, A&M 916
106. WE CALL ON HIM....Elvis Presley, RCA Victor 47-9600
107. IN THE MORNING....Marvellows, ABC 11011
108. CHAIN OF FOOLS....Jimmy Smith, Verve 10583
109. CHAIN GANG....Jackie Wilson & Count Basie, Brunswick 55373
110. YUMMY, YUMMY, YUMMY....Ohio Express, Buddah 38
111. CAN'T FIND THE TIME....Orpheus, MGM 13882
112. A STOP ALONG THE WAY....Timothy Carr, Hot Biscuit 1454
113. I AM THE MAN FOR YOU BABY....Edwin Starr, Gordy 7071
114. LOVE MACHINE....Roosters, Philips 40504
115. TRIBUTE TO A KING....William Bell, Stax 248
116. DR. JON (Medicine Man)....Jon & Robin & In-Crowd, Abnak 127
117. SO FINE....Ike & Tina & the Ikettes, Innis 6667
118. I FOUND YOU....Frankie Laine, ABC 11057
119. SOUL TRAIN....Classics IV, Imperial 66293
120. WHAT A DAY....Contrasts, featuring Bob Morrison, Monument 1058
121. I DON'T KNOW....Violinaires, Checker 5043
122. BONNIE & CLYDE....New Vaudeville Band, Fontana 1612
123. LEGEND OF XANADU..Dave Dee, Dozy, Beaky, Mick & Tich, Imperial 66287
124. TAKE ME IN YOUR ARMS (And Rock Me for a Little While)....Isley Brothers, Tamla 54164
125. LOOK AT WHAT I ALMOST MISSED....Parliaments, Revilot 217
126. HOLY MAN....Scott McKenzie, Ode 107
127. BY THE TIME I GET TO PHOENIX....Ace Cannon, Hi 2144
128. DON'T HURT ME NO MORE....Al Greene, Hot Line 15001
129. SHE WEARS MY RING....Solomon King, Capitol 2114
130. HOW'D WE EVER GET THIS WAY....Andy Kim, Steed 707

# Billboard HOT 100

FOR WEEK ENDING APRIL 27, 1968

★ STAR PERFORMER—Sides registering greatest proportionate upward progress this week.

(Seal) Record Industry Association of America seal of certification as million selling single.

| This Week | 1 Wk. Ago | 2 Wks. Ago | 3 Wks. Ago | TITLE Artist (Producer), Label & Number | Weeks On Chart |
|---|---|---|---|---|---|
| 1 (Billboard Award) (Seal) | 1 | 1 | 10 | HONEY — Bobby Goldsboro (Bob Montgomery & Bobby Goldsboro), United Artists 50283 | 6 |
| 2 | 3 | 4 | 6 | CRY LIKE A BABY — Box Tops (Dan Penn), Mala 593 | 9 |
| 3 (Seal) | 2 | 2 | 2 | YOUNG GIRL — Union Gap Featuring Gary Puckett (Jerry Fuller), Columbia 44450 | 9 |
| 4 (Seal) | 4 | 6 | 7 | LADY MADONNA — Beatles (George Martin), Capitol 2138 | 6 |
| 5 (Seal) | 5 | 5 | 5 | (Sweet Sweet Baby) SINCE YOU'VE BEEN GONE — Aretha Franklin (Jerry Wexler), Atlantic 2486 | 9 |
| ★6 | 9 | 11 | 18 | I GOT THE FEELIN' — James Brown & the Famous Flames (James Brown), King 6155 | 7 |
| 7 (Seal) | 6 | 3 | 1 | (Sittin' On) THE DOCK OF THE BAY — Otis Redding (Steve Cropper), Volt 157 | 14 |
| 8 | 8 | 14 | 14 | DANCE TO THE MUSIC — Sly & the Family Stone (Sly Stone), Epic 10256 | 12 |
| ★9 | 25 | 37 | 46 | TIGHTEN UP — Archie Bell & the Drells (L.J.F. Production), Atlantic 2478 | 5 |
| 10 | 7 | 7 | 8 | THE BALLAD OF BONNIE AND CLYDE — Georgie Fame (Manny Kellem), Epic 10283 | 11 |
| 11 | 14 | 16 | 16 | IF YOU CAN WAIT — Smokey Robinson and the Miracles ("Smokey" Cleveland), Tamla 54162 | 10 |
| ★12 | 20 | 26 | 27 | THE UNICORN — Irish Rovers (Charles Bud Dant), Decca 32254 | 6 |
| ★13 | 18 | 18 | 28 | COWBOYS TO GIRLS — Intruders (Gamble-Huff), Gamble 214 | 6 |
| 14 | 19 | 32 | 34 | THE GOOD, THE BAD AND THE UGLY — Hugo Montenegro, His Ork and Chorus (Neely Plumb), RCA Victor 9423 | 11 |
| 15 | 12 | 8 | 4 | LA-LA MEANS I LOVE YOU — Delfonics (Stan & Bell), Philly Groove 150 | 13 |
| 16 | 16 | 19 | 22 | SUMMERTIME BLUES — Blue Cheer (Abe "Voco" Kesh), Philips 40516 | 9 |
| 17 | 17 | 17 | 21 | PLAYBOY — Gene & Debbie (Don Gant), TRX 5006 | 11 |
| ★18 | 23 | 24 | 26 | SWEET INSPIRATION — Sweet Inspirations (Tom Dowd & Tommy Cogbill), Atlantic 2476 | 9 |
| ★19 | 31 | 56 | — | BEAUTIFUL MORNING — Rascals (Rascals), Atlantic 2493 | 3 |
| ★20 | 28 | 30 | 30 | TAKE TIME TO KNOW HER — Percy Sledge (Quin Ivy & Marlin Greene), Atlantic 2490 | 7 |
| ★21 | 21 | 21 | 78 | AIN'T NO WAY — Aretha Franklin (Jerry Wexler), Atlantic 2486 | 4 |
| 22 | 22 | 25 | 25 | LOVE IS ALL AROUND — Troggs (Page One), Fontana 1607 | 10 |
| ★23 | 30 | 31 | 35 | FUNKY STREET — Arthur Conley (Tom Dowd), Atco 6563 | 7 |
| 24 | 11 | 13 | 13 | SCARBOROUGH FAIR (/Canticle) — Simon & Garfunkel (Bob Johnston), Columbia 44465 | 9 |
| 25 (Seal) | 15 | 12 | 9 | LOVE IS BLUE — Paul Mauriat, Philips 40495 | 17 |
| 26 | 26 | 28 | 29 | JENNIFER JUNIPER — Donovan (Mickie Most), Epic 10300 | 8 |
| ★27 | 61 | 84 | — | DO YOU KNOW THE WAY TO SAN JOSE — Dionne Warwick (Bacharach-David), Scepter 12216 | 3 |
| 28 | 29 | 29 | 31 | FOREVER CAME TODAY — Diana Ross & the Supremes (Holland & Dozier), Motown 1122 | 7 |
| 29 | 10 | 10 | 11 | THE MIGHTY QUINN — Manfred Mann, Mercury 72770 | 9 |
| 30 | 27 | 23 | 23 | CAB DRIVER — Mills Brothers (Charles R. Grean & Tom Mack), Dot 17041 | 14 |
| ★31 | 47 | 57 | 74 | SHOO-BE-DOO-BE-DOO-DA-DAY — Stevie Wonder (H. Cosby), Tamla 54165 | 4 |
| 32 | 32 | 42 | 47 | U. S. MALE — Elvis Presley, RCA Victor 47-9465 | 6 |
| 33 | 33 | 36 | 51 | TAKE GOOD CARE OF MY BABY — Bobby Vinton (Billy Sherrill), Epic 10305 | 5 |
| ★34 | 34 | 34 | 53 | DELILAH — Tom Jones (Peter Sullivan), Parrot 40025 | 7 |
| 35 | 35 | 35 | 38 | SECURITY — Etta James (Rick Hall & Staff), Cadet 5594 | 9 |
| ★36 | 38 | 38 | 41 | SOUL SERENADE — Willie Mitchell (Willie Mitchell/Joe Cuoghi), Hi 2140 | 8 |
| 37 | 37 | 40 | 40 | SOUL COAXING (Ame Caline) — Raymond Lefevre, 4 Corners of the World 147 | 10 |
| 38 | 24 | 20 | 15 | KISS ME GOODBYE — Petula Clark (Tony Hatch), Warner Bros.-Seven Arts 7170 | 11 |
| ★39 | 56 | 75 | — | AIN'T NOTHING LIKE THE REAL THING — Marvin Gaye & Tammi Terrell (Ashford-Simpson), Tamla 54163 | 3 |
| 40 | 40 | 43 | 43 | THE SON OF HICKORY HOLLER'S TRAMP — O. C. Smith (Jerry Fuller), Columbia 44425 | 10 |
| ★41 | 45 | 66 | — | SHE'S LOOKIN' GOOD — Wilson Pickett (Tom Dowd & Tommy Cogbill), Atlantic 2504 | 3 |
| 42 | 42 | 44 | 44 | THE IMPOSSIBLE DREAM — Hesitations (Wiltshire-Banks-Victor), Kapp 899 | 7 |
| 43 | 43 | 47 | 54 | JENNIFER ECCLES — Hollies (Ron Richards), Epic 10298 Uni 55055 | 7 |
| 44 | 44 | 46 | 48 | I WILL ALWAYS THINK ABOUT YOU — New Colony Six (Senator Records Corp.), Mercury 72775 | 5 |
| 45 (Seal) | 13 | 9 | 3 | VALLERI — Monkees (Monkees), Colgems 66-1019 | 8 |
| 46 (Seal) | 36 | 15 | 12 | SIMON SAYS — 1910 Fruitgum Co. (J. Katz/J. Kasenetz/E. Chiprut), Buddah 24 | 14 |
| 47 | 49 | 53 | 57 | CALL ME LIGHTNING — The Who (Kit Lambert), Decca 32288 | 5 |
| 48 | 48 | 58 | 67 | UNKNOWN SOLDIER — Doors (Paul A. Rothchild), Elektra 45628 | 5 |
| 49 | 50 | 72 | 95 | MONY MONY — Tommy James & Shondells (Bo Gentry & Ritchie Cordell), Roulette 7008 | 4 |
| ★50 | 51 | 62 | 75 | LOOK TO YOUR SOUL — Johnny Rivers (Work), Imperial 66286 | 4 |
| ★51 | 67 | 90 | — | LOVING YOU HAS MADE ME BANANAS — Guy Marks (Peter De Angelis), ABC 11055 | 3 |
| 52 | 59 | 60 | 63 | SHERRY DON'T GO — Lettermen (Kelly Gordon), Capitol 2132 | 6 |
| 53 | 58 | 64 | 70 | GOODBYE BABY (I Don't Want to See You Cry) — Tommy Boyce & Bobby Hart (Boyce-Hart), A&M 919 | 4 |
| 54 | 39 | 39 | 39 | LITTLE GREEN APPLES — Roger Miller (Jerry Kennedy), Smash 2148 | 9 |
| 55 | 55 | 65 | 72 | FOGGY MOUNTAIN BREAKDOWN — Flatt & Scruggs (Bob Johnston), Columbia 44380/Mercury 72739 | 9 |
| ★56 | 73 | — | — | PAYING THE COST TO BE THE BOSS — B.B. King (Lou Zito & Johnny Pate), Bluesway 61015 | 2 |
| 57 | 57 | 71 | 90 | JUMBO — Bee Gees (Robert Stigwood & Bee Gees), Atco 6570 | 4 |
| ★58 | — | — | — | MRS. ROBINSON — Simon & Garfunkel (Simon, Garfunkel & Halee), Columbia 44511 | 1 |
| 59 | 52 | 52 | 52 | L. DAVID SLOANE — Michele Lee (Jack Gold), Columbia 44413 | 9 |
| 60 | 60 | 63 | 66 | YOU'VE STILL GOT A PLACE IN MY HEART — Dean Martin (Jimmy Bowen), Reprise 0672 | 6 |
| ★61 | 71 | — | — | LIKE TO GET TO KNOW YOU — Spanky & Our Gang (Scharf-Dorough), Mercury 72795 | 2 |
| 62 | 62 | 73 | — | RED RED WINE — Neil Diamond (Jeff Barry & Ellie Greenwich), Bang 556 | 3 |
| ★63 | 63 | 80 | 88 | I WANNA LIVE — Glen Campbell (Alyde Lory), Capitol 2146 | 4 |
| ★64 | 70 | 82 | — | WEAR IT ON OUR FACE — Dells (Bobby Miller), Cadet 5599 | 3 |
| 65 | 65 | 87 | — | I CAN'T BELIEVE I'M LOSING YOU — Frank Sinatra (Sonny Burks), Reprise 0677 | 3 |
| 66 | 66 | 69 | 79 | GENTLE ON MY MIND — Patti Page (Jack Gold), Columbia 44353 | 12 |
| 67 | 53 | 61 | 69 | ME, THE PEACEFUL HEART — Lulu (Mickie Most), Epic 10302 | 6 |
| 68 | 68 | 86 | 89 | CINDERELLA ROCKEFELLA — Esther & Abi Ofarim, Philips 40526 | 5 |
| 69 | 69 | 76 | 81 | 100 YEARS — Nancy Sinatra (Lee Hazlewood), Reprise 0670 | 6 |
| ★70 | 96 | — | — | FRIENDS — Beach Boys (Beach Boys), Capitol 2160 | 2 |
| 71 | 72 | — | — | IMPOSSIBLE MISSION (Mission Impossible) — Soul Survivors (Gamble-Huff), Crimson 1016 | 2 |
| ★72 | 82 | — | — | MEDLEY: MY GIRL, HEY GIRL — Bobby Vee (Dallas Smith), Liberty 56033 | 2 |
| 73 | 74 | 89 | — | FUNKY WALK, Part 1 — Dyke & the Blazers (East/Art Barrett), Original Sound 79 | 3 |
| 74 | 75 | 81 | 83 | I GOT A SURE THING — Ollie & the Nightingales (Booker T. Jones), Stax 245 | 4 |
| 75 | 76 | 93 | 94 | MASTER JACK — Four Jacks & A Jill, RCA Victor 47-9473 | 5 |
| 76 | 77 | 94 | — | IF YOU DON'T WANT MY LOVE — Robert John (David Rubinson), Columbia 44435 | 3 |
| 77 | 78 | — | — | WE'RE ROLLING ON — Impressions (Curtis Mayfield & Johnny Pate), ABC 11076 | 2 |
| ★78 | 97 | — | — | DOES YOUR MAMA KNOW ABOUT ME — Bobby Taylor & Vancouvers (B. Gordy Jr.), Gordy 7069 | 2 |
| 79 | 80 | 98 | — | GOIN' AWAY — Fireballs (Norman Petty), Atco 6569 | 3 |
| ★80 | 81 | 96 | — | ANYTHING — Eric Burdon & the Animals (Tom Wilson), MGM 13917 | 3 |
| ★81 | 83 | — | — | CABARET — Herb Alpert & the Tijuana Brass (Herb Alpert & Jerry Moss), A&M 925 | 2 |
| 82 | 85 | 88 | — | (You Keep Me) HANGIN' ON — Joe Simon (J.R. Enterprises), Sound Stage 7 2608 | 3 |
| ★83 | 84 | — | — | I PROMISE TO WAIT MY LOVE — Martha Reeves & Vandellas (Cosby & Brown), Gordy 7070 | 2 |
| 84 | 86 | — | — | MAY I TAKE A GIANT STEP — 1910 Fruitgum Co. (J. Katz/E. Chiprut/J. Kasenetz), Buddah 39 | 2 |
| ★85 | 87 | 95 | 96 | I LOVE YOU — People (Mikel Hunter), Capitol 2078 | 4 |
| ★86 | — | — | — | CHAIN GANG — Jackie Wilson & Count Basie (Nat Tarnopol & Teddy Reig), Brunswick 55373 | 1 |
| ★87 | — | — | — | THE HAPPY SONG (Dum Dum) — Otis Redding (Steve Cropper), Volt 163 | 1 |
| 88 | 92 | 99 | — | BABY MAKE OUR OWN SWEET MUSIC — Jay & the Techniques (Jerry Ross), Smash 2154 | 3 |
| 89 | 89 | 91 | 91 | SHOWTIME — Detroit Emeralds (Kent-Weems & Garrett), Ric Tic 135 | 5 |
| 90 | 90 | — | — | YOU'LL NEVER WALK ALONE — Elvis Presley, RCA Victor 47-9600 | 2 |
| 91 | 91 | 92 | 92 | YOUR HEART IS FREE JUST LIKE THE WIND — Vikki Carr (Dave Pell & Rob Bledsoe), Liberty 56026 | 5 |
| 92 | — | — | — | I'M SORRY — Delfonics (Stan & Bell), Philly Groove 151 | 1 |
| 93 | 93 | — | — | LOVE IN THEM THERE HILLS — Vibrations (Gamble-Huff), Okeh 7311 | 2 |
| 94 | — | — | — | I CAN REMEMBER — James & Bobby Purify (Papa Don), Bell 721 | 1 |
| 95 | 95 | — | — | NEVER GET ENOUGH OF YOUR LOVE — Oscar Toney Jr. (Papa Don), Bell 714 | 2 |
| 96 | — | — | — | LILI MARLENE — Al Martino (Tom Morgan), Capitol 2158 | 1 |
| 97 | 99 | — | — | UNWIND — Ray Stevens (Fred Foster & Ray Stevens), Monument 1048 | 2 |
| 98 | 98 | — | — | GREASY HEART — Jefferson Airplane (Al Schmitt), RCA Victor 47-9496 | 2 |
| 99 | — | — | — | IF I WERE A CARPENTER — Four Tops (Holland & Dozier), Motown 1124 | 1 |
| 100 | — | — | — | A TRIBUTE TO A KING — William Bell (Booker T. Jones), Stax 248 | 1 |

## HOT 100—A TO Z—(Publisher-Licensee)

Ain't Nothing Like the Real Thing (Jobete, BMI) .. 39
Ain't No Way (14th Hour/Cotillion, BMI) ........ 21
Anythnig (Sea-Lark/Slamina, BMI) ........ 80
Baby Make Your Own Sweet Music (Screen Gems-Columbia, BMI) ........ 88
Ballad of Bonnie and Clyde, The (Peer Int'l, BMI) 10
Beautiful Morning, A (Slacsar, BMI) ........ 19
Cab Driver (Blackhawk, BMI) ........ 30
Cabaret (Sunbeam, BMI) ........ 81
Call Me Lightning (Fabulous, ASCAP) ........ 47
Chain Gang (Kags, BMI) ........ 86
Cinderella Rockefella (Irving, BMI) ........ 68
Cowboys to Girls (Razor Sharp, BMI) ........ 13
Cry Like a Baby (Press, BMI) ........ 2
Dance to the Music (Daly City, BMI) ........ 8
Delilah (Francis, Day & Hunter, ASCAP) ........ 34
Do You Know the Way to San Jose (Jac/Blue Seas, ASCAP) ........ 27
Does Your Mama Know About Me (Stein & Van Stock, ASCAP) ........ 78
Foggy Mountain Breakdown (Peer Int'l, BMI) ... 55
Forever Came Today (Jobete, BMI) ........ 28
Friends (Sea of Tunes, BMI) ........ 70
Funky Street (Redwal, BMI) ........ 23
Funky Walk, Part I (Drive-In/Westward, BMI) ... 73
Gentle on My Mind (Sherman-DeVorzan, BMI) .... 66
Goin' Away (Dundee, BMI) ........ 79
Good, the Bad and the Ugly, The (Unart, BMI) .. 14
Goodbye Baby (I Don't Want to See You Cry) (Screen Gems-Columbia, BMI) ........ 53
Greasy Heart (Icebag, BMI) ........ 98
The Happy Song (Dum Dum) (East/Time/Redwal, BMI) ........ 87
Honey (Russell-Cason, ASCAP) ........ 1
I Can Remember (Big Seven, BMI) ........ 94
I Can't Believe I'm Losing You (Vogue/Hollyland, BMI) ........ 65
I Got a Sure Thing (East, BMI) ........ 74
I Got the Feelin' (Toccoa-Lois, BMI) ........ 6
I Love You (Mainstay, BMI) ........ 85
I Promise to Wait My Love (Jobete, BMI) ...... 83
I Wanna Live (Windward Side, BMI) ........ 63
I Will Alway Think About You (New Colony/T.M., BMI) ........ 44
If I Were a Carpenter (Faithful Virtue, BMI) ... 99
If You Can Want (Jobete, BMI) ........ 11
If You Don't Want My Love (Bornwin, BMI) ... 76
I'm Sorry (Mickel Shoe/Bellboy, BMI) ........ 92
Impossible Dream (Fox, ASCAP) ........ 42
Impossible Mission (Mission Impossible) (Double Diamond/Downstairs, BMI) ........ 71
Jennifer Eccles (Maribus, BMI) ........ 43
Jennifer Juniper (Peer Int'l, BMI) ........ 26
Jumbo (Nemperor, BMI) ........ 57
Kiss Me Goodbye (Donna, ASCAP) ........ 38
L. David Sloane (Meager, BMI) ........ 59
Lady Madonna (Maclen, BMI) ........ 4
La-La Means I Love You (Nickel Shoe, BMI) .... 15
Like to Get to Know You (Takya, ASCAP) ...... 61
Lili Marlene (Marks/G.E.M.A., ASCAP) ........ 96
Little Green Apples (Russell Cason, ASCAP) ..... 54
Look to Your Soul (Rivers, BMI) ........ 50
Loving You Has Made Me Bananas (Curtis, ASCAP) 51
Love In Them There Hills (Downstairs/Double Diamond, BMI) ........ 93
Love Is All Around (James, BMI) ........ 22
Love Is Blue (Croma, ASCAP) (Paul Mauriat) ..... 25
Master Jack (Milene, ASCAP) ........ 75
May I Take a Giant Step (Kaskat, BMI) ........ 84
Me, the Peaceful Heart (James, BMI) ........ 67
Medley: My Girl, Hey Girl (Jobete/Screen Gems-Columbia, BMI) ........ 72
Mighty Quinn, The (Dwarf, ASCAP) ........ 29
Mony, Mony (Patricia, BMI) ........ 49
Mrs. Robinson (Charing Cross, BMI) ........ 58
Never Get Enough of Your Love (East, BMI) .... 95
100 Years (Hazlewood, ASCAP) ........ 69
Paying the Cost to Be the Boss (Panco/LZMC, BMI) 56
Playboy (Acuff-Rose, BMI) ........ 17
Red Red Wine (Tallyrand, BMI) ........ 62
Scarborough Fair (/Canticle) (Charing Cross, BMI) 24
Security (East, BMI) ........ 35
She's Lookin' Good (Veytig, BMI) ........ 41
Sherry Don't Go (Grey Fox, BMI) ........ 52
Shoo-Be-Doo-Be-Doo-Da-Day (Jobete, BMI) ........ 31
Showtime (Wingate, BMI) ........ 89
Simon Says (Maskat, BMI) ........ 46
(Sittin' On) The Dock of the Bay (East/Pine/Redwal, BMI) ........ 7
Son of Hickory Holler's Tramp, The (Blue Crest, BMI) ........ 40
Soul Coaxing (Ame Caline) (Southern, ASCAP) ... 37
Soul Serenade (Kilyn, BMI) ........ 36
Summertime Blues (Viva, BMI) ........ 16
Sweet Inspiration (Press, BMI) ........ 18
(Sweet Sweet Baby) Since You've Been Gone (14th Hour/Cotillion, BMI) ........ 5
Take Good Care of My Baby (Screen Gems-Columbia, BMI) ........ 33
Take Time to Know Her (Gallico, BMI) ........ 20
Tighten Up (Cotillion/Orellis, BMI) ........ 9
A Tribute to a King (East, BMI) ........100
Unicorn, The (Hollis, BMI) ........ 12
Unknown Soldier (Nipper, ASCAP) ........ 48
Unwind (Ahab, BMI) ........ 97
U. S. Male (Vector, BMI) ........ 32
Valleri (Screen Gems-Columbia, BMI) ........ 45
We're Rolling On (Caman, BMI) ........ 77
Wear It on Our Face (Chevis, BMI) ........ 64
(You Keep Me) Hangin' On (Garpex/Alambo, BMI) 82
Young Girl (Viva, BMI) ........ 3
Your Heart Is Free Just Like the Wind (MRC, BMI) 91
You'll Never Walk Alone (Williamson, ASCAP) ... 90
You've Still Got a Place in My Heart (Acuff-Rose, BMI) ........ 60

## BUBBLING UNDER THE HOT 100

101. THE SHADOW OF YOUR LOVE ........Five Stairsteps & Cubie, Buddah 35
102. HERE'S TO YOU ..........Hamilton Camp, Warner Bros.-Seven Arts 7165
103. WIND SONG ..........Wes Montgomery, A&M 916
104. HONEY ..........Bob Shane, Decca 32275
105. YUMMY, YUMMY, YUMMY ..........Ohio Express, Buddah 38
106. IN THE MORNING ..........Mighty Marvelows, ABC 11011
107. LOUISIANA MAN ..........Bobbie Gentry, Capitol 2147
108. TIP-TOE THRU THE TULIPS WITH ME ..........Tiny Tim, Reprise 0679
109. YOU AIN'T GOING NOWHERE ..........Byrds, Columbia 44499
110. LOVE MACHINE ..........Roosters, Philips 40504
111. OH, I'LL NEVER BE THE SAME ..........Young Hearts, Minit 32039
112. A STOP ALONG THE WAY ..........Timothy Carr, Hot Biscuit 1454
113. I AM THE MAN FOR YOU BABY ..........Edwin Starr, Gordy 7071
114. BY THE TIME I GET TO PHOENIX ..........Ace Cannon, Hi 2144
115. HOW'D WE EVER GET THIS WAY ..........Andy Kim, Steed 707
116. LONELY IS THE NAME ..........Sammy Davis Jr., Reprise 0673
117. FACE IT GIRL, IT'S OVER ..........Nancy Wilson, Capitol 2136
118. SOUL TRAIN ..........Classics IV, Imperial 66293
119. DON'T TAKE YOUR LOVE FROM ME ..........Ben E. King, Atco 6571
120. THE SINGER SANG HIS SONG ..........Bee Gees, Atco 6570
121. SAN FRANCISCO GIRLS ..........Fever Tree, Uni 55060
122. TAKE ME IN YOUR ARMS (And Rock Me for a Little While) ..........Isley Brothers, Tamla 54164
123. ANGEL OF THE MORNING ..........Merrilee Rush, Bell 705
124. LOOK AT WHAT I ALMOST MISSED ..........Parliaments, Revilot 217
125. SLICK ..........Herb Alpert & the Tijuana Brass, A&M 925
126. FAT ALBERT ..........Fat Albert Ork & Chorus, Tetragrammaton 1500
127. DON'T HURT ME NO MORE ..........Al Greene, Hot Line 15001
128. SHE WEARS MY RING ..........Solomon King, Capitol 2114
129. SHE'S A HEARTBREAKER ..........Gene Pitney, Musicor 1306
130. WE CAN FLY/UP, UP & AWAY ..........Al Hirt, RCA Victor 47-9500
131. AS LONG AS I GOT YOU ..........Laura Lee, Chess 2041
132. WHY SAY GOODBYE ..........Connie Francis, MGM 13923
133. YESTERDAY, I HEARD THE RAIN ..........Tony Bennett, Columbia 44510
134. MAMAN ..........Arthur Prysock, Verve 10592
135. BILLY SUNSHINE ..........Evie Sands, Cameo 2002

Compiled from national retail sales and radio station airplay by the Music Popularity Dept. of Record Market Research, Billboard.

HOT 100

HOT 100

# Billboard HOT 100

FOR WEEK ENDING MAY 4, 1968

★ STAR PERFORMER—Sides registering greatest proportionate upward progress this week.

(Seal) Record Industry Association of America seal of certification as million selling single.

| THIS WEEK | 1 Wk. Ago | 2 Wks. Ago | 3 Wks. Ago | TITLE Artist (Producer), Label & Number | Weeks On Chart |
|---|---|---|---|---|---|
| 1 (Billboard Award) | 1 | 1 | 1 | HONEY — Bobby Goldsboro (Bob Montgomery & Bobby Goldsboro), United Artists 50283 | 7 |
| 2 | 2 | 3 | 4 | CRY LIKE A BABY — Box Tops (Dan Penn), Mala 593 | 10 |
| 3 | 3 | 2 | 2 | YOUNG GIRL — Union Gap Featuring Gary Puckett (Jerry Fuller), Columbia 44450 | 10 |
| 4 | 4 | 4 | 6 | LADY MADONNA — Beatles (George Martin), Capitol 2138 | 7 |
| ★ 5 | 9 | 25 | 37 | TIGHTEN UP — Archie Bell & the Drells (L.J.F. Production), Atlantic 2478 | 6 |
| 6 | 6 | 9 | 11 | I GOT THE FEELIN' — James Brown & the Famous Flames (James Brown), King 6155 | 8 |
| ★ 7 | 13 | 18 | 18 | COWBOYS TO GIRLS — Intruders (Gamble-Huff), Gamble 214 | 7 |
| ★ 8 | 14 | 19 | 32 | THE GOOD, THE BAD AND THE UGLY — Hugo Montenegro, His Ork and Chorus (Neely Plumb), RCA Victor 9423 | 12 |
| ★ 9 | 19 | 31 | 56 | BEAUTIFUL MORNING — Rascals (Rascals), Atlantic 2493 | 4 |
| 10 | 12 | 20 | 26 | THE UNICORN — Irish Rovers (Charles Bud Dant), Decca 32254 | 7 |
| 11 | 11 | 14 | 16 | IF YOU CAN WAIT — Smokey Robinson and the Miracles ("Smokey" Cleveland), Tamla 54162 | 11 |
| 12 | 8 | 8 | 14 | DANCE TO THE MUSIC — Sly & the Family Stone (Sly Stone), Epic 10256 | 13 |
| ★ 13 | 20 | 28 | 30 | TAKE TIME TO KNOW HER — Percy Sledge (Quin Ivy & Marlin Greene), Atlantic 2490 | 8 |
| 14 | 16 | 16 | 19 | SUMMERTIME BLUES — Blue Cheer (Abe "Voce" Kesh), Philips 40516 | 10 |
| 15 | 10 | 7 | 7 | THE BALLAD OF BONNIE AND CLYDE — Georgie Fame (Manny Kellem), Epic 10283 | 12 |
| ★ 16 | 21 | 21 | 21 | AIN'T NO WAY — Aretha Franklin (Jerry Wexler), Atlantic 2486 | 5 |
| ★ 17 | 22 | 22 | 25 | LOVE IS ALL AROUND — Troggs (Page One), Fontana 1607 | 11 |
| 18 | 18 | 23 | 24 | SWEET INSPIRATION — Sweet Inspirations (Tom Dowd & Tommy Cogbill), Atlantic 2476 | 10 |
| 19 | 7 | 6 | 3 | (Sittin' On) THE DOCK OF THE BAY — Otis Redding (Steve Cropper), Volt 157 | 15 |
| ★ 20 | 31 | 47 | 57 | SHOO-BE-DOO-BE-DOO DA-DAY — Stevie Wonder (H. Cosby), Tamla 54165 | 5 |
| ★ 21 | 27 | 61 | 84 | DO YOU KNOW THE WAY TO SAN JOSE — Dionne Warwick (Bacharach-David), Scepter 12216 | 4 |
| 22 | 5 | 5 | 5 | (Sweet Sweet Baby) SINCE YOU'VE BEEN GONE — Aretha Franklin (Jerry Wexler), Atlantic 2486 | 10 |
| 23 | 23 | 30 | 31 | FUNKY STREET — Arthur Conley (Tom Dowd), Atco 6563 | 8 |
| 24 | 17 | 17 | 17 | PLAYBOY — Gene & Debbie (Don Gant), TRX 5006 | 12 |
| ★ 25 | 39 | 56 | 75 | AIN'T NOTHING LIKE THE REAL THING — Marvin Gaye & Tammi Terrell (Ashford-Simpson), Tamla 54163 | 4 |
| 26 | 15 | 12 | 8 | LA-LA MEANS I LOVE YOU — Delfonics (Stan & Bell), Philly Groove 150 | 14 |
| ★ 27 | 34 | 34 | 34 | DELILAH — Tom Jones (Peter Sullivan), Parrot 40025 | 8 |
| 28 | 28 | 29 | 29 | FOREVER CAME TODAY — Diana Ross & the Supremes (Holland & Dozier), Motown 1122 | 8 |
| 29 | 29 | 10 | 10 | THE MIGHTY QUINN — Manfred Mann, Mercury 72770 | 10 |
| ★ 30 | 36 | 38 | 38 | SOUL SERENADE — Willie Mitchell (Willie Mitchell/Joe Cuoghi), Hi 2140 | 9 |
| 31 | 32 | 32 | 42 | U. S. MALE — Elvis Presley, RCA Victor 47-9465 | 7 |
| ★ 32 | 58 | — | — | MRS. ROBINSON — Simon & Garfunkel (Simon, Garfunkel & Halee), Columbia 44511 | 2 |
| 33 | 33 | 33 | 36 | TAKE GOOD CARE OF MY BABY — Bobby Vinton (Billy Sherrill), Epic 10305 | 6 |
| ★ 34 | 49 | 50 | 72 | MONY MONY — Tommy James & Shondells (Bo Gentry & Ritchie Cordell), Roulette 7008 | 5 |
| 35 | 25 | 15 | 12 | LOVE IS BLUE — Paul Mauriat, Philips 40495 | 18 |
| 36 | 24 | 11 | 13 | SCARBOROUGH FAIR (/Canticle) — Simon & Garfunkel (Bob Johnston), Columbia 44465 | 10 |
| 37 | 37 | 37 | 40 | SOUL COAXING (Ame Caline) — Raymond Lefevre, 4 Corners of the World 147 | 11 |
| 38 | 30 | 27 | 23 | CAB DRIVER — Mills Brothers (Charles R. Grean & Tom Mack), Dot 17041 | 15 |
| ★ 39 | 48 | 48 | 58 | UNKNOWN SOLDIER — Doors (Paul A. Rothchild), Elektra 45628 | 6 |
| ★ 40 | 47 | 49 | 53 | CALL ME LIGHTNING — The Who (Kit Lambert), Decca 32288 | 6 |
| 41 | 41 | 45 | 66 | SHE'S LOOKIN' GOOD — Wilson Pickett (Tom Dowd & Tommy Cogbill), Atlantic 2504 | 4 |
| 42 | 40 | 40 | 43 | THE SON OF HICKORY HOLLER'S TRAMP — O. C. Smith (Jerry Fuller), Columbia 44425 | 11 |
| 43 | 43 | 43 | 47 | JENNIFER ECCLES — Hollies (Ron Richards), Epic 10298 Uni 55055 | 8 |
| 44 | 44 | 44 | 46 | I WILL ALWAYS THINK ABOUT YOU — New Colony Six (Senator Records Corp.), Mercury 72775 | 6 |
| 45 | 45 | 13 | 9 | VALLERI — Monkees (Monkees), Colgems 66-1019 | 9 |
| ★ 46 | 61 | 71 | — | LIKE TO GET TO KNOW YOU — Spanky & Our Gang (Scharf-Dorough), Mercury 72795 | 3 |
| ★ 47 | 87 | — | — | THE HAPPY SONG (Dum Dum) — Otis Redding (Steve Cropper), Volt 163 | 2 |
| ★ 48 | 78 | 97 | — | DOES YOUR MAMA KNOW ABOUT ME — Bobby Taylor & Vancouvers (B. Gordy Jr.), Gordy 7069 | 3 |
| ★ 49 | 72 | 82 | — | MEDLEY: MY GIRL, HEY GIRL — Bobby Vee (Dallas Smith), Liberty 56033 | 3 |
| 50 | 50 | 51 | 62 | LOOK TO YOUR SOUL — Johnny Rivers (Work), Imperial 66286 | 5 |
| 51 | 51 | 67 | 90 | LOVING YOU HAS MADE ME BANANAS — Guy Marks (Peter De Angelis), ABC 11055 | 4 |
| 52 | 26 | 26 | 28 | JENNIFER JUNIPER — Donovan (Mickie Most), Epic 10300 | 9 |
| 53 | 53 | 58 | 64 | GOODBYE BABY (I Don't Want to See You Cry) — Tommy Boyce & Bobby Hart (Boyce-Hart), A&M 919 | 5 |
| 54 | 56 | 73 | — | PAYING THE COST TO BE THE BOSS — B.B. King (Lou Zito & Johnny Pate), Bluesway 61015 | 3 |
| 55 | 55 | 55 | 65 | FOGGY MOUNTAIN BREAKDOWN — Flatt & Scruggs (Bob Johnston), Columbia 44380/Mercury 72739 | 10 |
| 56 | 35 | 35 | 35 | SECURITY — Etta James (Rick Hall & Staff), Cadet 5594 | 10 |
| 57 | 57 | 57 | 71 | JUMBO — Bee Gees (Robert Stigwood & Bee Gees), Atco 6570 | 5 |
| 58 | 42 | 42 | 44 | THE IMPOSSIBLE DREAM — Hesitations (Wiltshire-Banks-Victor), Kapp 899 | 8 |
| ★ 59 | 77 | 78 | — | WE'RE ROLLING ON — Impressions (Curtis Mayfield & Johnny Pate), ABC 11076 | 3 |
| 60 | 60 | 60 | 63 | YOU'VE STILL GOT A PLACE IN MY HEART — Dean Martin (Jimmy Bowen), Reprise 0672 | 7 |
| 61 | 63 | 63 | 80 | I WANNA LIVE — Glen Campbell (Alyde Lory), Capitol 2146 | 5 |
| 62 | 64 | 70 | 82 | WEAR IT ON OUR FACE — Dells (Bobby Miller), Cadet 5599 | 4 |
| ★ 63 | 75 | 76 | 93 | MASTER JACK — Four Jacks & A Jill, RCA Victor 47-9473 | 6 |
| 64 | 52 | 59 | 60 | SHERRY DON'T GO — Lettermen (Kelly Gordon), Capitol 2132 | 7 |
| 65 | 65 | 65 | 87 | I CAN'T BELIEVE I'M LOSING YOU — Frank Sinatra (Sonny Burks), Reprise 0677 | 4 |
| 66 | 70 | 96 | — | FRIENDS — Beach Boys (Beach Boys), Capitol 2160 | 3 |
| 67 | 67 | 53 | 61 | ME, THE PEACEFUL HEART — Lulu (Mickie Most), Epic 10302 | 7 |
| 68 | 68 | 68 | 86 | CINDERELLA ROCKEFELLA — Esther & Abi Ofarim, Philips 40526 | 6 |
| ★ 69 | 99 | — | — | IF I WERE A CARPENTER — Four Tops (Holland & Dozier), Motown 1124 | 2 |
| 70 | 73 | 74 | 89 | FUNKY WALK, Part 1 — Dyke & the Blazers (East/Art Barrett), Original Sound 79 | 4 |
| 71 | 71 | 72 | — | IMPOSSIBLE MISSION (Mission Impossible) — Soul Survivors (Gamble-Huff), Crimson 1016 | 3 |
| 72 | 59 | 52 | 52 | L. DAVID SLOANE — Michele Lee (Jack Gold), Columbia 44413 | 10 |
| ★ 73 | 88 | 92 | 99 | BABY MAKES OUR OWN SWEET MUSIC — Jay & the Techniques (Jerry Ross), Smash 2154 | 4 |
| 74 | 74 | 75 | 81 | I GOT A SURE THING — Ollie & the Nightingales (Booker T. Jones), Stax 245 | 5 |
| ★ 75 | 97 | 99 | — | UNWIND — Ray Stevens (Fred Foster & Ray Stevens), Monument 1048 | 3 |
| 76 | 76 | 77 | 94 | IF YOU DON'T WANT MY LOVE — Robert John (David Rubinson), Columbia 44435 | 4 |
| ★ 77 | 92 | — | — | I'M SORRY — Delfonics (Stan & Bell), Philly Groove 151 | 2 |
| ★ 78 | 83 | 84 | — | I PROMISE TO WAIT MY LOVE — Martha Reeves & Vandellas (Cosby & Brown), Gordy 7070 | 3 |
| 79 | 79 | 80 | 98 | GOIN' AWAY — Fireballs (Norman Petty), Atco 6569 | 4 |
| 80 | 80 | 81 | 96 | ANYTHING — Eric Burdon & the Animals (Tom Wilson), MGM 13917 | 4 |
| 81 | 81 | 83 | — | CABARET — Herb Alpert & the Tijuana Brass (Herb Alpert & Jerry Moss), A&M 925 | 3 |
| 82 | 82 | 85 | 88 | (You Keep Me) HANGIN' ON — Joe Simon (J.R. Enterprises), Sound Stage 7 2608 | 4 |
| ★ 83 | 84 | 86 | — | MAY I TAKE A GIANT STEP — 1910 Fruitgum Co. (J. Katz/E. Chiprut/J. Kasenetz), Buddah 39 | 3 |
| 84 | 66 | 66 | 69 | GENTLE ON MY MIND — Patti Page (Jack Gold), Columbia 44353 | 13 |
| 85 | 85 | 87 | 95 | I LOVE YOU — People (Mikel Hunter), Capitol 2078 | 5 |
| 86 | 86 | — | — | CHAIN GANG — Jackie Wilson & Count Basie (Nat Tarnopol & Teddy Reig), Brunswick 55373 | 2 |
| ★ 87 | — | — | — | I COULD NEVER LOVE ANOTHER (After Loving You) — Temptations (Norman Whitfield), Gordy 7072 | 1 |
| ★ 88 | — | — | — | YUMMY, YUMMY, YUMMY — Ohio Express (Super X), Buddah 38 | 1 |
| ★ 89 | 100 | — | — | A TRIBUTE TO A KING — William Bell (Booker T. Jones), Stax 248 | 2 |
| ★ 90 | — | — | — | SOUL TRAIN — Classics IV (Bill Lowery), Imperial 66293 | 1 |
| 91 | — | — | — | NEVER GIVE YOU UP — Jerry Butler (Gamble-Huff), Mercury 72798 | 1 |
| 92 | — | — | — | I HAVE A DREAM — Rev. Martin Luther King Jr., Gordy 7023 | 1 |
| 93 | — | — | — | HE DON'T REALLY LOVE YOU — Delfonics (T. Bell), Moon Shot 6793 | 1 |
| 94 | 94 | — | — | I CAN REMEMBER — James & Bobby Purify (Papa Don), Bell 721 | 2 |
| 95 | — | — | — | I WISH I KNEW (How It Would Feel to Be Free) — Solomon Burke (Tom Dowd), Atlantic 2507 | 1 |
| 96 | 96 | — | — | LILLI MARLENE — Al Martino (Tom Morgan), Capitol 2158 | 2 |
| 97 | — | — | — | ANGEL OF THE MORNING — Merrilee Rush (T. Cogbill & C. Moman), Bell 705 | 1 |
| 98 | 98 | 98 | — | GREASY HEART — Jefferson Airplane (Al Schmitt), RCA Victor 47-9496 | 3 |
| 99 | — | — | — | HERE'S TO YOU — Hamilton Camp (Roy Silver & Felix Pappalardi), Warner Bros.-Seven Arts 7165 | 1 |
| 100 | — | — | — | HOW'D WE EVER GET THIS WAY? — Andy Kim (Jerry Barry), Steed 707 | 1 |

## HOT 100—A TO Z—(Publisher-Licensee)



## BUBBLING UNDER THE HOT 100

101. SHADOW OF YOUR LOVE — Five Stairsteps & Cubie, Buddah 35
102. LOVE IN THEM THERE HILLS — Vibrations, Okeh 7311
103. SAN FRANCISCO GIRLS — Fever Tree, Uni 55060
104. LOOK AT WHAT I ALMOST MISSED — Parliaments, Revilot 217
105. IN THE MORNING — Mighty Marvelows, ABC 11011
106. YOU AIN'T GOIN' NOWHERE — Byrds, Columbia 44499
107. LOUISIANA MAN — Bobbie Gentry, Capitol 2147
108. LOVE MACHINE — Roosters, Philips 40504
109. OH, I'LL NEVER BE THE SAME — Young Hearts, Minit 32039
110. BY THE TIME I GET TO PHOENIX — Ace Cannon, Hi 2144
111. TIP TOE THRU THE TULIPS WITH ME — Tiny Tim, Reprise 0679
112. I AM THE MAN FOR YOU BABY — Edwin Starr, Gordy 7071
113. YOU'LL NEVER WALK ALONE — Elvis Presley, RCA Victor 47-9600
114. LAZY SUNDAY — Small Faces, Immediate 5007
115. LONELY IS THE NAME — Sammy Davis Jr., Reprise 0673
116. FACE IT GIRL, IT'S OVER — Nancy Wilson, Capitol 2136
117. THE SINGER SANG HIS SONG — Bee Gees, Atco 6570
118. DON'T TAKE YOUR LOVE FROM ME — Ben E. King, Atco 6571
119. SLICK — Herb Alpert & the Tijuana Brass, A&M 925
120. SLEEPY JOE — Herman's Hermits, MGM 13934
121. FAT ALBERT — Fat Albert Ork & Chorus, Tetragrammaton 1500
122. TAKE ME IN YOUR ARMS (And Rock Me for a Little While) — Isley Brothers, Tamla 54164
123. ALONE AGAIN OR — Love, Elektra 45629
124. BROOKLYN ROADS — Neil Diamond, Uni 55065
125. SHE'S A HEARTBREAKER — Gene Pitney, Musicor 1306
126. ELEVATOR — Grapefruit, Equinox 70,005
127. DON'T HURT ME NO MORE — Al Greene, Hot Line 15001
128. AS LONG AS I GOT YOU — Laura Lee, Chess 2041
129. WE CAN FLY/UP UP & AWAY — Al Hirt, RCA Victor 47-9500
130. YESTERDAY I HEARD THE RAIN — Tony Bennett, Columbia 44510
131. PICTURES OF MATCHSTICK MEN — Status Quo, Cadet Concept 7001
132. CHAIN AROUND THE FLOWERS — Lewis & Clark Expedition, Colgems 66-1022
133. BILLY SUNSHINE — Evie Sands, Cameo 2002
134. MAMAN — Arthur Prysock, Verve 10592
135. I CAN'T MAKE IT ALONE — Bill Medley, MGM 13931

Compiled from national retail sales and radio station airplay by the Music Popularity Dept. of Record Market Research, Billboard.

# Billboard HOT 100

**FOR WEEK ENDING MAY 11, 1968**

★ STAR PERFORMER—Sides registering greatest proportionate upward progress this week.
● Record Industry Association of America seal of certification as million selling single.

| This Week | Wk. Ago | 2 Wk. Ago | 3 Wk. Ago | TITLE — Artist (Producer), Label & Number | Weeks On Chart |
|---|---|---|---|---|---|
| 1 | 1 | 1 | 1 | HONEY — Bobby Goldsboro (Bob Montgomery & Bobby Goldsboro), United Artists 50283 | 8 |
| 2 | 5 | 9 | 25 | TIGHTEN UP — Archie Bell & the Drells (L.J.F. Production), Atlantic 2478 | 7 |
| 3 | 3 | 3 | 2 | YOUNG GIRL — Union Gap Featuring Gary Puckett (Jerry Fuller), Columbia 44450 | 11 |
| 4 | 8 | 14 | 19 | THE GOOD, THE BAD AND THE UGLY — Hugo Montenegro, His Ork and Chorus (Neely Plumb), RCA Victor 9423 | 13 |
| 5 | 2 | 2 | 3 | CRY LIKE A BABY — Box Tops (Dan Penn), Mala 593 | 11 |
| 6 | 9 | 19 | 31 | BEAUTIFUL MORNING — Rascals (Rascals), Atlantic 2493 | 5 |
| 7 | 7 | 13 | 18 | COWBOYS TO GIRLS — Intruders (Gamble-Huff), Gamble 214 | 9 |
| 8 | 10 | 12 | 20 | THE UNICORN — Irish Rovers (Charles Bud Dant), Decca 32254 | 9 |
| 9 | 32 | 58 | — | MRS. ROBINSON — Simon & Garfunkel (Simon, Garfunkel & Halee), Columbia 44511 | 3 |
| 10 | 4 | 4 | 4 | LADY MADONNA — Beatles (George Martin), Capitol 2138 | 8 |
| 11 | 17 | 22 | 22 | LOVE IS ALL AROUND — Troggs (Page One), Fontana 1607 | 12 |
| 12 | 6 | 6 | 9 | I GOT THE FEELIN' — James Brown and the Famous Flames (James Brown), King 6155 | 8 |
| 13 | 13 | 20 | 28 | TAKE TIME TO KNOW HER — Percy Sledge (Quin Ivy & Marlin Greene), Atlantic 2490 | 9 |
| 14 | 23 | 23 | 30 | FUNKY STREET — Arthur Conley (Tom Dowd), Atco 6563 | 9 |
| 15 | 14 | 16 | 16 | SUMMERTIME BLUES — Blue Cheer (Abe "Voco" Kesh), Philips 40516 | 11 |
| 16 | 16 | 21 | 21 | AIN'T NO WAY — Aretha Franklin (Jerry Wexler), Atlantic 2486 | 6 |
| 17 | 15 | 10 | 7 | THE BALLAD OF BONNIE AND CLYDE — Georgie Fame (Manny Kellem), Epic 10283 | 13 |
| 18 | 18 | 18 | 23 | SWEET INSPIRATION — Sweet Inspirations (Tom Dowd & Tommy Cogbill), Atlantic 2476 | 11 |
| 19 | 21 | 27 | 61 | DO YOU KNOW THE WAY TO SAN JOSE? — Dionne Warwick (Bacharach-David), Scepter 12216 | 5 |
| 20 | 20 | 31 | 47 | SHOO-BE-DOO-BE-DOO-DA-DAY — Stevie Wonder (H. Cosby), Tamla 54165 | 6 |
| 21 | 12 | 8 | 8 | DANCE TO THE MUSIC — Sly & the Family Stone (Sly Stone), Epic 10256 | 11 |
| 22 | 34 | 49 | 50 | MONY MONY — Tommy James & Shondells (Kasenetz-Katz Associates), Roulette 7008 | 6 |
| 23 | 30 | 36 | 38 | SOUL SERENADE — Willie Mitchell (Willie Mitchell/Joe Cuoghi), Hi 2140 | 10 |
| 24 | 25 | 39 | 56 | AIN'T NOTHING LIKE THE REAL THING — Marvin Gaye & Tammi Terrell (Ashford-Simpson), Tamla 54163 | 5 |
| 25 | 22 | 5 | 5 | (Sweet Sweet Baby) SINCE YOU'VE BEEN GONE — Aretha Franklin (Jerry Wexler), Atlantic 2486 | 11 |
| 26 | 24 | 17 | 17 | PLAYBOY — Gene & Debbie (Don Gant), TRX 5006 | 13 |
| 27 | 27 | 34 | 34 | DELILAH — Tom Jones (Peter Sullivan), Parrot 40025 | 9 |
| 28 | 31 | 32 | 32 | U. S. MALE — Elvis Presley, RCA Victor 47-9465 | 8 |
| 29 | 44 | 44 | 44 | I WILL ALWAYS THINK ABOUT YOU — New Colony Six (Senator Records Corp.), Mercury 72775 | 7 |
| 30 | 41 | 41 | 45 | SHE'S LOOKIN' GOOD — Wilson Pickett (Tom Dowd & Tommy Cogbill), Atlantic 2504 | 6 |
| 31 | 29 | 29 | 10 | THE MIGHTY QUINN — Manfred Mann, Mercury 72770 | 11 |
| 32 | 26 | 15 | 12 | LA-LA MEANS I LOVE YOU — Delfonics (Stan & Bell), Philly Groove 150 | 15 |
| 33 | 11 | 11 | 14 | IF YOU CAN WANT — Smokey Robinson and the Miracles ("Smokey" Cleveland), Tamla 54162 | 12 |
| 34 | 33 | 33 | 33 | TAKE GOOD CARE OF MY BABY — Bobby Vinton (Billy Sherrill), Epic 10305 | 7 |
| 35 | 19 | 7 | 6 | (Sittin' On) THE DOCK OF THE BAY — Otis Redding (Steve Cropper), Volt 157 | 16 |
| 36 | 69 | 99 | — | IF I WERE A CARPENTER — Four Tops (Holland & Dozier), Motown 1124 | 3 |
| 37 | 47 | 87 | — | THE HAPPY SONG (Dum Dum) — Otis Redding (Steve Cropper), Volt 163 | 3 |
| 38 | 36 | 24 | 11 | SCARBOROUGH FAIR (/Canticle) — Simon & Garfunkel (Bob Johnston), Columbia 44465 | 11 |
| 39 | 39 | 48 | 48 | UNKNOWN SOLDIER — Doors (Paul A. Rathchild), Elektra 45628 | 7 |
| 40 | 40 | 43 | 49 | CALL ME LIGHTNING — The Who (Kit Lambert), Decca 32288 | 7 |
| 41 | 43 | 43 | 43 | JENNIFER ECCLES — Hollies (Ron Richards), Epic 10298/Uni 55055 | 6 |
| 42 | 42 | 40 | 40 | THE SON OF HICKORY HOLLER'S TRAMP — O. C. Smith (Jerry Fuller), Columbia 44425 | 12 |
| 43 | 63 | 75 | 76 | MASTER JACK — Four Jacks & A Jill, RCA Victor 47-9473 | 5 |
| 44 | 28 | 28 | 29 | FOREVER CAME TODAY — Diana Ross & the Supremes (Holland & Dozier), Motown 1122 | 9 |
| 45 | 46 | 61 | 71 | LIKE TO GET TO KNOW YOU — Spanky & Our Gang (Scharf-Dorough), Mercury 72795 | 4 |
| 46 | 48 | 78 | 97 | DOES YOUR MAMA KNOW ABOUT ME — Bobby Taylor & Vancouvers (B. Gordy Jr.), Gordy 7069 | 4 |
| 47 | 45 | 45 | 13 | VALLERI — Monkees (Monkees), Colgems 66-1019 | 10 |
| 48 | 49 | 72 | 82 | MEDLEY: MY GIRL, HEY GIRL — Bobby Vee (Dallas Smith), Liberty 56033 | 4 |
| 49 | 50 | 50 | 51 | LOOK TO YOUR SOUL — Johnny Rivers (Work), Imperial 66286 | 6 |
| 50 | 37 | 37 | 37 | SOUL COAXING (Ame Caline) — Raymond Lefevre, 4 Corners of the World 147 | 12 |
| 51 | 51 | 51 | 67 | LOVING YOU HAS MADE ME BANANAS — Guy Marks (Peter De Angelis), ABC 11055 | 4 |
| 52 | 54 | 56 | 73 | PAYING THE COST TO BE THE BOSS — B.B. King (Lou Zito & Johnny Pate), Bluesway 61015 | 4 |
| 53 | 62 | 64 | 70 | WEAR IT ON OUR FACE — Dells (Bobby Miller), Cadet 5599 | 5 |
| 54 | 61 | 63 | 63 | I WANNA LIVE — Glen Campbell (Alyde Lery), Capitol 2146 | 5 |
| 55 | 66 | 70 | 96 | FRIENDS — Beach Boys (Beach Boys), Capitol 2160 | 4 |
| 56 | 87 | — | — | I COULD NEVER LOVE ANOTHER (After Loving You) — Temptations (Norman Whitfield), Gordy 7072 | 2 |
| 57 | 57 | 57 | 57 | JUMBO — Bee Gees (Robert Stigwood & Bee Gees), Atco 6570 | 6 |
| 58 | 55 | 55 | 55 | FOGGY MOUNTAIN BREAKDOWN — Flatt & Scruggs (Bob Johnston), Columbia 44380/Mercury 72739 | 11 |
| 59 | 59 | 77 | 78 | WE'RE ROLLING ON — Impressions (Curtis Mayfield & Johnny Pate), ABC 11076 | 4 |
| 60 | 65 | 65 | 65 | I CAN'T BELIEVE I'M LOSING YOU — Frank Sinatra (Sonny Burks), Reprise 0677 | 4 |
| 61 | 85 | 85 | 87 | I LOVE YOU — People (Mikel Hunter), Capitol 2078 | 3 |
| 62 | 88 | — | — | YUMMY, YUMMY, YUMMY — Ohio Express (Kasenetz-Katz Associates), Buddah 38 | 2 |
| 63 | 53 | 53 | 58 | GOODBYE BABY (I Don't Want to See You Cry) — Tommy Boyce & Bobby Hart (Boyce-Hart), A&M 919 | 6 |
| 64 | 76 | 76 | 77 | IF YOU DON'T WANT MY LOVE — Robert John (David Rubinson), Columbia 44435 | 4 |
| 65 | 73 | 88 | 92 | BABY MAKES OUR OWN SWEET MUSIC — Jay & the Techniques (Jerry Ross), Smash 2154 | 5 |
| 66 | 78 | 83 | 84 | I PROMISE TO WAIT MY LOVE — Martha Reeves & Vandellas (Cosby & Brown), Gordy 7070 | 4 |
| 67 | 70 | 73 | 74 | FUNKY WALK, Part 1 — Dyke & the Blazers (East/Art Barrett), Original Sound 79 | 5 |
| 68 | 71 | 71 | 72 | IMPOSSIBLE MISSION (Mission Impossible) — Soul Survivors (Gamble-Huff), Crimson 1016 | 4 |
| 69 | 77 | 92 | — | I'M SORRY — Delfonics (Stan & Bell), Philly Groove 151 | 3 |
| 70 | 64 | 64 | 59 | SHERRY DON'T GO — Lettermen (Kelly Gordon), Capitol 2132 | 8 |
| 71 | 75 | 97 | 99 | UNWIND — Ray Stevens (Fred Foster & Ray Stevens), Monument 1048 | 4 |
| 72 | 72 | 59 | 52 | L. DAVID SLOANE — Michele Lee (Jack Gold), Columbia 44413 | 11 |
| 73 | 82 | 82 | 85 | (You Keep Me) HANGIN' ON — Joe Simon (J.R. Enterprises), Sound Stage 7 2608 | 5 |
| 74 | 74 | 74 | 75 | I GOT A SURE THING — Ollie & the Nightingales (Booker T. Jones), Stax 245 | 6 |
| 75 | 83 | 84 | 86 | MAY I TAKE A GIANT STEP — 1910 Fruitgum Co. (J. Katz/E. Chiprut/J. Kasenetz), Buddah 39 | 4 |
| 76 | 81 | 81 | 83 | CABARET — Herb Alpert & the Tijuana Brass (Herb Alpert & Jerry Moss), A&M 925 | 5 |
| 77 | — | — | — | THE LOOK OF LOVE — Sergio Mendes & Brasil '66 (Herb Alpert), A&M 924 | 1 |
| 78 | 94 | 94 | — | I CAN REMEMBER — James & Bobby Purify (Papa Don), Bell 721 | 3 |
| 79 | — | — | — | MacARTHUR PARK — Richard Harris (Jimmy Webb), Dunhill 4134 | 1 |
| 80 | 100 | — | — | HOW'D WE EVER GET THIS WAY? — Andy Kim (Jerry Barry), Steed 707 | 3 |
| 81 | — | — | — | LOVE IN EVERY ROOM (Meme Si Tu Revenais) — Paul Mauriat & His Ork (Paul Mauriat), Philips 40530 | 1 |
| 82 | 99 | — | — | HERE'S TO YOU — Hamilton Camp (Felix Pappalardi), Warner Bros.-Seven Arts 7165 | 2 |
| 83 | 97 | — | — | ANGEL OF THE MORNING — Merrilee Rush (T. Cogbill & C. Moman), Bell 705 | 2 |
| 84 | 84 | 66 | 66 | GENTLE ON MY MIND — Patti Page (Jack Gold), Columbia 44353 | 14 |
| 85 | 91 | — | — | NEVER GIVE YOU UP — Jerry Butler (Gamble-Huff), Mercury 72798 | 2 |
| 86 | 86 | 86 | — | CHAIN GANG — Jackie Wilson & Count Basie (Nat Tarnopol & Teddy Reig), Brunswick 55373 | 3 |
| 87 | — | — | — | A MAN WITHOUT LOVE (Quando M'Innamora) — Engelbert Humperdinck (Peter Sullivan), Parrot 40027 | 1 |
| 88 | 95 | — | — | I WISH I KNEW (How It Would Feel to Be Free) — Solomon Burke (Norman Whitfield), Atlantic 2507 | 2 |
| 89 | 89 | 100 | — | A TRIBUTE TO A KING — William Bell (Booker T. Jones), Stax 248 | 3 |
| 90 | 90 | — | — | SOUL TRAIN — Classics IV (Bill Lowery), Imperial 66293 | 2 |
| 91 | 92 | — | — | I HAVE A DREAM — Rev. Martin Luther King Jr. (Gamble-Huff), Gordy 7023 | 2 |
| 92 | 93 | — | — | HE DON'T REALLY LOVE YOU — Delfonics (T. Bell), Moon Shot 6793 | 2 |
| 93 | — | — | — | YOU AIN'T GOING NOWHERE — Byrds (Gary Usher), Columbia 44499 | 1 |
| 94 | 96 | 96 | — | LILI MARLENE — Al Martino (Tom Morgan), Capitol 2158 | 3 |
| 95 | — | — | — | SLEEPY JOE — Herman's Hermits (Mickie Most), MGM 13934 | 1 |
| 96 | — | — | — | FACE IT GIRL, IT'S OVER — Nancy Wilson (David Cavanaugh), Capitol 2136 | 1 |
| 97 | — | — | — | APOLOGIZE — Ed Ames (Jim Foglesong), RCA Victor 47-9517 | 1 |
| 98 | — | — | — | BROOKLYN ROADS — Neil Diamond (Chip Taylor), UNI 55065 | 1 |
| 99 | — | — | — | ANYONE FOR TENNIS (Savage Seven Theme) — Cream (Felix Pappalardi), Atco 6575 | 1 |
| 100 | — | — | — | SHE'S A HEARTBREAKER — Gene Pitney (Charlie Foxx), Musicor 1306 | 1 |

## HOT 100—A TO Z—(Publisher-Licensee)

Ain't Nothing Like the Real Thing (Jobete, BMI) .. 24
Ain't No Way (14th Hour/Cotillion, BMI) ........ 16
Angel of the Morning (Blackwood, BMI) ......... 83
Anyone For Tennis (Savage Seven Theme) (Dratleaf, BMI) .......... 99
Apologize (Stone Canyon, BMI) ................. 97
Baby Make Your Own Sweet Music (Screen Gems-Columbia, BMI) ........ 65
Ballad of Bonnie and Clyde, The (Peer Int'l, BMI) . 17
Beautiful Morning, A (Slacsar, BMI) ............. 6
Brooklyn Roads (Stonebridge, BMI) .............. 98
Cabaret (Sunbeam, BMI) ........................ 76
Call Me Lightning (Fabulous, ASCAP) ............ 40
Chain Gang (Kaga, BMI) ........................ 86
Cowboys to Girls (Razor Sharp, BMI) ............. 7
Cry Like a Baby (Press, BMI) ................... 5
Dance to the Music (Daly City, BMI) ........... 21
Delilah (Francis, Day & Hunter, ASCAP) ........ 27
Do You Know the Way to San Jose? (Jac/Blue Seas, ASCAP) .......... 19
Does Your Mama Know About Me (Stein & Van Stock, ASCAP) .............. 46
Face It Girl, It's Over (Meager, BMI) ........... 96
Foggy Mountain Breakdown (Peer Int'l, BMI) ..... 58
Forever Came Today (Jobete, BMI) .............. 44
Friends (Sea of Tunes, BMI) .................... 55
Funky Street (Redwal, BMI) ..................... 14
Funky Walk, Part 1 (Drive-In-Westward, BMI) .... 67
Gentle on My Mind (Sherman-DeVorzon, BMI) .... 84
Good, The Bad and The Ugly, The (Unart, BMI) .. 4
Goodbye Baby (I Don't Want to See You Cry) (Screen Gems-Columbia, BMI) .... 63
Happy Song (Dum Dum) (East/Time/Redwal, BMI) ...... 37
He Don't Really Love You (Grocalla, BMI) ....... 92
Here's to You (Royham, ASCAP) ................. 82
Honey (Russell-Cason, ASCAP) .................. 1
How'd We Ever Get This Way? (Unart, BMI) ...... 80
I Can Remember (Big Seven, BMI) ............... 78
I Can't Believe I'm Losing You (Vogue/Hollyland, BMI) ........ 60
I Could Never Love Another (Jobete, BMI) ....... 56
I Got a Sure Thing (Jobete, BMI) ................ 74
I Got the Feelin' (Toccoa-Lois, BMI) ............ 12
I Have a Dream (Mainstay, BMI) ................ 91
I Love You (Mainstay, BMI) ..................... 61
I Promise to Wait My Love (Jobete, BMI) ........ 66
I Will Always Think About You (New Colony/T.M., BMI) .......... 29
I Wish I Knew (Duane, BMI) .................... 88
If I Were a Carpenter (Faithful Virtue, BMI) .... 36
If You Can Want (Jobete, BMI) .................. 33
If You Don't Want My Love (Borwin, BMI) ....... 64
I'm Sorry (Nickel Shoe/Bellboy, BMI) ............ 69
Impossible Mission (Mission Impossible) (Double Diamond/Downstairs, BMI) ........ 68
Jennifer Eccles (Maribus, BMI) .................. 41
Jumbo (Nemperor, BMI) ........................ 57
L. David Sloane (Meager, BMI) .................. 72
Lady Madonna (Maclen, BMI) ................... 10
La-La Means I Love You (Nickel Shoe, BMI) .... 32
Like to Get to Know You (Rivers, BMI) .......... 45
Lili Marlene (Marks/E.T.M.A., BMI) ............. 94
Look to Your Soul (Rivers, BMI) ................. 49
Look of Love, The (Colgems, ASCAP) ........... 77
Loving You Has Made Me Bananas (Curtis, ASCAP) .... 51
Love in Every Room (Meme Si Tu Revenais) (Northern, ASCAP) ............ 81
Love Is All Around (James, BMI) ................ 11
MacArthur Park (Canopy, ASCAP) ............... 79
Man Without Love, A (Quando M'Innamora) (Leeds, ASCAP) .............. 87
Master Jack (Milene, ASCAP) ................... 43
May I Take a Giant Step (Kaskat, BMI) ......... 75
Medley: My Girl, Hey Girl (Jobete/Screen Gems-Columbia, BMI) .. 48
Mighty Quinn, The (Dwarf, ASCAP) ............. 31
Mony Mony (Patricia, BMI) ...................... 22
Mrs. Robinson (Charing Cross, BMI) ............. 9
Never Give You Up (Parabut/Double Diamond/Downstairs, BMI) ......... 85
Paying the Cost to Be the Boss (Panco/LZMC, BMI) ........ 52
Playboy (Acuff-Rose, BMI) ...................... 26
Scarborough Fair (/Canticle) (Charing Cross, BMI) . 38
She's a Heartbreaker (Catalogue/Cee & Eye, BMI) .. 100
She's Lookin' Good (Vertla, BMI) ................ 30
Sherry Don't Go (Grey Fox, BMI) ................ 70
Shoo-Be-Doo-Be-Do-Day (Jobete, BMI) .......... 20
(Sittin' On) The Dock of the Bay (East/Pine/Redwal, BMI) ........ 35
Sleepy Joe (Southern, ASCAP) ................... 95
Son of Hickory Holler's Tramp, The (Blue Crest, BMI) .. 42
Soul Coaxing (Ame Caline) (Southern, ASCAP) .. 50
Soul Serenade (Kilyn, BMI) ...................... 23
Soul Train (Lom-Sal, BMI) ...................... 90
Summertime Blues (Viva, BMI) .................. 15
Sweet Inspirations (Press, BMI) ................. 18
(Sweet, Sweet Baby) Since You've Been Gone (14th Hour/Cotillion, BMI) ........ 25
Take Good Care of My Baby (Screen Gems-Columbia, BMI) .............. 34
Take Time to Know Her (Gallico, BMI) .......... 13
Tighten Up (Cotillion/Orells, BMI) ............... 2
Tribute to a King, A (East, BMI) ................ 89
Unicorn, The (Hollis, ASCAP) .................... 8
Unknown Soldier (Nipper, ASCAP) ............... 39
Unwind (Ahab, BMI) ............................ 71
U. S. Male (Viva, BMI) ......................... 28
Valleri (Screen Gems-Columbia, BMI) ............ 47
We're Rolling On (Chevis, BMI) .................. 59
Wear It on Our Face (Chevis, BMI) ............... 53
You Ain't Going Nowhere (Dwarf, AFCAP) ....... 93
(You Keep Me) Hangin' On (Garpex/Alambo, BMI) . 73
Young Girl (Viva, BMI) ......................... 3
Yummy, Yummy, Yummy (TM, BMI) ............. 62

## BUBBLING UNDER THE HOT 100

101. JELLY JUNGLE (Of Orange Marmalade) ........... Lemon Pipers, Buddah 41
102. LOVE IN THEM THERE HILLS ................... Vibrations, Okeh 7311
103. SAN FRANCISCO GIRLS ...................... Fever Tree, Uni 55060
104. TIME FOR LIVING ................ Association, Warner Brothers-Seven Arts 7195
105. SHADOW OF YOUR LOVE ............. Five Stairsteps & Cubie, Buddah 35
106. LOVE MACHINE ........................ Roosters, Philips 40504
107. CLIMB EVERY MOUNTAIN ............... Hesitations, Kapp 911
108. THIS GUY'S IN LOVE WITH YOU ....... Herb Alpert, A&M 929
109. OH, I'LL NEVER BE THE SAME .......... Youngbeats, Minit 32039
110. BY THE TIME I GET TO PHOENIX ....... Redwal,
111. LONELY IS THE NAME ................. Sammy Davis Jr., Reprise 0673
112. DON'T SIGN THE PAPER ................ Jimmy Delphs, Immediate 5007
113. ELEVATOR ........................... Grapefruit, Equinox 70005
114. LAZY SUNDAY ........................ Small Faces, Immediate 5007
115. MY SHY VIOLET ...................... Mills Brothers, Dot 17094
116. THE SINGER SANG HIS SONG ........... Bee Gees, Atco 6570
117. FINDERS KEEPERS .................... Salt Water Taffy, Buddah 37
118. DON'T TAKE YOUR LOVE FROM ME ..... E. King, Atco 6571
119. SLICK ............. Herb Alpert & the Tijuana Brass, A&M 929
120. FAT ALBERT ......... Fat Albert Ork & Chorus, Tetragrammaton 1500
121. TAKE ME IN YOUR ARMS (And Rock Me for a Little While) ........ Isley Brothers, Tamla 54164
122. YOU'RE GOOD FOR ME ................ Lou Rawls, Capitol 2172
123. ALONE AGAIN OR .................... Love, Elektra 45629
124. RANDY ............................. B.T. Poppy 504
125. CAN I CARRY YOUR BALLOON ......... Swampseeds, Acta 805
126. LOOKING BACK ...................... Spencer Davis Group, United Artists 50286
127. READY, WILLIN' AND ABLE ........... American Breed, Acta 822
128. AS LONG AS I GOT YOU ............... Laura Lee, Chess 2041
129. I CAN'T MAKE IT ALONE ............. Bill Medley, MGM 13928
130. PICTURES OF MATCHSTICK MEN ....... Status Quo, Cadet Concept 7001
131. CHAIN AROUND THE FLOWERS ....... Lewis & Clark Expedition, Colgems 66-1022
132. FOLLOW ME ......................... Jack Jones, RCA Victor 47-9514
133. I CAN'T GO BACK TO DENVER ......... Gentrys, Bell 720
134. ONLY ME ........................... First Edition, Reprise 0683
135. HAVE A DRINK, A LITTLE LOVIN' ..... Los Bravos, Parrot 3020

Compiled from national retail sales and radio station airplay by the Music Popularity Dept. of Record Market Research, Billboard.

# Billboard HOT 100

FOR WEEK ENDING MAY 18, 1968

★ STAR PERFORMER—Sides registering greatest proportionate upward progress this week.

Ⓢ Record Industry Association of America seal of certification as million selling single.

| This Week | 1 Wk. Ago | 2 Wks. Ago | 3 Wks. Ago | TITLE Artist (Producer), Label & Number | Weeks On Chart |
|---|---|---|---|---|---|
| 1 (Billboard Award) | 2 | 5 | 9 | TIGHTEN UP — Archie Bell & the Drells (L.J.F. Production), Atlantic 2478 | 8 |
| ★ 2 | 9 | 32 | 58 | MRS. ROBINSON — Simon & Garfunkel (Simon, Garfunkel & Halee), Columbia 44511 | 4 |
| Ⓢ 3 | 1 | 1 | 1 | HONEY — Bobby Goldsboro (Bob Montgomery & Bobby Goldsboro), United Artists 50283 | 9 |
| 4 | 4 | 8 | 14 | THE GOOD, THE BAD AND THE UGLY — Hugo Montenegro, His Ork and Chorus (Neely Plumb), RCA Victor 9423 | 14 |
| ★ 5 | 6 | 9 | 19 | BEAUTIFUL MORNING — Rascals (Rascals), Atlantic 2493 | 6 |
| ★ 6 | 7 | 7 | 13 | COWBOYS TO GIRLS — Intruders (Gamble-Huff), Gamble 214 | 9 |
| 7 | 11 | 17 | 22 | LOVE IS ALL AROUND — Troggs (Page One), Fontana 1607 | 13 |
| 8 | 8 | 10 | 12 | THE UNICORN — Irish Rovers (Charles Bud Dant), Decca 32254 | 9 |
| Ⓢ 9 | 3 | 3 | 3 | YOUNG GIRL — Union Gap Featuring Gary Puckett (Jerry Fuller), Columbia 44450 | 12 |
| ★ 10 | 19 | 21 | 27 | DO YOU KNOW THE WAY TO SAN JOSE? — Dionne Warwick (Bacharach-David), Scepter 12216 | 6 |
| ★ 11 | 20 | 20 | 31 | SHOO-BE-DOO-BE-DOO-DA-DAY — Stevie Wonder (H. Cosby), Tamla 54165 | 7 |
| Ⓢ 12 | 5 | 2 | 2 | CRY LIKE A BABY — Box Tops (Dan Penn), Mala 593 | 12 |
| 13 | 13 | 13 | 20 | TAKE TIME TO KNOW HER — Percy Sledge (Quin Ivy & Marlin Greene), Atlantic 2490 | 10 |
| ★ 14 | 24 | 25 | 39 | AIN'T NOTHING LIKE THE REAL THING — Marvin Gaye & Tammi Terrell (Ashford-Simpson), Tamla 54163 | 6 |
| Ⓢ 15 | 10 | 4 | 4 | LADY MADONNA — Beatles (George Martin), Capitol 2138 | 9 |
| 16 | 15 | 14 | 16 | SUMMERTIME BLUES — Blue Cheer (Abe "Voce" Kesh), Philips 40516 | 12 |
| 17 | 12 | 6 | 6 | I GOT THE FEELIN' — James Brown & the Famous Flames (James Brown), King 6155 | 10 |
| 18 | 14 | 23 | 23 | FUNKY STREET — Arthur Conley (Tom Dowd), Atco 6563 | 10 |
| 19 | 22 | 34 | 49 | MONY MONY — Tommy James & Shondells (Kasenetz-Katz Associates), Roulette 7008 | 7 |
| ★ 20 | 45 | 46 | 61 | LIKE TO GET TO KNOW YOU — Spanky & Our Gang (Scharf-Dorough), Mercury 72795 | 5 |
| 21 | 16 | 16 | 21 | AIN'T NO WAY — Aretha Franklin (Jerry Wexler), Atlantic 2486 | 7 |
| 22 | 30 | 41 | 41 | SHE'S LOOKIN' GOOD — Wilson Pickett (Tom Dowd & Tommy Cogbill), Atlantic 2504 | 6 |
| 23 | 23 | 30 | 36 | SOUL SERENADE — Willie Mitchell (Willie Mitchell/Joe Cuoghi), Hi 2140 | 11 |
| 24 | 18 | 18 | 18 | SWEET INSPIRATION — Sweet Inspirations (Tom Dowd & Tommy Cogbill), Atlantic 2476 | 12 |
| ★ 25 | 56 | 87 | — | I COULD NEVER LOVE ANOTHER (After Loving You) — Temptations (Norman Whitfield), Gordy 7072 | 3 |
| 26 | 27 | 27 | 34 | DELILAH — Tom Jones (Peter Sullivan), Parrot 40025 | 10 |
| ★ 27 | 37 | 47 | 87 | THE HAPPY SONG (Dum Dum) — Otis Redding (Steve Cropper), Volt 163 | 4 |
| 28 | 29 | 44 | 44 | I WILL ALWAYS THINK ABOUT YOU — New Colony Six (Senator Records Corp.), Mercury 72775 | 8 |
| ★ 29 | 36 | 69 | 99 | IF I WERE A CARPENTER — Four Tops (Holland & Dozier), Motown 1124 | 4 |
| ★ 30 | 46 | 48 | 78 | DOES YOUR MAMA KNOW ABOUT ME — Bobby Taylor & Vancouvers (B. Gordy Jr.), Gordy 7069 | 5 |
| ★ 31 | 43 | 63 | 75 | MASTER JACK — Four Jacks & A Jill, RCA Victor 47-9473 | 8 |
| ★ 32 | 62 | 88 | — | YUMMY, YUMMY, YUMMY — Ohio Express (Kasenetz-Katz Associates), Buddah 38 | 3 |
| 33 | 21 | 12 | 8 | DANCE TO THE MUSIC — Sly & the Family Stone (Sly Stone), Epic 10256 | 15 |
| 34 | 17 | 15 | 10 | THE BALLAD OF BONNIE AND CLYDE — Georgie Fame (Manny Kellem), Epic 10283 | 14 |
| Ⓢ 35 | 25 | 22 | 5 | (Sweet Sweet Baby) SINCE YOU'VE BEEN GONE — Aretha Franklin (Jerry Wexler), Atlantic 2486 | 12 |
| ★ 36 | 48 | 49 | 72 | MEDLEY: MY GIRL, HEY GIRL — Bobby Vee (Dallas Smith), Liberty 56033 | 5 |
| 37 | 34 | 33 | 33 | TAKE GOOD CARE OF MY BABY — Bobby Vinton (Billy Sherrill), Epic 10305 | 8 |
| 38 | 26 | 24 | 17 | PLAYBOY — Gene & Debbie (Don Gant), TRX 5006 | 14 |
| 39 | 39 | 39 | 48 | UNKNOWN SOLDIER — Doors (Paul A. Rothchild), Elektra 45628 | 8 |
| 40 | 41 | 43 | 43 | JENNIFER ECCLES — Hollies (Ron Richards), Epic 10298 Uni 55055 | 10 |
| 41 | 28 | 31 | 32 | U. S. MALE — Elvis Presley, RCA Victor 47-9465 | 9 |
| 42 | 40 | 40 | 47 | CALL ME LIGHTNING — The Who (Kit Lambert), Decca 32288 | 8 |
| 43 | 42 | 42 | 40 | THE SON OF HICKORY HOLLER'S TRAMP — O. C. Smith (Jerry Fuller), Columbia 44425 | 13 |
| ★ 44 | 54 | 61 | 63 | I WANNA LIVE — Glen Campbell (Alyde Lory), Capitol 2146 | 7 |
| 45 | 53 | 62 | 64 | WEAR IT ON OUR FACE — Dells (Bobby Miller), Cadet 5599 | 6 |
| ★ 46 | 69 | 77 | 92 | I'M SORRY — Delfonics (Stan & Bell), Philly Groove 151 | 4 |
| 47 | 55 | 66 | 70 | FRIENDS — Beach Boys (Beach Boys), Capitol 2160 | 5 |
| ★ 48 | 79 | — | — | MacARTHUR PARK — Richard Harris (Jimmy Webb), Dunhill 4134 | 2 |
| 49 | 49 | 50 | 50 | LOOK TO YOUR SOUL — Johnny Rivers (Work), Imperial 66286 | 7 |
| ★ 50 | 61 | 85 | 85 | I LOVE YOU — People (Mikel Hunter), Capitol 2078 | 7 |
| ★ 51 | 78 | 94 | 94 | I CAN REMEMBER — James & Bobby Purify (Papa Don), Bell 721 | 4 |
| 52 | 52 | 54 | 56 | PAYING THE COST TO BE THE BOSS — B.B. King (Lou Zito & Johnny Pate), Bluesway 61015 | 5 |
| ★ 53 | 87 | — | — | A MAN WITHOUT LOVE (Quando M'Innamora) — Engelbert Humperdinck (Peter Sullivan), Parrot 40027 | 2 |
| ★ 54 | 80 | 100 | — | HOW'D WE EVER GET THIS WAY? — Andy Kim (Jerry Barry), Steed 707 | 3 |
| ★ 55 | 83 | 97 | — | ANGEL OF THE MORNING — Merrilee Rush (T. Cogbill & C. Moman), Bell 705 | 3 |
| ★ 56 | 71 | 75 | 97 | UNWIND — Ray Stevens (Fred Foster & Ray Stevens), Monument 1048 | 5 |
| 57 | 64 | 76 | 76 | IF YOU DON'T WANT MY LOVE — Robert John (David Rubinson), Columbia 44435 | 6 |
| 58 | 51 | 51 | 51 | LOVING YOU HAS MADE ME BANANAS — Guy Marks (Peter De Angelis), ABC 11055 | 6 |
| 59 | 58 | 55 | 55 | FOGGY MOUNTAIN BREAKDOWN — Flatt & Scruggs (Bob Johnston), Columbia 44380/Mercury 72739 | 12 |
| ★ 60 | 77 | — | — | THE LOOK OF LOVE — Sergio Mendes & Brasil '66 (Herb Alpert), A&M 924 | 2 |
| ★ 61 | 73 | 82 | 82 | (You Keep Me) HANGIN' ON — Joe Simon (J.R. Enterprises), Sound Stage 7 2608 | 6 |
| ★ 62 | 85 | 91 | — | NEVER GIVE YOU UP — Jerry Butler (Gamble-Huff), Mercury 72798 | 3 |
| 63 | 59 | 59 | 77 | WE'RE ROLLING ON — Impressions (Curtis Mayfield & Johnny Pate), ABC 11076 | 5 |
| 64 | 65 | 73 | 88 | BABY MAKE YOUR OWN SWEET MUSIC — Jay & the Techniques (Jerry Ross), Smash 2154 | 6 |
| ★ 65 | 100 | — | — | SHE'S A HEARTBREAKER — Gene Pitney (Charlie Foxx), Musicor 1306 | 2 |
| 66 | 66 | 78 | 83 | I PROMISE TO WAIT MY LOVE — Martha Reeves & Vandellas (Cosby & Brown), Gordy 7070 | 5 |
| ★ 67 | — | — | — | THINK — Aretha Franklin (Jerry Wexler), Atlantic 2518 | 1 |
| 68 | 68 | 71 | 71 | IMPOSSIBLE MISSION (Mission Impossible) — Soul Survivors (Gamble-Huff), Crimson 1016 | 5 |
| ★ 69 | 75 | 83 | 84 | MAY I TAKE A GIANT STEP — 1910 Fruitgum Co. (Kasenetz-Katz Associates), Buddah 39 | 5 |
| ★ 70 | — | — | — | JELLY JUNGLE (Of Orange Marmalade) — Lemon Pipers (Paul Leka), Buddah 41 | 1 |
| ★ 71 | 81 | — | — | LOVE IN EVERY ROOM (Meme Si Tu Revenais) — Paul Mauriat & His Ork (Paul Mauriat), Philips 40530 | 2 |
| ★ 72 | — | — | — | THIS GUY'S IN LOVE WITH YOU — Herb Alpert (Herb Alpert & Jerry Moss), A&M 929 | 1 |
| ★ 73 | — | — | — | TIME FOR LIVIN' — Association (Bones Howe), Warner Bros.-Seven Arts 7195 | 1 |
| 74 | 74 | 74 | 74 | I GOT A SURE THING — Ollie & the Nightingales (Booker T. Jones), Stax 245 | 7 |
| ★ 75 | 98 | — | — | BROOKLYN ROADS — Neil Diamond (Chip Taylor), UNI 55065 | 2 |
| 76 | 76 | 81 | 81 | CABARET — Herb Alpert & the Tijuana Brass (Herb Alpert & Jerry Moss), A&M 925 | 5 |
| ★ 77 | 88 | 95 | — | I WISH I KNEW (How It Would Feel to Be Free) — Solomon Burke (Tom Dowd), Atlantic 2507 | 3 |
| ★ 78 | 93 | — | — | YOU AIN'T GOING NOWHERE — Byrds (Gary Usher), Columbia 44499 | 2 |
| ★ 79 | 99 | — | — | ANYONE FOR TENNIS (Savage Seven Theme) — Cream (Felix Pappalardi), Atco 6575 | 2 |
| ★ 80 | 95 | — | — | SLEEPY JOE — Herman's Hermits (Mickie Most), MGM 13934 | 2 |
| ★ 81 | — | — | — | I'LL NEVER DO YOU WRONG — Joe Tex (Buddy Killen), Dial 4076 | 1 |
| 82 | 82 | 99 | — | HERE'S TO YOU — Hamilton Camp (Felix Pappalardi), Warner Bros.-Seven Arts 7165 | 3 |
| ★ 83 | — | — | — | TIP-TOE THRU' THE TULIPS WITH ME — Tiny Tim (Richard Perry), Reprise 0679 | 1 |
| ★ 84 | — | — | — | MY SHY VIOLET — Mills Brothers (Tom Mack), Dot 17096 | 1 |
| 85 | 86 | 86 | 86 | CHAIN GANG — Jackie Wilson & Count Basie (Nat Tarnopol & Teddy Reig), Brunswick 55373 | 4 |
| 86 | 89 | 89 | 100 | A TRIBUTE TO A KING — William Bell (Booker T. Jones), Stax 248 | 4 |
| 87 | 84 | 84 | 66 | GENTLE ON MY MIND — Patti Page (Jack Gold), Columbia 44353 | 15 |
| ★ 88 | — | — | — | I GOT YOU BABE — Etta James (Rick Hall & Staff), Cadet 5606 | 1 |
| ★ 89 | — | — | — | UNITED — Peaches & Herb (Gamble-Huff), Date 1603 | 1 |
| 90 | 90 | 90 | — | SOUL TRAIN — Classics IV (Bill Lowery), Imperial 66293 | 3 |
| 91 | 91 | 92 | — | I HAVE A DREAM — Rev. Martin Luther King Jr., Gordy 7023 | 3 |
| 92 | 92 | 93 | — | HE DON'T REALLY LOVE YOU — Delfonics (T. Bell), Moon Shot 6793 | 3 |
| 93 | 94 | 96 | 96 | LILLI MARLENE — Al Martino (Charles Calello), Capitol 2158 | 4 |
| 94 | 97 | — | — | APOLOGIZE — Ed Ames (Jim Foglesong), RCA Victor 47-9517 | 2 |
| 95 | 96 | — | — | FACE IT GIRL, IT'S OVER — Nancy Wilson (David Cavanaugh), Capitol 2136 | 2 |
| 96 | — | — | — | IT'S OVER — Eddy Arnold (Chet Atkins), RCA Victor 47-9525 | 1 |
| 97 | — | — | — | REACH OUT OF THE DARKNESS — Friend & Lover (Joe South & Bill Lowery), Verve Forecast 5069 | 1 |
| 98 | — | — | — | I CAN'T MAKE IT ALONE — Bill Medley (Bill Medley), MGM 13931 | 1 |
| 99 | — | — | — | PICTURES OF MATCHSTICK MEN — Status Quo (John Schroeder), Cadet Concept 7001 | 1 |
| 100 | — | — | — | THE DOCTOR — Mary Wells (C. & M. Womack), Jubilee 5621 | 1 |

## HOT 100—A TO Z—(Publisher-Licensee)

Ain't No Way (14th Hour/Cotillion, BMI) ...... 21
Angel of the Morning (Blackwood, BMI) ...... 55
Anyone For Tennis (Savage Seven Theme) (Dratleaf, BMI) ...... 79
Apologize (Stone Canyon, BMI) ...... 94
Baby Make Your Own Sweet Music (Screen Gems-Columbia, BMI) ...... 64
Ballad of Bonnie and Clyde, The (Peer Int'l, BMI) 34
Beautiful Morning, A (Slacsar, BMI) ...... 5
Brooklyn Roads (Stonebridge, BMI) ...... 75
Cabaret (Sunbeam, BMI) ...... 76
Call Me Lightning (Fabulous, ASCAP) ...... 42
Chain Gang (Kaga, BMI) ...... 85
Cowboys to Girls (Razor Sharp, BMI) ...... 6
Cry Like a Baby (Press, BMI) ...... 12
Dance to the Music (Daly City, BMI) ...... 33
Delilah (Francis, Day & Hunter, ASCAP) ...... 26
Do You Know the Way to San Jose? (Jac/Blue Seas, ASCAP) ...... 10
Doctor, The (Welwom, BMI) ...... 100
Does Your Mama Know About Me (Stein & Van Stock, ASCAP) ...... 30
Face It Girl, It's Over (Irwin, ASCAP) ...... 95
Foggy Mountain Breakdown (Peer Int'l, BMI) ...... 59
Friends (Sea of Tunes, BMI) ...... 47
Funky Street (Redwal, BMI) ...... 18
Gentle on My Mind (Sherman-DeVorzon, BMI) ...... 87
Good, the Bad, and the Ugly, The (Unart, BMI) ...... 4
Happy Song, The (Dum Dum) (East/Time/Redwal, BMI) ...... 27
He Doesn't Really Love You (Grocalla, BMI) ...... 92
Here's to You (Royham, ASCAP) ...... 82
Honey (Russell-Cason, ASCAP) ...... 3
How'd We Ever Get This Way (Unart, BMI) ...... 54
I Can Remember (Big Seven, BMI) ...... 51
I Can't Make It Alone (Screen Gems-Columbia, BMI) ...... 98
I Could Never Love Another (Jobete, BMI) ...... 25
I Got a Sure Thing (East, BMI) ...... 74
I Got the Feelin' (Toccoa-Lois, BMI) ...... 17
I Got You Babe (Cotillion/Chris Marc, BMI) ...... 88
I Have a Dream ...... 91
I Love You (Mainstay, BMI) ...... 50
I Promise to Wait My Love (Jobete, BMI) ...... 66
I Wanna Live (Windward Side, BMI) ...... 44
I Will Always Think About You (New Colony/T.M., BMI) ...... 28
I Wish I Knew (Duane, BMI) ...... 77
If I Were a Carpenter (Faithful Virtue, BMI) ...... 29
If You Don't Want My Love (Bornwin, BMI) ...... 57
I'll Never Do You Wrong (Tree, BMI) ...... 81
I'm Sorry (Nickel Shoe/Bellboy, BMI) ...... 46
Impossible Mission (Mission Impossible) (Double Diamond/Downstairs, BMI) ...... 68
It's Over (Honeycomb, ASCAP) ...... 96
Jelly Jungle (Of Orange Marmalade) (Kama Sutra, BMI) ...... 70
Jennifer Eccles (Maribus, BMI) ...... 40
Lady Madonna (Maclen, BMI) ...... 15
Like to Get to Know You (Takya, ASCAP) ...... 20
Lilli Marlene (Marks/G.E.M.A., BMI) ...... 93
Look to Your Soul (Rivers, BMI) ...... 49
Look of Love, The (Colgems, ASCAP) ...... 60
Loving You Has Made Me Bananas (Curtis, ASCAP) 58
Love In Every Room (Meme Si Tu Revenais) (Northern, ASCAP) ...... 71
Love Is All Around (James, BMI) ...... 7
MacArthur Park (Canopy, ASCAP) ...... 48
Man Without Love, A (Quando M'Innamora) (Leeds, ASCAP) ...... 53
Master Jack (Milene, ASCAP) ...... 31
May I Take a Giant Step (Kaskat, BMI) ...... 69
Medley: My Girl, Hey Girl (Jobete/Screen Gems-Columbia, BMI) ...... 36
Mony Mony (Patricia, BMI) ...... 19
Mrs. Robinson (Charing Cross, BMI) ...... 2
My Shy Violet (Pincus, ASCAP) ...... 84
Never Give You Up (Parabut/Double Diamond/Downstairs, BMI) ...... 62
Paying the Cost to Be the Boss (Panco/LZMC, BMI) ...... 52
Pictupres of Matchstick Men (Northern, ASCAP) ...... 99
Playboy (Acuff-Rose, BMI) ...... 38
Reach Out of the Darkness (Lowery, BMI) ...... 97
She's a Heartbreaker (Catalogue/Cee & Eye, BMI) 65
She's Lookin' Good (Veytig, BMI) ...... 22
Shoo-Be-Doo-Be-Do-Day (Jobete, BMI) ...... 11
Sleepy Joe (Southern, ASCAP) ...... 80
Son of Hickory Holler's Tramp, The (Blue Crest, BMI) ...... 43
Soul Serenade (Kilyn, BMI) ...... 23
Soul Train (Lom-Sal, BMI) ...... 90
Summertime Blues (Viva, BMI) ...... 16
Sweet Inspirations (Press, BMI) ...... 24
(Sweet, Sweet Baby) Since You've Been Gone (14th Hour/Cotillion, BMI) ...... 35
Take Good Care of My Baby (Screen Gems-Columbia, BMI) ...... 37
Take Time to Know Her (Gallico, BMI) ...... 13
Think (14th Hour, BMI) ...... 67
ASCAP) ...... 72
This Guy's In Love With You (Blue Seas/Jac, BMI) ...... 70
Tighten Up (Cotillion/Orelis, BMI) ...... 1
Time For Livin' (Tamerlane, BMI) ...... 73
Tip-Toe Thru' The Tulips With Me (Warner Bros.-Seven Arts, ASCAP) ...... 83
Tribute to a King, A (East, BMI) ...... 86
Unicorn, The (Hollis, BMI) ...... 8
United (Razor Sharp, BMI) ...... 89
Unknown Soldier (Nipper, ASCAP) ...... 39
Unwind (Ahab, BMI) ...... 56
U. S. Male (Vector, BMI) ...... 41
We're Rolling On (Caman, BMI) ...... 63
Wear It on Our Face (Chevis, BMI) ...... 45
You Ain't Going Nowhere (Dwarf, ASCAP) ...... 78
(You Keep Me) Hangin' On (Garpex/Alambo, BMI) 61
Young Girl (Viva, BMI) ...... 9
Yummy, Yummy, Yummy (T.M., BMI) ...... 32

## BUBBLING UNDER THE HOT 100

101. DON'T SIGN THE PAPERS ...... Jimmy Delphs, Karen 1538
102. READY, WILLING & ABLE ...... American Breed, Acta 824
103. LONELY IS THE NAME ...... Sammy Davis, Reprise 0673
104. CLIMB EVERY MOUNTAIN ...... Hesitations, Kapp 911
105. FUNKY FEVER ...... Clarence Carter, Atlantic 2508
106. UN-MUNDO ...... Buffalo Springfield, Atco 6572
107. BRING A LITTLE LOVIN' ...... Los Bravos, Parrot 3020
108. RUBY BABY ...... Mitch Ryder, New Voice 830
109. SKY PILOT ...... Eric Burdon & the Animals, MGM 13939
110. OPEN UP YOUR SOUL ...... Erma Franklin, Shout 230
111. FINDER'S KEEPERS ...... Salt Water Taffy, Buddah 37
112. IT'S MY TIME ...... Everly Brothers, Warner Bros.-Seven Arts 7192
113. ELEVATOR ...... Grapefruit, Equinox 70005
114. LOVER'S HOLIDAY ...... Peggy Scott & Jo Jo Benson, SSS International 736
115. LET'S GET TOGETHER ...... Sunshine Company, Imperial 66298
116. DIME A DOZEN ...... Carla Thomas, Stax 251
117. DON'T TAKE YOUR LOVE FROM ME ...... Ben E. King, Atco 6571
118. HAPPY WITH YOU ...... Kenny O'Dell, Vegas 724
119. LOOK OVER YOUR SHOULDER ...... O'Jays, Bell 704
120. YOU'RE GOOD FOR ME ...... Lou Rawls, Capitol 2172
121. LA LA LA (HE GIVES ME LOVE) ...... Raymond Lefevre & His Ork, 4 Corners of the World 149
122. FAITHFULLY ...... Margaret Whiting, London 122
123. RANDY ...... Happenings, B. T. Puppy 540
124. CAN I CARRY YOUR BALLOON ...... Swampseeds, Epic 10281
125. LOOKING BACK ...... Spencer Davis Group, United Artists 50286
126. PLEASE STAY ...... Dave Clark Five, Epic 10325
127. GOODNIGHT SWEET JOSEPHINE ...... Yardbirds, Epic 10303
128. AS LONG AS I GOT YOU ...... Laura Lee, Chess 2041
129. MECHANICAL WORLD ...... Spirit, Ode 108
130. FOLLOW ME ...... Jack Jones, RCA Victor 47-9510
131. CHAIN AROUND THE FLOWERS ...... Lewis & Clark Expedition, Colgems 66-1022
132. I CAN'T GO BACK TO DENVER ...... Gentrys, Bell 720
133. ONLY ME ...... First Edition, Reprise 0683
134. BACKWARDS & FORWARDS ...... Decembers Children, World Pacific 77887
135. I APOLOGIZE BABY ...... P.J. Proby, Liberty 56031

Compiled from national retail sales and radio station airplay by the Music Popularity Dept. of Record Market Research, Billboard.

# Billboard HOT 100

FOR WEEK ENDING MAY 25 1968

★ STAR PERFORMER—Sides registering greatest proportionate upward progress this week.

(Seal) Record Industry Association of America seal of certification as million selling single.

| This Week | 1 Wk. Ago | 2 Wks. Ago | 3 Wks. Ago | TITLE Artist (Producer), Label & Number | Weeks On Chart |
|---|---|---|---|---|---|
| 1 (Billboard Award) | 1 | 2 | 5 | **TIGHTEN UP** — Archie Bell & the Drells (L.J.F. Production), Atlantic 2478 | 9 |
| 2 | 2 | 9 | 32 | **MRS. ROBINSON** — Simon & Garfunkel (Simon, Garfunkel & Halee), Columbia 44511 | 5 |
| 3 | 5 | 6 | 9 | **BEAUTIFUL MORNING** — Rascals (Rascals), Atlantic 2493 | 7 |
| ★ 4 | 4 | 4 | 8 | **THE GOOD, THE BAD AND THE UGLY** — Hugo Montenegro, His Ork and Chorus (Neely Plumb), RCA Victor 9423 | 15 |
| 5 (RIAA seal) | 3 | 1 | 1 | **HONEY** — Bobby Goldsboro (Bob Montgomery & Bobby Goldsboro), United Artists 50283 | 10 |
| 6 (RIAA seal) | 6 | 7 | 7 | **COWBOYS TO GIRLS** — Intruders (Gamble-Huff), Gamble 214 | 10 |
| 7 | 8 | 8 | 10 | **THE UNICORN** — Irish Rovers (Charles Bud Dant), Decca 32254 | 10 |
| ★ 8 | 14 | 24 | 25 | **AIN'T NOTHING LIKE THE REAL THING** — Marvin Gaye & Tammi Terrell (Ashford-Simpson), Tamla 54163 | 7 |
| 9 | 11 | 20 | 20 | **SHOO-BE-DOO-BE-DOO-DA-DAY** — Stevie Wonder (H. Cosby), Tamla 54165 | 8 |
| 10 | 10 | 19 | 21 | **DO YOU KNOW THE WAY TO SAN JOSE?** — Dionne Warwick (Bacharach-David), Scepter 12216 | 7 |
| 11 | 13 | 13 | 13 | **TAKE TIME TO KNOW HER** — Percy Sledge (Quin Ivy & Marlin Greene), Atlantic 2490 | 11 |
| ★ 12 | 19 | 22 | 34 | **MONY MONY** — Tommy James & Shondells (Kasenetz-Katz Associates), Roulette 7008 | 8 |
| 13 (RIAA seal) | 9 | 3 | 3 | **YOUNG GIRL** — Union Gap Featuring Gary Puckett (Jerry Fuller), Columbia 44450 | 13 |
| 14 | 7 | 11 | 17 | **LOVE IS ALL AROUND** — Troggs (Page One), Fontana 1607 | 14 |
| 15 | 22 | 30 | 41 | **SHE'S LOOKIN' GOOD** — Wilson Pickett (Tom Dowd & Tommy Cogbill), Atlantic 2504 | 7 |
| ★ 16 | 67 | — | — | **THINK** — Aretha Franklin (Jerry Wexler), Atlantic 2518 | 2 |
| 17 | 17 | 12 | 6 | **I GOT THE FEELIN'** — James Brown & the Famous Flames (James Brown), King 6155 | 11 |
| 18 | 18 | 14 | 23 | **FUNKY STREET** — Arthur Conley (Tom Dowd), Atco 6563 | 11 |
| 19 (RIAA seal) | 12 | 5 | 2 | **CRY LIKE A BABY** — Box Tops (Dan Penn), Mala 593 | 13 |
| 20 | 20 | 45 | 46 | **LIKE TO GET TO KNOW YOU** — Spanky & Our Gang (Scharf-Dorough), Mercury 72795 | 6 |
| 21 | 26 | 27 | 27 | **DELILAH** — Tom Jones (Peter Sullivan), Parrot 40025 | 11 |
| ★ 22 | 25 | 56 | 87 | **I COULD NEVER LOVE ANOTHER (After Loving You)** — Temptations (Norman Whitfield), Gordy 7072 | 4 |
| ★ 23 | 23 | 23 | 30 | **SOUL SERENADE** — Willie Mitchell (Willie Mitchell/Joe Cuoghi), Hi 2140 | 12 |
| ★ 24 | 32 | 62 | 88 | **YUMMY, YUMMY, YUMMY** — Ohio Express (Kasenetz-Katz Associates), Buddah 38 | 4 |
| 25 | 27 | 37 | 47 | **THE HAPPY SONG (Dum Dum)** — Otis Redding (Steve Cropper), Volt 163 | 5 |
| 26 | 29 | 36 | 69 | **IF I WERE A CARPENTER** — Four Tops (Holland & Dozier), Motown 1124 | 5 |
| ★ 27 | 72 | — | — | **THIS GUY'S IN LOVE WITH YOU** — Herb Alpert (Herb Alpert & Jerry Moss), A&M 929 | 2 |
| 28 | 28 | 29 | 44 | **I WILL ALWAYS THINK ABOUT YOU** — New Colony Six (Senator Records Corp.), Mercury 72775 | 9 |
| 29 | 30 | 46 | 48 | **DOES YOUR MAMA KNOW ABOUT ME** — Bobby Taylor & Vancouvers (B. Gordy Jr.), Gordy 7069 | 6 |
| 30 | 31 | 43 | 63 | **MASTER JACK** — Four Jacks & A Jill, RCA Victor 47-9473 | 9 |
| 31 (RIAA seal) | 15 | 10 | 4 | **LADY MADONNA** — Beatles (George Martin), Capitol 2138 | 10 |
| 32 | 24 | 18 | 18 | **SWEET INSPIRATION** — Sweet Inspirations (Tom Dowd & Tommy Cogbill), Atlantic 2476 | 13 |
| 33 | 16 | 15 | 14 | **SUMMERTIME BLUES** — Blue Cheer (Abe "Voce" Kesh), Philips 40516 | 13 |
| ★ 34 | 48 | 79 | — | **MacARTHUR PARK** — Richard Harris (Jimmy Webb), Dunhill 4134 | 3 |
| 35 | 36 | 48 | 49 | **MEDLEY: MY GIRL, HEY GIRL** — Bobby Vee (Dallas Smith), Liberty 56033 | 6 |
| ★ 36 | 44 | 54 | 61 | **I WANNA LIVE** — Glen Campbell (Alyde Lory), Capitol 2146 | 8 |
| 37 | 21 | 16 | 16 | **AIN'T NO WAY** — Aretha Franklin (Jerry Wexler), Atlantic 2486 | 8 |
| 38 | 38 | 26 | 24 | **PLAYBOY** — Gene & Debbie (Don Gant), TRX 5006 | 15 |
| ★ 39 | 52 | 52 | 54 | **PAYING THE COST TO BE THE BOSS** — B.B. King (Lou Zito & Johnny Pate), Bluesway 61015 | 6 |
| 40 | 50 | 61 | 85 | **I LOVE YOU** — People (Mikel Hunter), Capitol 2078 | 8 |
| ★ 41 | 61 | 73 | 82 | **(You Keep Me) HANGIN' ON** — Joe Simon (J.R. Enterprises), Sound Stage 7 2608 | 7 |
| ★ 42 | 60 | 77 | — | **THE LOOK OF LOVE** — Sergio Mendes & Brasil '66 (Herb Alpert), A&M 924 | 3 |
| 43 | 46 | 69 | 77 | **I'M SORRY** — Delfonics (Stan & Bell), Philly Groove 151 | 5 |
| 44 | 45 | 53 | 62 | **WEAR IT ON OUR FACE** — Dells (Bobby Miller), Cadet 5599 | 7 |
| 45 | 43 | 42 | 42 | **THE SON OF HICKORY HOLLER'S TRAMP** — O. C. Smith (Jerry Fuller), Columbia 44425 | 14 |
| ★ 46 | 73 | — | — | **TIME FOR LIVIN'** — Association (Bones Howe), Warner Bros.-Seven Arts 7195 | 2 |
| 47 | 47 | 55 | 66 | **FRIENDS** — Beach Boys (Beach Boys), Capitol 2160 | 6 |
| 48 | 55 | 83 | 97 | **ANGEL OF THE MORNING** — Merrilee Rush (T. Cogbill & C. Moman), Bell 705 | 4 |
| 49 | 54 | 80 | 100 | **HOW'D WE EVER GET THIS WAY?** — Andy Kim (Jeff Barry), Steed 707 | 4 |
| ★ 50 | 62 | 85 | 91 | **NEVER GIVE YOU UP** — Jerry Butler (Gamble-Huff), Mercury 72798 | 4 |
| 51 | 51 | 78 | 94 | **I CAN REMEMBER** — James & Bobby Purify (Papa Don), Bell 721 | 5 |
| ★ 52 | 53 | 87 | — | **A MAN WITHOUT LOVE (Quando M'Innamora)** — Engelbert Humperdinck (Peter Sullivan), Parrot 40027 | 3 |
| 53 | 57 | 64 | 76 | **IF YOU DON'T WANT MY LOVE** — Robert John (David Rubinson), Columbia 44435 | 7 |
| 54 | 40 | 41 | 43 | **JENNIFER ECCLES** — Hollies (Ron Richards), Epic 10298 | 11 |
| 55 | 56 | 71 | 75 | **UNWIND** — Ray Stevens (Fred Foster & Ray Stevens), Monument 1048 | 6 |
| ★ 56 | 70 | — | — | **JELLY JUNGLE (Of Orange Marmalade)** — Lemon Pipers (Paul Leka), Buddah 41 | 2 |
| ★ 57 | 97 | — | — | **REACH OUT OF THE DARKNESS** — Friend & Lover (Joe South & Bill Lowery), Verve Forecast 5069 | 2 |
| 58 | 65 | 100 | — | **SHE'S A HEARTBREAKER** — Gene Pitney (Charlie Foxx), Musicor 1306 | 3 |
| ★ 59 | 89 | — | — | **UNITED** — Peaches & Herb (Gamble-Huff), Date 1603 | 2 |
| ★ 60 | 71 | 81 | — | **LOVE IN EVERY ROOM (Meme Si Tu Revenais)** — Paul Mauriat & His Ork (Paul Mauriat), Philips 40530 | 3 |
| ★ 61 | 81 | — | — | **I'LL NEVER DO YOU WRONG** — Joe Tex (Buddy Killen), Dial 4076 | 2 |
| 62 | 66 | 66 | 78 | **I PROMISE TO WAIT MY LOVE** — Martha Reeves & Vandellas (Cosby & Brown), Gordy 7070 | 6 |
| 63 | 63 | 59 | 59 | **WE'RE ROLLING ON** — Impressions (Curtis Mayfield & Johnny Pate), ABC 11076 | 6 |
| 64 | 64 | 65 | 73 | **BABY MAKES OUR OWN SWEET MUSIC** — Jay & the Techniques (Jerry Ross), Smash 2154 | 7 |
| ★ 65 | 79 | 99 | — | **ANYONE FOR TENNIS (Savage Seven Theme)** — Cream (Felix Pappalardi), Atco 6575 | 3 |
| 66 | 75 | 98 | — | **BROOKLYN ROADS** — Neil Diamond (Chip Taylor), UNI 55065 | 3 |
| ★ 67 | 80 | 95 | — | **SLEEPY JOE** — Herman's Hermits (Mickie Most), MGM 13934 | 3 |
| 68 | 69 | 75 | 83 | **MAY I TAKE A GIANT STEP** — 1910 Fruitgum Co. (Kasenetz-Katz Associates), Buddah 39 | 6 |
| ★ 69 | 83 | — | — | **TIP-TOE THRU' THE TULIPS WITH ME** — Tiny Tim (Richard Perry), Reprise 0679 | 2 |
| 70 | 68 | 68 | 71 | **IMPOSSIBLE MISSION (Mission Impossible)** — Soul Survivors (Gamble-Huff), Crimson 1016 | 6 |
| ★ 71 | — | — | — | **THE HORSE** — Cliff Nobles & Co. (Jesse James), Phil L. A. of Soul 313 | 1 |
| 72 | 76 | 76 | 81 | **CABARET** — Herb Alpert & the Tijuana Brass (Herb Alpert & Jerry Moss), A&M 925 | 6 |
| 73 | 74 | 74 | 74 | **I GOT A SURE THING** — Ollie & the Nightingales (Booker T. Jones), Stax 245 | 8 |
| 74 | 77 | 88 | 95 | **I WISH I KNEW (How It Would Feel to Be Free)** — Solomon Burke (Tom Dowd), Atlantic 2507 | 4 |
| ★ 75 | — | — | — | **LICKING STICK—LICKING STICK** — James Brown & the Famous Flames (James Brown), King 6166 | 1 |
| 76 | 82 | 82 | 99 | **HERE'S TO YOU** — Hamilton Camp (Felix Pappalardi), Warner Bros.-Seven Arts 7165 | 4 |
| ★ 77 | — | — | — | **YOU DON'T KNOW WHAT YOU MEAN TO ME** — Sam & Dave (Isaac Hayes & David Porter), Atlantic 2517 | 1 |
| 78 | 78 | 93 | — | **YOU AIN'T GOING NOWHERE** — Byrds (Gary Usher), Columbia 44499 | 3 |
| ★ 79 | 88 | — | — | **I GOT YOU BABE** — Etta James (Rick Hall & Staff), Cadet 5606 | 2 |
| ★ 80 | 84 | — | — | **MY SHY VIOLET** — Mills Brothers (Tom Mack), Dot 17096 | 2 |
| ★ 81 | 95 | 96 | — | **FACE IT GIRL, IT'S OVER** — Nancy Wilson (David Cavanaugh), Capitol 2136 | 3 |
| ★ 82 | 94 | 97 | — | **APOLOGIZE** — Ed Ames (Jim Foglesong), RCA Victor 47-9517 | 3 |
| ★ 83 | 100 | — | — | **THE DOCTOR** — Mary Wells (C. & M. Womack), Jubilee 5621 | 2 |
| 84 | 85 | 86 | 86 | **CHAIN GANG** — Jackie Wilson & Count Basie (Nat Tarnopol & Teddy Reig), Brunswick 55373 | 5 |
| 85 | 87 | 84 | 84 | **GENTLE ON MY MIND** — Patti Page (Jack Gold), Columbia 44353 | 16 |
| 86 | 86 | 89 | 89 | **A TRIBUTE TO A KING** — William Bell (Booker T. Jones), Stax 248 | 5 |
| 87 | 93 | 94 | 96 | **LILLI MARLENE** — Al Martino (Tom Morgan), Capitol 2158 | 5 |
| 88 | 91 | 91 | 92 | **I HAVE A DREAM** — Rev. Martin Luther King Jr., Gordy 7023 | 4 |
| ★ 89 | — | — | — | **AMERICA IS MY HOME** — James Brown & the Famous Flames (James Brown), King 6112 | 1 |
| ★ 90 | — | — | — | **CLIMB EVERY MOUNTAIN** — Hestitations (Wiltshire, Bangs & Victor), Kapp 911 | 1 |
| 91 | 96 | — | — | **IT'S OVER** — Eddy Arnold (Chet Atkins), RCA Victor 47-9525 | 2 |
| 92 | 92 | 92 | 93 | **HE DON'T REALLY LOVE YOU** — Delfonics (T. Bell), Moon Shot 6793 | 4 |
| 93 | — | — | — | **HOLD ON** — Radiants (Leonard Caston), Chess 2037 | 1 |
| 94 | — | — | — | **LONELY IS THE NAME** — Sammy Davis, Jr. (Jimmy Bowen), Reprise 0673 | 1 |
| 95 | 98 | — | — | **I CAN'T MAKE IT ALONE** — Bill Medley (Bill Medley), MGM 13931 | 2 |
| 96 | — | — | — | **FOLSOM PRISON BLUES** — Johnny Cash (Bob Johnston), Columbia 44513 | 1 |
| 97 | — | — | — | **BRING A LITTLE LOVIN'** — Los Bravos (Alain Milhaud), Parrot 3020 | 1 |
| 98 | 99 | — | — | **PICTURES OF MATCHSTICK MEN** — Status Quo (John Schroeder), Cadet Concept 7001 | 2 |
| 99 | — | — | — | **DON'T SIGN THE PAPER** — Jimmy Delphs (Ollie McLaughlin), Karen 1333 | 1 |
| 100 | — | — | — | **READY, WILLING AND ABLE** — American Breed (Bill Traut), Acta 324 | 1 |

## HOT 100—A TO Z—(Publisher-Licensee)



## BUBBLING UNDER THE HOT 100

101. SKY PILOT .. Eric Burdon & the Animals, MGM 13939
102. FUNKY FEVER .. Clarence Carter, Atlantic 2308
103. HERE I AM BABY .. Marvelettes, Tamla 54166
104. STONED SOUL PICNIC .. 5th Dimension, Soul City 7166
105. UN-MUNDO .. Buffalo Springfield, Atco 6572
106. RUBY BABY .. Mitch Ryder, New Voice 830
107. FINDER'S KEEPERS .. Salt Water Taffy, Buddah 37
108. OPEN UP YOUR SOUL .. Erma Franklin, Shout 230
109. AIN'T NOTHIN' BUT A HOUSE PARTY .. Showstoppers, Heritage 800
110. YOU'RE GOOD FOR ME .. Lou Rawls, Capitol 2172
111. LOOK OVER YOUR SHOULDER .. O'Jays, Bell 704
112. IT'S MY TIME .. Everly Brothers, Warner Bros.-7 Arts 7192
113. LOVER'S HOLIDAY .. Peggy Scott & Jo Jo Benson, SSS International 736
114. DIME A DOZEN .. Carla Thomas, Stax 251
115. LET'S GET TOGETHER .. Sunshine Company, Imperial 66298
116. INDIAN LAKE .. Cowsills, MGM 13944
117. FAITHFULLY .. Margaret Whiting, London 122
118. VALLEY OF THE DOLLS .. King Curtis & His Knights, Atco 6582
119. LA LA LA (He Gives Me Love) .. Raymond Lefevre & His Ork, 4 Corners of the World 149
120. PLEASE STAY .. Dave Clark Five, Epic 10325
121. FOLLOW ME .. Jack Jones, RCA Victor 47-9510
122. RANDY .. Happenings, B. T. Puppy 540
123. AS LONG AS I GOT YOU .. Laura Lee, Chess 2041
124. BACKWARDS AND FORWARDS .. December's Children, World Pacific 77887
125. CHOO CHOO TRAIN .. Box Tops, Mala 12005
126. WITH PEN IN HAND .. Johnny Darrell, United Artists 50292
127. LET IT BE ME .. Nino Tempo & April Stevens, White Whale 268
128. HERE COMES THE JUDGE .. Shorty Long, Soul 35044
129. A STONE GOOD LOVER .. Jo Armstead, Giant 704
130. WE PLAYED GAMES .. John Fred & His Playboy Band, Paula 303
131. BACK IN LOVE AGAIN .. Buckinghams, Columbia 44533
132. HANGIN' FROM YOUR LOVIN' TREE .. In Crowd, Abnak 129
133. SOCK IT TO ME SUNSHINE .. Curtin Calls, Dot 17093
134. ONLY ME .. First Edition, Reprise 0683
135. HERE COMES DA JUDGE .. Buena Vistas, Marquee 443
136. TURN AROUND, LOOK AT ME .. Vogues, Reprise 0686

Compiled from national retail sales and radio-station airplay by the Music Popularity Dept. of Record Market Research, Billboard.

# Billboard HOT 100

**FOR WEEK ENDING JUNE 1, 1968**

★ STAR PERFORMER—Sides registering greatest proportionate upward progress this week.
● Record Industry Association of America seal of certification as million selling single.

| This Week | Wk. Ago | 2 Wks. Ago | 3 Wks. Ago | TITLE, Artist (Producer), Label & Number | Weeks On Chart |
|---|---|---|---|---|---|
| 1 (Billboard Award) | 2 | 2 | 9 | MRS. ROBINSON — Simon & Garfunkel (Simon, Garfunkel & Halee), Columbia 44511 | 6 |
| 2 | 4 | 4 | 4 | THE GOOD, THE BAD AND THE UGLY — Hugo Montenegro, His Ork and Chorus (Neely Plumb), RCA Victor 9423 | 16 |
| 3 | 3 | 5 | 6 | BEAUTIFUL MORNING — Rascals (Rascals), Atlantic 2493 | 8 |
| 4 ● | 1 | 1 | 2 | TIGHTEN UP — Archie Bell & the Drells (L.J.F. Production), Atlantic 2478 | 10 |
| 5 ● | 5 | 3 | 1 | HONEY — Bobby Goldsboro (Bob Montgomery & Bobby Goldsboro), United Artists 50283 | 11 |
| 6 ★ | 24 | 32 | 62 | YUMMY, YUMMY, YUMMY — Ohio Express (Kasenetz-Katz Associates), Buddah 38 | 5 |
| 7 | 12 | 19 | 22 | MONY MONY — Tommy James & Shondells (Kasenetz-Katz Associates), Roulette 7008 | 9 |
| 8 | 8 | 14 | 24 | AIN'T NOTHING LIKE THE REAL THING — Marvin Gaye & Tammi Terrell (Ashford-Simpson), Tamla 54163 | 8 |
| 9 ● | 6 | 6 | 7 | COWBOYS TO GIRLS — Intruders (Gamble-Huff), Gamble 214 | 11 |
| 10 | 10 | 10 | 19 | DO YOU KNOW THE WAY TO SAN JOSE? — Dionne Warwick (Bacharach-David), Scepter 12216 | 8 |
| 11 ★ | 27 | 72 | — | THIS GUY'S IN LOVE WITH YOU — Herb Alpert (Herb Alpert & Jerry Moss), A&M 929 | 3 |
| 12 | 34 | 48 | 79 | MacARTHUR PARK — Richard Harris (Jimmy Webb), Dunhill 4134 | 4 |
| 13 | 16 | 67 | — | THINK — Aretha Franklin (Jerry Wexler), Atlantic 2518 | 3 |
| 14 | 14 | 7 | 11 | LOVE IS ALL AROUND — Troggs (Page One), Fontana 1607 | 15 |
| 15 | 15 | 22 | 30 | SHE'S LOOKIN' GOOD — Wilson Pickett (Tom Dowd & Tommy Cogbill), Atlantic 2504 | 8 |
| 16 | 9 | 11 | 20 | SHOO-BE-DOO-BE-DOO-DA-DAY — Stevie Wonder (H. Cosby), Tamla 54165 | 9 |
| 17 ● | 13 | 3 | 3 | YOUNG GIRL — Union Gap Featuring Gary Puckett (Jerry Fuller), Columbia 44450 | 14 |
| 18 | 7 | 8 | 8 | THE UNICORN — Irish Rovers (Charles Bud Dant), Decca 32254 | 11 |
| 19 | 20 | 20 | 45 | LIKE TO GET TO KNOW YOU — Spanky & Our Gang (Scharf-Dorough), Mercury 72795 | 7 |
| 20 | 22 | 25 | 56 | I COULD NEVER LOVE ANOTHER (After Loving You) — Temptations (Norman Whitfield), Gordy 7072 | 5 |
| 21 | 21 | 26 | 27 | DELILAH — Tom Jones (Peter Sullivan), Parrot 40025 | 12 |
| 22 ★ | 28 | 28 | 29 | I WILL ALWAYS THINK ABOUT YOU — New Colony Six (Senator Records Corp.), Mercury 72775 | 10 |
| 23 | 30 | 31 | 43 | MASTER JACK — Four Jacks & A Jill, RCA Victor 47-9473 | 10 |
| 24 | 11 | 13 | 13 | TAKE TIME TO KNOW HER — Percy Sledge (Quin Ivy & Martin Greene), Atlantic 2490 | 12 |
| 25 | 26 | 29 | 36 | IF I WERE A CARPENTER — Four Tops (Holland & Dozier), Motown 1124 | 6 |
| 26 | 23 | 23 | 23 | SOUL SERENADE — Willie Mitchell (Willie Mitchell/Joe Cuoghi), Hi 2140 | 13 |
| 27 ● | 19 | 12 | 5 | CRY LIKE A BABY — Box Tops (Dan Penn), Mala 593 | 14 |
| 28 | 25 | 27 | 37 | THE HAPPY SONG (Dum Dum) — Otis Redding (Steve Cropper), Volt 163 | 6 |
| 29 | 49 | 54 | 80 | HOW'D WE EVER GET THIS WAY? — Andy Kim (Jeff Barry), Steed 707 | 4 |
| 30 ★ | 48 | 55 | 83 | ANGEL OF THE MORNING — Merrilee Rush (T. Cogbill & C. Moman), Bell 705 | 5 |
| 31 | 40 | 50 | 61 | I LOVE YOU — People (Mikal Hunter), Capitol 2078 | 4 |
| 32 ★ | 75 | — | — | LICKING STICK—LICKING STICK — James Brown & the Famous Flames (James Brown), King 6166 | 2 |
| 33 | 32 | 24 | 18 | SWEET INSPIRATION — Sweet Inspirations (Tom Dowd & Tommy Cogbill), Atlantic 2476 | 14 |
| 34 ★ | 42 | 60 | 77 | THE LOOK OF LOVE — Sergio Mendes & Brasil '66 (Herb Alpert), A&M 924 | 4 |
| 35 | 35 | 36 | 48 | MEDLEY: MY GIRL, HEY GIRL — Bobby Vee (Dallas Smith), Liberty 56033 | 7 |
| 36 | 36 | 44 | 54 | I WANNA LIVE — Glen Campbell (Alyde Lory), Capitol 2146 | 9 |
| 37 | 18 | 18 | 14 | FUNKY STREET — Arthur Conley (Tom Dowd), Atco 6563 | 12 |
| 38 | 57 | 97 | — | REACH OUT OF THE DARKNESS — Friend & Lover (Joe South & Bill Lowery), Verve Forecast 5069 | 3 |
| 39 | 52 | 53 | 87 | A MAN WITHOUT LOVE (Quando M'Innamora) — Engelbert Humperdinck (Peter Sullivan), Parrot 40027 | 4 |
| 40 | 29 | 30 | 46 | DOES YOUR MAMA KNOW ABOUT ME — Bobby Taylor & Vancouvers (B. Gordy Jr.), Gordy 7069 | 7 |
| 41 | 41 | 61 | 73 | (You Keep Me) HANGIN' ON — Joe Simon (J.R. Enterprises), Sound Stage 7 2608 | 8 |
| 42 | 43 | 46 | 49 | I'M SORRY — Delfonics (Stan & Bell), Philly Groove 151 | 6 |
| 43 | 17 | 17 | 12 | I GOT THE FEELIN' — James Brown & the Famous Flames (James Brown), King 6155 | 12 |
| 44 ● | 31 | 15 | 10 | LADY MADONNA — Beatles (George Martin), Capitol 2138 | 11 |
| 45 | 46 | 73 | — | TIME FOR LIVIN' — Association (Bones Howe), Warner Bros.-Seven Arts 7195 | 3 |
| 46 ● | 69 | 83 | — | TIP-TOE THRU' THE TULIPS WITH ME — Tiny Tim (Richard Perry), Reprise 0679 | 3 |
| 47 | 38 | 38 | 26 | PLAYBOY — Gene & Debbie (Don Gant), TRX 5006 | 16 |
| 48 | 58 | 65 | 100 | SHE'S A HEARTBREAKER — Gene Pitney (Charlie Foxx), Musicor 1306 | 4 |
| 49 | 44 | 45 | 53 | WEAR IT ON OUR FACE — Dells (Bobby Miller), Cadet 5599 | 8 |
| 50 | 50 | 62 | 85 | NEVER GIVE YOU UP — Jerry Butler (Gamble-Huff), Mercury 72798 | 5 |
| 51 | 56 | 70 | — | JELLY JUNGLE (Of Orange Marmalade) — Lemon Pipers (Paul Leka), Buddah 41 | 3 |
| 52 | 55 | 56 | 71 | UNWIND — Ray Stevens (Fred Foster & Ray Stevens), Monument 1048 | 7 |
| 53 | 53 | 57 | 64 | IF YOU DON'T WANT MY LOVE — Robert John (David Rubinson), Columbia 44435 | 8 |
| 54 ★ | 71 | — | — | THE HORSE — Cliff Nobles & Co. (Jesse James), Phil L. A. of Soul 313 | 2 |
| 55 | 39 | 52 | 52 | PAYING THE COST TO BE THE BOSS — B.B. King (Lou Zito & Johnny Pate), Bluesway 61015 | 8 |
| 56 | 59 | 89 | — | UNITED — Peaches & Herb (Gamble-Huff), Date 1603 | 3 |
| 57 ★ | 77 | — | — | YOU DON'T KNOW WHAT YOU MEAN TO ME — Sam & Dave (Isaac Hayes & David Porter), Atlantic 2517 | 2 |
| 58 | 66 | 75 | 98 | BROOKLYN ROADS — Neil Diamond (Chip Taylor), UNI 55065 | 4 |
| 59 | 47 | 47 | 55 | FRIENDS — Beach Boys (Beach Boys), Capitol 2160 | 6 |
| 60 | 60 | 71 | 81 | LOVE IN EVERY ROOM (Meme Si Tu Revenais) — Paul Mauriat & His Ork (Paul Mauriat), Phillips 40530 | 5 |
| 61 | 61 | 81 | — | I'LL NEVER DO YOU WRONG — Joe Tex (Buddy Killen), Dial 4076 | 3 |
| 62 ★ | — | — | — | CHOO CHOO TRAIN — Box Tops (Dan Penn), Mala 12005 | 1 |
| 63 | 68 | 69 | 75 | MAY I TAKE A GIANT STEP — 1910 Fruitgum Co. (Kasenetz-Katz Associates), Buddah 39 | 7 |
| 64 | 65 | 79 | 99 | ANYONE FOR TENNIS (Savage Seven Theme) — Cream (Felix Pappalardi), Atco 6575 | 4 |
| 65 | 67 | 80 | 95 | SLEEPY JOE — Herman's Hermits (Mickie Most), MGM 13934 | 4 |
| 66 | 64 | 64 | 65 | BABY MAKE YOUR OWN SWEET MUSIC — Jay & the Techniques (Jerry Ross), Smash 2154 | 8 |
| 67 | 51 | 51 | 78 | I CAN REMEMBER — James & Bobby Purify (Papa Don), Bell 721 | 6 |
| 68 | 63 | 63 | 59 | WE'RE ROLLING ON — Impressions (Curtis Mayfield & Johnny Pate), ABC 11076 | 7 |
| 69 | 62 | 66 | 66 | I PROMISE TO WAIT MY LOVE — Martha Reeves & Vandellas (Cosby & Brown), Gordy 7070 | 7 |
| 70 | 83 | 100 | — | THE DOCTOR — Mary Wells (C. & M. Womack), Jubilee 5621 | 3 |
| 71 | 79 | 88 | — | I GOT YOU BABE — Etta James (Rick Hall & Staff), Cadet 5606 | 3 |
| 72 | 89 | — | — | AMERICA IS MY HOME — James Brown & the Famous Flames (James Brown), King 6112 | 2 |
| 73 | — | — | — | YESTER LOVE — Smokey Robinson & the Miracles ("Smokey"), Tamla 54167 | 1 |
| 74 | 74 | 77 | 88 | I WISH I KNEW (How It Would Feel to Be Free) — Solomon Burke (Tom Dowd), Atlantic 2507 | 5 |
| 75 | 97 | — | — | BRING A LITTLE LOVIN' — Los Bravos (Alain Milhaud), Parrot 3020 | 2 |
| 76 | 76 | 82 | 82 | HERE'S TO YOU — Hamilton Camp (Felix Pappalardi), Warner Bros.-Seven Arts 7165 | 5 |
| 77 | 78 | 78 | 93 | YOU AIN'T GOING NOWHERE — Byrds (Gary Usher), Columbia 44499 | 4 |
| 78 | 73 | 74 | 74 | I GOT A SURE THING — Ollie & the Nightingales (Booker T. Jones), Stax 245 | 9 |
| 79 | — | — | — | INDIAN LAKE — Cowsills (Wes Farrell), MGM 13944 | 1 |
| 80 | 80 | 84 | — | MY SHY VIOLET — Mills Brothers (Tom Mack), Dot 17094 | 3 |
| 81 | 81 | 95 | 98 | FACE IT GIRL, IT'S OVER — Nancy Wilson (David Cavanaugh), Capitol 2136 | 4 |
| 82 | 82 | 94 | 97 | APOLOGIZE — Ed Ames (Jim Foglesong), RCA Victor 47-9517 | 4 |
| 83 | — | — | — | HERE COMES THE JUDGE — Shorty Long (Shorty Long & B.J.), Soul 35044 | 1 |
| 84 | 96 | — | — | FOLSOM PRISON BLUES — Johnny Cash (Bob Johnston), Columbia 44513 | 2 |
| 85 | 100 | — | — | READY, WILLING AND ABLE — American Breed (Bill Traut), Acta 324 | 2 |
| 86 ★ | — | — | — | SKY PILOT — Eric Burdon & the Animals (Tom Wilson), MGM 13939 | 1 |
| 87 | 87 | 93 | 94 | LILLI MARLENE — Al Martino (Tom Morgan), Capitol 2158 | 6 |
| 88 | 91 | 96 | — | IT'S OVER — Eddy Arnold (Chet Atkins), RCA Victor 47-9525 | 3 |
| 89 | 86 | 86 | 89 | A TRIBUTE TO A KING — William Bell (Booker T. Jones), Stax 248 | 6 |
| 90 | 90 | — | — | CLIMB EVERY MOUNTAIN — Hesitations (Wiltshire, Bangs & Victor), Kapp 911 | 2 |
| 91 | — | — | — | SAN FRANCISCO GIRLS — Fever Tree (Scott & Vivian Holtzman), UNI 55060 | 1 |
| 92 | 93 | — | — | HOLD ON — Radiants (Leonard Caston), Chess 2037 | 2 |
| 93 | 94 | — | — | LONELY IS THE NAME — Sammy Davis, Jr. (Jimmy Bowen), Reprise 0673 | 2 |
| 94 | — | — | — | HERE COME DA JUDGE — Buena Vistas (Carl Cisco), Marquee 443 | 1 |
| 95 | — | — | — | STONED SOUL PICNIC — 5th Dimension (Bones Howe), Soul City 766 | 1 |
| 96 | — | — | — | FUNKY FEVER — Clarence Carter (Rick Hall & Staff), Atlantic 2508 | 1 |
| 97 | — | — | — | AIN'T NOTHIN' BUT A HOUSE PARTY — Show Stoppers (D. Sharah), Heritage 800 | 1 |
| 98 | 98 | 99 | — | PICTURES OF MATCHSTICK MEN — Status Quo (John Schroeder), Cadet Concept 7001 | 3 |
| 99 | 99 | — | — | DON'T SIGN THE PAPER — Jimmy Delphs (Ollie McLaughlin), Karen 1333 | 2 |
| 100 | — | — | — | HERE COMES THE JUDGE — Magistrates (Gross-Freda), MGM 13946 | 1 |

## HOT 100—A TO Z—(Publisher-Licensee)

Ain't Nothin' But a House Party (Dandelion, Clairlyn, BMI) ... 97
Ain't Nothing Like The Real Thing (Jobete, BMI) ... 8
America Is My Home (Blackwood, BMI) ... 72
Angel of the Morning (Roosevelt, BMI) ... 30
Anyone for Tennis (Savage Seven Theme) (Bratlief, BMI) ... 64
Apologize (Stone Canyon, BMI) ... 82
Baby Make Your Own Sweet Music (Screen Gems-Columbia, BMI) ... 66
Beautiful Morning, A (Slacsar, BMI) ... 3
Bring a Little Lovin' (Miller, ASCAP) ... 75
Brooklyn Roads (Stonebridge, BMI) ... 58
Choo Choo Train (Ruler/Mulji, BMI) ... 62
Climb Every Mountain (Williamson, ASCAP) ... 90
Cowboys to Girls (Razor Sharp, BMI) ... 9
Cry Like a Baby (Press, BMI) ... 27
Delilah (Francis, Day & Hunter, ASCAP) ... 21
Do You Know the Way to San Jose? (Jac/Blue Seas, ASCAP) ... 10
Does Your Mama Know About Me (Stein & Van Stock, BMI) ... 40
Doctor, The (Welvom, BMI) ... 70
Don't Sign the Paper (McLaughlin/Ala-King, BMI) ... 99
Face It Girl, It's Over (Pincus, ASCAP) ... 81
Folsom Prison Blues (Sea of Tunes, BMI) ... 84
Friends (Sea of Tunes, BMI) ... 59
Funky Fever (Fame-Beaik, BMI) ... 96
Funky Street (Redwal, BMI) ... 37
Good, the Bad and the Ugly, The (Unart, BMI) ... 2
Happy Song, The (Dum Dum) (East/Time/Redwal, BMI) ... 28
Here Come De Judge (Buena Vistas) (Timcal/Chetkay, BMI) ... 94
Here Comes the Judge (Shorty Long) (Jobete, BMI) ... 83
Here Comes the Judge (Magistrates) (Hastings/Sreeby, BMI) ... 100
Here's to You (Royham, ASCAP) ... 76
Hold On (Chevis, BMI) ... 92
Honey (Russell-Cason, ASCAP) ... 5
Horse, The (Dandelion/James Boy, BMI) ... 54
How'd We Ever Get This Way? (Unart, BMI) ... 29
I Can Remember (Big Seven, BMI) ... 67
I Could Never Love Another (Jobete, BMI) ... 20
I Got a Sure Thing (East, BMI) ... 78
I Got the Feelin' (Toccoa-Lois, BMI) ... 43
I Got You Babe (Cotillion/Chris Marc, BMI) ... 71
I Love You (Mainstay, BMI) ... 31
I Promise to Wait My Love (Jobete, BMI) ... 69
I Wanna Live (Windward Side, BMI) ... 36
I Will Always Think About You (New Colony T.M., BMI) ... 22
I Wish I Knew (Faithful Virtue, BMI) ... 74
If I Were a Carpenter (Faithful Virtue, BMI) ... 25
If You Don't Want My Love (Bornwin, BMI) ... 53
I'll Never Do You Wrong (Tree, BMI) ... 61
I'm Sorry (Nickel Shoe/Bellboy, BMI) ... 42
Indian Lake (Pocket Full of Tunes, BMI) ... 79
It's Over (Honeycomb, ASCAP) ... 88
Jelly Jungle (Of Orange Marmalade) (Kama Sutra, BMI) ... 51
Lady Madonna (Maclen, BMI) ... 44
Licking Stick—Licking Stick (Torrco/Lois, BMI) ... 32
Like to Get to Know You (Takya, ASCAP) ... 19
Lilli Marlene (Marks/G.E.M.A., ASCAP) ... 87
Lonely Is the Name (Hollis, BMI) ... 93
Look of Love, The (Colgems, ASCAP) ... 34
Love in Every Room (Meme Si Tu Revenais) (Northern, ASCAP) ... 60
Love Is All Around (James, BMI) ... 14
MacArthur Park (Canopy, ASCAP) ... 12
Man Without Love, A (Quando M'Innamora) (Leeds, ASCAP) ... 39
Master Jack (Allene, ASCAP) ... 23
May I Take a Giant Step (Kaskat, BMI) ... 63
Medley: My Girl, Hey Girl (Jobete/Screen Gems-Columbia, BMI) ... 35
Mony Mony (Patricia, BMI) ... 7
Mrs. Robinson (Charing Cross, BMI) ... 1
My Shy Violet (Hollis, BMI) ... 80
Never Give You Up (Parabut/Double Diamond/Downstairs, BMI) ... 50
Paying the Cost to Be the Boss (Pancro/LZMC, BMI) ... 55
Pictures of Matchstick Men (Northern, ASCAP) ... 98
Playboy (Acuff-Rose, BMI) ... 47
Reach Out of the Darkness (Lowery, BMI) ... 38
Ready, Willing and Able (Screen Gems-Columbia, BMI) ... 85
San Francisco Girls (Filigree, BMI) ... 91
She's a Heartbreaker (Catalogue/Cee & Eye, BMI) ... 48
She's Lookin' Good (Veytig, BMI) ... 15
Shoo-Be-Doo-Be-Doo-Da-Day (Jobete, BMI) ... 16
Sky Pilot (Slamina/Sea-Lark, BMI) ... 86
Sleepy Joe (Southern, ASCAP) ... 65
Soul Serenade (Kilyn, BMI) ... 26
Stoned Soul Picnic (Tuna Fish, BMI) ... 95
Sweet Inspirations (Press, BMI) ... 33
Take Time to Know Her (Gallico, BMI) ... 24
Think (14th Hour, BMI) ... 13
This Guy's in Love With You (Blue Seas/Jac, BMI) ... 11
Tighten Up (Cotillion/Orelis, BMI) ... 4
Time for Livin' (Tamerlane, BMI) ... 45
Tip-Toe Thru the Tulips With Me (Warner Bros.-Seven Arts, ASCAP) ... 46
Tribute to a King, A (East, BMI) ... 89
Unicorn, The (Hollis, BMI) ... 18
United (Razor Sharp, BMI) ... 56
Unwind (Ahab, BMI) ... 52
We're Rolling On (Chevis, BMI) ... 68
Wear It on Our Face (Chevis, BMI) ... 49
Yester Love (Jobete, BMI) ... 73
You Ain't Going Nowhere (Dwarf, ASCAP) ... 77
You Don't Know What You Mean to Me (Pronto/Walden, BMI) ... 57
(You Keep Me) Hangin' On (Garpax/Alambo, BMI) ... 41
Young Girl (Viva, BMI) ... 17
Yummy, Yummy, Yummy (T.M., BMI) ... 6

## BUBBLING UNDER THE HOT 100

101. HERE I AM BABY ... Marvelettes, Tamla 54166
102. SAFE IN MY GARDEN ... Mamas & the Papas, Dunhill 4125
103. TURN AROUND AND LOOK AT ME ... Vogues, Reprise 0686
104. BACK IN LOVE AGAIN ... Buckinghams, Columbia 44533
105. FINDER'S KEEPERS ... Salt Water Taffy, Buddah 33
106. IT SHOULD HAVE BEEN ME ... Gladys Knight & the Pips, Soul 35045
107. OPEN UP YOUR SOUL ... Erma Franklin, Shout 230
108. I CAN'T MAKE IT ALONE ... Bill Medley, MGM 13931
109. LOOK OVER YOUR SHOULDER ... D'Jays, Bell 704
110. LA LA LA (He Gives Me Love) ... Raymond LeFevre, 4 Corners of the World 149
111. LOVER'S HOLIDAY ... Peggy Scott & Jo Jo Benson, SSS International 736
112. LET'S GET TOGETHER ... Sunshine Company, Imperial 66298
113. CHAIN GANG ... Jackie Wilson & Count Basie, Brunswick 55372
114. I HAVE A DREAM ... Rev. Martin Luther King Jr., Cardo 7023
115. PLEASE STAY ... Dave Clark Five, Epic 10325
116. VALLEY OF THE DOLLS ... King Curtis & His Kingpins, Atco 6582
117. FOLLOW ME ... Jack Jones, RCA Victor 47-9510
118. RANDY ... Happenings, B.T. Puppy 540
119. MOUNTAIN OF LOVE ... Ronnie Dove, Diamond 244
120. SUGAR ... Jive Five Featuring Eugene Pitt, Musicor 1305
121. SOCK IT TO ME SUNSHINE ... Curtain Calls, Dot 17093
122. YOUNG BIRDS FLY ... Cryan Shames, Columbia 44545
123. CONGRATULATIONS ... Cliff Richard, Uni 55969
124. BACKWARDS AND FORWARDS ... December's Children, World Pacific 77887
125. EYES OF THE NEW YORK WOMAN ... B.J. Thomas, Scepter 12219
126. WITH PEN IN HAND ... Johnny Darrell, United Artists 50292
127. LOOK OVER YOUR SHOULDER ... Neil Sedaka, Scepter 1704
128. LET IT BE ME ... Nino Tempo & April Stevens, White Whale 269
129. LET ME BE LONELY ... American, Giant 704
130. THREE GOOD LOVERS ... Wayne Newton, Scepter 12216
131. HANGIN' FROM YOUR LOVIN' TREE ... In Crowd, Abnak 129
132. BE YOUNG, BE FOOLISH, BE HAPPY ... Tams, ABC 11066
133. HELULE, HELULE ... Tremeloes, Epic 10328
134. DAYS OF PEARLY SPENCER ... David McWilliams, Kapp 896

Compiled from national retail sales and radio station airplay by the Music Popularity Dept. of Record Market Research, Billboard.

# Billboard HOT 100
### For Week Ending June 8, 1968

★ STAR PERFORMER—Sides registering greatest proportionate upward progress this week.
® Record Industry Association of America seal of certification as million selling single.

| This Week | 1 Wk. Ago | 2 Wks. Ago | 3 Wks. Ago | TITLE, Artist (Producer), Label & Number | Weeks On Chart |
|---|---|---|---|---|---|
| 1 | 1 | 2 | 2 | MRS. ROBINSON — Simon & Garfunkel (Simon, Garfunkel & Halee), Columbia 44511 | 7 |
| 2 | 4 | 1 | 1 | TIGHTEN UP — Archie Bell & the Drells (L.J.F. Production), Atlantic 2478 | 11 |
| 3 | 11 | 27 | 72 | THIS GUY'S IN LOVE WITH YOU — Herb Alpert (Herb Alpert & Jerry Moss), A&M 929 | 4 |
| 4 | 2 | 4 | 4 | THE GOOD, THE BAD AND THE UGLY — Hugo Montenegro, His Ork and Chorus (Neely Plumb), RCA Victor 9423 | 17 |
| 5 | 7 | 12 | 19 | MONY MONY — Tommy James & Shondells (Kasenetz-Katz Associates), Roulette 7008 | 10 |
| 6 | 6 | 24 | 32 | YUMMY, YUMMY, YUMMY — Ohio Express (Kasenetz-Katz Associates), Buddah 38 | 6 |
| 7 | 12 | 34 | 48 | MacARTHUR PARK — Richard Harris (Jimmy Webb), Dunhill 4134 | 5 |
| 8 | 3 | 3 | 5 | BEAUTIFUL MORNING — Rascals (Jerry Wexler), Atlantic 2493 | 9 |
| 9 | 13 | 16 | 67 | THINK — Aretha Franklin (Jerry Wexler), Atlantic 2518 | 4 |
| 10 | 5 | 5 | 3 | HONEY — Bobby Goldsboro (Bob Montgomery & Bobby Goldsboro), United Artists 50283 | 12 |
| 11 | 8 | 14 | 18 | AIN'T NOTHING LIKE THE REAL THING — Marvin Gaye & Tammi Terrell (Ashford-Simpson), Tamla 54163 | 8 |
| 12 | 9 | 6 | 6 | COWBOYS TO GIRLS — Intruders (Gamble-Huff), Gamble 214 | 12 |
| 13 | 34 | 42 | 60 | THE LOOK OF LOVE — Sergio Mendes & Brasil '66 (Herb Alpert), A&M 924 | 5 |
| 14 | 30 | 48 | 55 | ANGEL OF THE MORNING — Merrilee Rush (T. Cogbill & C. Moman), Bell 705 | 6 |
| 15 | 21 | 21 | 26 | DELILAH — Tom Jones (Peter Sullivan), Parrot 40025 | 13 |
| 16 | 16 | 9 | 11 | SHOO-BE-DOO-BE-DOO-DA-DAY — Stevie Wonder (H. Cosby), Tamla 54165 | 10 |
| 17 | 19 | 20 | 20 | LIKE TO GET TO KNOW YOU — Spanky & Our Gang (Scharf-Dorough), Mercury 72795 | 8 |
| 18 | 23 | 30 | 31 | MASTER JACK — Four Jacks & A Jill, RCA Victor 47-9473 | 11 |
| 19 | 20 | 22 | 25 | I COULD NEVER LOVE ANOTHER (After Loving You) — Temptations (Norman Whitfield), Gordy 7072 | 6 |
| 20 | 25 | 26 | 29 | IF I WERE A CARPENTER — Four Tops (Holland & Dozier), Motown 1124 | 7 |
| 21 | 10 | 10 | 10 | DO YOU KNOW THE WAY TO SAN JOSE? — Dionne Warwick (Bacharach-David), Scepter 12216 | 10 |
| 22 | 31 | 40 | 50 | I LOVE YOU — People (Mikel Hunter), Capitol 2078 | 6 |
| 23 | 38 | 57 | 97 | REACH OUT OF THE DARKNESS — Friend & Lover (Joe South & Bill Lowery), Verve Forecast 5069 | 4 |
| 24 | 24 | 11 | 13 | TAKE TIME TO KNOW HER — Percy Sledge (Quin Ivy & Marlin Greene), Atlantic 2490 | 13 |
| 25 | 32 | 75 | — | LICKING STICK — James Brown and the Famous Flames (James Brown), King 6166 | 3 |
| 26 | 22 | 28 | 28 | I WILL ALWAYS THINK ABOUT YOU — New Colony Six (Senator Records Corp.), Mercury 72775 | 11 |
| 27 | 39 | 52 | 53 | A MAN WITHOUT LOVE (Quando M'Innamora) — Engelbert Humperdinck (Peter Sullivan), Parrot 40027 | 4 |
| 28 | 28 | 25 | 27 | THE HAPPY SONG (Dum Dum) — Otis Redding (Steve Cropper), Volt 163 | 7 |
| 29 | 29 | 49 | 54 | HOW'D WE EVER GET THIS WAY? — Andy Kim (Jeff Barry), Steed 707 | 6 |
| 30 | 15 | 15 | 22 | SHE'S LOOKIN' GOOD — Wilson Pickett (Tom Dowd & Tommy Cogbill), Atlantic 2504 | 8 |
| 31 | 14 | 14 | 7 | LOVE IS ALL AROUND — Troggs (Page One), Fontana 1607 | 16 |
| 32 | 26 | 23 | 23 | SOUL SERENADE — Willie Mitchell (Willie Mitchell/Joe Cuoghi), Hi 2140 | 14 |
| 33 | 46 | 69 | 83 | TIP-TOE THRU THE TULIPS WITH ME — Tiny Tim (Richard Perry), Reprise 0679 | 4 |
| 34 | 54 | 71 | — | THE HORSE — Cliff Nobles & Co. (Jesse James), Phil L.A. of Soul 313 | 3 |
| 35 | 35 | 35 | 36 | MEDLEY: MY GIRL, HEY GIRL — Bobby Vee (Dallas Smith), Liberty 56033 | 8 |
| 36 | 17 | 13 | 9 | YOUNG GIRL — Union Gap Featuring Gary Puckett (Jerry Fuller), Columbia 44450 | 15 |
| 37 | 41 | 41 | 61 | (You Keep Me) HANGIN' ON — Joe Simon (J.R. Enterprises), Sound Stage 7 2608 | 9 |
| 38 | 50 | 50 | 62 | NEVER GIVE YOU UP — Jerry Butler (Gamble-Huff), Mercury 72798 | 6 |
| 39 | 62 | — | — | CHOO CHOO TRAIN — Box Tops (Dan Penn), Mala 12005 | 2 |
| 40 | 40 | 29 | 30 | DOES YOUR MAMA KNOW ABOUT ME — Bobby Taylor & Vancouvers (B. Gordy Jr.), Gordy 7069 | 8 |
| 41 | 45 | 46 | 73 | TIME FOR LIVIN' — Association (Bones Howe), Warner Bros.-Seven Arts 7195 | 4 |
| 42 | 42 | 43 | 46 | I'M SORRY — Delfonics (Stan & Bell), Philly Groove 151 | 7 |
| 43 | 48 | 58 | 65 | SHE'S A HEARTBREAKER — Gene Pitney (Charlie Foxx), Musicor 1306 | 5 |
| 44 | 36 | 36 | 44 | I WANNA LIVE — Glen Campbell (Alyde Lory), Capitol 2146 | 10 |
| 45 | 18 | 7 | 8 | THE UNICORN — Irish Rovers (Charles Bud Dant), Decca 32254 | 12 |
| 46 | 27 | 19 | 12 | CRY LIKE A BABY — Box Tops (Dan Penn), Mala 593 | 15 |
| 47 | 73 | — | — | YESTER LOVE — Smokey Robinson & the Miracles ("Smokey"), Tamla 54167 | 2 |
| 48 | 56 | 59 | 89 | UNITED — Peaches & Herb (Gamble-Huff), Date 1603 | 4 |
| 49 | 53 | 57 | — | IF YOU DON'T WANT MY LOVE — Robert John (David Rubinson), Columbia 44435 | 3 |
| 50 | 83 | — | — | HERE COMES THE JUDGE — Shorty Long (Shorty Long & B.J.), Soul 35044 | 2 |
| 51 | 51 | 56 | 70 | JELLY JUNGLE (Of Orange Marmalade) — Lemon Pipers (Paul Leka), Buddah 41 | 4 |
| 52 | 79 | — | — | INDIAN LAKE — Cowsills (Wes Farrell), MGM 13944 | 2 |
| 53 | 95 | — | — | STONED SOUL PICNIC — 5th Dimension (Bones Howe), Soul City 766 | 2 |
| 54 | 86 | — | — | SKY PILOT — Eric Burdon & the Animals (Tom Wilson), MGM 13939 | 2 |
| 55 | 57 | 77 | — | YOU DON'T KNOW WHAT YOU MEAN TO ME — Sam & Dave (Isaac Hayes & David Porter), Atlantic 2517 | 3 |
| 56 | 52 | 55 | 56 | UNWIND — Ray Stevens (Fred Foster & Ray Stevens), Monument 1048 | 6 |
| 57 | 75 | 97 | — | BRING A LITTLE LOVIN' — Los Bravos (Alain Milhaud), Parrot 3020 | 3 |
| 58 | 58 | 66 | 75 | BROOKLYN ROADS — Neil Diamond (Chip Taylor), UNI 55065 | 4 |
| 59 | 61 | 61 | 81 | I'LL NEVER DO YOU WRONG — Joe Tex (Buddy Killen), Dial 4076 | 4 |
| 60 | 60 | 60 | 71 | LOVE IN EVERY ROOM (Meme Si Tu Revenais) — Paul Mauriat & His Ork (Paul Mauriat), Philips 40530 | 4 |
| 61 | 65 | 67 | 80 | SLEEPY JOE — Herman's Hermits (Mickie Most), MGM 13934 | 4 |
| 62 | — | — | — | JUMPIN' JACK FLASH — Rolling Stones (Jimmy Miller), London 908 | 1 |
| 63 | — | — | — | SOME THINGS YOU NEVER GET USED TO — Diana Ross & Supremes (Ashford & Simpson), Motown 1126 | 1 |
| 64 | — | — | — | LADY WILLPOWER — Gary Puckett & the Union Gap (Jerry Fuller), Columbia 44547 | 1 |
| 65 | 100 | — | — | HERE COMES THE JUDGE — Magistrates (Gross-Freda), MGM 13946 | 2 |
| 66 | — | — | — | IT SHOULD HAVE BEEN ME — Gladys Knight & the Pips (Norman Whitfield), Soul 35045 | 1 |
| 67 | 63 | 68 | 69 | MAY I TAKE A GIANT STEP — 1910 Fruitgum Co. (Kasenetz-Katz Associates), Buddah 39 | 8 |
| 68 | 74 | 74 | 77 | I WISH I KNEW (How It Would Feel to Be Free) — Solomon Burke (Tom Dowd), Atlantic 2507 | 6 |
| 69 | 72 | 89 | — | AMERICA IS MY HOME — James Brown and the Famous Flames (James Brown), King 6112 | 3 |
| 70 | 70 | 83 | 100 | THE DOCTOR — Mary Wells (C. & M. Womack), Jubilee 5621 | 4 |
| 71 | 71 | 79 | 88 | I GOT YOU BABE — Etta James (Rick Hall & Staff), Cadet 5606 | 4 |
| 72 | 64 | 65 | 79 | ANYONE FOR TENNIS (Savage Seven Theme) — Cream (Felix Pappalardi), Atco 6575 | 5 |
| 73 | 98 | 98 | 99 | PICTURES OF MATCHSTICK MEN — Status Quo (John Schroeder), Cadet Concept 7001 | 4 |
| 74 | 77 | 78 | 78 | YOU AIN'T GOING NOWHERE — Byrds (Gary Usher), Columbia 44499 | 5 |
| 75 | 84 | 96 | — | FOLSOM PRISON BLUES — Johnny Cash (Bob Johnston), Columbia 44513 | 3 |
| 76 | 80 | 80 | 84 | MY SHY VIOLET — Mills Brothers (Tom Mack), Dot 17096 | 4 |
| 77 | 81 | 81 | 95 | FACE IT GIRL, IT'S OVER — Nancy Wilson (David Cavanaugh), Capitol 2136 | 4 |
| 78 | — | — | — | BACK IN LOVE AGAIN — Buckinghams (Jimmy "Wiz" Wisner), Columbia 44533 | 1 |
| 79 | — | — | — | SAFE IN MY GARDEN — Mamas & Papas (Lou Adler), Dunhill 4125 | 1 |
| 80 | 88 | 91 | 96 | IT'S OVER — Eddy Arnold (Chet Atkins), RCA Victor 47-9525 | 4 |
| 81 | — | — | — | MOUNTAIN OF LOVE — Ronnie Dove (Phil Kahl), Diamond 244 | 1 |
| 82 | 82 | 82 | 94 | APOLOGIZE — Ed Ames (Jim Foglesong), RCA Victor 47-9517 | 4 |
| 83 | — | — | — | GRAZING IN THE GRASS — Hugh Masakela (Stewart Levine), Uni 55066 | 1 |
| 84 | 85 | 100 | — | READY, WILLING AND ABLE — American Breed (Bill Traut), Acta 324 | 3 |
| 85 | — | — | — | HERE I AM BABY — Marvelettes ("Smokey"), Tamla 54166 | 1 |
| 86 | — | — | — | ELEANOR RIGBY — Ray Charles (Joe Adams), ABC 11090 | 1 |
| 87 | — | — | — | LOVER'S HOLIDAY — Peggy Scott & Jo Jo Benson (Huey P. Meaux), SSS International 736 | 1 |
| 88 | 96 | — | — | FUNKY FEVER — Clarence Carter (Rick Hall & Staff), Atlantic 2508 | 2 |
| 89 | 97 | — | — | AIN'T NOTHIN' BUT A HOUSE PARTY — Show Stoppers (D. Sharah), Heritage 800 | 2 |
| 90 | 87 | 87 | 93 | LILLI MARLENE — Al Martino (Tom Morgan), Capitol 2158 | 7 |
| 91 | 91 | — | — | SAN FRANCISCO GIRLS — Fever Tree (Scott & Vivian Holtzman), UNI 55060 | 2 |
| 92 | 92 | 93 | — | HOLD ON — Radiants (Leonard Caston), Chess 2037 | 3 |
| 93 | — | — | — | LET ME BE LONELY — Dionne Warwick (Bacharach-David), Scepter 12216 | 1 |
| 94 | 94 | — | — | HERE COME DA JUDGE — Buena Vistas (Carl Cisco), Marquee 443 | 2 |
| 95 | — | — | — | BABY YOU COME ROLLIN' ACROSS MY MIND — Peppermint Trolley Company (Dan Dalton), Acta 815 | 1 |
| 96 | — | — | — | SWEET MEMORIES — Andy Williams (Nick DeCaro), Columbia 44527 | 1 |
| 97 | 90 | 90 | — | CLIMB EVERY MOUNTAIN — Hesitations (Wiltshire, Bangs & Victor), Kapp 911 | 3 |
| 98 | 99 | 99 | — | DON'T SIGN THE PAPER — Jimmy Delphs (Ollie McLaughlin), Karen 1533 | 3 |
| 99 | 93 | 94 | — | LONELY IS THE NAME — Sammy Davis, Jr. (Jimmy Bowen), Reprise 0673 | 3 |
| 100 | — | — | — | CONGRATULATIONS — Cliff Richard (Norrie Paramor), Uni 55069 | 1 |

## BUBBLING UNDER THE HOT 100

101. D. W. WASHBURN — Monkees, Colgems 66-1023
102. YOUR TIME HASN'T COME YET BABY — Elvis Presley, RCA Victor 47-9547
103. TURN AROUND, LOOK AT ME — Vogues, Reprise 0686
104. LET YOURSELF GO — Elvis Presley, RCA Victor 47-9547
105. IT'S NICE TO BE WITH YOU — Monkees, Colgems 66-1023
106. HANG 'EM HIGH — Hugo Montenegro, his Ork & Chorus, RCA Victor 9554
107. WHERE DO WE GO — Billy Vera & Judy Clay, Atlantic 2515
108. LOVIN' SEASON — Gene & Debbe, TRX 5010
109. ALL THE GRAY-HAIRED MEN — Lettermen, Capitol 2196
110. LA-LA-LA (He Gives Me Love) — Raymond Lefevre, 4 Corners of the World 149
111. LITTLE GREEN APPLES — Patti Page, Columbia 44556
112. UNDERSTANDING — Ray Charles, ABC 11090
113. LOOKING BACK — Spencer Davis Group, United Artists 50286
114. TURN ON YOUR LOVELIGHT — Bill Black's Combo, Hi 2141
115. PLEASE STAY — Dave Clark Five, Epic 10325
116. SOCK IT TO ME SUNSHINE — Curtain Calls, Dot 17092
117. YOUNG BIRDS FLY — Cryan' Shames, Columbia 44545
118. TIME FOR US — Tamerlane, Dot 17101
119. EYES OF A NEW YORK WOMAN — B. J. Thomas, Scepter 12219
120. SUGAR — Jive Five, Featuring Eugene Pitt, Musicor 1305
121. BE YOUNG, BE FOOLISH, BE HAPPY — Tams, ABC 11066
122. HELULE, HELULE — Tremeloes, Epic 10328
123. HE GIVES ME LOVE (La-La-La) — Lesley Gore, Mercury 72819
124. BACKWARDS AND FORWARDS — December's Children, World Pacific 77887
125. SOMETIMES YOU JUST CAN'T WIN — Mouse & the Traps, Fraternity 1005

Compiled from national retail sales and radio station airplay by the Music Popularity Dept. of Record Market Research, Billboard.

# Billboard HOT 100

FOR WEEK ENDING JUNE 15, 1968

★ STAR PERFORMER—Sides registering greatest proportionate upward progress this week.

Record Industry Association of America seal of certification as million selling single.

| THIS WEEK | 1 Wk. Ago | 2 Wks. Ago | 3 Wks. Ago | TITLE Artist (Producer), Label & Number | Weeks On Chart |
|---|---|---|---|---|---|
| Billboard Award | | 1 | 2 | MRS. ROBINSON — Simon & Garfunkel (Simon, Garfunkel & Halee), Columbia 44511 | 8 |
| ★ 2 | 3 | 11 | 27 | THIS GUY'S IN LOVE WITH YOU — Herb Alpert (Herb Alpert & Jerry Moss), A&M 929 | 5 |
| 3 | 5 | 7 | 12 | MONY MONY — Tommy James & Shondells (Kasenetz-Katz Associates), Roulette 7008 | 11 |
| 4 | 6 | 6 | 24 | YUMMY, YUMMY, YUMMY — Ohio Express (Kasenetz-Katz Associates), Buddah 38 | 7 |
| 5 | 7 | 12 | 34 | MacARTHUR PARK — Richard Harris (Jimmy Webb), Dunhill 4134 | 6 |
| 6 | 2 | 4 | 1 | TIGHTEN UP — Archie Bell & the Drells (L.J.F. Production), Atlantic 2478 | 12 |
| 7 | 9 | 13 | 16 | THINK — Aretha Franklin (Jerry Wexler), Atlantic 2518 | 5 |
| 8 | 8 | 3 | 3 | BEAUTIFUL MORNING — Rascals (Rascals), Atlantic 2493 | 10 |
| 9 | 4 | 2 | 4 | THE GOOD, THE BAD AND THE UGLY — Hugo Montenegro, His Ork and Chorus (Neely Plumb), RCA Victor 9423 | 18 |
| ★ 10 | 13 | 34 | 42 | THE LOOK OF LOVE — Sergio Mendes & Brasil '66 (Herb Alpert), A&M 924 | 6 |
| 11 | 11 | 8 | 8 | AIN'T NOTHING LIKE THE REAL THING — Marvin Gaye & Tammi Terrell (Ashford-Simpson), Tamla 54163 | 10 |
| 12 | 10 | 5 | 5 | HONEY — Bobby Goldsboro (Bob Montgomery & Bobby Goldsboro), United Artists 50283 | 13 |
| ★ 13 | 19 | 20 | 22 | I COULD NEVER LOVE ANOTHER (After Loving You) — Temptations (Norman Whitfield), Gordy 7072 | 7 |
| 14 | 14 | 30 | 48 | ANGEL OF THE MORNING — Merrilee Rush (T. Cogbill & C. Moman), Bell 705 | 7 |
| ★ 15 | 34 | 54 | 71 | THE HORSE — Cliff Nobles & Co. (Jesse James), Phil L. A. of Soul 313 | 4 |
| 16 | 15 | 21 | 21 | DELILAH — Tom Jones (Peter Sullivan), Parrot 40025 | 14 |
| ★ 17 | 25 | 32 | 75 | LICKING STICK — James Brown & the Famous Flames (James Brown), King 6166 | 4 |
| 18 | 22 | 31 | 40 | I LOVE YOU — People (Mikel Hunter), Capitol 2078 | 11 |
| ★ 19 | 50 | 83 | — | HERE COMES THE JUDGE — Shorty Long (Shorty Long & B.J.), Soul 35044 | 3 |
| 20 | 20 | 25 | 26 | IF I WERE A CARPENTER — Four Tops (Holland & Dozier), Motown 1124 | 8 |
| 21 | 21 | 10 | 10 | DO YOU KNOW THE WAY TO SAN JOSE? — Dionne Warwick (Bacharach-David), Scepter 12216 | 10 |
| 22 | 23 | 38 | 57 | REACH OUT OF THE DARKNESS — Friend & Lover (Joe South & Bill Lowery), Verve Forecast 5069 | 5 |
| 23 | 18 | 23 | 30 | MASTER JACK — Four Jacks & A Jill, RCA Victor 47-9473 | 12 |
| 24 | 17 | 19 | 20 | LIKE TO GET TO KNOW YOU — Spanky & Our Gang (Scharf-Dorough), Mercury 72795 | 9 |
| ★ 25 | 37 | 41 | 41 | (You Keep Me) HANGIN' ON — Joe Simon (J.R. Enterprises), Sound Stage 7 2608 | 10 |
| 26 | 27 | 39 | 52 | A MAN WITHOUT LOVE (Quando M'Innamora) — Engelbert Humperdinck (Peter Sullivan), Parrot 40027 | 6 |
| 27 | 29 | 29 | 49 | HOW'D WE EVER GET THIS WAY? — Andy Kim (Jeff Barry), Steed 707 | 7 |
| 28 | 16 | 16 | 9 | SHOO-BE-DOO-BE-DOO-DA-DAY — Stevie Wonder (H. Cosby), Tamla 54165 | 11 |
| 29 | 12 | 9 | 6 | COWBOYS TO GIRLS — Intruders (Gamble-Huff), Gamble 214 | 13 |
| 30 | 33 | 46 | 69 | TIP-TOE THRU THE TULIPS WITH ME — Tiny Tim (Richard Perry), Reprise 0679 | 5 |
| 31 | 30 | 15 | 15 | SHE'S LOOKIN' GOOD — Wilson Pickett (Tom Dowd & Tommy Cogbill), Atlantic 2504 | 10 |
| 32 | 26 | 22 | 28 | I WILL ALWAYS THINK ABOUT YOU — New Colony Six (Senator Records Corp.), Mercury 72775 | 12 |
| 33 | 32 | 26 | 23 | SOUL SERENADE — Willie Mitchell (Willie Mitchell/Joe Cuoghi), Hi 2140 | 15 |
| 34 | 39 | 62 | — | CHOO CHOO TRAIN — Box Tops (Den Penn), Mala 12005 | 3 |
| 35 | 38 | 50 | 50 | NEVER GIVE YOU UP — Jerry Butler (Gamble-Huff), Mercury 72798 | 7 |
| 36 | 40 | 40 | 29 | DOES YOUR MAMA KNOW ABOUT ME — Bobby Taylor & Vancouvers (B. Gordy Jr.), Gordy 7069 | 9 |
| 37 | 24 | 24 | 11 | TAKE TIME TO KNOW HER — Percy Sledge (Quin Ivy & Marlin Greene), Atlantic 2490 | 14 |
| ★ 38 | 62 | — | — | JUMPIN' JACK FLASH — Rolling Stones (Jimmy Miller), London 908 | 2 |
| 39 | 43 | 48 | 58 | SHE'S A HEARTBREAKER — Gene Pitney (Charlie Foxx), Musicor 1306 | 6 |
| ★ 40 | 77 | 81 | 81 | FACE IT GIRL, IT'S OVER — Nancy Wilson (David Cavanaugh), Capitol 2136 | 6 |
| 41 | 41 | 45 | 46 | TIME FOR LIVIN' — Association (Bones Howe), Warner Bros.-Seven Arts 7195 | 5 |
| 42 | 42 | 42 | 43 | I'M SORRY — Delfonics (Stan & Bell), Philly Groove 151 | 8 |
| 43 | 28 | 28 | 25 | THE HAPPY SONG (Dum Dum) — Otis Redding (Steve Cropper), Volt 163 | 8 |
| 44 | 44 | 36 | 36 | I WANNA LIVE — Glen Campbell (Alyde Lory), Capitol 2146 | 11 |
| ★ 45 | 64 | — | — | LADY WILLPOWER — Gary Puckett & the Union Gap (Jerry Fuller), Columbia 44547 | 2 |
| 46 | 48 | 56 | 59 | UNITED — Peaches & Herb (Gamble-Huff), Date 1603 | 5 |
| 47 | 47 | 73 | — | YESTER LOVE — Smokey Robinson & the Miracles ("Smokey"), Tamla 54167 | 3 |
| ★ 48 | 55 | 57 | 77 | YOU DON'T KNOW WHAT YOU MEAN TO ME — Sam & Dave (Isaac Hayes & David Porter), Atlantic 2517 | 4 |
| 49 | 49 | 53 | 53 | IF YOU DON'T WANT MY LOVE — Robert John (David Rubinson), Columbia 44435 | 10 |
| ★ 50 | 66 | — | — | IT SHOULD HAVE BEEN ME — Gladys Knight & the Pips (Norman Whitfield), Soul 35045 | 2 |
| ★ 51 | 52 | 79 | — | INDIAN LAKE — Cowsills (Wes Ferrell), MGM 13944 | 3 |
| ★ 52 | 83 | — | — | GRAZING IN THE GRASS — Hugh Masakela (Stewart Levine), Uni 55066 | 2 |
| 53 | 53 | 95 | — | STONED SOUL PICNIC — 5th Dimension (Bones Howe), Soul City 766 | 3 |
| ★ 54 | 54 | 86 | — | SKY PILOT — Eric Burdon & the Animals (Tom Wilson), MGM 13939 | 3 |
| ★ 55 | 75 | 84 | 96 | FOLSOM PRISON BLUES — Johnny Cash (Bob Johnston), Columbia 44513 | 4 |
| ★ 56 | 63 | — | — | SOME THINGS YOU NEVER GET USED TO — Diana Ross & Supremes (Ashford & Simpson), Motown 1126 | 2 |
| 57 | 57 | 75 | 97 | BRING A LITTLE LOVIN' — Los Bravos (Alain Milhaud), Parrot 3020 | 4 |
| ★ 58 | 73 | 98 | 98 | PICTURES OF MATCHSTICK MEN — Status Quo (John Schroeder), Cadet Concept 7001 | 5 |
| 59 | 59 | 61 | 61 | I'LL NEVER DO YOU WRONG — Joe Tex (Buddy Killen), Dial 4076 | 5 |
| ★ 60 | 87 | — | — | LOVER'S HOLIDAY — Peggy Scott & Jo Jo Benson (Huey P. Meaux), SSS International 736 | 2 |
| ★ 61 | — | — | — | D. W. WASHBURN — Monkees (Monkees), Colgems 66-1023 | 1 |
| 62 | 65 | 100 | — | HERE COMES THE JUDGE — Magistrates (Gross-Freda), MGM 13946 | 3 |
| 63 | 35 | 35 | 35 | MEDLEY: MY GIRL, HEY GIRL — Bobby Vee (Dallas Smith), Liberty 56033 | 9 |
| 64 | 69 | 72 | 89 | AMERICA IS MY HOME — James Brown & the Famous Flames (James Brown), King 6112 | 4 |
| 65 | 51 | 51 | 56 | JELLY JUNGLE (Of Orange Marmalade) — Lemon Pipers (Paul Leka), Buddah 41 | 5 |
| 66 | 56 | 52 | 55 | UNWIND — Ray Stevens (Fred Foster & Ray Stevens), Monument 1048 | 9 |
| 67 | 58 | 58 | 66 | BROOKLYN ROADS — Neil Diamond (Chip Taylor), UNI 55065 | 6 |
| 68 | 68 | 74 | 74 | I WISH I KNEW (How It Would Feel to Be Free) — Solomon Burke (Tom Dowd), Atlantic 2507 | 7 |
| 69 | 71 | 71 | 79 | I GOT YOU BABE — Etta James (Rick Hall & Staff), Cadet 5606 | 5 |
| 70 | 70 | 70 | 83 | THE DOCTOR — Mary Wells (C. & M. Womack), Jubilee 5621 | 5 |
| ★ 71 | 86 | — | — | ELEANOR RIGBY — Ray Charles (Joe Adams), ABC 11090 | 2 |
| ★ 72 | 85 | — | — | HERE I AM BABY — Marvelettes ("Smokey"), Tamla 54166 | 2 |
| 73 | 76 | 80 | 80 | MY SHY VIOLET — Mills Brothers (Tom Mack), Dot 17096 | 5 |
| 74 | 80 | 88 | 91 | IT'S OVER — Eddy Arnold (Chet Atkins), RCA Victor 47-9525 | 5 |
| ★ 75 | 81 | — | — | MOUNTAIN OF LOVE — Ronnie Dove (Phil Kahl), Diamond 244 | 2 |
| ★ 76 | 78 | — | — | BACK IN LOVE AGAIN — Buckinghams (Jimmy "Wiz" Wisner), Columbia 44533 | 2 |
| 77 | 60 | 60 | 60 | LOVE IN EVERY ROOM (Meme Si Tu Revenais) — Paul Mauriat & His Ork (Paul Mauriat), Philips 40530 | 6 |
| 78 | 79 | — | — | SAFE IN MY GARDEN — Mamas & Papas (Lou Adler), Dunhill 4125 | 2 |
| 79 | 82 | 82 | 82 | APOLOGIZE — Ed Ames (Jim Foglesong), RCA Victor 47-9517 | 6 |
| 80 | 61 | 65 | 67 | SLEEPY JOE — Herman's Hermits (Mickie Most), MGM 13934 | 6 |
| ★ 81 | — | — | — | YOU SEND ME — Aretha Franklin (Jerry Wexler), Atlantic 2518 | 1 |
| ★ 82 | — | — | — | HERE COMES THE JUDGE — Pigmeat Markham (Gene Barge), Chess 1049 | 1 |
| ★ 83 | 93 | — | — | LET ME BE LONELY — Dionne Warwick (Bacharach-David), Scepter 12216 | 2 |
| ★ 84 | — | — | — | IT'S NICE TO BE WITH YOU — Monkees (Monkees), Colgems 66-1023 | 1 |
| 85 | 96 | — | — | SWEET MEMORIES — Andy Williams (Nick DeCaro), Columbia 44527 | 2 |
| 86 | 92 | 92 | 93 | HOLD ON — Radiants (Leonard Caston), Chess 2037 | 4 |
| ★ 87 | — | — | — | UNDERSTANDING — Ray Charles (Joe Adams), ABC 11090 | 1 |
| 88 | 88 | 96 | — | FUNKY FEVER — Clarence Carter (Rick Hall & Staff), Atlantic 2508 | 3 |
| 89 | 89 | 97 | — | AIN'T NOTHIN' BUT A HOUSE PARTY — Show Stoppers (D. Sharah), Heritage 800 | 3 |
| ★ 90 | — | — | — | CAN'T YOU SEE ME CRY — New Colony Six (Sentar Records), Mercury 72817 | 1 |
| 91 | 91 | 91 | — | SAN FRANCISCO GIRLS — Fever Tree (Scott & Vivian Holtzman), UNI 55060 | 3 |
| 92 | 95 | — | — | BABY YOU COME ROLLIN' ACROSS MY MIND — Peppermint Trolley Company (Dan Dalton), Acta 815 | 2 |
| 93 | 94 | 94 | — | HERE COME DA JUDGE — Buena Vistas (Carl Cisco), Marquee 443 | 3 |
| 94 | — | — | — | LET YOURSELF GO — Elvis Presley (Douglas Laurence), RCA Victor 47-9547 | 1 |
| 95 | — | — | — | TURN AROUND, LOOK AT ME — Vogues (Dick Glasser), Reprise 0686 | 1 |
| 96 | 98 | 99 | 99 | DON'T SIGN THE PAPER — Jimmy Delphs (Ollie McLaughlin), Karen 1333 | 4 |
| 97 | — | — | — | LISTEN HERE — Eddie Harris (Joel Dorn), Atlantic 2487 | 1 |
| 98 | — | — | — | FORGET ME NOT — Martha Reeves & the Vandellas (R. Morris), Gordy 7070 | 1 |
| 99 | — | — | — | VALLEY OF THE DOLLS — King Curtis & His Kingpins (Arif Mardin), Atco 6582 | 1 |
| 100 | 100 | — | — | CONGRATULATIONS — Cliff Richard (Norrie Paramor), Uni 55069 | 2 |

## HOT 100—A TO Z—(Publisher-Licensee)



## BUBBLING UNDER THE HOT 100

101. YOUR TIME HASN'T COME YET .... Elvis Presley, RCA Victor 47-9547
102. CLASSICAL GAS .... Mason Williams, Warner Bros.-Seven Arts 7190
103. YOU'RE GOOD FOR ME .... Lou Rawls, Capitol 2172
104. HANG 'EM HIGH .... Hugo Montenegro, his Ork & Chorus, RCA Victor 47-9554
105. SHHHHHHHH (FOR A LITTLE WHILE) .... James Brown & His Famous Flames King 6164
106. LOVIN' SEASON .... Gene & Debbe, TRX 5010
107. WHERE DO WE GO .... Billy Vera & Judy Clay, Atlantic 2515
108. BE YOUNG, BE FOOLISH, BE HAPPY .... Tams, ABC 11066
109. EYES OF A NEW YORK WOMAN .... B. J. Thomas, Scepter 12219
110. TURN ON YOUR LOVELIGHT .... Bill Black's Combo, Hi 2141
111. LITTLE GREEN APPLES .... Patti Page, Columbia 44556
112. ALL THE GRAY HAIRED MEN .... Lettermen, Capitol 2196
113. YOUNG BOY .... Barbara Greene, Vivid 059
114. DON'T BREAK MY PRETTY BALLOON .... Vikki Carr, Liberty 56039
115. YOURS UNTIL TOMORROW .... Vivian Reed, EMC 10319
116. (The Puppet Song) WHISKEY ON A SUNDAY .... The Irish Rovers, Decca 32333
117. DON'T TAKE IT SO HARD .... Paul Revere & the Raiders Featuring Mark Lindsay, Columbia 44553
118. ..We're Gonna) ROCK AROUND THE CLOCK .... Bill Haley and His Comets, Decca 29124
119. SUGAR .... Jive Five Featuring Eugene Pitt, Musicor 1305
120. SEND MY BABY BACK .... Freddie Hughes, Wand 1182
121. HITCH IT TO THE HORSE .... The Fantastic Johnny C, Phil L.A. of Soul 315
122. HE GIVES ME LOVE (La-La-La) .... Lesley Gore, Mercury 72819
123. BACKWARDS AND FORWARDS .... December's Children, World-Pacific 77887
124. QUANDO M'INNAMORA .... Sandpipers, A&M 939
125. JOURNEY TO THE CENTER OF YOUR MIND .... Amboy Dukes, Mainstream 684
126. PEOPLE SURE ACT FUNNY .... Arthur Conley, Atco 6588
127. HURDY GURDY MAN .... Donovan, Epic 10345
128. SOCK IT TO ME BABY .... Bill Minkin as Senator Bobby, RCA Victor 41-9522
129. I GOT TO HAVE YA .... Trolls, U.S.A. 905
130. WITH PEN IN HAND .... Billy Vera, Atlantic 2526
131. SEALED WITH A KISS .... Gary Lewis & the Playboys, Liberty 56037
132. LIGHTS OF NIGHT .... Mitch Ryder, DynaVoice 916
133. BOTH SIDES NOW .... Harpers Bizarre, Warner Bros.-Seven Arts 7200
134. HAPPY MAN .... Perry Como, RCA Victor 47-9533
135. JUST A LITTLE BIT .... Blue Cheer, Philips 40541

Compiled from national retail sales and radio station airplay by the Music Popularity Dept. of Record Market Research, Billboard.

# Billboard HOT 100

**FOR WEEK ENDING JUNE 22, 1968**

★ STAR PERFORMER—Sides registering greatest proportionate upward progress this week.

Ⓡ Record Industry Association of America seal of certification as million selling single.

| This Week | 1 Wk. Ago | 2 Wks. Ago | 3 Wks. Ago | TITLE — Artist (Producer), Label & Number | Weeks on Chart |
|---|---|---|---|---|---|
| 1 ◆ Billboard Award | 2 | 3 | 11 | **THIS GUY'S IN LOVE WITH YOU** — Herb Alpert (Herb Alpert & Jerry Moss), A&M 929 | 6 |
| 2 | 5 | 7 | 12 | **MacARTHUR PARK** — Richard Harris (Jimmy Webb), Dunhill 4134 | 7 |
| 3 Ⓡ | 1 | 1 | 1 | **MRS. ROBINSON** — Simon & Garfunkel (Simon, Garfunkel & Halee), Columbia 44511 | 9 |
| 4 | 4 | 6 | 6 | **YUMMY, YUMMY, YUMMY** — Ohio Express (Kasenetz-Katz Associates), Buddah 38 | 8 |
| 5 | 10 | 13 | 34 | **THE LOOK OF LOVE** — Sergio Mendes & Brasil '66 (Herb Alpert), A&M 924 | 7 |
| 6 | 3 | 5 | 22 | **MONY MONY** — Tommy James & Shondells (Kasenetz-Katz Associates), Roulette 7008 | 12 |
| 7 | 7 | 9 | 13 | **THINK** — Aretha Franklin (Jerry Wexler), Atlantic 2518 | 6 |
| 8 | 14 | 14 | 30 | **ANGEL OF THE MORNING** — Merrilee Rush (T. Cogbill & C. Moman), Bell 705 | 8 |
| 9 Ⓡ | 6 | 2 | 4 | **TIGHTEN UP** — Archie Bell & the Drells (L.J.F. Production), Atlantic 2478 | 13 |
| 10 | 22 | 23 | 38 | **REACH OUT OF THE DARKNESS** — Friend & Lover (Joe South & Bill Lowery), Verve Forecast 5069 | 6 |
| 11 | 19 | 50 | 83 | **HERE COMES THE JUDGE** — Shorty Long (Shorty Long & B.J.), Soul 35044 | 4 |
| 12 | 38 | 62 | — | **JUMPIN' JACK FLASH** — Rolling Stones (Jimmy Miller), London 908 | 3 |
| 13 | 13 | 19 | 20 | **I COULD NEVER LOVE ANOTHER (After Loving You)** — Temptations (Norman Whitfield), Gordy 7072 | 8 |
| 14 | 18 | 22 | 31 | **I LOVE YOU** — People (Mikel Hunter), Capitol 2078 | 12 |
| 15 | 15 | 34 | 54 | **THE HORSE** — Cliff Nobles & Co. (Jesse James), Phil L.A. of Soul 313 | 5 |
| 16 | 8 | 8 | 3 | **BEAUTIFUL MORNING** — Rascals (Rascals), Atlantic 2493 | 11 |
| 17 | 17 | 25 | 32 | **LICKING STICK** — James Brown and the Famous Flames (James Brown), King 6166 | 5 |
| 18 | 9 | 4 | 2 | **THE GOOD, THE BAD AND THE UGLY** — Hugo Montenegro, His Ork and Chorus (Neely Plumb), RCA Victor 9423 | 19 |
| 19 | 26 | 27 | 39 | **A MAN WITHOUT LOVE (Quando M'Innamora)** — Engelbert Humperdinck (Peter Sullivan), Parrot 40027 | 7 |
| 20 | 45 | 64 | — | **LADY WILLPOWER** — Gary Puckett and the Union Gap (Jerry Fuller), Columbia 44547 | 3 |
| 21 | 27 | 29 | 29 | **HOW'D WE EVER GET THIS WAY?** — Andy Kim (Jeff Barry), Steed 707 | 8 |
| 22 | 30 | 33 | 46 | **TIP-TOE THRU THE TULIPS WITH ME** — Tiny Tim (Richard Perry), Reprise 0679 | 6 |
| 23 | 11 | 8 | 8 | **AIN'T NOTHING LIKE THE REAL THING** — Marvin Gaye & Tammi Terrell (Ashford-Simpson), Tamla 54163 | 11 |
| 24 | 24 | 17 | 19 | **LIKE TO GET TO KNOW YOU** — Spanky & Our Gang (Scharf-Dorough), Mercury 72795 | 10 |
| 25 | 25 | 37 | 41 | **(You Keep Me) HANGIN' ON** — Joe Simon (J.R. Enterprises), Sound Stage 7 2608 | 11 |
| 26 Ⓡ | 12 | 10 | 5 | **HONEY** — Bobby Goldsboro (Bob Montgomery & Bobby Goldsboro), United Artists 50283 | 14 |
| 27 | 34 | 39 | 62 | **CHOO CHOO TRAIN** — Box Tops (Dan Penn), Mala 12005 | 4 |
| 28 | 51 | 52 | 79 | **INDIAN LAKE** — Cowsills (Wes Farrell), MGM 13944 | 4 |
| 29 | 61 | — | — | **D. W. WASHBURN** — Monkees (Monkees), Colgems 66-1023 | 2 |
| 30 | 23 | 18 | 23 | **MASTER JACK** — Four Jacks & A Jill (Clive Calder), RCA Victor 47-9473 | 13 |
| 31 | 53 | 53 | 95 | **STONED SOUL PICNIC** — 5th Dimension (Bones Howe), Soul City 766 | 3 |
| 32 | 52 | 83 | — | **GRAZING IN THE GRASS** — Hugh Masakela (Stewart Levine), Uni 55066 | 3 |
| 33 | 39 | 43 | 48 | **SHE'S A HEARTBREAKER** — Gene Pitney (Charlie Foxx), Musicor 1306 | 7 |
| 34 | 35 | 38 | 50 | **NEVER GIVE YOU UP** — Jerry Butler (Gamble-Huff), Mercury 72798 | 8 |
| 35 | 21 | 21 | 10 | **DO YOU KNOW THE WAY TO SAN JOSE?** — Dionne Warwick (Bacharach-David), Scepter 12216 | 11 |
| 36 | 28 | 16 | 16 | **SHOO-BE-DOO-BE-DOO-DA-DAY** — Stevie Wonder (H. Cosby), Tamla 54165 | 12 |
| 37 | 16 | 15 | 21 | **DELILAH** — Tom Jones (Peter Sullivan), Parrot 40025 | 15 |
| 38 | 54 | 54 | 86 | **SKY PILOT** — Eric Burdon & the Animals (Tom Wilson), MGM 13939 | 4 |
| 39 | 41 | 41 | 45 | **TIME FOR LIVIN'** — Association (Bones Howe), Warner Bros.-Seven Arts 7195 | 6 |
| 40 | 40 | 77 | 81 | **FACE IT GIRL, IT'S OVER** — Nancy Wilson (David Cavanaugh), Capitol 2136 | 5 |
| 41 Ⓡ | 29 | 12 | 9 | **COWBOYS TO GIRLS** — Intruders (Gamble-Huff), Gamble 214 | 14 |
| 42 | 20 | 20 | 25 | **IF I WERE A CARPENTER** — Four Tops (Holland & Dozier), Motown 1124 | 9 |
| 43 | 32 | 26 | 22 | **I WILL ALWAYS THINK ABOUT YOU** — New Colony Six (Senator Records Corp.), Mercury 72775 | 13 |
| 44 | 55 | 75 | 84 | **FOLSOM PRISON BLUES** — Johnny Cash (Bob Johnston), Columbia 44513 | 5 |
| 45 ★ | 56 | 63 | — | **SOME THINGS YOU NEVER GET USED TO** — Diana Ross & Supremes (Ashford & Simpson), Motown 1126 | 3 |
| 46 | 46 | 48 | 56 | **UNITED** — Peaches & Herb (Gamble-Huff), Date 1603 | 6 |
| 47 | 47 | 47 | 73 | **YESTER LOVE** — Smokey Robinson and the Miracles ("Smokey"), Tamla 54167 | 6 |
| 48 | 48 | 55 | 57 | **YOU DON'T KNOW WHAT YOU MEAN TO ME** — Sam & Dave (Isaac Hayes & David Porter), Atlantic 2517 | 5 |
| 49 | 49 | 49 | 53 | **IF YOU DON'T WANT MY LOVE** — Robert John (David Robinson), Columbia 44435 | 11 |
| 50 | 50 | 66 | — | **IT SHOULD HAVE BEEN ME** — Gladys Knight and the Pips (Norman Whitfield), Soul 35045 | 3 |
| 51 | 57 | 57 | 75 | **BRING A LITTLE LOVIN'** — Los Bravos (Alain Milhaud), Parrot 3020 | 5 |
| 52 | 44 | 44 | 36 | **I WANNA LIVE** — Glen Campbell (Alyde Lory), Capitol 2146 | 12 |
| 53 | 58 | 73 | 98 | **PICTURES OF MATCHSTICK MEN** — Status Quo (John Schroeder), Cadet Concept 7001 | 6 |
| 54 | 84 | — | — | **IT'S NICE TO BE WITH YOU** — Monkees (Monkees), Colgems 66-1023 | 2 |
| 55 | 78 | 79 | — | **SAFE IN MY GARDEN** — Mamas & Papas (Lou Adler), Dunhill 4125 | 3 |
| 56 | 95 | — | — | **TURN AROUND, LOOK AT ME** — Vogues (Dick Glasser), Reprise 0686 | 2 |
| 57 | 36 | 40 | 40 | **DOES YOUR MAMA KNOW ABOUT ME** — Bobby Taylor & Vancouvers (B. Gordy Jr.), Gordy 7069 | 10 |
| 58 | 42 | 42 | 42 | **I'M SORRY** — Delfonics (Stan & Bell), Philly Groove 151 | 9 |
| 59 | 60 | 87 | — | **LOVER'S HOLIDAY** — Peggy Scott & Jo Jo Benson (Huey P. Meaux), SSS International 736 | 3 |
| 60 | 62 | 65 | 100 | **HERE COMES THE JUDGE** — Magistrates (Gross-Freda), MGM 13946 | 4 |
| 61 | 64 | 69 | 72 | **AMERICA IS MY HOME** — James Brown and the Famous Flames (James Brown), King 6112 | 5 |
| 62 | 81 | — | — | **YOU SEND ME** — Aretha Franklin (Jerry Wexler), Atlantic 2518 | 2 |
| 63 | 82 | — | — | **HERE COMES THE JUDGE** — Pigmeat Markham (Geno Barge), Chess 2049 | 2 |
| 64 | 72 | 85 | — | **HERE I AM BABY** — Marvelettes ("Smokey"), Tamla 54166 | 3 |
| 65 | 71 | 86 | — | **ELEANOR RIGBY** — Ray Charles (Joe Adams), ABC 11090 | 3 |
| 66 | 70 | 70 | 70 | **THE DOCTOR** — Mary Wells (C. & M. Womack), Jubilee 5621 | 6 |
| 67 | 90 | — | — | **CAN'T YOU SEE ME CRY** — New Colony Six (Sentar Records), Mercury 72817 | 2 |
| 68 | 75 | 81 | — | **MOUNTAIN OF LOVE** — Ronnie Dove (Phil Kahl), Diamond 244 | 3 |
| 69 | 76 | 78 | — | **BACK IN LOVE AGAIN** — Buckinghams (Jimmy "Wiz" Wisner), Columbia 44533 | 3 |
| 70 | 69 | 71 | 71 | **I GOT YOU BABE** — Etta James (Rick Hall & Staff), Cadet 5606 | 6 |
| 71 | — | — | — | **PEOPLE SURE ACT FUNNY** — Arthur Conley (Tom Dowd), Atco 6588 | 1 |
| 72 | — | — | — | **THE STORY OF ROCK AND ROLL** — Turtles (Chip Douglas), White Whale 273 | 1 |
| 73 | 73 | 76 | 80 | **MY SHY VIOLET** — Mills Brothers (Tom Mack), Dot 17096 | 6 |
| 74 | 74 | 80 | 88 | **IT'S OVER** — Eddy Arnold (Chet Atkins), RCA Victor 47-9525 | 5 |
| 75 | 85 | 96 | — | **SWEET MEMORIES** — Andy Williams (Nick DeCaro), Columbia 44527 | 3 |
| 76 | — | — | — | **HURDY GURDY MAN** — Donovan (Mickie Most), Epic 10345 | 1 |
| 77 | — | — | — | **DON'T TAKE IT SO HARD** — Paul Revere & The Raiders (Featuring Mark Lindsay) (Mark Lindsay), Columbia 4455 | 1 |
| 78 | 83 | 93 | — | **LET ME BE LONELY** — Dionne Warwick (Bacharach-David), Scepter 12216 | 3 |
| 79 | 87 | — | — | **UNDERSTANDING** — Ray Charles (Joe Adams), ABC 11090 | 2 |
| 80 | — | — | — | **BE YOUNG, BE FOOLISH, BE HAPPY** — Tams (Joe South), ABC 11066 | 1 |
| 81 | 92 | 95 | — | **BABY YOU COME ROLLIN' ACROSS MY MIND** — Peppermint Trolley Company (Dan Dalton), Acta 815 | 3 |
| 82 | 68 | 68 | 74 | **I WISH I KNEW (How It Would Feel to Be Free)** — Solomon Burke (Bert Berns), Atlantic 2507 | 8 |
| 83 | 99 | — | — | **VALLEY OF THE DOLLS** — King Curtis & His Kingpins (Arif Mardin), Atco 6582 | 2 |
| 84 | 97 | — | — | **LISTEN HERE** — Eddie Harris (Joel Dorn), Atlantic 2487 | 2 |
| 85 | — | — | — | **TURN ON YOUR LOVE LIGHT** — Bill Black's Combo (Joe Cuoghi), HI 2145 | 1 |
| 86 | 86 | 92 | 92 | **HOLD ON** — Radiants (Leonard Caston), Chess 2037 | 5 |
| 87 | 89 | 89 | 97 | **AIN'T NOTHIN' BUT A HOUSE PARTY** — Show Stoppers (D. Sharsh), Heritage 800 | 4 |
| 88 | 93 | 94 | 94 | **HERE COME DA JUDGE** — Buena Vistas (Carl Cisco), Marquee 443 | 4 |
| 89 | — | — | — | **D-I-V-O-R-C-E** — Tammy Wynette (Billy Sherrill), Epic 10315 | 1 |
| 90 | — | — | — | **(The Puppet Song) WHISKEY ON A SUNDAY** — Irish Rovers (Charles Bud Dant), Decca 32333 | 1 |
| 91 | — | — | — | **YOUNG BOY** — Barbara Greene, Renee 5001 | 1 |
| 92 | — | — | — | **YOUR TIME HASN'T COME YET, BABY** — Elvis Presley, RCA Victor 47-9547 | 1 |
| 93 | — | — | — | **CLASSICAL GAS** — Mason Williams (Mike Post), Warner Bros.-Seven Arts 7190 | 1 |
| 94 | 94 | — | — | **LET YOURSELF GO** — Elvis Presley (Douglas Laurence), RCA Victor 47-9547 | 2 |
| 95 | — | — | — | **I'M A MIDNIGHT MOVER** — Wilson Pickett (Tom Dowd), Atlantic 2528 | 1 |
| 96 | — | — | — | **THE EYES OF A NEW YORK WOMAN** — B.J. Thomas (Chips Moman), Scepter 12219 | 1 |
| 97 | — | — | — | **SEALED WITH A KISS** — Gary Lewis & Playboys (Snuff Garrett), Liberty 56037 | 1 |
| 98 | 98 | — | — | **FORGET ME NOT** — Martha Reeves & the Vandellas (R. Morris), Gordy | 2 |
| 99 | 100 | 100 | — | **CONGRATULATIONS** — Cliff Richard (Norrie Paramor), Uni 55069 | 3 |
| 100 | — | — | — | **YOUNG BIRDS FLY** — Cryan' Shames (Jim Golden & Robert Monaco), Columbia 44545 | 1 |

## BUBBLING UNDER THE HOT 100

101. LOVIN' SEASON — Gene & Debbe, TRX 5010
102. HANG 'EM HIGH — Hugo Montenegro, RCA Victor 47-9554
103. YOU'RE GOOD FOR ME — Lou Rawls, Capitol 2172
104. SHHHHHH (For a Little While) — James Brown & His Famous Flames, King 6164
105. APOLOGIZE — Ed Ames, RCA Victor 47-9517
106. WITH PEN IN HAND — Billy Vera, Atlantic 2526
107. COMPETITION AIN'T NOTHIN' — Little Carl Carlton, Back Beat 588
108. LOVE IN THEM THERE HILLS — Vibrations, Okeh 7311
109. LITTLE GREEN APPLES — Patti Page, Columbia 44556
110. YES SIR, THAT'S MY BABY — Julius Wechter & the Baja Marimba Band, A&M 937
111. VENUS — Johnny Mathis, Columbia 44517
112. SATURDAY'S FATHER — Four Seasons, Philips 40542
113. YOURS UNTIL TOMORROW — Vivian Reed, Epic 10319
114. DON'T BREAK MY PRETTY BALLOON — Vikki Carr, Liberty 56039
115. JOURNEY TO THE CENTER OF MY MIND — Amboy Dukes, Mainstream 684
116. HITCH IT TO THE HORSE — Fantastic Johnny C, Phil L.A. of Soul 315
117. SEND MY BABY BACK — Freddie Hughes, Wand 1182
118. (We're Gonna) ROCK AROUND THE CLOCK — Bill Haley and His Comets, Decca 29140
119. HE GIVES ME LOVE (La La La) — Lesley Gore, Mercury 72819
120. GEORGIA ON MY MIND — Wes Montgomery, A&M 940
121. ROCK AROUND THE CLOCK — Freddie Cannon, We Make Rock & Roll 1601
122. LIGHTS OF CINCINNATI — Mitch Ryder, DynaVoice 914
123. BOTH SIDES NOW — Harper's Bizarre, Warner Bros.-Seven Arts 7200
124. JUST A LITTLE BIT — Blue Cheer, Philips 40541

Compiled from national retail sales and radio station airplay by the Music Popularity Dept. of Record Market Research, Billboard.

# Billboard HOT 100

**For Week Ending June 29, 1968**

★ STAR PERFORMER—Sides registering greatest proportionate upward progress this week.
● Record Industry Association of America seal of certification as million selling single.

| This Week | 1 Wk. Ago | 2 Wks. Ago | 3 Wks. Ago | TITLE — Artist (Producer), Label & Number | Weeks on Chart |
|---|---|---|---|---|---|
| 1 | 1 | 2 | 3 | **THIS GUY'S IN LOVE WITH YOU** — Herb Alpert (Herb Alpert & Jerry Moss), A&M 929 | 7 |
| 2 | 2 | 15 | 15 | 34 | **THE HORSE** — Cliff Nobles & Co. (Jesse James), Phil L.A. of Soul 313 | 6 |
| 3 | 2 | 5 | 7 | **MacARTHUR PARK** — Richard Harris (Jimmy Webb), Dunhill 4134 | 8 |
| 4 | 4 | 4 | 6 | **YUMMY, YUMMY, YUMMY** — Ohio Express (Kasenetz-Katz Associates), Buddah 38 | 9 |
| 5 | 5 | 10 | 13 | **THE LOOK OF LOVE** — Sergio Mendes & Brasil '66 (Herb Alpert), A&M 924 | 8 |
| 6 | 6 | 3 | 5 | **MONY MONY** — Tommy James & Shondells (Kasenetz-Katz Associates), Roulette 7008 | 13 |
| 7 | 8 | 14 | 14 | **ANGEL OF THE MORNING** — Merrilee Rush (T. Cogbill & C. Moman), Bell 705 | 9 |
| 8 | 7 | 9 | 7 | **THINK** — Aretha Franklin (Jerry Wexler), Atlantic 2518 | 7 |
| 9 | 11 | 19 | 50 | **HERE COMES THE JUDGE** — Shorty Long (Shorty Long & B.J.), Soul 35044 | 5 |
| 10 | 10 | 22 | 23 | **REACH OUT OF THE DARKNESS** — Friend & Lover (Joe South & Bill Lowery), Verve Forecast 5069 | 7 |
| 11 | 12 | 38 | 62 | **JUMPIN' JACK FLASH** — Rolling Stones (Jimmy Miller), London 908 | 4 |
| 12 | 3 | 1 | 1 | **MRS. ROBINSON** — Simon & Garfunkel (Simon, Garfunkel & Halee), Columbia 44511 | 10 |
| 13 | 32 | 52 | 83 | **GRAZING IN THE GRASS** — Hugh Masekela (Stewart Levine), Uni 55066 | 4 |
| 14 | 17 | 17 | 25 | **LICKING STICK** — James Brown & the Famous Flames (James Brown), King 6166 | 3 |
| 15 | 20 | 45 | 64 | **LADY WILLPOWER** — Gary Puckett & the Union Gap (Jerry Fuller), Columbia 44547 | 4 |
| 16 | 14 | 18 | 22 | **I LOVE YOU** — People (Mikel Hunter), Capitol 2078 | 6 |
| 17 | 22 | 30 | 33 | **TIP-TOE THRU THE TULIPS WITH ME** — Tiny Tim (Richard Perry), Reprise 0679 | 5 |
| 18 | 28 | 51 | 52 | **INDIAN LAKE** — Cowsills (Wes Farrell), MGM 13944 | 4 |
| 19 | 31 | 53 | 53 | **STONED SOUL PICNIC** — 5th Dimension (Bones Howe), Soul City 766 | 4 |
| 20 | 13 | 13 | 19 | **I COULD NEVER LOVE ANOTHER (After Loving You)** — Temptations (Norman Whitfield), Gordy 7072 | 9 |
| 21 | 21 | 27 | 29 | **HOW'D WE EVER GET THIS WAY?** — Andy Kim (Jeff Barry), Steed 707 | 8 |
| 22 | 33 | 39 | 43 | **SHE'S A HEARTBREAKER** — Gene Pitney (Charlie Foxx), Musicor 1306 | 8 |
| 23 | 23 | 11 | 11 | **AIN'T NOTHING LIKE THE REAL THING** — Marvin Gaye & Tammi Terrell (Ashford-Simpson), Tamla 54163 | 12 |
| 24 | 18 | 9 | 4 | **THE GOOD, THE BAD AND THE UGLY** — Hugo Montenegro, His Orch and Chorus (Neely Plumb), RCA Victor 9423 | 20 |
| 25 | 25 | 25 | 37 | **(You Keep Me) HANGIN' ON** — Joe Simon (J.R. Enterprises), Sound Stage 7 2608 | 12 |
| 26 | 27 | 34 | 39 | **CHOO CHOO TRAIN** — Box Tops (Dan Penn), Mala 12005 | 5 |
| 27 | 16 | 8 | 8 | **BEAUTIFUL MORNING** — Rascals (Rascals), Atlantic 2493 | 9 |
| 28 | 9 | 6 | 2 | **TIGHTEN UP** — Archie Bell & the Drells (L.J.F. Production), Atlantic 2478 | 14 |
| 29 | 29 | 61 | — | **D. W. WASHBURN** — Monkees (Monkees), Colgems 66-1023 | 3 |
| 30 | 34 | 35 | 38 | **NEVER GIVE YOU UP** — Jerry Butler (Gamble-Huff), Mercury 72798 | 5 |
| 31 | 19 | 26 | 27 | **A MAN WITHOUT LOVE (Quando M'Innamora)** — Engelbert Humperdinck (Peter Sullivan), Parrot 40027 | 8 |
| 32 | 47 | 47 | 47 | **YESTER LOVE** — Smokey Robinson & the Miracles ("Smokey"), Tamla 54167 | 5 |
| 33 | 44 | 55 | 75 | **FOLSOM PRISON BLUES** — Johnny Cash (Bob Johnston), Columbia 44513 | 6 |
| 34 | 38 | 54 | 54 | **SKY PILOT** — Eric Burdon & the Animals (Tom Wilson), MGM 13939 | 5 |
| 35 | 24 | 24 | 17 | **LIKE TO GET TO KNOW YOU** — Spanky & Our Gang (Scharf-Dorough), Mercury 72795 | 11 |
| 36 | 53 | 58 | 73 | **PICTURES OF MATCHSTICK MEN** — Status Quo (John Schroeder), Cadet Concept 7001 | 7 |
| 37 | 76 | — | — | **HURDY GURDY MAN** — Donovan (Mickie Most), Epic 10345 | 2 |
| 38 | 30 | 23 | 18 | **MASTER JACK** — Four Jacks & A Jill, RCA Victor 47-9473 | 14 |
| 39 | 39 | 41 | 41 | **TIME FOR LIVIN'** — Association (Bones Howe), Warner Bros.-Seven Arts 7195 | 7 |
| 40 | 40 | 40 | 77 | **FACE IT GIRL, IT'S OVER** — Nancy Wilson (David Cavanaugh), Capitol 2136 | 8 |
| 41 | 26 | 12 | 10 | **HONEY** — Bobby Goldsboro (Bob Montgomery & Bobby Goldsboro), United Artists 50283 | 15 |
| 42 | 45 | 56 | 63 | **SOME THINGS YOU NEVER GET USED TO** — Diana Ross & Supremes (Ashford & Simpson), Motown 1126 | 4 |
| 43 | 36 | 28 | 16 | **SHOO-BE-DOO-BE-DOO-DA-DAY** — Stevie Wonder (H. Cosby), Tamla 54165 | 13 |
| 44 | 35 | 21 | 21 | **DO YOU KNOW THE WAY TO SAN JOSE?** — Dionne Warwick (Bacharach-David), Scepter 12216 | 12 |
| 45 | 56 | 95 | — | **TURN AROUND, LOOK AT ME** — Vogues (Dick Glasser), Reprise 0686 | 3 |
| 46 | 95 | — | — | **I'M A MIDNIGHT MOVER** — Wilson Pickett (Tom Dowd), Atlantic 2528 | 2 |
| 47 | 46 | 46 | 48 | **UNITED** — Peaches & Herb (Gamble-Huff), Date 1603 | 7 |
| 48 | 48 | 48 | 55 | **YOU DON'T KNOW WHAT YOU MEAN TO ME** — Sam & Dave (Isaac Hayes & David Porter), Atlantic 2517 | 7 |
| 49 | 42 | 20 | 20 | **IF I WERE A CARPENTER** — Four Tops (Holland & Dozier), Motown 1124 | 10 |
| 50 | 50 | 50 | 66 | **IT SHOULD HAVE BEEN ME** — Gladys Knight & the Pips (Norman Whitfield), Soul 35045 | 4 |
| 51 | 51 | 57 | 57 | **BRING A LITTLE LOVIN'** — Los Bravos (Alain Milhaud), Parrot 3020 | 6 |
| 52 | 61 | 64 | 69 | **AMERICA IS MY HOME** — James Brown & the Famous Flames (James Brown), King 6112 | 6 |
| 53 | 65 | 71 | 86 | **ELEANOR RIGBY** — Ray Charles (Joe Adams), ABC 11090 | 4 |
| 54 | 54 | 84 | — | **IT'S NICE TO BE WITH YOU** — Monkees (Monkees), Colgems 66-1023 | 3 |
| 55 | 55 | 78 | 79 | **SAFE IN MY GARDEN** — Mamas & Papas (Lou Adler), Dunhill 4125 | 4 |
| 56 | 60 | 62 | 65 | **HERE COMES THE JUDGE** — Magistrates (Gross-Freda), MGM 13946 | 5 |
| 57 | 69 | 76 | 78 | **BACK IN LOVE AGAIN** — Buckinghams (Jimmy "Wiz" Wisner), Columbia 44533 | 4 |
| 58 | 59 | 60 | 87 | **LOVER'S HOLIDAY** — Peggy Scott & Jo Jo Benson (Huey P. Meaux), SSS International 736 | 5 |
| 59 | 63 | 82 | — | **HERE COMES THE JUDGE** — Pigmeat Markham (Gene Barge), Chess 2049 | 3 |
| 60 | 77 | — | — | **DON'T TAKE IT SO HARD** — Paul Revere & the Raiders (Featuring Mark Lindsay) (Mark Lindsay), Columbia 44553 | 2 |
| 61 | 49 | 49 | 49 | **IF YOU DON'T WANT MY LOVE** — Robert John (David Rubinson), Columbia 44435 | 7 |
| 62 | 62 | 81 | — | **YOU SEND ME** — Aretha Franklin (Jerry Wexler), Atlantic 2518 | 3 |
| 63 | 71 | — | — | **PEOPLE SURE ACT FUNNY** — Amboy Conley (Tom Dowd), Atco 6588 | 2 |
| 64 | 64 | 72 | 85 | **HERE I AM BABY** — Marvelettes ("Smokey"), Tamla 54166 | 4 |
| 65 | 66 | 70 | 70 | **THE DOCTOR** — Mary Wells (C. & M. Womack), Jubilee 5621 | 5 |
| 66 | 67 | 90 | — | **CAN'T YOU SEE ME CRY** — New Colony Six (Sentar Records), Mercury 72817 | 3 |
| 67 | 68 | 75 | 81 | **MOUNTAIN OF LOVE** — Ronnie Dove (Phil Kahl), Diamond 244 | 4 |
| 68 | 72 | — | — | **THE STORY OF ROCK AND ROLL** — Turtles (Chip Douglas), White Whale 273 | 2 |
| 69 | 80 | — | — | **BE YOUNG, BE FOOLISH, BE HAPPY** — Tams (Joe South), ABC 11066 | 2 |
| 70 | 93 | — | — | **CLASSICAL GAS** — Mason Williams (Mike Post), Warner Bros.-Seven Arts 7190 | 2 |
| 71 | 78 | 83 | 93 | **LET ME BE LONELY** — Dionne Warwick (Bacharach-David), Scepter 12216 | 4 |
| 72 | 81 | 92 | 95 | **BABY YOU COME ROLLIN' ACROSS MY MIND** — Peppermint Trolley Company (Dan Dalton), Acta 815 | 4 |
| 73 | — | — | — | **HITCH IT TO THE HORSE** — Fantastic Johnny C (Jesse James), Phil L.A. of Soul 315 | 1 |
| 74 | 86 | 86 | 92 | **HOLD ON** — Radiants (Leonard Caston), Chess 2037 | 6 |
| 75 | 75 | 85 | 96 | **SWEET MEMORIES** — Andy Williams (Nick DeCaro), Columbia 44527 | 4 |
| 76 | 89 | — | — | **D-I-V-O-R-C-E** — Tammy Wynette (Billy Sherrill), Epic 10315 | 2 |
| 77 | 73 | 73 | 76 | **MY SHY VIOLET** — Mills Brothers (Tom Mack), Dot 17096 | 5 |
| 78 | 84 | 97 | — | **LISTEN HERE** — Eddie Harris (Joel Dorn), Atlantic 2487 | 3 |
| 79 | 79 | 87 | — | **UNDERSTANDING** — Ray Charles (Joe Adams), ABC 11090 | 3 |
| 80 | 74 | 74 | 80 | **IT'S OVER** — Eddy Arnold (Chet Atkins), RCA Victor 47-9525 | 7 |
| 81 | 70 | 69 | 71 | **I GOT YOU BABE** — Etta James (Rick Hall & Staff), Cadet 5606 | 7 |
| 82 | — | — | — | **WITH PEN IN HAND** — Billy Vera (Chip Taylor), Atlantic 2526 | 1 |
| 83 | 90 | — | — | **(The Puppet Song) WHISKEY ON A SUNDAY** — Irish Rovers (Charles Bud Dant), Decca 32333 | 2 |
| 84 | 85 | — | — | **TURN ON YOUR LOVE LIGHT** — Bill Black's Combo (Joe Cuoghi), Hi 2145 | 2 |
| 85 | 92 | — | — | **YOUR TIME HASN'T COME YET, BABY** — Elvis Presley, RCA Victor 47-9547 | 2 |
| 86 | 96 | — | — | **THE EYES OF A NEW YORK WOMAN** — B.J. Thomas (Chips Moman), Scepter 12219 | 2 |
| 87 | — | — | — | **BANG 'EM HIGH** — Hugo Montenegro, His Orch. & Chorus (Joe Reisman), RCA Victor 47-9554 | 1 |
| 88 | 91 | — | — | **YOUNG BOY** — Barbara Greene, Renee 5001 | 2 |
| 89 | — | — | — | **STAY IN MY CORNER** — Dells (Bobby Miller), Cadet 5612 | 1 |
| 90 | — | — | — | **AUTUMN OF MY LIFE** — Bobby Goldsboro (Bob Montgomery), United Artists 50318 | 1 |
| 91 | 97 | — | — | **SEALED WITH A KISS** — Gary Lewis & Playboys (Snuff Garrett), Liberty 56037 | 2 |
| 92 | 94 | 94 | — | **LET YOURSELF GO** — Elvis Presley (Douglas Laurence), RCA Victor 47-9547 | 3 |
| 93 | 98 | 98 | — | **FORGET ME NOT** — Martha Reeves & the Vandellas (R. Morris) | 3 |
| 94 | — | — | — | **DREAMS OF THE EVERYDAY HOUSEWIFE** — Wayne Newton (Jim Vienneau), MGM 13955 | 1 |
| 95 | — | — | — | **LOOK OVER YOUR SHOULDER** — O'Jays (George Kerr), Bell 704 | 1 |
| 96 | 87 | 89 | 89 | **AIN'T NOTHIN' BUT A HOUSE PARTY** — Show Stoppers (D. Sharah), Heritage 800 | 5 |
| 97 | — | — | — | **COMPETITION AIN'T NOTHIN'** — Little Carl Carlton, Back Beat 588 | 1 |
| 98 | — | — | — | **JOURNEY TO THE CENTER OF YOUR MIND** — Amboy Dukes (Bob Shad), Mainstream 684 | 1 |
| 99 | 100 | — | — | **YOUNG BIRDS FLY** — Cryan' Shames (Jim Golden & Robert Monaco), Columbia 44545 | 2 |
| 100 | 100 | — | — | **LOVIN' SEASON** — Gene & Debbe (Don Gant), TRX 5010 | 1 |

## BUBBLING UNDER THE HOT 100

101. SNOOPY FOR PRESIDENT ............ Royal Guardsmen, Laurie 3451
102. DREAMS OF THE EVERYDAY HOUSEWIFE ..... Glen Campbell, Capitol 2224
103. SEND MY BABY BACK .................. Freddie Hughes, Wand 1182
104. SLIP AWAY .......................... Clarence Carter, Atlantic 2508
105. TO LOVE SOMEBODY ............... Sweet Inspirations, Atlantic 2529
106. JUST A LITTLE BIT .................. Blue Cheer, Philips 40591
107. GEORGIA ON MY MIND ............... Wes Montgomery, A&M 940
108. HELLO, I LOVE YOU, WON'T YOU TELL ME YOUR NAME? ... Doors, Elektra 45635
109. SATURDAY'S FATHER ................. 4 Seasons, Philips 40542
110. ALICE LONG (You're Still My Favorite Girlfriend) .... Tommy Boyce & Bobby Hart, A&M 948
111. MRS. BLUEBIRD ................. Eternity's Children, Tower 416
112. BOY ............................ Lulu, Epic 10344
113. YES SIR, THAT'S MY BABY ........ Julius Wechter & the Baja Marimba Band, A&M 937

Compiled from national retail sales and radio station airplay by the Music Popularity Dept. of Record Market Research, Billboard.

# Billboard HOT 100

FOR WEEK ENDING JULY 6, 1968

★ STAR PERFORMER—Sides registering greatest proportionate upward progress this week.

Ⓢ Record Industry Association of America seal of certification as million selling single.

| This Week | 1 Wk. Ago | 2 Wks. Ago | 3 Wks. Ago | TITLE Artist (Producer), Label & Number | Weeks On Chart |
|---|---|---|---|---|---|
| 1 (Billboard Award) | 1 | 1 | 2 | THIS GUY'S IN LOVE WITH YOU — Herb Alpert (Herb Alpert & Jerry Moss), A&M 929 | 8 |
| 2 | 2 | 15 | 15 | THE HORSE — Cliff Nobles & Co. (Jesse James), Phil L. A. of Soul 313 | 7 |
| ★3 | 11 | 12 | 38 | JUMPIN' JACK FLASH — Rolling Stones (Jimmy Miller), London 908 | 5 |
| 4 | 5 | 5 | 10 | THE LOOK OF LOVE — Sergio Mendes & Brasil '66 (Herb Alpert), A&M 924 | 9 |
| ★5 | 13 | 32 | 52 | GRAZING IN THE GRASS — Hugh Masakela (Stewart Levine), Uni 55066 | 5 |
| ★6 | 15 | 20 | 45 | LADY WILLPOWER — Gary Puckett & the Union Gap (Jerry Fuller), Columbia 44547 | 5 |
| 7 | 7 | 8 | 14 | ANGEL OF THE MORNING — Merrilee Rush (T. Cogbill & C. Moman), Bell 705 | 10 |
| 8 | 9 | 11 | 19 | HERE COMES THE JUDGE — Shorty Long (Shorty Long & B.J.), Soul 35044 | 6 |
| 9 | 3 | 2 | 5 | MacARTHUR PARK — Richard Harris (Jimmy Webb), Dunhill 4134 | 9 |
| 10 | 10 | 10 | 22 | REACH OUT OF THE DARKNESS — Friend & Lover (Joe South & Bill Lowery), Verve Forecast 5069 | 8 |
| Ⓢ 11 | 4 | 4 | 4 | YUMMY, YUMMY, YUMMY — Ohio Express (Kasenetz-Katz Associates), Buddah 38 | 10 |
| 12 | 6 | 6 | 3 | MONY MONY — Tommy James & Shondells (Kasenetz-Katz Associates), Roulette 7008 | 14 |
| Ⓢ 13 | 12 | 3 | 1 | MRS. ROBINSON — Simon & Garfunkel (Simon, Garfunkel & Halee), Columbia 44511 | 11 |
| 14 | 8 | 7 | 7 | THINK — Aretha Franklin (Jerry Wexler), Atlantic 2518 | 8 |
| ★15 | 18 | 28 | 51 | INDIAN LAKE — Cowsills (Wes Ferrell), MGM 13944 | 6 |
| 16 | 16 | 14 | 18 | I LOVE YOU — People (Mikel Hunter), Capitol 2078 | 14 |
| ★17 | 19 | 31 | 53 | STONED SOUL PICNIC — 5th Dimension (Bones Howe), Soul City 766 | 6 |
| 18 | 14 | 17 | 17 | LICKING STICK — James Brown & the Famous Flames (James Brown), King 6166 | 7 |
| ★19 | 29 | 29 | 61 | D. W. WASHBURN — Monkees (Monkees), Colgems 66-1023 | 4 |
| 20 | 30 | 34 | 35 | NEVER GIVE YOU UP — Jerry Butler (Gamble-Huff), Mercury 72798 | 10 |
| 21 | 21 | 21 | 27 | HOW'D WE EVER GET THIS WAY? — Andy Kim (Jeff Barry), Steed 707 | 10 |
| 22 | 22 | 33 | 39 | SHE'S A HEARTBREAKER — Gene Pitney (Charlie Foxx), Musicor 1306 | 9 |
| ★23 | 37 | 76 | — | HURDY GURDY MAN — Donovan (Mickie Most), Epic 10345 | 3 |
| ★24 | 59 | 63 | 82 | HERE COMES THE JUDGE — Pigmeat Markham (Gene Barge), Chess 2049 | 4 |
| 25 | 25 | 25 | 25 | (You Keep Me) HANGING ON — Joe Simon (J.R. Enterprises), Sound Stage 7 2608 | 13 |
| 26 | 26 | 27 | 34 | CHOO CHOO TRAIN — Box Tops (Den Penn), Mala 12005 | 6 |
| 27 | 17 | 22 | 30 | TIP-TOE THRU THE TULIPS WITH ME — Tiny Tim (Richard Perry), Reprise 0679 | 8 |
| 28 | 24 | 18 | 9 | THE GOOD, THE BAD AND THE UGLY — Hugo Montenegro, His Ork and Chorus (Neely Plumb), RCA Victor 9423 | 21 |
| ★29 | 34 | 38 | 54 | SKY PILOT — Eric Burdon & the Animals (Tom Wilson), MGM 13939 | 6 |
| ★30 | 42 | 45 | 56 | SOME THINGS YOU NEVER GET USED TO — Diana Ross & Supremes (Ashford & Simpson), Motown 1126 | 5 |
| 31 | 32 | 47 | 47 | YESTER LOVE — Smokey Robinson & the Miracles ("Smokey"), Tamla 54167 | 6 |
| 32 | 33 | 44 | 55 | FOLSOM PRISON BLUES — Johnny Cash (Bob Johnston), Columbia 44513 Eric Burdon & the Animals | 7 |
| Ⓢ 33 | 28 | 9 | 6 | TIGHTEN UP — Archie Bell & the Drells (L.J.F. Production), Atlantic 2478 | 15 |
| 34 | 36 | 53 | 58 | PICTURES OF MATCHSTICK MEN — Status Quo (John Schroeder), Cadet Concept 7001 | 8 |
| 35 | 20 | 13 | 13 | I COULD NEVER LOVE ANOTHER (After Loving You) — Temptations (Norman Whitfield), Gordy 7072 | 10 |
| 36 | 23 | 23 | 11 | AIN'T NOTHING LIKE THE REAL THING — Marvin Gaye & Tammi Terrell (Ashford-Simpson), Tamla 54163 | 13 |
| ★37 | 46 | 95 | — | I'M A MIDNIGHT MOVER — Wilson Pickett (Tom Dowd), Atlantic 2528 | 3 |
| 38 | 40 | 40 | 40 | FACE IT GIRL, IT'S OVER — Nancy Wilson (David Cavanaugh), Capitol 2136 | 9 |
| ★39 | 58 | 59 | 60 | LOVER'S HOLIDAY — Peggy Scott & Jo Jo Benson (Huey P. Meaux), SSS International 736 | 5 |
| ★40 | 50 | 50 | 50 | IT SHOULD HAVE BEEN ME — Gladys Knight & the Pips (Norman Whitfield), Soul 35045 | 5 |
| 41 | 31 | 19 | 26 | A MAN WITHOUT LOVE (Quando M'Innamora) — Engelbert Humperdinck (Peter Sullivan), Parrot 40027 | 9 |
| ★42 | 60 | 77 | — | DON'T TAKE IT SO HARD — Paul Revere & The Raiders (Featuring Mark Lindsay) (Mark Lindsay), Columbia 4455 | 3 |
| ★43 | 45 | 56 | 95 | TURN AROUND, LOOK AT ME — Vogues (Dick Glasser), Reprise 0686 | 4 |
| ★44 | 90 | — | — | AUTUMN OF MY LIFE — Bobby Goldsboro (Bob Montgomery), United Artists 50318 | 2 |
| ★45 | 53 | 65 | 71 | ELEANOR RIGBY — Ray Charles (Joe Adams), ABC 11090 | 5 |
| 46 | 27 | 16 | 8 | BEAUTIFUL MORNING — Rascals (Rascals), Atlantic 2493 | 13 |
| ★47 | 89 | — | — | STAY IN MY CORNER — Dells (Bobby Miller), Cadet 5612 | 2 |
| 48 | 48 | 48 | 48 | YOU DON'T KNOW WHAT YOU MEAN TO ME — Sam & Dave (Isaac Hayes & David Porter), Atlantic 2517 | 7 |
| ★49 | 64 | 64 | 72 | HERE I AM BABY — Marvelettes ("Smokey"), Tamla 54166 | 5 |
| 50 | 39 | 39 | 41 | TIME FOR LIVIN' — Association (Bones Howe), Warner Bros.-Seven Arts 7195 | 8 |
| ★51 | 54 | 54 | 84 | IT'S NICE TO BE WITH YOU — Monkees (Monkees), Colgems 66-1023 | 4 |
| ★52 | — | — | — | SUNSHINE OF YOUR LOVE — Cream (Felix Pappalardi), Atco 6544 | 1 |
| 53 | 55 | 55 | 78 | SAFE IN MY GARDEN — Mamas & Papas (Lou Adler), Dunhill 4125 | 5 |
| 54 | 56 | 60 | 62 | HERE COMES THE JUDGE — Magistrates (Gross-Freda), MGM 13946 | 6 |
| ★55 | 70 | 93 | — | CLASSICAL GAS — Mason Williams (Mike Post), Warner-Bros.-Seven Arts 7190 | 3 |
| 56 | 47 | 46 | 46 | UNITED — Peaches & Herb (Gamble-Huff), Date 1603 | 8 |
| 57 | 57 | 69 | 76 | BACK IN LOVE AGAIN — Buckinghams (Jimmy "Wiz" Wisner), Columbia 44533 | 5 |
| ★58 | 63 | 71 | — | PEOPLE SURE ACT FUNNY — Arthur Conley (Tom Dowd), Atco 6588 | 3 |
| 59 | 52 | 61 | 64 | AMERICA IS MY HOME — James Brown & the Famous Flames (James Brown), King 6112 | 7 |
| 60 | 51 | 51 | 57 | BRING A LITTLE LOVIN' — Los Bravos (Alain Milhaud), Parrot 3020 | 7 |
| 61 | 62 | 62 | 81 | YOU SEND ME — Aretha Franklin (Jerry Wexler), Atlantic 2518 | 4 |
| ★62 | 66 | 67 | 90 | CAN'T YOU SEE ME CRY — New Colony Six (Sentar Records), Mercury 72817 | 4 |
| 63 | 68 | 72 | — | THE STORY OF ROCK AND ROLL — Turtles (Chip Douglas), White Whale 273 | 3 |
| ★64 | 98 | — | — | JOURNEY TO THE CENTER OF YOUR MIND — Amboy Dukes (Bob Shad), Mainstream 684 | 2 |
| 65 | 72 | 81 | 92 | BABY YOU COME ROLLIN' ACROSS MY MIND — Peppermint Trolley Company (Dan Dalton), Acta 815 | 5 |
| 66 | 69 | 80 | — | BE YOUNG, BE FOOLISH, BE HAPPY — Tams (Joe South), ABC 11066 | 3 |
| 67 | 67 | 68 | 75 | MOUNTAIN OF LOVE — Ronnie Dove (Phil Kahl), Diamond 244 | 5 |
| 68 | 65 | 66 | 70 | THE DOCTOR — Mary Wells (C. & M. Womack), Jubilee 5621 | 8 |
| 69 | 79 | 79 | 87 | UNDERSTANDING — Ray Charles (Joe Adams), ABC 11090 | 4 |
| ★70 | 82 | — | — | WITH PEN IN HAND — Billy Vera (Chip Taylor), Atlantic 2526 | 2 |
| 71 | 71 | 78 | 83 | LET ME BE LONELY — Dionne Warwick (Bacharach-David), Scepter 12216 | 5 |
| ★72 | 73 | — | — | HITCH IT TO THE HORSE — Fantastic Johnny C (Jesse Jmaes), Phil L.A. of Soul 315 | 2 |
| ★73 | — | — | — | DREAMS OF THE EVERYDAY HOUSEWIFE — Glen Campbell (Al de Lory), Capitol 2224 | 1 |
| 74 | 74 | 86 | 86 | HOLD ON — Radiants (Leonard Caston), Chess 2037 | 7 |
| 75 | 75 | 75 | 85 | SWEET MEMORIES — Andy Williams (Nick DeCaro), Columbia 44527 | 5 |
| 76 | 76 | 89 | — | D-I-V-O-R-C-E — Tammy Wynette (Billy Sherrill), Epic 10315 | 3 |
| ★77 | — | — | — | HELLO, I LOVE YOU, WON'T YOU TELL YOUR NAME — Doors (Paul Rothchild), Elektra 45635 | 1 |
| 78 | 78 | 84 | 97 | LISTEN HERE — Eddie Harris (Joel Dorn), Atlantic 2487 | 4 |
| ★79 | 91 | 97 | — | SEALED WITH A KISS — Gary Lewis & Playboys (Snuff Garrett), Liberty 56037 | 3 |
| 80 | 83 | 90 | — | (The Puppet Song) WHISKEY ON A SUNDAY — Irish Rovers (Charles Bud Dant), Decca 32333 | 3 |
| ★81 | 92 | 94 | 94 | LET YOURSELF GO — Elvis Presley (Douglas Laurence), RCA Victor 47-9547 | 4 |
| 82 | 85 | 92 | — | YOUR TIME HASN'T COME YET, BABY — Elvis Presley, RCA Victor 47-9547 | 3 |
| 83 | 84 | 85 | — | TURN ON YOUR LOVE LIGHT — Bill Black's Combo (Joe Cuoghi), Hi 2145 | 3 |
| ★84 | 100 | — | — | LOVIN' SEASON — Gene & Debbe (Don Gant), TRX 5010 | 2 |
| 85 | 86 | 96 | — | THE EYES OF A NEW YORK WOMAN — B.J. Thomas (Chips Moman), Scepter 12219 | 3 |
| 86 | 87 | — | — | HANG 'EM HIGH — Hugo Montenegro, His Orch. & Chorus (Joe Reisman), RCA Victor 47-9554 | 2 |
| 87 | 88 | 91 | — | YOUNG BOY — Barbara Greene, Renee 5001 | 3 |
| ★88 | — | — | — | ALICE LONG (You're Still My Favorite Girlfriend) — Tommy Boyce & Bobby Hart (Boyce & Hart), A&M 948 | 1 |
| 89 | 94 | — | — | DREAMS OF THE EVERYDAY HOUSEWIFE — Wayne Newton (Jim Vienneau), MGM 13955 | 2 |
| ★90 | 95 | — | — | LOOK OVER YOUR SHOULDER — O'Jays (George Kerr), Bell 704 | 2 |
| 91 | — | — | — | AMEN — Otis Redding (Steve Cropper), Atco 0592 | 1 |
| 92 | — | — | — | GEORGIA ON MY MIND — Wes Montgomery (Creed Taylor), A&M 940 | 1 |
| 93 | — | — | — | TO LOVE SOMEBODY — Sweet Inspirations (Tom Dowd), Atlantic 2529 | 1 |
| 94 | — | — | — | DREAM A LITTLE DREAM OF ME — Mama Cass with the Mamas & Papas (Lou Adler), Dunhill 4145 | 1 |
| 95 | — | — | — | WHAT'S MADE MILWAUKEE FAMOUS (Has Made a Loser Out of Me) — Jerry Lee Lewis (Jerry Kennedy), Smash 2164 | 1 |
| 96 | 97 | — | — | COMPETITION AIN'T NOTHIN' — Little Carl Carlton, Back Beat 588 | 2 |
| 97 | — | — | — | JUST A LITTLE BIT — Blue Cheer (Abe Kesh "Voco"), Philips 40541 | 1 |
| 98 | — | — | — | LITTLE GREEN APPLES — Patti Page (Costa), Columbia 44555 | 1 |
| 99 | — | — | — | (Love Is Like A) BASEBALL GAME — Intruders (Gamble Huff Prod.), Gamble 217 | 1 |
| 100 | — | — | — | SEND MY BABY BACK — Freddie Hughes (L. Hewitt), Wand 1182 | 1 |

## HOT 100—A TO Z—(Publisher-Licensee)

Ain't Nothing Like the Real Thing (Jobete, BMI).. 36
Alice Long (You're Still My Favorite Girlfriend) (Screen Gems-Columbia, BMI)... 88
Amen (East/Time/Redwal, BMI)... 91
America Is My Home (Dynatone, BMI)... 59
Angel of the Morning (Blackwood, BMI)... 7
Autumn of My Life (Unart, BMI)... 44
Baby You Come Rollin' Across My Mind (Bresnaban, BMI)... 65
Back in Love Again (Bucking-El, BMI)... 57
Be Young, Be Foolish, Be Happy (Low-Twi/Low-Sal, BMI)... 66
Beautiful Morning, A (Slacsar, BMI)... 46
Bring a Little Lovin' (Miller, ASCAP)... 60
Can't You See Me Cry (New Colony/T.M., BMI).. 62
Choo Choo Train (Ruler/Mulji, BMI)... 26
Classical Gas (Irving, BMI)... 55
Competition Ain't Nothin' (Don, BMI)... 96
D-I-V-O-R-C-E (Tree, BMI)... 76
Doctor, The (Welwom, BMI)... 68
Don't Take It So Hard (Boom, BMI)... 42
Dream a Little Dream of Me (Words & Music, Inc., ASCAP)... 94
Dreams of the Everyday Housewife (Glen Campbell) (Combine, BMI)... 73
Dreams of the Everyday Housewife (Wayne Newton) (Combine, BMI)... 89
D. W. Washburn (Screen Gems-Columbia, BMI)... 19
Eleanor Rigby (Maclen, BMI)... 45
Eyes of a New York Woman, The (Press, BMI)... 85
Face It Girl, It's Over (Morris, BMI)... 38
Folsom Prison Blues (Hilo, BMI)... 32
Georgia on My Mind (Peer Int'l, BMI)... 92
Good, the Bad and the Ugly, The (Unart, BMI)... 28
Grazing in the Grass (Chisa, BMI)... 5
Hang 'Em High (Unart, BMI)... 86
Hello, I Love You, Won't You Tell Your Name (Nipper, ASCAP)... 77
Here Comes the Judge (Shorty Long) (Jobete, BMI) 8
Here Comes the Judge (Magistrates) (Hastings/Sreeby, BMI)... 54
Here Comes the Judge (Pigmeat Markham) (Ara, BMI)... 24
Here I Am Baby (Jobete, BMI)... 49
Hitch It to the Horse (Dandelion/James Boy, BMI) 72
Hold On (Chevis, BMI)... 74
Horse, The (Dandelion/James Boy, BMI)... 2
How'd We Ever Get This Way (Unart, BMI)... 21
Hurdy Gurdy Man (Peer Int'l, BMI)... 23
I Could Never Love Another (Jobete, BMI)... 35
I Love You (Mainstay, BMI)... 16
I'm a Midnight Mover (Erva/Tracebob/Cotillion, BMI)... 37
Indian Lake (Pocket Full of Tunes, BMI)... 15
It Should Have Been Me (Jobete, BMI)... 40
It's Nice to Be With You (Screen Gems-Columbia, BMI)... 51
Journey to the Center of Your Mind (Brent, BMI) 64
Jumpin' Jack Flash (Gideon, BMI)... 3
Just a Little Bit (Blue Cheer, BMI)... 97
Lady Willpower (Viva, BMI)... 6
Let Me Be Lonely (Jac/Blue Seas, ASCAP)... 71
Let Yourself Go (Presley, BMI)... 81
Licking Stick (Toccoa/Lois, BMI)... 18
Listen Here (Hargrove, BMI)... 78
Little Green Apples (Russell-Cason, ASCAP)... 98
Look of Love, The (Colgems, ASCAP)... 4
Look Over Your Shoulder (Cinrick, BMI)... 90
(Love Is Like A) Baseball Game (Razor Sharp, BMI) 99
Lover's Holiday (Crazy Cajun, ASCAP)... 39
Lovin' Season (Acuff-Rose, BMI)... 84
MacArthur Park (Canopy, ASCAP)... 9
Man Without Love, A (Quando M'Innamora) (Leeds, ASCAP)... 41
Mony, Mony (Patricia, BMI)... 12
Mountain of Love (Wren, BMI)... 67
Mrs. Robinson (Charing Cross, BMI)... 13
My Shy Violet (Pincus, ASCAP)... 77
Never Give You Up (Parabut/Double Diamond/Downstairs, BMI)... 20
People Sure Act Funny (Bob-Dan, BMI)... 58
Pictures of Matchstick Men (Northern, ASCAP)... 34
(Puppet Song) Whiskey on a Sunday (Essex, ASCAP)... 80
Reach Out of the Darkness (Lowery, BMI)... 10
Safe in My Garden (Wingate/Honest John, ASCAP) 63
Sealed With a Kiss (Post, ASCAP)... 79
Send My Baby Back (Novice/Hackney, BMI)... 100
She's a Heartbreaker (Catalogue/Cee & Eye, BMI) 22
Sky Pilot (Slamina/Sea-Lark, BMI)... 29
Some Things You Never Get Used To (Jobete, BMI) 30
Stay in My Corner (Conrad, BMI)... 47
Stoned Soul Picnic (Tuna Fish, BMI)... 17
Story of Rock and Roll, The (Rock Music, BMI).. 63
Sunshine of Your Love (Dratleaf, BMI)... 52
Sweet Memories (Acuff-Rose, BMI)... 75
Think (14th Hour, BMI)... 14
This Guy's in Love With You (Blue Seas/Jac, ASCAP)... 1
Tighten Up (Cotillion/Orellia, BMI)... 33
Time for Livin' (Tamerlane, BMI)... 50
Tip-Toe Thru the Tulips With Me (Warner Bros.-Seven Arts/Witmark, ASCAP)... 27
To Love Somebody (Nemperor, BMI)... 93
Turn Around, Look at Me (Viva, BMI)... 43
Turn on Your Love Light (Don, BMI)... 83
Understanding (Metric, BMI)... 69
United (Razor Sharp, BMI)... 56
What's Made Milwaukee Famous (Has Made a Loser Out of Me) (Gallico, BMI)... 95
With Pen in Hand (Unart, BMI)... 70
Yester Love (Jobete, BMI)... 31
You Don't Know What You Mean to Me (East/Cotillion, BMI)... 48
(You Keep Me) Hangin' On (Garpax/Alambo, BMI).. 25
You Send Me (Kags, BMI)... 61
Young Boy (Conrad, BMI)... 87
Your Time Hasn't Come Yet, Baby (Presley, BMI).. 82
Yummy, Yummy, Yummy (T.M., BMI)... 11

## BUBBLING UNDER THE HOT 100

101. SNOOPY FOR PRESIDENT... Royal Guardsmen, Laurie 3451
102. SLIP AWAY... Clarence Carter, Atlantic 2508
103. SATURDAY'S FATHER... Four Seasons, Philips 40452
104. YOUNG BIRDS FLY... Cryan' Shames, Columbia 44545
105. NEVER GOIN' BACK... Lovin' Spoonful, Kama Sutra 250
106. TWO BIT MANCHILD... Neil Diamond, UNI 55075
107. ANYWAY YOU WANT ME... American Breed, Acta 827
108. BOY... Lulu, Epic 10346
109. YES SIR, THAT'S MY BABY... Julius Wechter & the Baja Marimba Band, A&M 937
110. MRS. BLUEBIRD... Eternity's Children, Tower 416
111. BORN TO BE WILD... Steppenwolf, Dunhill 4138
112. LIFE... Sly & the Family Stone, Epic 10353
113. PRAYER MEETIN'... Willie Mitchell, Hi 2147
114. BREAKING UP IS HARD TO DO... Happenings, B.T. Puppy 543
115. YOU GOT STYLE... Jon & Robin, Abnak 130
116. SOUL LIMBO... Booker T. & the M.G.'s, Stax 0001
117. I'VE NEVER FOUND A GIRL (To Love Me Like You Do)... Eddie Floyd, Stax 0002
118. WHO WILL ANSWER... Hesitations, Kapp 926
119. GIVE ME ONE MORE CHANCE... Wilmer Alexander & the Dukes, Aphrodisiac 260
120. SEALED WITH A KISS... Toys, Musicor 1319
121. YES SIR... Music Explosion, Laurie 3454
122. YOURS UNTIL TOMORROW... Vivian Reed, Epic 10319
123. MECHANICAL WORLD... Spirit, Ode 108
124. AND SUDDENLY... Cherry People, Heritage 801
125. I'M GONNA DO WHAT THEY DO TO ME... B.B. King, Bluesway 61018
126. WALK ON... Roy Orbison, MGM 13950
127. TUESDAY AFTERNOON... Moody Blues, Deram 85028
128. YOU CAN CRY IF YOU WANT TO... Troggs, Fontana 1622
129. ROCK AROUND THE CLOCK... Freddie Cannon, We Make Rock 'n Roll 1601
130. TAKE ME BACK... Frankie Laine, ABC 11097
131. WHAT A WONDERFUL WORLD... Louis Armstrong, ABC 10982
132. THE SNAKE... Al Wilson, Soul City 767
133. LIGHT MY FIRE... Jose Feliciano, RCA Victor 47-9550
134. I'LL BE YOUR BABY TONIGHT... Burl Ives, Columbia 44508

Compiled from national retail sales and radio station airplay by the Music Popularity Dept. of Record Market Research, Billboard.

HOT 100

# Billboard HOT 100
**For Week Ending July 13, 1968**

★ STAR PERFORMER—Sides registering greatest proportionate upward progress this week.
● Record Industry Association of America seal of certification as million selling single.

| This Week | Wk. Ago | 2 Wks. Ago | 3 Wks. Ago | TITLE, Artist (Producer), Label & Number | Weeks On Chart |
|---|---|---|---|---|---|
| 1 | 1 | 1 | | THIS GUY'S IN LOVE WITH YOU — Herb Alpert (Herb Alpert & Jerry Moss), A&M 929 | 9 |
| 2 | 2 | 2 | 15 | THE HORSE — Cliff Nobles & Co. (Jesse James), Phil L.A. of Soul 313 | 8 |
| ★3 | 3 | 11 | 12 | JUMPIN' JACK FLASH — Rolling Stones (Jimmy Miller), London 908 | 6 |
| 4 | 6 | 15 | 20 | LADY WILLPOWER — Gary Puckett & the Union Gap (Jerry Fuller), Columbia 44547 | 6 |
| 5 | 5 | 13 | 32 | GRAZING IN THE GRASS — Hugh Masekela (Stewart Levine), Uni 55066 | 6 |
| 6 | 4 | 5 | 5 | THE LOOK OF LOVE — Sergio Mendes & Brasil '66 (Herb Alpert), A&M 924 | 10 |
| 7 | 7 | 7 | 8 | ANGEL OF THE MORNING — Merrilee Rush (T. Cogbill & C. Moman), Bell 705 | 11 |
| ★8 | 17 | 19 | 31 | STONED SOUL PICNIC — 5th Dimension (Bones Howe), Soul City 766 | 7 |
| 9 | 8 | 9 | 11 | HERE COMES THE JUDGE — Shorty Long (Shorty Long & B.J.), Soul 35044 | 7 |
| 10 | 15 | 18 | 28 | INDIAN LAKE — Cowsills (Wes Ferrell), MGM 13944 | 7 |
| 11 | 10 | 10 | 10 | REACH OUT OF THE DARKNESS — Friend & Lover (Joe South & Bill Lowery), Verve Forecast 5069 | 9 |
| ★12 | 23 | 37 | 76 | HURDY GURDY MAN — Donovan (Mickie Most), Epic 10345 | 4 |
| 13 | 12 | 6 | 6 | MONY MONY — Tommy James & Shondells (Kasenetz-Katz Associates), Roulette 7008 | 15 |
| 14 | 9 | 3 | 2 | MacARTHUR PARK — Richard Harris (Jimmy Webb), Dunhill 4134 | 10 |
| ●15 | 11 | 4 | 4 | YUMMY, YUMMY, YUMMY — Ohio Express (Kasenetz-Katz Associates), Buddah 38 | 11 |
| ●16 | 13 | 12 | 3 | MRS. ROBINSON — Simon & Garfunkel (Simon, Garfunkel & Halee), Columbia 44511 | 12 |
| 17 | 16 | 16 | 14 | I LOVE YOU — People (Mikel Hunter), Capitol 2078 | 9 |
| 18 | 14 | 8 | 7 | THINK — Aretha Franklin (Jerry Wexler), Atlantic 2518 | 7 |
| 19 | 19 | 29 | 29 | D. W. WASHBURN — Monkees (Monkees), Colgems 66-1023 | 6 |
| 20 | 22 | 22 | 33 | SHE'S A HEARTBREAKER — Gene Pitney (Charlie Foxx), Musicor 1306 | 10 |
| ★21 | 43 | 45 | 56 | TURN AROUND, LOOK AT ME — Vogues (Dick Glasser), Reprise 0686 | 5 |
| ★22 | 77 | — | — | HELLO, I LOVE YOU, WON'T YOU TELL ME YOUR NAME — Doors (Paul Rothchild), Elektra 45635 | 2 |
| 23 | 20 | 30 | 34 | NEVER GIVE YOU UP — Jerry Butler (Gamble-Huff), Mercury 72798 | 11 |
| 24 | 24 | 59 | 63 | HERE COMES THE JUDGE — Pigmeat Markham (Gene Barge), Chess 2049 | 5 |
| 25 | 25 | 25 | 25 | (You Keep Me) HANGIN' ON — Joe Simon (J.R. Enterprises), Sound Stage 7 2608 | 14 |
| 26 | 26 | 26 | 27 | CHOO CHOO TRAIN — Box Tops (Dan Penn), Mala 12005 | 7 |
| 27 | 34 | 36 | 53 | PICTURES OF MATCHSTICK MEN — Status Quo (John Schroeder), Cadet Concept 7001 | 9 |
| ★28 | 29 | 34 | 38 | SKY PILOT — Eric Burdon & the Animals (Tom Wilson), MGM 13929 | 7 |
| 29 | 55 | 70 | 93 | CLASSICAL GAS — Mason Williams (Mike Post), Warner Bros.-Seven Arts 7190 | 4 |
| 30 | 30 | 42 | 45 | SOME THINGS YOU NEVER GET USED TO — Diana Ross & Supremes (Ashford & Simpson), Motown 1126 | 6 |
| 31 | 21 | 21 | 21 | HOW'D WE EVER GET THIS WAY? — Andy Kim (Jeff Barry), Steed 707 | 11 |
| 32 | 32 | 33 | 44 | FOLSOM PRISON BLUES — Johnny Cash (Bob Johnston), Columbia 44513 | 8 |
| 33 | 18 | 14 | 17 | LICKING STICK — James Brown & the Famous Flames (James Brown), King 6166 | 8 |
| 34 | 27 | 17 | 22 | TIP-TOE THRU THE TULIPS WITH ME — Tiny Tim (Richard Perry), Reprise 0679 | 9 |
| ★35 | 44 | 90 | — | AUTUMN OF MY LIFE — Bobby Goldsboro (Bob Montgomery), United Artists 50318 | 3 |
| 36 | 37 | 46 | 95 | I'M A MIDNIGHT MOVER — Wilson Pickett (Tom Dowd), Atlantic 2528 | 4 |
| 37 | 38 | 40 | 40 | FACE IT GIRL, IT'S OVER — Nancy Wilson (David Cavanaugh), Capitol 2136 | 10 |
| ★38 | 42 | 60 | 77 | DON'T TAKE IT SO HARD — Paul Revere & The Raiders (Featuring Mark Lindsay) (Mark Lindsay), Columbia 4455 | 4 |
| 39 | 39 | 58 | 59 | LOVER'S HOLIDAY — Peggy Scott & Jo Jo Benson (Huey P. Meaux), SSS International 736 | 6 |
| 40 | 31 | 32 | 47 | YESTER LOVE — Smokey Robinson and the Miracles ("Smokey"), Tamla 54167 | 7 |
| ★41 | 52 | — | — | SUNSHINE OF YOUR LOVE — Cream (Felix Pappalardi), Atco 6544 | 2 |
| 42 | 40 | 50 | 50 | IT SHOULD HAVE BEEN ME — Gladys Knight & the Pips (Norman Whitfield), Soul 35045 | 6 |
| 43 | 28 | 24 | 18 | THE GOOD, THE BAD AND THE UGLY — Hugo Montenegro, His Ork and Chorus (Neely Plumb), RCA Victor 9423 | 22 |
| 44 | 45 | 53 | 65 | ELEANOR RIGBY — Ray Charles (Joe Adams), ABC 11090 | 6 |
| ★45 | 73 | — | — | DREAMS OF THE EVERYDAY HOUSEWIFE — Glen Campbell (Al De Lory), Capitol 2224 | 2 |
| ★46 | 79 | 91 | 97 | SEALED WITH A KISS — Gary Lewis & Playboys (Snuff Garrett), Liberty 56037 | 3 |
| 47 | 47 | 89 | — | STAY IN MY CORNER — Dells (Bobby Miller), Cadet 5612 | 3 |
| 48 | 63 | 68 | 72 | THE STORY OF ROCK AND ROLL — Turtles (Chip Douglas), White Whale 273 | 4 |
| 49 | 49 | 64 | 64 | HERE I AM BABY — Marvelettes ("Smokey"), Tamla 54166 | 5 |
| 50 | 64 | 98 | — | JOURNEY TO THE CENTER OF YOUR MIND — Amboy Dukes (Bob Shad), Mainstream 684 | 3 |
| 51 | 51 | 54 | 54 | IT'S NICE TO BE WITH YOU — Monkees (Monkees), Colgems 66-1023 | 6 |
| 52 | 48 | 48 | 48 | YOU DON'T KNOW WHAT YOU MEAN TO ME — Sam & Dave (Isaac Hayes & David Porter), Atlantic 2517 | 8 |
| 53 | 94 | — | — | DREAM A LITTLE DREAM OF ME — Mama Cass with the Mamas & Papas (Lou Adler), Dunhill 4145 | 2 |
| 54 | 62 | 66 | 67 | CAN'T YOU SEE ME CRY — New Colony Six (Sentar Records), Mercury 72817 | 4 |
| 55 | 85 | 86 | 96 | THE EYES OF A NEW YORK WOMAN — B.J. Thomas (Chips Moman), Scepter 12219 | 4 |
| 56 | 61 | 62 | 62 | YOU SEND ME — Aretha Franklin (Jerry Wexler), Atlantic 2518 | 4 |
| 57 | 72 | 73 | — | HITCH IT TO THE HORSE — fantastic Johnny C (Jesse James), Phil L.A. of Soul 315 | 3 |
| 58 | 58 | 63 | 71 | PEOPLE SURE ACT FUNNY — Arthur Conley (Tom Dowd), Atco 6588 | 4 |
| 59 | 53 | 55 | 55 | SAFE IN MY GARDEN — Mamas & Papas (Lou Adler), Dunhill 4125 | 6 |
| 60 | 65 | 72 | 81 | BABY YOU COME ROLLIN' ACROSS MY MIND — Peppermint Trolley Company (Dan Dalton), Acta 815 | 6 |
| 61 | 54 | 56 | 60 | HERE COMES THE JUDGE — Magistrates (Gross-Freda), MGM 13946 | 5 |
| 62 | 91 | — | — | AMEN — Otis Redding (Steve Cropper), Atco 0592 | 2 |
| 63 | 70 | 82 | — | WITH PEN IN HAND — Billy Vera (Chip Taylor), Atlantic 2526 | 3 |
| 64 | 76 | 76 | 89 | D-I-V-O-R-C-E — Tammy Wynette (Billy Sherrill), Epic 10315 | 4 |
| 65 | 66 | 69 | 80 | BE YOUNG, BE FOOLISH, BE HAPPY — Tams (Joe South), ABC 11066 | 6 |
| ★66 | 88 | — | — | ALICE LONG (You're Still My Favorite Girlfriend) — Tommy Boyce & Bobby Hart (Boyce & Hart), A&M 948 | 2 |
| 67 | 67 | 67 | 68 | MOUNTAIN OF LOVE — Ronnie Dove (Phil Kahl), Diamond 244 | 6 |
| 68 | 57 | 57 | 69 | BACK IN LOVE AGAIN — Buckinghams (Jimmy "Wiz" Wisner), Columbia 44533 | 6 |
| 69 | 69 | 79 | 79 | UNDERSTANDING — Ray Charles (Joe Adams), ABC 11090 | 5 |
| ★70 | — | — | — | BORN TO BE WILD — Steppenwolf (Gabriel Mekler), Dunhill 4138 | 1 |
| ★71 | 81 | 92 | 94 | LET YOURSELF GO — Elvis Presley (Douglas Laurence), RCA Victor 47-9547 | 5 |
| 72 | 82 | 85 | 92 | YOUR TIME HASN'T COME YET, BABY — Elvis Presley, RCA Victor 47-9547 | 4 |
| 73 | — | — | — | (You Keep Me) HANGIN' ON — Vanilla Fudge (Shadow Morton), Atco 6495 | 7 |
| 74 | 74 | 74 | 86 | HOLD ON — Radiants (Leonard Caston), Chess 2037 | 8 |
| 75 | 80 | 83 | 90 | (The Puppet Song) WHISKEY ON A SUNDAY — Irish Rovers (Charles Bud Dant), Decca 32333 | 4 |
| ★76 | 89 | 94 | — | DREAMS OF THE EVERYDAY HOUSEWIFE — Wayne Newton (Jim Vienneau), MGM 13955 | 3 |
| 77 | — | — | — | THE IMPOSSIBLE DREAM — Roger Williams (Hy Grill), Kapp 907 | 1 |
| ★78 | 99 | — | — | (Love Is Like A) BASEBALL GAME — Intruders (Gamble Huff Prod.), Gamble 217 | 2 |
| 79 | 75 | 75 | 75 | SWEET MEMORIES — Andy Williams (Nick DeCaro), Columbia 44527 | 6 |
| 80 | 78 | 78 | 84 | LISTEN HERE — Eddie Harris (Joel Dorn), Atlantic 2487 | 5 |
| 81 | 84 | 100 | — | LOVIN' SEASON — Gene & Debbe (Don Gant), TRX 5010 | 3 |
| 82 | 86 | 87 | — | HANG 'EM HIGH — Hugo Montenegro, His Orch. & Chorus (Joe Reisman), RCA Victor 47-9554 | 3 |
| 83 | 83 | 84 | 85 | TURN ON YOUR LOVE LIGHT — Bill Black's Combo (Joe Cuoghi), Hi 2145 | 4 |
| ★84 | — | — | — | SOUL LIMBO — Booker T. & the M.G.'s (Booker T. Jones), Stax 0001 | 1 |
| 85 | 96 | 97 | — | COMPETITION AIN'T NOTHIN' — Little Carl Carlton, Back Beat 588 | 3 |
| 86 | — | — | — | PRAYER MEETIN' — Willie Mitchell (Joe Cuoghi), Hi 2147 | 1 |
| 87 | 87 | 88 | 91 | YOUNG BOY — Barbara Greene, Renee 5001 | 4 |
| 88 | — | — | — | HARD TO HANDLE — Otis Redding (Steve Cropper), Atco 6592 | 1 |
| 89 | — | — | — | SNOOPY FOR PRESIDENT — Royal Guardsmen (Phil Gernhard), Laurie 3451 | 1 |
| 90 | 90 | 95 | — | LOOK OVER YOUR SHOULDER — O'Jays (George Kerr), Bell 704 | 3 |
| 91 | 93 | — | — | TO LOVE SOMEBODY — Sweet Inspirations (Tom Dowd), Atlantic 2529 | 2 |
| 92 | 92 | — | — | GEORGIA ON MY MIND — Wes Montgomery (Creed Taylor), A&M 940 | 2 |
| 93 | 97 | — | — | JUST A LITTLE BIT — Blue Cheer (Abe Kesh "Voco"), Philips 40541 | 2 |
| 94 | — | — | — | MRS. BLUEBIRD — Eternity's Children (Curt Boettcher & Keith Olsen), Tower 416 | 1 |
| 95 | — | — | — | WHAT'S MADE MILWAUKEE FAMOUS (Has Made a Loser Out of Me) — Jerry Lee Lewis (Jerry Kennedy), Smash 2164 | 1 |
| 96 | 98 | — | — | LITTLE GREEN APPLES — Patti Page (Costa), Columbia 44556 | 2 |
| 97 | — | — | — | SLIP AWAY — Clarence Carter (Rick Hall & Staff), Atlantic 2508 | 1 |
| 98 | — | — | — | LOVE MAKES A WOMAN — Barbara Acklin (Carl Davis & Eugene Record), Brunswick 55379 | 1 |
| 99 | — | — | — | TWO-BIT MANCHILD — Neil Diamond (Tom Catalano & Neil Diamond), Uni 55075 | 1 |
| 100 | 100 | — | — | SEND MY BABY BACK — Freddie Hughes (L. Hewitt), Wand 1182 | 2 |

## BUBBLING UNDER THE HOT 100

101. TUESDAY AFTERNOON ... Moody Blues, Deram 85028
102. NEVER GOING BACK ... Lovin' Spoonful, Kama Sutra 250
103. SATURDAY'S FATHER ... 4 Seasons, Philips 40452
104. ANYWAY THAT YOU WANT ME ... American Breed, Acta 327
105. SOMEBODY CARES ... Tommy James & Shondells, Roulette 7016
106. YOU MET YOUR MATCH ... Stevie Wonder, Tamla 54163
107. PEOPLE GOT TO BE FREE ... Rascals, Atlantic 2537
108. HALFWAY TO PARADISE ... Bobby Vinton, Epic 10350
109. I LOVED AND LOST ... Impressions, ABC 11103
110. 1-2-3 RED LIGHT ... 1910 Fruitgum Co., Buddah 54
111. I'VE NEVER FOUND A GIRL (To Love Me Like You Do) ... Eddie Floyd, Stax 0002
112. LIFE ... Sly and Family Stone, Epic 10353
113. BREAKING UP IS HARD TO DO ... Happenings, B.T. Puppy 543
114. YOU GOT STYLE ... Jon & Robin, Abnak 127
115. YOURS UNTIL TOMORROW ... Gene Pitney, Musicor 1036
116. I'M GONNA DO WHAT THEY DO TO ME ... B.B. King, Bluesway 61018
117. WHO WILL ANSWER ... Hesitations, Kapp 926
118. GIVE ME ONE MORE CHANCE ... Wilmer Alexander & the Dukes, Aphrodisiac 260
119. SEALED WITH A KISS ... Toys, Musicor 1319
120. YES SIR ... Music Explosion, Laurie 3454
121. WALK ON ... Roy Orbison, MGM 13950
122. AND SUDDENLY ... Cherry People, Heritage 801
123. MR. BOJANGLES ... Jerry Jeff Walker, Atco 6594
124. SOUL MEETING ... Soul Clan, Atlantic 2537
125. THIS WHEEL'S ON FIRE ... Julie Driscoll, Brian Auger & Trinity, Atlantic 6593
126. MR. BOJANGLES ... Bobby Cole, Date 1613
127. YOU CAN CRY IF YOU WANT TO ... Troggs, Fontana 1622
128. WHAT A WONDERFUL WORLD ... Louis Armstrong, ABC 10982
129. TAKE ME BACK ... Frankie Laine, ABC 11097
130. MY NAME IS JACK ... Manfred Mann, Mercury 72822
131. YESTERDAYS DREAMS ... Four Tops, Motown 1127
132. LIGHT MY FIRE ... Jose Feliciano, RCA Victor 47-9550
133. ALL FOR YOUR BABY TONIGHT ... Bari Lou, Columbia 44508
134. DOWN IN TENNESSEE ... Kasenetz-Katz Singing Orchestral Circus, Buddah 52
135. I GET THE SWEETEST FEELING ... Jackie Wilson, Brunswick 55381

Compiled from national retail sales and radio station airplay by the Music Popularity Dept. of Record Market Research, Billboard.

# Billboard HOT 100

FOR WEEK ENDING JULY 20, 1968

★ STAR PERFORMER—Sides registering greatest proportionate upward progress this week.

(Seal) Record Industry Association of America seal of certification as million selling single.

| This Week | 1 Wk. Ago | 2 Wks. Ago | 3 Wks. Ago | TITLE Artist (Producer), Label & Number | Weeks On Chart |
|---|---|---|---|---|---|
| Billboard Award (1) | 5 | 5 | 13 | GRAZING IN THE GRASS — Hugh Masekela (Stewart Levine), Uni 55066 | 7 |
| 2 | 4 | 6 | 15 | LADY WILLPOWER — Gary Puckett & the Union Gap (Jerry Fuller), Columbia 44547 | 7 |
| 3 | 3 | 3 | 11 | JUMPIN' JACK FLASH — Rolling Stones (Jimmy Miller), London 908 | 7 |
| 4 | 1 | 1 | 1 | THIS GUY'S IN LOVE WITH YOU — Herb Alpert (Herb Alpert & Jerry Moss), A&M 929 | 10 |
| 5 | 2 | 2 | 2 | THE HORSE — Cliff Nobles & Co. (Jesse James), Phil L. A. of Soul 313 | 9 |
| 6 | 8 | 17 | 19 | STONED SOUL PICNIC — 5th Dimension (Bones Howe), Soul City 766 | 8 |
| ★7 | 12 | 23 | 37 | HURDY GURDY MAN — Donovan (Mickie Most), Epic 10345 | 5 |
| ★8 | 29 | 55 | 70 | CLASSICAL GAS — Mason Williams (Mike Post), Warner-Bros.-Seven Arts 7190 | 5 |
| ★9 | 22 | 77 | — | HELLO, I LOVE YOU — Doors (Paul Rothchild), Elektra 45635 | 3 |
| 10 | 10 | 15 | 18 | INDIAN LAKE — Cowsills (Wes Ferrell), MGM 13944 | 8 |
| 11 | 11 | 10 | 10 | REACH OUT OF THE DARKNESS — Friend & Lover (Joe South & Bill Lowery), Verve Forecast 5069 | 10 |
| 12 | 9 | 8 | 9 | HERE COMES THE JUDGE — Shorty Long (Shorty Long & B.J.), Soul 35044 | 8 |
| 13 | 7 | 7 | 7 | ANGEL IN THE MORNING — Merrilee Rush (T. Cogbill & C. Moman), Bell 705 | 12 |
| ★14 | 21 | 43 | 45 | TURN AROUND, LOOK AT ME — Vogues (Dick Glasser), Reprise 0686 | 6 |
| 15 | 6 | 4 | 5 | THE LOOK OF LOVE — Sergio Mendes & Brasil '66 (Herb Alpert), A&M 924 | 11 |
| 16 | 20 | 22 | 22 | SHE'S A HEARTBREAKER — Gene Pitney (Charlie Foxx), Musicor 1306 | 11 |
| 17 | 14 | 9 | 3 | MacARTHUR PARK — Richard Harris (Jimmy Webb), Dunhill 4134 | 11 |
| 18 (Seal) | 15 | 11 | 4 | YUMMY, YUMMY, YUMMY — Ohio Express (Kasenetz-Katz Associates), Buddah 38 | 12 |
| 19 | 17 | 16 | 16 | I LOVE YOU — People (Mikel Hunter), Capitol 2078 | 16 |
| 20 | 28 | 29 | 34 | SKY PILOT — Eric Burdon & the Animals (Tom Wilson), MGM 13939 | 8 |
| 21 | 27 | 34 | 36 | PICTURES OF MATCHSTICK MEN — Status Quo (John Schroeder), Cadet Concept 7001 | 10 |
| ★22 | 41 | 52 | — | SUNSHINE OF YOUR LOVE — Cream (Felix Pappalardi), Atco 6544 | 3 |
| 23 | 24 | 24 | 59 | HERE COMES THE JUDGE — Pigmeat Markham (Gene Barge), Chess 2049 | 6 |
| 24 | 13 | 12 | 6 | MONY MONY — Tommy James & Shondells (Kasenetz-Katz Associates), Roulette 7008 | 16 |
| 25 | 23 | 20 | 30 | NEVER GIVE YOU UP — Jerry Butler (Gamble-Huff), Mercury 72798 | 12 |
| 26 | 35 | 44 | 90 | AUTUMN OF MY LIFE — Bobby Goldsboro (Bob Montgomery), United Artists 50318 | 4 |
| 27 | 18 | 14 | 8 | THINK — Aretha Franklin (Jerry Wexler), Atlantic 2518 | 10 |
| 28 | 36 | 37 | 46 | I'M A MIDNIGHT MOVER — Wilson Pickett (Tom Dowd), Atlantic 2528 | 5 |
| 29 (Seal) | 16 | 13 | 12 | MRS. ROBINSON — Simon & Garfunkel (Simon, Garfunkel & Halee), Columbia 44511 | 13 |
| 30 | 30 | 30 | 42 | SOME THINGS YOU NEVER GET USED TO — Diana Ross & Supremes (Ashford & Simpson), Motown 1126 | 7 |
| 31 | 19 | 19 | 29 | D. W. WASHBURN — Monkees (Monkees), Colgems 66-1023 | 6 |
| 32 | 32 | 32 | 33 | FOLSOM PRISON BLUES — Johnny Cash (Bob Johnston), Columbia 44513 Eric Burdon & the Animals | 9 |
| ★33 | 39 | 39 | 58 | LOVER'S HOLIDAY — Peggy Scott & Jo Jo Benson (Huey P. Meaux), SSS International 736 | 7 |
| 34 | 38 | 42 | 60 | DON'T TAKE IT SO HARD — Paul Revere & The Raiders (Featuring Mark Lindsay) (Mark Lindsay), Columbia 44555 | 5 |
| 35 | 25 | 25 | 25 | (You Keep Me) HANGING ON — Joe Simon (J.R. Enterprises), Sound Stage 7 2608 | 15 |
| ★36 | 47 | 47 | 89 | STAY IN MY CORNER — Dells (Bobby Miller), Cadet 5612 | 4 |
| 37 | 37 | 38 | 40 | FACE IT GIRL, IT'S OVER — Nancy Wilson (David Cavanaugh), Capitol 2136 | 11 |
| 38 | 31 | 21 | 21 | HOW'D WE EVER GET THIS WAY? — Andy Kim (Jeff Barry), Steed 707 | 12 |
| ★39 | 70 | — | — | BORN TO BE WILD — Steppenwolf (Gabriel Mekler), Dunhill 4138 | 2 |
| 40 | 44 | 45 | 53 | ELEANOR RIGBY — Ray Charles (Joe Adams), ABC 11090 | 7 |
| ★41 | 53 | 94 | — | DREAM A LITTLE DREAM OF ME — Mama Cass with the Mamas & Papas (Lou Adler), Dunhill 4145 | 3 |
| 42 | 26 | 26 | 26 | CHOO CHOO TRAIN — Box Tops (Den Penn), Mala 12005 | 8 |
| ★43 | 63 | 70 | 82 | WITH PEN IN HAND — Billy Vera (Chip Taylor), Atlantic 2526 | 4 |
| ★44 | 62 | 91 | — | AMEN — Otis Redding (Steve Cropper), Atco 0592 | 3 |
| 45 | 45 | 73 | — | DREAMS OF THE EVERYDAY HOUSEWIFE — Glen Campbell (Al de Lory), Capitol 2224 | 3 |
| 46 | 46 | 79 | 91 | SEALED WITH A KISS — Gary Lewis & Playboys (Snuff Garrett), Liberty 56037 | 5 |
| 47 | 50 | 64 | 98 | JOURNEY TO THE CENTER OF YOUR MIND — Amboy Dukes (Bob Shad), Mainstream 684 | 4 |
| 48 | 48 | 63 | 68 | THE STORY OF ROCK AND ROLL — Turtles (Chip Douglas), White Whale 273 | 5 |
| 49 | 49 | 49 | 64 | HERE I AM BABY — Marvelettes ("Smokey"), Tamla 54166 | 7 |
| 50 | 42 | 40 | 50 | IT SHOULD HAVE BEEN ME — Gladys Knight & the Pips (Norman Whitfield), Soul 35045 | 7 |
| 51 | 51 | 51 | 54 | IT'S NICE TO BE WITH YOU — Monkees (Monkees), Colgems 66-1023 | 6 |
| ★52 | 84 | — | — | SOUL LIMBO — Booker T. & the M.G.'s (Booker T. Jones), Stax 0001 | 2 |
| 53 | 57 | 72 | 73 | HITCH IT TO THE HORSE — Fantastic Johnny C (Jesse James), Phil L.A. of Soul 315 | 4 |
| 54 | 54 | 62 | 66 | CAN'T YOU SEE ME CRY — New Colony Six (Sentar Records), Mercury 72817 | 6 |
| 55 | 55 | 85 | 86 | THE EYES OF A NEW YORK WOMAN — B.J. Thomas (Chips Moman), Scepter 12219 | 5 |
| ★56 | 73 | — | — | (You Keep Me) HANGIN' ON — Vanilla Fudge (Shadow Morton), Atco 6495 | 8 |
| 57 | 40 | 31 | 32 | YESTER LOVE — Smokey Robinson & the Miracles ("Smokey"), Tamla 54167 | 8 |
| 58 | 58 | 58 | 63 | PEOPLE SURE ACT FUNNY — Arthur Conley (Tom Dowd), Atco 6588 | 5 |
| ★59 | 66 | 88 | — | ALICE LONG (You're Still My Favorite Girlfriend) — Tommy Boyce & Bobby Hart (Boyce & Hart), A&M 948 | 3 |
| 60 | 60 | 65 | 72 | BABY YOU COME ROLLIN' ACROSS MY MIND — Peppermint Trolley Company (Dan Dalton), Acta 815 | 7 |
| 61 | 65 | 66 | 69 | BE YOUNG, BE FOOLISH, BE HAPPY — Tams (Joe South), ABC 11066 | 5 |
| ★62 | 86 | — | — | PRAYER MEETIN' — Willie Mitchell (Joe Coughi), Hi 2147 | 2 |
| 63 | 64 | 76 | 76 | D-I-V-O-R-C-E- — Tammy Wynette (Billy Sherrill), Epic 10315 | 5 |
| ★64 | — | — | — | PEOPLE GOT TO BE FREE — Rascals (Rascals), Atlantic 2537 | 1 |
| ★65 | — | — | — | HALFWAY TO PARADISE — Bobby Vinton (Billy Sherrill), Epic 10350 | 1 |
| 66 | 69 | 69 | 79 | UNDERSTANDING — Ray Charles (Joe Adams), ABC 11090 | 6 |
| 67 | 56 | 61 | 62 | YOU SEND ME — Aretha Franklin (Jerry Wexler), Atlantic 2518 | 6 |
| 68 | 74 | 74 | 74 | HOLD ON — Radiants (Leonard Caston), Chess 2037 | 9 |
| ★69 | 77 | — | — | THE IMPOSSIBLE DREAM — Roger Williams (Hy Grill), Kapp 907 | 2 |
| ★70 | 78 | 99 | — | (Love Is Like A) BASEBALL GAME — Intruders (Gamble Huff Prod.), Gamble 217 | 3 |
| ★71 | 98 | — | — | LOVE MAKES A WOMAN — Barbara Acklin (Carl Davis & Eugene Record), Brunswick 55379 | 2 |
| 72 | 72 | 82 | 85 | YOUR TIME HASN'T COME YET, BABY — Elvis Presley, RCA Victor 47-9547 | 5 |
| ★73 | — | — | — | YOU MET YOUR MATCH — Stevie Wonder (Don Hunter), Tamla 54168 | 1 |
| ★74 | 91 | 93 | — | TO LOVE SOMEBODY — Sweet Inspirations (Tom Dowd), Atlantic 2529 | 3 |
| 75 | 75 | 80 | 83 | (The Puppet Song) WHISKEY ON A SUNDAY — Irish Rovers (Charles Bud Dant), Decca 32333 | 5 |
| 76 | 76 | 89 | 94 | DREAMS OF THE EVERYDAY HOUSEWIFE — Wayne Newton (Jim Vienneau), MGM 13955 | 4 |
| ★77 | 99 | — | — | TWO-BIT MANCHILD — Neil Diamond (Tom Catalano & Neil Diamond), Uni 55075 | 2 |
| ★78 | — | — | — | I CAN'T STOP DANCING — Archie Bell & the Drells (Gamble-Huff), Atlantic 2534 | 1 |
| ★79 | 88 | — | — | HARD TO HANDLE — Otis Redding (Steve Cropper), Atco 6592 | 2 |
| ★80 | 94 | — | — | MRS. BLUEBIRD — Eternity's Children (Curt Boettcher & Keith Olsen), Tower 416 | 2 |
| 81 | 81 | 84 | 100 | LOVIN' SEASON — Gene & Debbe (Don Gant), TRX 5010 | 4 |
| 82 | 82 | 86 | 87 | HANG 'EM HIGH — Hugo Montenegro, His Orch. & Chorus (Joe Reisman), RCA Victor 47-9554 | 4 |
| 83 | 83 | 83 | 84 | TURN ON YOUR LOVE LIGHT — Bill Black's Combo (Joe Cuoghi), Hi 2145 | 5 |
| 84 | 85 | 96 | 97 | COMPETITION AIN'T NOTHIN' — Little Carl Carlton, Back Beat 588 | 4 |
| ★85 | 89 | — | — | SNOOPY FOR PRESIDENT — Royal Guardsmen (Phil Gernhard), Laurie 3451 | 2 |
| 86 | 87 | 87 | 88 | YOUNG BOY — Barbara Greene, Renee 5001 | 5 |
| ★87 | — | — | — | GOD BLESS OUR LOVE — Ballads (Jesse Mason & Willie Hutch), Venture 615 | 1 |
| ★88 | — | — | — | DON'T GIVE UP — Petula Clark (Tony Hatch), Warner Bros.-Seven Arts 7216 | 1 |
| 89 | 90 | 90 | 95 | LOOK OVER YOUR SHOULDER — O'Jays (George Kerr), Bell 704 | 4 |
| ★90 | — | — | — | I GET THE SWEETEST FEELING — Jackie Wilson (Carl Davis), Brunswick 55381 | 1 |
| 91 | 92 | 92 | — | GEORGIA ON MY MIND — Wes Montgomery (Creed Taylor), A&M 940 | 3 |
| 92 | 93 | 97 | — | JUST A LITTLE BIT — Blue Cheer (Abe Kesh "Voco"), Philips 40541 | 3 |
| 93 | 97 | — | — | SLIP AWAY — Clarence Carter (Rick Hall & Staff), Atlantic 2508 | 2 |
| 94 | 95 | 95 | — | WHAT'S MADE MILWAUKEE FAMOUS (Has Made a Loser Out of Me) — Jerry Lee Lewis (Jerry Kennedy), Smash 2164 | 3 |
| 95 | — | — | — | AND SUDDENLY — Cherry People (Ron Haffikine & Barry Oslander), Heritage 801 | 1 |
| 96 | — | — | — | YESTERDAY'S DREAMS — Four Tops (Ivy Hunter), Motown 1127 | 1 |
| 97 | — | — | — | I LOVED AND I LOST — Impressions (Johnny Pate), ABC 11103 | 1 |
| 98 | — | — | — | TUESDAY AFTERNOON (Forever Afternoon) — Moody Blues (Tony Clarke), Deram 85028 | 1 |
| 99 | 100 | 100 | — | SEND MY BABY BACK — Freddie Hughes (L. Hewitt), Wand 1182 | 3 |
| 100 | — | — | — | GIVE ME ONE MORE CHANCE — Wilmer Alexander Jr. & the Dukes (Dukes), Aphrodisiac 260 | 1 |

## HOT 100—A TO Z—(Publisher-Licensee)


Alice Long (You're Still My Favorite Girlfriend) (Screen Gems-Columbia, BMI) 59
Amen (East/Time/Redwal, BMI) 44
And Suddenly (Lazy Day, BMI) 95
Angel of the Morning (Blackwood, BMI) 13
Autumn of My Life (Unart, BMI) 26
Baby You Come Rollin' Across My Mind (Bresnaban, BMI) 60
Be Young, Be Foolish, Be Happy (Low-Twi/Low-Sal, BMI) 61
Born to Be Wild (Duchess, BMI) 39
Can't You See Me Cry (New Colony/T.M., BMI) 54
Choo Choo Train (Ruter/Mulji, BMI) 42
Classical Gas (Irving, BMI) 8
Competition Ain't Nothin' (Don, BMI) 84
D-I-V-O-R-C-E (Tree, BMI) 63
Don't Give Up (Duchess, BMI) 88
Don't Take It So Hard (Boom, BMI) 34
Dream a Little Dream of Me (Words & Music, Inc., ASCAP) 41
Dreams of the Everyday Housewife (Glen Campbell) (Combine, BMI) 45
Dreams of the Everyday Housewife (Wayne Newton) (Combine, BMI) 76
D. W. Washburn (Screen Gems-Columbia, BMI) 31
Eleanor Rigby (Maclen, BMI) 40
Eyes of a New York Woman, The (Press, BMI) 55
Face It Girl, It's Over (Morris, BMI) 37
Folsom Prison Blues (Hilo, BMI) 32
Georgia on My Mind (Peer Int'l, BMI) 91
Give Me One More Chance (Tupper, BMI) 100
God Bless Our Love (Jalynne, BMI) 87
Grazing in the Grass (Chisa, BMI) 1
Halfway to Paradise (Screen Gems-Columbia, BMI) 65
Hang 'Em High (Unart, BMI) 82
Hard to Handle (East/Time/Redwal, BMI) 79
Hello, I Love You (Nipper, ASCAP) 9
Here Comes the Judge (Pigmeat Markham) (Ara, BMI) 23
Here Comes the Judge (Shorty Long) (Jobete, BMI) 12
Here I Am Baby (Jobete, BMI) 49
Hitch It to the Horse (Dandelion/James Boy, BMI) 53
Hold On (Chevis, BMI) 68
Horse, The (Dandelion/James Boy, BMI) 5
How'd We Ever Get This Way (Unart, BMI) 38
Hurdy Gurdy Man (Peer Int'l, BMI) 7
I Can't Stop Dancing (Downstairs/Double Diamond, BMI) 78
I Get the Sweetest Feeling (T.M./McCoy, BMI) 90
I Love You (Mainstay, BMI) 19
I Loved and I Lost (Chi-Sound, BMI) 97
I'm a Midnight Mover (Erva/Tracebob/Cotillion, BMI) 28
Impossible Dream, The (Fox, ASCAP) 69
Indian Lake (Pocket Full of Tunes, BMI) 10
It Should Have Been Me (Jobete, BMI) 50
It's Nice to Be With You (Screen Gems-Columbia, BMI) 51
Journey to the Center of Your Mind (Brent, BMI) 47
Jumpin' Jack Flash (Gideon, BMI) 3
Just a Little Bit (Blue Cheer, BMI) 92
Lady Willpower (Viva, BMI) 2
Look of Love, The (Colgems, ASCAP) 15
Look Over Your Shoulder (Cinrick, BMI) 89
(Love Is Like A) Baseball Game (Razor Sharp, BMI) 70
Love Makes a Woman (Jalynne/BRC, BMI) 71
Lover's Holiday (Crazy Cajun, ASCAP) 33
Lovin' Season (Acuff-Rose, BMI) 81
MacArthur Park (Canopy, ASCAP) 17
Mony, Mony (Patricia, BMI) 24
Mrs. Bluebird (Crocked Foxx, ASCAP) 80
Mrs. Robinson (Charing Cross, BMI) 29
Never Give You Up (Parabut/Double Diamond/Downstairs, BMI) 25
People Got to Be Free (Slacsar, BMI) 64
People Sure Act Funny (Bob-Dan, BMI) 58
Pictures of Matchstick Men (Northern, ASCAP) 21
Prayer Meetin' (Edroy, BMI) 62
(Puppet Song) Whiskey on a Sunday (Essex, ASCAP) 75
Reach Out of the Darkness (Lowery, BMI) 11
Sealed With a Kiss (Post, ASCAP) 40
Send My Baby Back (Novice/Hackney, BMI) 99
She's a Heartbreaker (Catalogue/Cee & Eye, BMI) 16
Sky Pilot (Slamina/Sea-Lark, BMI) 20
Slip Away (Fame, BMI) 93
Snoopy for President (Roenique, BMI) 85
Some Things You Never Get Used To (Jobete, BMI) 30
Soul Limbo (East, BMI) 52
Stay in My Corner (Conrad, BMI) 36
Stoned Soul Picnic (Tuna Fish, BMI) 6
Story of Rock and Roll, The (Rock Music, BMI) 48
Sunshine of Your Love (Dratleaf, BMI) 22
Think (14th Hour, BMI) 27
This Guy's in Love With You (Blue Seas/Jac, ASCAP) 4
To Love Somebody (Nemperor, BMI) 74
Tuesday Afternoon (Forever Afternoon) (Essex, ASCAP) 98
Turn Around, Look at Me (Viva, BMI) 14
Turn on Your Love Light (Don, BMI) 83
Two-Bit Manchild (Stonebridge, BMI) 77
Understanding (Metric, BMI) 66
What's Made Milwaukee Famous (Has Made a Loser Out of Me) (Gallico, BMI) 94
With Pen in Hand (Unart, BMI) 43
Yesterday's Dreams (Jobete, BMI) 96
Yester Love (Jobete, BMI) 57
(You Keep Me) Hangin' On (Joe Simon) (Garpax/Alambo, BMI) 35
(You Keep Me) Hangin' On (Vanilla Fudge) (Jobete, BMI) 56
You Met Your Match (Jobete, BMI) 73
You Send Me (Kags, BMI) 67
Young Boy (Conrad, BMI) 86
Your Time Hasn't Come Yet, Baby (Presley, BMI) 72
Yummy, Yummy, Yummy (T.M., BMI) 18


## BUBBLING UNDER THE HOT 100

101. NEVER GOING BACK — Lovin' Spoonful, Kama Sutra 250
102. ANYWAY THAT YOU WANT ME — American Breed, Acta 327
103. SOMEBODY CARES — Tommy James & Shondells, Roulette 7216
104. 1-2-3 RED LIGHT — 1910 Fruitgum Co., Buddah 54
105. LIFE — Sly & Family Stone, Epic 10353
106. BREAKING UP IS HARD TO DO — Happenings, B.T. Puppy 543
107. MR. BOJANGLES — Jerry Jeff Walker, Atco 6594
108. I GUESS I'LL HAVE TO CRY CRY CRY — James Brown & His Famous Flames, King 6141
109. HAPPY — Nancy Sinatra, Reprise 0756
110. I'VE NEVER FOUND A GIRL (To Make Me Love You Like I Do) — Eddie Floyd, Stax 0002
111. YOU GOT STYLE — Jon & Robin, Abnak 130
112. I'M GONNA DO WHAT THEY DO TO ME — B.B. King, Bluesway 61018
113. MY NAME IS JACK — Manfred Mann, Mercury 72822
114. WHO WILL ANSWER — Hesitations, Kapp 926
115. DO IT AGAIN — Beach Boys, Capitol 2239
116. MR. BOJANGLES — Bobby Cole, Date 1613
117. SOUL MEETING — Soul Clan, Atlantic 2530
118. THE SNAKE — Al Wilson, Soul City 767
119. TAKE ME BACK — Frankie Laine, ABC 11097
120. YOU CAN CRY IF YOU WANT TO — Troggs, Fontana 1622
121. BOY — Lulu, Epic 10346
122. FUNNY MAN — Ray Stevens, Mercury 72816
123. BROWN-EYED WOMAN — Bill Medley, MGM 13959
124. SALLY HAD A PARTY — Flavor, Columbia 44521
125. THIS WHEEL'S ON FIRE — Julie Driscoll, Brian Auger & the Trinity, Atco 6593
126. WHAT A WONDERFUL WORLD — Louis Armstrong, ABC 10982
127. I AM YOUR MAN — Bobby Taylor & Vancouvers, Gordy 7073
128. SATURDAY'S FATHER — 4 Seasons, Philips 40452
129. LIGHT MY FIRE — Jose Feliciano, RCA Victor 47-9550
130. DOWN IN TENNESSEE — Kasenetz-Katz Singing Orchestral Circus, Buddah 52
131. DOWN AT LULU'S — Ohio Express, Buddah 56

Compiled from national retail sales and radio station airplay by the Music Popularity Dept. of Record Market Research, Billboard.

# Billboard HOT 100

**FOR WEEK ENDING JULY 27, 1968**

★ STAR PERFORMER—Sides registering greatest proportionate upward progress this week.

🅡 Record Industry Association of America seal of certification as million selling single.

| This Week | 1 Wk. Ago | 2 Wks. Ago | 3 Wks. Ago | TITLE Artist (Producer), Label & Number | Weeks On Chart |
|---|---|---|---|---|---|
| 1 (Billboard Award) | 1 | 5 | 5 | GRAZING IN THE GRASS — Hugh Masekela (Stewart Levine), Uni 55066 | 8 |
| ★2 | 2 | 4 | 6 | LADY WILLPOWER — Gary Puckett & the Union Gap (Jerry Fuller), Columbia 44547 | 8 |
| ★3 | 6 | 8 | 17 | STONED SOUL PICNIC — 5th Dimension (Bones Howe), Soul City 766 | 9 |
| ★4 | 3 | 3 | 3 | JUMPIN' JACK FLASH — Rolling Stones (Jimmy Miller), London 908 | 8 |
| 5 | 5 | 2 | 2 | THE HORSE — Cliff Nobles & Co. (Jesse James), Phil L.A. of Soul 313 | 10 |
| ★6 | 7 | 12 | 23 | HURDY GURDY MAN — Donovan (Mickie Most), Epic 10345 | 6 |
| 7 | 4 | 1 | 1 | THIS GUY'S IN LOVE WITH YOU — Herb Alpert (Herb Alpert & Jerry Moss), A&M 929 | 11 |
| ★8 | 29 | 55 | — | CLASSICAL GAS — Mason Williams (Mike Post), Warner Bros.-Seven Arts 7190 | 3 |
| ★9 | 22 | 77 | — | HELLO, I LOVE YOU — Doors (Paul Rothchild), Elektra 45635 | 4 |
| 10 | 10 | 15 | — | INDIAN LAKE — Cowsills (Wes Ferrell), MGM 13944 | 9 |
| 11 | 14 | 21 | 43 | TURN AROUND, LOOK AT ME — Vogues (Dick Glasser), Reprise 0686 | 7 |
| 12 | 9 | 8 | — | HERE COMES THE JUDGE — Shorty Long (Shorty Long & B.J.), Soul 35044 | 6 |
| 13 | 11 | 11 | 10 | REACH OUT OF THE DARKNESS — Friend & Lover (Joe South & Bill Lowery), Verve Forecast 5069 | 11 |
| ★14 | 20 | 28 | 29 | SKY PILOT — Eric Burdon & the Animals (Tom Wilson), MGM 13939 | 9 |
| 15 | 21 | 27 | 34 | PICTURES OF MATCHSTICK MEN — Status Quo (Jack Schroeder), Cadet Concept 7001 | 11 |
| 16 | 15 | 6 | 3 | THE LOOK OF LOVE — Sergio Mendes & Brasil '66 (Herb Alpert), A&M 924 | 12 |
| 17 | 13 | 7 | 7 | ANGEL IN THE MORNING — Merrilee Rush (T. Coghill & C. Moman), Bell 705 | 13 |
| 18 | 22 | 41 | 52 | SUNSHINE OF YOUR LOVE — Cream (Felix Pappalardi), Atco 6544 | 4 |
| 19 | 23 | 24 | 24 | HERE COMES THE JUDGE — Pigmeat Markham (Gene Barge), Chess 2049 | 7 |
| 20 | 16 | 20 | 22 | SHE'S A HEARTBREAKER — Gene Pitney (Charlie Foxx), Musicor 1306 | 12 |
| 21 | 26 | 35 | 44 | AUTUMN OF MY LIFE — Bobby Goldsboro (Bob Montgomery), United Artists 50318 | 5 |
| 22 | 19 | 17 | 16 | I LOVE YOU — People (Mikel Hunter), Capitol 2078 | 17 |
| 23 | 17 | 14 | 9 | MacARTHUR PARK — Richard Harris (Jimmy Webb), Dunhill 4134 | 12 |
| 24 | 28 | 36 | 37 | I'M A MIDNIGHT MOVER — Wilson Pickett (Tom Dowd), Atlantic 2528 | 6 |
| ★25 | 36 | 47 | 47 | STAY IN MY CORNER — Dells (Bobby Miller), Cadet 5612 | 6 |
| 26 | 25 | 23 | 20 | NEVER GIVE YOU UP — Jerry Butler (Gamble-Huff), Mercury 72798 | 13 |
| 27 | 34 | 38 | 42 | DON'T TAKE IT SO HARD — Paul Revere & The Raiders (Featuring Mark Lindsay) (Mark Lindsay), Columbia 44555 | 6 |
| ★28 | 18 | 15 | 11 | YUMMY, YUMMY, YUMMY — Ohio Express (Kasenetz-Katz Associates), Buddah 38 | 13 |
| 29 | 37 | 37 | 38 | FACE IT GIRL, IT'S OVER — Nancy Wilson (David Cavanaugh), Capitol 2136 | 12 |
| 30 | 41 | 53 | 94 | DREAM A LITTLE DREAM OF ME — Mama Cass with the Mamas & Papas (Lou Adler), Dunhill 4145 | 4 |
| ★31 | 39 | 70 | — | BORN TO BE WILD — Steppenwolf (Gabriel Mekler), Dunhill 4138 | 3 |
| ★32 | 64 | — | — | PEOPLE GOT TO BE FREE — Rascals (Rascals), Atlantic 2537 | 2 |
| 33 | 33 | 39 | 39 | LOVER'S HOLIDAY — Peggy Scott & Jo Jo Benson (Huey P. Meaux), SSS International 736 | 8 |
| 34 | 24 | 13 | 12 | MONY MONY — Tommy James & Shondells (Kasenetz-Katz Associates), Roulette 7008 | 17 |
| 35 | 40 | 44 | 45 | ELEANOR RIGBY — Ray Charles (Joe Adams), ABC 11090 | 8 |
| 36 | 44 | 62 | 91 | AMEN — Otis Redding (Steve Cropper), Atco 0592 | 4 |
| 37 | 32 | 32 | 32 | FOLSOM PRISON BLUES — Johnny Cash (Bob Johnston), Columbia 44513 | 10 |
| ★38 | 47 | 50 | 64 | JOURNEY TO THE CENTER OF YOUR MIND — Amboy Dukes (Bob Shad), Mainstream 684 | 5 |
| 39 | 31 | 19 | 19 | D. W. WASHBURN — Monkees (Monkees), Colgems 66-1023 | 7 |
| ★40 | 46 | 46 | 79 | SEALED WITH A KISS — Gary Lewis & Playboys (Snuff Garrett), Liberty 56037 | 6 |
| ★41 | 53 | 57 | 62 | HITCH IT TO THE HORSE — Fantastic Johnny C (Jesse James), Phil L.A. of Soul 315 | 7 |
| ★42 | 52 | 84 | — | SOUL LIMBO — Booker T. & the M.G.'s (Booker T. Jones), Stax 0001 | 3 |
| 43 | 43 | 63 | 70 | WITH PEN IN HAND — Billy Vera (Chip Taylor), Atlantic 2526 | 5 |
| 44 | 49 | 49 | 49 | HERE I AM BABY — Marvelettes ("Smokey"), Tamla 54166 | 7 |
| 45 | 45 | 45 | 73 | DREAM OF THE EVERYDAY HOUSEWIFE — Glen Campbell (Al de Lory), Capitol 2224 | 4 |
| 46 | 55 | 55 | 85 | THE EYES OF A NEW YORK WOMAN — B.J. Thomas (Chips Moman), Scepter 12219 | 4 |
| 47 | 56 | 73 | — | (You Keep Me) HANGIN' ON — Vanilla Fudge (Shadow Morton), Atco 6495 | 9 |
| ★48 | 73 | — | — | YOU MET YOUR MATCH — Stevie Wonder (Don Hunter), Tamla 54168 | 2 |
| ★49 | 78 | — | — | I CAN'T STOP DANCING — Archie Bell & the Drells (Gamble-Huff), Atlantic 2534 | 2 |
| 50 | 50 | 42 | 40 | IT SHOULD HAVE BEEN ME — Gladys Knight & the Pips (Norman Whitfield), Soul 35045 | 9 |
| 51 | 51 | 51 | 51 | IT'S NICE TO BE WITH YOU — Monkees (Monkees), Colgems 66-1023 | 6 |
| 52 | 54 | 54 | 62 | CAN'T YOU SEE ME CRY — New Colony Six (Sentar Records), Mercury 72817 | 7 |
| ★53 | 65 | — | — | HALFWAY TO PARADISE — Bobby Vinton (Billy Sherrill), Epic 10350 | 2 |
| ★54 | 96 | — | — | YESTERDAY'S DREAMS — Four Tops (Ivy Hunter), Motown 1127 | 2 |
| 55 | 48 | 48 | 63 | THE STORY OF ROCK AND ROLL — Turtles (Chip Douglas), White Whale 273 | 7 |
| 56 | 59 | 66 | 88 | ALICE LONG (You're Still My Favorite Girlfriend) — Tommy Boyce & Bobby Hart (Boyce & Hart), A&M 948 | 5 |
| 57 | 70 | 78 | 99 | (Love Is Like A) BASEBALL GAME — Intruders (Gamble Huff Prod.), Gamble 217 | 5 |
| 58 | 71 | 98 | — | LOVE MAKES A WOMAN — Barbara Acklin (Carl Davis & Eugene Record), Brunswick 55379 | 3 |
| 59 | 60 | 60 | 65 | BABY YOU COME ROLLIN' ACROSS MY MIND — Peppermint Trolley Company (Dan Dalton), Acta 815 | 8 |
| 60 | 62 | 86 | — | PRAYER MEETIN' — Willie Mitchell (Joe Cuoghi), Hi 2147 | 3 |
| 61 | 61 | 65 | 86 | BE YOUNG, BE FOOLISH, BE HAPPY — Tams (Joe South), ABC 11066 | 6 |
| ★62 | — | — | — | LIGHT MY FIRE — Jose Feliciano (Rick Jarrard), RCA Victor 47-9550 | 1 |
| 63 | 79 | 88 | — | HARD TO HANDLE — Otis Redding (Steve Cropper), Atco 6592 | 3 |
| 64 | 69 | 77 | — | THE IMPOSSIBLE DREAM — Roger Williams (Hy Grill), Kapp 907 | 3 |
| 65 | 66 | 69 | 69 | UNDERSTANDING — Ray Charles (Joe Adams), ABC 11090 | 7 |
| 66 | 90 | — | — | I GET THE SWEETEST FEELING — Jackie Wilson (Carl Davis), Brunswick 55381 | 2 |
| ★67 | 93 | 97 | — | SLIP AWAY — Clarence Carter (Rick Hall & Staff), Atlantic 2508 | 3 |
| 68 | 76 | 76 | 89 | DREAMS OF THE EVERYDAY HOUSEWIFE — Wayne Newton (Jim Vienneau), MGM 13955 | 5 |
| 69 | 63 | 64 | 76 | D-I-V-O-R-C-E — Tammy Wynette (Billy Sherrill), Epic 10315 | 6 |
| ★70 | 77 | 99 | — | TWO-BIT MANCHILD — Neil Diamond (Tom Catalano & Neil Diamond), Uni 55075 | 3 |
| ★71 | 98 | — | — | TUESDAY AFTERNOON (Forever Afternoon) — Moody Blues (Tony Clarke), Deram 85028 | 2 |
| 72 | 72 | 72 | 82 | YOUR TIME HASN'T COME YET, BABY — Elvis Presley, RCA Victor 47-9547 | 7 |
| ★73 | 80 | 94 | — | MRS. BLUEBIRD — Eternity's Children (Curt Boettcher & Keith Olsen), Tower 416 | 3 |
| 74 | 74 | 91 | 93 | TO LOVE SOMEBODY — Sweet Inspirations (Tom Dowd), Atlantic 2529 | 5 |
| 75 | 75 | 75 | 80 | (The Puppet Song) WHISKEY ON A SUNDAY — Irish Rovers (Charles Bud Dant), Decca 32333 | 6 |
| 76 | 84 | 85 | 96 | COMPETITION AIN'T NOTHIN' — Little Carl Carlton, Back Beat 588 | 5 |
| 77 | — | — | — | I GUESS I'LL HAVE TO CRY, CRY, CRY — James Brown and the Famous Flames (James Brown), King 6141 | 1 |
| 78 | 88 | — | — | DON'T GIVE UP — Petula Clark (Tony Hatch), Warner Bros. | 2 |
| 79 | — | — | — | HAPPY — Nancy Sinatra (Lee Hazlewood), Reprise 0756 | 1 |
| 80 | — | — | — | YOU'RE ALL I NEED TO GET BY — Marvin Gaye & Tammi Terrell (Ashford-Simpson), Tamla 54169 | 1 |
| 81 | 95 | — | — | AND SUDDENLY — Cherry People (Ron Haffkine & Barry Oslander), Heritage 801 | 2 |
| 82 | 83 | 83 | 83 | TURN ON YOUR LOVE LIGHT — Bill Black's Combo (Joe Cuoghi), Hi 2145 | 6 |
| 83 | 82 | 82 | 86 | HANG 'EM HIGH — Hugo Montenegro, His Orch. & Chorus (Joe Reisman), RCA Victor 47-9554 | 6 |
| ★84 | — | — | — | 1, 2, 3, RED LIGHT — 1910 Fruitgum Company (J. Katz, J. Kasenetz, S. Primachi), Buddah 54 | 1 |
| 85 | 87 | — | — | GOD BLESS OUR LOVE — Ballads (Jesse Mason & Willie Hutch), Venture 615 | 2 |
| 86 | — | — | — | BREAKING UP IS HARD TO DO — Happenings (Tokens), B.T. Puppy 543 | 1 |
| 87 | 86 | 87 | 87 | YOUNG BOY — Barbara Greene, Renee 5001 | 6 |
| 88 | — | — | — | DO IT AGAIN — Beach Boys (Brian Wilson), Capitol 2239 | 1 |
| 89 | 89 | 90 | 90 | LOOK OVER YOUR SHOULDER — O'Jays (George Kerr), Bell 704 | 5 |
| ★90 | — | — | — | SOMEBODY CARES — Tommy James & the Shondells (Neil Galligan & Gary Illingworth), Roulette 7016 | 1 |
| 91 | — | — | — | I'VE NEVER FOUND A GIRL (To Love Me Like You Do) — Eddie Floyd (Steve Cropper), Stax 0002 | 1 |
| 92 | 92 | 93 | 97 | JUST A LITTLE BIT — Blue Cheer (Abe Kesh "Voco"), Philips 40541 | 4 |
| 93 | — | — | — | LIFE — Sly & Family Stone (Stone Flower Prod.), Epic 10353 | 1 |
| 94 | — | — | — | I'M GONNA DO WHAT THEY DO TO ME — B.B. King (Lou Zito-Johnnie Pate), Blues Way 61018 | 1 |
| 95 | 97 | — | — | I LOVED AND I LOST — Impressions (Johnny Pate), ABC 11103 | 2 |
| 96 | — | — | — | MR. BOJANGLES — Jerry Jeff Walker (Tom Dowd & Dan Elliot), Atco 6594 | 1 |
| 97 | 99 | 100 | 100 | SEND MY BABY BACK — Freddie Hughes (L. Hewitt), Wand 1182 | 4 |
| 98 | — | — | — | NEVER GOING BACK — Lovin' Spoonful (Chip Douglas), Kama Sutra 250 | 1 |
| 99 | — | — | — | SOUL MEETING — Soul Clan (Don Covay), Atlantic 2530 | 1 |
| 100 | 100 | — | — | GIVE ME ONE MORE CHANCE — Wilmer Alexander Jr. & the Dukes (Dukes), Aphrodisiac 260 | 2 |

## BUBBLING UNDER THE HOT 100

101. ANYWAY THAT YOU WANT ME .......... American Breed, Acta 327
102. PLEASE RETURN YOUR LOVE TO ME .......... Temptations, Cordy 7074
103. WORKING ON A GROOVY THING .......... Patti Drew, Capitol 2197
104. THERE WAS A TIME .......... Dapps, Featuring Alfred Ellis, King 6169
105. MAIN STREET MISSION .......... O. C. Smith, Columbia 44555
106. ON A BEAUTIFUL DAY .......... Sunshine Company, Imperial 66308
107. DOWN AT LULU'S .......... Ohio Express, Buddah 56
108. MY NAME IS JACK .......... Manfred Mann, Mercury 72822
109. MR. BOJANGLES .......... Bobby Cole, Date 1613
110. THE SNAKE .......... Al Wilson, Soul City 767
111. YOU GOT STYLE .......... Jon & Robin, Abnak 130
112. SEALED WITH A KISS .......... Toys, Musicor 1319
113. THE WOMAN I LOVE .......... B. B. King, Kent 492
114. BROWN EYED WOMAN .......... Bill Medley, MGM 11097
115. TAKE ME BACK .......... Frankie Laine, ABC 11097
116. SALLY HAD A PARTY .......... Flavor, Columbia 44521
117. MONTAGE FROM HOW SWEET IT IS (I Knew That You Knew) .......... Love Generation, Imperial 66310
118. I'M YOUR MAN .......... Bobby Taylor & the Vancouvers, Gordy 7073
119. GIRL WATCHER .......... O'Kaysions, ABC 11094
120. YOU CRY IF YOU WANT TO .......... Troggs, Fontana 1622
121. MR. BUSINESSMAN .......... Ray Stevens, Monument 1083
122. THIS WHEEL'S ON FIRE .......... Julie Driscoll, Brian Auger & the Trinity, Atco 6593
123. WHAT A WONDERFUL WORLD .......... Louis Armstrong, ABC 10982
124. DOWN IN TENNESSEE .......... Kasenetz-Katz Singing Orchestral Circus, Buddah 52
125. TELL SOMEONE YOU LOVE THEM .......... Dino, Desi & Billy, Reprise 0698

# Billboard HOT 100

**FOR WEEK ENDING AUGUST 3, 1968**

★ STAR PERFORMER—Sides registering greatest proportionate upward progress this week.

Ⓡ Record Industry Association of America seal of certification as million selling single.

| This Week | 2 Wks. Ago | 3 Wks. Ago | TITLE Artist (Producer), Label & Number | Weeks On Chart |
|---|---|---|---|---|
| 1 ★ | 9 | 9 | 22 | HELLO, I LOVE YOU ... Doors (Paul Rothchild), Elektra 45635 | 5 |
| 2 | 8 | 8 | 29 | CLASSICAL GAS ... Mason Williams (Mike Post), Warner Bros.-Seven Arts 7190 | 7 |
| 3 | 3 | 6 | 8 | STONED SOUL PICNIC ... 5th Dimension (Bones Howe), Soul City 766 | 10 |
| 4 Ⓡ | 1 | 1 | 5 | GRAZING IN THE GRASS ... Hugh Masekela (Stewart Levine), Uni 55066 | 9 |
| 5 | 6 | 7 | 12 | HURDY GURDY MAN ... Donovan (Mickie Most), Epic 10345 | 7 |
| 6 | 4 | 3 | 3 | JUMPIN' JACK FLASH ... Rolling Stones (Jimmy Miller), London 908 | 9 |
| 7 Ⓡ | 2 | 2 | 4 | LADY WILLPOWER ... Gary Puckett & the Union Gap (Jerry Fuller), Columbia 44547 | 9 |
| 8 | 5 | 5 | 2 | THE HORSE ... Cliff Nobles & Co. (Jesse James), Phil L.A. of Soul 313 | 11 |
| 9 | 11 | 14 | 21 | TURN AROUND, LOOK AT ME ... Vogues (Dick Glasser), Reprise 0686 | 8 |
| 10 | 18 | 22 | 41 | SUNSHINE OF YOUR LOVE ... Cream (Felix Pappalardi), Atco 6544 | 5 |
| 11 | 31 | 39 | 70 | BORN TO BE WILD ... Steppenwolf (Gabriel Mekler), Dunhill 4138 | 4 |
| 12 | 15 | 21 | 27 | PICTURES OF MATCHSTICK MEN ... Status Quo (John Schroeder), Cadet Concept 7001 | 12 |
| 13 | 32 | 64 | — | PEOPLE GOT TO BE FREE ... Rascals (Rascals), Atlantic 2537 | 3 |
| 14 | 14 | 20 | 28 | SKY PILOT ... Eric Burdon & the Animals (Tom Wilson), MGM 13939 | 10 |
| 15 Ⓡ | 7 | 4 | 1 | THIS GUY'S IN LOVE WITH YOU ... Herb Alpert (Herb Alpert & Jerry Moss), A&M 929 | 12 |
| 16 | 47 | 56 | 73 | (You Keep Me) HANGIN' ON ... Vanilla Fudge (Shadow Morton), Atco 6495 | 10 |
| 17 | 38 | 47 | 50 | JOURNEY TO THE CENTER OF MY MIND ... Amboy Dukes (Bob Shad), Mainstream 684 | 6 |
| 18 | 25 | 36 | 47 | STAY IN MY CORNER ... Dells (Bobby Miller), Cadet 5612 | 6 |
| 19 | 21 | 26 | 35 | AUTUMN OF MY LIFE ... Bobby Goldsboro (Bob Montgomery), United Artists 50318 | 6 |
| 20 | 30 | 41 | 53 | DREAM A LITTLE DREAM OF ME ... Mama Cass with the Mamas & Papas (Lou Adler), Dunhill 4145 | 5 |
| 21 | 10 | 10 | 10 | INDIAN LAKE ... Cowsills (Wes Ferrell), MGM 13944 | 10 |
| 22 ★ | 42 | 52 | 84 | SOUL LIMBO ... Booker T. & the M.G.'s (Booker T. Jones), Stax 0001 | 4 |
| 23 | 16 | 15 | 8 | THE LOOK OF LOVE ... Sergio Mendes & Brasil '66 (Herb Alpert), A&M 924 | 13 |
| 24 | 17 | 13 | 7 | ANGEL IN THE MORNING ... Merrilee Rush (T. Coghill & C. Moman), Bell 705 | 14 |
| 25 | 12 | 12 | 9 | HERE COMES THE JUDGE ... Shorty Long (Shorty Long & B.J.), Soul 35044 | 10 |
| 26 | 13 | 11 | 11 | REACH OUT OF THE DARKNESS ... Friend & Lover (Joe South & Bill Lowery), Verve Forecast 5069 | 12 |
| 27 | 27 | 34 | 38 | DON'T TAKE IT SO HARD ... Paul Revere & The Raiders (Featuring Mark Lindsay) (Mark Lindsay), Columbia 44555 | 7 |
| 28 | 53 | 65 | — | HALFWAY TO PARADISE ... Bobby Vinton (Billy Sherrill), Epic 10350 | 3 |
| 29 | 29 | 37 | 37 | FACE IT GIRL, IT'S OVER ... Nancy Wilson (David Cavanaugh), Capitol 2136 | 13 |
| 30 | 40 | 46 | 46 | SEALED WITH A KISS ... Gary Lewis & Playboys (Snuff Garrett), Liberty 56037 | 7 |
| 31 | 33 | 33 | 39 | LOVER'S HOLIDAY ... Peggy Scott & Jo Jo Benson (Huey P. Meaux), SSS International 736 | 9 |
| 32 ★ | 62 | — | — | LIGHT MY FIRE ... Jose Feliciano (Rick Jarrard), RCA Victor 47-9550 | 2 |
| 33 ★ | 45 | 45 | 45 | DREAMS OF THE EVERYDAY HOUSEWIFE ... Glen Campbell (Al de Lory), Capitol 2224 | 5 |
| 34 ★ | 56 | 59 | 66 | ALICE LONG (You're Still My Favorite Girlfriend) ... Tommy Boyce & Bobby Hart (Boyce & Hart), A&M 948 | 5 |
| 35 | 35 | 40 | 44 | ELEANOR RIGBY ... Ray Charles (Joe Adams), ABC 11090 | 9 |
| 36 | 26 | 25 | 23 | NEVER GIVE YOU UP ... Jerry Butler (Gamble-Huff), Mercury 72798 | 14 |
| 37 | 37 | 32 | 32 | FOLSOM PRISON BLUES ... Johnny Cash (Bob Johnston), Columbia 44513 | 11 |
| 38 | 20 | 16 | 20 | SHE'S A HEARTBREAKER ... Gene Pitney (Charlie Foxx), Musicor 1306 | 13 |
| 39 ★ | 49 | 78 | — | I CAN'T STOP DANCING ... Archie Bell & the Drells (Gamble-Huff), Atlantic 2534 | 3 |
| 40 | 46 | 55 | 55 | THE EYES OF A NEW YORK WOMAN ... B.J. Thomas (Chips Moman), Scepter 12219 | 7 |
| 41 | 41 | 53 | 57 | HITCH IT TO THE HORSE ... Fantastic Johnny C (Jesse James), Phil L.A. of Soul 315 | 6 |
| 42 | 22 | 19 | 17 | I LOVE YOU ... People (Mikel Hunter), Capitol 2078 | 18 |
| 43 | 24 | 28 | 36 | I'M A MIDNIGHT MOVER ... Wilson Pickett (Tom Dowd), Atlantic 2528 | 7 |
| 44 | 48 | 73 | — | YOU MET YOUR MATCH ... Stevie Wonder (Don Hunter), Tamla 54168 | 3 |
| 45 | 19 | 23 | 24 | HERE COMES THE JUDGE ... Pigmeat Markham (Gene Barge), Chess 2049 | 8 |
| 46 | 23 | 17 | 14 | MacARTHUR PARK ... Richard Harris (Jimmy Webb), Dunhill 4134 | 13 |
| 47 Ⓡ | 28 | 18 | 15 | YUMMY, YUMMY, YUMMY ... Ohio Express (Kasenetz-Katz Associates), Buddah 38 | 14 |
| 48 | 71 | 98 | — | TUESDAY AFTERNOON (Forever Afternoon) ... Moody Blues (Tony Clarke), Deram 85028 | 3 |
| 49 | 57 | 70 | 78 | (Love Is Like A) BASEBALL GAME ... Intruders (Gamble Huff Prod.), Gamble 217 | 5 |
| 50 | 78 | 88 | — | DON'T GIVE UP ... Petula Clark (Tony Hatch), Warner Bros.-Seven Arts 7216 | 3 |
| 51 | 54 | 96 | — | YESTERDAY'S DREAMS ... Four Tops (Ivy Hunter), Motown 1127 | 3 |
| 52 | 36 | 44 | 62 | AMEN ... Otis Redding (Steve Cropper), Atco 0592 | 5 |
| 53 | 84 | — | — | 1, 2, 3, RED LIGHT ... 1910 Fruitgum Company (J. Katz, J. Kasenetz, S. Primeechi), Buddah 54 | 2 |
| 54 | 80 | — | — | YOU'RE ALL I NEED TO GET BY ... Marvin Gaye & Tammi Terrell (Ashford-Simpson), Tamla 54169 | 2 |
| 55 | 43 | 43 | 63 | WITH PEN IN HAND ... Billy Vera (Chip Taylor), Atlantic 2526 | 6 |
| 56 | 58 | 71 | 98 | LOVE MAKES A WOMAN ... Barbara Acklin (Carl Davis & Eugene Record), Brunswick 55379 | 4 |
| 57 | 60 | 62 | 86 | PRAYER MEETIN' ... Willie Mitchell (Joe Cough), Hi 2147 | 4 |
| 58 | 64 | 69 | 77 | THE IMPOSSIBLE DREAM ... Roger Williams (Hy Grill), Kapp 907 | 5 |
| 59 | 59 | 60 | 60 | BABY YOU COME ROLLIN' ACROSS MY MIND ... Peppermint Trolley Company (Dan Dalton), Acta 815 | 9 |
| 60 | 44 | 49 | 49 | HERE I AM BABY ... Marvelettes ("Smokey"), Tamla 54166 | 9 |
| 61 ★ | 88 | — | — | DO IT AGAIN ... Beach Boys (Beach Boys), Capitol 2239 | 2 |
| 62 | 68 | 76 | 76 | DREAMS OF THE EVERYDAY HOUSEWIFE ... Wayne Newton (Jim Vienneau), MGM 13955 | 6 |
| 63 | 63 | 79 | 88 | HARD TO HANDLE ... Otis Redding (Steve Cropper), Atco 6592 | 4 |
| 64 | 66 | 90 | — | I GET THE SWEETEST FEELING ... Jackie Wilson (Carl Davis), Brunswick 55381 | 3 |
| 65 | 65 | 66 | 69 | UNDERSTANDING ... Ray Charles (Joe Adams), ABC 11090 | 4 |
| 66 | 70 | 77 | 99 | TWO-BIT MANCHILD ... Neil Diamond (Tom Catalano & Neil Diamond), Uni 55075 | 4 |
| 67 | 67 | 93 | 97 | SLIP AWAY ... Clarence Carter (Rick Hall & Staff), Atlantic 2508 | 4 |
| 68 | 81 | 95 | — | AND SUDDENLY ... Cherry People (Ron Haffkine & Barry Oslander), Heritage 801 | 3 |
| 69 | 73 | 80 | 94 | MRS. BLUEBIRD ... Eternity's Children (Curt Boettcher & Keith Olsen), Tower 416 | 4 |
| 70 | 52 | 54 | 54 | CAN'T YOU SEE ME CRY ... New Colony Six (Sentar Records), Mercury 72817 | 8 |
| 71 ★ | 91 | — | — | I'VE NEVER FOUND A GIRL (To Love Me Like You Do) ... Eddie Floyd (Steve Cropper), Stax 0002 | 2 |
| 72 | 72 | 72 | 72 | YOUR TIME HASN'T COME YET, BABY ... Elvis Presley, RCA Victor 47-9547 | 9 |
| 73 | 98 | — | — | NEVER GOING BACK ... Lovin' Spoonful (Chip Douglas), Kama Sutra 250 | 2 |
| 74 | 77 | — | — | I GUESS I'LL HAVE TO CRY, CRY, CRY ... James Brown & the Famous Flames (James Brown), King 6141 | 2 |
| 75 | 79 | — | — | HAPPY ... Nancy Sinatra (Lee Hazlewood), Reprise 0756 | 2 |
| 76 | 76 | 84 | 85 | COMPETITION AIN'T NOTHIN' ... Little Carl Carlton, Back Beat 588 | 6 |
| 77 | 95 | 97 | — | I LOVE AND I LOST ... Impressions (Johnny Pate), ABC 11103 | 3 |
| 78 | 75 | 75 | 75 | (The Puppet Song) WHISKEY ON A SUNDAY ... Irish Rovers (Charles Bud Dant), Decca 32333 | 7 |
| 79 | 90 | — | — | SOMEBODY CARES ... Tommy James & the Shondells (Neil Galligan & Gary Illingworth), Roulette 7016 | 2 |
| 80 | — | — | — | BROWN EYED WOMAN ... Bill Medley (Bill Medley & Barry Mann), MGM 13959 | 1 |
| 81 | 86 | — | — | BREAKING UP IS HARD TO DO ... Happenings (Tokens), B.T. Puppy 543 | 2 |
| 82 | 85 | 87 | — | GOD BLESS OUR LOVE ... Ballads (Jesse Mason & Willie Hutch), Venture 615 | 3 |
| 83 | — | — | — | PLEASE RETURN YOUR LOVE TO ME ... Temptations (Norman Whitfield), Gordy 7074 | 1 |
| 84 | 100 | 100 | — | GIVE ME ONE MORE CHANCE ... Wilmer Alexander Jr. & the Dukes (Dukes), Aphrodisiac 260 | 3 |
| 85 | 94 | — | — | I'M GONNA DO WHAT THEY DO TO ME ... B.B. King (Lou Zito-Johnnie Pate), Blues Way 61018 | 2 |
| 86 | — | — | — | CAN'T YOU FIND ANOTHER WAY (Of Doing It) ... Sam & Dave (Isaac Hayes & David Porter), Atlantic 2540 | 1 |
| 87 | 96 | — | — | MR. BOJANGLES ... Jerry Jeff Walker (Tom Dowd & Dan Elliot), Atco 6594 | 2 |
| 88 | — | — | — | MR. BOJANGLES ... Bobby Cole (Bobby Cole), Date 1613 | 1 |
| 89 | — | — | — | DOWN AT LULU'S ... Ohio Express (Super K Prod.), Buddah 56 | 1 |
| 90 | — | — | — | MR. BUSINESSMAN ... Ray Stevens (Fred Foster & Ray Stevens), Monument 1083 | 1 |
| 91 | — | — | — | GIRLS CAN'T DO WHAT THE GUYS DO ... Betty Wright (Brad Shapiro & Steve Alaimo), Alston 4569 | 1 |
| 92 | — | — | — | ANYWAY YOU WANT ME ... American Breed (Bill Trout), Acta 827 | 1 |
| 93 | 93 | — | — | LIFE ... Sly & Family Stone (Stone Flower Prod.), Epic 10353 | 2 |
| 94 | 97 | 99 | 100 | SEND MY BABY BACK ... Freddie Hughes (L. Hewitt), Wand 1182 | 5 |
| 95 | — | — | — | GIVE A DAMN ... Spanky & Our Gang (Scharf/Derough, Edal), Mercury 72831 | 1 |
| 96 | — | — | — | WORKIN' ON A GROOVY THING ... Patti Drew (Carone Prod.), Capitol 2197 | 1 |
| 97 | 99 | — | — | SUDDEN STOP ... Percy Sledge (Quin Ivy & Marlin Greene), Atlantic 2539 | 2 |
| 98 | — | — | — | SOUL MEETING ... Soul Clan (Don Covay), Atlantic 2530 | 1 |
| 99 | — | — | — | MONTAGE FROM HOW SWEET IT IS (I Knew That You Knew) ... Love Generation (Tommy Oliver & Joe Saracene), Imperial 66310 | 1 |
| 100 | — | — | — | SALLY HAD A PARTY ... Flavor (Tim O'Brien), Columbia 44521 | 1 |

## BUBBLING UNDER THE HOT 100

101. SNOOPY FOR PRESIDENT ... Royal Guardsmen, Laurie 3451
102. MORNING DEW ... Lulu, Epic 10367
103. THERE WAS A TIME ... Dapps, King 6169
104. MY NAME IS JACK ... Manfred Mann, Mercury 72822
105. TO LOVE SOMEBODY ... Sweet Inspirations, Atlantic 2529
106. THIS WHEEL'S ON FIRE ... Julie Driscoll, Brian Auger & the Trinity, Atco 6593
107. GIRL WATCHER ... O'Kaysions, ABC 11094
108. THE SNAKE ... Al Wilson, Soul City 767
109. TELL SOMEONE YOU LOVE THEM ... Dino, Desi & Billy, Reprise 0698
110. YOU GOT STYLE ... Jon & Robin, Abnak 130
111. THE WOMAN I LOVE ... B.B. King, Kent 492
112. WHO WILL ANSWER ... Hesitations, Kapp 926
113. TURN ON YOUR LOVELIGHT ... Bill Black's Combo, Hi 2145
114. ON THE ROAD AGAIN ... Canned Heat, Liberty 55038
115. BREAKIN' DOWN THE WALLS OF HEARTACHE ... Bandwagon, Epic 10352
116. WHAT A WONDERFUL WORLD ... Louis Armstrong, ABC 10982
117. LULLABY FROM "ROSEMARY'S BABY" ... Mia Farrow, Dot 17126
118. LIFE TURNED HER THAT WAY ... James Carr, Goldwax 335

# Billboard HOT 100

FOR WEEK ENDING AUG. 10, 1968

★ STAR PERFORMER—Sides registering greatest proportionate upward progress this week.

(RIAA seal) Record Industry Association of America seal of certification as million selling single.

| This Week | 1 Wk. Ago | 2 Wks. Ago | 3 Wks. Ago | TITLE Artist (Producer), Label & Number | Weeks On Chart |
|---|---|---|---|---|---|
| 1 (Billboard Award) | 1 | 9 | 9 | HELLO, I LOVE YOU — Doors (Paul Rothchild), Elektra 45635 | 6 |
| 2 | 2 | 8 | 8 | CLASSICAL GAS — Mason Williams (Mike Post), Warner-Bros.-Seven Arts 7190 | 8 |
| 3 | 3 | 3 | 6 | STONED SOUL PICNIC — 5th Dimension (Bones Howe), Soul City 766 | 11 |
| 4 (RIAA seal) | 4 | 1 | 1 | GRAZING IN THE GRASS — Hugh Masekela (Stewart Levine), Uni 55066 | 10 |
| ★ 5 | 13 | 32 | 64 | PEOPLE GOT TO BE FREE — Rascals (Rascals), Atlantic 2537 | 4 |
| 6 | 5 | 6 | 7 | HURDY GURDY MAN — Donovan (Mickie Most), Epic 10345 | 8 |
| 7 (RIAA seal) | 7 | 2 | 2 | LADY WILLPOWER — Gary Puckett & the Union Gap (Jerry Fuller), Columbia 44547 | 10 |
| 8 | 9 | 11 | 14 | TURN AROUND, LOOK AT ME — Vogues (Dick Glasser), Reprise 0686 | 9 |
| 9 | 10 | 18 | 22 | SUNSHINE OF YOUR LOVE — Cream (Felix Pappalardi), Atco 6544 | 6 |
| 10 | 6 | 4 | 3 | JUMPIN' JACK FLASH — Rolling Stones (Jimmy Miller), London 908 | 10 |
| 11 | 11 | 31 | 39 | BORN TO BE WILD — Steppenwolf (Gabriel Mekler), Dunhill 4138 | 5 |
| 12 (RIAA seal) | 8 | 5 | 5 | THE HORSE — Cliff Nobles & Co. (Jesse James), Phil L. A. of Soul 313 | 12 |
| ★ 13 | 18 | 25 | 36 | STAY IN MY CORNER — Dells (Bobby Miller), Cadet 5612 | 7 |
| 14 | 12 | 15 | 21 | PICTURES OF MATCHSTICK MEN — Status Quo (John Schroeder), Cadet Concept 7001 | 13 |
| 15 | 16 | 47 | 56 | (You Keep Me) HANGIN' ON — Vanilla Fudge (Shadow Morton), Atco 6495 | 11 |
| 16 (RIAA seal) | 15 | 7 | 4 | THIS GUY'S IN LOVE WITH YOU — Herb Alpert (Herb Alpert & Jerry Moss), A&M 929 | 13 |
| 17 | 17 | 38 | 47 | JOURNEY TO THE CENTER OF MY MIND — Amboy Dukes (Bob Shad), Mainstream 684 | 7 |
| 18 | 20 | 30 | 41 | DREAM A LITTLE DREAM OF ME — Mama Cass with the Mamas & Papas (Lou Adler), Dunhill 4145 | 6 |
| 19 | 19 | 21 | 26 | AUTUMN OF MY LIFE — Bobby Goldsboro (Bob Montgomery), United Artists 50318 | 7 |
| ★ 20 | 32 | 62 | — | LIGHT MY FIRE — Jose Feliciano (Rick Jarrard), RCA Victor 47-9550 | 3 |
| 21 | 22 | 42 | 52 | SOUL LIMBO — Booker T. & the M.G.'s (Booker T. Jones), Stax 0001 | 5 |
| 22 | 14 | 14 | 20 | SKY PILOT — Eric Burdon & the Animals (Tom Wilson), MGM 13939 | 11 |
| ★ 23 | 39 | 49 | 78 | I CAN'T STOP DANCING — Archie Bell & the Drells (Gamble-Huff), Atlantic 2534 | 4 |
| 24 | 30 | 40 | 46 | SEALED WITH A KISS — Gary Lewis & Playboys (Snuff Garrett), Liberty 56037 | 8 |
| 25 | 21 | 10 | 10 | INDIAN LAKE — Cowsills (Wes Farrell), MGM 13944 | 11 |
| 26 | 26 | 13 | 11 | REACH OUT OF THE DARKNESS — Friend & Lover (Joe South & Bill Lowery), Verve Forecast 5069 | 13 |
| 27 | 28 | 53 | 65 | HALFWAY TO PARADISE — Bobby Vinton (Billy Sherrill), Epic 10350 | 4 |
| 28 | 24 | 17 | 13 | ANGEL IN THE MORNING — Merrilee Rush (T. Cogbill & C. Moman), Bell 705 | 15 |
| 29 | 23 | 16 | 15 | THE LOOK OF LOVE — Sergio Mendes & Brasil '66 (Herb Alpert), A&M 924 | 14 |
| ★ 30 | 49 | 57 | 70 | (Love Is Like A) BASEBALL GAME — Intruders (Gamble Huff Prod.), Gamble 217 | 6 |
| 31 | 31 | 33 | 33 | LOVER'S HOLIDAY — Peggy Scott & Jo Jo Benson (Huey P. Meaux), SSS International 736 | 10 |
| 32 | 33 | 45 | 45 | DREAMS OF THE EVERYDAY HOUSEWIFE — Glen Campbell (Al de Lory), Capitol 2224 | 6 |
| 33 | 27 | 27 | 34 | DON'T TAKE IT SO HARD — Paul Revere & The Raiders (Featuring Mark Lindsay) (Mark Lindsay), Columbia 44555 | 8 |
| 34 | 34 | 56 | 59 | ALICE LONG (You're Still My Favorite Girlfriend) — Tommy Boyce & Bobby Hart (Boyce & Hart), A&M 948 | 6 |
| 35 | 41 | 41 | 53 | HITCH IT TO THE HORSE — Fantastic Johnny C (Jesse James), Phil L.A. of Soul 315 | 7 |
| ★ 36 | 54 | 80 | — | YOU'RE ALL I NEED TO GET BY — Marvin Gaye & Tammi Terrell (Ashford-Simpson), Tamla 54169 | 3 |
| ★ 37 | 56 | 58 | 71 | LOVE MAKES A WOMAN — Barbara Acklin (Carl Davis & Eugene Record), Brunswick 55379 | 5 |
| 38 | 29 | 29 | 37 | FACE IT GIRL, IT'S OVER — Nancy Wilson (David Cavanaugh), Capitol 2136 | 14 |
| ★ 39 | 53 | 84 | — | 1, 2, 3, RED LIGHT — 1910 Fruitgum Company (Kasenetz-Katz Assoc.) Buddah 54 | 3 |
| 40 | 40 | 46 | 55 | THE EYES OF A NEW YORK WOMAN — B.J. Thomas (Chips Moman), Scepter 12219 | 8 |
| ★ 41 | 44 | 48 | 73 | YOU MET YOUR MATCH — Stevie Wonder (Don Hunter), Tamla 54168 | 4 |
| 42 | 35 | 35 | 40 | ELEANOR RIGBY — Ray Charles (Joe Adams), ABC 11090 | 10 |
| 43 | 25 | 12 | 12 | HERE COMES THE JUDGE — Shorty Long (Shorty Long & B.J.), Soul 35044 | 11 |
| ★ 44 | 83 | — | — | PLEASE RETURN YOUR LOVE TO ME — Temptations (Norman Whitfield), Gordy 7074 | 2 |
| ★ 45 | 57 | 60 | 62 | PRAYER MEETIN' — Willie Mitchell (Joe Coughi), Hi 2147 | 5 |
| 46 | 37 | 37 | 32 | FOLSOM PRISON BLUES — Johnny Cash (Bob Johnston), Columbia 44513 | 12 |
| 47 | 50 | 78 | 88 | DON'T GIVE UP — Petula Clark (Tony Hatch), Warner Bros.-Seven Arts 7216 | 4 |
| 48 | 48 | 71 | 98 | TUESDAY AFTERNOON (Forever Afternoon) — Moody Blues (Tony Clarke), Deram 85028 | 4 |
| ★ 49 | 51 | 54 | 96 | YESTERDAY'S DREAMS — Four Tops (Ivy Hunter), Motown 1127 | 4 |
| ★ 50 | 61 | 88 | — | DO IT AGAIN — Beach Boys (Beach Boys), Capitol 2239 | 3 |
| ★ 51 | 67 | 67 | 93 | SLIP AWAY — Clarence Carter (Rick Hall & Staff), Atlantic 2508 | 5 |
| ★ 52 | 89 | — | — | DOWN AT LULU'S — Ohio Express (Kasenetz-Katz Assoc.), Buddah 56 | 2 |
| 53 | 64 | 66 | 90 | I GET THE SWEETEST FEELING — Jackie Wilson (Carl Davis), Brunswick 55381 | 4 |
| 54 | 63 | 63 | 79 | HARD TO HANDLE — Otis Redding (Steve Cropper), Atco 6592 | 5 |
| ★ 55 | 79 | 90 | — | SOMEBODY CARES — Tommy James & the Shondells (Neil Galligan & Gary Illingworth), Roulette 7016 | 3 |
| ★ 56 | 86 | — | — | CAN'T YOU FIND ANOTHER WAY (Of Doing It) — Sam & Dave (Isaac Hayes & David Porter), Atlantic 2540 | 2 |
| 57 | 58 | 64 | 69 | THE IMPOSSIBLE DREAM — Roger Williams (Hy Grill), Kapp 907 | 5 |
| ★ 58 | 95 | — | — | GIVE A DAMN — Spanky & Our Gang (Scharf/Dorough, Edel), Mercury 72831 | 2 |
| ★ 59 | 74 | 77 | — | I GUESS I'LL HAVE TO CRY, CRY, CRY — James Brown & the Famous Flames (James Brown), King 6141 | 3 |
| 60 | 62 | 68 | 76 | DREAMS OF THE EVERYDAY HOUSEWIFE — Wayne Newton (Jim Vienneau), MGM 13955 | 7 |
| ★ 61 | — | — | — | THE FOOL ON THE HILL — Sergio Mendes & Brasil '66 (Sergio Mendes, Herb Alpert & Jerry Moss) | 1 |
| 62 | 59 | 59 | 60 | BABY, YOU COME ROLLIN' ACROSS MY MIND — Peppermint Trolley Company (Dan Dalton), Acta 815 | 10 |
| ★ 63 | 97 | — | — | SUDDEN STOP — Percy Sledge (Quin Ivy & Marlin Greene), Atlantic 2539 | 2 |
| ★ 64 | 80 | — | — | BROWN EYED WOMAN — Bill Medley (Bill Medley & Barry Mann), MGM 13959 | 2 |
| 65 | 65 | 65 | 66 | UNDERSTANDING — Ray Charles (Joe Adams), ABC 11090 | 9 |
| 66 | 66 | 70 | 77 | TWO-BIT MANCHILD — Neil Diamond (Tom Catalano & Neil Diamond), Uni 55075 | 5 |
| 67 | 71 | 91 | — | I'VE NEVER FOUND A GIRL (To Love Me Like You Do) — Eddie Floyd (Steve Cropper), Stax 0002 | 3 |
| 68 | 68 | 81 | 95 | AND SUDDENLY — Cherry People (Ron Haffkine, Barry Oslander & Jerry Ross), Heritage 801 | 4 |
| 69 | 69 | 73 | 80 | MRS. BLUEBIRD — Eternity's Children (Curt Boettcher & Keith Olsen), Tower 416 | 5 |
| ★ 70 | 81 | 86 | — | BREAKING UP IS HARD TO DO — Happenings (Tokens), B.T. Puppy 543 | 3 |
| ★ 71 | — | — | — | MORNING DEW — Lulu (Mickie Most), Epic 10367 | 1 |
| ★ 72 | — | — | — | KEEP THE ONE YOU GOT — Joe Tex (Buddy Killen), Dial 4083 | 1 |
| 73 | 73 | 98 | — | NEVER GOING BACK — Lovin' Spoonful (Chip Douglas), Kama Sutra 250 | 3 |
| 74 | 75 | 79 | — | HAPPY — Nancy Sinatra (Lee Hazlewood), Reprise 0756 | 3 |
| 75 | 76 | 76 | 84 | COMPETITION AIN'T NOTHIN' — Little Carl Carlton, Back Beat 588 | 7 |
| 76 | 77 | 95 | 97 | I LOVED AND I LOST — Impressions (Johnny Pate), ABC 11103 | 4 |
| 77 | 87 | 96 | — | MR. BOJANGLES — Jerry Jeff Walker (Tom Dowd & Dan Elliot), Atco 6594 | 3 |
| ★ 78 | 90 | — | — | MR. BUSINESSMAN — Ray Stevens (Fred Foster & Ray Stevens), Monument 1083 | 2 |
| 79 | 88 | — | — | MISTER BOJANGLES — Bobby Cole (Bobby Cole), Date 1613 | 2 |
| 80 | 82 | 85 | 87 | GOD BLESS OUR LOVE — Ballads (Jesse Mason & Willie Hutch), Venture 615 | 4 |
| 81 | 85 | 94 | — | I'M GONNA DO WHAT THEY DO TO ME — B.B. King (Lou Zito-Johnnie Pate), Blues Way 61018 | 3 |
| ★ 82 | 96 | — | — | WORKIN' ON A GROOVY THING — Patti Drew (Carone Prod.), Capitol 2197 | 2 |
| ★ 83 | — | — | — | MAGIC BUS — Who (Kit Lambert), Decca 32362 | 1 |
| 84 | 84 | 100 | 100 | GIVE ME ONE MORE CHANCE — Wilmer Alexander Jr. & the Dukes (Dukes), Aphrodisiac 260 | 4 |
| ★ 85 | — | — | — | HIP CITY—PART 2 — Jr. Walker & The All Stars (Lawrence Horn), Soul 35048 | 1 |
| 86 | 91 | — | — | GIRLS CAN'T DO WHAT THE GUYS DO — Betty Wright (Brad Shapiro & Steve Alaimo), Alston 4569 | 2 |
| 87 | 99 | — | — | MONTAGE FROM HOW SWEET IT IS (I Knew That You Knew) — Love Generation (Tommy Oliver & Joe Saraceno), Imperial 66310 | 2 |
| 88 | 92 | — | — | ANYWAY YOU WANT ME — American Breed (Bill Trout) Acta 827 | 2 |
| ★ 89 | — | — | — | I HEARD IT THROUGH THE GRAPEVINE — King Curtis & His Kingpins (Arif Mardin), Atco 6598 | 1 |
| ★ 90 | — | — | — | I CAN'T DANCE TO THE MUSIC YOU'RE PLAYIN' — Martha Reeves & The Vandellas (Deke Richards), Gordy 7075 | 1 |
| 91 | 98 | 99 | — | SOUL MEETING — Soul Clan (Don Covay), Atlantic 2530 | 3 |
| 92 | — | — | — | I AM YOUR MAN — Bobby Taylor & The Vancouvers (Frank Wilson), Gordy 7073 | 1 |
| 93 | 93 | 93 | — | LIFE — Sly & Family Stone (Stone Flower Prod.), Epic 10353 | 3 |
| 94 | 94 | 97 | 99 | SEND MY BABY BACK — Freddie Hughes (L. Hewitt), Wand 1182 | 6 |
| 95 | — | — | — | TIME HAS COME TODAY — Chambers Brothers (David Rubinson), Columbia 44414 | 1 |
| 96 | — | — | — | TELL SOMEONE YOU LOVE THEM — Dino, Desi & Billy (Martin & Hinsche), Reprise 0698 | 1 |
| 97 | — | — | — | M'LADY — Sly & The Family Stone (Stone Flower Prod.), Epic 10353 | 1 |
| 98 | — | — | — | MISTER NICO — Four Jacks & a Jill, RCA Victor 47-9572 | 1 |
| 99 | — | — | — | ON THE ROAD AGAIN — Canned Heat (Dallas Smith), Liberty 56038 | 1 |
| 100 | 100 | — | — | SALLY HAD A PARTY — Flavor (Tim O'Brien), Columbia 44521 | 2 |

## HOT 100—A TO Z—(Publisher-Licensee)



## BUBBLING UNDER THE HOT 100

101. I'VE GOTTA GET A MESSAGE TO YOU .... Bee Gees, Atco 6603
102. SUNSHINE GIRL .... Herman's Hermits, MGM 13973
103. THERE WAS A TIME .... Dapps, King 6169
104. THAT OLD TIME FEELING .... Dean Martin, Reprise 0761
105. TO LOVE SOMEBODY .... Sweet Inspirations, Atlantic 2529
106. FLY ME TO THE MOON .... Bobby Womack, Minit 32048
107. BREAK MY MIND .... Sammy Davis Jr., Reprise 0757
108. THE SNAKE .... Al Wilson, Soul City 767
109. APRIL AGAIN .... Dean Martin, Reprise 0761
110. SINCE YOU'VE BEEN GONE .... Ramsey Lewis, Cadet 5609
111. THE WOMAN I LOVE .... B.B. King, Kent 492
112. LIFE TURNED HER THAT WAY .... James Carr, Goldwax 335
113. TURN ON YOUR LOVELIGHT .... Bill Black's Combo, Hi 2145
114. MIDNIGHT CONFESSIONS .... Grassroots, Dunhill 4144
115. DO WHAT YOU GOTTA DO .... Bobby Vee, Liberty 56057
116. SINGLES GAME .... Jay & the Techniques, Smash 2171
117. LULLABY FROM "ROSEMARY'S BABY" .... Mia Farrow, Dot 17126
118. DO YOU WANNA DANCE .... Love Society, Scepter 12223
119. STORYBOOK CHILDREN .... Billy Joe Royal, Columbia 44574
120. HUSH .... Deep Purple, Tetragrammaton 102
121. HELP YOURSELF (To All of My Lovin') .... James & Bobby Purify, Bell 735
122. ME AND YOU .... Brenton Wood, Double Shot 130
123. ALL MY LOVE'S LAUGHTER .... Ed Ames, RCA Victor 47-9589
124. EVERYBODY'S TALKIN' .... Nilsson, RCA Victor 47-9544
125. ON A BEAUTIFUL DAY .... Sunshine Company, Imperial 66308
126. PEOPLE MAKE THE WORLD .... Roosevelt Grier, Amy 11029
127. SAN FRANCISCO (Wear Some Flowers in Your Hair) .... Paul Mauriat & his Ork, Philips 40550
128. WEIGHT .... Jackie DeShannon, Imperial 66313

Compiled from national retail sales and radio station airplay by the Music Popularity Dept. of Record Market Research, Billboard.

# Billboard HOT 100

**For Week Ending Aug. 17, 1968**

★ STAR PERFORMER—Sides registering greatest proportionate upward progress this week.

● Record Industry Association of America seal of certification as million selling single.

| This Week | Wk. Ago | 2 Wks. Ago | 3 Wks. Ago | TITLE — Artist (Producer), Label & Number | Weeks On Chart |
|---|---|---|---|---|---|
| 1 ● | 5 | 13 | 32 | PEOPLE GOT TO BE FREE — Rascals (Rascals), Atlantic 2537 | 5 |
| 2 | 1 | 1 | 9 | HELLO, I LOVE YOU — Doors (Paul Rothchild), Elektra 45635 | 7 |
| 3 | 2 | 2 | 8 | CLASSICAL GAS — Mason Williams (Mike Post), Warner Bros.-Seven Arts 7190 | 9 |
| 4 | 11 | 11 | 31 | BORN TO BE WILD — Steppenwolf (Gabriel Mekler), Dunhill 4138 | 6 |
| 5 ★ | 20 | 32 | 62 | LIGHT MY FIRE — Jose Feliciano (Rick Jarrard), RCA Victor 47-9550 | 4 |
| 6 | 3 | 3 | 3 | STONED SOUL PICNIC — 5th Dimension (Bones Howe), Soul City 766 | 12 |
| 7 | 8 | 9 | 11 | TURN AROUND, LOOK AT ME — Vogues (Dick Glasser), Reprise 0686 | 10 |
| 8 | 9 | 10 | 18 | SUNSHINE OF YOUR LOVE — Cream (Felix Pappalardi), Atco 6544 | 7 |
| 9 ● | 4 | 4 | 1 | GRAZING IN THE GRASS — Hugh Masekela (Stewart Levine), Uni 55066 | 11 |
| 10 | 6 | 5 | 6 | HURDY GURDY MAN — Donovan (Mickie Most), Epic 10345 | 9 |
| 11 ● | 7 | 7 | 2 | LADY WILLPOWER — Gary Puckett & the Union Gap (Jerry Fuller), Columbia 44547 | 11 |
| 12 | 18 | 20 | 30 | DREAM A LITTLE DREAM OF ME — Mama Cass with the Mamas & Papas (Lou Adler), Dunhill 4145 | 5 |
| 13 | 13 | 18 | 25 | STAY IN MY CORNER — Dells (Bobby Miller), Cadet 5612 | 8 |
| 14 | 15 | 16 | 47 | (You Keep Me) HANGIN' ON — Vanilla Fudge (Shadow Morton), Atco 6495 | 12 |
| 15 | 10 | 6 | 4 | JUMPIN' JACK FLASH — Rolling Stones (Jimmy Miller), London 908 | 11 |
| 16 ★ | 23 | 39 | 49 | I CAN'T STOP DANCING — Archie Bell & the Drells (Gamble-Huff), Atlantic 2534 | 5 |
| 17 | 17 | 17 | 38 | JOURNEY TO THE CENTER OF MY MIND — Amboy Dukes (Bob Shad), Mainstream 684 | 8 |
| 18 | 21 | 22 | 42 | SOUL LIMBO — Booker T. & the M.G.'s (Booker T. Jones), Stax 0001 | 6 |
| 19 | 24 | 30 | 40 | SEALED WITH A KISS — Gary Lewis & Playboys (Snuff Garrett), Liberty 56037 | 9 |
| 20 | 14 | 12 | 15 | PICTURES OF MATCHSTICK MEN — Status Quo (John Schroeder), Cadet Concept 7001 | 14 |
| 21 ● | 12 | 8 | 5 | THE HORSE — Cliff Nobles & Co. (Jesse James), Phil L.A. of Soul 313 | 13 |
| 22 | 22 | 14 | 14 | SKY PILOT — Eric Burdon & the Animals (Tom Wilson), MGM 13939 | 12 |
| 23 | 36 | 54 | 80 | YOU'RE ALL I NEED TO GET BY — Marvin Gaye & Tammi Terrell (Ashford-Simpson), Tamla 54169 | 4 |
| 24 | 37 | 56 | 58 | LOVE MAKES A WOMAN — Barbara Acklin (Carl Davis & Eugene Record), Brunswick 55379 | 6 |
| 25 | 27 | 28 | 53 | HALFWAY TO PARADISE — Bobby Vinton (Billy Sherrill), Epic 10350 | 5 |
| 26 | 19 | 19 | 21 | AUTUMN OF MY LIFE — Bobby Goldsboro (Bob Montgomery), United Artists 50318 | 8 |
| 27 | 30 | 49 | 57 | (Love Is Like A) BASEBALL GAME — Intruders (Gamble Huff Prod.), Gamble 217 | 7 |
| 28 | 34 | 34 | 56 | ALICE LONG (You're Still My Favorite Girlfriend) — Tommy Boyce & Bobby Hart (Boyce & Hart), A&M 948 | 6 |
| 29 | 51 | 67 | 67 | SLIP AWAY — Clarence Carter (Rick Hall & Staff), Atlantic 2508 | 6 |
| 30 | 25 | 21 | 10 | INDIAN LAKE — Cowsills (Wes Ferrell), MGM 13944 | 12 |
| 31 | 44 | 83 | — | PLEASE RETURN YOUR LOVE TO ME — Temptations (Norman Whitfield), Gordy 7074 | 3 |
| 32 | 39 | 53 | 84 | 1, 2, 3, RED LIGHT — 1910 Fruitgum Company (Kasenetz-Katz Assoc.), Buddah 54 | 4 |
| 33 | 50 | 61 | 88 | DO IT AGAIN — Beach Boys (Beach Boys), Capitol 2239 | 4 |
| 34 | 35 | 41 | 41 | HITCH IT TO THE HORSE — Fantastic Johnny C (Jesse James), Phil L.A. of Soul 315 | 8 |
| 35 | 41 | 44 | 48 | YOU MET YOUR MATCH — Stevie Wonder (Don Hunter), Tamla 54168 | 5 |
| 36 | 33 | 27 | 27 | DON'T TAKE IT SO HARD — Paul Revere & The Raiders (Featuring Mark Lindsay) (Mark Lindsay), Columbia 44555 | 9 |
| 37 | 31 | 31 | 33 | LOVER'S HOLIDAY — Peggy Scott & Jo Jo Benson (Huey P. Meaux), SSS International 736 | 11 |
| 38 | 40 | 40 | 46 | THE EYES OF A NEW YORK WOMAN — B.J. Thomas (Chips Moman), Scepter 12219 | 9 |
| 39 | 32 | 33 | 45 | DREAMS OF THE EVERYDAY HOUSEWIFE — Glen Campbell (Al de Lory), Capitol 2224 | 7 |
| 40 | 28 | 24 | 17 | ANGEL IN THE MORNING — Merrilee Rush (T. Cogbill & C. Moman), Bell 705 | 16 |
| 41 | 16 | 15 | 7 | THIS GUY'S IN LOVE WITH YOU — Herb Alpert (Herb Alpert & Jerry Moss), A&M 929 | 14 |
| 42 | 26 | 26 | 13 | REACH OUT OF THE DARKNESS — Friend & Lover (Joe South & Bill Lowery), Verve Forecast 5069 | 14 |
| 43 | 47 | 50 | 78 | DON'T GIVE UP — Petula Clark (Tony Hatch), Warner Bros.-Seven Arts 7216 | 5 |
| 44 | 48 | 48 | 71 | TUESDAY AFTERNOON (Forever Afternoon) — Moody Blues (Tony Clarke), Deram 85028 | 5 |
| 45 | 45 | 57 | 60 | PRAYER MEETIN' — Willie Mitchell (Joe Cough), Hi 2147 | 6 |
| 46 | 65 | 65 | 65 | UNDERSTANDING — Ray Charles (Joe Adams), ABC 11090 | 10 |
| 47 | 53 | 64 | 66 | I GET THE SWEETEST FEELING — Jackie Wilson (Carl Davis), Brunswick 55381 | 6 |
| 48 | 61 | — | — | THE FOOL ON THE HILL — Sergio Mendes & Brasil '66 (Sergio Mendes, Herb Alpert & Jerry Moss), A&M 961 | 2 |
| 49 | 49 | 51 | 54 | YESTERDAY'S DREAMS — Four Tops (Ivy Hunter), Motown 1127 | 5 |
| 50 | 68 | 68 | 81 | AND SUDDENLY — Cherry People (Jerry Ross, Ron Haffkine & Barry Oslander), Heritage 801 | 4 |
| 51 | 52 | 89 | — | DOWN AT LULU'S — Ohio Express (Kasenetz-Katz Assoc.), Buddah 56 | 3 |
| 52 | 54 | 63 | 63 | HARD TO HANDLE — Otis Redding (Steve Cropper), Atco 6592 | 5 |
| 53 | 55 | 79 | 90 | SOMEBODY CARES — Tommy James and the Shondells (Neil Galligan & Gary Illingworth), Roulette 7016 | 4 |
| 54 | 56 | 88 | — | CAN'T YOU FIND ANOTHER WAY (Of Doing It) — Sam & Dave (Isaac Hayes & David Porter), Atlantic 2540 | 3 |
| 55 | 57 | 58 | 64 | THE IMPOSSIBLE DREAM — Roger Williams (Hy Grill), Kapp 907 | 6 |
| 56 | 58 | 95 | — | GIVE A DAMN — Spanky & Our Gang (Scharf/Pomund, Edel), Mercury 72831 | 3 |
| 57 | 59 | 74 | 77 | I GUESS I'LL HAVE TO CRY, CRY, CRY — James Brown & the Famous Flames (James Brown), King 6141 | 4 |
| 58 | 78 | 90 | — | MR. BUSINESSMAN — Ray Stevens (Fred Foster & Ray Stevens), Monument 1083 | 3 |
| 59 | — | — | — | THE HOUSE THAT JACK BUILT — Aretha Franklin (Jerry Wexler), Atlantic 2546 | 1 |
| 60 | 72 | — | — | KEEP THE ONE YOU GOT — Joe Tex (Buddy Killen), Dial 4083 | 2 |
| 61 | 76 | 77 | 95 | I LOVED AND I LOST — Impressions (Johnny Pate), ABC 11103 | 4 |
| 62 | 64 | 80 | — | BROWN EYED WOMAN — Bill Medley (Bill Medley & Barry Mann), MGM 13959 | 3 |
| 63 | 63 | 97 | — | SUDDEN STOP — Percy Sledge (Quin Ivy & Marlin Greene), Atlantic 2539 | 3 |
| 64 | 83 | — | — | MAGIC BUS — Who (Kit Lambert), Decca 32362 | 2 |
| 65 | 80 | 82 | 85 | GOD BLESS OUR LOVE — Ballads (Jesse Mason & Willie Hutch), Venture 615 | 4 |
| 66 | 67 | 71 | 91 | I'VE NEVER FOUND A GIRL (To Love Me Like You Do) — Eddie Floyd (Steve Cropper), Stax 0002 | 4 |
| 67 | 70 | 81 | 86 | BREAKING UP IS HARD TO DO — Happenings (Tokens), B.T. Puppy 543 | 4 |
| 68 | 66 | 66 | 70 | TWO-BIT MANCHILD — Neil Diamond (Tom Catalano & Neil Diamond), Uni 55075 | 6 |
| 69 | 69 | 69 | 73 | MRS. BLUEBIRD — Eternity's Children (Curt Boettcher & Keith Olsen), Tower 416 | 5 |
| 70 | 71 | — | — | MORNING DEW — Lulu (Mickie Most), Epic 10367 | 2 |
| 71 | 86 | 91 | — | GIRLS CAN'T DO WHAT THE GUYS DO — Betty Wright (Brad Shapiro & Steve Alaimo), Alston 4569 | 3 |
| 72 | 90 | — | — | I CAN'T DANCE TO THE MUSIC YOU'RE PLAYIN' — Martha Reeves & The Vandellas (Deke Richards), Gordy 7075 | 2 |
| 73 | 73 | 78 | 98 | NEVER GOING BACK — Lovin' Spoonful (Chip Douglas), Kama Sutra 250 | 4 |
| 74 | 81 | 85 | 94 | I'M GONNA DO WHAT THEY DO TO ME — B.B. King (Lou Zito-Johnnie Pate), Blues Way 61018 | 4 |
| 75 | 75 | 76 | 76 | COMPETITION AIN'T NOTHIN' — Little Carl Carlton, Back Beat 588 | 5 |
| 76 | 85 | — | — | HIP CITY—PART 2 — Jr. Walker & The All Stars (Lawrence Horn), Soul 35048 | 2 |
| 77 | 77 | 87 | 96 | MR. BOJANGLES — Jerry Jeff Walker (Tom Dowd & Dan Elliot), Atco 6594 | 4 |
| 78 | 74 | 75 | 79 | HAPPY — Nancy Sinatra (Lee Hazlewood), Reprise 0756 | 5 |
| 79 | 79 | 88 | — | MISTER BOJANGLES — Bobby Cole (Bobby Cole), Date 1613 | 3 |
| 80 | 84 | 84 | 100 | GIVE ME ONE MORE CHANCE — Wilmer Alexander Jr. & the Dukes (Dukes), Aphrodisiac 26C | 5 |
| 81 | 82 | 96 | — | WORKIN' ON A GROOVY THING — Patti Drew (Carone Prod.), Capitol 2197 | 3 |
| 82 | — | — | — | I SAY A LITTLE PRAYER — Aretha Franklin (Jerry Wexler), Atlantic 2546 | 1 |
| 83 | — | — | — | HUSH — Deep Purple (Derek Lawrence), Tetragrammaton 1503 | 1 |
| 84 | 89 | — | — | I HEARD IT THROUGH THE GRAPEVINE — King Curtis & His Kingpins (Arif Mardin), Atco 6598 | 2 |
| 85 | 92 | — | — | I AM YOUR MAN — Bobby Taylor & The Vancouvers (Frank Wilson), Gordy 7073 | 2 |
| 86 | 87 | 99 | — | MONTAGE FROM HOW SWEET IT IS (I Knew That You Knew) — Love Generation (Tommy Oliver & Joe Saraceno), Imperial 66310 | 3 |
| 87 | — | — | — | SPECIAL OCCASION — Smokey Robinson & The Miracles (Smokey-Cleveland), Tamla 54172 | 1 |
| 88 | 88 | 92 | — | ANYWAY YOU WANT ME — American Breed (Bill Trout), Acta 827 | 3 |
| 89 | — | — | — | GIRL WATCHER — O'Kaysions (North State Music), ABC 11094 | 1 |
| 90 | 99 | — | — | ON THE ROAD AGAIN — Canned Heat (Dallas Smith), Liberty 56038 | 2 |
| 91 | 91 | 98 | 99 | SOUL MEETING — Soul Clan (Don Covay), Atlantic 2530 | 4 |
| 92 | 95 | — | — | TIME HAS COME TODAY — Chambers Brothers (David Robinson), Columbia 44414 | 2 |
| 93 | — | — | — | THE SNAKE — Al Wilson (Johnny Rivers), Soul City 767 | 1 |
| 94 | 97 | — | — | M'LADY — Sly & The Family Stone (Stone Flower Prod.), Epic 10353 | 2 |
| 95 | 96 | — | — | TELL SOMEONE YOU LOVE THEM — Dino, Desi & Billy (Martin & Hinsche), Reprise 0698 | 2 |
| 96 | 98 | — | — | MISTER NICO — Four Jacks & a Jill, RCA Victor 47-9572 | 2 |
| 97 | 100 | 100 | — | SALLY HAD A PARTY — Flavor (Tim O'Brien), Columbia 44521 | 3 |
| 98 | — | — | — | LITTLE GREEN APPLES — O.C. Smith (Jerry Fuller), Columbia 44616 | 1 |
| 99 | — | — | — | I'VE GOTTA GET A MESSAGE TO YOU — Bee Gees (Robert Stigwood), Atco 6603 | 1 |
| 100 | — | — | — | FLY ME TO THE MOON — Bobby Womack (Chips Moman), Minit 32048 | 1 |

## BUBBLING UNDER THE HOT 100

101. SUNSHINE GIRL .................... Herman's Hermits, MGM 13973
102. IF LOVE IS IN YOUR HEART ........ Friend & Lover, Verve Forecast 5091
103. BRING BACK THOSE ROCKABYE BABY DAYS ........ Tiny Tim, Reprise 0760
104. THAT OLD TIME FEELIN' ........... Dean Martin, Reprise 0761
105. TO LOVE SOMEBODY ........ Sweet Inspirations, Atlantic 2529
106. BREAK MY MIND ........ Sammy Davis Jr., Reprise 0757
107. THE WOMAN I LOVE ........ B.B. King, Kent 492
108. DO WHAT YOU GOTTA DO ........ Bobby Vee, Liberty 56057
109. APRIL AGAIN ........ Dean Martin, Reprise 0761
110. SINCE YOU'VE BEEN GONE ........ Ramsey Lewis, Cadet 5609
111. LULLABYE FROM ROSEMARY'S BABY ........ Mia Farrow, Dot 17126
112. MIDNIGHT CONFESSIONS ........ Grassroots, Dunhill 4144
113. TURN ON YOUR LOVELIGHT ........ Bill Black's Combo, Hi 2145
114. EVERYBODY'S TALKING ........ Nilsson, RCA Victor 47-9544
115. HELP YOURSELF (To All of My Lovin') ........ James & Bobby Purify, Bell 735
116. DO YOU WANNA DANCE ........ Love Society, Scepter 1223
117. STORYBOOK CHILDREN ........ Billy Joe Royal, Columbia 44574
118. WEIGHT ........ Jackie DeShannon, Imperial 66313
119. SIX MAN BAND ........ Association, Warner Bros.-Seven Arts 7229
120. DO THE BEST YOU CAN ........ Hollies, Epic 10361
121. ME AND YOU ........ Brenton Wood, Double Shot 130
122. ALL MY LOVE'S LAUGHTER ........ Ed Ames, RCA Victor 47-9580
123. SHE'S ABOUT A MOVER ........ Otis Clay, Cotillion 44001
124. SAN FRANCISCO (WEAR SOME FLOWERS IN YOUR HAIR) ........ Paul Mauriat, Philips 40550
125. LADY MADONNA ........ Fats Domino, Reprise 0763
126. HELP YOURSELF ........ Tom Jones, Parrot 40029

*Compiled from national retail sales and radio station airplay by the Music Popularity Dept. of Record Market Research, Billboard.*

# Billboard HOT 100

FOR WEEK ENDING AUG. 24, 1968

★ STAR PERFORMER—Sides registering greatest proportionate upward progress this week.

(Gold seal) Record Industry Association of America seal of certification as million selling single.

| This Week | 1 Wk. Ago | 2 Wks. Ago | 3 Wks. Ago | TITLE Artist (Producer), Label & Number | Weeks On Chart |
|---|---|---|---|---|---|
| 1 (Billboard Award) | 1 | 5 | 13 | PEOPLE GOT TO BE FREE — Rascals (Rascals), Atlantic 2537 | 6 |
| 2 ★ | 4 | 11 | 11 | BORN TO BE WILD — Steppenwolf (Gabriel Mekler), Dunhill 4138 | 7 |
| 3 | 2 | 1 | 1 | HELLO, I LOVE YOU — Doors (Paul Rothchild), Elektra 45635 | 8 |
| 4 ★ | 5 | 20 | 32 | LIGHT MY FIRE — Jose Feliciano (Rick Jarrard), RCA Victor 47-9550 | 5 |
| 5 | 3 | 2 | 2 | CLASSICAL GAS — Mason Williams (Mike Post), Warner-Bros.-Seven Arts 7190 | 10 |
| 6 | 8 | 9 | 10 | SUNSHINE OF YOUR LOVE — Cream (Felix Pappalardi), Atco 6544 | 8 |
| 7 | 7 | 8 | 9 | TURN AROUND, LOOK AT ME — Vogues (Dick Glasser), Reprise 0686 | 11 |
| 8 | 6 | 3 | 3 | STONED SOUL PICNIC — 5th Dimension (Bones Howe), Soul City 766 | 13 |
| 9 ★ | 16 | 23 | 39 | I CAN'T STOP DANCING — Archie Bell & the Drells (Gamble-Huff), Atlantic 2534 | 6 |
| 10 ★ | 13 | 13 | 18 | STAY IN MY CORNER — Dells (Bobby Miller), Cadet 5612 | 9 |
| 11 | 14 | 15 | 16 | (You Keep Me) HANGIN' ON — Vanilla Fudge (Shadow Morton), Atco 6495 | 13 |
| 12 | 12 | 18 | 20 | DREAM A LITTLE DREAM OF ME — Mama Cass with the Mamas & Papas (Lou Adler), Dunhill 4145 | 8 |
| 13 (Gold seal) | 11 | 7 | 7 | LADY WILLPOWER — Gary Puckett & the Union Gap (Jerry Fuller), Columbia 44547 | 12 |
| 14 | 10 | 6 | 5 | HURDY GURDY MAN — Donovan (Mickie Most), Epic 10345 | 10 |
| 15 ★ | 23 | 36 | 54 | YOU'RE ALL I NEED TO GET BY — Marvin Gaye & Tammi Terrell (Ashford-Simpson), Tamla 54169 | 5 |
| 16 | 17 | 17 | 17 | JOURNEY TO THE CENTER OF MY MIND — Amboy Dukes (Bob Shad), Mainstream 684 | 9 |
| 17 ★ | 24 | 37 | 56 | LOVE MAKES A WOMAN — Barbara Acklin (Carl Davis & Eugene Record), Brunswick 55379 | 7 |
| 18 | 18 | 21 | 22 | SOUL LIMBO — Booker T. & the M.G.'s (Booker T. Jones), Stax 0001 | 7 |
| 19 | 19 | 24 | 30 | SEALED WITH A KISS — Gary Lewis & Playboys (Snuff Garrett), Liberty 56037 | 10 |
| 20 (Gold seal) | 9 | 4 | 4 | GRAZING IN THE GRASS — Hugh Masekela (Stewart Levine), Uni 55066 | 12 |
| 21 ★ | 59 | — | — | THE HOUSE THAT JACK BUILT — Aretha Franklin (Jerry Wexler), Atlantic 2456 | 2 |
| 22 ★ | 32 | 39 | 53 | 1, 2, 3, RED LIGHT — 1910 Fruitgum Company (Kasenetz-Katz Assoc.) Buddah 54 | 5 |
| 23 | 25 | 27 | 28 | HALFWAY TO PARADISE — Bobby Vinton (Billy Sherrill), Epic 10350 | 6 |
| 24 | 29 | 51 | 67 | SLIP AWAY — Clarence Carter (Rick Hall & Staff), Atlantic 2508 | 7 |
| 25 | 20 | 14 | 12 | PICTURES OF MATCHSTICK MEN — Status Quo (John Schroeder), Cadet Concept 7001 | 15 |
| 26 | 27 | 30 | 49 | (Love Is Like A) BASEBALL GAME — Intruders (Gamble Huff Prod.), Gamble 217 | 8 |
| 27 | 28 | 34 | 34 | ALICE LONG (You're Still My Favorite Girlfriend) — Tommy Boyce & Bobby Hart (Boyce & Hart), A&M 948 | 8 |
| 28 | 31 | 44 | 83 | PLEASE RETURN YOUR LOVE TO ME — Temptations (Norman Whitfield), Gordy 7074 | 4 |
| 29 | 22 | 22 | 14 | SKY PILOT — Eric Burdon & the Animals (Tom Wilson), MGM 13939 | 13 |
| 30 | 15 | 10 | 6 | JUMPIN' JACK FLASH — Rolling Stones (Jimmy Miller), London 908 | 12 |
| 31 | 33 | 50 | 61 | DO IT AGAIN — Beach Boys (Beach Boys), Capitol 2239 | 5 |
| 32 ★ | 48 | 61 | — | THE FOOL ON THE HILL — Sergio Mendes & Brasil '66 (Sergio Mendes, Herb Alpert & Jerry Moss) | 3 |
| 33 (Gold seal) | 21 | 12 | 8 | THE HORSE — Cliff Nobles & Co. (Jesse James), Phil L. A. of Soul 313 | 14 |
| 34 | 38 | 40 | 40 | THE EYES OF A NEW YORK WOMAN — B.J. Thomas (Chips Moman), Scepter 12219 | 10 |
| 35 | 35 | 41 | 44 | YOU MET YOUR MATCH — Stevie Wonder (Don Hunter), Tamla 54168 | 6 |
| 36 | 26 | 19 | 19 | AUTUMN OF MY LIFE — Bobby Goldsboro (Bob Montgomery), United Artists 50318 | 9 |
| 37 | 43 | 47 | 50 | DON'T GIVE UP — Petula Clark (Tony Hatch), Warner Bros.-Seven Arts 7216 | 6 |
| 38 ★ | 83 | — | — | HUSH — Deep Purple (Derek Lawrence), Tetragrammaton 1503 | 2 |
| 39 ★ | 82 | — | — | I SAY A LITTLE PRAYER — Aretha Franklin (Jerry Wexler), Atlantic 2456 | 2 |
| 40 | 44 | 48 | 48 | TUESDAY AFTERNOON (Forever Afternoon) — Moody Blues (Tony Clarke), Deram 85028 | 6 |
| 41 ★ | 66 | 67 | 71 | I'VE NEVER FOUND A GIRL (To Love Me Like You Do) — Eddie Floyd (Steve Cropper), Stax 0002 | 5 |
| 42 | 47 | 53 | 64 | I GET THE SWEETEST FEELING — Jackie Wilson (Carl Davis), Brunswick 55381 | 6 |
| 43 ★ | 51 | 52 | 89 | DOWN AT LULU'S — Ohio Express (Kasenetz-Katz Assoc.), Buddah 56 | 4 |
| 44 | 37 | 31 | 31 | LOVER'S HOLIDAY — Peggy Scott & Jo Jo Benson (Huey P. Meaux), SSS International 736 | 12 |
| 45 | 39 | 32 | 33 | DREAMS OF THE EVERYDAY HOUSEWIFE — Glen Campbell (Al de Lory), Capitol 2224 | 8 |
| 46 | 46 | 65 | 65 | UNDERSTANDING — Ray Charles (Joe Adams), ABC 11090 | 11 |
| 47 | 30 | 25 | 21 | INDIAN LAKE — Cowsills (Wes Ferrell), MGM 13944 | 13 |
| 48 | 50 | 68 | 68 | AND SUDDENLY — Cherry People (Ron Haffkine, Barry Oslander & Jerry Ross), Heritage 801 | 6 |
| 49 | 34 | 35 | 41 | HITCH IT TO THE HORSE — Fantastic Johnny C (Jesse James), Phil L.A. of Soul 315 | 9 |
| 50 ★ | 58 | 78 | 90 | MR. BUSINESSMAN — Ray Stevens (Fred Foster & Ray Stevens), Monument 1083 | 4 |
| 51 | 52 | 54 | 63 | HARD TO HANDLE — Otis Redding (Steve Cropper), Atco 6592 | 7 |
| 52 ★ | 71 | 86 | 91 | GIRLS CAN'T DO WHAT THE GUYS DO — Betty Wright (Brad Shapiro & Steve Alaimo), Alston 4569 | 4 |
| 53 | 56 | 58 | 95 | GIVE A DAMN — Spanky & Our Gang (Scharf/Dorough, Edel), Mercury 72831 | 4 |
| 54 | 54 | 56 | 88 | CAN'T YOU FIND ANOTHER WAY (Of Doing It) — Sam & Dave (Isaac Hayes & David Porter), Atlantic 2540 | 4 |
| 55 | 57 | 59 | 74 | I GUESS I'LL HAVE TO CRY, CRY, CRY — James Brown & the Famous Flames (James Brown), King 6141 | 5 |
| 56 | 53 | 55 | 79 | SOMEBODY CARES — Tommy James & the Shondells (Neil Galligan & Gary Illingworth), Roulette 7016 | 5 |
| 57 ★ | 64 | 83 | — | MAGIC BUS — Who (Kit Lambert), Decca 32362 | 3 |
| 58 | 60 | 72 | — | KEEP THE ONE YOU GOT — Joe Tex (Buddy Killen), Dial 4083 | 3 |
| 59 ★ | 87 | — | — | SPECIAL OCCASION — Smokey Robinson & The Miracles (Smokey-Cleveland), Tamla 54172 | 2 |
| 60 | 62 | 64 | 80 | BROWN EYED WOMAN — Bill Medley (Bill Medley & Barry Mann), MGM 13959 | 4 |
| 61 | 61 | 76 | 77 | I LOVED AND I LOST — Impressions (Johnny Pate), ABC 11103 | 6 |
| 62 | 49 | 49 | 51 | YESTERDAY'S DREAMS — Four Tops (Ivy Hunter), Motown 1127 | 6 |
| 63 | 63 | 63 | 97 | SUDDEN STOP — Percy Sledge (Quin Ivy & Marlin Greene), Atlantic 2539 | 4 |
| 64 | 45 | 45 | 57 | PRAYER MEETIN' — Willie Mitchell (Joe Coughi), Hi 2147 | 7 |
| 65 | 65 | 80 | 82 | GOD BLESS OUR LOVE — Ballads (Jesse Mason & Willie Hutch), Venture 615 | 6 |
| 66 | 70 | 71 | — | MORNING DEW — Lulu (Mickie Most), Epic 10367 | 3 |
| 67 ★ | — | — | — | LISTEN HERE — Eddie Harris (Joel Dorn), Atlantic 2487 | 6 |
| 68 ★ | 99 | — | — | I'VE GOTTA GET A MESSAGE TO YOU — Bee Gees (Robert Stigwood), Atco 6603 | 2 |
| 69 ★ | 72 | 90 | — | I CAN'T DANCE TO THE MUSIC YOU'RE PLAYIN' — Martha Reeves & The Vandellas (Deke Richards), Gordy 7075 | 3 |
| 70 ★ | 76 | 85 | — | HIP CITY—PART 2 — Jr. Walker & The All Stars (Lawrence Horn), Soul 35048 | 3 |
| 71 ★ | 89 | — | — | GIRL WATCHER — O'Kaysions (North State Music), ABC 11094 | 2 |
| 72 ★ | 90 | 99 | — | ON THE ROAD AGAIN — Canned Heat (Dallas Smith), Liberty 56038 | 3 |
| 73 | 55 | 57 | 58 | THE IMPOSSIBLE DREAM — Roger Williams (Hy Grill), Kapp 907 | 7 |
| 74 | 67 | 70 | 81 | BREAKING UP IS HARD TO DO — Happenings (Tokens), B.T. Puppy 543 | 5 |
| 75 | 73 | 73 | 73 | NEVER GOING BACK — Lovin' Spoonful (Chip Douglas), Kama Sutra 250 | 5 |
| 76 | 69 | 69 | 69 | MRS. BLUEBIRD — Eternity's Children (Curt Boettcher & Keith Olsen), Tower 416 | 7 |
| 77 ★ | 81 | 82 | 96 | WORKIN' ON A GROOVY THING — Patti Drew (Carone Prod.), Capitol 2197 | 4 |
| 78 ★ | 98 | — | — | LITTLE GREEN APPLES — O. C. Smith (Jerry Fuller), Columbia 44616 | 2 |
| 79 | 77 | 77 | 87 | MR. BOJANGLES — Jerry Jeff Walker (Tom Dowd & Dan Elliot), Atco 6594 | 5 |
| 80 ★ | 93 | — | — | THE SNAKE — Al Wilson (Johnny Rivers), Soul City 767 | 2 |
| 81 ★ | — | — | — | HARPER VALLEY P.T.A. — Jeannie C. Riley (Shelby S. Singleton Jr.), Plantation 3 | 1 |
| 82 ★ | 100 | — | — | FLY ME TO THE MOON — Bobby Womack (Chips Moman), Minit 32048 | 2 |
| 83 | 84 | 89 | — | I HEARD IT THROUGH THE GRAPEVINE — King Curtis & His Kingpins (Arif Mardin), Atco 6598 | 3 |
| 84 ★ | — | — | — | I WISH IT WOULD RAIN — Gladys Knight & The Pips (N. Whitefield), Soul 35047 | 1 |
| 85 | 85 | 92 | — | I AM YOUR MAN — Bobby Taylor & The Vancouvers (Frank Wilson), Gordy 7073 | 3 |
| 86 | 80 | 84 | 84 | GIVE ME ONE MORE CHANCE — Wilmer Alexander Jr. & the Dukes (Dukes), Aphrodisiac 260 | 6 |
| 87 | 74 | 81 | 85 | I'M GONNA DO WHAT THEY DO TO ME — B.B. King (Lou Zito-Johnnie Pate), Blues Way 61018 | 5 |
| 88 | 88 | 88 | 92 | ANYWAY YOU WANT ME — American Breed (Bill Trout) Acta 827 | 4 |
| 89 ★ | — | — | — | SIX MAN BAND — Association (Association), Warner Bros.-Seven Arts 7229 | 1 |
| 90 ★ | — | — | — | DON'T CHANGE YOUR LOVE — Five Stairsteps & Cubie (Curtis Mayfield), Curtom 1931 | 1 |
| 91 | 92 | 95 | — | TIME HAS COME TODAY — Chambers Brothers (David Rubinson), Columbia 44414 | 3 |
| 92 | — | — | — | IN-A-GADDA-DA-VIDA — Iron Butterfly (Jim Hilton), Atco 6606 | 1 |
| 93 | 94 | 97 | — | M'LADY — Sly & The Family Stone (Stone Flower Prod.), Epic 10353 | 3 |
| 94 | — | — | — | THE WOMAN I LOVE — B.B. King, Kent 492 | 1 |
| 95 | 95 | 96 | — | TELL SOMEONE YOU LOVE THEM — Dino, Desi & Billy (Martin & Hinsche), Reprise 0698 | 3 |
| 96 | — | — | — | WHO IS GONNA LOVE ME? — Dionne Warwick (Bacharach-David), Scepter 12226 | 1 |
| 97 | — | — | — | BRING BACK THOSE ROCKABYE BABY DAYS — Tiny Tim (Richard Perry), Reprise 0760 | 1 |
| 98 | — | — | — | THE FUNKY JUDGE — Bull & The Matadors (Sherrel-Cross Prod.), Toddlin' Town 108 | 1 |
| 99 | — | — | — | SHE'S ABOUT A MOVER — Otis Clay (Rick Hall), Cotillion 44001 | 1 |
| 100 | — | — | — | THE WEIGHT — Jackie DeShannon (Charles Greene & Brian Stone), Imperial 66313 | 1 |

## HOT 100—A TO Z—(Publisher-Licensee)



## BUBBLING UNDER THE HOT 100

101. SUNSHINE GIRL .... Herman's Hermits, MGM 13973
102. IF LOVE IS IN YOUR HEART .... Friend & Lover, Verve Forecast 5091
103. DO WHAT YOU GOTTA DO .... Bobby Vee, Liberty 56057
104. MIDNIGHT CONFESSIONS .... Grassroots, Dunhill 4144
105. HELP YOURSELF .... Tom Jones, Parrot 40029
106. BREAK MY MIND .... Sammy Davis Jr., Reprise 0757
107. HELP YOURSELF (To All of My Lovin') .... James & Bobby Purify, Bell 735
108. LADY MADONNA .... Fats Domino, Reprise 0763
109. APRIL AGAIN .... Dean Martin, Reprise 0761
110. SINCE YOU'VE BEEN GONE .... Ramsey Lewis, Cadet 5609
111. SALLY HAD A PARTY .... Flavor, Columbia 44521
112. LIGHT MY FIRE .... Doors, Elektra 45615
113. EVERYBODY'S TALKING .... Nilsson, RCA Victor 47-9544
114. DO YOU WANNA DANCE .... Love Society, Scepter 12223
115. HANG 'EM HIGH .... Hugo Montenegro, RCA Victor 47-9554
116. THERE'S ALWAYS SOMETHING THERE TO REMIND ME .... Dionne Warwick, Scepter 12226
117. THAT KIND OF WOMAN .... Merrilee Rush, Bell 738
118. BAREFOOT IN BALTIMORE .... Strawberry Alarm Clock, UNI 55076
119. MY WAY OF LIFE .... Frank Sinatra, Reprise 0764
120. DO THE BEST YOU CAN .... Hollies, Epic 10361
121. SAN FRANCISCO—WEAR SOME FLOWERS IN YOUR HAIR .... Paul Mauriat & his Ork, Philips 40550
122. ALL MY LOVE'S LAUGHTER .... Ed Ames, RCA Victor 47-9589
123. BABY COME BACK .... Equals, RCA Victor 47-9583
124. THE MULE .... James Boys, Phil-L.A. of Soul 316
125. BREAK YOUR PROMISE .... Delfonics, Philly Groove 152
126. (The Lament of the Cherokee) INDIAN RESERVATION .... Don Fardon, GNP Crescendo 405
127. PRIVATE NUMBER .... Judy Clay & William Bell, Stax 0005
128. SHOOT 'EM UP BABY .... Andy Kim, Steed 710
129. HARD TO GET A THING CALLED LOVE .... Platters, Musicor 1322
130. (As I Went Down To) JERUSALEM .... Hello People, Philips 40531
131. HOLD ME TIGHT .... Johnny Nash, Jad 207
132. DOWN HERE ON THE GROUND .... Lou Rawls, Capitol 2252

Compiled from national retail sales and radio station airplay by the Music Popularity Dept. of Record Market Research, Billboard.

# Billboard HOT 100

FOR WEEK ENDING AUG. 31, 1968

★ STAR PERFORMER—Sides registering greatest proportionate upward progress this week.

(Seal) Record Industry Association of America seal of certification as million selling single.

| This Week | 1 Wk. Ago | 2 Wks. Ago | 3 Wks. Ago | TITLE Artist (Producer), Label & Number | Weeks On Chart |
|---|---|---|---|---|---|
| 1 (Billboard Award) | 1 | 1 | 5 | PEOPLE GOT TO BE FREE — Rascals (Rascals), Atlantic 2537 | 7 |
| 2 | 2 | 4 | 11 | BORN TO BE WILD — Steppenwolf (Gabriel Mekler), Dunhill 4138 | 8 |
| ★3 | 4 | 5 | 20 | LIGHT MY FIRE — Jose Feliciano (Rick Jarrard), RCA Victor 47-9550 | 6 |
| 4 | 3 | 2 | 1 | HELLO, I LOVE YOU — Doors (Paul Rothchild), Elektra 45635 | 9 |
| 5 | 6 | 8 | 9 | SUNSHINE OF YOUR LOVE — Cream (Felix Pappalardi), Atco 6544 | 9 |
| ★6 | 11 | 14 | 15 | (You Keep Me) HANGIN' ON — Vanilla Fudge (Shadow Morton), Atco 6495 | 14 |
| ★7 | 81 | — | — | HARPER VALLEY P.T.A. — Jeannie C. Riley (Shelby S. Singleton Jr.), Plantation 3 | 2 |
| ★8 | 15 | 23 | 36 | YOU'RE ALL I NEED TO GET BY — Marvin Gaye & Tammi Terrell (Ashford-Simpson), Tamla 54169 | 6 |
| 9 | 9 | 16 | 23 | I CAN'T STOP DANCING — Archie Bell & the Drells (Gamble-Huff), Atlantic 2534 | 7 |
| 10 | 10 | 13 | 13 | STAY IN MY CORNER — Dells (Bobby Miller), Cadet 5612 | 10 |
| 11 | 7 | 7 | 8 | TURN AROUND, LOOK AT ME — Vogues (Dick Glasser), Reprise 0686 | 12 |
| ★12 | 22 | 32 | 39 | 1, 2, 3, RED LIGHT — 1910 Fruitgum Company (Kasenetz-Katz Assoc.) Buddah 54 | 6 |
| 13 | 5 | 3 | 2 | CLASSICAL GAS — Mason Williams (Mike Post), Warner-Bros.-Seven Arts 7190 | 11 |
| ★14 | 38 | 83 | — | HUSH — Deep Purple (Derek Lawrence), Tetragrammaton 1503 | 3 |
| 15 | 17 | 24 | 37 | LOVE MAKES A WOMAN — Barbara Acklin (Carl Davis & Eugene Record), Brunswick 55379 | 8 |
| 16 | 16 | 17 | 17 | JOURNEY TO THE CENTER OF MY MIND — Amboy Dukes (Bob Shad), Mainstream 684 | 10 |
| 17 | 18 | 18 | 21 | SOUL LIMBO — Booker T. & the M.G.'s (Booker T. Jones), Stax 0001 | 8 |
| ★18 | 32 | 48 | 61 | THE FOOL ON THE HILL — Sergio Mendes & Brasil '66 (Sergio Mendes, Herb Alpert & Jerry Moss) | 4 |
| 19 | 19 | 19 | 24 | SEALED WITH A KISS — Gary Lewis & Playboys (Snuff Garrett), Liberty 56037 | 11 |
| ★20 | 21 | 59 | — | THE HOUSE THAT JACK BUILT — Aretha Franklin (Jerry Wexler), Atlantic 2456 | 3 |
| 21 | 12 | 12 | 18 | DREAM A LITTLE DREAM OF ME — Mama Cass with the Mamas & Papas (Lou Adler), Dunhill 4145 | 9 |
| 22 | 8 | 6 | 3 | STONED SOUL PICNIC — 5th Dimension (Bones Howe), Soul City 766 | 14 |
| 23 | 14 | 10 | 6 | HURDY GURDY MAN — Donovan (Mickie Most), Epic 10345 | 11 |
| ★24 | 31 | 33 | 50 | DO IT AGAIN — Beach Boys (Beach Boys), Capitol 2239 | 6 |
| ★25 | 39 | 82 | — | I SAY A LITTLE PRAYER — Aretha Franklin (Jerry Wexler), Atlantic 2456 | 3 |
| 26 | 28 | 31 | 44 | PLEASE RETURN YOUR LOVE TO ME — Temptations (Norman Whitfield), Gordy 7074 | 5 |
| 27 | 27 | 28 | 34 | ALICE LONG (You're Still My Favorite Girlfriend) — Tommy Boyce & Bobby Hart (Boyce & Hart), A&M 948 | 9 |
| 28 | 25 | 20 | 14 | PICTURES OF MATCHSTICK MEN — Status Quo (John Schroeder), Cadet Concept 7001 | 16 |
| 29 | 24 | 29 | 51 | SLIP AWAY — Clarence Carter (Rick Hall & Staff), Atlantic 2508 | 8 |
| 30 | 23 | 25 | 27 | HALFWAY TO PARADISE — Bobby Vinton (Billy Sherrill), Epic 10350 | 7 |
| 31 (seal) | 13 | 11 | 7 | LADY WILLPOWER — Gary Puckett & the Union Gap (Jerry Fuller), Columbia 44547 | 13 |
| ★32 | 57 | 64 | 83 | MAGIC BUS — Who (Kit Lambert), Decca 32362 | 4 |
| ★33 | 50 | 58 | 78 | MR. BUSINESSMAN — Ray Stevens (Fred Foster & Ray Stevens), Monument 1083 | 5 |
| 34 | 34 | 38 | 40 | THE EYES OF A NEW YORK WOMAN — B.J. Thomas (Chips Moman), Scepter 12219 | 11 |
| 35 | 42 | 47 | 53 | I GET THE SWEETEST FEELING — Jackie Wilson (Carl Davis), Brunswick 55381 | 7 |
| ★36 | 43 | 51 | 52 | DOWN AT LULU'S — Ohio Express (Kasenetz-Katz Assoc.), Buddah 56 | 5 |
| 37 | 40 | 44 | 48 | TUESDAY AFTERNOON (Forever Afternoon) — Moody Blues (Tony Clarke), Deram 85028 | 7 |
| 38 | 26 | 27 | 30 | (Love Is Like A) BASEBALL GAME — Intruders (Gamble Huff Prod.), Gamble 217 | 9 |
| ★39 | 59 | 87 | — | SPECIAL OCCASION — Smokey Robinson & The Miracles (Smokey-Cleveland), Tamla 54172 | 3 |
| 40 | 35 | 35 | 41 | YOU MET YOUR MATCH — Stevie Wonder (Don Hunter), Tamla 54168 | 7 |
| 41 | 41 | 66 | 67 | I'VE NEVER FOUND A GIRL (To Love Me Like You Do) — Eddie Floyd (Steve Cropper), Stax 0002 | 6 |
| ★42 | 68 | 99 | — | I'VE GOTTA GET A MESSAGE TO YOU — Bee Gees (Robert Stigwood), Atco 6603 | 3 |
| ★43 | 53 | 56 | 58 | GIVE A DAMN — Spanky & Our Gang (Scharf/Dorough, Edel), Mercury 72831 | 5 |
| ★44 | 69 | 72 | 90 | I CAN'T DANCE TO THE MUSIC YOU'RE PLAYIN' — Martha Reeves & The Vandellas (Deke Richards), Gordy 7075 | 4 |
| 45 | 48 | 50 | 68 | AND SUDDENLY — Cherry People (Ron Haffikine, Bary Oslander), Heritage 801 | 7 |
| ★46 | 72 | 90 | 99 | ON THE ROAD AGAIN — Canned Heat (Dallas Smith), Liberty 56038 | 4 |
| 47 | 37 | 43 | 47 | DON'T GIVE UP — Petula Clark (Tony Hatch), Warner Bros.-Seven Arts 7216 | 7 |
| 48 | 29 | 22 | 22 | SKY PILOT — Eric Burdon & the Animals (Tom Wilson), MGM 13939 | 14 |
| ★49 | 60 | 62 | 64 | BROWN EYED WOMAN — Bill Medley (Bill Medley & Barry Mann), MGM 13959 | 5 |
| ★50 | 70 | 76 | 85 | HIP CITY—PART 2 — Jr. Walker & The All Stars (Lawrence Horn), Soul 35048 | 4 |
| 51 | 52 | 71 | 86 | GIRLS CAN'T DO WHAT THE GUYS DO — Betty Wright (Brad Shapiro & Steve Alaimo), Alston 4569 | 5 |
| 52 | 58 | 60 | 72 | KEEP THE ONE YOU GOT — Joe Tex (Buddy Killen), Dial 4083 | 4 |
| ★53 | 96 | — | — | WHO IS GONNA LOVE ME? — Dionne Warwick (Bacharach-David), Scepter 12226 | 2 |
| 54 | 46 | 46 | 65 | UNDERSTANDING — Ray Charles (Joe Adams), ABC 11090 | 12 |
| 55 | 54 | 54 | 56 | CAN'T YOU FIND ANOTHER WAY (Of Doing It) — Sam & Dave (Isaac Hayes & David Porter), Atlantic 2540 | 5 |
| 56 | 55 | 57 | 59 | I GUESS I'LL HAVE TO CRY, CRY, CRY — James Brown & the Famous Flames (James Brown), King 6141 | 6 |
| ★57 | 89 | — | — | SIX MAN BAND — Association (Association), Warner Bros.-Seven Arts 7229 | 2 |
| ★58 | 84 | — | — | I WISH IT WOULD RAIN — Gladys Knight & The Pips (N. Whitefield), Soul 35047 | 2 |
| ★59 | 66 | 70 | 71 | MORNING DEW — Lulu (Mickie Most), Epic 10367 | 4 |
| ★60 | 71 | 89 | — | GIRL WATCHER — O'Kaysions (North State Music), ABC 11094 | 3 |
| 61 | 61 | 61 | 76 | I LOVED AND I LOST — Impressions (Johnny Pate), ABC 11103 | 7 |
| 62 | 67 | — | — | LISTEN HERE — Eddie Harris (Joel Dorn), Atlantic 2487 | 7 |
| ★63 | — | — | — | TO WAIT FOR LOVE — Herb Alpert (Herb Alpert & Jerry Moss), A&M 964 | 1 |
| 64 | 63 | 63 | 63 | SUDDEN STOP — Percy Sledge (Quin Ivy & Marlin Greene), Atlantic 2539 | 5 |
| ★65 | 80 | 93 | — | THE SNAKE — Al Wilson (Johnny Rivers), Soul City 767 | 3 |
| ★66 | 92 | — | — | IN-A-GADDA-DA-VIDA — Iron Butterfly (Jim Hilton), Atco 6606 | 2 |
| ★67 | — | — | — | HELP YOURSELF — Tom Jones (Peter Sullivan), Parrot 40029 | 1 |
| ★68 | 100 | — | — | THE WEIGHT — Jackie DeShannon (Charles Greene & Brian Stone), Imperial 66313 | 2 |
| 69 | 78 | 98 | — | LITTLE GREEN APPLES — O. C. Smith (Jerry Fuller), Columbia 44616 | 3 |
| 70 | 77 | 81 | 82 | WORKIN' ON A GROOVY THING — Patti Drew (Carone Prod.), Capitol 2197 | 5 |
| ★71 | 91 | 92 | 95 | TIME HAS COME TODAY — Chambers Brothers (David Rubinson), Columbia 44414 | 4 |
| ★72 | — | — | — | (The Lament of the Cherokee) INDIAN RESERVATION — Don Fardon (Miki Dallon), GNP Crescendo 405 | 1 |
| 73 | 65 | 65 | 80 | GOD BLESS OUR LOVE — Ballads (Jesse Mason & Willie Hutch), Venture 615 | 7 |
| ★74 | — | — | — | MIDNIGHT CONFESSIONS — Grassroots (Steve Barri), Dunhill 4144 | 1 |
| ★75 | — | — | — | BAREFOOT IN BALTIMORE — Strawberry Alarm Clock (F. Slay & Bill Holmes), Uni 55076 | 1 |
| ★76 | — | — | — | DOWN ON ME — Big Brother & the Holding Company (Bob Shad), Mainstream 662 | 1 |
| ★77 | — | — | — | UNCHAINED MELODY — Sweet Inspirations (Tom Dowd), Atlantic 2551 | 1 |
| ★78 | — | — | — | MY WAY OF LIFE — Frank Sinatra (Don Costa), Reprise 0764 | 1 |
| ★79 | — | — | — | DOWN HERE ON THE GROUND — Lou Rawls (David Axelrod), Capitol 2252 | 1 |
| ★80 | — | — | — | PIECE OF MY HEART — Big Brother & the Holding Company, Columbia 44626 | 1 |
| ★81 | — | — | — | PRIVATE NUMBER — Judy Clay & William Bell (Booker T. Jones), Stax 0005 | 1 |
| 82 | 82 | 100 | — | FLY ME TO THE MOON — Bobby Womack (Chips Moman), Minit 32048 | 3 |
| ★83 | — | — | — | HEY, WESTERN UNION MAN — Jerry Butler (Gamble-Huff), Mercury 72850 | 1 |
| ★84 | — | — | — | THE WEIGHT — The Band (John Simon), Capitol 2269 | 1 |
| ★85 | — | — | — | (There's) ALWAYS SOMETHING THERE TO REMIND ME — Dionne Warwick (Bacharach-David), Scepter 12226 | 1 |
| ★86 | — | — | — | BREAK YOUR PROMISE — Delfonics (Stan and Bell), Philly Groove 152 | 1 |
| ★87 | — | — | — | DO WHAT YOU GOTTA DO — Bobby Vee (Dallas Smith), Liberty 56057 | 1 |
| 88 | 90 | — | — | DON'T CHANGE YOUR LOVE — Five Stairsteps & Cubie (Curtis Mayfield), Curtom 1931 | 2 |
| ★89 | — | — | — | THAT KIND OF WOMAN — Merrilee Rush (Tommy Cogbill & Chips Moman), Bell 738 | 1 |
| ★90 | — | — | — | THE MULE — The James Boys (Jesse James), Phil L.A. of Soul 316 | 1 |
| 91 | — | — | — | LIGHT MY FIRE — Doors (Paul A. Rothchild), Elektra 45615 | 18 |
| 92 | 95 | 95 | 96 | TELL SOMEONE YOU LOVE THEM — Dino, Desi & Billy (Martin & Hinsche), Reprise 0698 | 4 |
| 93 | 98 | — | — | THE FUNKY JUDGE — Bull & The Matadors (Sherrel-Cross Prod.), Toddlin' Town 108 | 2 |
| 94 | 94 | — | — | THE WOMAN I LOVE — B.B. King, Kent 492 | 2 |
| 95 | 97 | — | — | BRING BACK THOSE ROCKABYE BABY DAYS — Tiny Tim (Richard Perry), Reprise 0760 | 2 |
| 96 | — | — | — | HELP YOURSELF (To All My Lovin') — James & Bobby Purify (Papa Don Prod.), Bell 735 | 1 |
| 97 | — | — | — | IF LOVE IS IN YOUR HEART — Friend & Lover (Joe South & Bill Lowery), Verve/Forecast 5091 | 1 |
| 98 | — | — | — | SINCE YOU'VE BEEN GONE — Ramsey Lewis, Cadet 5609 | 1 |
| 99 | 99 | — | — | SHE'S ABOUT A MOVER — Otis Clay (Rick Hall), Cotillion 44001 | 2 |
| 100 | — | — | — | NATURALLY STONED — Avant-Garde (Billy Sherril), Columbia [illegible] | 1 |

## HOT 100—A TO Z—(Publisher-Licensee)



## BUBBLING UNDER THE HOT 100

101. SUNSHINE GIRL .... Herman's Hermits, MGM 13973
102. BABY COME BACK .... Equals, RCA Victor 47-9583
103. LADY MADONNA .... Fats Domino, Reprise 0763
104. SAN FRANCISCO—WEAR SOME FLOWERS IN YOUR HAIR .... Paul Mauriat & His Ork, Philips 4055[illegible]
105. APRIL AGAIN .... Dean Martin, Reprise 076[illegible]
106. BREAK MY MIND .... Sammy Davis Jr., Reprise 075[illegible]
107. BATTLE OF NEW ORLEANS .... Harpers Bizarre, Warner Bros.-Seven Arts 722[illegible]
108. SHOOT 'EM UP BABY .... Andy Kim, Steed 71[illegible]
109. STREET FIGHTING MAN .... Rolling Stones, London 9[illegible]
110. DO YOU WANNA DANCE .... Love Society, Scepter 122[illegible]
111. MESSAGE FOR MARIA .... Joe Simon, Sound Stage 7 26[illegible]7
112. MY SPECIAL ANGEL .... Vogues, Reprise 07[illegible]6
113. DON'T LET HIM TAKE YOUR LOVE .... Jimmy Ruffin, Soul 35[illegible]6
114. SHAPE OF THINGS TO COME .... Max Frost & the Troopers, Tower [illegible]9
115. HARPER VALLEY P.T.A. .... Bobbi Martin, United Artists 50[illegible]43
116. SUN AIN'T GONNA SHINE ANYMORE .... Fuzzy Bunnies, Decca 32[illegible]4
117. DO THE BEST YOU CAN .... Hollies, Epic 10[illegible]61
118. YOU'VE HAD BETTER TIMES .... Peter & Gordon, Capitol [illegible]14
119. EVERYBODY'S TALKIN' .... Nilsson, RCA Victor 47-[illegible]44
120. SUZI Q PART II .... Credence Clearwater Revival, Fantasy [illegible]16
121. LOVE HEALS .... Colours, Dot 1[illegible]32
122. ALL MY LOVE'S LAUGHTER .... Ed Ames, RCA Victor 47-[illegible]589
123. (As I Went Down To) JERUSALEM .... Hello People, Philips 4[illegible]531
124. HOLD ME TIGHT .... Johnny Nash, Jad 207
125. HARD TO GET A THING CALLED LOVE .... Platters, Musicor [illegible]322
126. "BIPLANE EVERMORE" .... Irish Rovers, Decca [illegible]2371
127. THEN YOU CAN TELL ME GOODBYE .... Eddy Arnold, RCA Victor 47[illegible]9606

Compiled from national retail sales and radio station airplay by the Music Popularity Dept. of Record Market Research, Billboard.

# Billboard HOT 100

FOR WEEK ENDING SEPTEMBER 7, 1968

★ STAR PERFORMER—Sides registering greatest proportionate upward progress this week.

Record Industry Association of America seal of certification as million selling single.

| This Week | 1 Wk. Ago | 2 Wks. Ago | 3 Wks. Ago | TITLE Artist (Producer), Label & Number | Weeks On Chart |
|---|---|---|---|---|---|
| 1 (Billboard Award) | 1 | 1 | 1 | PEOPLE GOT TO BE FREE — Rascals (Rascals), Atlantic 2537 | 8 |
| 2 | 2 | 2 | 4 | BORN TO BE WILD — Steppenwolf (Gabriel Mekler), Dunhill 4138 | 9 |
| 3 | 3 | 4 | 5 | LIGHT MY FIRE — Jose Feliciano (Rick Jarrard), RCA Victor 47-9550 | 7 |
| 4 ★ | 7 | 81 | — | HARPER VALLEY P.T.A. — Jeannie C. Riley (Shelby S. Singleton Jr.), Plantation 3 | 3 |
| 5 | 4 | 3 | 2 | HELLO, I LOVE YOU — Doors (Paul Rothchild), Elektra 45635 | 10 |
| 6 ★ | 20 | 21 | 59 | THE HOUSE THAT JACK BUILT — Aretha Franklin (Jerry Wexler), Atlantic 2456 | 4 |
| 7 ★ | 12 | 22 | 32 | 1, 2, 3, RED LIGHT — 1910 Fruitgum Company (Kasenetz-Katz Assoc.) Buddah 54 | 7 |
| 8 | 8 | 15 | 23 | YOU'RE ALL I NEED TO GET BY — Marvin Gaye & Tammi Terrell (Ashford-Simpson), Tamla 54169 | 7 |
| 9 | 9 | 9 | 16 | I CAN'T STOP DANCING — Archie Bell & the Drells (Gamble-Huff), Atlantic 2534 | 8 |
| 10 | 10 | 10 | 13 | STAY IN MY CORNER — Dells (Bobby Miller), Cadet 5612 | 11 |
| 11 | 5 | 6 | 8 | SUNSHINE OF YOUR LOVE — Cream (Felix Pappalardi), Atco 6544 | 24 |
| 12 | 6 | 11 | 14 | (You Keep Me) HANGIN' ON — Vanilla Fudge (Shadow Morton), Atco 6495 | 14 |
| 13 ★ | 14 | 38 | 83 | HUSH — Deep Purple (Derek Lawrence), Tetragrammaton 1503 | 4 |
| 14 | 11 | 7 | 7 | TURN AROUND, LOOK AT ME — Vogues (Dick Glasser), Reprise 0686 | 13 |
| 15 | 15 | 17 | 24 | LOVE MAKES A WOMAN — Barbara Acklin (Carl Davis & Eugene Record), Brunswick 55379 | 9 |
| 16 | 13 | 5 | 3 | CLASSICAL GAS — Mason Williams (Mike Post), Warner Bros.-Seven Arts 7190 | 12 |
| 17 | 18 | 32 | 48 | THE FOOL ON THE HILL — Sergio Mendes & Brasil '66 (Sergio Mendes, Herb Alpert & Jerry Moss) | 5 |
| 18 ★ | 29 | 24 | 29 | SLIP AWAY — Clarence Carter (Rick Hall & Staff), Atlantic 2508 | 9 |
| 19 | 16 | 16 | 17 | JOURNEY TO THE CENTER OF YOUR MIND — Amboy Dukes (Bob Shad), Mainstream 684 | 11 |
| 20 | 17 | 18 | 18 | SOUL LIMBO — Booker T. & the M.G.'s (Booker T. Jones), Stax 0001 | 9 |
| 21 | 19 | 19 | 19 | SEALED WITH A KISS — Gary Lewis & Playboys (Snuff Garrett), Liberty 56037 | 12 |
| 22 | 24 | 31 | 33 | DO IT AGAIN — Beach Boys (Beach Boys), Capitol 2239 | 7 |
| 23 | 25 | 39 | 82 | I SAY A LITTLE PRAYER — Aretha Franklin (Jerry Wexler), Atlantic 2456 | 4 |
| 24 | 22 | 8 | 6 | STONED SOUL PICNIC — 5th Dimension (Bones Howe), Soul City 766 | 15 |
| 25 | 21 | 12 | 12 | DREAM A LITTLE DREAM OF ME — Mama Cass with the Mamas & Papas (Lou Adler), Dunhill 4145 | 10 |
| 26 | 26 | 28 | 31 | PLEASE RETURN YOUR LOVE TO ME — Temptations (Norman Whitfield), Gordy 7074 | 6 |
| 27 | 32 | 57 | 64 | MAGIC BUS — Who (Kit Lambert), Decca 32362 | 5 |
| 28 | 33 | 50 | 58 | MR. BUSINESSMAN — Ray Stevens (Fred Foster & Ray Stevens), Monument 1083 | 6 |
| 29 ★ | 37 | 40 | 44 | TUESDAY AFTERNOON (Forever Afternoon) — Moody Blues (Tony Clarke), Deram 85028 | 8 |
| 30 ★ | 42 | 68 | 99 | I'VE GOTTA GET A MESSAGE TO YOU — Bee Gees (Robert Stigwood), Atco 6603 | 4 |
| 31 | 28 | 25 | 20 | PICTURES OF MATCHSTICK MEN — Status Quo (John Schroeder), Cadet Concept 7001 | 17 |
| 32 | 34 | 34 | 38 | THE EYES OF A NEW YORK WOMAN — B.J. Thomas (Chips Moman), Scepter 12219 | 12 |
| 33 ★ | 51 | 52 | 71 | GIRLS CAN'T DO WHAT THE GUYS DO — Betty Wright (Brad Shapiro & Steve Alaimo), Alston 4569 | 6 |
| 34 | 35 | 42 | 47 | I GET THE SWEETEST FEELING — Jackie Wilson (Carl Davis), Brunswick 55381 | 8 |
| 35 ★ | 46 | 72 | 90 | ON THE ROAD AGAIN — Canned Heat (Dallas Smith), Liberty 56038 | 5 |
| 36 | 36 | 43 | 51 | DOWN AT LULU'S — Ohio Express (Kasenetz-Katz Assoc.), Buddah 56 | 6 |
| 37 | 39 | 59 | 87 | SPECIAL OCCASION — Smokey Robinson & The Miracles (Smokey-Cleveland), Tamla 54172 | 4 |
| 38 ★ | 60 | 71 | 89 | GIRL WATCHER — O'Kaysions (North State Music), ABC 11094 | 4 |
| 39 | 27 | 27 | 28 | ALICE LONG (You're Still My Favorite Girlfriend) — Tommy Boyce & Bobby Hart (Boyce & Hart), A&M 948 | 10 |
| 40 | 41 | 41 | 66 | I'VE NEVER FOUND A GIRL (To Love Me Like You Do) — Eddie Floyd (Steve Cropper), Stax 0002 | 7 |
| 41 | 23 | 14 | 10 | HURDY GURDY MAN — Donovan (Mickie Most), Epic 10345 | 12 |
| 42 | 44 | 69 | 72 | I CAN'T DANCE TO THE MUSIC YOU'RE PLAYIN' — Martha Reeves & The Vandellas (Deke Richards), Gordy 7075 | 5 |
| 43 | 43 | 53 | 56 | GIVE A DAMN — Spanky & Our Gang (Scharf/Dorough, Edel), Mercury 72831 | 6 |
| 44 ★ | 65 | 80 | 93 | THE SNAKE — Al Wilson (Johnny Rivers), Soul City 767 | 4 |
| 45 ★ | 69 | 78 | 98 | LITTLE GREEN APPLES — O. C. Smith (Jerry Fuller), Columbia 44616 | 4 |
| 46 | 50 | 70 | 76 | HIP CITY—PART 2 — Jr. Walker & The All Stars (Lawrence Horn), Soul 35048 | 5 |
| 47 | 49 | 60 | 62 | BROWN EYED WOMAN — Bill Medley (Bill Medley & Barry Mann), MGM 13959 | 6 |
| 48 ★ | 57 | 89 | — | SIX MAN BAND — Association (Association), Warner Bros.-Seven Arts 7229 | 3 |
| 49 ★ | 58 | 84 | — | I WISH IT WOULD RAIN — Gladys Knight & The Pips (N. Whitefield), Soul 35047 | 3 |
| 50 ★ | 67 | — | — | HELP YOURSELF — Tom Jones (Peter Sullivan), Parrot 40029 | 2 |
| 51 ★ | 71 | 91 | 92 | TIME HAS COME TODAY — Chambers Brothers (David Rubinson), Columbia 44414 | 5 |
| 52 | 53 | 96 | — | WHO IS GONNA LOVE ME? — Dionne Warwick (Bacharach-David), Scepter 12226 | 3 |
| 53 ★ | 59 | 66 | 70 | MORNING DEW — Lulu (Mickie Most), Epic 10367 | 5 |
| 54 | 45 | 48 | 50 | AND SUDDENLY — Cherry People (Ron Haffikine, Bary Oslander), Heritage 801 | 8 |
| 55 | 55 | 54 | 54 | CAN'T YOU FIND ANOTHER WAY (Of Doing It) — Sam & Dave (Isaac Hayes & David Porter), Atlantic 2540 | 6 |
| 56 ★ | 63 | — | — | TO WAIT FOR LOVE — Herb Alpert (Herb Alpert & Jerry Moss), A&M 964 | 2 |
| 57 | 62 | 67 | — | LISTEN HERE — Eddie Harris (Joel Dorn), Atlantic 2487 | 8 |
| 58 | 52 | 58 | 60 | KEEP THE ONE YOU GOT — Joe Tex (Buddy Killen), Dial 4083 | 5 |
| 59 ★ | 80 | — | — | PIECE OF MY HEART — Big Brother & the Holding Company, Columbia 44626 | 2 |
| 60 ★ | — | — | — | SAY IT LOUD (I'm Black And I'm Proud) — James Brown & His Famous Flames (James Brown), King 6187 | 1 |
| 61 ★ | 72 | — | — | (The Lament of the Cherokee) INDIAN RESERVATION — Don Fardon (Miki Dallon), GNP Crescendo 405 | 2 |
| 62 ★ | — | — | — | MY SPECIAL ANGEL — Vogues (Dick Glasser), Reprise 0766 | 1 |
| 63 | 70 | 77 | 81 | WORKIN' ON A GROOVY THING — Patti Drew (Carone Prod.), Capitol 2197 | 6 |
| 64 | 74 | — | — | MIDNIGHT CONFESSIONS — Grassroots (Steve Barri), Dunhill 4144 | 2 |
| 65 | 68 | 100 | — | THE WEIGHT — Jackie DeShannon (Charles Greene & Brian Stone), Imperial 66313 | 3 |
| 66 | 66 | 92 | — | IN-A-GADDA-DA-VIDA — Iron Butterfly (Jim Hilton), Atco 6606 | 3 |
| 67 ★ | 75 | — | — | BAREFOOT IN BALTIMORE — Strawberry Alarm Clock (F. Slay & Bill Holmes), Uni 55076 | 2 |
| 68 | 61 | 61 | 61 | I LOVED AND I LOST — Impressions (Johnny Pate), ABC 11103 | 8 |
| 69 ★ | 76 | — | — | DOWN ON ME — Big Brother & the Holding Company (Bob Shad), Mainstream 662 | 2 |
| 70 ★ | 85 | — | — | THERE'S ALWAYS SOMETHING THERE TO REMIND ME — Dionne Warwick (Bacharach-David), Scepter 12226 | 2 |
| 71 ★ | 86 | — | — | BREAK YOUR PROMISE — Delfonics (Stan and Bell), Philly Groove 152 | 2 |
| 72 ★ | — | — | — | BABY, COME BACK — Equals (President Records Prod.), RCA Victor 47-9583 | 1 |
| 73 ★ | 82 | 82 | 100 | FLY ME TO THE MOON — Bobby Womack (Chips Moman), Minit 32048 | 4 |
| 74 | 79 | — | — | DOWN HERE ON THE GROUND — Lou Rawls (David Axelrod), Capitol 2252 | 2 |
| 75 ★ | 81 | — | — | PRIVATE NUMBER — Judy Clay & William Bell (Booker T. Jones), Stax 0005 | 2 |
| 76 | 84 | — | — | THE WEIGHT — The Band (John Simon), Capitol 2269 | 2 |
| 77 | 77 | — | — | UNCHAINED MELODY — Sweet Inspirations (Tom Dowd), Atlantic 2551 | 2 |
| 78 | 78 | — | — | MY WAY OF LIFE — Frank Sinatra (Don Costa), Reprise 0764 | 2 |
| 79 ★ | 83 | — | — | HEY, WESTERN UNION MAN — Jerry Butler (Gamble-Huff), Mercury 72850 | 2 |
| 80 ★ | 89 | — | — | THAT KIND OF WOMAN — Merrilee Rush (Tommy Cogbill & Chips Moman), Bell 738 | 2 |
| 81 ★ | — | — | — | FIRE — Crazy World of Arthur Brown (Kit Lambert), Atlantic 2556 | 1 |
| 82 | 90 | — | — | THE MULE — The James Boys (Jesse James), Phil L.A. of Soul 316 | 2 |
| 83 | 88 | 90 | — | DON'T CHANGE YOUR LOVE — Five Stairsteps & Cubie (Curtis Mayfield), Curtom 1931 | 3 |
| 84 ★ | — | — | — | STREET FIGHTING MAN — Rolling Stones (Jimmy Miller), London 909 | 1 |
| 85 | 87 | — | — | DO WHAT YOU GOTTA DO — Bobby Vee (Dallas Smith), Liberty 56057 | 2 |
| 86 ★ | 97 | — | — | IF LOVE IS IN YOUR HEART — Friend & Lover (Joe South & Bill Lowery), Verve/Forecast 5091 | 2 |
| 87 ★ | — | — | — | THEN YOU TELL ME GOODBYE — Eddy Arnold (Chet Atkins), RCA Victor 47-9606 | 1 |
| 88 ★ | — | — | — | SHOOT 'EM UP BABY — Andy Kim (Jeff Barry), Steed 710 | 1 |
| 89 ★ | 100 | — | — | NATURALLY STONED — Avant-Garde (Billy Sherril), Columbia 44590 | 2 |
| 90 ★ | — | — | — | SHAPE OF THINGS TO COME — Max Frost & the Troopers (Mike Curb), Tower 419 | 1 |
| 91 | 91 | — | — | LIGHT MY FIRE — Doors (Paul A. Rothchild), Elektra 45615 | 19 |
| 92 | — | — | — | SUZIE Q — Creedence Clearwater Revival (Saul Zaentz), Fantasy 616 | 1 |
| 93 | 93 | 98 | — | THE FUNKY JUDGE — Bull & The Matadors (Sherrel-Cross Prod.), Toddlin' Town 108 | 3 |
| 94 | 94 | 94 | — | THE WOMAN I LOVE — B.B. King, Kent 492 | 3 |
| 95 | — | — | 97 | SALLY HAD A PARTY — Flavor (Tim O'Brien), Columbia 44521 | 4 |
| 96 | 96 | — | — | HELP YOURSELF (To All My Lovin') — James & Bobby Purify (Papa Don Prod.), Bell 735 | 2 |
| 97 | 99 | 99 | — | SHE'S ABOUT A MOVER — Otis Clay (Rick Hall), Cotillion 44001 | 3 |
| 98 | 98 | — | — | SINCE YOUVE BEEN GONE — Ramsey Lewis, Cadet 5609 | 2 |
| 99 | — | — | — | FOOL FOR YOU — Impressions (Curtis Mayfield), Curtom 1932 | 1 |
| 100 | — | — | — | LADY MADONNA — Fats Domino (Richard Perry), Reprise 0763 | 1 |

## HOT 100—A TO Z—(Publisher-Licensee)

Alice Long (You're Still My Favorite Girlfriend) (Screen Gems-Columbia, BMI) ... 39
And Suddenly (Lazy Day, BMI) ... 54
Baby, Come Back (Piccadilly, BMI) ... 72
Barefoot in Baltimore (Alarm Clock Claridge, ASCAP) ... 67
Born to Be Wild (Duchess, BMI) ... 2
Break Your Promise (Nickel Shoe/Bellboy, BMI) ... 71
Brown Eyed Woman (Screen Gems-Columbia, BMI) 47
Can't You Find Another Way (Of Doing It) (East/Pronto, BMI) ... 55
Classical Gas (Irving, BMI) ... 16
Do It Again (Sea of Tunes, BMI) ... 22
Do What You Gotta Do (Rivers, BMI) ... 85
Don't Change Your Love (Caned, BMI) ... 83
Down at Lulu's (Peanut Butter/Kaskat, BMI) ... 36
Down Here on the Ground (Warner Bros.-Seven Arts, BMI) ... 74
Down on Me (Brent, BMI) ... 69
Dream a Little Dream of Me (Words & Music, ASCAP) ... 25
Eyes of a New York Woman, The (Press, BMI) ... 32
Fire (New Action, BMI) ... 81
Fly Me to the Moon (Almanac, ASCAP) ... 73
Fool for You (Camad, BMI) ... 99
Fool on the Hill, The (Comet, ASCAP) ... 17
Funky Judge, The (Downstream/Napac/Flomar, BMI) ... 93
Girl Watcher (North State, ASCAP) ... 38
Girls Can't Do What the Guys Do (Sherlyn, BMI) ... 33
Give a Damn (Takya, ASCAP) ... 43
Harper Valley P.T.A. (Newkeys, BMI) ... 4
Hello, I Love You (Nipper, ASCAP) ... 5
Help Yourself (Famous, ASCAP) ... 50
Help Yourself (To All My Lovin') (Helios, BMI) ... 96
Hey, Western Union Man (Parabut/Double Diamond/Downstairs, BMI) ... 79
Hip City—Part 2 (Jobete, BMI) ... 46
House That Jack Built, The (Cotillion, BMI) ... 6
Hurdy Gurdy Man (Peer Int'l, BMI) ... 41
Hush (Lowery, BMI) ... 13
I Can't Dance to That Music You're Playin' (Jobete, BMI) ... 42
I Can't Stop Dancing (Downstairs/Double Diamond, BMI) ... 9
I Get the Sweetest Feeling (T.M./McCoy, BMI) ... 34
I Loved and I Lost (Chi-Sound, BMI) ... 68
I Say a Little Prayer (Jac/Blue Seas, ASCAP) ... 23
I Wish It Would Rain (Jobete, BMI) ... 49
If Love Is in Your Heart (Lowery, BMI) ... 86
In-a-Gadda-Da-Vida (Ten Last-Cotillion-Itasca, BMI) 66
I've Gotta Get a Message to You (Casserole, BMI) 30
I've Never Found a Girl (To Love Me Like You Do) (East, BMI) ... 40
Journey to the Center of Your Mind (Brent, BMI) ... 19
Keep The One You Got (Tree, BMI) ... 58
Lady Madonna (Maclen, BMI) ... 100
(Lament of the Cherokee) Indian Reservation (Acuff-Rose, BMI) ... 61
Light My Fire (Doors) (Nipper, ASCAP) ... 91
Light My Fire (Jose Feliciano) (Nipper, ASCAP) ... 3
Listen Here (Hargrove, BMI) ... 57
Little Green Apples (Russell-Cason, ASCAP) ... 45
Love Makes a Woman (Jalynne/BRC, BMI) ... 15
Magic Bus (Essex, ASCAP) ... 27
Midnight Confessions (Little Fugitive, BMI) ... 64
Mr. Businessman (Ahab, BMI) ... 28
Morning Dew (Nina, BMI) ... 53
The Mule (Dandelion/James, BMI) ... 82
My Special Angel (Viva, BMI) ... 62
My Way of Life (Roosevelt, BMI) ... 78
Naturally Stoned (Cedarwood, BMI) ... 89
On the Road Again (Lawn, BMI) ... 35
1, 2, 3 Red Light (Kaskat, BMI) ... 7
People Got to Be Free (Slacsar, ASCAP) ... 1
Pictures of Matchstick Men (Northern, ASCAP) ... 31
Piece of My Heart (Webb IV/Ragmar, BMI) ... 59
Please Return Your Love to Me (Jobete, BMI) ... 26
Private Number (East, BMI) ... 75
Sally Had a Party (125th Street, ASCAP) ... 95
Say It Loud—I'm Black and I'm Proud (Colo, BMI) 60
Sealed With a Kiss (Post, ASCAP) ... 21
Shape of Things to Come (Screen Gems-Columbia, BMI) ... 90
She's About a Mover (Crazy Cajun, BMI) ... 97
Shoot 'Em Up Baby (Unart/Joachim, BMI) ... 88
Since You've Been Gone (14th Hour/Cotillion, BMI) 98
Six Man Band (Beechwood, BMI) ... 48
Slip Away (Fame, BMI) ... 18
The Snake (Marks, BMI) ... 44
Soul Limbo (East, BMI) ... 20
Special Occasion (Jobete, BMI) ... 37
Stay in My Corner (Conrad, BMI) ... 10
Stoned Soul Picnic (Tuna Fish, BMI) ... 24
Street Fighting Man (Gideon, BMI) ... 84
Sunshine of Your Love (Dratleaf, BMI) ... 11
Suzie Q. (Arc, BMI) ... 92
That Kind of Woman (Screen Gems-Columbia, BMI) 80
Then You Tell Me Goodbye (Acuff-Rose, BMI) ... 87
There's Always Something There to Remind Me (Blue Seas/Jac/Rose Jungnickel, ASCAP) ... 70
Time Has Come Today (Spinmaker, BMI) ... 51
To Wait for Love (Blue Seas/Jac, ASCAP) ... 56
Tuesday Afternoon (Forever Afternoon) (Essex, ASCAP) ... 29
Turn Around, Look at Me (Viva, BMI) ... 14
Unchained Melody (Frank, ASCAP) ... 77
Weight, The (Jackie DeShannon) (Calla, ASCAP) ... 65
Weight, The (The Band) (Calla, ASCAP) ... 76
Who Is Gonna Love Me? (Blue Seas/Jac, BMI) ... 52
Woman I Love, The (Modern, BMI) ... 94
Workin' on a Groovy Thing (Screen Gems-Columbia, BMI) ... 63
(You Keep Me) Hangin' On (Jobete, BMI) ... 12
You're All I Need to Get By (Jobete, BMI) ... 8

## BUBBLING UNDER THE HOT 100

101. "BIPLANE EVERMORE" ... Irish Rovers, Decca 32371
102. MESSAGE FROM MARIA ... Joe Simon, Sound Stage 7 2617
103. SAN FRANCISCO—WEAR SOME FLOWERS IN YOUR HAIR ... Paul Mauriat, Philips 40550
104. FOR THE LOVE OF IVY ... Mamas & Papas, Dunhill 4150
105. BATTLE OF NEW ORLEANS ... Harper's Bizarre, Warner Bros.-Seven Arts 7223
106. I MET HER IN CHURCH ... Box Tops, Mala 12017
107. SPECIAL CARE ... Buffalo Springfield, Atco 6602
108. CHAINED ... Marvin Gaye, Tamla 54170
109. DO YOU WANNA DANCE? ... Love Society, Scepter 12223
110. POOR BABY ... Cowsills, MGM 13981
111. APPLE CIDER ... People, Capitol 2251
112. ICE IN THE SUN ... Status Quo, Cadet Concept 7006
113. DON'T LET HIM TAKE YOUR LOVE ... Jimmy Ruffin, Soul 35046
114. HARPER VALLEY P.T.A. ... Bobbi Martin, United Artists 50443
115. SUN AIN'T GONNA SHINE ANYMORE ... Fuzzie Bunnies, Decca 32364
116. DO THE BEST YOU CAN ... Hollies, Epic 10361
117. CHOICE ... O'Jays, Bell 737
118. YOU GOT THE LOVE ... Professor Morrison's Lollipop, White Whale 275
119. EVERYBODY'S TALKING ... Nilsson, RCA Victor 47-9544
120. LOVE RASCALS ... Colours, Dot 17132
121. THE B.B. JONES ... B.B. King, Bluesway 61019
122. SAN FRANCISCO GIRLS ... Fever Tree, Uni 55060
123. (As I Went Down To) JERUSALEM ... Hello People, Philips 40531
124. HOLD ME TIGHT ... Johnny Nash, Jad 207
125. OH LORD, WHY LORD ... Los Pop Tops, Calla 154
126. SOUL CLAPPIN' ... Buena Vistas, Marquee 445

Compiled from national retail sales and radio station airplay by the Music Popularity Dept. of Record Market Research, Billboard.

# Billboard HOT 100

**FOR WEEK ENDING SEPTEMBER 14, 1968**

★ STAR PERFORMER—Sides registering greatest proportionate upward progress this week.
Ⓡ Record Industry Association of America seal of certification as million selling single.

| This Week | 1 Wk. Ago | 2 Wks. Ago | 3 Wks. Ago | TITLE Artist (Producer), Label & Number | Weeks On Chart |
|---|---|---|---|---|---|
| 1 | 1 | 1 | 1 | PEOPLE GOT TO BE FREE — Rascals (Rascals), Atlantic 2537 | 9 |
| 2 | 4 | 7 | 81 | HARPER VALLEY P.T.A. — Jeannie C. Riley (Shelby S. Singleton Jr.), Plantation 3 | 4 |
| 3 | 3 | 3 | 4 | LIGHT MY FIRE — Jose Feliciano (Rick Jarrard), RCA Victor 47-9550 | 8 |
| 4 | 2 | 2 | 2 | BORN TO BE WILD — Steppenwolf (Gabriel Mekler), Dunhill 4138 | 10 |
| 5 | 7 | 12 | 22 | 1, 2, 3, RED LIGHT — 1910 Fruitgum Company (Kasenetz-Katz Assoc.), Buddah 54 | 8 |
| 6 | 6 | 20 | 21 | THE HOUSE THAT JACK BUILT — Aretha Franklin (Jerry Wexler), Atlantic 2456 | 5 |
| 7 | 8 | 8 | 15 | YOU'RE ALL I NEED TO GET BY — Marvin Gaye & Tammi Terrell (Ashford-Simpson), Tamla 54169 | 8 |
| 8 | 13 | 14 | 38 | HUSH — Deep Purple (Derek Lawrence), Tetragrammaton 1503 | 7 |
| 9 | 5 | 4 | 3 | HELLO, I LOVE YOU — Doors (Paul Rothchild), Elektra 45635 | 8 |
| 10 | — | — | — | HEY JUDE — Beatles (George Martin), Apple 2276 | 1 |
| 11 | 17 | 18 | 32 | THE FOOL ON THE HILL — Sergio Mendes & Brasil '66 (Sergio Mendes / Herb Alpert & Jerry Moss), A&M 961 | 6 |
| 12 | 12 | 6 | 11 | (You Keep Me) HANGIN' ON — Vanilla Fudge (Shadow Morton), Atco 6495 | 16 |
| 13 | 11 | 5 | 6 | SUNSHINE OF YOUR LOVE — Cream (Felix Pappalardi), Atco 6544 | 25 |
| 14 | 23 | 25 | 39 | I SAY A LITTLE PRAYER — Aretha Franklin (Jerry Wexler), Atlantic 2546 | 5 |
| 15 | 14 | 11 | 7 | TURN AROUND, LOOK AT ME — Vogues (Dick Glasser), Reprise 0686 | 14 |
| 16 | 9 | 9 | 9 | I CAN'T STOP DANCING — Archie Bell & the Drells (Gamble-Huff), Atlantic 2534 | 9 |
| 17 | 18 | 29 | 24 | SLIP AWAY — Clarence Carter (Rick Hall & Staff), Atlantic 2508 | 10 |
| 18 | 36 | 60 | 71 | GIRL WATCHER — O'Kaysions (North State Music), ABC 11094 | 5 |
| 19 | 10 | 10 | 10 | STAY IN MY CORNER — Dells (Bobby Miller), Cadet 5612 | 12 |
| 20 | 22 | 24 | 31 | DO IT AGAIN — Beach Boys (Beach Boys), Capitol 2239 | 6 |
| 21 | 15 | 15 | 17 | LOVE MAKES A WOMAN — Barbara Acklin (Carl Davis & Eugene Record), Brunswick 55379 | 10 |
| 22 | 16 | 13 | 5 | CLASSICAL GAS — Mason Williams (Mike Post), Warner Bros.-Seven Arts 7190 | 13 |
| 23 | 30 | 42 | 68 | I'VE GOTTA GET A MESSAGE TO YOU — Bee Gees (Robert Stigwood), Atco 6603 | 5 |
| 24 | 35 | 46 | 72 | ON THE ROAD AGAIN — Canned Heat (Dallas Smith), Liberty 56038 | 6 |
| 25 | 21 | 19 | 19 | SEALED WITH A KISS — Gary Lewis & Playboys (Snuff Garrett), Liberty 56037 | 13 |
| 26 | 27 | 32 | 57 | MAGIC BUS — Who (Kit Lambert), Decca 32362 | 5 |
| 27 | 51 | 71 | 91 | TIME HAS COME TODAY — Chambers Brothers (David Rubinson), Columbia 44414 | 6 |
| 28 | 32 | 34 | 34 | THE EYES OF A NEW YORK WOMAN — B.J. Thomas (Chips Moman), Scepter 12219 | 6 |
| 29 | 29 | 37 | 40 | TUESDAY AFTERNOON (Forever Afternoon) — Moody Blues (Tony Clarke), Deram 85028 | 9 |
| 30 | 20 | 17 | 18 | SOUL LIMBO — Booker T. & the M.G.'s (Booker T. Jones), Stax 0001 | 10 |
| 31 | 60 | — | — | SAY IT LOUD (I'm Black And I'm Proud) — James Brown & His Famous Flames (James Brown), King 6187 | 2 |
| 32 | 26 | 26 | 28 | PLEASE RETURN YOUR LOVE TO ME — Temptations (Norman Whitfield), Gordy 7074 | 7 |
| 33 | 33 | 51 | 52 | GIRLS CAN'T DO WHAT THE GUYS DO — Betty Wright (Brad Shapiro & Steve Alaimo), Alston 4569 | 7 |
| 34 | 36 | 36 | 43 | DOWN AT LULU'S — Ohio Express (Kasenetz-Katz Assoc.), Buddah 56 | 7 |
| 35 | 25 | 21 | 12 | DREAM A LITTLE DREAM OF ME — Mama Cass with the Mamas & Papas (Lou Adler), Dunhill 4145 | 11 |
| 36 | 28 | 33 | 50 | MR. BUSINESSMAN — Ray Stevens (Fred Foster & Ray Stevens), Monument 1083 | 7 |
| 37 | 37 | 39 | 59 | SPECIAL OCCASION — Smokey Robinson & The Miracles (Smokey-Cleveland), Tamla 54172 | 5 |
| 38 | — | — | — | REVOLUTION — Beatles (George Martin), Apple 2276 | 1 |
| 39 | 46 | 50 | 70 | HIP CITY—PART 2 — Jr. Walker & The All Stars (Lawrence Horn), Soul 35048 | 6 |
| 40 | 42 | 41 | 41 | I'VE NEVER FOUND A GIRL (To Love Me Like You Do) — Eddie Floyd (Steve Cropper), Stax 0002 | 8 |
| 41 | 45 | 69 | 78 | LITTLE GREEN APPLES — O. C. Smith (Jerry Fuller), Columbia 44616 | 6 |
| 42 | 42 | 44 | 69 | I CAN'T DANCE TO THE MUSIC YOU'RE PLAYIN' — Martha Reeves & The Vandellas (Deke Richards), Gordy 7075 | 6 |
| 43 | 43 | 43 | 53 | GIVE A DAMN — Spanky & Our Gang (Scharf/Dorough, Edel), Mercury 72831 | 7 |
| 44 | 44 | 65 | 80 | THE SNAKE — Al Wilson (Johnny Rivers), Soul City 767 | 5 |
| 45 | 49 | 58 | 84 | I WISH IT WOULD RAIN — Gladys Knight & The Pips (N. Whitefield), Soul 35047 | 4 |
| 46 | 47 | 49 | 60 | BROWN EYED WOMAN — Bill Medley (Bill Medley & Barry Mann), MGM 13959 | 7 |
| 47 | 48 | 57 | 89 | SIX MAN BAND — Association (Association), Warner Bros.-Seven Arts 7229 | 4 |
| 48 | 50 | 67 | — | HELP YOURSELF — Tom Jones (Peter Sullivan), Parrot 40029 | 3 |
| 49 | 52 | 53 | 96 | WHO IS GONNA LOVE ME? — Dionne Warwick (Bacharach-David), Scepter 12226 | 4 |
| 50 | 24 | 22 | 8 | STONED SOUL PICNIC — 5th Dimension (Bones Howe), Soul City 766 | 16 |
| 51 | 19 | 16 | 16 | JOURNEY TO THE CENTER OF MY MIND — Amboy Dukes (Bob Shad), Mainstream 684 | 12 |
| 52 | 64 | 74 | — | MIDNIGHT CONFESSIONS — Grassroots (Steve Barri), Dunhill 4144 | 3 |
| 53 | 53 | 59 | 66 | MORNING DEW — Lulu (Mickie Most), Epic 10367 | 6 |
| 54 | 56 | 63 | — | TO WAIT FOR LOVE — Herb Alpert (Herb Alpert & Jerry Moss), A&M 964 | 3 |
| 55 | 57 | 62 | 67 | LISTEN HERE — Eddie Harris (Joel Dorn), Atlantic 2487 | 9 |
| 56 | 59 | 80 | — | PIECE OF MY HEART — Big Brother and the Holding Company, Columbia 44626 | 3 |
| 57 | 62 | — | — | MY SPECIAL ANGEL — Vogues (Dick Glasser), Reprise 0766 | 2 |
| 58 | 66 | 66 | 92 | IN-A-GADDA-DA-VIDA — Iron Butterfly (Jim Hilton), Atco 6606 | 4 |
| 59 | 61 | 72 | — | (The Lament of the Cherokee) INDIAN RESERVATION — Don Fardon (Miki Dallon), GNP Crescendo 405 | 3 |
| 60 | 81 | — | — | FIRE — Crazy World of Arthur Brown (Kit Lambert), Atlantic 2556 | 2 |
| 61 | 65 | 68 | 100 | THE WEIGHT — Jackie DeShannon (Charles Greene & Brian Stone), Imperial 66313 | 4 |
| 62 | 63 | 70 | 77 | WORKIN' ON A GROOVY THING — Patti Drew (Carone Prod.), Capitol 2197 | 7 |
| 63 | 84 | — | — | STREET FIGHTING MAN — Rolling Stones (Jimmy Miller), London 909 | 2 |
| 64 | 79 | 83 | — | HEY, WESTERN UNION MAN — Jerry Butler (Gamble-Huff), Mercury 72850 | 3 |
| 65 | 71 | 86 | — | BREAK YOUR PROMISE — Delfonics (Stan and Bell), Philly Groove 152 | 3 |
| 66 | 72 | — | — | BABY, COME BACK — Equals (President Records Prod.), RCA Victor 47-9583 | 2 |
| 67 | 67 | 75 | — | BAREFOOT IN BALTIMORE — Strawberry Alarm Clock (F. Slay & Bill Holmes), Uni 55076 | 3 |
| 68 | 69 | 76 | — | DOWN ON ME — Big Brother and the Holding Company (Bob Shad), Mainstream 662 | 3 |
| 69 | 70 | 85 | — | THERE'S ALWAYS SOMETHING THERE TO REMIND ME — Dionne Warwick (Bacharach-David), Scepter 12226 | 3 |
| 70 | 76 | 84 | — | THE WEIGHT — The Band (John Simon), Capitol 2269 | 3 |
| 71 | 78 | 78 | — | MY WAY OF LIFE — Frank Sinatra (Don Costa), Reprise 0764 | 3 |
| 72 | 74 | 79 | — | DOWN HERE ON THE GROUND — Lou Rawls (David Axelrod), Capitol 2252 | 3 |
| 73 | 73 | 82 | 82 | FLY ME TO THE MOON — Bobby Womack (Chips Moman), Minit 32648 | 3 |
| 74 | 77 | 77 | — | UNCHAINED MELODY — Sweet Inspirations (Tom Dowd), Atlantic 2551 | 3 |
| 75 | 75 | 81 | — | PRIVATE NUMBER — Judy Clay & William Bell (Booker T. Jones), Stax 0005 | 3 |
| 76 | 80 | 89 | — | THAT KIND OF WOMAN — Merrilee Rush (Tommy Cogbill & Chips Moman), Bell 738 | 3 |
| 77 | 99 | — | — | FOOL FOR YOU — Impressions (Curtis Mayfield), Curtom 1932 | 2 |
| 78 | 83 | 88 | 90 | DON'T CHANGE YOUR LOVE — Five Stairsteps & Cubie (Curtis Mayfield), Curtom 1931 | 4 |
| 79 | — | — | — | CHAINED — Marvin Gaye (Frank Wilson), Tamla 54170 | 1 |
| 80 | — | — | — | I MET HER IN CHURCH — Box Tops (Dan Penn), Mala 12017 | 1 |
| 81 | 89 | 100 | — | NATURALLY STONED — Avant-Garde (Billy Sherrill), Columbia 44590 | 3 |
| 82 | 82 | 90 | — | THE MULE — The James Boys (Jesse James), Phil L.A. of Soul 316 | 3 |
| 83 | 85 | 87 | — | DO WHAT YOU GOTTA DO — Bobby Vee (Dallas Smith), Liberty 56057 | 3 |
| 84 | 90 | — | — | SHAPE OF THINGS TO COME — Max Frost & the Troopers (Mike Curb), Tower 419 | 2 |
| 85 | 87 | — | — | THEN YOU TELL ME GOODBYE — Eddy Arnold (Chet Atkins), RCA Victor 47-9606 | 2 |
| 86 | 88 | — | — | SHOOT 'EM UP BABY — Andy Kim (Jeff Barry), Steed 710 | 2 |
| 87 | — | — | — | POOR BABY — Cowsills (Wes Farrell), MGM 13981 | 1 |
| 88 | 92 | — | — | SUZIE Q — Creedence Clearwater Revival (Saul Zaentz), Fantasy 616 | 2 |
| 89 | — | — | — | GENTLE ON MY MIND — Glen Campbell (Al de Lory), Capitol 5939 | 8 |
| 90 | 91 | 91 | — | LIGHT MY FIRE — Doors (Paul A. Rothchild), Elektra 45615 | 20 |
| 91 | — | — | — | FOR THE LOVE OF IVY — Mamas & Papas (Lou Adler), Dunhill 4150 | 1 |
| 92 | 93 | 93 | 98 | THE FUNKY JUDGE — Bull & The Matadors (Sherrel-Cross Prod.), Toddlin' Town 108 | 4 |
| 93 | — | — | — | DO THE BEST YOU CAN — Hollies (Ron Richards), Epic 10361 | 1 |
| 94 | 96 | 96 | — | HELP YOURSELF (To All My Lovin') — James & Bobby Purify (Papa Don Prod.), Bell 735 | 3 |
| 95 | 95 | — | — | SALLY HAD A PARTY — Flavor (Tim O'Brien), Columbia 44521 | 2 |
| 96 | — | — | — | THE BIPLANE, EVERMORE — Irish Rovers (Charles Bud Dant), Decca 22371 | 1 |
| 97 | — | — | — | I CAN FEEL YOUR LOVE SLIPPING AWAY — Barbara Mason (Jimmy Bishop), Arctic 142 | 1 |
| 98 | — | — | — | HOLD ME TIGHT — Johnny Nash (Johnny Nash & Arthur Jenkins), JAD 207 | 1 |
| 99 | — | — | — | HORSE FEVER — Cliff Nobles & Company (Jesse James), Phil-L.A. of Soul 318 | 1 |
| 100 | 100 | — | — | LADY MADONNA — Fats Domino (Richard Perry), Reprise 0763 | 2 |

## BUBBLING UNDER THE HOT 100

101. ALL ALONG THE WATCHTOWER ... Jimi Hendrix Experience, Reprise 0767
102. MESSAGE FROM MARIA ... Joe Simon, Sound Stage 7 2617
103. ICE IN THE SUN ... Status Quo, Cadet Concept 7006
104. M'LADY ... Sly & the Family Stone, Epic 10353
105. BATTLE OF NEW ORLEANS ... Harper's Bizarre, Warner Bros.-Seven Arts 7223
106. OVER YOU ... Gary Puckett & the Union Gap, Columbia 44644
107. FIVE CARD STUD ... Dean Martin, Reprise 0765
108. DO YOU WANNA DANCE? ... Love Society, Scepter 12223
109. MONTAGE (From How Sweet It Is) ... Love Generation, Imperial 66310
110. I AM YOUR MAN ... Bobby Taylor & the Vancouvers, Gordy 7073
111. APPLE CIDER ... People, Capitol 2251
112. CHOICE ... O'Jays, Bell 737
113. DON'T LET HIM TAKE YOUR LOVE ... Jimmy Ruffin, Soul 35046
114. HARPER VALLEY P.T.A. ... Bobbi Martin, United Artists 50443
115. MEDLEY: YOU'VE LOST THAT LOVIN' FEELIN'/YOU'RE MY SOUL AND INSPIRATION ... Vivian Reed, Epic 10380
116. LOVE HEALS ... Colours, Dot 17132
117. SUNSHINE AMONG US ... Eternity's Children, Tower 429
118. YOU GOT THE LOVE ... Professor Morrison's Lollipop, White Whale 275
119. SAN FRANCISCO—WEAR SOME FLOWERS IN YOUR HAIR ... Paul Mauriat, Philips 40570
120. OH LORD, WHY LORD ... Los Pop Tops, Calla 154
121. THE B.B. JONES ... B.B. King, Bluesway 61019
122. SAN FRANCISCO GIRLS ... Fever Tree, Uni 55060
123. I'M GONNA MAKE YOU LOVE ME ... Aesop's Fables, Cadet Concept 7005
124. FIRE ... 5x5, Paula 302
125. BIRMINGHAM ... Movers, "123" 1700

# Billboard HOT 100

FOR WEEK ENDING SEPTEMBER 21, 1968

★ STAR PERFORMER—Sides registering greatest proportionate upward progress this week.

Record Industry Association of America seal of certification as million selling single.

| This Week | 1 Wk. Ago | 2 Wks. Ago | 3 Wks. Ago | TITLE | Artist (Producer), Label & Number | Weeks On Chart |
|---|---|---|---|---|---|---|
| 1 (Billboard Award) | 2 | 4 | 7 | HARPER VALLEY P.T.A. | Jeannie C. Riley (Shelby S. Singleton Jr.), Plantation 3 | 5 |
| 2 | 1 | 1 | 1 | PEOPLE GOT TO BE FREE | Rascals (Rascals), Atlantic 2537 | 10 |
| ★3 | 10 | — | — | HEY JUDE | Beatles (George Martin), Apple 2276 | 2 |
| ★4 | 8 | 13 | 14 | HUSH | Deep Purple (Derek Lawrence), Tetragrammaton 1503 | 6 |
| 5 | 5 | 7 | 12 | 1, 2, 3, RED LIGHT | 1910 Fruitgum Company (Kasenetz-Katz Assoc.) Buddah 54 | 9 |
| 6 | 3 | 3 | 3 | LIGHT MY FIRE | Jose Feliciano (Rick Jarrard), RCA Victor 47-9550 | 9 |
| 7 | 4 | 2 | 2 | BORN TO BE WILD | Steppenwolf (Gabriel Mekler), Dunhill 4138 | 11 |
| ★8 | 11 | 17 | 18 | THE FOOL ON THE HILL | Sergio Mendes & Brasil '66 (Sergio Mendes, Herb Alpert & Jerry Moss) | 7 |
| ★9 | 23 | 30 | 42 | I'VE GOTTA GET A MESSAGE TO YOU | Bee Gees (Robert Stigwood), Atco 6603 | 6 |
| 10 | 6 | 6 | 20 | THE HOUSE THAT JACK BUILT | Aretha Franklin (Jerry Wexler), Atlantic 2456 | 6 |
| ★11 | 27 | 51 | 71 | TIME HAS COME TODAY | Chambers Brothers (David Rubinson), Columbia 44414 | 7 |
| ★12 | 38 | — | — | REVOLUTION | Beatles (George Martin), Apple 2276 | 2 |
| 13 | 17 | 18 | 29 | SLIP AWAY | Clarence Carter (Rick Hall & Staff), Atlantic 2508 | 11 |
| 14 | 14 | 23 | 25 | I SAY A LITTLE PRAYER | Aretha Franklin (Jerry Wexler), Atlantic 2456 | 6 |
| ★15 | 60 | 81 | — | FIRE | Crazy World of Arthur Brown (Kit Lambert), Atlantic 2556 | 3 |
| ★16 | 18 | 36 | 60 | GIRL WATCHER | O'Kaysions (North State Music), ABC 11094 | 6 |
| 17 | 7 | 8 | 8 | YOU'RE ALL I NEED TO GET BY | Marvin Gaye & Tammi Terrell (Ashford-Simpson), Tamla 54169 | 9 |
| ★18 | 24 | 35 | 46 | ON THE ROAD AGAIN | Canned Heat (Dallas Smith), Liberty 56038 | 7 |
| ★19 | 57 | 62 | — | MY SPECIAL ANGEL | Vogues (Dick Glasser), Reprise 0766 | 3 |
| 20 | 20 | 22 | 24 | DO IT AGAIN | Beach Boys (Beach Boys), Capitol 2239 | 9 |
| ★21 | 52 | 64 | 74 | MIDNIGHT CONFESSIONS | Grassroots (Steve Barri), Dunhill 4144 | 4 |
| 22 | 12 | 12 | 6 | (You Keep Me) HANGIN' ON | Vanilla Fudge (Shadow Morton), Atco 6495 | 17 |
| 23 | 9 | 5 | 4 | HELLO, I LOVE YOU | Doors (Paul Rothchild), Elektra 45635 | 12 |
| 24 | 29 | 29 | 37 | TUESDAY AFTERNOON (Forever Afternoon) | Moody Blues (Tony Clarke), Deram 85028 | 10 |
| 25 | 13 | 11 | 5 | SUNSHINE OF YOUR LOVE | Cream (Felix Pappalardi), Atco 6544 | 26 |
| 26 | 26 | 27 | 32 | MAGIC BUS | Who (Kit Lambert), Decca 32362 | 7 |
| ★27 | 41 | 45 | 69 | LITTLE GREEN APPLES | O. C. Smith (Jerry Fuller), Columbia 44616 | 6 |
| 28 | 21 | 15 | 15 | LOVE MAKES A WOMAN | Barbara Acklin (Carl Davis & Eugene Record), Brunswick 55379 | 11 |
| ★29 | 59 | 61 | 72 | (The Lament of the Cherokee) INDIAN RESERVATION | Don Fardon (Miki Dallon), GNP Crescendo 405 | 4 |
| 30 | 22 | 16 | 13 | CLASSICAL GAS | Mason Williams (Mike Post), Warner-Bros.-Seven Arts 7190 | 14 |
| 31 | 31 | 60 | — | SAY IT LOUD (I'm Black and I'm Proud) | James Brown & His Famous Flames (James Brown), King 6187 | 3 |
| 32 | 15 | 14 | 11 | TURN AROUND, LOOK AT ME | Vogues (Dick Glasser), Reprise 0686 | 15 |
| 33 | 34 | 36 | 36 | DOWN AT LULU'S | Ohio Express (Kasenetz-Katz Assoc.), Buddah 56 | 8 |
| 34 | 37 | 37 | 39 | SPECIAL OCCASION | Smokey Robinson & The Miracles (Smokey-Cleveland), Tamla 54172 | 6 |
| 35 | 25 | 21 | 19 | SEALED WITH A KISS | Gary Lewis & Playboys (Snuff Garrett), Liberty 56037 | 14 |
| 36 | 19 | 10 | 10 | STAY IN MY CORNER | Dells (Bobby Miller), Cadet 5612 | 13 |
| 37 | 16 | 9 | 9 | I CAN'T STOP DANCING | Archie Bell & the Drells (Gamble-Huff), Atlantic 2534 | 10 |
| 38 | 39 | 46 | 50 | HIP CITY—PART 2 | Jr. Walker & The All Stars (Lawrence Horn), Soul 35048 | 7 |
| ★39 | 49 | 52 | 53 | WHO IS GONNA LOVE ME? | Dionne Warwick (Bacharach-David), Scepter 12226 | 5 |
| 40 | 44 | 44 | 65 | THE SNAKE | Al Wilson (Johnny Rivers), Soul City 767 | 6 |
| 41 | 28 | 32 | 34 | THE EYES OF A NEW YORK WOMAN | B.J. Thomas (Chips Moman), Scepter 12219 | 14 |
| ★42 | 58 | 66 | 66 | IN-A-GADDA-DA-VIDA | Iron Butterfly (Jim Hilton), Atco 6606 | 5 |
| 43 | 33 | 33 | 51 | GIRLS CAN'T DO WHAT THE GUYS DO | Betty Wright (Brad Shapiro & Steve Alaimo), Alston 4569 | 8 |
| ★44 | 88 | 92 | — | SUZIE Q | Creedence Clearwater Revival (Saul Zaentz), Fantasy 616 | 3 |
| ★45 | 56 | 59 | 80 | PIECE OF MY HEART | Big Brother & the Holding Company, Columbia 44626 | 4 |
| 46 | 46 | 47 | 49 | BROWN EYED WOMAN | Bill Medley (Bill Medley & Barry Mann), MGM 13959 | 8 |
| ★47 | 66 | 72 | — | BABY, COME BACK | Equals (President Records Prod.), RCA Victor 47-9583 | 3 |
| 48 | 48 | 50 | 67 | HELP YOURSELF | Tom Jones (Peter Sullivan), Parrot 40029 | 4 |
| 49 | 43 | 43 | 43 | GIVE A DAMN | Spanky & Our Gang (Scharf/Dorough, Edel), Mercury 72831 | 8 |
| 50 | 42 | 42 | 44 | I CAN'T DANCE TO THE MUSIC YOU'RE PLAYIN' | Martha Reeves & The Vandellas (Deke Richards), Gordy 7075 | 7 |
| ★51 | 54 | 56 | 63 | TO WAIT FOR LOVE | Herb Alpert (Herb Alpert & Jerry Moss), A&M 964 | 4 |
| 52 | 53 | 53 | 59 | MORNING DEW | Lulu (Mickie Most), Epic 10367 | 7 |
| 53 | 40 | 40 | 41 | I'VE NEVER FOUND A GIRL (To Love Me Like You Do) | Eddie Floyd (Steve Cropper), Stax 0002 | 9 |
| ★54 | — | — | — | OVER YOU | Gary Puckett & the Union Gap (Jerry Fuller), Columbia 44644 | 1 |
| 55 | 55 | 57 | 62 | LISTEN HERE | Eddie Harris (Joel Dorn), Atlantic 2487 | 10 |
| ★56 | 61 | 65 | 68 | THE WEIGHT | Jackie DeShannon (Charles Greene & Brian Stone), Imperial 66313 | 5 |
| ★57 | 63 | 84 | — | STREET FIGHTING MAN | Rolling Stones (Jimmy Miller), London 909 | 3 |
| 59 | 45 | 49 | 58 | I WISH IT WOULD RAIN | Gladys Knight & The Pips (N. Whitefield), Soul 35047 | 5 |
| 58 | 47 | 48 | 57 | SIX MAN BAND | Association (Association), Warner Bros.-Seven Arts 7229 | 5 |
| ★60 | 64 | 79 | 83 | HEY, WESTERN UNION MAN | Jerry Butler (Gamble-Huff), Mercury 72850 | 4 |
| 61 | 68 | 69 | 76 | DOWN ON ME | Big Brother & the Holding Company (Bob Shad), Mainstream 662 | 4 |
| 62 | 62 | 63 | 70 | WORKIN' ON A GROOVY THING | Patti Drew (Carone Prod.), Capitol 2197 | 8 |
| ★63 | 84 | 90 | — | SHAPE OF THINGS TO COME | Max Frost & the Troopers (Mike Curb), Tower 419 | 3 |
| 64 | 65 | 71 | 86 | BREAK YOUR PROMISE | Delfonics (Stan and Bell), Philly Groove 152 | 4 |
| 65 | 69 | 70 | 85 | THERE'S ALWAYS SOMETHING THERE TO REMIND ME | Dionne Warwick (Bacharach-David), Scepter 12226 | 4 |
| ★66 | — | — | — | ALL ALONG THE WATCHTOWER | Jimi Hendrix Experience (Jimi Hendrix), Reprise 0767 | 1 |
| 67 | 67 | 67 | 75 | BAREFOOT IN BALTIMORE | Strawberry Alarm Clock (F. Slay & Bill Holmes), Uni 55076 | 4 |
| ★68 | 80 | — | — | I MET HER IN CHURCH | Box Tops (Dan Penn), Mala 12017 | 2 |
| 69 | 72 | 74 | 79 | DOWN HERE ON THE GROUND | Lou Rawls (David Axelrod), Capitol 2252 | 4 |
| 70 | 70 | 76 | 84 | THE WEIGHT | The Band (John Simon), Capitol 2269 | 4 |
| 71 | 71 | 78 | 78 | MY WAY OF LIFE | Frank Sinatra (Don Costa), Reprise 0764 | 4 |
| 72 | 79 | — | — | CHAINED | Marvin Gaye (Frank Wilson), Tamla 54170 | 2 |
| 73 | 73 | 73 | 82 | FLY ME TO THE MOON | Bobby Womack (Chips Moman), Minit 32048 | 6 |
| 74 | 74 | 77 | 77 | UNCHAINED MELODY | Sweet Inspirations (Tom Dowd), Atlantic 2551 | 4 |
| 75 | 75 | 75 | 81 | PRIVATE NUMBER | Judy Clay & William Bell (Booker T. Jones), Stax 0005 | 4 |
| 76 | 76 | 80 | 89 | THAT KIND OF WOMAN | Merrilee Rush (Tommy Cogbill & Chips Moman), Bell 738 | 4 |
| 77 | 77 | 99 | — | FOOL FOR YOU | Impressions (Curtis Mayfield), Curtom 1932 | 3 |
| 78 | 78 | 83 | 88 | DON'T CHANGE YOUR LOVE | Five Stairsteps & Cubie (Curtis Mayfield), Curtom 1931 | 5 |
| ★79 | 89 | — | — | GENTLE ON MY MIND | Glen Campbell (Al de Lory), Capitol 5939 | 9 |
| ★80 | 81 | 89 | 100 | NATURALLY STONED | Avant-Garde (Billy Sherrill), Columbia 44590 | 4 |
| ★81 | 91 | — | — | FOR THE LOVE OF IVY | Mamas & Papas (Lou Adler), Dunhill 4150 | 2 |
| 82 | 82 | 82 | 90 | THE MULE | The James Boys (Jesse James), Phil L.A. of Soul 316 | 4 |
| 83 | 83 | 85 | 87 | DO WHAT YOU GOTTA DO | Bobby Vee (Dallas Smith), Liberty 56057 | 4 |
| 84 | 85 | 87 | — | THEN YOU TELL ME GOODBYE | Eddy Arnold (Chet Atkins), RCA Victor 47-9606 | 3 |
| ★85 | 86 | 88 | — | SHOOT 'EM UP BABY | Andy Kim (Jeff Barry), Steed 710 | 3 |
| ★86 | 87 | — | — | POOR BABY | Cowsills (Wes Farrell), MGM 13981 | 2 |
| ★87 | — | — | — | I FOUND A TRUE LOVE | Wilson Pickett (Tom Dowd), Atlantic 2558 | 1 |
| ★88 | 99 | — | — | HORSE FEVER | Cliff Nobles & Company (Jesse James), Phil.-L.A. of Soul 318 | 2 |
| 89 | 90 | 91 | 91 | LIGHT MY FIRE | Doors (Paul A. Rothchild), Elektra 45615 | 21 |
| ★90 | 98 | — | — | HOLD ME TIGHT | Johnny Nash (Johnny Nash & Arthur Jenkins), JAD 207 | 2 |
| 91 | 92 | 93 | 93 | THE FUNKY JUDGE | Bull & The Matadors (Sherrel-Cross Prod.), Toddlin' Town 108 | 5 |
| 92 | 96 | — | — | THE BIPLANE, EVERMORE | Irish Rovers (Charles Bud Dant), Decca 32371 | 2 |
| 93 | — | — | — | SAN FRANCISCO GIRLS | Fever Tree (Scott & Vivian Holtzman), Uni 55060 | 4 |
| 94 | — | — | — | THERE WAS A TIME | Gene Chandler (Carl Davis and Gene Chandler), Brunswick 55383 | 1 |
| 95 | — | — | — | BATTLE OF NEW ORLEANS | Harpers Bizarre (Lenny Waronker), Warner Bros.-Seven Arts 7223 | 1 |
| 96 | — | — | — | THE CHOICE | O'Jays (George Kerr), Bell 737 | 1 |
| 97 | — | — | — | ELENORE | Turtles (Chip Douglas), White Whale 276 | 1 |
| 98 | — | — | — | TOMBOY | Ronnie Dove (Phil Kahl & Bill Justis), Diamond 249 | 1 |
| 99 | — | — | — | I LOVE YOU MADLY | Fantastic Four (Mike Hanks), Ric Tic 144 | 1 |
| 100 | — | — | — | COURT OF LOVE | Unifics (Guy Draper), Kapp 935 | 1 |

## HOT 100—A TO Z—*(Publisher-Licensee)*

All Along the Watchtower (Dwarf, BMI) .......... 66
Baby, Come Back (Piccadilly, BMI) .......... 47
Barefoot in Baltimore (Alarm Clock Claridge, ASCAP) .......... 67
Battle of New Orleans (Warden, BMI) .......... 95
Biplane, Evermore, The (Little Darlin, BMI) .......... 92
Born to Be Wild (Duchess, BMI) .......... 7
Break Your Promise (Nickel Shoe/Bellboy, BMI) .......... 64
Brown Eyed Woman (Screen Gems-Columbia, BMI) .......... 46
Chained (Jobete, BMI) .......... 72
Choice, The (My/Bay-Wes, BMI) .......... 96
Classical Gas (Irving, BMI) .......... 30
Court of Love (Andjun, BMI) .......... 100
Do It Again (Sea of Tunes, BMI) .......... 20
Do What You Gotta Do (Rivers, BMI) .......... 83
Don't Change Your Love (Caned, BMI) .......... 78
Down at Lulu's (Peanut Butter/Kaskat, BMI) .......... 33
Down Here on the Ground (Warner Bros.-Seven Arts, BMI) .......... 69
Down on Me (Brent, BMI) .......... 61
Elenore (Ishmael/Blimp, BMI) .......... 97
Eyes of a New York Woman, The (Press, BMI) .......... 41
Fire (Track, BMI) .......... 15
Fly Me to the Moon (Almanac, ASCAP) .......... 73
Fool for You (Camad, BMI) .......... 77
Fool on the Hill, The (Comet, ASCAP) .......... 8
For the Love of Ivy (Wingate/Honest John, ASCAP) 81
Funky Judge, The (Downstream/Napac/Flomar, BMI) .......... 91
Gentle on My Mind (Glazer, BMI) .......... 79
Girl Watcher (North State, ASCAP) .......... 16
Girls Can't Do What the Guys Do (Sherlyn, BMI) .......... 43
Give a Damn (Takya, ASCAP) .......... 49
Harper Valley P.T.A. (Newkeys, BMI) .......... 1
Hello, I Love You (Nipper, ASCAP) .......... 23
Help Yourself (Famous, ASCAP) .......... 48
Hey Jude (Maclen, BMI) .......... 3
Hey, Western Union Man (Parabut/Double Diamond/Downstairs, BMI) .......... 60
Hip City—Part 2 (Jobete, BMI) .......... 38
Hold Me Tight (Nash, ASCAP) .......... 90
Horse Fever (Dandelion/James Boy, BMI) .......... 88
House That Jack Built, The (Cotillion, BMI) .......... 10
Hush (Lowery, BMI) .......... 4
I Can't Dance to That Music You're Playin' (Jobete, BMI) .......... 50
I Can't Stop Dancing (Downstairs/Double Diamond, BMI) .......... 37
I Found a True Love (Cotillion/Tracebob/Erva, BMI) 87
I Love You Madly (Ric Tic, BMI) .......... 99
I Met Her in Church (Press, BMI) .......... 68
I Say a Little Prayer (Jac/Blue Seas, ASCAP) .......... 14
I Wish It Would Rain (Jobete, BMI) .......... 59
In-a-Gadda-Da-Vida (Ten Last-Cotillion, Itasca, BMI) 42
I've Gotta Get a Message to You (Casserole, BMI) 9
I've Never Found a Girl (To Love Me Like You Do) (East, BMI) .......... 63
(Lament of the Cherokee) Indian Reservation (Acuff-Rose, BMI) .......... 29
Light My Fire (Doors) (Nipper, ASCAP) .......... 89
Light My Fire (Jose Feliciano) (Nipper, ASCAP) .......... 6
Listen Here (Hargrove, BMI) .......... 55
Little Green Apples (Russell-Cason, ASCAP) .......... 27
Love Makes a Woman (Jalynne/BRC, BMI) .......... 28
Magic Bus (Essex, ASCAP) .......... 26
Midnight Confessions (Little Fugitive, BMI) .......... 21
Morning Dew (Nina, BMI) .......... 52
The Mule (Dandelion/James, BMI) .......... 82
My Special Angel (Viva, BMI) .......... 19
My Way of Life (Roosevelt, BMI) .......... 71
Naturally Stoned (Cedarwood, BMI) .......... 80
On the Road Again (Lawn, BMI) .......... 18
1, 2, 3 Red Light (Kaskat, BMI) .......... 5
Over You (Viva, BMI) .......... 54
People Got to Be Free (Slacsar, ASCAP) .......... 2
Piece of My Heart (Webb IV/Ragmar, BMI) .......... 45
Poor Baby (Pocket Full of Tunes/Akbestal, BMI) .......... 86
Private Number (East, BMI) .......... 75
Revolution (Maclen, BMI) .......... 12
San Francisco Girls (Filigree, BMI) .......... 93
Say It Loud—I'm Black and I'm Proud (Colo, BMI) 31
Sealed With a Kiss (Post, ASCAP) .......... 35
Shape of Things to Come (Screen Gems-Columbia, BMI) .......... 63
Shoot 'Em Up Baby (Unart/Joachim, BMI) .......... 85
Six Man Band (Beechwood, BMI) .......... 58
Slip Away (Fame, BMI) .......... 13
Snake, The (Marks, BMI) .......... 40
Special Occasion (Jobete, BMI) .......... 34
Stay in My Corner (Conrad, BMI) .......... 36
Street Fighting Man (Gideon, BMI) .......... 57
Sunshine of Your Love (Dratleaf, BMI) .......... 25
Suzie Q. (Arc, BMI) .......... 44
That Kind of Woman (Screen Gems-Columbia, BMI) 76
Then You Tell Me Goodbye (Acuff-Rose, BMI) .......... 84
There's Always Something There to Remind Me (Blue Seas/Jac/Rose Jungnickel, ASCAP) .......... 65
There Was a Time (Golo, Lois, BMI) .......... 94
Time Has Come Today (Spinmaker, BMI) .......... 11
To Wait for Love (Blue Seas/Jac, ASCAP) .......... 51
Tomboy (Melrose, ASCAP) .......... 98
Tuesday Afternoon (Forever Afternoon) (Essex, ASCAP) .......... 24
Turn Around, Look at Me (Viva, BMI) .......... 32
Unchained Melody (Frank, ASCAP) .......... 74
Weight, The (Jackie DeShannon) (Calla, ASCAP) .......... 56
Weight, The (The Band) (Callee, ASCAP) .......... 70
Who Is Gonna Love Me? (Blue Seas/Jac, BMI) .......... 39
Workin' on a Groovy Thing (Screen Gems-Columbia, BMI) .......... 62
(You Keep Me) Hangin' On (Jobete, BMI) .......... 22
You're All I Need to Get By (Jobete, BMI) .......... 17

## BUBBLING UNDER THE HOT 100

101. I'VE GOT DREAMS TO REMEMBER .......... Otis Redding, Atco 6612
102. MESSAGE FROM MARIA .......... Joe Simon, Sound Stage 7 2617
103. ICE IN THE SUN .......... Status Quo, Cadet Concept 7006
104. I AM YOUR MAN .......... Bobby Taylor & the Vancouvers, Gordy 7073
105. SMELL OF INCENSE .......... Southwest F.O.B., Hip 8002
106. SALLY HAD A PARTY .......... Flavor, Columbia 44521
107. SWEET BLINDNESS .......... 5th Dimension, Soul City 768
108. PEACE OF MIND .......... Nancy Wilson, Capitol 2283
109. MONTAGE (From How Sweet It Is) .......... Love Generation, Imperial 66310
110. ALMOST IN LOVE .......... Elvis Presley, RCA Victor 47-9610
111. APPLE CIDER .......... People, Capitol 2251
112. OPEN MY EYES .......... Nazz, SGC 001
113. LOVE HEALS .......... Colours, Dot 17132
114. HARPER VALLEY P.T.A. .......... Bobbi Martin, United Artists 50443
115. MEDLEY: YOU'VE LOST THAT LOVIN' FEELIN'/YOU'RE MY SOUL & INSPIRATION .......... Vivian Reed, Epic 10382
116. WHAT'S EASY FOR TWO IS HARD FOR ONE .......... Marvelettes, Tamla 54171
117. SWEET YOUNG THING LIKE YOU .......... Ray Charles, ABC/TRC 11133
118. YOU GOT THE LOVE .......... Professor Morrison's Lollipop, White Whale 275
119. (I Can Feel Your Love) SLIPPING AWAY .......... Barbara Mason, Arctic 142
120. OH LORD, WHY LORD .......... Los Pop Tops, Calla 154
121. DO THE BEST YOU CAN .......... Hollies, Epic 10361
122. PUFFIN' DOWN THE TRACK .......... Hugh Masekela, Uni 55085
123. HELLO, HELLO .......... Tiny Tim, Reprise 0769
124. BIRMINGHAM .......... Movers, "123" 1700
125. IKE A ROLLING STONE .......... Flatt & Scruggs, Columbia 44623
126. MISSION: IMPOSSIBLE/NORWEGIAN WOOD .......... Alan Copeland Singers, ABC 11088
127. SUN AIN'T GONNA SHINE ANYMORE .......... Fuzzy Bunnies, Decca 32364
128. DESTINATION ANYWHERE .......... Marvelettes, Tamla 54171
129. (Till I) RUN WITH YOU .......... Lovin' Spoonful, Kama Sutra 251
130. PER-SON-ALLY .......... Bobby Paris, Tetragrammaton 1804
131. ISN'T IT LONELY TOGETHER .......... Robert Knight, EIF 90019
132. THOSE WERE THE DAYS .......... Mary Hopkins, Apple 1801
133. BANG-SHANG-A-LANG .......... Arenies, Calendar 63-1006
134. DON'T BOGART ME .......... Fraternity of Man, ABC 11106
135. CINAMMON .......... Lorek, Bang 558

Compiled from national retail sales and radio station airplay by the Music Popularity Dept. of Record Market Research, Billboard.

# Billboard HOT 100

**FOR WEEK ENDING SEPTEMBER 28, 1968**

★ STAR PERFORMER—Sides registering greatest proportionate upward progress this week.

Ⓢ Record Industry Association of America seal of certification as million selling single.

| This Week | 1 Wk. Ago | 2 Wks. Ago | 3 Wks. Ago | TITLE — Artist (Producer), Label & Number | Weeks On Chart |
|---|---|---|---|---|---|
| 1 | 3 | 10 | — | **HEY JUDE** — Beatles (George Martin), Apple 2276 | 3 |
| 2 | 1 | 2 | 4 | HARPER VALLEY P.T.A. — Jeannie C. Riley (Shelby S. Singleton Jr.), Plantation 3 | 6 |
| 3 | 2 | 1 | 1 | PEOPLE GOT TO BE FREE — Rascals (Rascals), Atlantic 2537 | 11 |
| 4 | 4 | 8 | 13 | HUSH — Deep Purple (Derek Lawrence), Tetragrammaton 1503 | 7 |
| 5 | 15 | 60 | 81 | ★ FIRE — Crazy World of Arthur Brown (Kit Lambert), Atlantic 2556 | 4 |
| 6 | 8 | 11 | 17 | THE FOOL ON THE HILL — Sergio Mendes & Brasil '66 (Sergio Mendes, Herb Alpert & Jerry Moss), A&M 961 | 8 |
| 7 | 5 | 5 | 7 | 1, 2, 3, RED LIGHT — 1910 Fruitgum Company (Kasenetz-Katz Assoc.), Buddah 54 | 10 |
| 8 | 9 | 23 | 30 | I'VE GOTTA GET A MESSAGE TO YOU — Bee Gees (Robert Stigwood), Atco 6603 | 7 |
| 9 | 16 | 18 | 36 | ★ GIRL WATCHER — O'Kaysions (North State Music), ABC 11094 | 7 |
| 10 | 13 | 17 | 18 | SLIP AWAY — Clarence Carter (Rick Hall & Staff), Atlantic 2508 | 12 |
| 11 | 11 | 27 | 51 | TIME HAS COME TODAY — Chambers Brothers (David Robinson), Columbia 44414 | 8 |
| 12 | 12 | 38 | — | REVOLUTION — Beatles (George Martin), Apple 2276 | 3 |
| 13 | 10 | 6 | 6 | THE HOUSE THAT JACK BUILT — Aretha Franklin (Jerry Wexler), Atlantic 2546 | 7 |
| 14 | 14 | 14 | 23 | I SAY A LITTLE PRAYER — Aretha Franklin (Jerry Wexler), Atlantic 2546 | 5 |
| 15 | 7 | 4 | 2 | BORN TO BE WILD — Steppenwolf (Gabriel Mekler), Dunhill 4138 | 12 |
| 16 | 18 | 24 | 35 | ★ ON THE ROAD AGAIN — Canned Heat (Dallas Smith), Liberty 56038 | 8 |
| 17 | 6 | 3 | 3 | LIGHT MY FIRE — Jose Feliciano (Rick Jarrard), RCA Victor 47-9550 | 10 |
| 18 | 21 | 52 | 64 | MIDNIGHT CONFESSIONS — Grassroots (Steve Barri), Dunhill 4144 | 5 |
| 19 | 19 | 57 | 62 | MY SPECIAL ANGEL — Vogues (Dick Glasser), Reprise 0766 | 4 |
| 20 | 27 | 41 | 45 | ★ LITTLE GREEN APPLES — O. C. Smith (Jerry Fuller), Columbia 44616 | 7 |
| 21 | 31 | 31 | 60 | ★ SAY IT LOUD (I'm Black and I'm Proud) — James Brown & His Famous Flames (James Brown), King 6187 | 3 |
| 22 | 17 | 7 | 8 | YOU'RE ALL I NEED TO GET BY — Marvin Gaye & Tammi Terrell (Ashford-Simpson), Tamla 54169 | 10 |
| 23 | 22 | 12 | 12 | (You Keep Me) HANGIN' ON — Vanilla Fudge (Shadow Morton), Atco 6495 | 18 |
| 24 | 45 | 56 | 59 | ★ PIECE OF MY HEART — Big Brother and The Holding Company, Columbia 44626 | 4 |
| 25 | 26 | 26 | 27 | MAGIC BUS — Who (Kit Lambert), Decca 32362 | 8 |
| 26 | 34 | 37 | 37 | SPECIAL OCCASION — Smokey Robinson & The Miracles (Smokey-Cleveland), Tamla 54172 | 7 |
| 27 | 44 | 88 | 92 | ★ SUZIE Q — Creedence Clearwater Revival (Saul Zaentz), Fantasy 616 | 4 |
| 28 | 29 | 59 | 61 | (The Lament of the Cherokee) INDIAN RESERVATION — Don Fardon (Miki Dallon), GNP Crescendo 405 | 5 |
| 29 | 54 | — | — | ★ OVER YOU — Gary Puckett & the Union Gap (Jerry Fuller), Columbia 44644 | 2 |
| 30 | 40 | 44 | 44 | THE SNAKE — Al Wilson (Johnny Rivers), Soul City 767 | 7 |
| 31 | 66 | — | — | ★ ALL ALONG THE WATCHTOWER — Jimi Hendrix Experience (Jimi Hendrix), Reprise 0767 | 2 |
| 32 | 24 | 29 | 29 | TUESDAY AFTERNOON (Forever Afternoon) — Moody Blues (Tony Clarke), Deram 85028 | 11 |
| 33 | 39 | 49 | 52 | WHO IS GONNA LOVE ME? — Dionne Warwick (Bacharach-David), Scepter 12226 | 6 |
| 34 | 47 | 66 | 72 | ★ BABY, COME BACK — Equals (President Records Prod.), RCA Victor 47-9583 | 4 |
| 35 | 38 | 39 | 46 | HIP CITY—PART 2 — Jr. Walker & The All Stars (Lawrence Horn), Soul 35048 | 8 |
| 36 | 63 | 84 | 90 | ★ SHAPE OF THINGS TO COME — Max Frost & The Troopers (Mike Curb), Tower 419 | 4 |
| 37 | 28 | 21 | 15 | LOVE MAKES A WOMAN — Barbara Acklin (Carl Davis & Eugene Record), Brunswick 55379 | 12 |
| 38 | 42 | 58 | 66 | IN-A-GADDA-DA-VIDA — Iron Butterfly (Jim Hilton), Atco 6606 | 6 |
| 39 | 20 | 20 | 22 | DO IT AGAIN — Beach Boys (Beach Boys), Capitol 2239 | 10 |
| 40 | 33 | 34 | 36 | DOWN AT LULU'S — Ohio Express (Kasenetz-Katz Assoc.), Buddah 56 | 9 |
| 41 | 59 | 45 | 49 | I WISH IT WOULD RAIN — Gladys Knight & The Pips (N. Whitfield), Soul 35047 | 5 |
| 42 | 60 | 64 | 79 | ★ HEY, WESTERN UNION MAN — Jerry Butler (Gamble-Huff), Mercury 72850 | 5 |
| 43 | 68 | 80 | — | ★ I MET HER IN CHURCH — Box Tops (Dan Penn), Mala 12017 | 3 |
| 44 | 64 | 65 | 71 | BREAK YOUR PROMISE — Delfonics (Stan and Bell), Philly Groove 152 | 5 |
| 45 | 55 | 55 | 57 | LISTEN HERE — Eddie Harris (Joel Dorn), Atlantic 2487 | 11 |
| 46 | 46 | 46 | 47 | BROWN EYED WOMAN — Bill Medley (Bill Medley & Barry Mann), MGM 13959 | 9 |
| 47 | 61 | 68 | 69 | DOWN ON ME — Big Brother & the Holding Company (Bob Shad), Mainstream 662 | 5 |
| 48 | 48 | 48 | 50 | HELP YOURSELF — Tom Jones (Peter Sullivan), Parrot 40029 | 5 |
| 49 | 87 | — | — | ★ I FOUND A TRUE LOVE — Wilson Pickett (Tom Dowd), Atlantic 2558 | 2 |
| 50 | 50 | 42 | 42 | I CAN'T DANCE TO THE MUSIC YOU'RE PLAYIN' — Martha Reeves & The Vandellas (Deke Richards), Gordy 7075 | 8 |
| 51 | 51 | 54 | 56 | TO WAIT FOR LOVE — Herb Alpert (Herb Alpert & Jerry Moss), A&M 964 | 6 |
| 52 | 72 | 79 | — | ★ CHAINED — Marvin Gaye (Frank Wilson), Tamla 54170 | 3 |
| 53 | 86 | 87 | — | ★ POOR BABY — Cowsills (Wes Farrell), MGM 13981 | 3 |
| 54 | 97 | — | — | ★ ELENORE — Turtles (Chip Douglas), White Whale 276 | 2 |
| 55 | 56 | 61 | 65 | THE WEIGHT — Jackie DeShannon (Charles Greene & Brian Stone), Imperial 66313 | 6 |
| 56 | 57 | 63 | 84 | STREET FIGHTING MAN — Rolling Stones (Jimmy Miller), London 909 | 4 |
| 57 | 80 | 81 | 89 | ★ NATURALLY STONED — Avant-Garde (Billy Sherrill), Columbia 44590 | 5 |
| 58 | 52 | 53 | 53 | MORNING DEW — Lulu (Mickie Most), Epic 10367 | 8 |
| 59 | 90 | 98 | — | ★ HOLD ME TIGHT — Johnny Nash (Johnny Nash & Arthur Jenkins), JAD 207 | 3 |
| 60 | 58 | 47 | 48 | SIX MAN BAND — Association (Association), Warner Bros.-Seven Arts 7229 | 6 |
| 61 | 77 | 77 | 99 | FOOL FOR YOU — Impressions (Curtis Mayfield), Curtom 1932 | 4 |
| 62 | 85 | 86 | 88 | ★ SHOOT 'EM UP BABY — Andy Kim (Jeff Barry), Steed 710 | 4 |
| 63 | 70 | 70 | 76 | THE WEIGHT — The Band (John Simon), Capitol 2269 | 5 |
| 64 | 71 | 71 | 78 | MY WAY OF LIFE — Frank Sinatra (Don Costa), Reprise 0764 | 5 |
| 65 | 62 | 62 | 63 | WORKIN' ON A GROOVY THING — Patti Drew (Carone Prod.), Capitol 2197 | 9 |
| 66 | 73 | 73 | 73 | FLY ME TO THE MOON — Bobby Womack (Chips Moman), Minit 32048 | 7 |
| 67 | 65 | 69 | 70 | THERE'S ALWAYS SOMETHING THERE TO REMIND ME — Dionne Warwick (Bacharach-David), Scepter 12226 | 5 |
| 68 | 91 | 92 | 93 | ★ THE FUNKY JUDGE — Bull & The Matadors (Sherrel-Cross Prod.), Toddlin' Town 108 | 6 |
| 69 | — | — | — | I'VE GOT DREAMS TO REMEMBER — Otis Redding (Steve Cropper), Atco 6612 | 1 |
| 70 | — | — | — | THOSE WERE THE DAYS — Mary Hopkin (Paul McCartney), Apple 1801 | 1 |
| 71 | — | — | — | BANG-SHANG-A-LANG — Archies (Don Kirshner), Calendar 63-1006 | 1 |
| 72 | — | — | — | ICE IN THE SUN — Status Quo (John Schroeder), Cadet Concept 7006 | 1 |
| 73 | 74 | 74 | 77 | UNCHAINED MELODY — Sweet Inspirations (Tom Dowd), Atlantic 2551 | 5 |
| 74 | 69 | 72 | 74 | DOWN HERE ON THE GROUND — Lou Rawls (David Axelrod), Capitol 2252 | 5 |
| 75 | 78 | 78 | 83 | DON'T CHANGE YOUR LOVE — Five Stairsteps & Cubie (Curtis Mayfield), Curtom 1936 | 6 |
| 76 | 100 | — | — | COURT OF LOVE — Unifics (Guy Draper), Kapp 935 | 2 |
| 77 | 75 | 75 | 75 | PRIVATE NUMBER — Judy Clay & William Bell (Booker T. Jones), Stax 0005 | 5 |
| 78 | 76 | 76 | 80 | THAT KIND OF WOMAN — Merrilee Rush (Tommy Coghill & Chips Moman), Bell 738 | 5 |
| 79 | 79 | 89 | — | GENTLE ON MY MIND — Glen Campbell (Al de Lory), Capitol 5939 | 10 |
| 80 | — | — | — | OH LORD, WHY LORD — Los Pop Tops (Alain Milhaud), Calla 154 | 1 |
| 81 | 81 | 91 | — | FOR THE LOVE OF IVY — Mamas & Papas (Lou Adler), Dunhill 4150 | 3 |
| 82 | — | — | — | MESSAGE FROM MARIA — Joe Simon (J.R. Ent.), Sound Stage 7 2617 | 1 |
| 83 | 94 | — | — | THERE WAS A TIME — Gene Chandler (Carl Davis and Gene Chandler), Brunswick 55383 | 2 |
| 84 | 88 | 99 | — | HORSE FEVER — Cliff Nobles & Company (Jesse James), Phil-L.A. of Soul 318 | 3 |
| 85 | — | — | — | DO THE CHOO CHOO — Archie Bell & the Drells (Gamble-Huff), Atlantic 2559 | 1 |
| 86 | — | — | — | SWEET YOUNG THING LIKE YOU — Ray Charles (Joe Adams), ABC/TRC 11133 | 1 |
| 87 | 89 | 90 | 91 | LIGHT MY FIRE — Doors (Paul A. Rothchild), Elektra 45615 | 22 |
| 88 | — | — | — | I AIN'T GOT TO LOVE NOBODY ELSE — Masqueraders (Tommy Coghill), Bell 733 | 1 |
| 89 | — | — | — | SWEET BLINDNESS — Fifth Dimension (Bones Howe), Soul City 768 | 1 |
| 90 | — | — | — | PUFFIN' DOWN THE TRACK — Hugh Masekela (Stewart Levine), Uni 55085 | 1 |
| 91 | 99 | — | — | I LOVE YOU MADLY — Fantastic Four (Mike Hanks), Ric Tic 144 | 2 |
| 92 | 92 | 96 | — | THE BIPLANE, EVERMORE — Irish Rovers (Charles Bud Dant), Decca 32371 | 3 |
| 93 | 93 | — | — | SAN FRANCISCO GIRLS — Fever Tree (Scott & Vivian Holtzman), Uni 55060 | 5 |
| 94 | 84 | 85 | 87 | THEN YOU TELL ME GOODBYE — Eddy Arnold (Chet Atkins), RCA Victor 47-9606 | 4 |
| 95 | 95 | — | — | BATTLE OF NEW ORLEANS — Harpers Bizarre (Lenny Waronker), Warner Bros.-Seven Arts 7223 | 2 |
| 96 | 96 | — | — | THE CHOICE — O'Jays (George Kerr), Bell 737 | 2 |
| 97 | 98 | — | — | TOMBOY — Ronnie Dove (Phil Kahl & Bill Justis), Diamond 249 | 2 |
| 98 | — | — | — | THE B.B. JONES — B.B. King (Quincy Jones), Bluesway 61019 | 1 |
| 99 | — | — | — | ALMOST IN LOVE — Elvis Presley, RCA Victor 47-9610 | 1 |
| 100 | — | — | — | PEACE OF MIND — Nancy Wilson (David Cavanaugh), Capitol 2283 | 1 |

## BUBBLING UNDER THE HOT 100

101. WHITE ROOM — Cream, Atco 6617
102. A LITTLE LESS CONVERSATION — Elvis Presley, RCA Victor 47-9610
103. HOLE IN MY POCKET — Barry Goldberg Reunion, Buddah 59
104. I AM YOUR MAN — Bobby Taylor & the Vancouvers, Gordy 7073
105. SMELL OF INCENSE — Southwest F.O.B., Hip 8002
106. ALFIE — Rivers Rednow, Gordy 7076
107. UP HARD — Willie Mitchell, Hi 2151
108. DESTINATION ANYWHERE — Marvelettes, Tamla 54171
109. YOU PUT IT ON ME — B.B. King, Bluesway 67019
110. LALENA — Donovan, Epic 10393
111. LOVE HEALS — Colours, Dot 17132
112. FUNKY BULL — Dyke & the Blazers, Original Sound 83
113. YOU GOT THE LOVE — Professor Morrison's Lollipop, White Whale 275
114. WHAT'S EASY FOR TWO IS HARD FOR ONE — Marvelettes, Tamla 54171
115. HARPER VALLEY P.T.A. — King Curtis & the Kingpins, Atco 6613
116. WHERE DO I GO — Carla Thomas, Stax 0011
117. SOUR MILK SEA — Jackie Lomax, Apple 1802
118. TROUBLE MAKER — Tams, ABC 11128
119. FIRE — Five by Five, Paula 302
120. PICKIN' WILD MOUNTAIN BERRIES — Peggy Scott & JoJo Benson, SSS Int'l 748
121. BIRMINGHAM — Movers, "123" 1700
122. HELLO, HELLO — Tiny Tim, Reprise 0769
123. I CLOSE MY EYES AND COUNT TO TEN — Dusty Springfield, Philips 40553
124. I'VE BEEN LOVING YOU TOO LONG — Billy Vera, Atlantic 2555
125. I GET THE BLUES WHEN IT RAINS — Rry Anthony, Kanwood 818
126. MISSION: IMPOSSIBLE/NORWEGIAN WOOD — Alan Copeland Singers, ABC 11088
127. YOU GOT IT — Etta James, Cadet 5620
128. I'LL RUN WITH YOU — Lovin' Spoonful, Kama Sutra 251
129. PER-SON-ALLY — Bobby Paris, Tetragrammaton 1504
130. CAN'T GET YOU OUT OF MY MIND — Margaret Whiting, London 124
131. ISN'T IT LONELY TOGETHER — Robert Knight, Elf 90019
132. CINNAMON — Derek, Bang 558
133. DON'T BOGART ME — Fraternity of Man, ABC 11106

Compiled from national retail sales and radio station airplay by the Music Popularity Dept. of Record Market Research, Billboard.

# Billboard HOT 100

FOR WEEK ENDING OCTOBER 5, 1968

★ STAR PERFORMER—Sides registering greatest proportionate upward progress this week.

Record Industry Association of America seal of certification as million selling single.

| This Week | 1 Wk. Ago | 2 Wks. Ago | 3 Wks. Ago | TITLE Artist (Producer), Label & Number | Weeks On Chart |
|---|---|---|---|---|---|
| 1 (Billboard Award) | 1 | 3 | 10 | HEY JUDE — Beatles (George Martin), Apple 2276 | 4 |
| 2 | 2 | 1 | 2 | HARPER VALLEY P.T.A. — Jeannie C. Riley (Shelby S. Singleton Jr.), Plantation 3 | 7 |
| ★3 | 5 | 15 | 60 | FIRE — Crazy World of Arthur Brown (Kit Lambert), Atlantic 2556 | 5 |
| ★4 | 20 | 27 | 41 | LITTLE GREEN APPLES — O. C. Smith (Jerry Fuller), Columbia 44616 | 8 |
| ★5 | 9 | 16 | 18 | GIRL WATCHER — O'Kaysions (North State Music), ABC 11094 | 8 |
| 6 | 10 | 13 | 17 | SLIP AWAY — Clarence Carter (Rick Hall & Staff), Atlantic 2508 | 13 |
| 7 | 3 | 2 | 1 | PEOPLE GOT TO BE FREE — Rascals (Rascals), Atlantic 2537 | 12 |
| 8 | 8 | 9 | 23 | I'VE GOTTA GET A MESSAGE TO YOU — Bee Gees (Robert Stigwood), Atco 6603 | 8 |
| 9 | 7 | 5 | 5 | 1, 2, 3, RED LIGHT — 1910 Fruitgum Company (Kasenetz-Katz Assoc.) Buddah 54 | 11 |
| ★10 | 14 | 14 | 14 | I SAY A LITTLE PRAYER — Aretha Franklin (Jerry Wexler), Atlantic 2456 | 8 |
| 11 | 11 | 11 | 27 | TIME HAS COME TODAY — Chambers Brothers (David Rubinson), Columbia 44414 | 9 |
| 12 | 12 | 12 | 38 | REVOLUTION — Beatles (George Martin), Apple 2276 | 4 |
| 13 | 6 | 8 | 11 | THE FOOL ON THE HILL — Sergio Mendes & Brasil '66 (Sergio Mendes, Herb Alpert & Jerry Moss), A&M 961 | 9 |
| ★14 | 21 | 31 | 31 | SAY IT LOUD (I'm Black and I'm Proud) — James Brown & His Famous Flames (James Brown), King 6187 | 5 |
| 15 | 13 | 10 | 6 | THE HOUSE THAT JACK BUILT — Aretha Franklin (Jerry Wexler), Atlantic 2456 | 8 |
| 16 | 4 | 4 | 8 | HUSH — Deep Purple (Derek Lawrence), Tetragrammaton 1503 | 8 |
| 17 | 18 | 21 | 52 | MIDNIGHT CONFESSIONS — Grassroots (Steve Barri), Dunhill 4144 | 6 |
| ★18 | 19 | 19 | 57 | MY SPECIAL ANGEL — Vogues (Dick Glasser), Reprise 0766 | 5 |
| 19 | 17 | 6 | 3 | LIGHT MY FIRE — Jose Feliciano (Rick Jarrard), RCA Victor 47-9550 | 11 |
| ★20 | 28 | 29 | 59 | (The Lament of the Cherokee) INDIAN RESERVATION — Don Fardon (Miki Dallon), GNP Crescendo 405 | 6 |
| 21 | 16 | 18 | 24 | ON THE ROAD AGAIN — Canned Heat (Dallas Smith), Liberty 56038 | 9 |
| 22 | 22 | 17 | 7 | YOU'RE ALL I NEED TO GET BY — Marvin Gaye & Tammi Terrell (Ashford-Simpson), Tamla 54169 | 11 |
| 23 | 15 | 7 | 4 | BORN TO BE WILD — Steppenwolf (Gabriel Mekler), Dunhill 4138 | 13 |
| 24 | 24 | 45 | 56 | PIECE OF MY HEART — Big Brother & the Holding Company, Columbia 44626 | 6 |
| ★25 | 29 | 54 | — | OVER YOU — Gary Puckett & the Union Gap (Jerry Fuller), Columbia 44644 | 3 |
| 26 | 27 | 44 | 88 | SUZIE Q — Creedence Clearwater Revival (Saul Zaentz), Fantasy 616 | 5 |
| ★27 | 30 | 40 | 44 | THE SNAKE — Al Wilson (Johnny Rivers), Soul City 767 | 8 |
| 28 | 26 | 34 | 37 | SPECIAL OCCASION — Smokey Robinson & The Miracles (Smokey-Cleveland), Tamla 54172 | 8 |
| ★29 | 42 | 60 | 64 | HEY, WESTERN UNION MAN — Jerry Butler (Gamble-Huff), Mercury 72850 | 6 |
| 30 | 25 | 26 | 26 | MAGIC BUS — Who (Kit Lambert), Decca 32362 | 9 |
| 31 | 31 | 66 | — | ALL ALONG THE WATCHTOWER — Jimi Hendrix Experience (Jimi Hendrix), Reprise 0767 | 3 |
| ★32 | 38 | 42 | 58 | IN-A-GADDA-DA-VIDA — Iron Butterfly (Jim Hilton), Atco 6606 | 7 |
| 33 | 33 | 39 | 49 | WHO IS GONNA LOVE ME? — Dionne Warwick (Bacharach-David), Scepter 12226 | 7 |
| 34 | 34 | 47 | 66 | BABY, COME BACK — Equals (President Records Prod.), RCA Victor 47-9583 | 5 |
| 35 | 35 | 38 | 39 | HIP CITY—PART 2 — Jr. Walker & The All Stars (Lawrence Horn), Soul 35048 | 9 |
| 36 | 36 | 63 | 84 | SHAPE OF THINGS TO COME — Max Frost & the Troopers (Mike Curb), Tower 419 | 5 |
| ★37 | 61 | 77 | 77 | FOOL FOR YOU — Impressions (Curtis Mayfield), Curtom 1932 | 5 |
| ★38 | 59 | 90 | 98 | HOLD ME TIGHT — Johnny Nash (Johnny Nash & Arthur Jenkins), JAD 207 | 4 |
| ★39 | 48 | 48 | 48 | HELP YOURSELF — Tom Jones (Peter Sullivan), Parrot 40029 | 6 |
| ★40 | 44 | 64 | 65 | BREAK YOUR PROMISE — Delfonics (Stan and Bell), Philly Groove 152 | 6 |
| 41 | 41 | 59 | 45 | I WISH IT WOULD RAIN — Gladys Knight & The Pips (N. Whitefield), Soul 35047 | 7 |
| 42 | 43 | 68 | 80 | I MET HER IN CHURCH — Box Tops (Dan Penn), Mala 12017 | 4 |
| 43 | 46 | 46 | 46 | BROWN EYED WOMAN — Bill Medley (Bill Medley & Barry Mann), MGM 13959 | 10 |
| ★44 | 54 | 97 | — | ELENORE — Turtles (Chip Douglas), White Whale 276 | 3 |
| 45 | 45 | 55 | 55 | LISTEN HERE — Eddie Harris (Joel Dorn), Atlantic 2487 | 12 |
| ★46 | 62 | 85 | 86 | SHOOT 'EM UP BABY — Andy Kim (Jeff Barry), Steed 710 | 5 |
| 47 | 47 | 61 | 68 | DOWN ON ME — Big Brother & the Holding Company (Bob Shad), Mainstream 662 | 6 |
| ★48 | 56 | 57 | 63 | STREET FIGHTING MAN — Rolling Stones (Jimmy Miller), London 909 | 5 |
| 49 | 49 | 87 | — | I FOUND A TRUE LOVE — Wilson Pickett (Tom Dowd), Atlantic 2558 | 3 |
| ★50 | 52 | 72 | 79 | CHAINED — Marvin Gaye (Frank Wilson), Tamla 54170 | 4 |
| 51 | 51 | 51 | 54 | TO WAIT FOR LOVE — Herb Alpert (Herb Alpert & Jerry Moss), A&M 964 | 6 |
| 52 | 53 | 86 | 87 | POOR BABY — Cowsills (Wes Farrell), MGM 13981 | 4 |
| 53 | 57 | 80 | 81 | NATURALLY STONED — Avant-Garde (Billy Sherril), Columbia 44590 | 6 |
| ★54 | 70 | — | — | THOSE WERE THE DAYS — Mary Hopkin (Paul McCartney), Apple 1801 | 2 |
| 55 | 55 | 56 | 61 | THE WEIGHT — Jackie DeShannon (Charles Greene & Brian Stone), Imperial 66313 | 7 |
| ★56 | 76 | 100 | — | COURT OF LOVE — Unifics (Guy Draper), Kapp 935 | 3 |
| ★57 | 69 | — | — | I'VE GOT DREAMS TO REMEMBER — Otis Redding (Steve Cropper), Atco 6612 | 2 |
| ★58 | — | — | — | WHITE ROOM — Cream (Felix Pappalardi), Atco 6617 | 1 |
| ★59 | 85 | — | — | DO THE CHOO CHOO — Archie Bell & the Drells (Gamble-Hutt), Atlantic 2559 | 2 |
| ★60 | 75 | 78 | 78 | DON'T CHANGE YOUR LOVE — Five Stairsteps & Cubie (Curtis Mayfield), Curtom 1931 | 7 |
| 61 | 68 | 91 | 92 | THE FUNKY JUDGE — Bull & The Matadors (Sherrel-Cross Prod.), Toddlin' Town 108 | 7 |
| ★62 | 89 | — | — | SWEET BLINDNESS — Fifth Dimension (Bones Howe), Soul City 768 | 2 |
| 63 | 66 | 73 | 73 | FLY ME TO THE MOON — Bobby Womack (Chips Moman), Minit 32048 | 8 |
| ★64 | 79 | 79 | 89 | GENTLE ON MY MIND — Glen Campbell (Al de Lory), Capitol 5939 | 11 |
| 65 | 65 | 62 | 62 | WORKIN' ON A GROOVY THING — Patti Drew (Carone Prod.), Capitol 2197 | 10 |
| 66 | 63 | 70 | 70 | THE WEIGHT — The Band (John Simon), Capitol 2269 | 6 |
| ★67 | 88 | — | — | I AIN'T GOT TO LOVE NOBODY ELSE — Masqueraders (Tommy Cogbill), Bell 733 | 2 |
| ★68 | 84 | 88 | 99 | HORSE FEVER — Cliff Nobles & Company (Jesse James), Phil.-L.A. of Soul 318 | 4 |
| ★69 | 100 | — | — | PEACE OF MIND — Nancy Wilson (David Cavanaugh), Capitol 2283 | 2 |
| 70 | 64 | 71 | 71 | MY WAY OF LIFE — Frank Sinatra (Don Costa), Reprise 0764 | 6 |
| 71 | 71 | — | — | BANG-SHANG-A-LANG — Archies (Don Kirshner), Calendar 63-1006 | 2 |
| 72 | 72 | — | — | ICE IN THE SUN — Status Quo (John Schroeder), Cadet Concept 7006 | 2 |
| ★73 | — | — | — | LALENA — Donovan (Mickie Most), Epic 10393 | 1 |
| ★74 | 90 | — | — | PUFFIN' DOWN THE TRACK — Hugh Masekela (Stewart Levine), Uni 55085 | 2 |
| 75 | 82 | — | — | MESSAGE FROM MARIA — Joe Simon (J.R. Ent.), Sound Stage 7 2617 | 2 |
| ★76 | — | — | — | DESTINATION: ANYWHERE — Marvelettes (Smokey), Tamla 54171 | 1 |
| 77 | 77 | 75 | 75 | PRIVATE NUMBER — Judy Clay & William Bell (Booker T. Jones), Stax 0005 | 6 |
| 78 | 78 | 76 | 76 | THAT KIND OF WOMAN — Merrilee Rush (Tommy Cogbill & Chips Moman), Bell 738 | 6 |
| ★79 | 91 | 99 | — | I LOVE YOU MADLY — Fantastic Four (Mike Hanks), Ric Tic 144 | 3 |
| 80 | 80 | — | — | OH LORD, WHY LORD — Los Pop Tops (Alain Milhaud), Calla 154 | 2 |
| 81 | 81 | 81 | 91 | FOR THE LOVE OF IVY — Mamas & Papas (Lou Adler), Dunhill 4150 | 4 |
| 82 | 83 | 94 | — | THERE WAS A TIME — Gene Chandler (Carl Davis and Gene Chandler), Brunswick 55383 | 3 |
| 83 | 86 | — | — | SWEET YOUNG THING LIKE YOU — Ray Charles (Joe Adams), ABC/TRC 11133 | 2 |
| ★84 | — | — | — | TAKE ME FOR A LITTLE WHILE — Vanilla Fudge (Shadow Morton), Atco 6616 | 1 |
| ★85 | — | — | — | ALFIE — Eivets Rednow (Henry Cosby), Gordy 7076 | 1 |
| ★86 | — | — | — | MAGIC CARPET RIDE — Steppenwolf (Gabriel Mekler), Dunhill 4160 | 1 |
| 87 | 87 | 89 | 90 | LIGHT MY FIRE — Doors (Paul A. Rothchild), Elektra 45615 | 23 |
| ★88 | — | — | — | YOU GOT THE LOVE — Professor Morrison's Lollipop (J. Levine & A. Resnick), White Whale 275 | 1 |
| ★89 | — | — | — | QUICK JOEY SMALL (Run Joey Run) — Kasenetz-Katz Singing Orchestral Circus (J. Katz-J. Kasenetz-J. Levine-A. Resnick), Buddah 64 | 1 |
| ★90 | — | — | — | YOU PUT IT ON ME — B.B. King (Quincy Jones), Bluesway 61019 | 1 |
| 91 | 93 | 93 | — | SAN FRANCISCO GIRLS — Fever Tree (Scott & Vivian Holtzman), Uni 55060 | 6 |
| 92 | 92 | 92 | 96 | THE BIPLANE EVERMORE — Irish Rovers (Charles Bud Dant), Decca 32371 | 4 |
| 93 | — | — | — | UP-HARD — Willie Mitchell (Joe Cuoghi), Hi 2151 | 1 |
| 94 | 96 | 96 | — | THE CHOICE — O'Jays (George Kerr), Bell 737 | 3 |
| 95 | 99 | — | — | ALMOST IN LOVE — Elvis Presley, RCA Victor 47-9610 | 2 |
| 96 | 97 | 98 | — | TOMBOY — Ronnie Dove (Phil Kahl & Bill Justis), Diamond 249 | 3 |
| 97 | — | — | — | NITTY GRITTY — Ricardo Ray (Neil Galligan), Alegre 4024 | 1 |
| 98 | — | — | — | I'M IN A DIFFERENT WORLD — Four Tops (R. Dean & Holland & Dozier), Motown 1132 | 1 |
| 99 | — | — | — | SMELL OF INCENSE — Southwest F.O.B., Hip 8002 | 1 |
| 100 | — | — | — | SUNDAY SUN — Neil Diamond (Tom Catalano & Neil Diamond), Uni 55084 | 1 |

## HOT 100—A TO Z—(Publisher-Licensee)



## BUBBLING UNDER THE HOT 100

101. LITTLE LESS CONVERSATION — Elvis Presley 47-9610
102. FUNKY BULL — Dyke & the Blazers, Original Sound 83
103. HOLE IN MY POCKET — Barry Goldberg Reunion, Buddah 59
104. I AM YOUR MAN — Bobby Taylor & the Vancouvers, Gordy 7073
105. RIDE MY SEE-SAW — Moody Blues, Deram 85033
106. HARPER VALLEY P.T.A. — King Curtis & the Kingpins, Atco 6613
107. WHERE DO I GO — Carla Thomas, Stax 0011
108. DON'T LEAVE ME — Robert John, Columbia 44639
109. PICKIN' WILD MOUNTAIN BERRIES — Peggy Scott & Jo Jo Benson, SSS Int'l 748
110. LOVE HEALS — Colours, Dot 17132
111. CINDERELLA SUNSHINE — Paul Revere & the Raiders, Columbia 44655
112. B.B. JONES — B.B. King, Bluesway 61019
113. YOU GOT IT — Etta James, Cadet 5620
114. LISTEN THEY'RE PLAYING MY SONG — Ray Charles, ABC/TRC 11133
115. ISN'T IT LONELY TOGETHER — Robert Knight, Elf 90019
116. BIRMINGHAM — Movers "123" 1700
117. SOUR MILK SEA — Jackie Lomax, Apple 1802
118. TROUBLE MAKER — Tams, ABC 11128
119. FIRE — Five by Five, Paula 302
120. MISSION IMPOSSIBLE/NORWEGIAN WOOD — Alan Copeland Singers, ABC 11088
121. I'VE BEEN LOVING YOU TOO LONG — Billy Vera, Atlantic 2555
122. I CLOSE MY EYES AND COUNT TO TEN — Dusty Springfield, Philips 40553
123. GREENBURG, GLICKSTEIN, CHARLES, DAVID SMITH & JONES — Cryan Shames, Columbia 44638
124. I GET THE BLUES WHEN IT RAINS — Ray Anthony, Ranwood 818
125. CAN'T GET YOU OUT OF MY MIND — Margaret Whiting, London 124
126. I COULDN'T SPELL!!*@! — Sam the Sham, MGM 13972
127. CINNAMON — Derek, Bang 558
128. BAROQUE-A-NOVA — Mason Williams, Warner Bros.-Seven Arts 7235
129. L.A. BREAK DOWN (And Take Me In) — Larry Marks, A&M 969
130. YOU GOT WHAT I NEED — Z.Z. Hill, Kent 494
131. STANDING ON THE OUTSIDE — Brenda Jo Harris, Roulette 7021
132. GOLDEN GATE PARK — Rejoice, Dunhill 4130
133. LOOK INTO MY TEARDROPS — Crispian St. Peters, Jamie 1350

Compiled from national retail sales and radio station airplay by the Music Popularity Dept. of Record Market Research, Billboard.

# Billboard HOT 100

FOR WEEK ENDING OCTOBER 12, 1968

★ STAR PERFORMER—Sides registering greatest proportionate upward progress this week.

Record Industry Association of America seal of certification as million selling single.

| This Week | 1 Wk. Ago | 2 Wks. Ago | 3 Wks. Ago | TITLE Artist (Producer), Label & Number | Weeks On Chart |
|---|---|---|---|---|---|
| 1 (Billboard Award) | 1 | 1 | 3 | **HEY JUDE** Beatles (George Martin), Apple 2276 | 5 |
| 2 | 2 | 2 | 1 | **HARPER VALLEY P.T.A.** Jeannie C. Riley (Shelby S. Singleton Jr.), Plantation 3 | 8 |
| 3 | 3 | 5 | 15 | **FIRE** Crazy World of Arthur Brown (Kit Lambert), Atlantic 2556 | 6 |
| 4 | 4 | 20 | 27 | **LITTLE GREEN APPLES** O. C. Smith (Jerry Fuller), Columbia 44616 | 9 |
| 5 | 5 | 9 | 16 | **GIRL WATCHER** O'Kaysions (North State Music), ABC 11094 | 9 |
| ★6 | 17 | 18 | 21 | **MIDNIGHT CONFESSIONS** Grassroots (Steve Barri), Dunhill 4144 | 7 |
| ★7 | 18 | 19 | 19 | **MY SPECIAL ANGEL** Vogues (Dick Glasser), Reprise 0766 | 6 |
| 8 | 8 | 8 | 9 | **I'VE GOTTA GET A MESSAGE TO YOU** Bee Gees (Robert Stigwood), Atco 6603 | 9 |
| ★9 | 25 | 29 | 54 | **OVER YOU** Gary Puckett & the Union Gap (Jerry Fuller), Columbia 44644 | 4 |
| 10 | 6 | 10 | 13 | **SLIP AWAY** Clarence Carter (Rick Hall & Staff), Atlantic 2508 | 14 |
| 11 | 11 | 11 | 11 | **TIME HAS COME TODAY** Chambers Brothers (David Rubinson), Columbia 44414 | 10 |
| 12 | 7 | 3 | 2 | **PEOPLE GOT TO BE FREE** Rascals (Rascals), Atlantic 2537 | 13 |
| 13 | 10 | 14 | 14 | **I SAY A LITTLE PRAYER** Aretha Franklin (Jerry Wexler), Atlantic 2456 | 9 |
| 14 | 14 | 21 | 31 | **SAY IT LOUD (I'm Black and I'm Proud)** James Brown & His Famous Flames (James Brown), King 6187 | 6 |
| 15 | 12 | 12 | 12 | **REVOLUTION** Beatles (George Martin), Apple 2276 | 5 |
| 16 | 16 | 4 | 4 | **HUSH** Deep Purple (Derek Lawrence), Tetragrammaton 1503 | 9 |
| ★17 | 26 | 27 | 44 | **SUZIE Q** Creedence Clearwater Revival (Saul Zaentz), Fantasy 616 | 6 |
| ★18 | 54 | 70 | — | **THOSE WERE THE DAYS** Mary Hopkin (Paul McCartney), Apple 1801 | 3 |
| 19 | 24 | 24 | 45 | **PIECE OF MY HEART** Big Brother & the Holding Company, Columbia 44626 | 7 |
| 20 | 20 | 28 | 29 | **(The Lament of the Cherokee) INDIAN RESERVATION** Don Fardon (Miki Dallon), GNP Crescendo 405 | 7 |
| 21 | 21 | 16 | 18 | **ON THE ROAD AGAIN** Canned Heat (Dallas Smith), Liberty 56038 | 10 |
| 22 | 13 | 6 | 8 | **THE FOOL ON THE HILL** Sergio Mendes & Brasil '66 (Sergio Mendes, Herb Alpert & Jerry Moss), A&M 961 | 10 |
| 23 | 9 | 7 | 5 | **1, 2, 3, RED LIGHT** 1910 Fruitgum Company (Kasenetz-Katz Assoc.), Buddah 54 | 12 |
| ★24 | 44 | 54 | 97 | **ELENORE** Turtles (Chip Douglas), White Whale 276 | 4 |
| 25 | 19 | 17 | 6 | **LIGHT MY FIRE** Jose Feliciano (Rick Jarrard), RCA Victor 47-9550 | 12 |
| ★26 | 36 | 36 | 63 | **SHAPE OF THINGS TO COME** Max Frost & the Troopers (Mike Curb), Tower 419 | 6 |
| 27 | 27 | 30 | 40 | **THE SNAKE** Al Wilson (Johnny Rivers), Soul City 767 | 9 |
| 28 | 29 | 42 | 60 | **HEY, WESTERN UNION MAN** Jerry Butler (Gamble-Huff), Mercury 72850 | 7 |
| ★29 | 31 | 31 | 66 | **ALL ALONG THE WATCHTOWER** Jimi Hendrix Experience (Jimi Hendrix), Reprise 0767 | 4 |
| 30 | 15 | 13 | 10 | **THE HOUSE THAT JACK BUILT** Aretha Franklin (Jerry Wexler), Atlantic 2456 | 9 |
| 31 | 35 | 35 | 38 | **HIP CITY—PART 2** Jr. Walker & The All Stars (Lawrence Horn), Soul 35048 | 10 |
| 32 | 32 | 38 | 42 | **IN-A-GADDA-DA-VIDA** Iron Butterfly (Jim Hilton), Atco 6606 | 8 |
| 33 | 22 | 17 | 7 | **YOU'RE ALL I NEED TO GET BY** Marvin Gaye & Tammi Terrell (Ashford-Simpson), Tamla 54169 | 12 |
| 34 | 34 | 34 | 47 | **BABY, COME BACK** Equals (President Records Prod.), RCA Victor 47-9583 | 6 |
| 35 | 39 | 48 | 48 | **HELP YOURSELF** Tom Jones (Peter Sullivan), Parrot 40029 | 7 |
| 36 | 37 | 61 | 77 | **FOOL FOR YOU** Impressions (Curtis Mayfield), Curtom 1932 | 6 |
| ★37 | 42 | 43 | 68 | **I MET HER IN CHURCH** Box Tops (Dan Penn), Mala 12017 | 5 |
| 38 | 38 | 59 | 90 | **HOLD ME TIGHT** Johnny Nash (Johnny Nash & Arthur Jenkins), JAD 207 | 5 |
| 39 | 33 | 33 | 39 | **WHO IS GONNA LOVE ME?** Dionne Warwick (Bacharach-David), Scepter 12226 | 8 |
| 40 | 40 | 44 | 64 | **BREAK YOUR PROMISE** Delfonics (Stan and Bell), Philly Groove 152 | 7 |
| 41 | 41 | 41 | 59 | **I WISH IT WOULD RAIN** Gladys Knight & The Pips (N. Whitefield), Soul 35047 | 8 |
| 42 | 28 | 26 | 34 | **SPECIAL OCCASION** Smokey Robinson & The Miracles (Smokey-Cleveland), Tamla 54172 | 9 |
| 43 | 47 | 47 | 61 | **DOWN ON ME** Big Brother & the Holding Company (Bob Shad), Mainstream 662 | 7 |
| ★44 | 52 | 53 | 86 | **POOR BABY** Cowsills (Wes Farrell), MGM 13981 | 5 |
| 45 | 46 | 62 | 85 | **SHOOT 'EM UP BABY** Andy Kim (Jeff Barry), Steed 710 | 6 |
| ★46 | 56 | 76 | 100 | **COURT OF LOVE** Unifics (Guy Draper), Kapp 935 | 4 |
| 47 | 50 | 52 | 72 | **CHAINED** Marvin Gaye (Frank Wilson), Tamla 54170 | 5 |
| 48 | 48 | 56 | 57 | **STREET FIGHTING MAN** Rolling Stones (Jimmy Miller), London 909 | 6 |
| 49 | 49 | 49 | 87 | **I FOUND A TRUE LOVE** Wilson Pickett (Tom Dowd), Atlantic 2558 | 4 |
| ★50 | 58 | — | — | **WHITE ROOM** Cream (Felix Pappalardi), Atco 6617 | 2 |
| ★51 | 59 | 85 | — | **DO THE CHOO CHOO** Archie Bell & the Drells (Gamble-Huff), Atlantic 2559 | 3 |
| ★52 | 62 | 89 | — | **SWEET BLINDNESS** Fifth Dimension (Bones Howe), Soul City 768 | 3 |
| 53 | 53 | 57 | 80 | **NATURALLY STONED** Avant-Garde (Billy Sherril), Columbia 44590 | 7 |
| 54 | 64 | 79 | 79 | **GENTLE ON MY MIND** Glen Campbell (Al de Lory), Capitol 5939 | 12 |
| 55 | 57 | 69 | — | **I'VE GOT DREAMS TO REMEMBER** Otis Redding (Steve Cropper), Atco 6612 | 3 |
| ★56 | 86 | — | — | **MAGIC CARPET RIDE** Steppenwolf (Gabriel Mekler), Dunhill 4160 | 2 |
| ★57 | 73 | — | — | **LALENA** Donovan (Mickie Most), Epic 10393 | 2 |
| ★58 | 84 | — | — | **TAKE ME FOR A LITTLE WHILE** Vanilla Fudge (Shadow Morton), Atco 6616 | 2 |
| 59 | 60 | 75 | 78 | **DON'T CHANGE YOUR LOVE** Five Stairsteps & Cubie (Curtis Mayfield), Curtom 1931 | 8 |
| ★60 | 71 | 71 | — | **BANG-SHANG-A-LANG** Archies (Don Kirshner), Calendar 63-1006 | 3 |
| 61 | 61 | 68 | 91 | **THE FUNKY JUDGE** Bull & The Matadors (Sherrel-Cross Prod.), Toddlin' Town 108 | 8 |
| 62 | 43 | 46 | 46 | **BROWN EYED WOMAN** Bill Medley (Bill Medley & Barry Mann), MGM 13959 | 11 |
| 63 | 63 | 66 | 73 | **FLY ME TO THE MOON** Bobby Womack (Chips Moman), Minit 32048 | 9 |
| 64 | 55 | 55 | 56 | **THE WEIGHT** Jackie DeShannon (Charles Greene & Brian Stone), Imperial 66313 | 8 |
| ★65 | 69 | 100 | — | **PEACE OF MIND** Nancy Wilson (David Cavanaugh), Capitol 2283 | 3 |
| 66 | 65 | 65 | 62 | **WORKIN' ON A GROOVY THING** Patti Drew (Carone Prod.), Capitol 2197 | 11 |
| 67 | 67 | 88 | — | **I AIN'T GOT TO LOVE NOBODY ELSE** Masqueraders (Tommy Cogbill), Bell 733 | 3 |
| 68 | 68 | 84 | 88 | **HORSE FEVER** Cliff Nobles & Company (Jesse James), Phil.-L.A. of Soul 318 | 5 |
| ★69 | — | — | — | **KEEP ON LOVIN' ME, HONEY** Marvin Gaye & Tammi Terrell (Ashford & Simpson), Tamla 54173 | 1 |
| ★70 | 72 | 72 | — | **ICE IN THE SUN** Status Quo (John Schroeder), Cadet Concept 7006 | 3 |
| 71 | 74 | 90 | — | **PUFFIN' DOWN THE TRACK** Hugh Masekela (Stewart Levine), Uni 55085 | 3 |
| ★72 | 98 | — | — | **I'M IN A DIFFERENT WORLD** Four Tops (R. Dean & Holland & Dozier), Motown 1132 | 2 |
| 73 | 66 | 63 | 70 | **THE WEIGHT** The Band (John Simon), Capitol 2269 | 7 |
| 74 | 45 | 45 | 55 | **LISTEN HERE** Eddie Harris (Joel Dorn), Atlantic 2487 | 13 |
| 75 | 75 | 82 | — | **MESSAGE FROM MARIA** Joe Simon (J.R. Ent.), Sound Stage 7 2617 | 3 |
| 76 | 76 | — | — | **DESTINATION: ANYWHERE** Marvelettes (Ashford-Simpson), Tamla 54171 | 2 |
| ★77 | — | — | — | **ALWAYS TOGETHER** Dells (Bobby Miller), Cadet 5621 | 1 |
| ★78 | 99 | — | — | **SMELL OF INCENSE** Southwest F.O.B., Hip 8002 | 2 |
| 79 | 79 | 91 | 99 | **I LOVE YOU MADLY** Fantastic Four (Mike Hanks), Ric Tic 144 | 4 |
| 80 | 80 | 80 | — | **OH LORD, WHY LORD** Los Pop Tops (Alain Milhaud), Calla 154 | 3 |
| 81 | 81 | 81 | 81 | **FOR THE LOVE OF IVY** Mamas & Papas (Lou Adler), Dunhill 4150 | 5 |
| ★82 | — | — | — | **HITCHCOCK RAILWAY** Jose Feliciano (Rick Jarrard), RCA Victor 47-9641 | 1 |
| ★83 | — | — | — | **A LITTLE LESS CONVERSATION** Elvis Presley, RCA Victor 47-9610 | 1 |
| 84 | 85 | — | — | **ALFIE** Eivets Rednow (Henry Cosby), Gordy 7076 | 2 |
| ★85 | — | — | — | **CINDERELLA SUNSHINE** Paul Revere & the Raiders, featuring Mark Lindsay (Mark Lindsay), Columbia 44655 | 1 |
| 86 | 89 | — | — | **QUICK JOEY SMALL (Run Joey Run)** Kasenetz-Katz Singing Orchestral Circus (Kasenetz-Katz Associates), Buddah 64 | 2 |
| ★87 | — | — | — | **ON THE WAY HOME** Buffalo Springfield (Jim Messina), Atco 6615 | 1 |
| 88 | 88 | — | — | **YOU GOT THE LOVE** Profesor Morrison's Lollipop (Kasenetz-Katz Associates), White Whale 275 | 2 |
| ★89 | — | — | — | **PORPOISE SONG** Monkees (Gerry Goffin), Colgems 66-1031 | 1 |
| 90 | 90 | — | — | **YOU PUT IT ON ME** B.B. King (Quincy Jones), Bluesway 61019 | 2 |
| 91 | 92 | 92 | 92 | **THE BIPLANE EVERMORE** Irish Rovers (Charles Bud Dant), Decca 32371 | 5 |
| 92 | 93 | — | — | **UP-HARD** Willie Mitchell (Joe Cuoghi), Hi 2151 | 2 |
| 93 | — | — | — | **HARPER VALLEY P.T.A.** King Curtis & the Kingpins (Tom Dowd), Atco 6613 | 1 |
| 94 | — | — | — | **CYCLES** Frank Sinatra (Don Costa), Reprise 0764 | 1 |
| 95 | 97 | — | — | **NITTY GRITTY** Ricardo Ray (Neil Galligan), Alegre 4024 | 2 |
| 96 | — | — | — | **BAROQUE-A-NOVA** Mason Williams (Dick Glasser), Warner Bros.-Seven Arts 7235 | 1 |
| 97 | — | — | — | **LITTLE ARROWS** Leapy Lee (Gordon Mills), Decca 32380 | 1 |
| 98 | — | — | — | **DO SOMETHING TO ME** Tommy James & the Shondells (Tommy James), Roulette 7024 | 1 |
| 99 | — | — | — | **YOU NEED ME, BABY** Joe Tex (Buddy Killen, Dial 4086) | 1 |
| 100 | — | — | — | **RIDE MY SEE-SAW** Moody Blues (Tony Clark), Deram 85033 | 1 |

## HOT 100—A TO Z—(Publisher-Licensee)


Alfie (Famous, ASCAP)............ 84
All Along the Watchtower (Dwarf, ASCAP)...... 29
Always Together (Chevis, BMI)........ 77

Baby Come Back (Piccadilly, BMI)........ 34
Bang-Shang-A-Lang (Kirshner, BMI)........ 60
Baroque-a-Nova (Irving, BMI)........ 96
Biplane Evermore, The (Little Darlin', BMI)...... 91
Break Your Promise (Nickel Shoe/Bellboy, BMI).. 40
Brown Eyed Woman (Screen Gems-Columbia, BMI).. 62

Chained (Jobete, BMI)........ 47
Cinderella Sunshine (Boom, BMI)........ 85
Court of Love (Andjun, BMI)........ 46
Cycles (Irving, BMI)........ 94

Destination: Anywhere (Jobete, BMI)........ 76
Do the Choo Choo (World War Three/Double Diamond/Downstairs, BMI)........ 51
Do Something to Me (Patricia/Kahoona Tunes, BMI) 98
Don't Change Your Love (Camad, BMI)........ 59
Down on Me (Brent, BMI)........ 43

Elenore (Ishmael/Blimp, BMI)........ 24

Fire (Track, BMI)........ 3
Fly Me to the Moon (Almanac, ASCAP)........ 63
Fool for You (Camad, BMI)........ 36
Fool on the Hill, The (Comet, ASCAP)........ 22
For the Love of Ivy (Wingate/Honest John, ASCAP) 81
Funky Judge, The (Downstream/Napac/Flomar, BMI) 61

Gentle on My Mind (Glaser, BMI)........ 54
Girl Watcher (North State, ASCAP)........ 5

Harper Valley P.T.A. (King Curtis & His Kingpins) (Newkeys, BMI)........ 93
Harper Valley P.T.A. (Jeannie C. Riley) (Newkeys, BMI)........ 2
Help Yourself (Famous, ASCAP)........ 35
Hey Jude (Maclen, BMI)........ 1
Hey, Western Union Man (Parabut/Double Diamond/Downstairs, BMI)........ 28
Hip City—Part 2 (Jobete, BMI)........ 31
Hitchcock Railway (Colgems, ASCAP)........ 82
Hold Me Tight (Nash, ASCAP)........ 38
Horse Fever (Dandelion/James Boy, BMI)........ 68
House That Jack Built, The (Cotillion, BMI)...... 30
Hush (Lowery, BMI)........ 16

I Ain't Got to Love Nobody Else (Press, BMI).... 67
I Found a True Love (Cotillion/Tracebob/Erva, BMI)........ 49
I Love You Madly (Ric Tic, BMI)........ 79
I Met Her in Church (Press, BMI)........ 37
I Say a Little Prayer (Jac/Blue Seas, ASCAP).... 13
I Wish It Would Rain (Jobete, BMI)........ 41
Ice in the Sun (Duchess, BMI)........ 70
In-a-Gadda-Da-Vida (Ten Last-Cotillion, Itasca, BMI) 32
I'm in a Different World (Jobete, BMI)........ 72
I've Got Dreams to Remember (East-Time-Redwal, BMI)........ 55
I've Gotta Get a Message to You (Casserole, BMI) 8

Keep on Loving Me, Honey (Jobete, BMI)...... 69

Lalena (Peer Int'l/Hi-Count, BMI)........ 57
(Lament of the Cherokee) Indian Reservation (Acuff-Rose, BMI)........ 20
Light My Fire (Jose Feliciano) (Nipper, ASCAP).. 4
Listen Here (Hargrove, BMI)........ 74
Little Arrows (Duchess, BMI)........ 97
Little Green Apples (Russell-Cason, ASCAP)...... 4
Little Less Conversation, A (Gladys, ASCAP)...... 83

Magic Carpet Ride (Trousdale, BMI)........ 56
Message From Maria (Cape Ann, BMI)........ 75
Midnight Confessions (Little Fugitive, BMI)...... 6
My Special Angel (Viva, BMI)........ 7

Naturally Stoned (Cedarwood, BMI)........ 53
Nitty Gritty (Gallico, BMI)........ 95

Oh Lord, Why Lord (Janf, BMI)........ 80
On the Road Again (Lawn, BMI)........ 21
On the Way Home (Springalo/Cotillion, BMI).... 87
1, 2, 3 Red Light (Kaskat, BMI)........ 23
Over You (Viva, BMI)........ 9

Peace of Mind (Almo, ASCAP)........ 65
People Got to Be Free (Slacsar, ASCAP)........ 12
Piece of My Heart (Webb IV/Ragmar, BMI)...... 19
Poor Baby (Pocket Full of Tunes/Akbestal, BMI).. 44
Porpoise Song (Screen Gems-Columbia, BMI).... 89
Puffin' Down the Track (Cherio, BMI)........ 71

Quick Joey Small (Run Joey Run) (T.M., BMI).... 86

Revolution (Maclen, BMI)........ 15
Ride My See-Saw (Felsted, BMI)........100

Say It Loud (I'm Black and I'm Proud) (Golo, BMI) 14
Shape of Things to Come (Screen Gems-Columbia, BMI)........ 26
Shoot 'Em Up Baby (Unart/Joachim, BMI)...... 45
Slip Away (Fame, BMI)........ 10
Snake, The (Marks, BMI)........ 27
Smell of Incense (Unart, BMI)........ 78
Special Occasion (Jobete, BMI)........ 42
Street Fighting Man (Gideon, BMI)........ 48
Suzie Q (Arc, BMI)........ 17
Sweet Blindness (Tuna Fish, BMI)........ 52

Take Me for a Little While (Lollipop, BMI)...... 58
Those Were the Days (T.R.O., ASCAP)........ 18
Time Has Come Today (Spinmaker, BMI)........ 11

Up Hard (Beaik, BMI)........ 92

Weight, The (Jackie DeShannon) (Callee, ASCAP).. 64
Weight, The (Band) (Callee, ASCAP)........ 73
White Room (Casserole, BMI)........ 50
Who Is Gonna Love Me (Blue Seas/Jac, BMI).... 39
Workin' on a Groovy Thing (Screen Gems-Columbia, BMI)........ 66
You Got the Love (Peanut Butter/Kaskat, BMI).... 88
You Need Me, Baby (Tree, BMI)........ 99
You Put It on Me (Ampco, ASCAP)........ 90
You're All I Need to Get By (Jobete, BMI)...... 33


## BUBBLING UNDER THE HOT 100

101. CHEWY CHEWY........Ohio Express, Buddah 70
102. FUNKY BULL........Dyke & the Blazers, Original Sound 83
103. HOLE IN MY POCKET........Barry Goldberg Reunion, Buddah 59
104. PICKIN' WILD MOUNTAIN BERRIES..Peggy Scott & Jo Jo Benson, SSS Int'l 748
105. FIRE........Five by Five, Paula 302
106. LOVE HEALS........Colours, Dot 17132
107. WHERE DO I GO........Carla Thomas, Stax 0041
108. DON'T LEAVE ME........Robert John, Columbia 44639
109. TOMBOY........Ronnie Dove, Diamond 249
110. SUNDAY SUN........Neil Diamond, Diamond 55084
111. SWEET YOUNG THING LIKE YOU........Ray Charles, ABC/TRC 11133
112. SOUL DRIPPIN'........Mauds, Mercury 72832
113. YOU GOT IT........Etta James, Cadet 5620
114. CINNAMON........Derek, Bang 558
115. GREENBURG, GLICKSTEIN, CHARLES, DAVID SMITH & JONES........Cryan Shames, Columbia 44638
116. BIRMINGHAM........Movers "123" 1700
117. 46 DRUMS—1 GUITAR........Little Carl Carlton, Back Beat 598
118. BATTLE HYMN OF THE REPUBLIC........Andy Williams with the Borromeo Choir, Columbia 44650
119. DO YOUR OWN THING........Brook Benton, Cotillion 44007
120. I COULDN'T SPELL!!*@!........Sam the Sham, MGM 13972
121. ARE MY THOUGHTS STILL WITH YOU........First Edition, Reprise 0773
122. 1432 FRANKLIN PIKE CIRCLE HERO........Bobby Russell, Elf 90020
123. AS WE GO ALONG........Monkees, Colgems 66-1031
124. CAN'T GET YOU OUT OF MY MIND........Margaret Whiting, London 124
125. HI-HEEL SNEAKERS........Jose Feliciano, RCA Victor 47-9641
126. SHAKE........Shadows of Knight, Team 520
127. STORMY........Classics IV, Imperial 66328
128. GETTING TO KNOW YOU........Sajid Khan, Colgems 66-1026
129. YOU GOT WHAT I NEED........Z.Z. Hill, Kent 494
130. FROM THE TEACHER TO THE PREACHER........Gene Chandler & Barbara Acklin, Brunswick 55387
131. THE MOST BEAUTIFUL THING IN THE WORLD..Herman's Hermits, MGM 13994
132. PAPER CASTLE........Rotary Connection, Cadet Concept 7007
133. LOOK INTO MY TEARDROPS........Crispian St. Peters, Jamie 1350
134. YOU TALK SUNSHINE I BREATHE FIRE......Amboy Dukes, Mainstream 693
135. HOW LUCKY (Can One Man Be)........Uniques, Paula 313

Compiled from national retail sales and radio station airplay by the Music Popularity Dept. of Record Market Research, Billboard.

HOT 100

HOT 100

# Billboard HOT 100

**FOR WEEK ENDING OCTOBER 19, 1968**

★ STAR PERFORMER—Sides registering greatest proportionate upward progress this week. ⓡ Record Industry Association of America seal of certification as million selling single.

| This Week | 1 Wk. Ago | 2 Wks. Ago | 3 Wks. Ago | TITLE, Artist (Producer), Label & Number | Weeks on Chart |
|---|---|---|---|---|---|
| 1 | 1 | 1 | 1 | **HEY JUDE** — Beatles (George Martin), Apple 2276 | 6 |
| 2 | 3 | 3 | 5 | **FIRE** — Crazy World of Arthur Brown (Kit Lambert), Atlantic 2556 | 7 |
| 3 | 4 | 4 | 20 | **LITTLE GREEN APPLES** — O. C. Smith (Jerry Fuller), Columbia 44616 | 10 |
| 4 | 2 | 2 | 2 | **HARPER VALLEY P.T.A.** — Jeannie C. Riley (Shelby S. Singleton Jr.), Plantation 3 | 9 |
| 5 | 5 | 5 | 9 | **GIRL WATCHER** — O'Kaysions (North State Music), ABC 11094 | 10 |
| 6 | 6 | 17 | 18 | **MIDNIGHT CONFESSIONS** — Grassroots (Steve Barri), Dunhill 4144 | 8 |
| 7 | 7 | 18 | 19 | **MY SPECIAL ANGEL** — Vogues (Dick Glasser), Reprise 0766 | 7 |
| 8 | 8 | 8 | 8 | **I'VE GOTTA GET A MESSAGE TO YOU** — Bee Gees (Robert Stigwood), Atco 6603 | 7 |
| 9 | 9 | 25 | 29 | **OVER YOU** — Gary Puckett & the Union Gap (Jerry Fuller), Columbia 44644 | 5 |
| 10 | 14 | 14 | 21 | **SAY IT LOUD (I'm Black and I'm Proud)** — James Brown & His Famous Flames (James Brown), King 6187 | 4 |
| 11 | 11 | 11 | 11 | **TIME HAS COME TODAY** — Chambers Brothers (David Rubinson), Columbia 44414 | 11 |
| 12 | 17 | 26 | 27 | **SUZIE Q** — Creedence Clearwater Revival (Saul Zaentz), Fantasy 616 | 7 |
| 13 | 18 | 54 | 70 | **THOSE WERE THE DAYS** — Mary Hopkin (Paul McCartney), Apple 1801 | 4 |
| 14 | 24 | 44 | 54 | **ELENORE** — Turtles (Jose Feliciano & Rick Jarrard), White Whale 276 | 5 |
| 15 | 19 | 24 | 24 | **PIECE OF MY HEART** — Big Brother & the Holding Company, Columbia 44626 | 7 |
| 16 | 10 | 6 | 10 | **SLIP AWAY** — Clarence Carter (Rick Hall & Staff), Atlantic 2508 | 15 |
| 17 | 15 | 12 | 12 | **REVOLUTION** — Beatles (George Martin), Apple 2276 | 6 |
| 18 | 28 | 29 | 42 | **HEY, WESTERN UNION MAN** — Jerry Butler (Gamble-Huff), Mercury 72850 | 4 |
| 19 | 38 | 38 | 59 | **HOLD ME TIGHT** — Johnny Nash (Johnny Nash & Arthur Jenkins), JAD 207 | 5 |
| 20 | 29 | 31 | 31 | **ALL ALONG THE WATCHTOWER** — Jimi Hendrix Experience (Jimi Hendrix), Reprise 0767 | 5 |
| 21 | 13 | 10 | 14 | **I SAY A LITTLE PRAYER** — Aretha Franklin (Jerry Wexler), Atlantic 2546 | 10 |
| 22 | 50 | 58 | — | **WHITE ROOM** — Cream (Felix Pappalardi), Atco 6617 | 3 |
| 23 | 36 | 37 | 61 | **FOOL FOR YOU** — Impressions (Curtis Mayfield), Curtom 1932 | 7 |
| 24 | 22 | 13 | 6 | **THE FOOL ON THE HILL** — Sergio Mendes & Brasil '66 (Sergio Mendes, Herb Alpert & Jerry Moss), A&M 961 | 11 |
| 25 | 20 | 20 | 28 | **(The Lament of the Cherokee) INDIAN RESERVATION** — Don Fardon (Miki Dallon), GNP Crescendo 405 | 8 |
| 26 | 26 | 36 | 36 | **SHAPE OF THINGS TO COME** — Max Frost & the Troopers (Mike Curb), Tower 419 | 6 |
| 27 | 12 | 7 | 3 | **PEOPLE GOT TO BE FREE** — Rascals (Rascals), Atlantic 2537 | 14 |
| 28 | 23 | 9 | 7 | **1, 2, 3, RED LIGHT** — 1910 Fruitgum Company (Kasenetz-Katz Assoc.), Buddah 54 | 13 |
| 29 | 16 | 16 | 4 | **HUSH** — Deep Purple (Derek Lawrence), Tetragrammaton 1503 | 10 |
| 30 | 27 | 27 | 30 | **THE SNAKE** — Al Wilson (Johnny Rivers), Soul City 767 | 10 |
| 31 | 21 | 21 | 16 | **ON THE ROAD AGAIN** — Canned Heat (Dallas Smith), Liberty 56038 | 11 |
| 32 | 32 | 32 | 38 | **IN-A-GADDA-DA-VIDA** — Iron Butterfly (Jim Hilton), Atco 6606 | 9 |
| 33 | 47 | 50 | 52 | **CHAINED** — Marvin Gaye (Frank Wilson), Tamla 54170 | 6 |
| 34 | 34 | 34 | 34 | **BABY, COME BACK** — Equals (President Records Prod.), RCA Victor 47-9583 | 7 |
| 35 | 31 | 35 | 35 | **HIP CITY—PART 2** — Jr. Walker & The All Stars (Lawrence Horn), Soul 35048 | 11 |
| 36 | 40 | 40 | 44 | **BREAK YOUR PROMISE** — Delfonics (Stan and Bell), Philly Groove 152 | 8 |
| 37 | 57 | 73 | — | **LALENA** — Donovan (Mickie Most), Epic 10393 | 3 |
| 38 | 69 | — | — | **KEEP ON LOVIN' ME, HONEY** — Marvin Gaye & Tammi Terrell (Ashford & Simpson), Tamla 54173 | 2 |
| 39 | 46 | 56 | 76 | **COURT OF LOVE** — Unifics (Guy Draper), Kapp 935 | 5 |
| 40 | 45 | 46 | 62 | **SHOOT 'EM UP BABY** — Andy Kim (Jeff Barry), Steed 710 | 7 |
| 41 | 41 | 41 | 41 | **I WISH IT WOULD RAIN** — Gladys Knight & The Pips (N. Whitefield), Soul 35047 | 7 |
| 42 | 52 | 62 | 89 | **SWEET BLINDNESS** — Fifth Dimension (Bones Howe), Soul City 768 | 4 |
| 43 | — | — | — | **LOVE CHILD** — Diana Ross & Supremes (Clan), Motown 1135 | 1 |
| 44 | 51 | 59 | 85 | **DO THE CHOO CHOO** — Archie Bell & the Drells (Gamble-Huff), Atlantic 2559 | 4 |
| 45 | 56 | 86 | — | **MAGIC CARPET RIDE** — Steppenwolf (Gabriel Mekler), Dunhill 4160 | 3 |
| 46 | 49 | 49 | 49 | **I FOUND A TRUE LOVE** — Wilson Pickett (Tom Dowd), Atlantic 2558 | 5 |
| 47 | 43 | 47 | 47 | **DOWN ON ME** — Big Brother & the Holding Company (Bob Shad), Mainstream 662 | 8 |
| 48 | 39 | 33 | 33 | **WHO IS GONNA LOVE ME?** — Dionne Warwick (Bacharach-David), Scepter 12226 | 9 |
| 49 | — | — | — | **HI-HEEL SNEAKERS** — Jose Feliciano (Rick Jarrard), RCA Victor 47-9641 | 1 |
| 50 | 37 | 42 | 43 | **I MET HER IN CHURCH** — Box Tops (Dan Penn), Mala 12017 | 6 |
| 51 | 53 | 53 | 57 | **NATURALLY STONED** — Avant-Garde (Billy Sherril), Columbia 44590 | 8 |
| 52 | 54 | 64 | 79 | **GENTLE ON MY MIND** — Glen Campbell (Al de Lory), Capitol 5939 | 13 |
| 53 | 35 | 39 | 48 | **HELP YOURSELF** — Tom Jones (Peter Sullivan), Parrot 40029 | 11 |
| 54 | 58 | 84 | — | **TAKE ME FOR A LITTLE WHILE** — Vanilla Fudge (Shadow Morton), Atco 6616 | 3 |
| 55 | 55 | 57 | 69 | **I'VE GOT DREAMS TO REMEMBER** — Otis Redding (Steve Cropper), Atco 6612 | 4 |
| 56 | 60 | 71 | 71 | **BANG-SHANG-A-LANG** — Archies (Don Kirshner), Calendar 63-1006 | 4 |
| 57 | 67 | 67 | 88 | **I AIN'T GOT TO LOVE NOBODY ELSE** — Masqueraders (Tommy Cogbill), Bell 733 | 4 |
| 58 | 63 | 63 | 66 | **FLY ME TO THE MOON** — Bobby Womack (Chips Moman), Minit 32048 | 10 |
| 59 | 59 | 60 | 75 | **DON'T CHANGE YOUR LOVE** — Five Stairsteps & Cubie (Curtis Mayfield), Curtom 1931 | 4 |
| 60 | 44 | 52 | 53 | **POOR BABY** — Cowsills (Wes Farrell), MGM 13981 | 7 |
| 61 | 61 | 61 | 68 | **THE FUNKY JUDGE** — Bull & The Matadors (Sherrel-Cross Prod.), Toddlin' Town 108 | 9 |
| 62 | 89 | — | — | **PORPOISE SONG** — Monkees (Gerry Goffin), Colgems 66-1031 | 2 |
| 63 | 76 | 76 | — | **DESTINATION: ANYWHERE** — Marvelettes (Ashford-Simpson), Tamla 54171 | 3 |
| 64 | 78 | 99 | — | **SMELL OF INCENSE** — Southwest F.O.B. (Hip 8002) | 3 |
| 65 | 65 | 69 | 100 | **PEACE OF MIND** — Nancy Wilson (David Cavanaugh), Capitol 2283 | 4 |
| 66 | 72 | 98 | — | **I'M IN A DIFFERENT WORLD** — Four Tops (R. Dean & Holland & Dozier), Motown 1132 | 3 |
| 67 | 77 | — | — | **ALWAYS TOGETHER** — Dells (Bobby Miller), Cadet 5621 | 2 |
| 68 | 85 | — | — | **CINDERELLA SUNSHINE** — Paul Revere & the Raiders, featuring Mark Lindsay (Mark Lindsay), Columbia 44655 | 2 |
| 69 | 83 | — | — | **A LITTLE LESS CONVERSATION** — Elvis Presley (J. Levine-A. Resnick), RCA Victor 47-9610 | 2 |
| 70 | 97 | — | — | **LITTLE ARROWS** — Leapy Lee (Gordon Mills), Decca 32380 | 2 |
| 71 | 71 | 74 | 90 | **PUFFIN' DOWN THE TRACK** — Hugh Masekela (Stewart Levine), Uni 55085 | 4 |
| 72 | — | — | — | **CHEWY CHEWY** — Ohio Express (J. Levine-A. Resnick), Buddah 70 | 1 |
| 73 | — | — | — | **PICKIN' WILD MOUNTAIN BERRIES** — Peggy Scott & Jo Jo Benson (Shelby S. Singleton Jr.), SSS Int'l 748 | 1 |
| 74 | 79 | 79 | 91 | **I LOVE YOU MADLY** — Fantastic Four (Mike Hanks), Soul 3505 | 5 |
| 75 | 75 | 75 | 82 | **MESSAGE FROM MARIA** — Joe Simon (J.R. Ent.), Sound Stage 7 2617 | 4 |
| 76 | 86 | 89 | — | **QUICK JOEY SMALL (Run Joey Run)** — Kasenetz-Katz Singing Orchestral Circus (Kasenetz-Katz Associates), Buddah 64 | 3 |
| 77 | 84 | 85 | — | **ALFIE** — Eivets Rednow (Henry Cosby), Gordy 7076 | 3 |
| 78 | 80 | 80 | 80 | **OH LORD, WHY LORD** — Los Pop Tops (Alain Milhaud), Calla 154 | 4 |
| 79 | — | — | — | **BRING IT ON HOME TO ME** — Eddie Floyd (Steve Cropper), Stax 0012 | 1 |
| 80 | 94 | — | — | **CYCLES** — Frank Sinatra (Don Costa), Reprise 0764 | 2 |
| 81 | 99 | — | — | **YOU NEED ME, BABY** — Joe Tex (Buddy Killen), Dial 4086 | 2 |
| 82 | 82 | — | — | **HITCHCOCK RAILWAY** — Jose Feliciano (Rick Jarrard), RCA Victor 47-9641 | 2 |
| 83 | 100 | — | — | **RIDE MY SEE-SAW** — Moody Blues (Tony Clark), Deram 85033 | 2 |
| 84 | 90 | 90 | — | **YOU PUT IT ON ME** — B.B. King (Quincy Jones), Bluesway 61019 | 3 |
| 85 | 98 | — | — | **DO SOMETHING TO ME** — Tommy James & the Shondells (Tommy James), Roulette 7024 | 2 |
| 86 | — | — | — | **WHERE DO I GO** — Carla Thomas (Al Bell), Stax 0011 | 1 |
| 87 | 87 | — | — | **ON THE WAY HOME** — Buffalo Springfield (Jim Messina), Atco 6615 | 2 |
| 88 | 88 | 88 | — | **YOU GOT THE LOVE** — Professor Morrison's Lollipop (Kasenetz-Katz Associates), White Whale 275 | 3 |
| 89 | — | — | — | **FROM THE TEACHER TO THE PREACHER** — Gene Chandler & Barbara Acklin (Carl Davis), Brunswick 55387 | 1 |
| 90 | 95 | 97 | — | **NITTY GRITTY** — Ricardo Ray (Neil Galligan), Alegre 4024 | 3 |
| 91 | 92 | 93 | — | **UP-HARD** — Willie Mitchell (Joe Cuoghi), Hi 2151 | 3 |
| 92 | — | — | — | **LISTEN, THEY'RE PLAYING MY SONG** — Ray Charles (Joe Adams), ABC/TRC 11133 | 1 |
| 93 | 93 | — | — | **HARPER VALLEY P.T.A.** — King Curtis & the Kingpins (Tom Dowd), Atco 6613 | 2 |
| 94 | — | — | — | **BATTLE HYMN OF THE REPUBLIC** — Andy Williams with the St. Charles Borromeo Choir (Andy Williams), Columbia 44650 | 1 |
| 95 | — | — | — | **SOUL DRIPPIN'** — Mauds (Badonsky & Bushor), Mercury 72832 | 1 |
| 96 | 96 | — | — | **BAROQUE-A-NOVA** — Mason Williams (Dick Glasser), Warner Bros. - Seven Arts 7235 | 2 |
| 97 | — | — | — | **LES BICYCLETTES DE BELSIZE** — Engelbert Humperdinck (Peter Sullivan), Parrot 40032 | 1 |
| 98 | — | — | — | **ISN'T IT LONELY TOGETHER** — Robert Knight (Buzz Cason & Mac Gayden), Elf 90019 | 1 |
| 99 | — | — | — | **NEVER MY LOVE** — Sandpebbles (Teddy Vann), Calla 155 | 1 |
| 100 | — | — | — | **DO WHAT YOU GOTTA DO** — Nina Simone (Stroud Prod.), RCA Victor 47-9602 | 1 |

## BUBBLING UNDER THE HOT 100

101. SWEET YOUNG THING LIKE YOU ........ Ray Charles, ABC/TRC 11133
102. SUNDAY SUN .......................... Neil Diamond, UNI 55084
103. FIRE ................................. Five by Five, Paula 302
104. HEARTACHE ............................ Roy Orbison, MGM 13991
105. I WALK ALONE ......................... Marty Robbins, Columbia 44633
106. AS WE GO ALONG ....................... Monkees, Colgems 66-1031
107. CINNAMON ............................. Derek, Bang 558
108. DO YOUR OWN THING .................... Brook Benton, Cotillion 44007
109. ABRAHAM, MARTIN & JOHN ............... Dion, Laurie 3464
110. YOU'RE ALL AROUND ME ................. Percy Sledge, Atlantic 2563
111. WILLIE JEAN .......................... Sunshine Company, Imperial 66324
112. GETTING TO KNOW YOU .................. Sajid Kahn, Colgems 66-1026
113. LOVE CITY (Postcards to Duluth) ...... Peter, Paul & Mary, Warner Bros.-Seven Arts 7232
114. YOU TALK SUNSHINE, I BREATHE FIRE .... Amboy Dukes, Mainstream 693
115. THE STRAIGHT LIFE .................... Bobby Goldsboro, United Artists 50461
116. 1432 FRANKLIN PIKE CIRCLE HERO ....... Bobby Russell, Elf 90020
117. JESSE BRADY .......................... McCoys, Mercury 72843
118. SHAKE ................................ Shadows of Knight, Team 520
119. ARE MY THOUGHTS STILL WITH YOU ....... First Edition, Reprise 0773
120. WAKE UP TO ME GENTLE ................. Al Martino, Capitol 2285
121. BABY LET'S WAIT ...................... Royal Guardsmen, Laurie 3461
122. STORMY ............................... Classics IV, Imperial 66328
123. HOOKED ON A FEELING .................. B. J. Thomas, Scepter 12230
124. SHAME, SHAME ......................... Magic Lanterns, Atlantic 2560
125. BILLY, YOU'RE MY FRIEND .............. Gene Pitney, Musicor 1331
126. LIVING IN THE U.S.A. ................. Steve Miller Band, Capitol 2287

*Compiled from national retail sales and radio station airplay by the Music Popularity Dept. of Record Market Research, Billboard.*

# Billboard HOT 100

For Week Ending October 26, 1968

★ STAR PERFORMER—Sides registering greatest proportionate upward progress this week.

® Record Industry Association of America seal of certification as million selling single.

| This Wk | 2 Wk Ago | 3 Wk Ago | TITLE Artist (Producer), Label & Number | Wks on Chart |
|---|---|---|---|---|
| 1 | 1 | 1 | HEY JUDE — Beatles (George Martin), Apple 2276 | 7 |
| 2 | 3 | 4 | LITTLE GREEN APPLES — O. C. Smith (Jerry Fuller), Columbia 44616 | 11 |
| 3 | 2 | 3 | FIRE — Crazy World of Arthur Brown (Kit Lambert), Track 2556 | 8 |
| ★4 | 13 | 18 | THOSE WERE THE DAYS — Mary Hopkin (Paul McCartney), Apple 1801 | 5 |
| 5 | 5 | 5 | GIRL WATCHER — O'Kaysions (North State Music), ABC 11094 | 11 |
| 6 | 6 | 6 | MIDNIGHT CONFESSIONS — Grassroots (Steve Barri), Dunhill 4144 | 9 |
| 7 | 9 | 9 | OVER YOU — Gary Puckett & the Union Gap (Jerry Fuller), Columbia 44644 | 6 |
| 8 | 4 | 2 | HARPER VALLEY P.T.A. — Jeannie C. Riley (Shelby S. Singleton Jr.), Plantation 3 | 10 |
| ★9 | 14 | 24 | ELENORE — Turtles (Chip Douglas), White Whale 276 | 4 |
| 10 | 8 | 8 | I'VE GOTTA GET A MESSAGE TO YOU — Bee Gees (Robert Stigwood), Atco 6603 | 11 |
| ★11 | 19 | 38 | HOLD ME TIGHT — Johnny Nash (Johnny Nash & Arthur Jenkins), JAD 207 | 5 |
| 12 | 12 | 17 | SUZIE Q — Creedence Clearwater Revival (Saul Zaentz), Fantasy 616 | 8 |
| ★13 | 15 | 19 | PIECE OF MY HEART — Big Brother & the Holding Company, Columbia 44626 | 9 |
| 14 | 7 | 7 | MY SPECIAL ANGEL — Vogues (Dick Glasser), Reprise 0766 | 8 |
| ★15 | 22 | 50 | WHITE ROOM — Cream (Felix Pappalardi), Atco 6617 | 4 |
| 16 | 10 | 14 | SAY IT LOUD (I'm Black and I'm Proud) — James Brown & His Famous Flames (James Brown), King 6187 | 8 |
| 17 | 17 | 15 | REVOLUTION — Beatles (George Martin), Apple 2276 | 7 |
| 18 | 18 | 28 | HEY, WESTERN UNION MAN — Jerry Butler (Gamble-Huff), Mercury 72850 | 9 |
| ★19 | 43 | — | LOVE CHILD — Diana Ross & Supremes (Clan), Motown 1135 | 2 |
| 20 | 20 | 29 | ALL ALONG THE WATCHTOWER — Jimi Hendrix Experience (Jimi Hendrix), Reprise 0767 | 6 |
| 21 | 11 | 11 | TIME HAS COME TODAY — Chambers Brothers (David Robinson), Columbia 44414 | 12 |
| ★22 | 26 | 26 | SHAPE OF THINGS TO COME — Max Frost & the Troopers (Mike Curb), Tower 419 | 8 |
| 23 | 23 | 36 | FOOL FOR YOU — Impressions (Curtis Mayfield), Curtom 1932 | 8 |
| 24 | 16 | 10 | SLIP AWAY — Clarence Carter (Rick Hall & Staff), Atlantic 2508 | 16 |
| ★25 | 45 | 56 | MAGIC CARPET RIDE — Steppenwolf (Gabriel Mekler), Dunhill 4161 | 4 |
| 26 | 21 | 13 | I SAY A LITTLE PRAYER — Aretha Franklin (Jerry Wexler), Atlantic 2546 | 8 |
| ★27 | 42 | 52 | SWEET BLINDNESS — Fifth Dimension (Bones Howe), Soul City 768 | 5 |
| 28 | 39 | 46 | COURT OF LOVE — Unifics (Guy Draper), Kapp 935 | 6 |
| 29 | 24 | 22 | THE FOOL ON THE HILL — Sergio Mendes & Brasil '66 (Sergio Mendes, Herb Alpert & Jerry Moss), A&M 961 | 12 |
| 30 | 32 | 32 | IN-A-GADDA-DA-VIDA — Iron Butterfly (Jim Hilton), Atco 6606 | 10 |
| 31 | 40 | 45 | SHOOT 'EM UP BABY — Andy Kim (Jeff Barry), Steed 710 | 8 |
| 32 | 34 | 34 | BABY, COME BACK — Equals (President Records Prod.), RCA Victor 47-9583 | 8 |
| 33 | 33 | 47 | CHAINED — Marvin Gaye (Frank Wilson), Tamla 54170 | 7 |
| ★34 | 49 | — | HI-HEEL SNEAKERS — Jose Feliciano (Rick Jarrard), RCA Victor 47-9641 | 2 |
| 35 | 36 | 40 | BREAK YOUR PROMISE — Delfonics (Stan and Bell), Philly Groove 152 | 9 |
| 36 | 38 | 69 | KEEP ON LOVIN' ME, HONEY — Marvin Gaye & Tammi Terrell (Ashford & Simpson), Tamla 54173 | 3 |
| 37 | 37 | 57 | LALENA — Donovan (Mickie Most), Epic 10393 | 4 |
| ★38 | 54 | 58 | TAKE ME FOR A LITTLE WHILE — Vanilla Fudge (Shadow Morton), Atco 6616 | 4 |
| 39 | 25 | 20 | (The Lament of the Cherokee) INDIAN RESERVATION — Don Farden (Miki Dallon), GNP Crescendo 405 | 9 |
| 40 | 51 | 53 | NATURALLY STONED — Avant-Garde (Billy Sherrill), Columbia 44590 | 9 |
| 41 | 41 | 41 | I WISH IT WOULD RAIN — Gladys Knight & The Pips (N. Whitfield), Soul 35047 | 10 |
| ★42 | 56 | 60 | BANG-SHANG-A-LANG — Archies (Don Kirshner), Calendar 63-1006 | 7 |
| 43 | 76 | 76 | QUICK JOEY SMALL (Run Joey Run) — Kasenetz-Katz Singing Orchestral Circus (Kasenetz-Katz Associates), Buddah 64 | 4 |
| 44 | 44 | 51 | DO THE CHOO CHOO — Archie Bell & the Drells (Gamble-Huff), Atlantic 2559 | 5 |
| 45 | — | — | WHO'S MAKING LOVE — Johnnie Taylor (Don Davis), Stax 0009 | 1 |
| 46 | 46 | 49 | I FOUND A TRUE LOVE — Wilson Pickett (Tom Dowd), Atlantic 2558 | 6 |
| 47 | 61 | 61 | THE FUNKY JUDGE — Bull & The Matadors (Sherral-Cross Prod.), Toddlin' Town 108 | 10 |
| ★48 | 72 | — | CHEWY CHEWY — Ohio Express (Kasenetz-Katz Associates), Buddah 70 | 2 |
| 49 | 55 | 55 | I'VE GOT DREAMS TO REMEMBER — Otis Redding (Steve Cropper), Atco 6612 | 5 |
| 50 | 52 | 54 | GENTLE ON MY MIND — Glen Campbell (Al de Lory), Capitol 5939 | 14 |
| ★51 | 66 | 72 | I'M IN A DIFFERENT WORLD — Four Tops (R. Dean & Holland & Dozier), Motown 1132 | 3 |
| 52 | 58 | 63 | FLY ME TO THE MOON — Bobby Womack (Chips Moman), Minit 32048 | 11 |
| ★53 | 94 | — | BATTLE HYMN OF THE REPUBLIC — Andy Williams with the St. Charles Borromeo Choir (Andy Williams), Columbia 44650 | 2 |
| 54 | 67 | 77 | ALWAYS TOGETHER — Dells (Bobby Miller), Cadet 5621 | 3 |
| 55 | 65 | 65 | PEACE OF MIND — Nancy Wilson (David Cavanaugh), Capitol 2283 | 5 |
| 56 | 64 | 78 | SMELL OF INCENSE — Southwest F.O.B., Hip 8002 | 4 |
| 57 | 57 | 67 | I AIN'T GOT TO LOVE NOBODY ELSE — Masqueraders (Tommy Cogbill), Bell 733 | 7 |
| 58 | 68 | 85 | CINDERELLA SUNSHINE — Paul Revere & the Raiders, featuring Mark Lindsay (Mark Lindsay), Columbia 44655 | 3 |
| 59 | 85 | 99 | DO SOMETHING TO ME — Tommy James & the Shondells (Tommy James), Roulette 7024 | 3 |
| 60 | 74 | 79 | I LOVE YOU MADLY — Fantastic Four (Mike Hanks), Soul 3505 | 6 |
| 61 | 83 | 100 | RIDE MY SEE-SAW — Moody Blues (Tony Clark), Deram 85030 | 3 |
| 62 | 62 | 89 | PORPOISE SONG — Monkees (Gerry Goffin), Colgems 66-1031 | 3 |
| 63 | 63 | 76 | DESTINATION: ANYWHERE — Marvelettes (Ashford-Simpson), Tamla 54171 | 3 |
| 64 | 79 | — | BRING IT ON HOME TO ME — Eddie Floyd (Steve Cropper), Stax 0012 | 2 |
| 65 | 70 | 97 | LITTLE ARROWS — Leapy Lee (Gordon Mills), Decca 32380 | 4 |
| 66 | — | — | ABRAHAM, MARTIN AND JOHN — Dion (Laurie Prod.-Phil Gernhard Prod.), Laurie 3464 | 1 |
| 67 | — | — | CINNAMON — Derek (George Tobin & Johnny Cymbal), Bang 558 | 1 |
| ★68 | 97 | — | LES BICYCLETTES DE BELSIZE — Engelbert Humperdinck (Peter Sullivan), Parrot 40032 | 2 |
| 69 | 69 | 83 | A LITTLE LESS CONVERSATION — Elvis Presley, RCA Victor 47-9610 | 3 |
| 70 | 80 | 94 | CYCLES — Frank Sinatra (Don Costa), Reprise 0764 | 3 |
| 71 | 71 | 74 | PUFFIN' DOWN THE TRACK — Hugh Masekela (Stewart Levine), Uni 55086 | 5 |
| 72 | 73 | — | PICKIN' WILD MOUNTAIN BERRIES — Peggy Scott & Jo Jo Benson (Shelby S. Singleton Jr.), SSS Int'l 748 | 3 |
| 73 | 77 | 84 | ALFIE — Eivets Rednow (Henry Cosby), Gordy 7076 | 4 |
| ★74 | — | — | SHAKE — Shadows of Knight (Kasenetz-Katz Associates), Team 520 | 1 |
| 75 | — | — | THE STRAIGHT LIFE — Bobby Goldsboro (Bob Montgomery & Bobby Goldsboro), United Artists 50461 | 1 |
| 76 | 89 | — | FROM THE TEACHER TO THE PREACHER — Gene Chandler & Barbara Acklin (Carl Davis), Brunswick 55387 | 2 |
| 77 | 82 | 82 | HITCHCOCK RAILWAY — Jose Feliciano (Rick Jarrard), RCA Victor 47-9641 | 3 |
| 78 | — | — | HARPER VALLEY P.T.A. (Later That Day) — Ben Colder (Jack Clement), MGM 13997 | 1 |
| 79 | — | — | 1432 FRANKLIN PIKE CIRCLE HERO — Bobby Russell (Buzz Cason & Bobby Russell), EM 90020 | 1 |
| 80 | — | — | STORMY — Classics IV (Buddy Buie), Imperial 66328 | 1 |
| 81 | 81 | 99 | YOU NEED ME, BABY — Joe Tex (Buddy Killen), Dial 4086 | 3 |
| 82 | 87 | 87 | ON THE WAY HOME — Buffalo Springfield (Jim Messina), Atco 6615 | 3 |
| 83 | 100 | — | DO WHAT YOU GOTTA DO — Nina Simone (Stroud Prod.), RCA Victor 47-9602 | 2 |
| 84 | 84 | 90 | YOU PUT IT ON ME — B.B. King (Quincy Jones), Bluesway 61019 | 4 |
| 85 | 95 | — | SOUL DRIPPIN' — Mauds (Badensky & Besher), Mercury 72832 | 2 |
| 86 | 86 | — | WHERE DO I GO — Carla Thomas (Al Bell), Stax 0011 | 2 |
| 87 | — | — | SHAME, SHAME — Magic Lanterns (Steve Rowland), Atlantic 2560 | 1 |
| 88 | — | — | IT'S CRAZY — Eddie Harris, Atlantic 2561 | 1 |
| 89 | — | — | GOODY GOODY GUMDROPS — 1910 Fruitgum Co. (Kasenetz-Katz Associates), Buddah 71 | 1 |
| 90 | — | — | I WALK ALONE — Marty Robbins (Bob Johnston), Columbia 44633 | 1 |
| 91 | 91 | 92 | UP-HARD — Willie Mitchell (Joe Cuoghi), Hi 2151 | 4 |
| 92 | 92 | — | LISTEN, THEY'RE PLAYING MY SONG — Ray Charles (Joe Adams), ABC/TRC 11133 | 2 |
| 93 | — | — | PEACE BROTHER PEACE — Bill Medley (Medley Prod.), MGM 14000 | 1 |
| 94 | — | — | AUNT DORA'S LOVE SOUL SHACK — Arthur Conley (Tom Dowd), Atco 6622 | 1 |
| 95 | — | — | MORNIN' GLORY — Bobbie Gentry & Glen Campbell (Kelly Gordon & Al de Lory), Capitol 2314 | 1 |
| 96 | — | — | GOLDEN GATE PARK — Rejoice (Steve Barri), Dunhill 4158 | 1 |
| 97 | 98 | — | ISN'T IT LONELY TOGETHER — Robert Knight (Buzz Cason & Mac Gayden), EM 90019 | 2 |
| 98 | 99 | — | NEVER MY LOVE — Sandpebbles (Teddy Vann), Calla 155 | 2 |
| 99 | — | — | DO YOUR OWN THING — Brook Benton (Leiber & Stoller), Cotillion 44007 | 1 |
| 100 | — | — | JESSE BRADY — McCoys (McCoys), Mercury 72843 | 1 |

## BUBBLING UNDER THE HOT 100

101. HOOKED ON A FEELING .... B. J. Thomas, Scepter 12230
102. I LOVE HOW YOU LOVE ME .... Bobby Vinton, Epic 10397
103. FIRE .... Five by Five, Paula 302
104. THERE WAS A TIME .... Gene Chandler, Brunswick 55383
105. 46 DRUMS—1 GUITAR .... Little Carl Carlton, Back Beat 596
106. PROMISES, PROMISES .... Dionne Warwick, Scepter 12231
107. SUNDAY SUN .... Neil Diamond, Uni 55084
108. NITTY GRITTY .... Ricardo Ray, Alegre 4024
109. AS WE GO ALONG .... Monkees, Colgems 66-1031
110. YOU'RE ALL AROUND ME .... Percy Sledge, Atlantic 2563
111. WILLIE JEAN .... Sunshine Company, Imperial 66324
112. GETTING TO KNOW YOU .... Sajid Khan, Colgems 66-1026
113. LOVE CITY .... Peter, Paul & Mary, Warner Bros.-Seven Arts 7222
114. YOU TALK SUNSHINE, I BREATHE FIRE .... Amboy Dukes, Mainstream 693
115. HOW LUCKY (Can One Man Be) .... Uniques, Paula 313
116. CALIFORNIA EARTHQUAKE .... Mama Cass, Dunhill 4166
117. I CAN GIVE YOU LOVE .... Diplomats, Dynamo 122
118. CRAZY RHYTHM .... Happenings, B. T. Puppy 545
119. LIVING IN THE U.S.A. .... Steve Miller Band, Capitol 2287
120. WAKE UP LITTLE GENTLE .... Al Martino, Capitol 2285
121. BABY LET'S WAIT .... Royal Guardsmen, Laurie 3461
122. RUN TO ME .... Montanas, Independence 87
123. BILLY, YOU'RE MY FRIEND .... Gene Pitney, Musicor 1331
124. TODAY .... Jimmie Rodgers, A&M 970
125. THE EAGLE LAUGHS AT YOU .... Jackie Lomax, Apple 1802
126. FEELIN' ALRIGHT? .... Traffic, United Artists 50460
127. MY LITTLE LADY .... Tremeloes, Epic 10376
128. NOT ENOUGH INDIANS .... Dean Martin, Reprise 0780
129. PAUL'S MIDNIGHT RIDE .... Delights Orch., Atco 6601

Compiled from national retail sales and radio station airplay by the Music Popularity Dept. of Record Market Research, Billboard.

# Billboard HOT 100

FOR WEEK ENDING NOVEMBER 2, 1968

★ STAR PERFORMER—Sides registering greatest proportionate upward progress this week.

(seal) Record Industry Association of America seal of certification as million selling single.

| This Week | 1 Wk. Ago | 2 Wks. Ago | 3 Wks. Ago | TITLE Artist (Producer), Label & Number | Weeks On Chart |
|---|---|---|---|---|---|
| 1 (Billboard Award) | 1 | 1 | 1 | HEY JUDE — Beatles (George Martin), Apple 2276 | 8 |
| ★ 2 | 4 | 13 | 18 | THOSE WERE THE DAYS — Mary Hopkin (Paul McCartney), Apple 1801 | 6 |
| 3 | 2 | 3 | 4 | LITTLE GREEN APPLES — O. C. Smith (Jerry Fuller), Columbia 44616 | 12 |
| 4 | 3 | 2 | 3 | FIRE — Crazy World of Arthur Brown (Kit Lambert), Track 2556 | 9 |
| 5 | 6 | 6 | 6 | MIDNIGHT CONFESSIONS — Grassroots (Steve Barri), Dunhill 4144 | 10 |
| 6 | 9 | 14 | 24 | ELENORE — Turtles (Chip Douglas), White Whale 276 | 7 |
| 7 | 7 | 9 | 9 | OVER YOU — Gary Puckett & the Union Gap (Jerry Fuller), Columbia 44644 | 7 |
| ★ 8 | 11 | 19 | 38 | HOLD ME TIGHT — Johnny Nash (Johnny Nash & Arthur Jenkins), JAD 207 | 8 |
| ★ 9 | 19 | 43 | — | LOVE CHILD — Diana Ross & Supremes (Clan), Motown 1135 | 3 |
| 10 | 15 | 22 | 50 | WHITE ROOM — Cream (Felix Pappalardi), Atco 6617 | 5 |
| 11 | 12 | 12 | 17 | SUZIE Q — Creedence Clearwater Revival (Saul Zaentz), Fantasy 616 | 9 |
| ★ 12 | 25 | 45 | 56 | MAGIC CARPET RIDE — Steppenwolf (Gabriel Mekler), Dunhill 4160 | 5 |
| 13 | 13 | 15 | 19 | PIECE OF MY HEART — Big Brother & the Holding Company, Columbia 44626 | 10 |
| (seal) 14 | 8 | 4 | 2 | HARPER VALLEY P.T.A. — Jeannie C. Riley (Shelby S. Singleton Jr.), Plantation 3 | 11 |
| 15 | 5 | 5 | 5 | GIRL WATCHER — O'Kaysions (North State Music), ABC 11094 | 12 |
| 16 | 10 | 8 | 8 | I'VE GOTTA GET A MESSAGE TO YOU — Bee Gees (Robert Stigwood), Atco 6603 | 12 |
| 17 | 14 | 7 | 7 | MY SPECIAL ANGEL — Vogues (Dick Glasser), Reprise 0766 | 9 |
| 18 | 18 | 18 | 28 | HEY, WESTERN UNION MAN — Jerry Butler (Gamble-Huff), Mercury 72850 | 10 |
| 19 | 17 | 17 | 15 | REVOLUTION — Beatles (George Martin), Apple 2276 | 8 |
| 20 | 16 | 10 | 14 | SAY IT LOUD (I'm Black and I'm Proud) — James Brown & His Famous Flames (James Brown), King 6187 | 9 |
| 21 | 27 | 42 | 52 | SWEET BLINDNESS — Fifth Dimension (Bones Howe), Soul City 768 | 6 |
| 22 | 22 | 26 | 26 | SHAPE OF THINGS TO COME — Max Frost & the Troopers (Mike Curb), Tower 419 | 9 |
| 23 | 23 | 23 | 36 | FOOL FOR YOU — Impressions (Curtis Mayfield), Curtom 1932 | 9 |
| 24 | 21 | 11 | 11 | TIME HAS COME TODAY — Chambers Brothers (David Rubinson), Columbia 44414 | 13 |
| 25 | 20 | 20 | 29 | ALL ALONG THE WATCHTOWER — Jimi Hendrix Experience (Jimi Hendrix), Reprise 0767 | 7 |
| 26 | 28 | 39 | 46 | COURT OF LOVE — Unifics (Guy Draper), Kapp 935 | 7 |
| 27 | 34 | 49 | — | HI-HEEL SNEAKERS — Jose Feliciano (Rick Jarrard), RCA Victor 47-9641 | 3 |
| ★ 28 | 42 | 56 | 60 | BANG-SHANG-A-LANG — Archies (Don Kirshner), Calendar 63-1006 | 6 |
| ★ 29 | 45 | — | — | WHO'S MAKING LOVE — Johnnie Taylor (Don Davis), Stax 0009 | 2 |
| 30 | 30 | 32 | 32 | IN-A-GADDA-DA-VIDA — Iron Butterfly (Jim Hilton), Atco 6606 | 11 |
| 31 | 31 | 40 | 45 | SHOOT 'EM UP BABY — Andy Kim (Jeff Barry), Steed 710 | 9 |
| 32 | 33 | 33 | 47 | CHAINED — Marvin Gaye (Frank Wilson), Tamla 54170 | 8 |
| ★ 33 | 37 | 37 | 57 | LALENA — Donovan (Mickie Most), Epic 10393 | 5 |
| 34 | 36 | 38 | 69 | KEEP ON LOVIN' ME, HONEY — Marvin Gaye & Tammi Terrell (Ashford & Simpson), Tamla 54173 | 4 |
| ★ 35 | 66 | — | — | ABRAHAM, MARTIN AND JOHN — Dion (Laurie Prod.-Phil Gernhard Prod.), Laurie 3464 | 2 |
| ★ 36 | 48 | 72 | — | CHEWY CHEWY — Ohio Express (Kasenetz-Katz Associates), Buddah 70 | 3 |
| ★ 37 | 54 | 67 | 77 | ALWAYS TOGETHER — Dells (Bobby Miller), Cadet 5621 | 4 |
| 38 | 38 | 54 | 58 | TAKE ME FOR A LITTLE WHILE — Vanilla Fudge (Shadow Morton), Atco 6616 | 5 |
| ★ 39 | 50 | 52 | 54 | GENTLE ON MY MIND — Glen Campbell (Al de Lory), Capitol 5939 | [illegible] |
| 40 | 32 | 34 | 34 | BABY, COME BACK — Equals (President Records Prod.), RCA Victor 47-9583 | 9 |
| 41 | 43 | 76 | 76 | QUICK JOEY SMALL (Run Joey Run) — Kasenetz-Katz Singing Orchestral Circus (Kasenetz-Katz Associates), Buddah 64 | 5 |
| 42 | 46 | 46 | 49 | I FOUND A TRUE LOVE — Wilson Pickett (Tom Dowd), Atlantic 2558 | 7 |
| ★ 43 | 70 | 80 | 94 | CYCLES — Frank Sinatra (Don Costa), Reprise 0764 | 4 |
| 44 | 44 | 44 | 51 | DO THE CHOO CHOO — Archie Bell & the Drells (Gamble-Huff), Atlantic 2559 | 6 |
| 45 | 35 | 36 | 40 | BREAK YOUR PROMISE — Delfonics (Stan and Bell), Philly Groove 152 | 10 |
| ★ 46 | 68 | 97 | — | LES BICYCLETTES DE BELSIZE — Engelbert Humperdinck (Peter Sullivan), Parrot 40032 | 3 |
| 47 | 47 | 61 | 61 | THE FUNKY JUDGE — Bull & The Matadors (Sherrel-Cross Prod.), Toddlin' Town 108 | 11 |
| 48 | 40 | 51 | 53 | NATURALLY STONED — Avant-Garde (Billy Sherril), Columbia 44590 | 10 |
| 49 | 49 | 55 | 55 | I'VE GOT DREAMS TO REMEMBER — Otis Redding (Steve Cropper), Atco 6612 | 6 |
| ★ 50 | 64 | 79 | — | BRING IT ON HOME TO ME — Eddie Floyd (Steve Cropper), Stax 0012 | 3 |
| 51 | 51 | 66 | 72 | I'M IN A DIFFERENT WORLD — Four Tops (R. Dean & Holland & Dozier), Motown 1132 | 5 |
| ★ 52 | 79 | — | — | 1432 FRANKLIN PIKE CIRCLE HERO — Bobby Russell (Buzz Cason & Bobby Russell), Elf 90020 | 2 |
| 53 | 53 | 94 | — | BATTLE HYMN OF THE REPUBLIC — Andy Williams with the St. Charles Borromeo Choir (Andy Williams), Columbia 44650 | 3 |
| ★ 54 | 75 | — | — | THE STRAIGHT LIFE — Bobby Goldsboro (Bob Montgomery & Bobby Goldsboro), United Artists 50461 | 2 |
| 55 | 55 | 65 | 65 | PEACE OF MIND — Nancy Wilson (David Cavanaugh), Capitol 2283 | 6 |
| ★ 56 | 72 | 73 | — | PICKIN' WILD MOUNTAIN BERRIES — Peggy Scott & Jo Jo Benson (Shelby S. Singleton Jr. & Bob McRee), SSS Int'l 748 | 3 |
| ★ 57 | 65 | 70 | 97 | LITTLE ARROWS — Leapy Lee (Gordon Mills), Decca 32380 | 4 |
| 58 | 58 | 68 | 85 | CINDERELLA SUNSHINE — Paul Revere & the Raiders, featuring Mark Lindsay (Mark Lindsay), Columbia 44655 | 4 |
| 59 | 59 | 85 | 99 | DO SOMETHING TO ME — Tommy James & the Shondells (Tommy James), Roulette 7024 | 4 |
| 60 | 67 | — | — | CINNAMON — Derek (George Tobin & Johnny Cymbal), Bang 558 | 2 |
| 61 | 61 | 83 | 100 | RIDE MY SEE-SAW — Moody Blues (Tony Clark), Deram 85033 | 4 |
| 62 | 62 | 62 | 89 | PORPOISE SONG — Monkees (Gerry Goffin), Colgems 66-1031 | 4 |
| 63 | 60 | 74 | 79 | I LOVE YOU MADLY — Fantastic Four (Mike Hanks), Soul 3505 | 7 |
| ★ 64 | — | — | — | I LOVE HOW YOU LOVE ME — Bobby Vinton (Billy Sherrill), Epic 10397 | 1 |
| ★ 65 | 76 | 89 | — | FROM THE TEACHER TO THE PREACHER — Gene Chandler & Barbara Acklin (Carl Davis), Brunswick 55387 | 3 |
| ★ 66 | — | — | — | PROMISES, PROMISES — Dionne Warwick (Burt Bacharach-Hal David), Scepter 12231 | 1 |
| ★ 67 | 80 | — | — | STORMY — Classics IV, (Buddy Buie), Imperial 66328 | 2 |
| 68 | 63 | 63 | 76 | DESTINATION: ANYWHERE — Marvelettes (Ashford-Simpson), Tamla 54171 | 5 |
| 69 | 56 | 64 | 78 | SMELL OF INCENSE — Southwest F.O.B., Hip 8002 | 5 |
| 70 | 52 | 58 | 63 | FLY ME TO THE MOON — Bobby Womack (Chips Moman), Minit 32048 | 12 |
| 71 | 74 | — | — | SHAKE — Shadows of Knight (Kasenetz-Katz Associates), Team 520 | 2 |
| ★ 72 | 89 | — | — | GOODY GOODY GUMDROPS — 1910 Fruitgum Co. (Kasenetz-Katz Associates), Buddah 71 | 2 |
| 73 | 73 | 77 | 84 | ALFIE — Eivets Rednow (Henry Cosby), Gordy 7076 | 5 |
| ★ 74 | 87 | — | — | SHAME, SHAME — Magic Lanterns (Steve Rowland), Atlantic 2560 | 2 |
| ★ 75 | — | — | — | WICHITA LINEMAN — Glen Campbell (Al de Lory), Capitol 2302 | 1 |
| ★ 76 | 93 | — | — | PEACE BROTHER PEACE — Bill Medley (Medley Prod.), MGM 14000 | 2 |
| 77 | 69 | 69 | 63 | A LITTLE LESS CONVERSATION — Elvis Presley, RCA Victor 47-9610 | 4 |
| 78 | 78 | — | — | HARPER VALLEY P.T.A. (Later That Day) — Ben Colder (Jack Clement), MGM 13997 | 2 |
| ★ 79 | — | — | — | FOR ONCE IN MY LIFE — Stevie Wonder (Henry Cosby), Tamla 54174 | 1 |
| ★ 80 | — | — | — | FOR ONCE IN MY LIFE — Jackie Wilson (Carl Davis), Brunswick 55392 | 1 |
| ★ 81 | — | — | — | EVERYBODY GOT TO BELIEVE IN SOMEBODY — Sam & Dave (Isaac Hayes & David Porter), Atlantic 2568 | 1 |
| 82 | 84 | 84 | 90 | YOU PUT IT ON ME — B.B. King (Quincy Jones), Bluesway 61019 | 5 |
| 83 | 83 | 100 | — | DO WHAT YOU GOTTA DO — Nina Simone (Straud Prod.), RCA Victor 47-9602 | 3 |
| ★ 84 | 95 | — | — | MORNIN' GLORY — Bobbie Gentry & Glen Campbell (Kelly Gordon & Al de Lory), Capitol 2314 | 2 |
| 85 | 85 | 95 | — | SOUL DRIPPIN' — Mauds (Badonsky & Busher), Mercury 72832 | 3 |
| ★ 86 | — | — | — | SWEET DARLIN' — Martha Reeves & the Vandellas (Richard Morris), Gordy 7080 | 1 |
| ★ 87 | — | — | — | FIRE — Five by Five (Gene Kent), Paula 302 | 1 |
| 88 | 88 | — | — | IT'S CRAZY — Eddie Harris, Atlantic 2561 | 2 |
| ★ 89 | — | — | — | THE STAR-SPANGLED BANNER — Jose Feliciano, RCA Victor 47-9665 | 1 |
| 90 | 90 | — | — | I WALK ALONE — Marty Robbins (Bob Johnston), Columbia 44633 | 2 |
| 91 | — | — | — | CROWN OF CREATION — Jefferson Airplane (Al Schmitt), RCA Victor 47-9644 | 1 |
| 92 | — | — | — | BILLY, YOU'RE MY FRIEND — Gene Pitney (Bob Schwartz), Musicor 1331 | 1 |
| 93 | — | — | — | NOT ENOUGH INDIANS — Dean Martin (Jimmy Bowen), Reprise 0780 | 1 |
| 94 | 94 | — | — | AUNT DORA'S LOVE SOUL SHACK — Arthur Conley (Tom Dowd), Atco 6622 | 2 |
| 95 | — | — | — | CALIFORNIA EARTHQUAKE — Mama Cass (John Simon), Dunhill 4166 | 1 |
| 96 | — | — | — | TALKING ABOUT MY BABY — Gloria Walker (Eugene Davis), Flaming Arrow 35 | 1 |
| 97 | — | — | — | THE YARD WENT ON FOREVER — Richard Harris (Jimmy Webb), Dunhill 4170 | 1 |
| 98 | 100 | — | — | JESSE BRADY — McCoys (McCoys), Mercury 72843 | 2 |
| 99 | 99 | — | — | DO YOUR OWN THING — Brook Benton (Leiber & Stoller), Cotillion 44007 | 2 |
| 100 | — | — | — | COME ON, REACT — Fireballs (Norman Petty), Atco 6614 | 1 |

## HOT 100—A TO Z —(Publisher-Licensee)



## BUBBLING UNDER THE HOT 100

101. HOOKED ON A FEELING — B. J. Thomas, Scepter 12230
102. UP-HARD — Willie Mitchell, Hi 2151
103. ISN'T IT LONELY TOGETHER — Robert Knight, Elf 90019
104. THERE WAS A TIME — Gene Chandler, Brunswick 55383
105. 46 DRUMS—1 GUITAR — Little Carl Carlton, Back Beat 598
106. LIVING IN THE U. S. A. — Steve Miller Band, Capitol 2287
107. SUNDAY SUN — Neil Diamond, Uni 55084
108. KENTUCKY WOMAN — Deep Purple, Tetragrammaton 1508
109. YOU'RE ALL AROUND ME — Percy Sledge, Atlantic 2563
110. GETTING TO KNOW YOU — Sajid Kahn, Colgems 66-1026
111. WILLIE JEAN — Sunshine Company, Imperial 66324
112. LET'S MAKE A PROMISE — Peaches & Herb, Date 2-1623
113. A WHITER SHADE OF PALE — Hesitations, Kapp 948
114. MAIN STREET — Gary Lewis & the Playboys, Liberty 56075
115. GREAT ESCAPE — Ray Stevens, Monument 1099
116. CRAZY RHYTHM — Happenings, B. T. Puppy 545
117. I CAN GIVE YOU LOVE — Diplomats, Dynamo 122
118. STAND BY YOUR MAN — Tammy Wynette, Epic 10398
119. OL' RACE TRACK — Mills Brothers, Dot 17162
120. BOTH SIDES NOW — Judy Collins, Elektra 45639
121. SLOW DRAG — Intruders, Gamble 221
122. RUN TO ME — Montanas, Independence 89
123. FEELIN' ALRIGHT? — Traffic, United Artists 50460
124. TODAY — Jimmie Rodgers, A&M 976
125. THE EAGLE LAUGHS AT YOU — Jackie Lomax, Apple 1802
126. COO COO — Big Brother & the Holding Company, Mainstream 678
127. TOO WEAK TO FIGHT — Clarence Carter, Atlantic 2569
128. PAUL'S M'DNIGHT RIDE — Delights Orch., Atco 6601
129. PUT YOUR HEAD ON MY SHOULDER — Lettermen, Capitol 2324

Compiled from national retail sales and radio station airplay by the Music Popularity Dept. of Record Market Research, Billboard.

HOT 100

# Billboard HOT 100

FOR WEEK ENDING NOVEMBER 9, 1968

★ STAR PERFORMER—Sides registering greatest proportionate upward progress this week.

Record Industry Association of America seal of certification as million selling single.

| This Week | 1 Wk. Ago | 2 Wks. Ago | 3 Wks. Ago | TITLE | Artist (Producer), Label & Number | Weeks On Chart |
|---|---|---|---|---|---|---|
| 1 (Billboard Award) | 1 | 1 | 1 | HEY JUDE | Beatles (George Martin), Apple 2276 | 9 |
| 2 | 2 | 4 | 13 | THOSE WERE THE DAYS | Mary Hopkin (Paul McCartney), Apple 1801 | 7 |
| 3 ★ | 9 | 19 | 43 | LOVE CHILD | Diana Ross & Supremes (Clan), Motown 1135 | 4 |
| 4 | 3 | 2 | 3 | LITTLE GREEN APPLES | O. C. Smith (Jerry Fuller), Columbia 44616 | 13 |
| 5 | 8 | 11 | 19 | HOLD ME TIGHT | Johnny Nash (Johnny Nash & Arthur Jenkins), JAD 207 | 9 |
| 6 ★ | 10 | 15 | 22 | WHITE ROOM | Cream (Felix Pappalardi), Atco 6617 | 6 |
| 7 ★ | 12 | 25 | 45 | MAGIC CARPET RIDE | Steppenwolf (Gabriel Mekler), Dunhill 4160 | 6 |
| 8 | 6 | 9 | 14 | ELENORE | Turtles (Chip Douglas), White Whale 276 | 8 |
| 9 | 4 | 3 | 2 | FIRE | Crazy World of Arthur Brown (Kit Lambert), Track 2556 | 10 |
| 10 | 5 | 6 | 6 | MIDNIGHT CONFESSIONS | Grassroots (Steve Barri), Dunhill 4144 | 11 |
| 11 | 7 | 7 | 9 | OVER YOU | Gary Puckett & the Union Gap (Jerry Fuller), Columbia 44644 | 8 |
| 12 | 13 | 13 | 15 | PIECE OF MY HEART | Big Brother & the Holding Company, Columbia 44626 | 11 |
| 13 ★ | 21 | 27 | 42 | SWEET BLINDNESS | Fifth Dimension (Bones Howe), Soul City 768 | 7 |
| 14 | 11 | 12 | 12 | SUZIE Q | Creedence Clearwater Revival (Saul Zaentz), Fantasy 616 | 10 |
| 15 | 14 | 8 | 4 | HARPER VALLEY P.T.A. | Jeannie C. Riley (Shelby S. Singleton Jr.), Plantation 3 | 12 |
| 16 | 15 | 5 | 5 | GIRL WATCHER | O'Kaysions (North State Music), ABC 11094 | 13 |
| 17 | 18 | 18 | 18 | HEY, WESTERN UNION MAN | Jerry Butler (Gamble-Huff), Mercury 72850 | 11 |
| 18 ★ | 35 | 66 | — | ABRAHAM, MARTIN AND JOHN | Dion (Laurie Prod.-Phil Gernhard Prod.), Laurie 3464 | 3 |
| 19 | 19 | 17 | 17 | REVOLUTION | Beatles (George Martin), Apple 2276 | 9 |
| 20 | 20 | 16 | 10 | SAY IT LOUD (I'm Black and I'm Proud) | James Brown & His Famous Flames (James Brown), King 6187 | 10 |
| 21 ★ | 29 | 45 | — | WHO'S MAKING LOVE | Johnnie Taylor (Don Davis), Stax 0009 | 3 |
| 22 | 22 | 22 | 26 | SHAPE OF THINGS TO COME | Max Frost & the Troopers (Mike Curb), Tower 419 | 10 |
| 23 | 23 | 23 | 23 | FOOL FOR YOU | Impressions (Curtis Mayfield), Curtom 1932 | 10 |
| 24 ★ | 34 | 36 | 38 | KEEP ON LOVIN' ME, HONEY | Marvin Gaye & Tammi Terrell (Ashford & Simpson), Tamla 54173 | 5 |
| 25 | 26 | 28 | 39 | COURT OF LOVE | Unifics (Guy Draper), Kapp 935 | 8 |
| 26 | 27 | 34 | 49 | HI-HEEL SNEAKERS | Jose Feliciano (Rick Jarrard), RCA Victor 47-9641 | 4 |
| 27 | 28 | 42 | 56 | BANG-SHANG-A-LANG | Archies (Don Kirshner), Calendar 63-1006 | 7 |
| 28 | 16 | 10 | 8 | I'VE GOTTA GET A MESSAGE TO YOU | Bee Gees (Robert Stigwood), Atco 6603 | 13 |
| 29 | 25 | 20 | 20 | ALL ALONG THE WATCHTOWER | Jimi Hendrix Experience (Jimi Hendrix), Reprise 0767 | 8 |
| 30 | 24 | 21 | 11 | TIME HAS COME TODAY | Chambers Brothers (David Rubinson), Columbia 44414 | 14 |
| 31 | 17 | 14 | 7 | MY SPECIAL ANGEL | Vogues (Dick Glasser), Reprise 0766 | 10 |
| 32 | 32 | 33 | 33 | CHAINED | Marvin Gaye (Frank Wilson), Tamla 54170 | 9 |
| 33 | 33 | 37 | 37 | LALENA | Donovan (Mickie Most), Epic 10393 | 6 |
| 34 ★ | 41 | 43 | 76 | QUICK JOEY SMALL (Run Joey Run) | Kasenetz-Katz Singing Orchestral Circus (Kasenetz-Katz Associates), Buddah 64 | 6 |
| 35 ★ | 79 | — | — | FOR ONCE IN MY LIFE | Stevie Wonder (Henry Cosby), Tamla 54174 | 2 |
| 36 ★ | 36 | 48 | 72 | CHEWY CHEWY | Ohio Express (Kasenetz-Katz Associates), Buddah 70 | 4 |
| 37 ★ | 37 | 54 | 67 | ALWAYS TOGETHER | Dells (Bobby Miller), Cadet 5621 | 5 |
| 38 ★ | 38 | 38 | 54 | TAKE ME FOR A LITTLE WHILE | Vanilla Fudge (Shadow Morton), Atco 6616 | 6 |
| 39 | 30 | 30 | 32 | IN-A-GADDA-DA-VIDA | Iron Butterfly (Jim Hilton), Atco 6606 | 12 |
| 40 ★ | 57 | 65 | 70 | LITTLE ARROWS | Leapy Lee (Gordon Mills), Decca 32380 | 5 |
| 41 | 49 | 49 | 55 | I'VE GOT DREAMS TO REMEMBER | Otis Redding (Steve Cropper), Atco 6612 | 7 |
| 42 | 50 | 64 | 79 | BRING IT ON HOME TO ME | Eddie Floyd (Steve Cropper), Stax 0012 | 4 |
| 43 ★ | 43 | 70 | 80 | CYCLES | Frank Sinatra (Don Costa), Reprise 0764 | 5 |
| 44 | 44 | 44 | 44 | DO THE CHOO CHOO | Archie Bell & the Drells (Gamble-Huff), Atlantic 2559 | 7 |
| 45 ★ | 46 | 68 | 97 | LES BICYCLETTES DE BELSIZE | Engelbert Humperdinck (Peter Sullivan), Parrot 40032 | 4 |
| 46 | 47 | 47 | 61 | THE FUNKY JUDGE | Bull & The Matadors (Sherrel-Cross Prod.), Toddlin' Town 108 | 12 |
| 47 ★ | 64 | — | — | I LOVE HOW YOU LOVE ME | Bobby Vinton (Billy Sherrill), Epic 10397 | 2 |
| 48 ★ | 66 | — | — | PROMISES, PROMISES | Dionne Warwick (Burt Bacharach-Hal David), Scepter 12231 | 2 |
| 49 | 31 | 31 | 40 | SHOOT 'EM UP BABY | Andy Kim (Jeff Barry), Steed 710 | 10 |
| 50 | 39 | 50 | 52 | GENTLE ON MY MIND | Glen Campbell (Al de Lory), Capitol 5939 | 16 |
| 51 | 51 | 51 | 66 | I'M IN A DIFFERENT WORLD | Four Tops (R. Dean & Holland & Dozier), Motown 1132 | 6 |
| 52 | 52 | 79 | — | 1432 FRANKLIN PIKE CIRCLE HERO | Bobby Russell (Buzz Cason & Bobby Russell), Elf 90020 | 3 |
| 53 | 53 | 53 | 94 | BATTLE HYMN OF THE REPUBLIC | Andy Williams with the St. Charles Borromeo Choir (Andy Williams), Columbia 44650 | 4 |
| 54 ★ | 54 | 75 | — | THE STRAIGHT LIFE | Bobby Goldsboro (Bob Montgomery & Bobby Goldsboro), United Artists 50461 | 3 |
| 55 | 55 | 55 | 65 | PEACE OF MIND | Nancy Wilson (David Cavanaugh), Capitol 2283 | 7 |
| 56 ★ | 56 | 72 | 73 | PICKIN' WILD MOUNTAIN BERRIES | Peggy Scott & Jo Jo Benson (Shelby S. Singleton Jr. & Bob McRee), SSS Int'l 748 | 4 |
| 57 ★ | 67 | 80 | — | STORMY | Classics IV, (Buddy Buie), Imperial 66328 | 3 |
| 58 | 58 | 58 | 68 | CINDERELLA SUNSHINE | Paul Revere & the Raiders, featuring Mark Lindsay (Mark Lindsay), Columbia 44655 | 5 |
| 59 ★ | 59 | 59 | 85 | DO SOMETHING TO ME | Tommy James & the Shondells (Tommy James), Roulette 7024 | 5 |
| 60 | 60 | 67 | — | CINNAMON | Derek (George Tobin & Johnny Cymbal), Bang 558 | 3 |
| 61 | 61 | 61 | 63 | RIDE MY SEE-SAW | Moody Blues (Tony Clark), Deram 85033 | 5 |
| 62 | 62 | 62 | 62 | PORPOISE SONG | Monkees (Gerry Goffin), Colgems 66-1031 | 5 |
| 63 | 63 | 60 | 74 | I LOVE YOU MADLY | Fantastic Four (Mike Hanks), Soul 3505 | 8 |
| 64 ★ | 65 | 76 | 89 | FROM THE TEACHER TO THE PREACHER | Gene Chandler & Barbara Acklin (Carl Davis), Brunswick 55387 | 4 |
| 65 ★ | 89 | — | — | THE STAR-SPANGLED BANNER | Jose Feliciano, RCA Victor 47-9665 | 2 |
| 66 | 73 | 73 | 77 | ALFIE | Eivets Rednow (Henry Cosby), Gordy 7076 | 6 |
| 67 ★ | 75 | — | — | WICHITA LINEMAN | Glen Campbell (Al de Lory), Capitol 2302 | 2 |
| 68 ★ | 72 | 89 | — | GOODY GOODY GUMDROPS | 1910 Fruitgum Co. (Kasenetz-Katz Associates), Buddah 71 | 3 |
| 69 ★ | 74 | 87 | — | SHAME, SHAME | Magic Lanterns (Steve Rowland), Atlantic 2560 | 3 |
| 70 | 70 | 52 | 58 | FLY ME TO THE MOON | Bobby Womack (Chips Moman), Minit 32048 | 13 |
| 71 | 71 | 74 | — | SHAKE | Shadows of Knight (Kasenetz-Katz Associates), Team 520 | 3 |
| 72 ★ | 76 | 93 | — | PEACE BROTHER PEACE | Bill Medley (Medley Prod.), MGM 14000 | 3 |
| 73 ★ | — | — | — | TOO WEAK TO FIGHT | Clarence Carter (Rick Hall & Staff), Atlantic 2569 | 1 |
| 74 ★ | — | — | — | BOTH SIDES NOW | Judy Collins (Mark Abramson), Elektra 45639 | 1 |
| 75 ★ | — | — | — | GOODBYE MY LOVE | James Brown (James Brown), King 6198 | 1 |
| 76 ★ | — | — | — | SLOW DRAG | Intruders (Gamble-Huff), Gamble 221 | 1 |
| 77 | 78 | 78 | — | HARPER VALLEY P.T.A. (Later That Day) | Ben Colder (Jack Clement), MGM 13997 | 3 |
| 78 ★ | 80 | — | — | FOR ONCE IN MY LIFE | Jackie Wilson (Carl Davis), Brunswick 55392 | 2 |
| 79 ★ | 93 | — | — | NOT ENOUGH INDIANS | Dean Martin (Jimmy Bowen), Reprise 0780 | 2 |
| 80 | 81 | — | — | EVERYBODY GOT TO BELIEVE IN SOMEBODY | Sam & Dave (Isaac Hayes & David Porter), Atlantic 2568 | 2 |
| 81 ★ | 97 | — | — | THE YARD WENT ON FOREVER | Richard Harris (Jimmy Webb), Dunhill 4170 | 2 |
| 82 ★ | 84 | 95 | — | MORNIN' GLORY | Bobbie Gentry & Glen Campbell (Kelly Gordon & Al de Lory), Capitol 2314 | 3 |
| 83 | 83 | 83 | 100 | DO WHAT YOU GOTTA DO | Nina Simone (Straud Prod.), RCA Victor 47-9602 | 4 |
| 84 | 87 | — | — | FIRE | Five by Five (Gene Kent), Paula 302 | 2 |
| 85 | 85 | 85 | 95 | SOUL DRIPPIN' | Mauds (Badonsky & Bushor), Mercury 72832 | 4 |
| 86 | 86 | — | — | SWEET DARLIN' | Martha Reeves & the Vandellas (Richard Morris), Gordy 7080 | 2 |
| 87 ★ | — | — | — | KENTUCKY WOMAN | Deep Purple (Derek Lawrence), Tetragrammaton 1508 | 1 |
| 88 | 90 | 90 | — | I WALK ALONE | Marty Robbins (Bob Johnston), Columbia 44633 | 3 |
| 89 ★ | 96 | — | — | TALKING ABOUT MY BABY | Gloria Walker (Eugene Davis), Flaming Arrow 35 | 2 |
| 90 ★ | 95 | — | — | CALIFORNIA EARTHQUAKE | Mama Cass (John Simon), Dunhill 4166 | 2 |
| 91 | 91 | — | — | CROWN OF CREATION | Jefferson Airplane (Al Schmitt), RCA Victor 47-9644 | 2 |
| 92 | 92 | — | — | BILLY, YOU'RE MY FRIEND | Gene Pitney (Bob Schwartz), Musicor 1331 | 2 |
| 93 | 94 | 94 | — | AUNT DORA'S LOVE SOUL SHACK | Arthur Conley (Tom Dowd), Atco 6622 | 3 |
| 94 | — | — | — | HANG 'EM HIGH | Booker T. & M.G.'s (Booker T. & M.G.'s), Stax 0013 | 1 |
| 95 | — | — | — | SUNDAY SUN | Neil Diamond (Tom Catalano & Neil Diamond), UNI 55084 | 2 |
| 96 | — | — | — | I PUT A SPELL ON YOU | Creedence Clearwater Revival (Saul Zaentz), Fantasy 617 | 1 |
| 97 | — | — | — | LET'S MAKE A PROMISE | Peaches & Herb (Gamble-Huff), Date 1623 | 1 |
| 98 | — | — | — | STAND BY YOUR MAN | Tammy Wynette (Billy Sherrill), Epic 10398 | 1 |
| 99 | 100 | — | — | COME ON, REACT | Fireballs (Norman Petty), Atco 6614 | 2 |
| 100 | — | — | — | A WHITER SHADE OF PALE | Hesitations (P. Robinson, T. Wiltshire, L. Banks), Kapp 948 | 1 |

## HOT 100—A TO Z—(Publisher-Licensee)

Abraham, Martin and John (Roznique/Sanphil, BMI) 18
Aifie (Famous, ASCAP) 66
All Along the Watchtower (Dwarf, ASCAP) 29
Always Together (Chevis, BMI) 37
Aunt Dora's Love Soul Shack (Redwal/Time, BMI) 93

Eang-Shang-A-Lang (Kirshner, BMI) 27
Battle Hymn of the Republic (Public Domain) 53
Billy, You're My Friend (Catalogue, BMI) 92
Both Sides Now (Siquomb, BMI) 74
Bring It on Home to Me (Kags, BMI) 42

California Earthquake (Glaser, BMI) 90
Chained (Jobete, BMI) 32
Chewy Chewy (Peanut Butter/Kaskat, BMI) 36
Cinderella Sunshine (Boom, BMI) 58
Cinnamon (Pamco, BMI) 60
Come On, React (Dundee, BMI) 99
Court of Love (Andjun, BMI) 25
Crown of Creation (Icebag, BMI) 91
Cycles (Irving, BMI) 43

Do the Choo Choo (World War Three/Double Diamond/Downstairs, BMI) 44
Do Something to Me (Patricia/Kahoona Tunes, BMI) 59
Do What You Gotta Do (Rivers, BMI) 83

Elenore (Ishmael/Blimp, BMI) 8
Everybody Got to Believe in Somebody (Birdees/Walden, ASCAP) 80
Fire (Crazy World of Arthur Brown) (Track, BMI) 9
Fire (Five by Five) (Sea-Lark, BMI) 84
Fly Me to the Moon (Almanac, ASCAP) 70
Fool for You (Camad, BMI) 23
For Once in My Life (Stevie Wonder) (Stein & Van Stock, ASCAP) 35
For Once in My Life (Jackie Wilson) (Stein & Van Stock, ASCAP) 78

1432 Franklin Pike Circle Hero (Russell-Cason, ASCAP) 52
From the Teacher to the Preacher (BRC/Jalynne, BMI) 64

Funky Judge, The (Downstream/Napac/Flomar, BMI) 46
Gentle on My Mind (Glaser, BMI) 50
Girl Watcher (North State, ASCAP) 16
Goodbye My Love (Dynatone, BMI) 75
Goody Goody Gumdrops (Kaskat, BMI) 68

Hang 'Em High (Unart, BMI) 94
Harper Valley P.T.A. (Jeannie C. Riley) (Newkeys, BMI) 15
Harper Valley P.T.A. (Later That Same Day) (Newkeys, ASCAP) 77
Hey Jude (Maclen, BMI) 1
Hey, Western Union Man (Parabut/Double Diamond/Downstairs, BMI) 17
Hi-Heel Sneakers (Medal, BMI) 26
Hold Me Tight (Nash, ASCAP) 5

I Love How You Love Me (Screen Gems-Columbia, BMI) 47
I Love You Madly (Ric Tic, BMI) 63
I Put a Spell on You (Shalimar, BMI) 96
I Walk Alone (Adams-Vee & Abbott, BMI) 88
In-a-Gadda-Da-Vida (Ten Last-Cotillion, Itasca, BMI) 39
I'm in a Different World (Jobete, BMI) 51
I've Got Dreams to Remember (East-Time-Redwal, BMI) 41
I've Gotta Get a Message to You (Casserole, BMI) 28

Keep on Loving Me, Honey (Jobete, BMI) 24
Kentucky Woman (Tallyrand, BMI) 87
Lalena (Peer Int'l/Hi-Count, BMI) 33
Les Bicyclettes de Belsize (W-7, ASCAP) 45
Let's Make a Promise (World War III/Downstairs, BMI) 97
Little Arrows (Duchess, BMI) 40
Little Green Apples (Russell-Cason, ASCAP) 4
Love Child (Jobete, BMI) 3

Magic Carpet Ride (Trousdale, BMI) 7
Midnight Confessions (Little Fugitive, BMI) 10
Mornin' Glory (Shayne, ASCAP) 82
My Special Angel (Viva, BMI) 31

Not Enough Indians (Pomona, BMI) 79
Over You (Viva, BMI) 11
Peace Brother Peace (Screen Gems-Columbia, BMI) 72
Peace of Mind (Almo, ASCAP) 55
Piece of My Heart (Webb IV/Ragmar, BMI) 12
Pickin' Wild Mountain Berries (Crazy Cajun, BMI) 56
Porpoise Song (Screen Gems-Columbia, BMI) 62
Promises, Promises (Blue Seas/Jac/Morris, ASCAP) 48

Quick Joey Small (Run Joey Run) (T.M., BMI) 34

Revolution (Maclen, BMI) 19
Ride My See-Saw (Felsted, BMI) 61

Say It Loud (I'm Black and I'm Proud) (Golo, BMI) 20
Shake (Kaskat/Peanut Butter, BMI) 71
Shame, Shame (4 Star, BMI) 69
Shape of Things to Come (Screen Gems-Columbia, BMI) 22
Shoot 'Em Up Baby (Unart/Joachim, BMI) 49
Slow Drag (Razor Sharp, BMI) 76
Soul Drippin' (Four Star, BMI) 85
Stand by Your Man (Gallico, BMI) 98
Star-Spangled Banner, The (Johi, BMI) 65
Stormy (Low-Sal, BMI) 57
Straight Life, The (Viva, BMI) 54
Sunday Sun (Stonebridge, BMI) 95
Suzie Q (Arc, BMI) 14
Sweet Blindness (Tuna Fish, BMI) 13
Sweet Darlin' (Jobete, BMI) 86

Take Me for a Little While (Lollipop, BMI) 38
Talking About My Baby (Flaming Arrow, BMI) 89
Those Were the Days (T.R.O., ASCAP) 2
Time Has Come Today (Chambro, BMI) 30
Too Weak to Fight (Fame, BMI) 73

White Room (Casserole, BMI) 6
Whiter Shade of Pale, A (Essex, ASCAP) 100
Who's Making Love (East, BMI) 21
Wichita Lineman (Canopy, ASCAP) 67

Yard Went on Forever, The (Canopy, ASCAP) 81

## BUBBLING UNDER THE HOT 100

101. HOOKED ON A FEELIN' — B. J. Thomas, Scepter 12230
102. UP-HARD — Willie Mitchell, Hi 2151
103. ISN'T IT LONELY TOGETHER — Robert Knight, Elf 90019
104. IT'S CRAZY — Eddie Harris, Atlantic 2561
105. MALINDA — Bobby Taylor & the Vancouvers, Gordy 7079
106. LIVIN' IN THE U. S. A. — Steve Miller Band, Capitol 2287
107. PEOPLE — Tymes, Columbia 44630
108. GETTING TO KNOW YOU — Sajid Khan, Colgems 66-1028
109. BORN TO BE WITH YOU — Sonny James, Capitol 2271
110. THE OL' RACE TRACK — Mills Brothers, Dot 17162
111. BABY LET'S WAIT — Royal Guardsmen, Laurie 3461
112. MAIN STREET — Gary Lewis & the Playboys, Liberty 56073
113. PUT YOUR HEAD ON MY SHOULDER — Lettermen, Capitol 2324
114. CRAZY RHYTHM — Happenings, B. T. Puppy 545
115. GREAT ESCAPE — Ray Stevens, Monument 1099
116. RIGHT RELATIONS — Johnny Rivers, Imperial 66335
117. COO COO — Big Brother & the Holding Company, Mainstream 678
118. HOW LUCKY (Can One Man Be) — Uniques, Paula 313
119. SCARBOROUGH FAIR — Sergio Mendes & Brasil '66, A&M 986
120. (She's) SOME KIND OF WONDERFUL — Fantastic Johnny C., Phil L.A. of Soul 320
121. STAND BY YOUR MAN — Patti Page, Columbia 44666
122. RUN TO ME — Montanas, Independence 89
123. FEELIN' ALRIGHT? — Traffic, United Artists 50460
124. TODAY — Jimmie Rodgers, A&M 976
125. THE EAGLE LAUGHS AT YOU — Jackie Lomax, Apple 1802
126. WITH A LITTLE HELP FROM MY FRIENDS — Joe Cocker, A&M 991
127. HE'S BAD, BAD, BAD — Betty Wright, Alston 4571
128. BOTH SIDES NOW — Johnstons, Tetragrammaton 1507
129. LISTEN TO ME — Hollies, Epic 10400
130. HEY MISTER — Four Jacks & a Jill, RCA Victor 47-9655
131. HARD TO HANDLE — Patti Drew, Capitol 2339
132. THE PATH OF LOVE — John Cowsill, MGM 14003

Compiled from national retail sales and radio station airplay by the Music Popularity Dept. of Record Market Research, Billboard.

HOT 100

# Billboard HOT 100
**For Week Ending November 16, 1968**

★ STAR PERFORMER—Sides registering greatest proportionate upward progress this week.
● Record Industry Association of America seal of certification as million selling single.

| This Week | Last Week | 2 Wks. Ago | 3 Wks. Ago | TITLE, Artist (Producer), Label & Number | Weeks on Chart |
|---|---|---|---|---|---|
| 1 | 1 | 1 | 1 | **HEY JUDE** — Beatles (George Martin), Apple 2276 | 10 |
| 2 | 2 | 2 | 4 | **THOSE WERE THE DAYS** — Mary Hopkin (Paul McCartney), Apple 1801 | 8 |
| 3 | 3 | 9 | 19 | **LOVE CHILD** — Diana Ross & Supremes (Clan), Motown 1135 | 5 |
| 4 | 7 | 12 | 25 | **MAGIC CARPET RIDE** — Steppenwolf (Gabriel Mekler), Dunhill 4160 | 7 |
| 5 | 5 | 8 | 11 | **HOLD ME TIGHT** — Johnny Nash (Johnny Nash & Arthur Jenkins), JAD 207 | 10 |
| 6 | 6 | 10 | 15 | **WHITE ROOM** — Cream (Felix Pappalardi), Atco 6617 | 8 |
| 7 | 4 | 3 | 2 | **LITTLE GREEN APPLES** — O. C. Smith (Jerry Fuller), Columbia 44616 | 14 |
| 8 | 21 | 29 | 45 | **WHO'S MAKING LOVE** — Johnnie Taylor (Don Davis), Stax 0009 | 4 |
| 9 | 18 | 35 | 66 | **ABRAHAM, MARTIN AND JOHN** — Dion (Laurie Prod.-Phil Gernhard Prod.), Laurie 3464 | 4 |
| 10 | 8 | 6 | 9 | **ELENORE** — Turtles (Chip Douglas), White Whale 276 | 9 |
| 11 | 9 | 4 | 3 | **FIRE** — Crazy World of Arthur Brown (Kit Lambert), Track 2556 | 11 |
| 12 | 11 | 7 | 7 | **OVER YOU** — Gary Puckett and the Union Gap (Jerry Fuller), Columbia 44644 | 9 |
| 13 | 13 | 21 | 27 | **SWEET BLINDNESS** — Fifth Dimension (Bones Howe), Soul City 768 | 8 |
| 14 | 35 | 79 | — | **FOR ONCE IN MY LIFE** — Stevie Wonder (Henry Cosby), Tamla 54174 | 3 |
| 15 | 10 | 5 | 6 | **MIDNIGHT CONFESSIONS** — Grassroots (Steve Barri), Dunhill 4144 | 12 |
| 16 | 17 | 18 | 18 | **HEY, WESTERN UNION MAN** — Jerry Butler (Gamble-Huff), Mercury 72850 | 12 |
| 17 | 36 | 36 | 48 | **CHEWY CHEWY** — Ohio Express (Kasenetz-Katz Associates), Buddah 70 | 5 |
| 18 | 37 | 37 | 54 | **ALWAYS TOGETHER** — Dells (Bobby Miller), Cadet 5621 | 6 |
| 19 | 14 | 11 | 12 | **SUZIE Q** — Creedence Clearwater Revival (Saul Zaentz), Fantasy 616 | 11 |
| 20 | 19 | 19 | 17 | **REVOLUTION** — Beatles (George Martin), Apple 2276 | 10 |
| 21 | 16 | 15 | 5 | **GIRL WATCHER** — O'Kaysions (North State Music), ABC 11094 | 14 |
| 22 | 23 | 23 | 23 | **FOOL FOR YOU** — Impressions (Curtis Mayfield), Curtom 1932 | 11 |
| 23 | 67 | 75 | — | **WICHITA LINEMAN** — Glen Campbell (Al de Lory), Capitol 2302 | 3 |
| 24 | 24 | 34 | 36 | **KEEP ON LOVIN' ME, HONEY** — Marvin Gaye & Tammi Terrell (Ashford & Simpson), Tamla 54173 | 6 |
| 25 | 26 | 27 | 34 | **HI-HEEL SNEAKERS** — Jose Feliciano (Rick Jarrard), RCA Victor 47-9641 | 5 |
| 26 | 47 | 64 | — | **I LOVE HOW YOU LOVE ME** — Bobby Vinton (Billy Sherrill), Epic 10397 | 3 |
| 27 | 27 | 28 | 42 | **BANG-SHANG-A-LANG** — Archies (Don Kirshner), Calendar 63-1006 | 7 |
| 28 | 20 | 20 | 16 | **SAY IT LOUD (I'm Black and I'm Proud)** — James Brown & His Famous Flames (James Brown), King 6187 | 11 |
| 29 | 12 | 13 | 13 | **PIECE OF MY HEART** — Big Brother & the Holding Company, Columbia 44626 | 12 |
| 30 | 42 | 50 | 64 | **BRING IT ON HOME TO ME** — Eddie Floyd (Steve Cropper), Stax 0012 | 4 |
| 31 | 40 | 57 | 65 | **LITTLE ARROWS** — Leapy Lee (Gordon Mills), Decca 32380 | 7 |
| 32 | 25 | 26 | 28 | **COURT OF LOVE** — Unifics (Guy Draper), Kapp 935 | 9 |
| 33 | 57 | 67 | 80 | **STORMY** — Classics IV (Buddy Buie), Imperial 66328 | 5 |
| 34 | 34 | 41 | 43 | **QUICK JOEY SMALL (Run Joey Run)** — Kasenetz-Katz Singing Orchestral Circus (Kasenetz-Katz Associates), Buddah 64 | 7 |
| 35 | 15 | 14 | 8 | **HARPER VALLEY P.T.A.** — Jeannie C. Riley (Shelby S. Singleton Jr.), Plantation 3 | 13 |
| 36 | 29 | 25 | 20 | **ALL ALONG THE WATCHTOWER** — Jimi Hendrix Experience (Jimi Hendrix), Reprise 0767 | 9 |
| 37 | 43 | 43 | 70 | **CYCLES** — Frank Sinatra (Don Costa), Reprise 0764 | 6 |
| 38 | 38 | 38 | 38 | **TAKE ME FOR A LITTLE WHILE** — Vanilla Fudge (Shadow Morton), Atco 6616 | 7 |
| 39 | 46 | 47 | 47 | **THE FUNKY JUDGE** — Bull & The Matadors (Sherrel-Cross Prod.), Toddlin' Town 108 | 13 |
| 40 | 22 | 22 | 22 | **SHAPE OF THINGS TO COME** — Max Frost & the Troopers (Mike Curb), Tower 419 | 11 |
| 41 | 48 | 66 | — | **PROMISES, PROMISES** — Dionne Warwick (Burt Bacharach-Hal David), Scepter 12231 | 3 |
| 42 | 56 | 56 | 72 | **PICKIN' WILD MOUNTAIN BERRIES** — Peggy Scott & Jo Jo Benson (Shelby S. Singleton Jr. & Bob McRee), SSS Int'l 748 | 5 |
| 43 | 45 | 46 | 68 | **LES BICYCLETTES DE BELSIZE** — Engelbert Humperdinck (Peter Sullivan), Parrot 40032 | 4 |
| 44 | 32 | 32 | 33 | **CHAINED** — Marvin Gaye (Frank Wilson), Tamla 54170 | 10 |
| 45 | — | — | — | **CLOUD NINE** — Temptations (Norman Whitfield), Gordy 7081 | 1 |
| 46 | 74 | — | — | **BOTH SIDES NOW** — Judy Collins (Mark Abramson), Elektra 45639 | 2 |
| 47 | 73 | — | — | **TOO WEAK TO FIGHT** — Clarence Carter (Rick Hall & Staff), Atlantic 2569 | 2 |
| 48 | 53 | 53 | 53 | **BATTLE HYMN OF THE REPUBLIC** — Andy Williams with the St. Charles Borromeo Choir (Andy Williams), Columbia 44650 | 5 |
| 49 | 54 | 54 | 75 | **THE STRAIGHT LIFE** — Bobby Goldsboro (Bob Montgomery & Bobby Goldsboro), United Artists 50461 | 4 |
| 50 | 60 | 60 | 67 | **CINNAMON** — Derek (George Tobin & Johnny Cymbal), Bang 558 | 4 |
| 51 | 69 | 74 | 87 | **SHAME, SHAME** — Magic Lanterns (Steve Rowland), Atlantic 2560 | 4 |
| 52 | 52 | 52 | 79 | **1432 FRANKLIN PIKE CIRCLE HERO** — Bobby Russell (Buzz Cason & Bobby Russell), Elf 90020 | 4 |
| 53 | 68 | 72 | 89 | **GOODY GOODY GUMDROPS** — 1910 Fruitgum Co. (Kasenetz-Katz Associates), Buddah 71 | 3 |
| 54 | 65 | 89 | — | **THE STAR-SPANGLED BANNER** — Jose Feliciano, RCA Victor 47-9665 | 3 |
| 55 | 59 | 59 | 59 | **DO SOMETHING TO ME** — Tommy James & the Shondells (Tommy James), Roulette 7024 | 5 |
| 56 | 63 | 63 | 60 | **I LOVE YOU MADLY** — Fantastic Four (Mike Hanks), Soul 3505 | 5 |
| 57 | 64 | 65 | 76 | **FROM THE TEACHER TO THE PREACHER** — Gene Chandler & Barbara Acklin (Carl Davis), Brunswick 55387 | 5 |
| 58 | 72 | 76 | 93 | **PEACE BROTHER PEACE** — Bill Medley (Medley Prod.), MGM 14000 | 3 |
| 59 | 58 | 58 | 58 | **CINDERELLA SUNSHINE** — Paul Revere & the Raiders, featuring Mark Lindsay (Mark Lindsay), Columbia 44655 | 5 |
| 60 | 75 | — | — | **GOODBYE MY LOVE** — James Brown (James Brown), King 6198 | 2 |
| 61 | 87 | — | — | **KENTUCKY WOMAN** — Deep Purple (Derek Lawrence), Tetragrammaton 1508 | 2 |
| 62 | 62 | 62 | 62 | **PORPOISE SONG** — Monkees (Gerry Goffin), Colgems 66-1031 | 5 |
| 63 | 84 | 87 | — | **FIRE** — Five by Five (Gene Kent), Paula 302 | 3 |
| 64 | 81 | 97 | — | **THE YARD WENT ON FOREVER** — Richard Harris (Jimmy Webb), Dunhill 4170 | 3 |
| 65 | 89 | 96 | — | **TALKING ABOUT MY BABY** — Gloria Walker (Eugene Davis), Flaming Arrow 35 | 3 |
| 66 | 94 | — | — | **HANG 'EM HIGH** — Booker T. & M.G.'s (Booker T. & M.G.'s), Stax 0013 | 2 |
| 67 | 77 | 78 | 78 | **HARPER VALLEY P.T.A. (Later That Day)** — Ben Colder (Jack Clement), MGM 13997 | 4 |
| 68 | 71 | 71 | 74 | **SHAKE** — Shadows of Knight (Kasenetz-Katz Associates), Team 520 | 4 |
| 69 | 79 | 93 | — | **NOT ENOUGH INDIANS** — Dean Martin (Jimmy Bowen), Reprise 0780 | 3 |
| 70 | 78 | 80 | — | **FOR ONCE IN MY LIFE** — Jackie Wilson (Carl Davis), Brunswick 55392 | 3 |
| 71 | 91 | 91 | — | **CROWN OF CREATION** — Jefferson Airplane (Al Schmitt), RCA Victor 47-9644 | 3 |
| 72 | 76 | — | — | **SLOW DRAG** — Intruders (Gamble-Huff), Gamble 221 | 2 |
| 73 | 80 | 81 | — | **EVERYBODY GOT TO BELIEVE IN SOMEBODY** — Sam & Dave (Isaac Hayes & David Porter), Atlantic 2568 | 3 |
| 74 | 95 | — | — | **SUNDAY SUN** — Neil Diamond (Tom Catalano & Neil Diamond), UNI 55084 | 2 |
| 75 | 97 | — | — | **LET'S MAKE A PROMISE** — Peaches & Herb (Gamble-Huff), Date 1623 | 2 |
| 76 | — | — | — | **SCARBOROUGH FAIR** — Sergio Mendes & Brasil '66 (Sergio Mendes), A&M 986 | 1 |
| 77 | — | — | — | **ROCKIN' IN THE SAME OLD BOAT** — Bobby Bland (Duke 440) | 1 |
| 78 | — | — | — | **A MAN AND A HALF** — Wilson Pickett (Tom Dowd), Atlantic 2575 | 1 |
| 79 | 98 | — | — | **STAND BY YOUR MAN** — Tammy Wynette (Billy Sherrill), Epic 10398 | 2 |
| 80 | 86 | 86 | — | **SWEET DARLIN'** — Martha Reeves & the Vandellas (Richard Morris), Gordy 7080 | 3 |
| 81 | — | — | — | **PUT YOUR HEAD ON MY SHOULDER** — Lettermen (Al de Lory), Capitol 2324 | 1 |
| 82 | 82 | 84 | 95 | **MORNIN' GLORY** — Bobbie Gentry & Glen Campbell (Kelly Gordon & Al de Lory), Capitol 2314 | 4 |
| 83 | 83 | 83 | 83 | **DO WHAT YOU GOTTA DO** — Nina Simone (Straud Prod.), RCA Victor 47-9602 | 5 |
| 84 | — | — | — | **PEOPLE** — Tymes (Jimmy "Wiz" Wisner), Columbia 44630 | 1 |
| 85 | 93 | 94 | 94 | **AUNT DORA'S LOVE SOUL SHACK** — Arthur Conley (Tom Dowd), Atco 6622 | 4 |
| 86 | — | — | — | **WITH A LITTLE HELP FROM MY FRIENDS** — Joe Cocker (Denny Cordell), A&M 991 | 1 |
| 87 | — | — | — | **(She's) SOME KIND OF WONDERFUL** — Fantastic Johnny C (Jesse James), Phil L.A. of Soul 320 | 1 |
| 88 | 88 | 90 | 90 | **I WALK ALONE** — Marty Robbins (Bob Johnston), Columbia 44633 | 4 |
| 89 | — | — | — | **JUST AIN'T NO LOVE** — Barbara Acklin (Carl Davis-Eugene Record), Brunswick 55388 | 1 |
| 90 | 90 | 95 | — | **CALIFORNIA EARTHQUAKE** — Mama Cass (John Simon), Dunhill 4166 | 3 |
| 91 | — | — | — | **BABY LET'S WAIT** — Royal Guardsmen (Gernard-Bromiege-Fuller), Laurie 3461 | 1 |
| 92 | 92 | 92 | — | **BILLY, YOU'RE MY FRIEND** — Gene Pitney (Bob Schwartz), Musicor 1331 | 3 |
| 93 | — | — | — | **BALLAD OF TWO BROTHERS** — Autry Inman (Glenn Sutton & Billy Sherrill), Epic 10389 | 1 |
| 94 | — | — | — | **HARD TO HANDLE** — Patti Drew (Carone Prod.), Capitol 2339 | 1 |
| 95 | — | — | — | **I'VE GOT LOVE FOR MY BABY** — Young Hearts (Bobby Sanders & Soultown Prod.), Minit 32049 | 1 |
| 96 | 96 | — | — | **I PUT A SPELL ON YOU** — Creedence Clearwater Revival (Saul Zaentz), Fantasy 617 | 2 |
| 97 | — | — | — | **HOOKED ON A FEELING** — B. J. Thomas (Chips Moman), Scepter 12230 | 1 |
| 98 | — | — | — | **I WORRY ABOUT YOU** — Joe Simon (J. R. Ent.), Sound Stage 7 2617 | 1 |
| 99 | 99 | 100 | — | **COME ON, REACT** — Fireballs (Norman Petty), Atco 6614 | 2 |
| 100 | 100 | — | — | **A WHITER SHADE OF PALE** — Hesitations (P. Robinson, T. Wiltshire, L. Banks), Kapp 948 | 2 |

## BUBBLING UNDER THE HOT 100

101. MAIN STREET .................. Gary Lewis & the Playboys, Liberty 56073
102. UP HARD .................. Willie Mitchell, Hi 2151
103. ISN'T IT LONELY TOGETHER .................. Robert Knight, Elf 90019
104. LIVIN' IN THE U.S.A. .................. Steve Miller Band, Capitol 2287
105. MALINDA .................. Bobby Taylor & Vancouvers, Gordy 7079
106. RIGHT RELATIONS .................. Johnny Rivers, Imperial 66335
107. SEE SAW .................. Aretha Franklin, Atlantic 2574
108. I HEARD IT THROUGH THE GRAPEVINE .................. Marvin Gaye, Tamla 5
109. BORN TO BE WITH YOU .................. Sonny James, Capitol 2271
110. THE OL' RACE TRACK .................. Mills Brothers, Dot 17162
111. HE'S BAD, BAD, BAD .................. Betty Wright, Alston 4571
112. LOVE MACHINE .................. O'Kaysions, ABC 11153
113. ALADDIN .................. Rotary Connection, Cadet 317
114. LO MUCHO QUE TE QUIERO .................. Rene & Rene, White Whale 287
115. GOODNIGHT MY LOVE .................. Duprees, Heritage 805
116. STORMY .................. Pigmeat Markham, Chess 2059
117. COO COO .................. Big Brother & the Holding Company, Mainstream 6
118. AMERICAN BOYS .................. Petula Clark, Warner Bros.-Seven Arts 724
119. WAY OVER THERE .................. Edwin Starr, Gordy 7078
120. YESTERDAY'S RAIN .................. Spanky & Our Gang, Mercury 72871
121. RUN TO ME .................. Montanas, Independence 84
122. TODAY .................. Jimmie Rodgers, A&M 991
123. WE'RE ALL GOING TO THE SAME PLACE .................. Tommy Boyce & Bobby Hart, A&M 992
124. WHERE DID YOU COME FROM .................. Buckinghams, Columbia 44672
125. SOCK IT TO 'EM JUDGE .................. Peanut Butter Conspiracy, Challenge
126. RELEASE ME .................. Johnny Adams, SSS Int'l 750
127. MAKE A NOISE LIKE LOVE .................. Gene & Debbe, TRX 5014

*Compiled from national retail sales and radio station airplay by the Music Popularity Dept. of Record Market Research, Billboard.*

# Billboard HOT 100

**FOR WEEK ENDING NOVEMBER 23, 1968**

★ STAR PERFORMER—Sides registering greatest proportionate upward progress this week.
Ⓡ Record Industry Association of America seal of certification as million selling single.

| This Week | Last Week | 2 Wks. Ago | 3 Wks. Ago | TITLE Artist (Producer), Label & Number | Weeks On Chart |
|---|---|---|---|---|---|
| 1 | 1 | 1 | 1 | HEY JUDE — Beatles (George Martin), Apple 2276 | 11 |
| 2 | 3 | 3 | 9 | LOVE CHILD — Diana Ross & Supremes (Clan), Motown 1135 | 6 |
| 3 | 2 | 2 | 2 | THOSE WERE THE DAYS — Mary Hopkin (Paul McCartney), Apple 1801 | 9 |
| 4 | 4 | 7 | 12 | MAGIC CARPET RIDE — Steppenwolf (Gabriel Mekler), Dunhill 4160 | 8 |
| 5 | 9 | 18 | 35 | ABRAHAM, MARTIN AND JOHN — Dion (Laurie Prod.-Phil Gernhard Prod.), Laurie 3464 | 5 |
| 6 | 6 | 6 | 10 | WHITE ROOM — Cream (Felix Pappalardi), Atco 6617 | 8 |
| 7 | 5 | 5 | 8 | HOLD ME TIGHT — Johnny Nash (Johnny Nash & Arthur Jenkins), JAD 207 | 11 |
| 8 | 8 | 21 | 29 | WHO'S MAKING LOVE — Johnnie Taylor (Don Davis), Stax 0009 | 5 |
| 9 | 7 | 4 | 3 | LITTLE GREEN APPLES — O. C. Smith (Jerry Fuller), Columbia 44616 | 15 |
| 10 | 23 | 67 | 75 | WICHITA LINEMAN — Glen Campbell (Al de Lory), Capitol 2302 | 4 |
| 11 | 33 | 57 | 67 | STORMY — Classics IV (Buddy Buie), Imperial 66328 | 5 |
| 12 | 10 | 8 | 6 | ELENORE — Turtles (Chip Douglas), White Whale 276 | 10 |
| 13 | 12 | 11 | 7 | OVER YOU — Gary Puckett & the Union Gap (Jerry Fuller), Columbia 44644 | 10 |
| 14 | 14 | 35 | 79 | FOR ONCE IN MY LIFE — Stevie Wonder (Henry Cosby), Tamla 54174 | 4 |
| 15 | 15 | 10 | 5 | MIDNIGHT CONFESSIONS — Grassroots (Steve Barri), Dunhill 4144 | 13 |
| 16 | 17 | 36 | 36 | CHEWY CHEWY — Ohio Express (Kasenetz-Katz Associates), Buddah 70 | 6 |
| 17 | 26 | 47 | 64 | I LOVE HOW YOU LOVE ME — Bobby Vinton (Billy Sherrill), Epic 10397 | 4 |
| 18 | 18 | 37 | 37 | ALWAYS TOGETHER — Dells (Bobby Miller), Cadet 5621 | 5 |
| 19 | 46 | 74 | — | BOTH SIDES NOW — Judy Collins (Mark Abramson), Elektra 45639 | 3 |
| 20 | 11 | 9 | 4 | FIRE — Crazy World of Arthur Brown (Kit Lambert), Track 2556 | 12 |
| 21 | 41 | 48 | 66 | PROMISES, PROMISES — Dionne Warwick (Burt Bacharach-Hal David), Scepter 12231 | 4 |
| 22 | 31 | 40 | 57 | LITTLE ARROWS — Leapy Lee (Gordon Mills), Decca 32380 | 7 |
| 23 | 37 | 43 | 43 | CYCLES — Frank Sinatra (Don Costa), Reprise 0764 | 7 |
| 24 | 27 | 27 | 28 | BANG-SHANG-A-LANG — Archies (Don Kirshner), Calendar 63-1006 | 9 |
| 25 | 25 | 26 | 27 | HI-HEEL SNEAKERS — Jose Feliciano (Rick Jarrard), RCA Victor 47-9641 | 9 |
| 26 | 13 | 13 | 21 | SWEET BLINDNESS — Fifth Dimension (Bones Howe), Soul City 768 | 9 |
| 27 | 30 | 42 | 50 | BRING IT ON HOME TO ME — Eddie Floyd (Steve Cropper), Stax 0012 | 7 |
| 28 | 34 | 34 | 41 | QUICK JOEY SMALL (Run Joey Run) — Kasenetz-Katz Singing Orchestral Circus (Kasenetz-Katz Associates), Buddah 64 | 8 |
| 29 | 20 | 19 | 19 | REVOLUTION — Beatles (George Martin), Apple 2276 | 11 |
| 30 | 16 | 17 | 18 | HEY, WESTERN UNION MAN — Jerry Butler (Gamble-Huff), Mercury 72850 | 13 |
| 31 | 19 | 14 | 11 | SUZIE Q — Creedence Clearwater Revival (Saul Zaentz), Fantasy 616 | 12 |
| 32 | 43 | 45 | 46 | LES BICYCLETTES DE BELSIZE — Engelbert Humperdinck (Peter Sullivan), Parrot 40032 | 6 |
| 33 | 24 | 24 | 34 | KEEP ON LOVIN' ME, HONEY — Marvin Gaye & Tammi Terrell (Ashford & Simpson), Tamla 54173 | 7 |
| 34 | — | — | — | I HEARD IT THROUGH THE GRAPEVINE — Marvin Gaye (Norman Whitfield), Tamla 54176 | 1 |
| 35 | — | — | — | SEE SAW — Aretha Franklin (Jerry Wexler), Atlantic 2574 | 1 |
| 36 | 52 | 52 | 52 | 1432 FRANKLIN PIKE CIRCLE HERO — Bobby Russell (Buzz Cason & Bobby Russell), Elf 90020 | 5 |
| 37 | 50 | 60 | 60 | CINNAMON — Derek (George Tobin & Johnny Cymbal), Bang 558 | 7 |
| 38 | 55 | 59 | 59 | DO SOMETHING TO ME — Tommy James & the Shondells (Tommy James), Roulette 7024 | 7 |
| 39 | 45 | — | — | CLOUD NINE — Temptations (Norman Whitfield), Gordy 7081 | 2 |
| 40 | 40 | 22 | 22 | SHAPE OF THINGS TO COME — Max Frost & the Troopers (Mike Curb), Tower 419 | 12 |
| 41 | 49 | 54 | 54 | THE STRAIGHT LIFE — Bobby Goldsboro (Bob Montgomery & Bobby Goldsboro), United Artists 50461 | 6 |
| 42 | 42 | 56 | 56 | PICKIN' WILD MOUNTAIN BERRIES — Peggy Scott & Jo Jo Benson (Shelby S. Singleton Jr. & Bob McRee), SSS Int'l 748 | 6 |
| 43 | 22 | 23 | 23 | FOOL FOR YOU — Impressions (Curtis Mayfield), Curtom 1932 | 12 |
| 44 | 61 | 87 | — | KENTUCKY WOMAN — Deep Purple (Derek Lawrence), Tetragrammaton 1508 | 3 |
| 45 | 53 | 68 | 72 | GOODY GOODY GUMDROPS — 1910 Fruitgum Co. (Kasenetz-Katz Associates), Buddah 71 | 4 |
| 46 | 51 | 69 | 74 | SHAME, SHAME — Magic Lanterns (Steve Rowland), Atlantic 2560 | 5 |
| 47 | 47 | 73 | — | TOO WEAK TO FIGHT — Clarence Carter (Rick Hall & Staff), Atlantic 2569 | 3 |
| 48 | 48 | 53 | 53 | BATTLE HYMN OF THE REPUBLIC — Andy Williams with the St. Charles Borromeo Choir (Andy Williams), Columbia 44650 | 6 |
| 49 | 38 | 38 | 38 | TAKE ME FOR A LITTLE WHILE — Vanilla Fudge (Shadow Morton), Atco 6616 | 8 |
| 50 | 76 | — | — | SCARBOROUGH FAIR — Sergio Mendes & Brasil '66 (Sergio Mendes), A&M 986 | 2 |
| 51 | 58 | 72 | 76 | PEACE BROTHER PEACE — Bill Medley (Medley Prod.), MGM 14000 | 4 |
| 52 | 69 | 79 | 93 | NOT ENOUGH INDIANS — Dean Martin (Jimmy Bowen), Reprise 0780 | 4 |
| 53 | — | — | — | TILL — Vogues (Dick Glasser), Reprise 0788 | 1 |
| 54 | 54 | 65 | 89 | THE STAR-SPANGLED BANNER — Jose Feliciano (RCA Victor), RCA Victor 47-9665 | 4 |
| 55 | 60 | 75 | — | GOODBYE MY LOVE — James Brown (James Brown), King 6198 | 3 |
| 56 | 81 | — | — | PUT YOUR HEAD ON MY SHOULDER — Lettermen (Al de Lory), Capitol 2324 | 2 |
| 57 | 39 | 46 | 47 | THE FUNKY JUDGE — Bull & The Matadors (Sherrel-Cross Prod.), Toddlin' Town 108 | 14 |
| 58 | 68 | 71 | 71 | SHAKE — Shadows of Knight (Kasenetz-Katz Associates), Team 7004 | 4 |
| 59 | 57 | 64 | 65 | FROM THE TEACHER TO THE PREACHER — Gene Chandler & Barbara Acklin (Carl Davis), Brunswick 55387 | 6 |
| 60 | 63 | 84 | 87 | FIRE — Five by Five (Gene Kent), Paula 302 | 4 |
| 61 | — | — | — | I CAN'T TURN YOU LOOSE — Chambers Brothers (Tim O'Brien), Columbia 44679 | 1 |
| 62 | 84 | — | — | PEOPLE — Tymes (Jimmy "Wiz" Wisner), Columbia 44630 | 2 |
| 63 | — | — | — | RIGHT RELATIONS — Johnny Rivers (Johnny Rivers), Imperial 66335 | 1 |
| 64 | 64 | 81 | 97 | THE YARD WENT ON FOREVER — Richard Harris (Jimmy Webb), Dunhill 4170 | 4 |
| 65 | 65 | 89 | 96 | TALKING ABOUT MY BABY — Gloria Walker (Eugene Davis), Flaming Arrow 35 | 4 |
| 66 | 66 | 94 | — | HANG 'EM HIGH — Booker T. & M.G.'s (Booker T. & M.G.'s), Stax 0013 | 3 |
| 67 | 90 | 90 | 95 | CALIFORNIA EARTHQUAKE — Mama Cass (John Simon), Dunhill 4166 | 4 |
| 68 | 74 | 95 | — | SUNDAY SUN — Neil Diamond (Tom Catalano & Neil Diamond), UNI 55084 | 4 |
| 69 | 97 | — | — | HOOKED ON A FEELING — B. J. Thomas (Chips Moman), Scepter 12230 | 2 |
| 70 | 88 | 88 | 90 | I WALK ALONE — Marty Robbins (Bob Johnston), Columbia 44633 | 5 |
| 71 | 71 | 91 | 91 | CROWN OF CREATION — Jefferson Airplane (Al Schmitt), RCA Victor 47-9644 | 4 |
| 72 | 72 | 76 | — | SLOW DRAG — Intruders (Gamble-Huff), Gamble 221 | 3 |
| 73 | 79 | 98 | — | STAND BY YOUR MAN — Tammy Wynette (Billy Sherrill), Epic 10398 | 3 |
| 74 | 82 | 82 | 84 | MORNIN' GLORY — Bobbie Gentry & Glen Campbell (Kelly Gordon & Al de Lory), Capitol 2314 | 4 |
| 75 | 75 | 97 | — | LET'S MAKE A PROMISE — Peaches & Herb (Gamble-Huff), Date 1623 | 3 |
| 76 | 78 | — | — | A MAN AND A HALF — Wilson Pickett (Tom Dowd), Atlantic 2575 | 2 |
| 77 | 77 | — | — | ROCKIN' IN THE SAME OLD BOAT — Bobby Bland (Don), Duke 440 | 2 |
| 78 | 67 | 77 | 78 | HARPER VALLEY P.T.A. (Later That Day) — Ben Colder (Jack Clement), MGM 13997 | 5 |
| 79 | — | — | — | AMERICAN BOYS — Petula Clark (Tony Hatch), Warner Bros.-Seven Arts 7244 | 1 |
| 80 | 80 | 86 | 86 | SWEET DARLIN' — Martha Reeves & the Vandellas (Richard Morris), Gordy 7080 | 4 |
| 81 | — | — | — | LOVE MACHINE — O'Kaysions (Johnny Pate), ABC 11153 | 1 |
| 82 | — | — | — | CHITTY CHITTY BANG BANG — Paul Mauriat (Philips 40574) | 1 |
| 83 | — | — | — | THE OL' RACE TRACK — Mills Brothers (Tom Mack), Dot 17162 | 1 |
| 84 | — | — | — | COO COO — Big Brother & the Holding Company (Bob Shad), Mainstream 678 | 1 |
| 85 | 86 | — | — | WITH A LITTLE HELP FROM MY FRIENDS — Joe Cocker (Denny Cordell), A&M 991 | 2 |
| 86 | 99 | 99 | 100 | COME ON, REACT — Fireballs (Norman Petty), Atco 6614 | 4 |
| 87 | 87 | — | — | (She's) SOME KIND OF WONDERFUL — Fantastic Johnny C (Jesse James), Phil L.A. of Soul 320 | 2 |
| 88 | — | — | — | DO YOU WANNA DANCE — Mamas & Papas (Lou Adler), Dunhill 4171 | 1 |
| 89 | 89 | — | — | JUST AIN'T NO LOVE — Barbara Acklin (Carl Davis-Eugene Record), Brunswick 55388 | 2 |
| 90 | — | — | — | KEEP ON DANCING — Alvin Cash (A. Williams & H. Scott), Toddlin' Town 111 | 1 |
| 91 | 91 | — | — | BABY LET'S WAIT — Royal Guardsmen (Gernard-Bromidge-Fuller), Laurie 3461 | 2 |
| 92 | 93 | — | — | BALLAD OF TWO BROTHERS — Autry Inman (Glenn Sutton & Billy Sherrill), Epic 10389 | 2 |
| 93 | 94 | — | — | HARD TO HANDLE — Patti Drew (Carone Prod.), Capitol 2339 | 2 |
| 94 | — | — | — | LIVING IN THE U.S.A. — Steve Miller Band (Steve Miller & Glyn Johns), Capitol 2287 | 1 |
| 95 | — | — | — | I'VE GOT LOVE FOR MY BABY — Young Hearts (Bobby Sanders & Soultown Prod.), Minit 32049 | 2 |
| 96 | 96 | 96 | — | I PUT A SPELL ON YOU — Creedence Clearwater Revival (Saul Zaentz), Fantasy 617 | 3 |
| 97 | — | — | — | BORN TO BE WITH YOU — Sonny James (Kelso Herston), Capitol 2271 | 1 |
| 98 | — | — | — | WHITE HOUSES — Eric Burdon & the Animals (Everyone of Us), MGM 14013 | 1 |
| 99 | — | — | — | DON'T CRY MY LOVE — Impressions (Johnny Pate), ABC 11135 | 1 |
| 100 | — | — | — | LO MUCHO QUE TE QUIERO (The More I Love You) — Rene & Rene, White Whale 287 | 1 |

## BUBBLING UNDER THE HOT 100

101. MAIN STREET — Gary Lewis & the Playboys, Liberty 56073
102. THEY DON'T MAKE LOVE LIKE THEY USED TO — Eddy Arnold, RCA Victor 47-9667
103. SOCK IT TO 'EM JUDGE — Pigmeat Markham, Chess 2059
104. MELINDA — Bobby Taylor & the Vancouvers, Gordy 7079
105. EVERYDAY PEOPLE — Sly & the Family Stone, Epic 10407
106. SMELL OF INCENSE — Southwest F.O.B., Hip 8002
107. DON'T MAKE THE GOOD GIRLS GO BAD — Della Humphrey, Arctic 144
108. TODAY — Jimmie Rodgers, A&M 991
109. ISN'T IT LONELY TOGETHER — Robert Knight, Elf 90019
110. GOOD TIME GIRL — Nancy Sinatra, Reprise 0789
111. THE CONTINUING STORY OF HARPER VALLEY P.T.A. — Dee Mullins, SSS Int'l 749
112. STAND BY ME — Quicksilver Messenger Service, Capitol 2320
113. IF I CAN DREAM — Elvis Presley, RCA Victor 47-9670
114. THE GREAT ESCAPE — Ray Stevens, Monument 1099
115. GOODNIGHT MY LOVE — Duprees, Heritage 805
116. REACH OUT — Merrilee Rush, AGP 107
117. YESTERDAY'S RAIN — Spanky and Our Gang, Mercury 72871
118. SON-OF-A PREACHER MAN — Dusty Springfield, Atlantic 2580
119. WHERE DID YOU COME FROM — Buckinghams, Columbia 44672
120. DON'T BE AFRAID — Frankie Karl & the Dreams, D.C. 180
121. HE'S BAD, BAD, BAD — Betty Wright, Alston 4571
122. HONEY DO — Strangeloves, Sire 4102
123. THE SPLIT — Lou Rawls, Capitol 2348
124. THE WORM — Jimmy McGriff, Solid State 2524
125. YUMMY, YUMMY, YUMMY — Julie London, Liberty 56074

Compiled from national retail sales and radio station airplay by the Music Popularity Dept. of Record Market Research, Billboard.

# Billboard HOT 100

FOR WEEK ENDING NOVEMBER 30, 1968

★ STAR PERFORMER—Sides registering greatest proportionate upward progress this week.

(Seal) Record Industry Association of America seal of certification as million selling single.

| This Week | 1 Wk. Ago | 2 Wks. Ago | 3 Wks. Ago | TITLE Artist (Producer), Label & Number | Weeks On Chart |
|---|---|---|---|---|---|
| 1 (Billboard Award) | 2 | 3 | 3 | **LOVE CHILD** — Diana Ross & Supremes (Clan), Motown 1135 | 7 |
| 2 (Seal) | 1 | 1 | 1 | **HEY JUDE** — Beatles (George Martin), Apple 2276 | 12 |
| 3 | 4 | 4 | 7 | **MAGIC CARPET RIDE** — Steppenwolf (Gabriel Mekler), Dunhill 4160 | 9 |
| 4 (Seal) | 3 | 2 | 2 | **THOSE WERE THE DAYS** — Mary Hopkin (Paul McCartney), Apple 1801 | 10 |
| 5 | 5 | 9 | 18 | **ABRAHAM, MARTIN AND JOHN** — Dion (Laurie Prod.-Phil Gernhard Prod.), Laurie 3464 | 6 |
| 6 ★ (Seal) | 8 | 8 | 21 | **WHO'S MAKING LOVE** — Johnnie Taylor (Don Davis), Stax 0009 | 6 |
| 7 ★ | 14 | 14 | 35 | **FOR ONCE IN MY LIFE** — Stevie Wonder (Henry Cosby), Tamla 54174 | 5 |
| 8 | 10 | 23 | 67 | **WICHITA LINEMAN** — Glen Campbell (Al de Lory), Capitol 2302 | 5 |
| 9 | 7 | 5 | 5 | **HOLD ME TIGHT** — Johnny Nash (Johnny Nash & Arthur Jenkins), JAD 207 | 12 |
| 10 | 6 | 6 | 6 | **WHITE ROOM** — Cream (Felix Pappalardi), Atco 6617 | 9 |
| 11 | 11 | 33 | 57 | **STORMY** — Classics IV (Buddy Buie), Imperial 66328 | 6 |
| 12 ★ | 17 | 26 | 47 | **I LOVE HOW YOU LOVE ME** — Bobby Vinton (Billy Sherrill), Epic 10397 | 5 |
| 13 ★ | 19 | 46 | 74 | **BOTH SIDES NOW** — Judy Collins (Mark Abramson), Elektra 45639 | 4 |
| 14 | 12 | 10 | 8 | **ELENORE** — Turtles (Chip Douglas), White Whale 276 | 11 |
| 15 | 16 | 17 | 36 | **CHEWY CHEWY** — Ohio Express (Kasenetz-Katz Associates), Buddah 70 | 7 |
| 16 ★ | 34 | — | — | **I HEARD IT THROUGH THE GRAPEVINE** — Marvin Gaye (Norman Whitfield), Tamla 54176 | 2 |
| 17 (Seal) | 9 | 7 | 4 | **LITTLE GREEN APPLES** — O. C. Smith (Jerry Fuller), Columbia 44616 | 16 |
| 18 | 15 | 15 | 10 | **MIDNIGHT CONFESSIONS** — Grassroots (Steve Barri), Dunhill 4144 | 14 |
| 19 ★ | 22 | 31 | 40 | **LITTLE ARROWS** — Leapy Lee (Gordon Mills), Decca 32380 | 8 |
| 20 | 21 | 41 | 48 | **PROMISES, PROMISES** — Dionne Warwick (Burt Bacharach-Hal David), Scepter 12231 | 5 |
| 21 | 27 | 30 | 42 | **BRING IT ON HOME TO ME** — Eddie Floyd (Steve Cropper), Stax 0012 | 7 |
| 22 ★ | 35 | — | — | **SEE SAW** — Aretha Franklin (Jerry Wexler), Atlantic 2574 | 2 |
| 23 | 23 | 37 | 43 | **CYCLES** — Frank Sinatra (Don Costa), Reprise 0764 | 8 |
| 24 | 24 | 27 | 27 | **BANG-SHANG-A-LANG** — Archies (Don Kirshner), Calendar 63-1006 | 10 |
| 25 | 25 | 25 | 26 | **HI-HEEL SNEAKERS** — Jose Feliciano (Rick Jarrard), RCA Victor 47-9641 | 7 |
| 26 ★ | 39 | 45 | — | **CLOUD NINE** — Temptations (Norman Whitfield), Gordy 7081 | 3 |
| 27 | 13 | 12 | 11 | **OVER YOU** — Gary Puckett & the Union Gap (Jerry Fuller), Columbia 44644 | 11 |
| 28 | 28 | 34 | 34 | **QUICK JOEY SMALL (Run Joey Run)** — Kasenetz-Katz Singing Orchestral Circus (Kasenetz-Katz Associates), Buddah 64 | 9 |
| 29 | 18 | 18 | 37 | **ALWAYS TOGETHER** — Dells (Bobby Miller), Cadet 5621 | 8 |
| 30 ★ | 46 | 51 | 69 | **SHAME, SHAME** — Magic Lanterns (Steve Rowland), Atlantic 2560 | 6 |
| 31 | 32 | 43 | 45 | **LES BICYCLETTES DE BELSIZE** — Engelbert Humperdinck (Peter Sullivan), Parrot 40032 | 7 |
| 32 | 20 | 11 | 9 | **FIRE** — Crazy World of Arthur Brown (Kit Lambert), Track 2556 | 13 |
| 33 | 26 | 13 | 13 | **SWEET BLINDNESS** — Fifth Dimension (Bones Howe), Soul City 768 | 10 |
| 34 | 37 | 50 | 60 | **CINNAMON** — Derek (George Tobin & Johnny Cymbal), Bang 558 | 6 |
| 35 ★ | 48 | 48 | 53 | **BATTLE HYMN OF THE REPUBLIC** — Andy Williams with the St. Charles Borromeo Choir (Andy Williams), Columbia 44650 | 7 |
| 36 | 41 | 49 | 54 | **THE STRAIGHT LIFE** — Bobby Goldsboro (Bob Montgomery & Bobby Goldsboro), United Artists 50461 | 6 |
| 37 ★ | 42 | 42 | 56 | **PICKIN' WILD MOUNTAIN BERRIES** — Peggy Scott & Jo Jo Benson (Shelby S. Singleton Jr. & Bob McRee), SSS Int'l 748 | 7 |
| 38 | 38 | 55 | 59 | **DO SOMETHING TO ME** — Tommy James & the Shondells (Tommy James), Roulette 7024 | 8 |
| 39 ★ | 47 | 47 | 73 | **TOO WEAK TO FIGHT** — Clarence Carter (Rick Hall & Staff), Atlantic 2569 | 4 |
| 40 | 36 | 52 | 52 | **1432 FRANKLIN PIKE CIRCLE HERO** — Bobby Russell (Buzz Cason & Bobby Russell), Elf 90020 | 6 |
| 41 ★ | 50 | 76 | — | **SCARBOROUGH FAIR** — Sergio Mendes & Brasil '66 (Sergio Mendes), A&M 986 | 3 |
| 42 ★ | 53 | — | — | **TILL** — Vogues (Dick Glasser), Reprise 0788 | 2 |
| 43 | 52 | 69 | 79 | **NOT ENOUGH INDIANS** — Dean Martin (Jimmy Bowen), Reprise 0780 | 5 |
| 44 | 44 | 61 | 87 | **KENTUCKY WOMAN** — Deep Purple (Derek Lawrence), Tetragrammaton 1508 | 4 |
| 45 | 45 | 53 | 68 | **GOODY GOODY GUMDROPS** — 1910 Fruitgum Co. (Kasenetz-Katz Associates), Buddah 71 | 6 |
| 46 ★ | 58 | 68 | 71 | **SHAKE** — Shadows of Knight (Kasenetz-Katz Associates), Team 520 | 6 |
| 47 | 56 | 81 | — | **PUT YOUR HEAD ON MY SHOULDER** — Lettermen (Al de Lory), Capitol 2324 | 3 |
| 48 | 51 | 58 | 72 | **PEACE BROTHER PEACE** — Bill Medley (Medley Prod.), MGM 14000 | 6 |
| 49 | 55 | 60 | 75 | **GOODBYE MY LOVE** — James Brown (James Brown), King 6198 | 4 |
| 50 | 54 | 54 | 65 | **THE STAR-SPANGLED BANNER** — Jose Feliciano, RCA Victor 47-9665 | 5 |
| 51 ★ | 66 | 66 | 94 | **HANG 'EM HIGH** — Booker T. & M.G.'s (Booker T. & M.G.'s), Stax 0013 | 4 |
| 52 ★ | 60 | 63 | 84 | **FIRE** — Five by Five (Gene Kent), Paula 302 | 5 |
| 53 | 61 | — | — | **I CAN'T TURN YOU LOOSE** — Chambers Brothers (Tim O'Brien), Columbia 44679 | 2 |
| 54 | 62 | 84 | — | **PEOPLE** — Tymes (Jimmy "Wiz" Wisner), Columbia 44630 | 3 |
| 55 ★ | 72 | 72 | 76 | **SLOW DRAG** — Intruders (Gamble-Huff), Gamble 221 | 4 |
| 56 ★ | 92 | 93 | — | **BALLAD OF TWO BROTHERS** — Autry Inman (Glenn Sutton & Billy Sherrill), Epic 10389 | 3 |
| 57 ★ | — | — | — | **PAPA'S GOT A BRAND NEW BAG** — Otis Redding, Atco 6636 | 1 |
| 58 | 69 | 97 | — | **HOOKED ON A FEELING** — B. J. Thomas (Chips Moman), Scepter 12230 | 3 |
| 59 | 59 | 57 | 64 | **FROM THE TEACHER TO THE PREACHER** — Gene Chandler & Barbara Acklin (Carl Davis), Brunswick 55387 | 7 |
| 60 | 65 | 65 | 89 | **TALKING ABOUT MY BABY** — Gloria Walker (Eugene Davis), Flaming Arrow 35 | 5 |
| 61 ★ | 100 | — | — | **LO MUCHO QUE TE QUIERO (The More I Love You)** — Rene & Rene, White Whale 287 | 2 |
| 62 ★ | — | — | — | **SON-OF-A PREACHER MAN** — Dusty Springfield (Jerry Wexler, Tom Dowd, Arif Mardin), Atlantic 2580 | 1 |
| 63 | 63 | — | — | **RIGHT RELATIONS** — Johnny Rivers (Johnny Rivers), Imperial 66335 | 2 |
| 64 | 64 | 64 | 81 | **THE YARD WENT ON FOREVER** — Richard Harris (Jimmy Webb), Dunhill 4170 | 5 |
| 65 ★ | — | — | — | **SOULFUL STRUT** — Young-Holt Unlimited (Carl Davis & Eugene Record), Brunswick 55391 | 1 |
| 66 | 70 | 88 | 88 | **I WALK ALONE** — Marty Robbins (Bob Johnston), Columbia 44633 | 6 |
| 67 | 67 | 90 | 90 | **CALIFORNIA EARTHQUAKE** — Mama Cass (John Simon), Dunhill 4166 | 5 |
| 68 | 68 | 74 | 95 | **SUNDAY SUN** — Neil Diamond (Tom Catalano & Neil Diamond), UNI 55084 | 5 |
| 69 | 77 | 77 | — | **ROCKIN' IN THE SAME OLD BOAT** — Bobby Bland, Duke 440 | 3 |
| 70 | 71 | 71 | 91 | **CROWN OF CREATION** — Jefferson Airplane (Al Schmitt), RCA Victor 47-9644 | 5 |
| 71 | 73 | 79 | 98 | **STAND BY YOUR MAN** — Tammy Wynette (Billy Sherrill), Epic 10398 | 4 |
| 72 ★ | 96 | 96 | 96 | **I PUT A SPELL ON YOU** — Creedence Clearwater Revival (Saul Zaentz), Fantasy 617 | 4 |
| 73 ★ | — | — | — | **CROSSTOWN TRAFFIC** — Jimi Hendrix Experience (Jimi Hendrix), Reprise 0792 | 1 |
| 74 | 74 | 82 | 82 | **MORNIN' GLORY** — Bobbie Gentry & Glen Campbell (Kelly Gordon & Al de Lory), Capitol 2314 | 6 |
| 75 | 76 | 78 | — | **A MAN AND A HALF** — Wilson Pickett (Tom Dowd), Atlanta 2575 | 3 |
| 76 | 79 | — | — | **AMERICAN BOYS** — Petula Clark (Tony Hatch), Warner Bros.-Seven Arts 7244 | 2 |
| 77 ★ | — | — | — | **MY SONG** — Aretha Franklin (Jerry Wexler), Atlantic 2574 | 1 |
| 78 ★ | 99 | — | — | **DON'T CRY MY LOVE** — Impressions (Johnny Pate), ABC 11135 | 2 |
| 79 | 75 | 75 | 97 | **LET'S MAKE A PROMISE** — Peaches & Herb (Gamble-Huff), Date 1623 | 4 |
| 80 | 85 | 86 | — | **WITH A LITTLE HELP FROM MY FRIENDS** — Joe Cocker (Denny Cordell), A&M 991 | 3 |
| 81 | 81 | — | — | **LOVE MACHINE** — O'Kaysions (Johnny Pate), ABC 11153 | 2 |
| 82 | 82 | — | — | **CHITTY CHITTY BANG BANG** — Paul Mauriat, Philips 40574 | 2 |
| 83 | 83 | — | — | **THE OL' RACE TRACK** — Mills Brothers (Tom Mack), Dot 17162 | 2 |
| 84 | 84 | — | — | **COO COO** — Big Brother & the Holding Company (Bob Shad), Mainstream 678 | 2 |
| 85 | 80 | 80 | 86 | **SWEET DARLIN'** — Martha Reeves & the Vandellas (Richard Morris), Gordy 7080 | 5 |
| 86 | 86 | 99 | 99 | **COME ON, REACT** — Fireballs (Norman Petty), Atco 6614 | 5 |
| 87 ★ | 89 | 89 | — | **JUST AIN'T NO LOVE** — Barbara Acklin (Carl Davis-Eugene Record), Brunswick 55388 | 3 |
| 88 | 88 | — | — | **DO YOU WANNA DANCE** — Mamas & Papas (Lou Adler), Dunhill 4171 | 2 |
| 89 | 90 | — | — | **KEEP ON DANCING** — Alvin Cash (A. Williams & H. Scott), Toddlin' Town 111 | 2 |
| 90 ★ | 91 | 91 | — | **BABY LET'S WAIT** — Royal Guardsmen (Gernard-Bromidge-Fuller), Laurie 3461 | 3 |
| 91 | — | — | — | **GOOD TIME GIRL** — Nancy Sinatra (Billy Strange), Reprise 0789 | 1 |
| 92 | — | — | — | **DON'T MAKE THE GOOD GIRLS GO BAD** — Della Humphrey (Reid-Corbitt), Arctic 144 | 1 |
| 93 | — | — | — | **EVERYDAY PEOPLE** — Sly & Family Stone (Sly Stone), Epic 10407 | 1 |
| 94 | 95 | 95 | — | **I'VE GOT LOVE FOR MY BABY** — Young Hearts (Bobby Sanders & Soultown Prod.), Minit 32049 | 3 |
| 95 | 94 | — | — | **LIVING IN THE U.S.A.** — Steve Miller Band (Steve Miller & Glyn Johns), Capitol 2287 | 2 |
| 96 | 97 | — | — | **BORN TO BE WITH YOU** — Sonny James (Kelso Herston), Capitol 2271 | 2 |
| 97 | 98 | — | — | **WHITE HOUSES** — Eric Burdon & the Animals (Everyone of Us), MGM 14013 | 2 |
| 98 | — | — | — | **THIS IS MY COUNTRY** — Impressions (Curtis Mayfield), Curtom 1934 | 1 |
| 99 | — | — | — | **BELLA LINDA** — Grassroots (Steve Barri), Dunhill 4162 | 1 |
| 100 | — | — | — | **IF I CAN DREAM** — Elvis Presley, RCA Victor 47-9670 | 1 |

## HOT 100—A TO Z —(Publisher-Licensee)

Abraham, Martin and John (Roznique/Sanphil, BMI) ... 5
Always Together (Chevis, BMI) ... 29
American Boys (Duchess, BMI) ... 76
Baby Let's Wait (Web IV, BMI) ... 90
Ballad of Two Brothers (Tree, BMI) ... 56
Bang-Shang-A-Lang (Kirshner, BMI) ... 24
Battle Hymn of the Republic (Public Domain) ... 35
Bella Linda (Vintage, ASCAP) ... 99
Both Sides Now (Siquomb, BMI) ... 13
Born to Be With You (Mayfair, ASCAP) ... 96
Bring It on Home to Me (Kags, BMI) ... 21
California Earthquake (Glaser, BMI) ... 67
Chewy Chewy (Peanut Butter/Kaskat, BMI) ... 15
Chitty Chitty Bang Bang (Unart, BMI) ... 82
Cinnamon (Pamco, BMI) ... 34
Cloud Nine (Jobete, BMI) ... 26
Come On, React (Dundee, BMI) ... 86
Coo Coo (Public Domain, BMI) ... 84
Crosstown Traffic (Bella Godive, BMI) ... 73
Crown of Creation (Icebag, BMI) ... 70
Cycles (Irving, BMI) ... 23
Do Something to Me (Patricia/Kahoona Tunes, BMI) 38
Do You Wanna Dance (Clockus, BMI) ... 88
Don't Cry My Love (Camad, BMI) ... 78
Don't Make the Good Girls Go Bad (Dandelion, BMI) 92
Elenore (Ishmael/Blimp, BMI) ... 14
Everyday People (Daly City, BMI) ... 93
Fire (Crazy World of Arthur Brown) (Track, BMI) .. 32
Fire (Five by Five) (Sea-Lark, BMI) ... 52
For Once in My Life (Stevie Wonder) (Stein & Van Stock, ASCAP) ... 7
1432 Franklin Pike Circle Hero (Russell-Cason, ASCAP) ... 40
From the Teacher to the Preacher (BRC/Jalynne, BMI) ... 59
Goodbye My Love (Dynatone, BMI) ... 49
Good Time Girl (Bootique, ASCAP) ... 91
Goody Goody Gumdrops (Kaskat, BMI) ... 45
Hang 'Em High (Unart, BMI) ... 51
Hey Jude (Maclen, BMI) ... 2
Hi-Heel Sneakers (Medal, BMI) ... 25
Hold Me Tight (Nash, ASCAP) ... 12
Hooked on a Feeling (Press, BMI) ... 58
I Can't Turn You Loose (East/Time/Redwel, BMI) .. 53
I Heard It Through the Grapevine (Jobete, BMI) ... 16
I Love How You Love Me (Screen Gems-Columbia, BMI) ... 12
I Put a Spell on You (Shalimar, BMI) ... 72
I Walk Alone (Adams-Vee & Abbott, BMI) ... 66
If I Can Dream (Gladys, ASCAP) ... 100
I've Got Love for My Baby (Metric/Lenoir, BMI) ... 94
Just Ain't No Love (Dakar/BRC, BMI) ... 87
Keep on Dancing (Vapac, BMI) ... 89
Kentucky Woman (Tallyrand, BMI) ... 44
Les Bicyclettes de Belsize (W-7, ASCAP) ... 31
Let's Make a Promise (World War III/Downstairs, BMI) ... 79
Little Arrows (Duchess, BMI) ... 19
Little Green Apples (Russell-Cason, ASCAP) ... 17
Living in the U.S.A. (Ohio River Valley, BMI) ... 95
Lo Mucho Que Te Quiero (The More I Love You) (Pecos, BMI) ... 61
Love Child (Jobete, BMI) ... 1
Love Machine (Pamco/Rascal/Yvonne, BMI) ... 81
Magic Carpet Ride (Trousdale, BMI) ... 3
A Man and a Half (Fame, BMI) ... 75
Midnight Confessions (Little Fugitive, BMI) ... 18
Mornin' Glory (Shayne, ASCAP) ... 74
My Song (Lion of Houston, BMI) ... 77
Not Enough Indians (Pomona, BMI) ... 43
Ol' Race Track, The (Notable, ASCAP) ... 83
Over You (Viva, BMI) ... 27
Papa's Got a Brand New Bag (Lois, Togoc, BMI) ... 57
Peace Brother Peace (Screen Gems-Columbia, BMI).. 48
People (Chappell, ASCAP) ... 54
Pickin' Wild Mountain Berries (Crazy Cajun, BMI).. 37
Promises, Promises (Blue Seas/Jac/Morris, ASCAP).. 20
Put Your Head on My Shoulder (Spanka, BMI) ... 47
Quick Joey Small (Run Joey Run) (T.M., BMI) ... 28
Right Relations (Rivers, BMI) ... 63
Rockin' in the Same Old Boat (Don, BMI) ... 69
Scarborough Fair (Charing Cross, BMI) ... 41
See Saw (Cotillion/East, BMI) ... 22
Shake (Kaskat/Peanut Butter, BMI) ... 46
Shame, Shame (4 Star, BMI) ... 30
Slow Drag (Razor Sharp, BMI) ... 55
Son-of-a Preacher Man (Tree, BMI) ... 62
Soulful Strut (Dakar/BRC, BMI) ... 65
Stand by Your Man (Gallico, BMI) ... 71
Star-Spangled Banner, The (Public Domain) ... 50
Stormy (Low-Sal, BMI) ... 11
Straight Life, The (Viva, BMI) ... 36
Sunday Sun (Stonebridge, BMI) ... 68
Sweet Blindness (Tuna Fish, BMI) ... 33
Sweet Darlin' (Jobete, BMI) ... 85
Talking About My Baby (Flaming Arrow, BMI) ... 60
This Is My Country (Camad, BMI) ... 98
Those Were the Days (T.R.O., ASCAP) ... 4
Till (Chappell, ASCAP) ... 42
Too Weak to Fight (Fame, BMI) ... 39
White Houses (Burdon/Noma, BMI) ... 97
White Room (Casserole, BMI) ... 10
Who's Making Love (East, BMI) ... 6
Wichita Lineman (Canopy, ASCAP) ... 8
With a Little Help From My Friends (Maclen, BMI).. 80
Yard Went on Forever, The (Canopy, ASCAP) ... 64

## BUBBLING UNDER THE HOT 100

101. MAIN STREET ... Gary Lewis & the Playboys, Liberty 56073
102. THEY DON'T MAKE LOVE LIKE THEY USED TO ... Eddy Arnold, RCA Victor 47-9667
103. SOCK IT TO 'EM JUDGE ... Pigmeat Markham, Chess 2059
104. MELINDA ... Bobby Taylor & the Vancouvers, Gordy 7079
105. YESTERDAY'S RAIN ... Spanky & Our Gang, Mercury 72871
106. A RAY OF HOPE ... Rascals, Atlantic 2584
107. TODAY ... Jimmie Rodgers, A&M 991
108. THE WORM ... Jimmy McGriff, Solid State 2524
109. GOING UP THE COUNTRY ... Canned Heat, Liberty 56077
110. STAND BY ME ... Quicksilver Messenger Service, Capitol 2320
111. CONTINUING STORY OF HARPER VALLEY P.T.A. ... Dee Mullins, SSS Int'l 749
112. EDGE OF REALITY ... Elvis Presley, RCA Victor 47-9670
113. GOODNIGHT MY LOVE ... Duprees, Heritage 805
114. DON'T BE AFRAID ... Frankie Karl & the Dreams, D.C. 180
115. REACH OUT ... Merrilee Rush, AGP 107
116. CALIFORNIA DREAMIN' ... Bobby Womack, Minit 32055
117. WHERE DID YOU COME FROM ... Buckinghams, Columbia 44672
118. GIRL MOST LIKELY ... Jeannie C. Riley, Plantation
119. LOOKING BACK ... Joe Simon, Sound Stage 78622
120. NIGHTMARE ... Crazy World of Arthur Brown, Track 2582
121. HE'S BAD, BAD, BAD ... Betty Wright, Alston 4571
122. HONEY DO ... Strangeloves, Sire 4102
123. THE SPLIT ... Lou Rawls, Capitol 2348
124. VANCE ... Roger Miller, Smash 2197
125. STAY CLOSE TO ME ... Five Stairsteps & Cubie, Curtom 1933
126. KING CROEBUS ... World of Oz, Deram 95034
127. PLEASE SEND ME SOMEONE TO LOVE ... B. B. King, Bluesway 61021
128. WHAT THE WORLD NEEDS NOW ... Sweet Inspirations, Atlantic 2571
129. THE THOUGHT OF LOVING YOU ... Crystal Mansion, Capitol 2275

HOT 100

HOT 100

Compiled from national retail sales and radio station airplay by the Music Popularity Dept. of Record Market Research, Billboard.

# Billboard HOT 100

**FOR WEEK ENDING DECEMBER 7, 1968**

★ STAR PERFORMER—Sides registering greatest proportionate upward progress this week.

● Record Industry Association of America seal of certification as million selling single.

| THIS WEEK | Last Week | 2 Wks. Ago | 3 Wks. Ago | TITLE — Artist (Producer), Label & Number | Weeks On Chart |
|---|---|---|---|---|---|
| 1 (Billboard Award) | 1 | 2 | 3 | LOVE CHILD — Diana Ross & Supremes (Clan), Motown 1135 | 8 |
| 2 ● | 2 | 1 | 1 | HEY JUDE — Beatles (George Martin), Apple 2276 | 13 |
| 3 ★ | 7 | 14 | 14 | FOR ONCE IN MY LIFE — Stevie Wonder (Henry Cosby), Tamla 54174 | 6 |
| 4 ★ | 16 | 34 | — | I HEARD IT THROUGH THE GRAPEVINE — Marvin Gaye (Norman Whitfield), Tamla 54176 | 3 |
| 5 ● | 6 | 8 | 8 | WHO'S MAKING LOVE — Johnnie Taylor (Don Davis), Stax 0009 | 8 |
| 6 | 3 | 4 | 4 | MAGIC CARPET RIDE — Steppenwolf (Gabriel Mekler), Dunhill 4160 | 10 |
| 7 | 5 | 5 | 9 | ABRAHAM, MARTIN AND JOHN — Dion (Laurie Prod.-Phil Gernhard Prod.), Laurie 3464 | 6 |
| 8 | 8 | 10 | 23 | WICHITA LINEMAN — Glen Campbell (Al de Lory), Capitol 2302 | 6 |
| 9 | 11 | 11 | 33 | STORMY — Classics IV (Buddy Buie), Imperial 66328 | 9 |
| 10 ● | 4 | 3 | 2 | THOSE WERE THE DAYS — Mary Hopkin (Paul McCartney), Apple 1801 | 11 |
| 11 | 12 | 17 | 26 | I LOVE HOW YOU LOVE ME — Bobby Vinton (Billy Sherrill), Epic 10397 | 6 |
| 12 | 9 | 7 | 5 | HOLD ME TIGHT — Johnny Nash (Johnny Nash & Arthur Jenkins), JAD 207 | 13 |
| 13 | 13 | 19 | 46 | BOTH SIDES NOW — Judy Collins (Mark Abramson), Elektra 45639 | 5 |
| 14 | 10 | 6 | 6 | WHITE ROOM — Cream (Felix Pappalardi), Atco 6617 | 10 |
| 15 ★ | 26 | 39 | 45 | CLOUD NINE — Temptations (Norman Whitfield), Gordy 7081 | 4 |
| 16 | 19 | 22 | 31 | LITTLE ARROWS — Leapy Lee (Gordon Mills), Decca 32380 | 9 |
| 17 | 22 | 35 | — | SEE SAW — Aretha Franklin (Jerry Wexler), Atlantic 2574 | 3 |
| 18 | 21 | 27 | 30 | BRING IT ON HOME TO ME — Eddie Floyd (Steve Cropper), Stax 0012 | 8 |
| 19 | 20 | 21 | 41 | PROMISES, PROMISES — Dionne Warwick (Burt Bacharach-Hal David), Scepter 12231 | 6 |
| 20 | 15 | 16 | 17 | CHEWY CHEWY — Ohio Express (Kasenetz-Katz Associates), Buddah 70 | 8 |
| 21 ● | 17 | 9 | 7 | LITTLE GREEN APPLES — O. C. Smith (Jerry Fuller), Columbia 44616 | 17 |
| 22 | 24 | 24 | 27 | BANG-SHANG-A-LANG — Archies (Don Kirshner), Calendar 63-1006 | 11 |
| 23 | 18 | 15 | 15 | MIDNIGHT CONFESSIONS — Grassroots (Steve Barri), Dunhill 4144 | 15 |
| 24 | 34 | 37 | 50 | CINNAMON — Derek (George Tobin & Johnny Cymbal), Bang 558 | 7 |
| 25 | 28 | 28 | 34 | QUICK JOEY SMALL (Run Joey Run) — Kasenetz-Katz Singing Orchestral Circus (Kasenetz-Katz Associates), Buddah 64 | 10 |
| 26 ★ | 41 | 50 | 76 | SCARBOROUGH FAIR — Sergio Mendes & Brasil '66 (Sergio Mendes), A&M 986 | 4 |
| 27 | 37 | 42 | 42 | PICKIN' WILD MOUNTAIN BERRIES — Peggy Scott & Jo Jo Benson (Shelby S. Singleton Jr. & Bob McRee), SSS Int'l 748 | 5 |
| 28 ★ | 39 | 47 | 47 | TOO WEAK TO FIGHT — Clarence Carter (Rick Hall & Staff), Atlantic 2569 | 5 |
| 29 | 23 | 23 | 37 | CYCLES — Frank Sinatra (Don Costa), Reprise 0764 | 6 |
| 30 | 30 | 46 | 51 | SHAME, SHAME — Magic Lanterns (Steve Rowland), Atlantic 2560 | 7 |
| 31 ★ | 65 | — | — | SOULFUL STRUT — Young-Holt Unlimited (Carl Davis & Eugene Record), Brunswick 55391 | 2 |
| 32 | 14 | 12 | 10 | ELENORE — Turtles (Chip Douglas), White Whale 276 | 12 |
| 33 | 35 | 48 | 48 | BATTLE HYMN OF THE REPUBLIC — Andy Williams with the St. Charles Borromeo Choir (Andy Williams), Columbia 44650 | 8 |
| 34 | 49 | 55 | 60 | GOODBYE MY LOVE — James Brown (James Brown), King 6198 | 5 |
| 35 | 42 | 53 | — | TILL — Vogues (Dick Glasser), Reprise 0788 | 3 |
| 36 | 36 | 41 | 49 | THE STRAIGHT LIFE — Bobby Goldsboro (Bob Montgomery & Bobby Goldsboro), United Artists 50461 | 7 |
| 37 | 25 | 25 | 25 | HI-HEEL SNEAKERS — Jose Feliciano (Rick Jarrard), RCA Victor 47-9641 | 9 |
| 38 ★ | 44 | 44 | 61 | KENTUCKY WOMAN — Deep Purple (Derek Lawrence), Tetragrammaton 1508 | 5 |
| 39 | 31 | 32 | 43 | LES BICYCLETTES DE BELSIZE — Engelbert Humperdinck (Peter Sullivan), Parrot 40032 | 8 |
| 40 | 45 | 45 | 53 | GOODY GOODY GUMDROPS — 1910 Fruitgum Co. (Kasenetz-Katz Associates), Buddah 71 | 5 |
| 41 ★ | 58 | 69 | 97 | HOOKED ON A FEELING — B. J. Thomas (Chips Moman), Scepter 12230 | 4 |
| 42 ★ | 51 | 66 | 66 | HANG 'EM HIGH — Booker T. & M.G.'s (Booker T. & M.G.'s), Stax 0013 | 5 |
| 43 | 43 | 52 | 69 | NOT ENOUGH INDIANS — Dean Martin (Jimmy Bowen), Reprise 0780 | 6 |
| 44 ★ | 61 | 100 | — | LO MUCHO QUE TE QUIERO (The More I Love You) — Rene & Rene (White Whale 287) | 3 |
| 45 | 53 | 61 | — | I CAN'T TURN YOU LOOSE — Chambers Brothers (Tim O'Brien), Columbia 44679 | 3 |
| 46 | 46 | 58 | 68 | SHAKE — Shadows of Knight (Kasenetz-Katz Associates), Team 520 | 7 |
| 47 | 47 | 56 | 81 | PUT YOUR HEAD ON MY SHOULDER — Lettermen (Al de Lory), Capitol 2324 | 4 |
| 48 | 48 | 51 | 58 | PEACE BROTHER PEACE — Bill Medley (Medley Prod.), MGM 14000 | 5 |
| 49 ★ | 62 | — | — | SON-OF-A PREACHER MAN — Dusty Springfield (Tom Dowd, Jerry Wexler & Arif Mardin), Atlantic 2580 | 2 |
| 50 | 57 | — | — | PAPA'S GOT A BRAND NEW BAG — Otis Redding (Steve Cropper), Atco 6636 | 2 |
| 51 | 40 | 36 | 52 | 1432 FRANKLIN PIKE CIRCLE HERO — Bobby Russell (Buzz Cason & Bobby Russell), Elf 90020 | 9 |
| 52 | 52 | 60 | 63 | FIRE — Five by Five (Gene Kent), Paula 302 | 5 |
| 53 | 38 | 38 | 55 | DO SOMETHING TO ME — Tommy James & the Shondells (Tommy James), Roulette 7024 | 9 |
| 54 | 54 | 62 | 84 | PEOPLE — Tymes (Jimmy "Wiz" Wisner), Columbia 44630 | 4 |
| 55 | 55 | 72 | 72 | SLOW DRAG — Intruders (Gamble-Huff), Gamble 221 | 5 |
| 56 | 56 | 92 | 93 | BALLAD OF TWO BROTHERS — Autry Inman (Glenn Sutton & Billy Sherrill), Epic 10389 | 4 |
| 57 ★ | — | — | — | I'M GONNA MAKE YOU LOVE ME — Diana Ross & Supremes & Temptations (F. Wilson & N. Ashford), Motown 1137 | 1 |
| 58 ★ | — | — | — | A RAY OF HOPE — Rascals (Felix Cavaliere & Arif Mardin), Atlantic 2584 | 1 |
| 59 | 77 | — | — | MY SONG — Aretha Franklin (Jerry Wexler), Atlantic 2574 | 2 |
| 60 | 60 | 65 | 65 | TALKING ABOUT MY BABY — Gloria Walker (Eugene Davis), Flaming Arrow 35 | 4 |
| 61 | 63 | 63 | — | RIGHT RELATIONS — Johnny Rivers (Johnny Rivers), Imperial 66335 | 3 |
| 62 | 59 | 59 | 57 | FROM THE TEACHER TO THE PREACHER — Gene Chandler & Barbara Acklin (Carl Davis), Brunswick 55387 | 8 |
| 63 ★ | 100 | — | — | IF I CAN DREAM — Elvis Presley, RCA Victor 47-9670 | 2 |
| 64 | 70 | 71 | 71 | CROWN OF CREATION — Jefferson Airplane (Al Schmitt), RCA Victor 47-9644 | 6 |
| 65 | 69 | 77 | 77 | ROCKIN' IN THE SAME OLD BOAT — Bobby Bland (Duke 440) | 4 |
| 66 | 66 | 70 | 88 | I WALK ALONE — Marty Robbins (Bob Johnston), Columbia 44633 | 7 |
| 67 | 71 | 73 | 79 | STAND BY YOUR MAN — Tammy Wynette (Billy Sherrill), Epic 10398 | 5 |
| 68 | 75 | 76 | 78 | A MAN AND A HALF — Wilson Pickett (Tom Dowd), Atlantic 2575 | 4 |
| 69 ★ | 98 | — | — | THIS IS MY COUNTRY — Impressions (Curtis Mayfield), Curtom 1934 | 2 |
| 70 | 64 | 64 | 64 | THE YARD WENT ON FOREVER — Richard Harris (Jimmy Webb), Dunhill 4170 | 6 |
| 71 | 78 | 99 | — | DON'T CRY MY LOVE — Impressions (Johnny Pate), ABC 11135 | 3 |
| 72 | 72 | 96 | 96 | I PUT A SPELL ON YOU — Creedence Clearwater Revival (Saul Zaentz), Fantasy 617 | 3 |
| 73 | 73 | — | — | CROSSTOWN TRAFFIC — Jimi Hendrix Experience (Jimi Hendrix), Reprise 0792 | 2 |
| 74 ★ | — | — | — | GOING UP THE COUNTRY — Canned Heat (Canned Heat & Skip Taylor), Liberty 56077 | 1 |
| 75 | 76 | 79 | — | AMERICAN BOYS — Petula Clark (Tony Hatch), Warner Bros.-Seven Arts 7244 | 3 |
| 76 | 80 | 85 | 86 | WITH A LITTLE HELP FROM MY FRIENDS — Joe Cocker (Denny Cordell), A&M 991 | 4 |
| 77 | 81 | 81 | — | LOVE MACHINE — O'Kaysions (Johnny Pate), ABC 11153 | 3 |
| 78 | 93 | — | — | EVERYDAY PEOPLE — Sly & Family Stone (Sly Stone), Epic 10407 | 2 |
| 79 | 89 | 90 | — | KEEP ON DANCING — Alvin Cash (A. Williams & H. Scott), Toddlin' Town 111 | 3 |
| 80 ★ | — | — | — | MALINDA — Bobby Taylor & Vancouvers (Robinson, Johnson, Cleveland), Gordy 7079 | 1 |
| 81 ★ | 96 | 97 | — | BORN TO BE WITH YOU — Sonny James (Kelso Herston), Capitol 2271 | 3 |
| 82 | 82 | 82 | — | CHITTY CHITTY BANG BANG — Paul Mauriat, Philips 40574 | 3 |
| 83 | 90 | 91 | 91 | BABY LET'S WAIT — Royal Guardsmen (Gernard-Bromidge-Fuller), Laurie 3461 | 4 |
| 84 | 84 | 84 | — | COO COO — Big Brother & the Holding Company (Bob Shad), Mainstream 678 | 3 |
| 85 ★ | — | — | — | THE GIRL MOST LIKELY — Jeannie C. Riley (Shelby S. Singleton Jr.), Plantation 7 | 1 |
| 86 | 86 | 86 | 99 | COME ON, REACT — Fireballs (Norman Petty), Atco 6614 | 6 |
| 87 | 97 | 89 | 89 | JUST AIN'T NO LOVE — Barbara Acklin (Carl Davis-Eugene Record), Brunswick 55388 | 4 |
| 88 | 88 | 88 | — | DO YOU WANNA DANCE — Mamas & Papas (Lou Adler), Dunhill 4171 | 3 |
| 89 ★ | — | — | — | REACH OUT — Merrilee Rush (Tommy Cogbill), AGP 107 | 1 |
| 90 | 99 | — | — | BELLA LINDA — Grassroots (Steve Barri), Dunhill 4162 | 2 |
| 91 | 91 | — | — | GOOD TIME GIRL — Nancy Sinatra (Billy Strange), Reprise 0789 | 2 |
| 92 | 92 | — | — | DON'T MAKE THE GOOD GIRLS GO BAD — Della Humphrey (Reid-Corbitt), Arctic 144 | 2 |
| 93 | 97 | 98 | — | WHITE HOUSES — Eric Burdon & the Animals (Everyone of Us), MGM 14013 | 3 |
| 94 ★ | — | — | — | READY OR NOT HERE I COME (Can't Hide From Love) — Delfonics (Stan & Bell Prod.), Philly Groove 154 | 1 |
| 95 ★ | — | — | — | YESTERDAY'S RAIN — Spanky & Our Gang (Schorf/Dorough), Mercury 72871 | 1 |
| 96 | — | — | — | ARE YOU HAPPY — Jerry Butler (Gamble-Huff), Mercury 72876 | 1 |
| 97 | — | — | — | CALIFORNIA DREAMIN' — Bobby Womack (Chips Moman), Minit 32055 | 1 |
| 98 | — | — | — | LOOKIN' BACK — Joe Simon (J.R. Enterprises), Sound Stage 7-2622 | 1 |
| 99 | — | — | — | THEY DON'T MAKE LOVE LIKE THEY USED TO — Eddy Arnold (Chet Atkins), RCA Victor 47-9667 | 1 |
| 100 | — | — | — | VANCE — Roger Miller (Jerry Kennedy), Smash 2197 | 1 |

## BUBBLING UNDER THE HOT 100

101. DON'T PAT ME ON THE BACK AND CALL ME BROTHER....Kasandra, Capitol 2342
102. PLEASE SEND ME SOMEBODY TO LOVE....Bluesway 61021
103. HE'S BAD BAD BAD....Betty Wright, Alston 4571
104. TODAY....Jimmie Rogers, A&M 991
105. I CAN'T HELP IT (If I'm Still in Love With You)....Al Martino, Capitol 2355
106. SHOUT Part I....Chambers Brothers, Vault 945
107. STAY CLOSE TO ME....Five Stairsteps and Cubie, Curtom 1933
108. THE WORM....Jimmy McGriff, Solid State 2524
109. BLUEBIRDS OVER THE MOUNTAIN....Beach Boys, Capitol 2360
110. NIGHTMARE....Crazy World of Arthur Brown, Track 2582
111. L.A. BREAKDOWN (And Take Me In)....Jack Jones, RCA Victor 47-9687
112. DON'T BE AFRAID (Do as I Say)....Frankie Carl & the Dreams, D.C. 180
113. THINGS I'D LIKE TO SAY....New Colony Six, Mercury 72858
114. RELEASE ME....Johnny Adams, SSS Int'l 750
115. YOU GOT THE POWER....Esquires, Wand 1193
116. THE THOUGHT OF LOVING YOU....Crystal Mansion, Capitol 2275
117. (I'm Into Looking For) SOMEONE TO LOVE ME....Bobby Vee, Liberty 56080
118. CANDY KID (From the Mission on the Bowery)....Cowsills, MGM 14001
119. ONLY FOR LOVERS....Roger Williams, Kapp 949
120. MY FAVORITE THINGS....Herb Alpert & the Tijuana Brass, A&M 1001
121. ISN'T IT LONELY TOGETHER....O. C. Smith, Columbia 4-44705
122. SEASON OF THE WITCH, Part I....Vanilla Fudge, Atco 6632
123. DANCE AT ST. FRANCIS....Barracuda, RCA 47-9660

Compiled from national retail sales and radio station airplay by the Music Popularity Dept. of Record Market Research, Billboard.

# Billboard HOT 100

FOR WEEK ENDING DECEMBER 14, 1968

★ STAR PERFORMER—Sides registering greatest proportionate upward progress this week.

(Seal) Record Industry Association of America seal of certification as million selling single.

| This Week | 1 Wk. Ago | 2 Wks. Ago | 3 Wks. Ago | TITLE Artist (Producer), Label & Number | Weeks On Chart |
|---|---|---|---|---|---|
| 1 (Billboard Award) | 4 | 16 | 34 | I HEARD IT THROUGH THE GRAPEVINE — Marvin Gaye (Norman Whitfield), Tamla 54176 | 4 |
| 2 | 1 | 1 | 2 | LOVE CHILD — Diana Ross & Supremes (Clan), Motown 1135 | 9 |
| 3 | 3 | 7 | 14 | FOR ONCE IN MY LIFE — Stevie Wonder (Henry Cosby), Tamla 54174 | 7 |
| 4 | 7 | 5 | 5 | ABRAHAM, MARTIN AND JOHN — Dion (Laurie Prod.-Phil Gernhard Prod.), Laurie 3464 | 8 |
| 5 (seal) | 5 | 6 | 8 | WHO'S MAKING LOVE — Johnnie Taylor (Don Davis), Stax 0009 | 8 |
| 6 (seal) | 2 | 2 | 1 | HEY JUDE — Beatles (George Martin), Apple 2276 | 14 |
| 7 | 8 | 8 | 10 | WICHITA LINEMAN — Glen Campbell (Al de Lory), Capitol 2302 | 7 |
| 8 | 9 | 11 | 11 | STORMY — Classics IV, (Buddy Buie), Imperial 66328 | 8 |
| 9 | 11 | 12 | 17 | I LOVE HOW YOU LOVE ME — Bobby Vinton (Billy Sherrill), Epic 10397 | 7 |
| 10 | 6 | 3 | 4 | MAGIC CARPET RIDE — Steppenwolf (Gabriel Mekler), Dunhill 4160 | 11 |
| 11 | 13 | 13 | 19 | BOTH SIDES NOW — Judy Collins (Mark Abramson), Elektra 45639 | 6 |
| 12 (seal) | 10 | 4 | 3 | THOSE WERE THE DAYS — Mary Hopkin (Paul McCartney), Apple 1801 | 12 |
| ★13 | 15 | 26 | 39 | CLOUD NINE — Temptations (Norman Whitfield), Gordy 7081 | 5 |
| ★14 | 17 | 22 | 35 | SEE SAW — Aretha Franklin (Jerry Wexler), Atlantic 2574 | 4 |
| 15 | 20 | 15 | 16 | CHEWY CHEWY — Ohio Express (Kasenetz-Katz Associates), Buddah 70 | 9 |
| ★16 | 26 | 41 | 50 | SCARBOROUGH FAIR — Sergio Mendes & Brasil '66 (Sergio Mendes), A&M 986 | 5 |
| ★17 | 24 | 34 | 37 | CINNAMON — Derek (George Tobin & Johnny Cymbal), Bang 558 | 8 |
| 18 | 18 | 21 | 27 | BRING IT ON HOME TO ME — Eddie Floyd (Steve Cropper), Stax 0012 | 9 |
| 19 | 12 | 9 | 7 | HOLD ME TIGHT — Johnny Nash (Johnny Nash & Arthur Jenkins), JAD 207 | 14 |
| ★20 | 57 | — | — | I'M GONNA MAKE YOU LOVE ME — Diana Ross & Supremes & Temptations (F. Wilson & N. Ashford), Motown 1137 | 2 |
| 21 | 16 | 19 | 22 | LITTLE ARROWS — Leapy Lee (Gordon Mills), Decca 32380 | 10 |
| 22 | 19 | 20 | 21 | PROMISES, PROMISES — Dionne Warwick (Burt Bacharach-Hal David), Scepter 12231 | 7 |
| ★23 | 41 | 58 | 69 | HOOKED ON A FEELING — B. J. Thomas (Chips Moman), Scepter 12230 | 5 |
| ★24 | 31 | 65 | — | SOULFUL STRUT — Young-Holt Unlimited (Carl Davis & Eugene Record), Brunswick 55391 | 3 |
| 25 | 22 | 24 | 24 | BANG-SHANG-A-LANG — Archies (Jeff Barry), Calendar 63-1006 | 12 |
| 26 | 14 | 10 | 6 | WHITE ROOM — Cream (Felix Pappalardi), Atco 6617 | 11 |
| 27 | 27 | 37 | 42 | PICKIN' WILD MOUNTAIN BERRIES — Peggy Scott & Jo Jo Benson (Shelby S. Singleton Jr. & Bob McRee), SSS Int'l 748 | 9 |
| 28 | 28 | 39 | 47 | TOO WEAK TO FIGHT — Clarence Carter (Bick Hall & Staff), Atlantic 2569 | 6 |
| 29 | 35 | 42 | 53 | TILL — Vogues (Dick Glasser), Reprise 0788 | 4 |
| 30 | 30 | 30 | 46 | SHAME, SHAME — Magic Lanterns (Steve Rowland), Atlantic 2560 | 8 |
| 31 | 34 | 49 | 55 | GOODBYE MY LOVE — James Brown (James Brown), King 6198 | 6 |
| ★32 | 44 | 61 | 100 | LO MUCHO QUE TE QUIERO (The More I Love You) — Rene & Rene, White Whale 287 | 4 |
| ★33 | 50 | 57 | — | PAPA'S GOT A BRAND NEW BAG — Otis Redding, Atco 6636 | 3 |
| 34 | 25 | 28 | 28 | QUICK JOEY SMALL (Run Joey Run) — Kasenetz-Katz Singing Orchestral Circus (Kasenetz-Katz Associates), Buddah 64 | 11 |
| 35 | 29 | 23 | 23 | CYCLES — Frank Sinatra (Don Costa), Reprise 0764 | 10 |
| ★36 | 49 | 62 | — | SON-OF-A PREACHER MAN — Dusty Springfield (Jerry Wexler, Tom Dowd, Arif Mardin), Atlantic 2580 | 3 |
| 37 | 40 | 45 | 45 | GOODY GOODY GUMDROPS — 1910 Fruitgum Co. (Kasenetz-Katz Associates), Buddah 71 | 8 |
| 38 | 38 | 44 | 44 | KENTUCKY WOMAN — Deep Purple (Derek Lawrence), Tetragrammaton 1508 | 6 |
| ★39 | 58 | — | — | A RAY OF HOPE — Rascals (Felix Cavaliere & Arif Mardin), Atlantic 2584 | 2 |
| ★40 | 63 | 100 | — | IF I CAN DREAM — Elvis Presley, RCA Victor 47-9670 | 3 |
| 41 | 42 | 51 | 66 | HANG 'EM HIGH — Booker T. & M.G.'s (Booker T. & M.G.'s), Stax 0013 | 6 |
| ★42 | 68 | 75 | 76 | A MAN AND A HALF — Wilson Pickett (Tom Dowd), Atlanta 2575 | 5 |
| 43 | 43 | 43 | 52 | NOT ENOUGH INDIANS — Dean Martin (Jimmy Bowen), Reprise 0780 | 7 |
| 44 | 45 | 53 | 61 | I CAN'T TURN YOU LOOSE — Chambers Brothers (Tim O'Brien), Columbia 44679 | 4 |
| 45 | 33 | 35 | 48 | BATTLE HYMN OF THE REPUBLIC — Andy Williams with the St. Charles Borromeo Choir (Andy Williams), Columbia 44650 | 9 |
| 46 | 47 | 47 | 56 | PUT YOUR HEAD ON MY SHOULDER — Lettermen (Al de Lory), Capitol 2324 | 5 |
| 47 | 39 | 31 | 32 | LES BICYCLETTES DE BELSIZE — Engelbert Humperdinck (Peter Sullivan), Parrot 40032 | 9 |
| 48 | 56 | 56 | 92 | BALLAD OF TWO BROTHERS — Autry Inman (Glenn Sutton & Billy Sherrill), Epic 10389 | 5 |
| 49 | 36 | 36 | 41 | THE STRAIGHT LIFE — Bobby Goldsboro (Bob Montgomery & Bobby Goldsboro), United Artists 50461 | 8 |
| ★50 | 69 | 98 | — | THIS IS MY COUNTRY — Impressions (Curtis Mayfield), Curtom 1934 | 3 |
| ★51 | 67 | 71 | 73 | STAND BY YOUR MAN — Tammy Wynette (Billy Sherrill), Epic 10398 | 6 |
| ★52 | 74 | — | — | GOING UP THE COUNTRY — Canned Heat (Canned Heat & Skip Taylor), Liberty 56077 | 2 |
| 53 | 54 | 54 | 62 | PEOPLE — Tymes (Jimmy "Wiz" Wisner), Columbia 44630 | 5 |
| 54 | 55 | 55 | 72 | SLOW DRAG — Intruders (Gamble-Huff), Gamble 221 | 6 |
| ★55 | 59 | 77 | — | MY SONG — Aretha Franklin (Jerry Wexler), Atlantic 2574 | 3 |
| 56 | 46 | 46 | 58 | SHAKE — Shadows of Knight (Kasenetz-Katz Associates), Team 520 | 8 |
| 57 | 52 | 52 | 60 | FIRE — Five by Five (Gene Kent), Paula 302 | 7 |
| ★58 | 90 | 99 | — | BELLA LINDA — Grassroots (Steve Barri), Dunhill 4162 | 3 |
| ★59 | 72 | 72 | 96 | I PUT A SPELL ON YOU — Creedence Clearwater Revival (Saul Zaentz), Fantasy 617 | 6 |
| 60 | 60 | 60 | 65 | TALKING ABOUT MY BABY — Gloria Walker (Eugene Davis), Flaming Arrow 35 | 7 |
| ★61 | 73 | 73 | — | CROSSTOWN TRAFFIC — Jimi Hendrix Experience (Jimi Hendrix), Reprise 0792 | 3 |
| ★62 | 75 | 76 | 79 | AMERICAN BOYS — Petula Clark (Tony Hatch), Warner Bros.-Seven Arts 7244 | 4 |
| ★63 | 86 | 86 | 86 | COME ON, REACT — Fireballs (Norman Petty), Atco 6614 | 7 |
| 64 | 65 | 69 | 77 | ROCKIN' IN THE SAME OLD BOAT — Bobby Bland, Duke 440 | 5 |
| 65 | 66 | 66 | 70 | I WALK ALONE — Marty Robbins (Bob Johnston), Columbia 44633 | 8 |
| ★66 | 94 | — | — | READY OR NOT HERE I COME (Can't Hide From Love) — Delfonics (Stan & Bell Prod.), Philly Groove 154 | 2 |
| ★67 | 80 | — | — | MALINDA — Bobby Taylor & Vancouvers (Robinson, Johnson, Cleveland), Gordy 7079 | 2 |
| 68 | 76 | 80 | 85 | WITH A LITTLE HELP FROM MY FRIENDS — Joe Cocker (Denny Cordell), A&M 991 | 5 |
| ★69 | 83 | 90 | 91 | BABY LET'S WAIT — Royal Guardsmen (Gernard-Bromidge-Fuller), Laurie 3461 | 5 |
| ★70 | 87 | 87 | 89 | JUST AIN'T NO LOVE — Barbara Acklin (Carl Davis-Eugene Record), Brunswick 55388 | 5 |
| 71 | 71 | 78 | 99 | DON'T CRY MY LOVE — Impressions (Johnny Pate), ABC 11135 | 4 |
| 72 | 78 | 93 | — | EVERYDAY PEOPLE — Sly & Family Stone (Sly Stone), Epic 10407 | 3 |
| 73 | 79 | 89 | 90 | KEEP ON DANCING — Alvin Cash (A. Williams & H. Scott), Toddlin' Town 111 | 4 |
| ★74 | — | — | — | BLUEBIRDS OVER THE MOUNTAIN — Beach Boys (Bruce Johnston-Carl Wilson), Capitol 2360 | 1 |
| ★75 | — | — | — | MY FAVORITE THINGS — Herb Alpert & Tijuana Brass (Herb Alpert-Jerry Moss) A&M 1001 | 1 |
| ★76 | 88 | 88 | 88 | DO YOU WANNA DANCE — Mamas & Papas (Lou Adler), Dunhill 4171 | 4 |
| 77 | 77 | 81 | 81 | LOVE MACHINE — O'Kaysions (Johnny Pate), ABC 11153 | 4 |
| ★78 | 96 | — | — | ARE YOU HAPPY — Jerry Butler (Gamble-Huff), Mercury 72876 | 2 |
| 79 | 92 | 92 | — | DON'T MAKE THE GOOD GIRLS GO BAD — Della Humphrey (Reid-Corbitt), Arctic 144 | 3 |
| ★80 | — | — | — | ISN'T IT LONELY TOGETHER — O. C. Smith (Jerry Fuller) Columbia 4-44705 | 1 |
| 81 | 81 | 96 | 97 | BORN TO BE WITH YOU — Sonny James (Kelso Herston), Capitol 2271 | 4 |
| 82 | 82 | 82 | 82 | CHITTY CHITTY BANG BANG — Paul Mauriat, Philips 40574 | 4 |
| 83 | 85 | — | — | THE GIRL MOST LIKELY — Jeannie C. Riley (Shelby S. Singleton Jr.), Plantation 7 | 2 |
| 84 | 91 | 91 | — | GOOD TIME GIRL — Nancy Sinatra (Billy Strange), Reprise 0789 | 3 |
| ★85 | — | — | — | CRIMSON & CLOVER — Tommy James & the Shondells (Tommy James) Roulette R-7028 | 1 |
| ★86 | — | — | — | THE BEGINNING OF MY END — Unifics (Guy Draper) Kapp 957 | 1 |
| ★87 | — | — | — | (There's Gonna Be a) SHOWDOWN — Archie Bell & the Drells (Gamble-Huff) Atlantic 2583 | 1 |
| 88 | 93 | 97 | 98 | WHITE HOUSES — Eric Burdon & the Animals (Everyone of Us), MGM 14013 | 4 |
| 89 | 89 | — | — | REACH OUT — Merrilee Rush (Tommy Cogbill), AGP 107 | 2 |
| ★90 | — | — | — | YOU GOT SOUL — Johnny Nash (Johnny Nash & Arthur Jenkins) Jad 209 | 1 |
| 91 | 98 | — | — | LOOKIN' BACK — Joe Simon (J.R. Enterprises), Sound Stage 7-2622 | 2 |
| 92 | 97 | — | — | CALIFORNIA DREAMIN' — Bobby Womack (Chips Moman), Minit 32055 | 2 |
| 93 | — | — | — | DON'T BE AFRAID (Do as I Say) — Frankie Karl & the Dreams (Gene Dozier) D.C. 180 | 1 |
| 94 | — | — | — | I'VE GOTTA BE ME — Sammy Davis Jr. (Jimmy Bowen) Reprise 0779 | 1 |
| 95 | 95 | — | — | YESTERDAY'S RAIN — Spanky & Our Gang (Schorf/Dorough), Mercury 72871 | 2 |
| 96 | — | — | — | RELEASE ME — Johnny Adams (Watch Record Co.) SSS International 750 | 1 |
| 97 | — | — | — | THE WORM — Jimmy McGriff (Sonny Lerster) Solid State 2524 | 1 |
| 98 | — | — | — | DON'T PAT ME ON THE BACK AND CALL ME BROTHER — Kasandra (Kelly Gordon) Capitol 2342 | 1 |
| 99 | 99 | — | — | THEY DON'T MAKE LOVE LIKE THEY USED TO — Eddy Arnold (Chet Atkins), RCA Victor 47-9667 | 2 |
| 100 | 100 | — | — | VANCE — Roger Miller (Jerry Kennedy), Smash 2197 | 2 |

## HOT 100—A TO Z—(Publisher-Licensee)

| | |
|---|---|
| Abraham, Martin and John (Roznique/Sanphil, BMI) | 4 |
| American Boys (Duchess, BMI) | 62 |
| Are You Happy (World War III/Parabut, BMI) | 78 |
| Baby Let's Wait (Web IV, BMI) | 69 |
| Ballad of Two Brothers (Tree, BMI) | 48 |
| Bang-Shang-A-Lang (Kirschner, BMI) | 25 |
| Battle Hymn of the Republic (Public Domain) | 45 |
| Bella Linda (Vintage, ASCAP) | 58 |
| The Beginning of My End (Cuydra, BMI) | 86 |
| Bluebirds Over the Mountain (Torpedo, BMI) | 74 |
| Both Sides Now (Siquomb, BMI) | 11 |
| Born to Be With You (Mayfair, ASCAP) | 81 |
| Bring It on Home to Me (Kags, BMI) | 18 |
| California Dreamin' (Honest John, ASCAP) | 92 |
| Chewy Chewy (Peanut Butter/Kaskat, BMI) | 15 |
| Chitty Chitty Bang Bang (Unart, BMI) | 82 |
| Cinnamon (Pamco, BMI) | 17 |
| Cloud Nine (Jobete, BMI) | 13 |
| Come On, React (Dundee, BMI) | 63 |
| Crimson & Clover (Big Seven Music, BMI) | 85 |
| Crosstown Traffic (Bella Godive, BMI) | 61 |
| Cycles (Irving, BMI) | 35 |
| Do You Wanna Dance (Clockus, BMI) | 76 |
| Don't Be Afraid (Do As I Say) (Proud Tunes, BMI) | 93 |
| Don't Cry My Love (Comad, BMI) | 71 |
| Don't Make the Good Girls Go Bad (Dandelion, BMI) | 78 |
| Don't Pat Me on the Back and Call Me Brother (Meaningful/Footboat, BMI) | 98 |
| Everyday People (Daly City, BMI) | 72 |
| Fire (Five by Five) (Sea-Lark, BMI) | 57 |
| For Once in My Life (Stevie Wonder) (Stein & Van Stock, ASCAP) | 3 |
| Girl Most Likely, The (Singleton, BMI) | 83 |
| Going Up the Country (Metric, BMI) | 52 |
| Goodbye My Love (Dynatone, BMI) | 31 |
| Good Time Girl (Bootique, ASCAP) | 84 |
| Goody Goody Gumdrops (Kaskat, BMI) | 37 |
| Hang 'Em High (Unart, BMI) | 41 |
| Hey Jude (Maclen, BMI) | 6 |
| Hold Me Tight (Nash, ASCAP) | 19 |
| Hooked on a Feeling (Press, BMI) | 23 |
| I Can't Turn You Loose (East/Time/Redwel, BMI) | 44 |
| I Heard It Through the Grapevine (Jobete, BMI) | 1 |
| I Love How You Love Me (Screen Gems-Columbia, BMI) | 9 |
| I Put a Spell on You (Shalimar, BMI) | 59 |
| I Walk Alone (Adams-Vee & Abbott, BMI) | 65 |
| If I Can Dream (Gladys, ASCAP) | 40 |
| Isn't It Lonely Together (Ahab, BMI) | 80 |
| I'm Gonna Make You Love Me (Act Three, BMI) | 20 |
| I've Gotta Be Me (Damila, ASCAP) | 94 |
| I've Got Love for My Baby (Metric/Lenoir, BMI) | 94 |
| Just Ain't No Love (Dakar/BRC, BMI) | 70 |
| Keep on Dancing (Vapac, BMI) | 73 |
| Kentucky Woman (Tallyrand, BMI) | 38 |
| Les Bicyclettes de Belsize (W-7, ASCAP) | 47 |
| Little Arrows (Duchess, BMI) | 21 |
| Lo Mucho Que Te Quiero (The More I Love You) (Pecos, BMI) | 32 |
| Looking Back (Eden/Sweco, BMI) | 91 |
| Love Child (Jobete, BMI) | 2 |
| Love Machine (Pamco/Rascal/Yvonne, BMI) | 77 |
| Magic Carpet Ride (Trousdale, BMI) | 10 |
| Malinda (Jobete, BMI) | 67 |
| Man and a Half, A (Fame, BMI) | 42 |
| My Favorite Things (Williamson, BMI) | 75 |
| My Song (Lion of Houston, BMI) | 55 |
| Not Enough Indians (Pomona, BMI) | 43 |
| Papa's Got a Brand New Bag (Lois, Togoc, BMI) | 33 |
| People (Chappell, ASCAP) | 53 |
| Pickin' Wild Mountain Berries (Crazy Cajun, BMI) | 27 |
| Promises, Promises (Blue Seas/Jac/Morris, ASCAP) | 22 |
| Put Your Head on My Shoulder (Spanka/BMI) | 46 |
| Quick Joey Small (Run Joey Run) (T.M., BMI) | 34 |
| Ray of Hope (Slascar, ASCAP) | 39 |
| Reach Out (Jobete, BMI) | 89 |
| Ready or Not Here I Come (Can't Hide From Love) (Nickel Shoe, BMI) | 66 |
| Release Me (4 Star Sales, BMI) | 96 |
| Rockin' in the Same Old Boat (Don, BMI) | 64 |
| Scarborough Fair (Charing Cross, BMI) | 16 |
| See Saw (Cotillion/East, BMI) | 14 |
| Shake (Kaskat/Peanut Butter, BMI) | 56 |
| Shame, Shame (4 Star, BMI) | 30 |
| Slow Drag (Razor Sharp, BMI) | 54 |
| Son-of-a Preacher Man (Tree, BMI) | 36 |
| Soulful Strut (Dakar/RC, BMI) | 24 |
| Stand by Your Man (Gallico, BMI) | 51 |
| Stormy (Low-Sal, BMI) | 8 |
| Straight Life, The (Viva, BMI) | 49 |
| Talking About My Baby (Flaming Arrow, BMI) | 60 |
| "There's Gonna Be a" Showdown (Downstairs/Double Diamond, BMI) | 87 |
| They Don't Make Love Like They Used To (Tree, BMI) | 99 |
| This Is My Country (Camad, BMI) | 50 |
| Those Were the Days (T.R.O., ASCAP) | 12 |
| Till (Chappell, ASCAP) | 29 |
| Too Weak to Fight (Fame, BMI) | 28 |
| Vance (Russell-Cason, ASCAP) | 100 |
| White Houses (Burdon/Noma, BMI) | 88 |
| White Room (Casserole, BMI) | 26 |
| Who's Making Love (East, BMI) | 5 |
| Wichita Lineman (Canopy, ASCAP) | 7 |
| With a Little Help From My Friends (Maclen, BMI) | 68 |
| The Worm (Jell, BMI) | 97 |
| Yesterday's Rain (Ridge, BMI) | 95 |
| You Got Soul (Johnny Nash, ASCAP) | 90 |

## BUBBLING UNDER THE HOT 100

101. RAMBLIN' GAMBLIN' MAN....Bob Seger, Capitol 2297
102. WORST THAT COULD HAPPEN....Brooklyn Bridge, Buddah 75
103. I STARTED A JOKE....Bee Gees, Atco 6639
104. AIN'T GOT NO/I GOT LIFE....Nina Simone, RCA 47-9686
105. I CAN'T HELP IT (If I'm Still in Love With You)...Al Martino, Capitol 2355
106. SHOUT PART I....Chambers Brothers, Vault 945
107. STAY CLOSE TO ME....Five Stairsteps & Cubie, Curtom 1933
108. NIGHTMARE....Crazy World of Arthur Brown, Track 2582
109. SEASON OF THE WITCH....Vanilla Fudge, Atco 6632
110. CAN I CHANGE MY MIND....Tyrone Davis, Dakar 602
111. L.A. BREAKDOWN (And Take Me In)....Jack Jones, RCA 47-9687
112. YOU GOT THE POWER....Esquires, Wand 1193
113. THINGS I'D LIKE TO SAY....New Colony Six, Mercury 72858
114. BY THE TIME I GET TO PHOENIX/SAY A LITTLE PRAYER....Dee Irwin & Mamie Galore, Imperial 66334
115. DANCE AT ST. FRANCIS....Barracuda, RCA 47-9660
116. THOUGHT OF LOVING YOU....Crystal Mansion, Capitol 2275
117. (I'm Into Looking For) SOMEONE TO LOVE ME....Bobby Vee, Liberty 56080
118. CANDY KID (From the Mission on the Bowery)....Cowsills, MGM 14001
119. ONLY FOR LOVERS....Roger Williams, Kapp 949
120. HONEY DO....Strangeloves, Sire 4102
121. SOCK IT TO ME, PART I....Deacons, Shama 102
122. IN A LONG WHITE ROOM....Nancy Wilson, Capitol 2361
123. FIFTY-TWO PERCENT....Max Frost & the Troopers, Tower 452
124. GAMES PEOPLE PLAY....Joe South, Capitol 2248
125. ELOISE....Barry Ryan, MGM 14010
126. I GOT A LINE ON YOU....Spirit, Ode 115
127. A MINUTE OF YOUR TIME....Tom Jones, Parrot 40035
128. RAINBOW RIDE....Andy Kim, Steed 711
129. KAY....John Wesley Ryles, Columbia 4-44682
130. FLY WITH ME....Avant Garde, Columbia 4-4470
131. ELECTRIC STORIES....Four Seasons, Philips 40577
132. SHE'S A LADY....John Sebastian, Kama Sutra 254

Compiled from national retail sales and radio station airplay by the Music Popularity Dept. of Record Market Research, Billboard.

# Billboard HOT 100

FOR WEEK ENDING DECEMBER 21, 1968

★ STAR PERFORMER—Sides registering greatest proportionate upward progress this week.

Record Industry Association of America seal of certification as million selling single.

| This Week | 1 Wk. Ago | 2 Wks. Ago | 3 Wks. Ago | TITLE Artist (Producer), Label & Number | Weeks On Chart |
|---|---|---|---|---|---|
| 1 (Billboard Award) | 1 | 4 | 16 | I HEARD IT THROUGH THE GRAPEVINE — Marvin Gaye (Norman Whitfield), Tamla 54176 | 5 |
| 2 | 2 | 1 | 1 | LOVE CHILD — Diana Ross & Supremes (Clan), Motown 1135 | 10 |
| 3 | 3 | 3 | 7 | FOR ONCE IN MY LIFE — Stevie Wonder (Henry Cosby), Tamla 54174 | 8 |
| 4 | 4 | 7 | 5 | ABRAHAM, MARTIN AND JOHN — Dion (Laurie Prod.-Phil Gernhard Prod.), Laurie 3464 | 9 |
| ★5 | 7 | 8 | 8 | WICHITA LINEMAN — Glen Campbell (Al de Lory), Capitol 2302 | 8 |
| ★6 | 8 | 9 | 11 | STORMY — Classics IV, (Buddy Buie), Imperial 66328 | 9 |
| 7 | 5 | 5 | 6 | WHO'S MAKING LOVE — Johnnie Taylor (Don Davis), Stax 0009 | 9 |
| ★8 | 11 | 13 | 13 | BOTH SIDES NOW — Judy Collins (Mark Abramson), Elektra 45639 | 7 |
| 9 | 9 | 11 | 12 | I LOVE HOW YOU LOVE ME — Bobby Vinton (Billy Sherrill), Epic 10397 | 8 |
| 10 | 10 | 6 | 3 | MAGIC CARPET RIDE — Steppenwolf (Gabriel Mekler), Dunhill 4160 | 12 |
| 11 | 6 | 2 | 2 | HEY JUDE — Beatles (George Martin), Apple 2276 | 15 |
| 12 | 13 | 15 | 26 | CLOUD NINE — Temptations (Norman Whitfield), Gordy 7081 | 6 |
| ★13 | 17 | 24 | 34 | CINNAMON — Derek (George Tobin & Johnny Cymbal), Bang 558 | 9 |
| 14 | 14 | 17 | 22 | SEE SAW — Aretha Franklin (Jerry Wexler), Atlantic 2574 | 5 |
| 15 | 15 | 20 | 15 | CHEWY CHEWY — Ohio Express (Kasenetz-Katz Associates), Buddah 70 | 10 |
| 16 | 16 | 26 | 41 | SCARBOROUGH FAIR — Sergio Mendes & Brasil '66 (Sergio Mendes), A&M 986 | 6 |
| ★17 | 20 | 57 | — | I'M GONNA MAKE YOU LOVE ME — Diana Ross & Supremes & Temptations (F. Wilson & N. Ashford), Motown 1137 | 3 |
| 18 | 18 | 18 | 21 | BRING IT ON HOME TO ME — Eddie Floyd (Steve Cropper), Stax 0012 | 10 |
| 19 | 12 | 10 | 4 | THOSE WERE THE DAYS — Mary Hopkin (Paul McCartney), Apple 1801 | 13 |
| ★20 | 24 | 31 | 65 | SOULFUL STRUT — Young-Holt Unlimited (Carl Davis & Eugene Record), Brunswick 55391 | 4 |
| 21 | 21 | 16 | 19 | LITTLE ARROWS — Leapy Lee (Gordon Mills), Decca 32380 | 11 |
| 22 | 23 | 41 | 58 | HOOKED ON A FEELING — B. J. Thomas (Chips Moman), Scepter 12230 | 6 |
| 23 | 22 | 19 | 20 | PROMISES, PROMISES — Dionne Warwick (Burt Bacharach-Hal David), Scepter 12231 | 8 |
| ★24 | 36 | 49 | 62 | SON-OF-A PREACHER MAN — Dusty Springfield (Jerry Wexler, Tom Dowd, Arif Mardin), Atlantic 2580 | 4 |
| 25 | 19 | 12 | 9 | HOLD ME TIGHT — Johnny Nash (Johnny Nash & Arthur Jenkins), JAD 207 | 15 |
| ★26 | 52 | 74 | — | GOING UP THE COUNTRY — Canned Heat (Canned Heat & Skip Taylor), Liberty 56077 | 3 |
| 27 | 29 | 35 | 42 | TILL — Vogues (Dick Glasser), Reprise 0788 | 5 |
| 28 | 28 | 28 | 39 | TOO WEAK TO FIGHT — Clarence Carter (Bick Hall & Staff), Atlantic 2569 | 7 |
| 29 | 30 | 30 | 30 | SHAME, SHAME — Magic Lanterns (Steve Rowland), Atlantic 2560 | 9 |
| ★30 | 32 | 44 | 61 | LO MUCHO QUE TE QUIERO (The More I Love You) — Rene & Rene, White Whale 287 | 5 |
| 31 | 33 | 50 | 57 | PAPA'S GOT A BRAND NEW BAG — Otis Redding, Atco 6636 | 4 |
| 32 | 25 | 22 | 24 | BANG-SHANG-A-LANG — Archies (Jeff Barry), Calendar 63-1006 | 13 |
| 33 | 27 | 27 | 27 | PICKIN' WILD MOUNTAIN BERRIES — Peggy Scott & Jo Jo Benson (Shelby S. Singleton Jr. & Bob McRee), SSS Int'l 748 | 10 |
| 34 | 45 | 33 | 35 | BATTLE HYMN OF THE REPUBLIC — Andy Williams with the St. Charles Borromeo Choir (Andy Williams), Columbia 44650 | 10 |
| ★35 | 39 | 58 | — | A RAY OF HOPE — Rascals (Felix Cavaliere & Arif Mardin), Atlantic 2584 | 3 |
| ★36 | 40 | 63 | 100 | IF I CAN DREAM — Elvis Presley, RCA Victor 47-9670 | 4 |
| ★37 | 44 | 45 | 53 | I CAN'T TURN YOU LOOSE — Chambers Brothers (Tim O'Brien), Columbia 44679 | 5 |
| 38 | 38 | 38 | 44 | KENTUCKY WOMAN — Deep Purple (Derek Lawrence), Tetragrammaton 1508 | 7 |
| ★39 | 85 | — | — | CRIMSON & CLOVER — Tommy James & the Shondells (Tommy James) Roulette R-7028 | 2 |
| 40 | 37 | 40 | 45 | GOODY GOODY GUMDROPS — 1910 Fruitgum Co. (Kasenetz-Katz Associates), Buddah 71 | 9 |
| 41 | 41 | 42 | 51 | HANG 'EM HIGH — Booker T. & M.G.'s (Booker T. & M.G.'s), Stax 0013 | 7 |
| 42 | 42 | 68 | 75 | A MAN AND A HALF — Wilson Pickett (Tom Dowd), Atlanta 2575 | 6 |
| 43 | 50 | 69 | 98 | THIS IS MY COUNTRY — Impressions (Curtis Mayfield), Curtom 1934 | 4 |
| 44 | 43 | 43 | 43 | NOT ENOUGH INDIANS — Dean Martin (Jimmy Bowen), Reprise 0780 | 8 |
| 45 | 31 | 34 | 49 | GOODBYE MY LOVE — James Brown (James Brown), King 6198 | 7 |
| 46 | 46 | 47 | 47 | PUT YOUR HEAD ON MY SHOULDER — Lettermen (Al de Lory), Capitol 2324 | 6 |
| ★47 | 75 | — | — | MY FAVORITE THINGS — Herb Alpert & Tijuana Brass (Herb Alpert-Jerry Moss) A&M 1001 | 2 |
| 48 | 48 | 56 | 56 | BALLAD OF TWO BROTHERS — Autry Inman (Glenn Sutton & Billy Sherrill), Epic 10389 | 6 |
| 49 | 58 | 90 | 99 | BELLA LINDA — Grassroots (Steve Barri), Dunhill 4162 | 4 |
| 50 | 69 | 83 | 90 | BABY LET'S WAIT — Royal, Guardsmen (Gernhard-Brumage-Fuller), Laurie 3461 | 6 |
| 51 | 51 | 67 | 71 | STAND BY YOUR MAN — Tammy Wynette (Billy Sherrill), Epic 10398 | 7 |
| 52 | 61 | 73 | 73 | CROSSTOWN TRAFFIC — Jimi Hendrix Experience (Jimi Hendrix), Reprise 0792 | 4 |
| 53 | 53 | 54 | 54 | PEOPLE — Tymes (Jimmy "Wiz" Wisner), Columbia 44630 | 6 |
| 54 | 55 | 59 | 77 | MY SONG — Aretha Franklin (Jerry Wexler), Atlantic 2574 | 4 |
| ★55 | 72 | 78 | 93 | EVERYDAY PEOPLE — Sly & Family Stone (Sly Stone), Epic 10407 | 4 |
| ★56 | 83 | 85 | — | THE GIRLS MOST LIKELY — Jeannie C. Riley (Shelby S. Singleton Jr.), Plantation 7 | 3 |
| 57 | 67 | 80 | — | MALINDA — Bobby Taylor & Vancouvers (Robinson, Johnson, Cleveland), Gordy 7079 | 3 |
| 58 | 54 | 55 | 55 | SLOW DRAG — Intruders (Gamble-Huff), Gamble 221 | 7 |
| 59 | 59 | 72 | 72 | I PUT A SPELL ON YOU — Creedence Clearwater Revival (Saul Zaentz), Fantasy 617 | 7 |
| 60 | 66 | 94 | — | READY OR NOT HERE I COME (Can't Hide From Love) — Delfonics (Stan & Bell Prod.), Philly Groove 154 | 3 |
| ★61 | — | — | — | I STARTED A JOKE — Bee Gees (Robert Stigwood, The Bee Gees), Atco 6639 | 1 |
| 62 | 62 | 75 | 76 | AMERICAN BOYS — Petula Clark (Tony Hatch), Warner Bros.-Seven Arts 7244 | 5 |
| 63 | 63 | 86 | 86 | COME ON, REACT — Fireballs (Norman Petty), Atco 6614 | 8 |
| 64 | 64 | 65 | 69 | ROCKIN' IN THE SAME OLD BOAT — Bobby Bland, Duke 440 | 6 |
| 65 | 84 | 91 | 91 | GOOD TIME GIRL — Nancy Sinatra (Billy Strange), Reprise 0789 | 4 |
| 66 | 73 | 79 | 89 | KEEP ON DANCING — Alvin Cash (A. Williams & H. Scott), Toddlin' Town 111 | 5 |
| 67 | 74 | — | — | BLUEBIRDS OVER THE MOUNTAIN — Beach Boys (Bruce Johnston-Carl Wilson), Capitol 2360 | 2 |
| 68 | 88 | 93 | 97 | WHITE HOUSES — Eric Burdon & the Animals (Everyone of Us), MGM 14013 | 5 |
| 69 | 68 | 76 | 80 | WITH A LITTLE HELP FROM MY FRIENDS — Joe Cocker (Denny Cordell), A&M 991 | 6 |
| 70 | 70 | 87 | 87 | JUST AIN'T NO LOVE — Barbara Acklin (Carl Davis-Eugene Record), Brunswick 55388 | 6 |
| ★71 | 92 | 97 | — | CALIFORNIA DREAMIN' — Bobby Womack (Chips Moman), Minit 32055 | 3 |
| ★72 | — | — | — | CALIFORNIA SOULED — 5th Dimension (Bones Howe), Soul City 770 | 1 |
| ★73 | — | — | — | SEASON OF THE WITCH, Part 1 — Vanilla Fudge (Shadow Morton), Atco 6632 | 1 |
| ★74 | — | — | — | CAN I CHANGE MY MIND — Tyrone Davis (Willie Henderson), Dakar 602 | 1 |
| 75 | 87 | — | — | (There's Gonna Be a) SHOWDOWN — Archie Bell & the Drells (Gamble-Huff) Atlantic 2583 | 2 |
| 76 | 80 | — | — | ISN'T IT LONELY TOGETHER — O. C. Smith (Jerry Fuller) Columbia 4-44705 | 2 |
| 77 | 77 | 77 | 81 | LOVE MACHINE — O'Kaysions (Johnny Pate), ABC 11153 | 5 |
| 78 | 78 | 96 | — | ARE YOU HAPPY — Jerry Butler (Gamble-Huff), Mercury 72876 | 3 |
| 79 | 79 | 92 | 92 | DON'T MAKE THE GOOD GIRLS GO BAD — Della Humphrey (Reid-Corbitt), Arctic 144 | 4 |
| 80 | 76 | 88 | 88 | DO YOU WANNA DANCE — Mamas & Papas (Lou Adler), Dunhill 4171 | 5 |
| ★81 | — | — | — | SOUL SISTER, BROWN SUGAR — Sam & Dave (Hayes & Porter), Atlantic 2590 | 1 |
| 82 | 89 | 89 | — | REACH OUT — Merrilee Rush (Tommy Cogbill), AGP 107 | 3 |
| 83 | 82 | 82 | 82 | CHITTY CHITTY BANG BANG — Paul Mauriat, Philips 40574 | 5 |
| ★84 | — | — | — | RAMBLIN' GAMBLIN' MAN — Bob Seger (Hideout), Capitol 2297 | 1 |
| 85 | 86 | — | — | THE BEGINNING OF MY END — Unifics (Guy Draper) Kapp 957 | 2 |
| 86 | 96 | — | — | RELEASE ME — Johnny Adams (Watch Record Co.) SSS International 750 | 2 |
| ★87 | — | — | — | RAINBOW RIDE — Andy Kim (Jeff Beard), Steed 711 | 1 |
| ★88 | — | — | — | A MINUTE OF YOUR TIME — Tom Jones (Peter Sullivan), Parrot 40035 | 1 |
| 89 | 90 | — | — | YOU GOT SOUL — Johnny Nash (Johnny Nash & Arthur Jenkins) Jad 209 | 2 |
| ★90 | — | — | — | HEY JUDE — Wilson Pickett (Rick Hall), Atlantic 2591 | 1 |
| 91 | 98 | — | — | DON'T PAT ME ON THE BACK AND CALL ME BROTHER — Kasandra (Kelly Gordon) Capitol 2342 | 2 |
| 92 | — | — | — | TIT FOR TAT (Ain't No Taking Back) — James Brown (James Brown), King 6204 | 1 |
| 93 | 94 | — | — | I'VE GOTTA BE ME — Sammy Davis Jr. (Jimmy Bowen) Reprise 0779 | 2 |
| 94 | 95 | 95 | — | YESTERDAY'S RAIN — Spanky & Our Gang (Schorf/Dorough), Mercury 72871 | 3 |
| 95 | — | — | — | STAY CLOSE TO ME — Five Stairsteps & Cubie (Curtis Mayfield), Curton 1933 | 1 |
| 96 | — | — | — | SHOUT, Part 1 — Chambers Brothers (Lucky Young), Vault 945 | 1 |
| 97 | 100 | 100 | — | VANCE — Roger Miller (Jerry Kennedy), Smash 2197 | 3 |
| 98 | — | — | — | WORST THAT COULD HAPPEN — Brooklyn Bridge (Wes Farrell), Buddah 75 | 1 |
| 99 | — | — | — | THOUGHT OF LOVING YOU — Crystal Mansion (Bob Cullen, Dave White, Arthur Kaplan) Capitol 2275 | 1 |
| 100 | — | — | — | CONDITION RED — Goodees (Davis, Briggs), HIP 8005 | 1 |

## HOT 100—A TO Z—(Publisher-Licensee)

A Minute of Your Time (Anne-Rachel, ASCAP) .... 88
Abraham, Martin and John (Roznique/Sanphil, BMI) .... 4
American Boys (Duchess, BMI) .... 62
Are You Happy (World War III/Parabut, BMI) .... 78
Baby Let's Wait (Web IV, BMI) .... 50
Ballad of Two Brothers (Tree, BMI) .... 48
Bang-Shang-A-Lang (Kirschner, BMI) .... 32
Battle Hymn of the Republic (Public Domain) .... 34
Bella Linda (Vintage, ASCAP) .... 49
The Beginning of My End (Cuydra, BMI) .... 85
Bluebirds Over the Mountain (Torpedo, BMI) .... 67
Both Sides Now (Siquomb, BMI) .... 8
Bring It on Home to Me (Kags, BMI) .... 18
Can I Change My Mind (Dakar, BMI) .... 74
California Dreamin' (Honest John, ASCAP) .... 71
California Souled (Mr. Bones, BMI) .... 72
Chewy Chewy (Peanut Butter/Kaskat, BMI) .... 15
Chitty Chitty Bang Bang (Unart, BMI) .... 83
Cinnamon (Pamco, BMI) .... 13
Cloud Nine (Jobete, BMI) .... 12
Come On, React (Dundee, BMI) .... 63
Crimson & Clover (Big Seven Music, BMI) .... 39
Condition Red (East Groovesville, BMI) .... 100
Crosstown Traffic (Bella Godive, BMI) .... 52
Cycles (Irving, BMI) .... 35
Do You Wanna Dance (Clockus, BMI) .... 80
Don't Make the Good Girls Go Bad (Dandelion, BMI) 79
Don't Pat Me on the Back and Call Me Brother (Meaningful/Footboat, BMI) .... 91
Everyday People (Daly City, BMI) .... 55
For Once in My Life (Stevie Wonder) (Stein & Van Stock, ASCAP) .... 3
Girl Most Likely, The (Singleton, BMI) .... 56
Going Up the Country (Metric, BMI) .... 26
Goodbye My Love (Dynatone, BMI) .... 45
Good Time Girl (Bootique, ASCAP) .... 65
Goody Goody Gumdrops (Kaskat, BMI) .... 40
Hang 'Em High (Unart, BMI) .... 41
Hey Jude (Maclen, BMI) (Beatles) .... 11
Hey Jude (Maclen, BMI) (Wilson Pickett) .... 90
Hold Me Tight (Nash, ASCAP) .... 25
Hooked on a Feeling (Press, BMI) .... 22
I Can't Turn You Loose (East/Time/Redwel, BMI) 37
I Heard It Through the Grapevine (Jobete, BMI) 1
I Love How You Love Me (Screen Gems-Columbia, BMI) .... 9
I Put a Spell on You (Shalimar, BMI) .... 59
I Started a Joke (Casserole, BMI) .... 61
If I Can Dream (Gladys, ASCAP) .... 36
Isn't It Lonely Together (Ahab, BMI) .... 76
I'm Gonna Make You Love Me (Act Three, BMI) .. 17
I've Gotta Be Me (Damila, ASCAP) .... 93
Just Ain't No Love (Dakar/BRC, BMI) .... 70
Keep on Dancing (Vapac, BMI) .... 66
Kentucky Woman (Tallyrand, BMI) .... 38
Little Arrows (Duchess, BMI) .... 21
Lo Mucho Que Te Quiero (The More I Love You) (Pecos, BMI) .... 30
Love Child (Jobete, BMI) .... 2
Love Machine (Pamco/Rascal/Yvonne, BMI) .... 77
Magic Carpet Ride (Trousdale, BMI) .... 10
Malinda (Jobete, BMI) .... 57
Man and a Half, A (Fame, BMI) .... 42
My Favorite Things (Williamson, BMI) .... 47
My Song (Lion of Houston, BMI) .... 54
Not Enough Indians (Pomona, BMI) .... 44
Papa's Got a Brand New Bag (Lois, Togoc, BMI).. 31
People (Chappell, ASCAP) .... 53
Pickin' Wild Mountain Berries (Crazy Cajun, BMI) 33
Promises, Promises (Blue Seas/Jac/Morris, ASCAP) 23
Put Your Head on My Shoulder (Spanka/BMI) ... 46
Ramblin' Gamblin' Man (Gear, ASCAP) .... 84
Rainbow Ride (Unart/Joachim, BMI) .... 87
Ray of Hope (Slascar, ASCAP) .... 35
Reach Out (Jobete, BMI) .... 82
Ready or Not Here I Come (Can't Hide From Love) (Nickel Shoe, BMI) .... 60
Release Me (4 Star Sales, BMI) .... 86
Rockin' in the Same Old Boat (Don, BMI) .... 64
Season of the Witch, Part 1 (Peer International, BMI) .... 73
Scarborough Fair (Charing Cross, BMI) .... 16
See Saw (Cotillion/East, BMI) .... 14
Shame, Shame (4 Star, BMI) .... 29
Shout, Part 1 (Wemar/Nom, BMI) .... 96
Slow Drag (Razor Sharp, BMI) .... 58
Son-of-a-Preacher Man (Tree, BMI) .... 24
Soul Sister, Brown Sugar (Walden-Birdees, ASCAP) 81
Soulful Strut (Dakar/RC, BMI) .... 20
Stand by Your Man (Gallico, BMI) .... 51
Stay Close to Me (Camad, BMI) .... 95
Stormy (Low-Sal, BMI) .... 6
"There's Gonna Be a" Showdown (Downstairs/Double Diamond, BMI) .... 75
This Is My Country (Camad, BMI) .... 43
Those Were the Days, (T.R.O., ASCAP) .... 19
Thought of Loving You (Golden Egg, BMI) .... 99
Till (Chappell, ASCAP) .... 27
Tit for Tat (Ain't No Taking Back) (Dynatone, BMI) 92
Too Weak to Fight (Fame, BMI) .... 28
Vance (Russell-Cason, ASCAP) .... 97
White Houses (Burdon/Noma, BMI) .... 68
Who's Making Love (East, BMI) .... 7
Wichita Lineman (Canopy, ASCAP) .... 5
With a Little Help From My Friends (Maclen, BMI) 69
Worst That Could Happen (Rivers, BMI) .... 98
Yesterday's Rain (Ridge, BMI) .... 94
You Got Soul (Johnny Nash, ASCAP) .... 89

## BUBBLING UNDER THE HOT 100

101. LOOKING BACK....Joe Simon, Sound Stage 7 2622
102. THINGS I'D LIKE TO SAY....New Colony Six, Mercury 72858
103. AIN'T GOT NO/I GOT LIFE....Nina Simone, RCA 47-9686
104. THE WORM....Jimmy McGriff, Solid State 2524
105. I CAN'T HELP IT IF I'M STILL IN LOVE WITH YOU....Al Martino, Capitol 2355
106. I FORGOT TO BE YOUR LOVER....William Bell, Stax 0015
107. NIGHTMARE....Crazy World of Arthur Brown, Track 2582
108. DON'T BE AFRAID....Frankie Karl & the Dreams, D.C. 180
109. TRAGEDY....Brian Hyland, Dot 17176
110. L.A. BREAKDOWN (And Let Me In)....Jack Jones, RCA 47-9687
111. I PUT A SPELL ON YOU....Crazy World of Arthur Brown, Track 2582
112. YOU GOT THE POWER....Esquires, Wand 1193
113. DANCE AT ST. FRANCIS....Barracuda, RCA 47-9660
114. SWEET CREAM LADIES....Box Tops, Mala 12,035
115. SATURDAY NIGHT AT THE WORLD....Mason Williams, Warner Bros.-Seven Arts 7248
116. (I'm Into Looking For) SOMEONE TO LOVE ME....Bobby Vee, Liberty 56080
117. THEY DON'T MAKE LOVE LIKE THEY USED TO....Eddy Arnold, RCA 47-9667
118. ELOISE....Barry Ryan, MGM 14010
119. ELECTRIC STORIES....Four Seasons, Philips 40577
120. HONEY DO....Strangeloves, Sire 4102
121. SHE'S A LADY....John Sebastian, Kama Sutra 254
122. GAMES PEOPLE PLAY....Joe South, Capitol 2248
123. FIFTY-TWO PERCENT....Max Frost & the Troopers, Tower 452
124. KAY....John Wesley Ryles, Columbus 4-44682
125. I GOT A LINE ON YOU....Spirit, Ode 115
126. IF IT WASN'T FOR BAD LUCK....Ray Charles & Jimmy Lewis, ABC/TRC 11170
127. GROOVIEST GIRL IN THE WORLD....Fun & Games, Uni 55098
128. I WHO HAVE NOTHING....Linda Jones, Loma 2105
129. THIS MAGIC MOMENT....Jay & the Americans, United Artists 50475
130. FLY WITH ME....Avant Garde, Columbia 4-4470
131. BILLY, YOU'RE MY FRIEND....Gene Pitney, Musicor 1331
132. LONG LINE RIDER....Bobby Darin, Direction 350
133. FEELIN' SO GOOD....Archies, Calendar 63-1007
134. TILL I CAN'T TAKE IT ANY MORE....Ben E. King, Atco 66637

Compiled from national retail sales and radio station airplay by the Music Popularity Dept. of Record Market Research, Billboard.

HOT 100

# Billboard HOT 100

FOR WEEK ENDING DECEMBER 28, 1968

★ STAR PERFORMER—Sides registering greatest proportionate upward progress this week.

◉ Record Industry Association of America seal of certification as million selling single.

| THIS WEEK | 1 Wk. Ago | 2 Wks. Ago | 3 Wks. Ago | TITLE Artist (Producer), Label & Number | Weeks On Chart |
|---|---|---|---|---|---|
| 1 (Billboard Award) | 1 | 1 | 4 | I HEARD IT THROUGH THE GRAPEVINE — Marvin Gaye (Norman Whitfield), Tamla 54176 | 6 |
| 2 | 3 | 3 | 3 | FOR ONCE IN MY LIFE — Stevie Wonder (Henry Cosby), Tamla 54174 | 9 |
| 3 | 2 | 2 | 1 | LOVE CHILD — Diana Ross & Supremes (Clan), Motown 1135 | 11 |
| 4 | 5 | 7 | 8 | WICHITA LINEMAN — Glen Campbell (Al de Lory), Capitol 2302 | 9 |
| 5 | 6 | 8 | 9 | STORMY — Classics IV, (Buddy Buie), Imperial 66328 | 10 |
| 6 | 4 | 4 | 7 | ABRAHAM, MARTIN AND JOHN — Dion (Laurie Prod.-Phil Gernhard Prod.), Laurie 3464 | 10 |
| ★7 | 17 | 20 | 57 | I'M GONNA MAKE YOU LOVE ME — Diana Ross & Supremes & Temptations (F. Wilson & N. Ashford), Motown 1137 | 4 |
| 8 | 7 | 5 | 5 | WHO'S MAKING LOVE — Johnnie Taylor (Don Davis), Stax 0009 | 10 |
| ◉9 | 9 | 9 | 11 | I LOVE HOW YOU LOVE ME — Bobby Vinton (Billy Sherrill), Epic 10397 | 9 |
| ★10 | 12 | 13 | 15 | CLOUD NINE — Temptations (Norman Whitfield), Gordy 7081 | 7 |
| 11 | 8 | 11 | 13 | BOTH SIDES NOW — Judy Collins (Mark Abramson), Elektra 45639 | 8 |
| 12 | 13 | 17 | 24 | CINNAMON — Derek (George Tobin & Johnny Cymbal), Bang 558 | 10 |
| ★13 | 22 | 23 | 41 | HOOKED ON A FEELING — B. J. Thomas (Chips Moman), Scepter 12230 | 7 |
| 14 | 14 | 14 | 17 | SEE SAW — Aretha Franklin (Jerry Wexler), Atlantic 2574 | 6 |
| ◉15 | 11 | 6 | 2 | HEY JUDE — Beatles (George Martin), Apple 2276 | 16 |
| ★16 | 20 | 24 | 31 | SOULFUL STRUT — Young-Holt Unlimited (Carl Davis & Eugene Record), Brunswick 55391 | 5 |
| 17 | 18 | 18 | 18 | BRING IT ON HOME TO ME — Eddie Floyd (Steve Cropper), Stax 0012 | 11 |
| 18 | 10 | 10 | 6 | MAGIC CARPET RIDE — Steppenwolf (Gabriel Mekler), Dunhill 4160 | 13 |
| 19 | 15 | 15 | 20 | CHEWY CHEWY — Ohio Express (Kasenetz-Katz Associates), Buddah 70 | 11 |
| ★20 | 26 | 52 | 74 | GOING UP THE COUNTRY — Canned Heat (Canned Heat & Skip Taylor), Liberty 56077 | 4 |
| ★21 | 24 | 36 | 49 | SON-OF-A PREACHER MAN — Dusty Springfield (Jerry Wexler, Tom Dowd, Arif Mardin), Atlantic 2580 | 5 |
| 22 | 21 | 21 | 16 | LITTLE ARROWS — Leapy Lee (Gordon Mills), Decca 32380 | 12 |
| ★23 | 28 | 28 | 28 | TOO WEAK TO FIGHT — Clarence Carter (Rick Hall & Staff), Atlantic 2569 | 8 |
| ★24 | 31 | 33 | 50 | PAPA'S GOT A BRAND NEW BAG — Otis Redding, Atco 6636 | 5 |
| ◉25 | 19 | 12 | 10 | THOSE WERE THE DAYS — Mary Hopkin (Paul McCartney), Apple 1801 | 14 |
| ★26 | 30 | 32 | 44 | LO MUCHO QUE TE QUIERO (The More I Love You) — Rene & Rene, White Whale 287 | 6 |
| 27 | 16 | 16 | 26 | SCARBOROUGH FAIR — Sergio Mendes & Brasil '66 (Sergio Mendes), A&M 986 | 7 |
| ★28 | 39 | 85 | — | CRIMSON & CLOVER — Tommy James & the Shondells (Tommy James) Roulette R-7028 | 3 |
| 29 | 29 | 30 | 30 | SHAME, SHAME — Magic Lanterns (Steve Rowland), Atlantic 2560 | 10 |
| ★30 | 36 | 40 | 63 | IF I CAN DREAM — Elvis Presley, RCA Victor 47-9670 | 5 |
| 31 | 27 | 29 | 35 | TILL — Vogues (Dick Glasser), Reprise 0788 | 6 |
| 32 | 35 | 39 | 58 | A RAY OF HOPE — Rascals (Felix Cavaliere & Arif Mardin), Atlantic 2584 | 4 |
| 33 | 34 | 45 | 33 | BATTLE HYMN OF THE REPUBLIC — Andy Williams with the St. Charles Borromeo Choir (Andy Williams), Columbia 44650 | 11 |
| ★34 | 51 | 51 | 67 | STAND BY YOUR MAN — Tammy Wynette (Billy Sherrill), Epic 10398 | 8 |
| 35 | 23 | 22 | 19 | PROMISES, PROMISES — Dionne Warwick (Burt Bacharach-Hal David), Scepter 12231 | 9 |
| ★36 | 54 | 55 | 59 | MY SONG — Aretha Franklin (Jerry Wexler), Atlantic 2574 | 5 |
| 37 | 37 | 44 | 45 | I CAN'T TURN YOU LOOSE — Chambers Brothers (Tim O'Brien), Columbia 44679 | 6 |
| ★38 | 43 | 50 | 69 | THIS IS MY COUNTRY — Impressions (Curtis Mayfield), Curtom 1934 | 5 |
| ★39 | 53 | 53 | 54 | PEOPLE — Tymes (Jimmy "Wiz" Wisner), Columbia 44630 | 7 |
| 40 | 41 | 41 | 42 | HANG 'EM HIGH — Booker T. & M.G.'s (Booker T. & M.G.'s), Stax 0013 | 8 |
| ★41 | 61 | — | — | I STARTED A JOKE — Bee Gees (Robert Stigwood, The Bee Gees), Atco 6639 | 2 |
| ★42 | 55 | 72 | 78 | EVERYDAY PEOPLE — Sly & Family Stone (Sly Stone), Epic 10407 | 5 |
| ★43 | 90 | — | — | HEY JUDE — Wilson Pickett (Rick Hall), Atlantic 2591 | 2 |
| 44 | 46 | 46 | 47 | PUT YOUR HEAD ON MY SHOULDER — Lettermen (Al de Lory), Capitol 2324 | 7 |
| 45 | 38 | 38 | 38 | KENTUCKY WOMAN — Deep Purple (Derek Lawrence), Tetragrammaton 1508 | 8 |
| ★46 | 49 | 58 | 90 | BELLA LINDA — Grassroots (Steve Barri), Dunhill 4162 | 5 |
| 47 | 47 | 75 | — | MY FAVORITE THINGS — Herb Alpert & Tijuana Brass (Herb Alpert-Jerry Moss) A&M 1001 | 3 |
| 48 | 50 | 69 | 83 | BABY LET'S WAIT — Royal Guardsmen (Gernhard-Brumage-Fuller), Laurie 3461 | 7 |
| ★49 | 75 | 87 | — | (There's Gonna Be a) SHOWDOWN — Archie Bell & the Drells (Gamble-Huff) Atlantic 2583 | 3 |
| ★50 | 60 | 66 | 94 | READY OR NOT HERE I COME (Can't Hide From Love) — Delfonics (Stan & Bell Prod.), Philly Groove 154 | 4 |
| 51 | 57 | 67 | 80 | MALINDA — Bobby Taylor & Vancouvers (Robinson, Johnson, Cleveland), Gordy 7079 | 4 |
| 52 | 44 | 43 | 43 | NOT ENOUGH INDIANS — Dean Martin (Jimmy Bowen), Reprise 0780 | 9 |
| ★53 | 98 | — | — | WORST THAT COULD HAPPEN — Brooklyn Bridge (Wes Farrell), Buddah 75 | 2 |
| 54 | 48 | 48 | 56 | BALLAD OF TWO BROTHERS — Autry Inman (Glenn Sutton & Billy Sherrill), Epic 10389 | 7 |
| 55 | 56 | 83 | 85 | THE GIRL MOST LIKELY — Jeannie C. Riley (Shelby S. Singleton Jr.), Plantation 7 | 4 |
| 56 | 52 | 61 | 73 | CROSSTOWN TRAFFIC — Jimi Hendrix Experience (Jimi Hendrix), Reprise 0792 | 5 |
| ★57 | 78 | 78 | 96 | ARE YOU HAPPY — Jerry Butler (Gamble-Huff), Mercury 72876 | 4 |
| 58 | 59 | 59 | 72 | I PUT A SPELL ON YOU — Creedence Clearwater Revival (Saul Zaentz), Fantasy 617 | 8 |
| 59 | 62 | 62 | 75 | AMERICAN BOYS — Petula Clark (Tony Hatch), Warner Bros.-Seven Arts 7244 | 6 |
| 60 | 64 | 64 | 65 | ROCKIN' IN THE SAME OLD BOAT — Bobby Bland, Duke 440 | 7 |
| 61 | 67 | 74 | — | BLUEBIRDS OVER THE MOUNTAIN — Beach Boys (Bruce Johnston-Carl Wilson), Capitol 2360 | 3 |
| ★62 | 72 | — | — | CALIFORNIA SOUL — 5th Dimension (Bones Howe), Soul City 770 | 2 |
| ★63 | 76 | 80 | — | ISN'T IT LONELY TOGETHER — O. C. Smith (Jerry Fuller) Columbia 4-44705 | 3 |
| ★64 | — | — | — | DADDY SANG BASS — Johnny Cash (Bob Johnson), Columbia 4-44689 | 1 |
| 65 | 73 | — | — | SEASON OF THE WITCH, Part 1 — Vanilla Fudge (Shadow Morton), Atco 6632 | 2 |
| 66 | 74 | — | — | CAN I CHANGE MY MIND — Tyrone Davis (Willie Henderson), Dakar 602 | 2 |
| 67 | 68 | 88 | 93 | WHITE HOUSES — Eric Burdon & the Animals (Everyone of Us), MGM 14013 | 6 |
| 68 | 70 | 70 | 87 | JUST AIN'T NO LOVE — Barbara Acklin (Carl Davis-Eugene Record), Brunswick 55388 | 7 |
| 69 | 71 | 92 | 97 | CALIFORNIA DREAMIN' — Bobby Womack (Chips Moman), Minit 32055 | 4 |
| ★70 | 81 | — | — | SOUL SISTER, BROWN SUGAR — Sam & Dave (Hayes & Porter), Atlantic 2590 | 2 |
| ★71 | 85 | 86 | — | THE BEGINNING OF MY END — Unifics (Guy Draper), Kapp 957 | 3 |
| ★72 | — | — | — | TOUCH ME — Doors (Paul A. Rothchild), Elektra 45646 | 1 |
| ★73 | 88 | — | — | A MINUTE OF YOUR TIME — Tom Jones (Peter Sullivan), Parrot 40035 | 2 |
| ★74 | 93 | 94 | — | I'VE GOTTA BE ME — Sammy Davis Jr. (Jimmy Bowen) Reprise 0779 | 3 |
| ★75 | 84 | — | — | RAMBLIN' GAMBLIN' MAN — Bob Seger (Hideout), Capitol 2297 | 2 |
| 76 | 77 | 77 | 77 | LOVE MACHINE — O'Kaysions (Johnny Pate), ABC 11153 | 6 |
| 77 | 65 | 84 | 91 | GOOD TIME GIRL — Nancy Sinatra (Billy Strange), Reprise 0789 | 5 |
| 78 | 83 | 82 | 82 | CHITTY CHITTY BANG BANG — Paul Mauriat, Philips 40574 | 6 |
| 79 | 82 | 89 | 89 | REACH OUT — Merrilee Rush (Tommy Cogbill), AGP 107 | 4 |
| ★80 | 97 | 100 | 100 | VANCE — Roger Miller (Jerry Kennedy), Smash 2197 | 4 |
| ★81 | 89 | 90 | — | YOU GOT SOUL — Johnny Nash (Johnny Nash & Arthur Jenkins) Jad 209 | 3 |
| 82 | 86 | 96 | — | RELEASE ME — Johnny Adams (Watch Record Co.) SSS International 750 | 3 |
| ★83 | — | — | — | ELECTRIC STORIES — 4 Seasons (Gaudio-Crewe), Philips 40577 | 1 |
| 84 | 87 | — | — | RAINBOW RIDE — Andy Kim (Jeff Beard), Steed 711 | 2 |
| ★85 | — | — | — | NOT ON THE OUTSIDE — Momcats (Sylvia & L. Roberts), Stang 5000 | 1 |
| 86 | 92 | — | — | TIT FOR TAT (Ain't No Taking Back) — James Brown (James Brown), King 6204 | 2 |
| ★87 | — | — | — | KAY — John Wesley Ryles (George Richey), Columbia 4-44682 | 1 |
| ★88 | — | — | — | FEELIN' SO GOOD — Archies (Jeff Barry), Calender 63-1007 | 1 |
| ★89 | — | — | — | SWEET CREAM LADIES — Box Tops (Chips Moxen/Tommy Cogbill), Mala 12035 | 1 |
| ★90 | — | — | — | THIS MAGIC MOMENT — Jay & the Americans (Jata Ent.), United Artists 50475 | 1 |
| 91 | 95 | — | — | STAY CLOSE TO ME — Five Stairsteps & Cubie (Curtis Mayfield), Curton 1933 | 2 |
| 92 | — | — | — | ELOISE — Barry Ryan (Bill Landis), MGM 14010 | 1 |
| 93 | — | — | — | YOU'VE GOT THE POWER — Esquires (Bunky Prod.), Wand 1193 | 1 |
| 94 | — | — | — | DOES ANYBODY KNOW I'M HERE — Dells (Bobby Miller), Cadet 5631 | 1 |
| 95 | 99 | — | — | THOUGHT OF LOVING YOU — Crystal Mansion (Bob Cullen, Dave White, Arthur Kaplan) Capitol 2275 | 2 |
| 96 | 96 | — | — | SHOUT, Part 1 — Chambers Brothers (Lucky Young), Vault 945 | 2 |
| 97 | 100 | — | — | CONDITION RED — Goodees (Davis, Briggs), HIP 8005 | 2 |
| 98 | — | — | — | (I'm Into Lookin' For) SOMEONE TO LOVE ME — Bobby Vee (Dallas Smith), Liberty 56080 | 1 |
| 99 | — | — | — | I CAN'T HELP IT IF I'M STILL IN LOVE WITH YOU — Al Martino, Capitol 2355 | 1 |
| 100 | — | — | — | THINGS I'D LIKE TO SAY — New Colony Six, Mercury 72858 | 1 |

## HOT 100—A TO Z—(Publisher-Licensee)


A Minute of Your Time (Anne-Rachel, ASCAP) .... 73
Abraham, Martin and John (Roznique/Sanphil, BMI) 6
American Boys (Duchess, BMI) .... 59
Are You Happy (World War III/Parabut, BMI) .... 57

Baby Let's Wait (Web IV, BMI) .... 48
Ballad of Two Brothers (Tree, BMI) .... 54
Battle Hymn of the Republic (Public Domain) .... 33
Bella Linda (Vintage, ASCAP) .... 46
Beginning of My End, The (Cuydra, BMI) .... 71
Bluebirds Over the Mountain (Torpedo, BMI) .... 61
Both Sides Now (Siquomb, BMI) .... 11
Bring It on Home to Me (Kags, BMI) .... 17

Can I Change My Mind (Dakar, BMI) .... 66
California Dreamin' (Honest John, ASCAP) .... 69
California Soul (Jobete, BMI) .... 62
Chewy Chewy (Peanut Butter/Kaskat, BMI) .... 19
Chitty Chitty Bang Bang (Unart, BMI) .... 78
Cinnamon (Pamco, BMI) .... 12
Cloud Nine (Jobete, BMI) .... 10
Crimson & Clover (Big Seven Music, BMI) .... 28
Condition Red (East Groovesville, BMI) .... 87
Crosstown Traffic (Bella Godive, BMI) .... 56

Daddy Sang Bass (House of Cash, BMI) .... 64
Does Anybody Know I'm Here (Chevis, BMI) .... 94

Electric Stories (Screen Gems-Columbia, BMI) .... 83
Eloise (Valley, BMI) .... 92
Everyday People (Daly City, BMI) .... 42

Feelin' So Good (Kirshner, BMI) .... 88
For Once in My Life (Stevie Wonder) (Stein & Van Stock, ASCAP) .... 2

Girl Most Likely, The (Singleton, BMI) .... 55
Going Up the Country (Metric, BMI) .... 20
Good Time Girl (Bootique, ASCAP) .... 77

Hang 'Em High (Unart, BMI) .... 40
Hey Jude (Maclen, BMI) (Beatles) .... 15
Hey Jude (Maclen, BMI) (Wilson Pickett) .... 43
Hooked on a Feeling (Press, BMI) .... 13

I Can't Help It If I'm Still In Love With You (Rose, BMI) .... 99
I Can't Turn You Loose (East/Time/Redwal, BMI) 37
I Heard It Through the Grapevine (Jobete, BMI) .. 1
I Love How You Love Me (Screen Gems-Columbia, BMI) .... 9
(I'm Into Lookin' For) Someone to Love Me (Columbia, BMI) .... 98
I Put a Spell on You (Shalimar, BMI) .... 58
I Started a Joke (Casserole, BMI) .... 41
If I Can Dream (Gladys, ASCAP) .... 30
Isn't It Lonely Together (Ahab, BMI) .... 63
I'm Gonna Make You Love Me (Act Three, BMI) .. 7
I've Gotta Be Me (Damila, ASCAP) .... 74

Just Ain't NB Love (Dakar/BRC, BMI) .... 68

Kay (Moss-Rose, BMI) .... 87
Kentucky Woman (Tallyrand, BMI) .... 45

Little Arrows (Duchess, BMI) .... 22
Lo Mucho Que Te Quiero (The More I Love You) (Pecos, BMI) .... 26
Love Child (Jobete, BMI) .... 3
Love Machine (Pamco/Rascal/Yvonne, BMI) .... 76

Magic Carpet Ride (Trousdale, BMI) .... 18
Malinda (Jobete, BMI) .... 51
My Favorite Things (Williamson, BMI) .... 47
My Song (Lion of Houston, BMI) .... 36

Not Enough Indians (Pomona, BMI) .... 52
Not On the Outside (Gambi, BMI) .... 85

Papa's Got a Brand New Bag (Lois, Togoc, BMI) .. 24
People (Chappell, ASCAP) .... 39
Promises, Promises (Blue Seas/Jac/Morris, ASCAP) 35
Put Your Head on My Shoulder (Spanka/BMI) .... 44

Ramblin' Gamblin' Man (Gear, ASCAP) .... 75
Rainbow Ride (Unart/Joachim, BMI) .... 84
Ray of Hope (Slascar, ASCAP) .... 32
Reach Out (Jobete, BMI) .... 79
Ready or Not Here I Come (Can't Hide From Love) (Nickel Shoe, BMI) .... 50
Release Me (4 Star Sales, BMI) .... 82
Rockin' in the Same Old Boat (Don, BMI) .... 60

Season of the Witch, Part 1 (Peer International, BMI) .... 65
Scarborough Fair (Charing Cross, BMI) .... 27
See Saw (Cotillion/East, BMI) .... 14
Shame, Shame (4 Star, BMI) .... 29
Shout, Part 1 (Wemar/Nom, BMI) .... 96
Son-of-a-Preacher Man (Tree, BMI) .... 21
Soul Sister, Brown Sugar (Walden-Birdees, ASCAP) 70
Soulful Strut (Dakar/RC, BMI) .... 16
Stand by Your Man (Gallico, BMI) .... 34
Stay Close to Me (Camad, BMI) .... 91
Stormy (Low-Sal, BMI) .... 5
Sweet Cream Ladies (Blackwood, BMI) .... 89

(There's Gonna Be a) Showdown (Downstairs/Double Diamond, BMI) .... 49
Things I'd Like to Say (New Colony, BMI) .... 100
This Is My Country (Camad, BMI) .... 38
This Magic Moment (Rumbalero/Progressive) .... 90
Those Were the Days, (T.R.O., ASCAP) .... 25
Thought of Loving Lou (Golden Egg, BMI) .... 95
Till (Chappell, ASCAP) .... 31
Tit for Tat (Ain't No Taking Back) (Dynatone, BMI) 86
Touch Me (Nipper, ASCAP) .... 72
Too Weak to Fight (Fame, BMI) .... 23

Vance (Russell-Cason, ASCAP) .... 80
White Houses (Burdon/Noma, BMI) .... 67
Who's Making Love (East, BMI) .... 8
Wichita Lineman (Canopy, ASCAP) .... 4
Worst That Could Happen (Rivers, BMI) .... 53

You Got Soul (Johnny Nash, ASCAP) .... 81
You've Got the Power (McLaughlin, BMI) .... 93


## BUBBLING UNDER THE HOT 100

101. LOOKING BACK ....Joe Simon, Sound Stage 7 2622
102. AIN'T GOT NO/I GOT LIFE ....Nina Simone, RCA Victor 47-9686
103. I FORGOT TO BE YOUR LOVER ....Wiliam Bell, Stax 0015
104. TRAGEDY ....Brian Hyland, Dot 17176
105. RAIN IN MY HEART ....Frank Sinatra, Reprise 0798
106. DON'T PAT ME ON THE BACK & CALL ME BROTHER ..Kasandra, Capitol 2342
107. THERE'LL COME A TIME ....Betty Everett, Uni 55100
108. L. A. BREAKDOWN (And Let Me In) ....Jack Jones, RCA 47-9687
109. SHE'S A LADY ....Sebastian, Kama Sutra 254
110. LONG LINE RIDER ....Bobby Darin, Direction 350
111. MY BABY SPECIALIZES ....William Bell & Judy Clay, Stax 0017
112. SATURDAY NIGHT AT THE WORLD..Mason Wiliams, Warner Bros.-7 Arts 7248
113. GOODNIGHT MY LOVE ....Paul Anka, RCA 47-9648
114. OB-LA-DI, OB-LA-DA ....Arthur Conley, Atco 6640
115. IF IT WASN'T FOR BAD LUCK ...Ray Charles & Jmmy Lewis, ABC/TRC 11170
116. GAMES PEOPLE PLAY ....Joe South, Capitol 2248
117. YOU SHOWED ME ....Turtles, White Whale 292
118. IN A LONG WHITE ROOM ....Nancy Wilson, Capitol 2361
119. GROOVIEST GIRL IN THE WORLD ....Fun & Games, Uni 55098
120. BUILD ME UP BUTTERCUP ....Foundations, Uni 55101
121. STONY END ....Peggy Lipton, Ode 114

Compiled from national retail sales and radio station airplay by the Music Popularity Dept. of Record Market Research, Billboard.

# Billboard HOT 100

FOR WEEK ENDING JANUARY 4, 1969

★ STAR PERFORMER—Sides registering greatest proportionate upward progress this week.

(Seal) Record Industry Association of America seal of certification as million selling single.

| This Week | 1 Wk. Ago | 2 Wks. Ago | 3 Wks. Ago | TITLE Artist (Producer), Label & Number | Weeks On Chart |
|---|---|---|---|---|---|
| 1 (Billboard Award) | 1 | 1 | 1 | I HEARD IT THROUGH THE GRAPEVINE — Marvin Gaye (Norman Whitfield), Tamla 54176 | 7 |
| 2 | 2 | 3 | 3 | FOR ONCE IN MY LIFE — Stevie Wonder (Henry Cosby), Tamla 54174 | 10 |
| ★3 | 7 | 17 | 20 | I'M GONNA MAKE YOU LOVE ME — Diana Ross & Supremes & Temptations (F. Wilson & N. Ashford), Motown 1137 | 5 |
| ★4 | 16 | 20 | 24 | SOULFUL STRUT — Young-Holt Unlimited (Carl Davis & Eugene Record), Brunswick 55391 | 6 |
| 5 | 4 | 5 | 7 | WICHITA LINEMAN — Glen Campbell (Al de Lory), Capitol 2302 | 10 |
| 6 | 10 | 12 | 13 | CLOUD NINE — Temptations (Norman Whitfield), Gordy 7081 | 8 |
| 7 | 3 | 2 | 2 | LOVE CHILD — Diana Ross & Supremes (Clan), Motown 1135 | 12 |
| 8 | 5 | 6 | 8 | STORMY — Classics IV, (Buddy Buie), Imperial 66328 | 11 |
| 9 (seal) | 8 | 7 | 5 | WHO'S MAKING LOVE — Johnnie Taylor (Don Davis), Stax 0009 | 11 |
| ★10 | 13 | 22 | 23 | HOOKED ON A FEELING — B. J. Thomas (Chips Moman), Scepter 12230 | 8 |
| 11 (seal) | 9 | 9 | 9 | I LOVE HOW YOU LOVE ME — Bobby Vinton (Billy Sherrill), Epic 10397 | 10 |
| 12 | 12 | 13 | 17 | CINNAMON — Derek (George Tobin & Johnny Cymbal), Bang 558 | 11 |
| ★13 | 23 | 28 | 28 | TOO WEAK TO FIGHT — Clarence Carter (Bick Hall & Staff), Atlantic 2569 | 9 |
| ★14 | 26 | 30 | 32 | LO MUCHO QUE TE QUIERO (The More I Love You) — Rene & Rene, White Whale 287 | 7 |
| ★15 | 20 | 26 | 52 | GOING UP THE COUNTRY — Canned Heat (Canned Heat & Skip Taylor), Liberty 56077 | 5 |
| 16 | 6 | 4 | 4 | ABRAHAM, MARTIN AND JOHN — Dion (Laurie Prod.-Phil Gernhard Prod.), Laurie 3464 | 11 |
| ★17 | 28 | 39 | 85 | CRIMSON & CLOVER — Tommy James & the Shondells (Tommy James) Roulette R-7028 | 4 |
| ★18 | 21 | 24 | 36 | SON-OF-A PREACHER MAN — Dusty Springfield (Jerry Wexler, Tom Dowd, Arif Mardin), Atlantic 2580 | 6 |
| 19 | 17 | 18 | 18 | BRING IT ON HOME TO ME — Eddie Floyd (Steve Cropper), Stax 0012 | 12 |
| 20 | 14 | 14 | 14 | SEE SAW — Aretha Franklin (Jerry Wexler), Atlantic 2574 | 7 |
| 21 | 24 | 31 | 33 | PAPA'S GOT A BRAND NEW BAG — Otis Redding, Atco 6636 | 6 |
| 22 | 11 | 8 | 11 | BOTH SIDES NOW — Judy Collins (Mark Abramson), Elektra 45639 | 9 |
| 23 (seal) | 15 | 11 | 6 | HEY JUDE — Beatles (George Martin), Apple 2276 | 17 |
| 24 | 18 | 10 | 10 | MAGIC CARPET RIDE — Steppenwolf (Gabriel Mekler), Dunhill 4160 | 14 |
| ★25 | 38 | 43 | 50 | THIS IS MY COUNTRY — Impressions (Curtis Mayfield), Curtom 1934 | 6 |
| ★26 | 30 | 36 | 40 | IF I CAN DREAM — Elvis Presley, RCA Victor 47-9670 | 6 |
| ★27 | 42 | 55 | 72 | EVERYDAY PEOPLE — Sly & Family Stone (Sly Stone), Epic 10407 | 6 |
| ★28 | 43 | 90 | — | HEY JUDE — Wilson Pickett (Rick Hall), Atlantic 2591 | 3 |
| ★29 | 66 | 74 | — | CAN I CHANGE MY MIND — Tyrone Davis (Willie Henderson), Dakar 602 | 3 |
| 30 | 27 | 16 | 16 | SCARBOROUGH FAIR — Sergio Mendes & Brasil '66 (Sergio Mendes), A&M 986 | 8 |
| 31 | 36 | 54 | 55 | MY SONG — Aretha Franklin (Jerry Wexler), Atlantic 2574 | 6 |
| 32 | 32 | 35 | 39 | A RAY OF HOPE — Rascals (Felix Cavaliere & Arif Mardin), Atlantic 2584 | 5 |
| ★33 | 34 | 51 | 51 | STAND BY YOUR MAN — Tammy Wynette (Billy Sherrill), Epic 10398 | 9 |
| ★34 | 40 | 41 | 41 | HANG 'EM HIGH — Booker T. & M.G.'s (Booker T. & M.G.'s), Stax 0013 | 9 |
| ★35 | 49 | 75 | 87 | (There's Gonna Be a) SHOWDOWN — Archie Bell & the Drells (Gamble-Huff) Atlantic 2583 | 4 |
| 36 | 19 | 15 | 15 | CHEWY CHEWY — Ohio Express (Kasenetz-Katz Associates), Buddah 70 | 12 |
| ★37 | 72 | — | — | TOUCH ME — Doors (Paul A. Rothchild), Elektra 45646 | 2 |
| ★38 | 53 | 98 | — | WORST THAT COULD HAPPEN — Brooklyn Bridge (Wes Farrell), Buddah 75 | 3 |
| ★39 | 48 | 50 | 69 | BABY LET'S WAIT — Royal Guardsmen (Gernhard-Brumage-Fulter), Laurie 3461 | 8 |
| 40 | 41 | 61 | — | I STARTED A JOKE — Bee Gees (Robert Stigwood, The Bee Gees), Atco 6639 | 3 |
| 41 | 33 | 34 | 35 | BATTLE HYMN OF THE REPUBLIC — Andy Williams with the St. Charles Borromeo Choir (Andy Williams), Columbia 44650 | 12 |
| 42 | 46 | 49 | 58 | BELLA LINDA — Grassroots (Steve Barri), Dunhill 4162 | 6 |
| ★43 | 57 | 78 | 78 | ARE YOU HAPPY — Jerry Butler (Gamble-Huff), Mercury 72876 | 5 |
| ★44 | 50 | 60 | 66 | READY OR NOT HERE I COME (Can't Hide From Love) — Delfonics (Stan & Bell Prod.), Philly Groove 154 | 5 |
| 45 | 22 | 21 | 21 | LITTLE ARROWS — Leapy Lee (Gordon Mills), Decca 32380 | 13 |
| 46 | 47 | 47 | 75 | MY FAVORITE THINGS — Herb Alpert & Tijuana Brass (Herb Alpert-Jerry Moss) A&M 1001 | 4 |
| ★47 | 74 | 93 | 94 | I'VE GOTTA BE ME — Sammy Davis Jr. (Jimmy Bowen) Reprise 0779 | 4 |
| 48 | 51 | 57 | 67 | MALINDA — Bobby Taylor & Vancouvers (Robinson, Johnson, Cleveland), Gordy 7079 | 5 |
| 49 | 39 | 53 | 53 | PEOPLE — Tymes (Jimmy "Wiz" Wisner), Columbia 44630 | 8 |
| 50 | 37 | 37 | 44 | I CAN'T TURN YOU LOOSE — Chambers Brothers (Tim O'Brien), Columbia 44679 | 7 |
| ★51 | 71 | 85 | 86 | THE BEGINNING OF MY END — Unifics (Guy Draper), Kapp 957 | 4 |
| 52 | 44 | 46 | 46 | PUT YOUR HEAD ON MY SHOULDER — Lettermen (Al de Lory), Capitol 2324 | 8 |
| ★53 | — | — | — | BABY, BABY DON'T CRY — Smokey Robinson 7 Miracles (Smokey, Moore, Johnson) Tamla 54178 | 1 |
| ★54 | 69 | 71 | 92 | CALIFORNIA DREAMIN' — Bobby Womack (Chips Moman), Minit 32055 | 5 |
| 55 | 55 | 56 | 83 | THE GIRL MOST LIKELY — Jeannie C. Riley (Shelby S. Singleton Jr.), Plantation 7 | 5 |
| 56 | 56 | 52 | 61 | CROSSTOWN TRAFFIC — Jimi Hendrix Experience (Jimi Hendrix), Reprise 0792 | 6 |
| 57 | 62 | 72 | — | CALIFORNIA SOUL — 5th Dimension (Bones Howe), Soul City 770 | 3 |
| 58 | 60 | 64 | 64 | ROCKIN' IN THE SAME OLD BOAT — Bobby Bland, Duke 440 | 8 |
| ★59 | 70 | 81 | — | SOUL SISTER, BROWN SUGAR — Sam & Dave (Hayes & Porter), Atlantic 2590 | 3 |
| 60 | 64 | — | — | DADDY SANG BASS — Johnny Cash (Bob Johnson), Columbia 4-44689 | 2 |
| 61 | 61 | 67 | 74 | BLUEBIRDS OVER THE MOUNTAIN — Beach Boys (Bruce Johnston-Carl Wilson), Capitol 2360 | 4 |
| 62 | 29 | 29 | 30 | SHAME, SHAME — Magic Lanterns (Steve Rowland), Atlantic 2560 | 11 |
| 63 | 63 | 76 | 80 | ISN'T IT LONELY TOGETHER — O. C. Smith (Jerry Fuller) Columbia 4-44705 | 4 |
| 64 | 58 | 59 | 59 | I PUT A SPELL ON YOU — Creedence Clearwater Revival (Saul Zaentz), Fantasy 617 | 9 |
| ★65 | 75 | 84 | — | RAMBLIN' GAMBLIN' MAN — Bob Seger (Hideout), Capitol 2297 | 3 |
| ★66 | 94 | — | — | DOES ANYBODY KNOW I'M HERE — Dells (Bobby Miller), Cadet 5631 | 2 |
| 67 | 68 | 70 | 70 | JUST AIN'T NO LOVE — Barbara Acklin (Carl Davis-Eugene Record), Brunswick 55388 | 8 |
| 68 | 73 | 88 | — | A MINUTE OF YOUR TIME — Tom Jones (Peter Sullivan), Parrot 40035 | 3 |
| 69 | 59 | 62 | 62 | AMERICAN BOYS — Petula Clark (Tony Hatch), Warner Bros.-Seven Arts 7244 | 7 |
| 70 | 65 | 73 | — | SEASON OF THE WITCH, Part 1 — Vanilla Fudge (Shadow Morton), Atco 6632 | 3 |
| 71 | 67 | 68 | 88 | WHITE HOUSES — Eric Burdon & the Animals (Everyone of Us), MGM 14013 | 7 |
| 72 | 81 | 89 | 90 | YOU GOT SOUL — Johnny Nash (Johnny Nash & Arthur Jenkins) Jad 209 | 4 |
| ★73 | 84 | 87 | — | RAINBOW RIDE — Andy Kim (Jeff Beard), Steed 711 | 3 |
| ★74 | 97 | 100 | — | CONDITION RED — Goodees (Davis, Briggs), HIP 8005 | 3 |
| ★75 | 85 | — | — | NOT ON THE OUTSIDE — Momcats (Sylvia & L. Roberts), Stang 5000 | 2 |
| 76 | 78 | 83 | 82 | CHITTY CHITTY BANG BANG — Paul Mauriat, Philips 40574 | 7 |
| 77 | 83 | — | — | ELECTRIC STORIES — 4 Seasons (Gaudic-Crewe), Philips 40577 | 2 |
| ★78 | 88 | — | — | FEELIN' SO GOOD — Archies (Jeff Barry), Calender 63-1007 | 2 |
| ★79 | 90 | — | — | THIS MAGIC MOMENT — Jay & the Americans (Jata Ent.), United Artists 50475 | 2 |
| 80 | 80 | 97 | 100 | VANCE — Roger Miller (Jerry Kennedy), Smash 2197 | 5 |
| ★81 | — | — | — | I FORGOT TO BE YOUR LOVER — William Bell (Booker T. Jones), Stax 0015 | 1 |
| ★82 | — | — | — | RAIN IN MY HEART — Frank Sinatra (Don Costa), Reprise 0798 | 1 |
| 83 | 96 | 96 | — | SHOUT, Part 1 — Chambers Brothers (Lucky Young), Vault 945 | 3 |
| ★84 | — | — | — | BUILD ME UP BUTTERCUP — The Foundations (Tony Macaulay), UNI 55101 | 1 |
| 85 | 89 | — | — | SWEET CREAM LADIES — Box Tops (Chips Moxen/Tommy Cogbill), Mala 12035 | 2 |
| 86 | 86 | 92 | — | TIT FOR TAT (Ain't No Taking Back) — James Brown (James Brown), King 6204 | 3 |
| 87 | 87 | — | — | KAY — John Wesley Ryles (George Richey), Columbia 4-44682 | 2 |
| ★88 | — | — | — | OB-LA-DI OB-LA-DA — Arthur Conley (Tom Dowd), Atco 6640 | 1 |
| ★89 | — | — | — | SHE'S A LADY — John Sebastian (Paul A. Rothchild), Kama Sutra 254 | 1 |
| ★90 | — | — | — | YOU SHOWED ME — Turtles (Chip Douglas), White Whale 292 | 1 |
| 91 | 92 | — | — | ELOISE — Barry Ryan (Bill Landis), MGM 14010 | 2 |
| 92 | — | — | — | IF IT WASN'T FOR BAD LUCK — Ray Charles & Jimmy Lewis (Tangerine Records), ABC 11170 | 1 |
| 93 | 93 | — | — | YOU'VE GOT THE POWER — Esquires (Bunky Prod.), Wand 1193 | 2 |
| 94 | — | — | — | LOOKING BACK — Joe Simon (J.R. Enterprises), Sound Stage 7-2622 | 3 |
| 95 | 95 | 99 | — | THOUGHT OF LOVING YOU — Crystal Mansion (Bob Cullen, Dave White, Arthur Kaplan) Capitol 2275 | 3 |
| 96 | 100 | — | — | THINGS I'D LIKE TO SAY — New Colony Six, Mercury 72858 | 2 |
| 97 | 99 | — | — | I CAN'T HELP IT IF I'M STILL IN LOVE WITH YOU — Al Martino, Capitol 2355 | 2 |
| 98 | 98 | — | — | (I'm Into Lookin' For) SOMEONE TO LOVE ME — Bobby Vee (Dallas Smith), Liberty 56080 | 2 |
| 99 | — | — | — | AIN'T GOT NO/I GOT LIFE — Nina Simone (Stroud), RCA 47-9686 | 1 |
| 100 | — | — | — | GOODNIGHT MY LOVE — Paul Anka (Don Costa), RCA Victor 47-9648 | 1 |

## HOT 100—A TO Z—(Publisher-Licensee)



## BUBBLING UNDER THE HOT 100

101. REACH OUT ....Merrilee Rush, AGP 107
102. TRAGEDY ....Brian Hyland, Dot 17176
103. BUT YOU KNOW I LOVE YOU ....First Edition, Reprise 0799
104. THIS OLD HEART OF MINE ....Tammi Terrell, Motown 1138
105. THERE'LL COME A TIME ....Betty Everett, Uni 55100
106. L.A. BREAKDOWN (And Let Me In) ....Jack Jones, RCA 47-9687
107. LONG LONE RIDER ....Bobby Darin, Direction 350
108. GROOVIEST GIRL IN THE WORLD ....Fun & Games, Uni 55098
109. MY BABY SPECIALIZES ....William Bell & Judy Clay, Stax 0017
110. I GOT A LINE ON YOU ....Spirit, Ode 115
111. SATURDAY NIGHT AT THE WORLD ....Mason Williams, Warner Bros./Seven Arts 7248
112. GAMES PEOPLE PLAY ....Joe South, Capitol 2248
113. BUBBLE GUM MUSIC ....Rock & Roll Double Bubble Trading Card Company of Philadelphia 19141, Buddah 78
114. FOX ON THE RUN ....Manfred Mann, Mercury 72879
115. HE CALLED ME BABY ....Ella Washington, Sound Stage 7 2621
116. I WHO HAVE NOTHING ....Linda Jones, Loma 2105
117. IN A LONG WHITE ROOM ....Nancy Wilson, Capitol 2361
118. DIZZY ....Tommy Roe, ABC 11164
119. ALMOST PERSUADED ....Etta James, Cadet 5630
120. RIOT ....Hugh Masekela, Uni 55102
121. MENDOCINO ....Sir Douglas Quintet, Smash 2191
122. MAY I ....Bill Deal, Heritage 803
123. I'M IN LOVE WITH YOU ....Kasenetz Katz Super Circus, Buddah 82
124. HONEY DO ....Strangeloves, Sire 4102
125. RING YOUR BELL ....Mitch Ryder, Dynavoice 934
126. SO TRUE ....Peaches & Herb, Date 2-1633
127. PLAY IT COOL ....Freddy King, Cotillion 44015
128. IF I ONLY HAD TIME ....Nick DeCaro, A&M 1000
129. LET'S GO ALL THE WAY ....Troy Shondell, TRX 5015

Compiled from national retail sales and radio station airplay by the Music Popularity Dept. of Record Market Research, Billboard.

# Billboard HOT 100

**For Week Ending January 11, 1969**

★ STAR PERFORMER—Sides registering greatest proportionate upward progress this week.
Ⓡ Record Industry Association of America seal of certification as million selling single.

| This Week | 1 Wk. Ago | 2 Wks. Ago | 3 Wks. Ago | TITLE – Artist (Producer), Label & Number | Weeks on Chart |
|---|---|---|---|---|---|
| 1 | 1 | 1 | 1 | **I HEARD IT THROUGH THE GRAPEVINE** – Marvin Gaye (Norman Whitfield), Tamla 54176 | 8 |
| 2 | 3 | 7 | 17 | **I'M GONNA MAKE YOU LOVE ME** – Diana Ross & Supremes & Temptations (F. Wilson & N. Ashford), Motown 1137 | 6 |
| 3 | 5 | 4 | 5 | **WICHITA LINEMAN** – Glen Campbell (Al de Lory), Capitol 2302 | 11 |
| 4 | 4 | 16 | 20 | **SOULFUL STRUT** – Young-Holt Unlimited (Carl Davis & Eugene Record), Brunswick 55391 | 7 |
| 5 | 10 | 13 | 22 | **HOOKED ON A FEELING** – B. J. Thomas (Chips Moman), Scepter 12230 | 9 |
| 6 | 6 | 10 | 12 | **CLOUD NINE** – Temptations (Norman Whitfield), Gordy 7081 | 9 |
| 7 | 2 | 2 | 3 | **FOR ONCE IN MY LIFE** – Stevie Wonder (Henry Cosby), Tamla 54174 | 11 |
| ★8 | 17 | 28 | 39 | **CRIMSON & CLOVER** – Tommy James & the Shondells (Tommy James), Roulette R-7028 | 5 |
| 9 | 7 | 3 | 2 | **LOVE CHILD** – Diana Ross & Supremes (Clan), Motown 1135 | 13 |
| Ⓡ10 | 11 | 9 | 9 | **I LOVE HOW YOU LOVE ME** – Bobby Vinton (Billy Sherrill), Epic 10397 | 11 |
| 11 | 12 | 12 | 13 | **CINNAMON** – Derek (George Tobin & Johnny Cymbal), Bang 558 | 12 |
| 12 | 15 | 20 | 26 | **GOING UP THE COUNTRY** – Canned Heat (Canned Heat & Skip Taylor), Liberty 56077 | 6 |
| ★13 | 18 | 21 | 24 | **SON-OF-A-PREACHER MAN** – Dusty Springfield (Jerry Wexler, Tom Dowd, Arif Mardin), Atlantic 2580 | 8 |
| 14 | 14 | 26 | 30 | **LO MUCHO QUE TE QUIERO (The More I Love You)** – Rene & Rene, White Whale 287 | 8 |
| 15 | 8 | 5 | 6 | **STORMY** – Classics IV (Buddy Buie), Imperial 66328 | 12 |
| 16 | 16 | 6 | 4 | **ABRAHAM, MARTIN AND JOHN** – Dion (Laurie Prod.-Phil Gernhard Prod.), Laurie 3464 | 12 |
| ★17 | 26 | 30 | 36 | **IF I CAN DREAM** – Elvis Presley, RCA Victor 47-9670 | 7 |
| 18 | 37 | 72 | — | **TOUCH ME** – Doors (Paul A. Rothchild), Elektra 45646 | 3 |
| ★19 | 40 | 41 | 61 | **I STARTED A JOKE** – Bee Gees (Robert Stigwood), Atco 6639 | 4 |
| Ⓡ20 | 9 | 8 | 7 | **WHO'S MAKING LOVE** – Johnnie Taylor (Don Davis), Stax 0009 | 12 |
| 21 | 13 | 23 | 28 | **TOO WEAK TO FIGHT** – Clarence Carter (Rick Hall & Staff), Atlantic 2569 | 10 |
| 22 | 22 | 11 | 8 | **BOTH SIDES NOW** – Judy Collins (Mark Abramson), Elektra 45639 | 10 |
| ★23 | 38 | 53 | 98 | **WORST THAT COULD HAPPEN** – Brooklyn Bridge (Wes Farrell), Buddah 75 | 4 |
| ★24 | 32 | 32 | 35 | **A RAY OF HOPE** – Rascals (Felix Cavaliere & Arif Mardin), Atlantic 2584 | 6 |
| 25 | 25 | 38 | 43 | **THIS IS MY COUNTRY** – Impressions (Curtis Mayfield), Curtom 1934 | 7 |
| 26 | 27 | 42 | 55 | **EVERYDAY PEOPLE** – Sly & Family Stone (Sly Stone), Epic 10407 | 7 |
| 27 | 28 | 43 | 90 | **HEY JUDE** – Wilson Pickett (Rick Hall), Atlantic 2591 | 4 |
| 28 | 29 | 66 | 74 | **CAN I CHANGE MY MIND** – Tyrone Davis (Willie Henderson), Dakar 602 | 4 |
| 29 | 24 | 18 | 10 | **MAGIC CARPET RIDE** – Steppenwolf (Gabriel Mekler), Dunhill 4160 | 15 |
| Ⓡ30 | 23 | 15 | 11 | **HEY JUDE** – Beatles (George Martin), Apple 2276 | 18 |
| 31 | 34 | 40 | 41 | **HANG 'EM HIGH** – Booker T. & M.G.'s (Booker T. & M.G.'s), Stax 0013 | 10 |
| 32 | 30 | 27 | 16 | **SCARBOROUGH FAIR** – Sergio Mendes & Brasil '66 (Sergio Mendes), A&M 986 | 9 |
| 33 | 33 | 34 | 51 | **STAND BY YOUR MAN** – Tammy Wynette (Billy Sherrill), Epic 10398 | 10 |
| ★34 | 57 | 62 | 72 | **CALIFORNIA SOUL** – 5th Dimension (Bones Howe), Soul City 770 | 4 |
| 35 | 35 | 49 | 75 | **(There's Gonna Be a) SHOWDOWN** – Archie Bell & the Drells (Gamble-Huff), Atlantic 2583 | 5 |
| 36 | 20 | 14 | 14 | **SEE SAW** – Aretha Franklin (Jerry Wexler), Atlantic 2574 | 8 |
| 37 | 21 | 24 | 31 | **PAPA'S GOT A BRAND NEW BAG** – Otis Redding, Atco 6636 | 7 |
| 38 | 42 | 46 | 49 | **BELLA LINDA** – Grassroots (Steve Barri), Dunhill 4162 | 7 |
| 39 | 39 | 48 | 50 | **BABY LET'S WAIT** – Royal Guardsmen (Gernhard-Brumage-Fuller), Laurie 3461 | 9 |
| ★40 | 19 | 17 | 18 | **BRING IT ON HOME TO ME** – Eddie Floyd (Steve Cropper), Stax 0012 | 13 |
| 41 | 31 | 36 | 54 | **MY SONG** – Aretha Franklin (Jerry Wexler), Atlantic 2574 | 7 |
| 42 | 43 | 57 | 78 | **ARE YOU HAPPY** – Jerry Butler (Gamble-Huff), Mercury 72876 | 6 |
| 43 | 44 | 50 | 60 | **READY OR NOT HERE I COME (Can't Hide From Love)** – Delfonics (Stan & Bell Prod.), Philly Groove 154 | 6 |
| 44 | 41 | 33 | 34 | **BATTLE HYMN OF THE REPUBLIC** – Andy Williams with the St. Charles Borromeo Choir (Andy Williams), Columbia 44650 | 13 |
| 45 | 46 | 47 | 47 | **MY FAVORITE THINGS** – Herb Alpert & Tijuana Brass (Herb Alpert-Jerry Moss), A&M 1001 | 8 |
| 46 | 47 | 74 | 93 | **I'VE GOTTA BE ME** – Sammy Davis Jr. (Jimmy Bowen), Reprise 0779 | 13 |
| 47 | 53 | — | — | **BABY, BABY DON'T CRY** – Smokey Robinson 7 Miracles (Smokey, Moore, Johnson), Tamla 54178 | 2 |
| ★48 | 84 | — | — | **BUILD ME UP BUTTERCUP** – The Foundations (Tony Macaulay), UNI 55101 | 2 |
| 49 | 36 | 19 | 15 | **CHEWY CHEWY** – Ohio Express (Kasenetz-Katz Associates), Buddah 70 | 13 |
| 50 | 45 | 22 | 21 | **LITTLE ARROWS** – Leapy Lee (Gordon Mills), Decca 32380 | 14 |
| 51 | 51 | 71 | 85 | **THE BEGINNING OF MY END** – Unifics (Guy Draper), Kapp 957 | 5 |
| 52 | 54 | 69 | 71 | **CALIFORNIA DREAMIN'** – Bobby Womack (Chips Moman), Minit 32055 | 6 |
| 53 | 56 | 56 | 52 | **CROSSTOWN TRAFFIC** – Jimi Hendrix Experience (Jimi Hendrix), Reprise 0792 | 7 |
| ★54 | 65 | 75 | 84 | **RAMBLIN' GAMBLIN' MAN** – Bob Seger (Hideout), Capitol 2297 | 5 |
| 55 | 68 | 73 | 88 | **A MINUTE OF YOUR TIME** – Tom Jones (Peter Sullivan), Parrot 40035 | 4 |
| ★56 | 88 | — | — | **OB-LA-DI OB-LA-DA** – Arthur Conley (Tom Dowd), Atco 6640 | 2 |
| 57 | 48 | 51 | 57 | **MALINDA** – Bobby Taylor & Vancouvers (Robinson, Johnson, Cleveland), Gordy 7079 | 6 |
| 58 | 59 | 70 | 81 | **SOUL SISTER, BROWN SUGAR** – Sam & Dave (Hayes & Porter), Atlantic 2590 | 4 |
| 59 | 60 | 64 | — | **DADDY SANG BASS** – Johnny Cash (Bob Johnson), Columbia 4-44689 | 3 |
| 60 | 73 | 84 | 87 | **RAINBOW RIDE** – Andy Kim (Jeff Beard), Steed 711 | 4 |
| 61 | 55 | 55 | 56 | **THE GIRL MOST LIKELY** – Jeannie C. Riley (Shelby S. Singleton Jr.), Plantation 7 | 6 |
| 62 | 61 | 61 | 67 | **BLUEBIRDS OVER THE MOUNTAIN** – Beach Boys (Bruce Johnston-Carl Wilson), Capitol 2360 | 5 |
| 63 | 78 | 88 | — | **FEELIN' SO GOOD** – Archies (Jeff Barry), Calender 63-1007 | 3 |
| 64 | 66 | 94 | — | **DOES ANYBODY KNOW I'M HERE** – Dells (Bobby Miller), Cadet 5631 | 3 |
| ★65 | 79 | 90 | — | **THIS MAGIC MOMENT** – Jay & the Americans (Jata Ent.), United Artists 50475 | 3 |
| 66 | 58 | 60 | 64 | **ROCKIN' IN THE SAME OLD BOAT** – Bobby Bland, Duke 440 | 9 |
| 67 | 50 | 37 | 37 | **I CAN'T TURN YOU LOOSE** – Chambers Brothers (Tim O'Brien), Columbia 44679 | 8 |
| 68 | 63 | 63 | 76 | **ISN'T IT LONELY TOGETHER** – O. C. Smith (Jerry Fuller), Columbia 4-44705 | 5 |
| 69 | 67 | 68 | 70 | **JUST AIN'T NO LOVE** – Barbara Acklin (Carl Davis-Eugene Record), Brunswick 55388 | 4 |
| 70 | 72 | 81 | 89 | **YOU GOT SOUL** – Johnny Nash (Johnny Nash & Arthur Jenkins), Jad 209 | 4 |
| 71 | 71 | 67 | 68 | **WHITE HOUSES** – Eric Burdon & the Animals (Everyone of Us), MGM 14013 | 8 |
| ★72 | 90 | — | — | **YOU SHOWED ME** – Turtles (Chip Douglas), White Whale 292 | 2 |
| 73 | 85 | 89 | — | **SWEET CREAM LADIES** – Box Tops (Chips Moxen/Tommy Cogbill), Mala 12035 | 3 |
| 74 | 74 | 97 | 100 | **CONDITION RED** – Goodees (Davis, Briggs), HIP 8005 | 4 |
| 75 | 75 | 85 | — | **NOT ON THE OUTSIDE** – Momcats (Sylvia & L. Roberts), Stang 5000 | 3 |
| 76 | 77 | 83 | — | **ELECTRIC STORIES** – 4 Seasons (Gaudic-Crewe), Philips 40577 | 3 |
| 77 | 76 | 78 | 83 | **CHITTY CHITTY BANG BANG** – Paul Mauriat, Philips 40574 | 4 |
| 78 | 81 | — | — | **I FORGOT TO BE YOUR LOVER** – William Bell (Booker T. Jones), Stax 0015 | 2 |
| 79 | 62 | 29 | 29 | **SHAME, SHAME** – Magic Lanterns (Steve Rowland), Atlantic 2560 | 12 |
| 80 | 69 | 59 | 62 | **AMERICAN BOYS** – Petula Clark (Tony Hatch), Warner Bros.-Seven Arts 7244 | 6 |
| 81 | 82 | — | — | **RAIN IN MY HEART** – Frank Sinatra (Don Costa), Reprise 0798 | 2 |
| 82 | 96 | 100 | — | **THINGS I'D LIKE TO SAY** – New Colony Six, Mercury 72858 | 3 |
| 83 | 100 | — | — | **GOODNIGHT MY LOVE** – Paul Anka (Don Costa), RCA Victor 47-9648 | 2 |
| 84 | 95 | 95 | 99 | **THOUGHT OF LOVING YOU** – Crystal Mansion (Bob Cullen, Dave White, Arthur Kaplan), Capitol 2275 | 4 |
| 85 | 89 | — | — | **SHE'S A LADY** – John Sebastian (Paul A. Rothchild), Kama Sutra 254 | 2 |
| 86 | 91 | 92 | — | **ELOISE** – Barry Ryan (Bill Landis), MGM 14010 | 3 |
| 87 | 86 | 86 | 92 | **TIT FOR TAT (Ain't No Taking Back)** – James Brown (James Brown), King 6204 | 4 |
| 88 | 80 | 80 | 97 | **VANCE** – Roger Miller (Jerry Kennedy), Smash 2197 | 6 |
| 89 | 87 | 87 | — | **KAY** – John Wesley Ryles (George Richey), Columbia 4-44682 | 3 |
| 90 | 92 | — | — | **IF IT WASN'T FOR BAD LUCK** – Ray Charles & Jimmy Lewis (Tangerine Records), ABC 11170 | 2 |
| 91 | — | — | — | **GAMES PEOPLE PLAY** – Joe South (Joe South), Capitol 2248 | 1 |
| 92 | 83 | 96 | 96 | **SHOUT, Part 1** – Chambers Brothers (Lucky Young), Vault 945 | 4 |
| 93 | 93 | 93 | — | **YOU'VE GOT THE POWER** – Esquires (Bunky Prod.), Wand 1193 | 3 |
| 94 | 94 | — | — | **LOOKING BACK** – Joe Simon (J.R. Enterprises), Sound Stage 7-2622 | 4 |
| 95 | — | — | — | **IF I ONLY HAD TIME** – Nick DeCaro (Tommy Lipuma & Nick DeCaro), A&M 1000 | 1 |
| 96 | 99 | — | — | **AIN'T GOT NO/I GOT LIFE** – Nina Simone (Stroud), RCA 47-9686 | 2 |
| 97 | — | — | — | **RIOT** – Hugh Masekela (Chisa Prod.), Uni 55102 | 1 |
| 98 | — | — | — | **TRAGEDY** – Brian Hyland (Ray Ruff), Dot 17176 | 1 |
| 99 | 98 | 98 | — | **(I'm Into Looking For) SOMEONE TO LOVE ME** – Bobby Vee (Dallas Smith), Liberty 56080 | 3 |
| 100 | 97 | 99 | — | **I CAN'T HELP IT IF I'M STILL IN LOVE WITH YOU** – Al Martino, Capitol 2355 | 3 |

## BUBBLING UNDER THE HOT 100

101. BUT YOU KNOW I LOVE YOU ............ First Edition, Reprise 0799
102. THIS OLE HEART OF MINE ............... Tammi Terrell, Motown 1138
103. SATURDAY NIGHT AT THE WORLD ..... Mason Williams, Seven Arts 7248
104. POOR SIDE OF TOWN ..................... Al Wilson, Soul City 771
105. THERE'LL COME A TIME .................. Betty Everett, ABC 55100
106. I'M GONNA HOLD ON AS LONG AS I CAN ... Marvellettes, Tamla 54177
107. LONG LINE RIDER ......................... Bobby Darin, Direction 350
108. GROOVIEST GIRL IN THE WORLD ........ Fun & Games, Uni 55098
109. BUBBLE GUM MUSIC ............ Rock & Roll Double Bubble Trading Card of Philadelphia 19141, Buddah 78
110. I GOT A LINE ON YOU ..................... Spirit, Ode 115
111. HE CALLED ME BABY ...................... Ella Washington, Sound Stage 7 2621
112. WHEN I STOP DREAMING ................. Ray Charles, ABC 11170
113. HOME COOKIN' .................... Jr. Walker & the All Stars, Soul 35055
114. KUM BA YAH .............................. Tommy Leonetti, Decca 32421
115. PROUD MARY ............... Creedence Clearwater Revival, Fantasy 619
116. THAT'S YOUR BABY ....................... Joe Tex, Dial 4089
117. MENDOCINO ................... Sir Douglas Quintet, Smash 2191
118. ALMOST PERSUADED ..................... Etta James, Cadet 5639

Compiled from national retail sales and radio station airplay by the Music Popularity Dept. of Record Market Research, Billboard.

# Billboard HOT 100

**FOR WEEK ENDING JANUARY 18, 1969**

★ STAR PERFORMER—Sides registering greatest proportionate upward progress this week.

® Record Industry Association of America seal of certification as million selling single.

| This Week | Last Week | 2 Wks. Ago | Title, Artist (Producer), Label & Number | Weeks on Chart |
|---|---|---|---|---|
| 1 | 1 | 1 | I HEARD IT THROUGH THE GRAPEVINE — Marvin Gaye (Norman Whitfield), Tamla 54176 | 9 |
| 2 | 2 | 3 | I'M GONNA MAKE YOU LOVE ME — Diana Ross & Supremes & Temptations (F. Wilson & N. Ashford), Motown 1137 | 7 |
| ★3 | 4 | 4 | SOULFUL STRUT — Young-Holt Unlimited (Carl Davis & Eugene Record), Brunswick 55391 | 8 |
| ★4 | 8 | 17 | CRIMSON & CLOVER — Tommy James & the Shondells (Tommy James), Roulette R-7028 | 6 |
| ★5 | 5 | 10 | HOOKED ON A FEELING — B. J. Thomas (Chips Moman), Scepter 12230 | 10 |
| 6 | 3 | 5 | WICHITA LINEMAN — Glen Campbell (Al de Lory), Capitol 2302 | 12 |
| 7 | 7 | 2 | FOR ONCE IN MY LIFE — Stevie Wonder (Henry Cosby), Tamla 54174 | 12 |
| ★8 | 18 | 37 | TOUCH ME — Doors (Paul A. Rothchild), Elektra 45646 | 4 |
| ★9 | 23 | 38 | WORST THAT COULD HAPPEN — Brooklyn Bridge (Wes Farrell), Buddah 75 | 5 |
| 10 | 13 | 18 | SON OF A PREACHER MAN — Dusty Springfield (Jerry Wexler, Tom Dowd, Arif Mardin), Atlantic 2580 | 8 |
| 11 | 11 | 12 | CINNAMON — Derek (George Tobin & Johnny Cymbal), Bang 558 | 13 |
| 12 | 12 | 15 | GOING UP THE COUNTRY — Canned Heat (Canned Heat & Skip Taylor), Liberty 56077 | 7 |
| 13 | 6 | 6 | CLOUD NINE — Temptations (Norman Whitfield), Gordy 7081 | 10 |
| 14 | 14 | 14 | LO MUCHO QUE TE QUIERO (The More I Love You) — Rene & Rene, White Whale 287 | 9 |
| ★15 | 26 | 27 | EVERYDAY PEOPLE — Sly & Family Stone (Sly Stone), Epic 10407 | 4 |
| 16 | 19 | 40 | I STARTED A JOKE — Bee Gees (Robert Stigwood, The Bee Gees), Atco 6639 | 5 |
| 17 | 17 | 26 | IF I CAN DREAM — Elvis Presley (Bones Howe & Steve Binder), RCA Victor 47-9670 | 9 |
| 18 | 9 | 7 | LOVE CHILD — Diana Ross & Supremes (Clan), Motown 1135 | 14 |
| ⓢ19 | 10 | 11 | I LOVE HOW YOU LOVE ME — Bobby Vinton (Billy Sherrill), Epic 10397 | 9 |
| 20 | 15 | 8 | STORMY — Classics IV (Buddy Buie), Imperial 66328 | 13 |
| ⓢ21 | 20 | 9 | WHO'S MAKING LOVE — Johnnie Taylor (Don Davis), Stax 0009 | 13 |
| 22 | 16 | 16 | ABRAHAM, MARTIN AND JOHN — Dion (Laurie Prod.-Phil Gernhard Prod.), Laurie 3464 | 13 |
| 23 | 21 | 13 | TOO WEAK TO FIGHT — Clarence Carter (Rick Hall & Staff), Atlantic 2569 | 11 |
| ★24 | 33 | 33 | STAND BY YOUR MAN — Tammy Wynette (Billy Sherrill), Epic 10398 | 11 |
| ★25 | 28 | 29 | CAN I CHANGE MY MIND — Tyrone Davis (Willie Henderson), Dakar 602 | 6 |
| 26 | 27 | 28 | HEY JUDE — Wilson Pickett (Rick Hall), Atlantic 2591 | 5 |
| ★27 | 31 | 34 | HANG 'EM HIGH — Booker T. & M.G.'s (Booker T. & M.G.'s), Stax 0013 | 11 |
| 28 | 38 | 42 | BELLA LINDA — Grassroots (Steve Barri), Dunhill 4162 | 8 |
| 29 | 34 | 57 | CALIFORNIA SOUL — 5th Dimension (Bones Howe), Soul City 770 | 5 |
| 30 | 25 | 25 | THIS IS MY COUNTRY — Impressions (Curtis Mayfield), Curtom 1934 | 8 |
| ★31 | 48 | 84 | BUILD ME UP BUTTERCUP — The Foundations (Tony Macaulay), UNI 55101 | 4 |
| 32 | 29 | 24 | MAGIC CARPET RIDE — Steppenwolf (Gabriel Mekler), Dunhill 4161 | 16 |
| 33 | 22 | 22 | BOTH SIDES NOW — Judy Collins (Mark Abramson), Elektra 45639 | 11 |
| 34 | 35 | 35 | (There's Gonna Be a) SHOWDOWN — Archie Bell and the Drells (Gamble-Huff), Atlantic 2583 | 6 |
| 35 | 24 | 32 | A RAY OF HOPE — Rascals (Felix Cavaliere & Arif Mardin), Atlantic 2584 | 7 |
| 36 | 39 | 39 | BABY LET'S WAIT — Royal Guardsmen (Gernhard-Brumage-Fuller), Laurie 3461 | 10 |
| 37 | 46 | 47 | I'VE GOTTA BE ME — Sammy Davis Jr. (Jimmy Bowen), Reprise 0779 | 8 |
| ⓢ38 | 30 | 23 | HEY JUDE — Beatles (George Martin), Apple 2276 | 19 |
| 39 | 51 | 51 | THE BEGINNING OF MY END — Unifics (Guy Draper), Kapp 957 | 6 |
| 40 | 42 | 43 | ARE YOU HAPPY — Jerry Butler (Gamble-Huff), Mercury 72876 | 7 |
| 41 | 43 | 44 | READY OR NOT HERE I COME (Can't Hide From Love) — Delfonics (Stan & Bell Prod.), Philly Groove 154 | 7 |
| 42 | 47 | 53 | BABY, BABY DON'T CRY — Smokey Robinson & Miracles (Smokey, Moore, Johnson), Tamla 54178 | 3 |
| 43 | 65 | 79 | THIS MAGIC MOMENT — Jay & the Americans (Jata Fat.), United Artists 50475 | 4 |
| 44 | 37 | 21 | PAPA'S GOT A BRAND NEW BAG — Otis Redding, Atco 6636 | 8 |
| 45 | 52 | 54 | CALIFORNIA DREAMIN' — Bobby Womack (Chips Moman), Minit 32055 | 7 |
| ★46 | 72 | 90 | YOU SHOWED ME — Turtles (Chip Douglas), White Whale 292 | 3 |
| ★47 | 83 | 100 | GOODNIGHT MY LOVE — Paul Anka (Don Costa), RCA Victor 47-9648 | 3 |
| 48 | 54 | 65 | RAMBLIN' GAMBLIN' MAN — Bob Seger (Hideout), Capitol 2297 | 5 |
| ★49 | 64 | 66 | DOES ANYBODY KNOW I'M HERE — Dells (Bobby Miller), Cadet 5631 | 4 |
| 50 | 60 | 73 | RAINBOW RIDE — Andy Kim (Jeff Barry), Steed 711 | 5 |
| 51 | 56 | 88 | OB-LA-DI OB-LA-DA — Arthur Conley (Tom Dowd), Atco 6640 | 3 |
| 52 | 58 | 59 | SOUL SISTER, BROWN SUGAR — Sam & Dave (Hayes & Porter), Atlantic 2590 | 5 |
| 53 | 59 | 60 | DADDY SANG BASS — Johnny Cash (Bob Johnson), Columbia 4-44689 | 5 |
| 54 | 45 | 46 | MY FAVORITE THINGS — Herb Alpert & Tijuana Brass (Herb Alpert-Jerry Moss), A&M 1001 | 6 |
| 55 | 55 | 68 | A MINUTE OF YOUR TIME — Tom Jones (Peter Sullivan), Parrot 40035 | 4 |
| 56 | 53 | 56 | CROSSTOWN TRAFFIC — Jimi Hendrix Experience (Jimi Hendrix), Reprise 0792 | 8 |
| 57 | 74 | 74 | CONDITION RED — Goodees (Davis, Briggs), HIP 8005 | 4 |
| 58 | 82 | 96 | THINGS I'D LIKE TO SAY — New Colony Six, Mercury 72858 | 4 |
| 59 | 70 | 72 | YOU GOT SOUL — Johnny Nash (Johnny Nash & Arthur Jenkins), Jad 209 | 5 |
| 60 | 75 | 75 | NOT ON THE OUTSIDE — Moments (Sylvia & L. Roberts), Stang 5000 | 5 |
| 61 | 63 | 78 | FEELIN' SO GOOD — Archies (Jeff Barry), Calendar 63-1007 | 4 |
| ★62 | — | 91 | GAMES PEOPLE PLAY — Joe South (Joe South), Capitol 2248 | 2 |
| 63 | 62 | 61 | BLUEBIRDS OVER THE MOUNTAIN — Beach Boys (Bruce Johnston-Carl Wilson), Capitol 2360 | 6 |
| 64 | 73 | 85 | SWEET CREAM LADIES — Box Tops (Chips Moman/Tommy Cogbill), Mala 12035 | 4 |
| 65 | 76 | 77 | ELECTRIC STORIES — 4 Seasons (Gaudio-Crewe), Philips 40577 | 4 |
| 66 | 81 | 82 | RAIN IN MY HEART — Frank Sinatra (Don Costa), Reprise 0798 | 3 |
| ★67 | — | — | TAKE CARE OF YOUR HOMEWORK — Johnnie Taylor (Al Jackson Jr. & Don Davis), Stax 0023 | 1 |
| 68 | 68 | 63 | ISN'T IT LONELY TOGETHER — O. C. Smith (Jerry Fuller), Columbia 4-44705 | 6 |
| 69 | 78 | 81 | I FORGOT TO BE YOUR LOVER — William Bell (Booker T. Jones), Stax 0015 | 3 |
| 70 | 66 | 58 | ROCKIN' IN THE SAME OLD BOAT — Bobby Bland, Duke 440 | 10 |
| ★71 | — | — | BUT YOU KNOW I LOVE YOU — First Edition (Jimmy Bowen), Reprise 0799 | 1 |
| 72 | 57 | 48 | MALINDA — Bobby Taylor & Vancouvers (Robinson, Johnson, Cleveland), Gordy 7079 | 7 |
| 73 | 94 | 94 | LOOKING BACK — Joe Simon (J.R. Enterprises), Sound Stage 7-2622 | 3 |
| 74 | — | — | I GOT A LINE ON YOU — Spirit (Lou Adler), Ode 115 | 1 |
| 75 | — | 98 | TRAGEDY — Brian Hyland (Ray Ruff), Dot 17176 | 2 |
| 76 | — | — | THERE'LL COME A TIME — Betty Everett (Archie Lee Hill Prod.), Uni 55100 | 1 |
| 77 | — | — | HOME COOKIN' — Jr. Walker & All Stars (Henry Cosby), Soul 35055 | 1 |
| 78 | — | — | HE CALLED ME BABY — Ella Washington (J.R. Enterprises), Sound Stage 7 2621 | 1 |
| 79 | 97 | — | RIOT — Hugh Masekela (Chisa Prod.), Uni 55102 | 2 |
| 80 | — | — | ALMOST PERSUADED — Etta James (Rick Hall & Staff), Cadet 5630 | 1 |
| 81 | 90 | 92 | IF IT WASN'T FOR BAD LUCK — Ray Charles & Jimmy Lewis (Tangerine Records), ABC 11170 | 3 |
| 82 | — | — | GETTING THE CORNERS — T.S.U. Tornadoes (A Frazier/McKay Production), Atlantic 2579 | 1 |
| 83 | 89 | 87 | KAY — John Wesley Ryles (George Richey), Columbia 4-44682 | 4 |
| 84 | 84 | 95 | THOUGHT OF LOVING YOU — Crystal Mansion (Bob Cullen, Dave White, Arthur Kaplan), Capitol 2275 | 5 |
| 85 | 85 | 89 | SHE'S A LADY — John Sebastian (Paul A. Rothchild), Kama Sutra 254 | 4 |
| 86 | 86 | 91 | ELOISE — Barry Ryan (Bill Landis), MGM 14010 | 4 |
| 87 | — | — | BUBBLE GUM MUSIC — Rock & Roll Dubble Bubble Trading Card Co. of Philadelphia 19141 (Jerry Goldstein), Buddah 78 | 1 |
| 88 | — | — | POOR SIDE OF TOWN — Al Wilson (Johnny Rivers & Marc Gordon), Soul City 771 | 1 |
| 89 | — | — | MAY I — Bill Deal & the Rhondels (Jerry Ross Prod.), Heritage 803 | 1 |
| ★90 | — | — | THE GROOVIEST GIRL IN THE WORLD — Fun & Games (Gary Zekley), Uni 55098 | 1 |
| 91 | 92 | 83 | SHOUT, Part 1 — Chambers Brothers (Lucky Young), Vault 945 | 5 |
| 92 | 93 | 93 | YOU'VE GOT THE POWER — Esquires (Bunky Prod.), Wand 1193 | 4 |
| 93 | — | — | KUM BA YAH — Tommy Leonetti (Bill Justis), Decca 32421 | 1 |
| 94 | — | — | I'M GONNA HOLD ON AS LONG AS I CAN — Marvelettes (Frank Wilson), Tamla 54177 | 1 |
| 95 | 96 | 99 | AIN'T GOT NO/I GOT LIFE — Nina Simone (Stroud), RCA 47-9686 | 3 |
| 96 | — | — | WILL YOU BE STAYING AFTER SUNDAY — Peppermint Rainbow (Paul Leka), Decca 32410 | 1 |
| 97 | — | — | THIS OLD HEART OF MINE — Tammi Terrell (Holland & Dozier), Motown 1138 | 1 |
| 98 | — | — | FOX ON THE RUN — Manfred Mann (Jerry Bron), Mercury 72879 | 1 |
| 99 | — | — | MENDOCINO — Sir Douglas Quintet (Amigos de Musica), Smash 2191 | 1 |
| 100 | — | — | THAT'S YOUR BABY — Joe Tex (Buddy Killen), Dial 4089 | 1 |

## BUBBLING UNDER THE HOT 100

101. SATURDAY NIGHT AT THE WORLD .. Mason Williams, Warner Bros.-7 Arts 7248
102. LONG LINE RIDER ............................ Bobby Darin, Direction 350
103. PRUPLE HAZE ..................................... Dion, Laurie 3478
104. MY BABY SPECIALIZES ........... William Bell and Judy Clay, Stax 0017
105. I'M IN LOVE WITH YOU . Kasenetz Katz Singing Orchestral Circus, Buddah 82
106. IF I ONLY HAD TIME ............................ Nick DeCaro, A&M 1000
107. PROUD MARY ................. Creedence Clearwater Revival, Fantasy 619
108. TIME OF THE SEASON ............................. Zombies, Date 2-1268
109. SOUL SHAKE ............. Peggy Scott & JoJo Benson, SSS International 761
110. DIZZY ............................................... Tommy Roe, ABC 11164
111. GREATEST LOVE .......................... Dorsey Burnette, Liberty 56087
112. WHEN I STOP DREAMING .................... Ray Charles, ABC 11170
113. LIGHT MY FIRE ......................... Rhetta Hughes, Tetragrammaton 1513
114. NO NOT MUCH ..................................... Smoke Ring, Buddah 77

Compiled from national retail sales and radio station airplay by the Music Popularity Dept. of Record Market Research, Billboard.

# Billboard HOT 100

FOR WEEK ENDING JANUARY 25, 1969

★ STAR PERFORMER—Sides registering greatest proportionate upward progress this week.

Record Industry Association of America seal of certification as million selling single.

| This Week | 1 Wk. Ago | 2 Wks. Ago | 3 Wks. Ago | TITLE Artist (Producer), Label & Number | Weeks On Chart |
|---|---|---|---|---|---|
| 1 (Billboard Award) | 1 | 1 | 1 | **I HEARD IT THROUGH THE GRAPEVINE** — Marvin Gaye (Norman Whitfield), Tamla 54176 | 10 |
| ★2 | 4 | 8 | 17 | **CRIMSON & CLOVER** — Tommy James & the Shondells (Tommy James), Roulette R-7028 | 7 |
| 3 | 2 | 2 | 3 | **I'M GONNA MAKE YOU LOVE ME** — Diana Ross & Supremes & Temptations (F. Wilson & N. Ashford), Motown 1137 | 8 |
| 4 | 3 | 4 | 4 | **SOULFUL STRUT** — Young-Holt Unlimited (Carl Davis & Eugene Record), Brunswick 55391 | 9 |
| ★5 | 15 | 26 | 27 | **EVERYDAY PEOPLE** — Sly & Family Stone (Sly Stone), Epic 10407 | 9 |
| 6 | 5 | 5 | 10 | **HOOKED ON A FEELING** — B. J. Thomas (Chips Moman), Scepter 12230 | 11 |
| 7 | 8 | 18 | 37 | **TOUCH ME** — Doors (Paul A. Rothchild), Elektra 45646 | 5 |
| 8 | 9 | 23 | 38 | **WORST THAT COULD HAPPEN** — Brooklyn Bridge (Wes Farrell), Buddah 75 | 6 |
| ★9 | 16 | 19 | 40 | **I STARTED A JOKE** — Bee Gees (Robert Stigwood, The Bee Gees), Atco 6639 | 6 |
| 10 | 10 | 13 | 18 | **SON OF A PREACHER MAN** — Dusty Springfield (Jerry Wexler, Tom Dowd, Arif Mardin), Atlantic 2580 | 9 |
| 11 | 12 | 12 | 15 | **GOING UP THE COUNTRY** — Canned Heat (Canned Heat & Skip Taylor), Liberty 56077 | 8 |
| ★12 | 25 | 28 | 29 | **CAN I CHANGE MY MIND** — Tyrone Davis (Willie Henderson), Dakar 602 | 6 |
| 13 | 6 | 3 | 5 | **WICHITA LINEMAN** — Glen Campbell (Al de Lory), Capitol 2302 | 13 |
| 14 | 7 | 7 | 2 | **FOR ONCE IN MY LIFE** — Stevie Wonder (Henry Cosby), Tamla 54174 | 13 |
| ★15 | 27 | 31 | 34 | **HANG 'EM HIGH** — Booker T. & M.G.'s (Booker T. & M.G.'s), Stax 0013 | 12 |
| 16 | 17 | 17 | 26 | **IF I CAN DREAM** — Elvis Presley (Bones Howe & Steve Binder), RCA Victor 47-9670 | 9 |
| 17 | 13 | 6 | 6 | **CLOUD NINE** — Temptations (Norman Whitfield), Gordy 7081 | 11 |
| 18 | 11 | 11 | 12 | **CINNAMON** — Derek (George Tobin & Johnny Cymbal), Bang 558 | 14 |
| 19 | 18 | 9 | 7 | **LOVE CHILD** — Diana Ross & Supremes (Clan), Motown 1135 | 15 |
| 20 | 19 | 10 | 11 | **I LOVE HOW YOU LOVE ME** — Bobby Vinton (Billy Sherrill), Epic 10397 | 13 |
| ★21 | 34 | 35 | 35 | **(There's Gonna Be a) SHOWDOWN** — Archie Bell & the Drells (Gamble-Huff), Atlantic 2583 | 7 |
| 22 | 24 | 33 | 33 | **STAND BY YOUR MAN** — Tammy Wynette (Billy Sherrill), Epic 10398 | 12 |
| 23 | 23 | 21 | 13 | **TOO WEAK TO FIGHT** — Clarence Carter (Rick Hall & Staff), Atlantic 2569 | 12 |
| 24 | 14 | 14 | 14 | **LO MUCHO QUE TE QUIERO (The More I Love You)** — Rene & Rene, White Whale 287 | 10 |
| 25 | 26 | 27 | 28 | **HEY JUDE** — Wilson Pickett (Rick Hall), Atlantic 2591 | 6 |
| 26 | 20 | 15 | 8 | **STORMY** — Classics IV, (Buddy Buie), Imperial 66328 | 14 |
| 27 | 21 | 20 | 9 | **WHO'S MAKING LOVE** — Johnnie Taylor (Don Davis), Stax 0009 | 14 |
| 28 | 31 | 48 | 84 | **BUILD ME UP BUTTERCUP** — The Foundations (Tony Macaulay), UNI 55101 | 4 |
| 29 | 29 | 34 | 57 | **CALIFORNIA SOUL** — 5th Dimension (Bones Howe), Soul City 770 | 6 |
| 30 | 30 | 25 | 25 | **THIS IS MY COUNTRY** — Impressions (Curtis Mayfield), Curtom 1934 | 9 |
| ★31 | 42 | 47 | 53 | **BABY, BABY DON'T CRY** — Smokey Robinson 7 Miracles (Smokey, Moore, Johnson), Tamla 54178 | 4 |
| 32 | 37 | 46 | 47 | **I'VE GOTTA BE ME** — Sammy Davis Jr. (Jimmy Bowen), Reprise 0779 | 7 |
| ★33 | 48 | 54 | 65 | **RAMBLIN' GAMBLIN' MAN** — Bob Seger (Hideout), Capitol 2297 | 6 |
| ★34 | 46 | 72 | 90 | **YOU SHOWED ME** — Turtles (Chip Douglas), White Whale 292 | 4 |
| 35 | 41 | 43 | 44 | **READY OF NOT HERE I COME (Can't Hide From Love)** — Delfonics (Stan & Bell Prod.), Philly Groove 154 | 8 |
| 36 | 36 | 39 | 39 | **BABY LET'S WAIT** — Royal Guardsmen (Gernhard-Brumage-Fuller), Laurie 3461 | 11 |
| 37 | 43 | 65 | 79 | **THIS MAGIC MOMENT** — Jay & the Americans (Jata Ent.), United Artists 50475 | 5 |
| 38 | 39 | 51 | 51 | **THE BEGINNING OF MY END** — Unifics (Guy Draper), Kapp 957 | 7 |
| 39 | 40 | 42 | 43 | **ARE YOU HAPPY** — Jerry Butler (Gamble-Huff), Mercury 72876 | 8 |
| ★40 | 67 | — | — | **TAKE CARE OF YOUR HOMEWORK** — Johnnie Taylor (Al Jackson Jr. & Don Davis), Stax 0023 | 2 |
| 41 | 28 | 38 | 42 | **BELLA LINDA** — Grassroots (Steve Barri), Dunhill 4162 | 9 |
| 42 | 22 | 16 | 16 | **ABRAHAM, MARTIN AND JOHN** — Dion (Laurie Prod.-Phil Gernhard Prod.), Laurie 3464 | 14 |
| 43 | 45 | 52 | 54 | **CALIFORNIA DREAMIN'** — Bobby Womack (Chips Moman), Minit 32055 | 8 |
| 44 | 44 | 37 | 21 | **PAPA'S GOT A BRAND NEW BAG** — Otis Redding, Atco 6636 | 9 |
| 45 | 47 | 83 | 100 | **GOODNIGHT MY LOVE** — Paul Anka (Don Costa), RCA Victor 47-9648 | 4 |
| 46 | 35 | 24 | 32 | **A RAY OF HOPE** — Rascals (Felix Cavaliere & Arif Mardin), Atlantic 2584 | 8 |
| ★47 | — | — | — | **I'M LIVIN' IN SHAME** — Diana Ross & the Supremes (The Clan), Motown 1139 | 1 |
| 48 | 49 | 64 | 66 | **DOES ANYBODY KNOW I'M HERE** — Dells (Bobby Miller), Cadet 5631 | 5 |
| 49 | 50 | 60 | 73 | **RAINBOW RIDE** — Andy Kim (Jeff Barry), Steed 711 | 6 |
| 50 | 52 | 58 | 59 | **SOUL SISTER, BROWN SUGAR** — Sam & Dave (Hayes & Porter), Atlantic 2590 | 6 |
| 51 | 51 | 56 | 88 | **OB-LA-DI OB-LA-DA** — Arthur Conley (Tom Dowd), Atco 6640 | 4 |
| ★52 | 62 | 91 | — | **GAMES PEOPLE PLAY** — Joe South (Joe South), Capitol 2248 | 3 |
| 53 | 53 | 59 | 60 | **DADDY SANG BASS** — Johnny Cash (Bob Johnson), Columbia 4-44689 | 5 |
| 54 | 55 | 55 | 68 | **A MINUTE OF YOUR TIME** — Tom Jones (Peter Sullivan), Parrot 40035 | 6 |
| 55 | 57 | 74 | 74 | **CONDITION RED** — Goodees (Davis, Briggs), HIP 8005 | 6 |
| 56 | 58 | 82 | 96 | **THINGS I'D LIKE TO SAY** — New Colony Six, Mercury 72858 | 5 |
| ★57 | 60 | 75 | 75 | **NOT ON THE OUTSIDE** — Momcats (Sylvia & L. Roberts), Stang 5000 | 5 |
| 58 | 59 | 70 | 72 | **YOU GOT SOUL** — Johnny Nash (Johnny Nash & Arthur Jenkins), Jad 209 | 7 |
| 59 | 61 | 63 | 78 | **FEELIN' SO GOOD** — Archies (Jeff Barry), Calender 63-1007 | 5 |
| ★60 | 69 | 78 | 81 | **I FORGOT TO BE YOUR LOVER** — William Bell (Booker T. Jones), Stax 0015 | 4 |
| ★61 | 64 | 73 | 85 | **SWEET CREAM LADIES** — Box Tops (Chips Moxen/Tommy Cogbill), Mala 12035 | 5 |
| ★62 | — | — | — | **PROUD MARY** — Creedence Clearwater Revival (John Fogerty), Fantasy 619 | 1 |
| ★63 | — | — | — | **GIVE IT UP OR TURNIT A LOOSE** — James Brown (James Brown), King 6213 | 1 |
| 64 | 65 | 76 | 77 | **ELECTRIC STORIES** — 4 Seasons (Gaudio-Crewe), Philips 40577 | 5 |
| 65 | 66 | 81 | 82 | **RAIN IN MY HEART** — Frank Sinatra (Don Costa), Reprise 0798 | 4 |
| ★66 | 71 | — | — | **BUT YOU KNOW I LOVE YOU** — First Edition (Jimmy Bowen), Reprise 0799 | 2 |
| ★67 | 97 | — | — | **THIS OLD HEART OF MINE** — Tammi Terrell (Holland & Dozier), Motown 1138 | 2 |
| ★68 | 77 | — | — | **HOME COOKIN'** — Jr. Walker & All Stars (Henry Cosby), Soul 35055 | 2 |
| ★69 | 76 | — | — | **THERE'LL COME A TIME** — Betty Everett (Archie Lee Hill Prod.), Uni 55100 | 2 |
| 70 | 73 | 94 | 94 | **LOOKING BACK** — Joe Simon (J.R. Enterprises), Sound Stage 7-2622 | 6 |
| ★71 | 79 | 97 | — | **RIOT** — Hugh Masekela (Chisa Prod.), Uni 55102 | 3 |
| ★72 | — | — | — | **RIVER DEEP—MOUNTAIN HIGH** — Deep Purple (Lawrence), Tetragrammaton 1514 | 1 |
| 73 | 74 | — | — | **I GOT A LINE ON YOU** — Spirit (Lou Adler), Ode 115 | 2 |
| 74 | 75 | 98 | — | **TRAGEDY** — Brian Hyland (Ray Ruff), Dot 17176 | 3 |
| ★75 | 88 | — | — | **POOR SIDE OF TOWN** — Al Wilson (Johnny Rivers & Marc Gordon), Soul City 771 | 2 |
| ★76 | 94 | — | — | **I'M GONNA HOLD ON AS LONG AS I CAN** — Marvelettes (Frank Wilson), Tamla 54177 | 2 |
| 77 | 78 | — | — | **HE CALLED ME BABY** — Ella Washington (J.R. Enterprises), Sound Stage 7 2621 | 2 |
| ★78 | — | — | — | **PURPLE HAZE** — Dion (Laurie Prod.), Laurie 3478 | 1 |
| 79 | 80 | — | — | **ALMOST PERSUADED** — Etta James (Rick Hall & Staff), Cadet 5630 | 2 |
| 80 | 81 | 90 | 92 | **IF IT WASN'T FOR BAD LUCK** — Ray Charles & Jimmy Lewis (Tangerine Records), ABC 11170 | 4 |
| 81 | 82 | — | — | **GETTING THE CORNERS** — T.S.U. Toronadoes (A Frazier/McKay Production), Atlantic 2579 | 2 |
| ★82 | — | — | — | **THE GREATEST LOVE** — Dorsey Burnette (Snuff Garrett), Liberty 56087 | 1 |
| 83 | 83 | 89 | 87 | **KAY** — John Wesley Ryles (George Richey), Columbia 4-44682 | 5 |
| 84 | 85 | 85 | 89 | **SHE'S A LADY** — John Sebastian (Paul A. Rothchild), Kama Sutra 254 | 4 |
| ★85 | — | — | — | **INDIAN GIVER** — 1910 Fruitgum Co. (Kasenetz, Katz), Buddah 91 | 1 |
| 86 | 90 | — | — | **THE GROOVIEST GIRL IN THE WORLD** — Fun & Games (Gary Zekley), Uni 55098 | 2 |
| 87 | 87 | — | — | **BUBBLE GUM MUSIC** — Rock & Roll Dubble Bubble Trading Card Co. of Philadelphia 19141 (Jerry Goldstein), Buddah 78 | 2 |
| ★88 | 100 | — | — | **THAT'S YOUR BABY** — Joe Tex (Buddy Killen), Dial 4089 | 2 |
| 89 | 89 | — | — | **MAY I** — Bill Deal & the Rhondels (Jerry Ross Prod.), Heritage 803 | 2 |
| ★90 | — | — | — | **LET IT BE ME** — Glen Campbell & Bobbie Gentry (Al DeLory & Kelly Gordon), Capitol 2387 | 1 |
| 91 | 92 | 93 | 93 | **YOU'VE GOT THE POWER** — Esquires (Bunky Prod.), Wand 1193 | 5 |
| 92 | 93 | — | — | **KUM BA YAH** — Tommy Leonetti (Bill Justis), Decca 32421 | 2 |
| 93 | — | — | — | **THE CARROLL COUNTY ACCIDENT** — Porter Wagoner (Bob Ferguson), RCA Victor 47-9651 | 1 |
| 94 | 95 | 96 | 99 | **AIN'T GOT NO/I GOT LIFE** — Nina Simone (Stroud), RCA 47-9686 | 4 |
| 95 | 96 | — | — | **WILL YOU BE STAYING AFTER SUNDAY** — Peppermint Rainbow (Paul Leka), Decca 32410 | 2 |
| 96 | 99 | — | — | **MENDOCINO** — Sir Douglas Quintet (Amigas de Musica), Smash 2191 | 2 |
| 97 | 98 | — | — | **FOX ON THE RUN** — Manfred Mann (Jerry Bron), Mercury 72879 | 2 |
| 98 | — | — | — | **PLEASE DON'T DESERT ME BABY** — Gloria Walker & Chevelles (Eugene Davis), Flaming Arrow 36 | 1 |
| 99 | — | — | — | **CROSSROADS** — Cream (Felix Pappalardi), Atco 6646 | 1 |
| 100 | — | — | — | **HEY! BABY** — Jose Feliciano (Rick Jarrard), RCA 47-9714 | 1 |

## HOT 100—A TO Z—(Publisher-Licensee)


Abraham, Martin and John (Roznique/Sanphil, BMI) ... 42
Ain't Got No/I Got Life (Rolly Royce, ASCAP) ... 94
Almost Persuaded (Gallico, BMI) ... 79
Are You Happy (World War III/Parabut, BMI) ... 39

Baby, Baby Don't Cry (Jobete, BMI) ... 31
Baby Let's Wait (Web IV, BMI) ... 36
Bella Linda (Vintage, ASCAP) ... 41
Beginning of My End, The (Cuydra, BMI) ... 38
Bubble Gum Music (Greyhound, BMI) ... 87
Build Me Up Buttercup (January Music, BMI) ... 28
But You Know I Love You (First Edition, BMI) ... 66

Can I Change My Mind (Dakar, BMI) ... 12
California Dreamin' (Honest John, ASCAP) ... 43
California Soul (Jobete, BMI) ... 29
Carroll County Accident, The (Warden, BMI) ... 93
Cinnamon (Pamco, BMI) ... 18
Cloud Nine (Jobete, BMI) ... 17
Crimson & Clover (Big Seven Music, BMI) ... 2
Condition Red (East Groovesville, BMI) ... 55
Crossroads (Noma, BMI) ... 99

Daddy Sang Bass (House of Cash, BMI) ... 53
Does Anybody Know I'm Here (Chevis, BMI) ... 48

Electric Stories (Screen Gems-Columbia, BMI) ... 64
Everyday People (Daly City, BMI) ... 5

Feelin' So Good (Kirshner, BMI) ... 59
For Once in My Life (Stein & Van Stock, ASCAP) ... 14
Fox on the Run (James, BMI) ... 97

Games People Play (Lowery, BMI) ... 52
Getting the Corners (Cotillion-Broken Soul, BMI) ... 81
Give It Up or Turnit a Loose (Brown & Sons, BMI) ... 63
Going Up the Country (Metric, BMI) ... 11
Goodnight My Love (Spanka, BMI) ... 45
Greatest Love, The (Lowery, BMI) ... 82
Grooviest Girl in the World, The (Teeny Bopper, ASCAP) ... 86

Hang 'Em High (Unart, BMI) ... 15
He Called Me Baby (Central Song, BMI) ... 77
Hey! Baby (LeBill, BMI) ... 100
Hey Jude (Maclen, BMI) ... 25
Home Cookin' (Jobete, BMI) ... 68
Hooked on a Feeling (Press, BMI) ... 6

I Forgot To Be Your Lover (Memphis, BMI) ... 60
If It Wasn't For Bad Luck (Tangerine Music Corp., BMI) ... 80
I Got a Line on You (Hollenbeck, BMI) ... 73
I Heard It Through the Grapevine (Jobete, BMI) ... 1
I Love How You Love Me (Screen Gems-Columbia, BMI) ... 20
I Started a Joke (Casserole, BMI) ... 9
If I Can Dream (Gladys, ASCAP) ... 16
Indian Giver (Kaskat/Kahoona, BMI) ... 85
I'm Gonna Hold on as Long as I Can (Jobete, BMI) 76
I'm Gonna Make You Love Me (M.R.C., BMI) ... 3
I'm Livin' in Shame (Jobete, BMI) ... 47
I've Gotta Be Me (Damila, ASCAP) ... 32

Kay (Moss-Rose, BMI) ... 83
Kum Ba Yah (Clinton, ASCAP) ... 92

Let It Be Me (Leeds, ASCAP) ... 90
Lo Mucho Que Te Quiero (The More I Love You) (Pecos, BMI) ... 24
Looking Back (Eden/Sweco, BMI) ... 70
Love Child (Jobete, BMI) ... 19

May I (Rhinelander, BMI) ... 89
Mendocino (Southern Love, BMI) ... 96
Minute of Your Time, A (Anne-Rachel, ASCAP) ... 54

Not On the Outside (Gambi, BMI) ... 57
Ob-La-Di Ob-La-Da (Maclen, BMI) ... 51

Papa's Got a Brand New Bag (Lois, Toga, BMI) ... 44
Please Don't Desert Me Baby (Cotillion/Flaming Arrow, BMI) ... 98
Poor Side of Town (Rivers, BMI) ... 75
Proud Mary (Jondora, BMI) ... 62
Purple Haze (Sea Lark, BMI) ... 78

Ramblin' Gamblin' Man (Gear, ASCAP) ... 33
Rain In My Heart (Razzle Dazzle Music, BMI) ... 65
Rainbow Ride (Unart-Joachim, BMI) ... 49
Ray of Hope (Slacsar, ASCAP) ... 46
Ready or Not Here I Come (Can't Hide From Love) (Nickel Shoe, BMI) ... 35
Riot (Cherio, BMI) ... 71
River Deep—Mountain High (Trio, BMI) ... 72

She's a Lady (Faithful Virtue, BMI) ... 84
Son of a Preacher Man (Tree, BMI) ... 10
Soul Sister, Brown Sugar (Walden-Birdees, ASCAP) ... 50
Soulful Strut (Dakar/RC, BMI) ... 4
Stand by Your Man (Gallico, BMI) ... 22
Stormy (Low-Sal, BMI) ... 26
Sweet Cream Ladies (Blackwood, BMI) ... 61

Take Care of Your Homework (East/Memphis, BMI) ... 40
That's Your Baby (Tree, BMI) ... 88
There'll Come a Time (Jalynne, BMI) ... 69
(There's Gonna Be a) Showdown (Downstairs/Double Diamond, BMI) ... 21
Things I'd Like to Say (New Colony, BMI) ... 56
This Is My Country (Camad, BMI) ... 30
This Magic Moment (Rumbalero/Progressive) ... 37
This Old Heart of Mine (Jobete, BMI) ... 67
Touch Me (Nipper, ASCAP) ... 7
Too Weak to Fight (Fame, BMI) ... 23
Tragedy (Bluff City, BMI) ... 74

Who's Making Love (East, BMI) ... 27
Wichita Lineman (Canopy, ASCAP) ... 13
Will You Be Staying After Sunday (Screen Gems-Columbia, BMI) ... 95
Worst That Could Happen (Rivers, BMI) ... 8

You Got Soul (Johnny Nash, ASCAP) ... 58
You've Got the Power (McLaughlin, BMI) ... 91
You Showed Me (Tickson, BMI) ... 34


## BUBBLING UNDER THE HOT 100

101. SATURDAY NIGHT AT THE WORLD..Mason Williams, Warner Bros.-7 Arts 7248
102. LONG LONE RIDER....Bobby Darin, Direction 350
103. SOUL SHAKE....Peggy Scott & JoJo Benson, SSS International 761
104. MY BABY SPECIALIZES....William Bell & Judy Clay, Stax 0017
105. I'M IN LOVE WITH YOU..Kasenetz Katz Singing Orchestral Circus, Buddah 82
106. DIZZY....Tommy Roe, ABC 11164
107. TIME OF THE SEASON....Zombies, Date 2-1268
108. WOMAN HELPING MAN....Vogues, Reprise 0802
109. LIGHT MY FIRE....Rhetta Hughes, Tetragrammaton 1513
110. ELOISE....Barry Ryan, MGM 14010
111. THE THOUGHT OF LOVING YOU....Crystal Mansion, Capitol 2275
112. NO NOT MUCH....Smoke Ring, Buddah 77
113. GREAT BALLS OF FIRE....Tiny Tim, Reprise 0802
114. SLEEP IN THE GRASS....Ann Margret-Lee Hazlewood, LHI 2
115. CARLIE....Bobby Russell, Elf 90-023
116. NOBODY....3 Dog Night, Dunhill 4168
117. I DON'T WANT TO CRY....Ruby Winters, Diamond 255
118. THE MEDITATION....T.N.T. Band, Cotique C-136
119. WHERE HAVE ALL THE FLOWERS GONE....Wes Montgomery, A&M 1008
120. JOHNNY ONE TIME....Brenda Lee, Decca 32428
121. YOU GAVE ME A MOUNTAIN....Frankie Laine, ABC 11174
122. A BROKEN MAN....Malibus, White Whale 289
123. CLASSICAL GAS/SCARBOROUGH FAIR ....Alan Copeland Singers, A&M 988
124. HOT SMOKE & SASSAFRASS....Bubble Puppy, International Artists 128
125. FLYIN' HIGH....Julius Wechter & the Baja Marimba Band, A&M 1005
126. (I'M INTO LOOKIN' FOR) SOMEONE TO LOVE ME...Bobby Vee, Liberty 56080
127. WITCHI TAI TO....Everything Is Everything, Vanguard 35028
128. SHE'S ALMOST YOU....Billy Harner, Open 1253

Compiled from national retail sales and radio station airplay by the Music Popularity Dept. of Record Market Research, Billboard.

# Billboard HOT 100

FOR WEEK ENDING FEBRUARY 1, 1969

★ STAR PERFORMER—Sides registering greatest proportionate upward progress this week.

Record Industry Association of America seal of certification as million selling single.

| THIS WEEK | 1 Wk. Ago | 2 Wks. Ago | 3 Wks. Ago | TITLE | Artist (Producer), Label & Number | Weeks On Chart |
|---|---|---|---|---|---|---|
| Billboard Award | 2 | 4 | 8 | CRIMSON & CLOVER | Tommy James & the Shondells (Tommy James), Roulette R-7028 | 8 |
| ★ 2 | 5 | 15 | 26 | EVERYDAY PEOPLE | Sly & Family Stone (Sly Stone), Epic 10407 | 10 |
| ★ 3 | 8 | 9 | 23 | WORST THAT COULD HAPPEN | Brooklyn Bridge (Wes Farrell), Buddah 75 | 7 |
| ★ 4 | 7 | 8 | 18 | TOUCH ME | Doors (Paul A. Rothchild), Elektra 45646 | 6 |
| 5 | 1 | 1 | 1 | I HEARD IT THROUGH THE GRAPEVINE | Marvin Gaye (Norman Whitfield), Tamla 54176 | 11 |
| 6 | 3 | 2 | 2 | I'M GONNA MAKE YOU LOVE ME | Diana Ross & Supremes & Temptations (F. Wilson & N. Ashford), Motown 1137 | 9 |
| 7 | 9 | 16 | 19 | I STARTED A JOKE | Bee Gees (Robert Stigwood, The Bee Gees), Atco 6639 | 7 |
| 8 | 6 | 5 | 5 | HOOKED ON A FEELING | B. J. Thomas (Chips Moman), Scepter 12230 | 12 |
| 9 | 4 | 3 | 4 | SOULFUL STRUT | Young-Holt Unlimited (Carl Davis & Eugene Record), Brunswick 55391 | 10 |
| ★ 10 | 28 | 31 | 48 | BUILD ME UP BUTTERCUP | The Foundations (Tony Macaulay), UNI 55101 | 5 |
| 11 | 12 | 25 | 28 | CAN I CHANGE MY MIND | Tyrone Davis (Willie Henderson), Dakar 602 | 7 |
| 12 | 16 | 17 | 17 | IF I CAN DREAM | Elvis Presley (Bones Howe & Steve Binder), RCA Victor 47-9670 | 10 |
| 13 | 15 | 27 | 31 | HANG 'EM HIGH | Booker T. & M.G.'s (Booker T. & M.G.'s), Stax 0013 | 13 |
| 14 | 10 | 10 | 13 | SON OF A PREACHER MAN | Dusty Springfield (Jerry Wexler, Tom Dowd, Arif Mardin), Atlantic 2580 | 10 |
| 15 | 11 | 12 | 12 | GOING UP THE COUNTRY | Canned Heat (Canned Heat & Skip Taylor), Liberty 56077 | 9 |
| ★ 16 | 37 | 43 | 65 | THIS MAGIC MOMENT | Jay & the Americans (Jata Ent.), United Artists 50475 | 6 |
| ★ 17 | 34 | 46 | 72 | YOU SHOWED ME | Turtles (Chip Douglas), White Whale 292 | 4 |
| 18 | 13 | 6 | 3 | WICHITA LINEMAN | Glen Campbell (Al de Lory), Capitol 2302 | 14 |
| 19 | 22 | 24 | 33 | STAND BY YOUR MAN | Tammy Wynette (Billy Sherrill), Epic 10398 | 13 |
| ★ 20 | 33 | 48 | 54 | RAMBLIN' GAMBLIN' MAN | Bob Seeger (Hideout), Capitol 2297 | 7 |
| 21 | 21 | 34 | 35 | (There's Gonna Be a) SHOWDOWN | Archie Bell & the Drells (Gamble-Huff), Atlantic 2583 | 8 |
| ★ 22 | 47 | — | — | I'M LIVIN' IN SHAME | Diana Ross & the Supremes (The Clan), Motown 1139 | 2 |
| 23 | 25 | 26 | 27 | HEY JUDE | Wilson Pickett (Rick Hall), Atlantic 2591 | 7 |
| ★ 24 | 32 | 37 | 46 | I'VE GOTTA BE ME | Sammy Davis Jr. (Jimmy Bowen), Reprise 0779 | 8 |
| 25 | 24 | 14 | 14 | LO MUCHO QUE TE QUIERO (The More I Love You) | Rene & Rene, White Whale 287 | 11 |
| 26 | 18 | 11 | 11 | CINNAMON | Derek (George Tobin & Johnny Cymbal), Bang 558 | 15 |
| 27 | 29 | 29 | 34 | CALIFORNIA SOUL | 5th Dimension (Bones Howe), Soul City 770 | 7 |
| 28 | 31 | 42 | 47 | BABY, BABY DON'T CRY | Smokey Robinson 7 Miracles (Smokey, Moore, Johnson), Tamla 54178 | 5 |
| 29 | 19 | 18 | 9 | LOVE CHILD | Diana Ross & Supremes (Clan), Motown 1135 | 16 |
| 30 | 17 | 13 | 6 | CLOUD NINE | Temptations (Norman Whitfield), Gordy 7081 | 12 |
| 31 | 14 | 7 | 7 | FOR ONCE IN MY LIFE | Stevie Wonder (Henry Cosby), Tamla 54174 | 14 |
| 32 | 20 | 19 | 10 | I LOVE HOW YOU LOVE ME | Bobby Vinton (Billy Sherrill), Epic 10397 | 14 |
| 33 | 23 | 23 | 21 | TOO WEAK TO FIGHT | Clarence Carter (Rick Hall & Staff), Atlantic 2569 | 13 |
| ★ 34 | 52 | 62 | 91 | GAMES PEOPLE PLAY | Joe South (Joe South), Capitol 2248 | 4 |
| ★ 35 | 36 | 36 | 39 | BABY LET'S WAIT | Royal Guardsmen (Gernhard-Brumage-Fuller), Laurie 3461 | 12 |
| ★ 36 | 45 | 47 | 83 | GOODNIGHT MY LOVE | Paul Anka (Don Costa), RCA Victor 47-9648 | 5 |
| 37 | 40 | 67 | — | TAKE CARE OF YOUR HOMEWORK | Johnnie Taylor (Al Jackson Jr. & Don Davis), Stax 0023 | 3 |
| 38 | 38 | 39 | 51 | THE BEGINNING OF MY END | Unifics (Guy Draper), Kapp 957 | 8 |
| 39 | 26 | 20 | 15 | STORMY | Classics IV (Buddy Buie), Imperial 66328 | 15 |
| 40 | 30 | 30 | 25 | THIS IS MY COUNTRY | Impressions (Curtis Mayfield), Curtom 1934 | 10 |
| ★ 41 | 50 | 52 | 58 | SOUL SISTER, BROWN SUGAR | Sam & Dave (Hayes & Porter), Atlantic 2590 | 7 |
| ★ 42 | 63 | — | — | GIVE IT UP OR TURNIT A LOOSE | James Brown (James Brown), King 6213 | 2 |
| 43 | 39 | 40 | 42 | ARE YOU HAPPY | Jerry Butler (Gamble-Huff), Mercury 72876 | 9 |
| ★ 44 | 66 | 71 | — | BUT YOU KNOW I LOVE YOU | First Edition (Jimmy Bowen), Reprise 0799 | 3 |
| 45 | 35 | 41 | 43 | READY OR NOT HERE I COME (Can't Hide From Love) | Delfonics (Stan & Bell Prod.), Philly Groove 154 | 9 |
| ★ 46 | — | — | — | SOUL SHAKE | Peggy Scott & JoJo Benson (Shelby Singleton Jr.), SSS International 761 | 1 |
| 47 | 48 | 49 | 64 | DOES ANYBODY KNOW I'M HERE | Dells (Bobby Miller), Cadet 5631 | 6 |
| ★ 48 | 68 | 77 | — | HOME COOKIN' | Jr. Walker & All Stars (Henry Cosby), Soul 35055 | 3 |
| ★ 49 | 54 | 55 | 55 | A MINUTE OF YOUR TIME | Tom Jones (Peter Sullivan), Parrot 40035 | 7 |
| 50 | 56 | 58 | 82 | THINGS I'D LIKE TO SAY | New Colony Six, Mercury 72858 | 6 |
| ★ 51 | 61 | 64 | 73 | SWEET CREAM LADIES | Box Tops (Chips Moxen/Tommy Cogbill), Mala 12035 | 6 |
| ★ 52 | 85 | — | — | INDIAN GIVER | 1910 Fruitgum Co. (Kasenetz, Katz), Buddah 91 | 2 |
| ★ 53 | 59 | 61 | 63 | FEELIN' SO GOOD | Archies (Jeff Barry), Calender 63-1007 | 6 |
| 54 | 55 | 57 | 74 | CONDITION RED | Goodees (Davis, Briggs), HIP 8005 | 7 |
| ★ 55 | 62 | — | — | PROUD MARY | Creedence Clearwater Revival (John Fogerty), Fantasy 619 | 2 |
| 56 | 53 | 53 | 59 | DADDY SANG BASS | Johnny Cash (Bob Johnson), Columbia 4-44689 | 6 |
| 57 | 51 | 51 | 56 | OB-LA-DI OB-LA-DA | Arthur Conley (Tom Dowd), Atco 6640 | 5 |
| 58 | 49 | 50 | 60 | RAINBOW RIDE | Andy Kim (Jeff Barry), Steed 711 | 7 |
| 59 | 60 | 69 | 78 | I FORGOT TO BE YOUR LOVER | William Bell (Booker T. Jones), Stax 0015 | 5 |
| 60 | 43 | 45 | 52 | CALIFORNIA DREAMIN' | Bobby Womack (Chips Moman), Minit 32055 | 9 |
| 61 | 64 | 65 | 76 | ELECTRIC STORIES | 4 Seasons (Gaudic-Crewe), Philips 40577 | 6 |
| ★ 62 | 65 | 66 | 81 | RAIN IN MY HEART | Frank Sinatra (Don Costa), Reprise 0798 | 5 |
| ★ 63 | 69 | 76 | — | THERE'LL COME A TIME | Betty Everett (Archie Lee Hill Prod.), Uni 55100 | 3 |
| 64 | 57 | 60 | 75 | NOT ON THE OUTSIDE | Momcats (Sylvia & L. Roberts), Stang 5000 | 6 |
| ★ 65 | 99 | — | — | CROSSROADS | Cream (Felix Pappalardi), Atco 6646 | 2 |
| 66 | 72 | — | — | RIVER DEEP—MOUNTAIN HIGH | Deep Purple (Lawrence), Tetragrammaton 1514 | 2 |
| 67 | 67 | 97 | — | THIS OLD HEART OF MINE | Tammi Terrell (Holland & Dozier), Motown 1138 | 3 |
| 68 | 71 | 79 | 97 | RIOT | Hugh Masekela (Chisa Prod.), Uni 55102 | 4 |
| ★ 69 | — | — | — | GOOD LOVIN' AIN'T EASY TO COME BY | Marvin Gaye & Tammi Terrell (Ashford & Simpson), Tamla 54179 | 1 |
| ★ 70 | 73 | 74 | — | I GOT A LINE ON YOU | Spirit (Lou Adler), Ode 115 | 3 |
| 71 | 78 | — | — | PURPLE HAZE | Dion (Laurie Prod.), Laurie 3478 | 2 |
| 72 | 74 | 75 | 98 | TRAGEDY | Brian Hyland (Ray Ruff), Dot 17176 | 4 |
| ★ 73 | 92 | 93 | — | KUM BA YAH | Tommy Leonetti (Bill Justis), Decca 32421 | 3 |
| ★ 74 | — | — | — | 30-60-90 | Willie Mitchell (Willie Mitchell), Hi 2154 | 1 |
| 75 | 75 | 88 | — | POOR SIDE OF TOWN | Al Wilson (Johnny Rivers & Marc Gordon), Soul City 771 | 3 |
| 76 | 76 | 94 | — | I'M GONNA HOLD ON AS LONG AS I CAN | Marvelettes (Frank Wilson), Tamla 54177 | 3 |
| 77 | 81 | 82 | — | GETTING THE CORNERS | T.S.U. Toronadoes (A Frazier/McKay Production), Atlantic 2579 | 3 |
| 78 | 80 | 81 | 90 | IF IT WASN'T FOR BAD LUCK | Ray Charles & Jimmy Lewis (Tangerine Records), ABC 11170 | 5 |
| 79 | 89 | 89 | — | MAY I | Bill Deal & the Rhondels (Jerry Ross Prod.), Heritage 803 | 3 |
| ★ 80 | 100 | — | — | HEY! BABY | Jose Feliciano (Rick Jarrard), RCA 47-9714 | 2 |
| 81 | 87 | 87 | — | BUBBLE GUM MUSIC | Rock & Roll Dubble Bubble Trading Card Co. of Philadelphia 19141 (Jerry Goldstein), Buddah 78 | 3 |
| 82 | 82 | — | — | THE GREATEST LOVE | Dorsey Burnette (Snuff Garrett), Liberty 56087 | 2 |
| 83 | 77 | 78 | — | HE CALLED ME BABY | Ella Washington (J.R. Enterprises), Sound Stage 7 2621 | 3 |
| 84 | 86 | 90 | — | THE GROOVIEST GIRL IN THE WORLD | Fun & Games (Gary Zekley), Uni 55098 | 3 |
| 85 | 79 | 80 | — | ALMOST PERSUADED | Etta James (Rick Hall & Staff), Cadet 5630 | 3 |
| ★ 86 | — | — | — | DIZZY | Tommy Roe (Steve Barri), ABC 11164 | 1 |
| 87 | 90 | — | — | LET IT BE ME | Glen Campbell & Bobbie Gentry (Al DeLory & Kelly Gordon), Capitol 2387 | 2 |
| 88 | 88 | 100 | — | THAT'S YOUR BABY | Joe Tex (Buddy Killen), Dial 4089 | 3 |
| ★ 89 | — | — | — | GRITS AIN'T GROCERIES | Little Milton (Calvin Carter), Checker 1212 | 1 |
| ★ 90 | — | — | — | WOMAN HELPING MAN | Vogues (Dick Glasser), Reprise 0803 | 1 |
| 91 | 96 | 99 | — | MENDOCINO | Sir Douglas Quintet (Amigas de Musica), Smash 2191 | 3 |
| 92 | — | — | — | THIS GIRL'S IN LOVE WITH YOU | Dionne Warwick (Bacharach-David), Scepter 12241 | 1 |
| 93 | 93 | — | — | THE CARROLL COUNTY ACCIDENT | Porter Wagoner (Bob Ferguson), RCA Victor 47-9651 | 2 |
| 94 | 95 | 96 | — | WILL YOU BE STAYING AFTER SUNDAY | Peppermint Rainbow (Paul Leka), Decca 32410 | 3 |
| 95 | — | — | — | DO YOUR OWN THING | Watts 103rd Street Band, Reprise 7250 | 1 |
| 96 | — | — | — | MY SPECIAL PRAYER | Percy Sledge, Atlantic 2594 | 1 |
| 97 | — | — | — | SOMEDAY SOON | Judy Collins (David Anderly) Elektra 45659 | 1 |
| 98 | 98 | — | — | PLEASE DON'T DESERT ME BABY | Gloria Walker & Chevelles (Eugene Davis), Flaming Arrow 36 | 2 |
| 99 | — | — | — | SATURDAY NIGHT AT THE WORLD | Mason Williams (Dick Glasser), Warner Bros.-Seven Arts 7248 | 1 |
| 100 | — | — | — | CLOUD NINE | Mongo Santamaria (David Rubinson), Columbia 4-44740 | 1 |

## HOT 100—A TO Z—(Publisher-Licensee)

Almost Persuaded (Gallico, BMI) .... 85
Are You Happy (World War III/Parabut, BMI) .... 43
Baby, Baby Don't Cry (Jobete, BMI) .... 28
Baby Let's Wait (Web IV, BMI) .... 35
Beginnnig of My End, The (Cuydra, BMI) .... 38
Bubble Gum Music (Greyhound, BMI) .... 81
Build Me Up Buttercup (January-Nice, BMI) .... 10
But You Know I Love You (First Edition, BMI) .... 44
Can I Change My Mind (Dakar, BMI) .... 11
California Dreamin' (Honest John, ASCAP) .... 60
California Soul (Jobete, BMI) .... 27
Carroll County Accident, The (Warden, BMI) .... 93
Cinnamon (Pamco, BMI) .... 26
Cloud Nine (Jobete, BMI) (Temptations) .... 30
Cloud Nine (Jobete, BMI) (Mongo Santamaria) .... 100
Crimson & Clover (Big Seven Music, BMI) .... 1
Condition Red (East Groovesville, BMI) .... 54
Crossroads (Noma, BMI) .... 65
Daddy Sang Bass (House of Cash-Cedarwood, BMI) .... 56
Dizzy (Low Twine, BMI) .... 86
Do Your Own Thing (Charles Wright & Fred Smith) (Wright-Gerstl-Tamerlan, BMI) .... 95
Does Anybody Know I'm Here (Chevis, BMI) .... 47
Electric Stories (Screen Gems-Columbia, BMI) .... 61
Everyday People (Daly City, BMI) .... 2
Feelin' So Good (Kirshner, BMI) .... 53
For Once in My Life (Stein & Van Stock, ASCAP) .... 31
Games People Play (Lowery, BMI) .... 34
Getting the Corners (Cotillion-Broken Soul, BMI) .... 77
Give It Up or Turnit a Loose (Brown & Sons, BMI) .... 42
Going Up the Country (Metric, BMI) .... 15
Good Lovin' Ain't Easy to Come By (Jobete, BMI) .... 69
Goodnight My Love (Spanka, BMI) .... 36
Greatest Love, The (Lowery, BMI) .... 82
Grits Ain't Groceries (Lois, BMI) .... 89
Grooviest Girl in the World, The (Teeny Bopper, ASCAP) .... 84
Hang 'Em High (Unart, BMI) .... 13
He Called Me Baby (Central Song, BMI) .... 83
Hey! Baby (LeBill, BMI) .... 80
Hey Jude (Maclen, BMI) .... 23
Home Cookin' (Jobete, BMI) .... 48
Hooked on a Feeling (Press, BMI) .... 8
I Forgot To Be Your Lover (Memphis, BMI) .... 59
If It Wasn't For Bad Luck (Tangerine Music Corp., BMI) .... 78
I Got a Line on You (Hollenbeck, BMI) .... 70
I Heard It Through the Grapevine (Jobete, BMI) .... 5
I Love How You Love Me (Screen Gems-Columbia, BMI) .... 32
I Started a Joke (Casserole, BMI) .... 7
If I Can Dream (Gladys, ASCAP) .... 12
Indian Giver (Kaskat/Kahoona, BMI) .... 52
I'm Gonna Hold On as Long as I Can (Jobete, BMI) .... 76
I'm Gonna Make You Love Me (M.R.C., BMI) .... 6
I'm Livin' in Shame (Jobete, BMI) .... 22
I've Gotta Be Me (Damila, ASCAP) .... 24
Kum Ba Yah (Clinton, ASCAP) .... 73
Let It Be Me (M.C.A., ASCAP) .... 87
Lo Mucho Que Te Quiero (The More I Love You) (Pecos, BMI) .... 25
Love Child (Jobete, BMI) .... 29
May I (Rhinelander, BMI) .... 79
Mendocino (Southern Love, BMI) .... 91
Minute of Your Time, A (Anne-Rachel, ASCAP) .... 49
My Special Prayer (Quin Ivy & Marlin Greene) (Maureen, BMI) .... 96
Not On the Outside (Gambi, BMI) .... 64
Ob-La-Di Ob-La-Da (Maclen, BMI) .... 57
Please Don't Desert Me Baby (Cotillion/Flaming Arrow, BMI) .... 98
Poor Side of Town (Rivers, BMI) .... 75
Proud Mary (Jondora, BMI) .... 55
Purple Haze (Sea Lark, BMI) .... 71
Ramblin' Gamblin' Man (Gear, ASCAP) .... 20
Rain In My Heart (Razzle Dazzle Music, BMI) .... 62
Rainbow Ride (Unart-Joachim, BMI) .... 58
Ready or Not Here I Come (Can't Hide From Love) (Nickel Shoe, BMI) .... 45
Riot (Cherio, BMI) .... 68
River Deep—Mountain High (Trio, BMI) .... 66
Saturday Night at the World (Irving, BMI) .... 99
Someday Soon (Witmark, BMI) .... 97
Son of a Preacher Man (Tree, BMI) .... 14
Soul Shake (Singleton, BMI) .... 46
Soul Sister, Brown Sugar (Walden-Birdees, ASCAP) .... 41
Soulful Strut (Dakar/RC, BMI) .... 9
Stand by Your Man (Gallico, BMI) .... 19
Stormy (Low-Sal, BMI) .... 39
Sweet Cream Ladies (Blackwood, BMI) .... 51
Take Care of Your Homework (East/Memphis, BMI) .... 37
That's Your Baby (Tree, BMI) .... 88
There'll Come a Time (Jalynne, BMI) .... 63
(There's Gonna Be a) Showdown (Downstairs/Double Diamond, BMI) .... 21
Things I'd Like to Say (New Colony-T.M., BMI) .... 50
30-60-90 (Jec, BMI) .... 74
This Girl's in Love With You (Blue Seas/Jac, ASCAP) .... 92
This Is My Country (Camad, BMI) .... 40
This Magic Moment (Rumbalero/Progressive) .... 16
This Old Heart of Mine (Jobete, BMI) .... 67
Touch Me (Nipper, ASCAP) .... 4
Too Weak to Fight (Fame, BMI) .... 33
Tragedy (Bluff City, BMI) .... 72
Wichita Lineman (Canopy, ASCAP) .... 18
Will You Be Staying After Sunday (Screen Gems-Columbia, BMI) .... 94
Woman Helping Man (Viva, BMI) .... 90
Worst That Could Happen (Rivers, BMI) .... 3
You Showed Me (Tickson, BMI) .... 17

## BUBBLING UNDER THE HOT 100

101. LONG LINE RIDER .... Bobby Darin, Direction 350
102. FOX ON THE RUN .... Manfred Mann, Mercury 72879
103. TIME OF THE SEASON .... Zombies, Date 2-1268
104. LIGHT MY FIRE .... Rhetta Hughes, Tetragrammaton 1513
105. GREAT BALLS OF FIRE .... Tiny Tim, Reprise 0802
106. WITCHI TAI TO .... Everything Is Everything, Vanguard Apostolic 35028
107. ME ABOUT YOU .... Lovin' Spoonful, Kama Sutra 255
108. SOPHISTICATED SISSY .... Meters, Josie 1001
109. SWEETER THAN SUGAR .... Ohio Express, Buddah 92
110. I DON'T WANT TO CRY .... Ruby Winters, Diamond 255
111. NO NOT MUCH .... Smoke Ring, Buddah 77
112. MY WORLD IS EMPTY WITHOUT YOU .... Jose Feliciano, RCA 47-9714
113. SLEEP IN THE GRASS .... Ann-Margret & Lee Hazlewood, LHI 2
114. HONEY (I MISS YOU TOO) .... O. C. Smith, Columbia 444751
115. CARLIE .... Bobby Russell, Elf 90-023
116. JOHNNY ONE TIME .... Brenda Lee, Decca 32428
117. YOU GAVE ME A MOUNTAIN .... Frankie Laine, ABC 11174
118. MEDITATION .... T.N.T. Band, Cotique C-136
119. DREAM .... Sajid Khan, Colgems 66-1034
120. HOT SMOKE & SASSAFRASS .... Bubble Puppy, International Artists 128
121. SWITCH IT ON .... Cliff Nobles & Co., Phil-L.A. of Soul 32
122. A BROKEN MAN .... Malibus, White Whale 289
123. ONLY THE LONELY .... Sonny James, Capitol 2370
124. TRACES .... Classics IV, Imperial 63652
125. FLYIN' H'GH .... Julius Wechter & the Baja Marimba Band, A&M 1005
126. WHERE HAVE ALL THE FLOWERS GONE .... Wes Montgomery, A&M 1008
127. DON'T WASTE MY TIME .... B. B. King, BluesWays 61022
128. SHE'S ALMOST YOU .... Billy Harner, Open 1253
129. HELLO, IT'S ME .... Nazz, SGC 001
130. TO SUSAN ON THE WEST COAST WAITING .... Donovan, Epic 5-10434
131. NOTHING BUT A HEARTACHE .... Flirtations, Deram 85036
132. SHE'S NOT THERE .... Road, Kama Sutra 256

Compiled from national retail sales and radio station airplay by the Music Popularity Dept. of Record Market Research, Billboard.

# Billboard HOT 100

FOR WEEK ENDING FEBRUARY 8, 1969

★ STAR PERFORMER—Sides registering greatest proportionate upward progress this week.

(seal) Record Industry Association of America seal of certification as million selling single.

| This Week | 1 Wk. Ago | 2 Wks. Ago | 3 Wks. Ago | TITLE | Artist (Producer), Label & Number | Weeks On Chart |
|---|---|---|---|---|---|---|
| 1 (Billboard Award) | 1 | 2 | 4 | CRIMSON & CLOVER | Tommy James & the Shondells (Tommy James), Roulette R-7028 | 9 |
| 2 | 2 | 5 | 15 | EVERYDAY PEOPLE | Sly & Family Stone (Sly Stone), Epic 10407 | 11 |
| 3 | 3 | 8 | 9 | WORST THAT COULD HAPPEN | Brooklyn Bridge (Wes Farrell), Buddah 75 | 8 |
| 4 ★ | 4 | 7 | 8 | TOUCH ME | Doors (Paul A. Rothchild), Elektra 45646 | 7 |
| 5 ★ | 10 | 28 | 31 | BUILD ME UP BUTTERCUP | The Foundations (Tony Macaulay), UNI 55101 | 6 |
| 6 | 7 | 9 | 16 | I STARTED A JOKE | Bee Gees (Robert Stigwood, The Bee Gees), Atco 6639 | 8 |
| 7 | 5 | 1 | 1 | I HEARD IT THROUGH THE GRAPEVINE | Marvin Gaye (Norman Whitfield), Tamla 54176 | 12 |
| 8 | 6 | 3 | 2 | I'M GONNA MAKE YOU LOVE ME | Diana Ross & Supremes & Temptations (F. Wilson & N. Ashford), Motown 1137 | 10 |
| 9 ★ | 13 | 15 | 27 | HANG 'EM HIGH | Booker T. & M.G.'s (Booker T. & M.G.'s), Stax 0013 | 14 |
| 10 | 11 | 12 | 25 | CAN I CHANGE MY MIND | Tyrone Davis (Willie Henderson), Dakar 602 | 8 |
| 11 | 8 | 6 | 5 | HOOKED ON A FEELING | B. J. Thomas (Chips Moman), Scepter 12230 | 13 |
| 12 | 12 | 16 | 17 | IF I CAN DREAM | Elvis Presley (Bones Howe & Steve Binder), RCA Victor 47-9670 | 11 |
| 13 ★ | 16 | 37 | 43 | THIS MAGIC MOMENT | Jay & the Americans (Jata Ent.), United Artists 50475 | 7 |
| 14 ★ | 17 | 34 | 46 | YOU SHOWED ME | Turtles (Chip Douglas), White Whale 292 | 5 |
| 15 ★ | 22 | 47 | — | I'M LIVIN' IN SHAME | Diana Ross & the Supremes (The Clan), Motown 1139 | 3 |
| 16 | 15 | 11 | 12 | GOING UP THE COUNTRY | Canned Heat (Canned Heat & Skip Taylor), Liberty 56077 | 10 |
| 17 (seal) | 9 | 4 | 3 | SOULFUL STRUT | Young-Holt Unlimited (Carl Davis & Eugene Record), Brunswick 55391 | 11 |
| 18 | 14 | 10 | 10 | SON OF A PREACHER MAN | Dusty Springfield (Jerry Wexler, Tom Dowd, Arif Mardin), Atlantic 2580 | 11 |
| 19 ★ | 24 | 32 | 37 | I'VE GOTTA BE ME | Sammy Davis Jr. (Jimmy Bowen), Reprise 0779 | 9 |
| 20 | 20 | 33 | 48 | RAMBLIN' GAMBLIN' MAN | Bob Seeger (Hideout), Capitol 2297 | 8 |
| 21 ★ | 28 | 31 | 42 | BABY, BABY DON'T CRY | Smokey Robinson 7 Miracles (Smokey, Moore, Johnson), Tamla 54178 | 6 |
| 22 ★ | 34 | 52 | 62 | GAMES PEOPLE PLAY | Joe South (Joe South), Capitol 2248 | 5 |
| 23 | 19 | 22 | 24 | STAND BY YOUR MAN | Tammy Wynette (Billy Sherrill), Epic 10398 | 14 |
| 24 | 21 | 21 | 34 | (There's Gonna Be a) SHOWDOWN | Archie Bell & the Drells (Gamble-Huff), Atlantic 2583 | 9 |
| 25 | 27 | 29 | 29 | CALIFORNIA SOUL | 5th Dimension (Bones Howe), Soul City 770 | 8 |
| 26 | 37 | 40 | 67 | TAKE CARE OF YOUR HOMEWORK | Johnnie Taylor (Al Jackson Jr. & Don Davis), Stax 0023 | 4 |
| 27 | 25 | 24 | 14 | LO MUCHO QUE TE QUIERO (The More I Love You) | Rene & Rene, White Whale 287 | 12 |
| 28 ★ | 55 | 62 | — | PROUD MARY | Creedence Clearwater Revival (John Fogerty), Fantasy 619 | 3 |
| 29 | 18 | 13 | 6 | WICHITA LINEMAN | Glen Campbell (Al de Lory), Capitol 2302 | 15 |
| 30 | 36 | 45 | 47 | GOODNIGHT MY LOVE | Paul Anka (Don Costa), RCA Victor 47-9648 | 6 |
| 31 ★ | 44 | 66 | 71 | BUT YOU KNOW I LOVE YOU | First Edition (Jimmy Bowen), Reprise 0799 | 4 |
| 32 ★ | 52 | 85 | — | INDIAN GIVER | 1910 Fruitgum Co. (Kasenetz, Katz), Buddah 91 | 3 |
| 33 ★ | 51 | 61 | 64 | SWEET CREAM LADIES | Box Tops (Chips Moxen/Tommy Cogbill), Mala 12035 | 7 |
| 34 ★ | 65 | 99 | — | CROSSROADS | Cream (Felix Pappalardi), Atco 6646 | 3 |
| 35 | 23 | 25 | 26 | HEY JUDE | Wilson Pickett (Rick Hall), Atlantic 2591 | 8 |
| 36 | 38 | 38 | 39 | THE BEGINNING OF MY END | Unifics (Guy Draper), Kapp 957 | 9 |
| 37 | 42 | 63 | — | GIVE IT UP OR TURNIT A LOOSE | James Brown (James Brown), King 6213 | 3 |
| 38 | 33 | 23 | 23 | TOO WEAK TO FIGHT | Clarence Carter (Rick Hall & Staff), Atlantic 2569 | 14 |
| 39 | 47 | 48 | 49 | DOES ANYBODY KNOW I'M HERE | Dells (Bobby Miller), Cadet 5631 | 7 |
| 40 ★ | 92 | — | — | THIS GIRL'S IN LOVE WITH YOU | Dionne Warwick (Bacharach-David), Scepter 12241 | 2 |
| 41 | 41 | 50 | 52 | SOUL SISTER, BROWN SUGAR | Sam & Dave (Hayes & Porter), Atlantic 2590 | 8 |
| 42 | 48 | 68 | 77 | HOME COOKIN' | Jr. Walker & All Stars (Henry Cosby), Soul 35055 | 4 |
| 43 | 46 | — | — | SOUL SHAKE | Peggy Scott & JoJo Benson (Shelby Singleton Jr.), SSS International 761 | 2 |
| 44 ★ | 86 | — | — | DIZZY | Tommy Roe (Steve Barri), ABC 11164 | 2 |
| 45 ★ | 69 | — | — | GOOD LOVIN' AIN'T EASY TO COME BY | Marvin Gaye & Tammi Terrell (Ashford & Simpson), Tamla 54179 | 2 |
| 46 | 54 | 55 | 57 | CONDITION RED | Goodees (Davis, Briggs), HIP 8005 | 8 |
| 47 | 50 | 56 | 58 | THINGS I'D LIKE TO SAY | New Colony Six, Mercury 72858 | 7 |
| 48 | 43 | 39 | 40 | ARE YOU HAPPY | Jerry Butler (Gamble-Huff), Mercury 72876 | 10 |
| 49 | 49 | 54 | 55 | A MINUTE OF YOUR TIME | Tom Jones (Peter Sullivan), Parrot 40035 | 8 |
| 50 | 35 | 36 | 36 | BABY LET'S WAIT | Royal Guardsmen (Gernhard-Brumage-Fuller), Laurie 3461 | 13 |
| 51 ★ | 63 | 69 | 76 | THERE'LL COME A TIME | Betty Everett (Archie Lee Hill Prod.), Uni 55100 | 4 |
| 52 | 56 | 53 | 53 | DADDY SANG BASS | Johnny Cash (Bob Johnson), Columbia 4-44689 | 7 |
| 53 ★ | 66 | 72 | — | RIVER DEEP—MOUNTAIN HIGH | Deep Purple (Lawrence), Tetragrammaton 1514 | 3 |
| 54 ★ | 70 | 73 | 74 | I GOT A LINE ON YOU | Spirit (Lou Adler), Ode 115 | 4 |
| 55 ★ | 68 | 71 | 79 | RIOT | Hugh Masekela (Chisa Prod.), Uni 55102 | 5 |
| 56 | 59 | 60 | 69 | I FORGOT TO BE YOUR LOVER | William Bell (Booker T. Jones), Stax 0015 | 6 |
| 57 | 57 | 51 | 51 | OB-LA-DI OB-LA-DA | Arthur Conley (Tom Dowd), Atco 6640 | 6 |
| 58 | 53 | 59 | 61 | FEELIN' SO GOOD | Archies (Jeff Barry), Calender 63-1007 | 7 |
| 59 ★ | 90 | — | — | WOMAN HELPING MAN | Vogues (Dick Glasser), Reprise 0803 | 2 |
| 60 ★ | — | — | — | TIME OF THE SEASON | Zombies (Rod Argent & Chris White), Date 2-1628 | 1 |
| 61 ★ | — | — | — | TRACES | Classics IV (Buddie Buie), Imperial 66352 | 1 |
| 62 | 62 | 65 | 66 | RAIN IN MY HEART | Frank Sinatra (Don Costa), Reprise 0798 | 6 |
| 63 | 71 | 78 | — | PURPLE HAZE | Dion (Laurie Prod.), Laurie 3478 | 3 |
| 64 | 64 | 57 | 60 | NOT ON THE OUTSIDE | Moments (Sylvia & L. Roberts), Stang 5000 | 7 |
| 65 ★ | 72 | 74 | 75 | TRAGEDY | Brian Hyland (Ray Ruff), Dot 17176 | 5 |
| 66 | 73 | 92 | 93 | KUM BA YAH | Tommy Leonetti (Bill Justis), Decca 32421 | 4 |
| 67 ★ | — | — | — | TO SUSAN ON THE WEST COAST WAITING | Donovan (Mickie Most), Epic 5-10434 | 1 |
| 68 | 87 | 90 | — | LET IT BE ME | Glen Campbell & Bobbie Gentry (Al DeLory & Kelly Gordon), Capitol 2387 | 3 |
| 69 ★ | — | — | — | YOU GAVE ME A MOUNTAIN | Frankie Laine (Jimmy Bowen), ABC 11174 | 1 |
| 70 | 79 | 89 | 89 | MAY I | Bill Deal & the Rhondels (Jerry Ross Prod.), Heritage 803 | 4 |
| 71 ★ | — | — | — | SOPHISTICATED SISSY | Meters (Marshall E. Sehorn & Allen Toussaint), Josie 1001 | 1 |
| 72 | 67 | 67 | 97 | THIS OLD HEART OF MINE | Tammi Terrell (Holland & Dozier), Motown 1138 | 4 |
| 73 | 74 | — | — | 30-60-90 | Willie Mitchell (Willie Mitchell), Hi 2154 | 2 |
| 74 | 81 | 87 | 87 | BUBBLE GUM MUSIC | Rock & Roll Dubble Bubble Trading Card Co. of Philadelphia 19141 (Jerry Goldstein), Buddah 78 | 4 |
| 75 | 77 | 81 | 82 | GETTING THE CORNERS | T.S.U. Toronadoes (A Frazier/McKay Production), Atlantic 2579 | 4 |
| 76 | 80 | 100 | — | HEY! BABY | Jose Feliciano (Rick Jarrard), RCA 47-9714 | 3 |
| 77 | 78 | 80 | 81 | IF IT WASN'T FOR BAD LUCK | Ray Charles & Jimmy Lewis (Tangerine Records), ABC 11170 | 6 |
| 78 | 84 | 86 | 90 | THE GROOVIEST GIRL IN THE WORLD | Fun & Games (Gary Zekley), Uni 55098 | 4 |
| 79 | 82 | 82 | — | THE GREATEST LOVE | Dorsey Burnette (Snuff Garrett), Liberty 56087 | 3 |
| 80 | 85 | 79 | 80 | ALMOST PERSUADED | Etta James (Rick Hall & Staff), Cadet 5630 | 4 |
| 81 ★ | — | — | — | LONG LINE RIDER | Bobby Darin (Bobby Darin), Direction 350 | 1 |
| 82 | 75 | 75 | 88 | POOR SIDE OF TOWN | Al Wilson (Johnny Rivers & Marc Gordon), Soul City 771 | 4 |
| 83 | 100 | — | — | CLOUD NINE | Mongo Santamaria (David Rubinson), Columbia 4-44740 | 2 |
| 84 | 91 | 96 | 99 | MENDOCINO | Sir Douglas Quintet (Amigas de Musica), Smash 2191 | 4 |
| 85 | 97 | — | — | SOMEDAY SOON | Judy Collins (David Anderly) Elektra 45659 | 2 |
| 86 ★ | — | — | — | HONEY | O. C. Smith (Jerry Fuller), Columbia 44751 | 1 |
| 87 ★ | — | — | — | MY WORLD IS EMPTY WITHOUT YOU | Jose Feliciano (Rick Jarrard), RCA 47-9714 | 1 |
| 88 ★ | — | — | — | JOHNNY ONE TIME | Brenda Lee (Mike Berniker), Decca 32428 | 1 |
| 89 | 89 | — | — | GRITS AIN'T GROCERIES | Little Milton (Calvin Carter), Checker 1212 | 2 |
| 90 ★ | — | — | — | HEAVEN | Rascals (Rascals), Atlantic 2599 | 1 |
| 91 | — | — | — | ME ABOUT YOU | The Lovin' Spoonful (Bob Finiz), Kama Sutra 255 | 1 |
| 92 | 93 | 93 | — | THE CARROLL COUNTY ACCIDENT | Porter Wagoner (Bob Ferguson), RCA Victor 47-9651 | 3 |
| 93 | — | — | — | WITCHI TAI TO | Everything Is Everything (Danny Weiss) Vanguard Apostolic 35082 | 1 |
| 94 | 95 | — | — | DO YOUR OWN THING | Watts 103rd Street Band, Reprise 7250 | 2 |
| 95 | 96 | — | — | MY SPECIAL PRAYER | Percy Sledge, Atlantic 2594 | 2 |
| 96 | — | — | — | THE TRA LA LA SONG (One Banana, Two Banana) | Banana Splits (David Nook), Decca 32429 | 1 |
| 97 | — | — | — | GREAT BALLS OF FIRE | Tiny Tim (Richard Perry), Reprise 0802 | 1 |
| 98 | — | — | — | GLAD SHE'S A WOMAN | Bobby Goldsboro (Bob Montgomery & Bobby Goldsboro), United Artists 50497 | 1 |
| 99 | — | — | — | TRY A LITTLE TENDERNESS | Three Dog Night (Gabriel Makler), Dunhill 4177 | 1 |
| 100 | — | — | — | ONLY THE LONELY | Sonny James (The Southern Gentleman) (Kelso Herston), Capitol 2370 | 1 |

## HOT 100—A TO Z—(Publisher-Licensee)

Almost Persuaded (Gallico, BMI) ........ 80
Are You Happy (World War III/Parabut, BMI) ........ 48

Baby, Baby Don't Cry (Jobete, BMI) ........ 21
Baby Let's Wait (Web IV, BMI) ........ 50
Beginning of My End, The (Cuydra, BMI) ........ 36
Bubble Gum Music (Greyhound, BMI) ........ 74
Build Me Up Buttercup (January-Nice, BMI) ........ 5
But You Know I Love You (First Edition, BMI) ........ 31

Can I Change My Mind (Dakar, BMI) ........ 10
California Soul (Jobete, BMI) ........ 25
Carroll County Accident, The (Warden, BMI) ........ 10
Cloud Nine (Jobete, BMI) ........ 83
Crimson & Clover (Big Seven Music, BMI) ........ 1
Condition Red (East Groovesville, BMI) ........ 46
Crossroads (Noma, BMI) ........ 34

Daddy Sang Bass (House of Cash-Cedarwood, BMI) ........ 52
Dizzy (Low Twine, BMI) ........ 44
Do Your Own Thing (Charles Wright & Fred Smith) (Wright-Gersti-Tamerlan, BMI) ........ 94
Does Anybody Know I'm Here (Chevis, BMI) ........ 39

Everyday People (Daly City, BMI) ........ 2
Feelin' So Good (Kirshner, BMI) ........ 58

Games People Play (Lowery, BMI) ........ 22
Getting the Corners (Cotillion-Broken Soul, BMI) ........ 75
Give It Up or Turnit a Loose (Brown & Sons, BMI) ........ 37
Glad She's a Woman (Tamerlane, BMI) ........ 98
Going Up the Country (Metric, BMI) ........ 16
Good Lovin' Ain't Easy to Come By (Jobete, BMI) ........ 45
Goodnight My Love (Spanka, BMI) ........ 30
Great Balls of Fire (BRS, BMI) ........ 97
Greatest Love, The (Lowery, BMI) ........ 79
Grits Ain't Groceries (Lois, BMI) ........ 89
Grooviest Girl in the World, The (Teeny Bopper, ASCAP) ........ 78

Hang 'Em High (Unart, BMI) ........ 9
Heaven (Slacsar, ASCAP) ........ 90
Hey! Baby (LeBill, BMI) ........ 76
Hey Jude (Maclen, BMI) ........ 35
Home Cookin' (Jobete, BMI) ........ 42
Honey (Russell-Cason, ASCAP) ........ 86
Hooked on a Feeling (Press, BMI) ........ 11

I Forgot To Be Your Lover (Memphis, BMI) ........ 56
If It Wasn't For Bad Luck (Tangerine Music Corp., BMI) ........ 77
I Got a Line on You (Hollenbeck, BMI) ........ 54
I Heard It Through the Grapevine (Jobete, BMI) ........ 7
I Started a Joke (Casserole, BMI) ........ 6
If I Can Dream (Gladys, ASCAP) ........ 12
Indian Giver (Kaskat/Kahoona, BMI) ........ 32
I'm Gonna Make You Love Me (M.R.C., BMI) ........ 8
I'm Livin' in Shame (Jobete, BMI) ........ 15
I've Gotta Be Me (Damila, ASCAP) ........ 19

Johnny One Time (Hill & Range/Blue Crest, BMI) ........ 88

Kum Ba Yah (Clinton, ASCAP) ........ 66
Let It Be Me (M.C.A., ASCAP) ........ 68
Lo Mucho Que Te Quiero (The More I Love You) (Pecos, BMI) ........ 27
Long Line Rider (Argent, BMI) ........ 81

May I (Rhinelander, BMI) ........ 70
Me About You (Charuon, BMI) ........ 91
Mendocino (Southern Love, BMI) ........ 84
Minute of Your Time, A (Anne-Rachel, ASCAP) ........ 49
My Special Prayer (Quin Ivy & Marlin Greene) (Maureen, BMI) ........ 95
My World Is Empty Without You (Jobete, BMI) ........ 87

Not On the Outside (Gambi, BMI) ........ 64

Ob-La-Di Ob-La-Da (Maclen, BMI) ........ 57
Only the Lonely (Acuff-Rose, BMI) ........ 100

Poor Side of Town (Rivers, BMI) ........ 82
Proud Mary (Jondora, BMI) ........ 28
Purple Haze (Sea Lark, BMI) ........ 63

Ramblin' Gamblin' Man (Gear, ASCAP) ........ 20
Rain In My Heart (Razzle Dazzle Music, BMI) ........ 62
Riot (Cherio, BMI) ........ 55
River Deep—Mountain High (Trio, BMI) ........ 53

Someday Soon (Witmark, BMI ) ........ 85
Son of a Preacher Man (Tree, BMI) ........ 18
Sophisticated Sissy (Marsaint, BMI) ........ 71
Soul Shake (Singleton, BMI) ........ 43
Soul Sister, Brown Sugar (Walden-Birdees, ASCAP) ........ 41
Soulful Strut (Dakar/RC, BMI) ........ 17
Stand by Your Man (Gallico, BMI) ........ 23
Sweet Cream Ladies (Blackwood, BMI) ........ 33

Take Care of Your Homework (East/Memphis, BMI) 26
There'll Come a Time (Jalynne, BMI) ........ 51
(There's Gonna Be a) Showdown (Downstairs/Double Diamond, BMI) ........ 24
Time of the Season (Mainstay, BMI) ........ 60
Things I'd Like to Say (New Colony-T.M., BMI) ........ 47
30-60-90 (Jec, BMI) ........ 73
This Girl's in Love With You (Blue Seas/Jac, ASCAP) ........ 40
This Magic Moment (Rumbalero/Progressive) ........ 13
This Old Heart of Mine (Jobete, BMI) ........ 72
To Susan on the West Coast Waiting (Peer Int'l, BMI) ........ 67
Touch Me (Nipper, ASCAP) ........ 4
Too Weak to Fight (Fame, BMI) ........ 38
Tra La La Song (One Banana, Two Banana) (Sea-Lark, BMI) ........ 96
Traces (Low-Sal, BMI) ........ 61
Tragedy (Bluff City, BMI) ........ 65
Try a Little Tenderness (Connelly & Robbins, ASCAP) ........ 99

Wichita Lineman (Canopy, ASCAP) ........ 29
Witchi Tai To (Lovetruth, BMI) ........ 93
Woman Helping Man (Viva, BMI) ........ 59
Worst That Could Happen (Rivers, BMI) ........ 3

You Gave Me a Mountain (Mojave, BMI) ........ 69
You Showed Me (Tickson, BMI) ........ 14

## BUBBLING UNDER THE HOT 100

101. FOX ON THE RUN........Manfred Mann, Mercury 72879
102. HE CALLED ME BABY........Ella Washington, Sound Stage 7 2621
103. LIGHT MY FIRE........Rhetta Hughes, Tetragrammaton 1513
104. WILL YOU BE STAYING AFTER SUNDAY....Peppermint Rainbow, Decca 32410
105. GIVE HER A TRANSPLANT........Intruders, Gamble G 223
106. I DON'T WANT TO CRY........Ruby Winters, Diamond 255
107. SATURDAY NIGHT AT THE WORLD........Mason Williams, Warner Bros.-Seven Arts 7248
108. ANYTHING YOU CHOOSE........Spanky & Our Gang, Mercury 72890
109. SWEETER THAN SUGAR........Ohio Express, Buddah 92
110. NO NOT MUCH........Smoke Ring, Buddah 77
111. HOT SMOKE & SASSAFRASS........Bubble Puppy, International Artists 128
112. GIVE IT AWAY........Chi-Lites, Brunswick 55398
113. SLEEP IN THE GRASS........Ann-Margret & Lee Hazlewood, LHI 2
114. SWITCH IT ON........Cliff Nobles & Co., Phil-L.A. of Soul 32
115. CHITTY CHITTY BANG BANG........New Christy Minstrels, Columbia 44631
116. IF........Al Hirt, RCA 47-9717
117. WHO'S GONNA MOW YOUR GRASS..Buck Owens & His Buckaroos, Capitol 2377
118. MEDITATION........T.N.T. Band, Cotique C-136
119. DREAM........Sajid Khan, Colgems 66-1034
120. AM I THE SAME GIRL........Barbara Acklin, Brunswick 55399
121. A BROKEN MAN........Malibus, White Whale 289
122. I'VE GOTTA HAVE YOUR LOVE........Eddie Floyd, Stax 0025
123. SHE'S ALMOST YOU........Billy Harner, Open 1253
124. HELLO, IT'S ME........Nazz, SGC 001
125. MR. SUN, MR. MOON........Paul Revere & the Raiders, Columbia 4-44744
126. DON'T WASTE MY TIME........B. B. King, BluesWays 61022
127. SHE'S NOT THERE........Road, Kama Sutra 256
128. NOTHING BUT A HEARTACHE........Flirtations, Deram 85036

Compiled from national retail sales and radio station airplay by the Music Popularity Dept. of Record Market Research, Billboard.

HOT 100

HOT 100

# Billboard HOT 100

FOR WEEK ENDING FEBRUARY 15, 1969

★ STAR PERFORMER—Sides registering greatest proportionate upward progress this week.

(Seal) Record Industry Association of America seal of certification as million selling single.

| THIS WEEK | 1 Wk. Ago | 2 Wks. Ago | 3 Wks. Ago | TITLE Artist (Producer), Label & Number | Weeks On Chart |
|---|---|---|---|---|---|
| Billboard Award (1) | 2 | 2 | 5 | EVERYDAY PEOPLE — Sly & Family Stone (Sly Stone), Epic 10407 | 12 |
| 2 | 1 | 1 | 2 | CRIMSON & CLOVER — Tommy James & the Shondells (Tommy James), Roulette R-7028 | 10 |
| 3 | 4 | 4 | 7 | TOUCH ME — Doors (Paul A. Rothchild), Elektra 45646 | 8 |
| 4 | 5 | 10 | 28 | BUILD ME UP BUTTERCUP — The Foundations (Tony Macaulay), UNI 55101 | 7 |
| 5 | 3 | 3 | 8 | WORST THAT COULD HAPPEN — Brooklyn Bridge (Wes Farrell), Buddah 75 | 9 |
| 6 | 10 | 11 | 12 | CAN I CHANGE MY MIND — Tyrone Davis (Willie Henderson), Dakar 602 | 9 |
| ★7 | 14 | 17 | 34 | YOU SHOWED ME — Turtles (Chip Douglas), White Whale 292 | 6 |
| 8 | 7 | 5 | 1 | I HEARD IT THROUGH THE GRAPEVINE — Marvin Gaye (Norman Whitfield), Tamla 54176 | 13 |
| 9 | 9 | 13 | 15 | HANG 'EM HIGH — Booker T. & M.G.'s (Booker T. & M.G.'s), Stax 0013 | 15 |
| 10 | 8 | 6 | 3 | I'M GONNA MAKE YOU LOVE ME — Diana Ross & Supremes & Temptations (F. Wilson & N. Ashford), Motown 1137 | 11 |
| 11 | 15 | 22 | 47 | I'M LIVING IN SHAME — Diana Ross & the Supremes (The Clan), Motown 1139 | 4 |
| 12 | 13 | 16 | 37 | THIS MAGIC MOMENT — Jay & the Americans (Jata Ent.), United Artists 50475 | 8 |
| 13 | 6 | 7 | 9 | I STARTED A JOKE — Bee Gees (Robert Stigwood, The Bee Gees), Atco 6639 | 9 |
| ★14 | 21 | 28 | 31 | BABY, BABY DON'T CRY — Smokey Robinson 7 Miracles (Smokey, Moore, Johnson), Tamla 54178 | 7 |
| ★15 | 22 | 34 | 52 | GAMES PEOPLE PLAY — Joe South (Joe South), Capitol 2248 | 6 |
| 16 | 12 | 12 | 16 | IF I CAN DREAM — Elvis Presley (Bones Howe & Steve Binder), RCA Victor 47-9670 | 12 |
| ★17 | 20 | 20 | 33 | RAMBLIN' GAMBLIN' MAN — Bob Seeger (Hideout), Capitol 2297 | 9 |
| (Seal) 18 | 17 | 9 | 4 | SOULFUL STRUT — Young-Holt Unlimited (Carl Davis & Eugene Record), Brunswick 55391 | 12 |
| 19 | 19 | 24 | 32 | I'VE GOTTA BE ME — Sammy Davis Jr. (Jimmy Bowen), Reprise 0779 | 10 |
| ★20 | 37 | 42 | 63 | GIVE IT UP OR TURNIT A LOOSE — James Brown (James Brown), King 6213 | 4 |
| ★21 | 28 | 55 | 62 | PROUD MARY — Creedence Clearwater Revival (John Fogerty), Fantasy 619 | 4 |
| 22 | 11 | 8 | 6 | HOOKED ON A FEELING — B. J. Thomas (Chips Moman), Scepter 12230 | 14 |
| 23 | 26 | 37 | 40 | TAKE CARE OF YOUR HOMEWORK — Johnnie Taylor (Al Jackson Jr. & Don Davis), Stax 0023 | 5 |
| 24 | 23 | 19 | 22 | STAND BY YOUR MAN — Tammy Wynette (Billy Sherrill), Epic 10398 | 15 |
| 25 | 24 | 21 | 21 | (There's Gonna Be a) SHOWDOWN — Archie Bell & the Drells (Gamble-Huff), Atlantic 2583 | 10 |
| ★26 | 40 | 92 | — | THIS GIRL'S IN LOVE WITH YOU — Dionne Warwick (Bacharach-David), Scepter 12241 | 3 |
| ★27 | 32 | 52 | 85 | INDIAN GIVER — 1910 Fruitgum Co. (Kasenetz, Katz), Buddah 91 | 4 |
| 28 | 30 | 36 | 45 | GOODNIGHT MY LOVE — Paul Anka (Don Costa), RGA Victor 47-9648 | 7 |
| 29 | 31 | 44 | 66 | BUT YOU KNOW I LOVE YOU — First Edition (Jimmy Bowen), Reprise 0799 | 5 |
| ★30 | 51 | 63 | 69 | THERE'LL COME A TIME — Betty Everett (Archie Lee Hill Prod.), Uni 55100 | 5 |
| ★31 | 47 | 50 | 56 | THINGS I'D LIKE TO SAY — New Colony Six, Mercury 72858 | 8 |
| 32 | 34 | 65 | 99 | CROSSROADS — Cream (Felix Pappalardi), Atco 6646 | 4 |
| 33 | 33 | 51 | 61 | SWEET CREAM LADIES — Box Tops (Chips Moman/Tommy Cogbill) Mala 12035 | 8 |
| 34 | 18 | 14 | 10 | SON OF A PREACHER MAN — Dusty Springfield (Jerry Wexler, Tom Dowd, Arif Mardin), Atlantic 2580 | 12 |
| 35 | 25 | 27 | 29 | CALIFORNIA SOUL — 5th Dimension (Bones Howe), Soul City 770 | 9 |
| ★36 | 45 | 69 | — | GOOD LOVIN' AIN'T EASY TO COME BY — Marvin Gaye & Tammi Terrell (Ashford & Simpson), Tamla 54179 | 3 |
| 37 | 16 | 15 | 11 | GOING UP THE COUNTRY — Canned Heat (Canned Heat & Skip Taylor), Liberty 56077 | 11 |
| 38 | 39 | 47 | 48 | DOES ANYBODY KNOW I'M HERE — Dells (Bobby Miller), Cadet 5631 | 8 |
| ★39 | 44 | 86 | — | DIZZY — Tommy Roe (Steve Barri), ABC 11164 | 3 |
| ★40 | 43 | 46 | — | SOUL SHAKE — Peggy Scott & JoJo Benson (Shelby Singleton Jr.), SSS International 761 | 3 |
| 41 | 35 | 23 | 25 | HEY JUDE — Wilson Pickett (Rick Hall), Atlantic 2591 | 9 |
| 42 | 42 | 48 | 68 | HOME COOKIN' — Jr. Walker & All Stars (Henry Cosby), Soul 35055 | 5 |
| 43 | 36 | 38 | 38 | THE BEGINNING OF MY END — Unifics (Guy Draper), Kapp 957 | 10 |
| 44 | 38 | 33 | 23 | TOO WEAK TO FIGHT — Clarence Carter (Rick Hall & Staff), Atlantic 2569 | 15 |
| ★45 | 52 | 56 | 53 | DADDY SANG BASS — Johnny Cash (Bob Johnson), Columbia 4-44689 | 8 |
| ★46 | 61 | — | — | TRACES — Classics IV (Buddie Buie), Imperial 66352 | 2 |
| ★47 | 56 | 59 | 60 | I FORGOT TO BE YOUR LOVER — William Bell (Booker T. Jones), Stax 0015 | 7 |
| 48 | 49 | 49 | 54 | A MINUTE OF YOUR TIME — Tom Jones (Peter Sullivan), Parrot 40035 | 9 |
| 49 | 41 | 41 | 50 | SOUL SISTER, BROWN SUGAR — Sam & Dave (Hayes & Porter), Atlantic 2590 | 9 |
| ★50 | — | — | — | MY WHOLE WORLD ENDED (The Moment You Left Me) — David Ruffin (Fuqua & Bristol), Motown 1140 | 1 |
| ★51 | 59 | 90 | — | WOMAN HELPING MAN — Vogues (Dick Glasser), Reprise 0803 | 3 |
| 52 | 60 | — | — | TIME OF THE SEASON — Zombies (Rod Argent & Chris White), Date 2-1628 | 2 |
| 53 | 53 | 66 | 72 | RIVER DEEP—MOUNTAIN HIGH — Deep Purple (Lawrence), Tetragrammaton 1514 | 4 |
| 54 | 54 | 70 | 73 | I GOT A LINE ON YOU — Spirit (Lou Adler), Ode 115 | 5 |
| 55 | 55 | 68 | 71 | RIOT — Hugh Masekela (Chisa Prod.), Uni 55102 | 6 |
| 56 | 46 | 54 | 55 | CONDITION RED — Goodees (Davis, Briggs), HIP 8005 | 9 |
| ★57 | 67 | — | — | TO SUSAN ON THE WEST COAST WAITING — Donovan (Mickie Most), Epic 5-10434 | 2 |
| ★58 | 70 | 79 | 89 | MAY I — Bill Deal & the Rhondels (Jerry Ross Prod.), Heritage 803 | 5 |
| ★59 | 90 | — | — | HEAVEN — Rascals (Rascals), Atlantic 2599 | 2 |
| ★60 | 68 | 87 | 90 | LET IT BE ME — Glen Campbell & Bobbie Gentry (Al DeLory & Kelly Gordon), Capitol 2387 | 4 |
| ★61 | 66 | 73 | 92 | KUM BA YAH — Tommy Leonetti (Bill Justis), Decca 32421 | 5 |
| 62 | 65 | 72 | 74 | TRAGEDY — Brian Hyland (Ray Ruff), Dot 17176 | 6 |
| 63 | 63 | 71 | 78 | PURPLE HAZE — Dion (Laurie Prod.), Laurie 3478 | 4 |
| ★64 | 71 | — | — | SOPHISTICATED SISSY — Meters (Marshall E. Sehorn & Allen Toussaint), Josie 1001 | 2 |
| 65 | 69 | — | — | YOU GAVE ME A MOUNTAIN — Frankie Laine (Jimmy Bowen), ABC 11174 | 2 |
| 66 | 58 | 53 | 59 | FEELIN' SO GOOD — Archies (Jeff Barry), Calender 63-1007 | 8 |
| ★67 | 83 | 100 | — | CLOUD NINE — Mongo Santamaria (David Rubinson), Columbia 4-44740 | 3 |
| ★68 | 94 | 95 | — | DO YOUR THING — Watts 103rd Street Band, Reprise 7250 | 3 |
| 69 | 73 | 74 | — | 30-60-90 — Willie Mitchell (Willie Mitchell), Hi 2154 | 3 |
| ★70 | — | — | — | RUN AWAY CHILD, RUNNING WILD — Temptations (Norman Whitfield), Gordy 7084 | 1 |
| 71 | 76 | 80 | 100 | HEY! BABY — Jose Feliciano (Rick Jarrard), RCA 47-9714 | 4 |
| ★72 | 93 | — | — | WITCHI TAI TO — Everything Is Everything (Danny Weiss) Vanguard Apostolic 35082 | 2 |
| ★73 | 89 | 89 | — | GRITS AIN'T GROCERIES — Little Milton (Calvin Carter), Checker 1212 | 3 |
| 74 | 79 | 82 | 82 | THE GREATEST LOVE — Dorsey Burnette (Snuff Garrett), Liberty 56087 | 4 |
| 75 | 75 | 77 | 81 | GETTING THE CORNERS — T.S.U. Toronadoes (A Frazier/McKay Production), Atlantic 2579 | 5 |
| 76 | 86 | — | — | HONEY — O. C. Smith (Jerry Fuller), Columbia 44751 | 2 |
| ★77 | — | — | — | I DON'T KNOW WHY — Stevie Wonder (D. Hunter and S. Wonder), Tamla 54180 | 1 |
| 78 | 85 | 97 | — | SOMEDAY SOON — Judy Collins (David Anderly) Elektra 45659 | 3 |
| 79 | 80 | 85 | 79 | ALMOST PERSUADED — Etta James (Rick Hall & Staff), Cadet 5630 | 5 |
| ★80 | 84 | 91 | 96 | MENDOCINO — Sir Douglas Quintet (Amigas de Musica), Smash 2191 | 5 |
| 81 | 81 | — | — | LONG LINE RIDER — Bobby Darin (Bobby Darin), Direction 350 | 2 |
| ★82 | — | — | — | MR. SUN, MR. MOON — Paul Revere & the Raiders (Mark Lindsay), Columbia 4-44744 | 1 |
| ★83 | — | — | — | LOVIN' THINGS — Grassroots (Steve Barri), Dunhill 4180 | 1 |
| ★84 | — | — | — | HOT SMOKE & SASSAFRASS — Bubble Puppy, International Artists 128 | 1 |
| 85 | 88 | — | — | JOHNNY ONE TIME — Brenda Lee (Mike Berniker), Decca 32428 | 2 |
| ★86 | — | — | — | MAYBE TOMORROW — Iveys, Apple 1803 | 1 |
| ★87 | — | — | — | HELLO, IT'S ME — Nazz (Nazz & Michael Friedman), SGC 001 | 1 |
| 88 | 97 | — | — | GREAT BALLS OF FIRE — Tiny Tim (Richard Perry), Reprise 0802 | 2 |
| ★89 | — | — | — | NO NOT MUCH — Smoke Ring (Rivertown), Buddah 77 | 1 |
| 90 | 98 | — | — | GLAD SHE'S A WOMAN — Bobby Goldsboro (Bob Montgomery & Bobby Goldsboro), United Artists 50497 | 2 |
| 91 | 91 | — | — | ME ABOUT YOU — The Lovin' Spoonful (Bob Finiz), Kama Sutra 255 | 2 |
| 92 | 92 | 93 | 93 | THE CARROLL COUNTY ACCIDENT — Porter Wagoner (Bob Ferguson), RCA Victor 47-9651 | 4 |
| 93 | 95 | 96 | — | MY SPECIAL PRAYER — Percy Sledge, Atlantic 2594 | 3 |
| 94 | 100 | — | — | ONLY THE LONELY — Sonny James (The Southern Gentleman) (Kelso Herston), Capitol 2370 | 2 |
| 95 | — | — | — | ANYTHING YOU CHOOSE — Spanky and Our Gang (Scharf/Dorough), Mercury 72890 | 1 |
| 96 | 99 | — | — | TRY A LITTLE TENDERNESS — Three Dog Night (Gabriel Makler), Dunhill 4177 | 2 |
| 97 | — | — | — | SWITCH IT ON — Cliff Nobles & Co. (Jesse James), Phil-L.A. of Soul 324 | 1 |
| 98 | — | — | — | I LIKE WHAT YOU'RE DOING (To Me) — Carla Thomas (Don Davis), Stax 0024 | 1 |
| 99 | — | — | — | I DON'T WANT TO CRY — Ruby Winters (Papa Don Prod.), Diamond 255 | 1 |
| 100 | — | — | — | TWENTY-FIVE MILES — Edwin Starr (Bristol & Fuqua), Gordy 7083 | 1 |

## HOT 100—A TO Z—(Publisher-Licensee)

| | |
|---|---|
| Almost Persuaded (Gallico, BMI) | 79 |
| Anything You Choose (Takya, ASCAP) | 95 |
| Baby, Baby Don't Cry (Jobete, BMI) | 14 |
| Beginning of My End, The (Cuydra, BMI) | 43 |
| Build Me Up Buttercup (January-Nice, BMI) | 4 |
| But You Know I Love You (First Edition, BMI) | 29 |
| Can I Change My Mind (Dakar, BMI) | 6 |
| California Soul (Jobete, BMI) | 35 |
| Carroll County Accident, The (Warden, BMI) | 92 |
| Cloud Nine (Jobete, BMI) | 67 |
| Crimson & Clover (Big Seven Music, BMI) | 2 |
| Condition Red (East Groovesville, BMI) | 56 |
| Crossroads (Noma, BMI) | 32 |
| Daddy Sang Bass (House of Cash-Cedarwood, BMI) | 45 |
| Dizzy (Low Twine, BMI) | 44 |
| Do Your Own Thing (Charles Wright & Fred Smith) (Wright-Gersti-Tamerlan, BMI) | 68 |
| Does Anybody Know I'm Here (Chevis, BMI) | 38 |
| Everyday People (Daly City, BMI) | 1 |
| Feelin' So Good (Kirshner, BMI) | 66 |
| Games People Play (Lowery, BMI) | 15 |
| Getting the Corners (Cotillion-Broken Soul, BMI) | 75 |
| Give It Up or Turnit a Loose (Brown & Sons, BMI) | 20 |
| Glad She's a Woman (Tamerlane, BMI) | 90 |
| Going Up the Country (Metric, BMI) | 37 |
| Good Lovin' Ain't Easy to Come By (Jobete, BMI) | 36 |
| Goodnight My Love (Spanka, BMI) | 28 |
| Great Balls of Fire (BRS, BMI) | 88 |
| Greatest Love, The (Lowery, BMI) | 74 |
| Grits Ain't Groceries (Lois, BMI) | 73 |
| Hang 'Em High (Unart, BMI) | 9 |
| Heaven (Slacsar, ASCAP) | 59 |
| Hello, It's Me (Screen Gems-Columbia, BMI) | 87 |
| Hey! Baby (LeBill, BMI) | 71 |
| Hey Jude (Maclen, BMI) | 41 |
| Home Cookin' (Jobete, BMI) | 42 |
| Honey (Russell-Cason, ASCAP) | 76 |
| Hooked on a Feeling (Press, BMI) | 22 |
| Hot Smoke & Sassafrass (Tapier, BMI) | 84 |
| I Don't Know Why (Jobete, BMI) | 77 |
| I Don't Want to Cry (Ludix/Betalbin, BMI) | 99 |
| I Forgot To Be Your Lover (Memphis, BMI) | 47 |
| I Got a Line on You (Hollenbeck, BMI) | 54 |
| I Heard It Through the Grapevine (Jobete, BMI) | 8 |
| I Like What You're Doing (to Me) (East/Memphis, BMI) | 98 |
| I Started a Joke (Casserole, BMI) | 13 |
| If I Can Dream (Gladys, ASCAP) | 16 |
| Indian Giver (Kaskat/Kahoona, BMI) | 27 |
| I'm Gonna Make You Love Me (M.R.C., BMI) | 10 |
| I'm Livin' in Shame (Jobete, BMI) | 11 |
| I've Gotta Be Me (Damila, ASCAP) | 19 |
| Johnny One Time (Hill & Range/Blue Crest, BMI) | 85 |
| Kum Ba Yah (Clinton, ASCAP) | 61 |
| Let It Be Me (M.C.A., ASCAP) | 60 |
| Long Line Rider (Argent, BMI) | 81 |
| Lovin' Things (Gallico, BMI) | 83 |
| Maybe Tomorrow (Apple, ASCAP) | 86 |
| May I (Rhinelander, BMI) | 58 |
| Me About You (Charuon, BMI) | 91 |
| Mendocino (Southern Love, BMI) | 80 |
| Minute of Your Time, A (Anne-Rachel, ASCAP) | 48 |
| Mr. Sun, Mr. Moon (Boom, BMI) | 82 |
| My Special Prayer (Quin Ivy & Marlin Greene) (Maureen, BMI) | 93 |
| My Whole World Ended (The Moment You Left Me) (Jobete, BMI) | 50 |
| No Not Much (Beaver, ASCAP) | 89 |
| Only the Lonely (Acuff-Rose, BMI) | 94 |
| Proud Mary (Jondora, BMI) | 21 |
| Purple Haze (Sea Lark, BMI) | 63 |
| Ramblin' Gamblin' Man (Gear, ASCAP) | 17 |
| Riot (Cherio, BMI) | 55 |
| River Deep—Mountain High (Trio, BMI) | 53 |
| Run Away Child, Running Wild (Jobete, BMI) | 70 |
| Someday Soon (Witmark, BMI) | 78 |
| Son of a Preacher Man (Tree, BMI) | 34 |
| Sophisticated Sissy (Marsaint, BMI) | 64 |
| Soul Shake (Singleton, BMI) | 40 |
| Soul Sister, Brown Sugar (Walden-Birdees, ASCAP) | 49 |
| Soulful Strut (Dakar/RC, BMI) | 18 |
| Stand by Your Man (Gallico, BMI) | 24 |
| Sweet Cream Ladies (Blackwood, BMI) | 33 |
| Switch It On (Dandelion/James Boy, BMI) | 97 |
| Take Care of Your Homework (East/Memphis, BMI) | 23 |
| There'll Come a Time (Jalynne, BMI) | 30 |
| (There's Gonna Be a) Showdown (Downstairs/Double Diamond, BMI) | 25 |
| Time of the Season (Mainstay, BMI) | 52 |
| Things I'd Like to Say (New Colony-T.M., BMI) | 31 |
| 30-60-90 (Jec, BMI) | 69 |
| This Girl's in Love With You (Blue Seas/Jac, ASCAP) | 26 |
| This Magic Moment (Rumbalero/Progressive) | 12 |
| To Susan on the West Coast Waiting (Peer Int'l, BMI) | 57 |
| Touch Me (Nipper, ASCAP) | 3 |
| Too Weak to Fight (Fame, BMI) | 44 |
| Traces (Low-Sal, BMI) | 46 |
| Tragedy (Bluff City, BMI) | 62 |
| Try a Little Tenderness (Connelly & Robbins, ASCAP) | 96 |
| Twenty-Five Miles (Jobete, BMI) | 100 |
| Witchi Tai To (Lovetruth, BMI) | 72 |
| Woman Helping Man (Viva, BMI) | 51 |
| Worst That Could Happen (Rivers, BMI) | 5 |
| You Gave Me a Mountain (Mojave, BMI) | 65 |
| You Showed Me (Tickson, BMI) | 7 |

## BUBBLING UNDER THE HOT 100

101. FOX ON THE RUN....Manfred Mann, Mercury 720879
102. LIGHT MY FIRE....Rhetta Hughes, Tetragrammaton 1513
103. WILL YOU BE STAYING AFTER SUNDAY....Peppermint Rainbow, Decca 32410
104. GIVE HER A TRANSPLANT....Intruders, Gamble 6223
105. GIVE IT AWAY....Chi-Lites, Brunswick 55398
106. WHO'S GONNA MOW YOUR GRASS..Buck Owens & His Buckaroos, Capitol 2377
107. THE GROOVIEST GIRL IN THE WORLD....Fun & Games, Uni 55098
108. SWEETER THAN SUGAR....Ohio Express, Buddah 92
109. AM I THE SAME GIRL....Barbara Acklin, Brunswick 55399
110. I'VE GOTTA HAVE YOUR LOVE....Eddie Floyd, Stax 0025
111. WHO'S MAKING LOVE....Young-Holt Unlimited, Brunswick 55400
112. TRA LA LA SONG....Banana Splits, Decca 32429
113. DON'T WASTE MY TIME....B. B. King, BluesWay 61022
114. SHE'S NOT THERE....Road, Kama Sutra 256
115. CHITTY CHITTY BANG BANG....New Christy Minstrels, Columbia 44631
116. IF....Al Hirt, RCA Victor 47-9717
117. MEDITATION....T.N.T. Band, Cotique C-136
118. MEMORIES ARE MADE OF THIS....Gene & Debb, TRX 5017
119. NOTHING BUT A HEARTACHE....Flirtations, Deram 85031
120. BABY MAKE ME FEEL SO GOOD....Five Stairsteps & Cubie, Curtom 1936
121. SHE'S ALMOST YOU....Billy Harner, Open 1253
122. KAWLIGA....Charley Pride, RCA 47-9716
123. I DO LOVE YOU....Billy Stewart, Chess 1922
124. GOOD VIBRATIONS....Hugo Montenegro, RCA 47-9712
125. DON'T TOUCH ME....Bettye Swann, Capitol 2382
126. I REALLY LOVE YOU....Ambassadors, Arctic 147
127. SOUL EXPERIENCE....Iron Butterfly, Atco 6647
128. I WOULDN'T CHANGE THE MAN HE IS....Blinky, Motown 1134
129. RED RED WINE....Jimmy James & the Vagabonds, Atco 6608
130. I SAW THE LIGHT....Nashville Brass, RCA 47-9705
131. LOVEY DOVEY....Johnny Nash, Jad 214
132. THE LETTER....Arbors, Date 2-1638
133. LILY THE PINK....Irish Rovers, Decca 32444
134. SOMEBODY LOVES YOU....Delphonics, Philly Groove 154
135. TOO LATE TO WORRY....Esther Philips, Roulette 7031

Compiled from national retail sales and radio station airplay by the Music Popularity Dept. of Record Market Research, Billboard.

# Billboard HOT 100

FOR WEEK ENDING FEBRUARY 22, 1969

★ STAR PERFORMER—Sides registering greatest proportionate upward progress this week.

Record Industry Association of America seal of certification as million selling single.

| THIS WEEK | 1 Wk. Ago | 2 Wks. Ago | 3 Wks. Ago | TITLE Artist (Producer), Label & Number | Weeks On Chart |
|---|---|---|---|---|---|
| 1 (Billboard Award) | 1 | 2 | 2 | **EVERYDAY PEOPLE** Sly & Family Stone (Sly Stone), Epic 10407 | 13 |
| 2 | 2 | 1 | 1 | **CRIMSON & CLOVER** Tommy James & the Shondells (Tommy James), Roulette R-7028 | 11 |
| 3 | 4 | 5 | 10 | **BUILD ME UP BUTTERCUP** The Foundations (Tony Macaulay), UNI 55101 | 8 |
| 4 | 3 | 4 | 4 | **TOUCH ME** Doors (Paul A. Rothchild), Elektra 45646 | 9 |
| 5 | 6 | 10 | 11 | **CAN I CHANGE MY MIND** Tyrone Davis (Willie Henderson), Dakar 602 | 10 |
| 6 | 5 | 3 | 3 | **WORST THAT COULD HAPPEN** Brooklyn Bridge (Wes Farrell), Buddah 75 | 10 |
| 7 | 7 | 14 | 17 | **YOU SHOWED ME** Turtles (Chip Douglas), White Whale 292 | 7 |
| ★ 8 | 12 | 13 | 16 | **THIS MAGIC MOMENT** Jay & the Americans (Jata Ent.), United Artists 50475 | 9 |
| ★ 9 | 21 | 28 | 55 | **PROUD MARY** Creedence Clearwater Revival (John Fogerty), Fantasy 619 | 5 |
| 10 | 11 | 15 | 22 | **I'M LIVING IN SHAME** Diana Ross & the Supremes (The Clan), Motown 1139 | 5 |
| 11 | 14 | 21 | 28 | **BABY, BABY DON'T CRY** Smokey Robinson & Miracles (Smokey, Moore, Johnson), Tamla 54178 | 8 |
| 12 | 9 | 9 | 13 | **HANG 'EM HIGH** Booker T. & M.G.'s (Booker T. & M.G.'s), Stax 0013 | 16 |
| ★ 13 | 15 | 22 | 34 | **GAMES PEOPLE PLAY** Joe South (Joe South), Capitol 2248 | 7 |
| 14 | 10 | 8 | 6 | **I'M GONNA MAKE YOU LOVE ME** Diana Ross & Supremes & Temptations (F. Wilson & N. Ashford), Motown 1137 | 12 |
| 15 | 8 | 7 | 5 | **I HEARD IT THROUGH THE GRAPEVINE** Marvin Gaye (Norman Whitfield), Tamla 54176 | 14 |
| 16 | 13 | 6 | 7 | **I STARTED A JOKE** Bee Gees (Robert Stigwood, The Bee Gees), Atco 6639 | 10 |
| 17 | 17 | 20 | 20 | **RAMBLIN' GAMBLIN' MAN** Bob Seeger (Hideout), Capitol 2297 | 10 |
| 18 | 19 | 19 | 24 | **I'VE GOTTA BE ME** Sammy Davis Jr. (Jimmy Bowen), Reprise 0779 | 11 |
| 19 | 20 | 37 | 42 | **GIVE IT UP OR TURNIT A LOOSE** James Brown (James Brown), King 6213 | 5 |
| 20 | 23 | 26 | 37 | **TAKE CARE OF YOUR HOMEWORK** Johnnie Taylor (Al Jackson Jr. & Don Davis), Stax 0023 | 6 |
| ★ 21 | 26 | 40 | 92 | **THIS GIRL'S IN LOVE WITH YOU** Dionne Warwick (Bacharach-David), Scepter 12241 | 4 |
| 22 | 22 | 11 | 8 | **HOOKED ON A FEELING** B. J. Thomas (Chips Moman), Scepter 12230 | 15 |
| ★ 23 | 46 | 61 | — | **TRACES** Classics IV (Buddie Buie), Imperial 66352 | 3 |
| ★ 24 | 27 | 32 | 52 | **INDIAN GIVER** 1910 Fruitgum Co. (Kasenetz, Katz), Buddah 91 | 5 |
| ★ 25 | 39 | 44 | 86 | **DIZZY** Tommy Roe (Steve Barri), ABC 11164 | 4 |
| ★ 26 | 29 | 31 | 44 | **BUT YOU KNOW I LOVE YOU** First Edition (Jimmy Bowen), Reprise 0799 | 6 |
| 27 | 28 | 30 | 36 | **GOODNIGHT MY LOVE** Paul Anka (Don Costa), RCA Victor 47-9648 | 8 |
| ★ 28 | 33 | 33 | 51 | **SWEET CREAM LADIES** Box Tops (Chips Moman/Tommy Cogbill) Mala 12035 | 9 |
| ★ 29 | 32 | 34 | 65 | **CROSSROADS** Cream (Felix Pappalardi), Atco 6646 | 5 |
| 30 | 30 | 51 | 63 | **THERE'LL COME A TIME** Betty Everett (Archie Lee Hill Prod.), Uni 55100 | 6 |
| 31 | 31 | 47 | 50 | **THINGS I'D LIKE TO SAY** New Colony Six, Mercury 72858 | 9 |
| 32 | 25 | 24 | 21 | **(There's Gonna Be a) SHOWDOWN** Archie Bell & the Drells (Gamble-Huff), Atlantic 2583 | 11 |
| 33 | 18 | 17 | 9 | **SOULFUL STRUT** Young-Holt Unlimited (Carl Davis & Eugene Record), Brunswick 55391 | 13 |
| 34 | 24 | 23 | 19 | **STAND BY YOUR MAN** Tammy Wynette (Billy Sherrill), Epic 10398 | 16 |
| 35 | 36 | 45 | 69 | **GOOD LOVIN' AIN'T EASY TO COME BY** Marvin Gaye & Tammi Terrell (Ashford & Simpson), Tamla 54179 | 4 |
| 36 | 16 | 12 | 12 | **IF I CAN DREAM** Elvis Presley (Bones Howe & Steve Binder), RCA Victor 47-9670 | 13 |
| ★ 37 | 52 | 60 | — | **TIME OF THE SEASON** Zombies (Rod Argent & Chris White), Date 2-1628 | 3 |
| ★ 38 | 70 | — | — | **RUN AWAY CHILD, RUNNING WILD** Temptations (Norman Whitfield), Gordy 7084 | 2 |
| 39 | 40 | 43 | 46 | **SOUL SHAKE** Peggy Scott & JoJo Benson (Shelby Singleton Jr.), SSS International 761 | 4 |
| ★ 40 | 50 | — | — | **MY WHOLE WORLD ENDED (The Moment You Left Me)** David Ruffin (Fuqua & Bristol), Motown 1140 | 2 |
| ★ 41 | 59 | 90 | — | **HEAVEN** Rascals (Rascals), Atlantic 2599 | 3 |
| 42 | 45 | 52 | 56 | **DADDY SANG BASS** Johnny Cash (Bob Johnson), Columbia 4-44689 | 9 |
| ★ 43 | 54 | 54 | 70 | **I GOT A LINE ON YOU** Spirit (Lou Adler), Ode 115 | 6 |
| 44 | 38 | 39 | 47 | **DOES ANYBODY KNOW I'M HERE** Dells (Bobby Miller), Cadet 5631 | 9 |
| 45 | 47 | 56 | 59 | **I FORGOT TO BE YOUR LOVER** William Bell (Booker T. Jones), Stax 0015 | 8 |
| ★ 46 | 58 | 70 | 79 | **MAY I** Bill Deal & the Rhondels (Jerry Ross Prod.), Heritage 803 | 6 |
| ★ 47 | 76 | 86 | — | **HONEY** O. C. Smith (Jerry Fuller), Columbia 44751 | 3 |
| 48 | 48 | 49 | 49 | **A MINUTE OF YOUR TIME** Tom Jones (Peter Sullivan), Parrot 40035 | 10 |
| ★ 49 | 67 | 83 | 100 | **CLOUD NINE** Mongo Santamaria (David Rubinson), Columbia 4-44740 | 4 |
| ★ 50 | 57 | 67 | — | **TO SUSAN ON THE WEST COAST WAITING** Donovan (Mickie Most), Epic 5-10434 | 3 |
| 51 | 51 | 59 | 90 | **WOMAN HELPING MAN** Vogues (Dick Glasser), Reprise 0803 | 4 |
| ★ 52 | — | — | — | **THE WEIGHT** Aretha Franklin (Jerry Wexler & Tom Dowd), Atlantic 2603 | 1 |
| 53 | 42 | 42 | 48 | **HOME COOKIN'** Jr. Walker & All Stars (Henry Cosby), Soul 35055 | 6 |
| 54 | 53 | 53 | 66 | **RIVER DEEP—MOUNTAIN HIGH** Deep Purple (Lawrence), Tetragrammaton 1514 | 5 |
| ★ 55 | 65 | 69 | — | **YOU GAVE ME A MOUNTAIN** Frankie Laine (Jimmy Bowen), ABC 11174 | 3 |
| 56 | 56 | 46 | 54 | **CONDITION RED** Goodees (Davis, Briggs), HIP 8005 | 10 |
| ★ 57 | 78 | 85 | 97 | **SOMEDAY SOON** Judy Collins (David Anderly) Elektra 45659 | 4 |
| 58 | 60 | 68 | 87 | **LET IT BE ME** Glen Campbell & Bobbie Gentry (Al DeLory & Kelly Gordon), Capitol 2387 | 5 |
| 59 | 55 | 55 | 68 | **RIOT** Hugh Masekela (Chisa Prod.), Uni 55102 | 7 |
| 60 | 61 | 66 | 73 | **KUM BA YAH** Tommy Leonetti (Bill Justis), Decca 32421 | 6 |
| ★ 61 | 82 | — | — | **MR. SUN, MR. MOON** Paul Revere & the Raiders (Mark Lindsay), Columbia 4-44744 | 2 |
| 62 | 62 | 65 | 72 | **TRAGEDY** Brian Hyland (Ray Ruff), Dot 17176 | 7 |
| 63 | 64 | 71 | — | **SOPHISTICATED SISSY** Meters (Marshall E. Sehorn & Allen Toussaint), Josie 1001 | 3 |
| ★ 64 | 90 | 98 | — | **GLAD SHE'S A WOMAN** Bobby Goldsboro (Bob Montgomery & Bobby Goldsboro), United Artists 50497 | 3 |
| ★ 65 | 84 | — | — | **HOT SMOKE & SASSAFRASS** Bubble Puppy, International Artists 128 | 2 |
| 66 | 68 | 94 | 95 | **DO YOUR THING** Watts 103rd Street Band, Reprise 7250 | 4 |
| ★ 67 | 74 | 79 | 82 | **THE GREATEST LOVE** Dorsey Burnette (Snuff Garrett), Liberty 56087 | 5 |
| ★ 68 | 77 | — | — | **I DON'T KNOW WHY** Stevie Wonder (D. Hunter and S. Wonder), Tamla 54180 | 2 |
| ★ 69 | 83 | — | — | **LOVIN' THINGS** Grassroots (Steve Barri), Dunhill 4180 | 2 |
| ★ 70 | 80 | 84 | 91 | **MENDOCINO** Sir Douglas Quintet (Amigas de Musica), Smash 2191 | 6 |
| 71 | 71 | 60 | 80 | **HEY! BABY** Jose Feliciano (Rick Jarrard), RCA 47-9714 | 5 |
| 72 | 72 | 93 | — | **WITCHI TAI TO** Everything Is Everything (Danny Weiss) Vanguard Apostolic 35082 | 3 |
| 73 | 73 | 89 | 89 | **GRITS AIN'T GROCERIES** Little Milton (Calvin Carter), Checker 1212 | 4 |
| 74 | 69 | 73 | 74 | **30-60-90** Willie Mitchell (Willie Mitchell), Hi 2154 | 4 |
| ★ 75 | 86 | — | — | **MAYBE TOMORROW** Iveys, Apple 1803 | 2 |
| 76 | 75 | 75 | 77 | **GETTING THE CORNERS** T.S.U. Toronadoes (A Frazier/McKay Production), Atlantic 2579 | 6 |
| ★ 77 | 87 | — | — | **HELLO, IT'S ME** Nazz (Nazz & Michael Friedman), SGC 001 | 2 |
| ★ 78 | 85 | 88 | — | **JOHNNY ONE TIME** Brenda Lee (Mike Berniker), Decca 32428 | 3 |
| 79 | 81 | 81 | — | **LONG LINE RIDER** Bobby Darin (Bobby Darin), Direction 350 | 3 |
| ★ 80 | — | — | — | **SOMEBODY LOVES YOU** Delfonics (Stan & Bell), Philly Groove 154 | 1 |
| ★ 81 | — | — | — | **SOUL EXPERIENCE** Iron Butterfly (Jim Hilton), Atco 6647 | 1 |
| ★ 82 | — | — | — | **APRICOT BRANDY** Rhinoceros (Paul A. Rothchild), Elektra 45647 | 1 |
| ★ 83 | — | — | — | **THE LETTER** The Arbors (Roy Cicala & Lorie Burton), Date 2-1638 | 1 |
| ★ 84 | — | — | — | **AM I THE SAME GIRL** Barbara Acklin (Carl Davis & Eugene Record), Brunswick 55399 | 1 |
| 85 | 88 | 97 | — | **GREAT BALLS OF FIRE** Tiny Tim (Richard Perry), Reprise 0802 | 3 |
| 86 | 89 | — | — | **NO NOT MUCH** Smoke Ring (Rivertown), Buddah 77 | 2 |
| ★ 87 | — | — | — | **TEAR DROP CITY** Monkees (Tommy Boyce & Bobby Hart), Colgems 66-5000 | 1 |
| ★ 88 | 95 | — | — | **ANYTHING YOU CHOOSE** Spanky and Our Gang (Scharf/Dorough), Mercury 72890 | 2 |
| ★ 89 | 96 | 99 | — | **TRY A LITTLE TENDERNESS** Three Dog Night (Gabriel Makler), Dunhill 4177 | 3 |
| ★ 90 | — | — | — | **BACK DOOR MAN** Derek (Cymbal-Tobin), Bang 566 | 1 |
| 91 | — | — | — | **LONG GREEN** The Fireballs (Norman Petty), Atco 6651 | 1 |
| 92 | 94 | 100 | — | **ONLY THE LONELY** Sonny James (The Southern Gentleman) (Kelso Herston), Capitol 2370 | 3 |
| 93 | 93 | 95 | 96 | **MY SPECIAL PRAYER** Percy Sledge, Atlantic 2594 | 4 |
| 94 | 100 | — | — | **TWENTY-FIVE MILES** Edwin Starr (Bristol & Fuqua), Gordy 7083 | 2 |
| 95 | 98 | — | — | **I LIKE WHAT YOU'RE DOING (To Me)** Carla Thomas (Don Davis), Stax 0024 | 2 |
| 96 | 97 | — | — | **SWITCH IT ON** Cliff Nobles & Co. (Jesse James), Phil-L.A. of Soul 324 | 2 |
| 97 | 99 | — | — | **I DON'T WANT TO CRY** Ruby Winters (Papa Don Prod.), Diamond 255 | 2 |
| 98 | — | — | — | **I DO LOVE YOU** Billy Stewart, Chess 13620 | 1 |
| 99 | — | — | — | **THESE ARE NOT MY PEOPLE** Johnny Rivers (Johnny Rivers), Imperial 66360 | 1 |
| 100 | — | — | — | **BROTHER LOVE'S TRAVELING SALVATION SHOW** Neil Diamond (Tommy Cogbill & Chips Moman), Uni 55109 | 1 |

## HOT 100—A TO Z—(Publisher-Licensee)

Am I the Same Girl (Dakar/BRC, BMI) .......... 84
Anything You Choose (Takya, ASCAP) .......... 88
Apricot Brandy (Nina, BMI) .......... 82
Baby, Baby Don't Cry (Jobete, BMI) .......... 11
Back Door Man (Cymto, BMI) .......... 90
Brother Love's Traveling Salvation Show (Stonebridge, BMI) .......... 100
Build Me Up Buttercup (January-Nice, BMI) .......... 3
But You Know I Love You (First Edition, BMI) .......... 26
Can I Change My Mind (Dakar, BMI) .......... 5
Cloud Nine (Jobete, BMI) .......... 49
Crimson & Clover (Big Seven Music, BMI) .......... 2
Condition Red (East Groovesville, BMI) .......... 56
Crossroads (Noma, BMI) .......... 29
Daddy Sang Bass (House of Cash-Cedarwood, BMI) .......... 42
Dizzy (Low Twine, BMI) .......... 28
Do Your Thing (Charles Wright & Fred Smith) (Wright-Gersti-Tamerlan, BMI) .......... 66
Does Anybody Know I'm Here (Chevis, BMI) .......... 44
Everyday People (Daly City, BMI) .......... 1
Games People Play (Lowery, BMI) .......... 13
Getting the Corners (Cotillion-Broken Soul, BMI) .......... 76
Give It Up or Turnit a Loose (Brown & Sons, BMI) .......... 19
Glad She's a Woman (Tamerlane, BMI) .......... 64
Good Lovin' Ain't Easy to Come By (Jobete, BMI) .......... 35
Goodnight My Love (Spanka, BMI) .......... 27
Great Balls of Fire (BRS, BMI) .......... 85
Greatest Love, The (Lowery, BMI) .......... 67
Grits Ain't Groceries (Lois, BMI) .......... 73
Hang 'Em High (Unart, BMI) .......... 12
Heaven (Slacsar, ASCAP) .......... 41
Hello, It's Me (Screen Gems-Columbia, BMI) .......... 77
Hey! Baby (LeBill, BMI) .......... 71
Home Cookin' (Jobete, BMI) .......... 53
Honey (Russell-Cason, ASCAP) .......... 47
Hooked on a Feeling (Press, BMI) .......... 22
Hot Smoke & Sassafrass (Tapier, BMI) .......... 65
I Do Love You (Chevis, BMI) .......... 98
I Don't Know Why (Jobete, BMI) .......... 68
I Don't Want to Cry (Ludix/Betalbin, BMI) .......... 97
I Forgot To Be Your Lover (Memphis, BMI) .......... 45
I Got a Line on You (Hollenbeck, BMI) .......... 43
I Heard It Through the Grapevine (Jobete, BMI) .......... 15
I Like What You're Doing (to Me) (East/Memphis, BMI) .......... 95
I Started a Joke (Casserole, BMI) .......... 16
If I Can Dream (Gladys, ASCAP) .......... 36
Indian Giver (Kaskat/Kahoona, BMI) .......... 24
I'm Gonna Make You Love Me (M.R.C., BMI) .......... 14
I'm Livin' in Shame (Jobete, BMI) .......... 10
I've Gotta Be Me (Damila, ASCAP) .......... 18
Johnny One Time (Hill & Range/Blue Crest, BMI) .......... 78
Kum Ba Yah (Cintom, ASCAP) .......... 60
Let It Be Me (M.C.A., ASCAP) .......... 58
The Letter (Burton, BMI) .......... 83
Long Green (Burdette, BMI) .......... 91
Long Line Rider (Argent, BMI) .......... 79
Lovin' Things (Gallico, BMI) .......... 69
Maybe Tomorrow (Apple, ASCAP) .......... 75
May I (Rhinelander, BMI) .......... 46
Mendocino (Southern Love, BMI) .......... 70
Minute of Your Time, A (Anne-Rachel, ASCAP) .......... 48
Mr. Sun, Mr. Moon (Boom, BMI) .......... 61
My Special Prayer (Quin Ivy & Marlin Greene) (Maureen, BMI) .......... 93
My Whole World Ended (The Moment You Left Me) (Jobete, BMI) .......... 40
No Not Much (Beaver, ASCAP) .......... 86
Only the Lonely (Acuff-Rose, BMI) .......... 92
Proud Mary (Jondora, BMI) .......... 9
Ramblin' Gamblin' Man (Gear, ASCAP) .......... 17
Riot (Cherio, BMI) .......... 59
River Deep—Mountain High (Trio, BMI) .......... 54
Run Away Child, Running Wild (Jobete, BMI) .......... 38
Somebody Loves You (Nickel Shoe, BMI) .......... 80
Someday Soon (Witmark, BMI) .......... 57
Sophisticated Sissy (Marsaint, BMI) .......... 63
Soul Experience (Cotillion-Ten-East-Itasca, BMI) .......... 81
Soul Shake (Singleton, BMI) .......... 39
Soulful Strut (Dakar/RC, BMI) .......... 33
Stand by Your Man (Gallico, BMI) .......... 34
Sweet Cream Ladies (Blackwood, BMI) .......... 28
Switch It On (Dandelion/James Boy, BMI) .......... 96
Take Care of Your Homework (East/Memphis, BMI) .......... 20
Tear Drop City (Screen Gems-Columbia) .......... 87
There'll Come a Time (Jalynne, BMI) .......... 30
(There's Gonna Be a Showdown (Downstairs/Double Diamond, BMI) .......... 32
These Are Not My People (Lowery, BMI) .......... 99
Time of the Season (Mainstay, BMI) .......... 37
Things I'd Like to Say (New Colony-T.M., BMI) .......... 31
30-60-90 (Jec, BMI) .......... 74
This Girl's in Love With You (Blue Seas/Jac, ASCAP) .......... 21
This Magic Moment (Rumbalero/Progressive) .......... 8
To Susan on the West Coast Waiting (Peer Int'l, BMI) .......... 50
Touch Me (Nipper, ASCAP) .......... 4
Traces (Low-Sal, BMI) .......... 23
Tragedy (Bluff City, BMI) .......... 62
Try a Little Tenderness (Connelly & Robbins, ASCAP) .......... 89
Twenty-Five Miles (Jobete, BMI) .......... 94
The Weight (Dwarf, ASCAP) .......... 52
Witchi Tai To (Lovetruth, BMI) .......... 72
Woman Helping Man (Viva, BMI) .......... 51
Worst That Could Happen (Rivers, BMI) .......... 6
You Gave Me a Mountain (Mojave, BMI) .......... 55
You Showed Me (Tickson, BMI) .......... 7

## BUBBLING UNDER THE HOT 100

101. A LOVER'S QUESTION..........Otis Redding, Atco 6654
102. I'VE GOTTA HAVE YOUR LOVE..........Eddie Floyd, Stax 0025
103. ROCK ME..........Steppenwolf, Dunhill 4182
104. GIVE HER A TRANSPLANT..........Intruders, Gamble 6223
105. GIVE IT AWAY..........Chi-Lites, Brunswick 55398
106. WHO'S GONNA MOW YOUR GRASS..Buck Owens & His Buckaroos, Capitol 2377
107. THE GROOVIEST GIRL IN THE WORLD..........Fun & Games, Uni 55098
108. SWEETER THAN SUGAR..........Ohio Express, Buddah 92
109. ONLY THE STRONG SURVIVE..........Jerry Butler, Mercury 72898
110. WHO'S MAKING LOVE..........Young-Holt Unlimited, Brunswick 55400
111. FOOLISH FOOL..........Dee Dee Warwick, Mercury 72880
112. THIS IS A LOVE SONG..........Bill Medley, MGM 14025
113. GENTLE ON MY MIND..........Dean Martin, Reprise 0812
114. CHITTY CHITTY BANG BANG..........New Christy Minstrels, Columbia 44631
115. GOOD VIBRATIONS..........Hugo Montenegro, RCA 47-9712
116. IF..........Al Hirt, RCA Victor 47-9717
117. MEMORIES ARE MADE OF THIS..........Gene & Debbe, TRX 5017
118. BABY MAKE ME FEEL SO GOOD..........5 Stairsteps & Cubie, Curtom 1936
119. NOTHING BUT HEARTACHE..........Flirtations, Deram 85031
120. KAWLIGA..........Charley Pride, RCA 47-9716
121. SHE'S ALMOST YOU..........Billy Harner, Open 1253
122. MY DECEIVING HEART..........Impressions, Curtom 1937
123. DON'T TOUCH ME..........Bettye Swan, Capitol 2382
124. I REALLY LOVE YOU..........Ambassadors, Arctic 147
125. UPTIGHT GOOD WOMAN..........Solomon Burke, Bell 759
126. WHEN HE TOUCHES ME..........Peaches & Herb, Date 2-1637
127. RED RED WINE..........Jimmy James & the Vagabonds, Atco 6608
128. THE WAY IT USED TO BE..........Engelbert Humperdinck, Parrott 40036
129. I SAW THE LIGHT..........Nashville Brass, RCA 47-9705
130. LOVEY DOVEY..........Johnny Nash, Jad 214
131. TOO LATE TO WORRY..........Esther Phillips, Roulette 7031
132. LILY THE PINK..........Irish Rovers, Decca 324444
133. CHANGING CHANGING..........Ed Ames, RCA 47-9722
134. SHOTGUN..........Vanilla Fudge, Atco 6665
135. COAL MAN..........Mac Rice, Atco 6645

Compiled from national retail sales and radio station airplay by the Music Popularity Dept. of Record Market Research, Billboard.

# Billboard HOT 100

FOR WEEK ENDING MARCH 1, 1969

★ STAR PERFORMER—Sides registering greatest proportionate upward progress this week.

(Seal) Record Industry Association of America seal of certification as million selling single.

| This Week | 1 Wk. Ago | 2 Wks. Ago | 3 Wks. Ago | TITLE Artist (Producer), Label & Number | Weeks On Chart |
|---|---|---|---|---|---|
| 1 (Billboard Award) | 1 | 1 | 2 | EVERYDAY PEOPLE — Sly & Family Stone (Sly Stone), Epic 10407 | 14 |
| 2 | 2 | 2 | 1 | CRIMSON & CLOVER — Tommy James & the Shondells (Tommy James), Roulette R-7028 | 12 |
| 3 | 3 | 4 | 5 | BUILD ME UP BUTTERCUP — The Foundations (Tony Macaulay), UNI 55101 | 9 |
| 4 (RIAA seal) | 4 | 3 | 4 | TOUCH ME — Doors (Paul A. Rothchild), Elektra 45646 | 10 |
| ★5 | 9 | 21 | 28 | PROUD MARY — Creedence Clearwater Revival (John Fogerty), Fantasy 619 | 6 |
| 6 | 7 | 7 | 14 | YOU SHOWED ME — Turtles (Chip Douglas), White Whale 292 | 8 |
| 7 | 8 | 12 | 13 | THIS MAGIC MOMENT — Jay & the Americans (Jata Ent.), United Artists 50475 | 10 |
| ★8 | 11 | 14 | 21 | BABY, BABY DON'T CRY — Smokey Robinson & Miracles (Smokey, Moore, Johnson), Tamla 54178 | 9 |
| 9 | 6 | 5 | 3 | WORST THAT COULD HAPPEN — Brooklyn Bridge (Wes Farrell), Buddah 75 | 11 |
| ★10 | 25 | 39 | 44 | DIZZY — Tommy Roe (Steve Barri), ABC 11164 | 5 |
| ★11 | 21 | 26 | 40 | THIS GIRL'S IN LOVE WITH YOU — Dionne Warwick (Bacharach-David), Scepter 12241 | 5 |
| 12 | 10 | 11 | 15 | I'M LIVING IN SHAME — Diana Ross & the Supremes (The Clan), Motown 1139 | 6 |
| 13 | 13 | 15 | 22 | GAMES PEOPLE PLAY — Joe South (Joe South), Capitol 2248 | 8 |
| 14 | 5 | 6 | 10 | CAN I CHANGE MY MIND — Tyrone Davis (Willie Henderson), Dakar 602 | 11 |
| 15 | 18 | 19 | 19 | I'VE GOTTA BE ME — Sammy Davis Jr. (Jimmy Bowen), Reprise 0779 | 12 |
| ★16 | 24 | 27 | 32 | INDIAN GIVER — 1910 Fruitgum Co. (Kasenetz, Katz), Buddah 91 | 6 |
| 17 | 17 | 17 | 20 | RAMBLIN' GAMBLIN' MAN — Bob Seeger (Hideout), Capitol 2297 | 11 |
| 18 | 19 | 20 | 37 | GIVE IT UP OR TURNIT A LOOSE — James Brown (James Brown), King 6213 | 6 |
| ★19 | 23 | 46 | 61 | TRACES — Classics IV (Buddie Buie), Imperial 66352 | 4 |
| 20 | 12 | 9 | 9 | HANG 'EM HIGH — Booker T. & M.G.'s (Booker T. & M.G.'s), Stax 0013 | 17 |
| ★21 | 26 | 29 | 31 | BUT YOU KNOW I LOVE YOU — First Edition (Jimmy Bowen), Reprise 0799 | 7 |
| ★22 | 38 | 70 | — | RUN AWAY CHILD, RUNNING WILD — Temptations (Norman Whitfield), Gordy 7084 | 3 |
| ★23 | 40 | 50 | — | MY WHOLE WORLD ENDED (The Moment You Left Me) — David Ruffin (Fuqua & Bristol), Motown 1140 | 3 |
| ★24 | 31 | 31 | 47 | THINGS I'D LIKE TO SAY — New Colony Six, Mercury 72858 | 10 |
| ★25 | 37 | 52 | 60 | TIME OF THE SEASON — Zombies (Rod Argent & Chris White), Date 2-1628 | 4 |
| ★26 | 30 | 30 | 51 | THERE'LL COME A TIME — Betty Everett (Archie Lee Hill Prod.), Uni 55100 | 7 |
| 27 | 20 | 23 | 26 | TAKE CARE OF YOUR HOMEWORK — Johnnie Taylor (Al Jackson Jr. & Don Davis), Stax 0023 | 7 |
| 28 | 15 | 8 | 7 | I HEARD IT THROUGH THE GRAPEVINE — Marvin Gaye (Norman Whitfield), Tamla 54176 | 15 |
| 29 | 29 | 32 | 24 | CROSSROADS — Cream (Felix Pappalardi), Atco 6646 | 6 |
| 30 | 27 | 28 | 30 | GOODNIGHT MY LOVE — Paul Anka (Don Costa), RCA Victor 47-9648 | 9 |
| 31 | 14 | 10 | 8 | I'M GONNA MAKE YOU LOVE ME — Diana Ross & Supremes & Temptations (F. Wilson & N. Ashford), Motown 1137 | 13 |
| ★32 | 35 | 36 | 45 | GOOD LOVIN' AIN'T EASY TO COME BY — Marvin Gaye & Tammi Terrell (Ashford & Simpson), Tamla 54179 | 5 |
| 33 | 16 | 13 | 6 | I STARTED A JOKE — Bee Gees (Robert Stigwood, The Bee Gees), Atco 6639 | 11 |
| ★34 | 52 | — | — | THE WEIGHT — Aretha Franklin (Jerry Wexler & Tom Dowd), Atlantic 2603 | 2 |
| ★35 | 50 | 57 | 67 | TO SUSAN ON THE WEST COAST WAITING — Donovan (Mickie Most), Epic 5-10434 | 4 |
| 36 | 22 | 22 | 11 | HOOKED ON A FEELING — B. J. Thomas (Chips Moman), Scepter 12230 | 16 |
| 37 | 39 | 40 | 43 | SOUL SHAKE — Peggy Scott & JoJo Benson (Shelby Singleton Jr.), SSS International 761 | 5 |
| 38 | 28 | 33 | 33 | SWEET CREAM LADIES — Box Tops (Chips Moman/Tommy Cogbill) Mala 12035 | 10 |
| 39 | 41 | 59 | 90 | HEAVEN — Rascals (Rascals), Atlantic 2599 | 4 |
| ★40 | 55 | 65 | 69 | YOU GAVE ME A MOUNTAIN — Frankie Laine (Jimmy Bowen), ABC 11174 | 4 |
| ★41 | 61 | 82 | — | MR. SUN, MR. MOON — Paul Revere & the Raiders (Mark Lindsay), Columbia 4-44744 | 3 |
| 42 | 43 | 54 | 54 | I GOT A LINE ON YOU — Spirit (Lou Adler), Ode 115 | 7 |
| ★43 | 68 | 77 | — | I DON'T KNOW WHY — Stevie Wonder (D. Hunter and S. Wonder), Tamla 54180 | 3 |
| 44 | 46 | 58 | 70 | MAY I — Bill Deal & the Rhondels (Jerry Ross Prod.), Heritage 803 | 7 |
| 45 | 49 | 67 | 83 | CLOUD NINE — Mongo Santamaria (David Rubinson), Columbia 4-44740 | 5 |
| 46 | 47 | 76 | 86 | HONEY — O. C. Smith (Jerry Fuller), Columbia 44751 | 4 |
| 47 | 51 | 51 | 59 | WOMAN HELPING MAN — Vogues (Dick Glasser), Reprise 0803 | 5 |
| 48 | 42 | 45 | 52 | DADDY SANG BASS — Johnny Cash (Bob Johnson), Columbia 4-44689 | 10 |
| ★49 | 70 | 80 | 84 | MENDOCINO — Sir Douglas Quintet (Amigas de Musica), Smash 2191 | 7 |
| ★50 | 63 | 64 | 71 | SOPHISTICATED SISSY — Meters (Marshall E. Sehorn & Allen Toussaint), Josie 1001 | 4 |
| 51 | 58 | 60 | 68 | LET IT BE ME — Glen Campbell & Bobbie Gentry (Al DeLory & Kelly Gordon), Capitol 2387 | 6 |
| 52 | 45 | 47 | 56 | I FORGOT TO BE YOUR LOVER — William Bell (Booker T. Jones), Stax 0015 | 9 |
| ★53 | 69 | 83 | — | LOVIN' THINGS — Grassroots (Steve Barri), Dunhill 4180 | 3 |
| ★54 | 65 | 84 | — | HOT SMOKE & SASSAFRASS — Bubble Puppy, International Artists 128 | 3 |
| 55 | 60 | 61 | 66 | KUM BA YAH — Tommy Leonetti (Bill Justis), Decca 32421 | 7 |
| 56 | 62 | 62 | 65 | TRAGEDY — Brian Hyland (Ray Ruff), Dot 17176 | 8 |
| 57 | 57 | 78 | 85 | SOMEDAY SOON — Judy Collins (David Anderly) Elektra 45659 | 5 |
| 58 | 66 | 68 | 94 | DO YOUR THING — Watts 103rd Street Band, Reprise 7250 | 5 |
| 59 | 59 | 55 | 55 | RIOT — Hugh Masekela (Chisa Prod.), Uni 55102 | 8 |
| 60 | 56 | 56 | 46 | CONDITION RED — Goodees (Davis, Briggs), HIP 8005 | 11 |
| 61 | 64 | 90 | 98 | GLAD SHE'S A WOMAN — Bobby Goldsboro (Bob Montgomery & Bobby Goldsboro), United Artists 50497 | 4 |
| ★62 | 89 | 96 | 99 | TRY A LITTLE TENDERNESS — Three Dog Night (Gabriel Makler), Dunhill 4177 | 4 |
| ★63 | — | — | — | ROCK ME — Steppenwolf (Gabriel Mekler), Dunhill 4182 | 1 |
| ★64 | — | — | — | WHO'S MAKING LOVE — Young-Holt Unlimited (Carl Davis & Eugene Record), Brunswick 55400 | 1 |
| ★65 | — | — | — | WHEN HE TOUCHES ME (Nothing Else Matters) — Peaches & Herb (Billy Sherrill & David Kapralik), Date 2-1637 | 1 |
| ★66 | 94 | 100 | — | TWENTY-FIVE MILES — Edwin Starr (Bristol & Fuqua), Gordy 7083 | 3 |
| 67 | 67 | 74 | 79 | THE GREATEST LOVE — Dorsey Burnette (Snuff Garrett), Liberty 56087 | 6 |
| ★68 | 87 | — | — | TEAR DROP CITY — Monkees (Tommy Boyce & Bobby Hart), Colgems 66-5000 | 2 |
| 69 | 72 | 72 | 93 | WITCHI TAI TO — Everything Is Everything (Danny Weiss) Vanguard Apostolic 35082 | 4 |
| ★70 | — | — | — | ONLY THE STRONG SURVIVE — Jerry Butler (Gamble & Huff), Mercury 72898 | 1 |
| ★71 | — | — | — | A LOVER'S QUESTION — Otis Redding (Steve Cropper), Atco 6654 | 1 |
| ★72 | 83 | — | — | THE LETTER — The Arbors (Roy Cicala & Lorie Burton), Date 2-1638 | 2 |
| 73 | 75 | 86 | — | MAYBE TOMORROW — Iveys, Apple 1803 | 3 |
| 74 | 74 | 69 | 73 | 30-60-90 — Willie Mitchell (Willie Mitchell), Hi 2154 | 5 |
| 75 | 78 | 85 | 88 | JOHNNY ONE TIME — Brenda Lee (Mike Berniker), Decca 32428 | 4 |
| 76 | 73 | 73 | 89 | GRITS AIN'T GROCERIES — Little Milton (Calvin Carter), Checker 1212 | 5 |
| 77 | 77 | 87 | — | HELLO, IT'S ME — Nazz (Nazz & Michael Friedman), SGC 001 | 3 |
| 78 | 81 | — | — | SOUL EXPERIENCE — Iron Butterfly (Jim Hilton), Atco 6647 | 2 |
| 79 | 80 | — | — | SOMEBODY LOVES YOU — Delfonics (Stan & Bell), Philly Groove 154 | 2 |
| 80 | 82 | — | — | APRICOT BRANDY — Rhinoceros (Paul A. Rothchild), Elektra 45647 | 2 |
| ★81 | 99 | — | — | THESE ARE NOT MY PEOPLE — Johnny Rivers (Johnny Rivers), Imperial 66360 | 2 |
| 82 | 84 | — | — | AM I THE SAME GIRL — Barbara Acklin (Carl Davis & Eugene Record), Brunswick 55399 | 2 |
| ★83 | 100 | — | — | BROTHER LOVE'S TRAVELING SALVATION SHOW — Neil Diamond (Tommy Cogbill & Chips Moman), Uni 55109 | 2 |
| ★84 | 90 | — | — | BACK DOOR MAN — Derek (Cymbal-Tobin), Bang 566 | 2 |
| 85 | 86 | 89 | — | NO NOT MUCH — Smoke Ring (Rivertown), Buddah 77 | 3 |
| 86 | 88 | 95 | — | ANYTHING YOU CHOOSE — Spanky and Our Gang (Scharf/Dorough), Mercury 72890 | 3 |
| ★87 | — | — | — | GALVESTON — Glen Campbell (Al De Lory), Capitol P-2428 | 1 |
| ★88 | — | — | — | DON'T FORGET ABOUT ME — Dusty Springfield (Jerry Wexler-Tom Dowd), Atlantic 45-2606 | 1 |
| ★89 | 95 | 98 | — | I LIKE WHAT YOU'RE DOING (To Me) — Carla Thomas (Don Davis), Stax 0024 | 3 |
| ★90 | — | — | — | SNATCHING IT BACK — Clarence Carter, Atlantic | 1 |
| 91 | 91 | — | — | LONG GREEN — The Fireballs (Norman Petty), Atco 6651 | 2 |
| 92 | 92 | 94 | 100 | ONLY THE LONELY — Sonny James (The Southern Gentleman) (Kelso Herston), Capitol 2370 | 4 |
| 93 | 96 | 97 | — | SWITCH IT ON — Cliff Nobles & Co. (Jesse James), Phil-L.A. of Soul 324 | 3 |
| 94 | — | — | — | GIMME GIMME GOOD LOVIN' — Crazy Elephant (J. Levine & A. Resnick), Bell 763 | 1 |
| 95 | — | — | — | YOU'VE MADE ME SO VERY HAPPY — Blood, Sweat & Tears (James Guerico), Columbia 4-44776 | 1 |
| 96 | — | — | — | SWEETER THAN SUGAR — Ohio Express (J. Levine & A. Resnick) Buddah 92 | 1 |
| 97 | — | — | — | DAY AFTER DAY (It's Slippin' Away) — Shango (Merry Rippelle), A&M 1014 | 1 |
| 98 | 98 | — | — | I DO LOVE YOU — Billy Stewart, Chess 13620 | 2 |
| 99 | — | — | — | GIVE IT AWAY — Chi-Lites (Carl Davis & Eugene Record), Brunswick 55398 | 1 |
| 100 | — | — | — | THE WAY IT USED TO BE — Engelbert Humperdinck (Peter Sullivan), Parrot 40036 | 1 |

## HOT 100—A TO Z—(Publisher-Licensee)

Am I the Same Girl (Dakar/BRC, BMI) ... 82
Anything You Choose (Takya, ASCAP) ... 86
Apricot Brandy (Nina, BMI) ... 80
Baby, Baby Don't Cry (Jobete, BMI) ... 8
Back Door Man (Cymto, BMI) ... 84
Brother Love's Traveling Salvation Show (Stonebridge, BMI) ... 83
Build Me Up Buttercup (January-Nice, BMI) ... 3
But You Know I Love You (First Edition, BMI) ... 21
Can I Change My Mind (Dakar, BMI) ... 14
Cloud Nine (Jobete, BMI) ... 45
Crimson & Clover (Big Seven Music, BMI) ... 2
Condition Red (East Groovesville, BMI) ... 60
Crossroads (Noma, BMI) ... 29
Daddy Sang Bass (House of Cash-Cedarwood, BMI) ... 48
Day After Day (It's Slippin' Away) (Goomby/Irving, BMI) ... 97
Dizzy (Low Twine, BMI) ... 10
Do Your Thing (Charles Wright & Fred Smith) (Wright-Gersti-Tamerlan, BMI) ... 58
Don't Forget About Me (Screen Gems-Columbia, BMI) 88
Everyday People (Daly City, BMI) ... 1
Galveston (Ja-Ma Music, ASCAP) ... 87
Games People Play (Lowery, BMI) ... 13
Gimme Gimme Good Lovin' (Peanut Butter/Kahoona, BMI) ... 94
Give It Away (Dakar/BRC, BMI) ... 99
Give It Up or Turnit a Loose (Brown & Sons, BMI) ... 18
Glad She's a Woman (Tamerlane, BMI) ... 61
Good Lovin' Aint Easy to Come By (Jobete, BMI) ... 32
Goodnight My Love (Spanka, BMI) ... 30
Greatest Love, The (Lowery, BMI) ... 67
Grits Ain't Groceries (Lois, BMI) ... 76
Hang 'Em High (Unart, BMI) ... 20
Heaven (Slacsar, ASCAP) ... 39
Hello, It's Me (Screen Gems-Columbia, BMI) ... 77
Honey (Russell-Cason, ASCAP) ... 46
Hooked on a Feeling (Press, BMI) ... 36
Hot Smoke & Sassafrass (Tapier, BMI) ... 54
I Do Love You (Chevis, BMI) ... 98
I Don't Know Why (Jobete, BMI) ... 43
I Forgot To Be Your Lover (Memphis, BMI) ... 52
I Got a Line on You (Hollenbeck, BMI) ... 42
I Heard It Through the Grapevine (Jobete, BMI) ... 28
I Like What You're Doing (to Me) (East/Memphis, BMI) ... 89
I Started a Joke (Casserole, BMI) ... 33
Indian Giver (Kaskat/Kahoona, BMI) ... 16
I'm Gonna Make You Love Me (M.R.C., BMI) ... 31
I'm Living in Shame (Jobete, BMI) ... 12
I've Gotta Be Me (Damila, ASCAP) ... 15
Johnny One Time (Hill & Range/Blue Crest, BMI) ... 75
Kum Ba Yah (Cintom, ASCAP) ... 55
Let It Be Me (M.C.A., ASCAP) ... 51
The Letter (Burton, BMI) ... 72
Long Green (Burdette, BMI) ... 91
Lover's Question, A (Progressive/Eden, BMI) ... 71
Lovin' Things (Gallico, BMI) ... 53
Maybe Tomorrow (Apple, ASCAP) ... 73
May I (Rhinelander, BMI) ... 44
Mendocino (Southern Love, BMI) ... 49
Mr. Sun, Mr. Moon (Boom, BMI) ... 41
My Whole World Ended (The Moment You Left Me) (Jobete, BMI) ... 23
No Not Much (Beaver, ASCAP) ... 85
Only the Lonely (Acuff-Rose, BMI) ... 92
Only the Strong Survive (Parabut/Double Diamond/Downstairs, BMI) ... 70
Proud Mary (Jondora, BMI) ... 5
Ramblin' Gamblin' Man (Gear, ASCAP) ... 17
Riot (Cherio, BMI) ... 59
Rock Me (Trousdale, BMI) ... 63
Run Away Child, Running Wild (Jobete, BMI) ... 22
Somebody Loves You (Nickel Shoe, BMI) ... 79
Someday Soon (Witmark, BMI) ... 57
Sophisticated Sissy (Marsaint, BMI) ... 50
Soul Experience (Cotillion-Ten-East-Itesca, BMI) ... 78
Soul Shake (Singleton, BMI) ... 37
Sweet Cream Ladies (Blackwood, BMI) ... 38
Sweeter Than Sugar (Kaskat/Peanut Butter, BMI) .. 96
Switch It On (Dandelion/James Boy, BMI) ... 93
Take Care of Your Homework (East/Memphis, BMI) 27
Tear Drop City (Screen Gems-Columbia) ... 68
There'll Come a Time (Jalynne, BMI) ... 26
These Are Not My People (Lowery, BMI) ... 81
Time of the Season (Mainstay, BMI) ... 25
Things I'd Like to Say (New Colony-T.M., BMI) ... 24
30-60-90 (Jec, BMI) ... 74
This Girl's in Love With You (Blue Seas/Jac, ASCAP) ... 11
This Magic Moment (Rumbalero/Progressive) ... 7
To Susan on the West Coast Waiting (Peer Int'l, BMI) ... 35
Touch Me (Nipper, ASCAP) ... 4
Traces (Low-Sal, BMI) ... 19
Tragedy (Bluff City, BMI) ... 56
Try a Little Tenderness (Connelly & Robbins, ASCAP) ... 62
Twenty-Five Miles (Jobete, BMI) ... 66
Way It Used to Be, The (Maribus, BMI) ... 100
The Weight (Dwarf, ASCAP) ... 34
When He Touches Me (Nothing Else Matters) (Painted Desert, BMI) ... 65
Who's Making Love (East/Memphis, BMI) ... 64
Witchi Tai To (Lovetruth, BMI) ... 69
Woman Helping Man (Viva, BMI) ... 47
Worst That Could Happen (Rivers, BMI) ... 9
You Gave Me a Mountain (Mojave, BMI) ... 40
You Showed Me (Tickson, BMI) ... 6
You've Made Me So Very Happy (Jobete, BMI) ... 95

## BUBBLING UNDER THE HOT 100

101. BABY MAKE ME FEEL SO GOOD ... Five Stairsteps & Cubie, Curtom 1936
102. I'VE GOTTA HAVE YOUR LOVE ... Eddie Floyd, Stax 0025
103. GENTLE ON MY MIND ... Dean Martin, Reprise 0812
104. MY DECEIVING HEART ... Impressions, Curtom 1937
105. HALLWAYS OF MY MIND ... Dells, Cadet 5636
106. WHO'S GONNA MOW YOUR GRASS .. Buck Owens & His Buckaroos, Capitol 2377
107. LONG LINE RIDER ... Bobby Darin, Direction 350
108. FOOLISH FOOL ... Dee Dee Warwick, Mercury 72880
109. TRACKS OF MY TEARS ... Aretha Franklin, Atlantic 2603
110. SHOTGUN ... Vanilla Fudge, Atco 6665
111. LIGHT MY FIRE ... Rhetta Hughes, Tetragrammaton 1513
112. GOOD VIBRATIONS ... Hugo Montenegro, RCA 47-9712
113. DON'T TOUCH ME ... Bettye Swann, Capitol 2382
114. MEMORIES ARE MADE OF THIS ... Gene & Debbe, TRX 5017 (S)
115. THIS IS A LOVE SONG ... Bill Medley, MGM 14025
116. UPTIGHT GOOD WOMAN ... Solomon Burke, Bell 759
117. WILL YOU BE STAYING AFTER SUNDAY ... Peppermint Rainbow, Decca 32410
118. PLAYGIRL ... Profits, Kapp K-962
119. NOTHING BUT A HEARTACHE ... Flirtations, Deram 85031
120. ONLY YOU ... Bobby Hatfield, Verve 10634
121. LILY THE PINK ... Irish Rovers, Decca 324444
122. WEDDING CAKE ... Connie Francis, MGM 14025
123. KAW-LIGA ... Charley Pride, RCA 47-9716
124. I REALLY LOVE YOU ... Ambassadors, Arctic 147
125. TOO LATE TO WORRY, TOO BLUE TO CRY ... Esther Phillips, Roulette 7031
126. HAIR ... Cowsills, MGM 14026
127. SING A SIMPLE SONG ... Sly & the Family Stone, Epic 10407
128. GOD KNOWS I LOVE YOU ... Nancy Sinatra, Reprise 0813
129. NO NOT MUCH ... Vogues, Reprise 0803
130. SOMETHING'S HAPPENING ... Herman's Hermits, MGM K-14035
131. I HAVE DREAMED ... Lettermen, Capitol 2414
132. CHANGING CHANGING ... Ed Ames, RCA 47-9722
133. VIRGINIA GIRL ... Michael Rabon & Five Americans, Abnak 134
134. WHAT'S WRONG WITH MY WORLD ... Ronnie Dove, Diamond 256
135. COAL MAN ... Mac Rice, Atco 6645

Compiled from national retail sales and radio station airplay by the Music Popularity Dept. of Record Market Research, Billboard.

# Billboard HOT 100

FOR WEEK ENDING MARCH 8 1969

★ STAR PERFORMER—Sides registering greatest proportionate upward progress this week.

Record Industry Association of America seal of certification as million selling single.

| This Week | 1 Wk. Ago | 2 Wks. Ago | 3 Wks. Ago | TITLE Artist (Producer), Label & Number | Weeks On Chart |
|---|---|---|---|---|---|
| 1 (Billboard Award) | 1 | 1 | 1 | EVERYDAY PEOPLE — Sly & Family Stone (Sly Stone), Epic 10407 | 15 |
| ★2 | 5 | 9 | 21 | PROUD MARY — Creedence Clearwater Revival (John Fogerty), Fantasy 619 | 7 |
| 3 | 3 | 3 | 4 | BUILD ME UP BUTTERCUP — The Foundations (Tony Macaulay), UNI 55101 | 10 |
| ★4 | 10 | 25 | 39 | DIZZY — Tommy Roe (Steve Barri), ABC 11164 | 6 |
| 5 | 2 | 2 | 2 | CRIMSON & CLOVER — Tommy James & the Shondells (Tommy James), Roulette R-7028 | 13 |
| 6 | 7 | 8 | 12 | THIS MAGIC MOMENT — Jay & the Americans (Jata Ent.), United Artists 50475 | 11 |
| 7 | 11 | 21 | 26 | THIS GIRL'S IN LOVE WITH YOU — Dionne Warwick (Bacharach-David), Scepter 12241 | 6 |
| 8 | 8 | 11 | 14 | BABY, BABY DON'T CRY — Smokey Robinson & Miracles (Smokey, Moore, Johnson), Tamla 54178 | 10 |
| 9 | 4 | 4 | 3 | TOUCH ME — Doors (Paul A. Rothchild), Elektra 45646 | 11 |
| ★10 | 16 | 24 | 27 | INDIAN GIVER — 1910 Fruitgum Co. (Kasenetz, Katz), Buddah 91 | 7 |
| ★11 | 15 | 18 | 19 | I'VE GOTTA BE ME — Sammy Davis Jr. (Jimmy Bowen), Reprise 0779 | 13 |
| ★12 | 22 | 38 | 70 | RUN AWAY CHILD, RUNNING WILD — Temptations (Norman Whitfield), Gordy 7084 | 4 |
| 13 | 13 | 13 | 15 | GAMES PEOPLE PLAY — Joe South (Joe South), Capitol 2248 | 9 |
| 14 | 14 | 5 | 6 | CAN I CHANGE MY MIND — Tyrone Davis (Willie Henderson), Dakar 602 | 12 |
| ★15 | 18 | 19 | 20 | GIVE IT UP OR TURNIT A LOOSE — James Brown (James Brown), King 6213 | 7 |
| ★16 | 23 | 40 | 50 | MY WHOLE WORLD ENDED (The Moment You Left Me) — David Ruffin (Fuqua & Bristol), Motown 1140 | 4 |
| 17 | 19 | 23 | 46 | TRACES — Classics IV (Buddie Buie), Imperial 66352 | 5 |
| 18 | 6 | 7 | 7 | YOU SHOWED ME — Turtles (Chip Douglas), White Whale 292 | 9 |
| 19 | 21 | 26 | 29 | BUT YOU KNOW I LOVE YOU — First Edition (Jimmy Bowen), Reprise 0799 | 8 |
| ★20 | 25 | 37 | 52 | TIME OF THE SEASON — Zombies (Rod Argent & Chris White), Date 2-1628 | 5 |
| 21 | 12 | 10 | 11 | I'M LIVING IN SHAME — Diana Ross & the Supremes (The Clan), Motown 1139 | 7 |
| 22 | 9 | 6 | 5 | WORST THAT COULD HAPPEN — Brooklyn Bridge (Wes Farrell), Buddah 75 | 12 |
| 23 | 24 | 31 | 31 | THINGS I'D LIKE TO SAY — New Colony Six, Mercury 72858 | 11 |
| ★24 | 34 | 52 | — | THE WEIGHT — Aretha Franklin (Jerry Wexler & Tom Dowd), Atlantic 2603 | 3 |
| 25 | 17 | 17 | 17 | RAMBLIN' GAMBLIN' MAN — Bob Seeger (Hideout), Capitol 2297 | 12 |
| 26 | 26 | 30 | 30 | THERE'LL COME A TIME — Betty Everett (Archie Lee Hill Prod.), Uni 55100 | 8 |
| 27 | 20 | 12 | 9 | HANG 'EM HIGH — Booker T. & M.G.'s (Booker T. & M.G.'s), Stax 0013 | 18 |
| 28 | 29 | 29 | 32 | CROSSROADS — Cream (Felix Pappalardi), Atco 6646 | 7 |
| 29 | 27 | 20 | 23 | TAKE CARE OF YOUR HOMEWORK — Johnnie Taylor (Al Jackson Jr. & Don Davis), Stax 0023 | 8 |
| 30 | 32 | 35 | 36 | GOOD LOVIN' AIN'T EASY TO COME BY — Marvin Gaye & Tammi Terrell (Ashford & Simpson), Tamla 54179 | 6 |
| ★31 | 70 | — | — | ONLY THE STRONG SURVIVE — Jerry Butler (Gamble & Huff), Mercury 72898 | 2 |
| ★32 | 45 | 49 | 67 | CLOUD NINE — Mongo Santamaria (David Rubinson), Columbia 4-44740 | 6 |
| 33 | 30 | 27 | 28 | GOODNIGHT MY LOVE — Paul Anka (Don Costa), RCA Victor 47-9648 | 10 |
| 34 | 38 | 28 | 33 | SWEET CREAM LADIES — Box Tops (Chips Moman/Tommy Cogbill) Mala 12035 | 11 |
| 35 | 35 | 50 | 57 | TO SUSAN ON THE WEST COAST WAITING — Donovan (Mickie Most), Epic 5-10434 | 5 |
| ★36 | 51 | 58 | 60 | LET IT BE ME — Glen Campbell & Bobbie Gentry (Al DeLory & Kelly Gordon), Capitol 2387 | 7 |
| 37 | 42 | 43 | 54 | I GOT A LINE ON YOU — Spirit (Lou Adler), Ode 115 | 8 |
| 38 | 40 | 55 | 65 | YOU GAVE ME A MOUNTAIN — Frankie Laine (Jimmy Bowen), ABC 11174 | 5 |
| 39 | 39 | 41 | 59 | HEAVEN — Rascals (Rascals), Atlantic 2599 | 5 |
| 40 | 41 | 61 | 82 | MR. SUN, MR. MOON — Paul Revere & the Raiders (Mark Lindsay), Columbia 4-44744 | 4 |
| ★41 | 50 | 63 | 64 | SOPHISTICATED SISSY — Meters (Marshall E. Sehorn & Allen Toussaint), Josie 1001 | 5 |
| 42 | 43 | 68 | 77 | I DON'T KNOW WHY — Stevie Wonder (D. Hunter and S. Wonder), Tamla 54180 | 4 |
| 43 | 44 | 46 | 58 | MAY I — Bill Deal & the Rhondels (Jerry Ross Prod.), Heritage 803 | 8 |
| 44 | 46 | 47 | 76 | HONEY — O. C. Smith (Jerry Fuller), Columbia 44751 | 5 |
| 45 | 49 | 70 | 80 | MENDOCINO — Sir Douglas Quintet (Amigas de Musica), Smash 2191 | 8 |
| 46 | 37 | 39 | 40 | SOUL SHAKE — Peggy Scott & JoJo Benson (Shelby Singleton Jr.), SSS International 761 | 6 |
| ★47 | 87 | — | — | GALVESTON — Glen Campbell (Al De Lory), Capitol P-2428 | 2 |
| ★48 | 63 | — | — | ROCK ME — Steppenwolf (Gabriel Mekler), Dunhill 4182 | 2 |
| ★49 | 53 | 69 | 83 | LOVIN' THINGS — Grassroots (Steve Barri), Dunhill 4180 | 4 |
| ★50 | 54 | 65 | 84 | HOT SMOKE & SASSAFRASS — Bubble Puppy, International Artists 128 | 4 |
| 51 | 58 | 66 | 68 | DO YOUR THING — Watts 103rd Street Band, Reprise 7250 | 6 |
| ★52 | 66 | 94 | 100 | TWENTY-FIVE MILES — Edwin Starr (Bristol & Fuqua), Gordy 7083 | 4 |
| ★53 | 71 | — | — | A LOVER'S QUESTION — Otis Redding (Steve Cropper), Atco 6654 | 2 |
| 54 | 55 | 60 | 61 | KUM BA YAH — Tommy Leonetti (Bill Justis), Decca 32421 | 8 |
| 55 | 57 | 57 | 78 | SOMEDAY SOON — Judy Collins (David Anderly) Elektra 45659 | 6 |
| 56 | 56 | 62 | 62 | TRAGEDY — Brian Hyland (Ray Ruff), Dot 17176 | 9 |
| 57 | 64 | — | — | WHO'S MAKING LOVE — Young-Holt Unlimited (Carl Davis & Eugene Record), Brunswick 55400 | 2 |
| 58 | 47 | 51 | 51 | WOMAN HELPING MAN — Vogues (Dick Glasser), Reprise 0803 | 6 |
| ★59 | 75 | 78 | 85 | JOHNNY ONE TIME — Brenda Lee (Mike Berniker), Decca 32428 | 5 |
| 60 | 62 | 89 | 96 | TRY A LITTLE TENDERNESS — Three Dog Night (Gabriel Makler), Dunhill 4177 | 5 |
| 61 | 61 | 64 | 90 | GLAD SHE'S A WOMAN — Bobby Goldsboro (Bob Montgomery & Bobby Goldsboro), United Artists 50497 | 5 |
| 62 | 68 | 87 | — | TEAR DROP CITY — Monkees (Tommy Boyce & Bobby Hart), Colgems 66-5000 | 3 |
| 63 | 65 | — | — | WHEN HE TOUCHES ME (Nothing Else Matters) — Peaches & Herb (Billy Sherrill & David Kapralik), Date 2-1637 | 2 |
| ★64 | 81 | 99 | — | THESE ARE NOT MY PEOPLE — Johnny Rivers (Johnny Rivers), Imperial 66360 | 3 |
| ★65 | 83 | 100 | — | BROTHER LOVES TRAVELLING SALVATION SHOW — Neil Diamond (Tommy Cogbill & Chips Moman), Uni 55109 | 3 |
| ★66 | 95 | — | — | YOU'VE MADE ME SO VERY HAPPY — Blood, Sweat & Tears (James William Guerico), Columbia 4-44776 | 2 |
| ★67 | — | — | — | BLESSED IS THE RAIN — Brooklyn Bridge (Wes Farrell), Buddah 95 | 1 |
| 68 | 73 | 75 | 86 | MAYBE TOMORROW — Iveys, Apple 1803 | 4 |
| ★69 | 84 | 90 | — | BACK DOOR MAN — Derek (Cymbal-Tobin), Bang 566 | 3 |
| 70 | 72 | 83 | — | THE LETTER — The Arbors (Roy Cicala & Lorie Burton), Date 2-1638 | 3 |
| ★71 | 77 | 77 | 87 | HELLO, IT'S ME — Nazz (Nazz & Michael Friedman), SGC 001 | 4 |
| 72 | 79 | 80 | — | SOMEBODY LOVES YOU — Delfonics (Stan & Bell), Philly Groove 154 | 3 |
| ★73 | 89 | 95 | 98 | I LIKE WHAT YOU'RE DOING (To Me) — Carla Thomas (Don Davis), Stax 0024 | 4 |
| ★74 | 88 | — | — | DON'T FORGET ABOUT ME — Dusty Springfield (Jerry Wexler-Tom Dowd), Atlantic 45-2606 | 2 |
| ★75 | 80 | 82 | — | APRICOT BRANDY — Rhinoceros (Paul A. Rothchild), Elektra 45647 | 3 |
| 76 | 69 | 72 | 72 | WITCHI TAI TO — Everything Is Everything (Danny Weiss) Vanguard Apostolic 35082 | 5 |
| ★77 | 90 | — | — | SNATCHING IT BACK — Clarence Carter, Atlantic | 2 |
| 78 | 78 | 81 | — | SOUL EXPERIENCE — Iron Butterfly (Jim Hilton), Atco 6647 | 3 |
| 79 | 82 | 84 | — | AM I THE SAME GIRL — Barbara Acklin (Carl Davis & Eugene Record), Brunswick 55399 | 3 |
| ★80 | 94 | — | — | GIMME GIMME GOOD LOVIN' — Crazy Elephant (J. Levine & A. Resnick), Bell 763 | 2 |
| ★81 | — | — | — | SHOTGUN — Vanilla Fudge (Vanilla Fudge), Atco 6655 | 1 |
| ★82 | 91 | 91 | — | LONG GREEN — The Fireballs (Norman Petty), Atco 6651 | 3 |
| ★83 | 97 | — | — | DAY AFTER DAY (It's Slippin' Away) — Shango (Merry Rippelle), A&M 1014 | 2 |
| ★84 | — | — | — | NO NOT MUCH — Vogues (Dick Glasser), Reprise 0803 | 1 |
| 85 | 85 | 86 | 89 | NO NOT MUCH — Smoke Ring (Rivertown), Buddah 77 | 4 |
| ★86 | — | — | — | I CAN HEAR MUSIC — Beach Boys (Carl Wilson), Capitol 2432 | 1 |
| ★87 | 100 | — | — | THE WAY IT USED TO BE — Engelbert Humperdinck (Peter Sullivan), Parrot 40036 | 2 |
| ★88 | — | — | — | DIDN'T YOU KNOW — Gladys Knight & the Pips (Ashford & Simpson), Soul 35057 | 1 |
| ★89 | — | — | — | AQUARIUS/LET THE SUNSHINE IN — Fifth Dimension (Bones Howe), Soul City 772 | 1 |
| ★90 | — | — | — | SING A SIMPLE SONG — Sly & the Family Stone (Sly Stone), Epic 5-10407 | 1 |
| 91 | — | — | — | DON'T TOUCH ME — Bettye Swan (Wayne Shuler), Capitol 2382 | 1 |
| 92 | — | — | — | WILL YOU BE STAYING AFTER SUNDAY — Peppermint Rainbow (Paul Leka), Decca 32410 | 4 |
| 93 | — | — | — | NOTHING BUT A HEARTACHE — Flirtations (Wayne Bickerton), Deram 85036 | 1 |
| 94 | 98 | 98 | — | I DO LOVE YOU — Billy Stewart, Chess 13620 | 3 |
| 95 | 99 | — | — | GIVE IT AWAY — Chi-Lites (Carl Davis & Eugene Record), Brunswick 55398 | 2 |
| 96 | — | — | — | PLAYGIRL — Thee Prophets (C. Bonafede, D. Belloc, L. Douglas), Kapp 962 | 1 |
| 97 | — | — | — | HALLWAYS OF MY MIND — Dells (Bobby Miller), Cadet 5636 | 1 |
| 98 | — | — | — | THE WEDDING CAKE — Connie Francis (Shelby S. Singleton Jr.), MGM 14034 | 1 |
| 99 | — | — | — | ONLY YOU — Bobby Hatfield (Dick Glasser), Verve 10634 | 1 |
| 100 | — | — | — | HAWAII FIVE-O — The Ventures (Joe Saraceno), Liberty 56068 | 1 |

## HOT 100—A TO Z—*(Publisher-Licensee)*

| | |
|---|---|
| Am I the Same Girl (Dakar/BRC, BMI) | 79 |
| Apricot Brandy (Nina, BMI) | 75 |
| Aquarius/Let the Sunshine In (United Artists, ASCAP) | 89 |
| Baby, Baby Don't Cry (Jobete, BMI) | 8 |
| Back Door Man (Symto, BMI) | 69 |
| Blessed Is the Rain (Pocket Full of Tunes, BMI) | 67 |
| Brother Love's Travelling Salvation Show (Stonebridge, BMI) | 65 |
| Build Me Up Buttercup (January-Nice, BMI) | 3 |
| But You Know I Love You (First Edition, BMI) | 19 |
| Can I Change My Mind (Dakar, BMI) | 14 |
| Cloud Nine (Jobete, BMI) | 32 |
| Crimson & Clover (Big Seven Music, BMI) | 5 |
| Crossroads (Noma, BMI) | 28 |
| Day After Day (It's Slippin' Away) (Goomby/Irving, BMI) | 83 |
| Didn't You Know (Jobete, BMI) | 88 |
| Dizzy (Low Twine, BMI) | 4 |
| Do Your Thing (Charles Wright & Fred Smith) (Wright-Gersti-Tamerlan, BMI) | 51 |
| Don't Forget About Me (Screen Gems-Columbia, BMI) | 74 |
| Don't Touch Me (Pamper, BMI) | 91 |
| Everyday People (Daly City, BMI) | 1 |
| Galveston (Ja-Ma Music, ASCAP) | 47 |
| Games People Play (Lowery, BMI) | 13 |
| Gimme Gimme Good Lovin' (Peanut Butter/Kahoona, BMI) | 80 |
| Give It Away (Dakar/BRC, BMI) | 95 |
| Give It Up or Turnit a Loose (Brown & Sons, BMI) | 15 |
| Glad She's a Woman (Tamerlane, BMI) | 61 |
| Good Lovin' Ain't Easy to Come By (Jobete, BMI) | 30 |
| Goodnight My Love (Spanka, BMI) | 33 |
| Hallways of My Mind (Chevis Music, BMI) | 97 |
| Hang 'Em High (Unart, BMI) | 27 |
| Hawaii Five-O (April, ASCAP) | 100 |
| Heaven (Slacsar, ASCAP) | 39 |
| Hello, It's Me (Screen Gems-Columbia, BMI) | 71 |
| Honey (Russell-Cason, ASCAP) | 44 |
| Hot Smoke & Sassafrass (Tapier, BMI) | 50 |
| I Can Hear Music (Trio Music Co. Inc., BMI) | 86 |
| I Do Love You (Chevis, BMI) | 94 |
| I Don't Know Why (Jobete, BMI) | 42 |
| I Got a Line on You (Hollenbeck, BMI) | 37 |
| I Like What You're Doing (to Me) (East/Memphis, BMI) | 73 |
| Indian Giver (Kaskat/Kahoona, BMI) | 10 |
| I'm Living in Shame (Jobete, BMI) | 21 |
| I've Gotta Be Me (Damila, ASCAP) | 11 |
| Johnny One Time (Hill & Range/Blue Crest, BMI) | 59 |
| Kum Ba Yah (Cintom, ASCAP) | 54 |
| Let It Be Me (M.C.A., ASCAP) | 36 |
| The Letter (Burton, BMI) | 70 |
| Long Green (Burdette, BMI) | 82 |
| Lover's Question, A (Progressive/Eden, BMI) | 53 |
| Lovin' Things (Gallico, BMI) | 49 |
| Maybe Tomorrow (Apple, ASCAP) | 68 |
| May I (Rhinelander, BMI) | 43 |
| Mendocino (Southern Love, BMI) | 45 |
| Mr. Sun, Mr. Moon (Boom, BMI) | 40 |
| My Whole World Ended (The Moment You Left Me) (Jobete, BMI) | 16 |
| No Not Much (Smoke Ring) (Beaver, ASCAP) | 85 |
| No Not Much (Vogues) (Budd, ASCAP) | 84 |
| Nothing But a Heartache (Feisted Music, BMI) | 93 |
| Only the Strong Survive (Parabut/Double Diamond/Downstairs, BMI) | 31 |
| Only You (Wildwood, BMI) | 99 |
| Playgirl (4 Star Music Co., BMI) | 96 |
| Proud Mary (Jondora, BMI) | 2 |
| Ramblin' Gamblin' Man (Gear, ASCAP) | 25 |
| Rock Me (Trousdale, BMI) | 48 |
| Run Away Child, Running Wild (Jobete, BMI) | 12 |
| Shotgun (Jobete, BMI) | 81 |
| Sing a Simple Song (Daly City, BMI) | 90 |
| Snatching It Back (Fame, BMI) | 77 |
| Somebody Loves You (Nickel Shoe, BMI) | 72 |
| Someday Soon (Witmark, BMI) | 55 |
| Sophisticated Sissy (Marsaint, BMI) | 41 |
| Soul Experience (Cotillion-Ten-East-Itasca, BMI) | 78 |
| Soul Shake (Singleton, BMI) | 46 |
| Sweet Cream Ladies (Blackwood, BMI) | 34 |
| Take Care of Your Homework (East/Memphis, BMI) | 29 |
| Tear Drop City (Screen Gems-Columbia) | 62 |
| There'll Come a Time (Jalynne, BMI) | 26 |
| These Are Not My People (Lowery, BMI) | 64 |
| Time of the Season (Mainstay, BMI) | 20 |
| Things I'd Like to Say (New Colony-T.M., BMI) | 23 |
| This Girl's in Love With You (Blue Seas/Jac, ASCAP) | 7 |
| This Magic Moment (Rumbalero/Progressive) | 6 |
| To Susan on the West Coast Waiting (Peer Int'l, BMI) | 35 |
| Touch Me (Nipper, ASCAP) | 9 |
| Traces (Low-Sal, BMI) | 17 |
| Tragedy (Bluff City, BMI) | 56 |
| Try a Little Tenderness (Connelly & Robbins, ASCAP) | 60 |
| Twenty-Five Miles (Jobete, BMI) | 52 |
| Way It Used to Be, The (Maribus, BMI) | 87 |
| Wedding Cake, The (Singleton, BMI) | 98 |
| The Weight (Dwarf, ASCAP) | 24 |
| When He Touches Me (Nothing Else Matters) (Painted Desert, BMI) | 63 |
| Who's Making Love (East/Memphis, BMI) | 57 |
| Will You Be Staying After Sunday (Screen Gems-Columbia, BMI) | 92 |
| Witchi Tai To (Lovetruth, BMI) | 76 |
| Woman Helping Man (Viva, BMI) | 58 |
| Worst That Could Happen (Rivers, BMI) | 22 |
| You Gave Me a Mountain (Mojave, BMI) | 38 |
| You Showed Me (Tickson, BMI) | 18 |
| You've Made Me So Vvry Happy (Jobete, BMI) | 66 |

## BUBBLING UNDER THE HOT 100

101. FOOLISH FOOL....Dee Dee Warwick, Mercury 72880
102. I'VE GOTTA HAVE YOUR LOVE....Eddie Floyd, Stax 0025
103. BABY MAKE ME FEEL SO GOOD....5 Stairsteps & Cubie, Curtom 1936
104. TRACKS OF MY TEARS....Aretha Franklin, Atlantic 2603
105. ONLY THE LONELY....Sonny James, Capitol 2370
106. WHO'S GONNA MOW YOUR GRASS..Buck Owens & His Buckaroos, Capitol 2377
107. LONG LINE RIDER....Bobby Darin, Direction 350
108. MY DECEIVING HEART....Impressions, Curtom 1937
109. 30-60-90....Willie Mitchell, Hi 2514
110. ALMOST PERSUADED....Etta James, Cadet 5630
111. GENTLE ON MY MIND....Dean Martin, Reprise 0812
112. GOOD VIBRATIONS....Hugo Montenegro, RCA 47-9712
113. I'LL TRY SOMETHING NEW....Diana Ross & Supremes & Temptations, Motown 1142
114. SWITCH IT ON....Cliff Nobles & Co., Phil-L.A. of Soul 324
115. GOODBYE COLUMBUS....Association, Warner Bros.-7 Arts 7267
116. UP TIGHT GOOD WOMAN....Solomon Burke, Bell 759
117. MEMORIES ARE MADE OF THIS....Gene & Debbe, TRX 5017
118. GOD KNOWS I LOVE YOU....Nancy Sinatra, Reprise 0813
119. ANYTHING YOU CHOOSE....Spanky & Our Gang, Mercury 72890
120. LILY THE PINK....Irish Rovers, Decca 324444
121. KAW-LIGA....Charlie Pride, RCA 47-9716
122. HAIR....Cowsills, MGM 14026
123. I REALLY LOVE YOU....Ambassadors, Arctic 147
124. TOO LATE TO WORRY, TOO BLUE TO CRY....Esther Phillips, Roulette 7031
125. TIME WAS....Canned Heat, Liberty 56097
126. IT'S YOUR THING....Isley Brothers, T Neck 901
127. NOVEMBER SNOW....Rejoice, Dunhill 4176
128. KICK OUT THE JAMS....MC 5, Elektra 45648
129. I HAVE DREAMED....Lettermen, Capitol 2414
130. SOMETHING HAPPENING....Herman's Hermits, MGM K-14035
131. CHANGING CHANGING....Ed Ames, RCA 47-9722
132. AS THE YEARS GO PASSING BY....Albert King, Atlantic 45-2604
133. APPLE CIDER....5X5, Paula 319
134. WHAT'S WRONG WITH MY WORLD....Ronnie Dove, Diamond 256
135. I DIDN'T KNOW WHAT TIME IT WAS....Ray Charles, ABC/TRC 11193

Compiled from national retail sales and radio station airplay by the Music Popularity Dept. of Record Market Research, Billboard.

# Billboard HOT 100

FOR WEEK ENDING MARCH 15, 1969

★ STAR PERFORMER—Sides registering greatest proportionate upward progress this week.

(seal) Record Industry Association of America seal of certification as million selling single.

| This Week | 1 Wk. Ago | 2 Wks. Ago | 3 Wks. Ago | TITLE | Artist (Producer), Label & Number | Weeks On Chart |
|---|---|---|---|---|---|---|
| Billboard Award | 4 | 10 | 25 | DIZZY | Tommy Roe (Steve Barri), ABC 11164 | 7 |
| 2 | 2 | 5 | 9 | PROUD MARY | Creedence Clearwater Revival (John Fogerty), Fantasy 619 | 8 |
| 3 (RIAA) | 1 | 1 | 1 | EVERYDAY PEOPLE | Sly & Family Stone (Sly Stone), Epic 10407 | 16 |
| 4 (RIAA) | 3 | 3 | 3 | BUILD ME UP BUTTERCUP | The Foundations (Tony Macaulay), UNI 55101 | 11 |
| 5 ★ | 17 | 19 | 23 | TRACES | Classics IV (Buddie Buie), Imperial 66352 | 6 |
| 6 | 5 | 2 | 2 | CRIMSON & CLOVER | Tommy James & the Shondells (Tommy James), Roulette R-7028 | 14 |
| 7 | 7 | 11 | 21 | THIS GIRL'S IN LOVE WITH YOU | Dionne Warwick (Bacharach-David), Scepter 12241 | 7 |
| 8 | 10 | 16 | 24 | INDIAN GIVER | 1910 Fruitgum Co. (Kasenetz-Katz, Assoc.), Buddah 91 | 8 |
| 9 ★ | 20 | 25 | 37 | TIME OF THE SEASON | Zombies (Rod Argent & Chris White), Date 2-1628 | 6 |
| 10 | 6 | 7 | 8 | THIS MAGIC MOMENT | Jay & the Americans (Jata Ent.), United Artists 50475 | 12 |
| 11 | 12 | 22 | 38 | RUN AWAY CHILD, RUNNING WILD | Temptations (Norman Whitfield), Gordy 7084 | 5 |
| 12 | 13 | 13 | 13 | GAMES PEOPLE PLAY | Joe South (Joe South), Capitol 2248 | 10 |
| 13 | 11 | 15 | 18 | I'VE GOTTA BE ME | Sammy Davis Jr. (Jimmy Bowen), Reprise 0779 | 14 |
| 14 | 16 | 23 | 40 | MY WHOLE WORLD ENDED (The Moment You Left Me) | David Ruffin (Fuqua & Bristol), Motown 1140 | 5 |
| 15 | 8 | 8 | 11 | BABY, BABY DON'T CRY | Smokey Robinson & Miracles (Smokey, Moore, Johnson), Tamla 54178 | 11 |
| 16 (RIAA) | 9 | 4 | 4 | TOUCH ME | Doors (Paul A. Rothchild), Elektra 45646 | 12 |
| 17 | 23 | 24 | 31 | THINGS I'D LIKE TO SAY | New Colony Six, Mercury 72858 | 12 |
| 18 ★ | 47 | 87 | — | GALVESTON | Glen Campbell (Al De Lory), Capitol P-2428 | 3 |
| 19 | 15 | 18 | 19 | GIVE IT UP OR TURNIT A LOOSE | James Brown (James Brown), King 6213 | 8 |
| 20 | 18 | 6 | 7 | YOU SHOWED ME | Turtles (Chip Douglas), White Whale 292 | 10 |
| 21 | 24 | 34 | 52 | THE WEIGHT | Aretha Franklin (Jerry Wexler & Tom Dowd), Atlantic 2603 | 4 |
| 22 | 14 | 14 | 5 | CAN I CHANGE MY MIND | Tyrone Davis (Willie Henderson), Dakar 602 | 13 |
| 23 | 19 | 21 | 26 | BUT YOU KNOW I LOVE YOU | First Edition (Jimmy Bowen), Reprise 0799 | 9 |
| 24 ★ | 40 | 41 | 61 | MR. SUN, MR. MOON | Paul Revere & the Raiders (Mark Lindsay), Columbia 4-44744 | 5 |
| 25 ★ | 37 | 42 | 43 | I GOT A LINE ON YOU | Spirit (Lou Adler), Ode 115 | 9 |
| 26 | 25 | 17 | 17 | RAMBLIN' GAMBLIN' MAN | Bob Seeger (Hideout), Capitol 2297 | 13 |
| 27 ★ | 38 | 40 | 55 | YOU GAVE ME A MOUNTAIN | Frankie Laine (Jimmy Bowen), ABC 11174 | 6 |
| 28 | 31 | 70 | — | ONLY THE STRONG SURVIVE | Jerry Butler (Gamble & Huff), Mercury 72898 | 3 |
| 29 | 21 | 12 | 10 | I'M LIVING IN SHAME | Diana Ross & the Supremes (The Clan), Motown 1139 | 8 |
| 30 | 34 | 38 | 28 | SWEET CREAM LADIES | Box Tops (Chips Moman/Tommy Cogbill) Mala 12035 | 12 |
| 31 ★ | 50 | 54 | 65 | HOT SMOKE & SASSAFRASS | Bubble Puppy, International Artists 128 | 5 |
| 32 | 32 | 45 | 49 | CLOUD NINE | Mongo Santamaria (David Rubinson), Columbia 4-44740 | 7 |
| 33 ★ | 48 | 63 | — | ROCK ME | Steppenwolf (Gabriel Mekler), Dunhill 4182 | 3 |
| 34 | 28 | 29 | 29 | CROSSROADS | Cream (Felix Pappalardi), Atco 6646 | 8 |
| 35 ★ | 45 | 49 | 70 | MENDOCINO | Sir Douglas Quintet (Amigas de Musica), Smash 2191 | 9 |
| 36 ★ | 66 | 95 | — | YOU'VE MADE ME SO VERY HAPPY | Blood, Sweat & Tears (James William Guerico), Columbia 4-44776 | 3 |
| 37 ★ | 89 | — | — | AQUARIUS/LET THE SUNSHINE IN | Fifth Dimension (Bones Howe), Soul City 772 | 2 |
| 38 | 26 | 26 | 30 | THERE'LL COME A TIME | Betty Everett (Archie Lee Hill Prod.), Uni 55100 | 9 |
| 39 | 43 | 44 | 46 | MAY I | Bill Deal & the Rhondels (Jerry Ross Prod.), Heritage 803 | 9 |
| 40 | 29 | 27 | 20 | TAKE CARE OF YOUR HOMEWORK | Johnnie Taylor (Al Jackson Jr. & Don Davis), Stax 0023 | 9 |
| 41 | 41 | 50 | 63 | SOPHISTICATED SISSY | Meters (Marshall E. Sehorn & Allen Toussaint), Josie 1001 | 6 |
| 42 | 42 | 43 | 68 | I DON'T KNOW WHY | Stevie Wonder (D. Hunter and S. Wonder), Tamla 54180 | 5 |
| 43 ★ | 52 | 66 | 94 | TWENTY-FIVE MILES | Edwin Starr (Bristol & Fuqua), Gordy 7083 | 5 |
| 44 | 30 | 32 | 35 | GOOD LOVIN' AIN'T EASY TO COME BY | Marvin Gaye & Tammi Terrell (Ashford & Simpson), Tamla 54179 | 7 |
| 45 | 51 | 58 | 66 | DO YOUR THING | Watts 103rd Street Band, Reprise 7250 | 7 |
| 46 | 39 | 39 | 41 | HEAVEN | Rascals (Rascals), Atlantic 2599 | 6 |
| 47 ★ | 60 | 62 | 89 | TRY A LITTLE TENDERNESS | Three Dog Night (Gabriel Makler), Dunhill 4177 | 6 |
| 48 | 36 | 51 | 58 | LET IT BE ME | Glen Campbell & Bobbie Gentry (Al DeLory & Kelly Gordon), Capitol 2387 | 8 |
| 49 | 49 | 53 | 69 | LOVIN' THINGS | Grassroots (Steve Barri), Dunhill 4180 | 5 |
| 50 | 35 | 35 | 50 | TO SUSAN ON THE WEST COAST WAITING | Donovan (Mickie Most), Epic 5-10434 | 6 |
| 51 ★ | 65 | 83 | 100 | BROTHER LOVE'S TRAVELLING SALVATION SHOW | Neil Diamond (Tommy Cogbill & Chips Moman), Uni 55109 | 4 |
| 52 | 53 | 71 | — | A LOVER'S QUESTION | Otis Redding (Steve Cropper), Atco 6654 | 3 |
| 53 ★ | 59 | 75 | 78 | JOHNNY ONE TIME | Brenda Lee (Mike Berniker), Decca 32428 | 6 |
| 54 ★ | — | — | — | I'LL TRY SOMETHING NEW | Diana Ross & the Supremes & the Temptations (F. Wilson & D. Richards), Motown 1142 | 1 |
| 55 ★ | 70 | 72 | 83 | THE LETTER | The Arbors (Roy Cicala & Lorie Burton), Date 2-1638 | 4 |
| 56 ★ | 62 | 68 | 87 | TEAR DROP CITY | Monkees (Tommy Boyce & Bobby Hart), Colgems 66-5000 | 4 |
| 57 | 57 | 64 | — | WHO'S MAKING LOVE | Young-Holt Unlimited (Carl Davis & Eugene Record), Brunswick 55400 | 3 |
| 58 | 44 | 46 | 47 | HONEY | O. C. Smith (Jerry Fuller), Columbia 44751 | 6 |
| 59 | 56 | 56 | 62 | TRAGEDY | Brian Hyland (Ray Ruff), Dot 17176 | 10 |
| 60 | 54 | 55 | 60 | KUM BA YAH | Tommy Leonetti (Bill Justis), Decca 32421 | 9 |
| 61 | 67 | — | — | BLESSED IS THE RAIN | Brooklyn Bridge (Wes Farrell), Buddah 95 | 2 |
| 62 | 63 | 65 | — | WHEN HE TOUCHES ME (Nothing Else Matters) | Peaches & Herb (Billy Sherrill & David Kapralik), Date 2-1637 | 3 |
| 63 | 64 | 81 | 99 | THESE ARE NOT MY PEOPLE | Johnny Rivers (Johnny Rivers), Imperial 66360 | 4 |
| 64 ★ | 75 | 80 | 82 | APRICOT BRANDY | Rhinoceros (Paul A. Rothchild), Elektra 45647 | 4 |
| 65 | 69 | 84 | 90 | BACK DOOR MAN | Derek (Cymbal-Tobin), Bang 566 | 4 |
| 66 ★ | 80 | 94 | — | GIMME GIMME GOOD LOVIN' | Crazy Elephant (Kasenetz-Katz Assoc.), Bell 763 | 3 |
| 67 | 68 | 73 | 75 | MAYBE TOMORROW | Iveys, Apple 1803 | 4 |
| 68 | 61 | 61 | 64 | GLAD SHE'S A WOMAN | Bobby Goldsboro (Bob Montgomery & Bobby Goldsboro), United Artists 50497 | 6 |
| 69 ★ | — | — | — | DON'T GIVE IN TO HIM | Gary Puckett & the Union Gap (Jerry Fuller), Columbia 4-44788 | 1 |
| 70 ★ | 86 | — | — | I CAN HEAR MUSIC | Beach Boys (Carl Wilson), Capitol 2432 | 2 |
| 71 | 71 | 77 | 77 | HELLO, IT'S ME | Nazz (Nazz & Michael Friedman), SGC 001 | 5 |
| 72 ★ | 81 | — | — | SHOTGUN | Vanilla Fudge (Vanilla Fudge), Atco 6655 | 2 |
| 73 | 73 | 89 | 95 | I LIKE WHAT YOU'RE DOING (To Me) | Carla Thomas (Don Davis), Stax 0024 | 5 |
| 74 | 74 | 88 | — | DON'T FORGET ABOUT ME | Dusty Springfield (Jerry Wexler-Tom Dowd), Atlantic 45-2606 | 3 |
| 75 | 78 | 78 | 81 | SOUL EXPERIENCE | Iron Butterfly (Jim Hilton), Atco 6647 | 4 |
| 76 | 77 | 90 | — | SNATCHING IT BACK | Clarence Carter, Atlantic | 3 |
| 77 ★ | 87 | 100 | — | THE WAY IT USED TO BE | Engelbert Humperdinck (Peter Sullivan), Parrot 40036 | 3 |
| 78 ★ | 91 | — | — | DON'T TOUCH ME | Bettye Swan (Wayne Shuler), Capitol 2382 | 2 |
| 79 | 84 | — | — | NO NOT MUCH | Vogues (Dick Glasser), Reprise 0803 | 2 |
| 80 ★ | — | — | — | GOODBYE COLUMBUS | Association (John Boylan), Warner Bros.-Seven Arts 7267 | 1 |
| 81 | 82 | 91 | 91 | LONG GREEN | The Fireballs (Norman Petty), Atco 6651 | 4 |
| 82 ★ | 92 | — | — | WILL YOU BE STAYING AFTER SUNDAY | Peppermint Rainbow (Paul Leka), Decca 32410 | 5 |
| 83 | 83 | 97 | — | DAY AFTER DAY (It's Slippin' Away) | Shango (Merry Rippelle), A&M 1014 | 3 |
| 84 ★ | — | — | — | HAIR | Cowsills (Bill & Bob Cowsill), MGM 14026 | 1 |
| 85 ★ | 96 | — | — | PLAYGIRL | Thee Prophets (C. Bonafede, D. Belloc, L. Douglas), Kapp 962 | 2 |
| 86 ★ | — | — | — | TIME IS TIGHT | Booker T. & the M.G.'s (B. T. Jones), Stax 0028 | 1 |
| 87 | 88 | — | — | DIDN'T YOU KNOW | Gladys Knight & the Pips (Ashford & Simpson), Soul 35057 | 2 |
| 88 | 93 | — | — | NOTHING BUT A HEARTACHE | Flirtations (Wayne Bickerton), Deram 85036 | 2 |
| 89 | 90 | — | — | SING A SIMPLE SONG | Sly & the Family Stone (Sly Stone), Epic 5-10407 | 2 |
| 90 ★ | — | — | — | KICK OUT THE JAMS | MC-5 (Jac Holzman & Bruce Botnick), Elektra 45648) | 1 |
| 91 | — | — | — | TRACKS OF MY TEARS | Aretha Franklin (Jerry Wexler & Tom Dowd), Atlantic 2603 | 1 |
| 92 | — | — | — | MOVE IN A LITTLE CLOSER, BABY | Mama Cass (Steve Barri), Dunhill 4184 | 1 |
| 93 | — | — | — | IT'S YOUR THING | Isley Brothers (R. Isley-O. Isley-R. Isley), T Neck 901 | 1 |
| 94 | — | — | — | TIME WAS | Canned Heat (Skip Taylor & Canned Heat), Liberty 56097 | 1 |
| 95 | 99 | — | — | ONLY YOU | Bobby Hatfield (Dick Glasser), Verve 10634 | 2 |
| 96 | — | — | — | THE PLEDGE OF ALLEGIANCE | Red Skelton, Columbia 4-44798 | 1 |
| 97 | 97 | — | — | HALLWAYS OF MY MIND | Dells (Bobby Miller), Cadet 5636 | 2 |
| 98 | 98 | — | — | THE WEDDING CAKE | Connie Francis (Shelby S. Singleton Jr.), MGM 14034 | 2 |
| 99 | 100 | — | — | HAWAII FIVE-O | The Ventures (Joe Saraceno), Liberty 56068 | 2 |
| 100 | — | — | — | GOD KNOWS I LOVE YOU | Nancy Sinatra (Billy Strange), Reprise 0813 | 1 |

## HOT 100—A TO Z—(Publisher-Licensee)

Apricot Brandy (Nina, BMI) .... 64
Aquarius/Let the Sunshine In (United Artists, ASCAP) 37
Baby, Baby Don't Cry (Jobete, BMI) .... 15
Back Door Man (Symto, BMI) .... 65
Blessed Is the Rain (Pocket Full of Tunes, BMI) .... 61
Brother Love's Travelling Salvation Show (Stonebridge, BMI) .... 51
Build Me Up Buttercup (January-Nice, BMI) .... 4
But You Know I Love You (First Edition, BMI) .... 23
Can I Change My Mind (Dakar, BMI) .... 22
Cloud Nine (Jobete, BMI) .... 32
Crimson & Clover (Big Seven Music, BMI) .... 6
Crossroads (Noma, BMI) .... 34
Day After Day (It's Slippin' Away) (Goomby/Irving, BMI) .... 83
Didn't You Know (Jobete, BMI) .... 87
Dizzy (Low Twine, BMI) .... 1
Do Your Thing (Charles Wright & Fred Smith) (Wright-Gersti-Tamerlan, BMI) .... 45
Don't Forget About Me (Screen Gems-Columbia, BMI) 74
Don't Give in to Him (Four Star, BMI) .... 69
Don't Touch Me (Pamper, BMI) .... 78
Everyday People (Daly City, BMI) .... 3
Galveston (Ja-Ma Music, ASCAP) .... 18
Games People Play (Lowery, BMI) .... 12
Gimme Gimme Good Lovin' (Peanut Butter/Kahoona, BMI) .... 66
Give It Up or Turnit a Loose (Brown & Sons, BMI) .... 19
Glad She's a Woman (Tamerlane, BMI) .... 68
God Knows I Love You (Metric, BMI) .... 100
Goodbye Columbus (Ensign, BMI) .... 80
Good Lovin' Ain't Easy to Come By (Jobete, BMI) .... 44
Hair (United Artists, ASCAP) .... 84
Hallways of My Mind (Chevis Music, BMI) .... 97
Hawaii Five-O (April, ASCAP) .... 99
Heaven (Slacsar, ASCAP) .... 46
Hello, It's Me (Screen Gems-Columbia, BMI) .... 71
Honey (Russell-Cason, ASCAP) .... 58
Hot Smoke & Sassafrass (Tapier, BMI) .... 31
I Can Hear Music (Trio Music Co. Inc., BMI) .... 70
I Don't Know Why (Jobete, BMI) .... 42
I Got a Line on You (Hollenbeck, BMI) .... 25
I Like What You're Doing (to Me) (East/Memphis, BMI) .... 73
Indian Giver (Kaskat/Kahoona, BMI) .... 8
I'll Try Something New (Jobete, BMI) .... 54
I'm Living in Shame (Jobete, BMI) .... 29
It's Your Thing (Brothers Three, BMI) .... 93
I've Gotta Be Me (Damila, ASCAP) .... 13
Johnny One Time (Hill & Range/Blue Crest, BMI) .... 53
Kick Out the Jams (Paradox, BMI) .... 90
Kum Ba Yah (Cintom, ASCAP) .... 60
Let It Be Me (M.C.A., ASCAP) .... 48
The Letter (Burton, BMI) .... 55
Long Green (Burdette, BMI) .... 81
Lover's Question, A (Progressive/Eden, BMI) .... 52
Lovin' Things (Gallico, BMI) .... 49
Maybe Tomorrow (Apple, ASCAP) .... 67
May I (Rhinelander, BMI) .... 39
Mendocino (Southern Love, BMI) .... 35
Move in a Little Closer, Baby (Arnold Jay, ASCAP) 92
Mr. Sun, Mr. Moon (Boom, BMI) .... 24
My Whole World Ended (The Moment You Left Me) (Jobete, BMI) .... 14
No Not Much (Beaver, ASCAP) .... 79
Nothing But a Heartache (Felsted Music, BMI) .... 88
Only the Strong Survive (Parabut/Double Diamond/Downstairs, BMI) .... 28
Only You (Wildwood, BMI) .... 95
Playgirl (4 Star Music Co., BMI) .... 85
Pledge of Allegiance, The (Valentina, ASCAP) .... 96
Proud Mary (Jondora, BMI) .... 2
Ramblin' Gamblin' Man (Gear, ASCAP) .... 26
Rock Me (Trousdale, BMI) .... 33
Run Away Child, Running Wild (Jobete, BMI) .... 11
Shotgun (Jobete, BMI) .... 72
Sing a Simple Song (Daly City, BMI) .... 89
Snatching It Back (Fame, BMI) .... 76
Sophisticated Sissy (Marsaint, BMI) .... 41
Soul Experience (Cotillion-Ten-East-Itasca, BMI) .... 75
Sweet Cream Ladies (Blackwood, BMI) .... 30
Take Care of Your Homework (East/Memphis, BMI) 40
Tear Drop City (Screen Gems-Columbia) .... 56
There'll Come a Time (Jalynne, BMI) .... 38
These Are Not My People (Lowery, BMI) .... 63
Time Is Tight (East/Memphis, BMI) .... 86
Time of the Season (Mainstay, BMI) .... 9
Time Was (Metric, BMI) .... 94
Things I'd Like to Say (New Colony-T.M., BMI) .... 17
This Girl's in Love With You (Blue Seas/Jac, ASCAP) .... 7
This Magic Moment (Rumbalero/Progressive) .... 10
To Susan on the West Coast Waiting (Peer Int'l, BMI) .... 50
Touch Me (Nipper, ASCAP) .... 16
Traces (Low-Sal, BMI) .... 5
Tracks of My Tears (Jobete, BMI) .... 91
Tragedy (Bluff City, BMI) .... 59
Try a Little Tenderness (Connelly & Robbins, ASCAP) .... 47
Twenty-Five Miles (Jobete, BMI) .... 43
Way It Used to Be, The (Maribus, BMI) .... 77
Wedding Cake, The (Singleton, BMI) .... 98
The Weight (Dwarf, ASCAP) .... 21
When He Touches Me (Nothing Else Matters) (Painted Desert, BMI) .... 62
Who's Making Love (East/Memphis, BMI) .... 57
Will You Be Staying After Sunday (Screen Gems-Columbia, BMI) .... 82
You Gave Me a Mountain (Mojave, BMI) .... 27
You Showed Me (Tickson, BMI) .... 20
You've Made Me So Very Happy (Jobete, BMI) .... 36

## BUBBLING UNDER THE HOT 100

101. FOOLISH FOOL .... Dee Dee Warwick, Mercury 72880
102. FIRST OF MAY .... Bee Gees, Atco 6657
103. IN THE STILL OF THE NIGHT .... Paul Anka, RCA 74-0126
104. GIVE IT AWAY .... Chi-Lites, Brunswick 55398
105. SOMEBODY LOVES YOU .... Delfonics, Philly Groove 154
106. BORN AGAIN .... Sam & Dave, Atlantic 2608
107. MEMORIES .... Elvis Presley, RCA 47-9731
108. NO NOT MUCH .... Smoke Ring, Buddah 77
109. WITCHI TAI TO .... Everything Is Everything, Vanguard Apostolic 35082
110. ALMOST PERSUADED .... Etta James, Cadet 5630
111. L.U.V. .... Tommy Boyce & Bobby Hart, A&M 1031
112. AM I THE SAME GIRL .... Barbara Acklin, Brunswick 55399
113. BABY MAKE ME FEEL SO GOOD .... Five Stairsteps & Cubie, Curtom 1936
114. BREAKFAST IN BED .... Dusty Springfield, Atlantic 2606
115. MORE TODAY THAN YESTERDAY .... Spiral Staircase, Columbia 4-44741
116. UP TIGHT GOOD WOMAN .... Solomon Burke, Bell 759
117. MEMORIES ARE MADE OF THIS .... Gene & Debbe, TRX 5017
118. LILY THE PINK .... Irish Rovers, Decca 32444
119. HEY JUDE .... Paul Mauriat, Philips 40594
120. THE CONSPIRACY OF HOMER JONES .... Dallas Frazier, Capitol 2402
121. I LEFT MY HEART IN SAN FRANCISCO .... Bobby Womack, Minit 32059
122. TRUCK STOP .... Jerry Smith, ABC 11162
123. TOO LATE TO WORRY, TOO BLUE TO CRY .... Esther Phillips, Roulette 7031
124. YOU'D BETTER GO .... Nancy Wilson, Capitol 2422
125. ARE YOU READY .... Chambers Brothers, Columbia 4-44779
126. CHOKIN' KIND .... Joe Simon, Sound Stage 7 2628
127. NOVEMBER SNOW .... Rejoice, Dunhill 4176
128. I DIDN'T KNOW WHAT TIME IT WAS .... Ray Charles, ABC/TRC 11193
129. LOS COSOS .... Rene & Rene, White Whale 298
130. CHANGING CHANGING .... Ed Ames, RCA 47-9722
131. WHAT'S WRONG WITH MY WORLD .... Ronnie Dove, Diamond 256
132. AS THE YEARS GO PASSING BY .... Albert King, Atlantic 45-2604
133. APPLE CIDER .... Five By Five, Paula 319
134. FEELINGS .... Cherry People, Heritage 810
135. A CHANGE IS GONNA COME .... Brenton Wood, Double Shot 137

Compiled from national retail sales and radio station airplay by the Music Popularity Dept. of Record Market Research, Billboard.

# Billboard HOT 100

FOR WEEK ENDING MARCH 22, 1969

★ STAR PERFORMER—Sides registering greatest proportionate upward progress this week.

(seal) Record Industry Association of America seal of certification as million selling single.

| This Week | 1 Wk. Ago | 2 Wks. Ago | 3 Wks. Ago | TITLE | Artist (Producer), Label & Number | Weeks On Chart |
|---|---|---|---|---|---|---|
| 1 (Billboard Award) | 1 | 4 | 10 | DIZZY | Tommy Roe (Steve Barri), ABC 11164 | 8 |
| 2 | 2 | 2 | 5 | PROUD MARY | Creedence Clearwater Revival (John Fogerty), Fantasy 619 | 9 |
| 3 | 5 | 17 | 19 | TRACES | Classics IV (Buddie Buie), Imperial 66352 | 7 |
| 4 (seal) | 4 | 3 | 3 | BUILD ME UP BUTTERCUP | The Foundations (Tony Macaulay), UNI 55101 | 12 |
| 5 | 8 | 10 | 16 | INDIAN GIVER | 1910 Fruitgum Co. (Kasenetz-Katz, Assoc.), Buddah 91 | 9 |
| 6 | 9 | 20 | 25 | TIME OF THE SEASON | Zombies (Rod Argent & Chris White), Date 2-1628 | 7 |
| 7 | 7 | 7 | 11 | THIS GIRL'S IN LOVE WITH YOU | Dionne Warwick (Bacharach-David), Scepter 12241 | 8 |
| 8 (seal) | 3 | 1 | 1 | EVERYDAY PEOPLE | Sly & Family Stone (Sly Stone), Epic 10407 | 17 |
| 9 | 6 | 5 | 2 | CRIMSON & CLOVER | Tommy James & the Shondells (Tommy James), Roulette R-7028 | 15 |
| 10 | 11 | 12 | 22 | RUN AWAY CHILD, RUNNING WILD | Temptations (Norman Whitfield), Gordy 7084 | 6 |
| ★11 | 18 | 47 | 87 | GALVESTON | Glen Campbell (Al De Lory), Capitol P-2428 | 4 |
| 12 | 12 | 13 | 13 | GAMES PEOPLE PLAY | Joe South (Joe South), Capitol 2248 | 11 |
| 13 | 14 | 16 | 23 | MY WHOLE WORLD ENDED (The Moment You Left Me) | David Ruffin (Fuqua & Bristol), Motown 1140 | 6 |
| ★14 | 37 | 89 | — | AQUARIUS/LET THE SUNSHINE IN | Fifth Dimension (Bones Howe), Soul City 772 | 3 |
| 15 | 13 | 11 | 15 | I'VE GOTTA BE ME | Sammy Davis Jr. (Jimmy Bowen), Reprise 0779 | 15 |
| 16 | 17 | 23 | 24 | THINGS I'D LIKE TO SAY | New Colony Six, Mercury 72858 | 13 |
| 17 | 15 | 8 | 8 | BABY, BABY DON'T CRY | Smokey Robinson & Miracles (Smokey, Moore, Johnson), Tamla 54178 | 12 |
| 18 | 10 | 6 | 7 | THIS MAGIC MOMENT | Jay & the Americans (Jata Ent.), United Artists 50475 | 13 |
| 19 | 21 | 24 | 34 | THE WEIGHT | Aretha Franklin (Jerry Wexler & Tom Dowd), Atlantic 2603 | 5 |
| ★20 | 33 | 48 | 63 | ROCK ME | Steppenwolf (Gabriel Mekler), Dunhill 4182 | 4 |
| ★21 | 36 | 66 | 95 | YOU'VE MADE ME SO VERY HAPPY | Blood, Sweat & Tears (James William Guerico), Columbia 4-44776 | 4 |
| ★22 | 31 | 50 | 54 | HOT SMOKE & SASSAFRASS | Bubble Puppy, International Artists 128 | 6 |
| 23 | 24 | 40 | 41 | MR. SUN, MR. MOON | Paul Revere & the Raiders (Mark Lindsay), Columbia 4-44744 | 6 |
| ★24 | 28 | 31 | 70 | ONLY THE STRONG SURVIVE | Jerry Butler (Gamble & Huff), Mercury 72898 | 4 |
| 25 | 25 | 37 | 42 | I GOT A LINE ON YOU | Spirit (Lou Adler), Ode 115 | 10 |
| 26 | 27 | 38 | 40 | YOU GAVE ME A MOUNTAIN | Frankie Laine (Jimmy Bowen), ABC 11174 | 7 |
| ★27 | 43 | 52 | 66 | TWENTY-FIVE MILES | Edwin Starr (Bristol & Fuqua), Gordy 7083 | 6 |
| 28 | 30 | 34 | 38 | SWEET CREAM LADIES | Box Tops (Chips Moman/Tommy Cogbill) Mala 12035 | 13 |
| 29 | 23 | 19 | 21 | BUT YOU KNOW I LOVE YOU | First Edition (Jimmy Bowen), Reprise 0799 | 10 |
| ★30 | 35 | 45 | 49 | MENDOCINO | Sir Douglas Quintet (Amigas de Musica), Smash 2191 | 10 |
| 31 (seal) | 16 | 9 | 4 | TOUCH ME | Doors (Paul A. Rothchild), Elektra 45646 | 13 |
| 32 | 20 | 18 | 6 | YOU SHOWED ME | Turtles (Chip Douglas), White Whale 292 | 11 |
| ★33 | 54 | — | — | I'LL TRY SOMETHING NEW | Diana Ross & the Supremes & the Temptations (F. Wilson & D. Richards), Motown 1142 | 2 |
| 34 | 41 | 41 | 50 | SOPHISTICATED SISSY | Meters (Marshall E. Sehorn & Allen Toussaint), Josie 1001 | 7 |
| 35 | 26 | 25 | 17 | RAMBLIN' GAMBLIN' MAN | Bob Seeger (Hideout), Capitol 2297 | 14 |
| 36 | 19 | 15 | 18 | GIVE IT UP OR TURNIT A LOOSE | James Brown (James Brown), King 6213 | 9 |
| 37 | 45 | 51 | 58 | DO YOUR THING | Watts 103rd Street Band, Reprise 7250 | 8 |
| 38 | 38 | 26 | 26 | THERE'LL COME A TIME | Betty Everett (Archie Lee Hill Prod.), Uni 55100 | 10 |
| 39 | 42 | 42 | 43 | I DON'T KNOW WHY | Stevie Wonder (D. Hunter and S. Wonder), Tamla 54180 | 6 |
| ★40 | 69 | — | — | DON'T GIVE IN TO HIM | Gary Puckett & the Union Gap (Jerry Fuller), Columbia 4-44788 | 2 |
| 41 | 39 | 43 | 44 | MAY I | Bill Deal & the Rhondels (Jerry Ross Prod.), Heritage 803 | 10 |
| ★42 | 93 | — | — | IT'S YOUR THING | Isley Brothers (R. Isley-O. Isley-R. Isley), T Neck 901 | 2 |
| ★43 | 79 | 84 | — | NO NOT MUCH | Vogues (Dick Glasser), Reprise 0803 | 3 |
| ★44 | 70 | 86 | — | I CAN HEAR MUSIC | Beach Boys (Carl Wilson), Capitol 2432 | 3 |
| 45 | 47 | 60 | 62 | TRY A LITTLE TENDERNESS | Three Dog Night (Gabriel Makler), Dunhill 4177 | 7 |
| 46 | 55 | 70 | 72 | THE LETTER | The Arbors (Roy Cicala & Lorie Burton), Date 2-1638 | 5 |
| 47 | 32 | 32 | 45 | CLOUD NINE | Mongo Santamaria (David Rubinson), Columbia 4-44740 | 8 |
| 48 | 52 | 53 | 71 | A LOVER'S QUESTION | Otis Redding (Steve Cropper), Atco 6654 | 4 |
| 49 | 51 | 65 | 83 | BROTHER LOVE'S TRAVELLING SALVATION SHOW | Neil Diamond (Tommy Cogbill & Chips Moman), Uni 55109 | 5 |
| 50 | 49 | 49 | 53 | LOVIN' THINGS | Grassroots (Steve Barri), Dunhill 4180 | 6 |
| 51 | 53 | 59 | 75 | JOHNNY ONE TIME | Brenda Lee (Mike Berniker), Decca 32428 | 7 |
| 52 | 48 | 36 | 51 | LET IT BE ME | Glen Campbell & Bobbie Gentry (Al DeLory & Kelly Gordon), Capitol 2387 | 9 |
| ★53 | 76 | 77 | 90 | SNATCHING IT BACK | Clarence Carter (Rick Hall), Atlantic 2605 | 4 |
| 54 | 61 | 67 | — | BLESSED IS THE RAIN | Brooklyn Bridge (Wes Farrell), Buddah 95 | 3 |
| 55 | 63 | 64 | 81 | THESE ARE NOT MY PEOPLE | Johnny Rivers (Johnny Rivers), Imperial 66360 | 5 |
| 56 | 56 | 62 | 68 | TEAR DROP CITY | Monkees (Tommy Boyce & Bobby Hart), Colgems 66-5000 | 5 |
| 57 | 62 | 63 | 65 | WHEN HE TOUCHES ME (Nothing Else Matters) | Peaches & Herb (Billy Sherrill & David Kapralik), Date 2-1637 | 4 |
| 58 | 66 | 80 | 94 | GIMME GIMME GOOD LOVIN' | Crazy Elephant (Kasenetz-Katz Assoc.), Bell 763 | 4 |
| 59 | 65 | 69 | 84 | BACK DOOR MAN | Derek (Cymbal-Tobin), Bang 566 | 5 |
| 60 | 64 | 75 | 80 | APRICOT BRANDY | Rhinoceros (Paul A. Rothchild), Elektra 45647 | 5 |
| ★61 | 78 | 91 | — | DON'T TOUCH ME | Bettye Swan (Wayne Shuler), Capitol 2382 | 3 |
| 62 | 57 | 57 | 64 | WHO'S MAKING LOVE | Young-Holt Unlimited (Carl Davis & Eugene Record), Brunswick 55400 | 4 |
| ★63 | 73 | 73 | 89 | I LIKE WHAT YOU'RE DOING (To Me) | Carla Thomas (Don Davis), Stax 0024 | 6 |
| ★64 | 74 | 74 | 88 | DON'T FORGET ABOUT ME | Dusty Springfield (Jerry Wexler-Tom Dowd), Atlantic 45-2606 | 4 |
| ★65 | 77 | 87 | 100 | THE WAY IT USED TO BE | Engelbert Humperdinck (Peter Sullivan), Parrot 40036 | 4 |
| ★66 | 96 | — | — | THE PLEDGE OF ALLEGIANCE | Red Skelton, Columbia 4-44798 | 2 |
| ★67 | — | — | — | MEMORIES | Elvis Presley, RCA 47-9731 | 1 |
| ★68 | 85 | 96 | — | PLAYGIRL | Thee Prophets (C. Bonafede, D. Belloc, L. Douglas), Kapp 962 | 3 |
| 69 | 67 | 68 | 73 | MAYBE TOMORROW | Iveys, Apple 1803 | 5 |
| ★70 | 84 | — | — | HAIR | Cowsills (Bill & Bob Cowsill), MGM 14026 | 2 |
| ★71 | — | — | — | CHOKIN' KIND | Joe Simon (J. R. Enterprises), SS7 2628 | 1 |
| 72 | 72 | 81 | — | SHOTGUN | Vanilla Fudge (Vanilla Fudge), Atco 6655 | 3 |
| 73 | 81 | 82 | 91 | LONG GREEN | The Fireballs (Norman Petty), Atco 6651 | 5 |
| 74 | 82 | 92 | — | WILL YOU BE STAYING AFTER SUNDAY | Peppermint Rainbow (Paul Leka), Decca 32410 | 6 |
| 75 | 75 | 78 | 78 | SOUL EXPERIENCE | Iron Butterfly (Jim Hilton), Atco 6647 | 5 |
| 76 | 83 | 83 | 97 | DAY AFTER DAY (It's Slippin' Away) | Shango (Merry Rippelle), A&M 1014 | 4 |
| ★77 | 87 | 88 | — | DIDN'T YOU KNOW | Gladys Knight & the Pips (Ashford & Simpson), Soul 35057 | 3 |
| 78 | 86 | — | — | TIME IS TIGHT | Booker T. & the M.G.'s (B. T. Jones), Stax 0028 | 2 |
| 79 | 71 | 71 | 77 | HELLO, IT'S ME | Nazz (Nazz & Michael Friedman), SGC 001 | 6 |
| 80 | 80 | — | — | GOODBYE COLUMBUS | Association (John Boylan), Warner Bros.-Seven Arts 7267 | 2 |
| ★81 | — | — | — | IS IT SOMETHING YOU GOT | Tyrone Davis (Willie Henderson), Dakar 605 | 1 |
| ★82 | — | — | — | FIRST OF MAY | Bee Gees (Robert Stigwood), Atco 6657 | 1 |
| 83 | 92 | — | — | MOVE IN A LITTLE CLOSER, BABY | Mama Cass (Steve Barri), Dunhill 4184 | 2 |
| ★84 | — | — | — | IT'S ONLY LOVE | B. J. Thomas (Chips Moman), Scepter 12244 | 1 |
| ★85 | — | — | — | IN THE STILL OF THE NIGHT | Paul Anka (Don Costa Prod.), RCA 74-0126 | 1 |
| ★86 | — | — | — | SWEET CHERRY WINE | Tommy James & Shondells (Chips Moman), Roulette 7039 | 1 |
| ★87 | — | — | — | ICE CREAM SONG | The Dynamics (Tommy Cogbill), Cotillion 44021 | 1 |
| 88 | 88 | 93 | — | NOTHING BUT A HEARTACHE | Flirtations (Wayne Bickerton), Deram 85036 | 3 |
| 89 | 89 | 90 | — | SING A SIMPLE SONG | Sly & the Family Stone (Sly Stone), Epic 5-10407 | 3 |
| 90 | 90 | — | — | KICK OUT THE JAMS | MC-5 (Jac Holzman & Bruce Botnick), Elektra 45648) | 2 |
| 91 | 91 | — | — | TRACKS OF MY TEARS | Aretha Franklin (Jerry Wexler & Tom Dowd), Atlantic 2603 | 2 |
| 92 | 99 | 100 | — | HAWAII FIVE-O | The Ventures (Joe Saraceno), Liberty 56068 | 3 |
| 93 | 94 | — | — | TIME WAS | Canned Heat (Skip Taylor & Canned Heat), Liberty 56097 | 2 |
| 94 | 97 | 97 | — | HALLWAYS OF MY MIND | Dells (Bobby Miller), Cadet 5636 | 3 |
| 95 | 95 | 99 | — | ONLY YOU | Bobby Hatfield (Dick Glasser), Verve 10634 | 3 |
| 96 | — | — | — | FOOLISH FOOL | Dee Dee Warwick (Ed Townsend), Mercury 72880 | 1 |
| 97 | — | — | — | BORN AGAIN | Sam & Dave (D. Porter & I. Hayes), Atlantic 2608 | 1 |
| 98 | 98 | 98 | — | THE WEDDING CAKE | Connie Francis (Shelby S. Singleton Jr.), MGM 14034 | 3 |
| 99 | — | — | — | GIVE IT AWAY | Chi-Lites (C. Davis & E. Record), Brunswick 55398 | 3 |
| 100 | 100 | — | — | GOD KNOWS I LOVE YOU | Nancy Sinatra (Billy Strange), Reprise 0813 | 2 |

## HOT 100—A TO Z—(Publisher-Licensee)



## BUBBLING UNDER THE HOT 100

101. MINI SKIRT MINNIE....Wilson Pickett, Atlantic 45-2611
102. MERCY....Ohio Express, Buddah 10
103. MY WAY....Frank Sinatra, Reprise 0817
104. MORNING GIRL....Neon Philharmonic, Warner Bros.-Seven Arts 7261
105. BREAKFAST IN BED....Dusty Springfield, Atlantic 2606
106. I DIDN'T KNOW WHAT TIME IT WAS....Ray Charles, ABC/TRC 11193
107. I'M STILL IN LOVE WITH YOU....Jackie Wilson, Brunswick 55402
108. ALBATROSS....Fleetwood Mac, Epic 5-10436
109. RHYTHM OF THE RAIN....Gary Lewis & the Playboys, Liberty 56093
110. WITH PEN IN HAND....Vicki Carr, Liberty 56092
111. L.U.V....Tommy Boyce & Bobby Hart, A&M 1031
112. THERE NEVER WAS A TIME....Jeannie C. Riley, Plantation 16
113. TRICIA TELL YOUR DADDY....Andy Kim, Steed 715
114. BUT IT'S ALRIGHT....J. J. Jackson, Calla 119
115. MORE TODAY THAN YESTERDAY....Spiral Staircase, Columbia 4-44747
116. ZAZUERA....Herb Alpert & the Tijuana Brass, A&M 1043
117. YOU'D BETTER GO....Nancy Wilson, Capitol 2422
118. LILY THE PINK....Irish Rovers, Decca 32444
119. HEY JUDE....Paul Mauriat, Philips 40594
120. CONSPIRACY OF HOMER JONES....Dallas Frazier, Capitol 2402
121. I LEFT MY HEART IN SAN FRANCISCO....Bobby Womack, Minit 32059
122. TRUCK STOP....Jerry Smith, ABC 11162
123. COME A LITTLE BIT CLOSER....Trini Lopez, Reprise 0814
124. SEATTLE....Perry Como, RCA 47-9722
125. ARE YOU READY....Chambers Brothers, Columbia 4-44779
126. NOVEMBER SNOW....Rejoice, Dunhill 4176
127. IT'S A GROOVY WORLD....Unifics, Kapp 985
128. LAS COSAS....Rene & Rene, White Whale 298
129. EMMERETTA....Deep Purple, Tetragrammaton 1519
130. IS THERE ANYTHING BETTER THAN MAKING LOVE....Fantastic Johnny C, Phil-L.A. of Soul 327
131. A CHANGE IS GONNA COME....Brenton Wood, Double Shot 137
132. GAMES PEOPLE PLAY....King Curtis & the Kingpins, Atco 6664
133. GRAZING IN THE GRASS....Friends of Distinction, RCA 74-0207
134. FEELINGS....Cherry People, Heritage 810
135. GITARZAN....Ray Stevens, Monument 1131

Compiled from national retail sales and radio station airplay by the Music Popularity Dept. of Record Market Research, Billboard.

# Billboard HOT 100

**FOR WEEK ENDING MARCH 29, 1969**

| This Week | Wk. Ago | 2 Wks. Ago | 3 Wks. Ago | TITLE — Artist (Producer), Label & Number | Weeks On Chart |
|---|---|---|---|---|---|
| 1 | 1 | 1 | 4 | DIZZY — Tommy Roe (Steve Barri), ABC 11164 | 9 |
| 2 | 3 | 5 | 17 | TRACES — Classics IV (Buddie Buie), Imperial 66352 | 8 |
| 3 | 6 | 9 | 20 | TIME OF THE SEASON — Zombies (Rod Argent & Chris White), Date 2-1628 | 8 |
| 4 | 14 | 37 | 89 | AQUARIUS/LET THE SUNSHINE IN — Fifth Dimension (Bones Howe), Soul City 772 | 4 |
| 5 | 2 | 2 | 2 | PROUD MARY — Creedence Clearwater Revival (John Fogerty), Fantasy 619 | 10 |
| 6 | 10 | 11 | 12 | RUN AWAY CHILD, RUNNING WILD — Temptations (Norman Whitfield), Gordy 7084 | 7 |
| 7 | 5 | 8 | 10 | INDIAN GIVER — 1910 Fruitgum Co. (Kasenetz-Katz Assoc.), Buddah 91 | 10 |
| 8 | 11 | 18 | 47 | GALVESTON — Glen Campbell (Al De Lory), Capitol P-2428 | 5 |
| 9 | 13 | 14 | 16 | MY WHOLE WORLD ENDED (The Moment You Left Me) — David Ruffin (Fuqua & Bristol), Motown 1140 | 5 |
| 10 | 24 | 28 | 31 | ONLY THE STRONG SURVIVE — Jerry Butler (Gamble & Huff), Mercury 72898 | 5 |
| 11 | 4 | 4 | 3 | BUILD ME UP BUTTERCUP — The Foundations (Tony Macaulay), UNI 55101 | 13 |
| 12 | 21 | 36 | 66 | YOU'VE MADE ME SO VERY HAPPY — Blood, Sweat & Tears (James William Guercio), Columbia 4-44776 | 5 |
| 13 | 7 | 7 | 7 | THIS GIRL'S IN LOVE WITH YOU — Dionne Warwick (Bacharach-David), Scepter 12241 | 9 |
| 14 | 8 | 3 | 1 | EVERYDAY PEOPLE — Sly & Family Stone (Sly Stone), Epic 10407 | 18 |
| 15 | 20 | 33 | 48 | ROCK ME — Steppenwolf (Gabriel Mekler), Dunhill 4182 | 5 |
| 16 | 16 | 17 | 23 | THINGS I'D LIKE TO SAY — New Colony Six, Mercury 72858 | 14 |
| 17 | 27 | 43 | 52 | TWENTY-FIVE MILES — Edwin Starr (Bristol & Fuqua), Gordy 7083 | 7 |
| 18 | 9 | 6 | 5 | CRIMSON & CLOVER — Tommy James & the Shondells (Tommy James), Roulette R-7028 | 16 |
| 19 | 22 | 31 | 50 | HOT SMOKE & SASSAFRASS — Bubble Puppy, International Artists 128 | 6 |
| 20 | 19 | 21 | 24 | THE WEIGHT — Aretha Franklin (Jerry Wexler & Tom Dowd), Atlantic 2603 | 6 |
| 21 | 17 | 15 | 8 | BABY, BABY DON'T CRY — Smokey Robinson & Miracles (Smokey, Moore, Johnson), Tamla 54178 | 13 |
| 22 | 12 | 12 | 13 | GAMES PEOPLE PLAY — Joe South (Joe South), Capitol 2248 | 12 |
| 23 | 23 | 24 | 40 | MR. SUN, MR. MOON — Paul Revere & the Raiders (Mark Lindsay), Columbia 4-44744 | 7 |
| 24 | 26 | 27 | 38 | YOU GAVE ME A MOUNTAIN — Frankie Laine (Jimmy Bowen), ABC 11174 | 8 |
| 25 | 18 | 10 | 6 | THIS MAGIC MOMENT — Jay & the Americans (Jata Ent.), United Artists 50475 | 14 |
| 26 | 42 | 93 | — | IT'S YOUR THING — Isley Brothers (R. Isley-O. Isley-R. Isley), T Neck 901 | 3 |
| 27 | 30 | 35 | 45 | MENDOCINO — Sir Douglas Quintet (Amigos de Musica), Smash 2191 | 11 |
| 28 | 37 | 45 | 51 | DO YOUR THING — Watts 103rd Street Band, Reprise 7250 | 9 |
| 29 | 33 | 54 | — | I'LL TRY SOMETHING NEW — Diana Ross & the Supremes & the Temptations (F. Wilson & D. Richards), Motown 1142 | 3 |
| 30 | 15 | 13 | 11 | I'VE GOTTA BE ME — Sammy Davis Jr. (Jimmy Bowen), Reprise 0779 | 16 |
| 31 | 40 | 69 | — | DON'T GIVE IN TO HIM — Gary Puckett & the Union Gap (Jerry Fuller), Columbia 4-44788 | 3 |
| 32 | 25 | 25 | 37 | I GOT A LINE ON YOU — Spirit (Lou Adler), Ode 115 | 11 |
| 33 | 28 | 30 | 34 | SWEET CREAM LADIES — Box Tops (Chips Moman/Tommy Cogbill), Mala 12035 | 14 |
| 34 | 43 | 79 | 84 | NO NOT MUCH — Vogues (Dick Glasser), Reprise 0803 | 4 |
| 35 | 70 | 84 | — | HAIR — Cowsills (Bill & Bob Cowsill), MGM 14026 | 3 |
| 36 | 49 | 51 | 65 | BROTHER LOVE'S TRAVELLING SALVATION SHOW — Neil Diamond (Tommy Cogbill & Chips Moman), Uni 55109 | 5 |
| 37 | 45 | 47 | 60 | TRY A LITTLE TENDERNESS — Three Dog Night (Gabriel Makler), Dunhill 4177 | 6 |
| 38 | 53 | 76 | 77 | SNATCHING IT BACK — Clarence Carter (Rick Hall), Atlantic 2605 | 5 |
| 39 | 71 | — | — | CHOKIN' KIND — Joe Simon (J. R. Enterprises), SS7 2628 | 2 |
| 40 | 29 | 23 | 19 | BUT YOU KNOW I LOVE YOU — First Edition (Jimmy Bowen), Reprise 0799 | 11 |
| 41 | 46 | 55 | 70 | THE LETTER — The Arbors (Roy Cicala & Lorie Burton), Date 2-1638 | 5 |
| 42 | 51 | 53 | 59 | JOHNNY ONE TIME — Brenda Lee (Mike Berniker), Decca 32428 | 8 |
| 43 | 44 | 70 | 86 | I CAN HEAR MUSIC — Beach Boys (Carl Wilson), Capitol 2432 | 5 |
| 44 | 78 | 86 | — | TIME IS TIGHT — Booker T. & the M.G.'s (B. T. Jones), Stax 0028 | 3 |
| 45 | 34 | 41 | 41 | SOPHISTICATED SISSY — Meters (Marshall E. Sehorn & Allen Toussaint), Josie 1001 | 8 |
| 46 | 38 | 38 | 26 | THERE'LL COME A TIME — Betty Everett (Archie Lee Hill Prod.), Uni 55100 | 11 |
| 47 | 39 | 42 | 42 | I DON'T KNOW WHY — Stevie Wonder (D. Hunter and S. Wonder), Tamla 54180 | 7 |
| 48 | 48 | 52 | 53 | A LOVER'S QUESTION — Otis Redding (Steve Cropper), Atco 6654 | 5 |
| 49 | 54 | 61 | 67 | BLESSED IS THE RAIN — Brooklyn Bridge (Wes Farrell), Buddah 95 | 4 |
| 50 | 57 | 62 | 63 | WHEN HE TOUCHES ME (Nothing Else Matters) — Peaches & Herb (Dave Kapralik), Date 2-1637 | 5 |
| 51 | 66 | 96 | — | THE PLEDGE OF ALLEGIANCE — Red Skelton, Columbia 4-44798 | 3 |
| 52 | 67 | — | — | MEMORIES — Elvis Presley, RCA 47-9731 | 2 |
| 53 | 58 | 66 | 80 | GIMME GIMME GOOD LOVIN' — Crazy Elephant (Kasenetz-Katz Assoc.), Bell 763 | 5 |
| 54 | 61 | 78 | 91 | DON'T TOUCH ME — Bettye Swan (Wayne Shuler), Capitol 2382 | 4 |
| 55 | 63 | 73 | 73 | I LIKE WHAT YOU'RE DOING (To Me) — Carla Thomas (Don Davis), Stax 0024 | 5 |
| 56 | 60 | 64 | 75 | APRICOT BRANDY — Rhinoceros (Paul A. Rothchild), Elektra 45647 | 6 |
| 57 | 81 | — | — | IS IT SOMETHING YOU GOT — Tyrone Davis (Willie Henderson), Dakar 605 | 2 |
| 58 | 56 | 56 | 62 | TEAR DROP CITY — Monkees (Tommy Boyce & Bobby Hart), Colgems 66-5000 | 6 |
| 59 | 50 | 49 | 49 | LOVIN' THINGS — Grassroots (Steve Barri), Dunhill 4180 | 7 |
| 60 | 65 | 77 | 87 | THE WAY IT USED TO BE — Engelbert Humperdinck (Peter Sullivan), Parrot 40036 | 4 |
| 61 | 86 | — | — | SWEET CHERRY WINE — Tommy James & Shondells (Chips Moman), Roulette 7039 | 2 |
| 62 | 82 | — | — | FIRST OF MAY — Bee Gees (Robert Stigwood), Atco 6657 | 2 |
| 63 | 68 | 85 | 96 | PLAYGIRL — Thee Prophets (C. Bonafede, D. Belloc, L. Douglas), Kapp 962 | 4 |
| 64 | 64 | 74 | 74 | DON'T FORGET ABOUT ME — Dusty Springfield (Jerry Wexler-Tom Dowd), Atlantic 45-2606 | 5 |
| 65 | 55 | 63 | 64 | THESE ARE NOT MY PEOPLE — Johnny Rivers (Johnny Rivers), Imperial 66360 | 5 |
| 66 | 59 | 65 | 69 | BACK DOOR MAN — Derek (Cymbal-Tobin), Bang 566 | 6 |
| 67 | 74 | 82 | 92 | WILL YOU BE STAYING AFTER SUNDAY — Peppermint Rainbow (Paul Leka), Decca 32410 | 7 |
| 68 | 72 | 72 | 81 | SHOTGUN — Vanilla Fudge (Vanilla Fudge), Atco 6655 | 4 |
| 69 | — | — | — | MY WAY — Frank Sinatra (Don Costa), Reprise 0817 | 1 |
| 70 | 92 | 99 | 100 | HAWAII FIVE-O — The Ventures (Joe Saraceno), Liberty 56068 | 4 |
| 71 | 84 | — | — | IT'S ONLY LOVE — B. J. Thomas (Chips Moman), Scepter 12244 | 2 |
| 72 | 76 | 83 | 83 | DAY AFTER DAY (It's Slippin' Away) — Shango (Merry Rippelle), A&M 1014 | 4 |
| 73 | 73 | 81 | 82 | LONG GREEN — The Fireballs (Norman Petty), Atco 6651 | 6 |
| 74 | 83 | 92 | — | MOVE IN A LITTLE CLOSER, BABY — Mama Cass (Steve Barri), Dunhill 4184 | 3 |
| 75 | 77 | 87 | 88 | DIDN'T YOU KNOW — Gladys Knight & the Pips (Ashford & Simpson), Soul 35057 | 4 |
| 76 | — | — | — | MINI SKIRT MINNIE — Wilson Pickett (Rick Hall), Atlantic 2611 | 1 |
| 77 | — | — | — | MERCY — Ohio Express (J. Levine-A. Resnick), Buddah 102 | 1 |
| 78 | 85 | — | — | IN THE STILL OF THE NIGHT — Paul Anka (Don Costa Prod.), RCA 74-0126 | 2 |
| 79 | — | — | — | WISHFUL SINFUL — Doors (Paul A. Rothchild), Elektra 45656 | 1 |
| 80 | 91 | 91 | — | TRACKS OF MY TEARS — Aretha Franklin (Jerry Wexler & Tom Dowd), Atlantic 2603 | 3 |
| 81 | 87 | — | — | ICE CREAM SONG — The Dynamics (Tommy Cogbill), Cotillion 44021 | 2 |
| 82 | 80 | 80 | — | GOODBYE COLUMBUS — Association (John Boylan), Warner Bros.-Seven Arts 7267 | 3 |
| 83 | 88 | 88 | 93 | NOTHING BUT A HEARTACHE — Flirtations (Wayne Bickerton), Deram 85038 | 4 |
| 84 | 93 | 94 | — | TIME WAS — Canned Heat (Skip Taylor & Canned Heat), Liberty 56097 | 3 |
| 85 | 90 | 90 | — | KICK OUT THE JAMS — MC-5 (Jac Holzman & Bruce Botnick), Elektra 45648 | 3 |
| 86 | — | — | — | THERE NEVER WAS A TIME — Jeannie C. Riley (Shelby S. Singleton Jr.), Plantation 16 | 1 |
| 87 | 79 | 71 | 71 | HELLO, IT'S ME — Nazz (Nazz & Michael Friedman), SGC 001 | 7 |
| 88 | 96 | — | — | FOOLISH FOOL — Dee Dee Warwick (Ed Townsend), Mercury 72880 | 2 |
| 89 | 99 | — | — | GIVE IT AWAY — Chi-Lites (C. Davis & E. Record), Brunswick 55398 | 4 |
| 90 | 89 | 89 | 90 | SING A SIMPLE SONG — Sly & the Family Stone (Sly Stone), Epic 5-10407 | 4 |
| 91 | 98 | 98 | 98 | THE WEDDING CAKE — Connie Francis (Shelby S. Singleton Jr.), MGM 14034 | 4 |
| 92 | 94 | 97 | 97 | HALLWAYS OF MY MIND — Dells (Bobby Miller), Cadet 5636 | 4 |
| 93 | 97 | — | — | BORN AGAIN — Sam & Dave (D. Porter & I. Hayes), Atlantic 2608 | 2 |
| 94 | — | — | — | GOOD TIMES BAD TIMES — Led Zeppelin (Jimmy Page), Atlantic 2613 | 1 |
| 95 | — | — | — | ONE EYE OPEN — Maskmen & Agents (BBC Prod.), Dynamo 125 | 1 |
| 96 | — | — | — | ZAZUERA — Herb Alpert & the Tijuana Brass (H. Alpert & Jerry Moss), A&M 1043 | 1 |
| 97 | 100 | 100 | — | GOD KNOWS I LOVE YOU — Nancy Sinatra (Billy Strange), Reprise 0813 | 3 |
| 98 | — | — | — | SOMETHING'S ON HER MIND — Four Seasons (Bob Gaudio), Phillips 40597 | 1 |
| 99 | 95 | 95 | 99 | ONLY YOU — Bobby Hatfield (Dick Glasser), Verve 10634 | 4 |
| 100 | — | — | — | I LOVE MY BABY — Archie Bell & the Drells (Gamble/Huff), Atlantic 2612 | 1 |

## BUBBLING UNDER THE HOT 100

101. TO KNOW YOU IS TO LOVE YOU — Bobby Vinton, Epic 5-10461
102. WHERE DO YOU GO TO (MY LOVELY) — Peter Sarstedt, World Pacific 77911
103. BREAKFAST IN BED — Dusty Springfield, Atlantic 2606
104. MORNING GIRL — Neon Philharmonic, Warner Bros.-Seven Arts 7261
105. I DIDN'T KNOW WHAT TIME IT WAS — Ray Charles, ABC/TRC 11193
106. WITH PEN IN HAND — Vikki Carr, Liberty 56092
107. I STILL LOVE YOU — Jackie Wilson, Brunswick 55402
108. ALBATROSS — Fleetwood Mac, Epic 5-10436
109. RHYTHM OF THE RAIN — Gary Lewis & the Playboys, Liberty 56093
110. CALIFORNIA GIRL — Tempali & the Glaser Brothers, MGM K 14036
111. TRICIA TELL YOUR DADDY — Andy Kim, Steed 715
112. YOU'D BETTER GO — Nancy Wilson, Capitol 2422
113. ARE YOU READY — Chambers Brothers, Columbia 4-44779
114. MORE TODAY THAN YESTERDAY — Spiral Staircase, Columbia 4-44747
115. LILY THE PINK — Irish Rovers, Decca 32444
116. GAMES PEOPLE PLAY — King Curtis & His Kingpins, Atco 6664
117. L.U.V. — Tommy Boyce & Bobby Hart, A&M 1031
118. GITARZAN — Ray Stevens, Monument 1131
119. I LEFT MY HEART IN SAN FRANCISCO — Bobby Womack, Minit 32059
120. GRAZIN' IN THE GRASS — Friends of Distinction, RCA 74-0107
121. COME A LITTLE BIT CLOSER — Trini Lopez, Reprise 0814
122. TOO LATE TO WORRY, TOO BLUE TO CRY — Esther Phillips, Roulette 7031
123. SEATTLE — Perry Como, RCA 47-9722
124. IT'S A GROOVY WORLD — Unifics, Kapp 985
125. IDAHO — Four Seasons, Phillips 40597
126. ATLANTIS — Donovan, Epic 5-10434
127. WHEN YOU DANCE — Jay & the Americans, United Artists 50510
128. HUSH — Deep Purple, Tetragrammaton 1519
129. PLEASE DON'T GO — Eddy Arnold, RCA Victor 74-0126
130. IS THE ANYTHING BETTER THAN MAKING LOVE — Fantastic Johnny C., Phil-L.A. of Soul 327

*Compiled from national retail sales and radio station airplay by the Music Popularity Dept. of Record Market Research, Billboard.*

# Billboard HOT 100

FOR WEEK ENDING APRIL 5, 1969

★ STAR PERFORMER—Sides registering greatest proportionate upward progress this week.

Record Industry Association of America seal of certification as million selling single.

| This Week | 1 Wk. Ago | 2 Wks. Ago | 3 Wks. Ago | TITLE Artist (Producer), Label & Number | Weeks On Chart |
|---|---|---|---|---|---|
| 1 (Billboard Award) | 1 | 1 | 1 | DIZZY — Tommy Roe (Steve Barri), ABC 11164 | 10 |
| ★ 2 | 4 | 14 | 37 | AQUARIUS/LET THE SUNSHINE IN — Fifth Dimension (Bones Howe), Soul City 772 | 5 |
| 3 | 3 | 6 | 9 | TIME OF THE SEASON — Zombies (Rod Argent & Chris White), Date 2-1628 | 9 |
| ★ 4 | 12 | 21 | 36 | YOU'VE MADE ME SO VERY HAPPY — Blood, Sweat & Tears (James William Guerico), Columbia 4-44776 | 6 |
| ★ 5 | 8 | 11 | 18 | GALVESTON — Glen Campbell (Al De Lory), Capitol P-2428 | 6 |
| 6 | 6 | 10 | 11 | RUN AWAY CHILD, RUNNING WILD — Temptations (Norman Whitfield), Gordy 7084 | 8 |
| ★ 7 | 10 | 24 | 28 | ONLY THE STRONG SURVIVE — Jerry Butler (Gamble & Huff), Mercury 72898 | 6 |
| 8 | 2 | 3 | 5 | TRACES — Classics IV (Buddie Buie), Imperial 66352 | 9 |
| 9 | 9 | 13 | 14 | MY WHOLE WORLD ENDED (The Moment You Left Me) — David Ruffin (Fuqua & Bristol), Motown 1140 | 8 |
| 10 | 5 | 2 | 2 | PROUD MARY — Creedence Clearwater Revival (John Fogerty), Fantasy 619 | 11 |
| ★ 11 | 15 | 20 | 33 | ROCK ME — Steppenwolf (Gabriel Mekler), Dunhill 4182 | 6 |
| 12 | 7 | 5 | 8 | INDIAN GIVER — 1910 Fruitgum Co. (Kasenetz-Katz, Assoc.), Buddah 91 | 11 |
| 13 | 17 | 27 | 43 | TWENTY-FIVE MILES — Edwin Starr (Bristol & Fuqua), Gordy 7083 | 8 |
| ★ 14 | 26 | 42 | 93 | IT'S YOUR THING — Isley Brothers (R. Isley-O. Isley-R. Isley), T Neck 901 | 4 |
| ★ 15 | 19 | 22 | 31 | HOT SMOKE & SASSAFRASS — Bubble Puppy, International Artists 128 | 8 |
| 16 | 11 | 4 | 4 | BUILD ME UP BUTTERCUP — The Foundations (Tony Macaulay), UNI 55101 | 14 |
| 17 | 13 | 7 | 7 | THIS GIRL'S IN LOVE WITH YOU — Dionne Warwick (Bacharach-David), Scepter 12241 | 10 |
| ★ 18 | 35 | 70 | 84 | HAIR — Cowsills (Bill & Bob Cowsill), MGM 14026 | 4 |
| ★ 19 | 23 | 23 | 24 | MR. SUN, MR. MOON — Paul Revere & the Raiders (Mark Lindsay), Columbia 4-44744 | 8 |
| ★ 20 | 41 | 46 | 55 | THE LETTER — The Arbors (Roy Cicala & Lorie Burton), Date 2-1638 | 7 |
| ★ 21 | 28 | 37 | 45 | DO YOUR THING — Watts 103rd Street Band, Warner Bros.-Seven Arts 7250 | 10 |
| 22 | 14 | 8 | 3 | EVERYDAY PEOPLE — Sly & Family Stone (Sly Stone), Epic 10407 | 19 |
| 23 | 21 | 17 | 15 | BABY, BABY DON'T CRY — Smokey Robinson & Miracles (Smokey, Moore, Johnson), Tamla 54178 | 14 |
| 24 | 24 | 26 | 27 | YOU GAVE ME A MOUNTAIN — Frankie Laine (Jimmy Bowen), ABC 11174 | 9 |
| 25 | 16 | 16 | 17 | THINGS I'D LIKE TO SAY — New Colony Six, Mercury 72858 | 15 |
| ★ 26 | 53 | 58 | 66 | GIMME GIMME GOOD LOVIN' — Crazy Elephant (Kasenetz-Katz Assoc.), Bell 763 | 6 |
| 27 | 27 | 30 | 35 | MENDOCINO — Sir Douglas Quintet (Amigas de Musica), Smash 2191 | 12 |
| 28 | 29 | 33 | 54 | I'LL TRY SOMETHING NEW — Diana Ross & the Supremes & the Temptations (F. Wilson & D. Richards), Motown 1142 | 4 |
| ★ 29 | 36 | 49 | 51 | BROTHER LOVE'S TRAVELLING SALVATION SHOW — Neil Diamond (Tommy Cogbill & Chips Moman), Uni 55109 | 7 |
| 30 | 31 | 40 | 69 | DON'T GIVE IN TO HIM — Gary Puckett & the Union Gap (Jerry Fuller), Columbia 4-44788 | 4 |
| ★ 31 | 37 | 45 | 47 | TRY A LITTLE TENDERNESS — Three Dog Night (Gabriel Makler), Dunhill 4177 | 9 |
| 32 | 20 | 19 | 21 | THE WEIGHT — Aretha Franklin (Jerry Wexler & Tom Dowd), Atlantic 2603 | 7 |
| ★ 33 | 44 | 78 | 86 | TIME IS TIGHT — Booker T. & the M.G.'s (B. T. Jones), Stax 0028 | 4 |
| ★ 34 | 61 | 86 | — | SWEET CHERRY WINE — Tommy James & Shondells (Chips Moman), Roulette 7039 | 3 |
| 35 | 32 | 25 | 25 | I GOT A LINE ON YOU — Spirit (Lou Adler), Ode 115 | 12 |
| ★ 36 | 43 | 44 | 70 | I CAN HEAR MUSIC — Beach Boys (Carl Wilson), Capitol 2432 | 5 |
| 37 | 38 | 53 | 76 | SNATCHING IT BACK — Clarence Carter (Rick Hall), Atlantic 2605 | 6 |
| 38 | 39 | 71 | — | CHOKIN' KIND — Joe Simon (J. R. Enterprises), SS7 2628 | 3 |
| 39 | 34 | 43 | 79 | NO NOT MUCH — Vogues (Dick Glasser), Reprise 0803 | 5 |
| 40 | 33 | 28 | 30 | SWEET CREAM LADIES — Box Tops (Chips Moman/Tommy Cogbill) Mala 12035 | 15 |
| ★ 41 | 69 | — | — | MY WAY — Frank Sinatra (Don Costa), Reprise 0817 | 2 |
| 42 | 42 | 51 | 53 | JOHNNY ONE TIME — Brenda Lee (Mike Berniker), Decca 32428 | 9 |
| ★ 43 | 62 | 82 | — | FIRST OF MAY — Bee Gees (Robert Stigwood), Atco 6657 | 3 |
| ★ 44 | 60 | 65 | 77 | THE WAY IT USED TO BE — Engelbert Humperdinck (Peter Sullivan), Parrot 40036 | 6 |
| 45 | 49 | 54 | 61 | BLESSED IS THE RAIN — Brooklyn Bridge (Wes Farrell), Buddah 95 | 5 |
| 46 | 51 | 66 | 96 | THE PLEDGE OF ALLEGIANCE — Red Skelton, Columbia 4-44798 | 4 |
| ★ 47 | 54 | 61 | 78 | DON'T TOUCH ME — Bettye Swan (Wayne Shuler), Capitol 2382 | 5 |
| ★ 48 | 52 | 67 | — | MEMORIES — Elvis Presley, RCA 47-9731 | 3 |
| 49 | 50 | 57 | 62 | WHEN HE TOUCHES ME (Nothing Else Matters) — Peaches & Herb (Billy Sherrill & David Kapralik), Date 2-1637 | 6 |
| ★ 50 | 63 | 68 | 85 | PLAYGIRL — Thee Prophets (C. Bonafede, D. Belloc, L. Douglas), Kapp 962 | 5 |
| ★ 51 | 70 | 92 | 99 | HAWAII FIVE-O — The Ventures (Joe Saraceno), Liberty 56068 | 5 |
| ★ 52 | 67 | 74 | 82 | WILL YOU BE STAYING AFTER SUNDAY — Peppermint Rainbow (Paul Leka), Decca 32410 | 8 |
| 53 | 57 | 81 | — | IS IT SOMETHING YOU GOT — Tyrone Davis (Willie Henderson), Dakar 605 | 3 |
| ★ 54 | 77 | — | — | MERCY — Ohio Express (Kasenetz-Katz Assoc.), Buddah 102 | 2 |
| 55 | 55 | 63 | 73 | I LIKE WHAT YOU'RE DOING (To Me) — Carla Thomas (Don Davis), Stax 0024 | 8 |
| 56 | 56 | 60 | 64 | APRICOT BRANDY — Rhinoceros (Paul A. Rothchild), Elektra 45647 | 7 |
| 57 | 48 | 48 | 52 | A LOVER'S QUESTION — Otis Redding (Steve Cropper), Atco 6654 | 6 |
| ★ 58 | 74 | 82 | 92 | MOVE IN A LITTLE CLOSER, BABY — Mama Cass (Steve Barri), Dunhill 4184 | 4 |
| ★ 59 | 72 | 76 | 83 | DAY AFTER DAY (It's Slippin' Away) — Shango (Merry Rippelle), A&M 1014 | 6 |
| ★ 60 | 79 | — | — | WISHFUL SINFUL — Doors (Paul A. Rothchild), Elektra 45656 | 2 |
| ★ 61 | — | — | — | I DON'T WANT NOBODY TO GIVE ME NOTHING (Open Up the Door, I'll Get It Myself) — James Brown (James Brown), King 6224 | 1 |
| ★ 62 | 83 | 88 | 88 | NOTHING BUT A HEARTACHE — Flirtations (Wayne Bickerton), Deram 85038 | 5 |
| ★ 63 | 71 | 84 | — | IT'S ONLY LOVE — B. J. Thomas (Chips Moman), Scepter 12244 | 3 |
| ★ 64 | 81 | 87 | — | ICE CREAM SONG — The Dynamics (Tommy Cogbill), Cotillion 44021 | 3 |
| ★ 65 | 75 | 77 | 87 | DIDN'T YOU KNOW — Gladys Knight & the Pips (Ashford & Simpson), Soul 35057 | 5 |
| 66 | 58 | 56 | 56 | TEAR DROP CITY — Monkees (Tommy Boyce & Bobby Hart), Colgems 66-5000 | 7 |
| ★ 67 | 84 | 93 | 94 | TIME WAS — Canned Heat (Skip Taylor & Canned Heat), Liberty 56097 | 4 |
| 68 | 68 | 72 | 72 | SHOTGUN — Vanilla Fudge (Vanilla Fudge), Atco 6655 | 5 |
| 69 | 76 | — | — | MINI SKIRT MINNIE — Wilson Pickett (Rick Hall), Atlantic 2611 | 2 |
| ★ 70 | 78 | 85 | — | IN THE STILL OF THE NIGHT — Paul Anka (Don Costa Prod.), RCA 74-0126 | 3 |
| 71 | 80 | 91 | 91 | TRACKS OF MY TEARS — Aretha Franklin (Jerry Wexler & Tom Dowd), Atlantic 2603 | 4 |
| ★ 72 | — | — | — | TO KNOW YOU IS TO LOVE YOU — Bobby Vinton (Billy Sherril), Epic 5-10461 | 1 |
| ★ 73 | — | — | — | PINBALL WIZARD — The Who (Baron Lambert), Decca 732465 | 1 |
| 74 | 73 | 73 | 81 | LONG GREEN — The Fireballs (Norman Petty), Atco 6651 | 7 |
| ★ 75 | — | — | — | ATLANTIS — Donovan (Mickie Most), Epic 5-10434 | 1 |
| 76 | 64 | 64 | 74 | DON'T FORGET ABOUT ME — Dusty Springfield (Jerry Wexler-Tom Dowd), Atlantic 45-2606 | 6 |
| ★ 77 | — | — | — | IN THE BAD BAD OLD DAYS — Foundations (Tony Macaulay), UNI 55117 | 1 |
| 78 | 86 | — | — | THERE NEVER WAS A TIME — Jeannie C. Riley (Shelby S. Singleton Jr.), Plantation 16 | 2 |
| ★ 79 | 96 | — | — | ZAZUERA — Herb Alpert & the Tijuana Brass (H. Alpert & Jerry Moss), A&M 1043 | 2 |
| ★ 80 | — | — | — | GRAZIN' IN THE GRASS — Friends of Distinction (John Florez), RCA 74-0207 | 1 |
| 81 | 88 | 96 | — | FOOLISH FOOL — Dee Dee Warwick (Ed Townsend), Mercury 72880 | 3 |
| 82 | 85 | 90 | 90 | KICK OUT THE JAMS — MC-5 (Jac Holzman & Bruce Botnick), Elektra 45648) | 4 |
| 83 | 82 | 80 | 80 | GOODBYE COLUMBUS — Association (John Boylan), Warner Bros.-Seven Arts 7267 | 4 |
| ★ 84 | 94 | — | — | GOOD TIMES BAD TIMES — Led Zeppelin (Jimmy Page), Atlantic 2613 | 2 |
| ★ 85 | — | — | — | WHERE DO YOU GO (My Lovely) — Peter Sarstedt (Ray Singer), World Pacific 7791 | 1 |
| ★ 86 | — | — | — | LOVE IS ALL I HAVE TO GIVE — Checkmates (Phil Spector), A&M 1039 | 1 |
| ★ 87 | — | — | — | BADGE — Cream (Felix Pappalardi), Atco 6668 | 1 |
| ★ 88 | — | — | — | MORE TODAY THAN YESTERDAY — Spiral Staircase (Sonny Knight), Columbia 4-44741 | 1 |
| 89 | 89 | 99 | — | GIVE IT AWAY — Chi-Lites (C. Davis & E. Record), Brunswick 55398 | 5 |
| ★ 90 | — | — | — | BACK IN THE U.S.S.R. — Chubby Checker (John Madera), Buddah 100 | 1 |
| 91 | — | — | — | THESE EYES — Guess Who (Nimbus 9), RCA 74-0102 | 1 |
| 92 | 93 | 97 | — | BORN AGAIN — Sam & Dave (D. Porter & I. Hayes), Atlantic 2608 | 3 |
| 93 | — | — | — | MORNING GIRL — Neon Philharmonic (T. Saussy, Don Gant & B. McCluskey), Warner Bros.-Seven Arts 7261 | 1 |
| 94 | — | — | — | GITARZAN — Ray Stevens (Fred Foster, Ray Stevens & Jim Malloy), Monument 1131 | 1 |
| 95 | — | — | — | WHEN YOU DANCE — Jay & the Americans (Jay & the Americans), United Artists 50510 | 1 |
| 96 | — | — | — | A MILLION TO ONE — Brian Hyland (Ray Ruff), Dot 17222 | 1 |
| 97 | — | — | — | CALIFORNIA GIRL (And the Tennessee Square) — Tompall and the Glaser Brothers (Jack Clement), MGM K-14036 | 1 |
| 98 | — | — | — | RHYTHM OF THE RAIN — Gary Lewis & the Playboys (Snuff Garrett), Liberty 56093 | 1 |
| 99 | — | — | — | IDAHO — 4 Seasons (Bob Gaudio), Philips 40597 | 1 |
| 100 | 100 | — | — | I LOVE MY BABY — Archie Bell & the Drells (Gamble/Huff), Atlantic 2612 | 2 |

## HOT 100—A TO Z—(Publisher-Licensee)



## BUBBLING UNDER THE HOT 100

101. BREAKFAST IN BED..........Dusty Springfield, Atlantic 2606
102. WEDDING CAKE..........Connie Francis, MGM 14034
103. ONLY YOU..........Bobby Hatfield, Verve 10634
104. ALBATROSS..........Fleetwood Mac, Epic 5-10436
105. I STILL LOVE YOU..........Jackie Wilson, Brunswick 55402
106. WITH PEN IN HAND..........Vicki Carr, Liberty 56092
107. I CAN'T DO ENOUGH..........Dells, Cadet 5636
108. SOMETHING'S ON HER MIND..........Four Seasons, Philips 40597
109. GOD KNOWS I LOVE YOU..........Nancy Sinatra, Reprise 0813
110. TRICIA TELL YOUR DADDY..........Andy Kim, Steed 715
111. YOU'D BETTER GO..........Nancy Wilson, Capitol 2422
112. RIVER IS WIDE..........Grassroots, Dunhill 4187
113. LILY THE PINK..........Irish Rovers, Decca 32444
114. HAPPY HEART..........Andy Williams, Columbia 4-44818
115. BABY MAKE ME FEEL SO GOOD..........5 Stairsteps & Cubie, Curtom 1936
116. THE BOXER..........Simon & Garfunkel, Columbia 4-44785
117. ONE EYE OPEN..........Maskman & the Agents, Dynamo 125
118. SOUL PRIDE..........James Brown, King 6222
119. SEATTLE..........Perry Como, RCA 47-9722
120. HAPPY HEART..........Petula Clark, Warner Bros.-Seven Arts 7275
121. TOO LATE TO WORRY, TOO BLUE TO CRY......Esther Phillips, Roulette 7031
122. LOVE (CAN MAKE YOU HAPPY)..........Mercy, Sundi 6811
123. IT'S A GROOVY WORLD..........Unifics, Kepp 985
124. MEDICINE MAN..........Buchanan Brothers, Event 3302
125. YOU CAME, YOU SAW, YOU CONQUERED..........Ronettes, A&M 1040
126. RHYTHM OF LIFE..........Sammy Davis Jr., Decca 732470
127. I'M ALIVE..........Johnny Thunder, Calla 161
128. EMERETTA..........Deep Purple, Tetragrammaton 1519
129. PLEASE DON'T GO..........Eddy Arnold, RCA Victor 74-0120
130. BUYING A BOOK..........Joe Tex, Dial 4090
131. SINGING MY SONG..........Tammy Wynette, Epic 5-10462
132. NEVER GONNA LET HIM KNOW..........Debbie Taylor, GWP 501

Compiled from national retail sales and radio station airplay by the Music Popularity Dept. of Record Market Research, Billboard.

# Billboard HOT 100

FOR WEEK ENDING APRIL 12, 1969

★ STAR PERFORMER—Sides registering greatest proportionate upward progress this week.

(seal) Record Industry Association of America seal of certification as million selling single.

| This Week | 1 Wk. Ago | 2 Wks. Ago | 3 Wks. Ago | TITLE Artist (Producer), Label & Number | Weeks On Chart |
|---|---|---|---|---|---|
| 1 (Billboard Award) | 2 | 4 | 14 | AQUARIUS/LET THE SUNSHINE IN — Fifth Dimension (Bones Howe), Soul City 772 | 6 |
| 2 | 4 | 12 | 21 | YOU'VE MADE ME SO VERY HAPPY — Blood, Sweat & Tears (James William Guerico), Columbia 4-44776 | 7 |
| (seal) 3 | 1 | 1 | 1 | DIZZY — Tommy Roe (Steve Barri), ABC 11164 | 11 |
| 4 | 5 | 8 | 11 | GALVESTON — Glen Campbell (Al De Lory), Capitol P-2428 | 7 |
| 5 | 3 | 3 | 6 | TIME OF THE SEASON — Zombies (Rod Argent & Chris White), Date 2-1628 | 10 |
| 6 | 7 | 10 | 24 | ONLY THE STRONG SURVIVE — Jerry Butler (Gamble & Huff), Mercury 72898 | 7 |
| ★7 | 14 | 26 | 42 | IT'S YOUR THING — Isley Brothers (R. Isley-O. Isley-R. Isley), T Neck 901 | 5 |
| ★8 | 18 | 35 | 70 | HAIR — Cowsills (Bill & Bob Cowsill), MGM 14026 | 5 |
| 9 | 6 | 6 | 10 | RUN AWAY CHILD, RUNNING WILD — Temptations (Norman Whitfield), Gordy 7084 | 9 |
| 10 | 13 | 17 | 27 | TWENTY-FIVE MILES — Edwin Starr (Bristol & Fuqua), Gordy 7083 | 9 |
| 11 | 11 | 15 | 20 | ROCK ME — Steppenwolf (Gabriel Mekler), Dunhill 4182 | 7 |
| 12 | 10 | 5 | 2 | PROUD MARY — Creedence Clearwater Revival (John Fogerty), Fantasy 619 | 12 |
| 13 | 8 | 2 | 3 | TRACES — Classics IV (Buddie Buie), Imperial 66352 | 10 |
| 14 | 15 | 19 | 22 | HOT SMOKE & SASSAFRASS — Bubble Puppy, International Artists 128 | 9 |
| (seal) 15 | 12 | 7 | 5 | INDIAN GIVER — 1910 Fruitgum Co. (Kasenetz-Katz, Assoc.), Buddah 91 | 12 |
| ★16 | 30 | 31 | 40 | DON'T GIVE IN TO HIM — Gary Puckett & the Union Gap (Jerry Fuller), Columbia 4-44788 | 5 |
| 17 | 17 | 13 | 7 | THIS GIRL'S IN LOVE WITH YOU — Dionne Warwick (Bacharach-David), Scepter 12241 | 11 |
| ★18 | 34 | 61 | 86 | SWEET CHERRY WINE — Tommy James & Shondells (Chips Moman), Roulette 7039 | 4 |
| 19 | 19 | 23 | 23 | MR. SUN, MR. MOON — Paul Revere & the Raiders (Mark Lindsay), Columbia 4-44744 | 9 |
| 20 | 20 | 41 | 46 | THE LETTER — The Arbors (Roy Cicala & Lorie Burton), Date 2-1638 | 8 |
| 21 | 21 | 28 | 37 | DO YOUR THING — Watts 103rd Street Band, Warner Bros.-Seven Arts 7250 | 11 |
| 22 | 9 | 9 | 13 | MY WHOLE WORLD ENDED (The Moment You Left Me) — David Ruffin (Fuqua & Bristol), Motown 1140 | 9 |
| (seal) 23 | 16 | 11 | 4 | BUILD ME UP BUTTERCUP — The Foundations (Tony Macaulay), UNI 55101 | 15 |
| 24 | 26 | 53 | 58 | GIMME GIMME GOOD LOVIN' — Crazy Elephant (Kasenetz-Katz Assoc.), Bell 763 | 7 |
| 25 | 28 | 29 | 33 | I'LL TRY SOMETHING NEW — Diana Ross & the Supremes & the Temptations (F. Wilson & D. Richards), Motown 1142 | 5 |
| 26 | 24 | 24 | 26 | YOU GAVE ME A MOUNTAIN — Frankie Laine (Jimmy Bowen), ABC 11174 | 10 |
| 27 | 29 | 36 | 49 | BROTHER LOVE'S TRAVELLING SALVATION SHOW — Neil Diamond (Tommy Cogbill & Chips Moman), Uni 55109 | 8 |
| ★28 | 38 | 39 | 71 | CHOKIN' KIND — Joe Simon (J. R. Enterprises), SS7 2628 | 4 |
| 29 | 33 | 44 | 78 | TIME IS TIGHT — Booker T. & the M.G.'s (B. T. Jones), Stax 0028 | 5 |
| 30 | 27 | 27 | 30 | MENDOCINO — Sir Douglas Quintet (Amigas de Musica), Smash 2191 | 13 |
| 31 | 31 | 37 | 45 | TRY A LITTLE TENDERNESS — Three Dog Night (Gabriel Makler), Dunhill 4177 | 10 |
| ★32 | 51 | 70 | 92 | HAWAII FIVE-O — The Ventures (Joe Saraceno), Liberty 56068 | 6 |
| 33 | 36 | 43 | 44 | I CAN HEAR MUSIC — Beach Boys (Carl Wilson), Capitol 2432 | 6 |
| ★34 | 53 | 57 | 81 | IS IT SOMETHING YOU GOT — Tyrone Davis (Willie Henderson), Dakar 605 | 4 |
| ★35 | 48 | 52 | 67 | MEMORIES — Elvis Presley (Bones Howe & Steve Binder), RCA 47-9731 | 4 |
| 36 | 37 | 38 | 53 | SNATCHING IT BACK — Clarence Carter (Rick Hall), Atlantic 2605 | 7 |
| 37 | 41 | 69 | — | MY WAY — Frank Sinatra (Don Costa), Reprise 0817 | 3 |
| 38 | 25 | 16 | 16 | THINGS I'D LIKE TO SAY — New Colony Six, Mercury 72858 | 16 |
| ★39 | 52 | 67 | 74 | WILL YOU BE STAYING AFTER SUNDAY — Peppermint Rainbow (Paul Leka), Decca 32410 | 9 |
| 40 | 43 | 62 | 82 | FIRST OF MAY — Bee Gees (Robert Stigwood), Atco 6657 | 4 |
| 41 | 42 | 42 | 51 | JOHNNY ONE TIME — Brenda Lee (Mike Berniker), Decca 32428 | 10 |
| 42 | 47 | 54 | 61 | DON'T TOUCH ME — Bettye Swan (Wayne Shuler), Capitol 2382 | 6 |
| 43 | 44 | 60 | 65 | THE WAY IT USED TO BE — Engelbert Humperdinck (Peter Sullivan), Parrot 40036 | 7 |
| 44 | 46 | 51 | 66 | THE PLEDGE OF ALLEGIANCE — Red Skelton, Columbia 4-44798 | 5 |
| ★45 | 60 | 79 | — | WISHFUL SINFUL — Doors (Paul A. Rothchild), Elektra 45656 | 3 |
| ★46 | 54 | 77 | — | MERCY — Ohio Express (Kasenetz-Katz Assoc.), Buddah 102 | 3 |
| 47 | 56 | 56 | 60 | APRICOT BRANDY — Rhinoceros (Paul A. Rothchild), Elektra 45647 | 8 |
| ★48 | 63 | 71 | 84 | IT'S ONLY LOVE — B. J. Thomas (Chips Moman), Scepter 12244 | 4 |
| 49 | 50 | 63 | 68 | PLAYGIRL — Thee Prophets (C. Bonafede, D. Belloc, L. Douglas), Kapp 962 | 6 |
| ★50 | 72 | — | — | TO KNOW YOU IS TO LOVE YOU — Bobby Vinton (Billy Sherril), Epic 5-10461 | 2 |
| ★51 | — | — | — | THE BOXER — Simon & Garfunkel (Simon & Garfunkel & Hales), Columbia 4-44785 | 1 |
| 52 | 55 | 55 | 63 | I LIKE WHAT YOU'RE DOING (To Me) — Carla Thomas (Don Davis), Stax 0024 | 9 |
| ★53 | 69 | 76 | — | MINI SKIRT MINNIE — Wilson Pickett (Rick Hall), Atlantic 2611 | 3 |
| 54 | 61 | — | — | I DON'T WANT NOBODY TO GIVE ME NOTHING (Open Up the Door, I'll Get It Myself) — James Brown (James Brown), King 6224 | 2 |
| 55 | 45 | 49 | 54 | BLESSED IS THE RAIN — Brooklyn Bridge (Wes Farrell), Buddah 95 | 6 |
| 56 | 49 | 50 | 57 | WHEN HE TOUCHES ME (Nothing Else Matters) — Peaches & Herb (Billy Sherrill & David Kapralik), Date 2-1637 | 7 |
| 57 | 59 | 72 | 76 | DAY AFTER DAY (It's Slippin' Away) — Shango (Merry Rippelle), A&M 1014 | 7 |
| 58 | 58 | 74 | 82 | MOVE IN A LITTLE CLOSER, BABY — Mama Cass (Steve Barri), Dunhill 4184 | 5 |
| 59 | 62 | 83 | 88 | NOTHING BUT A HEARTACHE — Flirtations (Wayne Bickerton), Deram 85038 | 6 |
| ★60 | 75 | — | — | ATLANTIS — Donovan (Mickie Most), Epic 5-10434 | 2 |
| ★61 | 73 | — | — | PINBALL WIZARD — The Who (Baron Lambert), Decca 732465 | 2 |
| 62 | 64 | 81 | 87 | ICE CREAM SONG — The Dynamics (Tommy Cogbill), Cotillion 44021 | 4 |
| 63 | 65 | 75 | 77 | DIDN'T YOU KNOW — Gladys Knight & the Pips (Ashford & Simpson), Soul 35057 | 6 |
| ★64 | 77 | — | — | IN THE BAD BAD OLD DAYS — Foundations (Tony Macaulay), UNI 55117 | 2 |
| 65 | 70 | 78 | 85 | IN THE STILL OF THE NIGHT — Paul Anka (Don Costa Prod.), RCA 74-0126 | 4 |
| ★66 | 91 | — | — | THESE EYES — Guess Who (Nimbus 9), RCA 74-0102 | 2 |
| 67 | 67 | 84 | 93 | TIME WAS — Canned Heat (Skip Taylor & Canned Heat), Liberty 56097 | 5 |
| ★68 | 94 | — | — | GITARZAN — Ray Stevens (Fred Foster, Ray Stevens & Jim Malloy), Monument 1131 | 2 |
| ★69 | 88 | — | — | MORE TODAY THAN YESTERDAY — Spiral Staircase (Sonny Knight), Columbia 4-44741 | 2 |
| 70 | 81 | 88 | 96 | FOOLISH FOOL — Dee Dee Warwick (Ed Townsend), Mercury 72880 | 4 |
| 71 | 71 | 80 | 91 | TRACKS OF MY TEARS — Aretha Franklin (Jerry Wexler & Tom Dowd), Atlantic 2603 | 5 |
| ★72 | — | — | — | LOVE (Can Make You Happy) — Mercy (Jamie-Guyden), Sundi 6811 | 1 |
| 73 | 80 | — | — | GRAZIN' IN THE GRASS — Friends of Distinction (John Florez), RCA 74-0207 | 2 |
| ★74 | 85 | — | — | WHERE DO YOU GO (My Lovely) — Peter Sarstedt (Ray Singer), World Pacific 7791 | 2 |
| ★75 | — | — | — | HAPPY HEART — Andy Williams (Jerry Fuller), Columbia 4-44818 | 1 |
| ★76 | 87 | — | — | BADGE — Cream (Felix Pappalardi), Atco 6668 | 2 |
| 77 | 78 | 86 | — | THERE NEVER WAS A TIME — Jeannie C. Riley (Shelby S. Singleton Jr.), Plantation 16 | 3 |
| ★78 | — | — | — | BUYING A BOOK — Joe Tex (Buddy Killen), Dial 4090 | 1 |
| 79 | 79 | 96 | — | ZAZUERA — Herb Alpert & the Tijuana Brass (H. Alpert & Jerry Moss), A&M 1043 | 3 |
| ★80 | — | — | — | STAND — Sly & the Family Stone (Sly Stone), Epic 5-10450 | 1 |
| 81 | 84 | 94 | — | GOOD TIMES BAD TIMES — Led Zeppelin (Jimmy Page), Atlantic 2613 | 3 |
| ★82 | — | — | — | SEATTLE — Perry Como (Chet Atkins & Andy Wiswell), RCA 47-9722 | 1 |
| 83 | 86 | — | — | LOVE IS ALL I HAVE TO GIVE — Checkmates (Phil Spector), A&M 1039 | 2 |
| ★84 | — | — | — | HAPPY HEART — Petula Clark, Warner Brothers-Seven Arts 7275 | 1 |
| 85 | 90 | — | — | BACK IN THE U.S.S.R. — Chubby Checker (John Madera), Buddah 100 | 2 |
| 86 | 93 | — | — | MORNING GIRL — Neon Philharmonic (T. Saussy, Don Gant & B. McCluskey), Warner Bros.-Seven Arts 7261 | 2 |
| ★87 | — | — | — | THE RIVER IS WIDE — The Grassroots (Steve Barri), Dunhill 4187 | 1 |
| 88 | 89 | 89 | 99 | GIVE IT AWAY — Chi-Lites (C. Davis & E. Record), Brunswick 55398 | 6 |
| ★89 | 95 | — | — | WHEN YOU DANCE — Jay & the Americans (Jay & the Americans), United Artists 50510 | 2 |
| ★90 | 96 | — | — | A MILLION TO ONE — Brian Hyland (Ray Ruff), Dot 17222 | 2 |
| 91 | — | — | — | BREAKFAST IN BED — Dusty Springfield (Jerry Wexler & Tom Dowd), Atlantic 45-2606 | 1 |
| 92 | — | — | — | ANY DAY NOW — Percy Sledge (Quin Ivy/Marlin Greene), Atlantic 2616 | 1 |
| 93 | — | — | — | CISSY STRUT — Meters (Marshall E. Schorn & Allen Toussaint), Josie 1005 | 1 |
| 94 | 100 | 100 | — | I LOVE MY BABY — Archie Bell & the Drells (Gamble/Huff), Atlantic 2612 | 3 |
| 95 | 99 | — | — | IDAHO — 4 Seasons (Bob Gaudio), Philips 40597 | 2 |
| 96 | 97 | — | — | CALIFORNIA GIRL (And the Tennessee Square) — Tompall and the Glaser Brothers (Jack Clement), MGM K-14036 | 2 |
| 97 | 98 | — | — | RHYTHM OF THE RAIN — Gary Lewis & the Playboys (Snuff Garrett), Liberty 56093 | 2 |
| 98 | — | — | — | IT'S A GROOVY WORLD — Unifics (Guy Draper), Kapp K 985 | 1 |
| 99 | — | — | — | I CAN'T DO ENOUGH — Dells (Bobby Miller), Cadet 5636 | 1 |
| 100 | — | — | — | SINGING MY SONG — Tammy Wynette (Billy Sherrill), Epic 5-10462 | 1 |

## HOT 100—A TO Z —(Publisher-Licensee)


Any Day Now (Plan Two, ASCAP) .... 92
Apricot Brandy (Nina, BMI) .... 47
Atlantis (Peer Int'l, BMI) .... 60
Aquarius/Let the Sunshine In (United Artists, ASCAP) .... 1
Back in the U.S.S.R. (Maclean, BMI) .... 85
Badge (Casserole, BMI) .... 76
Blessed Is the Rain (Pocket Full of Tunes, BMI) .... 55
Boxer, The (Charing Cross, BMI) .... 51
Breakfast in Bed (ScreenGems-Columbia, BMI) .... 91
Brother Love's Travelling Salvation Show (Stonebridge, BMI) .... 27
Build Me Up Buttercup (January-Nice, BMI) .... 23
Buying a Book (Tree, BMI) .... 78
California Girl (And the Tennessee Square) (Jack, BMI) .... 96
Chokin' Kind (Wilderness Music, BMI) .... 28
Cissy Strut (Marsaint, BMI) .... 93
Day After Day (It's Slippin' Away) (Goomby/Irving, BMI) .... 57
Didn't You Know (Jobete, BMI) .... 63
Dizzy (Low Twine, BMI) .... 3
Do Your Thing (Charles Wright & Fred Smith) (Wright-Gersti-Tamerlan, BMI) .... 21
Don't Give in to Him (Four Star, BMI) .... 16
Don't Touch Me (Pamper, BMI) .... 42
First of May (Casserole, BMI) .... 40
Foolish Fool (Chappell, ASCAP) .... 70
Galveston (Ja-Ma Music, ASCAP) .... 4
Gimme Gimme Good Lovin' (Peanut Butter/Kahoona, BMI) .... 24
Gitarzan (Ahab, BMI) .... 68
Give It Away (Darkar/BRC, BMI) .... 88
Good Times Bad Times (Superhype, ASCAP) .... 81
Grazin' in the Grass (Chisa, BMI) .... 73
Hair (United Artists, ASCAP) .... 8
Happy Heart (Miller, ASCAP) .... 75
Happy Heart (Miller, ASCAP) .... 84
Hawaii Five-O (April, ASCAP) .... 32
Hot Smoke & Sassafrass (Tapier, BMI) .... 14
I Can Hear Music (Trio Music Co. Inc., BMI) .... 33
I Can't Do Enough (Chevis Music, BMI) .... 99
I Don't Want Nobody to Give Me Nothing (Open Up the Door, I'll Get It Myself) (Dynatone, BMI) .... 54
I Like What You're Doing (to Me) (East/Memphis, BMI) .... 52
I Love My Baby (World War III/Downstairs, BMI) .... 94
Ice Cream Song (Dlief-Cotillion, BMI) .... 62
Idaho (Guvadima/Genius, ASCAP) .... 95
In the Bad Bad Old Days (January, BMI) .... 64
In the Still of the Night (Cherio, BMI) .... 65
Indian Giver (Kaskat/Kahoona, BMI) .... 15
I'll Try Something New (Jobete, BMI) .... 25
Is It Something You Got (Dakar, BMI) .... 34
It's a Groovy World (Andjun, ASCAP) .... 98
It's Only Love (Press, BMI) .... 48
It's Your Thing (Brothers Three, BMI) .... 7
Johnny One Time (Hill & Ranger/Blue Crest, BMI) .... 41
The Letter (Burton, BMI) .... 20
Love (Can Make You Happy) (Rendezvous/Tobac, BMI) .... 72
Love Is All I Have to Give (Irving, BMI) .... 83
Memories (Gladys, ASCAP) .... 35
Mendocino (Southern Love, BMI) .... 30
Mercy (Peanut Butter/Kaskat, BMI) .... 46
Million to One, A (Jobete, BMI) .... 90
Mini Skirt Minnie (New Research, BMI) .... 53
More Today Than Yesterday (Spiral, BMI) .... 69
Morning Girl (Acuff-Rose, BMI) .... 86
Move in a Little Closer Baby (Arnold Jay, ASCAP) .... 58
Mr. Sun, Mr. Moon (Boom, BMI) .... 19
My Way (Don C./Stanka, BMI) .... 37
My Whole World Ended (The Moment You Left Me) (Jobete, BMI) .... 22
Nothing But a Heartache (Felsted Music, BMI) .... 59
Only the Strong Survive (Parabut/Double Diamond/Downstairs, BMI) .... 6
Pinball Wizard (Track, BMI) .... 61
Playgirl (4 Star Music, Co., BMI) .... 49
Pledge of Allegiance, The (Valentina, ASCAP) .... 44
Proud Mary (Jondora, BMI) .... 12
River Is Wide, The (Saturday, BMI) .... 87
Rock Me (Trousdale, BMI) .... 11
Rhythm of the Rain (Tamerlane, BMI) .... 97
Run Away Child, Running Wild (Jobete, BMI) .... 9
Seattle (Screen Gems-Columbia, BMI) .... 82
Singing My Song (Al Gallico, BMI) .... 100
Snatching It Back (Fama, BMI) .... 36
Stand (Daly City, BMI) .... 80
Sweet Cherry Wine (Big Seven, BMI) .... 18
These Eyes (Dunbar, BMI) .... 66
Time Is Tight (East/Memphis, BMI) .... 29
Time of the Season (Mainstay, BMI) .... 5
Time Was (Metric, BMI) .... 67
There Never Was a Time (Singleton, BMI) .... 77
Things I'd Like to Say (New Colony-T.M., BMI) .... 38
This Girl's in Love With You (Blue Seas/Jac, ASCAP) .... 17
To Know You Is to Love You (Vogue, BMI) .... 50
Traces (Low-Sal, BMI) .... 13
Tracks of My Tears (Jobete, BMI) .... 71
Try a Little Tenderness (Connelly & Robbins, ASCAP) .... 31
Twenty-Five Miles (Jobete, BMI) .... 10
Way It Used to Be, The (Maribus, BMI) .... 43
When He Touches Me (Nothing Else Matters) (Painted Desert, BMI) .... 56
When You Dance (Angel, BMI) .... 89
Where Do You Go (My Lovely) (Unart, BMI) .... 74
Will You Be Staying After Sunday (Screen Gems-Columbia, BMI) .... 39
Wishful Sinful (Nipper Music, ASCAP) .... 45
You Gave Me A Mountain (Mojave, BMI) .... 26
You've Made Me So Very Happy (Jobete, BMI) .... 2
Zazuera (Rodra, BMI) .... 79


## BUBBLING UNDER THE HOT 100

101. JULY YOU'RE A WOMAN .... Pat Boone, Tetragrammaton 1516
102. BORN AGAIN .... Sam & Dave, Atlantic 2608
103. BABY DRIVER .... Simon & Garfunkel, Columbia 4-44785
104. ALBATROSS .... Fleetwood Mac, Epic 5-10436
105. WITH PEN IN HAND .... Vikki Carr, Liberty 56092
106. SORRY SUZANNE .... Hollies, Epic 5-10454
107. I STAND ACCUSED .... Al Wilson, Soul City 773
108. LONG WAYS FROM HOME .... Hugh Masekela, Uni
109. LOVE IS JUST A FOUR-LETTER WORD .... Joan Baez, Vanguard 35088
110. I WAS A BOY WHEN YOU NEEDED A MAN .... Billy Shields, Harbour 304
111. YOU CAME, YOU SAW, YOU CONQUERED .... Ronettes, A&M 1040
112. MOTHER WHERE'S YOUR DAUGHTER .... Royal Guardsmen, Laurie 3494
113. AREN'T YOU LONELY FOR ME, BABY .... Chuck Jackson, Motown 1144
114. GREENSLEEVES .... Mason Williams, Warner Bros.-Seven Arts 7272
115. HURTING EACH OTHER .... Ruby & the Romantics, A&M 1042
116. RUN ON .... Arthur Conley, Atco 6661
117. BABY MAKE ME FEEL SO GOOD .... 5 Stairsteps & Cubie, Curtom 1936
118. SOUL PRIDE .... James Brown, King 6222
119. CAROLINA ON MY MIND .... James Taylor, Apple 1805
120. EARTH ANGEL (WILL YOU BE MINE) .... Vogues, Reprise 0820
121. I FEEL LIKE I'M FALLING IN LOVE AGAIN .... Fantastic Four, Soul 35058
122. I'M AIVE .... Johnny Thunder, Calla 161
123. FOOT PATTIN' PART 2 .... King Curtis & His Kingpins, Atco 6664
124. MEDICINE MAN .... Buchanan Brothers, Event 3302
125. RHYTHM OF LIFE .... Sammy Davis Jr., Decca 732470
126. JUST A LITTLE BIT .... Little Milton, Checker 1217
127. NEVER GONNA LET HIM KNOW .... Debbie Taylor, GWP 501
128. (WE'VE GOT) HONEY LOVE .... Martha Reeves & the Vandellas, Gordy 7085
129. EVERY LITTLE BIT HURTS .... Peggy Scott, SSS International 767
130. IT'S A MIRACLE .... Willie Hightower, Capitol 2226
131. WE CAN'T GO ON TH'S WAY .... Unchained Mynds, Buddah 111
132. SING A SIMPLE SONG .... Noble Knights, Cotillion 44030

Compiled from national retail sales and radio station airplay by the Music Popularity Dept. of Record Market Research, Billboard.

# Billboard HOT 100

FOR WEEK ENDING APRIL 19, 1969

★ STAR PERFORMER—Sides registering greatest proportionate upward progress this week.

(RIAA seal) Record Industry Association of America seal of certification as million selling single.

| This Week | 1 Wk. Ago | 2 Wks. Ago | 3 Wks. Ago | TITLE Artist (Producer), Label & Number | Weeks On Chart |
|---|---|---|---|---|---|
| 1 (Billboard Award) | 1 | 2 | 4 | AQUARIUS/LET THE SUNSHINE IN — Fifth Dimension (Bones Howe), Soul City 772 | 7 |
| 2 | 2 | 4 | 12 | YOU'VE MADE ME SO VERY HAPPY — Blood, Sweat & Tears (James William Guerico), Columbia 4-44776 | 8 |
| ★ 3 (RIAA seal) | 7 | 14 | 26 | IT'S YOUR THING — Isley Brothers (R. Isley-O. Isley-R. Isley), T Neck 901 | 6 |
| ★ 4 | 6 | 7 | 10 | ONLY THE STRONG SURVIVE — Jerry Butler (Gamble & Huff), Mercury 72898 | 8 |
| 5 (RIAA seal) | 3 | 1 | 1 | DIZZY — Tommy Roe (Steve Barri), ABC 11164 | 12 |
| 6 | 4 | 5 | 8 | GALVESTON — Glen Campbell (Al De Lory), Capitol P-2428 | 8 |
| 7 | 8 | 18 | 35 | HAIR — Cowsills (Bill & Bob Cowsill), MGM 14026 | 6 |
| 8 | 10 | 13 | 17 | TWENTY-FIVE MILES — Edwin Starr (Bristol & Fuqua), Gordy 7083 | 10 |
| 9 | 5 | 3 | 3 | TIME OF THE SEASON — Zombies (Rod Argent & Chris White), Date 2-1628 | 11 |
| 10 | 11 | 11 | 15 | ROCK ME — Steppenwolf (Gabriel Mekler), Dunhill 4182 | 8 |
| 11 | 9 | 6 | 6 | RUN AWAY CHILD, RUNNING WILD — Temptations (Norman Whitfield), Gordy 7084 | 10 |
| ★ 12 | 18 | 34 | 61 | SWEET CHERRY WINE — Tommy James & Shondells (Tommy James), Roulette 7039 | 5 |
| ★ 13 | 21 | 21 | 28 | DO YOUR THING — Watts 103rd Street Band, Warner Bros.-Seven Arts 7250 | 12 |
| ★ 14 | 24 | 26 | 53 | GIMME GIMME GOOD LOVIN' — Crazy Elephant (Kasenetz-Katz Assoc.), Bell 763 | 8 |
| 15 | 16 | 30 | 31 | DON'T GIVE IN TO HIM — Gary Puckett & the Union Gap (Jerry Fuller), Columbia 4-44788 | 6 |
| 16 | 13 | 8 | 2 | TRACES — Classics IV (Buddie Buie), Imperial 66352 | 11 |
| ★ 17 | 32 | 51 | 70 | HAWAII FIVE-O — The Ventures (Joe Saraceno), Liberty 56068 | 7 |
| 18 | 19 | 19 | 23 | MR. SUN, MR. MOON — Paul Revere & the Raiders (Mark Lindsay), Columbia 4-44744 | 10 |
| 19 | 12 | 10 | 5 | PROUD MARY — Creedence Clearwater Revival (John Fogerty), Fantasy 619 | 13 |
| ★ 20 | 51 | — | — | THE BOXER — Simon & Garfunkel (Simon & Garfunkel & Hales), Columbia 4-44785 | 2 |
| 21 | 28 | 38 | 39 | CHOKIN' KIND — Joe Simon (J. R. Enterprises), SS7 2628 | 5 |
| 22 | 17 | 17 | 13 | THIS GIRL'S IN LOVE WITH YOU — Dionne Warwick (Bacharach-David), Scepter 12241 | 12 |
| 23 | 22 | 9 | 9 | MY WHOLE WORLD ENDED (The Moment You Left Me) — David Ruffin (Fuqua & Bristol), Motown 1140 | 10 |
| 24 | 29 | 33 | 44 | TIME IS TIGHT — Booker T. & the M.G.'s (B. T. Jones), Stax 0028 | 6 |
| 25 | 25 | 28 | 29 | I'LL TRY SOMETHING NEW — Diana Ross & the Supremes & the Temptations (F. Wilson & D. Richards), Motown 1142 | 6 |
| 26 | 27 | 29 | 36 | BROTHER LOVE'S TRAVELLING SALVATION SHOW — Neil Diamond (Tommy Cogbill & Chips Moman), Uni 55109 | 9 |
| 27 | 14 | 15 | 19 | HOT SMOKE & SASSAFRASS — Bubble Puppy, International Artists 128 | 10 |
| 28 (RIAA seal) | 15 | 12 | 7 | INDIAN GIVER — 1910 Fruitgum Co. (Kasenetz-Katz, Assoc.), Buddah 91 | 13 |
| 29 | 31 | 31 | 37 | TRY A LITTLE TENDERNESS — Three Dog Night (Gabriel Mekler), Dunhill 4177 | 11 |
| ★ 30 | 54 | 61 | — | I DON'T WANT NOBODY TO GIVE ME NOTHING (Open Up the Door, I'll Get It Myself) — James Brown (James Brown), King 6224 | 3 |
| 31 | 36 | 37 | 38 | SNATCHING IT BACK — Clarence Carter (Rick Hall), Atlantic 2605 | 8 |
| 32 | 33 | 36 | 43 | I CAN HEAR MUSIC — Beach Boys (Carl Wilson), Capitol 2432 | 7 |
| 33 | 37 | 41 | 69 | MY WAY — Frank Sinatra (Don Costa), Reprise 0817 | 4 |
| 34 | 34 | 53 | 57 | IS IT SOMETHING YOU GOT — Tyrone Davis (Willie Henderson), Dakar 605 | 5 |
| 35 | 35 | 48 | 52 | MEMORIES — Elvis Presley (Bones Howe & Steve Binder), RCA 47-9731 | 5 |
| 36 | 30 | 27 | 27 | MENDOCINO — Sir Douglas Quintet (Amigos de Musica), Smash 2191 | 14 |
| 37 | 40 | 43 | 62 | FIRST OF MAY — Bee Gees (Robert Stigwood), Atco 6657 | 5 |
| ★ 38 | 42 | 47 | 54 | DON'T TOUCH ME — Bettye Swan (Wayne Shuler), Capitol 2382 | 7 |
| 39 | 39 | 52 | 67 | WILL YOU BE STAYING AFTER SUNDAY — Peppermint Rainbow (Paul Leka), Decca 32410 | 10 |
| 40 | 20 | 20 | 41 | THE LETTER — The Arbors (Roy Cicala & Lorie Burton), Date 2-1638 | 9 |
| ★ 41 | 46 | 54 | 77 | MERCY — Ohio Express (Kasenetz-Katz Assoc.), Buddah 102 | 4 |
| 42 | 43 | 44 | 60 | THE WAY IT USED TO BE — Engelbert Humperdinck (Peter Sullivan), Parrot 40036 | 8 |
| 43 | 26 | 24 | 24 | YOU GAVE ME A MOUNTAIN — Frankie Laine (Jimmy Bowen), ABC 11174 | 10 |
| 44 | 45 | 60 | 79 | WISHFUL SINFUL — Doors (Paul A. Rothchild), Elektra 45656 | 4 |
| 45 | 50 | 72 | — | TO KNOW YOU IS TO LOVE YOU — Bobby Vinton (Billy Sherrill), Epic 5-10461 | 3 |
| 46 | 47 | 56 | 56 | APRICOT BRANDY — Rhinoceros (Paul A. Rothchild), Elektra 45647 | 9 |
| 47 | 48 | 63 | 71 | IT'S ONLY LOVE — B. J. Thomas (Chips Moman), Scepter 12244 | 5 |
| ★ 48 | 68 | 94 | — | GITARZAN — Ray Stevens (Fred Foster, Ray Stevens & Jim Malloy), Monument 1131 | 3 |
| 49 | 52 | 55 | 55 | I LIKE WHAT YOU'RE DOING (To Me) — Carla Thomas (Don Davis), Stax 0024 | 10 |
| 50 | 53 | 69 | 76 | MINI SKIRT MINNIE — Wilson Pickett (Rick Hall), Atlantic 2611 | 4 |
| ★ 51 | 61 | 73 | — | PINBALL WIZARD — The Who (Baron Lambert), Decca 732465 | 3 |
| ★ 52 | 60 | 75 | — | ATLANTIS — Donovan (Mickie Most), Epic 5-10434 | 3 |
| ★ 53 | — | — | — | THE COMPOSER — Diana Ross & the Supremes (Smokey), Motown 1146 | 1 |
| ★ 54 | 80 | — | — | STAND — Sly & the Family Stone (Sly Stone), Epic 5-10450 | 2 |
| 55 | 41 | 42 | 42 | JOHNNY ONE TIME — Brenda Lee (Mike Berniker), Decca 32428 | 11 |
| ★ 56 | 59 | 62 | 83 | NOTHING BUT A HEARTACHE — Flirtations (Wayne Bickerton), Deram 85038 | 7 |
| 57 | 49 | 50 | 63 | PLAYGIRL — Thee Prophets (C. Bonafede, D. Belloc, L. Douglas), Kapp 962 | 7 |
| ★ 58 | 69 | 88 | — | MORE TODAY THAN YESTERDAY — Spiral Staircase (Sonny Knight), Columbia 4-44741 | 3 |
| ★ 59 | 62 | 64 | 81 | ICE CREAM SONG — The Dynamics (Tommy Cogbill), Cotillion 44021 | 5 |
| 60 | 64 | 77 | — | IN THE BAD BAD OLD DAYS — Foundations (Tony Macaulay), UNI 55117 | 3 |
| 61 | 66 | 91 | — | THESE EYES — Guess Who (Nimbus 9), RCA 74-0102 | 3 |
| ★ 62 | 72 | — | — | LOVE (Can Make You Happy) — Mercy (Jamie-Guyden), Sundi 6811 | 2 |
| 63 | 63 | 65 | 75 | DIDN'T YOU KNOW — Gladys Knight & the Pips (Ashford & Simpson), Soul 35057 | 7 |
| 64 | 65 | 70 | 78 | IN THE STILL OF THE NIGHT — Paul Anka (Don Costa Prod.), RCA 74-0126 | 5 |
| ★ 65 | 73 | 80 | — | GRAZIN' IN THE GRASS — Friends of Distinction (John Florez), RCA 74-0207 | 3 |
| ★ 66 | 87 | — | — | THE RIVER IS WIDE — The Grassroots (Steve Barri), Dunhill 4187 | 2 |
| ★ 67 | 78 | — | — | BUYING A BOOK — Joe Tex (Buddy Killen), Dial 4090 | 2 |
| ★ 68 | 76 | 87 | — | BADGE — Cream (Felix Pappalardi), Atco 6668 | 3 |
| 69 | 70 | 81 | 88 | FOOLISH FOOL — Dee Dee Warwick (Ed Townsend), Mercury 72880 | 6 |
| 70 | 75 | — | — | HAPPY HEART — Andy Williams (Jerry Fuller), Columbia 4-44818 | 2 |
| 71 | 58 | 58 | 74 | MOVE IN A LITTLE CLOSER, BABY — Mama Cass (Steve Barri), Dunhill 4184 | 6 |
| ★ 72 | 82 | — | — | SEATTLE — Perry Como (Chet Atkins & Andy Wiswell), RCA 47-9722 | 2 |
| 73 | 74 | 85 | — | WHERE DO YOU GO (My Lovely) — Peter Sarstedt (Ray Singer), World Pacific 7791 | 3 |
| ★ 74 | — | — | — | I CAN'T SEE MYSELF LEAVING YOU — Aretha Franklin (Jerry Wexler), Atlantic 2619 | 1 |
| 75 | 44 | 46 | 51 | THE PLEDGE OF ALLEGIANCE — Red Skelton, Columbia 4-44798 | 6 |
| ★ 76 | 89 | 95 | — | WHEN YOU DANCE — Jay & the Americans (Jay & the Americans), United Artists 50510 | 3 |
| ★ 77 | 83 | 86 | — | LOVE IS ALL I HAVE TO GIVE — Checkmates (Phil Spector), A&M 1039 | 3 |
| 78 | 79 | 79 | 96 | ZAZUERA — Herb Alpert & the Tijuana Brass (H. Alpert & Jerry Moss), A&M 1043 | 4 |
| 79 | 84 | — | — | HAPPY HEART — Petula Clark, Warner Brothers-Seven Arts 7275 | 2 |
| 80 | 81 | 84 | 94 | GOOD TIMES BAD TIMES — Led Zeppelin (Jimmy Page), Atlantic 2613 | 4 |
| ★ 81 | 93 | — | — | CISSY STRUT — Meters (Marshall E. Sehorn & Allen Toussaint), Josie 1005 | 2 |
| 82 | 71 | 71 | 80 | TRACKS OF MY TEARS — Aretha Franklin (Jerry Wexler & Tom Dowd), Atlantic 2603 | 6 |
| 83 | 86 | 93 | — | MORNING GIRL — Neon Philharmonic (T. Saussy, Don Gant & B. McCluskey), Warner Bros.-Seven Arts 7261 | 3 |
| 84 | 85 | 90 | — | BACK IN THE U.S.S.R. — Chubby Checker (John Madera), Buddah 100 | 3 |
| ★ 85 | — | — | — | EARTH ANGEL — Vogues (Dick Glasser), Reprise 0820 | 1 |
| ★ 86 | — | — | — | GOODBYE — Mary Hopkin (Paul McCartney), Apple 1806 | 1 |
| ★ 87 | — | — | — | (We've Got) HONEY LOVE — Martha Reeves & the Vandellas (Richard Morris), Gordy 7085 | 1 |
| ★ 88 | 92 | — | — | ANY DAY NOW — Percy Sledge (Quin Ivy/Marlin Greene), Atlantic 2616 | 2 |
| ★ 89 | — | — | — | I'VE BEEN HURT — Bill Deal & the Rhondells (Jerry Ross), Heritage 812 | 1 |
| 90 | 90 | 96 | — | A MILLION TO ONE — Brian Hyland (Ray Ruff), Dot 17222 | 3 |
| 91 | 91 | — | — | BREAKFAST IN BED — Dusty Springfield (Jerry Wexler & Tom Dowd), Atlantic 45-2606 | 2 |
| 92 | 96 | 97 | — | CALIFORNIA GIRL (And the Tennessee Square) — Tompall and the Glaser Brothers (Jack Clement), MGM K-14036 | 3 |
| 93 | 77 | 78 | 86 | THERE NEVER WAS A TIME — Jeannie C. Riley (Shelby S. Singleton Jr.), Plantation 16 | 4 |
| 94 | 100 | — | — | SINGING MY SONG — Tammy Wynette (Billy Sherrill), Epic 5-10462 | 2 |
| 95 | 97 | 98 | — | RHYTHM OF THE RAIN — Gary Lewis & the Playboys (Snuff Garrett), Liberty 56093 | 3 |
| 96 | — | — | — | SORRY SUZANNE — Hollies (Ron Richards), Epic 5-10454 | 1 |
| 97 | 98 | — | — | IT'S A GROOVY WORLD — Unifics (Guy Draper), Kapp K 985 | 2 |
| 98 | 99 | — | — | I CAN'T DO ENOUGH — Dells (Bobby Miller), Cadet 5636 | 2 |
| 99 | — | — | — | I'M A DRIFTER — Bobby Goldsboro (Bob Montgomery & Bobby Goldsboro), United Artists 50525 | 1 |
| 100 | — | — | — | JULY YOU'RE A WOMAN — Pat Boone (Jerry Yester & Zal Yanovsky), Tetragrammaton 1516 | 1 |

## HOT 100—A TO Z—(Publisher-Licensee)


Any Day Now (Plan Two, ASCAP) .... 88
Apricot Brandy (Nina, BMI) .... 46
Atlantis (Peer Int'l, BMI) .... 52
Aquarius/Let the Sunshine In (United Artists, ASCAP) .... 1
Back in the U.S.S.R. (Maclean, BMI) .... 84
Badge (Casserole, BMI) .... 68
Boxer, The (Charing Cross, BMI) .... 20
Breakfast in Bed (Blackwood & Ruler), BMI) .... 91
Brother Love's Travelling Salvation Show (Stonebridge, BMI) .... 26
Buying a Book (Tree, BMI) .... 67
California Girl (And the Tennessee Square) (Jack, BMI) .... 92
Chokin' Kind (Wilderness Music, BMI) .... 21
Cissy Strut (Marsaint, BMI) .... 81
Composer, The (Jobete, BMI) .... 53
Didn't You Know (Jobete, BMI) .... 63
Dizzy (Low Twine, BMI) .... 6
Do Your Thing (Charles Wright & Fred Smith) (Wright-Gersti-Tamerlan, BMI) .... 13
Don't Give In to Him (Four Star, BMI) .... 15
Don't Touch Me (Pamper, BMI) .... 38
Earth Angel (Williams, BMI) .... 85
First of May (Casserole, BMI) .... 37
Foolish Fool (Chappell, ASCAP) .... 69
Galveston (Ja-Ma Music, ASCAP) .... 6
Gimme Gimme Good Lovin' (Peanut Butter/Kahoona, BMI) .... 14
Gitarzan (Ahab, BMI) .... 48
Goodbye (Maclen, BMI) .... 86
Good Times Bad Times (Superhype, ASCAP) .... 80
Grazin' in the Grass (Chisa, BMI) .... 65
Hair (United Artists, ASCAP) .... 7
Happy Heart (Andy Williams) (Miller, ASCAP) .... 70
Happy Heart (Petula Clark) (Miller, ASCAP) .... 79
Hawaii Five-O (April, ASCAP) .... 17
Hot Smoke & Sassafrass (Tapier, BMI) .... 27
I Can Hear Music (Trio Music Co. Inc., BMI) .... 32
I Can't Do Enough (Chevis Music, BMI) .... 98
I Can't See Myself Leaving You (Fourteenth Hour, BMI) .... 74
I Don't Want Nobody to Give Me Nothing (Open Up the Door, I'll Get It Myself) (Dynatone, BMI) 30
I Like What You're Doing (to Me) (East/Memphis, BMI) .... 49
Ice Cream Song (Dlief-Cotillion, BMI) .... 59
I'm a Drifter (Detail, BMI) .... 99
In the Bad Bad Old Days (January, BMI) .... 60
In the Still of the Night (Cherio, BMI) .... 64
Indian Giver (Kaskat/Kahoona, BMI) .... 28
I'll Try Something New (Jobete, BMI) .... 25
Is It Something You Got (Dakar, BMI) .... 34
It's a Groovy World (Andjun, ASCAP) .... 97
It's Only Love (Press, BMI) .... 47
It's Your Thing (Brothers Three, BMI) .... 3
I've Been Hurt (Low-Twy, BMI) .... 89
Johnny One Time (Hill & Ranger/Blue Crest, BMI).. 55
July You're a Woman (Great Montana, BMI) ....100
The Letter (Burton, BMI) .... 40
Love (Can Make You Happy) (Rendezvous/Tobac, BMI) .... 62
Love Is All I Have to Give (Irving, BMI) .... 77
Memories (Gladys, ASCAP) .... 35
Mendocino (Southern Love, BMI) .... 36
Mercy (Peanut Butter/Kaskat, BMI) .... 41
Million to One, A (Jobete, BMI) .... 90
Mini Skirt Minnie (New Research, BMI) .... 50
More Today Than Yesterday (Spiral, BMI) .... 58
Morning Girl (Acuff-Rose, BMI) .... 83
Move in a Little Closer Baby (Arnold Jay, ASCAP).. 71
Mr. Sun, Mr. Moon (Boom, BMI) .... 18
My Way (Don C./Stanka, BMI) .... 33
My Whole World Ended (The Moment You Left Me) (Jobete, BMI) .... 23
Nothing But a Heartache (Felsted Music, BMI) .... 56
Only the Strong Survive (Parabut/Double Diamond/Downstairs, BMI) .... 4
Pinball Wizard (Track, BMI) .... 51
Playgirl (4 Star Music Co., BMI) .... 57
Pledge of Allegiance, The (Valentina, ASCAP) .... 75
Proud Mary (Jondora, BMI) .... 19
River Is Wide, The (Saturday, BMI) .... 66
Rock Me (Trousdale, BMI) .... 10
Rhythm of the Rain (Tamerlane, BMI) .... 95
Run Away Child, Running Wild (Jobete, BMI) .... 11
Seattle (Screen Gems-Columbia, BMI) .... 72
Singing My Song (Al Gallico, BMI) .... 94
Snatching It Back (Fama, BMI) .... 31
Sorry Suzanne (January, BMI) .... 96
Stand (Daly City, BMI) .... 54
Sweet Cherry Wine (Big Seven, BMI) .... 12
These Eyes (Dunbar, BMI) .... 61
Time Is Tight (East/Memphis, BMI) .... 24
Time of the Season (Mainstay, BMI) .... 9
There Never Was a Time (Singleton, BMI) .... 93
This Girl's in Love With You (Blue Seas/Jac, ASCAP) .... 22
To Know You Is to Love You (Vogue, BMI) .... 45
Traces (Low-Sal, BMI) .... 16
Tracks of My Tears (Jobete, BMI) .... 82
Try a Little Tenderness (Connelly & Robbins, ASCAP) .... 29
Twenty-Five Miles (Jobete, BMI) .... 8
Way It Used to Be, The (Maribus, BMI) .... 42
(We've Got) Honey Love (Jobete, BMI) .... 87
When You Dance (Angel, BMI) .... 76
Where Do You Go (My Lovely) (Unart, BMI) .... 73
Will You Be Staying After Sunday (Screen Gems-Columbia, BMI) .... 39
Wishful Sinful (Nipper Music, ASCAP) .... 44
You Gave Me a Mountain (Mojave, BMI) .... 43
You've Made Me So Very Happy (Jobete, BMI) .... 2
Zazuera (Rodra, BMI) .... 78


## BUBBLING UNDER THE HOT 100

101. BABY DRIVER .... Simon & Garfunkel, Columbia 4-44785
102. GIVE IT AWAY .... Chi-Lites, Brunswick 55398
103. GENTLE ON MY MIND .... Aretha Franklin, Atlantic 2610
104. WITH PEN IN HAND .... Vikki Carr, Liberty 56092
105. LOVE IS JUST A FOUR-LETTER WORD .... Joan Baez, Vanguard 35088
106. I STAND ACCUSED .... Al Wilson, Soul City 773
107. LONG WAYS FROM HOME .... Hugh Masekela, Uni 55116
108. YOU CAME, YOU SAW, YOU CONQUERED .... Ronettes, A&M 1040
109. ARE YOU LONELY FOR ME BABY .... Chuck Jackson, Motown 1144
110. I WAS A BOY WHEN YOU NEEDED A MAN .... Billy Shields, Harbour 304
111. I FEEL LIKE I'M FALLING IN LOVE AGAIN .... Fantastic Four, Soul 3505
112. MOTHER WHERE'S YOUR DAUGHTER .... Royal Guardsmen, Laurie 2404
113. HURTING EACH OTHER .... Ruby & the Romantics, A&M 1042
114. GREENSLEEVES .... Mason Williams, Warner Bros.-7 Arts 7272
115. RUN ON .... Arthur Conley, Atco 6661
116. JUST A LITTLE BIT .... Little Milton, Checker 1217
117. SOUL PRIDE .... James Brown, King 6222
118. CAROLINA ON MY MIND .... James Taylor, Apple 1805
119. IDAHO .... Four Seasons, Phillips 40597
120. CRYING IN THE RAIN .... Sweet Impressions, Atlantic 2620
121. MEDICINE MAN .... Buchanan Brothers, Event 3302
122. TOO BUSY THINKING ABOUT MY BABY .... Marvin Gaye, Tamla 54181
123. FOOT PATIN' PART 2 .... King Curtis & the Kingpins, Atco 6664
124. RHYTHM OF LIFE .... Sammy Davis Jr., Reprise 732470
125. NEVER GONNA LET HIM KNOW .... Debbie Taylor, GWP 501
126. EVERY LITTLE BIT HURTS .... Peggy Scott, SSS International 767
127. I SHALL BE RELEASED .... Box Tops, Mala 12038
128. JUST A LITTLE BIT CLOSER .... Archie Bell & the Drells, Atlantic 2612
129. SEVEN YEARS .... Impressions, Curtom 1940
130. IT'S A MIRACLE .... Willie Hightower, Capitol 2226
131. WE CAN'T GO ON THIS WAY .... Unchained Mynd, Buddah 111
132. SING A SIMPLE SONG .... Noble Knights, Cotillion 44030
133. I CAN'T SAY NO .... Betty Everett, Uni 55122
134. WELCOME ME LOVE .... Brooklyn Bridge, Buddah 95
135. DAY IS DONE .... Peter, Paul & Mary, Warner Bros.-7 Arts 7279

Compiled from national retail sales and radio station airplay by the Music Popularity Dept. of Record Market Research, Billboard.

HOT 100

HOT 100

# Billboard HOT 100

FOR WEEK ENDING APRIL 26, 1969

★ STAR PERFORMER—Sides registering greatest proportionate upward progress this week.

◉ Record Industry Association of America seal of certification as million selling single.

| This Week | 1 Wk. Ago | 2 Wks. Ago | 3 Wks. Ago | TITLE | Artist (Producer), Label & Number | Weeks On Chart |
|---|---|---|---|---|---|---|
| 1 (Billboard Award) | 1 | 1 | 2 | AQUARIUS/LET THE SUNSHINE IN | Fifth Dimension (Bones Howe), Soul City 772 | 8 |
| 2 | 2 | 2 | 4 | YOU'VE MADE ME SO VERY HAPPY | Blood, Sweat & Tears (James William Guerico), Columbia 4-44776 | 9 |
| ◉ 3 | 3 | 7 | 14 | IT'S YOUR THING | Isley Brothers (R. Isley-O. Isley-R. Isley), T Neck 901 | 7 |
| ★ 4 | 7 | 8 | 18 | HAIR | Cowsills (Bill & Bob Cowsill), MGM 14026 | 7 |
| 5 | 4 | 6 | 7 | ONLY THE STRONG SURVIVE | Jerry Butler (Gamble & Huff), Mercury 72898 | 9 |
| 6 | 8 | 10 | 13 | TWENTY-FIVE MILES | Edwin Starr (Bristol & Fuqua), Gordy 7083 | 11 |
| 7 | 6 | 4 | 5 | GALVESTON | Glen Campbell (Al De Lory), Capitol P-2428 | 9 |
| ★ 8 | 24 | 29 | 33 | TIME IS TIGHT | Booker T. & the M.G.'s (B. T. Jones), Stax 0028 | 7 |
| ◉ 9 | 5 | 3 | 1 | DIZZY | Tommy Roe (Steve Barri), ABC 11164 | 13 |
| 10 | 12 | 18 | 34 | SWEET CHERRY WINE | Tommy James & Shondells (Tommy James), Roulette 7039 | 6 |
| 11 | 13 | 21 | 21 | DO YOUR THING | Watts 103rd Street Band, Warner Bros.-Seven Arts 7250 | 13 |
| 12 | 9 | 5 | 3 | TIME OF THE SEASON | Zombies (Rod Argent & Chris White), Date 2-1628 | 12 |
| ★ 13 | 17 | 32 | 51 | HAWAII FIVE-O | The Ventures (Joe Saraceno), Liberty 56068 | 8 |
| 14 | 14 | 24 | 26 | GIMME GIMME GOOD LOVIN' | Crazy Elephant (Kasenetz-Katz Assoc.), Bell 763 | 9 |
| 15 | 15 | 16 | 30 | DON'T GIVE IN TO HIM | Gary Puckett & the Union Gap (Jerry Fuller), Columbia 4-44788 | 7 |
| ★ 16 | 20 | 51 | — | THE BOXER | Simon & Garfunkel (Simon & Garfunkel & Hales), Columbia 4-44785 | 3 |
| 17 | 10 | 11 | 11 | ROCK ME | Steppenwolf (Gabriel Mekler), Dunhill 4182 | 9 |
| ★ 18 | 21 | 28 | 38 | CHOKIN' KIND | Joe Simon (J. R. Enterprises), SS7 2628 | 6 |
| 19 | 11 | 9 | 6 | RUNAWAY CHILD, RUNNING WILD | Temptations (Norman Whitfield), Gordy 7084 | 11 |
| 20 | 16 | 13 | 8 | TRACES | Classics IV (Buddie Buie), Imperial 66352 | 12 |
| 21 | 30 | 54 | 61 | I DON'T WANT NOBODY TO GIVE ME NOTHING (Open Up the Door, I'll Get It Myself) | James Brown (James Brown), King 6224 | 4 |
| 22 | 26 | 27 | 29 | BROTHER LOVE'S TRAVELLING SALVATION SHOW | Neil Diamond (Tommy Cogbill & Chips Moman), Uni 55109 | 10 |
| 23 | 19 | 12 | 10 | PROUD MARY | Creedence Clearwater Revival (John Fogerty), Fantasy 619 | 14 |
| 24 | 32 | 33 | 36 | I CAN HEAR MUSIC | Beach Boys (Carl Wilson), Capitol 2432 | 8 |
| ★ 25 | 52 | 60 | 75 | ATLANTIS | Donovan (Mickie Most), Epic 5-10434 | 4 |
| ★ 26 | 48 | 68 | 94 | GITARZAN | Ray Stevens (Fred Foster, Ray Stevens & Jim Malloy), Monument 1131 | 4 |
| 27 | 18 | 19 | 19 | MR. SUN, MR. MOON | Paul Revere & the Raiders (Mark Lindsay), Columbia 4-44744 | 11 |
| 28 | 27 | 14 | 15 | HOT SMOKE & SASSAFRASS | Bubble Puppy, International Artists 128 | 11 |
| 29 | 25 | 25 | 28 | I'LL TRY SOMETHING NEW | Diana Ross & the Supremes & the Temptations (F. Wilson & D. Richards), Motown 1142 | 7 |
| 30 | 33 | 37 | 41 | MY WAY | Frank Sinatra (Don Costa), Reprise 0817 | 5 |
| ★ 31 | 41 | 46 | 54 | MERCY | Ohio Express (Kasenetz-Katz Assoc.), Buddah 102 | 5 |
| ★ 32 | 53 | — | — | THE COMPOSER | Diana Ross & the Supremes (Smokey), Motown 1146 | 2 |
| 33 | 31 | 36 | 37 | SNATCHING IT BACK | Clarence Carter (Rick Hall), Atlantic 2605 | 9 |
| ★ 34 | 74 | — | — | I CAN'T SEE MYSELF LEAVING YOU | Aretha Franklin (Jerry Wexler), Atlantic 2619 | 2 |
| ★ 35 | 61 | 66 | 91 | THESE EYES | Guess Who (Nimbus 9), RCA 74-0102 | 4 |
| 36 | 65 | 73 | 80 | GRAZIN' IN THE GRASS | Friends of Distinction (John Florez), RCA 74-0207 | 4 |
| 37 | 37 | 40 | 43 | FIRST OF MAY | Bee Gees (Robert Stigwood), Atco 6657 | 6 |
| 38 | 38 | 42 | 47 | DON'T TOUCH ME | Bettye Swan (Wayne Shuler), Capitol 2382 | 8 |
| 39 | 39 | 39 | 52 | WILL YOU BE STAYING AFTER SUNDAY | Peppermint Rainbow (Paul Leka), Decca 32410 | 11 |
| ★ 40 | 54 | 80 | — | STAND | Sly & the Family Stone (Sly Stone), Epic 5-10450 | 3 |
| 41 | 35 | 35 | 48 | MEMORIES | Elvis Presley (Bones Howe & Steve Binder), RCA 47-9731 | 6 |
| 42 | 42 | 43 | 44 | THE WAY IT USED TO BE | Engelbert Humperdinck (Peter Sullivan), Parrot 40036 | 9 |
| 43 | 36 | 30 | 27 | MENDOCINO | Sir Douglas Quintet (Amigas de Musica), Smash 2191 | 15 |
| 44 | 44 | 45 | 60 | WISHFUL SINFUL | Doors (Paul A. Rothchild), Elektra 45656 | 5 |
| 45 | 45 | 50 | 72 | TO KNOW YOU IS TO LOVE YOU | Bobby Vinton (Billy Sherril), Epic 5-10461 | 4 |
| 46 | 51 | 61 | 73 | PINBALL WIZARD | The Who (Baron Lambert), Decca 732465 | 4 |
| 47 | 47 | 48 | 63 | IT'S ONLY LOVE | B. J. Thomas (Chips Moman), Scepter 12244 | 6 |
| ★ 49 | 70 | 75 | — | HAPPY HEART | Andy Williams (Jerry Fuller), Columbia 4-44818 | 3 |
| 48 | 40 | 20 | 20 | THE LETTER | The Arbors (Roy Cicala & Lorie Burton), Date 2-1638 | 10 |
| 50 | 50 | 53 | 69 | MINI SKIRT MINNIE | Wilson Pickett (Rick Hall), Atlantic 2611 | 5 |
| 51 | 34 | 34 | 53 | IS IT SOMETHING YOU GOT | Tyrone Davis (Willie Henderson), Dakar 605 | 6 |
| ★ 52 | 62 | 72 | — | LOVE (Can Make You Happy) | Mercy (Jamie-Guyden), Sundi 6811 | 3 |
| 53 | 46 | 47 | 56 | APRICOT BRANDY | Rhinoceros (Paul A. Rothchild), Elektra 45647 | 10 |
| 54 | 29 | 31 | 31 | TRY A LITTLE TENDERNESS | Three Dog Night (Gabriel Makler), Dunhill 4177 | 12 |
| 55 | 67 | 78 | — | BUYING A BOOK | Joe Tex (Buddy Killen), Dial 4090 | 3 |
| 56 | 56 | 59 | 62 | NOTHING BUT A HEARTACHE | Flirtations (Wayne Bickerton), Deram 85038 | 8 |
| 57 | 58 | 69 | 88 | MORE TODAY THAN YESTERDAY | Spiral Staircase (Sonny Knight), Columbia 4-44741 | 4 |
| 58 | 60 | 64 | 77 | IN THE BAD BAD OLD DAYS | Foundations (Tony Macaulay), UNI 55117 | 4 |
| 59 | 59 | 62 | 64 | ICE CREAM SONG | The Dynamics (Tommy Cogbill), Cotillion 44021 | 6 |
| 60 | 66 | 87 | — | THE RIVER IS WIDE | The Grassroots (Steve Barri), Dunhill 4187 | 3 |
| 61 | 49 | 52 | 55 | I LIKE WHAT YOU'RE DOING (To Me) | Carla Thomas (Don Davis), Stax 0024 | 11 |
| ★ 62 | 81 | 93 | — | CISSY STRUT | Meters (Marshall E. Schorn & Allen Toussaint), Josie 1005 | 3 |
| 63 | 69 | 70 | 81 | FOOLISH FOOL | Dee Dee Warwick (Ed Townsend), Mercury 72880 | 7 |
| ★ 64 | 86 | — | — | GOODBYE | Mary Hopkin (Paul McCartney), Apple 1806 | 2 |
| 65 | 57 | 49 | 50 | PLAYGIRL | Thee Prophets (C. Bonafede, D. Belloc, L. Douglas), Kapp 962 | 8 |
| ★ 66 | 85 | — | — | EARTH ANGEL | Vogues (Dick Glasser), Reprise 0820 | 2 |
| ★ 67 | — | — | — | TOO BUSY THINKING ABOUT MY BABY | Marvin Gaye (Norman Whitfield), Tamla 54181 | 1 |
| 68 | 68 | 76 | 87 | BADGE | Cream (Felix Pappalardi), Atco 6668 | 4 |
| 69 | 72 | 82 | — | SEATTLE | Perry Como (Chet Atkins & Andy Wiswell), RCA 47-9722 | 3 |
| 70 | 76 | 89 | 95 | WHEN YOU DANCE | Jay & the Americans (Jay & the Americans), United Artists 50510 | 4 |
| 71 | 79 | 84 | — | HAPPY HEART | Petula Clark, Warner Brothers-Seven Arts 7275 | 3 |
| ★ 72 | — | — | — | OH HAPPY DAY | Edwin Hawkins Singers (La Mont Bench), Pavillion 20001 | 1 |
| 73 | 73 | 74 | 85 | WHERE DO YOU GO (My Lovely) | Peter Sarstedt (Ray Singer), World Pacific 7791 | 4 |
| 74 | 77 | 83 | 86 | LOVE IS ALL I HAVE TO GIVE | Checkmates (Phil Spector), A&M 1039 | 4 |
| 75 | 83 | 86 | 93 | MORNING GIRL | Neon Philharmonic (T. Saussy, Don Gant & B. McCluskey), Warner Bros.-Seven Arts 7261 | 4 |
| ★ 76 | 89 | — | — | I'VE BEEN HURT | Bill Deal & the Rhondells (Jerry Ross), Heritage 812 | 2 |
| 77 | 64 | 65 | 70 | IN THE STILL OF THE NIGHT | Paul Anka (Don Costa Prod.), RCA 74-0126 | 6 |
| ★ 78 | 87 | — | — | (We've Got) HONEY LOVE | Martha Reeves & the Vandellas (Richard Morris), Gordy 7085 | 2 |
| ★ 79 | 96 | — | — | SORRY SUZANNE | Hollies (Ron Richards), Epic 5-10454 | 2 |
| 80 | 78 | 79 | 79 | ZAZUERA | Herb Alpert & the Tijuana Brass (H. Alpert & Jerry Moss), A&M 1043 | 5 |
| ★ 81 | 99 | — | — | I'M A DRIFTER | Bobby Goldsboro (Bob Montgomery & Bobby Goldsboro), United Artists 50525 | 2 |
| ★ 82 | 95 | 97 | 98 | RHYTHM OF THE RAIN | Gary Lewis & the Playboys (Snuff Garrett), Liberty 56093 | 4 |
| ★ 83 | — | — | — | DAY IS DONE | Peter, Paul & Mary (Phil Ramone), Warner Bros.-Seven Arts 7279 | 1 |
| 84 | 84 | 85 | 90 | BACK IN THE U.S.S.R. | Chubby Checker (John Madera), Buddah 100 | 4 |
| 85 | 94 | 100 | — | SINGING MY SONG | Tammy Wynette (Billy Sherrill), Epic 5-10462 | 3 |
| 86 | 88 | 92 | — | ANY DAY NOW | Percy Sledge (Quin Ivy/Marlin Greene), Atlantic 2616 | 3 |
| ★ 87 | — | — | — | HEATHER HONEY | Tommy Roe (Steve Barri), ABC 11211 | 1 |
| ★ 88 | — | — | — | LOVE IS JUST A FOUR LETTER WORD | Joan Baez (Maynard Solomon), Vanguard 35088 | 1 |
| ★ 89 | — | — | — | MR. WALKER, IT'S ALL OVER | Billie Jo Spears (Kelso Herston), Capitol 2436 | 1 |
| ★ 90 | — | — | — | I SHALL BE RELEASED | Box Tops (Chips Moman & Tommy Cogbill), Mala 12038 | 1 |
| 91 | — | — | — | BOTH SIDES NOW | Dion (Phil Gernhard), Laurie 3495 | 1 |
| 92 | 92 | 96 | 97 | CALIFORNIA GIRL (And the Tennessee Square) | Tompall and the Glaser Brothers (Jack Clement), MGM K-14036 | 4 |
| 93 | — | — | — | GREENSLEEVES | Mason Williams (Dick Glasser), Warner Bros.-Seven Arts 7272 | 1 |
| 94 | — | — | — | SEVEN YEARS | Impressions (Curtis Mayfield), Curtom 1940 | 1 |
| 95 | — | — | — | I CAN'T SAY NO TO YOU | Betty Everett (Archie Ros & Leo Austell & Hilary Johnson), UNI 55122 | 1 |
| 96 | — | — | — | I'VE BEEN LOVING YOU TOO LONG | Ike & Tina Turner (Bob Krasnow & Tina Turner), Blue Thumb 101 | 1 |
| 97 | — | — | — | HOME TO YOU | Earth Opera (Peter K. Siegel), Elektra 45650 | 1 |
| 98 | — | — | — | NEVER GONNA LET HIM KNOW | Debbie Taylor (George Kerr & Paul Robinson), GWP 501 | 1 |
| 99 | 90 | 90 | 96 | A MILLION TO ONE | Brian Hyland (Ray Ruff), Dot 17222 | 4 |
| 100 | 100 | — | — | JULY YOU'RE A WOMAN | Pat Boone (Jerry Yester & Zal Yanovsky), Tetragrammaton 1516 | 2 |

## HOT 100—A TO Z—*(Publisher-Licensee)*


Any Day Now (Plan Two, ASCAP) .... 86
Apricot Brandy (Nina, BMI) .... 53
Atlantis (Peer Int'l, BMI) .... 25
Aquarius/Let the Sunshine In (United Artists, ASCAP) .... 1
Back in the U.S.S.R. (Maclean, BMI) .... 84
Badge (Casserole, BMI) .... 68
Both Sides Now (Siquomb, BMI) .... 91
Boxer, The (Charing Cross, BMI) .... 16
Brother Love's Travelling Salvation Show (Stonebridge, BMI) .... 22
Buying a Book (Tree, BMI) .... 55
California Girl (And the Tennessee Square) (Jack, BMI) .... 92
Chokin' Kind (Wilderness Music, BMI) .... 18
Cissy Strut (Marsaint, BMI) .... 62
Composer, The (Jobete, BMI) .... 32
Day Is Done (Pepamar, ASCAP) .... 83
Dizzy (Low Twine, BMI) .... 9
Do Your Thing (Charles Wright & Fred Smith) (Wright-Gersti-Tamerlan, BMI) .... 11
Don't Give In to Him (Four Star, BMI) .... 15
Don't Touch Me (Pamper, BMI) .... 38
Earth Angel (Williams, BMI) .... 66
First of May (Casserole, BMI) .... 37
Foolish Fool (Chappell, ASCAP) .... 63
Galveston (Ja-Ma Music, ASCAP) .... 7
Gimme Gimme Good Lovin' (Peanut Butter/Kahoona, BMI) .... 14
Gitarzan (Ahab, BMI) .... 26
Goodbye (Maclen, BMI) .... 64
Grazin' in the Grass (Chisa, BMI) .... 36
Greensleeves (Irving, BMI) .... 93
Hair (United Artists, ASCAP) .... 4
Happy Heart (Andy Williams) (Miller, ASCAP) .... 49
Happy Heart (Petula Clark) (Miller, ASCAP) .... 71
Hawaii Five-O (April, ASCAP) .... 13
Heather Honey (Low-Twy, BMI) .... 87
Home to You (Nina, BMI) .... 97
Hot Smoke & Sassafrass (Tapier, BMI) .... 28
I Can Hear Music (Trio Music Co. Inc., BMI) .... 24
I Can't Say No to You (Screen Gems-Columbia, BMI) .... 95
I Can't See Myself Leaving You (Fourteenth Hour, BMI) .... 34
I Don't Want Nobody to Give Me Nothing (Open Up the Door, I'll Get It Myself) (Dynatone, BMI) .... 21
I Like What You're Doing (to Me) (East/Memphis, BMI) .... 61
Ice Cream Song (Dlief-Cotillion, BMI) .... 59
I'm a Drifter (Detail, BMI) .... 81
In the Bad Bad Old Days (January, BMI) .... 58
In the Still of the Night (Cherio, BMI) .... 77
I'll Try Something New (Jobete, BMI) .... 29
I Shall Be Released (Dwarft, ASCAP) .... 90
Is It Something You Got (Dakar, BMI) .... 51
It's Only Love (Press, BMI) .... 47
It's Your Thing (Brothers Three, BMI) .... 3
I've Been Hurt (Low-Twy, BMI) .... 76
I've Been Loving You Too Long (East/Time/Curton, BMI) .... 96
July You're a Woman (Great Montana, BMI) .... 100
The Letter (Burton, BMI) .... 48
Love (Can Make You Happy) (Rendezvous/Tobac, BMI) .... 52
Love Is All I Have to Give (Irving, BMI) .... 74
Love Is Just a Four Letter Word (Witmark, ASCAP) .... 88
Memories (Gladys, ASCAP) .... 41
Mendocino (Southern Love, BMI) .... 43
Mercy (Peanut Butter/Kaskat, BMI) .... 31
Million to One, A (Jobete, BMI) .... 99
Mini Skirt Minnie (New Research, BMI) .... 50
More Today Than Yesterday (Spiral, BMI) .... 57
Morning Girl (Acuff-Rose, BMI) .... 75
Mr. Sun, Mr. Moon (Boom, BMI) .... 27
Mr. Walker, It's All Over (Barmour, BMI) .... 89
My Way (Don C./Stanka, BMI) .... 30
Never Gonna Let Him Know (Green Light, BMI) .... 98
Nothing But a Heartache (Felsted Music, BMI) .... 56
Oh Happy Day (Kama Rippa/Hawkins, ASCAP) .... 72
Only the Strong Survive (Parabut/Double Diamond/Downstairs, BMI) .... 5
Pinball Wizard (Track, BMI) .... 46
Playgirl (4 Star Music Co., BMI) .... 65
Proud Mary (Jondora, BMI) .... 23
River Is Wide, The (Saturday, BMI) .... 60
Rock Me (Trousdale, BMI) .... 17
Rhythm of the Rain (Tamerlane, BMI) .... 82
Runaway Child, Running Wild (Jobete, BMI) .... 19
Seattle (Screen Gems-Columbia, BMI) .... 69
Seven Years (Camad, BMI) .... 94
Singing My Song (Al Gallico, BMI) .... 85
Snatching It Back (Fama, BMI) .... 33
Sorry Suzanne (January, BMI) .... 79
Stand (Daly City, BMI) .... 40
Sweet Cherry Wine (Big Seven, BMI) .... 10
These Eyes (Dunbar, BMI) .... 35
Time Is Tight (East/Memphis, BMI) .... 8
Time of the Season (Mainstay, BMI) .... 12
To Know You Is to Love You (Vogue, BMI) .... 45
Too Busy Thinking About My Baby (Jobete, BMI) .... 67
Traces (Low-Sal, BMI) .... 20
Try a Little Tenderness (Connelly & Robbins, ASCAP) .... 54
Twenty-Five Miles (Jobete, BMI) .... 6
Way It Used to Be, The (Maribus, BMI) .... 42
(We've Got) Honey Love (Jobete, BMI) .... 78
When You Dance (Angel, BMI) .... 70
Where Do You Go (My Lovely) (Unart, BMI) .... 73
Will You Be Staying After Sunday (Screen Gems-Columbia, BMI) .... 39
Wishful Sinful (Nipper Music, ASCAP) .... 44
You've Made Me So Very Happy (Jobete, BMI) .... 2
Zazuera (Rodra, BMI) .... 80


## BUBBLING UNDER THE HOT 100

101. MARLEY PURT DRIVE .... Jose Feliciano, RCA Victor 47-9739
102. EVERYDAY WITH YOU GIRL .... Classics IV, Imperial 66378
103. GENTLE ON MY MIND .... Aretha Franklin, Atlantic 2610
104. WITH PEN IN HAND .... Vikki Carr, Liberty 56092
105. I DON'T WANT TO HEAR IT ANYMORE .... Dusty Springfield, Atlantic 2623
106. I STAND ACCUSED .... Al Wilson, Soul City 773
107. ARE YOU LONELY FOR ME .... Chuck Jackson, Motown 1144
108. YOU CAME, YOU SAW, YOU CONQUERED .... Ronettes, A&M 1040
109. I WAS A BOY WHEN YOU NEEDED A MAN .... Billy Shields, Harbour 304
110. WHEN SOMETHING IS WRONG WITH MY BABY .... Otis Redding & Carla Thomas, Atco 6665
111. I FEEL LIKE I'M FALLING IN LOVE .... Fantastic Four, Soul 35038
112. MEDICINE MAN .... Buchanan Brothers, Event 3302
113. CHANGE YOUR MIND .... Jay & the Techniques, Smash 2217
114. IVORY .... Bob Seeger, Capitol 2480
115. JUST A LITTLE BIT .... Little Milton, Checker 1217
116. LOVE IS STRANGE .... Buddy Holly, Coral 62558
117. HOW GREAT THOU ART .... Elvis Presley, RCA Victor 74-0130
118. UNDER BRANCHES .... Association, Warner Bros.-Seven Arts 7277
119. CRYING IN THE RAIN .... Sweet Inspirations, Atlantic 2620
120. GO AWAY LITTLE GIRL & YOUNG GIRL .... Tokens, Warner Bros.-Seven Arts 7280
121. LOVE THEME FROM ROMEO & JULIET .... Henry Mancini & His Ork, RCA Victor 74-0131
122. TRUCK STOP .... Jerry Smith, ABC 1116
123. WELCOME ME LOVE .... Brooklyn Bridge, Buddah 95
124. REAL TRUE LOVING .... Steve & Eydie, RCA Victor 74-0123

Compiled from national retail sales and radio station airplay by the Music Popularity Dept. of Record Market Research, Billboard.

# Billboard HOT 100

FOR WEEK ENDING MAY 3, 1969

★ STAR PERFORMER—Sides registering greatest proportionate upward progress this week.

(seal) Record Industry Association of America seal of certification as million selling single.

| This Week | 1 Wk. Ago | 2 Wks. Ago | 3 Wks. Ago | TITLE — Artist (Producer), Label & Number | Weeks On Chart |
|---|---|---|---|---|---|
| 1 (Billboard Award) | 1 | 1 | 1 | **AQUARIUS/LET THE SUNSHINE IN** — Fifth Dimension (Bones Howe), Soul City 772 | 9 |
| 2 (seal) | 3 | 3 | 7 | **IT'S YOUR THING** — Isley Brothers (R. Isley-O. Isley-R. Isley), T Neck 901 | 8 |
| 3 (seal) | 4 | 7 | 8 | **HAIR** — Cowsills (Bill & Bob Cowsill), MGM 14026 | 8 |
| 4 | 2 | 2 | 2 | **YOU'VE MADE ME SO VERY HAPPY** — Blood, Sweat & Tears (James William Guerico), Columbia 4-44776 | 10 |
| 5 (seal) | 5 | 4 | 6 | **ONLY THE STRONG SURVIVE** — Jerry Butler (Gamble & Huff), Mercury 72898 | 10 |
| 6 ★ | 8 | 24 | 29 | **TIME IS TIGHT** — Booker T. & the M.G.'s (B. T. Jones), Stax 0028 | 8 |
| 7 ★ | 10 | 12 | 18 | **SWEET CHERRY WINE** — Tommy James & Shondells (Tommy James), Roulette 7039 | 7 |
| 8 ★ | 13 | 17 | 32 | **HAWAII FIVE-O** — The Ventures (Joe Saraceno), Liberty 56068 | 9 |
| 9 ★ | 16 | 20 | 51 | **THE BOXER** — Simon & Garfunkel (Simon & Garfunkel & Hales), Columbia 4-44785 | 4 |
| 10 | 7 | 6 | 4 | **GALVESTON** — Glen Campbell (Al De Lory), Capitol P-2428 | 10 |
| 11 (seal) | 9 | 5 | 3 | **DIZZY** — Tommy Roe (Steve Barri), ABC 11164 | 14 |
| 12 ★ | 14 | 14 | 24 | **GIMME GIMME GOOD LOVIN'** — Crazy Elephant (Kasenetz-Katz Assoc.), Bell 763 | 10 |
| 13 | 6 | 8 | 10 | **TWENTY-FIVE MILES** — Edwin Starr (Bristol & Fuqua), Gordy 7083 | 12 |
| 14 ★ | 35 | 61 | 66 | **THESE EYES** — Guess Who (Nimbus 9), RCA 74-0102 | 5 |
| 15 ★ | 52 | 62 | 72 | **LOVE (Can Make You Happy)** — Mercy (Jamie-Guyden), Sundi 6811 | 4 |
| 16 | 11 | 13 | 21 | **DO YOUR THING** — Watts 103rd Street Band, Warner Bros.-Seven Arts 7250 | 14 |
| 17 | 15 | 15 | 16 | **DON'T GIVE IN TO HIM** — Gary Puckett & the Union Gap (Jerry Fuller), Columbia 4-44788 | 8 |
| 18 | 18 | 21 | 28 | **CHOKIN' KIND** — Joe Simon (J. R. Enterprises), SS7 2628 | 7 |
| 19 ★ | 25 | 52 | 60 | **ATLANTIS** — Donovan (Mickie Most), Epic 5-10434 | 5 |
| 20 ★ | 26 | 48 | 68 | **GITARZAN** — Ray Stevens (Fred Foster, Ray Stevens & Jim Malloy), Monument 1131 | 5 |
| 21 | 21 | 30 | 54 | **I DON'T WANT NOBODY TO GIVE ME NOTHING (Open Up the Door, I'll Get It Myself)** — James Brown (James Brown), King 6224 | 5 |
| 22 | 22 | 26 | 27 | **BROTHER LOVE'S TRAVELLING SALVATION SHOW** — Neil Diamond (Tommy Cogbill & Chips Moman), Uni 55109 | 11 |
| 23 (seal) | 12 | 9 | 5 | **TIME OF THE SEASON** — Zombies (Rod Argent & Chris White), Date 2-1628 | 13 |
| 24 | 17 | 10 | 11 | **ROCK ME** — Steppenwolf (Gabriel Mekler), Dunhill 4182 | 10 |
| 25 ★ | 46 | 51 | 61 | **PINBALL WIZARD** — The Who (Baron Lambert), Decca 732465 | 5 |
| 26 | 19 | 11 | 9 | **RUNAWAY CHILD, RUNNING WILD** — Temptations (Norman Whitfield), Gordy 7084 | 12 |
| 27 ★ | 64 | 86 | — | **GOODBYE** — Mary Hopkin (Paul McCartney), Apple 1806 | 3 |
| 28 | 24 | 32 | 33 | **I CAN HEAR MUSIC** — Beach Boys (Carl Wilson), Capitol 2432 | 9 |
| 29 | 30 | 33 | 37 | **MY WAY** — Frank Sinatra (Don Costa), Reprise 0817 | 6 |
| 30 | 31 | 41 | 46 | **MERCY** — Ohio Express (Kasenetz-Katz Assoc.), Buddah 102 | 6 |
| 31 ★ | 32 | 53 | — | **THE COMPOSER** — Diana Ross & the Supremes (Smokey), Motown 1146 | 3 |
| 32 ★ | 39 | 39 | 39 | **WILL YOU BE STAYING AFTER SUNDAY** — Peppermint Rainbow (Paul Leka), Decca 32410 | 12 |
| 33 | 34 | 74 | — | **I CAN'T SEE MYSELF LEAVING YOU** — Aretha Franklin (Jerry Wexler), Atlantic 2619 | 3 |
| 34 ★ | 45 | 45 | 50 | **TO KNOW YOU IS TO LOVE YOU** — Bobby Vinton (Billy Sherril), Epic 5-10461 | 5 |
| 35 | 36 | 65 | 73 | **GRAZIN' IN THE GRASS** — Friends of Distinction (John Florez), RCA 74-0207 | 5 |
| 36 ★ | 40 | 54 | 80 | **STAND** — Sly & the Family Stone (Sly Stone), Epic 5-10450 | 4 |
| 37 ★ | 57 | 58 | 69 | **MORE TODAY THAN YESTERDAY** — Spiral Staircase (Sonny Knight), Columbia 4-44741 | 5 |
| 38 ★ | 49 | 70 | 75 | **HAPPY HEART** — Andy Williams (Jerry Fuller), Columbia 4-44818 | 4 |
| 39 | 27 | 18 | 19 | **MR. SUN, MR. MOON** — Paul Revere & the Raiders (Mark Lindsay), Columbia 4-44744 | 12 |
| 40 ★ | 72 | — | — | **OH HAPPY DAY** — Edwin Hawkins Singers (La Mont Bench), Pavillion 20001 | 2 |
| 41 | 41 | 35 | 35 | **MEMORIES** — Elvis Presley (Bones Howe & Steve Binder), RCA 47-9731 | 7 |
| 42 | 42 | 42 | 43 | **THE WAY IT USED TO BE** — Engelbert Humperdinck (Peter Sullivan), Parrot 40036 | 10 |
| 43 ★ | 60 | 66 | 87 | **THE RIVER IS WIDE** — The Grassroots (Steve Barri), Dunhill 4187 | 4 |
| 44 ★ | 69 | 72 | 82 | **SEATTLE** — Perry Como (Chet Atkins & Andy Wiswell), RCA 47-9722 | 4 |
| 45 | 47 | 47 | 48 | **IT'S ONLY LOVE** — B. J. Thomas (Chips Moman), Scepter 12244 | 7 |
| 46 | 37 | 37 | 40 | **FIRST OF MAY** — Bee Gees (Robert Stigwood), Atco 6657 | 7 |
| 47 ★ | 66 | 85 | — | **EARTH ANGEL** — Vogues (Dick Glasser), Reprise 0820 | 3 |
| 49 | 38 | 38 | 42 | **DON'T TOUCH ME** — Bettye Swan (Wayne Shuler), Capitol 2382 | 9 |
| 48 | 44 | 44 | 45 | **WISHFUL SINFUL** — Doors (Paul A. Rothchild), Elektra 45656 | 6 |
| 50 ★ | 56 | 56 | 59 | **NOTHING BUT A HEARTACHE** — Flirtations (Wayne Bickerton), Deram 85038 | 9 |
| 51 ★ | 75 | 83 | 86 | **MORNING GIRL** — Neon Philharmonic (T. Saussy, Don Gant & B. McCluskey), Warner Bros.-Seven Arts 7261 | 5 |
| 52 ★ | 58 | 60 | 64 | **IN THE BAD BAD OLD DAYS** — Foundations (Tony Macaulay), UNI 55117 | 5 |
| 53 | 55 | 67 | 78 | **BUYING A BOOK** — Joe Tex (Buddy Killen), Dial 4090 | 4 |
| 54 ★ | 67 | — | — | **TOO BUSY THINKING ABOUT MY BABY** — Marvin Gaye (Norman Whitfield), Tamla 54181 | 2 |
| 55 | 62 | 81 | 93 | **CISSY STRUT** — Meters (Marshall E. Schorn & Allen Toussaint), Josie 1005 | 4 |
| 56 | 28 | 27 | 14 | **HOT SMOKE & SASSAFRASS** — Bubble Puppy, International Artists 128 | 12 |
| 57 | 51 | 34 | 34 | **IS IT SOMETHING YOU GOT** — Tyrone Davis (Willie Henderson), Dakar 605 | 7 |
| 58 | 33 | 31 | 36 | **SNATCHING IT BACK** — Clarence Carter (Rick Hall), Atlantic 2605 | 10 |
| 59 ★ | — | — | — | **WHERE'S THE PLAYGROUND SUSIE** — Glen Campbell (Al De Lory), Capitol 2494 | 1 |
| 60 | 68 | 68 | 76 | **BADGE** — Cream (Felix Pappalardi), Atco 6668 | 5 |
| 61 | 50 | 50 | 53 | **MINI SKIRT MINNIE** — Wilson Pickett (Rick Hall), Atlantic 2611 | 6 |
| 62 ★ | 87 | — | — | **HEATHER HONEY** — Tommy Roe (Steve Barri), ABC 11211 | 2 |
| 63 | 63 | 69 | 70 | **FOOLISH FOOL** — Dee Dee Warwick (Ed Townsend), Mercury 72880 | 8 |
| 64 | 59 | 59 | 62 | **ICE CREAM SONG** — The Dynamics (Tommy Cogbill), Cotillion 44021 | 7 |
| 65 | 74 | 77 | 83 | **LOVE IS ALL I HAVE TO GIVE** — Checkmates (Phil Spector), A&M 1039 | 5 |
| 66 ★ | 83 | — | — | **DAY IS DONE** — Peter, Paul & Mary (Phil Ramone), Warner Bros.-Seven Arts 7279 | 2 |
| 67 ★ | 81 | 99 | — | **I'M A DRIFTER** — Bobby Goldsboro (Bob Montgomery & Bobby Goldsboro), United Artists 50525 | 3 |
| 68 | 71 | 79 | 84 | **HAPPY HEART** — Petula Clark, Warner Brothers-Seven Arts 7275 | 4 |
| 69 ★ | 79 | 96 | — | **SORRY SUZANNE** — Hollies (Ron Richards), Epic 5-10454 | 3 |
| 70 | 78 | 87 | — | **(We've Got) HONEY LOVE** — Martha Reeves & the Vandellas (Richard Morris), Gordy 7085 | 3 |
| 71 | 76 | 89 | — | **I'VE BEEN HURT** — Bill Deal & the Rhondells (Jerry Ross), Heritage 812 | 3 |
| 72 | 73 | 73 | 74 | **WHERE DO YOU GO (My Lovely)** — Peter Sarstedt (Ray Singer), World Pacific 7791 | 5 |
| 73 | 70 | 76 | 89 | **WHEN YOU DANCE** — Jay & the Americans (Jay & the Americans), United Artists 50510 | 5 |
| 74 ★ | — | — | — | **EVERYDAY WITHOUT YOU GIRL** — Classics IV (Buddy Blue), Imperial 66378 | 1 |
| 75 | 85 | 94 | 100 | **SINGING MY SONG** — Tammy Wynette (Billy Sherrill), Epic 5-10462 | 4 |
| 76 ★ | 90 | — | — | **I SHALL BE RELEASED** — Box Tops (Chips Moman & Tommy Cogbill), Mala 12038 | 2 |
| 77 ★ | — | — | — | **PROUD MARY** — Solomon Burke (Solomon Burke-Tamiko Jones), Bell 783 | 1 |
| 78 ★ | — | — | — | **LODI** — Creedence Clearwater Revival (John Fogerty), Fantasy 632 | 1 |
| 79 ★ | — | — | — | **IN THE GHETTO** — Elvis Presley (Felton Jarvis), RCA Victor 47-9741 | 1 |
| 80 ★ | — | — | — | **BAD MOON RISING** — Creedence Clearwater Revival (John Fogerty), Fantasy 632 | 1 |
| 81 | 82 | 95 | 97 | **RHYTHM OF THE RAIN** — Gary Lewis & the Playboys (Snuff Garrett), Liberty 56093 | 5 |
| 82 | 84 | 84 | 85 | **BACK IN THE U.S.S.R.** — Chubby Checker (John Madera), Buddah 100 | 5 |
| 83 ★ | — | — | — | **MEDICINE MAN** — Buchanan Brothers (Cashman, Pistilli & West), Event, 3302 | 1 |
| 84 ★ | — | — | — | **ONE** — Three Dog Night (Gabriel Mekler), Dunhill 4191 | 1 |
| 85 ★ | — | — | — | **PRETTY WORLD** — Sergio Mendes & Brasil '66 (Sergio Mendes & Herb Alpert), A&M 1049 | 1 |
| 86 | 86 | 88 | 92 | **ANY DAY NOW** — Percy Sledge (Quin Ivy/Marlin Greene), Atlantic 2616 | 4 |
| 87 | 88 | — | — | **LOVE IS JUST A FOUR LETTER WORD** — Joan Baez (Maynard Solomon), Vanguard 35088 | 2 |
| 88 | 89 | — | — | **MR. WALKER, IT'S ALL OVER** — Billie Jo Spears (Kelso Herston), Capitol 2436 | 2 |
| 89 ★ | — | — | — | **WITH PEN IN HAND** — Vikki Carr (Dave Pell & Rob Bledsoe), Liberty 56092 | 1 |
| 90 | 93 | — | — | **GREENSLEEVES** — Mason Williams (Dick Glasser), Warner Bros.-Seven Arts 7272 | 2 |
| 91 | 91 | — | — | **BOTH SIDES NOW** — Dion (Phil Gernhard), Laurie 3495 | 2 |
| 92 | 99 | 90 | 90 | **A MILLION TO ONE** — Brian Hyland (Ray Ruff), Dot 17222 | 5 |
| 93 | 95 | — | — | **I CAN'T SAY NO TO YOU** — Betty Everett (Archie Ros & Leo Austell & Hilary Johnson), UNI 55122 | 2 |
| 94 | 94 | — | — | **SEVEN YEARS** — Impressions (Curtis Mayfield), Curtom 1940 | 2 |
| 95 | 96 | — | — | **I'VE BEEN LOVING YOU TOO LONG** — Ike & Tina Turner (Bob Krasnow & Tina Turner), Blue Thumb 101 | 2 |
| 96 | — | — | — | **MARLEY PURT DRIVE** — Jose Feliciano (Rick Jarrard), RCA Victor 47-9739 | 1 |
| 97 | — | — | — | **I COULD NEVER LIE TO YOU** — New Colony Six, Mercury 72920 | 1 |
| 98 | 98 | — | — | **NEVER GONNA LET HIM KNOW** — Debbie Taylor (George Kerr & Paul Robinson), GWP 501 | 2 |
| 99 | — | — | — | **THE WINDMILLS OF YOUR MIND** — Dusty Springfield (Jerry Wexler), Atlantic 2623 | 1 |
| 100 | — | — | — | **I WANT TO LOVE YOU BABY** — Peggy Scott & Jo Jo Benson (Shelby Singleton), SSS International 769 | 1 |

## HOT 100—A TO Z—(Publisher-Licensee)

Any Day Now (Plan Two, ASCAP) .... 86
Atlantis (Peer Int'l, BMI) .... 19
Aquarius/Let the Sunshine In (United Artists, ASCAP) 1

Back in the U.S.S.R. (Maclean, BMI) .... 82
Bad Moon Rising (Jondora, BMI) .... 80
Badge (Casserole, BMI) .... 60
Both Sides Now (Siquomb, BMI) .... 91
Boxer, The (Charing Cross, BMI) .... 9
Brother Love's Travelling Salvation Show (Stonebridge, BMI) .... 22
Buying a Book (Tree, BMI) .... 53

Chokin' Kind (Wilderness Music, BMI) .... 18
Cissy Strut (Marsaint, BMI) .... 55
Composer, The (Jobete, BMI) .... 31

Day Is Done (Pepamar, ASCAP) .... 66
Dizzy (Low Twine, BMI) .... 11
Do Your Thing (Charles Wright & Fred Smith) (Wright-Gersti-Tamerlan, BMI) .... 16
Don't Give In to Him (Four Star, BMI) .... 17
Don't Touch Me (Pamper, BMI) .... 49

Earth Angel (Williams, BMI) .... 47
Everyday Without You Girl (Low-Sal, BMI) .... 74

First of May (Casserole, BMI) .... 46
Foolish Fool (Chappell, ASCAP) .... 63

Galveston (Ja-Ma Music, ASCAP) .... 10
Gimme Gimme Good Lovin' (Peanut Butter/Kahoona, BMI) .... 12
Gitarzan (Ahab, BMI) .... 20
Goodbye (Maclen, BMI) .... 27
Grazin' in the Grass (Chisa, BMI) .... 35
Greensleeves (Irving, BMI) .... 90

Hair (United Artists, ASCAP) .... 3
Happy Heart (Andy Williams) (Miller, ASCAP) .... 38
Happy Heart (Petula Clark) (Miller, ASCAP) .... 68
Hawaii Five-O (April, ASCAP) .... 8
Heather Honey (Low-Twy, BMI) .... 62
Hot Smoke & Sassafrass (Tapier, BMI) .... 56

I Can Hear Music (Trio Music Co. Inc., BMI) .... 28
I Can't Say No to You (Screen Gems-Columbia, BMI) 93
I Can't See Myself Leaving You (Fourteenth Hour, BMI) .... 33
I Could Never Lie to You (New Colony, BMI) .... 97
I Don't Want Nobody to Give Me Nothing (Open Up the Door, I'll Get It Myself) (Dynatone, BMI) 21
Ice Cream Song (Dlief-Cotillion, BMI) .... 64
I'm a Drifter (Detail, BMI) .... 67
In the Bad Bad Old Days (January, BMI) .... 52
In the Ghetto (B-N-B/Gladys, ASCAP) .... 79
I Shall Be Released (Dwarft, ASCAP) .... 76
I Want to Love You Baby (Green Owl, ASCAP) .... 100
Is It Something You Got (Roker, BMI) .... 57
It's Only Love (Press, BMI) .... 45
It's Your Thing (Brothers Three, BMI) .... 2
I've Been Hurt (Low-Twy, BMI) .... 71
I've Been Loving You Too Long (East/Time/Curton, BMI) .... 95

Lodi (Jondora, BMI) .... 78
Love (Can Make You Happy) (Rendezvous/Tobac, BMI) .... 15
Love Is All I Have to Give (Irving, BMI) .... 65
Love Is Just a Four Letter Word (Witmark, ASCAP) 87

Marley Purt Drive (Casserole, BMI) .... 96
Medicine Man (Sandbox, ASCAP) .... 83
Memories (Gladys, ASCAP) .... 41
Mercy (Peanut Butter/Kaskat, BMI) .... 30
Million to One, A (Jobete, BMI) .... 92
Mini Skirt Minnie (New Research, BMI) .... 61
More Today Than Yesterday (Spiral, BMI) .... 37
Morning Girl (Acuff-Rose, BMI) .... 51
Mr. Sun, Mr. Moon (Boom, BMI) .... 39
Mr. Walker, It's All Over (Barmour, BMI) .... 88
My Way (Don C./Spanka, BMI) .... 29
Never Gonna Let Him Know (Green Light, BMI) .... 98
Nothing But a Heartache (Felsted Music, BMI) .... 50

Oh Happy Day (Kama Rippa/Hawkins, ASCAP) .... 40
One (Dunbar, BMI) .... 84
Only the Strong Survive (Parabut/Double Diamond/Downstairs, BMI) .... 5

Pinball Wizard (Track, BMI) .... 25
Pretty World (Brava, ASCAP) .... 85
Proud Mary (Jondora, BMI) .... 77

River Is Wide, The (Saturday, BMI) .... 43
Rock Me (Trousdale, BMI) .... 24
Rhythm of the Rain (Tamerlane, BMI) .... 81
Runaway Child, Running Wild (Jobete, BMI) .... 26

Seattle (Screen Gems-Columbia, BMI) .... 44
Seven Years (Camad, BMI) .... 94
Singing My Song (Al Gallico, BMI) .... 75
Snatching It Back (Fama, BMI) .... 58
Sorry Suzanne (January, BMI) .... 69
Stand (Daly City, BMI) .... 36
Sweet Cherry Wine (Big Seven, BMI) .... 7

These Eyes (Dunbar, BMI) .... 14
Time Is Tight (East/Memphis, BMI) .... 6
Time of the Season (Mainstay, BMI) .... 23
To Know You Is to Love You (Vogue, BMI) .... 34
Too Busy Thinking About My Baby (Jobete, BMI) .. 54
Twenty-Five Miles (Jobete, BMI) .... 13

Way It Used to Be, The (Maribus, BMI) .... 42
(We've Got) Honey Love (Jobete, BMI) .... 70
When You Dance (Angel, BMI) .... 73
Where Do You Go (My Lovely) (Unart, BMI) .... 72
Where's the Playground Susie (Ja-Ma, ASCAP) .... 59
Will You Be Staying After Sunday (Screen Gems-Columbia, BMI) .... 32
Windmills of Your Mind, The (United Artists, ASCAP) 99
Wishful Sinful (Nipper Music, ASCAP) .... 48
With Pen in Hand (Unart, BMI) .... 89

You've Made Me So Very Happy (Jobete, BMI) .... 4

## BUBBLING UNDER THE HOT 100

101. HOW GREAT THOU ART .... Elvis Presley, RCA Victor 74-0130
102. GENTLE ON MY MIND .... Aretha Franklin, Atlantic 2610
103. WELCOME ME LOVE .... Brooklyn Bridge, Buddah 95
104. JUST A LITTLE BIT .... Little Milton, Checker 1217
105. TRUCK STOP .... Jerry Smith, ABC 1116
106. SUNDAY .... Moments, Stang 5003
107. WHAT IS A MAN .... Four Tops, Motown 1147
108. CHANGE YOUR MIND .... Jay & the Techniques, Smash 2217
109. WHEN SOMETHING IS WRONG WITH MY BABY .... Otis & Carla, Atco 6665
110. LOVE THEME FROM ROMEO & JULIET .... Henry Mancini & his Ork, RCA Victor 74-0131
111. SAUSILITO .... Al Martino, Capitol 2468
112. HERE WE GO AGAIN .... Nancy Sinatra, Reprise 0821
113. IVORY .... Bob Seeger, Capitol 2480
114. WHY I SING THE BLUES .... B. B. King, Bluesway 61024
115. LOVE IS STRANGE .... Buddy Holly, Coral 62558
116. CRYING IN THE RAIN .... Sweet Inspirations, Atlantic 2620
117. UNDER BRANCHES .... Association, Warner Bros.-Seven Arts 7277
118. HUNKY FUNKY .... American Breed, Acta 833
119. DEVIL OR ANGEL .... Tony Scotti, Liberty 56101
120. GO AWAY LITTLE GIRL/YOUNG GIRL .. Tokens, Warner Bros.-Seven Arts 7280
121. REAL TRUE LOVIN' .... Steve & Eydie, RCA Victor 74-0123
122. BLACK PEARL .... Sonny Charles, A&M 1053
123. TURN AROUND AND LOVE YOU .... Rita Coolidge, Pepper 443
124. TOO EXPERIENCED .... Eddie Lovette, Steady 124
125. CASTSCHOK .... Alexandrow Karazov, Jamie 1372
126. RUNAWAY CHILD RUNNING WILD .... Earl Van Dyke, Soul 35059
127. THE WINDMILLS OF YOUR MIND .... Jimmy Rodgers, A&M 1055
128. YOU DON'T NEED ME FOR ANYTHING ANYMORE .. Brenda Lee, Decca 732491
129. ROSE GARDEN .... Dobie Gray, White Whale 300
130. ROLLIN' TUMBLIN' .... Johnny Winter, Imperial 66376
131. SCOTCH & SODA .... Kingston Trio, Tetragrammaton 1526
132. HOME TO YOU .... Earth Opera, Elektra 45650
133. SOMEDAY MAN .... Monkees, Colgems 66-5004

Compiled from national retail sales and radio station airplay by the Music Popularity Dept. of Record Market Research, Billboard.

# Billboard HOT 100

FOR WEEK ENDING MAY 10, 1969

★ STAR PERFORMER—Sides registering greatest proportionate upward progress this week.

Record Industry Association of America seal of certification as million selling single.

| This Week | 1 Wk. Ago | 2 Wks. Ago | 3 Wks. Ago | TITLE Artist (Producer), Label & Number | Weeks On Chart |
|---|---|---|---|---|---|
| 1 (Billboard Award) | 1 | 1 | 1 | AQUARIUS/LET THE SUNSHINE IN — Fifth Dimension (Bones Howe), Soul City 772 | 10 |
| 2 | 3 | 4 | 7 | HAIR — Cowsills (Bill & Bob Cowsill), MGM 14026 | 9 |
| 3 | 2 | 3 | 3 | IT'S YOUR THING — Isley Brothers (R. Isley-O. Isley-R. Isley), T Neck 901 | 9 |
| 4 | 8 | 13 | 17 | HAWAII FIVE-O — The Ventures (Joe Saraceno), Liberty 56068 | 10 |
| 5 | 4 | 2 | 2 | YOU'VE MADE ME SO VERY HAPPY — Blood, Sweat & Tears (James William Guerico), Columbia 4-44776 | 11 |
| 6 | 6 | 8 | 24 | TIME IS TIGHT — Booker T. & the M.G.'s (B. T. Jones), Stax 0028 | 9 |
| 7 | 7 | 10 | 12 | SWEET CHERRY WINE — Tommy James & Shondells (Tommy James), Roulette 7039 | 8 |
| 8 | 9 | 16 | 20 | THE BOXER — Simon & Garfunkel (Simon & Garfunkel & Hales), Columbia 4-44785 | 5 |
| ★9 | 19 | 25 | 52 | ATLANTIS — Donovan (Mickie Most), Epic 5-10434 | 6 |
| ★10 | — | — | — | GET BACK — Beatles (George Martin), Apple 2490 | 1 |
| 11 | 15 | 52 | 62 | LOVE (Can Make You Happy) — Mercy (Jamie-Guyden), Sundi 6811 | 5 |
| 12 | 12 | 14 | 14 | GIMME GIMME GOOD LOVIN' — Crazy Elephant (Kasenetz-Katz Assoc.), Bell 763 | 11 |
| 13 | 14 | 35 | 61 | THESE EYES — Guess Who (Nimbus 9), RCA 74-0102 | 6 |
| 14 | 5 | 5 | 4 | ONLY THE STRONG SURVIVE — Jerry Butler (Gamble & Huff), Mercury 72898 | 11 |
| ★15 | 18 | 18 | 21 | CHOKIN' KIND — Joe Simon (J. R. Enterprises), SS7 2628 | 8 |
| 16 | 16 | 11 | 13 | DO YOUR THING — Watts 103rd Street Band, Warner Bros.-Seven Arts 7250 | 15 |
| 17 | 20 | 26 | 48 | GITARZAN — Ray Stevens (Fred Foster, Ray Stevens & Jim Malloy), Monument 1131 | 6 |
| ★18 | 40 | 72 | — | OH HAPPY DAY — Edwin Hawkins Singers (La Mont Bench), Pavillion 20001 | 3 |
| 19 | 10 | 7 | 6 | GALVESTON — Glen Campbell (Al De Lory), Capitol P-2428 | 11 |
| 20 | 21 | 21 | 30 | I DON'T WANT NOBODY TO GIVE ME NOTHING (Open Up the Door, I'll Get It Myself) — James Brown (James Brown), King 6224 | 6 |
| 21 | 13 | 6 | 8 | TWENTY-FIVE MILES — Edwin Starr (Bristol & Fuqua), Gordy 7083 | 13 |
| 22 | 11 | 9 | 5 | DIZZY — Tommy Roe (Steve Barri), ABC 11164 | 15 |
| ★23 | 35 | 36 | 65 | GRAZIN' IN THE GRASS — Friends of Distinction (John Florez), RCA 74-0207 | 6 |
| 24 | 27 | 64 | 86 | GOODBYE — Mary Hopkin (Paul McCartney), Apple 1806 | 4 |
| 25 | 25 | 46 | 51 | PINBALL WIZARD — The Who (Baron Lambert), Decca 732465 | 6 |
| 26 | 17 | 15 | 15 | DON'T GIVE IN TO HIM — Gary Puckett & the Union Gap (Jerry Fuller), Columbia 4-44788 | 9 |
| 27 | 29 | 30 | 33 | MY WAY — Frank Sinatra (Don Costa), Reprise 0817 | 7 |
| 28 | 31 | 32 | 53 | THE COMPOSER — Diana Ross & the Supremes (Smokey), Motown 1146 | 4 |
| ★29 | 54 | 67 | — | TOO BUSY THINKING ABOUT MY BABY — Marvin Gaye (Norman Whitfield), Tamla 54181 | 3 |
| ★30 | 33 | 34 | 74 | I CAN'T SEE MYSELF LEAVING YOU — Aretha Franklin (Jerry Wexler), Atlantic 2619 | 4 |
| 31 | 37 | 57 | 58 | MORE TODAY THAN YESTERDAY — Spiral Staircase (Sonny Knight), Columbia 4-44741 | 6 |
| 32 | 32 | 39 | 39 | WILL YOU BE STAYING AFTER SUNDAY — Peppermint Rainbow (Paul Leka), Decca 32410 | 13 |
| 33 | 38 | 49 | 70 | HAPPY HEART — Andy Williams (Jerry Fuller), Columbia 4-44818 | 5 |
| 34 | 34 | 45 | 45 | TO KNOW YOU IS TO LOVE YOU — Bobby Vinton (Billy Sherril), Epic 5-10461 | 6 |
| 35 | 36 | 40 | 54 | STAND — Sly & the Family Stone (Sly Stone), Epic 5-10450 | 5 |
| ★36 | 51 | 75 | 83 | MORNING GIRL — Neon Philharmonic (T. Saussy, Don Gant & B. McCluskey), Warner Bros.-Seven Arts 7261 | 6 |
| 37 | 28 | 24 | 32 | I CAN HEAR MUSIC — Beach Boys (Carl Wilson), Capitol 2432 | 10 |
| 38 | 22 | 22 | 26 | BROTHER LOVE'S TRAVELLING SALVATION SHOW — Neil Diamond (Tommy Cogbill & Chips Moman), Uni 55109 | 12 |
| 39 | 30 | 31 | 41 | MERCY — Ohio Express (Kasenetz-Katz Assoc.), Buddah 102 | 7 |
| ★40 | — | — | — | DON'T LET ME DOWN — Beatles (George Martin), Apple 2490 | 1 |
| ★41 | 79 | — | — | IN THE GHETTO — Elvis Presley (Felton Jarvis), RCA Victor 47-9741 | 2 |
| 42 | 43 | 60 | 66 | THE RIVER IS WIDE — The Grassroots (Steve Barri), Dunhill 4187 | 5 |
| 43 | 44 | 69 | 72 | SEATTLE — Perry Como (Chet Atkins & Andy Wiswell), RCA 47-9722 | 5 |
| ★44 | 59 | — | — | WHERE'S THE PLAYGROUND SUSIE — Glen Campbell (Al De Lory), Capitol 2494 | 2 |
| 45 | 47 | 66 | 85 | EARTH ANGEL — Vogues (Dick Glasser), Reprise 0820 | 4 |
| ★46 | 50 | 56 | 56 | NOTHING BUT A HEARTACHE — Flirtations (Wayne Bickerton), Deram 85038 | 10 |
| 47 | 55 | 62 | 81 | CISSY STRUT — Meters (Marshall E. Schorn & Allen Toussaint), Josie 1005 | 5 |
| ★48 | 53 | 55 | 67 | BUYING A BOOK — Joe Tex (Buddy Killen), Dial 4090 | 5 |
| 49 | 49 | 38 | 38 | DON'T TOUCH ME — Bettye Swan (Wayne Shuler), Capitol 2382 | 10 |
| ★50 | 66 | 83 | — | DAY IS DONE — Peter, Paul & Mary (Phil Ramone), Warner Bros.-Seven Arts 7279 | 3 |
| ★51 | 62 | 87 | — | HEATHER HONEY — Tommy Roe (Steve Barri), ABC 11211 | 3 |
| 52 | 52 | 58 | 60 | IN THE BAD BAD OLD DAYS — Foundations (Tony Macaulay), UNI 55117 | 6 |
| 53 | 77 | — | — | PROUD MARY — Solomon Burke (Solomon Burke-Tamiko Jones), Bell 783 | 2 |
| ★54 | 80 | — | — | BAD MOON RISING — Creedence Clearwater Revival (John Fogerty), Fantasy 632 | 2 |
| 55 | 42 | 42 | 42 | THE WAY IT USED TO BE — Engelbert Humperdinck (Peter Sullivan), Parrot 40036 | 11 |
| 56 | 45 | 47 | 47 | IT'S ONLY LOVE — B. J. Thomas (Chips Moman), Scepter 12244 | 8 |
| 57 | 63 | 63 | 69 | FOOLISH FOOL — Dee Dee Warwick (Ed Townsend), Mercury 72880 | 9 |
| ★58 | 84 | — | — | ONE — Three Dog Night (Gabriel Mekler), Dunhill 4191 | 2 |
| ★59 | 78 | — | — | LODI — Creedence Clearwater Revival (John Fogerty), Fantasy 632 | 2 |
| ★60 | 71 | 76 | 89 | I'VE BEEN HURT — Bill Deal & the Rhondells (Jerry Ross), Heritage 812 | 4 |
| 61 | 69 | 79 | 96 | SORRY SUZANNE — Hollies (Ron Richards), Epic 5-10454 | 4 |
| 62 | 68 | 71 | 79 | HAPPY HEART — Petula Clark, Warner Brothers-Seven Arts 7275 | 5 |
| ★63 | 74 | — | — | EVERYDAY WITHOUT YOU GIRL — Classics IV (Buddy Blue), Imperial 66378 | 2 |
| 64 | 67 | 81 | 99 | I'M A DRIFTER — Bobby Goldsboro (Bob Montgomery & Bobby Goldsboro), United Artists 50525 | 4 |
| 65 | 70 | 78 | 87 | (We've Got) HONEY LOVE — Martha Reeves & the Vandellas (Richard Morris), Gordy 7085 | 4 |
| ★66 | 83 | — | — | MEDICINE MAN — Buchanan Brothers (Cashman, Pistilli & West), Event, 3302 | 2 |
| ★67 | 99 | — | — | THE WINDMILLS OF YOUR MIND — Dusty Springfield (Jerry Wexler), Atlantic 2623 | 2 |
| 68 | 65 | 74 | 77 | LOVE IS ALL I HAVE TO GIVE — Checkmates (Phil Spector), A&M 1039 | 6 |
| 69 | 76 | 90 | — | I SHALL BE RELEASED — Box Tops (Chips Moman & Tommy Cogbill), Mala 12038 | 3 |
| 70 | 72 | 73 | 73 | WHERE DO YOU GO (My Lovely) — Peter Sarstedt (Ray Singer), World Pacific 7791 | 6 |
| ★71 | — | — | — | LOVE THEME FROM ROMEO & JULIET — Henry Mancini & Ork. (Joe Reisman), RCA Victor 74-0131 | 1 |
| ★72 | 81 | 82 | 95 | RHYTHM OF THE RAIN — Gary Lewis & the Playboys (Snuff Garrett), Liberty 56093 | 6 |
| ★73 | — | — | — | I WANNA TESTIFY — Johnnie Taylor (Don Davis), Stax 0033 | 1 |
| ★74 | 97 | — | — | I COULD NEVER LIE TO YOU — New Colony Six, Mercury 72920 | 2 |
| ★75 | — | — | — | BLACK PEARL — Sonny Charles with the Checkmates Ltd. (Phil Spector), A&M 1053 | 1 |
| ★76 | — | — | — | IT'S NEVER TOO LATE — Steppenwolf (Gabriel Mekler), Dunhill 4192 | 1 |
| ★77 | — | — | — | GENTLE ON MY MIND — Aretha Franklin (Jerry Wexler), Atlantic 2619 | 1 |
| ★78 | 93 | 95 | — | I CAN'T SAY NO TO YOU — Betty Everett (Archie Ros & Leo Austell & Hilary Johnson), UNI 55122 | 3 |
| ★79 | 96 | — | — | MARLEY PURT DRIVE — Jose Feliciano (Rick Jarrard), RCA Victor 47-9739 | 2 |
| 80 | 88 | 89 | — | MR. WALKER, IT'S ALL OVER — Billie Jo Spears (Kelso Herston), Capitol 2436 | 3 |
| 81 | 89 | — | — | WITH PEN IN HAND — Vikki Carr (Dave Pell & Rob Bladsoe), Liberty 56092 | 2 |
| ★82 | 100 | — | — | I WANT TO LOVE YOU BABY — Peggy Scott & Jo Jo Benson (Shelby Singleton), SSS International 769 | 2 |
| 83 | 85 | — | — | PRETTY WORLD — Sergio Mendes & Brasil '66 (Sergio Mendes & Herb Alpert), A&M 1049 | 2 |
| ★84 | 94 | 94 | — | SEVEN YEARS — Impressions (Curtis Mayfield), Curtom 1940 | 3 |
| ★85 | — | — | — | SOMEDAY MAN — Monkees (Bones Howe), Colgems 66-5004 | 1 |
| 86 | 87 | 88 | — | LOVE IS JUST A FOUR LETTER WORD — Joan Baez (Maynard Solomon), Vanguard 35088 | 3 |
| 87 | 75 | 85 | 94 | SINGING MY SONG — Tammy Wynette (Billy Sherrill), Epic 5-10462 | 5 |
| ★88 | — | — | — | FRIEND, LOVER, WOMAN, WIFE — O. C. Smith (Jerry Fuller), Columbia 44859 | 1 |
| ★89 | — | — | — | SPECIAL DELIVERY — 1910 Fruitgum Co. (Kasenetz-Katz Associates), Buddah 114 | 1 |
| ★90 | — | — | — | TRUCKSTOP — Jerry Smith (Paul Cohen), ABC 11116 | 1 |
| 91 | 95 | 96 | — | I'VE BEEN LOVING YOU TOO LONG — Ike & Tina Turner (Bob Krasnow & Tina Turner), Blue Thumb 101 | 3 |
| 92 | — | — | — | SUNDAY — Moments, Stang 5003 | 1 |
| 93 | — | — | — | WELCOME ME LOVE — Brooklyn Bridge (Wes Farrell), Buddah 95 | 1 |
| 94 | — | — | — | WHAT IS A MAN? — Four Tops (Fuqua), Motown 1147 | 1 |
| 95 | 98 | 98 | — | NEVER GONNA LET HIM KNOW — Debbie Taylor (George Kerr & Paul Robinson), GWP 501 | 3 |
| 96 | — | — | — | TURN AROUND AND LOVE YOU — Rita Coolidge (Ed Killis), Pepper 443 | 1 |
| 97 | — | — | — | IVORY — Bob Seeger System (Wayne Shuler), Capitol 2480 | 1 |
| 98 | — | — | — | JUST A LITTLE BIT — Little Milton (Calvin Carter), Checker 1217 | 1 |
| 99 | — | — | — | I'M GONNA DO ALL I CAN — Ike & Tina Turner (Ike Turner & Willie Mitchell), | 1 |
| 100 | — | — | — | BORN TO BE WILD — Wilson Pickett (Rick Hall), Atlantic 2631 | 1 |

## HOT 100—A TO Z—(Publisher-Licensee)

Atlantis (Peer Int'l, BMI) ... 9
Aquarius/Let the Sunshine In (United Artists, ASCAP) ... 1

Bad Moon Rising (Jondora, BMI) ... 54
Black Pearl (Irving, BMI) ... 75
Born to Be Wild (Duchess, BMI) ... 100
Boxer, The (Charing Cross, BMI) ... 8
Brother Love's Travelling Salvation Show (Stonebridge, BMI) ... 38
Buying a Book (Tree, BMI) ... 48

Chokin' Kind (Wilderness Music, BMI) ... 15
Cissy Strut (Marsaint, BMI) ... 47
Composer, The (Jobete, BMI) ... 28

Day Is Done (Pepamar, ASCAP) ... 50
Dizzy (Low Twine, BMI) ... 22
Do Your Thing (Charles Wright & Fred Smith) (Wright-Gersti-Tamerlan, BMI) ... 16
Don't Give In to Him (Four Star, BMI) ... 26
Don't Let Me Down (Maclen, BMI) ... 40
Don't Touch Me (Pamper, BMI) ... 49

Earth Angel (Williams, BMI) ... 45
Everyday Without You Girl (Low-Sal, BMI) ... 63

Foolish Fool (Chappell, ASCAP) ... 57
Friend, Lover, Woman, Wife (B 'n' B, ASCAP) ... 88

Galveston (Ja-Ma Music, ASCAP) ... 19
Gentle on My Mind (Glaser, BMI) ... 77
Get Back (Maclen, BMI) ... 10
Gimme Gimme Good Lovin' (Peanut Butter/Kahoona, BMI) ... 12
Gitarzan (Ahab, BMI) ... 17
Goodbye (Maclen, BMI) ... 24
Grazin' in the Grass (Chisa, BMI) ... 23

Hair (United Artists, ASCAP) ... 2
Happy Heart (Andy Williams) (Miller, ASCAP) ... 33
Happy Heart (Petula Clark) (Miller, ASCAP) ... 62
Hawaii Five-O (April, ASCAP) ... 4
Heather Honey (Low-Twy, BMI) ... 51

I Can Hear Music (Trio Music Co. Inc., BMI) ... 37
I Can't See Myself Leaving You (Fourteenth Hour, BMI) ... 30
I Could Never Lie to You (New Colony, BMI) ... 74
I Don't Want Nobody to Give Me Nothing (Open Up the Door, I'll Get It Myself) (Dynatone, BMI) 20
I'm a Drifter (Detail, BMI) ... 64
I'm Gonna Do All I Can (Barton, BMI) ... 99
In the Bad Bad Old Days (January, BMI) ... 52
In the Ghetto (B 'n' B/Gladys, ASCAP) ... 41
I Shall Be Released (Dwarft, ASCAP) ... 69
I Want to Love You Baby (Green Owl, ASCAP) ... 82
I Wanna Testify (Groovesville, BMI) ... 73
It's Never Too Late (Trousdale, BMI) ... 76
It's Only Love (Press, BMI) ... 56
It's Your Thing (Brothers Three, BMI) ... 3
I've Been Hurt (Low-Twy, BMI) ... 60
I've Been Loving You Too Long (East/Time/Curton, BMI) ... 91
Ivory (Gear, ASCAP) ... 97

Just a Little Bit (Armo, BMI) ... 98

Lodi (Jondora, BMI) ... 59
Love (Can Make You Happy) (Rendezvous/Tobac, BMI) ... 11
Love Is All I Have to Give (Irving, BMI) ... 68
Love Is Just a Four Letter Word (Witmark, ASCAP) 86
Love Theme From Romeo & Juliet (Famous, ASCAP) 71

Marley Purt Drive (Casserole, BMI) ... 79
Medicine Man (Sandbox, ASCAP) ... 66
Mercy (Peanut Butter/Kaskat, BMI) ... 39
More Today Than Yesterday (Spiral, BMI) ... 31
Morning Girl (Acuff-Rose, BMI) ... 36
Mr. Walker, It's All Over (Barmour, BMI) ... 80
My Way (Don C./Stanka, BMI) ... 27
Never Gonna Let Him Know (Green Light, BMI) ... 95
Nothing But a Heartache (Felsted Music, BMI) ... 46

Oh Happy Day (Kama Rippa/ Hawkins, ASCAP) ... 18
One (Dunbar, BMI) ... 58
Only the Strong Survive (Parabut/Double Diamond/Downstairs, BMI) ... 14

Pinball Wizard (Track, BMI) ... 25
Pretty World (Rodra, BMI) ... 83
Proud Mary (Jondora, BMI) ... 53

River Is Wide, The (Saturday, BMI) ... 42
Rhythm of the Rain (Tamerlane, BMI) ... 72

Seattle (Colgems, ASCAP) ... 43
Seven Years (Camad, BMI) ... 84
Singing My Song (Al Gallico, BMI) ... 87
Someday Man (Irving, BMI) ... 85
Sorry Suzanne (January, BMI) ... 61
Special Delivery (Kaskat/Kahoona, BMI) ... 89
Stand (Daly City, BMI) ... 35
Sunday (Gambi, BMI) ... 92
Sweet Cherry Wine (Big Seven, BMI) ... 7

These Eyes (Dunbar, BMI) ... 13
Time Is Tight (East/Memphis, BMI) ... 6
To Know You Is to Love You (Vogue, BMI) ... 34
Too Busy Thinking About My Baby (Jobete, BMI) ... 29
Truckstop (Papa Joe's Music House, BMI) ... 90
Turn Around and Love You (Screen Gems, BMI) ... 96
Twenty-Five Miles (Jobete, BMI) ... 21

Way It Used to Be, The (Maribus, BMI) ... 55
Welcome Me Love (Pocketful of Tunes, BMI) ... 93
(We've Got) Honey Love (Jobete, BMI) ... 65
What Is a Man? (Jobete, BMI) ... 94
Where Do You Go (My Lovely) (Unart, BMI) ... 70
Where's the Playground Susie (Ja-Ma, ASCAP) ... 44
Will You Be Staying After Sunday (Screen Gems-Columbia, BMI) ... 32
Windmills of Your Mind, The (United Artists, ASCAP) 67
With Pen in Hand (Unart, BMI) ... 81

You've Made Me So Very Happy (Jobete, BMI) ... 5

## BUBBLING UNDER THE HOT 100

101. BABY DRIVER ... Simon & Garfunkel, Columbia 44785
102. ANY DAY NOW ... Percy Sledge, Atlantic 2616
103. GREENSLEEVES ... Mason Williams, Warner Bros.-Seven Arts 7272
104. SAUSILITO ... Al Martino, Capitol 2468
105. LOVE IS STRANGE ... Buddy Holly, Coral 62558
106. IN-A-GADDA-DA-VIDA ... Iron Butterfly, Atco 6606
107. HUNKY FUNKY ... American Breed, Acta 833
108. CHANGE YOUR MIND ... Jay & the Techniques, Smash 2217
109. WHEN SOMETHING IS WRONG WITH MY BABY ... Otis & Carla, Atco 6665
110. HERE WE GO AGAIN ... Nancy Sinatra, Reprise 0821
111. LET ME ... Paul Revere & the Raiders featuring Mark Lindsay, Columbia 44854
112. CRYING IN THE RAIN ... Sweet Inspirations, Atlantic 2620
113. WHY I SING THE BLUES ... B. B. King, BluesWay 61024
114. RUNAWAY CHILD RUNNING WILD ... Earl Van Dyke, Soul 35059
115. MAMA SOUL ... Soul Survivors, Atco 6650
116. ISRAELITES ... Desmond Decker & the Aces, UNI 55129
117. DEVIL OR ANGEL ... Tony Scotti, Liberty 56101
118. GO AWAY LITTLE GIRL/YOUNG GIRL ... Tokens, Warner Bros.-Seven Arts 7280
119. REAL TRUE LOVIN' ... Steve & Eydie, RCA Victor 74-0123
120. NEVER COMES THE DAY ... Moody Blues, Deram 85044
121. YOU DON'T NEED ME FOR ANYTHING ANYMORE ... Brenda Lee, Decca 732491
122. TOO EXPERIENCED ... Eddie Lovette, Steady 124
123. WINDMILLS OF YOUR MIND ... Jimmy Rodgers, A&M 1055
124. SCOTCH & SODA ... Kingston Trio, Tetragrammaton 1526
125. CASTSCHOK ... Alexandrow Karazov, Jamie 1372
126. DENVER ... Ronnie Milsap, Scepter 246
127. I NEED YOU NOW ... Ronnie Dove, Diamond 260
128. ROSE GARDEN ... Dobie Gray, White Whale 300
129. ROLLIN' AND TUMBLIN' ... Johnny Winter, Imperial 66376
130. IT'S EASY TO BE HARD ... Jennifer, Parrot 336
131. GOOD MORNING STARSHINE ... Strawberry Alarm Clock, UNI 55125
132. ME AND MR. HOHNER ... Bobby Darin, Direction 351
133. DARKNESS DARKNESS ... Youngbloods, RCA Victor 74-0129
134. A-HA-HA DO YOUR THING ... Hit Parade, RCA Victor 47-9737
135. WE TRY HARDER ... Kim Weston & Johnny Nash, JAD 1001

Compiled from national retail sales and radio station airplay by the Music Popularity Dept. of Record Market Research, Billboard.

# Billboard HOT 100

FOR WEEK ENDING MAY 17, 1969

★ STAR PERFORMER—Sides registering greatest proportionate upward progress this week.

(Seal) Record Industry Association of America seal of certification as million selling single.

| This Week | 1 Wk. Ago | 2 Wks. Ago | 3 Wks. Ago | TITLE | Artist (Producer), Label & Number | Weeks On Chart |
|---|---|---|---|---|---|---|
| 1 (Billboard Award) | 1 | 1 | 1 | AQUARIUS/LET THE SUNSHINE IN | Fifth Dimension (Bones Howe), Soul City 772 | 11 |
| 2 (Seal) | 2 | 3 | 4 | HAIR | Cowsills (Bill & Bob Cowsill), MGM 14026 | 10 |
| ★ 3 (Seal) | 10 | — | — | GET BACK | Beatles (George Martin), Apple 2490 | 2 |
| 4 | 3 | 2 | 3 | IT'S YOUR THING | Isley Brothers (R. Isley-O. Isley-R. Isley), T Neck 901 | 10 |
| ★ 5 | 11 | 15 | 52 | LOVE (Can Make You Happy) | Mercy (Jamie-Guyden), Sundi 6811 | 6 |
| 6 | 4 | 8 | 13 | HAWAII FIVE-O | The Ventures (Joe Saraceno), Liberty 56068 | 11 |
| 7 | 8 | 9 | 16 | THE BOXER | Simon & Garfunkel (Simon & Garfunkel & Hales), Columbia 4-44785 | 6 |
| 8 | 9 | 19 | 25 | ATLANTIS | Donovan (Mickie Most), Epic 5-10434 | 7 |
| ★ 9 | 17 | 20 | 26 | GITARZAN | Ray Stevens (Fred Foster, Ray Stevens & Jim Malloy), Monument 1131 | 7 |
| 10 | 13 | 14 | 35 | THESE EYES | Guess Who (Nimbus 9), RCA 74-0102 | 7 |
| 11 | 5 | 4 | 2 | YOU'VE MADE ME SO VERY HAPPY | Blood, Sweat & Tears (James William Guerico), Columbia 4-44776 | 12 |
| ★ 12 | 18 | 40 | 72 | OH HAPPY DAY | Edwin Hawkins Singers (La Mont Bench), Pavillion 20001 | 4 |
| 13 | 6 | 6 | 8 | TIME IS TIGHT | Booker T. & the M.G.'s (B. T. Jones), Stax 0028 | 10 |
| ★ 14 | 24 | 27 | 64 | GOODBYE | Mary Hopkin (Paul McCartney), Apple 1806 | 5 |
| 15 | 15 | 18 | 18 | CHOKIN' KIND | Joe Simon (J. R. Enterprises), SS7 2628 | 9 |
| 16 (Seal) | 14 | 5 | 5 | ONLY THE STRONG SURVIVE | Jerry Butler (Gamble & Huff), Mercury 72898 | 12 |
| 17 | 12 | 12 | 14 | GIMME GIMME GOOD LOVIN' | Crazy Elephant (Kasenetz-Katz Assoc.), Bell 763 | 12 |
| 18 | 7 | 7 | 10 | SWEET CHERRY WINE | Tommy James & Shondells (Tommy James), Roulette 7039 | 9 |
| 19 | 23 | 35 | 36 | GRAZIN' IN THE GRASS | Friends of Distinction (John Florez), RCA 74-0207 | 7 |
| 20 | 25 | 25 | 46 | PINBALL WIZARD | The Who (Baron Lambert), Decca 732465 | 7 |
| 21 | 16 | 16 | 11 | DO YOUR THING | Watts 103rd Street Band, Warner Bros.-Seven Arts 7250 | 16 |
| ★ 22 | 35 | 36 | 40 | STAND | Sly & the Family Stone (Sly Stone), Epic 5-10450 | 6 |
| ★ 23 | 41 | 79 | — | IN THE GHETTO | Elvis Presley (Chips Moman), RCA Victor 47-9741 | 3 |
| 24 | 20 | 21 | 21 | I DON'T WANT NOBODY TO GIVE ME NOTHING (Open Up the Door, I'll Get It Myself) | James Brown (James Brown), King 6224 | 7 |
| 25 | 29 | 54 | 67 | TOO BUSY THINKING ABOUT MY BABY | Marvin Gaye (Norman Whitfield), Tamla 54181 | 4 |
| 26 | 31 | 37 | 57 | MORE TODAY THAN YESTERDAY | Spiral Staircase (Sonny Knight), Columbia 4-44741 | 7 |
| 27 | 28 | 31 | 32 | THE COMPOSER | Diana Ross & the Supremes (Smokey), Motown 1146 | 5 |
| 28 | 21 | 13 | 6 | TWENTY-FIVE MILES | Edwin Starr (Bristol & Fuqua), Gordy 7083 | 14 |
| 29 | 33 | 38 | 49 | HAPPY HEART | Andy Williams (Jerry Fuller), Columbia 4-44818 | 6 |
| 30 | 30 | 33 | 34 | I CAN'T SEE MYSELF LEAVING YOU | Aretha Franklin (Jerry Wexler), Atlantic 2619 | 5 |
| 31 | 19 | 10 | 7 | GALVESTON | Glen Campbell (Al De Lory), Capitol P-2428 | 12 |
| 32 | 27 | 29 | 30 | MY WAY | Frank Sinatra (Don Costa), Reprise 0817 | 8 |
| ★ 33 | 54 | 80 | — | BAD MOON RISING | Creedence Clearwater Revival (John Fogerty), Fantasy 622 | 3 |
| 34 | 44 | 59 | — | WHERE'S THE PLAYGROUND SUSIE | Glen Campbell (Al De Lory), Capitol 2494 | 3 |
| 35 | 36 | 51 | 75 | MORNING GIRL | Neon Philharmonic (T. Saussy, Don Gant & B. McCluskey), Warner Bros.-Seven Arts 7261 | 7 |
| 36 | 40 | — | — | DON'T LET ME DOWN | Beatles (George Martin), Apple 2490 | 2 |
| 37 | 42 | 43 | 60 | THE RIVER IS WIDE | The Grassroots (Steve Barri), Dunhill 4187 | 6 |
| ★ 38 | 50 | 66 | 83 | DAY IS DONE | Peter, Paul & Mary (Phil Ramone), Warner Bros.-Seven Arts 7279 | 4 |
| 39 | 39 | 30 | 31 | MERCY | Ohio Express (Kasenetz-Katz Assoc.), Buddah 102 | 8 |
| ★ 40 | 51 | 62 | 87 | HEATHER HONEY | Tommy Roe (Steve Barri), ABC 11211 | 4 |
| 41 | 38 | 22 | 22 | BROTHER LOVE'S TRAVELLING SALVATION SHOW | Neil Diamond (Tommy Cogbill & Chips Moman), Uni 55109 | 13 |
| 42 | 45 | 47 | 66 | EARTH ANGEL | Vogues (Dick Glasser), Reprise 0820 | 5 |
| 43 | 43 | 44 | 69 | SEATTLE | Perry Como (Chet Atkins & Andy Wiswell), RCA 47-9722 | 6 |
| 44 | 32 | 32 | 39 | WILL YOU BE STAYING AFTER SUNDAY | Peppermint Rainbow (Paul Leka), Decca 32410 | 14 |
| 45 | 46 | 50 | 56 | NOTHING BUT A HEARTACHE | Flirtations (Wayne Bickerton), Deram 85038 | 11 |
| 46 | 47 | 55 | 62 | CISSY STRUT | Meters (Marshall E. Schorn & Allen Toussaint), Josie 1005 | 6 |
| ★ 47 | 71 | — | — | LOVE THEME FROM ROMEO & JULIET | Henry Mancini & Ork. (Joe Reisman), RCA Victor 74-0131 | 2 |
| 48 | 48 | 53 | 55 | BUYING A BOOK | Joe Tex (Buddy Killen), Dial 4090 | 6 |
| 49 | 34 | 34 | 45 | TO KNOW YOU IS TO LOVE YOU | Bobby Vinton (Billy Sherril), Epic 5-10461 | 7 |
| 50 | 53 | 77 | — | PROUD MARY | Solomon Burke (Solomon Burke-Tamiko Jones), Bell 783 | 3 |
| 51 | 52 | 52 | 58 | IN THE BAD BAD OLD DAYS | Foundations (Tony Macaulay), UNI 55117 | 7 |
| ★ 52 | 63 | 74 | — | EVERYDAY WITH YOU GIRL | Classics IV (Buddy Blue), Imperial 66378 | 3 |
| 53 | 58 | 84 | — | ONE | Three Dog Night (Gabriel Mekler), Dunhill 4191 | 3 |
| ★ 54 | 60 | 71 | 76 | I'VE BEEN HURT | Bill Deal & the Rhondells (Jerry Ross), Heritage 812 | 5 |
| 55 | 59 | 78 | — | LODI | Creedence Clearwater Revival (John Fogerty), Fantasy 622 | 3 |
| 56 | 65 | 70 | 78 | (We've Got) HONEY LOVE | Martha Reeves & the Vandellas (Richard Morris), Gordy 7085 | 5 |
| ★ 57 | 67 | 99 | — | THE WINDMILLS OF YOUR MIND | Dusty Springfield (Jerry Wexler), Atlantic 2623 | 3 |
| ★ 58 | 75 | — | — | BLACK PEARL | Sonny Charles with the Checkmates Ltd. (Phil Spector), A&M 1053 | 2 |
| ★ 59 | 66 | 83 | — | MEDICINE MAN | Buchanan Brothers (Cashman, Pistilli & West), Event, 3302 | 3 |
| ★ 60 | 73 | — | — | I WANNA TESTIFY | Johnnie Taylor (Don Davis), Stax 0033 | 2 |
| 61 | 61 | 69 | 79 | SORRY SUZANNE | Hollies (Ron Richards), Epic 5-10454 | 5 |
| ★ 62 | 89 | — | — | SPECIAL DELIVERY | 1910 Fruitgum Co. (Kasenetz-Katz Associates), Buddah 114 | 2 |
| ★ 63 | 76 | — | — | IT'S NEVER TOO LATE | Steppenwolf (Gabriel Mekler), Dunhill 4192 | 2 |
| 64 | 64 | 67 | 81 | I'M A DRIFTER | Bobby Goldsboro (Bob Montgomery & Bobby Goldsboro), United Artists 50525 | 5 |
| 65 | 74 | 97 | — | I COULD NEVER LIE TO YOU | New Colony Six, Mercury 72920 | 3 |
| ★ 66 | 100 | — | — | BORN TO BE WILD | Wilson Pickett (Rick Hall), Atlantic 2631 | 2 |
| 67 | 69 | 76 | 90 | I SHALL BE RELEASED | Box Tops (Chips Moman & Tommy Cogbill), Mala 12038 | 4 |
| ★ 68 | 83 | 85 | — | PRETTY WORLD | Sergio Mendes & Brasil '66 (Sergio Mendes & Herb Alpert), A&M 1049 | 3 |
| 69 | 68 | 65 | 74 | LOVE IS ALL I HAVE TO GIVE | Checkmates (Phil Spector), A&M 1039 | 7 |
| ★ 70 | 81 | 89 | — | WITH PEN IN HAND | Vikki Carr (Dave Pell & Rob Bledsoe), Liberty 56092 | 3 |
| 71 | 72 | 81 | 82 | RHYTHM OF THE RAIN | Gary Lewis & the Playboys (Snuff Garrett), Liberty 56093 | 7 |
| 72 | 79 | 96 | — | MARLEY PURT DRIVE | Jose Feliciano (Rick Jarrard), RCA Victor 47-9739 | 3 |
| ★ 73 | — | — | — | IN-A-GADDA-DA-VIDA | Iron Butterfly (Jim Hilton), Atco 6606 | 13 |
| ★ 74 | 94 | — | — | WHAT IS A MAN? | Four Tops (Fuqua), Motown 1147 | 2 |
| ★ 75 | 91 | 95 | 96 | I'VE BEEN LOVING YOU TOO LONG | Ike & Tina Turner (Bob Krasnow & Tina Turner), Blue Thumb 101 | 4 |
| 76 | 77 | — | — | GENTLE ON MY MIND | Aretha Franklin (Jerry Wexler), Atlantic 2619 | 2 |
| ★ 77 | — | — | — | THE APRIL FOOLS | Dionne Warwick (Burt Bacharach, Hal David), Scepter 12249 | 1 |
| 78 | 78 | 93 | 95 | I CAN'T SAY NO TO YOU | Betty Everett (Archie Ros & Leo Austell & Hilary Johnson), UNI 55122 | 4 |
| 79 | 88 | — | — | FRIEND, LOVER, WOMAN, WIFE | O. C. Smith (Jerry Fuller), Columbia 44859 | 2 |
| 80 | 80 | 88 | 89 | MR. WALKER, IT'S ALL OVER | Billie Jo Spears (Kelso Herston), Capitol 2436 | 4 |
| 81 | 85 | — | — | SOMEDAY MAN | Monkees (Bones Howe), Colgems 66-5004 | 2 |
| 82 | 82 | 100 | — | I WANT TO LOVE YOU BABY | Peggy Scott & Jo Jo Benson (Shelby Singleton), SSS International 769 | 3 |
| ★ 83 | — | — | — | LET ME | Paul Revere & the Raiders Featuring Mark Lindsay, Columbia 4-44854 | 1 |
| 84 | 84 | 94 | 94 | SEVEN YEARS | Impressions (Curtis Mayfield), Curtom 1940 | 4 |
| 85 | 93 | — | — | WELCOME ME LOVE | Brooklyn Bridge (Wes Farrell), Buddah 95 | 2 |
| ★ 86 | — | — | — | WE GOT MORE SOUL | Dyke & the Blazers (Art Barrett), Original Sound 86 | 1 |
| ★ 87 | — | — | — | YOU DON'T NEED ME FOR ANYTHING ANYMORE | Brenda Lee (Mike Berniker), Decca 732491 | 1 |
| 88 | 95 | 98 | 98 | NEVER GONNA LET HIM KNOW | Debbie Taylor (George Kerr & Paul Robinson), GWP 501 | 4 |
| 89 | 86 | 87 | 88 | LOVE IS JUST A FOUR LETTER WORD | Joan Baez (Maynard Solomon), Vanguard 35088 | 4 |
| 90 | 90 | — | — | TRUCKSTOP | Jerry Smith (Paul Cohen), ABC 11116 | 2 |
| 91 | — | — | — | MY WIFE, MY DOG, MY CAT | Bethea the Masked Man & the Agents (BBC), Dynamo 131 | 1 |
| 92 | 92 | — | — | SUNDAY | Moments, Stang 5003 | 2 |
| 93 | — | — | — | WHAT DOES IT TAKE TO WIN YOUR LOVE | Jr. Walker & the All Stars (Fuqua & Bristol), Soul 35062 | 1 |
| 94 | — | — | — | WHY I SING THE BLUES | B. B. King (Bill Szymczyk), BluesWay 61034 | 1 |
| 95 | — | — | — | LET ME LOVE YOU | Ray Charles, ABC 11213 | 1 |
| 96 | — | — | — | THE ISRAELITES | Desmond Dekker & the Aces (A Pyramid Production), Uni 55129 | 1 |
| 97 | 98 | — | — | JUST A LITTLE BIT | Little Milton (Calvin Carter), Checker 1217 | 2 |
| 98 | 99 | — | — | I'M GONNA DO ALL I CAN | Ike & Tina Turner (Ike Turner & Willie Mitchell) | 2 |
| 99 | — | — | — | I THREW IT ALL AWAY | Bob Dylan (Bob Johnston), Columbia 4-44826 | 1 |
| 100 | — | — | — | SAUSALITO | Al Martino (Al De Lory), Capitol 2468 | 1 |

## HOT 100—A TO Z—(Publisher-Licensee)


April Fools, The (Blue Seas/Jac/April, ASCAP) .... 77
Atlantis (Peer Int'l, BMI) .... 8
Aquarius/Let the Sunshine In (United Artists, ASCAP) 1
Bad Moon Rising (Jondora, BMI) .... 33
Black Pearl (Irving, BMI) .... 58
Born to Be Wild (Duchess, BMI) .... 66
Boxer, The (Charing Cross, BMI) .... 7
Brother Love's Travelling Salvation Show (Stonebridge, BMI) .... 41
Buying a Book (Tree, BMI) .... 48
Chokin' Kind (Wilderness Music, BMI) .... 15
Cissy Strut (Marsaint, BMI) .... 46
Composer, The (Jobete, BMI) .... 27
Day Is Done (Pepamar, ASCAP) .... 38
Do Your Thing (Charles Wright & Fred Smith) (Wright-Gersti-Tamerlan, BMI) .... 21
Don't Let Me Down (Maclen, BMI) .... 36
Don't Touch Me (Pamper, BMI) .... 49
Earth Angel (Williams, BMI) .... 42
Everyday Without You Girl (Low-Sal, BMI) .... 52
Friend, Lover, Woman, Wife (B 'n' B, ASCAP) .... 79
Galveston (Ja-Ma Music, ASCAP) .... 31
Gentle on My Mind (Glaser, BMI) .... 76
Get Back (Maclen, BMI) .... 3
Gimme Gimme Good Lovin' (Peanut Butter/Kahoona, BMI) .... 17
Gitarzan (Ahab, BMI) .... 9
Goodbye (Maclen, BMI) .... 14
Grazin' in the Grass (Chisa, BMI) .... 19
Hair (United Artists, ASCAP) .... 2
Happy Heart (Miller, ASCAP) .... 29
Hawaii Five-O (April, ASCAP) .... 4
Heather Honey (Low-Twy, BMI) .... 40
I Can't Say No to You (Screen Gems-Columbia, BMI) 78
I Can't See Myself Leaving You (Fourteenth Hour, BMI) .... 30
I Could Never Lie to You (New Colony, BMI) .... 65
I Don't Want Nobody to Give Me Nothing (Open Up the Door, I'll Get It Myself) (Dynatone, BMI) 24
I'm a Drifter (Detail, BMI) .... 64
I'm Gonna Do All I Can (Barton, BMI) .... 98
In-a-Gadda-Da-Vida (Ten East/Cotillion/Itas, ASCAP) .... 73
In the Bad Bad Old Days (January, BMI) .... 51
In the Ghetto (B 'n' B/Gladys, ASCAP) .... 23
I Shall Be Released (Dwarft, ASCAP) .... 67
I Threw It All Away (Big Sky, ASCAP) .... 99
I Want to Love You Baby (Green Owl, ASCAP) .... 82
I Wanna Testify (Groovesville, BMI) .... 60
Israelites, The (Kenwood, BMI) .... 96
It's Never Too Late (Trousdale, BMI) .... 63
It's Your Thing (Brothers Three, BMI) .... 4
I've Been Hurt (Low-Twy, BMI) .... 54
I've Been Loving You Too Long (East/Time/Curton, BMI) .... 75
Just a Little Bit (Armo, BMI) .... 97
Let Me (Boom, BMI) .... 83
Let Me Love You (Asa/Racer, ASCAP) .... 95
Lodi (Jondora, BMI) .... 55
Love (Can Make You Happy) (Rendezvous/Tobac, BMI) .... 5
Love Is All I Have to Give (Irving, BMI) .... 69
Love Is Just a Four Letter Word (Witmark, ASCAP) 89
Love Theme From Romeo & Juliet (Famous, ASCAP) 47
Marley Purt Drive (Casserole, BMI) .... 72
Medicine Man (Sandbox, ASCAP) .... 59
Mercy (Peanut Butter/Kaskat, BMI) .... 39
More Today Than Yesterday (Spiral, BMI) .... 26
Morning Girl (Acuff-Rose, BMI) .... 35
Mr. Walker, It's All Over (Barmour, BMI) .... 80
My Wife, My Dog, My Cat (Catalogue, Clairbourne, BMI) .... 91
My Way (Don C./Stanka, BMI) .... 32
Never Gonna Let Him Know (Green Light, BMI) .... 88
Nothing But a Heartache (Felsted Music, BMI) .... 45
Oh Happy Day (Kama Rippa/Hawkins, ASCAP) .... 12
One (Dunbar, BMI) .... 53
Only the Strong Survive (Parabut/ Double Diamond/Downstairs, BMI) .... 16
Pinball Wizard (Track, BMI) .... 20
Pretty World (Rodra, BMI) .... 68
Proud Mary (Jondora, BMI) .... 50
River Is Wide, The (Saturday, BMI) .... 37
Rhythm of the Rain (Tamerlane, BMI) .... 71
Sausalito (Blendingwell, ASCAP) .... 100
Seattle (Screen Gems-Columbia, BMI) .... 43
Seven Years (Camad, BMI) .... 84
Someday Man (Irving, BMI) .... 81
Sorry Suzanne (January, BMI) .... 61
Special Delivery (Kaskat/Kahoona, BMI) .... 62
Stand (Daly City, BMI) .... 22
Sunday (Gambi, BMI) .... 92
Sweet Cherry Wine (Big Seven, BMI) .... 18
These Eyes (Dunbar, BMI) .... 10
Time Is Tight (East/Memphis, BMI) .... 13
To Know You Is to Love You (Vogue, BMI) .... 49
Too Busy Thinking About My Baby (Jobete, BMI) .. 25
Truckstop (Papa Joe's Music House, BMI) .... 90
Twenty-Five Miles (Jobete, BMI) .... 28
We Got More Soul (Drive-In/Westward, BMI) .... 86
Welcome Me Love (Pocketful of Tunes, BMI) .... 85
(We've Got) Honey Love (Jobete, BMI) .... 56
What Is a Man? (Jobete, BMI) .... 74
What Does It Take to Win Your Love (Jobete, BMI) 93
Where's the Playground Susie (Ja-Ma, ASCAP) .... 34
Why I Sing the Blues (Pamco/Sounds of Lucille, BMI) .... 94
Will You Be Staying After Sunday (Screen Gems-Columbia, BMI) .... 44
Windmills of Your Mind, The (United Artists, ASCAP) 57
With Pen in Hand (Unart, BMI) .... 70
You Don't Need Me for Anything Anymore (Pincus, ASCAP) .... 87
You've Made Me So Very Happy (Jobete, BMI) .... 11


## BUBBLING UNDER THE HOT 100

101. BABY DRIVER.... Simon & Garfunkel, Columbia 44785
102. TURN AROUND AND LOVE YOU.... Rita Coolidge, Pepper 443
103. IVORY.... Bob Seeger System, Capitol 2480
104. LEANIN' ON YOU.... Joe South, Capitol 2491
105. HURT SO BAD.... Lettermen, Capitol 2428
106. HERE WE GO AGAIN.... Nancy Sinatra, Reprise 0821
107. CHANGE YOUR MIND.... Jay & the Techniques, Smash 2217
108. BABY I LOVE YOU.... Andy Kim, Steed 1031
109. LOVE MAN.... Otis Redding, Atco 6677
110. I WANT TO TAKE YOU HIGHER.... Sly & the Family Stone, Epic 5-10450
111. RUNNING BEAR.... Sonny James, Capitol 2486
112. IT DIDN'T EVEN BRING ME DOWN.... Sir Douglas Quintet, Smash 2222
113. SEE.... Rascals, Atlantic 2634
114. MINOTAUR.... Dick Hyman & His Electric Electics, Command 5-4126
115. BUT IT'S ALL RIGHT.... J. J. Jackson, Warner Bros.-7 Arts 7276
116. IMAGINE THE SWAN.... Zombies, Date 2-1645
117. BIBLE SALESMAN.... Billy Vera, Atlantic 2628
118. NEVER COMES THE DAY.... Moody Blues, Deram 85044
119. REAL TRUE LOVIN'.... Steve & Eydie, RCA Victor 74-0123
120. BROWN ARMS IN HOUSTON.... Orpheus, MGM 14022
121. LIFE'S A DANCE.... Alexandro Karazov, Jamie 1372
122. SOME KINDA WONDERFUL.... Thee Prophets, Kapp 997
123. I NEED YOU NOW.... Ronnie Dove, Diamond 260
124. GOOD MORNING STARSHINE.... Strawberry Alarm Clock, Uni 55125
125. DENVER.... Ronnie Milsap, Scepter 246
126. ONCE AGAIN SHE'S ALL ALONE.... First Edition, Reprise 0822
127. ROSE GARDEN.... Dobie Gray, White Whale 300
128. EASY TO BE HARD.... Jennifer, Parrot 336
129. DARKNESS DARKNESS.... Youngbloods, RCA Victor 74-0129
130. ME & MR. HOHNER.... Bobby Darin, Direction 351
131. A-HA-HA DO YOUR THING.... Hit Parade, RCA Victor 47-9737

Compiled from national retail sales and radio station airplay by the Music Popularity Dept. of Record Market Research, Billboard.

# Billboard HOT 100

**FOR WEEK ENDING MAY 24, 1969**

★ STAR PERFORMER—Sides registering greatest proportionate upward progress this week.

(RIAA) Record Industry Association of America seal of certification as million selling single.

| This Week | Last Week | 2 Wks. Ago | 3 Wks. Ago | TITLE, Artist (Producer), Label & Number | Weeks On Chart |
|---|---|---|---|---|---|
| 1 | 3 | 10 | — | **GET BACK** — Beatles (George Martin), Apple 2490 | 3 |
| 2 | 1 | 1 | 1 | **AQUARIUS/LET THE SUNSHINE IN** — Fifth Dimension (Bones Howe), Soul City 772 | 12 |
| 3 | 5 | 11 | 15 | **LOVE (Can Make You Happy)** — Mercy (Jamie-Guyden), Sundi 6811 | 7 |
| 4 | 2 | 2 | 3 | **HAIR** — Cowsills (Bill & Bob Cowsill), MGM 14026 | 11 |
| ★5 | 12 | 18 | 40 | **OH HAPPY DAY** — Edwin Hawkins Singers (La Mont Bench), Pavillion 20001 | 5 |
| 6 | 4 | 3 | 2 | **IT'S YOUR THING** — Isley Brothers (R. Isley-O. Isley-R. Isley), T Neck 901 | 11 |
| 7 | 8 | 9 | 19 | **ATLANTIS** — Donovan (Mickie Most), Epic 5-10434 | 8 |
| 8 | 7 | 8 | 9 | **THE BOXER** — Simon & Garfunkel (Simon & Garfunkel & Hales), Columbia 4-44785 | 8 |
| 9 | 9 | 17 | 20 | **GITARZAN** — Ray Stevens (Fred Foster, Ray Stevens & Jim Malloy), Monument 1131 | 8 |
| 10 | 10 | 13 | 14 | **THESE EYES** — Guess Who (Nimbus 9), RCA 74-0102 | 8 |
| 11 | 6 | 4 | 8 | **HAWAII FIVE-O** — The Ventures (Joe Saraceno), Liberty 56068 | 12 |
| 12 | 19 | 23 | 35 | **GRAZIN' IN THE GRASS** — Friends of Distinction (John Florez), RCA 74-0207 | 8 |
| 13 | 15 | 15 | 18 | **CHOKIN' KIND** — Joe Simon (J. R. Enterprises), SS7 2628 | 10 |
| 14 | 14 | 24 | 27 | **GOODBYE** — Mary Hopkin (Paul McCartney), Apple 1806 | 6 |
| 15 | 13 | 6 | 12 | **TIME IS TIGHT** — Booker T. and the M.G.'s (B. T. Jones), Stax 0028 | 11 |
| ★16 | 25 | 29 | 54 | **TOO BUSY THINKING ABOUT MY BABY** — Marvin Gaye (Norman Whitfield), Tamla 54181 | 4 |
| 17 | 23 | 41 | 79 | **IN THE GHETTO** — Elvis Presley, RCA Victor 47-9741 | 4 |
| ★18 | 47 | 71 | — | **LOVE THEME FROM ROMEO & JULIET** — Henry Mancini & Ork. (Joe Reisman), RCA Victor 74-0131 | 3 |
| 19 | 20 | 25 | 25 | **PINBALL WIZARD** — The Who (Baron Lambert), Decca 732465 | 8 |
| ★20 | 33 | 54 | 80 | **BAD MOON RISING** — Creedence Clearwater Revival (John Fogerty), Fantasy 622 | 4 |
| 21 | 26 | 31 | 37 | **MORE TODAY THAN YESTERDAY** — Spiral Staircase (Sonny Knight), Columbia 4-44741 | 8 |
| 22 | 11 | 5 | 4 | **YOU'VE MADE ME SO VERY HAPPY** — Blood, Sweat & Tears (James William Guerico), Columbia 4-44776 | 13 |
| 23 | 29 | 33 | 38 | **HAPPY HEART** — Andy Williams (Jerry Fuller), Columbia 4-44818 | 6 |
| 24 | 46 | 47 | 55 | **CISSY STRUT** — Meters (Marshall E. Schorn & Allen Toussaint), Josie 1005 | 7 |
| 25 | 22 | 35 | 36 | **STAND** — Sly & the Family Stone (Sly Stone), Epic 5-10450 | 7 |
| 26 | 17 | 12 | 12 | **GIMME GIMME GOOD LOVIN'** — Crazy Elephant (Kasenetz-Katz Assoc.), Bell 763 | 13 |
| 27 | 18 | 7 | 7 | **SWEET CHERRY WINE** — Tommy James & Shondells (Tommy James), Roulette 7039 | 10 |
| 28 | 30 | 30 | 33 | **I CAN'T SEE MYSELF LEAVING YOU** — Aretha Franklin (Jerry Wexler), Atlantic 2619 | 6 |
| ★29 | 38 | 50 | 66 | **DAY IS DONE** — Peter, Paul & Mary (Phil Ramone), Warner Bros.-Seven Arts 7279 | 5 |
| 30 | 35 | 36 | 51 | **MORNING GIRL** — Neon Philharmonic (T. Saussy, Don Gant & B. Mc-Cluskey), Warner Bros.-Seven Arts 7261 | 4 |
| 31 | 27 | 28 | 31 | **THE COMPOSER** — Diana Ross & the Supremes (Smokey), Motown 1146 | 6 |
| ★32 | 40 | 51 | 62 | **HEATHER HONEY** — Tommy Roe (Steve Barri), ABC 11211 | 5 |
| 33 | 34 | 44 | 59 | **WHERE'S THE PLAYGROUND SUSIE** — Glen Campbell (Al De Lory), Capitol 2494 | 4 |
| ★34 | 45 | 46 | 50 | **NOTHING BUT A HEARTACHE** — Flirtations (Wayne Bickerton), Deram 85038 | 12 |
| 35 | 36 | 40 | — | **DON'T LET ME DOWN** — Beatles (George Martin), Apple 2490 | 3 |
| 36 | 37 | 42 | 43 | **THE RIVER IS WIDE** — The Grassroots (Steve Barri), Dunhill 4187 | 7 |
| 37 | 21 | 16 | 16 | **DO YOUR THING** — Watts 103rd Street Band, Warner Bros.-Seven Arts 7250 | 17 |
| 38 | 24 | 20 | 21 | **I DON'T WANT NOBODY TO GIVE ME NOTHING (Open Up the Door, I'll Get It Myself)** — James Brown (James Brown), King 6224 | 8 |
| 39 | 16 | 14 | 5 | **ONLY THE STRONG SURVIVE** — Jerry Butler (Gamble & Huff), Mercury 72898 | 13 |
| ★40 | 57 | 67 | 99 | **THE WINDMILLS OF YOUR MIND** — Dusty Springfield (Jerry Wexler), Atlantic 2623 | 4 |
| ★41 | 53 | 58 | 84 | **ONE** — Three Dog Night (Gabriel Mekler), Dunhill 4191 | 5 |
| 42 | 43 | 43 | 44 | **SEATTLE** — Perry Como (Chet Atkins & Andy Wiswell), RCA 47-9722 | 5 |
| 43 | — | — | — | **DON'T LET THE JONESES GET YOU DOWN** — Temptations (Norman Whitfield), Gordy 7086 | 1 |
| ★44 | 58 | 75 | — | **BLACK PEARL** — Sonny Charles with the Checkmates Ltd. (Phil Spector), A&M 1053 | 3 |
| 45 | 52 | 63 | 74 | **EVERYDAY WITH YOU GIRL** — Classics IV (Buddy Blue), Imperial 66378 | 5 |
| 46 | 50 | 53 | 77 | **PROUD MARY** — Solomon Burke (Solomon Burke-Tamiko Jones), Bell 783 | 4 |
| 47 | 48 | 48 | 53 | **BUYING A BOOK** — Joe Tex (Buddy Killen), Dial 4090 | 5 |
| 48 | 54 | 60 | 71 | **I'VE BEEN HURT** — Bill Deal & the Rhondells (Jerry Ross), Heritage 812 | 6 |
| 49 | 62 | 89 | — | **SPECIAL DELIVERY** — 1910 Fruitgum Co. (Kasenetz-Katz Associates), Buddah 114 | 3 |
| 50 | 59 | 66 | 83 | **MEDICINE MAN** — Buchanan Brothers (Cashman, Pistilli & West), Event, 3302 | 5 |
| 51 | 42 | 45 | 47 | **EARTH ANGEL** — Vogues (Dick Glasser), Reprise 0820 | 6 |
| 52 | 55 | 59 | 78 | **LODI** — Creedence Clearwater Revival (John Fogerty), Fantasy 622 | 4 |
| ★53 | 83 | — | — | **LET ME** — Paul Revere & the Raiders Featuring Mark Lindsay (Mark Lindsay), Columbia 4-44854 | 2 |
| 54 | 64 | 64 | 67 | **I'M A DRIFTER** — Bobby Goldsboro (Bob Montgomery & Bobby Goldsboro), United Artists 50525 | 6 |
| 55 | 60 | 73 | — | **I WANNA TESTIFY** — Johnnie Taylor (Don Davis), Stax 0033 | 3 |
| 56 | 77 | — | — | **THE APRIL FOOLS** — Dionne Warwick (Burt Bacharach, Hal David), Scepter 12249 | 2 |
| 57 | 65 | 74 | 97 | **I COULD NEVER LIE TO YOU** — New Colony Six, Mercury 72920 | 4 |
| 58 | 61 | 61 | 69 | **SORRY SUZANNE** — Hollies (Ron Richards), Epic 5-10454 | 6 |
| 59 | 63 | 76 | — | **IT'S NEVER TOO LATE** — Steppenwolf (Gabriel Mekler), Dunhill 4192 | 3 |
| 60 | 79 | 88 | — | **FRIEND, LOVER, WOMAN, WIFE** — O. C. Smith (Jerry Fuller), Columbia 44859 | 3 |
| 61 | — | — | — | **SEE** — Rascals (Rascals & Arif Mardin), Atlantic 2634 | 1 |
| 62 | 85 | 93 | — | **WELCOME ME LOVE** — Brooklyn Bridge (Wes Farrell), Buddah 95 | 3 |
| 63 | 74 | 94 | — | **WHAT IS A MAN?** — Four Tops (Fuqua), Motown 1147 | 3 |
| 64 | 70 | 81 | 89 | **WITH PEN IN HAND** — Vikki Carr (Dave Pell & Rob Bledsoe), Liberty 56092 | 4 |
| 65 | 66 | 100 | — | **BORN TO BE WILD** — Wilson Pickett (Rick Hall), Atlantic 2c | 3 |
| 66 | 68 | 83 | 85 | **PRETTY WORLD** — Sergio Mendes & Brasil '66 (Sergio Mendes & Herb Alpert), A&M 1049 | 4 |
| 67 | 69 | 76 | — | **I SHALL BE RELEASED** — Box Tops (Chips Moman & Tommy Cogbill), Mala 12038 | 5 |
| 68 | 56 | 65 | 70 | **(We've Got) HONEY LOVE** — Martha Reeves & the Vandellas (Richard Morris), Gordy 7085 | 6 |
| 69 | 75 | 91 | 95 | **I'VE BEEN LOVING YOU TOO LONG** — Ike & Tina Turner (Bob Krasnow & Tina Turner), Blue Thumb 101 | 5 |
| 70 | 72 | 79 | 96 | **MARLEY PURT DRIVE** — Jose Feliciano (Rick Jarrard), RCA Victor 47-9739 | 4 |
| 71 | 71 | 72 | 81 | **RHYTHM OF THE RAIN** — Gary Lewis and the Playboys (Snuff Garrett), Liberty 56093 | 8 |
| 72 | 73 | — | — | **IN-A-GADDA-DA-VIDA** — Iron Butterfly (Jim Hilton), Atco 6606 | 14 |
| ★73 | 86 | — | — | **WE GOT MORE SOUL** — Dyke & the Blazers (Art Barrett), Original Sound 86 | 2 |
| ★74 | 96 | — | — | **THE ISRAELITES** — Desmond Dekker & the Aces (A Pyramid Production), Uni 55129 | 2 |
| 75 | — | — | — | **SO I CAN LOVE YOU** — Emotions (Volt) | 1 |
| 76 | 76 | 77 | — | **GENTLE ON MY MIND** — Aretha Franklin (Jerry Wexler), Atlantic 2619 | 3 |
| 77 | — | — | — | **LOVE MAN** — Otis Redding (Steve Cropper), Atco 6677 | 1 |
| ★78 | 93 | — | — | **WHAT DOES IT TAKE TO WIN YOUR LOVE** — Jr. Walker and the All Stars (Fuqua & Bristol), Soul 35062 | 2 |
| 79 | — | — | — | **LOVE ME TONIGHT** — Tom Jones (Peter Sullivan), Parrot 40038 | 1 |
| 80 | — | — | — | **COLOR HIM FATHER** — Winstons (Don Carroll), Metromedia 117 | 1 |
| 81 | 82 | 82 | 100 | **I WANT TO LOVE YOU BABY** — Peggy Scott & Jo Jo Benson (Shelby Singleton), SSS International 769 | 4 |
| 82 | — | — | — | **MEDLEY: CAN SING A RAINBOW/LOVE IS BLUE** — Dells (Bobby Miller), Cadet 5641 | 1 |
| ★83 | — | — | — | **GOOD MORNING STARSHINE** — Oliver (Bob Crewe), Jubilee 5659 | 1 |
| ★84 | 94 | — | — | **WHY I SING THE BLUES** — B. B. King (Bill Szymczyk), BluesWay 61034 | 2 |
| 85 | 90 | 90 | — | **TRUCKSTOP** — Jerry Smith (Paul Cohen), ABC 11116 | 3 |
| 86 | 87 | — | — | **YOU DON'T NEED ME FOR ANYTHING ANYMORE** — Brenda Lee (Mike Berniker), Decca 732491 | 2 |
| ★87 | — | — | — | **GOOD MORNING STARSHINE** — Strawberry Alarm Clock (Julius Zababak), Uni 55125 | 1 |
| 88 | 88 | 95 | 98 | **NEVER GONNA LET HIM KNOW** — Debbie Taylor (George Kerr & Paul Robinson), GWP 501 | 5 |
| ★89 | — | — | — | **I WANT TO TAKE YOU HIGHER** — Sly & the Family Stone (Sly Stone), Epic 10450 | 1 |
| 90 | 92 | 92 | — | **SUNDAY** — Lettermen, Stang 5003 | 3 |
| 91 | 91 | — | — | **MY WIFE, MY DOG, MY CAT** — Bethea the Masked Man & the Agents (BBC), Dynamo 131 | 2 |
| 92 | — | 99 | — | **I THREW IT ALL AWAY** — Bob Dylan (Bob Johnston), Columbia 4-44826 | 1 |
| 93 | — | — | — | **LET'S DANCE** — Ola & the Janglers (Gunnar Bergstrom), GNP Crescendo 423 | 1 |
| 94 | 95 | — | — | **LET ME LOVE YOU** — Ray Charles, ABC 11213 | 2 |
| 95 | — | — | — | **BABY, I LOVE YOU** — Andy Kim (Jeff Barry), Steed 1031 | 1 |
| 96 | — | — | — | **BUT IT'S ALRIGHT** — J. J. Jackson (Lew Futterman), Warner Bros.-Seven Arts 7276 | 1 |
| 97 | — | — | — | **TOO EXPERIENCED** — Eddie Lovette (L. Dixon), Steady 124 | 1 |
| 98 | — | — | — | **HERE WE GO AGAIN** — Nancy Sinatra (Billy Strange), Reprise 0821 | 1 |
| 99 | 100 | — | — | **SAUSALITO** — Al Martino (Al De Lory), Capitol 2468 | 2 |
| 100 | — | — | — | **MEMPHIS UNDERGROUND** — Herbie Mann (Tom Dowd), Atlantic 2621 | 1 |

## HOT 100—A TO Z—(Publisher-Licensee)

April Fools, The (Blue Seas/Jac/April, ASCAP) .... 56
Atlantis (Peer Int'l, BMI) .... 7
Aquarius/Let the Sunshine In (United Artists, ASCAP) .... 2
Baby, I Love You (Trio/Mother Bertha, BMI) .... 95
Bad Moon Rising (Jondora, BMI) .... 20
Black Pearl (Irving, BMI) .... 44
Born to Be Wild (Duchess, BMI) .... 65
Boxer, The (Charing Cross, ASCAP) .... 8
Buying a Book (Tree, BMI) .... 47
But It's Alright (Pamelarosa, BMI) .... 96
Chokin' Kind (Wilderness Music, BMI) .... 13
Cissy Strut (Brothers Three, BMI) .... 24
Color Him Father (Holly Bee, BMI) .... 80
Composer, The (Jobete, BMI) .... 31
Day Is Done (Pepamar, ASCAP) .... 29
Do Your Thing (Charles Wright & Fred Smith) (Wright-Gersti-Tamerlan, BMI) .... 37
Don't Let Me Down (Maclen, BMI) .... 35
Don't Let the Joneses Get You Down (Jobete, BMI) .... 43
Earth Angel (Williams, BMI) .... 51
Everyday Without You Girl (Low-Sal, BMI) .... 45
Friend, Lover, Woman, Wife (B 'n' B, ASCAP) .... 60
Gentle On My Mind (Glaser, BMI) .... 76
Get Back (Maclen, BMI) .... 1
Gimme Gimme Good Lovin' (Peanut Butter/Kahoona, ASCAP) .... 26
Gitarzan (Ahab, BMI) .... 9
Goodbye (Maclen, BMI) .... 14
Good Morning Starshine (Oliver) (United Artists, ASCAP) .... 83
Good Morning Starshine (Strawberry Alarm Clock) (United Artists, ASCAP) .... 87
Grazin' in the Grass (Chisa, BMI) .... 12
Hair (United Artists, ASCAP) .... 4
Happy Heart (Miller, ASCAP) .... 23
Hawaii Five-O (April, ASCAP) .... 11
Heather Honey (Low-Twy, BMI) .... 32

Here We Go Again (Dirk, BMI) .... 98
I Can't See Myself Leaving You (Fourteenth Hour, BMI) .... 28
I Could Never Lie to You (New Colony/T.M., BMI) .... 57
I Don't Want Nobody to Give Me Nothing (Open Up the Door, I'll Get It Myself) (Dynatone, BMI) .... 38
I'm a Drifter (Detail, BMI) .... 54
In-A-Gadda-Da-Vida (Ten East/Cotillian/Itas, ASCAP) .... 72
In the Ghetto (B 'n' B/Gladys, ASCAP) .... 17
I Shall Be Released (Dwarf, ASCAP) .... 67
I Threw It All Away (Big Sky, ASCAP) .... 92
I Want to Love You Baby (Jobete, BMI) .... 81
I Want to Take You Higher (Daly City, BMI) .... 89
I Wanna Testify (Groovesville, BMI) .... 55
I've Been Hurt (Kenwood, BMI) .... 48
I've Been Loving You Too Long (East/Time/Curton, BMI) .... 69
Israelites, The (Trousdale, BMI) .... 74
It's Never Too Late (January, BMI) .... 59
It's Your Thing (Brothers Three, BMI) .... 6
Let Me (Boom, BMI) .... 53
Let Me Love You (Jax/Racer, ASCAP) .... 94
Let's Dance (Tamerlane/Rondell, ASCAP) .... 93
Lodi (Jondora, BMI) .... 52
Love (Can Make You Happy) (Rendezvous, BMI) .... 3
Love Me Tonight (Duchess, BMI) .... 79
Love Theme from Romeo & Juliet (Famous, ASCAP) .... 18
Marley Purt Drive (Casserole, BMI) .... 70
Medicine Man (Sandbox, ASCAP) .... 50
Medley: Can Sing a Rainbow/Love Is Blue (Mark VII/Croma, ASCAP) .... 82
Memphis Underground (Mann, BMI) .... 100
More Today Than Yesterday (Jobete, BMI) .... 21
Morning Girl (Acuff-Rose, BMI) .... 30
My Wife, My Dog, My Cat (Catalogue/Pincus, ASCAP) .... 91

Never Gonna Let Him Know (Green Light, BMI) .... 88
Nothing But a Heartache (Felsted Music, BMI) .... 34
Oh Happy Day (Kama Rippa/Hawkins, ASCAP) .... 5
One (Dunbar, BMI) .... 41
Only the Strong Survive (Parabut/Double Diamond/Downstairs, BMI) .... 39
Pinball Wizard (Track, BMI) .... 19
Pretty World (Rodra, BMI) .... 66
Proud Mary (Jondora, BMI) .... 46
River Is Wide, The (Saturday, BMI) .... 36
Rhythm of the Rain (Tamerlane, BMI) .... 71
Sausalito (Blendingwell, ASCAP) .... 99
Seattle (Screen Gems-Columbia, BMI) .... 42
See (Slacsar, ASCAP) .... 61
So I Can Love You (Pervis/Staples, BMI) .... 75
Sorry Suzanne (January, BMI) .... 58
Special Delivery (Kaskat/Kahoona, BMI) .... 49
Stand (Daly City, BMI) .... 25
Sunday (Gambi, BMI) .... 90
Sweet Cherry Wine (Big Seven, BMI) .... 27
These Eyes (East/Memphis, BMI) .... 10
Time Is Tight (East/Memphis, BMI) .... 15
Too Busy Thinking About My Baby (Jobete, BMI) .... 16
Too Experienced (Vee Vee/Jamerica, BMI) .... 97
Truckstop (Papa Joe's Music House, BMI) .... 85
We Got More Soul (Drive-In/Westward, BMI) .... 73
Welcome Me Love (Pocketful of Tunes, BMI) .... 62
(We've Got) Honey Love (Jobete, BMI) .... 68
What Does It Take to Win Your Love (Jobete, BMI) .... 78
What Is a Man? (Jobete, BMI) .... 63
Where's the Playground Susie (Ja-Ma, ASCAP) .... 33
Why I Sing the Blues (Pamco/Sounds of Lucille, BMI) .... 84
Windmills of Your Mind, The (United Artists, ASCAP) .... 40
With Pen in Hand (Unart, BMI) .... 64
You Don't Need Me for Anything Anymore (Pincus, ASCAP) .... 86
You've Made Me So Very Happy (Jobete, BMI) .... 22

## BUBBLING UNDER THE HOT 100

101. LISTEN TO THE BAND .................. Monkees, Colgems 66-5004
102. HURT SO BAD .......................... Lettermen, Capitol 2428
103. IVORY ................................ Bob Seeger System, Capitol 2480
104. LEANIN' ON YOU ....................... Joe South, Capitol 2491
105. TOMORROW, TOMORROW .................. Bee Gees, Atco 6682
106. BABY DRIVER ......................... Simon & Garfunkel, Columbia 44785
107. I NEED YOU NOW ...................... Ronnie Dove, Diamond 260
108. MINOTAUR ............................ Dick Hyman & His Electric Eclectics, Command 4126
109. RUNNING BEAR ........................ Sonny James, Capitol 2486
110. IT DIDN'T EVEN BRING ME DOWN ........ Sir Douglas Quintet, Smash 2227
111. SOMEDAY MAN ......................... Monkees, Colgems 66-5004
112. BROWN ARMS IN HOUSTON ............... Orpheus, MGM 14022
113. I'M GONNA DO ALL I CAN .............. Ike & Tina Turner, Minit 32060
114. BIBLE SALESMAN ...................... Billy Vera, Atlantic 2608
115. NEVER COMES THE DAY ................. Moody Blues, Deram 85044
116. IMAGINE THE SWAN .................... Zombies, Date 1644
117. MR. WALKER, IT'S ALL OVER ........... Billie Jo Spears, Capitol 2436
118. WITHOUT HER ......................... Herb Alpert, A&M 1065
119. SOME KIND-A WONDERFUL ............... The Prophets, Kapp 997
120. LIFE'S A DANCE ...................... Alexander Karazov, Jamie 1372
121. FEELIN' ALRIGHT .................... Joe Cocker, A&M 1063
122. MOODY WOMAN ......................... Jerry Butler, Mercury 72929
123. DENVER .............................. Ronnie Milsap, Scepter 246
124. DARKNESS DARKNESS ................... Youngbloods, RCA Victor 74-0129
125. ROSE GARDEN ......................... Dobie Gray, White Whale 300
126. SOME VELVET MORNING ................. Vanilla Fudge, Atco 6679
127. SINCERELY ........................... Paul Anka, RCA Victor 74-0164
128. JOHNNY B. GOODE .................... Buck Owens & His Buckaroos, Capitol 2485
129. ME & MR. HOHNER .................... Bobby Darin, Direction 351
130. SON OF A TRAVELLING MAN ............. Ed Ames, RCA Victor 74-0156
131. I CAN'T QUIT HER ................... Arbors, Date 1645
132. HUSHAPPYE ........................... Jay & the Americans, United Artists 50535
133. CAJUN BABY .......................... Hank Williams Jr., MGM 14040
134. MY PLEDGE OF LOVE ................... Joe Jeffrey Group, Wand 11200
135. EVERYDAY LIVIN' DAYS ................ Merrilee Rush, AGP 112

Compiled from national retail sales and radio station airplay by the Music Popularity Dept. of Record Market Research, Billboard.

# Billboard HOT 100

FOR WEEK ENDING MAY 31, 1969

★ STAR PERFORMER—Sides registering greatest proportionate upward progress this week.

Record Industry Association of America seal of certification as million selling single.

| This Week | 1 Wk. Ago | 2 Wks. Ago | 3 Wks. Ago | TITLE | Artist (Producer), Label & Number | Weeks On Chart |
|---|---|---|---|---|---|---|
| 1 | 1 | 3 | 10 | GET BACK | Beatles (George Martin), Apple 2490 | 4 |
| 2 | 3 | 5 | 11 | LOVE (Can Make You Happy) | Mercy (Jamie-Guyden), Sundi 6811 | 8 |
| 3 | 2 | 1 | 1 | AQUARIUS/LET THE SUNSHINE IN | Fifth Dimension (Bones Howe), Soul City 772 | 13 |
| 4 | 5 | 12 | 18 | OH HAPPY DAY | Edwin Hawkins Singers (La Mont Bench), Pavillion 20001 | 6 |
| 5 | 4 | 2 | 2 | HAIR | Cowsills (Bill & Bob Cowsill), MGM 14026 | 12 |
| ★6 | 10 | 10 | 13 | THESE EYES | Guess Who (Nimbus 9), RCA 74-0102 | 9 |
| 7 | 7 | 8 | 9 | ATLANTIS | Donovan (Mickie Most), Epic 5-10434 | 9 |
| 8 | 9 | 9 | 17 | GITARZAN | Ray Stevens (Fred Foster, Ray Stevens & Jim Malloy), Monument 1131 | 9 |
| ★9 | 17 | 23 | 41 | IN THE GHETTO | Elvis Presley, RCA Victor 47-9741 | 5 |
| 10 | 12 | 19 | 23 | GRAZIN' IN THE GRASS | Friends of Distinction (John Florez), RCA 74-0207 | 9 |
| ★11 | 18 | 47 | 71 | LOVE THEME FROM ROMEO & JULIET | Henry Mancini & Ork. (Joe Reisman), RCA Victor 74-0131 | 4 |
| 12 | 8 | 7 | 8 | THE BOXER | Simon & Garfunkel (Simon & Garfunkel & Hales), Columbia 4-44785 | 8 |
| 13 | 14 | 14 | 24 | GOODBYE | Mary Hopkin (Paul McCartney), Apple 1806 | 7 |
| ★14 | 20 | 33 | 54 | BAD MOON RISING | Creedence Clearwater Revival (John Fogerty), Fantasy 622 | 5 |
| 15 | 16 | 25 | 29 | TOO BUSY THINKING ABOUT MY BABY | Marvin Gaye (Norman Whitfield), Tamla 54181 | 6 |
| 16 | 6 | 4 | 3 | IT'S YOUR THING | Isley Brothers (R. Isley-O. Isley-R. Isley), T Neck 901 | 12 |
| 17 | 11 | 6 | 4 | HAWAII FIVE-O | The Ventures (Joe Saraceno), Liberty 56068 | 13 |
| 18 | 15 | 13 | 6 | TIME IS TIGHT | Booker T. & the M.G.'s (B. T. Jones), Stax 0028 | 12 |
| ★19 | 21 | 26 | 31 | MORE TODAY THAN YESTERDAY | Spiral Staircase (Sonny Knight), Columbia 4-44741 | 9 |
| 20 | 19 | 20 | 25 | PINBALL WIZARD | The Who (Baron Lambert), Decca 732465 | 9 |
| ★21 | 30 | 35 | 36 | MORNING GIRL | Neon Philharmonic (T. Saussy, Don Gant & B. McCluskey), Warner Bros.-Seven Arts 7261 | 9 |
| 22 | 23 | 29 | 33 | HAPPY HEART | Andy Williams (Jerry Fuller), Columbia 4-44818 | 8 |
| ★23 | 41 | 53 | 58 | ONE | Three Dog Night (Gabriel Mekler), Dunhill 4191 | 5 |
| 24 | 24 | 46 | 47 | CISSY STRUT | Meters (Marshall E. Schorn & Allen Toussaint), Josie 1005 | 8 |
| 25 | 13 | 15 | 15 | CHOKIN' KIND | Joe Simon (J. R. Enterprises), SS7 2628 | 11 |
| ★26 | 33 | 34 | 44 | WHERE'S THE PLAYGROUND SUSIE | Glen Campbell (Al De Lory), Capitol 2494 | 5 |
| 27 | 29 | 38 | 50 | DAY IS DONE | Peter, Paul & Mary (Phil Ramone), Warner Bros.-Seven Arts 7279 | 6 |
| 28 | 28 | 30 | 30 | I CAN'T SEE MYSELF LEAVING YOU | Aretha Franklin (Jerry Wexler), Atlantic 2619 | 7 |
| 29 | 32 | 40 | 51 | HEATHER HONEY | Tommy Roe (Steve Barri), ABC 11211 | 6 |
| ★30 | 45 | 52 | 63 | EVERYDAY WITH YOU GIRL | Classics IV (Buddy Blue), Imperial 66378 | 2 |
| ★31 | 36 | 37 | 42 | THE RIVER IS WIDE | The Grassroots (Steve Barri), Dunhill 4187 | 8 |
| ★32 | 44 | 58 | 75 | BLACK PEARL | Sonny Charles with the Checkmates Ltd. (Phil Spector), A&M 1053 | 4 |
| 33 | 25 | 22 | 35 | STAND | Sly & the Family Stone (Sly Stone), Epic 5-10450 | 8 |
| 34 | 34 | 45 | 46 | NOTHING BUT A HEARTACHE | Flirtations (Wayne Bickerton), Deram 85038 | 13 |
| ★35 | 43 | — | — | DON'T LET THE JONESES GET YOU DOWN | Temptations (Norman Whitfield), Gordy 7086 | 2 |
| ★36 | 48 | 54 | 60 | I'VE BEEN HURT | Bill Deal & the Rhondells (Jerry Ross), Heritage 812 | 7 |
| 37 | 40 | 57 | 67 | THE WINDMILLS OF YOUR MIND | Dusty Springfield (Jerry Wexler), Atlantic 2623 | 5 |
| 38 | 42 | 43 | 43 | SEATTLE | Perry Como (Chet Atkins & Andy Wiswell), RCA 47-9722 | 8 |
| ★39 | 50 | 59 | 66 | MEDICINE MAN | Buchanan Brothers (Cashman, Pistilli & West), Event, 3302 | 5 |
| ★40 | 55 | 60 | 73 | I WANNA TESTIFY | Johnnie Taylor (Don Davis), Stax 0033 | 4 |
| ★41 | 74 | 96 | — | THE ISRAELITES | Desmond Dekker & the Aces (A Pyramid Production), Uni 55129 | 3 |
| 42 | 35 | 36 | 40 | DON'T LET ME DOWN | Beatles (George Martin), Apple 2490 | 4 |
| ★43 | 61 | — | — | SEE | Rascals (Rascals & Arif Mardin), Atlantic 2634 | 2 |
| ★44 | 49 | 62 | 89 | SPECIAL DELIVERY | 1910 Fruitgum Co. (Kasenetz-Katz Associates), Buddah 114 | 4 |
| ★45 | 79 | — | — | LOVE ME TONIGHT | Tom Jones (Peter Sullivan), Parrot 40038 | 2 |
| 46 | 46 | 50 | 53 | PROUD MARY | Solomon Burke (Solomon Burke-Tamiko Jones), Bell 783 | 5 |
| ★47 | 56 | 77 | — | THE APRIL FOOLS | Dionne Warwick (Burt Bacharach, Hal David), Scepter 12249 | 3 |
| 48 | 53 | 83 | — | LET ME | Paul Revere & the Raiders Featuring Mark Lindsay, Columbia 4-44854 | 3 |
| ★49 | 62 | 85 | 93 | WELCOME ME LOVE | Brooklyn Bridge (Wes Farrell), Buddah 95 | 4 |
| 50 | 54 | 64 | 64 | I'M A DRIFTER | Bobby Goldsboro (Bob Montgomery & Bobby Goldsboro), United Artists 50525 | 7 |
| 51 | 59 | 63 | 76 | IT'S NEVER TOO LATE | Steppenwolf (Gabriel Mekler), Dunhill 4192 | 4 |
| 52 | 57 | 65 | 74 | I COULD NEVER LIE TO YOU | New Colony Six, Mercury 72920 | 5 |
| ★53 | 63 | 74 | 94 | WHAT IS A MAN? | Four Tops (Fuqua), Motown 1147 | 4 |
| 54 | 60 | 79 | 88 | FRIEND, LOVER, WOMAN, WIFE | O. C. Smith (Jerry Fuller), Columbia 44859 | 4 |
| 55 | 64 | 70 | 81 | WITH PEN IN HAND | Vikki Carr (Dave Pell & Rob Bledsoe), Liberty 56092 | 5 |
| 56 | 58 | 61 | 61 | SORRY SUZANNE | Hollies (Ron Richards), Epic 5-10454 | 7 |
| ★57 | 83 | — | — | GOOD MORNING STARSHINE | Oliver (Bob Crewe), Jubilee 5659 | 2 |
| 58 | 47 | 48 | 48 | BUYING A BOOK | Joe Tex (Buddy Killen), Dial 4090 | 8 |
| ★59 | 78 | 93 | — | WHAT DOES IT TAKE TO WIN YOUR LOVE | Jr. Walker & the All Stars (Fuqua & Bristol), Soul 35062 | 3 |
| ★60 | — | — | — | TOMORROW TOMORROW | Bee Gees (Robert Stigwood & the Bee Gees) Atco 6682 | 1 |
| ★61 | — | — | — | NO MATTER WHAT SIGN YOU ARE | Diana Ross & the Supremes (B. Gordy Jr. & H. Cosby, Motown 1148 | 1 |
| 62 | 66 | 68 | 83 | PRETTY WORLD | Sergio Mendes & Brasil '66 (Sergio Mendes & Herb Alpert), A&M 1049 | 5 |
| ★63 | — | — | — | I TURNED YOU ON | Isley Brothers (R. Isley-O. Isley-R. Isley), T-Neck 902 | 1 |
| 64 | 65 | 66 | 100 | BORN TO BE WILD | Wilson Pickett (Rick Hall), Atlantic 2[illegible] | 4 |
| ★65 | 71 | 71 | 72 | RHYTHM OF THE RAIN | Gary Lewis & the Playboys (Snuff Garrett), Liberty 56093 | 9 |
| ★66 | 82 | — | — | MEDLEY: CAN SING A RAINBOW/LOVE IS BLUE | Dells (Bobby Miller), Cadet 5641 | 2 |
| 67 | 73 | 86 | — | WE GOT MORE SOUL | Dyke & the Blazers (Art Barrett), Original Sound 86 | 3 |
| 68 | 69 | 75 | 91 | I'VE BEEN LOVING YOU TOO LONG | Ike & Tina Turner (Bob Krasnow & Tina Turner), Blue Thumb 101 | 6 |
| 69 | 72 | 73 | — | IN-A-GADDA-DA-VIDA | Iron Butterfly (Jim Hilton), Atco 6606 | 15 |
| ★70 | — | — | — | MY CHERIE AMOUR | Stevie Wonder (Hank Cosby), Tamla 54180 | 1 |
| ★71 | — | — | — | WITHOUT HER | Herb Alpert (Herb Alpert & Jerry Moss), A&M 1065 | 1 |
| ★72 | — | — | — | MOODY WOMAN | Jerry Butler (Gamble & Huff), Mercury 72929 | 1 |
| 73 | 75 | — | — | SO I CAN LOVE YOU | Emotions (Volt) | 2 |
| 74 | 80 | — | — | COLOR HIM FATHER | Winstons (Don Carroll), Metromedia 117 | 2 |
| 75 | 77 | — | — | LOVE MAN | Otis Redding (Steve Cropper), Atco 6677 | 2 |
| ★76 | 95 | — | — | BABY, I LOVE YOU | Andy Kim (Jeff Barry), Steed 1031 | 2 |
| 77 | 85 | 90 | 90 | TRUCKSTOP | Jerry Smith (Paul Cohen), ABC 11162 | 4 |
| ★78 | — | — | — | SPINNING WHEEL | Blood, Sweat & Tears (James William Guercio), Columbia 44871 | 1 |
| ★79 | — | — | — | THE MINOTAUR | Dick Hyman & His Electric Eclectics ( ), Command 4126 | 1 |
| ★80 | — | — | — | I CAN'T QUIT HER | Arbors (Lori Burton & Roy Cicola), Date 1645 | 1 |
| ★81 | — | — | — | THE POPCORN | James Brown (James Brown), King 6240 | 1 |
| ★82 | — | — | — | SINCERELY | Paul Anka (Don Costa), RCA 74-0164 | 1 |
| 83 | 84 | 94 | — | WHY I SING THE BLUES | B. B. King (Bill Szymczyk), BluesWay 61034 | 3 |
| 84 | 86 | 87 | — | YOU DON'T NEED ME FOR ANYTHING ANYMORE | Brenda Lee (Mike Berniker), Decca 732491 | 3 |
| ★85 | 96 | — | — | BUT IT'S ALRIGHT | J. J. Jackson (Lew Futterman), Warner Bros.-Seven Arts 7276 | 2 |
| 86 | 88 | 88 | 95 | NEVER GONNA LET HIM KNOW | Debbie Taylor (George Kerr & Paul Robinson), GWP 501 | 6 |
| 87 | 87 | — | — | GOOD MORNING STARSHINE | Strawberry Alarm Clock (Julius Zababak), Uni 55125 | 2 |
| 88 | 89 | — | — | I WANT TO TAKE YOU HIGHER | Sly & the Family Stone (Sly Stone), Epic 10450 | 2 |
| 89 | 92 | 99 | — | I THREW IT ALL AWAY | Bob Dylan (Bob Johnston), Columbia 4-44826 | 3 |
| ★90 | — | — | — | HUSHABYE | Jay & the Americans (Jay & the Americans), United Artists 50535 | 1 |
| 91 | 100 | — | — | MEMPHIS UNDERGROUND | Herbie Mann (Tom Dowd), Atlantic 2621 | 2 |
| 92 | — | — | — | BROWN ARMS IN HOUSTON | Orpheus (Alan Lorber), MGM 14022 | 1 |
| 93 | 93 | — | — | LET'S DANCE | Ola & the Janglers (Gunnar Bergstrom), GNP Crescendo 423 | 2 |
| 94 | — | — | — | I NEED YOU NOW | Ronnie Dove (Dick Glasser), Diamond 260 | 1 |
| 95 | — | — | — | RUNNING BEAR | Sonny James (Kelso Herston), Capitol 2486 | 1 |
| 96 | — | — | — | HURT SO BAD | Lettermen (Al DeLory), Capitol 2482 | 1 |
| 97 | 97 | — | — | TOO EXPERIENCED | Eddie Lovette (L. Dixon), Steady 124 | 2 |
| 98 | 98 | — | — | HERE WE GO AGAIN | Nancy Sinatra (Billy Strange), Reprise 0821 | 2 |
| 99 | 99 | 100 | — | SAUSALITO | Al Martino (Al De Lory), Capitol 2468 | 3 |
| 100 | — | — | — | SON OF A TRAVELIN' MAN | Ed Ames (Jim Fogelsong), RCA 74-0156 | 1 |

## HOT 100—A TO Z—(Publisher-Licensee)


April Fools, The (Blue Seas/Jac/April, ASCAP) .... 47
Atlantis (Peer Int'l, BMI) .... 7
Aquarius/Let the Sunshine In (United Artists, ASCAP) 3
Baby, I Love You (Trio/Mother Bertha, BMI) .... 76
Bad Moon Rising (Jondora, BMI) .... 14
Black Pearl (Irving, BMI) .... 32
Brown Arms in Houston (Interval, BMI) .... 92
Born to Be Wild (Duchess, BMI) .... 64
Boxer, The (Charing Cross, BMI) .... 12
Buying a Book (Tree, BMI) .... 58
But It's Alright (Pamelarosa, BMI) .... 85
Chokin' Kind (Wilderness Music, BMI) .... 25
Cissy Strut (Marsaint, BMI) .... 24
Color Him Father (Holly Bee, BMI) .... 74
Day Is Done (Pepamar, ASCAP) .... 27
Don't Let Me Down (Maclen, BMI) .... 42
Don't Let the Joneses Get You Down (Jobete, BMI) 35
Everyday Without You Girl (Low-Sal, BMI) .... 30
Friend, Lover, Woman, Wife (B 'n' B, ASCAP) .... 54
Get Back (Maclen, BMI) .... 1
Gitarzan (Ahab, BMI) .... 8
Goodbye (Maclen, BMI) .... 13
Good Morning Starshine (Oliver) (United Artists, ASCAP) .... 57
Good Morning Starshine (Strawberry Alarm Clock) (United Artists, ASCAP) .... 87
Grazin' in the Grass (Chisa, BMI) .... 10
Hair (United Artists, ASCAP) .... 5
Happy Heart (Miller, ASCAP) .... 22
Hawaii Five-O (April, ASCAP) .... 17
Heather Honey (Low-Twy, BMI) .... 29
Here We Go Again (Dirk, BMI) .... 98
Hurt So Bad (Vogue, BMI) .... 96
Hushabye (Brittany, BMI) .... 90
I Can't Quit Her (Sea-Lark, BMI) .... 80
I Can't See Myself Leaving You (Fourteenth Hour, BMI) .... 28
I Could Never Lie to You (New Colony/T.M., BMI).. 52
I'm a Drifter (Detail, BMI) .... 50
I Need You Now (Miller, ASCAP) .... 94
In-a-Gadda-Da-Vida (Ten East/Cotillion/Itas, ASCAP) .... 69
In the Ghetto (B 'n' B/Gladys, ASCAP) .... 9
I Threw It All Away (Big Sky, ASCAP) .... 89
I Turned You On (Triple 3, BMI) .... 63
I Want to Take You Higher (Daly City, BMI) .... 88
I Wanna Testify (Groovesville, BMI) .... 40
Israelites, The (Kenwood, BMI) .... 41
It's Never Too Late (Trousdale, BMI) .... 51
It's Your Thing (Brothers Three, BMI) .... 16
I've Been Hurt (Low-Twy, BMI) .... 36
I've Been Loving You Too Long (East/Time/Curton, BMI) .... 68
Let Me (Boom, BMI) .... 48
Let's Dance (Tamerlane/Rondell, BMI) .... 93
Love (Can Make You Happy) (Rendezvous/Tobac, BMI) .... 2
Love Man (East/Memphis/Time/Redwal, BMI) .... 75
Love Me Tonight (Duchess, BMI) .... 45
Love Theme From Romeo & Juliet (Famous, ASCAP) 11
Medicine Man (Sandbox, ASCAP) .... 39
Medley: Can Sing a Rainbow/Love Is Blue (Mark VII/Croma, ASCAP) .... 66
Memphis Underground (Mann, ASCAP) .... 91
Minotaur, The (Eastlake, ASCAP) .... 79
More Today Than Yesterday (Spiral/Red Dust, BMI) 19
Morning Girl (Acuff-Rose, BMI) .... 21
My Cherie Amour (Jobete, BMI) .... 70
Never Gonna Let Him Know (Green Light, BMI) .... 86
No Matter What Sign You Are (Jobete, BMI) .... 61
Nothing But a Heartache (Felsted Music, BMI) .... 34
Oh Happy Day (Kama Rippa/Hawkins, ASCAP) .... 4
One (Dunbar, BMI) .... 23
Pinball Wizard (Track, BMI) .... 20
Popcorn, The (Golo, BMI) .... 81
Pretty World (Rodra, BMI) .... 62
Proud Mary (Jondora, BMI) .... 46
River Is Wide, The (Saturday, BMI) .... 31
Rhythm of the Rain (Tamerlane, BMI) .... 65
Running Bear (Big Bopper, BMI) .... 95
Sausalito (Blendingwell, ASCAP) .... 99
Seattle (Screen Gems-Columbia, BMI) .... 38
See (Slacsar, ASCAP) .... 43
Sincerely (Arc, BMI) .... 82
Son of a Travelin' Man (Sunbury, ASCAP) .... 100
Sorry Suzanne (January, BMI) .... 56
Special Delivery (Kaskat/Kahoona, BMI) .... 44
Spinning Wheel (Blackwood/Minnesingers, BMI) .. 78
Stand (Daly City, BMI) .... 33
These Eyes (Dunbar, BMI) .... 6
Time Is Tight (East/Memphis, BMI) .... 18
Too Busy Thinking About My Baby (Jobete, BMI) .. 15
Too Experienced (Vee Vee/Jamerica, BMI) .... 97
Tomorrow Tomorrow (Casserole, BMI) .... 60
Truckstop (Papa Joe's Music House, ASCAP) .... 77
We Got More Soul (Drive-In/Westward, BMI) .... 67
Welcome Me Love (Pocketful of Tunes, BMI) .... 49
What Is a Man? (Jobete, BMI) .... 53
What Does It Take to Win Your Love (Jobete, BMI) 59
Where's the Playground Susie (Ja-Ma, ASCAP) .... 26
Why I Sing the Blues (Pamco/Sounds of Lucille, BMI) .... 83
Windmills of Your Mind, The (United Artists, ASCAP) 37
With Pen in Hand (Unart, BMI) .... 55
Without Her (Rock, BMI) .... 71
Moody Woman (Gold Forever, Parabut, BMI) .... 72
You Don't Need Me for Anything Anymore (Pincus, ASCAP) .... 84


## BUBBLING UNDER THE HOT 100

101. LISTEN TO THE BAND....Monkees, Colgems 66-5004
102. I SHALL BE RELEASED....Box Tops, Mala 12038
103. IVORY....Bob Seeger System, Capitol 2480
104. LEANIN' ON YOU....Joe South, Capitol 12491
105. MARLEY PURT DRIVE....Jose Feliciano, RCA 47-9739
106. SUNDAY....Moments, Stang 5003
107. CAJUN BABY....Hank Williams Jr., MGM 14047
108. IT DIDN'T EVEN BRING ME DOWN....Sir Douglas Quintet, Smash 2222
109. IMAGINE THE SWAN....Zombies, Date 1644
110. GALVESTON....Roger Williams, Kapp 2007
111. NEVER COMES THE DAY....Moody Blues, Deram 85044
112. BIBLE SALESMAN....Billy Vera, Atlantic 2628
113. IT'S GETTING BETTER....Mama Cass, Dunhill 4195
114. JOHNNY B. GOODE....Buck Owens & His Buckaroos, Capitol 2485
115. I WANT TO LOVE YOU BABY....Peggy Scott & Jo Jo Benson, SSS Int'l 769
116. THAT'S NOT LOVE....Dee Dee Warwick, Mercury 72927
117. SOME KIND-A WONDERFUL....Thee Prophets, Kapp 997
118. SOME VELVET MORNING....Vanilla Fudge, Atco 6679
119. ROSE GARDEN....Dobie Gray, White Whale 300
120. YOU DON'T HAVE TO WALK IN THE RAIN....Turtles, White Whale 308
121. FEELIN' ALRIGHT....Joe Cocker, A&M 1063
122. I HAVE BUT ONE LIFE TO LIVE....Sammy Davis Jr., Reprise 0827
123. TOUCH 'EM WITH LOVE....Bobbie Gentry, Capitol 2501
124. ME & MR. HOHNER....Bobby Darin, Direction 351
125. SHARE MY WORD WITH YOU....George Jones, Musicor 1351
126. MY PLEDGE OF LOVE....Joe Jeffrey Group, Wand 11200
127. ANGELS LISTENED IN....Percy Sledge, Atlantic 2616
128. HAPPY TOGETHER....Hugo Montenegro & His Ork., RCA 74-0160
129. INSTANT GROOVE....King Curtis & His Kingpins, Atco
130. EVERYDAY LIVIN' DAYS....Merrilee Rush, AGP 112
131. IF I HAD A REASON....Bubble Puppy, International Artists 133
132. GREEN DOOR....Jerms, Honor Brigade 1
133. PLASTIC FANTASTIC LOVER....Jefferson Airplane, RCA 74-0150
134. DON'T LET THE SUN CATCH YOU CRYIN'....Trini Lopez, Reprise 0825
135. IT'S IN YOUR POWER....Joe Odom, 1-2-3 1710

Compiled from national retail sales and radio station airplay by the Music Popularity Dept. of Record Market Research, Billboard.

# Billboard HOT 100

FOR WEEK ENDING JUNE 7, 1969

★ STAR PERFORMER—Sides registering greatest proportionate upward progress this week.

● Record Industry Association of America seal of certification as million selling single.

| This Week | 1 Wk. Ago | 2 Wks. Ago | 3 Wks. Ago | TITLE Artist (Producer), Label & Number | Weeks On Chart |
|---|---|---|---|---|---|
| ● 1 | 1 | 1 | 3 | **GET BACK** — Beatles (George Martin), Apple 2490 | 5 |
| 2 | 2 | 3 | 5 | **LOVE (Can Make You Happy)** — Mercy (Jamie-Guyden), Sundi 6811 | 9 |
| ★ 3 | 10 | 12 | 19 | **GRAZIN' IN THE GRASS** — Friends of Distinction (John Florez), RCA 74-0207 | 10 |
| 4 | 4 | 5 | 12 | **OH HAPPY DAY** — Edwin Hawkins Singers (La Mont Bench), Pavillion 20001 | 7 |
| ★ 5 | 14 | 20 | 33 | **BAD MOON RISING** — Creedence Clearwater Revival (John Fogerty), Fantasy 622 | 6 |
| ★ 6 | 9 | 17 | 23 | **IN THE GHETTO** — Elvis Presley, RCA Victor 47-9741 | 6 |
| ● 7 | 3 | 2 | 1 | **AQUARIUS/LET THE SUNSHINE IN** — Fifth Dimension (Bones Howe), Soul City 772 | 14 |
| ★ 8 | 11 | 18 | 47 | **LOVE THEME FROM ROMEO & JULIET** — Henry Mancini & Ork. (Joe Reisman), RCA Victor 74-0131 | 5 |
| 9 | 6 | 10 | 10 | **THESE EYES** — Guess Who (Nimbus 9), RCA 74-0102 | 10 |
| ★ 10 | 15 | 16 | 25 | **TOO BUSY THINKING ABOUT MY BABY** — Marvin Gaye (Norman Whitfield), Tamla 54181 | 7 |
| 11 | 8 | 9 | 9 | **GITARZAN** — Ray Stevens (Fred Foster, Ray Stevens & Jim Malloy), Monument 1131 | 10 |
| 12 | 7 | 7 | 8 | **ATLANTIS** — Donovan (Mickie Most), Epic 5-10434 | 10 |
| ● 13 | 5 | 4 | 2 | **HAIR** — Cowsills (Bill & Bob Cowsill), MGM 14026 | 13 |
| ★ 14 | 23 | 41 | 53 | **ONE** — Three Dog Night (Gabriel Mekler), Dunhill 4191 | 6 |
| 15 | 19 | 21 | 26 | **MORE TODAY THAN YESTERDAY** — Spiral Staircase (Sonny Knight), Columbia 4-44741 | 10 |
| 16 | 13 | 14 | 14 | **GOODBYE** — Mary Hopkin (Paul McCartney), Apple 1806 | 8 |
| 17 | 21 | 30 | 35 | **MORNING GIRL** — Neon Philharmonic (T. Saussy, Don Gant & B. McCluskey), Warner Bros.-Seven Arts 7261 | 10 |
| ★ 18 | 41 | 74 | 96 | **THE ISRAELITES** — Desmond Dekker & the Aces (A Pyramid Production), Uni 55129 | 4 |
| ● 19 | 16 | 6 | 4 | **IT'S YOUR THING** — Isley Brothers (R. Isley-O. Isley-R. Isley), T Neck 901 | 13 |
| 20 | 12 | 8 | 7 | **THE BOXER** — Simon & Garfunkel (Simon & Garfunkel & Hales), Columbia 4-44785 | 9 |
| 21 | 18 | 15 | 13 | **TIME IS TIGHT** — Booker T. & the M.G.'s (B. T. Jones), Stax 0028 | 13 |
| 22 | 22 | 23 | 29 | **HAPPY HEART** — Andy Williams (Jerry Fuller), Columbia 4-44818 | 9 |
| 23 | 24 | 24 | 46 | **CISSY STRUT** — Meters (Marshall E. Sehorn & Allen Toussaint), Josie 1005 | 9 |
| ★ 24 | 32 | 44 | 58 | **BLACK PEARL** — Sonny Charles with the Checkmates Ltd. (Phil Spector), A&M 1053 | 5 |
| ★ 25 | 35 | 43 | — | **DON'T LET THE JONESES GET YOU DOWN** — Temptations (Norman Whitfield), Gordy 7086 | 3 |
| 26 | 26 | 33 | 34 | **WHERE'S THE PLAYGROUND SUSIE** — Glen Campbell (Al De Lory), Capitol 2494 | 6 |
| 27 | 27 | 29 | 38 | **DAY IS DONE** — Peter, Paul & Mary (Phil Ramone), Warner Bros.-Seven Arts 7279 | 7 |
| 28 | 25 | 13 | 15 | **CHOKIN' KIND** — Joe Simon (J. R. Enterprises), SS7 2628 | 12 |
| 29 | 30 | 45 | 52 | **EVERYDAY WITH YOU GIRL** — Classics IV (Buddy Buie), Imperial 66378 | 3 |
| ★ 30 | 57 | 83 | — | **GOOD MORNING STARSHINE** — Oliver (Bob Crewe), Jubilee 5659 | 3 |
| 31 | 31 | 36 | 37 | **THE RIVER IS WIDE** — The Grassroots (Steve Barri), Dunhill 4187 | 9 |
| 32 | 17 | 11 | 6 | **HAWAII FIVE-O** — The Ventures (Joe Saraceno), Liberty 56068 | 14 |
| ★ 33 | 78 | — | — | **SPINNING WHEEL** — Blood, Sweat & Tears (James William Guercio), Columbia 44871 | 2 |
| 34 | 37 | 40 | 57 | **THE WINDMILLS OF YOUR MIND** — Dusty Springfield (Jerry Wexler), Atlantic 2623 | 6 |
| ★ 35 | 43 | 61 | — | **SEE** — Rascals (Rascals & Arif Mardin), Atlantic 2634 | 3 |
| 36 | 36 | 48 | 54 | **I'VE BEEN HURT** — Bill Deal & the Rhondells (Jerry Ross), Heritage 812 | 8 |
| 37 | 39 | 50 | 59 | **MEDICINE MAN** — Buchanan Brothers (Cashman, Pistilli & West), Event, 3302 | 6 |
| ★ 38 | 45 | 79 | — | **LOVE ME TONIGHT** — Tom Jones (Peter Sullivan), Parrot 40038 | 3 |
| 39 | 40 | 55 | 60 | **I WANNA TESTIFY** — Johnnie Taylor (Don Davis), Stax 0033 | 5 |
| ★ 40 | 47 | 56 | 77 | **THE APRIL FOOLS** — Dionne Warwick (Burt Bacharach, Hal David), Scepter 12249 | 4 |
| ★ 41 | 48 | 53 | 83 | **LET ME** — Paul Revere & the Raiders Featuring Mark Lindsay, Columbia 4-44854 | 4 |
| 42 | 20 | 19 | 20 | **PINBALL WIZARD** — The Who (Baron Lambert), Decca 732465 | 10 |
| 43 | 44 | 49 | 62 | **SPECIAL DELIVERY** — 1910 Fruitgum Co. (Kasenetz-Katz Associates), Buddah 114 | 5 |
| 44 | 29 | 32 | 40 | **HEATHER HONEY** — Tommy Roe (Steve Barri), ABC 11211 | 7 |
| 45 | 46 | 46 | 50 | **PROUD MARY** — Solomon Burke (Solomon Burke-Tamiko Jones), Bell 783 | 6 |
| ★ 46 | 61 | — | — | **NO MATTER WHAT SIGN YOU ARE** — Diana Ross & the Supremes (B. Gordy Jr. & H. Cosby, Motown 1148 | 2 |
| 47 | 38 | 42 | 43 | **SEATTLE** — Perry Como (Chet Atkins & Andy Wiswell), RCA 47-9722 | 9 |
| 48 | 49 | 62 | 85 | **WELCOME ME LOVE** — Brooklyn Bridge (Wes Farrell), Buddah 95 | 5 |
| 49 | 50 | 54 | 64 | **I'M A DRIFTER** — Bobby Goldsboro (Bob Montgomery & Bobby Goldsboro), United Artists 50525 | 8 |
| ★ 50 | 59 | 78 | 93 | **WHAT DOES IT TAKE TO WIN YOUR LOVE** — Jr. Walker & the All Stars (Fuqua & Bristol), Soul 35062 | 4 |
| 51 | 54 | 60 | 79 | **FRIEND, LOVER, WOMAN, WIFE** — O. C. Smith (Jerry Fuller), Columbia 44859 | 5 |
| 52 | 52 | 57 | 65 | **I COULD NEVER LIE TO YOU** — New Colony Six, Mercury 72920 | 6 |
| 53 | 53 | 63 | 74 | **WHAT IS A MAN?** — Four Tops (Fuqua), Motown 1147 | 5 |
| 54 | 55 | 64 | 70 | **WITH PEN IN HAND** — Vikki Carr (Dave Pell & Rob Bledsoe), Liberty 56092 | 6 |
| 55 | 60 | — | — | **TOMORROW TOMORROW** — Bee Gees (Robert Stigwood & the Bee Gees) Atco 6682 | 2 |
| 56 | 28 | 28 | 30 | **I CAN'T SEE MYSELF LEAVING YOU** — Aretha Franklin (Jerry Wexler), Atlantic 2619 | 8 |
| 57 | 34 | 34 | 45 | **NOTHING BUT A HEARTACHE** — Flirtations (Wayne Bickerton), Deram 85038 | 14 |
| ★ 58 | 63 | — | — | **I TURNED YOU ON** — Isley Brothers (R. Isley-O. Isley-R. Isley), T-Neck 902 | 2 |
| ★ 59 | 66 | 82 | — | **LOVE IS BLUE (I Can Sing a Rainbow)** — Dells (Bobby Miller), Cadet 5641 | 3 |
| ★ 60 | 70 | — | — | **MY CHERIE AMOUR** — Stevie Wonder (Hank Cosby), Tamla 54180 | 2 |
| ★ 61 | 74 | 80 | — | **COLOR HIM FATHER** — Winstons (Don Carroll), Metromedia 117 | 3 |
| 62 | 67 | 73 | 86 | **WE GOT MORE SOUL** — Dyke & the Blazers (Art Barrett), Original Sound 86 | 4 |
| 63 | 65 | 71 | 71 | **RHYTHM OF THE RAIN** — Gary Lewis & the Playboys (Snuff Garrett), Liberty 56093 | 10 |
| ★ 64 | 72 | — | — | **MOODY WOMAN** — Jerry Butler (Gamble & Huff), Mercury 72929 | 2 |
| ★ 65 | 73 | 75 | — | **SO I CAN LOVE YOU** — Emotions, Volt 4010 | 3 |
| ★ 66 | 79 | — | — | **THE MINOTAUR** — Dick Hyman & His Electric Eclectics, Command 4126 | 2 |
| ★ 67 | 76 | 95 | — | **BABY, I LOVE YOU** — Andy Kim (Jeff Barry), Steed 1031 | 3 |
| 68 | 69 | 72 | 73 | **IN-A-GADDA-DA-VIDA** — Iron Butterfly (Jim Hilton), Atco 6606 | 16 |
| 69 | 71 | — | — | **WITHOUT HER** — Herb Alpert (Herb Alpert & Jerry Moss), A&M 1065 | 2 |
| 70 | 51 | 59 | 63 | **IT'S NEVER TOO LATE** — Steppenwolf (Gabriel Mekler), Dunhill 4192 | 5 |
| 71 | 77 | 85 | 90 | **TRUCKSTOP** — Jerry Smith (Paul Cohen), ABC 11162 | 5 |
| 72 | 75 | 77 | — | **LOVE MAN** — Otis Redding (Steve Cropper), Atco 6677 | 3 |
| ★ 73 | 81 | — | — | **THE POPCORN** — James Brown (James Brown), King 6240 | 2 |
| ★ 74 | 85 | 96 | — | **BUT IT'S ALRIGHT** — J. J. Jackson (Lew Futterman), Warner Bros.-Seven Arts 7276 | 3 |
| ★ 75 | 91 | 100 | — | **MEMPHIS UNDERGROUND** — Herbie Mann (Tom Dowd), Atlantic 2621 | 3 |
| 76 | 80 | — | — | **I CAN'T QUIT HER** — Arbors (Lori Burton & Roy Cicola), Date 1645 | 2 |
| 77 | 68 | 69 | 75 | **I'VE BEEN LOVING YOU TOO LONG** — Ike & Tina Turner (Bob Krasnow & Tina Turner), Blue Thumb 101 | 7 |
| 78 | 56 | 58 | 61 | **SORRY SUZANNE** — Hollies (Ron Richards), Epic 5-10454 | 8 |
| 79 | 88 | 89 | — | **I WANT TO TAKE YOU HIGHER** — Sly & the Family Stone (Sly Stone), Epic 10450 | 3 |
| 80 | 62 | 66 | 68 | **PRETTY WORLD** — Sergio Mendes & Brasil '66 (Sergio Mendes & Herb Alpert), A&M 1049 | 6 |
| 81 | 82 | — | — | **SINCERELY** — Paul Anka (Don Costa), RCA 74-0164 | 2 |
| 82 | 83 | 84 | 94 | **WHY I SING THE BLUES** — B. B. King (Bill Szymczyk), BluesWay 61034 | 4 |
| ★ 83 | — | — | — | **DIDN'T WE** — Richard Harris (Jimmy Webb), Dunhill 4194 | 1 |
| ★ 84 | — | — | — | **MY PLEDGE OF LOVE** — The Joe Jeffrey Group (Jerry Meyers & Alan Klein), Wand 11200 | 1 |
| 85 | 89 | 92 | 99 | **I THREW IT ALL AWAY** — Bob Dylan (Bob Johnston), Columbia 4-44826 | 4 |
| 86 | 90 | — | — | **HUSHABYE** — Jay & the Americans (Jay & the Americans), United Artists 50535 | 2 |
| ★ 87 | — | — | — | **YOU DON'T HAVE TO WALK IN THE RAIN** — Turtles (Ray Davies), White Whale 308 | 1 |
| ★ 88 | — | — | — | **IT'S GETTING BETTER** — Mama Cass (Steve Barri), Dunhill 4195 | 1 |
| ★ 89 | — | — | — | **CRYSTAL BLUE PERSUASION** — Tommy James & the Shondells (Tommy James-Ritchie Cordell), Roulette 7050 | 1 |
| ★ 90 | — | — | — | **MRS. ROBINSON** — Booker T. & the M.G.'s (Booker T. & the M.G.'s), Stax 0037 | 1 |
| 91 | 92 | — | — | **BROWN ARMS IN HOUSTON** — Orpheus (Alan Lorber), MGM 14022 | 2 |
| 92 | 93 | 93 | — | **LET'S DANCE** — Ola & the Janglers (Gunnar Bergstrom), GNP Crescendo 423 | 3 |
| 93 | 94 | — | — | **I NEED YOU NOW** — Ronnie Dove (Dick Glasser), Diamond 260 | 2 |
| 94 | 95 | — | — | **RUNNING BEAR** — Sonny James (Kelso Herston), Capitol 2486 | 2 |
| 95 | 97 | 97 | — | **TOO EXPERIENCED** — Eddie Lovette (L. Dixon), Steady 124 | 3 |
| 96 | 96 | — | — | **HURT SO BAD** — Lettermen (Al DeLory), Capitol 2482 | 2 |
| 97 | — | — | — | **LISTEN TO THE BAND** — Monkees (Michael Nesmith), Colgems 66-5004 | 1 |
| 98 | — | — | — | **RUBY, DON'T TAKE YOUR LOVE TO TOWN** — Kenny Rogers and the First Edition (Jimmy Bowen), Reprise 0829 | 1 |
| 99 | 100 | — | — | **SON OF A TRAVELIN' MAN** — Ed Ames (Jim Fogelsong), RCA 74-0156 | 2 |
| 100 | — | — | — | **GALVESTON** — Roger Williams (Hy Grill), Kapp 2007 | 1 |

## HOT 100—A TO Z—(Publisher-Licensee)

April Fools, The (Blue Seas/Jac/April, ASCAP) 40
Aquarius/Let the Sunshine In (United Artists, ASCAP) 7
Atlantis (Peer Int'l, BMI) 12
Baby, I Love You (Trio/Mother Bertha, BMI) 67
Bad Moon Rising (Jondora, BMI) 5
Black Pearl (Irving, BMI) 24
Boxer, The (Charing Cross, BMI) 20
Brown Arms in Houston (Interval, BMI) 91
But It's Alright (Pamelarosa, BMI) 74
Chokin' Kind (Wilderness Music, BMI) 28
Cissy Strut (Marsaint, BMI) 23
Color Him Father (Holly Bee, BMI) 61
Crystal Blue Persuasion (Big Seven, BMI) 89
Day Is Done (Pepamar, ASCAP) 27
Didn't We (Ja-Ma, ASCAP) 83
Don't Let the Joneses Get You Down (Jobete, BMI) 25
Everyday With You Girl (Low-Sal, BMI) 29
Friend, Lover, Woman, Wife (B 'n' B, ASCAP) 51
Galveston (Ja-Ma, ASCAP) 100
Get Back (Maclen, BMI) 1
Gitarzan (Ahab, BMI) 11
Goodbye (Maclen, BMI) 16
Good Morning Starshine (United Artists, ASCAP) 30
Grazin' in the Grass (Chisa, BMI) 3
Hair (United Artists, ASCAP) 13
Happy Heart (Miller, ASCAP) 22
Hawaii Five-O (April, ASCAP) 32
Heather Honey (Low-Twy, BMI) 44
Hurt So Bad (Vogue, BMI) 96
Hushabye (Brittany, BMI) 86
I Can't Quit Her (Sea-Lark, BMI) 76
I Can't See Myself Leaving You (Fourteenth Hour, BMI) 56
I Could Never Lie to You (New Colony/T.M., BMI) 52
I'm a Drifter (Detail, BMI) 49
I Need You Now (Miller, ASCAP) 93
In-a-Gadda-Da-Vida (Ten East/Cotillion/Itas, ASCAP) 68
In the Ghetto (B 'n' B/Gladys, ASCAP) 6
I Threw It All Away (Big Sky, ASCAP) 85
I Turned You On (Triple 3, BMI) 58
I Want to Take You Higher (Daly City, BMI) 79
I Wanna Testify (Groovesville, BMI) 39
Israelites, The (Kenwood, BMI) 18
It's Getting Better (Screen Gems-Columbia, BMI) 88
It's Never Too Late (Trousdale, BMI) 70
It's Your Thing (Brothers Three, BMI) 19
I've Been Hurt (Low-Twy, BMI) 36
I've Been Loving You Too Long (East/Time/Curton, BMI) 77
Let Me (Boom, BMI) 41
Let's Dance (Tamerlane/Rondell, BMI) 92
Listen to the Band (Screen Gems-Columbia, BMI) 97
Love (Can Make You Happy) (Rendezvous/Tobac, BMI) 2
Love Is Blue (I Can Sing a Rainbow) (Mark VII/Croma, ASCAP) 59
Love Man (East/Memphis/Time/Redwal, BMI) 72
Love Me Tonight (Duchess, BMI) 38
Love Theme From Romeo & Juliet (Famous, ASCAP) 8
Medicine Man (Sandbox, ASCAP) 37
Memphis Underground (Mann, ASCAP) 75
Minotaur, The (Eastlake, ASCAP) 66
Moody Woman (Gold Forever/Parabut, BMI) 64
More Today Than Yesterday (Spiral/Red Dust, BMI) 15
Morning Girl (Acuff-Rose, BMI) 17
Mrs. Robinson (Charing Cross, BMI) 90
My Cherie Amour (Jobete, BMI) 60
My Pledge of Love (Wednesday Morn./Our Children's, BMI) 84
No Matter What Sign You Are (Jobete, BMI) 46
Nothing But a Heartache (Felsted Music, BMI) 57
Oh Happy Day (Kama Rippa/Hawkins, ASCAP) 4
One (Dunbar, BMI) 14
Pinball Wizard (Track, BMI) 42
Popcorn, The (Gola, BMI) 73
Pretty World (Rodra, BMI) 80
Proud Mary (Jondora, BMI) 45
Rhythm of the Rain (Tamerlane, BMI) 63
River Is Wide, The (Saturday, BMI) 31
Ruby, Don't Take Your Love to Town (Cedarwood, BMI) 98
Running Bear (Big Bopper, BMI) 94
Seattle (Screen Gems-Columbia, BMI) 47
See (Slacsar, ASCAP) 35
Sincerely (Arc, BMI) 81
So I Can Love You (Pervis/Staples, BMI) 65
Son of a Travelin' Man (Sunbury, ASCAP) 99
Sorry Suzanne (January, BMI) 78
Special Delivery (Kaskat/Kahoona, BMI) 43
Spinning Wheel (Blackwood/Minnesingers, BMI) 33
These Eyes (Dunbar, BMI) 9
Time Is Tight (East/Memphis, BMI) 21
Too Busy Thinking About My Baby (Jobete, BMI) 10
Too Experienced (Vee Vee/Jamerica, BMI) 95
Tomorrow Tomorrow (Casserole, BMI) 55
Truckstop (Papa Joe's Music House, ASCAP) 71
We Got More Soul (Drive-In/Westward, BMI) 62
Welcome Me Love (Pocketful of Tunes, BMI) 48
What Does It Take to Win Your Love (Jobete, BMI) 50
What Is a Man? (Jobete, BMI) 53
Where's the Playground Susie (Ja-Ma, ASCAP) 26
Why I Sing the Blues (Pamco/Sounds of Lucille, BMI) 82
Windmills of Your Mind, The (United Artists, ASCAP) 34
With Pen in Hand (Unart, BMI) 54
Without Her (Rock, BMI) 69
You Don't Have to Walk in the Rain (Ishmael/Blimp, BMI) 87

## BUBBLING UNDER THE HOT 100

101. NEVER COMES THE DAY — Moody Blues, Deram 85044
102. YOU DON'T NEED ME FOR ANYTHING ANYMORE — Brenda Lee, Decca 732491
103. SOME VELVET MORNING — Vanilla Fudge, Atco 6679
104. FEELIN' ALRIGHT — Joe Cocker, A&M 1063
105. SAUSALITO — Al Martino, Capitol 2468
106. BABY DRIVER — Simon & Garfunkel, Columbia 44785
107. THAT'S NOT LOVE — Dee Dee Warwick, Mercury 72927
108. MOTHER POPCORN — James Brown, King 6245
109. YESTERDAY WHEN I WAS YOUNG — Roy Clark, Dot 17246
110. IT'S IN YOUR POWER — Joe Odom, 1-2-3 1710
111. SOME KIND-A WONDERFUL — Thee Prophets, Kapp 997
112. STAY AND LOVE ME ALL SUMMER — Brian Hyland, Dot 17258
113. TOUCH 'EM WITH LOVE — Bobbie Gentry, Capitol 2501
114. JOHNNY B. GOODE — Buck Owens & His Buckaroos, Capitol 2485
115. WE CAN'T GO ON THIS WAY — Unchained Mynds, Buddah 111
116. I'LL NEVER FALL IN LOVE AGAIN — Burt Bacharach, A&M 1064
117. FUNNY FEELING — Delphonics, Philly Groove 156
118. SPRING — John Tipton, Date 2-1641
119. MANHATTAN SPIRITUAL — Sandy Nelson, Imperial 66375
120. YOUNG PEOPLE — Willie Mitchell, Hi 2158
121. I HAVE BUT ONE LIFE TO LIVE — Sammy Davis Jr., Reprise 0827
122. CROSSROADS OF THE STEPPING STONES — Elephant's Memory, Buddah 98
123. ME & MR. HOHNER — Bobby Darin, Direction 351
124. SHARE MY WORLD WITH YOU — George Jones, Musicor 1351
125. HAPPY TOGETHER — Hugo Montenegro & Ork, RCA 74-0160
126. ANGELS LISTENED IN — Percy Sledge, Atlantic 2616
127. GOTTA GET TO KNOW YOU — Bobby Bland, Duke 447
128. INSTANT GROOVE — King Curtis & His Kingpins, Atco 6680
129. IF I HAD A REASON — Bubble Puppy, International Artists 133
130. GREEN DOOR — Jerms, Honor Brigade 1
131. TEARS ON MY PILLOW — Johnny Tillotson, Amos 117
132. LAY LADY LAY — Byrds, Columbia 4-44868
133. DON'T WAKE ME IN THE MORNING, MICHAEL — Peppermint Rainbow, Decca 732498
134. DON'T LET THE SUN CATCH YOU CRYIN' — Trini Lopez, Reprise 0825
135. QUENTIN'S THEME — Charles Randolph Grean, Sounde, Ranwood 840

Compiled from national retail sales and radio station airplay by the Music Popularity Dept. of Record Market Research, Billboard.

# Billboard HOT 100

FOR WEEK ENDING JUNE 14, 1969

★ STAR PERFORMER—Sides registering greatest proportionate upward progress this week.

Record Industry Association of America seal of certification as million selling single.

| This Week | 1 Wk. Ago | 2 Wks. Ago | 3 Wks. Ago | TITLE Artist (Producer), Label & Number | Weeks On Chart |
|---|---|---|---|---|---|
| 1 | 1 | 1 | 1 | GET BACK — Beatles (George Martin), Apple 2490 | 6 |
| ★ 2 | 8 | 11 | 18 | LOVE THEME FROM ROMEO & JULIET — Henry Mancini & Ork. (Joe Reisman), RCA Victor 74-0131 | 6 |
| 3 | 6 | 9 | 17 | IN THE GHETTO — Elvis Presley, RCA Victor 47-9741 | 7 |
| 4 | 5 | 14 | 20 | BAD MOON RISING — Creedence Clearwater Revival (John Fogerty), Fantasy 622 | 7 |
| 5 | 2 | 2 | 3 | LOVE (Can Make You Happy) — Mercy (Jamie-Guyden), Sundi 6811 | 10 |
| 6 | 13 | 10 | 12 | GRAZIN' IN THE GRASS — Friends of Distinction (John Florez), RCA 74-0207 | 11 |
| 7 | 4 | 4 | 5 | OH HAPPY DAY — Edwin Hawkins Singers (La Mont Bench), Pavillion 20001 | 8 |
| 8 | 10 | 15 | 16 | TOO BUSY THINKING ABOUT MY BABY — Marvin Gaye (Norman Whitfield), Tamla 54181 | 8 |
| 9 | 9 | 6 | 10 | THESE EYES — Guess Who (Nimbus 9), RCA 74-0102 | 11 |
| ★ 10 | 14 | 23 | 41 | ONE — Three Dog Night (Gabriel Mekler), Dunhill 4191 | 7 |
| 11 | 7 | 3 | 2 | AQUARIUS/LET THE SUNSHINE IN — Fifth Dimension (Bones Howe), Soul City 772 | 15 |
| 12 | 15 | 19 | 21 | MORE TODAY THAN YESTERDAY — Spiral Staircase (Sonny Knight), Columbia 4-44741 | 11 |
| 13 | 11 | 8 | 9 | GITARZAN — Ray Stevens (Fred Foster, Ray Stevens & Jim Malloy), Monument 1131 | 11 |
| 14 | 12 | 7 | 7 | ATLANTIS — Donovan (Mickie Most), Epic 5-10434 | 11 |
| ★ 15 | 30 | 57 | 83 | GOOD MORNING STARSHINE — Oliver (Bob Crewe), Jubilee 5659 | 4 |
| ★ 16 | 18 | 41 | 74 | THE ISRAELITES — Desmond Dekker & the Aces (A Pyramid Production), Uni 55129 | 5 |
| 17 | 17 | 21 | 30 | MORNING GIRL — Neon Philharmonic (T. Saussy, Don Gant & B. McCluskey), Warner Bros.-Seven Arts 7261 | 11 |
| ★ 18 | 33 | 78 | — | SPINNING WHEEL — Blood, Sweat & Tears (James William Guercio), Columbia 44871 | 3 |
| ★ 19 | 29 | 30 | 45 | EVERYDAY WITH YOU GIRL — Classics IV (Buddy Blue), Imperial 66378 | 4 |
| ★ 20 | 24 | 32 | 44 | BLACK PEARL — Sonny Charles with the Checkmates Ltd. (Phil Spector), A&M 1053 | 6 |
| 21 | 3 | 5 | 4 | HAIR — Cowsills (Bill & Bob Cowsill), MGM 14026 | 14 |
| ★ 22 | 25 | 35 | 43 | DON'T LET THE JONESES GET YOU DOWN — Temptations (Norman Whitfield), Gordy 7086 | 4 |
| 23 | 16 | 13 | 14 | GOODBYE — Mary Hopkin (Paul McCartney), Apple 1806 | 9 |
| 24 | 22 | 22 | 23 | HAPPY HEART — Andy Williams (Jerry Fuller), Columbia 4-44818 | 10 |
| 25 | 27 | 27 | 29 | DAY IS DONE — Peter, Paul & Mary (Phil Ramone), Warner Bros.-Seven Arts 7279 | 8 |
| ★ 26 | 37 | 39 | 50 | MEDICINE MAN — Buchanan Brothers (Cashman, Pistilli & West), Event, 3302 | 7 |
| 27 | 20 | 12 | 8 | THE BOXER — Simon & Garfunkel (Simon & Garfunkel & Hales), Columbia 4-44785 | 10 |
| 28 | 19 | 16 | 6 | IT'S YOUR THING — Isley Brothers (R. Isley-O. Isley-R. Isley), T Neck 901 | 14 |
| ★ 29 | 41 | 48 | 53 | LET ME — Paul Revere & the Raiders Featuring Mark Lindsay, Columbia 4-44854 | 5 |
| ★ 30 | 35 | 43 | 61 | SEE — Rascals (Rascals & Arif Mardin), Atlantic 2634 | 4 |
| 31 | 34 | 37 | 40 | THE WINDMILLS OF YOUR MIND — Dusty Springfield (Jerry Wexler), Atlantic 2623 | 7 |
| 32 | 38 | 45 | 79 | LOVE ME TONIGHT — Tom Jones (Peter Sullivan), Parrot 40038 | 4 |
| ★ 33 | 46 | 61 | — | NO MATTER WHAT SIGN YOU ARE — Diana Ross & the Supremes (B. Gordy Jr. & H. Cosby, Motown 1148 | 3 |
| 34 | 26 | 26 | 33 | WHERE'S THE PLAYGROUND SUSIE — Glen Campbell (Al De Lory), Capitol 2494 | 7 |
| 35 | 36 | 36 | 48 | I'VE BEEN HURT — Bill Deal & the Rhondells (Jerry Ross), Heritage 812 | 9 |
| 36 | 31 | 31 | 36 | THE RIVER IS WIDE — The Grassroots (Steve Barri), Dunhill 4187 | 10 |
| 37 | 40 | 47 | 56 | THE APRIL FOOLS — Dionne Warwick (Burt Bacharach, Hal David), Scepter 12249 | 5 |
| 38 | 39 | 40 | 55 | I WANNA TESTIFY — Johnnie Taylor (Don Davis), Stax 0033 | 6 |
| ★ 39 | 61 | 74 | 80 | COLOR HIM FATHER — Winstons (Don Carroll), Metromedia 117 | 4 |
| 40 | 43 | 44 | 49 | SPECIAL DELIVERY — 1910 Fruitgum Co. (Kasenetz-Katz Associates), Buddah 114 | 6 |
| 41 | 50 | 59 | 78 | WHAT DOES IT TAKE TO WIN YOUR LOVE — Jr. Walker & the All Stars (Fuqua & Bristol), Soul 35062 | 5 |
| ★ 42 | 54 | 55 | 64 | WITH PEN IN HAND — Vikki Carr (Dave Pell & Rob Bledsoe), Liberty 56092 | 7 |
| ★ 43 | 59 | 66 | 82 | MEDLEY: CAN SING A RAINBOW/LOVE IS BLUE — Dells (Bobby Miller), Cadet 5641 | 4 |
| ★ 44 | 67 | 76 | 95 | BABY, I LOVE YOU — Andy Kim (Jeff Barry), Steed 1031 | 4 |
| 45 | 23 | 24 | 24 | CISSY STRUT — Meters (Marshall E. Schorn & Allen Toussaint), Josie 1005 | 10 |
| 46 | 49 | 50 | 54 | I'M A DRIFTER — Bobby Goldsboro (Bob Montgomery & Bobby Goldsboro), United Artists 50525 | 9 |
| 47 | 58 | 63 | — | I TURNED YOU ON — Isley Brothers (R. Isley-O. Isley-R. Isley), T-Neck 902 | 3 |
| 48 | 48 | 49 | 62 | WELCOME ME LOVE — Brooklyn Bridge (Wes Farrell), Buddah 95 | 6 |
| 49 | 51 | 54 | 60 | FRIEND, LOVER, WOMAN, WIFE — O. C. Smith (Jerry Fuller), Columbia 44859 | 6 |
| 50 | 52 | 52 | 57 | I COULD NEVER LIE TO YOU — New Colony Six, Mercury 72920 | 7 |
| 51 | 42 | 20 | 19 | PINBALL WIZARD — The Who (Baron Lambert), Decca 732465 | 11 |
| 52 | 60 | 70 | — | MY CHERIE AMOUR — Stevie Wonder (Hank Cosby), Tamla 54180 | 3 |
| 53 | 53 | 53 | 63 | WHAT IS A MAN? — Four Tops (Fuqua), Motown 1147 | 6 |
| 54 | 55 | 60 | — | TOMORROW TOMORROW — Bee Gees (Robert Stigwood & the Bee Gees) Atco 6682 | 3 |
| 55 | 44 | 29 | 32 | HEATHER HONEY — Tommy Roe (Steve Barri), ABC 11211 | 8 |
| ★ 56 | 64 | 72 | — | MOODY WOMAN — Jerry Butler (Gamble & Huff), Mercury 72929 | 3 |
| ★ 57 | 89 | — | — | CRYSTAL BLUE PERSUASION — Tommy James & the Shondells (Tommy James-Ritchie Cordell), Roulette 7050 | 2 |
| 58 | 47 | 38 | 42 | SEATTLE — Perry Como (Chet Atkins & Andy Wiswell), RCA 47-9722 | 10 |
| 59 | 62 | 67 | 73 | WE GOT MORE SOUL — Dyke & the Blazers (Art Barrett), Original Sound 86 | 5 |
| 60 | 45 | 46 | 46 | PROUD MARY — Solomon Burke (Solomon Burke-Tamiko Jones), Bell 783 | 7 |
| 61 | 73 | 81 | — | THE POPCORN — James Brown (James Brown), King 6240 | 2 |
| ★ 62 | 79 | 88 | 89 | I WANT TO TAKE YOU HIGHER — Sly & the Family Stone (Sly Stone), Epic 10450 | 4 |
| ★ 63 | 86 | 90 | — | HUSHABYE — Jay & the Americans (Jay & the Americans), United Artists 50535 | 3 |
| 64 | 66 | 79 | — | THE MINOTAUR — Dick Hyman & His Electric Eclectics, Command 4126 | 3 |
| 65 | 65 | 73 | 75 | SO I CAN LOVE YOU — Emotions, Volt 4010 | 4 |
| 66 | 69 | 71 | — | WITHOUT HER — Herb Alpert (Herb Alpert & Jerry Moss), A&M 1065 | 3 |
| 67 | 74 | 85 | 96 | BUT IT'S ALRIGHT — J. J. Jackson (Lew Futterman), Warner Bros.-Seven Arts 7276 | 4 |
| 68 | 68 | 69 | 72 | IN-A-GADDA-DA-VIDA — Iron Butterfly (Jim Hilton), Atco 6606 | 17 |
| 69 | 63 | 65 | 71 | RHYTHM OF THE RAIN — Gary Lewis & the Playboys (Snuff Garrett), Liberty 56093 | 11 |
| 70 | 90 | — | — | MRS. ROBINSON — Booker T. & the M.G.'s (Booker T. & the M.G.'s), Stax 0037 | 2 |
| ★ 71 | — | — | — | THE BALLAD OF JOHN AND YOKO — The Beatles (Lennon-McCartney), Apple 2531 | 1 |
| ★ 72 | 76 | 80 | — | I CAN'T QUIT HER — Arbors (Lori Burton & Roy Cicola), Date 1645 | 3 |
| 73 | 71 | 77 | 85 | TRUCKSTOP — Jerry Smith (Paul Cohen), ABC 11162 | 6 |
| 74 | 72 | 75 | 77 | LOVE MAN — Otis Redding (Steve Cropper), Atco 6677 | 4 |
| 75 | 75 | 91 | 100 | MEMPHIS UNDERGROUND — Herbie Mann (Tom Dowd), Atlantic 2621 | 4 |
| 76 | 84 | — | — | MY PLEDGE OF LOVE — The Joe Jeffrey Group (Jerry Meyers & Alan Klein), Wand 11200 | 2 |
| ★ 77 | 88 | — | — | IT'S GETTING BETTER — Mama Cass (Steve Barri), Dunhill 4195 | 2 |
| 78 | 83 | — | — | DIDN'T WE — Richard Harris (Jimmy Webb), Dunhill 4194 | 2 |
| 79 | 87 | — | — | YOU DON'T HAVE TO WALK IN THE RAIN — Turtles (Ray Davies), White Whale 308 | 2 |
| ★ 80 | — | — | — | PART I MOTHER POPCORN (You Got to Have a Mother for Me) — James Brown (James Brown), King 6245 | 1 |
| 81 | 81 | 82 | — | SINCERELY — Paul Anka (Don Costa), RCA 74-0164 | 3 |
| 82 | 82 | 83 | 84 | WHY I SING THE BLUES — B. B. King (Bill Szymczyk), BluesWay 61034 | 5 |
| ★ 83 | — | — | — | YESTERDAY WHEN I WAS YOUNG — Roy Clark (Joe Allison), Dot 17246 | 1 |
| ★ 84 | — | — | — | THE GIRL I'LL NEVER KNOW — Frankie Valli (Bob Crewe), Philips 40622 | 1 |
| ★ 85 | — | — | — | QUENTIN'S THEME — The Charles Randolph Grean Sounde (Charles R. Grean), Ranwood 840 | 1 |
| 86 | 85 | 89 | 92 | I THREW IT ALL AWAY — Bob Dylan (Bob Johnston), Columbia 4-44826 | 5 |
| ★ 87 | — | — | — | DAMMIT ISN'T GOD'S LAST NAME — Frankie Laine (Jimmy Bowen), ABC 11224 | 1 |
| ★ 88 | — | — | — | DON'T WAKE ME UP IN THE MORNING, MICHAEL — The Peppermint Rainbow (Paul Leka), Decca 732498 | 1 |
| 89 | 98 | — | — | RUBY, DON'T TAKE YOUR LOVE TO TOWN — Kenny Rogers and the First Edition (Jimmy Bowen), Reprise 0829 | 2 |
| ★ 90 | — | — | — | THE DAYS OF SAND AND SHOVELS — Bobby Vinton (Billy Sherrill), Epic 10485 | 1 |
| 91 | 91 | 92 | — | BROWN ARMS IN HOUSTON — Orpheus (Alan Lorber), MGM 14022 | 3 |
| 92 | 96 | 96 | — | HURT SO BAD — Lettermen (Al DeLory), Capitol 2482 | 3 |
| 93 | 99 | 100 | — | SON OF A TRAVELIN' MAN — Ed Ames (Jim Fogelsong), RCA 74-0156 | 3 |
| 94 | — | — | — | IT'S MY THING, PART I — Marva Whitney (......), King 6229 | 1 |
| 95 | — | — | — | FUNNY FEELING — The Delfonics (Stan & Bell Prod.), Philly Groove 156 | 1 |
| 96 | — | — | — | MOONFLIGHT — Vik Venus (Lewis Merenstein), Buddah 118 | 1 |
| 97 | 97 | — | — | LISTEN TO THE BAND — Monkees (Michael Nesmith), Colgems 66-5004 | 2 |
| 98 | — | — | — | GOTTA GET TO KNOW YOU — Bobby Bland (Broozier & Perry), Duke 447 | 1 |
| 99 | 100 | — | — | GALVESTON — Roger Williams (Hy Grill), Kapp 2007 | 2 |
| 100 | — | — | — | TELL ALL THE PEOPLE — Doors (Kreiger), Elektra 45663 | 1 |

## HOT 100—A TO Z—(Publisher-Licensee)

April Fools, The (Blue Seas/Jac/April, ASCAP) ... 37
Aquarius/Let the Sunshine In (United Artists, ASCAP) 11
Atlantis (Peer Int'l, BMI) ... 14
Baby, I Love You (Trio/Mother Bertha, BMI) ... 44
Bad Moon Rising (Jondora, BMI) ... 4
The Ballad of John and Yoko (Maclen, BMI) ... 71
Black Pearl (Irving, BMI) ... 20
Boxer, The (Charing Cross, BMI) ... 27
Brown Arms in Houston (Interval, BMI) ... 91
But It's Alright (Pamelarosa, BMI) ... 67
Cissy Strut (Marsaint, BMI) ... 45
Color Him Father (Holly Bee, BMI) ... 39
Crystal Blue Persuasion (Big Seven, BMI) ... 57
Dammit Isn't God's Last Name (Four Star, BMI) ... 87
Day Is Done (Pepamar, ASCAP) ... 25
The Days of Sand and Shovels (Lonzo&Oscar, BMI) 90
Didn't We (Ja-Ma, ASCAP) ... 78
Don't Let the Joneses Get You Down (Jobete, BMI) 22
Don't Wake Me Up in the Morning, Michael (M.R.C./Little Heather, BMI) ... 88
Everyday With You Girl (Low-Sal, BMI) ... 19
Friend, Lover, Woman, Wife (B 'n' B, ASCAP) ... 49
Funny Feeling (Nickel Shoe, BMI) ... 95
Galveston (Ja-Ma, ASCAP) ... 99
Get Back (Maclen, BMI) ... 1
The Girl I'll Never Know (Saturday, BMI) ... 84
Gitarzan (Ahab, BMI) ... 13
Goodbye (Maclen, BMI) ... 17
Good Morning Starshine (United Artists, ASCAP) ... 15
Gotta Get to Know You (Don, BMI) ... 98
Grazin' in the Grass (Chisa, BMI) ... 21
Hair (United Artists, ASCAP) ... 6
Happy Heart (Miller, ASCAP) ... 24
Heather Honey (Low-Twy, BMI) ... 55
Hurt So Bad (Vogue, BMI) ... 92
Hushabye (Brittany, BMI) ... 63
I Can't Quit Her (Sea-Lark, BMI) ... 72
I Could Never Lie to You (New Colony/T.M., BMI) 50
I'm a Drifter (Detail, BMI) ... 46
In-a-Gadda-Da-Vida (Ten East/Cotillion/Itas, ASCAP) ... 68
In the Ghetto (B 'n' B/Gladys, ASCAP) ... 3
I Threw It All Away (Big Sky, ASCAP) ... 86
I Turned You On (Triple 3, BMI) ... 47
I Want to Take You Higher (Daly City, BMI) ... 62
I Wanna Testify (Groovesville, BMI) ... 38
Israelites, The (Kenwood, BMI) ... 16
It's Getting Better (Screen Gems-Columbia, BMI) ... 77
It's My Thing, Part I (Dynatone, BMI) ... 94
It's Your Thing (Brothers Three, BMI) ... 28
I've Been Hurt (Low-Twy, BMI) ... 35
Let Me (Boom, BMI) ... 29
Listen to the Band (Screen Gems-Columbia, BMI) 97
Love (Can Make You Happy) (Rendezvous/Tobac, BMI) ... 5
Love Is Blue (I Can Sing a Rainbow) (Mark VII/Croma, ASCAP) ... 43
Love Man (East/Memphis/Time/Redwal, BMI) ... 74
Love Me Tonight (Duchess, BMI) ... 32
Love Theme From Romeo & Juliet (Famous, ASCAP) 2
Medicine Man (Sandbox, ASCAP) ... 26
Memphis Underground (Mann, ASCAP) ... 75
Minotaur, The (Eastlake, ASCAP) ... 64
Moody Woman (Gold Forever/Parabut, BMI) ... 56
Moonflight (Kaskat/Kahoona/Camad/T.M./Pocket Full of Tunes/Rivers/Peanut Butter/ Kama Sutra, BMI) ... 96
More Today Than Yesterday (Spiral/Red Dust, BMI) 12
Morning Girl (Acuff-Rose, BMI) ... 17
Part 1—Mother Popcorn (You Got to Have a Mother for Me) (Dynatone, BMI) ... 80
Mrs. Robinson (Charing Cross, BMI) ... 70
My Cherie Amour (Jobete, BMI) ... 52
My Pledge of Love (Wednesday Morn./Our Children's, BMI) ... 76
No Matter What Sign You Are (Jobete, BMI) ... 33
Oh Happy Day (Kama Rippa/Hawkins, ASCAP) ... 7
One (Dunbar, BMI) ... 10
Pinball Wizard (Track, BMI) ... 51
Popcorn, The (Gola, BMI) ... 61
Proud Mary (Jondora, BMI) ... 60
Quentin's Theme (Curnor, BMI) ... 85
Rhythm of the Rain (Tamerlane, BMI) ... 69
River Is Wide, The (Saturday, BMI) ... 36
Ruby, Don't Take Your Love to Town (Cedarwood, BMI) ... 89
Seattle (Screen Gems-Columbia, BMI) ... 58
See (Slacsar, ASCAP) ... 30
Sincerely (Arc, BMI) ... 81
So I Can Love You (Pervis/Staples, BMI) ... 65
Son of a Travelin' Man (Sunbury, ASCAP) ... 93
Special Delivery (Kaskat/Kahoona, BMI) ... 40
Spinning Wheel (Blackwood/Minnesingers, BMI) ... 18
Tell All the People (Nipper/Door, ASCAP) ... 100
These Eyes (Dunbar, BMI) ... 9
Too Busy Thinking About My Baby (Jobete, BMI) ... 8
Tomorrow Tomorrow (Casserole, BMI) ... 54
Truckstop (Papa Joe's Music House, ASCAP) ... 73
We Got More Soul (Drive-In/Westward, BMI) ... 59
Welcome Me Love (Pocketful of Tunes, BMI) ... 48
What Does It Take to Win Your Love (Jobete, BMI) 41
What Is a Man? (Jobete, BMI) ... 53
Where's the Playground Susie (Ja-Ma, ASCAP) ... 34
Why I Sing the Blues (Pamco/Sounds of Lucille, BMI) ... 82
Windmills of Your Mind, The (United Artists, ASCAP) 31
With Pen in Hand (Unart, BMI) ... 42
Without Her (Rock, BMI) ... 66
Yesterday When I Was Young (Tro-Dartmouth, ASCAP) ... 83
You Don't Have to Walk in the Rain (Ishmael/Blimp, BMI) ... 79

## BUBBLING UNDER THE HOT 100

101. NEVER COMES THE DAY ... Moody Blues, Deram 85044
102. PINCH ME ... Ohio Express, Buddah 117
103. SOME VELVET MORNING ... Vanilla Fudge, Atco 6679
104. FEELING ALRIGHT ... Joe Cocker, A&M 1063
105. LOLLIPOP ... Intruders, Gamble 231
106. TOO EXPERIENCED ... Eddie Lovette, Steady 124
107. THAT'S NOT LOVE ... Dee Dee Warwick, Mercury 72927
108. I NEED YOU NOW ... Ronnie Dove, Diamond 260
109. IT'S IN YOUR POWER ... Joe Odom, 1-2-3 1710
110. LET'S DANCE ... Ola & the Janglers, GNP Crescendo 423
111. STAY AND LOVE ME ALL SUMMER ... Brian Hyland, Dot 17258
112. I'LL NEVER FALL IN LOVE AGAIN ... Burt Bacharach, A&M 1064
113. TOUCH 'EM WITH LOVE ... Bobbie Gentry, Capitol 2501
114. AND SHE'S MINE ... Spanky & Our Gang, Mercury 72926
115. BABY DRIVER ... Simon & Garfunkel, Columbia 4-44785
116. EVERYTHING I DO GONN' BE FUNKY ... Lee Dorsey, Philly Groove 11055
117. GIRL YOU'RE TOO YOUNG ... Archie Bell & the Drells, Atlantic 2644
118. PUT A LITTLE LOVE IN YOUR HEART ... Jackie DeShannon, Imperial 66385
119. MANHATTAN SPIRITUAL ... Sandy Nelson, Imperial 66375
120. I HAVE BUT ONE LIFE TO LIVE ... Sammy Davis Jr., Reprise 0827
121. CROSSROADS OF THE STEPPING STONES ... Elephant's Memory, Buddah 98
122. I'M STILL A STRUGGLING MAN ... Edwin Starr, Gordy 7087
123. TAKE YOUR LOVE AND SHOVE IT ... Kane's Cousins, Shove Love 500
124. HAPPY TOGETHER ... Hugo Montenegro & His Ork., RCA 74-0160
125. WHILE YOU'RE OUT LOOKING FOR SUGAR ... Honey Cones, Hot Wax 6901
126. PROPHECY OF DANIEL & JOHN THE DIVINE ... Cowsills, MGM 14063
127. INSTANT GROOVE ... King Curtis & His Kingpins, Atco 6680
128. IF I HAD A REASON ... Bubble Puppy, International Artists 133
129. GREEN DOOR ... Jerms, Honor Brigade 1
130. TEARS ON MY PILLOW ... Johnny Tillotson, Amos 117
131. CAPT. GROOVY'S BUBBLE GUM ARMY ... Capt. Groovy's Bubble Gum Army, Super K 4
132. LAY LADY LAY ... Byrds, Columbia 4-44868
133. DON'T LET THE SUN CATCH YOU CRYIN' ... Trini Lopez, Reprise 0825
134. I'D RATHER BE AN OLD MAN'S SWEETHEART ... Candi Staton, Fame 1456
135. IN THE YEAR 2525 ... Zager & Evans, RCA 74-0174

Compiled from national retail sales and radio station airplay by the Music Popularity Dept. of Record Market Research, Billboard.

# Billboard HOT 100
**For Week Ending June 21, 1969**

★ STAR PERFORMER—Sides registering greatest proportionate upward progress this week.
● Record Industry Association of America seal of certification as million selling single.

| This Week | Wk. Ago | 2 Wk. Ago | 3 Wk. Ago | TITLE — Artist (Producer), Label & Number | Weeks On Chart |
|---|---|---|---|---|---|
| 1 | 1 | 1 | 1 | GET BACK — Beatles (George Martin), Apple 2490 | 7 |
| 2 | 2 | 8 | 11 | LOVE THEME FROM ROMEO & JULIET — Henry Mancini & Ork. (Joe Reisman), RCA Victor 74-0131 | 7 |
| 3 | 4 | 5 | 14 | BAD MOON RISING — Creedence Clearwater Revival (John Fogerty), Fantasy 622 | 8 |
| 4 | 3 | 6 | 9 | IN THE GHETTO — Elvis Presley, RCA Victor 47-9741 | 8 |
| 5 | 8 | 10 | 15 | TOO BUSY THINKING ABOUT MY BABY — Marvin Gaye (Norman Whitfield), Tamla 54181 | 8 |
| 6 | 10 | 14 | 23 | ONE — Three Dog Night (Gabriel Mekler), Dunhill 4191 | 6 |
| 7 | 5 | 2 | 2 | LOVE (Can Make You Happy) — Mercy (Jamie-Guyden), Sundi 6811 | 11 |
| 8 | 6 | 13 | 10 | GRAZIN' IN THE GRASS — Friends of Distinction (John Florez), RCA 74-0207 | 12 |
| ★9 | 15 | 30 | 57 | GOOD MORNING STARSHINE — Oliver (Bob Crewe), Jubilee 5659 | 5 |
| ★10 | 18 | 33 | 78 | SPINNING WHEEL — Blood, Sweat & Tears (James William Guercio), Columbia 44871 | 4 |
| 11 | 11 | 7 | 3 | AQUARIUS/LET THE SUNSHINE IN — Fifth Dimension (Bones Howe), Soul City 772 | 16 |
| 12 | 16 | 18 | 41 | THE ISRAELITES — Desmond Dekker & the Aces (A Pyramid Production), Uni 55129 | 6 |
| 13 | 7 | 4 | 4 | OH HAPPY DAY — Edwin Hawkins Singers (La Mont Bench), Pavillion 20001 | 9 |
| 14 | 9 | 9 | 6 | THESE EYES — Guess Who (Nimbus 9), RCA 74-0102 | 11 |
| 15 | 14 | 12 | 7 | ATLANTIS — Donovan (Mickie Most), Epic 5-10434 | 12 |
| 16 | 12 | 15 | 19 | MORE TODAY THAN YESTERDAY — Spiral Staircase (Sonny Knight), Columbia 4-44741 | 12 |
| 17 | 13 | 11 | 8 | GITARZAN — Ray Stevens (Fred Foster, Ray Stevens & Jim Malloy), Monument 1131 | 12 |
| ★18 | 32 | 38 | 45 | LOVE ME TONIGHT — Tom Jones (Peter Sullivan), Parrot 40038 | 4 |
| 19 | 19 | 29 | 30 | EVERYDAY WITH YOU GIRL — Classics IV (Buddy Buie), Imperial 66378 | 5 |
| 20 | 20 | 24 | 32 | BLACK PEARL — Sonny Charles with the Checkmates Ltd. (Phil Spector), A&M 1053 | 7 |
| 21 | 25 | 27 | 27 | DAY IS DONE — Peter, Paul & Mary (Phil Ramone), Warner Bros.-Seven Arts 7279 | 9 |
| 22 | 22 | 25 | 35 | DON'T LET THE JONESES GET YOU DOWN — Temptations (Norman Whitfield), Gordy 7086 | 5 |
| 23 | 21 | 3 | 5 | HAIR — Cowsills (Bill & Bob Cowsill), MGM 14026 | 15 |
| ★24 | 71 | — | — | THE BALLAD OF JOHN AND YOKO — The Beatles (Lennon-McCartney), Apple 2531 | 2 |
| 25 | 41 | 50 | 59 | WHAT DOES IT TAKE TO WIN YOUR LOVE — Jr. Walker & the All Stars (Fuqua & Bristol), Soul 35062 | 5 |
| 26 | 26 | 37 | 39 | MEDICINE MAN — Buchanan Brothers (Cashman, Pistilli & West), Event, 3302 | 6 |
| 27 | 29 | 41 | 48 | LET ME — Paul Revere & the Raiders Featuring Mark Lindsay, Columbia 4-44854 | 6 |
| ★28 | 39 | 61 | 74 | COLOR HIM FATHER — Winstons (Don Carroll), Metromedia 117 | 4 |
| 29 | 30 | 35 | 43 | SEE — Rascals (Rascals & Arif Mardin), Atlantic 2634 | 5 |
| 30 | 17 | 17 | 21 | MORNING GIRL — Neon Philharmonic (T. Saussy, Don Gant & B. McCluskey), Warner Bros.-Seven Arts 7261 | 12 |
| ★31 | 80 | — | — | MOTHER POPCORN, PART 1 (You Got to Have a Mother for Me) — James Brown (James Brown), King 6245 | 2 |
| 32 | 33 | 46 | 61 | NO MATTER WHAT SIGN YOU ARE — Diana Ross & the Supremes (B. Gordy Jr. & H. Cosby), Motown 1148 | 4 |
| 33 | 52 | 60 | 70 | MY CHERIE AMOUR — Stevie Wonder (Hank Cosby), Tamla 54180 | 4 |
| ★34 | 56 | 64 | 72 | MOODY WOMAN — Jerry Butler (Gamble & Huff), Mercury 72929 | 4 |
| ★35 | 47 | 58 | 63 | I TURNED YOU ON — Isley Brothers (R. Isley-O. Isley-R. Isley), T-Neck 902 | 4 |
| 36 | 38 | 39 | 40 | I WANNA TESTIFY — Johnnie Taylor (Don Davis), Stax 0033 | 5 |
| 37 | 37 | 40 | 47 | THE APRIL FOOLS — Dionne Warwick (Burt Bacharach, Hal David), Scepter 12249 | 6 |
| 38 | 40 | 43 | 44 | SPECIAL DELIVERY — 1910 Fruitgum Co. (Kasenetz-Katz Associates), Buddah 114 | 7 |
| 39 | 43 | 59 | 66 | LOVE IS BLUE (I Can Sing a Rainbow) — Dells (Bobby Miller), Cadet 5641 | 5 |
| 40 | 44 | 67 | 76 | BABY, I LOVE YOU — Andy Kim (Jeff Barry), Steed 1031 | 5 |
| 41 | 42 | 54 | 55 | WITH PEN IN HAND — Vikki Carr (Dave Pell & Rob Bledsoe), Liberty 56092 | 8 |
| 42 | 24 | 22 | 22 | HAPPY HEART — Andy Williams (Jerry Fuller), Columbia 4-44818 | 11 |
| 43 | 61 | 73 | 81 | THE POPCORN — James Brown (James Brown), King 6240 | 3 |
| ★44 | 57 | 89 | — | CRYSTAL BLUE PERSUASION — Tommy James & the Shondells (Tommy James-Ritchie Cordell), Roulette 7050 | 3 |
| 45 | 31 | 34 | 37 | THE WINDMILLS OF YOUR MIND — Dusty Springfield (Jerry Wexler), Atlantic 2623 | 8 |
| 46 | 45 | 23 | 24 | CISSY STRUT — Meters (Marshall E. Schorn & Allen Toussaint), Josie 1005 | 11 |
| 47 | 49 | 51 | 54 | FRIEND, LOVER, WOMAN, WIFE — O. C. Smith (Jerry Fuller), Columbia 44859 | 7 |
| 48 | 48 | 48 | 49 | WELCOME ME LOVE — Brooklyn Bridge (Wes Farrell), Buddah 95 | 7 |
| 49 | 34 | 26 | 26 | WHERE'S THE PLAYGROUND SUSIE — Glen Campbell (Al De Lory), Capitol 2494 | 8 |
| 50 | 76 | 84 | — | MY PLEDGE OF LOVE — The Joe Jeffrey Group (Jerry Meyers & Alan Klein), Wand 11200 | 3 |
| 51 | 70 | 90 | — | MRS. ROBINSON — Booker T. & the M.G.'s (Booker T. & the M.G.'s), Stax 0037 | 3 |
| 52 | 67 | 74 | 85 | BUT IT'S ALRIGHT — J. J. Jackson (Lew Futterman), Warner Bros.-Seven Arts 7276 | 4 |
| 53 | 36 | 31 | 31 | THE RIVER IS WIDE — The Grassroots (Steve Barri), Dunhill 4187 | 11 |
| 54 | 54 | 55 | 60 | TOMORROW TOMORROW — Bee Gees (Robert Stigwood & the Bee Gees), Atco 6682 | 4 |
| 55 | 35 | 36 | 36 | I'VE BEEN HURT — Bill Deal & the Rhondells (Jerry Ross), Heritage 812 | 10 |
| 56 | 65 | 65 | 73 | SO I CAN LOVE YOU — Emotions, Volt 4010 | 5 |
| 57 | 59 | 62 | 67 | WE GOT MORE SOUL — Dyke & the Blazers (Art Barrett), Original Sound 86 | 6 |
| ★58 | 85 | — | — | QUENTIN'S THEME — The Charles Randolph Grean Sounde (Charles R. Grean), Ranwood 840 | 2 |
| 59 | 64 | 66 | 79 | THE MINOTAUR — Dick Hyman & His Electric Eclectics, Command 4126 | 4 |
| 60 | 62 | 79 | 88 | I WANT TO TAKE YOU HIGHER — Sly & the Family Stone (Sly Stone), Epic 10450 | 5 |
| 61 | 53 | 53 | 53 | WHAT IS A MAN? — Four Tops (Fuqua), Motown 1147 | 6 |
| 62 | 63 | 86 | 90 | HUSHABYE — Jay & the Americans (Jay & the Americans), United Artists 50535 | 4 |
| 63 | 66 | 69 | 71 | WITHOUT HER — Herb Alpert (Herb Alpert & Jerry Moss), A&M 1065 | 6 |
| 64 | 50 | 52 | 52 | I COULD NEVER LIE TO YOU — New Colony Six, Mercury 72920 | 8 |
| 65 | 46 | 49 | 50 | I'M A DRIFTER — Bobby Goldsboro (Bob Montgomery & Bobby Goldsboro), United Artists 50525 | 10 |
| 66 | 79 | 87 | — | YOU DON'T HAVE TO WALK IN THE RAIN — Turtles (Ray Davies), White Whale 308 | 3 |
| 67 | 72 | 76 | 80 | I CAN'T QUIT HER — Arbors (Lori Burton & Roy Cicola), Date 1645 | 4 |
| ★68 | 78 | 83 | — | DIDN'T WE — Richard Harris (Jimmy Webb), Dunhill 4194 | 3 |
| 69 | 75 | 75 | 91 | MEMPHIS UNDERGROUND — Herbie Mann (Tom Dowd), Atlantic 2621 | 5 |
| ★70 | 89 | 98 | — | RUBY, DON'T TAKE YOUR LOVE TO TOWN — Kenny Rogers and the First Edition (Jimmy Bowen), Reprise 0829 | 3 |
| ★71 | 84 | — | — | THE GIRL I'LL NEVER KNOW — Frankie Valli (Bob Crewe), Philips 40622 | 2 |
| ★72 | — | — | — | IN THE YEAR 2525 (Exordium & Terminus) — Zager & Evans (Zager & Evans), RCA 74-0174 | 1 |
| 73 | 73 | 71 | 77 | TRUCKSTOP — Jerry Smith (Paul Cohen), ABC 11162 | 7 |
| 74 | 74 | 72 | 75 | LOVE MAN — Otis Redding (Steve Cropper), Atco 6677 | 5 |
| 75 | 77 | 88 | — | IT'S GETTING BETTER — Mama Cass (Steve Barri), Dunhill 4195 | 3 |
| ★76 | — | — | — | DOGGONE RIGHT — Smokey Robinson & the Miracles (Smokey), Tamla 54183 | 1 |
| 77 | 83 | — | — | YESTERDAY WHEN I WAS YOUNG — Roy Clark (Joe Allison), Dot 17246 | 2 |
| 78 | 82 | 82 | 83 | WHY I SING THE BLUES — B. B. King (Bill Szymczyk), BluesWay 61024 | 6 |
| 79 | 69 | 63 | 65 | RHYTHM OF THE RAIN — Gary Lewis & the Playboys (Snuff Garrett), Liberty 56093 | 12 |
| 80 | 81 | 81 | 82 | SINCERELY — Paul Anka (Don Costa), RCA 74-0164 | 4 |
| ★81 | — | — | — | THE DAYS OF SAND AND SHOVELS — Bobby Vinton (Billy Sherrill), Epic 10485 | 2 |
| 82 | 100 | — | — | TELL ALL THE PEOPLE — Doors (Kreiger), Elektra 45663 | 2 |
| 83 | 88 | — | — | DON'T WAKE ME UP IN THE MORNING, MICHAEL — The Peppermint Rainbow (Paul Leka), Decca 732498 | 2 |
| ★84 | — | — | — | MOMENTS TO REMEMBER — Vogues (Dick Glasser), Neprine 0831 | 1 |
| ★85 | — | — | — | THE PROPHECY OF DANIEL AND JOHN THE DEVINE — Cowsills (Bob Cowsill), MGM 14063 | 1 |
| ★86 | 92 | 96 | 96 | HURT SO BAD — Lettermen (Al DeLory), Capitol 2482 | 4 |
| 87 | 87 | — | — | DAMMIT ISN'T GOD'S LAST NAME — Frankie Laine (Jimmy Bowen), ABC 11224 | 2 |
| ★88 | — | — | — | I'D RATHERS BE AN OLD MAN'S SWEETHEART — Candi Staton (Rick Hall), Fame 1456 | 1 |
| ★89 | — | — | — | THE FEELING IS RIGHT — Clarence Carter (Rick Hall), Atlantic 2648 | 1 |
| ★90 | — | — | — | GIRL YOU'RE TOO YOUNG — Archie Bell & the Drells (Gamble & Huff), Atlantic 2644 | 1 |
| 91 | 97 | 97 | — | LISTEN TO THE BAND — Monkees (Michael Nesmith), Colgems 66-5004 | 3 |
| 92 | 93 | 99 | 100 | SON OF A TRAVELIN' MAN — Ed Ames (Jim Fogelsong), RCA 74-0156 | 4 |
| 93 | 94 | — | — | IT'S MY THING, PART I — Marva Whitney (........), King 6229 | 2 |
| 94 | 95 | — | — | FUNNY FEELING — The Delfonics (Stan & Bell Prod.), Philly Groove 156 | 2 |
| 95 | 96 | — | — | MOONFLIGHT — Vik Venus (Lewis Merenstein), Buddah 118 | 2 |
| 96 | — | — | — | BABY, DON'T BE LOOKING IN MY MIND — Joe Simon (J. B. Enterprises), Sound Stage 7 2634 | 1 |
| 97 | — | — | — | AND SHE'S MINE — Spanky & Our Gang (Scharf/Dorough), Mercury 72926 | 1 |
| 98 | — | — | — | GOTTA GET TO KNOW YOU — Bobby Bland (Broozier & Perry), Duke 447 | 1 |
| 99 | — | — | — | PINCH ME — Ohio Express (Katz/Kasenatz/Woods), Buddah 117 | 1 |
| 100 | — | — | — | FEELING ALRIGHT — Joe Cocker (Denny-Cordell), A&M 1063 | 1 |

## BUBBLING UNDER THE HOT 100

101. NEVER COMES THE DAY — Moody Blues, Deram 85044
102. LOLLIPOP — Intruders, Gamble 231
103. GALVESTON — Roger Williams, Kapp 2007
104. I'M STILL A STRUGGLING MAN — Edwin Starr, Gordy 7087
105. STAY AND LOVE ME ALL SUMMER — Brian Hyland, Dot 172926
106. THAT'S NOT LOVE — Dee Dee Warwick, Mercury 72927
107. I THREW IT ALL AWAY — Bob Dylan, Columbia 4-44826
108. GET TOGETHER — Youngbloods, RCA 47-9752
109. RECONSIDER ME — Johnny Adams, SSS International 770
110. (Sittin' On) THE DOCK OF THE BAY — Sergio Mendes & Brasil '66, A&M 1073
111. BIG BRUCE — Steve Greenburg, Trip 3000
112. I'LL NEVER FALL IN LOVE AGAIN — Burt DeShannon, Imperial 1064
113. PUT A LITTLE LOVE IN YOUR HEART — Jackie DeShannon, Imperial 66385
114. EVERYTHING I DO GONNA BE FUNKY — Lee Dorsey, Philly Groove 11055
115. CHOICE OF COLORS — Impressions, Curtom 1943
116. MY LITTLE CHICKADEE — Foundations, Uni 55137
117. FOREVER — Mercy, Warner Bros.-Seven Arts 7279
118. IN THE TIME OF OUR LIVES — Iron Butterfly, Atco 6647
119. I HAVE BUT ONE LIFE TO LIVE — Sammy Davis Jr., Reprise 0827
120. CROSSROADS OF THE STEPPING STONES — Elephant's Memory, Buddah 98
121. TAKE YOUR LOVE AND SHOVE IT — Kane's Cousins, Shove Love 500
122. HAPPY TOGETHER — Hugo Montenegro & His Orch., RCA 74-0160
123. WHILE YOU'RE OUT LOOKING FOR SUGAR — Honey Cone, Hot Wax 6901
124. SUGAR, SUGAR — Archies, Calendar 63-1008
125. FOLLOW THE LEADER — Major Lance, Dakar 608
126. ANGEL OF THE MORNING — Bettye Swann, Capitol 2515
127. THE HUNTER — Ike & Tina Turner, Blue Thumb 102
128. CAPTAIN GROOVY'S BUBBLE GUM ARMY — Captain Groovy's Bubble Gum Army, Super K 4
129. TEARS ON MY PILLOW — Johnny Tillotson, Amos 117
130. BUT FOR LOVE — Eddy Arnold, RCA 74-0175
131. COMIN' BACK TO ME — Del Shannon, Dunhill 4193

Compiled from national retail sales and radio station airplay by the Music Popularity Dept. of Record Market Research, Billboard.

# Billboard HOT 100

**FOR WEEK ENDING JUNE 28, 1969**

★ STAR PERFORMER—Sides registering greatest proportionate upward progress this week.

Ⓢ Record Industry Association of America seal of certification as million selling single.

| This Week | 1 Wk. Ago | 2 Wks. Ago | 3 Wks. Ago | TITLE Artist (Producer), Label & Number | Weeks On Chart |
|---|---|---|---|---|---|
| 1 | 2 | 2 | 8 | LOVE THEME FROM ROMEO & JULIET — Henry Mancini & Ork. (Joe Reisman), RCA Victor 74-0131 | 8 |
| 2 | 3 | 4 | 5 | BAD MOON RISING — Creedence Clearwater Revival (John Fogerty), Fantasy 622 | 9 |
| 3 | 1 | 1 | 1 | GET BACK — Beatles (George Martin), Apple 2490 | 8 |
| 4 | 5 | 8 | 10 | TOO BUSY THINKING ABOUT MY BABY — Marvin Gaye (Norman Whitfield), Tamla 54181 | 10 |
| ★5 | 6 | 10 | 14 | ONE — Three Dog Night (Gabriel Mekler), Dunhill 4191 | 9 |
| ★6 | 10 | 18 | 33 | SPINNING WHEEL — Blood, Sweat & Tears (James William Guercio), Columbia 44871 | 6 |
| 7 | 4 | 3 | 6 | IN THE GHETTO — Elvis Presley, RCA Victor 47-9741 | 9 |
| 8 | 9 | 15 | 30 | GOOD MORNING STARSHINE — Oliver (Bob Crewe), Jubilee 5659 | 6 |
| 9 | 12 | 16 | 18 | THE ISRAELITES — Desmond Dekker & the Aces (A Pyramid Production), Uni 55129 | 7 |
| Ⓢ10 | 8 | 6 | 13 | GRAZIN' IN THE GRASS — Friends of Distinction (John Florez), RCA 74-0207 | 13 |
| ★11 | 24 | 71 | — | THE BALLAD OF JOHN AND YOKO — The Beatles (Lennon-McCartney), Apple 2531 | 3 |
| 12 | 7 | 5 | 2 | LOVE (Can Make You Happy) — Mercy (Jamie-Guyden), Sundi 6811 | 12 |
| ★13 | 28 | 39 | 61 | COLOR HIM FATHER — Winstons (Don Carroll), Metromedia 117 | 6 |
| 14 | 20 | 20 | 24 | BLACK PEARL — Sonny Charles with the Checkmates Ltd. (Phil Spector), A&M 1053 | 8 |
| 15 | 18 | 32 | 38 | LOVE ME TONIGHT — Tom Jones (Peter Sullivan), Parrot 40038 | 6 |
| ★16 | 25 | 41 | 50 | WHAT DOES IT TAKE TO WIN YOUR LOVE — Jr. Walker & the All Stars (Fuqua & Bristol), Soul 35062 | 7 |
| 17 | 14 | 9 | 9 | THESE EYES — Guess Who (Nimbus 9), RCA 74-0102 | 13 |
| ★18 | 44 | 57 | 89 | CRYSTAL BLUE PERSUASION — Tommy James & the Shondells (Tommy James-Ritchie Cordell), Roulette 7050 | 4 |
| 19 | 31 | 80 | — | PART I MOTHER POPCORN (You Got to Have a Mother for Me) — James Brown (James Brown), King 6245 | 3 |
| 20 | 22 | 22 | 25 | DON'T LET THE JONESES GET YOU DOWN — Temptations (Norman Whitfield), Gordy 7086 | 6 |
| 21 | 16 | 12 | 15 | MORE TODAY THAN YESTERDAY — Spiral Staircase (Sonny Knight), Columbia 4-44741 | 13 |
| ★22 | 33 | 52 | 60 | MY CHERIE AMOUR — Stevie Wonder (Hank Cosby), Tamla 54180 | 5 |
| 23 | 19 | 19 | 29 | EVERYDAY WITH YOU GIRL — Classics IV (Buddy Blue), Imperial 66378 | 6 |
| 24 | 27 | 29 | 41 | LET ME — Paul Revere & the Raiders Featuring Mark Lindsay, Columbia 4-44854 | 7 |
| 25 | 26 | 26 | 37 | MEDICINE MAN — Buchanan Brothers (Cashman, Pistilli & West), Event, 3302 | 7 |
| Ⓢ26 | 11 | 11 | 7 | AQUARIUS/LET THE SUNSHINE IN — Fifth Dimension (Bones Howe), Soul City 772 | 17 |
| 27 | 34 | 56 | 64 | MOODY WOMAN — Jerry Butler (Gamble & Huff), Mercury 72929 | 5 |
| 28 | 29 | 30 | 35 | SEE — Rascals (Rascals & Arif Mardin), Atlantic 2634 | 6 |
| 29 | 13 | 7 | 4 | OH HAPPY DAY — Edwin Hawkins Singers (La Mont Bench), Pavillion 20001 | 10 |
| 30 | 15 | 14 | 12 | ATLANTIS — Donovan (Mickie Most), Epic 5-10434 | 13 |
| 31 | 32 | 33 | 46 | NO MATTER WHAT SIGN YOU ARE — Diana Ross & the Supremes (B. Gordy Jr. & H. Cosby), Motown 1148 | 5 |
| Ⓢ32 | 35 | 47 | 58 | I TURNED YOU ON — Isley Brothers (R. Isley-O. Isley-R. Isley), T-Neck 902 | 5 |
| 33 | 17 | 13 | 11 | GITARZAN — Ray Stevens (Fred Foster, Ray Stevens & Jim Malloy), Monument 1131 | 13 |
| 34 | 43 | 61 | 73 | THE POPCORN — James Brown (James Brown), King 6240 | 4 |
| ★35 | 72 | — | — | IN THE YEAR 2525 (Exordium & Terminus) — Zager & Evans (Zager & Evans), RCA 74-0174 | 3 |
| 36 | 41 | 42 | 54 | WITH PEN IN HAND — Vikki Carr (Dave Pell & Rob Bledsoe), Liberty 56092 | 9 |
| 37 | 40 | 44 | 67 | BABY, I LOVE YOU — Andy Kim (Jeff Barry), Steed 1031 | 6 |
| 38 | 39 | 43 | 59 | MEDLEY: CAN SING A RAINBOW/LOVE IS BLUE — Dells (Bobby Miller), Cadet 5641 | 6 |
| 39 | 21 | 25 | 27 | DAY IS DONE — Peter, Paul & Mary (Phil Ramone), Warner Bros.-Seven Arts 7279 | 10 |
| 40 | 36 | 38 | 39 | I WANNA TESTIFY — Johnnie Taylor (Don Davis), Stax 0033 | 8 |
| 41 | 50 | 76 | 84 | MY PLEDGE OF LOVE — The Joe Jeffrey Group (Jerry Meyers & Alan Klein), Wand 11200 | 4 |
| ★42 | 58 | 85 | — | QUENTIN'S THEME — The Charles Randolph Grean Sounde (Charles R. Grean), Ranwood 840 | 3 |
| 43 | 38 | 40 | 43 | SPECIAL DELIVERY — 1910 Fruitgum Co. (Kasenetz-Katz Associates), Buddah 114 | 8 |
| 44 | 37 | 37 | 40 | THE APRIL FOOLS — Dionne Warwick (Burt Bacharach, Hal David), Scepter 12249 | 7 |
| 45 | 51 | 70 | 90 | MRS. ROBINSON — Booker T. & the M.G.'s (Booker T. & the M.G.'s), Stax 0037 | 4 |
| ★46 | 59 | 64 | 66 | THE MINOTAUR — Dick Hyman & His Electric Eclectics, Command 4126 | 5 |
| 47 | 81 | 90 | — | THE DAYS OF SAND AND SHOVELS — Bobby Vinton (Billy Sherrill), Epic 10485 | 3 |
| ★48 | 76 | — | — | DOGGONE RIGHT — Smokey Robinson & the Miracles (Smokey), Tamla 54183 | 2 |
| 49 | 48 | 48 | 48 | WELCOME ME LOVE — Brooklyn Bridge (Wes Farrell), Buddah 95 | 8 |
| 50 | 77 | 83 | — | YESTERDAY WHEN I WAS YOUNG — Roy Clark (Joe Allison), Dot 17246 | 3 |
| 51 | 57 | 59 | 62 | WE GOT MORE SOUL — Dyke & the Blazers (Art Barrett), Original Sound 86 | 7 |
| 52 | 52 | 67 | 74 | BUT IT'S ALRIGHT — J. J. Jackson (Lew Futterman), Warner Bros.-Seven Arts 7276 | 6 |
| 53 | 47 | 49 | 51 | FRIEND, LOVER, WOMAN, WIFE — O. C. Smith (Jerry Fuller), Columbia 44859 | 6 |
| 54 | 69 | 75 | 75 | MEMPHIS UNDERGROUND — Herbie Mann (Tom Dowd), Atlantic 2621 | 5 |
| 55 | 70 | 89 | 98 | RUBY, DON'T TAKE YOUR LOVE TO TOWN — Kenny Rogers and the First Edition (Jimmy Bowen), Reprise 0829 | 4 |
| 56 | 56 | 65 | 65 | SO I CAN LOVE YOU — Emotions, Volt 4010 | 6 |
| 57 | 66 | 79 | 87 | YOU DON'T HAVE TO WALK IN THE RAIN — Turtles (Ray Davies), White Whale 308 | 5 |
| 58 | 54 | 54 | 55 | TOMORROW TOMORROW — Bee Gees (Robert Stigwood & the Bee Gees), Atco 6682 | 6 |
| ★59 | — | — | — | SWEET CAROLINE (Good Times Never Seemed So Good) — Neil Diamond (Tommy Cogbill, Tom Catalano, Neil Diamond), Uni 55136 | 1 |
| 60 | 60 | 62 | 79 | I WANT TO TAKE YOU HIGHER — Sly & the Family Stone (Sly Stone), Epic 10450 | 6 |
| ★61 | — | — | — | GOOD OLD ROCK 'N ROLL — Cat Mother and the All Night News Boys (Cat Mother & Jimi Hendrix), Polydor 14002 | 1 |
| 62 | 62 | 63 | 86 | HUSHABYE — Jay & the Americans (Jay & the Americans), United Artists 50535 | 5 |
| 63 | 63 | 66 | 69 | WITHOUT HER — Herb Alpert (Herb Alpert & Jerry Moss), A&M 1065 | 5 |
| 64 | 71 | 84 | — | THE GIRL I'LL NEVER KNOW — Frankie Valli (Bob Crewe), Philips 40622 | 3 |
| 65 | 75 | 77 | 88 | IT'S GETTING BETTER — Mama Cass (Steve Barri), Dunhill 4195 | 4 |
| 66 | 84 | — | — | MOMENTS TO REMEMBER — Vogues (Dick Glasser), Reprise 0831 | 2 |
| 67 | 68 | 78 | 83 | DIDN'T WE — Richard Harris (Jimmy Webb), Dunhill 4194 | 4 |
| 68 | 95 | 96 | — | MOONFLIGHT — Vik Venus (Lewis Merenstein), Buddah 118 | 3 |
| 69 | 82 | 100 | — | TELL ALL THE PEOPLE — Doors (Kreiger), Elektra 45663 | 3 |
| 70 | 78 | 82 | 82 | WHY I SING THE BLUES — B. B. King (Bill Szymczyk), BluesWay 61024 | 7 |
| ★71 | 88 | — | — | I'D RATHER BE AN OLD MAN'S SWEETHEART — Candi Staton (Rick Hall), Fame 1456 | 2 |
| ★72 | — | — | — | RECONSIDER ME — Johnny Adams (Shelby S. Singleton Jr.), SSS Int'l 770 | 1 |
| 73 | 91 | 97 | 97 | LISTEN TO THE BAND — Monkees (Michael Nesmith), Colgems 66-5004 | 4 |
| 74 | 83 | 88 | — | DON'T WAKE ME UP IN THE MORNING, MICHAEL — The Peppermint Rainbow (Paul Leka), Decca 732498 | 3 |
| 75 | 67 | 72 | 76 | I CAN'T QUIT HER — Arbors (Lori Burton & Roy Cicola), Date 1645 | 5 |
| ★76 | 85 | — | — | THE PROPHECY OF DANIEL AND JOHN THE DEVINE — Cowsills (Bob Cowsill), MGM 14063 | 2 |
| 77 | 86 | 92 | 96 | HURT SO BAD — Lettermen (Al DeLory), Capitol 2482 | 5 |
| 78 | 100 | — | — | FEELING ALRIGHT — Joe Cocker (Denny-Cordell), A&M 1063 | 2 |
| ★79 | — | — | — | I'M STILL A STRUGGLIN' MAN — Edwin Starr (Johnny Bristol), Gordy 7087 | 1 |
| 80 | 89 | — | — | THE FEELING IS RIGHT — Clarence Carter (Rick Hall), Atlantic 2648 | 2 |
| 81 | 93 | 94 | — | IT'S MY THING, PART I — Marva Whitney (King), King 6229 | 3 |
| 82 | 96 | — | — | BABY, DON'T BE LOOKING IN MY MIND — Joe Simon (J. B. Enterprises), Sound Stage 7 2634 | 2 |
| ★83 | 90 | — | — | GIRL YOU'RE TOO YOUNG — Archie Bell & the Drells (Gamble & Huff), Atlantic 2644 | 2 |
| ★84 | — | — | — | PUT A LITTLE LOVE IN YOUR HEART — Jackie DeShannon (VME), Imperial 66385 | 1 |
| 85 | 87 | 87 | — | DAMMIT ISN'T GOD'S LAST NAME — Frankie Laine (Jimmy Bowen), ABC 11224 | 3 |
| 86 | — | — | — | FOREVER — Mercy (Brad Shapiro & Steve Alaimo), Warner Bros.-Seven Arts 7297 | 1 |
| 87 | — | — | — | ON CAMPUS — Dickie Goodman (Dickie Goodman), Cotique 158 | 1 |
| 88 | — | — | — | ABRAHAM, MARTIN AND JOHN — Moms Mabley (Barry Oslander), Mercury 72935 | 1 |
| ★89 | — | — | — | WHILE YOU'RE OUT LOOKING FOR SUGAR? — Honey Cone (R. Dunbar), Hot Wax 6901 | 1 |
| 90 | 98 | 98 | — | GOTTA GET TO KNOW YOU — Bobby Bland (Broozier & Perry), Duke 447 | 3 |
| ★91 | — | — | — | NEVER COMES THE DAY — Moody Blues (Tony Clarke), Deram 85044 | 1 |
| 92 | — | — | — | GET TOGETHER — Youngbloods (Felix Pappalardi), RCA 47-9752 | 1 |
| 93 | — | — | — | ALONG CAME JONES — Ray Stevens (Ray Stevens, Jim Malloy), Monument 1150 | 1 |
| 94 | — | — | — | DON'T TELL YOU'VE BEEN — Eddie Floyd (Steve Cropper, B. T. Jones), Stax 0036 | 1 |
| 95 | — | — | — | EVERYTHING I DO GONNA BE FUNKY (From Now On) — Lee Dorsey (Marshall E. Sehorn & Allen R. Toussaint), Amy 11055 | 1 |
| 96 | — | — | — | MUDDY RIVER — Johnny Rivers (Johnny Rivers), Imperial 66386 | 1 |
| 97 | — | — | — | (Sittin' On) THE DOCK OF THE BAY — Sergio Mendes & Brasil '66 (Sergio Mendes & Herb Alpert), A&M 1073 | 1 |
| 98 | 99 | — | — | PINCH ME — Ohio Express (Katz/Kasenatz/Woods), Buddah 117 | 1 |
| 99 | — | — | — | THEME FROM 'A SUMMER PLACE' — Ventures (Joe Saraceno), Liberty 56115 | 1 |
| 100 | — | — | — | | |

## BUBBLING UNDER THE HOT 100

101. LOLLIPOP ............ Intruders, Gamble 231
102. STAY AND LOVE ME ALL SUMMER .... Brian Hyland, Dot 172926
103. IN THE TIME OF OUR LIVES ..... Iron Butterfly, Atco 6676
104. FUNNY FEELING ........ Delfonics, Philly Groove 156
105. I'D WAIT A MILLION YEARS ..... Grass Roots, Dunhill 4198
106. SINCERELY ............. Paul Anka, RCA 74-0164
107. ABRAHAM, MARTIN & JOHN . Smokey Robinson & the Miracles, Tamla 54184
108. SON OF A TRAVELING MAN ........ Ed Ames, RCA 74-0156
109. BIG BRUCE ........ Steve Greenberg, Trip 3000
110. I'LL NEVER FALL IN LOVE AGAIN ... Burt Bacharach, A&M 1064
111. PASS THE APPLE EVE ..... B. J. Thomas, Scepter 12255
112. ANGEL OF THE MORNING .... Bettye Swann, Capitol 2515
113. AND SHE'S MINE ... Spanky & Our Gang, Mercury 72926
114. SAINT PAUL ........ Terry Knight, Capitol 2506
115. MY LITTLE CHICKADEE .... Foundations, Uni 55137
116. HAPPY TOGETHER ... Hugo Montenegro & His Ork, RCA 74-0160
117. TAKE YOUR LOVE AND SHOVE IT ... Kanes Cousins, Shove Love 500
118. SUNSHINE RED WINE ..... Crazy Elephant, Bell 804
119. TEARS ON MY PILLOW .... Johnny Tillotson, Amos 117
120. WAKE UP .... Chambers Brothers, Columbia 4-44890
121. THE HUNTER ..... Ike & Tina Turner, Blue Thumb 102
122. STOMP ........... N.R.B.Q., Columbia 4-44865
123. SUGAR, SUGAR ........ Archies, Calendar 63-1008
124. BREAKAWAY .......... Beach Boys, Capitol 2530
125. OH HAPPY DAY ...... Billy Witchell, Calla 165
126. DID YOU SEE HER EYES .... Illusion, Steed 712
127. BUT FOR LOVE ........ Eddy Arnold, RCA 74-0175
128. COMIN' BACK TO ME ... Del Shannon, Dunhill 4193
129. THOU SHALT NOT STEAL .... Newbeats, Hickory 1539

Compiled from national retail sales and radio station airplay by the Music Popularity Dept. of Record Market Research, Billboard.

# Billboard HOT 100

FOR WEEK ENDING JULY 5, 1969

★ STAR PERFORMER—Sides registering greatest proportionate upward progress this week.

Record Industry Association of America seal of certification as million selling single.

| This Week | 1 Wk. Ago | 2 Wks. Ago | 3 Wks. Ago | TITLE Artist (Producer), Label & Number | Weeks On Chart |
|---|---|---|---|---|---|
| 1 | 1 | 2 | 2 | LOVE THEME FROM ROMEO & JULIET — Henry Mancini & Ork. (Joe Reisman), RCA Victor 74-0131 | 9 |
| 2 | 6 | 10 | 18 | SPINNING WHEEL — Blood, Sweat & Tears (James William Guercio), Columbia 44871 | 6 |
| 3 | 2 | 3 | 4 | BAD MOON RISING — Creedence Clearwater Revival (John Fogerty), Fantasy 622 | 10 |
| 4 | 8 | 9 | 15 | GOOD MORNING STARSHINE — Oliver (Bob Crewe), Jubilee 5659 | 7 |
| 5 | 5 | 6 | 10 | ONE — Three Dog Night (Gabriel Mekler), Dunhill 4191 | 10 |
| 6 | 3 | 1 | 1 | GET BACK — Beatles (George Martin), Apple 2490 | 9 |
| ★7 | 18 | 44 | 57 | CRYSTAL BLUE PERSUASION — Tommy James & the Shondells (Tommy James-Ritchie Cordell), Roulette 7050 | 5 |
| ★8 | 35 | 72 | — | IN THE YEAR 2525 (Exordium & Terminus) — Zager & Evans (Zager & Evans), RCA 74-0174 | 3 |
| 9 | 13 | 28 | 39 | COLOR HIM FATHER — Winstons (Don Carroll), Metromedia 117 | 7 |
| 10 | 4 | 5 | 8 | TOO BUSY THINKING ABOUT MY BABY — Marvin Gaye (Norman Whitfield), Tamla 54181 | 11 |
| 11 | 11 | 24 | 71 | THE BALLAD OF JOHN AND YOKO — The Beatles (Lennon-McCartney), Apple 2531 | 4 |
| 12 | 7 | 4 | 3 | IN THE GHETTO — Elvis Presley, RCA Victor 47-9741 | 10 |
| 13 | 14 | 20 | 20 | BLACK PEARL — Sonny Charles with the Checkmates Ltd. (Phil Spector), A&M 1053 | 9 |
| ★14 | 16 | 25 | 41 | WHAT DOES IT TAKE TO WIN YOUR LOVE — Jr. Walker & the All Stars (Fuqua & Bristol), Soul 35062 | 8 |
| 15 | 15 | 18 | 32 | LOVE ME TONIGHT — Tom Jones (Peter Sullivan), Parrot 40038 | 7 |
| ★16 | 22 | 33 | 52 | MY CHERIE AMOUR — Stevie Wonder (Hank Cosby), Tamla 54180 | 6 |
| 17 | 10 | 8 | 6 | GRAZIN' IN THE GRASS — Friends of Distinction (John Florez), RCA 74-0207 | 14 |
| 18 | 19 | 31 | 80 | PART I MOTHER POPCORN (You Got to Have a Mother for Me) — James Brown (James Brown), King 6245 | 4 |
| 19 | 9 | 12 | 16 | THE ISRAELITES — Desmond Dekker & the Aces (A Pyramid Production), Uni 55129 | 8 |
| ★20 | 24 | 27 | 29 | LET ME — Paul Revere & the Raiders Featuring Mark Lindsay, Columbia 4-44854 | 8 |
| 21 | 21 | 16 | 12 | MORE TODAY THAN YESTERDAY — Spiral Staircase (Sonny Knight), Columbia 4-44741 | 14 |
| 22 | 25 | 26 | 26 | MEDICINE MAN — Buchanan Brothers (Cashman, Pistilli & West), Event, 3302 | 10 |
| 23 | 12 | 7 | 5 | LOVE (Can Make You Happy) — Mercy (Jamie-Guyden), Sundi 6811 | 13 |
| 24 | 23 | 19 | 19 | EVERYDAY WITH YOU GIRL — Classics IV (Buddy Blue), Imperial 66378 | 7 |
| 25 | 17 | 14 | 9 | THESE EYES — Guess Who (Nimbus 9), RCA 74-0102 | 14 |
| 26 | 27 | 34 | 56 | MOODY WOMAN — Jerry Butler (Gamble & Huff), Mercury 72929 | 6 |
| 27 | 28 | 29 | 30 | SEE — Rascals (Rascals & Arif Mardin), Atlantic 2634 | 7 |
| ★28 | 42 | 58 | 85 | QUENTIN'S THEME — The Charles Randolph Grean Sounde (Charles R. Grean), Ranwood 840 | 4 |
| 29 | 37 | 40 | 44 | BABY, I LOVE YOU — Andy Kim (Jeff Barry), Steed 1031 | 7 |
| 30 | 32 | 35 | 47 | I TURNED YOU ON — Isley Brothers (R. Isley-O. Isley-R. Isley), T-Neck 902 | 6 |
| ★31 | 38 | 39 | 43 | LOVE IS BLUE/I CAN SING A RAINBOW — Dells (Bobby Miller), Cadet 5641 | 7 |
| 32 | 20 | 22 | 22 | DON'T LET THE JONESES GET YOU DOWN — Temptations (Norman Whitfield), Gordy 7086 | 7 |
| ★33 | 41 | 50 | 76 | MY PLEDGE OF LOVE — The Joe Jeffrey Group (Jerry Meyers & Alan Klein), Wand 11200 | 5 |
| 34 | 34 | 43 | 61 | THE POPCORN — James Brown (James Brown), King 6240 | 5 |
| ★35 | 51 | 57 | 59 | WE GOT MORE SOUL — Dyke & the Blazers (Art Barrett), Original Sound 86 | 8 |
| 36 | 36 | 41 | 42 | WITH PEN IN HAND — Vikki Carr (Dave Pell & Rob Bledsoe), Liberty 56092 | 10 |
| 37 | 55 | 70 | 89 | RUBY, DON'T TAKE YOUR LOVE TO TOWN — Kenny Rogers and the First Edition (Jimmy Bowen), Reprise 0829 | 5 |
| ★38 | 46 | 59 | 64 | THE MINOTAUR — Dick Hyman & His Electric Eclectics, Command 4126 | 6 |
| 39 | 31 | 32 | 33 | NO MATTER WHAT SIGN YOU ARE — Diana Ross & the Supremes (B. Gordy Jr. & H. Cosby, Motown 1148 | 6 |
| 40 | 45 | 51 | 70 | MRS. ROBINSON — Booker T. & the M.G.'s (Booker T. & the M.G.'s), Stax 0037 | 5 |
| 41 | 47 | 81 | 90 | THE DAYS OF SAND AND SHOVELS — Bobby Vinton (Billy Sherrill), Epic 10485 | 4 |
| 42 | 50 | 77 | 83 | YESTERDAY WHEN I WAS YOUNG — Roy Clark (Joe Allison), Dot 17246 | 4 |
| 43 | 48 | 76 | — | DOGGONE RIGHT — Smokey Robinson & the Miracles (Smokey), Tamla 54183 | 3 |
| ★44 | 56 | 56 | 65 | SO I CAN LOVE YOU — Emotions, Volt 4010 | 7 |
| 45 | 54 | 69 | 75 | MEMPHIS UNDERGROUND — Herbie Mann (Tom Dowd), Atlantic 2621 | 7 |
| 46 | 52 | 52 | 67 | BUT IT'S ALRIGHT — J. J. Jackson (Lew Futterman), Warner Bros.-Seven Arts 7276 | 7 |
| ★47 | 68 | 95 | 96 | MOONFLIGHT — Vik Venus (Lewis Merenstein), Buddah 118 | 4 |
| ★48 | 77 | — | — | CHOICE OF COLORS — Impressions (Curtis Mayfield), Curtom 1943 | 2 |
| ★49 | 66 | 84 | — | MOMENTS TO REMEMBER — Vogues (Dick Classer), Neprine 0831 | 3 |
| ★50 | 59 | — | — | SWEET CAROLINE (Good Times Never Seemed So Good) — Neil Diamond (Tommy Cogbill, Tom Catalano, Neil Diamond), Uni 55136 | 2 |
| ★51 | 61 | — | — | GOOD OLD ROCK 'N ROLL — Cat Mother and the All Night News Boys (Cat Mother & Jimi Hendrix), Polydor 14002 | 2 |
| ★52 | 64 | 71 | 84 | THE GIRL I'LL NEVER KNOW — Frankie Valli (Bob Crewe), Philips 40622 | 4 |
| ★53 | 57 | 66 | 79 | YOU DON'T HAVE TO WALK IN THE RAIN — Turtles (Ray Davies), White Whale 308 | 5 |
| 54 | 49 | 48 | 48 | WELCOME ME LOVE — Brooklyn Bridge (Wes Farrell), Buddah 95 | 9 |
| ★55 | 65 | 75 | 77 | IT'S GETTING BETTER — Mama Cass (Steve Barri), Dunhill 4195 | 5 |
| 56 | 43 | 38 | 40 | SPECIAL DELIVERY — 1910 Fruitgum Co. (Kasenetz-Katz Associates), Buddah 114 | 9 |
| ★57 | 89 | — | — | ABRAHAM, MARTIN AND JOHN — Moms Mabley (Barry Oslander), Mercury 72935 | 2 |
| 58 | 53 | 47 | 49 | FRIEND, LOVER, WOMAN, WIFE — O. C. Smith (Jerry Fuller), Columbia 44859 | 9 |
| ★59 | 71 | 88 | — | I'D RATHER BE AN OLD MAN'S SWEETHEART — Candi Staton (Rick Hall), Fame 1456 | 3 |
| 60 | 58 | 54 | 54 | TOMORROW TOMORROW — Bee Gees (Robert Stigwood & the Bee Gees) Atco 6682 | 6 |
| 61 | 40 | 36 | 38 | I WANNA TESTIFY — Johnnie Taylor (Don Davis), Stax 0033 | 9 |
| 62 | 69 | 82 | 100 | TELL ALL THE PEOPLE — Doors (Kreiger), Elektra 45663 | 4 |
| 63 | 60 | 60 | 62 | I WANT TO TAKE YOU HIGHER — Sly & the Family Stone (Sly Stone), Epic 10450 | 7 |
| ★64 | 85 | — | — | PUT A LITTLE LOVE IN YOUR HEART — Jackie DeShannon (VME), Imperial 66385 | 2 |
| 65 | 67 | 68 | 78 | DIDN'T WE — Richard Harris (Jimmy Webb), Dunhill 4194 | 5 |
| ★66 | 94 | — | — | ALONG CAME JONES — Ray Stevens (Ray Stevens, Jim Malloy), Monument 1150 | 2 |
| 67 | 73 | 91 | 97 | LISTEN TO THE BAND — Monkees (Michael Nesmith), Colgems 66-5004 | 5 |
| 68 | 72 | — | — | RECONSIDER ME — Johnny Adams (Shelby S. Singleton Jr.), SSS Int'l 770 | 2 |
| 69 | 62 | 62 | 63 | HUSHABYE — Jay & the Americans (Jay & the Americans), United Artists 50535 | 6 |
| 70 | 70 | 78 | 82 | WHY I SING THE BLUES — B. B. King (Bill Szymczyk), BluesWay 61024 | 8 |
| 71 | 74 | 83 | 88 | DON'T WAKE ME UP IN THE MORNING, MICHAEL — The Peppermint Rainbow (Paul Leka), Decca 732498 | 4 |
| ★72 | 98 | — | — | (Sittin On) THE DOCK OF THE BAY — Sergio Mendes & Brasil '66 (Sergio Mendes & Herb Alpert), A&M 1073 | 2 |
| ★73 | — | — | — | ABRAHAM, MARTIN & JOHN — Smokey Robinson & the Miracles (Smokey Robinson), Tamla 54184 | 1 |
| 74 | 84 | 90 | — | GIRL YOU'RE TOO YOUNG — Archie Bell & the Drells (Gamble & Huff), Atlantic 2644 | 3 |
| ★75 | 88 | — | — | ON CAMPUS — Dickie Goodman (Dickie Goodman), Cotique 158 | 2 |
| 76 | 76 | 85 | — | THE PROPHECY OF DANIEL AND JOHN THE DEVINE — Cowsills (Bob Cowsill), MGM 14063 | 3 |
| 77 | 78 | 86 | 92 | HURT SO BAD — Lettermen (Al DeLory), Capitol 2482 | 6 |
| 78 | 81 | 89 | — | THE FEELING IS RIGHT — Clarence Carter (Rick Hall), Atlantic 2648 | 3 |
| 79 | 79 | 100 | — | FEELING ALRIGHT — Joe Cocker (Denny-Cordell), A&M 1063 | 3 |
| 80 | 80 | — | — | I'M STILL A STRUGGLIN' MAN — Edwin Starr (Johnny Bristol), Gordy 7087 | 2 |
| 81 | 83 | 96 | — | BABY, DON'T BE LOOKING IN MY MIND — Joe Simon (J. B. Enterprises), Sound Stage 7 2634 | 3 |
| 82 | 82 | 93 | 94 | IT'S MY THING, PART I — Marva Whitney (......), King 6229 | 4 |
| 83 | 90 | — | — | WHILE YOU'RE OUT LOOKING FOR SUGAR — Honey Cone (R. Dunbar), Hot Wax 6901 | 2 |
| 84 | 63 | 63 | 66 | WITHOUT HER — Herb Alpert (Herb Alpert & Jerry Moss), A&M 1065 | 6 |
| ★85 | — | — | — | I'D WAIT A MILLION YEARS — Grassroots (Steve Barry), Dunhill 4198 | 1 |
| ★86 | — | — | — | POLK SALAD ANNIE — Tony Joe White (Billy Swan), Monument 1104 | 1 |
| 87 | 87 | — | — | FOREVER — Mercy (Brad Shapiro & Steve Alaimo), Warner Bros.-Seven Arts 7297 | 2 |
| ★88 | 97 | — | — | MUDDY RIVER — Johnny Rivers (Johnny Rivers), Imperial 66386 | 2 |
| 89 | 93 | — | — | GET TOGETHER — Youngbloods (Felix Pappalardi), RCA 47-9752 | 2 |
| ★90 | — | — | — | CLEAN UP YOUR OWN BACK YARD — Elvis Presley, RCA Vistor 47-9747 | 1 |
| 91 | 92 | — | — | NEVER COMES THE DAY — Moody Blues (Tony Clarke), Deram 85044 | 2 |
| 92 | — | — | — | DID YOU SEE HER EYES — Illusion (Jeff Barry), Steed 718 | 1 |
| 93 | — | — | — | BREAK AWAY — Beach Boys (Brian Wilson/Murray Wilson), Capitol 2530 | 1 |
| 94 | — | — | — | SOUL DEEP — Box Tops (Tommy Cogbill & Chips Moman), Mala 12040 | 1 |
| 95 | 95 | — | — | DON'T TELL YOUR MAMA WHERE YOU'VE BEEN — Eddie Floyd (Steve Cropper, B. T. Jones), Stax 0036 | 2 |
| 96 | 96 | — | — | EVERYTHING I DO GONNA BE FUNKY (From Now On) — Lee Dorsey (Marshall E. Sehorn & Allen R. Toussaint), Amy 11055 | 2 |
| 97 | 100 | — | — | THEME FROM A SUMMER PLACE — Ventures (Joe Saraceno), Liberty 56115 | 2 |
| 98 | — | — | — | I'LL NEVER FALL IN LOVE AGAIN — Burt Bacharach (Burt Bacharach & Phil Ramone), A&M 1064 | 1 |
| 99 | — | — | — | NOTHING CAN TAKE THE PLACE OF YOU — Brook Benton (Arif Mardin), Cotillion 44034 | 1 |
| 100 | — | — | — | MY LITTLE CHICKADEE — Foundations (Tony Macaulay & John Macleod), Uni 55137 | 1 |

## HOT 100—A TO Z—*(Publisher-Licensee)*



## BUBBLING UNDER THE HOT 100

101. PASS THE APPLE EVE ..... B. J. Thomas, Scepter 12255
102. STAY AND LOVE ME ALL SUMMER ..... Brian Hyland, Dot 172926
103. IN THE TIME OF OUR LIVES ..... Iron Butterfly, Atco 6676
104. WILLIE & LAURA MAE JONES ..... Dusty Springfield, Atlantic 2647
105. LOLLIPOP ..... Intruders, Gamble 231
106. BIRDS OF A FEATHER ..... Joe South, Capitol 2532
107. BIG BRUCE ..... Steve Greenberg, Trip 3000
108. DAMMIT ISN'T GOD'S LAST NAME ..... Frankie Laine, ABC 11224
109. HEY JOE ..... Wilson Pickett, Atlantic 2648
110. SUGAR, SUGAR ..... Archies, Calendar 63-1008
111. GOTTA GET TO KNOW YOU ..... Bobby Bland, Duke 447
112. ANGEL OF THE MORNING ..... Bettye Swann, Capitol 2515
113. HAPPY TOGETHER ..... Hugo Montenegro & His Ork., RCA 74-0160
114. ST. PAUL ..... Terry Knight, Capitol 2506
115. OH HAPPY DAY ..... Billy Mitchell Group, Calla 165
116. WAKE UP ..... Chambers Brothers, Columbia 4-44890
117. TAKE YOUR LOVE AND SHOVE IT ..... Kane's Cousins, Shove Love 500
118. SUNSHINE RED WINE ..... Crazy Elephant, Bell 804
119. TEARS ON MY PILLOW ..... Johnny Tillotson, Amos 117
120. THE HUNTER ..... Ike & Tina Turner, Blue Thumb 102
121. TILL YOU GET ENOUGH ..... Watts 103rd Street Rhythm Band, Warner Bros.-Seven Arts 7298
122. STOMP ..... N.R.B.Q., Columbia 444590
123. ME AND BOBBY McGEE ..... Roger Miller, Smash 2230
124. DELIA'S GONE ..... Waylon Jennings, RCA 74-0157
125. BUT FOR LOVE ..... Eddy Arnold, RCA 74-0175
126. THE RIB ..... Jeannie C. Riley, Plantation 22
127. COMIN' BACK TO ME ..... Del Shannon, Dunhill 4193
128. THOU SHALT NOT STEAL ..... Newbeats, Hickory 1539

Compiled from national retail sales and radio station airplay by the Music Popularity Dept. of Record Market Research, Billboard.

# Billboard HOT 100

FOR WEEK ENDING JULY 12, 1969

★ STAR PERFORMER—Sides registering greatest proportionate upward progress this week.

◉ Record Industry Association of America seal of certification as million selling single.

| This Week | 1 Wk. Ago | 2 Wks. Ago | 3 Wks. Ago | TITLE Artist (Producer), Label & Number | Weeks On Chart |
|---|---|---|---|---|---|
| ★ 1 | 8 | 35 | 72 | IN THE YEAR 2525 (Exordium & Terminus, — Zager & Evans (Zager & Evans), RCA 74-0174 | 4 |
| 2 | 2 | 6 | 10 | SPINNING WHEEL — Blood, Sweat & Tears (James William Guercio), Columbia 44871 | 7 |
| 3 | 4 | 8 | 9 | GOOD MORNING STARSHINE — Oliver (Bob Crewe), Jubilee 5659 | 8 |
| ◉ 4 | 1 | 1 | 2 | LOVE THEME FROM ROMEO & JULIET — Henry Mancini & Ork. (Joe Reisman), RCA Victor 74-0131 | 10 |
| 5 | 5 | 5 | 6 | ONE — Three Dog Night (Gabriel Mekler), Dunhill 4191 | 11 |
| 6 | 7 | 18 | 44 | CRYSTAL BLUE PERSUASION — Tommy James & the Shondells (Tommy James-Ritchie Cordell), Roulette 7050 | 6 |
| 7 | 3 | 2 | 3 | BAD MOON RISING — Creedence Clearwater Revival (John Fogerty), Fantasy 622 | 11 |
| ★ 8 | 11 | 11 | 24 | THE BALLAD OF JOHN AND YOKO — The Beatles (Lennon-McCartney), Apple 2531 | 5 |
| 9 | 9 | 13 | 28 | COLOR HIM FATHER — Winstons (Don Carroll), Metromedia 117 | 8 |
| 10 | 14 | 16 | 25 | WHAT DOES IT TAKE TO WIN YOUR LOVE — Jr. Walker & the All Stars (Fuqua & Bristol), Soul 35062 | 9 |
| 11 | 16 | 22 | 33 | MY CHERIE AMOUR — Stevie Wonder (Hank Cosby), Tamla 54180 | 7 |
| 12 | 6 | 3 | 1 | GET BACK — Beatles (George Martin), Apple 2490 | 10 |
| 13 | 10 | 4 | 5 | TOO BUSY THINKING ABOUT MY BABY — Marvin Gaye (Norman Whitfield), Tamla 54181 | 12 |
| 14 | 15 | 15 | 18 | LOVE ME TONIGHT — Tom Jones (Peter Sullivan), Parrot 40038 | 8 |
| ★ 15 | 18 | 19 | 31 | PART I MOTHER POPCORN (You Got to Have a Mother for Me) — James Brown (James Brown), King 6245 | 5 |
| ◉ 16 | 12 | 7 | 4 | IN THE GHETTO — Elvis Presley, RCA Victor 47-9741 | 11 |
| ★ 17 | 29 | 37 | 40 | BABY, I LOVE YOU — Andy Kim (Jeff Barry), Steed 1031 | 8 |
| 18 | 13 | 14 | 20 | BLACK PEARL — Sonny Charles with the Checkmates Ltd. (Phil Spector), A&M 1053 | 10 |
| 19 | 19 | 9 | 12 | THE ISRAELITES — Desmond Dekker & the Aces (A Pyramid Production), Uni 55129 | 9 |
| 20 | 20 | 24 | 27 | LET ME — Paul Revere & the Raiders Featuring Mark Lindsay, Columbia 4-44854 | 9 |
| ◉ 21 | 17 | 10 | 8 | GRAZIN' IN THE GRASS — Friends of Distinction (John Florez), RCA 74-0207 | 15 |
| ★ 22 | 28 | 42 | 58 | QUENTIN'S THEME — The Charles Randolph Grean Sounde (Charles R. Grean), Ranwood 840 | 5 |
| ★ 23 | 30 | 32 | 35 | I TURNED YOU ON — Isley Brothers (R. Isley-O. Isley-R. Isley), T-Neck 902 | 7 |
| 24 | 31 | 38 | 39 | MEDLEY: CAN SING A RAINBOW/LOVE IS BLUE — Dells (Bobby Miller), Cadet 5641 | 8 |
| 25 | 26 | 27 | 34 | MOODY WOMAN — Jerry Butler (Gamble & Huff), Mercury 72929 | 7 |
| ★ 26 | 37 | 55 | 70 | RUBY, DON'T TAKE YOUR LOVE TO TOWN — Kenny Rogers and the First Edition (Jimmy Bowen), Reprise 0829 | 6 |
| 27 | 22 | 25 | 26 | MEDICINE MAN — Buchanan Brothers (Cashman, Pistilli & West), Event, 3302 | 11 |
| 28 | 21 | 21 | 16 | MORE TODAY THAN YESTERDAY — Spiral Staircase (Sonny Knight), Columbia 4-44741 | 15 |
| 29 | 33 | 41 | 50 | MY PLEDGE OF LOVE — The Joe Jeffrey Group (Jerry Meyers & Alan Klein), Wand 11200 | 6 |
| ★ 30 | 50 | 59 | — | SWEET CAROLINE (Good Times Never Seemed So Good) — Neil Diamond (Tommy Cogbill, Tom Catalano, Neil Diamond), Uni 55136 | 3 |
| ★ 31 | 51 | 61 | — | GOOD OLD ROCK 'N ROLL — Cat Mother and the All Night News Boys (Cat Mother & Jimi Hendrix), Polydor 14002 | 3 |
| ★ 32 | 42 | 50 | 77 | YESTERDAY WHEN I WAS YOUNG — Roy Clark (Joe Allison), Dot 17246 | 5 |
| 33 | 34 | 34 | 43 | THE POPCORN — James Brown (James Brown), King 6240 | 6 |
| ★ 34 | 41 | 47 | 81 | THE DAYS OF SAND AND SHOVELS — Bobby Vinton (Billy Sherrill), Epic 10485 | 5 |
| 35 | 36 | 36 | 41 | WITH PEN IN HAND — Vikki Carr (Dave Pell & Rob Bledsoe), Liberty 56092 | 11 |
| 36 | 35 | 51 | 57 | WE GOT MORE SOUL — Dyke & the Blazers (Art Barrett), Original Sound 86 | 9 |
| 37 | 40 | 45 | 51 | MRS. ROBINSON — Booker T. & the M.G.'s (Booker T. & the M.G.'s), Stax 0037 | 6 |
| 38 | 38 | 46 | 59 | THE MINOTAUR — Dick Hyman & His Electric Eclectics, Command 4126 | 7 |
| 39 | 24 | 23 | 19 | EVERYDAY WITH YOU GIRL — Classics IV (Buddy Blue), Imperial 66378 | 8 |
| ★ 40 | 48 | 77 | — | CHOICE OF COLORS — Impressions (Curtis Mayfield), Curtom 1943 | 3 |
| 41 | 43 | 48 | 76 | DOGGONE RIGHT — Smokey Robinson & the Miracles (Smokey), Tamla 54183 | 4 |
| ★ 42 | 57 | 89 | — | ABRAHAM, MARTIN AND JOHN — Moms Mabley (Barry Oslander), Mercury 72935 | 3 |
| 43 | 47 | 68 | 95 | MOONFLIGHT — Vik Venus (Lewis Merenstein), Buddah 118 | 5 |
| 44 | 44 | 56 | 56 | SO I CAN LOVE YOU — Emotions, Volt 4010 | 8 |
| 45 | 45 | 54 | 69 | MEMPHIS UNDERGROUND — Herbie Mann (Tom Dowd), Atlantic 2621 | 8 |
| 46 | 46 | 52 | 52 | BUT IT'S ALRIGHT — J. J. Jackson (Lew Futterman), Warner Bros.-Seven Arts 7276 | 8 |
| 47 | 49 | 66 | 84 | MOMENTS TO REMEMBER — Vogues (Dick Classer), Neprine 0831 | 4 |
| ★ 48 | 73 | — | — | ABRAHAM, MARTIN & JOHN — Smokey Robinson & the Miracles (Smokey Robinson), Tamla 54184 | 2 |
| ★ 49 | 59 | 71 | 88 | I'D RATHER BE AN OLD MAN'S SWEETHEART — Candi Staton (Rick Hall), Fame 1456 | 4 |
| 50 | 27 | 28 | 29 | SEE — Rascals (Rascals & Arif Mardin), Atlantic 2634 | 8 |
| 51 | 53 | 57 | 66 | YOU DON'T HAVE TO WALK IN THE RAIN — Turtles (Ray Davies), White Whale 308 | 6 |
| 52 | 52 | 64 | 71 | THE GIRL I'LL NEVER KNOW — Frankie Valli (Bob Crewe), Philips 40622 | 5 |
| ★ 53 | 55 | 65 | 75 | IT'S GETTING BETTER — Mama Cass (Steve Barri), Dunhill 4195 | 6 |
| ★ 54 | 66 | 94 | — | ALONG CAME JONES — Ray Stevens (Ray Stevens, Jim Malloy), Monument 1150 | 3 |
| ★ 55 | 64 | 85 | — | PUT A LITTLE LOVE IN YOUR HEART — Jackie DeShannon (VME), Imperial 66385 | 3 |
| ★ 56 | 68 | 72 | — | RECONSIDER ME — Johnny Adams (Shelby S. Singleton Jr.), SSS Int'l 770 | 3 |
| ★ 57 | 86 | — | — | POLK SALAD ANNIE — Tony Joe White (Billy Swan), Monument 1104 | 2 |
| 58 | 32 | 20 | 22 | DON'T LET THE JONESES GET YOU DOWN — Temptations (Norman Whitfield), Gordy 7086 | 8 |
| ★ 59 | 85 | — | — | I'D WAIT A MILLION YEARS — Grassroots (Steve Barry), Dunhill 4198 | 2 |
| ★ 60 | 88 | 97 | — | MUDDY RIVER — Johnny Rivers (Johnny Rivers), Imperial 66386 | 3 |
| ★ 61 | 71 | 74 | 83 | DON'T WAKE ME UP IN THE MORNING, MICHAEL — The Peppermint Rainbow (Paul Leka), Decca 732498 | 5 |
| 62 | 62 | 69 | 82 | TELL ALL THE PEOPLE — Doors (Kreiger), Elektra 45663 | 5 |
| 63 | 65 | 67 | 68 | DIDN'T WE — Richard Harris (Jimmy Webb), Dunhill 4194 | 6 |
| 64 | 67 | 73 | 91 | LISTEN TO THE BAND — Monkees (Michael Nesmith), Colgems 66-5004 | 6 |
| ★ 65 | 90 | — | — | CLEAN UP YOUR OWN BACK YARD — Elvis Presley, RCA Vistor 47-9747 | 2 |
| 66 | 70 | 70 | 78 | WHY I SING THE BLUES — B. B. King (Bill Szymczyk), BluesWay 61024 | 9 |
| ★ 67 | 75 | 88 | — | ON CAMPUS — Dickie Goodman (Dickie Goodman), Cotique 158 | 3 |
| 68 | 74 | 84 | 90 | GIRL YOU'RE TOO YOUNG — Archie Bell & the Drells (Gamble & Huff), Atlantic 2644 | 4 |
| 69 | 72 | 98 | — | (Sittin' On) THE DOCK OF THE BAY — Sergio Mendes & Brasil '66 (Sergio Mendes & Herb Alpert), A&M 1073 | 3 |
| 70 | 79 | 79 | 100 | FEELING ALRIGHT — Joe Cocker (Denny-Cordell), A&M 1063 | 4 |
| 71 | 78 | 81 | 89 | THE FEELING IS RIGHT — Clarence Carter (Rick Hall), Atlantic 2648 | 4 |
| ★ 72 | 81 | 83 | 96 | BABY, DON'T BE LOOKING IN MY MIND — Joe Simon (J. B. Enterprises), Sound Stage 7 2634 | 4 |
| 73 | 77 | 78 | 86 | HURT SO BAD — Lettermen (Al DeLory), Capitol 2482 | 7 |
| ★ 74 | 89 | 93 | — | GET TOGETHER — Youngbloods (Felix Pappalardi), RCA 47-9752 | 3 |
| 75 | 76 | 76 | 85 | THE PROPHECY OF DANIEL AND JOHN THE DEVINE — Cowsills (Bob Cowsill), MGM 14063 | 4 |
| ★ 76 | 83 | 90 | — | WHILE YOU'RE OUT LOOKING FOR SUGAR — Honey Cone (R. Dunbar), Hot Wax 6901 | 3 |
| 77 | 69 | 62 | 62 | HUSHABYE — Jay & the Americans (Jay & the Americans), United Artists 50535 | 7 |
| ★ 78 | 92 | — | — | DID YOU SEE HER EYES — Illusion (Jeff Barry), Steed 718 | 2 |
| ★ 79 | 93 | — | — | BREAK AWAY — Beach Boys (Brian Wilson/Murray Wilson), Capitol 2530 | 2 |
| 80 | 87 | 87 | — | FOREVER — Mercy (Brad Shapiro & Steve Alaimo), Warner Bros.-Seven Arts 7297 | 3 |
| ★ 81 | — | — | — | HEY JOE — Wilson Pickett (Rick Hall), Atlantic 2648 | 1 |
| 82 | 80 | 80 | — | I'M STILL A STRUGGLIN' MAN — Edwin Starr (Johnny Bristol), Gordy 7087 | 3 |
| ★ 83 | — | — | — | LAUGHING — Guess Who (Jack Richardson), RCA 74-0195 | 1 |
| 84 | 97 | 100 | — | THEME FROM A SUMMER PLACE — Ventures (Joe Saraceno), Liberty 56115 | 3 |
| ★ 85 | — | — | — | WHERE DO I GO/BE-IN (Hare Krishna) — Happenings (Happenings), Jubilee 5666 | 1 |
| 86 | 95 | 95 | — | DON'T TELL YOUR MAMA WHERE YOU'VE BEEN — Eddie Floyd (Steve Cropper, B. T. Jones), Stax 0036 | 3 |
| ★ 87 | — | — | — | STAY AND LOVE ME ALL SUMMER — Brian Hyland (Ray Ruff), Dot 17258 | 1 |
| ★ 88 | — | — | — | WILLIE & LAURA MAE JONES — Dusty Springfield (Jerry Wexler, Tom Down, Arif Mardin), Atlantic 2647 | 1 |
| ★ 89 | 99 | — | — | NOTHING CAN TAKE THE PLACE OF YOU — Brook Benton (Arif Mardin), Cotillion 44034 | 2 |
| 90 | 94 | — | — | SOUL DEEP — Box Tops (Tommy Cogbill & Chips Moman), Mala 12040 | 2 |
| 91 | 91 | 92 | — | NEVER COMES THE DAY — Moody Blues (Tony Clarke), Deram 85044 | 3 |
| 92 | — | — | — | WAKE UP — Chambers Brothers (David Rubinson), Columbia 44890 | 1 |
| 93 | 98 | — | — | I'LL NEVER FALL IN LOVE AGAIN — Burt Bacharach (Burt Bacharach & Phil Ramone), A&M 1064 | 2 |
| 94 | — | — | — | LAY LADY LAY — Boy Dylan (Bob Johnson), Columbia 44926 | 1 |
| 95 | 96 | 96 | — | EVERYTHING I DO GONNA BE FUNKY (From Now On) — Lee Dorsey (Marshall E. Sehorn & Allen R. Toussaint), Amy 11055 | 3 |
| 96 | — | — | — | BIRDS OF A FEATHER — Joe South (Joe South), Capitol 2532 | 1 |
| 97 | — | — | — | IN THE TIME OF OUR LIVES — Iron Butterfly (Jim Hilton), Atco 6676 | 1 |
| 98 | — | — | — | PASS THE APPLE, EVE — B. J. Thomas (Chips Moman), Scepter 12255 | 1 |
| 99 | 100 | — | — | MY LITTLE CHICKADEE — Foundations (Tony Macaulay & John Macleod), Uni 55137 | 2 |
| 100 | — | — | — | ABERGAVENNY — Shannon ( ), Heritage 814 | 1 |

## HOT 100—A TO Z—(Publisher-Licensee)



## BUBBLING UNDER THE HOT 100

101. WORKIN' ON A GROOVY THING.......5th Dimension, Soul City 776
102. SUGAR, SUGAR.......Archies, Calendar 63-1008
103. BIG BRUCE.......Steve Greenberg, Trip 3000
104. SUNSHINE RED WINE.......Crazy Elephant, Bell 804
105. BIRTHDAY.......Underground Sunshine, Intrepid 75002
106. HERE I GO AGAIN.......Country Joe & the Fish, Vanguard 35090
107. DYNAMITE WOMAN.......Sir Douglas Quintet, Smash 2233
108. FIRST HYMN FROM GRAND TERRACE.......Mark Lindsay, Columbia 4-44875
109. ANGEL OF THE MORNING.......Bettye Swann, Capitol 2515
110. OUT OF SIGHT, OUT OF MIND.......Little Anthony & the Imperials, United Artists 50552
111. JACK AND JILL.......Tommy Roe, ABC 11229
112. HAPPY TOGETHER.......Hugo Montenegro & His Ork., RCA 74-0160
113. YOUR HUSBAND—MY WIFE.......Brooklyn Bridge, Buddah 126
114. I'M FREE.......Who, Decca 732519
115. OH HAPPY DAY.......Billy Mitchell Group, Calla 165
116. TAKE YOUR LOVE (AND SHOVE IT).......Kane's Cousins, Shove Love 500
117. A TIME FOR US.......Johnny Mathis, Columbia 4-44915
118. THE RIB.......Jeannie C. Riley, Plantation 22
119. TILL YOU GET ENOUGH.......Watts 103rd Street Rhythm Band, Warner Bros.-Seven Arts 7298
120. THE HUNTER.......Ike & Tina Turner, Blue Thumb 102
121. FROZEN ORANGE JUICE.......Peter Sarstedt, World Pacific 77919
122. ME AND BOBBY McGEE.......Roger Miller, Smash 2230
123. LOVE THAT A WOMAN SHOULD GIVE TO A MAN.......Patti Drew, Capitol 2473
124. DELIA'S GONE.......Waylon Jennings, RCA 74-0157
125. BUT FOR LOVE.......Eddy Arnold, RCA 74-0175
126. MY DARK HOUR.......Steve Miller Band, Capitol 2520
127. IN MY ROOM.......Saggitarius, Together 105
128. I'M GONNA MAKE YOU MINE.......Lou Christie, Buddah 116
129. I NEED YOU WOMAN.......William Bell & Carla Thomas, Stax 0044
130. EVERYBODY KNOWS MATILDA.......Duke Baxter, VMC 740
131. COLOR OF MY LOVE.......Jefferson, Decca 32501
132. NEVER, NEVER LET YOU GO.......Eddie Floyd & Mavis Staples, Stax 0041
133. THAT LUCKY OLD SUN.......Solomon Burke, Bell 806

Compiled from national retail sales and radio station airplay by the Music Popularity Dept. of Record Market Research, Billboard.

# Billboard HOT 100

FOR WEEK ENDING JULY 19, 1969

★ STAR PERFORMER—Sides registering greatest proportionate upward progress this week.

Record Industry Association of America seal of certification as million selling single.

| This Week | 1 Wk. Ago | 2 Wks. Ago | 3 Wks. Ago | TITLE — Artist (Producer), Label & Number | Weeks On Chart |
|---|---|---|---|---|---|
| 1 | 1 | 8 | 35 | IN THE YEAR 2525 (Exordium & Terminus) — Zager & Evans (Zager & Evans), RCA 74-0174 | 5 |
| 2 | 2 | 2 | 6 | SPINNING WHEEL — Blood, Sweat & Tears (James William Guercio), Columbia 44871 | 8 |
| 3 | 3 | 4 | 8 | GOOD MORNING STARSHINE — Oliver (Bob Crewe), Jubilee 5659 | 9 |
| ★4 | 6 | 7 | 18 | CRYSTAL BLUE PERSUASION — Tommy James & the Shondells (Tommy James-Ritchie Cordell), Roulette 7050 | 7 |
| ★5 | 10 | 14 | 16 | WHAT DOES IT TAKE TO WIN YOUR LOVE — Jr. Walker & the All Stars (Fuqua & Bristol), Soul 35062 | 10 |
| 6 | 5 | 5 | 5 | ONE — Three Dog Night (Gabriel Mekler), Dunhill 4191 | 12 |
| 7 | 9 | 9 | 13 | COLOR HIM FATHER — Winstons (Don Carroll), Metromedia 117 | 9 |
| 8 | 8 | 11 | 11 | THE BALLAD OF JOHN AND YOKO — The Beatles (Lennon-McCartney), Apple 2531 | 6 |
| ★9 | 11 | 16 | 22 | MY CHERIE AMOUR — Stevie Wonder (Hank Cosby), Tamla 54180 | 8 |
| 10 | 4 | 1 | 1 | LOVE THEME FROM ROMEO & JULIET — Henry Mancini & Ork. (Joe Reisman), RCA Victor 74-0131 | 11 |
| 11 | 7 | 3 | 2 | BAD MOON RISING — Creedence Clearwater Revival (John Fogerty), Fantasy 622 | 12 |
| ★12 | 15 | 18 | 19 | PART 1 MOTHER POPCORN (You Got to Have a Mother for Me) — James Brown (James Brown), King 6245 | 6 |
| 13 | 14 | 15 | 15 | LOVE ME TONIGHT — Tom Jones (Peter Sullivan), Parrot 40038 | 9 |
| 14 | 17 | 29 | 37 | BABY, I LOVE YOU — Andy Kim (Jeff Barry), Steed 1031 | 9 |
| 15 | 13 | 10 | 4 | TOO BUSY THINKING ABOUT MY BABY — Marvin Gaye (Norman Whitfield), Tamla 54181 | 13 |
| 16 | 12 | 6 | 3 | GET BACK — Beatles (George Martin), Apple 2490 | 11 |
| 17 | 16 | 12 | 7 | IN THE GHETTO — Elvis Presley, RCA Victor 47-9741 | 12 |
| 18 | 18 | 13 | 14 | BLACK PEARL — Sonny Charles with the Checkmates Ltd. (Phil Spector), A&M 1053 | 11 |
| ★19 | 26 | 37 | 55 | RUBY, DON'T TAKE YOUR LOVE TO TOWN — Kenny Rogers and the First Edition (Jimmy Bowen), Reprise 0829 | 7 |
| 20 | 22 | 28 | 42 | QUENTIN'S THEME — The Charles Randolph Grean Sounde (Charles R. Grean), Ranwood 840 | 6 |
| 21 | 20 | 20 | 24 | LET ME — Paul Revere & the Raiders Featuring Mark Lindsay, Columbia 4-44854 | 10 |
| 22 | 24 | 31 | 38 | LOVE IS BLUE (I Can Sing a Rainbow) — Dells (Bobby Miller), Cadet 5641 | 9 |
| 23 | 23 | 30 | 32 | I TURNED YOU ON — Isley Brothers (R. Isley-O. Isley-R. Isley), T-Neck 902 | 8 |
| ★24 | 30 | 50 | 59 | SWEET CAROLINE (Good Times Never Seemed So Good) — Neil Diamond (Tommy Cogbill, Tom Catalano, Neil Diamond), Uni 55136 | 4 |
| 25 | 25 | 26 | 27 | MOODY WOMAN — Jerry Butler (Gamble & Huff), Mercury 72929 | 8 |
| ★26 | 29 | 33 | 41 | MY PLEDGE OF LOVE — The Joe Jeffrey Group (Jerry Meyers & Alan Klein), Wand 11200 | 7 |
| ★27 | 31 | 51 | 61 | GOOD OLD ROCK 'N ROLL — Cat Mother and the All Night News Boys (Cat Mother & Jimi Hendrix), Polydor 14002 | 4 |
| 28 | 19 | 19 | 9 | THE ISRAELITES — Desmond Dekker & the Aces (A Pyramid Production), Uni 55129 | 10 |
| 29 | 21 | 17 | 10 | GRAZIN' IN THE GRASS — Friends of Distinction (John Florez), RCA 74-0207 | 16 |
| 30 | 33 | 34 | 34 | THE POPCORN — James Brown (James Brown), King 6240 | 7 |
| 31 | 32 | 42 | 50 | YESTERDAY WHEN I WAS YOUNG — Roy Clark (Joe Allison), Dot 17246 | 6 |
| ★32 | 40 | 48 | 77 | CHOICE OF COLORS — Impressions (Curtis Mayfield), Curtom 1943 | 4 |
| ★33 | 48 | 73 | — | ABRAHAM, MARTIN & JOHN — Smokey Robinson & the Miracles (Smokey Robinson), Tamla 54184 | 3 |
| 34 | 34 | 41 | 47 | THE DAYS OF SAND AND SHOVELS — Bobby Vinton (Billy Sherrill), Epic 10485 | 6 |
| 35 | 42 | 57 | 89 | ABRAHAM, MARTIN AND JOHN — Moms Mabley (Barry Oslander), Mercury 72935 | 4 |
| 36 | 36 | 35 | 51 | WE GOT MORE SOUL — Dyke & the Blazers (Art Barrett), Original Sound 86 | 10 |
| 37 | 41 | 43 | 48 | DOGGONE RIGHT — Smokey Robinson & the Miracles (Smokey), Tamla 54183 | 5 |
| 38 | 35 | 36 | 36 | WITH PEN IN HAND — Vikki Carr (Dave Pell & Rob Bledsoe), Liberty 56092 | 12 |
| 39 | 44 | 44 | 56 | SO I CAN LOVE YOU — Emotions, Volt 4010 | 9 |
| 40 | 37 | 40 | 45 | MRS. ROBINSON — Booker T. & the M.G.'s (Booker T. & the M.G.'s), Stax 0037 | 7 |
| ★41 | 54 | 66 | 94 | ALONG CAME JONES — Ray Stevens (Ray Stevens, Jim Malloy), Monument 1150 | 4 |
| 42 | 43 | 47 | 68 | MOONFLIGHT — Vik Venus (Lewis Merenstein), Buddah 118 | 6 |
| ★43 | 57 | 86 | — | POLK SALAD ANNIE — Tony Joe White (Billy Swan), Monument 1104 | 3 |
| 44 | 45 | 45 | 54 | MEMPHIS UNDERGROUND — Herbie Mann (Tom Dowd), Atlantic 2621 | 9 |
| 45 | 46 | 46 | 52 | BUT IT'S ALRIGHT — J. J. Jackson (Lew Futterman), Warner Bros.-Seven Arts 7276 | 9 |
| 46 | 49 | 59 | 71 | I'D RATHER BE AN OLD MAN'S SWEETHEART — Candi Staton (Rick Hall), Fame 1456 | 5 |
| ★47 | 56 | 68 | 72 | RECONSIDER ME — Johnny Adams (Shelby S. Singleton Jr.), SSS Int'l 770 | 4 |
| ★48 | 55 | 64 | 85 | PUT A LITTLE LOVE IN YOUR HEART — Jackie DeShannon (VME), Imperial 66385 | 4 |
| ★49 | 59 | 85 | — | I'D WAIT A MILLION YEARS — Grassroots (Steve Barry), Dunhill 4198 | 3 |
| 50 | 38 | 38 | 46 | THE MINOTAUR — Dick Hyman & His Electric Eclectics, Command 4126 | 8 |
| 51 | 51 | 53 | 57 | YOU DON'T HAVE TO WALK IN THE RAIN — Turtles (Ray Davies), White Whale 308 | 7 |
| 52 | 53 | 55 | 65 | IT'S GETTING BETTER — Mama Cass (Steve Barri), Dunhill 4195 | 7 |
| ★53 | 67 | 75 | 88 | ON CAMPUS — Dickie Goodman (Dickie Goodman), Cotique 158 | 4 |
| ★54 | 65 | 90 | — | CLEAN UP YOUR OWN BACK YARD — Elvis Presley, RCA Vistor 47-9747 | 3 |
| 55 | 52 | 52 | 64 | THE GIRL I'LL NEVER KNOW — Frankie Valli (Bob Crewe), Philips 40622 | 6 |
| ★56 | 60 | 88 | 97 | MUDDY RIVER — Johnny Rivers (Johnny Rivers), Imperial 66386 | 4 |
| 57 | 47 | 49 | 66 | MOMENTS TO REMEMBER — Vogues (Dick Classer), Neprine 0831 | 5 |
| ★58 | 62 | 62 | 69 | TELL ALL THE PEOPLE — Doors (Kreiger), Elektra 45663 | 6 |
| 59 | 68 | 74 | 84 | GIRL YOU'RE TOO YOUNG — Archie Bell & the Drells (Gamble & Huff), Atlantic 2644 | 5 |
| 60 | 61 | 71 | 74 | DON'T WAKE ME UP IN THE MORNING, MICHAEL — The Peppermint Rainbow (Paul Leka), Decca 732498 | 6 |
| 61 | 66 | 70 | 70 | WHY I SING THE BLUES — B. B. King (Bill Szymczyk), BluesWay 61024 | 10 |
| ★62 | 83 | — | — | LAUGHING — Guess Who (Jack Richardson), RCA 74-0195 | 2 |
| 63 | 64 | 67 | 73 | LISTEN TO THE BAND — Monkees (Michael Nesmith), Colgems 66-5004 | 7 |
| ★64 | 74 | 89 | 93 | GET TOGETHER — Youngbloods (Felix Pappalardi), RCA 47-9752 | 4 |
| ★65 | 71 | 78 | 81 | THE FEELING IS RIGHT — Clarence Carter (Rick Hall), Atlantic 2648 | 5 |
| 66 | 69 | 72 | 98 | (Sittin' On) THE DOCK OF THE BAY — Sergio Mendes & Brasil '66 (Sergio Mendes & Herb Alpert), A&M 1073 | 4 |
| ★67 | 73 | 77 | 78 | HURT SO BAD — Lettermen (Al DeLory), Capitol 2482 | 8 |
| ★68 | 79 | 93 | — | BREAK AWAY — Beach Boys (Brian Wilson/Murray Wilson), Capitol 2530 | 3 |
| 69 | 70 | 79 | 79 | FEELING ALRIGHT — Joe Cocker (Denny-Cordell), A&M 1063 | 5 |
| ★70 | — | — | — | WORKIN' ON A GROOVY THING — Fifth Dimension (Bones Howe), Soul City 776 | 1 |
| ★71 | 81 | — | — | HEY JOE — Wilson Pickett (Rick Hall), Atlantic 2648 | 2 |
| 72 | 72 | 81 | 83 | BABY, DON'T BE LOOKING IN MY MIND — Joe Simon (J. B. Enterprises), Sound Stage 7 2634 | 5 |
| ★73 | — | — | — | I'VE LOST EVERYTHING I'VE EVER LOVED — David Ruffin (Johnny Bristol), Motown 1149 | 1 |
| ★74 | 90 | 94 | — | SOUL DEEP — Box Tops (Tommy Cogbill & Chips Moman), Mala 12040 | 3 |
| 75 | 76 | 83 | 90 | WHILE YOU'RE OUT LOOKING FOR SUGAR — Honey Cone (R. Dunbar), Hot Wax 6901 | 4 |
| 76 | 78 | 92 | — | DID YOU SEE HER EYES — Illusion (Jeff Barry), Steed 718 | 3 |
| ★77 | 85 | — | — | WHERE DO I GO/BE-IN (Hare Krishna) — Happenings (Happenings), Jubilee 5666 | 2 |
| ★78 | 88 | — | — | WILLIE & LAURA MAE JONES — Dusty Springfield (Jerry Wexler, Tom Down, Arif Mardin), Atlantic 2647 | 2 |
| ★79 | — | — | — | HONKY TONK WOMEN — Rolling Stones (Jimmy Miller), London 910 | 1 |
| 80 | 80 | 87 | 87 | FOREVER — Mercy (Brad Shapiro & Steve Alaimo), Warner Bros.-Seven Arts 7297 | 4 |
| 81 | 82 | 80 | 80 | I'M STILL A STRUGGLIN' MAN — Edwin Starr (Johnny Bristol), Gordy 7087 | 4 |
| ★82 | 87 | — | — | STAY AND LOVE ME ALL SUMMER — Brian Hyland (Ray Ruff), Dot 17258 | 2 |
| 83 | 84 | 97 | 100 | THEME FROM A SUMMER PLACE — Ventures (Joe Saraceno), Liberty 56115 | 4 |
| 84 | 89 | 99 | — | NOTHING CAN TAKE THE PLACE OF YOU — Brook Benton (Arif Mardin), Cotillion 44034 | 3 |
| 85 | 86 | 95 | 95 | DON'T TELL YOUR MAMA WHERE YOU'VE BEEN — Eddie Floyd (Steve Cropper, B. T. Jones), Stax 0036 | 4 |
| ★86 | — | — | — | MARRAKESH EXPRESS — Crosby, Stills & Nash (Stephen Stills/David Crosby/Graham Nash), Atlantic 2652 | 1 |
| ★87 | — | — | — | YOUR GOOD THING (Is About to End) — Lou Rawls (David Axelrod), Capitol 2550 | 1 |
| ★88 | — | — | — | NITTY GRITTY — Gladys Knight & the Pips (Norman Whitfield), Soul 35063 | 1 |
| ★89 | 100 | — | — | ABERGAVENNY — Shannon, Heritage 814 | 2 |
| ★90 | — | — | — | I'M FREE — Who (Kit Lambert), Decca 732519 | 1 |
| 91 | 91 | 91 | 92 | NEVER COMES THE DAY — Moody Blues (Tony Clarke), Deram 85044 | 4 |
| 92 | 92 | — | — | WAKE UP — Chambers Brothers (David Rubinson), Columbia 44890 | 2 |
| 93 | 94 | — | — | LAY LADY LAY — Boy Dylan (Bob Johnson), Columbia 44926 | 2 |
| 94 | — | — | — | TILL YOU GET ENOUGH — Watts 103rd Street Rhythm Band (Charles Wright), Warner Bros.-Seven Arts 7298 | 1 |
| 95 | — | — | — | THAT'S THE WAY — Joe Tex (Buddy Killen), Dial 4093 | 1 |
| 96 | 97 | — | — | IN THE TIME OF OUR LIVES — Iron Butterfly (Jim Hilton), Atco 6676 | 2 |
| 97 | — | — | — | YOUR HUSBAND—MY WIFE — Brooklyn Bridge (Wes Farrell), Buddah 126 | 1 |
| 98 | 98 | — | — | PASS THE APPLE, EVE — B. J. Thomas (Chips Moman), Scepter 12255 | 2 |
| 99 | — | — | — | JACK AND JILL — Tommy Roe (Steve Barri), ABC 11229 | 1 |
| 100 | — | — | — | BIRTHDAY — Underground Sunshine (Underground Sunshine), Intrepid 75002 | 1 |

## HOT 100—A TO Z—*(Publisher-Licensee)*


Abergavenny (Mills, ASCAP) ... 89
Abraham, Martin & John (Rozniquet, BMI) ... 35
Abraham, Martin & John (Rozniquet, BMI) ... 33
Along Came Jones (Tiger, BMI) ... 41
Baby, Don't Be Looking in My Mind (Wilderness, BMI) ... 72
Baby, I Love You (Trio/Mother Bertha, BMI) ... 14
Bad Moon Rising (Jondora, BMI) ... 11
Ballad of John and Yoko, The (Maclen, BMI) ... 8
Birthday (Maclen, BMI) ... 100
Black Pearl (Irving, BMI) ... 18
Break Away (Bri-Mur, BMI) ... 68
But It's Alright (Pamelarosa, BMI) ... 45
Choice of Colors (Camad, BMI) ... 32
Clean Up Your Own Back Yard (Gladys, ASCAP) ... 54
Color Him Father (Holly Bee, BMI) ... 7
Crystal Blue Persuasion (Big Seven, BMI) ... 4
Days of Sand and Shovels, The (Lonzo & Oscar, BMI) ... 34
Did You See Her Eyes (Unart, BMI) ... 76
Doggone Right (Jobete, BMI) ... 37
Don't Tell Your Mama Where You've Been (East/Memphis, BMI) ... 85
Don't Wake Me Up in the Morning, Michael (M.R.C./Little Heather, BMI) ... 60
Feeling Alright (Almo, ASCAP) ... 69
Feeling Is Right, The (Fame, BMI) ... 65
Forever (Tree, BMI) ... 80
Get Back (Maclen, BMI) ... 16
Get Together (S.F.O., BMI) ... 64
Girl I'll Never Know, The (Saturday, BMI) ... 55
Girl You're Too Young (World War III, BMI) ... 59
Good Morning Starshine (United Artists, ASCAP) ... 3
Good Old Rock 'n' Roll (Cat Mother/Emm-Jay/Sea-Lark, BMI) ... 27
Grazin' in the Grass (Chisa, BMI) ... 29
Hey Joe (Third Story, BMI) ... 71
Honky Tonk Women (Gideon, BMI) ... 79
Hurt So Bad (Vogue, BMI) ... 67
I'd Rather Be an Old Man's Sweetheart (Fame, BMI) 46
I'd Wait a Million Years (Teenie Bopper, ASCAP) ... 49
I'm Free (Track, BMI) ... 90
I'm Still a Struggling Man (Jobete, BMI) ... 81
In the Ghetto (B 'n' B/Gladys, ASCAP) ... 17
In the Time of Our Lives (Cotillion/Ten/East/Itasca, BMI) ... 96
In the Year 2525 (Zelad, BMI) ... 1
I Turned You On (Triple 3, BMI) ... 23
Israelites, The (Kenwood, BMI) ... 28
It's Getting Better (Screen Gems-Columbia, BMI) ... 52
I've Lost Everything I've Ever Loved (Jobete, BMI) 73
Jack and Jill (Low-Twi, BMI) ... 99
Laughing (Dunbar, BMI) ... 62
Lay Lady Lay (Big Sky, ASCAP) ... 93
Let Me (Boom, BMI) ... 21
Listen to the Band (Screen Gems-Columbia, BMI) ... 63
Love Is Blue (I Can Sing a Rainbow) (Mark VII/Croma, ASCAP) ... 22
Love Me Tonight (Duchess, BMI) ... 13
Love Theme From Romeo & Juliet (Famous, ASCAP) 10
Marrakesh Express (Siquomb, BMI) ... 86
Memphis Underground (Mann, ASCAP) ... 44
Minotaur, The (Eastlake, ASCAP) ... 50
Moody Woman (Gold Forever/Parabut, BMI) ... 25
Moments to Remember (Spier, ASCAP) ... 57
Moonflight (Kaskat/Kahoona/Camad/T.M./Pocket Full of Tunes/Rivers/Peanut Butter/Kama Sutra, BMI) ... 42
Part 1—Mother Popcorn (You Got to Have a Mother for Me (Dynatone, BMI) ... 12
Mrs. Robinson (Charing Cross, BMI) ... 40
Muddy River (Rivers, BMI) ... 56
My Cherie Amour (Jobete, BMI) ... 9
My Pledge of Love (Wednesday Morn./Our Children's, BMI) ... 26
Never Comes the Day (Andover, ASCAP) ... 91
Nitty Gritty (Gallico, BMI) ... 88
Nothing Can Take the Place of You (Su-Ma, BMI) ... 84
One (Dunbar, BMI) ... 6
On Campus (Conique, BMI) ... 53
Pass the Apple Eve (Press, BMI) ... 98
Polk Salad Annie (Combine, BMI) ... 43
Popcorn, The (Gola, BMI) ... 30
Put a Little Love in Your Heart (Unart, BMI) ... 48
Quentin's Theme (Curnor, BMI) ... 20
Reconsider Me (Singleton, BMI) ... 47
Ruby, Don't Take Your Love to Town (Cedarwood, BMI) ... 19
(Sittin' On) The Dock of the Bay (East/Redwal/Time, BMI) ... 66
So I Can Love You (Pervis/Staples, BMI) ... 39
Soul Deep (Barton, BMI) ... 74
Spinning Wheel (Blackwood/Minnesingers, BMI) ... 2
Stay and Love Me All Summer (Saturday, BMI) ... 82
Sweet Caroline (Good Times Never Seemed So Good) (Stonebridge, BMI) ... 24
Tell All the People (Nipper/Door, ASCAP) ... 58
That's the Way (Tree, BMI) ... 95
Theme From "A Summer Place" (Warner Bros.-Seven Arts, ASCAP) ... 83
Till You Get Enough (Wright Gerstl/Tamerlane, BMI) ... 94
Too Busy Thinking About My Baby (Jobete, BMI) ... 15
Wake Up (Blackwood, BMI) ... 92
We Got More Soul (Drive-In/Westward, BMI) ... 36
What Does It Take to Win Your Love (Jobete, BMI) 5
Where Do I Go/Be-in (Hare Krishna) (United Artists, ASCAP) ... 77
While You're Out Looking for Sugar (Gold Forever, BMI) ... 75
Why I Sing the Blues (Pamco/Sounds of Lucille, BMI) ... 61
Willie & Laura Mae Jones (Combine, BMI) ... 78
With Pen in Hand (Unart, BMI) ... 38
Workin' on a Groovy Thing (Screen Gems-Columbia, BMI) ... 70
Yesterday When I Was Young (T.R.O.-Dartmouth, ASCAP) ... 31
You Don't Have to Walk in the Rain (Ishmael/Blimp, BMI) ... 51
Your Good Thing (Is About to End) (East, BMI) ... 87
Your Husband—My Wife (Pocketful of Tunes/Jill, BMI) ... 97


## BUBBLING UNDER THE HOT 100

101. SUGAR, SUGAR ... Archies, Calendar 63-1008
102. FIRST HYMN FROM GRAND TERRACE ... Mark Lindsay, Columbia 4-44875
103. BIG BRUCE ... Steve Greenberg, Trip 3000
104. OUT OF SIGHT, OUT OF MIND ... Little Anthony & the Imperials, United Artists 50552
105. DYNAMITE WOMAN ... Sir Douglas Quintet, Smash 2233
106. BIRDS OF A FEATHER ... Joe South, Capitol 2532
107. I'LL NEVER FALL IN LOVE AGAIN ... Burt Bacharach, A&M 1064
108. PROPHECY OF DANIEL AND JOHN THE DEVINE ... Cowsills, MGM 14063
109. ANGEL OF THE MORNING ... Bettye Swann, Capitol 2515
110. EVERYBODY KNOWS MATILDA ... Duke Baxter, VMC 740
111. COLOR OF MY LOVE ... Jefferson, Decca 32501
112. THE HUNTER ... Ike & Tina Turner, Blue Thumb 102
113. EASE BACK ... Meters, Josie 1008
114. CHELSEA MORNING ... Judy Collins, Elektra 45657
115. TRUE GRIT ... Glen Campbell, Capitol 2573
116. FROZEN ORANGE JUICE ... Peter Sarstedt, World Pacific 77919
117. A TIME FOR US ... Johnny Mathis, Columbia 4-44915
118. THE RIB ... Jeannie C. Riley, Plantation 22
119. LOVE THAT A WOMAN SHOULD GIVE TO A MAN ... Patti Drew, Capitol 2473
120. ODDS AND ENDS ... Dionne Warwick, Scepter 12256
121. YES I WILL ... Association, Warner Bros.-Seven Arts 7305
122. ME AND BOBBY McGEE ... Roger Miller, Smash 2230
123. HANDS OF THE CLOCK ... Life, Polydor 15003
124. IN MY ROOM ... Sagittarius, Together 105
125. NEVER, NEVER LET YOU GO ... Eddie Floyd & Mavis Staples, Stax 0041
126. MY DARK HOUR ... Steve Miller Band, Capitol 2520
127. I NEED YOU WOMAN ... William Bell & Carla Thomas, Stax 0044
128. I'M GONNA MAKE YOU MINE ... Lou Christie, Buddah 116
129. THAT LUCKY OLD SUN ... Solomon Burke, Bell 806
130. SIMPLE SONG OF FREEDOM ... Tim Hardin, Columbia 4-44920
131. EVERYBODY'S GOT A HANGUP ... Bobby Freeman, Double Shot 139
132. HOOK AND SLING ... Eddie Bo, Scram 117
133. RING OF BRIGHT WATER ... Dee Dee Warwick, Mercury 72940

Compiled from national retail sales and radio station airplay by the Music Popularity Dept. of Record Market Research, Billboard.

# Billboard HOT 100

FOR WEEK ENDING JULY 26, 1969

★ STAR PERFORMER—Sides registering greatest proportionate upward progress this week.

● Record Industry Association of America seal of certification as million selling single.

| This Week | 1 Wk. Ago | 2 Wks. Ago | 3 Wks. Ago | TITLE Artist (Producer), Label & Number | Weeks On Chart |
|---|---|---|---|---|---|
| 1 | 1 | 1 | 8 | IN THE YEAR 2525 (Exordium & Terminus) — Zager & Evans (Zager & Evans), RCA 74-0174 | 6 |
| ★2 | 4 | 6 | 7 | CRYSTAL BLUE PERSUASION — Tommy James & the Shondells (Tommy James-Ritchie Cordell), Roulette 7050 | 8 |
| 3 | 2 | 2 | 2 | SPINNING WHEEL — Blood, Sweat & Tears (James William Guercio), Columbia 44871 | 9 |
| ★4 | 9 | 11 | 16 | MY CHERIE AMOUR — Stevie Wonder (Hank Cosby), Tamla 54180 | 9 |
| 5 | 5 | 10 | 14 | WHAT DOES IT TAKE TO WIN YOUR LOVE — Jr. Walker & the All Stars (Fuqua & Bristol), Soul 35062 | 11 |
| 6 | 3 | 3 | 4 | GOOD MORNING STARSHINE — Oliver (Bob Crewe), Jubilee 5659 | 10 |
| 7 | 6 | 5 | 5 | ONE — Three Dog Night (Gabriel Mekler), Dunhill 4191 | 13 |
| ●8 | 8 | 8 | 11 | THE BALLAD OF JOHN AND YOKO — The Beatles (Lennon-McCartney), Apple 2531 | 7 |
| ★9 | 14 | 17 | 29 | BABY, I LOVE YOU — Andy Kim (Jeff Barry), Steed 1031 | 10 |
| ●10 | 10 | 4 | 1 | LOVE THEME FROM ROMEO & JULIET — Henry Mancini & Ork. (Joe Reisman), RCA Victor 74-0131 | 12 |
| 11 | 12 | 15 | 18 | PART I MOTHER POPCORN (You Got to Have a Mother for Me) — James Brown (James Brown), King 6245 | 7 |
| 12 | 7 | 9 | 9 | COLOR HIM FATHER — Winstons (Don Carroll), Metromedia 117 | 10 |
| ★13 | 24 | 30 | 50 | SWEET CAROLINE (Good Times Never Seemed So Good) — Neil Diamond (Tommy Cogbill, Tom Catalano, Neil Diamond), Uni 55136 | 5 |
| ★14 | 26 | 29 | 33 | MY PLEDGE OF LOVE — The Joe Jeffrey Group (Jerry Meyers & Alan Klein), Wand 11200 | 8 |
| ★15 | 19 | 26 | 37 | RUBY, DON'T TAKE YOUR LOVE TO TOWN — Kenny Rogers and the First Edition (Jimmy Bowen), Reprise 0829 | 8 |
| 16 | 11 | 7 | 3 | BAD MOON RISING — Creedence Clearwater Revival (John Fogerty), Fantasy 622 | 13 |
| 17 | 15 | 13 | 10 | TOO BUSY THINKING ABOUT MY BABY — Marvin Gaye (Norman Whitfield), Tamla 54181 | 14 |
| 18 | 18 | 18 | 13 | BLACK PEARL — Sonny Charles with the Checkmates Ltd. (Phil Spector), A&M 1053 | 12 |
| 19 | 20 | 22 | 28 | QUENTIN'S THEME — The Charles Randolph Grean Sounde (Charles R. Grean), Ranwood 840 | 7 |
| 20 | 13 | 14 | 15 | LOVE ME TONIGHT — Tom Jones (Peter Sullivan), Parrot 40038 | 10 |
| ★21 | 31 | 32 | 42 | YESTERDAY WHEN I WAS YOUNG — Roy Clark (Joe Allison), Dot 17246 | 7 |
| ★22 | 43 | 57 | 86 | POLK SALAD ANNIE — Tony Joe White (Billy Swan), Monument 1104 | 4 |
| 23 | 21 | 20 | 20 | LET ME — Paul Revere & the Raiders Featuring Mark Lindsay, Columbia 4-44854 | 11 |
| 24 | 25 | 25 | 26 | MOODY WOMAN — Jerry Butler (Gamble & Huff), Mercury 72929 | 9 |
| 25 | 27 | 31 | 51 | GOOD OLD ROCK 'N ROLL — Cat Mother and the All Night News Boys (Cat Mother & Jimi Hendrix), Polydor 14002 | 5 |
| ●26 | 17 | 16 | 12 | IN THE GHETTO — Elvis Presley, RCA Victor 47-9741 | 13 |
| ●27 | 16 | 12 | 6 | GET BACK — Beatles (George Martin), Apple 2490 | 12 |
| ★28 | 79 | — | — | HONKY TONK WOMEN — Rolling Stones (Jimmy Miller), London 910 | 2 |
| 29 | 32 | 40 | 48 | CHOICE OF COLORS — Impressions (Curtis Mayfield), Curtom 1943 | 5 |
| 30 | 23 | 23 | 30 | I TURNED YOU ON — Isley Brothers (R. Isley-O. Isley-R. Isley), T-Neck 902 | 9 |
| ★31 | 62 | 83 | — | LAUGHING — Guess Who (Jack Richardson), RCA 74-0195 | 3 |
| 32 | 37 | 41 | 43 | DOGGONE RIGHT — Smokey Robinson & the Miracles (Smokey), Tamla 54183 | 6 |
| 33 | 33 | 48 | 73 | ABRAHAM, MARTIN & JOHN — Smokey Robinson & the Miracles (Smokey Robinson), Tamla 54184 | 4 |
| ★34 | 48 | 55 | 64 | PUT A LITTLE LOVE IN YOUR HEART — Jackie DeShannon (VME), Imperial 66385 | 5 |
| 35 | 35 | 42 | 57 | ABRAHAM, MARTIN AND JOHN — Moms Mabley (Barry Oslander), Mercury 72935 | 5 |
| 36 | 22 | 24 | 31 | LOVE IS BLUE (I Can Sing a Rainbow) — Dells (Bobby Miller), Cadet 5641 | 10 |
| 37 | 30 | 33 | 34 | THE POPCORN — James Brown (James Brown), King 6240 | 8 |
| ★38 | 47 | 56 | 68 | RECONSIDER ME — Johnny Adams (Shelby S. Singleton Jr.), SSS Int'l 770 | 5 |
| ★39 | 41 | 54 | 66 | ALONG CAME JONES — Ray Stevens (Ray Stevens, Jim Malloy), Monument 1150 | 5 |
| ★40 | 42 | 43 | 47 | MOONFLIGHT — Vik Venus (Lewis Merenstein), Buddah 118 | 7 |
| 41 | 38 | 35 | 36 | WITH PEN IN HAND — Vikki Carr (Dave Pell & Rob Bledsoe), Liberty 56092 | 13 |
| ★42 | — | — | — | A BOY NAMED SUE — Johnny Cash (Bob Johnston), Columbia 4-44944 | 1 |
| ★43 | 49 | 59 | 85 | I'D WAIT A MILLION YEARS — Grassroots (Steve Barry), Dunhill 4198 | 4 |
| ★44 | 64 | 74 | 89 | GET TOGETHER — Youngbloods (Felix Pappalardi), RCA 47-9752 | 5 |
| 45 | 45 | 46 | 46 | BUT IT'S ALRIGHT — J. J. Jackson (Lew Futterman), Warner Bros.-Seven Arts 7276 | 10 |
| 46 | 46 | 49 | 59 | I'D RATHER BE AN OLD MAN'S SWEETHEART — Candi Staton (Rick Hall), Fame 1456 | 6 |
| ★47 | 54 | 65 | 90 | CLEAN UP YOUR OWN BACK YARD — Elvis Presley, RCA Vistor 47-9747 | 4 |
| 48 | 34 | 34 | 41 | THE DAYS OF SAND AND SHOVELS — Bobby Vinton (Billy Sherrill), Epic 10485 | 7 |
| 49 | 52 | 53 | 55 | IT'S GETTING BETTER — Mama Cass (Steve Barri), Dunhill 4195 | 8 |
| ★50 | 70 | — | — | WORKIN' ON A GROOVY THING — Fifth Dimension (Bones Howe), Soul City 776 | 2 |
| 51 | 53 | 67 | 75 | ON CAMPUS — Dickie Goodman (Dickie Goodman), Cotique 158 | 5 |
| 52 | 40 | 37 | 40 | MRS. ROBINSON — Booker T. & the M.G.'s (Booker T. & the M.G.'s), Stax 0037 | 8 |
| 53 | 39 | 44 | 44 | SO I CAN LOVE YOU — Emotions, Volt 4010 | 10 |
| 54 | 60 | 61 | 71 | DON'T WAKE ME UP IN THE MORNING, MICHAEL — The Peppermint Rainbow (Paul Leka), Decca 732498 | 7 |
| 55 | 56 | 60 | 88 | MUDDY RIVER — Johnny Rivers (Johnny Rivers), Imperial 66386 | 5 |
| ★56 | 93 | 94 | — | LAY LADY LAY — Boy Dylan (Bob Johnson), Columbia 44926 | 3 |
| ★57 | 86 | — | — | MARRAKESH EXPRESS — Crosby, Stills & Nash (Stephen Stills/David Crosby/Graham Nash), Atlantic 2652 | 2 |
| 58 | 58 | 62 | 62 | TELL ALL THE PEOPLE — Doors (Kreiger), Elektra 45663 | 7 |
| 59 | 59 | 68 | 74 | GIRL YOU'RE TOO YOUNG — Archie Bell & the Drells (Gamble & Huff), Atlantic 2644 | 6 |
| ★60 | 67 | 73 | 77 | HURT SO BAD — Lettermen (Al DeLory), Capitol 2482 | 9 |
| ★61 | — | — | — | TRUE GRIT — Glen Campbell (Al DeLory), Capitol 2573 | 1 |
| ★62 | — | — | — | GIVE PEACE A CHANCE — Plastic Ono Band (John & Yoko), Apple 1809 | 1 |
| 63 | 76 | 78 | 92 | DID YOU SEE HER EYES — Illusion (Jeff Barry), Steed 718 | 4 |
| ★64 | 74 | 90 | 94 | SOUL DEEP — Box Tops (Tommy Cogbill & Chips Moman), Mala 12040 | 4 |
| 65 | 65 | 71 | 78 | THE FEELING IS RIGHT — Clarence Carter (Rick Hall), Atlantic 2648 | 6 |
| 66 | 73 | — | — | I'VE LOST EVERYTHING I'VE EVER LOVED — David Ruffin (Johnny Bristol), Motown 1149 | 2 |
| 67 | 68 | 79 | 93 | BREAK AWAY — Beach Boys (Brian Wilson/Murray Wilson), Capitol 2530 | 4 |
| 68 | 71 | 81 | — | HEY JOE — Wilson Pickett (Rick Hall), Atlantic 2648 | 3 |
| 69 | 69 | 70 | 79 | FEELING ALRIGHT — Joe Cocker (Denny-Cordell), A&M 1063 | 6 |
| 70 | 44 | 45 | 45 | MEMPHIS UNDERGROUND — Herbie Mann (Tom Dowd), Atlantic 2621 | 10 |
| 71 | 66 | 69 | 72 | (Sittin' On) THE DOCK OF THE BAY — Sergio Mendes & Brasil '66 (Sergio Mendes & Herb Alpert), A&M 1073 | 5 |
| ★72 | 88 | — | — | NITTY GRITTY — Gladys Knight & the Pips (Norman Whitfield), Soul 35063 | 2 |
| 73 | 55 | 52 | 52 | THE GIRL I'LL NEVER KNOW — Frankie Valli (Bob Crewe), Philips 40622 | 7 |
| 74 | 75 | 76 | 83 | WHILE YOU'RE OUT LOOKING FOR SUGAR — Honey Cone (R. Dunbar), Hot Wax 6901 | 5 |
| 75 | 63 | 64 | 67 | LISTEN TO THE BAND — Monkees (Michael Nesmith), Colgems 66-5004 | 8 |
| ★76 | 100 | — | — | BIRTHDAY — Underground Sunshine (Underground Sunshine), Intrepid 75002 | 2 |
| 77 | 77 | 85 | — | WHERE DO I GO/BE-IN (Hare Krishna) — Happenings (Happenings), Jubilee 5666 | 3 |
| 78 | 78 | 88 | — | WILLIE & LAURA MAE JONES — Dusty Springfield (Jerry Wexler, Tom Down, Arif Mardin), Atlantic 2647 | 3 |
| 79 | 80 | 80 | 87 | FOREVER — Mercy (Brad Shapiro & Steve Alaimo), Warner Bros.-Seven Arts 7297 | 5 |
| ★80 | 97 | — | — | YOUR HUSBAND—MY WIFE — Brooklyn Bridge (Wes Farrell), Buddah 126 | 2 |
| ★81 | 89 | 100 | — | ABERGAVENNY — Shannon, Heritage 814 | 3 |
| 82 | 82 | 87 | — | STAY AND LOVE ME ALL SUMMER — Brian Hyland (Ray Ruff), Dot 17258 | 3 |
| 83 | 83 | 84 | 97 | THEME FROM A SUMMER PLACE — Ventures (Joe Saraceno), Liberty 56115 | 5 |
| 84 | 85 | 86 | 95 | DON'T TELL YOUR MAMA WHERE YOU'VE BEEN — Eddie Floyd (Steve Cropper, B. T. Jones), Stax 0036 | 5 |
| ★85 | 90 | — | — | I'M FREE — Who (Kit Lambert), Decca 732519 | 2 |
| ★86 | — | — | — | I'LL NEVER FALL IN LOVE AGAIN — Tom Jones (Peter Sullivan), Parrot 40018 | 1 |
| 87 | 87 | — | — | YOUR GOOD THING (Is About to End) — Lou Rawls (David Axelrod), Capitol 2550 | 2 |
| ★88 | 94 | — | — | TILL YOU GET ENOUGH — Watts 103rd Street Rhythm Band (Charles Wright), Warner Bros.-Seven Arts 7298 | 2 |
| ★89 | 99 | — | — | JACK AND JILL — Tommy Roe (Steve Barri), ABC 11229 | 2 |
| ★90 | — | — | — | ODDS AND ENDS — Dionne Warwick (Burt Bacharach & Hal David), Scepter 12256 | 1 |
| 91 | — | — | — | SUGAR, SUGAR — Archies (Jeff Barry), Calendar 63-1008 | 1 |
| 92 | — | — | — | EVERYBODY KNOWS MATILDA — Duke Baxter (Tony Harris), VMC 740 | 1 |
| 93 | — | — | — | FIRST HYMN FROM GRAND TERRACE — Mark Lindsay (Jerry Fuller), Columbia 4-44875 | 1 |
| 94 | — | — | — | LET YOURSELF GO — Friends of Distinction (John Florez), RCA 74-0204 | 1 |
| 95 | 95 | — | — | THAT'S THE WAY — Joe Tex (Buddy Killen), Dial 4093 | 2 |
| 96 | — | — | — | A TIME FOR US — Johnny Mathis (Jack Gold), Columbia 4-44915 | 1 |
| 97 | 98 | 98 | — | PASS THE APPLE, EVE — B. J. Thomas (Chips Moman), Scepter 12255 | 3 |
| 98 | — | — | — | EASE BACK — Meters (Allen Toussaint & Marshall E. Sehorn), Josie 1008 | 1 |
| 99 | — | — | — | OUT OF SIGHT, OUT OF MIND — Little Anthony & the Imperials (Bob Skaff), United Artists 50552 | 1 |
| 100 | — | — | — | BIG BRUCE — Steve Greenberg (Bill Smith & Bud Rensau), Trip 3000 | 1 |

## HOT 100—A TO Z—(Publisher-Licensee)

Abergavenny (Mills, ASCAP) ........ 81
Abraham, Martin & John (Rozniquet, BMI) ........ 35
Abraham, Martin & John (Rozniquet, BMI) ........ 33
Along Came Jones (Tiger, BMI) ........ 39
Baby, I Love You (Trio/Mother Bertha, BMI) ........ 9
Bad Moon Rising (Jondora, BMI) ........ 16
Ballad of John and Yoko, The (Maclen, BMI) ........ 8
Big Bruce (Rose, BMI) ........ 100
Birthday (Maclen, BMI) ........ 76
Black Pearl (Irving, BMI) ........ 18
Boy Named Sue, A (Evil Eye, BMI) ........ 42
Break Away (Bri-Mur, BMI) ........ 67
But It's Alright (Pamelarosa, BMI) ........ 45
Choice of Colors (Camad, BMI) ........ 29
Clean Up Your Own Back Yard (Gladys, ASCAP) ........ 47
Color Him Father (Holly Bee, BMI) ........ 12
Crystal Blue Persausion (Big Seven, BMI) ........ 2
Days of Sand and Shovels, The (Lonzo & Oscar, BMI) ........ 48
Did You See Her Eyes (Unart, BMI) ........ 63
Doggone Right (Jobete, BMI) ........ 32
Don't Tell Your Mama Where You've Been (East/Memphis, BMI) ........ 84
Don't Wake Me Up in the Morning, Michael (M.R.C./Little Heather, BMI) ........ 54
Ease Back (Marsaint, BMI) ........ 98
Everybody Knows Matilda (VSAV, BMI) ........ 92
Feeling Alright (Almo, ASCAP) ........ 69
Feeling Is Right, The (Fame, BMI) ........ 65
First Hymn From Grand Terrace (Ja-Ma, ASCAP) ........ 93
Forever (Tree, BMI) ........ 79
Get Back (Maclen, BMI) ........ 27
Get Together (S.F.O., BMI) ........ 44
Girl I'll Never Know, The (Saturday, BMI) ........ 73
Girl You're Too Young (World War III, BMI) ........ 59
Give Peace a Chance (Maclen, BMI) ........ 62
Good Morning Starshine (United Artists, ASCAP ........ 6
Good Old Rock 'n' Roll (Cat Mother/Emm-Jay/Sea Lark, BMI) ........ 25
Hey Joe (Third Story, BMI) ........ 68
Honky Tonk Women (Gideon, BMI) ........ 28
Hurt So Bad (Vogue, BMI) ........ 60
I'd Rather Be an Old Man's Sweetheart (Fame, BMI) 46
I'd Wait a Million Years (Teenie Bopper, ASCAP) ........ 43
I'll Never Fall in Love Again (Hollis, BMI) ........ 86
I'm Free (Track, BMI) ........ 85
In the Ghetto (B 'n' B/Gladys, ASCAP) ........ 26
In the Year 2525 (Zelad, BMI) ........ 1
I Turned You On (Triple 3, BMI) ........ 30
It's Getting Better (Screen Gems-Columbia, BMI) ........ 49
I've Lost Everything I've Ever Loved (Jobete, BMI) 66
Jack and Jill (Low-Twi, BMI) ........ 89
Laughing (Dunbar, BMI) ........ 31
Lay Lady Lay (Big Sky, ASCAP) ........ 56
Let Me (Boom, BMI) ........ 23
Let Yourself Go (Mavil, BMI) ........ 94
Listen to the Band (Screen Gems-Columbia, BMI) ........ 75
Love Is Blue (I Can Sing a Rainbow) (Mark VII/Croma, ASCAP) ........ 36
Love Me Tonight (Duchess, BMI) ........ 20
Love Theme From Romeo & Juliet (Famous, ASCAP) 10
Marrakesh Express (Siquomb, BMI) ........ 57
Memphis Underground (Mann, ASCAP) ........ 70
Moody Woman (Gold Forever/Parabut, BMI) ........ 24
Moonflight (Kaskat/Kahoona/Camad/T.M./Pocket Full of Tunes/Rivers/Peanut Butter/Kama Sutra, BMI) ........ 40
Part 1—Mother Popcorn (You Got to Have a Mother for Me (Dynatone, BMI) ........ 11
Mrs. Robinson (Charing Cross, BMI) ........ 52
Muddy River (Rivers, BMI) ........ 55
My Cherie Amour (Jobete, BMI) ........ 4
My Pledge of Love (Wednesday Morn./Our Children's, BMI) ........ 14
Nitty Gritty (Gallico, BMI) ........ 72
Odds and Ends (Blue Seas/Jac, ASCAP) ........ 90
One (Dunbar, BMI) ........ 7
On Campus (Conique, BMI) ........ 51
Out of Sight, Out of Mind (Nom, BMI) ........ 99
Pass the Apple Eve (Press, BMI) ........ 97
Polk Salad Annie (Combine, BMI) ........ 22
Popcorn, The (Gola, BMI) ........ 37
Put a Little Love in Your Heart (Unart, BMI) ........ 34
Quentin's Theme (Curnor, BMI) ........ 19
Reconsider Me (Singleton, BMI) ........ 38
Ruby, Don't Take Your Love to Town (Cedarwood, BMI) ........ 15
(Sittin' On) The Dock of the Bay (East/Redwal/Time, BMI) ........ 71
So I Can Love You (Pervis/Staples, BMI) ........ 53
Soul Deep (Barton, BMI) ........ 64
Spinning Wheel (Blackwood/Minnesingers, BMI) ........ 3
Stay and Love Me All Summer (Saturday, BMI) ........ 82
Sugar, Sugar (Kirshner, BMI) ........ 91
Sweet Caroline (Good Times Never Seemed So Good) (Stonebridge, BMI) ........ 13
Tell All the People (Nipper/Door, ASCAP) ........ 58
That's the Way (Tree, BMI) ........ 95
Theme From "A Summer Place" (Warner Bros.-Seven Arts, ASCAP) ........ 83
Till You Get Enough (Wright Gerstl/Tamerlane, BMI) ........ 88
Time for Us, A (Famous, ASCAP) ........ 96
Too Busy Thinking About My Baby (Jobete, BMI) ........ 17
True Grit (Famous, ASCAP) ........ 61
What Does It Take to Win Your Love (Jobete, BMI) 5
Where Do I Go/Be-in (Hare Krishna) (United Artists, ASCAP) ........ 77
While You're Out Looking for Sugar (Gold Forever, BMI) ........ 74
Willie & Laura Mae Jones (Combine, BMI) ........ 78
With Pen in Hand (Unart, BMI) ........ 41
Workin' on a Groovy Thing (Screen Gems-Columbia, BMI) ........ 50
Yesterday When I Was Young (TRO-Dartmouth, ASCAP) ........ 21
Your Good Thing (Is About to End) (East, BMI) ........ 87
Your Husband—My Wife (Pocketful of Tunes/Jill, BMI) ........ 80

## BUBBLING UNDER THE HOT 100

101. SHARE YOUR LOVE WITH ME........Aretha Franklin, Atlantic 2650
102. CHANGE OF HEART........Dennis Yost & the Classics IV, Imperial 66393
103. THAT'S THE WAY GOD PLANNED IT........Billy Preston, Apple 1808
104. NOTHING CAN TAKE THE PLACE OF YOU........Brook Benton, Cotillion 44034
105. DYNAMITE WOMAN........Sir Douglas Quintet, Smash 2233
106. COLOR OF MY LOVE........Jefferson, Decca 32501
107. I'LL NEVER FALL IN LOVE AGAIN........Burt Bacharach, A&M 1064
108. IN THE TIME OF OUR LIVES........Iron Butterfly, Atco 6676
109. CHELSEA MORNING........Judy Collins, Elektra 45657
110. IN MY ROOM........Sagittarius, Together 105
111. THEME FROM "A SUMMER PLACE"........Percy Faith Ork. & Chorus, Columbia 4-44932
112. THE HUNTER........Ike & Tina Turner, Blue Thumb 102
113. THESE ARE NOT MY PEOPLE........Freddy Weller, Columbia 4-44916
114. QUESTIONS 67 & 68........Chicago, Columbia 4-44909
115. SOUTH CAROLINA........Flirtations, Deram 85048
116. SIMPLE SONG OF FREEDOM........Tim Hardin, Columbia 4-44920
117. THE RIB........Jeannie C. Riley, Plantation 22
118. A GIFT OF SONG........Mason Williams, Warner Bros.-Seven Arts 7301
119. AGE (Where I Started Again)........Horatio, Event 3304
120. HANDS OF THE CLOCK........Life, Polydor 15003
121. YES, I WILL........Association, Warner Bros.-Seven Arts 7305
122. EVERYBODY'S GOT A HANGUP........Bobby Freeman, Double Shot 139
123. RING OF BRIGHT WATER........Dee Dee Warwick, Mercury 72490
124. NEVER, NEVER LET YOU GO........Eddie Floyd & Mavis Staples, Stax 0041
125. I NEED YOU WOMAN........William Bell & Carla Thomas, Stax 0044
126. I'M GONNA MAKE YOU MINE........Lou Christie, Buddah 116
127. I DON'T WANT TO WALK WITHOUT YOU........Julius Wechter & the Baja Marimba Band, A&M 1078
128. LODI........Al Wilson, Soul City 775
129. HOOK AND SLING........Eddie Bo, Scram 117

Compiled from national retail sales and radio station airplay by the Music Popularity Dept. of Record Market Research, Billboard.

HOT 100
HOT 100

# Billboard HOT 100

FOR WEEK ENDING AUGUST 2, 1969

★ STAR PERFORMER—Sides registering greatest proportionate sales progress this week.

Record Industry Association of America seal of certification as million selling single.

| This Week | 1 Wk. Ago | 2 Wks. Ago | 3 Wks. Ago | TITLE Artist (Producer), Label & Number | Weeks On Chart |
|---|---|---|---|---|---|
| ★1 | 1 | 1 | 1 | IN THE YEAR 2525 (Exordium & Terminus) — Zager & Evans (Zager & Evans), RCA 74-0174 | 7 |
| 2 | 4 | 6 | | CRYSTAL BLUE PERSUASION — Tommy James & the Shondells (Tommy James-Ritchie Cordell), Roulette 7050 | 9 |
| 3 | 2 | 2 | | SPINNING WHEEL — Blood, Sweat & Tears (James William Guercio), Columbia 44871 | 10 |
| 4 | 9 | 11 | | MY CHERIE AMOUR — Stevie Wonder (Hank Cosby), Tamla 54180 | 10 |
| 5 | 5 | 10 | | WHAT DOES IT TAKE TO WIN YOUR LOVE — Jr. Walker & the All Stars (Fuqua & Bristol), Soul 35062 | 12 |
| ★6 | 15 | 19 | 26 | RUBY, DON'T TAKE YOUR LOVE TO TOWN — Kenny Rogers and the First Edition (Jimmy Bowen), Reprise 0829 | 9 |
| 7 | 13 | 24 | 30 | SWEET CAROLINE (Good Times Never Seemed So Good) — Neil Diamond (Tommy Cogbill, Tom Catalano, Neil Diamond), Uni 55136 | 6 |
| ★8 | 28 | 79 | — | HONKY TONK WOMEN — Rolling Stones (Jimmy Miller), London 910 | 3 |
| 9 | 9 | 14 | 17 | BABY, I LOVE YOU — Andy Kim (Jeff Barry), Steed 1031 | 11 |
| 10 | 8 | 8 | 8 | THE BALLAD OF JOHN AND YOKO — The Beatles (Lennon-McCartney), Apple 2531 | 8 |
| 11 | 11 | 12 | 15 | PART I MOTHER POPCORN (You Got to Have a Mother for Me) — James Brown (James Brown), King 6245 | 8 |
| 12 | 12 | 7 | 9 | COLOR HIM FATHER — Winstons (Don Carroll), Metromedia 117 | 11 |
| ★13 | 19 | 20 | 22 | QUENTIN'S THEME — The Charles Randolph Grean Sounde (Charles R. Grean), Ranwood 840 | 8 |
| 14 | 14 | 26 | 29 | MY PLEDGE OF LOVE — The Joe Jeffrey Group (Jerry Meyers & Alan Klein), Wand 11200 | 9 |
| 15 | 6 | 3 | 3 | GOOD MORNING STARSHINE — Oliver (Bob Crewe), Jubilee 5659 | 11 |
| 16 | 10 | 10 | 4 | LOVE THEME FROM ROMEO & JULIET — Henry Mancini & Ork. (Joe Reisman), RCA Victor 74-0131 | 13 |
| 17 | 7 | 6 | 5 | ONE — Three Dog Night (Gabriel Mekler), Dunhill 4191 | 14 |
| ★18 | 22 | 43 | 57 | POLK SALAD ANNIE — Tony Joe White (Billy Swan), Monument 1104 | 5 |
| 19 | 21 | 31 | 32 | YESTERDAY WHEN I WAS YOUNG — Roy Clark (Joe Allison), Dot 17246 | 8 |
| ★20 | 42 | — | — | A BOY NAMED SUE — Johnny Cash (Bob Johnston), Columbia 4-44944 | 2 |
| 21 | 25 | 27 | 31 | GOOD OLD ROCK 'N ROLL — Cat Mother and the All Night News Boys (Cat Mother & Jimi Hendrix), Polydor 14002 | 6 |
| 22 | 16 | 11 | 7 | BAD MOON RISING — Creedence Clearwater Revival (John Fogerty), Fantasy 622 | 14 |
| 23 | 20 | 13 | 14 | LOVE ME TONIGHT — Tom Jones (Peter Sullivan), Parrot 40038 | 11 |
| ★24 | 29 | 32 | 40 | CHOICE OF COLORS — Impressions (Curtis Mayfield), Curtom 1943 | 6 |
| 25 | 34 | 48 | 55 | PUT A LITTLE LOVE IN YOUR HEART — Jackie DeShannon (VME), Imperial 66385 | 6 |
| 26 | 31 | 62 | 83 | LAUGHING — Guess Who (Jack Richardson), RCA 74-0195 | 4 |
| ★27 | 39 | 41 | 54 | ALONG CAME JONES — Ray Stevens (Ray Stevens, Jim Malloy), Monument 1150 | 6 |
| ★28 | 38 | 47 | 56 | RECONSIDER ME — Johnny Adams (Shelby S. Singleton Jr.), SSS Int'l 770 | 6 |
| ★29 | 44 | 64 | 74 | GET TOGETHER — Youngbloods (Felix Pappalardi), RCA 47-9752 | 6 |
| 30 | 30 | 23 | 23 | I TURNED YOU ON — Isley Brothers (R. Isley-O. Isley-R. Isley), T-Neck 902 | 10 |
| 31 | 17 | 15 | 13 | TOO BUSY THINKING ABOUT MY BABY — Marvin Gaye (Norman Whitfield), Tamla 54181 | 15 |
| 32 | 32 | 37 | 41 | DOGGONE RIGHT — Smokey Robinson & the Miracles (Smokey), Tamla 54183 | 7 |
| 33 | 24 | 25 | 25 | MOODY WOMAN — Jerry Butler (Gamble & Huff), Mercury 72929 | 10 |
| 34 | 18 | 18 | 18 | BLACK PEARL — Sonny Charles with the Checkmates Ltd. (Phil Spector), A&M 1053 | 13 |
| ★35 | 56 | 93 | 94 | LAY LADY LAY — Boy Dylan (Bob Johnston), Columbia 44926 | 4 |
| ★36 | 49 | 52 | 53 | IT'S GETTING BETTER — Mama Cass (Steve Barri), Dunhill 4195 | 9 |
| 37 | 47 | 54 | 65 | CLEAN UP YOUR OWN BACK YARD — Elvis Presley, RCA Victor 47-9747 | 5 |
| ★38 | 57 | 86 | — | MARRAKESH EXPRESS — Crosby, Stills & Nash (Stephen Stills/David Crosby/Graham Nash), Atlantic 2652 | 3 |
| 39 | 40 | 42 | 43 | MOONFLIGHT — Vik Venus (Lewis Merenstein), Buddah 118 | 8 |
| 40 | 23 | 21 | 20 | LET ME — Paul Revere & the Raiders Featuring Mark Lindsay, Columbia 4-44854 | 12 |
| 41 | 43 | 49 | 59 | I'D WAIT A MILLION YEARS — Grassroots (Steve Barry), Dunhill 4198 | 5 |
| 42 | 50 | 70 | — | WORKIN' ON A GROOVY THING — Fifth Dimension (Bones Howe), Soul City 776 | 3 |
| ★43 | 62 | — | — | GIVE PEACE A CHANCE — Plastic Ono Band (John & Yoko), Apple 1809 | 2 |
| ★44 | 61 | — | — | TRUE GRIT — Glen Campbell (Al DeLory), Capitol 2573 | 2 |
| 45 | 51 | 53 | 67 | ON CAMPUS — Dickie Goodman (Dickie Goodman), Cotique 158 | 6 |
| 46 | 33 | 33 | 48 | ABRAHAM, MARTIN & JOHN — Smokey Robinson & the Miracles (Smokey Robinson), Tamla 54184 | 5 |
| 47 | 35 | 35 | 42 | ABRAHAM, MARTIN AND JOHN — Moms Mabley (Barry Oslander), Mercury 72935 | 6 |
| ★48 | 60 | 67 | 73 | HURT SO BAD — Lettermen (Al DeLory), Capitol 2482 | 10 |
| 49 | 48 | 34 | 34 | THE DAYS OF SAND AND SHOVELS — Bobby Vinton (Billy Sherrill), Epic 10485 | 8 |
| ★50 | 64 | 74 | 90 | SOUL DEEP — Box Tops (Tommy Cogbill & Chips Moman), Mala 12040 | 5 |
| ★51 | 55 | 56 | 60 | MUDDY RIVER — Johnny Rivers (Johnny Rivers), Imperial 66386 | 6 |
| ★52 | 86 | — | — | I'LL NEVER FALL IN LOVE AGAIN — Tom Jones (Peter Sullivan), Parrot 40018 | 2 |
| 53 | 46 | 46 | 49 | I'D RATHER BE AN OLD MAN'S SWEETHEART — Candi Staton (Rick Hall), Fame 1456 | 7 |
| 54 | 54 | 60 | 61 | DON'T WAKE ME UP IN THE MORNING, MICHAEL — The Peppermint Rainbow (Paul Leka), Decca 732498 | 8 |
| ★55 | — | — | — | SHARE YOUR LOVE WITH ME — Aretha Franklin (Jerry Wexler-Tom Dowd-Arif Mardin), Atlantic 2650 | 1 |
| ★56 | 76 | 100 | — | BIRTHDAY — Underground Sunshine (Underground Sunshine), Intrepid 75002 | 3 |
| 57 | 58 | 58 | 62 | TELL ALL THE PEOPLE — Doors (Kreiger), Elektra 45663 | 8 |
| 58 | 63 | 76 | 78 | DID YOU SEE HER EYES — Illusion (Jeff Barry), Steed 718 | 5 |
| ★59 | 80 | 97 | — | YOUR HUSBAND—MY WIFE — Brooklyn Bridge (Wes Farrell), Buddah 126 | 3 |
| ★60 | 85 | 90 | — | I'M FREE — Who (Kit Lambert), Decca 732519 | 3 |
| ★61 | 87 | 87 | — | YOUR GOOD THING (Is About to End) — Lou Rawls (David Axelrod), Capitol 2550 | 3 |
| 62 | 68 | 71 | 81 | HEY JOE — Wilson Pickett (Rick Hall), Atlantic 2648 | 4 |
| 63 | 67 | 68 | 79 | BREAK AWAY — Beach Boys (Brian Wilson/Murray Wilson), Capitol 2530 | 5 |
| 64 | 59 | 59 | 68 | GIRL YOU'RE TOO YOUNG — Archie Bell & the Drells (Gamble & Huff), Atlantic 2644 | 7 |
| 65 | 72 | 88 | — | NITTY GRITTY — Gladys Knight & the Pips (Norman Whitfield), Soul 35063 | 3 |
| 66 | 66 | 73 | — | I'VE LOST EVERYTHING I'VE EVER LOVED — David Ruffin (Johnny Bristol), Motown 1149 | 3 |
| ★67 | 91 | — | — | SUGAR, SUGAR — Archies (Jeff Barry), Calendar 63-1008 | 2 |
| 68 | 74 | 75 | 76 | WHILE YOU'RE OUT LOOKING FOR SUGAR — Honey Cone (R. Dunbar), Hot Wax 6901 | 6 |
| ★69 | 92 | — | — | EVERYBODY KNOWS MATILDA — Duke Baxter (Tony Harris), VMC 740 | 1 |
| ★70 | — | — | — | GREEN RIVER — Creedence Clearwater Revival (J. C. Fogerty), Fantasy 625 | 1 |
| ★71 | — | — | — | COMMOTION — Creedence Clearwater Revival (J. C. Fogerty), Fantasy 625 | 1 |
| 72 | 81 | 89 | 100 | ABERGAVENNY — Shannon, Heritage 814 | 4 |
| ★73 | 77 | 77 | 85 | WHERE DO I GO/BE-IN (Hare Krishna) — Happenings (Happenings), Jubilee 5666 | 4 |
| ★74 | 88 | 94 | — | TILL YOU GET ENOUGH — Watts 103rd Street Rhythm Band (Charles Wright), Warner Bros.-Seven Arts 7298 | 3 |
| 75 | 84 | 85 | 86 | DON'T TELL YOUR MAMA WHERE YOU'VE BEEN — Eddie Floyd (Steve Cropper, B. T. Jones), Stax 0036 | 6 |
| ★76 | 98 | — | — | EASE BACK — Meters (Allen Toussaint & Marshall E. Sehorn), Josie 1008 | 2 |
| ★77 | — | — | — | NOBODY BUT YOU BABE — Clarence Reid (Brad Shapiro & Steve Alaimo), Alston 4574 | 1 |
| 78 | 89 | 99 | — | JACK AND JILL — Tommy Roe (Steve Barri), ABC 11229 | 3 |
| 79 | 90 | — | — | ODDS AND ENDS — Dionne Warwick (Burt Bacharach & Hal David), Scepter 12256 | 2 |
| ★80 | — | 84 | 89 | NOTHING CAN TAKE THE PLACE OF YOU — Brook Benton (Arif Mardin), Cotillion 44034 | 4 |
| ★81 | — | — | — | SIMPLE SONG OF FREEDOM — Tim Hardin (Gary Klein), Columbia 4-44920 | 1 |
| ★82 | — | — | — | CHANGE OF HEART — Dennis Yost & the Classics IV (Buddy Buie), Imperial 66393 | 1 |
| 83 | 93 | — | — | FIRST HYMN FROM GRAND TERRACE — Mark Lindsay (Jerry Fuller), Columbia 4-44875 | 2 |
| ★84 | — | — | — | THAT'S THE WAY GOD PLANNED IT — Billy Preston (George Harrison), Apple 1808 | 1 |
| 85 | 94 | — | — | LET YOURSELF GO — Friends of Distinction (John Florez), RCA 74-0204 | 2 |
| ★86 | — | — | — | BARABAJAGAL (Love Is Hot) — Donovan With the Jeff Beck Group (Mickie Most), Epic 5-10510 | 1 |
| ★87 | — | — | — | DYNAMITE WOMAN — Sir Douglas Quintet (Amigos de Musica), Smash 2233 | 1 |
| ★88 | — | — | — | THE YOUNG FOLKS — Diana Ross & the Supremes (George Gordy), Motown 1148 | 1 |
| ★89 | — | — | — | IN MY ROOM — Sagittarius (G. Usher-C. Boettcher-R. Olsen), Together 105 | 1 |
| ★90 | — | — | — | BY THE TIME I GET TO PHOENIX — Mad Lads (Al Jackson), Volt 4016 | 1 |
| 91 | — | — | — | KEEM-O-SABE — Electric Indian (Len Barry), United Artists 50563 | 1 |
| 92 | — | — | — | LET'S CALL IT A DAY GIRL — Bobby Vee (Snuff Garrett), Liberty 56124 | 1 |
| 93 | — | — | — | THE HUNTER — Ike & Tina Turner (Bob Krasnow & Friends), Blue Thumb 102 | 1 |
| 94 | 95 | 95 | — | THAT'S THE WAY — Joe Tex (Buddy Killen), Dial 4093 | 3 |
| 95 | — | — | — | HOOK AND SLING (Part 1) — Eddie Bo (Al Scramuzza), Scram 117 | 1 |
| 96 | — | — | — | YOU MADE A BELIEVER (Out of Me) — Ruby Andrews (Eaton-Knight & Bridges), Zodiac 1015 | 1 |
| 97 | — | — | — | LET ME BE THE MAN MY DADDY WAS — Chi-Lites (Carl Davis & Eugene Record), Brunswick 755414 | 1 |
| 98 | 99 | — | — | OUT OF SIGHT, OUT OF MIND — Little Anthony & the Imperials (Bob Skaff), United Artists 50552 | 2 |
| 99 | 100 | — | — | BIG BRUCE — Steve Greenberg (Bill Stith & Bud Reneau), Trip 3000 | 1 |
| 100 | — | — | — | IN A MOMENT — Intrigues (Martin & Bell), Yew 1001 | 1 |

## HOT 100—A TO Z—(Publisher-Licensee)

Abergavenny (Mills, ASCAP) ... 72
Abraham, Martin & John (Rozniquet, BMI) ... 47
Abraham, Martin & John (Rozniquet, BMI) ... 46
Along Came Jones (Tiger, BMI) ... 27
Baby, I Love You (Trio/Mother Bertha, BMI) ... 9
Bad Moon Rising (Jondora, BMI) ... 22
Ballad of John and Yoko, The (Maclen, BMI) ... 10
Barabajagal (Live Is Hot) (Peer Int'l, BMI) ... 86
Big Bruce (Rose, BMI) ... 99
Birthday (Maclen, BMI) ... 56
Black Pearl (Irving, BMI) ... 34
Boy Named Sue, A (Evil Eye, BMI) ... 20
Break Away (Bri-Mur, BMI) ... 63
By the Time I Get to Phoenix (Rivers, BMI) ... 90
Change of Heart (Low-Sal, BMI) ... 82
Choice of Colors (Camad, BMI) ... 24
Clean Up Your Own Back Yard (Gladys, ASCAP) ... 37
Color Him Father (Holly Bee, BMI) ... 12
Commotion (Jondora, BMI) ... 71
Crystal Blue Persuasion (Big Seven, BMI) ... 2
Days of Sand and Shovels, The (Lonzo & Oscar, BMI) ... 49
Did You See Her Eyes (Unart, BMI) ... 58
Doggone Right (Jobete, BMI) ... 32
Don't Tell Your Mama Where You've Been (East/Memphis, BMI) ... 75
Don't Wake Me Up in the Morning, Michael (M.R.C./Little Heather, BMI) ... 54
Dynamite Woman (Southern Love, BMI) ... 87
Ease Back (Marsaint, BMI) ... 76
Everybody Knows Matilda (VSAV, BMI) ... 69
First Hymn From Grand Terrace (Ja-Ma, ASCAP) ... 83
Get Together (S.F.O., BMI) ... 29
Girl You're Too Young (World War III, BMI) ... 64
Give Peace a Chance (Maclen, BMI) ... 43
Good Morning Starshine (United Artists, ASCAP) ... 15
Good Old Rock 'n' Roll (Cat Mother/Emmy-Jay/Sea Lark, BMI) ... 21
Green River (Jondora, BMI) ... 70
Hey Joe (Third Story, BMI) ... 62
Honky Tonk Women (Gideon, BMI) ... 8
Hook and Sling (Part 1) (Uzza, BMI) ... 95
Hunter, The (East, BMI) ... 93
Hurt So Bad (Vogue, BMI) ... 48
I'd Rather Be an Old Man's Sweetheart (Fame, BMI) 53
I'd Wait a Million Years (Teenie Bopper, ASCAP) ... 41
I'll Never Fall in Love Again (Hollis, BMI) ... 52
I'm Free (Track, BMI) ... 60
In a Moment (Odom & Neiburg, BMI) ... 100
In My Room (Sea of Tunes, BMI) ... 89
In the Year 2525 (Zelad, BMI) ... 1
I Turned You On (Triple 3, BMI) ... 30
It's Getting Better (Screen Gems-Columbia, BMI) ... 36
I've Lost Everything I've Ever Loved (Jobete, BMI) 66
Jack and Jill (Low-Twi, BMI) ... 78
Keem-O-Sabe (Binn/Elaine/United Artists, ASCAP) ... 91
Laughing (Dunbar, BMI) ... 26
Lay Lady Lay (Big Sky, ASCAP) ... 35
Let Me (Boom, BMI) ... 40
Let Me Be the Man My Daddy Was (Dakar/BRC, BMI) ... 97
Let Yourself Go (Mavil, BMI) ... 85
Let's Call It a Day Girl (Sea-Lark, BMI) ... 92
Love Me Tonight (Duchess, BMI) ... 23
Love Theme From Romeo & Juliet (Famous, ASCAP) 16
Marrakesh Express (Siquomb, BMI) ... 38
Moody Woman (Gold Forever/Parabut, BMI) ... 33
Moonflight (Kaskat/Kahoona/Camad/T.M./Pocket Full of Tunes/Rivers/Peanut Butter/Kama Sutra, BMI) ... 39
Part 1—Mother Popcorn (You Got to Have a Mother for Me (Dynatone, BMI) ... 11
Muddy River (Rivers, BMI) ... 51
My Cherie Amour (Jobete, BMI) ... 4
My Pledge of Love (Wednesday Morn./Our Children's, BMI) ... 14
Nitty Gritty (Gallico, BMI) ... 65
Nobody But You Babe (Sherlyn, BMI) ... 77
Nothing Can Take the Place of You (Su-Ma, BMI) ... 80
Odds and Ends (Blue Seas/Jac, ASCAP) ... 79
One (Dunbar, BMI) ... 17
On Campus (Conique, BMI) ... 45
Out of Sight, Out of Mind (Nom, BMI) ... 98
Polk Salad Annie (Combine, BMI) ... 18
Put a Little Love in Your Heart (Unart, BMI) ... 25
Quentin's Theme (Curnor, BMI) ... 13
Reconsider Me (Singleton, BMI) ... 28
Ruby, Don't Take Your Love to Town (Cedarwood, BMI) ... 6
Share Your Love With Me (Don, BMI) ... 55
Simple Song of Freedom (T.M., BMI) ... 81
Soul Deep (Barton, BMI) ... 50
Spinning Wheel (Blackwood/Minnesingers, BMI) ... 3
Sugar, Sugar (Kirshner, BMI) ... 67
Sweet Caroline (Good Times Never Seemed So Good) (Stonebridge, BMI) ... 7
Tell All the People (Nipper/Door, ASCAP) ... 57
That's the Way (Tree, BMI) ... 94
That's the Way God Planned It (Apple, ASCAP) ... 84
Till You Get Enough (Wright Gerstl/Tamerlane, BMI) ... 74
Too Busy Thinking About My Baby (Jobete, BMI) ... 31
True Grit (Famous, ASCAP) ... 44
What Does It Take to Win Your Love (Jobete, BMI) 5
Where Do I Go/Be-in (Hare Krishna) (United Artists, ASCAP) ... 73
While You're Out Looking for Sugar (Gold Forever, BMI) ... 68
Workin' on a Groovy Thing (Screen Gems-Columbia, BMI) ... 42
Yesterday When I Was Young (TRO-Dartmouth, ASCAP) ... 19
You Made a Believer (Out of Me) (WilRic,, BMI) ... 96
Young Folks, The (Jobete, BMI) ... 88
Your Good Thing (Is About to End) (East, BMI) ... 61
Your Husband—My Wife (Pocketful of Tunes/Jill, BMI) ... 59

## BUBBLING UNDER THE HOT 100

101. QUESTIONS 67 & 68 ... Chicago, Columbia 4-44909
102. COLOR OF MY LOVE ... Jefferson, Decca 32501
103. A TIME FOR US ... Johnny Mathis, Columbia 4-44915
104. HOT FUN IN THE SUMMERTIME ... Sly & the Family Stone, Epic 5-10497
105. FOREVER ... Mercy, Warner Bros.-Seven Arts 7297
106. I NEED YOU WOMAN ... William Bell & Carla Thomas, Stax 0044
107. NEVER, NEVER LET YOU GO ... Eddie Floyd & Mavis Staples, Stax 0041
108. LET ME BE THE ONE ... Peaches & Herb, Date 2-1649
109. HALLELUJAH (I Am the Preacher) ... Deep Purple, Tetragrammaton 1537
110. TOYS ARE MADE FOR CHILDREN ... Uniques, Paula 324
111. THE RIB ... Jeannie C. Riley, Plantation 22
112. CHELSEA MORNING ... Judy Collins, Elektra 45657
113. RING OF BRIGHT WATER ... Dee Dee Warwick, Mercury 72490
114. GOT IT TOGETHER ... Nancy Wilson, Capitol 2555
115. SOUTH CAROLINA ... Flirtations, Deram 85048
116. STRAIGHT AHEAD ... Young-Holt Unlimited, Brunswick 755417
117. JUST KEEP ON LOVING ME ... Johnny Taylor & Carla Thomas, Stax 0042
118. SHE'S A WOMAN ... Jose Feliciano, RCA Victor 47-9757
119. GOING IN CIRCLES ... Friends of Distinction, RCA 74-0204
120. YES, I WILL ... Association, Warner Bros.-Seven Arts 7305
121. I DON'T WANT TO WALK WITHOUT YOU ... Julius Wechter & the Baja Marimba Band, A&M 1078
122. MEMPHIS TRAIN ... Buddy Miles Express, Mercury 72945
123. FREE ME ... Otis Redding, Atco 6700
124. A GIFT OF SONG ... Mason Williams, Warner Bros.-Seven Arts 7301

Compiled from national retail sales and radio station airplay by the Music Popularity Dept. of Record Market Research, Billboard.

HOT 100

HOT 100

# Billboard HOT 100

**FOR WEEK ENDING AUGUST 9, 1969**

★ STAR PERFORMER—Sides registering greatest proportionate sales progress this week.
● Record Industry Association of America seal of certification as million selling single.

| This Week | Wk.Ago | 2 Wk.Ago | 3 Wk.Ago | TITLE — Artist (Producer), Label & Number | Weeks on Chart |
|---|---|---|---|---|---|
| ●1 | 1 | 1 | 1 | IN THE YEAR 2525 (Exordium & Terminus) — Zager & Evans (Zager & Evans), RCA 74-0174 | 8 |
| 2 | 2 | 2 | 4 | CRYSTAL BLUE PERSUASION — Tommy James & the Shondells (Tommy James-Ritchie Cordell), Roulette 7050 | 10 |
| ★3 | 8 | 28 | 79 | HONKY TONK WOMEN — Rolling Stones (Jimmy Miller), London 910 | 4 |
| 4 | 5 | 5 | 5 | WHAT DOES IT TAKE TO WIN YOUR LOVE — Jr. Walker & the All Stars (Fuqua & Bristol), Soul 35062 | 13 |
| 5 | 7 | 13 | 24 | SWEET CAROLINE (Good Times Never Seemed So Good) — Neil Diamond (Tommy Cogbill, Tom Catalano, Neil Diamond), Uni 55136 | 7 |
| 6 | 6 | 15 | 19 | RUBY, DON'T TAKE YOUR LOVE TO TOWN — Kenny Rogers and the First Edition (Jimmy Bowen), Reprise 0829 | 10 |
| ★7 | 20 | 42 | — | A BOY NAMED SUE — Johnny Cash (Bob Johnston), Columbia 4-44944 | 3 |
| 8 | 4 | 4 | 9 | MY CHERIE AMOUR — Stevie Wonder (Hank Cosby), Tamla 54180 | 11 |
| 9 | 25 | 34 | 48 | PUT A LITTLE LOVE IN YOUR HEART — Jackie DeShannon (VME), Imperial 66385 | 7 |
| 10 | 9 | 9 | 14 | BABY, I LOVE YOU — Andy Kim (Jeff Barry), Steed 1031 | 12 |
| ●11 | 3 | 3 | 2 | SPINNING WHEEL — Blood, Sweat & Tears (James William Guercio), Columbia 44871 | 11 |
| 12 | 11 | 11 | 12 | PART I MOTHER POPCORN (You Got to Have a Mother for Me) — James Brown (James Brown), King 6245 | 9 |
| 13 | 13 | 19 | 20 | QUENTIN'S THEME — The Charles Randolph Grean Sounde (Charles R. Grean), Ranwood 840 | 9 |
| 14 | 18 | 22 | 43 | POLK SALAD ANNIE — Tony Joe White (Billy Swan), Monument 1104 | 6 |
| ●15 | 12 | 12 | 7 | COLOR HIM FATHER — Winstons (Don Carroll), Metromedia 117 | 10 |
| 16 | 14 | 14 | 26 | MY PLEDGE OF LOVE — The Joe Jeffrey Group (Jerry Meyers & Alan Klein), Wand 11200 | 10 |
| ●17 | 15 | 6 | 3 | GOOD MORNING STARSHINE — Oliver (Bob Crewe), Jubilee 5659 | 12 |
| 18 | 17 | 7 | 6 | ONE — Three Dog Night (Gabriel Mekler), Dunhill 4191 | 15 |
| 19 | 35 | 56 | 93 | LAY LADY LAY — Bob Dylan (Bob Johnson), Columbia 44926 | 5 |
| 20 | 26 | 31 | 62 | LAUGHING — Guess Who (Jack Richardson), RCA 74-0195 | 5 |
| 21 | 29 | 44 | 64 | GET TOGETHER — Youngbloods (Felix Pappalardi), RCA 47-9752 | 5 |
| ●22 | 16 | 10 | 10 | LOVE THEME FROM ROMEO & JULIET — Henry Mancini & Ork. (Joe Reisman), RCA Victor 74-0131 | 14 |
| 23 | 43 | 62 | — | GIVE PEACE A CHANCE — Plastic Ono Band (John & Yoko), Apple 1809 | 3 |
| 24 | 24 | 29 | 32 | CHOICE OF COLORS — Impressions (Curtis Mayfield), Curtom 1943 | 7 |
| 25 | 19 | 21 | 31 | YESTERDAY WHEN I WAS YOUNG — Roy Clark (Joe Allison), Dot 17246 | 8 |
| 26 | 21 | 25 | 27 | GOOD OLD ROCK 'N ROLL — Cat Mother and the All Night News Boys (Cat Mother & Jimi Hendrix), Polydor 14002 | 7 |
| 27 | 27 | 39 | 41 | ALONG CAME JONES — Ray Stevens (Ray Stevens, Jim Malloy), Monument 1150 | 5 |
| 28 | 28 | 38 | 47 | RECONSIDER ME — Johnny Adams (Shelby S. Singleton Jr.), SSS Int'l 770 | 6 |
| 29 | 10 | 8 | 8 | THE BALLAD OF JOHN AND YOKO — The Beatles (Lennon-McCartney), Apple 2531 | 8 |
| 30 | 41 | 43 | 49 | I'D WAIT A MILLION YEARS — Grassroots (Steve Barry), Dunhill 4198 | 6 |
| 31 | 52 | 86 | — | I'LL NEVER FALL IN LOVE AGAIN — Tom Jones (Peter Sullivan), Parrot 40018 | 3 |
| ★32 | 42 | 50 | 70 | WORKIN' ON A GROOVY THING — Fifth Dimension (Bones Howe), Soul City 776 | 4 |
| 33 | 32 | 32 | 37 | DOGGONE RIGHT — Smokey Robinson & the Miracles (Smokey), Tamla 54183 | 8 |
| ★34 | 71 | — | — | COMMOTION — Creedence Clearwater Revival (J. C. Fogerty), Fantasy 625 | 2 |
| 35 | 37 | 47 | 54 | CLEAN UP YOUR OWN BACK YARD — Elvis Presley, RCA Victor 47-9747 | 6 |
| 36 | 36 | 49 | 52 | IT'S GETTING BETTER — Mama Cass (Steve Barri), Dunhill 4195 | 10 |
| 37 | 38 | 57 | 86 | MARRAKESH EXPRESS — Crosby, Stills & Nash (Stephen Stills/David Crosby/Graham Nash), Atlantic 2652 | 4 |
| 38 | 39 | 40 | 42 | MOONFLIGHT — Vik Venus (Lewis Merenstein), Buddah 118 | 9 |
| 39 | 65 | 72 | 88 | NITTY GRITTY — Gladys Knight & the Pips (Norman Whitfield), Soul 35063 | 4 |
| 40 | 55 | — | — | SHARE YOUR LOVE WITH ME — Aretha Franklin (Jerry Wexler-Tom Dowd-Arif Mardin), Atlantic 2650 | 2 |
| 41 | 67 | 91 | — | SUGAR, SUGAR — Archies (Jeff Barry), Calendar 63-1008 | 3 |
| 42 | 44 | 61 | — | TRUE GRIT — Glen Campbell (Al DeLory), Capitol 2573 | 4 |
| 43 | 50 | 64 | 74 | SOUL DEEP — Box Tops (Tommy Cogbill & Chips Moman), Mala 12040 | 6 |
| 44 | 48 | 60 | 67 | HURT SO BAD — Lettermen (Al DeLory), Capitol 2482 | 11 |
| 45 | 51 | 55 | 56 | MUDDY RIVER — Johnny Rivers (Johnny Rivers), Imperial 66386 | 7 |
| ★46 | 58 | 63 | 76 | DID YOU SEE HER EYES — Illusion (Jeff Barry), Steed 718 | 6 |
| 47 | 46 | 33 | 33 | ABRAHAM, MARTIN & JOHN — Smokey Robinson & the Miracles (Smokey Robinson), Tamla 54184 | 6 |
| 48 | 70 | — | — | GREEN RIVER — Creedence Clearwater Revival (J. C. Fogerty), Fantasy 625 | 2 |
| 49 | 45 | 51 | 53 | ON CAMPUS — Dickie Goodman (Dickie Goodman), Cotique 158 | 7 |
| 50 | 72 | 81 | 89 | ABERGAVENNY — Shannon, Heritage 814 | 4 |
| 51 | 61 | 87 | 87 | YOUR GOOD THING (Is About to End) — Lou Rawls (David Axelrod), Capitol 2550 | 4 |
| 52 | 60 | 85 | 90 | I'M FREE — Who (Kit Lambert), Decca 732519 | 4 |
| 53 | 56 | 76 | 100 | BIRTHDAY — Underground Sunshine (Underground Sunshine), Intrepid 75002 | 4 |
| 54 | 59 | 80 | 97 | YOUR HUSBAND—MY WIFE — Brooklyn Bridge (Wes Farrell), Buddah 126 | 4 |
| 55 | 53 | 46 | 46 | I'D RATHER BE AN OLD MAN'S SWEETHEART — Candi Staton (Rick Hall), Fame 1456 | 8 |
| 56 | 54 | 54 | 60 | DON'T WAKE ME UP IN THE MORNING, MICHAEL — The Peppermint Rainbow (Paul Leka), Decca 732498 | 9 |
| 57 | 57 | 58 | 58 | TELL ALL THE PEOPLE — Doors (Krieger), Elektra 45663 | 7 |
| 58 | 66 | 66 | 73 | I'VE LOST EVERYTHING I'VE EVER LOVED — David Ruffin (Johnny Bristol), Motown 1149 | 5 |
| 59 | 62 | 68 | 71 | HEY JOE — Wilson Pickett (Rick Hall), Atlantic 2648 | 5 |
| ★60 | 78 | 89 | 99 | JACK AND JILL — Tommy Roe (Steve Barri), ABC 11229 | 4 |
| ★61 | 86 | — | — | BARABAJAGAL (Love Is Hot) — Donovan with the Jeff Beck Group (Mickie Most), Epic 5-10510 | 2 |
| 62 | 68 | 74 | 75 | WHILE YOU'RE OUT LOOKING FOR SUGAR — Honey Cone (R. Dunbar), Hot Wax 6901 | 4 |
| 63 | 69 | 92 | — | EVERYBODY KNOWS MATILDA — Duke Baxter (Tony Harris), VMC 740 | 3 |
| ★64 | 77 | — | — | NOBODY BUT YOU BABE — Clarence Reid (Brad Shapiro & Steve Alaimo), Alston 4574 | 2 |
| 65 | 63 | 67 | 68 | BREAK AWAY — Beach Boys (Brian Wilson/Murray Wilson), Capitol 2530 | 5 |
| 66 | 73 | 77 | 77 | WHERE DO I GO/BE-IN (Hare Krishna) — Happenings (Happenings), Jubilee 5666 | 4 |
| 67 | 74 | 88 | 94 | TILL YOU GET ENOUGH — Watts 103rd Street Rhythm Band (Charles Wright), Warner Bros.-Seven Arts 7298 | 4 |
| ★68 | 82 | — | — | CHANGE OF HEART — Dennis Yost and the Classics IV (Buddy Buie), Imperial 66393 | 2 |
| 69 | 98 | 99 | — | OUT OF SIGHT, OUT OF MIND — Little Anthony & the Imperials (Bob Skaff), United Artists 50552 | 3 |
| 70 | 81 | — | — | SIMPLE SONG OF FREEDOM — Tim Hardin (Gary Klein), Columbia 4-44920 | 2 |
| 71 | 79 | 90 | — | ODDS AND ENDS — Dionne Warwick (Burt Bacharach & Hal David), Scepter 12256 | 3 |
| 72 | 85 | 94 | — | LET YOURSELF GO — Friends of Distinction (John Florez), RCA 74-0204 | 3 |
| 73 | 75 | 84 | 85 | DON'T TELL YOUR MAMA WHERE YOU'VE BEEN — Eddie Floyd (Steve Cropper, B. T. Jones), Stax 0036 | 7 |
| 74 | 80 | — | 84 | NOTHING CAN TAKE THE PLACE OF YOU — Brook Benton (Arif Mardin), Cotillion 44034 | 5 |
| 75 | 76 | 98 | — | EASE BACK — Meters (Allen Toussaint & Marshall E. Sehorn), Josie 1008 | 3 |
| ★76 | 84 | — | — | THAT'S THE WAY GOD PLANNED IT — Billy Preston (George Harrison), Apple 1808 | 2 |
| 77 | — | — | — | EASY TO BE HARD — Three Dog Night (Gabriel Mekler), Dunhill 4203 | 1 |
| 78 | 91 | — | — | KEEM-O-SABE — Electric Indian (Len Barry), United Artists 50563 | 2 |
| 79 | — | — | — | HOT FUN IN THE SUMMERTIME — Sly & the Family Stone (Sly Stone), Epic 5-10497 | 1 |
| 80 | — | — | — | WHEN I DIE — Motherlode (Mort Ross & Doug Riley), Buddah 131 | 1 |
| 81 | 83 | 93 | — | FIRST HYMN FROM GRAND TERRACE — Mark Lindsay (Jerry Fuller), Columbia 4-44875 | 3 |
| 82 | 88 | — | — | THE YOUNG FOLKS — Diana Ross and the Supremes (George Gordy), Motown 1148 | 2 |
| 83 | 87 | — | — | DYNAMITE WOMAN — Sir Douglas Quintet (Amigos de Musica), Smash 2233 | 2 |
| 84 | 90 | — | — | BY THE TIME I GET TO PHOENIX — Mad Lads (Al Jackson), Volt 4016 | 2 |
| 85 | — | — | — | I COULD NEVER BE PRESIDENT — Johnnie Taylor (Don Davis), Stax 0046 | 1 |
| 86 | 89 | — | — | IN MY ROOM — Sagittarius (G. Usher-C. Boettcher-R. Olsen), Together 105 | 2 |
| 87 | — | — | — | ONE NIGHT AFFAIR — O'Jays (Gamble-Huff), Neptune 12 | 1 |
| ★88 | 100 | — | — | I TAKE A LOT OF PRIDE IN WHAT I AM — Dean Martin (Jimmy Bowen), Reprise 0841 | 2 |
| 89 | 100 | — | — | IN A MOMENT — Intrigues (Martin & Andy), Yew 1001 | 2 |
| 90 | — | — | — | LOOK AT MINE — Petula Clark (Tony Hatch), Warner Bros.-Seven Arts 7310 | 1 |
| 91 | 92 | — | — | CHELSEA MORNING — Judy Collins (David Anderle), Elektra 45657 | 2 |
| 92 | 92 | — | — | LET'S CALL IT A DAY GIRL — Bobby Vee (Snuff Garrett), Liberty 56124 | 2 |
| 93 | 93 | — | — | THE HUNTER — Ike & Tina Turner (Bob Krasnow & Friends), Blue Thumb 102 | 2 |
| 94 | 95 | — | — | HOOK AND SLING (Part 1) — Eddie Bo (Al Scramuzza), Scram 117 | 2 |
| 95 | 97 | — | — | LET ME BE THE MAN MY DADDY WAS — Chi-Lites (Carl Davis & Eugene Record), Brunswick 755414 | 2 |
| 96 | — | — | — | YOU MADE A BELIEVER (Out of Me) — Ruby Andrews (Eaton-Knight & Bridges), Zodiac 1015 | 1 |
| 97 | 99 | 100 | — | BIG BRUCE — Steve Greenberg (Bill Stith & Bud Reneau), Trip 3800 | 3 |
| 98 | — | — | — | FAREWELL LOVE THEME — Romeo & Juliet Soundtrack (Neely Plumb), Capitol 2502 | 1 |
| 99 | — | — | — | QUESTIONS 67 & 68 — Chicago (James William Guercio), Columbia 4-44909 | 1 |
| 100 | — | — | — | WHO DO YOU LOVE — Quicksilver Messenger Service (Quicksilver Messenger Service), Capitol 2557 | 1 |

## BUBBLING UNDER THE HOT 100

101. AIN'T IT LIKE HIM — Edwin Hawkins Singers, Pavillion 20002
102. COLOR OF MY LOVE — Jefferson, Decca 22501
103. A TIME FOR US — Johnny Mathis, Columbia 4-44915
104. SHE'S A WOMAN — Jose Feliciano, RCA Victor 47-9757
105. LET ME BE THE ONE — Peaches & Herb, Date 2-1649
106. TRAIN — 1910 Fruitgum Co., Buddah 130
107. THE REAL THING — Russell Morriss, Diamond 263
108. HALLELUJAH (I Am the Preacher) — Deep Purple, Tetragrammaton 1537
109. TOYS ARE MADE FOR CHILDREN — Uniques, Paula 324
110. FREE ME — Otis Redding, Atco 6700
111. EVERYBODY'S TALKIN' — Nilsson, RCA 74-0161
112. STRAIGHT AHEAD — Young-Holt Unlimited, Brunswick 755417
113. SOUTH CAROLINA — Flirtations, Deram 85048
114. GOT IT TOGETHER — Nancy Wilson, Capitol 2555
115. JUST KEEP ON LOVING ME — Johnny Taylor & Carla Thomas, Stax 0042
116. GOING IN CIRCLES — Friends of Distinction, RCA 74-0204
117. MOONLIGHT SONATA — Henry Mancini & His Ork., RCA 74-0212
118. LOW DOWN — Percy Sledge, Atlantic 2646
119. RAIN — Jose Feliciano, RCA Victor 47-9757
120. LIVE AND LEARN — Andy Williams, Columbia 4-44929
121. MEMPHIS TRAIN — Buddy Miles Express, Mercury 72945
122. JEAN — Oliver, Crewe 334
123. NO ONE IS GOING TO HURT YOU — Neon Philharmonic, Warner Bros.-Seven Arts 7311
124. TIME TO MAKE A TURN — Andy Kim, Steed
125. SMILE A LITTLE SMILE FOR ME — Flying Machine, Congress 6000
126. YOU — Rugbys, Amazon 1
127. OH WHAT A NIGHT — Dells, Cadet
128. I WANT YOU SO BAD — B.B. King, BluesWay 61026
129. HAPPY — William Bell, Stax 0040
130. MUDDY MISSISSIPPI LINE — Bobby Goldsboro, United Artists 50565
131. LA JEANNE — King Curtis & His Kingpins, Atco 6695
132. ALL THE WAITING IS NOT IN VAIN — Tyrone Davis, Dakar 609
133. LOVE & PEACE — Johnny Nash, JAD 218

# Billboard HOT 100

FOR WEEK ENDING AUGUST 16, 1969

★ STAR PERFORMER—Sides registering greatest proportionate sales progress this week.

(RIAA) Record Industry Association of America seal of certification as million selling single.

| This Week | 1 Wk. Ago | 2 Wks. Ago | 3 Wks. Ago | TITLE Artist (Producer), Label & Number | Weeks On Chart |
|---|---|---|---|---|---|
| 1 (RIAA) | 1 | 1 | 1 | IN THE YEAR 2525 (Exordium & Terminus) — Zager & Evans (Zager & Evans), RCA 74-0174 | 9 |
| ★ 2 | 3 | 8 | 28 | HONKY TONK WOMEN — Rolling Stones (Jimmy Miller), London 910 | 5 |
| 3 | 2 | 2 | 2 | CRYSTAL BLUE PERSUASION — Tommy James & the Shondells (Tommy James-Ritchie Cordell), Roulette 7050 | 11 |
| 4 | 5 | 7 | 13 | SWEET CAROLINE (Good Times Never Seemed So Good) — Neil Diamond (Tommy Cogbill, Tom Catalano, Neil Diamond), Uni 55136 | 8 |
| ★ 5 | 7 | 20 | 42 | A BOY NAMED SUE — Johnny Cash (Bob Johnston), Columbia 4-44944 | 4 |
| ★ 6 | 9 | 25 | 34 | PUT A LITTLE LOVE IN YOUR HEART — Jackie DeShannon (VME), Imperial 66385 | 8 |
| 7 | 6 | 6 | 15 | RUBY, DON'T TAKE YOUR LOVE TO TOWN — Kenny Rogers and the First Edition (Jimmy Bowen), Reprise 0829 | 11 |
| 8 | 8 | 4 | 4 | MY CHERIE AMOUR — Stevie Wonder (Hank Cosby), Tamla 54180 | 12 |
| 9 | 4 | 5 | 5 | WHAT DOES IT TAKE TO WIN YOUR LOVE — Jr. Walker & the All Stars (Fuqua & Bristol), Soul 35062 | 14 |
| 10 | 10 | 9 | 9 | BABY, I LOVE YOU — Andy Kim (Jeff Barry), Steed 1031 | 13 |
| 11 (RIAA) | 11 | 3 | 3 | SPINNING WHEEL — Blood, Sweat & Tears (James William Guercio), Columbia 44871 | 12 |
| ★ 12 | 20 | 26 | 31 | LAUGHING — Guess Who (Jack Richardson), RCA 74-0195 | 6 |
| 13 | 14 | 19 | 22 | POLK SALAD ANNIE — Tony Joe White (Billy Swan), Monument 1104 | 7 |
| ★ 14 | 21 | 29 | 44 | GET TOGETHER — Youngbloods (Felix Pappalardi), RCA 47-9752 | 8 |
| ★ 15 | 48 | 70 | — | GREEN RIVER — Creedence Clearwater Revival (J. C. Fogerty), Fantasy 625 | 3 |
| ★ 16 | 19 | 35 | 56 | LAY LADY LAY — Boy Dylan (Bob Johnson), Columbia 44926 | 6 |
| 17 | 12 | 11 | 11 | PART I MOTHER POPCORN (You Got to Have a Mother for Me) — James Brown (James Brown), King 6245 | 10 |
| 18 | 13 | 13 | 19 | QUENTIN'S THEME — The Charles Randolph Grean Sounde (Charles R. Grean), Ranwood 840 | 10 |
| 19 | 16 | 14 | 14 | MY PLEDGE OF LOVE — The Joe Jeffrey Group (Jerry Meyers & Alan Klein), Wand 11200 | 11 |
| ★ 20 | 23 | 43 | 62 | GIVE PEACE A CHANCE — Plastic Ono Band (John & Yoko), Apple 1809 | 4 |
| ★ 21 | 24 | 24 | 29 | CHOICE OF COLORS — Impressions (Curtis Mayfield), Curtom 1943 | 8 |
| 22 | 32 | 42 | 50 | WORKIN' ON A GROOVY THING — Fifth Dimension (Bones Howe), Soul City 776 | 5 |
| 23 | 17 | 15 | 6 | GOOD MORNING STARSHINE — Oliver (Bob Crewe), Jubilee 5659 | 13 |
| ★ 24 | 41 | 67 | 91 | SUGAR, SUGAR — Archies (Jeff Barry), Calendar 63-1008 | 4 |
| ★ 25 | 31 | 52 | 86 | I'LL NEVER FALL IN LOVE AGAIN — Tom Jones (Peter Sullivan), Parrot 40018 | 4 |
| 26 | 25 | 19 | 21 | YESTERDAY WHEN I WAS YOUNG — Roy Clark (Joe Allison), Dot 17246 | 10 |
| 27 | 30 | 41 | 43 | I'D WAIT A MILLION YEARS — Grassroots (Steve Barry), Dunhill 4198 | 7 |
| 28 (RIAA) | 15 | 12 | 12 | COLOR HIM FATHER — Winstons (Don Carroll), Metromedia 117 | 13 |
| 29 (RIAA) | 18 | 17 | 7 | ONE — Three Dog Night (Gabriel Mekler), Dunhill 4191 | 16 |
| 30 | 36 | 36 | 49 | IT'S GETTING BETTER — Mama Cass (Steve Barri), Dunhill 4195 | 11 |
| ★ 31 | 37 | 38 | 57 | MARRAKESH EXPRESS — Crosby, Stills & Nash (Stephen Stills/David Crosby/Graham Nash), Atlantic 2652 | 5 |
| ★ 32 | 40 | 55 | — | SHARE YOUR LOVE WITH ME — Aretha Franklin (Jerry Wexler-Tom Dowd-Arif Mardin), Atlantic 2650 | 2 |
| 33 | 27 | 27 | 39 | ALONG CAME JONES — Ray Stevens (Ray Stevens, Jim Malloy), Monument 1150 | 8 |
| 34 | 34 | 71 | — | COMMOTION — Creedence Clearwater Revival (J. C. Fogerty), Fantasy 625 | 3 |
| 35 | 35 | 37 | 47 | CLEAN UP YOUR OWN BACK YARD — Elvis Presley, RCA Vistor 47-9747 | 7 |
| 36 | 26 | 21 | 25 | GOOD OLD ROCK 'N ROLL — Cat Mother and the All Night News Boys (Cat Mother & Jimi Hendrix), Polydor 14002 | 8 |
| ★ 37 | 44 | 48 | 60 | HURT SO BAD — Lettermen (Al DeLory), Capitol 2482 | 12 |
| 38 | 28 | 28 | 38 | RECONSIDER ME — Johnny Adams (Shelby S. Singleton Jr.), SSS Int'l 770 | 8 |
| 39 | 39 | 65 | 72 | NITTY GRITTY — Gladys Knight & the Pips (Norman Whitfield), Soul 35063 | 5 |
| ★ 40 | 77 | — | — | EASY TO BE HARD — Three Dog Night (Gabriel Mekler), Dunhill 4203 | 2 |
| 41 | 43 | 50 | 64 | SOUL DEEP — Box Tops (Tommy Cogbill & Chips Moman), Mala 12040 | 7 |
| 42 | 42 | 44 | 61 | TRUE GRIT — Glen Campbell (Al DeLory), Capitol 2573 | 4 |
| ★ 43 | 53 | 56 | 76 | BIRTHDAY — Underground Sunshine (Underground Sunshine), Intrepid 75002 | 5 |
| ★ 44 | 51 | 61 | 87 | YOUR GOOD THING (Is About to End) — Lou Rawls (David Axelrod), Capitol 2550 | 5 |
| 45 | 45 | 51 | 55 | MUDDY RIVER — Johnny Rivers (Johnny Rivers), Imperial 66386 | 8 |
| 46 | 46 | 58 | 63 | DID YOU SEE HER EYES — Illusion (Jeff Barry), Steed 718 | 7 |
| 47 | 50 | 72 | 81 | ABERGAVENNY — Shannon, Heritage 814 | 6 |
| 48 | 52 | 60 | 85 | I'M FREE — Who (Kit Lambert), Decca 732519 | 5 |
| ★ 49 | 61 | 86 | — | BARABAJAGAL (Love Is Hot) — Donovan With the Jeff Beck Group (Mickie Most), Epic 5-10510 | 3 |
| ★ 50 | 54 | 59 | 80 | YOUR HUSBAND—MY WIFE — Brooklyn Bridge (Wes Farrell), Buddah 126 | 5 |
| ★ 51 | 78 | 91 | — | KEEM-O-SABE — Electric Indian (Len Barry), United Artists 50563 | 3 |
| ★ 52 | 63 | 69 | 92 | EVERYBODY KNOWS MATILDA — Duke Baxter (Tony Harris), VMC 740 | 3 |
| 53 | 38 | 39 | 40 | MOONFLIGHT — Vik Venus (Lewis Merenstein), Buddah 118 | 10 |
| ★ 54 | 79 | — | — | HOT FUN IN THE SUMMERTIME — Sly & the Family Stone (Sly Stone), Epic 5-10497 | 1 |
| 55 | 49 | 45 | 51 | ON CAMPUS — Dickie Goodman (Dickie Goodman), Cotique 158 | 8 |
| 56 | 60 | 78 | 89 | JACK AND JILL — Tommy Roe (Steve Barri), ABC 11229 | 5 |
| ★ 57 | 68 | 82 | — | CHANGE OF HEART — Dennis Yost & the Classics IV (Buddy Buie), Imperial 66393 | 3 |
| 58 | 64 | 77 | — | NOBODY BUT THE BABE — Clarence Reid (Brad Shapiro & Steve Alaimo), Alston 4574 | 3 |
| ★ 59 | 71 | 79 | 90 | ODDS AND ENDS — Dionne Warwick (Burt Bacharach & Hal David), Scepter 12256 | 4 |
| 60 | 58 | 66 | 66 | I'VE LOST EVERYTHING I'VE EVER LOVED — David Ruffin (Johnny Bristol), Motown 1149 | 5 |
| ★ 61 | 70 | 81 | — | SIMPLE SONG OF FREEDOM — Tim Hardin (Gary Klein), Columbia 4-44920 | 3 |
| 62 | 62 | 68 | 74 | WHILE YOU'RE OUT LOOKING FOR SUGAR — Honey Cone (R. Dunbar), Hot Wax 6901 | 8 |
| 63 | 72 | 85 | 94 | LET YOURSELF GO — Friends of Distinction (John Florez), RCA 74-0204 | 4 |
| ★ 64 | 80 | — | — | WHEN I DIE — Motherlode (Mort Ross & Doug Riley), Buddah 131 | 2 |
| ★ 65 | — | — | — | OH, WHAT A NIGHT — Dells (Bobby Miller), Cadet 5649 | 1 |
| ★ 66 | 85 | — | — | I COULD NEVER BE PRESIDENT — Johnnie Taylor (Don Davis), Stax 0046 | 1 |
| 67 | 59 | 62 | 68 | HEY JOE — Wilson Pickett (Rick Hall), Atlantic 2648 | 6 |
| 68 | 69 | 98 | 99 | OUT OF SIGHT, OUT OF MIND — Little Anthony & the Imperials (Bob Skaff), United Artists 50552 | 4 |
| 69 | 75 | 76 | 98 | EASE BACK — Meters (Allen Toussaint & Marshall E. Sehorn), Josie 1008 | 4 |
| 70 | 66 | 73 | 77 | WHERE DO I GO/BE-IN (Hare Krishna) — Happenings (Happenings), Jubilee 5666 | 6 |
| 71 | 76 | 84 | — | THAT'S THE WAY GOD PLANNED IT — Billy Preston (George Harrison), Apple 1808 | 3 |
| ★ 72 | — | — | — | JEAN — Oliver (Bob Crewe), Crewe 334 | 1 |
| 73 | 82 | 88 | — | THE YOUNG FOLKS — Diana Ross & the Supremes (George Gordy), Motown 1148 | 3 |
| 74 | 67 | 74 | 88 | TILL YOU GET ENOUGH — Watts 103rd Street Rhythm Band (Charles Wright), Warner Bros.-Seven Arts 7298 | 5 |
| 75 | 74 | 80 | — | NOTHING CAN TAKE THE PLACE OF YOU — Brook Benton (Arif Mardin), Cotillion 44034 | 6 |
| ★ 76 | — | — | — | I DO — Moments (Sylvia, Edmounds & Ruffin), Stang 5005 | 1 |
| ★ 77 | — | — | — | MOVE OVER — Steppenwolf (Gabriel Mekler), Dunhill 4205 | 1 |
| ★ 78 | 99 | — | — | QUESTIONS 67 & 68 — Chicago (James William Guercio), Columbia 4-44909 | 2 |
| ★ 79 | — | — | — | EVERYBODY'S TALKIN' — Nilsson (Rick Jarrard), RCA 74-0161 | 1 |
| ★ 80 | 89 | 100 | — | IN A MOMENT — Intrigues (Martin & Bell), Yew 1001 | 3 |
| 81 | 81 | 83 | 93 | FIRST HYMN FROM GRAND TERRACE — Mark Lindsay (Jerry Fuller), Columbia 4-44875 | 4 |
| 82 | 87 | — | — | ONE NIGHT AFFAIR — O'Jays (Gamble-Huff), Neptune 12 | 2 |
| 83 | 91 | — | — | CHELSEA MORNING — Judy Collins (David Anderle), Elektra 45657 | 2 |
| ★ 84 | — | — | — | I CAN'T GET NEXT TO YOU — Temptations (Norman Whitfield), Gordy 7093 | 1 |
| ★ 85 | — | — | — | LET ME BE THE ONE — Peaches & Herb (Billy Sherrill/David Kapalik), Date 2-1649 | 1 |
| ★ 86 | — | — | — | THE COLOUR OF MY LOVE — Jefferson (John Schroeder), Decca 32501 | 1 |
| ★ 87 | — | — | — | WHAT KIND OF FOOL DO YOU THINK I AM — Bill Deal & the Rhondells (Jerry Ross), Heritage 817 | 1 |
| 88 | 88 | — | — | I TAKE A LOT OF PRIDE IN WHAT I AM — Dean Martin (Jimmy Bowen), Reprise 0841 | 2 |
| ★ 89 | — | — | — | MAYBE THE RAIN WILL FALL — Cascades (Andy Di Martino), Uni 551252 | 1 |
| 90 | 90 | — | — | LOOK AT MINE — Petula Clark (Tony Hatch), Warner Bros.-Seven Arts 7310 | 2 |
| 91 | — | — | — | MUDDY MISSISSIPPI LINE — Bobby Goldsboro (Bob Montgomery & Bobby Goldsboro), United Artists 50565 | 1 |
| 92 | — | — | — | GOING IN CIRCLES — Friends of Distinction (John Florez), RCA 74-0204 | 1 |
| 93 | 94 | 95 | — | HOOK AND SLING (Part 1) — Eddie Bo (Al Scramuzza), Scram 117 | 3 |
| 94 | 95 | 97 | — | LET ME BE THE MAN MY DADDY WAS — Chi-Lites (Carl Davis & Eugene Record), Brunswick 755414 | 3 |
| 95 | 100 | — | — | WHO DO YOU LOVE — Quicksilver Messenger Service (Quicksilver Messenger Service), Capitol 2557 | 2 |
| 96 | 98 | — | — | FAREWELL LOVE THEME — Romeo & Juliet Soundtrack (Neely Plumb), Capitol 2502 | 2 |
| 97 | — | — | — | YOU GOT YOURS AND I'LL GET MINE — Delfonics (Stan & Bell Prod.), Philly Groove 157 | 1 |
| 98 | — | — | — | GOODBYE COLUMBUS — Association (John Boylan), Warner Bros.-Seven Arts 7267 | 6 |
| 99 | — | — | — | OH HOW HAPPY — Blinky & Edwin Starr (Frank Wilson & B.J.), Gordy 7090 | 1 |
| 100 | — | — | — | ANY WAY THAT YOU WANT ME — Evie Sands (Chip Taylor-Al Gorgoni), A&M 1090 | 1 |

## HOT 100—A TO Z—(Publisher-Licensee)

Abergavenny (Mills, ASCAP) .... 47
Along Came Jones (Tiger, BMI) .... 33
Any Way That You Want Me (Blackwood, BMI) .... 100
Baby, I Love You (Trio/Mother Bertha, BMI) .... 10
Barabajagal (Love Is Hot) (Peer Int'l, BMI) .... 49
Birthday (Maclen, BMI) .... 43
Boy Named Sue, A (Evil Eye, BMI) .... 5
Change of Heart (Low-Sal, BMI) .... 57
Chelsea Morning (Siquomb, BMI) .... 83
Choice of Colors (Camad, BMI) .... 21
Clean Up Your Own Back Yard (Presley, ASCAP) .... 35
Color Him Father (Holly Bee, BMI) .... 28
Colour of My Love, The (Ann-Rachel, ASCAP) .... 86
Commotion (Jondora, BMI) .... 34
Crystal Blue Persuasion (Big Seven, BMI) .... 3
Did You See Her Eyes (Unart, BMI) .... 46
Ease Back (Marsaint, BMI) .... 69
Easy to Be Hard (United Artists, ASCAP) .... 40
Everybody Knows Matilda (VSAV, BMI) .... 52
Everybody's Talkin' (Coconut Grove/Story, BMI) .... 79
Farewell Love Theme (Famous, ASCAP) .... 96
First Hymn From Grand Terrace (Ja-Ma, ASCAP) .... 81
Get Together (S.F.O., BMI) .... 14
Give Peace a Chance (Maclen, BMI) .... 20
Going in Circles (Porpete, BMI) .... 92
Good Morning Starshine (United Artists, ASCAP) .... 23
Good Old Rock 'n' Roll (Cat Mother/Emmy-Jay/Sea Lark, Arc, BMI) .... 36
Goodbye Columbus (Ensign, BMI) .... 98
Green River (Jondora, BMI) .... 15
Hey Joe (Third Story, BMI) .... 67
Honky Tonk Women (Gideon, BMI) .... 2
Hook and Sling (Part 1) (Uzza, BMI) .... 93
Hot Fun in the Summertime (Stone Flower, BMI) .... 54
Hurt So Bad (Vogue, BMI) .... 37
I Can't Get Next to You (Jobete, BMI) .... 84
I Could Never Be President (East/Memphis, BMI) .... 66
I Do (Gambi, BMI) .... 76
I Take a Lot of Pride in What I Am (Blue Rock, BMI) .... 88
I'd Wait a Million Years (Teenie Bopper, ASCAP) .... 27
I'll Never Fall in Love Again (Hollis, BMI) .... 25
I'm Free (Track, BMI) .... 48
In a Moment (Odom & Neiburg, BMI) .... 80
In the Year 2525 (Zelad, BMI) .... 1
It's Getting Better (Screen Gems-Columbia, BMI) .... 30
I've Lost Everything I've Ever Loved (Jobete, BMI) .... 60
Jack and Jill (Low-Twi, BMI) .... 56
Jean (Twentieth Century, ASCAP) .... 72
Keem-O-Sabe (Binn/Elaine/United Artists, ASCAP) .... 51
Laughing (Dunbar, BMI) .... 12
Lay Lady Lay (Big Sky, ASCAP) .... 16
Let Me Be the Man My Daddy Was (Dakar/BRC, BMI) .... 94
Let Me Be the One (Screen Gems-Columbia, BMI) .... 85
Let Yourself Go (Mavil, BMI) .... 63
Look at Mine (Leeds, ASCAP) .... 90
Marrakesh Express (Siquomb, BMI) .... 31
Maybe the Rain Will Fall (Tupco, BMI) .... 89
Moonflight (Kaskat/Kahoona/Camad/T.M./Pocket Full of Tunes/Rivers/Peanut Butter/Kama Sutra, BMI) .... 53
Part 1—Mother Popcorn (You Got to Have a Mother for Me (Dynatone, BMI) .... 17
Move Over (Trousdale, BMI) .... 77
Muddy Mississippi Line (Detail, BMI) .... 91
Muddy River (Rivers, BMI) .... 45
My Cherie Amour (Jobete, BMI) .... 8
My Pledge of Love (Wednesday Morn./Our Children's, BMI) .... 19
Nitty Gritty (Gallico, BMI) .... 39
Nobody But You Babe (Sherlyn, BMI) .... 58
Nothing Can Take the Place of You (Su-Ma, BMI) .... 75
Odds and Ends (Blue Seas/Jac, ASCAP) .... 59
Oh How Happy (Jobete, BMI) .... 99
Oh, What a Night (Conrad, BMI) .... 65
On Campus (Conique, BMI) .... 55
One (Dunbar, BMI) .... 29
One Night Affair (Assorted, BMI) .... 82
Out of Sight, Out of Mind (Nom, BMI) .... 68
Polk Salad Annie (Combine, BMI) .... 13
Put a Little Love in Your Heart (Unart, BMI) .... 6
Quentin's Theme (Curnor, BMI) .... 18
Questions 67 & 68 (Aurelius, BMI) .... 78
Reconsider Me (Singleton, BMI) .... 38
Ruby, Don't Take Your Love to Town (Cedarwood, BMI) .... 7
Share Your Love With Me (Don, BMI) .... 32
Simple Song of Freedom (T.M., BMI) .... 61
Soul Deep (Barton, BMI) .... 41
Spinning Wheel (Blackwood/Minnesingers, BMI) .... 11
Sugar, Sugar (Kirshner, BMI) .... 24
Sweet Caroline (Good Times Never Seemed So Good) (Stonebridge, BMI) .... 4
That's the Way God Planned It (Apple, ASCAP) .... 71
Till You Get Enough (Wright Gerstl/Tamerlane, BMI) .... 74
True Grit (Famous, ASCAP) .... 42
What Does It Take to Win Your Love (Jobete, BMI) .... 9
What Kind of Fool Do You Think I Am (Whitley/Low Twi, BMI) .... 87
When I Die (Modo, BMI) .... 64
Where Do I Go/Be-in (Hare Krishna) (United Artists, ASCAP) .... 70
While You're Out Looking for Sugar (Gold Forever, BMI) .... 62
Who Do You Love (Arc, BMI) .... 95
Workin' on a Groovy Thing (Screen Gems-Columbia, BMI) .... 22
Yesterday When I Was Young (TRO-Dartmouth, ASCAP) .... 26
You Got Yours and I'll Get Mine (Nickel Shoe, BMI) .... 97
Young Folks, The (Jobete, BMI) .... 73
Your Good Thing (Is About to End) (East, BMI) .... 44
Your Husband—My Wife (Pocketful of Tunes/Jill, BMI) .... 50

## BUBBLING UNDER THE HOT 100

101. DADDY'S LITTLE MAN .... O. C. Smith, Columbia 4-44948
102. TRAIN .... 1910 Fruitgum Company, Buddah 130
103. SHE'S A WOMAN .... Jose Feliciano, RCA Victor 47-9757
104. AIN'T IT LIKE HIM .... Edwin Hawkins Singers, Pavillion 20002
105. TOYS ARE MADE FOR CHILDREN .... Uniques, Paula 324
106. MOONLIGHT SONATA .... Henry Mancini & His Orch., RCA 74-0212
107. THE REAL THING .... Russell Morriss, Diamond 263
108. HALLELUJAH (I Am the Preacher) .... Deep Purple, Tetragrammaton 1537
109. FREE ME .... Otis Redding, Atco 6700
110. STRAIGHT AHEAD .... Young-Holt Unlimited, Brunswick 755417
111. SOUTH CAROLINA .... Flirtations, Deram 85048
112. THIS GIRL IS A WOMAN NOW .... Gary Puckett & the Union Gap, Columbia 4-44967
113. I AM GONNA MAKE YOU MINE .... Lou Christy, Buddah 116
114. MEMPHIS TRAIN .... Buddy Miles Express, Mercury 72945
115. (Your Love Has Lifted Me) HIGHER AND HIGHER .... Otis Redding, Atco 6700
116. KIND WOMAN .... Percy Sledge, Atlantic 2646
117. YOU, I .... Rugbys, Amazon 1
118. RAIN .... Jose Feliciano, RCA Victor 47-9757
119. LIVE AND LEARN .... Andy Williams, Columbia 4-44929
120. OB-LA-DI OB-LA-DA .... Herb Alpert & the Tijuana Brass, A&M 1102
121. POOR MOON .... Canned Heat, Liberty 56127
122. NO ONE IS GOING TO HURT YOU .... Neon Philharmonic, Warner Bros.-Seven Arts 7311
123. TIME TO MAKE A TURN .... Crow, Amaret 106
124. SMILE A LITTLE SMILE FOR ME .... Flying Machine, Congress 6000
125. ALL THE WAITING IS NOT IN VAIN .... Tyrone Davis, Dakar 609
126. NO ONE FOR ME TO TURN TO .... Spiral Starecase, Columbia 4-44924
127. I WANT YOU SO BAD .... B. B. King, BluesWay 61026
128. LA JEANNE .... King Curtis & His Kingpins, Atco 6695
129. SPACE ODDITY .... David Bowie, Mercury 72949
130. ALL I HAVE TO OFFER YOU (Is Me) .... Charley Pride, RCA 74-0167
131. IT'S TRUE I'M GONNA MISS YOU .... Carolyn Franklin, RCA 74-0188
132. LOVE AND PEACE .... Johnny Nash, Jad 218
133. LODI .... Al Wilson, Soul City 775
134. AQUARIUS .... Dick Hyman, Command 4129
135. SHADOWS OF THE NIGHT (Quentin's Theme) .... Robert Cobert Orch., featuring Jonathan Frid & David Selby, Philips 40633

Compiled from national retail sales and radio station airplay by the Music Popularity Dept. of Record Market Research, Billboard.

# Billboard HOT 100

**For Week Ending August 23, 1969**

★ STAR PERFORMER—Sides registering greatest proportionate sales progress this week.
● Record Industry Association of America seal of certification as million selling single.

| This Week | Last Week | 2 Wks. Ago | TITLE — Artist (Producer), Label & Number | Weeks on Chart |
|---|---|---|---|---|
| 1 | 2 | 3 | HONKY TONK WOMEN — Rolling Stones (Jimmy Miller), London 910 | 6 |
| 2 | 5 | 7 | A BOY NAMED SUE — Johnny Cash (Bob Johnston), Columbia 4-44944 | 5 |
| 3 | 3 | 2 | CRYSTAL BLUE PERSUASION — Tommy James & the Shondells (Tommy James-Richie Cordell), Roulette 7050 | 12 |
| 4 | 4 | 5 | SWEET CAROLINE (Good Times Never Seemed So Good) — Neil Diamond (Tommy Cogbill, Tom Catalano, Neil Diamond), Uni 55136 | 9 |
| 5 | 1 | 1 | IN THE YEAR 2525 (Exordium & Terminus) — Zager & Evans (Zager & Evans), RCA 40-0174 | 10 |
| 6 | 6 | 9 | PUT A LITTLE LOVE IN YOUR HEART — Jackie DeShannon (VMG), Imperial 66385 | 8 |
| 7 | 15 | 48 | GREEN RIVER — Creedence Clearwater Revival (J. C. Fogerty), Fantasy 625 | 4 |
| 8 | 13 | 14 | POLK SALAD ANNIE — Tony Joe White (Billy Swan), Monument 1104 | 8 |
| 9 | 14 | 21 | GET TOGETHER — Youngbloods (Felix Pappalardi), RCA 47-9752 | 9 |
| 10 | 12 | 20 | LAUGHING — Guess Who (Jack Richardson), RCA 74-0195 | 7 |
| 11 | 7 | 6 | RUBY, DON'T TAKE YOUR LOVE TO TOWN — Kenny Rogers and the First Edition (Jimmy Bowen), Reprise 0829 | 12 |
| 12 | 16 | 19 | LAY LADY LAY — Bob Dylan (Bob Johnson), Columbia 44926 | 5 |
| 13 | 10 | 10 | BABY, I LOVE YOU — Andy Kim (Jeff Barry), Steed 1031 | 14 |
| 14 | 24 | 41 | SUGAR, SUGAR — Archies (Jeff Barry), Calendar 63-1008 | 5 |
| 15 | 20 | 23 | GIVE PEACE A CHANCE — Plastic Ono Band (John & Yoko), Apple 1809 | 5 |
| 16 | 8 | 8 | MY CHERIE AMOUR — Stevie Wonder (Hank Cosby), Tamla 54180 | 13 |
| 17 | 9 | 4 | WHAT DOES IT TAKE TO WIN YOUR LOVE — Jr. Walker & the All Stars (Fuqua & Bristol), Soul 35062 | 15 |
| 18 | 40 | 77 | EASY TO BE HARD — Three Dog Night (Gabriel Mekler), Dunhill 4203 | — |
| 19 | 25 | 31 | I'LL NEVER FALL IN LOVE AGAIN — Tom Jones (Peter Sullivan), Parrot 40018 | 5 |
| 20 | 22 | 32 | WORKIN' ON A GROOVY THING — Fifth Dimension (Bones Howe), Soul City 776 | 6 |
| 21 | 21 | 24 | CHOICE OF COLORS — Impressions (Curtis Mayfield), Curtom 1943 | 9 |
| 22 | 18 | 13 | QUENTIN'S THEME — The Charles Randolph Grean Sounde (Charles R. Grean), Ranwood 840 | 11 |
| 23 | 17 | 12 | PART 1 MOTHER POPCORN (You Got to Have a Mother for Me) — James Brown (James Brown), King 6245 | 11 |
| 24 | 41 | 43 | SOUL DEEP — Box Tops (Tommy Cogbill & Chips Moman), Mala 12040 | 8 |
| 25 | 11 | 11 | SPINNING WHEEL — Blood, Sweat & Tears (James William Guercio), Columbia 44871 | 13 |
| 26 | 27 | 30 | I'D WAIT A MILLION YEARS — Grassroots (Steve Barry), Dunhill 4198 | 5 |
| 27 | 43 | 53 | BIRTHDAY — Underground Sunshine (Underground Sunshine), Intrepid 75002 | 6 |
| 28 | 31 | 37 | MARRAKESH EXPRESS — Crosby, Stills & Nash (Stephen Stills/David Crosby/Graham Nash), Atlantic 2652 | 6 |
| 29 | 37 | 44 | HURT SO BAD — Lettermen (Al DeLory), Capitol 2482 | 13 |
| 30 | 39 | 39 | NITTY GRITTY — Gladys Knight and the Pips (Norman Whitfield), Soul 35063 | 6 |
| 31 | 32 | 40 | SHARE YOUR LOVE WITH ME — Aretha Franklin (Jerry Wexler-Tom Dowd-Arif Mardin), Atlantic 2650 | 3 |
| 32 | 34 | 34 | COMMOTION — Creedence Clearwater Revival (J. C. Fogerty), Fantasy 625 | 4 |
| 33 | 19 | 16 | MY PLEDGE OF LOVE — The Joe Jeffrey Group (Jerry Meyers & Alan Klein), Wand 11200 | 12 |
| 34 | 30 | 36 | IT'S GETTING BETTER — Mama Cass (Steve Barri), Dunhill 4195 | 12 |
| 35 | 42 | 42 | TRUE GRIT — Glen Campbell (Al DeLory), Capitol 2573 | 4 |
| 36 | 46 | 46 | DID YOU SEE HER EYES — Illusion (Jeff Barry), Steed 718 | 8 |
| 37 | 48 | 52 | I'M FREE — Who (Kit Lambert), Decca 732519 | 6 |
| 38 | 35 | 35 | CLEAN UP YOUR OWN BACK YARD — Elvis Presley, RCA Victor 47-9747 | 8 |
| 39 | 51 | 78 | KEEM-O-SABE — Electric Indian (Len Barry), United Artists 50563 | — |
| 40 | 65 | — | OH, WHAT A NIGHT — Dells (Bobby Miller), Cadet 5649 | 2 |
| 41 | 45 | 45 | MUDDY RIVER — Johnny Rivers (Johnny Rivers), Imperial 66386 | — |
| 42 | 54 | 79 | HOT FUN IN THE SUMMERTIME — Sly & the Family Stone (Sly Stone), Epic 5-10497 | — |
| 43 | 44 | 51 | YOUR GOOD THING (Is About to End) — Lou Rawls (David Axelrod), Capitol 2550 | 6 |
| 44 | 72 | — | JEAN — Oliver (Bob Crewe), Crewe 334 | 2 |
| 45 | 49 | 61 | BARABAJAGAL (Love Is Hot) — Donovan With the Jeff Beck Group (Mickie Most), Epic 5-10510 | 8 |
| 46 | 58 | 64 | NOBODY BUT THE BABE — Clarence Reid (Brad Shapiro & Steve Alaimo), Alston 4574 | — |
| 47 | 47 | 50 | ABERGAVENNY — Shannon, Heritage 814 | 7 |
| 48 | 84 | — | I CAN'T GET NEXT TO YOU — Temptations (Norman Whitfield), Gordy 7093 | — |
| 49 | 79 | — | EVERYBODY'S TALKIN' — Nilsson (Rick Jarrard), RCA 74-0161 | — |
| 50 | 50 | 54 | YOUR HUSBAND—MY WIFE — Brooklyn Bridge (Wes Farrell), Buddah 126 | 6 |
| 51 | 57 | 68 | CHANGE OF HEART — Dennis Yost & the Classics IV (Buddy Buie), Imperial 66393 | 4 |
| 52 | 52 | 63 | EVERYBODY KNOWS MATILDA — Duke Baxter (Tony Harris), VMC 740 | 4 |
| 53 | 59 | 71 | ODDS AND ENDS — Dionne Warwick (Burt Bacharach & Hal David), Scepter 12256 | — |
| 54 | 56 | 60 | JACK AND JILL — Tommy Roe (Steve Barri), ABC 11229 | 6 |
| 55 | 64 | 80 | WHEN I DIE — Motherlode (Mort Ross & Doug Riley), Buddah 131 | 3 |
| 56 | 68 | 69 | OUT OF SIGHT, OUT OF MIND — Little Anthony & the Imperials (Bob Skaff), United Artists 50552 | — |
| 57 | 61 | 70 | SIMPLE SONG OF FREEDOM — Tim Hardin (Gary Klein), Columbia 4-44920 | 4 |
| 58 | 77 | — | MOVE OVER — Steppenwolf (Gabriel Mekler), Dunhill 4205 | 2 |
| 59 | 66 | 85 | I COULD NEVER BE PRESIDENT — Johnnie Taylor (Don Davis), Stax 0046 | — |
| 60 | — | — | I'M A BETTER MAN — Engelbert Humperdinck (Peter Sullivan), Parrot 40040 | 1 |
| 61 | 69 | 75 | EASE BACK — Meters (Allen Toussaint & Marshall E. Seborn), Josie 1008 | 5 |
| 62 | 71 | 76 | THAT'S THE WAY GOD PLANNED IT — Billy Preston (George Harrison), Apple 1808 | 4 |
| 63 | 80 | 89 | IN A MOMENT — Intrigues (Martin & Bell), Yew 1001 | 4 |
| 64 | 63 | 72 | LET YOURSELF GO — Friends of Distinction (John Florez), RCA 74-0204 | 5 |
| 65 | 87 | — | WHAT KIND OF FOOL DO YOU THINK I AM — Bill Deal & the Rhondells (Jerry Ross), Heritage 817 | 2 |
| 66 | — | — | I'M GONNA MAKE YOU MINE — Lou Christie (Stan Vincent & Mike Duckman), Buddah 116 | 1 |
| 67 | — | — | THIS GIRL IS A WOMAN NOW — Gary Puckett & the Union Gap (Dick Glasser), Columbia 4-44967 | 1 |
| 68 | 76 | — | I DO — Moments (Sylvia, Edmonds & Ruffin), Stang 5005 | — |
| 69 | 73 | 82 | THE YOUNG FOLKS — Diana Ross and the Supremes (George Gordy), Motown 1148 | 4 |
| 70 | 91 | — | MUDDY MISSISSIPPI LINE — Bobby Goldsboro (Bob Montgomery & Bobby Goldsboro), United Artists 50546 | — |
| 71 | 78 | 99 | QUESTIONS 67 & 68 — Chicago (James William Guercio), Columbia 4-44909 | — |
| 72 | 82 | 87 | ONE NIGHT AFFAIR — O'Jays (Gamble-Huff), Neptune 12 | 3 |
| 73 | — | — | LITTLE WOMAN — Bobby Sherman (Jackie Mills), Metromedia 121 | 1 |
| 74 | — | — | LOWDOWN POPCORN — James Brown (James Brown), King 6250 | 1 |
| 75 | — | — | THAT'S THE WAY LOVE IS — Marvin Gaye (Norman Whitfield), Tamla 54185 | 1 |
| 76 | 88 | 88 | I TAKE A LOT OF PRIDE IN WHAT I AM — Dean Martin (Jimmy Bowen), Reprise 0841 | 3 |
| 77 | — | — | RAIN — Jose Feliciano (Rick Jarrard), RCA 47-9757 | 1 |
| 78 | 83 | 91 | CHELSEA MORNING — Judy Collins (David Anderle), Elektra 45657 | — |
| 79 | 89 | — | MAYBE THE RAIN WILL FALL — Cascades (Andy Di Martino), Uni 55125 | 2 |
| 80 | 85 | — | LET ME BE THE ONE — Peaches & Herb (Billy Sherrill/David Kapralik), Date 2-1649 | — |
| 81 | — | — | YOU, I — Rugbys (Steve McNicol), Amazon 1 | 1 |
| 82 | — | — | TRAIN — 1910 Fruitgum Co. (Kasenetz-Katz Assoc.), Buddah 130 | 1 |
| 83 | — | — | LODI — Al Wilson (Johnny Rivers), Soul City 775 | 1 |
| 84 | — | — | DON'T IT MAKE YOU WANT TO GO HOME — Joe South & the Believers (Joe South), Capitol 2592 | 1 |
| 85 | 86 | — | THE COLOUR OF MY LOVE — Jefferson (John Schroeder), Decca 32501 | — |
| 86 | 93 | 94 | HOOK AND SLING (Part 1) — Eddie Bo (Al Scramuzza), Scram 117 | 4 |
| 87 | 96 | 98 | FAREWELL LOVE THEME — Romeo & Juliet Soundtrack (Neely Plumb), Capitol 2502 | — |
| 88 | — | — | HERE I GO AGAIN — Smokey Robinson & the Miracles (W. Moore & T. Johnson), 7777 183 | 1 |
| 89 | 90 | 90 | LOOK AT MINE — Petula Clark (Tony Hatch), Warner Bros. Seven Arts 7310 | — |
| 90 | 92 | — | GOING IN CIRCLES — Friends of Distinction (John Florez), RCA 74-0204 | — |
| 91 | 95 | 100 | WHO DO YOU LOVE — Quicksilver Messenger Service (Quicksilver Messenger Service), Capitol 2557 | 3 |
| 92 | 99 | — | OH HOW HAPPY — Blinky & Edwin Starr (Frank Wilson & B.J.), Gordy 7090 | — |
| 93 | — | — | CAN'T FIND THE TIME — Orpheus (Alan Lorber), MGM 13882 | 1 |
| 94 | — | — | WALK ON BY — Isaac Hayes (Al Bell-Marvell Thomas-Allan Jones), Enterprise 9003 | 1 |
| 95 | 98 | — | GOODBYE COLUMBUS — Association (John Boylan), Warner Bros. Seven Arts 7267 | 7 |
| 96 | 100 | — | ANY WAY THAT YOU WANT ME — Evie Sands (Chip Taylor-Al Gorgoni), A&M 1090 | 2 |
| 97 | — | — | YOU GOT YOURS AND I'LL GET MINE — Delfonics (Stan & Bell Prod.), Philly Groove 157 | 2 |
| 98 | — | — | GREEN FIELDS — Vogues (Dick Glasser), Reprise 0844 | 1 |
| 99 | — | — | ALL I HAVE TO OFFER YOU (Is Me) — Charley Pride (Jack Clement), RCA 74-0167 | 1 |
| 100 | — | — | MEMPHIS TRAIN — Buddy Miles Express (Steve Cropper), Mercury 72945 | 1 |

## BUBBLING UNDER THE HOT 100

101. DADDY'S LITTLE MAN .... O. C. Smith, Columbia 4-44948
102. MOONLIGHT SONATA .... Henry Mancini & his Ork., RCA 74-0212
103. FREE ME .... Otis Redding, Atco 6700
104. GET OFF MY BACK, WOMAN .... B. B. King, BluesWay 61026
105. I WANT YOU TO KNOW .... New Colony Six, Mercury 72961
106. BLACK BERRIES .... Isley Brothers, T-Neck 106
107. SUGAR ON SUNDAY .... Clique, White Whale 323
108. SAUSALITO IS THE PLACE TO GO .... Ohio Express, Buddah 130
109. SAD GIRL .... Intruders, Gamble 235
110. (Your Love Has Taken Me) HIGHER & HIGHER .... Otis Redding, Atco 6700
111. NEED LOVE .... Vanilla Fudge, Atco 6703
112. THINGS GOT TO GET BETTER .... Marva Whitney, King 6249
113. CURLY .... Jimmy Clanton, Laurie 3508
114. LIVING IN THE U.S.A. .... Wilmer & the Dukes, Aphrodisiac 142
115. NOAH .... Bob Seeger System, Capitol 2576
116. PAIN .... Mystics, Metromedia 130
117. I'VE FALLEN IN LOVE AGAIN .... Carla Thomas, Stax 0011
118. OB LA DI, OB LA DA .... Herb Alpert & the Tijuana Brass, A&M 1102
119. POOR MOON .... Canned Heat, Liberty 56127
120. NO ONE IS GOING TO HURT YOU NOW .... Neon Philharmonic, Warner Bros.-Seven Arts 7311
121. BILLY, I'VE GOT TO GO TO TOWN .... Geraldine Stevens, World Pacific 77927
122. NO ONE FOR ME TO TURN TO .... Spiral Staircase, Columbia 4-44924
123. TIME TO MAKE A TURN .... Corn, Amaret 106
124. SPACE ODDITY .... David Bowie, Mercury 72949
125. SHADOWS OF THE NIGHT .... Robert Cobert Orch. featuring Jonathan Frid & David Selby, Philips 40633
126. AQUARIUS .... Dick Hyman, Command 4129
127. SAD BAG .... B. B. King, BluesWay 61026
128. IT'S TRUE I'M GONNA MISS YOU .... Carolyn Franklin, RCA 74-0188

*Compiled from national retail sales and radio station airplay by the Music Popularity Dept. of Record Market Research, Billboard.*

# Billboard HOT 100

FOR WEEK ENDING AUGUST 30, 1969

★ STAR PERFORMER—Sides registering greatest proportionate sales progress this week.

Record Industry Association of America seal of certification as million selling single.

| This Week | 1 Wk. Ago | 2 Wks. Ago | 3 Wks. Ago | TITLE Artist (Producer), Label & Number | Weeks On Chart |
|---|---|---|---|---|---|
| 1 | 1 | 2 | 3 | HONKY TONK WOMEN — Rolling Stones (Jimmy Miller), London 910 | 7 |
| 2 | 2 | 5 | 7 | A BOY NAMED SUE — Johnny Cash (Bob Johnston), Columbia 4-44944 | 6 |
| ★3 | 14 | 24 | 41 | SUGAR, SUGAR — Archies (Jeff Barry), Calendar 63-1008 | 6 |
| 4 | 6 | 6 | 9 | PUT A LITTLE LOVE IN YOUR HEART — Jackie DeShannon (VME), Imperial 66385 | 10 |
| 5 | 4 | 4 | 5 | SWEET CAROLINE (Good Times Never Seemed So Good) — Neil Diamond (Tommy Cogbill, Tom Catalano, Neil Diamond), Uni 55136 | 10 |
| ★6 | 9 | 14 | 21 | GET TOGETHER — Youngbloods (Felix Pappalardi), RCA 47-9752 | 10 |
| 7 | 7 | 15 | 48 | GREEN RIVER — Creedence Clearwater Revival (J. C. Fogerty), Fantasy 625 | 5 |
| 8 | 5 | 1 | 1 | IN THE YEAR 2525 (Exordium & Terminus) — Zager & Evans (Zager & Evans), RCA 74-0174 | 11 |
| 9 | 12 | 16 | 19 | LAY LADY LAY — Boy Dylan (Bob Johnson), Columbia 44926 | 8 |
| 10 | 3 | 3 | 2 | CRYSTAL BLUE PERSUASION — Tommy James & the Shondells (Tommy James-Ritchie Cordell), Roulette 7050 | 13 |
| 11 | 8 | 13 | 14 | POLK SALAD ANNIE — Tony Joe White (Billy Swan), Monument 1104 | 9 |
| 12 | 10 | 12 | 20 | LAUGHING — Guess Who (Jack Richardson), RCA 74-0195 | 8 |
| ★13 | 18 | 40 | 77 | EASY TO BE HARD — Three Dog Night (Gabriel Mekler), Dunhill 4203 | 4 |
| ★14 | 19 | 25 | 31 | I'LL NEVER FALL IN LOVE AGAIN — Tom Jones (Peter Sullivan), Parrot 40018 | 6 |
| 15 | 15 | 20 | 23 | GIVE PEACE A CHANCE — Plastic Ono Band (John & Yoko), Apple 1809 | 6 |
| 16 | 13 | 10 | 10 | BABY, I LOVE YOU — Andy Kim (Jeff Barry), Steed 1031 | 15 |
| ★17 | 26 | 27 | 30 | I'D WAIT A MILLION YEARS — Grassroots (Steve Barry), Dunhill 4198 | 9 |
| 18 | 24 | 41 | 43 | SOUL DEEP — Box Tops (Tommy Cogbill & Chips Moman), Mala 12040 | 9 |
| ★19 | 29 | 37 | 44 | HURT SO BAD — Lettermen (Al DeLory), Capitol 2482 | 14 |
| 20 | 20 | 22 | 32 | WORKIN' ON A GROOVY THING — Fifth Dimension (Bones Howe), Soul City 776 | 7 |
| 21 | 16 | 8 | 8 | MY CHERIE AMOUR — Stevie Wonder (Hank Cosby), Tamla 54180 | 6 |
| 22 | 11 | 7 | 6 | RUBY, DON'T TAKE YOUR LOVE TO TOWN — Kenny Rogers and the First Edition (Jimmy Bowen), Reprise 0829 | 13 |
| ★23 | 31 | 32 | 40 | SHARE YOUR LOVE WITH ME — Aretha Franklin (Jerry Wexler-Tom Dowd-Arif Mardin), Atlantic 2650 | 4 |
| 24 | 30 | 39 | 39 | NITTY GRITTY — Gladys Knight & the Pips (Norman Whitfield), Soul 35063 | 7 |
| 25 | 21 | 21 | 24 | CHOICE OF COLORS — Impressions (Curtis Mayfield), Curtom 1943 | 10 |
| 26 | 17 | 9 | 4 | WHAT DOES IT TAKE TO WIN YOUR LOVE — Jr. Walker & the All Stars (Fuqua & Bristol), Soul 35062 | 16 |
| 27 | 27 | 43 | 53 | BIRTHDAY — Underground Sunshine (Underground Sunshine), Intrepid 75002 | 7 |
| ★28 | 39 | 51 | 78 | KEEM-O-SABE — Electric Indian (Len Barry), United Artists 50563 | 5 |
| ★29 | 40 | 65 | — | OH, WHAT A NIGHT — Dells (Bobby Miller), Cadet 5649 | 3 |
| ★30 | 48 | 84 | — | I CAN'T GET NEXT TO YOU — Temptations (Norman Whitfield), Gordy 7093 | 3 |
| ★31 | 43 | 44 | 51 | YOUR GOOD THING (Is About to End) — Lou Rawls (David Axelrod), Capitol 2550 | 7 |
| 32 | 28 | 31 | 37 | MARRAKESH EXPRESS — Crosby, Stills & Nash (Stephen Stills/David Crosby/Graham Nash), Atlantic 2652 | 7 |
| ★33 | 44 | 72 | — | JEAN — Oliver (Bob Crewe), Crewe 334 | 3 |
| 34 | 36 | 46 | 46 | DID YOU SEE HER EYES — Illusion (Jeff Barry), Steed 718 | 9 |
| 35 | 32 | 34 | 34 | COMMOTION — Creedence Clearwater Revival (J. C. Fogerty), Fantasy 625 | 5 |
| ★36 | 42 | 54 | 79 | HOT FUN IN THE SUMMERTIME — Sly & the Family Stone (Sly Stone), Epic 5-10497 | 3 |
| 37 | 37 | 48 | 52 | I'M FREE — Who (Kit Lambert), Decca 732519 | 7 |
| 38 | 35 | 42 | 42 | TRUE GRIT — Glen Campbell (Al DeLory), Capitol 2573 | 6 |
| 39 | 45 | 49 | 61 | BARABAJAGAL (Love Is Hot) — Donovan With the Jeff Beck Group (Mickie Most), Epic 5-10510 | 5 |
| 40 | 34 | 30 | 36 | IT'S GETTING BETTER — Mama Cass (Steve Barri), Dunhill 4195 | 13 |
| 41 | 23 | 17 | 12 | PART I MOTHER POPCORN (You Got to Have a Mother for Me) — James Brown (James Brown), King 6245 | 12 |
| ★42 | 58 | 77 | — | MOVE OVER — Steppenwolf (Gabriel Mekler), Dunhill 4205 | 3 |
| ★43 | 67 | — | — | THIS GIRL IS A WOMAN NOW — Gary Pucket & the Union Gap (Dick Glasser), Columbia 4-44967 | 2 |
| 44 | 49 | 79 | — | EVERYBODY'S TALKIN' — Nilsson (Rick Jarrard), RCA 74-0161 | 3 |
| 45 | 46 | 58 | 64 | NOBODY BUT THE BABE — Clarence Reid (Brad Shapiro & Steve Alaimo), Alston 4574 | 5 |
| 46 | 50 | 50 | 54 | YOUR HUSBAND—MY WIFE — Brooklyn Bridge (Wes Farrell), Buddah 126 | 7 |
| ★47 | 55 | 64 | 80 | WHEN I DIE — Motherlode (Mort Ross & Doug Riley), Buddah 131 | 4 |
| 48 | 53 | 59 | 71 | ODDS AND ENDS — Dionne Warwick (Burt Bacharach & Hal David), Scepter 12256 | 6 |
| ★49 | 75 | — | — | THAT'S THE WAY LOVE IS — Marvin Gaye (Norman Whitfield), Tamla 54185 | 2 |
| 50 | 57 | 61 | 70 | SIMPLE SONG OF FREEDOM — Tim Hardin (Gary Klein), Columbia 4-44920 | 5 |
| 51 | 51 | 57 | 68 | CHANGE OF HEART — Dennis Yost & the Classics IV (Buddy Buie), Imperial 66393 | 5 |
| 52 | 41 | 45 | 45 | MUDDY RIVER — Johnny Rivers (Johnny Rivers), Imperial 66386 | 10 |
| 53 | 56 | 68 | 69 | OUT OF SIGHT, OUT OF MIND — Little Anthony & the Imperials (Bob Skaff), United Artists 50552 | 6 |
| 54 | 47 | 47 | 50 | ABERGAVENNY — Shannon, Heritage 814 | 8 |
| ★55 | 65 | 87 | — | WHAT KIND OF FOOL DO YOU THINK I AM — Bill Deal & the Rhondells (Jerry Ross), Heritage 817 | 3 |
| 56 | 59 | 66 | 85 | I COULD NEVER BE PRESIDENT — Johnnie Taylor (Don Davis), Stax 0046 | 3 |
| 57 | 63 | 80 | 89 | IN A MOMENT — Intrigues (Martin & Bell), Yew 1001 | 5 |
| 58 | 60 | — | — | I'M A BETTER MAN — Engelbert Humperdinck (Peter Sullivan), Parrot 40040 | 2 |
| ★59 | 66 | — | — | I'M GONNA MAKE YOU MINE — Lou Christie (Stan Vincent & Mike Duckman), Buddah 116 | 2 |
| ★60 | 74 | — | — | LOWDOWN POPCORN — James Brown (James Brown), King 6250 | 2 |
| 61 | 52 | 52 | 63 | EVERYBODY KNOWS MATILDA — Duke Baxter (Tony Harris), VMC 740 | 5 |
| 62 | 54 | 56 | 60 | JACK AND JILL — Tommy Roe (Steve Barri), ABC 11229 | 7 |
| ★63 | 79 | 89 | — | MAYBE THE RAIN WILL FALL — Cascades (Andy Di Martino), Uni 551252 | 3 |
| ★64 | — | — | — | WHAT'S THE USE OF BREAKING UP — Jerry Butler (Gamble-Huff), Mercury 72960 | 1 |
| 65 | 62 | 71 | 76 | THAT'S THE WAY GOD PLANNED IT — Billy Preston (George Harrison), Apple 1808 | 5 |
| 66 | 73 | — | — | LITTLE WOMAN — Bobby Sherman (Jackie Mills), Metromedia 121 | 2 |
| 67 | 68 | 76 | — | I DO — Moments (Sylvia, Edmounds & Ruffin), Stang 5005 | 3 |
| 68 | 70 | 91 | — | MUDDY MISSISSIPPI LINE — Bobby Goldsboro (Bob Montgomery & Bobby Goldsboro), United Artists 50565 | 3 |
| 69 | 72 | 82 | 87 | ONE NIGHT AFFAIR — O'Jays (Gamble-Huff), Neptune 12 | 4 |
| 70 | 61 | 69 | 75 | EASE BACK — Meters (Allen Toussaint & Marshall E. Sehorn), Josie 1008 | 6 |
| ★71 | 88 | — | — | HERE I GO AGAIN — Smokey Robinson & the Miracles (W. Moore & T. Johnson) ???? 183 | 2 |
| 72 | 69 | 73 | 82 | THE YOUNG FOLKS — Diana Ross & the Supremes (George Gordy), Motown 1148 | 5 |
| ★73 | 90 | 92 | — | GOING IN CIRCLES — Friends of Distinction (John Florez), RCA 74-0204 | 3 |
| 74 | 80 | 85 | — | LET ME BE THE ONE — Peaches & Herb (Billy Sherrill/David Kapalik), Date 2-1649 | 3 |
| 75 | 76 | 88 | 88 | I TAKE A LOT OF PRIDE IN WHAT I AM — Dean Martin (Jimmy Bowen), Reprise 0841 | 4 |
| ★76 | 97 | 97 | — | YOU GOT YOURS AND I'LL GET MINE — Delfonics (Stan & Bell Prod.), Philly Groove 157 | 3 |
| 77 | 77 | — | — | RAIN — Jose Feliciano (Rick Jarrard), RCA 47-9757 | 2 |
| ★78 | — | — | — | SUGAR ON SUNDAY — Clique (Gary Zekiey), White Whale 323 | 1 |
| 79 | 83 | — | — | LODI — Al Wilson (Johnny Rivers), Soul City 775 | 2 |
| 80 | 81 | — | — | YOU, I — Rugbys (Steve McNicol), Amazon 1 | 2 |
| 81 | 82 | — | — | TRAIN — 1910 Fruitgum Co. (Kasenetz-Katz Assoc.), Buddah 130 | 1 |
| 82 | 84 | — | — | DON'T IT MAKE YOU WANT TO GO HOME — Joe South & the Believers (Joe South), Capitol 2592 | 2 |
| ★83 | — | — | — | DADDY'S LITTLE MAN — O. C. Smith (Jerry Fuller), Columbia 4-44948 | 1 |
| 84 | 85 | 86 | — | THE COLOUR OF MY LOVE — Jefferson (John Schroeder), Decca 32501 | 3 |
| 85 | 86 | 93 | 94 | HOOK AND SLING (Part 1) — Eddie Bo (Al Scramuzza), Scram 117 | 5 |
| 86 | 87 | 96 | 98 | FAREWELL LOVE THEME — Romeo & Juliet Soundtrack (Neely Plumb), Capitol 2502 | 4 |
| 87 | 78 | 83 | 91 | CHELSEA MORNING — Judy Collins (David Anderle), Elektra 45657 | 4 |
| ★88 | — | — | — | BY THE TIME I GET TO PHOENIX — Isaac Hayes (Al Bell, Marvell Thomas, Allen Jones), Enterprise 9003 | 1 |
| ★89 | — | — | — | NO ONE FOR ME TO TURN TO — Spiral Starecase (Sonny Knight), Columbia 4-44924 | 1 |
| ★90 | — | — | — | I WANT YOU TO KNOW — New Colony Six (Sentar Record Prod.), Mercury 72961 | 1 |
| 91 | — | — | — | SAD GIRL — Intruders (Gamble-Huff), Gamble 235 | 1 |
| 92 | 96 | 100 | — | ANY WAY THAT YOU WANT ME — Evie Sands (Chip Taylor-Al Gorgoni), A&M 1090 | 3 |
| 93 | 93 | — | — | CAN'T FIND THE TIME — Orpheus (Alan Lorber), MGM 13882 | 2 |
| 94 | 94 | — | — | WALK ON BY — Isaac Hayes (Al Bell-Marvell Thomas-Allan Jones), Enterprise 9003 | 2 |
| 95 | 95 | 98 | — | GOODBYE COLUMBUS — Association (John Boylan), Warner Bros.-Seven Arts 7267 | 8 |
| 96 | — | — | — | THE WAYS TO LOVE A MAN — Tammy Wynette (Billy Sherrill), Epic 5-10512 | 1 |
| 97 | 99 | — | — | ALL I HAVE TO OFFER YOU (Is Me) — Charley Pride (Jack Clement), RCA 74-0167 | 2 |
| 98 | 98 | — | — | GREEN FIELDS — Vogues (Dick Glasser), Reprise 0844 | 2 |
| 99 | — | — | — | BLACK BERRIES — Isley Brothers (R. Isley/O. Isley/R. Isley), T Neck 906 | 1 |
| 100 | — | — | — | GET OFF MY BACK WOMAN — B. B. King (Bill Szymczyk), Bluesway 61026 | 1 |

## HOT 100—A TO Z —(Publisher-Licensee)


Abergavenny (Mills, ASCAP) .... 54
All I Have To Offer You (Is Me) (Hill & Range/Blue Crest, BMI) .... 97
Any Way That You Want Me (Blackwood, BMI) .... 92
Baby, I Love You (Trio/Mother Bertha, BMI) .... 16
Barabajagal (Love Is Hot) (Peer Int'l, BMI) .... 39
Birthday (Maclen, BMI) .... 27
Black Berries (Triple 3, BMI) .... 99
Boy Named Sue, A (Evil Eye, BMI) .... 2
By the Time I Get to Phoenix (Johnny Rivers, BMI) 88
Can't Find the Time (Interval, BMI) .... 93
Change of Heart (Low-Sal, BMI) .... 51
Chelsea Morning (Siquomb, BMI) .... 87
Choice of Colors (Camad, BMI) .... 25
Colour of My Love, The (Ramrac) .... 84
Commotion (Jondora, BMI) .... 35
Crystal Blue Persuasion (Big Seven, BMI) .... 10
Daddy's Little Man (BnB Music, ASCAP) .... 83
Did You See Her Eyes (Unart, BMI) .... 34
Don't It Make You Want To Go Home (Lowery, BMI) 82
Ease Back (Marsaint, BMI) .... 70
Easy to Be Hard (United Artists, ASCAP) .... 13
Everybody Knows Matilda (VSAV, BMI) .... 61
Everybody's Talkin' (Coconut Grove/Story, BMI) .... 44
Farewell Love Theme (Famous, ASCAP) .... 86
Get Off My Back Woman (Sounds of Lucille-Pampco, BMI) .... 100
Get Together (S.F.O., BMI) .... 6
Give Peace a Chance (Maclen, BMI) .... 15
Going in Circles (Porpete, BMI) .... 74
Goodbye Columbus (Ensign, BMI) .... 95
Green Fields (Blackwood, BMI) .... 98
Green River (Jondora, BMI) .... 7
Here I Go Again (Jobete, BMI) .... 71
Honky Tonk Women (Gideon, BMI) .... 1
Hook and Sling (Part 1) (Uzza, BMI) .... 85
Hot Fun in the Summertime (Stone Flower, BMI) .. 36
Hurt So Bad (Vogue, BMI) .... 19
In the Year 2525 (Zelad, BMI) .... 8
I Can't Get Next to You (Jobete, BMI) .... 30
I Could Never Be President (East/Memphis, BMI) .. 56
I Do (Gambi, BMI) .... 67
I Take a Lot of Pride in What I Am (Blue Rock, BMI) .... 75
I Want You to Know (New Colony, BMI) .... 90
I'd Wait a Million Years (Teenie Bopper, ASCAP) .... 17
I'll Never Fall in Love Again (Hollis, BMI) .... 14
I'm a Better Man (Blue Seas/Jac, ASCAP) .... 58
I'm Free (Track, BMI) .... 37
I'm Gonna Make You Mine (Pocketful of Tunes, BMI) .... 59
In a Moment (Odeom & Neiburg, BMI) .... 57
It's Getting Better (Screen Gems-Columbia, BMI) .. 40
Jack and Jill (Low-Twi, BMI) .... 62
Jean (Twentieth Century, ASCAP) .... 33
Keem-O-Sabe (Binn/Elaine/United Artists, ASCAP) .. 28
Laughing (Dunbar, BMI) .... 12
Lay Lady Lay (Big Sky, ASCAP) .... 9
Let Me Be the One (Screen Gems-Columbia, BMI) .. 74
Little Woman (Green Apple, BMI) .... 66
Lodi (Jondora, BMI) .... 79
Lowdown Popcorn (Golo, BMI) .... 60
Marrakesh Express (Siquomb, BMI) .... 32
Maybe the Rain Will Fall (Dunbar, BMI) .... 63
Part 1—Mother Popcorn (You Got to Have a Mother for Me (Dynatone, BMI) .... 41
Move Over (Trousdale, BMI) .... 42
Muddy Mississippi Line (Detail, BMI) .... 68
Muddy River (Rivers, BMI) .... 52
My Cherie Amour (Jobete, BMI) .... 21
Nitty Gritty (Gallico, BMI) .... 24
Nobody But You Babe (Sherlyn, BMI) .... 45
No One for Me to Turn to (Spiral, BMI) .... 89
Odds and Ends (Blue Seas/Jac, ASCAP) .... 48
Oh What a Night (Conrad, BMI) .... 29
One Night Affair (Assorted, BMI) .... 69
Out of Sight, Out of Mind (Nom, BMI) .... 53
Polk Salad Annie (Combine, BMI) .... 11
Put a Little Love in Your Heart (Unart, BMI) .... 4
Rain (Johi, BMI) .... 77
Ruby, Don't Take Your Love to Town (Cedarwood, BMI) .... 22
Sad Girl (IPC, BMI) .... 91
Share Your Love With Me (Don, BMI) .... 23
Simple Song of Freedom (T.M., BMI) .... 50
Soul Deep (Barton, BMI) .... 18
Sugar on Sunday (Big Seven, BMI) .... 78
Sugar, Sugar (Kirshner, BMI) .... 3
Sweet Caroline (Good Times Never Seemed So Good) (Stonebridge, BMI) .... 5
That's the Way God Planned It (Apple, ASCAP) .... 65
That's the Way Love Is (Jobete, BMI) .... 49
This Girl Is a Woman Now (Three Bridges, ASCAP) .. 43
Train (Kaskat, BMI) .... 81
True Grit (Famous, ASCAP) .... 38
Walk On By (Blue Seas/Jac, ASCAP) .... 94
Ways to Love a Man, The (Gallico, BMI) .... 96
What Does It Take to Win Your Love (Jobete, BMI) 26
What Kind of Fool Do You Think I Am (Whitley/Low Twi, BMI) .... 55
What's the Use of Breaking Up (Assorted/Parabut, BMI) .... 64
When I Die (M-do, BMI) .... 47
Workin' on a Groovy Thing (Screen Gems-Columbia, BMI) .... 20
You Got Yours and I'll Get Mine (Nickel Shoe, BMI) 76
You, I (Singleton, BMI) .... 80
Young Folks, The (Jobete, BMI) .... 72
Your Good Thing (Is About to End) (East, BMI) .... 31
Your Husband—My Wife (Pocketful of Tunes/Jill, BMI) .... 46


## BUBBLING UNDER THE HOT 100

| | | |
|---|---|---|
| 101. | OH HOW HAPPY | Blinky & Edwin Starr, Gordy 7090 |
| 102. | MOONLIGHT SONATA | Henry Mancini & His Ork., RCA 74-0212 |
| 103. | FREE ME | Otis Redding, Atco 6700 |
| 104. | WHO DO YOU LOVE | Quicksilver Messenger Service, Capitol 2557 |
| 105. | SAUSALITO (Is the Place to Go) | Ohio Express, Buddah 126 |
| 106. | DON'T FORGET TO REMEMBER | Bee Gees, Atco 6702 |
| 107. | MY BALLOON'S GOING UP | Archie Bell & the Drells, Atlantic 2663 |
| 108. | A TIME FOR US | Johnny Mathis, Columbia 4-44915 |
| 109. | BY THE TIME I GET TO PHOENIX | Mad Lads, Volt 4016 |
| 110. | THINGS GOT TO GET BETTER | Marva Whitney, King 6249 |
| 111. | NEED LOVE | Vanilla Fudge, Atco 6703 |
| 112. | CURLY | Jimmy Clanton, Laurie 3508 |
| 113. | WE GOTTA ALL GET TOGETHER | Paul Revere & the Raiders, Columbia 44970 |
| 114. | LIVING IN THE U.S.A. | Wilmer & the Dukes, Aphrodisiac 162 |
| 115. | NOAH | Bob Seeger System, Capitol 2576 |
| 116. | PAIN | Mystics, Metromedia 130 |
| 117. | I'VE FALLEN IN LOVE WITH YOU | Carla Thomas, Stax 0011 |
| 118. | OB-LA-DI OB-LA-DA | Herb Alpert & the Tijuana Brass, A&M 1102 |
| 119. | POOR MOON | Canned Heat, Liberty 56127 |
| 120. | BILLY, I'VE GOT TO GO TO TOWN | Geraldine Stevens, World Pacific 779275 |
| 121. | ARMSTRONG | John Stewart, Capitol 2605 |
| 122. | MAH-NA-MAH-NA | "Sweden Heaven & Hell" Soundtrack, Ariel 500 |
| 123. | IT'S TOO LATE | Ted Taylor, Ronn 34 |
| 124. | IT'S TRUE I'M GONNA MISS YOU | Carolyn Franklin, RCA 74-0188 |

Compiled from national retail sales and radio station airplay by the Music Popularity Dept. of Record Market Research, Billboard.

# Billboard HOT 100

**FOR WEEK ENDING SEPTEMBER 6, 1969**

★ STAR PERFORMER—Sides registering greatest proportionate sales progress this week.
● Record Industry Association of America seal of certification as million selling single.

| This Week | 1 Wk. Ago | 2 Wks. Ago | 3 Wks. Ago | TITLE Artist (Producer), Label & Number | Weeks On Chart |
|---|---|---|---|---|---|
| 1 | 1 | 1 | 2 | HONKY TONK WOMEN — Rolling Stones (Jimmy Miller), London 910 | 8 |
| 2 | 2 | 2 | 5 | A BOY NAMED SUE — Johnny Cash (Bob Johnston), Columbia 4-44944 | 7 |
| 3 | 3 | 14 | 24 | SUGAR, SUGAR — Archies (Jeff Barry), Calendar 63-1008 | 7 |
| 4 | 7 | 7 | 15 | GREEN RIVER — Creedence Clearwater Revival (J. C. Fogerty), Fantasy 625 | 6 |
| 5 | 6 | 9 | 14 | GET TOGETHER — Youngbloods (Felix Pappalardi), RCA 47-9752 | 11 |
| 6 | 4 | 6 | 6 | PUT A LITTLE LOVE IN YOUR HEART — Jackie DeShannon (VME), Imperial 66385 | 11 |
| 7 | 9 | 12 | 16 | LAY LADY LAY — Bob Dylan (Bob Johnson), Columbia 44926 | 7 |
| 8 | 13 | 18 | 40 | EASY TO BE HARD — Three Dog Night (Gabriel Mekler), Dunhill 4203 | 6 |
| 9 | 5 | 4 | 4 | SWEET CAROLINE (Good Times Never Seemed So Good) — Neil Diamond (Tommy Cogbill, Tom Catalano, Neil Diamond), Uni 55136 | 11 |
| 10 | 14 | 19 | 25 | I'LL NEVER FALL IN LOVE AGAIN — Tom Jones (Peter Sullivan), Parrot 40018 | 7 |
| 11 | 30 | 48 | 84 | I CAN'T GET NEXT TO YOU — Temptations (Norman Whitfield), Gordy 7093 | 4 |
| 12 | 12 | 10 | 12 | LAUGHING — Guess Who (Jack Richardson), RCA 74-0195 | 6 |
| 13 | 11 | 8 | 13 | POLK SALAD ANNIE — Tony Joe White (Billy Swan), Monument 1104 | 10 |
| 14 | 15 | 15 | 20 | GIVE PEACE A CHANCE — Plastic Ono Band (John & Yoko), Apple 1809 | 7 |
| 15 | 19 | 29 | 37 | HURT SO BAD — Lettermen (Al DeLory), Capitol 2482 | 15 |
| 16 | 17 | 26 | 27 | I'D WAIT A MILLION YEARS — Grassroots (Steve Barry), Dunhill 4198 | 10 |
| 17 | 10 | 3 | 3 | CRYSTAL BLUE PERSUASION — Tommy James & the Shondells (Tommy James-Ritchie Cordell), Roulette 7050 | 14 |
| 18 | 18 | 24 | 41 | SOUL DEEP — Box Tops (Tommy Cogbill & Chips Moman), Mala 12040 | 10 |
| 19 | 8 | 5 | 1 | IN THE YEAR 2525 (Exordium & Terminus) — Zager & Evans (R. Evans), RCA 74-0174 | 12 |
| 20 | 23 | 31 | 32 | SHARE YOUR LOVE WITH ME — Aretha Franklin (Jerry Wexler-Tom Dowd-Arif Mardin), Atlantic 2650 | 5 |
| 21 | 33 | 44 | 72 | JEAN — Oliver (Bob Crewe), Crewe 334 | 4 |
| 22 | 28 | 39 | 51 | KEEM-O-SABE — Electric Indian (Len Barry), United Artists 50563 | 6 |
| 23 | 24 | 30 | 39 | NITTY GRITTY — Gladys Knight & the Pips (Norman Whitfield), Soul 35063 | 5 |
| 24 | 20 | 20 | 22 | WORKIN' ON A GROOVY THING — Fifth Dimension (Bones Howe), Soul City 776 | 8 |
| 25 | 16 | 13 | 10 | BABY, I LOVE YOU — Andy Kim (Jeff Barry), Steed 1031 | 16 |
| 26 | 27 | 27 | 43 | BIRTHDAY — Underground Sunshine (Underground Sunshine), Intrepid 75002 | 8 |
| 27 | 29 | 40 | 65 | OH WHAT A NIGHT — Dells (Bobby Miller), Cadet 5649 | 6 |
| 28 | 44 | 49 | 79 | EVERYBODY'S TALKIN' — Nilsson (Rick Jarrard), RCA 74-0161 | 5 |
| 29 | 36 | 42 | 54 | HOT FUN IN THE SUMMERTIME — Sly & the Family Stone (Sly Stone), Epic 5-10497 | 4 |
| 30 | 31 | 43 | 44 | YOUR GOOD THING (Is About to End) — Lou Rawls (David Axelrod), Capitol 2550 | 8 |
| 31 | 25 | 21 | 21 | CHOICE OF COLORS — Impressions (Curtis Mayfield), Curtom 1943 | 11 |
| 32 | 34 | 36 | 46 | DID YOU SEE HER EYES — Illusion (Jeff Barry), Steed 718 | 10 |
| 33 | 32 | 28 | 31 | MARRAKESH EXPRESS — Crosby, Stills & Nash (Stephen Stills/David Crosby/Graham Nash), Atlantic 2652 | 8 |
| 34 | 66 | 73 | — | LITTLE WOMAN — Bobby Sherman (Jackie Mills), Metromedia 121 | 3 |
| 35 | 35 | 32 | 34 | COMMOTION — Creedence Clearwater Revival (J. C. Fogerty), Fantasy 625 | 6 |
| 36 | 39 | 45 | 49 | BARABAJAGAL (Love Is Hot) — Donovan With the Jeff Beck Group (Mickie Most), Epic 5-10510 | 6 |
| 37 | 42 | 58 | 77 | MOVE OVER — Steppenwolf (Gabriel Mekler), Dunhill 4205 | 4 |
| 38 | 43 | 67 | — | THIS GIRL IS A WOMAN NOW — Gary Puckett & the Union Gap (Dick Glasser), Columbia 4-44967 | 3 |
| 39 | 64 | — | — | WHAT'S THE USE OF BREAKING UP — Jerry Butler (Gamble-Huff), Mercury 72960 | 2 |
| 40 | 40 | 34 | 30 | IT'S GETTING BETTER — Mama Cass (Steve Barri), Dunhill 4195 | 14 |
| 41 | 49 | 75 | — | THAT'S THE WAY LOVE IS — Marvin Gaye (Norman Whitfield), Tamla 54185 | 3 |
| 42 | 47 | 55 | 64 | WHEN I DIE — Motherlode (Mort Ross & Doug Riley), Buddah 131 | 5 |
| 43 | 48 | 53 | 59 | ODDS AND ENDS — Dionne Warwick (Burt Bacharach & Hal David), Scepter 12256 | 7 |
| 44 | 55 | 65 | 87 | WHAT KIND OF FOOL DO YOU THINK I AM — Bill Deal & the Rhondells (Jerry Ross), Heritage 817 | 4 |
| 45 | 45 | 46 | 58 | NOBODY BUT YOU BABE — Clarence Reid (Brad Shapiro & Steve Alaimo), Alston 4574 | 8 |
| 46 | 78 | — | — | SUGAR ON SUNDAY — Clique (Gary Zekley), White Whale 323 | 2 |
| 47 | 59 | 66 | — | I'M GONNA MAKE YOU MINE — Lou Christie (Stan Vincent & Mike Duckman), Buddah 116 | 3 |
| 48 | 56 | 59 | 66 | I COULD NEVER BE PRESIDENT — Johnnie Taylor (Don Davis), Stax 0046 | 4 |
| 49 | 51 | 51 | 57 | CHANGE OF HEART — Dennis Yost & the Classics IV (Buddy Buie), Imperial 66393 | 6 |
| 50 | 50 | 57 | 61 | SIMPLE SONG OF FREEDOM — Tim Hardin (Gary Klein), Columbia 4-44920 | 6 |
| 51 | 38 | 35 | 42 | TRUE GRIT — Glen Campbell (Al DeLory), Capitol 2573 | 7 |
| 52 | 37 | 37 | 48 | I'M FREE — Who (Kit Lambert), Decca 732519 | 8 |
| 53 | 53 | 56 | 68 | OUT OF SIGHT, OUT OF MIND — Little Anthony & the Imperials (Bob Skaff), United Artists 50552 | 6 |
| 54 | 83 | — | — | DADDY'S LITTLE MAN — O. C. Smith (Jerry Fuller), Columbia 4-44948 | 2 |
| 55 | 58 | 60 | — | I'M A BETTER MAN — Engelbert Humperdinck (Peter Sullivan), Parrot 40040 | 3 |
| 56 | 57 | 63 | 80 | IN A MOMENT — Intrigues (Martin & Bell), Yew 1001 | 4 |
| 57 | 60 | 74 | — | LOWDOWN POPCORN — James Brown (James Brown), King 6250 | 3 |
| 58 | 46 | 50 | 50 | YOUR HUSBAND—MY WIFE — Brooklyn Bridge (Wes Farrell), Buddah 126 | 8 |
| 59 | 52 | 41 | 45 | MUDDY RIVER — Johnny Rivers (Johnny Rivers), Imperial 66386 | 11 |
| 60 | 80 | 81 | — | YOU, I — Rugbys (Steve McNicol), Amazon 1 | 3 |
| 61 | 76 | 97 | 97 | YOU GOT YOURS AND I'LL GET MINE — Delfonics (Stan & Bell Prod.), Philly Groove 157 | 4 |
| 62 | 67 | 68 | 76 | I DO — Moments (Sylvia, Edmonds & Ruffin), Stang 5005 | 4 |
| 63 | 63 | 79 | 89 | MAYBE THE RAIN WILL FALL — Cascades (Andy Di Martino), Uni 551252 | 4 |
| 64 | 68 | 70 | 91 | MUDDY MISSISSIPPI LINE — Bobby Goldsboro (Bob Montgomery & Bobby Goldsboro), United Artists 50565 | 4 |
| 65 | 65 | 62 | 71 | THAT'S THE WAY GOD PLANNED IT — Billy Preston (George Harrison), Apple 1808 | 6 |
| 66 | 73 | 90 | 92 | GOING IN CIRCLES — Friends of Distinction (John Florez), RCA 74-0204 | 4 |
| 67 | 71 | 88 | — | HERE I GO AGAIN — Smokey Robinson & the Miracles (W. Moore, S. T. Johnson), Tampa 54183 | 3 |
| 68 | 69 | 72 | 82 | ONE NIGHT AFFAIR — O'Jays (Gamble-Huff), Neptune 12 | 5 |
| 69 | 88 | — | — | BY THE TIME I GET TO PHOENIX — Isaac Hayes (Al Bell, Marvell Thomas, Allen Jones), Enterprise 9003 | 2 |
| 70 | — | — | — | CARRY ME BACK — Rascals (Rascals with Arif Mardin), Atlantic 2664 | 1 |
| 71 | 89 | — | — | NO ONE FOR ME TO TURN TO — Spiral Starecase (Sonny Knight), Columbia 4-44924 | 2 |
| 72 | 81 | 82 | — | TRAIN — 1910 Fruitgum Co. (Kasenetz-Katz Assoc.), Buddah 130 | 3 |
| 73 | 91 | — | — | SAD GIRL — Intruders (Gamble-Huff), Gamble 235 | 2 |
| 74 | 79 | 83 | — | LODI — Al Wilson (Johnny Rivers), Soul City 775 | 3 |
| 75 | — | — | — | ARMSTRONG — John Stewart (Chip Douglas), Capitol 2605 | 1 |
| 76 | 77 | 77 | — | RAIN — Jose Feliciano (Rick Jarrard), RCA 47-9757 | 3 |
| 77 | 74 | 80 | 85 | LET ME BE THE ONE — Peaches & Herb (Billy Sherrill/David Kapalik), Date 2-1649 | 4 |
| 78 | 85 | 86 | 93 | HOOK AND SLING (Part 1) — Eddie Bo (Al Scramuzza), Scram 117 | 6 |
| 79 | 82 | 84 | — | DON'T IT MAKE YOU WANT TO GO HOME — Joe South & the Believers (Joe South), Capitol 2592 | 3 |
| 80 | — | — | — | WE GOTTA ALL GET TOGETHER — Paul Revere & the Raiders (Mark Lindsay), Columbia 44970 | 1 |
| 81 | — | — | — | MAH-NA-MAH-NA — "Sweden Heaven and Hell" Soundtrack, Ariel 500 | 1 |
| 82 | — | — | — | SOMETHING IN THE AIR — Thunderclap Newman (Peter Townshend), Track 2656 | 1 |
| 83 | 90 | — | — | I WANT YOU TO KNOW — New Colony Six (Sentar Record Prod.), Mercury 72961 | 2 |
| 84 | 92 | 96 | 100 | ANY WAY THAT YOU WANT ME — Evie Sands (Chip Taylor-Al Gorgoni), A&M 1090 | 4 |
| 85 | 93 | 93 | — | CAN'T FIND THE TIME — Orpheus (Alan Lorber), MGM 13882 | 3 |
| 86 | — | — | — | SAUSALITO (Is the Place to Go) — Ohio Express (Kasenetz-Katz Associates), Buddah 129 | 1 |
| 87 | 99 | — | — | BLACK BERRIES — Isley Brothers (R. Isley/O. Isley/R. Isley), T. Neck 906 | 2 |
| 88 | 95 | 95 | 98 | GOODBYE COLUMBUS — Association (John Boylan), Seven Arts 7267 | 9 |
| 89 | — | — | — | RUNNIN' BLUE — Doors (Paul A. Rothchild), Elektra 45675 | 1 |
| 90 | — | — | — | MAKE BELIEVE — Wind (Bo Gentry), Life 200 | 1 |
| 91 | — | — | — | MOONLIGHT SONATA — Henry Mancini, His Ork. & Chorus (Joe Reisman), RCA 74-0212 | 1 |
| 92 | 98 | 98 | — | GREEN FIELDS — Vogues (Dick Glasser), Reprise 0844 | 3 |
| 93 | — | — | — | MacARTHUR PARK — Waylon Jennings & the Kimberlys (Chet Atkins & Danny Davis), RCA 74-0210 | 1 |
| 94 | — | — | — | BABY IT'S YOU — Smith (Joel Sill & Steve Barri), Dunhill 4206 | 1 |
| 95 | — | — | — | LUNA TRIP — Dickie Goodman (Dickie Goodman), Cotique 173 | 1 |
| 96 | 96 | — | — | THE WAYS TO LOVE A MAN — Tammy Wynette (Billy Sherrill), Epic 5-10512 | 2 |
| 97 | 97 | 99 | — | ALL I HAVE TO OFFER YOU (Is Me) — Charley Pride (Jack Clement), RCA 74-0167 | 3 |
| 98 | — | — | — | SLUM BABY — Booker T. & the M.G.'s (Booker T. & the M.G.'s), Stax 0049 | 1 |
| 99 | — | — | — | LIFE AND DEATH IN G & A — Abaco Dream (Ted Cooper), A&M 1081 | 1 |
| 100 | 100 | — | — | GET OFF MY BACK WOMAN — B. B. King (Bill Szymczyk), Bluesway 61026 | 2 |

## BUBBLING UNDER THE HOT 100

| 101 | ONE WOMAN | Steve Alaimo, Atco 6710 |
| 102 | TRACEY | Cufflinks, Decca 32533 |
| 103 | NOAH | Bob Seeger System, Capitol 2576 |
| 104 | COLOR OF MY LOVE | Jefferson, Decca 32501 |
| 105 | DON'T FORGET TO REMEMBER | Bee Gees, Atco 6702 |
| 106 | WALK ON BY | Isaac Hayes, Enterprise 9003 |
| 107 | MY BALLOON'S GOING UP | Archie Bell & the Drells, Atlantic 2663 |
| 108 | A TIME FOR US | Johnny Mathis, Columbia 4-44915 |
| 109 | BY THE TIME I GET TO PHOENIX | Mad Lads, Volt 4016 |
| 110 | THINGS GOT TO GET BETTER | Marva Whitney, King 6249 |
| 111 | JIVE | Bob Darin, Direction 352 |
| 112 | KOOL AND THE GANG | Kool and the Gang, Delite 519 |
| 113 | MY WOMAN'S GOOD TO ME | George Benson, A&M 1076 |
| 114 | HEIGHTY HI | Lee Michaels, A&M 1095 |
| 115 | WORLD | James Brown, King 6258 |
| 116 | GREEN ONIONS | Dick Hyman, Command 4129 |
| 117 | BILLY, I'VE GOT TO GO TO TOWN | Geraldine Stevens, World Pacific 779275 |
| 118 | IT'S TOO LATE | Ted Taylor, Ronn 34 |
| 119 | POOR MOON | Canned Heat, Liberty 56127 |
| 120 | IT'S TRUE I'M GONNA MISS YOU | Carolyn Franklin, RCA 74-0188 |

Compiled from national retail sales and radio station airplay by the Music Popularity Dept. of Record Market Research, Billboard.

# Billboard HOT 100

FOR WEEK ENDING SEPTEMBER 13, 1969

★ STAR PERFORMER—Sides registering greatest proportionate sales progress this week.

(seal) Record Industry Association of America seal of certification as million selling single.

| THIS WEEK | 1 Wk. Ago | 2 Wks. Ago | 3 Wks. Ago | TITLE Artist (Producer), Label & Number | Weeks On Chart |
| --- | --- | --- | --- | --- | --- |
| (seal) 1 | 1 | 1 | 1 | **HONKY TONK WOMEN** Rolling Stones (Jimmy Miller), London 910 | 9 |
| (seal) 2 | 3 | 3 | 14 | **SUGAR, SUGAR** Archies (Jeff Barry), Calendar 63-1008 | 8 |
| (seal) 3 | 2 | 2 | 2 | **A BOY NAMED SUE** Johnny Cash (Bob Johnston), Columbia 4-44944 | 8 |
| 4 | 4 | 7 | 7 | **GREEN RIVER** Creedence Clearwater Revival (J. C. Fogerty), Fantasy 625 | 7 |
| 5 | 5 | 6 | 9 | **GET TOGETHER** Youngbloods (Felix Pappalardi), RCA 47-9752 | 12 |
| ★ 6 | 10 | 14 | 19 | **I'LL NEVER FALL IN LOVE AGAIN** Tom Jones (Peter Sullivan), Parrot 40018 | 8 |
| 7 | 7 | 9 | 12 | **LAY LADY LAY** Bob Dylan (Bob Johnson), Columbia 44926 | 10 |
| 8 | 8 | 13 | 18 | **EASY TO BE HARD** Three Dog Night (Gabriel Mekler), Dunhill 4203 | 6 |
| 9 | 6 | 4 | 6 | **PUT A LITTLE LOVE IN YOUR HEART** Jackie DeShannon (VME), Imperial 66385 | 12 |
| ★ 10 | 11 | 30 | 48 | **I CAN'T GET NEXT TO YOU** Temptations (Norman Whitfield), Gordy 7093 | 5 |
| ★ 11 | 27 | 29 | 40 | **OH, WHAT A NIGHT** Dells (Bobby Miller), Cadet 5649 | 5 |
| (seal) 12 | 9 | 5 | 4 | **SWEET CAROLINE (Good Times Never Seemed So Good)** Neil Diamond (Tommy Cogbill, Tom Catalano, Neil Diamond), Uni 55136 | 12 |
| ★ 13 | 20 | 23 | 31 | **SHARE YOUR LOVE WITH ME** Aretha Franklin (Jerry Wexler-Tom Dowd-Arif Mardin), Atlantic 2650 | 6 |
| 14 | 15 | 19 | 29 | **HURT SO BAD** Lettermen (Al DeLory), Capitol 2482 | 16 |
| 15 | 16 | 17 | 26 | **I'D WAIT A MILLION YEARS** Grassroots (Steve Barry), Dunhill 4198 | 11 |
| ★ 16 | 34 | 66 | 73 | **LITTLE WOMAN** Bobby Sherman (Jackie Mills), Metromedia 121 | 4 |
| ★ 17 | 38 | 43 | 67 | **THIS GIRL IS A WOMAN NOW** Gary Puckett & the Union Gap (Dick Glasser), Columbia 4-44967 | 4 |
| ★ 18 | 21 | 33 | 44 | **JEAN** Oliver (Bob Crewe), Crewe 334 | 5 |
| 19 | 23 | 24 | 30 | **NITTY GRITTY** Gladys Knight & the Pips (Norman Whitfield), Soul 35063 | 9 |
| ★ 20 | 30 | 31 | 43 | **YOUR GOOD THING (Is About to End)** Lou Rawls (David Axelrod), Capitol 2550 | 9 |
| 21 | 17 | 10 | 3 | **CRYSTAL BLUE PERSUASION** Tommy James & the Shondells (Tommy James-Ritchie Cordell), Roulette 7050 | 15 |
| 22 | 22 | 28 | 39 | **KEEM-O-SABE** Electric Indian (Len Barry), United Artists 50563 | 7 |
| ★ 23 | 28 | 44 | 49 | **EVERYBODY'S TALKIN'** Nilsson (Rick Jarrard), RCA 74-0161 | 5 |
| 24 | 12 | 12 | 10 | **LAUGHING** Guess Who (Jack Richardson), RCA 74-0195 | 10 |
| 25 | 18 | 18 | 24 | **SOUL DEEP** Box Tops (Tommy Cogbill & Chips Moman), Mala 12040 | 11 |
| 26 | 29 | 36 | 42 | **HOT FUN IN THE SUMMERTIME** Sly & the Family Stone (Sly Stone), Epic 5-10497 | 5 |
| 27 | 24 | 20 | 20 | **WORKIN' ON A GROOVY THING** Fifth Dimension (Bones Howe), Soul City 776 | 9 |
| 28 | 13 | 11 | 8 | **POLK SALAD ANNIE** Tony Joe White (Billy Swan), Monument 1104 | 11 |
| 29 | 14 | 15 | 15 | **GIVE PEACE A CHANCE** Plastic Ono Band (John & Yoko), Apple 1809 | 8 |
| 30 | 35 | 35 | 32 | **COMMOTION** Creedence Clearwater Revival (J. C. Fogerty), Fantasy 625 | 7 |
| ★ 31 | 41 | 49 | 75 | **THAT'S THE WAY LOVE IS** Marvin Gaye (Norman Whitfield), Tamla 54185 | 4 |
| ★ 32 | 42 | 47 | 55 | **WHEN I DIE** Motherlode (Mort Ross & Doug Riley), Buddah 131 | 6 |
| 33 | 32 | 34 | 36 | **DID YOU SEE HER EYES** Illusion (Jeff Barry), Steed 718 | 11 |
| 34 | 26 | 27 | 27 | **BIRTHDAY** Underground Sunshine (Underground Sunshine), Intrepid 75002 | 9 |
| ★ 35 | 47 | 59 | 66 | **I'M GONNA MAKE YOU MINE** Lou Christie (Stan Vincent & Mike Duckman), Buddah 116 | 4 |
| ★ 36 | 44 | 55 | 65 | **WHAT KIND OF FOOL DO YOU THINK I AM** Bill Deal & the Rhondells (Jerry Ross), Heritage 817 | 5 |
| 37 | 37 | 42 | 58 | **MOVE OVER** Steppenwolf (Gabriel Mekler), Dunhill 4205 | 5 |
| 38 | 39 | 64 | — | **WHAT'S THE USE OF BREAKING UP** Jerry Butler (Gamble-Huff), Mercury 72960 | 3 |
| (seal) 39 | 19 | 8 | 5 | **IN THE YEAR 2525 (Exordium & Terminus)** Zager & Evans (Zager & Evans), RCA 74-0174 | 13 |
| ★ 40 | 45 | 45 | 46 | **NOBODY BUT THE BABE** Clarence Reid (Brad Shapiro & Steve Alaimo), Alston 4574 | 7 |
| ★ 41 | 54 | 83 | — | **DADDY'S LITTLE MAN** O. C. Smith (Jerry Fuller), Columbia 4-44948 | 3 |
| 42 | 40 | 40 | 34 | **IT'S GETTING BETTER** Mama Cass (Steve Barri), Dunhill 4195 | 15 |
| ★ 43 | 69 | 88 | — | **BY THE TIME I GET TO PHOENIX** Isaac Hayes (Al Bell, Marvell Thomas, Allen Jones), Enterprise 9003 | 3 |
| 44 | 46 | 78 | — | **SUGAR ON SUNDAY** Clique (Gary Zekley), White Whale 323 | 3 |
| ★ 45 | 57 | 60 | 74 | **LOWDOWN POPCORN** James Brown (James Brown), King 6250 | 4 |
| ★ 46 | 60 | 80 | 81 | **YOU, I** Rugbys (Steve McNicol), Amazon 1 | 4 |
| ★ 47 | 70 | — | — | **CARRY ME BACK** Rascals (Rascals with Arif Mardin), Atlantic 2664 | 2 |
| 48 | 48 | 56 | 59 | **I COULD NEVER BE PRESIDENT** Johnnie Taylor (Don Davis), Stax 0046 | 5 |
| ★ 49 | 55 | 58 | 60 | **I'M A BETTER MAN** Engelbert Humperdinck (Peter Sullivan), Parrot 40040 | 4 |
| ★ 50 | 56 | 57 | 63 | **IN A MOMENT** Intrigues (Martin & Bell), Yew 1001 | 7 |
| ★ 51 | 61 | 76 | 97 | **YOU GOT YOURS AND I'LL GET MINE** Delfonics (Stan & Bell Prod.), Philly Groove 157 | 5 |
| 52 | 53 | 53 | 56 | **OUT OF SIGHT, OUT OF MIND** Little Anthony & the Imperials (Bob Skaff), United Artists 50552 | 8 |
| ★ 53 | 67 | 71 | 88 | **HERE I GO AGAIN** Smokey Robinson & the Miracles (W. Moore & T. Johnson), Tampa 54183 | 4 |
| 54 | 36 | 39 | 45 | **BARABAJAGAL (Love Is Hot)** Donovan With the Jeff Beck Group (Mickie Most), Epic 5-10510 | 7 |
| ★ 55 | 66 | 73 | 90 | **GOING IN CIRCLES** Friends of Distinction (John Florez), RCA 74-0204 | 5 |
| 56 | 43 | 48 | 53 | **ODDS AND ENDS** Dionne Warwick (Burt Bacharach & Hal David), Scepter 12256 | 8 |
| 57 | 49 | 51 | 51 | **CHANGE OF HEART** Dennis Yost & the Classics IV (Buddy Buie), Imperial 66393 | 7 |
| ★ 58 | 64 | 68 | 70 | **MUDDY MISSISSIPPI LINE** Bobby Goldsboro (Bob Montgomery & Bobby Goldsboro), United Artists 50565 | 5 |
| ★ 59 | 73 | 91 | — | **SAD GIRL** Intruders (Gamble-Huff), Gamble 235 | 3 |
| ★ 60 | 80 | — | — | **WE GOTTA ALL GET TOGETHER** Paul Revere & the Raiders (Mark Lindsay), Columbia 44970 | 2 |
| 61 | 63 | 63 | 79 | **MAYBE THE RAIN WILL FALL** Cascades (Andy Di Martino), Uni 551252 | 5 |
| 62 | 62 | 67 | 68 | **I DO** Moments (Sylvia, Edmounds & Ruffin), Stang 5005 | 5 |
| 63 | 50 | 50 | 57 | **SIMPLE SONG OF FREEDOM** Tim Hardin (Gary Klein), Columbia 4-44920 | 7 |
| ★ 64 | 72 | 81 | 82 | **TRAIN** 1910 Fruitgum Co. (Kasenetz-Katz Assoc.), Buddah 130 | 3 |
| ★ 65 | 79 | 82 | 84 | **DON'T IT MAKE YOU WANT TO GO HOME** Joe South & the Believers (Joe South), Capitol 2592 | 4 |
| ★ 66 | 81 | — | — | **MAH-NA-MAH-NA** "Sweden Heaven and Hell" Soundtrack, Ariel 500 | 2 |
| ★ 67 | 74 | 79 | 83 | **LODI** Al Wilson (Johnny Rivers), Soul City 775 | 4 |
| 68 | 71 | 89 | — | **NO ONE FOR ME TO TURN TO** Spiral Starecase (Sonny Knight), Columbia 4-44924 | 3 |
| ★ 69 | — | — | — | **THE WEIGHT** Diana Ross & the Supremes & the Temptations (Frank Wilson), Motown 1153 | 1 |
| ★ 70 | — | — | — | **WORLD, Part 1** James Brown (James Brown), King 6258 | 1 |
| 71 | 68 | 69 | 72 | **ONE NIGHT AFFAIR** O'Jays (Gamble-Huff), Neptune 12 | 6 |
| ★ 72 | — | — | — | **AND THAT REMINDS ME (My Heart Reminds Me)** Four Seasons (Crewe-Gaudio), Crewe 333 | 1 |
| 73 | 78 | 85 | 86 | **HOOK AND SLING (Part 1)** Eddie Bo (Al Scramuzza), Scram 117 | 7 |
| ★ 74 | 83 | 90 | — | **I WANT YOU TO KNOW** New Colony Six (Sentar Record Prod.), Mercury 72961 | 3 |
| 75 | 75 | — | — | **ARMSTRONG** John Stewart (Chip Douglas), Capitol 2605 | 2 |
| 76 | 76 | 77 | 77 | **RAIN** Jose Feliciano (Rick Jarrard), RCA 47-9757 | 4 |
| ★ 77 | — | — | — | **SUSPICIOUS MINDS** Elvis Presley, RCA 47-9764 | 1 |
| ★ 78 | — | — | — | **JEALOUS KIND OF FELLOW** Garland Greene (Giant Enterprises Prod.), UNI 55143 | 1 |
| ★ 79 | 87 | 99 | — | **BLACK BERRIES** Isley Brothers (R. Isley/O. Isley/R. Isley), T Neck 906 | 3 |
| 80 | 82 | — | — | **SOMETHING IN THE AIR** Thunderclap Newman (Peter Townshend), Track 2656 | 2 |
| ★ 81 | 90 | — | — | **MAKE BELIEVE** Wind (Bo Gentry), Life 200 | 2 |
| ★ 82 | 100 | 100 | — | **GET OFF MY BACK WOMAN** B. B. King (Bill Szymczyk), Bluesway 61026 | 3 |
| 83 | 84 | 92 | 96 | **ANY WAY THAT YOU WANT ME** Evie Sands (Chip Taylor-Al Gorgoni), A&M 1090 | 5 |
| 84 | 85 | 93 | 93 | **CAN'T FIND THE TIME** Orpheus (Alan Lorber), MGM 13882 | 4 |
| 85 | 89 | — | — | **RUNNIN' BLUE** Doors (Paul A. Rothchild), Elektra 45675 | 2 |
| 86 | 86 | — | — | **SAUSALITO (Is the Place to Go)** Ohio Express (Kasenetz-Katz Associates), Buddah 129 | 2 |
| ★ 87 | 99 | — | — | **LIFE AND DEATH IN G & A** Abaco Dream (Ted Cooper), A&M 1081 | 2 |
| ★ 88 | — | — | — | **CHAINS OF LOVE** Bobby Bland (Andre Williams), Duke 449 | 1 |
| ★ 89 | — | — | — | **TRACY** Cuff Links (Paul Vance-Lee Pockriss), Decca 32533 | 1 |
| 90 | 94 | — | — | **BABY IT'S YOU** Smith (Joel Sill & Steve Barri), Dunhill 4206 | 2 |
| 91 | 91 | — | — | **MOONLIGHT SONATA** Henry Mancini, His Ork. & Chorus (Joe Reisman), RCA 74-0212 | 2 |
| 92 | — | 94 | 94 | **WALK ON BY** Isaac Hayes (Al Bell-Marvell Thomas-Allen Jones), Enterprise 9003 | 3 |
| 93 | 93 | — | — | **MacARTHUR PARK** Waylon Jennings & the Kimberlys (Chet Atkins & Danny Davis), RCA 74-0210 | 2 |
| 94 | 97 | 97 | 99 | **ALL I HAVE TO OFFER YOU (Is Me)** Charley Pride (Jack Clement), RCA 74-0167 | 4 |
| 95 | 95 | — | — | **LUNA TRIP** Dickie Goodman (Dickie Goodman), Cotique 173 | 2 |
| 96 | — | — | — | **MY BALLOON'S GOING UP** Archie Bell & the Drells (Gamble-Huff), Atlantic 2663 | 1 |
| 97 | 98 | — | — | **SLUM BABY** Booker T. & the M.G.'s (Booker T. & the M.G.'s), Stax 0049 | 2 |
| 98 | — | — | — | **LOVE'S BEEN GOOD TO ME** Frank Sinatra (Sonny Burke), Reprise 0852 | 1 |
| 99 | — | — | — | **A TIME FOR US** Johnny Mathis (Jack Gold), Columbia 4-44915 | 6 |
| 100 | — | — | — | **KOOL AND THE GANG** Kool and the Gang (Redd Coach Prod.), De-Lite 519 | 1 |

## HOT 100—A TO Z—*(Publisher-Licensee)*

A Time for Us (Famous, ASCAP) ... 99
All I Have to Offer You (Is Me) (Hill & Range/Blue Crest, BMI) ... 94
And That Reminds Me (My Heart Reminds Me) (Symphony House, ASCAP) ... 72
Any Way That You Want Me (Blackwood, BMI) ... 83
Armstrong (Great Montana, BMI) ... 75
Baby It's You (Dolfi, ASCAP) ... 90
Barabajagal (Love Is Hot) (Peer Int'l, BMI) ... 54
Birthday (Maclen, BMI) ... 34
Black Berries (Triple 3, BMI) ... 79
Boy Named Sue, A (Evil Eye, BMI) ... 3
By the Time I Get to Phoenix (Johnny Rivers, BMI) 43
Can't Find the Time (Interval, BMI) ... 84
Carry Me Back (Slacsar, ASCAP) ... 47
Chains of Love (Progressive, BMI) ... 88
Change of Heart (Low-Sal, BMI) ... 57
Commotion (Jondora, BMI) ... 30
Crystal Blue Persuasion (Big Seven, BMI) ... 21
Daddy's Little Man (BnB Music, ASCAP) ... 41
Did You See Her Eyes (Unart, BMI) ... 33
Don't It Make You Want To Go Home (Lowery, BMI) 65
Easy to Be Hard (United Artists, ASCAP) ... 8
Everybody's Talkin' (Coconut Grove/Story, BMI) ... 23
Get Off My Back Woman (Sounds of Lucille-Pampco, BMI) ... 82
Get Together (S.F.O., BMI) ... 5
Give Peace a Chance (Maclen, BMI) ... 29
Going in Circles (Porpete, BMI) ... 55
Green River (Jondora, BMI) ... 4
Here I Go Again (Jobete, BMI) ... 53
Honky Tonk Women (Gideon, BMI) ... 1
Hook and Sling (Part 1) (Uzza, BMI) ... 73
Hot Fun in the Summertime (Stone Flower, BMI) ... 26
Hurt So Bad (Vogue, BMI) ... 14
In the Year 2525 (Zelad, BMI) ... 39
I Can't Get Next to You (Jobete, BMI) ... 10
I Could Never Be President (East/Memphis, BMI) ... 48
I Do (Gambi, BMI) ... 62
I Want You to Know (New Colony, BMI) ... 74
I'd Wait a Million Years (Teenie Bopper, ASCAP) ... 15
I'll Never Fall in Love Again (Hollis, BMI) ... 6
I'm a Better Man (Blue Seas/Jac, ASCAP) ... 49
I'm Gonna Make You Mine (Pocketful of Tunes, BMI) ... 35
In a Moment (Odeom & Neiburg, BMI) ... 50
It's Getting Better (Screen Gems-Columbia, BMI) ... 42
Jealous Kind of Fellow (Colfam, BMI) ... 78
Jean (Twentieth Century, ASCAP) ... 18
Keem-O-Sabe (Binn/Elaine/United Artists, ASCAP) ... 22
Kool and the Gang (Stephayne, BMI) ... 100
Laughing (Dunbar, BMI) ... 24
Lay Lady Lay (Big Sky, ASCAP) ... 7
Life and Death in G & A (Daly City, BMI) ... 87
Little Woman (Green Apple, BMI) ... 16
Lodi (Jondora, BMI) ... 67
Love's Been Good to Me (Almo, ASCAP) ... 98
Lowdown Popcorn (Golo, BMI) ... 45
Luna Trip (Cotique, BMI) ... 95
MacArthur Park (Canopy, ASCAP) ... 93
Mah-Na-Mah-Na (E. B. Marks, BMI) ... 66
Make Believe (Love/Peanut Butter, BMI) ... 81
Maybe the Rain Will Fall (Dunbar, BMI) ... 61
Moonlight Sonata (Southdale, ASCAP) ... 91
Move Over (Trousdale, BMI) ... 37
Muddy Mississippi Line (Detail, BMI) ... 58
My Balloon's Going Up (Assorted, BMI) ... 96
Nitty Gritty (Gallico, BMI) ... 19
Nobody But You Babe (Sherlyn, BMI) ... 40
No One for Me to Turn To (Spiral, BMI) ... 68
Odds and Ends (Blue Seas/Jac, ASCAP) ... 56
Oh What a Night (Conrad, BMI) ... 11
One Night Affair (Assorted, BMI) ... 71
Out of Sight, Out of Mind (Nom, BMI) ... 52
Polk Salad Annie (Combine, BMI) ... 28
Put a Little Love in Your Heart (Unart, BMI) ... 9
Rain (Johi, BMI) ... 76
Runnin' Blue (Nippers/Doors, ASCAP) ... 85
Sad Girl (IPC, BMI) ... 59
Sausalito (Is the Place to Go) (Kaskat/Man-Ken, BMI) ... 86
Share Your Love With Me (Don, BMI) ... 13
Simple Song of Freedom (T.M., BMI) ... 63
Slum Baby (East/Memphis, BMI) ... 97
Something in the Air (Track, BMI) ... 80
Soul Deep (Barton, BMI) ... 25
Sugar on Sunday (Big Seven, BMI) ... 44
Sugar, Sugar (Kirshner, BMI) ... 2
Suspicious Minds (Press, BMI) ... 77
Sweet Caroline (Good Times Never Seemed So Good) (Stonebridge, BMI) ... 12
That's the Way Love Is (Jobete, BMI) ... 31
This Girl Is a Woman Now (Three Bridges, ASCAP) ... 17
Tracy (Vanlee/Emily, ASCAP) ... 89
Train (Kaskat, BMI) ... 64
Walk On By (Jac/Blue Seas, ASCAP) ... 92
We Gotta All Get Together (Equinox, BMI) ... 60
Weight, The (Dwarf, ASCAP) ... 69
What Kind of Fool Do You Think I Am (Whitley/Low Twi, BMI) ... 36
What's the Use of Breaking Up (Assorted/Parabut, BMI) ... 38
When I Die (Mode, BMI) ... 32
Workin' on a Groovy Thing (Screen Gems-Columbia, BMI) ... 27
World, Part 1 (Golo, BMI) ... 70
You Got Yours and I'll Get Mine (Nickel Shoe, BMI) 51
You, I (Singleton, BMI) ... 46
Your Good Thing (Is About to End) (East, BMI) ... 20

## BUBBLING UNDER THE HOT 100

101. ONE WOMAN ... Steve Alaimo, Atco 6710
102. SON OF A LOVIN' MAN ... Buchanan Brothers, Event 3305
103. LOVE OF THE COMMON PEOPLE ... Winstons, Metromedia 142
104. COLOUR OF MY LOVE ... Jefferson, Decca 32501
105. ECHO PARK ... Keith Barbour, Epic 5-10486
106. HARLAN COUNTY ... Jim Ford, Sundown 115
107. DON'T FORGET TO REMEMBER ... Bee Gees, Atco 6702
108. TAKING MY LOVE ... Martha Reeves & the Vandellas, Gordy 7094
109. BORN ON THE BAYOU ... Short Kuts, Pepper 445
110. NOAH ... Bob Seeger System, Capitol 2576
111. I'LL BET YOU ... Funkadelic, Westbound 150
112. BABY, I'M FOR REAL ... Originals, Soul 716
113. GOOD CLEAN FUN ... Monkees, Colgems 66-005
114. HEIGHTY HI ... Lee Michaels, A&M 1095
115. BY THE TIME I GET TO PHOENIX ... Mad Lads, Volt 4016
116. MAYBE ... Betty Everett, UNI 55141
117. LET A WOMAN BE A WOMAN—LET A MAN BE A MAN ... Dyke & the Blazers, Original Sound 89
118. HELPLESS ... Jackie Wilson, Brunswick 55418
119. IT'S TRUE I'M GONNA MISS YOU ... Carolyn Franklin, RCA 74-0188
120. THINGS GOT TO GET BETTER ... Marva Whitney, King 6249
121. THE WAYS TO LOVE A MAN ... Tammy Wynette, Epic 5-10512
122. THE BEST PART OF A LOVE AFFAIR ... Emotions, Volt 4021
123. IT'S TOO LATE ... Ted Taylor, Ronn 34
124. SAN FRANCISCO IS A LONELY TOWN ... Joe Simon, Sound Stage 7 2641
125. FOR WHAT IT'S WORTH ... Cher, Atco 6704
126. IT'S A BEAUTIFUL DAY ... Buckinghams, Columbia 44923
127. WE CAN MAKE IT ... Ray Charles, Tangerine 11239
128. HAPPY TOGETHER ... Hugo Montenegro, His Orch. & Chorus, RCA 74-0160
129. GIMME SOME MORE ... Crazy Elephant, Bell 817
130. SEPTEMBER SONG ... Roy Clark, Dot 17299
131. MY WOMAN'S GOOD TO ME ... George Benson, A&M 1076
132. GREEN ONIONS ... Dick Hyman, Command 4129
133. PENNY ARCADE ... Roy Orbison, MGM 14079
134. GROOVY GRUBWORM ... Harlow Wilcox, Plantation 28
135. BILLY, I'VE GOT TO GO TO TOWN ... Geraldine Stevens, World Pacific 77927

Compiled from national retail sales and radio station airplay by the Music Popularity Dept. of Record Market Research, Billboard.

# Billboard HOT 100

FOR WEEK ENDING SEPTEMBER 20, 1969

★ STAR PERFORMER—Sides registering greatest proportionate sales progress this week.

Record Industry Association of America seal of certification as million selling single.

| This Week | 1 Wk. Ago | 2 Wks. Ago | 3 Wks. Ago | TITLE Artist (Producer), Label & Number | Weeks On Chart |
|---|---|---|---|---|---|
| ★ 1 | 2 | 3 | 3 | **SUGAR, SUGAR** Archies (Jeff Barry), Calendar 63-1008 | 9 |
| 2 | 1 | 1 | 1 | **HONKY TONK WOMEN** Rolling Stones (Jimmy Miller), London 910 | 10 |
| 3 | 4 | 4 | 7 | **GREEN RIVER** Creedence Clearwater Revival (J. C. Fogerty), Fantasy 625 | 8 |
| 4 | 3 | 2 | 2 | **A BOY NAMED SUE** Johnny Cash (Bob Johnston), Columbia 4-44944 | 9 |
| ★ 5 | 8 | 8 | 13 | **EASY TO BE HARD** Three Dog Night (Gabriel Mekler), Dunhill 4203 | 7 |
| 6 | 6 | 10 | 14 | **I'LL NEVER FALL IN LOVE AGAIN** Tom Jones (Peter Sullivan), Parrot 40018 | 9 |
| 7 | 5 | 5 | 6 | **GET TOGETHER** Youngbloods (Felix Pappalardi), RCA 47-9752 | 13 |
| ★ 8 | 18 | 21 | 33 | **JEAN** Oliver (Bob Crewe), Crewe 334 | 6 |
| ★ 9 | 16 | 34 | 66 | **LITTLE WOMAN** Bobby Sherman (Jackie Mills), Metromedia 121 | 5 |
| 10 | 10 | 11 | 30 | **I CAN'T GET NEXT TO YOU** Temptations (Norman Whitfield), Gordy 7093 | 6 |
| 11 | 11 | 27 | 29 | **OH, WHAT A NIGHT** Dells (Bobby Miller), Cadet 5649 | 6 |
| 12 | 14 | 15 | 19 | **HURT SO BAD** Lettermen (Al DeLory), Capitol 2482 | 17 |
| 13 | 13 | 20 | 23 | **SHARE YOUR LOVE WITH ME** Aretha Franklin (Jerry Wexler-Tom Dowd-Arif Mardin), Atlantic 2650 | 7 |
| ★ 14 | 17 | 38 | 43 | **THIS GIRL IS A WOMAN NOW** Gary Puckett & the Union Gap (Dick Glasser), Columbia 4-44967 | 5 |
| 15 | 15 | 16 | 17 | **I'D WAIT A MILLION YEARS** Grassroots (Steve Barry), Dunhill 4198 | 12 |
| 16 | 7 | 7 | 9 | **LAY LADY LAY** Bob Dylan (Bob Johnson), Columbia 44926 | 11 |
| 17 | 12 | 9 | 5 | **SWEET CAROLINE (Good Times Never Seemed So Good)** Neil Diamond (Tommy Cogbill, Tom Catalano, Neil Diamond), Uni 55136 | 13 |
| ★ 18 | 23 | 28 | 44 | **EVERYBODY'S TALKIN'** Nilsson (Rick Jarrard), RCA 74-0161 | 6 |
| 19 | 9 | 6 | 4 | **PUT A LITTLE LOVE IN YOUR HEART** Jackie DeShannon (VME), Imperial 66385 | 13 |
| 20 | 20 | 30 | 31 | **YOUR GOOD THING (Is About to End)** Lou Rawls (David Axelrod), Capitol 2550 | 10 |
| ★ 21 | 26 | 29 | 36 | **HOT FUN IN THE SUMMERTIME** Sly & the Family Stone (Sly Stone), Epic 5-10497 | 6 |
| 22 | 22 | 22 | 28 | **KEEM-O-SABE** Electric Indian (Len Barry), United Artists 50563 | 8 |
| ★ 23 | 36 | 44 | 55 | **WHAT KIND OF FOOL DO YOU THINK I AM** Bill Deal & the Rhondells (Jerry Ross), Heritage 817 | 6 |
| ★ 24 | 32 | 42 | 47 | **WHEN I DIE** Motherlode (Mort Ross & Doug Riley), Buddah 131 | 7 |
| 25 | 25 | 18 | 18 | **SOUL DEEP** Box Tops (Tommy Cogbill & Chips Moman), Mala 12040 | 12 |
| 26 | 24 | 12 | 12 | **LAUGHING** Guess Who (Jack Richardson), RCA 74-0195 | 11 |
| ★ 27 | 35 | 47 | 59 | **I'M GONNA MAKE YOU MINE** Lou Christie (Stan Vincent & Mike Duckman), Buddah 116 | 5 |
| 28 | 31 | 41 | 49 | **THAT'S THE WAY LOVE IS** Marvin Gaye (Norman Whitfield), Tamla 54185 | 5 |
| 29 | 27 | 24 | 20 | **WORKIN' ON A GROOVY THING** Fifth Dimension (Bones Howe), Soul City 776 | 10 |
| 30 | 19 | 23 | 24 | **NITTY GRITTY** Gladys Knight & the Pips (Norman Whitfield), Soul 35063 | 10 |
| ★ 31 | 37 | 37 | 42 | **MOVE OVER** Steppenwolf (Gabriel Mekler), Dunhill 4205 | 6 |
| ★ 32 | 47 | 70 | — | **CARRY ME BACK** Rascals (Rascals with Arif Mardin), Atlantic 2664 | 3 |
| 33 | 33 | 32 | 34 | **DID YOU SEE HER EYES** Illusion (Jeff Barry), Steed 718 | 12 |
| 34 | 41 | 54 | 83 | **DADDY'S LITTLE MAN** O. C. Smith (Jerry Fuller), Columbia 4-44948 | 4 |
| 35 | 38 | 39 | 64 | **WHAT'S THE USE OF BREAKING UP** Jerry Butler (Gamble-Huff), Mercury 72960 | 4 |
| ★ 36 | 77 | — | — | **SUSPICIOUS MINDS** Elvis Presley, RCA 47-9764 | 2 |
| ★ 37 | 44 | 46 | 78 | **SUGAR ON SUNDAY** Clique (Gary Zekley), White Whale 323 | 4 |
| 38 | 34 | 26 | 27 | **BIRTHDAY** Underground Sunshine (Underground Sunshine), Intrepid 75002 | 10 |
| 39 | 30 | 35 | 35 | **COMMOTION** Creedence Clearwater Revival (J. C. Fogerty), Fantasy 625 | 8 |
| 40 | 40 | 45 | 45 | **NOBODY BUT THE BABE** Clarence Reid (Brad Shapiro & Steve Alaimo), Alston 4574 | 8 |
| 41 | 45 | 57 | 60 | **LOWDOWN POPCORN** James Brown (James Brown), King 6250 | 5 |
| 42 | 42 | 40 | 40 | **IT'S GETTING BETTER** Mama Cass (Steve Barri), Dunhill 4195 | 16 |
| 43 | 43 | 69 | 88 | **BY THE TIME I GET TO PHOENIX** Isaac Hayes (Al Bell, Marvell Thomas, Allen Jones), Enterprise 9003 | 4 |
| 44 | 28 | 13 | 11 | **POLK SALAD ANNIE** Tony Joe White (Billy Swan), Monument 1104 | 12 |
| 45 | 49 | 55 | 58 | **I'M A BETTER MAN** Engelbert Humperdinck (Peter Sullivan), Parrot 40040 | 5 |
| 46 | 46 | 60 | 80 | **YOU, I** Rugbys (Steve McNicol), Amazon 1 | 5 |
| 47 | 50 | 56 | 57 | **IN A MOMENT** Intrigues (Martin & Bell), Yew 1001 | 8 |
| 48 | 55 | 66 | 73 | **GOING IN CIRCLES** Friends of Distinction (John Florez), RCA 74-0204 | 6 |
| 49 | 29 | 14 | 15 | **GIVE PEACE A CHANCE** Plastic Ono Band (John & Yoko), Apple 1809 | 9 |
| 50 | 53 | 67 | 71 | **HERE I GO AGAIN** Smokey Robinson & the Miracles (W. Moore & T. Johnson), Tampa 54183 | 5 |
| 51 | 51 | 61 | 76 | **YOU GOT YOURS AND I'LL GET MINE** Delfonics (Stan & Bell Prod.), Philly Groove 157 | 6 |
| ★ 52 | 68 | 71 | 89 | **NO ONE FOR ME TO TURN TO** Spiral Starecase (Sonny Knight), Columbia 4-44924 | 4 |
| ★ 53 | 58 | 64 | 68 | **MUDDY MISSISSIPPI LINE** Bobby Goldsboro (Bob Montgomery & Bobby Goldsboro), United Artists 50565 | 6 |
| 54 | 52 | 53 | 53 | **OUT OF SIGHT, OUT OF MIND** Little Anthony & the Imperials (Bob Skaff), United Artists 50552 | 9 |
| 55 | 48 | 48 | 56 | **I COULD NEVER BE PRESIDENT** Johnnie Taylor (Don Davis), Stax 0046 | 6 |
| 56 | 65 | 79 | 82 | **DON'T IT MAKE YOU WANT TO GO HOME** Joe South & the Believers (Joe South), Capitol 2592 | 5 |
| 57 | 60 | 80 | — | **WE GOTTA ALL GET TOGETHER** Paul Revere & the Raiders (Mark Lindsay), Columbia 44970 | 3 |
| ★ 58 | 70 | — | — | **WORLD, Part 1** James Brown (James Brown), King 6258 | 2 |
| 59 | 59 | 73 | 91 | **SAD GIRL** Intruders (Gamble-Huff), Gamble 235 | 4 |
| ★ 60 | 72 | — | — | **AND THAT REMINDS ME (My Heart Reminds Me)** Four Seasons (Crewe-Gaudio), Crewe 333 | 2 |
| ★ 61 | — | — | — | **LOVE OF THE COMMON PEOPLE** The Winstons (Don Carroll), Metromedia 142 | 1 |
| ★ 62 | 90 | — | — | **BABY IT'S YOU** Smith (Joel Sill & Steve Barri), Dunhill 4206 | 3 |
| 63 | 66 | 81 | — | **MAH-NA-MAH-NA** "Sweden Heaven and Hell" Soundtrack, Ariel 500 | 3 |
| 64 | 64 | 72 | 81 | **TRAIN** 1910 Fruitgum Co. (Kasenetz-Katz Assoc.), Buddah 130 | 4 |
| 65 | 69 | — | — | **THE WEIGHT** Diana Ross & the Supremes & the Temptations (Frank Wilson), Motown 1153 | 2 |
| 66 | 62 | 62 | 67 | **I DO** Moments (Sylvia, Edmounds & Ruffin), Stang 5005 | 6 |
| 67 | 67 | 74 | 79 | **LODI** Al Wilson (Johnny Rivers), Soul City 775 | 5 |
| ★ 68 | 89 | — | — | **TRACY** Cuff Links (Paul Vance-Lee Pockriss), Decca 32533 | 2 |
| 69 | 61 | 63 | 63 | **MAYBE THE RAIN WILL FALL** Cascades (Andy Di Martino), Uni 551252 | 6 |
| ★ 70 | 81 | 90 | — | **MAKE BELIEVE** Wind (Bo Gentry), Life 200 | 3 |
| ★ 71 | — | — | 62 | **JACK AND JILL** Tommy Roe (Steve Barri), ABC 11229 | 8 |
| 72 | 78 | — | — | **JEALOUS KIND OF FELLOW** Garland Greene (Giant Enterprises Prod.), UNI 55143 | 2 |
| 73 | 74 | 83 | 90 | **I WANT YOU TO KNOW** New Colony Six (Sentar Record Prod.), Mercury 72961 | 4 |
| 74 | 75 | 75 | — | **ARMSTRONG** John Stewart (Chip Douglas), Capitol 2605 | 3 |
| 75 | 80 | 82 | — | **SOMETHING IN THE AIR** Thunderclap Newman (Peter Townshend), Track 2656 | 3 |
| 76 | 85 | 89 | — | **RUNNIN' BLUE** Doors (Paul A. Rothchild), Elektra 45675 | 3 |
| 77 | 76 | 76 | 77 | **RAIN** Jose Feliciano (Rick Jarrard), RCA 47-9757 | 5 |
| 78 | 73 | 78 | 85 | **HOOK AND SLING (Part 1)** Eddie Bo (Al Scramuzza), Scram 117 | 8 |
| 79 | 79 | 87 | 99 | **BLACK BERRIES** Isley Brothers (R. Isley/O. Isley/R. Isley), T Neck 906 | 4 |
| 80 | 83 | 84 | 92 | **ANY WAY THAT YOU WANT ME** Evie Sands (Chip Taylor-Al Gorgoni), A&M 1090 | 6 |
| ★ 81 | — | — | — | **SON OF A LOVIN' MAN** Buchanan Brothers (Cashman, Pistilli & West), Event 3305 | 1 |
| 82 | 82 | 100 | 100 | **GET OFF MY BACK WOMAN** B. B. King (Bill Szymczyk), Bluesway 61026 | 4 |
| 83 | 92 | — | 94 | **WALK ON BY** Isaac Hayes (Al Bell-Marvell Thomas-Allen Jones), Enterprise 9003 | 4 |
| 84 | 84 | 85 | 93 | **CAN'T FIND THE TIME** Orpheus (Alan Lorber), MGM 13882 | 5 |
| 85 | 98 | — | — | **LOVE'S BEEN GOOD TO ME** Frank Sinatra (Sonny Burke), Reprise 0852 | 2 |
| 86 | 88 | — | — | **CHAINS OF LOVE** Bobby Bland (Andre Williams), Duke 449 | 2 |
| 87 | 87 | 99 | — | **LIFE AND DEATH IN G & A** Abaco Dream (Ted Cooper), A&M 1081 | 3 |
| 88 | 91 | 91 | — | **MOONLIGHT SONATA** Henry Mancini, His Ork. & Chorus (Joe Reisman), RCA 74-0212 | 3 |
| ★ 89 | — | — | — | **LET A WOMAN BE A WOMAN LET A MAN BE A MAN** Dyke and the Blazers (Laboe/Barrette), Original Sound 89 | 1 |
| ★ 90 | — | — | — | **YOU'VE LOST THAT LOVIN' FEELING** Dionne Warwick (Chips Moman & Dionne Warwick), Scepter 12262 | 1 |
| 91 | 94 | 97 | 97 | **ALL I HAVE TO OFFER YOU (Is Me)** Charley Pride (Jack Clement), RCA 74-0167 | 5 |
| 92 | — | — | — | **DON'T FORGET TO REMEMBER** Bee Gees (Robert Stigwood & the Brothers Gibb), Atco 6702 | 1 |
| 93 | 96 | — | — | **MY BALLOON'S GOING UP** Archie Bell & the Drells (Gamble-Huff), Atlantic 2663 | 2 |
| 94 | — | — | — | **JESUS IS A SOUL MAN** Lawrence Reynolds (Don Davis), Warner Bros.-Seven Arts 7322 | 1 |
| 95 | — | 88 | 95 | **GOODBYE COLUMBUS** Association (John Boylan), Warner Bros.-Seven Bros. 7267 | 5 |
| 96 | 100 | — | — | **KOOL AND THE GANG** Kool and the Gang (Redd Coach Prod.), De-Lite 519 | 2 |
| 97 | — | — | — | **SINCE I MET YOU BABY** Sonny James (Kelso Herston), Capitol 2595 | 1 |
| 98 | — | — | — | **DRUMMER MAN** Nancy Sinatra (Billy Strange), Reprise 0851 | 1 |
| 99 | 99 | — | — | **A TIME FOR US** Johnny Mathis (Jack Gold), Columbia 4-44915 | 7 |
| 100 | — | — | — | **GOOD CLEAN FUN** The Monkees (Michael Nesmith), Colgems 66-5005 | 1 |

## HOT 100—A TO Z—(Publisher-Licensee)

A Time for Us (Famous, ASCAP) ... 99
All I Have to Offer You (Is Me) (Hill & Range/Blue Crest, BMI) ... 91
And That Reminds Me (My Heart Reminds Me) (Symphony House, ASCAP) ... 60
Any Way That You Want Me (Blackwood, BMI) ... 80
Armstrong (Great Montana, BMI) ... 74

Baby It's You (Dolfi, ASCAP) ... 62
Birthday (Maclen, BMI) ... 38
Black Berries (Triple 3, BMI) ... 79
Boy Named Sue, A (Evil Eye, BMI) ... 4
By the Time I Get to Phoenix (Johnny Rivers, BMI) 43

Can't Find the Time (Interval, BMI) ... 84
Carry Me Back (Slacsar, ASCAP) ... 32
Chains of Love (Progressive, BMI) ... 86
Commotion (Jondora, BMI) ... 39

Daddy's Little Man (BnB Music, ASCAP) ... 34
Did You See Her Eyes (Unart, BMI) ... 33
Don't It Make You Want to Go Home (Lowery, BMI) ... 56
Don't Forget to Remember (Casserole, BMI) ... 92
Drummer Man (Borwin, BMI) ... 98

Easy to Be Hard (United Artists, ASCAP) ... 5
Everybody's Talkin' (Coconut Grove/Story, BMI) ... 18

Get Off My Back Woman (Sounds of Lucille-Pampco, BMI) ... 82
Get Together (S.F.O., BMI) ... 7
Give Peace a Chance (Maclen, BMI) ... 49
Going in Circles (Porpete, BMI) ... 48
Good Clean Fun (Screen Gems-Columbia, BMI) ... 100
Goodbye Columbus (Ensign Music, BMI) ... 95
Green River (Jondora, BMI) ... 3

Here I Go Again (Jobete, BMI) ... 50
Honky Tonk Women (Gideon, BMI) ... 2
Hook and Sling (Part 1) (Uzza, BMI) ... 78
Hot Fun in the Summertime (Stone Flower, BMI) ... 21
Hurt So Bad (Vogue, BMI) ... 12

I Can't Get Next to You (Jobete, BMI) ... 10
I Could Never Be President (East/Memphis, BMI) ... 55
I Do (Gambi, BMI) ... 66
I Want You to Know (New Colony, BMI) ... 73
I'd Wait a Million Years (Teenie Bopper, ASCAP) ... 15
I'll Never Fall in Love Again (TRO-Hollis, BMI) ... 6
I'm a Better Man (Blue Seas/Jac, ASCAP) ... 45
I'm Gonna Make You Mine (Pocketful of Tunes, BMI) ... 27
In a Moment (Odeom & Neiburg, BMI) ... 47
It's Getting Better (Screen Gems-Columbia, BMI) ... 42

Jack and Jill (Low-Twi, BMI) ... 71
Jealous Kind of Fellow (Colfam, BMI) ... 72
Jean (Twentieth Century, ASCAP) ... 8
Jesus Is a Soul Man (Wilderness, BMI) ... 94

Keem-O-Sabe (Binn/Elaine/United Artists, ASCAP) ... 22
Kool and the Gang (Stephayne, BMI) ... 86

Laughing (Dunbar, BMI) ... 26
Lay Lady Lay (Big Sky, ASCAP) ... 16
Let a Woman Be a Woman, Let a Man Be a Man (Drive-In/Westward, BMI) ... 89
Life and Death in G & A (Daly City, BMI) ... 87
Little Woman (Green Apple, BMI) ... 9
Lodi (Jondora, BMI) ... 67
Love of the Common People (Tree, BMI) ... 61
Love's Been Good to Me (Almo, ASCAP) ... 85
Lowdown Popcorn (Golo, BMI) ... 41

Mah-Na-Mah-Na (E. B. Marks, BMI) ... 63
Make Believe (Love/Peanut Butter, BMI) ... 70
Maybe the Rain Will Fall (Dunbar, BMI) ... 69
Moonlight Sonata (Southdale, ASCAP) ... 88
Move Over (Trousdale, BMI) ... 31
Muddy Mississippi Line (Detail, BMI) ... 53
My Balloon's Going Up (Assorted, BMI) ... 93

Nitty Gritty (Gallico, BMI) ... 30
Nobody But You Babe (Sherlyn, BMI) ... 40
No One for Me to Turn To (Spiral, BMI) ... 52

Oh What a Night (Conrad, BMI) ... 11
Out of Sight, Out of Mind (Nom, BMI) ... 54

Polk Salad Annie (Combine, BMI) ... 44
Put a Little Love in Your Heart (Unart, BMI) ... 19

Rain (Johi, BMI) ... 77
Runnin' Blue (Nippers/Doors, ASCAP) ... 76

Sad Girl (IPC, BMI) ... 59
Share Your Love With Me (Don, BMI) ... 13
Since I Met You Baby (Marson, BMI) ... 97
Something in the Air (Track, BMI) ... 75
Son of a Lovin' Man (Blendingwell, ASCAP) ... 81
Soul Deep (Barton, BMI) ... 25
Sugar on Sunday (Big Seven, BMI) ... 37
Sugar, Sugar (Kirshner, BMI) ... 1
Suspicious Minds (Press, BMI) ... 36
Sweet Caroline (Good Times Never Seemed So Good) (Stonebridge, BMI) ... 17

That's the Way Love Is (Jobete, BMI) ... 28
This Girl Is a Woman Now (Three Bridges, ASCAP) ... 14
Tracy (Vanlee/Emily, ASCAP) ... 68
Train (Kaskat, BMI) ... 64

Walk On By (Jac/Seas, ASCAP) ... 83
We Gotta All Get Together (Equinox, BMI) ... 57
Weight, The (Dwarf, ASCAP) ... 65
What Kind of Fool Do You Think I Am (Whitley/Low Twi, BMI) ... 23
What's the Use of Breaking Up (Assorted/Parabut, BMI) ... 35
When I Die (Mode, BMI) ... 24
Workin' on a Groovy Thing (Screen Gems-Columbia, BMI) ... 29
World, Part 1 (Golo, BMI) ... 58

You Got Yours and I'll Get Mine (Nickel Shoe, BMI) 51
You, I (Singleton, BMI) ... 46
Your Good Thing (Is About to Eend) (East, BMI) ... 20
You've Lost That Lovin' Feeling (Screen Gems-Columbia, BMI) ... 90

## BUBBLING UNDER THE HOT 100

101. SO GOOD TOGETHER ... Andy Kim, Steed 720
102. SMILE A LITTLE SMILE FOR ME ... Flying Machine, Congress 6000
103. ECHO PARK ... Keith Barbour, Epic 5-10486
104. EVIL WOMAN ... Crow, Amaret 45112
105. THE WAYS TO LOVE A MAN ... Tammy Wynette, Epic 5-10512
106. HARLAN COUNTY ... Jim Ford, Sundown 115
107. THE COLOUR OF MY LOVE ... Jefferson, Decca 32501
108. DELTA LADY ... Joe Cocker, A&M 1112
109. ONE WOMAN ... Steve Alaimo, Atco 6710
110. MOMMY AND DADDY ... Monkees, Colgems 66-5005
111. I'LL BET YOU ... Funkadelic, Westbound 150
112. WE CAN MAKE IT ... Ray Charles, Tangerine 11239
113. BORN ON THE BAYOU ... Short Kuts, Pepper 445
114. DON'T WASTE MY TIME ... John Mayall, Polydor 14004
115. BABY I'M FOR REAL ... Originals, Soul 716
116. GIMME SOME MORE ... Crazy Elephant, Bell 817
117. GREEN ONIONS ... Dick Hyman, Command 4129
118. HELPLESS ... Jackie Wilson, Brunswick 55418
119. SAN FRANCISCO IS A LONELY TOWN ... Joe Simon, Sound Stage 7 2641
120. SLUM BABY ... Booker T. & the M.G.'s, Stax 0049
121. TAKING MY LOVE ... Martha Reeves & the Vandellas, Gordy 7094
122. THE BEST PART OF A LOVE AFFAIR ... Emotions, Volt 4021
123. WE'LL CRY TOGETHER ... Maxine Brown, Commonwealth United 3001
124. NEVER IN PUBLIC ... Candi Staton, Fame 1459
125. RUBEN JAMES ... Kenny Rodgers & the First Edition, Reprise 0854
126. THE 12th OF NEVER ... Chi-Lites, Brunswick 7-78030
127. IT'S A BEAUTIFUL DAY (For Loving) ... Buckinghams, Columbia 44923
128. SEPTEMBER SONG ... Roy Clark, Dot 17299
129. HAPPY TOGETHER ... Hugo Montenegro & His Orch. & Chorus, RCA 74-1076
130. GROOVY GRUBWORM ... Harlow Wilcox, Plantation 28
131. THESE ARE THE THINGS THAT MAKE ME KNOW YOU'RE GONE ... Howard Tate, Turntable 505
132. I STILL BELIEVE IN TOMORROW ... John & Ann Ryder, Decca 73256
133. HEIGHTY HI ... Lee Michaels, A&M 1095
134. WAS IT GOOD TO YOU ... Isley Brothers, T Neck 908

Compiled from national retail sales and radio station airplay by the Music Popularity Dept. of Record Market Research, Billboard.

# Billboard HOT 100

FOR WEEK ENDING SEPTEMBER 27, 1969

♫ Artist and/or Selection featured on "The Music Scene," ABC-TV Network

★ STAR PERFORMER—Sides registering greatest proportionate sales progress this week. (seal) Record Industry Association of America seal of certification as million selling single.

| This Week | 1 Wk. Ago | 2 Wks. Ago | 3 Wks. Ago | TITLE Artist (Producer), Label & Number | Weeks On Chart |
|---|---|---|---|---|---|
| ♫ 1 | 1 | 2 | 3 | SUGAR, SUGAR — Archies (Jeff Barry), Calendar 63-1008 | 10 (RIAA seal) |
| 2 | 3 | 4 | 4 | GREEN RIVER — Creedence Clearwater Revival (J. C. Fogerty), Fantasy 625 | 9 |
| 3 | 2 | 1 | 1 | HONKY TONK WOMEN — Rolling Stones (Jimmy Miller), London 910 | 11 (RIAA seal) |
| ♫ 4 | 5 | 8 | 8 | EASY TO BE HARD — Three Dog Night (Gabriel Mekler), Dunhill 4203 | 8 |
| ★ 5 | 9 | 16 | 34 | LITTLE WOMAN — Bobby Sherman (Jackie Mills), Metromedia 121 | 6 |
| ★ 6 | 10 | 10 | 11 | I CAN'T GET NEXT TO YOU — Temptations (Norman Whitfield), Gordy 7093 | 7 |
| ♫ 7 | 8 | 18 | 21 | JEAN — Oliver (Bob Crewe), Crewe 334 | 7 |
| ♫ 8 | 6 | 6 | 10 | I'LL NEVER FALL IN LOVE AGAIN — Tom Jones (Peter Sullivan), Parrot 40018 | 10 (RIAA seal) |
| ★ 9 | 21 | 26 | 29 | HOT FUN IN THE SUMMERTIME — Sly & the Family Stone (Sly Stone), Epic 5-10497 | 7 |
| 10 | 11 | 11 | 27 | OH, WHAT A NIGHT — Dells (Bobby Miller), Cadet 5649 | 7 |
| 11 | 4 | 3 | 2 | A BOY NAMED SUE — Johnny Cash (Bob Johnston), Columbia 4-44944 | 10 |
| ★ 12 | 14 | 17 | 38 | THIS GIRL IS A WOMAN NOW — Gary Puckett & the Union Gap (Dick Glasser), Columbia 4-44967 | 6 |
| 13 | 7 | 5 | 5 | GET TOGETHER — Youngbloods (Felix Pappalardi), RCA 47-9752 | 14 |
| 14 | 12 | 14 | 15 | HURT SO BAD — Lettermen (Al DeLory), Capitol 2482 | 18 |
| ★ 15 | 28 | 31 | 41 | THAT'S THE WAY LOVE IS — Marvin Gaye (Norman Whitfield), Tamla 54185 | 6 |
| ★ 16 | 22 | 22 | 22 | KEEM-O-SABE — Electric Indian (Len Barry), United Artists 50563 | 9 |
| 17 | 18 | 23 | 28 | EVERYBODY'S TALKIN' — Nilsson (Rick Jarrard), RCA 74-0161 | 7 |
| 18 | 20 | 20 | 30 | YOUR GOOD THING (Is About to End) — Lou Rawls (David Axelrod), Capitol 2550 | 11 |
| ★ 19 | 36 | 77 | — | SUSPICIOUS MINDS — Elvis Presley, RCA 47-9764 | 3 |
| 20 | 16 | 7 | 7 | LAY LADY LAY — Bob Dylan (Bob Johnson), Columbia 44926 | 12 |
| 21 | 24 | 32 | 42 | WHEN I DIE — Motherlode (Mort Ross & Doug Riley), Buddah 131 | 8 |
| ★ 22 | 35 | 38 | 39 | WHAT'S THE USE OF BREAKING UP — Jerry Butler (Gamble-Huff), Mercury 72960 | 5 |
| 23 | 23 | 36 | 44 | WHAT KIND OF FOOL DO YOU THINK I AM — Bill Deal & the Rhondells (Jerry Ross), Heritage 817 | 7 |
| 24 | 19 | 9 | 6 | PUT A LITTLE LOVE IN YOUR HEART — Jackie DeShannon (VME), Imperial 66385 | 14 |
| 25 | 15 | 15 | 16 | I'D WAIT A MILLION YEARS — Grassroots (Steve Barry), Dunhill 4198 | 13 |
| 26 | 27 | 35 | 47 | I'M GONNA MAKE YOU MINE — Lou Christie (Stan Vincent & Mike Duckman), Buddah 116 | 6 |
| 27 | 17 | 12 | 9 | SWEET CAROLINE (Good Times Never Seemed So Good) — Neil Diamond (Tommy Cogbill, Tom Catalano, Neil Diamond), Uni 55136 | 14 (RIAA seal) |
| 28 | 25 | 25 | 18 | SOUL DEEP — Box Tops (Tommy Cogbill & Chips Moman), Mala 12040 | 13 |
| 29 | 13 | 13 | 20 | SHARE YOUR LOVE WITH ME — Aretha Franklin (Jerry Wexler-Tom Dowd-Arif Mardin), Atlantic 2650 | 8 |
| ★ 30 | 46 | 46 | 60 | YOU, I — Rugbys (Steve McNicol), Amazon 1 | 6 |
| 31 | 31 | 37 | 37 | MOVE OVER — Steppenwolf (Gabriel Mekler), Dunhill 4205 | 7 |
| 32 | 32 | 47 | 70 | CARRY ME BACK — Rascals (Rascals with Arif Mardin), Atlantic 2664 | 4 |
| ★ 33 | 37 | 44 | 46 | SUGAR ON SUNDAY — Clique (Gary Zekley), White Whale 323 | 5 |
| 34 | 34 | 41 | 54 | DADDY'S LITTLE MAN — O. C. Smith (Jerry Fuller), Columbia 4-44948 | 5 |
| 35 | 30 | 19 | 23 | NITTY GRITTY — Gladys Knight & the Pips (Norman Whitfield), Soul 35063 | 11 |
| 36 | 33 | 33 | 32 | DID YOU SEE HER EYES — Illusion (Jeff Barry), Steed 718 | 13 |
| ♫ ★ 37 | 58 | 70 | — | WORLD, Part 1 — James Brown (James Brown), King 6258 | 3 |
| 38 | 45 | 49 | 55 | I'M A BETTER MAN — Engelbert Humperdinck (Peter Sullivan), Parrot 40040 | 6 |
| 39 | 43 | 43 | 69 | BY THE TIME I GET TO PHOENIX — Isaac Hayes (Al Bell, Marvell Thomas, Allen Jones), Enterprise 9003 | 5 |
| 40 | 42 | 42 | 40 | IT'S GETTING BETTER — Mama Cass (Steve Barri), Dunhill 4195 | 17 |
| 41 | 47 | 50 | 56 | IN A MOMENT — Intrigues (Martin & Bell), Yew 1001 | 9 |
| ★ 42 | 48 | 55 | 66 | GOING IN CIRCLES — Friends of Distinction (John Florez), RCA 74-0204 | 7 |
| 43 | 50 | 53 | 67 | HERE I GO AGAIN — Smokey Robinson & the Miracles (W. Moore & T. Johnson), Tampa 54183 | 6 |
| ★ 44 | 56 | 65 | 79 | DON'T IT MAKE YOU WANT TO GO HOME — Joe South & the Believers (Joe South), Capitol 2592 | 6 |
| 45 | 51 | 51 | 61 | YOU GOT YOURS AND I'LL GET MINE — Delfonics (Stan & Bell Prod.), Philly Groove 157 | 7 |
| 46 | 40 | 40 | 45 | NOBODY BUT YOU BABE — Clarence Reid (Brad Shapiro & Steve Alaimo), Alston 4574 | 9 |
| ♫ 47 | 41 | 45 | 57 | LOWDOWN POPCORN — James Brown (James Brown), King 6250 | 6 |
| ★ 48 | 65 | 69 | — | THE WEIGHT — Diana Ross & the Supremes & the Temptations (Frank Wilson), Motown 1153 | 3 |
| ★ 49 | 68 | 89 | — | TRACY — Cuff Links (Paul Vance-Lee Pockriss), Decca 32533 | 3 |
| ★ 50 | 62 | 90 | — | BABY IT'S YOU — Smith (Joel Sill & Steve Barri), Dunhill 4206 | 4 |
| ★ 51 | 57 | 60 | 80 | WE GOTTA ALL GET TOGETHER — Paul Revere & the Raiders (Mark Lindsay), Columbia 44970 | 4 |
| 52 | 52 | 68 | 71 | NO ONE FOR ME TO TURN TO — Spiral Starecase (Sonny Knight), Columbia 4-44924 | 5 |
| 53 | 53 | 58 | 64 | MUDDY MISSISSIPPI LINE — Bobby Goldsboro (Bob Montgomery & Bobby Goldsboro), United Artists 50565 | 7 |
| ★ 54 | 70 | 81 | 90 | MAKE BELIEVE — Wind (Bo Gentry), Life 200 | 4 |
| 55 | 60 | 72 | — | AND THAT REMINDS ME (My Heart Reminds Me) — Four Seasons (Crewe-Gaudio), Crewe 333 | 3 |
| 56 | 63 | 66 | 81 | MAH-NA-MAH-NA — "Sweden Heaven and Hell" Soundtrack, Ariel 500 | 4 |
| ★ 57 | 90 | — | — | YOU'VE LOST THAT LOVIN' FEELING — Dionne Warwick (Chips Moman & Dionne Warwick), Scepter 12262 | 2 |
| 58 | 55 | 48 | 48 | I COULD NEVER BE PRESIDENT — Johnnie Taylor (Don Davis), Stax 0046 | 7 |
| 59 | 61 | — | — | LOVE OF THE COMMON PEOPLE — The Winstons (Don Carroll), Metromedia 142 | 2 |
| ★ 60 | 72 | 78 | — | JEALOUS KIND OF FELLOW — Garland Greene (Giant Enterprises Prod.), UNI 55143 | 3 |
| 61 | 59 | 59 | 73 | SAD GIRL — Intruders (Gamble-Huff), Gamble 235 | 5 |
| ★ 62 | 75 | 80 | 82 | SOMETHING IN THE AIR — Thunderclap Newman (Peter Townshend), Track 2656 | 4 |
| ★ 63 | 83 | 92 | — | WALK ON BY — Isaac Hayes (Al Bell-Marvell Thomas-Allen Jones), Enterprise 9003 | 5 |
| 64 | 71 | — | — | JACK AND JILL — Tommy Roe (Steve Barri), ABC 11229 | 9 |
| 65 | 73 | 74 | 83 | I WANT YOU TO KNOW — New Colony Six (Sentar Record Prod.), Mercury 72961 | 5 |
| ★ 66 | 89 | — | — | LET A WOMAN BE A WOMAN LET A MAN BE A MAN — Dyke and the Blazers (Laboe/Barrette), Original Sound 89 | 2 |
| ★ 67 | — | — | — | WEDDING BELL BLUES — 5th Dimension (Bones Howe), Soul City 779 | 1 |
| 68 | 67 | 67 | 74 | LODI — Al Wilson (Johnny Rivers), Soul City 775 | 6 |
| 69 | 64 | 64 | 72 | TRAIN — 1910 Fruitgum Co. (Kasenetz-Katz Assoc.), Buddah 130 | 5 |
| ★ 70 | 94 | — | — | JESUS IS A SOUL MAN — Lawrence Reynolds (Don Davis), Warner Bros.-Seven Arts 7322 | 2 |
| 71 | 76 | 85 | 89 | RUNNIN' BLUE — Doors (Paul A. Rothchild), Elektra 45675 | 4 |
| 72 | 80 | 83 | 84 | ANY WAY THAT YOU WANT ME — Evie Sands (Chip Taylor-Al Gorgoni), A&M 1090 | 7 |
| ★ 73 | 92 | — | — | DON'T FORGET TO REMEMBER — Bee Gees (Robert Stigwood & the Brothers Gibb), Atco 6702 | 2 |
| ★ 74 | 87 | 87 | 99 | LIFE AND DEATH IN G & A — Abaco Dream (Ted Cooper), A&M 1081 | 4 |
| 75 | 85 | 98 | — | LOVE'S BEEN GOOD TO ME — Frank Sinatra (Sonny Burke), Reprise 0852 | 3 |
| ★ 76 | — | — | — | IS THAT ALL THERE IS — Peggy Lee (Lieber/Stoller), Capitol 2602 | 1 |
| ★ 77 | — | — | — | DOIN' OUR THING — Clarence Carter (Rick Hall), Atlantic 2660 | 1 |
| 78 | 78 | 73 | 78 | HOOK AND SLING (Part 1) — Eddie Bo (Al Scramuzza), Scram 117 | 9 |
| 79 | 82 | 82 | 100 | GET OFF MY BACK WOMAN — B. B. King (Bill Szymczyk), Bluesway 61026 | 5 |
| 80 | 81 | — | — | SON OF A LOVIN' MAN — Buchanan Brothers (Cashman, Pistilli & West), Event 3305 | 2 |
| 81 | 86 | 88 | — | CHAINS OF LOVE — Bobby Bland (Andre Williams), Duke 449 | 3 |
| ★ 82 | — | — | — | SO GOOD TOGETHER — Andy Kim (Jeff Barry), Steed 720 | 1 |
| 83 | 84 | 84 | 85 | CAN'T FIND THE TIME — Orpheus (Alan Lorber), MGM 13882 | 6 |
| ★ 84 | — | — | — | SAN FRANCISCO IS A LONELY TOWN — Joe Simon (John R.), Sound Stage 7 2641 | 1 |
| ★ 85 | — | — | — | ECHO PARK — Keith Barbour (Austin & Flemming), Epic 5-10486 | 1 |
| ★ 86 | — | — | — | BABY, I'M FOR REAL — Originals (Richard Morris), Soul 35066 | 1 |
| 87 | 88 | 91 | 91 | MOONLIGHT SONATA — Henry Mancini, His Ork. & Chorus (Joe Reisman), RCA 74-0212 | 4 |
| 88 | 93 | 96 | — | MY BALLOON'S GOING UP — Archie Bell & the Drells (Gamble-Huff), Atlantic 2663 | 3 |
| ★ 89 | — | 98 | 97 | SLUM BABY — Booker T. & the M.G.'s (Booker T. & the M.G.'s), Stax 0049 | 3 |
| 90 | 97 | — | — | SINCE I MET YOU BABY — Sonny James (Kelso Herston), Capitol 2595 | 2 |
| 91 | — | — | — | TIME MACHINE — Grand Funk Railroad (Terry Knight), Capitol 2567 | 1 |
| 92 | — | — | — | MIND, BODY & SOUL — Flaming Embers (R. Dunbar), Hot Wax 6902 | 1 |
| 93 | — | — | — | WAS IT GOOD TO YOU — Isley Brothers (R. O. & R. Isley), T-Neck 908 | 1 |
| 94 | 95 | — | 88 | GOODBYE COLUMBUS — Association (John Boylan), Warner Bros.-Seven Bros. 7267 | 6 |
| 95 | 96 | 100 | — | KOOL AND THE GANG — Kool and the Gang (Redd Coach Prod.), De-Lite 519 | 3 |
| 96 | — | — | — | WE'LL CRY TOGETHER — Maxine Brown (Charles Koppelman), Commonwealth United 3001 | 1 |
| 97 | — | — | — | JULIA — Ramsey Lewis (C. Stepney), Cadet 5640 | 1 |
| 98 | 98 | — | — | DRUMMER MAN — Nancy Sinatra (Billy Strange), Reprise 0851 | 2 |
| 99 | 100 | — | — | GOOD CLEAN FUN — The Monkees (Michael Nesmith), Colgems 66-5005 | 2 |
| 100 | — | — | — | RUBEN JAMES — Kenny Rogers & First Edition (Mike Post), Reprise 0854 | 1 |

## HOT 100—A TO Z—(Publisher-Licensee)


And That Reminds Me (My Heart Reminds Me) (Symphony House, ASCAP) .... 55
Any Way That You Want Me (Blackwood, BMI) .... 72

Baby, I'm For Real (Jobete, BMI) .... 86
Baby It's You (Dolfi-Mary Jane, ASCAP) .... 50
Boy Named Sue, A (Evil Eye, BMI) .... 11
By the Time I Get to Phoenix (Johnny Rivers, BMI) 39

Can't Find the Time (Interval, BMI) .... 83
Carry Me Back (Slacsar, ASCAP) .... 32
Chains of Love (Progressive, BMI) .... 81

Daddy's Little Man (BnB Music, ASCAP) .... 34
Did You See Her Eyes (Unart, BMI) .... 36
Doin' Our Thing (Fame, BMI) .... 77
Don't It Make You Want to Go Home (Lowery, BMI) .... 44
Don't Forget to Remember (Casserole, BMI) .... 73
Drummer Man (Borwin, BMI) .... 98

Easy to Be Hard (United Artists, ASCAP) .... 4
Echo Park (Hastings, BMI) .... 85
Everybody's Talkin' (Coconut Grove/Story, BMI) .... 17

Get Off My Back Woman (Sounds of Lucille-Pampco, BMI) .... 79
Get Together (S.F.O., BMI) .... 13
Going in Circles (Porpete, BMI) .... 42
Good Clean Fun (Screen Gems-Columbia, BMI) .... 99
Goodbye Columbus (Ensign Music, BMI) .... 94
Green River (Jondora, BMI) .... 2

Here I Go Again (Jobete, BMI) .... 43
Honky Tonk Women (Gideon, BMI) .... 3
Hook and Sling (Part 1) (Uzza, BMI) .... 78
Hot Fun in the Summertime (Stone Flower, BMI) .. 9
Hurt So Bad (Vogue, BMI) .... 14

I Can't Get Next to You (Jobete, BMI) .... 6
I Could Never Be President (East/Memphis, BMI) .. 58
I Want You to Know (New Colony, BMI) .... 65
I'd Wait a Million Years (Teenie Bopper, ASCAP) ... 25
I'll Never Fall in Love Again (TRO-Hollis, BMI) .... 8
I'm a Better Man (Blue Seas/Jac, ASCAP) .... 38
I'm Gonna Make You Mine (Pocketful of Tunes, BMI) .... 26
In a Moment (Odeom & Neiburg, BMI) .... 41
Is That All There Is (Trio, BMI) .... 76
It's Getting Better (Screen Gems-Columbia, BMI) .. 40

Jack and Jill (Low-Twi, BMI) .... 64
Jealous Kind of Fellow (Colfam, BMI) .... 60
Jean (Twentieth Century, ASCAP) .... 7
Jesus Is a Soul Man (Wilderness, BMI) .... 70
Julia (Maclen, BMI) .... 97

Keem-O-Sabe (Binn/Elaine/United Artists, ASCAP).. 16
Kool and the Gang (Stephayne, BMI) .... 8T

Lay Lady Lay (Big Sky, ASCAP) .... 20
Let a Woman Be a Woman, Let a Man Be a Man (Drive-In/Westward, BMI) .... 66
Life and Death in G & A (Daly City, BMI) .... 74
Little Woman (Green Apple, BMI) .... 5
Lodi (Jondora, BMI) .... 68
Love of the Common People (Tree, BMI) .... 59
Love's Been Good to Me (Almo, ASCAP) .... 75
Lowdown Popcorn (Golo, BMI) .... 47

Mah-Na-Mah-Na (E. B. Marks, BMI) .... 56
Make Believe (Love/Peanut Butter, BMI) .... 54
Mind, Body & Soul (Gold Forever, BMI) .... 92
Moonlight Sonata (Southdale, ASCAP) .... 87
Move Over (Trousdale, BMI) .... 31
Muddy Mississippi Line (Detail, BMI) .... 53
My Balloon's Going Up (Assorted, BMI) .... 88

Nitty Gritty (Gallico, BMI) .... 35
Nobody But You Babe (Sherlyn, BMI) .... 46
No One for Me to Turn To (Spiral, BMI) .... 52

Oh What a Night (Conrad, BMI) .... 10

Put a Little Love in Your Heart (Unart, BMI) .... 24

Ruben James (Unart, BMI) .... 100
Runnin' Blue (Nippers/Doors, ASCAP) .... 71

Sad Girl (IPC, BMI) .... 61
San Francisco Is a Lonely Town (Singleton, BMI) .. 84
Share Your Love With Me (Don, BMI) .... 29
Since I Met You Baby (Marson, BMI) .... 90
Slum Baby (East/Memphis, BMI) .... 89
So Good Together (Unart/Joachim, BMI) .... 82
Something in the Air (Track, BMI) .... 62
Son of a Lovin' Man (Blendingwell, ASCAP) .... 80
Soul Deep (Barton, BMI) .... 28
Sugar on Sunday (Big Seven, BMI) .... 33
Sugar, Sugar (Kirshner, BMI) .... 1
Suspicious Minds (Press, BMI) .... 19
Sweet Caroline (Good Times Never Seemed So Good) (Stonebridge, BMI) .... 27

That's the Way Love Is (Jobete, BMI) .... 15
This Girl Is a Woman Now (Three Bridges, ASCAP).. 12
Time Machine (Storybook, BMI) .... 91
Tracy (Vanlee/Emily, ASCAP) .... 49
Train (Kaskat, BMI) .... 69

Walk On By (Jac/Seas, ASCAP) .... 63
Was It Good to You (Triple 3, BMI) .... 93
We Gotta All Get Together (Equinox, BMI) .... 51
Wedding Bell Blues (Tuna Fish, BMI) .... 67
Weight, The (Dwarf, ASCAP) .... 48
We'll Cry Together (McCoy/Chevis, BMI) .... 96
What Kind of Fool Do You Think I Am (Whitley/Low Twi, BMI) .... 23
What's the Use of Breaking Up (Assorted/Parabut, BMI) .... 22
When I Die (Mode, BMI) .... 21
World, Part 1 (Golo, BMI) .... 37

You Got Yours and I'll Get Mine (Nickel Shoe, BMI) 45
You, I (Singleton, BMI) .... 30
Your Good Thing (Is About to End) (East, BMI) .... 18
You've Lost That Lovin' Feeling (Screen Gems-Columbia, BMI) .... 57


## BUBBLING UNDER THE HOT 100

101. THE BEST PART OF A LOVE AFFAIR ....Emotions, Volt 4021
102. SMILE A LITTLE SMILE FOR ME ....Flying Machine, Congress 6000
103. TAKING MY LOVE ....Martha Reeves & the Vandellas, Gordy 7094
104. GROOVY GRUBWORM ....Harlow Wilcox, Plantation 28
105. JUDY BLUE EYES ....Crosby/Stills/Nash, Atlantic 2676
106. DELTA LADY ....Joe Cocker, A&M 1112
107. COLOR OF MY LOVE ....Jefferson, Decca 32501
108. CHERRY HILL PARK ....Billy Joe Royal, Columbia 4-44902
109. MOMMY AND DADDY ....Monkees, Colgems 66-5005
110. EVIL WOMAN ....Crow, Amaret 45112
111. HARLAN COUNTY ....Jim Ford, Sundown 115
112. DON'T WASTE MY TIME ....John Mayall, Polydor 14004
113. I'LL BET YOU ....Funkadelic, Westbound 150
114. WE CAN MAKE IT ....Ray Charles, Tangerine 11239
115. HELPLESS ....Jackie Wilson, Brunswick 55418
116. GIMME SOME MORE ....Crazy Elephant, Bell 817
117. ETERNITY ....Vikki Carr, Liberty 56132
118. DARK EYED WOMAN ....Spirit, Ode 122
119. SEPTEMBER SONG ....Roy Clark, Dot 17299
120. THESE ARE THE THINGS THAT MAKE ME KNOW YOU'RE GONE ....Howard Tate, Turntable 505
121. CAN YOU DANCE TO IT ...Cat Mother & All Night Newsboys, Polydor 2-14007
122. 12th OF NEVER ....Chi-Lites, Brunswick 7-78030
123. I STILL BELIEVE IN TOMORROW ....John & Ann Ryder, Decca 73256
124. NEVER IN PUBLIC ....Candy Staton.., Fame 1459
125. HEIGHTY HI ....Lee Michaels, A&M 1095.

Compiled from national retail sales and radio station airplay by the Music Popularity Dept. of Record Market Research, Billboard.

# Billboard HOT 100
### FOR WEEK ENDING OCTOBER 4, 1969

♪ Artist and/or Selection featured on "The Music Scene," ABC-TV Network

★ STAR PERFORMER—Sides registering greatest proportionate sales progress this week.   ● Record Industry Association of America seal of certification as million selling single.

| This Week | 2 Wks. Ago | 3 Wks. Ago | TITLE  Artist (Producer), Label & Number | Weeks On Chart |
|---|---|---|---|---|
| ♪ 1 | 1 | 2 | SUGAR, SUGAR — Archies (Jeff Barry), Calendar 63-1008 | 11 |
| ♪ 2 | 7 | 8 | JEAN — Oliver (Bob Crewe), Crewe 334 | 8 |
| 3 | 5 | 9 | LITTLE WOMAN — Bobby Sherman (Jackie Mills), Metromedia 121 | 7 |
| ♪ 4 | 4 | 5 | EASY TO BE HARD — Three Dog Night (Gabriel Mekler), Dunhill 4203 | 9 |
| 5 | 6 | 10 | I CAN'T GET NEXT TO YOU — Temptations (Norman Whitfield), Gordy 7093 | 8 |
| 6 | 3 | 1 | HONKY TONK WOMEN — Rolling Stones (Jimmy Miller), London 910 | 12 |
| 7 | 2 | 3 | GREEN RIVER — Creedence Clearwater Revival (J. C. Fogerty), Fantasy 625 | 10 |
| ♪ 8 | 17 | 18 | EVERYBODY'S TALKIN' — Nilsson (Rick Jarrard), RCA 74-0161 | 8 |
| 9 | 9 | 21 | HOT FUN IN THE SUMMERTIME — Sly & the Family Stone (Sly Stone), Epic 5-10497 | 8 |
| 10 | 10 | 11 | OH, WHAT A NIGHT — Dells (Bobby Miller), Cadet 5649 | 8 |
| ♪ 11 | 12 | 14 | THIS GIRL IS A WOMAN NOW — Gary Puckett & the Union Gap (Dick Glasser), Columbia 4-44967 | 7 |
| ♪ 12 | 8 | 6 | I'LL NEVER FALL IN LOVE AGAIN — Tom Jones (Peter Sullivan), Parrot 40018 | 11 |
| 13 | 13 | 7 | GET TOGETHER — Youngbloods (Felix Pappalardi), RCA 47-9752 | 15 |
| ★ 14 | 19 | 36 | SUSPICIOUS MINDS — Elvis Presley, RCA 47-9764 | 4 |
| 15 | 15 | 28 | THAT'S THE WAY LOVE IS — Marvin Gaye (Norman Whitfield), Tamla 54185 | 7 |
| 16 | 16 | 22 | KEEM-O-SABE — Electric Indian (Len Barry), United Artists 50563 | 10 |
| 17 | 11 | 4 | A BOY NAMED SUE — Johnny Cash (Bob Johnston), Columbia 4-44944 | 11 |
| 18 | 14 | 12 | HURT SO BAD — Lettermen (Al DeLory), Capitol 2482 | 19 |
| 19 | 21 | 24 | WHEN I DIE — Motherlode (Mort Ross & Doug Riley), Buddah 131 | 9 |
| 20 | 26 | 27 | I'M GONNA MAKE YOU MINE — Lou Christie (Stan Vincent & Mike Duckman), Buddah 116 | 7 |
| 21 | 20 | 16 | LAY LADY LAY — Bob Dylan (Bob Johnson), Columbia 44926 | 13 |
| 22 | 22 | 35 | WHAT'S THE USE OF BREAKING UP — Jerry Butler (Gamble-Huff), Mercury 72960 | 6 |
| ♪ 23 | 18 | 20 | YOUR GOOD THING (Is About to End) — Lou Rawls (David Axelrod), Capitol 2550 | 12 |
| 24 | 50 | 62 | BABY IT'S YOU — Smith (Joel Sill & Steve Barri), Dunhill 4206 | 5 |
| 25 | 33 | 37 | SUGAR ON SUNDAY — Clique (Gary Zekley), White Whale 323 | 6 |
| 26 | 25 | 15 | I'D WAIT A MILLION YEARS — Grassroots (Steve Barry), Dunhill 4198 | 14 |
| 27 | 32 | 42 | CARRY ME BACK — Rascals (Rascals with Arif Mardin), Atlantic 2664 | 7 |
| 28 | 30 | 46 | YOU, I — Rugbys (Steve McNicol), Amazon 1 | 7 |
| 29 | 49 | 68 | TRACY — Cuff Links (Paul Vance-Lee Pockriss), Decca 32533 | 4 |
| 30 | 23 | 23 | WHAT KIND OF FOOL DO YOU THINK I AM — Bill Deal & the Rhondells (Jerry Ross), Heritage 817 | 8 |
| 31 | 29 | 13 | SHARE YOUR LOVE WITH ME — Aretha Franklin (Jerry Wexler-Tom Dowd-Arif Mardin), Atlantic 2650 | 9 |
| 32 | 28 | 25 | SOUL DEEP — Box Tops (Tommy Cogbill & Chips Moman), Mala 12040 | 14 |
| ★ 33 | 41 | 47 | IN A MOMENT — Intrigues (Martin & Bell), Yew 1001 | 10 |
| 34 | 31 | 31 | MOVE OVER — Steppenwolf (Gabriel Mekler), Dunhill 4205 | 8 |
| 35 | 67 | — | WEDDING BELL BLUES — 5th Dimension (Bones Howe), Soul City 779 | 2 |
| 36 | 54 | 70 | MAKE BELIEVE — Wind (Bo Gentry), Life 200 | 5 |
| ♪ 37 | 37 | 58 | WORLD, Part 1 — James Brown (James Brown), King 6258 | 4 |
| 38 | 43 | 50 | HERE I GO AGAIN — Smokey Robinson & the Miracles (W. Moore & T. Johnson), Tamla 54183 | 7 |
| 39 | 39 | 43 | BY THE TIME I GET TO PHOENIX — Isaac Hayes (Al Bell, Marvell Thomas, Allen Jones), Enterprise 9003 | 6 |
| 40 | 45 | 51 | YOU GOT YOURS AND I'LL GET MINE — Delfonics (Stan & Bell Prod.), Philly Groove 157 | 8 |
| 41 | 42 | 48 | GOING IN CIRCLES — Friends of Distinction (John Florez), RCA 74-0204 | 8 |
| 42 | 34 | 34 | DADDY'S LITTLE MAN — O. C. Smith (Jerry Fuller), Columbia 4-44948 | 6 |
| 43 | 40 | 42 | IT'S GETTING BETTER — Mama Cass (Steve Barri), Dunhill 4195 | 18 |
| 44 | 44 | 56 | DON'T IT MAKE YOU WANT TO GO HOME — Joe South & the Believers (Joe South), Capitol 2592 | 7 |
| ★ 45 | 70 | 94 | JESUS IS A SOUL MAN — Lawrence Reynolds (Don Davis), Warner Bros.-Seven Arts 7322 | 3 |
| 46 | 48 | 65 | THE WEIGHT — Diana Ross & the Supremes & the Temptations (Frank Wilson), Motown 1153 | 4 |
| 47 | 46 | 40 | NOBODY BUT YOU BABE — Clarence Reid (Brad Shapiro & Steve Alaimo), Alston 4574 | 10 |
| 48 | 60 | 72 | JEALOUS KIND OF FELLOW — Garland Greene (Giant Enterprises Prod.), UNI 55143 | 4 |
| 49 | 63 | 83 | WALK ON BY — Isaac Hayes (Al Bell-Marvell Thomas-Allen Jones), Enterprise 9003 | 6 |
| 50 | 76 | — | IS THAT ALL THERE IS — Peggy Lee (Lieber/Stoller), Capitol 2602 | 2 |
| 51 | 51 | 57 | WE GOTTA ALL GET TOGETHER — Paul Revere & the Raiders (Mark Lindsay), Columbia 44970 | 5 |
| 52 | 55 | 60 | AND THAT REMINDS ME (My Heart Reminds Me) — Four Seasons (Crewe-Gaudio), Crewe 333 | 4 |
| 53 | 57 | 90 | YOU'VE LOST THAT LOVIN' FEELING — Dionne Warwick (Chips Moman & Dionne Warwick), Scepter 12262 | 3 |
| 54 | 38 | 45 | I'M A BETTER MAN — Engelbert Humperdinck (Peter Sullivan), Parrot 40040 | 7 |
| 55 | 56 | 63 | MAH-NA-MAH-NA — "Sweden Heaven and Hell" Soundtrack, Ariel 500 | 6 |
| 56 | 62 | 75 | SOMETHING IN THE AIR — Thunderclap Newman (Peter Townshend), Track 2656 | 5 |
| 57 | 59 | 61 | LOVE OF THE COMMON PEOPLE — The Winstons (Don Carroll), Metromedia 142 | 3 |
| 58 | 64 | 71 | JACK AND JILL — Tommy Roe (Steve Barri), ABC 11229 | 10 |
| 59 | 61 | 59 | SAD GIRL — Intruders (Gamble-Huff), Gamble 235 | 6 |
| 60 | 52 | 52 | NO ONE FOR ME TO TURN TO — Spiral Starecase (Sonny Knight), Columbia 4-44924 | 6 |
| 61 | 80 | 81 | SON OF A LOVIN' MAN — Buchanan Brothers (Cashman, Pistilli & West), Event 3305 | 3 |
| 62 | 72 | 80 | ANY WAY THAT YOU WANT ME — Evie Sands (Chip Taylor-Al Gorgoni), A&M 1090 | 3 |
| 63 | 53 | 53 | MUDDY MISSISSIPPI LINE — Bobby Goldsboro (Bob Montgomery & Bobby Goldsboro), United Artists 50565 | 8 |
| 64 | 71 | 76 | RUNNIN' BLUE — Doors (Paul A. Rothchild), Elektra 45675 | 5 |
| ★ 65 | 66 | 89 | LET A WOMAN BE A WOMAN LET A MAN BE A MAN — Dyke and the Blazers (Labou/Barrette), Original Sound 89 | 3 |
| 66 | — | — | SMILE A LITTLE SMILE FOR ME — The Flying Machine (Tony MacAuley), Congress 6000 | 1 |
| 67 | 82 | — | SO GOOD TOGETHER — Andy Kim (Jeff Barry), Steed 720 | 2 |
| 68 | 65 | 73 | I WANT YOU TO KNOW — New Colony Six (Sentar Record Prod.), Mercury 72961 | 6 |
| 69 | 69 | 64 | TRAIN — 1910 Fruitgum Co. (Kasenetz-Katz Assoc.), Buddah 130 | 6 |
| 70 | — | — | YOU'LL NEVER WALK ALONE — Brooklyn Bridge (Wes Farrell), Buddah 139 | 1 |
| 71 | 81 | 86 | CHAINS OF LOVE — Bobby Bland (Andre Williams), Duke 449 | 4 |
| 72 | 77 | — | DOIN' OUR THING — Clarence Carter (Rick Hall), Atlantic 2660 | 2 |
| 73 | 73 | 92 | DON'T FORGET TO REMEMBER — Bee Gees (Robert Stigwood & the Brothers Gibb), Atco 6702 | 3 |
| 74 | 74 | 87 | LIFE AND DEATH IN G & A — Abaco Dream (Ted Cooper), A&M 1081 | 5 |
| 75 | 75 | 85 | LOVE'S BEEN GOOD TO ME — Frank Sinatra (Sonny Burke), Reprise 0852 | 4 |
| 76 | 90 | 97 | SINCE I MET YOU BABY — Sonny James (Kelso Herston), Capitol 2595 | 3 |
| 77 | 79 | 82 | GET OFF MY BACK WOMAN — B. B. King (Bill Szymczyk), Bluesway 61026 | 6 |
| 78 | 85 | — | ECHO PARK — Keith Barbour (Austin & Flemming), Epic 5-10486 | 2 |
| 79 | 86 | — | BABY, I'M FOR REAL — Originals (Richard Morris), Soul 35066 | 2 |
| 80 | 83 | 84 | CAN'T FIND THE TIME — Orpheus (Alan Lorber), MGM 13882 | 7 |
| 81 | 68 | 67 | LODI — Al Wilson (Johnny Rivers), Soul City 775 | 7 |
| 82 | — | — | BALL OF FIRE — Tommy James & the Shondells (Tommy James), Roulette 7060 | 1 |
| 83 | 91 | — | TIME MACHINE — Grand Funk Railroad (Terry Knight), Capitol 2567 | 2 |
| 84 | 84 | — | SAN FRANCISCO IS A LONELY TOWN — Joe Simon (John R.), Sound Stage 7 2641 | 2 |
| 85 | 92 | — | MIND, BODY & SOUL — Flaming Embers (R. Dunbar), Hot Wax 6902 | 2 |
| 86 | — | — | JUDY BLUE EYES — Crosby/Stills/Nash (Stephen Stills, David Crosby & Graham Nash), Atlantic 2676 | 1 |
| 87 | 88 | 93 | MY BALLOON'S GOING UP — Archie Bell & the Drells (Gamble-Huff), Atlantic 2663 | 4 |
| 88 | 89 | — | SLUM BABY — Booker T. & the M.G.'s (Booker T. & the M.G.'s), Stax 0049 | 4 |
| 89 | 100 | — | RUBEN JAMES — Kenny Rogers & First Edition (Mike Post), Reprise 0854 | 2 |
| 90 | — | — | THE WAYS TO LOVE A MAN — Tammy Wynette (Billy Sherrill), Epic 5010512 | 3 |
| 91 | 94 | 95 | GOODBYE COLUMBUS — Association (John Boylan), Warner Bros.-Seven Bros. 7267 | 7 |
| 92 | 93 | — | WAS IT GOOD TO YOU — Isley Brothers (R. O. & R. Isley), T-Neck 908 | 2 |
| 93 | 95 | 96 | KOOL AND THE GANG — Kool and the Gang (Redd Coach Prod.), De-Lite 519 | 4 |
| 94 | — | — | I'LL BET YOU — Funkadelic (Clinton/Baines/Lindsey), Westbound 130 | 1 |
| 95 | 96 | — | WE'LL CRY TOGETHER — Maxine Brown (Charles Koppelman), Commonwealth United 3001 | 2 |
| 96 | 97 | — | JULIA — Ramsey Lewis (C. Stepney), Cadet 5640 | 2 |
| 97 | 99 | 100 | GOOD CLEAN FUN — The Monkees (Michael Nesmith), Colgems 66-5005 | 3 |
| 98 | — | — | DELTA LADY — Joe Cocker (Denny Cordell), A&M 1112 | 1 |
| 99 | — | — | CHERRY HILL PARK — Billy Joe Royal (Buddy Buie), Columbia 4-44902 | 1 |
| 100 | — | — | ETERNITY — Vikki Carr (Bob Crewe), Liberty 56132 | 1 |

## BUBBLING UNDER THE HOT 100

101. WE CAN MAKE IT ............ Ray Charles, Tangerine 11239
102. TAKING MY LOVE ...... Martha Reeves & the Vandellas, Gordy 7094
103. SEPTEMBER SONG ........ Roy Clark, Dot 17299
104. GROOVY GRUBWORM ...... Harlow Wilcox, Plantation 28
105. COLOUR OF MY LOVE ........ Jefferson, Decca 32501
106. HEIGHTY HI ............ Lee Michaels, A&M 1095
107. BEST PART OF A LOVE AFFAIR ...... Emotions, Volt 4021
108. HELPLESS ............ Jackie Wilson, Brunswick 55418
109. GREEN ONIONS ............ Dick Hyman, Command 4129
110. EVIL WOMAN ............ Crow, Amaret 112
111. THINGS GO BETTER WITH LOVE ...... Jeannie C. Riley, Plantation 29
112. DON'T WASTE MY TIME ............ Hardy Boys, RCA 0228
113. IN THE LAND OF MAKE BELIEVE ...... Dusty Springfield, Atlantic 2673
114. ALL GOD'S CHILDREN GOT SOUL ...... Dorothy Morrison, Elektra 45671
115. CAN YOU DANCE TO IT ........ Cat Mother & the All Night Newsboys, Polydor 14007
116. GET RHYTHM ............ Johnny Cash, Sun 1103
117. I STILL BELIEVE IN TOMORROW ...... John & Ann Ryder, Decca 732256
118. NA NA HEY HEY KISS HIM GOODBYE ...... Steam, Fontana 1667
119. LOVE IN THE CITY ............ Turtles, White Whale 326
120. HOLD ME ............ Baskerville Hounds, Avco-Embassy 4504
121. HARLAM COUNTY ............ Jim Ford, Sundown 115
122. DARK EYED WOMAN ............ Spirit, Ode 122
123. THESE ARE THE THINGS THAT MAKE ME KNOW YOU'RE GONE ...... Howard Tate, Turntable 505
124. LOVE AND LET LOVE ...... Hardy Boys, Turntable 505
125. SIGN ON FOR THE GOOD TIMES ...... Marilee Rush, Diamond 265
126. ALWAYS DAVID ............ Ruby Winters, Diamond 265
127. WHITE BIRD ............ It's a Beautiful Day, Columbia 44928
128. SUNDAY MORNING COMING DOWN ...... Ray Stevens, Monument 1163
129. SILVER THREADS & GOLDEN NEEDLES ...... Cowsills, MGM 14084
130. CUPID ............ Johnny Nash, Jad 220
131. IT AIN'T SANITARY ............ Joe, Dot 4094
132. FEELIN' BAD ............ Spooky Tooth, A&M 1110
133. GET READY ............ Ella Fitzgerald, Reprise 0850
134. CURLY ............ Jimmy Clanton, Laurie 3508

Compiled from national retail sales and radio station airplay by the Music Popularity Dept. of Record Market Research, Billboard.

# Billboard HOT 100

FOR WEEK ENDING OCTOBER 11, 1969

♫ Artist and/or Selection featured on "The Music Scene" this week, ABC-TV Network. Those in black were featured on past programs.

★ STAR PERFORMER—Sides registering greatest proportionate sales progress this week. ◉ Record Industry Association of America seal of certification as million selling single.

| | This Week | 1 Wk. Ago | 2 Wks. Ago | 3 Wks. Ago | TITLE — Artist (Producer), Label & Number | Weeks On Chart |
|---|---|---|---|---|---|---|
| ♫ | 1 | 1 | 1 | 1 | SUGAR, SUGAR — Archies (Jeff Barry), Calendar 63-1008 | 12 ◉ |
| ♫ | 2 | 2 | 7 | 18 | JEAN — Oliver (Bob Crewe), Crewe 334 | 9 |
| ♫ | 3 | 3 | 5 | 9 | LITTLE WOMAN — Bobby Sherman (Jackie Mills), Metromedia 121 | 8 |
| | 4 | 5 | 6 | 10 | I CAN'T GET NEXT TO YOU — Temptations (Norman Whitfield), Gordy 7093 | 9 |
| ★ | 5 | 9 | 9 | 21 | HOT FUN IN THE SUMMERTIME — Sly & the Family Stone (Sly Stone), Epic 5-10497 | 9 |
| ♫ | 6 | 8 | 17 | 18 | EVERYBODY'S TALKIN' — Nilsson (Rick Jarrard), RCA 74-0161 | 9 |
| ♫ | 7 | 4 | 4 | 5 | EASY TO BE HARD — Three Dog Night (Gabriel Mekler), Dunhill 4203 | 10 |
| | 8 | 6 | 3 | 2 | HONKY TONK WOMEN — Rolling Stones (Jimmy Miller), London 910 | 13 ◉ |
| ♫ | 9 | 11 | 12 | 14 | THIS GIRL IS A WOMAN NOW — Gary Puckett & the Union Gap (Dick Glasser), Columbia 4-44967 | 8 |
| | 10 | 7 | 2 | 3 | GREEN RIVER — Creedence Clearwater Revival (J. C. Fogerty), Fantasy 625 | 11 |
| | 11 | 14 | 19 | 36 | SUSPICIOUS MINDS — Elvis Presley, RCA 47-9764 | 5 |
| | 12 | 15 | 15 | 28 | THAT'S THE WAY LOVE IS — Marvin Gaye (Norman Whitfield), Tamla 54185 | 8 |
| ★ | 13 | 20 | 26 | 27 | I'M GONNA MAKE YOU MINE — Lou Christie (Stan Vincent & Mike Duckman), Buddah 116 | 8 |
| ♫ | 14 | 10 | 10 | 11 | OH, WHAT A NIGHT — Dells (Bobby Miller), Cadet 5649 | 9 |
| ★ | 15 | 24 | 50 | 62 | BABY IT'S YOU — Smith (Joel Sill & Steve Barri), Dunhill 4206 | 6 |
| | 16 | 13 | 13 | 7 | GET TOGETHER — Youngbloods (Felix Pappalardi), RCA 47-9752 | 16 |
| ♫ | 17 | 12 | 8 | 6 | I'LL NEVER FALL IN LOVE AGAIN — Tom Jones (Peter Sullivan), Parrot 40018 | 12 |
| | 18 | 19 | 21 | 24 | WHEN I DIE — Motherlode (Mort Ross & Doug Riley), Buddah 131 | 10 |
| ★ | 19 | 29 | 49 | 68 | TRACY — Cuff Links (Paul Vance-Lee Pockriss), Decca 32533 | 5 |
| | 20 | 22 | 22 | 35 | WHAT'S THE USE OF BREAKING UP — Jerry Butler (Gamble-Huff), Mercury 72960 | 7 |
| | 21 | 18 | 14 | 12 | HURT SO BAD — Lettermen (Al DeLory), Capitol 2482 | 20 |
| | 22 | 17 | 11 | 4 | A BOY NAMED SUE — Johnny Cash (Bob Johnston), Columbia 4-44944 | 12 ◉ |
| | 23 | 16 | 16 | 22 | KEEM-O-SABE — Electric Indian (Len Barry), United Artists 50563 | 11 |
| | 24 | 25 | 33 | 37 | SUGAR ON SUNDAY — Clique (Gary Zekley), White Whale 323 | 7 |
| ★ | 25 | 35 | 67 | — | WEDDING BELL BLUES — 5th Dimension (Bones Howe), Soul City 779 | 3 |
| ♫ | 26 | 27 | 32 | 32 | CARRY ME BACK — Rascals (Rascals with Arif Mardin), Atlantic 2664 | 6 |
| | 27 | 28 | 30 | 46 | YOU, I — Rugbys (Steve McNicol), Amazon 1 | 8 |
| | 28 | 21 | 20 | 16 | LAY LADY LAY — Bob Dylan (Bob Johnson), Columbia 44926 | 14 |
| | 29 | 26 | 25 | 15 | I'D WAIT A MILLION YEARS — Grassroots (Steve Barry), Dunhill 4198 | 15 |
| ♫ | 30 | 23 | 19 | 20 | YOUR GOOD THING (Is About to End) — Lou Rawls (David Axelrod), Capitol 2550 | 13 |
| | 31 | 33 | 41 | 47 | IN A MOMENT — Intrigues (Martin & Bell), Yew 1001 | 11 |
| ★ | 32 | 41 | 42 | 48 | GOING IN CIRCLES — Friends of Distinction (John Florez), RCA 74-0204 | 9 |
| ★ | 33 | 50 | 76 | — | IS THAT ALL THERE IS — Peggy Lee (Lieber/Stoller), Capitol 2602 | 3 |
| | 34 | 30 | 23 | 23 | WHAT KIND OF FOOL DO YOU THINK I AM — Bill Deal & the Rhondells (Jerry Ross), Heritage 817 | 9 |
| | 35 | 36 | 54 | 70 | MAKE BELIEVE — Wind (Bo Gentry), Life 200 | 6 |
| ★ | 36 | 53 | 57 | 90 | YOU'VE LOST THAT LOVIN' FEELING — Dionne Warwick (Chips Moman & Dionne Warwick), Scepter 12262 | 4 |
| ♫ | 37 | 38 | 43 | 50 | HERE I GO AGAIN — Smokey Robinson & the Miracles (W. Moore & T. Johnson), Tamla 54183 | 8 |
| | 38 | 39 | 39 | 43 | BY THE TIME I GET TO PHOENIX — Isaac Hayes (Al Bell, Marvell Thomas, Allen Jones), Enterprise 9003 | 7 |
| ★ | 39 | 45 | 70 | 94 | JESUS IS A SOUL MAN — Lawrence Reynolds (Don Davis), Warner Bros.-Seven Arts 7322 | 4 |
| | 40 | 40 | 45 | 51 | YOU GOT YOURS AND I'LL GET MINE — Delfonics (Stan & Bell Prod.), Philly Groove 157 | 9 |
| | 41 | 44 | 44 | 56 | DON'T IT MAKE YOU WANT TO GO HOME — Joe South & the Believers (Joe South), Capitol 2592 | 8 |
| | 42 | 42 | 34 | 34 | DADDY'S LITTLE MAN — O. C. Smith (Jerry Fuller), Columbia 4-44948 | 7 |
| | 43 | 34 | 31 | 31 | MOVE OVER — Steppenwolf (Gabriel Mekler), Dunhill 4205 | 9 |
| ♫ | 44 | 37 | 37 | 58 | WORLD, Part 1 — James Brown (James Brown), King 6258 | 5 |
| | 45 | 43 | 40 | 42 | IT'S GETTING BETTER — Mama Cass (Steve Barri), Dunhill 4195 | 19 |
| | 46 | 48 | 60 | 72 | JEALOUS KIND OF FELLOW — Garland Greene (Giant Enterprises Prod.), UNI 55143 | 5 |
| ★ | 47 | 59 | 61 | 59 | SAD GIRL — Intruders (Gamble-Huff), Gamble 235 | 7 |
| | 48 | 49 | 63 | 83 | WALK ON BY — Isaac Hayes (Al Bell-Marvell Thomas-Allen Jones), Enterprise 9003 | 7 |
| | 49 | 52 | 55 | 60 | AND THAT REMINDS ME (My Heart Reminds Me) — Four Seasons (Crewe-Gaudio), Crewe 333 | 5 |
| | 50 | 51 | 51 | 57 | WE GOTTA ALL GET TOGETHER — Paul Revere & the Raiders (Mark Lindsay), Columbia 44970 | 6 |
| | 51 | 56 | 62 | 75 | SOMETHING IN THE AIR — Thunderclap Newman (Peter Townshend), Track 2656 | 6 |
| ★ | 52 | 82 | — | — | BALL OF FIRE — Tommy James & the Shondells (Tommy James), Roulette 7060 | 2 |
| ★ | 53 | 66 | — | — | SMILE A LITTLE SMILE FOR ME — The Flying Machine (Tony MacAuley), Congress 6000 | 2 |
| | 54 | 58 | 64 | 71 | JACK AND JILL — Tommy Roe (Steve Barri), ABC 11229 | 11 |
| | 55 | 57 | 59 | 61 | LOVE OF THE COMMON PEOPLE — The Winstons (Don Carroll), Metromedia 142 | 4 |
| ★ | 56 | 67 | 82 | — | SO GOOD TOGETHER — Andy Kim (Jeff Barry), Steed 720 | 3 |
| ★ | 57 | 69 | 69 | 64 | TRAIN — 1910 Fruitgum Co. (Kasenetz-Katz Assoc.), Buddah 130 | 7 |
| ★ | 58 | 78 | 85 | — | ECHO PARK — Keith Barbour (Austin & Flemming), Epic 5-10486 | 3 |
| ★ | 59 | 70 | — | — | YOU'LL NEVER WALK ALONE — Brooklyn Bridge (Wes Farrell), Buddah 139 | 2 |
| | 60 | 55 | 56 | 63 | MAH-NA-MAH-NA — "Sweden Heaven and Hell" Soundtrack, Ariel 500 | 6 |
| | 61 | 61 | 80 | 81 | SON OF A LOVIN' MAN — Buchanan Brothers (Cashman, Pistilli & West), Event 3305 | 4 |
| | 62 | 62 | 72 | 80 | ANY WAY THAT YOU WANT ME — Evie Sands (Chip Taylor-Al Gorgoni), A&M 1090 | 9 |
| | 63 | 63 | 53 | 53 | MUDDY MISSISSIPPI LINE — Bobby Goldsboro (Bob Montgomery & Bobby Goldsboro), United Artists 50565 | 9 |
| | 64 | 65 | 66 | 89 | LET A WOMAN BE A WOMAN LET A MAN BE A MAN — Dyke and the Blazers (Laboe/Barrette), Original Sound 89 | 4 |
| | 65 | 60 | 52 | 52 | NO ONE FOR ME TO TURN TO — Spiral Starecase (Sonny Knight), Columbia 4-44924 | 7 |
| ★ | 66 | 89 | 100 | — | RUBEN JAMES — Kenny Rogers & First Edition (Mike Post), Reprise 0854 | 3 |
| ★ | 67 | 79 | 86 | — | BABY, I'M FOR REAL — Originals (Richard Morris), Soul 35066 | 3 |
| | 68 | 72 | 77 | — | DOIN' OUR THING — Clarence Carter (Rick Hall), Atlantic 2660 | 3 |
| | 69 | 71 | 81 | 86 | CHAINS OF LOVE — Bobby Bland (Andre Williams), Duke 449 | 5 |
| | 70 | 46 | 48 | 65 | THE WEIGHT — Diana Ross & the Supremes & the Temptations (Frank Wilson), Motown 1153 | 5 |
| | 71 | 76 | 90 | 97 | SINCE I MET YOU BABY — Sonny James (Kelso Herston), Capitol 2595 | 4 |
| ♫ ★ | 72 | 86 | — | — | SUITE: JUDY BLUE EYES — Crosby/Stills/Nash (Stephen Stills, David Crosby & Graham Nash), Atlantic 2676 | 2 |
| ★ | 73 | 83 | 91 | — | TIME MACHINE — Grand Funk Railroad (Terry Knight), Capitol 2567 | 3 |
| | 74 | 77 | 79 | 82 | GET OFF MY BACK WOMAN — B. B. King (Bill Szymczyk), Bluesway 61026 | 7 |
| | 75 | 64 | 71 | 76 | RUNNIN' BLUE — Doors (Paul A. Rothchild), Elektra 45675 | 6 |
| | 76 | 74 | 74 | 87 | LIFE AND DEATH IN G & A — Abaco Dream (Ted Cooper), A&M 1081 | 6 |
| ★ | 77 | — | — | — | GROOVY GRUBWORM — Barlow Wilcox (Shelby Singleton), Plantation 28 | 1 |
| ♫ ★ | 78 | — | — | — | LET A MAN COME IN AND DO THE POPCORN (PART 1) — James Brown (James Brown), King 6255 | 1 |
| | 79 | 84 | 84 | — | SAN FRANCISCO IS A LONELY TOWN — Joe Simon (John R.), Sound Stage 7 2641 | 3 |
| | 80 | 85 | 92 | — | MIND, BODY & SOUL — Flaming Embers (R. Dunbar), Hot Wax 6902 | 3 |
| | 81 | 90 | — | — | THE WAYS TO LOVE A MAN — Tammy Wynette (Billy Sherrill), Epic 5010512 | 4 |
| ★ | 82 | — | — | — | THE SWEETER HE IS — Soul Children (Hayes/Porter), Stax ???? | 1 |
| ★ | 83 | 99 | — | — | CHERRY HILL PARK — Billy Joe Royal (Buddy Buie), Columbia 4-44902 | 2 |
| | 84 | 93 | 95 | 96 | KOOL AND THE GANG — Kool and the Gang (Redd Coach Prod.), De-Lite 519 | 5 |
| | 85 | 94 | — | — | I'LL BET YOU — Funkadelic (Clinton/Baines/Lindsey), Westbound 130 | 2 |
| ★ | 86 | — | — | — | SILVER THREADS AND GOLDEN NEEDLES — Cowsills (Bob Waschtel), MGM 14084 | 1 |
| ★ | 87 | — | — | — | COLOR OF MY LOVE — Jefferson (John Schroeder), Decca 32501 | 4 |
| ★ | 88 | — | — | — | HOLD ME — Baskerville Hounds (James M. Testa), Avco Embassy 1054 | 1 |
| ★ | 89 | — | — | — | TRY A LITTLE KINDNESS — Glen Campbell (Al De Lory), Capitol 2659 | 1 |
| ★ | 90 | — | — | — | DON'T WASTE MY TIME — John Mayall (John Mayall), Polydor 14004 | 1 |
| | 91 | 97 | 99 | 100 | GOOD CLEAN FUN — The Monkees (Michael Nesmith), Colgems 66-5005 | 4 |
| | 92 | 92 | 93 | — | WAS IT GOOD TO YOU — Isley Brothers (R. O. & R. Isley), T-Neck 908 | 3 |
| | 93 | 95 | 96 | — | WE'LL CRY TOGETHER — Maxine Brown (Charles Koppelman), Commonwealth United 3001 | 3 |
| | 94 | 96 | 97 | — | JULIA — Ramsey Lewis (C. Stepney), Cadet 5640 | 3 |
| | 95 | — | — | — | ALL GOD'S CHILDREN GOT SOUL — Dorothy Morrison (Delaney Bramlett/Leon Russell) Elektra 45671 | 1 |
| | 96 | — | — | — | I CAN'T BE ALL BAD — Johnny Adams (Shelby S. Singleton Jr.), SSS International 780 | 1 |
| | 97 | 100 | — | — | ETERNITY — Vikki Carr (Bob Crewe), Liberty 56132 | 2 |
| | 98 | 98 | — | — | DELTA LADY — Joe Cocker (Denny Cordell), A&M 1112 | 2 |
| | 99 | — | — | — | LOVE IN THE CITY — Turtles (Ray Davis), White Whale 326 | 1 |
| | 100 | — | — | — | SHE BELONGS TO ME — Rick Nelson (Rick Nelson), Decca 732550 | 1 |

## HOT 100—A TO Z—(Publisher-Licensee)

All God's Children Got Soul (East/Memphis, BMI) .. 95
And That Reminds Me (My Heart Reminds Me) (Symphony House, ASCAP) .. 49
Any Way That You Want Me (Blackwood, BMI) .. 62

Baby, I'm For Real (Jobete, BMI) .. 67
Baby It's You (Dolfi-Mary Jane, ASCAP) .. 15
Ball of Fire (Big Seven, BMI) .. 52
Boy Named Sue, A (Evil Eye, BMI) .. 22
By the Time I Get to Phoenix (Johnny Rivers, BMI) 35

Carry Me Back (Slacsar, ASCAP) .. 26
Chains of Love (Progressive, BMI) .. 69
Cherry Hill Park (Low-Sal, BMI) .. 83
Color of My Love (Ann-Rachel, ASCAP) .. 87

Daddy's Little Man (BnB Music, ASCAP) .. 42
Delta Lady (Skyhill, BMI) .. 98
Doin' Our Thing (Fame, BMI) .. 68
Don't It Make You Want to Go Home (Lowery, BMI) .. 41
Don't Waste My Time (St. George, BMI) .. 90

Easy to Be Hard (United Artists, ASCAP) .. 7
Echo Park (Hastings, BMI) .. 58
Eternity (Saturday, BMI) .. 97
Everybody's Talkin' (Coconut Grove/Story, BMI) .. 6

Get Off My Back Woman (Sounds of Lucille-Pampco, BMI) .. 74
Get Together (S.F.O., BMI) .. 16
Going in Circles (Porpete, BMI) .. 32
Good Clean Fun (Screen Gems-Columbia, BMI) .. 91
Green River (Jondora, BMI) .. 10
Groovy Grubworm (Little River, BMI) .. 77

Here I Go Again (Jobete, BMI) .. 37
Hold Me (Robbins, ASCAP) .. 88
Honky Tonk Women (Gideon, BMI) .. 8
Hot Fun in the Summertime (Stone Flower, BMI) .. 5
Hurt So Bad (Vogue, BMI) .. 21

I Can't Be All Bad (Singleton, BMI) .. 96
I Can't Get Next to You (Jobete, BMI) .. 4
I'd Wait a Million Years (Teenie Bopper, ASCAP) .. 29
I'll Bet You (Jobete, BMI) .. 85
I'll Never Fall in Love Again (TRO-Hollis, BMI) .. 17
I'm Gonna Make You Mine (Pocketful of Tunes, BMI) .. 13
In a Moment (Odeom & Neiburg, BMI) .. 31
Is That All There Is (Trio, BMI) .. 33
It's Getting Better (Screen Gems-Columbia, BMI) .. 45

Jack and Jill (Low-Twi, BMI) .. 54
Jealous Kind of Fellow (Colfam, BMI) .. 46
Jean (Twentieth Century, ASCAP) .. 2
Jesus Is a Soul Man (Wilderness, BMI) .. 39
Judy Blue Eyes (Gold Hill, BMI) .. 72
Julia (Maclen, BMI) .. 94

Keem-O-Sabe (Binn/Elaine/United Artists, ASCAP) .. 23
Kool and the Gang (Stephayne, BMI) .. 84

Lay Lady Lay (Big Sky, ASCAP) .. 28
Let a Man Come in and Do the Popcorn (Part 1) • (Dynatone, BMI) .. 78
Let a Woman Be a Woman, Let a Man Be a Man (Drive-In/Westward, BMI) .. 64
Life and Death in G & A (Daly City, BMI) .. 76
Little Woman (Green Apple, BMI) .. 3
Love in the City (Ishmael Music/Blimp, BMI) .. 99
Love of the Common People (Tree, BMI) .. 55

Mah-Na-Mah-Na (E. B. Marks, BMI) .. 60
Make Believe (Love/Peanut Butter, BMI) .. 35
Mind, Body & Soul (Gold Forever, BMI) .. 80
Move Over (Trousdale, BMI) .. 43
Muddy Mississippi Line (Detail, BMI) .. 63

No One for Me to Turn To (Spiral, BMI) .. 65

Oh What a Night (Conrad, BMI) .. 14

Ruben James (Unart, BMI) .. 66

Runnin' Blue (Nippers/Doors, ASCAP) .. 75

Sad Girl (IPC, BMI) .. 47
San Francisco Is a Lonely Town (Singleton, BMI) .. 79
She Belongs to Me (Warner Bros.-Seven Arts, ASCAP) .. 100
Silver Threads and Golden Needles (Central Songs, BMI) .. 86
Since I Met You Baby (Marson, BMI) .. 71
Smile a Little Smile for Me (January, BMI) .. 53
So Good Together (Unart/Joachim, BMI) .. 56
Something in the Air (Track, BMI) .. 51
Son of a Lovin' Man (Blendingwell, ASCAP) .. 61
Sugar on Sunday (Big Seven, BMI) .. 24
Sugar, Sugar (Kirshner, BMI) .. 1
Suspicious Minds (Press, BMI) .. 11
Sweeter He Is, The (Birdees, ASCAP) .. 82

That's the Way Love Is (Jobete, BMI) .. 12
This Girl Is a Woman Now (Three Bridges, ASCAP) .. 9
Time Machine (Storybrook, BMI) .. 73
Tracy (Vanlee/Emily, ASCAP) .. 19
Train (Kaskat, BMI) .. 57
Try a Little Kindness (Airfield/Glen Campbell, ASCAP) .. 89

Walk On By (Jac/Seas, ASCAP) .. 48
Was It Good to You (Triple 3, BMI) .. 92
Ways to Love a Man, The (Gallico, BMI) .. 81
We Gotta All Get Together (Equinox, BMI) .. 50
Wedding Bell Blues (Tuna Fish, BMI) .. 25
Weight, The (Dwarf, ASCAP) .. 70
We'll Cry Together (McCoy/Chevis, BMI) .. 93
What Kind of Fool Do You Think I Am (Whitley/Low Twi, BMI) .. 34
What's the Use of Breaking Up (Assorted/Parabut, BMI) .. 20
When I Die (Mode, BMI) .. 18
World, Part 1 (Golo, BMI) .. 44

You Got Yours and I'll Get Mine (Nickel Shoe, BMI) 40
You, I (Singleton, BMI) .. 27
Your Good Thing (Is About to End) (East, BMI) .. 30
You'll Never Walk Alone (Williamson, ASCAP) .. 59
You've Lost That Lovin' Feeling (Screen Gems-Columbia, BMI) .. 36

## BUBBLING UNDER THE HOT 100

101. TAKE A LETTER MARIA .. R. B. Greaves, Atco 6714
102. I STILL BELIEVE IN TOMORROW .. John & Ann Ryder, Decca 73256
103. LOVE AND LET LOVE .. Hardy Boys, RCA 74-0228
104. PROUD MARY .. Sonny Charles with the Checkmates, Ltd., A&M 1127
105. DON'T SHUT ME OUT .. Underground Sunshine, Intrepid 75012
106. LIKE A ROLLING STONE .. Phil Flowers, A&M 1122
107. TURN ON A DREAM .. Box Tops, Mala 12042
108. DREAMIN' TILL THEN .. Joe Jeffrey Group, Wand 11207
109. SHANGRI-LA .. Lettermen, Capitol 2643
110. NA NA HEY HEY KISS HIM GOODBYE .. Steam, Fontana 1667
111. SHE'S GOT LOVE .. Thomas & Richard Frost, Imperial 66405
112. SEPTEMBER SONG .. Roy Clark, Dot 17299
113. COMMENT .. Charles Wright/Watts 103rd Street Rhythm Band, Warner Bros.-7 Arts 7338
114. TODAY I SING THE BLUES .. Aretha Franklin, Columbia 4-44951
115. OKIE FROM MUSKOGEE .. Merle Haggard & the Strangers, Capitol 2626
116. SAY YOU LOVE ME .. Impressions, Curtom 1946
117. IT AIN'T SANITARY .. Joe Tex, Dial 4094
118. MIDNIGHT COWBOY .. John Barry, Columbia 4-44891
119. I CAN'T HELP BUT DECEIVE YOU LITTLE GIRL .. Iron Butterfly, Atco 6712
120. CRUMBS OFF THE TABLE .. Glass House, Invictus 9071
121. JUST A LITTLE LOVE .. B. B. King, BluesWay 61029
122. CURLY .. Jimmy Clanton, Laurie 3508
123. ALWAYS DAVID .. Ruby Winters, Diamond 265
124. SUNDAY MORNING COMING DOWN .. Ray Stevens, Monument 1163
125. WHITE BIRD .. It's a Beautiful Day, Columbia 4-44928
126. GET READY .. Ella Fitzgerald, Reprise 0850
127. THINGS GO BETTER WITH LOVE .. Jeannie C. Riley, Plantation 29
128. HOW DOES IT FEEL .. Illusion, Steed 721
129. MAKE YOUR OWN KIND OF MUSIC .. Mama Cass, Dunhill 4214
130. GET RHYTHM .. Johnny Cash, Sun 1103
131. CUPID .. Johnny Nash, Jad 220
132. MR. TURNKEY .. Zager & Evans, RCA 74-0246
133. POOR MAN .. Little Milton, Checker 1221

Compiled from national retail sales and radio station airplay by the Music Popularity Dept. of Record Market Research, Billboard.

# Billboard HOT 100

FOR WEEK ENDING OCTOBER 18, 1969

♫ Artist and/or Selection featured on "The Music Scene" this week, ABC-TV Network. Those in black were featured on past programs.

★ STAR PERFORMER—Sides registering greatest proportionate sales progress this week. Record Industry Association of America seal of certification as million selling single.

| This Week | 1 Wk. Ago | 2 Wks. Ago | 3 Wks. Ago | TITLE Artist (Producer), Label & Number | Weeks On Chart |
|---|---|---|---|---|---|
| ★ 1 | 4 | 5 | 6 | I CAN'T GET NEXT TO YOU — Temptations (Norman Whitfield), Gordy 7093 | 10 |
| ★ 2 | 5 | 9 | 9 | HOT FUN IN THE SUMMER-TIME — Sly & the Family Stone (Sly Stone), Epic 5-10497 | 10 |
| ♫ 3 | 1 | 1 | 1 | SUGAR, SUGAR — Archies (Jeff Barry), Calendar 63-1008 | 13 |
| ♫ 4 | 2 | 2 | 7 | JEAN — Oliver (Bob Crewe), Crewe 334 | 10 |
| ♫ 5 | 3 | 3 | 5 | LITTLE WOMAN — Bobby Sherman (Jackie Mills), Metromedia 121 | 9 |
| ★ 6 | 11 | 14 | 19 | SUSPICIOUS MINDS — Elvis Presley, RCA 47-9764 | 6 |
| ★ 7 | 12 | 15 | 15 | THAT'S THE WAY LOVE IS — Marvin Gaye (Norman Whitfield), Tamla 54185 | 9 |
| ★ 8 | 25 | 35 | 67 | WEDDING BELL BLUES — 5th Dimension (Bones Howe), Soul City 779 | 4 |
| ♫ 9 | 7 | 4 | 4 | EASY TO BE HARD — Three Dog Night (Gabriel Mekler), Dunhill 4203 | 11 |
| ★ 10 | 19 | 29 | 49 | TRACY — Cuff Links (Paul Vance-Lee Pockriss), Decca 32533 | 6 |
| 11 | 13 | 20 | 26 | I'M GONNA MAKE YOU MINE — Lou Christie (Stan Vincent & Mike Duckman), Buddah 116 | 9 |
| ♫ 12 | 9 | 11 | 12 | THIS GIRL IS A WOMAN NOW — Gary Puckett & the Union Gap (Dick Glasser), Columbia 4-44967 | 9 |
| ♫ 13 | 15 | 24 | 50 | BABY IT'S YOU — Smith (Joel Sill & Steve Barri), Dunhill 4206 | 7 |
| 14 | 8 | 6 | 3 | HONKY TONK WOMEN — Rolling Stones (Jimmy Miller), London 910 | 14 |
| ♫ 15 | 6 | 8 | 17 | EVERYBODY'S TALKIN' — Nilsson (Rick Jarrard), RCA 74-0161 | 10 |
| ♫ 16 | 14 | 10 | 10 | OH, WHAT A NIGHT — Dells (Bobby Miller), Cadet 5649 | 10 |
| ★ 17 | 33 | 50 | 76 | IS THAT ALL THERE IS — Peggy Lee (Lieber/Stoller), Capitol 2602 | 4 |
| ♫ 18 | 17 | 12 | 8 | I'LL NEVER FALL IN LOVE AGAIN — Tom Jones (Peter Sullivan), Parrot 40018 | 13 |
| 19 | 10 | 7 | 2 | GREEN RIVER — Creedence Clearwater Revival (J. C. Fogerty), Fantasy 625 | 12 |
| ♫ ★ 20 | — | — | — | SOMETHING — Beatles (George Martin), Apple 2654 | 1 |
| ★ 21 | 46 | 48 | 60 | JEALOUS KIND OF FELLOW — Garland Greene (Giant Enterprises Prod.), UNI 55143 | 6 |
| 22 | 24 | 25 | 33 | SUGAR ON SUNDAY — Clique (Gary Zekley), White Whale 323 | 8 |
| ♫ ★ 23 | — | — | — | COME TOGETHER — Beatles (George Martin), Apple 2654 | 1 |
| ♫ 24 | 20 | 22 | 22 | WHAT'S THE USE OF BREAKING UP — Jerry Butler (Gamble-Huff), Mercury 72960 | 8 |
| 25 | 27 | 28 | 30 | YOU, I — Rugbys (Steve McNicol), Amazon 1 | 9 |
| 26 | 18 | 19 | 21 | WHEN I DIE — Motherlode (Mort Ross & Doug Riley), Buddah 131 | 11 |
| ★ 27 | 32 | 41 | 42 | GOING IN CIRCLES — Friends of Distinction (John Florez), RCA 74-0204 | 10 |
| 28 | 16 | 13 | 13 | GET TOGETHER — Youngbloods (Felix Pappalardi), RCA 47-9752 | 17 |
| 29 | 21 | 18 | 14 | HURT SO BAD — Lettermen (Al DeLory), Capitol 2482 | 21 |
| ★ 30 | 36 | 53 | 57 | YOU'VE LOST THAT LOVIN' FEELING — Dionne Warwick (Chips Moman & Dionne Warwick), Scepter 12262 | 5 |
| ♫ 31 | 30 | 23 | 19 | YOUR GOOD THING (Is About to End) — Lou Rawls (David Axelrod), Capitol 2550 | 14 |
| ★ 32 | 48 | 49 | 63 | WALK ON BY — Isaac Hayes (Al Bell-Marvell Thomas-Allen Jones), Enterprise 9003 | 8 |
| ★ 33 | 67 | 79 | 86 | BABY, I'M FOR REAL — Originals (Richard Morris), Soul 35066 | 4 |
| 34 | 31 | 33 | 41 | IN A MOMENT — Intrigues (Martin & Bell), Yew 1001 | 12 |
| 35 | 35 | 36 | 54 | MAKE BELIEVE — Wind (Bo Gentry), Life 200 | 7 |
| ★ 36 | 39 | 45 | 70 | JESUS IS A SOUL MAN — Lawrence Reynolds (Don Davis), Warner Bros.-Seven Arts 7322 | 5 |
| 37 | 38 | 39 | 39 | BY THE TIME I GET TO PHOENIX — Isaac Hayes (Al Bell, Marvell Thomas, Allen Jones), Enterprise 9003 | 8 |
| ★ 38 | 53 | 66 | — | SMILE A LITTLE SMILE FOR ME — The Flying Machine (Tony MacAuley), Congress 6000 | 3 |
| ♫ 39 | 37 | 38 | 43 | HERE I GO AGAIN — Smokey Robinson & the Miracles (W. Moore & T. Johnson), Tamla 54183 | 9 |
| ♫ 40 | 26 | 27 | 32 | CARRY ME BACK — Rascals (Rascals with Arif Mardin), Atlantic 2664 | 7 |
| 41 | 41 | 44 | 44 | DON'T IT MAKE YOU WANT TO GO HOME — Joe South & the Believers (Joe South), Capitol 2592 | 9 |
| ★ 42 | 52 | 82 | — | BALL OF FIRE — Tommy James & the Shondells (Tommy James), Roulette 7060 | 3 |
| ♫ 43 | 44 | 37 | 37 | WORLD, Part 1 — James Brown (James Brown), King 6258 | 6 |
| ★ 44 | 58 | 78 | 85 | ECHO PARK — Keith Barbour (Austin & Flemming), Epic 5-10486 | 4 |
| 45 | 49 | 52 | 55 | AND THAT REMINDS ME (My Heart Reminds Me) — Four Seasons (Crewe-Gaudio), Crewe 333 | 6 |
| ★ 46 | 56 | 67 | 82 | SO GOOD TOGETHER — Andy Kim (Jeff Barry), Steed 720 | 4 |
| 47 | 47 | 59 | 61 | SAD GIRL — Intruders (Gamble-Huff), Gamble 235 | 8 |
| ★ 48 | — | — | — | BACKFIELD IN MOTION — Mel & Tim (Karl Tarleton), Bamboo 107 | 1 |
| 49 | 40 | 40 | 45 | YOU GOT YOURS AND I'LL GET MINE — Delfonics (Stan & Bell Prod.), Philly Groove 157 | 10 |
| ★ 50 | — | — | — | AND WHEN I DIE — Blood, Sweat & Tears (James William Guercio), Columbia 4-45008 | 1 |
| 51 | 51 | 56 | 62 | SOMETHING IN THE AIR — Thunderclap Newman (Peter Townshend), Track 2656 | 7 |
| ★ 52 | 59 | 70 | — | YOU'LL NEVER WALK ALONE — Brooklyn Bridge (Wes Farrell), Buddah 139 | 3 |
| 53 | 54 | 58 | 64 | JACK AND JILL — Tommy Roe (Steve Barri), ABC 11229 | 12 |
| 54 | 55 | 57 | 59 | LOVE OF THE COMMON PEOPLE — The Winstons (Don Carroll), Metromedia 142 | 5 |
| ★ 55 | 62 | 62 | 72 | ANY WAY THAT YOU WANT ME — Evie Sands (Chip Taylor-Al Gorgoni), A&M 1090 | 10 |
| ★ 56 | 66 | 89 | 100 | RUBEN JAMES — Kenny Rogers & First Edition (Mike Post), Reprise 0854 | 4 |
| 57 | 57 | 69 | 69 | TRAIN — 1910 Fruitgum Co. (Kasenetz-Katz Assoc.), Buddah 130 | 8 |
| 58 | 64 | 65 | 66 | LET A WOMAN BE A WOMAN LET A MAN BE A MAN — Dyke and the Blazers (Laboe/Barrette), Original Sound 89 | 5 |
| ★ 59 | 68 | 77 | 77 | DOIN' OUR THING — Clarence Carter (Rick Hall), Atlantic 2660 | 4 |
| 60 | 69 | 71 | 81 | CHAINS OF LOVE — Bobby Bland (Andre Williams), Duke 449 | 6 |
| ★ 61 | — | — | — | TAKE A LETTER MARIA — R. B. Greaves (Ahmet Ertegun), Atco 6714 | 1 |
| ★ 62 | 82 | — | — | THE SWEETER HE IS — Soul Children (Hayes/Porter), Stax ???? | 2 |
| ★ 63 | 83 | 99 | — | CHERRY HILL PARK — Billy Joe Royal (Buddy Buie), Columbia 4-44902 | 3 |
| ♫ ★ 64 | 72 | 86 | — | SUITE: JUDY BLUE EYES — Crosby/Stills/Nash (Stephen Stills, David Crosby & Graham Nash), Atlantic 2676 | 3 |
| ♫ ★ 65 | 78 | — | — | LET A MAN COME IN AND DO THE POPCORN (PART 1) — James Brown (James Brown), King 6255 | 2 |
| 66 | 50 | 51 | 51 | WE GOTTA ALL GET TOGETHER — Paul Revere & the Raiders (Mark Lindsay), Columbia 44970 | 7 |
| ★ 67 | 89 | — | — | TRY A LITTLE KINDNESS — Glen Campbell (Al De Lory), Capitol 2659 | 2 |
| 68 | 73 | 83 | 91 | TIME MACHINE — Grand Funk Railroad (Terry Knight), Capitol 2567 | 4 |
| ★ 69 | 80 | 85 | 92 | MIND, BODY & SOUL — Flaming Embers (R. Dunbar), Hot Wax 6902 | 4 |
| 70 | 61 | 61 | 80 | SON OF A LOVIN' MAN — Buchanan Brothers (Cashman, Pistilli & West), Event 3305 | 5 |
| ♫ 71 | 71 | 76 | 90 | SINCE I MET YOU BABY — Sonny James (Kelso Herston), Capitol 2595 | 5 |
| ★ 72 | 84 | 93 | 95 | KOOL AND THE GANG — Kool and the Gang (Redd Coach Prod.), De-Lite 519 | 6 |
| 73 | 77 | — | — | GROOVY GRUBWORM — Harlow Wilcox (Shelby Singleton), Plantation 28 | 2 |
| 74 | 74 | 77 | 79 | GET OFF MY BACK WOMAN — B. B. King (Bill Szymczyk), Bluesway 61026 | 8 |
| 75 | 85 | 94 | — | I'LL BET YOU — Funkadelic (Clinton/Baines/Lindsey), Westbound 130 | 3 |
| ★ 76 | — | — | — | NA NA HEY HEY KISS HIM GOODBYE — Steam (Paul Leka), Fontana 1667 | 1 |
| ★ 77 | 87 | — | — | COLOR OF MY LOVE — Jefferson (John Schroeder), Decca 32501 | 5 |
| ★ 78 | — | — | — | UNDUN — Guess Who (Jack Richardson), RCA 74-0195 | 1 |
| ★ 79 | — | — | — | TURN ON A DREAM — Box Tops (Tommy Cogbill), Mala 12042 | 1 |
| ★ 80 | — | — | — | MAKE YOUR OWN KIND OF MUSIC — Mama Cass Elliot (Steve Barri), Dunhill 4214 | 1 |
| ★ 81 | 94 | 96 | 97 | JULIA — Ramsey Lewis (C. Stepney), Cadet 5640 | 4 |
| 82 | 91 | 97 | 99 | GOOD CLEAN FUN — The Monkees (Michael Nesmith), Colgems 66-5005 | 5 |
| 83 | 92 | 92 | 93 | WAS IT GOOD TO YOU — Isley Brothers (R. O. & R. Isley), T-Neck 908 | 4 |
| 84 | 86 | — | — | SILVER THREADS AND GOLDEN NEEDLES — Cowsills (Bob Waschtel), MGM 14084 | 2 |
| ★ 85 | — | — | — | PROUD MARY — Checkmates, Ltd., featuring Sonny Charles (Phil Spector), A&M 1127 | 1 |
| 86 | 97 | 100 | — | ETERNITY — Vikki Carr (Bob Crewe), Liberty 56132 | 3 |
| 87 | 90 | — | — | DON'T WASTE MY TIME — John Mayall (John Mayall), Polydor 14004 | 2 |
| 88 | 88 | — | — | HOLD ME — Baskerville Hounds (James M. Testa), Avco Embassy 1054 | 2 |
| 89 | 96 | — | — | I CAN'T BE ALL BAD — Johnny Adams (Shelby S. Singleton Jr.), SSS International 780 | 2 |
| ★ 90 | — | — | — | IT'S HARD TO GET ALONG — Joe Simon (John R.), Sound Stage 7 2641 | 1 |
| 91 | 99 | — | — | LOVE IN THE CITY — Turtles (Ray Davis), White Whale 326 | 2 |
| 92 | — | — | — | SHANGRI-LA — Lettermen (Al De Lory), Capitol 2643 | 1 |
| 93 | 93 | 95 | 96 | WE'LL CRY TOGETHER — Maxine Brown (Koppelman & Rubin, Finiz), Commonwealth United 3001 | 4 |
| 94 | — | — | — | YESTER-ME, YESTER-YOU, YESTERDAY — Stevie Wonder (Fuqua & Bristol), Tamla 54188 | 1 |
| 95 | 98 | 98 | — | DELTA LADY — Joe Cocker (Denny Cordell), A&M 1112 | 3 |
| 96 | — | — | — | SAY YOU LOVE ME — Impressions (Curtis Mayfield), Curtom 1946 | 1 |
| 97 | — | — | — | CRUMBS OFF THE TABLE — Glass House (Holland-Dozier-Holland), Invictus 9071 | 1 |
| 98 | — | — | — | WE MUST BE IN LOVE — Five Stairsteps & Cubie (Curtis Mayfield), Curtom 1945 | 1 |
| 99 | 100 | — | — | SHE BELONGS TO ME — Rick Nelson (Rick Nelson), Decca 732550 | 2 |
| 100 | — | — | — | JUST A LITTLE LOVE — B. B. King (Bill Szymczyk), BluesWay 61029 | 1 |

## HOT 100—A TO Z—(Publisher-Licensee)


And That Reminds Me (My Heart Reminds Me) (Symphony House, ASCAP) ... 45
And When I Die (Tuna Fish, BMI) ... 50
Any Way That You Want Me (Blackwood, BMI) ... 55
Baby, I'm For Real (Jobete, BMI) ... 33
Baby It's You (Dolfi-Mary Jane, ASCAP) ... 13
Backfield in Motion (Cachand/Patcheal, BMI) ... 48
Ball of Fire (Big Seven, BMI) ... 42
By the Time I Get to Phoenix (Johnny Rivers, BMI) 37
Carry Me Back (Slacsar, ASCAP) ... 40
Chains of Love (Progressive, BMI) ... 60
Cherry Hill Park (Low-Sal, BMI) ... 63
Color of My Love (Ramraz, BMI) ... 77
Come Together (Maclen, BMI) ... 23
Crumbs Off the Table (Gold Forever, BMI) ... 97
Delta Lady (Skyhill, BMI) ... 95
Doin' Our Thing (Fame, BMI) ... 59
Don't It Make You Want to Go Home (Lowery, BMI) ... 41
Don't Waste My Time (St. George, BMI) ... 87
Easy to Be Hard (United Artists, ASCAP) ... 9
Echo Park (Hastings, BMI) ... 44
Eternity (Saturday, BMI) ... 86
Everybody's Talkin' (Coconut Grove/Story, BMI) ... 15
Get Off My Back Woman (Sounds of Lucille-Pampco, BMI) ... 74
Get Together (S.F.O., BMI) ... 28
Going in Circles (Porpete, BMI) ... 27
Good Clean Fun (Screen Gems-Columbia, BMI) ... 82
Green River (Jondora, BMI) ... 19
Groovy Grubworm (Little River, BMI) ... 73
Here I Go Again (Jobete, BMI) ... 39
Hold Me (Robbins, ASCAP) ... 88
Honky Tonk Women (Gideon, BMI) ... 14
Hot Fun in the Summertime (Stone Flower, BMI) ... 2
Hurt So Bad (Vogue, BMI) ... 29
I Can't Be All Bad (Singleton, BMI) ... 89
I Can't Get Next to You (Jobete, BMI) ... 1
I'll Bet You (Jobete, BMI) ... 75
I'll Never Fall in Love Again (TRO-Hollis, BMI) ... 18
I'm Gonna Make You Mine (Pocketful of Tunes, BMI) ... 11
In a Moment (Odeom & Nieburg, BMI) ... 34
Is That All There Is (Trio, BMI) ... 17
It's Hard to Get Along (Cape Ann, BMI) ... 90
Jack and Jill (Low-Twi, BMI) ... 53
Jealous Kind of Fellow (Colfam, BMI) ... 21
Jean (Twentieth Century, ASCAP) ... 4
Jesus Is a Soul Man (Wilderness, BMI) ... 36
Judy Blue Eyes (Gold Hill, BMI) ... 64
Julia (Maclen, BMI) ... 81
Just a Little Love (Sounds of Lucille-Pamco, BMI) ... 100
Kool and the Gang (Stephayne, BMI) ... 72
Let a Man Come in and Do the Popcorn (Part 1) (Dynatone, BMI) ... 65
Let a Woman Be a Woman, Let a Man Be a Man (Drive-In/Westward, BMI) ... 58
Little Woman (Green Apple, BMI) ... 5
Love in the City (Ishmael Music/Blimp, BMI) ... 91
Love of the Common People (Tree, BMI) ... 54
Mah-Na-Mah-Na (E. B. Marks, BMI) ... 60
Make Believe (Love/Peanut Butter, BMI) ... 35
Make Your Own Kind of Music (Screen Gems-Columbia, BMI) ... 80
Mind, Body & Soul (Gold Forever, BMI) ... 69
Na Na Hey Hey Kiss Him Goodbye (MRC/Little Heather, BMI) ... 76
Oh What a Night (Conrad, BMI) ... 16
Proud Mary (Jondora, BMI) ... 85
Ruben James (Unart, BMI) ... 56
Sad Girl (IPC, BMI) ... 47
Say You Love Me (Curtom, BMI) ... 96
Shangri-La (Robbins, ASCAP) ... 92
She Belongs to Me (Warner Bros.-Seven Arts, ASCAP) ... 99
Silver Threads and Golden Needles (Central Songs, BMI) ... 84
Since I Met You Baby (Marson, BMI) ... 71
Smile a Little Smile for Me (January, BMI) ... 38
So Good Together (Unart/Joachim, BMI) ... 46
Something (Harrisongs, BMI) ... 20
Something in the Air (Track, BMI) ... 51
Son of a Lovin' Man (Blendingwell, ASCAP) ... 70
Sugar on Sunday (Big Seven, BMI) ... 22
Sugar, Sugar (Kirshner, BMI) ... 3
Suspicious Minds (Press, BMI) ... 6
Sweeter He Is, The (Birdees, ASCAP) ... 62
Take a Letter Maria (Four Star Television, BMI) ... 61
That's the Way Love Is (Jobete, BMI) ... 7
This Girl Is a Woman Now (Three Bridges, ASCAP) .. 12
Time Machine (Storybrook, BMI) ... 68
Tracy (Vanlee/Emily, ASCAP) ... 10
Train (Kaskat, BMI) ... 57
Try a Little Kindness (Airfield/Glen Campbell, ASCAP) ... 67
Turn On a Dream (Press, BMI) ... 79
Undun (Friends of Mine, Ltd., Dunbar/Cirrus, BMI) 78
Walk On By (Jac/Seas, ASCAP) ... 32
Was It Good to You (Triple 3, BMI) ... 83
We Gotta All Get Together (Equinox, BMI) ... 66
We Must Be in Love (Gamad, BMI) ... 98
Wedding Bell Blues (Tuna Fish, BMI) ... 8
We'll Cry Together (McCoy/Chevis, BMI) ... 93
What's the Use of Breaking Up (Assorted/Parabut, BMI) ... 24
When I Die (Mode, BMI) ... 26
World, Part 1 (Golo, BMI) ... 43
Yester-Me, Yester-You, Yesterday (Stein/Van Stock, ASCAP) ... 94
You Got Yours and I'll Get Mine (Nickel Shoe, BMI) 49
You, I (Singleton, BMI) ... 25
Your Good Thing (Is About to End) (East, BMI) ... 31
You'll Never Walk Alone (Williamson, ASCAP) ... 52
You've Lost That Lovin' Feeling (Screen Gems-Columbia, BMI) ... 30


## BUBBLING UNDER THE HOT 100

101. WONDERFUL ... Blackwell, Astral 1000
102. DON'T SHUT ME OUT ... Underground Sunshine, Intrepid 75012
103. LOVE AND LET LOVE ... Hardy Boys, RCA 74-0228
104. LIKE A ROLLING STONE ... Phil Flowers & the Flowershop, A&M 1122
105. POOR MAN ... Little Milton, Checker 1221
106. I STILL BELIEVE IN TOMORROW ... John & Ann Ryder, Decca 73256
107. TODAY I SING THE BLUES ... Aretha Franklin, Columbia 4-44951
108. DREAMIN' TIL THEN ... Joe Jeffrey Group, Wand 11207
109. COMMENT ... Charles Wright/Watts 103rd Street Rhythm Band, Warner Bros.-7 Arts 7338
110. MR. TURNKEY ... Zager & Evans, RCA 74-0246
111. SHE'S GOT LOVE ... Thomas & Richard Frost, Imperial 66405
112. THE SEPTEMBER SONG ... Roy Clark, Dot 17299
113. ALL GOD'S CHILDREN GOT SOUL ... Dorothy Morrison, Elektra 45671
114. OKIE FROM MUSKOGEE ... Merle Haggard & the Strangers, Capitol 2626
115. HOW DOES IT FEEL ... Illusion, Steed 721
116. MIDNIGHT COWBOY ... John Barry, Columbia 4-44891
117. SUNDAY MORNIN' COMIN' DOWN ... Ray Stevens, Monument 1163
118. I CAN'T HELP BUT DECEIVE YOU LITTLE GIRL ... Iron Butterfly, Atco 6712
119. CUPID ... Johnny Nash, JAD 220
120. CURLY ... Jimmy Clanton, Laurie 3508
121. ALWAYS DAVID ... Ruby Winters, Diamond 265
122. WHITE BIRD ... It's a Beautiful Day, Columbia 4-44928
123. IT AIN'T SANITARY ... Joe Tex, Dial 4094
124. ROOSEVELT & IRA LEE ... Tony Joe White, Monument 1169
125. ONE TIN SOLDIER ... Original Caste, T.A. 186
126. I KNOW ... Ike & Tina Turner, Blue Thumb 104
127. BALLAD OF EASY RIDER ... Byrds, Columbia 4-44990
128. ONE WOMAN ... Johnny Rivers, Imperial 66418
129. LEAVING ON A JET PLANE ... Peter, Paul & Mary, Warner Bros.-7 Arts 7340
130. STONE FREE ... Jimi Hendrix Experience, Reprise 0853
131. RIVER DEEP—MOUNTAIN HIGH ... Ike & Tina Turner, A&M 1118
132. WE GOT LATIN SOUL ... Mongo Santamaria, Columbia 4-44998
133. GET IT FROM THE BOTTOM ... Steelers, Date 2-1642
134. SOME OF SHELLEY'S BLUES ... Nitty Gritty Dirt Band, Liberty 56134
135. UP ON CRIPPLE CREEK ... Band, Capitol 2635

Compiled from national retail sales and radio station airplay by the Music Popularity Dept. of Record Market Research, Billboard.

# Billboard HOT 100

FOR WEEK ENDING OCTOBER 25, 1969

♫ Artist and/or Selection featured on "The Music Scene" this week, ABC-TV Network. Those in black were featured on past programs.

★ STAR PERFORMER—Sides registering greatest proportionate sales progress this week. Record Industry Association of America seal of certification as million selling single.

| This Week | 1 Wk. Ago | 2 Wks. Ago | 3 Wks. Ago | TITLE | Artist (Producer), Label & Number | Weeks On Chart |
|---|---|---|---|---|---|---|
| ♫ 1 | 1 | 4 | 5 | I CAN'T GET NEXT TO YOU | Temptations (Norman Whitfield), Gordy 7093 | 11 |
| ♫ 2 | 2 | 5 | 9 | HOT FUN IN THE SUMMERTIME | Sly & the Family Stone (Sly Stone), Epic 5-10497 | 11 |
| ♫ 3 | 3 | 1 | 1 | SUGAR, SUGAR | Archies (Jeff Barry), Calendar 63-1008 | 14 |
| ♫ 4 | 4 | 2 | 2 | JEAN | Oliver (Bob Crewe), Crewe 334 | 11 |
| ★ 5 | 6 | 11 | 14 | SUSPICIOUS MINDS | Elvis Presley, RCA 47-9764 | 7 |
| ♫ 6 | 5 | 3 | 3 | LITTLE WOMAN | Bobby Sherman (Jackie Mills), Metromedia 121 | 10 |
| ★ 7 | 8 | 25 | 35 | WEDDING BELL BLUES | 5th Dimension (Bones Howe), Soul City 779 | 5 |
| ★ 8 | 13 | 15 | 24 | BABY IT'S YOU | Smith (Joel Sill & Steve Barri), Dunhill 4206 | 8 |
| ★ 9 | 10 | 19 | 29 | TRACY | Cuff Links (Paul Vance-Lee Pockriss), Decca 32533 | 7 |
| 10 | 11 | 13 | 20 | I'M GONNA MAKE YOU MINE | Lou Christie (Stan Vincent & Mike Duckman), Buddah 116 | 10 |
| ★ 11 | 20 | — | — | SOMETHING | Beatles (George Martin), Apple 2654 | 2 |
| 12 | 7 | 12 | 15 | THAT'S THE WAY LOVE IS | Marvin Gaye (Norman Whitfield), Tamla 54185 | 10 |
| ★ 13 | 23 | — | — | COME TOGETHER | Beatles (George Martin), Apple 2654 | 2 |
| ★ 14 | 17 | 33 | 50 | IS THAT ALL THERE IS | Peggy Lee (Lieber/Stoller), Capitol 2602 | 5 |
| ♫ 15 | 15 | 6 | 8 | EVERYBODY'S TALKIN' | Nilsson (Rick Jarrard), RCA 74-0161 | 11 |
| ★ 16 | 38 | 53 | 66 | SMILE A LITTLE SMILE FOR ME | The Flying Machine (Tony MacAuley), Congress 6000 | 4 |
| ♫ 17 | 12 | 9 | 11 | THIS GIRL IS A WOMAN NOW | Gary Puckett & the Union Gap (Dick Glasser), Columbia 4-44967 | 10 |
| ♫ 18 | 9 | 7 | 4 | EASY TO BE HARD | Three Dog Night (Gabriel Mekler), Dunhill 4203 | 12 |
| ♫ 19 | 18 | 17 | 12 | I'LL NEVER FALL IN LOVE AGAIN | Tom Jones (Peter Sullivan), Parrot 40018 | 14 |
| ★ 20 | 30 | 36 | 53 | YOU'VE LOST THAT LOVIN' FEELING | Dionne Warwick (Chips Moman & Dionne Warwick), Scepter 12262 | 6 |
| 21 | 21 | 46 | 48 | JEALOUS KIND OF FELLOW | Garland Greene (Giant Enterprises Prod.), UNI 55143 | 7 |
| 22 | 22 | 24 | 25 | SUGAR ON SUNDAY | Clique (Gary Zekley), White Whale 323 | 9 |
| 23 | 19 | 10 | 7 | GREEN RIVER | Creedence Clearwater Revival (J. C. Fogerty), Fantasy 625 | 13 |
| 24 | 25 | 27 | 28 | YOU, I | Rugbys (Steve McNicol), Amazon 1 | 10 |
| 25 | 27 | 32 | 41 | GOING IN CIRCLES | Friends of Distinction (John Florez), RCA 74-0204 | 11 |
| ★ 26 | 33 | 67 | 79 | BABY, I'M FOR REAL | Originals (Richard Morris), Soul 35066 | 5 |
| 27 | 14 | 8 | 6 | HONKY TONK WOMEN | Rolling Stones (Jimmy Miller), London 910 | 15 |
| 28 | 35 | 35 | 36 | MAKE BELIEVE | Wind (Bo Gentry), Life 200 | 8 |
| ★ 29 | 50 | — | — | AND WHEN I DIE | Blood, Sweat & Tears (James William Guercio), Columbia 4-45008 | 2 |
| 30 | 32 | 48 | 49 | WALK ON BY | Isaac Hayes (Al Bell-Marvell Thomas-Allen Jones), Enterprise 9003 | 9 |
| ♫ 31 | 16 | 14 | 10 | OH, WHAT A NIGHT | Dells (Bobby Miller), Cadet 5649 | 11 |
| 32 | 26 | 18 | 19 | WHEN I DIE | Motherlode (Mort Ross & Doug Riley), Buddah 131 | 12 |
| ★ 33 | 42 | 52 | 82 | BALL OF FIRE | Tommy James & the Shondells (Tommy James), Roulette 7060 | 4 |
| ♫ ★ 34 | 64 | 72 | 86 | SUITE: JUDY BLUE EYES | Crosby/Stills/Nash (Stephen Stills, David Crosby & Graham Nash), Atlantic 2676 | 4 |
| 35 | 36 | 39 | 45 | JESUS IS A SOUL MAN | Lawrence Reynolds (Don Davis), Warner Bros.-Seven Arts 7322 | 6 |
| ★ 36 | 56 | 66 | 89 | RUBEN JAMES | Kenny Rogers & First Edition (Mike Post), Reprise 0854 | 5 |
| ★ 37 | 61 | — | — | TAKE A LETTER MARIA | R. B. Greaves (Ahmet Ertegun), Atco 6714 | 2 |
| ★ 38 | 51 | 51 | 56 | SOMETHING IN THE AIR | Thunderclap Newman (Peter Townshend), Track 2656 | 8 |
| ♫ 39 | 24 | 20 | 22 | WHAT'S THE USE OF BREAKING UP | Jerry Butler (Gamble-Huff), Mercury 72960 | 9 |
| 40 | 34 | 31 | 33 | IN A MOMENT | Intrigues (Martin & Bell), Yew 1001 | 13 |
| ★ 41 | 46 | 56 | 67 | SO GOOD TOGETHER | Andy Kim (Jeff Barry), Steed 720 | 5 |
| 42 | 44 | 58 | 78 | ECHO PARK | Keith Barbour (Austin & Flemming), Epic 5-10486 | 5 |
| ★ 43 | 48 | — | — | BACKFIELD IN MOTION | Mel & Tim (Karl Tarleton), Bamboo 107 | 2 |
| ★ 44 | 67 | 89 | — | TRY A LITTLE KINDNESS | Glen Campbell (Al De Lory), Capitol 2659 | 3 |
| 45 | 41 | 41 | 44 | DON'T IT MAKE YOU WANT TO GO HOME | Joe South & the Believers (Joe South), Capitol 2592 | 10 |
| ♫ 46 | 43 | 44 | 37 | WORLD, Part 1 | James Brown (James Brown), King 6258 | 7 |
| ♫ 47 | 40 | 26 | 27 | CARRY ME BACK | Rascals (Rascals with Arif Mardin), Atlantic 2664 | 8 |
| ♫ ★ 48 | 58 | 64 | 65 | LET A WOMAN BE A WOMAN LET A MAN BE A MAN | Dyke and the Blazers (Laboe/Barrette), Original Sound 89 | 6 |
| ★ 49 | 63 | 83 | 99 | CHERRY HILL PARK | Billy Joe Royal (Buddy Buie), Columbia 4-44902 | 4 |
| ★ 50 | 68 | 73 | 83 | TIME MACHINE | Grand Funk Railroad (Terry Knight), Capitol 2567 | 5 |
| 51 | 52 | 59 | 70 | YOU'LL NEVER WALK ALONE | Brooklyn Bridge (Wes Farrell), Buddah 139 | 4 |
| ★ 52 | 76 | — | — | NA NA HEY HEY KISS HIM GOODBYE | Steam (Paul Leka), Fontana 1667 | 2 |
| 53 | 59 | 68 | 77 | DOIN' OUR THING | Clarence Carter (Rick Hall), Atlantic 2660 | 5 |
| 54 | 55 | 62 | 62 | ANY WAY THAT YOU WANT ME | Evie Sands (Chip Taylor-Al Gorgoni), A&M 1090 | 11 |
| 55 | 47 | 47 | 59 | SAD GIRL | Intruders (Gamble-Huff), Gamble 235 | 9 |
| 56 | 62 | 82 | — | THE SWEETER HE IS | Soul Children (Hayes/Porter), Stax ???? | 3 |
| ★ 57 | 69 | 80 | 85 | MIND, BODY & SOUL | Flaming Embers (R. Dunbar), Hot Wax 6902 | 5 |
| ♫ 58 | 65 | 78 | — | LET A MAN COME IN AND DO THE POPCORN (PART I) | James Brown (James Brown), King 6255 | 3 |
| ★ 59 | 94 | — | — | YESTER-ME, YESTER-YOU, YESTERDAY | Stevie Wonder (Fuqua & Bristol), Tamla 54188 | 2 |
| ★ 60 | 78 | — | — | UNDUN | Guess Who (Jack Richardson), RCA 74-0195 | 2 |
| ♫ ★ 61 | — | — | — | ELI'S COMING | Three Dog Night (Gabriel Mekler), Dunhill 4215 | 1 |
| 62 | 45 | 49 | 52 | AND THAT REMINDS ME (My Heart Reminds Me) | Four Seasons (Crewe-Gaudio), Crewe 333 | 7 |
| ★ 63 | 79 | — | — | TURN ON A DREAM | Box Tops (Tommy Cogbill), Mala 12042 | 2 |
| 64 | 57 | 57 | 69 | TRAIN | 1910 Fruitgum Co. (Kasenetz-Katz Assoc.), Buddah 130 | 9 |
| 65 | 72 | 84 | 93 | KOOL AND THE GANG | Kool and the Gang (Redd Coach Prod.), De-Lite 519 | 7 |
| 66 | 60 | 69 | 71 | CHAINS OF LOVE | Bobby Bland (Andre Williams), Duke 449 | 7 |
| ♫ 67 | 71 | 71 | 76 | SINCE I MET YOU BABY | Sonny James (Kelso Herston), Capitol 2595 | 6 |
| ★ 68 | 80 | — | — | MAKE YOUR OWN KIND OF MUSIC | Mama Cass Elliot (Steve Barri), Dunhill 4214 | 2 |
| 69 | 54 | 55 | 57 | LOVE OF THE COMMON PEOPLE | The Winstons (Don Carroll), Metromedia 142 | 6 |
| 70 | 70 | 61 | 61 | SON OF A LOVIN' MAN | Buchanan Brothers (Cashman, Pistilli & West), Event 3305 | 6 |
| 71 | 73 | 77 | — | GROOVY GRUBWORM | Harlow Wilcox (Shelby Singleton), Plantation 28 | 3 |
| 72 | 53 | 54 | 58 | JACK AND JILL | Tommy Roe (Steve Barri), ABC 11229 | 13 |
| ★ 73 | 95 | 98 | 98 | DELTA LADY | Joe Cocker (Denny Cordell), A&M 1112 | 4 |
| 74 | 75 | 85 | 94 | I'LL BET YOU | Funkadelic (Clinton/Baines/Lindsey), Westbound 130 | 4 |
| ★ 75 | 84 | 86 | — | SILVER THREADS AND GOLDEN NEEDLES | Cowsills (Bob Waschtel), MGM 14084 | 3 |
| ★ 76 | — | — | — | LEAVING ON A JET PLANE | Peter, Paul & Mary (Albert B. Grossman & Milt Okun), Warner Bros.-Seven Arts 7340 | 1 |
| 77 | 77 | 87 | — | COLOR OF MY LOVE | Jefferson (John Schroeder), Decca 32501 | 6 |
| 78 | 85 | — | — | PROUD MARY | Checkmates, Ltd., featuring Sonny Charles (Phil Spector), A&M 1127 | 2 |
| 79 | 86 | 97 | 100 | ETERNITY | Vikki Carr (Bob Crewe), Liberty 56132 | 4 |
| 80 | 81 | 94 | 96 | JULIA | Ramsey Lewis (C. Stepney), Cadet 5640 | 5 |
| 81 | 87 | 90 | — | DON'T WASTE MY TIME | John Mayall (John Mayall), Polydor 14004 | 3 |
| ★ 82 | 92 | — | — | SHANGRI-LA | Lettermen (Al De Lory), Capitol 2643 | 2 |
| 83 | 83 | 92 | 92 | WAS IT GOOD TO YOU | Isley Brothers (R. O. & R. Isley), T-Neck 908 | 5 |
| 84 | 93 | 93 | 95 | WE'LL CRY TOGETHER | Maxine Brown (Koppelman & Rubin, Finiz), Commonwealth United 3001 | 5 |
| ★ 85 | — | — | — | ROOSEVELT & IRA LEE | Tony Joe White (Billy Swann), Monument 1169 | 1 |
| ★ 86 | — | — | — | I STILL BELIEVE IN TOMORROW | John & Anne Ryder (Mark Edwards), Decca 734661 | 1 |
| ★ 87 | — | — | — | DOWN ON THE CORNER | Creedence Clearwater Revival (John Fogerty), Fantasy 634 | 1 |
| ★ 88 | — | — | — | EVIL WOMAN, DON'T PLAY YOUR GAMES WITH ME | Crow (Bob Monaco), Amaret 112 | 1 |
| ★ 89 | — | — | — | WONDERFUL | Blackwell (Doyle Jones), Astro 1000 | 1 |
| 90 | 90 | — | — | IT'S HARD TO GET ALONG | Joe Simon (John R.), Sound Stage 7 2641 | 2 |
| 91 | — | — | — | THESE EYES | Jr. Walker & the All Stars (Johnny Bristol), Soul 35067 | 1 |
| 92 | — | — | — | SHE'S GOT LOVE | Thomas & Richard Frost (Ted Glasser), Imperial 66405 | 1 |
| 93 | — | — | — | FRIENDSHIP TRAIN | Gladys Knight & the Pips (Norman Whitfield), Soul 35068 | 1 |
| 94 | — | — | — | SUNDAY MORNIN' COMIN' DOWN | Ray Stevens (Jim Malloy & Ray Stevens), Monument 1163 | 1 |
| 95 | 96 | — | — | SAY YOU LOVE ME | Impressions (Curtis Mayfield), Curtom 1946 | 2 |
| 96 | 97 | — | — | CRUMBS OFF THE TABLE | Glass House (Holland-Dozier-Holland), Invictus 9071 | 2 |
| 97 | — | — | — | JINGO | Santana [Brent Dangerfield (IT)], Columbia 4-45010 | 1 |
| 98 | — | — | — | ONE WOMAN | Johnny Rivers (Johnny Rivers), Imperial 66418 | 1 |
| 99 | 99 | 100 | — | SHE BELONGS TO ME | Rick Nelson (Rick Nelson), Decca 732550 | 3 |
| 100 | 100 | — | — | JUST A LITTLE LOVE | B. B. King (Bill Szymczyk), BluesWay 61029 | 2 |

## HOT 100—A TO Z—(Publisher-Licensee)


And That Reminds Me (My Heart Reminds Me) (Symphony House, ASCAP) .... 62
And When I Die (Tuna Fish, BMI) .... 29
Any Way That You Want Me (Blackwood, BMI) .... 54
Baby, I'm For Real (Jobete, BMI) .... 26
Baby It's You (Dolfi-Mary Jane, ASCAP) .... 8
Backfield in Motion (Cachand/Patcheal, BMI) .... 43
Ball of Fire (Big Seven, BMI) .... 33
Carry Me Back (Slacsar, ASCAP) .... 47
Chains of Love (Progressive, BMI) .... 66
Cherry Hill Park (Low-Sal, BMI) .... 49
Color of My Love (Ramrac, ASCAP) .... 77
Come Together (Maclen, BMI) .... 13
Crumbs Off the Table (Gold Forever, BMI) .... 96
Delta Lady (Skyhill, BMI) .... 73
Doin' Our Thing (Fame, BMI) .... 53
Don't It Make You Want to Go Home (Lowery, BMI) .... 45
Don't Waste My Time (St. George, BMI) .... 81
Down on the Corner (Jondora, BMI) .... 87
Easy to Be Hard (United Artists, ASCAP) .... 18
Echo Park (Hastings, BMI) .... 42
Eli's Coming (Tuna Fish, BMI) .... 61
Eternity (Saturday, BMI) .... 79
Everybody's Talkin' (Coconut Grove/Story, BMI) .... 15
Evil Woman, Don't Play Your Games With Me (Yoggoth, BMI) .... 88
Friendship Train (Jobete, BMI) .... 93
Going in Circles (Porpete, BMI) .... 25
Green River (Jondora, BMI) .... 23
Groovy Grubworm (Little River, BMI) .... 71
Honky Tonk Women (Gideon, BMI) .... 27
Hot Fun in the Summertime (Stone Flower, BMI) .... 2
I Can't Get Next to You (Jobete, BMI) .... 1
I Still Believe in Tomorrow (Leeds, ASCAP) .... 86
I'll Bet You (Jobete, BMI) .... 74
I'll Never Fall in Love Again (TRO-Hollis, BMI) .... 19
I'm Gonna Make You Mine (Pocketful of Tunes, BMI) .... 10
In a Moment (Odeom & Nieburg, BMI) .... 40
Is That All There Is (Trio, BMI) .... 14
It's Hard to Get Along (Cape Ann, BMI) .... 90
Jack and Jill (Low-Twi, BMI) .... 72
Jealous Kind of Fellow (Colfam, BMI) .... 21
Jean (Twentieth Century, ASCAP) .... 4
Jesus Is a Soul Man (Wilderness, BMI) .... 35
Jingo (Boosey/Hawkes, ASCAP) .... 97
Suite: Judy Blue Eyes (Gold Hill, BMI) .... 34
Julia (Maclen, BMI) .... 80
Just a Little Love (Sounds of Lucille-Pamco, BMI) .. 100
Kool and the Gang (Stephayne, BMI) .... 65
Leaving on a Jet Plane (Cherry Lane, ASCAP) .... 76
Let a Man Come in and Do the Popcorn (Part 1) (Dynatone, BMI) .... 58
Let a Woman Be a Woman, Let a Man Be a Man (Drive-In/Westward, BMI) .... 48
Little Woman (Green Apple, BMI) .... 6
Love of the Common People (Tree, BMI) .... 69
Make Believe (Love/Peanut Butter, BMI) .... 28
Make Your Own Kind of Music (Screen Gems-Columbia, BMI) .... 68
Mind, Body & Soul (Gold Forever, BMI) .... 57
Na Na Hey Hey Kiss Him Goodbye (MRC/Little Heather, BMI) .... 52
Oh What a Night (Conrad, BMI) .... 31
One Woman (Rhomers, BMI) .... 98
Proud Mary (Jondora, BMI) .... 78
Roosevelt & Ira Lee (Combine, BMI) .... 85
Ruben James (Unart, BMI) .... 36
Sad Girl (IPC, BMI) .... 55
Say You Love Me (Curtom, BMI) .... 95
Shangri-La (Robbins, ASCAP) .... 82
She Belongs to Me (Warner Bros.-Seven Arts, ASCAP) .... 99
She's Got Love (Claridge/Tons of Fun, ASCAP) .... 92
Silver Threads and Golden Needles (Central Songs, BMI) .... 75
Since I Met You Baby (Marson, BMI) .... 67
Smile a Little Smile for Me (January, BMI) .... 16
So Good Together (Unart/Joachim, BMI) .... 41
Something (Harrisongs, BMI) .... 11
Something in the Air (Track, BMI) .... 38
Son of a Lovin' Man (Blendingwell, ASCAP) .... 70
Sugar on Sunday (Big Seven, BMI) .... 22
Sugar, Sugar (Kirshner, BMI) .... 3
Sunday Mornin' Comin' Down (Combine, BMI) .... 94
Suspicious Minds (Press, BMI) .... 5
Sweeter He Is, The (Birdees, ASCAP) .... 56
Take a Letter Maria (Four Star Television, BMI) .... 37
That's the Way Love Is (Jobete, BMI) .... 12
These Eyes (Dunbar, BMI) .... 91
This Girl Is a Woman Now (Three Bridges, ASCAP) .... 17
Time Machine (Storybook, BMI) .... 50
Tracy (Vanlee/Emily, ASCAP) .... 9
Train (Kaskat, BMI) .... 64
Try a Little Kindness (Airfield/ Glen Campbell, BMI) .... 44
Turn On a Dream (Press, BMI) .... 63
Undun (Friends of Mine, Ltd./Dunbar/Cirrus, BMI) 60
Walk On By (Jac/Seas, ASCAP) .... 30
Was It Good to You (Triple 3, BMI) .... 83
Wedding Bell Blues (Tuna Fish, BMI) .... 7
We'll Cry Together (McCoy/Chevis, BMI) .... 84
What's the Use of Breaking Up (Assorted/Parabut, BMI) .... 39
When I Die (Mode, BMI) .... 32
Wonderful (Points West, BMI) .... 89
World, Part 1 (Golo, BMI) .... 46
Yester-Me, Yester-You, Yesterday (Stein/Van Stock, ASCAP) .... 59
You, I (Singleton, BMI) .... 24
You'll Never Walk Alone (Williamson, ASCAP) .... 51
You've Lost That Lovin' Feeling (Screen Gems-Columbia, BMI) .... 20


## BUBBLING UNDER THE HOT 100

101. FORTUNATE SON....Creedence Clearwater Revival, Fantasy 634
102. DON'T SHUT ME OUT....Underground Sunshine, Intrepid 75012
103. LOVE IN THE CITY....Turtles, White Whale 326
104. LIKE A ROLLING STONE....Phil Flowers & the Flowershop, A&M 1122
105. POOR MAN....Little Milton, Checker 1221
106. MR. TURNKEY....Zager & Evans, RCA 74-0246
107. TODAY I SING THE BLUES....Aretha Franklin, Columbia 4-44951
108. WE MUST BE IN LOVE....Five Stairsteps & Cubie, Curtom 1945
109. DREAMIN' TIL THEN....Joe Jeffrey Group, Wand 11207
110. OKIE FROM MUSKOGEE....Merle Haggard & the Strangers, Capitol 2626
111. ALL GOD'S CHILDREN GOT SOUL....Dorothy Morrison, Elektra 45671
112. MIDNIGHT COWBOY....Ferrante & Teicher, United Artists 50554
113. GIRLS IT AIN'T EASY....Honeycone, Hot Wax 6903
114. HOW DOES IT FEEL....Illusion, Steed 721
115. CUPID....Johnny Nash, JAD 220
116. MIDNIGHT COWBOY....John Barry, Columbia 4-44891
117. LOVE AND LET LOVE....Hardy Boys, RCA 74-0228
118. WHITE BIRD....It's a Beautiful Day, Columbia 4-44928
119. ONE TIN SOLDIER....Original Caste, T.A. 186
120. CURLY....Jimmy Clanton, Laurie 3508
121. WHY IS THE WINE SWEETER (On the Other Side)....Eddie Floyd, Stax 0051
122. BALLAD OF EASY RIDER....Byrds, Columbia 4-44990
123. UP ON CRIPPLE CREEK....Band, Capitol 2635
124. LOVE WILL FIND A WAY....Jackie DeShannon, Imperial 66419
125. TEN COMMANDMENTS OF LOVE....Little Anthony & the Imperials, United Artists 50598
126. I KNOW....Ike & Tina Turner, Blue Thumb 104
127. THE LORD MUST BE IN NEW YORK CITY....Nilsson, RCA 74-0216
128. MY IDEA....Creme Caramel, Janus 100
129. RIVER DEEP—MOUNTAIN HIGH....Ike & Tina Turner, A&M 1118
130. STONE FREE....Jimi Hendrix Experience, Reprise 0853
131. MOVIN'....Robbs, Dunhill 4208
132. GET IT FROM THE BOTTOM....Steelers, Date 2-1642
133. SOME OF SHELLEY'S BLUES....Nitty Gritty Dirt Band, Liberty 56134
134. ONE CUP OF HAPPINESS....Dean Martin, Reprise 0857
135. THE LORD MUST BE IN NEW YORK CITY....Sagittarius, Together 122

Compiled from national retail sales and radio station airplay by the Music Popularity Dept. of Record Market Research, Billboard.

HOT 100

HOT 100

# Billboard HOT 100
### For Week Ending November 1, 1969

♪ Artist and/or Selection featured on "The Music Scene" this week, ABC-TV Network. Those in black were featured on past programs.

★ STAR PERFORMER—Sides registering greatest proportionate sales progress this week.   ⓡ Record Industry Association of America seal of certification as million selling single.

| This Week | Wk. Ago | 2 Wks. Ago | 3 Wks. Ago | TITLE Artist (Producer), Label & Number | Weeks On Chart |
|---|---|---|---|---|---|
| 1 | 5 | 6 | 11 | SUSPICIOUS MINDS — Elvis Presley, RCA 47-9764 | 8 |
| 2 | 7 | 8 | 25 | WEDDING BELL BLUES — 5th Dimension (Bones Howe), Soul City 779 | 6 |
| 3 | 3 | 3 | 1 | SUGAR, SUGAR — Archies (Jeff Barry), Calendar 63-1008 | 15 |
| 4 | 1 | 1 | 4 | I CAN'T GET NEXT TO YOU — Temptations (Norman Whitfield), Gordy 7093 | 12 |
| 5 | 8 | 13 | 15 | BABY IT'S YOU — Smith (Joel Sill & Steve Barri), Dunhill 4206 | 9 |
| 6 | 2 | 2 | 5 | HOT FUN IN THE SUMMERTIME — Sly & the Family Stone (Sly Stone), Epic 5-10497 | 12 |
| 7 | 6 | 5 | 3 | LITTLE WOMAN — Bobby Sherman (Jackie Mills), Metromedia 121 | 11 |
| 8 | 4 | 4 | 2 | JEAN — Oliver (Bob Crewe), Crewe 334 | 12 |
| 9 | 9 | 10 | 19 | TRACY — Cuff Links (Paul Vance-Lee Pockriss), Decca 32533 | 8 |
| 10 | 13 | 23 | — | COME TOGETHER — Beatles (George Martin), Apple 2654 | 3 |
| 11 | 11 | 20 | — | SOMETHING — Beatles (George Martin), Apple 2654 | 3 |
| 12 | 16 | 38 | 53 | SMILE A LITTLE SMILE FOR ME — The Flying Machine (Tony MacAuley), Congress 6000 | 5 |
| 13 | 14 | 17 | 33 | IS THAT ALL THERE IS — Peggy Lee (Lieber/Stoller), Capitol 2602 | 6 |
| 14 | 12 | 7 | 12 | THAT'S THE WAY LOVE IS — Marvin Gaye (Norman Whitfield), Tamla 54185 | 11 |
| 15 | 10 | 11 | 13 | I'M GONNA MAKE YOU MINE — Lou Christie (Stan Vincent & Mike Duckman), Buddah 116 | 11 |
| 16 | 25 | 27 | 32 | GOING IN CIRCLES — Friends of Distinction (John Florez), RCA 74-0204 | 12 |
| 17 | 29 | 50 | — | AND WHEN I DIE — Blood, Sweat & Tears (James William Guercio), Columbia 4-45008 | 3 |
| 18 | 20 | 30 | 36 | YOU'VE LOST THAT LOVIN' FEELING — Dionne Warwick (Chips Moman & Dionne Warwick), Scepter 12262 | 7 |
| 19 | 19 | 18 | 17 | I'LL NEVER FALL IN LOVE AGAIN — Tom Jones (Peter Sullivan), Parrot 40018 | 15 |
| 20 | 21 | 21 | 46 | JEALOUS KIND OF FELLOW — Garland Greene (Giant Enterprises Prod.), UNI 55143 | 8 |
| 21 | 37 | 61 | — | TAKE A LETTER MARIA — R. B. Greaves (Ahmet Ertegun), Atco 6714 | 3 |
| 22 | 26 | 33 | 67 | BABY, I'M FOR REAL — Originals (Marvin Gaye), Soul 35066 | 6 |
| 23 | 18 | 9 | 7 | EASY TO BE HARD — Three Dog Night (Gabriel Mekler), Dunhill 4203 | 13 |
| 24 | 22 | 22 | 24 | SUGAR ON SUNDAY — Clique (Gary Zekley), White Whale 323 | 10 |
| 25 | 15 | 15 | 6 | EVERYBODY'S TALKIN' — Nilsson (Rick Jarrard), RCA 74-0161 | 12 |
| 26 | 33 | 42 | 52 | BALL OF FIRE — Tommy James & the Shondells (Tommy James), Roulette 7060 | 5 |
| 27 | 17 | 12 | 9 | THIS GIRL IS A WOMAN NOW — Gary Puckett & the Union Gap (Dick Glasser), Columbia 4-44967 | 11 |
| 28 | 35 | 36 | 39 | JESUS IS A SOUL MAN — Lawrence Reynolds (Don Davis), Warner Bros.-Seven Arts 7322 | 7 |
| 29 | 24 | 25 | 27 | YOU, I — Rugbys (Steve McNicol), Amazon 1 | 11 |
| 30 | 58 | 65 | 78 | LET A MAN COME IN AND DO THE POPCORN (PART I) — James Brown (James Brown), King 6255 | 4 |
| 31 | 30 | 32 | 48 | WALK ON BY — Isaac Hayes (Al Bell-Marvell Thomas-Allen Jones), Enterprise 9003 | 10 |
| 32 | 59 | 94 | — | YESTER-ME, YESTER-YOU, YESTERDAY — Stevie Wonder (John Bristol), Tamla 54188 | |
| 33 | 44 | 67 | 89 | TRY A LITTLE KINDNESS — Glen Campbell (Al De Lory), Capitol 2659 | 4 |
| 34 | 64 | 72 | — | SUITE: JUDY BLUE EYES — Crosby/Stills/Nash (Stephen Stills, David Crosby & Graham Nash), Atlantic 2676 | 5 |
| 35 | 36 | 56 | 66 | RUBEN JAMES — Kenny Rogers & First Edition (Mike Post), Reprise 0854 | 6 |
| 36 | 48 | 58 | 64 | LET A WOMAN BE A WOMAN LET A MAN BE A MAN — Dyke and the Blazers (Laboe/Barrette), Original Sound 89 | 7 |
| 37 | 38 | 51 | 51 | SOMETHING IN THE AIR — Thunderclap Newman (Peter Townshend), Track 2656 | 9 |
| 38 | 49 | 63 | 83 | CHERRY HILL PARK — Billy Joe Royal (Buddy Buie), Columbia 4-44902 | 5 |
| 39 | 39 | 24 | 20 | WHAT'S THE USE OF BREAKING UP — Jerry Butler (Gamble-Huff), Mercury 72960 | 10 |
| 40 | 42 | 44 | 58 | ECHO PARK — Keith Barbour (Austin & Flemming), Epic 5-10486 | 6 |
| 41 | 41 | 46 | 56 | SO GOOD TOGETHER — Andy Kim (Jeff Barry), Steed 720 | 6 |
| 42 | 43 | 48 | — | BACKFIELD IN MOTION — Mel & Tim (Karl Tarleton), Bamboo 107 | 3 |
| 43 | 32 | 26 | 18 | WHEN I DIE — Motherlode (Mort Ross & Doug Riley), Buddah 131 | 13 |
| 44 | 28 | 35 | 35 | MAKE BELIEVE — Wind (Bo Gentry), Life 200 | 9 |
| 45 | 52 | 76 | — | NA NA HEY HEY KISS HIM GOODBYE — Steam (Paul Leka), Fontana 1667 | 3 |
| 46 | 40 | 34 | 31 | IN A MOMENT — Intrigues (Martin & Bell), Yew 1001 | 14 |
| 47 | 45 | 41 | 41 | DON'T IT MAKE YOU WANT TO GO HOME — Joe South & the Believers (Joe South), Capitol 2592 | 11 |
| 48 | 53 | 59 | 68 | DOIN' OUR THING — Clarence Carter (Rick Hall), Atlantic 2660 | 6 |
| 49 | 50 | 68 | 73 | TIME MACHINE — Grand Funk Railroad (Terry Knight), Capitol 2567 | 6 |
| 50 | 61 | — | — | ELI'S COMING — Three Dog Night (Gabriel Mekler), Dunhill 4215 | 2 |
| 51 | 60 | 78 | — | UNDUN — Guess Who (Jack Richardson), RCA 74-0195 | 3 |
| 52 | 57 | 69 | 80 | MIND, BODY & SOUL — Flaming Embers (R. Dunbar), Hot Wax 6902 | 6 |
| 53 | 56 | 62 | 82 | THE SWEETER HE IS — Soul Children (Hayes/Porter), Stax 0050 | 4 |
| 54 | 54 | 55 | 62 | ANY WAY THAT YOU WANT ME — Evie Sands (Chip Taylor-Al Gorgoni), A&M 1090 | 12 |
| 55 | 51 | 52 | 59 | YOU'LL NEVER WALK ALONE — Brooklyn Bridge (Wes Farrell), Buddah 139 | 5 |
| 56 | 68 | 80 | — | MAKE YOUR OWN KIND OF MUSIC — Mama Cass Elliot (Steve Barri), Dunhill 4214 | 3 |
| 57 | 76 | — | — | LEAVING ON A JET PLANE — Peter, Paul & Mary (Albert B. Grossman & Milt Okun), Warner Bros.-Seven Arts 7340 | 2 |
| 58 | — | — | — | FORTUNATE SON — Creedence Clearwater Revival (John Fogerty), Fantasy 634 | 1 |
| 59 | 65 | 72 | 84 | KOOL AND THE GANG — Kool and the Gang (Redd Coach Prod.), De-Lite 519 | 8 |
| 60 | 87 | — | — | DOWN ON THE CORNER — Creedence Clearwater Revival (John Fogerty), Fantasy 634 | 2 |
| 61 | 63 | 79 | — | TURN ON A DREAM — Box Tops (Tommy Cogbill), Mala 12042 | 3 |
| 62 | 71 | 73 | 77 | GROOVY GRUBWORM — Harlow Wilcox (Shelby Singleton), Plantation 28 | 4 |
| 63 | 74 | 75 | 85 | I'LL BET YOU — Funkadelic (Clinton/Baines/Lindsey), Westbound 130 | 5 |
| 64 | 85 | — | — | ROOSEVELT & IRA LEE — Tony Joe White (Billy Swann), Monument 1169 | 2 |
| 65 | 67 | 71 | 71 | SINCE I MET YOU BABY — Sonny James (Kelso Herston), Capitol 2595 | 7 |
| 66 | 93 | — | — | FRIENDSHIP TRAIN — Gladys Knight & the Pips (Norman Whitfield), Soul 35068 | 2 |
| 67 | 82 | 92 | — | SHANGRI-LA — Lettermen (Al De Lory), Capitol 2643 | 4 |
| 68 | 91 | — | — | THESE EYES — Jr. Walker & the All Stars (Johnny Bristol), Soul 35067 | 2 |
| 69 | 78 | 85 | — | PROUD MARY — Checkmates, Ltd. featuring Sonny Charles (Phil Spector), A&M 1127 | 3 |
| 70 | 77 | 77 | 87 | COLOR OF MY LOVE — Jefferson (John Schroeder), Decca 32501 | 7 |
| 71 | — | — | — | HOLLY HOLY — Neil Diamond (Tom Catalano & Tom Cogbill), UNI 55175 | 1 |
| 72 | 86 | — | — | I STILL BELIEVE IN TOMORROW — John & Anne Ryder (Mark Edwards), Decca 734661 | 2 |
| 73 | 73 | 95 | 98 | DELTA LADY — Joe Cocker (Denny Cordell), A&M 1112 | 5 |
| 74 | — | — | — | UP ON CRIPPLE CREEK — The Band (John Simon), Capitol 2635 | 1 |
| 75 | 75 | 84 | 86 | SILVER THREADS AND GOLDEN NEEDLES — Cowsills (Bob Waschtel), MGM 14084 | 4 |
| 76 | 84 | 93 | 93 | WE'LL CRY TOGETHER — Maxine Brown (Koppelman & Rubin, Finiz), Commonwealth United 3001 | 6 |
| 77 | 88 | — | — | EVIL WOMAN, DON'T PLAY YOUR GAMES WITH ME — Crow (Bob Monaco), Amaret 112 | 2 |
| 78 | 95 | 96 | — | SAY YOU LOVE ME — Impressions (Curtis Mayfield), Curtom 1946 | 3 |
| 79 | 96 | 97 | — | CRUMBS OFF THE TABLE — Glass House (Holland-Dozier-Holland), Invictus 9071 | 3 |
| 80 | 80 | 81 | 94 | JULIA — Ramsey Lewis (C. Stepney), Cadet 5640 | 6 |
| 81 | 94 | — | — | SUNDAY MORNIN' COMIN' DOWN — Ray Stevens (Jim Malloy & Ray Stevens), Monument 1163 | 2 |
| 82 | — | — | — | (Sittin' On) THE DOCK OF THE BAY — Dells (Bobby Miller), Cadet 5658 | 1 |
| 83 | — | — | — | I GUESS THE LORD MUST BE IN NEW YORK CITY — Nilsson (Rick Jarrard), RCA 74-0261 | 1 |
| 84 | 92 | — | — | SHE'S GOT LOVE — Thomas & Richard Frost (Ted Glasser), Imperial 66405 | 2 |
| 85 | — | — | — | TONIGHT I'LL BE STAYING HERE WITH YOU — Bob Dylan (Bob Johnston), Columbia 4-45004 | 1 |
| 86 | — | — | — | RAINDROPS KEEP FALLIN' ON MY HEAD — B.J. Thomas (Burt Bacharach-Hal David), Scepter 12265 | 1 |
| 87 | 90 | 90 | — | IT'S HARD TO GET ALONG — Joe Simon (John R.), Sound Stage 7 2641 | 3 |
| 88 | — | 98 | — | WE MUST BE IN LOVE — Five Stairsteps & Cubie (Curtis Mayfield), Curtom 1945 | 2 |
| 89 | 89 | — | — | WONDERFUL — Blackwell (Doyle Jones), Astro 1000 | 2 |
| 90 | — | — | — | LOVE WILL FIND A WAY — Jackie DeShannon (VME Prod.), Imperial 66419 | 1 |
| 91 | — | — | — | OKIE FROM MUSKOGEE — Merle Haggard & the Strangers (Ken Nelson), Capitol 2626 | 1 |
| 92 | — | — | — | BALLAD OF EASY RIDER — Byrds (Terry Melcher), Columbia 4-44990 | 1 |
| 93 | — | — | — | WE LOVE YOU, CALL COLLECT — Art Linkletter (Irvin S. Arkins), Capitol 2678 | 1 |
| 94 | — | — | — | CUPID — Johnny Nash (Johnny Nash-Arthur Jenkins), JAD 220 | 1 |
| 95 | 98 | — | — | ONE WOMAN — Johnny Rivers (Johnny Rivers), Imperial 66418 | 4 |
| 96 | 99 | 99 | 100 | SHE BELONGS TO ME — Rick Nelson (Rick Nelson), Decca 732550 | 4 |
| 97 | — | — | — | JINGO — Santana (Brent Dangerfield [T]), Columbia 4-45010 | 1 |
| 98 | — | — | — | WHY IS THE WINE SWEETER (On the Other Side) — Eddie Floyd (Booker T. Jones), Stax 0051 | 1 |
| 99 | — | — | — | MIDNIGHT COWBOY — Ferrante & Teicher (George Butler), United Artists 50554 | 1 |
| 100 | — | — | — | I CAN'T MAKE IT ALONE — Lou Rawls (David Axelrod), Capitol 2668 | 1 |

## BUBBLING UNDER THE HOT 100

| | | |
|---|---|---|
| 101 | TODAY I SING THE BLUES | Aretha Franklin, Columbia 4-44951 |
| 102 | THAT'S HOW HEARTACHES ARE MADE | Marvelettes, Tamla 54186 |
| 103 | POOR MAN | Little Milton, Checker 1221 |
| 104 | JUST A LITTLE LOVE | B. B. King, BluesWay 61029 |
| 105 | GOODBYE COLUMBUS | Association, Warner Bros.-Seven Arts 7267 |
| 106 | GIRLS IT AIN'T EASY | Honeycone, Hot Wax 6903 |
| 107 | ONE CUP OF HAPPINESS | Dean Martin, Reprise 0857 |
| 108 | WHEN I'M IN YOUR ARMS | Dells, Cadet 5658 |
| 109 | BRAND NEW ME | Jerry Butler, Mercury 72960 |
| 110 | HOW DOES IT FEEL | Illusion, Steed 721 |
| 111 | GET IT FROM THE BOTTOM | Steelers, Date 2-1642 |
| 112 | RIVER DEEP—MOUNTAIN HIGH | Ike & Tina Turner, A&M 1118 |
| 113 | LOVE AND LET LOVE | Hardy Boys, RCA 74-0228 |
| 114 | LIKE A ROLLING STONE | Phil Flowers & the Flowershop, A&M 1122 |
| 115 | HOROSCOPE | Young Holt Unlimited, Brunswick 755421 |
| 116 | (I'm So) AFRAID OF LOSING YOU | Charley Pride, RCA 74-0265 |
| 117 | CURLY | Jimmy Clanton, Laurie 3508 |
| 118 | LADY JANE | Plastic Cow Goes Mooooog, Dot 17300 |
| 119 | A WOMAN'S WAY | Andy Williams, Columbia 4-45003 |
| 120 | TEN COMMANDMENTS OF LOVE | Little Anthony & the Imperials, United Artists 50598 |
| 121 | ST. LOUIS | Easy Beats, Rare Earth 5009 |
| 122 | HEAVEN KNOWS | Grassroots, Dunhill 4217 |
| 123 | BRAND NEW ME | Dusty Springfield, Atlantic 2685 |
| 124 | SOME OF SHELLEY'S BLUES | Nitty Gritty Dirt Band, Liberty 56134 |

Compiled from national retail sales and radio station airplay by the Music Popularity Dept. of Record Market Research, Billboard.

# Billboard HOT 100

FOR WEEK ENDING NOVEMBER 8, 1969

♫ Artist and/or Selection featured on "The Music Scene" this week, ABC-TV Network. Those in black were featured on past programs.

★ STAR PERFORMER—Sides registering greatest proportionate sales progress this week. (seal) Record Industry Association of America seal of certification as million selling single.

| This Week | 1 Wk. Ago | 2 Wks. Ago | 3 Wks. Ago | TITLE Artist (Producer), Label & Number | Weeks On Chart |
|---|---|---|---|---|---|
| ★1 | 2 | 7 | 8 | WEDDING BELL BLUES — 5th Dimension (Bones Howe), Soul City 779 | 7 |
| 2 | 1 | 5 | 6 | SUSPICIOUS MINDS — Elvis Presley, RCA 47-9764 | 9 |
| ♫ ★3 | 10 | 13 | 23 | COME TOGETHER — Beatles (George Martin), Apple 2654 | 4 (seal) |
| ♫ 4 | 4 | 1 | 1 | I CAN'T GET NEXT TO YOU — Temptations (Norman Whitfield), Gordy 7093 | 13 |
| ♫ 5 | 5 | 8 | 13 | BABY IT'S YOU — Smith (Joel Sill & Steve Barri), Dunhill 4206 | 10 |
| ♫ 6 | 3 | 3 | 3 | SUGAR, SUGAR — Archies (Jeff Barry), Calendar 63-1008 | 16 (seal) |
| ♫ 7 | 6 | 2 | 2 | HOT FUN IN THE SUMMER-TIME — Sly & the Family Stone (Sly Stone), Epic 5-10497 | 13 |
| ★8 | 17 | 29 | 50 | AND WHEN I DIE — Blood, Sweat & Tears (James William Guercio), Columbia 4-45008 | 4 |
| ♫ ★9 | 11 | 11 | 20 | SOMETHING — Beatles (George Martin), Apple 2654 | 4 (seal) |
| 10 | 12 | 16 | 38 | SMILE A LITTLE SMILE FOR ME — The Flying Machine (Tony MacAuley), Congress 6000 | 6 |
| 11 | 13 | 14 | 17 | IS THAT ALL THERE IS — Peggy Lee (Lieber/Stoller), Capitol 2602 | 7 |
| 12 | 9 | 9 | 10 | TRACY — Cuff Links (Paul Vance-Lee Pockriss), Decca 32533 | 9 |
| ♫ 13 | 7 | 6 | 5 | LITTLE WOMAN — Bobby Sherman (Jackie Mills), Metromedia 121 | 12 (seal) |
| ♫ 14 | 8 | 4 | 4 | JEAN — Oliver (Bob Crewe), Crewe 334 | 13 (seal) |
| 15 | 16 | 25 | 27 | GOING IN CIRCLES — Friends of Distinction (John Florez), RCA 74-0204 | 13 |
| 16 | 18 | 20 | 30 | YOU'VE LOST THAT LOVIN' FEELING — Dionne Warwick (Chips Moman & Dionne Warwick), Scepter 12262 | 8 |
| ★17 | 22 | 26 | 33 | BABY, I'M FOR REAL — Originals (Marvin Gaye), Soul 35066 | 7 |
| ♫ ★18 | 21 | 37 | 61 | TAKE A LETTER MARIA — R. B. Greaves (Ahmet Ertegun), Atco 6714 | 4 |
| ★19 | 26 | 33 | 42 | BALL OF FIRE — Tommy James & the Shondells (Tommy James), Roulette 7060 | 6 |
| ★20 | 42 | 43 | 48 | BACKFIELD IN MOTION — Mel & Tim (Karl Tarleton), Bamboo 107 | 4 |
| ♫ ★21 | 30 | 58 | 65 | LET A MAN COME IN AND DO THE POPCORN (PART I) — James Brown (James Brown), King 6255 | 5 |
| ★22 | 45 | 52 | 76 | NA NA HEY HEY KISS HIM GOODBYE — Steam (Paul Leka), Fontana 1667 | 4 |
| ♫ ★23 | 50 | 61 | — | ELI'S COMING — Three Dog Night (Gabriel Mekler), Dunhill 4215 | 3 |
| 24 | 15 | 10 | 11 | I'M GONNA MAKE YOU MINE — Lou Christie (Stan Vincent & Mike Duckman), Buddah 116 | 12 |
| ★25 | 38 | 49 | 63 | CHERRY HILL PARK — Billy Joe Royal (Buddy Buie), Columbia 4-44902 | 6 |
| ★26 | 33 | 44 | 67 | TRY A LITTLE KINDNESS — Glen Campbell (Al De Lory), Capitol 2659 | 5 |
| 27 | 14 | 12 | 7 | THAT'S THE WAY LOVE IS — Marvin Gaye (Norman Whitfield), Tamla 54185 | 12 |
| ♫ ★28 | 34 | 34 | 64 | SUITE: JUDY BLUE EYES — Crosby/Stills/Nash (Stephen Stills, David Crosby & Graham Nash), Atlantic 2676 | 6 |
| ★29 | 32 | 59 | 94 | YESTER-ME, YESTER-YOU, YESTERDAY — Stevie Wonder (John Bristol), Tamla 54188 | 4 |
| ★30 | 35 | 36 | 56 | RUBEN JAMES — Kenny Rogers & First Edition (Mike Post), Reprise 0854 | 7 |
| ♫ 31 | 31 | 30 | 32 | WALK ON BY — Isaac Hayes (Al Bell-Marvell Thomas-Allen Jones), Enterprise 9003 | 11 |
| ♫ 32 | 19 | 19 | 18 | I'LL NEVER FALL IN LOVE AGAIN — Tom Jones (Peter Sullivan), Parrot 40018 | 16 |
| ★33 | 58 | — | — | FORTUNATE SON — Creedence Clearwater Revival (John Fogerty), Fantasy 634 | 2 |
| 34 | 20 | 21 | 21 | JEALOUS KIND OF FELLOW — Garland Greene (Giant Enterprises Prod.), UNI 55143 | 9 |
| 35 | 28 | 35 | 36 | JESUS IS A SOUL MAN — Lawrence Reynolds (Don Davis), Warner Bros.-Seven Arts 7322 | 8 |
| 36 | 41 | 41 | 46 | SO GOOD TOGETHER — Andy Kim (Jeff Barry), Steed 720 | 7 |
| ★37 | 51 | 60 | 78 | UNDUN — Guess Who (Jack Richardson), RCA 74-0195 | 4 |
| ★38 | 60 | 87 | — | DOWN ON THE CORNER — Creedence Clearwater Revival (John Fogerty), Fantasy 634 | 3 |
| ★39 | 57 | 76 | — | LEAVING ON A JET PLANE — Peter, Paul & Mary (Albert B. Grossman & Milt Okun), Warner Bros.-Seven Arts 7340 | 3 |
| 40 | 40 | 42 | 44 | ECHO PARK — Keith Barbour (Austin & Flemming), Epic 5-10486 | 7 |
| ★41 | 52 | 57 | 69 | MIND, BODY & SOUL — Flaming Embers (R. Dunbar), Hot Wax 6902 | 7 |
| 42 | 24 | 22 | 22 | SUGAR ON SUNDAY — Clique (Gary Zekley), White Whale 323 | 11 |
| ★43 | 56 | 68 | 80 | MAKE YOUR OWN KIND OF MUSIC — Mama Cass Elliot (Steve Barri), Dunhill 4214 | 4 |
| ★44 | 71 | — | — | HOLLY HOLY — Neil Diamond (Tom Catalono & Tom Cogbill) UNI 55175 | 2 |
| 45 | 36 | 48 | 58 | LET A WOMAN BE A WOMAN, LET A MAN BE A MAN — Dyke and the Blazers (Laboe/Barrette), Original Sound 89 | 8 |
| 46 | 48 | 53 | 59 | DOIN' OUR THING — Clarence Carter (Rick Hall), Atlantic 2660 | 7 |
| 47 | 47 | 45 | 41 | DON'T IT MAKE YOU WANNA GO HOME — Joe South & the Believers (Joe South), Capitol 2592 | 12 |
| 48 | 49 | 50 | 68 | TIME MACHINE — Grand Funk Railroad (Terry Knight), Capitol 2567 | 7 |
| ★49 | 68 | 91 | — | THESE EYES — Jr. Walker & the All Stars (Johnny Bristol), Soul 35067 | 3 |
| ★50 | — | — | — | SOMEDAY WE'LL BE TOGETHER — Diana Ross & the Supremes (Johnny Bristol), Motown 1156 | 1 |
| 51 | 37 | 38 | 51 | SOMETHING IN THE AIR — Thunderclap Newman (Peter Townshend), Track 2656 | 10 |
| 52 | 53 | 56 | 62 | THE SWEETER HE IS — Soul Children (Hayes/Porter), Stax 0050 | 5 |
| 53 | 54 | 54 | 55 | ANY WAY THAT YOU WANT ME — Evie Sands (Chip Taylor-Al Gorgoni), A&M 1090 | 13 |
| ★54 | 93 | — | — | WE LOVE YOU, CALL COLLECT — Art Linkletter (Irvin S. Arkins), Capitol 2678 | 2 |
| ★55 | 64 | 85 | — | ROOSEVELT & IRA LEE — Tony Joe White (Billy Swann), Monument 1169 | 3 |
| ★56 | 66 | 93 | — | FRIENDSHIP TRAIN — Gladys Knight & the Pips (Norman Whitfield), Soul 35068 | 3 |
| ★57 | — | — | — | HEAVEN KNOWS — Grassroots (Steve Barri), Dunhill 4217 | 1 |
| ★58 | 74 | — | — | UP ON CRIPPLE CREEK — The Band (John Simon), Capitol 2635 | 2 |
| 59 | 59 | 65 | 72 | KOOL AND THE GANG — Kool and the Gang (Redd Coach Prod.), De-Lite 519 | 9 |
| 60 | 61 | 63 | 79 | TURN ON A DREAM — Box Tops (Tommy Cogbill), Mala 12042 | 4 |
| 61 | 62 | 71 | 73 | GROOVY GRUBWORM — Harlow Wilcox (Shelby Singleton), Plantation 28 | 5 |
| 62 | 55 | 51 | 52 | YOU'LL NEVER WALK ALONE — Brooklyn Bridge (Wes Farrell), Buddah 139 | 6 |
| 63 | 63 | 74 | 75 | I'LL BET YOU — Funkadelic (Clinton/Baines/Lindsey), Westbound 130 | 6 |
| 64 | 67 | 82 | 92 | SHANGRI-LA — Lettermen (Al De Lory), Capitol 2643 | 4 |
| ★65 | 83 | — | — | I GUESS THE LORD MUST BE IN NEW YORK CITY — Nilsson (Rick Jarrard), RCA 74-0261 | 2 |
| ♫ ★66 | 100 | — | — | I CAN'T MAKE IT ALONE — Lou Rawls (David Axelrod), Capitol 2668 | 2 |
| ★67 | 77 | 88 | — | EVIL WOMAN, DON'T PLAY YOUR GAMES WITH ME — Crow (Bob Monaco), Amaret 112 | 3 |
| 68 | 70 | 77 | 77 | COLOUR OF MY LOVE — Jefferson (John Schroeder), Decca 32501 | 8 |
| 69 | 73 | 73 | 95 | DELTA LADY — Joe Cocker (Denny Cordell), A&M 1112 | 6 |
| ★70 | 90 | — | — | LOVE WILL FIND A WAY — Jackie DeShannon (VME Prod.), Imperial 66419 | 2 |
| ♫ ★71 | 82 | — | — | (Sittin' On) THE DOCK OF THE BAY — Dells (Bobby Miller), Cadet 5658 | 2 |
| 72 | 72 | 86 | — | I STILL BELIEVE IN TOMORROW — John & Anne Ryder (Mark Edwards), Decca 734661 | 3 |
| 73 | 76 | 84 | 93 | WE'LL CRY TOGETHER — Maxine Brown (Koppelman & Rubin, Finiz), Commonwealth United 3001 | 7 |
| 74 | 75 | 75 | 84 | SILVER THREADS AND GOLDEN NEEDLES — Cowsills (Bob Waschtel), MGM 14084 | 5 |
| 75 | 78 | 95 | 96 | SAY YOU LOVE ME — Impressions (Curtis Mayfield), Curtom 1946 | 4 |
| 76 | 80 | 80 | 81 | JULIA — Ramsey Lewis (C. Stepney), Cadet 5640 | 7 |
| 77 | 69 | 78 | 85 | PROUD MARY — Checkmates, Ltd., featuring Sonny Charles (Phil Spector), A&M 1127 | 4 |
| 78 | 79 | 96 | 97 | CRUMBS OFF THE TABLE — Glass House (Holland-Dozier-Holland), Invictus 9071 | 4 |
| ★79 | 85 | — | — | TONIGHT I'LL BE STAYING HERE WITH YOU — Bob Dylan (Bob Johnston), Columbia 4-45004 | 2 |
| ★80 | 86 | — | — | RAINDROPS KEEP FALLIN' ON MY HEAD — B.J. Thomas (Burt Bacharach-Hal David), Scepter 12265 | 2 |
| 81 | 81 | 94 | — | SUNDAY MORNIN' COMIN' DOWN — Ray Stevens (Jim Malloy & Ray Stevens), Monument 1163 | 3 |
| ★82 | 92 | — | — | BALLAD OF EASY RIDER — Byrds (Terry Melcher), Columbia 4-44990 | 2 |
| ★83 | — | — | — | A BRAND NEW ME — Dusty Springfield (Roland Chambers), Atlantic 2685 | 1 |
| 84 | 84 | 92 | — | SHE'S GOT LOVE — Thomas & Richard Frost (Ted Glasser), Imperial 66405 | 3 |
| ★85 | — | — | — | GIRLS, IT AIN'T EASY — Honey Cone (Stagecoach Prod.), Hot Wax 6903 | 1 |
| ★86 | — | 100 | 100 | JUST A LITTLE LOVE — B. B. King (Bill Szymczyk), BluesWay 61029 | 4 |
| ★87 | 99 | — | — | MIDNIGHT COWBOY — Ferrante & Teicher (George Butler), United Artists 50554 | 2 |
| 88 | 88 | — | 98 | WE MUST BE IN LOVE — Five Stairsteps & Cubie (Curtis Mayfield), Curtom 1945 | 3 |
| 89 | 95 | 98 | — | ONE WOMAN — Johnny Rivers (Johnny Rivers), Imperial 66418 | 5 |
| ♫ 90 | 91 | — | — | OKIE FROM MUSKOGEE — Merle Haggard & the Strangers (Ken Nelson), Capitol 2626 | 2 |
| 91 | 97 | 97 | — | JINGO — Santana [Brent Dangerfield (IT)], Columbia 4-45010 | 3 |
| 92 | — | — | — | YOU GOT TO PAY THE PRICE — Gloria Taylor (S. Whisenhunt), Silver Fox 14 | 1 |
| 93 | — | — | — | THE TEN COMMANDMENTS OF LOVE — Little Anthony & the Imperials (Bob Skaff), United Artists 50598 | 1 |
| ♫ 94 | — | — | — | KOZMIC BLUES — Janis Joplin (Gabriel Mekler), Columbia 4-45023 | 1 |
| 95 | — | — | — | (I'm So) AFRAID OF LOSING YOU AGAIN — Charley Pride (Jack Clement), RCA 74-0265 | 1 |
| 96 | — | — | — | ELEANOR RIGBY — Aretha Franklin (Jerry Wexler-Tom Dowd-Arif Mardin), Atlantic 2683 | 1 |
| 97 | — | — | — | THAT'S THE WAY HEARTACHES ARE MADE — Marvelettes (Clay McMurray), Tamla 54186 | 1 |
| 98 | 98 | — | — | WHY IS THE WINE SWEETER (On the Other Side) — Eddie Floyd (Booker T. Jones), Stax 0051 | 2 |
| 99 | — | — | — | VOLUNTEERS — Jefferson Airplane (Al Schmitt), RCA 74-0245 | 1 |
| ♫ 100 | — | — | — | SEE RUBY FALL — Johnny Cash (Bob Johnston), Columbia 4-45020 | 1 |

## HOT 100—A TO Z—(Publisher-Licensee)


And When I Die (Tuna Fish, BMI) .... 8
Any Way That You Want Me (Blackwood, BMI) .... 53
Baby, I'm For Real (Jobete, BMI) .... 17
Baby It's You (Dolfi/Mary Jane, ASCAP) .... 5
Backfield in Motion (Cachand/Patcheal, BMI) .... 20
Ball of Fire (Big Seven, BMI) .... 19
Ballad of Easy Rider (Pation, BMI) .... 82
Brand New Me (Assorted/Parabut, BMI) .... 83
Cherry Hill Park (Low-Sal, BMI) .... 25
Colour of My Love (Ramrac) .... 68
Come Together (Maclen, BMI) .... 3
Crumbs Off the Table (Gold Forever, BMI) .... 78
Delta Lady (Skyhill, BMI) .... 69
Doin' Our Thing (Fame, BMI) .... 46
Don't It Make You Wanna Go Home (Lowery, BMI) 47
Down on the Corner (Jondora, BMI) .... 38
Echo Park (Hastings, BMI) .... 40
Eleanor Rigby (Maclen, BMI) .... 96
Eli's Coming (Tuna Fish, BMI) .... 23
Evil Woman, Don't Play Your Games With Me (Yoggoth, BMI) .... 67
Fortunate Son (Jondora, BMI) .... 33
Friendship Train (Jobete, BMI) .... 56
Girls, It Ain't Easy (Gold Forever, BMI) .... 85
Going in Circles (Porpete, BMI) .... 15
Groovy Grubworm (Little River, BMI) .... 61
Heaven Knows (Trousdale, BMI) .... 57
Holly Holy (Stonebridge, BMI) .... 44
Hot Fun in the Summertime (Stone Flower, BMI) .... 7
I Can't Get Next to You (Jobete, BMI) .... 4
I Can't Make It Alone (Screen Gems-Columbia, BMI) .... 66
I Guess the Lord Must Be in New York City (Dunbar, BMI) .... 65
I Still Believe in Tomorrow (Leeds, ASCAP) .... 72
I'll Bet You (Jobete, BMI) .... 63
I'll Never Fall in Love Again (TRO-Hollis, BMI) .... 32
I'm Gonna Make You Mine (Pocketful of Tunes, BMI) .... 24
(I'm So) Afraid of Losing You Again (Hill & Range/Blue Crest, BMI) .... 95
Is That All There Is (Trio, BMI) .... 11
Jealous Kind of Fellow (Colfam, BMI) .... 34
Jean (Twentieth Century, ASCAP) .... 14
Jesus Is a Soul Man (Wilderness, BMI) .... 35
Jingo (Blackwood, BMI) .... 91
Julia (Maclen, BMI) .... 76
Just a Little Love (Sound of Lucille/Pamco, BMI) .... 86
Kool and the Gang (Stephayne, BMI) .... 59
Kozmic Blues (Strong Arm/Wingate, ASCAP) .... 94
Leaving on a Jet Plane (Cherry Lane, ASCAP) .... 39
Let a Man Come in and Do the Popcorn (Part 1) (Dynatone, BMI) .... 21
Let a Woman Be a Woman, Let a Man Be a Man (Drive-In/Westward, BMI) .... 45
Little Woman (Green Apple, BMI) .... 13
Love Will Find a Way (Unart, BMI) .... 70
Make Your Own Kind of Music (Screen Gems-Columbia, BMI) .... 43
Midnight Cowboy (United Artists/Barwin, ASCAP) .... 87
Mind, Body & Soul (Gold Forever, BMI) .... 41
Na Na Hey Hey Kiss Him Goodbye (MRC/Little Heather, BMI) .... 22
Okie From Muskogee (Blue Book, BMI) .... 90
One Woman (Rhomers, BMI) .... 89
Proud Mary (Jondora, BMI) .... 77
Raindrops Keep Fallin' on My Head (Blue Seas/Jac/20th Century, ASCAP) .... 80
Roosevelt & Ira Lee (Combine, BMI) .... 55
Ruben James (Unart, BMI) .... 30
Say You Love Me (Curtom, BMI) .... 95
See Ruby Fall (House of Cash, BMI) .... 100
Shangri-La (Robbins, ASCAP) .... 64
She's Got Love (Claridge/Tons of Fun, ASCAP) .... 84
Silver Threads and Golden Needles (Central Songs, BMI) .... 74
(Sittin' On) The Dock of the Bay (East/Time/Redwall, BMI) .... 71
Smile a Little Smile for Me (January, BMI) .... 10
So Good Together (Unart/Joachim, BMI) .... 36
Someday We'll Be Together (Jobete, BMI) .... 50
Something (Harrisongs, BMI) .... 9
Something in the Air (Track, BMI) .... 51
Sugar on Sunday (Big Seven, BMI) .... 42
Sugar, Sugar (Kirshner, BMI) .... 6
Suite: Judy Blue Eyes (Gold Hill, BMI) .... 28
Sunday Mornin' Comin' Down (Combine, BMI) .... 81
Suspicious Minds (Press, BMI) .... 2
Sweeter He Is, The (Birdees, ASCAP) .... 52
Take a Letter Maria (Four Star Television, BMI) .... 18
Ten Commandments of Love, The (Arc, BMI) .... 93
That's the Way Heartaches Are Made (Sea Lark, BMI) .... 97
That's the Way Love Is (Jobete, BMI) .... 27
These Eyes (Dunbar, BMI) .... 49
Time Machine (Storybook, BMI) .... 48
Tonight I'll Be Staying With You (Big Sky, ASCAP) 79
Tracy (Vanlee/Emily, ASCAP) .... 12
Try a Little Kindness (Airfield/Campbell, BMI) .... 26
Turn On a Dream (Press, BMI) .... 60
Undun (Friends of Mine, Ltd./Dunbar/Cirrus, BMI) .... 37
Up on Cripple Creek (Canaan, ASCAP) .... 58
Volunteers (Icebag, BMI) .... 99
Walk On By (Blue Seas/Jac/ASCAP) .... 31
Wedding Bell Blues (Tuna Fish, BMI) .... 1
We Love You, Call Collect (World, BMI) .... 54
We Must Be In Love (Camad, BMI) .... 88
We'll Cry Together (McCoy/Chevis, BMI) .... 73
Why Is the Wine Sweeter (On the Other Side) (East/Memphis, BMI) .... 48
Yester-Me, Yester-You, Yesterday (Stein & Van Stock, ASCAP) .... 29
You Got to Pay the Price (Myto, BMI) .... 92
You'll Never Walk Alone (Williamson, ASCAP) .... 62
You've Lost That Lovin' Feeling (Screen Gems-Columbia, BMI) .... 16


## BUBBLING UNDER THE HOT 100

101. LOVE & LET LOVE .... Hardy Boys, RCA 74-0228
102. SHE BELONGS TO ME .... Rick Nelson, Decca 732550
103. ST. LOUIS .... Easybeats, Rare Earth 5009
104. ONE TIN SOLDIER .... Original Caste, T.A. 186
105. EARLY IN THE MORNING .... Vanity Fare, Page One 21-021
106. SOME OF SHELLEY'S BLUES .... Nitty Gritty Dirt Band, Liberty 56134
107. CURLY .... Jimmy Clanton, Laurie 3508
108. GET IT FROM THE BOTTOM .... Steelers, Date 2-1642
109. A WOMAN'S WAY .... Andy Williams, Columbia 4-45003
110. BABY YOU COME ROLLIN' CROSS MY MIND .... John Beland, Randwood 853
111. GROOVIN' (Out on Life) .... Newbeats, Hickory 1552
112. MIDNIGHT .... Dennis Yost & the Classics IV, Imperial 66424
113. CUPID .... Johnny Nash, JAD 220
114. SUNLIGHT .... Youngbloods, RCA 74-0270
115. MY BABE .... Willie Mitchell, HI 2167
116. MEMORIES ARE MADE OF BROKEN PROMISES .... Motherlode, Buddah 144
117. I WANT YOU BACK .... Jackson 5, Motown 1157
118. POOR MAN .... Little Milton, Checker 1221
119. TODAY I SING THE BLUES .... Aretha Franklin, Columbia 4-44951
120. I'M GONNA TEAR YOU A NEW HEART .... Clarence Reid, Alston 4578
121. A BRAND NEW ME .... Jerry Butler, Mercury 72960
122. WHEN I'M IN YOUR ARMS .... Dells, Cadet 5658
123. ONE CUP OF HAPPINESS .... Dean Martin, Reprise 0857
124. NO ONE BETTER THAN YOU .... Petula Clark, Warner Bros.-Seven Arts 7343

# Billboard HOT 100

FOR WEEK ENDING NOVEMBER 15, 1969

♫ Artist and/or Selection featured on "The Music Scene" this week, ABC-TV Network. Those in black were featured on past programs.

★ STAR PERFORMER—Sides registering greatest proportionate sales progress this week. (Seal) Record Industry Association of America seal of certification as million selling single.

| This Week | 1 Wk. Ago | 2 Wks. Ago | 3 Wks. Ago | TITLE Artist (Producer), Label & Number | Weeks On Chart | Notes |
|---|---|---|---|---|---|---|
| 1 | 1 | 2 | 7 | **WEDDING BELL BLUES** — 5th Dimension (Bones Howe), Soul City 779 | 8 | |
| 2 | 3 | 10 | 13 | **COME TOGETHER** — Beatles (George Martin), Apple 2654 | 5 | ♫ RIAA seal |
| 3 | 9 | 11 | 11 | **SOMETHING** — Beatles (George Martin), Apple 2654 | 5 | ♫ ★ RIAA seal |
| 4 | 8 | 17 | 29 | **AND WHEN I DIE** — Blood, Sweat & Tears (James William Guercio), Columbia 4-45008 | 5 | ★ |
| 5 | 5 | 5 | 8 | **BABY IT'S YOU** — Smith (Joel Sill & Steve Barri), Dunhill 4206 | 11 | ♫ |
| 6 | 4 | 4 | 1 | **I CAN'T GET NEXT TO YOU** — Temptations (Norman Whitfield), Gordy 7093 | 14 | ♫ |
| 7 | 2 | 1 | 5 | **SUSPICIOUS MINDS** — Elvis Presley, RCA 47-9764 | 10 | RIAA seal |
| 8 | 10 | 12 | 16 | **SMILE A LITTLE SMILE FOR ME** — The Flying Machine (Tony MacAuley), Congress 6000 | 7 | ★ |
| 9 | 6 | 3 | 3 | **SUGAR, SUGAR** — Archies (Jeff Barry), Calendar 63-1008 | 17 | ♫ RIAA seal |
| 10 | 18 | 21 | 37 | **TAKE A LETTER MARIA** — R. B. Greaves (Ahmet Ertegun), Atco 6714 | 5 | ♫ ★ |
| 11 | 22 | 45 | 52 | **NA NA HEY HEY KISS HIM GOODBYE** — Steam (Paul Leka), Fontana 1667 | 5 | ★ |
| 12 | 7 | 6 | 2 | **HOT FUN IN THE SUMMER-TIME** — Sly & the Family Stone (Sly Stone), Epic 5-10497 | 14 | ♫ |
| 13 | 12 | 9 | 9 | **TRACY** — Cuff Links (Paul Vance-Lee Pockriss), Decca 32533 | 10 | |
| 14 | 11 | 13 | 14 | **IS THAT ALL THERE IS** — Peggy Lee (Lieber/Stoller), Capitol 2602 | 8 | |
| 15 | 15 | 16 | 25 | **GOING IN CIRCLES** — Friends of Distinction (John Florez), RCA 74-0204 | 14 | |
| 16 | 33 | 58 | — | **FORTUNATE SON** — Creedence Clearwater Revival (John Fogerty), Fantasy 634 | 3 | ★ |
| 17 | 17 | 22 | 26 | **BABY, I'M FOR REAL** — Originals (Marvin Gaye), Soul 35066 | 8 | |
| 18 | 20 | 42 | 43 | **BACKFIELD IN MOTION** — Mel & Tim (Karl Tarleton), Bamboo 107 | 5 | ★ |
| 19 | 19 | 26 | 33 | **BALL OF FIRE** — Tommy James & the Shondells (Tommy James), Roulette 7060 | 7 | |
| 20 | 23 | 50 | 61 | **ELI'S COMING** — Three Dog Night (Gabriel Mekler), Dunhill 4215 | 4 | ♫ ★ |
| 21 | 21 | 30 | 58 | **LET A MAN COME IN AND DO THE POPCORN (PART I)** — James Brown (James Brown), King 6255 | 6 | ♫ |
| 22 | 29 | 32 | 59 | **YESTER-ME, YESTER-YOU, YESTERDAY** — Stevie Wonder (John Bristol), Tamla 54188 | 5 | ★ |
| 23 | 39 | 57 | 76 | **LEAVING ON A JET PLANE** — Peter, Paul & Mary (Albert B. Grossman & Milt Okun), Warner Bros.-Seven Arts 7340 | 4 | ★ |
| 24 | 25 | 38 | 49 | **CHERRY HILL PARK** — Billy Joe Royal (Buddy Buie), Columbia 4-44902 | 7 | |
| 25 | 26 | 33 | 44 | **TRY A LITTLE KINDNESS** — Glen Campbell (Al De Lory), Capitol 2659 | 6 | |
| 26 | 30 | 35 | 36 | **RUBEN JAMES** — Kenny Rogers & First Edition (Mike Post), Reprise 0854 | 8 | |
| 27 | 28 | 34 | 34 | **SUITE: JUDY BLUE EYES** — Crosby/Stills/Nash (Stephen Stills, David Crosby & Graham Nash), Atlantic 2676 | 7 | ♫ |
| 28 | 16 | 18 | 20 | **YOU'VE LOST THAT LOVIN' FEELING** — Dionne Warwick (Chips Moman & Dionne Warwick), Scepter 12262 | 9 | |
| 29 | 37 | 51 | 60 | **UNDUN** — Guess Who (Jack Richardson), RCA 74-0195 | 5 | ★ |
| 30 | 38 | 60 | 87 | **DOWN ON THE CORNER** — Creedence Clearwater Revival (John Fogerty), Fantasy 634 | 4 | ★ |
| 31 | 13 | 7 | 6 | **LITTLE WOMAN** — Bobby Sherman (Jackie Mills), Metromedia 121 | 13 | ♫ RIAA seal |
| 32 | 44 | 71 | — | **HOLLY HOLY** — Neil Diamond (Tom Catalono & Tom Cogbill) UNI 55175 | 3 | ★ |
| 33 | 14 | 8 | 4 | **JEAN** — Oliver (Bob Crewe), Crewe 334 | 14 | ♫ RIAA seal |
| 34 | 50 | — | — | **SOMEDAY WE'LL BE TOGETHER** — Diana Ross & the Supremes (Johnny Bristol), Motown 1156 | 2 | ★ |
| 35 | 31 | 31 | 30 | **WALK ON BY** — Isaac Hayes (Al Bell-Marvell Thomas-Allen Jones), Enterprise 9003 | 12 | ♫ |
| 36 | 41 | 52 | 57 | **MIND, BODY & SOUL** — Flaming Embers (R. Dunbar), Hot Wax 6902 | 8 | |
| 37 | 56 | 66 | 93 | **FRIENDSHIP TRAIN** — Gladys Knight & the Pips (Norman Whitfield), Soul 35068 | 4 | ★ |
| 38 | 35 | 28 | 35 | **JESUS IS A SOUL MAN** — Lawrence Reynolds (Don Davis), Warner Bros.-Seven Arts 7322 | 9 | |
| 39 | 43 | 56 | 68 | **MAKE YOUR OWN KIND OF MUSIC** — Mama Cass Elliot (Steve Barri), Dunhill 4214 | 5 | |
| 40 | 96 | — | — | **ELEANOR RIGBY** — Aretha Franklin (Jerry Wexler-Tom Dowd-Arif Mardin), Atlantic 2683 | 2 | ★ |
| 41 | 36 | 41 | 41 | **SO GOOD TOGETHER** — Andy Kim (Jeff Barry), Steed 720 | 8 | |
| 42 | 49 | 68 | 91 | **THESE EYES** — Jr. Walker & the All Stars (Johnny Bristol), Soul 35067 | 4 | ★ |
| 43 | 54 | 93 | — | **WE LOVE YOU, CALL COLLECT** — Art Linkletter (Irvin S. Arkins), Capitol 2678 | 3 | ★ |
| 44 | 65 | 83 | — | **I GUESS THE LORD MUST BE IN NEW YORK CITY** — Nilsson (Rick Jarrard), RCA 74-0261 | 3 | ★ |
| 45 | 45 | 36 | 48 | **LET A WOMAN BE A WOMAN, LET A MAN BE A MAN** — Dyke and the Blazers (Laboe/Barrette), Original Sound 89 | 9 | |
| 46 | 55 | 64 | 85 | **ROOSEVELT & IRA LEE** — Tony Joe White (Billy Swann), Monument 1169 | 4 | ★ |
| 47 | 57 | — | — | **HEAVEN KNOWS** — Grassroots (Steve Barri), Dunhill 4217 | 2 | ★ |
| 48 | 40 | 40 | 42 | **ECHO PARK** — Keith Barbour (Austin & Flemming), Epic 5-10486 | 8 | ♫ |
| 49 | 61 | 62 | 71 | **GROOVY GRUBWORM** — Harlow Wilcox (Shelby Singleton), Plantation 28 | 6 | ★ |
| 50 | 48 | 49 | 50 | **TIME MACHINE** — Grand Funk Railroad (Terry Knight), Capitol 2567 | 8 | |
| 51 | 58 | 74 | — | **UP ON CRIPPLE CREEK** — The Band (John Simon), Capitol 2635 | 3 | |
| 52 | 87 | 99 | — | **MIDNIGHT COWBOY** — Ferrante & Teicher (George Butler), United Artists 50554 | 3 | ★ |
| 53 | 53 | 54 | 54 | **ANY WAY THAT YOU WANT ME** — Evie Sands (Chip Taylor-Al Gorgoni), A&M 1090 | 14 | |
| 54 | 52 | 53 | 56 | **THE SWEETER HE IS** — Soul Children (Hayes/Porter), Stax 0050 | 6 | |
| 55 | 79 | 85 | — | **TONIGHT I'LL BE STAYING HERE WITH YOU** — Bob Dylan (Bob Johnston), Columbia 4-45004 | 3 | ★ |
| 56 | 46 | 48 | 53 | **DOIN' OUR THING** — Clarence Carter (Rick Hall), Atlantic 2660 | 8 | |
| 57 | 34 | 20 | 21 | **JEALOUS KIND OF FELLOW** — Garland Greene (Giant Enterprises Prod.), UNI 55143 | 10 | |
| 58 | 60 | 61 | 63 | **TURN ON A DREAM** — Box Tops (Tommy Cogbill), Mala 12042 | 5 | |
| 59 | 67 | 77 | 88 | **EVIL WOMAN, DON'T PLAY YOUR GAMES WITH ME** — Crow (Bob Monaco), Amaret 112 | 4 | |
| 60 | 59 | 59 | 65 | **KOOL AND THE GANG** — Kool and the Gang (Redd Coach Prod.), De-Lite 519 | 10 | |
| 61 | 70 | 90 | — | **LOVE WILL FIND A WAY** — Jackie DeShannon (VME Prod.), Imperial 66419 | 3 | |
| 62 | 80 | 86 | — | **RAINDROPS KEEP FALLIN' ON MY HEAD** — B.J. Thomas (Burt Bacharach-Hal David), Scepter 12265 | 3 | ★ |
| 63 | 71 | 82 | — | **(Sittin' On) THE DOCK OF THE BAY** — Dells (Bobby Miller), Cadet 5658 | 3 | ♫ |
| 64 | 66 | 100 | — | **I CAN'T MAKE IT ALONE** — Lou Rawls (David Axelrod), Capitol 2668 | 3 | ♫ |
| 65 | 75 | 78 | 95 | **SAY YOU LOVE ME** — Impressions (Curtis Mayfield), Curtom 1946 | 5 | |
| 66 | 63 | 63 | 74 | **I'LL BET YOU** — Funkadelic (Clinton/Baines/Lindsey), Westbound 130 | 7 | |
| 67 | 83 | — | — | **A BRAND NEW ME** — Dusty Springfield (Roland Chambers), Atlantic 2685 | 2 | ♫ ★ |
| 68 | 91 | 97 | 97 | **JINGO** — Santana [Brent Dangerfield (IT)], Columbia 4-45010 | 4 | ★ |
| 69 | 78 | 79 | 96 | **CRUMBS OFF THE TABLE** — Glass House (Holland-Dozier-Holland), Invictus 9071 | 5 | |
| 70 | 72 | 72 | 86 | **I STILL BELIEVE IN TOMORROW** — John & Anne Ryder (Mark Edwards), Decca 734661 | 4 | |
| 71 | 68 | 70 | 77 | **COLOUR OF MY LOVE** — Jefferson (John Schroeder), Decca 32501 | 9 | |
| 72 | 64 | 67 | 82 | **SHANGRI-LA** — Lettermen (Al De Lory), Capitol 2643 | 5 | |
| 73 | — | — | — | **MIDNIGHT** — Dennis Yost & the Classics IV (Buddy Buie), Imperial 66424 | 1 | ★ |
| 74 | 74 | 75 | 75 | **SILVER THREADS AND GOLDEN NEEDLES** — Cowsills (Bob Waschtel), MGM 14084 | 6 | |
| 75 | 92 | — | — | **YOU GOT TO PAY THE PRICE** — Gloria Taylor (S. Whisenhunt), Silver Fox 14 | 2 | ★ |
| 76 | 73 | 76 | 84 | **WE'LL CRY TOGETHER** — Maxine Brown (Koppelman & Rubin, Finiz), Commonwealth United 3001 | 8 | |
| 77 | 82 | 92 | — | **BALLAD OF EASY RIDER** — Byrds (Terry Melcher), Columbia 4-44990 | 3 | |
| 78 | 85 | — | — | **GIRLS, IT AIN'T EASY** — Honey Cone (Stagecoach Prod.), Hot Wax 6903 | 2 | |
| 79 | 76 | 80 | 80 | **JULIA** — Ramsey Lewis (C. Stepney), Cadet 5640 | 8 | |
| 80 | 86 | — | 100 | **JUST A LITTLE LOVE** — B. B. King (Bill Szymczyk), BluesWay 61029 | 5 | |
| 81 | — | 94 | — | **CUPID** — Johnny Nash (Johnny Nash-Arthur Jenkins), Jad 220 | 2 | ★ |
| 82 | — | — | — | **GET IT FROM THE BOTTOM** — Steelers (Calvin Carter-Al Smith), Date 2-1642 | 1 | ★ |
| 83 | 84 | 84 | 92 | **SHE'S GOT LOVE** — Thomas & Richard Frost (Ted Glasser), Imperial 66405 | 4 | |
| 84 | 93 | — | — | **THE TEN COMMANDMENTS OF LOVE** — Little Anthony & the Imperials (Bob Skaff), United Artists 50598 | 2 | ★ |
| 85 | 90 | 91 | — | **OKIE FROM MUSKOGEE** — Merle Haggard & the Strangers (Ken Nelson), Capitol 2626 | 3 | ♫ |
| 86 | — | — | — | **COLD TURKEY** — Plastic Ono Band (John & Yoko [Bag]) Apple 1813 | 1 | |
| 87 | 100 | — | — | **SEE RUBY FALL** — Johnny Cash (Bob Johnston), Columbia 4-45020 | 2 | ♫ ★ |
| 88 | — | — | — | **JAM UP JELLY TIGHT** — Tommy Roe (Steve Barri), ABC 11247 | 1 | ★ |
| 89 | 89 | 95 | 98 | **ONE WOMAN** — Johnny Rivers (Johnny Rivers), Imperial 66418 | 6 | |
| 90 | — | — | — | **I WANT YOU BACK** — The Jackson 5 (The Corporation), Motown 1157 | 1 | ★ |
| 91 | 94 | — | — | **KOZMIC BLUES** — Janis Joplin (Gabriel Mekler), Columbia 4-45023 | 2 | ♫ |
| 92 | 95 | — | — | **(I'm So) AFRAID OF LOSING YOU AGAIN** — Charley Pride (Jack Clement), RCA 74-0265 | 2 | |
| 93 | 99 | — | — | **VOLUNTEERS** — Jefferson Airplane (Al Schmitt), RCA 74-0245 | 2 | |
| 94 | — | — | — | **GET RHYTHM** — Johnny Cash (Sam Phillips), Sun 1103 | 1 | ♫ |
| 95 | — | — | — | **SWINGIN' TIGHT** — Bill Deal & the Rhondells (Jerry Ross), Heritage 818 | 1 | |
| 96 | — | 99 | 99 | **SHE BELONGS TO ME** — Rick Nelson (Rick Nelson), Decca 732550 | 3 | |
| 97 | — | — | — | **CURLY** — Jimmy Clanton (A Laurie), Laurie 3508 | 1 | |
| 98 | — | — | — | **DON'T LET LOVE HANG YOU UP** — Jerry Butler (Gamble-Huff), Mercury 72991 | 1 | ♫ |
| 99 | — | — | — | **ONE TIN SOLDIER** — The Original Caste (Dennis Lambert & Brian Potter), TA 186 | 1 | |
| 100 | — | — | — | **ST. LOUIS** — The Easybeats (Easy Beats), Rare Earth 5009 | 1 | |

## HOT 100—A TO Z—(Publisher-Licensee)

| | |
|---|---|
| And When I Die (Celestial, BMI) | 4 |
| Any Way That You Want Me (Blackwood, BMI) | 53 |
| Baby I'm For Real (Jobete, BMI) | 17 |
| Baby It's You (Dolfi/Mary Jane, ASCAP) | 5 |
| Backfield in Motion (Cachand/Patcheal, BMI) | 18 |
| Ball of Fire (Big Seven, BMI) | 19 |
| Ballad of Easy Rider (Blackwood/Last Minute/Patian, BMI) | 77 |
| Brand New Me (Assorted/Parabut, BMI) | 67 |
| Cherry Hill Park (Low-Sal, BMI) | 24 |
| Cold Turkey (Maclen, BMI) | 86 |
| Colour of My Love (Ramrac) | 71 |
| Come Together (Maclen, BMI) | 2 |
| Crumbs Off the Table (Gold Forever, BMI) | 69 |
| Cupid (Kags, BMI) | 81 |
| Curly (Dunbar, BMI) | 97 |
| Doin' Our Thing (Fame, BMI) | 56 |
| Don't Let Love Hang You Up (Assorted/Parabut, BMI) | 98 |
| Down on the Corner (Jondora, BMI) | 30 |
| Echo Park (Hastings, BMI) | 48 |
| Eleanor Rigby (Maclen, BMI) | 40 |
| Eli's Coming (Celestial, BMI) | 20 |
| Evil Woman, Don't Play Your Games With Me (Yoggoth, BMI) | 59 |
| Fortunate Son (Jondora, BMI) | 16 |
| Friendship Train (Jobete, BMI) | 37 |
| Get It From the Bottom (Alstin, BMI) | 82 |
| Get Rhythm (Hi-Lo, BMI) | 94 |
| Girls, It Ain't Easy (Gold Forever, BMI) | 78 |
| Going in Circles (Porpete, BMI) | 15 |
| Groovy Grubworm (Little River, BMI) | 49 |
| Heaven Knows (Trousdale, BMI) | 47 |
| Holly Holy (Stonebridge, BMI) | 32 |
| Hot Fun in the Summertime (Stone Flower, BMI) | 12 |
| I Can't Get Next to You (Jobete, BMI) | 6 |
| I Can't Make It Alone (Screen Gems-Columbia, BMI) | 64 |
| I Guess the Lord Must Be in New York City (Dunbar, BMI) | 44 |
| I Still Believe in Tomorrow (Leeds, ASCAP) | 70 |
| I Want You Back (Jobete, BMI) | 90 |
| I'll Bet You (Jobete, BMI) | 66 |
| (I'm So) Afraid of Losing You Again (Hill & Range/Blue Crest, BMI) | 92 |
| Is That All There Is (Trio, BMI) | 14 |
| Jam Up Jelly Tight (Low-Twi, BMI) | 88 |
| Jealous Kind of Fellow (Colfam, BMI) | 57 |
| Jean (Twentieth Century, ASCAP) | 33 |
| Jesus Is a Soul Man (Wilderness, BMI) | 38 |
| Jingo (Blackwood, BMI) | 68 |
| Julia (Maclen, BMI) | 79 |
| Just a Little Love (Sound of Lucille/Pamco, BMI) | 80 |
| Kool and the Gang (Stephayne, BMI) | 60 |
| Kozmic Blues (Strong Arm/Wingate, ASCAP) | 91 |
| Leaving on a Jet Plane (Cherry Lane, ASCAP) | 23 |
| Let a Man Come in and Do the Popcorn (Part 1) (Dynatone, BMI) | 21 |
| Let a Woman Be a Woman, Let a Man Be a Man (Drive-In/Westward, BMI) | 45 |
| Little Woman (Green Apple, BMI) | 31 |
| Love Will Find a Way (Unart, BMI) | 61 |
| Make Your Own Kind of Music (Screen Gems-Columbia, BMI) | 39 |
| Midnight (Low-Sal, BMI) | 73 |
| Midnight Cowboy (United Artists/Barwin, ASCAP) | 52 |
| Mind, Body & Soul (Gold Forever, BMI) | 36 |
| Na Na Hey Hey Kiss Him Goodbye (MRC/Little Heather, BMI) | 11 |
| Okie From Muskogee (Blue Book, BMI) | 85 |
| One Tin Soldier (Cents & Pence, BMI) | 99 |
| One Woman (Rhomers, BMI) | 89 |
| Raindrops Keep Fallin' on My Head (Blue Seas/Jac/20th Century, ASCAP) | 62 |
| Roosevelt & Ira Lee (Combine, BMI) | 46 |
| Ruben James (Unart, BMI) | 26 |
| Say You Love Me (Curtom, BMI) | 65 |
| See Ruby Fall (House of Cash, BMI) | 87 |
| Shangri-La (Robbins, ASCAP) | 72 |
| She Belongs to Me (Warner Bros.-Seven Arts, ASCAP) | 96 |
| She's Got Love (Claridge/Tons of Fun, ASCAP) | 83 |
| Silver Threads and Golden Needles (Central Songs, BMI) | 74 |
| Smile a Little Smile for Me (January, BMI) | 8 |
| So Good Together (Unart/Joachim, BMI) | 41 |
| Someday We'll Be Together (Jobete, BMI) | 34 |
| Something (Harrisongs, BMI) | 3 |
| St. Louis (Robbins, ASCAP) | 100 |
| Sugar, Sugar (Kirshner, BMI) | 9 |
| Suite: Judy Blue Eyes (Gold Hill, BMI) | 27 |
| Suspicious Minds (Press, BMI) | 7 |
| Sweeter He Is, The (Birdees, ASCAP) | 54 |
| Swingin' Tight (Pambar/Legacy, BMI) | 95 |
| Take a Letter Maria (Four Star Television, BMI) | 10 |
| Ten Commandments of Love, The (Arc, BMI) | 84 |
| These Eyes (Dunbar, BMI) | 42 |
| Time Machine (Storybook, BMI) | 50 |
| Tonight I'll Be Staying With You (Big Sky, ASCAP) | 55 |
| Tracy (Vanlee/Emily, ASCAP) | 13 |
| Try a Little Kindness (Airfield/Campbell, BMI) | 25 |
| Turn On a Dream (Press, BMI) | 58 |
| Undun (Friends of Mine, Ltd./Dunbar/Cirrus, BMI) | 29 |
| Up on Cripple Creek (Canaan, ASCAP) | 51 |
| Volunteers (Icebag, BMI) | 93 |
| Walk On By (Blue Seas/Jac, ASCAP) | 35 |
| Wedding Bell Blues (Celestial, BMI) | 1 |
| We Love You, Call Collect (World, BMI) | 43 |
| We'll Cry Together (McCoy/Chevis, BMI) | 76 |
| Yester-Me, Yester-You, Yesterday (Stein & Van Stock, ASCAP) | 22 |
| You Got to Pay the Price (Myto, BMI) | 75 |
| You've Lost That Lovin' Feeling (Screen Gems-Columbia, BMI) | 28 |

## BUBBLING UNDER THE HOT 100

101. BLISTERED — Johnny Cash, Columbia 4-45020
102. DON'T YOU EVER GET TIRED (Of Hurting Me) — Bettye Swann, Capitol 2606
103. IT'S A FUNKY THING—RIGHT ON (Part I) — Herbie Mann, Atlantic 2671
104. EARLY IN THE MORNING — Vanity Fare, Page One 21-021
105. CAN'T TAKE MY EYES OFF OF YOU — Nancy Wilson, Capitol 2644
106. THAT'S THE WAY HEARTACHES ARE MADE — Marvelettes, Tamla 54186
107. I CAN'T SEE YOU NO MORE (When Johnny Comes Marching Home Again) — Joe Tex, Dial 4095
108. LOVE AND LET LOVE — Hardy Boys, RCA 74-0228
109. WALKIN' IN THE RAIN — Jay & the Americans, United Artists 50605
110. I STARTED LOVING YOU AGAIN — Al Martino, Capitol 2674
111. SUNDAY'S GONNA COME ON TUESDAY — New Establishment, Colgems 5006
112. GOLDEN SLUMBERS/CARRY THAT WEIGHT — Trash, Apple 1811
113. LADY JANE — Plastic Cow Goes Moog, Dot 17300
114. A WOMAN'S WAY — Andy Williams, Columbia 4-45003
115. FORGET TO REMEMBER — Frank Sinatra, Reprise 0865
116. BLOWIN' IN THE WIND — Edwin Hawkins Singers, Buddah 145
117. SOME OF SHELLEY'S BLUES — Nitty Gritty Dirt Band, Liberty 56134
118. NO ONE BETTER THAN YOU — Petula Clark, Warner Bros.-7 Arts 7343
119. JENNIFER TOMKINS — Street People, Musicor 1365
120. I'M GONNA TEAR YOU A NEW HEART — Clarence Reid, Alston 4578
121. HAPPY — Paul Anka, RCA 47-9767
122. OH ME OH MY (I'm a Fool for You Baby) — Lulu, Atco 6722
123. SUNLIGHT — Youngbloods, RCA 74-0270
124. GROOVIN' (Out on Life) — Newbeats, Hickory 1552
125. CAMEL BACK — A. B. Skhy, MGM 14086

Compiled from national retail sales and radio station airplay by the Music Popularity Dept. of Record Market Research, Billboard.

# Billboard HOT 100

FOR WEEK ENDING NOVEMBER 22, 1969

♫ Artist and/or Selection featured on "The Music Scene" this week, ABC-TV Network. Those in black were featured on past programs.

★ STAR PERFORMER—Sides registering greatest proportionate sales progress this week. (Seal) Record Industry Association of America seal of certification as million selling single.

| This Week | 1 Wk. Ago | 2 Wks. Ago | 3 Wks. Ago | TITLE Artist (Producer), Label & Number | Weeks On Chart |
|---|---|---|---|---|---|
| 1 | 1 | 1 | 2 | WEDDING BELL BLUES — 5th Dimension (Bones Howe), Soul City 779 | 9 |
| ♫ ★ 2 | 10 | 18 | 21 | TAKE A LETTER MARIA — R. B. Greaves (Ahmet Ertegun), Atco 6714 | 6 |
| ♫ 3 | 3 | 9 | 11 | SOMETHING — Beatles (George Martin), Apple 2654 | 6 (Seal) |
| 4 | 4 | 8 | 17 | AND WHEN I DIE — Blood, Sweat & Tears (James William Guercio), Columbia 4-45008 | 6 |
| ★ 5 | 8 | 10 | 12 | SMILE A LITTLE SMILE FOR ME — The Flying Machine (Tony MacAuley), Congress 6000 | 8 |
| ★ 6 | 11 | 22 | 45 | NA NA HEY HEY KISS HIM GOODBYE — Steam (Paul Leka), Fontana 1667 | 6 |
| ♫ 7 | 2 | 3 | 10 | COME TOGETHER — Beatles (George Martin), Apple 2654 | 6 |
| ★ 8 | 22 | 29 | 32 | YESTER-ME, YESTER-YOU, YESTERDAY — Stevie Wonder (John Bristol), Tamla 54188 | 5 |
| 9 | 7 | 2 | 1 | SUSPICIOUS MINDS — Elvis Presley, RCA 47-9764 | 11 (Seal) |
| ♫ 10 | 6 | 4 | 4 | I CAN'T GET NEXT TO YOU — Temptations (Norman Whitfield), Gordy 7093 | 15 |
| ♫ 11 | 5 | 5 | 5 | BABY IT'S YOU — Smith (Joel Sill & Steve Barri), Dunhill 4206 | 12 |
| ★ 12 | 23 | 39 | 57 | LEAVING ON A JET PLANE — Peter, Paul & Mary (Albert B. Grossman & Milt Okun), Warner Bros.-Seven Arts 7340 | 5 |
| ★ 13 | 18 | 20 | 42 | BACKFIELD IN MOTION — Mel & Tim (Karl Tarleton), Bamboo 107 | 6 |
| 14 | 16 | 33 | 58 | FORTUNATE SON — Creedence Clearwater Revival (John Fogerty), Fantasy 634 | 4 |
| ★ 15 | 17 | 17 | 22 | BABY, I'M FOR REAL — Originals (Marvin Gaye), Soul 35066 | 9 |
| ♫ 16 | 9 | 6 | 3 | SUGAR, SUGAR — Archies (Jeff Barry), Calendar 63-1008 | 18 (Seal) |
| 17 | 15 | 15 | 16 | GOING IN CIRCLES — Friends of Distinction (John Florez), RCA 74-0204 | 15 |
| ♫ ★ 18 | 20 | 23 | 50 | ELI'S COMING — Three Dog Night (Gabriel Mekler), Dunhill 4215 | 5 |
| ★ 19 | 24 | 25 | 38 | CHERRY HILL PARK — Billy Joe Royal (Buddy Buie), Columbia 4-44902 | 8 |
| ★ 20 | 34 | 50 | — | SOMEDAY WE'LL BE TOGETHER — Diana Ross & the Supremes (Johnny Bristol), Motown 1156 | 3 |
| ★ 21 | 30 | 38 | 60 | DOWN ON THE CORNER — Creedence Clearwater Revival (John Fogerty), Fantasy 634 | 5 |
| 22 | 13 | 12 | 9 | TRACY — Cuff Links (Paul Vance-Lee Pockriss), Decca 32533 | 11 |
| 23 | 14 | 11 | 13 | IS THAT ALL THERE IS — Peggy Lee (Lieber/Stoller), Capitol 2602 | 9 |
| 24 | 25 | 26 | 33 | TRY A LITTLE KINDNESS — Glen Campbell (Al De Lory), Capitol 2659 | 7 |
| ♫ 25 | 12 | 7 | 6 | HOT FUN IN THE SUMMER-TIME — Sly & the Family Stone (Sly Stone), Epic 5-10497 | 15 |
| 26 | 26 | 30 | 35 | RUBEN JAMES — Kenny Rogers & First Edition (Mike Post), Reprise 0854 | 9 |
| ♫ 27 | 27 | 28 | 34 | SUITE: JUDY BLUE EYES — Crosby/Stills/Nash (Stephen Stills, David Crosby & Graham Nash), Atlantic 2676 | 8 |
| ★ 28 | 32 | 44 | 71 | HOLLY HOLY — Neil Diamond (Tom Catalono & Tom Cogbill) UNI 55175 | 4 |
| 29 | 29 | 37 | 51 | UNDUN — Guess Who (Jack Richardson), RCA 74-0195 | 6 |
| 30 | 28 | 16 | 18 | YOU'VE LOST THAT LOVIN' FEELING — Dionne Warwick (Chips Moman & Dionne Warwick), Scepter 12262 | 10 |
| 31 | 19 | 19 | 26 | BALL OF FIRE — Tommy James & the Shondells (Tommy James), Roulette 7060 | 8 |
| ♫ 32 | 21 | 21 | 30 | LET A MAN COME IN AND DO THE POPCORN (PART I) — James Brown (James Brown), King 6255 | 7 |
| ★ 33 | 40 | 96 | — | ELEANOR RIGBY — Aretha Franklin (Jerry Wexler-Tom Dowd-Arif Mardin), Atlantic 2683 | 3 |
| ★ 34 | 37 | 56 | 66 | FRIENDSHIP TRAIN — Gladys Knight & the Pips (Norman Whitfield), Soul 35068 | 5 |
| 35 | 36 | 41 | 52 | MIND, BODY & SOUL — Flaming Embers (R. Dunbar), Hot Wax 6902 | 9 |
| ★ 36 | 42 | 49 | 68 | THESE EYES — Jr. Walker & the All Stars (Johnny Bristol), Soul 35067 | 5 |
| ★ 37 | 62 | 80 | 86 | RAINDROPS KEEP FALLIN ON MY HEAD — B.J. Thomas (Burt Bacharach-Hal David), Scepter 12265 | 4 |
| 38 | 39 | 43 | 56 | MAKE YOUR OWN KIND OF MUSIC — Mama Cass Elliot (Steve Barri), Dunhill 4214 | 6 |
| ★ 39 | 49 | 61 | 62 | GROOVY GRUBWORM — Harlow Wilcox (Shelby Singleton), Plantation 28 | 7 |
| ★ 40 | 47 | 57 | — | HEAVEN KNOWS — Grassroots (Steve Barri), Dunhill 4217 | 3 |
| 41 | 41 | 36 | 41 | SO GOOD TOGETHER — Andy Kim (Jeff Barry), Steed 720 | 9 |
| 42 | 43 | 54 | 93 | WE LOVE YOU, CALL COLLECT — Art Linkletter (Irvin S. Arkins), Capitol 2678 | 4 |
| 43 | 44 | 65 | 83 | I GUESS THE LORD MUST BE IN NEW YORK CITY — Nilsson (Rick Jarrard), RCA 74-0261 | 4 |
| 44 | 46 | 55 | 64 | ROOSEVELT & IRA LEE — Tony Joe White (Billy Swann), Monument 1169 | 5 |
| ★ 45 | 59 | 67 | 77 | EVIL WOMAN, DON'T PLAY YOUR GAMES WITH ME — Crow (Bob Monaco), Amaret 112 | 5 |
| 46 | 52 | 87 | 99 | MIDNIGHT COWBOY — Ferrante & Teicher (George Butler), United Artists 50554 | 4 |
| 47 | 51 | 58 | 74 | UP ON CRIPPLE CREEK — The Band (John Simon), Capitol 2635 | 4 |
| 48 | 38 | 35 | 28 | JESUS IS A SOUL MAN — Lawrence Reynolds (Don Davis), Warner Bros.-Seven Arts 7322 | 10 |
| 49 | 45 | 45 | 36 | LET A WOMAN BE A WOMAN, LET A MAN BE A MAN — Dyke and the Blazers (Laboe/Barrette), Original Sound 89 | 10 |
| ♫ ★ 50 | 67 | 83 | — | A BRAND NEW ME — Dusty Springfield (Roland Chambers), Atlantic 2685 | 3 |
| ★ 51 | 61 | 70 | 90 | LOVE WILL FIND A WAY — Jackie DeShannon (VME Prod.), Imperial 66419 | 4 |
| 52 | 50 | 48 | 49 | TIME MACHINE — Grand Funk Railroad (Terry Knight), Capitol 2567 | 9 |
| ♫ 53 | 63 | 71 | 82 | (Sittin' On) THE DOCK OF THE BAY — Dells (Bobby Miller), Cadet 5658 | 4 |
| 54 | 55 | 79 | 85 | TONIGHT I'LL BE STAYING HERE WITH YOU — Bob Dylan (Bob Johnston), Columbia 4-45004 | 4 |
| 55 | 53 | 53 | 54 | ANY WAY THAT YOU WANT ME — Evie Sands (Chip Taylor-Al Gorgoni), A&M 1090 | 15 |
| ★ 56 | 75 | 92 | — | YOU GOT TO PAY THE PRICE — Gloria Taylor (S. Whisenhunt), Silver Fox 14 | 3 |
| 57 | 56 | 46 | 48 | DOIN' OUR THING — Clarence Carter (Rick Hall), Atlantic 2660 | 9 |
| 58 | 58 | 60 | 61 | TURN ON A DREAM — Box Tops (Tommy Cogbill), Mala 12042 | 6 |
| ♫ 59 | 48 | 40 | 40 | ECHO PARK — Keith Barbour (Austin & Flemming), Epic 5-10486 | 9 |
| 60 | 60 | 59 | 59 | KOOL AND THE GANG — Kool and the Gang (Redd Coach Prod.), De-Lite 519 | 11 |
| ♫ ★ 61 | 85 | 90 | 91 | OKIE FROM MUSKOGEE — Merle Haggard & the Strangers (Ken Nelson), Capitol 2626 | 4 |
| 62 | 69 | 78 | 79 | CRUMBS OFF THE TABLE — Glass House (Holland-Dozier-Holland), Invictus 9071 | 6 |
| ♫ 63 | 64 | 66 | 100 | I CAN'T MAKE IT ALONE — Lou Rawls (David Axelrod), Capitol 2668 | 4 |
| 64 | 65 | 75 | 78 | SAY YOU LOVE ME — Impressions (Curtis Mayfield), Curtom 1946 | 6 |
| 65 | 68 | 91 | 97 | JINGO — Santana [Brent Dangerfield (IT)], Columbia 4-45010 | 5 |
| 66 | 54 | 52 | 53 | THE SWEETER HE IS — Soul Children (Hayes/Porter), Stax 0050 | 7 |
| ★ 67 | 90 | — | — | I WANT YOU BACK — The Jackson 5 (The Corporation), Motown 1157 | 2 |
| 68 | 78 | 85 | — | GIRLS, IT AIN'T EASY — Honey Cone (Stagecoach Prod.), Hot Wax 6903 | 3 |
| ★ 69 | 88 | — | — | JAM UP JELLY TIGHT — Tommy Roe (Steve Barri), ABC 11247 | 2 |
| 70 | 73 | — | — | MIDNIGHT — Dennis Yost & the Classics IV (Buddy Buié), Imperial 66424 | 2 |
| ♫ ★ 71 | — | — | — | AIN'T IT FUNKY NOW — James Brown (James Brown Prod.), King 6280 | 1 |
| ★ 72 | 82 | — | — | GET IT FROM THE BOTTOM — Steelers (Calvin Carter-Al Smith), Date 2-1642 | 2 |
| ★ 73 | 81 | — | 94 | CUPID — Johnny Nash (Johnny Nash-Arthur Jenkins), Jad 220 | 3 |
| ★ 74 | 86 | — | — | COLD TURKEY — Plastic Ono Band (John & Yoko [Bag]) Apple 1813 | 2 |
| ♫ ★ 75 | 87 | 100 | — | SEE RUBY FALL — Johnny Cash (Bob Johnston), Columbia 4-45020 | 3 |
| ♫ 76 | 80 | 86 | — | JUST A LITTLE LOVE — B. B. King (Bill Szymczyk), BluesWay 61029 | 6 |
| ★ 77 | — | — | — | EARLY IN THE MORNING — Vanity Fare (Roger Easterby & Des Champ), Page One 21-027 | 1 |
| ♫ ★ 78 | — | — | — | SUNDAY MORNIN' — Oliver (Bob Crewe), Crewe 337 | 1 |
| ♫ ★ 79 | 94 | — | — | GET RHYTHM — Johnny Cash (Sam Phillips), Sun 1103 | 2 |
| ♫ ★ 80 | — | — | — | LA LA LA (If I Had You) — Bobby Sherman (Jackie Mills), Metromedia 150 | 1 |
| 81 | 70 | 72 | 72 | I STILL BELIEVE IN TOMORROW — John & Anne Ryder (Mark Edwards), Decca 734661 | 5 |
| ♫ 82 | 74 | 74 | 75 | SILVER THREADS AND GOLDEN NEEDLES — Cowsills (Bob Waschtel), MGM 14084 | 7 |
| ♫ 83 | 91 | 94 | — | KOZMIC BLUES — Janis Joplin (Gabriel Mekler), Columbia 4-45023 | 3 |
| 84 | 84 | 93 | — | THE TEN COMMANDMENTS OF LOVE — Little Anthony & the Imperials (Bob Skaff), United Artists 50598 | 3 |
| 85 | 92 | 95 | — | (I'm So) AFRAID OF LOSING YOU AGAIN — Charley Pride (Jack Clement), RCA 74-0255 | 3 |
| ★ 86 | — | — | — | I'LL HOLD OUT MY HAND — Clique (Gary Zekley), White Whale 333 | 1 |
| ★ 87 | 95 | — | — | SWINGIN' TIGHT — Bill Deal & the Rhondells (Jerry Ross), Heritage 818 | 2 |
| ★ 88 | 96 | — | 99 | SHE BELONGS TO ME — Rick Nelson (Rick Nelson), Decca 732550 | 4 |
| ★ 89 | — | — | — | WALKIN' IN THE RAIN — Jay & the Americans (Sandy Yogunda & Thomas Kaye), United Artists 50605 | 1 |
| ♫ 90 | 98 | — | — | DON'T LET LOVE HANG YOU UP — Jerry Butler (Gamble-Huff), Mercury 72991 | 2 |
| 91 | — | — | — | WHOLE LOTTA LOVE — Led Zeppelin (Jimmy Page), Atlantic 2590 | 1 |
| 92 | 77 | 82 | 92 | BALLAD OF EASY RIDER — Byrds (Terry Melcher), Columbia 4-44990 | 4 |
| 93 | 93 | 99 | — | VOLUNTEERS — Jefferson Airplane (Al Schmitt), RCA 74-0245 | 3 |
| 94 | — | — | — | FANCY — Bobbie Gentry (Rick Hall), Capitol 2675 | 1 |
| 95 | — | — | — | IT'S A FUNKY THING RIGHT ON — Herbie Mann (Herbie Mann), Atlantic 2671 | 1 |
| 96 | 99 | — | — | ONE TIN SOLDIER — The Original Caste (Dennis Lambert & Brian Potter), TA 186 | 2 |
| 97 | 97 | — | — | CURLY — Jimmy Clanton (A Laurie), Laurie 3508 | 2 |
| 98 | — | — | — | CAN'T TAKE MY EYES OFF OF YOU — Nancy Wilson (David D. Cavanaugh), Capitol 2644 | 1 |
| ♫ 99 | — | — | — | HAPPY — Paul Anka (Wes Farrell), RCA 47-9767 | 1 |
| ♫ 100 | — | — | — | BLISTERED — Johnnie Cash (Bob Johnston), Columbia 4-45020 | 1 |

## HOT 100—A TO Z—*(Publisher-Licensee)*

Ain't It Funky Now (Golo, BMI) ... 71
And When I Die (Tuna Fish, BMI) ... 4
Any Way That You Want Me (Blackwood, BMI) ... 55
Baby I'm For Real (Jobete, BMI) ... 15
Baby It's You (Dolfi/Mary Jane, ASCAP) ... 11
Backfield In Motion (Cachand/Patcheal, BMI) ... 13
Ball of Fire (Big Seven, BMI) ... 31
Ballad of Easy Rider (Blackwood/Last Minute/Patian, BMI) ... 92
Blistered (Quartet/Bexhill, ASCAP) ... 100
Brand New Me (Assorted/Parabut, BMI) ... 50
Can't Take My Eyes Off of You (Saturday/Seasons Four, BMI) ... 98
Cherry Hill Park (Low-Sal, BMI) ... 19
Cold Turkey (Maclen, BMI) ... 74
Come Together (Maclen, BMI) ... 7
Crumbs Off the Table (Gold Forever, BMI) ... 62
Cupid (Kags, BMI) ... 73
Curly (Dunbar, BMI) ... 97
Doin' Our Thing (Fame, BMI) ... 57
Don't Let Love Hang You Up (Assorted/Parabut, BMI) ... 90
Down on the Corner (Jondora, BMI) ... 21
Early in the Morning (Duchess, BMI) ... 77
Echo Park (Hastings, BMI) ... 59
Eleanor Rigby (Maclen, BMI) ... 33
Eli's Coming (Tuna Fish, BMI) ... 18
Evil Woman, Don't Play Your Games With Me (Yoggoth, BMI) ... 45
Fancy (Shayme, ASCAP) ... 94
Fortunate Son (Jondora, BMI) ... 14
Friendship Train (Jobete, BMI) ... 34
Get It From the Bottom (Alstin, BMI) ... 72
Get Rhythm (Hi-Lo, BMI) ... 79
Girls, It Ain't Easy (Gold Forever, BMI) ... 68
Going in Circles (Porpete, BMI) ... 17
Groovy Grubworm (Little River, BMI) ... 39
Happy (Pocketful of Tunes, BMI) ... 99
Heaven Knows (Trousdale, BMI) ... 40
Holly Holy (Stonebridge, BMI) ... 28
Hot Fun in the Summertime (Stone Flower, BMI) ... 25
I Can't Get Next to You (Jobete, BMI) ... 10
I Can't Make It Alone (Screen Gems-Columbia, BMI) 63
I Guess the Lord Must Be in New York City (Dunbar, BMI) ... 43
I'll Hold Out My Hand (Blackwood, BMI) ... 86
I Still Believe in Tommorow (Leeds, ASCAP) ... 81
It's a Funky Thing—Right On (Mann, ASCAP) ... 95
I Want You Back (Jobete, BMI) ... 67
(I'm So) Afraid of Losing You Again (Hill & Range/Blue Crest, BMI) ... 85
Is That All There Is (Trio, BMI) ... 23
Jam Up Jelly Tight (Low-Twi, BMI) ... 69
Jesus Is a Soul Man (Wilderness, BMI) ... 48
Jingo (Blackwood, BMI) ... 65
Just a Little Love (Sound of Lucille/Pamco, BMI) 76
Kool and the Gang (Stephayne, BMI) ... 60
Kozmic Blues (Strong Arm/Wingate, ASCAP) ... 83
La La La (If I Had You) (Green Apple, BMI) ... 80
Leaving on a Jet Plane (Cherry Lane, ASCAP) ... 12
Let a Man Come in and Do the Popcorn (Part 1) (Dynatone, BMI) ... 32
Let a Woman Be a Woman, Let a Man Be a Man (Drive-In/Westward, BMI) ... 49
Love Will Find a Way (Unart, BMI) ... 51
Make Your Own Kind of Music (Screen Gems-Columbia, BMI) ... 38
Midnight (Low-Sal, BMI) ... 70
Midnight Cowboy (United Artists/Barwin, ASCAP) 46
Mind, Body & Soul (Gold Forever, BMI) ... 35
Na Na Hey Hey Kiss Him Goodbye (MRC/Little Heather, BMI) ... 6
Okie From Muskogee (Blue Book, BMI) ... 61
One Tin Soldier (Cents & Pence, BMI) ... 96
Raindrops Keep Fallin' on My Head (Blue Seas/Jac/20th Century, ASCAP) ... 37
Roosevelt & Ira Lee (Combine, BMI) ... 44
Ruben James (Unart, BMI) ... 26
Say You Love Me (Curtom, BMI) ... 64
See Ruby Fall (House of Cash, BMI) ... 75
She Belongs to Me (Warner Bros.-Seven Arts, ASCAP) ... 88
Silver Threads and Golden Needles (Central Songs, BMI) ... 82
(Sittin' On) The Dock of the Bay (East/Time/Redwall, BMI) ... 53
Smile a Little Smile for Me (January, BMI) ... 5
So Good Together (Unart/Joachim, BMI) ... 41
Someday We'll Be Together (Jobete, BMI) ... 20
Something (Harrisongs, BMI) ... 3
Sugar, Sugar (Kirshner, BMI) ... 16
Sunday Mornin' (Blackwood, BMI) ... 78
Suite: Judy Blue Eyes (Gold Hill, BMI) ... 27
Suspicious Minds (Press, BMI) ... 9
Sweeter He Is, The (Birdees, ASCAP) ... 66
Swingin' Tight (Pambar/Legacy, BMI) ... 87
Take a Letter Maria (Four Star Television, BMI) .. 2
Ten Commandments of Love, The (Arc, BMI) ... 84
These Eyes (Dunbar, BMI) ... 36
Time Machine (Storybook, BMI) ... 52
Tonight I'll Be Staying With You (Big Sky, ASCAP) 54
Tracy (Vanlee/Emily, ASCAP) ... 22
Try a Little Kindness (Airfield/Campbell, BMI) ... 24
Turn On a Dream (Press, BMI) ... 58
Undun (Friends of Mine, Ltd./Dunbar/Cirrus, BMI) 29
Up on Cripple Creek (Canaan, ASCAP) ... 47
Volunteers (Icebag, BMI) ... 93
Walkin' in the Rain (Screen Gems-Columbia, BMI).. 89
Wedding Bell Blues (Tuna Fish, BMI) ... 1
We Love You, Call Collect (World, BMI) ... 42
Whole Lotta Love (Superhype, ASCAP) ... 91
Yester-Me, Yester-You, Yesterday (Stein & Van Stock, ASCAP) ... 8
You Got to Pay the Price (Myto, BMI) ... 56
You've Lost That Lovin' Feeling (Screen Gems-Columbia, BMI) ... 30

## BUBBLING UNDER THE HOT 100

101. WE MUST BE IN LOVE ... Five Stairsteps & Cubie, Curtom 1945
102. DON'T YOU EVER GET TIRED (Of Hurting Me) ... Bettye Swann, Capitol 2606
103. MUST BE YOUR THING ... Charles Wright & the Watts 103rd Street Band, Warner Bros.-Seven Arts 7338
104. FORGET TO REMEMBER ... Frank Sinatra, Reprise 0865
105. I CAN'T SEE YOU NO MORE (When Johnny Comes Marching Home) ... Joe Tex, Dial 4095
106. ME AND YOU ... O. C. Smith, Columbia 4-45038
107. I STARTED LOVING YOU AGAIN ... Al Martino, Capitol 2674
108. GOIN' OUT OF MY HEAD ... Frank Sinatra, Reprise 0865
109. BLOWIN' IN THE WIND ... Edwin Hawkins Singers, Buddah 145
110. TONIGHT I'LL SAY A PRAYER ... Eydie Gorme, RCA 74-0250
111. TOO MANY COOKS (SPOIL THE SOUP) ... 100% Proof Aged In Soul, Hot Wax 6904
112. COWBOY CONVENTION ... Ohio Express, Buddah 147
113. I'M TIRED ... Savoy Brown, Parrot 40042
114. SHE LETS HER HAIR DOWN ... Gene Pitney, Musicor 1384
115. TURN TURN TURN—To Everything There Is A Season ... Judy Collins, Elektra 45680
116. I LOVE YOU ... Otis Leavill, Dakar 614
117. OH ME OH MY (I'm A Fool For You) ... Lulu, Atco 6722
118. WHEN WE GET MARRIED ... 1910 Fruitgum Company, Buddah 146
119. SOME OF SHELLEY'S BLUES ... Nitty Gritty Dirt Band, Liberty 56134
120. SUNDAY'S GONNA COME ON TUESDAY ... New Establishment, Colgems 5006
121. YOU ARE MY LIFE ... Herb Alpert & the Tijuana Brass, A&M 1143
122. HEY GIRL ... Panhandle, Happy Tiger 523
123. WICHITA LINEMAN ... Sergio Mendes & Brasil '66, A&M 1132
124. CAMEL BACK ... A. B. Skye, MGM 14086

Compiled from national retail sales and radio station airplay by the Music Popularity Dept. of Record Market Research, Billboard.

# Billboard HOT 100

FOR WEEK ENDING NOVEMBER 29, 1969

♫ Artist and/or Selection featured on "The Music Scene" this week, ABC-TV Network. Those in black were featured on past programs.

★ STAR PERFORMER—Sides registering greatest proportionate sales progress this week. ● Record Industry Association of America seal of certification as million selling single.

| THIS WEEK | 1 Wk. Ago | 2 Wks. Ago | 3 Wks. Ago | TITLE Artist (Producer), Label & Number | Weeks On Chart |
|---|---|---|---|---|---|
| ♫ ★ 1 | 3 | 3 | 9 | COME TOGETHER/SOMETHING — Beatles (George Martin), Apple 2654 | 7 |
| ★ 2 | 4 | 4 | 8 | AND WHEN I DIE — Blood, Sweat & Tears (James William Guercio), Columbia 4-45008 | 7 |
| 3 | 1 | 1 | 1 | WEDDING BELL BLUES — 5th Dimension (Bones Howe), Soul City 779 | 10 |
| ♫ 4 | 2 | 10 | 18 | TAKE A LETTER MARIA — R. B. Greaves (Ahmet Ertegun), Atco 6714 | 7 |
| ★ 5 | 6 | 11 | 22 | NA NA HEY HEY KISS HIM GOODBYE — Steam (Paul Leka), Fontana 1667 | 7 |
| 6 | 5 | 8 | 10 | SMILE A LITTLE SMILE FOR ME — The Flying Machine (Tony MacAuley), Congress 6000 | 9 |
| ★ 7 | 12 | 23 | 39 | LEAVING ON A JET PLANE — Peter, Paul & Mary (Albert B. Grossman & Milt Okun), Warner Bros.-Seven Arts 7340 | 6 |
| 8 | 8 | 22 | 29 | YESTER-ME, YESTER-YOU, YESTERDAY — Stevie Wonder (John Bristol), Tamla 54188 | 6 |
| ★ 9 | 14 | 16 | 33 | DOWN ON THE CORNER/FORTUNATE SON — Creedence Clearwater Revival (John Fogerty), Fantasy 634 | 5 |
| ♫ ★ 10 | 18 | 20 | 23 | ELI'S COMING — Three Dog Night (Gabriel Mekler), Dunhill 4215 | 6 |
| ★ 11 | 20 | 34 | 50 | SOMEDAY WE'LL BE TOGETHER — Diana Ross & the Supremes (Johnny Bristol), Motown 1156 | 4 |
| ♫ 12 | 11 | 5 | 5 | BABY IT'S YOU — Smith (Joel Sill & Steve Barri), Dunhill 4206 | 13 |
| 13 | 13 | 18 | 20 | BACKFIELD IN MOTION — Mel & Tim (Karl Tarleton), Bamboo 107 | 7 |
| 14 | 15 | 17 | 17 | BABY, I'M FOR REAL — Originals (Marvin Gaye), Soul 35066 | 10 |
| ★ 15 | 19 | 24 | 25 | CHERRY HILL PARK — Billy Joe Royal (Buddy Buie), Columbia 4-44902 | 9 |
| 16 | 9 | 7 | 2 | SUSPICIOUS MINDS — Elvis Presley, RCA 47-9764 | 12 |
| ♫ 17 | 10 | 6 | 4 | I CAN'T GET NEXT TO YOU — Temptations (Norman Whitfield), Gordy 7093 | 16 |
| ★ 18 | 28 | 32 | 44 | HOLLY HOLY — Neil Diamond (Tom Catalano & Tom Cogbill), UNI 55175 | 5 |
| ♫ 19 | 16 | 9 | 6 | SUGAR, SUGAR — Archies (Jeff Barry), Calendar 63-1008 | 19 |
| 20 | 17 | 15 | 15 | GOING IN CIRCLES — Friends of Distinction (John Florez), RCA 74-0204 | 16 |
| ♫ 21 | 27 | 27 | 28 | SUITE: JUDY BLUE EYES — Crosby/Stills/Nash (Stephen Stills, David Crosby & Graham Nash), Atlantic 2676 | 9 |
| 22 | 29 | 29 | 37 | UNDUN — Guess Who (Jack Richardson), RCA 74-0195 | 7 |
| 23 | 24 | 25 | 26 | TRY A LITTLE KINDNESS — Glen Campbell (Al De Lory), Capitol 2659 | 8 |
| ★ 24 | 33 | 40 | 96 | ELEANOR RIGBY — Aretha Franklin (Jerry Wexler-Tom Dowd-Arif Mardin), Atlantic 2683 | 4 |
| ★ 25 | 37 | 62 | 80 | RAINDROPS KEEP FALLING ON MY HEAD — B.J. Thomas (Burt Bacharach-Hal David), Scepter 12265 | 5 |
| ★ 26 | 35 | 36 | 41 | MIND, BODY & SOUL — Flaming Embers (R. Dunbar), Hot Wax 6902 | 10 |
| 27 | 22 | 13 | 12 | TRACY — Cuff Links (Paul Vance-Lee Pockriss), Decca 32533 | 12 |
| 28 | 23 | 14 | 11 | IS THAT ALL THERE IS — Peggy Lee (Lieber/Stoller), Capitol 2602 | 10 |
| 29 | 34 | 37 | 56 | FRIENDSHIP TRAIN — Gladys Knight & the Pips (Norman Whitfield), Soul 35068 | 6 |
| 30 | 36 | 42 | 49 | THESE EYES — Jr. Walker & the All Stars (Johnny Bristol), Soul 35067 | 6 |
| ★ 31 | 47 | 51 | 58 | UP ON CRIPPLE CREEK — The Band (John Simon), Capitol 2635 | 5 |
| ★ 32 | 40 | 47 | 57 | HEAVEN KNOWS — Grassroots (Steve Barri), Dunhill 4217 | 4 |
| 33 | 26 | 26 | 30 | RUBEN JAMES — Kenny Rogers & First Edition (Mike Post), Reprise 0854 | 10 |
| ★ 34 | 43 | 44 | 65 | I GUESS THE LORD MUST BE IN NEW YORK CITY — Nilsson (Rick Jarrard), RCA 74-0261 | 5 |
| ★ 35 | 39 | 49 | 61 | GROOVY GRUBWORM — Harlow Wilcox (Shelby Singleton), Plantation 28 | 8 |
| 36 | 38 | 39 | 43 | MAKE YOUR OWN KIND OF MUSIC — Mama Cass Elliot (Steve Barri), Dunhill 4214 | 7 |
| ★ 37 | 46 | 52 | 87 | MIDNIGHT COWBOY — Ferrante & Teicher (George Butler), United Artists 50554 | 5 |
| 38 | 45 | 59 | 67 | EVIL WOMAN, DON'T PLAY YOUR GAMES WITH ME — Crow (Bob Monaco), Amaret 112 | 6 |
| ♫ 39 | 32 | 21 | 21 | LET A MAN COME IN AND DO THE POPCORN (Part I) — James Brown (James Brown), King 6255 | 8 |
| ♫ ★ 40 | 50 | 67 | 83 | A BRAND NEW ME — Dusty Springfield (Roland Chambers), Atlantic 2685 | 4 |
| ★ 41 | 51 | 61 | 70 | LOVE WILL FIND A WAY — Jackie DeShannon (VME Prod.), Imperial 66419 | 5 |
| ♫ ★ 42 | 53 | 63 | 71 | (Sittin' On) THE DOCK OF THE BAY — Dells (Bobby Miller), Cadet 5658 | 5 |
| ★ 43 | 69 | 88 | — | JAM UP JELLY TIGHT — Tommy Roe (Steve Barri), ABC 11247 | 3 |
| 44 | 44 | 46 | 55 | ROOSEVELT & IRA LEE — Tony Joe White (Billy Swann), Monument 1169 | 6 |
| ★ 45 | 91 | — | — | WHOLE LOTTA LOVE — Led Zeppelin (Jimmy Page), Atlantic 2690 | 2 |
| ♫ ★ 46 | 83 | 91 | 94 | KOZMIC BLUES — Janis Joplin (Gabriel Mekler), Columbia 4-45023 | 4 |
| ★ 47 | 74 | 86 | — | COLD TURKEY — Plastic Ono Band (John & Yoko [Bag]) Apple 1813 | 3 |
| 48 | 42 | 43 | 54 | WE LOVE YOU, CALL COLLECT — Art Linkletter (Irvin S. Arkins), Capitol 2678 | 5 |
| ♫ ★ 49 | 71 | — | — | AIN'T IT FUNKY NOW — James Brown (James Brown Prod.), King 6280 | 2 |
| 50 | 54 | 55 | 79 | TONIGHT I'LL BE STAYING HERE WITH YOU — Bob Dylan (Bob Johnston), Columbia 4-45004 | 5 |
| ★ 51 | 67 | 90 | — | I WANT YOU BACK — The Jackson 5 (The Corporation), Motown 1157 | 3 |
| 52 | 52 | 50 | 48 | TIME MACHINE — Grand Funk Railroad (Terry Knight), Capitol 2567 | 10 |
| 53 | 56 | 75 | 92 | YOU GOT TO PAY THE PRICE — Gloria Taylor (S. Whisenhunt), Silver Fox 14 | 4 |
| ♫ ★ 54 | 80 | — | — | LA LA LA (If I Had You) — Bobby Sherman (Jackie Mills), Metromedia 150 | 2 |
| 55 | 55 | 53 | 53 | ANY WAY THAT YOU WANT ME — Evie Sands (Chip Taylor-Al Gorgoni), A&M 1090 | 16 |
| 56 | 49 | 45 | 45 | LET A WOMAN BE A WOMAN, LET A MAN BE A MAN — Dyke and the Blazers (Laboe/Barrette), Original Sound 89 | 11 |
| ♫ ★ 57 | 78 | — | — | SUNDAY MORNIN' — Oliver (Bob Crewe), Crewe 337 | 2 |
| 58 | 64 | 65 | 75 | SAY YOU LOVE ME — Impressions (Curtis Mayfield), Curtom 1946 | 7 |
| 59 | 62 | 69 | 78 | CRUMBS OFF THE TABLE — Glass House (Holland-Dozier-Holland), Invictus 9071 | 7 |
| 60 | 65 | 68 | 91 | JINGO — Santana [Brent Dangerfield (IT)], Columbia 4-45010 | 6 |
| ♫ 61 | 61 | 85 | 90 | OKIE FROM MUSKOGEE — Merle Haggard & the Strangers (Ken Nelson), Capitol 2626 | 5 |
| ★ 62 | 77 | — | — | EARLY IN THE MORNING — Vanity Fare (Roger Easterby & Des Champ), Page One 21-027 | 2 |
| 63 | 60 | 60 | 59 | KOOL AND THE GANG — Kool and the Gang (Redd Coach Prod.), De-Lite 519 | 12 |
| 64 | 58 | 58 | 60 | TURN ON A DREAM — Box Tops (Tommy Cogbill), Mala 12042 | 7 |
| 65 | 73 | 81 | — | CUPID — Johnny Nash (Johnny Nash-Arthur Jenkins), Jad 220 | 4 |
| ★ 66 | 92 | 77 | 82 | BALLAD OF EASY RIDER — Byrds (Terry Melcher), Columbia 4-44990 | 5 |
| 67 | 70 | 73 | — | MIDNIGHT — Dennis Yost & the Classics IV (Buddy Buie), Imperial 66424 | 3 |
| 68 | 68 | 78 | 85 | GIRLS, IT AIN'T EASY — Honey Cone (Stagecoach Prod.), Hot Wax 6903 | 4 |
| ♫ 69 | 75 | 87 | 100 | BLISTERED/SEE RUBY FALL — Johnny Cash (Bob Johnston), Columbia 4-45020 | 4 |
| 70 | 72 | 82 | — | GET IT FROM THE BOTTOM — Steelers (Calvin Carter-Al Smith), Date 2-1642 | 3 |
| ♫ 71 | 79 | 94 | — | GET RHYTHM — Johnny Cash (Sam Phillips), Sun 1103 | 3 |
| ★ 72 | 86 | — | — | I'LL HOLD OUT MY HAND — Clique (Gary Zekley), White Whale 333 | 2 |
| ★ 73 | — | — | — | DON'T CRY DADDY/RUBBERNECKIN' — Elvis Presley, RCA 47-9768 | 1 |
| ★ 74 | 98 | — | — | CAN'T TAKE MY EYES OFF OF YOU — Nancy Wilson (David D. Cavanaugh), Capitol 2644 | 2 |
| ★ 75 | 94 | — | — | FANCY — Bobbie Gentry (Rick Hall), Capitol 2675 | 2 |
| ♫ ★ 76 | 90 | 98 | — | DON'T LET LOVE HANG YOU UP — Jerry Butler (Gamble-Huff), Mercury 72991 | 3 |
| ★ 77 | — | — | — | WHAT YOU GAVE ME — Marvin Gaye & Tammi Terrell (Ashford & Simpson), Tamla 54187 | 1 |
| ♫ 78 | 63 | 64 | 66 | I CAN'T MAKE IT ALONE — Lou Rawls (David Axelrod), Capitol 2668 | 5 |
| 79 | 88 | 96 | — | SHE BELONGS TO ME — Rick Nelson (Rick Nelson), Decca 732550 | 5 |
| 80 | 89 | — | — | WALKIN' IN THE RAIN — Jay & the Americans (Sandy Yogunda & Thomas Kaye), United Artists 50605 | 2 |
| ★ 81 | — | — | — | I'M TIRED — Savoy Brown (Mike Vernon Prod.), Parrot 40042 | 1 |
| 82 | 84 | 84 | 93 | THE TEN COMMANDMENTS OF LOVE — Little Anthony & the Imperials (Bob Skaff), United Artists 50598 | 4 |
| 83 | 85 | 92 | 95 | (I'm So) AFRAID OF LOSING YOU AGAIN — Charley Pride (Jack Clement), RCA 74-0265 | 4 |
| ♫ ★ 84 | — | — | — | TURN TURN TURN (To Everything There Is a Season) — Judy Collins (Mark Abramson), Elektra 45680 | 1 |
| ★ 85 | 93 | 93 | 99 | VOLUNTEERS — Jefferson Airplane (Al Schmitt), RCA 74-0245 | 4 |
| 86 | 87 | 95 | — | SWINGIN' TIGHT — Bill Deal & the Rhondells (Jerry Ross), Heritage 818 | 3 |
| ★ 87 | — | — | — | JE T'AIME . . . MOI NON PLUS — Jane Birkin & Serge Gainsbourg (Jack Baverstock), Fontana 1665 | 1 |
| 88 | 96 | 99 | — | ONE TIN SOLDIER — The Original Caste (Dennis Lambert & Brian Potter), TA 186 | 3 |
| ♫ 89 | 99 | — | — | HAPPY — Paul Anka (Wes Farrell), RCA 47-9767 | 2 |
| ♫ ★ 90 | — | — | — | JINGLE JANGLE — The Archies (Jeff Barry), Kirshner 63-5002 | 1 |
| ♫ 91 | — | — | — | TONIGHT I'LL SAY A PRAYER — Eydie Gorme (Don Costa), RCA 74-0250 | 1 |
| 92 | — | — | — | I LOVE YOU — Otis Leavill (Willie Henderson), Dakar 614 | 1 |
| 93 | — | — | — | NO ONE BETTER THAN YOU — Petula Clark (Claude Wolff), Warner Bros.-Seven Arts 7343 | 1 |
| 94 | — | — | — | YOU KEEP ME HANGING ON — Wilson Pickett (W. Pickett & D. Crawford—C. Grits), Atlantic 2682 | 1 |
| 95 | 95 | — | — | IT'S A FUNKY THING—RIGHT ON — Herbie Mann (Herbie Mann), Atlantic 2671 | 2 |
| 96 | — | — | — | (One of These Days) SUNDAY'S GONNA COME ON TUESDAY — The New Establishment (Ernie Sheldon/Jack Keller), Colgems 66-5006 | 1 |
| 97 | — | — | — | FEELING ALRIGHT — Mongo Santamaria (Tom Dowd), Atlantic 2689 | 1 |
| 98 | 97 | 97 | — | CURLY — Jimmy Clanton (A Laurie), Laurie 3508 | 3 |
| 99 | — | — | — | WICHITA LINEMAN — Sergio Mendes & Brasil '66 (Sergio Mendes), A&M 1132 | 1 |
| 100 | — | — | — | GOIN' OUT OF MY HEAD/FORGET TO REMEMBER — Frank Sinatra (Frank Sinatra), Reprise 0865 | 1 |

## HOT 100—A TO Z—*(Publisher-Licensee)*

Ain't It Funky Now (Golo, BMI) . . . 49
And When I Die (Tuna Fish,* BMI) . . . 2
Any Way That You Want Me (Blackwood, BMI) . . . 55
Baby I'm For Real (Jobete, BMI) . . . 14
Baby It's You (Dolfi/Mary Jane, ASCAP) . . . 12
Backfield In Motion (Cachand/Patcheal, BMI) . . . 13
Ballad of Easy Rider (Blackwood/Last Minute/Patian, BMI) . . . 66
Blistered (Quartet/Bexhill, ASCAP) . . . 69
Brand New Me (Assorted/Parabut, BMI) . . . 40
Can't Take My Eyes Off of You (Saturday/Seasons Four, BMI) . . . 74
Cherry Hill Park (Low-Sal, BMI) . . . 15
Cold Turkey (Maclen, BMI) . . . 47
Come Together (Maclen, BMI) . . . 1
Crumbs Off the Table (Gold Forever, BMI) . . . 59
Cupid (Kags, BMI) . . . 65
Curly (Dunbar, BMI) . . . 98
Don't Cry Daddy (Gladys/BnB, ASCAP) . . . 73
Don't Let Love Hang You Up (Assorted/Parabut, BMI) . . . 76
Down on the Corner (Jondora, BMI) . . . 9
Early in the Morning (Duchess, BMI) . . . 62
Eleanor Rigby (Maclen, BMI) . . . 24
Eli's Coming (Tuna Fish, BMI) . . . 10
Evil Woman, Don't Play Your Games With Me (Yoggoth, BMI) . . . 38
Fancy (Shayme, ASCAP) . . . 75
Feeling Alright (Almo, ASCAP) . . . 97
Fortunate Son (Jondora, BMI) . . . 9
Friendship Train (Jobete, BMI) . . . 29
Get It From the Bottom (Alstin, BMI) . . . 70
Get Rhythm (Hi-Lo, BMI) . . . 71
Girls, It Ain't Easy (Gold Forever, BMI) . . . 68
Going in Circles (Porpete, BMI) . . . 20
Goin' Out of My Head/Forget to Remember (Vogue/Razzle Dazzle, BMI) . . . 100
Groovy Grubworm (Little River, BMI) . . . 35
Happy (Pocketful of Tunes, BMI) . . . 89
Heaven Knows (Trousdale, BMI) . . . 32
Holly Holy (Stonebridge, BMI) . . . 18
I Can't Get Next to You (Jobete, BMI) . . . 17
I Can't Make It Alone (Screen Gems-Columbia, BMI) 78
I Guess the Lord Must Be in New York City (Dunbar, BMI) . . . 34
I Love You (Dakar, BMI) . . . 92
I'll Hold Out My Hand (Blackwood, BMI) . . . 72
I'm Tired (Cool Water, ASCAP) . . . 81
It's a Funky Thing—Right On (Mann, ASCAP) . . . 95
I Want You Back (Jobete, BMI) . . . 51
(I'm So) Afraid of Losing You Again (Hill & Range/Blue Crest, BMI) . . . 83
Is That All There Is (Trio, BMI) . . . 28
Jam Up Jelly Tight (Low-Twi, BMI) . . . 43
Je T'Aime . . . Moi Non Plus (Monday Morning, BMI) . . . 87
Jingle Jangle (Don Kirshner, BMI) . . . 90
Jingo (Blackwood, BMI) . . . 60
Kool and the Gang (Stephayne, BMI) . . . 63
Kozmic Blues (Strong Arm/Wingate, ASCAP) . . . 46
La La La (If I Had You) (Green Apple, BMI) . . . 54
Leaving on a Jet Plane (Cherry Lane, ASCAP) . . . 7
Let a Man Come in and Do the Popcorn (Part 1) (Dynatone, BMI) . . . 39
Let a Woman Be a Woman, Let a Man Be a Man (Drive-In/Westward, BMI) . . . 56
Love Will Find a Way (Unart, BMI) . . . 41
Make Your Own Kind of Music (Screen Gems-Columbia, BMI) . . . 36
Midnight (Low-Sal, BMI) . . . 67
Midnight Cowboy (United Artists/Barwin, ASCAP) . . 37
Mind, Body & Soul (Gold Forever, BMI) . . . 26
Na Na Hey Hey Kiss Him Goodbye (MRC/Little Heather, BMI) . . . 5
No One Better Than You (Anne-Rachel, ASCAP) . . . 93
Okie From Muskogee (Blue Rock, BMI) . . . 61
One Tin Soldier (Cents & Pence, BMI) . . . 88
Raindrops Keep Fallin' on My Head (Blue Seas/Jac/20th Century, ASCAP) . . . 25
Roosevelt & Ira Lee (Combine, BMI) . . . 44
Rubberneckin' (Elvis Presley, BMI) . . . 73
Ruben James (Unart, BMI) . . . 33
Say You Love Me (Curtom, BMI) . . . 58
See Ruby Fall (House of Cash, BMI) . . . 69
She Belongs to Me (Warner Bros.-Seven Arts, ASCAP) . . . 79
(Sittin' On) The Dock of the Bay (East/Time/Redwall, BMI) . . . 42
Smile a Little Smile for Me (January, BMI) . . . 6
Someday We'll Be Together (Jobete, BMI) . . . 11
Something (Harrisongs, BMI) . . . 1
Sugar, Sugar (Kirshner, BMI) . . . 19
Sunday Mornin' (Blackwood, BMI) . . . 57
(One of These Days) Sunday's Gonna' Come on Tuesday (Colgems Music, ASCAP) . . . 96
Suite: Judy Blue Eyes (Gold Hill, BMI) . . . 21
Suspicious Minds (Press, BMI) . . . 16
Swingin' Tight (Pambar/Legacy, BMI) . . . 86
Take a Letter Maria (Four Star Television, BMI) . . . 4
Ten Commandments of Love, The (Arc, BMI) . . . 82
These Eyes (Dunbar, BMI) . . . 30
Time Machine (Storybook, BMI) . . . 52
Tonight I'll Be Staying With You (Big Sky, ASCAP) 50
Tonight I'll Say a Prayer (Sunbury, ASCAP) . . . 91
Tracy (Vanlee/Emily, ASCAP) . . . 27
Try a Little Kindness (Airfield/Campbell, BMI) . . . 23
Turn On a Dream (Press, BMI) . . . 64
Turn Turn Turn (To Everything There Is a Season) (Melody Trails, BMI) . . . 84
Undun (Friends of Mine, Ltd./Dunbar/Cirrus, BMI) 22
Up on Cripple Creek (Canaan, ASCAP) . . . 31
Volunteers (Icebag, BMI) . . . 85
Walkin' in the Rain (Screen Gems-Columbia, BMI) . . 80
Wedding Bell Blues (Tuna Fish,* BMI) . . . 3
We Love You, Call Collect (World, BMI) . . . 48
What You Gave Me (Jobete, BMI) . . . 77
Whole Lotta Love (Superhype, ASCAP) . . . 45
Wichita Lineman (Canopy, ASCAP) . . . 99
Yester-Me, Yester-You, Yesterday (Stein & Van Stock, ASCAP) . . . 8
You Got to Pay the Price (Myto, BMI) . . . 53
You Keep Me Hanging On (Jobete, BMI) . . . 94

*In litigation

## BUBBLING UNDER THE HOT 100

101. OH ME OH MY (I'm a Fool for You) . . . Lulu, Atco 6722
102. SIX WHITE HORSES . . . Tommy Cash, Epic 5-10540
103. ME & YOU . . . O. C. Smith, Columbia 4-45038
104. BALLAD OF PAUL . . . Mystery Tour, MGM 14097
105. MUST BE YOUR THING . . . Charles Wright & the Watts 103rd Street Rhythm Band, Warner Bros.-Seven Arts 7338
106. I CAN'T SEE YOU NO MORE (When Johnny Comes Marching Home) . . . Joe Tex, Dial 4095
107. I STARTED LOVING YOU AGAIN . . . Al Martino, Capitol 2674
108. I'M GONNA LOVE YOU . . . Intrigues, Yew 1002
109. LET'S WORK TOGETHER . . . Wilbert Harrison, Sue 11
110. TOO MANY COOKS (Spoil the Soup) . . 100% Proof Aged In Soul, Hot Wax 6904
111. WHAT DOES IT TAKE/MEMORIES ARE MADE OF BROKEN PROMISES . . . Motherlode, Buddah 144
112. JET SONG . . . The Group, Bell 822
113. VOODO WOMAN . . . Simon Stokes & the Nighthawks, Elektra 45670
114. VENUS . . . Shockin' Blue, Colossus 108
115. YOU ARE MY LIFE . . . Herb Alpert & the Tijuana Brass, A&M 1143
116. COWBOY CONVENTION . . . Ohio Express, Buddah 147
117. ARIZONA . . . Mark Lindsay, Columbia 4-45037
118. MORNING DEW . . . Sound Foundation, Smobro 401
119. WHEN WE GET MARRIED . . . 1910 Fruitgum Company, Buddah 146
120. ARE YOU GETTING ANY SUNSHINE . . . Lou Christie, Buddah 149
121. GROOVIN' (Out On Life) . . . Newbeats, Hickory 1552
122. CAMEL BACK . . . A. B. Skye, MGM 14086
123. COW PIE . . . Masked Marauders, Deity 0870
124. LAND OF 1000 DANCES . . . Electric Indian, United Artists 50613
125. RIGHT OR LEFT ON OAK STREET . . . Roy Clark, Dot 17324

Compiled from national retail sales and radio station airplay by the Music Popularity Dept. of Record Market Research, Billboard.

HOT 100

HOT 100

# Billboard HOT 100

FOR WEEK ENDING DECEMBER 6, 1969

♫ Artist and/or Selection featured on "The Music Scene" this week, ABC-TV Network. Those in black were featured on past programs.

★ STAR PERFORMER—Sides registering greatest proportionate sales progress this week. (RIAA seal) Record Industry Association of America seal of certification as million selling single.

| THIS WEEK | 1 Wk. Ago | 2 Wks. Ago | 3 Wks. Ago | TITLE | Artist (Producer), Label & Number | Weeks On Chart |
|---|---|---|---|---|---|---|
| ★ 1 | 5 | 6 | 11 | NA NA HEY HEY KISS HIM GOODBYE | Steam (Paul Leka), Fontana 1667 | 8 |
| ★ 2 | 7 | 12 | 23 | LEAVING ON A JET PLANE | Peter, Paul & Mary (Albert B. Grossman & Milt Okun), Warner Bros.-Seven Arts 7340 | 7 |
| (RIAA seal) ♫ 3 | 1 | 3 | 3 | COME TOGETHER/SOMETHING | Beatles (George Martin), Apple 2654 | 8 |
| ♫ 4 | 4 | 2 | 10 | TAKE A LETTER MARIA | R. B. Greaves (Ahmet Ertegun), Atco 6714 | 8 |
| ♫ ★ 5 | 9 | 14 | 16 | DOWN ON THE CORNER/FORTUNATE SON | Creedence Clearwater Revival (John Fogerty), Fantasy 634 | 6 |
| 6 | 2 | 4 | 4 | AND WHEN I DIE | Blood, Sweat & Tears (James William Guercio), Columbia 4-45008 | 8 |
| 7 | 3 | 1 | 1 | WEDDING BELL BLUES | 5th Dimension (Bones Howe), Soul City 779 | 11 |
| 8 | 8 | 8 | 22 | YESTER-ME, YESTER-YOU, YESTERDAY | Stevie Wonder (John Bristol), Tamla 54188 | 7 |
| ★ 9 | 11 | 20 | 34 | SOMEDAY WE'LL BE TOGETHER | Diana Ross & the Supremes (Johnny Bristol), Motown 1156 | 5 |
| ♫ 10 | 10. | 18 | 20 | ELI'S COMING | Three Dog Night (Gabriel Mekler), Dunhill 4215 | 7 |
| ★ 11 | 13 | 13 | 18 | BACKFIELD IN MOTION | Mel & Tim (Karl Tarleton), Bamboo 107 | 8 |
| 12 | 6 | 5 | 8 | SMILE A LITTLE SMILE FOR ME | The Flying Machine (Tony MacAuley), Congress 6000 | 10 |
| ★ 13 | 25 | 37 | 62 | RAINDROPS KEEP FALLING ON MY HEAD | B.J. Thomas (Burt Bacharach-Hal David), Scepter 12265 | 6 |
| 14 | 14 | 15 | 17 | BABY, I'M FOR REAL | Originals (Marvin Gaye), Soul 35066 | 11 |
| 15 | 15 | 19 | 24 | CHERRY HILL PARK | Billy Joe Royal (Buddy Buie), Columbia 4-44902 | 10 |
| ♫ ★ 16 | 18 | 28 | 32 | HOLLY HOLY | Neil Diamond (Tom Catalono & Tom Cogbill) UNI 55175 | 6 |
| (RIAA seal) 17 | 16 | 9 | 7 | SUSPICIOUS MINDS | Elvis Presley, RCA 47-9764 | 13 |
| ♫ 18 | 12 | 11 | 5 | BABY IT'S YOU | Smith (Joel Sill & Steve Barri), Dunhill 4206 | 14 |
| ★ 19 | 24 | 33 | 40 | ELEANOR RIGBY | Aretha Franklin (Jerry Wexler-Tom Dowd-Arif Mardin), Atlantic 2683 | 5 |
| 20 | 20 | 17 | 15 | GOING IN CIRCLES | Friends of Distinction (John Florez), RCA 74-0204 | 17 |
| ♫ 21 | 21 | 27 | 27 | SUITE: JUDY BLUE EYES | Crosby/Stills/Nash (Stephen Stills, David Crosby & Graham Nash), Atlantic 2676 | 10 |
| ★ 22 | 30 | 36 | 42 | THESE EYES | Jr. Walker & the All Stars (Johnny Bristol), Soul 35067 | 7 |
| ★ 23 | 29 | 34 | 37 | FRIENDSHIP TRAIN | Gladys Knight & the Pips (Norman Whitfield), Soul 35068 | 7 |
| ★ 24 | 37 | 46 | 52 | MIDNIGHT COWBOY | Ferrante & Teicher (George Butler), United Artists 50554 | 6 |
| ★ 25 | 32 | 40 | 47 | HEAVEN KNOWS | Grassroots (Steve Barri), Dunhill 4217 | 5 |
| 26 | 26 | 35 | 36 | MIND, BODY & SOUL | Flaming Embers (R. Dunbar), Hot Wax 6902 | 11 |
| ★ 27 | 51 | 67 | 90 | I WANT YOU BACK | The Jackson 5 (The Corporation), Motown 1157 | 4 |
| ★ 28 | 45 | 91 | — | WHOLE LOTTA LOVE | Led Zeppelin (Jimmy Page), Atlantic 2690 | 3 |
| 29 | 31 | 47 | 51 | UP ON CRIPPLE CREEK | The Band (John Simon), Capitol 2635 | 6 |
| 30 | 22 | 29 | 29 | UNDUN | Guess Who (Jack Richardson), RCA 74-0195 | 8 |
| ♫ 31 | 17 | 10 | 6 | I CAN'T GET NEXT TO YOU | Temptations (Norman Whitfield), Gordy 7093 | 17 |
| ♫ 32 | 19 | 16 | 9 | SUGAR, SUGAR | Archies (Jeff Barry), Calendar 63-1008 | 20 |
| 33 | 35 | 39 | 49 | GROOVY GRUBWORM | Harlow Wilcox (Shelby Singleton), Plantation 28 | 9 |
| 34 | 34 | 43 | 44 | I GUESS THE LORD MUST BE IN NEW YORK CITY | Nilsson (Rick Jarrard), RCA 74-0261 | 6 |
| ♫ ★ 35 | 40 | 50 | 67 | A BRAND NEW ME | Dusty Springfield (Roland Chambers), Atlantic 2685 | 5 |
| ★ 36 | 38 | 45 | 59 | EVIL WOMAN, DON'T PLAY YOUR GAMES WITH ME | Crow (Bob Monaco), Amaret 112 | 7 |
| ★ 37 | 43 | 69 | 88 | JAM UP JELLY TIGHT | Tommy Roe (Steve Barri), ABC 11247 | 4 |
| 38 | 23 | 24 | 25 | TRY A LITTLE KINDNESS | Glen Campbell (Al De Lory), Capitol 2659 | 9 |
| ♫ ★ 39 | 54 | 80 | — | LA LA LA (If I Had You) | Bobby Sherman (Jackie Mills), Metromedia 150 | 3 |
| 40 | 41 | 51 | 61 | LOVE WILL FIND A WAY | Jackie DeShannon (VME Prod.), Imperial 66419 | 6 |
| ★ 41 | 73 | — | — | DON'T CRY DADDY/RUBBERNECKIN' | Elvis Presley, RCA 47-9768 | 2 |
| ♫ 42 | 42 | 53 | 63 | (Sittin' On) THE DOCK OF THE BAY | Dells (Bobby Miller), Cadet 5658 | 6 |
| ♫ ★ 43 | 49 | 71 | — | AIN'T IT FUNKY NOW | James Brown (James Brown Prod.), King 6280 | 3 |
| 44 | 47 | 74 | 86 | COLD TURKEY | Plastic Ono Band (John & Yoko [Bag]) Apple 1813 | 4 |
| 45 | 33 | 26 | 26 | RUBEN JAMES | Kenny Rogers & First Edition (Mike Post), Reprise 0854 | 11 |
| ♫ 46 | 46 | 83 | 91 | KOZMIC BLUES | Janis Joplin (Gabriel Mekler), Columbia 4-45023 | 5 |
| ♫ ★ 47 | 57 | 78 | — | SUNDAY MORNIN' | Oliver (Bob Crewe), Crewe 337 | 3 |
| ★ 48 | 62 | 77 | — | EARLY IN THE MORNING | Vanity Fare (Roger Easterby & Des Champ), Page One 21-027 | 3 |
| ♫ 49 | 36 | 38 | 39 | MAKE YOUR OWN KIND OF MUSIC | Mama Cass Elliot (Steve Barri), Dunhill 4214 | 8 |
| ♫ ★ 50 | 69 | 75 | 87 | BLISTERED/SEE RUBY FALL | Johnny Cash (Bob Johnston), Columbia 4-45020 | 5 |
| ★ 51 | 72 | 86 | — | I'LL HOLD OUT MY HAND | Clique (Gary Zekley), White Whale 333 | 3 |
| 52 | 53 | 56 | 75 | YOU GOT TO PAY THE PRICE | Gloria Taylor (S. Whisenhunt), Silver Fox 14 | 5 |
| ♫ ★ 53 | 90 | — | — | JINGLE JANGLE | The Archies (Jeff Barry), Kirshner 63-5002 | 2 |
| ♫ ★ 54 | 76 | 90 | 98 | DON'T LET LOVE HANG YOU UP | Jerry Butler (Gamble-Huff), Mercury 72991 | 4 |
| 55 | 48 | 42 | 43 | WE LOVE YOU, CALL COLLECT | Art Linkletter (Irvin S. Arkins), Capitol 2678 | 6 |
| 56 | 60 | 65 | 68 | JINGO | Santana [Brent Dangerfield (IT)], Columbia 4-45010 | 7 |
| ♫ 57 | 61 | 61 | 85 | OKIE FROM MUSKOGEE | Merle Haggard & the Strangers (Ken Nelson), Capitol 2626 | 6 |
| 58 | 65 | 73 | 81 | CUPID | Johnny Nash (Johnny Nash-Arthur Jenkins), Jad 220 | 5 |
| ★ 59 | 70 | 72 | 82 | GET IT FROM THE BOTTOM | Steelers (Calvin Carter-Al Smith), Date 2-1642 | 4 |
| ♫ ★ 60 | 71 | 79 | 94 | GET RHYTHM | Johnny Cash (Sam Phillips), Sun 1103 | 4 |
| ★ 61 | 67 | 70 | 73 | MIDNIGHT | Dennis Yost & the Classics IV (Buddy Buie), Imperial 66424 | 4 |
| 62 | 55 | 55 | 53 | ANY WAY THAT YOU WANT ME | Evie Sands (Chip Taylor-Al Gorgoni), A&M 1090 | 17 |
| 63 | 59 | 62 | 69 | CRUMBS OFF THE TABLE | Glass House (Holland-Dozier-Holland), Invictus 9071 | 8 |
| ★ 64 | 74 | 98 | — | CAN'T TAKE MY EYES OFF OF YOU | Nancy Wilson (David D. Cavanaugh), Capitol 2644 | 3 |
| 65 | 66 | 92 | 77 | BALLAD OF EASY RIDER | Byrds (Terry Melcher), Columbia 4-44990 | 6 |
| 66 | 52 | 52 | 50 | TIME MACHINE | Grand Funk Railroad (Terry Knight), Capitol 2567 | 11 |
| 67 | 58 | 64 | 65 | SAY YOU LOVE ME | Impressions (Curtis Mayfield), Curtom 1946 | 8 |
| 68 | 44 | 44 | 46 | ROOSEVELT & IRA LEE | Tony Joe White (Billy Swann), Monument 1169 | 7 |
| 69 | 50 | 54 | 55 | TONIGHT I'LL BE STAYING HERE WITH YOU | Bob Dylan (Bob Johnston), Columbia 4-45004 | 6 |
| 70 | 75 | 94 | — | FANCY | Bobbie Gentry (Rick Hall), Capitol 2675 | 3 |
| ★ 71 | — | — | — | DON'T LET HIM TAKE YOUR LOVE FROM ME | Four Tops (Norman Whitfield), Motown 1159 | 1 |
| 72 | 68 | 68 | 78 | GIRLS, IT AIN'T EASY | Honey Cone (Stagecoach Prod.), Hot Wax 6903 | 5 |
| 73 | 77 | — | — | WHAT YOU GAVE ME | Marvin Gaye & Tammi Terrell (Ashford & Simpson), Tamla 54187 | 2 |
| 74 | 83 | 85 | 92 | (I'm So) AFRAID OF LOSING YOU AGAIN | Charley Pride (Jack Clement), RCA 74-0265 | 5 |
| 75 | 79 | 88 | 96 | SHE BELONGS TO ME | Rick Nelson (Rick Nelson), Decca 732550 | 6 |
| ★ 76 | 88 | 96 | 99 | ONE TIN SOLDIER | The Original Caste (Dennis Lambert & Brian Potter), TA 186 | 4 |
| 77 | 85 | 93 | 93 | VOLUNTEERS | Jefferson Airplane (Al Schmitt), RCA 74-0245 | 5 |
| ♫ 78 | 78 | 63 | 64 | I CAN'T MAKE IT ALONE | Lou Rawls (David Axelrod), Capitol 2668 | 6 |
| 79 | 80 | 89 | — | WALKIN' IN THE RAIN | Jay & the Americans (Sandy Yogunda & Thomas Kaye), United Artists 50605 | 3 |
| 80 | 81 | — | — | I'M TIRED | Savoy Brown (Mike Vernon Prod.), Parrot 40042 | 2 |
| ★ 81 | — | — | — | WONDERFUL WORLD, BEAUTIFUL PEOPLE | Jimmy Cliff (Larry Fallon-Leslie Kong), A&M 1146 | 1 |
| ★ 82 | 100 | — | — | GOIN' OUT OF MY HEAD/FORGET TO REMEMBER | Frank Sinatra (Frank Sinatra), Reprise 0865 | 2 |
| ♫ 83 | 84 | — | — | TURN TURN TURN (To Everything There Is a Season) | Judy Collins (Mark Abramson), Elektra 45680 | 2 |
| ★ 84 | — | — | — | WINTER WORLD OF LOVE | Engelbert Humperdinck (Peter Sullivan), Parrot 40044 | 1 |
| 85 | 86 | 87 | 95 | SWINGIN' TIGHT | Bill Deal & the Rhondells (Jerry Ross), Heritage 818 | 4 |
| ♫ 86 | 89 | 99 | — | HAPPY | Paul Anka (Wes Farrell), RCA 47-9767 | 3 |
| 87 | 87 | — | — | JE T'AIME . . . MOI NON PLUS | Jane Birklin & Serge Gainsbourg (Jack Baverstock), Fontana 1665 | 2 |
| 88 | 92 | — | — | I LOVE YOU | Otis Leavill (Willie Henderson), Dakar 614 | 2 |
| ♫ 89 | 91 | — | — | TONIGHT I'LL SAY A PRAYER | Eydie Gorme (Don Costa), RCA 74-0250 | 2 |
| ★ 90 | — | — | — | LADY-O | Turtles (Bob Harris-John Beck), White Whale 334 | 1 |
| 91 | — | — | — | LOOK-KA PY PY | Meters (Marshall Sehorn-Allan R. Toussaint), Josie 1015 | 1 |
| 92 | 96 | — | — | (One of These Days) SUNDAY'S GONNA COME ON TUESDAY | The New Establishment (Ernie Sheldon/Jack Keller), Colgems 66-5006 | 2 |
| 93 | 94 | — | — | YOU KEEP ME HANGING ON | Wilson Pickett (W. Pickett & D. Crawford—C. Grits), Atlantic 2682 | 2 |
| ♫ 94 | — | — | — | SHE CAME IN THROUGH THE BATHROOM WINDOW | Joe Cocker (Denny Cordell-Leon Russell), A&M 1147 | 1 |
| ♫ 95 | 99 | — | — | WICHITA LINEMAN | Sergio Mendes & Brasil '66 (Sergio Mendes), A&M 1132 | 2 |
| 96 | 97 | — | — | FEELING ALRIGHT | Mongo Santamaria (Tom Dowd), Atlantic 2689 | 2 |
| 97 | — | — | — | ARIZONA | Mark Lindsay (Jerry Fuller), Columbia 4-45037 | 1 |
| 98 | — | — | — | LET'S WORK TOGETHER | Wilbert Harrison (Juggy Murray), Sue 11 | 1 |
| 99 | — | — | — | I STARTED LOVING YOU AGAIN | Al Martino (Voyle Gilmore), Capitol 2674 | 1 |
| 100 | — | — | — | CAMEL BACK | A. B. Skhy (Richard Delvey), MGM 14086 | 1 |

## HOT 100—A TO Z—(Publisher-Licensee)

| | |
|---|---|
| Ain't It Funky Now (Golo, BMI) | 43 |
| And When I Die (Tuna Fish,* BMI) | 6 |
| Any Way That You Want Me (Blackwood, BMI) | 62 |
| Arizona (Kangaroo, BMI) | 97 |
| Baby I'm for Real (Jobete, BMI) | 14 |
| Baby It's You (Dolfi/Mary Jane, ASCAP) | 18 |
| Backfield In Motion (Cachand/Patcheal, BMI) | 11 |
| Ballad of Easy Rider (Blackwood/Last Minute/Patian, BMI) | 65 |
| Blistered (Quartet/Bexhill, ASCAP) | 50 |
| Brand New Me (Assorted/Parabut, BMI) | 35 |
| Camel Back (Skhy Blue, ASCAP) | 100 |
| Can't Take My Eyes Off of You (Saturday/Seasons Four, BMI) | 64 |
| Cherry Hill Park (Low-Sal, BMI) | 15 |
| Cold Turkey (Maclen, BMI) | 44 |
| Come Together (Maclen, BMI) | 3 |
| Crumbs Off the Table (Gold Forever, BMI) | 63 |
| Cupid (Kags, BMI) | 58 |
| Don't Cry Daddy (Gladys/BnB, ASCAP) | 41 |
| Don't Let Him Take Your Love From Me (Jobete, BMI) | 71 |
| Don't Let Love Hang You Up (Assorted/Parabut, BMI) | 54 |
| Down on the Corner (Jondora, BMI) | 5 |
| Early in the Morning (Duchess, BMI) | 48 |
| Eleanor Rigby (Maclen, BMI) | 19 |
| Eli's Coming (Tuna Fish, BMI) | 10 |
| Evil Woman, Don't Play Your Games With Me (Yoggoth, BMI) | 36 |
| Fancy (Shayme, ASCAP) | 70 |
| Feeling Alright (Almo, ASCAP) | 96 |
| Fortunate Son (Jondora, BMI) | 5 |
| Friendship Train (Jobete, BMI) | 23 |
| Get It From the Bottom (Alstin, BMI) | 59 |
| Get Rhythm (Hi-Lo, BMI) | 60 |
| Girls, It Ain't Easy (Gold Forever, BMI) | 72 |
| Going in Circles (Porpete, BMI) | 20 |
| Goin' Out of My Head (Vogue, BMI) | 82 |
| Groovin' (Out on Life) (Grand Teton, BMI) | 100 |
| Groovy Grubworm (Singleton, BMI) | 33 |
| Happy (Pocketful of Tunes, BMI) | 86 |
| Heaven Knows (Trousdale, BMI) | 25 |
| Holly Holy (Stonebridge, BMI) | 16 |
| I Can't Get Next to You (Jobete, BMI) | 31 |
| I Can't Make It Alone (Screen Gems-Columbia, BMI) | 78 |
| I Guess the Lord Must Be in New York City (Dunbar, BMI) | 34 |
| I Love You (Dakar, BMI) | 88 |
| I Started Loving You Again (Blue Book, BMI) | 99 |
| I'll Hold Out My Hand (Blackwood, BMI) | 51 |
| I'm Tired (Cool Water, ASCAP) | 80 |
| I Want You Back (Jobete, BMI) | 27 |
| (I'm So) Afraid of Losing You Again (Hill & Range/Blue Crest, BMI) | 74 |
| Jam Up Jelly Tight (Low-Twi, BMI) | 37 |
| Je T'Aime . . . Moi Non Plus (Monday Morning, BMI) | 87 |
| Jingle Jangle (Don Kirshner, BMI) | 53 |
| Jingo (Blackwood, BMI) | 56 |
| Kozmic Blues (Strong Arm/Wingate, ASCAP) | 46 |
| La La La (If I Had You) (Green Apple, BMI) | 39 |
| Lady-O (Blimp, BMI) | 90 |
| Leaving on a Jet Plane (Cherry Lane, ASCAP) | 2 |
| Let's Work Together (Sagittarius, BMI) | 98 |
| Look-Ka Py Py (Marsaint, BMI) | 91 |
| Love Will Find a Way (Unart, BMI) | 40 |
| Make Your Own Kind of Music (Screen Gems-Columbia, BMI) | 49 |
| Midnight (Low-Sal, BMI) | 61 |
| Midnight Cowboy (United Artists/Barwin, ASCAP) | 24 |
| Mind, Body & Soul (Gold Forever, BMI) | 26 |
| Na Na Hey Hey Kiss Him Goodbye (MRC/Little Heather, BMI) | 1 |
| Okie From Muskogee (Blue Rock, BMI) | 57 |
| One Tin Soldier (Cents & Pence, BMI) | 76 |
| Raindrops Keep Fallin' on My Head (Blue Seas/Jac/20th Century, ASCAP) | 13 |
| Roosevelt & Ira Lee (Combine, BMI) | 68 |
| Rubberneckin' (Presley, BMI) | 41 |
| Ruben James (Unart, BMI) | 45 |
| Say You Love Me (Curtom, BMI) | 67 |
| See Ruby Fall (House of Cash, BMI) | 50 |
| She Belongs to Me (Warner Bros.-Seven Arts, ASCAP) | 75 |
| She Came In Through the Bathroom Window (Maclen, BMI) | 94 |
| (Sittin' On) The Dock of the Bay (East/Time/Redwall, BMI) | 42 |
| Smile a Little Smile for Me (January, BMI) | 12 |
| Someday We'll Be Together (Jobete, BMI) | 9 |
| Something (Harrisongs, BMI) | 3 |
| Sugar, Sugar (Kirshner, BMI) | 32 |
| Sunday Mornin' (Blackwood, BMI) | 47 |
| (One of These Days) Sunday's Gonna' Come on Tuesday (Colgems Music, ASCAP) | 92 |
| Suite: Judy Blue Eyes (Gold Hill, BMI) | 21 |
| Suspicious Minds (Press, BMI) | 17 |
| Swingin' Tight (Pambar/Legacy, BMI) | 85 |
| Take a Letter Maria (Four Star Television, BMI) | 4 |
| These Eyes (Dunbar, BMI) | 22 |
| Time Machine (Storybook, BMI) | 66 |
| Tonight I'll Be Staying With You (Big Sky, ASCAP) | 69 |
| Tonight I'll Say a Prayer (Sunbury, ASCAP) | 89 |
| Try a Little Kindness (Airfield/Campbell, BMI) | 38 |
| Turn Turn Turn (To Everything There Is a Season) (Melody Trails, BMI) | 83 |
| Undun (Friends of Mine, Ltd./Dunbar/Cirrus, BMI) | 30 |
| Up on Cripple Creek (Canaan, ASCAP) | 29 |
| Volunteers (Icebag, BMI) | 77 |
| Walkin' in the Rain (Screen Gems-Columbia, BMI) | 79 |
| Wedding Bell Blues (Tuna Fish,* BMI) | 7 |
| We Love You, Call Collect (World, BMI) | 55 |
| What You Gave Me (Jobete, BMI) | 73 |
| Whole Lotta Love (Superhype, ASCAP) | 28 |
| Wichita Lineman (Canopy, ASCAP) | 95 |
| Winter World of Love (Donna, ASCAP) | 84 |
| Wonderful World, Beautiful People (Irving, BMI) | 81 |
| Yester-Me, Yester-You, Yesterday (Stein & Van Stock, ASCAP) | 8 |
| You Got to Pay the Price (Myto, BMI) | 52 |
| You Keep Me Hanging On (Jobete, BMI) | 93 |

*In litigation

## BUBBLING UNDER THE HOT 100

101. COWBOY CONVENTION .......... Ohio Express, Buddah 147
102. SIX WHITE HORSES .......... Tommy Cash, Epic 5-10540
103. VOODOO WOMAN .......... Simon Stokes & the Nighthawks, Elektra 45670
104. FREE .......... Pearly Gate, Decca 732573
105. OH ME OH MY .......... Lulu, Atco 6722
106. CURLY .......... Jimmy Clanton, Laurie 3508
107. NO ONE BETTER THAN YOU .......... Petula Clark, Warner Bros.-Seven Arts 7343
108. I'M GONNA LOVE YOU .......... Intrigues, Yew 1002
109. YOU ARE MY LIFE .......... Herb Alpert & the Tijuana Brass, A&M 1143
110. TOGETHER .......... Illusion, Steed 722
111. GROOVIN' (Out On Life) .......... Newbeats, Hickory 1552
112. VENUS .......... Shocking Blue, Colossus 108
113. VICTORIA .......... Kinks, Reprise 0863
114. TO BE YOUNG, GIFTED AND BLACK .......... Nina Simone, RCA 74-0269
115. LAND OF 1,000 DANCES .......... Electric Indian, United Artists 50613
116. MAYBE .......... Chantels, Roulette 7064
117. POINT IT OUT .......... Smokey Robinson & the Miracles, Tamla 54189
118. I'M SO GLAD I FELL FOR YOU .......... David Ruffin, Motown 1158
119. I FALL TO PIECES .......... Diana Trask, Dot 17316
120. ARE YOU GETTING ANY SUNSHINE .......... Lou Christie, Buddah 149
121. COME SATURDAY MORNING .......... Sandpipers, A&M 1134
122. SHE .......... Tommy James & Shondells, Roulette 7066
123. RIGHT OR LEFT AT OAK STREET .......... Roy Clark, Dot 17324
124. BLESS YOUR HEART .......... Isley Brothers, T-Neck 912
125. ME AND YOU .......... O. C. Smith, Columbia 4-45038
126. MORNIN' MORNIN' .......... Bobby Goldsboro, United Artists 50614

# Billboard HOT 100

FOR WEEK ENDING DECEMBER 13, 1969

♫ Artist and/or Selection featured on "The Music Scene" this week, ABC-TV Network. Those in black were featured on past programs.

★ STAR PERFORMER—Sides registering greatest proportionate sales progress this week. ◉ Record Industry Association of America seal of certification as million selling single.

| THIS WEEK | 1 Wk. Ago | 2 Wks. Ago | 3 Wks. Ago | TITLE Artist (Producer), Label & Number | Weeks On Chart |
|---|---|---|---|---|---|
| 1 | 1 | 5 | 6 | NA NA HEY HEY KISS HIM GOODBYE — Steam (Paul Lekai, Fontana 1667 | 9 |
| 2 | 2 | 7 | 12 | LEAVING ON A JET PLANE — Peter, Paul & Mary (Albert B. Grossman & Milt Okun), Warner Bros.-Seven Arts 7340 | 8 |
| ★ 3 | 9 | 11 | 20 | SOMEDAY WE'LL BE TOGETHER — Diana Ross & the Supremes (Johnny Bristol), Motown 1156 | 6 |
| ♫ 4 | 3 | 1 | 3 | COME TOGETHER/SOMETHING — Beatles (George Martin), Apple 2654 | 9 |
| ♫ 5 | 5 | 9 | 14 | DOWN ON THE CORNER/ FORTUNATE SON — Creedence Clearwater Revival (John Fogerty), Fantasy 634 | 7 |
| ♫ 6 | 4 | 4 | 2 | TAKE A LETTER MARIA — R. B. Greaves (Ahmet Ertegun), Atco 6714 | 9 |
| ♫ 7 | 8 | 8 | 8 | YESTER-ME, YESTER-YOU, YESTERDAY — Stevie Wonder (John Bristol), Tamla 54188 | 8 |
| 8 | 6 | 2 | 4 | AND WHEN I DIE — Blood, Sweat & Tears (James William Guercio), Columbia 4-45008 | 9 |
| ★ 9 | 13 | 25 | 37 | RAINDROPS KEEP FALLING ON MY HEAD — B.J. Thomas (Burt Bacharach-Hal David), Scepter 12265 | 7 |
| 10 | 11 | 13 | 13 | BACKFIELD IN MOTION — Mel & Tim (Karl Tarleton), Bamboo 107 | 9 |
| ♫ 11 | 10 | 10 | 18 | ELI'S COMING — Three Dog Night (Gabriel Mekler), Dunhill 4215 | 8 |
| 12 | 7 | 3 | 1 | WEDDING BELL BLUES — 5th Dimension (Bones Howe), Soul City 779 | 12 ◉ |
| ♫ 13 | 16 | 18 | 28 | HOLLY HOLY — Neil Diamond (Tom Catalono & Tom Cogbill) UNI 55175 | 7 |
| 14 | 12 | 6 | 5 | SMILE A LITTLE SMILE FOR ME — The Flying Machine (Tony MacAuley), Congress 6000 | 11 |
| 15 | 14 | 14 | 15 | BABY, I'M FOR REAL — Originals (Marvin Gaye), Soul 35066 | 12 |
| 16 | 15 | 15 | 19 | CHERRY HILL PARK — Billy Joe Royal (Buddy Buie), Columbia 4-44902 | 11 |
| 17 | 19 | 24 | 33 | ELEANOR RIGBY — Aretha Franklin (Jerry Wexler-Tom Dowd-Arif Mardin), Atlantic 2683 | 6 |
| ★ 18 | 23 | 29 | 34 | FRIENDSHIP TRAIN — Gladys Knight & the Pips (Norman Whitfield), Soul 35068 | 8 |
| ★ 19 | 27 | 51 | 67 | I WANT YOU BACK — The Jackson 5 (The Corporation), Motown 1157 | 5 |
| 20 | 22 | 30 | 36 | THESE EYES — Jr. Walker & the All Stars (Johnny Bristol), Soul 35067 | 8 |
| ★ 21 | 28 | 45 | 91 | WHOLE LOTTA LOVE — Led Zeppelin (Jimmy Page), Atlantic 2690 | 4 |
| ★ 22 | 24 | 37 | 46 | MIDNIGHT COWBOY — Ferrante & Teicher (George Butler), United Artists 50554 | 7 |
| 23 | 20 | 20 | 17 | GOING IN CIRCLES — Friends of Distinction (John Florez), RCA 74-0204 | 18 |
| ♫ 24 | 25 | 32 | 40 | HEAVEN KNOWS — Grassroots (Steve Barri), Dunhill 4217 | 6 |
| ♫ ★ 25 | 35 | 40 | 50 | A BRAND NEW ME — Dusty Springfield (Roland Chambers), Atlantic 2685 | 6 |
| ♫ 26 | 18 | 12 | 11 | BABY IT'S YOU — Smith (Joel Sill & Steve Barri), Dunhill 4206 | 15 |
| ♫ 27 | 21 | 21 | 27 | SUITE: JUDY BLUE EYES — Crosby/Stills/Nash (Stephen Stills, David Crosby & Graham Nash), Atlantic 2676 | 11 |
| 28 | 17 | 16 | 9 | SUSPICIOUS MINDS — Elvis Presley, RCA 47-9764 | 14 |
| 29 | 29 | 31 | 47 | UP ON CRIPPLE CREEK — The Band (John Simon), Capitol 2635 | 7 |
| 30 | 33 | 35 | 39 | GROOVY GRUBWORM — Harlow Wilcox (Shelby Singleton), Plantation 28 | 10 |
| ★ 31 | 37 | 43 | 69 | JAM UP JELLY TIGHT — Tommy Roe (Steve Barri), ABC 11247 | 5 |
| ♫ 32 | 32 | 19 | 16 | SUGAR, SUGAR — Archies (Jeff Barry), Calendar 63-1008 | 21 ◉ |
| 33 | 30 | 22 | 29 | UNDUN — Guess Who (Jack Richardson), RCA 74-0195 | 9 |
| ♫ ★ 34 | 39 | 54 | 80 | LA LA LA (If I Had You) — Bobby Sherman (Jackie Mills), Metromedia 150 | 4 |
| 35 | 36 | 38 | 45 | EVIL WOMAN, DON'T PLAY YOUR GAMES WITH ME — Crow (Bob Monaco), Amaret 112 | 8 |
| ★ 36 | 41 | 73 | — | DON'T CRY DADDY/ RUBBERNECKIN' — Elvis Presley, RCA 47-9768 | 3 |
| 37 | 26 | 26 | 35 | MIND, BODY & SOUL — Flaming Embers (R. Dunbar), Hot Wax 6902 | 12 |
| 38 | 38 | 23 | 24 | TRY A LITTLE KINDNESS — Glen Campbell (Al De Lory), Capitol 2659 | 10 |
| ★ 39 | 44 | 47 | 74 | COLD TURKEY — Plastic One Band (John & Yoko [Bag]) Apple 1813 | 5 |
| ♫ 40 | 43 | 49 | 71 | AIN'T IT FUNKY NOW — James Brown (James Brown Prod.), King 6280 | 4 |
| ♫ ★ 41 | 47 | 57 | 78 | SUNDAY MORNIN' — Oliver (Bob Crewe), Crewe 337 | 4 |
| ★ 42 | 48 | 62 | 77 | EARLY IN THE MORNING — Vanity Fare (Roger Easterby & Des Champ), Page One 21-027 | 4 |
| ♫ ★ 43 | 46 | 46 | 83 | KOZMIC BLUES — Janis Joplin (Gabriel Mekler), Columbia 4-45023 | 6 |
| ♫ 44 | 42 | 42 | 53 | (Sittin' On) THE DOCK OF THE BAY — Dells (Bobby Miller), Cadet 5658 | 7 |
| 45 | 51 | 72 | 86 | I'LL HOLD OUT MY HAND — Clique (Gary Zekley), White Whale 333 | 4 |
| 46 | 45 | 33 | 26 | RUBEN JAMES — Kenny Rogers & First Edition (Mike Post), Reprise 0854 | 12 |
| ♫ ★ 47 | 57 | 61 | 61 | OKIE FROM MUSKOGEE — Merle Haggard & the Strangers (Ken Nelson), Capitol 2626 | 7 |
| ♫ ★ 48 | 53 | 90 | — | JINGLE JANGLE — The Archies (Jeff Barry), Kirshner 63-5002 | 3 |
| 49 | 52 | 53 | 56 | YOU GOT TO PAY THE PRICE — Gloria Taylor (S. Whisenhunt), Silver Fox 14 | 6 |
| ♫ 50 | 50 | 69 | 75 | BLISTERED/SEE RUBY FALL — Johnny Cash (Bob Johnston), Columbia 4-45020 | 6 |
| ♫ 51 | 54 | 76 | 90 | DON'T LET LOVE HANG YOU UP — Jerry Butler (Gamble-Huff), Mercury 72991 | 5 |
| ★ 52 | 58 | 65 | 73 | CUPID — Johnny Nash (Johnny Nash-Arthur Jenkins), Jad 220 | 6 |
| ★ 53 | 71 | — | — | DON'T LET HIM TAKE YOUR LOVE FROM ME — Four Tops (Norman Whitfield), Motown 1159 | 2 |
| ★ 54 | 73 | 77 | — | WHAT YOU GAVE ME — Marvin Gaye & Tammi Terrell (Ashford & Simpson), Tamla 54187 | 3 |
| ★ 55 | 64 | 74 | 98 | CAN'T TAKE MY EYES OFF OF YOU — Nancy Wilson (David D. Cavanaugh), Capitol 2644 | 4 |
| 56 | 59 | 70 | 72 | GET IT FROM THE BOTTOM — Steelers (Calvin Carter-Al Smith), Date 2-1642 | 5 |
| ♫ 57 | 49 | 36 | 38 | MAKE YOUR OWN KIND OF MUSIC — Mama Cass Elliot (Steve Barri), Dunhill 4214 | 9 |
| 58 | 34 | 34 | 43 | I GUESS THE LORD MUST BE IN NEW YORK CITY — Nilsson (Rick Jarrard), RCA 74-0261 | 7 |
| 59 | 40 | 41 | 51 | LOVE WILL FIND A WAY — Jackie DeShannon (VME Prod.), Imperial 66419 | 7 |
| ★ 60 | 81 | — | — | WONDERFUL WORLD, BEAUTIFUL PEOPLE — Jimmy Cliff (Larry Fallon-Leslie Kong), A&M 1146 | 2 |
| 61 | 61 | 67 | 70 | MIDNIGHT — Dennis Yost & the Classics IV (Buddy Buie), Imperial 66424 | 5 |
| ★ 62 | 70 | 75 | 94 | FANCY — Bobbie Gentry (Rick Hall), Capitol 2675 | 4 |
| 63 | 63 | 59 | 62 | CRUMBS OFF THE TABLE — Glass House (Holland-Dozier-Holland), Invictus 9071 | 9 |
| ★ 64 | 75 | 79 | 88 | SHE BELONGS TO ME — Rick Nelson (Rick Nelson), Decca 732550 | 7 |
| ★ 65 | — | — | — | SHE — Tommy James & the Shondells (Tommy James & Bob King), Roulette 7066 | 1 |
| 66 | 56 | 60 | 65 | JINGO — Santana [Brent Dangerfield (IT)], Columbia 4-45010 | 8 |
| 67 | 67 | 58 | 64 | SAY YOU LOVE ME — Impressions (Curtis Mayfield), Curtom 1946 | 9 |
| ♫ 68 | 60 | 71 | 79 | GET RHYTHM — Johnny Cash (Sam Phillips), Sun 1103 | 5 |
| 69 | 69 | 50 | 54 | TONIGHT I'LL BE STAYING HERE WITH YOU — Bob Dylan (Bob Johnston), Columbia 4-45004 | 7 |
| 70 | 76 | 88 | 96 | ONE TIN SOLDIER — The Original Caste (Dennis Lambert & Brian Potter), TA 186 | 5 |
| ★ 71 | 84 | — | — | WINTER WORLD OF LOVE — Engelbert Humperdinck (Peter Sullivan), Parrot 40044 | 2 |
| 72 | 72 | 68 | 68 | GIRLS, IT AIN'T EASY — Honey Cone (Stagecoach Prod.), Hot Wax 6903 | 6 |
| 73 | 77 | 85 | 93 | VOLUNTEERS — Jefferson Airplane (Al Schmitt), RCA 74-0245 | 6 |
| ★ 74 | 79 | 80 | 89 | WALKIN' IN THE RAIN — Jay & the Americans (Sandy Yogunda & Thomas Kaye), United Artists 50605 | 4 |
| ♫ ★ 75 | 83 | 84 | — | TURN TURN TURN (To Everything There Is a Season) — Judy Collins (Mark Abramson), Elektra 45680 | 3 |
| ♫ ★ 76 | — | — | — | POINT IT OUT — Smokey Robinson & the Miracles ("Smokey" & Cleveland), Tamla 54189 | 1 |
| ★ 77 | — | — | — | VENUS — Shocking Blue (Robert van Leeuwen), Colossus 108 | 1 |
| 78 | 80 | 81 | — | I'M TIRED — Savoy Brown (Mike Vernon Prod.), Parrot 40042 | 3 |
| 79 | 88 | 92 | — | I LOVE YOU — Otis Leavill (Willie Henderson), Dakar 614 | 3 |
| 80 | 98 | — | — | LET'S WORK TOGETHER — Wilbert Harrison (Juggy Murray), Sue 11 | 2 |
| ★ 81 | — | — | — | SHE LETS HER HAIR DOWN (Early in the Morning) — Tokens (Tokens), Buddah 151 | 1 |
| 82 | 82 | 100 | — | GOIN' OUT OF MY HEAD/ FORGET TO REMEMBER — Frank Sinatra (Frank Sinatra), Reprise 0865 | 3 |
| ♫ ★ 83 | 94 | — | — | SHE CAME IN THROUGH THE BATHROOM WINDOW — Joe Cocker (Denny Cordell-Leon Russell), A&M 1147 | 2 |
| ♫ 84 | 78 | 78 | 63 | I CAN'T MAKE IT ALONE — Lou Rawls (David Axelrod), Capitol 2668 | 7 |
| 85 | 85 | 86 | 87 | SWINGIN' TIGHT — Bill Deal & the Rhondells (Jerry Ross), Heritage 818 | 5 |
| 86 | 74 | 83 | 85 | (I'm So) AFRAID OF LOSING YOU AGAIN — Charley Pride (Jack Clement), RCA 74-0265 | 6 |
| 87 | 90 | — | — | LADY-O — Turtles (Bob Harris-John Beck), White Whale 334 | 2 |
| ♫ 88 | 89 | 91 | — | TONIGHT I'LL SAY A PRAYER — Eydie Gorme (Don Costa), RCA 74-0250 | 3 |
| ★ 89 | 97 | — | — | ARIZONA — Mark Lindsay (Jerry Fuller), Columbia 4-45037 | 2 |
| ★ 90 | — | — | — | WHEN JULIE COMES AROUND — Cuff Links (Paul Vance-Lee Pockriss), Decca 732592 | 1 |
| 91 | 91 | — | — | LOOK-KA PY PY — Meters (Marshall Sehorn-Allan R. Toussaint), Josie 1015 | 2 |
| 92 | 93 | 94 | — | YOU KEEP ME HANGING ON — Wilson Pickett (W. Pickett & D. Crawford—C. Grits), Atlantic 2682 | 3 |
| 93 | — | — | — | TO BE YOUNG, GIFTED & BLACK — Nina Simone (Stroud Prods. & Enterprises, Inc.), RCA 74-0269 | 1 |
| 94 | — | — | — | IS IT BECAUSE I'M BLACK — Syl Johnson (Pieces of Peace), Twinight 125 | 1 |
| 95 | — | — | — | LAND OF 1,000 DANCES — Electric Indian (Len Barry-Tom Sellers), United Artists 50613 | 1 |
| 96 | — | — | — | SIX WHITE HORSES — Tommy Cash (Glenn Sutton), Epic 5-10540 | 1 |
| 97 | — | — | — | SHE LETS HER HAIR DOWN — Gene Pitney (Paul Vance-Lee Pockriss), Musicor 1384 | 1 |
| 98 | — | — | — | ALICE'S ROCK & ROLL RESTAURANT — Arlo Guthrie (Lenny Waronker-Van Dyke Parks), Reprise 0877 | 1 |
| 99 | — | — | — | HOW I MISS YOU BABY — Bobby Womack (Chips Moman), Minit 32081 | 1 |
| ♫ 100 | — | — | — | BIG IN VEGAS — Buck Owens and the Buckaroos (Ken Nelson), Capitol 2646 | 1 |

## HOT 100—A TO Z—*(Publisher-Licensee)*

Ain't It Funky Now (Golo, BMI) .... 40
Alice's Rock & Roll Restaurant (Appleseed, ASCAP) 98
And When I Die (Tuna Fish,* BMI) .... 8
Arizona (Kangaroo, BMI) .... 89
Baby I'm for Real (Jobete, BMI) .... 15
Baby It's You (Dolfi/Mary Jane, ASCAP) .... 26
Backfield In Motion (Cachand/Patcheal, BMI) .... 10
Big in Vegas (Blue Book/Exbrook/Mike Curb, BMI)..100
Blistered (Quartet/Bexhill, ASCAP) .... 50
Brand New Me (Assorted/Parabut, BMI) .... 25
Can't Take My Eyes Off of You (Saturday/ Seasons Four, BMI) .... 55
Cherry Hill Park (Low-Sal, BMI) .... 16
Cold Turkey (Maclen, BMI) .... 39
Come Together (Maclen, BMI) .... 4
Crumbs Off the Table (Gold Forever, BMI) .... 63
Cupid (Kags, BMI) .... 52
Don't Cry Daddy (Gladys/BnB, ASCAP) .... 36
Don't Let Him Take Your Love From Me (Jobete, BMI) .... 53
Don't Let Love Hang You Up (Assorted/ Parabut, BMI) .... 51
Down on the Corner (Jondora, BMI) .... 5
Early in the Morning (Duchess, BMI) .... 42
Eleanor Rigby (Maclen, BMI) .... 17
Eli's Coming (Tuna Fish, BMI) .... 11
Evil Woman, Don't Play Your Games With Me (Yoggoth, BMI) .... 35
Fancy (Shayme, ASCAP) .... 62
Fortunate Son (Jondora, BMI) .... 5
Friendship Train (Jobete, BMI) .... 18
Get It From the Bottom (Alstin, BMI) .... 56
Get Rhythm (Hi-Lo, BMI) .... 68
Girls, It Ain't Easy (Gold Forever, BMI) .... 72
Going in Circles (Porpete, BMI) .... 23
Goin' Out of My Head (Vogue, BMI) .... 82
Groovy Grubworm (Singleton, BMI) .... 30
Heaven Knows (Trousdale, BMI) .... 24
Holly Holy (Stonebridge, BMI) .... 13
How I Miss You Baby (Tracebob/Unart, BMI) .... 99
I Can't Make It Alone (Screen Gems-Columbia, BMI) 84
I Guess the Lord Must Be in New York City (Dunbar, BMI) .... 58
I Love You (Dakar, BMI) .... 79
Is It Because I'm Black (Nuddato Syl/Zel Hightone, BMI) .... 94
I'll Hold Out My Hand (Blackwood, BMI) .... 45
I'm Tired (Cool Water, ASCAP) .... 78
I Want You Back (Jobete, BMI) .... 19
(I'm So) Afraid of Losing You Again (Hill & Range/Blue Crest, BMI) .... 86
Jam Up Jelly Tight (Low-Twi, BMI) .... 31
Jingle Jangle (Don Kirshner, BMI) .... 48
Jingo (Blackwood, BMI) .... 66
Kozmic Blues (Strong Arm/Wingate, ASCAP) .... 43
La La La (If I Had You) (Green Apple, BMI) .... 34
Lady-O (Blimp, BMI) .... 87
Land of 1,000 Dances (Tune-Kel/Aantole, BMI) .... 95
Leaving on a Jet Plane (Cherry Lane, ASCAP) .... 2
Let's Work Together (Sagittarius, BMI) .... 80
Look-Ka Py Py (Marsaint, BMI) .... 91
Love Will Find a Way (Unart, BMI) .... 59
Make Your Own Kind of Music (Screen Gems-Columbia, BMI) .... 57
Midnight (Low-Sal, BMI) .... 61
Midnight Cowboy (United Artists/Barwin, ASCAP).. 22
Mind, Body & Soul (Gold Forever, BMI) .... 7
Na Na Hey Hey Kiss Him Goodbye (MRC/Little Heather, BMI) .... 1
Okie From Muskogee (Blue Rock, BMI) .... 47
One Tin Soldier (Cents & Pence, BMI) .... 70
Point It Out (Jobete, BMI) .... 76
Raindrops Keep Fallin' on My Head (Blue Seas/ Jac/20th Century, ASCAP) .... 9
Rubberneckin' (Presley, BMI) .... 36
Ruben James (Unart, BMI) .... 46
Say You Love Me (Curtom, BMI) .... 67
See Ruby Fall (House of Cash, BMI) .... 50
She (Big Seven, BMI) .... 65
She Belongs to Me (Warner Bros.- Seven Arts, ASCAP) .... 64
She Came In Through the Bathroom Window (Maclen, BMI) .... 83
She Lets Her Hair Down (Early in the Morning) (Moon Beam, ASCAP) .... 81
She Lets Her Hair Down (Moon Beam, ASCAP) .... 97
(Sittin' On) The Dock of the Bay (East/ Time/Redwall, BMI) .... 44
Six White Horses (Peer Int'l, BMI) .... 96
Smile a Little Smile for Me (January, BMI) .... 14
Someday We'll Be Together (Jobete, BMI) .... 3
Something (Harrisongs, BMI) .... 4
Sugar, Sugar (Kirshner, BMI) .... 32
Sunday Mornin' (Blackwood, BMI) .... 41
Suite: Judy Blue Eyes (Gold Hill, BMI) .... 27
Suspicious Minds (Press, BMI) .... 28
Swingin' Tight (Pambar/Legacy, BMI) .... 85
Take a Letter Maria (Four Star Television, BMI)... 6
These Eyes (Dunbar, BMI) .... 20
To Be Young, Gifted & Black (Ninandy, BMI) .... 93
Tonight I'll Be Staying With You (Big Sky, ASCAP) 69
Tonight I'll Say a Prayer (Sunbury, ASCAP) .... 88
Try a Little Kindness (Airfield/Campbell, BMI) .... 38
Turn Turn Turn (To Everything There Is a Season) (Melody Trails, BMI) .... 75
Undun (Friends of Mine, Ltd./Dunbar/Cirrus, BMI).. 33
Up on Cripple Creek (Canaan, ASCAP) .... 29
Venus (Fat Zach, BMI) .... 77
Volunteers (Icebag, BMI) .... 73
Walkin' in the Rain (Screen Gems-Columbia, BMI).. 74
Wedding Bell Blues (Tuna Fish,* BMI) .... 12
What You Gave Me (Jobete, BMI) .... 54
When Julie Comes Around (Emily/Vanlee, ASCAP).. 90
Whole Lotta Love (Superhype, ASCAP) .... 21
Winter World of Love (Donna, ASCAP) .... 71
Wonderful World, Beautiful People (Irving, BMI)... 60
Yester-Me, Yester-You, Yesterday (Stein & Van Stock, ASCAP) .... 7
You Got to Pay the Price (Myto, BMI) .... 49
You Keep Me Hanging On (Jobete, BMI) .... 92
*In litigation

## BUBBLING UNDER THE HOT 100

101. MORNIN' MORNIN'....Bobby Goldsboro, United Artists 50614
102. BEEN A LONG TIME....Betty Everett, Uni 55174
103. VOODOO WOMAN....Simon Stokes & the Nighthawks, Elektra 45670
104. FAREWELL IS A LONELY SOUND....Jimmy Ruffin, Soul 35060
105. I'M SO GLAD I FELL FOR YOU....David Ruffin, Motown 1158
106. BLESS YOUR HEART....Isley Brothers, T-Neck 912
107. ME AND YOU....O. C. Smith, Columbia 4-45038
108. COMPARED TO WHAT....Les McCann & Eddie Harris, Atlantic 2694
109. FEELING ALRIGHT....Mongo Santamaria, Atlantic 2689
110. I STARTED LOVING YOU AGAIN....Al Martino, Capitol 2674
111. GUESS WHO....Ruby Winters, Diamond 269
112. ALICE'S RESTAURANT MASSACREE....Gary Sherman, United Artists 50589
113. I'M JUST A PRISONER (Of Your Good Lovin')....Candi Staton, Fame 1460
114. I FALL TO PIECES....Diana Trask, Dot 17316
115. CAMEL BACK....A. B. Skhy, MGM 14086
116. GROOVIN' (Out on Life)....Newbeats, Hickory 1552
117. COWBOY CONVENTION....Ohio Express, Buddah 147
118. LOVE BONES....Johnny Taylor, Stax 0055
119. THEME FROM 2001: A SPACE ODYSSEY...Berlin Philharmonic, Polydor 2-15009
120. HE AIN'T HEAVY HE'S MY BROTHER....Hollies, Epic 5-10532
121. I'M GONNA LOVE YOU....Intrigues, Yew 1002
122. MAYBE....Chantels, Roulette 7064
123. ARE YOU GETTING ANY SUNSHINE....Lou Christie, Buddah 149
124. HAVE A LITTLE TALK WITH MYSELF....Ray Stevens, Monument 1171
125. TROUBLEMAKER....Lee Hazlewood, LHI 20
126. FUNK #48....James Gang, BluesWay 61030
127. FREE....Pearly Gate, Decca 732573
128. READY TO RIDE....Southwind, Blue Thumb 108
129. JENNIFER TOMPKINS....Street People, Musicor 1365
130. NO TIME....Guess Who, RCA 74-0030
131. SHE'S READY....Spiral Starecase, Columbia 4-45048
132. BABY TAKE ME IN YOUR ARMS....Jefferson, Janus 106
133. TOGETHER....Illusion, Steed 722

Compiled from national retail sales and radio station airplay by the Music Popularity Dept. of Record Market Research, Billboard.

# Billboard HOT 100

FOR WEEK ENDING DECEMBER 20, 1969

♫ Artist and/or Selection featured on "The Music Scene" this week, ABC-TV Network. Those in black were featured on past programs.

★ STAR PERFORMER—Sides registering greatest proportionate sales progress this week. ◉ Record Industry Association of America seal of certification as million selling single.

| THIS WEEK | 1 Wk. Ago | 2 Wks. Ago | 3 Wks. Ago | TITLE Artist (Producer), Label & Number | Weeks On Chart |
|---|---|---|---|---|---|
| 1 | 2 | 2 | 7 | LEAVING ON A JET PLANE — Peter, Paul & Mary (Albert B. Grossman & Milt Okun), Warner Bros.-Seven Arts 7340 | 9 |
| 2 | 3 | 9 | 11 | SOMEDAY WE'LL BE TOGETHER — Diana Ross & the Supremes (Johnny Bristol), Motown 1156 | 7 |
| ♫ ★ 3 | 5 | 5 | 9 | DOWN ON THE CORNER/FORTUNATE SON — Creedence Clearwater Revival (John Fogerty), Fantasy 634 | 8 |
| 4 | 1 | 1 | 5 | NA NA HEY HEY KISS HIM GOODBYE — Steam (Paul Leka), Fontana 1667 | 10 ◉ |
| ★ 5 | 9 | 13 | 25 | RAINDROPS KEEP FALLING ON MY HEAD — B.J. Thomas (Burt Bacharach-Hal David), Scepter 12265 | 8 |
| ♫ 6 | 4 | 3 | 1 | COME TOGETHER/SOMETHING — Beatles (George Martin), Apple 2654 | 10 ◉ |
| ♫ 7 | 7 | 8 | 8 | YESTER-ME, YESTER-YOU, YESTERDAY — Stevie Wonder (John Bristol), Tamla 54188 | 9 |
| ♫ 8 | 6 | 4 | 4 | TAKE A LETTER MARIA — R. B. Greaves (Ahmet Ertegun), Atco 6714 | 10 |
| ♫ ★ 9 | 13 | 16 | 18 | HOLLY HOLY — Neil Diamond (Tom Catalono & Tom Cogbill) UNI 55175 | 8 |
| 10 | 8 | 6 | 2 | AND WHEN I DIE — Blood, Sweat & Tears (James William Guercio), Columbia 4-45008 | 10 |
| ♫ 11 | 11 | 10 | 10 | ELI'S COMING — Three Dog Night (Gabriel Mekler), Dunhill 4215 | 9 |
| ★ 12 | 21 | 28 | 45 | WHOLE LOTTA LOVE — Led Zeppelin (Jimmy Page), Atlantic 2690 | 5 |
| 13 | 10 | 11 | 13 | BACKFIELD IN MOTION — Mel & Tim (Karl Tarleton), Bamboo 107 | 10 |
| ♫ ★ 14 | 34 | 39 | 54 | LA LA LA (If I Had You) — Bobby Sherman (Jackie Mills), Metromedia 150 | 5 |
| ★ 15 | 22 | 24 | 37 | MIDNIGHT COWBOY — Ferrante & Teicher (George Butler), United Artists 50554 | 8 |
| 16 | 16 | 15 | 15 | CHERRY HILL PARK — Billy Joe Royal (Buddy Buie), Columbia 4-44902 | 12 |
| 17 | 19 | 27 | 51 | I WANT YOU BACK — The Jackson 5 (The Corporation), Motown 1157 | 6 |
| 18 | 18 | 23 | 29 | FRIENDSHIP TRAIN — Gladys Knight & the Pips (Norman Whitfield), Soul 35068 | 9 |
| 19 | 12 | 7 | 3 | WEDDING BELL BLUES — 5th Dimension (Bones Howe), Soul City 779 | 13 ◉ |
| 20 | 20 | 22 | 30 | THESE EYES — Jr. Walker & the All Stars (Johnny Bristol), Soul 35067 | 9 |
| 21 | 14 | 12 | 6 | SMILE A LITTLE SMILE FOR ME — The Flying Machine (Tony MacAuley), Congress 6000 | 12 |
| 22 | 15 | 14 | 14 | BABY, I'M FOR REAL — Originals (Marvin Gaye), Soul 35066 | 13 |
| ★ 23 | 31 | 37 | 43 | JAM UP JELLY TIGHT — Tommy Roe (Steve Barri), ABC 11247 | 6 |
| ♫ 24 | 25 | 35 | 40 | A BRAND NEW ME — Dusty Springfield (Roland Chambers), Atlantic 2685 | 7 |
| ★ 25 | 36 | 41 | 73 | DON'T CRY DADDY/RUBBERNECKIN' — Elvis Presley, RCA 47-9768 | 4 |
| ★ 26 | 29 | 29 | 31 | UP ON CRIPPLE CREEK — The Band (John Simon), Capitol 2635 | 8 |
| ♫ 27 | 24 | 25 | 32 | HEAVEN KNOWS — Grassroots (Steve Barri), Dunhill 4217 | 7 |
| ★ 28 | 35 | 36 | 38 | EVIL WOMAN, DON'T PLAY YOUR GAMES WITH ME — Crow (Bob Monaco), Amaret 112 | 9 |
| 29 | 17 | 19 | 24 | ELEANOR RIGBY — Aretha Franklin (Jerry Wexler-Tom Dowd-Arif Mardin), Atlantic 2683 | 7 |
| 30 | 23 | 20 | 20 | GOING IN CIRCLES — Friends of Distinction (John Florez), RCA 74-0204 | 19 |
| ★ 31 | 77 | — | — | VENUS — Shocking Blue (Robert van Leeuwen), Colossus 108 | 2 |
| ♫ 32 | 27 | 21 | 21 | SUITE: JUDY BLUE EYES — Crosby/Stills/Nash (Stephen Stills, David Crosby & Graham Nash), Atlantic 2676 | 12 |
| 33 | 30 | 33 | 35 | GROOVY GRUBWORM — Harlow Wilcox (Shelby Singleton), Plantation 28 | 11 |
| ♫ ★ 34 | 48 | 53 | 90 | JINGLE JANGLE — The Archies (Jeff Barry), Kirshner 63-5002 | 4 |
| 35 | 39 | 44 | 47 | COLD TURKEY — Plastic Ono Band (John & Yoko [Bag]) Apple 1813 | 6 |
| ♫ 36 | 40 | 43 | 49 | AIN'T IT FUNKY NOW — James Brown (James Brown Prod.), King 6280 | 5 |
| ★ 37 | 42 | 48 | 62 | EARLY IN THE MORNING — Vanity Fare (Roger Easterby & Des Champ), Page One 21-027 | 5 |
| ♫ 38 | 41 | 47 | 57 | SUNDAY MORNIN' — Oliver (Bob Crewe), Crewe 337 | 5 |
| 39 | 37 | 26 | 26 | MIND, BODY & SOUL — Flaming Embers (R. Dunbar), Hot Wax 6902 | 13 |
| ★ 40 | 65 | — | — | SHE — Tommy James & the Shondells (Tommy James & Bob King), Roulette 7066 | 2 |
| ♫ 41 | 43 | 46 | 46 | KOZMIC BLUES — Janis Joplin (Gabriel Mekler), Columbia 4-45023 | 7 |
| ♫ 42 | 47 | 57 | 61 | OKIE FROM MUSKOGEE — Merle Haggard & the Strangers (Ken Nelson), Capitol 2626 | 8 |
| ★ 43 | 52 | 58 | 65 | CUPID — Johnny Nash (Johnny Nash-Arthur Jenkins), Jad 220 | 7 |
| ♫ ★ 44 | 51 | 54 | 76 | DON'T LET LOVE HANG YOU UP — Jerry Butler (Gamble-Huff), Mercury 72991 | 6 |
| 45 | 45 | 51 | 72 | I'LL HOLD OUT MY HAND — Clique (Gary Zekley), White Whale 333 | 5 |
| ★ 46 | 53 | 71 | — | DON'T LET HIM TAKE YOUR LOVE FROM ME — Four Tops (Norman Whitfield), Motown 1159 | 3 |
| ★ 47 | 60 | 81 | — | WONDERFUL WORLD, BEAUTIFUL PEOPLE — Jimmy Cliff (Larry Fallon-Leslie Kong), A&M 1146 | 3 |
| ★ 48 | 71 | 84 | — | WINTER WORLD OF LOVE — Engelbert Humperdinck (Peter Sullivan), Parrot 40044 | 3 |
| 49 | 49 | 52 | 53 | YOU GOT TO PAY THE PRICE — Gloria Taylor (S. Whisenhunt), Silver Fox 14 | 7 |
| 50 | 54 | 73 | 77 | WHAT YOU GAVE ME — Marvin Gaye & Tammi Terrell (Ashford & Simpson), Tamla 54187 | 4 |
| ♫ 51 | 44 | 42 | 42 | (Sittin' On) THE DOCK OF THE BAY — Dells (Bobby Miller), Cadet 5658 | 8 |
| ♫ 52 | 50 | 50 | 69 | BLISTERED/SEE RUBY FALL — Johnny Cash (Bob Johnston), Columbia 4-45020 | 7 |
| 53 | 32 | 32 | 19 | SUGAR, SUGAR — Archies (Jeff Barry), Calendar 63-1008 | 22 ◉ |
| ★ 54 | 62 | 70 | 75 | FANCY — Bobbie Gentry (Rick Hall), Capitol 2675 | 5 |
| 55 | 55 | 64 | 74 | CAN'T TAKE MY EYES OFF OF YOU — Nancy Wilson (David D. Cavanaugh), Capitol 2644 | 5 |
| ★ 56 | 64 | 75 | 79 | SHE BELONGS TO ME — Rick Nelson (Rick Nelson), Decca 732550 | 8 |
| 57 | 28 | 17 | 16 | SUSPICIOUS MINDS — Elvis Presley, RCA 47-9764 | 15 ◉ |
| ★ 58 | 61 | 61 | 67 | MIDNIGHT — Dennis Yost & the Classics IV (Buddy Buie), Imperial 66424 | 6 |
| 59 | 38 | 38 | 23 | TRY A LITTLE KINDNESS — Glen Campbell (Al De Lory), Capitol 2659 | 11 |
| ♫ ★ 60 | 83 | 94 | — | SHE CAME IN THROUGH THE BATHROOM WINDOW — Joe Cocker (Denny Cordell-Leon Russell), A&M 1147 | 3 |
| 61 | 33 | 30 | 22 | UNDUN — Guess Who (Jack Richardson), RCA 74-0195 | 10 |
| 62 | 59 | 40 | 41 | LOVE WILL FIND A WAY — Jackie DeShannon (VME Prod.), Imperial 66419 | 8 |
| 63 | 70 | 76 | 88 | ONE TIN SOLDIER — The Original Caste (Dennis Lambert & Brian Potter), TA 186 | 6 |
| ♫ ★ 64 | 76 | — | — | POINT IT OUT — Smokey Robinson & the Miracles ("Smokey" & Cleveland), Tamla 54189 | 2 |
| 65 | 73 | 77 | 85 | VOLUNTEERS — Jefferson Airplane (Al Schmitt), RCA 74-0245 | 7 |
| ♫ ★ 66 | 89 | 97 | — | ARIZONA — Mark Lindsay (Jerry Fuller), Columbia 4-45037 | 3 |
| 67 | 56 | 59 | 70 | GET IT FROM THE BOTTOM — Steelers (Calvin Carter-Al Smith), Date 2-1642 | 6 |
| ★ 68 | 80 | 98 | — | LET'S WORK TOGETHER — Wilbert Harrison (Juggy Murray), Sue 11 | 3 |
| 69 | 74 | 79 | 80 | WALKIN' IN THE RAIN — Jay & the Americans (Sandy Yogunda & Thomas Kaye), United Artists 50605 | 5 |
| ♫ 70 | 68 | 60 | 71 | GET RHYTHM — Johnny Cash (Sam Phillips), Sun 1103 | 6 |
| ★ 71 | 90 | — | — | WHEN JULIE COMES AROUND — Cuff Links (Paul Vance-Lee Pockriss), Decca 732592 | 2 |
| ♫ ★ 72 | — | — | — | LET A MAN COME IN AND DO THE POPCORN (Part II) — James Brown (J. Brown), King 6275 | 1 |
| ★ 73 | — | — | — | BABY TAKE ME IN YOUR ARMS — Jefferson (John Schroeder), Janus 106 | 1 |
| 74 | 78 | 80 | 81 | I'M TIRED — Savoy Brown (Mike Vernon Prod.), Parrot 40042 | 4 |
| ♫ 75 | 75 | 83 | 84 | TURN TURN TURN (To Everything There Is a Season) — Judy Collins (Mark Abramson), Elektra 45680 | 4 |
| 76 | 79 | 88 | 92 | I LOVE YOU — Otis Leavill (Willie Henderson), Dakar 614 | 4 |
| 77 | 81 | — | — | SHE LETS HER HAIR DOWN (Early in the Morning) — Tokens (Tokens), Buddah 151 | 2 |
| 78 | 87 | 90 | — | LADY-O — Turtles (Bob Harris-John Beck), White Whale 334 | 3 |
| 79 | 82 | 82 | 100 | GOIN' OUT OF MY HEAD/FORGET TO REMEMBER — Frank Sinatra (Frank Sinatra), Reprise 0865 | 4 |
| ★ 80 | — | — | — | I'M SO GLAD I FELL FOR YOU — David Ruffin (Berry Gordy, Jr.), Motown 1158 | 1 |
| ★ 81 | — | — | — | NO TIME — The Guess Who (Jack Richardson), RCA 74-0300 | 1 |
| ★ 82 | 91 | 91 | — | LOOK-KA PY PY — Meters (Marshall Sehorn-Allan R. Toussaint), Josie 1015 | 3 |
| ★ 83 | — | — | — | ARE YOU GETTING ANY SUNSHINE? — Lou Christie (Stan Vincent-Mike Duckman), Buddah 149 | 1 |
| ★ 84 | — | — | — | COME SATURDAY MORNING — The Sandpipers (Allen Stanton), A&M 1134 | 1 |
| ♫ 85 | 88 | 89 | 91 | TONIGHT I'LL SAY A PRAYER — Eydie Gorme (Don Costa), RCA 74-0250 | 4 |
| ★ 86 | 96 | — | — | SIX WHITE HORSES — Tommy Cash (Glenn Sutton), Epic 5-10540 | 2 |
| ★ 87 | — | — | — | TOGETHER — The Illusion (Jeff Barry), Steed 722 | 1 |
| ★ 88 | — | — | — | GROOVIN' (Out on Life) — Newbeats (Don Gant), Hickory 1552 | 1 |
| ★ 89 | — | — | — | I'M GONNA LOVE YOU — The Intrigues (Martin & Bell), Yew 1002 | 1 |
| 90 | 93 | — | — | TO BE YOUNG, GIFTED & BLACK — Nina Simone (Stroud Prods. & Enterprises, Inc.), RCA 74-0269 | 2 |
| 91 | — | — | — | VOODOO WOMAN — Simon Stokes & the Nighthawks (Linda Perry), Elektra 45670 | 1 |
| 92 | — | — | — | BOLD SOUL SISTER — Ike & Tina Turner (Bob Krasnow), Blue Thumb 104 | 1 |
| 93 | 99 | — | — | HOW I MISS YOU BABY — Bobby Womack (Chips Moman), Minit 32081 | 2 |
| 94 | 94 | — | — | IS IT BECAUSE I'M BLACK — Syl Johnson (Pieces of Peace), Twinight 125 | 2 |
| 95 | — | — | — | LOVE BONES — Johnny Taylor (Don Davis), Stax 0055 | 1 |
| 96 | — | — | — | BEEN A LONG TIME — Betty Everett (Leo Austell), Uni 55174 | 1 |
| 97 | 98 | — | — | ALICE'S ROCK & ROLL RESTAURANT — Arlo Guthrie (Lenny Waronker-Van Dyke Parks), Reprise 0877 | 2 |
| 98 | — | — | — | MR. LIMOUSINE DRIVER — Grand Funk Railroad (Terry Knight), Capitol 2691 | 1 |
| 99 | — | — | — | TOO MANY COOKS (Spoil the Soup) — 100 Proof Aged In Soul (Stagecoach Prod.), Hot Wax 6904 | 1 |
| 100 | — | — | — | HE AIN'T HEAVY, HE'S MY BROTHER — Hollies (Ron Richards), Epic 5-10532 | 1 |

## HOT 100—A TO Z—(Publisher-Licensee)



*In litigation

## BUBBLING UNDER THE HOT 100

101. WORLD WITHOUT MUSIC....Archie Bell & the Drells, Atlantic 2693
102. SHE'S READY....Spiral Starecase, Columbia 4-45048
103. TRACES/MEMORIES MEDLEY....Lettermen, Capitol 2697
104. AT THE CROSSROADS....Sir Douglas Quintet, Smash 2253
105. BLESS YOUR HEART....Isley Brothers, T-Neck 912
106. FEELIN' ALRIGHT....Mongo Santamaria, Atlantic 2689
107. THRILL IS GONE....B. B. King, BluesWay 61032
108. COMPARED TO WHAT....Les McCann & Eddie Harris, Atlantic 2694
109. MORNIN' MORNIN'....Bobby Goldsboro, United Artists 50614
110. GUESS WHO....Ruby Winters, Diamond 269
111. ANY WAY THAT YOU WANT ME....Walter Jackson, Cotillion 44053
112. CLAUDIE MAE....Ray Charles, ABC 11251
113. AMEN (1970)....Impressions, Curtom 1948
114. LAND OF 1,000 DANCES....Electric Indian, United Artists 50613
115. JENNIFER TOMPKINS....Street People, Musicor 1365
116. TROUBLEMAKER....Lee Hazlewood, LHI 20
117. THEME FROM 2001: A SPACE ODYSSEY....Berlin Philharmonic, Polydor 2-15009
118. THE GANG IS BACK AGAIN....Kool & the Gang, De-Lite 523
119. SHE LETS HER HAIR DOWN....Gene Pitney, Musicor 1384
120. HEY THERE LONELY GIRL....Eddie Holman, ABC 11240
121. BARBARA I LOVE YOU....New Colony Six, Mercury 73004
122. ELECTRIC SURFBOARD....Brother Jack McDuff, Blue Note BN 1953
123. HAVE A LITTLE TALK WITH MYSELF....Ray Stevens, Monument 1171
124. (Gotta Find) A BRAND NEW LOVER....Sweet Inspirations, Atlantic 2686
125. HELLO SUNSHINE....Rev. Maceo Woods, Volt 4025
126. FUNK #48....James Gang, BluesWay 61030
127. READY TO RIDE....Southwind, Blue Thumb 108
128. MY BABY LOVES ME....David T. Walker, Revue 11060
129. ME AND YOU....O. C. Smith, Columbia 4-45038
130. FAREWELL IS A LONELY SOUND....Jimmy Ruffin, Soul 35260
131. OH ME OH MY (I'm a Fool for You Baby)....Lulu, Atco 6722
132. WON'T FIND BETTER THAN ME....New Hope, Jamie 1381
133. WHAT A BEAUTIFUL FEELING....California Earthquake, World Pacific 779

Compiled from national retail sales and radio station airplay by the Music Popularity Dept. of Record Market Research, Billboard.

# Billboard HOT 100

**FOR WEEK ENDING DECEMBER 27, 1969**

♪ Artist and/or Selection featured on "The Music Scene" this week, ABC-TV Network. Those in black were featured on past programs.

★ STAR PERFORMER—Sides registering greatest proportionate sales progress this week.   ● Record Industry Association of America seal of certification as million selling single.

| This Week | Wks. Ago 1 | Wks. Ago 2 | Wks. Ago 3 | TITLE  Artist (Producer), Label & Number | Weeks On Chart |
|---|---|---|---|---|---|
| 1 | 2 | 3 | 9 | SOMEDAY WE'LL BE TOGETHER — Diana Ross & the Supremes (Johnny Bristol), Motown 1156 | 8 |
| 2 | 1 | 2 | 2 | LEAVING ON A JET PLANE — Peter, Paul & Mary (Albert B. Grossman & Milt Okun), Warner Bros.-Seven Arts 7340 | 10 |
| 3 | 5 | 9 | 13 | RAINDROPS KEEP FALLING ON MY HEAD — B.J. Thomas (Burt Bacharach-Hal David), Scepter 12265 | 9 |
| ♪ 4 | 3 | 5 | 5 | DOWN ON THE CORNER/FORTUNATE SON — Creedence Clearwater Revival (John Fogerty), Fantasy 634 | 9 |
| 5 | 4 | 1 | 1 | NA NA HEY HEY KISS HIM GOODBYE — Steam (Paul Leka), Fontana 1667 | 14 |
| ♪ 6 | 9 | 13 | 16 | HOLLY HOLY — Neil Diamond (Tom Catalano & Tom Cogbill), UNI 55175 | 9 |
| ♪ 7 | 6 | 4 | 3 | COME TOGETHER/SOMETHING — Beatles (George Martin), Apple 2654 | 11 |
| ★ 8 | 17 | 19 | 27 | I WANT YOU BACK — The Jackson 5 (The Corporation), Motown 1157 | 7 |
| 9 | 12 | 21 | 28 | WHOLE LOTTA LOVE — Led Zeppelin (Jimmy Page), Atlantic 2690 | 6 |
| ♪ 10 | 8 | 6 | 4 | TAKE A LETTER MARIA — R. B. Greaves (Ahmet Ertegun), Atco 6714 | 11 |
| 11 | 15 | 22 | 24 | MIDNIGHT COWBOY — Ferrante & Teicher (George Butler), United Artists 50554 | 9 |
| ♪ 12 | 11 | 11 | 10 | ELI'S COMING — Three Dog Night (Gabriel Mekler), Dunhill 4215 | 11 |
| ♪ 13 | 7 | 7 | 8 | YESTER-ME, YESTER-YOU, YESTERDAY — Stevie Wonder (John Bristol), Tamla 54188 | 10 |
| ♪ 14 | 14 | 34 | 39 | LA LA LA (If I Had You) — Bobby Sherman (Jackie Mills), Metromedia 150 | 6 |
| 15 | 10 | 8 | 6 | AND WHEN I DIE — Blood, Sweat & Tears (James William Guercio), Columbia 4-45008 | 11 |
| 16 | 20 | 20 | 22 | THESE EYES — Jr. Walker & the All Stars (Johnny Bristol), Soul 35067 | 9 |
| 17 | 18 | 18 | 23 | FRIENDSHIP TRAIN — Gladys Knight & the Pips (Norman Whitfield), Soul 35068 | 10 |
| 18 | 13 | 10 | 11 | BACKFIELD IN MOTION — Mel & Tim (Karl Tarleton), Bamboo 107 | 11 |
| ★ 19 | 31 | 77 | — | VENUS — Shocking Blue (Robert van Leeuwen), Colossus 108 | 3 |
| 20 | 23 | 31 | 37 | JAM UP JELLY TIGHT — Tommy Roe (Steve Barri), ABC 11247 | 7 |
| 21 | 16 | 16 | 15 | CHERRY HILL PARK — Billy Joe Royal (Buddy Buie), Columbia 4-44902 | 13 |
| ★ 22 | 34 | 48 | 53 | JINGLE JANGLE — The Archies (Jeff Barry), Kirshner 63-5002 | 5 |
| 23 | 25 | 36 | 41 | DON'T CRY DADDY/RUBBERNECKIN' — Elvis Presley, RCA 47-9768 | 5 |
| 24 | 21 | 14 | 12 | SMILE A LITTLE SMILE FOR ME — The Flying Machine (Tony MacAuley), Congress 6000 | 13 |
| 25 | 22 | 15 | 14 | BABY, I'M FOR REAL — Originals (Marvin Gaye), Soul 35066 | 14 |
| 26 | 26 | 29 | 29 | UP ON CRIPPLE CREEK — The Band (John Simon), Capitol 2635 | 9 |
| ♪ 27 | 24 | 25 | 35 | A BRAND NEW ME — Dusty Springfield (Roland Chambers), Atlantic 2685 | 8 |
| 28 | 28 | 36 | 35 | EVIL WOMAN, DON'T PLAY YOUR GAMES WITH ME — Crow (Bob Monaco), Amaret 112 | 10 |
| 29 | 19 | 12 | 7 | WEDDING BELL BLUES — 5th Dimension (Bones Howe), Soul City 779 | 14 |
| 30 | 37 | 42 | 48 | EARLY IN THE MORNING — Vanity Fare (Roger Easterby & Des Champ), Page One 21-027 | 6 |
| ♪ 31 | 27 | 24 | 25 | HEAVEN KNOWS — Grassroots (Steve Barri), Dunhill 4217 | 8 |
| 32 | 29 | 17 | 19 | ELEANOR RIGBY — Aretha Franklin (Jerry Wexler-Tom Dowd-Arif Mardin), Atlantic 2683 | 8 |
| 33 | 35 | 39 | 44 | COLD TURKEY — Plastic Ono Band (John & Yoko [Bag]), Apple 1813 | 7 |
| ★ 34 | 40 | 65 | — | SHE — Tommy James & the Shondells (Tommy James & Bob King), Roulette 7066 | 3 |
| ♪ 35 | 38 | 41 | 47 | SUNDAY MORNIN' — Oliver (Bob Crewe), Crewe 337 | 6 |
| ♪ 36 | 36 | 40 | 43 | AIN'T IT FUNKY NOW — James Brown (James Brown Prod.), King 6280 | 6 |
| 37 | 30 | 23 | 20 | GOING IN CIRCLES — Friends of Distinction (John Florez), RCA 74-0204 | 20 |
| 38 | 33 | 30 | 33 | GROOVY GRUBWORM — Harlow Wilcox (Shelby Singleton), Plantation 28 | 12 |
| 39 | 47 | 60 | 81 | WONDERFUL WORLD, BEAUTIFUL PEOPLE — Jimmy Cliff (Larry Fallon-Leslie Kong), A&M 1146 | 4 |
| ★ 40 | 64 | 76 | — | POINT IT OUT — Smokey Robinson & the Miracles ("Smokey" & Cleveland), Tamla 54189 | 3 |
| 41 | 48 | 71 | 84 | WINTER WORLD OF LOVE — Engelbert Humperdinck (Peter Sullivan), Parrot 40044 | 4 |
| ♪ 42 | 42 | 47 | 57 | OKIE FROM MUSKOGEE — Merle Haggard & the Strangers (Ken Nelson), Capitol 2626 | 8 |
| 43 | 43 | 52 | 58 | CUPID — Johnny Nash (Johnny Nash-Arthur Jenkins), Jad 220 | 8 |
| ♪ 44 | 44 | 51 | 54 | DON'T LET LOVE HANG YOU UP — Jerry Butler (Gamble-Huff), Mercury 72991 | 7 |
| 45 | 46 | 53 | 71 | DON'T LET HIM TAKE YOUR LOVE FROM ME — Four Tops (Norman Whitfield), Motown 1159 | 4 |
| 46 | 39 | 37 | 26 | MIND, BODY & SOUL — Flaming Embers (R. Dunbar), Hot Wax 6902 | 14 |
| 47 | 66 | 89 | 97 | ARIZONA — Mark Lindsay (Jerry Fuller), Columbia 4-45037 | 4 |
| 48 | 41 | 43 | 46 | KOZMIC BLUES — Janis Joplin (Gabriel Mekler), Columbia 4-45023 | 8 |
| 49 | 50 | 54 | 73 | WHAT YOU GAVE ME — Marvin Gaye & Tammi Terrell (Ashford & Simpson), Tamla 54187 | 5 |
| ♪ 50 | — | — | — | WITHOUT LOVE (There Is Nothing) — Tom Jones (Peter Sullivan), Parrot 40045 | 1 |
| ★ 51 | — | — | — | I'LL NEVER FALL IN LOVE — Dionne Warwick (Burt Bacharach-Hal David), Scepter 12273 | 1 |
| 52 | 55 | 55 | 64 | CAN'T TAKE MY EYES OFF OF YOU — Nancy Wilson (David D. Cavanaugh), Capitol 2644 | 6 |
| 53 | 54 | 62 | 70 | FANCY — Bobbie Gentry (Rick Hall), Capitol 2675 | 7 |
| 54 | 69 | 74 | 79 | WALKIN' IN THE RAIN — Jay & the Americans (Sandy Yogunda & Thomas Kaye), United Artists 50605 | 6 |
| 55 | 68 | 80 | 98 | LET'S WORK TOGETHER — Wilbert Harrison (Juggy Murray), Sue 11 | 4 |
| 56 | 56 | 64 | 75 | SHE BELONGS TO ME — Rick Nelson (Rick Nelson), Decca 732550 | 9 |
| 57 | 45 | 45 | 51 | I'LL HOLD OUT MY HAND — Clique (Gary Zekley), White Whale 333 | 7 |
| ♪ 58 | 60 | 83 | 94 | SHE CAME IN THROUGH THE BATHROOM WINDOW — Joe Cocker (Denny Cordell-Leon Russell), A&M 1147 | 4 |
| 59 | 49 | 49 | 52 | YOU GOT TO PAY THE PRICE — Gloria Taylor (S. Whisenhunt), Silver Fox 14 | 8 |
| ♪ 60 | 52 | 50 | 50 | BLISTERED/SEE RUBY FALL — Johnny Cash (Bob Johnston), Columbia 4-45020 | 8 |
| 61 | 58 | 61 | 61 | MIDNIGHT — Dennis Yost & the Classics IV (Buddy Buie), Imperial 66424 | 7 |
| 62 | 63 | 70 | 76 | ONE TIN SOLDIER — The Original Caste (Dennis Lambert & Brian Potter), TA 186 | 10 |
| 63 | 71 | 90 | — | WHEN JULIE COMES AROUND — Cuff Links (Paul Vance-Lee Pockriss), Decca 732592 | 3 |
| 64 | 73 | — | — | BABY TAKE ME IN YOUR ARMS — Jefferson (John Schroeder), Janus 106 | 2 |
| 65 | 65 | 73 | 77 | VOLUNTEERS — Jefferson Airplane (Al Schmitt), RCA 74-0245 | 8 |
| ♪ 66 | 72 | — | — | LET A MAN COME IN AND DO THE POPCORN (Part II) — James Brown (J. Brown), King 6275 | 2 |
| 67 | 80 | — | — | I'M SO GLAD I FELL FOR YOU — David Ruffin (Berry Gordy, Jr.), Motown 1158 | 2 |
| 68 | 77 | 81 | — | SHE LETS HER HAIR DOWN (Early in the Morning) — Tokens (Tokens), Buddah 151 | 3 |
| ♪ 69 | 75 | 75 | 83 | TURN TURN TURN (To Everything There Is a Season) — Judy Collins (Mark Abramson), Elektra 45680 | 5 |
| 70 | 81 | — | — | NO TIME — The Guess Who (Jack Richardson), RCA 74-0300 | 2 |
| 71 | — | — | — | MONSTER — Steppenwolf (Gabriel Makler), Dunhill 4221 | 1 |
| ♪ 72 | 85 | 88 | 89 | TONIGHT I'LL SAY A PRAYER — Eydie Gorme (Don Costa), RCA 74-0250 | 5 |
| 73 | — | — | — | HEY THERE LONELY GIRL — Eddie Holman (Peter DeAngelis), ABC 11240 | 1 |
| 74 | 74 | 78 | 80 | I'M TIRED — Savoy Brown (Mike Vernon Prod.), Parrot 40042 | 4 |
| 75 | — | — | — | TRACES/MEMORIES MEDLEY — The Lettermen (Al De Lory), Capitol 2697 | 1 |
| 76 | 76 | 79 | 88 | I LOVE YOU — Otis Leavill (Willie Henderson), Dakar 614 | 5 |
| 77 | 95 | — | — | LOVE BONES — Johnny Taylor (Don Davis), Stax 0055 | 2 |
| 78 | 78 | 87 | 90 | LADY-O — Turtles (Bob Harris-John Beck), White Whale 334 | 4 |
| 79 | 94 | 94 | — | IS IT BECAUSE I'M BLACK — Syl Johnson (Pieces of Peace), Twinight 125 | 3 |
| 80 | 82 | 91 | 91 | LOOK-KA PY PY — Meters (Marshall Sehorn-Allan R. Toussaint), Josie 1015 | 4 |
| 81 | 83 | — | — | ARE YOU GETTING ANY SUNSHINE? — Lou Christie (Stan Vincent-Mike Duckman), Buddah 149 | 2 |
| 82 | 87 | — | — | TOGETHER — The Illusion (Jeff Barry), Steed 722 | 2 |
| 83 | 86 | 96 | — | SIX WHITE HORSES — Tommy Cash (Glenn Sutton), Epic 5-10540 | 3 |
| 84 | 84 | — | — | COME SATURDAY MORNING — The Sandpipers (Allen Stanton), A&M 1134 | 2 |
| 85 | 90 | 93 | — | TO BE YOUNG, GIFTED & BLACK — Nina Simone (Stroud Prods. & Enterprises, Inc.), RCA 74-0269 | 3 |
| 86 | 92 | — | — | BOLD SOUL SISTER — Ike & Tina Turner (Bob Krasnow), Blue Thumb 104 | 2 |
| 87 | 88 | — | — | GROOVIN' (Out on Life) — Newbeats (Don Gant), Hickory 1552 | 2 |
| ♪ 88 | — | — | — | OH ME OH MY (I'm a Fool for You Baby) — Lulu (Jerry Wexler, Tom Bowa, Arif Mardin), Atco 6722 | 1 |
| 89 | 89 | — | — | I'M GONNA LOVE YOU — The Intrigues (Martin & Bell), Yew 1002 | 2 |
| 90 | 91 | — | — | VOODOO WOMAN — Simon Stokes & the Nighthawks (Linda Perry), Elektra 45670 | 2 |
| 91 | — | — | 99 | I STARTED LOVING YOU AGAIN — Al Martino (Voyle Gilmore), Capitol 2674 | 2 |
| 92 | — | — | — | A WORLD WITHOUT MUSIC — Archie Bell & the Drells (Gamble & Huff), Atlantic 2693 | 1 |
| 93 | 100 | — | — | HE AIN'T HEAVY, HE'S MY BROTHER — Hollies (Ron Richards), Epic 5-10532 | 2 |
| 94 | 99 | — | — | TOO MANY COOKS (Spoil the Soup) — 100 Proof Aged In Soul (Stagecoach Prod.), Hot Wax 6904 | 2 |
| 95 | — | — | — | THEME FROM ELECTRIC SURFBOARD — Brother Jack McDuff (Lew Futterman/Larry Rogers), Blue Note 1953 | 1 |
| 96 | 96 | — | — | BEEN A LONG TIME — Betty Everett (Leo Austell), Uni 55174 | 2 |
| 97 | 98 | — | — | MR. LIMOUSINE DRIVER — Grand Funk Railroad (Terry Knight), Capitol 2691 | 2 |
| 98 | — | — | — | THE GANG'S BACK AGAIN — Kool & the Gang (Gene Redd), De-lite 523 | 1 |
| 99 | — | — | — | GUESS WHO — Ruby Winters (Marlin Greene), Diamond 269 | 1 |
| ♪ 100 | — | — | — | THE THRILL IS GONE — B. B. King (Bill Szymczyk), BluesWay 61032 | 1 |

## BUBBLING UNDER THE HOT 100

101. WALK A MILE IN MY SHOES .... Joe South, Capitol 2704
102. JENNIFER TOMKINS .... Street People, Musicor 1365
103. SHE'S READY .... Spiral Starecase, Columbia 4-45048
104. MORNIN' MORNIN' .... Bobby Goldsboro, United Artists 50614
105. BARBARA I LOVE YOU .... New Colony Six, Mercury 73004
106. THE LAST TIME .... Buchanan Brothers, Event 3307
107. SHE LETS HER HAIR DOWN (Early in the Morning) .... Gene Pitney, Musicor 1384
108. WANT YOU TO KNOW .... Rotary Connection, Cadet Concept 7018
109. HEY HEY WOMAN .... Joe Jeffrey, Wand 11213
110. HOLD ON .... Rascals, Atlantic 2695
111. AMEN (1970) .... Impressions, Curtom 1948
112. CLAUDIE MAE .... Ray Charles, ABC 1125
113. SHE LETS HER HAIR DOWN (Early in the Morning) .... Don Young, Bang 574
114. ANYWAY THAT YOU WANT ME .... Walter Jackson, Cotillion 44053
115. HOW CAN I TELL MY MOM AND DAD .... Lovelites, Lock 723
116. THEME FROM 2001: A SPACE ODYSSEY .... Berlin Philharmonic, Polydor 2-15009
117. TROUBLEMAKER .... Lee Hazlewood, LHI 20
118. DON'T THINK THAT I'M A VIOLENT GUY .... Garland Green, Uni 55188
119. WON'T FIND BETTER (Than Me) .... New Hope, Jamie 1381
120. GOTTA FIND A BRAND NEW LOVER .... Sweet Inspirations, Atlantic 2686
121. HELLO SUNSHINE .... Rev. Maceo Woods, Volt 4025

Compiled from national retail sales and radio station airplay by the Music Popularity Dept. of Record Market Research, Billboard.

# THE SONG TITLES

Lists, alphabetically by song title, all titles shown on the *Hot 100* charts from 1960-1969. Next to each title is the date it *debuted* on the *Hot 100*, based on the magazine's issue date.

A song with more than one charted version is listed once, with the artists' names listed below. The artist with the earliest charted version is shown first. Songs that have the same title, but are different tunes, are listed separately, with the song that charted earliest shown first.

All titles listed on the first chart of the Sixties (January 4, 1960) are included in this section, even though most debuted prior to this date. For those that debuted earlier, an asterisk follows the date (ex.: 1/4/60*).

It should be pointed out that the titles in this section are listed exactly as they appear on the actual records. Unfortunately, the charts were not always as precise, and therefore, you will occasionally notice a difference in the way a title is listed in this section versus the charts.

Cross-references are used throughout this section to aid in finding a title. If you have trouble, please keep the following rules in mind: titles in which an apostrophe is used within a word come before titles using the complete spelling (Lovin' comes before Loving); titles beginning with a contraction follow titles that begin with a similar non-contracted word (Can't follows Can); titles such as "G.T.O." and "U.S. Male" are found at the beginning of their respective letters, however, initialed titles which actually spell out a word like "D-I-V-O-R-C-E" or "L-O-N-E-L-Y" are sorted with the normal spelling of the word.

During the Sixties many records hit the charts, fell off, and then re-charted within a short period of time. In a few instances, months went by before a record re-charted. To aid in following each record's chart history, a list was compiled of records which re-charted after more than an eight-week absence, but less than one year, from their last chart appearance. That list was placed at the end of this section, and includes the date each record re-charted. Please note that records which re-charted after more than a one-year absence, are listed, with a new debut date, in the main song title section.

# A

| Date | Title | Artist |
|---|---|---|
| 4/23/66 | "A" Team | SSgt Barry Sadler |
| 7/12/69 | Abergavenny | Shannon |
| 2/1/64 | Abigail Beecher | Freddy Cannon |
| 6/22/63 | Abilene | George Hamilton IV |
| 2/29/60 | About This Thing Called Love | Fabian |
| 7/14/62 | Above The Stars | Mr. Acker Bilk |
|  | **Abraham, Martin And John** |  |
| 10/26/68 | Dion |  |
| 6/28/69 | Moms Mabley |  |
| 7/5/69 | Miracles |  |
| 5/30/64 | Across The Street | Lenny O'Henry |
| 9/25/65 | Act Naturally | Beatles |
| 8/14/65 | Action | Freddy Cannon |
| 4/4/60 | Adam And Eve | Paul Anka |
| 12/12/60 | Adeste Fideles | Bing Crosby |
| 5/5/62 | Adios Amigo | Jim Reeves |
|  | Adventures In Paradise..see: Theme From |  |
|  | Afraid Of Losing You..see: (I'm So) |  |
| 4/10/61 | African Waltz | Cannonball Adderley |
| 1/20/62 | Afrikaan Beat | Bert Kaempfert |
| 7/31/65 | After Loving You | Della Reese |
| 12/5/60 | Age For Love | Jimmy Charles |
| 8/7/65 | Agent Double-O-Soul | Edwin Starr |
| 6/30/62 | Ahab, The Arab | Ray Stevens |
| 10/24/64 | Ain't Doing Too Bad | Bobby Bland |
| 5/30/60 | Ain't Gonna Be That Way | Marv Johnson |
| 7/2/66 | Ain't Gonna Cry No More | Brenda Lee |
|  | Ain't Gonna Eat Out My Heart Anymore..see: I Ain't Gonna |  |
| 2/2/63 | Ain't Gonna Kiss Ya | Ribbons |
| 9/17/66 | Ain't Gonna Lie | Keith |
| 4/15/67 | Ain't Gonna Rest (Till I Get You) | Five Stairsteps |
| 3/14/64 | Ain't Gonna Tell Anybody | Jimmy Gilmer & The Fireballs |
| 1/4/69 | Ain't Got No; I Got Life | Nina Simone |
| 6/5/65 | Ain't It A Shame | Major Lance |
| 3/27/61 | Ain't It, Baby | Miracles |
| 11/22/69 | Ain't It Funky Now | James Brown |
| 10/31/64 | Ain't It The Truth | Mary Wells |
| 9/4/65 | Ain't It True | Andy Williams |
| 5/13/67 | Ain't No Mountain High Enough | Marvin Gaye & Tammi Terrell |
| 4/24/65 | Ain't No Telling | Bobby Bland |
| 4/6/68 | Ain't No Way | Aretha Franklin |
| 8/20/66 | Ain't Nobody Home | Howard Tate |
| 6/1/68 | Ain't Nothin' But A House Party | Show Stoppers |
| 4/13/68 | Ain't Nothing Like The Real Thing | Marvin Gaye & Tammi Terrell |
| 3/7/64 | Ain't Nothing You Can Do | Bobby Bland |
| 7/18/64 | Ain't She Sweet | Beatles |
| 3/5/66 | Ain't That A Groove | James Brown |
| 4/20/63 | Ain't That A Shame! | 4 Seasons |
| 1/23/61 | Ain't That Just Like A Woman | Fats Domino |
| 4/18/64 | Ain't That Just Like Me | Searchers |
| 7/31/65 | Ain't That Love | Four Tops |
| 3/31/62 | Ain't That Loving You | Bobby Bland |
| 10/10/64 | Ain't That Loving You Baby | Elvis Presley |
| 10/9/65 | Ain't That Peculiar | Marvin Gaye |
| 5/28/66 | Ain't Too Proud To Beg | Temptations |
| 6/23/62 | Air Travel | Ray & Bob |
| 6/17/67 | Airplane Song (My Airplane) | Royal Guardsmen |
|  | **Al Di La'** |  |
| 5/19/62 | Emilio Pericoli |  |
| 1/5/63 | Connie Francis |  |
| 7/11/64 | Ray Charles Singers |  |
| 4/17/65 | Al's Place | Al Hirt |
|  | **Alabam** |  |
| 9/26/60 | Cowboy Copas |  |
| 10/24/60 | Pat Boone |  |
| 10/27/62 | Aladdin | Bobby Curtola |
|  | Alamo..see: Ballad Of The |  |
|  | **Alfie** |  |
| 7/30/66 | Cher |  |
| 8/27/66 | Cilla Black |  |
| 4/8/67 | Dionne Warwick |  |
| 10/5/68 | Eivets Rednow |  |
| 2/2/63 | Alice In Wonderland | Neil Sedaka |
| 7/6/68 | Alice Long (You're Still My Favorite Girlfriend) | Tommy Boyce & Bobby Hart |
| 12/13/69 | Alice's Rock & Roll Restaurant | Arlo Guthrie |
| 1/14/67 | All | James Darren |
| 1/5/63 | All About My Girl | Jimmy McGriff |
| 9/29/62 | All Alone Am I | Brenda Lee |
| 9/21/68 | All Along The Watchtower | Jimi Hendrix |
| 9/26/64 | All Cried Out | Dusty Springfield |
| 12/26/64 | All Day And All Of The Night | Kinks |
| 10/11/69 | All God's Children Got Soul | Dorothy Morrison |
| 8/1/64 | All Grown Up | Crystals |
| 5/2/60 | All I Could Do Was Cry | Etta James |
|  | **All I Have To Do Is Dream** |  |
| 7/24/61 | Everly Brothers |  |
| 2/9/63 | Richard Chamberlain |  |
| 8/23/69 | All I Have To Offer You (Is Me) | Charley Pride |
| 4/29/67 | All I Need | Temptations |
|  | **All I Really Want To Do** |  |
| 7/3/65 | Byrds |  |
| 7/3/65 | Cher |  |
| 9/17/66 | All I See Is You | Dusty Springfield |
| 12/31/60 | All In My Mind | Maxine Brown |
|  | All My Love..see: (You Were Made For) |  |
|  | **All My Loving** |  |
| 3/28/64 | Beatles |  |
| 7/4/64 | Hollyridge Strings |  |
| 2/22/64 | All My Trials | Dick & DeeDee |
| 7/14/62 | All Night Long | Sandy Nelson |
| 10/30/65 | (All Of A Sudden) My Heart Sings | Mel Carter |
| 2/27/61 | All Of Everything | Frankie Avalon |
| 3/27/65 | All Of My Life | Lesley Gore |
| 12/4/65 | All Or Nothing | Patti LaBelle & The Bluebells |
| 3/2/63 | All Over The World | Nat "King" Cole |
| 9/10/66 | All Strung Out | Nino Tempo & April Stevens |
| 10/8/66 | All That I Am | Elvis Presley |
| 6/13/60 | All The Love I've Got | Marv Johnson |
| 7/2/66 | All These Things | Uniques |
| 7/22/67 | All You Need Is Love | Beatles |
| 10/14/67 | All Your Goodies Are Gone (The Loser's Seat) | Parliaments |
|  | **Alley Cat** |  |
| 7/28/62 | Bent Fabric |  |
| 10/20/62 | David Thorne |  |
|  | **Alley-Oop** |  |
| 5/30/60 | Dante & the Evergreens |  |
| 5/30/60 | Hollywood Argyles |  |
| 6/6/60 | Dyna-Sores |  |
| 11/4/67 | Alligator Bogaloo | Lou Donaldson |
| 11/23/63 | Ally Ally Oxen Free | Kingston Trio |
| 9/28/68 | Almost In Love | Elvis Presley |
|  | **Almost Persuaded** |  |
| 7/16/66 | David Houston |  |
| 10/1/66 | Ben Colder |  |
| 1/18/69 | Etta James |  |
| 11/14/64 | Almost There | Andy Williams |
| 6/6/64 | Alone | Four Seasons |
| 10/10/60 | Alone At Last | Jackie Wilson |
| 6/13/64 | Alone With You | Brenda Lee |
| 6/28/69 | Along Came Jones | Ray Stevens |
|  | **Along Comes Mary** |  |
| 6/4/66 | Association |  |
| 8/5/67 | Baja Marimba Band |  |
| 9/5/60 | Alvin For President | Chipmunks |
| 3/3/62 | Alvin Twist | Chipmunks |
| 11/26/66 | Alvin's Boo-Ga-Loo | Alvin Cash & The Registers |
|  | **Alvin's Harmonica** |  |
| 12/25/61 | Chipmunks |  |
| 12/22/62 | Chipmunks |  |
| 2/22/60 | Alvin's Orchestra | Chipmunks |
| 1/04/60* | Always | Sammy Turner |
| 3/14/64 | Always In My Heart | Los Indios Tabajaras |
| 5/16/60 | Always It's You | Everly Brothers |
|  | Always Something There To Remind Me..see: (There's) |  |
| 8/15/64 | Always Together | Al Martino |
| 10/12/68 | Always Together | Dells |
| 5/13/67 | Am I Grooving You | Freddie Scott |
| 10/24/60 | Am I Losing You | Jim Reeves |
|  | **Am I That Easy To Forget** |  |
| 1/18/60 | Debbie Reynolds |  |
| 12/16/67 | Engelbert Humperdinck |  |
| 10/24/60 | Am I The Man | Jackie Wilson |
| 2/22/69 | Am I The Same Girl | Barbara Acklin |
|  | (also see: Soulful Strut) |  |
| 1/18/60 | Amapola | Jacky Noguez |
| 2/24/68 | Ame Caline (Soul Coaxing) | Raymond Lefevre |
|  | **Amen** |  |
| 11/21/64 | Impressions |  |
| 7/6/68 | Otis Redding |  |
| 5/25/68 | America Is My Home | James Brown |
| 11/23/68 | American Boys | Petula Clark |
| 1/4/60* | Among My Souvenirs | Connie Francis |
|  | **Amor** |  |
| 7/31/61 | Ben E. King |  |
| 3/10/62 | Roger Williams |  |
| 3/30/63 | Amy | Paul Petersen |
| 10/3/64 | Anaheim, Azusa & Cucamonga Sewing Circle, Book Review And Timing Association | Jan & Dean |
| 11/25/67 | And Get Away | Esquires |
|  | **And I Love Her (Him)** |  |
| 7/25/64 | Beatles |  |
| 5/8/65 | Esther Phillips |  |
| 9/5/60 | And Now | Della Reese |
| 4/3/65 | And Roses And Roses | Andy Williams |
| 6/21/69 | And She's Mine | Spanky & Our Gang |
| 7/20/68 | And Suddenly | Cherry People |
| 9/13/69 | And That Reminds Me (My Heart Reminds Me) | 4 Seasons |
| 1/9/61 | And The Heavens Cried | Ronnie Savoy |
| 9/22/62 | And Then There Were Drums | Sandy Nelson |
| 10/18/69 | And When I Die | Blood, Sweat & Tears |
| 1/22/66 | Andrea | Sunrays |
| 2/13/65 | Angel | Johnny Tillotson |
| 12/12/60 | Angel Baby | Rosie & The Originals |
| 5/4/68 | Angel Of The Morning | Merrilee Rush |
| 12/26/60 | Angel On My Shoulder | Shelby Flint |
| 2/22/69 | Angela Jones | Johnny Ferguson |
| 7/11/64 | Angelito | Rene & Rene |
| 4/20/63 | Ann-Marie | Belmonts |
| 5/22/61 | Anna | Jorgen Ingmann |
| 10/27/62 | Anna (Go To Him) | Arthur Alexander |
| 8/7/65 | Annie Fanny | Kingsmen |
| 3/10/62 | Annie Get Your Yo-Yo | Little Junior Parker |
| 9/11/61 | Anniversary Of Love | Caslons |
| 5/16/64 | Another Cup Of Coffee | Brook Benton |
| 4/29/67 | Another Day, Another Heartache | 5th Dimension |
| 12/24/66 | Another Night | Dionne Warwick |
| 3/30/68 | Another Place Another Time | Jerry Lee Lewis |
| 4/20/63 | Another Saturday Night | Sam Cooke |
| 4/25/60 | Another Sleepless Night | Jimmy Clanton |
| 2/5/66 | Answer To My Prayer | Neil Sedaka |
| 6/29/63 | Antony And Cleopatra Theme | Ferrante & Teicher |
|  | **Any Day Now** |  |
| 4/28/62 | Chuck Jackson |  |
| 4/12/69 | Percy Sledge |  |
| 11/2/63 | Any Other Way | Chuck Jackson |
|  | **Any Way That You Want Me** |  |
| 12/24/66 | Liverpool Five |  |
| 8/3/68 | American Breed |  |
| 8/16/69 | Evie Sands |  |
| 11/14/64 | Any Way You Want It | Dave Clark Five |
| 10/2/61 | Anybody But Me | Brenda Lee |
| 8/8/60 | Anymore | Teresa Brewer |
| 5/11/68 | Anyone For Tennis (The Savage Seven Theme) | Cream |
| 12/7/63 | Anyone Who Had A Heart | Dionne Warwick |
| 7/4/64 | Anyone Who Knows What Love Is (Will Understand) | Irma Thomas |
| 4/13/68 | Anything | Animals |
| 8/19/67 | Anything Goes | Harpers Bizarre |
| 3/17/62 | Anything That's Part Of You | Elvis Presley |
| 2/15/69 | Anything You Choose | Spanky & Our Gang |
| 3/13/65 | Anytime At All | Frank Sinatra |
| 2/22/60 | Anyway The Wind Blows | Doris Day |

|     |     |
| --- | --- |
|  | **Apache** |
| 1/23/61 | Jorgen Ingmann |
| 3/6/61 | Sonny James |
| 2/13/65 | Arrows/Davie Allan ('65) |
|  | **Apartment**..see: Theme From The |
| 5/11/68 | **Apologize** Ed Ames |
| 3/7/60 | **Apple Green** June Valli |
| 11/20/65 | **Apple Of My Eye** Roy Head |
| 4/10/65 | **Apples And Bananas** Lawrence Welk |
| 7/15/67 | **Apples, Peaches, Pumpkin Pie** Jay & The Techniques |
| 2/22/69 | **Apricot Brandy** Rhinoceros |
| 5/17/69 | **April Fools** Dionne Warwick |
| 3/8/69 | **Aquarius/Let The Sunshine In** 5th Dimension |
| 9/25/65 | **Are You A Boy Or Are You A Girl** Barbarians |
| 12/20/69 | **Are You Getting Any Sunshine?** Lou Christie |
| 12/7/68 | **Are You Happy** Jerry Butler |
| 12/24/66 | **Are You Lonely For Me** Freddie Scott |
| 11/14/60 | **Are You Lonesome To-night?** Elvis Presley (also see: Yes, I'm Lonesome Tonight) |
| 10/21/67 | **Are You Never Coming Home** Sandy Posey |
| 6/12/65 | **Are You Sincere** Trini Lopez |
| 12/26/64 | **Are You Still My Baby** Shirelles |
| 12/11/65 | **Are You There (With Another Girl)** Dionne Warwick |
| 12/6/69 | **Arizona** Mark Lindsay |
|  | (**Armen's Theme**)..see: Yesterday And You |
| 9/6/69 | **Armstrong** John Stewart |
| 7/24/65 | **Around The Corner** Duprees |
| 9/26/60 | **Artificial Flowers** Bobby Darin |
| 7/24/61 | **As If I Didn't Know** Adam Wade |
| 11/9/63 | **As Long As I Know He's Mine** Marvelettes |
| 1/26/63 | **As Long As She Needs Me** Sammy Davis Jr. |
|  | **As Tears Go By** |
| 11/28/64 | Marianne Faithfull |
| 12/25/65 | Rolling Stones |
| 12/14/63 | **As Usual** Brenda Lee |
| 8/13/66 | **Ashes To Ashes** Mindbenders |
| 2/20/61 | **Asia Minor** Kokomo |
| 4/6/63 | **Ask Me** Maxine Brown |
| 1/25/64 | **Ask Me** Inez Foxx |
| 10/10/64 | **Ask Me** Elvis Presley |
| 2/6/65 | **Ask The Lonely** Four Tops |
| 7/10/61 | **Astronaut** Jose Jimenez |
| 1/16/61 | **At Last** Etta James |
| 3/14/60 | **At My Front Door** Dee Clark |
| 3/31/62 | **At The Club** Ray Charles |
| 1/30/65 | **At The Club** Drifters |
| 2/5/66 | **At The Scene** Dave Clark Five |
| 8/3/63 | **At The Shore** Johnny Caswell |
| 3/16/68 | **At The Top Of The Stairs** Formations |
| 3/18/67 | **At The Zoo** Simon & Garfunkel |
| 4/5/69 | **Atlantis** Donovan |
| 12/18/65 | **Attack** Toys |
| 10/26/68 | **Aunt Dora's Love Soul Shack** Arthur Conley |
| 10/16/65 | **Autumn Leaves - 1965** Roger Williams |
| 6/29/68 | **Autumn Of My Life** Bobby Goldsboro |
| 1/27/62 | **Aw Shucks, Hush Your Mouth** Jimmy Reed |

## B

|     |     |
| --- | --- |
| 9/28/68 | **B.B. Jones** B.B. King |
| 8/20/66 | **B-A-B-Y** Carla Thomas |
| 10/3/64 | **Baby Baby All The Time** Superbs |
| 2/2/63 | **Baby, Baby, Baby** Sam Cooke |
| 4/4/64 | **Baby Baby Baby** Anna King-Bobby Byrd |
| 1/4/69 | **Baby, Baby Don't Cry** Miracles |
| 9/26/64 | **Baby Be Mine** Jelly Beans |
| 3/6/61 | **Baby Blue** Echoes |
| 9/7/68 | **Baby, Come Back** Equals |
| 7/18/64 | **Baby Come Home** Ruby & The Romantics |
| 1/8/66 | **Baby Come On Home** Solomon Burke |
| 10/1/66 | **Baby, Do The Philly Dog** Olympics |
| 6/21/69 | **Baby, Don't Be Looking In My Mind** Joe Simon |
| 8/21/65 | **Baby Don't Go** Sonny & Cher |
| 2/22/64 | **Baby, Don't You Cry** Ray Charles |

|     |     |
| --- | --- |
| 9/19/64 | **Baby Don't You Do It** Marvin Gaye |
| 11/16/63 | **Baby Don't You Weep** Garnet Mimms & The Enchanters |
|  | **Baby Elephant Walk** |
| 6/9/62 | Miniature Men |
| 6/9/62 | Lawrence Welk |
| 9/29/62 | **Baby Face** Bobby Darin |
| 9/21/63 | **Baby Get It (And Don't Quit It)** Jackie Wilson |
| 11/17/62 | **Baby Has Gone Bye Bye** George Maharis |
| 2/18/67 | **Baby, Help Me** Percy Sledge |
| 2/1/60 | **(Baby) Hully Gully** Olympics |
| 11/23/63 | **Baby I Do Love You** Galens |
|  | **Baby, I Love You** |
| 12/21/63 | Ronettes |
| 5/24/69 | Andy Kim |
| 9/3/66 | **Baby I Love You** Jimmy Holiday |
| 7/22/67 | **Baby I Love You** Aretha Franklin |
| 3/19/66 | **Baby I Need You** Manhattans |
|  | **Baby I Need Your Loving** |
| 8/15/64 | Four Tops |
| 2/4/67 | Johnny Rivers |
| 9/27/69 | **Baby, I'm For Real** Originals |
| 9/16/67 | **Baby I'm Lonely** Intruders |
| 6/19/65 | **Baby, I'm Yours** Barbara Lewis |
| 3/3/62 | **Baby It's Cold Outside** Ray Charles & Betty Carter |
|  | **Baby It's You** |
| 12/18/61 | Shirelles |
| 9/6/69 | Smith |
| 11/16/68 | **Baby Let's Wait** Royal Guardsmen |
| 10/3/64 | **Baby Love** Supremes |
| 4/13/68 | **Baby Make Your Own Sweet Music** Jay & The Techniques |
| 12/23/67 | **Baby, Now That I've Found You** Foundations |
| 12/19/60 | **Baby Oh Baby** Shells |
| 5/20/67 | **Baby Please Come Back Home** J.J. Barnes |
| 1/29/66 | **Baby Scratch My Back** Slim Harpo |
| 1/9/61 | **Baby Sittin' Boogie** Buzz Clifford |
| 12/20/69 | **Baby Take Me In Your Arms** Jefferson |
| 3/13/65 | **Baby The Rain Must Fall** Glenn Yarbrough |
| 9/3/66 | **Baby Toys** Toys |
| 11/30/63 | **Baby, We've Got Love** Johnnie Taylor |
| 10/29/66 | **Baby What Do You Want Me To Do** Barbara Lewis |
| 12/3/66 | **Baby What I Mean** Drifters |
|  | **Baby What You Want Me To Do** |
| 2/15/60 | Jimmy Reed |
| 2/1/64 | Etta James |
| 11/30/63 | **Baby, What's Wrong** Lonnie Mack |
| 3/9/63 | **Baby Workout** Jackie Wilson |
| 6/8/68 | **Baby You Come Rollin' Across My Mind** Peppermint Trolley Company |
| 11/25/67 | **Baby You Got It** Brenton Wood |
| 7/29/67 | **Baby You're A Rich Man** Beatles |
| 2/16/63 | **Baby, You're Driving Me Crazy** Joey Dee |
| 8/21/61 | **Baby, You're Right** James Brown |
| 8/21/61 | **Baby You're So Fine** Mickey & Sylvia |
| 3/16/68 | **Baby You're So Right For Me** Brenda & The Tabulations |
| 1/25/60 | **Baby (You've Got What It Takes)** Dinah Washington & Brook Benton |
| 12/11/61 | **Baby's First Christmas** Connie Francis |
| 11/16/63 | **Baby's Gone** Gene Thomas |
| 8/1/64 | **Bachelor Boy** Cliff Richard |
| 1/4/60* | **Baciare Baciare (Kissing Kissing)** Dorothy Collins |
| 3/9/63 | **Back At The Chicken Shack** Jimmy Smith |
| 8/14/61 | **Back Beat No. 1** Rondels |
| 2/22/69 | **Back Door Man** Derek |
| 6/8/68 | **Back In Love Again** Buckinghams |
| 5/1/65 | **Back In My Arms Again** Supremes |
| 4/5/69 | **Back In The U.S.S.R.** Chubby Checker |
| 3/9/68 | **Back On My Feet Again** Foundations |
| 10/21/67 | **Back On The Street Again** Sunshine Company |
| 12/11/65 | **Back Street** Edwin Starr |
| 9/18/61 | **Back To The Hop** Danny & The Juniors |
| 12/9/67 | **Back Up Train** Al Greene |
| 10/18/69 | **Backfield In Motion** Mel & Tim |
| 4/23/66 | **Backstage** Gene Pitney |

|     |     |
| --- | --- |
| 10/16/61 | **Backtrack** Faron Young |
| 2/8/60 | **Bad Boy** Marty Wilde |
| 5/7/66 | **Bad Eye** Willie Mitchell |
| 11/16/63 | **Bad Girl** Neil Sedaka |
| 9/10/66 | **Bad Little Woman** Shadows Of Knight |
| 6/20/60 | **Bad Man Blunder** Kingston Trio |
| 12/3/66 | **Bad Misunderstanding** Critters |
| 5/3/69 | **Bad Moon Rising** Creedence Clearwater Revival |
| 5/30/64 | **Bad To Me** Billy J. Kramer |
| 4/5/69 | **Badge** Cream |
| 7/27/63 | **Baja** Astronauts |
| 4/28/62 | **Balboa Blue** Marketts |
| 10/4/69 | **Ball Of Fire** Tommy James & The Shondells |
|  | **Ballad Of Bonnie And Clyde** |
| 2/17/68 | Georgie Fame |
| 3/2/68 | Flatt & Scruggs |
| 11/1/69 | **Ballad Of Easy Rider** Byrds |
|  | **Ballad Of Francis Powers**..see: There's A Star Spangled Banner Waving |
| 4/16/66 | **Ballad Of Irving** Frank Gallop |
| 12/8/62 | **Ballad Of Jed Clampett** Lester Flatt & Earl Scruggs |
| 6/14/69 | **Ballad Of John And Yoko** Beatles |
| 7/7/62 | **Ballad Of Paladin** Duane Eddy |
|  | **Ballad Of The Alamo** |
| 10/17/60 | Bud & Travis |
| 10/17/60 | Marty Robbins |
| 2/5/66 | **Ballad Of The Green Berets** SSgt Barry Sadler |
| 2/24/62 | **Ballad Of Thunder Road** Robert Mitchum |
| 11/16/68 | **Ballad Of Two Brothers** Autry Inman |
| 9/2/67 | **Ballad Of You & Me & Pooneil** Jefferson Airplane |
| 7/18/64 | **Bama Lama Bama Loo** Little Richard |
| 4/9/66 | **Band Of Gold** Mel Carter |
| 9/9/67 | **Banda, A** Herb Alpert |
| 1/27/62 | **Bandit Of My Dreams** Eddie Hodges |
| 10/22/66 | **Bang Bang** Joe Cuba Sextet |
| 3/12/66 | **Bang Bang (My Baby Shot Me Down)** Cher |
| 9/28/68 | **Bang-Shang-A-Lang** Archies |
|  | **Banjo Boy** |
| 6/6/60 | Jan & Kjeld |
| 6/13/60 | Dorothy Collins |
| 6/13/60 | Art Mooney |
| 6/22/63 | **Banzai Pipeline** Henry Mancini |
| 4/18/60 | **Barbara** Temptations |
|  | **Barbara-Ann** |
| 5/15/61 | Regents |
| 1/1/66 | Beach Boys |
| 8/31/68 | **Barefoot In Baltimore** Strawberry Alarm Clock |
| 4/23/66 | **Barefootin'** Robert Parker |
| 10/12/68 | **Baroque-A-Nova** Mason Williams |
| 3/27/65 | **Barracuda, The** Alvin Cash & The Crawlers |
|  | **Baseball Game**..see: (Love Is Like A) |
| 1/13/62 | **Basie Twist** Count Basie |
| 2/12/66 | **Batman** Jan & Dean |
| 5/28/66 | **Batman & His Grandmother** Dickie Goodman |
|  | **Batman Theme** |
| 2/5/66 | Marketts |
| 2/12/66 | Neal Hefti |
| 10/19/68 | **Battle Hymn Of The Republic** Andy Williams |
| 2/27/61 | **Battle Of Gettysburg** Fred Darian |
| 9/21/68 | **Battle Of New Orleans** Harpers Bizarre |
|  | **Be Anything (But Be Mine)** |
| 4/4/64 | Gloria Lynne |
| 5/9/64 | Connie Francis |
| 7/11/60 | **Be Bop A-Lula** Everly Brothers |
| 7/6/63 | **Be Careful Of Stones That You Throw** Dion |
| 7/12/69 | **Be-In (medley)** Happenings |
| 11/23/63 | **Be Mad Little Girl** Bobby Darin |
| 8/31/63 | **Be My Baby** Ronettes |
| 3/13/65 | **Be My Baby** Dick & Dee Dee |
| 4/24/65 | **Be My Boy** Paris Sisters |
| 5/30/64 | **Be My Girl** Four-Evers |
| 1/4/60* | **Be My Guest** Fats Domino |
| 11/2/63 | **Be True To Your School** Beach Boys |
| 6/22/63 | **Be True To Yourself** Bobby Vee |
| 6/22/68 | **Be Young, Be Foolish, Be Happy** Tams |

| Date | Title | Artist |
|---|---|---|
| 9/26/64 | Beach Girl | Pat Boone |
| 7/21/62 | Beach Party | King Curtis |
| 8/25/62 | Beach Party | Dave York |
| 9/5/60 | Beachcomber | Bobby Darin |
| 5/23/64 | Beans In My Ears | Serendipity Singers |
| 1/14/67 | Beat Goes On | Sonny & Cher |
| 5/13/67 | Beat The Clock | McCoys |
|  | Beatles E.P.'s..see: Four By The Beatles | |
| 2/15/60 | Beatnik Fly | Johnny & The Hurricanes |
| 11/7/64 | Beautician Blues | B.B. King |
| 4/13/68 | Beautiful Morning | Rascals |
| 4/25/60 | Beautiful Obsession | Sir Chauncey |
|  | Beautiful People | |
| 11/18/67 |  | Kenny O'Dell |
| 11/18/67 |  | Bobby Vee |
| 4/29/67 | Beautiful Story | Sonny & Cher |
| 8/20/66 | Beauty Is Only Skin Deep | Temptations |
| 8/1/64 | Because | Dave Clark Five |
| 1/22/66 | Because I Love You | Billy Stewart |
| 3/4/67 | Because Of You | Chris Montez |
| 5/23/60 | Because They're Young | Duane Eddy |
| 8/11/62 | Beechwood 4-5789 | Marvelettes |
| 4/3/65 | (Bees Are For The Birds) The Birds Are For The Bees | Newbeats |
| 5/15/65 | Before And After | Chad & Jeremy |
| 5/9/60 | Before I Grow Too Old | Fats Domino |
| 5/15/65 | Before You Go | Buck Owens |
| 10/7/67 | Beg, Borrow And Steal | Ohio Express |
| 5/23/64 | Beg Me | Chuck Jackson |
| 3/4/67 | Beggin' | 4 Seasons |
| 11/30/63 | Begging To You | Marty Robbins |
| 3/18/67 | Beginning Of Loneliness | Dionne Warwick |
| 12/14/68 | Beginning Of My End | Unifics |
| 11/26/66 | Behind The Door | Cher |
| 10/21/67 | Believe In Me Baby | Jesse James |
| 1/4/60* | Believe Me | Royal Teens |
| 11/30/68 | Bella Linda | Grass Roots |
| 11/14/60 | Bells, The | James Brown |
| 7/31/61 | Bells Are Ringing | Van Dykes |
|  | Ben Casey..see: Theme From | |
|  | Ben Crazy - Dr. Ben Basey | |
| 6/16/62 |  | Mickey Shorr & The Cutups |
| 7/14/62 |  | Dickie Goodman |
|  | (also see: Callin' Doctor Casey) | |
| 12/2/67 | Bend Me, Shape Me | American Breed |
| 9/18/61 | Berlin Melody | Billy Vaughn |
| 2/10/62 | Bermuda | Linda Scott |
| 3/11/67 | Bernadette | Four Tops |
| 5/2/60 | Besame Mucho | Coasters |
| 12/16/67 | Best Of Both Worlds | Lulu |
| 4/4/64 | (Best Part Of) Breakin' Up | Ronettes |
| 4/24/61 | Better Tell Him No | Starlets |
| 10/12/63 | Better To Give Than Receive | Joe Hinton |
| 5/14/66 | Better Use Your Head | Little Anthony & The Imperials |
| 8/31/63 | Betty In Bermudas | Dovells |
|  | Beverly Hillbillies..see: Ballad Of Jed Clampett | |
| 2/27/61 | Bewildered | James Brown |
| 1/18/60 | Beyond The Sea | Bobby Darin |
| 10/2/61 | Big Bad John | Jimmy Dean |
| 5/1/61 | Big Big World | Johnny Burnette |
| 12/15/62 | Big Boat | Peter, Paul & Mary |
| 5/23/64 | Big Boss Line | Jackie Wilson |
|  | Big Boss Man | |
| 5/29/61 |  | Jimmy Reed |
| 5/2/64 |  | Gene Chandler (Soul Hootenanny) |
| 10/14/67 |  | Elvis Presley |
| 5/23/60 | Big Boy Pete | Olympics |
|  | (also see: Jolly Green Giant) | |
| 7/26/69 | Big Bruce | Steve Greenberg |
| 8/21/61 | Big Cold Wind | Pat Boone |
| 3/31/62 | Big Draft (medley) | Four Preps |
| 10/20/62 | Big Girls Don't Cry | 4 Seasons |
|  | Big Hurt | |
| 1/4/60* |  | Miss Toni Fisher |
| 5/7/66 |  | Del Shannon |
| 12/13/69 | Big In Vegas | Buck Owens |
| 3/14/60 | Big Iron | Marty Robbins |
| 10/2/61 | Big John | Shirelles |
| 9/8/62 | Big Love | Joe Henderson |
| 11/7/64 | Big Man In Town | 4 Seasons |
| 5/2/64 | Big Party | Barbara & The Browns |
| 7/17/61 | Big River, Big Man | Claude King |
| 3/19/66 | Big Time | Lou Christie |
| 11/14/60 | Big Time Spender | Cornbread & Biscuits |
| 1/26/63 | Big Wide World | Teddy Randazzo |
| 4/24/61 | Bilbao Song | Andy Williams |
|  | Bill Bailey..see: Won't You Come Home | |
| 1/11/64 | Billie Baby | Lloyd Price |
| 6/18/66 | Billy And Sue | B.J. Thomas |
|  | Billy Jack..see: One Tin Soldier | |
| 11/2/68 | Billy You're My Friend | Gene Pitney |
| 6/6/60 | Biology | Danny Valentino |
| 9/14/68 | Biplane, Ever More | Irish Rovers |
|  | Bird..also see: (Bossa Nova) | |
| 2/8/64 | Bird Dance Beat | Trashmen |
| 7/14/62 | Bird Man | Highwaymen |
| 3/30/63 | Bird's The Word | Rivingtons |
|  | (also see: Surfin' Bird) | |
| 5/18/63 | Birdland | Chubby Checker |
| 1/23/65 | Birds And The Bees | Jewel Akens |
|  | Birds Are For The Bees..see: (Bees Are For The Birds) | |
| 7/12/69 | Birds Of A Feather | Joe South |
| 10/28/67 | Birds Of Britain | Bob Crewe Generation |
| 2/24/69 | Birth Of The Beat | Sandy Nelson |
| 7/19/69 | Birthday | Underground Sunshine |
| 8/17/63 | Birthday Party | Pixies Three |
| 4/4/64 | Bits And Pieces | Dave Clark Five |
| 8/30/69 | Black Berries | Isley Brothers |
| 6/15/63 | Black Cloud | Chubby Checker |
| 8/13/66 | Black Is Black | Los Bravos |
|  | Black Land Farmer | |
| 7/10/61 |  | Frankie Miller |
| 8/21/61 |  | Wink Martindale |
| 1/2/65 | Black Night | Bobby Bland |
| 12/25/65 | Black Nights | Lowell Fulsom |
| 5/10/69 | Black Pearl | Checkmates, Ltd. |
| 6/17/67 | Black Sheep | Sam The Sham & The Pharoahs |
| 1/19/63 | Blame It On The Bossa Nova | Eydie Gorme |
| 9/26/64 | Bless Our Love | Gene Chandler |
| 8/14/61 | Bless You | Tony Orlando |
| 1/20/68 | Blessed Are The Lonely | Robert Knight |
| 3/8/69 | Blessed Is The Rain | Brooklyn Bridge |
|  | Blind Man | |
| 1/2/65 |  | Little Milton |
| 1/9/65 |  | Bobby Bland |
| 11/22/69 | Blistered | Johnny Cash |
| 3/20/61 | Blizzard | Jim Reeves |
|  | Blowin' In The Wind | |
| 6/29/63 |  | Peter, Paul & Mary |
| 7/23/66 |  | Stevie Wonder |
| 9/19/60 | Blue Angel | Roy Orbison |
| 12/10/66 | Blue Autumn | Bobby Goldsboro |
| 9/14/63 | Blue Bayou | Roy Orbison |
| 12/19/60 | Blue Christmas | Browns |
| 9/28/63 | Blue Guitar | Richard Chamberlain |
|  | Blue Moon | |
| 3/6/61 |  | Herb Lance |
| 3/6/61 |  | Marcels |
| 10/23/61 |  | Ventures |
| 5/18/63 | Blue On Blue | Bobby Vinton |
| 1/1/66 | Blue River | Elvis Presley |
| 7/3/65 | Blue Shadows | B.B. King |
| 8/27/66 | Blue Side Of Lonesome | Jim Reeves |
| 11/28/60 | Blue Tango | Bill Black's Combo |
| 6/12/61 | Blue Tomorrow | Billy Vaughn |
|  | Blue Velvet | |
| 8/8/60 |  | Statues |
| 8/10/63 |  | Bobby Vinton |
| 1/20/62 | Blue Water Line | Brothers Four |
| 2/15/64 | Blue Winter | Connie Francis |
| 7/15/67 | Bluebird | Buffalo Springfield |
| 12/14/68 | Bluebirds Over The Mountain | Beach Boys |
| 4/14/62 | Blues (Stay Away From Me) | Ace Cannon |
| 4/22/67 | Blue's Theme | Davie Allan & The Arrows |
| 6/12/61 | Bobby | Neil Scott |
| 10/20/62 | Bobby's Girl | Marcie Blane |
| 12/20/69 | Bold Soul Sister | Ike & Tina Turner |
| 5/15/61 | Boll Weevil Song | Brook Benton |
| 12/14/63 | Bon-Doo-Wah | Orlons |
|  | Bonanza | |
| 4/3/61 |  | Al Caiola |
| 9/15/62 |  | Johnny Cash |
| 8/15/60 | Bongo Bongo Bongo | Preston Epps |
| 6/16/62 | Bongo Stomp | Little Joey & The Flips |
|  | Bonnie And Clyde..see: Ballad Of | |
| 1/4/60* | Bonnie Came Back | Duane Eddy |
|  | (also see: My Bonnie) | |
| 3/30/63 | Bony Moronie | Appalachians |
| 5/1/65 | Boo-Ga-Loo | Tom & Jerrio |
| 10/7/67 | Boogaloo Down Broadway | Fantastic Johnny C |
| 3/19/66 | Boogaloo Party | Flamingos |
| 7/10/61 | Boogie Woogie | B. Bumble & The Stingers |
| 3/14/64 | Book Of Love | Raindrops |
|  | Boom Boom | |
| 5/26/62 |  | John Lee Hooker |
| 12/5/64 |  | Animals |
|  | Boomerang..see: Do The | |
| 6/5/65 | Boot-Leg | Booker T. & The MG's |
| 7/23/66 | Born A Woman | Sandy Posey |
| 3/22/69 | Born Again | Sam & Dave |
|  | Born Free | |
| 8/27/66 |  | Roger Williams |
| 1/6/68 |  | Hesitations |
| 2/6/65 | Born To Be Together | Ronettes |
|  | Born To Be Wild | |
| 7/13/68 |  | Steppenwolf |
| 5/10/69 |  | Wilson Pickett |
| 11/23/68 | Born To Be With You | Sonny James |
|  | Born To Cry..see: (I was) | |
| 5/12/62 | Born To Lose | Ray Charles |
| 2/16/63 | Boss | Rumblers |
| 2/9/63 | Boss Guitar | Duane Eddy |
| 10/19/63 | Bossa Nova Baby | Elvis Presley |
| 12/22/62 | (Bossa Nova) Bird | Dells |
| 1/5/63 | Bossa Nova U.S.A. | Dave Brubeck Quartet |
|  | Both Sides Now | |
| 11/9/68 |  | Judy Collins |
| 4/26/69 |  | Dion |
| 12/30/67 | Bottle Of Wine | Fireballs |
| 4/27/63 | Bounce, The | Olympics |
| 5/27/67 | Bowling Green | Everly Brothers |
| 4/12/69 | Boxer, The | Simon & Garfunkel |
| 1/16/65 | Boy From New York City | Ad Libs |
|  | Boy I'm Gonna Marry..see: (Today I Met) | |
| 7/26/69 | Boy Named Sue | Johnny Cash |
| 11/9/63 | Boy Next Door | Secrets |
| 2/29/64 | Boy With The Beatle Hair | Swans |
| 8/4/62 | Boys' Night Out | Patti Page |
| 11/8/69 | Brand New Me | Dusty Springfield |
| 3/27/61 | Brass Buttons | String-A-Longs |
| 8/15/64 | Bread And Butter | Newbeats |
| 7/5/69 | Break Away | Beach Boys |
| 1/23/65 | Break Away (From That Boy) | Newbeats |
| 1/13/62 | Break It To Me Gently | Brenda Lee |
| 5/28/66 | Break Out | Mitch Ryder & The Detroit Wheels |
| 5/22/65 | Break Up | Del Shannon |
| 8/31/68 | Break Your Promise | Delfonics |
| 4/12/69 | Breakfast In Bed | Dusty Springfield |
| 4/17/61 | Breakin' In A Brand New Broken Heart | Connie Francis |
|  | Breakin' Up..also see: (Best Part Of) | |
| 1/22/66 | Breakin' Up Is Breakin' My Heart | Roy Orbison |
|  | Breaking Up Is Hard To Do | |
| 6/30/62 |  | Neil Sedaka |
| 7/27/68 |  | Happenings |
| 6/22/63 | Breakwater | Lawrence Welk |
| 7/27/63 | Breath Taking Guy | Supremes |
| 7/6/63 | Brenda | Cupids |
| 10/16/61 | Bridge Of Love | Joe Dowell |
| 8/8/60 | Brigade Of Broken Hearts | Paul Evans |
| 9/18/61 | Bright Lights Big City | Jimmy Reed |
| 3/9/63 | Brightest Smile In Town | Ray Charles |
| 5/25/68 | Bring A Little Lovin' | Los Bravos |
| 5/22/65 | Bring A Little Sunshine (To My Heart) | Vic Dana |
| 7/30/66 | Bring Back The Time | B.J. Thomas |
| 8/24/68 | Bring Back Those Rockabye Baby Days | Tiny Tim |
|  | Bring It On Home To Me | |
| 6/23/62 |  | Sam Cooke |
| 5/15/65 |  | Animals |
| 10/19/68 |  | Eddie Floyd |
|  | (also see: I'll Bring It Home To You) | |
| 1/7/67 | Bring It Up | James Brown |
| 1/30/65 | Bring Your Love To Me | Righteous Brothers |

| Date | Title | Artist |
|---|---|---|
| 10/21/67 | **Brink Of Disaster** | Lesley Gore |
| 9/11/61 | **Bristol Stomp** | Dovells |
| 5/19/62 | **Bristol Twistin' Annie** | Dovells |
| 8/25/62 | **Broken Heart** | Fiestas |
| 10/2/61 | **Broken Heart And A Pillow Filled With Tears** | Patti Page |
| 7/3/61 | **Broken Hearted** | Miracles |
| 9/12/60 | **Brontosaurus Stomp** | Piltdown Men |
| 5/11/68 | **Brooklyn Roads** | Neil Diamond |
| 12/18/65 | **Broomstick Cowboy** | Bobby Goldsboro |
| 5/15/61 | **Brother-In-Law (He's A Moocher)** | Paul Peek |
| 2/22/69 | **Brother Love's Travelling Salvation Show** | Neil Diamond |
| 5/31/69 | **Brown Arms In Houston** | Orpheus |
| 7/15/67 | **Brown Eyed Girl** | Van Morrison |
| 8/3/68 | **Brown Eyed Woman** | Bill Medley |
| 1/18/69 | **Bubble Gum Music** | Rock & Roll Dubble Bubble Trading Card Co. |
| 11/13/65 | **Buckaroo** | Buck Owens |
| 12/19/64 | **Bucket "T"** | Ronny & The Daytonas |
| 1/4/69 | **Build Me Up Buttercup** | Foundations |
| 1/11/60 | **Bulldog** | Fireballs |
|  | **Bumble Bee** |  |
| 11/14/60 | | LaVern Baker |
| 3/20/65 | | Searchers |
| 3/27/61 | **Bumble Boogie** | B. Bumble & The Stingers |
| 4/18/60 | **Burning Bridges** | Jack Scott |
| 10/6/62 | **Burning Of Atlanta** | Claude King |
| 2/3/68 | **Burning Spear** | Soulful Strings |
| 7/23/66 | **Bus Stop** | Hollies |
| 9/7/63 | **Bust Out** | Busters |
| 9/7/63 | **Busted** | Ray Charles |
| 7/17/65 | **Buster Browne** | Willie Mitchell |
| 2/20/61 | **But I Do** | Clarence Henry |
|  | **But It's Alright** |  |
| 10/1/66 | | J.J. Jackson |
| 5/24/69 | | J.J. Jackson |
| 6/23/62 | **But Not For Me** | Ketty Lester |
| 12/11/61 | **But On The Other Hand Baby** | Ray Charles |
| 1/18/69 | **But You Know I Love You** | First Edition |
| 10/9/65 | **But You're Mine** | Sonny & Cher |
| 2/9/63 | **Butterfly Baby** | Bobby Rydell |
| 4/8/67 | **Buy For Me The Rain** | Nitty Gritty Dirt Band |
| 4/12/69 | **Buying A Book** | Joe Tex |
| 5/1/61 | **Buzz Buzz A-Diddle-It** | Freddy Cannon |
| 2/10/62 | **B'wa Nina (Pretty Girl)** | Tokens |
|  | **By The Time I Get To Phoenix** |  |
| 10/28/67 | | Glen Campbell |
| 8/2/69 | | Mad Lads |
| 8/30/69 | | Isaac Hayes |
| 1/30/61 | **Bye Bye Baby** | Mary Wells |
| 1/16/65 | **Bye, Bye, Baby (Baby Goodbye)** | 4 Seasons |
| 2/1/64 | **Bye Bye Barbara** | Johnny Mathis |
| 1/22/66 | **Bye Bye Blues** | Bert Kaempfert |

# C

|  | **C.C. Rider** |  |
|---|---|---|
| 12/1/62 | | LaVern Baker |
| 12/4/65 | | Bobby Powell |
| 9/17/66 | | Animals |
|  | (also see: Jenny Take A Ride!) |  |
| 1/27/68 | **Cab Driver** | Mills Brothers |
| 4/20/68 | **Cabaret** | Herb Alpert |
| 1/27/62 | **Cajun Queen** | Jimmy Dean |
|  | **Calcutta** |  |
| 12/12/60 | | Lawrence Welk |
| 2/6/61 | | Four Preps |
| 5/2/64 | **Caledonia** | James Brown |
| 12/19/60 | **Calendar Girl** | Neil Sedaka |
| 11/7/64 | **California Bound** | Ronny & The Daytonas |
|  | **California Dreamin'** |  |
| 1/8/66 | | Mamas & The Papas |
| 12/7/68 | | Bobby Womack |
| 11/2/68 | **California Earthquake** | Mama Cass |
| 4/5/69 | **California Girl (And The Tennessee Square)** | Tompall & The Glaser Brothers |
| 7/24/65 | **California Girls** | Beach Boys |
| 2/4/67 | **California Nights** | Lesley Gore |
| 12/21/68 | **California Soul** | 5th Dimension |
|  | **California Sun** |  |
| 4/3/61 | | Joe Jones |
| 1/25/64 | | Rivieras |
| 1/8/66 | **Call Me** | Chris Montez |
|  | **Call Me Irresponsible** |  |
| 4/6/63 | | Frank Sinatra |
| 5/4/63 | | Jack Jones |
| 3/30/68 | **Call Me Lightning** | Who |
| 7/21/62 | **Call Me Mr. In-Between** | Burl Ives |
| 1/5/63 | **Call On Me** | Bobby Bland |
| 7/28/62 | **Callin' Doctor Casey** | John D. Loudermilk |
| 12/6/69 | **Camel Back** | A.B. Skhy |
| 9/3/66 | **Campfire Girls** | Billy Joe Royal |
| 12/21/68 | **Can I Change My Mind** | Tyrone Davis |
| 10/19/63 | **Can I Get A Witness** | Marvin Gaye |
| 10/29/66 | **Can I Get To Know You Better** | Turtles |
| 7/2/66 | **Can I Trust You?** | Bachelors |
| 4/4/64 | **Can You Do It** | Contours |
| 12/19/64 | **Can You Jerk Like Me** | Contours |
| 1/1/66 | **Can You Please Crawl Out Your Window?** | Bob Dylan |
| 2/1/64 | **Can Your Monkey Do The Dog** | Rufus Thomas |
| 3/28/64 | **Can't Buy Me Love** | Beatles |
| 8/23/69 | **Can't Find The Time** | Orpheus |
| 3/25/67 | **Can't Get Enough Of You, Baby** | ? & The Mysterians |
| 8/29/64 | **Can't Get Over (The Bossa Nova)** | Eydie Gorme |
| 3/2/63 | **Can't Get Used To Losing You** | Andy Williams |
| 11/25/67 | **Can't Help But Love You** | Standells |
| 12/4/61 | **Can't Help Falling In Love** | Elvis Presley |
| 6/5/61 | **Can't Help Lovin' That Girl Of Mine** | Excels |
| 8/21/65 | **Can't Let You Out Of My Sight** | Chuck Jackson & Maxine Brown |
| 7/20/63 | **Can't Nobody Love You** | Solomon Burke |
| 9/3/66 | **Can't Satisfy** | Impressions |
| 4/29/67 | **Can't Seem To Make You Mine** | Seeds |
| 10/21/67 | **Can't Stop Loving You** | Last Word |
|  | **Can't Take My Eyes Off You** |  |
| 5/20/67 | | Frankie Valli |
| 12/9/67 | | Lettermen (medley) |
| 11/22/69 | | Nancy Wilson |
| 8/3/68 | **Can't You Find Another Way (Of Doing It)** | Sam & Dave |
| 1/30/65 | **Can't You Hear My Heartbeat** | Herman's Hermits |
| 1/30/65 | **Can't You Just See Me** | Aretha Franklin |
| 6/15/68 | **Can't You See Me Cry** | New Colony Six |
| 6/13/64 | **Can't You See That She's Mine** | Dave Clark Five |
| 1/22/67 | **Can't You See (You're Losing Me)** | Mary Wells |
|  | **Canadian Sunset** |  |
| 3/13/61 | | Etta Jones |
| 7/31/61 | | Sounds Orchestral |
| 7/10/65 | **Candy** | Astors |
| 7/6/63 | **Candy Girl** | Four Seasons |
| 8/7/61 | **Candy Man** | Roy Orbison |
| 8/22/60 | **Candy Sweet** | Pat Boone |
| 8/29/64 | **Candy To Me** | Eddie Holland |
| 9/18/65 | **Cara-Lin** | Strangeloves |
| 6/5/65 | **Cara, Mia** | Jay & The Americans |
| 3/14/60 | **Caravan** | Santo & Johnny |
| 7/28/62 | **Careless Love** | Ray Charles |
| 1/13/68 | **Carmen** | Herb Alpert |
| 4/25/64 | **Carol** | Tommy Roe |
| 3/26/68 | **Caroline, No** | Brian Wilson |
| 2/3/68 | **Carpet Man** | 5th Dimension |
| 6/17/67 | **Carrie-Anne** | Hollies |
| 1/25/69 | **Carroll County Accident** | Porter Wagoner |
| 9/6/69 | **Carry Me Back** | Rascals |
| 4/8/67 | **Casino Royale** | Herb Alpert |
| 8/26/67 | **Casonova (Your Playing Days Are Over)** | Ruby Andrews |
|  | **Cast Your Fate To The Wind** |  |
| 12/8/62 | | Vince Guaraldi |
| 3/20/65 | | Sounds Orchestral |
| 6/26/65 | | Steve Alaimo |
| 8/13/66 | | Shelby Flint |
| 2/29/64 | **Castles In The Sand** | Stevie Wonder |
| 9/5/64 | **Cat, The** | Jimmy Smith |
| 9/2/67 | **Cat In The Window (The Bird In The Sky)** | Petula Clark |
| 5/15/65 | **Catch The Wind** | Donovan |
| 8/21/65 | **Catch Us If You Can** | Dave Clark Five |
| 3/31/62 | **Caterina** | Perry Como |
| 4/18/60 | **Cathy's Clown** | Everly Brothers |
| 11/13/61 | **Certain Girl** | Ernie K-Doe |
| 2/6/61 | **Cerveza** | Bert Kaempfert |
| 12/31/60 | **C'est Si Bon (It's So Good)** | Conway Twitty |
| 10/13/62 | **Cha-Cha-Cha** | Bobby Rydell |
|  | **Chain Gang** |  |
| 8/15/60 | | Sam Cooke |
| 4/27/68 | | Jackie Wilson & Count Basie |
|  | **Chain Of Fools** |  |
| 12/9/67 | | Aretha Franklin |
| 4/6/68 | | Jimmy Smith |
| 9/14/68 | **Chained** | Marvin Gaye |
| 10/24/64 | **Chained And Bound** | Otis Redding |
| 11/10/62 | **Chains** | Cookies |
| 4/24/65 | **Chains Of Love** | Drifters |
| 9/13/69 | **Chains Of Love** | Bobby Bland |
| 1/30/65 | **Change Is Gonna Come** | Sam Cooke |
| 8/2/69 | **Change Of Heart** | Classics IV |
| 9/17/66 | **Changes** | Crispian St. Peters |
|  | **Chantilly Lace**..see: (You've Got) Personality |  |
| 3/17/62 | **Chapel By The Sea** | Billy Vaughn |
|  | **Chapel In The Moonlight** |  |
| 10/9/65 | | Bachelors |
| 7/8/67 | | Dean Martin |
| 5/2/64 | **Chapel Of Love** | Dixie Cups |
|  | **Charade** |  |
| 12/7/63 | | Henry Mancini |
| 1/18/64 | | Andy Williams |
| 4/4/64 | | Sammy Kaye |
| 4/10/61 | **Charanga** | Merv Griffin |
| 1/23/61 | **Charlena** | Sevilles |
| 6/19/61 | **Charleston** | Ernie Fields |
| 3/30/63 | **Charms** | Bobby Vee |
|  | **Chattanooga Choo Choo** |  |
| 2/29/60 | | Ernie Fields |
| 1/20/62 | | Floyd Cramer |
| 11/18/67 | | Harpers Bizarre |
| 2/22/60 | **Chattanooga Shoe Shine Boy** | Freddy Cannon |
| 1/29/66 | **Cheater, The** | Bob Kuban |
| 11/30/63 | **Cheer Leader** | Paul Petersen |
| 8/9/69 | **Chelsea Morning** | Judy Collins |
| 2/13/61 | **Cherie** | Bobby Rydell |
| 8/27/66 | **Cherish** | Association |
| 2/27/61 | **Cherry Berry Wine** | Charlie McCoy |
| 8/20/66 | **Cherry, Cherry** | Neil Diamond |
| 10/4/69 | **Cherry Hill Park** | Billy Joe Royal |
| 4/4/60 | **Cherry Pie** | Skip & Flip |
| 12/26/60 | **Cherry Pink And Apple Blossom White** | Harmonicats |
| 10/19/68 | **Chewy Chewy** | Ohio Express |
| 1/12/63 | **Chicken Feed** | Bent Fabric |
| 9/23/67 | **Child Of Clay** | Jimmie Rodgers |
| 12/26/60 | **Child Of God** | Bobby Darin |
| 11/6/65 | **Child Of Our Times** | Barry McGuire |
| 1/9/61 | **Chills And Fever** | Ronnie Love |
| 4/24/65 | **Chim, Chim, Cheree** | New Christy Minstrels |
| 2/1/60 | **China Doll** | Ames Brothers |
| 8/24/63 | **China Nights (Shina No Yoru)** | Kyu Sakamoto |
| 7/27/63 | **Chinese Checkers** | Booker T. & The MG's |
| 1/20/62 | **Chip Chip** | Gene McDaniels |
|  | **Chipmunk Song** |  |
| 1/4/60* | | Chipmunks |
| 12/12/60 | | Chipmunks |
| 12/18/61 | | Chipmunks |
| 12/8/62 | | Chipmunks |
| 11/23/68 | **Chitty Chitty Bang Bang** | Paul Mauriat |
| 9/21/68 | **Choice, The** | O'Jays |
| 6/28/69 | **Choice Of Colors** | Impressions |
| 3/22/69 | **Chokin' Kind** | Joe Simon |
|  | **Choo Choo**..also see: Do The |  |
| 6/1/68 | **Choo Choo Train** | Box Tops |
| 12/19/60 | **Christmas Auld Lang Syne** | Bobby Darin |

**Christmas Song**
12/12/60  Nat "King" Cole
12/15/62  Nat "King" Cole
9/5/64    **Chug-A-Lug**  Roger Miller
3/16/63   **Cigarettes And Coffee Blues**
          Marty Robbins
9/11/61   **Cinderella**  Paul Anka
3/17/62   **Cinderella**  Jack Ross
3/30/68   **Cinderella Rockefella**
          Esther & Abi Ofarim
10/12/68  **Cinderella Sunshine**
          Paul Revere & The Raiders
5/12/62   **Cindy's Birthday**  Johnny Crawford
9/7/63    **Cindy's Gonna Cry**  Johnny Crawford
10/26/68  **Cinnamon**  Derek
12/29/62  **Cinnamon Cinder (It's A Very Nice Dance)**  Pastel Six
4/12/69   **Cissy Strut**  Meters
4/10/61   **City Girl Stole My Country Boy**
          Patti Page
5/2/60    **City Lights**  Debbie Reynolds
          **Clam**..see: Do The
5/16/61   **Clap Your Hands**  Beau-Marks
3/20/65   **Clapping Song (Clap Pat Clap Slap)**
          Shirley Ellis
6/22/68   **Classical Gas**  Mason Williams
7/5/69    **Clean Up Your Own Back Yard**
          Elvis Presley
          **Clementine**
2/8/60    Jan & Dean
3/21/60   Bobby Darin
10/9/65   **Cleo's Back**  Jr. Walker & The All Stars
1/15/66   **Cleo's Mood**  Jr. Walker & The All Stars
10/10/60  **(Clickity Clack Song) Four Little Heels**  Brian Hyland
5/8/65    **Climb, The**  Kingsmen
          **Climb Every Mountain**
1/4/60*   Tony Bennett
5/25/68   Hesitations
8/8/64    **Clinging Vine**  Bobby Vinton
9/19/64   **Clock, The**  Baby Washington
9/15/62   **Close To Cathy**  Mike Clifford
1/30/61   **Close Together**  Jimmy Reed
3/25/67   **Close Your Eyes**  Peaches & Herb
          **Closer Walk**..see: Just A Closer Walk
          **Cloud Nine**
11/16/68  Temptations
2/1/69    Mongo Santamaria
1/4/60*   **Clouds, The**  Spacemen
5/21/66   **Cloudy Summer Afternoon (Raindrops)**  Barry McGuire
          **C'mon**..see: Come On
11/17/62  **Cold, Cold Heart**  Dinah Washington
12/14/63  **Cold Cold Winter**  Pixies Three
2/3/68    **Cold Feet**  Albert King
7/15/67   **Cold Sweat**  James Brown
11/15/69  **Cold Turkey**  Plastic Ono Band
5/24/69   **Color Him Father**  Winstons
12/24/66  **Color My World**  Petula Clark
8/16/69   **Colour Of My Love**  Jefferson
8/14/65   **Colours**  Donovan
11/13/61  **Comancheros**  Claude King
9/12/64   **Come A Little Bit Closer**
          Jay & The Americans
4/10/61   **Come Along**  Maurice Williams
5/28/66   **Come And Get Me**  Jackie de Shannon
4/6/63    **Come And Get These Memories**
          Martha & The Vandellas
2/27/65   **Come And Stay With Me**
          Marianne Faithfull
8/22/60   **Come Back**  Jimmy Clanton
10/12/63  **Come Back**  Johnny Mathis
11/5/66   **Come Back**  Five Stairsteps
3/20/65   **Come Back Baby**  Roddie Joy
2/17/62   **Come Back Silly Girl**  Lettermen
7/22/67   **Come Back When You Grow Up**
          Bobby Vee
11/30/63  **Come Dance With Me**
          Jay & The Americans
6/15/63   **Come Go With Me**  Dion
2/6/65    **Come Home**  Dave Clark Five
1/4/60*   **Come Into My Heart**  Lloyd Price
1/18/64   **Come On**  Tommy Roe
5/28/66   **Come On And See Me**  Tammi Terrell
7/11/64   **C'mon And Swim**  Bobby Freeman
7/28/62   **Come On Baby**  Bruce Channel
12/12/64  **Come On Do The Jerk**  Miracles

5/6/67    **Come On Down To My Boat**
          Every Mothers' Son
4/23/66   **Come On Let's Go**  McCoys
7/21/62   **Come On Little Angel**  Belmonts
6/10/67   **C'mon Marianne**  4 Seasons
4/10/61   **Come On Over**  Strollers
4/24/65   **Come On Over To My Place**  Drifters
11/2/68   **Come On, React!**  Fireballs
8/19/67   **Come On Sock It To Me**  Syl Johnson
9/24/66   **Come On Up**  Young Rascals
          **Come Rain Or Come Shine**
11/28/60  Ray Charles
1/20/68   Ray Charles
11/5/66   **(Come 'Round Here) I'm The One You Need**  Miracles
5/7/66    **Come Running Back**  Dean Martin
12/20/69  **Come Saturday Morning**  Sandpipers
3/6/65    **Come See**  Major Lance
          **Come See About Me**
11/14/64  Nella Dodds
11/14/64  Supremes
11/25/67  Jr. Walker & The All Stars
10/9/61   **Come September**  Billy Vaughn
8/20/66   **Come Share The Good Times With Me**  Julie Monday
3/21/64   **Come To Me**  Otis Redding
3/23/68   **Come To Me Softly**  Jimmy James
5/20/67   **Come To The Sunshine**
          Harpers Bizarre
10/18/69  **Come Together**  Beatles
2/20/65   **Come Tomorrow**  Manfred Mann
5/30/60   **Comin' Down With Love**  Mel Gadson
11/3/62   **Comin' Home Baby**  Mel Torme
12/21/63  **Comin' In The Back Door**
          Baja Marimba Band
2/1/64    **Comin' On**  Bill Black's Combo
1/30/65   **Comin' On Too Strong**  Wayne Newton
1/4/64    **Coming Back To You**  Maxine Brown
11/19/66  **Coming Home Soldier**  Bobby Vinton
10/1/66   **Coming On Strong**  Brenda Lee
8/2/69    **Commotion**
          Creedence Clearwater Revival
          (also see: Kommotion)
12/10/66  **Communication Breakdown**
          Roy Orbison
6/29/68   **Competition Ain't Nothin'**  Carl Carlton
4/19/69   **Composer, The**  Supremes
          **Concrete And Clay**
5/1/65    Eddie Rambeau
5/1/65    Unit Four plus Two
12/21/68  **Condition Red**  Goodees
11/24/62  **Coney Island Baby**  Excellents
3/14/64   **Congratulations**  Rick Nelson
6/8/68    **Congratulations**  Cliff Richard
4/14/62   **Conscience**  James Darren
12/24/66  **Constant Rain**
          Sergio Mendes & Brasil '66
          **Continental Walk**
4/3/61    Hank Ballard
4/10/61   Rollers
          (also see: Do The New)
11/23/68  **Coo Coo**
          Big Brother & The Holding Company
4/7/62    **Cookin'**  Al Casey Combo
4/30/66   **Cool Jerk**  Capitols
7/25/60   **Cool Water**  Jack Scott
8/25/62   **Copy Cat**  Gary (U.S.) Bonds
11/21/60  **Corinna, Corinna**  Ray Peterson
11/5/66   **Corner In The Sun**  Walter Jackson
5/9/60    **Cottage For Sale**  Little Willie John
4/11/64   **Cotton Candy**  Al Hirt
          **Cotton Fields**
11/27/61  Highwaymen
6/22/63   Ace Cannon
6/4/66    **Count Down**  Dave "Baby" Cortez
          **Count Every Star**
5/1/61    Donnie & The Dreamers
4/7/62    Linda Scott
4/3/65    **Count Me In**  Gary Lewis & The Playboys
          **Count The Days**..see: (1-2-3-4-5-6-7)
2/1/60    **Country Boy**  Fats Domino
2/17/68   **Country Girl - City Man**
          Billy Vera & Judy Clay
9/21/68   **Court Of Love**  Unifics
9/26/64   **Cousin Of Mine**  Sam Cooke
11/25/67  **Cover Me**  Percy Sledge
10/12/63  **Cowboy Boots**  Dave Dudley
2/6/61    **Cowboy Jimmy Joe**  Lolita

3/23/68   **Cowboys To Girls**  Intruders
3/28/60   **Cradle Of Love**  Johnny Preston
11/6/65   **Crawling Back**  Roy Orbison
10/23/61  **Crazy**  Patsy Cline
1/4/60    **Crazy Arms**  Bob Beckham
          **Crazy Downtown**..see: Downtown
4/29/67   **Creeque Alley**  Mamas & The Papas
12/14/68  **Crimson And Clover**
          Tommy James & The Shondells
          **(Crooked Little Man)**..see: Don't Let The Rain Come Down
9/28/63   **Cross Fire!**  Orlons
2/6/65    **Cross My Heart**  Bobby Vee
12/2/67   **Cross My Heart**  Billy Stewart
5/1/61    **Cross Stands Alone**  Jimmy Witter
11/2/63   **Crossfire Time**  Dee Clark
1/25/69   **Crossroads**  Cream
11/30/68  **Crosstown Traffic**  Jimi Hendrix
6/2/62    **Crowd, The**  Roy Orbison
11/2/68   **Crown Of Creation**  Jefferson Airplane
4/23/66   **Cruel War**  Peter, Paul & Mary
10/18/69  **Crumbs Off The Table**  Glass House
1/9/65    **Crusher, The**  Novas
          **Cry**
2/6/65    Ray Charles
11/26/66  Ronnie Dove
8/17/63   **Cry Baby**
          Garnet Mimms & The Enchanters
2/17/62   **Cry Baby Cry**  Angels
11/7/60   **Cry Cry Cry**  Bobby Bland
3/2/68    **Cry Like A Baby**  Box Tops
1/18/60   **Cry Me A River**  Janice Harper
6/30/62   **Cry Myself To Sleep**  Del Shannon
10/8/66   **Cry Softly**  Nancy Ames
7/29/67   **Cry Softly Lonely One**  Roy Orbison
          **Cry To Me**
1/27/62   Solomon Burke
9/21/63   Betty Harris
3/25/67   Freddie Scott
          **Crying**
8/14/61   Roy Orbison
5/28/66   Jay & The Americans
1/9/65    **Crying Game**  Brenda Lee
          **Crying In The Chapel**
1/30/65   Adam Wade
4/24/65   Elvis Presley
1/13/62   **Crying In The Rain**  Everly Brothers
12/11/65  **Crying Time**  Ray Charles
6/7/69    **Crystal Blue Persuasion**
          Tommy James & The Shondells
12/4/65   **Crystal Chandelier**  Vic Dana
          **Cuando Calienta El Sol**..see: Love Me With All Of Your Heart
          **Cupid**
6/5/61    Sam Cooke
2/20/65   Johnny Rivers
11/1/69   Johnny Nash
11/15/69  **Curly**  Jimmy Clanton
2/22/64   **Custom Machine**  Bruce & Terry
10/12/68  **Cycles**  Frank Sinatra

# D

6/15/68   **D. W. Washburn**  Monkees
4/27/63   **Da Doo Ron Ron**  Crystals
12/28/68  **Daddy Sang Bass**  Johnny Cash
          **Daddy's Home**
3/27/61   Shep & The Limelites
5/6/67    Chuck Jackson & Maxine Brown
1/28/67   **Daddy's Little Girl**  Al Martino
8/30/69   **Daddy's Little Man**  O.C. Smith
12/14/63  **Daisy Petal Pickin'**
          Jimmy Gilmer/Fireballs
6/14/69   **Dammit Isn't God's Last Name**
          Frankie Laine
12/5/60   **Dance By The Light Of The Moon**
          Olympics
7/20/63   **Dance, Dance, Dance**  Joey Dee
11/7/64   **Dance, Dance, Dance**  Beach Boys
8/24/63   **Dance, Everybody, Dance**  Dartells
5/29/61   **Dance On Little Girl**  Paul Anka
4/24/61   **Dance The Mess Around**
          Chubby Checker
2/10/68   **Dance To The Music**
          Sly & The Family Stone
1/4/60*   **Dance With Me**  Drifters
10/30/65  **Dance With Me**  Mojo Men
10/24/60  **Dance With Me Georgie**  Bobbettes

| Date | Title | Artist |
|---|---|---|
| 7/21/62 | Dance With Mr. Domino | Fats Domino |
| 10/6/62 | (Dance With The) Guitar Man | Duane Eddy |
| 7/6/63 | Dancin' Holiday | Olympics |
| 12/16/67 | Dancin' Out Of My Heart | Ronnie Dove |
| 6/23/62 | Dancin' Party | Chubby Checker |
| 6/9/62 | Dancin' The Strand | Maureen Gray |
| 12/9/67 | Dancing Bear | Mamas & The Papas |
|  | **Dancing In The Street** |  |
| 8/22/64 |  | Martha & The Vandellas |
| 12/17/66 |  | Mamas & The Papas |
| 9/23/67 |  | Ramsey Lewis |
| 9/9/67 | Dandelion | Rolling Stones |
| 10/1/66 | Dandy | Herman's Hermits |
| 6/13/64 | Dang Me | Roger Miller |
| 5/25/63 | Danger | Vic Dana |
| 8/14/65 | Danger Heartbreak Dead Ahead | Marvelettes |
| 1/14/67 | Danger! She's A Stranger | Five Stairsteps |
| 8/6/66 | Dangling Conversation | Simon & Garfunkel |
| 7/13/63 | Danke Schoen | Wayne Newton |
|  | **Danny Boy** |  |
| 1/4/60* |  | Conway Twitty |
| 10/30/61 |  | Andy Williams |
| 12/19/64 |  | Patti LaBelle & Her Bluebells |
| 2/27/65 |  | Jackie Wilson |
| 3/25/67 |  | Ray Price |
|  | Dark At The Top Of The Stairs ..see: Theme From The |  |
| 2/25/67 | Dark End Of The Street | James Carr |
| 1/5/63 | Darkest Street In Town | Jimmy Clanton |
| 12/23/67 | Darlin' | Beach Boys |
| 3/19/66 | Darling Baby | Elgins |
|  | **Darling Be Home Soon** |  |
| 2/11/67 |  | Lovin' Spoonful |
| 7/29/67 |  | Bobby Darin |
| 1/4/60* | Darling Lorraine | Knockouts |
| 6/26/65 | Darling Take Me Back | Lenny Welch |
| 10/3/64 | Dartell Stomp | Mustangs |
| 7/6/63 | Daughter | Blenders |
| 11/9/63 | Dawn | David Rockingham Trio |
| 2/1/64 | Dawn (Go Away) | Four Seasons |
| 9/18/65 | Dawn Of Correction | Spokesmen |
| 3/1/69 | Day After Day (It's Slippin' Away) | Shango |
| 6/11/66 | Day For Decision | Johnny Sea |
| 10/29/66 | Day In The Life Of A Fool | Jack Jones |
| 4/26/69 | Day Is Done | Peter, Paul & Mary |
|  | **Day Tripper** |  |
| 12/18/65 |  | Beatles |
| 9/3/66 |  | Vontastics |
| 12/24/66 |  | Ramsey Lewis |
| 2/26/66 | Daydream | Lovin' Spoonful |
| 11/18/67 | Daydream Believer | Monkees |
| 6/12/61 | Daydreams | Johnny Crawford |
| 6/17/67 | Daylight Savin' Time | Keith |
| 6/14/69 | Days Of Sand And Shovels | Bobby Vinton |
|  | **Days Of Wine And Roses** |  |
| 1/26/63 |  | Henry Mancini |
| 3/16/63 |  | Andy Williams |
| 3/25/67 | Dead End Street | Lou Rawls |
| 1/7/67 | Deadend Street | Kinks |
| 3/7/64 | Dead Man's Curve | Jan & Dean |
| 10/19/63 | Dear Abby | Hearts |
| 4/3/65 | Dear Dad | Chuck Berry |
| 3/2/68 | Dear Delilah | Grapefruit |
| 12/2/67 | Dear Eloise | Hollies |
|  | **Dear Heart** |  |
| 11/28/64 |  | Jack Jones |
| 11/28/64 |  | Andy Williams |
| 12/12/64 |  | Henry Mancini |
| 11/3/62 | Dear Hearts And Gentle People | Springfields |
| 1/6/62 | Dear Ivan | Jimmy Dean |
| 10/24/60 | Dear John | Pat Boone |
| 12/11/61 | Dear Lady Twist | Gary (U.S.) Bonds |
| 11/10/62 | Dear Lonely Hearts | Nat "King" Cole |
| 2/12/66 | Dear Lover | Mary Wells |
| 9/18/61 | Dear Mr. D.J. Play It Again | Tina Robin |
| 8/20/66 | Dear Mrs. Applebee | Flip Cartridge |
| 2/24/62 | Dear One | Larry Finnegan |
| 3/9/63 | Dearer Than Life | Brook Benton |
| 9/12/64 | Death Of An Angel | Kingsmen |
| 1/4/60* | Deck Of Cards | Wink Martindale |

| Date | Title | Artist |
|---|---|---|
| 5/21/66 | Dedicated Follower Of Fashion | Kinks |
|  | **Dedicated To The One I Love** |  |
| 1/23/61 |  | "5" Royales |
| 1/23/61 |  | Shirelles |
| 2/25/67 |  | Mamas & The Papas |
| 7/31/61 | Dedicated (To The Songs I Love) | 3 Friends |
| 2/19/66 | Dedication Song | Freddy Cannon |
| 1/4/64 | Deep In The Heart Of Harlem | Clyde McPhatter |
| 4/21/62 | Deep In The Heart Of Texas | Duane Eddy |
| 9/14/63 | Deep Purple | Nino Tempo & April Stevens |
| 2/8/60 | Delaware | Perry Como |
| 8/22/60 | Delia Gone | Pat Boone |
| 3/16/68 | Delilah | Tom Jones |
| 10/4/69 | Delta Lady | Joe Cocker |
| 6/15/63 | Denise | Randy & The Rainbows |
|  | **Desafinado** |  |
| 9/29/62 |  | Stan Getz/Charlie Byrd |
| 12/8/62 |  | Pat Thomas |
| 8/3/63 | Desert Pete | Kingston Trio |
| 10/28/67 | Desiree' | Left Banke |
| 10/5/68 | Destination: Anywhere | Marvelettes |
|  | **Detroit City** |  |
| 6/15/63 |  | Bobby Bare |
| 10/12/63 |  | Ben Colder |
| 3/11/67 |  | Tom Jones |
|  | Devil In Disguise ..see: (You're the) |  |
| 8/1/60 | Devil Or Angel | Bobby Vee |
| 10/8/66 | Devil With A Blue Dress On (medley) | Mitch Ryder & The Detroit Wheels |
| 7/28/62 | Devil Woman | Marty Robbins |
| 7/29/67 | Devil's Angels | Davie Allen & The Arrows |
| 1/30/65 | Diamond Head | Ventures |
| 8/22/60 | Diamonds And Pearls | Paradons |
| 2/13/65 | Diana | Bobby Rydell |
|  | **Diane** |  |
| 4/20/63 |  | Joe Harnell |
| 4/18/64 |  | Bachelors |
| 9/3/66 | Dianne, Dianne | Ronny & The Daytonas |
| 2/13/65 | Did You Ever | Hullaballoos |
| 5/7/66 | Did You Ever Have To Make Up Your Mind? | Lovin' Spoonful |
| 10/6/62 | Did You Ever See A Dream Walking | Fats Domino |
| 12/14/63 | Did You Have A Happy Birthday? | Paul Anka |
| 7/5/69 | Did You See Her Eyes | Illusion |
| 11/17/62 | Diddle-Dee-Dum (What Happens When Your Love Has Gone) | Belmonts |
| 6/7/69 | Didn't We | Richard Harris |
| 3/8/69 | Didn't You Know (You'd Have To Cry Sometime) | Gladys Knight & The Pips |
| 11/11/67 | Different Drum | Stone Poneys/Linda Ronstadt |
| 10/14/67 | Different Strokes | Syl Johnson |
| 5/9/60 | Ding-A-Ling | Bobby Rydell |
| 5/20/67 | Ding Dong! The Witch Is Dead | Fifth Estate |
| 9/23/67 | Dirty Man | Laura Lee |
| 4/23/66 | Dirty Water | Standells |
| 2/4/67 | Dis-Advantages Of You | Brass Ring |
| 4/9/66 | Distant Drums | Jim Reeves |
| 7/9/66 | Distant Shores | Chad & Jeremy |
| 6/22/68 | D-I-V-O-R-C-E | Tammy Wynette |
|  | Dixie ..see: Theme From |  |
| 2/1/69 | Dizzy | Tommy Roe |
| 11/14/64 | Do Anything You Wanna | Harold Betters |
| 6/20/64 | Do I Love You? | Ronettes |
| 12/18/65 | Do I Make Myself Clear | Etta James & Sugar Pie DeSanto |
| 7/27/68 | Do It Again | Beach Boys |
| 5/6/67 | Do It Again A Little Bit Slower | Jon & Robin & The In Crowd |
| 4/27/63 | Do It - Rat Now | Bill Black's Combo |
| 12/19/64 | Do It Right | Brook Benton |
| 1/4/60* | Do-Re-Mi | Mitch Miller |
| 12/18/61 | Do-Re-Mi | Lee Dorsey |
| 10/12/68 | Do Something To Me | Tommy James & The Shondells |
| 9/14/68 | Do The Best You Can | Hollies |
| 3/2/63 | Do The Bird | Dee Dee Sharp |

| Date | Title | Artist |
|---|---|---|
| 6/5/65 | Do The Boomerang | Jr. Walker & The All Stars |
| 9/28/68 | Do The Choo Choo | Archie Bell & The Drells |
| 2/27/65 | Do The Clam | Elvis Presley |
| 4/24/65 | Do The Freddie | Freddie & The Dreamers (also see: Let's Do The Freddie) |
|  | (Do The) Mashed Potatoes ..see: Mashed Potatoes |  |
| 8/24/63 | Do The Monkey | King Curtis |
| 1/27/62 | Do The New Continental | Dovells |
| 4/8/67 | Do The Thing | Lou Courtney |
| 1/13/68 | Do Unto Me | James & Bobby Purify |
| 11/28/64 | Do-Wacka-Do | Roger Miller |
|  | **Do Wah Diddy Diddy** |  |
| 1/4/64 |  | Exciters |
| 9/5/64 |  | Manfred Mann |
| 12/26/64 | Do What You Do Do Well | Ned Miller |
|  | **Do What You Gotta Do** |  |
| 8/31/68 |  | Bobby Vee |
| 10/19/68 |  | Nina Simone |
|  | **Do You Believe In Magic** |  |
| 8/21/65 |  | Lovin' Spoonful |
| 2/10/62 | Do You Know How To Twist | Hank Ballard |
| 4/13/68 | Do You Know The Way To San Jose | Dionne Warwick |
|  | **Do You Love Me** |  |
| 8/11/62 |  | Contours |
| 5/2/64 |  | Dave Clark Five |
|  | **Do You Mind?** |  |
| 7/4/60 |  | Andy Williams |
| 7/18/60 |  | Anthony Newley |
|  | **Do You Want To Dance** |  |
| 9/19/64 |  | Del Shannon |
| 2/27/65 |  | Beach Boys |
| 11/23/68 |  | Mamas & The Papas |
| 3/28/64 | Do You Want To Know A Secret | Beatles |
| 10/26/68 | Do Your Own Thing | Brook Benton |
| 2/1/69 | Do Your Thing | Watts 103rd St. Band |
|  | Dock Of The Bay ..see: (Sittin' On) |  |
| 5/18/68 | Doctor, The | Mary Wells |
|  | Dr. Ben Basey ..see: Ben Crazy |  |
| 4/21/62 | Doctor Feel-Good | Dr. Feelgood & The Interns |
| 3/16/68 | Dr. Jon (The Medicine Man) | Jon & Robin & The In Crowd |
|  | Doctor Kildare ..see: Theme From |  |
|  | Dr. Zhivago ..see: Somewhere My Love |  |
| 11/7/64 | Dodo, The | Jumpin' Gene Simmons |
| 12/28/68 | Does Anybody Know I'm Here | Dells |
| 12/22/62 | Does He Mean That Much To You? | Eddy Arnold |
| 2/20/65 | Does He Really Care For Me | Ruby & The Romantics |
| 8/7/61 | Does Your Chewing Gum Lose It's Flavor (On The Bedpost Over Night) | Lonnie Donegan |
| 4/20/68 | Does Your Mama Know About Me | Bobby Taylor |
| 2/9/63 | Dog, The | Rufus Thomas |
| 4/4/60 | Doggin' Around | Jackie Wilson |
| 6/21/69 | Doggone Right | Miracles |
| 9/27/69 | Doin' Our Thing | Clarence Carter |
| 4/14/62 | Doin' The Continental Walk | Danny & The Juniors |
| 4/25/60 | (Doin' The) Lovers Leap | Webb Pierce |
| 11/28/60 | Doll House | Donnie Brooks |
| 4/24/61 | Dollar Down | Limeliters |
| 11/9/63 | Dominique | Singing Nun |
|  | **Dommage, Dommage (Too Bad, Too Bad)** |  |
| 10/8/66 |  | Jerry Vale |
| 10/8/66 |  | Paul Vance |
| 10/22/66 | Don't Answer The Door | B.B. King |
| 10/20/62 | Don't Ask Me To Be Friends | Everly Brothers |
| 10/8/66 | Don't Be A Drop-Out | James Brown |
| 12/14/68 | Don't Be Afraid (Do As I Say) | Frankie Karl |
| 3/9/63 | Don't Be Afraid, Little Darlin' | Steve Lawrence |
|  | **Don't Be Cruel** |  |
| 9/12/60 |  | Bill Black's Combo |
| 2/23/63 |  | Barbara Lynn |
| 12/31/60 | Don't Believe Him, Donna | Lenny Miles |

| Date | Title | Artist |
|---|---|---|
| 7/3/61 | **Don't Bet Money Honey** | Linda Scott |
| 9/25/61 | **Don't Blame Me** | Everly Brothers |
| 5/27/67 | **Don't Blame The Children** | Sammy Davis, Jr. |
| 2/10/62 | **Don't Break The Heart That Loves You** | Connie Francis |
| 5/21/66 | **Don't Bring Me Down** | Animals |
| 8/24/68 | **Don't Change Your Love** | Five Stairsteps |
| 6/27/60 | **Don't Come Knockin'** | Fats Domino |
| 1/30/65 | **Don't Come Running Back To Me** | Nancy Wilson |
|  | **Don't Cry, Baby** |  |
| 8/7/61 |  | Etta James |
| 7/21/62 |  | Aretha Franklin |
| 1/29/69 | **Don't Cry Daddy** | Elvis Presley |
| 1/23/68 | **Don't Cry My Love** | Impressions |
| 8/7/61 | **Don't Cry No More** | Bobby Bland |
| 3/14/60 | **Don't Deceive Me** | Ruth Brown |
| 3/4/67 | **Don't Do It** | Micky Dolenz |
| 10/20/62 | **Don't Ever Leave Me** | Bob & Earl |
| 10/24/64 | **Don't Ever Leave Me** | Connie Francis |
|  | **Don't Fence Me In** |  |
| 2/22/60 |  | Tommy Edwards |
| 2/23/63 |  | George Maharis |
| 11/6/65 | **Don't Fight It** | Wilson Pickett |
|  | **Don't Forget About Me** |  |
| 1/29/66 |  | Barbara Lewis |
| 3/1/69 |  | Dusty Springfield |
| 7/31/61 | **Don't Forget I Love You** | Butanes |
| 1/28/64 | **Don't Forget I Still Love You** | Bobbi Martin |
| 9/20/69 | **Don't Forget To Remember** | Bee Gees |
| 9/4/61 | **Don't Get Around Much Anymore** | Belmonts |
| 3/15/69 | **Don't Give In To Him** | Union Gap |
| 7/20/68 | **Don't Give Up** | Petula Clark |
| 1/24/62 | **Don't Go Near The Eskimos** | Ben Colder |
| 9/15/62 | **Don't Go Near The Indians** | Rex Allen |
| 6/24/67 | **Don't Go Out Into The Rain (You're Going To Melt)** | Herman's Hermits |
| 11/7/60 | **Don't Go To Strangers** | Etta Jones |
| 10/13/62 | **Don't Hang Up** | Orlons |
| 10/23/65 | **Don't Have To Shop Around** | Mad Lads |
| 8/23/69 | **Don't It Make You Want To Go Home** | Joe South |
| 6/26/65 | **Don't Just Stand There** | Patty Duke |
| 4/6/63 | **Don't Let Her Be Your Baby** | Contours |
| 2/6/61 | **Don't Let Him Shop Around** | Debbie Dean (also see: Shop Around) |
| 12/6/69 | **Don't Let Him Take Your Love From Me** | Four Tops |
| 11/15/69 | **Don't Let Love Hang You Up** | Jerry Butler |
| 10/10/60 | **Don't Let Love Pass Me By** | Frankie Avalon |
| 2/6/65 | **Don't Let Me Be Misunderstood** | Animals |
| 2/9/63 | **Don't Let Me Cross Over** | Carl Butler |
| 5/10/69 | **Don't Let Me Down** | Beatles |
| 5/24/69 | **Don't Let The Joneses Get You Down** | Temptations |
| 2/29/64 | **Don't Let The Rain Come Down (Crooked Little Man)** | Serendipity Singers |
| 7/8/67 | **Don't Let The Rain Fall Down On Me** | Critters |
| 2/8/60 | **Don't Let The Sun Catch You Cryin'** | Ray Charles |
| 5/23/64 | **Don't Let The Sun Catch You Crying** | Gerry & The Pacemakers |
| 4/10/65 | **Don't Let Your Left Hand Know** | Joe Tex |
| 12/18/65 | **Don't Look Back** | Temptations |
| 12/8/62 | **Don't Make Me Over** | Dionne Warwick |
| 5/11/63 | **Don't Make My Baby Blue** | Frankie Laine |
| 11/30/68 | **Don't Make The Good Girls Go Bad** | Della Humphrey |
| 3/9/63 | **Don't Mention My Name** | Shepherd Sisters |
| 2/6/65 | **Don't Mess Up A Good Thing** | Fontella Bass & Bobby McClure |
| 1/1/66 | **Don't Mess With Bill** | Marvelettes |
| 12/14/68 | **Don't Pat Me On The Back And Call Me Brother** | Kasandra |
| 11/6/65 | **Don't Pity Me** | Peter & Gordon |
| 4/21/62 | **Don't Play That Song** | Ben E. King |
| 12/31/60 | **Don't Read The Letter** | Patti Page |
| 7/1/67 | **Don't Rock The Boat** | Eddie Floyd |
| 6/15/63 | **Don't Say Goodnight And Mean Goodbye** | Shirelles |
| 3/2/63 | **Don't Say Nothin' Bad (About My Baby)** | Cookies |
| 2/23/63 | **Don't Set Me Free** | Ray Charles |
| 5/25/68 | **Don't Sign The Paper Baby (I Want You Back)** | Jimmy Delphs |
| 6/3/67 | **Don't Sleep In The Subway** | Petula Clark |
| 10/3/64 | **Don't Spread It Around** | Barbara Lynn |
| 11/24/62 | **Don't Stop The Wedding** | Ann Cole |
| 6/22/68 | **Don't Take It So Hard** | Paul Revere & The Raiders |
| 7/4/64 | **Don't Take Your Love From Me** | Gloria Lynne |
| 10/9/65 | **Don't Talk To Strangers** | Beau Brummels |
| 6/28/69 | **Don't Tell Your Mama (Where You've Been)** | Eddie Floyd |
|  | **Don't Think Twice, It's All Right** |  |
| 9/14/63 |  | Peter, Paul & Mary |
| 11/6/65 |  | Wonder Who? |
| 3/14/60 | **Don't Throw Away All Those Teardrops** | Frankie Avalon |
| 5/30/64 | **Don't Throw Your Love Away** | Searchers |
|  | **Don't Touch Me** |  |
| 5/28/66 |  | Jeannie Seely |
| 3/8/69 |  | Bettye Swann |
| 6/1/63 | **Don't Try To Fight It, Baby** | Eydie Gorme |
| 10/12/63 | **Don't Wait Too Long** | Tony Bennett |
| 6/14/69 | **Don't Wake Me Up In The Morning, Michael** | Peppermint Rainbow |
| 3/16/63 | **Don't Wanna Think About Paula** | Dickey Lee |
| 10/11/69 | **Don't Waste My Time** | John Mayall |
| 1/30/61 | **Don't Worry** | Marty Robbins |
| 5/30/64 | **Don't Worry Baby** | Beach Boys |
| 8/11/62 | **Don't Worry 'Bout Me** | Vincent Edwards |
| 10/1/66 | **Don't Worry Mother, Your Son's Heart Is Pure** | McCoys |
| 9/15/62 | **Don't You Believe It** | Andy Williams |
| 3/11/67 | **Don't You Care** | Buckinghams |
|  | **Don't You Forget It**..see: (I Love You) |  |
| 1/4/60* | **Don't You Know** | Della Reese |
| 7/22/67 | **Don't You Miss Me A Little Bit Baby** | Jimmy Ruffin |
| 8/25/62 | **Don't You Worry** | Don Gardner & Dee Dee Ford |
|  | **(Don't You Worry 'Bout Me)**..see: Opus 17 |  |
| 8/21/61 | **Donald Where's Your Troosers?** | Andy Stewart |
| 9/14/63 | **Donna The Prima Donna** | Dion |
| 4/18/64 | **Donnie** | Bermudas |
| 6/19/61 | **Dooley** | Olympics |
| 1/27/62 | **Door Is Open** | Tommy Hunt |
| 9/26/64 | **Door Is Still Open To My Heart** | Dean Martin |
| 10/9/61 | **Door To Paradise** | Bobby Rydell |
| 3/20/65 | **Double-O-Seven** | Detergents |
| 4/23/66 | **Double Shot (Of My Baby's Love)** | Swingin' Medallions |
| 8/3/68 | **Down At Lulu's** | Ohio Express |
| 9/28/63 | **(Down At) Papa Joe's** | Dixiebelles |
| 3/7/60 | **Down By The Riverside** | Les Compagnons De La Chanson |
| 1/4/60* | **Down By The Station** | Four Preps |
| 8/31/68 | **Down Here On The Ground** | Lou Rawls |
| 7/3/65 | **Down In The Boondocks** | Billy Joe Royal |
| 5/26/62 | **Down In The Valley** | Solomon Burke |
| 8/31/68 | **Down On Me** | Big Brother & The Holding Company |
| 10/25/69 | **Down On The Corner** | Creedence Clearwater Revival |
| 5/23/60 | **Down The Aisle** | Ike Clanton |
| 9/14/63 | **Down The Aisle (Wedding Song)** | Patti LaBelle & The Blue Belles |
| 7/11/60 | **Down The Street To 301** | Johnny Cash |
| 5/30/60 | **Down Yonder** | Johnny & The Hurricanes |
|  | **Downtown** |  |
| 12/19/64 |  | Petula Clark |
| 3/27/65 |  | Allan Sherman (Crazy Downtown) |
| 4/30/66 |  | Mrs. Miller |
|  | **Dr.**..see: Doctor |  |
| 12/7/63 | **Drag City** | Jan & Dean |
|  | **Dream** |  |
| 6/26/61 |  | Etta James |
| 5/12/62 |  | Dinah Washington |
| 7/6/68 | **Dream A Little Dream Of Me** | Mama Cass |
| 2/17/62 | **Dream Baby (How Long Must I Dream)** | Roy Orbison |
| 2/20/61 | **Dream Boy** | Annette |
| 6/13/64 | **Dream Lover** | Paris Sisters |
|  | **Dream Merchant**..see: Mr. Dream Merchant |  |
| 4/10/65 | **Dream On Little Dreamer** | Perry Como |
|  | **Dreamboat**..see: (He's My) |  |
| 7/27/63 | **Dreamer, The** | Neil Sedaka |
| 7/25/60 | **Dreamin'** | Johnny Burnette |
|  | **Dreams Of The Everyday Housewife** |  |
| 6/29/68 |  | Wayne Newton |
| 7/6/68 |  | Glen Campbell |
| 12/4/65 | **Dreamy Eyes** | Johnny Tillotson |
| 3/9/68 | **Driftin' Blues** | Bobby Bland |
| 12/18/65 | **Drinking Man's Diet** | Allan Sherman |
| 11/6/65 | **Drip Drop** | Dion |
| 7/16/66 | **Drive My Car** | Bob Kuban |
| 7/17/61 | **Drivin' Home** | Duane Eddy |
| 5/22/61 | **Driving Wheel** | Little Junior Parker |
| 1/6/62 | **Drown In My Own Tears** | Don Shirley |
| 8/10/63 | **Drownin' My Sorrows** | Connie Francis |
| 5/26/62 | **Drum Stomp** | Sandy Nelson |
| 9/20/69 | **Drummer Man** | Nancy Sinatra |
| 4/28/62 | **Drummin' Up A Storm** | Sandy Nelson |
| 8/19/67 | **Drums** | Jon & Robin |
| 2/10/62 | **Drums Are My Beat** | Sandy Nelson |
| 2/25/67 | **Dry Your Eyes** | Brenda & The Tabulations |
| 3/10/62 | **Duchess Of Earl** | Pearlettes |
| 11/20/65 | **Duck, The** | Jackie Lee |
| 1/13/62 | **Duke Of Earl** | Gene Chandler |
|  | **Dum-De-Da**..see: She Understands Me |  |
| 6/19/61 | **Dum Dum** | Brenda Lee |
| 8/3/63 | **Dum Dum Dee Dum** | Johnny Cymbal |
| 11/16/63 | **Dumb Head** | Ginny Arnell |
| 1/23/65 | **Dusty** | Rag Dolls |
| 4/25/60 | **Dutchman's Gold** | Walter Brennan/Billy Vaughn |
| 8/2/69 | **Dynamite Woman** | Sir Douglas Quintet |

# E

| Date | Title | Artist |
|---|---|---|
| 3/13/61 | **Early Every Morning (Early Every Evening Too)** | Dinah Washington |
| 11/22/69 | **Early In The Morning** | Vanity Fare |
| 10/9/65 | **Early Morning Rain** | Peter, Paul & Mary |
|  | **Earth Angel** |  |
| 4/11/60 |  | Johnny Tillotson |
| 4/19/69 |  | Vogues |
| 7/26/69 | **Ease Back** | Meters |
| 6/8/63 | **Easier Said Than Done** | Essex |
| 12/3/66 | **East West** | Herman's Hermits |
| 4/25/60 | **Easy Lovin'** | Wade Flemons |
|  | **Easy Question**..see: (Such An) |  |
|  | **Easy Rider**..see: Ballad Of |  |
| 8/9/69 | **Easy To Be Hard** | Three Dog Night |
|  | **Ebb Tide** |  |
| 5/16/60 |  | Platters |
| 3/21/64 |  | Lenny Welch |
| 12/4/65 |  | Righteous Brothers |
| 1/30/61 | **Ebony Eyes** | Everly Brothers |
| 12/1/62 | **Echo** | Emotions |
| 9/27/69 | **Echo Park** | Keith Barbour |
| 2/3/62 | **Ecstasy** | Ben E. King |
| 11/26/66 | **Eggplant That Ate Chicago** | Dr. West's Medicine Show & Junk Band |
| 8/24/63 | **8 X 10** | Bill Anderson |
| 2/20/65 | **Eight Days A Week** | Beatles |
| 5/13/67 | **Eight Men, Four Women** | O.V. Wright |
| 4/9/66 | **Eight Miles High** | Byrds |
| 5/11/63 | **18 Yellow Roses** | Bobby Darin |
| 11/21/64 | **81, The** | Candy & The Kisses |
|  | **Ein Schiff Wird Kommen**..see: Never On Sunday |  |
| 2/22/60 | **El Matador** | Kingston Trio |
| 1/4/60* | **El Paso** | Marty Robbins |

| Date | Title | Artist |
|---|---|---|
| 3/6/65 | **El Pussy Cat** | Mongo Santamaria |
| 4/27/63 | **El Watusi** | Ray Barretto |
| | (also see: Wah Watusi & Watusi) | |
| | **Eleanor Rigby** | |
| 8/27/66 | | Beatles |
| 6/8/68 | | Ray Charles |
| 11/8/69 | | Aretha Franklin |
| 12/28/68 | **Electric Stories** | 4 Seasons |
| | **Electric Surfboard**..see: Theme From | |
| 9/21/68 | **Elenore** | Turtles |
| | **Elephant Walk**..see: (Native Girl) | |
| 10/25/69 | **Eli's Coming** | Three Dog Night |
| 12/28/68 | **Eloise** | Barry Ryan |
| 1/22/66 | **Elusive Butterfly** | Bob Lind |
| 4/30/66 | **Elvira** | Dallas Frazier |
| 12/31/60 | **Emotions** | Brenda Lee |
| 9/14/63 | **Enamorado** | Keith Colley |
| 2/10/68 | **End Of Our Road** | |
| | | Gladys Knight & The Pips |
| 1/26/63 | **End Of The World** | Skeeter Davis |
| 12/5/64 | **Endless Sleep** | Hank Williams, Jr. |
| 5/8/65 | **Engine Engine #9** | Roger Miller |
| 11/6/65 | **England Swings** | Roger Miller |
| 3/27/65 | **Entertainer, The** | Tony Clarke |
| 2/11/67 | **Epistle To Dippy** | Donovan |
| 11/3/62 | **Eso Beso (That Kiss!)** | Paul Anka |
| | **Eternally** | |
| 2/8/60 | | Sarah Vaughan |
| 3/23/63 | | Chantels |
| | (also see: Limelight) | |
| 10/4/69 | **Eternity** | Vikki Carr |
| 8/21/65 | **Eve Of Destruction** | Barry McGuire |
| 9/30/67 | **Even The Bad Times Are Good** | |
| | | Tremeloes |
| 7/3/61 | **Eventually** | Brenda Lee |
| 10/10/60 | **Everglades** | Kingston Trio |
| 9/30/67 | **Everlasting Love** | Robert Knight |
| 10/2/61 | **Everlovin'** | Rick Nelson |
| | **Every**..also see: Ev'ry | |
| | **Every Beat Of My Heart** | |
| 5/15/61 | | Pips |
| 5/15/61 | | Gladys Knight & The Pips |
| 2/9/63 | | James Brown |
| 8/7/61 | **Every Breath I Take** | Gene Pitney |
| | **Every Day**..also see: Everyday | |
| 10/22/66 | **Every Day And Every Night** | Trolls |
| 2/11/67 | **Every Day I Have The Blues** | |
| | | Billy Stewart |
| | **Every Day I Have To Cry Some** | |
| 1/5/63 | | Steve Alaimo |
| 5/14/66 | | Gentrys |
| 5/2/64 | **Every Little Bit Hurts** | Brenda Holloway |
| | **Every Little Move You Make**..see: (I'm Watching) | |
| 4/10/65 | **Every Night, Every Day** | |
| | | Jimmy McCracklin |
| 8/25/62 | **Every Night (Without You)** | Paul Anka |
| 5/25/63 | **Every Step Of The Way** | Johnny Mathis |
| 10/12/63 | **Everybody** | Tommy Roe |
| 11/27/65 | **Everybody Do The Sloopy** | |
| | | Johnny Thunder |
| 9/28/63 | **Everybody Go Home** | Eydie Gorme |
| 11/2/68 | **Everybody Got To Believe In Somebody** | Sam & Dave |
| 5/30/64 | **Everybody Knows** | Steve Lawrence |
| 12/16/67 | **Everybody Knows** | Dave Clark Five |
| 10/3/64 | **Everybody Knows (I Still Love You)** | |
| | | Dave Clark Five |
| 7/26/69 | **Everybody Knows Matilda** | |
| | | Duke Baxter |
| 9/25/65 | **Everybody Loves A Clown** | |
| | | Gary Lewis & The Playboys |
| 12/1/62 | **Everybody Loves A Lover** | Shirelles |
| 7/2/66 | **Everybody Loves A Nut** | Johnny Cash |
| 4/15/67 | **Everybody Loves A Winner** | |
| | | William Bell |
| 4/14/62 | **Everybody Loves Me But You** | |
| | | Brenda Lee |
| 6/27/64 | **Everybody Loves Somebody** | |
| | | Dean Martin |
| 8/3/63 | **Everybody Monkey** | Freddy Cannon |
| 7/8/67 | **Everybody Needs Love** | |
| | | Gladys Knight & The Pips |
| | **Everybody Needs Somebody To Love** | |
| 7/18/64 | | Solomon Burke |
| 2/4/67 | | Wilson Pickett |
| 12/25/61 | **Everybody's Cryin'** | Jimmie Beaumont |
| 10/23/61 | **Everybody's Gotta Pay Some Dues** | |
| | | Miracles |
| 5/9/60 | **Everybody's Somebody's Fool** | |
| | | Connie Francis |
| 8/16/69 | **Everybody's Talkin'** | Nilsson |
| 4/7/62 | **Everybody's Twistin'** | Frank Sinatra |
| 11/30/68 | **Everyday People** | |
| | | Sly & The Family Stone |
| 5/3/69 | **Everyday With You Girl** | Classics IV |
| 9/25/65 | **Everyone's Gone To The Moon** | |
| | | Jonathan King |
| 6/28/69 | **Everything I Do Gohn Be Funky (From Now On)** | Lee Dorsey |
| 2/3/68 | **Everything That Touches You** | |
| | | Association |
| 10/24/64 | **Everything's Alright** | Newbeats |
| 10/25/69 | **Evil Woman Don't Play Your Games With Me** | Crow |
| 4/16/66 | **Evol-Not Love** | Five Americans |
| | **Ev'ry Little Bit Hurts**..see: (There'll Come A Day When) | |
| 5/16/60 | **Exclusively Yours** | Carl Dobkins, Jr. |
| | **Exodus** | |
| 11/14/60 | | Ferrante & Teicher |
| 11/21/60 | | Mantovani |
| 1/23/61 | | Pat Boone |
| 4/10/61 | | Eddie Harris |
| 1/13/68 | **Expecting To Fly** | Buffalo Springfield |
| 12/23/67 | **Explosion In Your Soul** | Soul Survivors |
| 9/2/67 | **Expressway To Your Heart** | |
| | | Soul Survivors |
| 6/22/68 | **Eyes Of A New York Woman** | |
| | | B.J. Thomas |

# F

| Date | Title | Artist |
|---|---|---|
| 10/1/66 | **Fa-Fa-Fa-Fa-Fa (Sad Song)** | |
| | | Otis Redding |
| 5/11/68 | **Face It Girl, It's Over** | Nancy Wilson |
| | **Faded Love** | |
| 2/23/63 | | Jackie de Shannon |
| 8/31/63 | | Patsy Cline |
| 7/29/67 | **Fakin' It** | Simon & Garfunkel |
| 9/23/67 | **Fall In Love With Me** | Bettye Swann |
| 11/21/60 | **Fallen Angel** | Webb Pierce |
| 6/8/63 | **Falling** | Roy Orbison |
| 4/11/60 | **Fame And Fortune** | Elvis Presley |
| 11/22/69 | **Fancy** | Bobbie Gentry |
| 1/16/65 | **Fancy Pants** | Al Hirt |
| 2/1/60 | **Fannie Mae** | Buster Brown |
| 8/1/60 | **Far, Far Away** | Don Gibson |
| 9/25/61 | **Faraway Star** | Chordettes |
| 8/9/69 | **Farewell Love Scene** | |
| | | Romeo & Juliet Soundtrack |
| 6/20/64 | **Farmer John** | Premiers |
| 11/3/62 | **Father Knows Best** | Radiants |
| 3/16/68 | **Father Of Girls** | Perry Como |
| 8/8/64 | **Father Sebastian** | Ramblers |
| | **Feel It** | |
| 9/25/61 | | Sam Cooke |
| 2/19/66 | | Sam Cooke |
| | **Feel So Bad**..see: I Feel So Bad | |
| | **Feel So Fine (Good)** | |
| 6/20/60 | | Johnny Preston |
| 6/24/67 | | Bunny Sigler (medley) |
| | **Feelin' Groovy**..see: 59th Street Bridge | |
| 12/28/68 | **Feelin' So Good (S.k.o.o.b.y-D.o.o)** | |
| | | Archies |
| | **Feeling Alright** | |
| 6/21/69 | | Joe Cocker |
| 11/29/69 | | Mongo Santamaria |
| 12/28/63 | **Feeling Is Gone** | Bobby Bland |
| 6/21/69 | **Feeling Is Right** | Clarence Carter |
| 11/18/67 | **Felicidad** | Sally Field |
| 3/20/61 | **Fell In Love On Monday** | Fats Domino |
| 2/6/65 | **Ferris Wheel** | Everly Brothers |
| 2/6/65 | **Ferry Across The Mersey** | |
| | | Gerry & The Pacemakers |
| 11/13/65 | **Fever** | McCoys |
| 9/3/66 | **Fiddle Around** | Jan & Dean |
| 12/5/64 | **Fiddler On The Roof** | Village Stompers |
| 11/17/62 | **Fiesta** | Dave "Baby" Cortez |
| 9/3/66 | **Fife Piper** | Dynatones |
| 2/18/67 | **59th Street Bridge Song (Feelin' Groovy)** | Harpers Bizarre |
| 3/6/61 | **Find Another Girl** | Jerry Butler |
| 3/13/65 | **Find My Way Back Home** | |
| | | Nashville Teens |
| 1/9/65 | **Finders Keepers, Losers Weepers** | |
| | | Nella Dodds |
| 10/19/63 | **Fine Fine Boy** | Darlene Love |
| 5/16/60 | **Finger Poppin' Time** | Hank Ballard |
| 6/22/63 | **Fingertips** | Little Stevie Wonder |
| 9/7/68 | **Fire** | Crazy World Of Arthur Brown |
| 11/2/68 | **Fire** | Five By Five |
| 10/5/63 | **First Day Back At School** | Paul & Paula |
| 7/26/69 | **First Hymn From Grand Terrace** | |
| | | Mark Lindsay |
| 8/14/65 | **First I Look At The Purse** | Contours |
| 1/4/60* | **First Name Initial** | Annette |
| 5/30/64 | **First Night Of The Full Moon** | |
| | | Jack Jones |
| 3/22/69 | **First Of May** | Bee Gees |
| 6/1/63 | **First Quarrel** | Paul & Paula |
| 12/31/60 | **First Taste Of Love** | Ben E. King |
| 6/26/65 | **First Thing Ev'ry Morning (And The Last Thing Ev'ry Night)** | Jimmy Dean |
| 7/3/61 | **Fish, The** | Bobby Rydell |
| 9/12/60 | **Five Brothers** | Marty Robbins |
| 7/16/66 | **5 D (Fifth Dimension)** | Byrds |
| 10/5/63 | **500 Miles Away From Home** | |
| | | Bobby Bare |
| 11/27/65 | **Five O'Clock World** | Vogues |
| 4/17/61 | **Flaming Star** | Elvis Presley |
| 9/3/66 | **Flamingo** | Herb Alpert |
| 1/16/61 | **Flamingo Express** | Royaltones |
| 6/19/61 | **Float, The** | Hank Ballard |
| 11/13/65 | **Flowers On The Wall** | Statler Brothers |
| 9/25/61 | **Fly, The** | Chubby Checker |
| 11/6/61 | **Fly By Night** | Andy Williams |
| | **Fly Me To The Moon** | |
| 12/29/62 | | Joe Harnell (Bossa Nova) |
| 2/13/65 | | LaVern Baker |
| 7/24/65 | | Tony Bennett |
| 1/29/66 | | Sam & Bill |
| 8/17/68 | | Bobby Womack |
| 12/11/61 | **Flying Circle** | Frank Slay |
| | **Foggy Mountain Breakdown**..see: Ballad Of Bonnie & Clyde | |
| 5/4/63 | **Folk Singer** | Tommy Roe |
| 7/3/65 | **Follow Me** | Drifters |
| 3/19/66 | **Follow Me** | Lyme & Cybelle |
| 5/12/62 | **Follow That Dream** | Elvis Presley |
| 3/2/63 | **Follow The Boys** | Connie Francis |
| 1/1/66 | **Follow Your Heart** | Manhattans |
| 5/25/68 | **Folsom Prison Blues** | Johnny Cash |
| 9/7/68 | **Fool For You** | Impressions |
| | (also see: I'm Just A) | |
| 8/29/60 | **Fool In Love** | Ike & Tina Turner |
| 1/11/64 | **Fool Never Learns** | Andy Williams |
| 10/2/61 | **Fool #1** | Brenda Lee |
| 8/10/68 | **Fool On The Hill** | |
| | | Sergio Mendes & Brasil '66 |
| 6/12/61 | **Fool That I Am** | Etta James |
| 3/20/61 | **Foolin' Around** | Kay Starr |
| 3/22/69 | **Foolish Fool** | Dee Dee Warwick |
| 3/23/63 | **Foolish Little Girl** | Shirelles |
| | **Fools Rush In** | |
| 11/14/60 | | Brook Benton |
| 10/13/62 | | Etta James |
| 9/14/63 | | Rick Nelson |
| 9/4/61 | **Foot Stomping** | Flares |
| 3/7/60 | **Footsteps** | Steve Lawrence |
| 8/25/62 | **For All We Know** | Dinah Washington |
| 3/18/67 | **For He's A Jolly Good Fellow** | |
| | | Bobby Vinton |
| 5/2/60 | **For Love** | Lloyd Price |
| 1/23/65 | **For Lovin' Me** | Peter, Paul & Mary |
| | **For Mama** | |
| 3/6/65 | | Connie Francis |
| 3/6/65 | | Jerry Vale |
| 4/1/67 | **For Me** | Sergio Mendes & Brasil '66 |
| 10/16/61 | **For Me And My Gal** | Freddy Cannon |
| 2/6/61 | **For My Baby** | Brook Benton |
| | **For Once In My Life** | |
| 10/28/67 | | Tony Bennett |
| 11/2/68 | | Jackie Wilson |
| 11/2/68 | | Stevie Wonder |
| 9/4/61 | **For Sentimental Reasons** | Cleftones |
| | **For The Love Of Ivy** | |
| 9/14/68 | | Mamas & The Papas |
| | **For What It's Worth** | |
| 1/28/67 | | Buffalo Springfield |
| 9/23/67 | | Staple Singers |
| 11/25/67 | | King Curtis |
| 12/28/63 | **For You** | Rick Nelson |

| Date | Title / Artist |
|---|---|
| 11/27/65 | **For You** *Spellbinders* |
| | **For Your Love** |
| 5/15/61 | *Wanderers* |
| 9/18/65 | *Sam & Bill* |
| 6/24/67 | *Peaches & Herb* |
| 5/15/65 | **For Your Love** *Yardbirds* |
| | **For Your Precious Love** |
| 11/23/64 | *Garnet Mimms & The Enchanters* |
| 3/26/66 | *Jerry Butler* |
| 5/27/67 | *Oscar Toney, Jr.* |
| 2/17/68 | *Jackie Wilson & Count Basie* |
| 12/28/63 | **For Your Sweet Love** *Cascades* |
| | **Forever** |
| 1/25/60 | *Little Dippers* |
| 2/15/60 | *Billy Walker* |
| 3/7/64 | *Pete Drake* |
| 6/28/69 | *Mercy* |
| 5/4/63 | **Forever** *Marvelettes* |
| 9/22/62 | **Forever And A Day** *Jackie Wilson* |
| 3/16/68 | **Forever Came Today** *Supremes* |
| | **Forget Domani** |
| 6/26/65 | *Connie Francis* |
| 6/26/65 | *Frank Sinatra* |
| 11/9/63 | **Forget Him** *Bobby Rydell* |
| 9/9/67 | **Forget It** *Sandpebbles* |
| 6/15/68 | **Forget Me Not** *Martha & The Vandellas* |
| 11/29/69 | **Forget To Remember** *Frank Sinatra* |
| 10/16/65 | **Forgive Me** *Al Martino* |
| 11/1/69 | **Fortunate Son** |
| | *Creedence Clearwater Revival* |
| 12/31/66 | **Fortune Teller** *Hardtimes* |
| 5/5/62 | **Fortuneteller** *Bobby Curtola* |
| 5/23/60 | **Found Love** *Jimmy Reed* |
| | **4-By The Beatles [E.P.]** |
| 6/13/64 | *Beatles* |
| 2/27/65 | *Beatles* |
| | **Four Little Heels**..see: (Clickity Clack Song) |
| 10/31/64 | **Four Strong Winds** *Bobby Bare* |
| 10/27/62 | **Four Walls** *Kay Starr* |
| 10/13/62 | **409** *Beach Boys* |
| 1/18/64 | **442 Glenwood Avenue** *Pixies Three* |
| 10/26/68 | **1432 Franklin Pike Circle Hero** |
| | *Bobby Russell* |
| 1/18/69 | **Fox On The Run** *Manfred Mann* |
| 12/23/67 | **Foxey Lady** *Jimi Hendrix* |
| | **Francis Powers, Ballad Of**..see: There's A Star Spangled Banner Waving |
| | **Frankie And Johnny** |
| 8/21/61 | *Brook Benton* |
| 7/27/63 | *Sam Cooke* |
| 8/1/64 | *Greenwood County Singers* |
| 3/19/66 | *Elvis Presley* |
| | **Freddie**..also see: Do The & Let's Do The |
| 7/16/66 | **Freddie Feelgood (and His Funky Little Five Piece Band)** *Ray Stevens* |
| 10/15/66 | **Free Again** *Barbra Streisand* |
| 12/25/61 | **Free Me** *Johnny Preston* |
| 5/16/64 | **French Song** *Lucille Starr* |
| 3/18/67 | **Friday On My Mind** *Easybeats* |
| 7/9/66 | **Friday's Child** *Nancy Sinatra* |
| 5/10/69 | **Friend, Lover, Woman, Wife** |
| | *O.C. Smith* |
| | **Friendly World**..see: This Friendly World |
| 4/20/68 | **Friends** *Beach Boys* |
| 10/25/69 | **Friendship Train** |
| | *Gladys Knight & The Pips* |
| 4/10/61 | **Frogg** *Brothers Four* |
| 12/29/62 | **From A Jack To A King** *Ned Miller* |
| | **From A Window** |
| 8/22/64 | *Billy J. Kramer* |
| 7/10/65 | *Chad & Jeremy* |
| | **From All Over The World**..see: (Here They Come) |
| | **From Both Sides Now**..see: Both Sides Now |
| | **From Me To You** |
| 6/29/63 | *Del Shannon* |
| 3/7/64 | *Beatles* |
| 4/25/64 | **From Russia With Love** |
| | *Village Stompers* |
| 12/1/62 | **From The Bottom Of My Heart (Dammi, Dammi, Dammi)** *Dean Martin* |
| 6/5/65 | **From The Bottom Of My Heart (I Love You)** *Moody Blues* |
| 10/19/68 | **From The Teacher To The Preacher** *Gene Chandler & Barbara Acklin* |

| Date | Title / Artist |
|---|---|
| 1/7/67 | **Full Measure** *Lovin' Spoonful* |
| 2/15/64 | **Fun, Fun, Fun** *Beach Boys* |
| 9/24/66 | **Function At The Junction** *Shorty Long* |
| | **Funky Broadway** |
| 4/15/67 | *Dyke & The Blazers* |
| 8/5/67 | *Wilson Pickett* |
| 9/23/67 | **Funky Donkey** *Pretty Purdie* |
| 6/1/68 | **Funky Fever** *Clarence Carter* |
| 8/24/68 | **Funky Judge** *Bull & The Matadors* |
| 3/2/68 | **Funky North Philly** *Bill Cosby* |
| 3/16/68 | **Funky Street** *Arthur Conley* |
| 4/13/68 | **Funky Walk** *Dyke & The Blazers* |
| 1/13/68 | **Funky Way** *Calvin Arnold* |
| 3/27/61 | **Funny** *Maxine Brown* |
| 4/21/62 | **Funny** *Gene McDaniels* |
| 5/20/67 | **Funny Familiar Forgotten Feelings** *Tom Jones* |
| 6/14/69 | **Funny Feeling** *Delfonics* |
| 9/12/64 | **Funny Girl** *Barbra Streisand* |
| | **Funny How Time Slips Away** |
| 11/13/61 | *Jimmy Elledge* |
| 10/19/63 | *Johnny Tillotson* |
| 8/15/64 | *Joe Hinton* |
| 9/25/65 | **Funny Little Butterflies** *Patty Duke* |
| 3/30/63 | **Funny Man** *Ray Stevens* |
| 4/7/62 | **Funny Way Of Laughin'** *Burl Ives* |
| 10/13/62 | **Further More** *Ray Stevens* |

## G

| Date | Title / Artist |
|---|---|
| 8/1/64 | **G.T.O.** *Ronny & The Daytonas* |
| 12/24/66 | **Gallant Men** |
| | *Senator Everett McKinley Dirksen* |
| | **Galveston** |
| 3/1/69 | *Glen Campbell* |
| 6/7/69 | *Roger Williams* |
| 3/20/65 | **Game Of Love** |
| | *Wayne Fontana & The Mindbenders* |
| 1/11/69 | **Games People Play** *Joe South* |
| | **Games That Lovers Play** |
| 10/22/66 | *Wayne Newton* |
| 10/29/66 | *Eddie Fisher* |
| 12/27/69 | **Gangs Back Again** *Kool & The Gang* |
| 10/17/64 | **Garden In The Rain** *Vic Dana* |
| 9/26/64 | **Gator Tails And Monkey Ribs** *Spats* |
| | **Gee** |
| 11/14/60 | *Jan & Dean* |
| 4/18/64 | *Pixies Three* |
| 3/6/65 | **Gee Baby (I'm Sorry)** *Three Degrees* |
| 11/21/60 | **Gee Whiz** *Innocents* |
| 1/30/61 | **Gee Whiz (Look At His Eyes)** *Carla Thomas* |
| | **Gentle On My Mind** |
| 7/8/67 | *Glen Campbell* |
| 2/10/68 | *Patti Page* |
| 9/14/68 | *Glen Campbell* |
| 5/10/69 | *Aretha Franklin* |
| | **Georgia On My Mind** |
| 9/26/60 | *Ray Charles* |
| 2/5/66 | *Righteous Brothers* |
| 7/6/68 | *Wes Montgomery* |
| 11/18/67 | **Georgia Pines** *Candymen* |
| 7/23/66 | **Georgia Rose** *Tony Bennett* |
| 5/1/65 | **Georgie Porgie** *Jewel Akens* |
| | **Georgy Girl** |
| 12/3/66 | *Seekers* |
| 4/29/67 | *Baja Marimba Band* |
| 8/20/66 | **Get Away** *Georgie Fame* |
| 1/15/66 | **Get Back** *Roy Head* |
| 5/10/69 | **Get Back** *Beatles* |
| 10/14/67 | **Get Down** *Harvey Scales* |
| 6/22/63 | **Get Him** *Exciters* |
| 11/15/69 | **Get It From The Bottom** *Steelers* |
| 10/28/67 | **Get It Together** *James Brown* |
| 4/1/67 | **Get Me To The World On Time** *Electric Prunes* |
| 8/30/69 | **Get Off My Back Woman** *B.B. King* |
| 10/9/65 | **Get Off Of My Cloud** *Rolling Stones* |
| 8/19/67 | **Get On Up** *Esquires* |
| 1/27/68 | **Get Out Now** |
| | *Tommy James & The Shondells* |
| 1/1/66 | **Get Out Of My Life, Woman** *Lee Dorsey* |
| 2/26/66 | **Get Ready** *Temptations* |
| 11/15/69 | **Get Rhythm** *Johnny Cash* |
| 8/12/67 | **Get The Message** *Brian Hyland* |

| Date | Title / Artist |
|---|---|
| | **Get Together** |
| 11/13/65 | *We Five* |
| 9/2/67 | *Youngbloods* |
| 6/28/69 | *Youngbloods* |
| 8/26/67 | **Gettin' Together** |
| | *Tommy James & The Shondells* |
| 11/28/64 | **Getting Mighty Crowded** *Betty Everett* |
| 11/17/62 | **Getting Ready For The Heartbreak** *Chuck Jackson* |
| 1/18/69 | **Getting The Corners** |
| | *T.S.U. Toronadoes* |
| | **(Ghost) Riders In The Sky** |
| 1/9/61 | *Ramrods* |
| 9/25/61 | *Lawrence Welk* |
| 11/26/66 | *Baja Marimba Band* |
| 1/8/66 | **Giddyup Go** *Red Sovine* |
| 1/16/61 | **Gift Of Love** *Van Dykes* |
| 3/1/69 | **Gimme Gimme Good Lovin'** |
| | *Crazy Elephant* |
| 8/12/67 | **Gimme Little Sign** *Brenton Wood* |
| 12/31/66 | **Gimme Some Lovin'** |
| | *Spencer Davis Group* |
| 9/22/62 | **Gina** *Johnny Mathis* |
| 1/23/61 | **Ginnie Bell** *Paul Dino* |
| 3/10/62 | **Ginny Come Lately** *Brian Hyland* |
| 6/19/65 | **Girl Come Running** *4 Seasons* |
| 2/25/67 | **Girl Don't Care** *Gene Chandler* |
| 3/6/65 | **Girl Don't Come** *Sandie Shaw* |
| 6/6/64 | **Girl From Ipanema** |
| | *Stan Getz/Astrud Gilberto* |
| 9/4/65 | **Girl From Peyton Place** *Dickey Lee* |
| 3/10/62 | **Girl Has To Know** *G-Clefs* |
| 3/25/67 | **Girl I Knew Somewhere** *Monkees* |
| 3/18/67 | **Girl I Need You** *Artistics* |
| 6/14/69 | **Girl I'll Never Know (Angels Never Fly This Low)** *Frankie Valli* |
| 5/14/66 | **Girl In Love** *Outsiders* |
| 9/18/61 | **Girl In My Dreams** *Capris* |
| 7/15/67 | **Girl Like You** *Young Rascals* |
| 12/7/68 | **Girl Most Likely** *Jeannie C. Riley* |
| 4/17/61 | **Girl Of My Best Friend** *Ral Donner* |
| 9/10/66 | **Girl On A Swing** |
| | *Gerry & The Pacemakers* |
| 6/26/65 | **Girl On The Billboard** *Del Reeves* |
| 12/10/66 | **Girl That Stood Beside Me** |
| | *Bobby Darin* |
| 8/17/68 | **Girl Watcher** *O'Kaysions* |
| 9/12/64 | **Girl (Why You Wanna Make Me Blue)** *Temptations* |
| 10/17/60 | **Girl With The Story In Her Eyes** |
| | *Safaris* |
| 6/10/67 | **Girl (You Captivate Me)** |
| | *? & The Mysterians* |
| 4/8/67 | **Girl, You'll Be A Woman Soon** *Neil Diamond* |
| 6/21/69 | **Girl You're Too Young** |
| | *Archie Bell & The Drells* |
| 6/27/64 | **Girls** *Major Lance* |
| 5/15/61 | **Girl's A Devil** *Dukays* |
| 2/11/67 | **Girls Are Out To Get You** *Fascinations* |
| 8/3/68 | **Girls Can't Do What The Guys Do** *Betty Wright* |
| 8/14/61 | **Girls Girls Girls** *Coasters* |
| 6/23/62 | **(Girls, Girls, Girls) Made To Love** *Eddie Hodges* |
| 11/30/63 | **Girls Grow Up Faster Than Boys** *Cookies* |
| 5/13/67 | **Girls In Love** |
| | *Gary Lewis & The Playboys* |
| 11/8/69 | **Girls It Ain't Easy** *Honey Cone* |
| 4/5/69 | **Gitarzan** *Ray Stevens* |
| 8/3/68 | **Give A Damn** *Spanky & Our Gang* |
| 8/14/65 | **Give All Your Love To Me** |
| | *Gerry & The Pacemakers* |
| 10/14/67 | **Give Everybody Some** *Bar-Kays* |
| 12/26/64 | **Give Him A Great Big Kiss** |
| | *Shangri-Las* |
| 3/1/69 | **Give It Away** *Chi-Lites* |
| 1/25/69 | **Give It Up Or Turnit A Loose** |
| | *James Brown* |
| | **Give Me**..also see: Gimme |
| 7/20/68 | **Give Me One More Chance** |
| | *Wilmer & The Dukes* |
| 7/1/67 | **Give Me Time** *Dusty Springfield* |
| 1/20/68 | **Give My Love A Try** *Linda Jones* |
| 7/26/69 | **Give Peace A Chance** |
| | *Plastic Ono Band* |

**Give Us Your Blessings**
6/1/63 Ray Peterson
5/29/65 Shangri-Las
5/9/64 **Giving Up** Gladys Knight & The Pips
4/4/64 **Giving Up On Love** Jerry Butler
2/15/64 **Glad All Over** Dave Clark Five
2/8/69 **Glad She's A Woman** Bobby Goldsboro
10/28/67 **Glad To Be Unhappy**
Mamas & The Papas
**Gloria**
5/22/65 Them
3/19/66 Shadows Of Knight
11/21/60 **Gloria's Theme** Adam Wade
**Glory Of Love**
4/10/61 Roommates
8/11/62 Don Gardner & Dee Dee Ford
7/29/67 Otis Redding
8/6/66 **Go Ahead And Cry** Righteous Brothers
12/11/65 **Go Away From My World**
Marianne Faithfull
**Go Away Little Girl**
11/10/62 Steve Lawrence
10/1/66 Happenings
10/21/67 **Go-Go Girl** Lee Dorsey
1/4/60* **Go, Jimmy, Go** Jimmy Clanton
2/20/65 **Go Now!** Moody Blues
12/25/61 **Go On Home** Patti Page
1/14/67 **Go Where You Wanna Go**
5th Dimension
10/14/67 **Go With Me** Gene & Debbe
1/4/60* **God Bless America** Connie Francis
7/20/68 **God Bless Our Love** Ballads
10/16/61 **God, Country And My Baby**
Johnny Burnette
3/15/69 **God Knows I Love You** Nancy Sinatra
8/13/66 **God Only Knows** Beach Boys
4/13/68 **Goin' Away** Fireballs
11/18/67 **Goin' Back** Byrds
**Goin' Out Of My Head**
11/7/64 Little Anthony & The Imperials
12/9/67 Lettermen (medley)
11/29/69 Frank Sinatra
2/29/64 **Going Back To Louisiana**
Bruce Channel
1/25/64 **Going Going Gone** Brook Benton
8/16/69 **Going In Circles** Friends Of Distinction
12/17/66 **Going Nowhere** Los Bravos
12/25/65 **Going To A Go-Go** Miracles
12/7/68 **Going Up The Country** Canned Heat
10/26/68 **Golden Gate Park** Rejoice!
**Goldfinger**
1/23/65 Billy Strange
1/30/65 Shirley Bassey
1/30/65 Jack Laforge
3/13/65 John Barry
8/17/63 **Gone** Rip Chords
10/17/64 **Gone, Gone, Gone** Everly Brothers
3/23/63 **Gone With The Wind** Duprees
(Gong-Gong Song)..see: I'm Blue
**Gonna' Get Along Without You Now**
4/25/64 Tracey Dey
5/2/64 Skeeter Davis
2/18/67 Trini Lopez
3/18/67 **Gonna Give Her All The Love I've Got** Jimmy Ruffin
12/1/62 **Gonna Raise A Rukus Tonight**
Jimmy Dean
**Gonna Send You Back To Georgia**
1/25/64 Timmy Shaw
9/12/64 Animals (Walker)
11/7/60 **Gonzo** James Booker
8/2/69 **Goo Goo Barabajagal (Love Is Hot)**
Donovan
9/20/69 **Good Clean Fun** Monkees
12/16/67 **Good Combination** Sonny & Cher
8/5/67 **Good Day Sunshine** Claudine Longet
**Good Golly Miss Molly**
5/9/64 Swinging Blue Jeans
10/8/66 Mitch Ryder & The Detroit Wheels (medley)
4/17/61 **Good, Good Lovin'** Chubby Checker
5/11/63 **Good Life** Tony Bennett
6/23/62 **Good Lover** Jimmy Reed
**Good Lovin'**
5/1/65 Olympics
3/12/66 Young Rascals
2/1/69 **Good Lovin' Ain't Easy To Come By**
Marvin Gaye & Tammi Terrell
3/17/62 **Good Luck Charm** Elvis Presley

**Good Morning Starshine**
5/24/69 Oliver
5/24/69 Strawberry Alarm Clock
1/25/64 **Good News** Sam Cooke
9/12/64 **Good Night Baby** Butterflys
6/28/69 **Good Old Rock 'N Roll (medley)**
Cat Mother & the All Night News Boys
2/17/68 **Good, The Bad And The Ugly**
Hugo Montenegro
12/3/66 **Good Thing** Paul Revere & The Raiders
1/23/61 **Good Time Baby** Bobby Rydell
5/21/66 **Good Time Charlie** Bobby Bland
11/30/68 **Good Time Girl** Nancy Sinatra
12/25/65 **Good Time Music** Beau Brummels
6/13/64 **Good Time Tonight** Soul Sisters
6/6/64 **Good Times** Sam Cooke
3/6/65 **Good Times** Jerry Butler
8/21/65 **Good Times** Gene Chandler
3/29/69 **Good Times Bad Times** Led Zeppelin
4/18/60 **Good Timin'** Jimmy Jones
10/22/66 **Good Vibrations** Beach Boys
4/19/69 **Goodbye** Mary Hopkin
**Goodbye Again**..see: Theme From
4/18/64 **Goodbye Baby (Baby Goodbye)**
Solomon Burke
4/6/68 **Goodbye Baby (I Don't Want To See You Cry)** Tommy Boyce & Bobby Hart
3/15/69 **Goodbye Columbus** Association
10/16/61 **Goodbye Cruel World** James Darren
7/21/62 **Goodbye Dad** Castle Sisters
11/9/68 **Goodbye My Love** James Brown
4/3/65 **Goodbye My Lover Goodbye**
Searchers
2/13/65 **Goodnight** Roy Orbison
(also see: Good Night)
6/30/62 **Goodnight, Irene** Jerry Reed
**Goodnight My Love**
6/1/63 Fleetwoods
1/8/66 Ben E. King
1/4/69 Paul Anka
12/10/66 **Goodnight My Love** Happenings
10/26/68 **Goody Goody Gumdrops**
1910 Fruitgum Co.
4/18/60 **Got A Girl** Four Preps
4/2/66 **Got My Mojo Working** Jimmy Smith
3/6/65 **Got To Get You Off My Mind**
Solomon Burke
5/6/67 **Got To Have You Back** Isley Brothers
2/10/68 **Got What You Need**
Fantastic Johnny C
5/4/63 **Got You On My Mind**
Cookie & His Cupcakes
6/14/69 **Gotta Get To Know You** Bobby Bland
5/1/65 **Gotta Have Your Love** Sapphires
11/16/63 **Gotta Lotta Love** Steve Alaimo
10/12/63 **Gotta Travel On** Timi Yuro
**Graduation Day**
6/22/63 Bobby Pickett
6/17/67 Arbors
6/26/61 **Graduation Song...Pomp And Circumstance** Adrian Kimberly
7/3/61 **Granada** Frank Sinatra
9/28/63 **Grass Is Greener** Brenda Lee
6/16/62 **Gravy (For My Mashed Potatoes)**
Dee Dee Sharp
4/27/63 **Gravy Waltz** Steve Allen
**Grazing In The Grass**
6/8/68 Hugh Masekela
4/5/69 Friends Of Distinction
4/20/68 **Greasy Heart** Jefferson Airplane
10/1/66 **Great Airplane Strike**
Paul Revere & The Raiders
2/8/69 **Great Balls Of Fire** Tiny Tim
**Great Imposter**..see: (He's) The & Theme From The
1/13/62 **Greatest Hurt** Jackie Wilson
1/25/69 **Greatest Love** Dorsey Burnette
**Green Berets**..see: Ballad Of
**Green Fields**..see: Greenfields
5/14/66 **Green Grass**
Gary Lewis & The Playboys
3/27/61 **Green Grass Of Texas** Texans
6/29/63 **Green, Green** New Christy Minstrels
12/24/66 **Green, Green Grass Of Home**
Tom Jones
**Green Leaves Of Summer**
10/31/60 Brothers Four
6/2/62 Kenny Ball

2/24/68 **Green Light** American Breed
8/11/62 **Green Onions** Booker T. & The MG's
8/2/69 **Green River**
Creedence Clearwater Revival
12/16/67 **Green Tambourine** Lemon Pipers
1/26/63 **Greenback Dollar** Kingston Trio
**Greenfields**
2/22/60 Brothers Four
8/23/69 Vogues
4/26/69 **Greensleeves** Mason Williams
(also see: Stay Away)
**Greetings (This Is Uncle Sam)**
11/20/61 Valadiers
4/16/66 Monitors
6/18/66 **Grim Reaper Of Love** Turtles
2/1/69 **Grits Ain't Groceries (All Around The World)** Little Milton
12/17/66 **Grizzly Bear** Youngbloods
1/18/69 **Grooviest Girl In The World**
Fun & Games
**Groovin'**
4/22/67 Rascals
8/5/67 Booker T. & The M.G.'s
12/20/69 **Groovin' (Out On Life)** Newbeats
7/20/63 **Groovy Baby** Billy Abbott
10/11/69 **Groovy Grubworm** Harlow Wilcox
4/16/66 **Groovy Kind Of Love** Mindbenders
6/24/67 **Groovy Summertime** Love Generation
12/5/60 **Groovy Tonight** Bobby Rydell
4/10/61 **Ground Hog** Browns
2/17/62 **Grow Closer Together** Impressions
7/30/66 **Guantanamera** Sandpipers
12/27/69 **Guess Who** Ruby Winters
6/29/63 **Guilty** Jim Reeves
10/9/61 **Guilty Of Loving You** Jerry Fuller
3/24/62 **Guitar Boogie Shuffle Twist** Virtues
1/27/68 **Guitar Man** Elvis Presley
(also see: Dance With The)
7/3/61 **Guns Of Navarone** Joe Peisman
1/5/63 **Gypsy Cried** Lou Christie
11/6/61 **Gypsy Rover** Highwaymen
10/16/61 **Gypsy Woman** Impressions
5/18/63 **Gypsy Woman** Rick Nelson

# H

8/5/67 **Ha Ha Said The Clown** Yardbirds
10/13/62 **Hail To The Conquering Hero**
James Darren
3/15/69 **Hair** Cowsills
10/1/66 **Hair On My Chinny Chin Chin**
Sam The Sham & The Pharoahs
12/15/62 **Half Heaven - Half Heartache**
Gene Pitney
**Halfway To Paradise**
5/1/61 Tony Orlando
7/20/68 Bobby Vinton
3/8/69 **Hallways Of My Mind** Dells
3/28/64 **Hand It Over** Chuck Jackson
6/18/66 **Hand Jive** Strangeloves
**Handy Man**
1/4/60* Jimmy Jones
7/4/64 Del Shannon
**Hang 'Em High**
6/29/68 Hugo Montenegro
11/9/68 Booker T. & The MGs
10/2/61 **Hang On** Floyd Cramer
**Hang On Sloopy**
3/28/64 Vibrations (My Girl)
8/14/65 Little Caesar & The Consuls (My Girl)
8/14/65 McCoys
11/20/65 Ramsey Lewis Trio
**Hangin' On**..see: (You Keep Me)
6/4/66 **Hanky Panky**
Tommy James & The Shondells
**Happening, The**
4/8/67 Supremes
7/8/67 Herb Alpert
11/26/66 **Happenings Ten Years Time Ago**
Yardbirds
10/1/66 **Happiness** Shades Of Blue
**Happy**
7/15/67 Blades Of Grass
7/15/67 Sunshine Company
7/27/68 **Happy** Nancy Sinatra
11/22/69 **Happy** Paul Anka
7/29/67 **Happy And Me** Don & The Goodtimes
1/4/60* **Happy Anniversary** Jane Morgan

| | | | | | |
|---|---|---|---|---|---|
| 2/20/61 | **Happy Birthday Blues** Kathy Young with The Innocents | | **He Don't Love You (Like I Love You)** | 1/9/65 | **Hello Pretty Girl** Ronnie Dove |
| 11/13/61 | **Happy Birthday, Sweet Sixteen** Neil Sedaka | 10/31/60 | Jerry Butler | 5/4/63 | **Hello Stranger** Barbara Lewis |
| | | 6/4/66 | Righteous Brothers | 4/10/61 | **Hello Walls** Faron Young |
| 12/12/60 | **Happy Days** Marv Johnson | 5/4/68 | **He Don't Really Love You** Delfonics | 8/1/60 | **Hello Young Lovers** Paul Anka |
| 5/2/60 | **Happy-Go-Lucky-Me** Paul Evans | 1/27/62 | **He Knows I Love Him Too Much** Paris Sisters | 8/7/65 | **Help!** Beatles |
| 11/28/64 | **Happy Guy** Rick Nelson | | | 11/19/66 | **Help Me (Get Myself Back Together Again)** Spellbinders |
| | **Happy Heart** | 1/25/64 | **He Says The Same Things To Me** Skeeter Davis | | **Help Me Girl** |
| 4/12/69 | Petula Clark | | | 10/29/66 | Outsiders |
| 4/12/69 | Andy Williams | 10/6/62 | **He Thinks I Still Care** Connie Francis | 11/26/66 | Animals |
| 4/15/67 | **Happy Jack** Who | 10/2/65 | **He Touched Me** Barbra Streisand | 4/17/65 | **Help Me, Rhonda** Beach Boys |
| 1/13/62 | **Happy Jose (Ching, Ching)** Jack Ross | 2/8/64 | **He Walks Like A Man** Jody Miller | 6/27/64 | **Help The Poor** B.B. King |
| 1/18/60 | **Happy Muleteer** Ivo Robic | 1/30/65 | **He Was Really Sayin' Somethin'** Velvelettes | 8/31/68 | **Help Yourself** Tom Jones |
| 1/4/60* | **Happy Reindeer** Dancer, Prancer & Nervous | | **He Will Break Your Heart**...see: **He Don't Love You** | 8/31/68 | **Help Yourself (To All Of My Lovin')** James & Bobby Purify |
| 7/25/60 | **Happy Shades Of Blue** Freddie Cannon | 3/19/66 | **He Wore The Green Beret** Nancy Ames | 3/12/66 | **Helpless** Kim Weston |
| 4/27/68 | **Happy Song (Dum-Dum)** Otis Redding | | | 2/3/62 | **Her Royal Majesty** James Darren |
| 6/18/66 | **Happy Summer Days** Ronnie Dove | | **He'll Have To Go (Stay)** | 12/2/67 | **Here Comes Heaven** Eddy Arnold |
| 11/27/61 | **Happy Times (Are Here To Stay)** Tony Orlando | 1/4/60* | Jim Reeves | 4/8/67 | **Here Comes My Baby** Tremeloes |
| | | 5/2/60 | Jeanne Black | 4/28/62 | **Here Comes That Feelin'** Brenda Lee |
| 2/11/67 | **Happy Together** Turtles | 2/8/64 | Solomon Burke | 12/28/63 | **Here Comes The Boy** Tracey Dey |
| 10/13/62 | **Happy Weekend** Dave "baby" Cortez | 4/27/63 | **He's A Bad Boy** Carole King | | **Here Comes The Judge** |
| 1/25/60 | **Harbor Lights** Platters | 2/22/64 | **He's A Good Guy (Yes He Is)** Marvelettes | 6/1/68 | Buena Vistas |
| | **Hard Day's Night** | | | 6/1/68 | Shorty Long |
| 7/18/64 | Beatles | 6/19/65 | **He's A Lover** Mary Wells | 6/1/68 | Magistrates |
| 1/22/66 | Ramsey Lewis | 9/8/62 | **He's A Rebel** Crystals | 6/15/68 | Pigmeat Markham |
| 1/21/67 | **Hard Lovin' Loser** Judy Collins | 7/31/65 | **He's Got No Love** Searchers | 10/9/61 | **Here Comes The Night** Ben E. King |
| | **Hard To Handle** | 3/2/64 | **He's Got The Power** Exciters | 5/29/65 | **Here Comes The Night** Them |
| 7/13/68 | Otis Redding | 8/8/64 | **He's In Town** Tokens | 2/10/68 | **Here Comes The Rain, Baby** Eddy Arnold |
| 11/16/68 | Patti Drew | 9/14/63 | **He's Mine (I Love Him, I Love Him, I Love Him)** Alice Wonder Land | | |
| 11/21/60 | **Hardhearted Hannah** Ray Charles | | | 7/3/65 | **Here I Am** Dionne Warwick |
| 7/12/69 | **Hare Krishna (medley)** Happenings | 9/25/61 | **(He's My) Dreamboat** Connie Francis | 6/8/68 | **Here I Am Baby** Marvelettes |
| | **Harlem Nocturne** | 12/19/64 | **He's My Guy** Irma Thomas | 8/23/69 | **Here I Go Again** Miracles |
| 1/4/60* | Viscounts | 11/26/66 | **(He's) Raining In My Sunshine** Jay & The Americans | 3/30/63 | **Here I Stand** Rip Chords |
| 10/30/65 | Viscounts | | | 7/24/61 | **Here In My Heart** Al Martino |
| | **Harlem Shuffle** | 2/23/63 | **He's So Fine** Chiffons | 11/6/65 | **Here It Comes Again** Fortunes |
| 12/21/63 | Bob & Earl | 4/13/63 | **He's So Heavenly** Brenda Lee | 11/21/64 | **Here She Comes** Tymes |
| 11/12/66 | Traits | 12/29/62 | **He's Sure The Boy I Love** Crystals | 3/13/65 | **(Here They Come) From All Over The World** Jan & Dean |
| | **Harlow**...see: **Theme From** | 9/11/61 | **(He's) The Great Impostor** Fleetwoods | | |
| 10/10/60 | **Harmony** Billy Bland | 5/7/66 | **Headline News** Edwin Starr | | **Here We Go Again** |
| | **Harper Valley P.T.A.** | 8/24/63 | **Hear The Bells** Tokens | 5/20/67 | Ray Charles |
| 8/24/68 | Jeannie C. Riley | | **Heart** | 5/24/69 | Nancy Sinatra |
| 10/12/68 | King Curtis | 4/6/63 | Kenny Chandler | 2/1/64 | **Here's A Heart** Diplomats |
| 10/26/68 | Ben Colder | 4/27/63 | Wayne Newton | 5/15/61 | **Here's My Confession** Wyatt (Earp) McPherson |
| 6/15/63 | **Harry The Hairy Ape** Ray Stevens | | **Heart And Soul** | | |
| | **Hatari**...see: **Theme From** | 5/22/61 | Cleftones | 5/4/63 | **Here's To You** Hamilton Camp |
| 6/5/61 | **Hats Off To Larry** Del Shannon | 6/26/61 | Jan & Dean | 8/5/67 | **Heroes And Villains** Beach Boys |
| 8/8/64 | **Haunted House** Gene Simmons | 10/7/67 | **Heart Be Still** Lorraine Ellison | | **Hey! Baby** |
| 6/16/62 | **Have A Good Time** Sue Thompson | 11/3/62 | **Heart Breaker** Dean Christie | 1/27/62 | Bruce Channel |
| 3/9/68 | **Have A Little Faith** David Houston | 7/31/65 | **Heart Full Of Soul** Yardbirds | 1/25/69 | Jose Feliciano |
| 5/16/64 | **Have I Stayed Away Too Long** Bobby Bare | 7/6/62 | **Heart In Hand** Brenda Lee | 9/9/67 | **Hey Baby (They're Playing Our Song)** Buckinghams |
| | | 1/9/65 | **Heart Of Stone** Rolling Stones | | |
| 6/4/66 | **Have I Stayed Too Long** Sonny & Cher | 5/21/66 | **Heart's Desire** Billy Joe Royal | 3/14/64 | **Hey, Bobba Needle** Chubby Checker |
| 9/19/64 | **Have I The Right?** Honeycombs | | **Heartaches** | 1/20/68 | **Hey Boy Take A Chance On Love** Ruby Andrews |
| | **Have Mercy Baby** | 10/9/61 | Marcels | | |
| 10/10/60 | Bobbettes | 10/13/62 | Patsy Cline | 12/19/64 | **Hey-Da-Da-Dow** Dolphins |
| 12/26/64 | James Brown | | **Heartaches By The Number** | | **Hey, Girl** |
| | **Have You Ever Been Lonely (Have You Ever Been Blue)** | 1/4/60* | Guy Mitchell | 7/27/63 | Freddie Scott |
| | | 8/28/65 | Johnny Tillotson | 4/20/68 | Bobby Vee (medley) |
| 11/28/60 | Teresa Brewer | 10/31/64 | **Heartbreak Hill** Fats Domino | 7/18/64 | **Hey Girl Don't Bother Me** Tams |
| 2/8/64 | Caravelles | 11/5/66 | **Heartbreak Hotel** Roger Miller | 6/13/64 | **Hey Harmonica Man** Stevie Wonder |
| 11/26/66 | **Have You Ever Loved Somebody** Searchers | | **Heartbreak (It's Hurtin' Me)** | 2/24/68 | **Hey Hey Bunny** John Fred |
| | | 5/30/60 | Little Willie John | 2/22/64 | **Hey Jean, Hey Dean** Dean & Jean |
| 11/9/63 | **Have You Heard** Duprees | 6/6/60 | Jon Thomas | | **Hey Joe** |
| 12/19/64 | **Have You Looked Into Your Heart** Jerry Vale | 4/28/62 | **Hearts** Jackie Wilson | 5/21/66 | Leaves |
| | | 2/20/61 | **Hearts Of Stone** Bill Black's Combo | 9/9/67 | Cher |
| 6/10/67 | **Have You Seen Her Face** Byrds | 8/3/63 | **Heat Wave** Martha & The Vandellas | 7/12/69 | Wilson Pickett |
| | **Have You Seen My Wife, Mr. Jones**...see: **New York Mining Disaster 1941** | 4/26/69 | **Heather Honey** Tommy Roe | | **Hey Jude** |
| | | 2/8/69 | **Heaven** Rascals | 9/14/68 | Beatles |
| | | 11/8/69 | **Heaven Knows** Grass Roots | 12/21/68 | Wilson Pickett |
| 10/8/66 | **Have You Seen Your Mother, Baby, Standing In The Shadow?** Rolling Stones | 10/22/66 | **Heaven Must Have Sent You** Elgins | 12/31/66 | **Hey, Leroy, Your Mama's Callin' You** Jimmy Castor |
| | | | **Hello, Dolly!** | | |
| 2/6/61 | **Havin' Fun** Dion | 2/15/64 | Louis Armstrong | 2/17/62 | **Hey, Let's Twist** Joey Dee |
| 5/26/62 | **Having A Party** Sam Cooke | 2/6/65 | Bobby Darin | 12/14/63 | **Hey Little Cobra** Rip Chords |
| 3/8/69 | **Hawaii Five-O** Ventures | 12/2/67 | **Hello Goodbye** Beatles | 11/27/61 | **Hey! Little Girl** Del Shannon |
| 4/3/65 | **Hawaii Honeymoon** Waikikis | 9/7/63 | **Hello Heartache, Goodbye Love** Little Peggy March | 10/19/63 | **Hey Little Girl** Major Lance |
| 12/5/64 | **Hawaii Tattoo** Waikikis | | | | **Hey Little One** |
| 11/5/66 | **Hazy Shade Of Winter** Simon & Garfunkel | | **Hello Hello** | 6/6/60 | Dorsey Burnette |
| | | 12/24/66 | Sopwith "Camel" | 11/28/64 | J. Frank Wilson |
| 6/4/66 | **He** Righteous Brothers | 5/27/67 | Claudine Longet | 1/20/68 | Glen Campbell |
| 11/11/67 | **He Ain't Give You None** Freddie Scott | 7/6/68 | **Hello, I Love You** Doors | 10/12/63 | **Hey Lonely One** Baby Washington |
| 12/20/69 | **He Ain't Heavy, He's My Brother** Hollies | 2/15/69 | **Hello It's Me** Nazz | 4/22/67 | **Hey Love** Stevie Wonder |
| | | 6/29/63 | **Hello Jim** Paul Anka | 11/16/63 | **Hey Lover** Debbie Dovale |
| 5/1/65 | **He Ain't No Angel** Ad Libs | 5/1/61 | **Hello Mary Lou** Ricky Nelson | 4/4/64 | **Hey, Mr. Sax Man** Boots Randolph |
| 1/18/69 | **He Called Me Baby** Ella Washington | | **Hello Mudduh, Hello Fadduh! (A Letter From Camp)** | 10/17/64 | **Hey Now** Lesley Gore |
| | **He Cried**...see: **She Cried** | 8/3/63 | Allan Sherman | 12/29/62 | **Hey Paula** Paul & Paula |
| | | 7/25/64 | Allan Sherman (1964) | | |

| | | | | | | |
|---|---|---|---|---|---|---|
| | **Hey There Lonely Girl (Boy)** | 9/25/61 | **Honky Train** Bill Black's Combo | 3/20/61 | **Hundred Pounds Of Clay** |
| 8/10/63 | Ruby & The Romantics | 9/7/63 | **Honolulu Lulu** Jan & Dean | | Gene McDaniels |
| 12/27/69 | Eddie Holman | 12/5/60 | **Hoochi Coochi Coo** Hank Ballard | 7/17/65 | **Hung On You** Righteous Brothers |
| 8/31/68 | **Hey, Western Union Man** Jerry Butler | 8/2/69 | **Hook And Sling** Eddie Bo | 2/18/67 | **Hung Up In Your Eyes** Brian Hyland |
| 7/2/66 | **Hey You! Little Boo-Ga-Loo** | 12/7/63 | **Hooka Tooka** Chubby Checker | 6/18/66 | **Hungry** Paul Revere & The Raiders |
| | Chubby Checker | 11/16/68 | **Hooked On A Feeling** B.J. Thomas | 9/11/65 | **Hungry For Love** |
| 12/7/63 | **Hi Diddle Diddle** Inez Foxx | 9/17/66 | **Hooray For Hazel** Tommy Roe | | San Remo Golden Strings |
| | **Hi-Heel Sneakers** | 12/2/67 | **Hooray For The Salvation Army** | 8/2/69 | **Hunter, The** Ike & Tina Turner |
| 2/8/64 | Tommy Tucker | | **Band** Bill Cosby | 1/21/67 | **Hunter Gets Captured By The Game** |
| 11/21/64 | Jerry Lee Lewis | 6/15/63 | **Hootenanny** Glencoves | | Marvelettes |
| 8/28/65 | Stevie Wonder | 12/14/63 | **Hootenanny Saturday Night** | 6/22/68 | **Hurdy Gurdy Man** Donovan |
| 3/26/66 | Ramsey Lewis | | Brothers Four | | **Hurt** |
| 10/19/68 | Jose Feliciano | 4/17/63 | **Hop Scotch** Santo & Johnny | 7/24/61 | Timi Yuro |
| | (also see: Slip-In Mules) | 6/22/63 | **Hopeless** Andy Williams | 1/1/66 | Little Anthony & The Imperials |
| 11/19/66 | **Hi Hi Hazel** Gary & The Hornets | 5/25/68 | **Horse, The** Cliff Nobles & Co. | 4/25/64 | **Hurt By Love** Inez Foxx |
| 2/16/63 | **Hi-Lili, Hi-Lo** Richard Chamberlain | 9/14/68 | **Horse Fever** Cliff Nobles & Co. | | **Hurt So Bad** |
| 5/30/64 | **Hickory, Dick And Doc** Bobby Vee | 4/13/63 | **Hot Cakes! 1st Serving** | 2/6/65 | Little Anthony & The Imperials |
| | **Hide & Go Seek** | | Dave "Baby" Cortez | 5/31/69 | Lettermen |
| 8/25/62 | Bunker Hill | 8/9/69 | **Hot Fun In The Summertime** | | **Hurt Yourself**...see: (You're Gonna) |
| 1/29/66 | Sheep | | Sly & The Family Stone | 2/19/66 | **Husbands And Wives** Roger Miller |
| 3/6/61 | **Hide Away** Freddy King | 4/13/63 | **Hot Pastrami** Dartells | | **Hush** |
| 4/7/62 | **Hide 'Nor Hair** Ray Charles | 4/27/63 | **Hot Pastrami With Mashed Potatoes** | 9/30/67 | Billy Joe Royal |
| | **High-Heel**...see: Hi-Heel | | Joey Dee | 8/17/68 | Deep Purple |
| 2/22/64 | **High On A Hill** Scott English | 7/7/62 | **Hot Pepper** Floyd Cramer | 10/10/60 | **Hush-Hush** Jimmy Reed |
| 7/2/66 | **High On Love** Knickerbockers | | **Hot Rod Lincoln** | 4/24/65 | **Hush, Hush, Sweet Charlotte** |
| 1/4/60* | **High School U.S.A.** Tommy Facenda | 5/9/60 | Charlie Ryan | | Patti Page |
| | **Higher And Higher**...see: (Your Love | 8/8/60 | Johnny Bond | 5/31/69 | **Hushabye** Jay & The Americans |
| | Keeps Lifting Me) | 7/2/66 | **Hot Shot** Buena Vistas | 6/24/67 | **Hypnotized** Linda Jones |
| 4/29/67 | **Him Or Me - What's It Gonna Be?** | 2/15/69 | **Hot Smoke & Sasafrass** Bubble Puppy | | |
| | Paul Revere & The Raiders | 11/24/62 | **Hotel Happiness** Brook Benton | | **I** |
| 8/10/68 | **Hip City** Jr. Walker & The All Stars | 8/4/62 | **Houdini** Walter Brennan | | |
| 3/25/67 | **Hip Hug-Her** Booker T. & The M.G.'s | 1/4/60* | **Hound Dog Man** Fabian | 10/26/63 | **I Adore Him** Angels |
| 3/7/64 | **Hippy Hippy Shake** | | **House Is Not A Home** | 12/25/65 | **I Ain't Gonna Eat Out My Heart** |
| | Swinging Blue Jeans | 7/18/64 | Brook Benton | | **Anymore** Young Rascals |
| 1/4/64 | **His Kiss** Betty Harris | 8/1/64 | Dionne Warwick | 9/28/68 | **I Ain't Got To Love Nobody Else** |
| | **His Latest Flame**...see: (Marie's the | 3/28/60 | **House Of Bamboo** Earl Grant | | Masqueraders |
| | Name) | 8/8/64 | **House Of The Rising Sun** Animals | 5/7/66 | **I Am A Rock** Simon & Garfunkel |
| | **History Repeats Itself** | 8/17/68 | **House That Jack Built** Aretha Franklin | 11/9/63 | **I Am A Witness** Tommy Hunt |
| 4/9/66 | Buddy Starcher | 8/7/65 | **Houston** Dean Martin | 12/9/67 | **I Am The Walrus** Beatles |
| 4/16/66 | Cab Calloway | 1/4/60* | **How About That** Dee Clark | 8/10/68 | **I Am Your Man** Bobby Taylor |
| 5/5/62 | **Hit Record** Brook Benton | 3/28/64 | **How Blue Can You Get** B.B. King | 10/9/61 | **I Apologize** Timi Yuro |
| 9/11/61 | **Hit The Road Jack** Ray Charles | 9/9/67 | **How Can I Be Sure** Young Rascals | 6/27/64 | **I Believe** Bachelors |
| 1/12/63 | **Hitch Hike** Marvin Gaye | | **How Can I Forget** | 10/23/65 | **I Believe I'll Love On** Jackie Wilson |
| 6/29/68 | **Hitch It To The Horse** | 3/16/63 | Jimmy Holiday | 7/23/66 | **I Believe I'm Gonna Make It** Joe Tex |
| | Fantastic Johnny C | 3/16/63 | Ben E. King | 5/6/67 | **I Believed It All** Pozo-Seco Singers |
| 10/12/68 | **Hitchcock Railway** Jose Feliciano | 5/26/62 | **How Can I Meet Her?** Everly Brothers | 12/23/67 | **I Call It Love** Manhattans |
| 4/18/60 | **Hither And Thither And Yon** | 12/4/61 | **(How Can I Write On Paper) What I** | 9/14/68 | **(I Can Feel Your Love) Slipping** |
| | Brook Benton | | **Feel In My Heart** Jim Reeves | | **Away** Barbara Mason |
| 5/11/63 | **Hobo Flats** Jimmy Smith | 8/26/67 | **How Can You Mistreat The One You** | | **I Can Hear Music** |
| 6/5/61 | **Hold Back The Tears** Delacardos | | **Love** Jean & The Darlings | 10/29/66 | Ronettes |
| | **Hold Me** | 4/11/60 | **How Deep Is The Ocean** | 3/8/69 | Beach Boys |
| 9/5/64 | P.J. Proby | | Miss Toni Fisher | | **I Can Make It With You** |
| 10/11/69 | Baskerville Hounds | 12/24/66 | **How Do You Catch A Girl** | 9/10/66 | Jackie DeShannon |
| 6/26/65 | **Hold Me, Thrill Me, Kiss Me** | | Sam The Sham & The Pharoahs | 9/10/66 | Pozo-Seco Singers |
| | Mel Carter | 7/11/64 | **How Do You Do It?** | 11/6/65 | **I Can Never Go Home Anymore** |
| 9/14/68 | **Hold Me Tight** Johnny Nash | | Gerry & The Pacemakers | | Shangri-Las |
| 5/25/68 | **Hold On** Radiants | 4/23/66 | **How Does That Grab You, Darlin'?** | 4/27/68 | **I Can Remember** James & Bobby Purify |
| | **Hold On! I'm A Comin'** | | Nancy Sinatra | 10/14/67 | **I Can See For Miles** Who |
| 4/23/66 | Sam & Dave | | **How Glad I Am**...see: (You Don't Know) | 5/24/69 | **I Can Sing A Rainbow (medley)** Dells |
| 2/18/67 | Chuck Jackson & Maxine Brown | 8/15/60 | **How High The Moon** Ella Fitzgerald | 1/13/68 | **I Can Take Or Leave Your Loving** |
| 12/19/64 | **Hold What You've Got** Joe Tex | 12/13/69 | **How I Miss You Baby** Bobby Womack | | Herman's Hermits |
| 11/13/65 | **Hole In The Wall** Packers | 5/12/62 | **How Is Julie?** Lettermen | 10/11/69 | **I Can't Be All Bad** Johnny Adams |
| 9/30/67 | **Holiday** Bee Gees | 7/20/63 | **How Many Teardrops** Lou Christie | 4/13/68 | **I Can't Believe I'm Losing You** |
| 5/27/67 | **Holiday For Clowns** Brian Hyland | 5/29/61 | **How Many Tears** Bobby Vee | | Frank Sinatra |
| 11/1/69 | **Holly Holy** Neil Diamond | 2/22/64 | **How Much Can A Lonely Heart** | 10/3/64 | **I Can't Believe What You Say (For** |
| 9/25/61 | **Hollywood** Connie Francis | | **Stand** Skeeter Davis | | **Seeing What You Do)** |
| 10/22/66 | **Holy Cow** Lee Dorsey | 1/5/63 | **How Much Is That Doggie In The** | | Ike & Tina Turner |
| 10/28/67 | **Homburg** Procol Harum | | **Window** Baby Jane & The Rockabyes | 1/8/66 | **I Can't Believe You Love Me** |
| 1/18/69 | **Home Cookin'** Jr. Walker & The All Stars | 9/18/65 | **How Nice It Is** Billy Stewart | | Tammi Terrell |
| | **Home Of The Brave** | 8/3/68 | **How Sweet It Is, Montage From** | 10/15/66 | **I Can't Control Myself** Troggs |
| 8/28/65 | Bonnie & The Treasures | | **Love Generation** | 8/10/68 | **I Can't Dance To That Music You're** |
| 8/28/65 | Jody Miller | | **How Sweet It Is (To Be Loved By You)** | | **Playin'** Martha & The Vandellas |
| 4/26/69 | **Home To You** Earth Opera | 11/21/64 | Marvin Gaye | 4/12/69 | **I Can't Do Enough** Dells |
| 2/12/66 | **Homeward Bound** Simon & Garfunkel | 7/30/66 | Jr. Walker & The All Stars | 5/15/61 | **I Can't Do It By Myself** Anita Bryant |
| 8/15/60 | **Honest I Do** Innocents | 12/26/60 | **How To Handle A Woman** | 3/27/65 | **I Can't Explain** Who |
| | **Honey** | | Johnny Mathis | 8/16/69 | **I Can't Get Next To You** Temptations |
| 3/23/68 | Bobby Goldsboro | 5/4/68 | **How'd We Ever Get This Way** | | **(I Can't Get No) Satisfaction** |
| 2/8/69 | O.C. Smith | | Andy Kim | 6/12/65 | Rolling Stones |
| 11/18/67 | **Honey Chile** Martha & The Vandellas | 10/10/60 | **Hucklebuck, The** Chubby Checker | 3/5/66 | Otis Redding |
| 1/4/60* | **Honey Hush** Joe Turner | | **Hully Gully**...also see: (Baby) | 8/15/64 | **I Can't Get You Out Of My Heart** |
| 2/8/60 | **Honey Love** Narvel Felts | 8/7/61 | **Hully Gully Again** | | Al Martino |
| | (also see: We've Got) | | Little Caesar & The Romans | 10/15/66 | **I Can't Give You Anything But Love** |
| | **Honky Tonk** | 8/11/62 | **Hully Gully Baby** Dovells | | Bert Kaempfert |
| 1/30/61 | Bill Doggett | 10/13/62 | **Hully Gully Guitar** Jerry Reed | 7/22/67 | **I Can't Go On Livin' Baby Without** |
| 10/30/65 | Lonnie Mack | | **Hully Gully Twist**...see: (Let's Do) | | **You** Nino Tempo & April Stevens |
| 7/25/60 | **Honky-Tonk Girl** Johnny Cash | 9/4/61 | **Human** Tommy Hunt | 3/12/66 | **I Can't Grow Peaches On A Cherry** |
| 3/31/62 | **Honky-Tonk Man** Johnny Horton | 10/10/60 | **Humdinger** Freddy Cannon | | **Tree** Just Us |
| 7/19/69 | **Honky Tonk Women** Rolling Stones | | | 6/27/64 | **I Can't Hear You** Betty Everett |

| | | | | | | |
|---|---|---|---|---|---|---|
| | **I Can't Help It (If I'm Still In Love With You)** | 9/4/61 | **I Don't Like It Like That** Bobbettes (also see: I Like It Like That) | 11/23/63 | **I Gotta Dance To Keep From Crying** Miracles |
| 6/20/60 | Adam Wade | | | 11/14/60 | **I Gotta Know** Elvis Presley |
| 10/27/62 | Johnny Tillotson | 6/16/62 | **I Don't Love You No More (I Don't Care About You)** Jimmy Norman | | **I Gotta Woman**..see: I Got A Woman |
| 5/13/67 | B.J. Thomas | 5/15/61 | **I Don't Mind** James Brown | 7/16/66 | **I Guess I'll Always Love You** Isley Brothers |
| 12/28/68 | Al Martino | 11/26/66 | **I Don't Need No Doctor** Ray Charles | | |
| 5/15/65 | **I Can't Help Myself** Four Tops | 5/23/64 | **I Don't Wanna Be A Loser** Lesley Gore | 7/27/68 | **I Guess I'll Have To Cry, Cry, Cry** James Brown |
| 8/22/60 | **(I Can't Help You) I'm Falling Too** Skeeter Davis (also see: Please Help Me, I'm Falling) | 8/7/65 | **I Don't Wanna Lose You Baby** Chad & Jeremy | 8/22/64 | **I Guess I'm Crazy** Jim Reeves |
| | | 4/5/69 | **I Don't Want Nobody To Give Me Nothing** James Brown | 11/1/69 | **I Guess The Lord Must Be In New York City** Nilsson |
| 3/19/66 | **I Can't Let Go** Hollies | | | 8/19/67 | **I Had A Dream** Paul Revere & The Raiders |
| 5/18/68 | **I Can't Make It Alone** Bill Medley | 12/31/60 | **I Don't Want Nobody (To Have My Love But You)** Ella Johnson with Buddy Johnson | | |
| 11/1/69 | Lou Rawls | | | 9/26/64 | **I Had A Talk With My Man** Mitty Collier |
| 3/25/67 | **I Can't Make It Anymore** Spyder Turner | 4/25/64 | **I Don't Want To Be Hurt Anymore** Nat "King" Cole | 12/10/66 | **I Had Too Much To Dream (Last Night)** Electric Prunes |
| 5/31/69 | **I Can't Quit Her** Arbors | | **I Don't Want To Cry** | 11/16/63 | **I Have A Boyfriend** Chiffons |
| 1/25/60 | **I Can't Say Goodbye** Fireflies | 2/20/61 | Chuck Jackson | 5/4/68 | **I Have A Dream** Rev. Martin Luther King |
| 2/24/62 | **I Can't Say Goodbye** Bobby Vee | 2/15/69 | Ruby Winters | | |
| 4/26/69 | **I Can't Say No To You** Betty Everett | 6/27/64 | **I Don't Want To Hear Anymore** Jerry Butler | 10/30/65 | **I Have Dreamed** Chad & Jeremy |
| 4/19/69 | **I Can't See Myself Leaving You** Aretha Franklin | 3/4/67 | **I Don't Want To Lose You** Jackie Wilson | 10/30/65 | **I Hear A Symphony** Supremes |
| | | | | 3/19/66 | **I Hear Trumpets Blow** Tokens |
| 2/29/64 | **I Can't Stand It** Soul Sisters | 9/19/64 | **I Don't Want To See Tomorrow** Nat "King" Cole | 12/4/61 | **I Hear You Knocking** Fats Domino |
| 12/9/67 | **I Can't Stand Myself (When You Touch Me)** James Brown | | | | **I Heard It Through The Grapevine** |
| | | 10/3/64 | **I Don't Want To See You Again** Peter & Gordon | 10/21/67 | Gladys Knight & The Pips |
| 9/2/67 | **I Can't Stay Away From You** Impressions | | | 8/10/68 | King Curtis |
| | | | **(I Don't Want To See You Cry)**..see: Goodbye Baby | 11/23/68 | Marvin Gaye |
| 9/7/63 | **I Can't Stay Mad At You** Skeeter Davis | | | 12/12/60 | **I Idolize You** Ike & Tina Turner |
| 12/19/64 | **I Can't Stop** Honeycombs | 2/20/65 | **I Don't Want To Spoil The Party** Beatles | 7/7/62 | **I Just Can't Help It** Jackie Wilson |
| 7/20/68 | **I Can't Stop Dancing** Archie Bell & The Drells | | | 12/19/64 | **I Just Can't Say Goodbye** Bobby Rydell |
| | | 7/17/61 | **I Don't Want To Take A Chance** Mary Wells | | |
| | **I Can't Stop Loving You** | | | 10/1/66 | **I Just Don't Know What To Do With Myself** Dionne Warwick |
| 5/5/62 | Ray Charles | 12/5/64 | **I Don't Want To Walk Without You** Phyllis McGuire | | |
| 6/1/63 | Count Basie | | | 7/24/61 | **I Just Don't Understand** Ann-Margret |
| 12/21/63 | **I Can't Stop Talking About You** Steve & Eydie | 7/3/61 | **I Dreamed Of A Hill-Billy Heaven** Tex Ritter | 9/1/62 | **I Keep Forgettin'** Chuck Jackson |
| | | | | 4/25/64 | **I Knew It All The Time** Dave Clark Five |
| 3/13/65 | **I Can't Stop Thinking Of You** Bobbi Martin | 5/22/61 | **I Fall To Pieces** Patsy Cline | 9/18/65 | **I Knew You When** Billy Joe Royal |
| | | 4/9/66 | **I Feel A Sin Coming On** Solomon Burke | 3/20/65 | **I Know A Place** Petula Clark |
| 8/28/61 | **I Can't Take It** Mary Ann Fisher | | | 5/25/63 | **I Know I Know** "Pookie" Hudson |
| 11/23/68 | **I Can't Turn You Loose** Chambers Brothers | 12/5/64 | **I Feel Fine** Beatles | 11/19/66 | **(I Know) I'm Losing You** Temptations |
| | | 8/26/67 | **I Feel Good (I Feel Bad)** Lewis & Clarke Expedition | 7/25/60 | **I Know One** Jim Reeves |
| 3/21/64 | **I Can't Wait Until I See My Baby** Baby Washington | | | 2/8/60 | **I Know What God Is** Perry Como |
| | | | **I Feel So Bad** | | |
| 7/3/65 | **I Can't Work No Longer** Billy Butler | 5/15/61 | Elvis Presley | 5/14/66 | **I Know You Better Than That** Bobby Goldsboro |
| 9/3/66 | **I Chose To Sing The Blues** Ray Charles | 2/4/67 | Little Milton | | |
| | | 11/26/66 | **I Fooled You This Time** Gene Chandler | 11/13/61 | **I Know (You Don't Love Me No More)** Barbara George |
| 2/19/66 | **I Confess** New Colony Six | 1/18/60 | **I Forgot More Than You'll Ever Know** Sonny James | | |
| 4/22/67 | **I Could Be So Good To You** Don & The Goodtimes | | | 8/11/62 | **I Left My Heart In San Francisco** Tony Bennett |
| | | 1/4/69 | **I Forgot To Be Your Lover** William Bell | | |
| 7/15/67 | **I Could Be So Happy** Magnificent Men | 1/29/66 | **I Fought The Law** Bobby Fuller Four | 9/22/62 | **I Left My Heart In The Balcony** Linda Scott |
| 11/2/63 | **I Could Have Danced All Night** Ben E. King | 10/16/65 | **I Found A Girl** Jan & Dean | 3/6/61 | **I Lied To My Heart** Enchanters |
| | | | **I Found A Love** | 9/26/64 | **I Like It** Gerry & The Pacemakers |
| 12/18/61 | **I Could Have Loved You So Well** Ray Peterson | 3/31/62 | Falcons | | **I Like It Like That** |
| | | 4/1/67 | Wilson Pickett | 5/29/61 | Chris Kenner |
| 8/9/69 | **I Could Never Be President** Johnnie Taylor | 12/12/64 | **I Found A Love Oh What A Love** Jo Ann & Troy | 6/19/65 | Dave Clark Five (also see: I Don't Like It Like That) |
| 5/3/69 | **I Could Never Lie To You** New Colony Six | 12/15/62 | **I Found A New Baby** Bobby Darin | 6/27/64 | **I Like It Like That** Miracles |
| | | 9/21/68 | **I Found A True Love** Wilson Pickett | 7/1/67 | **I Like The Way** Tommy James & The Shondells |
| 5/4/68 | **I Could Never Love Another (After Loving You)** Temptations | 4/21/62 | **I Found Love** Jackie Wilson & Linda Hopkins | | |
| | | | | 2/15/69 | **I Like What You're Doing (To Me)** Carla Thomas |
| 7/16/66 | **I Couldn't Live Without Your Love** Petula Clark | 5/23/64 | **I Get Around** Beach Boys | 9/4/65 | **I Live For The Sun** Sunrays |
| | | 7/20/68 | **I Get The Sweetest Feeling** Jackie Wilson | 11/3/62 | **I Lost My Baby** Joey Dee |
| 12/19/60 | **I Count The Tears** Drifters | | | | **I Love How You Love Me** |
| 8/17/63 | **I Cried** Tammy Montgomery | 1/9/65 | **I Go To Pieces** Peter & Gordon | 9/4/61 | Paris Sisters |
| 8/10/63 | **(I Cried at) Laura's Wedding** Barbara Lynn | 1/18/69 | **I Got A Line On You** Spirit | 11/2/68 | Bobby Vinton |
| | | 4/6/68 | **I Got A Sure Thing** Ollie & The Nightingales | 3/29/69 | **I Love My Baby** Archie Bell & The Drells |
| 11/6/61 | **I Cried My Last Tear** Ernie K-Doe | | | 6/11/66 | **I Love Onions** Susan Christie |
| 2/8/64 | **I Didn't Know What Time It Was** Crampton Sisters | | **I Got A Woman** | 3/7/60 | **I Love The Way You Love** Marv Johnson |
| | | 10/13/62 | Jimmy McGriff | | |
| 12/31/66 | **I Dig Girls** J.J. Jackson | 3/16/63 | Rick Nelson | 4/28/62 | **I Love You** Volume's |
| 8/19/67 | **I Dig Rock And Roll Music** Peter, Paul & Mary | 11/2/63 | Freddie Scott | 4/6/68 | **I Love You** People |
| | | 4/17/65 | Ray Charles | 11/29/69 | **I Love You** Otis Leavill |
| 1/21/67 | **I Dig You Baby** Jerry Butler | | **I Got Life**..see: Ain't Got No | 4/6/63 | **I Love You Because** Al Martino |
| 5/15/65 | **I Do** Marvelows | 4/8/67 | **I Got Rhythm** Happenings | 6/1/63 | **(I Love You) Don't You Forget It** Perry Como |
| 8/16/69 | **I Do** Moments | 3/16/68 | **I Got The Feelin'** James Brown | | |
| | **I Do Love You** | 11/12/66 | **I Got The Feelin' (Oh No No)** Neil Diamond | 5/7/66 | **I Love You Drops** Vic Dana |
| 3/27/65 | Billy Stewart | | | | **(I Love You) For Sentimental Reasons**..see: For Sentimental Reasons |
| 2/22/69 | Billy Stewart | 1/7/67 | **I Got To Go Back (And Watch That Little Girl Dance)** McCoys | | |
| | **(I Do The)**..see: Shimmy Shimmy | | | 8/1/60 | **I Love You In The Same Old Way** Paul Anka |
| 8/22/64 | **I Don't Care (Just As Long As You Love Me)** Buck Owens | 8/27/66 | **I Got To Handle It** Capitols | | |
| | | 3/16/63 | **I Got What I Wanted** Brook Benton | 9/21/68 | **I Love You Madly** Fantastic Four |
| 1/4/60* | **I Don't Know What It Is** Bluenotes | 4/29/67 | **I Got What You Need** Kim Weston | 2/1/64 | **I Love You More And More Every Day** Al Martino |
| 11/27/65 | **I Don't Know What You've Got But It's Got Me** Little Richard | | **I Got You Babe** | | |
| | | 7/10/65 | Sonny & Cher | 4/8/67 | **I Love You More Than Words Can Say** Otis Redding |
| 10/30/61 | **I Don't Know Why** Linda Scott | 5/18/68 | Etta James | | |
| 2/15/69 | **I Don't Know Why** Stevie Wonder (also see: But I Do) | 11/13/65 | **I Got You (I Feel Good)** James Brown | 4/30/66 | **I Love You 1000 Times** Platters |
| | | | | 5/29/65 | **I Love You So** Bobbi Martin |

| | | | | | |
|---|---|---|---|---|---|
| 8/11/62 | I Love You The Way You Are<br>Bobby Vinton | 12/25/61 | I Told The Brook   Marty Robbins | | I Wish It Would Rain |
| 9/11/61 | I Love You Yes I Do<br>Bull Moose Jackson | 3/27/61 | I Told You So   Jimmy Jones | 1/13/68 | Temptations |
| | | 5/31/69 | I Turned You On   Isley Brothers | 8/24/68 | Gladys Knight & The Pips |
| 7/20/68 | I Loved And I Lost   Impressions | | I Understand (Just How You Feel) | 3/31/62 | I Wish That We Were Married<br>Ronnie & The Hi-Lites |
| 8/26/67 | I Make A Fool Of Myself   Frankie Valli | 9/18/61 | G-Clefs | 2/4/67 | I Wish You Could Be Here   Cyrkle |
| 11/24/62 | I May Not Live To See Tomorrow<br>Brian Hyland | 3/13/65 | Freddie & The Dreamers | 1/11/64 | I Wish You Love   Gloria Lynne |
| | | 8/21/61 | I Wake Up Crying   Chuck Jackson | 11/21/64 | I Won't Forget You   Jim Reeves |
| 9/14/68 | I Met Her In Church   Box Tops | 10/26/68 | I Walk Alone   Marty Robbins | 12/4/65 | I Won't Love You Anymore (Sorry)<br>Lesley Gore |
| 10/2/65 | I Miss You So<br>Little Anthony & The Imperials | 8/29/60 | I Walk The Line   Jaye P. Morgan | | |
| | | 1/12/63 | I Wanna Be Around   Tony Bennett | 7/13/63 | I Wonder   Brenda Lee |
| 11/14/60 | I Missed Me   Jim Reeves | 1/4/60* | I Wanna Be Loved   Ricky Nelson | 10/30/61 | I Wonder (If Your Love Will Ever<br>Belong To Me)   Pentagons |
| 2/27/65 | I Must Be Seeing Things   Gene Pitney | 5/30/64 | I Wanna Be Loved   Dean & Jean | | |
| 6/11/66 | I Need Love   Barbara Mason | | I Wanna Be With You | 10/19/63 | I Wonder What She's Doing Tonight<br>Barry & The Tamerlanes |
| 12/25/61 | I Need Some One   Belmonts | 10/3/64 | Nancy Wilson | | |
| 11/19/66 | I Need Somebody   ? & The Mysterians | 8/27/66 | Dee Dee Warwick | 12/23/67 | I Wonder What She's Doing Tonite<br>Tommy Boyce & Bobby Hart |
| 12/22/62 | I Need You   Rick Nelson | 1/16/65 | I Wanna Be (Your Everything)<br>Manhattans | | |
| 4/24/65 | I Need You   Chuck Jackson | | | 3/7/64 | I Wonder Who's Kissing Her Now<br>Bobby Darin |
| 8/14/65 | I Need You   Impressions | 4/6/68 | I Wanna Live   Glen Campbell | | |
| | I Need You Now | 6/20/64 | I Wanna Love Him So Bad   Jelly Beans | 11/16/68 | I Worry About You   Joe Simon |
| 3/28/60 | Joni James | 1/30/61 | (I Wanna) Love My Life Away<br>Gene Pitney | 9/1/62 | I Wouldn't Know (What To Do)<br>Dinah Washington |
| 5/31/69 | Ronnie Dove | | | | |
| 10/23/65 | I Need You So<br>Chuck Jackson & Maxine Brown | 11/26/66 | I Wanna Meet You   Cryan Shames | 9/12/64 | I Wouldn't Trade You For The World<br>Bachelors |
| | | | (I Wanna) Testify | | |
| 6/2/62 | I Need Your Loving<br>Don Gardner & Dee Dee Ford | 7/1/67 | Parliaments | 6/21/69 | I'd Rather Be An Old Man's<br>Sweetheart   Candi Staton |
| | | 5/10/69 | Johnnie Taylor | | |
| 7/24/61 | I Never Knew   Clyde McPhatter | 10/16/61 | I Wanna Thank You   Bobby Rydell | 1/26/63 | I'd Rather Be Here In Your Arms<br>Duprees |
| 3/4/67 | I Never Loved A Man (The Way I Love<br>You)   Aretha Franklin | 9/5/64 | I Wanna Thank You   Enchanters | | |
| | | 6/26/65 | I Want Candy   Strangeloves | 7/5/69 | I'd Wait A Million Years   Grass Roots |
| 6/18/66 | I Only Have Eyes For You   Lettermen | 1/30/65 | I Want My Baby Back   Jimmy Cross | 6/17/67 | I'll Always Have Faith In You<br>Carla Thomas |
| 1/25/64 | I Only Want To Be With You<br>Dusty Springfield | 3/5/66 | I Want Someone   Mad Lads | | |
| | | | I Want To .. also see: I Wanna | 8/8/64 | I'll Always Love You   Brenda Holloway |
| 2/20/61 | I Pity The Fool   Bobby Bland | 8/18/62 | I Want To Be Loved   Dinah Washington | 7/17/65 | I'll Always Love You   Spinners |
| 4/20/68 | I Promise To Wait My Love<br>Martha & The Vandellas | 9/12/60 | I Want To Be Wanted   Brenda Lee | 3/20/65 | I'll Be Doggone   Marvin Gaye |
| | | 8/28/65 | I Want To (Do Everything For You)<br>Joe Tex | 6/18/66 | I'll Be Gone   Pozo-Seco Singers |
| | I Put A Spell On You | | | 12/3/66 | I'll Be Home   Platters |
| 7/30/66 | Alan Price Set | 2/5/66 | I Want To Go With You   Eddy Arnold | 5/30/64 | I'll Be In Trouble   Temptations |
| 11/9/68 | Creedence Clearwater Revival | | I Want To Hold Your Hand | | I'll Be Seeing You |
| | I Really Don't Want To Know | 1/18/64 | Beatles | 5/9/60 | Five Satins |
| 5/23/60 | Tommy Edwards | 7/4/64 | Boston Pops Orchestra | 10/16/61 | Frank Sinatra |
| 9/8/62 | Solomon Burke | 5/3/69 | I Want To Love You Baby<br>Peggy Scott & Jo Jo Benson | 11/25/67 | I'll Be Sweeter Tomorrow   O'Jays |
| 2/9/63 | Esther Phillips | | | | I'll Be There |
| 9/3/66 | Ronnie Dove | 8/5/67 | I Want To Love You For What You<br>Are   Ronnie Dove | 7/11/60 | Bobby Darin |
| 9/25/61 | I Really Love You   Stereos | | | 12/12/64 | Gerry & The Pacemakers |
| 11/6/65 | I Really Love You   Dee Dee Sharp | 11/6/65 | I Want To Meet Him   Royalettes | 7/3/61 | I'll Be There   Damita Jo |
| 1/16/61 | I Remember   Maurice Williams | 7/20/63 | I Want To Stay Here   Steve & Eydie | | (also see: Stand By Me) |
| 9/8/62 | I Remember You   Frank Ifield | 5/24/69 | I Want To Take You Higher<br>Sly & The Family Stone | 5/22/65 | I'll Be With You In Apple Blossom<br>Time   Wayne Newton |
| 5/2/64 | I Rise, I Fall   Johnny Tillotson | | | | |
| 7/2/66 | I Saw Her Again   Mamas & The Papas | 3/18/67 | I Want To Talk About You<br>Ray Charles | 10/4/69 | I'll Bet You   Funkadelic |
| 2/8/64 | I Saw Her Standing There   Beatles | | | 10/13/62 | I'll Bring It Home To You<br>Carla Thomas |
| 12/8/62 | I Saw Linda Yesterday   Dickey Lee | 7/2/66 | I Want You   Bob Dylan | | |
| | I Say A Little Prayer | 11/15/69 | I Want You Back   Jackson 5 | | (also see: Bring It On Home To Me) |
| 10/21/67 | Dionne Warwick | 6/26/65 | I Want You Back Again   Zombies | 8/1/64 | I'll Cry Instead   Beatles |
| 8/17/68 | Aretha Franklin | 5/6/67 | I Want You To Be My Baby<br>Ellie Greenwich | 7/1/67 | I'll Do It For You   Toussaint McCall |
| 2/17/68 | I Say Love   Royal Guardsmen | | | 2/19/66 | I'll Go Crazy   James Brown |
| 11/4/67 | I Second That Emotion   Miracles | 1/16/65 | I Want You To Be My Boy   Exciters | 11/22/69 | I'll Hold Out My Hand   Clique |
| 1/1/66 | I See The Light   Five Americans | 8/30/69 | I Want You To Know   New Colony Six | 4/10/61 | I'll Just Have A Cup Of Coffee (Then<br>I'll Go)   Claude Gray |
| 10/10/64 | I See You   Cathy & Joe | 7/25/64 | I Want You To Meet My Baby<br>Eydie Gorme | | |
| 4/26/69 | I Shall Be Released   Box Tops | | | 5/29/65 | I'll Keep Holding On   Marvelettes |
| 7/4/60 | I Shot Mr. Lee   Bobbettes | 4/21/62 | (I was) Born To Cry   Dion | 7/25/64 | I'll Keep You Satisfied   Billy J. Kramer |
| 4/4/64 | I Should Care   Gloria Lynne | 4/29/67 | I Was Kaiser Bill's Batman<br>Whistling Jack Smith | 5/7/66 | I'll Love You Forever   Holidays |
| 7/25/64 | I Should Have Known Better   Beatles | | | 8/28/65 | I'll Make All Your Dreams Come<br>True   Ronnie Dove |
| 4/21/62 | I Sold My Heart To The Junkman<br>Blue-Belles | | I Was Made To Love Her | | |
| | | 6/10/67 | Stevie Wonder | 4/22/67 | I'll Make Him Love Me   Barbara Lewis |
| 3/19/66 | I Spy (For The FBI)   Jamo Thomas | 12/30/67 | King Curtis | 3/30/63 | I'll Make It Alright   Valentinos |
| 8/1/64 | I Stand Accused   Jerry Butler | | I Was Such A Fool (To Fall In Love<br>With You) | 2/22/64 | I'll Make You Mine   Bobby Vee |
| 6/17/67 | I Stand Accused (Of Loving You)<br>Glories | | | 6/19/61 | I'll Never Be Free   Kay Starr |
| | | 1/25/60 | Flamingos | 6/2/62 | I'll Never Dance Again   Bobby Rydell |
| 12/21/68 | I Started A Joke   Bee Gees | 10/6/62 | Connie Francis | 5/18/68 | I'll Never Do You Wrong   Joe Tex |
| 12/6/69 | I Started Loving You Again   Al Martino | 6/11/66 | (I Washed My Hands In) Muddy<br>Water   Johnny Rivers | | I'll Never Fall In Love Again |
| 10/25/69 | I Still Believe In Tomorrow<br>John & Anne Ryder | | | 9/9/67 | Tom Jones |
| | | | I (Who Have Nothing) | 7/26/69 | Tom Jones |
| 6/20/64 | I Still Get Jealous   Louis Armstrong | 6/29/63 | Ben E. King | | I'll Never Fall In Love Again |
| 10/23/65 | I Still Love You   Vejtables | 11/12/66 | Terry Knight | 7/5/69 | Burt Bacharach |
| 9/17/66 | I Struck It Rich   Len Barry | | I Will | 12/27/69 | Dionne Warwick |
| 3/26/66 | I Surrender   Fontella Bass | 3/31/62 | Vic Dana | | I'll Never Find Another You |
| 2/3/62 | I Surrender, Dear   Aretha Franklin | 10/30/65 | Dean Martin | 3/27/65 | Seekers |
| 8/9/69 | I Take A Lot Of Pride In What I Am<br>Dean Martin | 3/30/68 | I Will Always Think About You<br>New Colony Six | 7/22/67 | Sonny James |
| | | | | 7/31/65 | I'll Never Smile Again   Platters |
| 6/10/67 | I Take It Back   Sandy Posey | 3/23/63 | I Will Follow Him   Little Peggy March | 11/27/61 | I'll Never Stop Wanting You<br>Brian Hyland |
| 7/15/67 | I Take What I Want<br>James & Bobby Purify | 1/5/63 | I Will Live My Life For You<br>Tony Bennett | | |
| | | | | | (I'll Remember) .. also see: In The Still Of<br>The Nite |
| 7/15/67 | I Thank The Lord For The Night<br>Time   Neil Diamond | 7/6/63 | I Will Love You   Richard Chamberlain | | |
| | | 5/4/68 | I Wish I Knew   Solomon Burke | 10/13/62 | I'll Remember Carol   Tommy Boyce |
| 1/27/68 | I Thank You   Sam & Dave | 6/1/63 | I Wish I Were A Princess<br>Little Peggy March | 10/24/60 | I'll Save The Last Dance For You<br>Damita Jo |
| 2/11/67 | I Think We're Alone Now<br>Tommy James & The Shondells | | | | |
| | | 10/3/60 | I Wish I'd Never Been Born   Patti Page | | (also see: Save The Last Dance For Me) |
| 5/17/69 | I Threw It All Away   Bob Dylan | | | 3/9/68 | I'll Say Forever My Love   Jimmy Ruffin |

| Date | Song | Artist |
|---|---|---|
| 12/14/63 | I'll Search My Heart | Johnny Mathis |
| 1/27/62 | I'll See You In My Dreams | Pat Boone |
| 1/25/60 | I'll Take Care Of You | Bobby Bland |
| 1/21/67 | I'll Take Care Of Your Cares | Frankie Laine |
| 3/26/66 | I'll Take Good Care Of You | Garnet Mimms |
| 4/14/62 | I'll Take You Home | Corsairs |
| 9/7/63 | I'll Take You Home | Drifters |
| 8/14/65 | I'll Take You Where The Music's Playing | Drifters |
| 5/23/64 | I'll Touch A Star | Terry Stafford |
| 3/18/67 | I'll Try Anything | Dusty Springfield |
| | I'll Try Something New | |
| 5/12/62 | | Miracles |
| 3/15/69 | | Supremes & Temptations |
| 7/15/67 | I'll Turn To Stone | Four Tops |
| 12/10/66 | I'm A Believer | Monkees |
| 8/23/69 | I'm A Better Man | Engelbert Humperdinck |
| 4/19/69 | I'm A Drifter | Bobby Goldsboro |
| 6/26/65 | I'm A Fool | Dino, Desi & Billy |
| 9/23/67 | I'm A Fool For You | James Carr |
| | I'm A Fool To Care | |
| 4/24/61 | | Joe Barry |
| 4/24/61 | | Oscar Black |
| 7/17/65 | | Ray Charles |
| 8/14/65 | I'm A Happy Man | Jive Five |
| 10/30/65 | I'm A Man | Yardbirds |
| 3/25/67 | I'm A Man | Spencer Davis Group |
| 6/22/68 | I'm A Midnight Mover | Wilson Pickett |
| 6/25/66 | I'm A Nut | Leroy Pullins |
| 4/9/66 | (I'm A) Road Runner | Jr. Walker & The All Stars |
| 7/24/61 | I'm A Telling You | Jerry Butler |
| 1/5/63 | I'm A Woman | Peggy Lee |
| 6/29/63 | I'm Afraid To Go Home | Brian Hyland |
| 1/13/62 | I'm Blue (The Gong-Gong Song) | Ikettes |
| 4/9/66 | I'm Comin' Home, Cindy | Trini Lopez |
| 6/12/61 | I'm Comin' On Back To You | Jackie Wilson |
| 8/25/62 | I'm Coming Home | Paul Anka |
| 12/30/67 | I'm Coming Home | Tom Jones |
| | I'm Confessin' (That I Love You) | |
| 9/7/63 | | Frank Ifield |
| 4/25/64 | | Nino Tempo & April Stevens |
| 10/19/63 | I'm Crazy 'Bout My Baby | Marvin Gaye |
| 9/26/64 | I'm Crying | Animals |
| 11/9/63 | I'm Down To My Last Heartbreak | Wilson Pickett |
| | I'm Falling Too..see: (I Can't Help You) | |
| 7/19/69 | I'm Free | Who |
| 6/20/60 | I'm Gettin' Better | Jim Reeves |
| 10/6/62 | I'm Going Back To School | Dee Clark |
| 10/24/64 | I'm Gonna Be Strong | Gene Pitney |
| 12/15/62 | I'm Gonna' Be Warm This Winter | Connie Francis |
| 10/13/62 | I'm Gonna Change Everything | Jim Reeves |
| 5/10/69 | I'm Gonna Do All I Can (To Do Right By My Man) | Ike & Tina Turner |
| 7/27/68 | I'm Gonna Do What They Do To Me | B.B. King |
| 1/18/69 | I'm Gonna Hold On Long As I Can | Marvelettes |
| 6/19/61 | I'm Gonna Knock On Your Door | Eddie Hodges |
| 12/20/69 | I'm Gonna Love You | Intrigues |
| 11/28/64 | I'm Gonna Love You Too | Hullaballoos |
| | I'm Gonna Make You Love Me | |
| 11/26/66 | | Dee Dee Warwick |
| 2/10/68 | | Madeline Bell |
| 12/7/68 | | Supremes & Temptations |
| 12/24/66 | I'm Gonna Make You Mine | Shadows Of Knight |
| 8/23/69 | I'm Gonna Make You Mine | Lou Christie |
| 12/17/66 | I'm Gonna Miss You | Artistics |
| 6/19/61 | I'm Gonna Move To The Outskirts Of Town | Ray Charles |
| 7/7/62 | I'm Hanging Up My Heart For You | Solomon Burke |
| 8/1/64 | I'm Happy Just To Dance With You | Beatles |
| 7/3/65 | I'm Henry VIII, I Am | Herman's Hermits |
| 10/13/62 | I'm Here To Get My Baby Out Of Jail | Everly Brothers |
| 12/12/60 | I'm Hurtin' | Roy Orbison |
| 2/17/68 | I'm Hypnotized | Anthony & The Imperials |
| 10/5/68 | I'm In A Different World | Four Tops |
| 12/2/67 | I'm In Love | Wilson Pickett |
| 2/23/63 | I'm In Love Again | Rick Nelson |
| 3/27/61 | I'm In The Mood For Love | Chimes |
| 4/15/67 | I'm Indestructible | Jack Jones |
| 12/28/68 | I'm Into Lookin' For Someone To Love Me | Bobby Vee |
| | I'm Into Somethin' Good | |
| 6/27/64 | | Earl-Jean |
| 10/17/64 | | Herman's Hermits |
| 3/2/63 | I'm Just A Country Boy | George McCurn |
| 3/19/66 | (I'm Just A) Fool For You | Gene Chandler |
| 1/30/61 | I'm Learning About Love | Brenda Lee |
| 10/5/63 | I'm Leaving It Up To You | Dale & Grace |
| 1/25/69 | I'm Livin' In Shame | Supremes |
| 4/2/66 | I'm Living In Two Worlds | Bonnie Guitar |
| | I'm Losing You..see: (I Know) | |
| | I'm Movin' On | |
| 1/4/60* | | Ray Charles |
| 5/4/63 | | Matt Lucas |
| 8/17/63 | I'm Not A Fool Anymore | T.K. Hulin |
| 9/5/60 | I'm Not Afraid | Ricky Nelson |
| 12/17/66 | (I'm Not Your) Steppin' Stone | Monkees |
| 4/11/64 | I'm On Fire | Jerry Lee Lewis |
| 4/14/62 | I'm On My Way | Highwaymen |
| 8/22/64 | I'm On The Outside (Looking In) | Little Anthony & The Imperials |
| 2/6/65 | I'm Over You | Jan Bradley |
| 10/29/66 | I'm Ready For Love | Martha & The Vandellas |
| 11/27/65 | I'm Satisfied | San Remo Golden Strings |
| 5/11/63 | I'm Saving My Love | Skeeter Davis |
| 11/8/69 | (I'm So) Afraid Of Losing You Again | Charley Pride |
| 12/20/69 | I'm So Glad I Fell For You | David Ruffin |
| | I'm So Lonesome I Could Cry | |
| 12/1/62 | | Johnny Tillotson |
| 2/19/66 | | B.J. Thomas |
| 4/4/64 | I'm So Proud | Impressions |
| 10/9/65 | I'm So Thankful | Ikettes |
| 5/30/60 | I'm Sorry | Brenda Lee |
| 4/27/68 | I'm Sorry | Delfonics |
| 6/28/69 | I'm Still A Struggling Man | Edwin Starr |
| 3/13/65 | I'm Telling You Now | Freddie & The Dreamers |
| 8/18/62 | (I'm The Girl On) Wolverton Mountain | Jo Ann Campbell |
| 4/18/64 | I'm The Lonely One | Cliff Richard |
| 7/11/64 | I'm The One | Gerry & The Pacemakers |
| 2/9/63 | I'm The One Who Loves You | Impressions (also see: Remember Me) |
| | I'm The One You Need..see: (Come 'Round Here) | |
| 11/29/69 | I'm Tired | Savoy Brown |
| 1/8/66 | I'm Too Far Gone (To Turn Around) | Bobby Bland |
| 7/28/62 | I'm Tossin' And Turnin' Again | Bobby Lewis |
| | I'm Walking The Floor Over You..see: Walking The Floor | |
| 2/1/64 | (I'm Watching) Every Little Move You Make | Little Peggy March |
| 10/7/67 | I'm Wondering | Stevie Wonder |
| 8/27/66 | I'm Your Hoochie Cooche Man | Jimmy Smith |
| 9/24/66 | I'm Your Puppet | James & Bobby Purify |
| 8/28/65 | I'm Yours | Elvis Presley |
| 9/29/62 | I've Been Everywhere | Hank Snow |
| 4/19/69 | I've Been Hurt | Bill Deal |
| 1/28/67 | I've Been Lonely Too Long | Young Rascals |
| 6/27/60 | I've Been Loved Before | Shirley & Lee |
| | I've Been Loving You Too Long (To Stop Now) | |
| 5/15/65 | | Otis Redding |
| 4/26/69 | | Ike & Tina Turner |
| 8/7/65 | I've Cried My Last Tear | O'Jays |
| 1/23/65 | I've Got A Tiger By The Tail | Buck Owens |
| | I've Got A Woman..see: I Got A Woman | |
| 2/17/62 | I've Got Bonnie | Bobby Rydell |
| 9/28/68 | I've Got Dreams To Remember | Otis Redding |
| 4/17/65 | I've Got Five Dollars And It's Saturday Night | George Jones & Gene Pitney |
| 11/16/68 | I've Got Love For My Baby | Young Hearts |
| 6/19/61 | I've Got News For You | Ray Charles |
| 8/1/64 | I've Got No Time To Lose | Carla Thomas |
| 9/26/64 | I've Got Sand In My Shoes | Drifters |
| 5/15/61 | (I've Got) Spring Fever | Little Willie John |
| 11/14/64 | I've Got The Skill | Jackie Ross |
| | I've Got To..also see: I've Gotta | |
| 12/4/65 | I've Got To Be Somebody | Billy Joe Royal |
| 10/8/66 | I've Got To Do A Little Bit Better | Joe Tex |
| 1/7/67 | I've Got To Have A Reason | Dave Clark Five |
| 9/3/66 | I've Got You Under My Skin | 4 Seasons |
| 12/14/68 | I've Gotta Be Me | Sammy Davis, Jr. |
| 8/17/68 | I've Gotta Get A Message To You | Bee Gees |
| 7/19/69 | I've Lost Everything I've Ever Loved | David Ruffin |
| 5/6/67 | I've Lost You | Jackie Wilson |
| 7/27/68 | I've Never Found A Girl (To Love Me Like You Do) | Eddie Floyd |
| 12/3/66 | I've Passed This Way Before | Jimmy Ruffin |
| 3/13/61 | I've Told Every Little Star | Linda Scott |
| 3/22/69 | Ice Cream Song | Dynamics |
| 9/28/68 | Ice In The Sun | Status Quo |
| 3/3/62 | Ida Jane | Fats Domino |
| 4/5/69 | Idaho | 4 Seasons |
| 7/17/61 | If | Paragons |
| 9/29/62 | If A Man Answers | Bobby Darin |
| 3/10/62 | If A Woman Answers (Hang Up The Phone) | Leroy Van Dyke |
| 11/30/68 | If I Can Dream | Elvis Presley |
| 8/1/60 | If I Can't Have You | Etta & Harvey |
| 12/2/67 | If I Could Build My Whole World Around You | Marvin Gaye & Tammi Terrell |
| 4/21/62 | If I Cried Every Time You Hurt Me | Wanda Jackson |
| 1/9/61 | If I Didn't Care | Platters |
| 9/1/62 | If I Didn't Have A Dime (To Play The Jukebox) | Gene Pitney |
| 8/7/65 | If I Didn't Love You | Chuck Jackson |
| 8/1/64 | If I Fell | Beatles |
| 1/4/60* | If I Had A Girl | Rod Lauren |
| | If I Had A Hammer | |
| 8/18/62 | | Peter, Paul & Mary |
| 7/27/63 | | Trini Lopez |
| 12/31/60 | If I Knew | Nat "King" Cole |
| 2/20/65 | If I Loved You | Chad & Jeremy |
| 1/11/69 | If I Only Had Time | Nick DeCaro |
| 2/13/65 | If I Ruled The World | Tony Bennett |
| 6/30/62 | If I Should Lose You | Dreamlovers |
| | If I Were A Carpenter | |
| 9/24/66 | | Bobby Darin |
| 4/27/68 | | Four Tops |
| 8/8/64 | If I'm A Fool For Loving You | Bobby Wood |
| 1/4/69 | If It Wasn't For Bad Luck | Ray Charles & Jimmy Lewis |
| 8/31/68 | If Love Is In Your Heart | Friend & Lover |
| 3/2/63 | If Mary's There | Brian Hyland |
| 5/18/63 | If My Pillow Could Talk | Connie Francis |
| | If She Should Come To You (La Montana) | |
| 5/16/60 | | Frank DeVol |
| 6/6/60 | | Roger Williams |
| 10/10/60 | | Anthony Newley |
| 1/4/64 | If Somebody Told You | Anna King |
| 10/7/67 | If This Is Love (I'd Rather Be Lonely) | Precisions |
| 3/2/68 | If This World Were Mine | Marvin Gaye & Tammi Terrell |

| Date | Title | Artist |
|---|---|---|
| 2/24/68 | If You Can Want | Miracles |
| 4/20/63 | If You Can't Rock Me | Rick Nelson |
| 1/4/60* | (If You Cry) True Love, True Love | Drifters |
| 11/6/65 | If You Don't (Love Me, Tell Me So) | Barbara Mason |
| 4/13/68 | If You Don't Want My Love | Robert John |
| 2/17/68 | If You Ever Leave Me | Jack Jones |
| 12/10/66 | If You Go Away | Damita Jo |
|  | If You Gotta Make A Fool Of Somebody |  |
| 11/20/61 |  | James Ray |
| 12/11/65 |  | Maxine Brown |
| 2/15/60 | If You Need Me | Fats Domino |
|  | If You Need Me |  |
| 4/20/63 |  | Solomon Burke |
| 5/4/63 |  | Wilson Pickett |
| 7/24/65 | If You Really Want Me To, I'll Go | Ron-Dels |
| 7/4/64 | If You See My Love | Lenny Welch |
| 8/21/65 | If You Wait For Love | Bobby Goldsboro |
| 3/30/63 | If You Wanna Be Happy | Jimmy Soul |
| 10/10/64 | If You Want This Love | Sonny Knight |
| 11/10/62 | If You Were A Rock And Roll Record | Freddy Cannon |
| 9/25/65 | If You've Got A Heart | Bobby Goldsboro |
| 4/3/65 | Iko Iko | Dixie Cups |
| 10/9/61 | Image | Hank Levine |
| 6/6/60 | Image Of A Girl | Safaris |
| 5/12/62 | Imagine That | Patsy Cline |
| 9/11/61 | Impossible | Gloria Lynne |
|  | Impossible Dream |  |
| 6/4/66 |  | Jack Jones |
| 3/16/68 |  | Hesitations |
| 7/13/68 |  | Roger Williams |
| 11/23/63 | Impossible Happened | Little Peggy March |
| 4/20/68 | Impossible Mission (Mission Impossible) | Soul Survivors |
| 8/24/68 | In-A-Gadda-Da-Vida | Iron Butterfly |
| 8/2/69 | In A Moment | Intrigues |
| 11/11/67 | In And Out Of Love | Supremes |
| 12/16/67 | In Another Land | Bill Wyman |
| 5/8/61 | In Between Tears | Lenny Miles |
|  | "In" Crowd |  |
| 1/9/65 |  | Dobie Gray |
| 7/31/65 |  | Ramsey Lewis Trio |
| 2/9/63 | In Dreams | Roy Orbison |
| 5/8/61 | In My Heart | Timetones |
| 7/11/60 | In My Little Corner Of The World | Anita Bryant |
| 4/11/64 | In My Lonely Room | Martha & The Vandellas |
|  | In My Room |  |
| 11/2/63 |  | Beach Boys |
| 8/2/69 |  | Sagittarius |
| 2/5/66 |  | Verdelle Smith |
| 3/16/68 | In Need Of A Friend | Cowsills |
| 9/17/66 | In Our Time | Nancy Sinatra |
|  | In Real Life..see: (It Never Happens) |  |
| 3/16/68 | In Some Time | Ronnie Dove |
| 8/27/66 | In The Arms Of Love | Andy Williams |
| 4/5/69 | In The Bad, Bad Old Days | Foundations |
| 8/13/66 | In The Basement | Etta James & Sugar Pie DeSanto |
|  | In The Chapel In The Moonlight..see: Chapel |  |
| 5/3/69 | In The Ghetto | Elvis Presley |
| 8/26/67 | In The Heat Of The Night | Ray Charles |
| 5/1/65 | In The Meantime | Georgie Fame |
| 10/16/61 | In The Middle Of A Heartache | Wanda Jackson |
|  | In The Midnight Hour |  |
| 7/10/65 |  | Wilson Pickett |
| 2/17/68 |  | Mirettes |
|  | In The Misty Moonlight |  |
| 7/25/64 |  | Jerry Wallace |
| 12/2/67 |  | Dean Martin |
| 1/4/60* | In The Mood | Ernie Fields |
| 7/18/60 | In The Still Of The Night | Dion & The Belmonts |
|  | In The Still Of The Nite |  |
| 1/4/60 |  | Five Satins |
| 1/23/61 |  | Five Satins |
| 1/18/64 |  | Santo & Johnny |
| 3/22/69 |  | Paul Anka |
| 12/28/63 | In The Summer Of His Years | Connie Francis |
| 7/12/69 | In The Time Of Our Lives | Iron Butterfly |
| 6/21/69 | In The Year 2525 (Exordium & Terminus) | Zager & Evans |
| 8/14/61 | In Time | Steve Lawrence |
| 9/30/67 | Incense And Peppermints | Strawberry Alarm Clock |
| 1/28/67 | Indescribably Blue | Elvis Presley |
| 1/25/69 | Indian Giver | 1910 Fruitgum Co. |
| 6/1/68 | Indian Lake | Cowsills |
| 8/31/68 | Indian Reservation | Don Fardon |
| 10/23/65 | Inky Dinky Spider | Kids Next Door |
| 3/30/68 | Inner Light | Beatles |
| 2/26/66 | Inside-Looking Out | Animals |
| 3/30/63 | Insult To Injury | Timi Yuro |
| 7/18/64 | Invisible Tears | Ray Conniff Singers |
|  | Irresistable You |  |
| 10/31/60 |  | Bobby Peterson |
| 12/11/61 |  | Bobby Darin |
|  | Irving..see: Ballad Of |  |
| 6/13/60 | Is A Blue Bird Blue | Conway Twitty |
| 12/13/69 | Is It Because I'm Black | Syl Johnson |
| 1/29/66 | Is It Me? | Barbara Mason |
| 8/14/65 | Is It Really Over? | Jim Reeves |
| 3/22/69 | Is It Something You've Got | Tyrone Davis |
| 10/17/64 | Is It True | Brenda Lee |
| 5/2/60 | Is It Wrong (For Loving You) | Webb Pierce |
| 9/27/69 | Is That All There Is | Peggy Lee |
| 6/20/60 | Is There Any Chance | Marty Robbins |
| 1/9/61 | Is There Something On Your Mind | Jack Scott |
| 5/29/65 | Is This What I Get For Loving You? | Ronettes |
| 9/19/60 | Is You Is Or Is You Ain't My Baby | Buster Brown |
| 1/13/62 | Island In The Sky | Troy Shondell |
| 10/24/60 | Isn't It Amazing | Crests |
|  | Isn't It Lonely Together |  |
| 10/19/68 |  | Robert Knight |
| 12/14/68 |  | O.C. Smith |
| 5/17/69 | Israelites | Desmond Dekker & The Aces |
|  | It Ain't Me, Babe |  |
| 10/31/64 |  | Johnny Cash |
| 8/7/65 |  | Turtles |
| 5/8/65 | It Ain't No Big Thing | Radiants |
| 6/6/64 | It Ain't No Use | Major Lance |
| 8/5/67 | It Could Be We're In Love | Cryan' Shames |
| 3/28/60 | It Could Happen To You | Dinah Washington |
| 11/13/61 | It Do Me So Good | Ann-Margret |
| 6/19/65 | It Feels So Right | Elvis Presley |
| 2/29/64 | It Hurts Me | Elvis Presley |
| 9/3/66 | It Hurts Me | Bobby Goldsboro |
| 7/18/64 | It Hurts To Be In Love | Gene Pitney |
| 7/20/63 | It Hurts To Be Sixteen | Andrea Carroll |
| 5/15/61 | It Keeps Rainin' | Fats Domino |
| 5/12/62 | It Keeps Right On A-Hurtin' | Johnny Tillotson |
| 1/14/67 | It May Be Winter Outside (But In My Heart It's Spring) | Felice Taylor |
| 8/25/62 | It Might As Well Rain Until September | Carole King |
| 9/2/67 | It Must Be Him | Vikki Carr |
| 4/10/61 | (It Never Happens) In Real Life | Chuck Jackson |
| 8/1/60 | It Only Happened Yesterday | Jack Scott |
| 6/8/68 | It Should Have Been Me | Gladys Knight & The Pips |
| 6/30/62 | It Started All Over Again | Brenda Lee |
| 1/7/67 | It Takes Two | Marvin Gaye & Kim Weston |
| 10/22/66 | It Tears Me Up | Percy Sledge |
|  | It Was A Very Good Year |  |
| 12/25/65 |  | Frank Sinatra |
| 9/10/66 |  | Della Reese |
|  | It Will Stand |  |
| 11/13/61 |  | Showmen |
| 7/4/64 |  | Showmen |
| 8/17/63 | It Won't Be This Way (Always) | King Pins |
| 2/12/66 | It Won't Be Wrong | Byrds |
| 11/28/64 | It'll Never Be Over For Me | Baby Washington |
| 8/15/64 | It's A Cotton Candy World | Jerry Wallace |
|  | It's A Funky Thing..see: Memphis Underground |  |
| 4/12/69 | It's A Groovy World! | Unifics |
| 11/12/66 | It's-A-Happening | Magic Mushrooms |
| 3/11/67 | It's A Happening Thing | Peanut Butter Conspiracy |
| 7/22/67 | It's A Happening World | Tokens |
| 8/10/63 | It's A Lonely Town | Gene McDaniels |
| 10/19/63 | It's A Mad, Mad, Mad, Mad World | Shirelles |
| 8/7/65 | It's A Man Down There | G.L. Crockett |
| 4/30/66 | It's A Man's Man's Man's World | James Brown |
| 7/11/64 | It's A Sin To Tell A Lie | Tony Bennett |
| 11/13/61 | It's All Because | Linda Scott |
| 12/7/63 | It's All In The Game | Cliff Richard |
| 9/12/64 | It's All Over | Ben E. King |
| 11/21/64 | It's All Over | Walter Jackson |
|  | It's All Over Now |  |
| 6/27/64 |  | Valentinos |
| 7/25/64 |  | Rolling Stones |
| 4/29/67 | It's All Over Now | Casinos |
| 9/25/61 | It's All Right | Sam Cooke |
| 9/28/63 | It's All Right | Impressions |
| 4/4/64 | It's All Right (You're Just In Love) | Tams |
| 5/29/65 | It's Almost Tomorrow | Jimmy Velvet |
| 1/16/65 | It's Alright | Adam Faith |
| 6/4/66 | It's An Uphill Climb To The Bottom | Walter Jackson |
| 7/29/67 | It's Been A Long Long Time | Elgins |
| 12/20/69 | It's Been A Long Time | Betty Everett |
| 1/9/65 | It's Better To Have It | Barbara Lynn |
| 6/3/67 | It's Cold Outside | Choir |
| 10/26/68 | It's Crazy | Eddie Harris |
| 9/19/64 | It's For You | Cilla Black |
| 6/7/69 | It's Getting Better | Mama Cass |
| 2/13/65 | It's Gonna Be Alright | Maxine Brown |
| 4/10/65 | It's Gonna Be Alright | Gerry & The Pacemakers |
| 7/17/65 | It's Gonna Be Fine | Glenn Yarbrough |
| 7/17/65 | It's Gonna Take A Miracle | Royalettes |
| 7/31/61 | It's Gonna Work Out Fine | Ike & Tina Turner |
| 12/4/65 | It's Good News Week | Hedgehoppers Anonymous |
| 4/10/65 | It's Got The Whole World Shakin' | Sam Cooke |
| 8/12/67 | It's Got To Be Mellow | Leon Haywood |
| 2/6/65 | It's Gotta Last Forever | Billy J. Kramer |
| 4/3/65 | It's Growing | Temptations |
| 10/18/69 | It's Hard To Get Along | Joe Simon |
|  | (It's In His Kiss)..see: Shoop Shoop Song |  |
| 10/2/61 | It's Just A House Without You | Brook Benton |
| 6/12/65 | It's Just A Little Bit Too Late | Wayne Fontana & The Mindbenders |
| 2/17/62 | It's Magic | Platters |
| 11/6/65 | It's My Life | Animals |
| 5/11/63 | It's My Party | Lesley Gore |
| 6/14/69 | It's My Thing | Marva Whitney |
| 5/10/69 | It's Never Too Late | Steppenwolf |
| 6/15/68 | It's Nice To Be With You | Monkees |
| 1/25/64 | (It's No) Sin | Duprees |
| 2/3/68 | It's Not Easy | Will-O-Bees |
| 10/10/60 | It's Not The End Of Everything | Tommy Edwards |
| 11/12/66 | It's Not The Same | Anthony & The Imperials |
| 4/10/65 | It's Not Unusual | Tom Jones |
| 7/18/64 | It's Now Or Never | Elvis Presley |
| 12/24/66 | It's Now Winters Day | Tommy Roe |
| 11/5/66 | It's Only Love | Tommy James & The Shondells |
| 3/22/69 | It's Only Love | B.J. Thomas |
| 4/11/64 | It's Over | Roy Orbison |
|  | It's Over |  |
| 5/14/66 |  | Jimmie Rodgers |
| 5/18/68 |  | Eddy Arnold |
| 4/15/67 | It's So Hard Being A Loser | Contours |
| 6/18/66 | It's That Time Of The Year | Len Barry |
| 8/12/67 | It's The Little Things | Sonny & Cher |
| 7/31/65 | It's The Same Old Song | Four Tops |

| Date | Title | Artist |
|---|---|---|
| 1/4/60* | **It's Time To Cry** | Paul Anka |
| 7/27/63 | **It's Too Late** | Wilson Pickett |
| 2/19/66 | **It's Too Late** | Bobby Goldsboro |
| 7/17/65 | **It's Too Late, Baby Too Late** Arthur Prysock | |
| | **It's Too Soon To Know** | |
| 11/6/61 | | Etta James |
| 8/6/66 | | Roy Orbison |
| 3/6/61 | **It's Unbelievable** | Larks |
| 12/15/62 | **It's Up To You** | Rick Nelson |
| 12/9/67 | **It's Wonderful** | Rascals |
| 5/22/65 | **It's Wonderful To Be In Love** | Ovations |
| | **It's You That I Need**..see: (Loneliness Made Me Realize) | |
| 3/15/69 | **It's Your Thing** | Isley Brothers |
| 9/11/61 | **It's Your World** | Marty Robbins |
| 11/11/67 | **Itchycoo Park** | Small Faces |
| 7/4/60 | **Itsy Bitsy Teenie Weenie Yellow Polkadot Bikini** | Brian Hyland |
| 4/7/62 | **Itty Bitty Pieces** | James Ray |
| 5/10/69 | **Ivory** | Bob Seger System |

## J

| Date | Title | Artist |
|---|---|---|
| 2/27/61 | **Ja-Da** | Johnny & The Hurricanes |
| 7/19/69 | **Jack And Jill** | Tommy Roe |
| 6/15/63 | **Jack The Ripper** | Link Wray |
| 6/24/67 | **Jackson** | Nancy Sinatra & Lee Hazlewood |
| 3/21/64 | **Jailer, Bring Me Water** | Trini Lopez |
| 3/17/62 | **Jam, The** | Bobby Gregg |
| 11/15/69 | **Jam Up Jelly Tight** | Tommy Roe |
| 7/11/64 | **Jamaica Ska** | Ska Kings |
| | **Jambalaya (On The Bayou)** | |
| 3/7/60 | | Bobby Comstock |
| 12/11/61 | | Fats Domino |
| 8/22/64 | **James Bond Theme** | Billy Strange |
| 9/29/62 | **James (Hold The Ladder Steady)** | Sue Thompson |
| 1/20/62 | **Jamie** | Eddie Holland |
| 5/19/62 | **Jane, Jane, Jane** | Kingston Trio |
| | **Java** | |
| 12/29/62 | | Floyd Cramer |
| 1/4/64 | | Al Hirt |
| 11/29/69 | **Je T'Aime...Moi Non Plus** | Jane Birkin & Serge Gainsbourg |
| 11/27/65 | **Jealous Heart** | Connie Francis |
| 9/13/69 | **Jealous Kind Of Fella** | Garland Green |
| 2/17/68 | **Jealous Love** | Wilson Pickett |
| 5/23/60 | **Jealous Of You** | Connie Francis |
| 8/16/69 | **Jean** | Oliver |
| | **Jed Clampett**..see: Ballad Of | |
| 5/18/68 | **Jelly Jungle (Of Orange Marmalade)** | Lemon Pipers |
| 12/22/62 | **Jellybread** | Booker T. & The MG's |
| 3/16/68 | **Jennifer Eccles** | Hollies |
| 3/9/68 | **Jennifer Juniper** | Donovan |
| 9/28/63 | **Jenny Brown** | Smothers Brothers |
| 4/11/60 | **Jenny Lou** | Sonny James |
| 12/11/65 | **Jenny Take A Ride!** | Mitch Ryder & The Detroit Wheels |
| 8/21/61 | **Jeremiah Peabody's Poly Unsaturated Pills** | Ray Stevens |
| 11/14/64 | **Jerk, The** | Larks |
| 1/30/65 | **Jerk And Twine** | Jackie Ross |
| 10/26/68 | **Jesse Brady** | McCoys |
| 9/20/69 | **Jesus Is A Soul Man** | Lawrence Reynolds |
| 8/12/67 | **Jill** | Gary Lewis & The Playboys |
| 2/25/67 | **Jimmy Mack** | Martha & The Vandellas |
| 5/29/61 | **Jimmy Martinez** | Marty Robbins |
| 1/9/61 | **Jimmy's Girl** | Johnny Tillotson |
| | **Jingle Bell Rock** | |
| 12/12/60 | | Bobby Helms |
| 12/11/61 | | Bobby Helms |
| 12/11/61 | | Bobby Rydell/Chubby Checker |
| 12/8/62 | | Bobby Helms |
| 12/15/62 | | Bobby Rydell/Chubby Checker |
| 11/29/69 | **Jingle Jangle** | Archies |
| 10/25/69 | **Jingo** | Santana |
| 11/24/62 | **Jitterbug, The** | Dovells |
| 2/16/63 | **Jive Samba** | Cannonball Adderley |
| 7/28/62 | **Jivin' Around** | Al Casey Combo |
| 6/12/61 | **Joanie** | Frankie Calen |
| 2/17/62 | **Joey Baby** | Anita & Th' So-And-So's |
| | **John And Yoko**..see: Ballad Of | |
| 5/19/62 | **John Birch Society** | Chad Mitchell Trio |
| 3/3/62 | **Johnny Angel** | Shelley Fabares |
| 8/22/64 | **Johnny B. Goode** | Dion |
| 7/4/60 | **Johnny Freedom** | Johnny Horton |
| 5/26/62 | **Johnny Get Angry** | Joanie Sommers |
| 3/17/62 | **Johnny Jingo** | Hayley Mills |
| 6/9/62 | **Johnny Loves Me** | Shelley Fabares |
| 2/8/69 | **Johnny One Time** | Brenda Lee |
| 11/13/61 | **Johnny Will** | Pat Boone |
| 9/25/61 | **Johnny Willow** | Fred Darian |
| 7/16/66 | **Joker Went Wild** | Brian Hyland |
| 6/24/67 | **Jokers, The** | Peter & Gordon |
| 1/9/65 | **Jolly Green Giant** | Kingsmen |
| | (also see: Big Boy Pete) | |
| 6/27/60 | **Josephine** | Bill Black's Combo |
| 9/12/60 | **Journey Of Love** | Crests |
| 6/29/68 | **Journey To The Center Of The Mind** | Amboy Dukes |
| 7/1/67 | **Joy** | Mitch Ryder |
| 7/31/65 | **Ju Ju Hand** | Sam The Sham & The Pharoahs |
| 3/12/66 | **Juanita Banana** | Peels |
| 9/9/67 | **Judy** | Elvis Presley |
| | **Judy Blue Eyes**..see: Suite | |
| 11/25/67 | **Judy In Disguise (With Glasses)** | John Fred |
| 1/11/64 | **Judy Loves Me** | Johnny Crawford |
| 7/6/63 | **Judy's Turn To Cry** | Lesley Gore |
| 9/4/61 | **Juke Box Saturday Night** | Nino & The Ebb Tides |
| 9/27/69 | **Julia** | Ramsey Lewis |
| 4/19/69 | **July You're A Woman** | Pat Boone |
| 4/6/68 | **Jumbo** | Bee Gees |
| | **Jump Back** | |
| 10/10/64 | | Rufus Thomas |
| 5/13/67 | | King Curtis |
| 5/9/60 | **Jump Over** | Freddy Cannon |
| 6/8/68 | **Jumpin' Jack Flash** | Rolling Stones |
| 4/1/67 | **Jungle, The** | B.B. King |
| 4/24/61 | **Jura (I Swear I Love You)** | Les Paul & Mary Ford |
| | **Just A Closer Walk With Thee** | |
| 2/8/60 | | Pete Fountain |
| 4/11/60 | | Jimmie Rodgers |
| 10/3/60 | **Just A Little** | Brenda Lee |
| 4/17/65 | **Just A Little** | Beau Brummels |
| | **Just A Little Bit** | |
| 2/15/60 | | Rosco Gordon |
| 10/30/65 | | Roy Head |
| 7/6/68 | **Just A Little Bit** | Blue Cheer |
| 5/10/69 | **Just A Little Bit** | Little Milton |
| 9/18/65 | **Just A Little Bit Better** | Herman's Hermits |
| 10/18/69 | **Just A Little Love** | B.B. King |
| 5/28/66 | **Just A Little Misunderstanding** | Contours |
| 10/10/64 | **Just A Moment Ago** | Soul Sisters |
| 5/23/64 | **Just Ain't Enough Love** | Eddie Holland |
| 11/16/68 | **Just Ain't No Love** | Barbara Acklin |
| | **Just As Much As Ever** | |
| 1/4/60* | | Bob Beckham |
| 12/30/67 | | Bobby Vinton |
| 2/11/67 | **Just Be Sincere** | Jackie Wilson |
| 7/11/64 | **Just Be True** | Gene Chandler |
| 11/6/61 | **Just Because** | McGuire Sisters |
| 9/12/60 | **Just Call Me (And I'll Understand)** | Lloyd Price |
| 1/4/60* | **Just Come Home** | Hugo & Luigi |
| 2/10/68 | **Just Dropped In (To See What Condition My Condition Was In)** | First Edition |
| 3/13/61 | **Just For Old Time's Sake** | McGuire Sisters |
| 2/29/60 | **Just Give Me A Ring** | Clyde McPhatter |
| 12/11/61 | **Just Got To Know** | Jimmy McCracklin |
| 9/10/66 | **Just Like A Woman** | Bob Dylan |
| 12/4/65 | **Just Like Me** | Paul Revere & The Raiders |
| 4/11/64 | **(Just Like) Romeo & Juliet** | Reflections |
| 4/22/67 | **Just Look What You've Done** | Brenda Holloway |
| 8/12/67 | **Just Once In A Lifetime** | Brenda & The Tabulations |
| 4/10/65 | **Just Once In My Life** | Righteous Brothers |
| 10/2/65 | **Just One Kiss From You** | Impressions |
| | **Just One Look** | |
| 6/8/63 | | Doris Troy |
| 5/16/64 | | Hollies |
| 9/30/67 | | Hollies |
| 12/4/65 | **Just One More Day** | Otis Redding |
| 12/24/66 | **Just One Smile** | Gene Pitney |
| 3/7/60 | **Just One Time** | Don Gibson |
| | **Just Out Of Reach (Of My Two Open Arms)** | |
| 9/18/61 | | Solomon Burke |
| 9/2/67 | | Percy Sledge |
| 8/11/62 | **Just Tell Her Jim Said Hello** | Elvis Presley |
| 10/9/65 | **Just Yesterday** | Jack Jones |
| 8/6/66 | **Just Yesterday** | Al Martino |
| 8/28/65 | **Just You** | Sonny & Cher |
| 7/3/65 | **Justine** | Righteous Brothers |

## K

| Date | Title | Artist |
|---|---|---|
| | **Kansas City** | |
| 11/16/63 | | Trini Lopez |
| 3/4/67 | | James Brown |
| 9/11/65 | **Kansas City Star** | Roger Miller |
| 12/3/66 | **Karate** | Emperor's |
| 9/16/67 | **Karate-Boo-Ga-Loo** | Jerryo |
| 12/28/68 | **Kay** | John Wesley Ryles, I |
| 8/2/69 | **Keem-O-Sabe** | Electric Indian |
| 2/11/67 | **Keep A Light In The Window Till I Come Home** | Solomon Burke |
| 8/21/61 | **Keep On Dancing** | Hank Ballard |
| 9/11/65 | **Keep On Dancing** | Gentrys |
| 11/23/68 | **Keep On Dancing** | Alvin Cash |
| 10/12/68 | **Keep On Lovin' Me Honey** | Marvin Gaye & Tammi Terrell |
| 6/6/64 | **Keep On Pushing** | Impressions |
| 3/5/66 | **Keep On Running** | Spencer Davis Group |
| 5/8/65 | **Keep On Trying** | Bobby Vee |
| 11/21/64 | **Keep Searchin'** | Del Shannon |
| | **Keep The Ball Rollin'** | |
| 10/21/67 | | Jay & The Techniques |
| 1/27/68 | | Al Hirt |
| 8/10/68 | **Keep The One You Got** | Joe Tex |
| 7/14/62 | **Keep Your Hands In Your Pockets** | Playmates |
| 11/3/62 | **Keep Your Hands Off My Baby** | Little Eva |
| 2/6/61 | **Keep Your Hands Off Of Him** | Damita Jo |
| 6/9/62 | **Keep Your Love Locked (Deep In Your Heart)** | Paul Petersen |
| | **Kentucky Woman** | |
| 10/14/67 | | Neil Diamond |
| 11/9/68 | | Deep Purple |
| 3/15/69 | **Kick Out The Jams** | MC5 |
| 5/30/64 | **Kick That Little Foot Sally Ann** | Round Robin |
| 3/19/66 | **Kicks** | Paul Revere & The Raiders |
| 8/8/60 | **Kiddio** | Brook Benton |
| 5/16/64 | **Kiko** | Jimmy McGriff |
| | **Killer Joe** | |
| 3/23/63 | | Rocky Fellers |
| 4/2/66 | | Kingsmen |
| 12/31/66 | **Kind Of A Drag** | Buckinghams |
| 8/10/63 | **Kind Of Boy You Can't Forget** | Raindrops |
| 10/7/67 | **King Midas In Reverse** | Hollies |
| 3/31/62 | **King Of Clowns** | Neil Sedaka |
| 1/30/65 | **King Of The Road** | Roger Miller |
| | (also see: Queen Of The House) | |
| 9/22/62 | **King Of The Whole Wide World** | Elvis Presley |
| 11/6/65 | **Kiss Away** | Ronnie Dove |
| 2/17/68 | **Kiss Me Goodbye** | Petula Clark |
| 5/2/64 | **Kiss Me Quick** | Elvis Presley |
| 4/4/64 | **Kiss Me Sailor** | Diane Renay |
| 10/31/60 | **Kissin' And Twistin'** | Fabian |
| 2/22/64 | **Kissin' Cousins** | Elvis Presley |
| 5/1/61 | **Kissin' Game** | Dion |
| 8/28/61 | **Kissin' On The Phone** | Paul Anka |
| 12/24/66 | **Knight In Rusty Armour** | Peter & Gordon |
| 8/29/64 | **Knock! Knock! (Who's There?)** | Orlons |
| | **Knock On Wood** | |
| 9/10/66 | | Eddie Floyd |
| 8/12/67 | | Otis & Carla |

| | | | | | |
|---|---|---|---|---|---|
| | Know What You're Doin'..see: (You Better) | | Lawdy Miss Clawdy | | Let's Call It A Day Girl |
| 9/2/67 | Knucklehead Bar-Kays | 2/22/60 | Gary Stites | 7/30/66 | Razor's Edge |
| 3/13/61 | Kokomo Flamingos | 3/11/67 | Buckinghams | 8/2/69 | Bobby Vee |
| 8/22/60 | Kommotion Duane Eddy | | Lawrence Of Arabia..see: Theme From | | Let's Dance |
| | Kookie Little Paradise | 7/12/69 | Lay Lady Lay Bob Dylan | 8/4/62 | Chris Montez |
| 8/15/60 | Jo Ann Campbell | 4/29/67 | Lay Some Happiness On Me Dean Martin | 5/24/69 | Ola & The Janglers |
| 8/15/60 | Tree Swingers | 10/14/67 | Lazy Day Spanky & Our Gang | 4/3/65 | Let's Do The Freddie Chubby Checker (also see: Do The Freddie) |
| 9/13/69 | Kool And The Gang Kool & The Gang | 6/6/64 | Lazy Elsie Molly Chubby Checker | 12/26/60 | (Let's Do) The Hully Gully Twist Bill Doggett |
| 11/8/69 | Kozmic Blues Janis Joplin | 2/29/64 | Lazy Lady Fats Domino | 12/31/66 | Let's Fall In Love Peaches & Herb |
| 1/18/69 | Kum Ba Yah Tommy Leonetti | | Lazy River | 9/4/61 | Let's Get Together Hayley Mills (also see: Get Together) |
| | **L** | 2/6/61 | Bobby Darin | 2/3/62 | Let's Go Floyd Cramer |
| | | 11/13/61 | Si Zentner | 11/3/62 | Let's Go Routers |
| 3/2/68 | L. David Sloane Michele Lee | 12/5/64 | Leader Of The Laundromat Detergents | 2/20/61 | Let's Go Again Hank Ballard |
| | La Bomba | 10/10/64 | Leader Of The Pack Shangri-Las | 5/28/66 | Let's Go Get Stoned Ray Charles |
| 6/30/62 | Tokens | 10/6/62 | Leah Roy Orbison | 9/19/60 | Let's Go, Let's Go, Let's Go Hank Ballard |
| 6/25/66 | Trini Lopez | 4/9/66 | Leaning On The Lamp Post Herman's Hermits | | |
| 7/3/61 | La Dolce Vita (The Sweet Life) Ray Ellis | 7/20/63 | Leave Me Alone Baby Washington | 4/27/63 | Let's Go Steady Again Neil Sedaka |
| 4/2/66 | La La La Gerry & The Pacemakers | | Leave My Kitten Alone | 4/30/66 | Let's Go Steady Again Sam Cooke |
| 11/22/69 | La La La (If I Had You) Bobby Sherman | 1/23/61 | Little Willie John | 11/27/61 | Let's Go Trippin' Dick Dale |
| | | 1/30/61 | Johnny Preston | 10/9/65 | Let's Hang On! 4 Seasons |
| 9/12/64 | La La La La La Blendells | 1/26/63 | Leavin' On Your Mind Patsy Cline | | Let's Have A Party |
| 2/3/68 | La-La Means I Love You Delfonics | 2/8/64 | Leaving Here Eddie Holland | 8/29/60 | Wanda Jackson |
| | La Montana..see: If She Should Come To You | 10/25/69 | Leaving On A Jet Plane Peter, Paul & Mary | 5/30/64 | Rivieras |
| 4/10/61 | La Pachanga Audrey Arno | | (Legend Of Billy Jack)..see: One Tin Soldier | 12/1/62 | Let's Kiss And Make Up Bobby Vinton |
| 3/17/62 | La Paloma Twist Chubby Checker | | Lemon Tree | 2/16/63 | Let's Limbo Some More Chubby Checker |
| 1/21/67 | Lady Jack Jones | 5/5/62 | Peter, Paul & Mary | 5/13/67 | Let's Live For Today Grass Roots |
| 10/21/67 | Lady Bird Nancy Sinatra & Lee Hazlewood | 1/23/65 | Trini Lopez | 12/26/64 | Let's Lock The Door Jay & The Americans |
| 4/8/67 | Lady Came From Baltimore Bobby Darin | 5/20/67 | Leopard-Skin Pill-Box Hat Bob Dylan | 11/9/68 | Let's Make A Promise Peaches & Herb |
| 8/19/67 | Lady Friend Byrds | 10/19/68 | Les Bicyclettes De Belsize Engelbert Humperdinck | 9/28/63 | Let's Make Love Tonight Bobby Rydell |
| 10/8/66 | Lady Godiva Peter & Gordon | 12/23/67 | Lesson, The Vikki Carr | 9/25/65 | Let's Move & Groove (Together) Johnny Nash |
| 7/23/66 | Lady Jane Rolling Stones | | Let A Man Come In And Do The Popcorn | 1/21/67 | Let's Spend The Night Together Rolling Stones |
| 2/1/60 | Lady Luck Lloyd Price | 10/11/69 | James Brown (Part One) | 4/16/66 | Let's Start All Over Again Ronnie Dove |
| | Lady Madonna | 12/20/69 | James Brown (Part Two) | 2/16/63 | Let's Stomp Bobby Comstock |
| 3/23/68 | Beatles | 9/20/69 | Let A Woman Be A Woman - Let A Man Be A Man Dyke & The Blazers | 9/5/60 | Let's Think About Living Bob Luman |
| 9/7/68 | Fats Domino | | Let It Be Me | 1/4/60* | Let's Try Again Clyde McPhatter |
| 12/6/69 | Lady-O Turtles | 1/11/60 | Everly Brothers | 2/2/63 | Let's Turkey Trot Little Eva |
| 6/8/68 | Lady Willpower Union Gap | 9/5/64 | Betty Everett & Jerry Butler | 6/19/61 | Let's Twist Again Chubby Checker |
| 10/5/68 | Lalena Donovan | 7/22/67 | Sweet Inspirations | 12/6/69 | Let's Work Together Wilbert Harrison |
| | Lament Of Cherokee..see: Indian Reservation | 1/25/69 | Glen Campbell & Bobbie Gentry | 10/23/65 | Letter, The Sonny & Cher |
| 6/4/66 | Land Of Milk And Honey Vogues | 9/16/67 | Let It Out (Let It All Hang Out) Hombres | | Letter, The |
| | Land Of 1000 Dances | 2/1/60 | Let It Rock Chuck Berry | 8/12/67 | Box Tops |
| 6/29/63 | Chris Kenner | 9/9/67 | Let Love Come Between Us James & Bobby Purify | 2/22/69 | Arbors |
| 2/27/65 | Cannibal & The Headhunters | 5/17/69 | Let Me Paul Revere & The Raiders | 6/29/63 | Letter From Betty Bobby Vee |
| 3/13/65 | Thee Midniters | 10/30/65 | Let Me Be Turtles | 12/28/63 | Letter From Sherry Dale Ward |
| 7/30/66 | Wilson Pickett | 4/30/66 | Let Me Be Good To You Carla Thomas | 12/11/61 | Letter Full Of Tears Gladys Knight & The Pips |
| 12/13/69 | Electric Indian | 6/8/68 | Let Me Be Lonely Dionne Warwick | | Letter Song..see: S.Y.S.L.J.F.M. |
| 11/6/61 | Language Of Love John D. Loudermilk | 8/2/69 | Let Me Be The Man My Daddy Was Chi-Lites | 11/25/67 | Letter To Dad Every Father's Teenage Son (also see: Open Letter To My Teenage Son) |
| 10/28/67 | Lapland Baltimore & Ohio Marching Band | | Let Me Be The One | 3/21/64 | Letter To The Beatles Four Preps |
| | Lara's Theme..see: Somewhere My Love | 5/12/62 | Paris Sisters | 8/14/65 | Liar, Liar Castaways |
| 4/25/64 | Last Chance Collay & the Satellites | 8/16/69 | Peaches & Herb | | Liberty Valance..see: (Man Who Shot) |
| 5/8/65 | Last Chance To Turn Around Gene Pitney | 8/7/61 | Let Me Belong To You Brian Hyland | | Lickin' Stick..see: (Mama Come Quick, And Bring Your) |
| 8/15/60 | Last Dance McGuire Sisters | 2/3/62 | Let Me Call You Sweetheart Timi Yuro | 5/25/68 | Licking Stick - Licking Stick James Brown |
| | Last Date | 12/15/62 | Let Me Entertain You Ray Anthony | 8/25/62 | Lie To Me Brook Benton |
| 10/10/60 | Floyd Cramer | 12/8/62 | Let Me Go The Right Way Supremes | 12/4/65 | Lies Knickerbockers |
| 10/24/60 | Lawrence Welk (also see: My Last Date With You) | 1/6/62 | Let Me In Sensations | 7/27/68 | Life Sly & The Family Stone |
| 9/5/64 | Last Kiss J. Frank Wilson | 5/17/69 | Let Me Love You Ray Charles | 9/6/69 | Life And Death In G & A Abaco Dream |
| 5/11/63 | Last Leaf Cascades | 8/6/66 | Let Me Tell You, Babe Nat "King" Cole | 5/8/61 | Life's A Holiday Jerry Wallace |
| 5/25/63 | Last Minute Jimmy McGriff | 7/24/61 | Let The Four Winds Blow Fats Domino | 7/21/62 | Life's Too Short Lafayettes |
| 8/19/67 | Last Minute Miracle Shirelles | | Let The Good Times In..see: (Open Up The Door) | 10/2/65 | Lifetime Of Loneliness Jackie DeShannon |
| 7/3/61 | Last Night Mar-Keys | | Let The Good Times Roll | | Light My Fire |
| 10/17/60 | Last One To Know Fleetwoods | 1/11/60 | Ray Charles | 6/3/67 | Doors |
| 3/27/65 | Last Time Rolling Stones | 9/5/60 | Shirley & Lee | 7/27/68 | Jose Feliciano |
| 9/10/66 | Last Train To Clarksville Monkees | 11/13/65 | Roy Orbison | 8/31/68 | Doors |
| 9/23/67 | Last Waltz Engelbert Humperdinck | 6/24/67 | Bunny Sigler (medley) | 12/25/65 | Lightnin' Strikes Lou Christie |
| 5/14/66 | Last Word In Lonesome Is Me Eddy Arnold | 1/13/68 | Let The Heartaches Begin Long John Baldry | 9/23/67 | Lightning's Girl Nancy Sinatra |
| 10/9/61 | Late Date Parkays | 2/15/60 | Let The Little Girl Dance Billy Bland | 11/11/67 | (Lights Went Out In) Massachusetts Bee Gees |
| 10/9/61 | Laugh Velvets | | Let The Sunshine In..see: Aquarius | 1/1/66 | Like A Baby Len Barry |
| 8/21/65 | Laugh At Me Sonny | 2/22/60 | Let Them Talk Little Willie John | 2/13/65 | Like A Child Julie Rogers |
| 1/2/65 | Laugh, Laugh Beau Brummels | 10/30/61 | Let There Be Drums Sandy Nelson | 7/24/65 | Like A Rolling Stone Bob Dylan |
| 7/12/69 | Laughing Guess Who | 9/18/61 | Let True Love Begin Nat "King" Cole | 10/21/67 | Like An Old Time Movie Scott McKenzie |
| 2/23/63 | Laughing Boy Mary Wells | 5/6/67 | Let Yourself Go James Brown | | |
| | Laura, What's He Got That I Ain't Got | 6/15/68 | Let Yourself Go Elvis Presley | | |
| 8/12/67 | Frankie Laine | 7/26/69 | Let Yourself Go Friends Of Distinction | | |
| 8/19/67 | Brook Benton | | | | |
| | Laura's Wedding..see: (I Cried at) | | | | |
| 5/15/65 | Laurie (Strange Things Happen) Dickey Lee | | | | |

| Date | Title | Artist |
|---|---|---|
| 7/11/64 | Like Columbus Did | Reflections |
| 3/27/61 | Like, Long Hair | Paul Revere & The Raiders |
| 10/31/60 | Like Strangers | Everly Brothers |
| 6/29/63 | Like The Big Guys Do | Rocky Fellers |
| 4/20/68 | Like To Get To Know You | Spanky & Our Gang |
| 6/11/66 | Lil' Red Riding Hood | Sam The Sham & The Pharoahs |
| 4/27/68 | Lili Marlene | Al Martino |
| 8/18/62 | Limbo | Capris |
| 10/20/62 | Limbo Dance | Champs |
| | **Limbo Rock** | |
| 5/26/62 | | Champs |
| 9/8/62 | | Chubby Checker |
| 12/1/62 | Limelight | Mr. Acker Bilk |
| | (also see: Eternally) | |
| 10/2/61 | Linda | Adam Wade |
| 2/23/63 | Linda | Jan & Dean |
| 3/6/61 | Ling-Ting-Tong | Buddy Knox |
| 11/13/61 | Lion Sleeps Tonight | Tokens |
| 5/29/65 | Lip Sync (To The Tongue Twisters) | Len Barry |
| | **Lipstick Traces (On A Cigarette)** | |
| 5/5/62 | | Benny Spellman |
| 5/8/65 | | O'Jays |
| 7/25/60 | Lisa | Jeanne Black |
| 6/16/62 | Lisa | Ferrante & Teicher |
| 6/15/68 | Listen Here | Eddie Harris |
| 10/24/64 | Listen Lonely Girl | Johnny Mathis |
| 2/19/66 | Listen People | Herman's Hermits |
| 10/19/68 | Listen, They're Playing My Song | Ray Charles |
| 6/7/69 | Listen To The Band | Monkees |
| | Little..also see: Lil' | |
| 11/27/61 | Little Altar Boy | Vic Dana |
| 10/12/68 | Little Arrows | Leapy Lee |
| 3/23/63 | Little Band Of Gold | James Gilreath |
| 12/19/64 | Little Bell | Dixie Cups |
| 3/25/67 | Little Bit Me, A Little Bit You | Monkees |
| | **Little Bit Now** | |
| 11/17/62 | | Majors |
| 8/12/67 | | Dave Clark Five |
| 6/5/65 | Little Bit Of Heaven | Ronnie Dove |
| | **Little Bit Of Soap** | |
| 7/31/61 | | Jarmels |
| 1/2/65 | | Garnet Mimms |
| 1/29/66 | | Exciters |
| 5/13/67 | Little Bit O' Soul | Music Explosion |
| 2/1/60 | Little Bitty Girl | Bobby Rydell |
| | **Little Bitty Pretty One** | |
| 8/6/60 | | Frankie Lymon |
| 6/16/62 | | Clyde McPhatter |
| | **Little Bitty Tear** | |
| 12/18/61 | | Burl Ives |
| 1/20/62 | | Wanda Jackson |
| 9/15/62 | Little Black Book | Jimmy Dean |
| 1/21/67 | Little Black Egg | Nightcrawlers |
| | **Little Boxes** | |
| 1/11/64 | | Pete Seeger |
| 4/18/64 | | Womenfolk |
| 12/21/63 | Little Boy | Tony Bennett |
| 2/1/64 | Little Boy | Crystals |
| 12/25/65 | Little Boy (In Grown Up Clothes) | Four Seasons |
| 2/6/61 | Little Boy Sad | Johnny Burnette |
| 4/18/64 | Little Children | Billy J. Kramer |
| 1/4/60 | Little Coco Palm | Jerry Wallace |
| 8/20/66 | Little Darling, I Need You | Marvin Gaye |
| 8/17/63 | Little Deuce Coupe | Beach Boys |
| 5/1/61 | Little Devil | Neil Sedaka |
| 7/7/62 | Little Diane | Dion |
| 9/4/61 | Little Dog Cried | Jimmie Rodgers |
| 5/2/64 | Little Donna | Rivieras |
| | **Little Drummer Boy** | |
| 1/4/60* | | Johnny Cash |
| 1/4/60* | | Harry Simeone Chorale |
| 12/12/60 | | Harry Simeone Chorale |
| 12/11/61 | | Harry Simeone Chorale |
| 1/6/62 | | Jack Halloran Singers |
| 12/8/62 | | Harry Simeone Chorale |
| 9/28/63 | Little Eeefin Annie | Joe Perkins |
| 4/24/61 | Little Egypt (Ying-Yang) | Coasters |
| 5/29/61 | Little Feeling (Called Love) | Jack Scott |
| 4/22/67 | Little Games | Yardbirds |
| 6/4/66 | Little Girl | Syndicate Of Sound |
| 11/27/65 | Little Girl I Once Knew | Beach Boys |
| | **Little Green Apples** | |
| 3/2/68 | | Roger Miller |
| 7/6/68 | | Patti Page |
| 8/17/68 | | O.C. Smith |
| | **Little Honda** | |
| 9/12/64 | | Hondells |
| 10/17/64 | | Beach Boys |
| | **Little Latin Lupe Lu** | |
| 5/11/63 | | Righteous Brothers |
| 7/11/64 | | Kingsmen |
| 3/5/66 | | Mitch Ryder & The Detroit Wheels |
| 10/12/68 | Little Less Conversation | Elvis Presley |
| 5/29/65 | Little Lonely One | Tom Jones |
| 10/1/66 | Little Man | Sonny & Cher |
| 10/24/64 | Little Marie | Chuck Berry |
| 12/5/60 | Little Miss Blue | Dion |
| 9/11/65 | Little Miss Sad | Five Emprees |
| 3/6/61 | Little Miss Stuck-Up | Playmates |
| 6/10/67 | Little Miss Sunshine | Tommy Roe |
| 6/27/64 | Little Old Lady (From Pasadena) | Jan & Dean |
| | **Little Old Wine Drinker Me** | |
| 8/12/67 | | Robert Mitchum |
| 8/19/67 | | Dean Martin |
| 9/2/67 | Little Ole Man (Uptight-Everything's Alright) | Bill Cosby |
| 3/27/61 | Little Pedro | Olympics |
| 10/3/64 | Little Queenie | Bill Black's Combo |
| 12/16/67 | Little Rain Must Fall | Epic Splendor |
| 6/23/62 | Little Red Rented Rowboat | Joe Dowell |
| 10/26/63 | Little Red Rooster | Sam Cooke |
| 8/21/61 | Little Sister | Elvis Presley |
| 3/16/63 | Little Star | Bobby Callender |
| 1/23/65 | Little Things | Bobby Goldsboro |
| 1/4/60* | Little Things Mean A Lot | Joni James |
| 12/29/62 | Little Tin Soldier | Toy Dolls |
| 1/13/62 | Little Too Much | Clarence Henry |
| 12/22/62 | Little Town Flirt | Del Shannon |
| 6/20/64 | Little Toy Balloon | Danny Williams |
| 3/13/61 | Little Turtle Dove | Otis Williams/Charms |
| 5/2/64 | Little White Cloud That Cried | Wayne Newton |
| 8/23/69 | Little Woman | Bobby Sherman |
| 7/31/65 | Little You | Freddie & The Dreamers |
| 7/28/62 | Little Young Lover | Impressions |
| 4/29/67 | Live | Merry-Go-Round |
| 12/2/67 | Live For Life | Jack Jones |
| 2/8/64 | Live Wire | Martha & The Vandellas |
| 7/30/66 | Livin' Above Your Head | Jay & The Americans |
| 1/25/60 | Livin' Dangerously | McGuire Sisters |
| 10/26/63 | Living A Lie | Al Martino |
| 11/19/66 | Living For You | Sonny & Cher |
| 11/23/68 | Living In The U.S.A. | Steve Miller Band |
| 1/27/62 | Lizzie Borden | Chad Mitchell Trio |
| 11/23/68 | Lo Mucho Que Te Quiero | Rene & Rene |
| 3/23/63 | Locking Up My Heart | Marvelettes |
| 6/30/62 | Loco-Motion | Little Eva |
| 11/2/63 | Loddy Lo | Chubby Checker |
| | **Lodi** | |
| 5/3/69 | | Creedence Clearwater Revival |
| 8/23/69 | | Al Wilson |
| 8/4/62 | Lolita Ya-Ya | Ventures |
| | **Lollipops And Roses** | |
| 3/3/62 | | Jack Jones |
| 8/25/62 | | Paul Petersen |
| 1/19/63 | Lone Teen Ranger | Jerry Landis |
| 5/2/64 | Loneliest Night | Dale & Grace |
| 10/14/67 | (Loneliness Made Me Realize) It's You That I Need | Temptations |
| 5/8/65 | L-O-N-E-L-Y | Bobby Vinton |
| 3/18/67 | Lonely Again | Eddy Arnold |
| 1/4/60* | Lonely Blue Boy | Conway Twitty |
| 3/13/61 | Lonely Blue Nights | Rosie |
| 5/18/63 | Lonely Boy, Lonely Guitar | Duane Eddy |
| 10/27/62 | Lonely Bull | Tijuana Brass |
| 6/5/61 | Lonely Crowd | Teddy Vann |
| | **Lonely Drifter** | |
| 9/14/63 | | O'Jays |
| 6/24/67 | | Pieces Of Eight |
| 5/25/68 | Lonely Is The Name | Sammy Davis, Jr. |
| 6/12/61 | Lonely Life | Jackie Wilson |
| 2/27/61 | Lonely Man | Elvis Presley |
| 7/9/66 | Lonely Soldier | Mike Williams |
| 8/7/61 | Lonely Street | Clarence Henry |
| 7/30/66 | Lonely Summer | Shades Of Blue |
| 8/10/63 | Lonely Surfer | Jack Nitzsche |
| 10/17/60 | Lonely Teenager | Dion |
| 3/14/60 | Lonely Weekends | Charlie Rich |
| 5/23/60 | Lonely Winds | Drifters |
| 12/4/61 | Lonesome Number One | Don Gibson |
| 7/29/67 | Lonesome Road | Wonder Who? |
| 5/22/61 | Lonesome Whistle Blues | Freddy King |
| 8/25/62 | Long As The Rose Is Red | Florraine Darlin |
| 2/1/64 | Long Gone Lonesome Blues | Hank Williams, Jr. |
| 2/22/69 | Long Green | Fireballs |
| 5/20/67 | Long Legged Girl (With The Short Dress On) | Elvis Presley |
| 2/8/69 | Long Line Rider | Bobby Darin |
| 6/12/65 | Long Live Love | Sandie Shaw |
| 2/5/66 | Long Live Our Love | Shangri-Las |
| 3/6/65 | Long Lonely Nights | Bobby Vinton |
| 5/16/64 | Long Tall Shorty | Tommy Tucker |
| 11/9/63 | Long Tall Texan | Murry Kellum |
| 12/24/66 | Look At Granny Run, Run | Howard Tate |
| 1/12/63 | Look At Me | Dobie Gray |
| 7/9/66 | Look At Me Girl | Bobby Vee |
| 8/9/69 | Look At Mine | Petula Clark |
| 10/17/64 | Look Away | Garnet Mimms |
| | **Look For A Star** | |
| 6/20/60 | | Deane Hawley |
| 6/20/60 | | Garry Miles |
| 6/20/60 | | Garry Mills |
| 6/20/60 | | Billy Vaughn |
| 2/10/68 | Look, Here Comes The Sun | Sunshine Company |
| 2/22/64 | Look Homeward Angel | Monarchs |
| | **Look In My Eyes** | |
| 8/28/61 | | Chantels |
| 1/1/66 | | Three Degrees |
| 12/6/69 | Look-Ka Py Py | Meters |
| 12/26/64 | Look Of Love | Lesley Gore |
| | **Look Of Love** | |
| 7/22/67 | | Dusty Springfield |
| 5/11/68 | | Sergio Mendes & Brasil '66 |
| 6/29/68 | Look Over Your Shoulder | O'Jays |
| 11/20/65 | Look Through Any Window | Hollies |
| 10/22/66 | Look Through My Window | Mamas & The Papas |
| 4/6/68 | Look To Your Soul | Johnny Rivers |
| 12/17/66 | Look What You've Done | Pozo-Seco Singers |
| 8/18/62 | Lookin' For A Love | Valentinos |
| 10/8/66 | Lookin' For Love | Ray Conniff |
| 12/7/68 | Looking Back | Joe Simon |
| 1/20/68 | Looking For A Fox | Clarence Carter |
| 7/18/64 | Looking For Love | Connie Francis |
| 7/24/65 | Looking Through The Eyes Of Love | Gene Pitney |
| 10/2/65 | Looking With My Eyes | Dionne Warwick |
| 1/22/66 | Loop, The | Johnny Lytle |
| 12/22/62 | Loop De Loop | Johnny Thunder |
| 2/17/62 | Lose Her | Bobby Rydell |
| 7/17/65 | Loser, The | Skyliners |
| 3/11/67 | Loser (With A Broken Heart) | Gary Lewis & The Playboys |
| 4/6/63 | Losing You | Brenda Lee |
| 3/13/65 | Losing You | Dusty Springfield |
| 11/6/61 | Losing Your Love | Jim Reeves |
| 12/30/67 | Lost | Jerry Butler |
| 1/9/61 | Lost Love | H.B. Barnum |
| 1/13/62 | Lost Penny | Brook Benton |
| | **Lost Someone** | |
| 12/18/61 | | James Brown |
| 2/5/66 | | James Brown |
| | **Louie Louie** | |
| 11/9/63 | | Kingsmen |
| 5/14/66 | | Kingsmen |
| 10/22/66 | | Sandpipers |
| | **Louisiana Man** | |
| 9/16/67 | | Pozo-Seco Singers |
| 4/20/68 | | Bobbie Gentry |
| 9/26/64 | L-O-V-E | Nat "King" Cole |
| 7/30/66 | Love Attack | James Carr |
| 12/20/69 | Love Bones | Johnnie Taylor |
| 12/11/65 | Love Bug | Jack Jones |
| 8/19/67 | Love Bug Leave My Heart Alone | Martha & The Vandellas |
| 11/10/62 | Love Came To Me | Dion |
| 4/12/69 | Love (Can Make You Happy) | Mercy |

| Date | Title / Artist |
|---|---|
| 4/28/62 | **Love Can't Wait**  Marty Robbins |
| 10/19/68 | **Love Child**  Supremes |
| 2/17/68 | **Love Explosion**  Troy Keyes |
| 3/25/67 | **Love Eyes**  Nancy Sinatra |
| 2/2/63 | **Love For Sale**  Arthur Lyman Group |
| 2/18/67 | **Love I Saw In You Was Just A Mirage**  Miracles |
| 11/20/61 | **Love (I'm So Glad) I Found You**  Spinners |
| 5/11/68 | **Love In Every Room**  Paul Mauriat |
| 10/11/69 | **Love In The City**  Turtles |
| 4/20/68 | **Love In Them There Hills**  Vibrations |
| 8/26/67 | **Love Is A Doggone Good Thing**  Eddie Floyd |
| 5/8/65 | **Love Is A 5-Letter Word**  James Phelps |
| 9/10/66 | **Love Is A Hurtin' Thing**  Lou Rawls |
| 2/24/68 | **Love Is All Around**  Troggs |
| 4/5/69 | **Love Is All I Have To Give**  Checkmates, Ltd. |
|  | **Love Is All We Need** |
| 7/11/64 | Vic Dana |
| 1/22/66 | Mel Carter |
|  | **Love Is Blue** |
| 1/6/68 | Paul Mauriat |
| 2/10/68 | Al Martino |
| 2/24/68 | Manny Kellem |
| 2/24/68 | Claudine Longet |
| 5/24/69 | Dells (medley) |
| 1/28/67 | **Love Is Here And Now You're Gone**  Supremes |
| 4/26/69 | **Love Is Just A Four-Letter Word**  Joan Baez |
| 7/6/68 | **(Love Is Like A) Baseball Game**  Intruders |
| 4/30/66 | **Love Is Like An Itching In My Heart**  Supremes |
| 3/19/66 | **Love Is Me, Love Is You**  Connie Francis |
| 9/30/67 | **Love Is Strange**  Peaches & Herb |
| 1/27/62 | **Love Is The Sweetest Thing**  Saverio Saridis |
|  | **Love Letters** |
| 2/24/62 | Ketty Lester |
| 7/2/66 | Elvis Presley |
| 11/23/68 | **Love Machine**  O'Kaysions |
| 7/13/68 | **Love Makes A Woman**  Barbara Acklin |
| 12/11/65 | **Love (Makes Me Do Foolish Things)**  Martha & The Vandellas |
| 1/19/63 | **Love (Makes The World Go 'Round)**  Paul Anka |
| 1/22/66 | **Love Makes The World Go Round**  Deon Jackson |
| 5/24/69 | **Love Man**  Otis Redding |
| 12/31/66 | **Love Me**  Bobby Hebb |
| 7/6/63 | **Love Me All The Way**  Kim Weston |
| 8/4/62 | **Love Me As I Love You**  George Maharis |
| 2/6/65 | **Love Me As Though There Were No Tomorrow**  Sonny Knight |
| 4/11/64 | **Love Me Do**  Beatles |
| 5/6/67 | **Love Me Forever**  Roger Williams |
| 7/3/65 | **Love Me Now**  Brook Benton |
|  | **Love Me Tender** |
| 10/6/62 | Richard Chamberlain |
| 6/17/67 | Percy Sledge |
| 5/24/69 | **Love Me Tonight**  Tom Jones |
| 12/9/67 | **Love Me Two Times**  Doors |
| 2/24/62 | **Love Me Warm And Tender**  Paul Anka |
|  | **Love Me With All Your Heart** |
| 10/12/63 | Steve Allen (Cuando Calienta) |
| 4/11/64 | Ray Charles Singers |
| 4/16/66 | Bachelors |
|  | **Love My Life Away**..see: (I Wanna) |
| 12/1/62 | **Love Of A Boy**  Timi Yuro |
| 4/20/63 | **Love Of My Man**  Theola Kilgore |
| 5/8/61 | **Love Of My Own**  Carla Thomas |
| 9/20/69 | **Love Of The Common People**  Winstons |
|  | **Love Potion Number Nine** |
| 1/4/60* | Clovers |
| 11/28/64 | Searchers |
| 11/25/67 | **Love Power**  Sandpebbles |
| 3/30/63 | **Love She Can Count On**  Miracles |
| 9/7/63 | **Love So Fine**  Chiffons |
| 4/30/66 | **Love Takes A Long Time Growing**  Deon Jackson |
| 12/2/67 | **Love That's Real**  Intruders |

| Date | Title / Artist |
|---|---|
| 3/20/61 | **Love Theme From One Eyed Jacks**  Ferrante & Teicher |
|  | **Love Theme From Romeo & Juliet** |
| 5/10/69 | Henry Mancini |
| 7/26/69 | Johnny Mathis |
|  | **Love Theme From The Sandpiper**..see: Shadow Of Your Smile |
| 10/3/60 | **Love Walked In**  Dinah Washington |
| 11/1/69 | **Love Will Find A Way**  Jackie DeShannon |
| 2/15/64 | **Love With The Proper Stranger**  Jack Jones |
| 3/5/66 | **Love You Save (May Be Your Own)**  Joe Tex |
| 4/4/60 | **Love You So**  Ron Holden |
| 2/18/67 | **Love You So Much**  New Colony Six |
| 9/13/69 | **Loves Been Good To Me**  Frank Sinatra |
| 4/16/66 | **Love's Made A Fool Of You**  Bobby Fuller Four |
| 8/7/61 | **Lovedrops**  Mickey & Sylvia |
| 1/2/65 | **Lovely, Lovely (Loverly, Loverly)**  Chubby Checker |
| 4/7/62 | **Lover Come Back**  Doris Day |
| 12/29/62 | **Lover Come Back To Me**  Cleftones |
| 3/3/62 | **Lover Please**  Clyde McPhatter |
|  | **Lover's Concerto** |
| 9/11/65 | Toys |
| 4/2/66 | Sarah Vaughan |
| 5/7/66 | Mrs. Miller |
| 6/8/68 | **Lover's Holiday**  Peggy Scott & Jo Jo Benson |
| 8/14/61 | **Lover's Island**  Blue Jays |
| 8/29/64 | **Lover's Prayer**  Wallace Brothers |
|  | **Lover's Question** |
| 2/27/61 | Ernestine Anderson |
| 3/1/69 | Otis Redding |
| 8/22/64 | **Lovers Always Forgive**  Gladys Knight & The Pips |
| 10/13/62 | **Lovers By Night, Strangers By Day**  Fleetwoods |
|  | **Lovers Leap**..see: (Doin' The) |
| 4/21/62 | **Lovers Who Wander**  Dion |
|  | **Lovesick Blues** |
| 4/14/62 | Floyd Cramer |
| 12/22/62 | Frank Ifield |
|  | **Lovey Dovey** |
| 12/19/60 | Buddy Knox |
| 10/14/67 | Bunny Sigler (medley) |
| 2/10/68 | Otis & Carla |
| 3/9/68 | **Lovey Dovey Kinda Lovin'**  Brenton Wood |
| 12/5/64 | **Lovin' Place**  Gale Garnett |
| 6/29/68 | **Lovin' Season**  Gene & Debbe |
| 2/15/69 | **Lovin' Things**  Grass Roots |
| 8/22/60 | **Lovin' Touch**  Mark Dinning |
| 1/14/67 | **Lovin' You**  Bobby Darin |
| 4/13/68 | **Loving You Has Made Me Bananas**  Guy Marks |
| 5/28/66 | **Loving You Is Sweeter Than Ever**  Four Tops |
| 4/18/64 | **Loving You More Every Day**  Etta James |
| 8/23/69 | **Lowdown Popcorn**  James Brown |
| 9/5/60 | **Lucille**  Everly Brothers |
| 1/4/60* | **Lucky Devil**  Carl Dobkins, Jr. |
| 8/3/63 | **Lucky Lips**  Cliff Richard |
| 4/10/61 | **Lullaby Of Love**  Frank Gari |
| 3/5/66 | **Lullaby Of Love**  Poppies |
| 4/24/61 | **Lullaby Of The Leaves**  Ventures |
| 10/3/64 | **Lumberjack**  Brook Benton |
| 9/6/69 | **Luna Trip**  Dickie Goodman |

## M

| Date | Title / Artist |
|---|---|
| 2/2/63 | **M.G. Blues**  Jimmy McGriff |
|  | **MacArthur Park** |
| 5/11/68 | Richard Harris |
| 9/6/69 | Waylon Jennings |
|  | **Mack The Knife** |
| 1/4/60* | Bobby Darin |
| 5/2/60 | Ella Fitzgerald |
|  | **Made To Love**..see: (Girls, Girls, Girls) |
| 4/4/60 | **Madison, The**  Al Brown's Tunetoppers |
| 4/11/60 | **Madison Time**  Ray Bryant Combo |
| 8/10/68 | **Magic Bus**  Who |
| 10/5/68 | **Magic Carpet Ride**  Steppenwolf |
| 9/18/61 | **Magic Is The Night**  Kathy Young with The Innocents |

| Date | Title / Artist |
|---|---|
| 8/14/61 | **Magic Moon**  Rays |
| 6/13/64 | **Magic Of Our Summer Love**  Tymes |
| 2/26/66 | **Magic Town**  Vogues |
| 10/27/62 | **Magic Wand**  Don & Juan |
| 12/5/60 | **Magnificent Seven**  Al Caiola |
| 9/6/69 | **Mah-Na-Mah-Na**  Piero Umiliani |
|  | **Main Theme From Exodus**..see: Exodus |
| 3/4/67 | **Mairzy Doats**  Innocence |
| 12/4/61 | **Majestic, The**  Dion |
| 4/1/67 | **Make A Little Love**  Lowell Fulsom |
| 9/6/69 | **Make Believe**  Wind |
| 10/9/61 | **Make Believe Wedding**  Castells |
|  | **Make It Easy On Yourself** |
| 7/7/62 | Jerry Butler |
| 10/16/65 | Walker Bros. |
| 4/15/67 | **Make Love To Me**  Johnny Thunder & Ruby Winters |
| 7/23/66 | **Make Me Belong To You**  Barbara Lewis |
| 3/28/64 | **Make Me Forget**  Bobby Rydell |
| 9/11/65 | **Make Me Your Baby**  Barbara Lewis |
| 5/13/67 | **Make Me Yours**  Bettye Swann |
| 12/26/60 | **Make Someone Happy**  Perry Como |
| 8/3/63 | **Make The Music Play**  Dionne Warwick |
|  | **Make The World Go Away** |
| 7/20/63 | Timi Yuro |
| 8/31/63 | Ray Price |
| 10/16/65 | Eddy Arnold |
| 10/18/69 | **Make Your Own Kind Of Music**  Mama Cass Elliot |
| 12/12/64 | **Makin' Whoopee**  Ray Charles |
| 8/19/67 | **Making Every Minute Count**  Spanky & Our Gang |
| 4/8/67 | **Making Memories**  Frankie Laine |
| 8/22/60 | **Malaguena**  Connie Francis |
| 1/27/68 | **Malayisha**  Miriam Makeba |
| 12/7/68 | **Malinda**  Bobby Taylor |
| 2/22/60 | **Mama**  Connie Francis |
| 5/14/66 | **Mama**  B.J. Thomas |
| 2/17/68 | **(Mama Come Quick, And Bring Your) Lickin' Stick**  George Torrence |
| 1/5/63 | **Mama Didn't Lie**  Jan Bradley |
| 7/20/63 | **Mama Don't Allow**  Rooftop Singers |
| 9/8/62 | **Mama (He Treats Your Daughter Mean)**  Ruth Brown |
| 4/17/61 | **Mama Said**  Shirelles |
|  | **Mama Sang A Song** |
| 10/13/62 | Stan Kenton |
| 10/20/62 | Walter Brennan |
| 10/27/62 | Bill Anderson |
|  | **Mame** |
| 4/30/66 | Bobby Darin |
| 5/21/66 | Louis Armstrong |
| 11/19/66 | Herb Alpert |
| 1/30/65 | **Man, The**  Lorne Greene |
| 11/16/68 | **Man And A Half**  Wilson Pickett |
| 11/12/66 | **Man And A Woman**  Tamiko Jones with Herbie Mann |
|  | **Man In You**..see: (You Can't Let The Boy Overpower) |
| 1/6/68 | **Man Needs A Woman**  James Carr |
| 4/28/62 | **(Man Who Shot) Liberty Valance**  Gene Pitney |
| 5/11/68 | **Man Without Love**  Engelbert Humperdinck |
| 8/10/63 | **Man's Temptation**  Gene Chandler |
| 8/29/60 | **Many A Wonderful Moment**  Rosemary Clooney |
| 11/7/60 | **Many Tears Ago**  Connie Francis |
| 5/14/66 | **Marble Breaks And Iron Bends**  Drafi |
| 4/14/62 | **March Of The Siamese Children**  Kenny Ball |
| 3/30/63 | **Marching Thru Madrid**  Herb Alpert |
|  | **Maria** |
| 5/30/60 | Johnny Mathis |
| 12/11/61 | Johnny Mathis |
| 12/11/61 | Roger Williams |
| 9/21/63 | **Maria Elena**  Los Indios Tabajaras |
| 6/16/62 | **Marianna**  Johnny Mathis |
| 6/12/65 | **Marie**  Bachelors |
| 8/28/61 | **(Marie's the Name) His Latest Flame**  Elvis Presley |
|  | **Marina** |
| 1/4/60* | Willy Alberti |
| 1/4/60* | Rocco Granata |
| 7/13/63 | **Marlena**  Four Seasons |
| 5/3/69 | **Marley Purt Drive**  Jose Feliciano |

| | | | | | |
|---|---|---|---|---|---|
| 7/19/69 | **Marrakesh Express** | | **Mercy, Mercy, Mercy** | 6/12/61 | **Mom And Dad's Waltz**  Patti Page |
| | Crosby, Stills & Nash | 1/7/67 | "Cannonball" Adderley | 3/24/62 | **Moments**  Jennell Hawkins |
| 1/30/65 | **Married Man**  Richard Burton | 2/25/67 | Larry Williams & Johnny Watson | 6/21/69 | **Moments To Remember**  Vogues |
| 8/3/63 | **Martian Hop**  Ran-Dells | 3/11/67 | Marlena Shaw | 4/9/66 | **Monday, Monday**  Mamas & The Papas |
| 11/30/63 | **Marvelous Toy**  Chad Mitchell Trio | 6/17/67 | Buckinghams | 1/6/68 | **Money**  Lovin' Spoonful |
| 11/3/62 | **Mary Ann Regrets**  Burl Ives | 3/13/61 | **Merry-Go-Round**  Marv Johnson | | **Money (That's What I Want)** |
| 1/4/60* | **Mary Don't You Weep** | 4/17/61 | **Mess Around**  Bobby Freeman | 2/1/60 | Barrett Strong |
| | Stonewall Jackson | 7/25/60 | **Mess Of Blues**  Elvis Presley | 3/14/64 | Kingsmen |
| 5/27/67 | **Mary In The Morning**  Al Martino | 9/28/68 | **Message From Maria**  Joe Simon | 11/19/66 | Jr. Walker & The All Stars |
| 6/30/62 | **Mary's Little Lamb**  James Darren | 4/2/66 | **Message To Michael**  Dionne Warwick | 7/30/66 | **Money Won't Change You** |
| 9/24/66 | **Mas Que Nada** | 3/28/64 | **Mexican Drummer Man**  Herb Alpert | | James Brown |
| | Sergio Mendes & Brasil '66 | 4/17/65 | **Mexican Pearls**  Billy Vaughn | | **Monkee**..see: Do The |
| 3/3/62 | **Mashed Potato Time**  Dee Dee Sharp | 6/27/64 | **Mexican Shuffle**  Herb Alpert | 10/5/63 | **Monkey-Shine**  Bill Black's Combo |
| | **Mashed Potatoes** | 8/14/61 | **Mexico**  Bob Moore | 7/13/63 | **Monkey Time**  Major Lance |
| 2/15/60 | Nat Kendrick | | **Michael** | 12/27/69 | **Monster**  Steppenwolf |
| 3/17/62 | Steve Alaimo | 7/10/61 | Highwaymen | 9/8/62 | **Monster Mash**  Bobby "Boris" Pickett |
| 9/29/62 | **Mashed Potatoes U.S.A.**  James Brown | 10/5/63 | Steve Alaimo | 12/8/62 | **Monsters' Holiday** |
| | **Massachusetts**..see: (Lights Went Out In) | 8/22/64 | Trini Lopez | | Bobby "Boris" Pickett |
| | | 11/27/65 | **Michael**  C.O.D.'s | | **Montage From**..see: How Sweet It Is |
| 3/30/68 | **Master Jack**  Four Jacks & A Jill | | **Michelle** | 12/16/67 | **Monterey**  Animals |
| 10/26/63 | **Matador, The**  Johnny Cash | 1/8/66 | David & Jonathan | 4/6/68 | **Mony Mony** |
| 3/28/64 | **Matador, The**  Major Lance | 1/8/66 | Billy Vaughn | | Tommy James & The Shondells |
| 9/5/64 | **Matchbox**  Beatles | 1/22/66 | Bud Shank | 5/1/61 | **Moody River**  Pat Boone |
| 1/18/69 | **May I**  Bill Deal | 8/17/63 | **Mickey's Monkey**  Miracles | 5/31/69 | **Moody Woman**  Jerry Butler |
| 4/20/68 | **May I Take A Giant Step (Into Your Heart)**  1910 Fruitgum Co. | 2/3/62 | **Midnight**  Johnny Gibson | 7/10/65 | **Moon Over Naples**  Bert Kaempfert |
| | | 11/15/69 | **Midnight**  Classics IV | | (also see: Spanish Eyes) |
| 4/2/66 | **May My Heart Be Cast Into Stone** | 8/31/68 | **Midnight Confessions**  Grass Roots | | **Moon River** |
| | Toys | 11/1/69 | **Midnight Cowboy**  Ferrante & Teicher | 10/9/61 | Jerry Butler |
| 10/16/65 | **May The Bird Of Paradise Fly Up Your Nose**  "Little" Jimmy Dickens | | **Midnight Hour**..see: In The | 10/9/61 | Henry Mancini |
| | | 2/3/62 | **Midnight In Moscow**  Kenny Ball | 3/17/62 | **Moon Was Yellow**  Frank Sinatra |
| 12/26/64 | **Maybe**  Shangri-Las | | **Midnight Lace** | 6/14/69 | **Moonflight**  Vik Venus |
| 7/25/64 | **Maybe I Know**  Lesley Gore | 10/17/60 | Ray Conniff | 8/7/65 | **Moonlight And Roses**  Vic Dana |
| 2/10/68 | **Maybe Just Today**  Bobby Vee | 10/17/60 | Ray Ellis | 9/6/69 | **Moonlight Sonata**  Henry Mancini |
| 8/16/69 | **Maybe The Rain Will Fall**  Cascades | 10/24/60 | David Carroll | | **More** |
| 2/15/69 | **Maybe Tomorrow**  Iveys | 11/9/63 | **Midnight Mary**  Joey Powers | 7/6/63 | Kai Winding |
| 10/31/64 | **Maybe Tonight**  Shirelles | | **Midnight Special** | 8/10/63 | Vic Dana |
| 8/15/64 | **Maybelline**  Johnny Rivers | 1/25/60 | Paul Evans | 7/8/67 | **More And More**  Andy Williams |
| | **Me About You** | 2/6/65 | Johnny Rivers | 4/16/66 | **More I See You**  Chris Montez |
| 5/27/67 | Mojo Men | 3/3/62 | **Midnight Special**  Jimmy Smith | 6/17/67 | **More Love**  Miracles |
| 2/8/69 | Lovin' Spoonful | 1/4/60* | **Mighty Good**  Ricky Nelson | 8/14/61 | **More Money For You And Me** |
| 12/1/62 | **Me And My Shadow** | 7/10/61 | **Mighty Good Lovin'**  Miracles | | Four Preps |
| | Frank Sinatra & Sammy Davis Jr. | 3/2/68 | **Mighty Quinn (Quinn The Eskimo)** | 2/27/61 | **More Than I Can Say**  Bobby Vee |
| 8/8/64 | **Me Japanese Boy I Love You** | | Manfred Mann | 9/23/67 | **More Than The Eye Can See** |
| | Bobby Goldsboro | 12/31/60 | **Milk Cow Blues**  Ricky Nelson | | Al Martino |
| 3/23/68 | **Me, The Peaceful Heart**  Lulu | 2/8/64 | **Miller's Cave**  Bobby Bare | 4/5/69 | **More Today Than Yesterday** |
| 9/11/65 | **Me Without You**  Mary Wells | | **Million And One** | | Spiral Starecase |
| 3/20/65 | **Mean Old World**  Rick Nelson | 7/23/66 | Dean Martin | 10/26/68 | **Mornin' Glory** |
| 9/7/63 | **Mean Woman Blues**  Roy Orbison | 8/6/66 | Vic Dana | | Bobbie Gentry & Glen Campbell |
| 3/23/63 | **Mecca**  Gene Pitney | | **Million To One** | 10/9/61 | **Morning After**  Mar-Keys |
| 5/3/69 | **Medicine Man**  Buchanan Brothers | 8/22/60 | Jimmy Charles | 8/10/68 | **Morning Dew**  Lulu |
| | **Meditation (Meditacao)** | 1/27/68 | Five Stairsteps | 4/5/69 | **Morning Girl**  Neon Philharmonic |
| 1/26/63 | Charlie Byrd | 4/5/69 | Brian Hyland | 2/18/67 | **Morningtown Ride**  Seekers |
| 3/9/63 | Pat Boone | | **Milord** | 2/6/61 | **Most Beautiful Words**  Della Reese |
| 11/5/66 | Claudine Longet | 3/6/61 | Edith Piaf | 4/21/62 | **Most People Get Married**  Patti Page |
| 1/25/60 | **Mediterranean Moon**  Rays | 5/22/61 | Teresa Brewer | 3/27/61 | **Mother-In-Law**  Ernie K-Doe |
| 4/14/62 | **Meet Me At The Twistin' Place** | 5/16/64 | Bobby Darin | | (also see: Son-In-Law) |
| | Johnnie Morisette | 9/27/69 | **Mind, Body and Soul**  Flaming Ember | 11/13/65 | **Mother Nature, Father Time** |
| 6/5/65 | **Meeting Over Yonder**  Impressions | 9/3/66 | **Mind Excursion**  Trade Winds | | Brook Benton |
| 4/22/67 | **Melancholy Music Man** | 4/30/66 | **Mine Exclusively**  Olympics | 4/27/63 | **Mother, Please!**  Jo Ann Campbell |
| | Righteous Brothers | 3/29/69 | **Mini-Skirt Minnie**  Wilson Pickett | 6/14/69 | **Mother Popcorn**  James Brown |
| 12/30/67 | **Mellow Moonlight**  Leon Haywood | 5/31/69 | **Minotaur, The**  Dick Hyman | 7/9/66 | **Mothers Little Helper**  Rolling Stones |
| | **Mellow Yellow** | 12/21/68 | **Minute Of Your Time**  Tom Jones | 1/6/62 | **Motorcycle**  Tico & The Triumphs |
| 11/12/66 | Donovan | 8/10/63 | **Minute You're Gone**  Sonny James | 2/26/66 | **Moulty**  Barbarians |
| 3/11/67 | Senator Bobby & Senator McKinley | 7/18/60 | **Mio Amore**  Flamingos | | **Mountain Of Love** |
| 9/24/66 | **Melody For An Unknown Girl** | 7/14/62 | **Miracle, A**  Frankie Avalon | 2/29/60 | Harold Dorman |
| | Unknowns | 4/29/67 | **Mirage**  Tommy James & The Shondells | 10/31/64 | Johnny Rivers |
| 3/22/69 | **Memories**  Elvis Presley | 11/2/63 | **Misery**  Dynamics | 6/8/68 | Ronnie Dove |
| 3/19/66 | **Memories Are Made Of This**  Drifters | 5/15/61 | **Miss Fine**  New Yorkers | 1/1/66 | **Mountain Of Love**  Billy Stewart |
| 3/17/62 | **Memories Of Maria**  Jerry Byrd | 7/31/61 | **Missing You**  Ray Peterson | 7/31/61 | **Mountain's High**  Dick & DeeDee |
| 4/13/63 | **Memory Lane**  Hippies | 6/13/60 | **Mission Bell**  Donnie Brooks | 4/24/65 | **Mouse, The**  Soupy Sales |
| 3/13/61 | **Memphis**  Donnie Brooks | 1/6/68 | **Mission-Impossible**  Lalo Schifrin | 3/15/69 | **Move In A Little Closer, Baby** |
| | **Memphis** | | **Mister**..see: Mr. | | Mama Cass |
| 6/8/63 | Lonnie Mack | | **Misty** | 8/16/69 | **Move Over**  Steppenwolf |
| 5/30/64 | Johnny Rivers | 1/4/60* | Johnny Mathis | | **Move Two Mountains**..see: (You've Got To) |
| 8/26/67 | **Memphis Soul Stew**  King Curtis | 10/5/63 | Lloyd Price | | |
| 8/23/69 | **Memphis Train**  Buddy Miles | 10/23/65 | Vibrations | 9/25/61 | **Movin'**  Bill Black's Combo |
| | **Memphis Underground** | 6/25/66 | Richard "Groove" Holmes | 2/16/63 | **Mr. Bass Man**  Johnny Cymbal |
| 5/24/69 | Herbie Mann | 5/6/67 | **Misty Blue**  Eddy Arnold | 1/4/60* | **Mr. Blue**  Fleetwoods |
| 11/22/69 | Herbie Mann | 6/20/64 | **Mixed-Up, Shook-Up, Girl** | | **Mr. Bojangles** |
| 2/10/68 | **Men Are Gettin' Scarce**  Joe Tex | | Patty & The Emblems | 7/27/68 | Jerry Jeff Walker |
| 12/25/65 | **Men In My Little Girl's Life** | 2/22/64 | **Mo-Onions**  Booker T. & The MG's | 8/3/68 | Bobby Cole |
| | Mike Douglas | | **Mockingbird** | 12/23/67 | **Mr. Bus Driver**  Bruce Channel |
| 1/18/69 | **Mendocino**  Sir Douglas Quintet | 6/22/63 | Inez Foxx | 8/3/68 | **Mr. Businessman**  Ray Stevens |
| 3/29/69 | **Mercy**  Ohio Express | 12/23/67 | Aretha Franklin | 8/29/60 | **Mr. Custer**  Larry Verne |
| 9/5/64 | **Mercy, Mercy**  Don Covay | 2/6/61 | **Model Girl**  Johnny Maestro | 8/13/66 | **Mr. Dieingly Sad**  Critters |
| | | 8/28/65 | **Mohair Sam**  Charlie Rich | 10/21/67 | **Mr. Dream Merchant**  Jerry Butler |
| | | 5/16/60 | **Mojo Workout**  Larry Bright | 3/11/67 | **Mr. Farmer**  Seeds |
| | | 12/22/62 | **Molly**  Bobby Goldsboro | 7/24/61 | **Mr. Happiness**  Johnny Maestro |

| Date | Title | Artist |
|---|---|---|
| 12/20/69 | **Mr. Limousine Driver** | Grand Funk Railroad |
| 12/19/60 | **Mr. Livingston** | Larry Verne |
| 6/13/60 | **Mister Lonely** | Videls |
| | **Mr. Lonely** | |
| 9/22/62 | | Buddy Greco |
| 10/31/64 | | Bobby Vinton |
| 4/4/60 | **Mr. Lucky** | Henry Mancini |
| 8/10/68 | **Mr. Nico** | Four Jacks & A Jill |
| 2/20/65 | **Mr. Pitiful** | Otis Redding |
| 7/1/67 | **Mr. Pleasant** | Kinks |
| 4/10/61 | **Mr. Pride** | Chuck Jackson |
| 8/4/62 | **Mr. Songwriter** | Connie Stevens |
| 9/24/66 | **Mr. Spaceman** | Byrds |
| 2/15/69 | **Mr. Sun, Mr. Moon** | Paul Revere & The Raiders |
| 5/15/65 | **Mr. Tambourine Man** | Byrds |
| 4/26/69 | **Mr. Walker, It's All Over** | Billie Jo Spears |
| 9/14/63 | **Mr. Wishing Well** | Nat "King" Cole |
| 7/13/68 | **Mrs. Bluebird** | Eternity's Children |
| 4/17/65 | **Mrs. Brown You've Got A Lovely Daughter** | Herman's Hermits |
| | **Mrs. Robinson** | |
| 4/27/68 | | Simon & Garfunkel |
| 6/7/69 | | Booker T. & The M.G.'s |
| 8/16/69 | **Muddy Mississippi Line** | Bobby Goldsboro |
| 6/28/69 | **Muddy River** | Johnny Rivers |
| | **Muddy Water**..see: (I Washed My Hands In) | |
| 8/31/68 | **Mule, The** | James Boys |
| 5/23/60 | **Mule Skinner Blues** | Fendermen |
| 12/18/61 | **Multiplication** | Bobby Darin |
| 2/15/60 | **Mumblin' Mosie** | Johnny Otis Show |
| 8/26/67 | **Museum** | Herman's Hermits |
| | **Music, Music, Music** | |
| 8/14/61 | | Sensations |
| 2/17/68 | | Happenings |
| | **Music To Watch Girls By** | |
| 12/31/66 | | Bob Crewe Generation |
| 3/25/67 | | Andy Williams |
| 10/2/61 | **Muskrat** | Everly Brothers |
| 1/9/61 | **Muskrat Ramble** | Freddy Cannon |
| 12/25/65 | **Must To Avoid** | Herman's Hermits |
| 11/26/66 | **Mustang Sally** | Wilson Pickett |
| | **My Airplane**..see: Airplane Song | |
| 1/29/66 | **My Answer** | Jimmy McCracklin |
| 9/7/63 | **My Babe** | Righteous Brothers |
| 3/12/66 | **My Babe** | Roy Head |
| 4/22/67 | **My Babe** | Ronnie Dove |
| 10/23/65 | **My Baby** | Temptations |
| 5/30/64 | **My Baby Don't Dig Me** | Ray Charles |
| 1/22/66 | **My Baby Loves Me** | Martha & The Vandellas |
| 12/16/67 | **My Baby Must Be A Magician** | Marvelettes |
| | **(My Baby Shot Me Down)**..see: Bang Bang | |
| 4/1/67 | **My Back Pages** | Byrds |
| 9/13/69 | **My Balloon's Going Up** | Archie Bell & The Drells |
| 6/22/63 | **My Block** | Four Pennies |
| 8/28/61 | **My Blue Heaven** | Duane Eddy |
| 2/15/64 | **My Bonnie** | Beatles/Tony Sheridan |
| | (also see: Bonnie Came Back) | |
| 1/13/62 | **My Boomerang Won't Come Back** | Charlie Drake |
| 5/23/64 | **My Boy Lollipop** | Millie Small |
| 2/22/64 | **My Boyfriend Got A Beatle Haircut** | Donna Lynn |
| 8/3/63 | **My Boyfriend's Back** | Angels |
| | (also see: Your Boyfriend's Back) | |
| 12/12/64 | **My Buddy Seat** | Hondells |
| 6/12/65 | **My Cherie** | Al Martino |
| 5/31/69 | **My Cherie Amour** | Stevie Wonder |
| 7/17/61 | **My Claire De Lune** | Steve Lawrence |
| | **My Coloring Book** | |
| 12/22/62 | | Kitty Kallen |
| 12/29/62 | | Sandy Stewart |
| 1/21/67 | **My Cup Runneth Over** | Ed Ames |
| 11/17/62 | **My Dad** | Paul Petersen |
| 7/7/62 | **My Daddy Is President** | Little Jo Ann |
| 8/3/63 | **My Daddy Knows Best** | Marvelettes |
| 9/19/60 | **My Dearest Darling** | Etta James |
| 8/28/61 | **My Dream Come True** | Jack Scott |
| 6/6/64 | **My Dreams** | Brenda Lee |
| 7/8/67 | **My Elusive Dreams** | David Houston & Tammy Wynette |
| 1/9/61 | **My Empty Arms** | Jackie Wilson |
| 4/18/60 | **My Empty Room** | Little Anthony & The Imperials |
| 12/14/68 | **My Favorite Things** | Herb Alpert |
| 3/2/63 | **My Foolish Heart** | Demensions |
| 1/15/66 | **My Generation** | Who |
| | **My Girl** | |
| 1/16/65 | | Temptations |
| 4/20/68 | | Bobby Vee (medley) |
| 10/9/65 | **My Girl Has Gone** | Miracles |
| | **My Girl Josephine** | |
| 10/24/60 | | Fats Domino |
| 4/15/67 | | Jerry Jaye |
| | **(My Girl) Sloopy**..see: Hang On Sloopy | |
| 4/4/64 | **My Guy** | Mary Wells |
| | **My Heart Belongs To Only You** | |
| 10/23/61 | | Jackie Wilson |
| 2/29/64 | | Bobby Vinton |
| 2/29/64 | **My Heart Cries For You** | Ray Charles |
| 8/15/60 | **My Heart Has A Mind Of Its Own** | Connie Francis |
| | **My Heart Reminds Me**..see: And That Reminds Me | |
| | **My Heart Sings**..see: (All Of A Sudden) | |
| 7/4/64 | **My Heart Skips A Beat** | Buck Owens |
| 1/16/65 | **My Heart Would Know** | Al Martino |
| 8/7/61 | **My Heart's On Fire** | Billy Bland |
| 7/30/66 | **My Heart's Symphony** | Gary Lewis & The Playboys |
| 10/3/60 | **My Hero** | Blue Notes |
| 5/23/60 | **My Home Town** | Paul Anka |
| 5/29/61 | **My Kind Of Girl** | Matt Monro |
| 8/10/68 | **M'Lady** | Sly & The Family Stone |
| | **My Last Date (With You)** | |
| 12/12/60 | | Skeeter Davis |
| 12/19/60 | | Joni James |
| | (also see: Last Date) | |
| 7/5/69 | **My Little Chickadee** | Foundations |
| 1/25/60 | **My Little Marine** | Jamie Horton |
| 4/30/66 | **My Little Red Book** | Love |
| 8/1/60 | **My Love** | Nat "King" Cole |
| 12/25/65 | **My Love** | Petula Clark |
| 8/29/60 | **My Love For You** | Johnny Mathis |
| 10/24/64 | **My Love, Forgive Me** | Robert Goulet |
| 6/4/66 | **My Lover's Prayer** | Otis Redding |
| 7/15/67 | **My Mammy** | Happenings |
| 7/3/65 | **My Man** | Barbra Streisand |
| 2/3/62 | **My Melancholy Baby** | Marcels |
| 7/17/61 | **My Memories Of You** | Donnie & The Dreamers |
| 5/13/67 | **My Old Car** | Lee Dorsey |
| 12/28/63 | **My One And Only, Jimmy Boy** | Girlfriends |
| 10/20/62 | **My Own True Love** | Duprees |
| 6/7/69 | **My Pledge Of Love** | Joe Jeffrey Group |
| 5/12/62 | **My Real Name** | Fats Domino |
| 1/29/66 | **My Ship Is Comin' In** | Walker Bros. |
| 7/11/60 | **My Shoes Keep Walking Back To You** | Guy Mitchell |
| 5/18/68 | **My Shy Violet** | Mills Brothers |
| 11/30/68 | **My Song** | Aretha Franklin |
| 9/7/68 | **My Special Angel** | Vogues |
| | **My Special Prayer** | |
| 2/4/67 | | Joe Simon |
| 2/1/69 | | Percy Sledge |
| 5/18/63 | **My Summer Love** | Ruby & The Romantics |
| 9/3/66 | **My Sweet Potato** | Booker T. & The M.G.'s |
| 7/4/60 | **My Tani** | Brothers Four |
| | **My Three Sons**..see: Theme From | |
| 6/30/62 | **My Time For Cryin'** | Maxine Brown |
| 9/11/65 | **My Town, My Guy And Me** | Lesley Gore |
| 2/22/64 | **My True Carrie, Love** | Nat "King" Cole |
| 6/15/63 | **My True Confession** | Brook Benton |
| 7/3/61 | **My True Story** | Jive Five |
| 9/17/66 | **My Uncle Used To Love Me But She Died** | Roger Miller |
| 3/29/69 | **My Way** | Frank Sinatra |
| 8/31/68 | **My Way Of Life** | Frank Sinatra |
| 2/15/69 | **My Whole World Ended (The Moment You Left Me)** | David Ruffin |
| 7/6/63 | **My Whole World Is Falling Down** | Brenda Lee |
| 12/8/62 | **My Wife Can't Cook** | Lonnie Russ |
| 5/17/69 | **My Wife, My Dog, My Cat** | Maskman & The Agents |
| 6/24/67 | **My World Fell Down** | Sagittarius |
| | **My World Is Empty Without You** | |
| 1/15/66 | | Supremes |
| 2/8/69 | | Jose Feliciano |
| 10/30/65 | **Mystic Eyes** | Them |

# N

| Date | Title | Artist |
|---|---|---|
| 10/18/69 | **Na Na Hey Hey Kiss Him Goodbye** | Steam |
| 3/7/64 | **Nadine (Is It You?)** | Chuck Berry |
| 7/17/61 | **"Nag"** | Halos |
| 12/12/64 | **Name Game** | Shirley Ellis |
| 12/17/66 | **Nashville Cats** | Lovin' Spoonful |
| 5/16/60 | **National City** | Joiner, Arkansas Junior High School Band |
| 9/14/63 | **(Native Girl) Elephant Walk** | Donald Jenkins |
| 10/31/60 | **Natural Born Lover** | Fats Domino |
| 9/30/67 | **Natural Woman** | Aretha Franklin |
| 8/31/68 | **Naturally Stoned** | Avant-Garde |
| 6/12/61 | **Nature Boy** | Bobby Darin |
| 1/25/64 | **Navy Blue** | Diane Renay |
| 7/29/67 | **Nearer To You** | Betty Harris |
| 11/23/63 | **Need To Belong** | Jerry Butler |
| 10/17/64 | **Needle In A Haystack** | Velvelettes |
| | **Needles And Pins** | |
| 5/18/63 | | Jackie deShannon |
| 3/7/64 | | Searchers |
| 6/4/66 | **Neighbor, Neighbor** | Jimmy Hughes |
| | **Nel Blu Dipinto Di Blu**..see: Volare | |
| 11/11/67 | **Neon Rainbow** | Box Tops |
| 9/4/65 | **N-E-R-V-O-U-S!** | Ian Whitcomb |
| 6/28/69 | **Never Comes The Day** | Moody Blues |
| 4/20/68 | **Never Get Enough Of Your Love** | Oscar Toney, Jr. |
| 5/4/68 | **Never Give You Up** | Jerry Butler |
| 7/27/68 | **Never Going Back** | Lovin' Spoonful |
| 4/26/69 | **Never Gonna Let Him Know** | Debbie Taylor |
| 6/16/62 | **Never In A Million Years** | Linda Scott |
| 3/7/60 | **Never Let Me Go** | Lloyd Price |
| 12/28/63 | **Never Love A Robin** | Bobby Vee |
| | **Never My Love** | |
| 8/26/67 | | Association |
| 10/19/68 | | Sandpebbles |
| 11/13/61 | **Never, Never** | Jive Five |
| 3/20/65 | **Never, Never Leave Me** | Mary Wells |
| | **Never On Sunday** | |
| 8/8/60 | | Don Costa |
| 4/24/61 | | Lale Anderson (Ein Schiff) |
| 6/19/61 | | Chordettes |
| 11/7/64 | **Never Trust A Woman** | B.B. King |
| 3/21/64 | **New Girl In School** | Jan & Dean |
| 1/4/60* | **(New In) The Ways Of Love** | Tommy Edwards |
| | **New Lovers**..see: (Welcome) | |
| 10/5/63 | **New Mexican Rose** | Four Seasons |
| | **New Orleans** | |
| 10/17/60 | | U.S. Bonds |
| 7/3/65 | | Eddie Hodges |
| 1/6/68 | | Neil Diamond |
| 5/27/67 | **New York Mining Disaster 1941** | Bee Gees |
| 2/6/65 | **New York's A Lonely Town** | Trade Winds |
| 10/6/62 | **Next Door To An Angel** | Neil Sedaka |
| 10/13/62 | **Next Door To The Blues** | Etta James |
| 4/3/61 | **Next Kiss (Is The Last Goodbye)** | Conway Twitty |
| 10/21/67 | **Next Plane To London** | Rose Garden |
| 8/29/60 | **Nice 'N' Easy** | Frank Sinatra |
| 9/28/63 | **Nick Teen And Al K. Hall** | Rolf Harris |
| 3/21/60 | **Night** | Jackie Wilson |
| | (also see: Nite) | |
| 6/3/67 | **Night And Day** | Sergio Mendes & Brasil '66 |
| 2/17/68 | **Night Fo' Last** | Shorty Long |
| 12/8/62 | **Night Has A Thousand Eyes** | Bobby Vee |
| 9/28/63 | **Night Life** | Rusty Draper |
| 10/17/60 | **Night Theme** | Mark II |
| 12/8/62 | **Night Time** | Pete Antell |
| 1/15/66 | **Night Time** | Strangeloves |
| 6/20/64 | **Night Time Is The Right Time** | Rufus & Carla |

| | | | | | | | |
|---|---|---|---|---|---|---|---|
| | **Night Train** | 7/31/65 | **Nothing But Heartaches** Supremes | 6/28/69 | **On Campus** Dickie Goodman |
| 7/18/60 | Viscounts | 9/29/62 | **Nothing Can Change This Love** | 1/25/60 | **On The Beach** Frank Chacksfield |
| 9/18/61 | Richard Hayman | | Sam Cooke | 7/2/66 | **On The Good Ship Lollipop** |
| 4/14/62 | James Brown | 4/17/65 | **Nothing Can Stop Me** Gene Chandler | | Wonder Who? |
| 1/28/67 | **Niki Hoeky** P.J. Proby | 7/5/69 | **Nothing Can Take The Place Of You** | 3/6/61 | **On The Rebound** Floyd Cramer |
| 9/23/67 | **Nine Pound Steel** Joe Simon | | Brook Benton | 8/10/68 | **On The Road Again** Canned Heat |
| 10/22/66 | **Nineteen Days** Dave Clark Five | 3/2/63 | **Nothing Goes Up (Without Coming** | 9/12/64 | **On The Street Where You Live** |
| 2/26/66 | **19th Nervous Breakdown** | | **Down)** Nat "King" Cole | | Andy Williams |
| | Rolling Stones | 6/30/62 | **Nothing New (Same Old Thing)** | 10/12/68 | **On The Way Home** Buffalo Springfield |
| | **96 Tears** | | Fats Domino | 10/29/66 | **On This Side Of Goodbye** |
| 9/3/66 | ? & The Mysterians | 3/25/67 | **Nothing Takes The Place Of You** | | Righteous Brothers |
| 1/14/67 | Big Maybelle | | Toussaint McCall | 6/1/63 | **On Top Of Spaghetti** Tom Glazer |
| 12/10/66 | **98.6** Keith | 4/16/66 | **Nothing's Too Good For My Baby** | 10/31/60 | **Once In Awhile** Chimes |
| 5/28/66 | **Ninety-Nine And A Half (Won't Do)** | | Stevie Wonder | 2/6/61 | **Once Upon A Time** |
| | Wilson Pickett | 11/23/63 | **Now!** Lena Horne | | Rochell & The Candles |
| 3/16/68 | **1941** Tom Northcott | 7/31/61 | **Now And Forever** Bert Kaempfert | 5/2/64 | **Once Upon A Time** |
| 1/20/62 | **Nite Owl** Dukays | 6/10/67 | **Now I Know** Jack Jones | | Marvin Gaye & Mary Wells |
| | **Nitty Gritty** | 4/24/65 | **Now That You've Gone** | 5/3/69 | **One** Three Dog Night |
| 11/16/63 | Shirley Ellis | | Connie Stevens | | **(One Banana, Two Banana)**..see: Tra |
| 10/5/68 | Ricardo Ray | 7/17/61 | **Now You Know** Little Willie John | | La La Song |
| 7/19/69 | Gladys Knight & The Pips | 3/5/66 | **Nowhere Man** Beatles | 7/4/60 | **One Boy** Joanie Sommers |
| 8/8/60 | **No** Dodie Stevens | 2/27/65 | **Nowhere To Run** | 5/11/63 | **One Boy Too Late** Mike Clifford |
| 12/26/64 | **No Arms Can Ever Hold You** | | Martha & The Vandellas | 2/16/63 | **One Broken Heart For Sale** |
| | Bachelors | 4/28/62 | **Number One Man** Bruce Channel | | Elvis Presley |
| 2/4/67 | **No Fair At All** Association | 3/3/62 | **Nutrocker** B. Bumble & The Stingers | 6/10/67 | **One By One** Blues Magoos |
| 1/9/65 | **No Faith, No Love** Mitty Collier | | | 7/10/65 | **One Dyin' And A Buryin'** Roger Miller |
| 5/27/67 | **No Good To Cry** Wildweeds | | **O** | 3/29/69 | **One Eye Open** Maskman & The Agents |
| 4/25/60 | **No If's - No And's** Lloyd Price | | | | **One Eyed Jacks**..see: Love Theme From |
| 1/4/60* | **No Love Have I** Webb Pierce | 2/22/60 | **O Dio Mio** Annette | 6/1/63 | **One Fine Day** Chiffons |
| 4/2/66 | **No Man Is An Island** Van Dykes | 1/4/69 | **Ob-La-Di, Ob-La-Da** Arthur Conley | 5/16/64 | **One Girl** Garnet Mimms |
| 12/11/65 | **No Matter What Shape (Your** | 7/26/69 | **Odds And Ends** Dionne Warwick | 11/6/65 | **One Has My Name (The Other Has My** |
| | **Stomach's In)** T-Bones | | **Ode To Billie Joe** | | **Heart)** Barry Young |
| 5/31/69 | **No Matter What Sign You Are** | 8/5/67 | Bobbie Gentry | 3/23/68 | **100 Years** Nancy Sinatra |
| | Supremes | 9/23/67 | Kingpins | | (also see: Hundred) |
| 2/18/67 | **No Milk Today** Herman's Hermits | 9/30/67 | Ray Bryant | 4/15/67 | **One Hurt Deserves Another** Raeletts |
| 6/19/61 | **No, No, No** Chanters | 1/2/65 | **Ode To The Little Brown Shack Out** | 3/13/65 | **One Kiss For Old Times' Sake** |
| | **No Not Much** | | **Back** Billy Edd Wheeler | | Ronnie Dove |
| 2/15/69 | Smoke Ring | 9/24/66 | **Off To Dublin In The Green** | | **One Mint Julep** |
| 3/8/69 | Vogues | | Abbey Tavern Singers | 1/4/60 | Chet Atkins |
| | **No One** | | **Oh**..also see: O | 3/6/61 | Ray Charles |
| 1/16/61 | Connie Francis | 6/20/64 | **Oh! Baby** Barbara Lynn | 6/26/65 | **One Monkey Don't Stop No Show** |
| 6/22/63 | Ray Charles | 1/25/64 | **Oh Baby Don't You Weep** | | Joe Tex |
| 5/29/65 | Brenda Lee | | James Brown | 1/4/60* | **One More Chance** Rod Bernard |
| 11/29/69 | **No One Better Than You** Petula Clark | 1/4/60* | **Oh! Carol** Neil Sedaka | 2/19/66 | **One More Heartache** Marvin Gaye |
| 8/30/69 | **No One For Me To Turn To** | 4/26/69 | **Oh Happy Day** Edwin Hawkins' Singers | 2/18/67 | **One More Mountain To Climb** |
| | Spiral Starecase | | **Oh How Happy** | | Ronnie Dove |
| 1/27/68 | **No One Knows** Every Mother's Son | 5/7/66 | Shades Of Blue | 9/12/64 | **One More Tear** Raindrops |
| 7/18/64 | **No One To Cry To** Ray Charles | 8/16/69 | Edwin Starr & Blinky | 11/14/64 | **One More Time** Ray Charles Singers |
| 9/1/62 | **No One Will Ever Know** | 12/26/60 | **Oh, How I Miss You Tonight** | 10/27/62 | **One More Town** Kingston Trio |
| | Jimmie Rodgers | | Jeanne Black | 8/9/69 | **One Night Affair** O'Jays |
| 5/23/64 | **No Particular Place To Go** | 12/23/67 | **Oh, How It Hurts** Barbara Mason | 10/10/60 | **One Of The Lucky Ones** Anita Bryant |
| | Chuck Berry | 5/2/60 | **Oh, Little One** Jack Scott | 11/29/69 | **(One Of These Days) Sunday's Gonna'** |
| 7/3/65 | **No Pity (In The Naked City)** | 12/31/60 | **Oh Lonesome Me** Johnny Cash | | **Come On Tuesday** |
| | Jackie Wilson | 9/28/68 | **Oh Lord, Why Lord** Los Pop Tops | | New Establishment |
| 1/6/68 | **No Sad Songs** Joe Simon | 12/27/69 | **Oh Me Oh My (I'm A Fool For You** | 6/6/60 | **One Of Us (Will Weep Tonight)** |
| 12/20/69 | **No Time** Guess Who | | **Baby)** Lulu | | Patti Page |
| 4/1/67 | **No Time Like The Right Time** | 3/13/61 | **Oh Mein Papa** Dick Lee | 2/26/66 | **One On The Right Is On The Left** |
| | Blues Project | 5/5/62 | **Oh My Angel** Bertha Tillman | | Johnny Cash |
| 12/9/67 | **Nobody But Me** Human Beinz | 10/24/64 | **Oh No Not My Baby** Maxine Brown | 8/8/64 | **One Piece Topless Bathing Suit** |
| 8/2/69 | **Nobody But You Babe** Clarence Reid | 8/29/64 | **Oh, Pretty Woman** Roy Orbison | | Rip Chords |
| 4/24/61 | **Nobody Cares (about me)** | 6/27/64 | **Oh, Rock My Soul** Peter, Paul & Mary | 7/3/65 | **One Step At A Time** Maxine Brown |
| | Baby Washington | 3/18/67 | **Oh That's Good, No That's Bad** | 7/3/61 | **One Summer Night** Diamonds |
| 6/27/64 | **Nobody I Know** Peter & Gordon | | Sam The Sham & The Pharoahs | 11/15/69 | **One Tin Soldier (The Legend Of Billy** |
| 6/19/65 | **Nobody Knows What's Goin' On** | 8/16/69 | **Oh, What A Night** Dells | | **Jack)** Original Caste |
| | Chiffons | 8/25/62 | **Oh! What It Seemed To Be** Castells | 6/4/66 | **One Too Many Mornings** |
| 9/5/60 | **Nobody Knows You When You're** | 6/4/66 | **Oh Yeah** Shadows Of Knight | | Beau Brummels |
| | **Down And Out** Nina Simone | 1/7/67 | **Oh Yeah!** Joe Cuba Sextet | 8/28/61 | **One Track Mind** Bobby Lewis |
| 4/18/60 | **Nobody Loves Me Like You** Flamingos | 11/1/69 | **Okie From Muskogee** Merle Haggard | 3/19/66 | **One Track Mind** Knickerbockers |
| 10/8/66 | **Nobody's Baby Again** Dean Martin | 11/25/67 | **Okolona River Bottom Band** | | **1-2-3** |
| 12/4/61 | **Norman** Sue Thompson | | Bobbie Gentry | 9/25/65 | Len Barry |
| 9/19/60 | **North To Alaska** Johnny Horton | 11/7/60 | **Ol' MacDonald** Frank Sinatra | 2/11/67 | Ramsey Lewis |
| 11/2/68 | **Not Enough Indians** Dean Martin | 9/1/62 | **Ol' Man River** Jimmy Smith | 7/27/68 | **1, 2, 3, Red Light** 1910 Fruitgum Co. |
| 5/2/64 | **Not Fade Away** Rolling Stones | 11/23/68 | **Ol' Race Track** Mills Brothers | 1/13/68 | **(I-2-3-4-5-6-7) Count The Days** |
| 4/13/63 | **Not For All The Money In The World** | 5/4/63 | **Old Enough To Love** Rick Nelson | | Inez & Charlie Foxx |
| | Shirelles | 3/14/60 | **Old Lamplighter** Browns | 5/2/64 | **One Way Love** Drifters |
| 6/15/63 | **Not Me** Orlons | 8/22/60 | **Old Oaken Bucket** Tommy Sands | 3/24/62 | **One Who Really Loves You** |
| 12/28/68 | **Not On The Outside** Moments | 2/29/60 | **Old Payola Roll Blues** Stan Freberg | | Mary Wells |
| 1/4/60* | **Not One Minute More** Della Reese | 4/7/62 | **Old Rivers** Walter Brennan | 10/25/69 | **One Woman** Johnny Rivers |
| 6/18/66 | **Not Responsible** Tom Jones | 6/1/63 | **Old Smokey Locomotion** Little Eva | 8/17/63 | **Only In America** Jay & The Americans |
| 8/5/67 | **Not So Sweet Martha Lorraine** | 6/5/61 | **Ole Buttermilk Sky** Bill Black's Combo | | **Only Love Can Break A Heart** |
| | Country Joe & The Fish | 1/20/62 | **Oliver Twist** Rod McKuen | 9/15/62 | Gene Pitney |
| 9/18/65 | **Not The Lovin' Kind** Dino, Desi & Billy | 7/8/67 | **Omaha** Moby Grape | 6/3/67 | Margaret Whiting |
| 3/20/65 | **Not Too Long Ago** Uniques | 3/18/67 | **On A Carousel** Hollies | 11/27/65 | **Only Love (Can Save Me Now)** |
| 6/8/63 | **Not Too Young To Get Married** | 12/18/65 | **On A Clear Day You Can See** | | Solomon Burke |
| | Bob B. Soxx & The Blue Jeans | | **Forever** Johnny Mathis | | **Only The Lonely** |
| | **Nothin' Yet**..see: (We Ain't Got) | 10/28/67 | **On A Saturday Night** Eddie Floyd | 6/6/60 | Roy Orbison |
| 3/8/69 | **Nothing But A Heartache** Flirtations | 10/30/61 | **On Bended Knees** Clarence Henry | 2/8/69 | Sonny James |
| 8/21/61 | **Nothing But Good** Hank Ballard | 3/23/63 | **On Broadway** Drifters | 3/1/69 | **Only The Strong Survive** Jerry Butler |

| Date | Title | Artist |
|---|---|---|
| 7/24/65 | Only Those In Love | Baby Washington |
| 9/10/66 | Only When You're Lonely | Grass Roots |
| | Only You | |
| 2/2/63 |   Mr. Acker Bilk | |
| 3/8/69 |   Bobby Hatfield | |
| 11/4/67 | O-O, I Love You | Dells |
| 1/19/63 | Oo-La-La-Limbo | Danny & The Juniors |
| 5/29/65 | Oo Wee Baby, I Love You | Fred Hughes |
| 4/15/67 | Oogum Boogum Song | Brenton Wood |
| 1/21/67 | Ooh Baby | Bo Diddley |
| 11/18/67 | Ooh Baby | Deon Jackson |
| | Ooh Baby Baby | |
| 3/27/65 |   Miracles | |
| 5/27/67 |   Five Stairsteps | |
| 3/28/60 | Ooh Poo Pah Doo | Jessie Hill |
| 7/31/65 | Oowee, Oowee | Perry Como |
| 11/11/67 | Open Letter To My Teenage Son | Victor Lundberg |
| | (also see: Letter To Dad) | |
| 7/23/66 | Open The Door To Your Heart | Darrell Banks |
| 12/17/66 | (Open Up The Door) Let The Good Times In | Dean Martin |
| 9/24/66 | Open Up Your Door | Richard & The Young Lions |
| 4/14/62 | Operator | Gladys Knight & The Pips |
| 6/5/65 | Operator | Brenda Holloway |
| 10/10/64 | Opportunity | Jewels |
| 5/21/66 | Opus 17 (Don't You Worry 'Bout Me) | 4 Seasons |
| | Orange Blossom Special | |
| 2/20/61 |   Billy Vaughn | |
| 2/13/65 |   Johnny Cash | |
| 10/2/65 | Organ Grinder's Swing | Jimmy Smith, Kenny Burrell, Grady Tate |
| 8/24/63 | Organ Shout | Dave "Baby" Cortez |
| 12/2/67 | Other Man's Grass Is Always Greener | Petula Clark |
| 9/24/66 | Other Side Of This Life | Peter, Paul & Mary |
| 2/17/62 | Our Anniversary | Shep & The Limelites |
| 2/9/63 | Our Day Will Come | Ruby & The Romantics |
| 3/21/64 | Our Everlasting Love | Ruby & The Romantics |
| 5/8/61 | Our Love Is Here To Stay | Dinah Washington |
| 9/9/67 | Our Song | Jack Jones |
| | Our Winter Love | |
| 2/2/63 |   Bill Pursell | |
| 1/28/67 |   Lettermen | |
| 11/20/65 | Our World | Johnny Tillotson |
| 7/15/67 | Out & About | Tommy Boyce & Bobby Hart |
| 4/3/65 | Out In The Streets | Shangri-Las |
| 4/8/67 | Out Of Left Field | Percy Sledge |
| 12/7/63 | Out Of Limits | Marketts |
| 3/2/63 | Out Of My Mind | Johnny Tillotson |
| 8/15/64 | Out Of Sight | James Brown |
| | Out Of Sight - Out Of Mind | |
| 2/22/64 |   Sunny & The Sunliners | |
| 7/26/69 |   Little Anthony & The Imperials | |
| 10/28/67 | Out Of The Blue | Tommy James & The Shondells |
| 8/6/66 | Out Of This World | Chiffons |
| 2/15/64 | Outside My Window | Fleetwoods |
| 3/5/66 | Outside The Gates Of Heaven | Lou Christie |
| 11/13/65 | Over And Over | Dave Clark Five |
| | Over The Mountain; Across The Sea | |
| 9/26/60 |   Johnnie & Joe | |
| 3/9/63 |   Bobby Vinton | |
| 7/4/60 | Over The Rainbow | Demensions |
| 6/25/66 | Over Under Sideways Down | Yardbirds |
| 9/21/68 | Over You | Union Gap |

## P

| Date | Title | Artist |
|---|---|---|
| 5/9/64 | P.S. I Love You | Beatles |
| 3/31/62 | P.T. 109 | Jimmy Dean |
| 1/15/66 | Pain Gets A Little Deeper | Darrow Fletcher |
| 11/23/63 | Pain In My Heart | Otis Redding |
| 5/14/66 | Paint It, Black | Rolling Stones |
| | Paint Me A Picture..see: (You Don't Have To) | |
| 7/27/63 | Painted, Tainted Rose | Al Martino |
| 6/25/66 | Painter | Lou Christie |
| | Paladin..see: Ballad Of | |
| 5/12/62 | Palisades Park | Freddy Cannon |
| 11/26/66 | Pandora's Golden Heebie Jeebies | Association |
| 9/18/61 | Panic | Otis Williams & His Charms |
| | Papa Joe's..see: (Down At) | |
| 8/18/62 | Papa-Oom-Mow-Mow | Rivingtons |
| 12/17/66 | Papa Was Too | Joe Tex |
| | Papa's Got A Brand New Bag | |
| 7/17/65 |   James Brown | |
| 11/30/68 |   Otis Redding | |
| 11/4/67 | Paper Cup | 5th Dimension |
| 4/11/60 | Paper Roses | Anita Bryant |
| 9/2/67 | Paper Sun | Traffic |
| 1/2/65 | Paper Tiger | Sue Thompson |
| 6/11/66 | Paperback Writer | Beatles |
| 2/15/60 | Paradise | Sammy Turner |
| 8/17/63 | Part Time Love | Little Johnny Taylor |
| 5/16/64 | Party Girl | Bernadette Carroll |
| 12/5/64 | Party Girl | Tommy Roe |
| 6/30/62 | Party Lights | Claudine Clark |
| 2/27/65 | Pass Me By | Peggy Lee |
| 7/12/69 | Pass The Apple Eve | B.J. Thomas |
| 6/25/66 | Past, Present And Future | Shangri-Las |
| 10/7/67 | Pata Pata | Miriam Makeba |
| 8/25/62 | Patches | Dickey Lee |
| 4/7/62 | Patricia - Twist | Perez Prado |
| 10/17/60 | Patsy | Jack Scott |
| 3/3/62 | Patti Ann | Johnny Crawford |
| 5/4/63 | Patty Baby | Freddy Cannon |
| 8/10/63 | Pay Back | Etta James |
| 6/3/67 | Pay You Back With Interest | Hollies |
| 4/20/68 | Paying The Cost To Be The Boss | B.B. King |
| 10/26/68 | Peace Brother Peace | Bill Medley |
| 2/1/60 | Peace Of Mind | Teresa Brewer |
| 11/18/67 | Peace Of Mind | Paul Revere & The Raiders |
| 9/28/68 | Peace Of Mind | Nancy Wilson |
| 3/13/65 | Peaches "N" Cream | Ikettes |
| 12/10/66 | Peak Of Love | Bobby McClure |
| 4/24/61 | Peanut Butter | Marathons |
| 7/3/61 | Peanuts | Rick & The Keens |
| 8/5/65 | Peanuts | Sunglows |
| 7/29/67 | Pearl Time | Andre Williams |
| 9/12/64 | Pearly Shells | Burl Ives |
| 10/7/67 | Peas 'N' Rice | Freddie McCoy |
| 2/18/67 | Peek-A-Boo | New Vaudeville Band |
| 6/20/64 | Peg O' My Heart | Robert Maxwell |
| 2/1/64 | Penetration | Pyramids |
| 5/9/60 | Pennies From Heaven | Skyliners |
| 9/2/67 | Penny Arcade | Cyrkle |
| 2/25/67 | Penny Lane | Beatles |
| | People | |
| 4/4/64 |   Barbra Streisand | |
| 4/11/64 |   Nat "King" Cole | |
| 11/16/68 |   Tymes | |
| 9/23/67 | People Are Strange | Doors |
| 2/13/65 | People Get Ready | Impressions |
| 7/20/68 | People Got To Be Free | Rascals |
| 1/28/67 | People In Me | Music Machine |
| 2/11/67 | People Like You | Eddie Fisher |
| 7/18/64 | People Say | Dixie Cups |
| 6/22/68 | People Sure Act Funny | Arthur Conley |
| 2/3/68 | People World | Jim & Jean |
| 12/19/60 | "Pepe" | Duane Eddy |
| 12/8/62 | Pepino The Italian Mouse | Lou Monte |
| 3/9/63 | Pepino's Friend Pasqual (The Italian Pussy-Cat) | Lou Monte |
| | Peppermint Twist | |
| 11/20/61 |   Joey Dee | |
| 12/4/61 |   Danny Peppermint | |
| 12/19/64 | Percolatin' | Willie Mitchell |
| 1/13/62 | Percolator | Billy Joe & The Checkmates |
| 12/12/60 | Perfect Love | Frankie Avalon |
| 10/31/60 | Perfidia | Ventures |
| | Personality..see: (You've Got) | |
| 10/10/60 | Peter Gunn | Duane Eddy |
| 5/7/66 | Peter Rabbit | Dee Jay & The Runaways |
| | (Petite Fleur)..see: Time To Love-A Time To Cry | |
| 8/6/66 | Petticoat White (Summer Sky Blue) | Bobby Vinton |
| | Philly Dog | |
| 3/5/66 |   Mar-Keys | |
| 10/1/66 |   Herbie Mann | |
| |   (also see: Baby, Do The Philly Dog) | |
| 7/30/66 | Philly Freeze | Alvin Cash & The Registers |
| 3/12/66 | Phoenix Love Theme | Brass Ring |
| 5/22/61 | Pick Me Up On Your Way Down | Pat Zill |
| 12/30/67 | Pick Up The Pieces | Carla Thomas |
| 10/19/68 | Pickin' Wild Mountain Berries | Peggy Scott & Jo Jo Benson |
| 2/10/62 | Pictures In The Fire | Pat Boone |
| 7/1/67 | Pictures Of Lily | Who |
| 5/18/68 | Pictures Of Matchstick Men | Status Quo |
| | Piece Of My Heart | |
| 11/4/67 |   Erma Franklin | |
| 8/31/68 |   Big Brother & The Holding Company | |
| | Pied Piper | |
| 11/13/65 |   Changin' Times | |
| 6/11/66 |   Crispian St. Peters | |
| 2/9/63 | Pin A Medal On Joey | James Darren |
| 4/16/66 | Pin The Tail On The Donkey | Paul Peek |
| 4/5/69 | Pinball Wizard | Who |
| 6/21/69 | Pinch Me (Baby, Convince Me) | Ohio Express |
| 8/15/60 | Pineapple Princess | Annette |
| 5/9/60 | Pink Chiffon | Mitchell Torok |
| 12/28/63 | Pink Dominos | Crescents |
| 4/4/64 | Pink Panther Theme | Henry Mancini |
| 3/18/67 | Pipe Dream | Blues Magoos |
| 3/2/63 | Pipeline | Chantay's |
| 8/14/61 | Pitter-Patter | Four Sportsmen |
| 11/12/66 | Place In The Sun | Stevie Wonder |
| 6/10/67 | Plastic Man | Sonny & Cher |
| 3/31/62 | Play The Thing | Marlowe Morris Quintet |
| 5/22/65 | Play With Fire | Rolling Stones |
| 5/5/62 | Playboy | Marvelettes |
| 2/17/68 | Playboy | Gene & Debbe |
| 3/8/69 | Playgirl | Thee Prophets |
| 7/22/67 | Pleasant Valley Sunday | Monkees |
| 12/14/63 | Please | Frank Ifield |
| 12/25/61 | Please Come Home For Christmas | Charles Brown |
| 2/24/62 | Please Don't Ask About Barbara | Bobby Vee |
| 1/25/69 | Please Don't Desert Me Baby | Gloria Walker |
| 12/3/66 | Please Don't Ever Leave Me | Cyrkle |
| 12/11/65 | Please Don't Fight It | Dino, Desi & Billy |
| 9/25/61 | Please Don't Go | Ral Donner |
| 11/23/63 | Please Don't Kiss Me Again | Charmettes |
| 4/30/66 | Please Don't Sell My Daddy No More Wine | Greenwoods |
| 3/19/66 | Please Don't Stop Loving Me | Elvis Presley |
| 8/3/63 | Please Don't Talk To The Lifeguard | Diane Ray |
| | Please Help Me, I'm Falling | |
| 5/23/60 |   Hank Locklin | |
| 7/18/60 |   Rusty Draper | |
| |   (also see: I Can't Help You) | |
| 3/6/65 | Please Let Me Wonder | Beach Boys |
| | Please Love Me Forever | |
| 2/27/61 |   Cathy Jean & The Roommates | |
| 9/30/67 |   Bobby Vinton | |
| 9/4/61 | Please Mr. Postman | Marvelettes |
| 9/24/66 | Please Mr. Sun | Vogues |
| 2/1/64 | Please Please Me | Beatles |
| 2/15/64 | Please, Please, Please | James Brown |
| 8/3/68 | Please Return Your Love To Me | Temptations |
| 11/12/66 | Please Say You're Fooling | Ray Charles |
| 6/5/61 | Please Stay | Drifters |
| 3/13/61 | Please Tell Me Why | Jackie Wilson |
| 6/11/66 | Please Tell Me Why | Dave Clark Five |
| 3/15/69 | Pledge Of Allegiance | Red Skelton |
| 4/11/60 | Pledging My Love | Johnny Tillotson |
| 12/18/61 | Pocketful Of Miracles | Frank Sinatra |
| 10/2/61 | Pocketful Of Rainbows | Deane Hawley |
| 10/10/60 | Poetry In Motion | Johnny Tillotson |
| 12/13/69 | Point It Out | Miracles |
| 6/19/61 | Point Of No Return | Adam Wade |
| 8/4/62 | Point Of No Return | Gene McDaniels |
| 9/28/63 | Point Panic | Surfaris |
| 7/5/69 | Polk Salad Annie | Tony Joe White |
| | Pomp & Circumstance..see: Graduation Song | |

| Date | Song | Artist |
|---|---|---|
| 2/20/61 | **Pony Express** | Danny & The Juniors |
|  | **Pony Time** |  |
| 1/23/61 | Chubby Checker |  |
| 1/23/61 | Goodtimers |  |
| 11/11/67 | **Pony With The Golden Mane** |  |
|  | Every Mothers' Son |  |
| 9/14/68 | **Poor Baby** | Cowsills |
| 11/27/61 | **Poor Fool** | Ike & Tina Turner |
| 8/4/62 | **Poor Little Puppet** | Cathy Carroll |
| 5/25/63 | **Poor Little Rich Girl** | Steve Lawrence |
| 3/13/65 | **Poor Man's Son** | Reflections |
|  | **Poor Side Of Town** |  |
| 9/17/66 | Johnny Rivers |  |
| 1/18/69 | Al Wilson |  |
| 2/17/62 | **Pop-Eye** | Huey Smith |
| 3/31/62 | **Pop-Eye Stroll** | Mar-Keys |
| 12/4/61 | **Pop Goes The Weasel** | Anthony Newley |
| 10/6/62 | **Pop Pop Pop-Pie** | Sherrys |
| 5/31/69 | **Popcorn, The** | James Brown |
| 2/24/62 | **Popeye Joe** | Ernie K-Doe |
|  | **Popeye The Hitchhiker** |  |
| 9/15/62 | Chubby Checker |  |
| 12/29/62 | **Popeye Waddle** | Don Covay |
| 6/4/66 | **Popsicle** | Jan & Dean |
| 11/23/63 | **Popsicles And Icicles** | Murmaids |
| 10/12/68 | **Porpoise Song** | Monkees |
| 1/20/62 | **Portrait Of A Fool** | Conway Twitty |
|  | **Portrait Of My Love** |  |
| 3/6/61 | Steve Lawrence |  |
| 4/15/67 | Tokens |  |
| 10/2/65 | **Positively 4th Street** | Bob Dylan |
| 4/1/67 | **Postcard From Jamaica** |  |
|  | Sopwith "Camel" |  |
| 6/30/62 | **Potato Peeler** | Bobby Gregg |
| 10/22/66 | **Pouring Water On A Drowning Man** |  |
|  | James Carr |  |
| 9/17/66 | **Poverty** | Bobby Bland |
| 7/13/68 | **Prayer Meetin'** | Willie Mitchell |
| 3/30/63 | **Preacherman** | Charlie Russo |
| 4/1/67 | **Precious Memories** | Romeos |
| 12/5/64 | **Pretend You Don't See Her** |  |
|  | Bobby Vee |  |
| 1/7/67 | **Pretty Ballerina** | Left Banke |
| 1/4/60* | **Pretty Blue Eyes** | Steve Lawrence |
| 3/9/63 | **Pretty Boy Lonely** | Patti Page |
| 7/2/66 | **Pretty Flamingo** | Manfred Mann |
| 7/3/61 | **Pretty Little Angel Eyes** | Curtis Lee |
| 7/10/65 | **Pretty Little Baby** | Marvin Gaye |
| 12/14/63 | **Pretty Paper** | Roy Orbison |
| 5/3/69 | **Pretty World** | Sergio Mendes & Brasil '66 |
| 11/28/64 | **Price, The** | Solomon Burke |
| 5/18/63 | **Pride And Joy** | Marvin Gaye |
| 1/4/60* | **Primrose Lane** | Jerry Wallace |
| 7/3/61 | **Princess** | Frank Gari |
| 11/20/65 | **Princess In Rags** | Gene Pitney |
| 4/20/63 | **Prisoner Of Love** | James Brown |
| 8/31/68 | **Private Number** |  |
|  | Judy Clay & William Bell |  |
| 2/19/66 | **Promise Her Anything** | Tom Jones |
| 1/4/60* | **Promise Me A Rose (A Slight Detail)** |  |
|  | Anita Bryant |  |
| 12/12/64 | **Promised Land** | Chuck Berry |
| 11/2/68 | **Promises, Promises** | Dionne Warwick |
| 6/21/69 | **Prophecy Of Daniel and John The Divine (Six-Six-Six)** Cowsills |  |
| 1/5/63 | **Proud** | Johnny Crawford |
|  | **Proud Mary** |  |
| 1/25/69 | Creedence Clearwater Revival |  |
| 5/3/69 | Solomon Burke |  |
| 10/18/69 | Checkmates, Ltd. |  |
| 11/12/66 | **Proud One** | Frankie Valli |
| 11/7/60 | **Psycho** | Bobby Hendricks |
| 9/10/66 | **Psychotic Reaction** | Count Five |
| 2/11/67 | **Pucker Up Buttercup** |  |
|  | Jr. Walker & The All Stars |  |
| 1/12/63 | **Puddin N' Tain (Ask Me Again, I'll Tell You The Same)** Alley Cats |  |
| 3/16/63 | **Puff The Magic Dragon** |  |
|  | Peter, Paul & Mary |  |
| 9/28/68 | **Puffin' On Down The Track** |  |
|  | Hugh Masekela |  |
| 9/1/62 | **Punish Her** | Bobby Vee |
| 11/13/65 | **Puppet On A String** | Elvis Presley |
| 12/12/60 | **Puppet Song** | Frankie Avalon |
| 6/22/68 | **(Puppet Song) Whiskey On A Sunday** Irish Rovers |  |
| 2/22/60 | **Puppy Love** | Paul Anka |
| 1/11/64 | **Puppy Love** | Barbara Lewis |
|  | **Purple Haze** |  |
| 8/26/67 | Jimi Hendrix |  |
| 1/25/69 | Dion |  |
| 11/10/62 | **Push And Kick** | Mark Valentino |
| 11/14/60 | **Push Push** | Austin Taylor |
| 12/24/66 | **Pushin' Too Hard** | Seeds |
| 12/18/61 | **Pushin' Your Luck** | Sleepy King |
| 4/20/63 | **Pushover** | Etta James |
| 6/28/69 | **Put A Little Love In Your Heart** |  |
|  | Jackie DeShannon |  |
|  | **Put Your Arms Around Me Honey** |  |
| 5/9/60 | Ray Smith |  |
| 9/5/60 | Fats Domino |  |
| 11/16/68 | **Put Your Head On My Shoulder** |  |
|  | Lettermen |  |
| 8/26/67 | **Put Your Mind At Ease** |  |
|  | Every Mothers' Son |  |
| 2/19/66 | **Put Yourself In My Place** | Elgins |
| 5/29/65 | **Puzzle Song (A Puzzle In Song)** |  |
|  | Shirley Ellis |  |

## Q

| Date | Song | Artist |
|---|---|---|
| 5/19/62 | **Quando, Quando, Quando (Tell Me When)** Pat Boone |  |
| 3/3/62 | **Quarter To Four Stomp** | Stompers |
| 5/22/61 | **Quarter To Three** | U.S. Bonds |
| 7/27/63 | **Que Sera, Sera (Whatever Will Be, Will Be)** High Keys |  |
| 6/9/62 | **Queen Of My Heart** | Rene & Ray |
| 4/24/65 | **Queen Of The House** | Jody Miller |
|  | (also see: King Of The Road) |  |
| 6/14/69 | **Quentin's Theme** |  |
|  | Charles Randolph Greane Sounde |  |
| 6/27/60 | **Question** | Lloyd Price |
| 2/24/68 | **Question Of Temperature** |  |
|  | Balloon Farm |  |
| 8/9/69 | **Questions 67 And 68** | Chicago |
| 12/10/66 | **Questions And Answers** | In Crowd |
| 10/5/68 | **Quick Joey Small (Run Joey Run)** |  |
|  | Kasenetz-Katz Singing Orchestral Circus |  |
| 11/23/63 | **Quicksand** | Martha & The Vandellas |
| 12/4/65 | **Quiet Nights Of Quiet Stars** |  |
|  | Andy Williams |  |
| 7/18/64 | **Quiet Place** |  |
|  | Garnet Mimms & The Enchanters |  |
| 6/26/61 | **Quite A Party** | Fireballs |

## R

| Date | Song | Artist |
|---|---|---|
|  | **Race Is On** |  |
| 1/23/65 | George Jones |  |
| 2/27/65 | Jack Jones |  |
| 6/20/64 | **Rag Doll** | 4 Seasons |
| 11/16/63 | **Rags To Riches** | Sunny & The Sunliners |
| 6/11/66 | **Rain** | Beatles |
| 8/23/69 | **Rain** | Jose Feliciano |
| 1/4/69 | **Rain In My Heart** | Frank Sinatra |
| 10/15/66 | **Rain On The Roof** | Lovin' Spoonful |
| 8/25/62 | **Rain Rain Go Away** | Bobby Vinton |
| 9/30/67 | **Rain, The Park & Other Things** |  |
|  | Cowsills |  |
|  | **Rainbow** |  |
| 2/23/63 | Gene Chandler |  |
| 11/27/65 | Gene Chandler ('65) |  |
| 11/24/62 | **Rainbow At Midnight** | Jimmie Rodgers |
| 12/21/68 | **Rainbow Ride** | Andy Kim |
| 5/1/61 | **Raindrops** | Dee Clark |
|  | (also see: Cloudy Summer Afternoon) |  |
| 11/1/69 | **Raindrops Keep Fallin' On My Head** |  |
|  | B.J. Thomas |  |
| 5/29/61 | **Rainin' In My Heart** | Slim Harpo |
|  | **Raining In My Sunshine** ..see: (He's) |  |
|  | **Rains Came** |  |
| 3/10/62 | Big Sambo |  |
| 1/29/66 | Sir Douglas Quintet |  |
| 4/16/66 | **Rainy Day Women #12 & 35** |  |
|  | Bob Dylan |  |
| 2/4/67 | **Raise Your Hand** | Eddie Floyd |
| 1/23/61 | **Ram-Bunk-Shush** | Ventures |
| 5/1/61 | **Rama Lama Ding Dong** | Edsels |
| 12/21/68 | **Ramblin' Gamblin' Man** | Bob Seger |
| 8/4/62 | **Ramblin' Rose** | Nat "King" Cole |
| 12/5/60 | **Rambling** | Ramblers |
| 11/28/60 | **Ramona** | Blue Diamonds |
| 6/15/63 | **Rat Race** | Drifters |
| 12/7/68 | **Ray Of Hope** | Rascals |

| Date | Song | Artist |
|---|---|---|
|  | **Reach Out For Me** |  |
| 10/19/63 | Lou Johnson |  |
| 10/24/64 | Dionne Warwick |  |
|  | **Reach Out I'll Be There** |  |
| 9/3/66 | Four Tops |  |
| 12/7/68 | Merrilee Rush |  |
| 5/18/68 | **Reach Out Of The Darkness** |  |
|  | Friend & Lover |  |
| 7/10/61 | **Ready For Your Love** |  |
|  | Shep & The Limelites |  |
| 12/7/68 | **Ready Or Not Here I Come (Can't Hide From Love)** Delfonics |  |
| 5/25/68 | **Ready, Willing and Able** |  |
|  | American Breed |  |
| 4/9/66 | **Real Humdinger** | J.J. Barnes |
| 3/6/65 | **Real Live Girl** | Steve Alaimo |
| 7/21/62 | **Reap What You Sow** | Billy Stewart |
| 6/28/69 | **Reconsider Me** | Johnny Adams |
| 4/3/65 | **Record, The (Baby I Love You)** |  |
|  | Ben E. King |  |
| 12/25/65 | **Recovery** | Fontella Bass |
| 11/18/67 | **Red And Blue** | Dave Clark Five |
| 2/5/66 | **Red Hot** | Sam The Sham & The Pharoahs |
| 1/5/63 | **Red Pepper I** |  |
|  | Roosevelt Fountain & Pens Of Rhythm |  |
| 4/13/68 | **Red Red Wine** | Neil Diamond |
|  | **Red Roses For A Blue Lady** |  |
| 1/23/65 | Bert Kaempfert |  |
| 2/6/65 | Vic Dana |  |
| 2/27/65 | Wayne Newton |  |
| 5/20/67 | **Red Roses For Mom** | Bobby Vinton |
| 5/21/66 | **Red Rubber Ball** | Cyrkle |
|  | **Red Sails In The Sunset** |  |
| 8/1/60 | Platters |  |
| 9/21/63 | Fats Domino |  |
| 4/17/65 | **Reelin' And Rockin'** | Dave Clark Five |
| 8/12/67 | **Reflections** | Supremes |
|  | **Release Me** |  |
| 10/27/62 | Esther Phillips |  |
| 4/8/67 | Engelbert Humperdinck |  |
| 6/3/67 | Esther Phillips |  |
| 12/14/68 | Johnny Adams |  |
| 2/9/63 | **Remember Baby** | Shep & The Limelites |
| 4/13/63 | **Remember Diana** | Paul Anka |
| 6/6/64 | **Remember Me** | Rita Pavone |
| 5/22/65 | **(Remember Me) I'm The One Who Loves You** Dean Martin |  |
| 4/23/66 | **Remember The Rain** | Bob Lind |
| 12/15/62 | **Remember Then** | Earls |
| 8/22/64 | **Remember (Walkin' In The Sand)** |  |
|  | Shangri-Las |  |
| 10/16/65 | **Remember When** | Wayne Newton |
| 9/2/67 | **Requiem For The Masses** | Association |
| 10/2/65 | **Rescue Me** | Fontella Bass |
|  | **Respect** |  |
| 9/4/65 | Otis Redding |  |
| 11/12/66 | Rationals |  |
| 4/29/67 | Aretha Franklin |  |
| 8/6/66 | **Respectable** | Outsiders |
| 2/25/67 | **Return Of The Red Baron** |  |
|  | Royal Guardsmen |  |
| 10/20/62 | **Return To Sender** | Elvis Presley |
| 1/4/60* | **Reveille Rock** | Johnny & The Hurricanes |
| 11/20/61 | **Revenge** | Brook Benton |
| 4/6/63 | **Reverend Mr. Black** | Kingston Trio |
| 8/29/60 | **Revival** | Johnny & The Hurricanes |
| 9/14/68 | **Revolution** | Beatles |
| 11/27/65 | **Revolution Kind** | Sonny |
| 3/26/66 | **Rhapsody In The Rain** | Lou Christie |
| 8/22/64 | **Rhythm** | Major Lance |
|  | **Rhythm Of The Rain** |  |
| 1/12/63 | Cascades |  |
| 4/5/69 | Gary Lewis & The Playboys |  |
| 1/29/66 | **Rib Tip's** | Andre Williams |
| 3/9/68 | **Rice Is Nice** | Lemon Pipers |
| 10/20/62 | **Ride!** | Dee Dee Sharp |
| 8/21/65 | **Ride Away** | Roy Orbison |
| 10/12/68 | **Ride My See-Saw** | Moody Blues |
| 1/14/67 | **Ride, Ride, Ride** | Brenda Lee |
| 9/19/64 | **Ride The Wild Surf** | Jan & Dean |
| 7/3/65 | **Ride Your Pony** | Lee Dorsey |
|  | **Riders In The Sky** ..see: (Ghost) |  |
| 2/16/63 | **Ridin' The Wind** | Tornadoes |
| 5/2/60 | **Right By My Side** | Ricky Nelson |
| 10/9/65 | **Right Now And Not Later** | Shangri-Las |
|  | **Right Or Wrong** |  |
| 6/5/61 | Wanda Jackson |  |
| 10/24/64 | Ronnie Dove |  |

| Date | Title / Artist |
|---|---|
| 11/23/68 | **Right Relations** Johnny Rivers |
| 8/4/62 | **Right String But The Wrong Yo-Yo** Dr. Feelgood & The Interns |
| 10/9/65 | **Ring Dang Doo** Sam The Sham & The Pharoahs |
| 5/29/61 | **Ring Of Fire** Duane Eddy |
| 6/1/63 | **Ring Of Fire** Johnny Cash |
| 10/31/64 | **Ringo** Lorne Greene |
| 7/25/64 | **Ringo's Theme (This Boy)** George Martin |
| 7/14/62 | **Rinky Dink** Baby Cortez |
| 1/11/69 | **Riot** Hugh Masekela |
| 2/8/64 | **Rip Van Winkle** Devotions |
| | **River Deep-Mountain High** |
| 5/28/66 | Ike & Tina Turner |
| 1/25/69 | Deep Purple |
| | **River Is Wide** |
| 7/8/67 | Forum |
| 4/12/69 | Grass Roots |
| 5/30/60 | **River, Stay 'Way From My Door** Frank Sinatra |
| 6/1/63 | **River's Invitation** Percy Mayfield |
| 1/4/60 | **Riverboat** Faron Young |
| 12/1/62 | **Road Hog** John D. Loudermilk |
| | **Road Runner** |
| 2/29/60 | Bo Diddley |
| 9/25/65 | Gants (also see: I'm A) |
| 10/9/61 | **Rock-A-Bye Your Baby With A Dixie Melody** Aretha Franklin |
| 12/4/61 | **Rock-A-Hula Baby** Elvis Presley |
| | **Rock And Roll**..see: Rock 'N' Roll |
| 3/1/69 | **Rock Me** Steppenwolf |
| 5/9/64 | **Rock Me Baby** B.B. King |
| 6/29/63 | **Rock Me In The Cradle Of Love** Dee Dee Sharp |
| 9/30/67 | **Rock 'N' Roll Woman** Buffalo Springfield |
| | **Rockin' Around The Christmas Tree** |
| 12/12/60 | Brenda Lee |
| 12/11/61 | Brenda Lee |
| 12/15/62 | Brenda Lee |
| 10/16/61 | **Rockin' Bicycle** Fats Domino |
| 4/27/63 | **Rockin' Crickets** Rockin' Rebels |
| 5/23/60 | **Rockin' Good Way (To Mess Around And Fall In Love)** Dinah Washington & Brook Benton |
| 11/16/68 | **Rockin' In The Same Old Boat** Bobby Bland |
| 1/4/60 | **Rockin' Little Angel** Ray Smith |
| 4/4/60 | **Rockin' Red Wing** Sammy Masters |
| 9/5/64 | **Rockin' Robin** Rivieras |
| 12/5/60 | **Rockin', Rollin' Ocean** Hank Snow |
| 9/5/60 | **Rocking Goose** Johnny & The Hurricanes |
| | **Roll Over Beethoven** |
| 8/14/61 | Velaires |
| 3/21/64 | Beatles |
| 9/10/66 | **Roller Coaster** Ides Of March |
| 3/10/62 | **Roly Poly** Joey Dee |
| 12/5/64 | **Rome Will Never Leave You** Richard Chamberlain |
| 8/28/61 | **Romeo** Janie Grant |
| | **Romeo & Juliet**..see: Love Theme, (Just Like), & Farewell Love Theme |
| 5/22/61 | **Ronnie** Marcy Joe |
| 4/11/64 | **Ronnie** 4 Seasons |
| 4/27/63 | **Ronnie, Call Me When You Get A Chance** Shelley Fabares |
| 12/18/61 | **Room Full Of Tears** Drifters |
| 10/25/69 | **Roosevelt And Ira Lee (Night Of The Mossacin)** Tony Joe White |
| 1/27/68 | **Rosanna's Going Wild** Johnny Cash |
| 10/16/65 | **Roses And Rainbows** Danny Hutton |
| | **Roses And Roses**..see: And Roses |
| 6/9/62 | **Roses Are Red (My Love)** Bobby Vinton |
| 11/28/64 | **Roses Are Red My Love** "You Know Who" Group! (also see: Long As The Rose Is Red) |
| 2/10/62 | **Rough Lover** Aretha Franklin |
| 10/9/65 | **Round Every Corner** Petula Clark |
| 9/11/65 | **Roundabout** Connie Francis |
| 6/2/62 | **Route 66 Theme** Nelson Riddle |
| 11/28/60 | **Rubber Ball** Bobby Vee |
| 11/29/69 | **Rubberneckin'** Elvis Presley |
| 9/27/69 | **Ruben James** Kenny Rogers & The First Edition |

| Date | Title / Artist |
|---|---|
| | **Ruby** |
| 3/14/60 | Adam Wade |
| 11/21/60 | Ray Charles |
| 11/17/62 | **Ruby Ann** Marty Robbins |
| 1/19/63 | **Ruby Baby** Dion |
| 6/7/69 | **Ruby, Don't Take Your Love To Town** Kenny Rogers & The First Edition |
| | **Ruby Duby Du** |
| 10/31/60 | Tobin Mathews & Co. |
| 10/31/60 | Charles Wolcott |
| 1/21/67 | **Ruby Tuesday** Rolling Stones |
| | **Rudolph The Red Nosed Reindeer** |
| 12/19/60 | Chipmunks |
| 12/19/60 | Melodeers |
| 12/18/61 | Chipmunks |
| 12/15/62 | Chipmunks |
| 5/16/64 | **Rules Of Love** Orlons |
| 11/23/63 | **Rumble** Jack Nitzsche |
| 11/3/62 | **Rumors** Johnny Crawford |
| 8/20/66 | **Rumors** Syndicate Of Sound |
| 2/15/69 | **Run Away Child, Running Wild** Temptations |
| 10/2/65 | **Run, Baby Run (Back Into My Arms)** Newbeats |
| 1/4/60* | **Run Red Run** Coasters |
| 10/22/66 | **Run, Run, Look And See** Brian Hyland |
| 7/31/61 | **Run, Run, Run** Ronny Douglas |
| 3/14/64 | **Run, Run, Run** Supremes |
| 11/14/64 | **Run, Run, Run** Gestures |
| 8/5/67 | **Run, Run, Run** Third Rail |
| 8/8/60 | **Run Samson Run** Neil Sedaka |
| 11/13/61 | **Run To Him** Bobby Vee |
| 12/4/65 | **Run To My Lovin' Arms** Lenny Welch |
| 5/23/60 | **Runaround** Fleetwoods |
| 7/10/61 | **Runaround** Regents |
| 9/25/61 | **Runaround Sue** Dion |
| | **Runaway** |
| 3/6/61 | Del Shannon |
| 4/7/62 | Lawrence Welk (also see: Run Away) |
| 9/6/69 | **Runnin' Blue** Doors |
| 9/19/64 | **Runnin' Out Of Fools** Aretha Franklin |
| | **Running Bear** |
| 1/4/60* | Johnny Preston |
| 5/31/69 | Sonny James |
| 4/10/61 | **Running Scared** Roy Orbison |
| 10/9/65 | **Rusty Bells** Brenda Lee |

# S

| Date | Title / Artist |
|---|---|
| 5/14/66 | **S.Y.S.L.J.F.M. (The Letter Song)** Joe Tex |
| 5/29/61 | **Sacred** Castells |
| 6/12/61 | **Sad Eyes (Don't You Cry)** Echoes |
| 8/30/69 | **Sad Girl** Intruders |
| 12/5/60 | **Sad Mood** Sam Cooke |
| | **Sad Movies (Make Me Cry)** |
| 9/4/61 | Sue Thompson |
| 9/25/61 | Lennon Sisters |
| 8/7/65 | **Sad, Sad Girl** Barbara Mason |
| 5/25/63 | **Sad, Sad Girl And Boy** Impressions |
| 5/1/65 | **Sad Tomorrows** Trini Lopez |
| 8/27/66 | **Safe And Sound** Fontella Bass |
| 6/8/68 | **Safe In My Garden** Mamas & The Papas |
| 1/18/64 | **Saginaw, Michigan** Lefty Frizzell |
| 9/10/66 | **Said I Wasn't Gonna Tell Nobody** Sam & Dave |
| 8/1/64 | **Sailor Boy** Chiffons |
| 10/24/60 | **Sailor (Your Home Is The Sea)** Lolita |
| | **Saint**..see: St. |
| 8/31/63 | **Sally, Go 'Round The Roses** Jaynetts |
| 8/3/68 | **Sally Had A Party** Flavor |
| | **Sally Was A Good Old Girl** |
| 9/19/64 | Fats Domino |
| 3/2/68 | Trini Lopez |
| 11/9/63 | **Saltwater Taffy** Morty Jay |
| 5/21/66 | **Sam, You Made The Pants Too Long** Barbra Streisand |
| 4/15/67 | **Sam's Place** Buck Owens |
| 12/22/62 | **Sam's Song** Dean Martin & Sammy Davis Jr. |
| 1/26/63 | **Same Old Hurt** Burl Ives |
| 2/29/60 | **Same Old Me** Guy Mitchell |
| 8/22/60 | **Same One** Brook Benton |
| 6/5/61 | **San Antonio Rose** Floyd Cramer |
| 8/5/67 | **San Franciscan Nights** Animals |

| Date | Title / Artist |
|---|---|
| 5/27/67 | **San Francisco (Be Sure To Wear Flowers In Your Hair)** Scott McKenzie |
| 6/1/68 | **San Francisco Girls (Return of the Native)** Fever Tree |
| 9/27/69 | **San Francisco Is A Lonely Town** Joe Simon |
| 8/7/61 | **San-Ho-Zay** Freddy King |
| | **Sandpiper, Love Theme From**..see: Shadow Of Your Smile |
| 1/4/60* | **Sandy** Larry Hall |
| 3/2/63 | **Sandy** Dion |
| 12/4/65 | **Sandy** Ronny & The Daytonas |
| 12/25/61 | **Santa & The Touchables** Dickie Goodman |
| 12/15/62 | **Santa Claus Is Coming To Town** 4 Seasons |
| 12/15/62 | **Santa Claus Is Watching You** Ray Stevens |
| 12/4/65 | **Satin Pillows** Bobby Vinton |
| | **Satisfaction**..see: (I Can't Get No) |
| 10/8/66 | **Satisfied Mind** Bobby Hebb |
| 8/13/66 | **Satisfied With You** Dave Clark Five |
| 10/26/63 | **Saturday Night** New Christy Minstrels |
| 11/14/64 | **Saturday Night At The Movies** Drifters |
| 2/1/69 | **Saturday Night At The World** Mason Williams |
| 7/27/63 | **Saturday Sunshine** Burt Bacharach |
| | **Sausalito** |
| 5/17/69 | Al Martino |
| 9/6/69 | Ohio Express |
| 9/22/62 | **Save All Your Lovin' For Me** Brenda Lee |
| 8/29/64 | **Save It For Me** 4 Seasons |
| 9/5/60 | **Save The Last Dance For Me** Drifters (also see: I'll Save The Last Dance) |
| 7/3/65 | **Save Your Heart For Me** Gary Lewis & The Playboys |
| 4/10/61 | **Saved** LaVern Baker |
| 3/2/63 | **Sax Fifth Avenue** Johnny Beecher |
| 8/6/66 | **Say I Am (What I Am)** Tommy James & The Shondells |
| 9/7/68 | **Say It Loud - I'm Black And I'm Proud** James Brown |
| 10/2/65 | **Say Something Funny** Patty Duke |
| | **Say Wonderful Things** |
| 6/1/63 | Patti Page |
| 6/8/63 | Ronnie Carroll |
| 7/18/64 | **Say You** Ronnie Dove |
| 10/18/69 | **Say You Love Me** Impressions |
| 7/10/65 | **(Say) You're My Girl** Roy Orbison |
| | **Scarborough Fair** |
| 3/2/68 | Simon & Garfunkel |
| 11/16/68 | Sergio Mendes & Brasil '66 |
| 1/4/60* | **Scarlet Ribbons (For Her Hair)** Browns |
| 6/29/63 | **Scarlett O'Hara** Lawrence Welk |
| 10/26/63 | **Scavenger, The** Dick Dale |
| 10/23/61 | **School Is In** Gary (U.S.) Bonds |
| 7/24/61 | **School Is Out** Gary (U.S.) Bonds |
| 4/28/62 | **Scotch And Soda** Kingston Trio |
| 4/3/61 | **Scottish Soldier (Green Hills of Tyrol)** Andy Stewart |
| 11/21/64 | **Scratchy** Travis Wammack |
| 6/19/61 | **Sea Of Heartbreak** Don Gibson |
| | **Sealed With A Kiss** |
| 6/9/62 | Brian Hyland |
| 6/22/68 | Gary Lewis & The Playboys |
| | **Searching** |
| 11/27/61 | Jack Eubanks |
| 3/14/64 | Ace Cannon |
| 6/25/66 | **Searching For My Love** Bobby Moore |
| 11/24/62 | **Searching Is Over** Joe Henderson |
| 12/21/68 | **Season Of The Witch** Vanilla Fudge |
| 4/12/69 | **Seattle** Perry Como |
| 9/22/62 | **Second Fiddle Girl** Barbara Lynn |
| 5/12/62 | **Second Hand Love** Connie Francis |
| 12/18/65 | **Second Hand Rose** Barbra Streisand |
| 7/4/60 | **Second Honeymoon** Johnny Cash |
| 3/6/61 | **Second Time Around** Frank Sinatra |
| | **Secret Agent Man** |
| 2/26/66 | Ventures |
| 3/19/66 | Johnny Rivers |
| | **Secret Love** |
| 10/1/66 | Richard "Groove" Holmes |
| 10/15/66 | Billy Stewart |
| 1/25/60 | **Secret Of Love** Elton Anderson |

| Date | Song / Artist |
|---|---|
| 10/2/65 | **Secretly** Lettermen |
|  | **Security** |
| 5/23/64 | Otis Redding |
| 3/2/68 | Etta James |
| 5/24/69 | **See** Rascals |
| 11/8/69 | **See Ruby Fall** Johnny Cash |
|  | **See Saw** |
| 11/13/65 | Don Covay |
| 11/23/68 | Aretha Franklin |
|  | **See See**..see: C.C. |
| 1/11/64 | **See The Funny Little Clown** Bobby Goldsboro |
| 4/3/65 | **See You At The "Go-Go"** Dobie Gray |
| 7/9/66 | **See You In September** Happenings |
| 6/12/65 | **Seein' The Right Love Go Wrong** Jack Jones |
| 8/1/64 | **Selfish One** Jackie Ross |
| 9/8/62 | **Send For Me (If you need some Lovin')** Barbara George |
| 1/26/63 | **Send Me Some Lovin'** Sam Cooke |
|  | **Send Me The Pillow You Dream On** |
| 11/14/60 | Browns |
| 8/11/62 | Johnny Tillotson |
| 2/20/65 | Dean Martin |
| 7/6/68 | **Send My Baby Back** Freddie Hughes |
| 11/7/60 | **Senza Mamma (With No One)** Connie Francis |
| 10/16/61 | **September In The Rain** Dinah Washington |
| 9/7/63 | **September Song** Jimmy Durante |
| 10/10/60 | **Serenata** Sarah Vaughan |
| 6/12/65 | **Set Me Free** Kinks |
| 2/5/66 | **Set You Free This Time** Byrds |
| 1/19/63 | **Settle Down (Goin' Down That Highway)** Peter, Paul & Mary |
| 7/30/66 | **7 And 7 Is** Love |
| 12/18/61 | **Seven Day Fool** Etta James |
| 6/23/62 | **Seven Day Weekend** Gary (US) Bonds |
| 12/19/64 | **Seven Letters** Ben E. King |
| 1/4/60* | **Seven Little Girls Sitting In The Back Seat** Paul Evans |
| 5/20/67 | **7 Rooms Of Gloom** Four Tops |
| 4/26/69 | **Seven Years** Impressions |
| 6/5/65 | **Seventh Son** Johnny Rivers |
| 3/20/61 | **Seventeen** Frankie Ford |
| 1/27/68 | **7:30 Guided Tour** Five Americans |
|  | **Sha-La-La** |
| 3/21/64 | Shirelles |
| 11/14/64 | Manfred Mann |
| 4/20/68 | **Shadow Of Your Love** 5 Stairsteps |
|  | **Shadow Of Your Smile** |
| 11/13/65 | Tony Bennett |
| 12/24/66 | Boots Randolph |
| 5/23/60 | **Shadows Of Love** LaVern Baker |
| 1/13/62 | **Shadrack** Brook Benton |
| 10/10/64 | **Shaggy Dog** Mickey Lee Lane |
|  | **Shake** |
| 1/9/65 | Sam Cooke |
| 5/20/67 | Otis Redding |
| 10/26/68 | **Shake** Shadows Of Knight |
|  | **Shake A Hand** |
| 6/23/62 | Ruth Brown |
| 5/25/63 | Jackie Wilson & Linda Hopkins |
|  | **Shake A Tail Feather** |
| 5/18/63 | Five Du-Tones |
| 4/15/67 | James & Bobby Purify |
| 7/31/65 | **Shake And Fingerpop** Jr. Walker & The All Stars |
| 2/26/66 | **Shake Hands (And Come Out Crying)** Newbeats |
| 4/29/67 | **Shake Hands And Walk Away Cryin'** Lou Christie |
| 12/29/62 | **Shake Me I Rattle (Squeeze Me I Cry)** Marion Worth |
| 2/19/66 | **Shake Me, Wake Me (When It's Over)** Four Tops |
| 6/10/67 | **Shake, Rattle & Roll** Arthur Conley |
| 7/13/63 | **Shake! Shake! Shake!** Jackie Wilson |
| 12/22/62 | **Shake Sherry** Contours |
| 5/8/65 | **Shakin' All Over** Guess Who |
|  | **Shame On Me** |
| 7/21/62 | Bobby Bare |
| 10/14/67 | Chuck Jackson |
| 10/26/68 | **Shame, Shame** Magic Lanterns |
| 4/13/63 | **Shame, Shame, Shame** Jimmy Reed |

| Date | Song / Artist |
|---|---|
|  | **Shangri-La** |
| 3/21/64 | Robert Maxwell |
| 3/28/64 | Vic Dana |
| 10/18/69 | Lettermen |
| 9/7/68 | **Shape Of Things To Come** Max Frost |
| 3/19/66 | **Shapes Of Things** Yardbirds |
|  | **Share Your Love With Me** |
| 6/13/64 | Bobby Bland |
| 8/2/69 | Aretha Franklin |
| 5/19/62 | **Sharing You** Bobby Vee |
| 3/19/66 | **Sharing You** Mitty Collier |
| 3/21/60 | **Shazam!** Duane Eddy |
| 12/13/69 | **She** Tommy James & The Shondells |
| 10/11/69 | **She Belongs To Me** Rick Nelson |
| 3/19/66 | **She Blew A Good Thing** Poets |
| 12/6/69 | **She Came In Through The Bathroom Window** Joe Cocker |
| 3/3/62 | **She Can't Find Her Keys** Paul Petersen |
|  | **She Comes To Me**..see: (When She Needs Good Lovin') |
|  | **She Cried** |
| 3/17/62 | Jay & The Americans |
| 4/9/66 | Shangri-Las (He Cried) |
| 8/20/66 | **She Drives Me Out Of My Mind** Swingin' Medallions |
| 10/28/67 | **She Is Still A Mystery** Lovin' Spoonful |
|  | **She Lets Her Hair Down (Early In The Morning)** |
| 12/13/69 | Gene Pitney |
| 12/13/69 | Tokens |
|  | **She Loves You** |
| 1/25/64 | Beatles |
| 6/27/64 | Die Beatles (Sie Liebt Dich) |
| 12/4/61 | **She Really Loves You** Timi Yuro |
| 5/6/67 | **She Shot A Hole In My Soul** Clifford Curry |
| 3/25/67 | **She Took You For A Ride** Aaron Neville |
|  | **She Understands Me** |
| 10/31/64 | Johnny Tillotson |
| 4/30/66 | Bobby Vinton (Dum-De-Da) |
| 8/29/64 | **She Wants T' Swim** Chubby Checker |
| 5/13/67 | **She'd Rather Be With Me** Turtles |
| 3/23/68 | **She'll Be There** Vikki Carr |
| 1/26/63 | **She'll Never Know** Brenda Lee |
| 9/28/63 | **She's A Fool** Lesley Gore |
| 5/11/68 | **She's A Heartbreaker** Gene Pitney |
| 1/4/69 | **She's A Lady** John Sebastian |
| 12/30/67 | **She's A Rainbow** Rolling Stones |
| 11/24/62 | **She's A Troublemaker** Majors |
|  | **She's A Very Lovely Woman**..see: You're A |
| 12/5/64 | **She's A Woman** Beatles |
|  | **She's About A Mover** |
| 4/3/65 | Sir Douglas Quintet |
| 8/24/68 | Otis Clay |
| 4/10/65 | **She's Coming Home** Zombies |
| 12/25/61 | **She's Everything (I Wanted You To Be)** Ral Donner |
| 11/16/63 | **She's Got Everything** Essex |
| 10/25/69 | **She's Got Love** Thomas & Richard Frost |
| 1/27/62 | **She's Got You** Patsy Cline |
| 7/25/60 | **She's Just A Whole Lot Like You** Hank Thompson |
| 12/11/65 | **She's Just My Style** Gary Lewis & The Playboys |
| 4/13/68 | **She's Lookin' Good** Wilson Pickett |
| 8/8/60 | **She's Mine** Conway Twitty |
| 7/18/64 | **She's My Girl** Bobby Shafto |
| 11/11/67 | **She's My Girl** Turtles |
| 10/17/64 | **She's Not There** Zombies |
| 8/4/62 | **She's Not You** Elvis Presley |
|  | **(She's) Some Kind Of Wonderful**..see: Some Kind |
| 7/11/64 | **She's The One** Chartbusters |
| 11/20/65 | **She's With Her Other Love** Leon Haywood |
| 7/28/62 | **Sheila** Tommy Roe |
| 11/30/63 | **Shelter Of Your Arms** Sammy Davis Jr. |
| 8/25/62 | **Sherry** 4 Seasons |
| 3/23/68 | **Sherry Don't Go** Lettermen |
| 9/12/60 | **Shimmy Like Kate** Olympics |
|  | **Shimmy Shimmy** |
| 8/15/60 | Bobby Freeman |
| 2/1/64 | Orlons |

| Date | Song / Artist |
|---|---|
| 1/4/60* | **Shimmy, Shimmy, Ko-Ko-Bop** Little Anthony & The Imperials |
| 1/27/62 | **Shimmy, Shimmy Walk** Megatons |
|  | **(Ship Will Come)**..see: Never On Sunday |
| 10/26/63 | **Shirl Girl** Wayne Newton |
|  | **Shoo**..also see: Shu |
| 4/6/68 | **Shoo-Be-Doo-Be-Doo-Da-Day** Stevie Wonder |
| 2/29/64 | **Shoop Shoop Song (It's In His Kiss)** Betty Everett |
| 7/22/67 | **Shoot Your Shot** Jr. Walker & The All Stars |
| 9/7/68 | **Shoot'em Up, Baby** Andy Kim |
| 12/12/60 | **Shop Around** Miracles (also see: Don't Let Him Shop Around) |
| 10/3/60 | **Shoppin' For Clothes** Coasters |
|  | **Shortnin' Bread** |
| 8/29/60 | Bell Notes |
| 8/29/60 | Paul Chaplain |
| 7/18/64 | **Shot In The Dark** Henry Mancini |
|  | **Shotgun** |
| 2/13/65 | Jr. Walker & The All Stars |
| 3/8/69 | Vanilla Fudge |
| 6/12/61 | **Should I** String-A-Longs |
|  | **Shout** |
| 3/24/62 | Joey Dee |
| 3/24/62 | Isley Brothers |
| 8/1/64 | LuLu |
| 12/9/67 | Lulu |
| 12/21/68 | Chambers Brothers |
| 7/7/62 | **Shout And Shimmy** James Brown |
| 10/7/67 | **Shout Bamalama** Mickey Murray |
| 3/31/62 | **Shout! Shout! (Knock Yourself Out)** Ernie Maresca |
| 7/1/67 | **Show Business** Lou Rawls |
| 3/4/67 | **Show Me** Joe Tex |
| 3/30/68 | **Show Time** Detroit Emeralds |
| 3/20/61 | **Shu Rah** Fats Domino |
| 4/27/63 | **Shut Down** Beach Boys |
| 11/17/62 | **Shutters And Boards** Jerry Wallace |
| 4/24/61 | **Shy Away** Jerry Fuller |
| 4/27/63 | **Shy Girl** Cascades |
| 10/17/60 | **Side Car Cycle** Charlie Ryan |
| 10/31/64 | **Sidewalk Surfin'** Jan & Dean |
| 12/19/64 | **Sidewinder, The** Lee Morgan |
|  | **Sie Liebt Dich**..see: She Loves You |
| 3/26/66 | **Sign Of The Times** Petula Clark |
|  | **Signed, Sealed And Delivered** |
| 9/11/61 | Rusty Draper |
| 10/12/63 | James Brown |
| 9/11/65 | **Silence, The (Il Silenzio)** Al Hirt |
| 6/17/67 | **Silence Is Golden** Tremeloes |
|  | **Silent Night** |
| 12/19/60 | Bing Crosby |
| 12/29/62 | Mahalia Jackson |
| 4/3/65 | **Silhouettes** Herman's Hermits |
| 8/18/62 | **Silly Boy (She Doesn't Love You)** Lettermen |
| 11/28/64 | **Silly Little Girl** Tams |
| 8/8/64 | **Silly Ol' Summertime** New Christy Minstrels |
|  | **Silver City**..see: (Theme From) |
|  | **Silver Threads And Golden Needles** |
| 8/4/62 | Springfields |
| 6/26/65 | Jody Miller |
| 10/11/69 | Cowsills |
| 1/27/68 | **Simon Says** 1910 Fruitgum Co. |
| 9/4/65 | **Simpel Gimpel** Horst Jankowski |
| 8/2/69 | **Simple Song Of Freedom** Tim Hardin |
|  | **Sin**..see: (It's No) |
| 11/14/64 | **Since I Don't Have You** Chuck Jackson |
| 10/26/63 | **Since I Fell For You** Lenny Welch |
| 1/4/64 | **Since I Found A New Love** Little Johnny Taylor |
| 7/24/65 | **Since I Lost My Baby** Temptations |
| 2/5/66 | **Since I Lost The One I Love** Impressions |
| 1/18/60 | **Since I Made You Cry** Rivieras |
|  | **Since I Met You Baby** |
| 9/12/60 | Bobby Vee |
| 9/20/69 | Sonny James |
| 11/25/67 | **Since You Showed Me How To Be Happy** Jackie Wilson |
|  | **Since You've Been Gone**..see: (Sweet Sweet Baby) |

| | | | | | |
|---|---|---|---|---|---|
| | **Sincerely** | 1/15/66 | **Snow Flake**  *Jim Reeves* | 5/30/60 | **Something Happened**  *Paul Anka* |
| 8/29/64 | Four Seasons | 1/13/62 | **So Deep**  *Brenda Lee* | 1/22/66 | **Something I Want To Tell You** |
| 5/31/69 | Paul Anka | 1/18/64 | **So Far Away**  *Hank Jacobs* | | Johnny & The Expressions |
| 3/8/69 | **Sing A Simple Song** | | **So Good**..also see: (You Make Me Feel) | 9/6/69 | **Something In The Air** |
| | Sly & The Family Stone | 9/27/69 | **So Good Together**  *Andy Kim* | | Thunderclap Newman |
| 4/8/67 | **Sing Along With Me**  *Tommy Roe* | 5/24/69 | **So I Can Love You**  *Emotions* | 8/24/63 | **Something Old, Something New** |
| 4/12/69 | **Singing My Song**  *Tammy Wynette* | 10/16/65 | **So Long Babe**  *Nancy Sinatra* | | Paul & Paula |
| 11/19/66 | **Single Girl**  *Sandy Posey* | 9/18/61 | **So Long Baby**  *Del Shannon* | | **Something You Got** |
| 3/7/60 | **Sink The Bismarck**  *Johnny Horton* | 10/3/64 | **So Long Dearie**  *Louis Armstrong* | 6/6/64 | Alvin Robinson |
| 10/16/65 | **Sinner Man**  *Trini Lopez* | 1/4/60* | **So Many Ways**  *Brook Benton* | 10/10/64 | Ramsey Lewis Trio |
| 9/25/65 | **Sins Of A Family**  *P.F. Sloan* | 6/1/63 | **So Much In Love**  *Tymes* | 4/24/65 | Chuck Jackson & Maxine Brown |
| 3/26/66 | **Sippin' 'N Chippin'**  *T-Bones* | | **So Much Love** | 2/24/62 | **Something's Got A Hold On Me** |
| 2/4/67 | **Sit Down, I Think I Love You** | 5/21/66 | Steve Alaimo | | Etta James |
| | Mojo Men | 5/21/66 | Ben E. King | 12/2/67 | **Something's Missing**  *5 Stairsteps* |
| 3/16/68 | **Sit With The Guru** | 9/5/60 | **So Sad (To Watch Good Love Go Bad)**  *Everly Brothers* | 3/29/69 | **Something's On Her Mind**  *4 Seasons* |
| | Strawberry Alarm Clock | 4/14/62 | **So This Is Love**  *Castells* | 10/30/61 | **Sometime**  *Gene Thomas* |
| | **(Sittin' On) The Dock Of The Bay** | | **So What** | 8/13/66 | **Sometimes Good Guys Don't Wear White**  *Standells* |
| 1/27/68 | Otis Redding | 8/11/62 | Bill Black's Combo | 10/31/64 | **Sometimes I Wish I Were A Boy** |
| 3/9/68 | King Curtis | 1/2/65 | Bill Black's Combo | | Lesley Gore |
| 6/28/69 | Sergio Mendes & Brasil '66 | 8/25/62 | **So Wrong**  *Patsy Cline* | 12/5/64 | **Sometimes I Wonder**  *Major Lance* |
| 11/1/69 | Dells | 1/28/67 | **So You Want To Be A Rock 'N' Roll Star**  *Byrds* | 7/20/63 | **Sometimes You Gotta Cry A Little**  *Bobby Bland* |
| 6/19/65 | **Sitting In The Park**  *Billy Stewart* | 9/12/64 | **Society Girl**  *Rag Dolls* | 12/7/63 | **Somewhere**  *Tymes* |
| 6/8/63 | **Six Days On The Road**  *Dave Dudley* | 5/27/67 | **Society's Child (Baby I've Been Thinking)**  *Janis Ian* | | **Somewhere** |
| 8/24/68 | **Six Man Band**  *Association* | 2/4/67 | **Sock It To Me-Baby!** | 2/13/65 | P.J. Proby |
| 4/29/67 | **Six O'Clock**  *Lovin' Spoonful* | | Mitch Ryder & The Detroit Wheels | 3/19/66 | Len Barry |
| 2/12/66 | **634-5789 (Soulsville, U.S.A.)** | 12/2/67 | **Sockin' 1-2-3-4**  *John Roberts* | 10/23/61 | **Somewhere Along The Way** |
| | Wilson Pickett | 9/5/64 | **Softly, As I Leave You**  *Frank Sinatra* | | Steve Lawrence |
| | (also see: Beechwood 4-5789) | 3/24/62 | **Soldier Boy**  *Shirelles* | 12/19/64 | **Somewhere In Your Heart** |
| 12/13/69 | **Six White Horses**  *Tommy Cash* | 7/18/64 | **Sole Sole Sole** | | Frank Sinatra |
| 2/1/60 | **Sixteen Reasons**  *Connie Stevens* | | Siw Malmkvist/Umberto Marcato | | **Somewhere, My Love** |
| 8/12/67 | **Sixteen Tons**  *Tom Jones* | 5/21/66 | **Solitary Man**  *Neil Diamond* | 6/18/66 | Ray Conniff |
| 1/28/67 | **Skate Now**  *Lou Courtney* | 8/15/64 | **Some Day We're Gonna Love Again**  *Searchers* | 6/25/66 | Roger Williams (Lara's Theme) |
| 10/28/67 | **Skinny Legs And All**  *Joe Tex* | 9/4/65 | **Some Enchanted Evening** | 2/12/66 | **Somewhere There's A Someone**  *Dean Martin* |
| 12/23/67 | **Skip A Rope**  *Henson Cargill* | | Jay & The Americans | 5/8/61 | **Son-In-Law**  *Louise Brown* |
| 1/4/60 | **Skokiaan (South African Song)** | 3/20/61 | **Some Kind Of Wonderful**  *Drifters* | 5/8/61 | **Son-In-Law**  *Blossoms* |
| | Bill Haley & His Comets | | **Some Kind Of Wonderful** | 9/20/69 | **Son Of A Lovin' Man** |
| 6/1/68 | **Sky Pilot**  *Animals* | 6/24/67 | Soul Brothers Six | | Buchanan Brothers |
| 10/24/64 | **Slaughter On Tenth Avenue**  *Ventures* | 11/16/68 | Fantastic Johnny C | 11/30/68 | **Son-Of-A Preacher Man** |
| 9/5/60 | **Sleep**  *Little Willie John* | 12/8/62 | **Some Kinda Fun**  *Chris Montez* | | Dusty Springfield |
| | **Sleeping Beauty**..see: To A | 6/8/68 | **Some Things You Never Get Used To**  *Supremes* | 5/31/69 | **Son Of A Travelin' Man**  *Ed Ames* |
| 3/27/61 | **Sleepy-Eyed John**  *Johnny Horton* | 1/6/68 | **Some Velvet Morning** | 2/24/68 | **Son Of Hickory Holler's Tramp**  *O.C. Smith* |
| 5/11/68 | **Sleepy Joe**  *Herman's Hermits* | | Nancy Sinatra & Lee Hazlewood | 1/4/64 | **Son Of Rebel Rouser**  *Duane Eddy* |
| 2/22/60 | **Sleepy Lagoon**  *Platters* | 7/27/68 | **Somebody Cares** | 5/11/63 | **Soon (I'll Be Home Again)**  *4 Seasons* |
| 7/29/67 | **Slim Jenkin's Place** | | Tommy James & The Shondells | 9/12/64 | **Soon I'll Wed My Love**  *John Gary* |
| | Booker T. & The M.G.'s | 3/27/65 | **Somebody Else Is Taking My Place**  *Al Martino* | 9/7/63 | **Sooner Or Later**  *Johnny Mathis* |
| 7/13/68 | **Slip Away**  *Clarence Carter* | 10/27/62 | **Somebody Have Mercy**  *Sam Cooke* | | **Soothe Me** |
| 4/18/64 | **Slip-In Mules (No High Heel Sneakers)**  *Sugar Pie DeSanto* | 6/17/67 | **Somebody Help Me**  *Spencer Davis Group* | 10/23/61 | Sims Twins |
| | **Slipin' And Slidin'** | 10/15/66 | **Somebody Like Me**  *Eddy Arnold* | 6/17/67 | Sam & Dave |
| 1/18/64 | Jim & Monica | 2/22/69 | **Somebody Loves You**  *Delfonics* | 2/8/69 | **Sophisticated Cissy**  *Meters* |
| 7/22/67 | Willie Mitchell | 10/3/64 | **Somebody New**  *Chuck Jackson* | 4/19/69 | **Sorry Suzanne**  *Hollies* |
| | **Slipping Away**..see: (I Can Feel Your Love) | 10/15/66 | **Somebody (Somewhere) Needs You**  *Darrell Banks* | | **Soul And Inspiration**..see: (You're My) |
| | **Sloop John B** | 4/11/64 | **Somebody Stole My Dog**  *Rufus Thomas* | | **(Soul Coaxing)**..see: Ame Caline |
| 8/1/60 | Jimmie Rodgers | 9/26/60 | **Somebody To Love**  *Bobby Darin* | 6/17/67 | **Soul Dance Number Three**  *Wilson Pickett* |
| 4/2/66 | Beach Boys | 4/1/67 | **Somebody To Love**  *Jefferson Airplane* | 7/5/69 | **Soul Deep**  *Box Tops* |
| | **Sloopy**..see: Hang | 12/16/67 | **Somebody's Sleeping In My Bed**  *Johnnie Taylor* | 8/15/64 | **Soul Dressing**  *Booker T. & The MG's* |
| 1/12/63 | **Slop Time**  *Sherry* | | **Someday**..also see: Some Day | 10/19/68 | **Soul Drippin'**  *Mauds* |
| 9/5/64 | **Slow Down**  *Beatles* | 5/10/69 | **Someday Man**  *Monkees* | 2/22/69 | **Soul Experience**  *Iron Butterfly* |
| 11/9/68 | **Slow Drag**  *Intruders* | 2/1/69 | **Someday Soon**  *Judy Collins* | 5/20/67 | **Soul Finger**  *Bar-Kays* |
| 3/3/62 | **Slow Twistin'**  *Chubby Checker* | 11/8/69 | **Someday We'll Be Together**  *Supremes* | 9/4/65 | **Soul Heaven**  *Dixie Drifter* |
| 9/6/69 | **Slum Baby**  *Booker T. & The M.G.'s* | 9/22/62 | **Someday (When I'm Gone From You)**  *Bobby Vee* | | **Soul Hootenanny**..see: Big Boss Man |
| 9/26/64 | **Smack Dab In The Middle**  *Ray Charles* | | **Someday (You'll Want Me To Want You)** | 7/13/68 | **Soul-Limbo**  *Booker T. & The M.G.'s* |
| 12/4/61 | **Small Sad Sam**  *Phil McLean* | 3/21/60 | Della Reese | | **Soul Man** |
| 10/5/68 | **Smell Of Incense**  *Southwest F.O.B.* | 12/26/60 | Brook Benton | 9/9/67 | Sam & Dave |
| | **Smile** | 8/21/65 | **Someone Is Watching**  *Solomon Burke* | 11/11/67 | Ramsey Lewis |
| 11/6/61 | Timi Yuro | 4/18/60 | **Someone Loves You, Joe** | 7/27/68 | **Soul Meeting**  *Soul Clan* |
| 3/17/62 | Ferrante & Teicher | | Singing Belles | 6/5/65 | **Soul Sauce (Guacha Guaro)** |
| 12/5/64 | Betty Everett & Jerry Butler | 9/12/64 | **Someone, Someone**  *Brian Poole* | | Cal Tjader |
| 10/4/69 | **Smile A Little Smile For Me** | 1/12/63 | **Someone Somewhere** | | **Soul Serenade** |
| | Flying Machine | | Little Junior Parker | 3/7/64 | King Curtis |
| 2/26/66 | **Smokey Joe's La La** | 3/18/67 | **Somethin' Stupid** | 3/9/68 | Willie Mitchell |
| | Googie Rene Combo | | Nancy & Frank Sinatra | 2/1/69 | **Soul Shake** |
| | **Smokie** | 10/18/69 | **Something**  *Beatles* | | Peggy Scott & Jo Jo Benson |
| 1/4/60* | Bill Black's Combo | 11/13/65 | **Something About You**  *Four Tops* | 12/21/68 | **Soul Sister, Brown Sugar**  *Sam & Dave* |
| 1/4/60 | Bill Doggett | 1/14/67 | **Something Good (Is Going To Happen To You)**  *Carla Thomas* | 2/25/67 | **Soul Time**  *Shirley Ellis* |
| 12/25/61 | **Smoky Places**  *Corsairs* | | | 5/4/68 | **Soul Train**  *Classics IV* |
| 8/17/68 | **Snake, The**  *Al Wilson* | | | 2/17/62 | **Soul Twist**  *King Curtis* |
| | **Snap Your Fingers** | | | 11/30/68 | **Soulful Strut**  *Young-Holt Unlimited* |
| 5/19/62 | Joe Henderson | | | | (also see: Am I The Same Girl) |
| 12/28/63 | Barbara Lewis | | | | **(Soulsville, U.S.A.)**..see: 634-5789 |
| 3/1/69 | **Snatching It Back**  *Clarence Carter* | | | | **Soulville** |
| 7/13/68 | **Snoopy For President** | | | 5/25/63 | Dinah Washington |
| | Royal Guardsmen | | | 2/24/68 | Aretha Franklin |
| 12/17/66 | **Snoopy Vs. The Red Baron** | | | 3/2/68 | **Sound Asleep**  *Turtles* |
| | Royal Guardsmen | | | | |
| | (also see: Return Of The Red Baron) | | | | |

| Date | Song | Artist |
|---|---|---|
| 5/20/67 | **Sound Of Love** | Five Americans |
| 1/4/60* | **Sound Of Music** | Patti Page |
| 1/16/61 | **Sound-Off** | Titus Turner |
| 11/20/65 | **Sounds Of Silence** | Simon & Garfunkel |
| 2/16/63 | **South Street** | Orlons |
| 1/18/64 | **Southtown, U.S.A.** | Dixiebelles |
| 12/4/65 | **Spanish Eyes** | Al Martino |
|  | (also see: Moon Over Naples) | |
| 3/19/66 | **Spanish Flea** | Herb Alpert |
|  | **Spanish Harlem** | |
| 12/31/60 | | Ben E. King |
| 12/25/65 | | King Curtis |
| 11/10/62 | **Spanish Lace** | Gene McDaniels |
| 11/5/66 | **Spanish Nights And You** | |
|  | | Connie Francis |
| 4/15/67 | **Speak Her Name** | Walter Jackson |
| 5/10/69 | **Special Delivery** | 1910 Fruitgum Co. |
| 8/17/68 | **Special Occasion** | Miracles |
| 10/12/63 | **Speed Ball** | Ray Stevens |
| 6/16/62 | **Speedy Gonzales** | Pat Boone |
| 5/31/69 | **Spinning Wheel** | Blood, Sweat & Tears |
| 10/8/66 | **Spinout** | Elvis Presley |
|  | **Spooky** | |
| 1/28/67 | | Mike Sharpe |
| 12/23/67 | | Classics IV |
| 12/26/60 | **Spoonful** | Etta & Harvey |
| 1/1/66 | **Spread It On Thick** | Gentrys |
| 9/9/67 | **Spreadin' Honey** | |
|  | | Watts 103rd St. Rhythm Band |
| 7/6/63 | **Spring** | Birdlegs & Pauline |
|  | **Spring Fever**..see: (I've Got) | |
| 6/8/63 | **Spring In Manhattan** | Tony Bennett |
| 5/30/60 | **Spring Rain** | Pat Boone |
| 2/24/68 | **Springfield Plane** | Kenny O'Dell |
| 8/22/64 | **Squeeze Her-Tease Her (But Love Her)** | Jackie Wilson |
| 11/15/69 | **St. Louis** | Easybeats |
| 11/4/67 | **Stag-O-Lee** | Wilson Pickett |
| 3/28/60 | **Stairway To Heaven** | Neil Sedaka |
| 4/12/69 | **Stand!** | Sly & The Family Stone |
|  | **Stand By Me** | |
| 5/8/61 | | Ben E. King |
| 10/23/65 | | Earl Grant |
| 12/17/66 | | Spyder Turner |
|  | (also see: I'll Be There) | |
| 11/9/68 | **Stand By Your Man** | Tammy Wynette |
| 10/22/66 | **Stand In For Love** | O'Jays |
| 12/17/66 | **Standing In The Shadows Of Love** | |
|  | | Four Tops |
| 4/18/60 | **Star Is Born (A Love Has Died)** | |
|  | | Mark Dinning |
| 11/2/68 | **Star-Spangled Banner** | Jose Feliciano |
| 2/29/60 | **Starbright** | Johnny Mathis |
|  | **Stardust** | |
| 3/24/62 | | Frank Sinatra |
| 2/22/64 | | Nino Tempo & April Stevens |
| 8/14/61 | **Starlight** | Preludes Five |
| 7/17/61 | **Starlight, Starbright** | Linda Scott |
|  | **Stay** | |
| 10/3/60 | | Maurice Williams |
| 2/15/64 | | 4 Seasons |
| 7/12/69 | **Stay And Love Me All Summer** | |
|  | | Brian Hyland |
| 3/16/68 | **Stay Away ('Greensleeves' melody)** | |
|  | | Elvis Presley |
| 12/4/65 | **Stay Away From My Baby** | Ted Taylor |
| 3/28/64 | **Stay Awhile** | Dusty Springfield |
| 12/21/68 | **Stay Close To Me** | Five Stairsteps |
| 6/29/68 | **Stay In My Corner** | Dells |
| 5/20/67 | **Stay Together Young Lovers** | |
|  | | Brenda & The Tabulations |
| 1/18/64 | **Stay With Me** | Frank Sinatra |
| 10/8/66 | **Stay With Me** | Lorraine Ellison |
| 2/13/61 | **Stayin' In** | Bobby Vee |
| 6/20/64 | **Steal Away** | Jimmy Hughes |
| 5/26/62 | **Steel Guitar And A Glass Of Wine** | |
|  | | Paul Anka |
| 6/23/62 | **Steel Men** | Jimmy Dean |
| 2/29/60 | **Step By Step** | Crests |
| 6/3/67 | **Step Out Of Your Mind** | |
|  | | American Breed |
| 9/18/65 | **Steppin' Out** | Paul Revere & The Raiders |
|  | **Steppin' Stone**..see: (I'm Not Your) | |
| 11/6/61 | **Steps 1 And 2** | Jack Scott |
| 11/30/63 | **Stewball** | Peter, Paul & Mary |
| 9/11/61 | **Stick Shift** | Duals |
| 6/5/61 | **Stick With Me Baby** | Everly Brothers |
| 6/27/60 | **Sticks And Stones** | Ray Charles |

| Date | Song | Artist |
|---|---|---|
|  | **Still** | |
| 4/13/63 | | Bill Anderson |
| 7/20/63 | | Ben Colder |
| 5/7/66 | | Sunrays |
| 12/8/62 | **Still Waters Run Deep** | Brook Benton |
| 4/27/63 | **Sting Ray** | Routers |
| 3/14/64 | **Stockholm** | Lawrence Welk |
| 6/1/68 | **Stoned Soul Picnic** | 5th Dimension |
| 4/2/66 | **Stop!** | Moody Blues |
| 1/27/68 | **Stop** | Howard Tate |
| 1/25/64 | **Stop And Think It Over** | Dale & Grace |
| 5/20/67 | **Stop! And Think It Over** | Perry Como |
| 6/25/66 | **Stop! Get A Ticket** | |
|  | | Clefs Of Lavender Hill |
| 2/19/66 | **Stop Her On Sight (S.O.S.)** | |
|  | | Edwin Starr |
| 2/20/65 | **Stop! In The Name Of Love** | Supremes |
| 10/1/66 | **Stop, Look And Listen** | Chiffons |
| 7/3/65 | **Stop! Look What You're Doing** | |
|  | | Carla Thomas |
| 11/9/63 | **Stop Monkeyin' Aroun'** | Dovells |
| 10/29/66 | **Stop Stop Stop** | Hollies |
| 11/7/64 | **Stop Takin' Me For Granted** | |
|  | | Mary Wells |
| 9/8/62 | **Stop The Music** | Shirelles |
| 7/28/62 | **Stop The Wedding** | Etta James |
| 10/26/68 | **Stormy** | Classics IV |
| 9/8/62 | **Stormy Monday Blues** | Bobby Bland |
| 1/16/61 | **Story Of My Love** | Paul Anka |
| 6/22/68 | **Story Of Rock And Roll** | Turtles |
| 3/14/64 | **(Story Of) Woman, Love And A Man** | |
|  | | Tony Clarke |
| 12/2/67 | **Storybook Children** | |
|  | | Billy Vera & Judy Clay |
| 8/26/67 | **Stout-Hearted Men** | Barbra Streisand |
| 3/14/60 | **Straight A's In Love** | Johnny Cash |
| 10/26/68 | **Straight Life** | Bobby Goldsboro |
| 8/17/63 | **Straighten Up Your Heart** | |
|  | | Barbara Lewis |
| 9/30/67 | **Stranded In The Middle Of Noplace** | |
|  | | Righteous Brothers |
| 2/10/62 | **Strange** | Patsy Cline |
| 9/28/63 | **Strange Feeling** | Billy Stewart |
| 12/1/62 | **Strange I Know** | Marvelettes |
| 2/8/64 | **Strange Things Happening** | |
|  | | Little Junior Parker |
| 11/21/60 | **Stranger From Durango** | Richie Allen |
| 2/27/65 | **Stranger In Town** | Del Shannon |
| 1/25/64 | **Stranger In Your Arms** | Bobby Vee |
| 5/11/63 | **Stranger In Your Town** | Shacklefords |
|  | **Stranger On The Shore** | |
| 3/17/62 | | Mr. Acker Bilk |
| 5/12/62 | | Drifters |
| 6/9/62 | | Andy Williams |
| 5/7/66 | **Strangers In The Night** | Frank Sinatra |
| 2/25/67 | **Strawberry Fields Forever** | Beatles |
| 1/20/68 | **Strawberry Shortcake** | |
|  | | Jay & The Techniques |
| 9/7/68 | **Street Fighting Man** | Rolling Stones |
|  | **String Along** | |
| 2/22/60 | | Fabian |
| 5/25/63 | | Rick Nelson |
| 5/12/62 | **Stripper, The** | David Rose |
| 10/20/62 | **Stubborn Kind Of Fellow** | Marvin Gaye |
| 4/4/60 | **Stuck On You** | Elvis Presley |
| 4/3/65 | **Subterranean Homesick Blues** | |
|  | | Bob Dylan |
| 7/25/64 | **Such A Night** | Elvis Presley |
| 7/2/66 | **Such A Sweet Thing** | Mary Wells |
| 6/19/65 | **(Such An) Easy Question** | Elvis Presley |
| 8/3/68 | **Sudden Stop** | Percy Sledge |
| 3/7/60 | **Suddenly** | Nickey DeMatteo |
| 2/13/65 | **Suddenly I'm All Alone** | Walter Jackson |
| 2/17/68 | **Suddenly You Love Me** | Tremeloes |
| 11/2/63 | **Sue's Gotta Be Mine** | Del Shannon |
|  | **Sugar And Spice** | |
| 5/2/64 | | Searchers |
| 7/23/66 | | Cryan Shames |
| 2/3/62 | **Sugar Babe** | Buster Brown |
| 12/31/60 | **Sugar Bee** | Cleveland Crochet |
| 4/14/62 | **Sugar Blues** | Ace Cannon |
| 7/24/65 | **Sugar Dumpling** | Sam Cooke |
| 7/11/64 | **Sugar Lips** | Al Hirt |
| 8/30/69 | **Sugar On Sunday** | Clique |
| 8/4/62 | **Sugar Plum** | Ike Clanton |
| 9/21/63 | **Sugar Shack** | Jimmy Gilmer/Fireballs |
| 7/26/69 | **Sugar, Sugar** | Archies |
| 11/19/66 | **Sugar Town** | Nancy Sinatra |

| Date | Song | Artist |
|---|---|---|
| 10/4/69 | **Suite: Judy Blue Eyes** | |
|  | | Crosby, Stills & Nash |
| 5/11/63 | **Sukiyaki** | Kyu Sakamoto |
| 6/10/67 | **Summer And Sandy** | Lesley Gore |
| 7/16/66 | **Summer In The City** | Lovin' Spoonful |
| 7/25/64 | **Summer Means Fun** | Bruce & Terry |
| 8/14/65 | **Summer Nights** | Marianne Faithfull |
|  | **Summer Place**..see: Theme From A | |
| 11/18/67 | **Summer Rain** | Johnny Rivers |
| 8/27/66 | **Summer Samba (So Nice)** | |
|  | | Walter Wanderley |
| 2/29/60 | **Summer Set** | Monty Kelly |
| 8/15/64 | **Summer Song** | Chad & Jeremy |
| 6/5/65 | **Summer Sounds** | Robert Goulet |
| 7/31/61 | **Summer Souvenirs** | Karl Hammel, Jr. |
|  | **Summer Wind** | |
| 8/7/65 | | Wayne Newton |
| 9/3/66 | | Frank Sinatra |
| 3/4/67 | **Summer Wine** | |
|  | | Nancy Sinatra with Lee Hazlewood |
| 6/15/63 | **Summer's Comin'** | Kirby St. Romain |
| 9/26/60 | **Summer's Gone** | Paul Anka |
|  | **Summertime** | |
| 5/29/61 | | Marcels |
| 3/10/62 | | Rick Nelson |
| 6/29/63 | | Chris Columbo Quintet |
| 7/16/66 | | Billy Stewart |
| 3/2/68 | **Summertime Blues** | Blue Cheer |
| 6/23/62 | **Summertime, Summertime** | Jamies |
| 4/16/66 | **Sun Ain't Gonna Shine (Anymore)** | |
|  | | Walker Bros. |
| 3/16/63 | **Sun Arise** | Rolf Harris |
| 5/10/69 | **Sunday** | Moments |
| 11/20/65 | **Sunday And Me** | Jay & The Americans |
| 3/25/67 | **Sunday For Tea** | Peter & Gordon |
| 1/20/62 | **Sunday Kind Of Love** | Jan & Dean |
|  | **Sunday Mornin'** | |
| 1/6/68 | | Spanky & Our Gang |
| 11/22/69 | | Oliver |
| 10/25/69 | **Sunday Morning Coming Down** | |
|  | | Ray Stevens |
| 10/5/68 | **Sunday Sun** | Neil Diamond |
| 5/20/67 | **Sunday Will Never Be The Same** | |
|  | | Spanky & Our Gang |
|  | **Sunday's Gonna' Come On Tuesday**..see: (One Of These Days) | |
|  | **Sundowners**..see: Theme From The | |
| 7/25/64 | **Sunny** | Neil Sedaka |
| 6/25/66 | **Sunny** | Bobby Hebb |
| 8/6/66 | **Sunny Afternoon** | Kinks |
| 1/28/67 | **Sunrise, Sunset** | Roger Williams |
| 9/9/67 | **Sunshine Games** | Music Explosion |
| 4/15/67 | **Sunshine Girl** | Parade |
| 6/19/65 | **Sunshine, Lollipops And Rainbows** | |
|  | | Lesley Gore |
| 1/13/68 | **Sunshine Of Your Love** | Cream |
| 7/30/66 | **Sunshine Superman** | Donovan |
| 4/24/65 | **Super-cali-fragil-istic-expi-ali-docious** | Julie Andrews-Dick Van Dyke |
| 3/5/66 | **Superman** | Dino, Desi & Billy |
| 3/5/66 | **Sure Gonna Miss Her** | |
|  | | Gary Lewis & The Playboys |
| 6/15/63 | **Surf City** | Jan & Dean |
| 7/13/63 | **Surf Party** | Chubby Checker |
| 8/3/63 | **Surfer Girl** | Beach Boys |
| 8/31/63 | **Surfer Joe** | Surfaris |
| 12/14/63 | **Surfer Street** | Allisons |
| 1/13/62 | **Surfer's Stomp** | Mar-Kets |
| 2/17/62 | **Surfin'** | Beach Boys |
| 12/7/63 | **Surfin' Bird** | Trashmen |
|  | (also see: Bird's The Word) | |
| 7/13/63 | **Surfin' Hootenanny** | Al Casey |
| 8/11/62 | **Surfin' Safari** | Beach Boys |
| 3/23/63 | **Surfin' U.S.A.** | Beach Boys |
| 2/20/61 | **Surrender** | Elvis Presley |
| 12/9/67 | **Susan** | Buckinghams |
| 10/6/62 | **Susie Darlin'** | Tommy Roe |
| 2/22/64 | **Suspicion** | Terry Stafford |
| 8/6/66 | **Suspicions** | Sidekicks |
| 9/13/69 | **Suspicious Minds** | Elvis Presley |
| 10/28/67 | **Suzanne** | Noel Harrison |
| 9/7/68 | **Suzie Q.** | Creedence Clearwater Revival |
| 11/7/60 | **Sway** | Bobby Rydell |
| 7/7/62 | **Sweet And Lovely** | |
|  | | April Stevens & Nino Tempo |
| 9/28/68 | **Sweet Blindness** | 5th Dimension |
| 6/28/69 | **Sweet Caroline (Good Times Never Seemed So Good)** | Neil Diamond |

| | | | | | | | |
|---|---|---|---|---|---|---|---|
| 3/22/69 | **Sweet Cherry Wine** *Tommy James & The Shondells* | 4/13/63 | **Take These Chains From My Heart** *Ray Charles* | 3/18/67 | **Tell Me To My Face**  *Keith* |
| 12/28/68 | **Sweet Cream Ladies, Forward March** *Box Tops* | 5/21/66 | **Take This Heart Of Mine**  *Marvin Gaye* | 5/22/61 | **Tell Me Why**  *Belmonts* |
| 11/2/68 | **Sweet Darlin'**  *Martha & The Vandellas* | 12/26/64 | **Take This Hurt Off Me**  *Don Covay* | 5/23/64 | **Tell Me Why**  *Bobby Vinton* |
| | **Sweet Dreams** | 3/16/68 | **Take Time To Know Her**  *Percy Sledge* | 1/1/66 | **Tell Me Why**  *Elvis Presley* |
| 11/14/60 | *Don Gibson* | 7/30/66 | **Takin' All I Can Get** *Mitch Ryder & The Detroit Wheels* | 7/4/64 | **Tell Me (You're Coming Back)** *Rolling Stones* |
| 4/20/63 | *Patsy Cline* | 4/17/65 | **Talk About Love**  *Adam Faith* | 8/10/68 | **Tell Someone You Love Them** *Dino, Desi & Billy* |
| 6/25/66 | *Tommy McLain* | 11/9/63 | **Talk Back Trembling Lips** *Johnny Tillotson* | 11/3/62 | **Telstar**  *Tornadoes* |
| 8/18/62 | **Sweet Georgia Brown**  *Carroll Bros.* | 11/12/66 | **Talk Talk**  *Music Machine* | | **Temptation** |
| 9/28/63 | **Sweet Impossible You**  *Brenda Lee* | 1/4/60* | **Talk That Talk**  *Jackie Wilson* | 9/26/60 | *Roger Williams* |
| 3/2/68 | **Sweet Inspiration**  *Sweet Inspirations* | 9/7/63 | **Talk To Me**  *Sunny & The Sunglows* | 5/29/61 | *Everly Brothers* |
| 4/3/61 | **Sweet Little Kathy**  *Ray Peterson* | 12/26/60 | **Talk To Me Baby**  *Annette* | 7/8/67 | *Boots Randolph* |
| 9/15/62 | **Sweet Little Sixteen**  *Jerry Lee Lewis* | 12/5/64 | **Talk To Me Baby**  *Barry Mann* | 6/12/65 | **Temptation 'Bout To Get Me** *Knight Bros.* |
| 8/28/61 | **Sweet Little You**  *Neil Sedaka* | 1/18/64 | **Talking About My Baby**  *Impressions* | 2/4/67 | **Ten Commandments**  *Prince Buster* |
| 6/8/68 | **Sweet Memories**  *Andy Williams* | 11/2/68 | **Talking About My Baby**  *Gloria Walker* | | **Ten Commandments Of Love** |
| 1/4/60* | **Sweet Nothin's**  *Brenda Lee* | 4/11/64 | **Tall Cool One**  *Wailers* | 6/22/63 | *James MacArthur* |
| 6/11/66 | **Sweet Pea**  *Tommy Roe* | | **Tall Oak Tree**..see: (There Was A) | 2/24/68 | *Peaches & Herb* |
| 9/8/62 | **Sweet Sixteen Bars**  *Earl Grant* | 3/9/68 | **Tapioca Tundra**  *Monkees* | 11/8/69 | *Little Anthony & The Imperials* |
| 9/9/67 | **Sweet Soul Medley**  *Magnificent Men* | 7/9/66 | **Tar And Cement**  *Verdelle Smith* | 3/13/65 | **10 Little Bottles**  *Johnny Bond* |
| 3/11/67 | **Sweet Soul Music**  *Arthur Conley* | | **Taras Bulba**..see: Theme From | 12/1/62 | **Ten Little Indians**  *Beach Boys* |
| | **(Sweet Sweet Baby) Since You've Been Gone** | | **Taste Of Honey** | 11/18/67 | **Ten Little Indians**  *Yardbirds* |
| 3/2/68 | *Aretha Franklin* | 7/14/62 | *Martin Denny* | 9/22/62 | **Ten Lonely Guys**  *Pat Boone* |
| 8/31/68 | *Ramsey Lewis* | 9/1/62 | *Victor Feldman Quartet* | | **Tender, Love and Care**..see: T.L.C. |
| 10/21/67 | **Sweet, Sweet Lovin'**  *Platters* | 8/22/64 | *Tony Bennett* | 7/3/61 | **Tender Years**  *George Jones* |
| 5/7/66 | **Sweet Talkin' Guy**  *Chiffons* | 9/25/65 | *Herb Alpert* | 3/27/61 | **Tenderly**  *Bert Kaempfert* |
| 3/17/62 | **Sweet Thursday**  *Johnny Mathis* | 6/20/64 | **Taste Of Tears**  *Johnny Mathis* | 5/26/62 | **Tennessee**  *Jan & Dean* |
| 8/8/64 | **Sweet William**  *Millie Small* | 6/26/61 | **Te-Ta-Te-Ta-Ta**  *Ernie K-Doe* | 11/13/61 | **Tennessee Flat-Top Box**  *Johnny Cash* |
| 12/4/65 | **Sweet Woman Like You**  *Joe Tex* | 5/2/64 | **Tea For Two** *Nino Tempo & April Stevens* | 6/13/64 | **Tennessee Waltz**  *Sam Cooke* |
| 9/28/68 | **Sweet Young Thing Like You** *Ray Charles* | 4/21/62 | **Teach Me Tonight**  *George Maharis* | | **Tequila** |
| 10/11/69 | **Sweeter He Is**  *Soul Children* | 7/3/61 | **Tear, A**  *Gene McDaniels* | 2/3/62 | *Champs (Twist)* |
| 3/1/69 | **Sweeter Than Sugar**  *Ohio Express* | 1/4/60* | **Tear Drop**  *Santo & Johnny* | 5/16/64 | *Bill Black's Combo* |
| 1/14/67 | **Sweetest One**  *Metros* | 2/22/69 | **Tear Drop City**  *Monkees* | | **Testify**..see: (I Wanna) |
| 7/22/67 | **Sweetest Thing This Side Of Heaven**  *Chris Bartley* | 8/1/64 | **Tear Fell**  *Ray Charles* | 2/13/61 | **Texan And A Girl From Mexico** *Anita Bryant* |
| 9/11/61 | **Sweets For My Sweet**  *Drifters* | 1/23/61 | **Tear Of The Year**  *Jackie Wilson* | 2/10/68 | **Thank U Very Much**  *Scaffold* |
| 10/31/64 | **S-W-I-M**  *Bobby Freeman* | 7/31/61 | **Teardrops In My Heart**  *Joe Barry* | 12/7/63 | **Thank You And Goodnight**  *Angels* |
| 8/1/60 | **Swingin' Down The Lane** *Jerry Wallace* | 2/26/66 | **Tears**  *Bobby Vinton* | 7/18/64 | **Thank You Baby**  *Shirelles* |
| 5/26/62 | **Swingin' Gently**  *Earl Grant* | 2/10/62 | **Tears And Laughter**  *Dinah Washington* | 4/4/64 | **Thank You Girl**  *Beatles* |
| 1/4/60* | **Swingin' On A Rainbow**  *Frankie Avalon* | 5/16/64 | **Tears And Roses**  *Al Martino* | 1/16/65 | **Thanks A Lot**  *Brenda Lee* |
| 7/21/62 | **Swingin' Safari**  *Billy Vaughn* | 12/25/61 | **Tears From An Angel**  *Troy Shondell* | 3/11/67 | **That Acapulco Gold**  *Rainy Daze* |
| 5/9/60 | **Swingin' School**  *Bobby Rydell* | 5/22/65 | **Tears Keep On Falling**  *Jerry Vale* | 11/30/63 | **That Boy John**  *Raindrops* |
| 11/15/69 | **Swingin' Tight**  *Bill Deal* | 7/6/63 | **Tears Of Joy**  *Chuck Jackson* | 1/18/64 | **That Girl Belongs To Yesterday** *Gene Pitney* |
| 5/25/63 | **Swinging On A Star** *Big Dee Irwin/Little Eva* | 7/24/61 | **Tears On My Pillow**  *McGuire Sisters* | 6/23/62 | **That Greasy Kid Stuff**  *Janie Grant* |
| 9/15/62 | **Swiss Maid**  *Del Shannon* | 4/22/67 | **Tears, Tears, Tears**  *Ben E. King* | 5/19/62 | **That Happy Feeling**  *Bert Kaempfert* |
| 6/26/61 | **Switch-A-Roo**  *Hank Ballard* | 4/30/66 | **Teaser, The**  *Bob Kuban* | 8/31/68 | **That Kind Of Woman**  *Merrilee Rush* |
| 2/15/69 | **Switch It On**  *Cliff Nobles & Co.* | 3/20/65 | **Teasin' You**  *Willie Tee* | | **(That Kiss!)**..see: Eso Beso |
| 10/15/66 | **Symphony For Susan**  *Arbors* | 2/29/60 | **Teddy**  *Connie Francis* | 12/7/63 | **That Lucky Old Sun**  *Ray Charles* |
| | | | **Teen Age**..also see: Teenage | 5/1/61 | **That Old Black Magic**  *Bobby Rydell* |
| | **T** | 8/11/62 | **Teen Age Idol**  *Rick Nelson* | 2/1/60 | **That Old Feeling**  *Kitty Kallen* |
| | | 1/4/60* | **Teen Angel**  *Mark Dinning* | 10/20/62 | **That Stranger Used To Be My Girl** *Trade Martin* |
| | | 9/19/64 | **Teen Beat '65**  *Sandy Nelson* | | |
| | | 3/28/60 | **Teen-Ex**  *Browns* | 8/31/63 | **That Sunday, That Summer** *Nat "King" Cole* |
| 1/11/60 | **T.L.C. Tender Love And Care** *Jimmie Rodgers* | 2/3/62 | **Teen Queen Of The Week** *Freddy Cannon* | 2/24/68 | **That's A Lie**  *Ray Charles* |
| 7/18/60 | **Ta Ta**  *Clyde McPhatter* | 9/14/63 | **Teenage Cleopatra**  *Tracey Dey* | 3/2/63 | **That's All**  *Rick Nelson* |
| 3/28/64 | **T'ain't Nothin' To Me**  *Coasters* | 1/11/60 | **Teenage Hayride**  *Tender Slim* | 6/6/60 | **That's All You Gotta Do**  *Brenda Lee* |
| 6/26/61 | **Take A Fool's Advice**  *Nat "King" Cole* | 5/11/63 | **Teenage Heaven**  *Johnny Cymbal* | 8/6/66 | **That's Enough**  *Roscoe Robinson* |
| 10/18/69 | **Take A Letter Maria**  *R.B. Greaves* | 3/14/60 | **Teenage Sonata**  *Sam Cooke* | | **That's How Heartaches Are Made** |
| 9/2/67 | **Take A Look**  *Aretha Franklin* | 8/29/60 | **Teenager Feels It Too**  *Denny Reed* | 3/23/63 | *Baby Washington* |
| 1/18/69 | **Take Care Of Your Homework** *Johnnie Taylor* | 6/18/66 | **Teenager's Prayer**  *Joe Simon* | 11/8/69 | *Marvelettes* |
| 9/11/61 | **Take Five**  *Dave Brubeck Quartet* | 2/15/60 | **Teensville**  *Chet Atkins* | 9/21/63 | **That's How It Goes**  *George Maharis* |
| | **Take Good Care Of Her** | 6/14/69 | **Tell All The People**  *Doors* | 10/24/60 | **That's How Much**  *Brian Hyland* |
| 3/13/61 | *Adam Wade* | | **Tell Her**..also see: Tell Him | 1/30/65 | **That's How Strong My Love Is** *Otis Redding* |
| 10/1/66 | *Mel Carter* | 1/11/60 | **Tell Her For Me**  *Adam Wade* | | |
| | **Take Good Care Of My Baby** | 1/9/65 | **Tell Her No**  *Zombies* | 3/6/61 | **That's It-I Quit-I'm Movin' On** *Sam Cooke* |
| 8/7/61 | *Bobby Vee* | 5/22/65 | **Tell Her (You Love Her Every Day)** *Frank Sinatra* | 11/19/66 | **That's Life**  *Frank Sinatra* |
| 3/30/68 | *Bobby Vinton* | | **Tell Him** | 11/10/62 | **That's Life (That's Tough)** *Gabriel & The Angels* |
| 6/26/65 | **Take Me Back** *Little Anthony & The Imperials* | 12/1/62 | *Exciters* | 4/28/62 | **That's My Desire** *Yvonne Baker & The Sensations* |
| | **Take Me For A Little While** | 7/16/66 | *Dean Parrish (Her)* | | |
| 12/31/65 | *Patti LaBelle & The Bluebelles* | | **Tell Him** | 1/6/62 | **That's My Pa**  *Sheb Wooley* |
| 10/5/68 | *Vanilla Fudge* | 2/8/64 | *Drew-Vels* | 5/12/62 | **That's Old Fashioned (That's The Way Love Should Be)**  *Everly Brothers* |
| 1/29/66 | **Take Me For What I'm Worth** *Searchers* | 8/26/67 | *Patti Drew* | | |
| 5/6/67 | **Take Me In Your Arms And Love Me** *Gladys Knight & The Pips* | 2/2/63 | **Tell Him I'm Not Home**  *Chuck Jackson* | 6/6/64 | **That's Really Some Good** *Rufus & Carla* |
| 10/2/65 | **Take Me In Your Arms (Rock Me)** *Kim Weston* | 12/3/66 | **Tell It Like It Is**  *Aaron Neville* | 5/27/67 | **That's Someone You Never Forget** *Elvis Presley* |
| 7/1/67 | **Take Me (Just As I Am)** *Solomon Burke* | 3/7/64 | **Tell It On The Mountain** *Peter, Paul & Mary* | 10/5/63 | **That's The Only Way**  *Four Seasons* |
| 9/18/61 | **Take My Love (I Want To Give It All To You)**  *Little Willie John* | 12/10/66 | **Tell It To The Rain**  *4 Seasons* | 12/24/66 | **That's The Tune**  *Vogues* |
| 5/28/66 | **Take Some Time Out For Love** *Isley Brothers* | 6/13/67 | **Tell Laura I Love Her**  *Ray Peterson* | 7/19/69 | **That's The Way**  *Joe Tex* |
| | | 11/11/67 | **Tell Mama**  *Etta James* | 3/28/64 | **That's The Way Boys Are**  *Lesley Gore* |
| | | 3/17/62 | **Tell Me**  *Dick & DeeDee* | 8/2/69 | **That's The Way God Planned It** *Billy Preston* |
| | | 2/15/64 | **Tell Me Baby**  *Garnet Mimms* | | |
| | | 5/23/64 | **Tell Me Mamma**  *Christine Quaite* | 1/19/63 | **That's The Way Love Is**  *Bobby Bland* |
| | | 4/25/60 | **Tell Me That You Love Me** *Fats Domino* | | |
| | | 8/24/63 | **Tell Me The Truth**  *Nancy Wilson* | | |

| Date | Title | Artist |
|---|---|---|
| 8/23/69 | That's The Way Love Is | Marvin Gaye |
| 4/24/61 | That's The Way With Love | Piero Soffici |
| 6/26/61 | That's What Girls Are Made For | Spinners |
| 9/19/64 | That's What Love Is Made Of | Miracles |
| 2/22/64 | (That's) What The Nitty Gritty Is | Shirley Ellis |
| 7/11/60 | That's When I Cried | Jimmy Jones |
| 4/4/64 | That's When It Hurts | Ben E. King |
| 10/10/64 | That's Where It's At | Sam Cooke |
| 1/18/69 | That's Your Baby | Joe Tex |
| 1/16/61 | Them That Got | Ray Charles |
| 5/9/60 | Theme For Young Lovers | Percy Faith |
|  | Theme From A Summer Place |  |
| 1/11/60 | Percy Faith |  |
| 8/4/62 | Dick Roman |  |
| 6/26/65 | Lettermen |  |
| 6/28/69 | Ventures |  |
| 8/1/60 | Theme From Adventures In Paradise | Jerry Byrd |
| 11/2/63 | Theme From Any Number Can Win | Jimmy Smith |
| 5/19/62 | Theme From Ben Casey | Valjean |
| 3/20/61 | Theme From Dixie | Duane Eddy |
| 6/2/62 | Theme From Dr. Kildare (Three Stars Will Shine Tonight) | Richard Chamberlain |
| 12/27/69 | Theme From Electric Surfboard | Brother Jack McDuff |
| 6/12/61 | Theme From Goodbye Again | Ferrante & Teicher |
| 7/10/65 | Theme From Harlow (Lonely Girl) | Bobby Vinton |
| 7/14/62 | Theme From Hatari! | Henry Mancini |
| 2/2/63 | Theme From Lawrence Of Arabia | Ferrante & Teicher |
| 3/20/61 | Theme From My Three Sons | Lawrence Welk |
|  | Theme From Pink Panther ..see: Pink Panther Theme |  |
| 8/28/61 | (Theme From) Silver City | Ventures |
| 12/15/62 | Theme From Taras Bulba (The Wishing Star) | Jerry Butler |
| 7/25/60 | Theme From The Apartment | Ferrante & Teicher |
| 10/24/60 | Theme From The Dark At The Top Of The Stairs | Ernie Freeman |
| 4/3/61 | Theme From The Great Imposter | Henry Mancini |
|  | Theme From The Sundowners |  |
| 10/3/60 | Felix Slatkin |  |
| 10/3/60 | Billy Vaughn |  |
| 11/7/60 | Mantovani |  |
|  | Theme From The Three Penny Opera ..see: Mack The Knife |  |
| 5/2/60 | Theme From The Unforgiven (The Need For Love) | Don Costa |
| 11/12/66 | Theme From The Wild Angels | Davie Allan & The Arrows |
|  | Theme From Tunes Of Glory |  |
| 2/13/61 | Cambridge Strings & Singers |  |
| 2/27/61 | Mitch Miller |  |
|  | Theme From Valley Of The Dolls |  |
| 1/20/68 | Dionne Warwick |  |
| 6/15/68 | King Curtis |  |
| 8/17/63 | Then He Kissed Me | Crystals |
| 6/5/65 | Then I'll Count Again | Johnny Tillotson |
|  | Then You Can Tell Me Goodbye |  |
| 1/14/67 | Casinos |  |
| 9/7/68 | Eddy Arnold |  |
| 9/11/65 | There But For Fortune | Joan Baez |
|  | There Goes My Everything |  |
| 1/7/67 | Jack Greene |  |
| 6/24/67 | Engelbert Humperdinck |  |
| 5/18/63 | There Goes (My Heart Again) | Fats Domino |
| 9/2/67 | There Goes The Lover | Gene Chandler |
| 11/30/63 | There! I've Said It Again | Bobby Vinton |
| 1/20/68 | There Is | Dells |
| 8/12/67 | There Is A Mountain | Donovan |
| 8/25/62 | There Is No Greater Love | Wanderers |
| 8/12/67 | There Must Be A Way | Jimmy Roselli |
| 3/29/69 | There Never Was A Time | Jeannie C. Riley |
| 12/26/60 | There She Goes | Jerry Wallace |
| 2/1/60 | (There Was A) Tall Oak Tree | Dorsey Burnette |
|  | There Was A Time |  |
| 1/20/68 | James Brown |  |
| 9/21/68 | Gene Chandler |  |
| 8/13/66 | There Will Never Be Another You | Chris Montez |
| 1/20/62 | There'll Be No Next Time | Jackie Wilson |
| 12/12/64 | (There'll Come A Day When) Ev'ry Little Bit Hurts | Bobby Vee |
| 1/18/69 | There'll Come A Time | Betty Everett |
| 4/8/67 | There's A Chance We Can Make It | Blues Magoos |
| 2/11/67 | There's A Kind Of Hush (All Over The World) | Herman's Hermits |
| 12/31/60 | There's A Moon Out Tonight | Capris |
| 4/11/64 | There's A Place | Beatles |
| 6/27/60 | There's A Star Spangled Banner Waving #2 (The Ballad Of Francis Powers) | Red River Dave |
| 8/26/67 | There's Always Me | Elvis Presley |
|  | (There's) Always Something There To Remind Me |  |
| 8/22/64 | Lou Johnson |  |
| 11/28/64 | Sandie Shaw |  |
| 8/31/68 | Dionne Warwick |  |
| 12/14/68 | There's Gonna Be A Showdown | Archie Bell & The Drells |
| 12/3/66 | There's Got To Be A Word! | Innocence |
| 5/7/66 | There's No Living Without Your Loving | Peter & Gordon |
| 11/20/61 | There's No Other (Like My Baby) | Crystals |
| 8/22/64 | There's Nothing I Can Say | Rick Nelson |
|  | There's Something On Your Mind |  |
| 6/13/60 | Bobby Marchan |  |
| 12/3/66 | Baby Ray |  |
| 2/22/69 | These Are Not My People | Johnny Rivers |
| 5/25/63 | These Arms Of Mine | Otis Redding |
| 1/22/66 | These Boots Are Made For Walkin' | Nancy Sinatra |
|  | These Eyes |  |
| 4/5/69 | Guess Who |  |
| 10/25/69 | Jr. Walker & The All Stars |  |
| 7/27/63 | These Foolish Things | James Brown |
| 8/28/65 | These Hands (Small But Mighty) | Bobby Bland |
| 12/7/68 | They Don't Make Love Like They Used To | Eddy Arnold |
| 2/23/63 | They Remind Me Too Much Of You | Elvis Presley |
| 7/23/66 | They're Coming To Take Me Away, Ha-Haaa! | Napoleon XIV |
| 6/10/67 | They're Here | Boots Walker |
|  | Thing..also see: Do The Thing |  |
| 7/10/61 | Thing Of The Past | Shirelles |
| 7/7/62 | Things | Bobby Darin |
| 8/12/67 | Things I Should Have Said | Grass Roots |
| 12/28/68 | Things I'd Like To Say | New Colony Six |
| 10/3/64 | Things In This House | Bobby Darin |
| 7/4/64 | Things That I Used To Do | James Brown |
| 9/15/62 | Things We Did Last Summer | Shelley Fabares |
|  | Think |  |
| 5/2/60 | James Brown |  |
| 4/8/67 | Vicki Anderson & James Brown |  |
| 3/7/64 | Think | Brenda Lee |
| 10/23/65 | Think | Jimmy McCracklin |
| 5/18/68 | Think | Aretha Franklin |
| 3/12/66 | Think I'll Go Somewhere And Cry Myself To Sleep | Al Martino |
| 4/4/60 | Think Me A Kiss | Clyde McPhatter |
| 5/28/66 | Think Of Me | Buck Owens |
| 3/27/65 | Think Of The Good Times | Jay & The Americans |
|  | Think Twice |  |
| 2/13/61 | Brook Benton |  |
| 1/15/66 | Jackie Wilson & LaVern Baker |  |
| 9/11/65 | 3rd Man Theme | Herb Alpert |
| 2/1/69 | 30-60-90 | Willie Mitchell |
| 11/2/63 | 31 Flavors | Shirelles |
| 6/20/60 | This Bitter Earth | Dinah Washington |
|  | (This Boy)..see: Ringo's Theme |  |
| 1/15/66 | This Can't Be True | Eddie Holman |
| 1/16/65 | This Diamond Ring | Gary Lewis & The Playboys |
| 7/9/66 | This Door Swings Both Ways | Herman's Hermits |
| 3/23/63 | This Empty Place | Dionne Warwick |
| 1/4/60* | This Friendly World | Fabian |
| 8/23/69 | This Girl Is A Woman Now | Union Gap |
| 2/19/66 | This Golden Ring | Fortunes |
|  | This Guy's (Girl's) In Love With You |  |
| 5/18/68 | Herb Alpert |  |
| 2/1/69 | Dionne Warwick |  |
|  | This Is All I Ask |  |
| 7/20/63 | Tony Bennett |  |
| 8/3/63 | Burl Ives |  |
| 3/13/65 | This Is It | Jim Reeves |
| 11/30/68 | This Is My Country | Impressions |
| 8/10/63 | This Is My Prayer | Theola Kilgore |
| 2/27/65 | This Is My Prayer | Ray Charles Singers |
| 3/4/67 | This Is My Song | Petula Clark |
| 12/31/60 | This Is My Story | Mickey & Sylvia |
| 2/17/68 | This Is The Thanks I Get | Barbara Lynn |
|  | This Land Is Your Land |  |
| 12/1/62 | Ketty Lester |  |
| 12/1/62 | New Christy Minstrels |  |
| 6/5/65 | This Little Bird | Marianne Faithfull |
| 4/20/63 | This Little Girl | Dion |
|  | This Magic Moment |  |
| 2/22/60 | Drifters |  |
| 12/28/68 | Jay & The Americans |  |
| 8/29/60 | This Old Heart | James Brown |
|  | This Old Heart Of Mine |  |
| 2/19/66 | Isley Brothers |  |
| 1/18/69 | Tammi Terrell |  |
| 3/13/65 | This Sporting Life | Ian Whitcomb |
| 9/18/61 | This Time | Troy Shondell |
| 1/4/60* | This Time Of The Year | Brook Benton |
| 10/28/67 | This Town | Frank Sinatra |
| 5/8/61 | This World We Live In | Mina |
| 5/11/63 | Those Lazy-Hazy-Crazy Days Of Summer | Nat "King" Cole |
| 5/1/61 | Those Oldies But Goodies (Remind Me Of You) | Little Caesar & The Romans |
| 9/28/68 | Those Were The Days | Mary Hopkin |
|  | Thou Shalt Not Steal |  |
| 4/7/62 | John D. Loudermilk |  |
| 11/21/64 | Dick & DeeDee |  |
| 12/21/68 | Thought Of Loving You | Crystal Mansion |
| 11/7/60 | Thousand Miles Away | Heartbeats |
| 7/15/67 | Thousand Shadows | Seeds |
| 10/24/60 | Thousand Stars | Kathy Young with The Innocents |
| 6/24/67 | Thread The Needle | Clarence Carter |
|  | Three Hearts In A Tangle |  |
| 4/10/61 | Roy Drusky |  |
| 12/8/62 | James Brown |  |
| 4/29/67 | Three Little Fishes (medley) | Mitch Ryder & The Detroit Wheels |
| 9/5/60 | Three Nights A Week | Fats Domino |
|  | Three O'Clock In The Morning |  |
| 5/1/65 | Bert Kaempfert |  |
| 6/5/65 | Lou Rawls |  |
|  | Three Penny Opera..see: Mack The Knife |  |
| 10/2/61 | Three Steps From The Altar | Shep & The Limelites |
| 4/25/64 | Three Window Coupe | Rip Chords |
| 4/16/66 | 3000 Miles | Brian Hyland |
| 12/27/69 | Thrill Is Gone | B.B. King |
|  | Thunder Road..see: Ballad Of |  |
| 12/11/65 | Thunderball | Tom Jones |
| 4/24/65 | Ticket To Ride | Beatles |
| 7/10/65 | Tickle Me | Elvis Presley |
| 6/8/63 | Tie Me Kangaroo Down, Sport | Rolf Harris |
| 4/11/60 | Ties That Bind | Brook Benton |
| 3/30/68 | Tighten Up | Archie Bell & The Drells |
| 12/25/65 | Tijuana Taxi | Herb Alpert |
|  | 'Til |  |
| 10/16/61 | Angels |  |
| 11/23/68 | Vogues |  |
| 7/21/62 | Till Death Do Us Part | Bob Braun |
| 3/26/66 | Till The End Of The Day | Kinks |
| 9/19/64 | Till The End Of Time | Ray Charles Singers |

| | | | | | | |
|---|---|---|---|---|---|---|
| 6/22/63 | **Till Then**  Classics | | **Tonight** | | 7/31/61 | **Transistor Sister**  Freddy Cannon |
| 8/25/62 | **Till There Was You**  Valjean | 10/16/61 | Ferrante & Teicher | | 4/24/61 | **Travelin' Man**  Ricky Nelson |
| 7/19/69 | **Till You Get Enough** | 11/6/61 | Eddie Fisher | | 3/4/67 | **Travlin' Man**  Stevie Wonder |
| | Watts 103rd Street Rhythm Band | | (also see: Tonite) | | 9/4/65 | **Treat Her Right**  Roy Head |
| 2/26/66 | **Time**  Pozo-Seco Singers | 5/29/61 | **Tonight (Could Be The Night)**  Velvets | 8/24/63 | **Treat My Baby Good**  Bobby Darin |
| | **Time After Time** | 3/6/61 | **Tonight I Fell In Love**  Tokens | 4/3/61 | **Trees**  Platters |
| 1/18/60 | Frankie Ford | 9/18/61 | **Tonight I Won't Be There**  Adam Wade | 3/27/61 | **Triangle**  Janie Grant |
| 10/29/66 | Chris Montez | 11/1/69 | **Tonight I'll Be Staying Here With** | 4/27/68 | **Tribute To A King**  William Bell |
| 4/15/67 | **Time Alone Will Tell**  Connie Francis | | **You**  Bob Dylan | 1/28/67 | **Trouble Down Here Below**  Lou Rawls |
| 2/1/60 | **Time And The River**  Nat "King" Cole | 11/29/69 | **Tonight I'll Say A Prayer**  Eydie Gorme | 6/6/64 | **Trouble I've Had**  Clarence Ashe |
| 5/18/68 | **Time For Livin'**  Association | 3/13/61 | **Tonight My Love, Tonight**  Paul Anka | | **Trouble In Mind** |
| | **(Time For Us)**..see: Love Theme From | 1/11/64 | **Tonight You're Gonna Fall In Love** | 1/23/61 | Nina Simone |
| | Romeo & Juliet | | **With Me**  Shirelles | 12/15/62 | Aretha Franklin |
| 8/10/68 | **Time Has Come Today** | | **Tonight's The Night** | 6/13/60 | **Trouble In Paradise**  Crests |
| | Chambers Brothers | 9/12/60 | Chiffons | 12/8/62 | **Trouble Is My Middle Name** |
| 10/17/64 | **Time Is On My Side**  Rolling Stones | 9/12/60 | Shirelles | | Bobby Vinton |
| 3/15/69 | **Time Is Tight**  Booker T. & The M.G.'s | 5/29/65 | **Tonight's The Night**  Solomon Burke | 5/10/69 | **Truck Stop**  Jerry Smith |
| 9/12/60 | **Time Machine**  Dante & the Evergreens | 1/23/61 | **Tonite, Tonite**  Mello-Kings | 7/27/63 | **True Blue Lou**  Tony Bennett |
| 9/27/69 | **Time Machine**  Grand Funk Railroad | 12/2/67 | **Tony Rome**  Nancy Sinatra | 7/26/69 | **True Grit**  Glen Campbell |
| 2/8/69 | **Time Of The Season**  Zombies | 8/11/62 | **Too Bad**  Ben E. King | 7/27/63 | **True Love**  Richard Chamberlain |
| 9/16/67 | **Time Seller**  Spencer Davis Group | 4/26/69 | **Too Busy Thinking About My Baby** | 12/28/63 | **True Love Goes On And On**  Burl Ives |
| 5/6/67 | **Time, Time**  Ed Ames | | Marvin Gaye | 7/6/63 | **True Love Never Runs Smooth** |
| 11/13/65 | **Time To Love-A Time To Cry (Petite** | 5/24/69 | **Too Experienced**  Eddie Lovette | | Gene Pitney |
| | **Fleur)** · Lou Johnson | 8/28/65 | **Too Hot To Hold**  Major Lance | | **True Love, True Love**..see: (If You Cry) |
| 7/3/61 | **Time Was**  Flamingos | 5/9/64 | **Too Late To Turn Back Now** | 4/17/65 | **True Love Ways**  Peter & Gordon |
| 3/15/69 | **Time Was**  Canned Heat | | Brook Benton | 9/25/61 | **True, True Love**  Frankie Avalon |
| 2/19/66 | **Time Won't Let Me**  Outsiders | 8/25/62 | **Too Late To Worry - Too Blue To** | 5/7/66 | **Truly Julie's Blues (I'll Be There)** |
| 11/7/64 | **Times Have Changed**  Irma Thomas | | **Cry**  Glen Campbell | | Bob Lind |
| 3/16/68 | **Tin Soldier**  Small Faces | 12/20/69 | **Too Many Cooks (Spoil The Soup)** | 4/3/65 | **Truly, Truly, True**  Brenda Lee |
| 11/26/66 | **Tiny Bubbles**  Don Ho & The Aliis | | 100 Proof Aged In Soul | 3/13/61 | **Trust In Me**  Etta James |
| | **Tip Of My Fingers** | | **Too Many Fish In The Sea** | 10/11/69 | **Try A Little Kindness**  Glen Campbell |
| 6/29/63 | Roy Clark | 11/7/64 | Marvelettes | | **Try A Little Tenderness** |
| 7/23/66 | Eddy Arnold | 4/29/67 | Mitch Ryder & The Detroit Wheels (medley) | 9/29/62 | Aretha Franklin |
| 1/21/67 | **Tip Toe**  Robert Parker | 5/29/65 | **Too Many Rivers**  Brenda Lee | 12/3/66 | Otis Redding |
| 5/18/68 | **Tip-Toe Thru' The Tulips With Me** | 7/17/61 | **Too Many Rules**  Connie Francis | 2/8/69 | Three Dog Night |
| | Tiny Tim | 11/25/67 | **Too Much Of Nothing** | 2/3/68 | **Try It**  Ohio Express |
| 3/12/66 | **Tippy Toeing**  Harden Trio | | Peter, Paul & Mary | 6/6/64 | **Try It Baby**  Marvin Gaye |
| 1/15/66 | **Tired Of Being Lonely**  Sharpees | 2/10/68 | **Too Much Talk** | | **Try Me** |
| 3/13/65 | **Tired Of Waiting For You**  Kinks | | Paul Revere & The Raiders | 9/26/64 | Jimmy Hughes |
| 12/21/68 | **Tit For Tat (Ain't No Taking Back)** | 1/18/60 | **Too Much Tequila**  Champs | 11/20/65 | James Brown |
| | James Brown | 2/15/60 | **Too Pooped To Pop ("Casey")** | 12/17/66 | **Try My Love Again** |
| | **To**..also see: Too | | Chuck Berry | | Bobby Moore's Rhythm Aces |
| 1/20/62 | **To A Sleeping Beauty**  Jimmy Dean | 4/2/66 | **Too Slow**  Impressions | | **Try To Remember** |
| 6/10/67 | **To Be A Lover**  Gene Chandler | | **Too Soon To Know**..see: It's Too Soon | 1/23/61 | Ed Ames |
| 2/20/61 | **To Be Loved (Forever)**  Pentagons | 11/9/68 | **Too Weak To Fight**  Clarence Carter | 4/10/65 | Roger Williams |
| 12/13/69 | **To Be Young, Gifted And Black** | 7/4/60 | **Too Young To Go Steady** | 11/6/65 | Brothers Four |
| | Nina Simone | | Connie Stevens | 4/2/66 | **Try Too Hard**  Dave Clark Five |
| | **To Each His Own** | 2/20/61 | **Top Forty, News, Weather And** | 7/20/68 | **Tuesday Afternoon (Forever** |
| 10/10/60 | Platters | | **Sports**  Mark Dinning | | **Afternoon)**  Moody Blues |
| 3/14/64 | Tymes | 9/1/62 | **Torture**  Kris Jensen | 12/25/61 | **Tuff**  Ace Cannon |
| 1/20/68 | Frankie Laine | 4/24/61 | **Tossin' And Turnin'**  Bobby Lewis | | **Tunes Of Glory**..see: Theme From |
| | **(To Everything There Is A** | 9/18/65 | **Tossing & Turning**  Ivy League | 11/23/63 | **Turn Around**  Dick & DeeDee |
| | **Season)**..see: Turn! Turn! Turn! | 12/28/68 | **Touch Me**  Doors | 5/10/69 | **Turn Around And Love You** |
| 12/30/67 | **To Give (The Reason I Live)** | 2/20/61 | **Touchables, The**  Dickie Goodman | | Rita Coolidge |
| | Frankie Valli | 4/24/61 | **Touchables In Brooklyn** | | **Turn Around, Look At Me** |
| | **To Know You Is To Love You** | | Dickie Goodman | 10/30/61 | Glen Campbell |
| 7/10/65 | Peter & Gordon | | **Tough**..also see: Tuff | 6/15/68 | Vogues |
| 4/5/69 | Bobby Vinton | 10/2/61 | **Tower Of Strength**  Gene McDaniels | 8/13/66 | **Turn-Down Day**  Cyrkle |
| | **To Love Somebody** | | (also see: You Don't Have To Be A) | 10/18/69 | **Turn On A Dream**  Box Tops |
| 7/15/67 | Bee Gees | 10/30/61 | **Town Without Pity**  Gene Pitney | | **Turn On Your Love Light** |
| 7/6/68 | Sweet Inspirations | 4/10/65 | **Toy Soldier**  4 Seasons | 12/4/61 | Bobby Bland |
| | **To Love Someone**..see: (What A Sad | | **Toys In The Attic** | 8/12/67 | Oscar Toney, Jr. |
| | Way) | 10/5/63 | Jack Jones | 3/9/68 | Human Beinz |
| 9/17/66 | **To Make A Big Man Cry**  Roy Head | 10/5/63 | Joe Sherman | 6/22/68 | Bill Black's Combo |
| 9/23/67 | **To Share Your Love**  Fantastic Four | 3/24/62 | **Tra La La La La**  Ike & Tina Turner | 8/19/67 | **Turn The World Around**  Eddy Arnold |
| 7/30/66 | **To Show I Love You**  Peter & Gordon | 11/2/63 | **Tra La La La Suzy**  Dean & Jean | | **Turn! Turn! Turn!** |
| | **To Sir With Love** | 2/8/69 | **Tra La La Song (One Banana, Two** | 10/23/65 | Byrds |
| 9/9/67 | Lulu | | **Banana)**  Banana Splits | 11/29/69 | Judy Collins |
| 10/21/67 | Herbie Mann | | **Traces** | 6/13/60 | **Tuxedo Junction**  Frankie Avalon |
| 2/8/69 | **To Susan On The West Coast** | 2/8/69 | Classics IV | 8/26/67 | **Twelve Thirty (Young Girls Are** |
| | **Waiting**  Donovan | 12/27/69 | Lettermen (medley) | | **Coming To The Canyon)** |
| 8/31/68 | **To Wait For Love**  Herb Alpert | | **Tracks Of My Tears** | | Mamas & The Papas |
| 9/12/64 | **Tobacco Road**  Nashville Teens | 7/17/65 | Miracles | 2/23/63 | **Twenty Miles**  Chubby Checker |
| 4/18/64 | **Today**  New Christy Minstrels | 6/3/67 | Johnny Rivers | 8/29/64 | **20-75**  Willie Mitchell |
| 4/6/63 | **(Today I Met) The Boy I'm Gonna** | 3/15/69 | Aretha Franklin | 10/19/63 | **Twenty Four Hours From Tulsa** |
| | **Marry**  Darlene Love | 9/13/69 | **Tracy**  Cuff Links | | Gene Pitney |
| 11/30/63 | **Today's Teardrops**  Rick Nelson | 1/4/60 | **Tracy's Theme**  Spencer Ross | 2/15/69 | **Twenty-Five Miles**  Edwin Starr |
| | **Together** | | **Tragedy** | 12/8/62 | **Twilight Time**  Andy Williams |
| 6/26/61 | Connie Francis | 4/17/61 | Fleetwoods | 1/2/65 | **Twine Time**  Alvin Cash & The Crawlers |
| 4/29/67 | Intruders | 1/11/69 | Brian Hyland | 4/30/66 | **Twinkle Toes**  Roy Orbison |
| 12/20/69 | Illusion | 8/23/69 | **Train, The**  1910 Fruitgum Co. | | **Twist** |
| 3/26/66 | **Together Again**  Ray Charles | 6/6/60 | **Train Of Love**  Annette | 7/18/60 | Hank Ballard |
| 9/19/60 | **Togetherness**  Frankie Avalon | | **Trains And Boats And Planes** | 8/1/60 | Chubby Checker |
| 3/23/63 | **Tom Cat**  Rooftop Singers | 6/26/65 | Billy J. Kramer with The Dakotas | 11/13/61 | Chubby Checker |
| 9/21/63 | **Tomboy**  Ronnie Dove | 7/2/66 | Dionne Warwick | 1/6/62 | Ernie Freeman |
| 5/8/65 | **Tommy**  Reparata & The Delrons | | **Tramp** | | **Twist And Shout** |
| 12/30/67 | **Tomorrow**  Strawberry Alarm Clock | 1/14/67 | Lowell Fulsom | 6/2/62 | Isley Brothers |
| 9/10/66 | **Tomorrow Never Comes**  B.J. Thomas | 5/6/67 | Otis & Carla | 3/14/64 | Beatles |
| 5/31/69 | **Tomorrow Tomorrow**  Bee Gees | | | | |

| Date | Title | Artist |
|---|---|---|
| 12/18/61 | **Twist-Her** | Bill Black's Combo |
| 7/20/63 | **Twist It Up** | Chubby Checker |
| 3/31/62 | **Twist, Twist Senora** | Gary "U.S." Bonds |
| 1/6/62 | **Twistin' All Night Long** | Danny & The Juniors/Freddy Cannon |
| 12/19/60 | **Twistin' Bells** | Santo & Johnny |
| 3/31/62 | **Twistin' Matilda** | Jimmy Soul |
|  | (also see: Waltzing Matilda) |  |
| 1/27/62 | **Twistin' Postman** | Marvelettes |
| 2/3/62 | **Twistin' The Night Away** | Sam Cooke |
|  | **Twistin' U.S.A.** |  |
| 9/19/60 | Danny & The Juniors |  |
| 12/11/61 | Chubby Checker |  |
|  | **Twistin' White Silver Sands**..see: White Silver Sands |  |
| 9/22/62 | **Twistin' With Linda** | Isley Brothers |
| 7/13/68 | **Two-Bit Manchild** | Neil Diamond |
|  | **Two Brothers**..see: Ballad Of |  |
| 8/21/65 | **Two Different Worlds** | Lenny Welch |
| 3/30/63 | **Two Faces Have I** | Lou Christie |
| 6/17/67 | **Two In The Afternoon** | Dino, Desi & Billy |
| 4/13/63 | **Two Kind Of Teardrops** | Del Shannon |
| 12/16/67 | **Two Little Kids** | Peaches & Herb |
| 12/1/62 | **Two Lovers** | Mary Wells |
| 3/17/62 | **Two Of A Kind** | Sue Thompson |
| 10/5/63 | **Two Sides (To Every Story)** | Etta James |
| 10/12/63 | **Two-Ten, Six-Eighteen (Doesn't Anybody Know My Name)** | Jimmie Rodgers |
| 9/7/63 | **Two Tickets To Paradise** | Brook Benton |
| 3/23/63 | **Two Wrongs Don't Make A Right** | Mary Wells |
| 12/29/62 | **2,000 Pound Bee** | Ventures |
| 4/25/60 | **Two Thousand, Two Hundred, Twenty-Three Miles** | Patti Page |

## U

| Date | Title | Artist |
|---|---|---|
| 3/23/68 | **U.S. Male** | Elvis Presley |
|  | **Uh! Oh!** |  |
| 1/4/60* | Nutty Squirrels (Part 1) |  |
| 1/4/60* | Nutty Squirrels (Part 2) |  |
| 1/4/64 | **Um, Um, Um, Um, Um, Um** | Major Lance |
|  | **Unchain My Heart** |  |
| 11/27/61 | Ray Charles |  |
| 2/17/68 | Herbie Mann |  |
|  | **Unchained Melody** |  |
| 10/26/63 | Vito & The Salutations |  |
| 7/17/65 | Righteous Brothers |  |
| 8/31/68 | Sweet Inspirations |  |
| 6/27/64 | **Under The Boardwalk** | Drifters |
| 10/16/61 | **Under The Moon Of Love** | Curtis Lee |
| 12/18/65 | **Under Your Spell Again** | Johnny Rivers |
| 2/15/64 | **Understand Your Man** | Johnny Cash |
| 6/15/68 | **Understanding** | Ray Charles |
| 4/3/61 | **Underwater** | Frogmen |
| 10/18/69 | **Undun** | Guess Who |
|  | **Unforgiven**..see: Theme From The |  |
| 3/23/68 | **Unicorn, The** | Irish Rovers |
|  | **United** |  |
| 7/16/66 | Intruders |  |
| 12/30/67 | Music Makers |  |
| 5/18/68 | Peaches & Herb |  |
|  | **Universal Soldier** |  |
| 9/25/65 | Glen Campbell |  |
| 9/25/65 | Donovan |  |
| 3/30/68 | **Unknown Soldier** | Doors |
| 11/21/64 | **Unless You Care** | Terry Black |
| 12/4/61 | **Unsquare Dance** | Dave Brubeck Quartet |
| 10/20/62 | **Untie Me** | Tams |
| 4/20/68 | **Unwind** | Ray Stevens |
|  | **Up A Lazy River**..see: Lazy River |  |
| 10/10/64 | **Up Above My Head (I Hear Music In The Air)** | Al Hirt |
| 2/12/66 | **Up And Down** | McCoys |
| 3/16/68 | **Up From The Skies** | Jimi Hendrix |
| 10/5/68 | **Up-Hard** | Willie Mitchell |
| 11/1/69 | **Up On Cripple Creek** | Band |
|  | **Up On The Roof** |  |
| 11/3/62 | Drifters |  |
| 4/6/68 | Cryan' Shames |  |
| 12/23/67 | **Up Tight, Good Man** | Laura Lee |
| 3/30/68 | **Up To My Neck In High Muddy Water** | Linda Ronstadt |
| 1/18/60 | **Up Town** | Roy Orbison |
| 3/31/62 | **Uptown** | Crystals |
|  | **Up-Up And Away** |  |
| 6/3/67 | 5th Dimension |  |
| 6/24/67 | Johnny Mann Singers |  |
| 12/9/67 | Hugh Masekela |  |
| 2/18/67 | **Ups And Downs** | Paul Revere & The Raiders |
|  | **Uptight**..also see: Up Tight |  |
|  | **Uptight (Everything's Alright)** |  |
| 12/18/65 | Stevie Wonder |  |
| 4/2/66 | Jazz Crusaders |  |
| 7/16/66 | Nancy Wilson |  |
| 10/15/66 | Ramsey Lewis |  |
|  | (also see: Little Ole Man) |  |
| 5/16/60 | **Urge, The** | Freddy Cannon |
| 1/2/65 | **Use Your Head** | Mary Wells |
| 12/19/60 | **Utopia** | Frank Gari |

## V

| Date | Title | Artist |
|---|---|---|
| 7/28/62 | **Vacation** | Connie Francis |
| 3/9/68 | **Valleri** | Monkees |
|  | **Valley Of The Dolls**..see: Theme From |  |
| 12/7/68 | **Vance** | Roger Miller |
| 3/28/64 | **Vanishing Point** | Marketts |
| 8/29/60 | **Vaquero (Cowboy)** | Fireballs |
| 2/1/64 | **Vaya Con Dios** | Drifters |
| 12/13/69 | **Venus** | Shocking Blue |
| 8/18/62 | **Venus In Blue Jeans** | Jimmy Clanton |
|  | **Very Thought Of You** |  |
| 3/13/61 | Little Willie John |  |
| 4/25/64 | Rick Nelson |  |
| 4/28/62 | **Village Of Love** | Nathaniel Mayer |
| 1/4/60* | **Village Of St. Bernadette** | Andy Williams |
|  | **Viva Las Vegas** |  |
| 5/9/64 | Elvis Presley |  |
| 7/4/64 | Elvis Presley |  |
| 12/9/67 | **Voice In The Choir** | Al Martino |
| 12/26/64 | **Voice Your Choice** | Radiants |
| 7/18/60 | **Volare** | Bobby Rydell |
| 11/8/69 | **Volunteers** | Jefferson Airplane |
| 5/1/65 | **Voodoo Woman** | Bobby Goldsboro |
| 12/20/69 | **Voodoo Woman** | Simon Stokes |

## W

| Date | Title | Artist |
|---|---|---|
| 12/5/60 | **Wabash Blues** | Viscounts |
| 12/17/66 | **Wack Wack** | Young Holt Trio |
|  | **Wade In The Water** |  |
| 7/9/66 | Ramsey Lewis |  |
| 3/11/67 | Herb Alpert |  |
| 6/9/62 | **Wah Watusi** | Orlons |
|  | (also see: El Watusi & Watusi) |  |
| 9/26/60 | **Wait** | Jimmy Clanton |
| 1/30/61 | **Wait A Minute** | Coasters |
| 3/5/66 | **Wait A Minute** | Tim Tam & The Turn-Ons |
| 10/24/60 | **Wait For Me** | Playmates |
| 7/20/63 | **Wait Til' My Bobby Gets Home** | Darlene Love |
| 1/29/66 | **Waitin' In Your Welfare Line** | Buck Owens |
| 6/20/60 | **Wake Me, Shake Me** | Coasters |
| 3/21/60 | **Wake Me When It's Over** | Andy Williams |
| 7/12/69 | **Wake Up** | Chambers Brothers |
| 10/28/67 | **Wake Up, Wake Up** | Grass Roots |
| 11/28/64 | **Walk Away** | Matt Monro |
|  | **Walk Away Renee** |  |
| 9/10/66 | Left Banke |  |
| 2/3/68 | Four Tops |  |
|  | **Walk Don't Run** |  |
| 7/18/60 | Ventures |  |
| 7/11/64 | Ventures ('64) |  |
| 5/8/65 | **Walk In The Black Forest** | Horst Jankowski |
| 1/26/63 | **Walk Like A Man** | 4 Seasons |
| 10/30/61 | **Walk On By** | Leroy Van Dyke |
|  | **Walk On By** |  |
| 4/25/64 | Dionne Warwick |  |
| 8/23/69 | Isaac Hayes |  |
|  | **Walk On The Wild Side** |  |
| 2/17/62 | Brook Benton |  |
| 5/12/62 | Jimmy Smith |  |
| 4/28/62 | **Walk On With The Duke** | Duke Of Earl |
| 2/6/61 | **Walk Right Back** | Everly Brothers |
|  | **Walk Right In** |  |
| 1/5/63 | Rooftop Singers |  |
| 1/12/63 | Moments |  |
| 11/28/66 | **Walk Slow** | Little Willie John |
| 3/18/67 | **Walk Tall** | 2 Of Clubs |
| 1/7/67 | **Walk With Faith In Your Heart** | Bachelors |
| 12/4/61 | **Walkin' Back To Happiness** | Helen Shapiro |
|  | **Walkin' In The Rain** |  |
| 10/24/64 | Ronettes |  |
| 11/22/69 | Jay & The Americans |  |
|  | **Walkin' In The Sand**..see: Remember |  |
| 3/25/67 | **Walkin' In The Sunshine** | Roger Miller |
| 8/24/63 | **Walkin' Miracle** | Essex |
| 2/26/66 | **Walkin' My Cat Named Dog** | Norma Tanega |
| 10/7/67 | **Walkin' Proud** | Pete Klint Quintet |
| 11/27/61 | **Walkin' With My Angel** | Bobby Vee |
| 10/19/63 | **Walking Proud** | Steve Lawrence |
| 10/5/63 | **Walking The Dog** | Rufus Thomas |
| 5/23/60 | **Walking The Floor Over You** | Pat Boone |
| 6/20/60 | **Walking To New Orleans** | Fats Domino |
| 1/6/62 | **Waltz You Saved For Me** | Ferlin Husky |
| 1/18/60 | **Waltzing Matilda** | Jimmie Rodgers |
|  | (also see: Twistin' Matilda) |  |
| 12/4/61 | **Wanderer, The** | Dion |
| 4/23/66 | **Wang Dang Doodle** | Koko Taylor |
| 12/2/67 | **Wanted: Lover, No Experience Necessary** | Laura Lee |
| 7/23/66 | **Warm And Tender Love** | Percy Sledge |
| 9/22/62 | **Warmed Over Kisses (Left Over Love)** | Brian Hyland |
| 9/27/69 | **Was It Good To You** | Isley Brothers |
| 7/1/67 | **Washed Ashore (On A Lonely Island In The Sea)** | Platters |
| 9/21/63 | **Washington Square** | Village Stompers |
| 10/23/61 | **Wasn't The Summer Short?** | Johnny Mathis |
| 12/16/67 | **Watch Her Ride** | Jefferson Airplane |
| 10/28/67 | **Watch The Flowers Grow** | 4 Seasons |
| 6/12/61 | **Watch Your Step** | Bobby Parker |
| 12/14/63 | **Watch Your Step** | Brooks O'Dell |
| 7/17/61 | **Water Boy** | Don Shirley Trio |
|  | **Watermelon Man** |  |
| 3/16/63 | Mongo Santamaria |  |
| 6/26/65 | Gloria Lynne |  |
| 2/20/61 | **Watusi, The** | Vibrations |
|  | (also see: El Watusi & Wah Watusi) |  |
| 1/4/60* | **Way Down Yonder In New Orleans** | Freddy Cannon |
| 10/23/61 | **Way I Am** | Jackie Wilson |
| 3/1/69 | **Way It Used To Be** | Engelbert Humperdinck |
| 4/18/60 | **Way Of A Clown** | Teddy Randazzo |
| 9/18/65 | **Way Of Love** | Kathy Kirby |
| 9/15/62 | **Way Over There** | Miracles |
| 2/29/64 | **Way You Do The Things You Do** | Temptations |
| 9/4/61 | **Way You Look Tonight** | Lettermen |
|  | **Ways Of Love**..see: (New In) |  |
| 8/30/69 | **Ways To Love A Man** | Tammy Wynette |
| 4/24/61 | **Wayward Wind** | Gogi Grant |
| 12/10/66 | **(We Ain't Got) Nothin' Yet** | Blues Magoos |
| 12/14/63 | **We Belong Together** | Jimmy Velvet |
| 1/13/68 | **We Can Fly** | Cowsills |
| 12/18/65 | **We Can Work It Out** | Beatles |
| 11/7/64 | **We Could** | Al Martino |
| 8/1/60 | **We Go Together** | Jan & Dean |
| 11/12/66 | **We Got A Thing That's In The Groove** | Capitols |
| 1/4/60* | **We Got Love** | Bobby Rydell |
| 5/17/69 | **We Got More Soul** | Dyke & The Blazers |
| 2/12/66 | **We Got The Winning Hand** | Little Milton |
| 9/6/69 | **We Gotta All Get Together** | Paul Revere & The Raiders |
| 8/14/65 | **We Gotta Get Out Of This Place** | Animals |
| 5/13/67 | **We Had A Good Thing Goin'** | Cyrkle |
| 12/26/60 | **We Have Love** | Dinah Washington |
| 2/5/66 | **We Know We're In Love** | Lesley Gore |
| 9/16/67 | **We Love You** | Rolling Stones |
| 3/21/64 | **We Love You Beatles** | Carefrees |
| 11/1/69 | **We Love You, Call Collect** | Art Linkletter |

| Date | Title | Artist |
|---|---|---|
| 10/18/69 | We Must Be In Love | Five Stairsteps |
| 11/9/63 | We Shall Overcome | Joan Baez |
| | (We'll Be) United ..see: United | |
| 9/27/69 | We'll Cry Together | Maxine Brown |
| 8/8/64 | We'll Sing In The Sunshine | Gale Garnett |
| 12/30/67 | We're A Winner | Impressions |
| 8/7/65 | We're Doing Fine | Dee Dee Warwick |
| 3/27/65 | We're Gonna Make It | Little Milton |
| 4/20/68 | We're Rolling On | Impressions |
| 4/19/69 | (We've Got) Honey Love | Martha & The Vandellas |
| 4/13/68 | Wear It On Our Face | Dells |
| 11/25/67 | Wear Your Love Like Heaven | Donovan |
| 11/21/64 | Wedding, The | Julie Rogers |
| 9/27/69 | Wedding Bell Blues | 5th Dimension |
| 3/8/69 | Wedding Cake | Connie Francis |
| 9/9/67 | Wednesday | Royal Guardsmen |
| | Weight, The | |
| 8/24/68 | | Jackie DeShannon |
| 8/31/68 | | Band |
| 2/22/69 | | Aretha Franklin |
| 9/13/69 | | Suprêmes & Temptations |
| 4/3/61 | Welcome Home | Sammy Kaye |
| 6/12/65 | Welcome Home | Walter Jackson |
| 6/23/62 | Welcome Home Baby | Shirelles |
| 5/10/69 | Welcome Me Love | Brooklyn Bridge |
| 2/22/60 | (Welcome) New Lovers | Pat Boone |
| 8/7/61 | Well-A, Well-A | Shirley & Lee |
| 11/13/61 | Well. I Told You | Chantels |
| 12/4/65 | Well Respected Man | Kinks |
| 10/17/64 | Wendy | Beach Boys |
| 2/29/60 | Werewolf | Frantics |
| 5/26/62 | West Of The Wall | Toni Fisher |
| 3/4/67 | Western Union | Five Americans |
| 8/24/63 | Wham! | Lonnie Mack |
| 7/20/63 | What A Fool I've Been | Carla Thomas |
| 4/27/63 | What A Guy | Raindrops |
| 10/2/61 | What A Party | Fats Domino |
| 1/23/61 | What A Price | Fats Domino |
| 3/24/62 | (What A Sad Way) To Love Someone | Ral Donner |
| 4/24/61 | What A Surprise | Johnny Maestro |
| 7/17/61 | What A Sweet Thing That Was | Shirelles |
| 11/20/61 | What A Walk | Bobby Lewis |
| 3/11/67 | What A Woman In Love Won't Do | Sandy Posey |
| 2/13/61 | What About Me | Don Gibson |
| 1/4/60* | What About Us | Coasters |
| 6/11/66 | What Am I Going To Do Without Your Love | Martha & The Vandellas |
| 1/9/61 | What Am I Gonna Do | Jimmy Clanton |
| | What Am I Living For | |
| 3/28/60 | | Conway Twitty |
| 7/8/67 | | Percy Sledge |
| 3/24/62 | What Am I Supposed To Do | Ann-Margret |
| 3/30/63 | What Are Boys Made Of | Percells |
| 8/14/65 | What Are We Going To Do? | David Jones |
| 8/20/66 | What Becomes Of The Brokenhearted | Jimmy Ruffin |
| | What Cha ..see: What You & Whatcha | |
| 9/18/65 | What Color (Is A Man) | Bobby Vinton |
| 6/30/62 | What Did Daddy Do | Shep & The Limelites |
| 4/4/60 | What Do You Want? | Bobby Vee |
| 4/10/65 | What Do You Want With Me | Chad & Jeremy |
| 2/23/63 | What Does A Girl Do? | Marcie Blane |
| 9/7/63 | What Does A Girl Do? | Shirelles |
| 5/17/69 | What Does It Take (To Win Your Love) | Jr. Walker & The All Stars |
| 3/12/66 | What Goes On | Beatles |
| 10/24/64 | What Good Am I Without You | Marvin Gaye & Kim Weston |
| 5/9/64 | What Have I Got Of My Own | Trini Lopez |
| 1/30/65 | What Have They Done To The Rain | Searchers |
| | What I Feel In My Heart ..see: (How Can I Write On Paper) | |
| 1/11/60 | What In The World's Come Over You | Jack Scott |
| 5/10/69 | What Is A Man | Four Tops |
| | What Kind Of Fool Am I | |
| 9/1/62 | | Sammy Davis Jr. |
| 9/22/62 | | Anthony Newley |
| 10/6/62 | | Robert Goulet |
| | What Kind Of Fool Do You Think I Am | |
| 12/14/63 | | Tams |
| 8/16/69 | | Bill Deal |
| 8/25/62 | What Kind Of Love Is This | Joey Dee |
| 12/5/64 | What Now | Gene Chandler |
| | What Now My Love | |
| 1/29/66 | | Sonny & Cher |
| 3/19/66 | | Herb Alpert |
| 10/1/66 | | "Groove" Holmes |
| 9/9/67 | | Mitch Ryder |
| | What The Nitty Gritty Is ..see: (That's) | |
| 5/22/65 | What The World Needs Now Is Love | Jackie DeShannon |
| 9/15/62 | What Time Is It? | Jive Five |
| 12/29/62 | What To Do With Laurie | Mike Clifford |
| 5/8/61 | What Will I Tell My Heart | Harptones |
| 1/26/63 | What Will Mary Say | Johnny Mathis |
| 12/31/60 | What Would I Do | Mickey & Sylvia |
| 7/10/61 | What Would You Do? | Jim Reeves |
| | What You ..also see: Whatcha | |
| 11/29/69 | What You Gave Me | Marvin Gaye & Tammi Terrell |
| | What'd I Say | |
| 4/3/61 | | Jerry Lee Lewis |
| 3/31/62 | | Bobby Darin |
| 5/23/64 | | Elvis Presley |
| 7/14/62 | What's A Matter Baby | Timi Yuro |
| 10/19/63 | What's Easy For Two Is So Hard For One | Mary Wells |
| 9/8/62 | What's Gonna Happen When Summer's Done | Freddy Cannon |
| 2/15/60 | What's Happening | Wade Flemons |
| 5/15/65 | What's He Doing In My World | Eddy Arnold |
| 11/18/67 | What's It Gonna Be | Dusty Springfield |
| 7/6/68 | What's Made Milwaukee Famous (Has Made A Loser Out Of Me) | Jerry Lee Lewis |
| 6/19/65 | What's New Pussycat? | Tom Jones |
| 1/13/62 | What's So Good About Good-By | Miracles |
| 5/16/64 | What's The Matter With You Baby | Marvin Gaye & Mary Wells |
| 1/13/62 | What's The Reason | Bobby Edwards |
| 8/30/69 | What's The Use Of Breaking Up | Jerry Butler |
| 2/10/62 | What's Your Name | Don & Juan |
| 9/30/67 | What've I Done (To Make You Mad) | Linda Jones |
| | Whatcha ..also see: What You | |
| 3/7/60 | Whatcha Gonna Do | Nat "King" Cole |
| | Whatever Will Be, Will Be ..see: Que Sera, Sera | |
| 3/30/63 | Whatever You Want | Jerry Butler |
| 5/2/60 | Wheel Of Fortune | LaVern Baker |
| | Wheel Of Hurt | |
| 10/8/66 | | Margaret Whiting |
| 10/15/66 | | Al Martino |
| | Wheels | |
| 1/9/61 | | String-A-Longs |
| 2/6/61 | | Billy Vaughn |
| | When A Boy Falls In Love | |
| 7/6/63 | | Mel Carter |
| 6/5/65 | | Sam Cooke |
| | When A Man (Woman) Loves A Woman (Man) | |
| 4/9/66 | | Percy Sledge |
| 6/4/66 | | Esther Phillips |
| 3/1/69 | When He Touches Me (Nothing Else Matters) | Peaches & Herb |
| 8/9/69 | When I Die | Motherlode |
| | When I Fall In Love | |
| 1/16/61 | | Etta Jones |
| 11/20/61 | | Lettermen |
| 5/19/62 | When I Get Thru With You (You'll Love Me Too) | Patsy Cline |
| 9/5/64 | When I Grow Up (To Be A Man) | Beach Boys |
| 4/8/67 | When I Was Young | Animals |
| 3/6/65 | When I'm Gone | Brenda Holloway |
| 3/21/64 | When Joanna Loved Me | Tony Bennett |
| 12/13/69 | When Julie Comes Around | Cuff Links |
| 1/22/66 | When Liking Turns To Loving | Ronnie Dove |
| 5/6/67 | When Love Slips Away | Dee Dee Warwick |
| 2/24/64 | When My Little Girl Is Smiling | Drifters |
| 11/5/66 | (When She Needs Good Lovin') She Comes To Me | Chicago Loop |
| 2/25/67 | When Something Is Wrong With My Baby | Sam & Dave |
| 11/20/61 | When The Boy In Your Arms (Is The Boy In Your Heart) | Connie Francis |
| 11/9/63 | When The Boy's Happy (The Girl's Happy Too) | Four Pennies |
| 10/6/62 | When The Boys Get Together | Joanie Sommers |
| 6/3/67 | When The Good Sun Shines | Elmo & Almo |
| 11/30/63 | When The Lovelight Starts Shining Through His Eyes | Supremes |
| 5/15/65 | When The Ship Comes In | Peter, Paul & Mary |
| 9/30/67 | When The Snow Is On The Roses | Ed Ames |
| 5/6/67 | When Tomorrow Comes | Carla Thomas |
| 7/31/61 | When We Get Married | Dreamlovers |
| 5/30/60 | When Will I Be Loved | Everly Brothers |
| 4/5/69 | When You Dance | Jay & The Americans |
| 8/8/64 | When You Loved Me | Brenda Lee |
| | When You Walk In The Room | |
| 1/25/64 | | Jackie de Shannon |
| 10/17/64 | | Searchers |
| 4/25/60 | When You Wish Upon A Star | Dion & The Belmonts |
| 11/4/67 | When You're Gone | Brenda & The Tabulations |
| | When You're Young And In Love | |
| 10/3/64 | | Ruby & The Romantics |
| 4/22/67 | | Marvelettes |
| 1/9/65 | Whenever A Teenager Cries | Reparata & The Delrons |
| | Whenever He (She) Holds You | |
| 4/18/64 | | Bobby Goldsboro |
| 2/26/66 | | Patty Duke |
| 2/19/66 | Where Am I Going? | Barbra Streisand |
| 6/13/60 | Where Are You | Frankie Avalon |
| 5/19/62 | Where Are You | Dinah Washington |
| 2/1/64 | Where Did I Go Wrong | Dee Dee Sharp |
| 7/11/64 | Where Did Our Love Go | Supremes |
| 10/5/63 | Where Did The Good Times Go | Dick & DeeDee |
| | Where Do I Go | |
| 10/19/63 | | Carla Thomas |
| 7/12/69 | | Happenings (medley) |
| 10/27/62 | Where Do You Come From | Elvis Presley |
| 10/16/65 | Where Do You Go | Cher |
| 4/5/69 | Where Do You Go To (My Lovely) | Peter Sarstedt |
| 3/14/64 | Where Does Love Go | Freddie Scott |
| | Where Have All The Flowers Gone | |
| 1/20/62 | | Kingston Trio |
| 10/2/65 | | Johnny Rivers |
| 5/26/62 | Where Have You Been (All My Life) | Arthur Alexander |
| 3/27/61 | Where I Fell In Love | Capris |
| 2/10/68 | Where Is My Mind | Vanilla Fudge |
| 11/11/67 | Where Is The Party | Helena Ferguson |
| 8/15/64 | Where Love Has Gone | Jack Jones |
| | Where Or When | |
| 1/4/60* | | Dion & The Belmonts |
| 12/28/63 | | Lettermen |
| | Where The Action Is ..see: Action | |
| 1/16/61 | Where The Boys Are | Connie Francis |
| 1/15/66 | Where The Sun Has Never Shone | Jonathan King |
| 8/7/65 | Where Were You When I Needed You | Jerry Vale |
| 6/18/66 | Where Were You When I Needed You | Grass Roots |
| 12/17/66 | Where Will The Words Come From | Gary Lewis & The Playboys |
| 5/3/69 | Where's The Playground Susie | Glen Campbell |
| 2/1/60 | Whiffenpoof Song | Bob Crewe |
| 6/28/69 | While You're Out Looking For Sugar? | Honey Cone |
| 7/25/60 | Whip It On Me | Jessie Hill |
| 2/20/65 | Whipped Cream | Herb Alpert |
| | Whiskey On A Sunday ..see: (Puppet Song) | |

| Date | Title / Artist |
|---|---|
| 12/21/63 | **Whispering** *Nino Tempo & April Stevens* |
| 10/15/66 | **Whispers (Gettin' Louder)** *Jackie Wilson* |
| | **White Christmas** |
| 12/12/60 | *Bing Crosby* |
| 12/19/60 | *Drifters* |
| 12/11/61 | *Bing Crosby* |
| 12/15/62 | *Bing Crosby* |
| 12/22/62 | *Drifters* |
| 11/23/68 | **White Houses** *Animals* |
| 3/7/64 | **White On White** *Danny Williams* |
| 6/24/67 | **White Rabbit** *Jefferson Airplane* |
| 10/5/68 | **White Room** *Cream* |
| 2/24/62 | **White Rose Of Athens** *David Carroll* |
| | **White Silver Sands** |
| 3/7/60 | *Bill Black's Combo* |
| 5/5/62 | *Bill Black's Combo (Twistin')* |
| | **Whiter Shade Of Pale** |
| 6/24/67 | *Procol Harum* |
| 11/9/68 | *Hesitations* |
| 10/22/66 | **Who Am I** *Petula Clark* |
| 10/23/61 | **Who Can I Count On** *Patsy Cline* |
| | **Who Can I Turn To** |
| 10/3/64 | *Tony Bennett* |
| 2/27/65 | *Dionne Warwick* |
| 1/4/64 | **Who Cares** *Fats Domino* |
| 1/11/64 | **Who Do You Love** *Sapphires* |
| | **Who Do You Love** |
| 3/11/67 | *Woolies* |
| 8/9/69 | *Quicksilver Messenger Service* |
| 9/3/66 | **Who Do You Think You Are** *Shindogs* |
| 5/29/61 | **Who Else But You** *Frankie Avalon* |
| 8/24/68 | **Who Is Gonna Love Me?** *Dionne Warwick* |
| 8/7/61 | **Who Put The Bomp (In The Bomp, Bomp, Bomp)** *Barry Mann* |
| 1/19/63 | **Who Stole The Keeshka?** *Matys Bros.* |
| 12/16/67 | **Who Will Answer?** *Ed Ames* |
| 3/31/62 | **Who Will The Next Fool Be** *Bobby Bland* |
| 8/14/65 | **Who'll Be The Next In Line** *Kinks* |
| 4/25/64 | **Who's Afraid Of Virginia Woolf?** *Jimmy Smith* |
| 1/25/64 | **Who's Been Sleeping In My Bed?** *Linda Scott* |
| 6/12/65 | **Who's Cheating Who?** *Little Milton* |
| 6/10/67 | **Who's Lovin' You** *Brenda & The Tabulations* |
| | **Who's Making Love** |
| 10/26/68 | *Johnnie Taylor* |
| 3/1/69 | *Young-Holt Unlimited* |
| | **Whole Lot Of Shakin' Goin' On** |
| 10/10/60 | *Chubby Checker* |
| 10/31/60 | *Conway Twitty* |
| 6/18/66 | **Whole Lot Of Shakin' In My Heart (Since I Met You)** *Miracles* |
| 1/22/69 | **Whole Lotta Love** *Led Zeppelin* |
| 11/4/67 | **Whole Lotta Woman** *Arthur Conley* |
| 3/25/67 | **Whole World Is A Stage** *Fantastic Four* |
| 1/23/65 | **Whose Heart Are You Breaking Tonight** *Connie Francis* |
| 1/4/60* | **Why** *Frankie Avalon* |
| 4/18/64 | **Why** *Beatles/Tony Sheridan* |
| | **Why? (Am I Treated So Bad)** |
| 4/8/67 | *"Cannonball" Adderley* |
| 6/3/67 | *Staple Singers* |
| 6/3/67 | *Sweet Inspirations* |
| 6/17/67 | *Bobby Powell* |
| 2/19/66 | **Why Can't You Bring Me Home** *Jay & The Americans* |
| 4/3/65 | **Why Did I Choose You** *Barbra Streisand* |
| 7/7/62 | **Why Did You Leave Me?** *Vince Edwards* |
| 1/23/67 | **Why Do Fools Fall In Love** *Happenings* |
| 1/18/60 | **Why Do I Love You So** *Johnny Tillotson* |
| 9/14/63 | **Why Do Kids Grow Up** *Randy & The Rainbows* |
| 2/16/63 | **Why Do Lovers Break Each Other's Heart?** *Bob B. Soxx & The Blue Jeans* |
| 8/24/63 | **Why Don't You Believe Me** *Duprees* |
| 3/14/64 | **Why (Doncha Be My Girl)** *Chartbusters* |
| 5/17/69 | **Why I Sing The Blues** *B.B. King* |
| 2/28/60 | **Why I'm Walkin'** *Stonewall Jackson* |
| 1/1/69 | **Why Is The Wine Sweeter (On The Other Side)** *Eddie Floyd* |
| 9/16/61 | **Why Not Now** *Matt Monro* |
| 3/18/67 | **Why Not Tonight** *Jimmy Hughes* |
| 10/22/66 | **Why Pick On Me** *Standells* |
| 5/5/62 | **Why'd You Wanna Make Me Cry** *Connie Stevens* |
| | **Wichita Lineman** |
| 11/2/68 | *Glen Campbell* |
| 11/29/69 | *Sergio Mendes & Brasil '66* |
| 5/28/66 | **Wiederseh'n** *Al Martino* |
| 10/6/62 | **Wiggle Wobble** *Les Cooper* |
| 10/5/63 | **Wild!** *Dee Dee Sharp* |
| | **Wild Angels**..see: Theme From The |
| 11/4/67 | **Wild Honey** *Beach Boys* |
| 6/5/61 | **Wild In The Country** *Elvis Presley* |
| 2/1/60 | **Wild One** *Bobby Rydell* |
| 12/5/64 | **Wild One** *Martha & The Vandellas* |
| | **Wild Thing** |
| 6/25/66 | *Troggs* |
| 1/7/67 | *Senator Bobby* |
| 12/29/62 | **Wild Weekend** *Rebels* |
| 5/11/63 | **Wildwood Days** *Bobby Rydell* |
| 7/6/63 | **Will Power** *Cookies* |
| 1/18/69 | **Will You Be Staying After Sunday** *Peppermint Rainbow* |
| | **Will You Love Me Tomorrow** |
| 11/21/60 | *Shirelles* |
| 2/24/68 | *4 Seasons* |
| 7/12/69 | **Willie & Laura Mae Jones** *Dusty Springfield* |
| | **Willie And The Hand Jive**..see: Hand Jive |
| 1/12/63 | **Willie Can** *Sue Thompson* |
| 11/14/64 | **Willow Weep For Me** *Chad & Jeremy* |
| 2/29/64 | **Willyam, Willyam** *Dee Dee Sharp* |
| | **Winchester Cathedral** |
| 10/29/66 | *New Vaudeville Band* |
| 11/5/66 | *Dana Rollin* |
| 5/3/69 | **Windmills Of Your Mind** *Dusty Springfield* |
| 7/29/67 | **Windows Of The World** *Dionne Warwick* |
| | **Windy** |
| 5/27/67 | *Association* |
| 11/25/67 | *Wes Montgomery* |
| 11/28/60 | **Wings Of A Dove** *Ferlin Husky* |
| 4/25/64 | **Winkin', Blinkin' And Nod** *Simon Sisters* |
| 12/6/69 | **Winter World Of Love** *Engelbert Humperdinck* |
| | **Wipe Out** |
| 6/22/63 | *Surfaris* |
| 7/30/66 | *Surfaris* |
| 12/24/66 | **Wish Me A Rainbow** *Gunter Kallmann Chorus* |
| 3/28/64 | **Wish Someone Would Care** *Irma Thomas* |
| 1/28/67 | **Wish You Didn't Have To Go** *James & Bobby Purify* |
| 10/22/66 | **Wish You Were Here, Buddy** *Pat Boone* |
| 3/29/69 | **Wishful Sinful** *Doors* |
| 6/20/64 | **Wishin' And Hopin'** *Dusty Springfield* |
| 7/10/61 | **Wishin' On A Rainbow** *Phill Wilson* |
| 5/1/65 | **Wishing It Was You** *Connie Francis* |
| 10/19/63 | **Witchcraft** *Elvis Presley* |
| 2/8/69 | **Witchi Tai To** *Everything is Everything* |
| 8/6/66 | **With A Girl Like You** *Troggs* |
| 11/16/68 | **With A Little Help From My Friends** *Joe Cocker* |
| | **With Pen In Hand** |
| 6/29/68 | *Billy Vera* |
| 5/3/69 | *Vikki Carr* |
| 8/28/65 | **With These Hands** *Tom Jones* |
| 2/25/67 | **With This Ring** *Platters* |
| 5/31/69 | **Without Her** *Herb Alpert* |
| | **Without Love (There Is Nothing)** |
| 6/22/63 | *Ray Charles* |
| 1/13/68 | *Oscar Toney, Jr.* |
| 12/27/69 | *Tom Jones* |
| 11/28/64 | **Without The One You Love (Life's Not Worth While)** *Four Tops* |
| 8/7/61 | **Without You** *Johnny Tillotson* |
| 11/2/63 | **Wives And Lovers** *Jack Jones* |
| 8/21/61 | **Wizard Of Love** *Ly-Dells* |
| 5/26/62 | **Wolverton Mountain** *Claude King* (also see: I'm The Girl On) |
| 2/12/66 | **Woman** *Peter & Gordon* |
| 7/11/60 | **Woman, A Lover, A Friend** *Jackie Wilson* |
| 4/10/65 | **Woman Can Change A Man** *Joe Tex* |
| 2/1/69 | **Woman Helping Man** *Vogues* |
| 8/24/68 | **Woman I Love** *B.B. King* |
| 5/19/62 | **Woman Is A Man's Best Friend** *Teddy & The Twilights* |
| 6/3/67 | **Woman Like That, Yeah** *Joe Tex* |
| | **Woman, Love And A Man**..see: (Story Of) |
| 11/18/67 | **Woman, Woman** *Union Gap* |
| 4/3/65 | **Woman's Got Soul** *Impressions* |
| 8/5/67 | **Woman's Hands** *Joe Tex* |
| 11/28/64 | **Woman's Love** *Carla Thomas* |
| 2/27/65 | **Won't Be Long** *Aretha Franklin* |
| | **Won't You Come Home Bill Bailey** |
| 5/23/60 | *Bobby Darin* |
| 4/24/61 | *Della Reese* |
| 4/6/63 | *Ella Fitzgerald* |
| 10/2/61 | **Wonder Like You** *Rick Nelson* |
| 4/25/64 | **Wonder Of You** *Ray Peterson* |
| 10/25/69 | **Wonderful** *Blackwell* |
| 8/11/62 | **Wonderful Dream** *Majors* |
| 11/2/63 | **Wonderful Summer** *Robin Ward* |
| 8/17/63 | **Wonderful! Wonderful!** *Tymes* |
| | **Wonderful World** |
| 5/9/60 | *Sam Cooke* |
| 5/29/65 | *Herman's Hermits* |
| 12/6/69 | **Wonderful World, Beautiful People** *Jimmy Cliff* |
| 3/24/62 | **Wonderful World Of The Young** *Andy Williams* |
| | **Wonderland By Night** |
| 11/14/60 | *Bert Kaempfert* |
| 11/14/60 | *Louis Prima* |
| 12/5/60 | *Anita Bryant* |
| 1/4/60* | **Wont'cha Come Home** *Lloyd Price* |
| 6/26/61 | **Wooden Heart** *Joe Dowell* |
| 4/3/65 | **Wooly Bully** *Sam The Sham & The Pharoahs* |
| 3/21/60 | **Words** *Pat Boone* |
| 7/22/67 | **Words** *Monkees* |
| 1/20/68 | **Words** *Bee Gees* |
| 12/3/66 | **Words Of Love** *Mamas & The Papas* |
| 7/2/66 | **Work Song** *Herb Alpert* |
| 9/22/62 | **Workin' For The Man** *Roy Orbison* |
| | **Workin' On A Groovy Thing** |
| 8/3/68 | *Patti Drew* |
| 7/19/69 | *5th Dimension* |
| 7/23/66 | **Working In The Coal Mine** *Lee Dorsey* |
| 1/6/68 | **Working Man's Prayer** *Arthur Prysock* |
| 1/29/66 | **Working My Way Back To You** *4 Seasons* |
| 10/5/63 | **Workout Stevie, Workout** *Stevie Wonder* |
| 9/13/69 | **World** *James Brown* |
| 5/30/64 | **World I Used To Know** *Jimmie Rodgers* |
| 8/6/66 | **World Of Fantasy** *Five Stairsteps* |
| 5/16/64 | **World Of Lonely People** *Anita Bryant* |
| 5/29/65 | **World Of Our Own** *Seekers* |
| 8/28/65 | **World Through A Tear** *Neil Sedaka* |
| 8/5/67 | **World We Knew (Over And Over)** *Frank Sinatra* |
| | **World Without Love** |
| 5/9/64 | *Peter & Gordon* |
| 5/9/64 | *Bobby Rydell* |
| 12/27/69 | **World Without Music** *Archie Bell & The Drells* |
| 12/14/68 | **Worm, The** *Jimmy McGriff* |
| 2/22/64 | **Worried Guy** *Johnny Tillotson* |
| 6/30/62 | **Worried Mind** *Ray Anthony* |
| 7/18/64 | **Worry** *Johnny Tillotson* |
| 12/21/68 | **Worst That Could Happen** *Brooklyn Bridge* |
| 1/12/63 | **Would It Make Any Difference To You** *Etta James* |
| 7/30/66 | **Wouldn't It Be Nice** *Beach Boys* |
| 1/18/64 | **Wow Wow Wee (He's The Boy For Me)** *Angels* |
| | **Wreck Of The "John B"**..see: Sloop John B |
| 5/15/61 | **Writing On The Wall** *Adam Wade* |
| 4/18/64 | **Wrong For Each Other** *Andy Williams* |

# Y

| | |
|---|---|
| 9/11/61 | **Ya Ya** *Lee Dorsey* |

## Yakety Sax (Axe)
- 2/23/63 Boots Randolph
- 7/17/65 Chet Atkins
- 11/2/68 **Yard Went On Forever** Richard Harris
- 1/4/60* **Year Ago Tonight** Crests
- 8/21/61 **Years From Now** Jackie Wilson
- **Yeh, Yeh**
- 6/22/63 Mongo Santamaria
- 2/13/65 Georgie Fame
- 4/1/67 **Yellow Balloon** Yellow Balloon
- **Yellow Bird**
- 5/29/61 Arthur Lyman Group
- 6/12/61 Lawrence Welk
- 8/20/66 **Yellow Submarine** Beatles
- 6/6/60 **Yen Yet Song** Gary Cane
- 10/10/64 **Yes I Do** Solomon Burke
- **Yes, I'm Lonesome Tonight**
- 12/31/60 Thelma Carpenter
- 12/31/60 Dodie Stevens
  (also see: Are You Lonesome To-night?)
- 5/15/65 **Yes, I'm Ready** Barbara Mason
- 2/24/62 **Yes Indeed** Pete Fountain
- 5/1/65 **Yes It Is** Beatles
- 9/12/60 **Yes Sir, That's My Baby** Ricky Nelson
- 2/10/62 **Yessiree** Linda Scott
- 6/1/68 **Yester Love** Miracles
- 10/18/69 **Yester-Me, Yester-You, Yesterday** Stevie Wonder
- **Yesterday**
- 9/25/65 Beatles
- 11/11/67 Ray Charles
- 11/9/63 **Yesterday And You (Armen's Theme)** Bobby Vee
- 1/1/66 **Yesterday Man** Chris Andrews
- 6/14/69 **Yesterday, When I Was Young** Roy Clark
- 7/20/68 **Yesterday's Dreams** Four Tops
- **Yesterday's Gone**
- 5/23/64 Chad & Jeremy
- 5/23/64 Overlanders
- 5/9/64 **Yesterday's Hero** Gene Pitney
- 12/7/68 **Yesterday's Rain** Spanky & Our Gang
- 8/29/64 **Yet...I Know** Steve Lawrence
- 8/11/62 **Yield Not To Temptation** Bobby Bland
- 8/8/60 **Yogi** Ivy Three
- 1/13/68 **You** Marvin Gaye
- 5/11/68 **You Ain't Going Nowhere** Byrds
- 3/4/67 **You Always Hurt Me** Impressions
- 5/15/61 **You Always Hurt The One You Love** Clarence Henry
- **You & Me & Pooneil**..see: Ballad Of
- 3/24/62 **You Are Mine** Frankie Avalon
- **You Are My Sunshine**
- 12/5/60 Johnny & The Hurricanes
- 11/17/62 Ray Charles
- 10/28/67 Mitch Ryder
- 10/8/66 **You Are She** Chad & Jeremy
- 12/26/66 **You Are The Only One** Ricky Nelson
- 2/5/66 **You Baby** Turtles
- 8/11/62 **You Beat Me To The Punch** Mary Wells
- 8/4/62 **You Belong To Me** Duprees
- 2/20/65 **You Better Get It** Joe Tex
- 7/31/65 **You Better Go** Derek Martin
- 12/5/60 **(You Better) Know What You're Doin'** Lloyd Price
- 2/24/62 **You Better Move On** Arthur Alexander
- 6/18/66 **You Better Run** Rascals
- 10/28/67 **You Better Sit Down Kids** Cher
- 11/26/66 **You Can Bring Me All Your Heartaches** Lou Rawls
- 3/27/61 **You Can Depend On Me** Brenda Lee
- **You Can Have Her (Him)**
- 1/30/61 Roy Hamilton
- 2/20/65 Timi Yuro
- 3/13/65 Dionne Warwick
- 5/8/65 Righteous Brothers
- 8/10/63 **You Can Never Stop Me Loving You** Johnny Tillotson
- 10/13/62 **You Can Run (But You Can't Hide)** Jerry Butler
- 9/11/65 **You Can't Be True, Dear** Patti Page
- 4/4/64 **You Can't Do That** Beatles
- 8/13/66 **You Can't Hurry Love** Supremes
- 3/6/65 **You Can't Hurt Me No More** Gene Chandler
- 8/18/62 **You Can't Judge A Book By The Cover** Bo Diddley

## (You Can't Let The Boy Overpower) The Man In You
- 3/7/64 Miracles
- 3/9/68 Chuck Jackson
- 10/13/62 **You Can't Lie To A Liar** Ketty Lester
- 6/25/66 **You Can't Roller Skate In A Buffalo Herd** Roger Miller
- **You Can't Sit Down**
- 6/19/61 Philip Upchurch Combo
- 4/27/63 Dovells
- 5/27/67 **You Can't Stand Alone** Wilson Pickett
- 9/25/65 **You Can't Take It Away** Fred Hughes
- 11/27/65 **You Didn't Have To Be So Nice** Lovin' Spoonful
- 11/2/63 **You Don't Have To Be A Baby To Cry** Caravelles
- 12/18/61 **You Don't Have To Be A Tower Of Strength** Gloria Lynne
- 10/8/66 **(You Don't Have To) Paint Me A Picture** Gary Lewis & The Playboys
- **You Don't Have To Say You Love Me**
- 5/21/66 Dusty Springfield
- 2/10/68 Four Sonics
- 6/7/69 **You Don't Have To Walk In The Rain** Turtles
- 6/27/64 **(You Don't Know) How Glad I Am** Nancy Wilson
- 1/15/66 **You Don't Know Like I Know** Sam & Dave
- **You Don't Know Me**
- 2/29/60 Lenny Welch
- 7/28/62 Ray Charles
- 10/14/67 Elvis Presley
- 10/2/61 **You Don't Know What It Means** Jackie Wilson
- 5/25/68 **You Don't Know What You Mean To Me** Sam & Dave
- 7/10/61 **You Don't Know What You've Got (Until You Lose It)** Ral Donner
- 3/9/63 **You Don't Love Me Anymore (And I Can Tell)** Rick Nelson
- 4/28/62 **You Don't Miss Your Water** William Bell
- 5/17/69 **You Don't Need Me For Anything Anymore** Brenda Lee
- 12/28/63 **You Don't Own Me** Lesley Gore
- 12/12/60 **You Don't Want My Love** Andy Williams
- 2/8/69 **You Gave Me A Mountain** Frankie Laine
- 5/27/67 **You Gave Me Something (And Everything's Alright)** Fantastic Four
- 12/3/66 **You Got Me Hummin'** Sam & Dave
- 12/14/68 **You Got Soul** Johnny Nash
- 10/5/68 **You Got The Love** Professor Morrison's Lollipop
- 1/28/67 **You Got To Me** Neil Diamond
- **You Got To Pay The Price**..see: You've Got
- **You Got What It Takes**
- 1/4/60* Marv Johnson
- 4/1/67 Dave Clark Five
- 2/27/65 **You Got What It Takes** Joe Tex
- 8/16/69 **You Got Yours And I'll Get Mine** Delfonics
- 8/23/69 **You, I** Rugbys
- **You Keep Me Hangin' On**
- 10/29/66 Supremes
- 7/8/67 Vanilla Fudge
- 7/13/68 Vanilla Fudge
- 11/29/69 Wilson Pickett
- 4/13/68 **(You Keep Me) Hangin' On** Joe Simon
- 9/16/67 **You Keep Running Away** Four Tops
- 6/1/63 **You Know It Ain't Right** Joe Hinton
- 8/5/67 **You Know What I Mean** Turtles
- 3/21/64 **You Lied To Your Daddy** Tams
- 9/28/63 **You Lost The Sweetest Boy** Mary Wells
- 8/2/69 **You Made A Believer (Out Of Me)** Ruby Andrews
- 7/30/66 **(You Make Me Feel) So Good** McCoys
- 8/8/60 **You Mean Everything To Me** Neil Sedaka
- 10/7/67 **You Mean The World To Me** David Houston
- 7/20/68 **You Met Your Match** Stevie Wonder
- 9/5/64 **You Must Believe Me** Impressions

## You Must Have Been A Beautiful Baby
- 9/4/61 Bobby Darin
- 6/10/68 Dave Clark Five
- 10/12/68 **You Need Me, Baby** Joe Tex
- 8/1/64 **You Never Can Tell** Chuck Berry
- 4/27/63 **You Never Miss Your Water (Till The Well Runs Dry)** "Little Esther" Phillips & "Big Al" Downing
- 10/7/67 **You, No One But You** Frankie Laine
- 6/24/67 **You Only Live Twice** Nancy Sinatra
- 10/5/68 **You Put It On Me** B.B. King
- 9/26/64 **You Really Got Me** Kinks
- 5/22/65 **You Really Know How To Hurt A Guy** Jan & Dean
- 6/15/68 **You Send Me** Aretha Franklin
- 10/24/64 **You Should Have Seen The Way He Looked At Me** Dixie Cups
- 6/30/62 **You Should'a Treated Me Right** Ike & Tina Turner
- 1/4/69 **You Showed Me** Turtles
- 3/31/62 **You Talk About Love** Barbara George
- **You Talk Too Much**
- 9/19/60 Joe Jones
- 9/26/60 Frankie Ford
- 7/24/65 **You Tell Me Why** Beau Brummels
- 11/24/62 **You Threw A Lucky Punch** Gene Chandler
- 5/22/65 **You Turn Me On** Ian Whitcomb
- 5/21/66 **You Waited Too Long** Five Stairsteps
- 6/17/67 **You Wanted Someone To Play With (I Wanted Someone To Love)** Frankie Laine
- 6/27/60 **You Were Born To Be Loved** Billy Bland
- 7/11/60 **(You Were Made For) All My Love** Jackie Wilson
- 5/1/65 **You Were Made For Me** Freddie & The Dreamers
- **You Were On My Mind**
- 7/24/65 We Five
- 7/1/67 Crispian St. Peters
- 4/17/65 **You Were Only Fooling (While I Was Falling In Love)** Vic Damone
- 3/7/64 **You Were Wrong** Z.Z. Hill
- 2/24/62 **You Win Again** Fats Domino
- 6/25/66 **You Wouldn't Listen** Ides Of March
- 7/16/66 **You You You** Mel Carter
- 5/8/61 **You'd Better Come Home** Russell Byrd
- 7/10/65 **You'd Better Come Home** Petula Clark
- 12/26/64 **You'll Always Be The One I Love** Dean Martin
- 6/26/61 **You'll Answer To Me** Patti Page
- 6/16/62 **You'll Lose A Good Thing** Barbara Lynn
- 5/29/65 **You'll Miss Me (When I'm Gone)** Fontella Bass & Bobby McClure
- 8/15/64 **You'll Never Get To Heaven (If You Break My Heart)** Dionne Warwick
- **You'll Never Walk Alone**
- 1/4/64 Patti LaBelle & Her Blue Belles
- 6/5/65 Gerry & The Pacemakers
- 4/20/68 Elvis Presley
- 10/4/69 Brooklyn Bridge
- **You're**..also see: Your
- 11/24/62 **You're A Sweetheart** Dinah Washington
- 9/9/67 **You're A Very Lovely Woman** Merry-Go-Round
- 3/14/64 **You're A Wonderful One** Marvin Gaye
- 4/22/67 **You're All I Need** Bobby Bland
- 7/27/68 **You're All I Need To Get By** Marvin Gaye & Tammi Terrell
- 11/20/61 **You're Following Me** Perry Como
- 1/15/66 **(You're Gonna) Hurt Yourself** Frankie Valli
- 8/7/65 **You're Gonna Make Me Cry** O.V. Wright
- 8/20/66 **You're Gonna Miss Me** Thirteenth Floor Elevators
- 5/1/61 **You're Gonna Need Magic** Roy Hamilton
- 12/15/62 **You're Gonna Need Me** Barbara Lynn
- 11/2/63 **You're Good For Me** Solomon Burke
- 3/26/66 **You're Just About To Lose Your Clown** Ray Charles
- 8/15/60 **You're Looking Good** Dee Clark

| Date | Title | Artist |
|---|---|---|
| 2/15/60 | **You're My Baby** | Sarah Vaughan |
| 7/24/65 | **You're My Baby (And Don't You Forget It)** | Vacels |
| 7/29/67 | **You're My Everything** | Temptations |
| | **You're My Girl** ..see: (Say) | |
| 7/4/64 | **You're My Remedy** | Marvelettes |
| 3/5/66 | **(You're My) Soul And Inspiration** | Righteous Brothers |
| 7/4/64 | **You're My World** | Cilla Black |
| 3/6/65 | **You're Next** | Jimmy Witherspoon |
| | **You're No Good** | |
| 11/23/63 | Betty Everett | |
| 8/1/64 | Swinging Blue Jeans | |
| | **You're Nobody 'Til Somebody Loves You** | |
| 5/12/62 | Dinah Washington | |
| 12/12/64 | Dean Martin | |
| 7/16/66 | Wonder Who? | |
| 10/31/60 | **You're Sixteen** | Johnny Burnette |
| 10/14/67 | **You're So Fine (medley)** | Bunny Sigler |
| 2/13/61 | **You're The Boss** | LaVern Baker & Jimmy Ricks |
| 6/29/63 | **(You're the) Devil In Disguise** | Elvis Presley |
| 9/18/65 | **You're The One** | Vogues |
| 4/23/66 | **You're The One** | Marvelettes |
| 11/28/64 | **You're The Only World I Know** | Sonny James |
| | **You're The Reason** | |
| 8/28/61 | Bobby Edwards | |
| 8/28/61 | Joe South | |
| 1/19/63 | **You're The Reason I'm Living** | Bobby Darin |
| 11/20/65 | **You've Been Cheatin'** | Impressions |
| 8/14/65 | **You've Been In Love Too Long** | Martha & The Vandellas |
| 4/9/66 | **You've Got My Mind Messed Up** | James Carr |
| 2/3/68 | **(You've Got) Personality & Chantilly Lace** | Mitch Ryder |
| 6/27/68 | **You've Got The Power** | James Brown |
| 12/28/68 | **You've Got The Power** | Esquires |
| 3/2/68 | **You've Got To Be Loved** | Montanas |
| 10/16/65 | **You've Got To Hide Your Love Away** | Silkie |
| 1/9/61 | **You've Got To Love Her With A Feeling** | Freddy King |
| 9/5/60 | **(You've Got To) Move Two Mountains** | Marv Johnson |
| | **You've Got To Pay The Price** | |
| 8/19/67 | Al Kent | |
| 11/8/69 | Gloria Taylor | |
| | **(You've Got What It Takes)** ..see: Baby | |
| 8/21/65 | **You've Got Your Troubles** | Fortunes |
| | **You've Lost That Lovin' Feelin'** | |
| 12/12/64 | Righteous Brothers | |
| 9/20/69 | Dionne Warwick | |
| | **You've Made Me So Very Happy** | |
| 9/9/67 | Brenda Holloway | |
| 3/1/69 | Blood, Sweat & Tears | |
| 7/17/65 | **You've Never Been In Love Like This Before** | Unit Four plus Two |
| 12/8/62 | **You've Really Got A Hold On Me** | Miracles |
| 3/23/68 | **You've Still Got A Place In My Heart** | Dean Martin |
| 3/16/63 | **Young And In Love** | Dick & DeeDee |
| 2/15/64 | **Young And In Love** | Chris Crosby |
| 6/22/68 | **Young Birds Fly** | Cryan' Shames |
| 6/22/68 | **Young Boy** | Barbara Greene |
| 10/16/61 | **Young Boy Blues** | Ben E. King |
| 4/25/60 | **Young Emotions** | Ricky Nelson |
| 8/2/69 | **Young Folks** | Supremes |
| 12/4/65 | **Young Girl** | Noel Harrison |
| 3/2/68 | **Young Girl** | Union Gap |
| 3/26/66 | **Young Love** | Lesley Gore |
| 3/16/63 | **Young Lovers** | Paul & Paula (also see: Theme For) |
| 10/26/63 | **Young Wings Can Fly (Higher Than You Know)** | Ruby & The Romantics |
| 3/3/62 | **Young World** | Rick Nelson |
| | **Younger Girl** | |
| 5/28/66 | Critters | |
| 5/28/66 | Hondells | |
| | **Your** ..also see: You're | |
| 8/24/63 | **Your Baby's Gone Surfin'** | Duane Eddy |
| 9/14/63 | **Your Boyfriend's Back** | Bobby Comstock (also see: My Boyfriend's Back) |
| 11/17/62 | **Your Cheating Heart** | Ray Charles |
| 2/6/61 | **Your Friends** | Dee Clark |
| | **Your Good Thing (Is About To End)** | |
| 8/6/66 | Mable John | |
| 7/19/69 | Lou Rawls | |
| 8/11/62 | **Your Heart Belongs To Me** | Supremes |
| 3/30/68 | **Your Heart Is Free Just Like The Wind** | Vikki Carr |
| 7/19/69 | **Your Husband - My Wife** | Brooklyn Bridge |
| 9/25/61 | **Your Last Goodbye** | Floyd Cramer |
| 8/12/67 | **(Your Love Keeps Lifting Me) Higher And Higher** | Jackie Wilson |
| 11/6/61 | **Your Ma Said You Cried In Your Sleep Last Night** | Kenny Dino |
| 8/11/62 | **Your Nose Is Gonna Grow** | Johnny Crawford |
| 5/25/63 | **Your Old Stand By** | Mary Wells |
| 3/13/61 | **Your One And Only Love** | Jackie Wilson |
| 12/19/60 | **Your Other Love** | Flamingos |
| 10/19/63 | **Your Other Love** | Connie Francis |
| 9/9/67 | **Your Precious Love** | Marvin Gaye & Tammi Terrell (also see: For Your Precious Love) |
| 10/12/63 | **Your Teenage Dreams** | Johnny Mathis |
| 6/22/68 | **Your Time Hasn't Come Yet, Baby** | Elvis Presley |
| 7/1/67 | **Your Unchanging Love** | Marvin Gaye |
| 1/26/63 | **Your Used To Be** | Brenda Lee |
| 5/4/68 | **Yummy Yummy Yummy** | Ohio Express |

# Z

| Date | Title | Artist |
|---|---|---|
| 1/6/68 | **Zabadak** | Dave Dee, Dozy, Beaky, Mick & Tich |
| 3/29/69 | **Zazueira** | Herb Alpert |
| 12/8/62 | **Zero-Zero** | Lawrence Welk |
| 2/9/63 | **Zing! Went The Strings Of My Heart** | Furys |
| 11/17/62 | **Zip-A-Dee Doo-Dah** | Bob B. Soxx & The Blue Jeans |
| 8/12/67 | **Zip Code** | Five Americans |
| 12/25/65 | **Zorba The Greek** | Herb Alpert |

# RE-ENTRYS

Records which re-charted after more than an eight-week absence, but less than one year. These re-entry dates are not shown in the title section.

| Date Re-Charted | Weeks Off Chart | Title | Artist |
|---|---|---|---|
| 7/13/68 | 48 | **You Keep Me Hangin' On** | Vanilla Fudge |
| 4/23/66 | 47 | **Gloria** | Them |
| 5/17/69 | 26 | **In-A-Gadda-Da-Vida** | Iron Butterfly |
| 5/8/61 | 24 | **Never On Sunday** | Don Costa |
| 8/16/69 | 18 | **Goodbye Columbus** | The Association |
| 7/6/68 | 11 | **Sunshine Of Your Love** | Cream |
| 11/20/61 | 10 | **Let's Twist Again** | Chubby Checker |
| 5/5/62 | 9 | **Moon River** | Henry Mancini |
| 1/16/65 | 8 | **Cousin Of Mine** | Sam Cooke |
| 6/19/61 | 8 | **A Scottish Soldier** | Andy Stewart |

See the introduction to the song title section for a complete explanation of the above listing.

# The RECORD RESEARCH Collection

| BOOK TITLE | Quantity | Price | Total |
|---|---|---|---|
| 1. Billboard Pop Charts 1955-1959 (hardcover) | _____ | $95 | _____ |
| 2. Billboard Hot 100 Charts — The Sixties (hardcover) | _____ | $95 | _____ |
| 3. Billboard Hot 100 Charts — The Seventies (hardcover) | _____ | $95 | _____ |
| 4. Billboard Hot 100 Charts — The Eighties (hardcover) | _____ | $95 | _____ |
| 5. Top Pop Albums 1955-1992 (hardcover)* | _____ | $95 | _____ |
| *Anticipated publication date: December, 1992 | | | |
| 6. Top Pop Singles 1955-1990 (hardcover) | _____ | $70 | _____ |
| 7. Top Pop Singles 1955-1990 (softcover) | _____ | $60 | _____ |
| 8. Pop Singles Annual 1955-1990 (hardcover) | _____ | $70 | _____ |
| 9. Pop Singles Annual 1955-1990 (softcover) | _____ | $60 | _____ |
| 10. Top Country Singles 1944-1988 (hardcover) | _____ | $60 | _____ |
| 11. Top Country Singles 1944-1988 (softcover) | _____ | $50 | _____ |
| 12. Top R&B Singles 1942-1988 (hardcover) | _____ | $60 | _____ |
| 13. Top R&B Singles 1942-1988 (softcover) | _____ | $50 | _____ |
| 14. Pop Memories 1890-1954 (hardcover) | _____ | $60 | _____ |
| 15. Top 10 Charts 1958-1988 (softcover) | _____ | $50 | _____ |
| 16. Bubbling Under The Hot 100 1959-1985 (hardcover) | _____ | $45 | _____ |
| 17. Billboard #1s 1950-1991 (softcover) | _____ | $35 | _____ |
| 18. Top 3000+ 1955-1990 (softcover) | _____ | $25 | _____ |

19. Yearbooks (all softcover) ............................................. $35 each  _____
 ☐ 1991  ☐ 1990  ☐ 1989  ☐ 1988  ☐ 1987  ☐ 1986  ☐ 1985  ☐ 1984  ☐ 1983

**Subtotal** ............... $ _____

**Shipping & Handling** ............................................................................. $ _____

**All U.S. orders add $5 for the first book ordered and $2 for each additional book.**

**All Canadian and foreign orders add $6 for the first book ordered and $3 for each additional book.** Canadian and foreign orders are shipped via surface mail and must be paid in **U.S. dollars**. Call or write for air mail shipping rates.

**Total Payment** ............ $ _____

**Payment Method**
☐ Check  ☐ Money Order
☐ MasterCard  ☐ VISA

MasterCard or VISA # ____ ____ ____ ____
Expiration Date _____ / _____
                    Mo.       Yr.
Signature _____

To Charge Your Order By Phone, Call 414-251-5408 or
Fax 414-251-9452 (office hours: 8AM-5PM CST)

Name _____
Company Name _____
Address _____ Apt/Suite # _____
City _____ State/Province _____
ZIP/Postal Code _____ Country _____

For complete book descriptions and ordering information, call write or fax today.

Record Research Inc.
P.O. Box 200
Menomonee Falls, WI 53052-0200
U.S.A.

Phone: 414-251-5408
Fax: 414-251-9452

*Record Research*
**The World's Leading Authority On Recorded Entertainment**